Who's Who in the Midwest

Biographical Titles Currently Published by Marquis Who's Who

- Who's Who in America
  - Who's Who in America supplements:
    - Geographic/Professional Area Index
    - Supplement to Who's Who in America
    - Who's Who in America Classroom Project Book
- Who Was Who in America
  - Historical Volume (1607–1896)
  - Volume I (1897–1942)
  - Volume II (1943–1950)
  - Volume III (1951–1960)
  - Volume IV (1961–1968)
  - Volume V (1969–1973)
  - Volume VI (1974–1976)
  - Volume VII (1977–1981)
  - Volume VIII (1982–1985)
  - Index Volume (1607–1985)
- Who's Who in the World
- Who's Who in the East
- Who's Who in the Midwest
- Who's Who in the South and Southwest
- Who's Who in the West
- Who's Who in American Law
- Who's Who of American Women
- Who's Who of Emerging Leaders in America
- Who's Who in Finance and Industry
- Index to Who's Who Books
- Directory of Medical Specialists

Who's Who in the Midwest®

Including Illinois, Indiana, Iowa, Kansas, Michigan, Minnesota, Missouri, Nebraska, North Dakota, Ohio, South Dakota, and Wisconsin; and in Canada, Manitoba and western Ontario

21st edition 1988-1989

MARQUIS
Who'sWho

Macmillan Directory Division
3002 Glenview Road
Wilmette, Illinois 60091 U.S.A.

For information, address Marquis Who's Who, 3002 Glenview Road, Wilmette, Illinois 60091.

James J. Pfister—President
Paul E. Rose—Executive Vice President
A. Robert Weicherding—Vice President, Publisher
Sandra S. Barnes—Vice President, Marketing
Timothy J. Sullivan—Vice President, Finance
Paul Canning—Operations Manager

Library of Congress Catalog Card Number 50-289
International Standard Book Number 0-8379-0721-7
Product Code Number 030466

Distributed in Asia by
United Publishers Services Ltd.
Kenkyu-Sha Bldg.
9, Kanda Surugadai 2-Chome
Chiyoda-Ku, Tokyo, Japan

Manufactured in the United States of America

Table of Contents

Preface

The twenty-first edition of *Who's Who in the Midwest* represents our most recent effort to provide biographical information on men and women of distinction whose influence is concentrated in the midwestern sector of North America. Such individuals are of decided reference interest locally and, to an increasing degree, nationally.

The volume contains more than 23,000 names from the midwestern region of the United States including Illinois, Indiana, Iowa, Kansas, Michigan, Minnesota, Missouri, Nebraska, North Dakota, Ohio, South Dakota, and Wisconsin in the United States and the provinces of Manitoba and western Ontario in Canada. The twenty-first edition offers up-to-the-minute coverage of a broad range of Midwesterners based on position or individual achievement.

The persons sketched in this volume represent virtually every important field of endeavor. Included are executives and officials in government, business, education, religion, the press, civic affairs, the arts, cultural affairs, law, and other fields. This edition also includes significant contributors in such fields as contemporary art, music, and science.

Most biographees have furnished their own data, thus assuring a high degree of accuracy. In some cases where individuals failed to supply information, Marquis staff members compiled the data through independent research. Such sketches are denoted by an asterisk. Brief key information is provided in the sketches of selected individuals, new to this edition, who did not submit data. As in previous editions, biographees were given the opportunity to review prepublication proofs of their sketches to make sure they were correct.

The question is often asked, "How do people get into a Who's Who volume?" Name selection is based on one fundamental principle: reference value. Biographees of *Who's Who in the Midwest* can be classified in two basic categories: (1) Persons who are of regional reference importance to colleagues, librarians, researchers, scholars, the press, historians, biographers, participants in business and civic affairs, and others with specific or general inquiry needs; (2) Individuals of national reference interest who are also of such regional or local importance that their inclusion in the book is essential.

Marquis Who's Who editors exercise the utmost care in preparing each biographical sketch for publication. Occasionally, however, errors do occur. Users of this directory are requested to draw to the attention of the publisher any errors found so that corrections can be made in a subsequent edition.

Board of Advisors

Marquis Who's Who gratefully acknowledges the following distinguished individuals who have made themselves available for review, evaluation, and general comment with regard to the publication of the twenty-first edition of *Who's Who in the Midwest.* The advisors have enhanced the reference value of this edition by the nomination of outstanding individuals for inclusion. However, the Board of Advisors, either collectively or individually, is in no way responsible for the final selection of names appearing in this volume, nor does the Board of Advisors bear responsibility for the accuracy or comprehensiveness of the biographical information or other material contained herein.

Steven C. Beering
President
Purdue University

Gwendolyn Brooks
Poet Laureate of Illinois
Publisher
The David Company

Thomas J. Clifford
President
The University of North Dakota

George A. Drake
President
Grinnell College

Reverend Theodore M. Hesburgh, C.S.C.
President Emeritus
University of Notre Dame

Roger H. Hull
President
Beloit College

Helmut Jahn
President and Chief Executive Officer
Murphy/Jahn

Martin A. Massengale
Chancellor
University of Nebraska-Lincoln

Reverend John P. Raynor, S.J.
President
Marquette University

Norman Ross
Senior Vice President Retired
The First National Bank of Chicago

Irving Shain
Former Chancellor
University of Wisconsin-Madison

Richard H. Stanley
Chairman
Stanley Consultants, Inc.

Charles E. Stoltz
President and Chief Executive Officer
Dubuque Packing Company

Maria Tallchief
Artistic Director
School of Chicago City Ballet

Marc F. Wilson
Director
The Nelson-Atkins Museum of Art

Board of Nominators

Marquis Who's Who gratefully acknowledges the following distinguished nominators for their assistance with regard to the publication of the twenty-first edition of *Who's Who in the Midwest.* They have enhanced the reference value of this edition by the recommendation of outstanding individuals from their respective states or local areas. However, the Board of Nominators, either collectively or individually, is in no way responsible for the final selection of names appearing in this volume, nor does the Board of Nominators bear responsibility for the accuracy or comprehensiveness of the biographical information or other material contained herein.

Rodney F. Benson
President
Ann Arbor Area Chamber of Commerce
Ann Arbor, Michigan

Robert W. Brennan
President
Greater Madison Chamber of Commerce
Madison, Wisconsin

William H. Bryant
President
Greater Cleveland Growth Association
Cleveland, Ohio

Jerry M. Mallot
President
Wichita Area Chamber of Commerce
Wichita, Kansas

David L. May
President
Independence Chamber of Commerce
Independence, Missouri

Frank D. McMullen, Jr.
President
Greater Omaha Chamber of Commerce
Omaha, Nebraska

J. Michael Porter
President
Toledo Area Chamber of Commerce
Toledo, Ohio

Larry S. Reed
President
Davenport Chamber of Commerce
Davenport, Iowa

Frank E. Smith
President
Greater Detroit Chamber of Commerce
Detroit, Michigan

Duane S. Vicary
President
Lincoln Chamber of Commerce
Lincoln, Nebraska

Larry J. Waller
President
Cedar Rapids Area Chamber of Commerce
Cedar Rapids, Iowa

Standards of Admission

The foremost consideration in selecting biographees for *Who's Who in the Midwest* is the extent of an individual's reference interest. Such reference interest is judged on either of two factors: (1) the position of responsibility held, or (2) the level of significant achievement attained.

Admissions based on the factor of position include:

Members of the U.S. Congress

Federal judges

Governors of states covered by this volume

Premiers of Canadian provinces covered by this volume

State attorneys general

Judges of state and territorial courts of highest appellate jurisdiction

Mayors of major cities

Heads of major universities and colleges

Heads of leading philanthropic, educational, cultural, and scientific institutions and associations

Chief ecclesiastics of the principal religious denominations

Principal officers of national and international businesses

Others chosen because of incumbency or membership

Admission for individual achievement is based on objective qualitative criteria. To be selected, a person must have attained conspicuous achievement. The biographee may scarcely be known in the local community but may be recognized in some field of endeavor for noteworthy accomplishment.

Key to Information

❶ **BURKE, JAMES ALLEN,** ❷ toy manufacturing company executive; ❸ b. Highland Park, Ill., Mar. 23, 1947; ❹ s. Miles Benjamin and Thelma (Allen) B.; ❺ m. Lynne Gruber, Jan. 28, 1971; ❻ children: Jennifer Marie, Joseph Paul, Michael Scott. ❼ BS, Northwestern U., 1971; MBA, U. Chgo., 1973. ❽ CPA, Ill. ❾ With Millington Toy Mfg. Co., Peoria, Ill. 1973—, sales mgr., 1975-79, v.p., 1979-80, v.p., asst. treas., 1980-82, v.p., treas., 1982-86, sr. v.p., 1986—; lectr. Peoria Community Coll., 1977-79. ❿ Author: Corporate Accounting Standards, 1983. ⓫ Active Boy Scouts Am.; mem. Peoria Heights Bd. Edn., 1983-86. ⓬ Served USNR, 1965-67. ⓭ Named One of Outstanding Young Men of Am., U.S. Jaycees, 1983. ⓮ Mem. Am. Inst. CPA's, AIM, NAM, Beta Theta Pi. ⓯ Republican. ⓰ Presbyterian. ⓱ Clubs: Peoria Lake Country, Chgo. Athletic. ⓲ Lodges: Masons, Shriners. ⓳ Avocations: camping, skiing, gardening. ⓴ Home: 903 Spring Dr Peoria Heights IL 61613 ㉑ Office: Millington Toy Mfg Co 1912 Main St Peoria IL 60606

KEY

❶ Name
❷ Occupation
❸ Vital statistics
❹ Parents
❺ Marriage
❻ Children
❼ Education
❽ Professional certifications
❾ Career
❿ Writings and creative works
⓫ Civic and political activities
⓬ Military
⓭ Awards and fellowships
⓮ Professional and association memberships
⓯ Political affiliation
⓰ Religion
⓱ Clubs
⓲ Lodges
⓳ Avocations
⓴ Home address
㉑ Office address

Table of Abbreviations

The following abbreviations and symbols are frequently used in this book.

*An asterisk following a sketch indicates that it was researched by the Marquis Who's Who editorial staff and has not been verified by the biographee.

AA, A.A. Associate in Arts
AAAL American Academy of Arts and Letters
AAAS American Association for the Advancement of Science
AAHPER Alliance for Health, Physical Education and Recreation
AAU Amateur Athletic Union
AAUP American Association of University Professors
AAUW American Association of University Women
AB, A.B. Arts, Bachelor of
AB Alberta
ABA American Bar Association
ABC American Broadcasting Company
AC Air Corps
acad. academy, academic
acct. accountant
acctg. accounting
ACDA Arms Control and Disarmament Agency
ACLU American Civil Liberties Union
ACP American College of Physicians
ACS American College of Surgeons
ADA American Dental Association
a.d.c. aide-de-camp
adj. adjunct, adjutant
adj. gen. adjutant general
adm. admiral
adminstr. administrator
adminstrn. administration
adminstrv. administrative
ADP Automatic Data Processing
adv. advocate, advisory
advt. advertising
AE, A.E. Agricultural Engineer
A.E. and P. Ambassador Extraordinary and Plenipotentiary
AEC Atomic Energy Commission
aero. aeronautical, aeronautic
aerodyn. aerodynamic
AFB Air Force Base
AFL-CIO American Federation of Labor and Congress of Industrial Organizations
AFTRA American Federation of TV and Radio Artists
agr. agriculture
agrl. agricultural
agt. agent
AGVA American Guild of Variety Artists
agy. agency
A&I Agricultural and Industrial
AIA American Institute of Architects
AIAA American Institute of Aeronautics and Astronautics
AID Agency for International Development
AIEE American Institute of Electrical Engineers
AIM American Institute of Management
AIME American Institute of Mining, Metallurgy, and Petroleum Engineers
AK Alaska
AL Alabama
ALA American Library Association
Ala. Alabama
alt. alternate
Alta. Alberta
A&M Agricultural and Mechanical
AM, A.M. Arts, Master of
Am. American, America
AMA American Medical Association
A.M.E. African Methodist Episcopal
Amtrak National Railroad Passenger Corporation
AMVETS American Veterans of World War II, Korea, Vietnam
anat. anatomical
ann. annual
ANTA American National Theatre and Academy
anthrop. anthropological
AP Associated Press
APO Army Post Office
apptd. appointed
Apr. April
apt. apartment
AR Arkansas
ARC American Red Cross
archeol. archeological
archtl. architectural
Ariz. Arizona
Ark. Arkansas
ArtsD, ArtsD. Arts, Doctor of
arty. artillery
AS American Samoa
AS Associate in Science
ASCAP American Society of Composers, Authors and Publishers
ASCE American Society of Civil Engineers
ASHRAE American Society of Heating, Refrigeration, and Air Conditioning Engineers
ASME American Society of Mechanical Engineers
assn. association
assoc. associate
asst. assistant
ASTM American Society for Testing and Materials
astron. astronomical
astrophys. astrophysical
ATSC Air Technical Service Command
AT&T American Telephone & Telegraph Company
atty. attorney
Aug. August
AUS Army of the United States
aux. auxiliary
Ave. Avenue
AVMA American Veterinary Medical Association
AZ Arizona

B. Bachelor
b. born
BA, B.A. Bachelor of Arts
BAgr, B.Agr. Bachelor of Agriculture
Balt. Baltimore
Bapt. Baptist
BArch, B.Arch. Bachelor of Architecture
BAS, B.A.S. Bachelor of Agricultural Science
BBA, B.B.A. Bachelor of Business Administration
BBC British Broadcasting Corporation
BC, B.C. British Columbia
BCE, B.C.E. Bachelor of Civil Engineering
BChir, B.Chir. Bachelor of Surgery
BCL, B.C.L. Bachelor of Civil Law
BCS, B.C.S. Bachelor of Commercial Science
BD, B.D. Bachelor of Divinity
bd. board
BE, B.E. Bachelor of Education
BEE, B.E.E. Bachelor of Electrical Engineering
BFA, B.F.A. Bachelor of Fine Arts
bibl. biblical
bibliog. bibliographical
biog. biographical
biol. biological
BJ, B.J. Bachelor of Journalism
Bklyn. Brooklyn
BL, B.L. Bachelor of Letters
bldg. building
BLS, B.L.S. Bachelor of Library Science
Blvd. Boulevard
bn. battalion
B.&O.R.R. Baltimore & Ohio Railroad
bot. botanical
BPE, B.P.E. Bachelor of Physical Education
BPhil, B.Phil. Bachelor of Philosophy
br. branch
BRE, B.R.E. Bachelor of Religious Education
brig. gen. brigadier general
Brit. British, Brittanica
Bros. Brothers
BS, B.S. Bachelor of Science
BSA, B.S.A. Bachelor of Agricultural Science
BSD, B.S.D. Bachelor of Didactic Science
BST, B.S.T. Bachelor of Sacred Theology
BTh, B.Th. Bachelor of Theology
bull. bulletin
bur. bureau
bus. business
B.W.I. British West Indies

CA California
CAA Civil Aeronautics Administration
CAB Civil Aeronautics Board
Calif. California
C.Am. Central America
Can. Canada, Canadian
CAP Civil Air Patrol
capt. captain
CARE Cooperative American Relief Everywhere
Cath. Catholic
cav. cavalry
CBC Canadian Broadcasting Company
CBI China, Burma, India Theatre of Operations
CBS Columbia Broadcasting System
CCC Commodity Credit Corporation
CCNY City College of New York
CCU Cardiac Care Unit
CD Civil Defense
CE, C.E. Corps of Engineers, Civil Engineer
cen. central
CENTO Central Treaty Organization
CERN European Organization of Nuclear Research
cert. certificate, certification, certified
CETA Comprehensive Employment Training Act
CFL Canadian Football League
ch. church
ChD, Ch.D. Doctor of Chemistry
chem. chemical
ChemE, Chem.E. Chemical Engineer

Chgo. Chicago
chirurg. chirurgical
chmn. chairman
chpt. chapter
CIA Central Intelligence Agency
CIC Counter Intelligence Corps
Cin. Cincinnati
cir. circuit
Cleve. Cleveland
climatol. climatological
clin. clinical
clk. clerk
C.L.U. Chartered Life Underwriter
CM, C.M. Master in Surgery
CM Northern Mariana Islands
C.&N.W.Ry. Chicago & North Western Railway
CO Colorado
Co. Company
COF Catholic Order of Foresters
C. of C. Chamber of Commerce
col. colonel
coll. college
Colo. Colorado
com. committee
comd. commanded
comdg. commanding
comdr. commander
comdt. commandant
commd. commissioned
comml. commercial
commn. commission
commr. commissioner
condr. conductor
Conf. Conference
Congl. Congregational, Congressional
Conglist. Congregationalist
Conn. Connecticut
cons. consultant, consulting
consol. consolidated
constl. constitutional
constn. constitution
constrn. construction
contbd. contributed
contbg. contributing
contbn. contribution
contbr. contributor
Conv. Convention
coop. cooperative
CORDS Civil Operations and Revolutionary Development Support
CORE Congress of Racial Equality
corp. corporation, corporate
corr. correspondent, corresponding, correspondence
C.&O.Ry. Chesapeake & Ohio Railway
CPA, C.P.A. Certified Public Accountant
C.P.C.U. Chartered Property and Casualty Underwriter
CPH, C.P.H. Certificate of Public Health
cpl. corporal
C.P.R. Cardio-Pulmonary Resuscitation
C.P.Ry. Canadian Pacific Railway
C.S. Christian Science
CSB, C.S.B. Bachelor of Christian Science
C.S.C. Civil Service Commission
CSD, C.S.D. Doctor of Christian Science
CT Connecticut
ct. court
ctr. center
CWS Chemical Warfare Service
C.Z. Canal Zone

D. Doctor
d. daughter
DAgr, D.Agr. Doctor of Agriculture
DAR Daughters of the American Revolution
dau. daughter
DAV Disabled American Veterans
DC, D.C. District of Columbia
DCL, D.C.L. Doctor of Civil Law
DCS, D.C.S. Doctor of Commercial Science
DD, D.D. Doctor of Divinity
DDS, D.D.S. Doctor of Dental Surgery
DE Delaware
Dec. December
dec. deceased
def. defense
Del. Delaware
del. delegate, delegation
Dem. Democrat, Democratic
DEng, D.Eng. Doctor of Engineering
denom. denomination, denominational
dep. deputy
dept. department
dermatol. dermatological
desc. descendant
devel. development, developmental
DFA, D.F.A. Doctor of Fine Arts
D.F.C. Distinguished Flying Cross
DHL, D.H.L. Doctor of Hebrew Literature
dir. director
dist. district
distbg. distributing
distbn. distribution
distbr. distributor
disting. distinguished
div. division, divinity, divorce
DLitt, D.Litt. Doctor of Literature
DMD, D.M.D. Doctor of Medical Dentistry
DMS, D.M.S. Doctor of Medical Science
DO, D.O. Doctor of Osteopathy
DPH, D.P.H. Diploma in Public Health
DPhil, D.Phil. Doctor of Philosophy
D.R. Daughters of the Revolution
Dr. Drive, Doctor
DRE, D.R.E. Doctor of Religious Education
DrPH, Dr.P.H. Doctor of Public Health, Doctor of Public Hygiene
D.S.C. Distinguished Service Cross
DSc, D.Sc. Doctor of Science
D.S.M. Distinguished Service Medal
DST, D.S.T. Doctor of Sacred Theology
DTM, D.T.M. Doctor of Tropical Medicine
DVM, D.V.M. Doctor of Veterinary Medicine
DVS, D.V.S. Doctor of Veterinary Surgery

E. East
ea. eastern
E. and P. Extraordinary and Plenipotentiary
Eccles. Ecclesiastical
ecol. ecological
econ. economic
ECOSOC Economic and Social Council (of the UN)
ED, E.D. Doctor of Engineering
ed. educated
EdB, Ed.B. Bachelor of Education
EdD, Ed.D. Doctor of Education
edit. edition
EdM, Ed.M. Master of Education
edn. education
ednl. educational
EDP Electronic Data Processing
EdS, Ed.S. Specialist in Education
EE, E.E. Electrical Engineer
E.E. and M.P. Envoy Extraordinary and Minister Plenipotentiary
EEC European Economic Community
EEG Electroencephalogram
EEO Equal Employment Opportunity
EEOC Equal Employment Opportunity Commission
E.Ger. German Democratic Republic
EKG Electrocardiogram
elec. electrical
electrochem. electrochemical
electrophys. electrophysical
elem. elementary
EM, E.M. Engineer of Mines
ency. encyclopedia
Eng. England
engr. engineer
engring. engineering
entomol. entomological
environ. environmental
EPA Environmental Protection Agency
epidemiol. epidemiological
Episc. Episcopalian
ERA Equal Rights Amendment
ERDA Energy Research and Development Administration
ESEA Elementary and Secondary Education Act
ESL English as Second Language
ESSA Environmental Science Services Administration
ethnol. ethnological
ETO European Theatre of Operations
Evang. Evangelical
exam. examination, examining
exec. executive
exhbn. exhibition
expdn. expedition
expn. exposition
expt. experiment
exptl. experimental

F.A. Field Artillery
FAA Federal Aviation Administration
FAO Food and Agriculture Organization (of the UN)
FBI Federal Bureau of Investigation
FCA Farm Credit Administration
FCC Federal Communications Commission
FCDA Federal Civil Defense Administration
FDA Food and Drug Administration
FDIA Federal Deposit Insurance Administration
FDIC Federal Deposit Insurance Corporation
FE, F.E. Forest Engineer
FEA Federal Energy Administration
Feb. February
fed. federal
fedn. federation
FERC Federal Energy Regulatory Commission
fgn. foreign
FHA Federal Housing Administration
fin. financial, finance
FL Florida
Fla. Florida
FMC Federal Maritime Commission
FOA Foreign Operations Administration
found. foundation
FPC Federal Power Commission
FPO Fleet Post Office
frat. fraternity
FRS Federal Reserve System
FSA Federal Security Agency
Ft. Fort
FTC Federal Trade Commission

G-1 (or other number) Division of General Staff

GA, Ga. Georgia
GAO General Accounting Office
gastroent. gastroenterological
GATT General Agreement of Tariff and Trades
gen. general
geneal. genealogical
geod. geodetic
geog. geographic, geographical
geol. geological
geophys. geophysical
gerontol. gerontological
G.H.Q. General Headquarters
G.N. Ry. Great Northern Railway
gov. governor
govt. government
govtl. governmental
GPO Government Printing Office
grad. graduate, graduated
GSA General Services Administration
Gt. Great
GU Guam
gynecol. gynecological

hdqrs. headquarters
HEW Department of Health, Education and Welfare
HHD, H.H.D. Doctor of Humanities
HHFA Housing and Home Finance Agency
HHS Department of Health and Human Services
HI Hawaii
hist. historical, historic
HM, H.M. Master of Humanics
homeo. homeopathic
hon. honorary, honorable
Ho. of Dels. House of Delegates
Ho. of Reps. House of Representatives
hort. horticultural
hosp. hospital
HUD Department of Housing and Urban Development
Hwy. Highway
hydrog. hydrographic

IA Iowa
IAEA International Atomic Energy Agency
IBM International Business Machines Corporation
IBRD International Bank for Reconstruction and Development
ICA International Cooperation Administration
ICC Interstate Commerce Commission
ICU Intensive Care Unit
ID Idaho
IEEE Institute of Electrical and Electronics Engineers
IFC International Finance Corporation
IGY International Geophysical Year
IL Illinois
Ill. Illinois
illus. illustrated
ILO International Labor Organization
IMF International Monetary Fund
IN Indiana
Inc. Incorporated
Ind. Indiana
ind. independent
Indpls. Indianapolis
indsl. industrial
inf. infantry
info. information
ins. insurance
insp. inspector
insp. gen. inspector general
inst. institute
instl. institutional
instn. institution
instr. instructor
instrn. instruction
intern. international
intro. introduction
IRE Institute of Radio Engineers
IRS Internal Revenue Service
ITT International Telephone & Telegraph Corporation

JAG Judge Advocate General
JAGC Judge Advocate General Corps
Jan. January
Jaycees Junior Chamber of Commerce
JB, J.B. Jurum Baccalaureus
JCB, J.C.B. Juris Canoni Baccalaureus
JCD, J.C.D. Juris Canonici Doctor, Juris Civilis Doctor
JCL, J.C.L. Juris Canonici Licentiatus
JD, J.D. Juris Doctor
jg. junior grade
jour. journal
jr. junior
JSD, J.S.D. Juris Scientiae Doctor
JUD, J.U.D. Juris Utriusque Doctor
jud. judicial

Kans. Kansas
K.C. Knights of Columbus
K.P. Knights of Pythias
KS Kansas
K.T. Knight Templar
KY, Ky. Kentucky

LA, La. Louisiana
lab. laboratory
lang. language
laryngol. laryngological
LB Labrador
lectr. lecturer
legis. legislation, legislative
LHD, L.H.D. Doctor of Humane Letters
L.I. Long Island
lic. licensed, license
L.I.R.R. Long Island Railroad
lit. literary, literature
LittB, Litt.B. Bachelor of Letters
LittD, Litt.D. Doctor of Letters
LLB, LL.B. Bachelor of Laws
LLD, LL.D. Doctor of Laws
LLM, LL.M. Master of Laws
Ln. Lane
L.&N.R.R. Louisville & Nashville Railroad
LS, L.S. Library Science (in degree)
lt. lieutenant
Ltd. Limited
Luth. Lutheran
LWV League of Women Voters

M. Master
m. married
MA, M.A. Master of Arts
MA Massachusetts
mag. magazine
MAgr, M.Agr. Master of Agriculture
maj. major
Man. Manitoba
Mar. March
MArch, M.Arch. Master in Architecture
Mass. Massachusetts
math. mathematics, mathematical
MATS Military Air Transport Service
MB, M.B. Bachelor of Medicine
MB Manitoba
MBA, M.B.A. Master of Business Administration
MBS Mutual Broadcasting System
M.C. Medical Corps
MCE, M.C.E. Master of Civil Engineering
mcht. merchant
mcpl. municipal
MCS, M.C.S. Master of Commercial Science
MD, M.D. Doctor of Medicine
MD, Md. Maryland
MDip, M.Dip. Master in Diplomacy
mdse. merchandise
MDV, M.D.V. Doctor of Veterinary Medicine
ME, M.E. Mechanical Engineer
ME Maine
M.E.Ch. Methodist Episcopal Church
mech. mechanical
MEd, M.Ed. Master of Education
med. medical
MEE, M.E.E. Master of Electrical Engineering
mem. member
meml. memorial
merc. mercantile
met. metropolitan
metall. metallurgical
MetE, Met.E. Metallurgical Engineer
meteorol. meteorological
Meth. Methodist
Mex. Mexico
MF, M.F. Master of Forestry
MFA, M.F.A. Master of Fine Arts
mfg. manufacturing
mfr. manufacturer
mgmt. management
mgr. manager
MHA, M.H.A. Master of Hospital Administration
M.I. Military Intelligence
MI Michigan
Mich. Michigan
micros. microscopic, microscopical
mid. middle
mil. military
Milw. Milwaukee
mineral. mineralogical
Minn. Minnesota
Miss. Mississippi
MIT Massachusetts Institute of Technology
mktg. marketing
ML, M.L. Master of Laws
MLA Modern Language Association
M.L.D. Magister Legnum Diplomatic
MLitt, M.Litt. Master of Literature
MLS, M.L.S. Master of Library Science
MME, M.M.E. Master of Mechanical Engineering
MN Minnesota
mng. managing
MO, Mo. Missouri
moblzn. mobilization
Mont. Montana
M.P. Member of Parliament
MPE, M.P.E. Master of Physical Education
MPH, M.P.H. Master of Public Health
MPhil, M.Phil. Master of Philosophy
MPL, M.P.L. Master of Patent Law
Mpls. Minneapolis
MRE, M.R.E. Master of Religious Education
MS, M.S. Master of Science
MS, Ms. Mississippi
MSc, M.Sc. Master of Science
MSF, M.S.F. Master of Science of Forestry
MST, M.S.T. Master of Sacred Theology
MSW, M.S.W. Master of Social Work

MT Montana
Mt. Mount
MTO Mediterranean Theatre of Operations
mus. museum, musical
MusB, Mus.B. Bachelor of Music
MusD, Mus.D. Doctor of Music
MusM, Mus.M. Master of Music
mut. mutual
mycol. mycological

N. North
NAACP National Association for the Advancement of Colored People
NACA National Advisory Committee for Aeronautics
NAD National Academy of Design
N.Am. North America
NAM National Association of Manufacturers
NAPA National Association of Performing Artists
NAREB National Association of Real Estate Boards
NARS National Archives and Record Service
NASA National Aeronautics and Space Administration
nat. national
NATO North Atlantic Treaty Organization
NATOUSA North African Theatre of Operations
nav. navigation
NB, N.B. New Brunswick
NBC National Broadcasting Company
NC, N.C. North Carolina
NCCJ National Conference of Christians and Jews
ND, N.D. North Dakota
NDEA National Defense Education Act
NE Nebraska
NE Northeast
NEA National Education Association
Nebr. Nebraska
NEH National Endowment for Humanities
neurol. neurological
Nev. Nevada
NF Newfoundland
NFL National Football League
Nfld. Newfoundland
NG National Guard
NH, N.H. New Hampshire
NHL National Hockey League
NIH National Institutes of Health
NIMH National Institute of Mental Health
NJ, N.J. New Jersey
NLRB National Labor Relations Board
NM New Mexico
N. Mex. New Mexico
No. Northern
NOAA National Oceanographic and Atmospheric Administration
NORAD North America Air Defense
Nov. November
NOW National Organization for Women
N.P.Ry. Northern Pacific Railway
nr. near
NRC National Research Council
NS, N.S. Nova Scotia
NSC National Security Council
NSF National Science Foundation
N.T. New Testament
NT Northwest Territories
numis. numismatic
NV Nevada
NW Northwest
N.W.T. Northwest Territories
NY, N.Y. New York
N.Y.C. New York City
NYU New York University
N.Z. New Zealand

OAS Organization of American States
ob-gyn obstetrics-gynecology
obs. observatory
obstet. obstetrical
Oct. October
OD, O.D. Doctor of Optometry
OECD Organization of European Cooperation and Development
OEEC Organization of European Economic Cooperation
OEO Office of Economic Opportunity
ofcl. official
OH Ohio
OK Oklahoma
Okla. Oklahoma
ON Ontario
Ont. Ontario
ophthal. ophthalmological
ops. operations
OR Oregon
orch. orchestra
Oreg. Oregon
orgn. organization
ornithol. ornithological
OSHA Occupational Safety and Health Administration
OSRD Office of Scientific Research and Development
OSS Office of Strategic Services
osteo. osteopathic
otol. otological
otolaryn. otolaryngological

PA, Pa. Pennsylvania
P.A. Professional Association
paleontol. paleontological
path. pathological
P.C. Professional Corporation
PE Prince Edward Island
P.E.I. Prince Edward Island (text only)
PEN Poets, Playwrights, Editors, Essayists and Novelists (international association)
penol. penological
P.E.O. women's organization (full name not disclosed)
pfc. private first class
PHA Public Housing Administration
pharm. pharmaceutical
PharmD, Pharm.D. Doctor of Pharmacy
PharmM, Pharm.M. Master of Pharmacy
PhB, Ph.B. Bachelor of Philosophy
PhD, Ph.D. Doctor of Philosophy
PhM, Ph.M. Master of Philosophy
Phila. Philadelphia
philharm. philharmonic
philol. philological
philos. philosophical
photog. photographic
phys. physical
physiol. physiological
Pitts. Pittsburgh
Pkwy. Parkway
Pl. Place
P.&L.E.R.R. Pittsburgh & Lake Erie Railroad
P.O. Post Office
PO Box Post Office Box
polit. political
poly. polytechnic, polytechnical
PQ Province of Quebec
PR, P.R. Puerto Rico
prep. preparatory
pres. president
Presbyn. Presbyterian
presdl. presidential
prin. principal
proc. proceedings
prod. produced (play production)
prodn. production
prof. professor
profl. professional
prog. progressive
propr. proprietor
pros. atty. prosecuting attorney
pro tem pro tempore
PSRO Professional Services Review Organization
psychiat. psychiatric
psychol. psychological
PTA Parent-Teachers Association
ptnr. partner
PTO Pacific Theatre of Operations, Parent Teacher Organization
pub. publisher, publishing, published
pub. public
publ. publication
pvt. private

quar. quarterly
qm. quartermaster
Q.M.C. Quartermaster Corps
Que. Quebec

radiol. radiological
RAF Royal Air Force
RCA Radio Corporation of America
RCAF Royal Canadian Air Force
RD Rural Delivery
Rd. Road
REA Rural Electrification Administration
rec. recording
ref. reformed
regt. regiment
regtl. regimental
rehab. rehabilitation
Rep. Republican
rep. representative
Res. Reserve
ret. retired
rev. review, revised
RFC Reconstruction Finance Corporation
RFD Rural Free Delivery
rhinol. rhinological
RI, R.I. Rhode Island
RN, R.N. Registered Nurse
roentgenol. roentgenological
ROTC Reserve Officers Training Corps
R.R. Railroad
Ry. Railway

S. South
s. son
SAC Strategic Air Command
SALT Strategic Arms Limitation Talks
S.Am. South America
san. sanitary
SAR Sons of the American Revolution
Sask. Saskatchewan
savs. savings
SB, S.B. Bachelor of Science
SBA Small Business Administration
SC, S.C. South Carolina
SCAP Supreme Command Allies Pacific
ScB, Sc.B. Bachelor of Science
SCD, S.C.D. Doctor of Commercial Science
ScD, Sc.D. Doctor of Science
sch. school
sci. science, scientific
SCLC Southern Christian Leadership Conference
SCV Sons of Confederate Veterans
SD, S.D. South Dakota

SE Southeast
SEATO Southeast Asia Treaty Organization
SEC Securities and Exchange Commission
sec. secretary
sect. section
seismol. seismological
sem. seminary
Sept. September
s.g. senior grade
sgt. sergeant
SHAEF Supreme Headquarters Allied Expeditionary Forces
SHAPE Supreme Headquarters Allied Powers in Europe
S.I. Staten Island
S.J. Society of Jesus (Jesuit)
SJD Scientiae Juridicae Doctor
SK Saskatchewan
SM, S.M. Master of Science
So. Southern
soc. society
sociol. sociological
S.P. Co. Southern Pacific Company
spl. special
splty. specialty
Sq. Square
S.R. Sons of the Revolution
sr. senior
SS Steamship
SSS Selective Service System
St. Saint, Street
sta. station
stats. statistics
statis. statistical
STB, S.T.B. Bachelor of Sacred Theology
stblzn. stabilization
STD, STD Doctor of Sacred Theology
subs. subsidiary
SUNY State University of New York
supr. supervisor
supt. superintendent
surg. surgical
SW Southwest

TAPPI Technical Association of the Pulp and Paper Industry
Tb Tuberculosis
tchr. teacher
tech. technical, technology
technol. technological
Tel.&Tel. Telephone & Telegraph
temp. temporary
Tenn. Tennessee
Ter. Territory
Terr. Terrace
Tex. Texas
ThD, Th.D. Doctor of Theology
theol. theological
ThM, Th.M. Master of Theology
TN Tennessee
tng. training
topog. topographical
trans. transaction, transferred
transl. translation, translated
transp. transportation
treas. treasurer
TT Trust Territory
TV television
TVA Tennessee Valley Authority
twp. township
TX Texas
typog. typographical

U. University
UAW United Auto Workers
UCLA University of California at Los Angeles
UDC United Daughters of the Confederacy
U.K. United Kingdom
UN United Nations
UNESCO United Nations Educational, Scientific and Cultural Organization
UNICEF United Nations International Children's Emergency Fund
univ. university
UNRRA United Nations Relief and Rehabilitation Administration
UPI United Press International
U.P.R.R. United Pacific Railroad
urol. urological
U.S. United States
U.S.A. United States of America
USAAF United States Army Air Force
USAF United States Air Force
USAFR United States Air Force Reserve
USAR United States Army Reserve
USCG United States Coast Guard
USCGR United States Coast Guard Reserve
USES United States Employment Service
USIA United States Information Agency
USMC United States Marine Corps
USMCR United States Marine Corps Reserve
USN United States Navy
USNG United States National Guard
USNR United States Naval Reserve
USO United Service Organizations
USPHS United States Public Health Service
USS United States Ship
USSR Union of the Soviet Socialist Republics
USV United States Volunteers
UT Utah

VA Veterans' Administration
VA, Va. Virginia
vet. veteran, veterinary
VFW Veterans of Foreign Wars
VI, V.I. Virgin Islands
vice pres. vice president
vis. visiting
VISTA Volunteers in Service to America
VITA Volunteers in Technical Service
vocat. vocational
vol. volunteer, volume
v.p. vice president
vs. versus
VT, Vt. Vermont

W. West
WA Washington (state)
WAC Women's Army Corps
Wash. Washington (state)
WAVES Women's Reserve, US Naval Reserve
WCTU Women's Christian Temperance Union
we. western
W.Ger. Germany, Federal Republic of
WHO World Health Organization
WI Wisconsin
W.I. West Indies
Wis. Wisconsin
WSB Wage Stabilization Board
WV West Virginia
W.Va. West Virginia
WY Wyoming
Wyo. Wyoming

YK Yukon Territory
YMCA Young Men's Christian Association
YMHA Young Men's Hebrew Association
YM & YWHA Young Men's and Young Women's Hebrew Association
yr. year
YT, Y.T. Yukon Territory
YWCA Young Women's Christian Association

zool. zoological

Alphabetical Practices

Names are arranged alphabetically according to the surnames, and under identical surnames according to the first given name. If both surname and first given name are identical, names are arranged alphabetically according to the second given name. Where full names are identical, they are arranged in order of age—with the elder listed first.

Surnames beginning with De, Des, Du, however capitalized or spaced, are recorded with the prefix preceding the surname and arranged alphabetically under the letter D.

Surnames beginning with Mac and Mc are arranged alphabetically under M.

Surnames beginning with Saint or St. appear after names that begin Sains, are arranged according to the second part of the name, e.g. St. Clair before Saint Dennis.

Surnames beginning with Van, Von or von are arranged alphabetically under letter V.

Compound hyphenated surnames are arranged according to the first member of the compound. Compound unhyphenated surnames are treated as hyphenated names.

Parentheses used in connection with a name indicate which part of the full name is usually deleted in common usage. Hence Abbott, W(illiam) Lewis indicates that the usual form of the given name is W. Lewis. In such a case, the parentheses are ignored in alphabetizing. However, if the name is recorded Abbott, (William) Lewis, signifying that the entire name William is not commonly used, the alphabetizing would be arranged as though the name were Abbott, Lewis.

Who's Who in the Midwest

AAL, IRVIN E., tractor manufacturing company executive. Student, U. Minn. V.p., gen. mgr. Sperry New Holland, Pa., 1962-83; sr. v.p. Internat. Harvester Co., Chgo., 1983-85; pres., chief exec. officer Steiger Tractor Inc., Fargo, N.D., 1985—. Office: Steiger Tractor Inc 406 Main Fargo ND 58126 *

AANERUD, MELVIN BERNARD, government agency administrator; b. Spring Lake Park, Minn., Jan. 7, 1943; s. Bernard Melvin and Margaret Agnes (Beck) A.; B.A., U. Minn., 1964; m. Kathleen Dipprey, Aug. 19, 1978; children—Adam Curtis, Eric Christopher. Prodn. analyst Honeywell, Inc., New Brighton, Minn., 1966-68; plant mgr. Ault, Inc., Mpls., 1968-71; gen. mgr. Mille Lacs Reservation Bus. Enterprise, Vineland, Minn., 1971-74; bus. devel. specialist SBA, Mpls., 1974-78; asst. dist. dir. SBA, Mpls., 1978-80, dep. dist. dir., 1980-85, portfolio mgr., 1986—. Pres. Columbia Hts. Charter Commn., 1971-82; chmn. Minn. Minority Bus. Opportunity Com. 1976-79; treas. edn. adv. bd. McKinley Sch. Community; vice chmn., pres. park bd. Ham Lake; pres. Rodeo Days, Inc. . Served with Signal Corps, AUS, 1964-66. Recipient Gold Key Man award Minn. Jaycees, 1971, 76, Silver Key, 1973; Columbia Heights Disting. Service award, 1970, Columbia Hgts. Outstanding Civil Servant award, 1970; named One of 10 Outstanding Young Minnesotans, 1978. Mem. Minn. (dir. Minn. Jaycee Found. 1976-82), Columbia Heights (nat. U.S. dir. 1972-73) jaycees, U. Minn. Alumni Assn. Mem. Democratic Farm Labor party. Home: 15041 Fillmore NE Ham Lake MN 55304 Office: 100 N 6th St Butler Square Minneapolis MN 55402

AARON, R., movie theatre company executive. Pres. Plitt Theatres Inc., Chgo. Office: Plitt Theatres Inc 175 N State St Chicago IL 60601 *

AARONSON, ARTHUR LEE, psychologist; b. Detroit, Dec. 31, 1946; s. Max and Beatrice P. Aaronson; m. Ann Schroeder, June 10, 1978; children: Jacob Mathew, Adam Victor. BS, U. Mich., 1968; MA, Claremont Grad. Sch., 1971; postgrad., Wright State U., 1985—. Lic. psychologist, Ohio. Instr. Oakland Community Coll., Union Lake, Mich., 1971, Urbana (Ohio) Coll., 1971; psychology asst. Logan-Champaign Guidance Clinic, Urbana, 1971-73; psychologist II Lima (Ohio) State Hosp., 1973-83; psychology supr. Oakwood Forensic Ctr., Lima, 1983—; asst. clin. prof. Wright State U., Dayton, Ohio, 1984—. Contbr. articles to profl. jours. Mem. Am. Psychology Assn. (assoc.), Ohio Psychology Assn. (trustee 1984-86), State Assn. Psychologist and Psychology Assts. (pres. 1984-85). Democrat. Jewish. Avocations: ham radio, skiing. Home: 1005 Orders Ave Ada OH 45810 Office: Oakwood Forensic Ctr 3200 Northwest St Lima OH 45802

ABADI, JOSEPH, surgeon; b. Charleston, W.Va., Feb. 23, 1938; s. Samuel and Esther (Misseri)A.; m. Mary Ann Mustari, June 26, 1983; 1 child, Samuel. AA, Wright Jr. Coll., 1958; postgrad., Loyola U., Chgo., 1958-61, Roosevelt U., Chgo., 1963-64; DO, Chgo. Coll. Osteo. Medicine, 1968. Intern Chgo. Osteo. Hosp., 1968-69; resident in surgery Art Centre Hosp., Detroit, 1969-70, Met. Hosp., Phila., 1970-71; practice osteo. medicine specializing in surgery Detroit, 1971-82, Chgo., 1982—. Home and Office: 4139 W Suffield Ct Skokie IL 60076

ABBASI, TARIQ AFZAL, psychiatrist, educator; b. Hyderabad, India, Aug. 13, 1946; came to U.S., 1976, naturalized, 1983; s. Shujaat Ali and Salma Khatoon (Siddiqui) A.; m. Kashifa Khatoon, Nov. 10, 1972; children—Sameena, Omar, Osman. B.S., Madrasa-I-Aliya, Hyderabad, 1964; M.B.B.S., Osmania Med. Coll., Hyderabad, 1970; Diploma in Psychol. Medicine, St. John's Hosp., U. Sheffield (Eng.), 1976. Diplomate Am. Bd. Psychiatry and Neurology; diplomate in psychiatry Royal Coll. Physicians of Eng. Sr. house officer St. John's Hosp., Lincoln, Eng., 1972-73, registrar, 1973-76; resident in psychiatry Rutgers Med. Sch., Piscataway, N.J., 1976-79, chief resident, 1979, dir. adult in-patient services Community Mental Health Ctr., Rutgers Med. Sch., also asst. prof. psychiatry, 1979-82; staff psychiatrist Northville Regional Psychiat. Hosp. (Mich.), 1982-83, sect. dir., 1983—; cons. psychiatrist Rahway State Prison (N.J.), 1979-82; clin. instr. psychiatry Wayne State U. Med. Sch., Detroit. Mem. Am. Psychiat. Assn., Mich. Psychiat. Soc. Office: Northville Regional Psychiat Hosp 41001 Seven Mile Rd Northville MI 48167 also: Personal Dynamics Ctr 22646 Michigan Ave Dearborn MI 48124

ABBASY, IFTIKHARUL H., surgeon; b. Pakistan, Oct. 28, 1935; s. Ikramul Haque and Mumtaz Begum; came to U.S., 1964, naturalized, 1970; M.B., B.S., Dow Med. Coll., Karachi, Pakistan, 1961; m. Karen Gaye Hampton, Feb. 14, 1969; 1 dau., Shameem Ara. Intern, Civil Hosp., Karachi, Pakistan, 1961-62, St. Olaves Hosp., London, 1962-63; resident in surgery E. Ham Meml. Hosp., London, 1963, Michael Reese Hosp., Chgo., 1965-69; practice medicine specializing in gen. surgery and peripheral vascular surgery, Villa Park, Ill., 1969—; mem. staff Meml. Hosp., Elmhurst, Ill., McHenry (Ill.) Hosp., Good Samaritan Hosp., Downers Grove, Ill., Harvard (Ill.) Community Hosp. Diplomate Am. Bd. Surgery. Fellow A.C.S., Internat. Coll. Surgeons, Royal Coll. Surgeons Can.; mem. AMA (Physicians's Recognition award 1974-77). Home: 905 Burroak Ct Oak Brook IL 60521 Office: 10 E Central Blvd Villa Park IL 60181

ABBATE, SANDRA JEAN REED, educational administrator; b. Warren, Ohio, Apr. 20, 1941; d. Gilbert Vernon and Clara Helen (Mount) Reed; m. Ciro F. Abbate, Dec. 21, 1984. Student Kent (Ohio) State U., 1959-62; BS in Edn., Youngstown (Ohio) State U., 1964; postgrad. Purdue U., 1969-70; MS in Edn., No. Ill. U., 1977. Tchr. elem. sch., Mineral Ridge, Ohio, 1962-66, Kent pub. schs., 1966-68, Duneland Sch. Corp., Chesterton, Ind., 1969-70, Overseas Dependent Schs., Germany, 1971-73; coordinator career edn. Thornton Area Pub. Sch. Corp., 1973-76; dir. DuPage Career Edn. Center, Wheaton, Ill., 1976-83; dir. No. Ill. U. Office for Computer Learning, MIS dir., DeKalb, 1983—; sex equity cons. Ill. Bd. Edn.; mem. teaching staff Nat. Coll. Edn., Evanston, Ill., Governors State U., Park Forest, Ill., No. Ill. U., DeKalb; cons. to Cook and DuPage Counties, SBA, U.S. Office of Career Edn., Washington. Office: No Ill U Office for Computer Learning Coll Continuing Edn DeKalb IL 60115

ABBOTT, DAVID HENRY, manufacturing company executive; b. Milton, Ky., July 6, 1936; s. Carl and Rachael (Miles) A.; m. Joan Shefchik, Aug. 14, 1976; children—Kristine, Gina, Beth, Linsey. B.S., U. Ky., 1960, M.B.A., 1961. With Ford Motor Co., Louisville, Mpls. and Dearborn, Mich., 1961-69; div. controller J I Case Co., Racine, Wis., 1970-73, gen. mgr. service parts supply, 1973-75, v.p., 1975-81, v.p. and gen. mgr. constrn. equipment, 1975-77; v.p., gen. mgr. Drott div. J I Case Co., Wausau, Wis., 1977-79, exec. v.p. worldwide constrn. equipment, 1979-81; pres., chief operating officer Portec, Inc., Oak Brook, Ill., 1981—, also dir.; dir. Oak Brook Bank, 1982—. Served with U.S. Army, 1958. Mem. Constrn. Industry Mfrs. Assn. (bd. dirs. 1979-81, 82—). Republican. Home: 41 Steeple Ridge Ct Oak Brook IL 60521 Office: Portec Inc 300 Windsor Dr Oak Brook IL 60521

ABBOTT, DAVID WARREN, psychiatrist. m. ViAnn M. Carlson, June 21, 1969 (div. May 1985); children: Mark Benjamin, Natalie Marina; m. Jane C. Voglewede, May 30, 1982. BA, Concordia Coll., 1970; MD, Tulane U., 1973. Cert. Am. Bd. Psychiatry and Neurology. Resident in psychiatry Tulane U. Hosps., La., 1973-74, U. Minn. Hosps., Mpls., 1974-76; psychiatrist Southeast Human Service Ctr., Fargo, N.D., 1979-81; psychiatrist Fargo Clinic, Ltd., 1977-79, 81—, dir. eating disorders program, 1985—; asst. prof. dept. neuroscience U. N.D. Sch. Medicine, Fargo, 1979-81; cons. St. Luke's Hosp., Fargo, 1978-80, N.D. State Hosp., Jamestown, 1980-83; med. dir. Southeast Human Service Ctr., Fargo, 1979-83, adult psychiatry St. Ansgar Hosp., Moorhead, Minn., 1984-87. Mem. AMA, Am. Acad. Med. Dirs., Am. Psychiat. Assn., N.D. Med. Assn. Office: Fargo Clinic Ltd Dept Psychiatry 700 S 1st Ave Fargo ND 58103

ABBOTT, MARY ANN, tobacco company executive; b. Indpls., Sept. 29, 1955; d. Elwood L. and Shirley (Kirch) McElhiney; m. Theodore L. Abbott, Sept. 4, 1982; 1 child, Lindsey. BS, Ball State U., 1977; postgrad., Eastern Mich. U., 1984-85. Tchr. Northview Jr. High Sch., Indpls., 1977-79; sales rep. Brown & Williamson Tobacco Co., Indpls., 1979-80; field sales asst. Brown & Williamson Tobacco Co., Columbus, Ohio, 1980-81; div. sales mgr. Brown & Williamson Tobacco Co., Peoria, Ill., 1981-82; key accounts mgr. Brown & Williamson Tobacco Co., Detroit, 1982—. Mem. Tobacco Action Network. Republican. Roman Catholic. Avocations: aerobics, needlepoint, reading, skiing. Office: Brown & Williamson Tobacco Corp 31313 Northwestern Hwy Suite 124 Farmington Hills MI 48108

ABBOTT, ROBERT ELLIOTT, management analyst; b. Concord, N.H., Feb. 4, 1946; s. Robert Elliot Abbott and Ruth Gertrude (Bent) Bombera; m. Roswitha Maria Dotzel, Nov. 9, 1980; children: Michelle, Robert. Machine design degree, Wentworth Inst., 1964; BS in Mgmt., Park Coll., 1985. Commd. U.S. Army, 1971, advanced through ranks to capt., engr. officer, ret., 1985; mgmt. analyst U.S. Army, Ft. Leavenworth, Kans., 1986; rep. Mutual of Omaha, Nebr., 1985—; cons. Leavenworth County, 1986. Mem. Soc. Am. Mil. Engrs., Am. Legion (judge adv. 1978-79, vice comdr. 1980-81), MENSA. Republican. Avocations: auto and boat restoration. Home: 1311 Olive St Leavenworth KS 66048 Office: Comptroller Meddac Fort Leavenworth KS 66027

ABBOUD, A. ROBERT, consultant and investor, former banker and oil company executive; b. Boston, May 29, 1929; s. Alfred and Victoria (Karam) A.; m. Joan Grover, June 11, 1955; children: Robert, Jeanne Frances, Katherine Jane. B.S. cum laude, Harvard U., 1951, LL.B., 1956, M.B.A., 1958. Asst. cashier First Nat. Bank of Chgo., 1960-62, asst. v.p., 1962-64, v.p., 1964-69, sr. v.p., 1969-72, exec. v.p., 1972-73, vice chmn. bd., 1973-74, dep. chmn. bd., 1974-75, chmn. bd., chief exec. officer, 1975-80; pres., chief operating officer Occidental Petroleum Corp., Los Angeles, 1980-84; pres. A. Robert Abboud and Co., Fox River Grove, Ill., Braeburn Capital, Inc.; bd. dirs. Hart Schaffner & Marx, Inland Steel Co., ICN Pharm., Inc., AAR Corp., Washington Bankcorp. Served with USMCR, 1951-53. Clubs: Econ, Chicago, Comml, Barrington Hills Country. Office: A Robert Abboud and Co 212 Stone Hill Ctr Fox River Grove IL 60021

ABBOUD, CHRISTOPHER WILLIAM, state senator; b. Omaha, Aug. 29, 1956; s. Fred Abboud and Bonny Burgess. B.A., Creighton U., 1978; J.D., U. Nebr., 1982. Mem. Nebr. Senate, 1983—. Mem. German-Am. Soc., ABA, Nebr. Bar Assn., Ralston Area C. of C., Phi Alpha Theta, Sigma Alpha Epsilon. Republican. Lodge: Rotary. Office: 7515 Highland St Ralston NE 68127

ABDALLA, LAWRENCE HAMADI, personnel resources executive; b. Kansas City, Mo., Apr. 13, 1954. Cert. in Indsl. Adminstrn., Gen. Motors Inst., 1978. Sr. specification analyst Gen. Motors Corp., Warren, Mich., 1978-82; pres. World Aid Assn., Kansas City, 1982-83; chief exec. Exec. Service Corp., Kansas City, Mo., 1983—; trade cons. Mich. Fast Food Supply Corp., Detorit, 1980-82. Author: Tips on Buying Used Cars, 1981. Mem. Rep. Nat. Com., Washington, 1980—. Mem. Agora Internat., Trans-World Nat. Resources (exec. bd. dirs. 1985-86).

ABDOLLAHIAN, AMIR, orthopedic surgeon; b. Khorasan, Iran, Sept. 7, 1933; came to U.S., 1972, naturalized, 1973; s. Abdoghasam and Massoumeh (Fazel) A.; m. Karen G. Ostergard, July 16, 1966; children: Mark Andrew, Neil Peiman. Diploma Natural Sci., Ferdowsi Coll., Meshed, Iran, 1951; MD, U. Meshed, 1957. Practice medicine specializing in orthopaedic surgery Cuyahoga Falls, Ohio, 1969—; asst. prof. orthopedics Northeast Ohio U., Rootstown, 1980—. Fellow AMA, Summit County Med. Soc., Ohio State Med. Assn., Am. Acad. Orthopedic Surgeons, Am. Trauma Soc. (founding mem.), Cleve. Orthopedic Club. Office: 275 Graham Rd Suite 4 Cuyahoga Falls OH 44313

ABEC, JAMES MARTIN, psychologist; b. Tangiers, Morroco, Nov. 4, 1944; came to U.S., 1957; s. Maurice and Margareta (Juhasz) A. BA, Rutgers U., 1967; MS, Ill. Inst. Tech., 1973, PhD, 1975. Registered psychologist, Ill. Staff psychologist Dupage Mental Health, Wheaton, Ill., 1975-78, supr. mental health, 1978-79; asst. dir. Chgo. Stress Ctr., 1979—; pvt. practice psychology Chgo., 1979—. Served to capt. U.S. Army, 1968-72, Vietnam. Fellow Am. Orthopsychiat. Assn.; mem. Am. Psychol. Assn. Republican. Unitarian. Avocations: skiing, travel. Home: 4630 N Virginia Ave Chicago IL 60625 Office: 477 E Butterfield Rd Suite 204 Lombard IL 60148

ABEL, JOHN PHILLIP, firefighter; b. Pekin, Ill., Nov. 28, 1947; s. Erven George and Eleanor Kay (Graber) A.; m. Alma Jean Buffington; children: Susan, Steven, Shane. AAS, Ill. Cen. Coll., 1983. Firefighter City of Pekin, Ill., 1977—. Chmn. Tazewell County br. ARC, 1985—. Served to sgt. USAF, 1966-70. Mem. Internat. Assn. Firefighters, Nat. Assn. Emergency Med. Technicians, Ill. Emergency Med. Technicians. Republican. Lodges: Optimists, Elks. Avocations: jogging, reading, volunteer work, gardening. Home: 217 Indian Creek Dr Pekin IL 61554

ABEL, RAYMOND JOSEPH, programmer, system analyst, electrical technician, engineering analyst; b. Darby, Penn., Nov. 22, 1960; s. Paul Raymond and Elizabeth Ann (Smith) A. Student, Pa. State U., 1979-82; BA in Math. and Computer Sci., Shippensburg U., 1983. Engring. analyst Farrall Instruments Inc., Grand Island, Nebr., 1984—. Home: 1021 W John St Grand Island NE 68801 Office: Farrall Instruments Inc Arch Ave & W Hwy 30 Grand Island NE 68802

ABELE, TED MERL, management company executive; b. Nevada, Mo., Feb. 21, 1951; s. Calvin C. and Wanda F. (Smith) A.; m. Heddy Marie Rekieta, May 1, 1978 (div. May 1986); children: Justin Grady, Ashley Elizabeth. BS in Agrl. Econs. with honors, U. Mo., 1973; MS in Agrl. Econs. with honors, Tex. A&M U., 1976. Fieldman Fed. Intermediate Credit Bank, St. Louis, 1973; asst. v.p. Ozark Prodn. Credit, Springfield, Mo., 1973-74; credit examiner Farm Credit Adminstrn., Bloomington, Minn., 1976-77; sr. ptnr. Abele Farms, El Dorado Springs, Mo., 1977-82; chief exec. officer Am. Agrinomics Mgmt. Co., Nevada, 1979-82, pres., chmn. bd. dirs., 1982—; arbitrator Commodity Futures Assn., Chgo., 1984-86; bd. dirs. Agrl. Leaders of Tomorrow, Columbia, Mo., The Blair Found., Kansas City, Mo. Author: Limited Partnerships: Impact on Texas Agriculture, 1976; editor Am. Farmarket Letter, 1984-86. Council pres. St. Paul's Luth. Ch., Nevada, 1984; chmn. Vernon County (Mo.) Rep. Com., 1979-80; mem. Gov.'s Com. on Agriculture, Mo., 1980-84; advisor Congressmen Skeltons Com. on Agriculture, Mo., 1982-84. Named one of Outstanding Young Men of Am., 1985. Mem. Am. Soc. Agrl. Cons. (sr.), Mo. Soc. Farm Mgrs. and Rural Appraisors, Nat. Futures Assn. Club: Know Not Investment (chmn. investment com. 1985-86) (Nevada). Avocations: flying, tennis, racquetball, guitar, poetry. Home: 2017 N Washington Nevada MO 64772 Office: Am Agrinomics Mgmt Co Inc PO Drawer 638 Nevada MO 64772

ABEL HOROWITZ, MICHELLE SUSAN, advertising agency executive; b. Detroit, Mar. 31, 1950; d. Martin Louis and Phyllis (Berkowitz) A.; m. H. Jay Abel Horowitz, July 11, 1976; children—Jordan Michael, Stefanie Jennifer. Student Goucher Coll., 1967-70; B.A. in Econs., U. Mich., 1971; postgrad. in econs. U. Calif.-San Diego, 1973; M.A. in Econs., U. Detroit, 1974-76. Planning group supr. Hill Holliday Connors, Cosmopolus, Mass., 1974-78; econ. analyst Data Resources, Boston, 1978-79; v.p., media dir. Barkley & Evergreen, Southfield, Mich., 1979-80; v.p., dir. mktg. and media Yaffe/Berline, Southfield, Mich., 1980-82; sr. v.p., dir. client services, corp. treas. Berline Group, Birmingham, Mich., 1982—; instr. Oakland U., Rochester, Mich., 1982; trustee, chairperson mktg. com. Harbinger Dance Co., Farmington, Mich., 1983—. Named Advt. Woman of Yr., Women's Ad Club Detroit, 1982. Mem. Adcraft Club Detroit, Women in Communications. Democrat. Jewish. Office: The Berline Group 31600 Telegraph Rd #100 Birmingham MI 48010-3439

ABELN, JAMES MEAGHER, management consultant; b. Holdingford, Minn., Jan. 27, 1925; s. Bennedict Aloise and Katherine (Meagher) A.; m. Bernice Sogolik, Nov. 24, 1950 (div. Jan. 1976); children: Michael, Nancy, Julie, Elizabeth, Emily; m. Ethel Hennerita Peterson, Sept. 2, 1978. BA, U. Minn., 1949. Indsl. engr. Gen. Mills Inc., Mpls., 1950-51; quality engr. Northrop Aircraft, Hawthorne, Calif., 1951-52, Honeywell, Mpls., 1952-62; pres. A&G Engring., Mpls., 1962—. Served with U.S. Army, 1943-46. Mem. Am. Soc. Quality Control (sr.), Minn. Soc. Indsl. Engrs. (sr.), Sales and Mktg. Execs., Tower Investment Club. Lodges: Sertoma, KC, Lions. Avocations: golfing, tennis, travelling. Home: 10511 Cedar Lake Rd #210 Minnetonka MN 55343 Office: A&G Engring 7515 Wayzata Blvd #208 Minneapolis MN 55426

ABELOV, STEPHEN LAWRENCE, manufacturing company executive; b. N.Y.C., Apr. 1, 1923; s. Saul S. and Ethel (Esterman) A.; B.S., NYU, 1945, M.B.A., 1950; m. Phyllis S. Lichtenson, Nov. 18, 1945; children—Patricia C. (Mrs. Marvin Demoff), Gary M. Asst. div. mgr. Nat. Silver Co., N.Y., 1945; sales rep. Angelica Uniform Co., N.Y., 1945-50; asst. sales mgr., 1950-56, western regional mgr., Los Angeles, 1956-66, v.p. Angelica Uniform Co. of Calif., 1958-66, nat. v.p. sales, 1966-72, v.p. Angelica Corp. 1968—group v.p. mktg., 1972-80, exec. v.p., chief mktg. officer Angelica Uniform Group, 1980—; vis. lectr. mktg. NYU Grad. Sch. Bus. Adminstrn. Vice comdr. Am. Legion; mem. vocational adv. bd. VA.; adv. bd. Woodcraft Rangers; bd. dirs. Univ. Temple. Mem. Am. Assn. Contamination Control (dir.), Am. Soc. for Advancement Mgmt. (chpt. pres.), Am. Mktg. Assn., Health Industries Assn. Am. (dir.), Inst. Environ. Scis., various trade assns., St. Louis Council on World Affairs, NYU Alumni Assn., Phi Epsilon Pi (treas.). Mem. B'nai B'rith (past pres.). Clubs: Men's (exec. v.p.); Town Hall, NYU, Aqua Sierra Sportsmen, Clayton. Contbr. articles to profl. jours. Home: 9821 Log Cabin Ct Ladue MO 63124 Office: Angelica Corp 10176 Corporate Square Dr Saint Louis MO 63132

ABEND, STEPHEN NEIL, architect; b. Kansas City, Mo., Sept. 19, 1939; s. Joseph S. and Esther (Greenfeld) A.; m. Sherri Grossman, 1962 (div. 1970); m. Barbara A. Alport, Sept. 2, 1972; children: Sarah Heather, Lynda Joelle. BArch, Washington U., St. Louis, 1962; MArch, U. Pa., 1965; course in Japanese garden design, Harvard U., 1985. Lic. architect, Mo., Kans., Tex., Colo., Utah, Ark., Nebr., Okla. Architect Kivett & Myers, Kansas City, 1965-67, Marshall & Brown, Kansas City, 1967-68; ptnr. Urban Architects, Kansas City, 1968-72; pres. Abend Singleton Assocs. Inc., Kansas City, 1972—; assoc. prof. Kans. U. Sch. of Architecture and Design, Lawrence, 1968-70, bd. advisor, 1974-75; critic/juror U. Kans., 1981-86; teaching fellow U. Pa., 1964-65; lectr. Kans. State Sch. of Architecture, Manhattan, 1980-86, "Beyond Fascades" series U. Kans., 1981, "Architecture of the Plains" series, 1984; guest speaker "Skylines" pub. TV series, 1987. Prin. works include Clay County Govt. Complex, State of Mo. Ct. Appeals, Grace Holy Trinity Cathedrals, Shalom Plaza, Westport House, Nev. State Sch. and Hosp. Med. Clinic, United Mo. Bank Hdqrs., Command & Gen. Staff Coll. Bell Hall, Jeanne Jugan Ctr., Yellow Freight Corp. Hdqrs., Whitaker Cable Corp. Hdqrs., Prairie View Park & Recreation Facilities, UMKC Recreation & Athlete Bldg., Pembroke Hill Auditorium & Student Ctr.; founding sponsor Louis I KAHN Meml. Archives U. Pa.; illustrator: Ford Found. Anthology of City Planning, 1965; contbr. articles to profl. jours. Bd. dirs. Jewish Geriatric and Convalescent Ctr., Kansas City, Kehilath Israel Synagogue, Kansas City; active Hist. Kansas City Found., Clay County Devel. Commn. Kans. State Hist. Soc.; founding mem. Kansas City Consensus; mem. Kansas Capitol Bldg. Art Selection Com.; Am. Jewish Com., Am. Arbitration Soc., social service budget com. Jewish Fedn. & Council of Kansas City, Jewish Family & Children's Services Agy., Kansas City Mus. Recipient 1st Place award Ruberoid Nat. Competition, 1962, 2d Place award Wainwright Nat. Competition, 1975, Urban Design awards Mcpl. Art Commn., 1980, 84. Mem. AIA (pres. Kansas City chpt. 1985, Craftsmanship award 1969, 71, 73, 75, 77, 79, 81, Design award 1986), Mo. Council Architects (bd. dirs. 1984-87), Pres.'s Rountable. Club: Friends of Art. Avocations: travel, gardening, art collecting. Office: Abend Singleton Assocs Inc 20 West 9 Kansas City MO 64105

ABERDEEN, JEFFERY, accountant; b. Chgo., Mar. 6, 1954; s. Donald Edward and Lois Carolyn (Peterson) A.; m. Kathleen Joan Johnson, Oct. 27, 1979; children: Jill, Steven, Michelle. BA, Augustana Coll., Rock Island, Ill., 1976. CPA, Iowa. Sr. mgr. auditing Peat, Marwick & Mitchell, Davenport, Iowa, 1976-85; dir. internal auditing Davenport Bank and Trust Co., Davenport, 1985—. Mem. Am. Inst. CPA's, Iowa Soc. CPA's, Bettendorf (Iowa) C. of C. Republican. Lutheran. Home: 3132 Willowwood Dr Bettendorf IA 52722 Office: Davenport Bank and Trust Co 201 W 3d Davenport IA 52801

ABERNATHY, MAX ROLAND, pharmaceutical company executive; b. St. Louis, Nov. 15, 1931; med. technician diploma, Gradwohl Sch. Lab. Technique, St. Louis, 1956; student Stowe Tchrs. Coll., St. Louis; m. Georgia M. Taylor; 9 children. Mem. staff Washington U. Hosps., 1956-68, chief med. technologist Outpatient Clinic and Barnes Hosp. Labs., 1961-68; instr. clin. and lab. medicine Washington U. Med. Sch., 1964-68; clin. systems sales rep., then asso. research scientist tech. services lab. Ames div. Miles Labs. Inc., Elkhart, Ind., 1968-74, various positions, 1974-77, sr. project mgr. blood chemistry systems, growth and devel., 1977-78, sr. tech. tng. specialist, 1978, mgr. tech. tng., 1978-83, mgr. tech. services and tng. internat., 1983, supr. customer services, 1983-84, pub. relations prodn. coordinator, 1984-85, supr. customer services, 1985—. Past pres. Elkhart County NAACP, producer Outreach radio show. Recipient Best Tech. Paper award Internat. Soc. Clin. Lab. Technologists, 1966; Gov.'s award Volunteerism. Mem. Am. Soc. Med. Technologists, Nat. Soc. Histotech. (charter), Ind. Soc. Med. Technologists, Internat. Soc. Clin. Lab. Technologists, Alumni Assn. Gradwohl Sch. (past pres.; Honor Soc. Key 1965). Home: 19 Sunrise Dr Elkhart IN 46517 Office: Miles Labs Inc PO Box 40 Elkhart IN 46515

ABINGTON, EUGENE BRYANT, management consultant; b. Chgo., Aug. 5, 1937; s. Homer Oregon and Petronia Christine (Bryant) A.; B.S., Roosevelt U., 1977, M.S., 1981; m. Michelle Stevens, Jan. 30, 1979; children by previous marriage—Tarra, Carla, Brian, Kimberly. Investigator, Chgo. Police Force, 1964—; chmn. bd. Abington Enterprises, Inc., Chgo., 1978—; pres. AEI Mgmt. & Cons. Co., 1979—; pres. Char-Gene, Ltd., 1982—. Owner, founder Ida B. Wells Barnett Mus., 1981—; pres. Near South Coalition Community Orgns., 1983—, A Growing Concern, 1984—. Democrat. Methodist.

ABLAHAT, NEWTON ANDRE, business consultant; b. Chgo.; s. Haidow and Katie (Samuels) A.; B.S., Northwestern U., 1937; postgrad. U. Chgo.,

1940, U. Colo., 1943, Johns Hopkins U., 1953-55, Syracuse U., 1961, Am. U., 1965-67; m. Ella May Cason, June 14, 1947; 1 son, Roger Haydon. Mgr. mdse. research, mgr. credit research Spiegel, Inc., Chgo., 1938-41, mgr. market research, 1946-47, dir. policy, 1948-50; economist WPB, Washington, 1941-42; econ. intelligence officer, Yenan, China, 1943-45; exporter Trans World Assos., 1947; cons. Bur. Labor Stats., Washington, 1950-53; analyst ORO, Johns Hopkins U., 1953-56; head ops. research Gen. Electric Co., Phila., 1956-58; cons. Haskins & Sells, Chgo., 1958; cons. Gen. Electric Co., Syracuse, Europe and Washington, 1959-67; v.p. corp. planning dept. Investors Diversified Services, Inc., Mpls., 1967-80; pres. The Stratcon Group Inc., Mpls., 1980—; bus. cons. to fgn. firms; past cons. U.S. Dept. Transp.; dir. New Beginning Funds, Sherlock's Book Home. Bd. dirs. Suburban Community Services. Served with USNR, 1943; CBI. Mem. Council Ind. Profl. Cons. (dir.), Am. Finance Assn., Nat. Assn. Bus. Economists, Ops. Research Soc., Inst. Mgmt. Scis., N.Am. Soc. Corp. Planners, Assn. Corp. Growth. Home: 5200 Chantrey Rd Edina MN 55436 Office: Stratcon Group Inc 7600 Parklawn Ave Suite 257 Minneapolis MN 55435

ABLE, WARREN WALTER, natural resource company executive; b. Seymour, Ind., Mar. 3, 1932; s. Walter Cudwith and Edith (Harmon) A.; m. Joan Graham, May 6, 1956; children: Susan, Nancy, Cynthia, Wally. AB, Ind. U., 1953, MD, 1956, JD, 1968. Bar: Ind. 1968. Physician Columbus (Ind.) Med. Soc., 1960-76; pres. Able Energy Co. Inc., Evansville, Ind., 1968—. Editor: Lawyer's Medical Cyclopedia, 1967-68. Bd. dirs. Bartholomew Consol. Sch. Corp., Columbus, Ind., 1970-74. Served as surgeon USPHS, 1957-59. Mem. AMA, Ind. Med. Soc., ABA, Ind. Bar Soc. Democrat. Mem. Disciples of Christ Ch. Avocations: aviation, farming. Home: 4253 Windsor Ln Columbus IN 47201 Office: Able Energy Co Inc 101 Court Street Evansville IN 47708

ABLER, JOYCE LESCELIUS, systems analyst; b. Owosso, Mich., Oct. 13, 1941; d. Toivo Joseph and Agdrina I. (Tahtinen) Lescelius; B.S., Central Mich. U., 1963, M.B.A., 1973. Acct., Dow Chem. Co., Midland, Mich., 1963-64, Sterling Nat. Industries, Milw., 1965; with Molson's Breweries Ont., Ltd. (Can.), 1965-67, B.F. Goodrich Can. Ltd., Kitchener, Ont., 1967-71; systems analyst Central Mich. U., Mt. Pleasant, 1971—; faculty Northwood Inst., Midland, Mich., 1976-78, Central Mich. U., 1978—; sec.-treas. Data Basic Inc., 1980-81. Mem. computer adv. com. Mt. Pleasant High Sch., 1976-79; treas. ch. council Zion Luth. Ch., Mt. Pleasant, 1977—. Mem. Data Processing Mgmt. Assn. (sec. 1972-78, v.p. 1978, pres. 1979, newsletter editor 1980-84), Alpha Sigma Alpha (province dir. 1976—, collegiate sorority advisor 1971-80, dir. 1980-83, scholarship chmn. 1982-84). Home: 1018 Main St Mount Pleasant MI 48858 Office: 10 Foust Hall Central Mich Univ Mount Pleasant MI 48859

ABNEE, A. VICTOR, III, information systems executive; b. Cin., Feb. 11, 1952; s. A. Victor Jr. and Doris (Heuck) A.; m. Nina Louise Heagstedt, Mar. 1, 1986; 1 child, Louise Heagstedt. BA, Williams Coll., 1974. Mgr. data processing Strick Corp., Fairless Hills, Pa., 1979-81; mgr. cost acctg. Strick Corp., Fairless Hills, 1981, dir. market research, 1981-82; comptroller Balimoy Mfg., Kinross, Mich., 1982-83; v.p. mgmt. info. systems Baird & Warner, Inc., Chgo., 1983—; cons. in field. Mem. Phi Beta Kappa. Club: East Bank (Chgo.). Home: 2512 N Burling St Chicago IL 60614 Office: Baird & Warner Inc 200 W Madison St Chicago IL 60606

ABNEY, CHARLOTTE MAXINE, school counselor, librarian; b. Courtois, Mo., May 9, 1936; d. Grayfer Leo and Isla (Evans) A.; student (Valedictorian scholar, Delta Kappa Gamma scholar) Flat River Jr. Coll., 1953-54; B.S. in Edn. cum laude, SW Mo. State U., 1962, M.S. in Guidance and Counseling, 1970. Mgr., Abneys' Restaurant, Caledonia, Mo., 1954-55; tchr. Grandview R-II Sch., Ware, Mo., 1955-60; tchr., librarian Bismarck (Mo.) R-V Sch., 1960-67, 1969-74, counselor, librarian, 1974—; lectr. edn. and child devel.; tchr. rep. Bd. Edn., 1972-75; cons. to Mo. Dept. Edn. Certified tchr., sch. psychol. examiner, counselor, librarian. Mem. Am. Assn. Counseling and Devel., Am. Sch. Counselors Assn., Mo. Sch. Counselor Assn., Southeast Mo. Sch. Counselor Assn. Southeast Mo. Dept. Sch. Librarians, St. Francois County Edn. Assn. (sec. 1965-66), Mo. Assn. Sch. Librarians, Bismarck R-V Community, Mo. State tchrs. assns. Methodist. Home: Box 707 Bismarck MO 63624 Office: Bismarck Sch Dist Campus Dr Bismarck MO 63624

ABRAHAM, BETTE HAVENS, business consultant; b. Meriden, Conn., June 19, 1946; d. John Joseph and Abina Dorothy (Walsh) Havens; B.A. with honors, Lake Erie Coll., 1968; M.A., U. N.D., 1970; postgrad. M.B.A. program U. Minn., 1981; m. Alden A. Abraham, Aug. 29, 1970. Tchr., Chgo. Sch. for Retarded, 1971; supr. psychology dept. London Meml. Hosp., Chgo., 1971-75; pvt. practice psychotherapy, Chgo., 1975-77, Mpls., 1977—; cons. Paul Cekan, M.D., 1975-77, Anil Godbole, M.D., 1976-77; assoc. Transculture Center for Human Relations, 1974-76, Chgo. Med. Sch. Faculty, 1974-76, Ill. Psychol. Assn., 1974-77; group psychotherapist Abbott Northwestern Hosp., Mpls., 1977-78; family therapist Exodus, St. Paul, 1978; reach coordinator Mental Health Assn. Minn., 1979; fin. analyst Pillsbury Corp., 1981-82; sr. strategic planner First Bank Mpls., 1982-84; v.p. mktg. and strategic planning Glengarry Co., 1984-85; pres. Bus. Matters, 1985—; adj. faculty Coll. St. Thomas, 1986—. Chmn. alumni adv. council Carlson Sch. Mgmt. Mem. N.Am. Soc. Corporate Planning (v.p. programs), Alumnae Soc. U. Minn. (bd. dirs., pres.), Assn. for Corporate Growth (bd. dirs.), U. Chgo. Library Soc., ACLU, Common Cause, Center for Study of Democratic Instns. Minn. Zool. Gardens, Mpls. Inst. Art, Minn. Hist. Soc., Smithsonian Instn., Sci. Mus. Minn., M.B.A. Assn. Home: 3526 W 28th St Minneapolis MN 55416 Office: Business Matters Inc 100 N 7th Minneapolis MN 55403

ABRAHAM, GERSHEN MARK, manufacturing executive; b. Tarrytown, N.Y., Dec. 27, 1935; s. Leonard and Sylvia Helen (Projansky) A.; m. Sally Ann Ginsberg, Feb. 12, 1961; children: Marcelle Beth, David Benjamin. AB, Dartmouth Coll., 1958, MSME, 1959; MBA, NYU, 1968. V.p. Swingline, Inc., Long Island City, N.Y., 1975-78; pres. Spotnails, Inc., Rolling Meadows, Ill., 1979-81; corp. v.p. mfg. and engring. Acco Internat., Northbrook, Ill., 1981—. Served to maj. USAF, 1960-64, N.Y. Air NG, 1959-80. Mem. Soc. Plastics Engrs., Am. Soc. Metals. Jewish. Avocations: tennis, jogging, gardening. Home: 584 Cherokee Rd Highland Park IL 60035 Office: ACCO World Corp 2215 Sanders Rd Northbrook IL 60062

ABRAHAM, HASSEN JACOB, accountant; b. Bremen, Ind., Aug. 7, 1918; s. Jacob Hassen and Jennie Lee (Nick) A.; widower; children: Diane, Semia, Marian, Jeffrey. AA, South Bend (Ind.) Coll., 1946. CPA, Ind. Sr. auditor Price, Flatley and Co., CPA's, South Bend, 1963-73; v.p. Michiana Coll. Commerce, South Bend, 1973-78, pres., 1970-78; pvt. practice acct. South Bend, 1978—; adj. prof. U. Notre Dame, Ind., 1978—. Author: (book) Five Major Prophets of Islam, 1956. Served to col. U.S. Army, 1941-46. Mem. Am. Inst. Accts., Nat. Assn. Accts., Army Res. (past pres. council oaks chpt.), Fedn. Islamic Assn. (past. pres. U.S., Can. 1955-57). Home: 1959 Thornhill Dr South Bend IN 46614 Office: U Notre Dame Dept Accountancy Coll Bus Adminstrn Notre Dame IN 46556

ABRAHAMS, LLOYD ALAN, accountant; b. Chgo., Sept. 30, 1952; s. Robert and Helen (Silverstein) A.; m. Lori Robin Nathanson, June 9, 1974; children: Bradley, Jason. BS, U. Ill., 1984. CPA, Ill. Staff acct. Doty, Jarrow & Co., Chgo., 1978-83; controller Fin. Corp. of Ga., Peachtree City, 1978-79; mgr. Doty Jarrow & Co., Chgo., 1979-82, Schwartz, Bayer, Herzog, Kolof & Lev, Chgo., 1982-85; ptnr. Bayer, Kolof & Lev, Chgo., 1986—. Mem. Am. Inst. CPA's, Ill. CPA Soc. Office: Bayer Kolof & Lev 180 N LaSalle Suite 2020 Chicago IL 60601

ABRAHAMSEN, CATHERINE ELLEN, psychiatric hospital and management consultant; b. Chgo., July 28, 1950; d. Phillip Michael and Doris Catherine (Foster) Gearon; m. Paul Carl Abrahamsen, Sept. 24, 1974; children: Jena Marget, Kyra Ellen. AA, Mayfair Jr. Coll., 1974; BS in Nursing, No. Ill. U., 1978, MS in Nursing, 1980. Staff nurse U. Ill. Hosp., Chgo., 1974-75; staff nurse Chgo. Read/Henry Horner Childrens Ctr., 1976-77, head nurse, after-care coordinator, asst. dir. social skills program, 1978-79; head nurse Chgo. Lake Shore Hosp., 1977-78; instr. Northwestern U., Chgo., 1980-81; pvt. practice nursing Chgo., 1981-83; unit nurse adminstr. Riveredge Hosp., 1982-84; head nurse Old Orchard Hosp., Skokie, Ill., 1984—; participant Soviet-Am. psychiatric nursing clin. tour to USSR, 1979; adj. instr. community health, psychiatric field instr., Elmhurst Coll., 1982-84; unit nurse adminstr. Riveredge Hosp., 1982-84. Vol. ARC, 1979. Mem. Am. Nurse Assn., Ill. Nurse Assn. (pres. Chgo. Read local unit 1976-77, chairperson labor-mgmt. com. 1977, state wide steering com. for contract negotiations 1977), Advs. for Child Psychiatric Nursing, Am. Assn. Univ. Women, Assn. Female Execs. Home and Office: 112 W Garden Palatine IL 60067

ABRAHAMSON, PAUL RICHARD, dentist; b. Devils Lake, N.Dak., Feb. 24, 1938; s. Paul Eskel Richard and Mary Jeannette (Penny) A.; m. Connie Faye Johnson, June 19, 1966; children: Donna Maria, Susan Leigh. BS, Jamestown Coll., 1960; DDS, U. Iowa, 1966. Asst. scientist Salsbury's Labs., Charles City, Iowa, 1960-62; gen. practice resident Denver Gen. Hosp., 1966-67; pvt. practice dentistry Fargo, N.Dak., 1967—; courtesy staff mem. Dakota Hosp., Fargo, 1967—, St. Ansgar Hosp., Moorhead, Minn., 1977—. Rep. precinct chmn., mem. com. 46th and 51st dist., Fargo, 1979—; trustee Jamestown (N.Dak.) Coll., 1972-82. Served with U.S. Army, 1962. Recipient Minger award Coll. Dentistry U. Iowa, 1964; named one of Outstanding Young Men Am., 1971. Fellow Acad. Gen. Dentistry, Am. Coll. Dentists; mem. ADA (del. 1985-86), N.Dak. Dental Assn. (trustee 1979, pres. 1986), Am. Acad. Dental Practice Adminstrn. (bd. dirs. 1975—), Am. Acad. Dental Practice Adminstrn. Found. (bd. dirs. 1982—), Fargo C. of C., Greater N.Dak. Assn., U. Iowa Alumni Assn. (life), Jamestown Coll. Alumni Assn. (bd. dirs. 1969-72). Presbyterian. Lodges: Elks, Masons, Kiwanis (bd.dirs. Fargo club 1970—). Avocations: gardening, photography, playing in dance band, amateur radio operator. Office: 118 Broadway Suite 711 Fargo ND 58102

ABRAHAMSON, SHIRLEY SCHLANGER, justice Supreme Court Wisconsin; b. N.Y.C., Dec. 17, 1933; d. Leo and Ceil (Sauerteig) Schlanger; m. Seymour Abrahamson, Aug. 26, 1953; 1 son, Daniel Nathan. A.B., NYU, 1953; J.D., Ind. U., 1956; S.J.D., U. Wis., 1962. Bar: Wis. 1962. Asst. dir. Legis. Drafting Research Fund, Columbia U. Law Sch., 1957-60; since practiced in Madiso; mem. firm LaFollette, Sinykin, Anderson & Abrahamson, 1962-76; justice Supreme Ct. Wis., Madison, 1976—; prof. U. Wis. Sch. Law, 1966—, currently on leave; Mem. Wis. Bd. Bar Commrs.; mem. adv. bd. Nat. Inst. Justice, U.S. Dept. Justice, 1980-82; mem. Mayor's Adv. Com., Madison, 1968-70, Gov.'s Study Com. on Jud. Orgn., 1970-72; bd. visitors Ind. U. Sch. Law, 1972—, U. Miami Sch. Law, 1982—, Brigham Young U. Sch. Law, 1986—; bd. dirs. LWV, Madison, 1963-65; Union council Wis. Union, U. Wis., 1970-71. Editor: Constitutions of the United States (National and State) 2 vols, 1962. Bd. dirs. Wis. Civil Liberties Union, 1968-72, chmn. Capital Area chpt., 1969. Mem. ABA (council, sect. of legal edn. and admissions to the bar 1976-86, mem. commn. on undergrad. edn. in law and the humanities 1978-79), Wis. Bar Assn., Dane County Bar Assn., 7th Cir. Bar Assn., Nat. Assn. Women Judges, Am. Law Inst. (council), Order of Coif, Phi Beta Kappa. Home: 2012 Waunona Way Madison WI 53713 Office: Wis Supreme Ct PO Box 1688 Madison WI 53701

ABRAM, LEON JAY, orthopaedic surgeon; b. Duluth, Minn., July 10, 1956; s. Richard Wolfe and Muriel (Sadoff) A.; m. DeAnne Goldetsky, Aug. 24, 1980. BA, Colo. Coll., 1977; MD, U. Minn., 1982. Diplomate Nat. Bd. Med. Examiners. Intern St. Joseph Hosp., Denver; resident Mt. Sinai Med. Ctr., Cleve.; practice medicine specializing in orthopaedic surgery Cleve., 1984—. Contbr. articles to profl. jours. Mem. AMA, ACS, Am. Acad. Orthopaedic Surgeons (candidate), Ohio State Med. Assn., Cleve. Med. Soc., Am. Heart Assn., Nat. Eagle Scout Assn., Nat. Ski Patrol, Colo. Doctor's Ski Patrol, Phi Delta Epsilon, Kappa Sigma. Jewish. Office: One Mount Sinai Dr Cleveland OH 44106

ABRAMS, ALAN EDWIN, journalist, author; b. Detroit, Feb. 19, 1941; s. Harry J. and Mildred (Volod) A.; student public schs., Detroit. Pub. relations dir. Motown Record Corp., Detroit, 1959-66; Pub. relations dir. Gale Research Co., Detroit, 1974-76, editor journalism projects, 1976-81; contbg. editor Contemporary Authors, Detroit, 1976-81; book reviewer, spl. feature writer, paperback columnist The Windsor, (Ont., Can.) Star, 1980-85, gen. assignment reporter, 1985—; book reviewer Newsday, L.I., N.Y., 1980—; free-lance journalist, 1981—; spl. writer Detroit Free Press, 1983-85, Globe and Mail, Toronto, Ont., 1984-85, Balt. Jewish Times, 1984—, Jewish News, Detroit, 1983—; contbr. sects. to 1987 Ont. Red Book; contbr. to various publs.; appraiser rare books and autographs, IRS, 1978-79; author: Special Treatment: The Untold Story ofThe Survival of Thousands of Jews in Hitler's Third Reich, 1985; Why Windsor? An Anecdotal History of the Jews of Windsor and Essex County, 1981; Journalist Biographies Master Index, 1979; Media Personnel Guide, 1979; The Fourth Estate: Gale 1980 Literary Date Book. Recipient award of merit U.S. Dept. Labor, 1969; writing grantee Ont. Arts Council, 1980, 81, 82; Western Ont. Newspaper award, 1984; Simon Rockower Meml. Award for Jewish Journalism, 1986. Mem. Ontario Reporters Assn. (awards for features and commentary 1987), Essex County Hist. Soc. Jewish. Clubs: Detroit Press, Algonquin. Office: The Windsor Star, City Desk, 167 Ferry St, Windsor, ON Canada N8Y 2K3

ABRAMS, MARLENE RAE, lawyer; b. Albany, N.Y., May 16, 1949; d. Hyman and Charlotte (Rosenblum) A. B.S. summa cum laude, Boston U., 1971; J.D., Georgetown U., 1974. Bar: Ill. 1974, U.S. Dist. Ct. (no. dist.) Ill., 1974. Assoc. Isham, Lincoln & Beale, Chgo., 1974-77; asst. regional atty. Dept. Health and Human Services, Chgo., 1977—. Mem. cabinet Young Leadership div. Anti-Defamation League, vice-chmn. Nat. leadership com., mem. regional bd. dirs.; jr. governing bd. Chgo. Symphony Orch.; mem. friends com. Hubbard St. Dance Co., Alliance of Art Inst. Recipient Spl. Citation for Exemplary Service Pub. Health Service Adminstrs., 1984. Mem. Beta Gamma Sigma. Office: Dept Health and Human Services 300 S Wacker Dr Suite 1800 Chicago IL 60606

ABRAMS, MICHAEL, real estate executive, developer; b. Chgo., Oct. 19, 1949; s. Albert and Sally (Joseph) A.; Josephine Meninger, Nov. 1974. BSc, DePaul U., 1971. CPA, Ill. Acct. VA, Chgo., 1971-79, Ralph Picker & Assocs., Rosemont, Ill., 1979-80; asst. v.p., asst. controller Robert Sheridan & Ptnrs., Chgo., 1980—. Mem. Am. Inst CPA's, Ill. CPA Soc. Office: Robert Sheridan & Ptnrs 311 W Superior Suite 504 Chicago IL 60610

ABRAMS, RICHARD BRILL, lawyer; b. Mpls., Nov. 2, 1931; s. Joseph E. and Nettie (Brill) A.; m. Myrna Carole Noodleman, Dec. 5, 1965; children—Jennifer, Adam. B.B.A., U. Minn., 1958, B.S.L., 1958, J.D., 1958. Bar: Minn. 1958, U.S. Ct. Appeals (8th cir.) 1981, U.S. Dist. Ct. Minn. 1981, Wis. 1983. Sole practice Mpls., 1958-64; pres. Abrams & Spector, P.A., Mpls., 1964—; ad hoc instr. labor edn. U. Minn. Bd. dirs. Mpls. United Way; bd. dirs., v.p. Courage Ctr., 1977-83, 85-86; mem pain com. Nat. Acad. Sci., Nat. Inst. Medicine, 1986. Served with U.S. Army, 1955-57. Recipient Disting. and Devoted Service award Human Rights Com., Mpls. Central Labor Union Council, 1975; Meritorious Service award Minn. Rehab. Assn., 1978; Disting. Service award Courage Ctr., 1983. Mem. ABA, Minn. State Bar Assn., Wis. State Bar Assn., Assn. Trial Lawyers Am., Minn. Trial Lawyers Assn., Nat. Acad. Scis. (pain com.), Nat. Inst. Medicine. Office: Abrams & Spector PA 6800 France Ave S Suite 435 Minneapolis MN 55435

ABRAMS, SYLVIA FLECK, religious educator; b. Buffalo, Apr. 5, 1942; d. Abraham and Ann (Hanf) Fleck; m. Ronald M. Abrams, June 30, 1963; children—Ruth, Sharon. B.A. magna cum laude, Western Res. U., 1963, M.A., 1964, now postgrad.; B.H.L., Cleve. Coll. Jewish Studies, 1976, M.H.L., 1983; postgrad. U. Haifa, 1975, Yad Va Shem Summer Inst., Hebrew U., 1983. Hebrew tchr. The Temple, 1959-77, Hebrew coordinator, 1973-77; tchr. Beachwood High Sch., 1964-66; tchr. Hebrew and social studies Agnon Sch., Cleve., 1975-77, social studies resource tchr., 1976-77; ednl. dir. Temple Emanu El, Cleve., 1977-85; asst. dir. Cleve. Bur. Jewish Edn., 1985—; chmn. ednl. dirs. council Cleve. Bd. Jewish Edn., 1982-85. Appointed to Ohio Council Holocaust Edn., 1986. Recipient Elbert J. Benton award Western Res. U., 1963; Fred and Rose Rosenwasser Bible award Coll. Jewish Studies, 1974; Emmanuel Gamoran Meml. Curriculum award Nat. Assn. Temple Educator, 1978; Samuel Lipson Meml. award Coll. Jewish Studies, 1981 Bingham fellow Case Western Res. U., 1984-86. Mem. Nat. Assn. Temple Educators (bd. dirs. 1984—), Assn. Supervision and Curriculum Devel., Nat. Council Jewish Edn., Coalition for Alternative in Jewish Edn., Union Am. Hebrew Congregations (Israel curriculum task force), Cleve. Bur. Jewish Edn. (chmn. ednl. dirs. council 1982-85), Phi Beta Kappa. Jewish. Club: Hadassah (life). Editor: You and Your Schools, 1972. Office: Cleve Bur Jewish Edn 2030 S Taylor Rd Cleveland OH 44118

ABRAMSON, HERBERT FRANCIS, superintendent schools; b. Chgo., Dec. 16, 1930; s. Maurice P. and Rose (Harris) A.; B.S., Ind. U., 1953; M.Ed., Loyola U., 1961; postgrad. Roosevelt, Purdue, Ind. univs.; m. Sylvia Linde, June 29, 1958; children—Marcia Beth, Jacquelyn, Rachel. Tchr. pub. secondary schs., Lake Ridge, 1955—, prin. Calumet Jr. High Sch., Lake Ridge Sch. System, 1961-69; prin. Lake Jr. High Sch., 1969-74; supt. Lake Ridge Schs., Gary, 1974—; mem. State Supt. Schs. Adv. Com., 1978—, Ind. Planning Com. for Adult and Community Edn., 1979. Prin. Temple Israel Religious Sch., Gary; dir. Gary Sch. Employee Fed. Credit Union; mem. adv. council N.W. Ind. Urban League; mem. President's Roundtable, Meth. Hosp. Served with AUS, 1953-55; bd. dirs. N.W. Ind. Jewish Welfare Fedn.; bd. dirs. Temple Israel, Gary, 1971-72, pres. 1973-75; cons. Hebrew Acad. N.W. Ind. Mem. Am. Fedn. Tchrs. (past pres. No. 662), Nat. Assn. Secondary Sch. Prins., Lake County Jr. and Sr. High Prins. Assn., Ind. Assn. Pub. Sch. Supts. (state policies and resolutions com.), Ind. Assn. Sch. Bus. Ofcls., N.W. Ind. Pub. Sch. Study Council (pres. 1982-83), Am. Assn. Sch. Adminstrs., ACLU. Lodge: B'nai B'rith. Contbr. articles to profl. jours. Home: 7210 Polk St Merrillville IN 46410 Office: Lake Ridge Schs 6111 W Ridge Rd Gary IN 46408

ABRAMSON, HONEY, small business manager; b. Detroit, Nov. 27, 1927; d. Edward and Sarah (Farber) Fisher; m. Marlin Philip Abramson, Oct. 9, 1955; children: Debra A., Lisa W. Student, Ohio State U., 1945-47. Sec. to editor Chem. Abstracts, Columbus, Ohio, 1959-63; sec., treas. Thistle Class Assn., Columbus, Highland Park (Ill.), 1960—. Home: 1811 Cavell Ave Highland Park IL 60035

ABT, SYLVIA HEDY, dentist; b. Chgo., Oct. 7, 1957; s. Wendel Peter and Hedi Lucie (Wieder) A. Student, Loyola U., Chgo., 1975-77, cert. dental hygiene, 1979; DDS, Loyola U., 1983. Registered dental hygienist. Dental asst. Office Dr. Baran and Dr. O'Neill, DDS, Chgo., 1977-78; dental hygienist Drs. Spiro, Sudakoff, Kadens, Weidman, DDS, Skokie, Ill., 1979-80, Dr. Laudando, DiFranco, Rosemont, Ill., 1980-83; gen. practice dentistry Chgo., 1983—. Vol. Community Health Rotations, VA Hosps. and Convalescent Ctrs., Mental Health Ctrs., grammar schs., Maywood, Ill. and Chgo., 1978-82. Recipient 1st Place award St. Apollonia Art Show, Loyola U., 1982. Mem. ADA, Ill. State Dental Soc., Chgo. Dental Soc., Psi Omega (historian, editor). Avocations: art, singing, dancing, bicycling, jogging. Office: 6509 W Higgins Chicago IL 60656

ABUHL, JEANNE MARIE, realtor; b. Des Moines, May 13, 1946; d. Albert James and Marjorie Jeanette (Larson) A.; student Moody Bible Inst., 1966, local community colls. Exec. sec. to v.p. Scripture Press Found., Glen Ellyn, Ill., 1967-73; asst. to nat. field dir. Youth for Christ/USA, Wheaton, Ill., 1973-75; office mgr. Youth for Christ Internat., Geneva, Switzerland, 1975-78; dir. adminstrv. services Follett Coll. Stores, Elmhurst, Ill., 1978-83; mgr. client services McKay-Doerschuk & Co., Wheaton, Ill., 1983-84; sales assoc. Baird & Warner, Wheaton, 1984—; cons. Performax Systems. Bd. dirs. campign bd. Fox Valley Youth for Christ, 1981-82. Mem. Nat. Assn. Female Execs. Republican. Evangelical. Club: Zonta. Home: 27W370 Geneva Rd #138 West Chicago IL 60185 Office: Baird & Warner 400 W Roosevelt Rd Wheaton IL 60187

ACCORSI, ERNEST WILLIAM, JR., professional football team executive; b. Hershey, Pa., Oct. 29, 1941; s. Ernest William Sr. and Mary Doris (Nardi) A.; m. Judy Ann Nangle, Sept. 9, 1967 (div. Aug. 1985); children: Michael Ryan, Sherlyn Paige, Patrick Vincent. BA, Wake Forest U., 1963; postgrad., Temple U., 1967. Sportswriter Phila. Inquirer, 1966-69; with sports info. dept. Pa. State U., University Park, 1969-70; pub. relations dir. Balt. Colts, Owings Mill, Md., 1970-75, asst. gen. mgr., 1977-82, gen. mgr., 1982-84; asst. to pres. NFL, N.Y.C., 1975-77; asst. to pres. Cleve. Browns, 1984-85, exec. v.p. football ops., 1985—. Bd. dirs. Nat. Football Found., N.Y.C., 1983. Served with U.S. Army N.G., 1964. Recipient Columbia award Italian-Am. Orgns. Md., Balt., 1982; named Grand Marshall Conv. Council Colts' Corrals, 1983. Mem. Advt. Club Balt. (bd. dirs. 1978—). Democrat. Roman Catholic. Home: 6270 Greenwwod Pkwy Sagamore Hills OH 44067 Office: Cleve Browns Cleve Stadium Cleveland OH 44114

ACH, J. WICKLIFFE, architectural and engineering design firm executive; b. Cin., May 24, 1948; s. Roger Workum and Dorothy (Johnson) A.; m. Marlin Bachman, Jan. 24, 1970; 2 children. BA, Hillsdale Coll., 1970. Sales mgr. Chester Products Inc., Middletown, Ohio, 1970-73, corp. v.p., 1973-77; bus. mgr. Hixson Architects/Engrs., Cin., 1977-82, chief operating officer, 1982-83, pres., chief exec. officer, 1983—; bd. dirs. Glendale Youth Sports, Cin. Trustee, v.p. Hamilton County Devel. Co., Ohio, 1984—; com. mem. Cin. C. of C., 1982-84. Mem. Profl. Services Mgmt. Assn., Soc. for Mktg. Profl. Services (com. dir. 1978-84), Dairy and Food Industries Assn. (bd. dirs.), Young Pres.'s Orgn. Episcopalian. Clubs: Lyceum (Glendale, Ohio); Banker's (Cin.). Avocations: tennis, home renovation. Office: Hixson Architects/Engrs Inc 25 Merchant St Suite 400 Cincinnati OH 45246

ACHARYA, USHA SUMANT, physician; b. Mombasa, Kenya, Jan. 10, 1941; d. Ambalal Bhailalbhai and Shanta Ambalal (Desai) Patel; m. Sumant Acharya, July 4, 1968; children: Pinak, Shital. MB, BS, Grand Med. Coll., Bombay, 1964. Intern Nazareth Hosp., Phila., 1970; resident Schwab Rehab. Hosp., Chgo., 1972-73; gen. practice medicine Northlake, Ill., 1976—; mem. staff Elmhurst (Ill.) Meml. Hosp., 1978—, St. Anne's West Hosp., North Lake, Ill., 1980—. Home: 126 Tomlin Cir Burr Ridge IL 60521

ACHILLES, CHARLES ALBERT, association executive; b. Berwyn, Ill., Sept. 29, 1946; s. Charles Laddie and Mildred Antonette (Volmut) A.; B.S. in Chemistry, No. Ill. U., 1968; M.B.A., Loyola U., Chgo., 1972; m. Sharon Lee Lullo, May 23, 1970 (div.); children—Amber Lee, Brylan Charles. Tchr., Woodridge (Ill.) Sch. System, 1968-69, asst. prin., 1969-72; dir. membership services Inst. Real Estate Mgmt., Chgo., 1972-76, staff v.p. membership services and communications, 1976-81, staff v.p. legis. and spl. services, 1981—. Active Community Affairs Com., 1977-79; pres. Oakwood Community Assn., 1978, bd. dirs., 1979; bd. dirs. Oakwood Homeowners Assn., 1979, v.p., 1981, pres., 1982-83; active Community Party of Westmont, 1978, 80, 82 Mem. Am. Mktg. Assn., Am. Soc. Assn. Execs., Community Assns. Inst., Am. Statis. Assn., Nat. Housing Conf. (dir.), Nat. Inst. Bldg. Scis., Assn. MBA Execs., Cavaliers, Phi Eta Sigma. Congregationalist. Clubs: 71; Downtown; Capitol Hill. Home: 17 W 521 Portsmouth Dr Westmont IL 60559 Office: Inst Real Estate Mgmt 430 N Michigan Ave Chicago IL 60611

ACHTEMEIER, GARY LYNN, atmospheric scientist; b. Wichita, Kans., Mar. 1, 1943; s. Walter John and Phyllis (Norman) A.; m. (Mildred) Sue Dicus, June 15, 1968; children—Cheryl Ann, Scott Alan. B.S., Fla. State U., 1965, M.S., 1969, Ph.D., 1972. NRC grantee Nat. Severe Storms Lab., Norman, Okla., 1972-73; assoc. research scientist Ill. State Water Survey, Champaign, 1973-82; profl. research scientist, vis. assoc. prof. Lab. for Atmospheric Research, U. Ill., 1981-82; cons. Nat. Forest Expt. Sta., Macon, Ga., 1975—; cons. U. Ill. M.B.A. Program; proposal reviewer NSF, 1976—, NASA, 1982—. Contbr. articles to profl. jours. Tech. paper reviewer for three jours., 1976—. Publicity chmn. Full Gospel Businessmen's Fellowship Internat. Rally, 1979, rally co-chmn., 1981, 83, 85, v.p. Champaign-Urbana chpt. #5 1982-84, pres., 1985—; vol. petition drive coordinator for East Cen. Ill. Pat Robertson Campaign, 1986—. NSF grantee, 1976-77, NASA grantee, 1982—. Mem. Am. Meteorol. Soc. (com. on severe storms 1980-81), AAAS, Sigma Xi, Chi Epsilon Pi. Republican. Lodge: Kiwanis. Office: Ill State Water Survey 2204 Griffith Dr Champaign IL 61820

ACHTENBERG, JOEL FRANKLIN, data processing executive, educator; b. Kansas City, Mo., Oct. 21, 1946; s. Irving and Gail (Wiener) A. AB, Washington U., 1968; postgrad., U. Wis., 1968-71. Project dir. Midwest Council of Model Cities, Kansas City, 1971-73; pvt. cons. Kansas City, 1973-75; research analyst Wash. U., St. Louis, 1975-80, dir. med. computing, 1980—, instr. occupational therapy, 1984—; cons. Rand Corp., Washington, 1973, City of Kansas City, 1974. Contbr. articles to profl. jours. Bd. dirs. Am. Youth Hostels, St. Louis, 1983—, Jewish Cen. Reform Congregation, 1987—. Avocations: jewelery, gemology, bicycling. Home: 4015 Magnolia

Pl Saint Louis MO 63110 Office: Washington U Lindell & Skinker Saint Louis MO 63130

ACHTERMAN, JAMES WILLIAM, management consultant; b. Cin., May 27, 1945; s. Hubert Lewis and Alberta (Moore) A.; B.B.A., U. Cin., 1968; m. Janet C. Gibbs; children—Nicole Lee, Jeffrey Scott. Mgmt. analyst City of Cin., 1968-70; budget dir. Hamilton County Ohio, Cin., 1970-72, asst. county adminstr., 1972-74; controller Cin. Public Schs., 1974-76; mng. cons. Ernst & Whinney, Cin., 1976-77, mgr. services to local govt., 1977-82; sr. mgr. services to local govt. for State of Ohio, Peat, Marwick, Mitchell & Co., 1982—, also dir. mgmt. cons. office, Columbus. Chmn. found. com. United Negro Coll. Fund, 1979-81; councilman City of Wyoming, Ohio, 1979-84; chmn. adv. com. on state acctg. policy State of Ohio. Mem. Ohio-Ky.-Ind. Regional Council Govts. (trustee 1971-74, 81-84), Internat. City Mgmt. Assn., Mcpl. Finance Officers Assn., Ohio Mcpl. Finance Officers Assn. Office: Peat Marwick Main and Co 2 Nationwide Plaza Columbus OH 43215

ACHTERMAN, JANET GIBBS, university controller; b. Cin., July 19, 1956; d. Orville Louis and Betty Louise (Pope) Gibbs; m. James William Achterman, Mar. 16, 1985. BBA, U. Cin., 1979. CPA, Ohio. Mgr. Ernst & Whinney, Cin., 1978-83; sr. mgr. Arthur Young & Co., Cin., 1983-85; portfolio mgr. The Investment Club, Columbus, Ohio, 1986—. V.p. Ville Charmante Condominium Assn., 1985—, Worthington, Ohio, 1985—; mem. fin. com. Life Care Alliance, Columbus, 1986—, relocation com., capital campaign steering com., 1986—. Mem. Nat. Assn. Coll. and Univ. Bus. Officers, Am. Inst. CPA's, Cen. Assn. Coll. and Univ. Bus. Officers, Ohio Soc. CPA's, Ohio State U. Faculty Women's Club (treas.). Avocations: racquetball, walking, snow-skiing. Home: 250 St Antoine Worthington OH 43085 Office: Ohio State U 1800 Cannon Dr Columbus OH 43210

ACKER, JOHN D., chemical company executive; b. Cleve., Mar. 12, 1935; s. Frank H. and Lenabelle (Thompson) A.; m. D. Jean Endres, July 21, 1956; children: Cynthia J., Daniel S. BBA, Kent (Ohio) State U., 1959. Salesman U.S. Gypsum Co., Cleve., 1959-65; sales mgr. Gen. Electric Co., St. Louis, Dallas, Saratoga Springs (Fla.), 1965-72; nat. mktg. mgr. Stauffer Chem. Co., Adrian, Mich., 1972-77, Schuld Mfg. Co., Cape Girardo, Mo., 1977-78; v.p. Perstorp Polyols Inc., Toledo, 1978—. Served as cpl. U.S. Army, 1954-56. Episcopalian. Clubs: Toledo, Sylvania (Oh.) Country, Anchor Point Yacht (Curtice, Oh.) (bd. dirs.). Avocation: power boating. Office: Perstorp Polyols Inc 600 Matzinger Rd Toledo OH 43612

ACKERMAN, LOUISE MAGAW, writer, civic worker; b. Topeka, July 9, 1904; d. William Glenn and Anna Mary (Shaler) Magaw; BS, Kans. State U., 1926; MA, U. Nebr., 1942; m. Grant Albert Ackerman, Dec. 27, 1926; children—Edward Shaler, Anita Louise. Free lance writer, 1930—. Mem. Nat. Soc. Daus. Colonial Wars (nat. pres. 1977-80), Daus. Am. Colonists (regent Nebr. 1970-72), DAR (past v.p. gen.), Americans of Armorial Ancestry (sec. 1976-82), Nat. Huguenot Soc. (2d v.p. 1977-81), Nebr. Writers Guild (past sec.-treas.), Nat. League Am. Pen Women, Colonial Lords in Am., Nat. Gavel Soc., Soc. Descs. of Founders of Hartford, Conn., Phi Kappa Phi. Republican. Club: Nat. Writers. Lodge: Order Eastern Star. Home: Eastmont Towers III Apt 428 6335 O St Lincoln NE 68510

ACKERMAN, NORMAN ALVIN, electronics executive; b. Chgo., Sept. 22, 1924; s. Herman Rae (Spiegel) A.; m. Ruth Renberg, Oct. 19, 1947 (div. 1969); children: David Paul, Janice Lee; m. Shirley Wohlman, Mar. 26, 1970. BEE, Northwestern U., 1946; MEE, Chgo. Tech. Coll., 1949; post-grad., U. Ill. Registered profl. engr., Ill. Engr. Gen. Transformer Corp., Chgo., 1947-52; pres., engr. Perma Power Mfg. Co., Chgo., 1952-68; dir. sales Perma Power div. Chamberlain Mfg. Co., Elmhurst, Ill., 1968-77; pres. Perma Power Electronics, Inc., Niles, Ill., 1977—; bd. dirs. Electronics Show Corp., Chgo., 1986—. Inventor TV tube brightener, 1954, multiple outlet strip, 1973, flourescent lamp ballast, 1953. Mem. neighborhood com. northwest suburban council Boy Scouts Am., Des Plaines, Ill., 1955-67. Served as lt. commdr. USNR, 1942-46, PTO. Recipient Hall of Fame award Electronic Distbr. Research Inst., 1976, Founding Fathers award Door Opener and Remote Control Mfrs. Assn., 1979, Cert. of Appreciation, Assn. Electronic Mfrs., Inc., 1969, Cert. of Service, Boy Scouts Am., 1967. Mem. IEEE, Electronics Industry Assn., Nat. Electronics Distbrs. Assn., Am. Mgmt. Assn. Club: Electronics VIP (Chgo.). Avocation: tennis. Home: 7615 Church St Morton Grove IL 60053 Office: Perma Power Electronics Inc 5601 W Howard St Niles IL 60048

ACKERMAN, ORA RAY, hospital superintendent; b. Mapleton, Minn., Jan. 13, 1931; s. Ora R. and Minnie T. (Quam) A.; m. Barbara Singley, Mar. 25, 1951; children—Bruce, David, Cindy. B.S. with distinction, U. Minn., 1953; M.Ed., 1955; M.Ed. certificate dir. recreation, Ind. U., 1961; Ed.D., 1963; Ed.D. certificate recreation techniques in rehab, N.Y. U., 1966; grad. exec. devel. program, Ind. U., 1968. Mental health coordinator in Calif., Md., Ind., 1953-63; dir. edn. and activity therapy Ind. Dept. Mental Health, 1963-66; supt. Ft. Wayne (Ind.) State Hosp. and Tng. Center, 1966—; Vis. prof. psychology Ind. U. (Purdue-Ft. Wayne campus), 1967—; Mem. adv. council title IV-A, Ind. State Library, 1968—; mem. gov.'s tech. planning com. for devel. plans for Correction Center, 1970—; mem. Ind. Mental Health-Mental Retardation Commn., 1970—, Gov.'s Com. to Study Mental Health Laws. Contbr. to profl. jours. Mem. Nat. Recreation Assn. (dist. adv. com. 1965-68), Nat. Therapeutic Recreation Soc. (div. 1966-69), Am. Soc. Mental Hosp. Bus. Adminstrs., Am. Soc. Mental Deficiency, Am. Cancer Soc. (mem. nat. house dels., bd. dirs. Ind. div.), Am. Recreation Soc., Ind. Park and Recreation Assn. Methodist (chmn. bd. 1967, mem. commn. social concerns 1958-69). Club: Kiwanian. Home: 802 Northwood Blvd Fort Wayne IN 46805 Office: Fort Wayne State Hosp 4900 Saint Joe Rd Fort Wayne IN 46815

ACKERMAN, PAUL DENNIS, psychology educator; b. St. Francis, Kans., Dec. 26, 1941; s. Robert Anson and Erma Elizabeth (McDaniel) A.; m. Betty Ann Melick, Sept. 9, 1962; children: Robert, Bryan, Sally. BA, U. Kans., 1964, MA, 1966, PhD, 1968. Lic. psychologist, Kans. Asst. prof. psychology Wichita (Kans.) State U., 1968—. Author It's A Young World After All: Exciting Evidences for Recent Creation, 1986. Mem. Bible-Sci. Assn. (bd. dirs. 1980—), Creation Social Sci. and Humanities Soc. (pres. 1978—, editor jour. 1978—). Republican. Home: 4726 E 25 Wichita KS 67220 Office: Wichita State U Dept Psychology #34 Wichita KS 67208

ACKERMAN, ROBERT ALAN, health center administrator; b. Springfield, Ill., Aug. 9, 1951; s. Harold Henry and Hermina Marie (Wims) A.; m. Deborah Susan Litwiller, Feb. 12, 1972; children: Scott Ryan, Tara Lianne, Ian Nathaniel. AS, Lincoln Land Community Coll., Springfield, 1971; BS in Acctg., U. Ill., 1974; postgrad., U. Iowa, 1987—. CPA, Ill., Iowa. Health planner State of Ill., Springfield, 1974-76; mgmt. cons. McGladrey, Hendrickson & Pullen, Springfield, 1977-81; dir. fin. and planning Henry County Health Ctr., Mount Pleasant, Iowa, 1981—; mem. New Ventures Com. Vol. Hosps. Iowa, Cedar Rapids, 1985—; cons. Health Software Mount Pleasant, Inc., 1982—, Sangamon County (Ill.) Govt., 1979, Henry County Govt., 1986. Mem. Am. Inst. CPA's, Iowa Soc. CPA's, Ill. CPA Soc. (Mems. in Industry com. 1986—), Healthcare Fin. Mgrs. Assn., Soc. for Hosp. Planning and Mktg., Iowa Soc. for Hosp. Mgmt. Services (bd. dirs. 1985-86). Republican. Lodges: Kiwanis (bd. dirs. Mt. Pleasant club 1986—), Masons (officer 1977-81), Shriners. Office: Henry County Health Ctr Saunders Park Mount Pleasant IA 52641

ACKERSON, CHARLES STANLEY, clergyman, social worker; b. St. Louis, June 19, 1935; s. Charles Albert and Glenda Mae (Brown) A.; m. Carol Jean Stehlick, Aug. 18, 1957; children—Debra Lynn, Charles Mark, Heather Sue. A.B., William Jewell Coll., 1957; M.Div., Colgate Rochester Div. Sch., 1961. Ordained to ministry Baptist Ch., 1961. Pastor, Glens Falls (N.Y.) Friends Meeting, 1961-65; assoc. pastor Delmar Bapt. Ch., St. Louis, 1965-68; resource dir. Block Partnership, St. Louis, 1968-71; group home dir. North Side YMCA, St. Louis, 1971-72; group home supr. St. Louis Juvenile Ct., 1973-74; program dir. Youth Opportunities Unltd., casework supr. St. Louis County Juvenile Ct., 1974-83; human resource specialist St. Louis County Dept. Human Resources, 1985—; instr. adminstrn. of justice Mo. Bapt. Coll., St. Louis, 1980—; mem. ordination council area V, Great Rivers region Am. Bapt. Chs. U.S.A., 1982-84; chmn. youth focus group Interfaith Partnership Met. St. Louis, 1985—, St. Louis Area Youth Services Network, 1987—. Chmn. group home com. Mo. Council on Criminal Justice, 1973-75; chmn. cts. and instns. subcom. Juvenile Delinquency Task Force for Gov. Mo. Action Plan for Pub. Safety, 1976. Mem. Nat. Council Juvenile and Family Ct. Judges, Mo. Juvenile Justice Assn. (v.p., chmn. tng. com.), Cairn Terrier Assn. Am., Three Rivers Kennel Club of Mo. (pres.), Mo. Conservation Fedn., Nat. Rifle Assn., Nat. Muzzle Loading Rifle Assn., Trappers of Starved Rock, Lambda Chi Alpha. Democrat. Baptist. Home: 1221 Havenhurst St Manchester MO 63011

ACKERSON, LAIRD DOUGLAS, optometrist; b. Ridley Park, Pa., June 11, 1956; s. Herbert D. and Rosemary (Kraus) A.; m. Jacqueline Ann Fallon, Sept. 8, 1979; children—Natalie Fallon, Kenneth Herbert William. B.S., Ohio State U., 1978, O.D., 1982. Lic. optometrist, Ohio. Practice optometry, Hilliard, Ohio, 1982—; co-owner, mgr. Sportsoptic, Hilliard, 1982—; lectr. Hilliard High Sch., 1983—. Bd. dirs. Hilliard Athletic Boosters, 1983-85, mem. 1983—; coach Hilliard Baseball Assn., 1975—; vision screener Hilliard Community Ctr., 1982—. Mem. Am. Optometric Assn., Ohio Optometric Assn., Am. Optometric Assn. (sports vision sect.), Hilliard C. of C., Ohio State U. Alumni Assn. Republican. Lutheran. Lodges: Lions (bd. dirs. 1983—), Optimist. Home and Office: 4939 Cemetery Rd Hilliard OH 43026

ACKLEY, ROBERT RADCLIFFE, JR., health care company executive; b. Jersey City, Aug. 3, 1938; s. Robert R. and Edith A. (Adolfson) A.; m. Sharon Premo, Sept. 13, 1965 (div. Mar. 1974); children: Robert R. III, Jennifer E.; m. Eleanor L. Truesdell, June 15, 1974. BSBA, U. Mass., 1964. Mktg. mgr. NCR Corp., Dayton, Ohio, 1969-84; product mgr. Mead Data Cen., Dayton, 1984, mktg. mgr., 1985; v.p. Micromedex, Inc., Dayton, 1986—. Served to U.S. Army, 1957-60. Mem. Electronic Computing-Health Oriented. Republican. Episcopalian. Avocations: scuba diving, bridge. Home: 231 Forrer Blvd Dayton OH 45419 Office: Micromedex Inc PO Box 933 Dayton OH 45401

ACKLEY, RON DEAN, corporate training specialist; b. Canton, Ohio, Feb. 13, 1952; s. Ronald Dean Sr. and Betty Ruth (Ream) A.; m. Nancy Louise Gable, Apr. 12, 1980; children: Andrew Michael, Erin Christine. AA, Kent (Ohio) State U., 1974, BS, 1975; MBA, Lindenwood Coll., 1986. Dist. exec. Boy Scouts Am., Mansfield, Ohio, 1976-80, program dir., 1980; rep. employee relations Therm-O-Disk div. Emerson Electric Co., Mansfield, 1980-84; sr. corp. tng. specialist Emerson Electric Co., St. Louis, 1984—. Scoutmaster Boy Scouts Am., Nankin, Ohio, 1976-84, asst. scoutmaster, St. Peters, Mo.; instr. Am. Red Cross, Mansfield, 1979-84. Mem. Am. Soc. Tng. and Devel., Mansfield Safety Council, Ctr. Ohio Self-Insured Council. Club: Lions. Avocations: camping, winter survival, bicycling, cross-country skiing. Home: 18 Heather Valley Circle Saint Peters MO 63376 Office: Emerson Electric Co 8000 W Florissant Ave Saint Louis MO 63136

ACKMANN, LOWELL EUGENE, electrical engineer; b. Elgin, Ill., July 2, 1923; s. Henry C. and Matilda (Rineck) A.; m. Dorothy Collier, July 26, 1948; children: Robert, Lee, Barbara. B.S.E.E., U. Ill., 1944. Engr. Allis-Chalmers Mfg. Co., Milw., 1946-48; sales engr. Allis-Chalmers Mfg. Co., Chgo., 1948-52, Peoria, Ill., 1952-54; v.p. Roland Constrn. Co., Dallas, 1954-56; elec. engr. Sargent & Lundy, Chgo., 1956-68, ptnr., 1966, mgr. electric dept., 1968-76, dir. services, 1976-84, sr. ptnr., 1984-87, ret., 1987. Served with USN, 1943-46. Recipient Disting. Alumnus award Elec. Engring. Alumni Assn., U. Ill., 1979. Mem. Atomic Indsl. Forum, Western Soc. Engrs., Ill. Soc. Profl. Engrs., IEEE, Nat. Soc. Profl. Engrs. Clubs: Inverness Golf, Chgo. Athletic Assn. Home: 200 Dover Circle Inverness IL 60067 Office: Sargent & Lundy 55 E Monroe St Chicago IL 60603 *

ACOTT, RICHARD THOMAS, architect; b. Baraboo, Wis., Feb. 23, 1927; s. Thomas H. and Lila (Meyer) A.; m. Isabel Agnes Wirtz, Dec. 26, 1976; children: James, John. BArch, U. Minn., 1952. Project designer Magney, Tusler, Setter, Mpls., 1952, Victor Gruen, Architect, Los Angeles, 1952-56, Holabird & Root, Chgo., 1956-59, Perkins & Will, Chgo., 1959-60, Samuelson & Sanquist, Chgo., 1960-62; pres. Richard Acott & Assoc., Chgo., 1962-73, Wisconsin Rapids, Wis., 1973—; pres. Nekoosa (Wis.) Plaza Corp., 1969—; mem. Tech. Housing Adv. Com., Wausau, Wis., North Cen. Wis. Regional Planning Commn., 1976-78. Served with USN, 1944-46. Recipient Design Citation, Progressive Architecture mag., 1956, design award Soc. Am. Registered Architects, 1963, 64, 65, 66, 67, 69, Design award Archtl. Record mag., 1972. Mem. AIA, Wis. Soc. Architects. Home: 175 N Section St Nekoosa WI 54457 Office: 410 Daly Ave Wisconsin Rapids WI 54494

ACUFF, CHARLES DAVIS, data processing executive; b. Louisiana, Mo., Aug. 25, 1934; s. Davis Halliburton Acuff and Anna Mae (McGahen) McCuskey; m. Shirley Ann Vincent, Dec. 18, 1954; children—Suzanne Rose, Charles Davis, Jr. B.S., N.E. Mo. State U., Kirksville, 1956, M.A., 1961. Cert. tchr., Mo. Systems analyst Ford Motor Co., Dearborn, Mich., 1966-67; supr. adminstrn. program MCAUTO, St. Louis, 1967-69; dir. EDP, Peabody Coal Co., St. Louis, 1969-80; data processing cons., instr. St. Charles pub. schs., Mo., 1980-81; systems coordination mgr. Emerson Electric, St. Louis, 1982-83, mgr. computer services, 1983—; adj. prof. Lindenwood Coll., St. Charles, 1977—. Asst. cubmaster St. Louis Area council Boy Scouts Am., St. Charles, 1976-77, troop chmn., 1978. Served with U.S. Army, 1956-58. Mem. Inst. Cert. Systems Profls. (cert.), Assn. Systems Mgmt., Data Processing Mgmt. Assn. Methodist. Club: Spanish Lake Quadrils (Mo.). Avocations: bridge, gardening, square dancing. Home: 2420 Westminster Dr Saint Charles MO 63301 Office: Emersons Electric E & S Div 8100 W Florissant St Saint Louis MO 63136

ADAIR, BRUCE JAMES, publishing company official; b. Phila., Apr. 19, 1947; s. Francis and Marion Frances (Kosek) A.; B.A. in Sociology, Eastern Coll., St. David's, Pa., 1969; M.A. in Religious Edn., Eastern Baptist Theol. Sem., Phila., 1971; m. Linda Kushman, Oct. 15, 1982: children—Kenneth, Kristina Marie, Amy Lynne. Asst. pastor Jacobstown (N.J.) Bapt. Ch., 1966-67; dir. youth Upper Merion (Pa.) Bapt. Ch., 1967-68; minister edn. United Presbyn. Ch. of Manoa, Havertown, Pa., 1969-74; instr. phys. edn., head varsity soccer coach Eastern Coll., 1969-73; field cons., then asst. curriculum product mgr. David C. Cook Pub. Co., Elgin, Ill., 1974-76, curriculum product mgr., 1976-79, curriculum market mgr., 1979-82, curriculum mktg. dir., 1982—, dir. curriculum div., 1987—. Recipient Good Citizenship award Phila. Union League, 1968; named Christian Educator of Year, Phila. Sunday Sch. Assn., 1973. Office: David C Cook Pub Co 850 N Grove St Elgin IL 60120

ADAIR, CHARLES VALLOYD, retired physician; b. Lorain, Ohio, Apr. 20, 1923; s. Waite and Ella Jane (Robertson) A.; m. Contance Dean, Apr. 1, 1944; children—Allen V., Richard D. A.B., Hobart Coll, Geneva, N.Y., 1944; M.D., Western Res. U., 1947. Diplomate Am. Bd. Internal Medicine. Intern, then asst. resident in medicine Rochester Gen. Hosp., N.Y., 1947-49; fellow in medicine Univ. Hosps., Syracuse, N.Y., 1949-51; practice medicine specializing in internal medicine Mansfield, Ohio, 1953-85; ret. 1985; mem. staffs Mansfield Gen. Hosp., Peoples Hosp., Richland Neuropsychiat. Hosp.; mem. Mansfield City Bd. Health to 1985; trustee, past. pres. Mansfield Meml. Homes. Served to capt. AUS, 1943-46, 51-53. Fellow ACP; mem. Am. Soc. Internal Medicine, AMA, Ohio Med. Assn., Richland County Med. Soc. Republican. Congregationalist. Clubs: Our, Westbrook Country, University. Home: 1010 Woodland Rd Mansfield OH 44907

ADAM, KEN L., ceramic engineer; b. Fairfield, Iowa, Nov. 22, 1957; s. Elmer A. and Helen L. (Pacha) A.; m. Peggy S. Ashland, Aug. 6, 1983; 1 child, Angela S. BS in Ceramic Engring., Iowa State U., 1982. Process engr. E.F. Johnson, Waseca, Minn., 1982-86, Converter Concepts, Inc., Pardeeville, Wis., 1986—; computer instr. Wasela Elementary Schs., 1983. Patentee pig restraining device. Roman Catholic. Avocations: woodworking, water skiing. Home: Rural Rt 2 Box 85 Wells MN 56097 Office: Converter Concepts Inc Industrial Pkwy Pardeeville WI 53954

ADAM, PAUL JAMES, engineering company executive, mechanical engineer; b. Kansas City, Mo., Oct. 26, 1934; s. Paul James and Adrienne (Zimmerman) A.; m. Barbara Ann Mills, Dec. 18, 1956; children: Paul James, Blair Dodderidge, Matthew Mills. B.S. in Mech. Engring., U. Kans., 1956. Registered profl. engr., 16 states. Mech. engr. Black & Veatch, Cons. Engrs., Kansas City, Mo., 1956, 59-74, ptnr. asst. head power div., 1975-78, exec. ptnr., head power div., 1978—; dir. First Continental Bank & Trust Co. Mem. engring. adv. bd. U. Kans., 1982—; mem. WEC/UNIPEPE Com. on Thermal Generating Plant Availability, 1985—. Served to 1st lt. USAF, 1956-59. Mem. Nat. Soc. Profl. Engrs., Mo. Soc. Profl. Engrs., ASME, Am. Nuclear Soc., Atomic Indsl. Forum, Tau Beta Pi, Sigma Tau, Pi Tau Sigma, Omicron Delta Kappa, Alpha Tau Omega. Episcopalian. Club: Mission Hills Country. Office: Black & Veatch 1500 Meadow Lake Pkwy Kansas City MO 64114

ADAMANY, DAVID WALTER, university president; b. Janesville, Wis., Sept. 23, 1936; s. Walter Joseph and Dora Marie (Mutter) A. AB, Harvard U., 1958, JD, 1961; MS, U. Wis., 1963, PhD in Polit. Sci., 1967; LLD (hon.), Adrian Coll., 1984; AAS (hon.), Schoolcraft Coll., 1986. Bar: Wis. 1961. Spl. asst. to atty. gen. State of Wis., Madison, 1961-63, exec. pardon counsel, 1963; commr. Wis. Public Service Commn., 1963-65; instr. polit. sci. Wis. State U., Whitewater, 1965-67; asst. prof., then assoc. prof. Wesleyan U., Middletown, Conn., 1967-72; dean coll. Wesleyan U., 1969-71; assoc. prof., then prof. polit. sci. U. Wis., Madison, 1972-77; sec. of revenue State of Wis., 1974-76; v.p. acad. affairs, prof. Calif. State U., Long Beach, 1977-80, U. Md., College Park, 1980-82; prof. law and polit. sci. Wayne State U., Detroit, 1982—, pres., 1982—; chmn. Wis. Council Criminal Justice, 1973-75, Wis. Elections Bd., 1976-77, sec. Wis. Dept. Revenue; advisor to Gov. Patrick J. Lucey, State of Wis., 1972. Author: Financing Politics, 1969, Campaign Finance in America, 1972, Borzoi Reader in American Politics, 1972; co-author: American Government: Democracy and Liberty in Balance, 1975, Political Money, 1975; editorial bd.: Social Sci. Quarterly, 1973—, State and Local Govt. Rev, 1974-80; contbr. articles to profl. jours. Mem. exec. com. Detroit Med. Ctr., Met. Ctr. High Tech.; chmn. Mich. Bicentennial of Constn. Commn., 1986—; bd. dirs. Detroit Econ. Growth Corp., Detroit Inst. Arts Founders Soc., Detroit Symphony Orch., Mich. Cancer Found., New Detroit, United Found., Gov.'s Commn. on Jobs and Econ. Devel. Mem. Pres.' Council State Colls. and Univs. (chmn.), Am. Polit. Sci. Assn., ACLU, Wis. Bar Assn. Democrat. Office: Wayne State U Office of Pres Detroit MI 48202

ADAMKIEWICZ, JOSEPH JULIAN, physician, neurosurgeon, educator; b. Milw., Dec. 24, 1932; s. Joseph Julian Adamkiewicz and Sylvia Veronica Marlewski. Diplomate Am. Bd. Radiology, Am. Bd. Neurosurgery. Resident in neurosurgy Johns Hopkins U., Balt., 1961-65, asst. prof. neurosurgery, 1967-68; resident in radiology St. Luke's Hosp., Milw., 1977-80; assoc. prof. neurosurgery Med. Coll. Wis., Milw., 1980—; chmn. dept. radiology St. Lukes Hosp., Milw., 1982—. Served to lt. comdr. USPHS, 1959-61. Fellow ACS, Assn. University Radiologists; mem. Am. Coll. Radiology, Congress Neurol. Surgeons, Am. Assn. Neurol. Surgeons, Radiol. Soc. N.Am.; Alpha Omega Alpha. Club: Atheletic (Milw.). Avocations: gardening, sailing, skiing. Home: 3062 S Superior St Milwaukee WI 53207 Office: Dept Radiology St Louke's Hosp 2900 W Oklahoma Milwaukee WI 53215

ADAMS, ALLAN WILFRED, business consultant, lawyer; b. Beloit, Wis., Aug. 23, 1910; s. Harry Wilfred and Prudence Mary (Bennett) A.; A.B., Harvard Coll., 1932; LL.B., U. Wis., 1935; m. Charlotte Amy Ray, Nov. 26, 1936; children—Allan Wilfred, Prudence B., Polly H., John B. Admitted to Wis. bar, 1935; partner firm Adams & Adams, Beloit, Wis., 1935-61; of counsel firm Hansen, Eggers, Berres & Kelley, Beloit, 1961—; pres. Adams Corp., Beloit, 1946-62; sec. Flakall Corp., Beloit, 1945-61; pres. Dell Foods, Beloit, 1957-61; pres. Adams Internat. div. Beatrice Foods Co., Beloit, 1962-75, cons., 1975-79; corp. sec., gen. counsel Regal-Beloit Corp., 1979-82; dir. Regal-Beloit Corp., 1955-81, corp. sec., 1979-82. Pres., Beloit YMCA, 1955-64, dir., 1950-72; dir. Wis. Taxpayers Alliance, 1963-85 ; bd. dirs. Beloit ARC, 1958-70, United Givers, 1978-83, Greater Beloit Steering Com., 1978-81; with OPA-Rent Div., 1942-45; mem. Young Pres. Orgn., 1949-59, Wis. Pres. Orgn. Paul Harris Rotary fellow, 1978. Fellow Am. Coll. Probate Counsel, Am. Bar Found., Wis. Bar Found.; mem. Rock County Bar Assn. (pres. 1946), Am., Wis. bar assns., U. Wis. Bascom Hill Soc., Beloit Coll. Chapin Soc. Republican. Congregationalist. Clubs: Rotary, Beloit Country, Madison, Elks, Wis. 49ers. Home: 1628 Emerson St Beloit WI 53511 Office: Regal Beloit Co 419 Pleasant St Beloit WI 53511

ADAMS, ANDREA COLLEEN, civic organization administrator; b. Chgo., June 27, 1953; d. Hunter H. and Lorraine V. (McAfee) A. BA in Music Therapy, Lincoln U., 1975. Adminstrv. aide State Rep. Phillip Curls, Jefferson City, Mo., 1974; personnel adminstr. Standard Encyclopedias, Chgo., 1975; rehab. counselor State of Ill. Dept. Rehab. Services, Chgo., 1975-81; asst. dir. INROADS Chgo. Inc., 1981-87, mgr. Cen. region, 1987—; workshop facilitator Antioch Bapt. Ch., Chgo., 1983-84, New Covenant Bapt. Ch., Chgo., 1983-84, Christian Hope Bapt. Ch., Chgo., 1985, Progressive Community Ch., Chgo., 1984-86. Bd. dirs. Greater Grand Crossing Organizing Com., Chgo., 1982-85, chmn. community fest, 1983-84; mem. re-election campaign com. Charles Hayes, Chgo., 1985—; mem. Ill. Ethnic Cons., Chgo., 1985—; mem. Operation Push, Chgo., 1986—; bd. dirs. Chgo. Health Systems Agy., vice chmn. 1984—; bd. dirs. Chgo. Ctr. Health Systems Devel., Statewide Health Coordinating Council. Recipient Cert. Appreciation, New Covenant Miss. Bapt. Ch., Chgo., 1983, Cert. Recognition, Salem Luth. Ch., Chgo., 1982, Cert. Recognition, Luth. Ch. of Holy Spirit, Chgo., 1981; named Chgo.'s Up and Coming Black Bus. and Prof. Woman, Dollars and Sense Mag., 1985, one of Outstanding Young Women of Am., 1986. Mem. NAACP, Nat. Assn. Female Execs., Nat. Assn. Media Women, Women's Christian Fellowship (2d v.p. 1985-86), Delta Sigma Theta. Avocations: reading, politics, board games, cycling. Office: INROADS Chgo Inc 1313 S Michigan Ave Suite 601 Chicago IL 60604

ADAMS, ANNIE JENE, educator, consultant; b. Hopkinsville, Ky., Feb. 25, 1947; d. Robert Fulton and Jeanette Juanita (Johnson) Pollard; m. Elijah Harold Adams, Apr. 13, 1968; children—Angela, Norman. M.A. in Recreation Therapy, Wayne State U., 1981, Cert. Ed. S., 1984, doctoral candidate, 1985—. Cert. tchr., Mich. Tchr. adult edn. Hazel Park, Mich., 1974-75, St. Mary Magdalen, Hazel Park, Mich., 1974-75; tchr. spl. edn. Washington Careers Ctr. Detroit Bd. Edn., 1977—; host radio show Women of Power. Mem. Assn. Supervision and Curriculum Devel., Detroit Fedn. Tchrs., Nat. Coalition of 100 Black Women (Detroit chpt. bd. dirs., chmn. edn. com.), NAACP, Phi Delta Kappa. Home: 6433 Sheridan Ave Detroit MI 4821 Office: Poe Consortium Ctr 1200 W Canfield Detroit MI 48212

ADAMS, ARLIE, manufacturing company executive; b. Louisa, Ky 22, 1935; s. George and Effie Josephine (Davis) A.; m. Peggy Jo B Sept. 1, 1956; children—Arlie, James Richard. Mgr. systems Ga div. Dresser Industries (Ohio), 1983—. Mem. Hilliard (Ohio) Pl Zoning Commn., 1978-83. Club: Tosastmasters (past pres.). Lo Home: 988 N Biddle Rd Galion OH 44833 Office: Galion M Industries 352 South St Galion OH 44833

ADAMS, BRADLEY HASSAN, civil engineer; b. Roche 1953; s. Elee James and Alease Rebekah A.; m. Mary 25, 1954; children—Bradley Kennedy, Brenda Renee. Ohio U., 1976; postgrad. Cleve. State U., 1981-82. Ohio. Engr. Factory Mut., Cleve., 1976-78; safety sions, constrn. project engr. Polytech Inc., Cle Ozanne Constrn. Inc., 1984—; engring. cons. fo tion. Mem. ASCE. Home: 2449 Channing Rd Office: Ozanne Constrn Co 1744 Payne Ave

ADAMS, BRUCE ROGER, chemist; b. Roger Pierson and Lorraine Amelia 1973. BS, Colo. State U., 1978; PhD, Wis. Chemistry Dept., Madison, 1984 jours. Mem. Am. Chem. Soc., AAA Phi Beta Kappa. Avocations: ch Sheridan Dr Madison WI 53704

ADAMS, BUEL THOMAS, Ohio, Feb. 8, 1933; s. Olive Phyllis Joan Flahive, Apr Timothy, Christopher. B v.p. adminstrn. Blue C Playboy Enterprises,

Lincolnwood, Ill., 1976-78, Blount, Inc., Montgomery, Ala., 1978-81; v.p. fin. The Richardson Co., Des Plaines, Ill., 1981-83; v.p., treas. CBI Industries, Oak Brook, Ill., 1983—. Mem. Fin. Execs. Inst. (pres. Chgo. chpt. 1986-87), The Chgo. Forum, 1975-76, Machinery and Allied Products Inst.(fin. council). Roman Catholic. Avocations: sports, music, reading. Home: 233 Meadowbrook Ln Hinsdale IL 60521 Office: CBI Industries Inc 800 Jorie Blvd Oak Brook IL 60521

ADAMS, CHARLES HENRY, retired animal scientist, educator; b. Burdick, Kans., Nov. 7, 1918; s. Henry Lory and Bertha Frances (Westbrook) A.; m. Eula Mae Peters, Apr. 29, 1943. B.S., Kans. State U., 1941, M.S., 1942; Ph.D., Mich. State U., 1964. Instr. Kans. State U., Manhattan, 1946-47; asst. prof. U. Nebr., Lincoln, 1947-64, assoc. prof., 1964-70, prof. animal sci., 1970-83, prof. emeritus, 1983—; asst. dean Coll. Agr., U. Nebr., Lincoln, 1973-83. Contbr. articles to profl. jours. Served to 1st lt. AUS, 1943-46. Recipient Disting. Teaching awards Gamma Sigma Delta, 1969, U. Nebr., 1971, Am. Meat Sci. Assn., 1969, Am. Soc. Animal Sci., 1972. Fellow Am. Soc. Animal Sci., AAAS; mem. Am. Meat Sci. Assn., Inst. Food Technologists, Nebr. Acad. Sci., Am. Legion, VFW, Sigma Xi, Gamma Sigma Delta, Alpha Zeta, Alpha Gamma Rho. Republican. Mem. Christian Ch. (Disciples of Christ). Lodge: Rotary. Home: 7101 Colby St Lincoln NE 68505

ADAMS, CLAIRE ROBERTS, travel agency owner, educator; b. Jenkins, Ky., Oct. 31, 1940; d. Jack Andrews and Martha Claire (Drinkard) Roberts; m. James E. Adams, July 25, 1965; children: Keith Andrews, David Rush. BS, U. Ala., Tuscaloosa, 1962. Cert. travel counselor. With United Airlines, Chgo., 1962-65; tchr. Mt. Vernon (Ill.) Jr. High Sch., 1965-67; owner, mgr. Windjammer Travel, St. Louis, 1973—; Instr. Forrest Park Coll., St. Louis, 1980—. Mem. Inst. Cert. Travel Agts. (life, adv. bd., trustee 1987—), St. Louis Gateway Cert. Travel Counselors Forum (chmn. 1981-83). Republican. Mem. Ch. of Christ. Home: 2604 Bopp Rd Saint Louis MO 63131 Office: Windjammer Travel 9989 Manchester Saint Louis MO 63122

ADAMS, DAVID KYLE, architect; b. Washington Court House, Ohio, Mar. 28, 1930; s. Gilbert Gustin and Lois (Kyle) A.; m. Barbara Trueland, Sept. 20, 1957 (div. 1973); children: Deborah, Kimberly, Shawn, Kyle. Student, Muskingum Coll., 1947-49; BArch, Ohio State U., 1953. Project architect Dan A. Carmichael Architects, Columbus, Ohio, 1956-66, Dan A. Carmichael & Assocs., Columbus, Ohio, 1956-66; prin. David Kyle Adams, Architect, Columbus, 1966-69; pres. Adams Harder Kincheloe Swearingen, Architects, Columbus, 1969-80, Swearingen/Adams, Inc., Columbus, 1980—. Served to cpl. U.S. Army, 1953-55. Mem. AIA, Ohio Soc. Architects, Beta Theta Pi. Lodge: Optimists (local pres. 1971-72). Avocation: golf. Home: 584 Franklin Ave Columbus OH 43215 Office: Swearingen/Adams Inc 960 Kingsmill Pkwy Columbus OH 43229

ADAMS, EDMUND JOHN, lawyer; b. Lansing, Mich., June 6, 1938; s. John Edmund and Helen Kathryn (Pavlick) A.; m. Mary Louise Riegler, Aug. 11, 1962. B.A., Xavier U., 1960; LL.B., U. Notre Dame, 1963. Bar: Ohio 1963. Assoc. Paxton & Seasongood, Cin., 1965-70; assoc. Frost & Jacobs, 1970-71, ptnr., 1971—, exec. com., 1985—. Author: Founding Families of Loretto, 1983. Trustee, Southwest Ohio Regional Transit Authority, 1980—; chmn. Cin. Sister City Program, 1984—; mem. Hamilton County Republican Exec. Com., 1982—. Served to 1st lt. U.S. Army, 1963-65. Mem. ABA, Ohio Bar Assn., Cin. Bar Assn., Greater Cin. C. of C. (chmn. ballot issues com.). Roman Catholic. Clubs: Cin. Tennis, Hyde Park Country. Home: 1346 Park Ridge Place Cincinnati OH 45208 Office: Frost & Jacobs 2500 Central Trust Ctr Cincinnati OH 45202

ADAMS, GEORGE EMERY, mathematician, educator; b. Gary, Ind., Mar. 9, 1942; s. John Emery and Katherine Ellen (Cassiday) A.; m. Elvira Elizabeth Bene, June 24, 1967; children: Robert Edward Lee, Kelly Elizabeth. B.A. in Math., Manchester Coll., 1963; M.A., U. Ill., 1967; postgrad. (univ. fellow) Fla. State U., 1969-71; postgrad. U. N.C.-Asheville, 1983-84, Clemson U., 1984-85, Bowling Green State U., 1985—; Math. tchr. public schs., Cleve., 1963-66; asst. prof. math. Manchester Coll., N. Manchester, Ind., 1967-69, 71-72; prof. math. and computer sci. Montreat-Anderson Coll., Montreat, N.C., 1972-85, chmn. dept. math. and computer sci., chmn. div. natural sci.; teaching asst. Fla. State U., 1970-71; asst. prof. computer sci. Heidelberg Coll., Tiffin, Ohio, 1985—. Deacon, Montreat Presbyn. Ch., 1976-83; vestry Old Trinity Episc. Ch., 1987—. Recipient Tchr. of Year award, 1976, 78, 82. Mem. Math. Assn. Am., Am. Math. Assn. of Two-Yr. Colls. Republican. Home: 20 Sherwood Ct Tiffin OH 44883 Office: Dept Computer Sci Heidelberg Coll Tiffin OH 44883

ADAMS, HERBERT RICHARDS, publishing executive, clergyman; b. Phila., Apr. 19, 1932; s. Leander Hampton and Helen Marguerite (Richards) A.; m. Carol Anne Levine, Aug. 27, 1956; children—Ashley Pozefsky, Joshua, Lee Hampton, Rachel Ellis; m. 2d, Mary Ryan, Aug. 20, 1977. A.B., Colby Coll., 1954; Ed.D., Harvard U., 1972; student Harvard Divinity Sch., 1955-56, Kent State U., 1957, Boston U., 1963. Ordained to ministry Congregationalist Ch., 1952, Unitarian Universalist Assn., 1968; minister Fairfield and Pine Point, Maine, 1950-56, Chelsea, Mass., 1962-66; Lexington, Mass., 1967-75, Winnetka, Ill., 1978—; editor Allyn and Bacon, Boston, 1959-62; sr. editor Ginn and Co., Boston, 1962-68; v.p. mktg. Visual Learning Corp., Cambridge, Mass., 1968-71; dir. Sci. Research Assocs. subs. IBM, Chgo., 1975-83; v.p. Laidlaw Bros., River Forest, Ill., 1983-84, pres., 1984—; tchr. Greenville (Pa.) High Sch., 1956-58, Euclid (Ohio) High Sch., 1958-59, Lexington (Mass.) High Sch., 1968-69, Harvard Grad. Sch. Edn., 1971-72. Sponsor The Hunger Project. Recipient Coe Found. award DePauw U., 1958. Mem. Soc. Scholarly Publishing, Assn. Supervision and Curriculum Devel., Chgo. Book Clinic, Nat. Council Tchrs. English, SANE, ACLU. Clubs: Harvard of Chgo., Caxton. Author: Poetry on Film, 1970; Project Listening, 1975; Listening Your Way to Management Success, 1983; contbr. [illegible]erous articles to profl. jours. Home: 2679 Stewart Ave Evanston IL [illegible] Office: Laidlaw Educational Pub Thatcher & Madison Sts River [illegible]0305

ADAMS, [illegible]D GLEN, education association administrator; b. [illegible], 1940; s. Daniel Boone and Delsia Mae (Waller) A.; [illegible]n. 30, 1965; 1 child, Stephanie Glen. BS, Norfolk State U., 1970; PhD, Syracuse U., 1979. Biology [illegible] 1964-70; dir. alumni affairs Norfolk State U., 1970- [illegible] Nat. Consortium Minorities in Engring., Notre [illegible] Black Collegian Publs., New Orleans, 1986—. [illegible]ting the Graduate School Process, 1985; contbr. [illegible] Bd. dirs. YMCA Community Service Br., [illegible]stee Meadville Lombard Theol. Sch., Chgo., [illegible] Grants Panel, Boston, 1981—.. Mem. Nat. [illegible] 1986), Nat. Assn. Minority Program Ad- [illegible]), Nat. Alumni Assn. Norfolk State (nat. [illegible]qual Opportunity in Higher Edn. (corp. [illegible]me: 11061 Al-Vir Ct Osceola IN 46556 [illegible]n Engring Box 537 Notre Dame IN [illegible]

[illegible]hool district official; b. Isom, Ky., [illegible]lenda C. O'Connell, Apr. 8, 1958; [illegible]Morehead State U., 1958, M.A., [illegible]upt., Ind. Tchr. Simon Kenton [illegible] Central Jr. High Sch., Xenia, [illegible] Sch., Xenia, Ohio, 1961-65, [illegible]dminstr. asst. to supt. Xenia [illegible]naw City Sch., Mich., 1967- [illegible]c. Office Acad. Affairs and [illegible] 1969-70; supt. The Pub. [illegible]ch., 1974-76; supt. Win- [illegible]N.C., 1976-82, Indpsl. [illegible]d. dirs. Green County [illegible], Indpls. Conv. and [illegible]of Am. council Boy [illegible]ons. to bd. Central [illegible]n and Curriculum [illegible]SA, NCEA, Phi [illegible]e: 1206 Golden Hill Dr Indianapolis IN 46208 Office: Indpls Pub Schs 120 E Walnut St Indianapolis IN 46204 *

ADAMS, JANET KAY, computer scientist; b. McKeesport, Pa., Oct. 17, 1935; d. William John and Irene Pearl (Craven) Smith; m. Ralph Emerson Adams, Sept. 8, 1962; 1 child, Richard. RN, Presbyn. Hosp., Pitts., 1956; BS in Computer Sci. cum laude, Wright State U., 1985. Staff nurse Bur. Indian Affairs, Anchorage, 1961-62, Alaska Psychiat. Inst., Anchorage, 1962-64; vice-chmn. Profl. Nurses Registry, Wichita, Kans., 1964-66; instr. Wright State U., Dayton, Ohio, 1983-85; systems analyst NCR Corp., Dayton, 1985—. Served to 1st lt. USAF, 1957-61. Mormon. Avocations: reading, gardening, swimming, walking. Office: NCR Corp 1700 S Patterson Blvd Dayton OH 45479

ADAMS, JOHN CARTER, accounting firm executive; b. Bismark, N.D., Apr. 20, 1919; s. John Bennett and Olive Hazel (Procter) A.; student Wilson Jr. Coll., 1946, Walton Sch. Commerce, Chgo., 1947-48, LaSalle U., 1954-55; C.P.A., U. Ill., 1956; children—John, Judith Fitzgerald, Paul, William; m. Harriet N. Hall, May 1, 1976. With John E. Burke & Co., 1946-48, Gen. Motors Corp., 1948-51; with Wynn M. Wagner & Co. (now Wagner Sim & Co.), pub. accts., Chgo., 1951-79, partner, 1956-79; ptnr. Lester Witte & Co., C.P.A.s Chgo., 1979-82; pres. John C. Adams & Co. P.C., 1982—; v.p. Naperville (Ill.) Elderly Homes, Inc., 1972-75, pres., 1975-76, also dir.; partner Mill Ogden Venture. Served with USAAF, 1942-46. C.P.A., Ill. Mem. Am. Inst. C.P.A.s., Ill. Soc. C.P.A.s. Club: Union League (vice chmn; mem. fin. com.) (Chgo.). Lodge: Rotary. Home: 1001 Belaire Ct Naperville IL 60540 Office: 604 N Washington Naperville IL 60540

ADAMS, JOHN DAVID VESSOT, manufacturing company executive; b. Ottawa, Ont., Can., Jan. 7, 1934; s. Albert Oliver and Estelle Priscilla (Vessot) A.; m. Dorothy Marion Blyth, June 27, 1959; children—Nancy, Joel, Louis. Student Carleton U., 1950-51; B.Eng., McGill U., 1955; M.B.A., U. Western Ont., 1958. Registered profl. engr., Ont. Project engr. Abitibi Paper Co., Toronto, Ont., 1962-63, Cockshutt Farm Equipment Co. Ltd., Brantford, Ont., 1958-62, Can. Industries Ltd., Kingston, Ont., 1955-58; mgr. fin. analysis and planning Rio Tinto Zinc Group, London, 1963-66; mgr. adminstrn. and planning Can. Gypsum Co. Ltd., Toronto, 1966-72; mgr. logistics and fin. Massey Ferguson Co. Ltd., Toronto, 1972-79; pres. Can. Spool & Bobbin Co. Ltd., Walkerton, Ont., 1979—; dir. Knechtel Furniture Ltd. Mem. Assn. Profl. Engrs. Province Ont. Mem. United Ch. of Can. Clubs: Walkerton Golf and Curling, Rotary. Home: 386 14th Ave, Hanover, ON Canada N4N 2Y1 Office: Canadian Spool & Bobbin Co, 604 Durham, Walkerton, ON Canada N0G 2V0

ADAMS, JOHN TAYLOR, II, real estate developer; b. Dubuque, Iowa, Nov. 13, 1941; s. Paul Livermore and Lassie (Culling) A.; m. Ann Lundy, July 20, 1963 (div. 1971); children John Taylor III, Paul Livermore II; m. Wendy Storck, Aug. 19, 1978; 1 child, Samuel Townsend. BA, DePauw U., 1964; postgrad. in architecture, Clemson U., 1972; MBC, U. Fla., 1973. Editor Attica Ledger Tribune, 1964-65; pres. Empresa Tropica, S.A., Tegucigalpa, Honduras, 1967-71; v.p. Palmas del Mar, Humacao, P.R., 1973-75; pres. J.T. Adams Properties, Inc., West Chester, Ohio, 1979—; bd. dirs. Spahn & Rose Lumber Co., Dubuque. Mem. Nat. Assn. Realtors, Nat. Assn. Home Builders (bd. dirs. 1985), Home Buildres Assn. Greater Cin. (bd. dirs.), Urban Land Inst., ASCE. Republican. Avocations: sailing, archeology. Office: 8300 Princeton-Glendale Rd West Chester OH 45069

ADAMS, JOSEPH JOHN, historical photography specialist, consultant; b. Springfield, Ill., Apr. 8, 1944; s. Grant D. and Margaret Marie (Bogenschutz) A.; m. Mary Ann Wilkerson, Sept. 10, 1977; children: Jason, Christina. Grad. high sch., Springfield, Ill., 1963. Gen. mgr. Midwest Microfilm Co., Springfield, 1963-84; microfilm operator Ill. State Hist. Soc. Library, Springfield, 1985, specialist hist. photography, 1985—. V.p. St. Joseph Sch. Parent-Tchrs. Club, Springfield, 1984. Served with U.S. Army, 1964-66, Vietnam. Republican. Roman Catholic. Home: Rural Rt 5 Box 307A Springfield IL 62707 Office: Ill State Hist Library Old State Capitol Springfield IL 62701

ADAMS, JOSEPH MERLE, accountant; b. Florence, S.C., July 4, 1961; s. Thomas Louie and Joann (Goff) A.; m. Gail Patricia Masterson, May 18, 1985. BS in Accountancy, No. Ill. U., 1983. CPA, Ill. Sec.-treas. Goff Enterprises, Glen Ellyn, Ill., 1979-82; internal auditor Household Internat., Prospect Heights, Ill., 1982; staff acct. Arthur Andersen & Co., Chgo., 1983—. Mem. No. Ill. U. Council, DeKalb, 1982-83. Mem. Am. Inst. CPA's, Ill. CPA Soc. (Elijah Watts Sells award 1983), Beta Alpha Psi. Republican. Methodist. Club: Glen Oak Country (Glen Ellyn). Avocations: golf, tennis. Office: Arthur Andersen & Co 33 W Monroe Chicago IL 60603

ADAMS, JUDITH ANN, educator; b. Dayton, Nov. 18, 1948; d. Robert Lewis and Elizabeth Jean (List) Myers; m. Keith Guy Adams, Aug. 13, 1977; 1 child, Collin Matthew. Student, Am. U., Washington, 1970; BA magna cum laude, Franklin Coll., 1971; MEd., Xavier U., 1974. Tchr. Rodger O. Borror Sch., Wilmington, Ohio, 1971—, advisor student council, 1972-85; guest lectr. Ohio Dept. Edn. Jennings Found. Character Edn. Conf., 1987. Co-author: Peer Tutoring the Multiply Handicapped Public School Student, 1985; columnist: Washington Close Up (Best Column award 1970); author: A + For Positive Living! Sec. Christian Women's Fellowship, Wilmington, 1985—; counselor , dir. China Lake (Maine) Conf. Ctr., 1974-76; coordinator Robert F. Kennedy for President, Johnson County, Ind., 1968. Named Outstanding Young Educator Wilmington Area Jaycees, 1976, All-Ohio Student Council Advisor Ohio Assn. Student Councils, 1984, 85; recipient Outstanding Educators citation Ohio Ho. Rep., 1985; Exceptional Achievement award Hopewell Special Edn. Regional Resource Ctr., 1985. Mem. NEA, Wilmington Edn. Assn. (sec. 1973-74, Disting. Service award 1985), Ohio Edn. Assn., Assn. Supervision Curriculum Devel., Nat. Assn. Student Activities Advisors, Phi Alpha Theta. Mem. Christian Ch. Lodge: Order of Eastern Star (marshal 1976-77, chaplain 1973-75). Avocations: flower gardening, reading, photography. Home: 689 Hiatt Ave Wilmington OH 45177-1570 Office: Rodger O Borror Sch 365 W Locust St Wilmington OH 45177

ADAMS, KEITH EDWARD, food products executive; b. Waukesha, Wis., Jan. 24, 1959; s. Mike and Rosemary (Blessington) A. BBA in Acctg., U. Wis., Oshkosh, 1981. CPA, Wis.; cert. mgmt. acct., Wis. Cost acct. Square D Co., Oshkosh, 1982-83, gen. acct., 1983-84; sr. fin. acct. Anaquest div. BOC Health Care, Madison, 1984-86, supr. internat. acctg., 1986; mgr. fin. planning Beatrice Food Ingredients div. Beatrice Foods Co., Beloit, Wis., 1986—. Mem. Nat. Assn. Accts., Wis. Inst. CPA's, Am. Inst. CPA's. Republican. Roman Catholic. Office: Beatrice Food Ingredients 352 E Grand Ave Beloit WI 53511

ADAMS, LESLIE, composer; b. Cleve., 1932. B.Mus., Oberlin (Ohio) Coll., 1955; M.A., Calif. State U., Long Beach, 1967; Ph.D., Ohio State U., 1973. Mem. faculty Kans. U., 1970-78; composer-in-residence Karamu House, Cleve., 1979-81, Cleve. Music Sch. Settlement, 1981—; Rockefeller Found. fellow, Bellagio, Italy, summer 1979; fellow Yaddo, Saratoga Springs, N.Y., summer 1980, winter 1984; del. Gt. Lakes Assembly for Future Performing Arts, 1980; composer: A Kiss in Xanadu (ballet), 1954, 73; Piano Concerto, 1974; Ode to Life for Orch. (performed by Buffalo Philharm. 1983) 1979; Symphony No. 1, 1980; Dunbar Songs (commd. by Ohio Chamber Orch), 1982; Blake (opera), 1985; The Righteous Man (cantata), 1986; also works for piano, horn, cello, brass ensemble, solo voice chorus. Winner nat. choral composition competition Christian Arts, 1974. Mem. Am. Composers Alliance, Am. Choral Dirs. Assn., Am. Music Center, Pi Kappa Lambda, Phi Delta Kappa, Phi Mu Alpha Sinfonia, Phi Kappa Phi. Contbr. articles to profl. jours. Address: 9409 Kempton Ave Cleveland OH 44108

ADAMS, LUCILLE JOAN, psychotherapist, health administrator; b. Hartford, Conn., Apr. 2, 1933; d. Charles William and Catherine Therese (Messmer) A. AS, Hartford Coll. for Women, 1958; BA, Wheaton Coll., 1960; MSW, Smith Coll., 1962; cert. child psychotherapy, Inst. Psychoanalysis, 1972. Cert. social Worker, Ill. Caseworker I and II Family Service of Milw., 1962-66; child therapist Lakeside Children's Ctr., Milw., 1966-69; dist. dir. Jewish Children's Bur., Chgo., 1969—; pvt. practice psychotherapy Chgo., 1976—; field instr. U. Chgo., 1970-72; clin. instr. Smith Coll. Sch. Social Work, Northampton, Mass., 1979-81; faculty postgrad. edn. Inst. Psychoanalysis, Chgo., 1978-82;. Mem. Nat. Acad. Social Workers (sec. 1965-66, cert.), Assn. Child Psychotherapists (sec. 1972-73), Ill. Soc. Clin. Social Workers, Photographic Soc. Am. Avocation: color slide photography. Home: 1455 N Sandburg Terr #1104 Chicago IL 60610 Office: Jewish Childrens Bur 5050 Church St Skokie IL 60077

ADAMS, NINA M., insurance company executive; b. N.Y.C., Mar. 14, 1945; d. D. Howard and Celia (Schneider) Magid. BS in Math., SUNY, Cortland, 1966. Resident advisor Grinnell (Iowa) Coll., 1972-74; spl. project coordinator Stadiums Unltd., Grinnell, 1974-77; product mgr. CNA Ins., Chgo., 1977-79, systems analyst, 1979-83, systems mgr., 1983—; lectr. in field, 1983-85. Vol. St. Nicks Theater, Chgo., 1983-84, Organic Theater, Chgo., 1984-85, Chgo. Theater, 1986. Home: 6342 N Sheridan Rd Chicago IL 60660 Office: CNA Ins CNA Plaza Chicago IL 60660

ADAMS, PAUL, company executive, consultant; b. Elyria, Ohio, Aug. 19, 1955; s. Paul and Pauline (Bougioukle) A.; m. Beth Sutter, Oct. 13, 1979. B.B.A., Cleve. State U., 1982. Sales engr. Meriam Instrument, Cleve., 1976-78; tech. rep. Gibson Homans Co., Cleve., 1978-83; nat. mktg. mgr. Fred Wilson Co., Lathrup Village, Mich., 1983; pres., founder R-Tech Protective Coatings, Inc., Elyria, Ohio, 1983—; pvt. practice cons. comml. roof systems. Mem. Sales and Mktg. Execs. of Cleve., Greater Cleve. Growth Assn. Republican. Home: 732 University Elyria OH 44035 Office: R-Tech Protective Coatings Inc PO Box 1045 Elyria OH 44036

ADAMS, ROBERT JAY, technical training manager; b. Wheelersburg, Ohio, June 8, 1935; s. John Benton and Phoebe Jane (Kraft) A.; m. Alice Ann Boyer, Apr. 10, 1961; children: Michael Jay, Cheryl Ann. AA magna cum laude, Hillsborough Community Coll., 1977; student indsl. tech., U. of South Fla., 1977-79. Cert. secondary tchr. Enlist USN, 1953, advanced through ranks to warrant officer, 1967, commd. ensign, 1969, advanced through grades to lt., 1971, retired, 1973; service mgr. Ohdt-Waring Corp., Tampa, Fla., 1973-79; supr. instrumentation Goodyear Atomic Corp., Piketon, Ohio, 1980-82; tchr. electronics Telemedia Corp., Jubail, Saudi Arabia, 1982-84; tng. mgr. Liebert Corp., Columbus, Ohio, 1984—. Pres. Western Australia Kindergarten Assn., Exmouth, West Australia, 1969-71, Minford (Ohio) Band Boosters Assn., 1979-82; trustee Tanglewood Home Owners Assn., Wheelersburg, 1980-82. Mem. Ohio Edn. Assn., Assn. Field Service Mgrs. Republican. Lodge: Rotary. Avocations: woodworking, fishing. Home: 6158 Northgate Rd Columbus OH 43229 Office: Liebert Corp 1050 Dearborn Dr Columbus OH 43229

ADAMS, RONALD BRENT, manufacturing executive; b. Atlanta, June 8, 1949; s. Horace George and Carrie (Drake) A.; m. Peggy Elise Gault, Apr. 24, 1970; children: Michelle, Brent. BSMET with highest honors, So. Tech. Inst., 1973; postgrad. in bus., Ga. State U., 1973-74. Project engr. Southwire Co., Carrolton, Ga., 1970-72; application engr. Ingersoll-Rand Co., Atlanta, 1973-74; sales engr. Ingersoll-Rand Co., Raleigh, N.C., 1974-76; utility sales exec. Ingersoll-Rand Co., Charlotte, N.C., 1976-80; petroleum energy specialist Ingersoll-Rand Co., Houston, 1980-84; mgr. mktg. Ingersoll-Rand Co., Baxter Springs, Kans., 1984—. Mem. Soc. Mfg. Engrs. (composites group, cert. appreciation 1985-86). Republican. Presbyterian. Club: Candlelight Hills Recreation (Houston) (bd. dirs.). Avocations: water skiing, tennis. Office: Ingersoll-Rand Waterjet Cutting 635 W 12th St Baxter Springs KS 66713

ADAMS, THOMAS JOSEPH, food company executive; real estate developer; b. Portsmouth, Ohio, Sept. 2, 1923; s. Allen Willard and Clara Audry (Jones) A.; m. Andree Claudine Jaccard, Sept. 9, 1946; children—Christelle Claire Frost, Paul Allen, Patrick Stephen. BA, Ohio State U., 1949. With Ideal Bakery, Inc., Jackson, Ohio, 1946-72, Tops Cleaners, Inc., Chillicothe, Ohio, 1953-73; owner, operator Adams Baking Co., Portsmouth, Ohio, 1973-78; with Phoenix Pies, Inc., Portsmouth, 1973-85; pres., owner Adams Holdings, Inc., Portsmouth, 1978—. Served with U.S. Army, 1943-45, ETO. Recipient Golden Shovel award State of Ohio House Reps., 1985. Mem. Ohio Bakers Assn. (bd. dirs. 1976). Republican. Club: Columbus Athletic. Lodges: Rotary (Portsmouth); Masons. Avocations: reading; swimming; walking. Home: 826 Gay St Portsmouth OH 45662 also: 5875 Cactus Way La Jolla CA 92037 Office: Adams Holdings Inc PO Box 1481 Portsmouth OH 45662

ADAMS, THOMAS WALTON, probation agent; b. Midland, Mich., Apr. 15, 1947; s. Lawrence Walton and Elizabeth (Miller) A.; m. Karen Lynn Perry. BS with honors, Mich. State U., 1973, MS, 1987. Probation agt. 75th Dist. Ct., Midland, 1973—. Mem. Midland County Alcohol Services Bd., 1975-78, Midland-Gladwin County Community Mental Health Bd., 1978-87, chmn. 1980-82. Named One of Outstanding Young Men Am., 1982; recipient Liberty Bell award, Midland Bar Assn., 1983. Mem. Am. Correctional Assn., Alpha Phi Sigma. Avocations: stereo equipment, music, photography. Home: 5823 Leeway Dr Midland MI 48640 Office: Adult Probation Courthouse Midland MI 48640

ADAMS, TIMOTHY RAYMOND, EDP training and quality specialist; b. Chgo., July 23, 1951; s. Roy and Norine (Hendrickson) A. BS in Psychology, Loyola U., Chgo., 1973, MS in Indsl. Relations, 1977. Employment counselor West Personnel Service, Oak Brook, Ill., 1973-74; personnel asst., human resource rep. Helene Curtis Industries, Inc., Chgo., 1974-79; exec. recruiter Ill. Dept. Personnel, Springfield, 1979-80; manpower coordinator Ill. Dept. Mental Health, Chgo., 1980; mgr. personnel resources Chgo. Bd. Options Exchange, 1980-83, mgr. employee relations, 1983-85, mgr. staff devel., 1985, mgr. quality adminstrn., edn., 1985—; part-time instr. Morton Coll., 1983—; mem. bus. occupation adv. bd. Dawson Skill Ctr., Chgo. City Colls., 1975-79; guest lectr. personnel Loyola U., 1976-78. Chmn. 1st aid com. West Cook County dist. Mid-Am. chpt. ARC, 1978-79, 81-82, chmn. dist. bd., 1983-86, supr. disaster services, 1980—, instr. 1st aid, 1969-85 instr. CPR, 1975-85, bd. dirs. 1983-86. Recipient service awards ARC, 1974, 79, 81, 83-84, 86. Mem. Am. Soc. Tng. and Devel. Office: Chgo Bd Options Exchange La Salle at Van Buren Chicago IL 60605

ADAMS, WILLIAM CHARLES, manufacturing company executive; b. Reynoldsville, Pa., 1923; married. B.S., UCLA, 1950. With Federal-Mogul Corp., Southfield, Mich., 1950; various positions Arrowhead Products div. Federal-Mogul Corp., Southfield, Mich., 1950-60; gen. mfr. microtech. div. Federal-Mogul Corp., Southfield, Mich., 1960-65, gen. mgr. Arrowhead products div., 1965-68; gen. mgr. Nat. Seal div. Federal-Mogul Corp., Southfield, Mich, 1968-71; group mgr. rubber and plastics group Federal-Mogul Corp., Southfield, Mich., 1971-72, group mgr. products group, 1973-76, exec. v.p., 1976-77, pres., chief operating officer, 1977—, also dir. Office: Fed-Mogul Corp PO Box 1966 Southfield MI 48235 *

ADAMS, WILLIAM JOHNSTON, accounting firm executive; b. Detroit, Nov. 24, 1934; s. William Montgomery and Sara Emogene (Johnston) A.; m. Lynn Laviolette, Aug. 24, 1957 (div. Sept. 1976); 1 child, William David; m. Donna Wolcott, Apr. 24, 1977. BBA, U. Mich., 1957, MBA, 1958. CPA, Mich. Staff acct. Arthur Andersen & Co., Detroit, 1958-62, tax mgr., 1962-70, tax ptnr., 1970—. Trustee, sec., treas., pres. Grosse Pointe (Mich.) Pub. Schs., 1969-72; chmn. Greater Detroit Fgn. Trade Zone, Inc., 1983—; bd. dirs. Civic Searchlight, Detroit, 1985—. Named Outstanding Young Man of Yr. Grosse Pointe Jaycees, 1970; named to Pres.' Club U. Mich., Ann Arbor, 1975. Mem. Mich. Assn. CPA's, Mich. Inst. CPA's. Congregationalist. Clubs: Detroit, Detroit Boat (bd. dirs., treas. 1985—), Indian Village Tennis (Detroit). Home: 2480 Iroquois Detroit MI 48214

ADAMS, WILLIAM RICHARD, zooarcheologist; b. Bloomington, Ind., Feb. 21, 1923; s. William Baker and Mildred Florence (Dingle) A.; A.B., Ind. U., 1945, M.A., 1949, S.O.P.A., 1980; m. Connie Marie Christie, Oct. 20, 1968; children—William H., James E., Richard B., Margaret E., Scott C., Teresa M. Archeologist, Ind. Hist. Bur., 1945-47; instr., embalmer Sch. Medicine, Ind. U., Bloomington, 1947-49; ethnozoologist Central Miss. Valley Archaeol. Expdn., St. Louis, 1949; field archaeologist Royal Ont. Museum, 1955-56; dir. Ind. Ethnozoological Lab., Bloomington, 1947—; curator Ind. U. Museums, Bloomington, 1949—, instr. ethnozoology, 1956—; pres., chmn. bd. Bloomington Nat. Bank, 1973-80. Mem. Soc. Am.

Archaeology, Southwestern Archaeol. Assn., Wilderness Soc., Sierra Club, Audubon Soc., Ind. Hist. Soc., Ind. Acad. Sci., Monroe County Aux. Police. Republican. Clubs: Trowel and Brush, Elks, Ind. Police League, Ind. Chiefs Police. Office: Ind Univ Dept Ethnozoology 407 Rawles Hall Bloomington IN 47401

ADAMSHICK, DONALD RAYMOND, psychologist; b. Toledo, Mar. 10, 1930; s. Christopher and Joanna A. (Fry) A.; m. Carolyn M. Vandekerkhoff, Aug. 10, 1957; children: Mary Helen, Michael R., Margaret A., Elizabeth T., Jane K. BA, U. Toledo, 1954, MEd, 1960. Lic. psychologist, Ohio. Psychologist Adams Twp. Local Schs., Toledo, 1960-61, Ohio Dept. of Edn. Blind-Deaf, Columbus, 1961-83; dean personal formation Pontifical Coll. Josephinum, Columbus, 1983—; cons. in mental retardation and low incidence handicaps; cons. clin. medicine team, Dept. Edn., Columbus, 1961-75, psychologist edn. clin. team, 1961-83; dir. sem. evaluation of handicapped, Taichung, Taiwan, Republic of China, 1979; dir. sem. teaching mentally retarded using behavior objectives, Tainan, Taiwan, 1983; dir. sem. implementing behavior objectives in classroom Nat. Taiwan Normal U., Taipei, Taiwan, 1987. Author: Teaching with Behavorial Objectives, 1979 (Chinese award). Served with M.C., U.S. Army, 1950-53. Recipient Cert. Appreciation Phillipine Nat. Sch. Deaf and Blind, Quezon City, 1979, Republic of China Assn. for Mentally Retarded, 1983; awarded Key to City, Mayor of Tainan, 1983. Mem. Ohio Psychol. Assn. (spl. recognition of service award 1972), Cen. Ohio Psychol. Assn., Ohio Sch. Psychologists Assn., Phi Delta Kappa. Democrat. Roman Catholic. Avocations: writing, fishing, boating.

ADAMSON, JAMES CANTWELL, automotive engring. co. exec.; b. Kenosha, Wis., May 21, 1935; s. Harry Richard and Esther Taaffe (Cantwell) A.; B.E.E., Marquette U., Milw., 1959; m. Rita Marie Ruffolo, June 24, 1961; children—Michael, Paula, Gregory, Patrick, Margaret, Catherine (dec.). With Am. Motors Corp., Kenosha, 1959—, sr. product devel. engr., 1967-75, resident engr., 1975—. Served with AUS, 1954-56. Mem. Soc. Automotive Engrs., Wis. Hist. Soc., Kenosha County Hist. Soc., Nat. Rifle Assn., Wis. Sportsman's Assn., Triangle frat. Roman Catholic. Clubs: Shamrock, Elks, Southport Gun, Ausblick Ski. Home: 1518 Harmony Dr Racine WI 53402 Office: Am Motors Corp 5626 25th Ave Kenosha WI 53140

ADAMSONS-SCHRANZ, GLORIA, dentist; b. Liepaja, Latvia, Oct. 29, 1929; came to U.S., 1951; s. Eugene and Sofia (Keister) A.; m. William R. Schranz, Feb. 17, 1961. BA, Milw.-Downer Coll., 1953; DDS, Marquette U., 1957. Pvt. practice dentistry Milw., 1957—. Bd. dirs. Am. Cancer Soc., Milw., 1985—. Mem. ADA, Wis. Dental Assn., Greater Milw. Dental Assn., Assn. Am. Women Dentists (pres. 1975), Marquette U. Dental Alumni Assn. (pres. 1984), Altrusa Internat. (bd. dirs. 1984—). Club: Women's of Wis. Avocations: travel, golf. Home: 1626 N Prospect Ave Milwaukee WI 53202 Office: 2266 N Prospect Ave Milwaukee WI 53202

ADAN, ADELBERTO JOSE, hospital administrator; b. Camaguey, Cuba, Aug. 21, 1951; came to U.S. 1965, naturalized 1976; s. Adelberto and Bertha (Cepeda) A.; m. Nancy Sue Shepard, June 2, 1979; 1 child, Ashley Sue. B.A., Grand Valley State Colls., 1974; M.B.A., Central Mich. U., 1980. Health care worker Health Delivery, Inc., Saginaw, Mich., 1971-76; adminstrv. asst./div. mgr. Midland Hosp. Ctr. (Mich.), 1977-79, asst. v.p. support services, 1979-82, asst. v.p. profl. services, 1982-84, v.p., 1984—. Ex-officio mem. bd. dirs. Ernie Wallace Meml. Blood Bank; bd. dirs. Saginaw Valley Blood Program. Am. Coll. Healthcare Execs. Republican. Baptist. Home: 1800 Sylvan Ln Midland MI 48640 Office: Midland Hosp Ctr 4005 Orchard Dr Midland MI 48640

ADDERLEY, TERENCE E., corporate executive. married. B.M.A., U. Minn., 1956. Former fin. analyst Standard Oil Co. of N.J.; with Kelly Services, Inc., Troy, Mich., 1957—, v.p., 1961-65, exec. v.p., 1965-67, pres., 1967—, also dir. Office: Kelly Services Inc 999 W Big Beaver Rd Troy MI 48084 *

ADDINGTON, JAMES EDWARD, anthropologist; b. Detroit, Mar. 1, 1947; s. Jack Elwood and Virginia Lucille (Tucker) A.; BS, Western Mich. U., 1969, MA, 1972; ABD, Ohio State U., 1975; m. Nancy Louise Salchow, Sept. 6, 1969; children: Timothy Finley, Peter Henry. Instr., Ohio State U., Columbus, 1972-75; sr. research asso. Ohio State Mus., Columbus, 1972—; field archaeologist W. Va. Geol. Survey, 1974; cultural resource sect. head Ohio Dept. Transp., Columbus, 1975—; cons. archaeologist Ohio Cultural Resource Cons., Columbus, 1976—; cultural resource cons. Active, Indian Guides, YMCA, Columbus, 1977—, program coordinator, 1984—. Recipient Cert. of Appreciation, Columbus Pub. Schs., 1974, 86, 87, Kiwanis, 1978-79, Ohio Transp. Engrs. Assn., 1977, 79, YMCA of Columbus, 1986; commendation Columbus Police Dept., 1983; Hist. Preservation Survey grantee, 1978-79. Mem. Ohio Archaeol. Council (treas., dir. 1978-84), Nat. Trust for Hist. Preservation, Am. Assn. State and Local History, Northeast Anthrop. Assn., Eastern States Archaeol. Fedn., Soc. Hist. Archaeology, Soc. Indsl. Archaeology, Nat. Hist. Soc., Ohio Hist. Soc., Soc. Am. Archaeology, Central State Anthropol. Assn., Sigma Xi, Alpha Phi Omega. Contbr. articles in field to profl. jours. Home: 2590 Dibblee Ave Columbus OH 43204 Office: Ohio Dept Transp Bur Environ Services 25 S Front St Columbus OH 43215

ADDINGTON, KEENE HARWOOD, banker; b. Chgo., May 28, 1932; s. James Rol and Sarah Stires (Wood) A.; m. Constance Goldsmith, Nov. 16, 1968; children: Sarah Lee, Keene Harwood, II, Leslie, Margo, Pamela, Elinor, Brooks. B.A., Amherst Coll., 1954; postgrad., U. Chgo. Bus. Sch. Vice pres. mktg. Miehle Goss Dexter Inc., Chgo., 1959-72; pres. Pandrick Press Midwest Inc., Chgo., 1972-75; adminstrv. v.p., then exec. v.p. Am. Nat. Bank & Trust Co., Chgo., 1975-78; pres. Am. Nat. Bank & Trust Co., 1978—; also dir.; sr. v.p., dir. Walter E. Heller Internat. Adv. group Opportunities Industrialization Center, Chgo.; treas. Met. Housing and Planning Council; adv. bd. Center Sports Medicine; trustee Glenwood (Ill.) Sch. Boys. Served to capt. USAF, 1954-58. Mem. Am. Bankers Assn., Assn. Res. City Bankers, Robert Morris Assos., Ill. Bankers Assn. Republican. Episcopalian. Clubs: Shoreacreas, Chicago, Economic, Onwentsia. Home: 877 N Woodbine Pl Lake Forest IL 60045

ADDISON, ROBERT A., manufacturingcompany executive. Pres. Kirsch Co., Sturgis, Mich. Office: Kirsch Co 309 N Prospect St Sturgis MI 49091 *

ADDUCCI, JOSEPH EDWARD, obstetrician, gynecologist; b. Chgo., Dec. 1, 1934; s. Dominee Edward and Harriet Evelyn (Kneppreth) A.; m. Mary Ann Tiertje, 1958; children—Christopher, Gregory, Steven, Jessica, Tobias. B.S., U. Ill., 1955; M.D., Loyola U., Chgo., 1959. Diplomate Am. Bd. Ob-Gyn., Nat. Bd. Med. Examiners. Intern Cook County Hosp, Chgo., 1959-60; resident in ob-gyn Mt. Carmel Hosp., Detroit, 1960-64; practice medicine specializing in obstetrics and gynecology Williston, N.D., 1966—; chief staff, chmn. obstetrics dept. Mercy Hosp., Williston; clin. prof. U. N.D. Med. Sch., 1973—. Mem. N.D. Bd. Med. Examiners, 1974—, past chmn.; project dir. Tri County Family Planning Service; past pres. Tri County Health Planning Council; chmn. Williams County Welfare Bd., 1966—. Served with M.C., AUS, 1964-66. Fellow Am. Soc. Abdominal Surgeons, A.C.S., Am. Coll. Obstetrics and Gynecologists (sect. chmn. N.D.), Internat. Coll. Surgeons (regent 1972-74), Am. Fertility Soc., Am. Assn. Internat. Lazar Soc., Gynecol. Lataropists, N.D. Obstetricians and Gynecologists Soc. (pres. 1966, 76); mem. Am. Soc. for Colposcopy and Colpomicroscopy, Am. soc. Cryosurgery, Am. Soc. Contemporary Medicine and Surgery, Am. Assn. Profl. Ob-Gyn., Pan Am. Med. Assn. Lodge: Elks. Home: 1717 Mian St Williston ND 58801 Office: Med Ctr Williston ND 58801

ADDY, ALVA LEROY, mechanical engineer; b. Dallas, S.D., Mar. 29, 1936; s. Alva Isaac and Nellie Amelia (Brumbaugh) A.; m. Sandra Ruth Turney, June 8, 1958. B.S., S.D. Sch. Mines and Tech., 1958; M.S., U. Cin., 1960; Ph.D., U. Ill., 1963. Engr. Gen. Electric Co., Cin., also Lancaster, Calif., 1958-60; prof. mech. engring. U. Ill., Urbana, 1963—, dir. mech. engring. lab., 1965—, assoc. head mech. engring. dept., 1980-87, head, 1987—; aerodynamics cons. U.S. Army Missile Command, Redstone Arsenal, Ala., summers 1965—; cons. U.S. Army Research Office, 1964—; cons. in high-speed fluid dynamics to indsl. firms, 1963—; vis. research prof. U.S. Army, 1976; lectr. Von Karman Inst. Fluid Dynamics, Brussels, 1968, 75, 76. Fellow ASME; assoc. fellow AIAA; mem. Am. Soc. for Engring. Edn., Sigma Xi, Pi Tau Sigma, Sigma Tau. Home: 1706 Golfview Dr Urbana IL 61801 Office: U Ill 208 Mech Engring Lab Urbana IL 61801

ADELL, STANLEY DEAN, art director; b. Lawrence, Kans., June 14, 1954; s. Charles Stanley and Donna Marie (Mayer) A.; m. Peggy Ann Cox, May 29, 1976; children: Adrienne Marie, Joel Stephen, Eric James. Student, San Antonio Coll., 1976-79; cert. tech. illustration, Platt Coll., 1980-81. Art dir. Allied/Signal King Radio Corp., Olathe, Kans., 1980-87; owner, operator On-Line Design, Olathe, 1986—. Served as sgt. USAF, 1976-79. Republican. Mem. Bible Ch. Home: 15310 Summertree Dr Olathe KS 66062 Office: On Line Design 100 E Park Suite 8 Olathe KS 66061

ADELMAN, RAPHAEL MARTIN, physician; b. Plainfield, N.J., May 4, 1915; s. Samuel and Betty (Taich) A.; m. Charlotte M. Koepke, Aug. 25, 1945 (dec. July, 1985); children—Karen Rae, Robert John. DDS, U. Pa., 1939; MSc, Northwestern U., 1940; BM, Chgo. Med. Sch., 1943, MD, 1944. Intern Norwegian-Am. Hosp., Chgo., 1943-44; assoc. in surgery Chgo. Med. Sch., 1945-50; assoc. in plastic surgery Dr. A.M. Brown, Chgo., 1946-50; gen. practice medicine Wauconda, Ill., 1950—; chief of staff St. Therese Hosp., 1963—, chief exec. com., 1965, asst. adminstr., med. dir., 1965—, v.p. med. affairs, 1973, dir., 1974—, dir. med. edn.; chief sect. ear, nose, throat Victory Meml. Hosp., Waukegan, Ill., 1963, 65-66; clin. asst. prof. family medicine U. Health Scis.-Chgo. Med. Sch., 1979—; med. dir. Am. Hosp. Supply Corp.; cons. physician Coll. Lake County Health Services Trust; physian cons. utilization rev. Region V HEW, 1973-75, cons. quality and standards, 1975; physician cons. Lake County Bd. Health, 1974-76; cons. continuing med. edn. Downey VA Hosp., 1974-76; authorized agt. Lake County Dept. Pub. Health, 1974-76; sr. examiner FAA, 1973—; mem. Am. Bd. Quality Assurance and Utilization Rev. Physicians, 1978—; mem. ancillary services rev. Crescent Counties for Med. Care, 1979—. Mem. exec. com. Lake County chpt. Am. Cancer Soc., 1963—; pres. Wauconda High Sch. Bd. Edn., 1954-60; mem. Wauconda Grade Sch. Bd. Edn., 1952-60; chmn. health and safety N.W. Dist., North Suburban council Boy Scouts Am., 1964-65, vice chmn. N.W. dist. North Shore council, 1967, 75, mem. exec. com. Northeastern Ill. council; mem. Lake County Health Services Com., 1969—; mem. profl. adv. com. United Community Services Planning Div., 1969—; mem. exec. com., exec. bd. Evanston-North Shore Area Council, 1969; mem. mgmt. com. Lake County Mental Health Clinic, 1967-69; mem. budget and fin. com., 1968-69, program chmn. Regional Conf. on Health Care Costs, Health,-Edn. and Welfare, Cleve., 1968; del. Hosp. Planning Council Chgo., 1967-69; chmn. subcom. Ill. Hosp. Licensing Bd. Com., 1969; pres. 1968-69 class U. Ala. Health Service Adminstrs. Devel. Program; chmn. Lake County Health Services Planning Council, Inc.; mem. regional com. Hosp. Admission Surveillance Program, State of Ill., 1972-77; mem. Lake County Drug Commn., 1972-73; mem. Lake County Bd. Health, 1973-77; chmn. orgn. and search com. for exec. dir. Lake County Health Dept.; mem. com. on search for dean Univ. Health Scis-Chgo. Med. Sch., 1975; mem. Lake County Coroner's Adv. Commn., 1977; mem. adv. council health edn. programs Coll. Lake County, 1970-77; bd. dirs. Blumberg Blood Bank, St. Therese Nurse Scholarship Fund, 1962, Lake County Health Planning Council, 1969-72. Fellow Am. Pub. Health Assn. (life mem., community health edn. accreditation panel 1975-76), AAAS, Chgo. Inst. Medicine, Royal Soc. Health, Am. Acad. Med. Adminstrs., Soc. Acad. Achievement (life), Am. Coll. Hosp. Adminstrs.; mem. Am. Acad. Family Practice, Ill. Acad. Family Practice (state del. 1960-63, dir.), Lake County Acad. Family Practice (past pres.), AMA, ADA, Assn. Mil. Surgeons U.S. (life), Ill. Hosp. Assn., Ill. Soc. Med. Research, Ill. Med. Soc. (com. physician-hosp. relationship 1974-75), Am. Acad. Dental Radiology, Ill. Pub. Health Anns. (exec. council 1976-78), Assn. Hosp. Med. Assn., Ill. Found. Med. Care, Am. Coll. Preventive Medicine, Am. Soc. Law and Medicine, Chgo. and Acad. Legal Medicine, Ill. Hosp. Attys., Am. Legion (life), Sigma Xi, Alpha Omega, Phi Lambda Kappa. Home: 1600 Wedgewood Dr Gurnee IL 60031

ADELMAN, ROBERT PAUL, construction company executive, lawyer; b. N.Y.C., Dec. 7, 1930; s. Saul and Eva (Ochs) A.; m. Renee Gratum, June 7, 1953; children: Michael, Susan, John. BA, Columbia U., 1952, JD, 1954. Bar: N.Y. 1954, U.S. Supreme Ct. 1960. Assoc. Winthrop, Stimson, Putnam & Roberts, N.Y.C., 1956-64; with Celanese Corp., N.Y.C., 1964-71; v.p., treas., gen. counsel Calina Industries, Inc., N.Y.C., 1971-73; chief fin. officer Rockefeller Group, Inc., N.Y.C., 1975-84; chmn. and chief exec. officer Rogers Group, Inc., Bloomington, Ind., 1984—; trustee N. European Oil Royalty Trust. Treas. and chief fin. officer N.Y. State Urban Devel. Corp., N.Y.C., 1973-75. Served with U.S. Army, 1954-56. Mem. Conf. Bd. Exec. Council. Club: University (N.Y.C.). Avocations: sailing, tennis.

ADELSON, EDWARD, physicist, musician; b. Bklyn., Aug. 19, 1934; s. Barnet and Sarah (Strongin) A.; m. Juliane A.W. Riedel, Aug. 5, 1961 (div. June, 1982); BA, N.Y.U., 1956; student (Woodrow Wilson fellow), Eastman Sch. of Music, 1956-57; MS, Ohio State U., 1965, PhD, 1974. Prin. physicist Battelle Mem. Inst., Columbus, Ohio, 1957-71; lectr. Ohio State U., Columbus, 1974—. Organist, choirmaster St. Alban's Episcopal Ch., Bexley, Ohio. Mem. Am. Phys. Soc., Am. Assn. Physics Tchrs., Am. Guild Organists, Phi Beta Kappa, Sigma Pi Sigma. Contbr. numerous articles to various profl. jours. Home: 6384 Falkirk Pl Columbus OH 43229 Office: Smith Lab Ohio State Univ Columbus OH 43210

ADELSON, MARGERY JEAN, psychologist, educator; b. N.Y.C., Jan. 10, 1945; d. Emanuel George and Greta (Weingartner) Gross; m. Joseph Bernard Adelson, May 24, 1981; children: Eric Daniel, David Seth, Gretchen Diana. AB magna cum laude, U. Rochester, 1966; PhD, U. Mich., 1971. Lic. psychologist, Mich. Clin. psychologist U. Mich., Ann Arbor, 1971—; pvt. practice psychology Ann Arbor, 1971—. Mem. Am. Psychol. Assn., Phi Beta Kappa. Home: 3743 Meadow Ln Saline MI 48176 Office: U Mich Psychol Clinic 1027 E Huron Ann Arbor MI 48109

ADELSTEIN, LINDY M., lawyer; b. Cleve., Feb. 24, 1934; s. Adolph M. and Rickie (Berger) A.; m. Harriet P. Hepner, June 12, 1960; children—Terri, Steven, Brian. B.A., Adelbert Coll., Western Res. U., 1955; J.D., Ohio No. U., 1958. Bar: Ohio 1958. Ptnr. Adelstein & Adelstein, Cleve., 1967—; advisor-selective service U.S. Govt., Cleve., 1967—; prof. law Lakeland Community Coll., Mentor, Ohio, 1971—; pres., chief exec. Printing Industries, Cleve., 1980-81. Recipient cert. Appreciation Printing Industries Assn. of No. Ohio, Inc., 1981, cert. Appreciation Pres. of U.S.A., 1972, numerous photo awards. Mem. Cleve. Bar Assn., Cuyahoga Bar Assn., Ohio State Bar Assn. Lodge: Masons. Avocation: photography. Home: 24118 E Baintree Beachwood OH 44122 Office: Adelstein & Adelstein Co L P A 925 Euclid Ave Suite 758 Cleveland OH 44115

ADENWALLA, SHABBIR TAHER, orthodontist; b. Cambay, Gujarat, India, Jan. 11, 1954; came to U.S., 1979; s. Taher Mohammedali and Banu T. (Poonawalla) A.; m. Durriya R. Parekh, Oct. 5, 1978; children: Muneera, Maria. B in Dental Surgery, Mysore U., Manipal, India, 1978; MS, Tufts U., 1983; DMD, Boston U., 1983. Lic. dentist Ohio, Mass., Northeastern U.S., Hong Kong, India. Research fellow Tufts U., Boston, 1981-83; orthodontist Orthodontic Assocs., Inc., Lowell, Mass., 1983-84; orthodontic dir. Horizon Dental Group, Lorain, Ohio, 1984—. Contbr. articles to profl. jours. Recipient Cert. Indian Soc. Periodontology, 1978-79, Cert. Supreme Governing Body of Acad. Gen. Edn., 1978-79; fellow Supreme Governing Body of Acad. Gen. Edn., 1978; C.V. Mosby scholar Boston U., 1983. Mem. Jaycees. Moslem. Avocations: tennis, reading, coin and stamp collection. Home: 1580 Prospect St #E6 Elyria OH 44035 Office: Horizon Dental Group 1300 Cooper Foster Park Rd Lorain OH 44053

ADERMAN, MORRIS, psychology educator; b. Bklyn., June 29, 1927; s. Isidore and Frieda (Augenstein) A.; m. Marlene Rose Towbin, Feb. 1, 1959; children: Elisa Hope, Carla Fran, Richard Evan. BA, Bklyn. Coll., 1950; MA, U. Oreg., 1952; PhD, U. Tex., 1956. Lic. psychologist, Ill.; diplomate indsl. and organizational psychology Am. Bd. Profl. Psychology. Teaching asst. U. Tex., Austin, 1954-56; instr. psychology Ill. Inst. Tech., Chgo., 1956-58, asst. prof., 1958-61, assoc. prof., 1961—; dir. grad. indsl./organizational psychology program, 1970-80; mem. Ill. Psychol. Examining Com., 1971-74; cons. in field. Contbr. articles to profl. jours. Served with USAF, 1945-46. Mem. Am. Psychol. Assn., Acad. Mgmt., Sigma Xi. Home: 4038 Tower Circle Skokie IL 60076 Office: Ill Inst Tech Psychology Dept 3100 S Dearborn St Chicago IL 60616

ADISESH, RAMASWAMY CHIKKANAYANAHALLI, computer software engineer; b. Bangalore, India, June 6, 1953; came to U.S., 1974; s. Ramaswamy K. Chikkanayanahalli and Kaveramma L. Turuvekere; m. Jamuna Nanjappa, Aug. 15, 1982. BS, U. Agrl. Sci., Bangalore, 1973; PhD, Kans. State U., 1978. Instr. Kans. State U., Manhattan, 1978-80; systems analyst C.I.S., Inc., Manhattan, 1979-82; software engr. Am. Satellite Co., Rockville, Md., 1982-83; supr. software engring. Astronautics Corp. of Am., Milw., 1983—. Mem. Assn. for Computing Machinery. Avocations: swimming, jogging. Office: Astronautics Corp of Am 4115 N Teutonia Milwaukee WI 53209

ADKINS, MEREDITH C., infosystems specialist, consultant; b. Cin., Sept. 6, 1953; s. W.C. and Mildred Althea (Byrd) A.; m. Carolyn Jean Wolf, Oct. 20, 1978; children: Nathanial C., Andrew Jordan. B in Bus., Xavier Coll., 1978. Cert. data processor. Programmer Clopay Corp., Cin., 1978-79; system analyst Regional Computer Ctr., Cin., 1979—. Mem. Am. Inst. for Certification of Computer Profls. Office: Regional Computer Ctr 138 E Court St Cincinnati OH 45202

ADKINS, TIMOTHY ARTHUR, educator; b. Newark, Ohio, May 28, 1945; s. Philip and Thelma A.; A.A., Lorain County Community Coll., 1971; B.S., Ohio State U., 1972; M.Ed., Kent State U., 1978, Ed.S., 1979; postgrad. Bowling Green State U., 1980, Mt. St. Joseph, 1980, Lesley Coll., 1980, U. South Fla., 1984. Tchr. history, Lorain (Ohio) City Schs., 1972-73; tchr., coordinator occupational work experience Elyria (Ohio) Schs., 1973-75; component coordinator career edn. Parma (Ohio) City Schs., 1978-80, occupational work adjustment coordinator, 1975—; adj. prof. Grad. Sch. Edn., Coll. Mt. St. Joseph, 1980—. Served with USAF, 1965-69; Vietnam. Mem. Am. Vocat. Assn., Ohio Vocat. Assn., NEA, Ohio Edn. Assn., N.E. Ohio Edn. Assn., Parma Edn. Assn., Career Edn. Assn., Ohio Parent Tchrs. Assn., Ohio State Alumni Assn., Kent State U. Alumni Assn. Republican. Methodist. Home: 454 Georgia Ave Elyria OH 44035 Office: Parma City Schools 6726 Ridge Rd Parma OH 44130

ADLER, BENARD CHARLES, otolaryngologist, educator; b. St. Louis, June 21, 1913; s. Louis B. and Rose (Young) A.; m. Phyllis Frankle, Oct. 19, 1946; children: Alan Richard, Diane Lynne Baker Adler. BS, MD, Washington U., St. Louis, 1937. Diplomate Am. Bd. Otolaryngology. Practice medicine specializing in otolaryngology St. Louis, 1948-83; clin. prof. emeritus Washington U. Sch. Medicine, 1983—. Contbg. editor (book) Diseases of the External Ear, 1957, Dermatology, 1963. Served to maj. U.S. Army, 1941-46, PTO. Fellow Am. Acad. Otolaryngology, Head and Neck Surgery, St. Louis Ear Nose and Throat Club (pres. 1974-75). Home: 100 Aberdeen Pl Saint Louis MO 63105 Office: Washington U Med Sch 4911 Barnes Hosp Plaza Room 817 McMillan Saint Louis MO 63110

ADLER, GERSON, business executive; b. Berlin, Germany, Oct. 2, 1927; s. Max and Rosy (Lange) A.; came to U.S., 1939, naturalized, 1945; student CCNY, 1946-56, Western Res. U., 1954-63, Rabbinical Coll. Telshe, 1950-51; m. Naomi Samuel, Aug. 1, 1950; children—Don, Samson, Nathan, Eli, Hillel, Ezra, Zahava Sarah. Owner, operator Eagle Day Camp, N.Y.C., 1948-50; dir. Hebrew Acad. Cleve., 1951-61; inventory controller Am. Greetings Corp., Cleve., 1961-62, dir. audits, 1962-65, asst. v.p., 1965-68, v.p. audit and research, 1968-71; exec. v.p. Courtland Group and affiliated cos., 1971-74; pres., dir. Courtland Communications Corp., 1971-74; exec. v.p. Andover Crest & Co., Inc., Courtland Capital Corp., Courtland Hosp. Systems Corp., 1971-74; mgmt. cons. Gerson Adler and Assocs., Cleveland Heights, Ohio, 1974-78; sr. v.p., dir. Waxman Industries, Inc., Cleve., 1978-81; sr. v.p., treas. Continental Alloy Steel Corp., Solon, Ohio, 1982-86; v.p. fin., HGM Hilltop Corp., Lyndhurst, Ohio, 1986—; lectr. Am. Mgmt. Assn., 1970; cons. audit standards U.S. Gen. Accounting Office, 1970-72. Bd. dirs. Bur. Jewish Edn. Mem. Ohio Sch. Survey Commn., 1966-67; chmn. com. legislative auditor, State of Ohio, 1970-72; pres. Agudath Israel Orgn., 1961-72; chmn. bd. Rabbinical Coll. Telshe; bd. dirs. Citizens for Ednl. Freedom, Hebrew Acad. Cleve., 1952—, Bur. Jewish Fedn. Mem. Inst. Internal Auditors (pres. 1967, internat. v.p. 1977-79). Home: 3595 Severn Rd Cleveland Heights OH 44118

ADLER, MARK, television and film producer, consultant; b. Detroit, Aug. 18, 1955. Student, Oakland Community Coll., 1974, Wayne State U., 1976; BA in Telecommunication, Mich. State U., 1978. Mgr. legal sect. Legal Tapes, Inc., Southfield, Mich., 1978-80; program mgr. McClean Hunter, East Detroit, Mich., 1980-82; ind. video film specialist Royal Oak, Mich., 1982-83; owner, chief exec. officer Video Assist, Inc., Farmington Hills, Mich., 1983—; co-founder Metro Sensory Media, Detroit, 1978—; cons. Sierra Clubs, Detroit, 1984-85. Dir. (documentary) Is Your Water Safe ?, 1985; producer series outdoor programs, 1986; contbr. articles to trade mag., 1985. Mem. Am. Film Inst., Detroit Producers Assn. Avocations: backpacking, photography, music, swimming, cross country skiing.

ADLER, MILTON LEON, psychologist; b. Bronx, N.Y., June 11, 1926; s. Siegmund and Josephine (Eppsteiner) A.; B.S., Rutgers U., 1951; M.S., City U. N.Y., 1952; postgrad. N.Y. U., 1952-53; Ph.D., U. Ill., 1963; m. Margrit Klein, Mar. 5, 1948; children—Sandra Ellen, Mark Lawrence. Psychiat. case worker N.J. Neuropsychiat. Inst., Blauenberg, 1953; clin. psychology intern, staff psychologist Manteno (Ill.) State Hosp., 1953-57; regional psychologist Ill. Inst. Juvenile Research, Champaign, 1957-66; sr. psychologist, clin. supr., subregion dir. Herman M. Adler Children's Center, Champaign, 1966-74; cons. psychologist Frederic Chusid and Co., Chgo., 1963-64; lectr. psychology Ill. State U., Normal, 1974-75; instr. psychology Parkland Coll., Champaign, Ill., 1979-80; pvt. practice clin. counseling, cons. psychology, Urbana, Ill., 1965—; mem. staff Cole Hosp., 1985—; med. cons. Ill. Dept. Rehab. Services and Disability Determination Services, 1986—; presenter growth in groups seminars and workshops on personal growth and interpersonal relationships, Stress Mgmt. Services. Served with USAAF, 1944-47. Registered psychologist, Ill. Fellow Am. Group Psychotherapy Assn. (mem. fellowship com. 1982—, dir. 1974-76, instr. tng. inst., mem. inst. com.); mem. Internat. Group Psychotherapy Assn., Ill. Assn. Maternal and Child Health (dir. bd. dirs. 1975-83, v.p. 1980-81, pres-elect 1981-82 pres. 1982-83, workshop, seminar presenter), Champaign-Urbana State Employees Assn. (past v.p., pres.), Ill. Group Psychotherapy Soc. (workshop presenter, council rep., awards of distinction 1977, 83, v.p., pres.-elect 1980-81, pres. 1982), Am. Psychol. Assn. (divs. psychotherapy, ind. practice, cons., community, humanistic and family psychology), Nat. Assn. Sch. Psychologists, Am. Assn. for Counseling and Devel., Am. Assn. Mental Health Counselors, Ill. Psychol. Assn. (clin. sect.), Ill. Acad. Criminology, Ill. Assn. for Counseling and Devel., Ill. Assn. Mental Health Counselors, Nat. Assn. Disability Examiners, Am. Acad. Psychotherapists, Saab Club Am., N. Am. Hunting Club, Phi Delta Kappa. Democrat. Unitarian-Universalist. Contbr. workshops/seminars for community groups on anxiety, risk-taking/and interpersonal relationships, and personal growth, workshops on group psychotherapy to profl. insts. Home: 1507 W University Ave Champaign IL 61821 Office: 404 W Green St Urbana IL 61801

ADLER, PHILIP, osteopathic physician; b. N.Y.C., Jan. 2, 1925; s. Willie and Ethel (Zichler) A.; m. Ethel Kugler, Sept. 23, 1948; 1 dau., Deborah. B.S., N.Y. U., 1944; D.O., Phila. Coll. Osteo. Medicine, 1947. Diplomate: Nat. Bd. Osteo. Medicine and Surgery, Am. Osteo. Bd. Obstetrics and Gynecology. Intern Detroit Osteo. Hosp., 1947-48, resident obstetrics and gynecology, 1948-50, mem. profl. staff, 1950-72, sec. intern/resident tng. com., 1960-63, chmn. dept. obstetrics and gynecology, 1964-67; practice osteo. medicine specializing in obstetrics and gynecology Farmington, Mich., 1950—; med. dir., dir. med. edn. Zieger/Botsford Osteo. Hosp., 1970-76, med. dir., 1970—; clin. prof. obstetrics and gynecology Mich. State U., Coll. Osteo. Medicine; cons. MIST Program; bd. dirs. Blue Shield of Mich., 1963-69; mem. adv. com. for teaching hosps. for social security studies HEW; mem. Mich. adv. com. Third Nat. Cancer Survey, Fed. Govt.; apptd. by gov. to Mich. State Health Coordinating Com., 1980-83; mem. State Health Coordinating Com. of Mich., 1984-87, vice chmn., 1987; coordinator for clin. clk. Mich. State U. Coll. Osteopathic Medicine, 1983—. Contbr. articles to med. jours. Recipient Walter F. Patenge medal of pub. service Mich. Coll. Osteo. Medicine at Mich. State U., 1973, Medal of Pub. Service Ohio U. Coll. Osteo. Medicine, 1977, medal of Pub. Service Okla. Coll. Osteo. Medicine and Surgery, 1977. Fellow Am. Coll. Osteo. Obstetricians and Gynecologists; mem. Am. Osteo. Assn. (trustee 1968—, pres. 1977-78, chmn. dept. ednl. affairs 1976—), Mich. Assn. Osteo. Physicians and Surgeons (trustee 1963-68, pres. 1966-67), Wayne County Assn. Osteo. Physicians and Surgeons (trustee 1955-64, pres. 1961-62), Detroit Cancer Club, Am., Mich. Assns. Osteo. Dirs. Med. Edn., Am., Mich. Assns. For Hosp. Med. Edn., Mich. Assn. Regional Med. Programs (profl. adv. com.). Clubs: B'nai B'rith; Carlton (Chgo.). Home: 31020 McKinney Dr Franklin MI 48025

ADLER, SEYMOUR JACK, social services administrator; b. Chgo., Oct. 22, 1930; s. Michael L. and Sarah (Pasnick) A.; B.S., Northwestern U., 1952; M.A., U. Chgo., 1958; m. Barbara Fingold, Mar. 24, 1958; children—Susan Lynn, Karen Sandra, Michelle Lauren. Caseworker, Cook County Dept. Pub. Aid, Chgo., 1955; juvenile officer Cook County Sheriff's Office, 1955-56; U.S. probation-parole officer U.S. Dist. Ct., Chgo., 1958-68; exec. dir. Youth Guidance, Chgo., 1968-73; dir. court services Juvenile Ct. Cook County, Chgo., 1973-75; exec. dir. Methodist Youth Services, Chgo., 1975-85; program mgr. Dept. Social Services, Kenosha, Wis., 1985—; mem. Ill. Law Enforcement Commn., 1969-72; instr. corrections program Chgo. State U., 1972-75; instr. Harper Coll., 1977, St. Joseph's Coll., 1978; case developer Nat. Ctr. on Instns. and Alternatives, 1985-86. Bd. dirs. Child Care Assn. Ill., 1979-84. Served to 1st lt. USMCR, 1952-55. Recipient Morris J. Wexler award Ill. Acad. Criminology, 1975, Meritorious Service award Chgo. City Colls., 1968. Mem. Ill. Acad. Criminology (pres. 1972), Nat. Assn. Social Workers (del. Assembly 1977, 79, 81, 84, chmn. Chgo. dist. 1978-80, chmn. group for action planning childrens services 1980-84, Disting. Service award Criminal Justice Council 1978), Ill. Probation, Parole and Correctional Assn., Internat. Half-way House Assn. (Ill. dir.), Alpha Kappa Delta, Tau Delta Phi. Contbr. articles to profl. jours. Home: 232 Grandview Ln Twin Lakes WI 53181 Office: Kenosha Dept Social Services 714 52d St Kenosha WI 53140

ADRIAN, PATRICIA LEE GRIMSHAW, association executive; b. Reliance, S.D., July 20, 1938; d. Walter George and Dorthy Veronica (Zastrow) Grimshaw; student Sinte Gleska U., 1973; m. Robert Earl Adrian, Oct. 12, 1957; children—James Robert, Thomas Edward, Kevin Patrick, David Duane. Sec., Cherry Todd Electric, 1956-57; tchr. White River (S.D.) Ind. Sch. Dist., 1970-71; dir. S.D. Beef Industry Council, 1970-73, pres., 1972-73, exec. v.p., 1973—; exec. sec., lobbyist S.D. Livestock Assn., part-time 1977—; pres. Mktg. Internat., Inc., 1981—; ptnr. Prairie Press; dir. Nat. Livestock and Meat Bd. Gov.'s rep. to nutrition symposium Old West Regional Commn., 1979-80; elected chmn. Beef Industry Council of Nat. Livestock and Meat Bd., 1986—; mem. S.D. Indsl. Devel. Commn., 1979-82; mem. S.D. Agrl. Mktg. Commn., 1980-82; mem. adv. com. S.D. Vocat. Tech. Edn. Commn. for Agr.; bd. dirs. S.D. Livestock Expansion Found., 1981—; vice-chmn. Cattleman's Beef Promotion and Research Bd. Operating com., 1986—. Recipient Disting. Service award S.D. Stockgrowers Assn., 1974, S.D. State U., 1976, S.D. State U. Alumni Assn., 1987. Mem. Nat. Fedn. Press Women, Am. Soc. Assn. Execs., Nat. Cattlemen's Assn., S.D. Livestock Assn., Am. Agri-Women, U.S. Meat Export Fedn. (dir. 1980-82), S.D. Press Women's Assn., S.D. CowBelles (pres.). Republican. Roman Catholic. Home: Star Route Box 222 White River SD 57579 Office: SD Beef Industry Council 110 W Capitol St Pierre SD 57501

ADRIANOPOLI, BARBARA CATHERINE, librarian; b. Ft. Dodge, Iowa, Jan. 27, 1943; d. Daniel Joseph and Mary Dolores (Coleman) Hogan; m. Carl David Adrianopoli, June 28, 1968; children—Carlin, Laurie. B.S., Mundeline Coll., 1966; M.L.S., Rosary Coll., 1975. Tchr., Father Bertrand High Sch., Memphis, 1966-68; caseworker Cook County Dept. Pub. Aid Chgo., 1968; tchr. North Chicago Jr. High Sch. (Ill.), 1968-70, Austin Middle Sch., Chgo., 1970-73; librarian Barrington Pub. Library (Ill.), 1976-79, Schaumburg Twp. Pub. Library (Ill.), 1979—; adv. com. Suburban AudioVisual N. Suburban/Suburban Library Systems, LaGrange, Ill., 1981-84, NEH grants for N. Suburban Library System, Wheeling, Ill., 1981-86. Contbr. articles to jours. Mem. Com. Schaumburg Twp. Disabled, 1981—; pres. Lakeview Pub. Sch. PTA, Hoffman Estates, Ill., 1983-84; mem. Armstrong PTA; historian Village of Hoffman Estates, 1986—; mem. Sch. Dist. 54-Citizens Adv. Com., Schaumburg, 1983—; advisor Boy Scout Am. handicapped badge, Schaumburg Twp., 1981—. N. Suburban Library System grantee, 1983. Mem. ALA, Ill. Library Assn., Library Assn. No. Ill. (v.p. 1981-84), NOW, Polit. Majority, Common Cause. Democrat. Roman Catholic. Home: 1105 Kingsdale Rd Hoffman Estates IL 60194 Office: Schaumburg Twp Pub Library 21 W Library Ln Schaumburg IL 60194

ADSIT, GORDON EDWIN, city official, educator; b. Lansing, Mich., Apr. 3, 1930; s. Guy Everett and Matilda (Montanye) A.; m. Patricia Lavey, Feb. 3, 1951; children—Constance L., Douglas G., Judith K., Susanne M. A.S. in Fire Sci. Tech., Lansing Community Coll., 1972; postgrad. Mich. State U. With fire fighting div. Lansing (Mich.) Fire Dept., 1953-64, insp. II, 1964-65, insp. IV, 1965-72, fire marshal, 1972-83; chief charter Twp. of Lansing, 1983—; mem. faculty Lansing Community Coll.; tech. adv. arson assistance program U.S. Fire Adminstrn.; cons. ins. cos., architects, gen. contractors, real estate cos.; speaker at confs., seminars. With U.S. Army, 1948-50, USAR, 1950-56. Named Insp. of Yr. Mich. Fire Inspector Soc., 1980. Mem. Nat. Fire Protection Assn., Fire Marshal's Assn. N.Am., Am. Soc. Safety Engrs., Internat. Assn. Arson Investigators, Mich. Fire Insps. Soc., Lansing Safety Council, Internat. Assn. Fire Chiefs, Mich. Fire Chiefs Assn. Roman Catholic. Lodge: Elks. Home: 1600 Boston Blvd Lansing MI 48910 Office: Twp of Lansing 3301 W Michigan Ave Lansing MI 48917

ADUDDLE, LARRY STEVEN, marketing and sales executive, consultant; b. Miami Beach, Fla., Oct. 21, 1946; s. William Allen and Bernice Elizabeth (Newlon) A.; m. Susan Carol Dominiak, Nov. 27, 1982; 1 child, Melissa Sue. BBA, Lake Forest Coll., 1982; MBA, Lake Forest Sch. Mgmt., 1984. Supr. Rexnord, Inc., Milw., 1974-77, product mgr., 1977-79, sales mgr., 1979-81; mktg. mgr. V/R Wesson, Fansteel, Inc., Waukegan, Ill., 1981-82; v.p. Metropolymer Labs, Inc., Milw., 1983—, bd. dirs.; cons. in field, Milw., 1982-83. Patentee insert for drill stabilizers. vice chmn. United Fund Campaign, Milw., 1975; adv. Jr. Achievement, Milw., 1980.Served to capt. U.S. Army, 1965-69, Vietnam. Decorated Bronze Star. Mem. Reserve Officers Assn. (sec. 1977-78), Assn. Internat. Mktg. Execs. Republican. Lutheran. Avocations: golf, tennis, boating. Home: 10234 W Beacon Hill Dr Franiklin WI 53132 Office: Metropolymer Labs Inc 2400 W Clybourn Milwaukee WI 53233

AEH, RICHARD KENT, telecommunications executive, organization effectiveness consultant; b. Jackson, Ohio, Aug. 3, 1939; s. Richard Clayton and Julia (Bryan) A.; m. Sandra Leigh Magruder, June 28, 1969; children—Jennifer Kristin, Allison Leslie, Meridith Courtney. B.S. in Bus. Adminstrn., Ohio State U., 1966. Dist. mgr. info. mgmt. AT&T Communications, Cin., 1966—; mem. adv. council Miami U. Sch. Applied Sci., Oxford, Ohio, 1982-85. Vol. mgmt. cons. Community Chest, Cin., 1979—; trustee Housing for Older Ams., 1984—, Better Housing League, Cin., 1982-83, Lower River Nursing Assn., Cin., 1980-83; mem. Citizens Adv. Com. on Cable TV, Cin., 1979; chairperson adv. council minority programs U. Cin., 1987. Served with U.S. Army, 1959-62. Recipient Community Service award Community Chest and United Appeal, 1985. Mem. Assn. for Systems Mgmt. (chpt. v.p. 1984-85, chpt. pres. 1985—, mem. internat. pub. policy com. 1985—). Republican. Episcopalian. Avocations: running, camping. Home: 7059 Royalgreen Dr Cincinnati OH 45244 Office: AT&T Communications 221 E 4th St 11th St Atrium II Cincinnati OH 45202

AERY, SHAILA ROSALIE, state educational administrator; b. Tulsa, Dec. 4, 1938; d. Silas Cleveland and Billie (Brewer) A. B.S., U. Okla., 1964; M.S., Okla. State U., 1972, Ed.D., 1975. Spl. asst., chancellor Okla. Regents for Higher Edn., Oklahoma City, 1977; spl. asst., chancellor U. Mo., Columbia, 1978-80, asst. provost acad. affairs, 1980-81; dep. commr. higher edn. State of Mo., Jefferson City, 1981, commr., 1982—; dir. Mo. Higher Edn. Loan Authority, St. Louis, 1982—; commr. Edn. Commn. of the States, Denver, 1983—; mem. exec. bd. State Higher Edn. Offices, Denver, 1983—. Contbr. articles to profl. jours. Mem. AAUW. Democrat. Episcopalian. Office: Mo Dept of Higher Edn 600 Monroe Jefferson City MO 65102

AFT, LARRY NORMAN, accountant; b. St. Louis, Apr. 5, 1957; s. Leo and Irene Bess (Hartstein) A.; m. Sandra Lee, Dec. 23, 1980; children: Jason, Jennifer, Ryan. BSBA, U. Mo., 1980. CPA, Mo. With Clifton Gunderson, St. Joseph, Mo., 1980-82; supr., instr. Parnell Kerr Forster, St. Louis, 1982—. Mem. Am. Inst. CPA's, Mo. Soc. CPA's (strategic planning com.). Clubs: Missouri Athletic (St. Louis); Olivette Athletic Assn. (bd dirs.). Avocations: running, racquetball, weightlifting. Home: 931 Floradale Saint Louis MO 63132 Office: Parrell Kerr Forster 720 Olive Saint Louis MO 63101

AFTERMAN, ALLAN B., accounting educator, writer; b. Chgo., Jan. 25, 1944; s. Joseph and Ruth Gertrude (Jacobson) A.; m. Joan Elaine Hoffman, Apr. 30, 1974; children: Debra, Lori, Julie, Robin. BBA, Roosevelt U., 1964. CPA, Ill. Staff acct. Alexander Grant & Co., Chgo., 1967-70; nat. staff mgr. Touche Ross & Co., Chgo., 1970-73; nat. tech. dir. Practice Devel. Inst., Chgo., 1977-82; acctg. prof. U. Ill., Chgo., 1983—, dir. exec. edn.; pres. CPA Cons. Group, Evanston, Ill., 1983—; bd. dirs. Ctr. for Continuing Study in Accountancy and Fin., Chgo., 1986—. Author: Accounting and Auditing Disclosures, 1982, Compilation and Review, 1983, Accounting and Auditing Update, 1984, SEC Accounting and Reporting Update, 1985, GAAP Practice Manual 1985 (best looseleaf bus. reference award profl. and scholastic div. Assn. Am. Pubs. 1985), Accounting Tax Highlights 1986, Handbook of SEC Accounting and Reporting, 1987, Financial Analysts Report, 1987. Mem. Am. Inst. CPA's, Am. Acctg. Assn., Practicing Law Inst., Calif. Soc. CPA's, N.Y. Soc. CPA's. Jewish. Home: 3900 S Mission Hills Rd #302 Northbrook IL 60062 Office: U Ill Dept Acctg PO Box 4348 Chicago IL 60680

AFUH, JERRY ADEM, construction executive, consultant; b. Batibo, Cameroon, Dec. 23, 1950; m. Bernice Marilyn Belgrave, May 6, 1979; children: Jerry II, Joseph, Chantal. BS in Agrl. Engring., Nat. Agrl. Coll., Deventer, The Netherlands, 1973; MS in Agrl. Econs., U. Nebr., 1976. Research asst. State of Nebr., Lincoln, 1974-79; pres. Lincoln Constrn. Group, Lincoln, 1980—; bd. dirs. Malone Housing Corp., Lincoln; sec., treas. Service Assn. Nebr., Lincoln, 1981—; mem. task force City of Lincoln, 1984—. Contbr. articles to profl. jours. Mem. cen. com. State Rep. Mem. Am. Assn. Agrl. Econs., Am. Econs. Assn., Am. Mgmt. Assn., Internat. Mgmt. Assn., Associated Gen. Contractors Am., Omicron Delta Epsilon, Gamma Sigma Delta.

AGBORUCHE, WILLIAM, auditor; b. South Bend, Ind., Apr. 24, 1954; s. Jacob and Alice (Anderson) A.; m. Jacqueline D. Martin, Aug. 5, 1986. BS in Acctg., Eastern Mich. U., 1980; MEd, Wayne State U., 1982, postgrad., 1985—; MS in Acctg., Walsh Coll., 1985. Staff acct. Charles Co., Detroit, 1979-81; supr. acctg. Shaw Coll., Detroit, 1981-84; audit mgr. Wilkerson & Co. CPA's, Detroit, 1984-86; internal auditor Electronic Data Systems Corp., Southfield, Mich., 1986—; tng. cons. Human Energy Am., Grosse Pointe, Mich., 1984—; audit cons. Wilkerson & Co., Detroit, 1986—. Mem. Nat. Assn. Accts. (council mem.), Assn. Govt. Accts. (assoc.), Assn. MBA Execs., Phi Theta Kappa. Lodge: Rosicrucian Order. Avocations: tennis, bowling, poetry, writing and reading philosophy. Office: Electronic Data Systems Corp 26533 Evergreen Southfield MI 48086

AGGARWAL, SHIV KUMAR, business executive; b. New Delhi; s. Ishwari Prasad and Bhagwati Devi A.; came to U.S., 1956, naturalized, 1975; B.A., U. Delhi, 1953; M.S.W., U. Baroda, India, 1955; M.B.A., U. Mo., 1957. Pres., Imperial Cycle & Motor Co., Bombay, India, 1959-62; dir. neighborhood services East End Neighborhood House, Cleve., 1962-67; founder, exec. dir. Collinwood Community Services Center, Cleve., 1967-80; pres. Century Bus. Systems, Cleve., 1980-82, Macon Internat. Inc., Cleve., 1982-85, Profl. Weight Control Systems, Inc., 1985-86, Unicorn Ltd., 1986—. Mem. Gerontol. Soc., India Assn. Greater Cleve. Home: 2595 Hickory Ln Cleveland OH 44124 Office: Unicorn Ltd 16360 Broadway Ave Cleveland OH 44137

AGIN, GARY PAUL, physics educator, researcher; b. Kansas City, Mo., Dec. 22, 1940; s. George Franklin and Minnie Irene (Holt) A. BS in Engring. Physics, U. Kans., 1963; MS in Physics, Kans. State U., 1967, PhD in Physics, 1968. Asst. prof. physics Mich. Tech. U., Houghton, 1968-87, assoc. prof., 1987—; presenter numerous papers in nuclear physics at profl. meetings. Mem. AAAS, Am. Assn. Physics Tchrs., Am. Phys. Soc., Mensa, Tau Beta Pi, Sigma Pi Sigma (councillor zone 8 soc. physics students 1982—), Sigma Xi. Home: 717 Cedar Bluff Dr Houghton MI 49931 Office: Dept Physics Mich Technol U Houghton MI 49931

AGIN, JAMES EUGENE, health care company executive; b. Salina, Kans., Feb. 16, 1943; s. Harold F. and Agnes E. (Curry) A.; m. Sally Sue White, May 15, 1972; children—Robert A., Scott C. B.S. in Bus., Fort Hays State U., 1970, M.B.A., 1971. Dist. sales mgr. Frito-Lay, Inc., Indpls., 1971-72; exec. asst. Kans. Med. Soc., Topeka, 1972-74; exec. dir. Kans. Found. Med. Care, Topeka, 1974-82; v.p. Health Care Plus, Inc., Wichita, Kans., 1983-84; dir. planning, radiology and nuclear medicine, P.A., Topeka, Kans., 1985; pres., chief exec. officer Physicians Health Plan of Kans., Topeka, 1985—; vice chmn. bd. Dave Fisher Jr. Prodns. Inc., Topeka, 1986—; adj. instr. Coll. Health Sci. Wichita State U., 1979-82; speaker confs. Mem. Topeka Police Chief's Com. Police-Community Relations, 1972; mem. exec. staff Kans. Med. Polit. Action Com., Topeka, 1972-74; mem. Christ the King Fund Dr. Com., Topeka, 1983. Served with USMC, 1963-66. Fort Hays State U. fellow, 1970-71; recipient Cert. of Commendation, Kans. Found. Med. Care, Topeka, 1982; Resolution of Commendation, Kans. Med. Soc., 1982; Exec. Dir. Testimonial award Am. Assn. Profl. Standards Rev. Orgns., 1979. Mem. Am. Assn. Med. Soc. Execs., Am. Assn. Profl. Standards Rev. Orgns., Am. Mgmt. Assn., Am. Legion. Republican. Roman Catholic. Lodge: Elks. Home: 2601 Ashworth Pl Topeka KS 66614 Office: Physicians Health Plan of Kans Capitol Towers 400 SW 8th St Topeka KS 66603

AGINIAN, RICHARD DICRAN, communications company executive; b. N.Y.C., Sept. 13, 1941; s. Hrant and Virginia (Solakian) A.; m. Diana Carol Tashjian, July 31, 1966; children: Dawn, Marla. B in Philosophy, Wayne State U., 1963; MBA, Rutgers U., 1964. CPA, Mich. Audit mgr. Arthur Andersen, Detroit, 1964-75; asst. to pres. Falvey Motors, Troy, Mich., 1975-76; treas. Suburban Communications, Livonia, Mich., 1976-77; pres., chief exec. officer Suburban Communications Corp., Livonia, Mich., 1977—. Bd. dirs., chmn. Henry Ford Hosp., West Bloomfield, Mich., 1978-84; bd. dirs. Community House of Birmingham , Mich., 1985, Walsh Coll., Troy, 1985. Mem. Mich. Press Assn. (bd. dirs. 1982—), Suburban Newspapers of Am. (pres. 1985-86), Young Pres. Orgn. Clubs: Oakland Hills Country, Econ. Club. Avocations: golf, tennis. Home: 835 Westwood Birmingham MI 48009 Office: Suburban Communications Corp 36251 Schoolcraft Rd Livonia MI 48150

AGNEW, JAMES LAMBERT, financial consultant; b. Macon, Ga., Apr. 17, 1944; s. James L. and Margaret M. (Shebilsky) A. BA with distinction, Peru (Nebr.) State Coll., 1965; MA, Stanford U., 1972; postgrad., Drake U., U. No. Colo. Tchr. Hamburg (Iowa) High Sch., 1965-69, Urbandale (Iowa) High Sch., 1969-73; pres. Agnew-Tunink Assocs., West Des Moines, Iowa, 1973—, Assoc. Fin. Planners, West Des Moines, 1983—. Grantee NSF, 1969-72. Mem. Nat. Soc. Pub. Accts., Nat. Assn. Enrolled Agents, Inst. Cert. Fin. Planners, Internat. Assn. Fin. Planning (v.p. edn. Iowa chpt. 1986—), Alpha Mu Omega. Avocations: reading, travel, photography. Office: Agnew Tunink & Assocs 1233 8th St West Des Moines IA 50265

AGNEW, NETTIE LOU, nurse, administrator; b. Jasper, Mo., Jan. 23, 1948; d. Andrew J. and Mary Marie (Burton) Butler; m. Edwin John Agnew, Oct. 23, 1973; 1 dau., Rhian Mallorie. Diploma Burge Sch. Nursing, 1969; B.S. magna cum laude, Drury Coll., 1970; M.S., No. Ill. U., 1977. Staff nurse Cox. Med. Ctr., Springfield, Mo., 1969-70; staff nurse U.S. Air Force, Mather AFB, Calif., 1970-71, aero-med. staging nurse Scott AFB, Ill., 1971-73, Flight Nurse Sch., Brooks AFB, Tex., 1972; vis. nurse St. Clair County Vis. Nurse Assn., East St. Louis, Ill., 1973-75; staff nurse North Kansas City (Mo.) Meml. Hosp., 1975, clin. nurse specialist, 1978-79, dir. nursing, v.p. nursing, v.p. clin. services, 1979—; instr. Research Med. Ctr. Sch. Nursing, Kansas City, Mo., 1975-76. Mem. adv. council St. Mary Coll. Sch. Nursing, Leavenworth, Kans., 1981—; bd. advisors dept. nursing William Jewell Coll. 1983. Served with USAF, 1969-73. Mem. Dirs. Nursing Greater Kansas City Area Hosp. Assn., Mo. Orgn. Nurse Execs., Am. Assn. Nurse Execs., Sigma Theta Tau. Club: Soroptimist. Office: North Kansas City Meml Hosp 2800 Hospital Dr North Kansas City MO 64116

AGNO, JOHN G., marketing executive; b. Gloversville, N.Y., Dec. 8, 1940; s. John G. and Margaretta (Luff) Anagnostopulos; m. Lynn Airey Mar. 30, 1968 (div. Oct. 1979); children; J. Robert, Constance Blythe; m. Karen Clark Mikus, June 29, 1985; 1 stepchild, Luke Ravlin-Mikus. BBA, U. Fla., 1962. Mktg. specialist Eastman Kodak Co., Rochester, N.Y., 1965-73; gen. mgr. sanitation appliance div. Thetford Corp., Ann Arbor, Mich., 1973-80; v.p. mktg. and adminstrn. Stirling Power Systems Corp. div. McDonnell Douglas Corp., Ann Arbor, 1980—; pres. Signature, Inc., Ann Arbor, 1983—. Contbr. tech. papers to profl. jours. Deacon First Presbyterian Ch., Ann Arbor. Served to 1st lt. U.S. Army, 1963-65. Mem. Elect. Engring. Systems Assn., Recreational Vehicle Industry Assn. (chmn. mktg. commn. 1978-82, bd. dirs. 1981-83), Am. Defense Preparedness, Internat. Cogeneration Soc. Republican. Club: Travis Point Country (Ann Arbor). Avocations: golf, camping. Home: 2222 Gerogetown Blvd Ann Arbor MI 48105 Office: Stirling Powers Systems Corp 7101 Jackson Rd Ann Arbor MI 48103

AGRUSS, NEIL STUART, physician; b. Chgo., June 2, 1939; s. Meyer and Frances (Spector) A.; B.S., U. Ill., 1960, M.D., 1963; m. Teresa Marie Stafford; children—David, Lauren, Michael, Joshua, Susan. Intern, U. Ill. Hosp., Chgo., 1963-64, resident in internal medicine, 1964-65, 67-68; fellow in cardiology, Cin. Gen. Hosp., 1968-70, dir. coronary care unit, 1971-74, dir. echocardiography lab., 1972-74; dir. cardiac diagnostic labs., Central DuPage Hosp., Winfield, Ill., 1974—; asst. prof. medicine, U. Cin., 1970-74, Rush Med. Coll., 1976—. Chmn. coronary care com. Heart Assn. DuPage County, 1974-76; active Congregation Beth Shalom, Naperville, Ill. Served to capt. M.C. U.S. Army, 1965-67. Diplomate Am. Bd. Internal Medicine. Fellow ACP, Am. Coll. Cardiology, Am. Coll. Chest Physicians, Council Clin. Cardiology, Am. Heart Assn.; mem. AMA, DuPage County, Ill. State Med. Socs., Am. Fedn. Clin. Research, Chgo. Heart Assn. Author and coauthor publs. in field. Office: Neil Stuart Agruss MD 454 Pennsylvania Ave Glen Ellyn IL 60137

AGUAS, RUBEN TECH, otolaryngologist; b. Manila, Philippines, Feb. 10, 1941; came to U.S., 1969; s. Francisco Calaguas and Lydia (Tech) A.; m. Aida Raymundo, June 12, 1967; 1 child, Ruben R. Jr. Student premedicine, U. Philippines, Quezon City, 1956-59; MD, U. Philippines, Manilla, 1964. Diplomate Am. Bd. Otolaryngology. Resident in otolaryngology Philippines Gen. Hosp., 1964-68, Bellevue Hosp. Ctr., N.Y.C., 1969-71; resident gen. surgery Columbus Hosp., N.Y.C., 1971-72; resident in otolaryngology Met. Hosp. Ctr., N.Y.C., 1972-73; staff physician specializing in otolaryngology Marshfield (Wis.) Clinic, 1973—. Mem. AMA, ACS, Am. Acad. Otolaryngology Head and Neck Surgery, State Med. Soc. Wis. Roman Catholic. Avocations: tennis, chess, fishing. Office: Marshfield Clinic 1000 N Oak Marshfield WI 54449

AHEE, DAVID LYNN, accountant; b. Ottumwa, Iowa, Dec. 4, 1946; s. Donald Winfred and Thelma Roberteen (Beaty) A.; m. Suzanne Lorelei Koetting, June 22, 1969; children: Bradley Jamison, Tracey Lynnette, Nicole Janette. BS in Acctg., Drake U., 1973. CPA, Nebr., Iowa. Sr. mgr. Peat, Marwick, Main and Co., Lincoln, Nebr., 1974—. Served with USMC, 1967-69, Vietnam. Mem. Am. Inst. CPA's, Nebr. Soc. CPA's, Lincoln Jaycees (treas. 1976, pres. found. 1984). Lodge: Sertoma. Avocations: golf, outdoor sports, water skiing, swimming. Home: 3811 Raspberry Circle Lincoln NE 68516 Office: Peat Marwick Main & Co Firstier Bank Bldg Suite 1600 Lincoln NE 68508

AHERN, JOSEPH JAMES, JR., television station executive; b. Phila., June 9, 1945; s. Joseph James Ahern Sr. and Frances E. Murray; m. Lynn Barbara Pettit, Apr. 5, 1969; 1 child, Meredith Lynn. Student, St. Joseph's U., Phila., 1964-68. Salesman Phila. Evening Bull., 1968-70, Sta. WDVR-FM, Phila., 1970-73, Sta. WPVI-TV, Phila., 1973-75; sales mgr. Sta. WLS-TV, Chgo., 1975-77, sta. mgr., 1981-85, v.p., gen. mgr., 1985-86, pres., gen. mgr., 1986—; nat. sales mgr. spot sales ABC-TV, Detroit, 1977-78; gen. sales mgr. Sta. WABC-TV, N.Y.C., 1978-81. Bd. dirs., gen. chmn. United Cerebral Palsy, Chgo., 1981-86; bd. dirs., sec. Spl. Children's Charities, Chgo., 1983-86; bd. dirs., exec. bd. State St. Council, Chgo., 1985-86; bd. dirs., v.p. Starlight Found., Chgo., 1985-86; bd. dirs. library bd. Northwestern U., Evanston, Ill., 1985-86; bd. dirs. Childrens Meml. Found., 1987. Named Man of Yr., WE-TIP, Inc., 1984, Gen. Mgr. of Yr., Pub. Affairs Drs. Chgo., 1985, Media Man of yr., 1986; recipient One Ch. One Child award Dept. Children and Family Services, Chgo., 1986, Spirit of Life award City of Hope, Distng. Vol. award Chgo. Pub Schs., citation U.S. Dept. Health and Human Services Regional, 1987. Mem. Acad. TV Arts and Scis. (bd. dirs. Chgo. chpt. 1982-86), Ill. Film Inst., Chgo. Urban League (bus. adv. council 1986). Republican. Presbyterian. Clubs: Broadcast Ad, East Bank (Chgo.). Avocations: running, weightlifting, wine. Office: Sta WLS-TV 190 N State St Chicago IL 60601

AHERN, PETER LAWRENCE, computer information systems specialist; b. Meriden, Conn., Dec. 12, 1947; s. Lawrence James and Nathalie (Houdlette) A.; m. Brenda Darlene Pollinger, Feb. 1, 1969 (div. Feb. 1978); m. Mary Barbara Mechling, Nov. 22, 1980 (div. July 1986). A in Applied Sci., Waterbury (Conn.) State Tech. Coll., 1968; BS in Computer Sci., Monmouth Coll., West Long Branch, N.J., 1976. Programmer Bell Labs., Holmdel, N.J., 1968-76; systems programmer Dun & Bradstreet Inc., Berkeley Heights, N.J., 1976-80; cons. Computer Scis. Corp., El Segundo, Calif., 1980-84, dept. mgr. software devel., 1984—; contracting cons. Bell Labs., Piscataway, N.J., 1980-84; contracting cons., dept. mgr. AT&T, Cin., 1984-86. Mem. Assn. for Computing Machinery (Cin. chpt.). Congregationalist. Club: Western Hills Athletic (Cin.). Avocations: tennis, golf, bicycling, photography. Home: 5505 Revmal Ln Cincinnati OH 45238 Office: Computer Scis Corp 221 E 4th St 10th floor Cincinnati OH 45202

AHLBERG, DANIEL B., neurosurgeon; b. St. Paul, May 29, 1945; s, Herbert C. and Helen Mae (Haugen) A.; m. Linda Ann Olbergm July 28, 1979; children: Ryan Herbert, Braden Daniel. BA, U. Minn., 1967, MD, 1970, PhD, 1977, cert. neurosurgery, 1978. Diplomate Am. Bd. Neurol. Surgery. Pres. Met. Neurosurgery, P.A., Mpls., 1978—. Pres. Northwestern Edn1. Found., 1975-77. Served to lt. commdr. USHPS, 1972-74. Mem. AMA, Minn. Med. ASsn., Hennepin County Med. Soc., Minn. Neurosurg. Soc., Am. ASsn. Neurol. Surgeons. Home: 4410 Tyrol Crest Golden Valley MN 55416 Office: Met Neurosurgery PA 606 24th Ave S Suite 815 Minneapolis MN 55454

AHMAD, ANWAR, radiologist; b. Peshawar, Pakistan, Apr. 15, 1945; s. Shams and Amtulaziz (Lateef) A.; m. Amtur R. Hameed, May 20, 1970; children: Attiya, Ghazala, Iftekhar. FSc, Islamia Coll., Peshawar, 1962; MBBS, Khyber Med. Sch., Peshawar, 1968. Cert. Am. Bd. Radiology. Gen. practice medicine Govt. Pakistan, Peshawar, 1968-71; med. missionary Ahmadiyya Mission, Banjul, The Gambia, 1971-75; attending physician VA Hosp., Hines, Ill., 1975-85, Mercy Hosp., Benton Harbor, Mich., 1985—; clin. instr. Chgo. Med. Sch., North Chicago, Ill., 1978—; program dir. residency tng., VA Hosp., Hines, 1982-85. Pres. suburban chpt. Ahmadiyya Muslim Mission, Glen Ellyn, Ill., 1982-85. Mem. AMA, Am. Soc. Therapeutic Radiology and Oncology, Am. Soc. Clin. Oncology, Am. Coll. Radiology, Radiol. Soc. N.Am., Am. Endocurie Therapy Soc., European Soc. Therapeutic Radiology and Oncology, Am. Endocurietherapy Soc. Avocations: tennis, photography, reading. Home: 1515 Cardinal Dr Saint Joseph MI 49085 Office: PO Box 273 Saint Joseph MI 49085

AHMADI, SAÏD, engineering executive; b. Kashan, Iran, Feb. 17, 1934; came to U.S., 1963; S. Ali Ahmadi and Zahra (Haeri) A.; m. Lina Castellano, Jan. 2, 1965 (div. Jan 1979); children: Dariush, Nader, Kayvan. BSME, U. Tehran, 1956. Cert. mfg. engr. Mgr. engring. Civil Constrn. Co., Tehran, 1956-63; pres. Gesco Ltd., N.Y.C., 1963-66; materials control mgr. Kerr Lakeside Inc., Cleve., 1966—; pres., chief exec. officer Internat. Sci. Group, Inc., Cleve. 1986—. Author: Estimating Manual, 1972; editor: Ravash Mag., 1977-78. Mem. ASTM, Soc. Mfg. Engrs. (sr.), Am. Inst. Indsl. Engrs. (sr.). Democrat. Muslim. Avocations: chess, tennis. Home: 30901 Lakeshore Blvd #915 Willowick OH 44094 Office: Kerr Lakeside Inc 22841 Tungsten Rd Cleveland OH 44132

AHRENS, DALE ELMER, manufacturing company executive; b. Wausau, Wis., June 10, 1949; s. Elmer Gustave and Lydia Clara (Hemmerich) A.; m. Montine Avis Luedtke, May 27, 1979; children: Austin Emerson, Preston Whitney, Collin Chandler. Student. U. Wis., 1967-68; BSME, Cornell U., 1972; MBA, Hofstra U., 1976. Registered profl. engr., N.Y., Minn. Mgr. advanced research and devel. Grumman Corp., Beth Page, N.Y., 1972-73, dir. advanced research and devel., 1973-79; dir. advanced med. tech. 3M, St. Paul, 1979-81; dir. ops. AVI Inc., St. Paul, 1981-83, Wagner Corp., Mpls., 1983-85; v.p., gen. mgr. Plastics Products Co., Lindstrom, Minn., 1985—; cons. Dayton/Hudson Co., Mpls., 1981-84, Ford Co., St. Paul, 1984-87. Patentee in field. Mem. NSPE, Am. Mgmt. Assn., Am. Soc. for Quality Control. Lodge: Masons. Avocations: creative writing, golf, music. Home: 7211 Sherwood Echo Woodbury MN 55125 Office: Plastic Products Co Inc 30355 Akerson St Lindstrom MN 55045

AHRENS, RICHARD C., pediatrician, educator; b. Waukesha, Wis., May 28, 1947; s. Ora Earl and Evelyn Alice (Hardacker) A.; m. Janice Ann Weber, Aug. 1, 1970; children: Kym Reneé, Scott Richard. BS, U. Wis., 1969; MD, Med. Coll. Wis., 1973; MS, U. Iowa, 1980. Cert. Am. Bd. Pediatrics, Am. Bd. Allergy and Immunology. Assoc. prof. U. Iowa, Iowa City, 1980—. Contbr. articles to med. jours. Mem. Am. Acad. Pediatrics, Am. Thoracic Soc., Am. Acad. Allergy and Immunology, Am. Coll. Allergy, Am. Bd. Pediatric Pulmonology, Sierra Club. Mem. United Ch. of Christ. Avocations: hiking, rock climbing. Home: 1426 Oaklawn Ave Iowa City IA 52240 Office: U Iowa Dept Pediatrics Iowa City IA 52242

AHSTROM, JAMES PETER, JR., orthopaedic surgeon; b. Chgo., Dec. 3, 1925; s. James Peter and Anna (Berg) A.; m. Harriet Jane White, Aug. 3, 1949; children: James David, Jill Daly. BS, U. Richmond, 1946; B in Medicine, Northwestern U., Chgo., 1948, MD, 1949. Diplomate Am. Bd. Orthopaedic Surgeons. Practice medicine specializing orthopaedic surgery Downers Grove, Ill., 1955—; clin. asst. Shriners Hosp. Crippled Children, Chgo., 1955-57, orthopaedic surgeon, cons. staff. 1957—; mem. staff Gottlieb Meml. Hosp., Melrose Park, Ill., 1961-65, Good Samaritan Hosp., Downers Grove, Ill., 1974—; attending physician orthopaedic surgery, VA Hosp., Hines, Ill., 1965—; clin. instr. Abraham Lincoln Sch. Medicine, U. Ill., Chgo., 1958-67, clin. asst. prof., 1967-79, 85-86, clin. assoc. prof. 1986—. Contbr. numerous articles to profl. jours. Served to lt. USNR, 1950-52, Korea. Mem. AMA, ACS, Am. Acad. Orthopaedic Surgeons, Am. Orthopaedic Assn., chgo. med. Soc., Ill. State Med. Soc., Clin. Orthopaedic Soc., Internat. Soc. Orthopaedic Surgery and Traumatology, Russell Hibbs Soc., Pan Pacific Surgical Assn., Pan Am. Med. Assn., Chgo. Orthopaedic Soc., Am. Coll. Surgeons (chgo. Com. on trauma), Am. Geriatrics Soc., Am. Soc. Surgery of Hand, Chgo. Soc. Surgery of Hand, Am. Orthopaedic Soc. Sports Medicine, Mid-Am. Orthopaedic Assn. Republican. Presbyterian. Clubs: River Forest Tennis, Oak Park Country (River Grove, Ill.). Home: 821 Bonnie Brae River Forest IL 60305 Office: 3825 Highland Suite 2M Downers Grove IL 60515

AIENA, PETER PAUL, systems engineering development manager; b. Bklyn., Nov. 12, 1951; s. Peter P. and Nettie (Miceli) A.; m. Theresa Hochwalt, May 22, 1982. BS in Computer Sci., U. Dayton, 1979. Software engr. NCR Corp., Dayton, Ohio, 1974-79, project leader, 1979-81, mgr. devel., 1981-84; sr. mgr. interactive video systems Reynolds and Reynolds, Dayton, 1984-87, sr. mgr. systems mgmt. and systems hardware, 1987—. Patentee in field. Avocations: automobile restoration, skiing. Office: Reynolds & Reynolds 800 Germantown St Dayton OH 45407

AIG, DENNIS IRA, writer, film producer; b. Bklyn., Jan. 15, 1950; s. Irving and Judith (Gran) A.; m. Ann Therese Bertagnolli, Nov. 26, 1983; 1 child, Aaron Anthony (dec.). BA, CUNY, Flushing, 1971; MA, Ohio State U., 1973, PhD, 1983. Lectr. Ohio State U., 1978-81; co-exec. dir., pres. bd. dirs. Community Film Assn., Columbus, Ohio, 1979-81, writer, producer, 1981; sr. mktg. writer Staff Chem. Abstracts Service, Columbus, 1983—; instr. continuing edn., Ohio State U., 1978; writer Frontier Press, Columbus, 1980-81;media cons. Ridihalgh and Eggers, 1981-82. producer films including CAS-The World Resource, 1986. Trustee Nat. Hall Fame for Persons with Disabilities, 1981-84; co-chmn. Anne Frank In The World Project, 1986-87. Mem. Univ. Film and Video Assn., Assn. Ind. Video and Filmmakers. Avocations: photography, reading, weight training. Home: 1520B Bradshire Dr Columbus OH 43220 Office: Chem Abstracts Service PO Box 3012 2540 Olentangy River Rd Columbus OH 43210

AIKEN, ROGER GEORGE, energy systems research analyst; b. Feilding, N.Z., Jan. 12, 1933; came to U.S., 1973; s. Henry George and Muriel Christine A.; m. Susan Graham Hamilton, July 14, 1962 (div. 1980); children: Andrew Graham, David George; m. Connie Lynn Haugen, Feb. 19, 1983; 1 child, Julie Christine. BSc, U. Canterbury, Christchurch, N.Z., 1954, BE with honors, 1956, ME with distinction, 1958; postgrad. in mech. engring., U. Minn., 1973-83. Sci. officer physics and engring. labs., Dept. Sci. and Indsl. Research, Lower Hutt, N.Z., 1958-59; devel. engr. Collier and Beale Ltd., Wellington, N.Z., 1959-61; sr. sci. staff Hirst Research Centre, Brit. Gen. Electric Co., Wembley, England, 1961-65; mem. sci. staff Bell No. Research, Ottawa, Ont., Can., 1965-67; temporary engr. transmission dept. N.Z. Post Office, Wellington, 1968; research scientist, engr. Communications Research Centre, Can. Fed. Dept. Communications, Ottawa, Ont., 1968-73; research fellow Center for Studies of Phys. Environment, Inst. Tech., U. Minn., Mpls., 1974-76; energy research analyst research div. Minn. Energy Agy., St. Paul, 1976-78; research fellow Underground Space Ctr., U. Minn., Mpls., 1978-79, Bio Energy Coordinating Office, 1980, instr. energy, honors program Coll. Liberal Arts, 1982-83; prin. energy systems analyst Synergistic Design and Engring., Mpls., 1981-82; bldg. mgmt. systems analyst Honeywell, Inc., Mpls., 1982-83; tng. supr. MTS Systems Corp., Mpls., 1984—. Contbr. articles to profl. jours. and meetings. Recipient Minn. Energy Design award 1979, Honeywell Futurist Competition award 1983. Coordinator Future Lifestyle Planners program U. Minn. YMCA, 1978-80; elder Bethany Presbyn. Ch., 1985—; mem. edn. subcom. Mayor Latimer's Com. 100, 1979. Mem. Instn. Elec. Engrs. (U.K.), IEEE, Biomass Energy Inst. (Can.), AIAA, Internat. Solar Energy Soc., Minn. Renewable Energy Soc. (chmn. policy com. 1978-79, treas. 1984—), Twin Cities Energy Engrs., Phi Kappa Phi. Clubs: U. Minn., YMCA. Home: 1589 Hollywood Ct Falcon Heights MN 55108-2130

AILSLIEGER, ROSS EDWARD, aircraft company manager, flight instructor; b. Hays, Kans., Sept. 24, 1937; s. Herbert George and Mary May (Pizinger) A.; m. Sharon Marie Shue, June 12, 1965; children—Paul Edward, Kristafer Ross, Alex Mathew. A.B. in Psychology, Ft. Hays State U., 1964, M.S. in Exptl. Psychology, 1965. Cert. flight instr., FAA. Human factors engr. N.Am. Rockwell, Los Angeles, 1966-68; human factors and maintainability lead engr. Spartan Missile program McDonnell-Douglas Astronautics Co., Huntington Beach, Calif., 1968-76; sr. human factors engr. AH-64 attack helicopter program Hughes Helicopters, Culver City, Calif., 1976-77; supr. human factors engring., and flight simulation Boeing Mil. Airplane Co., Wichita, Kans., 1977—; cons. aircraft cockpit design requirements, Wichita, Kans., 1977—; mgr. crew systems tech., 1986—. Served with U.S. Army, 1955-59. Mem. Tri-Service Aircrew Sta. Standardization Panel. Republican. Lutheran. Patentee in field. Home: 303 Wheatland Pl Wichita KS 67235 Office: Boeing Mil Airplane Co PO Box 7730 Wichita KS 67277

AIMONE, MICHAEL DENNIS, treasurer; b. St. Louis, June 24, 1943; s. Bartholomew and Mildred V. (Hargett) A.; m. H. Eileen Decker, Dec. 18, 1965; children: Michael S., Steven D. BBA, U. Mo., 1967, MA in Acctg., 1968. CPA, Mo. Audit mgr. Ernst & Whinney, St. Louis, 1968-73; asst. treas. Miss. Lime Co., Alton, Ill., 1973-83, treas., 1984—; mem. corp. assembly Blue Cross Health Services, Inc., St. Louis, 1984—. dir. Alton Wood River Jr. Achievement Dist. Bd., 1982—; chmn. Boy Scout Troop Adv. Com., Alton, 1983—. Mem. Am. Inst CPA's, Mo. Soc. CPA's, Am. Assn. Indsl. Mgmt. (exec. roundtable), Future Bus. Leaders Am. (adv. counsil 1984—). Republican. Avocations: golf, racquetball, duck hunting. Home: 5210 Dover Dr Godfrey IL 62035 Office: Miss Lime Co 7 Alby St Alton IL 62002

AINLEY, ROBERT WALLACE, advertising executive; b. Perry, Iowa, Aug. 18, 1922; s. Oscar Albert and Goldie May (Beatty) A.; m. Ila June Inman, Apr. 15, 1949; children: Robert Kent, Leslie Ann. Student, Kemper Mil. Sch., 1940-41, State U. of Iowa, 1941-43; AB, Drake U., 1947. Internal sales rep. The Maytag Co., Newton, Iowa, 1947-48; sales rep. The Upson Co., Des Moines, 1948-54; advt. sales rep. Wallaces Farmer, Des Moines, 1954-65; advt. mgr. Prairie Farmer Pub. Co., Chgo., 1965-76; mgr. advt. sales Farmer Progress Publs., Indpls., 1976—; supr. Midwest Unit Farm Publs., Chgo., 1968-74, promotion mgr., 1974-76; bd. dirs. Plans Bd. State Farm Mag. Bur., 1971-76. Past bd. dirs., pres. Churchill and Hawthorn Grade Sch. PTA, Glen Ellyn, Ill., 1965-75; trustee Prairie Farmer Pension Trust, Chgo., 1970-73; bd. dirs. Greenwood (Ind.) High Sch. Band Parents Assn., 1976-80. Served to master sgt. AUS, 1943-46, ETO, Res. 1950-51. Decorated 2 Bronze Stars. Mem. Nat. Agrl. Mktg. Assn. (charter, bd. dirs. 1976-78), N.Am. Farm Show Council (pres. 1975-76), 69th Infantry Div. Assn. Republican. Methodist. Home: 754 Colonial Way Greenwood IN 46142 Office: Farmer Progress Publs 2346 S Lynhurst Dr Indianapolis IN 46241

AITCHISON, GARY L., business and management educator, academic administrator; b. Corwith, Iowa, May 21, 1935; s. Clarence E. and Alta Bernice (Jacobs) A.; m. Kathryn Jean Quinn, Aug. 4, 1956; children: Steven, Brent, Jon, Peter, Matthew. BA, U. No. Iowa, 1956; MA, U. No. Colo., 1961; PhD, Iowa State U., 1972. Instr. Garrison (Iowa) Sch., 1956-61, Marshalltown Community Coll., 1961-65; assoc. prof. Iowa State U., 1961—, assoc. dean Coll. Bus., 1983-87, dean, 1987—. Co-author: Work, Money in the Family, 1976, Your Marriage: The Great Adventure, 1979; contbr. articles on marriage, family and small bus. mgmt. to profl. jours. Mayor appointee Bus. Devel. Com., Ames, 1979—; past pres., sec, v.p. USA Christian Family Movement, Ames, 1977-85. Recipient Outstanding Service award Christian Family Movement, 1985; named Outstanding Advisor, Iowa State U., 1979. Mem. Nat. Assn. Mgmt. and Mktg. Educators (pres. 1983—, bd. dirs. 1985—, Outstanding Service award 1986). Democrat. Roman Catholic. Avocation: woodworking. Home: 922 9th St Ames IA 50010 Office: Iowa State U Carver Hall Rm 300 Ames IA 50010

AITKEN, ROSEMARY THERESA, financial planner and consultant; b. Phila., June 26, 1946; d. John Francis and Mary Helen (Kinslow) A.; m. Frank Furch, June 24, 1983. A.A., Mundelein Coll., 1976. C.L.U. Mktg. cons. Anchor Orgn., Chgo., 1974-76; assoc. dir. Big Bros.-Big Sisters of Chgo., 1975-76; fin. planner Phoenix Co., Chgo., 1976—; chmn bd. Lincoln Equities, Inc., Chgo., 1985—, also bd. dirs.; pres. Capital Interests, Inc., Chgo., 1984—, Aitken Assocs., Chgo., 1980—; speaker, instr. Chgo. Women's Network, 1984—; cons., columnist Chgo. Tribune, 1980—, Chgo. Sun-Times, 1981—; lectr. Midwest Life Underwriters Assns., 1982—, lectr., instr. Mundelein Coll., Northwestern Univ., Oakton Community Coll., Loyola U. Contbr. articles to profl. jours. Bd. dirs. Loop YWCA, 1974-81. Mem. Women Life Underwriters Conf. (bd. dirs., 1st v.p. 1984-85), Chgo. Life Underwriters Assn. (chmn. membership com. 1984-85), Million Dollar Roundtable (life and qualifying mem.), Internat. Assn. Fin. Planners. Republican. Roman Catholic. Club: East Bank. Avocations: marathon running, sailing, photography. Home: 2462 W Estes Chicago IL 60645 Office: Aitken Assocs 10 S Riverside Plaza Suite 1250 Chicago IL 60606

AJANS, Z. A., psychiatrist, internist; b. Aleppo, Syria, July 28, 1937; came to U.S., 1965; s. Karam and Nabiha M. (Dawly) A.; m. Mona S. Salloum, Sept. 4, 1966; children: Lena, Leile, Amy, Anthony. Student, Aleppo Coll., 1953-55; BS, Am. U., Beirut, 1957, MD, 1961. Resident in internal medicine Am. U. Hosp., Beirut, 1961-63, asst. instr., 1963-65; postdoctoral fellow U. Mo., Columbia, 1966-69; asst. prof. U. Mo., Columbus, 1969-72; med. dir. Audrain Med. Ctr., Mexico, Mo., 1972—; cons. psychiatrist Dept. Human Resources, Jefferson City, Mo., 1972—, Dept. Mental Health, Fulton, Mo., 1978—. Served to lt. col. USAR, 1970-80. Fellow Am. Psychiat. Assn. (physicians recognition award 1985); mem. AMA , Cen. Mo. Psychiat. Soc. (pres. 1979), Alpha Omega Alpha. Mem. Christian Eastern Orthodox Ch. Avocations: tennis, reading, travel.

AKAHA, TSUNEO, political science educator; b. Chino, Japan, July 30, 1949; s. Keisaku and Shime (Hirabayashi) A.; m. Janet Louise Billstein, Jan. 30, 1977; children: Yoshio Michael, Mitsuko Katherine. BA in Polit. Sci., Oreg. State U., 1974, Waseda U., Tokyo, Japan, 1975; MA in Internat. Relations, U. So. Calif., 1977, PhD in Internat. Relations, 1981. Cert. tourist guide, Japan. Asst. prof. polit. sci. Kans. State U., Manhattan, 1981-83; asst. prof. Bowling Green (Ohio) State U., 1983-86, assoc. prof., 1986—. Author: Japan in Global Ocean Politics, 1985; contbr. articles to profl. jours. Grantee Bowling Green State U., 1984-85, U.S. Dept. Edn. grantee, 1986; fellow Japan Found., 1985. Mem. Internat. Peace Research Assn., Am. Polit. Sci. Assn., Internat. Studies Assn., Japan Assn. Internat. Relations, Am. Soc. Pub. Adminstrn. Home: 879 Brookfield Ln Perrysburg OH 43551 Office: Bowling Green State U Dept Polit Sci Bowling Green OH 43403

AKE, MONTIE RALPH, hotel exec.; b. San Angelo, Tex., July 10, 1931; s. William Raleigh and Lorraine (Elliott) A.; B.A., Lamar U., 1949, B.S., 1953. Trainee, front office mgr. Sheraton Corp. Am., St. Louis, 1956-61; sales mgr. Tan-Tar-A Resort, Osage Beach, Mo., 1962-63, gen. mgr., 1963-69, v.p., 1969-78; exec. v.p. Regency Park Resort, Overland Park, Kans., 1978-80; gen. mgr. Rancho Bernardo Inn, San Diego, 1981-84; gen. mgr. Pheasant Run, St. Charles, Ill., 1984—; past sec.-treas., dir., v.p. Dickinson Operating Co., Dickinson, Inc.; sec.-treas. Le Jardin, Inc.; dir. M.D.H. Theatre Corp. Sustaining mem. Gt. Rivers council Boy Scouts Am. Past pres., bd. dirs. Lake Ozarks Assn., 1967-77. Served with U.S. Army, 1953-55. Mem. Am. Hotel-Motel Assn. (past dir.), Greater Kansas City Restaurant Assn. (dir.), Greater Kansas City Hotel Assn. (dir.), Kans. Hotel and Motel Assn. (dir.), San Diego Conv. and Visitors Bur., Kans. Cavalry (col.), AMKO Assn. (dir.), San Diego C. of C. Republican. Presbyterian. Clubs: Variety Internat. (2d asst. barker), Rotary of Rancho Bernardo. Home: 111 Whittington Course Saint Charles IL 60174

AKENHEAD, JAMES ELLIS, school system administrator; b. Alliance, Ohio, Feb. 9, 1943; s. Robert E. and Elizabeth (Brunt) A.; m. Charlene A. Akenhead, July 12, 1965; 1 child, Matthew. EdB, Bowling Green State U., 1965; MEd, Kent (Ohio) State U., 1969, ednl. specialist, 1972; MS, U. Dayton, 1980; EdD, U. Akron, 1983. County sch. supr. Stark County Schs., Canton, Ohio, 1969-70; supt. New Riegel (Ohio) Schs., 1970-73, Seneca County Schs., Tiffin, Ohio, 1973-76, Bellaire (Ohio) City Schs., 1976-79, Marlington Schs., Alliance, Ohio, 1979—; ptnr. People Tech Cons., Alliance, 1985—, People Stuff Cons., Alliance, 1985—. Recipient Edit. Commendation, Times Leader, 1979, Exemplary Leadership Salute, Stark County Bd. Edn., 1984. Mem. Am. Assn. Sch. Adminstrs. (group facilitator Nat. Convention), Buckeye Assn. Sch. Adminstrs. (speaker various coms.), Belmont-Harrison Supts. Assn. (pres. 1978), Nat. Orgn. Legal Problems in Edn., Phi Delta Kappa. Lodge: Rotary. Avocations: boating, sports cars, weightlifting. Home: 14143 Ravenna Ave NE Alliance OH 44601 Office: Marlington Public Schs 10320 Moulin Ave NE Alliance OH 44601

AKERS, DENNIS LYNN, electronics company executive; b. Lima, Ohio, Dec. 3, 1946; s. John Henry and Mary Alice (Conway) A.; m. Juanita Parrigan; children: James Gregory, Brandon Scott. BSEE, U. Cin., 1970. Registered profl. engr., Ohio. With Westinghouse, various locations, 1966-77; dist. mgr. sales RTE Corp., Portland, Oreg., 1977; mgr. mktg. RTE Corp., Milw., 1979; v.p. mktg., sales Alloy Tek, Inc., Grand Rapids, Mich., 1979-81; mgr. mktg. Eaton Corp., Sarasota, Fla., 1981-85; v.p. mktg., sales CTS Corp., Beane, Ind., 1985—. Served with USMCR, 1970-76. Mem. Internat. Soc. Hybrid Electronics, Am. Mktg. Assn. (exec.). Home: 6610 Sweetwood Ct Fort Wayne IN 46804 Office: CTS Corp 406 Parr Rd Beane IN 46711

AKIN, CAVIT, biotechnologist, research scientist; b. Nigde, Turkey, Feb. 28, 1931; came to U.S., 1957; s. Ahmet and Fatma Kenan (Yuceeren) A.; m. Ingeborg Katharina Tange, Feb. 24, 1978; children—Deniz Leyla, Suzan Sema, Tulin Selma, Aylin Neva. M.S.Chem.E., U. Ankara, 1954; M.S. in Food Tech., U. Ill., 1959, Ph.D., 1961; postdoctoral U. Mass., 1962. Research scientist Sugar Research Inst., Turkey, 1956-57; sr. bioengr. Falstaff Research Lab., St. Louis, 1962-67; sr. research engr. Am. Oil Co., Whiting, Ind., 1967-70; sr. research engr. Standard Oil Co., Naperville, Ill., 1971-73, research assoc., supr. biotech. research, 1979-87; research supr. Amoco Chems., Naperville, Ill., 1973-77; mgr. foods exploratory research Amoco Foods, Naperville, 1978-79; assoc. dir. biotech. research Inst. Gas Tech., Chgo., 1987—. Served to lt. Signal Corps, Turkish Armed Forces, 1955-56. Fulbright scholar U. Ill., 1957-61. Mem. Am. Chem. Soc., Am. Soc. Microbiology, Soc. Indsl. Microbiologists, Inst. Food Technologists, AAAS. Moslem. Patentee in field; contbr. articles to profl. jours. Home: 1462 Inverary Dr Naperville IL 60540 Office: Inst Gas Tech Chicago IL 60616

AKIN, DANIEL PHILLIP, otolaryngologist; b. Greensburg, Ky., Nov. 25, 1944; s. Leonard Taft and Mary L. (Gerdon) A.; m. Margaret Ann Jacobi, June 8, 1968; children: Brian Daniel, Scott Bradley, Kyndra Ann, Jodi Marie. AB in Zoology, Ind. U., 1967, PhD in Gross Anatomy, 1972, MD, 1973. Diplomate Am. Bd. Otolaryngology. Intern Meth. Hosp., Indpls., 1973-74; resident in otorhinolaryngology Ind. U. Med. Ctr., Bloomington, Ind., 1974-78; practice medicine specializing in otorhinolaryngology New Albany, Ind., 1978—. Mem. ACS, Am. Coll. Facial, Plastic and Reconstructive Surgery, Am. Soc. Outpatient Surgeons, Floyd County Med. Soc., Louisville Ear Nose and Throat Soc., Midwest Bio-laser Inst., Am. Soc. Laser Medicine and Surgery, Ind. Med. Assn. Home: Rt #2 Box 445D New Albany IN 47150 Office: Akin Med Ctr 2019 State St New Albany IN 47150

ALADJEM, SILVIO, obstetrician and gynecologist, educator; b. Bucharest, Romania, June 16, 1928; came to U.S., 1964, naturalized, 1969; s. Nahman and Lea (Campus) A. M.D. summa cum laude, U. Uruguay, 1961. Diplomate: Am. Bd. Obstetrics and Gynecology; cert. subsplty. in maternal-fetal medicine. Intern Uruguay Pub. Health Service, Montevideo, 1961-62; resident in obstetrics and gynecology U. Uruguay, 1962-63, Cleve. Met. Gen. Hosp., 1964-67; fellow in obstetrics and gynecology Western Res. U., 1967, asst. prof., attending obstetrician and gynecologist, 1969-74; instr. Med. Coll. Ga., 1967-68, asst. prof., 1968-69; assoc. prof. U. Ill., Chgo., 1975-76; prof. U. Ill., 1976-78, head div. perinatal medicine, 1976-78; prof., chmn. dept. obstetrics and gynecology Stritch Sch. Medicine, Loyola U., Chgo., 1978-84; dir. perinatal ctr. Bronson Hosp., Kalamazoo, 1984—; practice medicine specializing in obstetrics and gynecology; cons. Nat. Found. March of Dimes, Cleve., Chgo. Author: Risks in the Practice of Modern Obstetrics, 1972, 75, (with Audrey Brown) Clinical Perinatology, 1975, 79, Perinatal Intensive Care, 1976, Obstetrical Practice, 1980; contbr. (with Audrey Brown) articles to med. jours. Mem. Am. Coll. Obstetricians and Gynecologists (E. McDowell award 1967), Am. Fertility Soc. (C. Hartman award 1968), Soc. Gynecologic Investigation, Am. Soc. Anatomists, N.Y. Acad. Scis., Chgo. Gynecol. Soc., Chgo. Med. Soc., AMA, Ill. Med. Assn., Perinatal Group of Ill. (pres. 1976), Am. Assn. Maternal Neonatal Health (pres. 1978—). Office: Bronson Hosp 252 E Lovell Kalamazoo MI 49007

AL-'ARABY, WAHEED S., historian; b. Jerusalem, May 27, 1927; s. 'Awdah and Ilanah (Muhr) Shawiriyyah; divorced; children: Guhaynah, Gihad. BA in Arabic Lit., An-Nahda Coll., Jerusalem, 1947; PhD in History, Univ. de Chile, Santiago, 1957. Asst. sec. gen. Arab Tarde Union Congress, Jerusalem, 1944-49; asst. editor Arab affairs An-Nasr, Damascus, Syria, 1949-50; editor-in-chief Al-Balad, 1950-52; dir. press. cultural and political depts. Embassy Arab Rep., Santiago, Chile, 1953-58; founder, editor, pub. Al-Watan, Santiago, 1957-60; sales mgr. Combined Ins. Co. of Am., N.J., 1962-65; real estate broker Palm Beach and Miami, Fla., 1967-78; cons. Arab-Am., African-Am. affairs Washington, 1979-81; dir. Jana News Agy., N.Y.C and Washington, 1981-82; founder, pres. Internat. Inst. for Arab-Am. Relations, N.Y.C and Washington, 1983-85; founder, dir. English sect. Syrian Broadcasting Service, Damascus, 1950-52; founder, chmn. bd. Arab-Am. Devel. Corp., 1967-78; lectr. Arab-Am. affairs 1978—. Co-editor Al-Ittihad, 1944-49; contbg. editor Al-Ghad, 1944-49; sr. columnist Arab News, Jedda, Saudi Arabia, 1983-85; author: Al-Quds "Jerusalem": The Untold History, 1985, Human Rights and Israel; founder, pub., editor-in-chief Ency. Arabica. Home: 510 E Schantz Ave Dayton OH 45409

ALBAN, ROGER CHARLES, construction equipment distribution executive; b. Columbus, Ohio, Aug. 3, 1948; s. Charles Ellis and Alice Jacqueline (Hosfeld) A.; student pub. schs.; m. 2d Rebecca Lynn Gallicchio, Aug. 12, 1978; children—: Roger Charles II, Charles Michael; 1 dau. by previous marriage, Allison Ann. With Alban Equipment Co., Columbus, 1963—, sales mgr., 1972-75, gen. mgr., 1975-85, treas., 1978-85, v.p., 1980-85, pres. 1985—. Mem. Grandview Heights Bd. Edn., Columbus, 1978-85, pres., 1979, v.p., 1982, legis. liaison, 1978-79, 83-84; elected Grandview Heights City Council, 1986; mem. Met. Ednl. Council, Columbus Area Leadership Program, 1982-83. Mem. Assoc. Equipment Distbrs. (lt. dir. region 6 1980, 85, 86, chmn. light equipment dist. com. 1985, chmn. sales and mktg. com. 1987), Ohio Sch. Bds. Assn. (mem. all cen. region bd. 1984), Bldg. Industry Assn. Cen. Ohio, Internat. Platform Assn., Am. Rental Assn., Builders Exchange Cen. Ohio (trustee 1987—), Am. Mgmt. Assn., Nat. Right To Work Com., Nat. Fedn. Ind. Bus., Ohio Equipment Distbrs. Assn. (dir. 1982, 84—, pres. 1983), Am. Mensa Ltd. (chpt. exec. com. 1979-80). Roman Catholic. Clubs: Rotary, Downtown Columbus. Home: 1430 Cambridge Blvd Marble Cliff OH 43212 Office: 1825 McKinley Ave Columbus OH 43222

ALBANI, THOMAS J., manufacturing company executive; b. Hartford, Conn., May 3, 1942; s. Charles A. and Marie F. Albani; m. Suzanne Beardsley, Sept. 3, 1966; children: Karin, Steven. B.A., Amherst Coll., 1964; M.B.A., Wharton Sch. U. Pa., 1967. Asst. product mgr. Gen. Mills, Inc., Mpls., 1967-69; dir. mktg. Am. Can Co., Greenwich, Conn., 1969-73; mgmt. cons. McKinsey and Co., Inc., N.Y.C., 1973-78; gen. mgr. Gen. Electric Corp., Bridgeport, Conn., 1978-84; group v.p. Black & Decker, Inc., Bridgeport, 1984; pres., corp. v.p. Sunbeam No. Am. Appliance Div. Allegheny Internat., Pitts., 1984-86; exec. v.p., chief operating officer Allegheny Internat., Oak Brook, Ill., 1986—. Mem. Nat. Housewares Mfrs. Assn. (bd. dirs. 1985—), Assn. Home Appliance Mfrs. (bd. dirs. 1985—), Chgo. Assn. Commerce and Industry (bd. dirs. 1986).

ALBANO, JILL, savings and loan training manager; b. Chgo., June 15, 1959; d. Valentine Peter and Mary Lorraine (Zdrojewski) Szydlowski; m. Robert Joseph Albano, May 15, 1982. AS in Commerce, Morton Coll., 1979; BA in Bus. Mgmt., U. Ill., Chgo., 1981. Teller, asst. disbursing teller Cen. Fed. Savs. and Loan, Cicero, Ill., 1977-81; supr. Lyons Savings and Loan, Stickney, Ill., 1981-82; br. Lyons (Ill.) Savings and Loan, 1982-84; corp. trainer Lyons Savings and Loan, Hinsdale, Ill., 1984—, asst. v.p., 1985—; mem. Chgo. Area Fin. Tng. Network, 1984—. Mem. Nat. Assn. Women in Careers. Avocations: cooking, sewing, crafts. Home: 1618 W 54th St La Grange Highlands IL 60525 Office: Lyons Fed Trust & Savs Bank 911 N Elm Hinsdale IL 60521

ALBAZZAZ, FAIQ JABER, physician, researcher, educator; b. Baghdad, Iraq, July 1, 1939; s. Jaber Mehdi and Fadela (Hassoun) AlBazzaz; children—Alexandra Nesreen, Michael Basheer, Brian Senan. M.B., Ch.B., U. Baghdad, 1962. Diplomate Am. Bd. Internal Medicine, Am. Bd. Pulmonary Diseases. Intern, Teaching Hosp., Mosul, Iraq, 1965-66; resident in medicine U. Miss. Med. Ctr., 1966-68, Mpls. VA Hosp.-U. Minn. Hosp., 1968-69; pulmonary fellow Mass. Gen. Hosp.-Harvard Med. Sch., Boston, 1969-71; asst. prof. medicine U. Ill.-Chgo., 1971-78, assoc. prof., 1978-86, prof., 1986—; dir. pulmonary lab. VA Westside Med. Ctr., Chgo., 1971—, chief respiratory and critical care sect., 1977—. Contbr. articles to profl. jours. Fellow Royal Coll. Physicians and Surgeons (Can.), Am. Fedn. Clin. Research, Cen. Soc. Clin. Research, ACP, Am. Coll. Chest Physicians; mem. Am. Physiol. Soc., Am. Thoracic Soc. Avocation: photography. Home: 930 North Blvd Oak Brook IL 60301 Office: VA 820 S Damen Ave Chicago IL 60612

ALBERDING, CHARLES HOWARD, petroleum and hotel executive; b. Clayville, N.Y., Mar. 5, 1901; s. Charles and Doris (Roberts) A.; m. Bethine Wolverton, May 2, 1930; children: Beth Ann, Mary Katherine, Melissa Linda. EE, Cornell U., 1923. Lab. asst., draftsman, operator Producers & Refiners Corp., Parco, Wyo., 1923-25; engr., cracking plant supt. Imperial Refineries, Ardmore, Okla., Eldorado, Ark., 1925-27; head fgn. operating dept. Universal Oil Products Co., London, Eng., Ploesti, Roumania, Rangoon, Burma, Venice, Italy, 1927-33; head operating, service depts., Chgo. hdqrs. Universal Oil Products Co., 1933-42; pres., dir. Paradise Inn, Inc., Jokake Inn, Inc., Vinoy Park Hotel Co., Holiday Hotel Corp., Alsonett Hotels, Sabine Irrigation Co., Sabine Canal Co., Tides Hotel Corp., Harmony Oil Corp., London Square Corp., Petroleum Spltys., Lincoln Lodge Corp., Peabody Hotel Corp., Memphis, Hermitage Hotel Co., Nashville, Royal Palms Inn, Inc., Torrey Pines Inn, La Jolla, Calif., Charleston First Corp.; petroleum cons., dollar-per-yr. man WPB, 1942-43; dist. dir. petroleum refining Petroleum Adminstrn. for War, 1943-45. Presdl. councilor Cornell U.; bd. govs. Endowment Found., Heritage Trust. Mem. Scorpion. Republican. Congregationalist. Clubs: Valley (Phoenix); Kenilworth (Chgo.), Cornell (Chgo.); Sunset Country (St. Petersburg, Fla.), Bath (St. Petersburg, Fla.); Tides Country (pres., dir.), Rolling Greens Golf (pres., dir.), Sunrise Golf (Sarasota, Fla.) (pres., dir.). Home: 99 Tudor Pl Kenilworth IL 60043 Office: 9 E Huron Chicago IL 60611

ALBERS, LOIS HELEN, nurse; b. Peotone, Ill., Oct. 30, 1926; d. Carl John and Florence Magdalene (Pries) Schneeweis; R.N., St. Luke's Hosp., 1948; B.S., St. Francis Coll., 1978; m. John Albers, Feb. 14, 1948; children—Steven John, Linda Susan. With Westlake Community Hosp., Melrose Park, Ill., 1948—, dir. nursing services, 1968-76, adminstrv. coordinator for health programming services, 1976—. Mem. Presbyn.-St. Luke's Alumni Assn. Republican. Lutheran. Home: 465 Fairview Ave Elmhurst IL 60126 Office: Westlake Community Hosp 1225 Superior St Melrose Park IL 60160

ALBERT, JANYCE LOUISE, banker; b. Toledo, July 27, 1932; d. Howard C. and Glenola Mae (Masters) Blessing; m. John R. Albert, Aug. 7, 1954; children: John R., James H. Student Ohio Wesleyan U., 1949-51; BA, Mich. State U., 1953; MS, Iowa State U., 1980. Asst. personnel mgr./tng. supr. Sears, Roebuck & Co., Toledo, 1953-56; tchr. adult edn. Tenafly Pub. Schs. (N.J.), 1966-70; personnel officer, tng. officer, tng. and edn. mgr. Iowa Dept. Transp., Ames, 1974-77; coll. recruiting coordinator Rockwell Internat., Cedar Rapids, Iowa, 1977-79, engring. adminstrn. mgr., 1979-80; employee relations and job evaluation analyst Phillips Petroleum Co., Bartlesville, Okla., 1980-81; v.p., dir. personnel Republic Bancorp, Tulsa, 1981-83; v.p. and dir. human resources First Nat. Bank, Rockford, Ill., 1983—; advisor to Nat. Profl. Secs. Assn. Bd. dirs. Rocvale Children's Home, United Way of Ames, 1976-77; mem. adv. council Rockford br. Ill. Job Service; publicity chmn. Tenafly 300th Ann. Celebration, 1969; bd. deacons Presbyn. Ch., Ames, 1972-75; mem. adv. council Rockford YWCA, bd. dirs., 1986; co-chmn. YWCA Leader Luncheon, 1985; sec. Bravo council Rockford Dance Co., advisor Rockford chpt. ARC; mem. Mayor's Task Force for Rockford Project Self-Sufficiency. Pres.'s scholar, 1951-53; recipient YWCA Kate O'Connor award for Women in Labor Force 1985. Mem. Rockford Network (chairperson 1985, pres. 1986), Rockford C. of C. (transp. com.), Rockford Personnel Assn. (co-chmn. programs 1985-86, adv. council), Am. Soc. Personnel Adminstrn., Rockford Personnel Assn., Employee Benefits Assn. No. Ill. (membership chmn.), Rockford Council Affordable Health Care, P.E.O., Sigma Epsilon, Alpha Gamma Delta, Phi Kappa Phi. Home: 5587 Thunderidge Dr Rockford IL 61107 Office: First Nat Bank Rockford 401 E State St Rockford IL 61110

ALBERT, JOHN LEE, media specialist; b. Akron, Ohio, July 11, 1942; s. John Samuel and Helen Irene (Decker) A.; m. Sarah Mosser, Apr. 10, 1966; children: John Mathew, Susan Larissa. BSED, Ohio U., 1966, MA, 1968. Media specialist Parkersburg (W.Va.) Cath. High Sch., 1966-68, Bloom-Carroll High Sch., Carroll, Ohio, 1968-70, Licking Valley High Sch., Newark, Ohio, 1970-76, Lancaster (Ohio) High Sch., 1976—. Chairperson Educators Polit. Action Com., Senate Dist. 31, House Dist. 78, 1982—. Martha Holden Jennings Found. grantee, 1974, 75. Mem. NEA (Congl. Contact Team 1982—), Ohio Edn. Assn. (chairperson Soc. Uniserv Council 1980-86), Lancaster Edn. Assn. (pres. 1981-86). Democrat. Avocations: cooking, canoeing, photography, computers. Home: 12919 Claylick Rd Newark OH 43056 Office: Lancaster High School 1312 Granville Pike Lancaster OH 43130

ALBERTELLI, GUY LEO, computer systems programmer; b. Phila., Aug. 26, 1950; s. Guido and Anne (Michelotti) A.; m. Ruth Dzintra Williamson, May 6, 1972; children: Sylvia, Guy II, Ruth Angela. BS, U. Dayton, 1972; MS, SUNY, Buffalo, 1974. Sr. mgmt. info. systems specialist BF Goodrich, Akron, Ohio, 1980-84, mgmt. info. systems cons., 1985—. Roman Catholic.

ALBERTS, MARION EDWARD, physician; b. Hastings, Nebr., Mar. 14, 1923; s. Eddie and Mary Margaret (Hilbers) A.; m. Jeannette McDaniel, Dec. 25, 1944; children—Kathryn, Brian, Deborah, Timothy. B.A., U. Nebr., 1944, M.D., 1948. Licenciate Am. Bd. Pediatrics. Intern Iowa Methodist Hosp., Des Moines, 1948-49; resident in pediatrics Raymond Blank Hosp. Children, Des Moines, 1949-50, 52-53; practice medicine specializing in pediatrics Des Moines, 1953—; chief pediatrics Mercy Hosp., 1953—; mem. med. staff Iowa Luth. Hosp., 1953—, Iowa Meth. Hosp., 1953—, Broadlawns Polk County Hosp., 1953—; instr. clin. pediatrics Coll. Osteo. Medicine and Surgery, 1970-82. Sci. editor Iowa Medicine, 1971—. Contbr. articles to profl. jours. Pres. Polk County Tb and Respiratory Diseases Assn., 1965, 66, 70. Served to comdr. USNR, 1943-45, 50-52. Recipient Whitaker Interstate Teaching award Interstate Postgrad. Med. Assn., 1980; Service award Sisters of Mercy, 1978. Fellow Am. Acad. Pediatrics, Internat. Coll. Pediatrics; mem. AMA (recognition awards 1969—), Iowa Med. Soc. Republican. Presbyterian (elder). Lodge: Masons. Home: 5104 Ashworth Rd West Des Moines IA 50265 Office: 1071 5th Ave Des Moines IA 50314

ALBERTS, SUSAN, social worker; b. Flint, Mich., July 11, 1947; d. Charles and Anne (Lande) Weinstein; m. Barry Alberts; 1 child, Jaime. Student, London Sch. Econs., 1967; BA cum laude, U. Mich., 1968, MSW, 1972. Social worker Michael Reese Hosp., Chgo., 1972-74, Northwest Mental Health Ctr., Arlington Heights, Ill., 1974-79; pvt. practice social worker Evanston, Ill., 1979—; Instr. Northwestern U., Chgo., 1982-86; workshop leader. Chair Commn. Women's Equality, Am. Jewish Congress, 1985; organizer Feldenkrais Parents, Chgo., 1985—. Mem. Nat. Assn. Social Workers. Jewish. Avocation: following psychology of women through literature. Home: 200 Dempster Evanston IL 60202

ALBERTSON, DAVID EDWIN, banker; b. Evanston, Ill., Mar. 7, 1937; s. Walter S. and Frances M. (Coon) A.; m. Carol E. Coolidge, Sept. 16, 1961; children: Robert Coolidge, David Stanley. B.S. in Bus. Adminstrn., Miami U., Ohio, 1959, M.A. in Econs., 1961. Vice pres. No. Trust Co., Chgo., 1961-71; pres., chief exec. officer State Nat. Bank, Evanston, 1971—. Served with II. N.G., 1961-67. Mem. Bankers Club of Chgo. (exec. com. 1983-85, pres. 1986—), Evanston C. of C. (pres. 1984-86), Econ. Club of Chgo., Ill. Bankers Assn. (bd. dirs. 1983-86), Am. Bankers Assn. (leadership council), Phi Beta Kappa. Republican. Congregationalist. Clubs: University; Skokie Country. Home: 770 Bryant St Winnetka IL 60093 Office: State Nat Corp 1603 Orrington Ave Evanston IL 60204

ALBIN, JOAN ELIZABETH, social services administrator; b. Waterloo, N.Y., Nov. 18, 1948; d. John Martin and Elizabeth (Young) Pontius; m. Ronald James Albin, June 30, 1979; children: Elizabeth Marie, Michael Ronald. BA, Elmira Coll., 1970; MSW, U. Md., Balt., 1974. Social worker Balt. City Dept. Social Services, 1970-79; therapist Assoc. Cath. Charities, Luth. Social Services, Balt., 1976-79; cons. Luth. Social Services, Balt., 1978-79; dist. adminstr. Nebr. Dept. Social Services, Norfolk, 1983—; mem. adv. bd. Monroe Mental Health Ctr., Norfolk, 1985-87, Liberty Centre, Norfolk, 1985-87. Mem. Nat. Assn. Social Workers (cert.), Am. Pub. Welfare Assn. Democrat. Episcopalian. Home: 1602 Norfolk Ave Norfolk NE 68701 Office: Dept Social Services PO Box 339 Norfolk NE 68701

ALBIN, JOHN SANFORD, farmer; b. Newman, Ill., Oct. 28, 1928; s. Leonard Bruce and Grace Nettie (Herrington) A.; B.S. with honors, U. Ill., 1950; m. Marjorie Ann Martin, Sept. 10, 1949; children—Perry S., David A. Farmer, Newman, 1951—; operator Albin Farm; pres. Albin Pork Farm, Inc., Plants Pals Inc.; chmn. bd. Longview State Bank (Ill.); bd. dirs. Castillo Rio, Inc.; pres. Longview Capital Corp., 1977-86. Pres., Newman Community Unit 303 Sch. Bd., 1958-66; trustee Parkland Coll., Champaign, Ill., 1968-87, v.p., 1977-87; chmn. bd. 1st Nat. Bank of Ogden (Ill.). Recipient Ill. 4H Alumni award, 1968, Master Farmer award Prairie Farmer mag., 1970, award of merit U. Ill. Coll. Agr. Alumni Assn., 1977. Mem. Am. Shropshire Registry Assn. (pres. 1962-65), Ill. Farm Bus. Farm Mgrs. Assn. (pres. 1968-83), E. Central Farm Bus. Farm Mgrs. Assn. (pres. 1965-72), Douglas County Farm Bur. (bd. dirs. 1968-87), Top Farmers Assn. Am., Farm House, Alpha Zeta. Republican. Clubs: Villa Grove Country, Masons. Home: PO Box 377 Newman IL 61942

ALBOR, LARRY JOHN, marketing professional; b. Chgo., Jan. 15, 1948; s. Enedino John and MAry Eve (Kaminski) A. BA, Quincy Coll., 1971; MA, St. Louis U., 1974. Sales rep. Garner Sales, St. Louis, 1976-78; coordinator Inroads/Chgo., 1978-80; acct. exec. Ill. Bell, Chgo., 1980-83, mgr. mktg., 1983-87; adminstr. market research Contel Service Corp., St. Louis, 1987—. Pres. Buena Park Neighbors Assn.; bd. dirs. Uptown Chgo. Commn. Grad. fellow St. Louis U., 1971-75, Fulbright-Hays fellow, 1976. Mem. Am. Mgmt. Assn., Chgo. Computer Soc., Hispanic Bell Mgmt. Assn. Republican. Roman Catholic. Lodge: Kiwanis. Avocations: theatre, travel, personal computers. Office: Contel Service Corp 600 Mason Ridge Ctr Dr Saint Louis MO 63141

ALBRECHT, EDWARD DANIEL, metals manufacturing company executive; b. Kewanee, Ill., Feb. 11, 1937; s. Edward Albert and Mary Jane (Horner) A.; B.S. in Metall. Engring., U. Ariz., 1959, M.S., 1961, Ph.D., 1964, Metal. Engr. (hon.), 1973; m. Mignon Y. Buehler, Jan. 1, 1973; 1 child, Deborah J. Research metallurgist, U. Calif. Los Alamos Lab., 1959-61; sr. physicist, project mgr. U. Calif. Lawrence Radiation Lab., Livermore, 1964-71; founder, pres. Metall. Innovations Inc., Pleasanton, Calif., 1969-71; chmn. bd., 1971-73; gen. mgr. Buehler Ltd. & Adolph I. Buehler, Inc., Lake Bluff, Ill., 1972, v.p., gen. mgr., 1973-76, chmn., pres., 1976, also dir.; pres. bd. dirs. Buehler-Met AG Basel, Switzerland, 1983-87; pres. Mowlem Tech. Inc., Lake Bluff, 1984-86; founder, pres., chief exec. officer, Buehler Internat. Inc., 1985—; bd. dirs. Mowlem Tech. Ltd., London; chmn. bd. Soiltest, Inc., Evanston, Ill., 1984—, CPN Corp., Pacheco, Calif., 1984—; bd. dirs. Tech Met Canada Ltd., Toronto, Ont., Banner Sci. Ltd. (now Buehler UK ltd.), Coventry, Eng., Coal Gasification, Inc., Hinsdale, Ill., Sauk Southwest Steel, Inc., Tulsa. Bd. dirs. Danville (Calif.) Homeowners Inc., treas., 1966-68; trustee Lake Forest Acad. - Ferry Hall Prep Sch., 1977-81; mem. nat. adv. bd. Heard Mus. Anthropology, Phoenix, 1980—; trustee Millicent Rogers Mus., Taos, N.Mex., 1982—, chmn. devel. com., 1983-85. NDEA fellow, 1959-62. Fellow Am. Soc. Metals (chmn. Tucson 1961), Royal Micros. Soc. Eng.; mem. Internat. Metallographic Soc. (pres. 1973-75, dir. 1975-81 chmn. gen. tech. meeting San Francisco 1969, Chgo. 1972, Brighton, Eng., 1980), Deutsche Gesellschaft für Metallkunde, Sigma Gamm Epsilon, Delta Upsilon. Clubs: Chicago, Onwentsia, Desert Highlands. Contbr. articles to profl. jours. Patentee in field. Office: Buehler Internat Inc PO Box 1 Lake Bluff IL 60044

ALBRECHT, FRANK WAYNE, data processor; b. Bloomington, Ill., May 30, 1936; s. Frank Peter and Ellen May (Middlekauff) A.; A.A. in Computer Sci., Lincoln Land Community Coll., Springfield, Ill., 1972; divorced; children: Michelle Rae, Traci Lynn; m. Nona B. Albrecht, July 16, 1987. Computer operator Franklin Life Ins. Co., Springifeld, 1957-61; with State of Ill., 1961—, mgr. data preparation ops. Dept. Public Aid, 1979-83, mgr. prodn. ops., 1983-86, computer security mgr., 1986—; adv. bd. Capitol Area Vocat. Tng. Center, Springfield. Mem. Sangamon County Sheriff's Patrol, 1968-80, Springfield/Sangamon County CD Group, 1968-80. Served with USN, 1954-57, Korea. Cert. in data mgmt., 1983. Mem. Data Entry Mgmt. Assn., Optical Character Reader Users Assn., Ill. Welfare Assn. Roman Catholic. Club: Moose. Office: State of Ill Data Processing 100 S Grand Ave E Springfield IL 62704

ALBRECHT, ROBERT F., management consultant; b. Rock Island, Ill., Nov. 24, 1926; s. Arthur A. and Marie J. (Kruse) A.; m. Shirley J. Sammon, Oct. 29, 1949; children: Sheryl, Katherine, Nancy. BS, Northwestern U., 1947. Indsl. engr. Deere & Co., Moline, Ill., 1952-59, sr. div. mgr., 1963-86; chief indsl. engr. Red Jacket Mfg. Co., Davenport, Iowa, 1959-62; plant mgr. Long Mfg. Co., Davenport, 1962-63; prin. Robert F. Albrecht, Inc., Rock Island, Ill., 1986—. Served to lt. USN, 1950-52. Mem. Inst. Indsl. Engrs. Republican. Lutheran. Avocations: sports, woodworking. Home and Office: 3108 35th St Rock Island IL 61201

ALBRIGHT, JUSTIN W., lawyer; b. Lisbon, Iowa, Oct. 14, 1908; m. Mildred Carlton, 1935; 1 child, Carlton J. B.S.C., U. Iowa, 1931, J.D., 1933. Bar: Iowa 1933. Now of counsel firm Simmons, Perrine, Albright & Ellwood, Cedar Rapids., Iowa. Editor: Iowa Law Rev, 1932-33. Trustee YMCA of Met. Cedar Rapids; bd. dirs. Cedar Rapids Symphony Orch.; past pres. St. Paul's United Meth. Ch. Found., Cedar Rapids. Served with AUS, World War II. Mem. Am., Iowa, Linn County bar assns., Cedar Rapids C. of C., Phi Delta Phi. Clubs: Cedar Rapids Country, Pickwick (Cedar Rapids). Lodges: Mason (33 deg.), (Shriner), Rotarian. Office: 12th Floor Mchts Nat Bank Bldg Cedar Rapids IA 52401

ALBRIGHT, KATHERINE JEAN, controller; b. LaGrange, Ill., Mar. 12, 1958; d. W. Kenneth and Jean Catherine (Mazzarella) Nank; m. Rodney E. Albright, Apr. 3, 1982. EdB, Ill. State U., 1980; postgrad., Ill. Benedictine Coll., 1981-85; CPA, U. Ill., 1985. Asst. head teller, bookkeeper, customer service West Suburban Bank Darian, Ill., 1974-80; tchr. reading Elwood (Ill.) Grade Sch., 1980-81; acct. First Penn Pacific Life Ins., Oak Brook, Ill., 1981-85; asst. controller, data processing mgr. Subaru Mid Am., Addison, Ill., 1985—; controller Albright Constrn., Joliet, Ill., 1987—; cons. Harbor Enterprises, Balt., 1985-87, Md. Undercoating, Balt., 1985-87, Automotive Mgmt. Services, Addison, 1987—. Mem. Am. Inst. CPA's. Methodist. Avocations: scuba diving, snow mobiling, water skiing, gardening. Office: Subaru Mid Am 301 Mitchell Ct Addison IL 60101

ALBRIGHT, LAURIE JO, school psychologist; b. Toledo, Jan. 14, 1952; d. Lawrence Ray and Josephine Amelia (Knott) A.; m. Brian Lee Larson, Sept. 24, 1983; children: Timothy Martin, Bradley Roy. BA in Psychology magna cum laude, Cleve. State U., 1973, MA in Psychology, 1975. Lic. sch. psychologist, Ohio. Staff sch. psychologist Positive Edn. Program Early Intervention Ctr. East, Cleve., 1975-80, program coordinator, 1980—. Mem. Nat. Assn. Sch. Psychologists, Am. Psychol. Assn., Am. Orthopsychiat. Assn., Ohio Sch. Psychologist Assn., Cleve. Assn. Sch. Psychologists (pres. 1983-84). Office: Early Intervention Ctr East 5442 Rae Rd Lyndhurst OH 44124

ALBRIGHT, TOWNSEND SHAUL, investment banker; b. Anderson, Ind., May 1, 1942; s. Townsend S. and Maxine Aree (Zimmerman) A.; m. Eileen Therese Argent, Aug. 30, 1968; children—Megan Eileen, Alexandra Michele. B.A., Wabash Coll., 1964; M.B.A., U. Mich., 1966. With Mead Corp., Cin. and Chgo., 1966-69; mcpl. bond underwriter No. Trust Co., Chgo., 1969-71; v.p. Channer Newman Securities Co., Chgo., 1971-80; v.p., treas., dir., Croake Roberts, Inc., Chgo., 1980-86; v.p. instl. sales John Nuveen & Co., Chgo., 1986—. Bd. dirs., mem. adv. council Urban Gateways, Chgo., 1976—; v.p., bd. dirs. Wilmette Jaycees, 1979-80. Served with USAR, 1966-72. Mem. Mcpl. Bond Club Chgo., Chgo. Assn. Wabash Men, U. Mich. Alumni Assn. Presbyterian. Clubs: Economic (Chgo.); Wilmette Sailing Assn. (dir.-treas. 1980-81), Michigan Shores (Wilmette, Ill.). Home: 2019 Beechwood Ave Wilmette IL 60091 Office: Croake Roberts Inc 135 S LaSalle St Chicago IL 60603

ALBRITTON, KEVIN WEBB, financial consultant; b. St. Louis, May 2, 1954; s. Wallace E. and Betty M. (Webb) A.; m. Linda Susan Mueller, Jan. 7, 1978; children: Neal M., Katharine M. BA in Biology, St. Louis U., 1976. Salesperson Curtin Matheson Scientific, St. Louis, 1976-79; assoc. Siegfried & Assocs., St. Louis, 1979-84; prin. First Fin. Group, St. Louis, 1985—; adult edn. instr. Jefferson Coll., Arnold, Mo., 1982-86. Baseball coach Rockwood Sch. Dist., 1986; coach West County Soccer Assn., St. Louis, 1986, 87; pres. St. Claire of Assisi PTO, St. Louis, 1986-87. Mem. Nat. Assn. Life Underwriters, Am. Soc. CLU's, St. Louis Life Underwriters (bd. dirs. 1984-86, sec. 1987), Life Underwriters Tng. Council (moderator 1985-86), Internat. Assn. Fin. Planners (cert. fin. planner), Nat. Assn. Security Dealers (registered rep.). Republican. Roman Catholic. Avocations: hunting, fishing, family activities. Home: 2702 Hillcroft Dr Chesterfield MO 63017 Office: First Fin Group 100 S Brentwood Blvd #300 Clayton MO 63105

ALBY, JAMES FRANCIS PAUL, priest, educator; b. Milw., July 16, 1936; s. Francis Joseph and Sarah Sophie (Hansen) A.; B.A., Gallaudet U., 1963, M.S. in Edn., 1964; M.Div., Va. Theol. Sem., 1971; m. Jan Lorraine Peplinski, Aug. 2, 1980; 1 child. Ordained priest Episcopal Ch., 1971; priest to the deaf St. James Mission of the Deaf, Milw., 1971-76; priest assoc. St. Peter's Ch., West Allis, Wis., 1972-83; asst. to rector: Ministry of the Deaf, St. James Parish, Milw., 1983—; tchr. high sch. hearing impaired Milw. Pub. Schs., 1972—; priest assoc. Holy House of Our Lady of Walsingham, Norfolk, Eng., 1984—; instr. interpreting for deaf U. Wis., Milw., 1975-77; sr. high sch. boys dorm supr.-counselor St. John's Sch. for the Deaf, St. Francis, Wis., 1971-72; tchr. lang. of signs Milw. Area Tech. Coll., 1974-75; mem. adv. com. continuing edn. deaf adults, Milw., 1976-84, mem. adv. com. on edn. hearing impaired Milw. Pub. Schs., 1977—; mem. sect. 504 com. Southeastern Wis. Disabilities Coalition, 1979-81, mem. adult edn. adv. com. Milw. Hearing Soc., 1976-83. Contbr. articles to profl. jours. Mem. Nashotah House Sem. Alumni Assn. (assoc.), Nat. Fraternal Soc. Deaf, Nat. Assn. of Deaf, Wis. Assn. Deaf, WDanish Brotherhood in Am., Gallaudet U. Alumni Assn., Alpha Sigma Pi. Lodges: Lions (charter pres.), Lioness (liaison 1980-84). Office: St James Episcopal Ch 833 W Wisconsin Ave Milwaukee WI 53233

ALCOTT, JAMES ARTHUR, communications executive; b. Stillwater, Okla., Oct. 24, 1930; s. Arthur Bernard and Dorothy Laura (Hopkins) A.; m. Marilynn Hill, June 14, 1952; children—David, Thomas, Tobin, Anne. B.S. in Econs, Okla. State U., 1952; M.B.A., Stanford U., 1956. Credit analyst Republic Nat. Bank, Dallas, 1956-58; dir. econs. and mgmt. scis. Midwest Research Inst., Kansas City, Mo., 1958-69; trustee Midwest Research Inst., 1969—; v.p. Heald, Hobson & Assos., N.Y.C., 1969-71; gen. mgr. Minn. Exptl. City Project, Mpls., 1971-74; pres., pub. Harper's mag., N.Y.C., 1975-80; v.p. Cowles Media Co., 1978—; Adv. com. AIA Research Corp., 1977-78; adv. bd. Carnegie-Mellon Inst. Research, 1975-80; mem. commn. ecumenical missions and relations and program agy. United Presbyn. Ch., 1964-74; exec. com. Urban Coalition Greater Kansas City, Mo., 1968-69, Jackson County (Mo.) Govtl. Reorgn. Commn., 1968-69; chmn. research conf. Engring. Found., 1964-65; cons. Citizens Conf. on State Legislatures, 1971-72, Nat. Council Juvenile Ct. Judges, 1971-72. Pres. Minn. Ctr. for Book Arts, 1983-86, bd. dirs., 1983—; trustee Twin Cities Pub. TV, Inc., 1983—; trustee Minn. Charities Rev. Council, 1984—; mem. Gov.'s Adv. Com., 1985-87, Minn. Adult Reading Campaign, 1985—; bd. dirs. Technology for Literary Project Donor Rev. Bd., 1985—. Served to 1st lt. USAF, 1952-54. Recipient Disting. Alumnus award Okla. State U., 1978; Named to Coll. Bus. Adminstrn. Hall of Fame Okla. State U., 1978. Mem. Phi Delta Theta, Phi Kappa Phi, Beta Gamma Sigma. Office: Cowles Media Co 329 Portland Ave Minneapolis MN 55415

ALDEN, DON EDWARD, cosmetics company executive; b. Long Beach, Calif., Oct. 29, 1937; s. John James and Nathell (Larson) A.; B.S., Okla. State U., 1962; cert., honor grad. Inst. for Mgmt., Ill. Benedictine Coll., 1971; m. Sandra Jean Horn, July 6, 1963; children—Laura Marie, John Vincent. With Swift & Co., Oak Brook, Ill., 1963—, ind. investigator in research, 1963-71, div. head vegetable protein research, 1971-76, research mgr. new product devel., 1978-80, grocery product devel., 1980-84; dir. research Alberto-Culver Corp., Melrose Park, Ill., 1984—. Served with M.C., U.S. Army, 1960-66. Mem. Inst. for Mgmt. (v.p. bd. dirs. 1979-81, pres. 1982), Am. Assn. Cereal Chemists, Internat. Food Technologists, Peanut Butter Mfrs. Assn. Democrat. Roman Catholic. Developer texturized vegetable protein, 1971; patentee flavor-free undenatured legume seeds, 1976, vegetable oil extraction, 1980, process for prodn. of flavored protein foods, 1971. Home: 3143 Everglade St Woodridge IL 60517 Office: Alberto-Culver Corp 2525 Armitage Melrose Park IL 60160

ALDER, ALTHEA ALICE, marketing service agency executive; b. Wilmore, Kans., Jan. 4, 1933; d. Lloyd Lewis and Margaret Mae (Baldwin) A.; student Ft. Hays State U., 1952-55. Owner, operator 2 beauty shops, 1961-67; quality control mgr., supr. women Solo Cup Co., 1967-70; v.p. purchasing, prodn. and premiums William A. Robinson, Inc., Northbrook, Ill., 1970-79; pres. A-three Services Agy., Ltd., Northbrook, Ill., 1980—, Lake Forest Tng. Salon, Ltd., 1979-80. Served with W.A.C., AUS, 1951-53, 55-61; Korea. Decorated Army Commendation medal. Mem. Am. Legion. Lodge: Eastern Star. Home: 1116 Greenwood Ave Deerfield IL 60015 Office: A-three Services 3125 Commercial Ave Northbrook IL 60062

ALDERFER, OWEN HIRAM, bishop, educator; b. Upland, Calif., June 7, 1923; s. Hiram R. and Mary Rebecca (Frymire) A.; m. Ardis W. Witter, June 15, 1945; children: Jill Annette, Eric Ray. AB, Upland (Calif.) Coll., 1945; BD, Asbury Theol. Sem., Wilmore, Ky., 1951; PhD, Claremont (Calif.) Grad. Sch., 1964. Ordained minister Brethren in Christ Ch., 1946. Pastor Brethren In Christ Ch., Springfield, Ohio, 1951-55; prof. religion Upland Coll., 1955-65; prof. ch. history Ashland (Ohio) Theol. Sem., 1965-80; prof. religion Messiah Coll., Grantham, Pa., 1980-84, C.N. Hostetter prof. theology, 1980-84; bishop Brethren in Christ Ch., West Milton, Ohio, 1984—. Author: Called to Obedience, 1974; editor Ashland Theol. Bull., 1969-79; contbr. articles to profl. jours. Recipient Disting. Alumnus award Messiah Coll., 1983; Danforth Found. grantee, 1961-63. Mem. Am. Soc. Ch. History, Conf. on Faith and History. Home: 6336 S Jay Rd West Milton OH 45383 Office: Brethren in Christ Ch PO Box 57 West Milton OH 45383

ALDERFER, RONALD GODSHALL, environmental consultant; b. Harleysville, Pa., July 14, 1943; s. Allen and Eva (Godshall) A.; m. Constance Joan Beachy, Aug. 21, 1965; children: Philip Wendell, Kristin Nicole. AB, Washington U., St. Louis, 1965, PhD, 1969. Asst. prof. U. Chgo., 1969-75; chief ecologist Harland Bartholomew, St. Louis, 1975-80; mgr. midwest region Environ. Sci. and Engring., St. Louis, 1981—. Mem. AAAS, Ecol. Soc. Am., Air Pollution Control Assn., Soc. Environ. Toxicology and Chemistry, Nat. Assn. Environ. Profls. (bd. trustees 1982-84), Regional Commerce and Growth Assn. (chmn. environ. com. 1984). Lodge: Rotary. Avocations: skiing, hiking, sailing, cycling. Home: 15574 Highcroft Dr Chesterfield MO 63017 Office: Environ Sci and Engring Inc 11665 Lilburn Park Rd Saint Louis MO 63146

ALDERSON, KENNETH ALLEN, state association executive; b. Decatur, Ill.. BA, So. Ill. U., 1971. Asst. to dir. Ill. EPA, 1972-73; mgr. membership services Ill. Mcpl. League, Springfield, 1973—; mem. econ. tech. adv. com. Ill. Pollution Control Bd., 1976—. Served with U.S. Army, 1960-63, Vietnam. Mem. Ill. Environ. Consensus Forum (exec. com. 1980—), Assn. Ill. Soil and Water Conservation Dists. (tech. advisor). Republican. Avocation: sailboat racing. Home: 2639 Yale Springfield IL 62703 Office: Ill Mcpl League 1220 S 7th St Springfield IL 62703

ALDIS, HENRY, gynecologist; b. Basim, Berar, India, Nov. 3, 1913; s. Steadman and Ethel Rebecca (Fry) A. (parents Am. citizens); A.B., U. Kans., 1938, M.D., 1941; m. Margaret Elizabeth Warner, June 24, 1941; children—John Warner, Henry Weeks (dec.), William Leggett, David Fry. Intern, City Hosp., Winston-Salem, N.C., 1941-42; resident, Gorgas Hosp., C.Z., 1942-43, asst. resident in surgery U. Kans., 1943-44, asst. resident in ob-gyn., Balt. City Hosps., 1954-56, chief resident in ob-gyn., 1956-57; asso. Walter Sheeley, M.D., Shepherdstown, W.Va., 1946-52; gen. practice medicine, Ft. Scott, Kans., 1952-54; practice medicine specializing in ob-gyn., Ft. Scott, 1957—; mem. staff Newman-Young Clinic, Mercy Hosp., Ft. Scott, Bourbon County. Served with AUS, 1944-46; ETO; served to col. M.C. Kans. N.G., 1956-73. Diplomate Am. Bd. Ob-Gyn (also recert.). Mem. AMA, Bourbon County Med. Soc., Kansas City Gynecol. Soc. Republican. Methodist. Home: 501 S Main St Fort Scott KS 66701 Office: 6 E 13th St Fort Scott KS 66701

ALDRICH, ANN, federal judge; b. Providence, R.I., June 28, 1927; d. Allie C. and Ethel M. (Carrier) A.; m. Chester Aldrich, 1960 (dec.); children: Martin, William; children by previous marriage: James, Allen. B.A.; cum laude, Columbia U., 1948; LL.B. cum laude, N.Y. U., 1950, LL.M., 1964, S.J.D. Bar: D.C. bar, N.Y. bar 1952, Conn. bar 1966, Ohio bar 1973, Supreme Ct. bar 1956. Research asst. to mem. faculty N.Y. U. Sch. Law; asso. firm Samuel Nakasian, Washington, 1952-53; mem. gen. counsel's staff FCC, Washington, 1953-60; U.S. del. to Internat. Radio Conf., Geneva, 1959; practice law Darien, Conn.; asso. prof. law Cleve. State U., 1968-71, prof., 1971-80; also chmn. curriculum com.; U.S. Dist. Ct. (no. dist.) Ohio, 1980—; bd. govs. Citizens' Communications Center, Inc., Washington; mem. litigation com.; guest lectr. Calif. Inst. Tech., Pasadena, summer 1971. Mem. Fed. Bar Assn., Nat. Assn. of Women Judges, Fed. Communications Bar Assn. Episcopalian. Office: U S Dist Ct 210 US Courthouse 201 Superior Ave NE Cleveland OH 44114 *

ALDRICH, MARILYN JEAN, pharmacist; b. Akron, Ohio, July 2, 1955; d. Robert L. and Sarah C. (Moulton) Minkler; m. Warren Charles Aldrich, Sept. 8, 1984. B.S. in Pharmacy, Drake U., 1977. Registered pharmacist, Iowa. Switchboard operator Sta. KCCI-TV, Des Moines, 1972-75; pharmacy clk. Target, Des Moines, 1975-76; pharmacy intern Hammer Pharmacy, Des Moines, 1976-77; pharmacist Easter's, Creston, Iowa, 1977; pharmacist/asst. mgr. Dahl's Foods, Inc., West Des Moines, Iowa, 1977—. State of Iowa scholar, 1973; Drake U. Presdl. scholar, 1973; U.S. Govt. grantee, 1973, 74. Mem. Iowa Pharmacists Assn., Polk County Pharmacists Assn. (sec. 1981-82), Chi Omega Alumni. Republican. Presbyterian. Lodge: Hon. Order of Blue Goose Internat. (women's auxiliary 1985—). Avocations: reading; sewing; knitting; racquetball; swimming. Home: 1414 68th St Des Moines IA 50311 Office: Dahl's Pharmacy 1819 Beaver Des Moines IA 50310

ALDRICH, THOMAS LEO, petroleum products manufacturing company executive; b. Akron, Ohio, Nov. 2, 1931; s. George Leo and Bernadine June (McGuire) A.; m. Patricia Ann Mills, Dec. 26, 1955; children: Pamela, Timothy, Michael, Gregory, Terrence, Lori, Matthew. BS in Engring., U.S. Naval Acad., 1955; MBA, U. Ill., 1985. Commd. USN, 1955, advanced through grades to lt., 1959, resigned, 1960; engr. Firestone Tire and Rubber, Akron, 1960-64; tech. mgr. Firestone Tire and Rubber, Joliette, Quebec, Can., 1965-67, plant mgr., 1968-74; plant mgr. Firestone Tire and Rubber, Whitby, Ont., Can., 1974-77; prodn. mgr. Firestone Tire and Rubber, Decatur, Ill., 1978—. Bd. dirs. Jr. Achievement, Decatur, 1978-82. Mem. U.S Naval Inst., Sch. Assn. (Joliette treas. 1967-74, Decatur v.p. 1980-82), Richland Community Coll. Alumni. Roman Catholic. Avocation: swimming. Home: 849 Harold Circle Decatur IL 62526 Office: Firestone Tire and Rubber PO Box 1320 Decatur IL 62525

ALEKSY, RONALD JAMES, engineering educator; b. Milw., June 22, 1947; s. Stanley and Suzanne (Neubauer) A. BS, U. Wis., 1970, MS, 1971. Registered profl. engr., Wis. Fire protection engr. Indsl. Risk Insurers, Hartford, Conn., 1971-78; asst. prof. Milw. Sch. Engring., 1978—. Author: Computer Program Replication, 1971, Process of Special Relativity, 1985, Life and Cosmos, 1987. Mem. IEEE, Engrs. and Scientists of Milw., Wis. Soc. Profl. Engrs. (v.p. Milw. south chpt. 1984—), U.S. Chess Fedn. (life). Avocations: chess, real estate. Home: 3812 E Bottsford Ave Cudahy WI 53110 Office: Milw Sch Engring 1025 N Milwaukee St Milwaukee WI 53201

ALEMAN, MINDY R., advertising and public relations executive, freelance writer; b. N.Y.C., Nov. 23, 1950; d. Lionel and Jocelyn (Cohen) Luskin; m. Gary Aleman, Aug. 27, 1983. B.A., U. Akron, 1972, M.A., 1975. Instr. speech U. Akron, 1973-83; car salesperson Dave Towell Cadillac, Akron, 1977-79, mgr. fin. and ins., 1979; account exec., pub. relations dir. Loos, Edwards & Sexauer, Akron, 1980-82; mktg. services coordinator Century Products, Stow, Ohio, 1982-83; mgr. advt., pub. relations Century Products, Gerber Furniture Group, Stow, 1983-86, Macedonia, Ohio, 1986—. Author: (play) Danny's Choice, 1972. Mem. Am. Mktg. Assn., Pub. Relations Soc. Am.(cert.), Akron Advt. Club (various awards 1983-86), Akron Women's Network, Sales and Mktg. Execs. of Cleve. Office: Century Products Inc 9600 Valley View Rd Macedonia OH 44056

ALESHIRE, CHARLES THOMAS, comptroller; b. Macomb, Ill., Nov. 18, 1959; s. Charles Theodore and Donna Bell (Roberts) A.; m. Rebecca Louise Timmons, Oct. 18, 1978 (div. Jan. 1980); m. Monica Marie Jones, Dec. 30, 1985; 1 child, Katelyn Adele. BBA, Western Ill. U., 1984. CPA, Iowa. Profl. staff McGladrey, Hendrickson& Pullen, Inc., Davenport, Iowa, 1984-86; comptroller 1st Bank, Davenport, Iowa, 1986—. Mem. Am. Inst. CPA's, Iowa Soc. CPA's. Lodge: Kiwanis. Avocations: fishing, motorcycling. Home: 2607 2d St Moline IL 61265 Office: 1st Bank 201 W 2d St Davenport IA 52801

ALESSI, NORMAN EMIL, child psychiatrist; b. Birmingham, Ala., Mar. 25, 1950; s. Joseph Samual and Lucy (D'zuana) A.; m. Barbara McCaslin, May 28, 1983; 1 child, Jacqualine Regina. Student, Auburn U., 1968-70; BS in Biology, Emory U., 1972, MD, 1976. Diplomate Am. Bd. Psychiatry and Child Psychiatry. Intern U. Mich., Ann Arbor, 1976-77, resident in psychiatry, 1977-80, fellow in child psychiatry, 1978-81, research fellow, 1981-83, dir. diagnostic and research unit, 1986—; med. dir. Octagon House, Ann Arbor, 1979-80; cons. psychiatrist Maxey Boys Tng. Sch., Whitmore Lake, Mich., 1979-84; research cons. State of Mich., 1981-82. Contbr. articles to profl. jours. Mem. AMA, Am. Psychiat. Assn., Am. Acad. Child Psychiatry, Soc. Neurosci., Internat. Soc. Psychoneuroendocrinology, Phi Beta Kappa. Home: 2009 Carhart Ann Arbor MI 48104 Office: U Mich Hosp Dept Psychiatry 1500 E Medical Center Dr Ann Arbor MI 48109-0706

ALEXANDER, ARISTOTLE ALEX, psychiatry educator, psychologist; b. Milw., May 25, 1933; s. Alex M. and Grace A. (Stamos) A.; m. Virginia Haskins, Oct. 24, 1981. BS, U. Wis., 1957, MS, 1959, PhD, 1962. Predoctoral fellow USPHS, Madison, Wis., 1961-62; postdoctoral fellow dept. psychiatry U. Wis., Madison, 1962-63, prof. psychiatry Sch. Medicine, 1965—, dir. psychophysiology labs., 1965-83, dir. Health Maintenance Orgn. Services, 1983—, dir. psychiat. outpatient clinics, 1985—; cons. Wis. State Prisons, Waupun, 1965-72. Contbr. articles to profl. jours. Served to capt. USAF, 1963-65. Grantee NIMH, Madison, 1966-71, Ford Found., Madison, 1971. Mem. Am. Psychol. Assn., Soc. Psychophysiol. Research, Transcultural Psychiatry, World Psychiat. Assn. Avocation: sailing. Office: U Wis Med Schs Dept Psychiatry B6/274-CSC Madison WI 53792

ALEXANDER, BARBARA LEAH SHAPIRO, psychiatric social worker; b. St. Louis, May 6, 1943; d. Harold Albert and Dorothy Miriam (Leifer) Shapiro; m. Richard E. Alexander. B in Music Edn., Washington U., St. Louis, 1964; postgrad., U. Ill., 1964-66; MSW, Smith Coll., 1970; postgrad., Inst. Psychoanalysis, Chgo., 1971-73, child therapy program, 1976-80; cert. therapist Sex Dysfunction Clinic, Loyola U., Chgo., 1975. Research asst., NIMH grantee Smith Coll., 1968-70; probation officer Juvenile Ct. Cook County, Chgo., 1966-68, 70; therapist Madden Mental Health Center, Hines, Ill., 1970-72; supr., therapist, field instr. U. Chgo., U. Ill. Grad. Schs. Social Work, also Pritzker Children's Hosp., Chgo., 1972—; therapist, cons., also pvt. practice, 1973—; instr. tng. and advanced tng. Effectiveness Tng. Assocs., Chgo., 1974; instr. psychology Northeastern U., Chgo., 1975; intern Divorce Conciliation Service, Circuit Ct. Cook County, 1976-77. Contbr. articles to profl. jours. Bd. dirs. North Am. Found., Grant Park Concerts Soc. Recipient Sterling Achievement award Mu Phi Epsilon, 1964. Mem. Acad. Cert. Social Workers (cert.), Nat. Assn. Social Workers (pres. 1987—), Ill. Soc. Clin. Social Work (bd. dirs., chmn. services to mems. com., dir. pvt. practitioners' referral service), Am. Assn. Marriage and Family Therapy, Assn. Child Psychotherapists, Am. Assn. Sex Educators and Counselors, Amateur Chamber Music Players Assn., Jewish Geneal. Soc., Smith Coll. Alumni Assn. (bd. dirs.). Democrat. Home: 179 E Lake Shore Dr Chicago IL 60611 Office: 919 N Michigan Ave #3012 Chicago IL 60611

ALEXANDER, BRUCE KIRBY, information resource specialist; b. Elkhart, Ind., Apr. 19, 1948; s. Kirby Vernon and Josephine Alyce (Mullett) A.; m. Mary Jo Hardy, July 7, 1979; 1 child, Benjamin. BS, Mich. State U., 1973, MA, 1983. Cert. systems profl. Systems analyst Mich. State U., East Lansing, 1979-84, mgr. data base & info. ctr., 1984—. Data processing cons. Ingham County Dem. Party, Lansing, Mich. Mem. Assn. Systems Mgmt., Cause (coordinator spl. interest group 1986). Democrat. Presbyterian. Club: Fast Break (Okemos, Mich.) (bd. dirs. 1985—). Home: 1231 Wolf Ct East Lansing MI 48823 Office: Mich State U Adminstrv Info Services Room 2 Adminstrn Bldg East Lansing MI 48824

ALEXANDER, COLLIN HERBERT, consulting company executive; b. Carsonville, Mich., Dec. 27, 1916; s. George Herbert and Emma Louise (Strong) A.; m. Mary Elizabeth Horrall (dec.); m. 2d, Suzanne Revier, Dec. 28, 1977; children—Graham, Carolyn, Nancy, Katherine, Alice, Jonathan, Robert. B.S., Alma Coll., 1937; postgrad. MIT, 1937-39. With Kimberly Clark Co., Niagara Falls, N.Y., 1940-41, Bausch & Lomb Optical Co., Rochester, N.Y., 1941-51, Minn. Mining & Mfg. Co., St. Paul, 1951-70; pres. Tech. Enterprises Co., St. Paul, 1970—. Mem. Am. Optical Soc., Am. Chem. Soc., Am. Phys. Soc., Am. Vacuum Soc. Republican. Presbyterian. Club: St. Paul. Patentee. Office: Box 13122 Saint Paul MN 55113

ALEXANDER, JAMES WESLEY, surgeon, educator; b. El Dorado, Kans., May 23, 1934; s. Rossiter Wells and Merle Lydia Alexander; m. Maureen L. Strohofer; children: Joseph, Judith, Elizabeth, Randolph, John Charles, Lori, Molly. Student, Tex. Technol. Coll., 1951-53; M.D., U. Tex., 1957; postgrad., U. Cin., 1958-64, U. Minn., 1966-67. Diplomate Am. Bd. Surgery, Am. Bd. Thoracic Surgery; lic. physician, Tex., Ohio. Intern Cin. Gen. Hosp., 1957-58; resident U. Cin.-Cin. Gen. Hosp., 1958-64; mem. faculty Coll. Medicine, U. Cin., 1962-64, 66—, prof. surgery, 1975—, dir. transplantation div., dept. surgery, 1967—, dir. surg. immunology lab., 1967—; dir. research Shriners Burns Inst. Coll. Medicine U. Cin., 1979—; practice medicine and surgery Cin., 1966—; mem. staff Cin. U., Cin. Hosp., VA Hosp., Christian R. Holmes Hosp., Cin. Children's Hosp., Christ Hosp., Cin. Shriners Burns Inst., Good Samaritan Hosp., Jewish Hosp. Author: (with R.A. Good) Fundamentals of Clinical Immunology, 1977; mem. editorial bd. Annals of Surgery, 1975—, Jour. Burn Care and Rehabilitation, 1979,Circulatory Shock, 1979—, Burns, Including Thermal Injury, 1985— ; contbr. articles to profl. jours. Served as capt. M.C., U.S. Army, 1964-66. Mem. AAAS, Am. Assn. for Surgery of Trauma, Am. Assn. Immunologists, Am. Assn. Tissue Banks, Am. Burn Assn. (pres. 1984-85), ACS, Am. Soc. Transplant Surgeons (sec. 1985-87), Am. Soc. Parenteral and Enteral Nutrition, Am. Surg. Assn., Assn. for Acad. Surgery, Central Surg. Assn., Cin. Acad. Medicine, Cin. Surg. Soc., Halsted Soc., Internat. Soc. for Burn Injuries, Internat. Soc. Surgery, Colombian Coll. Surgeons (hon.), Peruvian Acad. Surgery (hon.), St. Paul Surg. Soc. (hon.), Ohio Med. Assn., Reticuloendothelial Soc., Soc. Univ. Surgeons, Surg. Biology Club, Surg. Infection Soc. (sec. 1981-84, pres.-elect 1985-86, pres. 1986-87), Transplantation Soc., Alpha Omega Alpha, Alpha Chi, Alpha Epsilon Delta, Phi Eta Sigma. Home: 2869 Grandin Rd Cincinnati OH 45208 Office: U Cin Coll Medicine 231 Bethesda Ave Cincinnati OH 45267-0558

ALEXANDER, JOANN SAYRE, nurse, educator; b. Evansville, Ind., Dec. 24, 1934; d. Joseph Sayres and Evelyn Catherine (Schmitt) Coughlin; B.S. in Nursing, St. Louis U., 1956; M.S. in Nursing, U. Evansville, 1976; m. James Edward Alexander, Oct. 11, 1958; children—James Edward, Laurie Ann, Mary E., Jan R. Asst. head nurse Marion (Ill.) VA Hosp., 1956-57; staff nurse Firmin Desloge Hosp., St. Louis, 1957-58; staff nurse Herrin (Ill.) Hosp., 1963-64; staff nurse Byron (Ill.) Clinic, 1966-67; sch. nurse Vanderburgh Sch. Corp., Evansville, Ind., 1968-69; asst. prof. nursing U. Evansville, 1973—; inservice edn. program cons. Welborn Hosp., Evansville; reviewer Ind. Continuing Edn. for Nursing, 1978-79. Tchr., Confraternity of Christian Doctrine, 1973-77, Service award, 1977; active Women's Service Guild, 1968-72; nursing del. Ind. State Conv., 1977, 79. Mem. Am. Nurses Assn., Ind. Nurses Assn., Dist. #4 Nurses Assn. (chmn. nomination com.), Nat. League Nursing, Ind. Citizens League for Nursing, Bus. and Profl. Women's Club (treas. 1958), Beta Sigma Phi, Sigma Theta Tau. Clubs: Holy Rosary Women's; Horseshoe Bend. Home: 5801 Monroe Ave Evansville IN 47715 Office: Box 329 Evansville IN 47702

ALEXANDER, JOHN J., chemistry educator; b. Indpls., Apr. 13, 1940; s. John Gregory and Inez Helene (Snedaker) A. A.B. summa cum laude, Columbia U., 1962, M.A., 1963, Ph.D., 1967. Postdoctoral fellow Ohio State U., Columbus, 1967-69, research assoc., 1977-78; asst. prof. chemistry U. Cin., 1969-73, assoc. prof., 1973-79, prof., 1979—, faculty fellow, 1972-74; vis. prof. Ohio State U., 1985-86. Author: (with M.J. Steffel) Chemistry in the Laboratory, 1976, (with B.E. Douglas, D.H. McDaniel) Concepts and Models of Inorganic Chemistry, 1983, Problems in Inorganic Chemistry, 1983; contbr. articles to profl. jours., chpts. to books. Mem. Clifton Town Meeting. Woodrow Wilson fellow, NSF fellow Columbia U., 1963-65, faculty fellow, 1966. Mem. Am. Chem. Soc. (past chmn., trustee), Phi Beta Kappa, Sigma Xi, Phi Lambda Upsilon. Democrat. Home: 3446 Whitfield Ave Cincinnati OH 45220 Office: U Cin Dept Chemistry Cincinnati OH 45221

ALEXANDER, J(OSEPH) EDWARD, manufacturing company executive; b. Eugene, Oreg., Mar. 17, 1948; s. Joseph Edward and Opal Marie (Robison) A.; B.S. in Mech. Engring., Oreg. State U., 1970; M.S. in Mech. Engring., Carnegie-Mellon U., 1973; m. Judith Elaine Koharik, July 26, 1980. Mech. design engr. Westinghouse Corp.-Bettis Atomic Power Lab., Pitts., 1970-75, Bettis resident mgr. at FMC Corp., 1976-78; mil. mktg. engr. No. Ordnance div. FMC Corp., Mpls., 1978-79, mgr. concepts devel., 1979—. Registered profl. engr., Pa. Mem. ASME, Am. Def. Preparedness Assn., Phi Kappa Phi, Tau Beta Pi, Pi Tau Sigma, Sigma Tau, Phi Eta Sigma. Home: 2633 Natchez Ave S Minneapolis MN 55416 Office: No Ordnance Div FMC Corp 4800 E River Rd Minneapolis MN 55421

ALEXANDER, ZENON L., industrial executive; b. Ukraine, USSR, May 29, 1943; m. Jean A. Alexander. BCE, Rensselaer Poly. Inst., 1966; MBA in Mktg. and Internat. Bus., Mich. State U., 1968. With sales Gen. Electric Co., N.Y.C., 1968-69; mgr. mktg. Advanced Digital Systems, Mohawk, N.Y., 1969-72; mgr. planning, market research and devel., products Rexnord Inc., Milw., 1972—. Rep. village chmn., Bayside, Wis.; chmn. 9th Dist. Rep. Resolutions Com.; del. Wis. Rep. Conv. Mem. Am. Mktg. Assn. (activities chair), Power Transp. Dist. Assn. (chmn. mfg., digital processing). Home: 8936 N King Rd Bayside WI 53217 Office: Rexnord Inc PO Box 2022 Milwaukee WI 53202

ALEXANDROFF, MIRRON (MIKE), academic administrator; b. Chgo., Mar. 3, 1923; s. Norman and Cherrie (Phillips) A.; m. Anna C. Avgerin, Dec. 22, 1947 (dec.); children: Niki Alexandroff Gray, Pam Alexandroff Eidenberg; m. Jane Ann Legnard, Jan. 27, 1962; 1 child, Norman. BA, Roosevelt U., 1947; MA, Columbia Coll., Chgo., 1948. Pres. Columbia Coll., 1961—; chmn. Chgo. Met. Higher Edn. Council, 1982—. Adv. com. Chgo. Dept. Cultural Affairs, 1985—; pres. Grant Park Cultural and Ednl. Community, 1985—. Served to sgt. U.S. Army, 1942-45, PTO. Mem. Am. Assn. Urban Universities (chmn. 1986—). Clubs: University, Arts (Chgo.). Home: 199 E Lake Shore Dr Chicago IL 60611 Office: Columbia Coll 600 S Michigan Ave Chicago IL 60605

ALF, JOHN JAMES, chem. co. exec.; b. Aurora, Ill., May 7, 1936; s. Frank Peter and Anne Mary (Urlaub) A.; B.S., St. Mary's Coll., Winona, Minn., 1958; M.B.A., U. Mich., Ann Arbor, 1966; m. Marianne E. Schmidt, Jan. 24, 1959; children—Christine, Julie, Elizabeth, Eric. Chemist, Chemetron Corp., Rockhill Labs., Newport, Tenn., 1960-63, sr. chemist N.W. Chem. div., Detroit, 1963-65; mgr. adminstrv. services Vulcan Labs., Inc., Pontiac, Mich., 1965-68; v.p. ops. water mgmt. div. Clow Corp., Pontiac, 1968—. Mem. Am. Chem. Soc., Mensa. Home: 35306 Lancashire Ct Livonia MI 48152 Office: Clow Corp 408 Auburn Ave Pontiac MI 48058

ALFATHER, ROBERT BRUCE, manufacturing company executive; b. Detroit, May 2, 1930; s. Frank George and Goldie Ofer (Miller) A.; m. Lois Anne Madigan, Jan. 7, 1953; children: Michael, Patricia. BS in Indsl. Engring., Lawrence Inst. Tech., 1959. Registered profl. engr., Calif. Mgr. automation Ford Motor, Dearborn, Mich., 1956-66; facilities mgr. Fruehauf Corp., Detroit, 1966-70; corp. dir. engring. Key Internat., Dearborn, 1970-78; pres. Roblo Corp., Livonia, Mich., 1978-81; dep. mgr. Kintech Services, Cin., 1981-84; mgr. mfg. engring. Mac Tools, Washington Court House, Ohio, 1984—; cons. W. Spink & Assocs., Mich., 1975-80. Author: Best on Record, 1982. Served with USCG, 1953-55. Mem. Soc. Mfg. Engrs. (sec. 1974-75, vice chmn. 1975-76, chmn. elect 1976-77), Robotics Internat. (sr.), Engring. Soc. Detroit, Kappa Sigma Kappa (v.p. Mich. 1950-51). Avocations: backpacking, sailing, jazz history. Home: 12377 Ridgeway Rd Orient OH 43146 Office: Mac Tools Inc S Fayette St PO Box 370 Washington Court House OH 43160

ALFIE, SALOMON, psychoanalyst, child and general psychiatrist; b. Buenos Aires, Sept. 15, 1933; came to U.S., 1960.; s. Roberto and Margarita (Intebi) A.; m. Maria Teresa Moltifiori, May 27, 1957; children: Sebastian, Fabian Robert. MD, Buenos Aires U., 1957; cert. psychoanalyst, Boston Psychoanalytical Inst., 1973. Diplomate Am. Bd. Psychiatry and Neurology. Resident in gen. psychiatry Menninger Found., Topeka, 1961-64, psychiatry resident, 1961-63; psychoanalysis trainee Boston Psychoanalytic Inst., 1965-73; dir. dept. psychiatry Bradley Hosp., Providence, 1968-76; prof. psychiatry U. Mo., Kansas City, 1977—; practice medicine specializing in psychoanalysis Prairie Village, Kans.; cons. Greater Kansas City Mental Health Found., 1975—. Fellow Am. Psychiat. Assn.; mem. AMA, Am. Psychoanalytical Assn., Am. Acad. Child Psychiatry, Topeka Psychoanalytical Soc. (v.p. 1985—). Club: Lake Quivara. Lodge: Masons. Avocations: music, art history, American and European literature. Office: 7301 Mission Rd #328 Prairie Village KS 66208

ALFRED, KARL SVERRE, orthopedic surgeon; b. Stavanger, Norway, July 10, 1917; s. Aldred Bjarne Abrahamsen Floen and Thora Garpestad; m. Amalia Leona Bombach, July 26, 1951; children—Patricia (Mrs. Dennis Alleman) Richard Lincoln, Peter Karl. Student, U. Va., 1935-38; M.D., L.I. Coll. Medicine, 1942. Intern Mountainside Hosp., Montclair, N.J., 1942-43; resident orthopedics Univ. Hosps., Cleve., 1947-50; practice medicine specializing in orthopedic surgery Cleve., 1950—; chief orthopedic surgery St. Vincent Charity Hosp., Cleve., 1955-81, chief orthopedic surgery emeritus, 1981—, chief of staff, 1971-75; assoc. staff Euclid Gen. Hosp., Cleve., mem. cons. staff; courtesy staff Univ., St. Luke's hosps., Cleve., Geauga Community Hosp., Chardon, O.; orthopedic cons. Norfolk & Western R.R.; affiliate tchr. orthopedics Bunts Edn. Inst., Cleve. Contbr. articles to profl. jours. Trustee, St. Vincent Charity Hosp., Cleve. Served with M.C., USNR, 1942-47. Episcopalian. Lodges: Masons, Rotary. Home: 20 Brandywood Dr Pepper Pike OH 44124 Office: 2475 E 22d St Cleveland OH 44115

ALGER, CHADWICK FAIRFAX, educator, political scientist; b. Chambersburg, Pa., Oct. 9, 1924; s. Herbert and Thelma (Drawbaugh) A.; m. Elinor Reynolds, Aug. 28, 1948; children: Mark, Scott, Laura, Craig. BA, Ursinus Coll., 1949, LLD, 1979; MA, Johns Hopkins U., 1950; PhD, Princeton, 1958. Internat. relations specialist Dept. Navy, 1950-54; instr. Swarthmore Coll., 1957; faculty Northwestern U., Evanston, Ill., 1958-71; prof. polit. sci. Northwestern U., 1966-71, dir. internat. relations program, 1967-71; Mershon prof. polit. sci. and pub. policy Ohio State U., 1971—, dir. transnat. intellectual cooperation program, 1971-80, dir. world affairs program, Mershon Ctr., 1980—; vis. prof. UN affairs N.Y.U., 1962-63. Author: Internationalization form Local Areas: Beyond Interstate Relations, 1987; co-author: Simulation in International Relations, 1963, You and Your Community in the World, 1978, Conflicts and Crisis of International Order: New Tasks for Peace Research, 1985; contbr. articles profl. jours. Served with USNR, 1943-46. Recipient Disting. Scholar award Internat. Soc. for Ednl., Cultural and Sci. Interchanges, 1980. Mem. Am. Polit. Sci. Assn. (council 1970-72), Internat. Polit. Sci. Assn., AAAS, Internat. Studies Assn. (pres. 1978-79), Internat. Peace Research Assn. (council 1971-77, sec.-gen. 1983-87), Midwest Conf. Polit. Scis. (recipient prize 1966), Consortium on Peace Research, Edn. and Devel. (exec. com. 1971-77, chmn. 1976-77), Union Internat. Assns., Ohio Trade Council. Home: 2674 Westmont Blvd Columbus OH 43221 Office: Ohio State U Mershon Ctr 199 W Tenth Ave Columbus OH 43201

ALI, MIR MASOOM, educator; b. Bangladesh, Feb. 1, 1937; s. Mir Muazzam and Azifa Khatoon (Chowdhury) A.; came to U.S., 1969; B.Sc. with honors, U. Dacca, 1956, M.Sc., 1957; M.Sc., U. Toronto, 1967, Ph.D., 1969; m. Firoza Chowdhury, June 25, 1959; children—Naheed, Fahima, Farah, Mir Ishtiaque. Research officer Ministry of Food and Agriculture, Ministry of Commerce, Central Pub. Service Commn., Govt. of Pakistan, 1958-66; teaching asst. U. Toronto (Ont., Can.), 1966-69; asst. prof. math. scis. Ball State U., Muncie, Ind., 1969-74, assoc. prof., 1974-78, prof., 1978—; vis. prof. U. Dhaka, 1983-84, Jahangirnagar U., 1983-84; vis. spl. lectr. U. Windsor (Can.), 1972-73; cons., researcher. Grantee Ball State U., 1974-85, Ind. Com. for Humanities, 1976-77. Recipient Outstanding Researcher award Ball State U., 1984-85. Fellow Royal Statis. Soc. London; mem. Am. Statis. Assn. (meritorius service award from biopharm. sect. 1987), Inst. Math. Statistics. Moslem. Mem. editorial bd., overseas coordinator Jour. Statis. Research; mem. editorial bd. Aligarh Jour. Stats., Jour. Statis. Studies; mem. exec. editorial bd. South Asian Population Dilemma; cons. editor Daktar; contbr. articles to profl. jours. Home: 3003 Riverside Ave Muncie IN 47304 Office: Ball State U Dept Math Scis Muncie IN 47306

ALI, NIAZ, accountant; b. Nalagadh, India, Oct. 10, 1940; came to U.S., 1969; d. Noor Ud and Hurmat Din; m. Jamila Niaz Ali, Sept. 4, 1965; children: Mohammad, Farah, Saba. BA, Panjab U., Lahore, Pakistan, 1963; BBA, Detroit Inst. Tech., 1977; M in Pub. Adminstrn., Cen. Mich. U., 1984. Adminstr. U.S. Embassy, Islamabad, Pakistan, 1965-69; acct. Hutzel Hosp., Detroit, 1969-75, Wayne County Community Coll., Detroit, 1975—. Trustee Brownstown (Mich.) Citizen's Council, 1984-85. Mem. Nat. Assn. Accts., Profl. and Adminstrn. Assn. (treas. 1984-85), Pakistan Assn. Am. (pres. Detroit chpt. 1981-83), Mich. Islamic Assn. (gen. sec. Wyandotte, Mich. chpt. 1981-82). Home: 18130 Doncaster Court Wyandotte MI 48192 Office: Wayne County Community Coll 801 Fort St Detroit MI 48226

ALI, SYED IRFAN, forensic and general psychiatrist; b. Bombay, India, Jan. 25, 1948; came to U.S., 1973; m. Fatima Zehra Ali, 1984; 1 child, Hassan. BS, U. Karachi, Pakistan, 1966; BS, MD, Dow Med. Coll., Karachi, 1972; postgrad., Adamjee Sci. Coll., Karachi, 1974. Intern Augustana Hosp., Chgo., 1973-74; resident in neurology Cook County Hosp., Chgo., 1974-75; resident in psychiatry Ill. State Psychiat. Inst., Chgo., 1975-78; gen. practice psychiatry Glendale Heights, Ill., 1978—; attending psychiatrist Hartgrove Hosp. (formerly Ridgeway Hosp.), Chgo., 1978—; forensic psychiatrist Pontiac (Ill.) Correctional Ctr., 1981-84, Dwight (Ill.) Correctional Ctr., 1982-84, Joliet (Ill.) Correctional Ctr., 1982-85, Stateville Correctional Ctr., Joliet, 1984—; emergency physician St. Mary's Hosp., Decatur, Ill., Lincoln (Ill.) Meml. Hosp., Freeport (Ill.) Meml. Hosp., Iroquois Meml. Hosp., Watseka, Ill., Shapiro Devel. Ctr., Kankakee, Ill., Lincoln Devel. Ctr., 1976-78; cons. Greater Lawn Mental Ctr., Chgo., 1978; asst. prof. psychiatry U. Ill., Chgo., 1985—, instr. clin. psychiatry, 1977-78. Contbr. articles to profl. jours. Mem. mental health adv. com. DuPage County Bd. Health. Mem. Am. Psychiat. Assn., AMA, Ill. State Med. Soc., DuPage County Med. Soc. (communication com., legal liaison com.), Am. Coll. Forensic Psychiatry, Am. Acad. Psychiatry and Law, U. Ill. Alumni Assn., Ill. State Psychiat. Inst. Alumni Assn. (pres.-elect), Am. Coll. Emergency Physicians. Avocations: racquetball, tennis, traveling, guitar, bicycling. Office: DuPage Mental Health Services Ltd 1793 Bloomingdale Rd Suite 9 Glendale Heights IL 60139

ALIAS, AIKARAKUDY G., psychiatrist; b. Mavattupuzhaa, India, Apr. 6, 1936; came to U.S., 1971; s. Pailey and Kunjamma (Kuzhikandathil) G.; m. Susy Thekkekkara, Dec. 28, 1969; 1 child, Subash George. BS, St. Thomas Coll., Palai, India, 1959; MD, Calicut Med. Coll., Kozhikode, India, 1963; MD in Biochemistry, Trivandrum (India) Med. Coll., 1970. Diplomate Am. Bd. Psychiatry and Neurology. Tutor in biochemistry Calicut Med. Coll., 1965-68, asst. prof., 1970-71; resident in psychiatry Taunton State Hosp., Mass., 1971-73; resident in psychiatry St. Louis State Hosp., 1973-74, staff psychiatrist, 1974-87; sr. psychiatrist S.E. Mo. Mental Health Ct., Farmington, 1987—. Contbr. numerous articles to profl. jours. Mem. Am. Psychiat. Assn., Internat. Soc. Psychoneuroendocrinology, The N.Y. Acad. Scis., Am. Fertility Soc., Am. Andrology Soc. Home: 15 Maryhill Saint Louis MO 63124 Office: SE Mo Mental Health Ctr Farmington MO 63640

ALIBER, JAMES A., bank executive; b. 1925; married. BA, U. Mich., 1947. Asst. buyer J.L. Hudson Co., Detroit, 1947-49; with advt. sales dept. R.L. Polk & Co., Detroit, 1949-54; asst. cashier Nat. Bank Detroit, 1954-57; exec. asst. First Fed. Mich., Detroit, 1957-58, v.p., 1958-65, treas., 1960-66, exec. v.p., 1965-69, pres., 1969-79, chief exec. officer, 1977—, chmn., 1979—, also bd. dirs. Served to lt. (j.g.) USN, 1943-46. Office: First Fed of Mich 1001 Woodward Detroit MI 48226 *

ALIG, FRANK DOUGLAS STALNAKER, construction company executive; b. Indpls., Oct. 10, 1921; s. Clarence Schirmer and Marjory (Stalnaker) A.; student U. Mich., 1939-41; B.S., Purdue U., 1948; m. Ann Bobbs, Oct. 22, 1949; children—Douglas, Helen, Barbara. Project engr. Ind. State Hwy. Commn., Indpls., 1948; pres. Alig-Stark Constrn. Co., Inc., 1949-57, Frank S. Alig, Inc., 1957—; chmn. bd. Concrete Structures Corp., Indpls.; v.p., dir. Bo-Wit Products Corp., Edinburg, Ind.; pres. dir. Home Stove Realty Co.; pres, dir. Home Land Investment Co., Inc. Served with AUS, 1943-46. Registered profl. engr., Ind. Mem. U.S., Ind. Socs. Profl. Engrs., Indpls. C. of C. Republican. Presbyterian. (deacon). Clubs: Woodstock, Dramatic, Lambs (Indpls.). Home: 8080 N Pennsylvania St Indianapolis IN 46240 Office: 4849 W 96th St Indianapolis IN 46268

AL-JADDA, SOUHEIL, surgeon; b. Souwera, Iraq, June 27, 1946; came to U.S., 1971; s. Muhammad Aadel and Souheila (Dassouki) Al-J.; M.D., Damascus (Syria) U., 1971; m. Sahar Dassouki, Aug. 5, 1971; children—Souheila, Aadel, Omar. Intern, Fairview Gen. Hosp., Cleve., 1971-72, surg. resident, 1972-76; practice medicine, specializing in gen. surgery, Norwalk, Ohio, 1976—; staff Fisher Titus Meml. Hosp., Norwalk, 1976—. Diplomate Am. Bd. Surgery. Fellow A.C.S., Internat. Coll. Surgeons; mem. AMA, Ohio Med. Assn., Huron County Med. Soc. Home: 115 Sycamore Dr Norwalk OH 44857 Office: 34 Executive Dr Norwalk OH 44857

ALKIRE, BETTY JO, artist, marketing consultant; b. Kansas City, Mo., June 20, 1942; d. Robert Emmitt and Gladys Faye (Craigg) Sharp; m. Daniel Wayne Hedrick, Nov. 15, 1958 (div.); children—Diane Laurie, Lisa Kay, Brett, Darin, Julie; m. William Edgar Alkire, Sept. 23, 1975. Tchr. art

Independence Adult Edn., Mo., 1967—; portrait artist Silver Dollar City Nat. Crafts Festival, 1971—; owner, operator portrait artist's concession Kansas City Worlds of Fun, 1972—; tchr. pvt. art classes, 1970—; tchr., lectr. mktg. art U. Mo. Extension Program, 1982—; cons. mktg. and life-planning for artists; broker and cons. comml. investment real estate. Contbr. articles in field to various mags. Mem. Mo. Arts Council, Table Rock Art Guild, Independent Profl. Artists Assn. (pres. 1980—). Methodist. Clubs: Rockaway Beach Ladies, Rockaway Beach Booster (Mo.). Avocations: local art and history, antiques, real estate. Home: Historic Taneywood Rockaway Beach MO 65740

ALLABACH, DAISY MARIE, educator, author, illustrator; b. Monroe, Mich., Aug. 24, 1932; d. Marceilus Francis and Grace Daisy (McCrow) DuVall; m. Graydon Duncan Allabach, Mar. 18, 1950; children: Ken, Denise, Crystal, Scot. AA, Glen Oaks Coll., 1968; BA, Western Mich. U., 1970, MA, 1971, MA in Counseling, 1976, Ed.S in Edn. Leadership, 1977. Cert. tchr., counselor. Instr. White Pigeon (Mich.) Community Schs., 1970—; counselor in field, Sturgis, Mich. Author/illustrator: Beachy Amish, 1976, What is a Watermelon, 1977, Constantine By Noon, 1986, Herbs in the Bible, also family bus. It's a Daisy; contbr. articles to profl. jours. Fellow Royal Soc. Promotion of Health; mem. Nat. Edn. Assn., Mich. Edn. Assn., White Pigeon Edn. Assn. Avocations: philately, coin shooting, creative arts, music. Home: 25019 Featherstone Sturgis MI 49091

ALLBRIGHT, CECIL ROY, automotive company executive; b. Richmond, Ind., Feb. 17, 1949; s. Cecil Fredric and Carolyn M. (Byrne) A.; m. Jacqueline A. Hodapp, Jan. 17, 1970 (div. June 1978); m. Gail Toney, Oct. 12, 1978; children: David, William, Michael, Lani. Student, Miami Jacobs Coll., Dayton, Ohio, 1972. Buyer Rexarc, Inc., West Alexandria, Ohio, 1968-73, Midwest Graphic, Dayton, 1973-76; purchasing agt. Mechaneer, Inc., Dayton, 1976-84, Sheffield Machine Tool, Dayton, 1984-85; material mgr. Advanced Assy Automation, Dayton, 1985—. Mem. Nat. Assn. Purchasing Mgrs., Ducks Unltd. Lutheran. Avocations: hunting, bldg. and flying kites, outdoor activities. Home: 867 State Rt 726 Eaton OH 45320 Office: Advanced Assembly Automation 314 Leo St Dayton OH 45404

ALLEGO, MELQUIADITO MAAMBONG, diagnostic radiologist, nuclear medicine specialist, poet; b. Cebu, Apalan Tuburan, Philippines, Mar. 21, 1944; came to U.S., 1974.; s. Melquiades Alinas Allego and Emiliana Artajo Maambong; m. Maria Thelma Desquitado, Jan. 26, 1974; children: Carmel Thelangela, Meljun Bathalad, Melanee Sonrisa. BS summa cum laude, Southwestern U., Cebu City, Philippines, 1963, MD, 1968. Diplomate Am. Bd. Nuclear Medicine. Intern De Paul Hosp., Norfolk, Va., 1974-75; resident in radiology Michael Reese Hosp., Chgo., 1975-78; resident in nuclear medicine Harry Truman Vets. Hosp., Columbia, Mo., 1978-80, also lectr., 1979-81; jr. mem. staff U. Mo. Med. Ctr., Columbia, Mo., 1980-81; chief of staff nuclear medicine div. Lucy Lee Hosp., Poplar Bluff, Mo., 1982-83; chmn. radiology dept. Perry County Meml. Hosp., Perryville, Mo., 1983-87; reviewer, coach med. bd. examinees Southwestern U. Med. Coll., Cebu City, 1972-73. Author poems; contbr. articles to profl. jours. Recipient Young Citizen award YMCA, 1972. Fellow Soc. Nuclear Medicine; mem. AMA (Physicians Recognition award 1985), Philippine Practicing Physicians, Am. Assn., Perry-St. Genevieve Med. Soc. (pres. 1985), Nancy Reagan's Crusade Against Drugs & Alcohol (mem. publ. com. local chpt. 1983-84), Am. Legion. Roman Catholic. Lodges: Lions, KC. Avocations: writing poems and articles, singing, dancing, playing chess, tennis. Office: Perry County Meml Hosp North West St Perryville MO 63775

ALLEGRUCCI, DONALD L., state supreme court justice; b. Pittsburg, Kans., Sept. 19, 1936; s. Nello and Josephine Marie (Funaro) A.; m. Joyce Ann Thompson, Nov. 30, 1963; children: Scott David, Bowen Jay. AB, Pittsburg State U., 1959; JD, Washburn U., 1963. Asst. county atty. Butler County, El Dorado, Kans., 1963-67; state senator Kans. Legislature, Topeka, 1976-80; mem. Kans. Pub. Relations Bd., 1981-82; dist. judge Kans. 11th Jud. Dist., Pittsburg, 1982-87, adminstrv. judge, 1983-87; justice Kans. Supreme Ct., Topeka, 1987—; instr. Pittsburg State U., 1969-72; exec. dir. Mid-Kans. CAP, Inc. Mem. Dem. State Com., 1974-80; candidate 5th Congl. Dist., 1978; past pres. Heart Assn.; bd. dirs. YMCA. Served with USAF, 1959-60. Mem. Kans. Bar Assn. Democrat. Office: Kansas Supreme Court Kansas Jud Ctr 301 W 10th St Topeka KS 66612

ALLEN, ANNA MARIE, financial consultant; b. Ft. Scott, Kans., Aug. 3, 1955; d. Harold Laverne and Dorothy Arlene Kirk; m. John Leroy Allen, Sept. 18, 1982. AA, Johnson County Community Coll., Overland Park, Kans., 1976; BSBA in Fin., Pittsburg (Kans.) State U., 1979. CPA, Kans. Asst. teller supr. Kans. Nat. Bank & Trust, Prairie Village, 1975-77; bookkeeper Foodtown, Pittsburg, 1978-79; sr. tax cons. GRA, Inc., Merriam, Kans., 1979—. Mem. com. bd. Kansas City (Mo.) Ballet Guild, 1985—. Mem. Am. Inst. CPA's, Cen. Exchange, AAUW (bd. dirs. Shawnee Mission, Kans. chpt. 1979—), Womens's Resource Ctr. Johnson County (bd. dirs. 1986—, charter mem.), Am. Legion Aux., Phi Kappa Phi, Delta Mu Delta. Baptist. Club: Woodside Racquet (Westwood, Kans.). Lodge: P.E.O. Avocations: running, tatting, the flute.

ALLEN, ARNOLD, medical educator; b. N.Y.C.; s. Maxwell and Evelyn (Friedland) A.; m. Phyllis Karesh, Oct. 2, 1945; children: Barbara, Michael. BS, U. Cin., 1939, MD, 1943. Diplomate Am. Bd. Psychiatry and Neurology. Intern Harlem Hosp., N.Y.C., 1943-44; resident in Psychiatry U. Pa. and Jefferson Med. Coll., Temple U., 1946-48; mem. faculty U. Cin. Med. Sch., 1948-75, clin. prof. psychiatry, 1970-75; prof. chmn. dept. psychiatry Wright State U. Med. Sch., Dayton, Ohio, 1979—. Contbr. articles to profl. jours. Served to capt. AUS, 1943-45. Mem. AMA, Am. Psychiat. Assn. Office: Wright State U PO Box 927 Dayton OH 45401

ALLEN, BELLE, management consulting firm executive, communications company executive; b. Chgo.; d. Isaac and Clara (Friedman) A. Ed., U. Chgo. Cons., v.p., treas., dir. William Karp Cons. Co. Inc., Chgo., 1961-79, chmn. bd., pres., treas., 1979—; pres. Belle Allen Communications, Chgo., 1961—; v.p., treas., bd. dirs. Cultural Arts Survey Inc., Chgo., 1965-79; cons., bd. dirs. Am. Diversified Research Corp., Chgo., 1967-70; v.p., sec., bd. dirs. Mgmt. Performance Systems Inc., 1976-77; cons. City Club Chgo., 1962-65, Ill. Commn. on Tech. Progress, 1965-67; mem. Ill. Gov.'s Grievance Panel for State Employees, 1979—; mem. grievance panel Ill. Dept. Transp., 1985—; mem. adv. governing bd. Ill. Coalition on Employment of Women, 1980—; spl. program advisor President's Project Partnership, 1980—; mem. consumer adv. council FRS, 1979—. Editor, contbr.: Operations Research and the Management of Mental Health Systems, 1968; editor, contbr. articles to profl. jours. Mem. campaign staff Adlai E. Stevenson II, 1952, 56, John F. Kennedy, 1960; founding mem. women's bd. United Cerebral Palsy Assn., Chgo., 1954, bd. dirs., 1954-58; pres. Democratic Fedn. Ill., 1958-61; pres. conf. staff Eleanor Roosevelt, 1960; mem. Welfare Pub. Relations Forum, 1960-61; bd. dirs., mem. exec. com., chmn. pub. relations com. Regional Ballet Ensemble, Chgo., 1961-63; bd. dirs. Soc. Chgo. Strings, 1963-64; mem. Ind. Dem. Coalition, 1968-69; bd. dirs. Citizens for Polit. Change, 1969; campaign mgr. aldermanic election 42d ward Chgo. City Council, 1969. Recipient Outstanding Service award United Cerebral Palsy Assn., Chgo., 1954, 55, Chgo. Lighthouse for Blind, 1986; Spl. Communications award The White House, 1961; cert. of appreciation Ill. Dept. Human Rights, 1985, Internat. Assn. Ofcl. Human Rights Agys., 1985; selected as reference source Am. Bicentennial Research Inst. Library Human Resources, 1973; named Hon. Citizen, City of Alexandria, Va., 1985. Mem. Affirmative Action Assn. (bd. dirs. 1981—, chmn. mem. and program coms. 1981—, pres. 1983—), Fashion Group (bd. dirs. 1981-83, chmn. Retrospective View of An Historical Decade 1960-70, editor The Bull. 1981), Indsl. Relations Research Assn. (bd. dirs., chmn. personnel placement com. 1960-61), AAAS, NOW, Sarah Siddons Soc., Soc. Personnel Adminstrs., Women's Equity Action League, Nat. Assn. Inter-Group Relations Ofcls. (nat. conf. program 1959), Publicity Club Chgo. (chmn. inter-city relations com. 1960-61, disting. service award 1968), Ill. C. of C. (community relations com., alt. mem. labor relations com. 1971-74), Chgo. C. of C. and Industry (merit employment com. 1961-63). Club: Chgo. Press (chmn. women's activities 1969-71). Office: 111 E Chestnut St Chicago IL 60611

ALLEN, DARRYL FRANK, industrial company executive; b. Detroit, Sept. 7, 1943; s. Hairston Ulysses and Frances (Akers) A.; m. Sharon Mae Baines, Aug. 27, 1966; children: Richard Baines, James Bretten, Michael Jeffery. B.A., Mich. State U., 1965; M.B.A., U. Mich., 1966. Mgr. Arthur Andersen & Co., Detroit, 1965-72; corporate controller Aeroquip Corp., Jackson, Mich., 1972-76, v.p. finance, 1976-78, v.p. fin. and adminstrn., 1978-79; v.p. fin. services Libbey-Owens-Ford Co., Toledo, 1980-81, chief fin. officer, 1981-83, group v.p., 1983-84, pres., 1984-86, chief operating officer; pres., chief exec. officer Trinova Corp. (formerly Libbey-Owens-Ford Co.), Toledo, 1986—; bd. dirs. First Ohio Bancshares. Mem. Am. Inst. C.P.A.s, Mich. Assn. C.P.A.s. Home: 2808 Westchester Toledo OH 43615 Office: Trinova Corp 1705 Indian Wood Circle Maumee OH 43537

ALLEN, DEBORAH RUDISILL, clinical psychologist, educator, university administrator; b. Port Chester, N.Y., Oct. 31, 1951; d. Stewart Ellwood and Sarah Louise (Rudisill) A.; m. Howard Schein, Nov. 24, 1984. BA in Psychology summa cum laude, U. Vt., 1972; MA in Clin. Psychology, Mich. State U., 1974, PhD in Clin. Psychology, 1977. Lic. psychologist, Ill. Asst. prof. psychology Olin health services and counseling ctr. Mich. State U., East Lansing, 1977-78; clin. counselor counseling ctr. U. Ill., Urbana, 1978—, asst. dir. counseling ctr., 1981-84, assoc. dir. counseling ctr., 1984—; pvt. practice psychology, Urbana, 1979—; cons. employee assistance program Control Data Inst., Urbana, 1984—. Contbr. articles to profl. jours.; co-author: (book) Giving Advice to Students: A Roadmap for College Professionals, 1987, (brochures) numerous self-help publications, 1984—. Mem. Am. Psychol. Assn., Am. Assn. Counseling and Devel., Am. Coll. Personnel Assn., Phi Beta Kappa, Phi Kappa Phi, Psi Chi. Home: 608 W Nevada St Urbana IL 61801 Office: U Ill Counseling Ctr 610 E John St Champaign IL 61820

ALLEN, DONALD RAY, physician; b. Evansville, Ind., Dec. 6, 1932; s. William Delmar and Mildred Adelaide (Ashworth) A.; A.B. cum laude, U. Evansville, 1957; M.D., Ind. U., 1960. Intern, Marion County Gen. Hosp., Indpls., 1960-61; resident VA Hosp., Louisville, 1963, St. Louis City Hosp., 1964, Washington U. Barnes Hosp., St. Louis, 1965; practice medicine specializing in family practice, Evansville. Diplomate Am. Bd. Family Practice. Fellow Am. Acad. Family Physicians; mem. AMA, Ind. Med. Assn., Vanderburgh County Med. Soc., Alpha Omega Alpha, Phi Chi. Office: VA Outpatient Clinic Evansville IN 47708

ALLEN, DOUGLAS MARK, materials engineer; b. Dayton, Ohio, May 31, 1958; s. George Thomas and Lillie Mae (Daniels) A. BSME, U. Dayton, 1980; MSME, U. Dayton, 1982. Project engr. USAF Wright Aero Labs., Wright Patterson AFB, Ohio, 1980—; cons. Corning Glass, Greenville, Ohio, 1982-84, U. Dayton Sch. Engring., 1981—. Contbr. articles to profl. jours. Bd. dirs. Shaping the 80's, Dayton, 1982, Creativitiy 80's, Dayton, 1983. Mem. AIEE, Mensa. Republican. Clubs: Dayton Dressage and Combines Tng. Assn. Avocations: horse riding, basketball, softball. Home: 11588 Sweet Potato Ridge Rd Brookville OH 45309 Office: Air Force Wright Aeronautical Labs AFWAL/POOS Wright Patterson AFB OH 45449

ALLEN, ERNIE ALBERT, JR., chemical company executive; b. Decatur, Ill., Jan. 16, 1950; s. Ernie Albert and Luise Hefner A.; B.S. in Fin.-Acctg., So. Ill. U., Carbondale, 1972; m. Lynda Ishee, Dec. 1, 1972; children—Christina, Carla, Eric. Jr. acct. Kaiser Agrl. Chems., Inc., Sullivan, Ill., 1972-76, acct. supr. III, 1976-77, regional acctg. mgr., 1978, regional controller, 1978-85, adminstrv. mgr., 1985-86; dir. adminstrs. Vigoro Industries, Inc., 1986—. Bd. dirs. United Way Moultrie County, 1980-86; pres. citizens adv. council Sullivan High Sch., 1983-84, Sullivn Township Library Bd., 1985-86. Mem. So. Ill. U. Alumni Assn., Beta Alpha Psi. Democrat. Methodist. Clubs: Am. Business (v.p. 1979-80, pres.-elect 1980-81, pres. 1981-82), Sno-n-Go Snowmobile. Home: 1977 Maple Leaf Collinsville IL 62234 Office: Vigoro Industries Inc PO Box 4139 Fairview Heights IL 62208

ALLEN, EUGENE, JR., mfg. co. exec.; b. Chgo., Nov. 7, 1937; s. Eugene and Pearl (Smith) A.; B.S., Ill. Inst. Tech., 1970; M.B.A., U. Chgo., 1976; m. Ledell Fields, Apr. 16, 1961; children—Sheryl, Karla, Nicole, Eugene M. Chemist, formulator and paint technologist Sherwin-Williams Co., 1963-67; materials engr. Libby, McNeill & Libby, 1967-69; prodn. supr., div. sales mgr. Avon Products Inc., 1969-74; exec. trainee, ops. mgr. Jewel Cos. Inc., Chgo., 1974-75; v.p. mktg. and sales Valeer Industries Inc., Mundelein, Ill., 1975-76; sr. v.p., dir. mktg. and sales HUB States Corp., Indpls., 1976-79; pres., chief operating officer Clinitemp, Inc., Indpls., 1979-81; pres., chief exec. officer Aquamint Labs., Inc., Indpls., 1981—. Pres., Stoney Island Heights Civic Assn., Chgo., 1968-70; chmn. investment com., dir. Indpls. Bus. Devel. Council, 1985—; bd. dirs. Jr. Achievement of Cen. Ind., 1985—; bd. dirs. Ivy Hill Civic Assn., Arlington Heights, Ill., 1972-76, Youth for Christ, Indpls.; adv. bd. Lawrence Twp. Sch. Dist., Ind., 1977-78; mem. Dist. Export Council for Ind., 1979—. Served with U.S. Army, 1961-63. Recipient Paint Technologist award Nat. Paint Industry Ednl. Bur., 1966. Club: Exec. Program (U. Chgo.). Home: 7527 N Cape Cod Ln Indianapolis IN 46250 Office: 6256 La Pas Trail Indianapolis IN 46268

ALLEN, FLORENCE AMELIA, motel company executive; b. Warrington, England, Sept. 15, 1933; d. David Owen and Florence (Richardson) D.; m. Gerald Stewart, Sept. 19, 1953; children: Michelle, Gerald Jr. Grad. high sch., Penketh, England. Customer service specialist AAFES, Panama Canal Zone, 1970-72; desk clk. Newport (Ark.) Travelodge, 1972-76; liquor store mgr. Hitching Post Inn, Cheyenne, Wyo., 1976-78; mgr. Super 8 Motel, Cheyenne, 1978-83, Bloomington, Minn., 1983-84; dir. tng. Super 8 Motels Inc., Aberdeen, S.D., 1984—. Mem. S.D. Innkeepers Assn. (bd. dirs. 1985—), Bus. and Profl. Womens Club. Republican. Lutheran. Lodge: Zonta Internat. Home: 916 18th Ave NE Aberdeen SD 57401 Office: Super 8 Motels Inc 1910 8th Ave NE PO Box 4090 Aberdeen SD 57402-4090

ALLEN, FRANKLIN GLENN, corporation executive, lawyer; b. Athens, Ohio, Sept. 12, 1925; s. George Samuel and Lola Elma (Davis) A. BA in Physics, Ohio State U., 1950, JD, 1952; LL.M, NYU, 1959; MBA, U. Chgo., 1963. Bar: Ill., Ohio, 1952, N.Y., 1956. Assoc. Vedder, Price, Kaufman & Kammholz, Chgo., 1952-53, Byron, Hume, Groen & Clement, Chgo., 1953-55, Davis, Polk, Wardwell, Sunderland & Kiendl, N.Y.C., 1955-57; corp. counsel Hubbard & Co., Chgo. and Pitts., 1957-64, Dyson-Kissner Corp., N.Y.C., 1960-64, The Marmon Group, Inc., Chgo., 1964-69, Pritzker & Pritzker, Chgo., 1965-69; ptnr., of counsel Sachnoff, Weaver, Rubenstein Ltd., Chgo., 1969—; chmn. bd., pres. Pantera's Corp., St. Louis, 1978—. Served to Sgt. U.S. Army, 1943-46. Mem. ABA, Ill. Bar Assn., Chgo. Bar Assn., Delta Theta Phi. Republican. Presbyterian. Club: Chicago. Avocation: boating. Home: 1321 W Berwyn Ave Chicago IL 60640 Office: Pantera's Corp 30 S Wacker Dr 29th Floor Chicago IL 60606

ALLEN, GEORGE WHITAKER, physician, educator; b. Milledgeville, Ga., Feb. 8, 1928; s. Henry Dawson and Caroline (Reynolds) A.; m. Lis Margaret Jensen, Oct. 1, 1951 (div. 1973); 1 son, John Whitaker; m. 2d., Janice Alene Mandabach, Apr. 26, 1980. A.B., Harvard U., 1948; M.D., Columbia U., 1952. Diplomate Am. Bd. Otolaryngology. Intern, Presbyn. Hosp., N.Y.C., 1952-53; Jr. asst. resident in otolaryngology U. Chgo. Clinics, 1955-56, sr. asst. resident, 1956-57, resident, 1957-58, NIH spl. trainee, 1958-59; instr. dept. otolaryngology Northwestern U. Med. Sch., Chgo., 1959-60, asst. prof., 1961-64, assoc. prof., 1964—, dir. teaching and research, 1959-63, acting chmn. dept. otolaryngology, 1964-67; sole practice otolaryngology, Chgo., 1967—; attending physician Northwestern Meml. Hosp., Chgo., 1959—; attending physician in surgery Children's Meml. Hosp., Chgo., 1979—; Chgo., 1981—; vis. prof. U. Colo. Med. Sch., 1965; vis. prof. Emory U. Med. Sch., 1967; cons. Nat. Ctr. for Devices and Radiol. Health, FDA, 1983—. Served to 1st lt. M.C., U.S. Army, 1953-55. Recipient research award Am. Acad. Otolaryngology, 1960. Mem. AMA, Ill. Med. Soc., Chgo. Med. Soc., Chgo. Laryngological and Otological Soc., ACS, Pan Am. Med. Assn., Triological Soc., Inst. Medicine Chgo., Am. Acad. Facial Plastic and Reconstructive Surgery, Am. Council of Otolaryngology, Nu Sigma Nu, Alpha Omega Alpha, Sigma Xi. Republican. Methodist. Club: Carlton (Chgo.). Contbr. articles to med. jours.; mem. editorial bd. Archives of Otolaryngology, 1960-69; co-author: (movie) Carcinoma of the Tonsil, 1960. Office: 150 E Huron St Suite 801 Chicago IL 60611

ALLEN, HENRY SERMONES, JR., lawyer; b. Bronxville, N.Y., Aug. 26, 1947; s. Henry S. and Cecelia Marie (Chartrand) A.; A.B. magna cum laude, Washington U., St. Louis, 1969; M.P.A., Cornell U., 1973, J.D., 1974; m. Louann Beckman, June 25, 1976; children—David Beckman, Amy Louise, Jeffrey Roy. Bar: Ill. 1974. Adminstrv. resident Montefiore Hosp. and Med. Center, Bronx, N.Y., 1971; research trainee Nat. Center Health Services Research, HEW, 1974-75; adj. asst. prof. hosp. law Ithaca (N.Y.) Coll., 1974-75; lectr., adj. asst. prof. health services adminstrn. and law Sangamon State U., Springfield, Ill., 1975-82; adj. asst. prof. hosp. law Coll. of St. Francis, Joliet, Ill., 1980-81; assoc. firm Vedder, Price, Kaufman & Kammholz, Chgo., 1975-79; ind. practice law, health care cons., Chgo. and Springfield, 1979-81; ptnr. Allen & Reed, Chgo., 1981-86, McBride, Baker & Coles, 1986—; lectr. in field. Bd. dirs. Dr. Deepak K. Merchant Found. HUD fellow, 1969-71. Mem. Am. Soc. Hosp. Attys., Am. Acad. Hosp. Attys., Ill. Soc. Hosp. Attys., Nat. Health Lawyers Assn., Phi Beta Kappa, Omicron Delta Epsilon. Club: Cornell U. of Chgo. Home: 5223 Carpenter St Chicago IL 60515 Office: 3 First National Plaza 38th Floor Chicago IL 60602

ALLEN, HERBERT JOSEPH, hospital social work administrator; b. Jersey City, May 19, 1922; s. Benjamin James and Jeanetta Gladys (Casey) A.; m. Gwen Cann, July 26, 1949 (div.); 1 child, Deborah Allen Kane. B.S. in Edn., U. Cin., 1946; M.S. in Social Work, Case Western Res. U., 1948. Lic. ind. social worker. Dir. social work dept. Barney Children's Med. Center, Dayton, Ohio, 1967; supr. Family and Children's Service, Dayton, 1968; dir. social work dept. Good Samaritan Hosp., Dayton, 1968; field service asso. prof., dir. social work dept. Cin. Gen. Hosp.-U. Cin. Med. Center, 1970—; adj. asst. prof. Thomas More Coll., Ft. Mitchell, Ky., 1978; field service assoc. prof. Coll. Community Services, U. Cin., 1979; adj. assoc. prof., dir. dept. social work U. Cin. Pres., Central Community Health Bd. Catchment Area 11, 1976, Mt. Auburn Health Center, 1977; lectr. Am. Hosp. Assn., Soc. for Dirs. Hosp. Social Work Depts. Pres. Cin. chpt. Nat. Friends of Amistad, 1976—. Served with U.S. Army, 1942-46. Named Cin. Social Worker of Year, Social Service Assn. Greater Cin., 1952, Nat. Assn. Black Social Workers, 1973; Recipient award Pride mag., Cin., 1979, Key to City City of Cincinnati, 1987, Ida M. Cannon award Soc. Hosp. Social Work Dirs. Am. Hosp. Assn., 1987. Mem. Nat. Assn. Social Workers (cert.), Ohio Hosp. Soc. Workers (pres. 1982), Nat. Soc. Hosp. Social Work Dirs. (pres. 1983), Soc. Dirs. Hosp. Social Work Depts., Am. Hosp. Assn. (dir. 1975-77, v.p. personal membership com. 1984-85), Soc. Hosp. Social Work Dirs. (pres.-elect 1982), Ohio Hosp. Assn. (pres. 1982-83), Kappa Alpha Psi (Community Service award Cin. chpg. 1985, 87). Democrat. Roman Catholic. Home: 144 Dorsey St Cincinnati OH 45210 Office: Univ Hosp U Cin Med Center 234 Goodman St ML 743 Cincinnati OH 45267

ALLEN, IRENE AMILHAT, teacher educator, consultant; b. Highgate, Va., July 2; d. Guilliaume Joseph and Ida Marie (Garceau) Amilhat; m. Roger Frank Allen, Nov. 29, 1958 (dec. 1965). B.S. in Edn., Johnson Tchrs. Coll., 1957; student U. Vt., summer 1959, U. Mich., 1973; M.A. in Edn., Ball State Tchrs. Coll., 1962; Ed.D. in Reading Ball State U., 1968. Elem. sch. tchr. Morristown Pub. Schs., Vt., 1957-59, Ft. Wayne Pub. Schs., Ind., 1959-66; doctoral fellow Ball State U., Muncie, Ind., 1966-68; asst. to full prof. Eastern Mich. U., Ypsilanti, 1968-77; vis. prof. Bulmershe Coll. Higher Edn., Reading, Eng., summer 1975; vis. exchange prof. U. Warwick, Coventry, Eng., 1980-81; prof., chief-of-party Swaziland Primary Curriculum Project, Manzini, Swaziland, 1982-84, prof. Eastern Mich. U., 1984—; presentor papers at profl. association meetings, U.S., Africa and Europe. Co-author: Kollection of Kues from Kids, 1975; The Reading Skills Inventory, 1980; Effective Reading Instruction, 1984. Mem. editorial rev. bds. Fla. Reading Research Jour., 1981—, Jour. Edn. in Reading, 1984—. Bd. dirs. Cliffs on the Bay Condominium Assn., Ypsilanti, 1984—; mem. St. Ursula's choir, Ypsilanti, 1983—. Named Woman of Yr., Eastern Mich. U. Women's Commn., 1980, Outstanding Tchr. in Reading, Orgn. Tchr. Educators in Reading, 1979; recipient Josephine Nevins Keal Endowment award, 1980, 84, 85. Mem. Orgn. Tchr. Educators in Reading (pres.), Internat. Reading Assn., Assn. for Supervision and Curriculum Devel., Assn. Tchr. Educators, Mich. Reading Assn., Phi Delta Kappa (pres. Ea. Mich. U. chpt.1979-80), Delta Kappa Gamma (pres. Beta). . Avocations: reading; traveling; mountain climbing, in U.S., Japan, Africa; bicycling; alpine skiing. Office: Eastern Mich U 234-P Boone Hall Ypsilanti MI 48197

ALLEN, JAMES ALVIN, SR., safety supervisor; b. Camp Hill, Ala., Apr. 9, 1934; s. Forest and Alva (Vines) A.; m. Audrey Burris, Nov. 21, 1958; children—James Alvin, Tamra Denise. B.S., Tuskegee Inst., 1958; M.Ed., S.C. State Coll., 1969; M.B.A., Western Mich. U., 1980. Tech. specialist Uniroyal, Inc., 1967-68, quality control supr., 1968-69, acting supt. texturizing, 1968-69; asst. plant supt. Coca-Cola U.S.A., 1970-74; processing shift supr. infant formula Ross Labs/Abbott Labs., Sturgis, Mich., 1974-81, safety supr., 1981—. Bd. dirs. St. Joseph County Substance Abuse Council, 1982—; v.p. Sturgis (Mich.) Bd. Edn. Served to capt. inf., U.S. Army, 1959-65. Mem. Am. Soc. Safety Engrs., Am. Chem. Soc., Internat. Platform Assn., Assn. MBA Execs. Republican. Mem. African Methodist Ch. Club: Nat. Exchange. Lodge: Masons. Home: 316 S Clay St PO Box 372 Sturgis MI 49091 Office: 700 W Lafayette St Sturgis MI 49091

ALLEN, JAMES CURTIS, manufacturing company executive; b. Winston, Mo., June 7, 1922; s. Vernon and Carrie Belle (Palmer) A.; grad. Chillicothe Bus. Coll., (Mo.), 1942, Internat. Corr. Schs., 1946; m. Juanita G. Kennedy, Dec. 4, 1944; children—Daryl C., Karen A., Marti L., Jimmie, Randy. Accountant, Nat. Bellas Hess, Kansas City, Mo., 1946-48; controller Lawn-Boy div. Outboard Marine Corp., Lamar, Mo., 1948-63; sec.-treas. EFCO Corp., Monett, Mo., 1963-66; co-owner, sec-treas. F.M. Thorpe Mfg. Co., Lamar, Mo., 1966-84; pres. Allen Investments, 1984—; dir. Barton County State Bank. Pres., United Fund, 1970-71; pres. Community Betterment, 1968-70; dist. chmn. Sowemco council Boy Scouts Am., 1964-66, Arrowhead council, 1972 Big 3 dist., 1982-83, v.p. Mo-Kans Area council, 1975-79; mem. Lamar Sch. Bd., 1969-71; mem. Lamar Park Bd., 1955—, pres., 1973-84. Served with USNR, 1942-45. Recipient Outstanding Leadership award Mo. Municipal League, 1971; Distinguished Service award Kiwanis Club Monett, Mo., 1965; Leadership award Mo. Community Betterment, 1970; Golden Sun Silver Beaver, Order Arrow awards Boy Scouts Am. chpt. farmer award Future Farmers Am., 1979; Boss of Yr. award Am. Bus. Womens Assn., 1980. Mem. Lamar C. of C. (Person of Yr. 1981), Mo. C. of C. Methodist (chmn. bd. 1971, del. conf. 1968-71, treas. 1966—, supt. 1955-63). Mason (Shriner), Rotarian (pres. 1971-72, Man of Yr. award 1979, Paul Harris award), Kiwanian (pres. 1968). Home: 400 W 1st St Lamar MO 64759 Office: 1801 Gulf St Lamar MO 64759

ALLEN, JEAN ELLEN (MRS. WILLIAM L.), computer technical analyst; b. Saginaw, Mich., Aug. 11, 1949; d. Albert Arthur and Gladys Pearl (Simon) Geiersbach; m. William Leroy Allen, Nov. 19, 1983; children: Margaret, Jeffrey. BA, Anderson Coll., 1971; MA, Cen. Mich. U., 1974. Tchr. math. Vanderbilt (Mich.) High Sch., 1971-76; mathematician Newark (Ohio) AFB, 1976-81; computer analyst Gen. Tire, Akron, Ohio, 1981-83, tech. analyst, 1983—; cons. David Wills Tax Service, Newark, 1981-83. Mem. Bus. and Profl. Women. Home: 543 Treeside Dr Stow OH 44224

ALLEN, JOHN TREVETT, JR., lawyer; b. Ill., Apr. 9, 1939; s. John Trevett and Elinor Rose (Hatfield) A.; m. Marguerite DeHuszar, Jan 18, 1969; children—John Trevett, Samuel DeHuszar. AB in English summa cum laude and Spanish cum laude (double major), Williams Coll., 1961; LLB, Harvard U., 1964; postgrad., Central U. Ecuador, Quito, 1964-65. Bar: Ill. 1964, U.S. Supreme Ct., U.S. Ct. Appeals (7th cir.), U.S. Dist. Ct. (no. dist.) Ill., U.S. Dist. Ct. (ea. dist.) Ill. Assoc. Goodrich, Dalton, Little & Riquelme, Mexico City, 1962; assoc. Graham, James & Rolph, San Francisco, 1963; assoc. MacLeish, Spray, Price & Underwood, Chgo., 1963-71, ptnr., 1973-80; gen. atty. U.S. Gypsum Co., Chgo., 1971-73; ptnr. McBride, Baker & Coles, Chgo., 1980-86; assoc. Burditt, Bowles & Radzius, Ltd., Chgo., 1986—. Contbr. articles to profl. jours. Alderman City of Evanston, 1977-81; governing mem. Orchestral Assn. Chgo., 1980—; pres. Internat. Bus. Council MidAm., 1982-84, also mem. bd. dirs.; trustee Library Internat. Relations, 1983—, pres. 1986-87; vice chmn. Ill. Export Council, 1983—; counsel and dir. Ill. 4-H Found. Fulbright scholar, 1964-65. Mem. ABA, Ill. Bar Assn., Chgo. Bar Assn. (past chmn. internat. and fgn. law com., founder and past chmn. agri-bus. law com.), Vermilion County Bar Assn., Legal Club Chgo., Law Club Chgo., Phi Beta Kappa (exec. com. Chgo. area assn.). Republican. Presbyterian. Club: Union League (Chgo.). Office: Burditt Bowles & Radzins 333 W Wacker Dr Suite 1900 Chicago IL 60606

ALLEN, JULIUS OLU, alcoholism and mental health counselor; b. Cape Coast, Ghana, Feb. 6, 1930; came to U.S., 1962, naturalized, 1970; s. James Akerele and Dorcas Ade (Ejide) Ale; B.A. with high honors, Lewis U., Lockport, Ill., 1975; diploma Chgo. Counseling Center, 1978; M.A., Internat. U., 1979; m. Prudence Addy, Jan. 20, 1957; children—Coni, Moumi, Rotimi, Sonya, Aku. Lic. ins. broker, 1965-75; counselor, dir. drug abuse and prevention program Garfield Counseling Center, Chgo., 1977—; counselor Northwestern Meml. Hosp., 1977-80, Volta House Corp., 1980-83, Spiegel Inc., 1983-86 ; vol. Peoples Community Outreach Mission. Recipient Citizen's award Chgo. Police Dept., 1978. Mem. Am. Assn. Mental Deficiency, Center Counseling and Psychotherapy, Afro-Am. Corrections Officers Movement (pres.). Mormon. Club: Human Growth Book; editor Shegun 1975. Research on mentally health persons, better prison systems. Home: 4028 S King Dr Chicago IL 60653

ALLEN, LEATRICE DELORICE, psychologist; b. Chgo., July 15, 1948; d. Burt and Mildred Floy (Taylor) Hawkins; m. Allen Moore, Jr., July 30, 1965 (div. Oct. 1975); children—Chandra, Valarie, Allen; m. Armstead Allen, May 11, 1978. A.A. in Bus. Edn., Olive Harvey Coll., Chgo., 1975; B.A. in Psychology cum laude, Chgo. State U., 1977; M.Clin. Psychology, Roosevelt U., 1980. Clk., U.S. Post Office, Chgo., 1967-72; clin. therapist Bobby Wright Mental Health Ctr., Chgo., 1979-80; clin. therapist Community Mental Health Council, Chgo., 1980-83, assoc. dir., 1983—; cons. Edgewater Mental Health, Chgo., 1984—, Project Pride, Chgo., 1985—; victim services coordinator Community Mental Health Council, Chgo., 1986-87; mgr. youth family services Mile Square Health Ctr., Chgo., 1987—. Scholar Chgo. State U., 1976, Roosevelt U., 1978; fellow Menninger Found., 1985; mem. treatment innovation task force Soc. Traumatic Stress Studies. Fellow Internat. Biographical Assn.; mem. Nat. Orgn. for Victim Assistance, Ill. Coalition Against Sexual Assault (del. 1985—). Avocations: aerobics; reading; theatre; dining. Home: 16603 S Paulina St Markham IL 60426

ALLEN, LEONARD BROWN, tax manager; b. Longmont, Colo., Sept. 5, 1932; s. Victor Brown and Anna Catherine (Cottrell) A.; m. Virginia Lee Harvey, May 27, 1960; children: Susan Ann, Denise Diane. BS, Colo. A&M Coll., 1954; MS, Colo. State U., 1967. CPA, Ill. Office mgr. Walco Distbg., Craig, Colo., 1962-65; teaching asst. Colo. State U., Ft. Collins, 1965-67; internal auditor Deere & Co., Moline, Ill., 1967-68, acct. consolidations dept., 1968-70, tax acct., 1970-73, mgr. state and local taxes, 1973—. Served to capt. USAF, 1954-57, with Res. 1967. Mem. Ill. CPA Soc., Chgo. Tax Club (bd. dirs.), Iowa Taxpayers Assn. (bd. dirs., mem. exec. com.), Taxpayers Fedn. Ill. (mem. adv. com.), Ill. State C. of C. (chmn. state and local tax com.). Republican. Mem. United Ch. Christ. Lodge: AF & AM (master 1964-65). Home: 38 Crestview Dr Geneseo IL 61254 Office: Deere & Co John Deere Rd Moline IL 61265

ALLEN, LOIS ARLENE HEIGHT (MRS. JAMES PIERPONT ALLEN), musician; b. Kenton, Ohio, Sept. 2, 1932; d. Robert Harold and Frances (Sims) Height; B.S., Ohio State U., 1954, M.A., 1958; m. James Pierpont Allen, June 14, 1953; children—Daniel Pierpont, Carole Elizabeth. Tchr. jr. and sr. high music, Upper Arlington High Sch., Columbus, O., 1954-56; high sch. music supr., Westerville, Ohio, 1956-67; tchr. music Ohio State U. Sch., 1957-59; pvt. tchr. music, Columbus, 1960—; exec. dir. Battelle Scholars Program Trust Fund, 1983-86; ch. organist, choir dir. Mountview Bapt. Ch., Upper Arlington, Ohio, 1960-77; ednl. radio interviewer WOSU, 1970, 71, 72. Mem. Project Hope, Central Ohio, 1967-73; mem. sustaining bd. Maryhaven House for Alcoholic Women, 1969-73, 1st v.p.; mem. women's bd. Columbus Symphony, 1965-79, chmn. youth council, 1965-68, pres.-elect women's assn., 1973, pres., 1974-76; pres.-elect vol. council Am. Symphony Orch. League, 1986-87; chmn. juried art competition Central Ohio Arts Festival, 1969, 70, chmn. fine and applied arts, 1971, gen. chmn. of festival, 1972; area chmn. United Appeals Franklin County, 1966-68, Heart drive, 1968-85; pres. Ohio State U. Soc. Friends Sch. Music, 1977-78; trustee Columbus Symphony Orch., 1973-81, Opera/Columbus, 1981-85; v.p. women's guild Opera/Columbus, 1986-87, pres., 1987-88; mem. vol. council Am. Symphony Orch. League, 1981—, v.p., 1983-84, pres., 1987-88; organist, choir dir. North Congregational Ch., 1979-85; area leader Republican party, 1966-68; mem. Mayor's Award Council Com., 1981-84; active Conexions, Columbus Literacy Council. Mem. Am. Guild Organists, Choristers Guild Am., Fedn. Am. Bapt. Musicians, Center Sci. and Industry, Ohio State Hist. Soc., Ohio Orgn. Orchs. (treas. 1976-79, sec. 1979-82), Nat. Trust U.S.A., Tau Beta Sigma, Delta Omicron, Kappa Delta (Central Ohio Woman of Yr. 1970). Mem. Order Eastern Star, White Shrine of Jerusalem. Clubs: Ohio State U. Alumnae of Franklin County (pres. 1962-64, 71-72). Home: 3355 Somerford Rd Columbus OH 43221

ALLEN, MARION CARROLL, clergyman; b. Spartanburg, S.C., Dec. 12, 1914; s. Albert Mayfield and Caroline May (Rogers) A.; B.A., Furman U., 1937; M.Div., Yale, 1940; M.A., Kans. U., 1960; m. Eleanor Earl Burt, July 31, 1943; children—Marian, Burt, Robert, Louise. Ordained to ministry Am. Bapt. Conv., 1940, received into United Ch. of Christ; pastor Bapt. chs., Bristol, Conn., 1940-47, Beaufort, S.C., 1947-50, Clemson, S.C., 1950-56, Lawrence, Kans., 1956-76; pastor First Congregational Ch., Topeka, 1976, Central Congregational Ch., 1977-80, Pilgrim Congregational Ch., Wichita, Kans., 1980—; instr. religion Clemson U., 1951-56, instr. homiletics Central Sem., Kansas City, Kans., 1959-61, English, Kans. U., 1958, 76—. Bd. dirs. YMCA, U. Kans., 1956-60; v.p. Lawrence Friends of Music, 1968-75; sec. adv. bd. Kans. Sch. Religion, 1970-76. Mem. Topeka Ministerial Alliance, Lawrence Ministerial Alliancce, Topeka Council Chs., Consultation of Cooperating Chs. Kans., Kans. Okla. Conf. United Ch. of Christ. Clubs: Masons. Author: A Voice Not Our Own, 1963. Editor: The Springs of Learning, 1969. Editor: Serving in the Armed Forces, monthly 1972-74. Home: 3508 Riverview Rd Lawrence KS 66044

ALLEN, RICHARD HERBERT, orthopaedic surgeon; b. Janesville, Wis., Aug. 4, 1926; s. Herbert William and Helen Marie (Taylor) A.; m. Patricia Warner Allen, Oct. 23, 1955; children: Douglas, Elizabeth, David. Undergrad., Dartmouth Coll., 1944-46; MD, Harvard U., 1950. Diplomate Am. Bd. Orhtopaedic Surgery. Orthopaedic surgeon Coll. St. Orthopaedics, Battle Creek, Mich., 1956—, pres., 1971—; clin. assoc. prof. health scis. Western Mich U., Kalamazoo; orthopaedic cons. VA, Ft. Custer, Mich., 1956—; bd. dirs. Mercy Pavillion, Battle Creek, 1986. Trustee Southwestern Mich. Rehab. Hosp., Battle Creek, 1968—, Leila Hosp., Battle Creek, 1979—, Lakeview Gen. Hosp. Assn., Battle Creek, 1984—; Served to lt. MC USN, 1952-54. Mem. AMA, ACS, Latin Am. Soc. for Orthopaedics and Trauma, Am. Acad. Orthopaedic Surgery, Clin. Orthopaedic Soc., Mid-Am. Orthopaedic Assn., Mich. Orthopaedic Soc. (past pres., rep.), Mich. State Med. Soc., Detroit Acad. Orthopaedic Surgery, Calhoun Med. Soc., Phi Beta Kappa. Republican. Club: Battle Creek Country. Avocation: golf. Home: 227 E Emmett Battlecreek MI 49017 Office: Coll St Orthopaedics PC 191 College St Battle Creek MI 49017

ALLEN, ROBERT SHAW, chemical engineer; b. Providence, Nov. 12, 1931; s. Ray Spencer and Madeline (Shaw) A.; B.S. in Chem. Engring., Worcester Poly. Inst., 1956; m. Norma Elaine Porter, Nov. 8, 1958; children—Trudi Lynn, Ronald Shaw. With Am. Cyanamid Co., 1956-59; with Dewey & Almy Chem. div. W.R. Grace Co., 1959-62, Monroe Mfg. Co., 1962-67; Neutron Produ- cts, Inc., 1967-68, Continental Oil Co., 1968-72, Allen-Herzog Asso., Framingham, Mass., 1972-73, World-Wide Constrn. Services, Inc., Wichita, Kans., 1973-76; prin. Allen Assos., engrs. and consultants, Wichita, 1976—. Chmn., Sedgwick County Republican Central Com., 1977-82. Served with U.S. Army, 1953-55. Mem. Am. Inst. Chem. Engrs., Instrument Soc. Am., Nat. Soc. Profl. Engrs., Kans. Engring. Soc., Wichita Soc. Profl. Engrs., Wichita Area C. of C. Home: 9003 E Harry Apt 111 Wichita KS 67207 Office: 250 N Rock Rd Suite 350 Wichita KS 67206

ALLEN, SARA ELLSWORTH, lawyer; b. Detroit, Oct. 5, 1958; d. Frank and Joan Elizabeth (Ellsworth) A.; m. Lucius Bogdan Allen, Dec. 29, 1984. BA in History with high distinction, Wayne State U., 1980; JD, U. Mich., 1983. Atty. Clark, Klein & Beaumont, Detroit, 1983-86, Simpson & Morgan, PC, Birmingham, Mich., 1986—. Mem. ABA, Mich. Bar Assn., Christian Legal Soc. Republican. Presbyterian. Avocations: travel, English lit. Home: 8426 Oak Tree Ln Warren MI 48093 Office: Simpson & Morgan PC 555 S Woodward 5th floor Birmingham MI 48011

ALLEN, TERRY WAYNE, hospital administrator, accountant; b. Frankfort, Ind., Jan. 23, 1949; s. Billie Calvin and Marilyn Jane (Allen) Shires; m. Cheryl Elaine Utter, Dec. 16, 1972; 1 child, Heather. Student, U. Ky., 1970; BS in Bus., Ind. U., Indpls., 1977; postgrad., Ball State U., 1984—. CPA, Ind. Staff acct. Cleon Point & Assocs., Kokomo, Ind., 1977-78; acct. S.P.E.D.Y.-O.I.C./O.D.C., Kokomo, 1978; asst. comptroller Kolux div. Gen. Indicator Corp., Kokomo, 1978-79; staff acct. Bergstrom & Bergstrom Pub. Accts., Kokomo, 1979-82; dir. fiscal services Duke's Meml. Hosp., Peru, Ind., 1982-87; v.p. mgmt. info. systems Howard Community Hosp., Kokomo, 1987—; cons. Kokomo Creative Arts Council, 1978; cons. tax and fin., Kokomo, 1982-87. Served to 1st lt., U.S. Army, 1968-71. Mem. Am. Inst. CPA's, Ind. CPA Soc., Healthcare Fin. Mgmt. Assn., Nat. Fedn. Intersholastic Ofcls. Assn., Howard County Vietnam Vets., Ind. U. Alumni Assn. Methodist. Club: Ind. U. Varsity (Bloomington). Lodge: Elks. Avocations: basketball, photography. Home: 1903 Olds Ct Kokomo IN 46902 Office: Howard Community Hospital 3500 S LaFountain St Kokomo IN 46902

ALLEN, THOMAS ERNEST, lawyer; b. Salt Lake City, Sept. 30, 1939; s. Kenneth L. and Joyce Catherine (Thompson) A.; m. Elizabeth Harker Curtis, June 26, 1965; children: Kenneth, Susan, Gregory. AB, Dartmouth Coll., 1961; JD, U. Mich., 1967. Bar: Minn., 1967, U.S. Dist. Ct. Minn., 1968, U.S. Tax Ct., 1970, Mo., 1976, U.S. Dist. Ct. (ea. dist.) Mo., 1977. Assoc. Peterson, Peterson & Peterson, Albert Lea, Minn., 1967-69; ptnr. Peterson, Peterson & Allen, Albert Lea, Minn., 1969-76; assoc. Curtis, Casserly & Barnes, St. Louis, 1976-77; ptnr. Curtis & Crossen, St. Louis, 1977-84; of counsel Curtis, Bamburg & Crossen, St. Louis, 1984-87, Curtis, Bamburg, Oetting et al, St. Louis, 1987—; bd. dirs. Brooking Park Geriatrics, Inc., Sedalia, Mo., Geriatric Mgmt. Inc., Sedalia. Chmn. Freeborn County Rep. Com., Albert Lea, 1970-74. Served to 1st lt. U.S. Army, 1962-64. Mem. ABA, Mo. Bar Assn., Minn. Bar Assn., Bar Assn. Met. St. Louis, Phi Kappa Psi. Republican. Episcopalian. Club: Mo. Athletic (St. Louis). Lodge: Masons. Home: 423 Miriam Kirkwood MO 63122 Office: Curtis Bamburg & Oetting 325 N Kirkwood Rd Suite 203 Kirkwood MO 63122

ALLEN, WALTER RECHARDE, sociology educator; b. Kansas City, Mo., Feb. 3, 1949; s. Grady Lee and Freddie Mae (Clayton) A.; m. Wilma Jean Sharber, Sept. 26, 1970; children: Rena Marie, Binti Tamarra, Bryan Recharde. BA, Beloit (Wis.) Coll., 1971; MA, U. Chgo., 1973, PhD, 1975. Asst. prof. sociology U. N.C., Chapel Hill, 1974-79; from asst. to assoc. prof. sociology, Afro-Am. and African studies U. Mich., Ann Arbor, 1979—, assoc. prof. sociology, Afro-Am. and African studies, 1985—, assoc. dir. Cen. for Afro-Am. Studies, 1985—, bd. dirs. Nat. Study Black Coll. Students, 1979—. Co-author: The Colorline and the Quality of Life, 1987; co-editor: (book) Beginnings: Development of Black Children, 1985; (bibliography) Black Families, 1965-80, 1986. Recipient distinguished leadership award United Negro Coll. Fund, 1985; Rockefeller Found. fellow, 1982-83, Fulbright scholar, 1984, 86-87. Mem. Internat. Sociol. Assn., Am. Sociol. Assn., Am. Ednl. Research Assn. (distinguished scholar 1987), Assn. Black Sociologists, Phi Delta Kappa. Baptist. Avocations: reading, travel, swimming, gardening. Office: U Mich Dept Sociology 3515 LSA Bldg Ann Arbor MI 48109

ALLEN, WARREN WILLIAM, JR., brick co. exec.; b. St. Louis, Jan. 2, 1924; s. Warren William and Edith (Eilers) A.; student Purdue U., 1942-43; B.S. in Chem. Engring., Wash. U., 1948; m. Ruth Reddish, June 11, 1949; children—William Reddish, Margaret, John Warren. Sales engr. Presstite Engr. Co., 1948-51; with Hydraulic Press Brick Co., St. Louis, 1951—, sales engr., Cleve., 1951-52, sales mgr., Cleve., 1952-55, mgr. Haydite div., 1955-63, v.p., St. Louis, 1963-67, pres., Cleve., 1967—, also dir.; dir. St. Louis Steel Casting Inc. Dir. Expanded Shale Clay and Slate Inst. Served with AUS, 1943-46. Mem. Am. Ceramic Soc., Am. Concrete Inst., ASTM, Alpha Chi Sigma, Phi Delta Theta. Home: 1690 E Shore Dr Martinsville IN 46151 Office: PO Box 7 Brooklyn IN 46111

ALLEN, WILLIAM CECIL, physician, educator; b. LaBelle, Mo., Sept. 8, 1919; s. William H. and Viola O. (Holt) A.; m. Madge Marie Gehardt, Dec. 25, 1943; children: William Walter, Linda Diane Allen Deardeuff, Robert Lee, Leah Denise. A.B., U. Nebr., 1947, M.D., 1951; M.P.H., Johns Hopkins U., 1960. Diplomate Am. Bd. Preventive Medicine, Am. Bd. Family Practice. Intern Bishop Clarkson Meml. Hosp., Omaha, 1952; practice medicine specializing in family practice Glasgow, Mo., 1952-59; specializing in preventive medicine Columbia, Mo., 1960—; dir. sect. chronic diseases Mo. Div. Health, Jefferson City, 1960-65; asst. med. dir. U. Mo. Med. Ctr., 1965-75; assoc. coordinator Mo. Regional Med. Program, 1968-73, coordinator health programs, 1969—, clin. asst. prof. community health and med. practice, 1962-65, asst. prof. community health and med. practice, 1965-69, assoc. prof., 1969-75, prof., 1975-76, prof. dept. family and community medicine, 1976-87, prof. emeritus, 1987—; cons. Mo. Regional Med. Program, 1966-67, Norfolk Area Med. Sch. Authority, Va., 1965-66; governing body Area II Health Systems Agy., 1977-79, mem. coordinating com., 1977-79; founding dir. Mid-Mo. PSRO Corp., 1974-79, dir., 1976-84. Contbr. articles to profl. jours. Mem. Gov.'s Adv Council for Comprehensive Health Planning, 1970-73; trustee U. Mo. Med. Sch. Found., 1976—. Served with USMC, 1943-46. Fellow Am. Coll. Preventive Medicine, Am. Acad. Family Physicians (sci. program com. 1972-75, commn. on edn. 1975-80), Royal Soc. Health; mem. Mo. Acad. Family Physicians (dir. 1956-59, 76-82, alt. del. 1982—, pres. 1985-86), Mo. Med. Assn., Howard County Med. Soc. (pres. 1958-59), Boone County Med. Soc. (pres. 1974-75), Am. Diabetes Assn. (pres. 1978, dir. 1974-77), Mo. Diabetes Assn. (pres. 1972-73), Soc. Tchrs. Family Medicine, AMA, Mo. Public Health Assn., Am. Heart Assn. (program com. 1979-82), Am. Heart Assn. of Mo. (sec. 1980-81), Mo. Heart Assn. (sec. 1979-82, pres.-elect 1982-84, pres. 1984-86). Methodist. Club: Optimists. Office: Univ Mo Regional Med Program M234 Medical Center Columbia MO 65212

ALLERS, MARLENE ELAINE, law office business manager; b. Crosby, Minn., Dec. 29, 1931; d. Robert Prudent and Tressa Ida May (Hiller) Huard; m. Herbert Dodge Allers, Aug. 29, 1950 (dec. Aug. 1977); children—Melanie Lynn, Geoffrey Brian. B.S. in Math., U. Minn.-Mpls., 1966, B.A. in Acctg., 1968, M.B.A. in Personnel and Fin. Mgmt., 1972. Bus. mgr., Earl Clinic, St. Paul, 1959-68, Lindquist & Vennum, Mpls., 1968-79, Stacker, Ravich & Simon, Mpls., 1979-82, Wagner, Johston & Falconer, Ltd., Mpls., 1983—; lectr. Inst. of Continuing Legal Edn., Mpls., 1977. Recipient Outstanding Achievement award in Bus. Young Women's Christian Assn., Mpls., 1978. Mem. Minn. Legal Adminstrs. Assn., Mensa. Avocations: bridge; reading. Home: 608 Queen Ave S Minneapolis MN 55405

ALLERY, ALAN J., health science association administrator, consultant; b. Cando, N.D., July 29, 1947; s. Louis E. and Ermaline P. (Krebsback) A.; m. Margaret J. DeMers, Aug. 2, 1969; children: Chris, Aaron, Gina. BS in Physical Edn., Bus., Mayville State U., 1970; M in Sch. Adminstrn., Northern State U., 1975; MHA, U. Minn., 1981. Educator Lansford (N.D.) Pub. Sch., 1970-72; adminstr. United Tribes N.D., Bismarck, 1972-73; educator Northern State Coll., Aberdeen, N.D., 1973-75; health adminstr. Indian Health, Aberdeen, 1975-84, Bemidji, Minn., 1984—. Republican. Roman Catholic. Office: Indian Health Services Bemidji MN 56601

ALLEY, WILLIS DAVID, architect, military officer; b. Laramie, Wyo., Nov. 18, 1954; s. Harold Pugmire and Nadra Jeanne (Dayton) A.; m. Eva Jennine Poljanec, Aug. 15, 1979; children: Julie Jeanne, John Harold, Lewis Michael. BS with honor, U. Wyo., 1979; MArch, Ohio State U., 1986. Commd. 2d lt. USAF, 1979, advanced through grades to capt., 1984; archtl. engr. 35th civil engring. squadron USAF, George AFB, Calif., 1980-81; base architect 1605th civil engring. squadron USAF, Lajes Field AFB, Azores, 1981-83; instr. architecture Air Force Inst. Tech. USAF, Wright-Patterson AFB, Ohio, 1986—; Computer Aided Design/Drafting implementation officer Air Force Logistics Command, Wright-Patterson AFB, Ohio, 1986—. Fellow Am. Computing Machinery Assn.; mem. Soc. Am. Mil. Engrs. Avocations: raquetball, tennis, skiing.

ALLIE, MICHAEL DUANE, computer services company manager, consultant; b. Dearborn, Mich., Feb. 14, 1954; s. Mike and Dorothy Mae (Cadry) A.; m. Louise Henriette Pinvidic, Apr. 24, 1976; children—Cheryl Ann, Alan Michael. B.S. in Bus. Adminstrn., Detroit Coll. Bus., 1975; M.B.A., U. Mich., 1981. Computer programmer Bundy Tubing Co., Warren, Mich., 1974-76; project leader Chevrolet div. Gen. Motors Corp., Warren, 1976-80, 1981-84; cons. Ernst & Whinney, Detroit, 1980-81; mgr. Electronic Data System, Troy, Mich., 1985—; adv. DCB Curricula Adv. Com., Dearborn, 1982—. Mem. Assn. Systems Mgmt. (chmn. program com. 1984-85). Avocation: photography.

ALLINGHAM, DENNIS JOHN, health care industry executive, accountant; b. Escanaba, Mich., Sept. 29, 1950; s. William Hubert and Evelyn Mae (Stockemer) A.; m. Claudette Ann Vanlerberghe, Nov. 30, 1968; children: Michelle, Brian. BA in Bus. Adminstrn., U. Mich., 1972. CPA, Mich. Sr. acct. Deloitte, Haskins & Sells, Detroit, 1972-76; div. controller Household Mfg., Albert Lea, Minn., 1976-80; corp. controller Krelitz Industries, Mpls., 1980-81, v.p. fin., 1981—, also bd. dirs.; chmn., treas. James Phillips Co. sub. Krelitz Industries, Inc.; guest lectr. U. Minn., 1983; speaker Ky. Soc. CPA's, 1984. Vol. St. Joseph's Home for Children, Mpls., 1982-83. Recipient Hon. Order Ky. Cols. award, Louisville, 1984. Mem. Am. Inst. CPA's (speaker Las Vegas, Nev. 1985), Minn. Soc. CPA's (chmn. mems. in industry 1984, 1985, named outstanding chmn. 1984). Republican. Roman Catholic. Club: Calhoun Beach (Mpls.). Lodge: Elks. Avocations: reading, skiing, music, boating, camping. Office: Krelitz Industries Inc 900 N 3d St Minneapolis MN 55401

ALLINSON, JULIE ANN, banker; b. Cedar Rapids, Iowa, May 18, 1958; d. Hilbert John and Mary Ann (Schlotterback) Lorenz; m. George Allinson, Aug. 18, 1979. BBA, U. Iowa, 1980. Lic. stock broker, N.Y., Minn. Stock broker, ops. mgr. Piper, Jaffray & Hopwood, Mpls., 1980-85; product mgr. First Banks, Mpls., 1985—. Vol. Pub. Radio Action Auction, Mpls. and St. Paul, 1980-85, Twin Cities Paintathon, 1985-86, Twin Cities Secret Santa, 1985-86, Twin Cities United Way, 1986. Mem. Kappa Kappa Gamma (Twin Cities chpt. v.p. 1985-86, pres. 1986-87). Avocation: antiques. Home: 1423 W 27th St Minneapolis MN 55408 Office: First Banks 1st Bank Pl Minneapolis MN 55480

ALLISON, BRENDA DENISE, benefits administrator; b. Macomb, Ill., Mar. 3, 1953; d. George M. and Anna Ruth (McGaughey) A. B.S., Western Ill. U., 1976, postgrad., 1977-83; cert. Harvard Bus. Sch., 1981, postgrad. Sangamon State U., 1984—. Dir. field services, pub. relations dir. Two Rivers Council Girl Scouts, Quincy, Ill., 1977-82; apprentice pharmacist Jack Stites Pharmacy, Macomb, Ill., 1976-77; program/camp services dir. Shining Trail Council Girl Scouts, Burlington, Iowa, 1975-77; apprentice pharmacist Christy Apothecary Shop, Pekin, Ill., 1972-74; pub. relations cons., farm mgr., Macomb, Ill., 1983-84; asst. adminstr. Central Laborers Pension, Annuity and Welfare Funds, 1984—. Mem. WIBC Child Advocacy Interagy. Council; past pres. Parents Anonymous; bd. dirs. Girl Scouts U.S.A. Recipient Cert. of Honor, Girl Scouts, 1977, Appreciation Pin, 1977; Cert. Recognition, Mayor of Macomb, 1981, 82; Ill. state scholar, 1972-76. Mem. Assn. Girl Scout Exec. Staff, Am. Camping Assn., Am. Mgmt. Assn., Pub. Relations Soc., Internat. Platform Assn., Farm Bur., Am. Polled Herefords, Am. Quarter Horse Assn., Home Extension, Social Welfare Assn., Ill. Quarter Horse Assn. Republican. Clubs: Rushville Saddle (sec., treas.); Lamoine Trails Saddle (Macomb). Home: PO Box 802 Jacksonville IL 62651 Office: PO Box 1246 Jacksonville IL 62650

ALLISON, DAVID NEAL, accountant; b. Kansas City, Mo., Aug. 7, 1957; s. Kenneth and Daisy (Bilyeu) A.; m. Sheryl Lynn Amos, May 22, 1982; 1 child, Meaghen Ashley. AA, Kansas City Community Coll., 1977; BS, Kans. State U., 1980. CPA, Kans. Staff acct. Aubrey E. Richardson, CPA, Kansas City, Mo., 1980-83; staff acct. Braunsdorf, Carlson & Clinkinbeard, Topeka, 1983-86, ptnr., 1986—. Bd. dirs. Kansas City Vaccine Co., 1985—. Mem. Am. Inst. CPA's, Kans. Soc. CPA's, Kans. Contractors Soc., Constrn. Fin. Mgmt. Assn. Avocation: sports, collectibles. Home: 3700 SW Arvonia Pl Topeka KS 66610 Office: Braunsdorf Carlson and Clinkinbeard 990 SW Fairlawn Topeka KS 66606

ALLISON, DEBRA HUST, systems analyst, university official; b. Cin., Feb. 10, 1951; d. Elmer George and Laverne Marie (Guckiean) Hust; m. Christopher E. Allison, Sept. 3, 1977; 1 child, Brian Douglas. B.A. (Howard White award 1973), Miami U., Oxford, Ohio, 1973, M.S., 1983; Cert. systems profl.; Congl. intern, 1972-73; congl. aide, 1973-75; systems analyst Miami U., 1975-83, mgr. Info. Ctr., 1983—; project officer SHARE, Inc. Info Ctr. Project, 1982-86. Mem. Miami U. IBM Personal Computer Users Group (founder, pres.), Nat. Fedn. Bus. and Profl. Women (named Young Career Woman, Oxford chpt. 1979), Oxford C. of C. (charter), Phi Kappa Phi. Republican. Episcopalian. Club: Order Eastern Star. Home: 7 Quail Ridge Dr Oxford OH 45056 Office: Miami U 137 Hoyt Hall Oxford OH 45056

ALLISON, RICHARD DRING, government official; b. Murphysboro, Ill., Sept. 21, 1944; s. Reuel Dring and Ruby Francis (Jungewaelter) A.; student So. Ill. U., 1973-78, Belleville Area Coll., 1974-78; m. Beverly Lindsey, Oct. 17, 1968; children: Billy Wayne, Jay Dean. Land surveyor R.M. Harrison Co., St. Louis, 1967-70; license examiner Office Sec. of State, Sparta, Ill., 1970-75; corrections clk. Menard (Ill.) Correctional Center, 1975-84, correctional counselor, 1984—. Chmn. Bicentennial Wagon Train, Chester, Ill., 1976; pres., treas. Menard Credit Union, 1980—; coordinator Randolph County Reagan-Bush Campaign, Jim Edgar Sec. State Campaign, 1986; mem. Cohen Ho. com. Served with U.S. Army, 1965-67. Mem. Ill. Jaycees (John H. Armbruster award 1978, Outstanding Local V.P. 1977-78), Chester Jaycees (pres. 1978-79, mem. internat. senate 1979—), Am. Legion (comdr. 1983-83, jr. vice-comdr. 1984-85, sr. vice comdr. 1985-86), VFW (life). Republican. Roman Catholic. Clubs: KC, Elks. Home: 1735 Swanwick St Chester IL 62233 Office: Menard Correctional Center Menard IL 62259

ALLMAN, TOMMY LYNN, chemical company executive; b. Maryville, Tenn., Mar. 16, 1951; s. John Luther and Marion Imogene (Borin) A.; m. Elizabeth Ann Helms, June 9, 1973; children: Timothy John, Amanda Lee, Mary Ann, Joseph Thomas. BSBA, U. Tenn., 1973. Indsl. engr. Colgate-Palmolive Co., Jeffersonville, Ind., 1973-74, shipping prodn. foreman, 1974-78, traffic mgr., 1983—; transp. analyst Colgate-Palmolive Co., N.Y.C., 1978-80, customer service, systems coordinator, 1980-82; distbg. supr. Colgate-Palmolive Co., Los Angeles, 1982-83. Scouting coordinator Boy Scouts Am., New Albany, Ind., 1985—; sponsor, GOP Victory Fund, Washington, 1985—. Mem. Nat. Indsl. Transp. League, Pvt. Truck Council, Transp. Club Louisville, Delta Nu Alpha. Mormon. Avocations: basketball, camping, ch. related activities. Home: 1216 Lexington Dr New Albany IN 47150 Office: Colgate Palmolive Co State and Woerner Sts Jeffersonville IN 47130

ALLMON, JUDITH LYNN, interior designer; b. St. Louis, Nov. 11, 1955; d. Joseph Francis and Pearl Elizabeth (Enderson) Gentili; m. Arlen Dale Allmon, Apr. 29, 1983; 1 child, Cody Bryan. BS in Home Econs., U. Mo., 1977. Material control engr. Daniel Internat., Reform, Mo., 1978-79; design specialist Mo. Dept. Conservation, Jefferson City, Mo., 1979-83; designer Mo. Dept. Nat. Resources, Jefferson City and Lebanon, Mo., 1983—; instr. Nicholas Career Ctr., Jefferson City, 1981-82; co-owner Inside/Out, Willard, Mo., 1983—. Illustrator to profl. jours. Cons. Cole County Hist. Soc., Jefferson City, 1981. Avocations: landscaping, photography, travel, reading, piano. Home: 6915 Blackjack Ct Willard MO 65781 Office: Mo Dept Natural Resources Div Parks Recreation and Hist PO Box 951 Lebanon MO 65536

ALLTON, JUDITH A. SCHROEDER, guidance counselor; b. Findlay, Ohio, Apr. 13, 1948; d. Harold J. and Esther A. (Kuhlman) Schroeder; m. John D. Allton, June 21, 1969; children: Michael, Melissa. BS, Bowling Green State U., 1968, postgrad., 1978-82; MEd, U. N.C., 1972; postgrad., Ohio U., 1973-76, Ashland Coll., 1982—. Nat. cert. career counselor; nat. cert. counselor; cert. counselor, Ohio. Tchr. Findlay City Schs., 1968-69, Chapel Hill Schs., N.C., 1969-72; counselor Fairfield Union High Sch., Lancaster, Ohio, 1972-76, Norwalk (Ohio) High Sch., 1977—. Pres. Norwalk Child Study Club, 1983, St. Mary's Sch. Bd., 1985—; bd. dirs. Huron County Chpt. Am. Diabetic Assn., 1986—. Mem. Am. Sch. Counselor's Assn., Ohio Sch. Counselors' Assn. (Career Edn. award 1976, Innovative Program award 1986), Ohio Coll. Admissions Counselors Assn., Am. Assn. Counseling and Devel., Ohio Assn. Counseling and Devel., NEA, Ohio Edn. Assn., North Cen. Ohio Edn. Assn., Norwalk Tchrs. Assn. (v.p. 1986—), Bowling Green State U. Alumni Assn. (bd. dirs. 1983—). Democrat.

Roman Catholic. Avocations: reading, gourmet cooking, tennis, bicycling. Home: 210 W Main St Norwalk OH 44857 Office: Norwalk High Sch 80 E Main Norwalk OH 44857

ALLY, RONALD NASSER, controller; b. Elgin, Ill., Mar. 31, 1958; s. Syed R. W. and Bettie A. (Craddock) A.; m. Carol A. Muhr, Oct. 10, 1980; children: Amy, Susan. BS, Elmhurst Coll., 1983. CPA, Ill. Acct. Midco Chgo. Co., Schaumburg, Ill., 1983-84; acctg. mgr. Meadows Credit Union, Rolling Meadows, Ill., 1984-87; controller Am. Law Enforcement Credit Union, Wheeling, Ill., 1987—, Combined Counties Police Assn., Wheeling, Ill., 1987—. Mem. Am. Inst. CPA's, Ill. CPA Soc. Lutheran. Home: 230 Stonehurst Dr Elgin IL 60120 Office: Am Law Enforcement Credit Union 39 S Milwaukee Ave Wheeling IL 60090

ALM, BRIAN ROBERT, public relations executive; b. Kewanee, Ill., Feb. 10, 1944; s. Leslie Clifford and Marie (Ponte) A.; m. Diana Jean Wolff, Oct. 26, 1969; children: Eric C., David G. BA in English, Augustana Coll., 1966; MA in English, U. Chgo., 1971. English and journalism instr. Western Mich. U., Kalamazoo, 1971-74; news editor Daily Jour., Kankakee, Ill., 1974-78; product info. specialist Deere and Co., Moline, Ill., 1978-84; mgr. media relations Deere and Co., Moline, 1984—; pub. relations lectr. U. Iowa, 1985-86. Pres. bd. dirs. Briarcliff Estates Community Assn., Bourbonnais, Ill., 1977-78. Served to lt. USN, 1967-70, USNR, 1970-81. Home: 2709 35th St Rock Island IL 61201 Office: Deere and Co John Deere Rd Moline IL 61265

ALMEIDA, JAMES ANTHONY, military officer; b. Newark, Sept. 7, 1950; s. John Lopes and Mary (Dacunha) A.; m. Genevieve Mary Archer; children: John, Scott, Eric. BS in History, USAF, 1973; MBA, Rensselaer Poly. Inst., 1977; MS in Logistics Mgmt., USAF, 1979. Cert. profl. logistician. Commd. 2d lt. USAF, 1973, advanced through grades to maj., 1984, mgr. B-52 acquisition support div. Strategic Systems Program Office, 1979-81, chief logistics programs br. div. B-1 Program Office, 1981-83, officer instr. electronic warfare div. 28th Bomb Wing, 1983-84, chief B-52 def. system br. div. 28th Bomb Wing, 1984-86, chief eletronic combat br. div. 28th Bomb Wing, 1986—. Asst. Den leader Cub Scouts Am., Rapid City, S.D., 1986. Mem. Soc. Logistics Engrs. Lodge: Assn. Old Crows (pres. Rushmore Roost chpt. 1986). Avocations: running, tennis.

ALMONY, ROBERT ALLEN, JR., librarian, businessman; b. Charleston, W.Va., Oct. 14, 1945; s. Robert Allen and Margaret Elizabeth (Morrison) A.; m. Carol A. Krzeminski, May 6, 1972; children—Robby, Michael, Chandra, Rachel. A.A., Grossmont Coll., 1965; B.A., San Diego State U., 1968; M.L.S., U. Calif.-Berkeley, 1977. Sr. div. clk. San Diego State U. Library, 1965-68; acct. Calif. Tchrs. Fin. Services, Orange County, 1968-70, v.p., gen. mgr., 1971-76; research asst. library sch. U. Calif.-Berkeley, 1976-77; reference librarian Oberlin Coll. Library, Ohio, 1977-79; asst. dir. libraries U. Mo., Columbia, 1980—; owner Almony & Assocs. Tax and Fin. Planning, Columbia, 1980—; distbr. USA Today, Columbia, 1984—. Contbr. articles to profl. jours. Treas. Bahai's of Columbia, 1982-86, sec. 1987—; coach Columbia Youth Soccer League, 1981—; cubmaster Boy Scouts Am., Columbia, 1983-85, asst. scoutmaster, 1985—, hon. warrior, Mic-O-Say, 1986—. Mem. ALA, Mo. Library Assn., Assn. Coll. and Research Libraries (exec. com. 1983-86), Mo. Assn. Coll. and Research Libraries (vice chmn., chmn. 1982-84). Avocations: camping; reading; gardening. Home: 301 Rothwell Dr Columbia MO 65203 Office: U Mo 104 Ellis Library Columbia MO 65201

ALONSO, LOU JOHNSON, counseling and educational psychology educator; b. Mason, Mich.; d. James Reginald and Mabel Elizabeth (Reid) Johnson; B.A., Mich. State U., 1947, M.A., 1950, postgrad., 1951-54; m. Noah Alonso, Dec. 17, 1948; 1 son, Jose Gregory II (dec.). Speech, language pathologist Flint (Mich.) Pub. Schs., 1947-48; tchr., then asst. prin. Mich. Sch. for Blind, Lansing, 1949-56; prof. spl. edn., coordinator programs preparing personnel for visually handicapped and deaf-blind pupils, 1959—; dir. Gt. Lakes Region Spl. Edn. Instl. Materials Ctr., Mich. State U., East Lansing, 1967-84; cons. Office Spl. Edn., U.S. Dept. Edn.; mem. adv. bd. numerous agy.; co-owner Riggers' Den, 1978—, Yankee Art Co., 1975—. Mem. Council for Exceptional Children, Am. Assn. Workers for the Blind, Assn. Educators Visually Handicapped, Mich. Restaurant Assn., Delta Zeta, Theta Alpha Phi. Author books, research reports, numerous articles, brochures and instrnl. media. Home: PO Box 1562 East Lansing MI 48826 Office: 331 Erickson Hall Michigan State U East Lansing MI 48824

ALOTTO, ANTHONY LEE, communications company executive; b. Detroit, Oct. 3, 1950; s. Frank Paul Alotto and Mildred Pauline (Theron) Screws; m. Sherry Lynn Parker, Oct. 21, 1971 (div. 1975); 1 child, Kristina Michelle; m. Daluh Ann Wyrick, Nov. 18, 1977; 1 child, Brandia LeAnn. AS, Henderson County Jr. Coll., 1973; BS, Tex. A&M U., 1983; postgrad., Amber U., 1985, Webster U. Technician United Telephone of Tex., Athens, 1971-77; trainer Tex. A&M U., College Station, 1977-83; tng. developer U.S. Telephone, Dallas, 1983-84; mgr. tng. US Telecom, Kansas City, Mo., 1984-86; mgr. network quality US Sprint, Kansas City, 1986, dir. nat. account mgmt., 1986—; cons. Data Loss Prevention, Houston, 1980-83. Author: Basic Electricity For The Security And Alarm Industry, 1982, Transmission Testing, 1984, Basic Telecommunications, 1985. Mem. Am. Mgmt. Assn. Republican. Avocations: scuba diving, computers, robotics, tennis, swimming. Home: 10110 El Monte Overland Park KS 66207 Office: US Sprint 9300 Metcalf Suite 100 Overland Park KS 66212

ALSCHULER, MARJORIE DION, medical educator; b. Chgo., July 4, 1934; d. Milton D. and Rosaline K. (Takiff) Traxler; m. Frank S. Alschuler, July 24, 1960; children: Matthew, Miriam. BA, Northwestern U., 1955; MS, Sanford U., 1958; PhD, Northwestern U., 1980. Research chemist Internat. Minerals and Chems., Skokie, Ill., 1957-58; instr. chemistry Lake Forest Coll., Chgo., 1958-59, U. Ill., Chgo., 1959-62; lectr. chem. North Park Coll., Chgo., 1966-68; staff assoc. Ill. region 2 Am. Health Edn. System, Chgo., 1974-76; asst. prof., med. educator U. Ill., Chgo., 1976-84; med. educator Am. Osteopathic Assn., Chgo., 1984—; chmn. program evaluation Dept. Nutrition, U. Ill., Chgo., 1983—. Contbr. articles to profl. jours., 1957—. founding pres. Walt Disney Sch. Parent Adv. Com., Chgo., 1968-69; mem. dist. 24 council Chgo. Bd. Edn., 1968-70, Uptown Model Cities Edn. Com., Chgo., 1968-70; mem. State Rep. Ellis Levin's Citizen Com., Chgo., 1977—. Fulbright grantee U. Frankfurt, Main, Fed. Republic of Germany, 1955-56; Edward Bayer Franklin fellow, Stanford U., 1956-57. Mem. AAAS (chmn. mus. sci. and industry, 1984—), Am. Ednl. Research Assn., Phi Delta Kappa. Avocations: travel, photography, collecting art, music. Home: 832 Junior Terr Chicago IL 60613 Office: Am Osteopatic Assn 212 E Ohio St Chicago IL 60611

ALSOP, DONALD DOUGLAS, federal judge; b. Duluth, Minn., Aug. 28, 1927; s. Robert Alvin and Mathilda (Aaseng) A.; m. Jean Lois Tweeten, Aug. 16, 1952; children: David, Marcia, Robert. BS, U. Minn., 1950, LLB, 1952. Bar: Minn. 1952. Sole practice New Ulm, Minn., 1952-75; ptnr. Gislason, Alsop, Dosland & Hunter, 1954-75; judge U.S. Dist. Ct. Minn., 1975—, now chief judge; mem. Jud. Conf. Com. to Implement Criminal Justice Act, 1979—. Chmn. Brown County (Minn.) Republican Com., 1960-64, 2d Congl. Dist. Rep. Com., 1968-72, Brown County chpt. ARC, 1968-74. Served with AUS, 1945-46. Mem. ABA, Minn. Bar Assn., 8th Circuit Dist. Judges Assn. (pres. 1982-84, New Ulm C. of C. (pres. 1974-75), Order of Coif. Office: U S Dist Ct 760 Fed Bldg 316 N Robert St Saint Paul MN 55101

ALSTON, ROBERT MERRITT, brewery company executive; b. Greenwood, S.C., Nov. 26, 1949; s. William C. and Frances Albertine (Reynolds) A.; m. Mary Frances Phillips, May 19, 1972; children: Stephanie, Douglas, Kristine. BA in Math., DePauw U., 1972; MBA, U. Mich., 1974. Sr. mgr., mgmt. info. cons. div. Arthur Andersen & Co., Detroit, 1973-83; dir. data processing The Stroh Brewery Co., Detroit, 1983—. Vice chmn. info. tech. planning com. Detroit United Found.; mem. info. systems exec. forum U. Mich. Bus. Sch. Mem. Soc. Info. Mgmt. (founder Detroit chpt.), Beta Gamma Sigma, Phi Beta Kappa. Avocations: bicycle touring, 35mm photography, tropical fish. Office: The Stroh Brewery Co 100 River Pl Detroit MI 48207

ALSUM, LAWRENCE ALLEN, produce marketing executive; b. Beaver Dam, Wis., June 18, 1953; s. Newton and Theresa Alberta (Homan) A.; m. Paula Jean DeYoung, Sept. 6, 1975; children: Timothy Paul, Heidi Lynn, Wendy Jo, Chad Ryan. BBA in Acctg., U. Wis., 1975. CPA, Wis. Acct., mgr. Houghton, Taplick and Co., CPA's, Madison, Wis., 1975-81; pres., gen. mgr. Alsum Produce, Inc., Friesland, Wis., 1981—. Vol. fireman Friesland Fire Dept., 1983—. Mem. Am. Inst. CPA's, Wis. Inst. CPA's (com. chmn. 1978-80), Nat. Assn. Accts., Produce Mktg. Assn., United Fresh Fruit and Vegetable Assn., Friesland C. of C. (pres. 1985—). Republican. Avocations: basketball, volleyball, golf, hunting, travel. Home: Hwy EF PO Box 205 Friesland WI 53935 Office: Alsum Produce Inc Hwys E & EF PO Box 188 Friesland WI 53935

ALT, ROBERT NICHOLAS, JR., lawyer, wire company executive; b. Grand Rapids, Mich., Dec. 30, 1942; s. Robert Nicholas and Catherine Rita (McInerney) A.; m. Mary Houseman, Sept. 11, 1963 (div. 1969); children—Andrew E., Margaret R.; m. Lucinda Dewey, Dec. 29, 1977; 1 dau., Emily Catherine. Bar: Calif. 1978, Mich. 1979, U.S. dist. ct. (we. dist.) Mich. 1979. Assoc. Lascher & Wilner, Ventura, Calif., 1978-79, Hillman, Baxter & Hammond, Grand Rapids, 1979-80, Baxter & Hammond, Grand Rapids, 1980-84; founding ptnr. Bremer, Wade, Nelson & Alt, Grand Rapids, 1984—; mem. litigation sect. Mich. State Bar; mem. adv. com. Mich. State Bar Jour., 1983-86; chmn. bd., sec. McInerney Spring and Wire Co., Grand Rapids, 1984—, chief exec. officer, 1985—. Co-editor column: Litigation Strategies, 1984-86. Chmn. City of Grand Rapids Urban Homestead Commn., 1982-84; mem. lay adv. bd. Cath. Info. Ctr., 1984-86. Recipient 2 1st prizes Mich. Newspaper Assn., 1968; editor-in-chief U. Detroit Law Rev., 1977-78; presdl. scholar U. Detroit, 1977-78; Clarence M. Burton scholar Burton Found., 1977-78; named to honor roll Best Am. Short Stories, Houghton-Mifflin Pub. Co., 1971. Mem. ABA, Mich. Bar Assn., Calif. Bar Assn., Grand Rapids Bar Assn., Mich. Def. Trial Lawyers. Roman Catholic. Home: 728 Cambridge Blvd SE East Grand Rapids MI 49506 Office: Bremer Wade Nelson & Alt 190 Monroe NW 5th Floor Grand Rapids MI 49503 also: 655 Godfrey SW Grand Rapids MI 49503

ALTAN, TAYLAN, engineering educator, mechanical engineer, consultant; b. Trabzon, Turkey, Feb. 12, 1938; came to U.S., 1962; s. Seref and Sadife (Baysal) Kadioglu; m. Susan Borah, July 18, 1964; children—Peri Michele, Aylin Elisabeth. Diploma in engring., Tech. U., Hannover, Fed. Republic Germany, 1962; M.S. in Mech. Engring., U. Calif.-Berkeley, 1964, Ph.D. in Mech. Engring., 1966. Research engr. DuPont Co., Wilmington, Del., 1966-68; research scientist Battelle Columbus Labs, Ohio, 1968-72, research fellow, 1972-75, sr. research leader, 1975-86; prof. mech. engring. Ohio State U., Columbus, 1985—; chmn. sci. com. N.Am. Mfg. Research Inst./Soc. Mfg. Engrs., Detroit, 1982-86. Co-author: Forging Equipment, 1973, Metal Forming, 1983; assoc. editor Jour. Mech. Working Tech., Eng., 1978—; contbr. over 150 tech. articles to profl. jours. Fellow Am. Soc. Metals (chmn. forging com. 1978—), Soc. Mfg. Engrs. (Gold medal 1985), ASME. Avocations: languages: travel. Office: Ohio State U 210 Baker Bldg 1971 Neil Ave Columbus OH 43210

ALTEMUS, JAMES ROY, farm bureau official; b. West Frankfort, Ill., Jan. 12, 1946; s. Harold and Grace Marie (Chick) A.; B.S. in Edn., Ill. State U., 1969; m. Allida Frisch, Feb. 4, 1967; children—Sarah, Emily. Info. services mgr. Ill. Farm Bur., Bloomington, 1969-73, dir. public relations, 1973-78, dir. public info., 1978—; communications cons. Am. Coll. Testing, Nat. Inst. Fin. Aid. Mem. Dist. 87 Sch. Adv. Com., 1978-79; bd. dirs. Central Ill. Jr. Achievement, 1977-79; bd. dirs. McLean County ARC, 1977-81, 1st v.p., 1979, chmn. bd., 1980-81. Served with Chem. Corps, USAR, 1969-75. Mem. Public Relations Soc. Am. (accredited; chpt. pres. 1981, dist. sec. 1982, treas. 1983, dist. chmn. 1985), Bloomington-Normal Advt., Mktg. and Pub. Relations Assn. (pres. 1984). Home: 319 Hillside Ln Bloomington IL 61701 Office: 1701 Towanda Ave Bloomington IL 61701

ALTER, ALBERT JERVISS, JR., radiologist; b. Durham, N.C., July 23, 1942; s. Albert Jerviss and Caroline J. (Morgan) A.; m. Karen Ruth Lentz, Aug. 4, 1966; 1 child, Robert A. BS in Molecular Biology, Yale U., 1964; MD, Case Western Reserve U., 1969; MS in Med. Physics, U. Wis., 1984. Diplomate Am. Bd. Radiology. Intern U. N.Mex. Hosp., Albuquerque, 1969-70; resident in diagnostis radiology McGill-Royal Victoria Hosp., Montreal, Que., Can., 1972-75; asst. prof. U. Wis., Madison, 1976-79, assoc. prof. radiology, 1979—; chief of radiology VA Hosp., Madison, 1979-83; cons. Jackson Clinic, Madison, 1984—; staff Meth. Hosp., Madison, 1984—; mem. chest radiographic task group Ctrs. Radiologic Physics, 1982-86; bd. dirs. Radiation Measurements, Inc. Served with USPHS, 1970-72. Mem. Am. Coll. Radiology, Radiol. Soc. N.Am., Can. Assn. Radiologists, Wis. Soc. Radiologists, Wis. Radiol. Soc. (chmn. com. radiation safety 1984-87), Am. Assn. Physicists in Medicine. Office: Jackson Clinic 345 W Washington Ave Madison WI 53703

ALTER, JOHN, otolaryngologist, facial cosmetic surgeon, educator; b. Hoffgastein, Austria, Feb. 6, 1946; came to U.S., 1948; s. Irving Israel and Clara Klara (Scotchinsky) A.; m. Denise Mary Webber, Apr. 17, 1982; children—Andrea Leah, Geoffrey Ian. B.S., Wayne State U., 1967; D.O., Des Moines Coll. Osteo. Medicine and Surgery, 1971. Diplomate Am. Bd. Otolaryngology, Am. Bd. Osteo. Otolaryngology & Facial Cosmetic Surgery. Intern, Botsford Hosp., Farmington, Mich., 1971-72; resident in surgery Providence Hosp., Southfield, Mich., 1972-73; resident in otolaryngology, facial cosmetic surgery Wayne State U., Detroit, 1973-76; practice medicine specializing in otolaryngology and facial cosmetic surgery, Pontiac, Mich., 1976—, Henry Ford Hosp., West Bloomfield, Mich., 1981—; clin. instr. Wayne State U. Med. Ctr., also local hosps.; past chmn. dept. otolaryngology and ophthalmology Pontiac (Mich.) Gen. Hosp., Huron Valley Hosp., Milford, St. Joseph Mercy Hosp. Mem. Simon Weisenthal Found., Zionist Orgn. Am., Sierra Club (West Bloomfield, Mich.). Fellow Am. Acad. Otolaryngology, Am. Facial Plastic and Reconstructive Soc., Osteo. Coll. Ophthalmalogy and Otohinolaryngology, Am. Acad. Cosmetic Surgery; mem. Am. Osteo. Assn., Oakland County Osteo. Assn., Mich. Osteo. Assn. Physicians and Surgeons, Mich. Otolaryn. Soc. Democrat. Jewish. Office: 7001 Orchard Lake Rd West Bloomfield MI 48033

ALTER, JOSEPH DINSMORE, physician, educator; b. Lawrence, Kans., Apr. 19, 1923; s. David Emmet and Martha (Payne) A.; M.D., Hahnemann Med. Coll., 1950; M.P.H., U. Calif.-Berkeley, 1961; m. Marian Elizabeth Wengert, May 31, 1946 (div. Feb. 1981); children—Robert Emmet, Janet Lynn; m. Joyce Ellen Willis, Apr. 10, 1981; 1 son, Joseph Leslie. Intern, Huntington Meml. Hosp., Pasadena, Calif., 1950-51; mem. med. staff Group Health Coop. Puget Sound (Wash.), 1951-60, chmn. family practice dept., 1956-57; field dir. Houses for Korea, Coordinated Community Devel. Project, 1953-54; lectr. med. care adminstrn. Sch. Pub. Health, U. Calif., Berkeley, 1961-62; lectr. Sch. Hygiene and Pub. Health, Johns Hopkins U., Balt., 1962-65, asst. prof., 1965-67, dep. dir. rural health research projects, dept. internat. health Sch. Hygiene and Pub. Health, Narangwal Village, Punjab, India, 1962-67, asst. prof. dept. internat. health Sch. Hygiene and Pub. Health, Balt., 1965-68; assoc. prof., field prof. community medicine, dept. community medicine Coll. Medicine, U. Ky. Med. Center, 1968-70; med. dir. Pilot City Health Center, Cin., 1970-73, HealthCare of Louisville, 1973-75; chief domiciliary med. service VA Center, Dayton, Ohio, 1975-77, assoc. chief staff for extended care, 1977; prof., chmn. dept. community medicine Wright State U. Sch. Medicine, 1977—. Chmn. Dayton regional exec. com., mem. nat. bd. Am. Friends Service Com., 1977-78; pres. bd. trustees Sr. Citizens Ctr. of Greater Dayton, 1984-87; trustee Quaker Heights, Waynesville, Ohio. Recipient Physician's Recognition award AMA, 1976, 79, 82; diplomate Am. Bd. Preventive Medicine. Mem. Am. Pub. Health Assn., AMA, Am. Acad. Family Physicians, Am. Coll. Preventive Medicine, Gerontol. Soc., Aerospace Med. Assn., Ohio, Montgomery County med. assns. Quaker. Author: Narrowing Our Medical Care Gap, 1972; (with others) The Health Center Doctor in India, 1967, Doctors for the Villages, 1976; Life After Fifty-Your Guide to Health and Happiness, 1983; contbr. articles to profl. jours. Home: 4160 Willow Creek Dr Dayton OH 45415 Office: Dept Community Medicine Wright State U Sch Medicine Box 927 Dayton OH 45401

ALTHEIMER, ALAN MILTON, messenger company executive; b. Chgo., July 25, 1940; s. Milton Louis and Rena (Cohen) A.; student Drake U., 1959-61; children—Amy, Marcy. Pres., Altheimer & Baer, Inc., Chgo., 1968-80; pres. v.p. Fast Messenger Service, Inc., Chgo., 1976-83; v.p. Cannonball Inc., Chgo., 1983—. Chmn. Chgo. dist., disaster services ARC, 1980-83; vice chmn. Mid-Am. Disaster Services, ARC, 1983-87, chmn., 1987—; bd. dirs. Midwest Epilepsy Center, 1980-82. Mem. Ill. Messenger Service Assn. Home: 3200 N Lake Shore Dr Chicago IL 60657 Office: Cannonball Inc 400 N Orleans St Chicago IL 60610

ALTMAN, HARVEY JAY, psychobiologist, researcher; b. Bklyn., June 28, 1949; s. David and Audrey Sydell (Garfield) A.; m. Barbara Nan Hefter, June 12, 1974; children—Jill Robyn, Paul Todd, Stefanie Nicole. BS in Biology, N.Y. Inst. Tech., 1973; postgrad. in Biology, L.I. U., 1976; PhD in Biology, NYU, 1986. Researcher dept. neurology Sch. Medicine, NYU, N.Y.C., 1976-77, supr., research asst. div. behavioral neurology, 1977-79, research asst. dept. neurology, 1979-80; instr. Mercy Coll., Dobbs Ferry, N.Y., 1979-80; dir. animal resources facility and dept. behavioral animal research, Lafayette Clinic, Detroit, 1980—; dir. Nat. Conf. on Alzheimer's Disease: Problems, Prospects and Perspectives, 1983—. Contbr. articles to profl. publs. Mem. med. adv. bd. Alzheimer's Disease and Related Disorders Assn., Southfield, Mich., 1982—. A.H. Robins Co. grantee, 1984-86; Wayne State U. Sch. Medicine grantee 1982-83, 83-84, 84-85; Nat. Inst. Aging grantee, 1983, NIH/Nat. Inst. Aging grantee, 1982—. Mem. AAAS, Soc. for Neurosci., Gerontol. Soc. Am., N.Y. Acad. Sci. Republican. Office: Lafayette Clinic Dept Behavioral Animal Research 951 E Lafayette Detroit MI 48207

ALTMAN, LOUIS, lawyer, author, educator; b. N.Y.C., Aug. 6, 1933; s. Benjamin and Jean (Zimmerman) A.; m. Eleanor H. Silver, Oct. 30, 1966; children—Cynthia, Robert. A.B., Cornell U., 1955; LL.B., Harvard U., 1958. Bar: N.Y. 1959, Conn. 1970, Ill. 1973. Assoc. Amster & Levy, N.Y.C., 1958-60; patent atty. Sperry Rand, N.Y.C., 1960-63; chief patent csl. Gen. Time Corp., N.Y.C., 1963-67; ptnr. Altman & Reens, Stamford, Conn., 1967-72; chief patent csl. Baxter-Travenol Labs., Deerfield, Ill., 1972-76; assoc. prof. John Marshall Law Sch., 1976-79, adj. prof., 1979—; of counsel Gerlach, O'Brien & Kleinke, Chgo., 1981-83; ptnr. Laff, Whitesel, Conte & Saret, Chgo., 1983—. Author: Callmann on Unfair Competition, Trademarks & Monopolies, 4th edit., 1981; editor Business Competition Law Adviser, 1983, Construction Law, 1986. Contbr. articles to legal jours. Home: 3005 Manor Dr Northbrook IL 60062 Office: Laff Whitesel et al 401 N Michigan Ave Suite 2000 Chicago IL 60611

ALTMAN, MILTON HUBERT, lawyer; b. Mpls., July 18, 1917; s. Harry Edmund and Lee (Cohen) A.; m. Helen Horwitz, May 21, 1942; children—Neil, Robert, James. B.S., U. Minn., 1938, LL.B., 1947. Bar: Minn. bar 1947. Ptnr. firm Altman, Weiss & Bearmon, St. Paul, 1947-85; Mem. Minn. Gov.'s adv. com. on Constl. Revision, 1950, on Gift and Inheritance Tax Regulations, 1961-65; chmn. atty. gen.'s adv. com. on Consumer Protection, 1961-65; mem. U.S. Dist. Ct. Nominating Commn., 1979; spl. atty. Minn. Bd. Med. Examiners, 1963-75, U. Minn., 1963-75; dir. SPH Hotel Co.; Mem. nat. emergency com. Nat. Council on Crime and Delinquency, 1967-69; mem. Minn.-Wis. small bus. advisory council SBA, 1968-70; mem., v.p. Citizens' Council on Delinquency and Crime, 1968-76; bd. dirs. Correctional Service Minn., 1968-76; mem. Lawyers Com. for Civil Rights Under Law, 1965—; Chmn. Minn. Lawyers for Johnson and Humphrey, 1968. Author: Estate Planning, 1966. Bd. dirs. St. Paul Jewish Fund and Council, 1966-69, Minn. Soc. Crippled Children and Adults. Mem. Minn. Bar Assn. (chmn tax sect. 1960-62), Ramsey County Bar Assn. (exec. council 1968-71), Am. Arbitration Assn. (nat. panel arbitrators), Fgn. Policy Assn. (nat. council 1969), U. Minn. Law Sch. Alumni Assn. (dir. 1967-70), UN Assn. (nat. legacies com. 1967). Clubs: Minn. (dir. 1975-78), St. Paul Athletic. Home: Galtier Plaza Apt 1702 172 E 6th St Saint Paul MN 55101 Office: 310 Cedar St Suite 200 Saint Paul MN 55101

ALTSCHUL, ALFRED SAMUEL, transportation company executive; b. Chgo., Oct. 16, 1939; s. Herman and Lillian (Ginsburg) A.; m. Lynn Silverman, Sept. 8, 1968; children: Howard, Steven, Mark. B.S., U. Wis., 1961; M.B.A., U. Chgo., 1963. C.P.A., Ill. With G.A.T.X. Corp., Chgo., 1964-81; asst. treas. G.A.T.X. Corp., 1967-70, treas., 1970-81; v.p. fin., chief fin. officer Midway Airlines, Chgo., 1981—. Lectr. fin. mgmt. Active Talent Assistance Program. Served with AUS, 1963-69. Mem. Financial Mgrs. Assn. (pres.), Alpha Epsilon Pi. Jewish religion. Club: Standard (Chgo.). Home: 8824 N Lowell Skokie IL 60076 Office: 5700 S Cicero Chicago IL 60638

ALTSCHUL, JOEL HENRY, communications company executive; b. Chgo., Apr. 16, 1948; s. Gilbert I. and Esther G. (Sager) A.; m. Lynn Harriet Feldman, Dec. 28, 1969; children: Jason, Sarah, Jonathan. BA, Harvard U., 1970; MEd, U. Ill., 1973. Account exec. Gilbert Altschul Prodns., Inc., Evanston, Ill., 1973-76; gen. mgr. Jour. Films, Inc., Evanston, 1976-79; v.p. Altschul Group, Evanston, 1979-82, exec. v.p., 1982-86, chmn. bd., 1986—. Office: Altschul Group 930 Pitner Ave Evanston IL 60202

ALTVATER, PHILIP C., JR., marketing executive; b. Upland, Pa., Jan. 16, 1945; s. Philip C. and Elsie C. (Moore) A.; B.A., Pa. State U., 1966. Sales rep. Westvaco Corp., N.Y.C., 1969-73, Oxford Paper Co., Chgo., 1974; product mgr. Hobart McIntosh Paper Co., Elk Grove, Ill., 1975-76; dist. mktg. mgr. Consol. Papers, Inc., Chgo., 1976—. Served with U.S. Army, 1967-69. Home: 21 W 754 Huntington Rd Glen Ellyn IL 60137 Office: 200 W Madison St Chicago IL 60606

ALUKAL, VARGHESE GEORGE, technical director; b. Chengal, India, Jan. 3, 1945; came to U.S., 1967; s. Kunjipaulo and Elizabeth Lizy (Alapat) A.; m. Lyla Chandy, July 11, 1976. B in Tech., Indian Inst. Tech., Madras, 1965; MS, Marquette U., 1969; postgrad., Cornell U., 1969-72. Cert. quality engr. Sci. pool officer Nat. Metall. Labs., Jamshedpur, India, 1973-74; metall. engr. Internat. harvester Corp., Melrose Park, Ill., 1975; quality control mgr. Charles E. Larson & Sons, Chgo., 1976-85, tech. dir., 1985—, also bd. dirs.; lectr. metallurgy Calicut (India) Univ., 1965-67; adj. faculty mem. Triton Coll., River Grove, Ill., 1984-85; instr. Affiliated Ednl. Cons., Harwood Heights, ill., 1985—; cons. mettalurgy, 1984—; quality cons., 1981—. Counselor Crossroads Student Ctr. U. Chgo., 1981—. Mem. ASTM, Am. Soc. Metals, Am. Soc. for Non-Destructive Testing, Am. Soc. Quality Control (assoc. dir. Chgo. chpt. 1983—), Mensa. Roman Catholic. Club: Toastmasters (adminstrv. v.p. Park Ridge chpt. 1986—). Avocations: bridge, tennis. Home: 1801 S Courtland Ave Park Ridge IL 60068 Office: Charles E Larson & Sons 2645 N Keeler Ave Chicago IL 60639

ALVARADO, ARTURO ROCHA, social worker, educator; b. Edenburgh, Tex., Nov. 11, 1941; s. Lorenzo Jaramillo and Trinidad (Rocha) A. BA, St. Edwards U., 1967; MA, Sam Houston State U., 1968; PhD, Columbia Pacific U., 1981. Tchr. Lansing (Mich.) Pub. Schs., 1968-69, Grand Rapids (Mich.) Pub. Schs., 1971-72, Latin Am. Council, Grand Rapids, 1973-78; with Little Mexico Cafe, Grand Rapids, 1979-82, State of Mich., Grand Rapids, 1983—. Author: Cronica de Aztlan: Tales of a Migrant, 1973. Mem. St. Joseph's Ch.; rep. to bd. dirs. Latin Am. Council, Grand Rapids, 1973-78; bd. dirs. Econ. Devel., Grand Rapids, 1973-74.. Democrat. Roman Catholic. Avocations: writing, reading. Home: 4486 Forest Park Dr SW Wyoming MI 49509

ALVAREZ, RONALD, hospital administrator, consultant; b. Columbus, Ohio, Aug. 25, 1944; s. Ralph and Mildred Ann (Stout) A.; m. Linda Kay Williams, Aug. 27, 1966; children—Ronda Lynn, Brenda Lee. B.S. in Bus. Adminstrn., Ohio State U., 1967; M.B.A., Xavier U., Cin., 1978. Inventory control mgr. Borden Inc./Columbus Coated (Ohio), 1969-73, Lunkenheimer Value/Condec Corp., Cin., 1973-74; prodn. and inventory control mgr. Sybron/Liebel-Flarsheim, Cin., 1974-77; v.p. Jewish Hosp. Cin., 1977—, also cons. material mgmt.; instr. master's program and continuing edn. Xavier U.; frequent seminar speaker. Served to 1st lt. U.S. Army, 1967-69. Vietnam. Decorated Bronze Star, Mem. Am. Prodn. and Inventory Control Soc., Internat. Material Mgmt. Soc., Health Care Materiel Mgmt. Soc. (pres. Cin. chpt. 1983-84, internat. dir. 1983-85, cert. profl. in health care mgmt.; Health Care Materiel Mgr. of Yr. award 1983), Ohio State U. Alumni Assn., Alpha Kappa Psi (life). Lutheran. Contbr. numerous articles to profl. jours. Office: 3200 Burnet Ave Cincinnati OH 45229

ALVINO, SYLVIA MARIE, reading educator, educational company executive, consultant; b. Chicago Heights, Ill., Oct. 17, 1948; d. John Joseph and

Diana (Urbinati) A. BA in English, Loyola U., Chgo., 1970, MEd in Reading, 1977. Reading specialist Project Upward Bound, Loyola U., Chgo., 1972—; v.p. fin., cons. Assocs. for Career Devel., Inc., Chgo., 1980—, The Phoenix Group, Inc., Chgo., 1982—; mgr. High Sch. Renaissance Program, Chgo. Bd. Edn., 1984—. Author: (with others) Tutorial Supervisor's Manual, 1977; Cable TV Training Manual, 1981; editor Vineyard, 1971-73. Recipient plaques Rush Med. Ctr., 1982, Loyola U. Upward Bound Program, 1982, Calumet High Sch., 1978. Mem. Mid-Am. Equal Ednl. Opportunity Program Personnel, Assn. Supervision and Curriculum Devel.; Ind. Voters Ill., Ill. Guidance and Personnel Assn., Internat. Reading Assn., Nat. Council Tchrs. of English, Phi Delta Kappa, Phi Chi Theta (officer Beta Psi chpt.). Roman Catholic. Home: 915 W Margate Terr Chicago IL 60640 Office: Loyola U Project Upward Bound 1041 W Loyola Ave Chicago IL 60626 Office: 6101 N Sheridan Rd Chicago IL 60660

ALWIN, LEROY VINCENT, JR., mechanical engineer; b. Mpls., Sept. 23, 1931; s. LeRoy Vincent and Norma Constance (Hartmuth) A.; B.M.E., U. Minn., 1958; m. Barbara June Hecker, Sept. 23, 1972; children—Elizabeth Ann, Anthony Jay; stepchildren—Pamela Jeanne Bohach, Joel Edward Bohach. Engring. designer, asst. ' ' Linac Project", Dept. Physics, U. Minn., Mpls., 1953-58; weather observer, forecaster, USN, Coco Solo, Canal Zone, 1954-56; design mech. engr. Temperature Control Div., Honeywell, Inc., Mpls., 1958-71; cons. mech. engr., pres. Park Engring., Mpls., 1971-83; pres., owner Alwin Engring., Inc., Mound, Minn., 1983—; v.p. Scantec, Inc., heating cons., St. Paul, 1984—; propr. Sugar Wood Farm, Mound, Minn., 1959—. Chmn., N. Am. Maple Syrup Council, 1975-77; chmn. Mound, Minn. Park Commn., 1968-71. Served with USNR, 1954-56. Registered profl. engr., Minn., Wis., Iowa, S.D., Mich., N.D., Ga., La., Nebr. Mem. ASME, Am. Meteorol. Soc. Republican. Club: Engrs. Patentee in field; contbr. articles to profl. jours. Home: Robin Ln Mound MN 55364 Office: Robin Ln Mound MN 55364

ALWIS, SRI KANTHA, physician, psychiatrist; b. Galle, Sri Lanka, June 19, 1939; s. Carlo and Gerti Alwis; m. Shantie Ramya Dealwis, Jan. 29, 1969; children: Sanji, Ruwan. MD, U. Ceylon, 1966. Pvt. practice psychiatry Hamilton, Ohio, 1976—; dir. dept. psychiatry Ft. Hamilton (Ohio) Hosp., 1985-86; med. dir. Drug Counseling Services, Hamilton, 1979—; cons. psychiatrist M.H.C., Hamilton, 1976—. Mem. AMA, Am. Psychiat. Assn., Ohio State Med. Assn., Ohio Psychiat. Assn., Acad. Medicine Hamilton. Home: 360 Hill Top Ln Cincinnati OH 45215 Office: Psychiat Assocs Inc 1000 Dayton St Hamilton OH 45011

AMADIO, BARI ANN, metal fabrication executive; b. Phila., Mar. 26, 1949; d. Fred Deutscher and Celena (Lusky) Garber; m. Peter Colby Amadio, June 24, 1973; children: P. Grant, Jamie Blair. BA in Psychology, U. Miami, 1970; diploma in Nursing, Thomas Jefferson U., 1973, Johnston-Willis Sch. Nursing, 1974; BS in Nursing, Northeastern U., 1977; MS in Nursing, Boston U., 1978; JD, U. Bridgeport, 1983. Faculty Johnston-Willis Sch. Nursing, Richmond, Va., 1974-75; staff, charge nurse Mass. Gen. Hosp., Boston, 1975-78; faculty New England Deaconess, Boston, 1978-80, Lankenau Hosp. Sch. of Nursing, Phila., 1980-81; pres. Original Metals, Inc., Phila., 1985—, also bd. dirs.; owner Silver Carousel Antiques, Rochester, Minn. Treas. Women's Assn. Minn. Orch., Rochester, 1986-87, pres., 1987—, newsnotes editor, 1985-87; fin. chmn. Zumbro Valley Med. Soc. Aux., Rochester, 1986; mem. mayor's com. All. Am. City Award Com., Rochester, 1984—. Mem. Am. Soc. Law and Medicine, Nat. Assn. Female Execs., Nat. Assn. Food Equipment Manufacturers, Phi Alpha Delta, Sigma Theta Tau. Avocations: fencing, painting, writing poetry, piano, squash. Home: 816 9th Ave SW Rochester MN 55902

AMADO, RICHARD STEVEN, psychologist; b. Chgo., May 1, 1948; s. David Samuel and Goldie (Simon) A. AB in Psychology, U. Ill., 1970, MA in Ednl. Psychology, 1974, PhD in Ednl. Psychology, 1981. Lic. psychologist, Minn. Cons. HEED Sch., Champaign, Ill., 1971-74; group leader Ill. Supt. Pub. Instrn., Springfield, 1974; behavior mgmt. specialist Black Hawk Edn. Ctr., East Moline, Ill., 1976-77; devel. workshop supr. Devel. Services Ctr., Champaign, 1977-78; bldg. dir. Brainerd (Minn.) State Hosp., 1978-83; chief exec. officer Human Services Support Network, St. Paul, 1984—; adj. instr. psychology St. Cloud State U., 1979, asst. prof. 1982; mem. Gov.'s Council Devel. Disabilities, 1979-81, Task Force Crisis Intervention Hennepin County, Minn. Dept. Pub. Welfare Task Force; bd. dirs. Assn. Retarded Citizens, Hennepin County. Author: (with E.H. Rudrud and R. Hirschenberger) Behavior Analysis for People With Developmental Disabilities, 1984; contbg. author to book, 1986. Mem. adult services com. Jewish Community Ctr., 1983-84, chmn. annual book fair com.; bd. dirs. Big Bros. and Big Sisters of Brainerd, 1979-81, pres. bd. dirs., 1981. Mem. Am. Psychol. Assn., Assn. Behavior Analysis (clin. spl. interest group past co-chmn., interbehaviorism spl. interest group sec., treas.), Minn. Assn. Behavior Analysis, Minn. Assn. Severely Handicapped, Assn. Persons Severe Handicaps, Phi Kappa Phi, Phi Delta Kappa, Psi Chi.

AMAN, REINHOLD ALBERT, philologist, publisher; b. Fuerstenzell, Bavaria, Apr. 8, 1936; came to U.S., 1959, naturalized, 1963; s. Ludwig and Anna Margarete (Waindinger) A.; m. Shirley Ann Beischel, Apr. 9, 1960; 1 child, Susan. Student, Chem. Engring. Inst., Augsburg, Germany, 1953-54; B.S. with high honors, U. Wis., 1965; Ph.D., U. Tex., 1968. Chem. engr. Munich and Frankfurt, Ger., 1954-57; petroleum chemist Shell Oil Co., Montreal, Que., Can., 1957-59; chem. analyst A. O. Smith Corp., Milw., 1959-62; prof. German U. Wis., Milw., 1968-74; editor, pub. Maledicta Jour., Maledicta Press Publs., Waukesha, Wis., 1976—; pres. Maledicta Press, Waukesha, 1976—; dir. Internat. Maledicta Archives, Waukesha, 1975—. Author: Der Kampf in Wolframs Parzival, 1968, Bayrisch-oesterreichisches Schimpfwoerterbuch, 1973, 86; gen. editor Mammoth Cod (Mark Twain), 1976, Dictionary of International Slurs (A. Roback), 1979, Graffiti (A. Read), 1977; editor Maledicta: The Internat. Jour. Verbal Aggression, 1977—; contbr. articles to profl. jours. U. Wis. scholar, 1963-65; U. Wis. research grantee, 1973, 74; NDEA Title IV fellow, 1965-68. Mem. Internat. Maledicta Soc. (pres.), Am. Dialect Soc., Am. Name Soc., Dictionary Soc. N.Am. Home and Office: 331 S Greenfield Ave Waukesha WI 53186

AMANKWAH, KOFI SARPONG, obstetrics-gynecology educator; b. Ghana, Aug. 31, 1939; s. Kwasi and Abena Birago (Juantoah) A.; m. Sheila Amankwah; children: Kwame, Kofi, Kwasi. BS, U. Alta., Can., MD. Cert. Am. Bd. Ob-Gyn. Intern Ottawa (Can.) Civic Hosp., 1967-68; resident in ob-gyn Meth. Hosp., Bklyn., 1968-72; resident in gynecology Downstate Med. Ctr., Bklyn., 1970; resident in surgery U. Ottawa Hosp.; prof. ob-gyn., chief div. maternal fetal medicine So. Ill. U., Springfield, 1973—, mem. perinatal adv. com.; cons. in field. Contbr. articles to profl. jours. Grantee Ctr. for Disease Control, 1985-86, Ill. Dept. Pub. Health, 1985. Fellow Royal Coll. Physicians and Surgeons; mem. AMA, Can. Med. Assn., Cen. Assn. Ob-Gyn, Ill. State Med. Soc., Sangamon County Med. Soc., Nat. Perinatal Assn., Perinatal Assn. Ill., Soc. Perinatal Obstetricians. Office: Southern Ill U PO Box 3926 Springfield IL 62708

AMARKUMAR, BASAULINGA SADASIVAIAH, physician; b. Tumkur, India, Nov. 2, 1948; s. Sadasivaiah and Sharada A. Markumar; m. Mangala Prabha, Nov. 13, 1981; children: Chatan, Aashik. MD, Bangalore Med. Coll., 1973. Intern Cook County Hosp., Chgo., 1973-74; resident U. Ill. Hosp., Chgo., 1975-80; attending physician Oak Forest (Ill.) Hosp., 1981—, dir. continuing edn., 1986—; urologist South Suburban Hosp., Homewood, 1985—. Avocations: skiing, tennis, jogging, swimmer. Home: 12906 Westgate Dr Palos Heights IL 60463

AMATANGELO, NICHOLAS S., financial printing company executive; b. Monessen, Pa., Feb. 12, 1935; s. Sylvester and Lucy Amatangelo; m. Kathleen Driscoll, May 3, 1964; children: Amy Kathleen, Holly Megan. BA, Duquesne U., 1957; MBA, U. Pitts., 1958. Indsl. engr. U.S. Steel Co., Pitts., 1959-61; indsl. engr. mgr. Anaconda Co., N.Y.C., 1961-63; product mktg. mgr., Xerox Corp., N.Y.C., 1965-68; dir. mktg. MacMillan Co., N.Y.C., 1968-70; dir. product planning Philco-Ford Corp., Phila., 1970-72; pres. Bowne of San Francisco, Inc., 1972-79; pres. Bowne of Houston, 1979-83, Bowne of Chgo. Inc., 1982—; instr. U. Pitts., 1959-61; asst. prof. Westchester Community Coll., N.Y.C., 1961-64, 70-72. Contbr. articles in field to profl. jours. Bd. dirs. San Francisco Boys Club, 1974-79, Boys Towns Italy, 1973-79; mem. pres. council Houston Grand Opera, 1980-83. Served with U.S. Army, 1958-59, 61-62. Mem. Printing Industries Am. (bd. dirs.), Am. Soc. Corp. Secs., Am. Mgmt. Assn.-Pres. Assn., Am. Inst. Indsl. Engrs., Am. Soc. Tng. and Devel. Clubs: Forest, Houston, University (Houston); Executive, Economic (Chgo.); Olympic (San Francisco). Lodge: Kiwanis. Office: Bowne of Chgo 325 W Ohio St Chicago IL 60610

AMATO, JUDY KAY, computer programmer analyst; b. Beech Grove, Ind., Nov. 7, 1958; d. William Logan Sr. and Shirley Mae (Tuttle) Linhart; m. Pasquale Amato Jr., Nov. 5, 1983. BS, Butler U., 1981, postgrad., 1982—. Computer operator Holcomb Research Inst., Indpls., 1980-81; programmer analyst Alverno Adminstrv. Services Inc., Beech Grove, 1981-85, AFNB, Indpls., 1985-86; programmer, analyst Polygram Records, Inc., Indpls., 1987—. Mem. Kappa Mu Epsilon, Delta Delta Delta (corresponding sec. Indpls. chpt. 1986—). Democrat. Mem. Wesleyan Ch. Avocations: skiing, needlecrafts. Home: 709 North Bend Rd Beech Grove IN 46107

AMATOS, BARBARA HANSEN, accounting executive; b. Toledo, Aug. 30, 1944; d. John Richard and Irene Emily (Greunke) Hansen; m. James David Mokren, Sept. 12, 1964 (div. Feb. 1974); children: Frederic Hansen Mokren, Jennifer Joy Mokren; m. David Michael Amatos, Dec. 27, 1975; 1 stepchild, Anthony Steven. Student, Capital U., 1962-64, Cen. Mich. U., 1965-66; BBA, Franklin U., 1979. CPA, Ohio. Account clk. Buckeye Mart, Columbus, Ohio, 1971-73, SCOA Industries Inc., Columbus, 1973-75; payroll mgr. City of Columbus Auditor's Office, 1975-86; mgmt. adv. cons. State of Ohio Auditor's Office, Columbus, 1986—, acctg. mgr., 1987—; ptnr. McGuiness Amatos Properties, Amatos & Amatos, CPA's. Mem. Am. Inst. CPA's, Ohio Soc. CPA's, Assn. Govt. Accts. Office: Auditor State of Ohio 88 E Broad St Columbus OH 43212

AMBELANG, JOEL RAYMOND, social worker; b. Milw., Aug. 23, 1939; s. Raymond Frank and Clara Ottilie (Alft) A.; student Concordia Coll., Milw., 1953-59; B.S., Concordia Sr. Coll., Ft. Wayne, Ind., 1961; M.S. in Community Devel., U. Mo., 1971; m. Lois Jean Yarbrough, Aug. 15, 1964; children—Joel Mark, Kimi Lee, Elizabeth Jean. Chief officer juvenile ct. 11th Jud. Circuit Mo., St. Charles, 1968-74, dir. juvenile ct. services, 1974-76; dir., owner Counseling and Clin. Services, St. Charles, 1976-80; exec. dir. Luth. Family Services N.W. Ind., Inc., Merrillville, 1980—; field instr., part-time asst. prof. dept. social work Valparaiso (Ind.) U., 1981—; instr. sociology and adminstrn. of justice evening coll. Lindenwood Colls., St. Charles, 1975-80; co-founder Youth in Need, Inc., 1973, bd. dirs., 1974-78, pres., 1976-78; cons. Mo. Council on Criminal Justice, Juvenile Tech. Adv. Com., 1973-75; cons., tng. chmn. Mo. Juvenile Justice Assn., 1972-74; mem. St. Charles County Child Welfare Adv. Bd., St. Charles County Child Abuse Task Force; mem. U.S. Cycling Fedn.; chmn. Nat. Bicycle Safety Program, 1979-80. Recipient awards Nat. Dist. Attys. Assn., 1974, Nat. Council Juvenile Ct. Judges, 1979, Juvenile Ct. Services Adminstrn. Nat. Coll. Juvenile Justice, 1971; cert. advanced alcoholism counselor Mo. Dept. Mental Health. Mem. Acad. Cert. Social Workers, Nat. Council Juvenile and Family Ct. Judges, St. Charles Community Council (award 1978), Nat. Assn. Social Workers, Legal Services Eastern Mo. (adv. com.). Lutheran. Originator, host program Lean On Me, sta. KCLC-FM, 1973-80; participant seminars in field; designer, author courses of study in field. Home: 2606 Sears St Valparaiso IN 46383 Office: Merrillville Rd Suite 1 Merrillville IN 46410

AMBRE, JOHN JOSEPH, physician, toxicologist, clinical pharmacologist, researcher; b. Aurora, Ill., Sept. 14, 1937; s. Frederick Mathias and Cecelia Angela (Petit) A.; m. Anita Marie Sievert, Nov. 3, 1962; children—Susan, Peter, Denise, Matthew. B.S., Notre Dame U., 1959; M.D., Loyola U., Chgo., 1963; Ph.D. in Pharmacology, U. Iowa, 1972. Fellow Mayo Clinic, Rochester, Minn., 1966-68; asst. prof. medicine U. Iowa, Iowa City, 1972-75, assoc. prof., 1975-78; med. dir. CBT Labs., Highland Park, Ill., 1978—; assoc. prof. medicine Northwestern U. Med. Sch., 1980—; cons. MetPath Labs., Teterboro, N.J., Abbott Labs., North Chicago, Time, Inc., Chgo., Motorola, Inc., Schaumburg, Ill., Fermi Lab, Batavia, Ill., Velsicol Chem. Corp., Chgo.; expert witness; testifier various govt. congrl. hearings and subcoms. on drug testing. Served as capt. U.S. Army, 1964-66. Recipient Nat. Research award Nat. Inst. on Drug Abuse. Mem. Am. Fedn. Clin. Research, Am. Soc. Pharmacology and Exptl. Therapeutics. Democrat. Author: Drug Assay, 1983; mem. editorial bd. Jour. Analytical Toxicology; contbr. articles to profl. jours., chpts. to books. Home: 1210 Walden Ln Deerfield IL 60015 Office: 303 E Superior St Room 209 Chicago IL 60611

AMBROSE, CHARLES THOMAS, probation officer; b. Springfield, Ill., Apr. 14, 1951; s. Archie and Mae Ambrose; m. Denise Maria Paul, Oct. 6, 1984. BA in Social Sci. and Sociology, Blackburn Coll., 1973. Child welfare worker Ill. Dept. Children and Family Services, 1978-82; probation officer Macoupin County (Ill.) Probation, 1983, 84—; case worker Ill. Dept. Pub. Aid, 1984; cons. in field. Active fund drive Carlinville (Ill.) Area Hosp., 1979, Blackburn Coll Phone-a-thon, Carlinville, 1979, 81, 82, 83, 86; reader St. Mary's Cath. Ch., Carlinville, 1985. Named one of Outstanding Young Men Am., Montgomery, 1985. Home: 327 S Broad Carlinville IL 62626 Office: Macoupin County Probation Office 203 S East Carlinville IL 62626

AMBROSIUS, G. RICHARD, marketing company executive; b. Huron, S.D., Apr. 25, 1946; s. George Norman and Lillian Fern (McGaughey) A.; children: Jennifer Joanne, Matthew Logan; m. Karen Anne Derr, Sept. 8, 1984. BA, U. S.D., 1968, MA, 1975. Asst. city mgr. City of Vermillion, S.D., 1973-74; ct. service officer Woodbury County, Sioux City, Iowa, 1974-75; security supr. Iowa Beef Processor, South Sioux City, Nebr., 1975-76; exec. dir. Iowa Lakes Area Agy. on Aging, Spencer, Iowa, 1976-83; owner, pres. Phoenix Systems, Inc., Sioux Falls, S.D., 1983—. Author: Marketing Is Not A Four Letter Word, 1983. Mem. mktg. com. United Way; bd. dirs. Girls Club. U.S. Adminstrn. on Aging grantee, 1982, 84-86. Mem. Nat. Speakers Assn., Am. Soc. Aging, Mid-Am. Congress on Aging, Am. Soc. Tng. and Devel., Sioux Falls C. of C. Republican. Methodist. Lodge: Rotary Internat. Home: 1901 S Main Ave Sioux Falls SD 57105 Office: Phoenix Systems Inc 601 S Minnesota Ave Suite L102 Sioux Falls SD 57104

AMBROZIAK, SHIRLEY ANN, communication specialist; b. Saginaw, Mich., July 8, 1953; d. John Joseph and Stella Mary (Wasik) A.; B.A. with honors, Mich. State U., 1975; M.A. (grantee), Purdue U., 1977. Speech instr. Purdue U., West Lafayette, Ind., 1975-77, Hammond, Ind., 1977-78; journalism instr. West Side High Sch., Gary, Ind., 1977-78; dir. communications Northwestern U. Transp. Center, Evanston, Ill., 1978, asst. dir., 1978-83; account exec. Arthur Andersen & Co., St. Charles, Ill., 1983-85, mktg. officer, The Old Second Nat. Bank, Aurora, Ill., 1985—; speech instr. Northeastern Ill. U., 1979-80. Bd. dirs. Cook County Am. Cancer Soc., 1977-79; chmn. Gov.'s Commn. on Higher Edn. Student Adv. Com., East Lansing, Mich., 1973-75. Mem. Women's Transp. Assn. (chmn. seminar and Chgo. program 1980-81). Internat. Assn. Bus. Communications, Women in Communications (co-chmn. job placement 1980-82), Transp. Research Forum, Speech Communication Assn. Am., Purdue Alumni Assn. Author: Organizational Communication, 1974; Human Communications, 1975; (with L. Stewart) The Relationship Between Adherence to Traditional Sex Roles and Communication Apprehension, 1976; (with Leon N. Moses) Corporate Planning under Deregulation: The Case of the Airline, 1980; (with Robert P. Neuschel) Managing Effectively under Deregulation, 1981; contbr. articles to profl. jours. and newspapers. Home: 107-C N 15th St Saint Charles IL 60174 Office: 37 S River St Aurora IL 60507

AMDAHL, DOUGLAS KENNETH, justice Supreme Court; b. Mabel, Minn., Jan. 23, 1919. B.B.A., U. Minn., 1945; J.D. summa cum laude, William Mitchell Coll. Law, 1951. Bar: Minn. 1951, Fed. Dist. Ct. 1952. Ptnr. Amdahl & Scott, Mpls., 1951-55; asst. county atty. Hennepin County, Minn., 1955-61; judge Mcpl. Ct., Mpls., 1961-62, Dist. Ct. 4th Dist., Minn., 1962-80; chief judge Dist. Ct. 4th Dist., 1973-75; assoc. justice Minn. Supreme Ct., 1980-81, chief justice, 1981—; asst. registrar, then registrar Mpls. Coll. Law, 1948-55; prof. law William Mitchell Coll. Law, 1951-65; moot ct. instr. U. Minn.; faculty mem. and advisor Nat. Coll. State Judiciary; mem. Nat. Bd. Trial Advocacy. Mem. ABA, Minn., Hennepin County bar assns., Internat. Acad. Trial Judges, State Dist. Ct. Judges Assn. (pres. 1976-77). Home: 2322 W 53d St Minneapolis MN 55155 Office: Minn Supreme Ct 230 State Capitol Saint Paul MN 55155

AMENDT, ROXANNE SUE BEALE, utilities executive; b. Waterloo, Iowa, Jan. 5, 1955; d. Marion Evelyn (Minish) Beale; 1 child, Marcy Ann. BS, Iowa State U., 1978. Dist. mgr. Ralston Purina Co., St. Louis, 1979-83; dir. customer relations and communications Iowa So. Utilities Co., Centerville, 1983—. Named Outstanding Young Woman of Am., 1978. Mem. Mo. Valley Electric Assn. (pub. relations com., 1986—), Iowa Utility Assn. (chmn. pub. info. com. 1986), Am. Hereford Aux. (nat. sec. 1984-85, nat. v.p. 1985), Iowa Jr. Hereford Assn. (advisor 1981-84, Outstanding Nat. Advisor of the Yr. 1985), Iowa Cattlemen's Assn. (beef team speaker, 1982-85), Iowa State Alumni Assn. (bd. dirs. 1983—, pres.-elect 1987), Mortar Bd., Sister of Farmhouse, Alpha Zeta, Alpha Xi Delta. Republican. Methodist. Avocations: sewing, cooking, showing cattle. Home: Rural Rt 1 Cincinnati IA 52549 Office: Iowa Southern Utilities Co 300 Sheridan Ave Centerville IA 52544

AMENT, RICHARD RAND, psychologist; b. Merrill, Wis., Aug. 5, 1950; s. Jacob John and Edith Jean (Selner) A.; m. Mary Elizabeth Beau, Aug. 5, 1978; children: Adrianne Beth, Jacob John III. BS, U. Wis., Eau Claire, 1972; MSEd, U. Wis., Stout of Menominee, 1974. Sch. psychologist Wausau (Wis.) Sch. Dist., 1974—. Campaign mgr. Kasten for Assembly, Wausau, 1982; treas. Marathon County Reps., Wausau, 1977-86; v.p. personnel, bd. dirs. Montessori Presch., Inc., Wausau, 1986, pres. bd. dirs., 1987—. Mem. Wis. Sch. Psychologists Assn. (mem. exec. bd. 1983-85), Sch. Psychologists of Wis.'s North (v.p. 1976-77, 81-82, pres. 1983-85). Republican. Lutheran. Avocations: golf, fishing. Home: 3722 Troy St Wausau WI 54401 Office: Wausau Pub Schs 1018 S 12th Ave Wausau WI 54401

AMES, BRUCE CHARLES, machinery company executive; b. Elgin, Ill., June 27, 1925; s. Daniel Franklin and Ruth Maude (Wright) A.; m. Joyce Grace Eichhorn, Sept. 9, 1950; children: Paula, Richard, Cynthia. Ph.B., Ill. Wesleyan U., 1950; M.B.A., Harvard U., 1954. Service engr. Ill. Bell Telephone Co., 1950-52; gen. comml. mgr. Gen. Telephone Co. N.Y., 1954-56; dir. mktg. Cin. Telephone Co., 1956-57; dir. McKinsey & Co., 1957-71; pres. Reliance Electric Co., Cleve., 1971-80; pres. Acme-Cleve. Corp., Cleve., 1981-83, chief exec. officer, 1981—, chmn., 1983—; dir. Diamond Shamrock Corp., Warner-Lambert Co., M.A. Hanna Mining Co., Harris Graphics Corp., Progressive Corp., Cleve. Center for Econ. Edn. Author articles. Served with U.S. Army, 1943-46. Office: Acme-Cleve Corp 30195 Chagrin Blvd Cleveland OH 44124 *

AMES, CLINTON G., JR., manufacturing company executive; b. Norfolk, Va., 1922; married. B.S., Va. Poly Inst., 1946. With Calvert Distilling Co., 1946-47; plant project engr. Eli Lilly & Co., 1948-51; staff engr. Merck & Co., 1951-54; mgr. tech. services Scott Paper Co., 1954-63; v.p. engring. Rice Barton Corp., 1963-68; asst. to gen. mgr. Continental Can Co., 1968; gen. mgr. ops. and engring. Inland Container Corp., Indpls., 1968-70, v.p. container bd. div., 1970-71, sr. v.p. ops., 1971-72, exec. v.p. ops., 1972-77, pres., 1977—, chief exec. officer, 1979—, dir. Served with 1st lt. USAAF, 1942-45. Office: Inland Container Corp 151 N Delaware St Indianapolis IN 46206 *

AMES, EDWARD RUSSELL, veterinary education administrator, veterinary parasitologist; b. Denver, Apr. 10, 1935; s. Edward Russell Ames and June Virginia (Nixon) Ames Heckendorf; m. Janice Elaine Painter, June 9, 1957; children: Denise Virginia, Marjorie Sue, Susan Deanne. BS, Colo. A&M Coll., 1957, DVM, 1959; PhD, Colo. State U., 1968. Pvt. practice vet. medicine Littleton, Colo., 1959; research veterinarian Merck & Co., Rahway, N.J. and Ft. Collins., Colo., 1960-65; post doctoral resident Colo. State U., Ft. Collins, 1965-68; assoc. prof. U. Mo., Columbia, 1968-73; dir. div. sci. Am. Vet. Medicine Assn., Schaumburg, Ill., 1973—; cons. Merck & Co., Inc., Rahway, 1971-73; staff coordinator Vet. Coll. Accreditation Program, 1986—. Contbg. author Merck Veterinary Manual, 4th ed., 1973; editor and author Continuing Edn. News, 1975-86; editor Am. Vet. Medicine Assn. Panel Reports, 1978-86; contbr. over 25 articles on vet. parasitology to profl. jours. Ruling elder Christian Ch., Oak Park, Ill., 1982—. Mem. Am. Vet. Med. Assn., Ill. Vet. Med. Assn., Health Scis. Communication Assn. (bd. dirs. 1972—), Phi Kappa Phi. Republican. Avocations: distance running, skiing, tennis, golf, vol. Heifer Project Internat. Home: 600 N Taylor Oak Park IL 60302 Office: Am Vet Med Assn 930 N Keacham Rd Schaumburg IL 60196

AMES, JANE IRENE, higher education administrator; b. Lafayette, Ind., Aug. 27, 1950; s. John James and Adena Irene (Booker) Wilkerson; divorced; 1 child, Brian Dale. BS in Acctg., St. Joseph's Coll., Rensselaer, Ind., 1973; postgrad. in bus. adminstrn., Ind. U., 1976-82, Northwestern U., Chgo., 1980-82. CPA. Intern Ernst & Ernst, Ft. Wayne, Indiana, 1972-73; staff acct. Coopers and Lybrand, Indpls., 1973-74; fin. analyst Westinghouse Electric Corp., Bloomington, Ind., 1974-78; mgr. fin. ops. G.D. Searle & Co., Skokie, Ill., 1979-84; dir. bus. affairs U. Ill., Chgo., 1984—, affirmative action officer, 1984-86; treas., bd. dirs. Ind. Credit Union League, Bloomington, 1976-78. Youth dir. Bethany Chapel Christian Ch., Fowler, Ind., 1968. Recipient Cert. Appreciation Outstanding Young Women of Am., 1985. Mem. Am. Inst. CPA's, Chgo. Council Fgn. Affairs. Republican. Home: 617 Dalton Pl Northbrook IL 60062

AMICE, CAROL RIZZARDI, marketing and merchandising manager, public relations copywriter; b. Chambersburg, Pa., Aug. 11, 1955; d. Carl J. and Angela A. (Zagrosky) Rizzardi; m. Thierry Thymen Amice, June 12, 1980. Student U. Ill.-Chgo., 1983, U. Md., Munich, 1979-80; B.S.J., Northwestern U., 1978, student Simpson Coll., 1987—. Staff reporter Dayton (Ohio) Jour.-Herald, 1977, Pottsville (Pa.) Republican, 1976; asst. personnel and logistics U. Md., 1979-80; copy editor Stars and Stripes, Griesheim, W.Ger., 1980; asst. advt. mgr., pub. relations specialist Chas. Levy Circulating Co., Chgo., 1981-83; copywriter, mktg. and merchandising mgr. Better Homes and Gardens mag., Des Moines, 1983—; instr. part-time Drake U., 1987—; copy editor Comparative Law Yearbook, 1978; contbr. article to Women's mag. Recipient Internat. Relations award Holzkirchen Internat. Volkssport Festival, Ministry of Fgn. Affairs, Fed. Republic Germany, 1985. Vol. internat. exchange program Youth for Understanding. Mem. Women in Communications (v.p. membership/communications chpt. 1984-85, pres. 1986, mem. nat. First Amendment com. 1986-87, regional meeting planning com. 1988, Cora award 1987), Advt. Profls. Des Moines (Gridiron producer 1985, sec.-treas. 1986-87), ACLU, Iowa Civil Liberties Union, greater Des Moines Volkssport Assn. (founder 1984, pres. 1985-86), Am. Volkssport Assn. (pub. relations and spl. events com. 1986), Amnesty Internat., Democrat. Home: 9009 Maplecrest Dr Norwalk IA 50211 Office: Better Homes and Gardens Advt 17th and Locust Sts Des Moines IA 50336

AMICK, SHIRLEY MARILYN, marketing services executive; b. Armour, S.D., Dec. 4, 1925; d. Robert and Bertha Breen; student pub. schs. Eastern and Madison, S.D.; children—Sally, Matthew, James, Terry, Darlene. Supr. credit card acquisitions A.J. Wood Corp., Milw., 1968—. Mem. Internat. Traders Guild, Internat. Entrepreneurs Assn., Consumer Credit Assn. Jehovah's Witness. Home: 2927 S Logan Ave Milwaukee WI 53207 Office: A J Wood Corp 405 E Lincoln Ave Milwaukee WI 53207

AMIDON, BLAINE FRANKLIN, physician; b. Lafayette, N.Y., Sept. 9, 1917; s. Blaine F. and Cora Floy (Morningstar) A.; m. Virginia Mae Neff, Aug. 6, 1943; children: Diana, Sheryl, Cathy, Blaine. BA, Syracuse U., 1938, MD, 1942. Diplomate Am. Bd. Ob-Gyn. Intern Welfare Island City Hosp., N.Y.C., 1942-43, asst. resident in pathology, 1947, asst. resident in ob-gyn, 1948, resident in ob-gyn, 1948-49; resident in ob-gyn Lakewood (Ohio) Hosp., 1949-50; ptnr. Dakota Clinic Ltd., Fargo, N.D., 1950—. Served with U.S. Army, 1943-45, ETO. Fellow Am. Coll. Ob-Gyn; mem. AMA, Am. Soc. Colposcopy, Gynecol. Laser Soc. Office: Dakota Clinic Ltd 1702 S University Dr Fargo ND 58103

AMIDON, PAUL CHARLES, pub. co. exec.; b. St. Paul, July 23, 1932; s. Paul Samuel and Eleanor Ruth (Simons) A.; B.A., U. Minn., 1954; m. Patricia Jean Winjum, May 7, 1960; children—Karen, Michael, Susan. Bus. mgr. Paul S. Amidon & Assos., Inc., St. Paul, 1956-66, pres., 1966—. Served with AUS, 1954-56. Home: 1582 Hillcrest Ave Saint Paul MN 55116 Office: 1966 Benson Ave Saint Paul MN 55116

AMIDON, WILLIAM DOUGLAS, retail executive; b. Ashtabula, Ohio, Mar. 23, 1954; s. Douglas B. and Velma J. Amidon; student Kent State U., 1973; B.B.A., U. Toledo, 1976; m. Nancy Ann Kingston, Aug. 26, 1978. With Ashtabula Office Equipment Inc., 1970—, salesman, 1977-78, v.p.,

1978—. Mem. Am. Fedn. Musicians. Club: Exchange (past pres.). Home: 3231 Plymouth Ridge Rd Ashtabula OH 44004 Office: 5402 Main Ave Ashtabula OH 44004

AMIRIKIA, HASSAN, obstetrician-gynecologist; b. Tehran, Iran, Dec. 10, 1937; came to U.S., 1966; d. Ahmad and Showkat (Asgari) Cheftsaz; m. Mino Vassigh Amirikia, Apr. 4, 1964; children: Arezo, Omid. MD, Tehran U., 1964. Cert. Am. Bd. Ob-Gyn. Intern Cook County Hosp., Chgo., 1966-67; resident Wayne State U., Detroit, 1967-71, fellow, 1971-72; practice medicine specializing in infertility Detroit, 1972—; asst. prof. Wayne State U., Detroit, 1972—; dir. infertility Oakwood Hosp., Dearborn, Mich., 1979—; researcher effects of androgens on the ovary. Contbr. articles to profl. jours. Fellow ACS, Am. Coll. Ob-Gyn (Mich. sect.), Royal Coll. Physicians and Surgeons. Home: 5384 Provincial Dr Bloomfield Hills MI 48013 Office: 4727 Saint Antoine Blvd Detroit MI 48201

AMIRJAHED, ABDOLREZA KASRA, pharmacist, educator; b. Tehran, Iran, Dec. 15, 1940; s. Mohammad Ali and Khadijeh Kutchak (Bananshahi) A.; came to U.S., 1958; B.S., Am. U. Beirut, 1965; M.S., U. Ill. at Med. Center, Chgo., 1969, Ph.D., 1972. Instr. pharmacy U. Ill. at Med. Center, Chgo., 1969-72, resident in pharmacy research and devel. hosp., 1972; asst. prof. pharmacy U. Toledo, 1972-77, assoc. prof., 1977—. Am. Field Service scholar, 1958-59, AID scholar, 1960-65. Mem. Am. Pharm. Assn., Am. Assn. Colls. Pharmacy, Acad. Pharm. Scis., Internat. Transactional Analysis Assn., Sigma Xi, Phi Kappa Phi, Rho Chi. Office: U Toledo Coll Pharmacy 2801 W Bancroft Ave Toledo OH 43606

AMIS, ROBERT WALTER, equipment leasing executive, consultant; b. Canton, Ohio, Feb. 24, 1923; s. Everett Lynes and Mary (Orme) A.; m. Lucille Hamer, Oct. 20, 1949; children—Robert Walter, Allan W. B.A. Southwestern U. (now Rhodes Coll.), 1948. Asst. dir. Nat. Cotton Council, Memphis, 1948-54; v.p. Advance Machine Co., Spring Pk., Minn., 1954-78; pres. World Floor Machine Co., Mpls., 1966-74; mng. dir. Advance Internat., Luxembourg, 1977-78; sr. v.p. Advance Machine Co., Plymouth, Minn., 1978—; pres. Advance Acceptance Corp., Plymouth, 1973—; dir. Advance Machine Co., 1957-74, Dyersburg (Tenn.) Fabrics, Inc., 1967—, First Bank of the Lakes, Navarre, Minn., 1970—. Elder Presbyn. Ch., Memphis and Edina, Minn., 1960—. Served to lt. (j.g.) USN, 1943-46; PTO. Mem. Southwestern Alumni Assn. (pres. 1950). Republican. Presbyterian. Clubs: Minikahda (Mpls.); Mill Reef (Antigua, W.I.). Home: 358 Ferndale Rd S Wayzata MN 55391 Office: Advance Acceptance Corp 14576 21st Ave N Plymouth MN 55441-3443

AMLADI, PRASAD GANESH, management consulting executive, health care consultant, researcher; b. Mudhol, India, Sept. 12, 1941; came to U.S., 1967, naturalized, 1968; s. Ganesh L. and Sundari G. Amladi; m. Chitra G. Panje, Dec. 20, 1970; children—Amita, Amol. B.Tech. with honors, Indian Inst. Tech., Bombay, 1963; M.S., Stanford U., 1968; M.B.A. with high distinction U. Mich., 1975. Sr. research engr. Ford Motor Co., Dearborn, Mich., 1968-75; mgr. strategic planning Mich. Consol. Gas Co., Detroit, 1975-78; mgr. planning services The Resources Group, Bloomfield Hills, Mich., 1978-80; project mgr., sr. cons. Mediflex Systems Corp., Bloomfield Hills, 1980-85; mgr. strategic planning services Mersco Corp., Bloomfield Hills, 1985-86, mgr. corp. planning and research Diversified Techs., Inc., New Hudson, Mich., 1986—. Author numerous research papers. Recipient Kodama Meml. Gold medal, 1957; India Merit scholar, 1959-63, K.C. Mahindra scholar, 1967, R.D. Sethna Grad. scholar, 1968. Mem. Inst. Indsl. Engrs. (sr.), N.Am. Soc. Corp. Planning, Economic Club Detroit, Beta Gamma Sigma. Office: 53200 Grand River New Hudson MI 48165

AMMAR, RAYMOND GEORGE, physicist, educator; b. Kingston, Jamaica, July 15, 1932; came to U.S., 1961, naturalized, 1965; s. Elias George and Nellie (Khaleel) A.; m. Carroll Ikerd, June 17, 1961; children—Elizabeth, Robert, David. A.B., Harvard U., 1953; PhD., U. Chgo., 1959. Research assoc. Enrico Fermi Inst., U. Chgo., 1959-60; asst. prof. physics Northwestern U., Evanston, Ill., 1960-64; assoc. prof. Northwestern U., 1964-69; prof. physics U. Kans., Lawrence, 1969—; (on sabbatical leave Fermilab and Deutsches Elektronen Synchrotron, 1984-85); cons. Argonne (Ill.) Nat. Lab., 1965-69, vis. scientist, 1971-72; vis. scientist Fermilab, Batavia, Ill., summers 1976-81, Deutsches Elektronen Synchrotron, Hamburg, Fed. Republic Germany, summers 1982-86; project dir. NSF grant for research in high energy physics, 1962—. Contbr. articles to sci. jours. Fellow Am. Phys. Soc.; mem. AAUP. Home: 1651 Hillcrest Rd Lawrence KS 66044 Office: U Kans Dept Physics Lawrence KS 66045

AMMER, WILLIAM, common pleas judge; b. Circleville, Ohio, May 21, 1919; s. Moses S. and Mary (Schallas) A.; B.S. in Bus. Adminstrn., Ohio State U., 1941, J.D., 1946. Admitted to Ohio bar, 1947; atty., examiner Ohio Indsl. Commn. Columbus, 1947-51; asst. atty. gen. State of Ohio, Columbus, 1951-52; practiced in Circleville, 1953-57, pros. atty. Pickaway County, Circleville, 1953-57, common pleas judge, 1957—; asst. city solicitor Circleville, 1955-57. Past pres. Pickaway County ARC, Am. Cancer Soc. Served with inf., AUS, 1942-46. Mem. Am., Ohio (chmn. criminal law com. 1964-67), Pickaway County (pres. 1955-56) bar assns., Ohio Common Pleas Judges Assn. (pres. 1968). Methodist. Mason (K.T., Shriner), Kiwanian (Ohio dist. chmn., past lt. gov.). Home: 141 Pleasant St Circleville OH 43113 Office: Courthouse PO Box 87 Circleville OH 43113

AMMERMAN, JAY NEIL, bar association technology executive; b. Richmond, Ind., Aug. 21, 1945; s. Francis Andrew and Pollyanna (Kitchel) A.; B.S. in Mathematics, U. Chgo., 1967, M.B.A. in Fin., 1977; M.S. in Mathematics (NSF fellow), Northwestern U., 1968; m. Paula Jean Lorig, Dec. 19, 1969; 1 son, Jason Lorig. Sr. programmer Vapor Corp., Chgo., 1969, systems analyst, 1970, sr. systems analyst, 1970-72, asst. mgr. systems and programming, 1972-75; mgr. systems and programming Am. Bar Assn., Chgo., 1975-77, asst. dir. data processing, 1977-81, dir. data processing, 1981-87, dir. tech. services group, 1987—. Mem. supervisory com. Hyde Park Co-op Credit Union; sec. 5227 S. Blackstone Corp.; treas. The Manor Condominium Assn. Mem. GUIDE, (assn. for large scale IBM computer users), Sigma Xi, Beta Gamma Sigma. Home: 5222 S Blackstone Ave Chicago IL 60615 Office: 750 N Lake Shore Dr Chicago IL 60611

AMMONS, EDSEL ALBERT, bishop; b. Chgo., Feb. 17, 1924; s. Albert Clifton and Lila Kay (Sherrod) A.; m. June Billingsley, Aug. 18, 1951; children—Marilyn, Edsel, Carol, Kenneth, Carlton, Lila. B.A., Roosevelt U., 1948; B.D., Garrett Theol. Sem., 1956; D.Min., Chgo. Theol. Sem., 1975; D.D. (hon.), Westmar Coll., 1975. Social case worker Dept. Welfare Cook County, Chgo., 1951-56; ordained to ministry Meth. Ch., 1949; pastor Whitfield Meth. Ch., Chgo., 1957-60, Ingleside-Whitfield Meth. Ch., Chgo., 1960-63; dist. dir. urban work Rockford dist. No. Ill. Conf. United Meth. Ch., 1963-66; council staff ann. conf. No. Ill. Conf., 1966-68; urban ch. cons., prof. ch. and soc., dir. basic degree studies Garrett Evang. Theol. Sem., Evanston, Ill., 1968-76; bishop United Meth. Ch., Mich. area, 1976-84; bishop United Meth. Ch., West Ohio area 1984—; exec. dir. Ednl. and Cultural Inst. Black Clergy, Chgo., 1972-73. Vice pres. Chatham-Avalon Community Council, Chgo., 1958-61; pres. W. Avalon Community Council, 1959-60. Served with U.S. Army, 1943-46. Mem. Alpha Phi Alpha. Office: United Meth Ch 471 Broad St Suite 1106 Columbus OH 43215

AMOS, EUNICE CARRIE, home economist, educator; b. Atwater, Minn., Jan. 20, 1936; d. Arnold and Irene (Martine) Paulson; B.S., U. Minn., 1958; M.S., Mankato State U., 1982; m. Marlin Amos, July 19, 1959; 1 son, Paul. Instr. home econs. Lake Crystal (Minn.) Pub. Schs., 1958-64, dept. head adult evening sch., 1958-64; free-lance work with home econs. occupations and edn., 1964-67; tchr. and supr. home health aides Nicollet County (Minn.) Pub. Health Nursing Service, 1967-68; tchr. and coordinator home econs. Mankato (Minn.) Area Vocat. Tech. Inst., North Mankato, 1968-75; instr. home econs., dept. lead tchr. St. Peter (Minn.) Pub. Schs., 1975—, instr. adult tailoring, tutor teenage program for pregnant girls, 1975—, mem. supt.'s adv. council, 1976-78; guest instr. Minn. State Dept. Edn., 1970, 71; mem. Minn. Dept. Vocat. Edn. Evaluation and North Central Assn. Schs. and Colls. teams, 1979-81. Judge, 4-H County Fairs, Minn., 1965-67; sec. exec. bd. St. Peter Play Group for Children, 1967-69; active Cub Scouts, Boy Scouts Am., 1969-70; bd. dirs. Citizens Scholarship Found., Community Edn. Adv. Council St. Peter-Kasota Area, Minn., 1977-80. Mem. NEA, Minn. Edn. Assn., St. Peter Edn. Assn., Am. Home Econs. Assn., Minn. Home Econs. Assn., Am. Vocat. Assn., Minn. Vocat. Assn., Minn. Home Economists in Edn., Minn., Lake Crystal High Sch., St. Peter High Sch. assns. future homemakers Am. (hon. mem.), Gustavus Adolphus Coll. Library Assos., Phi Upsilon Omicron, Delta Kappa Gamma, Phi Kappa Phi. Lutheran. Club: Order Eastern Star (St. Peter, Minn.). Contbr. articles on home econs. to profl. publs. Home: 323 S 7th St Saint Peter MN 56082 Office: Lincoln Dr Saint Peter MN 56082

AMPEL, LEON LOUIS, anesthesiologist; b. Kansas City, Mo., Oct. 29, 1936; s. Joseph and Eva (Resnick) A.; m. Jane Lee Isador, June 21, 1959; children—Jill, Ross, Jackie. B.A. in Chemistry, U. Mo., 1958, M.D., 1962. Diplomate Am. Bd. Anesthesiology. Intern Evanston Hosp., Ill., 1962-63, resident in anesthesiology, 1965-67, attending anesthesiology, 1967-74, sr. attending anesthesiologist, 1974—; head dept. anesthesiology Glenbrook Hosp., Glenview, Ill., 1977—; asst. prof. clin. anesthesiology Northwestern U. Contbr. articles to publs. Active Northbrook Sch. Caucus, Ill., 1975-76. Served to lt. M.C., USN, 1963-65. Fellow Am. Coll. Anesthesiologists; mem. AMA, Ill. Med. Assn., Am. Coll. Legal Medicine, Chgo. Med. Assn., N. Surburban Med. Soc. (pres. 1974), Am. Soc. Anesthesiology, Ill. Soc. Anesthesiology, Chgo. Soc. Anesthesiology. Clubs: Old Willow, U.S. Lawn Tennis Assn., Chgo. Dist. Tennis Assn. (v.p., bd. dirs. 1976—). Home: 2701 Oak St Northbrook IL 60062 Office: 2100 Pfingsten St Glenview IL 60025

AMROMIN, GEORGE DAVID, pathologist, educator; b. Gomel, USSR, Feb. 27, 1919; came to U.S., 1923, naturalized, 1929; s. David Rachmiel and Fannie (Simonoff) Amromin; m. Elaine Barbara Sabath, June 13, 1942; children—Joel, Richard, Barbara, Steven, James. B.S., Northwestern U., 1940, M.D., 1943. Diplomate Am. Bd. Pathology. Intern Michael Reese Hosp., Chgo., 1943, resident in pathology, 1946-48, asst. pathologist, 1949, asst. dir., assoc. pathologist, 1954-56; rotating gen. resident Edgewater Hosp., Chgo., 1944; practice medicine specializing in pathology, Tulare, Calif., 1950-54; clin. instr. U. Ill. Med. Sch., Chgo., 1954-56; chmn. dept. pathology City of Hope Nat. Med. Ctr., Duarte, Calif., 1956-71, chmn. dept. neuropathology and research pathology, 1971-76, mem. hon. staff, cons. neuropathologist, 1976-77, pathologist emeritus, 1976—; asst. prof. pathology Loma Linda U., Calif., 1958-70, clin. prof., 1970-77; prof. pathology U. Mo., Columbia, 1977-84, emeritus, 1984—. Author: The Pathology of Leukemia, 1968. Contbr. articles to profl. jours., chpts. to books. Pathologist, Project Hope, Ecuador, South Am., 1963, 64. Neuropathology research fellow Nat. Inst. Neurologic Diseases and Blindness, Belleview Hosp., N.Y.C., 1968. Fellow ACS, Coll. Am. Pathologists (emeritus), Am. Soc. Clin. Pathologists (emeritus); mem. Boone County Med. Soc., Mo. State Med. Soc., AMA, Am. Assn. Neuropathologists, Sigma Xi, Alpha Omega Alpha. Jewish. Avocation: painting. Home: 104 Defoe Ct Columbia MO 65203

AMSBERRY, KENT EUGENE, small business owner, educational scholarship consultant; b. Des Moines, Sept. 9, 1948; s. Kenneth Elsworth and Fern (Risinger) A.; m. Susan Lee, July 5, 1970. AA, Waldorf Jr. Coll., Forest City, Iowa, 1968; student, Simpson Coll., Indianola, Iowa, 1968-76. Owner The Jewelry Ctr., Indianola, 1976-80; mgr. Clover Jewelers, Las Vegas, Nev., 1980-84; broker J&D Appraisal and Realty, Indianola, 1984—; owner Barrett & Amsberry Jewelers, Indianola, 1984—, Barrett & Amsberry Ednl. Services, Indianola, 1986—, Barrett & Amsberry Real Estate Appraisal, Indianola, 1987—. Bd. dirs. Carousel Theatre, Indianola, 1984—. Mem. Iowa Retail Jewelers Assn., Warren County Bd. Realtors (ethics com.). Republican. Lutheran. Lodges: Lions, Masons. Avocations: golf, boating, hunting, trap shooting. Office: PO Box 474 Indianola IA 50125

AMSTER, CARYN MERIS, marketing professional; b. Warren, Ohio, Mar. 2, 1941; d. Emanuel and Belle (Rosen Hyman) Lazar; m. Ronald Harr, July, 1961 (div.); children: Kimberlee, Ian; m. William Amster, Oct. 17, 1982. Cert. in med. tech., Am. Acad. Med. Tech., 1959-60; student, S.E. Jr. Coll., Chgo., 1960-64, Northwestern U., 1965-66. Lic. real estate salesman, Ill. With pediatric research Michael Reese Hosp., Chgo., 1960-62; with bacteriological research Rush Presbyn.-St. Luke's Hosp., Chgo., 1962-63; dir. pub. relations and fund raising Happiday Ctrs., Chicago Heights, Ill., 1976-78; mgr., mktg. dir. shopping ctr. Jacobs Kahn, Chgo., 1978-79, Fifield Palmer, Park Forest, Ill., 1979-82; mktg. specialist Mt. Sinai Hosp., Chgo., 1982-83; mgr., mktg. dir. shopping ctr. The Tucker Cos., Northbrook, Ill., 1983—; corp. mktg. dir. Tucker Co., Northbrook, Ill. Mem. bd. Elk Grove Village (Ill.) United Way, 1986-87. Mem. Internat. Council Shopping Ctrs. (cert.), NW Suburban Assn. Commerce and Industry, Chgo. Area Mktg. Dirs. (lectr. 1980—). Jewish. Avocation: racquetball. Home: 1564 Columbia Ct Elk Grove Village IL 60007 Office: The Tucker Cos 40 Skokie Blvd Northbrook IL 60007

AMUNDSON, DUANE MELVIN, gas company executive; b. Niagara, Wis., Apr. 3, 1925; s. Melvin Oscar and Thalia (McSweeny) A.; m. Marian Force, Nov. 21, 1948; children: Melvin, Robert, Jeffrey, Kimberly. B.S. in Civil Engring., Purdue U., 1950. With Ind. Gas Co., Inc., Indpls., 1950—; v.p. ops. engring. Ind. Gas Co., Inc., 1963-74, sr. v.p. ops. engring., 1974-77, exec. v.p., 1977-80, pres. and chief exec. officer, 1980-84, chmn., chief exec. officer, 1984—; also dir.; chmn., chief exec. officer IGC Energy, Inc.; pres. Ohio River Pipeline Corp., 1980-84, chmn., chief exec. officer, 1984—; dir. En Trade Corp. Served with USNR, 1943-46, 51-52. Mem. Nat., Ind. socs. profl. engrs., Am., Ind. gas assns. Clubs: Masons, Lions, Elks. Home: 19720 Allisonville Ave Noblesville IN 46060 Office: Ind Gas Co Inc 1630 N Meridian St Indianapolis IN 46202

AMUNDSON, JAY PATRICK, architect; b. St. Paul, May 12, 1959; s. Leo James and Genavive P. (Rutherford) A.; m. Cynthia Ann Raymond, Sept. 22, 1984. Student, N.D. State U., BS, 1982, BArch, 1983. Intern KBM Inc., Grand Forks, N.D., 1983-84, Archtl. Coalition Inc., Mpls., 1985, Paul Pink & Assocs. Inc., Mpls., 1984-85, 85—. Mem. AIA, Nat. Trust for Hist. Preservation. Home: 2254 F Benson Ave Saint Paul MN 55116 Office: Paul Pink and Assocs Inc 425 Oak Grove St Minneapolis MN 55403

AMUNDSON, KEVIN ERIC, oral surgeon; b. New Ulm, Minn., Aug. 3, 1949; s. Alfred Arnold and Agnes Pearl (Finnberg) A.; m. Joy Marie Erickson, June 25, 1975; children: Erik Matthew, Kierin Joy. BA, Gustavus Adolphus Coll., 1971; DDS, U. Minn., 1975, MSD, 1979. Diplomate Am. Bd. Oral and Maxillofacial Surgery. Practice oral and maxillofacial Lowell Graves DDS, Stevens Point, Wis., 1979-80, Ogle and Amundson PA, Owatonna and Rochester, Minn., 1980—. Fellow Am. Assn. Oral and Maxillofacial Surgery; mem. ADA, Minn. Dental Assn. (v.p. southeastern dist. 1983-84, 86—). Republican. Lutheran. Avocations: golf, skiing, sailing. Home: 1414 Woodland Dr SW Rochester MN 55902 Office: Ogle & Amundson PA Atrium Profl Bldg 401 16th St SE Rochester MN 55904

ANAGNOSTOPOULOS, CONSTANTINE EMMANUEL, venture capitalist, former company executive; b. Athens, Greece, Nov. 1, 1922; came to U.S., 1946; s. Emmanuel Constantine A. and Helen (Michaelides) Kefalas; m. Maria Tsagarakis, July 10, 1949; 1 son, Paul Constantine. Sc.B. in Chemistry, Brown U., 1949; M.S. in Chemistry, Harvard U., 1950, Ph.D. in Chemistry, 1952; postgrad. in bus. adminstrn., Columbia U., 1964. Dir. research and devel. organic div. Monsanto Co., St. Louis, 1962-67, research scientist, 1952-61, bus. dir., 1967-71, gen. mgr. New Enterprise div., 1971-75, gen. mgr. rubber chem. div., 1975-80; v.p. mng. dir. Monsanto Europe-Africa, Brussels, 1980-82; corp. v.p., vice chmn. corp. devel. and growth com. Monsanto Co., St. Louis, 1982-85; cons. 1986-87; mng. gen. ptnr. Gateway Venture Ptnrs., L.P., St. Louis, 1987—; chmn. bd. Monsanto Europe S.A., Brussels, 1980-82, Kinetek Corp.; dir. Advent Capital Ltd., Invitron Corp., U.S.A., Advent Internat. Corp., Genzyme Corp., Aspect Systems, F.I.T. Corp.; mem. com. on patent system Nat. Acad. Engring., 1971; mem. nat. inventors council Dept. Commerce, 1964-72. Patentee in organic and polymer chemistry, 1953-67; contbr. articles to profl. jours. Bd. dirs. Am. C. of C., Brussels, 1981-82; mem. European Govt. Bus. Council, Strasbourg, France, 1981-82; pres. United Fund Belgium, 1982; mem. presdl. com. prizes for innovation, Washington, 1972, U.S.-USSR Trade and Econ. Council, 1980-82; chmn. bd. St. Louis Tech. Ctr. Served to capt. Brit. Army, 1944-46. Recipient chemistry prize Brown U., 1949, teaching award Harvard U., 1950, 51, 52, St. Louis Tech. award Regional Comml. and Growth Assn., 1987. Mem. Research Soc. Am., Indsl. Research Inst., Comml. Devel. Assn., Am. Chem. Soc., St. Louis Art Mus. Republican. Episcopalian. Club: Bellerive Country (St. Louis). Home: 13003 Starbuck Rd Saint Louis MO 63141 Office: Gateway Venture Ptnrs 8000 Maryland Ave Suite 1190 Saint Louis MO 63105

ANAND, YOGINDRA NATH, structural engineer; b. Peshawar, India, Dec. 5, 1939; came to U.S., 1967; s. Amar Nath and Prakash (Chaddah) A.; m. Helga Tieves, Jan. 9, 1971 (div. 1980); children: Lara, Martin; m. Pancharathna Anand, Sept. 25, 1980. MSCE, Wayne State U., 1968; D in Engring., U. Detroit, 1972. Registered profl. engr., Mich. Apprentice Stein, Chattertee and Polk, New Delhi, 1959-62; structural designer R. Reiser Co., New Delhi, 1962-65, Arthur G. McKee Co., Toronto, Ont., Can., 1965, Stelco, Hamilton, Ont., 1966; sr. project engr. Harley Ellington Co., Detroit, 1968-71; staff civil engr. Detroit Edison Co., 1972—. Editor: Seismic Experience Data, Nuclear and Other Plants, 1985, Structural Design Cementitions, Products and Case Histories, 1985. Mem. ASCE (pres. southeastern br. 1986—), Am. Soc. Engrs. from India (pres. 1984-85), Am. Concrete Inst., Engg Soc. of Detroit. Home: 308 Longford Dr Rochester Hills MI 48063 Office: Detroit Edison Co 2000 2d Ave Detroit MI 48226

ANANTHESWARAN, RAMASWAMY CHELAKARA, engineer, educator, researcher; b. Trichur, Kerala, India, Jan. 3, 1955; came to U.S., 1977; s. Chelakara R. and Eswari Anantheswaran. BS, Indian Inst. Tech., Kharagpur, India, 1977; MS, U. Ga., 1979; PhD, Cornell U., 1984. Research assoc. N.Y. State Agrl. Experiment Sta., Geneva, 1983-84, Pa. State U., University Park, 1984-85; asst. prof. engring. U. Nebr., Lincoln, 1985—. Contbr. articles to profl. jours. Mem. Am. Soc. Agrl. Engrs., Am. Inst. Chem. Engrs., Inst. Food Technologists, Sigma Xi, Phi Kappa Phi, Gamma Sigma Delta, Alpha Phi Omega, Tau Beta Pi, Phi Tau Sigma. Avocations: swimming, photography, hiking, listening to classical and jazz music. Office: U Nebr 134 Filley Hall Lincoln NE 68583-0919

ANAST, NICK JAMES, lawyer; b. Gary, Ind., Apr. 4, 1947; s. James Terry and Kiki (Pappas) A.; m. Linda K. Skirvin, Oct. 28, 1972; children: Jason, Nicole. AB, Ind. U., 1969, JD, 1972. Bar: Ind. 1972, U.S. Dist. Ct. (no. and so. dists.) Ind. 1972, U.S Ct. Appeals (7th cir.) 1975, U.S. Supreme Ct. 1976. Ptnr. Pappas, Tokarski & Anast, Gary, 1972-74; ptnr. Tokarski & Anast, Gary, 1974-85, Schererville, Ind., 1985—; dep. pros. atty. Lake County Prosecutors Office, Crown Point, Ind., 1973-74; pub. defender Lake County Superior Ct., Gary, 1974-78; atty. Town of Schererville, 1982, Lowell, 1983, City of Lake Station, Ind., 1978. Pres. St. John (Ind.) Twp. Young Dems., 1980. Recipient Service to Youth award YMCA, 1980, Outstanding Service award Schererville Soccer Club, 1985. Fellow Ind. Bar Found.; mem. ABA, Ind. Bar Assn., Lake County Bar Assn. (bd. dirs.) 1983-85, Outstanding Service award 1985). Democrat. Greek Orthodox. Lodge: Lions (pres. Schererville chpt. 1985-86). Avocations: gardening, wood crafts, assisting children. Office: Tokarski & Anast 7803 W 75th Ave Suite 1 Schererville IN 46375

ANASTOS, JOHN GEORGE, advertising executive; b. Chgo., Apr. 15, 1921; s. George J. and Sofia (Gnatek) A.; m. Adeline Glab, Mar. 3, 1923; children: George, Gregory, David, Maryann, William. BS in Commerce, De Paul U., 1940. V.p. J. Walter Thompson Co., Chgo., 1950-83; owner The Drummers, Chgo., 1983—. Chmn. Mundelein Police Pension Bd., 1978—, Boy Scouts Am., Mundelein, 1970-80; pres. Santa Maria Del Popolo Sch. Bd., Mundelein, 1974-76. Served to lt. USN, 1943-45. Mem. Internat. Food Service Mfg. Assn. (founder 1950), Am. Logistics Assn. (pres. Chgo. chpt. 1980-83), Am. Assn. Advt. Agys. Republican. Roman Catholic. Avocations: golf, swimming, fishing, reading. Home: 1149 Lomond Dr Mundelein IL 60060 Office: The Drummers 405 N Wabash Chgo IL 60611

ANCELL, ROBERT M., publisher; b. Phoenix, Oct. 16, 1942; s. Robert M. and Alice (Lovett) A.; m. Janet C. Neuber, Dec. 21, 1966 (div. 1984); children: Kevin, Kristin; m. Christine Marie Miller, Mar. 30, 1985. BA, U. N.Mex., 1971. Announcer KDEF Radio, Albuquerque, 1966-67; reporter KOB TV, Albuquerque, 1967-72; sr. sales representative Xerox Corp., Albuquerque, 1972-78; gen. sales mgr. Sta. KRDO-TV, Colorado Springs, Colo., 1978-79; publisher Titsch Pub., Denver, 1979-82; publ. dir. Denver Bus. Mag., 1982-83; advt. mgr. U.S. Naval Res. (recalled to active duty), New Orleans, 1984-85; publisher Endless Vacation Pubs., Indpls., 1985—; cons. Media Masters, Denver, 1983-84. Contbr. articles to mags., profl. jours., newspapers, 1960—. Served to lt. comdr. USNR, 1980. Recipient First Place award N.Mex. Broadcasters, 1970; First Place award UPI, 1970, Pres. Club award Xerox Corp., 1973, 75-76. Mem. Reserve Officers Assn. of U.S. (tng. officer 1980-81, Cert. of Appreciation 1981), U.S. Naval. Inst., Pub. Relations Soc. U.S., Air Force Assn., Manuscript Soc. Republican. Presbyterian. Avocations: private pilot, bicycling, bridge, writing, photography. Office: Endless Vacations Pubs One RCI Plaza Trace 3502 Woodview Trace Indianapolis IN 46268

ANDERKIN, MICHAEL SCOTT, government contract negotiator, analyst; b. Dayton, Ohio, Sept. 20, 1961; s. Renus Belvin and Geneva Lea (Harrison) A. BS, U. Dayton, 1982. Contract negotiator Wright-Patterson AFB, Dayton, Ohio, 1983—, chmn. copper-CHP adv. council aeronautical systems div., 1985, publicity chmn., 1986. Mem. Am. Assn. MBA's. Home: 715 Red Deer Ln Miamisburg OH 45342 Office: ASD/YPKSB Wright Patterson AFB Dayton OH 45433

ANDERL, STEPHEN, clergyman; b. Chippewa Falls, Wis., July 13, 1910; s. Henry A. and Katherine (Schneider) A.; B.A. magna cum laude St. John's U., 1932, M.Div., 1974; postgrad. Catholic U. Am., 1940; Ph.D., World U., 1982; D.D., Partasarathy Acad., Madras, India, 1984. Ordained priest Roman Catholic Ch., 1936; curate in Wisconsin Rapids, Wis., 1936-37; chaplain Villa St. Joseph, LaCrosse, Wis., 1942-49; pastor in Spring Valley, Wis., 1949-52, Hewitt, Wis., 1952-53, Assumption Parish, Durand, Wis., 1953-82; tchr., guidance counselor, vice prin. Aquinas High Sch., La Crosse, Wis., 1937-49. Censor books, clergy examiner, vicar gen. for religious Diocese of La Crosse, 1951-66; vicar forane Durand Deanery, 1953-82; mem. commn. on worship and sacraments 3d Diocesan Synod, 1955; spl. research cons. 4th Diocesan Synod, 1985-86; diocesan chaplain Boy Scouts Am., Girl Scouts U.S.A., 1936-49; diocesan dir. Young Christian Workers, 1940-50; chaplain XII World Jamboree Boy Scouts, 1967, Nat. Jamboree Boy Scouts Am., 1969, 73; Wis. state chaplain COF, 1986—; mem. Diocesan Clergy Personnel Bd., 1970-74; exec. sec. Cath. Youth Orgn., Diocese of La Crosse, 1938-49; diocesan dir. Sodality, 1938-49; cons. Central Commn. of Diocese of LaCrosse for Implementation of Vatican Council. Mem. exec. com. Chippewa Valley council Boy Scouts Am., mem. nat. Cath. com. on scouting, 1974—, vice chmn. diocesan Cath. com. on scouting; housing commr., La Crosse, 1948-49; mem. Gov.'s Com. on Children and Youth, 1957-63; adviser Wis. Youth Com., 1960—; mem. State Comprehensive Mental Health and Retardation Planning Com., Durand Community Council; dir. West Central Wis. Community Action Agy., OEO; bd. dirs. La Crosse Diocesan Bd. Edn., La Crosse Diocesan Cath. Social Agy., Inc., Silver Waters council Girl Scouts U.S.A.; founder, dir. West Central Wis. Community Action Agy. Created domestic prelate with title of right reverend msgr. by Pope John XXIII, 1962; recipient Silver Beaver award Boy Scouts Am., 1968; St. George award, 1969; St. Ann. award Girl Scouts U.S., 1980, citation West Cap, 1975. Mem. Wis. Geneol. Soc., Am. Acad. Religion, Wis. Acad. Arts, Sci. and Letters, Am. Numis. Soc., Collectors of Religion on Stamps, Christian Writers Assn. Lodge: K.C. (4th degree; chaplain Durand council 1953-82, John F. Kennedy council 1984—, faithful friar Pope John XXIII gen. assembly 1960-82, Bishop Sheen assembly 1984—). Author: Technique. of the Catholic Action Cell, 1942; Papal Teaching on Catholic Action, 1946; The Religious and Catholic Action, 1947; Catholic Action, a Responsibility of the School, 1948; Parish of the Assumption, Life and Times of the Mystical Christ in Durand, 1960. Contbr. articles to religious mags. and jours. Address: Ramsgate II Apt 309 2214 Peters Dr Eau Claire WI 54701

ANDERS, LESLIE, history educator; b. Admire, Kans., Jan. 22, 1922; s. Ray Leslie and Bertie Mae (Hasson) A.; A.B., Coll. Emporia, 1949; A.M. (Allen Cook White, Jr. fellow), U. Mo., 1950, Ph.D., 1954; m. Mardellya Mary Soles, Oct. 17, 1942; children—Geraldine (Mrs. Robert C. Hunt), Charlotte (Mrs. Alexander Wilson). Historian, Office of Chief of Engrs., Dept. Army, Balt., 1951-55; faculty history Central Mo. State U., Warrensburg, 1955—, prof., 1963—. Hon. commr. Mo. Am. Revolutionary Bicentennial Commn., 1974. Served with AUS, 1940-45. Recipient Merit award Am. Assn. for State and Local History, 1976, Disting. Service award State Hist. Soc. Mo., 1986. Mem. Am. Mil. Inst., Sons of Union Vets. of

Civil War, Scabbard and Blade, Phi Kappa Phi. Republican. Presbyn. Author: The Ledo Road, 1965; The Eighteenth Missouri, 1968; Education for Service, 1971; The Twenty-First Missouri, 1975; Gentle Knight, 1985. Home: 318 Goodrich Dr Warrensburg MO 64093

ANDERS, MICHEAL FRED, vocal music educator; b. Kountze, Tex., Nov. 20, 1954; s. Fred and Mae Bertie (Basar) A.; m. Denise Kay Reno, July 5, 1986. B.S. in Vocal Music Edn. with highest honors, Lamar U., Beaumont, Tex., 1976, M.M. in Music Lit. and Vocal Performance, 1979. Instr. music Port Arthur (Tex.) Ind. Sch. Dist., 1977; instr. choral and vocal music, music coordinator Silsbee (Tex.) Ind. Sch. Dist., 1977-81; minister of music Calvary Baptist Ch., Beaumont, 1981; prin. roles Beaumont Civic Opera, 1974-81; dir. choral activities, asst. prof. music Findlay (Ohio) Coll., 1981—; choir dir. First Christian Ch., Findlay, 1983—; vocal recitalist. Mem. Interfaith Choral Soc., 1977-81, v.p., 1980-81, bd. dirs., 1978-81; mem. Beaumont Jr. Forum LUV Follies, 1977-81, Silsbee Bicentennial Musical Prodn. Co., 1976, Heidelburg Summer Theatre, 1983. Lamar U. Summer Opera Workshop, 1974-82, others. Recipient Cert. of Recognition for disting. achievement by a graduating senior Lamar U., 1976. Mem. Tex. Music Educators Assn., Tex. Classroom Tchrs. Assn. Am. Choral Dirs. Assn., So. Bapt. Ch. Music Conf., Phi Eta Sigma, Phi Kappa Phi. Appeared in My Fair Lady, 1776, Funny Girl, Kismet, George M, Once Upon a Mattress, The Best Little Whorehouse in Texas, The Most Happy Fellow, Trial by Jury, Fiddler on the Roof, Gianni Schicchi, Cavalleria Rusticana, Madama Butterfly, Der Zigeunerbaron, La Traviata, La Fille du Regiment, Amahl and the Night Visitors; also solo appearances in maj. choral works; producer, mus. dir. No, No, Nanette, The Sound of Music, The King and I. Home: 421 E Lima St Findlay OH 45840 Office: Findlay Coll 1000 N Main St Findlay OH 45840

ANDERS, PAUL EUGENE, computer systems executive; b. Detroit, Nov. 11, 1943; s. Paul Eugene and Beulah Cecelia (Murray) A.; m. Judith Adele LaCroix, Sept. 16, 1965; children: Paul Eugene III, Patrick Nicholas. BS in Physics, U. Mich., 1965, BA in Econs., 1966; MBA in Mgmt., Wayne State U., 1970. Mgmt. trainee Jones & Laughlin, Detroit, 1966-67; sr. indsl. engr. Chrysler Corp., Detroit, 1967-70, mgr. parts systems, 1970-78, mgr. mfg. plant systems, 1978-80, mgr. end user computing, 1980-85, mgr. assembly and material systems, 1985—. Roman Catholic. Office: Chrysler Corp 6565 E 8 Mile Rd Warren MI 48091

ANDERSEN, A. L., chemical company execuitve; b. 1909. Student, Muskegon Community Coll.; BBA, U. Minn., 1931. Salesman E.H. Sheldon Co., 1928-34; gov. State of Minn., St. Paul, 1961-63; with H.B. Fuller Co., St. Paul, 1934—; sales mgr. 1937-41, pres., 1941-66, chmn. bd., pres., chief exec. officer, 1966-71, chmn. bd., chief exec. officer, 1971-74, chmn. bd., dir., 1974—. Office: H B Fuller Co 2400 Energy Park Dr Saint Paul MN 55108 *

ANDERSEN, DALE JAY, sales marketing executive; b. Omaha, Sept. 26, 1939; s. Ernest Jay and Helen Irene (Grabowski) A.; children: Travis Jay, Kye L. BA, U. Nebr., 1965. Sales mgr. wine div. Ed Phillips & Sons Importers & Distbr., Omaha, 1974-81; gen. mgr. Crown Services, Omaha, 1981-83; pres., co-owner INC. Services Inc., Omaha, 1983—; bd. dirs. U. Nebr. Coll. Arts & Scis. Alumni Bd., Lincoln, Nebr. Asst. scout master Boy Scouts Am., Omaha, 1980-83. Served as chief warrant officer USN, Vietnam, with Res. 1962—. Mem. Nebr. Assn. Temp. Services (past pres. 1982), Met. Area Planning Agy. (bd. dirs. 1982-84), Sales Mktg. Execs. of Midlands, Adminstrv. Mgmt. Soc. Greater Omaha (pres. 1987—), Naval Enlisted Res. Assn. (pres. 1979-81), Naval Res. Assn., Fleet Res. Assn., VFW (adj. Omaha Post 2503 1986-87), Am. Legion (Omaha Post 1), Res. Officers Assn., U.S. Naval Inst., Phi Gamma Delta (Omaha alumni pres. 1972, bd. dirs. 1982-83). Republican. Lutheran. Lodges: Optimist Club (local pres.), Optimist Clubs of Dist. (Lt. Gov. State of Nebr. 1974), Optimist Internat. (disting. pres. W. Omaha 1971-72). Avocations: hunting, reading, wine collecting. Home: 8101 Boyd St Omaha NE 68134 Office: INC Services Inc Temp Personnel 7701 Pacific St Suite 10 Omaha NE 68114-5422

ANDERSEN, DAVID LEE, architect; b. June 13, 1951; s. Richard Axel and Janette May (Iverson) A.; m. Gail S. Swenson, Apr. 16, 1983. Tech. degree, Hawkeye Inst., 1972; BA, Iowa State U., 1974, MArch, 1977. Registered architect, Iowa, Wis., Minn. Project mgr. Savage & Ver Ploeg, West Des Moines, 1975-79, Miller Hanson Westerbeck Bell Architects, Mpls., 1979-84; pres. Andersen Group Architects, Mpls., 1984—. Contbr. articles to profl. jours. Mem. profl. devel. bd. dept. architecture Iowa State U., 1987—; founder Mainstream Living Inc., 1974-78, v.p. Wooddale Luth. Ch. Bd., 1984-85, bd. dirs; bd. dirs. Story County Devel. Ctr., 1975-78. Mem. AIA (pres. Mpls. 1987, commr. pub. relations, pub. edn. and hist. resources com.), Minn. Soc. Architects (bd. dirs. 1986-87). Office: Andersen Group Architects ltd 7601 Wayzata Blvd Suite 211 Minneapolis MN 55426

ANDERSEN, ELMER L., manufacturing executive, governor of Minnesota; b. Chgo., June 17, 1909; s. Arne and Jennie (Johnson) A.; m. Eleanor Johnson, 1932; children: Anthony L., Julian L., Emily E. BBA, U. Minn., 1931; LLD (hon.), Macalester College, St. Paul, 1965; LHD, Carleton Coll., 1972; D of Mgmt. (hon.), U. Minn., 1984. With H.B. Fuller Co. (mfrs. indsl. adhesives), 1934—, sales mgr., 1937-41, pres., 1941-61, 63-71, chmn., 1961-63, 71—, chief exec. officer, 1971-74, chmn. bd., 1974—; dir. Davis Consol. Industries, Sydney, Australia, Prenor Group Ltd., Montreal, Que., 1972-76, Geo. A. Hormel & Co., Austin, 1971-75, First Trust Co., St. Paul, 1969-74; mem. Minn. Senate, 1949-58; gov. of Minn. 1961-63; pub. Princeton (Minn.) Union Eagle, 1976—, Sun Newspapers, 1978-84. Campaign chmn. St. Paul Community Chest, 1959—; exec. com. Boy Scouts Am.; mem. Nat. Parks Centennial Commn., 1971, Gov.'s Voyageurs Nat. Park Adv. Commn., Select Com. on Minn. Jud. System; chmn. Minn. Constl. Study Commn.; Bd. dirs., pres. Child Welfare League Am., 1965-67; past pres. St. Paul Gallery and Sch. of Art; past trustee Augsburg Coll., Mpls.; pres. Charles A. Lindbergh Meml. Fund, 1978—; regent U. Minn., 1967-75; chmn. bd., 1971-75; chmn. Bush Found., St. Paul; bd. dirs. Council on Founds., N.Y.C; chmn. U. Minn. Found.; chmn. bd. Alliss Found., 1982—; mem. exec. council Minn. Hist. Soc. Decorated Order of Lion Finland; recipient Outstanding Achievement award U. Minn., 1959; award of merit Izaak Walton League; Silver Beaver award; Silver Antelope award Boy Scouts Am.; Conservation award Mpls. C. of C.; Taconite award Minn. chpt. Am. Inst. Mining Engrs., 1976; Nat. Phi Kappa Phi award U. Minn., 1977; Minn. Bus. Hall Fame award, 1977; Greatest Living St. Paulite award St. Paul C. of C., 1980; award Adhesive and Sealant Council, 1980; others. Fellow Morgan Library (N.Y.C); Mem. Adhesive Mfrs. Assn. Am. (past pres.), Voyageurs Nat. Park Assn. (past pres.), Minn. Hist. Soc. (exec. com., pres. 1966-70), Am. Antiquarian Soc. Republican. Lutheran. Clubs: Rotarian (N.Y.C.) (past pres. St. Paul, past dist. gov.), Grolier, Univ. (N.Y.C.); St. Paul Gavel (past pres.). Home and Office: 1483 Bussard Ct Arden Hills MN 55112

ANDERSEN, HAROLD WAYNE, newspaper publisher; b. Omaha, July 30, 1923; s. Andrew B. and Grace (Russell) A.; m. Marian Louise Battey, Apr. 19, 1952; children: David, Nancy. B.S. in Edn., U. Nebr., Lincoln, 1945; D.H.L. (hon.), U. Nebr., Omaha, 1975; L.H.D. (hon.), Dana Coll., 1983, Doane Coll., 1984; LL.D. (hon.), Creighton U., 1986; D.Internat. Communications, Bellevue Coll., 1986. Reporter Lincoln (Nebr.) Star, 1945-46; with Omaha World-Herald, 1946—, pres., 1966-85, chmn., pub., 1985—; dir. Raleigh (N.C.) News & Observer, Newspaper Advt. Bur.; chmn. World Press Freedom Com.; past chmn. Fed. Res. Bank, Kansas City (Mo.); bd. dirs. Great Lakes Forest Products, Ltd. Bd. dirs., past pres. United Arts/Omaha; bd. govs. Ak-Sar-Ben; trustee U. Nebr. Found., Nebr. Nature Conservancy; trustee, past pres. Jr. Achievement Omaha; chmn. Nebr. Game and Parks Found.; bd. dirs. Bellevue Coll. Found., Creighton U. Recipient Disting. Journalist award U. Nebr. chpt. Kappa Tau Alpha, 1972, Americanism citation Henry Monsky lodge B'nai B'rith, 1972, Nebr. Builder award U. Nebr., Lincoln, 1976, award Nat. Soc. Parks Resources, 1984, Communications award Nat. Assn. Resource Dists., 1987; named Omaha Health Citizen of Yr., 1986, Citizen of Yr. United Way of Midlands, 1987. Mem. Am. Newspapers Pubs. Assn. (past chmn., dir.), Internat. Fedn. Newspapers Pubs. (past pres.), Nebr. Press Assn. (Master Editor-Pub. award 1979), Council Fgn. Relations, Omaha C. of C. (bd. dirs., chmn.-elect 1987)), Phi Beta Kappa, Phi Gamma Delta. Republican. Presbyterian. Home: 6545 Prairie Ave Omaha NE 68132 Office: Omaha World-Herald World-Herald Sq Omaha NE 68102

ANDERSEN, HARRY EDWARD, oil equipment co. exec.; b. Omaha, Apr. 25, 1906; s. John Anton and Caroline (Ebbensgaard) A.; student pub. schs. and spl. courses, including Ohio State U., 1957, U. Okla., 1959; Ph.D. in Bus. Adminstrn. (hon.), Colo. State Christian Coll., 1972; m. Alma Theora Vawter, June 12, 1931; children—Jeanenne Dee (Mrs. Gaylord Fernstrom) and Maureen Lee (Mrs. Roger Podany) (twins), John Harry. Founder N.W. Service Sta. Equipment Co., Mpls., 1934, pres., treas., 1956—; owner Joint Ops. Co., real estate mgmt.; dir. Franklin Nat. Bank, Mpls. Spl. dep. sheriff Hennepin County, 1951—; hon. fire chief of Mpls., 1951—; pres. Washington Lake Improvement Assn., 1955. Mem. Shrine Directors Assn. (N.W. gov.), Nat. Assn. Oil Equipment Jobbers (pres. 1957-58, dir. 1954-56), C. of C., Upper Midwest Oil Mans Club. Lutheran. Mason (32deg., K.T., Shriner), Jester. Clubs: Viking (pres.), Engineers, Toastmasters, Minneapolis Athletic, Golden Valley Golf, Le Mirador Country (Lake Geneva, Switzerland). Home: 2766 W River Pkwy Minneapolis MN 55406 Office: 2520 Nicollet Ave Minneapolis MN 55404

ANDERSEN, JAMES L., chemical executive; b. Mauston, Wis., May 8, 1949; s. Einer M. and Alice (Sorensen) A.; m. Julieann A. Vogel, Dec. 31, 1984; stepchildren: Joshua Rhein, Rachel Rhein. BBA, U. Wis., Whitewater, 1971. Bus. mgr. Custofoam Corp., Mauston, 1971-74; sales mgr. Empro Corp., Mpls., 1974-78, Empire Foam Corp., Mpls., 1978-80; v.p. Foam Enterprises, Inc., Mpls., 1980—. Rep. campaign co-chmn. Thompson for State Assembly, Mauston, 1973. Served with USAR, 1971—. Named one of Outstanding Young Men Am., Jaycees, 1973. Mem. Soc. Plastics (mktg. com.), Urethane Foam Contractors Assn. (assoc.), Reserve Officers Assn., Am. Legion, Soc. Plastics, Mauston Jaycees. Lutheran. Home: 4400 Goldenrod Ln Plymouth MN 55442 Office: Foam Enterprises Inc 13630 Watertower Cir Minneapolis MN 55441

ANDERSEN, JUDITH MARIE, pharmacist, educator, consultant; b. Des Moines, Apr. 1, 1953; d. Robert Lee and Dolores Bethine (Madsen) A.; m. Romualdas Mickevicius, Nov. 11, 1978; 1 child, Kristina Marie. B.S. in Pharmacy, Creighton U., 1976; Pharm.D., U. Minn., 1978. Registered pharmacist, Iowa, Nebr., Minn. Asst. prof. Creighton U., Omaha, 1978-85; cons. pharmacist Omaha Devel. Ctr., 1981—; clin. pharmacist St. Joseph Ctr. for Mental Health, Omaha, 1980—, Omaha Psychiat. Assocs., 1983—. Author (with others) MICRODID (drug interaction detection computer program), 1981. Contbr. (with others) articles to profl. jours. Mem. Nebr. Democratic Party; bd. dirs. Nebr. Council Continuing Pharmacy Edn. Grantee Upjohn, 1983. Mem. Am. Coll. Clin. Pharmacy, Am. Soc. Cons. Pharmacists, Am. Soc. Hosp. Pharmacists, Nebr. Pharmacists Assn. (mem. polit. action com. 1980—), Greater Omaha Pharmacists Assn. (bd. dirs. 1981—), Rho Chi, Lambda Kappa Sigma (chpt. advisor 1978—). Lutheran. Lodges: FOE Auxiliary, Danish Brotherhood, Danish Sisterhood. Home: 3660 S 44th Ave Omaha NE 68105

ANDERSEN, LEE DIXON, automobile dealership manager, accountant; b. Sioux Falls, S.D., Feb. 7, 1952; s. Vernon Benedict and Beverly June (Paulson) A.; m. Carol Ranae Oakland, June 4, 1977; 1 child, Darin. BSBA, U. S.D., 1975. Auditor Eide Helmeke & Co., Sioux Falls, 1977-86; bus. mgr. Frank Stinson Chevrolet, Sioux Falls, 1986—. Mem. Am. Inst. CPA's, S.D. Soc. CPA's. Republican. Lutheran. Club: Westward Ho Country (Sioux Falls). Lodge: Rotary. Avocations: reading, golf, woodworking. Home: 4413 Hickory Hill Rd Sioux Falls SD 57103 Office: Frank Stinson Chevrolet Inc 4200 W 12th St Sioux Falls SD 57107

ANDERSEN, LEONARD CHRISTIAN, former state legislator, real estate investor; b. Waukegan, Ill., May 30, 1911; s. Lauritz Frederick and Meta Marie (Jacobsen) A.; B.A., Huron (S.D.) Coll., 1933; M.A., U. S.D., 1937; m. Charlotte O. Ritland, June 30, 1937; children: Karen (Mrs. Fred Schneider), Paul R., Charlene (Mrs. Kurt Olsson), Mark Luther. Tchr., Onida (S.D.) High Sch., 1934-35; dir. bus. tng. Waldorf Coll., Forest City, Iowa, 1935-39; ins. salesman, 1939-41; tchr. econs., current history Morningside Coll., Sioux City, Iowa, 1941-43; engaged in ins. and real estate, Sioux City, 1943-76; mem. Iowa Ho. of Reps. from Woodbury County, 1961-64, 66-71; mem. Iowa Senate from 26th Dist., 1972-76, chmn. rules and adminstrn. com. Mem. Iowa Commn. on Aging; mem. cen. com. Woodbury County Reps.; v.p. housing com., project rev. com. Siouxland Interstate Met. Planning Council; mem. Simpco Projects Rev. Com.; chmn. bd. Siouxland Rental Assn.; past mem. Sioux City Housing Appeals Bd., Siouxland Council on Alcoholism; bd. regents Augustana Coll., Sioux Falls, S.D., 12 yrs., now mem. Augustana Fellows; chmn. Morningside Lutheran Ch. Mem. UN Assn. (past pres. Siouxland chpt.), Siouxland Rental Assn. (pres. 1984, chmn. bd. dirs.), Sioux City C. of C. (legis. com. 1986—), United Comml. Travelers. Republican. Lodges: Masons, Lions. Home and Office: 712 S Glass St Sioux City IA 51106

ANDERSEN, SHEREE HILTON, research analyst, educator; b. Provo, Utah, Aug. 28, 1954; d. Lynn Mathers and Annalee Hope (Averall) Hilton; m. Blaine Perkes Andersen, Sept. 19, 1979; children: Ashlee Brynn, Reghan Yael. BS, Brigham Young U., 1975; MS, U. Utah, 1980. Assoc. systems analyst ITEL Corp., Salt Lake City, 1977-78; programmer analyst State of Utah, Salt Lake City, 1980-81; research analyst Ford Motor Co., Dearborn, Mich., 1982—; adj. instr. Madonna Coll., Livonia, Mich., 1986—; systems cons. Young & Rubicam, Detroit, 1986—; speaker Ford Motor Co., Dearborn, Mich., 1986; system cons., instr. R.L. Polk & Co., Detroit, 1987—. asst. dir. Multi-Congl. Youth Program, Southeast Mich., 1984-85; troop leader Girl Scouts U.S., 1986—; mem. cen. com. Bush for Pres., Utah, 1979-80; staff Headlee for Gov., Mich., 1982. Nat. Merit scholar, 1972, Deseret Newspaper Sterling scholar 1972. Mem. SAS Users Group Internat., Detroit SAS Users Group, Am. Statis. Assn. (speaker 1986), Am. Mothers (speaker 1985—). Republican. Mormon. Avocations: world traveler, skiing, interior decorating, aerobic exercise, Scuba diving. Home: 3939 McNichol Trail West Bloomfield MI 48033 Office: Ford Motor Co 17101 Rotunda Dr Dearborn MI 48121

ANDERSON, ALAN MARSHALL, lawyer; b. Postville, Iowa, Oct. 23, 1955; s. Hilbert Emil and Wilma Althea (Zummack) A.; m. Ann Marie Luken, Aug. 9, 1980. BA magna cum laude, Coe Coll., 1974-78; MBA with distinction, Cornell U., 1981, JD magna cum laude, 1982. Bar: Minn. 1983, U.S. Dist. Ct. Minn. 1983, U.S. Ct. Appeals (4th cir.) 1983, U.S. Ct. Appeals (8th cir.) 1983. Law clk. to presiding judge U.S. Ct. Appeals (4th cir.), Richmond, Va., 1982-83; assoc. Faegre & Benson, Mpls., 1983—. Contbr. articles to law revs. Recipient Chatman Labor Law Prize Cornell Law Sch. Faculty, 1982. Mem. ABA, Minn. Bar Assn., Assn. Trial Lawyers of Am., Order of Coif, Phi Beta Kappa, Phi Kappa Phi. Republican. Lutheran. Avocation: judo. Office: Faegre & Benson 2300 Multifood Tower Minneapolis MN 55402

ANDERSON, ALAN R., department store executive; b. 1935. Div. mdse. mgr. Dayton's Dept. Store Group, Mpls., 1959-70; v.p. gen. mdse. Davison's Dept. Store, Atlanta, 1970-75; pres., chief exec. officer Howland, Steinbach, Hochschild, White Plains, N.Y., 1975-83; chmn. bd. P.A. Bergner & Co., Peoria, 1983—. Office: P A Bergner & Co 331 W WisconsinAve Milwaukee WI 53203 *

ANDERSON, ALLAN EUGENE, civil engineer; b. Chgo., Aug. 13, 1936; s. Carl Victor and Florence Josephine (Erickson) A.; m. Susan Elizabeth Hastings, June 28, 1958; children: Elisabeth, Mark, Philip. BSCE, U. Ill., 1958. Registered profl. engr., Iowa, Minn., Nebr., Ohio. Bridge engr. Ill. Cen. R.R., Chgo., 1956-57; gas engr. Dayton (Ohio) Power & Light, 1958-66, HD&R Engring., Omaha, 1966-73; chief engr. Gt. Plains Natural Gas, Fergus Falls, Minn., 1973—. Mem. grants evaluation com. S.W. Minn. Arts & Humanities Council, Marshall, 1984—; deacon Evang. Free Ch.; sec. Marshall Cable TV Commn., 1983—, chmn. 1986—. Mem. NSPE (s.w. dist. pres., v.p., sec. 1983-85), Nat. Assn. Corrosion Engrs., Midwest Gas Assn., Soc. for Preservation and Encouragement of Barber Shop Quartet Singing in Am. (sec., v.p., pres. local chpt. 1968-72). Republican. Club: Engineers (Dayton, Omaha). Avocations: chorale singing, barbershop quartet singing. Office: Gt Plains Natural Gas Co PO Box 310 Marshall MN 56258

ANDERSON, ALLAN JEFFREY, systems analyst; b. Anchorage, Feb. 10, 1950; s. Arthur Oscar and Thelma Marie (Montgomery) A. BS, U. Ariz., 1974, MS, 1983. Chemist Jones Blair Co., Dallas, 1976-80; mem. tech. staff Hughes Aircraft Co., Tucson, 1983-86; with Boeing Mil. Aircraft Co., Wichita, Kans., 1986—. Vol. Murphy for Mayor campaign, Tucson, 1971; Rep. precinct capt., Tucson, 1972-74. Mem. Am. Chem. Soc., Assn. Computing Machinery. Club: SUNHUG (Tucson)(treas. 1983-85). Avocations: home computers, electronics, cryptology. Mailing Address: 5337 E Bellevue Tucson AZ 85712

ANDERSON, AMOS ROBERT, chemical company executive; b. Delavan, Wis., Feb. 11, 1920; s. Oscar and Bertha (Ives) A.; m. Charlotte Maxine Bourland, Nov. 4, 1945; children: Dabney Jo, Mark Valdis. BS in Chemistry, Adrian (Mich.) Coll., 1942, PhD (hon.), 1965; MS, Ohio State U., 1943. Research chemist Girdler Corp., Louisville, 1943-44; with Manhattan Project, 1944-46; pres. Anderson Chem. Co., Adrian, 1946-58; v.p. and head of various divs. Stauffer Chem. Co., Weston, Mich., 1958-66; pres. Valjo Corp., 1966-87; v.p. Aquaphase Labs., 1967-86; pres. Interam. Zinc, Inc., 1974—, Anderson Devel. Co., Adrian, 1966—; bd. dirs. Comml. Savs. Bank, Gulf Bio-Systems, Dallas; mem. research adv. com., mgmt. com., operating com. Stauffer Chem. Co., 1960-66. Patentee in field; contbr. numerous articles to profl. jours. Mem. Lenawee County Planning Commn., 1965-76, Lenawee County Econ. Devel. Commn., 1971-82; trustee Adrian Coll., 1963—, mem. exec. com., 1964—, chmn. fin. com., 1967—; mem. Adrian Coll.-Siena Heights Coll. Cooperation Com., 1975-80. Recipient Adrian Bootstrap award, Outstanding Alumni award Adrian Coll. Mem. Am. Chem. Soc. Club: Lenawee Country. Lodge: Elks. Avocations: music, woodworking, architecture, gardening, painting. Home: 11 Lakeridge Dr Adrian MI 49221 Office: Anderson Devel Co 1415 E Michigan St Adrian MI 49221-3499

ANDERSON, ARTHUR RODNEY, vocat. educator; b. Oak Park, Ill., Feb. 14, 1930; s. Arthur J. and Hilda Marie (Fauske) A.; B.S., So. Ill. U., 1981, M.S., 1983; m. Marjorie Raglin, June 23, 1965. Carpenter, Wade Constrn. Co., Itasca, Ill., 1962-72, foreman, 1962-65, supt., 1965-72; tchr. bldg. trades Lockport (Ill.) Twp. High Sch., 1972—, developer vocat. bldg. trades course; lectr. secondary edn. workshops, 1968—. Recipient Outstanding Service award James McKinnon Smith chpt. Nat. Honor Soc., 1975; citation for outstanding contbn. to vocat. edn. studies So. Ill. U., 1981. Mem. Am. Vocat. Assn., Ill. Vocat. Assn., Ill. Indsl. Edn. Assn. (pres. Roundtable 4, 1983-84), United Brotherhood of Carpenters and Joiners (pres. local 558, Elmhurst, Ill. 1967-76), Iota Lambda Sigma. Lutheran. Club: Sons of Norway. Home: 603 S Dunston Ave Arlington Heights IL 60005 Office: Lockport Twp High Sch 12th and Jefferson Sts Lockport IL 60441

ANDERSON, AUSTIN GOTHARD, university adminstrator, lawyer; b. Calumet, Minn., June 30, 1931; s. Hugo Gothard and Turna Marie (Johnson) A.; m. Catherine Antoinette Spellacy, Jan. 2. 1954; children: Todd, Susan, Timothy, Linda, Mark. B.A., U. Minn., 1954, J.D., 1958. Bar: Minn. 1958, Ill. 1962, Mich. 1974. Mem. Spellacy, Spellacy, Lano & Anderson, Marble, Minn., 1958-62; dir. Ill. Inst. Continuing Legal Edn., Springfield, 1962-64; dir. dept. continuing legal edn. U. Minn., Mpls., 1964-70, assoc. dean gen. extension div., 1968-70; mem. Dorsey, Marquart, Windhorst, West & Halladay, Mpls., 1970-73; assoc. dir. Nat. Ctr. State Cts., St. Paul, 1973-74; dir. Inst. Continuing Legal Edn. U. Mich., Ann Arbor, 1973—; project dir. Select Com. on Judiciary State of Minn., 1974-76; adj. faculty U. Minn., 1974, Wayne State U., 1974-75, William Mitchell Coll. Law, 1973-74; mem. Am. Inst. Law Tng. within the Office, 1985—; cons. in field. Co-editor, contbg. author: Lawyer's Handbook, 1975; author: A Plan for Lawyer Development, 1986, Client Development: The Key to Successful Law Practice, 1986; cons. editor, contbg. author: Webster's Legal Secretaries Handbook, 1981; contbr. chpt. to book. Chmn. City of Bloomington Park and Recreation Adv. Commn., Minn., 1970-72; mem. adv. com. Ferris State Coll.; mem. Ann Arbor Citizens Recreation Adv. Com., 1983—, Ann Arbor Parks Adv. Com., 1983—. Served with U.S. Navy, 1950-51. Fellow Am. Bar Found., State Bar Mich. Found.; mem. Assn. Legal Adminstrs. (pres. 1969-70), ABA (chmn. sect. econ. of law practice 1981-82), Mich. Bar Assn., Ill. Bar Assn., Minn. Bar Assn., Washtenaw County Bar Assn., Am. Mgmt. Assn., Assn. Continuing Legal Edn. Adminstrs. Home: 3617 Larchmont Dr Ann Arbor MI 48105 Office: U Mich 1020 Greene St Ann Arbor MI 48109-1444

ANDERSON, BARRIE, gynecologist/obstetrician; b. Syracuse, N.Y., Apr. 17, 1942; d. Eric Albert and Edna (Barrie) A.; m. George Joel Wine, June 15, 1985. BS, U. Wis., 1963; MD, SUNY, Syracuse, 1967. Diplomate Am. Bd. Ob-Gyn; Nat. Bd. Med. Examiners (ob-gyn com.). Intern New Eng. Med. Ctr. Hosp., Boston, 1967-68; resident in ob-gyn Tufts Affiliated Hosp., Boston, 1968-71, fellow in gynecol. oncology, 1971-72, 74-75, asst. prof. ob-gyn, 1972-82, assoc. prof. ob-gyn, 1982, instr. radiation therapy, 1975-82; assoc. prof. ob-gyn U. Iowa Hosps. and Clinics, Iowa City, 1982—, dir. gynecol. oncology, 1982—. Contbr. articles to profl. jours. Galloway fellow Meml. Hosp. Cancer and Allied Diseases, 1971, Am. Cancer Soc. Clin. fellow, 1974-75, Am. Cancer Soc. Jr. Faculty Clin. fellow, 1977-80. Mem. Am. Coll. Ob-Gyn, Western Assn. Gynecol. Oncologists (v.p. 1985), Soc. Gynecol. Oncologists (v.p. 1986), New England Assn. Gynecol. Oncologists (sec., treas. 1980-83), Mass. Med. Soc., Iowa Med. Soc. Office: U Iowa Hosps & Clinics Dept Ob Gyn div Gynecol Oncology Iowa City IA 52242

ANDERSON, BARRY STANLEY, health care executive; b. Atlanta, Sept. 6, 1942; s. Rex and Virginia A.; m. Katherine Krupp, Dec. 26, 1966 (div. 1973); 1 child, Jon Robert; m. Patricia Ann O'Neil, May 25, 1974; children: Russell Barry, Robert Bruce. AA, Foothill Coll., 1968; BA, San Francisco State U., 1976; MBA, U. N.D., 1984. V.p. Ventilation Assocs., Inc., Houston, 1971-74; program dir. Inst. Med. Studies, Berkeley, Calif., 1976-78; program dir. Sch. Respiratory Care, St. Alexius Med. Ctr., Bismarck, N.D., 1978-84, dir. edn., 1984—; chmn. bd. dirs., pres. Creative Mktg., Inc., Bismarck, 1982—; v.p. Baby Products Ltd., 1987—; asst. prof. U. of Mary, 1982-85. Author: (with D. Quesinberry) Blood Gas Interpretations, 1974; mem. editorial adv. bd. Respiratory Mgmt.; contbr. articles to profl. jours. Nominee Am. Coll. Healthcare Execs. Mem. Am. Mktg. Assn., Am. Mgmt. Assn., Am. Hosp. Assn., Acad. for Health Services Mktg., Assn. MBA Execs., Ctr. for Entrepreneurial Mgmt., U. N.D. Alumni Assn. Lodge: Elks. Avocations: computer programming, writing, reading, lecturing, sailing. Office: St Alexius Med Ctr 900 E Broadway Bismarck ND 58501

ANDERSON, BOB, state legislator, business executive; b. Wadena, Minn., Jan. 16, 1932; s. Alfred Emmanuel and Frances Agnes (Hassler) A.; m. Janet Lynn Hemquist, Aug. 3, 1967. B.B.A., U. Miami, 1959. Small businessman, Minn., 1954—; mem. Minn. Ho. of Reps., 1976—, mem. appropriations com. mem. exec. com.; Nat. Conf. State Legislatures; sec. Minn. Legis. Commn. on Waste Mgmt. Past pres. Viking-Land, U.S.A., Explorers Highroad Found., Ottertail Lake Property Owners Assn.; mem. Minn. Fuel Alcohol Assn., Fergus Falls N.G. Citizens Com. Served with U.S. Army, 1952-54. Decorated D.S.M. Named Hon. Citizen, City of Winnipeg; recipient Highroad Explorer award, Hon. Viking award. Mem. Minn. Meat Processors Assn. (past pres.), Otter Tail County Hist. Soc., Am. Legion, VFW. Republican. Clubs: Bal Moral Golf, Fergus Falls Fish and Game, Pelican River Sportsmen, St. Paul Athletic. Lodges: Elks, Masons, Shriners.

ANDERSON, CARL HENRY, insurance company executive; b. Primghar, Iowa, Mar. 29, 1938; s. Claude Franklin and Clementine Elizabeth (Burns) A.; m. Rebecca Dorothy Hintze, May 31, 1959; children: Jeffrey Lee, Steven Allan, Robin Renee. BA in Math. and Acctg., U. No. Iowa, 1960. Agt. Equitable Life of Iowa, Cedar Falls, 1960-62; pvt. practice ins. agt. Cedar Falls, 1962-66; regional agy. supr. Provident Life and Accident Ins. Co., Chattanooga, 1966-68, supr. sales devel., 1968-72, asst. v.p., 1972-77, v.p., 1977-81; v.p. Vol. State Life Ins. Co., 1982-85; v.p. prodn. mgmt. div. Gen. Am. Life Ins. Co., St. Louis, 1985-86, pres., chief exec. officer, 1986—; bd. dirs. Enterprise Life Inc. Co.; instr. life underwriters tng. course, part III. Chmn. Young Reps. Blackhawk County, Iowa, 1962-64; chmn. rebldg. fund Luth. Sch., Chattanooga, 1972, chmn. bd. dirs., 1975, 81; div. bd. dirs. United Fund of Chattanooga, 1979. Mem. Sales and Mktg. Execs. Chattanooga (bd. dirs. 1977, 79, 1st v.p. 1978), Am. Coll. Life Underwriters (CLU, chartered fin. cons.), Am. Mgmt. Assn., Life Ins. Mktg. and Research Assn. (mktg. com., speaker regional and nat. meetings), Am. Soc. Tng. and Devel. (bd. dirs. Chattanooga chpt. 1970). Lodge: Rotary. Home: 16703 Kehrsgrove Dr Chesterfield MO 63017

ANDERSON, CATHERINE LOUISE, psychologist, consultant, therapist; b. Omaha, Jan. 8, 1956; d. Clarence W. and Louise M. (Shannon) James; m.

William L. Anderson, Mar. 25, 1978; children: Nathaniel W., Amanda Daigh. BA in Psychology, Hendrix Coll., 1975; MS in Psychology, U. Cen. Ark., 1977. Lic. psychologist, Minn. Psychologist Ark. Children's Colony, Conway, 1977-78; program dir. Riverview Homes, Brookston, Mich., 1978-79; psychologist Goodwill Industries, Duluth, Minn., 1981-84, Human Devel. Ctr., Duluth, 1983—; cons. Miller Dwan Comprehensive Evaluation Clinic, Duluth, 1984-85, St. Louis County Juvenile Ct., Duluth, 1985—, Arrowhead Juvenile Ctr., Duluth, 1985—. Bd. dirs. U. Minn. Child Care Ctr., Duluth, 1984-85; mem. legis. com. Coalition Adolescent Sex Therapists, Mpls., 1985, mem. planning com. Regional Juvenile Sex Offender Task Force, Duluth, 1985—. Mem. Adolescent Perpatrator Network, Coalition Adolescent Sexual Therapists (coordinator 1985-86), Twin Ports Area Psychologist. Democrat. Office: Human Devel Ctr 1401 E 1st St Duluth MN 55805

ANDERSON, CHARLES VAN HORN, audiology educator, speech and hearing clinic director; b. Little Sioux, Iowa, Aug. 18, 1933; s. Paul A. and Clarissa (Snover) A.; m. Jane E. Middleton, Aug. 20, 1966; 1 child, Mary E. BS in Edn., U. Nebr., 1955, MA, 1957; PhD, U. Pitts., 1962. Instr., dir. hearing conservation U. Nebr., Lincoln, 1956-58; instr. U. Pitts., 1960; asst. prof. Purdue U., West Lafayette, Ind., 1962-66; assoc. prof. U. Iowa, Iowa City, 1968—, dir. Speech and Hearing Clinic, 1986—. Contbr. 15 articles to profl. jours., 4 chpts. to books. Served to 1st lt. U.S. Army. Mem. Am. Speech-Lang.-Hearing Assn. (legis. counselor 1974-80, 83-86). Home: 16 Woodland Heights Iowa City IA 52240 Office: Wendell Johnson Speech and Hearing Ctr Iowa City IA 52242

ANDERSON, CLARENCE AXEL FREDERICK, retired mechanical engineer; b. Muskegon, Mich., Dec. 14, 1909; s. Axel Robert and Anna Victoria (Wikman) A.; student Muskegon Jr. Coll., 1929, Internat. Corr. Schs., 1934; m. Frances K. Swem, Apr. 9, 1934; children—Robert Curtis, Clarelyn Christine Anderson Schmelling, Stanley Herbert. With Shaw-Walker Co., Muskegon, Mich., 1928-78, mech. engr., 1940-65, project engr., 1965-70, chief engr., 1970-78; ret., 1978. Mem. Christian edn. bd. Forest Park Covenant Ch., 1959-61, 67-73, usher, 1953—, trustee, 1985—, chmn. bd. trustees 1986, co-chmn. Jackson Hill Oldtimers Reunion, 1982, 83, 85, usher 1953-86. Mem. Nat. Rifle Assn. Club: Holland (Mich.) Beagle (life, pres. 1966-68, 70-73, 75—). Home: 5757 E Sternberg Rd Fruitport MI 49415

ANDERSON, CRAIG BARRY, bishop Episcopal Church; b. Glendale, Calif., Feb. 12, 1942. BA, Valparaiso U., 1963; grad., U. of South Sch. Theology; MA, Vanderbilt U., 1981, PhD, 1985. Ordained priest, Episcopal Ch., 1975. With mktg. div. Procter and Gamble, 1965-71; faculty U. of the South Sch. of Theology, Sewanee, Tenn.; bishop Diocese of S.D., Rapid City, 1984—. Served with AUS, 1963-65. Office: Episc Ch 200 W 18th St PO Box 517 Sioux Falls SD 57101 *

ANDERSON, CRAIG EARL, manufacturing company executive; b. Seneca Falls, N.Y., Sept. 17, 1941; s. Robert D. and Eva Kate (Cowen) A.; m. Mary Lou Baldasarie, May 25, 1960; children: Stephanie, Robert, Eric, David. AAS in Bus., Auburn Community Coll., 1961; BS in Mktg., Mich. State U., 1963; postgrad. in Consumer Behavior, Ohio State U., 1968-72. Mktg. mgr. Fidesta, Columbus, 1966-72, Seiberling, Barberton, Ohio, 1972-75; mgr. internat. mktg. Firestone, Akron, Ohio, 1975-76; v.p. mktg. Hercules Tire and Rubber, Findlay, Ohio, 1976-81, exec. v.p., 1981-86, pres., 1987—; bd. dirs., pres. Tread Rubber Mfg. Group, Washington. Bd. dirs. Findlay Amateur Hockey Assn., 1980-87, Hancock Recreation Ctr., Findlay, 1985-87. Mem. Private Brands Group (bd. dirs.), Am. Retreaders Assn., Nat. Tire Dealers and Retreaders Assn., Jaycees (past bd. dirs., pres.). Republican. Methodist. Lodge: Elks. Avocations: golf, snow skiing, coaching youth sports, boating, speaking. Home: 1723 Windsor Dr Findlay OH 45840 Office: Hercules Tire and Rubber Co 1300 Morrical Blvd Findlay OH 45840

ANDERSON, DANITA RUTH, minister; b. Chgo., Nov. 5, 1956; d. Walter and Doris E. (Terrell) A. B.S.B.A., Chgo. State U., 1978; M.Div., Gammon Theol. Sem., Atlanta, 1983. Ordained deacon United Methodist Ch., 1983, elder, 1985. Ch. sec. Grace-Calvary Ch., Chgo., 1976-78; parish sec. Ingleside-Whitfield Meth. Ch., Chgo., 1978-79; computer programmer trainee Sears, Roebuck & Co., Chgo., 1979-80; ch. sec. Gorham United Meth. Ch., Chgo., 1980; asst. pastor Cascade United Meth. C., Atlanta, 1980-83; assoc. minister St. Mark Ch., Chgo., 1983-86; pastor Neighborhood United Meth. Ch., Maywood Ill., 1986—. Former mem. NAACP, Atlanta Assn. Black Journalists; sec. Black Methodists for Ch. Renewal, Chgo., 1979. Bd. Global Ministries Crusade scholar, 1981-83; Women's Div. United Meth. Ch. grantee, 1982; recipient Joseph W. Queen award Gammon Sem., 1982, James and Emma Todd award, 1983. Mem. Black Chgo. United Meth. Clergy Orgn., Chgo. Black Methodists for Ch. Renewal (corr. sec. 1984). Home: 431 S 19th Ave Maywood IL 60153 Office: P O Box 605 Maywood IL 60153-0605

ANDERSON, DARREL JAMES, insurance company executive; b. Oak Park, Ill., Aug. 30, 1950; s. Vivian Martha (Carlson) A.; m. Mary Therese Gedeon, Feb. 14, 1976 (div. Mar. 1980); 1 child, David James. Student, Robert Morris Coll., 1969-71, U. Iowa, 1971-73. Ins. salesman State Mut. of Am., Des Plaines, Ill., 1977-78, W.M. Mercer, Inc., Chgo., 1978-80; ins. sales W.B. Brockford, Inc., Oak Brook, Ill., 1980-83; pres. Anderson Assocs., Northbrook, Ill., 1983—. Chmn. rules com. Youth Baseball Wheeling (Ill.) Park Dist., 1986; bd. dirs. Horizon Children's Ctr., 1983—. Named one of Outstanding Young Men Am., 1985, 86. Mem. Wheeling Jaycees (pres. 1983-84, JC of Yr. 1983, Outstanding Pres. 1984). Lodge: Rotary (Wheeling) (sr. citizen chmn. 1986). Avocations: woodworking, boating, coaching youth athletics, photography. Home: 375 Plum Creek Dr #501 Wheeling IL 60090 Office: 60 Revere Dr Suite 360 Northbrook IL 60002

ANDERSON, DAVID DANIEL, author, educator, editor; b. Lorain, Ohio, June 8, 1924; s. David and Nora Marie (Foster) A.; m. Patricia Ann Rittenhour, Feb. 1, 1953. B.S., Bowling Green State U., 1951, M.A., 1952; Ph.D., Mich. State U., 1960; D. Litt., Wittenberg U., 1986. From instr. to prof. dept. Am. thought and lang. Mich. State U., East Lansing, 1957—; lectr. Am. Mus., Bath, Eng., 1980; editor U. Coll. Quar., 1971-80; Fulbright prof. U. Karachi, Pakistan, 1963-64; Am. del. to Internat. Fedn. Modern Langs. and Lit., 1969-84, Internat. Congress Orientalists, 1971-79. Author: Sherwood Anderson, 1968 (Book Manuscript award 1961), Louis Bromfield, 1964, Critical Studies in American Literature, 1964, Sherwood Anderson's Winesburg, Ohio, 1967, Brand Whitlock, 1968, Abraham Lincoln, 1970, Suggestions for the Instructor, 1971, Robert Ingersoll, 1972, Woodrow Wilson, 1978, Ignatius Donnelly, 1980, William Jennings Bryan, 1981; editor: The Black Experience, 1969, The Literary Works of Abraham Lincoln, 1970, Sunshine and Smoke: American Writers and the American Environment, 1971, (with others) The Dark and Tangled Path, 1971, MidAmerica I, 1974, II, 1975, III, 1976, IV, 1977, V, 1978, VI, 1979, VII, 1980, VIII, 1981, IX, 1982, X, 1983, XI, 1984, XII, 1985, XIII, 1986, XIV, 1987, Sherwood Anderson: Dimensions of his Literary Art, 1976, Sherwood Anderson: The Writer at His Craft, 1979, Critical Essays on Sherwood Anderson, 1981, Michigan: A State Anthology, 1983; editor Midwestern Miscellany, 1974—; also numerous articles, essays, short stories, poems. Served with USN, 1942-45; with AUS, 1952-53. Decorated Silver Star, Purple Heart; recipient Disting. Alumnus award Bowling Green State U., 1976, Disting. Faculty award Mich. State U., 1974. Mem. AAUP, MLA, Popular Culture Assn., Soc. Study Midwestern Lit. (founder, exec. sec., Disting. Service award 1982), Assn. Gen. and Liberal Edn. Am. Assn. Advancement Humanities. Club: University. Home: 6555 Lansdown Dr Dimondale MI 48821 Office: Mich State U Dept Am Thought and Lang East Lansing MI 48824

ANDERSON, DAVID GOTFRIED, orthopaedic surgeon; b. Rockford, Ill., Sept. 20, 1935; s. Gotfried Theodore and Edith Marie Victoria (Leaf) A.; m. Karen Elizabeth Barner, June 10, 1961; children: Christian (dec.), Victoria, Lauren, Heather. BA, St. Olaf Coll., 1957; MD, U. Chgo., 1961. Diplomate Am. Bd. Orthopaedic Surgery. Intern Rockford Meml. Hosp., 1961-62; resident N.Y. Hosp., 1964-65; resident in orthopaedic surgery Hosp. for Special Surgery, N.Y.C., 1965-69; practice medicine specializing in orthopaedic surgery Hutchinson, Kans., 1969—; resident in orthopaedic surgery Hosp. for Spl. Surgery, Hutchinson, 1965-69. Served to capt. U.S Army, 1962-64. Mem. Kans. Orthopaedic Soc., Mid-Cen. States Orthopaedic Soc. Lutheran. Home: Lone Eagle Ranch Rt #5 Hutchinson KS 67502 Office: 2020 N Waldron St Hutchinson KS 67502

ANDERSON, DAVID MICHAEL, sales executive; b. Ft. Wayne, Ind., May 18, 1942; s. C. Wayne and Dorothy M. (Ueber) A.; m. Frances Lee Clement, June 27, 1970; children: Christopher M., Michele M. AB in Acctg., Internat. Coll., Ft. Wayne, 1964; BS in Acctg., Defiance (Ohio) Coll., 1977. Mgmt. trainee Kent-Moore Corp., Jackson, Mich., 1964-67, corp. systems analyst, 1978-80; credit mgr. Robinair Mfg. Corp., Montpelier, Ohio, 1967-68, data processing mgr., 1969-78; data processing mgr. Pyles Industries, Wixom, Mich., 1968-69; asst. to pres. Ohio Gas Co., Bryan, 1980-87; sales mgr. Legal Shield, Bryan, 1987—. Councilman Village of Montpelier, 1974-77, mayor, 1977-83, mem. Montpelier Fair Found., 1977-83. Served with U.S. Army, 1964-66. Mem. Ohio Gas Assn., Williams City Mayors Assn. (pres. 1980), Montpelier Jaycees (bd. dirs. 1973-76). Republican. Roman Catholic. Lodge: Lions (Montpelier) (pres. 1985-86). Avocations: gardening, bowling, golf. Home: 915 Linden St Montpelier OH 43543 Office: Nat Legal Shield 202 S Union St Bryan OH 43506

ANDERSON, DAVID SIDNEY, accountant; b. Highland Park, Mich., Aug. 17, 1954; s. Carl S. and Joyce F. (Meeks) A.; m. Mary C. Halloran, Aug. 25, 1979; children: David J., Megan C. BBA, U. Mich., 1978; MBA, Wayne State U., 1986. CPA, Mich. Audit sr. Touche Ross & Co., Detroit, 1978-80; acctg. mgr. Mich. Nat. Corp., Bloomfield Hills, 1981-83, mgr. fin. reporting, 1984-85; dir. fin. reporting Mich. Nat. Corp., Farmington Hills, 1986, 1st v.p., dir. bank acctg., controller, 1987—. Mem. Bank Adminstrn. Inst., Am. Inst. CPA's, Mich. Assn. CPA's. Home: 37131 Highlite Sterling Heights MI 48310

ANDERSON, DENNIS ALBIN, bishop; b. Glenwood, Minn., July 8, 1937; s. Albin G. and Florence Elizabeth (Larson) A.; m. Barbara Ann Forse, Dec. 30, 1960; children: Kristin, Charles. B.A., Gustavus Adolphus Coll., 1959; M.Div., Luth. Sch. Theology, Chgo., 1963; D.Div. hon., Gustavus Adolphus Coll., 1978; D.H.L. (hon.), Midland Luth. Coll., Fremont, Nebr., 1980. Ordained to minstry Lutheran Ch. Am., 1963. Mission developer Luth. Ch. in Am., Austin, Tex., 1963-64; pastor Holy Cross Luth. Ch., Austin, 1964-66, Luth. Ch. Good Shepherd, Prospect Heights, Ill., 1966-71, St. Paul Luth. Ch., Grand Island, Nebr., 1973-78; bishop Nebr. synod Luth. Ch. in Am., Omaha, 1978—, mem. exec. council, 1976-84. Author: Searching for Faith, 1975, Baptism and ..., 1976, Jesus My Brother in Suffering, 1977. Office: Nebr Synod Lutheran Ch in Am 124 S 24th St Suite 204 Omaha NE 68131

ANDERSON, DENNIS KEITH, molecular biologist, computer scientist; b. Moorhead, Minn., Mar. 21, 1956; s. Alvin Eugene and Eileen Catherine (Wilkinson) A. BS with scholastic honors, N.D. State U., 1978; MS, Kans. State U., 1981. Research assoc. Molecular Genetics, Inc., Minnetonka, Minn., 1981, mgr. support services, 1981-83, dir. data mgmt. and info. systems, 1983-85, tech. devel. and sci. info. systems specialist, 1985-86, mgr. tech. applications-corp. devel., 1986—. Recipient Cora M. Downs award Mo. Valley chpt., 1980. Presdl. fellow Am. Soc. Microbiology, 1977. Mem. IEEE (posix standards com. 1986—), Assn. for Computing Machinery, N.Y. Acad. Scis., Minn. Acad. Scis., Sigma Xi, Phi Kappa Phi. Lutheran. Office: 10320 Bren Rd E Minnetonka MN 55343

ANDERSON, DERWYN LEROY, psychology educator, psychotherapist; b. Storm Lake, Iowa, Jan. 10, 1940; s. LeRoy Edward and Elvera Hilda (Bjorklund) A.; m. Jacquelyn Grace Erickson, Aug. 25, 1962; children: Mark John, Karen Marie. BA, North Park Coll., 1965; MA, U. N.D., 1967, PhD, 1968. Assoc. prof. St. Cloud (Minn.) State U., 1968—; bd. dirs. therapist Dynalife Counseling Ctr., St. Cloud, 1977—. Contbr. articles to profl. jours. Mem. Am. Psychol. Assn., Cen. Minn. Psychol. Assn., Phi Delta Kappa. Baptist. Home: 9431 Crestview Ct Saint Joseph MN 56374 Office: St Cloud State U Psychology Dept Saint Cloud MN 56301

ANDERSON, DORRINE ANN PETERSEN (MRS. HAROLD EDWARD ANDERSON), librarian; b. Ishpeming, Mich., Feb. 24, 1923; d. Herbert Nathaniel and Dorothy (Eman) Petersen; B.S. with distinction, No. Mich. U., 1944; postgrad. Northwestern U., summer 1945, U. Wash., summer 1967, U. Mich. Extension, 1958-65; M.S. in L.S., Western Mich. U., 1970; m. Harold Edward Anderson, Aug. 23, 1947; children—Brian Peter, Kent Harold, Bruce Herbert, David (dec.), Timothy Jon. Tchr. English jr. high sch., Eaton Rapids, Mich., 1944-45; tchr. English, speech Arlington Heights (Ill.) High Sch., 1945-48; tchr. English high sch., Nahma, Mich., 1948-49, 54-61, Gladstone, Mich., 1961-62; librarian Gladstone Sch. and Pub. Library, 1962-70; dir. library services Gladstone Area Pub. Schs., 1971-87, Bicentennial coordinator, 1975-76, ret., 1987; mem. planning com. Upper Peninsula Region Library Cooperation, 1982—; rep.-at-large Mich. Citizens for Libraries. Acting dir. Mid-Peninsula Library Fedn., 1965-66; chmn. Region 21 Media Advisory Council, 1972-85; chmn. adv. com. Regional Ednl. Materials Center 21, 1973—; regional del. Mich. White House Conf. on Libraries and Info. Services, 1979. Pres., Delta County League Woman Voters, 1970-72; mem. human resources subcom. Upper Peninsula Com. for Area Progress, 1964—; mem. com. for library devel. Upper Peninsula, chmn. Delta County Library Bd., 1967-76; mem. region 17, Polit. Action Team, 1968-70, Upper Peninsula Region of Library Cooperation Council, 1983-85, 86—; history chmn. Gladstone City Centennial Com., 1982—. County del. Delta County Democratic Com., 1968; trustee Library of Mich., 1984—; bd. dirs. Library of Mich. Found., 1985—. Named Tchr. of Year, Region 17 (Mich.), 1969. Mem. NEA, Mich. Edn. Assn. (pres. region 17 council 1967-68, chmn. Upper Peninsula dels. to rep. assembly 1966-68), ALA, Mich. Library Assn., Internat. Reading Assn., Mich. Assn. Media in Edn. (state Library Week chmn. 1973-74; recipient leadership award 1977), Mich. Assn. Sch. Library Suprs., Upper Peninsula Reading Conf. (program chmn. Leadership award planning com. 1981), AAUW, Assn. Ednl. Communications and Tech., Kappa Delta Pi, Phi Epsilon, Beta Phi Mu, Delta Kappa Gamma (recipient citation for seminars in mgmt. for women 1977, v.p., program chmn. Beta Sigma chpt. 1980-82). Home: 1723 Montana Ave Gladstone MI 49837

ANDERSON, DOUGLAS WILLIAM, engine company executive; b. Sylacauga, Ala., Aug. 7, 1943; s. Francis Douglas and Sarah Sabra (Key) A.; m. Carol Ann Bandos, Nov. 25, 1967; children: Shannon, Kristin, Ashley. BBA, Memphis State U., 1967. Area mgr. lighting dept. Gen. Electric, Hendersonville, N.C., 1974-77; mgr. distbr. sales small AC motor dept. Gen. Electric, Hendersonville, Tenn., 1977-83; dir. sales Am. meter div. Singer Co., Phila., 1983; dir. sales controls div. Singer Co., Schiller Park, Ill., 1983-84, v.p. mktg. controls div., 1984-86; v.p. sales, officer of corp. Briggs and Stratton, Milw., 1986—. Republican. Roman Catholic. Office: Briggs and Stratton PO Box 702 Milwaukee WI 53201

ANDERSON, DWAYNE RICHARD, bank examiner, accountant; b. Moline, Ill., Aug. 5, 1956. BA, Augustana Coll., 1978. CPA, Ill.; lic. real estate broker; auctioneer. Nat. bank examiner Comptroller of Currency, Peoria, Ill., 1978—. Mem. Am. Inst. CPA's, Ill. CPA Soc. (banking com. 1986), Nat. Auctioneers Assn., Ill. Auctioneers Assn., Ill. Farm Bur. Avocations: golf, horseback riding, racquetball.

ANDERSON, EDWARD MARSHALL, manufacturing company executive; b. Nyack, N.Y., Jan. 19, 1931; s. Edward Martin and Hulda Bertina (Hanson) A.; m. Gloria Wetherald, June 15, 1962 (div. July 1971); m. Patricia Lee Stamper, July 21, 1971; children: Merritt, Catherine. AB, Gettysburg (Pa.) Coll. Owner Anderson Co., Phila., 1956-60; pres. Micronics Corp., Phila., 1960-63, Edwards-Roberts, Phila., 1963-70, Lil' Orbits, Inc., Mpls., Anderson-Stepwell Inc., Mpls., 1974—. Inventor automatic donut machine, automatic oil/water separator. Mem. Nat. Sanitation Found., Spill Control Assn. Am. Republican. Lutheran. Avocations: advt. and publicity writing, snowmobiling, developing new products.

ANDERSON, EUGENE I., retired auto parts company exec.; b. Crothersville, Ind., Oct. 5, 1917; s. Irving and Grace (Rawlings) A.; m. Rosemary Tulley, Oct. 9, 1941; children—David E., John F., Carol, Judy J. B.S. in Indsl. Engring, Purdue U., 1939. Indsl. engr. Goodyear Tire & Rubber Co., Akron, O., 1939-43, P.R. Mallory Co., Indpls., 1946-47; indsl. engr., plant mgr., works mgr., gen. mgr., exec. v.p., pres., retired chmn. Arvin Industries; dir. Irwin Union Bank & Trust Co., Columbus, Ind. Gas. Co., Indpls. Served with USNR, 1943-46. Home: 4011 Shoshonee Dr Columbus IN 47203

ANDERSON, FRANCES SWEM, nuclear medical technologist; b. Grand Rapids, Mich., Nov. 27, 1913; d. Frank Oscar and Carrie (Strang) Swem; student Muskegon Sch. Bus., 1959-60; cert. Muskegon Community Coll., 1964; m. Clarence A.F. Anderson, Apr. 9, 1934; children—Robert Curtis, Clarelyn Christine (Mrs. Roger L. Schmelling), Stanley Herbert. X-ray file clk., film librarian Hackley Hosp., Muskegon, Mich., 1957-59; student refresher course in nuclear med. tech. Chgo. Soc. Nuclear Med. Techs., 1966; radioisotope technologist and sec. Hackley Hosp., 1959-65; nuclear med. technologist Butler Meml. Hosp., Muskegon Heights, Mich., 1966-70, Mercy Hosp., Muskegon, 1970-79; ret., 1979. Mem. Muskegon Civic A Capella choir, 1932-39; mem. Mother-Tch. Singers, PTA, Muskegon, 1941-48, treas. 1944-48; with Muskegon Civic Opera Assn., 1950-51. Soc. Nuclear Medicine Cert. nuclear medicine technologist Soc. Nuclear Medicine. Mem. Am. Registry Radiologic Technologists. Mem. Forest Park Covenant Ch. (mem. choir 1953-79, 83—, choir sec. 1963-69, Sunday sch. tchr. 1954-75, supt. Sunday sch. 1975-78, treas. Sunday sch. 1981-86, chmn. master planning council, coordinator centennial com. to 1981, ch. sec. 1982-84, 87—); co-chmn. Jackson Hill Old Timers Reunion, 1982, 83, 85; mem. Muskegon Body Building Assn. Health and Wellness Ctr. (permanent, member of month Mar., 1985). Home: 5757 E Sternberg Rd Fruitport MI 49415

ANDERSON, FRANK RUSSELL, writer, editor; b. Jerseyville, Ill., Sept. 19, 1923; s. Carl Hjalmer and Irene Victoria (Sandahl) A.; m. Doris Jeanne Butler, Feb. 12, 1946; children: Jill Elaine, Beth Eileen. AB magna cum laude, Princeton U., 1947. Ptnr. Daff and Phelps, Inc., Chgo., 1947-59; v.p. Bus. Capital Corp., Chgo., 1959-67; acquisitions officer Sci. Research div. IBM, Chgo., 1967-70, Canteen Corp., Chgo., 1970-74; free-lance writer, editor Frank Comments and others, Oconomowoc, Wis., 1974—. Author: Quality Controlled Investing, 1978; contbr. articles to investment/fin. jours. Active Winnetka (Ill.) Congl. Ch., 1952-86. Served to sgt. U.S. Army, 1943-46, ETO. Mem. Am. Acad. Polit. Sci., Nat. Writers Club, Nat. Assn. Bus. Economists. Avocations: tennis, church work. Home and Office: 1165-2 Lowell Dr Oconomowoc WI 53066

ANDERSON, GARY ALLAN, transportation manager; b. Duluth, Minn., Apr. 8, 1942; s. Arnold and Bernice (LeRoux) A.; m. Mary Cecil Kostik, Aug. 4, 1962; children: Steven, Jeffrey, Sheryl. BA, Met. State U., St. Paul, 1984. Clerk No. Pacific R.R., St. Paul, 1961-69; programmer, analyst Burlington No. R.R., St. Paul, 1970-80, system staff specialist, 1981-85, mgr., 1985—; rail industry rep. Transp. Data Coordinating Com., Washington, 1985—. Mem. Nat. Campers and Hikers Assn. (pres. St. Paul 1972-73, asst. state dir. 1974-76). Roman Catholic. Avocations: cross-country skiing, waterskiing, boating. Office: Burlington No RR 176 E 5th St PO Box 64962 Saint Paul MN 55164

ANDERSON, GARY LEE, utility company executive; b. Harlan, Iowa, Feb. 3, 1946; s. Lake Nels and Helen Margaret Anderson; A.B., Creighton U., Omaha, 1969; M.P.A., U. Nebr., 1975; m. Jeanne Kwapiszeski, Oct. 15, 1977; children—Gary Lee, John Nicholas. Supr., Panganerix, Omaha, 1969-71; asst. adminstr. Doctors' Hosp., Omaha, 1971-73; mem. research team Social Security Adminstrn., Omaha, 1974; dir. Nebr. Dept. Public Instns., Lincoln, 1975-80; systems analyst Mut. of Omaha, Omaha, 1980-84, No. Natural Gas, Omaha, 1984—. Home: 6006 N 109 Plaza Omaha NE 68164

ANDERSON, GEOFFREY ALLEN, lawyer; b. Chgo., Aug. 3, 1947; s. Roger Allen and Ruth (Teninga) A.; B.A. cum laude, Yale U., 1969; J.D., Columbia U., 1972. Bar: Ill. 1972. Assoc., Isham, Lincoln & Beale, Chgo., 1972-79, ptnr., 1980-81; ptnr. Reuben & Proctor, Chgo., 1981-85; dep. gen. counsel Tribune Co., Chgo., 1985—; gen. counsel Chgo. Cubs, 1986— . Mem. bd. deacons Fourth Presbyn Ch., Chgo. Recipient Citizenship award Am. Legion, 1965. Mem. Chgo. Bar Assn. (chmn. entertainment com. 1981-82, best performance award, 1977), Phi Delta Phi. Clubs: Yale (N.Y.C.); Attic (Chgo.). Office: Tribune Co 435 N Michigan Ave Chicago IL 60611

ANDERSON, GEORGE ELI, engineering executive; b. Mpls., Mar. 24, 1946; s. Clifford Hawkins and Katharine (Irving) A.; m. Barbara Jean Kredit, Mar. 31, 1973; 2 children. B.S. in Mech. Engring., Stanford U., 1969. Draftsman, Crown Iron Works Co., Mpls., 1969-70, engr., 1970-72, project mgr., 1972-75, chief engr., 1975-84, v.p. engring., 1984—, sec., 1974—, dir., 1979—; dir. Crown Holdings, Inc. Contbr. articles to profl. jours. Inventor in field. Adult tchr. Redeemer Covenant Ch., Bklyn. Park, Minn., 1977—; del. Rep. County Conv., 1984; trustee Redeemer Covenant Ch., 1978-80, deacon, 1986—. Recipient Cert. of Merit Nat. Merit Scholarship program, 1964, others. Mem. ASME, Nat. Soc. Profl. Engrs., Minn. Soc. Profl. Engrs., Am. Oilseed Chemists Soc., Internat. Oil Mill Supts. Assn., Nat. Fire Protection Assn. Republican. Avocations: Classic autos.; computers; comparative religions. Office: Crown Iron Works Co PO Box 1364 Minneapolis MN 55440

ANDERSON, GEORGE LEE (SPARKY ANDERSON), professional baseball team manager; b. Bridgewater, S.D., Feb. 22, 1934. Profl. baseball player Phila. Phillies, 1959; mgr. Cin. Reds, 1970-78, Detroit Tigers, 1979—. Named Nat. League Mgr. of Year, 1972; first baseball mgr. to achieve 100 wins ina season in both Nat. and Am. Leagues (Cincinnati Reds-1970, 75, 76; Detroit Tigers-1984). Winner Nat. League championship, 1970, 72, 75, 76; mgr. Nat. League All Star Team, 1971, 73, 76, 77; Winner World Series, 1975-76, Am. League and World Series, 1984. Office: care Detroit Tigers Tiger Stadium Detroit MI 48216 *

ANDERSON, GERALDINE LOUISE, clinical laboratory scientist; b. Mpls., July 7, 1941; d. George M. and Viola Julia-Mary (Abel) Havrilla; B.S., U. Minn., 1963; m. Henry Clifford Anderson, May 21, 1966; children—Bruce Henry, Julie Lynne. Med. technologist Swedish Hosp., Mpls., 1963-68; hematology supr. Glenwood Hills Hosp. lab., Golden Valley, Minn., 1968-70; asso. scientist dept. pediatrics U. Minn. Hosps., Mpls., 1970-74; instr. health occupations and med. lab. asst. Suburban Hennepin County Area Vocat. Tech. Center, Brooklyn Park, Minn., 1974-81, St. Paul Tech. Vocat. Inst., 1978—; research med. technologist Miller Hosp., St. Paul, 1975-78; research asso. Children's and United Hosps., St. Paul, 1979—; mem. health occupations adv. com. Hennepin Tech. Centers, 1975—, chairperson, 1978-79; mem. hematology slide edn. rev. bd. Am. Soc. Hematology, 1976—. Mem. Med. Lab. Tech. Polit. Action Com., 1978—; resource person lab. careers Robbinsdale Sch. Dist., Minn., 1970-79; del. Crest View Home Assn., 1981—; mem. sci. and math. subcom. Minn. High Tech. Council. Recipient service awards and honors Omicron Sigma. Mem. Minn. Soc. Med. Tech. (sec. 1969-71), Am. Soc. of Profl. and Exec. Women, Am. Soc. Med. Tech. (del. to ann. meetings 1972—, chmn. hematology sci. assembly 1977-79, nomination com. 1979-81, bd. dirs. 1985-88), Twin City Soc. Med. Technologists, Twin Cities Hosp. Assn. (speakers bur. 1968-70), Assn. Women in Sci., World Future Soc., AAAS, AAUW, Minn. Med. Tech. Alumni, Am. Soc. Hematology, Soc. Analytical Cytology, Nat. Assn. Female Execs., Sigma Delta Epsilon (corr. sec. Xi chpt. 1980-82, pres. 1982-84), Alpha Mu Tau Lutheran. Contbr. articles to profl. publs. Office: United Hosps Inc Harris Cancer Research Lab 333 Smith Ave N Saint Paul MN 55102

ANDERSON, GORDON MACKENZIE, petroleum service contractors executive; b. Los Angeles, Mar. 25, 1932; s. Kenneth C.M. and Edith (King) A.; m. Elizabeth Ann Pugh, Mar. 21, 1959; children: Michael James, Greg Mark, Jeffrey Stevens. AA, Glendale Coll., 1951; BSME, U. So. Calif., 1954; grad., Officers Candidate Sch., Newport, R.I., 1955; student, various Navy Schs. including CIC Sch. Mgr. Santa Fe Drilling Co., Chile, 1960-63, Libya, 1963-67; mgr. contracts adminstrn. Santa Fe Drilling Co., Calif., 1967-70; pres. Santa Fe Drilling Co., Orange, Calif., from 1970; sr. v.p. Santa Fe Internat. Corp., Alhambra, Calif., 1974-80, pres., chief operating officer, 1980—, also dir.; bd. dirs. Baker Internat., Orange. Mem. adv. bd. U. So. Calif. Sch. Engring.; bd. dirs. St. Jude Hosp., Fullerton, Calif. Served to lt. (j.g.) USN, 1955-58. Mem. Young Pres.'s Orgn. (chmn. 1978-79), Internat. Assn. Oilwell Drilling Contractors. Office: Santa Fe Internat Corp 100 S Fremont Ave Box 4000 Alhambra CA 91802 *

ANDERSON, GREGORY ALAN, accountant; b. Rockford, Ill., Aug. 31, 1957; s. Robert Warren and Geneva Lea (Hudson) A.; m. Anita Maria D'Souza, Sept. 5, 1982. BA in Acctg., Westminster, 1979; JD, U. Mo., 1982. Tax specialist Peat Marwick and Co., Tulsa, 1982-83, Stanfield and O'Dell, Tulsa, 1983-86; sr. acct. F.B. Kubik and Co., Wichita, Kans., 1986—. Tchr. project bus. Jr. Achievement, Wichita, 1986. Churchill scholar Westminster Coll., 1975. Mem. Okla. Soc. CPA's, Okla. Bar Assn., Tulsa Chpt. CPA's. Democrat. Home: 6747 Par Ln #1204 Wichita KS 67212 Office: FB Kubik & Co 125 N Market Suite 925 Wichita KS 67212

ANDERSON, GREGORY JAMES, professional society administrator; b. Postville, Iowa, Jan. 20, 1950; s. Roger Allen and Joan Pearl (Wainwright) A.; m. Beth Ann Davies, July 30, 1977; children: Kaaren, Whitney, Mackenzie. BS, USAF Acad., 1972; MA, Fletcher Sch. Law and Diplomacy, 1973. Exec. staff Wausau (Wis.) C. of C., 1979-81; office adminstr., liason to local govt. State of Wis. Govs. Office, 1981-82; dir. devel. EAA Aviation Found. Inc., Oshkosh, Wis., 1983—. Contbr. articles to profl. jours. Served to capt. USAF, 1972-79. Mem. Exptl. Aircraft Assn., Air Force Assn. Republican. Lutheran. Lodge: Rotary. Avocations: flying, sports, reading, writing. Office: EAA Aviation Found INc Wittman Airfield Oshkosh WI 54903-3065

ANDERSON, H. RICHARD, economic development specialist; b. Detroit, Nov. 10, 1953; s. Harold Richard and Lois Marie (Blondal) A.; m. Nancy Lee Usitalo, Oct. 9, 1982. BS in Urban Planning, Mich. State U., 1975; MA in Administrv. Services, No. Mich. U., 1979. Cons. Marquette, Mich., 1978; assoc. Planning Analysis and Devel., San Francisco, 1984-85; cons., dir.No. Econ. Initiatives Ctr. No. Mich. U., Marquette, 1985—; Mich. del. White House Conf. on Small Bus., Washington, 1986. Mem. Am. Planning Assn., Am. Inst. Cert. Planners (cert.), Small Bus. Assn. Mich. (bd. dirs. 1987—). Office: No Mich U 206 Cohodas Adminstrv Ctr Marquette MI 49855

ANDERSON, HAROLD EDWARD, dermatologist; b. Battle Creek, Mich., Dec. 1, 1913; s. Olaf Andrew and Ethel Margaret (Stephan) Andersen; B.S., Battle Creek Coll., 1937; M.D., Loma Linda (Calif.) U., 1940; M.S., Wayne State U., Detroit, 1943; m. Mary Vivian Spomer, June 12, 1939; children—Robert, Nancy, Kent. Intern Henry Ford Hosp., Detroit, 1939-40; resident in dermatology Wayne State U., Detroit, 1940-43; practice medicine specializing in dermatology, Long Beach, Calif., 1943-50, Battle Creek, 1950—; mem. staff Leila Y. Post Montgomery Hosp., Community Hosp., Battle Creek Sanitarium Hosp.; cons. VA Hosp., Battle Creek; instr. Loma Linda U. Med. Sch., 1943-50. Diplomate Am. Bd. Dermatology. Mem. Am. Acad. Dermatology, AMA, Mich. Dermatol. Soc., Mich., Calhoun County med. socs., Mich., Central states dermatol. socs. Contbr. med. jours. Home: 951 Riverside Dr Battle Creek MI 49015 Office: 131 E Columbia Ave Battle Creek MI 49015

ANDERSON, HOWARD DOUGLAS, health association administrator; b. Lumpkin, Ga., Feb. 28, 1936; s. James M. and Lila M. (Glenn) A.; B.A., Morehouse Coll., 1968; m. Louise Clapp, Sept. 13, 1958; 1 son, Howard D.; m. 2d, Susan Benson, Oct. 10, 1975; stepchildren—Deborah, Robert Taylor. Postal clk., 1958-66; sales rep. Merck Sharp & Dohme, Chgo., 1969-70; staff writer U. Chgo. Office Pub. Info., 1970-72; exec. dir. Midwest Assn. Sickle Cell Anemia, Chgo., 1972-82, pres., 1982—. Former bd. dirs. Chgo. Regional Blood Program; former mem. citizens adv. council U. Chgo. Sickle Cell Center, now mem. adv. council; mem. adv. council Chgo. State U. Coll. Nursing, 1983—. Served with U.S. Army, 1958-60. Mem. Nat. Assn. Sickle Cell Disease (founder). Home: 2231 E 67th St Chicago IL 60649 Office: 65 E Wacker Pl Suite 2200 Chicago IL 60601

ANDERSON, JAMES ALBIN, minister; b. Jackson, Minn., Apr. 13, 1936; s. Hans Albin and Phylinda Anine (Madsen) A.; m. Corrine Joyce Lyon, Aug. 22, 1958; children: Phylinda, Laurie, Allen. BS, Mankato (Minn.) State U., 1958; BD, U. Dubuque, 1961, STM, 1970. Pastor 1st Presbyn. Ch., Rochester, Minn., 1961-68; fellow Menninger Found., Topeka, Kans., 1968-70; chaplain supr. Hennepin County Med. Ctr., Mpls., 1970-77; Dir. Clin. Pastoral Edn. Met. Med. Ctr., Mpls., 1977—; stated clk. Sheldon Jackson Presbytery, Rochester, 1963-68. Fellow Am. Assn. Pastoral Counselors, Assn. Mental Health Clergy; mem Assn. Clin. Pastoral Edn. (supr., Researcher of Yr. 1981). Democrat. Presbyterian. Avocations: cooking, baking, poetry. Home: 1913 Dupont Ave S #5 Minneapolis MN 55403 Office: Met Med Ctr 900 S Eight St Minneapolis MN 55404

ANDERSON, JAMES DONALD, financial institution executive; b. Vinton, Iowa, June 10, 1952; s. Donald Arvid and Irene Dorothea (Jones) A.; m. Patricia Rae Vaupel, Dec. 22, 1973; children—Krista Rene, Lori Jolene, Amy Marie, Betsy Ellen. B.A. with honors, Luther Coll., 1974. C.P.A., Iowa. Staff acct. McGladrey, Hendrickson & Pullen, Cedar Rapids, Iowa, 1974-77; controller Perpetual Savs. and Loan, Cedar Rapids, 1977, asst. v.p., 1978-79, v.p., 1980, sr. v.p., 1981-83, exec. v.p., 1983-84, sr. exec. v.p. fin. and planning, corp sec., 1985—; dir. Perpetual Savs., Cedar Rapids, 1986—; pres. Perpetual Diversified Services, Inc. subs. Perpetual Savs. Cedar Rapids, 1983—; dir. Perpetual Investment Assocs., Cedar Rapids. Deacon, Cedar Valley Bible Ch., Cedar Rapids, 1977-85, elder, 1985-87; chmn. sch. bd. Cedar Valley Christian Sch., 1983-87; participant Leadership for Five Seasons, Cedar Rapids, 1983. Mem. Am. Inst. C.P.A.s, Iowa Inst. C.P.A.s, C.P.A.s in Industry Orgn. Republican. Clubs: Christian Businessmen's (sec. 1983-84), Elmcrest Country. Home: 216 22d St NE Cedar Rapids IA 52402 Office: Perpetual Savs & Loan 3730 Williams Blvd SW Cedar Rapids IA 52404

ANDERSON, JAMES FRANCIS, JR., management consultant; b. Peoria, Ill., May 6, 1954; s. James Francis and Ruby (Hawkins) A.; m. Judith Margo Schmidt, Oct. 2, 1976 (June 1982); m. Sarah Louise Rossing, Sept. 28, 1985; 1 child, Courtney Elizabeth. BBA in Mgmt. with distinction, U. Wis., Madison, 1975; MBA, U. Minn., 1981. V.p. Caterpillar Employees Credit Union, Peoria, 1976-79; staff cons. Arthur Andersen & Co., Mpls., 1981-83, sr. cons., 1983-85, cons. mgr., 1985—. Mem. Phi Kappa Phi, Phi Gamma Delta. Avocations: golf, music. Home: 5215 James Ave S Minneapolis MN 55419 Office: Arthur Andersen & Co 801 Nicollet Mall Suite 1200 Minneapolis MN 55402

ANDERSON, JAMES HARRY, utility engineer; b. Mpls., Aug. 30, 1927; s. Harry Aden and Leilah Betty (Anderson) A.; B. Civil Engring., U. Minn., 1952; m. Marilyn Louise Graaf, Sept. 7, 1951; children—Christine, Richard, Mark, Susan. Cadet engr. Mpls. Gas Co., 1952-54, engr., 1954-56, coordinator suburban div. main and service, 1956-58, asst. chief engr., 1958-68, chief design engr., 1968-72; chief design engr. Minn. Gas Co., Mpls., 1972-76, chief engr., 1977-80, mgr. operating services, 1980-82, mgr. Mpls. region ops., 1982-85, mgr. pub. affairs adminstrn., 1985—; mem. utility com. Nat. Transp. Research Bd.; lectr. in field. Chmn. Mpls.-St. Paul Met. Utilities Coordinating Com., 1973-80; planning commr. City of Bloomington, 1962-68, city councilman, 1971-75. Bd. dirs. Martin Luther Manor, 1985—; chmn. bd. dirs. South Hennepin County Human Service Council. Served with AUS, 1945-47; PTO. Registered profl. engr., Minn., Iowa, S.D., Nebr. Mem. Minn. Pub. Works Assn. (dir. 1966-72), Am. Gas Assn. (chmn. com. distbn. design 1968-69, chmn. com. system protection 1980, gas industry rep. to Am. Pub. Works Assn. 1975-80, operating sect. award of merit 1964, Silver award of merit 1982), Midwest Gas Assn., Nat., Minn. socs. profl. engrs., Mpls. Engrs. Club (pres. 1966, Engr. of Year award 1976), Internat. Right-of-Way Assn. (pres. Tri State chpt. 1979, internat. liaison com.), Bloomington (Minn.) C. of C. (pres. 1970), ASCE. Contbr. articles to trade mags. Home: 1400 E 100th St Bloomington MN 55420 Office: Minnagasco Inc 700 Linden Ave Minneapolis MN 55403

ANDERSON, JAMES NORMAN, marketing executive; b. Norristown, Pa., May 24, 1955; s. James Edward Anderson and Francis Jean (Garrett) Brawley; m. Deborah Ann Lehmann, Oct. 31, 1980; 1 child, Brandon-James Andrew. Prodn. asst. CBS Sports, N.Y.C., 1977-79; broker Dawson Sales Co., Oak Brook, Ill., 1979-83; mktg., sales mgr. CFC, Inc., Chgo., 1983-86; mktg. cons. J. Norman Anderson & Assocs., Chgo., 1983—; acct. exec. The Waxler Co., Chgo., 1986-87; dir. sales Greene's Ingredients, Inc., Chgo., 1987—; mktg. cons. motorsports. Pub. info. officer La Grange Park, Ill., 1983—; commr. W. Cen. Cable Commn., La Grange Park, 1984—. Mem. Inst. Food Technologists, Sugar Trade Assn., Nat. Soybean Processors Assn., Inst. Shortenings and Oils, Nat. Restaurant Assn. Republican. Episcopalian. Avocations: chess, board games, photography, video prodn., tennis. Office: J Norman Anderson & Assocs Lock Box 356 Western Springs IL 60558

ANDERSON, JAMES NORMAN, educational administrator; b. Hudson, S.D., Sept. 27, 1947; s. Norman and Mavis (Sogge) A.; m. Andrea Kathleen Arnold, Dec. 27, 1970; children—Matthew James, Lora Colleen. B.S., Northern State, Aberdeen, S.D., 1969, M.S., 1971; Ed.D., U. Wyo., 1975. Cert. supt., prin., tchr., Colo., Minn., S.D. Tchr., Faulkton Sch. Dist. (S.D.), 1969-71; high sch. prin. Bowdle Sch. Dist. (S.D.), 1971-73; dir. Wyo. Ednl. Needs Assessment Project, Laramie, 1973-75; supt. schs. Houston Ind. Sch. Dist. (Minn.), 1975-78, Gunnison Watershed Sch. Dist. (Colo.), 1978-86; supt. Spearfish (S.D.) Sch. Dist., 1986—. Mem. Am. Assn. Sch. Adminstrs. (adv. council 1983—), S.D. Assn. Sch. Adminstrn., Gunnison C. of C., Phi Delta Kappa, Phi Kappa Phi. Republican. Lodge: Kiwanis.

ANDERSON, JAMES ROBERT, architectural researcher; b. Sioux City, Iowa, Apr. 2, 1943; s. Vincint Emanuel and Harriet Virginia (Paulson) A.; m. Ruth Ann Wolfmeyer, June 2, 1968; 1 child, Sara Beth. BArch, U. Nebr., 1968; M in Urban Planning, U Ill., Champaign, 1972. Asst. prof. Sch. Arch. U. Ill., Urbana and Champaign, 1974-77, assoc. prof., 1977-84, prof., 1984—; cons. Can. Mortgage and Housing Corp., Ottawa, 1982-83. Co-author: Residents' Satisfaction in HUD Assisted Housing, 1979. Recipient Applied Research award Progressive Architecture, 1980-82, Merit Research award Am. Soc. Landscape Architects, 1982, 85. Mem. Environ. Design Research Assn., Internat. Assn. Housing Sci. Lutheran. Home: 1107 W Charles Champaign IL 61821

ANDERSON, JAMES WILLIAM, savings and loan executive; b. Storm Lake, Iowa, Oct. 11, 1954; s. William Andrew and Vivian Margene (Carlburg) A.; m. Lisa Beth Watkins, Dec. 2, 1979; children: Kristen, Jennifer. BS, Northwest Mo. State U., 1978. Product mgr. Wilson Foods, Albert Lea, Minn., 1979-84; office mgr., loan officer First Fed. Savs. and Loan, Ida Grove, Iowa, 1984—. Treas. Boy Scouts Am., Ida Grove, 1986, Miss Ida County Scholarship Pageant, Ida Grove, 1986. Named Outstanding Young Man of Am., 1985. Mem. Ida Grove C. of C. (v.p. 1986, pres. 1987), Delta Chi. Lodges: Lions (treas. 1985-86), Kiwanis (v.p. Ida Grove 1986, pres.-elect 1987). Avocations: golf, tennis, bike riding, canoeing. Home: 702 Circle Dr Ida Grove IA 51445

ANDERSON, JEFFREY LYNN, stone company executive; b. Rochester, Minn., Dec. 3, 1955; s. Rolland Mayo and Lenora A. (Damann) A.; m. Renee Elizabeth Stanley, Apr. 22, 1977; children: Cimarron, Chelsea, William. AA in Bus. Adminstrn., Rochester Community Coll., 1978; student, Brigham Young U., 1980, Winona State U., 1980-86. With Rochester Granite Co., 1970-76, gen. mgr., 1985—; bus. teller, bookkeeper Marquette Bank, Rochester, 1974-76; mgr., owner Anderson Memls., Austin, Minn., 1979—; trustee Monument Industry Edn. Found., 1987—. Designer, carver meml. art. Mem. N.W. Monument Builders Assn. (pres. 1985—), Monument Builders N.Am. (com. chmn. 1984—, Archie L. Green award 1986, Grand prize Expert div. 1987). Republican. Mormon. Club: Exchange. Avocations: woodworking, skiing, hunting, fishing. Home: 306 S Main St Austin MN 55912 Office: Anderson Memls 1805 4th St NW Austin MN 55912 Office: Rochester Granite Co 2843 Broadway Hwy 63 S Rochester MN 55904

ANDERSON, JERRY WILLIAM, JR., electronics co. exec.; b. Stow, Mass., Jan. 14, 1926; s. Jerry William and Heda Charlotte (Petersen) A.; B.S. in Physics, U. Cin., 1949, Ph.D. in Econs., 1976; M.B.A., Xavier U., 1959; m. Joan Hukill Balyeat, Sept. 13, 1947; children—Katheleen, Diane. Research and test project engr. meteorol. equipment, Wright-Patterson AFB, Ohio, 1949-53; project engr., electronics div. AVCO Corp., Cin., 1953-70, program mgr., 1970-73; program mgr. Cin. Electronics Corp. (successor to electronics div. AVCO Corp.), 1973-78; pres. Anderson Industries Unltd., 1978; chmn. dept. mgmt. and mgmt. info. services Xavier U., 1980—; lectr. No. Ky. U., 1977-78; tech. adviser Cin. Tech. Coll., 1971—. Served with USNR, 1943-46. Mem. Madeira (Ohio) City Planning Commn., 1962—; founder, pres. Grassroots, Inc., 1964; active United Appeal, Heart Fund, Multiple Sclerosis Fund; co-founder, tech. Presbyterian Ch., Cin., 1964. Named Man of Year, City of Madeira, 1964. Mem. Assn. Energy Engrs. (charter), Soc. Non-Destructive Testing, Nat. Wood Carvers Assn., Am. Legion (past comdr.), Acad. Mgmt., Madeira Civic Assn. (past v.p.), Omicron Delta Epsilon. Republican. Contbr. articles on lasers, infrared detection equipment, air pollution to govt. publs. and profl. jours. Home and Office: 7208 Sycamorehill Ln Cincinnati OH 45243

ANDERSON, JOEL TODD, architect; b. Erie, Pa., July 25, 1941; s. John Andrew Anderson and Charlotte (Boehm) Rosenzweig; m. Penelope Jean Miller, July 8, 1966 (div. June 1978); children: Jeremy Todd, Bethany Jean; m. Patricia Ann Fralick, May 20, 1983. BArch cum laude, Case Western Res. U., 1972. Registered architect, Ohio, Tenn., Colo., Tex. Project architect Andre Buehler Assocs., Cleve., 1972-73; design architect William Dorsky Assocs., Cleve., 1973; sr. space analyst E.F. Hauserman, Cleve., 1973-80; corp. architect Standard Oil Co. (name now BP Am. Inc.), Cleve., 1980—. Mem. AIA, Internat. Facilities Mgmt. Assn. (founder). Avocation: golf. Office: BP Am Inc 200 Public Sq Cleveland OH 44114

ANDERSON, JOHN A(LFRED), JR., data processing executive, consultant; b. Cin., Dec. 10, 1930; s. John Alfred and Beatrice (Evans) A.; m. Helen Hutzler, Aug. 27, 1967; children: John Schuholz, Shauna Schuholz, Joe Anderson, Steve Schuholz. BS in Chemistry, U. Ill., 1953. Product devel. chemist Procter & Gamble, Cin., 1955-74, sr. systems analyst, 1974—. Patentee in field. Served with U.S. Army, 1953-55. Recipient Silver Beaver award Boy Scouts Am. Mem. Assn. Computing Machinery, AAAS. Unitarian. Avocations: music, scouting. Home: 644 Hilltop Ln Wyoming OH 45215-2533 Office: Procter & Gamble PO Box 599 TR-GO Cincinnati OH 45201

ANDERSON, JOHN FREEMAN, marketing executive; b. St. Paul, July 15, 1945; s. William Freeman and Mildred (Zerine) A. BS with distinction, U. Minn., 1967, MA, 1969, PhD, 1974. Music tchr. Mpls. Pub. Schs., 1968-70; mem. faculty U. MInn., Mpls., 1974-76; pres. Anderson, Niebuhr & Assoc., St. Paul, 1974—. Contbr. articles to profl jours. Bd. mgmt. YMCA, St. Paul, 1977-83, chmn., 1983. Mem. Am. Ednl. Research Assn., Am. Mktg. Assn., Spl. Interest Group Survey Research (founder), Phi Delta Kappa, Phi Mu Alpha. Avocations: running, music, singing, water skiing. Home: 860 Dodd Rd West Saint Paul MN 55107 Office: Anderson Niebuhr & Assoc Inc 1885 University Ave Saint Paul MN 55104

ANDERSON, JOHN ROBERT, mathematics educator; b. Stromsburg, Nebr., Aug. 1, 1928; s. Norris Merton and Violet Charlotte (Stromberg) A.; m. Bertha Margery Nore, Aug. 27, 1950; children: Eric Jon, Mary Lynn. Student, Midland Coll., 1945-46; A.A., Luther Jr. Coll., 1949; B.S. (Regents scholar), U. Nebr., Lincoln, 1951, M.A. in Math, 1954; Ph.D., Purdue U., 1970. Tchr. math., coach Bloomfield (Nebr.) High Sch., 1951-52; control systems analyst, Allison div. Gen. Motors Corp., Indpls., 1954-60; prof. math. Depauw U., Greencastle, Ind., 1960, asst. dean, dir. grad. studies, 1973-76, dir. grad. studies, 1976-84, chmn. math. dept., 1984—; resident dir. W. European studies program Depauw U., Fed. Republic Germany, France, 1975; resident dir. Mediterrenean Studies program Depauw U., 1982; dir. NSF Coop. Coll. Sch., Sci. Inst., 1969-70; instr. NSF summer inst., 1972; instr. Challenge sci. and math. program U.S. Students in Europe, 1976, 77, 78, 80, 82; bd. dirs. Law Focused Edn., Indpls., 1975-77, Ind. Regional Math. Consortium, 1977—. Bd. dirs. Luth. Brotherhood; officer Peace Evangel. Luth. Ch., 1960—. Served with U.S. Army, 1946-48. Danforth Tchr. fellow, 1963-64; NSF sci. faculty fellow, 1964-65; Lilly Found. edn. grantee, summers 1961-63. Mem. Math. Assn. Am., Nat. Council Tchrs. Math., North Central Assn. ((commr. 1974-78)), Sigma Xi, Pi Mu Epsilon, Kappa Delta Pi, Beta Sigma Psi. Club: Rotary Internat. (sec. 1976-77, v.p. 1977-78, pres. 1978-79). Home: 1560 Bloomington St Greencastle IN 46135

ANDERSON, JOHN ROBERT, tire and rubber manufacturing executive; b. Boston, June 26, 1936; s. Robert Elmer and Alma Evelyn (Webster) A.; m. Carole Kilgore, Jan. 5, 1980; 1 child, Christine Anne; m. Sherry Floe, June 4, 1958 (div. 1979); children—Robin Evelyn, Douglas Carl, Dana Katharine, Judith Carol. A.B., U. S.C., 1958; M.B.A., Stanford U., 1963. Asst. controller Ford Motor Co., Dearborn, Mich., 1972-73, dir. diversified products analysis, 1973-74, asst. treas., 1974-77, fin. ops. planning dir., 1977-78; pres. Ford Motor Land Devel. Corp., Dearborn, 1978-83; sr. v.p., chief fin. officer Firestone Tire & Rubber Co., Akron, Ohio, 1983—, also bd. dirs. Trustee United Way Summit County, Akron, 1983—, Childrens Hosp., Akron, 1986; bd. dirs., mem. exec. com. Mich. Statewide Health Coordinating Council, 1975-77. Served to lt. USN, 1958-61. Mem. Fin. Execs. Inst., Nat. Planning Assn. (com. on changing internat. realities). Republican. Methodist. Clubs: Firestone Country, Mentor Harbor Yacht (Mentor, Ohio). Office: Firestone Tire & Rubber Co 1200 Firestone Pkwy Akron OH 44317

ANDERSON, JUDITH ANN, academic administrator; b. Evansville, Ind., Aug. 28, 1948; d. Elmer and Edna Irene (Kinney) Jaggers; m. Haldon L. Anderson, Nov. 29, 1969; children: Ryan Jason, Renee Michelle. BS, Ind. State U., 1970, MA, 1972, PhD, 1977. Registered psychologist, Ill. Asst. prof. Fla. State U., Tallahassee, Fla., 1977-78; dir. career devel. UCP Fla., Tallahassee, 1979-80; psychologist Human Services Ctr., Toledo, 1981-82; pvt. practice psychology Charleston, Ill., 1982—; dir. affirmative action Eastern Ill. U., Charleston, Ill., 1982—; cons. Dept. Rehabilitation Services, mattoon, Ill., 1982-86; Dept. Children and Family Services, Charleston, Ill., 1982—. Contbr. articles to profl. jour. Pres. bd. dirs. Coalition Against Domestic Violence, several counties, Ill., 1985-86. Fla. Dept. Labor grantee, 1979-81; Univ. scholar Bryn Mawr Inst., 1984. Mem. Am. Psychol. Assn., Am. Assn. Affirmative Action, Am. Assn. U. Adminstrs., Am. Assn. Higher Edn. Democrat. Avocations: hiking, canoeing, aerobics. Home: 513 Ashby Dr Charleston IL 61920 Office: Eastern Ill U 108 Old Main Charleston IL 61920

ANDERSON, JUDITH HELENA, English language educator; b. Worcester, Mass., Apr. 21, 1940; d. Oscar William and Beatrice Marguerite (Beaudry) A.; m. E. Talbot Donaldson, May 18, 1971 (dec. Apr. 1987). A.B. magna cum laude, Radcliffe Coll., 1961; M.A., Yale U., 1962, Ph.D., 1965. Instr. Cornell U., Ithaca, N.Y., 1964-66, asst. prof., 1966-72; vis. lectr. Yale U., New Haven, 1973; vis. asst. prof. U. Mich., Ann Arbor, 1973-74; assoc. prof. Ind. U., Bloomington, 1974-79, prof. English, 1979—, dir. grad. studies, 1986—; mem. governing bd. Ind. U. Inst. Advanced Study, 1983-85, 86-87. Author: The Growth of a Personal Voice, 1976, Biographical Truth, 1984; mem. editorial bd. Spenser Ency., 1979—, Duquesne Studies in Lang. and Lit., 1976—, Spenser Studies, 1986—. Woodrow Wilson fellow 1961-62, 63-64; NEH summer fellow and sr. research fellow, 1979, 81-82; Huntington Library research grantee, 1978, vis. fellow, 1985-86. Mem. Spenser Soc. (pres. 1980), MLA (exec. com. Renaissance div. 1973-78, 86—), Renaissance Soc. Am., Milton Soc., Shakespeare Assn., AAUP, Phi Beta Kappa. Home: 2525 E 8th St Bloomington IN 47401 Office: Dept English Ind U Bloomington IN 47405

ANDERSON, KARL STEPHEN, newspaper executive; b. Chgo., Nov. 10, 1933; s. Karl William and Eleanore (Grell) A.; m. Saralee Hegland, Nov. 5, 1977; children by previous marriage: Matthew, Douglas, Eric. BS in Editorial Journalism, U. Ill., 1955. Successively advt. mgr., asst. to pub., plant mgr. Pioneer Press, Oak Park and St. Charles, Ill., 1955-71; asst. to pub., then pub. Crescent Newspapers, Downers Grove, Ill., 1971-73; assoc. pub. and editor Chronicle Pub. Co., St. Charles, 1973-80; assoc. pub. Chgo. Daily Law Bull., 1981—. Trustee Chi Psi Ednl. Trust; mem. courts com. Chgo. Crime Commn.; bd. overseers Ctr. for Freedom of Info. Studies, Loyola U.; mem. fair trial free press com. Ill. State Bar, now co-chmn. Editor: The Purple and Gold Chi Psi. Recipient C.V. Amenoff award No. Ill. U. Dept. Journalism, 1976, Ill. State Bd. of Govs. award, 1987, Coalition of Sub Bar Assns. Print Media Humanitarian award, 1987. Mem. Ill. Press Assn. (mem. pub. bd., Will Loomis award 1977, 80), Nat. Newspaper Assn., No. Ill. Newspaper Assn., Sigma Delta Chi, Chi Psi. Clubs: Headline (past pres.). Home: 3180 N Lake Shore Dr Unit 14-D Chicago IL 60657 Office: 415 N State St Chicago IL 60610

ANDERSON, KAY CLIFTON, manufacturing company executive; b. Washington, Dec. 8, 1952; d. Ernest Ridley and Marjorie (Bowyer) Clifton; m. LeRoy E. Anderson, Nov. 26, 1978; children: LeRoy, Eric, David. BE, Pittsburg (Kans.) State U., 1974. Cost estimator labor and material Cessna Aircraft Co., Wichita, Kans., 1974-78; subcontract buyer Boeing Mil. Airplane Co., Wichita, 1978—. Avocations: outdoor activities, fishing, camping, flying. Home: 327 W 58th St S Wichita KS 67217 Office: Boeing Mil Airplane Co PO Box 7730 Wichita KS 67277

ANDERSON, KIM EDWARD, manufacturing company executive; b. Okarche, Okla., Nov. 6, 1950; s. Kermit E. and Zeta F. (Crawford) A.; m. Rebecca Cogwell, May 29, 1976; children—Kristin Lain, Courtney Lynn. B.S., East Central U., Ada, Okla., 1972; M.S., Okla. U., 1973, PhD, Okla. U., 1986. Engr. Okla. Health Dept., Ada, 1971-72; indsl. hygienist Johnson Space Ctr., NASA, Houston, 1973-74; supervisory indsl. hygienist U.S. Dept. Labor, Little Rock, 1974-78; corp. dir. environ. and occupational safety and health A.O. Smith Corp., Milw., 1978—; asst. prof. U. Ark., Little Rock and Fayetteville, U. Central Ark., 1976—. Author: Fundamentals of Industrial Toxicology, 1981. Contbr. articles to profl. jours. Chmn. indsl. environ. com. Ark. Fedn. Water and Air Users, 1979-81, chmn. hazardous waste com., 1983-85, chmn. annual meeting, 1983—, bd. dirs., 1983—, v.p., 1983-85; mem. clean air com. Am. Lung Assn., Little Rock, 1980—; mem. workers compensation com. Ark. State C. of C., Little Rock, 1983—, chmn. right to know com. USPHS grantee, 1972-73, EPA grantee, 1980-82; Okla. Frontiers Sci. scholar, 1972-73; recipient Environ. award Merit Okla. Health Dept., 1973, Skylab Achievement award Johnson Space Ctr., 1973; named Ark. Safety Profl. of Yr., 1984, Region IV Safety Profl. of Yr. (Ark., Mo., Okla., Kans., Nebr., Iowa), 1984, Nat. Safety Profl. of Yr., 1984-85. Mem. Am. Soc. Safety Engrs. (pres. Ark. chpt. 1982-83, v.p. 1981-82, sec.-treas. Gulf Coast sect. 1973, sec.-treas. Wis. chpt. 1986—), Am. Indsl Hygiene Assn. (pres. Ark. sect. 1979, toxicology com. 1978-81, workroom environ. exposure level com. 1979-81), Am. Welding Soc. (co-chmn safety and health com. 1980-81). Republican. Methodist. Avocations: athletics. Office: A O Smith Corp PO Box 23974 Milwaukee WI 53223

ANDERSON, KIRBY VERN, obstetrician-gynecologist; b. Effingham, Ill., Oct. 1, 1934; s. Lester Vern and Venonah (Shelley) A.; m. Mary Bischof, Aug. 29, 1954 (div. Sept. 1969); children: Kathy, Stephen, Kevin, Karen; m. Priscilla Ann Branch, Feb. 5, 1973; children: Gina, Nathan. BA, U. Colo., Colorado Springs, 1956; MD, U. Colo., Denver, 1960. Diplomate Am. Bd. Ob-Gyn. Practice medicine specializing in ob-gyn Lima; chmn. dept. ob-gyn. St. Rita's Med. Ctr., Lima, Ohio, 1978-84, chmn. med. staff, 1985—. Served to maj. U.S. Army, 1960-69, Vietnam. Decorated Legion of Merit. Fellow Am. Coll. Obstetricians and Gynecologists; mem. Phi Beta Kappa, Delta Epsilon. Republican. Methodist. Home: 1500 Fairway View Dr Lima OH 45805 Office: 825 W Market St Lima OH 45805

ANDERSON, LEE GREG, electrical engineer; b. Mpls., May 26, 1950; s. Robert William and Helen Mureen (Petersen) A.; m. Delores Ann Barstad, Sept. 16, 1972; children: Joshua Michael, Joanna Lee. BEE, U. Minn., 1973. Cert. quality engr., Minn. Product engr. Minco Products, Inc., Fridley, Minn., 1972-77; quality engr. Honeywell, Inc., Mpls., 1977-82; quality mgr. Rosemount, Inc., Mpls., 1982—. Mem. Am. Soc. Quality Control (sec. 1983-84, treas. 1984-85, Young Engr. of Yr. 1984), Kappa Eta Kappa (pres.

1983-85, v.p. 1986). Avocation: amateur radio. Home: 2513 Westcliffe Dr Burnsville MN 55337 Office: Rosemount Inc 14300 Judicial Rd Burnsville MN 55337

ANDERSON, LINDA JEAN FULLER, candy and gum manufacturing company executive; b. Chgo., Sept. 24, 1948; d. Otmar and Delores (Newman) Fuller; student No. Ill. U., 1966-68; m. John Richard Anderson, Mar. 20, 1971. Budget dir. Leo Burnett Inc., Chgo., 1968-70; controller Leaf-Donruss div. Leaf, Inc., Chgo., 1970-86, dir. cash mgmt. Leaf, Inc., Bannockburn, Ill., 1986—. Mem. Am. Mgmt. Assn., Ill. Mfrs. Assn. Lutheran. Office: 2345 Waukegan Rd Bannockburn IL 60015

ANDERSON, LOIS MARILYN, psychologist; b. Cambridge, Minn., Mar. 19, 1934; d. Oliver Ferdinand and Marjorie Constance (Strait) Ledin; m. Malcolm Charles Anderson, July 9, 1960; 1 son, Andrew. B.S., Gustavus Adolphus Coll., 1956; Ph.D., U. Minn., 1969. Intern counseling Student Counseling Bur., Univ. Hosps. dept. of phys. medicine and rehab. U. Minn., 1959-60; research fellow Indsl. Relations Center, U. Minn., 1960-65; research psychologist InterStudy, Mpls., 1969-73; state program mgmt. coordinator Minn. Dept. Adminstrn., St. Paul, 1973-77, projects coordinator Mgmt. Analysis div., 1977-79; staff psychologist Minn. State Services for the Blind, St. Paul, 1979—; pvt. practice psychologist, Mpls., 1985—. Governing mem. YMCA of Met. Mpls., 1971-79; bd. mgmt. Northwest (Mpls.) YMCA, 1970-76; bd. dirs., chmn. Camden Community Theater, 1981-83; lectr. U. Minn. Grad. Schs. of Pub. Affairs and Social Work, 1975, 76; mem. Twin City Met. Council Advisory com. on Waste Mgmt. and Water Quality, 1976-78. Mem. Am. Psychol. Assn., Minn. Psychol. Assn., Am. Assn. for Counseling and Devel., Minn. Assn. for Counseling and Devel., Psi Chi, Pi Lamdba Theta. Recipient Annual Research award, Am. Rehab. Counseling Assn., 1965. Author: (with others) AFDC Employment and Referral Guidelines, 1973; Impact of Welfare Reform on the Elderly Poor, 1973; Medicaid Cost Containment and Long Term Care, 1976. Home: 4400 Victory Ave Minneapolis MN 55412 Office: 1745 University Ave Saint Paul MN 55104

ANDERSON, LORNA KATHRYN, federal agency administrator; b. Harrisonville, Mo., May 9, 1942; d. Loran Francis and Mary Louise (Russell) Honley; m. Thomas Jerald Anderson, Mar. 5, 1962; children: Jerome William, Benjamin Joseph. Student, Cen. Mo. State U., 1960-62, postgrad., 1976-79; BA summa cum laude, U. No. Colo., 1972, postgrad., 1972; postgrad., U. Mo., Kansas City, 1986—. Dep. Cass County Recorder of Deeds, Harrisonville, 1966-68; coordinator abstract dept. Stewart Title Co., Greeley, Colo., 1972-73; benefit authorizer Social Secutiry Adminstrn., Kansas City, Mo., 1973-77; recovery reviewer Social Secutiry Adminstrn., Kansas City, 1977-80, claims authorizer, 1980—; asst. coordinator women's issues Local 1336 Am. Fedn. Govt. Employees, Kansas City, 1985—. Mem. Community Coll. Support com., Blue Springs, Mo., 1984; dist. chmn. Am. Cancer Soc., Independence, Mo., 1982; committeewoman Dem. Cen. Com., Weld County, Colo., 1972; pres. Dem. Women's Club, Harrisonville, 1968; bd. dirs. 5th Congl. Dist. Dem. Women's Cub, Kansas City, 1968. Mem. AAUW (v.p. Independence br. 1981-83, pres. 1983-85), Jackson County Hist. Soc., Cass County Hist. Soc., Sigma Sigma Sigma. Democrat. Avocations: writing, editing, walking, jogging, reading. Home: 3924 Crackerneck Rd Independence MO 64055 Office: MidAm Program Service Ctr 601 E 12th St Kansas City MO 64016

ANDERSON, LOYAL EDWARD, oil jobber, farmer; b. Hugoton, Kans., Aug. 24, 1931; s. Webb Huitt and Lucille Caroline (Flummerfelt) A.; student Mt. Carmel (Ill.) public schs.; m. Mary Ann Baumgart, June 24, 1953; children—Ray, Randy, Ricky, Rose Ann. Pres., Anderson Bros. Oil Co., Mt. Carmel, 1953—; farmer, 1974—; dir. Security Bank & Trust Co. Bd. dirs. Ill. Jaycees, 1953-56; 4-H leader, 1953—; pres. 4-H Youth Found., 1970—; bd. dirs. Wabash County Retarded Children, 1975, Fair Bd., 1954—; pres. Extension Council, 1973—, St. Mary Sch. Bd., 1970-76. Served with USAF, 1950-53. Recipient Community Service award Phillips Petroleum Co., 1975. Mem. Nat. Fedn. Ind. Bus., Am. Legion, Mt. Carmel C. of C. (dir. 1974). Roman Catholic. Clubs: K.C., Elks, Moose. Home: Rural Route 1 Mount Carmel IL 62863 Office: 909 W 9th St Mount Carmel IL 62863

ANDERSON, LYLE ARTHUR, manufacturing company executive; b. Jewell, Kans., Dec. 29, 1931; s. Arvid Herman and Clara Vera (Herman) A.; m. Harriet Virginia Robson, June 12, 1953; children—Brian, Karen, Eric. B.S., U. Kans., 1953; M.S., Butler U., 1961. C.P.A., Mo., Kans. Mgmt. trainee, internal auditor RCA, Camden, N.J. and Indpls., 1955-59; auditor Ernst & Ernst (C.P.A.'s), Kansas City, Mo., 1959-63; v.p. fin. and adminstrn., treas., dir. Affiliated Hosp. Products, Inc., St. Louis, 1963-71; sr. v.p. Consol. Foods Corp., Deerfield, Ill., 1971-74; exec. v.p. fin. Consol. Foods Corp., Chgo., 1974-76; chmn. bd. Valley Electromagnetics Corp., Spring Valley, Ill.; pres. Happy Baby, Inc., Crystal Lake. Bd. dirs. Meml. Hosp. of McHenry County. Served with AUS, 1953-55. Mem. Am. Inst. C.P.A.'s, Ill. Mfrs. Assn. (bd. dirs.), Omicron Delta Kappa. Republican. Methodist. Home: 9804 Partridge Ln Crystal Lake IL 60014 Office: Electromagnetics Corp 365 E Prairie St Crystal Lake IL 60014

ANDERSON, MARY ANN, hospital nursing administrator, nurse; b. Sparta, Wis., Nov. 22, 1939; d. Harold C. and Laura R. (DeWitt) Woolley; m. James A. Anderson, Aug. 26, 1960; children—Sandra, Julianne, Mark, Janine. Diploma St. Francis Sch. Nursing, LaCrosse, Wis., 1960; student Viterbo Coll., 1962-65, U. Wis.-LaCrosse, 1972-82, Milton Coll./Mt. Senario Coll., 1982-84. R.N., Wis. Staff nurse St. Francis Hosp., LaCrosse, Wis., 1961-63, LaCrosse Lutheran Hosp., 1963-72; head nurse emergency dept. LaCrosse Luth. Hosp., 1972-76, nursing coordinator, 1976-84, assoc. dir. nursing, 1984—; nat. LaCrosse sexual assault area counselor coordinator; chmn. LaCrosse County Emergency Med. Services, bd. dirs. Western Wis. Emergency Med. Services Inc. Mem. Western Wis. Emergency Dept. Nurses Assn. (past pres.), Nat. Emergency Dept. Nurses Assn. (cert.), Wis. Council Emergency Dept. Nurses Assn. (pres.), Am. Trauma Soc. (Wis. chpt.), Am. Heart Assn. (Wis. chpt.) Roman Catholic. Contbr. chpt. to book. Home: 508 11th Ave N Onalaska WI 54650 Office: La Crosse Lutheran Hosp 1910 South Ave LaCrosse WI 54601

ANDERSON, MARY ANN, psychologist; b. Gary, Ind., Dec. 22, 1928; d. Antonio Mario and Palma Elizabeth (Marino) De Nicola; m. James Ernest Anderson, Dec. 19, 1954 (div. Feb. 1967); 1 child, Melanie Wynne. BS, Ind. U., 1953, MS in Ednl. Psychology, 1965. Cert. elem. tchr., Ind. Elem. tchr. Hobart (Ind.) Schs., 1953-55, Gary, 1955-59; sch. psychologist Gary Pub. Schs., 1965—. Mem. Nat. Assn. Sch. Psychologists, Ind. Sch. Psychology Assn., Ind. Civil Liberties Union (bd. dirs. Calumet chpt. 1975—), Ind. Assn. Sch. Psychologists (charter, sec., bd. dirs. 1987—). Home: 9215 Lake Shore Dr Gary IN 46403 Office: MADA Computer Programs for Psychologists PO Box 2744 Gary IN 46403

ANDERSON, MARY VIRGINIA, actuary; b. Washington, Apr. 14, 1941; d. Bascom Slemp and Mary Ellen (Long) Damron. A.A., Nat. Bus. Coll., Roanoke, Va., 1960. Bookkeeper Alexander Grant & Co., Roanoke, 1960-61; math. aid NASA, Hampton, Va., 1962-64; statis. clk. Blue Cross Blue Shield, Indpls., 1967-74, asst. actuary, 1974-75, actuary, 1975-78, sr. actuary, 1978-80, asst. corp. actuary, 1980-86; v.p. Brougher Ins. Group, Greenwood, Ind., 1986—. Fellow Soc. Actuaries; mem. Am. Acad. Actuaries, Indpls. Actuaries (chmn. membership com. 1984-85), Am. Statis. Assn. (chpt. treas. 1982), Casualty Actuarial Soc. (assoc.). Republican. Episcopalian. Avocations: hiking, bicycling, reading. Office: Brougher Ins Group PO Box BAI Greenwood IN 46142

ANDERSON, MAX ELLIOT, television film production company executive; b. St. Charles, Ill., Nov. 3, 1946; s. Kenneth O. and Doris I. (Jones) A.; B.A. in Psychology, Grace Coll., 1973; m. Claudia Lynd, Aug. 17, 1968; children—James Brightman, Sarah Lynd. Cinematographer, Ken Anderson Films, Winona Lake, Ind., 1968-78; partner Q Media Group, Rockford, Ill., 1978-82, assoc. producer TV, films, 1978—, also cinematographer, since 1963—, advt. exec., 1965—; pres. Philip Lasz Gallery, 1973—, The Market Place; ptnr. Thunderbolt Prodns.; producer nat. TV spots for True Valu Hardware, 1985—; nat. distbr. inspirational home video cassettes, 1985—. Assoc. producer Gospel at the Symphony, 1979. Served with U.S. Army, 1971-73. Recipient Best Cinematography award Christian Film Distbrs. Assn., 1978. Mem. Christian Film Distributor Assn., Internat. Christian Video Assn., Christian Booksellers Assn. Republican. Mem. Evang. Free Ch. Home and Office: 4112 Marsh Ave Rockford IL 61111

ANDERSON, MICHAEL STEVEN, lawyer; b. Mpls., May 25, 1954; s. Wesley James and Lorraine Kathryn (Sword) A.; m. Gail Karin Miller, June 18, 1977; children: Mark, Steven. BA magna cum laude, Cornell U., 1976; JD, Washington U., St. Louis, 1980. Bar: Wis. 1980, U.S. Dist. Ct. (ea. and we. dists.) Wis. 1980, U.S. Ct. Appeals (7th cir.) 1986. Ptnr. Brynelson, Herrick, Bucaida, Dorschel & Armstrong, Madison, Wis., 1980—. Editor, author Washington U. Law Quarterly, 1979-80. Mem. exec. com. Dane County Reps., Madison, 1984. Mem. ABA, Order of Coif. Mem. Evangelical Free Ch. Avocation: family. Home: 6421 Portage Rd DeForest WI 53532 Office: Brynelson Herrick et al 122 W Washington Ave Madison WI 53701

ANDERSON, PAMELA JO, architect; b. Pomona, Calif., June 29, 1955; d. Roger Alan and Pauline Virginia (Harzler) A.; m. Robert Keith Humbert, Oct. 1, 1981 (div. 1985). BArch, U. Ariz., Tucson, 1978. Registered architect. Architect, draftsman, designer Perkins & Will, Chgo., 1978-81; architect Jacobs & Kahan, Chgo., 1981-82; pres. P.J. Anderson Assocs., Inc., Chgo., 1982—. Mem. AIA. Republican. Methodist. Club: Chgo Yacht. Avocations: golf, yachting. Office: P J Anderson Assocs Inc 403 W North Ave Chicago IL 60610

ANDERSON, PAUL SIMON, geography educator; b. Chgo., Sept. 27, 1943; s. Paul Simon and Merle Marie (Fink) A.; stepson of Joseph Kenneth A.; m. Noeli Vettori, June 27, 1970; children: Lily Emma, Merle Veronica, Sarah Noeli, Simon Paul. BA in Biology, Augustana Coll., Rock Island, Ill., 1965; grad. diploma, Centro Interamericano de Fotointerpretación, Bogotá, Colombia, 1971; MA in Geography, U. Calif., Berkeley, 1972; PhD in Demography, Australian Nat. U., Canberra, 1979. Tchg. fellow in geography U. New England, Armidale, Australia, 1972-74; lectr. Canberra Coll. Advanced Edn., Australia, 1974-77; asst. prof. Universidade de Brasilia, Brazil, 1978-82; assoc. prof. Ill. State U., Normal, 1982—; founder, owner, chief exec. officer Anderson Group, Inc., Normal, 1983—, Multi-Digit Techs. Corp., Normal, 1985—; co-founder Great Australian Ice Creameries, 1976—; v.p., part owner Colonial Ice Cream, Inc., St. Charles, Ill. Author, editor textbooks; developer testing method; contbr. articles to profl. jours. Served with U.S. Army, 1967-69, Vietnam. Fulbright-Hays scholarship, 1970-71; grantee Inventure Tech. Commercialization Ctr., 1985. Mem. Assn. Am. Geographers, Conf. Latin Americanist Geographers, Soc. for History Discoveries, Ill. Conf. Latin Americanists, Nat. Council for Geog. Edn., Ill. Geog. Soc., Geog. Assn., Midwest Assn. for Latin Am. Studies, Am. Cartographic Assn., Am. Soc. Photogrammery and Remote Sensing, Remote Sensing Assn. Australia, Am. Congress Surveying and Mapping, N.Am. Cartographic Info. Soc., Can. Cartographic Assn., Am. Ednl. Research Assn., Midwestern Ednl. Research Assn., Internat. Council for Distance Edn., Ill. Sci. Tchrs. Assn., Assn. for Supervision and Curriculum Devel., Associaćo de Geógrafos Brasileiros, Asociación de Geógrafos Latino Americanos, Sociedade Brasileira de Cartografia, Associaćo Brasileira de Tecnologia Educacional. Lodge: Rotary Internat. Avocations: creative writing, distance edn., practical inventions. Home: 227 S Orr Dr Normal IL 61761 Office: Dept Geography-Geology Ill State U Normal IL 61761

ANDERSON, PAUL STEVEN, optometrist; b. Cherokee, Iowa, Nov. 14, 1947; s. Verland Joseph and Georgia Louise (Heaney) A.; m. Lynette Young, Oct. 15, 1967; children: Heather, Brent. BS, OD, Ill. Coll. Optometry, 1976. Pvt. practice optometry Yankton, S.D., 1976—. Pres. Community Concert Assn., Yankton, 1986—. Mem. Am. Optometric Assn., Southeast Dist. Optometric Soc. (sec. 1980, pres. 1985), S.D. Optometric Assn., S.D. Optometric Soc. (pres. 1987). Republican. Lodge: Optimists (sec.-treas. Yankton club 1981, pres. 1983-85). Home: 304 Valley Dr Yankton SD 57078 Office: 1213 W 9th St Box 649 Yankton SD 57078

ANDERSON, PHILIP ALDEN, physician; b. Cambridge, Mass., June 11, 1948; s. David L. and Madeleine (Mather) A.; m. Mary Sterrett, Sept. 8, 1973; children: William, Anne. BA, Harvard U., 1970; MDiv, Episcopal Divinity Sch., Cambridge, 1973; MD, Case Western Res. U., 1978. Diplomate Am. Bd. Internal Medicine. Resident physician Univ. Hosp., Cleve., 1978-81; physician Hough Norwood Health Care Ctr., Cleve., 1982-83, chief adult medicine, 1983-86, asst. med. dir., 1986—; asst. clin. prof. Case Western Res. U., Cleve., 1982—. Deacon Episcopal Diocese Ohio, 1976—. Mem. Am. Coll. Physicians, Alpha Omega Alpha. Office: Hough Norwood Health Care Ctr 1465 E 55th St Cleveland OH 44103

ANDERSON, PHYLLIS REINHOLD, business executive, management consultant, engineer; b. Denver, July 29, 1936; d. Floyd Reinhold and Minerva Eva (Needham) A.; children: Kristin Elizabeth, Michele Ann. Metall. Engr., Colo. Sch. Mines, 1962; MBA, U. Chgo., 1968. Mill metallurgist, supr. U.S. Steel Corp., 1962-66; research and devel. sr. metallurgist, supr., planner Continental Can Co., 1966-73; mgr. corp. planning B.F. Goodrich Co., 1973-76; regional assoc. Strategic Planning Inst., Cambridge, Mass., 1975-76; project mgr. corp. planning, sales engring., then project mgr. corp. devel. Signode Corp., Glenview, Ill., 1976-80; mgmt. cons., 1974—; pres., prin. cons. Corp. Devel. Assocs., Inc., mgmt. cons. in strategic planning, mktg., product and systems devel., CAD/CAM/CAE, Oak Brook, Ill., 1980—; assoc. Strategic Planning Inst., 1982—, initial exec. com., chmn. membership com., 1975-76; bd. dirs. Quest Assocs. Mgmt. and Quality Cons.; instr. bus. analysis methods. Author: Corporate Strategic Planning: An Integrated Approach, 1981; contbr. articles to profl. jours. Active psychiat. support services, career counseling women's groups and individuals. Recipient Leadership award Chgo. YWCA, 1977. Mem. Am. Soc. Metals, Soc. Women Engrs., Am. Mktg. Assn., N.Y. Acad. Scis., Women in Mgmt., Nat. Assn. Women Bus. Owners, AAAS, Mensa. Clubs: Execs. of Chgo., Whitehall. Home: 2201 S Highland Ave Lombard IL 60148 Office: 55 W 22nd St Suite 111 Lombard IL 60148

ANDERSON, RANDALL SCOTT, accountant; b. Roselle, Ill., Oct. 14, 1955; s. Marvin Arthur and Verna Frieda (Koehler) A.; m. Sharon Louise Swanson, May 26, 1979; children: Randall Scott II, Seth Robert Marvin. Student, MacMurray Coll., 1973-74; BA, North Cen. Coll., 1977; postgrad., Roosevelt U., 1984—. CPA, Ill. Staff acct. MacMillan & Co., Arlington Heights, Ill., 1977-78, Switches, Inc., Northbrook, Ill., 1978-79, Donald Bark, CPA, Arlington Heights, 1979-81; controller Complete Equity Markets, Wheeling, Ill., 1981-83; staff acct. Weiss, Simon & Co., Arlington Heights, 1983—; educator income tax Community Edn. Dist. 214, Arlington Heights, 1985-86; pres. RASA, Inc., Arlington Heights, 1987—. Asst. treas. Our Redeemer Luth. Ch., Prospect Heights, Ill., 1985—; actor St. James Theater, Arlington Heights, 1986-87. Mem. Am. Inst. CPA's, Ill. CPA Soc. Republican. Avocations: sports. Home: 2420 Cornell Ave Arlington Heights IL 60004 Office: Weiss Simon & Co 2015 S Arlington Heights Rd Suite 101 Arlington Heights IL 60005

ANDERSON, ROBERT CHARLES, writer, magazine editor; b. Sault Ste. Marie, Mich., May 22, 1930; s. James Orville and Nesta Grace (Cottle) A.; student Mich. Coll. Mining and Tech., 1954-55; B.A. (Winthrop Burr Chamberlain scholar), U. Mich., 1957; postgrad. Chgo.-Kent Coll. Law, 1969-70; m. Frances Theresa Merimee, July 25, 1952; children—James Russell, Helen Christine Anderson Doepel. Reporter, Evening News, Sault Ste. Marie, 1954-55, Ypsilanti (Mich.) Press, 1957; circulation worker Ann Arbor (Mich.) News, 1956; reporter, TV columnist, mag. editor Chgo. Tribune, 1957-72; mng. editor Oui mag., Chgo., 1972-75; free-lance writer, editor Profl. Photographer, Chgo., 1976-78; editor Success mag., Chgo., 1978-84, editor-at-large, 1984—; editorial cons., author PMA Books div. W. Clement Stone PMA Communications, Inc.; lectr. to writers groups, tchr. workshops. Mem. Winnetka (Ill.) Caucus Selection Com., 1968; leader, merit badge counselor Boy Scouts Am. Served with U.S. Army, 1948-52; Korea. Mem. Am. Soc. Journalists and Authors, Midwest Writers (co-chmn.), Kappa Tau Alpha, Phi Eta Sigma. Republican. Unitarian. Author: (with Ray Kroc) Grinding It Out: The Making of McDonald's, 1977, (with Thomas Monaghan) Pizza Tiger, 1986; contbr. numerous articles to various mags. Office: 401 N Wabash Ave Suite 530 Chicago IL 60611

ANDERSON, ROBERT FERDINAND, mining company executive; b. Hibbing, Minn., Apr. 26, 1921; s. A.G. and Anna (Tanquist) A.; m. Marjorie Mahon, Mar. 9, 1944; children: Judith A., Christopher R., Mark M. B. Engring., Mich. Tech. U., 1946. With M.A. Hanna Co., Cleve., 1947—, chmn., chief exec. officer, 1978-86, chmn., pres., chief exec. officer, 1982-86, also dir., chmn. exec. com., 1986—, chmn., dir. Iron Ore Co. Can.; dir. Que. N. Shore and Labrador Ry. Co., Midland SouthWest Corp., Soc. Corp., Soc. Nat. Bank. Served with USAAF, 1943-46. Mem. AIME, Am. Iron and Steel Inst., Am. Iron Ore Assn., Am. Mining Congress. Clubs: Union (Cleve.), Pepper Pike (Cleve.), Westwood Country (Cleve.); Mt. Royal (Montreal, Que., Can.); Laurel Valley Golf (Ligonier, Pa.), Rolling Rock (Ligonier, Pa.); Duquesne (Pitts.). Home: 3585 Eldorado Dr Rocky River OH 44116 Office: M A Hanna Co 100 Erieview Plaza Cleveland OH 44114

ANDERSON, ROBERT HUNTER, data processing and data communications consultant; b. Duluth, Minn., Sept. 17, 1941; s. Herbert Andrew and Mildred May (Hunter) A.; student public schs., Duluth; m. Nancy Jeanne Overland, May 23, 1970; children—Christina Jeanne, John Robert. Programmer, Litton Industries, Duluth, 1967-69; programmer/analyst Paper Calmenson & Co., St. Paul, 1970-71, State of Minn., St. Paul, 1971-74, Apache Corp., Mpls., 1974-76; EDP auditor Coopers & Lybrand, Mpls., 1976-78; data communications cons. AT&T, Mpls., 1978-85; tech. cons. Contel Info. Systems, 1985—. Served with Minn. Air N.G., 1963-69. Address: 9867 Dakota Rd Bloomington MN 55438

ANDERSON, ROBERT LEROY, educator; b. Wadena, Minn., Nov. 22, 1940; s. Eddie Irvin and Elsie Amelia (Winter) A.; B.S., U. Minn., 1966, in bus. mgmt., 1974. County extension dir. U. Minn., Walker, 1970-71; vets. farm mgmt. instr. Little Falls (Minn.) Community Schs., 1971-74, Area Vo-Tech. Inst., Staples, Minn., 1974-76; adult farm bus. mgmt. instr. Woodland Coop. Center, Staples, 1976—; mgmt. cons. Served with U.S. Army, 1962-64. Mem. NEA, Minn. Edn. Assn., Nat. Agrl. Edn. Instrs. Assn., Minn. Agrl. Educators Assn., Nat. Hort. Therapy Assn. Home: PO Box 281 Rural Route 2 Staples MN 56479 Office: Woodland Coop Center Clarissa MN 56440

ANDERSON, ROBERT MARSHALL, bishop; b. S.I., N.Y., Dec. 18, 1933; s. Arthur Harold and Hazel Schneider A.; m. Mary Artemis Evans, Aug. 24, 1960; children: Martha, Elizabeth, Catherine, Thomas. B.A., Colgate U., 1955; S.T.B., Berkeley Div. Sch., 1961; D.D. (hon.), Seabury Western Sem., 1978, Berkeley Divinity Sch., Yale U., 1977. Ordained priest Episcopal Ch.; curate St. John's Ch., Stamford, Conn., 1961-63; vicar St. John's Ch., 1963-67; priest in charge Middle Haddan, Conn., 1963-67; rector 1967-68; asso. rector St. John's Ch., Stamford, 1968-72; dean St. Mark's Cathedral, Salt Lake City, 1972-78; bishop Episcopal Diocese of Minn., Mpls., 1978—. Served with U.S. Army.; Danforth fellow, 1959-60. Mem. Berkeley Alumni (pres. 1972-76). Democrat. Clubs: Mpls, Minikahda. Office: Episc Diocese of Minn 309 Clifton Ave Minneapolis MN 55403 *

ANDERSON, RONALD REGIS, manufacturing executive; b. Youngstown, Ohio, Jan. 27, 1942; s. Harold M. and Mary (Harris) A.; m. Gayle Ann Fergus, June 20, 1970; children: Brian A., Melissa L. BBA, Youngstown State U., 1966. V.p. Mid-States Electric Inc., Brookfield, Ohio, 1967-70; pres., chmn. bd. Universal Devel. Enterprises, Inc., Girard, Ohio, 1970—; pres., chief exec. officer, chmn. bd. Universal Inns of Am., Inc., Girard, 1972—; chief exec. officer, chmn. GF Corp., Youngstown, 1982—; vice chmn. franchise adv. bd. Days Inn Am., 1976, chmn. 1977-78. Mem. Internat. Franchise Assn. (Disting. Achievement award 1976), Mfrs. Assn. (bd. dirs. Eastern Ohio and Western Pa. 1986), Youngstown Area C. of C. (bd. dirs. 1984-86). Republican. Roman Catholic. Office: GF Corp 4944 Belmont Ave Youngstown OH 44505

ANDERSON, RUTH NATHAN, syndicated columnist, TV news host, writer, recording artist; b. N.Y.C., Jan. 28, 1934; d. Solomon and Anna (Cornick) Gans; student N.Y. U., George Washington U., evenings 1952-56; m. Arthur Aksel Anderson, Jr., Sept. 11, 1971; stepchildren—Jack Anderson, Barbara Anderson-Rouse, Terri Anderson-Sarli. Newsletter editor Washington Post, 1952-53; chief med. writer, press officer Nat. Multiple Sclerosis Soc., N.Y.C., 1953-55; feature editor Crusade for Freedom, Radio Free Europe, N.Y.C., 1955-58; editor jr. TV dept. TV Revue, N.Y.C., 1958-61; feature-series reporter N.Am. Newspaper Alliance, Women's News Service, N.Y.C., 1961-79; writer, originator Doctor's Grapevine column Nat. Features Syndicate, Chgo., 1969-73; author-owner syndicated column VIP Med. Grapevine, Round Lake, Ill., 1973—; feature news corr. Waukegan (Ill.) News-Sun, 1977-82; writer, host Celebrity Health News, Cablenet TV, Chgo., 1985—; feature writer Scripps-Howard News Service, Chgo.; Chgo. contbg. editor Music City Entertainer, Nashville, 1976—; tchr. journalism, creative writing, speech arts Fla. State Bd. Adult Edn., 1968-69; lectr. writing seminars for faculty U. Ill. at Chgo. Circle Campus, 1970-80. Trustee, v.p. bd. Round Lake Pub. Library, 1977—; Right-to-Read vol. tutor jr. high schs., Round Lake, 1977-86; singer ARC entertainment com. Bedside Network, 1974—. Mem. Chgo. Women in Broadcasting, Am. Med. Writers Assn., Am. Mus. Women in the Arts (charter), Lake County Assn. Journalists, Nat. Assn. for Female Execs., Chgo. Unltd., Press Vets. Assn., Internat. Platform Assn., Future Physicians Am. (hon.), Nat. Acad. Recording Arts and Scis. Clubs: Chgo. Press, Chgo. Advt. Author booklet: How You Can Be a Part of Your United Nations, 1959; contbg. writer Woman's World mag.; contbr. articles to various mags. including Parents, Pageant, Mademoiselle, Science Digest, Reader's Digest, TV Guide, TV Radio Mirror, This Week, Am. Weekly, Am. Home, others; features on U.S. presidents in archives of Hoover, Truman, Eisenhower, Kennedy and Johnson presdl. libraries. Rec. artist mus. comedy songs, pop for Am. Sound label. Home: 161 Nasa Circle Round Lake IL 60073

ANDERSON, STEFAN STOLEN, banker; b. Madison, Wis., Apr. 1934; s. Theodore M. and Siri (Stolen) A.; m. Joan Timmermann, Sept. 19, 1959; children - Sharon Jill, Theodore Peter. A.B. magna cum laude, Harvard, 1956; M.B.A., U. Chgo., 1960. With Am. Nat. Bank & Trust Co. of Chgo., 1960-74, v.p., 1966-68, group v.p., 1968, exec v.p. 1969-74; exec. v.p., dir.Mchts. Nat. Bank, Muncie Ind., 1974-79, pres., dir., 1979 -, chmn. bd. dirs., 1987 -; pres., dir. First Mchts. Corp., Muncie, 1983-87, chmn. bd. dirs., pres., 1987 -; dir. Maxon Corp., Del. Advancement Corp.; pres., dir. BMH Health Services, Inc. bd. dirs. Delaware County C. of C., Delaware County United Way , Muncie Symphony Orch., pres.; trustee Roosevelt U., 1970-74, George Francis Ball Found., 1987 -, Muncie Family YMCA, 1987 -; nat. chmn. ann. fund Ball State U., 1985 -86. Served with USNR, 1956 -58. Mem. Independent Bankers Assn. Ind. (dir.), Ind. Bankers Assn. (dir.), Phi Beta Kappa, Beta Gamma Sigma. Clubs: Delaware Country (Muncie), Rotary (past pres.) (Muncie). Home: 2705 W Twickingham Dr Muncie IN 47304 Office: Merchants Nat Bank 200 E Jackson St Muncie IN 47305

ANDERSON, STEPHEN JOEL, engineer, manufacturing company executive; b. Des Moines, Feb. 9, 1953; s. Noel Merrill and Mary Mabel A.; m Jacqueline Rae Fagen, July 26, 1975; children: Matthew Joel, Joel Justin, Holly Jo. BSCE, Iowa State U., 1975. Engr. Black and Veatch, Kansas City, Mo., 1975-76; engr., gen. mgr., pres. Merrill Mfg. Co., Storm Lake, Iowa, 1976-80, pres., 1980—, also bd. dirs. Patentee yard hydrant. Mem. Nat. Water Well Assn., Iowa Assn. Bus. and Industry (minuteman 1982). Republican. Methodist. Home: 132 Mallard Ave Box 1214 Storm Lake IA 50588 Office: Merrill Mfg Co 315 Flindt Dr Storm Lake IA 50588

ANDERSON, STEVEN KEITH, musical entertainer, writer; b. New Rockford, N.D., Apr. 18, 1948; s. Keith Elmo and Ida (Noraker) A.; m. Helen Christine Eastman, Mar. 9, 1968; children: Kevin Patrick, Kia Kristine. BS in Music Edn., N.D. State U., 1970; postgrad., U. No. Colo., 1972. Tchr. Newburg (N.D.) Pub. Sch., 1970-72, Kennedy (Minn.) Pub. Sch., 1972-74; entertainer The Steve Anderson Show, Thief River Falls, Minn., 1974—; repair tech. musical instruments Anderson Instrument Repair, Thief River Falls, 1983—; instr. tuba Northland Community Coll., Thief River Falls, 1977—; guest conductor N.D. State U. Alumni Band, Fargo, 1984. Artist and composer (record albums) Steve Anderson: On His Best Behavior, 1984, Steve Anderson: Pushin' 40, 1987; writer various songs. Mem. bd. dirs. Thief River Falls Arts Council, 1981-83, also com. chmn. Mem. Am. Fedn. Musicians. Lutheran. Home and Office: 501 S Kendall Thief River Falls MN 56701

ANDERSON, SUSAN BARBARA, academic administrator; b. N.Y.C., Mar. 21, 1946; d. Allen John Jr. and Barbara V. de Castro; 1 child, Sonja

Denise. Student, Lake Erie Coll., 1965-66; AA, Cuyahoga Community Coll., 1976; BS, MS, Kent (Ohio) State U., 1978. Placement officer Cuyahoga Community Coll., Cleve., 1974-76, displaced homemakers counselor, 1977-80, dir. women's programs, 1980-82, dist. dir. continuing edn., 1982-84, asst. dean continuing edn., 1984—; talk show host Cable TV, Cleve., 1984-85; instr. Cuyahoga Community Coll., Cleve.; cons. Shaker Heights, Ohio Library System., 1984. Cons., vol. United Way Cleve., 1984—; fundraiser Am. Cancer Soc., 1986—. Named Career Woman of Achievement YWCA, Cleve., 1985; recipient Jefferson award for Community Service, City of Cleve., 1984. Mem. Am. Soc. Tng. and Devel., Am. Assn. Community Edn. Adminstrs. Club: Scandanavian Health Nut (Cleve.). Avocations: aerobics, music, cross country skiing, swimming, weaving. Home: 891 Spicers Ln Sagamore Hills OH 44067 Office: Cuyahoga Community Coll 4250 Richmond Rd Warrensville Township OH 44122

ANDERSON, THEODORE EDMUND, chemical company executive, researcher; b. Dallas, Nov. 27, 1929; s. Theodore Edmund and Agnes Amelia (Hagman) A.; m. Phyllis Jane Beacom, Sept. 8, 1956; children—Mary, Joan. Student Augustana Coll., 1948-49; B.S., U. Mich., 1953; M.S., Mich. State U., 1958, Ph.D., 1963. Research chemist Union Carbide, Pitts., 1958-59; research sect. head Dow Chem. Co., Midland, Mich., 1963-69; quality control devel. mgr. Miles Labs., Elkhart, Ind., 1969-76, quality assurance dir., 1976-79; research mgr. Badische Anilin & Soda Fabrik Co., Diversey-Wyandotte Corp., Wyandotte, Mich., 1979—. Inventor in field. Vice pres. St. Thomas Lutheran Ch., 1983-84; fund raiser Republican Party, East Lansing, Mich., 1960. Served with U.S. Army, 1954-55. Recipient Sigma Xi Research award, 1963; Pickle Packers Assn. grantee, 1959-61. Mem. Am. Chem. Soc., U. Mich. Alumni Assn. (pres. Midland chpt. 1966-67). Club: Grosse Ile Yacht. Lodges: Masons, Rotary. Avocations: tennis; downhill skiing; boating; music; reading. Home: 8534 Manchester Rd Grosse Ile MI 48138 Office: Diversey-Wyandotte Corp 1532 Biddle Ave Wyandotte MI 48192

ANDERSON, THOMAS ELLSWORTH, building service company executive, retail executive; b. Moline, Ill., Nov. 11, 1947; s. Harold Ellsworth and Mildred (Lofgren) A.; m. Paulette Sue Mataya, June 19, 1976; children: Jennifer Lynn, Amy Sue. BA, Augustana Coll., Rock Island, Ill., 1969. Salesman State Mut. Ins., Davenport, Iowa, 1970-73; territory mgr. Duracell Batteries, Bethel, Conn., 1973-78, Acco Industries, York, Pa., 1980-82; systems engr. R.V. Evans Co., Decatur, Ill., 1978-80; v.p. Sani-Pro Maintenance Systems Inc., Moline, 1984—. Mem. Bldg. Service Contractor Assn., Am. Gem Soc., Jaycees (sec. 1984). Methodist. Avocations: golf, bowling, boys' baseball, girls' fastpitch softball. Home: 872 38th Ave East Moline IL 61244 Office: Sani-Pro Maintenance Systems Inc 2452 53d St Moline IL 61265

ANDERSON, THOMAS RALPH, financial services company executive; b. Aurora, Ill., Feb. 12, 1938; s. Ralph A. and Jeannette C. (Malmer) A.; m. Carol Tremaine, Oct. 6, 1962; children: Brian, Rodney, Nicole. B.S., U. Ill., 1961. C.P.A., Ill. Auditor Arthur Young & Co., Chgo., 1961-66; comptroller Kemper Fin. Services, Inc., Chgo., 1966-71, v.p., comptroller, 1971-75, exec. v.p., 1975-77, pres., chief exec. officer, bd. dirs., 1977-83, chmn., chief exec. officer, bd. dirs., 1983—13; chmn., treas. Kemper Investors Life Ins. Co., Chgo., 1976-78, chmn., chief exec. officer, treas., 1978-79, chmn., chief exec. officer, 1979—, mgr., dir. separate accounts, 1983—; sr. v.p., bd. dirs. Kemper Corp., Long Grove, Ill., 1983-86, exec. v.p., bd. dirs., 1986—; sr. v.p., bd. dirs. Lumbermens Mut. Casualty Co., Chgo., 1983-86, exec. v.p., bd. dirs., 1986—; sr. v.p., bd. dirs. Am. Motorists Ins. Co., Long Grove, 1983-86, exec. v.p., bd. dirs., 1986; sr. v.p., bd. dirs. Am. Mfrs. Mut. Ins. Co., Long Grove, 1983-86, now exec. v.p., bd. dirs., 1986—; chmn. bd. dirs. Kemper/Cymrot, Inc., Chgo., 1983—; chmn. bd. dirs., pres. and chief exec. officer Kemper Fin. Cos., Inc., Chgo., 1986—; v.p., bd. dirs. Tech. Fund, Inc., Kemper Growth Fund, Inc., Kemper Summit Fund, Inc., Kemper Total Return Fund, Inc., Kemper Income & Capital Preservation Fund, Inc., Kemper Money Market Fund, Inc., Kemper Mcpl. Bond Fund, Inc., Kemper Option Income Fund, Inc., Kemper U.S. Govt. Securities Fund, Inc., Kemper High Yield Fund, Inc., Cash Equivalent Fund, Inc., Kemper Internat. Fund, Inc., Kemper Govt. Money Market Fund, Inc., Tax-Exempt Money Market Fund, Inc., Kemper Calif. Tax-Free Income Fund, Inc., Investment Portfolios, Inc.; bd. dirs. Fin. Guaranty Ins. Co., Bateman Eichler Hill Richards, Inc., Blunt, Ellis & Loewi, Inc., Prescott, Ball & Turben, Inc., Lovett Mitchell Webb & Garrison, Inc., Boettcher & Co., Inc., Peers & Co., Plymouth Place, Inc., FGIC Corp.. Trustee, chmn. fin. com. Ill. chpt. Leukemia Soc. Am., 1980-86; trustee James S. Kemper Found., 1983—; bd. dirs. Robert Crown Ctr. Health Edn., 1986—, Plymouth Pl., Inc., 1986—. Mem. Am. Inst. C.P.A.s, Ill. Soc. C.P.A.s, Am. Inst. Corp. Controllers, Alpha Tau Omega. Congregationalist. Clubs: Economics (LaGrange, Ill.), LaGrange Country (LaGrange, Ill.); University (Chgo.), Attic (Chgo.), Whitehall (Chgo.). Lodge: Masons. Home: 209 S Blackstone Ave LaGrange IL 60525 Office: Kemper Fin Serivces 120 S LaSalle St Chicago IL 60603

ANDERSON, TIMOTHY LEE, real estate and finance executive; b. Indpls., July 5, 1948; s. Jack Miller and Barbara Lee (Price) A.; m. Mary Jane Wiltgen, Feb. 21, 1970; children: Aaron Lee, Adrienne Lynn. BA, Ind. U., 1975. CPA, Ind. Field auditor Ind. Farm Bur. Cooperative, Indpls., 1978-80, account supr., 1980-82, tax adminstr., 1982-84, mgr. acctg., 1984-85; controller, sec., treas. Crossroads Rentals, Indpls., 1985—, also bd. dirs. Served with USN, 1967-71. Mem. Am. Inst. CPA's, Ind. CPA Soc. Home: 2215 N 600 E Lebanon IN 46502 Office: Crossroads Rentals Inc 8225 W Washington Indianapolis IN 46231

ANDERSON, WARREN LEE, marketing professional; b. Kansas City, Mo., Jan. 27, 1952; s. Warren Lee and Helen Jesse (Dundas) A.; m. Kathleen Ann Benson, Jan. 6, 1979; children: Jessica Lee, Ryan Joseph. BS in Biology, U. Mo., Kansas City, 1979; MA in Mktg. with distinction, Webster U., 1986. Lab. tech. Curts Labs., Kansas City, 1975-77; analytical chemist Marion Labs., Inc., Kansas City, 1977-81, mktg. adminstr., 1981-84, mgr. sales adminstrn., 1984-86, mktg. mgr., 1986—; contbr. Marion Labs. Polit. Action Com., 1985-86. Active United Way, Kansas City, 1983—; mem. River Oaks South Home Owners Assn., 1986—. Named one of Outstanding Young Men Am., 1985. Mem. Phi Kappa Phi. Lutheran. Club: Toastmasters. Avocations: outdoor sports, woodworking, poetry.

ANDERSON, WENDELL WILLIAM, JR., metal and plastic products maufacturing company executive; b. Pitts., 1925; married. Student, Yale U., 1945. With Bundy Corp., Warren, Mich., 1945—; asst. gen. mgr. Bundy Corp., Detroit, 1951-52; v.p., gen. mgr. Bundy Corp., 1952-59, pres., 1959-66; chmn., chief exec. officer, dir. Bundy Corp., Detroit, 1966—; dir. Detroit Edison Co., Ex-Coll-O Corp., Mfrs. Nat. Bank, Detroit. Office: Bundy Corp 333 W Fort St Detroit MI 48226 also: Bundy Corp 12345 E Nine Mile Rd Warren MI 48090

ANDERSON, WILLIAM ARTHUR, school superintendent; b. Page County, Iowa, May 7, 1922; s. Arthur and Martha Anderson; m. Joyce (Peg) Nesbit; children: Kathy, Kerry. BA magna cum laude, Tarkio Coll., 1943, LHD (hon.), 1963; postgrad., Ala. Poly. Inst., 1943, Vanderbilt U., 1944; MS, Iowa State U., 1951; EdD, U. Nebr., 1960; D of Pedagogy (hon.), Buena Vista Coll., 1973; LLD (hon.), Morningside Coll., 1975. Tchr. sci. and math. Villisca (Iowa) High Sch., 1946-48, prin., 1946-48; supt. Villisca Community Schs., 1951-57, Clarinda (Iowa) Community Schs., 1957-61, Cedar Falls (Iowa) Community Schs., 1961-66, Sioux City (Iowa) Community Schs., 1966-76, Hampton City (Va.) Pub. Schs., 1976-80, Des Moines Community Ind. Sch. Dist., 1980—; mem. gov.'s commn. intergovtl. relations, 1963-66, Title III state adv. com., 1968, task force on tchr. edn. and cert., 1984; chmn. ednl. TV com. Northwest Iowa, 1966-68; adminstr. rep. State Merit Pay Com., 1968; bd. dirs. Iowa Ctr. Research in Sch. adminstrn., 1962-66, Upper Midwest Regional Edn. Lab., 1969-71, Tchrs. Corps Policy, 1980-81. Mem. adv. com. State Fire Marshall, 1964-66; edn. div. leader United Way, 1981, bd. dirs., 1984; chmn. Goals for Sioux City Study, 1974-75; trustee Briar Cliff Coll., Sioux City, 1981, Des Moines Sci. Ctr., 1982; bd. dirs. Hampton City Library, Jr. Achievement Cen. Iowa, 1980-81, Hampton Employees Retirement System, vice chmn., Morningside Coll., 1975-78, 81-84. Recipient Laureate award Iowa State U., 1983, Iowa High Sch. Athletic Assn. award, 1987; named Educator of Yr., Phi Delta Kappa, 1986. Mem. Am. Assn. Sch. Adminstrs. (exec. com. 1975-78, com. advancement sch. adminstrn. 1985-87), Iowa Assn. Sch. Adminstrs. (pres. 1961-62), Iowa State Edn. Assn. (exec. bd. dirs. 1960-65, pres. 1962-63, named one of Top 100 Educators in U.S. 1984, 87). Methodist. Avocations: music, hunting, fishing, traveling, sports. Home: 2917 Fleur Dr Des Moines IA 50321 Office: Des Moines Ind Community Sch Dist 1800 Grand Ave Des Moines IA 50307

ANDERSON, WILLIAM JUDSON, engineering educator; b. Yale, Iowa, Nov. 18, 1935; s, Frank Albert and Agnes Delores (Leo) A.; m. Elizabeth Maurine Kruse, June 21, 1957; children: Anne Christine, Ellen Carol, Glen Richard. BS, Iowa State U., 1957, MS, 1958; PhD, Calif. Inst. Tech., 1963. Registered profl. engr., Mich. Prof. U. Mich., Ann Arbor, 1965—; pres. Automated Analysis Corp., Ann Arbor, 1983—. Author: MSC/Interactive Training, 1983, (video lecture series) Finite Elements in Design, 1984; editor: (video lecture series) DMAP Programming, 1986. Served with USAF, 1962-65. Mem. AIAA. Presbyterian. Avocations: volleyball, woodworking. Home: 2692 Byington Ann Arbor MI 48105 Office: U Mich Aerospace Engring Dept Ann Arbor MI 48109

ANDERSON, WILLIAM MILLER, educational administrator; b. Pulaski, Va., Nov. 26, 1940; s. William Miller and Fary Virginia (Wyrick) A.; m. Lee Ann Stephens, Apr. 13, 1968; children: David Ryan, Grant Michael. MusB with distinction, U. Rochester, 1963, MusM, 1964; PhD, U. Mich., 1970. Tchr. Gates Chili High Sch., Rochester, N.Y., 1963-64, Penfield (N.Y.) Cen. Schs., 1964-66; instr. music Macalester Coll., St. Paul, 1970-71, U. Mich., Ann Arbor, 1971; prof. music Kent (Ohio) State U., 1971—, asst. dean grad. coll., 1978—, dir. Ctr. for Study of World Music, 1980—, dir. Liberal Studies Program, 1985—; dir. Ctr. for Study of World Music, Kent State U., 1980—, Liberal STudies Program, Kent State U., 1985—. Author: Teaching Asian Musics in Elementary and Secondary School, 1976; (with others) Music and Related Arts for the Classroom, 1978, Integrating Music into the Classroom, 1985. Mem. Internat. Soc. Music Edn., Music Educators Nat. Conf., Soc. Ethnomusicology, Soc. Asian Musics, Coll. Music Soc. Avocation: waterskiing. Home: 855 Nautilis Trail Aurora OH 44202 Office: Kent State U Grad Coll Kent OH 44242

ANDERSON-GRANT, ANGELA THEODORA, dentist; b. Louisville, Oct. 17, 1955; s. Mentoria Annesse (Wiggins) Anderson; m. Owen Essex Grant, May 8, 1982. Student, Miami U., Oxford, Ohio, 1974-76; BS in Zoology, Ohio State U., 1978, cert. dental hygiene, 1978; DDS, Case-Western Res. U., 1983. Dentist Dr. E. Jordan, Cleve., 1983-85, Dr. J. Greene, Cleve., 1985—; dentist, mgr. Convenient Dental Ctr., Warrensville, Ohio, 1985—. Career day speaker., various schs., Cleve., 1984-86. Named Outstanding Young Woman of Am., 1982, 83. Mem. ADA, Ohio Dental Soc., Cleve. Dental Soc., Forest City Dental Soc., Delta Sigma Theta. Methodist. Home: 1000 Pennfield Rd Cleveland Heights OH 44121 Office: Convenient Dental Ctr 4411 Northfield Rd Warrensville OH 44128

ANDONIAN, ELISA MARIE, retail executive; b. Garfield Heights, Ohio, Apr. 14, 1960; d. Edward Serg and Elaine Joy (Draeger) A. BA, Cleve. State U., 1983. Asst. dir. pub. relations and advt. Cleve. Tux Hdqrs., Macedonia, Ohio, 1983; mgr. Gold Circle Stores, Parma, Ohio, 1984; mgr. women's wear Paul Harris, North Randall, Ohio, 1984—. Profl. figure skater. Avocations: fashion shows. Home: 11310 Briarclift Dr Garfield Heights OH 44125 Office: Paul Harris #143 North Randall Mall North Randall OH 44125

ANDRE, ELLEN CAROL, business educator; b. Parkston, S.D., Jan. 17, 1945; d. Leonard David and Fern Carol (Fox) Hanson; m. William Elmer Andre, June 27, 1969; children—Marcus William, Erica Ellen. B.S. in Ed., U. S.D.-Springfield, 1967; M.A. in Adult and Higher Edn., U. S.D.-Vermillion, 1980. Permanent profl. cert. edn., Iowa. Tchr., Akron (Iowa) Community High Sch., 1967-69; sec. Pacific Ordnance and Electronics Co., Long Beach, Calif., 1969-70; tchr. Andes Central High Sch., Lake Andes, S.D., 1970-74; adminstrv. asst. Fed. Land Bank Assn., Sioux City, Iowa, 1974-76; instr. Bus. and Office Occupations div. Western Iowa Tech. Community Coll., Sioux City, 1976—, advisor Office Edn. Assn., 1978-83. Mobile dep. registrar for Woodbury County, Iowa, 1982; Americanism chmn. VFW Aux., 1970-74; mem., treas. Sioux City Civic New Comers, 1974-77; mem., sec. parent adv. com. Nodland Elem. Sch., Sioux City, 1981-82, 84-86. Mem. Profl. Secs. Internat., Iowa Vocat. Assn., NEA, Iowa State Edn. Assn., Am. Vocat. Assn., Western Iowa Tech. Community Coll. Edn. Assn. (sec., treas.). Democrat. Lutheran. Developer Competency Based Instructional Learning Materials, 1978-80.

ANDREAS, BRUCE FREDERICK, pathologist; b. Cleve., May 10, 1925; s. Frederick William and Edna Louise (Buehler) A.; m. Jean Bobbitt, Aug. 28, 1954; children—Karen Louise Podojil, Frederick William II, Patricia Marie Driver, Jonathan Bruce; m. Marie Greder Nimietz, July 4, 1976. A.B., Heidelberg Coll., 1949; M.D., Ohio State U., 1953. Diplomate Am. Bd. Pathology. Intern Miami Valley Hosp., Dayton, Ohio, 1953-54; resident in pathology Miami Valley Hosp., 1954-58; pathologist, dir. lab. Geauga Community Hosp., Chardon, Ohio, 1959—; chief of staff Geauga Community Hosp., 1969-70, med. dir., 1985—; pres. Geauga Lab. Services, Inc.; trustee Cancer Data Systems Inc., 1987—; cancer liaison physician Am. Coll. Surgeons, 1980—. Served with U.S. Army, 1943-46. Decorated Bronze Star with two oak leaf clusters. Fellow Coll. Am. Pathologists (lab. insp. accreditation program 1976—), Am. Acad. Med. Dirs., Am. Soc. Clin. Pathologists; mem. AMA, Ohio Soc. Pathologists, Cleve. Soc. Pathologists (pres. 1971), Ohio Med. Assn. (del.), Geauga County Med. Soc. (pres. 1966), Cleve. Acad. Medicine, Am. Acad. Med. Dirs. Home: 11296 Brookside Rd Chardon OH 44024 Office: Geauga Community Hosp Box 249 Chardon OH 44024

ANDREAS, DWAYNE ORVILLE, corporation executive; b. Worthington, Minn., Mar. 4, 1918; s. Reuben P. and Lydia (Stoltz) A.; m. Bertha Benedict, 1938 (div.); 1 dau., Sandra Ann Andreas McMurtie; m. Dorothy Inez Snyder, Dec. 21, 1947; children: TerryHerbert-Burns, Michael D. Student, Wheaton (Ill.) Coll., 1935-36; hon. degree, Barry U. Vice pres., dir. Honeymead Products Co., Cedar Rapids, Iowa, 1936-46; chmn. bd., chief exec. officer Honeymead Products Co. (now Nat. City Bancorp.), Mankato, Minn., 1952-72; v.p. Cargill, Inc., Mpls., 1946-52; exec. v.p. Farmers Union Grain Terminal Assn., St. Paul, 1960-66; chmn. bd., chief exec. officer Archer-Daniels-Midland Co., Decatur, Ill., 1970—, also mem. exec. com., dir.; pres. Seaview Hotel Corp., 1958—; dir. Salomon, Inc., Lone Star Industries, Inc., Greenwich, Conn.; mem. Pres.'s Gen. Adv. Commn. on Fgn. Assistance Programs, 1965-68, Pres.'s Adv. Council on Mgmt. Improvement, 1969-73; chmn. Pres.'s Task Force on Internat. Pvt. Enterprise. Pres. Andreas Found.; trustee U.S. Naval Acad. Found., Freedom from Hunger Found., Woodrow Wilson Internat. Ctr. Scholars; nat. bd. dirs. Boys' Club Am.; chmn. U.S.-USSR Trade and Econ. Council; chmn. Exec. Council on Fgn. Diplomats; trustee Hoover Inst. on War, Revolution and Peace, Woodrow Wilson Internat. Ctr. for Scholars; mem. Trilateral Commn.; chmn. Found. for Commemoration of the U.S. Constitution, 1986. Mem. Fgn. Policy Assn. N.Y. (dir.). Clubs: Union League (Chgo.); Indian Creek Country (Miami Beach, Fla.); Mpls., Minikahda (Mpls.); Blind Brook Country (Purchase, N.Y.); Economic of N.Y. (chmn.), Links, Knickerbocker, Friars (N.Y.C.). Office: Archer Daniels Midland Co PO Box 1470 Decatur IL 62525

ANDREASEN, GEORGE FREDRICK, dentist; b. Fremont, Nebr., Feb. 16, 1934; s. George T. and Laura Mae (Hynek) A.; m. Nancy Coover, June 13, 1959; children—Susan, Robin. B.S. (Regents scholar), U. Nebr., 1959; D.D.S., 1959, M.S. (NIH fellow), 1963. Research fellow Worcester Coll., Oxford, Eng., 1960-61; asst. prof. orthodontics U. Iowa Coll. Dentistry, Iowa City, 1963-67; asso. prof., acting head dept. orthodontics U. Iowa Coll. Dentistry, 1967, asso. prof., head dept., 1968, prof., head dept. orthodontics, 1968—; practice dentistry Iowa City, 1963—; cons. to various dental corps. on dental materials. Contbr. articles to profl. jours. U. Nebr. alumnus master, 1974; Jarabek award nominee, 1985. Fellow Am. Coll. Dentists, Royal Soc. Health (Eng.); mem. Am. Assn. Orthodontists (chmn. sci. com. 1971-72, nat. com. on research 1976-79, leader roundtable 1970—), Iowa Orthodontic Soc. (pres. 1972-73), Am., Iowa dental assns., Univ. Dist. Dental Assn., Iowa Alumni Assn. (life), U. Iowa Med. Center (life), Orthodontic Edn. and Research Found., Fedn. Dentmire Internat., Iowa Acad. Scis., AAAS, Am. Oxonion, Phalanx Blue Print Key, Sigma Xi, Pi Tau Sigma, Omicron Kappa Upsilon, Delta Tau Delta, Xi Psi Phi. Club: Athletic (Iowa City). Patentee in field. Home: 1104 Penkridge St Iowa City IA 52240 Office: Room 5221 DSB U Iowa Iowa City IA 52240

ANDREE, ROBERT GLEN, information system executive; b. Rensselaer, Ind., Dec. 1, 1934; s. George William and Marie Irene (Johnson) A.; m. Linda Lou Tilton, Feb. 22, 1957; children: Robert Jr., Scott, Anne. BS, U.S. Mil. Acad., 1956; MBA, U. Ga., 1972. Commd. 2d lt. U.S. Army, 1956, advanced through grades to lt. col., 1970, ret., 1977; dir. computer systems Ind. U., Gary, 1977—. Mem. Am. Mgmt. Assn., Data Processing Mgmt. Assn. Lodge: Rotary. Avocation: bicycling. Home: 5290 W 85th Pl Crown Point IN 46307 Office: Ind U NW Campus 3400 Broadway Gary IN 46408

ANDREOFF, CHRISTOPHER ANDON, lawyer; b. Detroit, July 15, 1947; s. Andon Anastas and Mildred Dimitry (Kolinoff) A.; m. Nancy Anne Krochmal, Jan. 12, 1980; 1 child, Alison Brianne. B.A., Wayne State U., 1969; postgrad. in law Washington U., St. Louis, 1969-70; J.D., U. Detroit, 1972. Bar: Mich. 1972, U.S. Dist. Ct. (ea. dist.) Mich. 1972, U.S. Ct. Appeals (6th cir.) 1974, Fla. 1978, U.S. Supreme Ct. 1980. Legal intern Wayne County Prosecutor's Office, Detroit, 1970-72; law clk. Wayne County Cir. Ct., Detroit, 1972-73; asst. U.S. atty. U.S. Dept. Justice, Detroit, 1973-80, asst. chief Criminal Div., U.S. Atty.'s Office, 1977-80, spl. atty. Organized Crime and Racketeering sect. U.S. Dept. Justice, 1980-84, dep. chief Detroit Organized Crime Strike Force, 1982-85, mem. narcotics adv. com. U.S. Dept. Justice, 1979-80; ptnr. Evans & Luptak, Detroit, 1985—; lectr. U.S. Atty. Gen. Advocacy Inst., 1984. Recipient numerous spl. commendations FBI, U.S. Drug Enforcement Adminstrn., U.S. Dept. Justice, U.S. Atty. Gen. Mem. ABA, Fed. Bar Assn. (speaker criminal law sect. Detroit 1983—), Mich. Bar Assn., Fla. Bar Assn., Detroit Bar Assn. Greek Orthodox. Home: 4661 Rivers Edge Dr Troy MI 48098 Office: Evans & Luptak 2500 Buhl Bldg Detroit MI 48226

ANDREOLI, CHARLES ANTHONY, designer, sculptor; b. Kenosha, Wis., Aug. 26, 1928; s. Ralph and Jenny Andreoli; student Am. Acad. Art, 1946-48, DePaul U., 1948-49; student of Alexandre Zlatoff-Mierski, 1947-51; m. Mary Celebre, Nov. 28, 1953. Portrait painter, 1949—; interior designer DaPrato Studio, Chgo., 1954-56, J. Cotey Co., Chgo.; free lance designer to home furnishing trade, including Hillenbrand Industries (Ind.), Sandel Lamps, Chgo., U.S. Industries Lamp div., Chgo., L.C.A. Lamp div., (Ky.); lamp design cons. McGraw Edison Co., Chgo.; product designer Stiffel Co.; important works include Mayan Room Restaurant, Rockefeller Centre, sculptured arches Emerald Door Restaurant, New Orleans; created Andreoli Porcelaine Sculptures Ltd. Edition. Address: 1340 N Astor St Chicago IL 60610

ANDREOLI, PAUL NELSON, financial executive; b. Dayton, Ohio, Sept. 10, 1948; s. Louis and Mary Betty Jane (Bensley) A.; m. Cynthia Sue Goldberg, Sept. 3, 1970 (div. July 1985); children: Philip N., Joshua David; m. Flavia Angela Maria Musto, Dec. 1985. BS in Acctg., U. Md., 1974; MS in Mgmt., MIT, 1975. CPA, Md. Asst. to controller Baxter Travenol Labs., Deerfield, Ill., 1976-76; mgr. fin. Travenal Group Baster Travenol Labs., Deerfield, Ill., 1976-77; mgr. long-range planning Playboy Enterprise, Chgo., 1977-79; mgr. fin. control Brunswick Corp., Skokie, Ill., 1979-82; treas., v.p. Vapor Corp., Niles, Ill., 1986—. Served to sgt. U.S. Army, 1966-72, Vietnam. Republican. Avocations: wargame, history, languages. Office: Vapor Corp 6420 W Howard St Niles IL 60648

ANDRES, ERNEST HERMAN, restaurateur; b. Chgo., Feb. 27, 1941; s. Herman Ernest and Mary Eileen (Nolan) A.; m. Barbara Jean Shannon, Nov. 5, 1966; children: Edward, Diane. Grad. high sch., Chgo. Owner Andres Steak and Seafood, Richmond, Ill., 1964—. Named Citizen of Yr., Genoa City (Wis.) Lions Club, 1985, Patriotic Citizen of Yr. Richmond (Ill.) VFW, 1985. Mem. McHenry County Restaurant Assn. (pres. 1980-81), Nat. Tour Assn., Am. Bus Assn., No. Ill. Tourism Assn., Ont. Motorcoach Assn., Ill. Restaurant Assn., Nat. Restaurant Assn., United Bus. Owners of Am., Twin Lakes Businessman's Assn., Twin Lakes C. of C., Richmond C. of c., Richmond Mchts. Assn. Republican. Roman Catholic. Avocations: golf, boating, fishing, bowling. Home: 1926 Esch Rd Twin Lakes WI 53181 Office: Andres Steak and Seafood 11106 US 12 N Richmond IL 60071

ANDREW, ROBERT HARRY, agronomist; b. Platteville, Wis., Aug. 2, 1916; s. Harry Roscoe and Lu (Howery) A.; B.A., U. Wis., Madison, 1938; Ph.D., 1942; m. Nancy H. Wright, Apr. 15, 1944; children—Stephen, Elizabeth, Sarah, Martha, Charles. Agronomist Wis. Expt. Sta., 1942-46; asst. prof. agronomy U. Wis., Madison, 1946-52, asso. prof., 1952-58, prof., 1958—; vis. Fulbright lectr. U. Wageningen (Netherlands), 1953-54. Fellow AAAS, Am. Soc. Agronomy, Crop Sci. Soc. Am.; mem. Sigma Xi, Phi Sigma, Gamma Sigma Delta, Phi Beta Kappa, Gamma Alpha. Methodist. Contbr. articles to profl. jours. Home: 3809 Hillcrest Dr Madison WI 53705

ANDREWS, CATHERINE JOANNE, vocational administrator, consultant; b. Moline, Ill., Dec. 5, 1950; d. Earl Buzz and Mary Lucille (McCartey) A.; m. Steven George Andrews, June 12, 1970 (div. Dec., 1973); 1 child, Joseph Harrison. AA in Psychology, Black Hawk Coll., 1970; BBA, St. Ambrose Coll., 1985; postgrad., U. Iowa, 1986. Truant officer United Twnshp. High Sch., East Moline, Ill., 1972-73; employment counselor/planner to asst. dir. Ptnrs. in Job Tng., Rock Island, Ill., 1973-85; assoc. dir. job tng. Eastern Iowa Community Coll., Davenport, 1985-86, assoc. personnel dir., 1986—; mem. Women's Ednl. Needs, Davenport, 1985-86; chmn. Dislocated Worker task force, Rock Island, 1984-85; leader seminar Youth Employment Competencies for U.S. Dept. Labor, Bus., Nat.Govs. Assn., 1984—; presenter at pub. hearing Sen. subcom. on Employment Needs of Rural Areas, Des Moines, 1986. Editor, mem. review group Youth Employment Competencies, 1985; cons., editor Special Needs Students/Employment, 1986. Mem. Pres. Task Force on Youth Employment, Washington, 1979. Recipient award for Contbns. to Youth Employment Policy Devel., U.S. Dept. Labor, 1982. Mem. Am. Personnel Assn. Avocations: reading, jogging, housing renovation, horseback riding. Home: 629 18th St Silvis IL 61282 Office: Eastern Iowa Community Coll Job Tng 1606 Brady St Suite 306 Davenport IA 52803

ANDREWS, DIANN LOUISE, sales account executive; b. Spencer, Iowa, July 12, 1958; d. George Robert and Marilyn Ann (English) Graham; m. David Marshall Andrews, May 28, 1983. BS in Engring Ops., Iowa State U., 1980; MBA, U. Chgo., 1983. Trainee Detroit Diesel Allison, Indpls., 1980, plant floor supr., 1980-81; market planner GMF Robotics, Troy, Mich., 1983, product planner, 1983-84, bus. devel. mgr., 1984-86, Ford accounts mgr., 1986—. Precinct del. Troy Reps., 1984. Recipient Troy Community award Troy C. of C., 1986. Mem. Soc. Mfg. Engrs. Methodist. Lodge: Zonta (pres. Troy chpt. 1986). Avocations: aerobics, hiking, cross-country skiing. Office: GMF Robotics Corp 2000 S Adams Rd Auburn Hills MI 48057

ANDREWS, DONALD FREDERICK, architect; b. Moline, Ill., June 20, 1929; s. Norman Frederick and Marie Margaret (Mitchell) A.; m. Phyllis Kay Paine, June 15, 1957; children: Michael Frederick, Kathryn Jo. BArch, U. Minn., 1957. Architect Gingold and Assocs., Mpls., 1958-59; project architect Thorsen & Thorsen, Mpls., 1959-79, Setter Leach & Lindstrom, Mpls., 1979-80, Smiley, Glotter & Assocs., Mpls., 1980-85, Korsunsky, Krank, Erickson, Mpls., 1985—. Vol. Minn. Zool. Soc., Dakota County, 1983-86. Served with USN, 1949-53. Mem. AIA. Avocations: chess, duplicate bridge, bicycling, sports cars. Home: 50 Birnamwood Dr Burnsville MN 55337 Office: Korsunsky Krank Erickson 300 1st Ave Minneapolis MN 55401

ANDREWS, HOWARD, telephone company executive; b. Ft. Worth, Dec. 26, 1928; s. Howard Goddard and Vivian (Newsom) A.; m. Joyce June Tennison, Dec. 31, 1947; children: Gerald Wayne, Kathryn Michele. Student, Tex. Christian U., 1957-60. Mem. tech. staff Bell Telephone Lab., Holmdel, N.J., 1970-71; dist. plant supt. Southwestern Bell Telephone Co., St. Louis, 1971-75, dist. mgr., 1975-77, plant supr., 1977-79, div. mgr.-NCOO, 1979-85, div. staff mgr., 1985-86; v.p. ops. SystemOne Telecommunication, Houston, 1987—; cons. Bell Telephone Lab., Holmdel, 1970-71. Contbr. tech. papers to industry publs. (recognition award 1971). Recipient SWB's Chas W. Rider award, 1987. Republican. Avocations: amateur radio, fly fishing, sports cars, family activities.

ANDREWS, KAY ZIMMERMAN, family therapist; b. Sioux Falls, S.D., May 15, 1942; d. Erick Raynhold and Edna Charlotte (Anderson) Zimmerman; divorced; children: Joseph Steven, Peter Jay, Andrew Erich. BA, Macalester Coll., 1964; MDiv, McCormick Theol. Sem., 1967; postgrad., U. Minn., Mankato (Minn.) State U., 1978-80; clin., Am. Assn. Marriage and Family Therapy, 1978-80. Assoc. pastor Community Presbyn. Ch., Grand Rapids, Minn., 1967-69; exec. dir. Cannon Valley Counseling and Learning Problems Ctr., Inc., Northfield and Lakeville, Minn., 1972-76; youth and family counselor N.W. Suburban Youth Services, Roseville, Minn., 1976—; pvt. practice marriage and family therapy St. Paul, 1978—; program asst., counselor Camp Clearwater, Deerwood, Minn., 1964; dir. recreation and personality devel. program 5th Presbyn. Ch., Springfield, Ill., 1965; assoc. chaplain Ill. State Children's Hosp. Sch., Chgo., 1965-67; coordinator of vols. Assn. for the Promotion of Adoption of Children with Special Needs, Fargo, N.D., 1969-72; youth services coordinator 1st Presbyn. Ch., United Ch. Christ, 1969-71; counselor Clay County Assn. Retarded Citizens, Moorhead, Minn., Vanguard Sch., Fargo, 1970-71; cons. Profl. Assn. Treatment Homes, Inc., Mpls., 1975-77, Ramsey County Emergency Shelter Foster Care, St. Paul, 1978-81; instr. St. Cloud State U., 1983—, Roseville Community Edn., 1980-81. Bd. dirs. Family Tree, St. Paul, 1982-85. Named Notable Am. of the Bicentennial Era Am. Biog. Inst., 1976, one of Outstanding Young Women Minn., 1968; recipient WCCO Good Neighbor award, 1968, Phillips award Minn. Soc. Crippled Children and Adults, 1974, Leadership award Midwest Biog. Inst., 1972. Mem. Internat. Council Sex Edn. and Parenthood, Nat. Wellness Assn., Minn. Health Promotion Network, Am. Assn. Marriage and Family Therapy, Upper Midwest Assn. Marriage and Family Therapy, Ski for Light Internat. Democratic Farm Labor. Avocations: cross country skiing, hiking, reading, listening to music.

ANDREWS, MARK LEE, quality assurance director, consultant; b. Muskegon, Mich., July 3, 1948; s. Kenneth Lee and Colleen Marie (Bolduc) A.; m. Linda Marie Darling, Oct. 7, 1978; children: Jason, Eric, Ryan, Casey. BS, Mich. State U., 1970. Gen. supr. Valley Tow Rite, Lansing, Mich., 1970-74; dept. supr. Grand Haven (Mich.) Stamped Products, 1977-79, quality assurance mgr., 1979-82, quality assurance dir., 1982—; Cons. Muskegon (Mich.) Community Coll., 1986, State of Mich., Lansing, 1986. Mem. Am. Metal Stamping Assn. (vice chmn. 1985-86, chmn. 1986—), Soc. Mfg. Engrs. (Resolution of Appreciation 1985). Avocations: bridge, coaching soccer. Home: 18382 Country Ave Spring Lake MI 49456 Office: Grand Haven Stamped Products 1250 S Beech Tree Grand Haven MI 49417

ANDREWS, MARY LYNN, employment search and training executive; b. Detroit, Mar. 23, 1948; d. Albert Nathan and Mae Ruth (Tringali) Andrews; divorced; 1 child Seana Jonelle. BS, Mich. State U., 1970. Sales supr. Winkelman's, Detroit, 1970-72; sales rep. V-G Supply, Morton Grove, Ill., 1978-79; mfrs. rep. Total Mktg., Rolling Meadows, Ill., 1979-80; employment specialist Chicagoland PWI, Inc., 1980-82, dir., 1982-85, pres., 1985—; instr. Thornton Coll., South Holland, Ill., 1982—. Mem. Rehab. Inst. Chgo. (TEAM com.), Profl. Career Counselors Network, Nat. Assn. Female Execs., The Nat. Disting. Service Registry: Med. and Vocat. Rehab. Republican. Lodge: Rotary-One (DEED com.). Avocations: computer programming, reading, poetry. Home: PO Box 2613 Homewood IL 60430 Office: Chicagoland PWI Inc 345 E Superior Chicago IL 60611

ANDREWS, SUSAN BETH, psychologist; b. Danville, Ill., Aug. 5, 1948; d. Jack Arthur and Rosemary (Haywood) Kuhlman; m. Bruce Rolf Andrews, Mar. 22, 1970. BS in Psychology, U. Ill., Champaign, 1970; PhD, U. Ill., Chgo., 1975. Registered clin. psychologist. Clin. psychology program Assocs. in Adolescent Psychiatry, Skokie, Ill., 1975-85; pres. Assocs. in Clin. Psychology, Westchester, Ill., 1985—; assoc. prof. Rush Presbyn. St. Lukes Hosp., Chgo., 1985—. Mem. Am. Psychol. Assn., Ill. Psychol. Assn., Nat. Register of Health Service Providers. Avocations: cross country skiing, horseback riding, yoga.

ANDREWS, WAYNE WILLIAM, manufacturing engineer; b. Cleve., Nov. 4, 1936; s. William George and Isabella Marie (Mako) A.; m. Gail Alfather, Oct. 13, 1956 (div. July 1973); children: Kim Michelle, Deena Marie, Nicalene Ann; m. Kay Lyn Swartz, Apr. 19, 1974; 1 child, Christine Michelle. Grad. in tool and die, Chrysler Corp. Howard Adult Vocat. Sch., 1963. Lic. profl. engr., Ind., Colo., Calif. Mfg. engr. Franklin Electric, Bluffton, Ind., 1972-75; dir. mfg. Synthes Ltd., Monument, Colo., 1978-79; mfg. engring. mgr. Depuy, Warsaw, Ind., 1975-78, 79-81; chief engr. Am. Tool & Engrs., Ft. Wayne, Ind., 1981-82; research and devel. project engr. Orthopedic Equipment Co., Warsaw, Ind., 1983-84; mfg. engr. Spicer Axle div. Dana Corp., Syracuse, Ind., 1984—. Served with USCGR, 1954-62. Mem. Soc. Mfg. Engrs. (cert.). Republican. Roman Catholic. Lodge: Elks. Avocations: boating, woodwork. Home: PO Box 366 North Webster IN 46555 Office: Dana Corp 100 Railroad Ave Syracuse IN 46567

ANDRIST, JOHN M., publishing company executive; b. Crosby, N.D., Aug. 1, 1931; s. Calvin L. and Lela G. (Revis) A.; m. Elaine G. Thvedt, June 17, 1951; children: Pamela, Paula, Steve, Stan, Penny. Owner, pres. Jour. Pubs. Co., Crosby, N.D., 1961. Mem. N.D. Newspaper Assn. (chmn. legis. com. 1968-86), Nat. Newspaper Assn. (N.D. state chmn. 1970-82, bd. dirs., representing Iowa, N.D., S.D., Minn. 1982-87), Bus. Builders (pres.), Crosby Jaycees (past pres.), N.D. Jaycees (state sec.), Sigma Delta Chi (past pres.). Presbyterian. Lodges: Kiwanis, Moose. Avocations: golf, running. Office: PO Box E Crosby ND 58730

ANDRLA, VALERIE ETTA, manufacturing company executive; b. Wichita, Kans., June 27, 1948; d. William Francis and Barbara June (Ballance) A.; m. James Edward Baxter, Aug. 4, 1968 (div. Apr. 1975); 1 child, Janell Renee. Student, Wichita State U., 1969-71; BSME, U. Kans., 1978; MBA in Fin. and Internat. Bus., U. Chgo., 1982. Registered profl. engr., Kans., Ill. Meat packer Cudahy Co., Wichita, 1968-75; mgr. AB Sand & Rock Co., Wichita, 1975-76; plant engr. Food, Machinery & Chem. Co., Inc., Lawrence, Kans., 1976-78; engring. liaison Internat. Harvester Corp. (name changed to Navistar), Chgo., 1979-80, purchasing engr., 1981-82, supr. purchasing research, 1983-84, corp. buyer, 1985—. Contbr. Kans. Engineer mag., 1976-78. Tutor math. Community Service Ctr., Rolling Meadows, Ill., 1982—; council mem. Sister Cities, Rolling Meadows, 1984—. Mem. ASME, Soc. Mfg. Engrs., Chgo. Rubber Group, AAUW (chair ways and means com. 1984—, newsletter editor 1984-87), U. Chgo. Women's Bus. Group. Republican. Methodist. Avocations: tennis, writing. Home: 4735 Calvert Apt 107 Rolling Meadows IL 60008 Office: Navistar Internat Corp 600 Woodfield Dr Schaumburg IL 60196

ANDROW, MARK ROBERT, TV commercial producer; b. Chgo., Sept. 21, 1954; s. Samuel D. and Alice (Wright) A. BFA, NYU, 1974; JD, DePaul U., 1979. Bar: Ill., 1979. Prodn. mgr. Filmack Studios, Chgo., 1974-78; producer The Movie House, N.Y.C., 1978-79; exec. producer Freese & Friends, Chgo., 1979—; bd. dirs. Chgo. Coalition. Columnist Screen mag., 1982, Millimeter mag., 1981. Recipient Addy award Chgo. Ad Club, 1985. Mem. Assn. Ind. Comml. Producers (pres. 1985—, sec.-treas. 1983-85), chgo. Film Council (bd. dirs. 1981-83). Home: 445 Wellington Chicago IL 60610 Office: Freese & Friends 1429 N Wells Chicago IL 60610

ANDRZEJEWSKI, THOMAS STANLEY, journalist, lecturer; b. Cleve., Oct. 19, 1945; s. Stanley Vincent and Cecilia Helen (Ciechanowicz) A.; m. Leslie Kay, Sept. 9, 1973; 1 child, David Aaron. Student Cuyahoga Community Coll., 1963-65; B.A., Cleve. State U., 1968. Copy boy The Plain Dealer, Cleve., 1963-66, news reporter, 1966-75, writer, columnist urban affairs, 1975—; dir. Cleve. Newspaper Guild Local 1, 1971-85. Served with U.S. Army, 1968-70, Vietnam. Decorated Bronze Star; named best series writer Ohio A.P., 1980; recipient Spl. Media award Nat. Assn. Criminal Def. Lawyers, 1979; Silver Gavel, ABA, 1979. Avocation: running, swimming. Office: 1801 Superior Ave Cleveland OH 44114

ANGE, CONSTANCE ELIZABETH, psychiatrist; b. Plymouth, N.C., Sept. 24, 1949; d. Mack West and Irma (Perry) A.; m. Richard Jay Fryman, Sept. 9, 1978. D.O., Chgo. Coll. Osteo. Medicine, 1974. Intern, Grandview Hosp., Dayton, Ohio, 1974-75; resident U. Cin., 1977-79, fellow in child psychiatry, 1979-81; gen. practice family medicine, Springboro, Ohio, 1975-77; practice adult and child psychiatry, Dayton, Ohio, 1981—; faculty Ohio U., Athens, 1982-83; cons. Contbr. articles to profl. jours. Robert Wood Johnson scholar, 1973. Mem. Am. Osteo. Assn., Ohio Osteo. Assn., Am. Coll. Neuropsychiatry, Am. Psychiat. Assn., Am. Acad. Child Psychiatry, Sigma Sigma Phi. Avocations: reading; horticulture. Office: 1410 Talbott Tower 131 N Ludlow Dayton OH 45402

ANGELL, JOHN FREDERICK, newspaper editor, consultant; b. Greensburg, Ind., Oct. 10, 1944; s. Claude Merle and Viola Veronica (Amrhein) A.; m. Margaret Diana Angell, July 13, 1974 (div. Sept. 1978); children: Deborah Ann, Karlee Donica. Degree in bus. mgmt. (hon.), Porter Bus. Coll., 1964. Cert. mech. technician. Mgr. ops. Marathon Oil Co., Findlay, Ohio, 1964-70; gen. mgr. Louis Lazacoff, Inc., Indpls., 1970-78, Warren Radio Co., Davenport, Iowa, 1978-85; mng. editor and chmn. bd. dirs. Indpls. Outlook, 1986—; pres. Marketing Acts, Inc., Indpls., 1978—, Comco Internat., Ltd., Indpls., 1981—; chmn. bd. dirs. J. Fredericks & Assocs., Indpls., 1986—. Ind. Party candidate for mayor Davenport, Iowa, 1984. Recipient Presdl. Sports Award Pres. of U.S., 1975, Outstanding Citizenship City of Davenport, 1983. Mem. Nat. Small Bus. Assn. (Outstanding Sales Achievement award 1976), Ind. Conv. and Visitors Assn., Commn. for Downtown, Cen. Ind. Newspapers Alliance, Commn. for Downtown, Iowa State Policemans' Assn. (hon.). Roman Catholic. Lodge: Moose. Avocations: water skiing, photography, horseback riding. Office: Indpls Outlook Inc 4475 Allisonville Rd Suite 575 Indianapolis IN 46205

ANGELL, LYNN ELIZABETH, accountant; b. Gallipolis, Ohio, June 20, 1960; d. Cordie E. Smith Jr. and Roma F. Wood; m. Bill E. Angell, Jan. 9, 1985. BS, Ohio State U., Columbus, 1981; MS, Ohio State U., Athens, 1984. CPA, Ohio. Resdl. area planner Gallipolis Devel. Ctr., 1981-83; acct. Am. Electric Power, New Haven, W.Va., 1984; pvt. practice acctg. Gallipolis, 1985—; instr. Rio Grande (Ohio) Coll., 1984-87; trustee Gallia County Farm Bur., Gallipolis, 1986-87. Travelors scholar Travelors Ins., 1981-83, Regents scholar Ohio State U. Bd. Regents, 1980-81. Mem. Am. Inst. CPA's, Ohio Soc. CPA's. Lodge: Eastern Star. Home: Rt 2 Box 146 Crown City OH 45623 Office: 444 2d Ave PO Box 1135 Gallipolis OH 45631

ANGELL, MADELINE (MRS. KENNETH F. JOHNSON), writer; b. Devils Lake, N.D., Jan. 6, 1919; d. Bernard Oscar and Evelyn May (Smith) Angell; student Stephens Coll., 1936-37; B.S., U. Minn., 1940; m. Kenneth Frederick Johnson, Aug. 31, 1940; children—Mark Frederick, Randall David. Works include: 120 Questions and Answers about Birds, 1973; America's Best Loved Wild Animals, 1975; The Fantastic Variety of Marine Animals, 1976; Red Wing, Minnesota, Saga of a River Town, 1977; Snakes and Frogs and Turtles and Such, 1979; (with Mary Cavaness Miller) Joseph Woods Hancock: The Life and Times of a Minnesota Pioneer, 1980; A Field Guide to Berries and Berrylike Fruits, 1981; contbr. articles to publs. including Parents' Mag., Better Homes and Gardens, Sci. World. Mem. Mayor's Citizens Com. for Red Wing Tng. Sch., co-chmn., 1970-72. Recipient McKnight Found. Humanities award for novel, 1966, Blue Flame Ecology Salute, 1974. Mem. AAUW (co-pres. 1956-58), Audubon Soc., Goodhue County Hist. Soc., Minn. Hist. Soc., Authors Guild, Alpha Chi Omega, Phi Upsilon Omicron, Omicron Nu (pres. 1939-40). Lutheran. Home and Office: Route 4 Cardinal Dr Red Wing MN 55066

ANGLE, ANN ZEHNER, fraternal organization adminstrator; b. Evansville, Ind., July 10, 1951; d. Darwin Berl and Julia Ellyn (Hudelson) Zehner; m. Richard Allen Angle, July 14, 1974. B.S. in Pharmacy, Purdue U., 1974. Registered pharmacist, Ind., Va., N.C. Staff pharmacist Braeburn Pharmacy, Salem, Va., 1974, Edmonds Pharmacy, Greensboro, N.C., 1975, Rite-Aid Pharmacies, Greensboro, 1975, Scottie Pharmacy, Kernersville, N.C., 1976-78, West Side Pharmacy, Bowling Green, Ohio, 1978-80; pharmacist, mgr., owner Lucas Pharmacy, Inc., Rensselaer, Ind., 1980-85; staff pharmacist Walgreen's, 1985-86; exec. dir. Kappa Epsilon Frat. Nat. Office, 1986—. Pres. Am. Cancer Soc., Jasper County Unit, Rensselaer, 1982-84, treas., 1984-86. Named Young Career Woman, Rensselaer Bus. and Profl. Women's Club, 1981. Mem. Acad. Pharmacy N.C. Pharmacists, Am. Pharm. Assn., Ind. Pharmacists Assn. (employers com. 1981—), Am. Bus. Women's Assn. (pres. 1984-85, Woman of Yr. 1984), Kappa Epsilon (nat. pres. 1977-81, nat. adviser 1981—), Alpha Gamma Delta (province dir.-alumnae 1983—, Arc of Epsilon Pi 1979, Arc of Epsilon Pi with Diamond 1985), Psi Iota Xi (v.p. 1983-84, treas. 1984-86). Club: United Methodist Women. Home: 602 E 6th St Fowler IN 47944 Office: Purdue U Sch Pharmacy Kappa Epsilon Frat 162 Robert Heine Bldg West Lafayette IN 47907

ANGLE, MARGARET SUSAN, lawyer; b. Lincoln, Nebr., Feb. 20, 1948; d. John Charles and Catherine (Sellers) A. BA with distinction in Polit. Sci., U. Wis., Madison, 1970, MA in Scandinavian Studies (scholarship, NDEA fellow), 1972, JD cum laude, 1976. Bar: Wis. 1977, Minn. 1978. Law clk., Madison, Mpls., Chgo., 1974-76; law clk. U.S. Dist. Ct., Mpls., 1977-78; mem. firm Faegre & Bensen, Mpls., 1978-84; sr. atty. Nat. Car Rental System, Inc., Mpls., 1984—. Note and comment editor U. Wis. Law Rev.; contbr. articles to profl. publs. Mem. ABA, Minn. Bar Assn., Wis. Bar Assn., Hennepin County Bar Assn., Order of Coif, ACRA. Home: 4340 Fox Ridge Ct Eagan MN 55122 Office: Nat Car Rental System Inc 7700 France Ave S Minneapolis MN 55435

ANGLEMYER, ROMA KATHLEEN, teacher; b. Wakarusa, Ind., Sept. 17, 1932; d. Wayne Douglas and Evelyn Virginia (Weldy) Wyman; m. Keith Alois Anglemyer, June 10, 1956; children: Debra Anglemyer McNally, Linda Anglemyer Stolley. BE, Goshen (Ind.) Coll., 1955; MA, St. Mary's Coll., Notre Dame, Ind., 1966. Lic. real estate rep. Tchr. Bremen (Ind.) Pub. Sch., 1955-59; tchr. Wa-Nee Schs., Nappanee, Ind., 1960—, instr. enrichment classes, 1984-86; instr. mentally retarded Concord Schs., Elkhart, Ind., 1967; instructional asst. Coll. of the Gifted and Talented, Ind. U., Bloomington, 1984, Kids-on-Campus, Goshen Coll., 1985. Contbr. curriculum Wa-Nee Ind. History, 1980-86. Sponsor Wakarusa 4-H Clubs Elkhart County, 1974-76; pres. Progressive Homemakers, Elkhart County, 1984-85; sch. rep. Wa-Nee Sch. Reorgn. 25th Anniversary, Nappanee, 1987; mem. steering com. Gifted and Talented Program Wa-Nee, Nappanee, 1985-86; mem. curriculum devel. team for gifted and talented Elkhart Schs., 1984-86. Instr. Mem. NEA, Ind. State Tchrs. Assn., Wa-Nee Tchrs. Assn. (exec. mem. 1984-85), Wakarusa Tchrs. Assn. (pres. 1981-82), Elkhart County Reading Assn., Pi Lambda Theta (membership chmn. No. Ind. 1985-87, pres. 1987—, del. Great Lakes Region II 1987—, del. Biennial Council 1987). Avocations: antique cars, traveling, collecting candlewick crystal. Home: 28584 County Rd 38 Rt 1 Wakarusa IN 46573 Office: Wakarusa Elem Sch Box 367 Wakarusa IN 46573

ANIXTER, ALAN B., electrical manufacturing company executive; b. Chgo., July 25, 1920; s. Julius B. and Zelda (Rogoff) A.; m. Gail Annenberg, Nov. 6, 1943; children: James, Scott. B.S. in Econs., U. Pa., 1941, M.B.A., 1943. With Webster-Chgo. Corp., 1941-43; ptnr. Telmor Engring. Co., Chgo., Il, 1943-46; v.p. sales R.I. Insulated Wire Co., Cranston, 1946-52; ptnr. Mfrs. Agy., Chgo., Il, 1953-57; pres. Anixter Bros., Inc., Skokie, Ill., 1957-85; chmn., chief exec. officer Anixter Bros., Inc., Skokie, 1985—; dir. Cregier Elec. Mfrs. Co., Mark Products, Royal Elec. Co., Turmac, Ltd. Clubs: Standard (Chgo.); Northmoor Country (Highland Park, Ill.). Home: 1111 Turicum Rd Lake Forest IL 60045 Office: Anixter Bros Inc 4711 Golf Rd Skokie IL 60076 *

ANIXTER, EDWARD FRANKLIN, retired electronics company executive; b. Chgo., Dec. 11, 1917; s. Arthur Nathenial and Sadie (Novey) A.; B.S., U. Pa., 1939; m. Edith Pearl, Nov. 19, 1941; children—Barbara, Steven, Jo Ann (Mrs. Luis Silva). With Englewood Elec. Supply Co., Chgo., 1939-67, v.p., 1958-67; v.p. Potter-Englewood Corp., Chgo., 1967-71; pres. Pemcor, Inc., Westchester, Ill., 1971-78; pres. Internat. Jensen, Inc., subs. Esmark, Inc., 1979-80; pres. Estronics, Inc., subs. Esmark, Inc., from 1980-84, chmn., dir., vice pres. Schwab Rehab. Hosp., Chgo., 1953-62. Served with AUS, 1941-45. Decorated Bronze Star medal. Mem. Nat. Assn. Elec. Distbrs. (pres. 1972), Electric Assn. Chgo. (pres. 1962-63). Clubs: Standard (Chgo.), Idlewild Country (pres. Flossmoor, Ill. 1969-70), Tamarisk Country (Rancho Mirage, Calif.).

ANKENY, DEWALT HOSMER, JR., banker; b. Mpls., Dec. 29, 1932; s. DeWalt and Marie Josephine (Hamm) A.; B.A. summa cum laude, Dartmouth Coll., 1954, M.B.A., Amos Tuck Sch. Bus. Adminstrn., 1955; M.S. in Mech. Engring., Thayer Sch. Engring., 1955; m. Margaret Dayton, June 24, 1955; children: Donald, Harriett, Sarah, Charles, Phillip. With Theo. Hamm Brewing Co., 1955-66; with 1st Nat. Bank Mpls., 1967-82, pres., 1976-82, chmn., 1980-82, also dir.; vice chmn. 1st Bank System, 1983, pres., 1984-85, chmn., chief exec. officer, 1985—. Bd. dirs. United Way Mpls., Greater Mpls. Met. Housing Corp. Mem. Minn. Bankers Assn., Assn. Reserve City Bankers, Am. Bankers Assn. Clubs: Woodhill Country, Mpls. Home: Wayzata MN 55391 Office: First Bank System Inc 1200 1st Bank Pl E Minneapolis MN 55402 *

ANKOVIAK, WILLIAM GERARD, accountant, controller; b. Saginaw, Mich., Feb. 9, 1955; s. John Henry and Mary M. (Wydra) A.; m. Cindy Lou Klement, Nov. 17, 1979; children: kelly Rene, Christopher Jacob. BS, Saginaw Valley State Coll., 1978. CPA, Mich. Newscarrier Saginaw (Mich.) News, 1968-73; various positions held Second Nat. Bank, Saginaw, 1973-78; acct. Rehmann, Robson and Osborn, Saginaw, 1978-82, Auburn Bean & Grain, Auburn, Mich., 1982—. Mem. Am. Inst. CPA's, Mich. Assn. CPA's. Avocations: softball, bowling. Office: Auburn Bean & Grain 321 N Auburn PO Box 67 Auburn MI 48611

ANNESLEY, THOMAS MICHAEL, clinical chemist, pathology educator; b. Kewanee, Ill., Nov. 21, 1953; s. Charles Louis and Betty Jane Elsbecker; m. Linda Meeker, June 21, 1975. BA, Gustavus Adolphus, 1975; PhD, Rice U., 1979. Diplomate Am. Bd. Clin. Chemistry. Resident Mayo Clinic, Rochester, Minn., 1979-81; asst. prof. pathology U. Mich., Ann Arbor, Mich., 1981—; lab. dir. U. Mich., Ann Arbor, 1981—. Contbr. articles to profl. jours. Ch. sch. tchr. St. Clare Ch., Ann Arbor, 1982-84, vestry mem., 1985—. Recipient Young Investigator award Acad. Clin. Lab. Physicians, 1981, 1st Decade award Gustavus Adolphus Coll., 1985. Fellow Nat. Acad. Clin. Biochemistry; mem. Am. Assn. Clin. Chemistry (chmn. Mich. 1986, Clin. Chemist Recognition award, 1985), Am. Assn. Pathology, Fedn. Am. Socs., Assn. Clin. Scientists. Avocation: scuba diving. Home: 2530 Powell Ann Arbor MI 48104 Office: U Mich Hosp 1500 E Med Ctr Dr Ann Arbor MI 48109

ANNETT, RICHARD BROOKS, marketing executive; b. Bethlehem, Pa., Dec. 2, 1947; s. Edward and Mary (Luch) A.; m. Cynthia Perin Annett, Nov. 24, 1973; children—Julie Brooks, Lindsay Brooks. Grad. Marietta Coll., 1970; diploma Internat. Mgmt. Devel. Inst., 1985. Sales supr. Stouffer Foods, Boston, 1973-74, area sales mgr., Hartford, Conn., 1974-75, regional sales mgr., Boston, 1975-78, asst. plant mgr., Solon, Ohio, 1978-80, plant mgr., 1980-82, mktg. mgr. Lean Cuisine, 1982—. Named Outstanding Young Alumnus, Marietta Coll., 1983. Home: 2096 Edgeview Dr Hudson OH 44236 Office: Stouffer Foods Corp 5750 Harper Rd Solon OH 44139

ANNUNZIO, FRANK, congressman; b. Chgo., Jan. 12, 1915; m. Angeline Alesia, Dec. 28, 1935; children: Jacqueline (Mrs. Frank Lato), Linda (Mrs. William O'Donnell), Susan (Mrs. Kevin Tynan). B.S., M.Ed., DePaul U. Asst. supr. Nat. Def. Tng. Program Austin Evening Sch., Chgo.; legislative, ednl. dir. United Steelworkers of Am., Chgo.; mem. 89th-100th congresses from Ill. 11th Dist.; chmn. consumer affairs and coinage subcom. of banking, fin. and urban affairs com., chmn. House adminstrn. com.; Dir. Ill. Dept. Labor; chmn. War Ration Bd. 40-20; mem. adv. com. on Unemployment Compensation; mem. adv. com. to Ill. Indsl. Commn. on Health and Safety; mem. adv. bd. Cook County (Ill.) Health and Survey; gen. chmn. Villa Scalabrini Devel. Fund; v.p., lay adv. bd. Villa Scalabrini Italian Old People's Home. Mem. Catholic Youth Orgn., K.C. (4 deg.). Office: Rayburn Bldg Washington DC 20515

ANSHUTZ, WILLIAM MAURICE, radiologist; b. Somerton, Ohio, Sept. 16, 1917; s. Harvey and Atrella (Tomlinson) A.; A.B., Ohio State U., 1942; M.D., 1948; m. Betty Millisor, Sept. 10, 1944; children—Wendy Lee, Cathy Jo. Intern Lima (Ohio) Meml. Hosp., 1949; resident in radiology Henry Ford Hosp., Detroit, 1956-59; gen. practice medicine, Ohio, 1953-56; practice medicine specializing in radiology, Ind., 1959-64; mem. staffs St. Francis Hosp., Beech Grove, Ind., 1959-61; radiologist Meth. Hosp., Indpls., 1961-69, Witham Meml. Hosp., Lebanon, Ind., 1959-61, 70-83, Clinton County Hosp., Frankfort, Ind., 1969-79. Served with U.S. Army, 1942-44; USAF, 1951-53. Decorated Bronze Star. Mem. AMA, Radiol. Soc. N.Am., Am. Coll. Radiology, Ind. Roentgen Soc. Republican. Methodist. Home and Office: 6340 Breamore Rd Indianapolis IN 46220

ANTHIS, BILL CLINTON, school superintendent; b. Patoka, Ind., Oct. 4, 1926; s. George W. and Safrona Wallis (Morrison) A.; m. Patricia Mae Weaver, May 23, 1952; 1 child, Clinton Weaver. BS, Ind. State U., 1948, MS, 1950; EdD, Ind. U., 1962. Lic. psychologist, Ind. Tchr. Pub. Schs., Rockville and Orleans, Ind., 1948-52; asst. prin. Princeton (Ind.) Community Schs., 1952-57, N. Side High Sch., Ft. Wayne, Ind., 1957-63; prin. N. Side High Sch., Ft. Wayne, 1963-72; asst. supt. Ft. Wayne Community Schs., 1972-80, supt., 1980—; bd. dirs. Ind. Council Econ. Edn., Lafayette, 1976—, Ind. Congress on Edn., Indpls., 1985—. Contbr. articles to profl. jours. Mem. Corp. Council Ft. Wayne, 1982—; pres. Boy Scouts Am., Ft. Wayne, 1985-87; trustee Ind. State U., Terre Haute, 1985—; bd. dirs. Ind., Purdue, Ft. Wayne Adv. Com., 1973—, ARC Youth Com., Ft. Wayne, 1976—, Ft. Wayne Philharm., 1980—, Jr. Achievement, Ft. Wayne, 1980—, Leadership Ft. Wayne, 1982—, St. Joseph's Hosp., Ft. Wayne, 1983—, United Way Ft. Wayne/Allen County, 1983—, campaign chmn., 1984. Served with USN, 1945-46. Named to Hon. Legion Honor, Internat. Supreme Council Order of Demolay, 1986; recipient Disting. Alumni award Ind. State U., 1977, Ralph E. Broyles medal Ind. U., 1981, Silver Beaver award Boy Scouts Am., 1981, Liberty Bell award Allen County Bar Assn., 1985. Mem. Am. Assn. Sch. Adminstrs. (life), Nat. Assn. Secondary Sch. Prins. (life), Ind. Assn. Pub. Sch. Supts., Ind. Assn. Supervision and Curriculum Devel., Internat. Reading Assn., Assn. Childhood Edn. Internat., Greater Ft. Wayne C. of C., Ind. Council Deliberation (prior 1981-87), Phi Delta Kappa (life, pres. Ft. Wayne chpt. 1977-78, Service Key 1981). Methodist. Club: Quest. Lodges: Rotary (pres. Ft. Wayne chpt. 1971-72, Paul Harris fellow 1982), Masons (33 degree), Shriners, Order Eastern Star, Red Cross of Constantine (sentinel 1986-87). Avocations: golf, poetry, electronics, photography. Home: 3939 Evergreen Ln PO Box 13364 Fort Wayne IN 46868-3364 Office: Ft Wayne Community Schs 1230 S Clinton St Fort Wayne IN 46802

ANTHONY, DONALD BARRETT, petroleum corporation executive; b. Kansas City, Kans., Jan. 28, 1948; s. Donald W. and Marjorie (Lifsey) A.; m. Darla S. Donovan, Dec. 16, 1972; children—Jennifer L., Danielle S. B.S. in Chem. Engring., U. Toledo, 1970; M.S., MIT, 1971, Sc.D., 1974. Asst. prof., practice sch. dir. dept. chem. engring. MIT, Cambridge, Mass., 1974-75; group supr. coal research and devel. Standard Oil Co. Ohio, Cleve., 1976-77, mgr. marine planning, 1978-79, mgr. synthetic fuels devel., 1980-83; v.p. Sohio Shale Oil Co., Salt Lake City, 1980-83, Sohio Coal Conversion Co., Cleve., 1981-83; dir. White River Shale Oil Corp., Salt Lake City, 1980-83; v.p., gen. mgr. Pfandler Co., Rochester, N.Y., 1983-85; v.p. research and devel. Standard Oil Co., Cleve., 1985—. Contbr. articles in field to profl. jours.; patentee. Served to capt. AUS, 1970-78. MIT Esso fellow, 1970-71, Little research/devel. fellow, 1971-72, Procter & Gamble fellow, 1972-73. Mem. Am. Inst. Chem. Engrs., Am. Chem. Soc., Sigma Xi, Phi Kappa Phi, Tau Beta Pi, Pi Mu Epsilon, Phi Eta Sigma. Lutheran. Home: 105 Fox Trace Ln Hudson OH 44236 Office: Standard Oil Research & Devel 4440 Warrensville Ctr Rd Cleveland OH 44128

ANTHONY, DONALD HAROLD, rancher, farmer; b. Lexington, Nebr., July 1, 1950; s. Harold Alfred and Eva Karoline (Jensen) A.; m. Linda Marie Hofferber, July 29, 1972; children: Phillip John, Kirsten Marie, David Jacob. BS, U. Nebr., 1973. V.P. Anthony Land Co., Lexington, 1973—; Councillor Nebr. Coop. Council, 1985—; bd. dirs. Lexington Coop. Oil Co., 1985—. Sec. Dawson County Farm Bur., Lexington, 1975-76, 82-84; pres. Dawson County Extension Service, 1976-77, Sch. Dist. 17, Dawson County, 1982—. Served as staff sgt. USAR, 1970-73, Nebr. NG, 1973-76. Mem. U.S. Jaycees (Outstanding Young Farmer 1986), Nebr. Jaycees (Outstanding Young Farmer 1985), Alpha Zeta, Gamma Sigma Delta, Farmhouse Frat. Republican. Presbyterian. Home and Office: Route 1 Box 90 Lexington NE 68850

ANTHONY, GEORGE MARTIN, transportation executive; b. Savannah, Ga., Aug. 27, 1953; s. Joseph John and Clara Maria (Martin) A.; m. Gayle Lynn Shelton, June 17, 1978; children: Adam Christian, Aaron Scott, Abby Lynn. Student, Cen. Drafting Coll., 1977-78; BA with Graduating Honors, Wichita (Kans.) State U., 1985. Draftsman Cessna, Wichita, 1978-79; design draftsman Boeing Mil. Airplane Co., Wichita, 1979-86, quality auditor,

1986—. Served with U.S. Army, 1972-75; with USNR, 1986—. Mem. Soc. Mfg. Engrs., Nat. Assn. S Gaugers, Am. Legion. Republican. Avocations: model train collecting, model airplane bldg., coaching softball. Office: Boeing Mil Airplane Co 3801 S Oliver PO Box 7730 Wichita KS 67277

ANTHONY, JOSEPH HARRY, accounting educator; b. York, Pa., Sept. 28, 1949; s. Frederick Rutter and Mary Rose (Finnegan) A.; m. Madeline De Paulis, June 24, 1972. BA in Political Sci., Pa. State U., 1971, MS in Acctg., 1974; PhD in Acctg., Ohio State U., 1984. CPA. Sr. acct. Ernst & Whinney, Orlando, Fla., 1973-76, Louisville, Ky., 1976-77; instr. U. Louisville, 1977-79; asst. prof. Mich. State U., East Lansing, 1983—. Contbr. articles to profl. jours. Bd. dirs. Carriage Hills Condominium Assoc., 1987. Mem. Am. Acctg. Assn., Am. Inst. CPAS, Pa. State Alumni CLub (pres. 1984—). Avocations: golf, oenology, gourmet cooking. Home: 6223 Cobblers Dr East Lansing MI 48823 Office: Mich State U 339 Eppley Ctr East Lansing MI 48824

ANTIA, KERSEY H., industrial and clinical psychologist, consultant; b. Surat, Gujarat, India, Jan. 7, 1936; came to U.S. 1965; s. Hormasji and Dinsi R. (Mistry) A.; m. Dilshad K. Khambatta, Dec. 18, 1966; children: Anahita, Mazda, Jimmy. AB with honors, U. Bombay, 1958; MS, Tata Inst. Social Scis., Bombay, 1960, N.C. State U., 1969; PhD, Ind. No. U., 1976. Lic. psychologist, Ill.; cert. social worker, Ill. Personnel mgr., welfare officer Tata Steel and Tata Chem., 1960-65; research asst. psychology dept. N.C. State U., 1966-67, U. N.C., 1967-69; project dir. Behavior Systems, Inc., Raleigh, N.C., 1969-70; dir. Midwest Inst. Human Resources, Tinley Park, Ill., 1972—. Lang. scholar U. Bombay, 1954-56. Mem. Chgo. Psychol. Assn., Ill. Psychol. Assn. (health service adv. bd.), N.Y. Acad. Sci., Nat. Forensic Ctr., Orland Park C. of C., Am. Jaycees. Zoroastrian. Lodge: Masons. Avocations: photography, yoga, jogging, hiking, traveling. Home: 8318 W 138th Pl Orland Park IL 60462 Office: Tinley Center 17730B S Oak Park Ave Tinley Park IL 60477

ANTONACCI, ANTHONY EUGENE, beer corporation engineer; b. Sept. 21, 1949; s. Salvatore Natali and Odile Estella (Stanton) A.; m. Sherry Lee Kessler, Mar. 6, 1971; children—Don Warren, Lance Anthony. Student U.S. Air Force Acad., 1968-69; Assoc. in Sci., Forest Park Coll., St. Louis, 1971. Lic. stationary engr. Asst. supr. data processing ops. First Nat. Bank, St. Louis, 1969-71; engr. Installation and Service Engring. (Mech. and Nuclear) div. Gen. Electric Corp., St. Louis, 1971-76; engr. Anheuser-Busch Corp., St. Louis, 1976—; software author. Trustee, treas. Antonette Hills Trusteeship, Affton, Mo., 1976-80. Recipient Spl. Performance awards Gen. Electric Co., 1972, 74. Mem. Brewers and Maltsters Local 6 (del. 1982, 83), Nat. Aerospace Edn. Council, Internat. Platform Assn., Apple Programmers and Developers Assn. Republican. Roman Catholic. Avocations: classic auto restoration; music (trumpet). Home: 8971 Antonette Hills Saint Louis MO 63123

ANTONIC, JAMES PAUL, international marketing consultant; b. Milw., Mar. 29, 1943; s. George Paul and Betti Ware (Littler) A.; m. Irene Robson, Dec. 26, 1970; 1 child, Glenn. BS in Metallurgy, U. Wis., 1964; MBA, Boston U., 1976. Owner JPA Supply and Warehouse Co., Milw., 1966-68; product mgr., market mgr. Delta Oil Products, Milw., 1968-74; v.p. internat. ops., Brussels, 1974-76; pres. Internat. Market Devel. Group, Barrington, Ill., 1976—; exec. v.p. J & M, Ltd., Okazaki, Japan; lectr. Cast Metals Inst., Am. Mgmt. Assn., various colls. Served with U.S. Army, 1964-66. Mem. Licensing Execs. Soc., Internat. Trade Club Chgo. Episcopalian. Home: 655 Plum Tree Rd Barrington Hills IL 60010 also: 7F Seto Bldg 3-3-10 Yamamoto-Dori, 3 Chrome Chuo-Ku, Kobe 650, Japan Office: PO Box 751 Barrington IL 60010

ANTONIU, ADRIAN, retail executive, investment banker; b. Bucharest, Romania, July 26, 1946; s. Alexander and Sofia Antoniu; divorced. B in Engring., NYU, 1969, MEE, 1970; MBA, Harvard U., 1972. Assoc. corp. fin. Morgan Stanley & Co., N.Y.C., 1972-75; v.p. Lehman Kuhn Loeb, N.Y.C., 1975-78; prin. Egon Zehnder Internat., Milan, Italy, 1978-84; pres. Sport About Inc., Mpls., 1984—; cons. Computerland, Mpls., 1984; cons. Island Courier, Miami, Fla., 1984-86. Mem. Internat. Franchise Assn., Harvard. Club: Mpls. Athletic. Home: 1117 Marquette Ave Minneapolis MN 55403 Office: Sport About Inc 1557 Coon Rapids Blvd Minneapolis MN 55403

ANUM, ISAAC BOYE, social scientist; b. Accra, Ghana, Nov. 13, 1943; came to U.S., 1974; s. James Osabu and Augustina (Osae) A.; m. Naa Laatele Anum, Jan. 6, 1978 (dec. June 1985); children: Mildred, Daniel. AA in Bus. Adminstrn., Cen. YMCA Coll., Chgo., 1982; BA in Polit. Sci., Chgo. State U., 1984; MA in Internat. Relations, Northeastern Ill. U., 1986. Analysist, cons. Tyler Co., Chgo., 1980-86. Mem. Am. Polit. Sci. Soc. Baptist. Avocations: golf, tennis, traveling. Home: 810 W Grace St Chicago IL 60613 Office: Tyler Co 863 N LaSalle Chicago IL 60613

ANVARI, SAYYED TAHA, neurologist; b. Ardabil, Iran, Oct. 19, 1926; came to U.S., 1952; s. Mohammed and Mariam (Akbar) A.; m. Joyce V. Davis, Dec. 8, 1956; children: Shahla, Soheyla. BS, AlborzU., Tehran, Iran, 1944; MD, U. Tehran, 1950. Diplomate Am. Bd. Psychiatry and Neurology. Intern U. Tehran Hosp., 1950; resident in internal medicine U. Louisville, 1953-55; resident in neurology U. Louisville, Ky., 1955-58, from asst. prof. to assoc. prof. neurology, 1971-75; practice medicine specializing in neurology Jasper, Ind., 1984—. Fellow Am. Acad. Neurology; mem. Ky. Med. Assn. Republican. Moslem. Home: PO Box 2574 Clarksville IN 47131

ANWAR, ZEENAT ALI, gynecologist; b. Quetta, Pakistan, Oct. 10, 1932; came to U.S., 1965; d. Ferman and Jan Ali; married; 1 child, Mohsen. MBBS, Fatima Jinnah Med. Coll., Lahore, Pakistan, 1957. Diplomate Am. Bd. Ob-Gyn. Intern Port Huron Gen. Hosp.; resident Mercy Hosp. P.H.; chief resident in ob-gyn Med. Coll. Toledo, Ohio, 1969; fellow in oncology Hutzel Hosp., Detroit, 1970; practice medicine specializing in ob-gyn Port Huron, Mich., 1973—; staff Port Huron Hosp., 1973—. Fellow Royal Coll Ob-Gyn; mem. Mich. Med. Soc., St. Clair Med. Soc. Republican. Moslem. Office: 1201 Stone St Port Huron MI 48060

APMANN, WILLIAM FREDERICK, mathematics teacher; b. Waukesha, Wis., Oct. 5, 1953; s. Gerald D. and Golden Emma (Hehnke) A. BSE, U. Wis., Whitewater, 1975; MS, U. Wis., Milw., 1983. Math. tchr. Unified Sch. Dist., Racine, Wis., 1975—, educator of gifted, talented, 1983—; ednl. planning cons., Racine, 1985—. Mem. NEA, Nat. Council Tchrs. Math., Racine Edn. Assn. (sub-council pres. 1981), Wis. Edn. Assn., Gamma Theta Upsilon (v.p. 1974). Lutheran. Avocations: sports, reading, music. Home: 816 W Lawn Ave Racine WI 53405

APPEL, FREDERICK, JR, reading educator; b. Youngstown, Ohio, Jan. 23, 1947; s. Frederick and Mildred Elizabeth (Stanley) A.; m. Wendy Jean Warner, Aug. 28, 1974; children: Jeffrey V., Amanda B. BA, Kent State U., 1970; MEd, U. Fla., 1976. Cert. tchr., Ill., Iowa, Ind. Tchr. social studies and reading Cen. Jr. High Sch., Rock Island, Ill., 1975-76; tchr. remedial reading J.B. Young Jr. High Sch., Davenport, Iowa, 1976-77, Niemann Elem. Sch., Michigan City, Ind., 1977—; instr. computer assisted instrn. Purdue U. North Cen. Campus, Westville, Ind., 1983—. Cubmaster Cub Pack 871. Mem. Mich. City Computer Using Educators (pres. 1984-86), Internat. Council for Computers in Edn. Mem. Baha'i Faith. Home: 4303 N Wozniak Rd Michigan City IN 46360 Office: Niemann Elem Sch 811 Royal Rd Michigan City IN 46360

APPELSON, WALLACE BERTRAND, college president; b. Bklyn., June 9, 1930. B.S., NYU, 1951, M.A., 1952; Ed.D., Columbia U., 1959. Chief X-ray technician Samaritan Hosp., Bklyn., 1951-52; tchr. art White Plains Pub. Schs., N.Y., 1954-57; research asst. Inst. Adminstrv. Research (Columbia U.), 1957-58; asst. prof. ednl. adminstrn. Rutgers U., 1958-60; coordinator terminal program N.J. State Dept. Higher Edn., 1960-65; dean acad. affairs Bucks County Community Coll., Newton, Pa., 1965-70; pres. Atlantic Community Coll., Mays Landing, N.J., 1970-73; dean faculty LaGuardia Community Coll., CUNY, 1973-76; pres. Truman Coll., Chgo., 1976—. Editor: Associated Public Schools System Yearbook, 1958, Toward Higher Education Newsletter, N.J. Div. Higher Edn., 1960-65; contbr. articles to profl. jours. Pres. bd. dirs. North Bus. and Indsl. Council Chgo., Orchard Mental Health Ctr., Skokie, Ill.; bd. dirs. Ravenswood Hosp. Med. Ctr., Chgo., Uptown Chgo. Commn. Mem. Am. Assn. Sch. Adminstrs., Am. Assn. Higher Edn., Am. Assn. Community and Jr. Colls., Uptown C. of C. (pres. bd. dirs.), Phi Delta Kappa, Kappa Delta Pi. Office: Truman Coll 1145 W Wilson Ave Chicago IL 60640

APPLE, JOHN PHILIP, marketing executive; b. Oaklandon, Ind., June 9, 1930; s. John Howard and Edna Geneva (McConnell) A.; m. Julietta Beeler, Sept. 5, 1959; children: Denise, Tracy. BS in Mktg., Ind. U., 1952. Dist. mgr. Reynolds Metals, Peoria, Ill., 1954-56; pension cons. Conn. Gen. Ins. Co., Chgo., 1957-63; regional mgr. Wallace Computer Services, N.Y.C., 1963-79; gen. sales mgr. Wallace Computer Services, Hillside, Ill., 1979-81, dir. mktg., 1981—. Served to 1st lt. USAF, 1952-54, Korea. Republican. Methodist. Avocations: tennis, travel. Home: 763 Fox Hunt Trail Deerfield IL 60015

APPLEBAUM, EDWARD LEON, otolaryngologist, editor, educator; b. Detroit, Jan. 14, 1940; s. M. Lawrence and Frieda (Millman) A.; m. Marilyn Novetsky, June 21, 1966; children: Daniel Ira, Rachel Anne. A.B., Wayne State U., 1961, M.D., 1964. Diplomate: Am. Bd. Otolaryngology. Intern Univ. Hosp., Ann Arbor, Mich., 1964-65; resident Mass. Eye and Ear Infirmary Harvard Med. Sch., Boston, 1966-69; practice medicine specializing in otolaryngology Chgo., 1972—; assoc. prof. Northwestern U. Med. Sch., 1972-79; prof., head dept. otolaryngology, head and neck surgery Coll. Medicine, U. Ill., 1979—; mem. staffs U. Ill. Hosp., Westside VA Med. Ctr., Children's Meml. Hosp. Author: Tracheal Intubation, 1976; editor: Am. Jour. Otolaryngology, 1982. Served as maj. U.S. Army, 1969-71. Recipient Anna Albert Keller Research award Wayne State U. Coll. Medicine, 1964; recipient William Beaumont Soc. Orig. Research award, 1964. Fellow ACS, Am. Soc. for Head and Neck Surgery, Am. Acad. Facial Plastic and Reconstructive Surgery, Am. Acad. Otolaryngology, Head and Neck Surgery, Am. Laryngol. Rhinol. and Otol. Soc., Am. Laryngol. Assn., Am. Otol. Soc. Office: Ill Coll Medicine Dept Otolaryngology-Head and Neck Surgery 1855 W Taylor St Chicago IL 60612

APPLEBAUM, MYRON DAVID, construction company executive; b. Pitts., Aug. 27, 1937; s. Aaron Samuel and Bessie (Rader) A.; divorced; children: Bari, Bart, Martin. BBA, U. Miami, Fla., 1959. Pres. Applebaum & Assocs., St. Louis, 1963-85, Westwood Condominium, St. Louis, 1981-85; treas. Rit-Lan, St. Louis, 1983—; sec. Gold Apple Investment, St. Louis, 1984—; v.p. San Rol, St. Louis, 1980—, Myro San, St. Louis, 1984—; bd. dirs. All Dade Driveway, Miami;. Bd. dirs. Olivette (Mo.) Athletic Assn. (outstanding service award 1984). Served with USAF, 1960-67. Mem. Beta Sigma Rho (pres. Miami chpt.). Democrat. Jewish. Lodge: B'nai B'rith (pres. St. Louis chpt.). Avocations: collecting and restoring antiques. Home and Office: Applebaum & Assocs Inc 6601 Olive Blvd University City MO 63130

APPLEBERRY, JAMES BRUCE, university president; b. Waverly, Mo., Feb. 22, 1938; s. James Earnest and Bertha Viola (Lane) A.; m. Patricia Ann Trent, June 5, 1960; children: John Mark, Timothy David. BS in Edn., Central Mo. State Coll., 1960; MS, Cen. Mo. State Coll., 1963, EdS, 1967; postgrad., U. Kans., 1967; Ed.D., Okla. State U., 1969. Tchr. Knob Noster (Mo.) Pub. Sch., 1960-62; prin. Knob Noster Elem. Sch., 1962-63, Knob Noster Jr. High Sch., 1963-64; minister edn. Wornall Rd. Bapt. Ch., Kansas City, Mo., 1964-65; grad. fellow Cen. Mo. State Coll., Warrensburg, 1965-66, asst. dir. field service, 1966-67; grad. asst. Okla. State U., 1967-68, asst. prof. ednl. adminstrn., 1967-71, assoc. prof., 1971-73, prof., head dept. adminstrn. and higher edn., 1973-75; Am. Council on Edn. fellow acad. adminstrn. internship program U. Kans., Lawrence, 1973-74, dir. planning, prof. adminstrn., founds. and higher edn., 1975-76, asst. to chancellor, prof., 1976-77; pres. Pittsburg (Kans.) State U., 1977-83, No. Mich. U., Marquette, 1983—; plenary rep. Univ. Council for Ednl. Adminstrn., 1968-72, mem. exec. com., 1973-76; ednl. adminstrn. rep. Council on Tchr. Edn., 1968-75; chmn. Am. Council Edn. Commn. Leadership Devel. and Acad. Adminstrn.; abstracter Univ. Council for Ednl. Adminstrn., Columbus, Ohio, 1969-75; asst. state liaison rep. to Am. Assn. Colls. for Tchr. Edn., 1971; coordinator Interested Profs. Ednl. Adminstrn.; cons. North Cen. Okla. Assn. Sch. Adminstrs.; mem. adv. council Nat. Council Edn. Stats., 1980-83; Kans. rep. to Am. Assn. State Colls. and Univs., 1980-81. Contbr. articles to ednl. jours. Trustee Marquette Gen. Hosp. Mem. Am. Assn. for Higher Edn., Am. Assn. State Colls. and Univs. (policy and purposes com.), Am. Ednl. Research Assn., NEA, Nat. Conf. Profs. Ednl. Adminstrn. (co-chmn. Great Lakes sports commn.), Internat. Platform Assn., Newcomen Soc. U.S., Mace and Torch, Phi Delta Kappa, Phi Kappa Phi, Kappa Delta Pi, Phi Sigma Phi, Kappa Mu Epsilon., Alpha Kappa Psi. Lodges: Rotary, Masons (33d degree). Home: 1440 Center St Marquette MI 49855 Office: Northern Michigan Univ Office of the President Marquette MI 49855

APPLEGATE, DOUGLAS, congressman; b. Steubenville, Ohio, Mar. 27, 1928; s. Earl Douglas and Mary Margaret (Longacre) A.; m. Betty Jean Engstrom, Aug. 25, 1950; children: Kirk Douglas, David Allen. Student pub. schs., Steubenville. Real estate salesman and broker Steubenville, 1950—; mem. Ohio Ho. of Reps. from 33d Dist., 1961-68, Ohio Senate, 1969-76; mem. 95th-100th Congresses from 18th Dist. Ohio, Washington, 1977—; Del.-at-large Democratic Nat. Conv., 1964; past pres. Jefferson County Young Dems. Named One of 10 Outstanding Young Men U.S. C. of C.; Outstanding Ohio Legislator DAV, 1975. Mem. Young Dems., Farm Bur., Pine Valley, Mingo Sportsmen, Sons of Italy, Polish-Am. Citizens, League Women Voters. Presbyterian. Clubs: Elks (Steubenville), Eagles (Steubenville), Polish Athletic (Steubenville). Home: Route 3 Berkeley Pl Steubenville OH 43952 Office: US House of Reps 2183 Rayburn House Office Bldg Washington DC 20515

APPLEGATE, SARA JOAN, insurance executive; b. Knoxville, Tenn., Aug. 2, 1938; d. Kenneth C. and Elizabeth Winsor (Snead) A.; B.S. in Bus. Adminstrn., Ohio U., 1960; postgrad. U. Cin., 1962. With Hartford Ins. Group, 1960-82, property and package underwriting mgr., Cleve., 1974-77, asst. gen. mgr., Milw., 1977-82; v.p. U.S. Counseling Services, Inc., Milw., 1982—; tchr. profl. courses. Active Cystic Fibrosis Assn., Jerry Lewis Telethon. Mem. C.P.C.U. Soc. (past pres. Milw. chpt.), Ins. Women Milw. (past pres.; named Ins. Woman of Yr. 1980), Am. Mgmt. Soc., Nat. Assn. Ins. Women. Home: 4912F S 19th St Milwaukee WI 53221 Office: 120 Bishops Way Brookfield WI 53008

APPLEMAN, TODD EDSEL, public relations executive; b. Auburn, Ind., Sept. 23, 1958; s. Thomas Edsel and Judith Ann (Boger) A. BA, Anderson (Ind.) Coll., 1982; MA, Ball State U., 1984. Pub. relations specialist Ball Corp., Muncie, Ind., 1983-85; account exec. Bozell, Jacobs, Kenyon & Eckhardt Pub. Relations, Chgo., 1985—; pres. T.E. Appleman & Assoc., Inc., Chgo., 1985—. Pub. relations vol. United Way Delaware County, Ind., 1983-85; bd. dirs. Epilepsy Edn. Group E. Cen. Ind., Muncie, 1984-85. Recipient 1st Place Corp. Pub. Relations award Nat. Agri-Mktg. Assn. Mem. Pub. Relations Soc. Am., Internat. Assn. Bus. Communicators (external councils mem. 1985—, Silver Quill award 1983, Epic award 1985). Republican. Mem. Ch. of God. Avocations: writing, boating, snow skiing, water skiing. Home: 525 W Barry Ave Chicago IL 60614 Office: Bozell Jacobs Kenyon & Eckhardt Pub Relations 625 N Michigan Ave 23d Floor Chicago IL 60611

APPOLD, JAMES MARTIN, baking company executive; b. Saginaw, Mich., Apr. 10, 1939; s. Martin J. and Louise S. Appold; B.S., Gen. Motors Inst., 1962; M.B.A., U. Toledo, 1977; M.S. in Indsl. Engring., 1978; m. Patricia J. Kirchner, Aug. 20, 1960; children—Jonn, Karen, Melinda, Caitlin, Andrew. Engr., maintenance foreman, maintenance dept. Chevrolet Saginaw (Mich.) Grey Iron, 1957-66; sales engr. Honeywell, Inc., Saginaw, 1966-68; plant supt./engring. mgr. A T. Ferrell & Co., Saginaw, 1968-75; mgr. tech. services The Andersons, Maumee, Ohio, 1975-82; pres. gen. mgr. Consol. Biscuit Co., McComb, Ohio. Mem. Am. Soc. Agrl. Engrs., Biscuit and Cracker Mfrs. Assn., Am. Inst. Plant Engrs., Air Pollution Control Assn., Internat. Maintenance Inst., Nat. Grain and Feed Assn. Home: 2049 Scottwood Ave Toledo OH 43620 Office: PO Box 847 McComb OH 45858

APPS, JEROLD WILLARD, educator; b. Wild Rose, Wis., July 25, 1934; s. Herman E. and Eleanor S. (Witt) A.; m. Ruth Ellen Olson, May 20, 1961; children: Susan, Steven, Jeffrey. BS, U. Wis., 1955, MS, 1957, PhD, 1967. Extension agt. U. Wis., Green Lake, 1957-60, Green Bay, 1960-62; asst. prof. U. Wis., Madison, 1962-67, assoc. prof., 1967-69, prof. adult and continuing edn., 1969—; vis. prof. N.C. State U., Raleigh, 1979, U. Guelph, Ont., CAn., 1980, U. Alta., Can., 1982, U. Man., Can., 1986. Author: The Land Still Lives, 1970, How To Improve Adult Education in Your Church, 1972, Cabin in the Country, 1972, Toward a Working Philosophy of Adult Education, 1973, Ideas for Better Church Meetings, 1975, Barns of Wisconsin, 1977, Problems in Continuing Education, 1979, Spanish edit., 1983, Mills of Wisconsin and the Midwest, 1980, The Adult Learner on Campus: A Guide for Instructors and Administrators, 1981, Study Skills: For Adults Returning to School, 1981, Improving Your Writing Skills, 1982, Improving Practice in Continuing Education, 1985, Skiing Into Wisconsin: A Celebration of Winter, 1985. Served to capt. U.S. Army, 1956. Recipient Non-Fiction Book Award of Merit, Wis. Hist. Soc., 1978, 81. Mem. Am. Assn. for Adult and Continuing Edn. (exec. com. 1975-76, Research to Practice award 1982), Commn. Profs. of Adult Edn. (pres. 1972-74), Wis. Acad. Scis. Arts and Letters (pres. 1987), Wis. Assn. Adult and Continuing Edn. (pres. 1969, Outstanding Adult Educator of Yr. award 1986), Wis. Council Writers (pres. 1978-80, Best Non-Fiction Book award 1977). Office: U Wis 225 N Mills St Madison WI 53706

AQUINO, NICOLAS ANTONIO, architect; b. Concepcion, Paraguay; came to U.S., 1980; s. Antonio L. and Deolinda (Medina) A.; m. M. Magdalena Triguöis, July 30, 1970; children: Jorge Antonio, Nicolas Alejandro, Andrea Raquel. BArch, U. Tex., 1974. Registered architect, Paraguay. Architect Bryan Adams & Co., Austin, Tex., 1973-75, CIPA, SA, Asuncion, Paraguay, 1975-79, Am. Constrn., Buenos Aires, Argentina, 1979-80, Leo A. Daly Co., Omaha, 1980-84, Henningson, Durham & Richardson, Omaha, 1984—. Foster father Nebr. Children's Home, Omaha, 1981-85; active Big Bros. Am., Omaha, 1981-82. Recipient Outstanding Service to Profession Architure award Pan Am. Fedn. Assns. Architects, Brazil, 1978. Mem. AIA (assoc., chmn. profl. devel. com. 1982-84), Nebr. Soc. Architects, Assn. Paraguayan Architects (sec. 1978-80), Young Men Christian Assn. Democrat. Roman Catholic. Club: West Omaha Soccer. Avocations: soccercoach, foreign langs. Home: 13055 Taylor Circle Omaha NE 68164 Office: Henningson Durham & Richardson 8404 Indian Hills Dr Omaha NE 68114

ARAI, HAROLD YUTAKA, orthodontist; b. Los Angeles, Feb. 1, 1936; s. Akira B. and Joan Fusako (Fujisawa) A.; B.A., Ohio Wesleyan U., 1957; D.D.S., Loyola U., 1961, M.S., 1966; m. Irene Shigihara, Aug. 27, 1961; children—David Andrew, Shaunna Lynn. Pvt. practice orthodontics, Park Ridge, Ill., 1967—; Lectr. Loyola U., 1966-73, 77, Ind. U., 1975, Emory U., 1975, La. State U., 1977. Pres., U. Chgo. Jarabak Orthodontic Found., 1975-76; v.p. Denver Orthodontic Summer Seminar, 1974, pres., 1975-76; lectr. Fox River Valley Dental Soc. meeting, Greater Miami Midwinter Dental meeting, 1977, Mid-Atlantic Soc. Orthodontists, 1978, Pacific Coast Soc. Orthodontists, 1978, Rocky Mountain Provocative Discussion Seminar, 1979, Cleve. Soc. Orthodontists, 1979, Colo. Orthodontic Assn., 1979. Served to capt. USAF, 1961-63. Mem. ADA (orthodontic chmn. sci. sessions 1974—), Japanese Civic Assn., Am. Assn. Orthodontics (clinician, chmn. round table programs 1979 meeting), Eastern Orthodontic Study Club, Midwestern Orthodontic Soc., Japanese Orthodontic Soc., Mexican Orthodontic Soc., Southwestern Soc. Orthodontists, Japanese Citizens League, Blue Key, Alpha Sigma Phi, Omicron Delta Kappa, Omicron Kappa Upsilon, Delta Sigma Delta. Author: Welcome to the World of Orthodontics, 1973. Home: 2026 Abbotsford Dr Barrington IL 60010 Office: 101 S Washington Park Ridge IL 60068

ARAKAWA, KASUMI, physician, educator; b. Toyohashi, Japan, Feb. 19, 1926; came to U.S., 1954, naturalized, 1963; s. Masumi and Fayuko (Hattori) A.; m. Juen Hope Takahara, Aug. 27, 1956; children—Jane Riet, Kenneth Luke, Amy Kathryn. M.D., Tokyo Med. Coll., 1953; Ph.D., Showa U. Sch. Med., Tokyo, 1984. Diplomate: Am. Bd. Anesthesiology. Intern Iowa Meth. Hosp., Des Moines, 1954-56; resident U. Kans. Med. Center, Kansas City, 1956-58; practice medicine specializing in anesthesiology Kansas City, 1958—; instr. anesthesiology U. Kans. Med Center, Kansas City, 1961-64; asst. prof. U. Kans. Med Center, 1964-71, assoc. prof., 1971-77, prof., 1977—, chmn. dept. anesthesiology, 1977—; clin. asso. prof. U. Mo.-Kans. City Sch. Dentistry, 1973—; dir. Kansas City Health Care, Inc. Fulbright scholar, 1954. Recipient Outstanding Faculty award Student AMA, 1970. Fellow Am. Coll. Anesthesiology; mem. Asso. Univ. Anesthesiologists (sec.-treas. 1969—), Acad. Anesthesiology (pres. 1986-87), Japan-Am. Soc. Midwest (v.p. 1965, 71). Home: 7917 El Monte St Shawnee Mission KS 66208 Office: Univ Med Ctr 39 Rainbow St Kansas City KS 66103

ARAND, FREDERICK FRANCIS, accountant, finance executive; b. Chgo., Mar. 14, 1954; s. Bernard Anthony and Millicent Catherine (Schweizer) A.; m. Judith Mary Utz, May 22, 1982; children: Joseph, Diana, Thomas. AB, Dartmouth Coll., 1976; MBA, U. Mich., 1978. CPA, Ill. Staff acct. Ernst & Whinney, Chgo., 1978-79, advanced staff, 1979-80, sr. staff, 1980-82, supr., 1982-85, sr. mgr., 1985—. Leader Jr. Achievement, Wheaton, Ill., 1981-83. Mem. Math. Assn. Am., Ill. CPA Soc., Am. Inst. CPA's, Fin. Mgr. Soc. (fin. mgmt. com. 1986—), Dartmouth Alumni Club. Club: Metropolitan (Chgo.). Lodge: Toastmasters (area gov. 1985-86). Avocations: soccer, golf, tennis, softball. Home: 8023 N Merrill Niles IL 60648 Office: Ernst & Whinney 150 S Wacker Chicago IL 60606

ARASMITH, NEIL HARVEY, state senator, insurance agent; b. Jewell, Kans., Feb. 23, 1930; s. James H. and Jessie M. (Fields) A.; B.A., U. Kans., 1951; m. Donna Schindler, July 1, 1951; children—David, Jeffrey, Susan, Timothy. Adjustor, Mason Investment Co., Salina, Kans., 1951-54, br. mgr., Garden City, Kans., 1954, Philipsburg, Kans., 1955-68; with Interstate Securities, Philipsburg, 1968-77; ins. agt. Central Nat. Life Ins. Co., Philipsburg, 1977—; mem. Kans. State Senate, 1972—. Past chmn. bd. Phillips County Hosp., Phillipsburg Community Found. Served in USAF, 1951. Mem. C. of C. (past dir.). Republican. Methodist. Clubs: Elks, Masons, Shriners.

ARAZAN, VIRGINIA, psychiatrist; b. Limerick, Sask., Can., Nov. 20, 1924; came to U.S., 1969.; d. George and Maria (Mihai) Olteanu; m. George Berca, Feb. 19, 1950 (dec. Aug. 1966); 1 child, Florin; m. George S. Arazan, Oct. 1968. MD, Medico-Pharmaceutic Inst., Bucharest, Romania, 1951. Diplomate Am. Bd. Psychiatry, Am. Bd. Child-Adolescent Psychiatry. Internship Grace Hosp., Detroit, 1970; resident Lafayette Clinic, Detroit, 1970-74; cons. child psychiatist Bd. Edn., Detroit, 1975-77, Macomb Child Guidance Ctr., Mt. Clenence, Mich., 1974-86, Children's Ctr., Detroit, 1975—. Mem. Am. Psychiatric Assn., Am. Acad. Child Psychiatry, Mich. Psychiatric Assn., Warren and Fraser Warercolor Soc. Greek Orthodox. Avocation: needlepoint (artistic award 1984, 85). Office: Childrens Ctr 101 E Alexandrine Detroit MI 48201

ARBAUGH, ROBERT BRUCE, data processing executive; b. Charleston, W.Va., Dec. 31, 1948; a. William Harry and Peggy Jane (Pitts) A.; B.S. in Elec. Engring., Milw. Sch. Engring., 1971; postgrad. (Asso. Western Univs. fellow) U. Ariz., 1971-73. With PolySystems, Inc., Chgo., 1973-85, dir. data center, 1974—, v.p. ops., 1978-85; mgr. EDP ops. Beaven/Inter Am. Cos., Chgo., 1985—. Mem. Am. Theater Organ Soc. Episcopalian. Office: 901 W Jackson Blvd Chicago IL 60607

ARBIT, HARVEY MARVIN, pharmaceutical company executive; b. Schenectady, N.Y., Jan. 17, 1947; s. Joseph Abraham and Ruth (Sherman) A.; m. Judith Sue Engel, May 13, 1971; children: Julie Pamela, Alexander Ron. BS in Pharmacy, Union U., 1970; PharmD, Duquesne U, 1972; MBA, No. Ill. U., 1979. Staff pharmacist Homer G. Phillips Hosp., St. Louis, 1970; staff pharmacist Mercy Hosp., Pitts., 1970-71, pharmacy resident, 1971-72; sr. clin. research coordinator Travenol Labs., Inc., Deerfield, Ill., 1972-76; supr. regulatory documentation Travenol Labs., Inc., Deerfield, 1976-79; mgr. regulatory affairs and clin. devel. Hyland Diagnostics div. Travenol Labs, Inc., Deerfield, 1979-82; mgr. clin. research and regulatory affairs med. products div. 3M Co., St. Paul, 1982-84; dir. sci. affairs Upsher-Smith Labs., Inc., Mpls., 1984—. Contbr. articles to profl. jours. Mem. com. United Way Agy. Mem. Am. Pharm. Assn., Am. Soc. Hosp. Pharmacists, AMA (spl. affiliate), Regulatory Affairs Profls. Soc., Assn. Clin. Pharmacology, Rho Pi Phi. Jewish. Lodges: Shriners, Masons. Home:

1782 Trail Rd Saint Paul MN 55118 Office: 14905 23d Ave N Minneapolis MN 55441

ARBUCKLE, PHILIP WAYNE, travel company executive; b. West Memphis, Ark., Feb. 9, 1954; s. Wayne C. and Betty Jo (Atkins) A. B.B.A., Mid-Am. Nazarene Coll., 1976; M.A., North Am. Sch. of Travel, 1979. Asst. to pres. Medco Inc., Overland Park, Kans., 1976-80; v.p. ops. Group Travel Service Ltd., Overland Park, 1980—; cons. travel Ozark Council of Govs., Jefferson City, Mo., 1983-84, Internat. Congress of Radiology, Kans. City, Kans., 1983—. Author: Paris for Little or Nothing, 1972. Mem. community development City of Olathe, Kans. 1982-83; mem. bi-centennial com. County of Johnson, Kansas, 1976. Mem. Am. Mgmt. Assn., Olathe C. of C. (community affairs com. 1983-84), Olathe Hist. Soc. Republican. Mem. Nazarene Ch. Club: Kans. City Friends of Art (Mo.). Avocations: computers; genealogy; archaeology. Office: Group Travel Service Ltd 6340 Glenwood St Overland Park KS 66202

ARBUTHNOT, JACK BRAEDEN, psychology educator; b. Hartford, Conn., Dec. 3, 1943; s. Gordon Delane and Breta (Atkins) A.; 1 child, Skylar Braeden. BA, U. Mich., 1966; MS, Cornell U., 1968, PhD, 1971. Lic. psychologist, Ohio. Asst. prof. Ohio U., Athens, 1971-77, assoc. prof., 1977-84; prof. Ohio State U., Athens, 1984—; owner, cons. Devel. Services, Amesville, Ohio, 1982—, Psycholegal Systems, Athens, 1984—; co-founder Ctr. Psychol. Family Law Alternatives. Author: Teaching Moral Reasoning, 1981; contbr. articles and papers to profl. jours. and confs. Mem. ACLU, Am. Psychol. Assn., Am. Psychology Law Soc., Soc. Psychol. Study of Social Issues, Assn. Moral Edn. Avocations: carpentry, farming, whitewater canoeing. Home: 1441 McDaniel Dr Amesville OH 45711 Office: Ohio Univ Dept Psychology Athens OH 45701

ARCHAMBAULT, BENNETT, corp. exec.; b. Oakland, Calif.; s. Albert Joseph and May (Smales) A.; m. Margaret Henrietta Morgan; children—Suzanne Morgan, Michele Lorraine, Steven Bennett. Student, Ga. Inst. Tech.; S.B., Mass. Inst. Tech. Vice pres., gen. mgr. M.W. Kellogg Co., N.Y.C., 1946-54; pres. Stewart-Warner Corp., Chgo., 1954—; chmn. bd. Stewart-Warner Corp., 1959—; pres., dir. Thor Power Tool Co.; exec. com., dir. Kemper Corp., Lumbermens Mut. Casualty Co., Am. Motorists Ins. Co., Am. Mfrs. Mut. Ins. Co., Lawter Chems., Inc.; head London Mission for OSRD, 1942-45. Mem. Mayor's Com. Econ. And Cultural Devel. Chgo.; bd. govs. United Republican Fund Ill.; former chmn. for Ill. Rep. Nat. Fin. Com.; trustee, mem. exec. com. Ill. Inst. Tech.; trustee Ill. Inst. Tech. Research Inst.; trustee, mem. exec. com., nominating com. Mus. Sci. and Industry; mem. com. on devel., past mem. corp. Mass. Inst. Tech.; adv. council Grad. Sch. Mgmt. Northwestern U.; trustee Better Govt. Assn.; bd. dirs. Protestant Found. Greater Chgo. Decorated Medal Merit U.S.; His Majesty's Medal for Service in Cause of Freedom Brit.). Mem. Employers Assn. Greater Chgo. (dir.), Newcomen Soc. N.Am., Research Soc. Am., C. of C. U.S., Ill. Mfrs. Assn. (adv. bd.), NAM. Republican. Clubs: Racquet (Chgo.), Saddle and Cycle (Chgo.), Commercial (Chgo.), MIT of Chgo. (Chgo.), Executives (Chgo.), Chicago (Chgo.), Economic (Chgo.); Glen View, Westmoreland. Home: 3240 Lake Shore Dr Chicago IL 60657 Office: Stewart-Warner Corp 1826 Diversey Pkwy Chicago IL 60614

ARCHER, ALFORD, geographer; b. Garrettsville, Ohio, Apr. 11, 1908; s. John Clark and Cathaline (Alford) A.; m. Barbara Kathleen Dietrich, Oct. 14, 1938 (dec.); children: John Clark, Joan Elizabeth. Student, Hiram Coll., 1925-26, Carnegie Inst. Tech., 1927-29; BS, Columbia U., 1935, MS, 1936; PhD, Ohio State U., 1962. Asst. dept. geography Ohio State U., Columbus, 1936-41; instr. geology and geography Ind. State Tchrs. Coll., 1941-42; asst. prof. commerce and geography Toledo U., 1942-46, asst. dir. summer session, 1946; geographer geography div. U.S. Bur. Census, Washington, 1946-49, 55-59, 68-71, chief cartographic methods br., 1959-61; census geography advisor Internat. Statis. programs loaned to Agy. Internat. Devel., assigned to census and stats. offices of U.S. Bur. Census, Panama, 1949-50, Bolivia, 1950, Honduras, 1951-55, 60, Costa Rica, 1952-54, El Salvador, 1953-55, 61, Thailand, 1961-63, Iran, 1966-68, Argentina, 1969, Paraguay, 1971-72, 74; chief fgn. census research br. U.S. Bur. Census, 1963-66, staff geographer, 1972-74; geog. advisor to census and stats. office population lab. U. N.C., Kenya, 1975; cartography adviser cen. bur. stats. devel. programme UN, Indonesia, 1978; adj. instr. George Washington U., Am. U., U.S. Dept. Agr. Grad. Sch.; mem. adv. com. Pan-Am. Inst. Geography and History, Nat. Acad. Scis., 1959-62. Pres. Rolling Terr. Civic Assn., Silver Spring, Md., 1958-59, 64-65. Recipient Meritorious Service award U.S. Sec. Commerce, 1956. Mem. Assn. Am. Geographers, Congress Surveying and Mapping. Home: 6800 A St Apt 217 Lincoln NE 68510

ARCHER, BERNARD THOMAS, radiologist; b. Rock Island, Ill., Dec. 8, 1935; s. Marcus Matthew and Janet Christita (Rank) A.; student St. Ambrose Coll., 1953-56; M.D., U. Iowa, 1960; m. Doreen Mary Smith, Aug. 26, 1961; children—Martha, Amy, Christopher, Stephen, Megan, Matthew. Intern, Milw. County Gen. Hosp., 1960-61; resident Univ. Hosps. Cleve., 1963-66, fellow in radiology, 1966-67; practice medicine specializing in radiology, 1967—; pres. Huron Rd. Radiologists, Cleve., 1970—; dir. dept. radiology Huron Road Hosp., East Cleveland, Ohio, 1970-85; asst. clin. prof. Case Western Res. U., 1977—. Served with USAF, 1961-63. Certified Am. Bd. Radiology. Mem. AMA, Ohio Med. Assn., Acad. Medicine Cleve., Radiol. Soc. N. Am., Am. Col. Radiology, Ohio State, Cleve. Radiol. Socs. Roman Catholic. Home: 1009 Hillcreek Ln Gates Mills OH 44040 Office: 13951 Terrace Rd Cleveland OH 44112

ARCHER, BRIDGET ISA, systems analyst; b. Georgetown, Guyana, May 21, 1940; came to U.S., 1971; d. Ivelaw and Elsie (Osborn) Miranda; m. Walter Errol Archer, July 30, 1966 ; children: Dean Walter, Duane Lyle. Cert. office automation profl. Supr. word processing U. Ill., Chgo., 1978-81, mgr. word processing, 1981-82, system and proced planner, 1982-83, systems analyst, 1983—; lectr. Oakton Community Coll., DesPlaines, Ill., 1984—; cons. in field, Chgo., 1982—. Mem. advisory bd. Kennedy King Coll., Chgo., 1986, Triton Coll., River Grove, Ill., 1983—, Norell Temporary Services, Chgo., 1984; presenter Kennedy King Coll., 1981, Malcolm X City Coll., Chgo., 1983-84. Mem. Assn. Info. Systems Profls. (bd. dirs. 1986—, pres. Chgo. chpt. 1981-83, v.p. membership Chgo. chpt. 1981-84, v.p. 1987—), Internat. Soc. Wang Users, Big Ten Wang Users Group (steering com. 1984—). Roman Catholic. Avocations: racquetball, travelling. Office: U Ill Chgo Sch Pub Health 2121 W Taylor St MC 922 Chicago IL 60612

ARCHER, DENNIS WAYNE, judge; b. Detroit, Jan. 1, 1942; s. Ernest James and Frances (Carroll) A.; B.S., Western Mich. U., 1965; J.D., Detroit Coll. Law, 1970; m. Trudy Ann DunCombe, June 17, 1967; children—Dennis Wayne, Vincent DunCombe. Tchr. spl. edn. Detroit Bd. Edn., 1965-70; admitted to Mich. bar, 1970, assoc. Gragg & Gardner, 1970-71; ptnr. Hall, Stone, Allen & Archer, 1971-73; ptnr. Charfoos, Christensen & Archer, P.C., 1973-85; assoc. justice Mich. Supreme Ct. 1986—. Assoc. prof. Detroit Coll. Law, 1972-78; adj. prof. Wayne State U. Law Sch., Detroit, 1984-85. mem. Mich. Bd. Ethics, 1979-83; bd. dirs. Legal Aid and Defenders Assn. Detroit, 1980-82. Trustee Mich. Cancer Found., 1980-84, bd. dirs., 1985—; co-chmn. Met. Detroit Community Coalition for Democratic Party, 1979-80; active numerous local Dem. campaigns, 1970-85; host local public service radio programs. Mem. ABA (ho. dels. 1979—, chmn. elect gen. practice sect. 1986-87, chair commn. on opportunities for minorities in the profession 1986-87, sect. legal edn. and admissions to the bar law sch. accreditation com. 1982-87, chmn. spl. com. prepaid legal services 1981-83), Nat. Bar Assn. (spl. asst. to pres. 1981-82, pres. 1983-84), Detroit Bar Assn., Am. Judicature Soc. (dir. 1977-81), State Bar Mich. (pres. 1984-85), Wolverine Bar Assn. (pres. 1979-80), Detroit Bar Assn. (dir. 1973-75), Mich. Trial Lawyers Assn. (exec. bd. 1973-74), Am. Trial Lawyers Assn., Alpha Phi Alpha. Roman Catholic. Club: Economic. Contbr. articles to legal jours. Office: Mich Supreme Ct 1425 Lafayette Bldg Detroit MI 48226

ARCHER, MARTHA JANE, psychologist; b. Cambridge, Ohio, Nov. 30, 1933; d. Ralph Herbert and Edith Sarah (Lemmon) Heller; m. Robert Dale Archer, Sept. 26, 1953; children—Robert, Gregory, Richard. M.Ed., Kent State U., 1969. Lic. psychologist, Ohio. Coordinator inpatient adolescent program Fallsview Psychiat. Hosp., Cuyahoga Falls, Ohio, 1970-72; counselor Hawthornden State Hosp., Northfield, Ohio, 1972; counselor-coordinator Residential Intervention Ctr.-YWCA, Akron, Ohio, 1973-74; dir. rehab. treatment Portage County (Ohio) Juvenile Ct., 1974-76; family counseling psychologist Portage Family Counseling and Mental Health Ctr., Ravenna, Ohio, 1976-78; pvt. practice psychology, Ravenna, 1978—; cons. Portage County Juvenile Ct. HEW grantee, 1968. Mem. Am. Psychol. Assn., Ohio Psychol. Assn., Acad. for Edn. and Research in Profl. Psychology. Home: 1102 Ledgeview Rd Macedonia OH 44056 Office: 830 W Main St Ravenna OH 44266

ARCHER, ROBERT EARL, controller; b. Canton, Ohio, July 30, 1955; s. Bernard Michael and Florence Matilda (Blake) A.; m. Patricia Lynn McCaskey, July 2, 1977; children: Kelly Lynn, Lyndsey Ann, Holly Ann, Kevin Robert. BS in Acctg., U. Akron, 1977. CPA, Ohio. Staff acct. Price Waterhouse, Cleve., 1977-80, sr. staff acct., 1980-83; mgr. Bober & Markey CPA's, Akron, 1983-84; internal auditor Mohawk Rubber Co., Akron, Ohio, 1984-86, corp. controller, 1986—. Mem. Am. Inst. CPA's. Roman Catholic. Lodge: Masons. Avocations: golf, softball, bowling, reading, collector. Home: 2473 Silver Springs Dr Stow OH 44224 Office: Mohawk Rubber Co 3560 W Market St Akron OH 44313

ARCHIBALD, CHARLES ARNOLD, holding company executive; b. Louisville, Aug. 21, 1936; s. James Henry and Phyllis Maxine (Rice) A.; m. Rosa Jane Cusano, July 11, 1959; children: James Henry II (dec.), Diane Marie. BBA, U. Cin., 1959; postgrad., Xavier U., 1963-65. V.p., bd. dirs. J.H. Archibald Co., Cin., 1963-75; pres. J.H. Archibald Co., Springfield, Mo., 1975—; also chmn. bd. dirs. J.H. Archibald Co., Springfield; pres. C/D/R Assocs., Inc., Springfield, 1987—; v.p., The Oasis, Inc., Southgate, Ky., 1963-73, Crawford Sales of So. Ohio, Cin., 1965-73, Mid-western Bldg. Systems, Norwood, Ohio, 1968-73; ptnr. TGA Publ. Palm Springs, Calif., 1985—, The Graphic Arts Ctr., Cathedral City, Calif., 1985— (all affiliates of J.H. Archibald Co.). Mem. Dem. Cen. Com., Hamilton County, Ohio, 1968-70. Served to lt. commdr. USN, 1959-62. Mem. Springfield C. of C., Pi Kappa Alpha (pres. local alumni chpt. 1980—), U. Cin. Alumni Assn. Methodist. Home: 1224 W Highland Springfield MO 65807 Office: JH Archibald Co Plaza Towers Suite 414 Springfield MO 65804

ARCHIBALD, ERWIN ROGER, osteopathic physician, educator; b. East Hiram, Maine, Oct. 7, 1922; s. Roy Archibald and Evelyn Matilda (Douglas) Archibald Day; m. Katherine Agnes Pesek, Feb. 19, 1944 (div. 1970); children: Susan K., Philip R., Kathleen E., Linda A., Gail L., Judy M.; m. Muriel Laura Bryant, June 16, 1972. Student, Bowdoin Coll., 1941-42; AB, U. Calif., Berkeley, 1950, PhD, 1964; DO, Kansas City (Mo.) Coll. Osteo. Medicine, 1973. Diplomate Osteo. Nat. Bd. Exmainers; cert. Am. Osteo. Bd. Gen. practice osteo. medicine Eliot, Maine, 1974-75; asst. prof. Kirksville (Mo.) Coll. Osteo. Medicine, 1975-78; assoc. physician HES, Inc., Kansas City, 1978-79; med. cons. Social Security Adminstrn., Kansas City, 1979-80; gen. practice osteo. medicine Pomme de Terre Clinic, Hermitage, Mo., 1980-82; asst. prof. U. Osteo. Medicine and Health Scis., Des Moines, 1982—; med. dir. Adair County Nursing Home, Kirksville, 1975-78, nursing home programs, Kirksville Coll. Osteo. Medicine, 1975-78; clin. dir. Dietz FP Clinic, Des Moines, 1982-83, Polk City (Iowa) Clinic, 1983—. Sustaining mem. Mid Iowa Council Boy Scouts Am., Des Moines, 1986; mem. Civic Ctr. Assn., Des Moines, 1986. Served to maj. USAF, 1942-46, 52-68. Mem. AAUP, Iowa Acad. Osteopathy, Am. Coll. Gen. Practitioners Osteo. Medicine and Surgery, Nat. Retired Officers Assn., Iowa Retired Officers Assn., Polk City C. of C., Sigma Xi. Avocations: gardening, bicycling, hunting, fishing, bird watching. Office: Polk City Clinic 308 N 3d St Polk City IA 50226

ARDT, THOMAS EDWARD, accountant, systems analyst; b. Columbus, Ohio, Sept. 10, 1957; s. Edward William and Emily Jeanette (Korodi) A.; m. Diana Lynn Moran, June 28, 1980; children: Charity Lynn, Thomas Edward Jr., Andrea Faith. BS in Mgmt., Bob Jones U., 1980; MBA in Acct., Loyola U., Chgo., 1985. Accounts payable supr. Ill. Bell Telephone Co., Chgo., 1980-82, systems analyst, 1982-86, acctg. analyst, 1986—. Bd. deacons Marquette Manor Bapt. Ch., Downers Grove, Ill., 1985—. Republican. Home: 1540 Bolson Dr Downers Grove IL 60516 Office: Ill Bell Telephone Co 225 W Randolph HQ5B Chicago IL 60606

AREDDY, RICHARD DANIEL, JR., insurance company executive; b. Detroit, Feb. 13, 1955; s. Richard Daniel and Rita Susan (Gombos) A.; m. Claudette M. Torpey, Nov. 17, 1979; children: Richard III, Ashley. BS in Psychology, Mich. State U., 1977; MBA, U. Detroit, 1984. Agy. rep. Ticor Title Ins., Birmingham, Mich., 1977-80, agy. mgr., 1980-84; mgr. Ticor Title Ins., Cleve., 1984—. Mem. Nat. Assn. Corp. Real Estate Execs., Nat. Assn. Indsl. Office Parks, Ohio Land Title Assn., Growth Assn. of Cleve. Club: Tanglewood Country (Chagrin Falls, Ohio). Avocations: golf, racquet sports. Office: Ticor Title Co 100 Erieview Plaza Suite 1220 Cleveland OH 44114

AREKAPUDI, VIJAYALAKSHMI, obstetrician-gynecologist; b. Davajigudem, Andhra Pradesh, India, Sept. 28, 1948; came to U.S., 1974; d. Subba Rao and Ramatulasamma (Ravi) Gondi; m. Bapu P. Arekapudi, May 5, 1974; children: Smitha, Swathi. MBBS, Guntur Med. Coll., Andhra Pradesh, India, 1970; DGO, Coll. Physicians and Surgeons Bombay, 1973. Intern Ill. Masonic Med. Ctr., Chgo., 1975-76, resident in ob-gyn, 1976-79, jr. attending staff, 1979-82, assoc. attending staff, 1982-84, attending physician, 1985—; practice medicine specializing in ob-gyn Lake Shore Med. Assocs., Ltd., Chgo., 1979—, sec., treas., 1981—. Fellow Am. Coll. Obstetricians-Gynecologists. Democrat. Hindu. Office: Lake Shore Med Assocs Ltd 2734 N Lincoln Ave Chicago IL 60614

ARENDALE, DAVID RAY, learning skills center director; b. Olathe, Kans., Mar. 5, 1956; s. John L. and Leota L. (Potter) A. BS, Emporia (Kans.) State U., 1978, MA, 1985. Cert. HRD cons. Social sci. instr. Pratt (Kans.) Community Coll., 1979-82, learning skills ctr. dir., 1982-86; learning skills ctr. dir. Highland (Kans.) Community Coll., 1986—; public speaker various orgns., Kans., 1979—; speech judge various high schs. Kans. 1979—; human relations devel. cons. Personal Growth Assocs., St. Joseph, Mo. Author Church Computer Software Directory; contbr. articles and book reviews to profl. jours. Tech. support Miss Kans. Pagent, Pratt, 1983-85; small group leader Great Commn. Internat. Ch., Kansas City, Mo., 1986. Recipient Cert. Appreciation, Kans. State High Sch. Activity Assn., 1982; named one of Outstanding Young Men Am., 1983-86; teaching fellow Emporia State U., 1978. Mem. Internat. Reading Assn., NEA (supporter polit. action com. Washington 1985-86), Nat. Assn. Devel. Edn., Western Coll. Reading and Learning Assn., Performax Systems Internat. (cons.), Doniphan County C. of C. Republican. Avocations: reading, tropical fish, classical music, church activities. Home: 3515 Gene Field Bldg 8 Apt 8 Saint Joseph MO 64506 Office: Highland Community Coll PO Box 68 Highland KS 66035

ARENDS, DAVID ANTHONY, accountant, consultant, business executive, farmer; b. Marshalltown, Iowa, Nov. 26, 1939; s. Jesse E. and Phyllis J. (Pace) A.; m. Linda E. Templeton, Sept. 20, 1967 (div. Mar. 1983). B.A. in History, Elmhurst Coll., 1965; LL.B., Blackstone Sch. Law, Chgo., 1969. Enrolled agt., U.S. Treasury Dept.; pub. acct., Iowa. Asst. corp. controller Coleman Cable & Wire Co., Broadview, Ill., 1971-72; chief corp. acctg. Wieboldt Stores, Inc., Chgo., 1972-73; corp. controller Foremost-McKesson, Skokie, Ill., 1979-84; acct., tax cons. Toledo, Iowa, 1984—; exec. officer China Trade Inc., Toledo, 1977—. Del. Democratic State Conv., 1980. Served to maj. U.S. Army, 1960-63; USAR, 1963—. Mem. Am. Assn. Astronautics, Assn. Old Crows. Democrat. Lutheran. Club: Baker Street Irregulars (Chgo.). Lodges: Masons, Shriners. Avocations: video collecting; pulp magazines; high tech.

ARENS, THEODORE GERARD, electrical controls company executive; b. Groesbeek, Netherlands, Sept. 23, 1947; s. Theodore Gerard and Theodora Francisca (Berenbroek) A.; m. Pamela Jean Nessel, Aug. 1, 1970; 1 child, Jaimie Elizabeth. BSEE, Lawrence Inst. Tech., 1974. Registered profl. engr., Mich. Jr. engr. Maxitrol Co., Southfield, Mich., 1969-72, Chrysler Corp., Highland Park, Mich., 1972-73; chief engr. Stegner Electric, Livonia, Mich., 1973-78, pres., 1978—; chmn. bd. Stegner Engring., Livonia, 1985—; bd. dirs. Tool Mfg. Ins., Bermuda, 1981—; v.p. Digital Controls, Milford, Mich., 1978—. Served with USMC, 1967-69, Vietnam. Republican. Roman Catholic. Home: 2861 Tamwood Ct Milford MI 48042 Office: Stegner Electric Controls Inc 35432 Industrial Livonia MI 48150

ARENSMAN, CRAIG LOUIS, mechanical engineer; b. lima, Ohio, May 12, 1955; s. George Louis and Beulah Ernestine (Brunson) A. BS in Mech. Engring., Ohio No. U., 1978. Registered profl. engr., Mich. Plant engr. Consumers Power, Bay City, Mich., 1978-81; thermal performance engr. Detroit Edison, 1982—; cons. Arensman Assocs., Lima, 1980—. Mem. ASME, NSPE, Am. Soc. Naval Engrs. (assoc.), Engring. Soc. Detroit, Ops. Research Soc. Am. (assoc.). Mthodist. Cb: Mich. Apple. Home: 6172 N Norborne Ct Dearborn MI 48127 Office: Detroit Edison 6200 W Warren Detroit MI 48210

ARENTZ, ANDREW ALBERT, management consultant; b. Chgo., May 12, 1928; s. Andrew A. and Ruth J. (Gulbransen) A.; B.S.C.E., Ill. Inst. Tech., 1950; J.D., John Marshall Law Sch., 1960; m. Lillian Regina Ivanovsky, Sept. 1, 1950; children—Andrew Anton, Alethea Ruth, Paul David. Supr. ops. research AMF, Niles, Ill., 1959-62; assoc. dir. advanced transp. planning Gen. Am. Transp. Corp., Chgo., 1963-66, asst. to v.p. corp. planning, 1966-68; pres., chief exec. officer GARD, Inc., Niles, 1968-77; dir. planning and devel. GATX Corp., Chgo., 1977-83, spl. asst. to v.p. fin., 1983-84, dir. personnel research and benefits planning, 1984-86; pres. Arentz and Assocs., 1986—; Bd. dirs. Chgo. Bot. Garden, 1979-82, Luth. Sch. Theology, Chgo., 1972-78; trustee Village of Riverwoods, 1969-73, 87—. Served with AUS, 1952-54. Home and Office: 333 Juneberry Rd Riverwoods IL 60015

ARETZ, TONYA MARIE, lawyer; b. Lafayette, Ind., Nov. 6, 1959; d. Donald T. and Ruth M. (Crone) A. BA, Ind. U., 1982; JD, U. Dayton, 1985. Police officer Ind. U. Police Dept., Bloomington, 1980-82; law clk. to presiding justice Montgomery County Common Pleas Ct., Dayton, Ohio, 1984-85; dep. atty. gen. State of Ind., Indpls., 1986—. Named one of Outstanding Young Women Am., 1983. Mem. ABA (liaison 1984-85), Ind. Bar Assn., Assn. Trial Lawyers Am., Phi Delta Phi. Republican. Roman Catholic. Home: 7112 Islander Dr Apt E Indianapolis IN 46214 Office: Office of Atty Gen 219 State House Indianapolis IN 46204

AREY, HUGH CUSTER, sales professional; b. Mpls., Feb. 3, 1927; s. Hugh Custer and Mabel (Lane) A.; m. Barbara Teachout, Aug. 3, 1951 (div. July 1964); children: Molly Arey Snyder, Cynthia Arey Brinkhaus, Thomas John Arey; m. Kathryn Kay, July 9, 1966. BA in Psychology, U. Minn., 1951. Time study analyst Kickernick, Inc., Mpls., 1955-56; outside salesman Heinrich Envelope Co., Mpls., 1956-68; regional sales mgr. Advance Floor Machine Co., Cleve., 1968-71; outside salesman Envelope div. St. Regis Paper Co., Cleve., 1971-76, Atlantic Envelope Co. Div. Nat. Service Industries, Berea, Ohio, 1976—. Councilman City of Berea, 1982—. Served with USN, 1945-46; served to 2d lt. USAF, 1952-55, chief warrant officer Res. ret. Mem. U.S. Power Squadron. Republican. Episcopalian. Lodges: Rotary, Masons, Shriners. Avocations: hunting, skiing, sailing. Home: 356 Brockton Circle Berea OH 44017-2201 Office: Atlantic Envelope Co PO Box 380 Berea OH 44017-0380

AREY, LEO BETRAM, clin. psychologist; b. Richfield, N.C., June 19, 1913; s. Nathan Green and Nina (Trexler) A.; m. Jennie Lind Mitchell, Dec. 31, 1941; A.B., Lenoir Rhyne Coll., 1935; Ph.D., U. Chgo., 1952. Registered psychologist, Ill., 1964; diplomate Am. Bd. Profl. Psychology. Psychology intern VA Hosp., Hines, Ill., 1947-51, staff clin. psychologist, 1952-61, research psychologist, 1962-66, asst. chief, psychology service, supervisory psychologist, psychiatry service, 1966-80, pvt. practice, 1981—. Mem. Am., Midwest, Ill. psychol. assns., Assn. Psychophysiol. Study Sleep, Assn. Psychophysiol. Study of Sleep, Am. Acad. Psychotherapists, Assn. Advancement Psychology, Sigma Xi. Contbr. to psychol. jours. and book. Home: 5532 South Shore Dr Chicago IL 60637

AREY, RICHARD EVERETT, hotel executive; b. Shelby, N.C., June 4, 1927, s. William Griffin and Catherine (Roberts) A.; m. Anice Miller, Sept. 2, 1950; 1 child, Ann Rochelle Arey Mason. Student Davidson Coll., 1944-45, Mcht. Marine Acad., 1945-46; cert. hotel adminstrn., Ech. Inst. of Am. Hotel and Motel Assn. From mgmt. trainee to dept. head Robert E. Lee Hotel, Winston-Salem, N.C., 1950-58; gen. mgr. Washington Duke Hotel, Durham, N.C., 1958-60; v.p., gen. mgr. Jack Tar Hotel, Durham, 1960-70, Hilton Plaza Inns, Kansas City, Mo., 1970—; treas. N.C. Travel Council, 1960-61; Pres. Durham Mchts. Assn., 1968; mem. faculty dept. food and lodging Penn Valley Coll.; commr. Planned Indsl. Expansion Authority, Kansas City, Mo.; bd. dirs., vice chmn. Kansas City Tourist and Conv. Bur.; bd. dirs. Country Club Plaza Assn. Served as midshipman USNR and USMC, 1945-46. Recipient Rocamora award N.C., 1967, Salut Au Restaurateur award Fla. State U., 1967. Mem. Hotel Sales Mgrs. Assn., Am. Soc. Travel Agts., Am. Hotel Motel Career Devel. Assn., Hotel Motel Greeters Assn., Hotel and Motel Assn. Greater Kansas City, (pres. 1977), Mo. Restaurant Assn. (pres. Kansas City chpt. 1978, Kansas City Restaurateur of Yr. 1983), N.C. Hotel Motel Assn. (pres.), N.C. Restaurant Assn. (pres. 1966), So. Innkeepers Assn. (v.p. 1962), Am. Hotel Motel Assn. (bd. dirs. 1960-70). Presbyterian. Office: Hilton Plaza Inns 45th and Main Kansas City MO 64111

ARGABRITE, JOHN WILLIAM, allergist; b. Watertown, S.D., June 13, 1917; s. Lewis Hiram and Margaret Elizabeth (Shields) A.; m. Volga Dorothy Lehmberg, Dec. 18, 1943; children: Michele, Francene, Colleen, Nannette. B in Pharmacy, S.D. State Coll., 1940; PharmM, Western Res. U., 1942; MD, U. Ill., Chgo., 1945. Med. License, S.D., Ill., Calif. Practice medicine specializing in allergies Watertown, 1946—; pres. St. Ann's Hosp.; instr. S.D. Med. Sch., Vermillion; adv. State of S.D. bd. dirs. United Fund Dr., Watertown. Served to capt. MC, 1945-48. Mem. Am. Coll. Allergy (bd. dirs.), Am. Acad. Environ. Medicine (pres.), S.D. Heart Assn. (pres.), S.D. Internal Medicine Assn. (pres.), North Cen. Allergy Assn. (pres.). Republican. Roman Catholic. Lodge: Lions (pres.). Avocations: golf, hunting, dancing, tennis. Office: 3 E Kemp Ave Watertown SD 57201

ARGANIAN, MOURAD PETER, psychotherapist, family life educator; b. Racine, Wis., June 14, 1935; s. Hovsep and Mary (Jananian) A.; m. Roberta Sigman, Aug. 22, 1959; children: Jean Laura, John Michael. BS, U. Wis., Madison, 1959; MA, U. Chgo., 1962. Child welfare specialist Racine County Human Services Ctr., 1962-64; staff social worker Wis. Children's Treatment Ctr., Madison, 1964-67; coordinator child psychiatry clinic U. Wis. Hosps., Madison, 1967-75, staff social worker, 1975-78; coordinator mental health services and programs Group Health Coop. of S. Cen. Wis., Madison, 1978—; pvt. practice marriage and family therapy, Madison, 1981—; clin. instr. dept. family medicine U. Wis. Med. Sch., 1984—; leader workshops on marriage and couple retreats, 1981—. Bd. dirs. Friends of Madison Pub. Library, 1971, 84. Served with U.S. Army, 1954-56. Mem. Acad. Cert. Social Workers, Am. Group Psychotherapy Assn. Avocations: walking, boating, photography. Home: 3709 Paus St Madison WI 53714

ARJONA, JOSE RAFAEL, university business officer, accountant; b. Fajardo, P.R., Feb. 11, 1958; s. Efrain Sr. and Nilda (De Celis) A.; m. Tracy Lynn Reeves, May 2, 1981; children: Jason Michael Jarvis, Christina Lynn, Kara Michele. BBA with honors, U. Puerto Rico, 1979. CPA, Ind. Bus. office intern Purdue U., West Lafayette, Ind., 1980, jr. acct., 1980-83, sr. acct., 1983-85, mgr. fed. costing studies, 1985—; pvt. practice acctg. Lafayette, Ind., 1987—; cons. Pete's Place, West Lafayette, 1985-86; mem. esprit com. Purdue U., 1984-86, supervisory com. Purdue Employees Fed. Credit Union, 1985-87, bd. dirs., 1987—. Attache to protocol div. Paraguay PAX Indpls., Inc., 10th Pan-Am. games, 1986-87. Mem. Am. Inst. CPA's, Ind. CPA Soc. (non-profit orgn. com. 1987—), Am. Express Centurion Council. Roman Catholic. Avocations: fishing, reading, physical fitness. Office: PO Box 2416 West Lafayette IN 47906

ARKING, LUCILLE MUSSER, nurse epidemiologist; b. Centre County, Pa., Jan. 26, 1936; d. Boyd Albert and Marion Anna (Merryman) Musser; m. Robert Arking, May 8, 1959; children—Henry David, Jonathan Jacob. R.N., Episcopal Sch. Nursing, 1958; BS in Nursing, U. Pa., 1968; MS in Nursing, Wayne State U., 1985. Psychiat. research nurse Boston City Hosp., 1958; hosp. supr. Phila. Psychiat. Ctr., 1959-61; pub. health nurse Community Nursing Service, Phila., 1961-64; dir. nursing Green Acres Nursing Ctr., Phila., 1966-67; head nurse U. Va., Charlottesville, 1967-68; asst. dir. nursing U. Ky., Lexington, 1968-70; asst. dir. nursing edn. Rio Hondo Hosp., Downey, Calif., 1973-75; dir. nursing Bellwood Hosp., Bellflower, Calif., 1974-75; nurse epidemiologist Henry Ford Hosp., Detroit, 1975-84, dir. hosp. epidemiology, 1984—; instr. Santa Ana Coll., 1971-73; lectr. drug abuse Fountain Valley, Calif., 1970-75. Co-founder Parents and Friends Learning Disabilities Orgn., 1968-70; den leader Cub Scouts, Fountain Valley, Calif. 1968-75; bd. dirs. Wellness Networks, Detroit, 1982—. Women's Club of Centre County scholar, 1954-58; grantee Community Nursing Service Edn., 1963-64; USPHS nursing trainee, 1965; mem. Mich. Gov. AIDS task force, 1985-86, Mich. Med. Soc. AIDS task force, 1986. Mem. Am. Nurse's Assn., Mich. Nurse's Assn. (AIDS task force 1987), Am. Pub. Health Assn. (mem. epidemiology sect. 1975—), Assn. Practitioners of Infection Control, Mich. Infection Control Soc., Nat. League of Nursing. Contbr. articles to profl. jours. Home: 4705 Stoddard Troy MI 48098 Office: Henry Ford Hosp Dept Epidemiology 2799 W Grand Blvd Detroit MI 48202

ARKING, ROBERT, geneticist, gerontologist, educator; b. Bklyn., July 1, 1936; s. Henry and Mollie (Levinson) A.; B.S., Dickinson Coll., 1958; Ph.D., Temple U., 1967; m. Lucille Mae Musser, May 8, 1959; children—Henry David, Jonathan Jacob. Sci. tchr. Phila. Public Schs., 1959-61; asst. prof. zoology U. Ky., Lexington, 1968-70; research biologist Ctr. for Pathology, U. Calif., Irvine, 1970-75; asst. prof. biology Wayne State U., Detroit, 1975-81, assoc. prof. 1981—; faculty assoc. Inst. Gerontology Wayne State U. NSF fellow, 1964-66, NIH fellow, 1967-68; NIH and NSF grantee, 1970—. Mem. AAAS, Am. Soc. Zoologists, Genetics Soc. Am., Soc. for Developmental Biology, Gerontology Soc. Am., Sigma Xi. Contbr. articles to profl. jours. Office: Wayne State University Dept Biological Sciences Detroit MI 48202

ARKINS, JOHN A., physician; b. Milw., Sept. 13, 1926; s. Alex and Marguerite (Newhouse) A.; m. Carolyn Lois Babush, June 27, 1948; children: Debra, James, Jeffrey. BS, U. Wis., 1950, MD, 1952. Diplomate Am. Bd. Allergy and Immunology. Intern Rochester (N.Y.) Gen. Hosp., 1952-53; resident in internal medicine Milw. County Hosp., 1953-56, fellow-allergy, 1956-58; prof. medicine U. Wis. Med. Coll., Milw., 1965-86, coordinator of undergrad. edn., 1975-86; pres. profl. staff Milw. County Med. Ctr., 1978-80; bd. dirs. Wis. Indo-Chinese Refugee Relief, Milw.; mem. Surgeon Gen.'s Adv. Council, U.S. Army, Washington, 1981-84. Contbr. articles to profl. jours. Served to brig. gen. USAR, 1954-86. Grantee USPHS, 1965, 68, NIH, 1965, 68. Fellow ACP, Am. Acad. Allergy and Immunology; mem. N.Y. Acad. Sci., Am. Thoracic Soc. Jewish. Avocations: golf, travel, photography. Office: Milw County Hosp 8700 W Wisconsin Ave Milwaukee WI 53226

ARLINGHAUS, EDWARD JAMES, health administration educator; b. Cin., Jan. 6, 1925; s. Edward A. and Irene (Custer) A.; B.B.A., U. Cin., 1948, Ph.D., 1981; M.B.A., Xavier U., 1958, M.Ed., 1971, M.S., 1973; m. Ilse Denninger, Aug. 10, 1974; 1 dau., Toni Gail. Dir. personnel tng. Mabley & Carew Co., Cin., 1948-51; sales researcher John Shillito Co., Cin., 1951-53; personnel devel. specialist Gen. Elec. Co., Cin., 1953-57; dir. personnel, pub. relations and security Jewish Hosp. of Cin., 1957-66; dir. grad. program in hosp. and health adminstrn. Xavier U., Cin., 1966—; mem. health care sect. Cath. Conf. Ohio; sec. bd. trustees Providence Hosp., 1968-77, St. Francis Hosp., 1968-75, St. Mary's Hosp., 1968-72 (all Cin.); trustee Epp Meml. Hosp., 1983—, Otterbeni Homes, 1981—; chmn. health manpower com. CORVA, Cin., 1970-75; mem. Ohio Bd. Examiners Nursing Home Adminstrs., 1974-76. Served with AUS, 1943-45; col. Res. (ret.). Fellow Royal Soc. Health; Am. Coll. Healthcare Execs., Am. Acad. Med. Adminstrs.; mem. Assn. Mental Health Adminstrs., Cath. Hosp. Assn., Am. Public Health Assn., Scarbard and Blade, Phi Delta Kappa. Home: 8060 Indian Hill Rd Cincinnati OH 45243 Office: Xavier University Cincinnati OH 45207

ARLOOK, IRA ARTHUR, public interest association executive; b. N.Y.C., Apr. 7, 1943; s. George G. and Shirley (Meyers) A.; m. Karen Beth Nussbaum, July 9, 1978; children: Gene, Jack. BA, Tufts U., 1964; MA in History, Stanford U., 1966; PhD in Pub. Policy, Union Grad. Sch., 1978. Asst. prof. Cleve. State U., 1975-80; exec. dir. Ohio Pub. Interest Campaign, Cleve., 1976—, Citizen Action, Cleve., Chgo., 1980—. Woodrow Wilson Nat. fellow, 1965, NSF fellow, 1980. Mem. Citizens for Tax Justice (pres. Washington 1980—), Nat. Conf. Alternative State and Local Pub. Policies (bd. dirs. 1976-80), Citizen Labor Energy Coalition (bd. dirs. Washington 1978—), Nat. Campaign Against Toxic Hazards (bd. dirs. 1983—). Avocations: sports, music. Office: Citizen Action Burgess Bldg 1406 W 6th St 2d Floor Cleveland OH 44113

ARLOOK, THEODORE DAVID, dermatologist; b. Boston, Mar. 12, 1910; s. Louis and Rebecca (Sakansky) A.; B.S., U. Ind. Sch. Medicine, 1932, M.D., 1934; postgrad. dermatology U. So. Calif., 1946-47. Intern, Luth. Meml. Hosp., Chgo., 1934-35; resident in dermatology Indpls. Gen. Hosp., 1947-49; practice medicine specializing in dermatology, Elkhart, Ind., 1950—; mem. staff Elkhart Gen. Hosp.; assoc. mem. dermatology dept. Wishard Meml. Hosp., Indpls, 1950-86, Regenstrief Hosp., Indpls., 1987—. Pres., Temple Israel, Elkhart, 1963-64; pres. B'nai B'rith, 1955. Served to capt. M.C. AUS, 1941-46; PTO. Diplomate Am. Bd. Dermatology. Mem. AMA, Ill. State Med. Assn., Am. Acad. Dermatology, Elkhart County Med. Soc. (pres. 1967), Noah Worcester Dermatol. Soc. Contbr. articles to med. jours. Office: 912 W Franklin St Elkhart IN 46516

ARMACOST, ROBERT LEO, management educator, former coast guard officer, educator; b. Balt., July 17, 1942; s. Leo Mathias and Margaret Virginia (Ruth) A.; m. Susan Marie Danesi, Jan. 16, 1965; children—Robert Leo, Andrew Paul, Kathleen Erin. B.S. with honors, U.S. Coast Guard Acad., 1964; M.S., U.S. Naval Postgrad. Sch., 1970; D.Sc. in Ops. Research, George Washington U., 1976. Engring. officer USCG Cutter Mendota, Wilmington, N.C., 1964-66; ops. officer USCGC Cook Inlet, Portland, Maine, 1966-68; ops. research analyst, ops. planning staff USCG Hdqrs., Washington, 1970-75; planning officer, aids to navigation div., 1976-78; comdr. Coast Guard Group, Milw., 1978-81; comdg. officer USCG Marine Safety Office, Milw., 1981-84, capt. of port, 1981-84, officer in charge of marine inspection, 1981-84; ret., 1984; instr. computer sci. Milw. Area Tech. Coll., 1982-83; asst. prof. mgmt. sci. Marquette U., Milw., 1984—. First v.p. Md. Right to Life, 1976-78; active Wis. Marine Hist. Soc., Manitowoc Maritime Mus., Little League, Glendale, Wis.; mem. Archdiocese Mils. Pastoral Council, 1984—, vice chmn., 1986-87, chmn., 1987—. Contbr. articles to profl. jours. Recipient USCG commendation award, 1972, 74, 78, 81, 84; named Outstanding Civic Vol., Bowie, Md., 1976; nat. finalist White House fellow, 1977-78. Mem. Ops. Research Soc. Am. (mem. com. 1983-84), Math. Programming Soc., Inst. Mgmt. Sci. Roman Catholic. Home: 7012 N Bethmaur Ln Glendale WI 53209 Office: Marquette Univ Coll Bus Adminstrn Milwaukee WI 53233

ARMAGOST, ELSA GAFVERT, computer industry communications consultant; b. Duluth, Minn., Jan. 26, 1917; d. Axel Justus and Martina Emelia (Magnuson) Gafvert; m. Byron William Armagost, Dec. 8, 1945; children: David Byron, Laura Martina. Grad. with honors, Duluth Jr. Coll., 1936; BJ, U. Minn., 1938, postgrad. in public relations, bus. mgmt. and computer tech., 1965-81; PhD in Computer Communication Cons. Sci. (hon.), Internat. U. Found. Freelance editor, Duluth, 1939-42; procedure editor and analyst U.S. Steel, Duluth, 1942-45; fashion advt. staff Dayton Co., Mpls., 1945-48; systems applications and documentation mgr. Control Data Corp., Mpls., 1969-74, promotion specialist, mktg. editor, 1974-76, corp. staff coordinator info. on edn., 1976-78; instr. communications, publ. specialist, 1978-79, communication cons. peripheral products group, 1979-83; communications cons., 1983—; mem. steering com. U.S. Senatorial Bus. Adv. Bd., 1962-68; mem. Am. Security Council, U.S. Congl. Adv. Bd., 1958-62; adv. bd. Process Mgmt. Inst., Inc., Optional Care Systems, Inc.; bd. dirs. N. Cen. Deming Mgmt. Forum. V.p. Sewickley Valley Hosp. Aux., Sewickley Valley Mental Health Council; dir. publicity Sacred Arts Expo, World Affairs Council radio program, Pitts., 1962-68. Recipient Medal of Merit Rep. Presdl. Task Force. Mem. AAUW (1st v.p. Caracas, Venezuela), Women in Communication (job mart dir.), Am. Security Council, Internat. Platform Assn., Friends of Mpls. Inst. Art., Walker Art Inst., LWV (bd. dirs. Pitts. chpt.), Phi Beta Music Soc., Minn. Alumni Assn., Am. Swedish Inst. Club: Toastmasters (Communications award 1984). Home and Office: 9500 Collegeview Rd Bloomington MN 55437

ARMON, GARY LEO, educational counselor; b. Winnebago, Minn., Sept. 24, 1950; s. Woodrow Charles and Mary (Michelau) A.; m. Elizabeth Louise Willmert, Aug. 11, 1973; children: Emily, Elizabeth Ann. BS, Mankato State U., 1972, MS, 1977. Tchr. Amboy (Minn.) Pub. Sch., 1972-77; counselor Blue Earth (Minn.) Pub. Sch., 1977—, also mem. planning, evaluation and report com. Dept. chmn. Blue Earth High Sch., 1983-87; adv. bd. Winnebago Treatment Ctr., 1981-85, Albert Lea (Minn.) Vocat. Ctr., 1981-87; sec.,treas. Campaign for County Commr., Fairbault County, Minn., 1986; chmn. community task force; mem. ch. council Saints Peter and Paul's Cath. Ch., Blue Earth, 1980-82, pres. 1982. Mem. NEA, Minn. Edn. Assn., Minn. Sch. Counselors Assn. (bd. dirs. 1984-85 southeast div., Service award 1985), Blue Earth Edn. Assn. (pres. 1983). Lodges: K.C., Lions (v.p. Blue Earth club 1983-85, pres. 1986). Avocations: cross country, skiing, golf, bow hunting. Office: Blue Earth High Sch Counseling Ctr E 6th St Blue Earth MN 56013

ARMOUR, SUZANNE BURTON, pharmaceutical manufacturing executive; b. Akron, Ohio, Jan. 24, 1931; d. Robert Lawrence and Vivian Laconia (Butts) B.; m. Leslie Armour Jr., July 14, 1950 (div. June 1965). BS in Edn., Akron U., 1950; MA in Biology, Case Western Res. U., 1959. Research asst. Harvard Med. Sch., Boston, 1962-65, Med. Research Council, London, 1965-66, U. Geneva, 1966-70; research asst. The Upjohn Co., Kalamazoo, 1970-74, supr., 1974-76, ops. mgr., 1977—. Author Cooking with Fresh Herbs, 1986. adv. Jr. Achievement, Kalamazoo, 1978; bd. dirs. Douglass Community Assn., 1974, Kalamazoo Alcohol and Drug Abuse Council, 1981-84. Mem. Am. Mgmt. Assn., Parenteral Drug Assn., Herb Marketers and Growers Assn., Black Career Women, Inc. Democrat. Baptist. Avocations: music, travel, reading, photography, growing orchids. Home: 3907 Cricket Ln Kalamazoo MI 49008 Office: The Upjohn Co 7171 Portage Rd Kalamazoo MI 49008

ARMSTRONG, CLIFFORD BURTON, JR., chemical engineer; b. Detroit, May 20, 1920; s. Clifford B. and Lucile Helen (Mabie) A.; m. Lydia E. Hargrove, Mar. 12, 1949; children: Paul Gerald, Warren Burton. BS in Chem. Engring., Mich. Tech. Inst., 1942. Registered profl. engr., Mich. Chem. engr. Hooker Chems., Niagara Falls, N.Y., 1942-44, Sharples Chems., Wyandotte, Mich., 1946-50; material engr. Wyandotte Chems., 1950-53; mfrs. rep., owner C. Armstrong Co., Detroit, 1953—. Served with USN, 1944-46. Mem. Nat. Assn. Corrosion Engrs. (chpt. chmn. 1987—), Assn. Finishing Processes (bulletin editor 1985—), Am. Inst. Chem. Engrs., Mfrs. Agts. Nat. Assn. Republican. Methodist. Club: Tandem. Avocations: health and fitness. Home: 7053 Cathedral Birmingham MI 48010 Office: Clifford Armstrong Co 24634 Five Mile Rd Detroit MI 48239

ARMSTRONG, GARY EDWARD, advertising executive; b. New Castle, Pa., Mar. 11, 1952; s. Robert P. and Jean (Wadding) A.; m. Elaine Green, Oct. 25, 1975; children: Colin, Christene. BS, Ashland (Ohio) Coll., 1974. V.p. Topper Assoc., Inc., Ashland, 1974-78; account exec. Lord Sullivan & Yoder, Marion, Ohio, 1978-80, dir. bus. devel., 1980-82, v.p. bus devel., 1983-85, v.p., dir. mktg., 1986—; cons. in field. Bd. dirs. Ashland County United Appeal, 1979. Republican. Presbyterian. Club: Muirfield Village Golf (Dublin, Ohio). Avocations: piloting, restoring antique autos, collecting tinplate trains. Home: 6753 Amur Dr Worthington OH 43085 Office: Lord Sullivan & Yoder Inc 250 Old Wilson Bridge Rd Columbus OH 43085

ARMSTRONG, HART REID, minister, editor, publisher; b. St. Louis, May 11, 1912; s. Hart Champlin and Zora Lillian (Reid) A.; m. Iona Rhoda Mehl, Feb. 21, 1932; 1 son, Hart Reed. Grad. Life Bible Coll., 1931; A.B., Christian Temples U., 1936; Litt.D., Geneva Theol. Coll., 1967; D.D. (hon.) Central Sch. Religion, Surrey, Eng., 1972; Th.M., Central Christian Coll., 1968, Th.D., 1970; Ph.D. in Religion, Berean Christian Coll., 1980. Ordained to ministry Assembly of God, 1932; pastor, 1932-34; dean Bible Standard Coll., Eugene, Oreg., 1935-40; missionary, Indonesia, 1941-42; editor Open Bible Pubs., Des Moines, 1944-46, Gospel Pub. House, Springfield, Mo., 1947-53, Gospel Light Pubs., Glendale, Calif., 1954; crusade adminstr. Oral Roberts Assn., Tulsa, 1955-62; exec. dir. Assembly Homes, Inc., Glenwood, Minn., 1963-66; pres. Defenders Christian Faith, Kansas City, Mo., 1967-80; founder, pres., editor Christian Communications, Inc., Wichita, Kans., 1981—; editor Communicare mag. Fellow London Royal Soc. Arts; mem. Nat. Sunday Sch. Assn., Pope County Hist. Soc., Sigma Delta Chi. Lodge: Rotary (past charter pres. Glenwood, Minn.). Author: To Those Who Are Left, 1950; You Should Know, 1951; The Rebel, 1967; The Beast, 1967; How Do I Pray, 1968; All Things for Life, 1969; What Will Happen to the United States, 1969; Impossible Events of Bible Prophecy, 1979; All You Need to Know about Bible Prophecy, 1980; Thoughts at Three Score and Ten, 1981; The A-B-C of Last Day Events, 1982. Home: 6436 N Hillside Ave Wichita KS 67219 Office: 6450 N Hillside Ave Wichita KS 67219

ARMSTRONG, JERRY RAY, agricultural business executive; b. Elwood, Ind., Feb. 12, 1951; s. Zelotes George and Martha Lucille (Samuels) A.; m. Nancy May Hobbs, June 20, 1971; children: Jason, Jill. BS cum laude, Ball State U., 1973. CPA, Ind. Acct. Pioneer Hi-Bred Inc., Tipton, Ind., 1973-77; office and acctg. coordinator Pioneer Hi-Bred Internat., Inc., Tipton, Ind., 1977-80, controller, treas., 1980-84, dir. fin., adminstrn., 1984—; chmn. community investment com. Pioneer Hi-Bred Internat., Tipton, 1982—; mem. bus., econ. adv. bd. Ind. U. at Kokomo, 1983—. Mem. adv. bd. Twp. of Madison, Tipton, 1980-83, State Future Bus. Leaders Am., Indpls., 1983-84; pres. Tipton Community Fund, 1982-83; founder Tipton County Found., 1985, v.p., 1987; mem. gifted and talented task force Tipton Community Sch., 1985-86; bd. dirs. Tipton Econ. Devel. Corp., 1987. Mem. Am. Inst. CPA's, Ind. Assn. CPA's, Nat. Assn. Accts., Friends of Indpls. Museum of Art. Republican. Lodge: Elks. Home: Rural Rt 1 Box 64 Atlanta IN 46031 Office: Pioneer Hi-Bred Internat Inc 1000 W Jefferson St Tipton IN 46072

ARMSTRONG, KAY DIANE, teacher, librarian; b. Detroit; d. Charles Hubert and Frankye Alida (Harberd) A.; m. Julius Kenton Armstrong, Feb. 7, 1964; children: Julius, Chad. BS in Edn., Wayne State U., 1965, MA, 1976. Cert. tchr., Mich. Tchr. Franklin Elementary Sch., Detroit, 1965-67, Custer Elementary Sch., Detroit, 1967, Bagley Elementary Sch., Detroit, 1967-76, Redford High Sch., Detroit, 1976—; owner Kay's Creation, 1982-85. commr. Parent Youth Guidance Commn., Southfield, Mich., 1982-85. Recipient Outstanding Pioneer award, 1982, cert. Recognition LWV, Livonia, Mich., 1983, cert. Appreciation Oakland County Juvenile Ct., 1984, 85, plaque of Appreciation Redford's Parent Club, 1986. Mem. Jack and Jill Am. (pres. Oakland County 1984-86), Delta Sigma Theta. Democrat. Cert. scuba diver. Avocations: down hill skiing, arts and crafts. Home: 23926 Plumbrooke Southfield MI 48075

ARMSTRONG, LOREN DOYLE, pastor; b. Enid, Okla., Nov. 10, 1947; s. Loren Ray and Veda Marcine (West) A.; m. Donna Marie Badger, June 30, 1966; children: Denny, Tammy. Student, Clark Coll., 1966-67; BTh., Bethany Bible Coll. Cert. electric engr. Electronics technician Am. Music, Vancouver, Wash., 1966-67, Armstrong Enterprises, Palmer, Ak., 1968-71; electronics engr. Internat. Tools Co., Newark, Ohio, 1974-75; pastor The Ch. of God, Bradford, Ark., 1972-73, Dayton, Ohio, 1975—; group leader Cambridge Sales Orgn., San Francisco, 1981-83; tchr. Sword and Trumpet Library, West Carrollton, Ohio, 1975—; spkr. Bible Truth Video Library, Dayton, 1985—. Author 28 books; contbr. articles to profl. jours. Clark Coll. scholar, 1966. Mem. Montgomery County Ministerial. Club: Photo (Anchorage) (pres. 1964-65). Avocations: music, building houses, hunting, farming, boating, writing. Home: 4500 Crains Run Rd Franklin OH 45005 Office: Church of God 851 S Elm St West Carrollton OH 45449

ARMSTRONG, NAOMI YOUNG, retired educator; b. Dermott, Ark., Oct. 17, 1918; d. Allen Wesley and Sarah Elizabeth (Fluker) Young; B.S., Northwestern U., 1961; L.H.D. (hon.), U. Libre, Karachi, Pakistan, 1974; Ph.D. (hon.), World U., Tucson, 1979; D.LiH. (hon.), Universal Orthodox Coll., Iperu-Remo, Ogun State, Nigeria, 1980; Litt.D. (hon.) World Acad. Arts and Culture, Taipei, Taiwan, 1981; m. Joe Leslie Armstrong, July 17, 1938; 1 dau., Betty-Jo Armstrong Dunbar. Actress, Skyloft Players, also Center Aisle Players, Chgo., 1945-59; silk dress operator Rue-Ann Originals, Chgo., 1947-55; clk. Bur. Pub. Debt, 1955-56, IRS, 1956-59; caseworker Cook County Dept. Pub. Aid, Chgo., 1961-62; tchr. Chgo. pub. schs., 1962-83, creative writing instr., 1975-77, instr. Social Center, 1965-67; dramatic instr. Crerar Meml. Presbyn. Ch., Chgo., 1972; real estate salesman Century 21 Maner, 1978—. Mem. exec. bd., membership chmn. Northwestern U. Young Alumni Council, 1971-72; trustee World U., 1973-74. Recipient Hon. Gold diploma, spl. award 3d World Congress Poets, 1976; named Internat. Woman of 1975, United Poets Laureate Internat. others; lic. real estate salesman. Mem. United Poets Laureate Internat. (exec. bd.), Internat. Platform Assn. (life; bd. govs.); 3d Preview winner 1976), World Poets Resource Center, Poetry Soc. London, Centro Studi e Scambi Internat., Intercontinental Biog. Assn. (life), World Poetry Soc., NAACP (life, chpt. chmn. edn. com. 1983), Sigma Gamma Rho. Author: A Child's Easter, 1971; Expression I, 1973; Expression III, 1976; Naomi's Two Line Sillies (A Guide for Living) Expression IV, 1985. Address: 9257 S Burnside Ave Chicago IL 60619

ARMSTRONG, RANDOLPH KERRY, automation systems designer; b. Lititz, Pa., July 20, 1962; s. Robert Keith and Helen Louise (Blackburn) A.; m. Beth Ann Stephens, Oct. 4, 1986. BEE, BS in Biomed. Engring., Duke U., 1984. Engr. Picker Internat., Cleve., 1984-86; sr. systems engr. Xetron Corp., Cin., 1986—; cons. in field. Patentee in field. Mem. IEEE. Presbyterian. Avocation: songwriter. Office: Xetron Corp 40 W Crescentville Cincinnati OH 45246

ARMSTRONG, THEODORE MORELOCK, corporate executive; b. St. Louis, July 22, 1939; s. Theodore Roosevelt and Vassar Fambrough (Morelock) A.; m. Carol Mercer Robert, Sept. 7, 1963; children: Evelyn Anne, Robert Theodore. BA, Yale U., 1961; LLB, Duke U., 1964. Bar: Mo. 1964. With Miss. River Transmission Corp. and affiliated cos., 1964-85; corp. sec. Mo. Pacific Corp., 1971-75, River Cement Co., 1968-75; asst. v.p. Miss. River Transmission Corp., 1974-75, v.p. gas supply, 1975-79, exec. v.p., 1979-83, pres., chief exec. officer, 1983-85; exec. v.p. Natural Gas Pipeline of Am., 1985; sr. v.p. fin. and adminstrn. Angelica Corp., St. Louis, 1986—. Bd. dirs. Cen. Inst. for the Deaf. Mem. ABA, Mo. Bar, Met. St. Louis Bar Assn., Phi Alpha Delta. Republican. Presbyterian. Clubs: Bellerive, St. Louis, Yale (St. Louis); Yale (N.Y.C.). Home: 43 Countryside Ln Saint Louis MO 63131 Office: Angelica Corp 10176 Corporate Sq Dr Saint Louis MO 63132

ARMSTRONG, WARREN BRUCE, university president, historian, educator; b. Tidioute, Pa., Oct. 16, 1933; s. Mead C. and Mary (Griffin) A.; m. Elizabeth Ann Fowler, Aug. 7, 1954 (div. 1973); children: Linda Susan, Heidi Jo; m. Joan Elizabeth Gregory, Apr. 19, 1974; children: Susan Elizabeth, Pamela Anne. Th.B., Bapt. Coll. Pa., 1956; A.M., U. Mich., 1958, Ph.D., 1964. Instr. history Olivet Coll., 1961-63, asst. prof., 1963-65, chmn. dept., 1964-65; asst. prof. U. Wis.-Whitewater, 1965-66, asso. prof., 1966-69, prof., 1969-70, asst. dean Coll. Arts and Scis., 1966-69, asso. dean, 1969-70; dean St. Cloud (Minn.) State U., 1970-75, prof. history, 1970-75; pres. Eastern N.Mex. U., Portales, 1975-83; pres. Wichita State U. (Kans.), 1983—, prof. history, 1983—; bd. dirs. The Coleman Co., Bank IV-Wichita. Author: (with Dae Hong Chang) The Prison: Voices from the Inside, 1972; Contbr. articles to profl. jours. Councilman, Whitewater, 1968-70; bd. visitors Air U., Maxwell AFB, Montgomery, Ala. Mem. AAUP, Orgn. Am. Historians, Am. Conf. Acad. Deans., Am. Assn. Higher Edn., Phi Kappa Phi. Democrat. Home: 1820 N Hillside Wichita KS 67214 Office: Wichita State Univ Office of the Pres Wichita KS 67208

ARN, KENNETH DALE, city official, physician; b. Dayton, Ohio, July 19, 1921; s. Elmer R. and Minna Marie (Wannagat) A.; m. Vivien Rose Fontini, Sept. 24, 1966; children—Christine H. Hulme, Laura P. Hafstad, Kevin D., Kimmel R. B.A., Miami U., Oxford, Ohio, 1943; M.D., U. Mich., 1946. Intern Miami Valley Hosp., Dayton, Ohio, 1947-48; resident in pathology U. Mich., 1948-49, fellow in renal research, 1949-50; fellow in internal medicine Cleve. Clinic, 1950-52; practice medicine specializing in internal medicine, pub. health and vocat. rehab. Dayton, 1952—; commr. of health City of Oakwood, Ohio, 1953—; assoc. clin. prof. medicine Wright State U., 1975—; mem. staffs Kettering Med. Ctr., Dayton, Miami Valley Hosp.; adj. assoc. prof. edn. Wright State U.; field med. cons. Bur. Vocat. Rehab., 1958—, Bur. Services to Blind, 1975—; med. dir. Ohio Rehab. Services Commn., 1979—; mem. Pres.'s Com. on Employment of Handicapped, 1971—; chmn. med. adv. com. Goodwill Industries, 1960-75, chmn. bd. trustees 1985-87; mem., chmn. lay adv. com. vocat. edn. Dayton Pub. Schs., 1973-82; exec. com. Gov.'s Com. on Employment Handicapped; bd. dirs. Vis. Nurses Assn. Greater Dayton; chmn. profl. adv. com. Combined Gen. Health Dist. Montgomery County. Named City of Dayton's Outstanding Young Man, Jr. C. of C., 1957; 1 of 5 Outstanding Young Men of State, Ohio Jr. C. of C., 1958; Physician of Yr., Pres.'s Com. on Employment of Handicapped, 1971; Bishop's medal for meritorious service Miami U., 1972. Mem. AMA, Ohio Med. Assn., Montgomery County Med. Soc. (chmn. com. on diabetic detection 1955-65, chmn. polio com. 1954-58), Nat. Rehab. Assn., Am. Diabetes Assn., Am. Profl. Practice Assn., Am. Heart Assn., Am. Pub. Health Assn., Ohio Pub. Health Assn., Aerospace Med. Assn., Fraternal Order Police, Nu Sigma Nu, Sigma Chi. Lutheran. Club: Dayton Country. Lodges: Kiwanis, Royal Order Jesters, Masons (past potentate), Shriners, K.T. Home: 167 Lookout Dr Dayton OH 45409 Office: 55 Park Ave Dayton OH 45419

ARNASON, J. J., electrical supply company executive. Pres., chief exec. officer Man. Hydro, Winnipeg, Can. Office: Manitoba Hydro, PO Box 815, Winnipeg, MB Canada *

ARNDT, ROBERT GORDON, educator, psychologist; b. Flint, Mich., Apr. 29, 1938; s. Gordon and Charlotte A.; B.S., Carroll Coll., Waukesha, Wis., 1961; M.S., Bradley U., 1962; m. Judith Ann Nissley, June 26, 1965; children—Nicole M., Dean R. In-patient dir. alcoholism unit Singer Zone Center, Rockford, Ill., 1966-68; chief psychologist Stephenson County (Ill.) Mental Health, Freeport, Ill., 1968-74; dir. adult clinic Saginaw County (Mich.) Mental Health, 1974-77; adminstr. Planning for Living, Bay City, Mich., 1977-78; coordinator developmental disability asso. degree Delta Coll., University Center, Mich., 1978—, asst. prof. dept. psychology, 1979—; chmn. spl. edn. com. Saginaw Twp. Sch. Parent Adv. Com., 1982-83; pres. Saginaw County Inter. Agy. Coordinating Com., 1977-79; cons. Saginaw Valley Rehab. Center. Mem. adult edn. com. First Congregational Ch., Saginaw, 1975—; mgr. Little League, 1977-80. Served to lt. (j.g.) USN, 1963-66. Ill. State fellow, 1968-76; cert. psychologist, Ill.; lic. psychologist, Mich. Mem. Am. Psychol.Ass Psychol. Assn., Mich. Psychol. Assn., Mid-Mich. Psychol. Assn. (past pres.). Author tng. manual. Home: 2905 Reppuhn St Saginaw MI 48603 Office: Delta College University Center MI 48710

ARNDT, ROBERT PHILLIP, community services administrator, finance executive; b. Detroit, Mar. 11, 1952; s. William Robert and Margaret Ann (Breen) A.; m. Mary Ann Gronda, Aug. 17, 1973; children: Robert P. Jr., Blair M., Melissa A. BBA, Western Mich. U., 1974; MBA, Eastern Mich. U., 1979. Adminstrv. trainee Comerica Bank, Detroit, 1975; fin. and spl. projects mgr. Ford Motor Co., Dearborn, Mich., 1975-79; tchr. Henry Ford Community Coll., Dearborn, 1979-83; comml. loan officer Mfrs. Nat. Bank of Detroit, 1984-85; v.p. fin. and adminstrn. United Community Services Met. Detroit, 1985—; adj. prof. Jordan Coll., Detroit, 1986—; adj. prof. econs., Madonna Coll., Livonia, Mich. Past mem. allocation and review com. United Found. of Detroit; chmn. fundraising bd. dirs. Mich. Human Services, Inc., Livonia; bd. advisors Internat. Assn. Students in Econs. and Bus. Mgmt. at U. Mich., Ann Arbor; bd. dirs. Mich. Voluntary Agy. Group Plan for Unemployment Compensation, Inc., Detroit, Mich. Ins. Coalition, Inc. Lansing; bd. dirs., sec./asst. treas. exec. bd. World Med. Relief, Inc., Detroit. Mem. Detroit Personnel Mgmt. Assn., Greater Detroit C. of C. (past chmn. bus. contributions com.). Republican. Roman Catholic. Club: Serra (Dearborn) (v.p.). Lodge: KC. Avocation: fitness. Home: 23810 E River Rd Grosse Ile MI 48138 Office: United Community Services Met Detroit 51 W Warren Detroit MI 48201

ARNELL, PAULA ANN YOUNGBERG, pathologist; b. Moline, Ill., Nov. 25, 1938; d. Paul Phillip and Mabel Eleanor (Arnell) Youngberg; B.A. summa cum laude, Augustana Coll., 1960; M.D., U. Iowa, 1964; m. Richard Anthony Arnell, June 28, 1969; children—Carla Ann, Paula Marie, Paul Anthony. Intern, St. Lukes-Mercy Hosp., Cedar Rapids, Iowa, 1964-65; resident pathology U. Iowa, Iowa City, 1965-68; chief resident State U. Iowa Hosp., Iowa City, 1968-69; pathologist, dir. labs. Luth. Hosp., Moline, Ill., 1970—; mem. staffs Moline Pub. Hosp., Franciscan Hosp., Rock Island, Ill. Sec., Rock Island County Blood Bank, 1972-73, v.p., 1973-74; cons. Rock Island Tb Center, 1970-72; profl. del. Am. Cancer Soc., 1971-73; tchr. Luth. Hosp. Sch. Inhalation Therapy, Sch. Nursing, 1970-80 ; med. dir. Royal Neighbors of Am. Ins. Co., Rock Island; asso dir. Met. Med. Lab., Moline, Quad-Cities Pathologists Group Sch. of Med. Tech.; dir. 7th Street Realty

Co.; founder Quad Cities Regional Screening and Diagnostic Breast Ctr., 1984. Pres. Rock Island County Cancer Soc., 1970-78; mem. alumni bd. Augustana Coll., Rock Island, 1972-75, bd. dirs., 1976-83, chmn. bd. dirs., 1977-83; sec. med. sect. Nat. Fraternal Congress, 1976—; bd. dirs. Mississippi Valley Regional Blood Bank, 1973—, Ill. div. Am. Cancer Soc., 1980—; bd. govs. Luth. Social Services Ill., 1985—. Fellow Coll. Am. Pathologists (insp.), Am. Soc. Clin. Pathologists; cons. pathologist, ICON, 1981—; mem. Internat. Acad. Pathologists, Am. Assn. Cytologists, Am. Assn. Blood Banks, Am. Assn. Clin. Scientists, Am. Womans Med. Assn., AMA, Iowa Ill. med. socs., Ill. Pathologists Asso., Rock Island County Hist. Soc., Phi Beta Kappa, Beta Beta Beta. Home: 3904 7th Ave Rock Island IL 61201 Office: Luth Hosp 501 10th Ave Moline IL 61265

ARNELL, RICHARD ANTHONY, radiologist, nuclear medicine physician; b. Chgo., Aug. 21, 1938; s. Tony Frank and Mary Martha (Oberman) Yaki; B.A. (Younker Achievement scholar), Grinnell Coll., 1960; M.D., U. Iowa, 1964; m. Paula Ann Youngberg, June 28, 1964; children—Carla Ann, Paula Marie, Paul Anthony. Intern, Mercy and St. Luke's hosps., Cedar Rapids, Iowa, 1964-65; resident in radiology and nuclear medicine U. Iowa Hosps., 1965-68; practice medicine specializing in radiology and nuclear medicine, Moline, Ill., 1968—; mem. Moline Radiology Assos., 1968—, v.p., 1970-78, sec., 1978—, trustee pension and profit plan, 1979—; mem. staff Luth. Hosp., Moline, dir. continuing med. edn. program for physicians, 1979-83, bd. dirs., 1977-83; mem. staff Moline Pub. Hosp., Hammond-Henry Dist. Ill., Geneseo, Ill.; trustee Midstate Found. for Med. Care, 1975-79, exec. com., 1976-79; v.p. Quad City HMO Health Plan, 1979; clin. lectr. U. Iowa, 1980—. Supt. Sunday Ch. Sch. St. John's Luth. Ch., Rock Island, Ill., 1974-79, mem. ch. cabinet, 1975-76; del. Chs. United of Scott and Rock Island counties, Ill., 1977; mem. nat. exec. com. Augustana Coll., Rock Island, Ill., 1977-81; assoc. chmn. profl. div. United Way, 1985; bd. dirs. Luth. Hosp. Found., 1981-84, pres., 1982-84; bd. dirs. Quad Cities Health Care Resources, Inc., 1984—; chmn. Luth. Health Care Found., 1984—. Recipient David Theophillus trophy for outstanding athlete Grinnell Coll., 1960; diplomate Am. Bd. Radiology, Am. Bd. Nuclear Medicine. Mem. Am. Coll. Radiology, Ill. Radiol. Soc., Am. Coll. Nuclear Medicine, Soc. Nuclear Medicine, AMA, Ill. (ho. of dels. 1974-79), Rock Island County (exec. com. 1974-79, peer-rev. com. 1975-79), Iowa-Ill. Central (pres.-elect 1977, pres. 1978) med. socs., Central Ill. Med. Assn. (v.p. 1977, pres. 1978), Ind. Physicians Assn. Western Ill. (dir. 1984-86, v.p. 1985, pres. 1986), World Med. Assn., Tri-City Med. Jour. Club (sec.-treas. 1972-77), Am. Coll. Med. Imaging. Club: Short Hills Country. Home: 3904 7th Ave Rock Island IL 61201 Office: 1505 7th St Moline IL 61265

ARNESON, GEORGE STEPHEN, manufacturing company executive; b. St. Paul, Apr. 3, 1925; s. Oscar and Louvia Irene (Clare) A.; children: George Stephen Fernando, Deborah Clare Fernanda, Diane Elizabeth Fernanda, Frederick Oscar Fernando. BEE, U. Minn., 1949; BS in Marine Transp., U.S. Mcht. Marine Acad., 1945. Certified mgmt. cons. Sales engr. Hubbard & Co., Chgo., 1949-54; cons. Booz, Allen & Hamilton, Chgo., 1954-57; mgr. mktg. cons. services, dir. mktg., plant mgr. Borg-Warner Corp., Chgo., 1957-60; asst. gen. mgr., then v.p., gen. mgr. Delta-Star Electric div. H.K. Porter Co., Inc., Pitts., 1960-63; v.p., gen. mgr. elec. divs. Delta-Star Electric div. H.K. Porter Co., Inc., 1963-65; v.p. mktg. Wheeling Steel Corp., 1965-66; pres., chief exec. officer Vendo Co., Kansas City, Mo., 1966-72, also dir., chmn. exec. com.; pres., chmn. Dun-Lap Mfg. Co., Newton, Iowa, 1973-77; pres. Arneson & Co., Kansas City, Mo., 1974—; bd. dirs. TelCon Assocs., Shawnee Mission, Kans. Chmn. adv. bd. Kans. Dept. Corrections. Served to lt. (j.g.) USNR, 1943-46. Recipient Outstanding Achievement award U.S. Mcht. Marine Acad.; Past Dir. award Automatic Merchandising Assn. Mem. Am. Soc. Appraisers (sr.), Phi Gamma Delta (life), Alpha Phi Omega (life). Republican. Presbyterian. Clubs: Masons, K.T, Shriners. Home: 12715 High Dr Leawood KS 66209 Office: Arneson & Co Leawood KS 66209

ARNESON, PHILLIP WILLIAM, manufacturing executive; b. Mpls., Oct. 20, 1936; s. Esther (Thompson) A.; m. Dolores Ann Arneson, Apr. 20, 1954; children: Ann, Susan, Kay. BSEE, U. Minn., 1962. Gen. mgr. Control Data Corp., Mpls., 1973-76, v.p., 1976-78, group v.p., 1978-83; pres. Computer Peripherals Inc., Mpls., 1978-79, Allied Amphenol, Lisle, Ill., 1983-86; bd. dirs. Microelectronics and Computer Tech. Corp., Austin, Dai-Ichi Denshi Kogyo, Tokyo, Durafilm Materials Corp., Computer Pathways, Inc.; pres. Allied Far East Asia Ltd., Hong Kong, 1983-86; v.p., officer Bunker Ramo Electra Corp., Chgo., 1983-86. Served to sgt. USMC, 1953-58. Mem. IEEE, Am. Mgmt. Assn. Republican. Club: Morningside Country (Rancho Mirage, Calif.). Avocations: cattle breeding, hunting, painting. Home: 6 Oak Brook Club Oak Brook IL 60521 Office: Allied Amphenol 4300 Commerce Ct Lisle IL 60532

ARNETT, JAMES EDWARD, educator, ins. co. dir.; b. Gullett, Ky., Oct. 3, 1912; s. Haden and Josephine (Risner) A.; A.B., San Jose State Coll., 1947, M.A., 1955; Ed.S., Stanford, 1959; m. Helen Mae Vallish, Mar. 23, 1943. Tchr., prin. pub. schs., Salyersville, Ky., 1930-41; tchr., administr. pub. schs., Salinas, Calif., 1947-52; owner-mgr. Arnett Apts., Salinas, 1950-53; tchr., Innes High Sch., Akron, Ohio, 1953-73; owner-mgr. Arnett Apts., Akron, 1953-72; dir. Educator & Exec. Co., 1962-73, Educator and Exec. Insurers, 1957-76, Educator and Exec. Life Ins. Co., 1962-76, Great Am. of Dallas Fire and Casualty Co., 1974-76, Great Am. of Dallas Ins. Co., 1974-76, J.C. Penney Casualty Ins. Co., 1976; cons., 1976-77. Mem. county, state central coms. Democratic party, 1952. Served with AUS, 1942-45. Mem. NEA (life mem.; del. conv. 1957-65), Ohio (del. convs. 1957-73), Akron (1st v.p. 1964-65, parliamentarian 1965-72), edn. assns., San Jose State Coll., Stanford alumni assns., Phi Delta Kappa. Home: 691 Payne Ave Akron OH 44302-1347 Office: 800 Brooksedge Blvd Westerville OH 43081

ARNETTE, HAROLD LEE, infosystems company executive; b. Columbus, Ohio, Feb. 21, 1941; s. C. A. and O. Mary (Tucker) A.; m. Janet L. Orr, Aug. 5, 1961; children: Debbi, Jeff. BS, Ohio State U., 1968, MS, 1970, postgrad., 1970-75. Cert. data processor, cert. system profl. Staff N.Am. Rockwell Corp., Columbus, 1967-69, Bell Telephone Lab., Columbus, 1969-70; prof. Mt. Vernon (Ohio) Nazarene Coll., 1970-76; cons. Arnette & Assocs., Gambier, Ohio, 1976-78; pres. Info. Control, Mt. Vernon, 1978—; cons. ITT, Delaware, Ohio, 1971-73, Mgmt. Decisions Devel. Corp., Cin., 1973-75. Fellow Mt. Vernon Nazarene Coll., 1982—. Mem. Am. Mgmt. Assn., Assn. Computing Machinery (sr.), Soc. Mfg. Engrs. (sr.), Soc. Cert. Computer Profls., Door and Hardware Inst. Mem. Ch. of the Nazarene. Office: Info Control Corp 8337 Martinsburg Rd Mount Vernon OH 43050-9506

ARNHOLD, THOMAS DEAN, lawyer; b. Hays, Kans., Dec. 1, 1954; s. Richard A. and Ann (Dechant) A.; m. Joleen Marie McNeive, Aug. 11, 1979; children: Colleen Marie, Kevin Thomas. BS in Polit. Sci., Ft. Hays State U., Kans., 1975; JD, Washburn U., 1978. Bar: Kans. 1979, U.S. Dist. Ct. Kans. 1979, U.S. Ct. Appeals (10th cir.) 1979. Assoc. McPherson Brown & Brown, Great Bend, Kans., 1978-79, Reno County Legal Aid Soc., Hutchinson, Kans., 1979-80; ptnr. Arnhold & McEwen, Hutchinson, 1980—. V.p. Hutchinson Human Rights Commn., 1982, Big Bros. for Boys, Hutchinson, 1982; sec. Downtown Devel. Bd., Hutchinson, 1986. Served as capt. Kans. Army N.G., 1983—. Mem. ABA, Kans. Bar Assn., Reno County Bar Assn. Democrat. Roman Catholic. Lodge: KC (recorder Hutchinson 1986). Avocations: golf, cross-country skiing, basketball. Home: 81 Faircrest Hutchinson KS 67502 Office: Arnhold & McEwen PO Box 703 Hutchinson KS 67504-0703

ARNOLD, ANDREW J., temperature control company executive; b. Elmhurst, Ill., Dec. 1, 1953; s. Richard C. and Geraldine C. (Gray) A.; m. Susan M. O'Brian, Aug. 7, 1976. BS in Materials Engring., Brown U., 1976. Sales engr. Johnson Controls, Lansing, Ill., 1976-80; v.p. Precision Control Systems, Inc., Hammond, Ind., 1980-85, pres., 1985—. Mem. Nat. Assn. Power Engrs., South Suburban Schs. Maintenance Assn. Clubs: Sports Illus. (Highland, Ind.), Gary (Ind.) Rugby (capt. 1979). Avocations: golf, racquetball, rugby. Home: 18930 Avers Ave Flossmoor IL 60422 Office: Precision Control Systems Inc 6829 Grand Ave Hammond IN 46323

ARNOLD, CONSTANCE GIDCUMB, plastic surgeon; b. Harrisburg, Ill., Dec. 12, 1948; d. Wayne Bertram and Sarah Kathleen (Coffee) Gidcumb; m. Daniel Jack Arnold, June 21, 1970; children: David, Elizabeth. BS of Medicine, Northwestern U., 1968, MD, 1972. Cert. Am. Bd. Surgery, Am. Bd. Plastic Surgery. Resident in gen. surgery NorthShore U. Hosp., Manhasset, N.Y., 1972-77; resident in plastic surgery N.Y. Hosp., N.Y.C., 1977-79; gen. practice medicine specializing in plastic surgery Marquette, Mich., 1979—; attending plastic surgeon Marquette Gen. Hosp., 1979—; burn and replantation cons. Upper Peninsula Emergency Med. Services, Marquette, 1983-86; premedical adv. bd. No. Mich. U., Marquette, 1982—. Fellow ACS; mem. Am. Soc. Plastic and Reconstructive Surgeons, Am. Cleft Palate Assn., Mich. Cleft Palate Assn. (treas. 1986), Mich. Acad. Plastic Surgeons, Marquette-Algier Med. Soc. Jewish. Avocations: painting, sculpture, cross country and downhill skiing. Home: 111 Lakewood Ln Marquette MI 49855 Office: 1414 W Fair Marquette MI 49855

ARNOLD, DAVID PAUL, sales professional; b. Pitts., May 11, 1942; s. Arthur and Elizabeth (Novak) A.; m. Patricia Arda Graham, Sept. 3, 1966; children: Nichelle, Bret, Janelle. BA in Bus., Ohio No. U., 1964. Sales engr. Reliance Electric, various cities, 1964-70; sales dir. Columbia Nat., Columbus, Ohio, 1970-73; owner Mint Lake Valley Lumber, Ashtabula, Ohio, 1973-76; v.p. sales Preformed Line Products, Cleve., 1976—. Republican. Methodist. Avocations: farming, architecture, private pilot. Office: Preformed Line Products 660 Beta Dr Mayfield Village OH 44143

ARNOLD, DEAN EDWARD, anthropology educator; b. Sioux Falls, S.D., Aug. 2, 1942; s. Eldon Earl and Reva Iola (Marquette) A.; m. June Ann Trottier, June 22, 1968; children—Michelle Reneé, Andrea Celeste. B.A. in Anthropology, Wheaton Coll., 1964; M.A. in Anthropology, U. Ill., 1967, Ph.D., 1970. Asst. prof. anthropology Pa. State U., University Park, 1969-72; Fulbright lectr., vis. prof. anthropology Universidad Nacional San Antonio Abad del Cuzco, Cuzco, Peru, 1972-73; asst. prof. Wheaton Coll. (Ill.), 1973-77, assoc. prof., 1977-82, prof., 1982—; vis. fellow Clare Hall, Cambridge U., Eng., 1985. Nat. Def. Fgn. Lang. fellow, 1966-69; Fulbright research fellow, Yucatan, Mex., 1984. Fellow AAAS; mem. Am. Anthrop. Assn., Soc. Am. Archaeology, Ill. Archaeol. Survey, Chgo. Anthrop. Soc. (sec. 1975-77), Inst. Andean Studies, Fulbright Alumni Assn., Sigma Xi. Democrat. Presbyterian. Author: Ceramic Theory and Cultural Process, 1985. Contbr. numerous articles to profl. jours. Office: Wheaton Coll Dept Sociology-Anthropology Wheaton IL 60187

ARNOLD, FERRIS LUCIEN, lawyer; b. Saginaw, Mich., Aug. 16, 1946; s. Ferris Chester and Betty Lou (Pol) A. A Bus. Adminstrn., Delta Coll., 1971; BA in Psychology, Mich. State U., 1973; JD, Thomas M. Cooley Law Sch., 1980. Bar: Mich. 1981, U.S. Dist. Ct. (ea. dist.) Mich. 1981. Bargaining rep. UAW, Saginaw, 1973-75, benefits rep., 1975-78; with Workers Compensation Appeal Bd., Mich., 1979-84; assoc. Davidson, Breen & Doud, Saginaw, 1984—. Bd. mem. Underground RR Women's Shelter, Saginaw, 1984-85, Saginaw City Substance Abuse, 1986. Mem. Assn. Trial Lawyers Assn., Mich. Trial Lawyers Assn., Mich. Bar Assn., Saginaw County Bar Assn. Democrat. Lutheran. Avocations: travel, photography. Home: 418 Foxboro Rd Saginaw MI 48603 Office: Davidson Breen & Doud 1121 N Michigan Ave Saginaw MI 48602

ARNOLD, HELEN PAXTON, banker; b. Columbus, Ohio, Dec. 3, 1949; d. Edmund Bernard and Helen Marie (Jefferson) Paxton; m. L. Patrick Arnold, Apr. 17, 1971; 1 child, Aaron Paxton. BS in Edn., Cen. State U., Wilberforce, Ohio, 1971. Tchr. English lit., journalism Chgo. and Columbus (Ohio) Pub. Schs., 1970-73; tchr. English lit., acting prin. Acad. St. James Coll. Preparatory Sch., Chgo., 1973-74; editorial asst. ABA, Chgo., 1975-76; research asst. Ky. State U., Frankfort, 1977-78; fin. services rep. Citicorp Savs. Ill., Chgo., 1978-81, tng. specialist, 1981-83; mgr. tng. and devel. Skokie (Ill.) Fed. Savs. & Loan Assn., 1983—; industry cons. Tng. Service div. Inst. Fin. Edn., Chgo. Fundraiser St. Marker's for Harold Washington, Chgo., 1983, 87; mem. Jack & Jill of Am., Inc. Named one of Outstanding Young Women Am., Jaycees, 1977. Mem. Am. Mgmt. Assn., Am. Soc. Tng. and Devel., Chgo. Area Fin. Trainers' Network, Delta Sigma Theta. Methodist. Avocations: swimming, reading, singing classical music, civic activities. Home: 585 S Cornell Chicago IL 60615 Office: Skokie Fed Savs & Loan 7952 Lincoln Ave Skokie IL 60077

ARNOLD, LAWRENCE EUGENE, child psychiatrist; b. Zanesville, Ohio, Feb. 16, 1936; s. Carl Andrew and Carrie Agnes (Untied) A.; m. Billie Marie Crowley, Dec. 26, 1961; children: Ann, Laurie, Matt, Mark, Paul. BS, U. Dayton, 1959; MD, Ohio State U., 1963; MEd, John Hopkins U., Balt., 1969. Diplomate Am. Bd. Psychiatry and Neurology. Resident John Hopkins U. Hosp., 1964-66, 68-70; med. staff St. Elizabeth's Hosp., Wash., 1966-68; asst. prof. Ohio State U., 1970-73, assoc. prof., 1973-78, dir. child psychiatry, 1973-85, prof., 1978—, vice chmn. psychiatry, 1985—; cons. peer review com. NIMH, 1981; mem. Mental Health Ad Hoc Prevention Com, 1981; Marburn Acad. Adv. Bd., 1981-84; examiner Am. Bd. Psychiatry and Neurology. Author: Parents' Survival Handbook, 1983, Parent-child Group Therapy, 1985; editor: Helping Parents to Help their Children, 1978, Preventing Adolescent Alienation, 1983, Parents, Children, and Change, 1985. Active Big Walnut Sch. Bd., Sunbury, Ohio, 1981—; Cen. Ohio Coalition Children, Columbus, 1982—; Ctr. Pub. Edn. Adv. Com., Franklin, Colo., 1983-84; co-chmn. Franklin County Com. to Rev. Juvenile Facilities, 1985. Served to surgeon USPHS, 1966-68. Ohio Dept. Mental Health grantee, 1973, 74, 78, 80, 82, Efamol Research Inst. grantee, Nova Scotia, Can., 1985. Fellow Am. Psychiatry Assn., Am. Acad. Child Psychiatry; mem. AMA, Am. Orthopsychiat. Assn., Soc. Pediatric Psychology. Roman Catholic. Avocations: gardening, bridge, family. Office: The Ohio State U 473 W 12th Ave Columbus OH 43210

ARNOLD, LYNN ELLIS, metallurgical engineer; b. Nov. 17, 1934; s. Leslie Lee and Emma R. (Betscher) A. Metall. Engr., U. Cin., 1957; M.S. in Mech. Engring., U. Ill., 1959. Registered profl. engr., Ohio. Grad. asst. U. Ill., Urbana, 1957-59; with Xtek, Inc., Cin., 1959—, mgr. tech. services, 1984-86, research engr., 1986—. Author articles in field. Served with USAF, 1958-59. Fellow AAAS, Am. Soc. Metals (past pres. Cin. chpt., past mem. tech. div. bd., Wm. H. Eisenman Meml. award 1979); mem. NSPE (past chmn. indsl. div., past v.p.), Ohio Soc. Profl. Engrs. (past pres. Cin. chpt., Young Engr. award 1965), ASME (past pres. Cin. sect., past pres. Ohio council), Soc. Mfg. Engrs. (past pres. Cin. chpt.), Cin. Tech. and Sci. Socs. Council (past pres., Community Service award 1979), Engring. Soc. Cin. (past pres.), Soc. Advancement of Mgmt. (v.p. Cin. chpt.), Cin. Mgmt. Assn. (past pres.), Cin. Editors Assn. (past pres.), Tool Steel Mgmt. Club (past pres.), U. Cin. Engring. Alumni Assn. (past pres., Disting. Alumnus award 1979), SAR (past pres. Cin. chpt.), Audubon Soc. Ohio (past pres.), Ohio Audubon Council (past pres.), Am. Gear Mfg. Assn. (chmn. metallurgy and materials com.), AIME-ISS (co-chmn. roll Tech. com.), Tau Beta Pi, Alpha Sigma Mu, Alpha Phi Omega, Pi Delta Epsilon, Alpha Chi Sigma. Republican. Methodist. Home: 5154 Montgomery Rd Cincinnati OH 45212 Office: 11451 Reading Rd Cincinnati OH 45241

ARNOLD, MICHAEL FREDERICK, dentist; b. Indpls., Oct. 28, 1955; s. Lyman Frederick and Mary Ann (Meincken) A.; m. Ann Elaine Irwin, May 20, 1978; children: Eric Michael, Alicia Ann. BA in Biology, Ind. U., 1977, DDS, 1982. Gen. practice dentistry Indpls., 1982—. Sec., treas., pres. Perry Dental Study Club, 1983—; treas., v.p., pres. Greater Southside Study Club, 1984—. Republican. Lutheran. Lodge: Kiwanis (sec., v.p. Perry Twp. chpt. 1984—). Avocations: golf, bowling, racquetball, basketball. Home: 3826 Pine View Ln Greenwood IN 46142 Office: 6745 S Gray Rd Indianapolis IN 46237

ARNOLD, MICHAEL ROBERT, sales executive; b. Ft. Wayne, Ind., May 6, 1960; s. John Ford and Marjorie Marie (Browne) A.; m. Ann Marie Geary, June 11, 1983; 1 child, Christine Marie. BA in English and Mass Communication with high honors, St. Francis Coll., Ft. Wayne, 1972-82, postgrad. in bus., 1984—. Dist. sales rep. Fram div. Allied Automotive, Ft. Wayne, 1982-85, sr. sales rep., 1985-86, ter. mgr., 1986—. Mem. Nat. Intercollegiate Soccer Officials Assn. (referee 1982—), U.S. Soccer Fedn. (referee 1982—), Am. Indoor Soccer Assn. (referee 1986—). Republican. Avocations: soccer coaching, playing and refereeing. Home: 6236 Landmark Dr Fort Wayne IN 46815 Office: Allied Automotive 3436 N Kennicott Suite 260 Arlington Heights IL 60004

ARNOLD, ORVILLE EDWARD, consulting engineer; b. Sparta, Wis., Sept. 30, 1933; s. Donald E. and Lenice K. (Reilly) A.; m. Judith A. Schmidt, Feb. 14, 1987; children: Donald E., David C., Beth A., Sandra M. BSCE, U. Wis., 1955. Registered profl engr., Wis. Engr. Inland Steel Co., Chgo., 1955-56; chief structural engr. Flad Architects, Madison, Wis., 1956-63; pres. Arnold & O'Sheridan, Inc. Cons. Engrs., Madison, 1964—; mem. Wis. Examining Bd. Architects, Engrs., Designers and Surveyors, 1974-77, pub. works and lake problems com. City of Middleton, Wis., 1964-71, pub. works com. Village of Shorewood Hills, Wis., 1978-82; chmn. Wis. Bldg. Code Com., 1975-87. Pres. Mendota Monona Lake Property Owners Assn., Madison, 1974; trustee Madison Art Ctr.; bd. dirs. Madison Opportunity Ctr., 1980-86. Served with U.S. Army, 1956. Named Engr. of Yr. in Pvt. Practice in Wis. Wis. Soc. Profl. Engrs., 1978; recipient Disting. Service citation U. Wis. Coll. Engring., 1982. Mem. ASCE, Nat. Soc. Profl. Engrs., Wis. Soc. Profl. Engrs., Am. Concrete Inst., Cons. Engrs. Council. Roman Catholic. Home: 531 N Pinckney St Madison WI 53703 Office: 815 Forward Dr Madison WI 53711

ARNOLD, ROBERT EDWIN, chaplain, marriage and family therapist; b. Ages, Ky., Feb. 19, 1948; s. Jasper E. and Zenna I. (Greer) A.; m. Karen Ann Villafarra, July 28, 1979; 1 child, Julie Ann. AA, Sinclair Community Coll., 1968; BS in Edn., Wright State U., 1971; MA, Southwestern Bapt. Theol. Sem., 1973; EdD, New Orleans Bapt. Theol. Sem., 1982. Ordained to ministry Bapt. Ch., 1972; lic. marriage and family therapist, Iowa; cert. secondary edn. tchr., N.J. Youth minister First Bapt. Ch., Englewood, Ohio, 1972, Madison (N.J.) Bapt. Ch., 1973-75; assoc. pastor Lakeland Bapt. Chapel, Sparta, N.J., 1974-77; minister of edn. United Meth. Ch., Kenner, La., 1979-80; family therapist De Paul Hosp., New Orleans, 1980-82; clin. social worker Assn. Cath. Charities, New Orleans, 1982; chaplain VA Med. Ctr., Knoxville, Iowa, 1983—; cons. marriage and family therapy Iowa State U., 1987—. Trustee First So. Bapt. Ch., Newton, Iowa, 1986. Fellow Am. Orthopsychiat. Assn.; mem. Am. Assn. Marriage and Family Therapists (clin., approved supr.), N.Am. Assn. Christians in Social Work, Am. Assn. Sex Educators, Counselors and Therapists (life., cert.). Home: Rural Rt 2 Bittersweet Estates Newton IA 50208

ARNOLD, ROY GARY, food science and technology educator; b. Lyons, Nebr., Feb. 20, 1941; m. Jane Kay Price, 1963; children: Jana Lynn, Julie Kay. BS, U. Nebr., 1962; MS, Oreg. State U., 1965, PhD in Food Sci. and Tech., 1967. Research and devel. project leader Fairmont Foods Co., Omaha, 1962-63; asst. prof. food sci. and tech. U. Nebr., Lincoln, 1967-71, assoc. prof., 1971-74, asst. dir. resident instrn., 1971-72, acting dir. resident instrn., 1972-73, prof., 1974-87, head dept. food sci. and tech., 1973-79, coordinator food protein research group, 1975-79, dean, dir. agrl. expt. sta., 1980-82, vice chancellor inst. agr. and natural resources, 1982-87; dean Coll. Agrl. Scis. Oregon State U., Corvallis, 1987—; cons. in field; interviewer Sta. KRVN-AM; participant numerous workshops, 1977—; del., devel. com. Imo (Nigeria) State U., 1981; mem. Ralston Purina Grad. Food Sci. Fellowship com., 1976-78, rev. team dept. food sci. U. Ill., 1979, adminstrv. site visit com. to Mid-Am. Internat. Agriculture Consortium Agy. for Internat. Devel. Morocco project, 1983, exec. com. agr. 2001 com. U. Nebr. Bd. Regents, 1982-83; program chmn. corn and sorghum industry research conf. Am. Seed Trade Assn., 1985. Mem. editorial bd. Jour. Dairy Sci., 1976-82, Jour. Agrl. and Food Chemistry, 1978-81; contbr. numerous articles to profl jours.; patentee in field. Mem. adminstrv. bd. St. Mark's United Meth. Ch., Lincoln, 1975-78, chmn. long range planning com., 1977-78, chmn. bldg. com. 1978-82. Recipient William V. Cruess award Inst. Food Technologists, 1980; grantee Nutrition Found., FDA, Nebr. Soybean Bd., Am. Soybean Assn. Research Found., Am. Egg Bd; Gen. Foods fellow, 1963-66. Fellow AAAS; mem. Inst. Food Technologists (nat. orgn. chmn. forward planning subco. of exec. com. 1976-79, expert panel food safety and nutrition 1979-82, chmn. 1980-81, nominations and elections com. 1981-83, exec. com. 1985—, William V. Cruess award 1980; Ak-Sar-Ben sect. past treas., sec., chmn.-elect, chmn. nat. councilor), Am. Chem. Soc., Nat. Assn. Colls. and Tchrs. Agr., Univ. Assn. Adminstrv. Devel. (exec. com. 1973-74, 76-77, pres. 1978-79), MidAm. Internat. Agrl. Consortium (bd. dirs. 1982—, chmn.-elect. 1985-86), N. Cen. Adminstrv. Heads Agr. (chmn.-elect 1985-86), Nat. Assn. State Univs. and Land Grant Colls. (div. agr.council adminstrv. heads agr. exec. com. 1985-87), Coll. Agr. Alumni Assn. (v.p. 1977-79), Innocents Soc. (pres. 1961-62), Sigma Xi (Nebr. chpt. sec. 1979-81), Phi Kappa Phi, Alpha Zeta, Gamma Sigma Delta (Nebr. chpt. past treas., sec., v.p., pres., Merit Teaching award 1975), Phi Tau Sigma, FarmHouse Frat. (Doane award Nebr. chpt. 1962). Club: Crucibles (Lincoln). Home: 1811 Buckingham Dr Lincoln NE 68506 Office: U Nebr Dept Food Sci and Tech 310 Administration Bldg Lincoln NE 68588-0422

ARNOLD, SCOTT GREGORY, computer information systems specialist; b. Wabash, Ind., June 23, 1961; s. Don H. and Martha S. (Gregor) A. BS in Computer Sci., Ball State U., 1983; postgrad., Dale Carnegie Inst., 1985, St. Francis Coll., 1985, Ind. U./Purdue U., 1985, Ind. Voc. Tech. Coll., 1985. Programmer Slater Steel Corp., Ft. Wayne, Ind., 1983-85; programmer II N.Am. Van Lines, Ft. Wayne, 1985-86; programmer, analyst Speed Queen Co., Ripon, Wis., 1986—. Mem. Assn. for Computing Machinery. Republican. Lutheran. Home: 511 Metomen Ripon WI 54971 Office: Speed Queen Co Shepard St Ripon WI 54971

ARNOLD, THOMAS BURTON, physician; b. Mpls., May 29, 1939; s. Duma Carroll and Ann (Whelan) A.; m. Janet Onstad, June 16, 1957 (div. 1977); children—Pamela, Thomas, Virginia Ann. B.A., Dartmouth Coll., 1951; M.D., U. Pa., 1955. Diplomate Am. Bd. Internal Medicine. Rotating intern U. Chgo. Clinics, 1955-56; fellow in internal medicine Mayo Found., Rochester, Minn., 1960-63; practice medicine specializing in internal medicine, Mpls., 1963-77, Edina, Minn., 1977—; mem. staffs Abbott Hosp., Northwestern Hosp., Fairview Hosp., Southdale Hosp.; regional med. dir. Standard Oil Co. Ind., Chgo., 1966—; sr. aviation med. examiner FAA, 1963—; asst. prof. medicine U. Minn., Mpls., 1970—. Served to capt. USAF, 1956-59. Fellow ACP; mem. AMA, Minn. Med. Assn., Hennepin County Med. Soc. Republican. Advocation: gardening. Office: Thomas Arnold & Assocs 681 Southdale Med Bldg 6545 France Ave S Edina MN 55435

ARNOLDT, ROBERT PATRICK, historian, international economist; b. Chgo., Oct. 16, 1944; s. Frederick Werner and Margaret (O'Callaghan) A.; AA, Chgo. City Coll., 1970; BA in History, Elmhurst (Ill.) Coll., 1973; MA in History, Northeastern Ill. U., 1979; m. Patricia Ellen Ruh, Dec. 27, 1970; children: Robert Kevin Patrick, James Matthew Patrick, Kathleen Patricia Maureen, Thomas Michael Patrick, Brian Joseph Patrick. Dist. exec. Boy Scouts Am., Oak Park, Ill., 1970-71; supr. trust dept. Continental Ill. Nat. Bank, Chgo., 1972-77, analyst internat. banking dept., 1977-84, sr. internat. analyst econ. research dept., 1985-86; internat. economist, 1986—; mil. historian and writer, 1975—. Served with U.S. Army, 1965-68. Decorated Bronze Star medal, Air medal, Combat Infantryman's badge. Home: 1134 S Scoville Ave Oak Park IL 60304 Office: 231 S LaSalle St Chicago IL 60693

ARNOLDY, JAMES PETER, hospital facilities manager; b. Rollingstone, Minn., Aug. 18, 1928; s. Theo M. and Margaret O. (Maus) A.; ed. high sch.; m. Johanna Gullickson, Jan. 15, 1954; children—Gilbert, Mary Ann, Jane. Operating engr. Owatonna (Minn.) State Sch., 1956-61; supt. maintenance St. Elizabeth Hosp., Wabasha, Minn., from 1961, now facilities mgr.; tchr. steam engring. course vocat. sch., Winona, Minn., 3 yrs.; lectr. in field. Mem. Wabasha City Council, 1976-78, 83—, elected pres., 1987. Served with U.S. Army, 1951-53; Korea. Mem. Nat. Assn. Power Engrs. (pres.'s award 1977, trustee Minn. assn., dir. Minn. assn. 1981—, merit award 1971), So. Minn. Hosp. Engrs. (pres.'s award 1979), Am. Soc. Hosp. Engring., Am. Legion, VFW. Roman Catholic. Home: 124 E Grant Blvd Wabasha MN 55981 Office: St Elizabeth Hosp 1200 5th Grant Blvd W Wabasha MN 55981

ARNOTT, JAMES S., management consultant; b. Mankato, Minn., Sept. 1, 1944. BA, Mankato (Minn.) State U., 1967, BS, 1971; MA, U. Minn., 1979; postgrad., U. San Francisco, 1982—. Dept. chmn. The Blake Schs., Mpls., 1971-79; regional dir. State Dept. Edn., St. Paul, 1979-82; orgnl. devel. specialist U. Minn., Mpls., 1985—; Cons. Minn. Youth Debates, 1984-86, various corps. and agys., Minn., 1983—; guest speaker various locations. Contbr. articles to profl. jours. Mem. Am. Soc. Tng. and Devel., Speech Assn. Am., Minn. Debate Tchrs. Assn., Speech Assn. of Minn. Office: 1770 Bryant Ave S Minneapolis MN 55403

ARNSDORF, DAVID ROBERT, structural engineer; b. Chester, Pa., Apr. 17, 1951; s. Robert Ernest and Mary (Roberts) A.; m. Linda Lou Kerfman,

Sept. 8, 1979; children: Lisa Anne, Rachel Elizabeth. B in Archtl. Engring., Pa. State U., 1974; postgrad., UCLA, 1979-80; MSCE, U. Mich., 1984. Registered profl. engr., Wash., Calif., Mich. Jr. engr. Setter, Leach & Lindstrom, Mpls., 1974-75; engr. The Austin Co., Los Angles and Seattle, 1975-77, KPFF Cons. Engrs., Seattle, 1977-80, Bechtel Power Corp., Los Angeles, 1980-81; sr. engr. Bechtel Power Corp., Ann Arbor, Mich., 1981-84; sr. staff engr. Indsl. Tech. Inst., Ann Arbor, 1984—. Mem. library bd. Manchester (Mich.) Twp. Library, 1985—. Mem. Engring. Soc. Detroit. Republican. Methodist. Home: 406 W Main St Manchester MI 48158 Office: Indsl Tech Inst 1101 Beal St Ann Arbor MI 48106

ARNSDORF, MORTON FRANK, cardiologist, educator; b. Chgo., Aug. 7, 1940; s. Selmar N. and Irmgard C. (Steinmann) A.; m. Mary Hunter Tower, Dec. 26, 1963 (div. 1982). B.A. magna cum laude, Harvard U., 1962; M.D., Columbia U., 1966. Diplomate Am. Bd. Internal Medicine. House staff officer U. Chgo., 1966-69; fellow cardiology Columbia-Presbyn. Med. Ctr., N.Y.C., 1969-71; asst. prof. medicine U. Chgo., 1973-79, assoc. prof., 1979-83, prof., 1983—, chief sect. cardiology, 1981—; mem. pharmacology study sect. NIH, 1981-84. Contbr. articles to profl. jours. Served to maj. USAF, 1971-73. Recipient Research Career Devel. award NIH, 1976-81; research grantee Chgo. Heart Assn., 1976-78, NIH, 1977—. Fellow ACP, Am. Coll. Cardiology, Am. Coll. Physicians; mem. Am. Heart Assn. (dir. 1981-83, chmn. exec. com. basic sci. council 1981-83, steering com. 1983-86), Chgo. Heart Assn. (v.p. 1986, pres.-elect 1987—, bd. govs., chmn. research council), AMA, Am. Fedn. Clin. Research, Assn. Univ. Cardiologists, Cen. Soc. Clin. Research (chmn. cardiovascular council 1986-87), Chgo. Med. Soc., Ill. Med. Soc., Cardiac Electrophysiology Soc. (sec.-treas. 1984-86, pres. 1986—). Club: Quadrangle. Office: Chief Sect Cardiology Univ Chgo Hosps and Clinics Box 423 5841 S Maryland Chicago IL 60637

ARON, BERNARD STEPHEN, oncologist; b. N.Y.C., July 11, 1932; s. Mannie and Ruth (Baer) A.; m. Janice Levine, June 30, 1956; children: Melanie, Marc. BA, NYU, 1953, MD, 1957; Diploma in Med.-Radio Therapy, Christie Hosp., Manchester, Eng., 1961. Diplomate Am. Bd. Radiology, Am. Coll. Radiology,. Intern Beth-El Hosp., Bklyn., 1957-58; resident in radiology Mt. Sinai Hosp., N.Y.C., 1958-61; fellow Christie Hosp. and Holt Radium Inst., Manchester, Eng., 1962-63; clin. dir. Univ. Hosp. Downstate Med. Ctr., Bklyn., 1967-68; prof. clin. oncology U. Cin. Med. Ctr., 1973, 80-85, prof. radiology, 1973—, dir. div. radiation oncology, 1976—; attending radiology therapist Children's Hosp. Med. Ctr., Cin., 1969—; attending radiologist Univ. Hosp., Cin., 1969—; cons. radiation therapy VA Med. Ctr., Cin., 1972. Contbr. 47 articles to profl. jours. Recipient Golden Apple award U. Cin. Coll. Medicine, 1971; fellow Am. Coll. Radiology, 1983. Mem. AMA, Am. Assn. Cancer Edn., Am. Soc. Therapeutic Radiology and Oncology, Am. Soc. Clin. Oncology, Am. Radium Soc. Home: 4130 Rose Hill Ave Cincinnati OH 45229 Office: U Cin Coll Medicine Div Radiation Oncology 234 Goodman St Cincinnati OH 45267-0757

ARON, GRETCHEN MARLINSKY, computer consultant; b. Tblisi, Georgia, USSR, Jan. 20, 1956; came to U.S., 1983; d. Vladimir Ivan and Mira (Kirzner) Krasinovich; m. Stewart H. Aron, Jan. 1, 1987. PhD in Biology, Shevchenko State U., Kiev, USSR, 1979; PhD in Computer Sci., Kiev Inst., 1981. Prof. Kiev Inst., 1981-83; cons. computer sci. Toledo, 1983—. Author: Programming Software for Use in Liver Transplants, 1983 (Kiev medal 1983). Sec. profl. sect. Communist Party, Kiev, 1983, mem. cen. com., 1983, mem. 1981-83. Democrat. Lutheran. Club: Roadrunners (Toledo). Avocations: mountain climbing, running. Home and Office: 4122 Terrace View N Toledo OH 43607

ARONIN, SANFORD LOUIS, accountant; b. Milw., July 29, 1938; s. Jacob and Sadie Lillian (Epstein) A.; m. Margaret Sylvia Frand, June 11, 968; children: Shmuel, Shelley, Shoshanna, Dovid. BBA, Roosevelt U., 1963. CPA, Ill. Jr. acct. Checkers, Simon & Rosner, Chgo., 1963, semi sr. acct., sr. acct., supr., audit mgr. Pres. Yeshiva Parents Assn., Skokie, Ill., 1985—; mem. bd. edn. Arie Crown Hebrew Day Sch., Skokie, 1980—, Hebrew Theol. Coll., Skokie, 1985—; v.p. Congregation Kehilath Jacob Beth Samuel, Chgo., 1980, instr. Talmud, 1971—, lay minister, 1975. Mem. Am. Inst. CPA's, Ill. CPA Soc. Avocation: collecting Judaica. Home: 6308 N Monticello Chicago IL 60659 Office: Checkers Simon & Rosner One South Wacker Dr Chicago IL 60606

ARONSON, DAVID EMMERT, clinical psychologist, consulting psychologist; b. Syracuse, N.Y., May 2, 1953; s. Manuel and Ruth (Hammer) A.; m. Dee A. Emmert, July 19, 1980; 1 child, Benjamin Owen Emmert-Aronson. B.A., SUNY-Buffalo, 1975; M.A., Kent State U., 1977, Ph.D., 1980. Lic. psychologist, Ohio, N.J.; diplomate Am. Bd. Profl. Psychology. Intern in psychology Albany (N.Y.) Med. Coll., 1978-79; asst. dir. Kent State U. psychology clinic, 1979-80; clin. psychologist Alliance Mental Health Clinic (Ohio), 1980-82; adj. asst. prof. psychology Kent State U., 1980—; cons. psychologist Massillon (Ohio) State Hosp., 1981-85, dir. psychology, 1985—; pvt. practice psychology, Cuyahoga Falls, Ohio, 1981—; psychologist supr. Child and Adolescent Service Center, Canton, Ohio, 1982-87. Mem. Am. Psychol. Assn., Midwest Psychol. Assn., Eastern Psychol. Assn., Ohio Psychol. Assn., N.J. Psychol. Assn., State Assn. Psychologists and Psychology Assts., Contbr. articles to profl. jours. Avocations: reading, photography, taking walks, child care, family. Office: 2125 Front St PO Box 71 Cuyahoga Falls OH 44222-0071

ARRATHOON, LEIGH ADELAIDE, medievalist, editor; b. N.Y.C., Nov. 30, 1942; d. Henry and Peggy Adelaide (Weed) A.; m. Raymond Arrathoon, June 10, 1967. Cours de Vacances at U. de Genève, Lausanne, Lille at Boulogne, 1961-63; AB in French and Spanish, Hunter Coll., 1963; MA in French, Stanford U., 1966, MA in Spanish, 1968; MA in Medieval French Lit., Princeton U., 1975, PhD in Medieval French Lit., 1975. With UN Secretariat, N.Y.C., 1963-64; teaching asst., Stanford U., 1964-66; tchr. Spanish and French, Convent of Sacred Heart, Menlo Park, Calif., 1966-67; asst. prof. Spanish, Rider Coll., Trenton, N.J., 1970-71; pub. editor-in-chief Solaris Press, Troy, Idaho, 1975-80, Rochester, Mich., 1980-86; pres. Solaris Press II, 1986—, advt. and mktg. cons. A.D. Agy., 1986. Scholar, Centre d'Art Dramatique, 1957. Mem. MLA, Medieval Acad. Am., Courtly Lit. Soc., Sigma Delta Pi, Alpha Gamma Delta. Editor and contbr. The Craft of Fiction: Essays in Medieval Poetics, 1984; editor, translator The Lady of Vergi, 1984; editor: Chaucer and the Craft of Fiction, 1986; contbr. articles and book revs. to profl. jours. Office: PO Box 1009 Rochester MI 48063

ARRINGTON, DOROTHY M. CHRISTIAN, dietitian; b. Birmingham, Ala., July 25, 1929; d. Noah and Maggie Louise (Cook) Christian; B.S. (scholar), Tuskegee Inst., 1950; m. W.C. Arrington, Apr. 25, 1950; children—Kathleen Yvonne, William Curtis, Maragret Elaine, Christopher Jay. Dietary technician Michael Reese Hosp., Chgo., 1952-53; library clk. Chgo. Public Library, 1959-61; lunchroom mgr. Chgo. Bd. Edn., 1961-62; dietitian-mgr. St. Peter Lutheran Sch., 1962-64; adminstrv. dietitian Mercy Hosp., Chgo., 1965-77, nutritionist Mercy Hosp. Diagnostic and Treatment Center, 1977—, nutritionist Calorie Anonymous; clin. instr. U. Ill.-Chgo. Mem. parent-tchr. leagues St. Peter Luth. Sch., 1957-76, Luther High Sch. S., 1964-74, Morgan Park High Sch., 1974-76; mem. fund raising com. Whitney Young High Sch. Band Booster Club, 1977-79; active Beverly Area Planning Assn., 1974—. Mem. Am. Dietetics Assn., Ill. Dietetics Assn., Chgo. Dietetic Assn., Dietitians in Gen. Clin. Practice, Diabetes Educators of Chgo Area. Democrat. Lutheran. Club: Tuskegee Inst. Alumni. Office: Mercy Hosp Diagnostic and Treatment Ctr at King Dr Chicago IL 60616

ARROYAVE, CARLOS MARIANO, physician; b. Mexico City, Aug. 18, 1939; came to U.S., 1969, naturalized, 1985.; s. Mariano Arroyave and Helena Hernandez; m. Josefa Delaluz Cardenas, Dec. 6, 1964; children: Monica, Elizabeth. BS, Universidad Nacional Autonoma Mexico, 1956; MD, UNAM, 1963. Intern Gen. Hosp., Mex., 1962; resident Hosp. de Enfermedades de la Nutricion, Mex., 1963-64; resident in pediatrics Children's Hosp. de Mex., 1964-66, resident in pediatrics and nephrology, 1966-67; asst. research vol. Inst. Nacional de Cardiologia, Mex., 1967-69; Rogers Found. fellow Scripps Clinic and Research Found., La Jolla, Calif., 1969-70, research fellow, 1970-72, research assoc., 1972-73, asst. div. allergy and immunology, 1973-74, assoc. div. allergy and immunology, 1974-77; asst. clin. prof. pediatrics U. Calif., San Diego, 1972-77; assoc. prof. medicine and pediatrics div. rheumatology U. Colo., Denver, 1977-78; assoc. prof., head div. ummunology and cen. labs. NIMH, Mex., 1978-80; prof. basic sci. and immunology Inst. Tech. y de Estudios Superiores de Monterrey, Mex., 1980-83; asst. prof. dept. pediatrics Northwestern U., Chgo., 1983-84, assoc. prof., 1984-85; clin. immunologist Cook County Hosp., Chgo., 1985—; instr. microteaching course, adminstrn. course Inst. Tech. y Estudios Superiores de Monterrey, 1980, adminstrn. course Dinamica, Monterrey, 1981; head clin. research and div. allergy and immunology Clin. Nova de Monterrey, 1980-83; guest profl. allergy and immunology U. Autonoma de Neuvo Leon, Monterrey, 1980-83; clin. dir. diagnostic immunology/rheumatology lab. Children's Meml. Hosp., Chgo., 1983-85, mem. hazardouse subcom. 1983-84, chmn. 1984-85, mem. radiation safety com. 1984-85, research com. 1983-85; chmn. med. evaluation Clinica Nova, 1980-82; mem. med. promotion com. U. colo., 1977-78; mem. human research com. Scripps Clinic Research Found., 1975-77, radioisotopes com. 1974-76; observer Nat. Com. Clin. Lab. Standards, 1985—; mem. Inst. Mex. de Investigaciones Nefrologicas Sci. Com., 1969-74. Author: What To Do If My Child Is Sick, 1983; contbr. articles to profl. jours.; chpts. to books. Mem. Am. Assn. Immunologists, Am. Rheumatism Assn., Am. Acad. Allergy and Immunology (lab. and diagnostic immunology com. 1985—), Soc. Pediatric Research, Academia Mexicana de Pediatria, Sociedad Mexicana de Alergia e Inmunologia, Sociedad Mexicana de Inmunologia. Home: 4712-B Church St Skokie IL 60076 Office: Cook County Hosp 1835 W Harrison Chicago IL 60612

ARSLAN, ORHAN ENAYET OMAR, anatomist, veterinary scientist; b. Kirkuk, Iraq, May 15, 1951; came to U.S., 1981; s. Enayet Omar and Zubeydeh (Ahmed) A. BVMS, DVM, U. Baghdad (Iraq), 1973; PhD, Hacettepe U., Ankara, Turkey, 1979. Postdoctoral fellow Med. Sch., 1981-82; postgrad. asst. anatomist Hacettepe U., Ankara, Turkey, 1975-79, instr., 1979-81; asst. prof. Nat. Coll. Chiropractic, Lombard, Ill., 1982-86, dept. biol. chemistry and structure U. Health Scis. Chgo. Med. Sch., North Chicago, Ill., 1986—. Mem. AVMA, Found. for Advancement Edn. in Scis., N.Y. Acad. Scis., Am. Assn. Anatomists, Internat. Soc. Drs. Sci., Internat. Platform Assn. Home: 1115 Lorraine Rd Apt 139 Wheaton IL 60187 Office: Univ Health Scis Chgo Med Sch 3333 Green Bay Rd North Chicago IL 60064

ARTES, JAMES ALLEN, restaurant owner; b. Mason City, Iowa, Sept. 25, 1950; s. Robert Berdell Artes and Kathleen Mary Arrenos; m. Monica Maribeth Kehoe; children: Meghann, Katie, Erin. BBA, U. Iowa, 1973. Asst. buyer Famous Barr, St. Louis, 2974-75; gen. mgr. Continental Restaurant Systems div. Ralston Purina, North Olmsted, Ohio, 1975-81, Barvarian Inn Restaurant, Des Moines, Iowa, 1981-84; owner, gen. mgr., pres. Pheasant Run Restaurant Corp., Mason City, 1984—; broker N.C. Real Estate Commn., Charlotte, 1979—; pres. Etra Mgmt. Corp., Clear Lake, Iowa, 1984—. Mem. Mason City C. of C. (ambassador 1986). Republican. Roman Catholic. Avocations: fishing, hunting, golf. Home: 811 W 10th Ave N Clear Lake IA 50428 Office: Pheasant Run Restaurant W Hwy 18 Mason City IA 50401

ARTHUR, JAMES WILLIAM, constrn., fin., devel. co. exec.; b. Akron, Ohio, Jan. 29, 1940; s. William L. and Ethel H. A.; B.A., Kent State U., 1963; m. Nancy L. Sage, June 28, 1964; children—William, Walter, Jennifer. Broker, Merrill Lynch Pierce Fenner & Smith, Akron, 1964-71; owner, pres. Arthur Constrn. Co., Kent, Ohio, 1971-73; pres. Trans Ohio Land Corp., Kent, 1972—; pres. Mahoning River Valley Corp., Kent, 1978—; owner, pres. Kent Limousine Service, 1986—; treas. Downtown Kent Redevel. Corp, 1985—, Intertraternity Housing Corp., Kent, 1987. Mem. Village Council, Sugar Bush Knolls, 1981—, pres., 1986; mem. adv. com. Kent Environ. Council, 1986-87; mem. deans council Kent State U.; former scoutmaster Troop 3250, Boy Scouts Am. Served with U.S. Army, 1957. Mem. Ohio Hist. Soc., Am. Legion, Phi Gamma Delta. Home: 1515 Lake Martin Dr Kent OH 44240 Office: 1640 Franklin Ave Kent OH 44240

ARTLEY, NANCY LILLIAN MARIE, psychologist; b. Saginaw, Mich., Apr. 24, 1948; d. Bernerd and Alice Anna (Stoeckle) H.; divorced; children: Sean, Paul. BS, Cen. Mich. U., 1975, MA, 1978. Lic. psychologist, Minn., Mich. (ltd.). Psychologist State Prison S. Mich., Jackson, 1979-81; psychologist, clin. case coordinator Northwestern Mental Health Ctr., Crookston, Minn., 1981-82; psychologist, program dir. Cass County Social Services, Walker, Minn., 1982—; psychology instr. Jackson Community Coll., 1979-81; psychologist Dept. Jobs and Tng., St. Paul, 1982—; program dir. Mental Health Outreach Program. Mem. Minn. Lic. Psychologists. Avocations: fiction writing, cross country skiing, sewing, reading, traveling. Office: Cass County Social Services Box 519 Walker MN 56484

ARVEDSON, PETER FREDRICK, clergyman; b. Peoria, Ill., Apr. 15, 1937; s. Fredrick St. Clair and Dorothy Evelyn (Young) A.; m. Joan Carol Swiggum, Aug. 17, 1963; children: Stephen, Mark. BS, U. Ill., 1959; PhD, U. Wis., 1964; MDiv., Gen. Theol. Sem., N.Y.C., 1967. Ordained priest Episcopal Ch., 1967. Vicar St. Laurence's Ch., Effingham, Ill., 1967-72; rector All Souls' Ch., Okinawa, Japan, 1972-78, St. Andrew's Ch., Madison, Wis., 1978—; dir. Inst. For Christian Studies, Milw., 1984—. V.p. Assn. of Attending Clergy, Madison Gen. Hosp., 1983-86. Avocation: running. Home: 9 Rye Circle Madison WI 53717 Office: St Andrew's Episcopal Ch 1833 Regent St Madison WI 53705

ARVIN, CHARLES STANFORD, librarian; b. Loogootee, Ind., Apr. 17, 1931; s. Leland Stanford and Mary Hope (Armstrong) A.; A.B., Wayne State U., 1953, postgrad., 1956-57; M.A. in Library Sci., U. Mich. 1960. Asst. divisional Librarian U. Mich. Natural Sci. Library, 1960-62; head reference Genesee County Library, Flint, Mich., 1962-67, 77-83, head central services, 1967-77, head acquisitions, 1983—. Served with AUS, 1953-56. Mem. ALA, Mich. Library Assn., Mich., Ind., Genesee County hist. socs., ACLU. Club: Flint Library. Editor: Flint Geneal. Quar., 1981—. Home: 702 W Oliver St Owosso MI 48867 Office: 4195 W Pasadena St Flint MI 48504

ARZOUMANIDIS, GREGORY G., chemist; b. Thessaloniki, Greece, Aug. 16, 1936; came to U.S., 1964, naturalized, 1976; s. Gerasimos and Sophia A.; m. Anastasia Anastasopoulos, Jan. 2, 1966; children: Sophia, Alexis. B.S. in Chemistry, U. Thessaloniki, 1959, M.S. in Chemistry, 1959; Ph.D. in Inorganic Chemistry, U. Stuttgart, (Germany), 1964; M.B.A., U. Conn., 1979. Research assoc. MIT, 1964-66; research chemist Monsanto, Everett, Mass., 1966-69; sr. research chemist Am. Cyanamid Co., Stamford, Conn., 1969-72, Stauffer Chem. Co., Dobbs Ferry, N.Y., 1972-79; research assoc. Amoco Chems. Corp., Naperville, Ill., 1979—. Inventor comml. catalysts for polypropylene plastics, new processes; patentee (U.S. and fgn.); contbr. articles to profl. jours. Served to 2d lt. Greek Army, 1959-61. Recipient acad. award Govt. of W.Ger., 1963. Mem. AAAS, Am. Chem. Soc., Sigma Xi. Greek Orthodox. Home: 7 S 610 Carriage Way Naperville IL 60540 Office: PO Box 400 Naperville IL 60566

ASCHAUER, CHARLES JOSEPH, JR., health products company executive; b. Decatur, Ill., July 23, 1928; s. Charles Joseph and Beulah Diehl (Kniple) A.; m. Elizabeth Claire Meagher, Apr. 28, 1962; children: Karen Claire, Thomas Arthur, Susan Jean, Karl Andrew. B.B.A., Northwestern U., 1950; certificate internat. bus. adminstr., Centre d'Etudes Industrielles, Geneva, Switzerland, 1951. Prin. McKinsey & Co., Chgo., 1955-62; v.p. mktg. Mead Johnson Labs. div. Mead Johnson & Co., Evansville, Ind., 1962-67; v.p., pres. automotive group Maremont Corp., Chgo., 1967-70; v.p., group exec. Whittaker Corp., Los Angeles, 1970-71; v.p., pres. hosp. products div. Abbott Labs., North Chicago, Ill., 1971-76; v.p., group exec. Abbott Labs., 1976-79, exec. v.p., dir., 1979—; dir. Benefit Trust Life Ins. Co., Chgo., Rust-Oleum Corp., Vernon Hills, Ill., Marine Corp., Milw., Marine Bank N.A., Evanston (Ill.) Hosp. Corp. Bd. dirs. Evanston Hosp. Corp. Served to lt. Supply Corps USNR, 1951-55. Mem. Chgo. Pres.'s Orgn., Proprietary Assn. (bd. dirs.), Sigma Nu. Clubs: University (Chgo.), Economics (Chgo.); Sunset Ridge Country (Northbrook, Ill.); Fairbanks Ranch Country (Rancho Santa Fe, Calif.). Office: Abbott Labs Abbott Park North Chicago IL 60064

ASCHER, JAMES JOHN, pharmaceutical executive; b. Kansas City, Mo., Oct. 2, 1928; s. Bordner Fredrick and Helen (Barron) A.; student Bergen Jr. Coll., 1947-48, U. Kans., 1946-47, 49-51; m. Mary Ellen Robitsch, Feb. 27, 1954; children—Jill Denise, James John, Christopher Bordner. Rep., B.F. Ascher & Co., Inc., Memphis, 1954-55, asst. to pres., Kansas City, Mo., 1956-57, v.p., 1958-64, pres., 1965—. Bd. dirs. Childrens Cardiac Center, 1964-70, pres., 1968-70; mem. central governing bd. Children's Mercy Hosp., 1968-80; bd. dirs. Jr. Achievement of Middle Am., 1970—, pres., 1973-76, chmn., 1979-81; edn. chmn. Young Pres.'s Orgn. 6th Internat. Univ. for Pres., Athens, 1975. Served to 1st. lt. inf., U.S. Army, 1951-53; Korea. Decorated Bronze Star, Combat Infantryman's Badge. Mem. Pharm. Mfrs. Assn., Drug, Chem. and Allied Trades Assn., World Bus. Council, Proprietary Assn., Chief Execs. Orgn., Midwest Pharm. Advt. Club, Sales and Advt. Execs. Club, Am. Mgmt. Assn. (pres.'s assn.), Kansas City C. of C., Am. Legion, VFW, Delta Chi. Clubs: Lotos, N.Y. Athletic; Kansas City; Mercury; Indian Hills Country (Prairie Village, Kans.); Rotary. Home: 6706 Glenwood Shawnee Mission KS 66204 Office: 15501 W 109th St Lenexa KS 66219

ASCHLIMAN, PATRICIA EILEEN, nurse; b. Evergreen Park, Ill., July 10, 1957; d. Cecil Francis and Patricia Mary (McGuire) Hasbrouck; m. Mark Randall Aschliman, Oct. 20, 1984. Nursing degree, Michael Reese Hosp., 1978. Staff nurse Michael Reese Hosp., Chgo., 1978-85, Med. Personnel Pool, Dallas, 1985-86, St. Mary's Hosp., Milw., 1986—; Registered nurse. Mem. Am. Assn. Critical Care Nurses. Roman Catholic. Avocation: gardening, woodworking.

ASGAR, KAMAL, dentistry educator, consultant; b. Tabriz, Iran, Aug. 28, 1922; s. Salmon and Rogheye Asgarzadeh; m. Safieh Seyedi, Sept. 4, 1948; children—Alexander, Andrew. B.A. in Chemistry, Tech. Coll. Tehran, 1945; M.S., U. Mich., 1948, B.S. in Chem. Engring., 1950, Ph.D., 1959. Paint chemist, Tehran, 1945-46; research asst. U. Mich., Ann Arbor, 1949-56, research assoc., asst. prof., 1956-62, assoc. prof., 1962-66, prof. dentistry, 1966—; cons. U.S. Army, U.S. Navy. Recipient Gibbon award U. Mich., 1963, 70, 80, Hollenback Meml. prize Acad. Operative Dentistry, 1984. Fellow Internat. Coll. Dentistry; mem. Internat. Assn. Dental Research (Souder award 1970), Am. Electron Probe Assn., Am. Soc. Metals, Fedn. Dentaire Internationale. Contbr. articles to sci. jours.; patentee in field. Home: 2240 Belmont St Ann Arbor MI 48104 Office: Univ Mich Sch Dentistry Ann Arbor MI 48109

ASH, GALEN LOWELL, police officer, security consultant; b. Bowling Green, Ohio, Feb. 16, 1939; s. Ernest M. and Opel (Kidwell) A.; m. Carol J. Orwig, May 5, 1979; children: Kim, Pam, Marcia, Tom. Student Owens Tech. Coll., Bowling Green State U., U. Va.-Quantico, Ohio State U. Chief of police City of Bowling Green, 1961—; security cons. Continental Distbg. Co., Findlay, Ohio, 1978—, C.W.C. Cos., Findlay, 1978—, Great Scot, Findlay, 1978—, Community Markets, Marysville, Ohio, 1978—; adj. asst. prof. criminal justice Bowling Green State U. Contbr. articles to profl. jours. Chmn., Bowling Green Traffic Commn., 1978—; v.p. Wood County Council on Alcoholism (Ohio), 1978—; nat. chmn. law enforcement com. Nat. Safety Council, 1982-84; appointed mem. Ohio Organized Crime Commn., 1986—. Active adv. com. Bowling Green State U.; active law adv. com. Owens Tech. Coll. Recipient Community Service award C. of C. Bowling Green, 1976, 77, 78, Service Above Self award Rotary Club, 1976, award citation 112th Gen. Assembly Ohio, 1978, award citation 116th Gen. Assembly Ohio Senate, 1986, two award citations 116th Assembly Ohio Ho. Reps., 1986, Outstanding Service Community award Bowling Green Kiwanis Club, 1985, Jefferson award WTVG, Toledo, 1985, Gov.'s Spl. Recognition award 1986; named Bus. Assoc. of Yr., Am. Bus. Women's Assn., 1980, Ky. Col., Gov. Ky. Mem. Fraternal Order of Police (v.p. 1965-66), Am. Criminal Justice Assn., Internat. Assn. Chiefs of Police, Ohio Assn. Chiefs of Police (exec. com. 1982—, v.p. 1984-85, pres. 1986-87), Nat. FBI Acad. Assocs., Ohio Crime Prevention Assn., Alpha Phi Sigma. Lutheran. Club: Falcon (Bowling Green). Home: 719 Rosalind Dr Bowling Green OH 43402 Office: Bowling Green Police Div 175 W Wooster St Bowling Green OH 43402

ASHBACH, DAVID LAURENCE, internist, nephrologist; b. Chgo., Nov. 17, 1942; s. Sol Henry and Lila Mae A.; A.B., Knox Coll., 1964; M.S., Case Western Reserve U., 1969, M.D., 1970; m. Arlene Rosenthal Nov. 28, 1963; children—Barbara, Deborah, Robert. Intern, Presbyterian-St. Luke's Hosp., Chgo., 1970-71, resident, 1971-73, fellow in nephrology, 1973-75; practice medicine specializing in nephrology, Hammond, Ind., 1975—; mem. staffs St. Margaret's Hosp., Hammond, Ind., Presbyterian-St. Luke's Hosp., Chgo., Meth. Hosp., Gary, Ind., St. Anthony's Hosp., Crown Point, Ind.; asst. clin. prof. medicine Ind. U.; asst. prof. health sci. Purdue U. Diplomate Am. Bd. Internal Medicine. Mem. A.C.P., Am. Internat. socs. nephrology. Jewish. Home: 20457 Ithaca St Olympia Fields IL 60461 Office: 5500 Hohman Ave Hammond IN 46320

ASHBECK, KAREN RAE, communications executive; b. Marshfield, Wis., Aug. 3, 1955; d. Raymond Clarence and Catherine (Haasl) A. BS in Tech. Communications, U. Wis., Platteville, 1977. Engring. writer Control Data Corp., Mpls., 1977-79; copywriter Campbell Mithun, Mpls., 1979-80, copycontact, 1980, creative dir., 1980-81; pres. Ashbeck & Assocs., St. Paul, 1981—. Chmn. communications task team Minn. Literacy Council, Mpls., 1986; vol. Nat. Kidney Found., Mpls., 1986. Recipient Volunteerism award Am. Lung Assn., 1986. Mem. Internat. Assn. Bus. Communications. Republican. Avocations: piano, fishing, weightlifting, reading. Office: Ashbeck & Assocs 450 N Syndicate # 122 Saint Paul MN 55104

ASHBROOK, JAMES BARBOUR, theology educator; b. Adrian, Mich., Nov. 1, 1925; s. Milan Forest and Elizabeth (Barbour) A.; m. Patricia Jane Cober, Aug. 14, 1948; children: Peter, Susan, Martha, Karen. A.B. with honors, Denison U., 1947, LL.D., 1976; B.D., Colgate Rochester Div. Sch., 1950; M.A., Ohio State U., 1962, Ph.D., 1964; postdoctoral fellow, U. Rochester, 1971-73; postgrad., Union Theol. Sem., 1954-55. Diplomate: Am. Assn. Pastoral Counselors, Am. Bd. Profl. Psychology (subsplty. clin. psychology). Ordained to ministry Am. Bapt. Ch., 1950; asst. chaplain U. Rochester, 1948-50; pastor South Congl. Ch., Rochester, N.Y., 1950-54, First Baptist Ch., Granville, Ohio, 1955-60; asso. prof. pastoral theology Colgate Rochester Div. Sch., 1960-65, prof., 1965-69, prof. psychology and theology, 1969-81; prof. religion and personality Garrett-Evang. Sem., 1981—; atv. mem. Grad. Faculty Northwestern U., 1982—; vis. lectr. Denison U., 1958-60; vis. asso. prof. Ohio State U., 1966; vis. prof. Princeton Theol. Sem., 1970-71. Author: Become Community, 1971, In Human Presence-Hope, 1971, Humanitas, 1973, The Old Me and A New i, 1974, Responding to Human Pain, 1975; co-author: Christianity for Pious Skeptics, 1977; The Human Mind and the Mind of God, 1984; contbr. chpts. to Religion and Medicine, 1967, Psychological Testing for Ministerial Selection, 1970, Explorations in Ministry, 1971. Bd. mgrs. ministers and missionaries benefit bd. Am. Bapt. Chs., 1962-71, 72-80. Faculty fellow Am. Assn. Theol. Schs., 1963-64, 71-72; recipient W.C. and J.V. Stone Found. grants, 1969-72; Alumni citation Denison U., 1972. Mem. Am. Psychol. Assn., Am. Assn. Pastoral Counselors, Soc. Sci. Study Religion, Am. Acad. Religion, Phi Beta Kappa. Home: 1205 Wesley Ave Evanston IL 60202 Office: 2121 Sheridan Rd Evanston IL 60201

ASHBY, JOHN FORSYTHE, bishop; b. Tulsa, Mar. 26, 1929; s. Thomas Albert and Margaret (Mote) A.; m. Mary Carver, Aug. 12, 1954; children: Anne Carver Ashby Jones, Elizabeth Ashby McBride. B.A., Okla. State U., 1952; M.Div., Episcopal Theol. Sem. Southwest, Austin, Tex., 1955, D.D. hon., 1981; M.A., Cambridge U., Eng., 1967. Ordained to minstry Episcopal Ch., 1955. Vicar St. John's Episcopal Ch., Burant, Okla., 1955-59; rector St. Luke's Episcopal Ch., Ada, Okla., 1959-81; bishop Episcopal Diocese of Western Kans., Salina, 1981—. Served to lt. col. USAR, 1960-81. Home: 512 Sunset Dr Salina KS 67401 Office: Diocese of Western Kans 142 S 8th St PO Box 1383 Salina KS 67401 *

ASHBY, ROBERT SAMUEL, lawyer; b. Crawfordsville, Ind., July 9, 1916; s. William Wallace and Nellie (Graybill) A.; m. Susan Gatch, June 4, 1949; children: Jean G., Willis G. A.B. with highest honors, Ind. U., 1938; LL.B. magna cum laude, Harvard, 1941. Bar: Ind. 1941, N.Y. 1942. Assoc. firm Carter, Ledyard & Milburn, N.Y.C., 1941-42; partner firm Barnes & Thornburg, Indpls., 1946—; dir. Ind. Nat. Corp., Danner's, Inc. Editor: Harvard Law Rev, 1941; Contbr. articles to tax and legal jours. Chmn. bd. of govs. Indpls. Mus. Art, 1960—. Served to lt. comdr. USNR, 1942-46. Mem. Am., Ind., Indpls. bar assns., Assn. Bar City N.Y., Bar Assn. 7th Fed. Circuit, Phi Beta Kappa, Sigma Nu. Clubs: Indianapolis Dramatic, Contemporary, University. Home: 7248 Pennsylvania St Indianapolis IN 46240 Office: 1313 Merchants Bank Bldg Indianapolis IN 46204

ASHCRAFT, LAURIE CRAGG, marketing executive; b. Washington, May 28, 1945; d. Richard Edwards and Dorothy (Shawhan) Cragg; B.A., Northwestern U., 1967; m. C. Brian Pendleton, May 20, 1972 (div.); m. 2d, W. Dale Ashcraft, Sept. 3, 1977. Psychol. research analyst Allstate Ins. Co., Northbrook, Ill., 1968-70; project supr. Marsteller, Inc., Chgo., 1970-74; mktg. research mgr. corporate mktg. research dept. Internat. Harvester, Chgo., 1974-76; assoc. dir. mktg. research Libby, McNeill & Libby, Chgo., 1976-78; project mgr. mktg. research S.C. Johnson & Son (Johnson Wax), Racine, Wis., 1978-80; mktg. research mgr. Minnetonka Inc. (Minn.), 1980-82; v.p. Custom Research Inc., 1982—; guest lectr. market research various univs. and assns. Research collaborator: The Coming Matriarchy, 1981. Mem. Am. Mktg. Assn. (chmn. career conf. 1976, pres. chpt. 1986-87), Jr. League, Alliance Francaise, Alpha Delta Pi. Club: Woman's Athletic (Chgo.). Office: Custom Research Inc 625 N Michigan Ave Chicago IL 60611

ASHCROFT, JOHN DAVID, governor of Missouri b. Chgo., May 9, 1942; s. J. Robert and Grace Pauline (Larson) A.; m. Janet Elise Roede, Dec. 23, 1967; children: Martha, Jay, Andrew. BA in History cum laude, Yale U., 1964; JD, U. Chgo., 1967. Bar: Mo. Assoc. prof. bus. law S.W. Mo. State U., Springfield, 1968-72; auditor State of Mo., Jefferson City, 1972-75, asst. atty. gen., 1975-76, atty. gen., 1976-85, governor State of Mo., 1985—. Bd. dirs. Greene County chpt. ARC, Sunshine Children's Home, Greater Ozarks chpt. Cystic Fibrosis Found.; appointed mem. task force family violence U.S. Atty. Gen.'s Office, 1983, task force on coll. quality Nat. Gov.'s Assn., chmn. task force on adulty literacy; mem. adv. council Intergovtl. Affairs; chmn. Edn. Commn. of States. Mem. ABA, Mo. Bar Assn., Cole County Bar Assn., Nat. Assn. Attys. Gen. (pres. 1980-81, chmn. budget com., Wyman award 1983). Republican. Mem. Assembly of God Ch. Author (with wife), College Law for Business, It's the Law; co-rec. artist albums Truth, In the Spirit of Liberty; contbr. articles to profl. jours. Office: Office Governor PO Box 720 Jefferson City MO 65102

ASHFORD, CAROLYN KAY, publishing executive; b. Kansas City, Mo., July 1, 1946; d. Milton Jennings and Virginia Caroline (Ford) Marquette; m. John Edward Ashford, Aug. 11, 1973 (div. Aug. 1982). BA in Polit. Sci., BJ, U. Mo., 1968, MA in Journalism, 1969. Dir. Mo. Dept. Natural Resoruces, Jefferson City, 1976-77; chief staff Gov. State Govt., Jefferson City, 1977-81; corp. dir. communications Payless Cashways, Kansas City, Mo., 1981-84; pub. Bus. First, Columbus, Ohio, 1984-1985; v.p. ops. Am. City Bus. Jours., Kansas City, 1985-87, exec. v.p., chief operating officer, 1987—. Democrat. Mem. Unity Sch. of Christianity. Home: 8329 Northern Blvd Kansas City MO 64138 Office: Am City Bus Jours 3535 Broadway Kansas City MO 64111

ASHHURST, ANNA WAYNE, educator; b. Phila., Jan. 5, 1933; d. Astley Paston Cooper and Anne Pauline (Campbell) Ashhurst; A.B., Vassar Coll., 1954; M.A., Middlebury Coll., 1956; Ph.D., U. Pitts., 1967; m. Ronald G. Gerber, July 22, 1978. English tchr. Internat. Inst. Spain, Madrid, 1954-56; asst. prof. Juniata Coll., Huntingdon, Pa., 1961-63; asst. prof. Spanish dept. Franklin and Marshall Coll., Lancaster, Pa., 1964-74, acting chmn. Spanish dept., 1972, convenor, fgn. lang. council, 1972-74; asso. prof. dept. modern fgn. langs. U. Mo., St. Louis, 1974-78. Mem. Welcome Wagon Wagon of Lancaster, Pa., 1968-70, 71-74. Fulbright-Hays grantee, Colombia, S.Am., summer 1963; Ford Humanities fellow, summer 1970; Mellon fellow, 1970-71. Mem. Internat. Inst. in Spain, Instituto Internacional de Literatura Iberoamericana, Am. Assn. Tchrs. Spanish and Portuguese, Women's Equity Action League (pres. Mo. div. 1975-76). Author: La literatura hispano-americana en la crítica española, 1980. Home: 2105 Barcelona Dr Florissant MO 63033

ASHLAND, EMELYNE IDA ANDREA, educator; b. Chgo., Oct. 29, 1910; d. Gustav A. and Ida Frances (Alex) A.; B.S., U. Chgo., 1931, S.M., 1933; postgrad. U. Calif. at Berkeley, 1939, U. Colo., 1940. Silhouette artist Century of Progress World's Fair, Chgo., 1933; trade mark artist Colgate-Palmolive Peet Co., Chgo., 1933-34; artist non-verbal Test I.J.R., 1934; med. social worker Unemployment Relief Services, Chgo., 1934-35; tchr. Sterling Twp. (Ill.) High Sch., 1936-37, Chgo. Pub. High Schs., 1937-76; adv., chmn. sci. dept. Gage Park High Sch., 1939-48, Morgan Park High Sch., 1948-54, Senn High Sch., 1954-76; pioneer in traffic safety edn., 1948-51; evaluator sci. materials representing Chgo. South Side schs., 1948-51. Recipient certificate of appreciation Lake County Health Dept., 1976. Mem. Chgo. Tchrs. Union (charter), Soc. Circumnavigators (mem. Marco Polo club). Baptist. Researcher tomato canker incitant: Aplanobactor Michiganese; author (with Tsu-kiang Yen) Devel. of Flower and Fruit of Myrica Rubra, pub. China, 1950. Home: 773 Marion Ave Highland Park IL 60035

ASHLEY-CAMERON, SYLVIA ELAINE, psychologist; b. St. Paul, June 12, 1955; s. Allen O. and Bernice S. (Rossbach) Ashley; m. David J. Cameron, June 18, 1977; 1 child, Shawn. BA, Gustavus Adolphus Coll., 1977; MS in Psychology, Iowa State U., 1980, PhD, 1982. Lic. psychologist. Asst. prof. Hamline U., St. Paul, 1981—; child psychologist North Meml. Med. Ctr., Robbinsdale, Minn., 1982—; cons. Van Wagner & Assocs., Mpls., 1983—, Opportunity Workshop, Mpls., 1985—; bd. dirs. Learning Link Found., Mpls. Mem. Am. Psychol. Assn., Am. Orthopsychiat. Assn., Soc. Clin. Child Psychologists, Phi Kappa Phi. Office: North Meml Child Guidance Clinic 3401 Oakdale Ave N Robbinsdale MN 55422

ASHLOCK, KENNETH RAY, lawyer; b. Lebanon, Mo., June 17, 1956; s. Darrell Ray and Nadean W. (Stewart) Asklock; m. Karan Diana Tripp, Dec. 26, 1982; children: Kimberly, Kristen. BS, Southwest Bapt. U., Bolivar, Mo., 1977; JD, U. Mo., 1980. Bar: Mo. 1980. Ptnr. Douglas, Lynch & Ashlock, Bolivar, 1980-85; sole practice Springfield and Bolivar, Mo., 1985—; prof. bus. and real estate law Southwest Bapt. U., 1980—. Mem. Bolivar Musical Arts Assn. Community Concerts,1986; bd. dirs. Bolivar Sheltered Workshop, 1986. Mem. ABA (software div., real property, probate and trust sec.), Green County Bar Assn., Nat. Assn. Trial Lawyers, Bolivar C. of C. Republican. Lodge: Lions (v.p. Bolivar chpt. 1984-86). Avocations: computers, farming. Home: 816 E Lindon Bolivar MO 65613 Office: 1800 S Glenstone Springfield MO 65804

ASHMORE, KARLA LYNN, computer training coordinator; b. West Point, N.Y., Nov. 3, 1956; d. Fred D. and Margaret Erika (Buckmann) Spinks; m. David Jefferson Ashmore, Feb. 19, 1977 (div. Dec. 17, 1979); 1 child, Erika Margaret Augusta. BA, Ind. U.-Purdue U. at Indpls., 1982; MS, Ind. U., 1986. Mgr. Eastside Chiropractic Clinic, Indpls., 1978-80; English tutor univ. div. Ind. U.-Purdue U. at Indpls., 1980-82, composition instr. English dept., 1982-83, tech. writer computing services, 1983-84; tech. writer Ind. U. Adminstrv. Computing, 1984-87; computer tng. coordinator Melvin Simon and Assocs., Inc., Indpls., 1987—. Author 4 articles, 5 book revs. and 20 pub. poems; editor: Literary Jour., Genesis, All-Am. Mag., Am. Collegiate Press Assn., 1983. Mem. Indpls. Nuclear Weapons Freeze, Inc. Mem. Soc. Tech. Communication (Cert. of Achievement 1985), Soc. Profl. Journalists, Writer's Ctr. of Indpls., Ind. U. Alumni Assn., Sigma Delta Chi, Pi Lambda Theta. Democrat. Unitarian. Avocations: operatic singing, watercolor painting, poetry writing, swimming, yoga. Office: Melvin Simon & Assocs Inc 2 West Washington Indianapolis IN 46207

ASKEGAARD, ERIC ARTHUR, manufacturing engineer; b. Fargo, N.D., July 5, 1960; s. John Burkee and Darlene Hope (Finney) A. BS in Indsl. Engring., N.D. State U., 1982. Field engr. Houston Engring. Co., Fargo, 1982-84; mfg. engring. specialist The Toro Co., Windom, Minn., 1984—. Mem. Am. Inst. Indsl. Engrs., Soc. Mfg. Engrs., Soc. for Preservation and Encouragement of Barber Shop Quartet Singing in Am. (S.W. div. quartet champion). Republican. Lutheran. Home: 1453 6th Ave Windom MN 56101 Office: The Toro Co 174 16th St Windom MN 56101

ASKEN, EVIE (YVONNE WARNER), architect; b. Kans. City, Kans., Oct. 27, 1936; d. Floyd B. Warner and Frances (Kalinich) W.; m. Eugene J. Asken, Apr. 10, 1960; children—Gregory, Linda, Richard. B.Arch., Kans. State U., 1959. Registered architect, Mich. Architect, Kingscott Assos., Inc., Kalamazoo, 1980—; cons.; chair Mich. Bd. Architects, 1985-87; mem. Mich. Constrn. Code Commn., 1984-88. Mem. Kalamazoo Econ. Devel. Corp., treas. 1979-81; mem. Kalamazoo County Overall Econ. Expansion, Portage City Planners Commn., 1977-80, Kalamazoo 2000 Com., 1982, Downtown Devel. Authority Com. on Arcadia Creek, 1982 . Fellow Kans. State U. Alumni; mem. AIA (pres. task force affirmative action, pres. Western Mich. chpt. 1976-77, fellowship 1984), Mich. Soc. Architects (dir. 1978-82, sec. 1978-80, pres. 1981, Gold Medal award 1986, Kalamazoo Women Aware award 1986), Kalamazoo C. of C. (dir. 1978-82, pres. Portage div. 1981, 82). Office: PO Box 671 Kalamazoo MI 49005

ASMA, JOHN WILLIAM, accountant; b. Andyk, The Netherlands, July 13, 1928; came to U.S., 1948; s. William and Winnie (Trompetter) A.; m. Donna Helen Vander Ploeg, Jan. 21, 1954; children: Robin J., Wendy A., Calvin J., Daniel J. AB, Calvin Coll., Grand Rapids, Mich., 1957; MBA, U. Mich., 1958. CPA, Mich., Ind. Staff acct. Scovell Wellington, Niles, Mich., 1958-62; auditor 1st Nat. Bank, Mishawaka, Ind., 1962-64; chief acct., dir. audits Western Mich. U., Kalamazoo, 1964-73; controller, v.p., treas. Continental Linen, Kalamazoo, 1973-80; pvt. practice acctg. Kalamazoo, 1980—. Bd. dirs. Sr. Services, Kalamazoo, 1981-84. Served as cpl. Signal Corps, U.S. Army, 1951-53. Mem. Am. Inst. CPA's, Mich. Assn. CPA's. Republican. Mem. Christian Reformed Ch. Lodge: Kiwanis. Home: 6691 Hayward Dr Indian Lake Vicksburg MI 49097 Office: 535 S Burdick Suite 255 Kalamazoo MI 49007

ASMAN, ROBERT JOSEPH, lawyer; b. St. Louis, Feb. 7, 1924; s. Robert J. and Anna M. (Spaeth) A.; student Holy Cross Coll., 1941-43; A.B., Cath. U. Am., 1948; LL.B., Georgetown U., 1951; m. Mary Elizabeth Kane, Sept. 8, 1948; children—Kathryn Anne, Robert Joseph III, Peter Kane, Teresa Elizabeth, Suzanne Marie, Elizabeth Jane. Admitted to D.C. bar, 1952, Ohio bar, 1961; asso. firm Cummings, Truitt & Reeves, Washington, 1956; trial atty. anti-trust div. Dept. Justice, 1952-53; asst. U.S. atty. D.C., 1953-60; counsel flight propulsion lab. dept. Gen. Electric Co., 1960-63; v.p., sec., gen. counsel Pneumo Dynamics Corp., Cleve., 1963-70; pres., chief exec. officer Ohio State Bar Assn. Automated Research, Cleve.; mem. firm Van Aken, Bond, Withers, Asman & Smith, Cleve. Mem. Bd. Zoning Appeals, Cleveland Heights, Ohio; mem. Ohio Mental Health and Mental Retardation Adv. Council, 1972—, mem. com. Met. Health Planning Corp.; mem. Cuyahoga County Community Mental Health and Retardation Bd., 1972—. Pres. Hill House, Cleve., 1964; trustee Cleve. Mental Health Assn., 1966-68, St. John's Coll., Hill House. Served with AUS, 1943-45; ETO. Decorated Bronze Star. Mem. Am., Fed., D.C., Ohio bar assns., Greater Cleve. Growth Assn., Phi Delta Phi. Clubs: Clevelander, Union, Rowfant Skating (Cleve.). Home: 2676 Berkshire Rd Cleveland Heights OH 44106 Office: 1519 Nat City Bank Bldg Cleveland OH 44114

ASPEN, MARVIN EDWARD, U.S. dist. judge; b. Chgo., July 11, 1934; s. George Abraham and Helen (Adelson) A.; m. Susan Alona Tubbs, Dec. 18, 1966; children: Jennifer Marion, Jessica Maile, Andrew Joseph. B.S. in Law, Northwestern U., 1956, J.D., 1958. Bar: Ill. bar 1958. Individual practice Chgo., 1958-59; draftsman joint com. to draft new Ill. criminal code Chgo. Bar Assn.-Ill. Bar Assn., 1959-60; asst. state's atty. Cook County, Ill., 1960-63; asst. corp. counsel City of Chgo., 1963-71; individual practice 1971; judge Circuit Ct. Cook County, 1971-79; U.S. dist. judge No. Dist. Ill., Eastern div., Chgo., 1979—; mem. part-time faculty Northwestern U. Law Sch.; chmn. adv. bd. Inst. Criminal Justice, John Marshall Sch. Law; mem. Ill. Law Enforcement Commn., Gov. Ill. Adv. Commn. Criminal Justice, Cook County Bd. Corrections; chmn. coms. Commn. Ill. Supreme Ct. Appointments; mem. faculty Nat. Inst. Trial Advocacy, Nat. Jud. Coll.; past chmn. coms. Ill. Jud. Conf. Programs. Co-author: Criminal Law for the Layman-A Citizen's Guide, 2d edit, 1977, Criminal Evidence for the Police, 1972; Contbr. articles legal publns. Served with USAF, 1958-59. Mem. ABA Judicature Soc., Ill. Bar Assn. (past chmn. coms.), Chgo. Bar Assn. (bd. mgrs. 1978-79), Decalogue Soc. Lawyers (past chmn. coms.), John Howard Assn. (dir.). Jewish. Office: US Dist Ct 219 S Dearborn St Chicago IL 60604

ASPER, BERNICE VICTORIA, editor; b. Luck, Wis., Apr. 1, 1920; d. Harry L. and Christine Marie (Hilseth) Johansen; m. Verdie Sanford Asper, Dec. 23, 1942 (dec. 1944); 1 dau., Victoria Sharon Asper Johnson. Student Mpls. Bus. Coll., 1939. Office worker, Fed. Agr. Agy., Balsam Lake, Wis., 1942; bookkeeper Enterprise-Herald, Luck, 1942-44; cashier Thorp Fin. Corp., Frederic, Wis., 1946-51; bookkeeper Rudell Motor Co., Frederic, 1951-57; billing clk. Frederic Telephone Co., 1958-63; editor Inter-County Leader, Frederic, 1963—. Author: 75 Years in Frederic, 1976; 100 Years at St. Peter's, 1980. Bd. dirs. Western Wis. Health Systems Agy., LaCrosse, 1976-82, Frederic Municipal Hosp., 1981—; sec. Frederic Citizens Adv. Com., 1968-83; supt. St. Peter's Luth. Sunday Sch., Luck, 1948-78; sec. Frederic Devel. Corp., 1982-84. Named Frederic Citizen of Yr., C. of C., 1980. Mem. Wis. Press Assn., Polk County Jury Commn. Democrat. Lutheran. Home: 302 N Wisconsin Ave Frederic WI 54837 Office: Inter County Leader 303 N Wisconsin Ave Frederic WI 54837

ASPIN, LES, congressman; b. Milw., July 21, 1938; s. Leslie and Marie (Orth) A. B.A. summa cum laude, Yale U., 1960; M.A., Oxford (Eng.) U., 1962; Ph.D., MIT, 1965. Mem. staff Sen. William Proxmire, 1960, campaign dir., 1964; staff asst. to Walter Heller; chmn. Pres. Kennedy's Council Econ. Advisers, 1963; mem. 92d-100th congresses from 1st Wis. Dist., chmn. sub-com. mil. personnel and compensation, chmn. HAS com. 99th-100th Congress. Served to capt. AUS, 1966-68. Mem. Jr. C. of C., Am. Legion, Phi Beta Kappa. Episcopalian. Office: 2336 Rayburn Office Bldg Washington DC 20515

ASPLIN, EDWARD WILLIAM, packaging company executive; b. Mpls., June 25, 1922; s. John E. and Alma (Carlbom) A.; m. Eleanor Young Rodgers, Oct. 20, 1951; children—Sarah L., William R., Lynn E. B.B.A., U. Minn., 1943; postgrad., U. Mich., 1947-48, Wayne State, 1949-50, Rutgers U. Sch. Banking, 1957-59. Cost accountant Nat. Bank Detroit, 1947-50; asst. v.p. adminstrn. Northwest Bancorp., Mpls., 1950-59; v.p. mktg. Northwestern Nat. Bank, Mpls., 1959-67; chmn. exec. com. Bemis Co., Inc., Mpls., 1967—; also dir. Bemis Co., Inc.; dir. Cin. Milacron Inc., DeLuxe Check Printers, Inc. Advisor Opportunity Workshop, Inc.; chmn. bd. dirs. Mpls. YMCA; bd. dirs. Minn. Hist. Soc. Served with USNR, 1943-46. Clubs: Minikahda, Minneapolis; University (N.Y.C.). Office: Bemis Co 800 Northstar Center Minneapolis MN 55402

ASSAD, LETICIA BELTRÁN, university program administrator; b. El Paso, Tex., Dec. 31, 1959; d. Rafael and Antonia (Esquivel) Beltrán. BS, U. Tex., El Paso, 1979. Tchr. Ysleta Sch. Dist., El Paso, 1979-81; social worker Cath. Charities, St. Paul, 1981-82; student personnel worker U. Minn., Mpls., 1982-83, student support services officer, 1983—; translator/receptionist Hispanic Agy., St. Paul, 1981. Role model Hispanic Community in St. Paul, 1982—; bd. dirs. Minn. Hispanic Tech. and Profl. Edn. Project, St. Paul, 1983084; mem. adv. bd. Met. Council, St. Paul, 1985. Office: U Minn Health Scis 614 Delawane St SE W-61 Centennial Hall Minneapolis MN 55427

ASSEL, BARBARA GAIL, obstetrician, gynecologist; b. Minot, N.D., Dec. 18, 1951; d. Conrad Orville and Gladys Irene (Goodrich) Juelke; m. Thomas George Assel, May 27, 1972; children: Christopher George, Nathan Thomas. BS, N.D. State U., 1973; BS in Medicine, U. N.D., 1977; MD, U. Nebr., 1979. Diplomate Am. Bd. Obstetrics and Gynecology. Resident U. Minn. Affiliated Hosps., Mpls., 1979-83; staff physician Dakota Med. Ctr., Fargo, N.D., 1983—; clin. staff U. N.D. Sch. Medicine, Grand Forks, 1983—. Fellow Am. Coll. Ob/gyn; mem. AMA, Am. Soc. Colposcopy and Cervical Pathology. Methodist. Avocations: skiing, racquetball. Office: Dakota Clinic 1702 S University Dr Fargo ND 58103

ASSELIN, PAUL JOSEPH, interior designer; b. Bay City, Mich., July 20, 1953; s. Francis John and Alice (Lanouette) A. Cert. Kendall Sch. Design, Grand Rapids, 1977. Prin., Free Lance Design Assocs., Grand Rapids, Mich., 1977-78; sr. designer Contract Interiors, Grand Rapids, 1978-81; sr. designer Custer Office Environments, Grand Rapids, 1981-83; instr. Kendall Sch. Design, Grand Rapids, 1983—; prin. P. Asselin & Assocs., Grand Rapids, Mich., 1983-85; sr. designer Interphase, 1985-86; mgr. Interior Design, Daverman Assocs., Inc., Grand Rapids, 1986—. Mem. Am. Soc. Interior Designers (v.p. chpt. 1982-83, v.p. Mich. 1983-85). Roman Catholic.

ASSIMACOPOULOS, LYNN ANN, nurse; b. Ft. Dodge, Iowa, Apr. 23, 1939; d. Jay A. and Clara M. (Lind) Soppeland; m. Costas A. Assimacopoulos, Apr. 7, 1962; children: Aristides, Paul, Christopher. BS in Nursing, U. Minn., 1962. Nurse intensive care U. Minn. Hosp., Mpls., 1962-69; dir. nurses Nursing Care Services, Sioux Falls, S.D., 1978-79; nurse surgical staff Sioux Valley Hosp., Sioux Falls, 1979-80, staff nurse intensive care, 1980-81, instr. staff devel., 1981-84, spl. project coordinator pub. affairs, 1984—; editor nursing newsletter Sioux Valley Hosp., 1987—. Contbr. articles to profl. jours. Vol. dir. nurses S.D. Red Cross, Sioux Falls, 1975-78; vol. Pub. Schs., Sioux Falls, 1975-79. Mem. Am. Nurses Assn. (bd. dirs. S.D. dist. 9 1986-87), S.D. Nurses Assn. (bd. dirs. 1986—), Nat. League for Nursing, Transcultural Nursing Soc. (S.D. liasion). Democrat. Greek Orthodox. Avocations: reading, collecting nurse figurines, writing, fossil hunting. Home: 2800 W 23 St Sioux Falls SD 57105 Office: Sioux Valley Hosp Pub Affairs Dept 1100 S Euclid Ave Box 5039 Sioux Falls SD 57117-5039

ASTON, KENNETH PRESTON, JR., real estate salesman and investments; b. St. Louis, Mar. 29, 1959; s. Kenneth Preston and Carol Audrey (Dependahl) A.; m. Lori Ann Shikany, Apr. 17, 1982; children: Andrea Roxanne, Elizabeth René. A.B. in Polit. Sci., U. Mo., 1981. Mgr., cons. Oliver Realty Inc., St. Louis, 1981-82; apt./investment salesman Coldwell Banker Comml. Real Estate Services, St. Louis, 1982—; pres. Aston & Aston Properties, St. Louis, 1982—. Fund raiser Dream Factory, Inc., St. Louis, 1983-84. Recipient awards apt. investment salesperson Coldwell Banker, North Central Region U.S.A., 1983, 84. Mem. Phi Delta Theta. Republican. Mem. United Ch. of Christ. Clubs: Jaycees (pres. Chesterfield 1985-86, chmn. 1986), Toastmasters. Avocations: wrestling; golf. Home: 1372 White Rd Chesterfield MO 63017 Office: Coldwell Banker 222 S Central Ave 1104 Saint Louis MO 63105

ATANASOFF, DONN ANTHONY, retail executive, lawyer; b. Iron River, Mich., Feb. 8, 1958; s. Stanley E. and Cecelia Ann Atanasoff; m. Faye Dawn Atanasoff, Sept. 14, 1985. BSBA, Marquette U., 1981; JD, Thomas M. Cooley Law Sch., 1984. Bar: Wis. 1985, Mich. 1987. V.p., gen. mgr. Krist Oil Co., Iron River, 1984—; bd. dirs. Convenience Store Assn. Mich., Lansing, 1986—. Mem. Wis. Petroleum Assn., Mich. Petroleum Assn., Wis. Convenience Store Assn., Wis. Bar Assn. Lodge: Kiwanis. Avocations: hunting, fishing, skiing. Office: Krist Oil Co 303 Seldon Rd Iron River MI 49935

ATCHER, ROBERT WHITEHILL, medical researcher; b. Chgo., June 12, 1951; s. Robert Owen and Marguerite Alice (Whitehill) A. BA in Chemistry, Washington U., St. Louis, 1972; MS in Chemistry, U. Rochester, 1974, PhD in Nuclear Chemistry, 1980; MA in Journalism, U. Mo., 1976. Research fellow Brigham Women's Hosp., Boston, 1979-81, research assoc., 1981-83; cancer expert Nat. Cancer Inst., Bethesda, Md., 1983-86; group leader nuclear medicine research Argonne (Ill.) Nat. Lab., 1986—; adj. prof. U. Md., College Park, 1984-86; asst. prof. radiation oncology U. Chgo., 1986—; cons. in field, 1981—. Patentee in field; contbr. articles to profl. jours. Fellow Am. Inst. Chemists; mem. Soc. Nuclear Medicine, Am. Chem. Soc., AAAS. Roman Catholic. Avocations: music, fishing, bicycling, travel. Home: 1560 N Sandburg Terrace Apt 915 Chicago IL 60610 Office: Argonne Nat Lab 9700 S Cass Ave Argonne IL 60439

ATEN, ORLEY ROGER, marketing professional; b. Canton, Ill., June 3, 1937; s. Fremont Allison and Norma Lee (Meyer) A.; m. Julia Adele Friederich, Nov. 1, 1959; children: Timothy L., Jeffrey R., Gregory T., Bradley J., Stanley D. BSBA, Bradley U., 1963. Nat. account mgr. Caterpillar Indsl., Mentor, Ohio, 1973-85; N.Am. mktg. mgr. Volvo Automated Systems, Sterling Heights, Mich., 1985—; bd. dirs. Sportstyme Ltd., Rochester, Mich., 1986. Mem. Indsl. Material Mgmt. Tech. Soc. Republican. Club: Mentor Bantam Football (bd. dirs. 1976-84, pres. 1983). Lodges: Optimists (pres. 1975), Masons (jr. steward 1972). Avocations: tennis, golf. Home: 4585 Torrington Dr Sterling Heights MI 48310 Office: Volvo Automated Systems 7000 19 Mile Rd Sterling Heights MI 48310

ATKINS, CHARLES GILMORE, medical school administrator; b. Stambaugh, Mich., July 4, 1939; s. Howard B. and Bernice M. (Gilmore) A.; m. Kay Roberta Bueschen, Dec. 28, 1958 (div. 1983); children—Robert Howard, Karla Marie, James Charles. B.A., Albion Coll., 1961; postgrad. Med. Sch., U. Mich., 1960-62; M.S., Eastern Mich. U., 1963; Ph.D., N.C. State U., 1969. Instr. Coe Coll., 1963-66; lectr. genetics Cornell Coll., Mt. Vernon, Iowa, 1964-65; NIH predoctoral genetics trainee N.C. State U., Raleigh, 1966-69; asst. prof. microbiology Ohio U., Athens, 1969-74, assoc. prof., 1974—, dir. Appalachian life sci. coll. tng. program, 1972-74, dir. willed body program, 1976-77, assoc. dean for basic scis., 1976—, del. to state-level Ohio faculty senate, 1970-73; cons. in field. Elder 1st Presbyn. Ch., Athens, 1977—; scoutmaster Boy Scouts Am., 1972-82, dist. and council commr., 1979-86. Served to lt. col. USAR, 1981—. Dist. Award of Merit, Boy Scouts Am., 1976; Silver Wreath award, Nat. Eagle Scout Assn., 1981; Alfred E. Noyes scholar, 1957-60. Mem. Genetics Soc. Am., AAAS, Assn. Am. Med. Colls., Am. Soc. Microbiology, Ohio Acad. Sci., Nat. Eagle Scout Assn., Order of the Arrow, Sigma Xi. Lodge: Rotary, Contbr. articles to profl. jours. Home: 6 Riverview Dr Athens OH 45701 Office: Ohio Univ 226 Irvine Hall Athens OH 45701

ATKINS, EDWARD MORRIS, anesthesiologist; b. Milw., June 20, 1954; s. Julius Robert and Mildred (Smith) A.; m. Cathy Gilford; 1 child, Lisa. BA in Polit. Sci. with honors, U. Wis., 1975, MD, 1980. Diplomate Am. Bd. Anesthesiology. Intern, then resident Presbyn. St. Lukes Hosp., Chgo., 1980-83; attending physician Alexian Bros. Med. Ctr., Elk Grove Village, Ill., 1983—; cons. Inst. for Pain Therapy, Highland Park, Ill., 1987—; med. dir., owner North Suburban Surgicenter, Schaumburg, Ill., 1987—, Creekside Surgicenter, Hoffman Estates, Ill., 1987—. Bd. dirs. Camp Chi-Chgo. Jewish Community Ctr., 1984—. Mem. Am. Soc. Anesthesiology, Ill. Soc. Anesthesiology, Chgo. Soc. Anesthesiology, Internat. Anesthesia Research Soc. Club: Green Acres Country (Northbrook, Ill.). Avocations: golf, tennis, basketball, football, water skiing. Home: 1279 Pine Ct Glencoe IL 60022

ATKINS, JAMES ALBERT, food services administration consultant; b. Washington, Apr. 24, 1945; s. James Earl and Dorothy (Mix) A.; A.A. in Applied Sci., Ferris State Coll., 1966; student health care mgmt. program U. Ill., 1978-79; m. Joan Marie Pierce, Nov. 7, 1976; children—James Norman, Katherine Marie, Michael William, Daniel Mathew. Food service mgr., Fred Harvey Restaurants, Chgo., 1966-69; food and beverage mgr. Quality Motels, Jackson, Mich., 1969-70, St. Louis, 1970; food service mgr. Venture Stores, St. Ann, Mo., 1971; asst. dir. food services St. Francis Hosp., Evanston, Ill., 1971-72; gen. mgr. Food Mgmt. Assos., Glen Ellyn, Ill., 1973; asso. dir. of food services St. Annes Hosp., Chgo., 1973-79, St. Elizabeth's Hosp., Chgo., 1973-79; dir. food and nutrition services U. Chgo. Med. Center, 1979-82; account exec. Superin Lottee and Foods, 1985—, Superior Coffee and Foods; instr. (part-time) in food service curriculum Coll. of Du Page, Glen Ellyn, Ill., 1976—, adv. coll. food service curriculum, 1979—; chmn. food service com. Ancilla Domini Health Services, 1977-79; cons. food services, 1975—; pres. Atkins & Assos., 1976—; instr. restaurant mgmt. tng. program Triton Jr. Coll., 1978—; coll. curriculum adv. U. Ill., 1979—; lectr., key speaker at food service and mgmt. seminars, 1978—; chmn. Tri-State Conv. for Health Care Food Service, 1979; seminar leader food service tng. programs. Served with USN, 1967-68; Vietnam. Recipient cert. of recognition Evanston Sch. System and Chgo. Food Service Mktg. Club, 1973; designated disting. healthcare food service adminstr. Mem. Internat. Food Service Execs. Assn. (1st v.p.), Am. Soc. for Hosp. Food Service Adminstrs. (past pres.), Am. Hosp. Assn. Assn. Catering Execs. Clubs Am. Roman Catholic. Club: Lion. Home and Office: 105 Garden Ave Roselle IL 60172-1713

ATKINS, THOMAS LEE, human resources development specialist; b. Chgo., Dec. 4, 1921; s. Samuel Merritt and Alphonsine Marie (La Londe) A.; B.A., U. Notre Dame, 1943; postgrad. Cath. U. Am., 1947-51; m. Marylin E. Bowman, Dec. 19, 1966; children—Elizabeth Ann, Catherine Marie. Ordained priest, Roman Cath. Ch., 1951; asst. pastor Saginaw (Mich.) Sts. Peter & Paul Ch., 1951-54, St. Helen Ch., Saginaw, 1954-58; chaplain VA Hosp., Saginaw, 1954-58, USNR Tng. Ctr., Bay City, Mich., 1958-64; pastor Sebewaing (Mich.) St. Mary's Nativity Ch., 1958-63; tng. specialist Bur. Personnel Services, Mich. Employment Security Commn., 1974—. Bd. dirs. Saginaw Valley Indian Assn., 1972—, pres., 1981-87. Served with USNR, 1943-46. Mem. Social Workers Roundtable (pres. 1969-74), SAR. Portrait editor, Notre Dame DOME, 1942; lit. editor Sacred

Heart Gothic, 1946-47. Home: PO Box 616 Sunny Acres Ranch 1501 Clear Lake Rd West Branch MI 48661 Office: 7310 Woodward St Detroit MI 48202

ATKINSON, ARTHUR JOHN, JR., clinical pharmacologist, educator; b. Chgo., Mar. 22, 1938; s. Arthur John and Inez (Hill) A.; A.B. in Chemistry, Harvard U., 1959; M.D., Cornell U., 1963. Intern and asst. resident in medicine Mass. Gen. Hosp., Boston, 1963-65, chief resident and Howard Carroll fellow in medicine Passavant Meml. Hosp., Chgo., instr. in medicine Northwestern U., Chgo., 1967-68; fellow in clin. pharmacology U. Cin., 1968-69, asst. prof. pharmacology, 1969; vis. scientist dept. toxicology Karolinska Inst., Stockholm, Sweden, 1970; asst. prof. medicine and pharmacology Northwestern U., Chgo., 1970-73, assoc. prof., 1973-76, prof., 1976—. Served with NIH, USPHS, 1965-67. Recipient Faculty Devel. award in clin. pharmacology Pharm. Mfrs. Assn., 1970-72; Burroughs Wellcome scholar in clin. pharmacology, 1972-77. Fellow ACP; mem. Am. Fedn. Clin. Research, Central Soc. Clin. Research, Am. Soc. for Clin. Investigation, Am. Soc. Pharmacology and Exptl. Therapeutics, Am. Soc. Clin. Pharmacology and Therapeutics (Rawls Palmer award 1983), Assn. Am. Physicians, Chgo. Soc. Internal Medicine, Alpha Omega Alpha. Club: Chgo. Yacht. Mem. editorial bd. jours. Rational Drug Therapy, 1972-83, Clin. Pharmacology and Therapeutics, 1973—, Pharm. Revs., 1977—, Therapeutic Drug Monitoring, 1979—. Home: 175 E Delaware Pl Chicago IL 60611 Office: 303 E Superior St Chicago IL 60611

ATKINSON, GEORGE DUANE, sales executive; b. Creighton, Pa., Nov. 22, 1950; s. George Dae and Jean M. (McMurdo) A.; m. Patricia Kramer, May 1, 1976; children: Trisha Jane, Sara Elizabeth. BBA, Ohio No. U., 1972. Customer service expeditor Hobert Corp., Troy, Ohio, 1973-74, sales adminstr., 1975-78; indsl. markets coordinator Hartzell Fan Inc., Piqua, Ohio, 1979-83, regional sales mgr., 1984—; nat. sales mgr., mktg. mgr. Barry Blower Co., Mpls., 1983-84. Served to sgt. USAR, 1972-78. Mem. Am. Mgmt. Assn., Dayton Sales and Mktg. Execs. Assn. Republican. Methodist. Lodges: Masons, Elks. Avocations: racquetball, bicycling, tennis, golf, fishing. Home: 115 Finsbury Ln Troy OH 45373 Office: Hartzell Fan Inc 910 S Downing St Piqua OH 45356

ATKINSON, G(EORGE) LESLIE, accountant; b. Doncaster, Eng., Jan. 22, 1942; came to U.S., 1963; s. Norman Pearson and Iris Mary (Hawson) A.; m. Linda Beth Stein, June 1, 1969; children: David, Ian. BA, U. Nottingham, Eng., 1963. CPA. Internal auditor Nat. Dairy Products Co., N.Y.C., 1963-68; acct. Sealtest Foods, Pitts., 1968-70; acctg. mgr. Sealtest Foods, Cleve., 1970-74; ptnr. Sherwood A. Goldfarb & Co., Cleve., 1974-85; mgr. Laventhol & Horwath, Cleve., 1985—. Trustee Temple Emanu El, Cleve., 1977—, treas., v.p., 1981-86, pres., 1986; treas., trustee Mayfield Schs. Ednl. Excellence Found., 1986—. Mem. Am. Inst. CPA's, Nat. Assn. Accts., Ohio Soc. CPA's. Club: City (Cleve.). Home: 920 Rose Blvd Highland Heights OH 44143 Office: Laventhol & Horwath 1900 E 9th St 14th Floor Cleveland OH 44114

ATKINSON, HAROLD DENNIS, dentist; b. Ft. Wayne, Ind., Feb. 4, 1955; s. Lewis Lester and Jeanne Ann (Mahoney) A.; m. Jenna Kay Moon, Apr. 17, 1982; 1 child, Benjamin Todd. BA in Chemistry, Ind. U., 1977, DDS, 1981. Registered profl. dentist. Gen. practice dentistry Ft. Wayne, 1982—. Mem. ADA, Acad. Gen. Dentistry, Ind. Dental Assn., Isaac Knaap Dental Soc., Nat. Wildlife Fedn. Roman Catholic. Club: Ft. Wayne Ski. Avocations: canoeing, camping, skiing, running, travel. Office: 4111 Diplomat Plaza Ctr Fort Wayne IN 46806

ATKINSON, JEFF JOHN FREDERICK, lawyer, educator, writer; b. Mpls., Nov. 12, 1948; s. Frederick Melville Atkinson and Patricia (Bauman) Atkinson Farnes; m. Janis Pressendo, Dec. 22, 1982; children: Tara, Abigail, Grant. BS, Northwestern U., 1974; J.D. summa cum laude, DePaul U., 1977. Bar: Ill. 1977, U.S. Ct. Appeals (7th cir.) 1977, U.S. Dist. Ct. (no. dist.) Ill. 1978, U.S. Supreme Ct. 1982. Editor, reporter various Chgo. area newspapers and radio stas., 1967-71; assoc., Jenner & Block, Chgo., 1977-80; sole practice, Evanston and Chgo., 1980-83; instr. Loyola U. Law Sch., Chgo., 1982—. Author Modern Child Custody Practice, (2 vols.) 1986; contbr. articles on criminal, family, and constl. law to various publs. Mem. ABA (chmn. child custody com. 1983-84, 86—, mem. publs. devel. bd. 1984—, mem. task force on needs of children 1983-85, mem. research com. 1984—, chmn., 1987—, Merit award 1984, 86), Ill. Bar Assn., Chgo. Bar Assn., Chgo. Council Lawyers, Am. Trial Lawyers Assn., ACLU (bd. dirs. Ill. div. 1972-74), Northwestern U. Coll. Alumni Assn. (v.p. 1987—). Home: 525 Grove St Apt 2-D Evanston IL 60201

ATKINSON, ROBERT WILMER, trade association executive; b. Norristown, Pa., Sept. 26, 1928; s. Paul Gregory and Pauline Mary (Beckman) A.; m. Willea Lenora Cason, Sept. 18, 1955; children: Wendy Sue, Robert Alan, William Andrew (dec.), Richard Lee. BBA, Rutgers U., 1950; MBA in Mktg., Case Western Res. U., 1959. Sales trainee Continental Can Co., Phila., Chgo., N.Y., Balt., 1950-52; sales rep. Continental Can Co., Phila. and Cleve., 1954-55; market analyst Brush Electronics Co., Cleve., 1956-58; staff rep. Forging Industry Assn., Cleve., 1958-64, exec. sec., treas., 1964-68, exec. v.p., 1968—. Scoutmaster Boy Scouts Am., Cleve., 1965-74; elder Presbyterian Ch. 1985—). Served to 1st lt. USAF, 1952-54, Korea. Mem. Am. Soc. Assn. Execs. (pres. Cleve. chpt. 1968, Key award 1979), Insts. for Orgn. Mgmt. (mem. bd. trustees 1970-79, chmn. 1974). Republican. Avocations: hiking, genealogy, cross-country skiing. Home: 185 Canyon Rd Chagrin Falls OH 44022 Office: Forging Industry Assn 55 Public Sq Cleveland OH 44113

ATREYA, SUSHIL KUMAR, science educator, researcher; b. Ajmer, India, Apr. 15, 1946; came to U.S., 1966, naturalized, 1975; s. Harvansh Lal and Kailash Vati (Sharma) A.; m. Evelyn M. Bruckner, Dec. 31, 1970; 1 dau., Chloé E. Sc.B., U Rajasthan, India, 1963, M.Sc., 1965; M.S., Yale U., 1968; Ph.D., U. Mich., 1973. Research assoc. physics U. Pitts., 1973-74; asst. to assoc. research scientist Space Physics Research Lab., U. Mich., Ann Arbor, 1974-78, asst. prof., 1978-81, assoc. prof. atmospheric sci., 1981-87, prof., 1987—; prof. associé U. Paris, 1984-85; mem. sci. teams Voyager, Galileo, Space Lab I and Comet Rendezvous Asteroid Flyby Projects; prin. guest investigator Copernicus Orbiting Astron. Observatory; guest investigator Internat. Ultraviolet Explorer Satellite; mem. sci. working groups NASA and Jet Propulsion Lab. Recipient NASA award for exceptional sci. contbns. Voyager Project, 1981, Group Achievement award for Voyager Ultraviolet Spectrometer Investigations, 1981, 86. Author: Atmospheres and Ionospheres of the Outer Planets and their Satellites, 1986; contbr. numerous articles to books and profl. jours. Mem. Am. Geophys. Union, AAAS, Internat. Astron. Union, Am. Astron. Soc. Office: Dept Atmospheric & Oceanic Sci Space Research Bldg 2 455 Hayward U Mich Ann Arbor MI 48109

ATTANASIO, JOHN BAPTIST, law educator; b. Jersey City, Oct. 19, 1954; s. Gaetano and Madeline (Germinario) A.; m. Kathleen Mary Spartana, Aug. 20, 1977; 1 child, Thomas. BA, U. Va., 1976; JD, NYU, 1979; diploma in law, Oxford U., 1982; LLM, Yale U., 1985. Bar: Md. 1979, U.S. Dist. Ct. Md. 1980, U.S. Ct. Appeals (4th cir.) 1980, U.S. Supreme Ct. 1983. Pvt. practice Balt., 1979-81; vis. asst. prof. law U. Pitts., 1982-84; assoc. prof. U. Notre Dame Law Sch., South Bend, Ind., 1985—. Mem. Phi Beta Kappa. Democrat. Roman Catholic. Office: Univ Notre Dame Law Sch Notre Dame IN 46556

ATTEMA, LEONARD, marketing executive; b. Rock Valley, Iowa, July 31, 1940; s. Lane and Henrietta (Moerman) A.; m. Shirley Mae Passick, July 5, 1942; children: Michael, Deborah, Kim, Jody. Mgr. nat. sales Dyna Tech., Mpls., 1974-78, v.p. mktg., 1978-80, sr. v.p., 1980-85; v.p. mktg. Earth Energy Systems, Eden Prarie, Minn., 1985-86, Energx, Eden Prarie, 1986—. Office: Energx Corp 245 E 6th St Saint Paul MN 55101-1988

ATTERBURY, WILLIAM GODWIN, research engineer; b. Columbus, Ohio, Nov. 29, 1958; s. Thomas J. and Jean (Godwin) A. BSME, Rose-Hulman Inst. Tech., Terre Haute, Ind., 1980; MSME, U. Calif., Berkeley, 1981. Registered profl. engr., Ohio. Researcher Battelle Meml. Inst., Columbus, 1981-83, research engr., 1983—. Patentee in field. Mem. Soc. Automotive Engrs. Republican. Home: 4927 Godown Rd Columbus OH 43220 Office: Battelle Meml Inst 505 King Ave Columbus OH 43201

ATTIA, SABRY M., state official; b. Damanhour, Egypt, Apr. 25, 1927; s. Hassan and Galila A. (El-Sayed) A.; came to U.S., 1970, naturalized, 1975; B.S.W., Cairo Sch. Social Work, 1956; M.S.W., Wayne State U., 1973, PhD, 1985; M.Public Adminstrn. U. Detroit, 1979; m. Serria Moustafa Rashid, June 9, 1951; children—Mervat, Mona, Madiha, Mayssa. Social planning cons. The Egyptian Govt., 1961-70; instr. social work Cairo Sch. Social Work, 1958-61; cons. Egyptian Nat. Planning Com., 1961-70; unit mgr. Henry Ford Hosp., Detroit, 1970-72; program dir. Catholic Youth Orgn., Detroit, 1972; med. social worker Hutzel Hosp., Detroit, 1973-75; welfare services supr. Wayne County Dept. Social Services, State of Mich., Detroit, 1975-78, program specialist, central adminstr., 1979-81, dist. dir. N.E. Med. Dist., 1981—; pvt. practice social work, St. Clair Shores, Mich.; dir. Profl. Counseling Services, P.C., Grosse Pointe; dir. The Council Social Agys., Cairo. Recipient Exceptional Achievement award CASE, 1981; cert. social worker, Mich. Mem. Nat. Assn. Social Workers, Acad. Cert. Social Workers, Am. Hosp. Assn., Mich. Unit Mgmt. Assn., Brit. Council Social Workers, Egyptian Assn. Social Workers, Wayne State U. Social Work Alumni Assn. (pres.). Home: 19777 E Ida Ln Grosse Pointe Woods MI 48236 Office: Wayne County Social Services 14060 Maddelein Detroit MI 48205 also: 23915 E Jefferson St Saint Clair Shores MI 48080

ATTNER, PAUL THOMAS, correspondent; b. Concord, Mass., May 9, 1947; s. Raymond Francis and Florence (Robinson) A.; m. Mary Ellen McGuire, June 14, 1969. BA in Communications with high honors, Calif. State U., Fullerton, 1969. Staff writer Washington Post, 1969-84; nat. corr. The Sporting News, St. Louis, 1984—. Author: The Terrapins: History of Football at the Univ. Md., 1975, Fat Lady Sings, 1979, Redskin Country, 1984. Mem. Soc. Profl. Journalists, Prof. Football Writers Am. (four 1st Pl. awards), Profl. Basketball Writers Am., Baseball Writers Assn. Am. Methodist. Avocations: indoor-outdoor gardening, joggging, golf. Office: The Sporting News PO Box 56 Saint Louis MO 63166

ATWATER, HORACE BREWSTER, JR., food company executive; b. Mpls., Apr. 19, 1931; s. Horace Brewster and Eleanor (Cook) A.; m. Martha Joan Clark, May 8, 1955; children—Elizabeth C., Mary M., John C., Joan P. A.B., Princeton U., 1952; M.B.A., Stanford U., 1954. Divisional v.p., dir. mktg. Gen. Mills. Inc., Mpls., 1958-65, mktg. v.p., 1965-70, exec. v.p., 1970-76, chief operating officer, 1976-81, pres., 1977-82, chief exec. officer, 1981—, chmn. bd., 1982—, also dir.; dir. Northwestern Nat. Life Ins. Co., Honeywell Inc., N.W. Bancorp. Trustee Princeton U., MacAlester Coll., Walker Art Ctr.; mem. adv. council Stanford U. Grad. Sch. Bus. Served to lt. USNR, 1955-58. Club: Woodhill Country (Wayzata, Minn.). Office: Gen Mills Inc 9200 Wayzata Blvd Minneapolis MN 55426 *

ATWOOD, H(ARRY) MASON, educator; b. Marshfield, Wis., Oct. 19, 1916; s. Henry Harrison and Anna Rosetta (Mason) A.; m. Opal Thompson Tellman, June 5, 1959; children: Carol Tellman Clark, Diane Tellman Baker, Peggy Tellman Davis, Amy Doris Atwood Birmingham. BS, U. Wis., Stevens Point, 1940; MS, U. Wis., Madison, 1953, PhD, 1958. Tchr. Florence (Wis.) High Sch., 1941-42; instr. chemistry U. Wis., Racine, Milw., Green Bay, Wausau, Marinette, 1946-55, grad. asst., Madison, 1955-57; asst. prof. adult edn. Ind. U., 1957-71; prof. adult and community edn. Ball State U., Muncie, Ind., 1971-83, prof. emeritus, dir. Inst. Gerontology, 1976-83, dir. emeritus, 1983—; mem. Ind. Health Facility Adminstrs. Bd. Registration and Edn., 1976-86; cons. in field. Book rev. editor: Adult Leadership, 1973-77, Lifelong Learning: The Adult Years, 1977-78, The AGHE Newsletter, 1978-81; contbr. chpts. to books and articles to profl. jours. Mem. homes for aging div. Ind. Health Facilities Council, 1964-82; bd. dirs. Delaware County (Ind.) Council on Aging, 1973-80. Served with AUS, 1942-46. Mem. Gerontol. Soc., Assn. Gerontology in Higher Edn., Am. Assn. Adult and Continuing Edn., Ind. Assn. Adult and Continuing Edn., Am. Soc. Aging. Episcopalian. Club: Exchange. Lodge: Elks. Home: 220 Alden Rd Muncie IN 47304

AUBE, RANDY ALAN, accountant; b. Alpena, Mich., Sept. 27, 1957; s. Robert E. Aube and Marsha L. (Jacobs) Wise. Grad., Tiffin U., 1982. CPA, Ohio. Staff acct. Arthur Young & Co., Toledo, 1982-87, mgr., 1987—. Mem. Am. Inst. CPA's, Ohio Soc. CPA's. Republican. Roman Catholic. Club: Toastmasters Internat. (pres. Toledo club 1984-85). Office: Arthur Young & Co 3130 Executive Pkwy Toledo OH 43606

AUBLE, DONALD CARLTON, advertising executive; b. Lodi, Ohio, Apr. 29, 1944; s. Donald C. and Julia C. (Toth) A.; m. Judith F. Fathauer, Aug. 10, 1974; children: Kathryn, Karen, Lauren. BA, Baldwin-Wallace Coll., 1966; MS, Ohio U., 1976. Asst. to the exec. v.p. Am. Soc. Personnel Adminstrn., Berea, Ohio, 1967-70, mng. editor, 1968-70; account exec. Jaeger Adv., Berea, 1971-75, v.p., 1975-80, exec. v.p., 1980—; faculty evening div. Baldwin-Wallace Coll., Berea. Mem. Employment Mgmt. Assn., Berea C. of C. (exec. trustee 1984-86). Republican. Unitarian Universalist. Club: Cleve. Yachting (Rocky River, Ohio) (various offices). Lodge: Masons. Avocations: sailing, photography, flying. Office: Jaeger Adv Two Berea Commons Berea OH 44017

AUBREY, GERTRUDE MARIAN, manufacturing company executive; b. Huntley, Ill., June 4, 1921; s. Harry C. and Mamie Natalie (Hegberg) Sarbaugh; m. Donald Miles Aubrey, June 27, 1972; children: Connie, Robert. Student, Ellis Bus. Coll., 1938-39. Pres. Nat. Inds. Inc., Ocala, Fla., 1972-78, Aubrey Inc., Union, Ill., 1978-81; v.p. Air-Care Ind., Union, 1981-83, Aubrey Nat., Arlington, Tex., 1983; pres. Aubrey Mfg., Inc., Union, 1972—. Mem. Gen. Fedn. of Women's Clubs (Profl. Woman of Yr. 1985). Club: Marengo (Ill.) Woman's (pres. 1968-70).

AUERBACH, MARSHALL JAY, lawyer; b. Chgo., Sept. 5, 1932; s. Samuel M. and Sadie (Miller) A.; m. Carole Landsberg, July 3, 1960; children—Keith Alan, Michael Ward. Student, U. Ill.; J.D., John Marshall Law Sch., 1955. Bar: Ill. 1955. Sole practice Evanston, Ill., 1955-72; ptnr. in charge matrimonial law sect. Jenner & Block, Chgo., 1972-80; mem. firm Marshall J. Auerbach & Assocs., Ltd., Chgo., 1980—; mem. faculty Ill. Inst. Continuing Legal Edn. Author Illinois Marriage and Dissolution of Marriage Act, enacted into law, 1977; (with Albert E. Jenner, Jr.) Historical and Practice Notes to Illinois Marriage and Dissolution of Marriage Act, 1980—; contbr. chpts. to Family Law, Vol. 2. Fellow Am. Acad. Matrimonial Lawyers; mem. Ill. State Bar Assn. (chmn. family law sect. 1971-72), ABA (vice-chmn. family law sect. com. for liaison with tax sect. 1974-76). Home: 2314 Orrington Ave Evanston IL 60201 Office: 180 N LaSalle St Chicago IL 60601

AUFFERT, FRANCIS EUGENE, financial executive; b. Maryville, Mo., July 7, 1949. BS, N.W. Mo. State U., 1972. CPA, Mo. Staff acct. Lester Witte Co., Kansas City, Mo., 1972-76, Troupe, Kehoe, Whiteaker & Kent, Kansas City, Mo., 1976-79; pvt. practice acctg. Gladstone, Mo., 1979-86; chief fin. officer Am. Laminates, Inc., Kansas City, 1986—. Served with USAR, 1972-78. Mem. Am. Inst. CPA's, Mo. Soc. CPA's, Gladstone C. of C. (treas. 1981-86). Republican. Roman Catholic. Lodge: Elks. Avocations: reading, boating, fishing. Home: 1310 NW Vivion Rd Kansas City MO 64118 Office: Am Laminates Inc 655 Sunshine Rd Kansas City KS 66115

AUGUSTIN, ANN SUTHERLAND, author, realtor; b. Evergreen Park, Ill., Aug. 11, 1934; d. Donald A. and Helen E. (Dorsey) Sutherland; m. Edward J. Augustin Jr., Jan. 8, 1955 (div. 1974); children: Edward J. III, Kathryn, Donald J., Suzanne. Student Iowa State U., 1951-53. Exec. sec. Standard Register Co., Chgo., 1953-55; tchr. adult edn. Maine Twp. Sch., Park Ridge, Ill., 1961-68; now realtor Century 21, Arlington Heights, Ill., monthly columnist regional Century 21 newsletter; free-lance writer. Republican. Roman Catholic. Author: Help! I Want to Remodel My Home, 1975; contbr. articles to Reader's Digest, MacFadden-Bartell, Playboy, Chgo. Daily News, Chgo. Tribune, Mt. Prospect Herald, others. Home: 1655 N Arlington Heights Rd Arlington Heights IL 60004 Office: 1635 N Arlington Hts Rd Arlington Heights IL 60004

AUGUSTINE, SANTHOSH, auditor, consultant; b. Alleppey, Kerala, India, Apr. 14, 1950; came to U.S., 1971; s. Davis and Claramma (Michael) A.; m. Mary Margaret Chacko, Dec. 10, 1978; 1 child, David Jude. BS in Hotel Mgmt., U. Houston, 1975; postgrad., U. Ill., Northeastern Ill. U., 1982-83. CPA, Ill. Mgr. restaurant 1976-82; auditor State of Fla., Hillside, Ill., 1985—. Auditor Syro Malabar Ch., Forest Park, Ill., 1987; adv. com. Jyoti Children's Devel., Inc., Skokie, Ill., 1986—. Mem. Am. Inst. CPA's, Ill. CPA Soc. Avocations: chess, reading. Office: State of Fla 4415 W Harrison Suite 448 Hillside IL 60162

AUKAMP, MERLE LOUIS, hospital administrator; b. St. Peter, Ill., Nov. 16, 1932; s. George H. and Lela M. (Niehaus) A.; B.S. in Phys. Edn., U. Ill., 1957; M.H.A., Washington U., St. Louis, 1968; m. Joyce H. Metter, Nov. 16, 1957; children—Regina, Donna, Craig. Coach, tchr. Armstrong (Ill.) Twp. High Sch., 1957-58; recreational dir. Barnes Hosp. Med. Ctr., St. Louis, 1958-67; mem. adminstrv. staff Meml. Hosp., Belleville, Ill., 1967-72, asso. dir., 1971-72; adminstr. Jane Lamb Meml. Hosp., Clinton, Iowa, 1972-75, Alton (Ill.) Meml. Hosp., 1975-82, Marion (Ill.) Meml. Hosp., 1982—; preceptor health care adminstrn. U. Minn., 1976-78, Washington U., St. Louis, 1983—; mem. health adv. council Clinton Community Coll.; mem. part-time faculty Belleville Area Coll.; bd. dirs. Madison County Cancer Soc., Upper Madison County Heart Assn. Served with AUS, 1953-55. Mem. Am. Coll. Hosp. Adminstrs. (regents adv. council 1985-87), Am. Hosp. Assn., Am. Assn. Hosp. Planning, Am. Protestant Hosp. Assn., Ill. Hosp. Assn. (regional pres. 1978-79, 85-86), Southwestern Ill. Hosp. Assn., Greater Alton C. of C. (bd. dirs.), Greater Marion area C. of C. (bd. dirs.). Lutheran. Lodge: Rotary. Office: Marion Meml Hosp 917 W Main St Marion IL 62959

AULABAUGH, NORMAN RICHARD, manufacturing company executive; b. Geneva, Ill., Oct. 29, 1944; s. Norman Lee and Vivian (Savatson) A.; B.S. in Mgmt., No. Ill. U., 1966, M.B.A. in Mgmt., 1968; m. Carol Grace Topel, June 6, 1970. Systems analyst Parker Pen Co., Janesville, Wis., 1972-77, system and programming mgr., 1978-79, then dir. mgmt. info., 1980-85; mgr. materials/mfg. SSI Techs., Janesville, 1985—. Public Expenditure Survey County Budget review chmn., 1978-80. Served with USN, 1968-72. Mem. Assn. for System Mgmt. (pres. Madison chpt.). Republican. Home: Rural Route 4 Janesville WI 53545 Office: PO Box 5002 Janesville WI 53547

AULD, FRANK, psychologist, educator; b. Denver, Aug. 9, 1923; s. Benjamin Franklin and Marion Leland (Evans) A.; m. Elinor James, June 29, 1946; children—Mary, Robert, Margaret. A.B., Drew U., 1946; M.A., Yale U., 1948, Ph.D., 1950. Diplomate: certified psychologist, Mich., Conn., Ont. Instr. psychology Yale U., New Haven; 1950-52, asst. prof. Yale U., 1952-59; assoc. prof. Wayne State U., Detroit, 1959-61; prof. Wayne State U., 1961-67, dir. clin. psychology tng. program, 1960-66; prof. U. Detroit, 1967-70, dir. psychol. clinic, 1967-69; prof. U. Windsor, Ont., Can., 1970—; cons. in field. Author: Steps in Psychotherapy, 1953, Scoring Human Motives, 1959; contbr. articles to profl. jours. Chmn. Dearborn (Mich.) Community Council, 1962; mem. adv. com. on coll. work Episcopal Diocese Mich., 1962-71. Recipient Alumni Achievement award Drew U., 1965. Fellow Am. Psychol. Assn. (evaluation com. 1961-66); mem. Can. Assn. U. Tchrs., Can., Mich. psychol. assns., Ont. Psychol. Assn. (edn. and tng. bd. 1976—), Conn. State Psychol. Soc. (pres. 1958), Soc. Psychotherapy Research, Econ. Club Detroit, Sigma Xi. Home: 1340 Pierce St Birmingham MI 48009 Office: Dept Psychology, U Windsor, Windsor, ON Canada N9B 3P4

AULERT, ROBERT H., JR., software development analyst; b. Chgo., Dec. 28, 1951; s. Robert H. Sr. and Mary Rose (Bianchi) A.; m. Vicki L. Deman, Aug. 7, 1976; 1 child, Alison. Student, U. Ill., 1969-73; BA in Computer Sci., Sangamon State U., 1982; postgrad., U. Minn. Grad Sch. Bus., 1986—. Field agt. Underwriter's Salvage, Chgo., 1974-75; announcer, producer Sta. WDBR Radio, Springfield, Ill., 1975-76; ops. mgr. Sta. WLDS/WEAI Radio, Jacksonville, Ill., 1976-80; programmer, analyst Ill. Dept. Pub. Aid, Springfield, 1980-84; application devel. analyst 3M Co., St. Paul, 1984—. Mem. Data Processing Mgmt. Assn., Mensa. Lutheran. Home: 6664 Homestead Ave S Cottage Grove MN 55016 Office: 3M Co 3M Ctr 224 4N 02 Saint Paul MN 55144

AULL, ELIZABETH BERRYMAN, property management specialist; b. Independence, Mo., Feb. 2, 1951; d. Homer Hayter and Mary Elizabeth (Wulfert) A. AA, Christian Coll., 1971; BS, U. Mo., 1973. With Mo. Senate Staff and Dept. Revenue, Jefferson City, 1973-74; adminstrv. asst. B. State Devel. Agy., St. Louis, 1974-76, Bingham Sketches, Inc., St. Louis, 1976; rate/routing analyst Mo. Pacific R.R., St. Louis, 1976-78; sr. property mgmt. specialist Burlington No. Inc., St. Louis and Springfield, Mo., 1978—. Bd. dirs. Independence Ctr., St. Louis, 1982-83, Mental Health Assn. Greater St. Louis, 1982-83, Mental Health Assn. of Ozarks, Springfield, 1983—; mem. Jr. League St. Louis, 1980-83, property com. Nat. Ave. Christian Ch., Springfield, 1985—; chmn. bldg. subcommittee Ozark Food Harvest Springfield Council of Chs., 1987—. Named one of Outstanding Young Women Am., 1978, 80, 81. Mem. Mineral Area Bd. Realtors, Jr. League Springfield (sec. bldg. com. 1986-87). Republican. Club: Network. Lodge: Soroptimists. Avocations: travelling, art, herb gardening. Home: 2391 E Wayland Springfield MO 65804

AULT, JOHN BRADY, insurance broker; b. Washington, July 18, 1951; s. John Miller and Beatrice Ann (Brady) A.; m. Alice Patricia Rowan, Apr. 14, 1973 (div. Jan. 1983); 1 child, Rebecca Marie. AB in Econs., St. Louis U., 1973, MBA in Fin., 1976. Underwriter Reliance Ins. Co., St. Louis, 1973-76; v.p. Lawton, Byrne and Bruner, St. Louis, 1976-83; asst. v.p. Marsh & McLennan Inc., St. Louis, 1983—. Mem. Ind. Ins. Agts. Clubs: Mo. Athletic (St. Louis); Glen Echo Country (Normandie, Mo.). Home: 4 Hull Ave Webster Groves MO 63119 Office: Marsh & McLennan Inc 515 Olive Saint Louis MO 63101

AUSBURN, KEVIN ROSS, controller; b. Oceanside, Calif., Dec. 29, 1955; s. Ross Buford and Mary Ann (Nilson) A.; m. Lynn Michele Holmes, Aug. 11, 1979; Matthew Ross, Melissa Lynn. BBA in Fin., U. Mo., 1978, MBA in Acctg., 1979. CPA, Mo. Staff acct. Mayer, Hoffman & McCann, Kansas City, Mo., 1980-82; controller So. Mo. Containers, Springfield, 1982—. Active Leadership Springfield, 1985-86; group chmn. United Way of Ozarks, Springfield, 1985-86; bd. dirs., treas. Parenting Pl., Springfield, 1987—; bd. dirs., asst. treas. Springfield Family YMCA, 1987—. Mem. Am. Inst. CPA's, Mo. Soc. CPA's. Republican. Presbyterian. Avocations: fishing, canoeing, golf. Office: So Mo Containers Inc PO Box 4306 Springfield MO 65808

AUSMAN, GARY DAVID, real estate executive; b. Merrill, Wis., Dec. 24, 1955; s. Irving Milton Ausman and Helen Lucille (Feldman) Radke; m. Mary Jo Flynn, May 17, 1986. BBA, U. Wis., 1980. Prin. Ausman Fire Equipment, Madison, Wis., 1978-80; indsl. sales rep. Boise Cascade, Inc., Itasca, Ill., 1980-83; account exec. Autex div. Xerox Corp., Oak Brook, Ill., 1983-85; sales mgr. FreshNet, Inc., Cleve., 1985-86; v.p. Realcorp, Inc., Chgo., 1986—; real estate cons. Hanson Realty, Inc., Chgo., 1986—. Mgmt. cons., bd. dirs. Madison Area Safety Council, 1980. Mem. North Side Real Estate Bd. Republican. Methodist. Avocations: financial planning, tennis, racketball.

AUSNEHMER, JOHN EDWARD, lawyer; b. Youngstown, Ohio, June 26, 1954; s. John Louis and Patricia Jean (Liguore) A.; m. Margaret Mary Kane, Oct. 17, 1981; 1 child, Jill Ellen. BS, Ohio State U., 1976; JD, U. Dayton, 1980. Bar: Ohio 1980, U.S. Dist. Ct. (no. dist.) Ohio 1981, U.S. Supreme Ct. 1984, U.S. Ct. Appeals (6th cir.) 1984. Law clk. Ohio Atty. Gen., Columbus, 1978, Green, Schiavoni, Murphy, Haines & Sgambati Co., L.P.A., 1978; assoc. Dickson Law Office, Petersburg, Ohio, 1979-85 ; sole practice, Youngstown, Ohio, 1984—; asst. prosecuting atty. Mahoning County, Ohio, 1986—. Mem. Am. Trial Lawyers Assn., Ohio Acad. Trial Lawyers, ABA, Ohio State Bar Assn., Nat. Assn. Criminal Def. Lawyers, Mahoning County Bar Assn., Columbiana County Bar Assn., Phi Alpha Delta. Democrat. Roman Catholic. Club: Mahoning Valley Soccer (rep. 1982-84). Home: 51 S Shore Dr Youngstown OH 44512 Office: 14 Boardman-Poland Rd Youngstown OH 44512-4601

AUSTAD, OSCAR, recreational supplies company executive. Pres. Austad Co., Sioux Falls, S.D. Office: The Austad Co 4500 E 10th St Sioux Falls SD 57101 *

AUSTIFF, GERALD ALLYN, state agency manager; b. Jacksonville, Ill., Dec. 23, 1951; s. Ralph Norman and Rita Marie (Moran) A.; m. Sarah Elizabeth Houston, Feb. 14, 1975; children: Joseph, Carrie, Brent and Blake (twins). BA, Western Ill. U., 1974. Cert. records mgr. Records analyst Ill. State Archives, Springfield, 1975-76, state records mgmt. mgr., 1976—. Author: Records Management Manual for Ill. State Agencies, 1985. Mem. Soc. Am. Archivists, Cen. Ill. Assn. Records Mgrs. and Adminstrs. (chmn. budget and fin. com. 1985—, Outstanding Achievement award 1985), Jaycees (sec. Chatham, Ill. chpt. 1983-84). Avocation: golf. Home: 1527 E Walnut Chatham IL 62629 Office: Ill State Archives Capitol Complex Springfield IL 62756

AUSTIN, CAROL JEAN, dentist; b. Detroit Lakes, Minn., May 5, 1938; d. Fred Christian and Vivian Hazel (DiMarco) Fredrickson; m. Jack Fecht, Sept. 6, 1958 (div. April 1972); children: Kay, Randi. DDS, U. Minn., 1976. Clin. instr. dental anatomy and occlusion U. Minn., Mpls., 1976-78; practice dentistry specializing in cosmetic dentistry Mpls., 1977—; cons., lectr. Excel Lab., Mpls., 1986—. Mem. dental mission Christian Med. Soc., Govt. of Honduras, 1982. Mem. ADA, Internat. Acad. Oral Medicine and Toxicology, Acad. Gen. Dentistry (citation Minn. Women's Yearbook, 1983), Acad. Cosmetic Dentistry. Avocations: windsurfing, waterskiing, snowskiing, running, rollerskating. Home: 2925 Dean Pkwy #905 Minneapolis MN 55416 Office: Cross Dentalcare 121 S 8th St #150 Minneapolis MN 55402

AUSTIN, DANIEL WILLIAM, lawyer; b. Springfield, Ill., Feb. 24, 1949; s. Daniel D. and Ruth A. (Ahrenkiel) A.; m. Lois Ann Austin, June 12, 1971; 1 child, Elizabeth Ann. BA, Millikin U., 1971; JD, Washington U., 1974. Bar: Ill. 1974, U.S. Dist. Ct. (cen. dist.) Ill. 1979, U.S. Ct. Appeals (7th cir.) 1980, U.S. Supreme Ct. 1980, U.S. Tax Ct. 1986. Assoc. Miley & Meyer, Taylorville, Ill., 1974-78; ptnr. Miley, Meyer & Austin, Taylorville, 1978-81; v.p. Miley, Meyer, Austin, Spears & Romano P.C., Taylorville, 1981—. Pres. United Fund, Taylorville, 1980, Christian County YMCA, Taylorville, 1983-85. Named one of Outstanding Young Men Am., 1985. Mem. ABA, Ill. Bar Assn., Christian County Bar Assn., Ill. Appellate Lawyers Assn., Order of Barristers. Democrat. Presbyterian. Club: Taylorville Country (pres. 1985). Lodge: Sertoma (Taylorville pres. 1976). Avocations: golf, photography. Home: 14 Westhaven Ct Taylorville IL 62568 Office: Miley Meyer Austin Spears Romano PC 210 S Washington Taylorville IL 62568

AUSTIN, DAVID GEORGE, dentist; b. Dayton, Ohio, Sept. 11, 1951; s. Donald Edward and Mary Josephine (Thompson) A.; m. Mary Allene Allen, Dec. 23, 1977; children: Jonathon David, Jennifer Mary. BA, Ohio Wesleyan U., 1973; DDS, Ohio State U., 1977. Diplomate Nat. Bd. Dental Examiners. Sr. assoc. dentist Dr. Deeds and Assocs., Inc., Columbus, Ohio, 1980-82, clinic dir., 1982-85; gen. practice dentistry Columbus, 1981—; dental cons. Franklin County Dept. Human Services, Columbus, 1982—; bd. dirs. Found. Pedodontique d'Haiti, Port-au-Prince; pres. Brineserve, Inc., Columbus, 1985—. Pres., founder Volunteer Health Services Found., Columbus, 1982—. Served to capt. U.S. Army, 1977-80. Mem. ADA, Ohio Dental Assn. (Humanitarian of Yr. 1986, mem. speakers bur. 1983—,pub. relations council 1984—, vice chmn. radio com. 1985—), Ohio Oil and Gas Assn., Columbus Dental Assn., Xi Psi Phi (pres. Kappa chpt. 1976-77). Home: 4826 McBane St Columbus OH 43220 Office: 3142 Allegheny Ave Columbus OH 43209

AUSTIN, DAVID LAWRENCE, steel company executive; b. Alton, Ill., Oct. 26, 1946; s. Anthony Bernard and Rena Firn (Landon) A.; m. Kathleen Chyrl, Dec. 31, 1966; children: Ginger, David II. BFA and BBA, SIU, Alton, Ill., 1965; BS in Math., SIU, East St. Louis, Ill., 1966; BS in Engring., SIU, Edwardsville, Ill., 1973. Design engr. Emerson Electric Co., St. Louis, 1966-68; salesman J. T. Ryerson and Son, St. Louis, 1968-69; mgr. contract sales U.S. Steel Supply Div., St. Louis, 1969-71; v.p. sales S. J. Iron and Steel Corp., St. Louis, 1971-77; pres. D. L. Austin Steel Supply, Collinsville, Ill., 1977—. Author: (computer program) Sequel, 1984 (T.M. award 1987). Bd. dirs. Boy Scouts Am., Collinsville, 1983; zoning bd. appeals, Collinsville, 1983; Gov. J. Thompson Small Bus. Adv. Com., Springfield, Ill. 1983. Mem. St. Louis Purchasing Mgmt. (Cert. 1982); Visiting Nurse Assn. (bd. dirs. 1979, 86). Republican. Roman Catholic. Lodge: Rotary, KC. Avocations: golf, intergallactic conceptions. Office: D L Austin Steel Supply Corp 1701 Golfview Collinsville IL 62234

AUSTIN, JACK KENNETH, banker; b. Anderson, Mo., Sept. 28, 1923; s. Chester Andrew and Edna Sue (Eddins) A.; B.S., U. Denver, 1952, postgrad., 1953; m. Vivian Lenore Bell, July 21, 1966; children—Kathleen, Mary Ann, Debra. Escrow officer, office mgr., acct. Titles Inc., 1954-58; asst. trust officer Am. Nat. Bank, Denver, 1958-65; asst. account adminstr. 1st Nat. Bank, Denver, 1965-69; trust officer Bank of Commerce, Sheridan, Wyo., 1969-73; v.p., trust officer Wyo. Nat. Bank, Casper, 1973-75; v.p., trust officer Central Trust & Savs. Bank, Geneseo, Ill., 1975—; cons. estate planning, taxation. Served with AUS, 1943-46, ETO. Mem. Quad City Estate Planning Council, Rock Island County Assn. Life Underwriters, Am. Bankers Assn., Henry County Bankers Assn., Henry County Bar Assn. Republican. Congregationalist. Clubs: Elks, Kiwanis. Home: 26 Geneseo Hills Geneseo IL 61254 Office: 101 N State St Geneseo IL 61254

AUSTIN, KENNETH RALPH, insurance executive; b. Keosauqua, Iowa, Mar. 15, 1920; s. James Clayton and Nancy M. (Landreth) A.; m. LaVerne Eleanor Turin, May 9, 1942; children: Marilyn Ruth, Alan Karl. B.C.S., Drake U., 1941; M.S., U. Iowa, 1942. With Equitable Life Ins. Co. Iowa, Des Moines, 1947-85; asst. sec. Equitable Life Ins. Co. Iowa, 1953-59, supt. policy issue, 1959-60, agy. v.p., 1960-64, v.p., controller, 1964-66, exec. v.p., 1966-69, pres., 1969-81, chief exec. officer, 1970-83, chmn., 1981-85. Bd. dirs. Drake U.; past bd. dirs. Simpson Coll., Marycrest Coll., South Iowa Methodist Homes, Am. Assn. Homes for Aging; bd. govs. Iowa Coll. Found. Served to comdr. USNR, 1942-45. Fellow Life Mgmt. Inst.; mem. Life Office Mgmt. Assn. (past dir.), Am. Council Life Ins. (past dir.). Home: 2880 Grand Apt 402 Des Moines IA 50312 Office: PO Box 1635 Des Moines IA 50306

AUSTIN, OTIS GENE, medical director; b. Alliance, Ohio, Sept. 12, 1917; s. John Sherwood and Mary Frances (Walker) A.; m. Ruth Elizabeth Burrus, Dec. 24, 1944 (dec. Mar. 1983); children: John S. II, Frances A., William B.; m. Betty Jo Perrine, Sept. 17, 1983. BS, Mt. Union Coll., Alliance, 1940; MD, Vanderbilt U., 1943. Diplomate Am. Bd. Obstetrics and Gynecology. Pvt. practice obstetrics Ohio, 1947-65; pres. Austin, Welty, Knochs & Kuehn, Inc., Medina, Ohio, 1965-83, Medina Gynecologists Inc., 1965-83; med. dir. Medina Community Hosp., 1984—; bd. dirs. Emerald Health Network Preferred Provider Orgn., Cleve. Contbr. numerous articles to profl. jours. Served to capt. AUS, 1944-46, ETO. Fellow Am. Coll. Surgeons; mem. Am. Coll. Obstetricians and Gynecologists (life), Medina C. of C. (bd. dirs. 1984—), Alpha Omega Alpha. Republican. Methodist. Avocations: golf, reading, music, gardening. Home: 33 Squire's Ct Medina OH 44256 Office: Medina Community Hosp 990 E Washington Medina OH 44256

AUSTIN, RICHARD HENRY, state official; b. Ala., May 6, 1913; s. Richard H. and Lelia (Hill) A.; m. Ida B. Dawson, Aug. 19, 1939; 1 dau., Hazel. B.S., Detroit Inst. Tech., 1937; LL.D. (hon.), Detroit Coll. Bus., 1971, Mich. State U., 1985. Pvt. practice accounting Detroit, 1941-71; auditor Wayne County, Mich., 1967-70; sec. of state Mich. Lansing, 1971—; del. Mich. Constl. Conv., 1961-62. Bd. dirs. Harper-Grace Hosp., Detroit, Met. Detroit United Found., Community Found. S.E. Mich., Detroit YMCA, Detroit council Boy Scouts Am. Mem. Am. Inst. C.P.A.s, Mich. Assn. C.P.A.s (Distinguished Achievement award 1972). Democrat. Home: 3374 Oakman Blvd Detroit MI 48238 Office: Office of Sec of State State Capitol Lansing MI 48913

AUSTIN-LETT, GENELLE, educator; b. Chgo.; d. Howard Joseph and Evelyn Gene (Reynolds) Blomquist. B.A., U. Ill., Chgo., 1969; M.A., No. Ill. U., 1972. Teaching and research asst. No. Ill. U., 1970-71; TV prodn. asst. Nat. Coll. Edn. High Sch. Workshop, 1972; prof. mass media and critical consumer Principia Coll., summer 1975; reviewer in interpersonal communication, media and behavioral scis. Houghton Mifflin, Harper & Row, William C. Brown, and Wadsworth Pub., 1972—, also asso. prof. speech communication and media Ill. Central Coll., East Peoria, 1971-79; editorial cons. Concordia Pub. House, 1978-82; program dir. Clayton (Mo.) U., 1978-82; tchr. English, Principia Upper Sch., 1983—; asst. prof. communications Meramec Community Coll.; coordinator performing arts multimedia presentations, publicity and recruitment; lectr. media consumerism, psychopolitics and advt.; instr. communications, cons. crisis intervention Fed. Police Tng., 1974-75. Group leader Community Devel. Council, 1974; organizer 9th Ward Teenage Republicans, Chgo., 1963, coordinator, 1967-69; adviser to Ill. Central Coll. Young Reps., 1971-75; clk., dir. exec. bd., chmn. bd. 1st Ch. of Christ, Scientist, Peoria; nat. advisory bd. Am. Security Council; mem. Rep. Nat. Com. Recipient Honors Day recognition U. Ill., 1968, hon. mention Nat. Arts and Letters playwriting contest, 1972; lic. life ins. agt., Mo. Mem. Ill. Speech and Theatre Assn., Speech Communication Assn., Central States Speech Assn., Internat. Data Speak. Clubs: U.S. Senatorial, Bible Investigation, Racquet. Author: (with others) Instructor's Manual for Mass Communication and Human Interaction, 1977; (with Jan Sprague) Talk to Yourself, 1976; contbr. articles to Christian Sci. periodicals.

AUW, DOROTHY BABETTE, psychologist, health care administrator; b. Chgo., Mar. 13, 1935; d. John Robert and Elise Anna (Tietz) A. BA, DePaul U., 1956; MA, Loyola U., Chgo., 1965. Psychologist guidance ctr. Loyola U., Chgo., 1956-65; psychologist Cath. Charities Child Mental Health Ctr., Chgo., 1965-78; dir. Cath. Charities Family Counseling Ctr., Chgo., 1978—. Council chairperson St. Nicolai United Ch. of Christ, 1975-76, 84-87; sec. Ill. Conf. United Ch. Christ, 1987—. Mem. Am. Psychol. Assn., Am. Orthopsychiat. Assn., Ill. Psychol. Assn., Ill. United Ministries for Higher Edn. (treas. 1986—). Avocations: knitting, sewing, reading, opera. Office: Catholic Charities 126 N Desplaines St Chicago IL 60606

AVEDON, BRUCE, business consultant; b. Atlantic City, Dec. 31, 1928; s. N. Jay and Rosalie Ann (Sholtz) A.; B.S., Yale U., 1950; m. Shirlee Florence Young, May 19, 1951; children—Linda Michele, Bruce Frederick. Vice pres. Sholtz Ins. Agy., Inc., Miami, Fla., 1950-51; various positions to dir. planning State Mut. Life Assurance Co. Am., Worcester, Mass., 1953-69, also sec. Am. Variable Annuity Life Assurance Co., Worcester, 1967-69; v.p. equity products Ohio Nat. Life Ins. Co., Cin., 1969-83, also v.p., dir. O.N. Equity Sales Co., Cin, 1973-83; pres., dir. Ohio Nat. Fund, Inc., 1978-83; ins./investment products cons. to fin. services industry, 1983—. Served to lt. AUS, 1951-53; maj. Finance Corps Res. ret. Mem. Investment Co. Inst. (pension com.), Life Office Mgmt. Assn. (equity products and annuity com.), Nat. Assn. Securities Dealers (qualifications com. 1982—), Res. Officers Assn., Mil. Order World Wars. Republican. Methodist. Clubs: Yale (Cin.), Masons, Order Eastern Star. Home: 6601 Hitching Post Ln Cincinnati OH 45230 Office: PO Box 30324 Cincinnati OH 45230

AVELLONE, FRANCIS PAUL, actuarial and pension consulting firm exec.; b. St. Louis, Mar. 5, 1926; s. Salvatore Carmelo and Mary Amanda (Gingrich) A.; B.B.A., Miami U., 1947; M.B.A., Roosevelt U., 1964; m. Elizabeth Therese Byrne, Apr. 26, 1947; children—Mary Eichmann, Richard, William, Francis, Thomas, Anne. Joined U.S. Navy, 1943, commd. ensign, 1945, advanced through grades to comdr.; ret., 1966; with Louis Behr Orgn., Inc., Chgo., 1966—, exec. vice-pres., 1972-76, pres., 1976—. Mem. Am. Acad. Actuaries, Am. Soc. Chartered Life Underwriters, Am. Soc. Pension Actuaries, Am. Legion, Navy League. Roman Catholic. Rotarian. Home and Office: 650 Green Bay Rd #200 Lake Bluff IL 60044

AVENSON, DONALD D., state legislator; b. Mpls., Sept. 16, 1944; s. Donald Conrad and Wilma (Morey) A.; m. Diane Duda, 1964; children: Eric, Clay, Nicolle. Student, U. No. Iowa; BS, U. Wis., River Falls, 1970. Office mgr. Oelwein Tool and Die, Iowa, 1970-84, pres., 1984—; state rep. 15th dist. State of Iowa House Reps., Des Moines, 1973-82, state rep. 23d dist., 1982—, asst. majority leader, 1975-78, minority floor leader, 1979-82, speaker, 1983—. Office: House of Reps State Capitol Des Moines IA 50319 *

AVERILL, STUART CARSON, psychiatry educator; b. Sacramento, Calif., May 31, 1924; s. Harry Weston and Elizabeth Alice (Carson) A.; m. Elizabeth Kathryn Walter, Aug. 10, 1946; children: Timothy, Thomas, Richard, Elizabeth. Student, Johns Hopkins U., 1942-43; pre-med. student, U. Calif., Berkeley, 1946-48, MA in Anatomy, 1950; MD, U. Calif., San Francisco, 1952; grad., The Menninger Sch. Psychiatry, Topeka, 1958; hon. grad. career tng. in child psychiatry, The Menninger Sch. Psychiatry, 1975; grad., The Topeka Inst. Psychoanalysis, 1973, grad. child psycholanalysis, 1975. Cert. Am. Bd. Psychiatry and Neurology. Intern San Francisco County Hosp., 1952-53; resident Topeka State Hosp., 1953-54, 1956-58; clin. dir. Boys Indsl. Sch., Topeka, 1958-72; faculty adult and child tng. programs Menninger Sch. Psychiatry The Menninger Found., 1958—; med. dir. C.F. Menninger Meml. Hosp., 1984—; staff psychiatrist adult outpatient clinic The Menninger Found., 1972-76; dir. diagnostic and consultation service adult outpatient dept., 1976-84; tng. and supr. analyst Topeka Inst. Psychoanalysis, 1982—. Contr. articles to profl. jours. Served with USNR. Fellow Am. Psychiat. Assn.; mem. AMA, Kans. Psychiat. Assn., Kans. Med. Soc., Shawnee County Med. Soc. (past. pres.), Am. Group Psychotherapy Assn., Kans. Group Psychotherapy Assn., Topeka Psychoanalytic Soc. (past pres.), Am. Psychoanalytic Assn. (cert.), Assn. Child Psychoanalysis. Democrat. Mem. United Ch. Christ. Avocations: bagpipng, fishing, singing, bicycling. Home: 4404 Holly Ln Topeka KS 66604 Office: The Menninger Found Box 829 Topeka KS 66601

AVERY, GERALD KENNETH, oil company executive; b. Petoskey, Mich., Aug. 14, 1953; s. Kenneth James Avery and Marilyn Fay (Stoneham) Blauman; m. Carie Sue Fowler, Aug. 26, 1978; children: Krysten, Jeremiah, Taylor. Pres. Oil Trust Corp., Benzonia, Mich., 1983—; v.p. Peninsula Oil Co., Traverse City, Mich., 1985—; gen. ptnr., cons. Peninsula Oil & Gas, Ltd., Traverse City, 1985—. Avocations: architecture, law, karate. Home and Office: 6312 Demerly Rd Benzonia MI 49616

AVERY, MARY EMERSON, management consultant; b. Indpls., July 30, 1953; s. John Thomas and Patricia Mae (Campbell) Emerson; m. Thomas Emerson Avery, Nov. 25, 1983; children: Katharine Lauren, Dylan Emerson, Ryan Thomas. BA, U. Wis., Milw., 1975; MBA, U. Wis., Whitewater, 1979. Br. banking officer First Wis. Bank, Milw., 1976-77, asst. br. mgr., 1977-79, comml. banking officer, 1979-80; dir. adminstrv. Coulee Region C.A.P., Inc., 1980-82; exec. dir. C.A.P., Inc., Westby, Wis., 1982-86; owner Bus. Devel. Services, Ripon, Wis., 1986—. vice chmn. United Way of Greater Milw., 1979-80; regional dir. Community Devel. Soc., 1980-82; sec. Douglas Mental Health Clinic, Viroqua, Wis., 1981—; v.p. Wis. Community Action Program, 1982-86; Wis. Bus. Devel. Fin. Corp., Madison, 1982—; bd. dirs. State Job Tng. Coordinating Council, Madison, 1982—. Mem. Am. Inst. Bankers (bd. govs. 1977-79), LWV. Methodist. Club: MSPAC (La Crosse) (sec. 1985-86). Avocations: cross-country skiing, racquetball, bicycling, birding. Home: Route 3 Box 343 Ripon WI 54971 Office: Bus Devel Services PO Box 461 Ripon WI 54971

AVERY, WILLIAM PAUL, political scientist, educator; b. Erwin, N.C., Feb. 7, 1942; s. Sherrill William and Vida (Parker) A.; BS, U. Tenn., Knoxville, 1968, MA, 1971; PhD Tulane U., 1975; children: Paul Kevin, Amanda Kay. Instr. polit. sci. Tulane U., New Orleans, 1972-74; asst. prof. polit. sci. U. Nebr., Lincoln, 1974-78, assoc. prof., 1978-83, prof., 1983—, vice chmn. dept. polit. sci., 1977-79; vis. prof. Warsaw U., Poland, 1980-81. Nebr. chmn. Com. of Ams. for Canal Treaties, 1978; U. Nebr. coordinating com. United Way, 1979; mem. state steering com. Common Cause Nebr., 1984—; exec. com. Lancaster County Dem. Party, 1984-86; state chmn. Common Cause, 1986—; bd. dirs. Nebraskans for Peace, 1985-86. Served with USAF, 1960-64. U.S. Office Edn. grantee, 1976-78. Mem. Am. Polit. Sci. Assn., Internat. Studies Assn., Peace Sci. Soc., Midwest Polit. Sci. Assn., So. Polit. Sci. Assn., Latin Am. Studies Assn., Midwest Assn. Latin Am. Studies. Editor: The Process of Rural Transformations, 1979, Rural Change and Pub. Policy, 1980, America in a Changing World Political Economy, 1982; co-editor: Internat. Political Economy Yearbook, 1986—; contbr. articles to profl. jours. Home: 1925 E St Lincoln NE 68510 Office: Dept Polit Sci U Nebr Lincoln NE 68588

AVISCHIOUS, RAYMOND, food distribution company executive; b. Chgo., Oct. 23, 1931; m. Arlene Lentner; children—Tom, Gary. B.S. in Mktg, U. Ill., 1953. With Kroger Co., 1953; with Shurfine Central Corp., Northlake, Ill., 1955—; pres., gen. mgr. Shurfine Central Corp., 1971—, also dir. Bd. dirs. Aid Assn. Lutherans, Appleton, Wis. Served with AUS, 1953-55. Office: Shurfine Cen Corp 2100 N Mannheim Rd Northlake IL 60164

AVNET, ALLAN, construction company owner, engineering consultant; b. Detroit, June 16, 1939; m. Jane Ann Simpson, Mar. 12, 1977; children—Jeff Wayne, Jay Robert. B.S. M.E., Am. Western U., 1972. Pvt. practice cons. mech. engr. Boardman, Ohio, 1970-77; mech. engr. BASF Video Corp., Fountain Valley, Calif., 1977-80, Gen. Monitors, Costa Mesa, Calif., 1980-82; prin. mech. engr. MAI/Basic Four, Tustin, Calif., 1982-84; owner Tri-County Diecor Built, Salem, Ohio, 1984—; cons. engr. Trans Com, Costa Mesa, 1980. Mem. ASME, Soc. Plastic Engrs. Jewish. Club: Outspoken Wheelmen. Avocation: Photography. Home: 11615 Beaver Creek Rd Salem OH 44460

AVRIL, ARTHUR CHRISTIAN, manufacturing executive; b. Cin., Jan. 8, 1901; s. John Anton and Florentine (Conver) A.; m. Mary Elizabeth Joyce, June 18, 1930. B in Engring., Ohio State U., 1925. Registered profl. engr., Ohio. Mining engr. France Stone Co., Toledo, 1925-28; pres. Avril Tru-Batch Concrete Co., Cin., 1928-36, Sakrete Inc., Cin., 1936—, A&T Devel. Co., Cin., 1951—, Sakrete Sales Inc., Cin., 1953—, Sakrete of Ind. Inc., Westfield, 1964—; ptnr. Sakret Trockenbaustoffe, Giessen, Fed. Republic Germany, 1966—. Inventor concrete processing and blending equipment. Mem. bldg. com. Children's Hosp., com. of 100-Ohio State U. Mem. ASTM, Delta Tau Delta. Clubs: Cincinnati; Queen City; Brown's Run. Lodges: Rotary, Masons. Avocations: golf, photography, travel. Home: 111 Congress Run Rd Cincinnati OH 45215 Office: Sakrete Inc PO Box 17087 St Bernard Fischer Ave and B&O RR Cincinnati OH 45217

AWAIS, GEORGE MUSA, obstetrician, gynecologist; b. Ajloun, Jordan, Dec. 15, 1929; s. Musa and Meha (Koury) A.; m. Nabila Rizk, June 24, 1970. A.B., Hope Coll., 1955; M.D., U. Toronto, 1960. Diplomate Am. Bd. Obstetrics and Gynecology. Intern U. Toronto Hosps., Ont., Can., 1960-61, resident in obstetrics and gynecology, 1961-64, chief resident, 1965; chief resident Harlem Hosp., Columbia U., N.Y.C., 1966; asst. obstetrician and gynecologist Cleve. Met. Gen. Hosp., 1967, assoc. obstetrician and gynecologist, 1969; instr. obstetrics and gynecology Case Western Res. U., Cleve., 1967-70, asst. obstetrician and gynecologist MacDonald House, 1970, asst. prof., 1970, asst. clin. prof. dept. reproductive biology, 1971, asst. obstetrician and gynecologist Univ. Hosps., 1971; mem. staff, dept. gynecology Cleve. Clinic Found., 1971—; chmn. dept. obstetrics and gynecology King Faisal Specialist Hosp. and Research Ctr., Riyadh, 1975-76; cons. panel mem. Internat. Corr. Soc. Obstetricians and Gynecologists, 1971. Contbr. articles to publs. in field, papers, reports to confs., TV appearances, Saudi Arabia. Fellow ACS, Am. Coll. Obstetricians and Gynecologists, Royal Coll. Surgeons Can.; mem. AMA, AAAS, Acad. Medicine of Cleve., Am. Infertility Soc. Office: Cleveland Clinic Dept Gynecology Cleveland OH 44106

AWL, CHARLOTTE JANE, nursing educator; b. St. Louis, Apr. 28, 1935; d. Herbert Vincent and Elizabeth Edwards (White) Pate; diploma Presbyn. Hosp. Sch. Nursing, Phila., 1956; student U. Pa., 1957-58; B.S. with distinction in Gen. Nursing, U. Ind., 1960, M.S. in Nursing Edn., 1961; postgrad. (Ada Belle Clark Welsh scholar), Ill. State U., 1978—; cert. CPR instr.; m. Richard Allen Awl, Sept. 2, 1962; children—Deborah Jane, David Allen, Stephen Scott. Team leader Presbyn. Hosp., Phila., 1956-57, head nurse women's surg. ward, 1957-58; staff nurse Bloomington (Ind.) Hosp., part-time 1958-60; pvt. duty nurse Robert Long Hosp., Indpls., spring 1960, Nursing Service Bur. Dist. 5, Ind. State Nurses Assn., Indpls., summer 1962; instr. med.-surg. nursing De Pauw U. Sch. Nursing, Greencastle and Indpls., 1961-63; instr. Meth. Med. Center Sch. Nursing, Peoria, Ill., 1963-64, part-time staff nurse Meth. Med. Center of Ill., 1964-66; cons. dept nursing Bradley U., Peoria, 1966-67, asst. prof., 1967-74, asso. prof., 1974—, assoc. chmn. dept. nursing, 1972-78, assoc. dir. div. nursing, 1978—, standard first aid instr. Am. Red Cross Multimedia. Mem. AAUP, Am. Nurses Assn., Nat. League Nursing, Assn. Operating Room Nurses, Council on Grad. Edn. for Adminstrn. in Nursing, AAUW, Sigma Theta Tau, Pi Lambda Theta, Kappa Delta Pi, Phi Kappa Phi. Presbyterian. Office: Bradley Univ Div Nursing Peoria IL 61625

AX, TONI SUE, lawyer; b. Evansville, Ind., Oct. 1, 1940; d. John R. and Kathryn M. (Steinkamp) A. BA cum laude, Butler U., 1962, EdS, 1966; MAT, Harvard U., 1963; JD magna cum laude, Ind. U., 1970. Bar: Ind. 1970, U.S. Dist. Ct. (so. dist.) Ind. 1970, U.S. Tax Ct. 1971, U.S. Ct. Appeals (7th cir.) 1972, U.S. Supreme Ct. 1978. High sch. tchr. Indpls. Pub. Schs., 1963-64; jr. high sch. tchr. MSD of Washington Twp., Indpls., 1964-65; cons. English Dept. Pub. Instrn. State of Ind., Indpls., 1965-67; contract adminstr. Naval Avionics Ctr., Indpls., 1967-70; assoc. Barnes, Hickam, Pantzer & Boyd, Indpls., 1970-76; ptnr. Barnes & Thornburg, Indpls., 1977—; mem. com. on character and fitness Ind. Supreme Ct., Indpls., 1982—. Contbr. articles to profl. jours. Pres. Butler U. Alumni Assn., Indpls., 1984-86, v.p. 1982-84, trustee, 1987—; past. pres., v.p., treas. Ind. U. Sch. Law Indpls. Alumni Assn.; chmn. atty.'s div. United Way Greater Indpls., 1976; mem. task force on student activities, Commn. on the Future of Butler U.; past bd. dirs., sec., parliamentarian Cen. Ind. Counicl Camp Fire Girls; mem. Devon Civic League; com. mem. 500 Festival of the Arts Sch. Exhibit. Recipient Citation for Outstanding Contributions, Ind. Council Tchrs. English, 1967, Alumni Achievement award Butler U., 1986. Fellow Ind. Bar Found. (charter), Indpls. Bar Found. (charter disting.); mem. ABA (taxation sect., adj. mem. employee benefits com.), Ind. Bar Assn. (bd. mgrs. 1984-86, taxation sect., scholarship chmn., membership chmn., past co-chmn. written publs. com., House of Dels.), Indpls. Bar Assn. (v.p. 1984, treas. 1980-83, bd. mgrs. 1978-84, exec. com., del. to taxation sect., Presdl. Citation 1981, Spl. Recognition award 1984), Ind. Bar Ctr. (master donor, co-chmn. 11th dist. fund raising drive), Midwest Pension Conf. (Ind. chpt., chmn. 1983, vice chmn. 1982, membership com. chmn.), Am. Arbitration Assn. (arbitrator 1977-86), Internat. Found. Employee Benefits Plan, Montgolfier Soc. Ind. (sec.), Aircraft Owners and Pilots Assn. Democrat. Club: Mercedes Benz of Am. First female in Ind. licensed by FAA as comml. hot air balloon pilot. Office: Barnes & Thornburg 1313 Merchants Bank Bldg 11 S Meridian St Indianapolis IN 46204

AXDAHL, LEE OLIN, radio broadcasting executive; b. St. Paul, May 12, 1957; s. Lester Glenn and Evelyn Irene (Smith) A.; m. Roanne Mary Tardy, Oct., 1981; 1 child, Erik Lee. BA, Augustana Coll., Sioux Falls, S.D., 1975. Gen. mgr. Minn. Pub. Radio, Inc., St. Paul, 1979—; pres., treas. Kirkwood Broadcasting, Inc., Sioux Falls, 1985—; council head KRSD and KRSW Regional Adv. Council, Sioux Falls, 1984—. Mem. Pub. Radio in MidAm., Sioux Falls Advt. Fedn. (membership com. 1986—), Sioux Falls C. of C. (com. mem. 1985—). Avocations: electronic design, woodworking, old home restoration. Home: 628 W 20th St Sioux Falls SD 57105 Office: Kirkwood Broadcasting Inc Box 1580 Sioux Falls SD 57101-1580

AXELROD, BARRY LEON, real estate financier; b. N.Y.C., Apr. 25, 1947; s. John and Frances Virginia (Cohen) A.; m. Holly Beth Golding, July 19, 1970; children—Rebecca Elyse, Jessica Gayle. B.A., No. Mich. U., 1969; M.A., Northeastern Ill. U., 1970. Producer, dir. New Trier Twp. Instructional TV, Winnetka, Ill., 1969-71; mortgage analyst Heitman Mortgage Co., Chgo., 1971-74; loan officer B.B. Cohen & Co., Chgo., 1974-75; asst. v.p. Banco Mortgage Co., Chgo., 1975-79; v.p. Cohen Fin. Corp., Chgo., 1979-83; pres. Golding Axelrod & Co., Chgo., 1983-86; Axelrod & Co., Park Ridge, Ill., 1983. Sportcaster, football, basketball and hockey, high sch. and colls. Chgo. area, 1981—. Bd. dirs. Young Men's Jewish Council, Chgo., 1972-79, v.p. 1979; mem. Jr. Real Estate Bd. Chgo., pres. 1978. Mem. Internat. Council Shopping Ctrs., Assn. Ind. Real Estate Brokers, Aircraft Owners and Pilots Assn., No. Mich. U. Alumni Assn. (co-chmn. Chgo. chpt.), Pal-Waukee Airport Assn. (bd. dirs.). Office: Axelrod & Co 1300 Higgins Rd Park Ridge IL 60068

AXELROD, LEONARD, management consultant; b. Boston, Oct. 27, 1950; s. Morris and Doris S. Axelrod. BA, Ind. U., 1972; MPA, U. So. Calif., 1974; JD, Hamline U., 1982. Asst. dir. Ind. Jud. Ctr. Ind. U. Sch. Law, Indpls., 1974-76; cons. Booz, Allen & Hamilton, Washington, 1976-77; staff assoc. Nat. Ctr. State Cts., St. Paul, 1977-82; ptnr. Ct. Mgmt. Cons., Mpls., 1982-87; ptnr. Friedman, Farrar & Axelrod, Mpls., 1984-86; cons. Ctr. Jury Studies, Vienna, Va., 1979-82, Calif. Atty. Gen., 1972-73, Control Data Bus. Advisers, Mpls., 1982—; prin. Ct. Mgmt. Concepts, Mpls.,1987—; mem. presdl. search com. Hamline U., 1980-81. Author: North Dakota Bench Book, 1982; contbr. articles to profl. jours.; assoc. editor Law Rev. Digest, 1982. Mem. exec. bd. Am. Jewish Com., Mpls.-St. Paul, 1980; reporter Minn. Citizen Conf. on Cts., 1980. Samuel Miller scholar, 1981. Mem. ABA, Am. Soc. Pub. Adminstrn., So. Calif. Soc. Public Adminstrn., Am. Judicature Soc., Booz, Allen & Hamilton Alumni (pres. Minn. 1980), Brandeis Soc. (exec. dir. Mpls. 1980), U. So. Calif. Midwest Alumni (exec. bd. Chgo. 1974), Phi Alpha Alpha. Republican. Jewish. Home: 2051 Loop Station Minneapolis MN 55402 Office: Ct Mgmt Concepts 11868 Airmail Facility Minneapolis MN 55111

AXELSON, CARL MARK, management consultant; b. Omaha, Nebr., Apr. 2, 1948; s. Kjell and Arlene Frances (Walters) A.; m. Nancy Marian Petersen, Sept. 2, 1972; children: Emily Anne, Erik Kjell. BS in Indsl. Mgmt., Purdue U., 1971; MBA, U. Ill., 1973. Systems analyst Chgo. Title and Trust, 1973-75, mgr., 1975-78; cons. Benton, Schneider & Assocs., Naperville, Ill., 1978-80, prin., 1980-82, v.p., ptnr., 1982—. Author: (software system) Micro Inventory System, 1985, Telcom Cost Allocation Program, 1982, Telcom Network Optimizer, 1979, System Failure Simulator, 1978. Mem. Am. Mgmt. Assn., MBA Assn., Soc. for Computer Simulation, Purdue Alumni Assn. Republican. Home: 328 Brooklea Ct Naperville IL 60565 Office: Benton Schneider & Assocs 100 Park St Naperville IL 60540

AYERS, GEORGE EDWARD LEWIS, university president; b. Quincy, Ill., Nov. 20, 1938; s. David Lewis and Mary Elizabeth (Wheeler) A.; m. Carolyn Sue Wasson, May 5, 1960; children: Deanne, Danita, Darryl. BS, Western Ill. U., 1961; MA, U. No. Colo., 1963, EdD, 1965; LHD (hon.), SUNY. Prof. Mankato State U., Minn., 1969-71; asst. v.p. acad. affairs Met. State U., St. Paul, 1971-73, v.p. adminstrv. affairs, 1973-74, v.p., dean acad affairs, 1974-78; pres. Massasoit Community Coll., Brockton, Mass., 1978-82, Chgo. State U., 1982—; adv. bd. Inst. Mgmt. Lifelong Edn., Prednl. Coouncil Employment of Handicapped. Co-author: Conflict Management: A 1976 Human Relations Training Guide, 1976; ednl. reports; editor: Recruitment and Selection of Support Personnel, 1969. Chmn. adv. com. Blcak Creativity; trustee Milton Acad.; bd. dirs. Chgo. Cable Access, Roseland Community Hosp., S. Cen. Community Services, Chgo. Symphony Orch. Recipient Nat. Rehab. Assn. Cordelia Shelving Ellis award, 1969; recipient Western Ill. U. Alumni Achievement award, 1981. Mem. Am. Assn. Higher Edn., Am. Personnel and Guidance Assn., Am. Council Edn., Assn. Am. Colls. (bd. dirs.), Am. Assn. Univ. Adminstrs. (bd.dirs.), Assn. Urban Univs. (sec. bd. dirs.). Home: 10400 Longwood Dr Chicago IL 60643 Office: Chicago State Univ 95th St at King Dr Chicago IL 60628

AYERS, LEONA WESTON, pathologist, physician, educator; b. Garner, N.C., Jan. 14, 1940; d. William Albert and Ida Bertha (Bell) Weston; B.S., Duke, 1962, M.D., 1967; m. James Cordon Ayers, Aug. 1, 1965; children—Ashley Albert, Alan Andrew. Intern, Duke U. Med. Center, Durham, N.C., 1967-68, resident in pathology, 1968-69; resident in pathology Univ. Hosps., Columbus, Ohio, 1969-71; individual practice medicine, specializing in pathology Columbus, Ohio, 1970—; dir. div. clin. microbiology Univ. Hosp., Columbus, 1970—; attending staff, 1971—; asst. prof. allied health professions Ohio State U., Columbus, 1974-78, pathology, 1971-77, assoc. prof. pathology, 1977—, allied health professions, 1978—; cons. in field. Diplomate Am. Bd. Pathology. Fellow Am. Soc. Clin. Pathologists, Coll. Am. Pathologists (mem. microbiology resource com.). Contbr. articles to profl. publs. Home: 3870 Lyon Dr Columbus OH 43220 Office: 410 W 10th Ave Columbus OH 43210

AYERS, RICHARD WAYNE, electrical manufacturing company official; b. Atlanta, Aug. 23, 1945; s. Harold Richard and Martha Elizabeth (Vaughan) A.; B.B.A., Ga. State Coll., 1967; M.B.A., Ind. U., 1969; m. Nancy Katherine Martin, Aug. 9, 1969. Specialist mktg. communications research Gen. Electric Co., Schenectady, 1969-70, copywriter Lamp div., Cleve., 1970-73, supr., distbr. advt. and sales promotion, 1973-75, supr. comml. and indsl. promotional programs Gen. Electric Lighting Bus. Group, 1975-79, mgr. comml. and indsl. market distbr. and promotional programs, 1979-87, mgr. comml and indsl. sales communications, 1987—; lectr. in field. Author: Winning Through Promotion, 1987. Recipient Best Indsl. Promotion award Advt. Age, 1974, Premium Showcase award Nat. Premium Sales Execs., 1975, 76, 87, Gold Key award Nat. Premium Mfrs. Reps., 1976, 77, 87 Golden Key Communicators award Factory mag., 1976; Leader award Direct Mktg. Assn., 1983. Dir.-at-large Ga. Young Reps., 1966-67. Mem. Blue Key, Delta Sigma Pi, Beta Gamma Sigma. Office: Nela Park Building 307 Cleveland OH 44112

AYERS, WILLIAM THOMAS, analytical chemist; b. Akron, Ohio, Apr. 11, 1940; s. William Thomas and Rose Mary (Fostyk) A.; m. Terry Lee Allen, Feb. 6, 1965; 1 child, Kimberly Jacqueline. BS, U. Akron, 1966, MS, 1969, PhD, 1978. Alanlytical chemist Norton Co., Stow, Ohio, 1970-75; sr. chemist Edmont Wilson Co., Canton, Ohio, 1975-79, McGean Co., Cleve., 1979-80; chief chemist Harshaw Chem. Co., Cleve., 1981-83; lab. mgr. Clevite Industries, Inc., Milan, Ohio, 1984—. Contbr. articles to profl. jours. Served with USNR, 1958-62. Mem. Am. Chem. Soc., Soc. Applied Spectroscopy, Akron Rubber Group, Northeast Ohio Rubber Group. Republican. Lodges: Moose, Masons. Home: 4154 Ellsworth Rd Stow OH 44224 Office: Clevite Industries Inc 33 Lockwood Rd Milan OH 44486

AYLWARD, PATRICIA MARIE, personnel director; b. Milton, Mass., Feb. 11, 1955; d. Matthew Thomas and Margaret Marie (O'Donnell) A. BA, DePaul U., 1983. Personnel interviewer Great Lakes Mortgage Corp., Chgo., 1979-80; placement specialist First Fed. Savs. & Loan, Chgo., 1980; personnel dir. Ryan Ins. Group, Chgo., 1980-84; asst. dir. human resources Mass. Eye & Ear Infirmary, Boston, 1984-85; mgr. benefits and spl. projects The Balcor Co., Skokie, Ill., 1985-86; personnel dir. William Blair & Co., Chgo., 1986—. Active vol. mgmt. services com. Chgo. Heart Assn., 1980-81; vol. Santa Claus Anonymous, Chgo., 1986—; vol. community and hospitality com. St. Clement Ch., Chgo., 1987—; bd. dirs. Baywick Repertory Theater Co., Chgo., 1986—. Mem. Am. Assn. Personnel Adminstrn., Human Resources Mgmt. Assn. Chgo. (mem. planning and devel. com. 1983-84, benefits and compensation com. 1987—). Roman Catholic. Avocations: theater, films, travel, reading, hiking.

AYRES, ROBERT FRANKLIN, superintendent schools; b. nr. Warren, Ind., Apr. 29, 1925; s. James Madison and Dora Evelyn (Lucas) A.; B.S., Butler U., 1949, M.S., 1952; postgrad. Purdue U., 1958-62; m. Helen Denton, Mar. 7, 1947; children—James Michael, Robert William, John David, Christopher Allen, Carolyn Ann. Tchr., Orchard Country Day Sch., Indpls., 1948-50; tchr., dean of boys Frankfort High Sch. (Ind.), 1950-59, prin., 1959-65; asst. supt. schs. Huntington County, Ind., 1965-70; supt. schs. Rensselaer Sch. System, 1970-75; supt. Community Schs. Frankfort, 1975—; instr. Huntington Coll., 1967-70; lectr. Butler U.; mem. overseas evaluation group Dept. Def. Dependent Schs., Panama, 1983, Philippines, 1985, Mediterranean region; bd. dirs. Citizen's Savs. and Loan. Exec. bd. Anthony Wayne council Boy Scouts Am.; bd. dirs. Huntington Coll. Found., Rensselaer chpt. Red Cross, Big Bros. Am., Retarded Children's Assn.; mem. Clinton County Area Plan Commn., 1976-78; pres. Clinton County Commn. Pub. Records, 1980-88; v.p. and campaign drive chmn. Clinton County United Way. Served to lt. AUS, 1943-46. Nat. Defense Edn. Act fellow, 1960; St. Joseph's Coll. fellow, 1974. Mem. Ind. Assn. Pub. Sch. Supts., N.E.A., Am. Legion, V.F.W., Ind. Schoomen's Club, Am. Assn. Sch. Adminstrs., Clinton County C. of C. (dir. 1977—), Phi Delta Kappa, Lambda Chi Alpha, Tau Kappa Alpha, Alpha Phi Omega. Methodist. Optimist (pres. 1970), Rotarian, Lion. Home: 709 Williams Rd Frankfort IN 46041 Office: 50 S Maish Rd Frankfort IN 46041

AZAR, CYRUS, inventor, artist; b. Boston, May 3, 1958; s. Sam Azar and Cynthia (Eulenberg) Weisz; m. Laura Jean Wentz, Sept. 10, 1982; 1 child, Daniel. BS in Computer Sci., U. Ill., 1980. Research asst. U. Ill., Urbana, 1978-80; softwre engr. Ampex Corp., Redwood City, Calif., 1980-83; founder, inventor Symplex Communications, Belmont, Calif. and Ann Arbor, Mich., 1982—; founder, pres. Compusound, Ann Arbor, 1987—; computer cons. Azar Enterprises, Belmont, Ann Arbor, 1981-86. Author (computer program) algebra calculator, 1978; author/inventor datamizer SDC-4, 1982, quantum 24K modem, 1985. Avocations: camping, hiking, music. Office: Symplex Communications 5 Research Dr Ann Arbor MI 48103

AZARNOFF, DANIEL LESTER, pharmaceutical company consultant; b. Bklyn., Aug. 4, 1926; s. Samuel J. and Kate (Asarnow) A.; m. Joanne Stokes, Dec. 26, 1951; children: Rachel, Richard, Martin. B.S., Rutgers U., 1947, M.S., 1948; M.D., U. Kans., 1955. Asst. instr. anatomy U. Kans. Med. Sch., 1949-50, research fellow, 1950-52, intern, 1955-56, resident, Nat. Heart Inst. research fellow, 1956-58, asst. prof. medicine, 1962-64, assoc. prof., 1964-68, dir. clin. pharmacology study unit, 1964-68, assoc. prof. pharmacology, 1965-68, prof. medicine and pharmacology, 1968, dir. Clin. Pharmacology-Toxicology Ctr., 1967-78, Disting. prof., 1973-78, also prof. medicine, 1965-67, pres. Sigma Xi Club, 1968-69; Nat. Inst. Neurol. Diseases and Blindness spl. trainee Washington U. Sch. Medicine, St. Louis, 1958-60; asst. prof. medicine St. Louis U. Sch. Medicine, 1960-62; vis. scientist Fulbright scholar Karolinska Inst., Stockholm, Sweden, 1968; sr. v.p. worldwide research and devel. G.D. Searle & Co., Chgo., 1978; pres. Searle Research and Devel., Skokie, Ill., 1979-85, D.L. Azarnoff Assocs., Inc., Evanston, Ill., 1986—; prof. pathology, clin. prof. pharmacology Northwestern U. Med. Sch., 1978—; professorial lectr. U. Chgo., 1979; dir. Second Workshop on Prins. Drug Evaluation in Man, 1970; chmn. com. on problems of drug safety NRC-Nat. Acad. Sci., 1972-76; cons. numerous govtl. agys. Editor: Dev. of Drug Interactions, 1974-77, Yearbook of Drug Therapy, 1977-79; series editor: Monographs in Clin. Pharmacology, 1977—; mem. editorial and adv. bds. various jours. Mem. commn. on orphan diseases Health and Human Services, 1986—. Served with U.S. Army, 1945-46. Recipient Ginsburg award in phys. diagnosis U. Kans. Med. Center, 1953; Outstanding Intern award, 1956, Ciba award for gerontol. research, 1958, Rectors medal U. Helsinki, 1968; John and Mary R. Markle scholar, 1962; Burroughs Wellcome scholar, 1964; William N. Creasy vis. prof. clin. pharmacology Med. Coll. Va., 1975; Bruce Hall Meml. lectr. St. Vincents Hosp., Sydney, 1976; 7th Sir Henry Hallett Dale lectr. Johns Hopkins U. Med. Sch., 1978. Fellow A.C.P., N.Y. Acad. Scis.; mem. Am. Soc. Clin. Nutrition, Am. Nutrition Instn., Am. Soc. Pharmacology and Exptl. Therapeutics (chmn. clin. pharmacology div. 1969-71, mem. exec. com. 1966-73, 78-81, del. 1975-78, bd. publ. trustees), Am. Soc. Clin. Pharmacology and Therapeutics, Am. Fedn. Clin. Research, Brit. Pharmacol. Soc., AMA (vice chmn. council on drugs 1971-72, editorial bd. Jour.), Central Soc. Clin. Research, Royal Soc. for Promotion Health, Inst. Medicine of Nat. Acad. Scis., Soc. Exptl. Biology and Medicine (councillor 1976-80), Internat. Union Pharmacologists (sec. clin. pharmacology sect. 1975-81, internat. adv. com. Paris Congress 1978), Sigma Xi.

BAALMAN, KATHRYN MARGARET, mathematics and computer science educator; b. Liebenthal, Kans., Sept. 22, 1939; d. Lawrence and Elizabeth (Leiker) Herman; m. Anthony Baalman, Sept. 13, 1969; children: Theresa, Michael, Angela. BA, Alverno Coll., Milw., 1960; MS, Emporia (Kans.) State U., 1965. Cert. secondary tchr., Mo. Tchr. and dept. chmn. Sacred Heart High Sch., Walls, Miss., 1960-65; tchr. Alvernia High Sch., Chgo., 1965-67, Plymouth Jr. High Sch., Webster Groves, Mo., 1967-68; programmer McDonnell-Douglas Electronics, St. Charles, Mo., 1968-71; tchr. Ft. Zumwalt Schs., O'Fallon, Mo., 1971-85; instr. and dept. chmn. St. Mary's Coll., O'Fallon, 1985—; dept. chmn. Ft. Zumwalt Schs., 1978-80; pres. Impact Ednl. Software Co. Mem. Am. Soc. Educators, Nat. Council Tchrs. Math., Internat. Council Computers in Edn., Assn. Computers in Mat. and Sci. Teaching, Assn. Ednl. Data Systems, Assn. Small Computer Usres in Edn., Assn. Computing Machinery. Home: 605 Lorene Dr O'Fallon MO 63366 Office: St Mary's Coll 200 N Main O'Fallon MO 63366

BAALMANN, RICHARD FENTON, retail hardware executive; b. St. Louis, Oct. 30, 1935; s. Roderick Oliver and Melba (Bertholdt) B.; student St. Louis U., 1953-57; m. Kathleen Felke, June 12, 1957; children—Richard Fenton, Mary Kathleen, Margaret Grace, Anne Patricia. Vice pres. Mars Enders, Inc., retail hardware, St. Louis, 1956-68, pres., 1968-79; pres. Hardware Center, Inc., retail hardware, St. Louis, 1956-79, Markat, Inc., St. Louis, 1970-79, Bramm, Inc., 1979—. Past pres., chmn. bd. trustees Nat. Cystic Fibrosis Research Found.; chmn. St. Louis chpt. Jesuit Program for Living and Learning, nat. chmn., 1979-83; mem. Mo. Air Conservation Commn., 1980-83; bd. commrs. Bi-State Devel. Agy., 1982—, chmn., 1982-83; bd. dirs. East-West Gateway Coordinating Council, Glennon Children's Hosp., 1985—. Served as 1st lt. USAF, 1958-59. Mem. Brentwood C. of C. (pres. 1966), St. Louis Regional Commerce and Growth Assn., Advt. Club St. Louis, Delta Sigma Pi. Clubs: Univ. St. Louis, St. Louis Counts. Lodge: Rotary (pres. 1972). Home: 458 Bambury Way Saint Louis MO 63131 Office: 11767 Manchester Saint Louis MO 63131

BABA, MARIETTA LYNN, university official, business anthropologist, b. Flint, Mich., Nov. 9, 1949; d. David and Lillian (Joseph) Baba; m. David Smokler, Feb. 14, 1977 (div. 1982); 1 dau., Alexia Baba Smokler. B.A. with highest distinction, Wayne State U., 1971, M.A. in Anthropology, 1973, Ph.D. in Phys. Anthropology, 1975. Asst. prof. sci. and tech. Wayne State U., Detroit, Mich., 1975-80, assoc. prof., 1980—, assoc. prof. anthropology, 1980—, spl. asst. to pres., 1980-82, econ. devel. officer, 1982-83, asst. provost, 1983-85; assoc. provost, 1985—; founder, corp. officer Applied Research Teams Mich., Inc., Detroit, Intelligent Techs., Inc., Detroit; evolution researcher Wayne State U., 1975-82; research collaborator operating scis. dept. unit Gen. Motors Research Labs.; lectr. nat. and internat. symposia, profl. conferences. Contbr. numerous papers and abstracts to profl. jours, tech. publs. Bd. dirs. City-Univ. Consortium, Detroit, 1980-83; v.p. Neighborhood Service Orgn., Detroit, 1980-85; mem. State Research Fund Feasibility Rev. Panel, 1982-86; active Leadership Detroit Class IV, 1982-83; dir. Mich. Tech. Council (SE div.), 1984-85. Job Partnership Tng. Act grantee, 1981-87; NSF grantee, 1982, 84-85. Fellow Am. Anthrop. Assn. (exec. com. 1986—), Nat. Assn. Practice Anthropology (pres. 1986—), Soc. Applied Anthropology, Phi Beta Kappa, Sigma Xi. Office: Wayne State U 1050 Mackenzie Hall Detroit MI 48202

BABAD, YAIR MOSHE, information systems and accounting educator, consultant; b. Gedera, Israel, Jan. 12, 1941; came to U.S., 1969; s. Jacob and Janet S. (Davis) B.; m. Naomi Waldman, Sept. 12, 1963; children: Galit, Orna. BS in Math., Hebrew U., Jerusalem, 1965, diploma in Actuarial Sci., 1968; MS in Ops. Research, Cornell U., 1972, PhD in Ops. Research, 1973. CPA, Ill. Actuary Mivtahim Social Ins. Co., Tel Aviv, 1966-69; info. mgmt. cons. Shiloah Ins. Co., Tel Aviv, 1968-75; asst. prof. mgmt. and info. scis. Grad. Sch. Bus. U. Chgo., 1973-77; project mgr. Arthur Andersen & Co., Chgo., 1977-80; prof. info. and decision scis. U. Ill., Chgo., 1981—; cons. various corps. Contbr. numerous articles to profl. jours. Bd. dirs., fin. sec. Or Torah Congregation, Skokie, Ill., 1985—. Served to lt. Engring. Corps, Israeli Army, 1958-63. Mem. Am. Inst. CPA's, Ill. CPA Soc. (chmn. com. on info. scis. 1985-87), Ops. Research Soc. Am., Inst. Mgmt. Sci., Assn. for Computing Machinery. Jewish. Avocations: music, racquetball. Home: 1628 South Blvd Evanston IL 60202 Office: U Ill Coll Bus Adminstrn Dept Info and Decision Scis Box 4348 Chicago IL 60680

BABAI, MASSOOD REZA, psychiatrist; b. Zahedan, Iran, Jan. 27, 1939; s. Gholam Reza and Fatomeh G. B.; came to U.S., 1968; M.D., U. Tehran, 1965; m. Simin Soltanzadeh, May 6, 1963; children—Mojgan, Sarah, Dora. Pvt. practice medicine, Tehran, 1965-66; intern Misericordia Hosp., N.Y.C., 1968-69; resident Rollman Psychiat. Inst., Cin., 1969-72; pvt. practice medicine, specializing in psychiatry, Cuyahoga Falls, Ohio, 1973—; dir. ambulatory services Fallsview Psychiat. Hosp., 1972-74, dir. med. edn., 1974-77; dir., div. psychiatry St. Thomas Hosp., Akron, Ohio, 1976—; tchr. interns and residents St. Thomas Hosp., Fallsview Psychiat. Hosp. Med. Sch.; clin. prof. psychiatry N.E. Ohio U. Coll. Medicine. Served as 2d lt., Health Corps, Iranian Imperial Army, 1966-68. Diplomate Am. Bd. Psychiatry and Neurology. Mem. Am. Psychiat. Assn., Ohio Psychiat. Assn. Translator from English to Persian, Applied Physiology, 1965. Office: 275 Graham Rd Suite 8 Cuyahoga Falls OH 44223

BABAR, RAZA ALI, industrial engineer, utility consultant and management educator; b. Shujabad, Punjab, Pakistan, May 29, 1947; came to U.S., 1972, naturalized, 1978; s. Syeed Mohammad Ali Shah and Syeda Hafeeza (Gilani) Bukhari; m. Sufia K. Durrett, July 23, 1974 (div. 1983); children: Azra Yasmeen, Imran Ali, Amenah Andaleep; m. Syeda Afshan Gilani, Aug. 23, 1983; children: Abdullah Ali, Hammad Ali. BS in Mining Engring., U. Engring. and Tech., Lahore, Pakistan, 1969; MS in Indsl. Engring., Wayne State U., 1978; postgrad Detroit Coll. Law, 1982, U. Mich., 1977-84. Engr., planner Bukhari Elec. Concern, Multan, Pakistan, 1969-70; mgr. mining operations Felezzate Yazd Co., Iran, 1970-72; salesman Great Books, Inc., Chgo., 1972-73; field underwriter N.Y. Life Insurance Co., 1972-73; indsl. engr. Ellis/Naeyaert Assocs., Inc., Warren, Mich., 1973-74; grad. asst. dept. indsl. engring. and ops. research Wayne State U., Detroit, 1974-75; prin. engr., work leader project services div. Generation Constrn. Dept., Detroit Edison Co., 1975-79; tech. advisor Ministry of Prodn., Govt. Pakistan, Islamabad, 1979-80; chmn. dept. bus. adminstrn. Zakariya U., Multan, Pakistan, 1980-82; prin. engr. project controls Enrico Fermi 2 Detroit Edison Co., 1981-82, supr. Fermi 2 rate case task force, 1982-84, mgr. econ. support service Syndeco, Inc., 1985—; vis. prof. grad. Sch. Bus. Adminstrn., Wayne State U., 1987—; spl. projects engr. planning, Detroit Edison Co., 1984—. Author research papers, papers presentations to Am. Assn. of Cost Engrs., Am. Power Conf., Internat. Assn. of Energy, Power and Environ. Systems. Founder Fedn. Engring. Assns. Pakistan, 1969; pres. acad. staff assn., mem. chancellor's com. Zakariya U., Pakistan, 1980-81; pres. Pakistan Cultural Group, Detroit, 1975-76; bd. dirs. Detroit Islamic Library, 1976-77; mem. Econ. Outlook Conf., U. Mich., Ann Arbor, 1977-84, Rep. Presdl. Task Force. Recipient Pride of Performance medal Engring. U., Pakistan, 1967; Acad. Merit scholar Detroit Coll. Law, 1982. Mem. Am. Mgmt. Assn., Am. Mgmt. Assn. Internat., Econ. Club Detroit, Am. Inst. Indsl. Engrs., Am. Assn. Cost Engrs., Engring. Soc. Detroit, ESD Profl. Activities Council, Pakistan Engring. Congress, Pakistan Inst. Mining Engrs., ABA (student chpt.), Am. Assn. of MBA Execs., Assn. Muslims Scientists and Engrs., Assn. Muslim Social Scientists, Internat. Platform Assn., Islamic Soc. N.Am., Am. Moslem Soc., Islamic Cultural Inst. Avocations: reading, writing, photography, sports, travel. Home: 15581 Plaza South Dr Taylor MI 48180 Office: 2000 Second Ave Detroit MI 48226

BABB, KEITH FRANKLIN, utilities executive; b. Salzburg, Austria, Apr. 9, 1955; came to U.S., 1956; s. Earl Franklin and Alta Lorraine (Dannels) B.; m. Pamela Jeannette Stipp, June 26, 1976; children: Nathaniel Franklin, Joshua Raymond, Hailee Jeannette. AA, Crowder Coll., 1977; BBA, Mo. So. State Coll., 1979; MBA, S.W. Mo. State U., 1984. Rate analyst Empire Dist. Electric Co., Joplin, Mo., 1979-82, planning analyst, 1983-85, corp. planner, 1985—; prof. econs. Pittsburg (Kans.) State U., 1985. Mem. Ch. Christ. Avocations: running, golf. Home: 113 W South St Neosho MO 64850 Office: Empire Dist Electric Co 602 Joplin St Joplin MO 64802

BABBINI, VICTOR LAWRENCE, educational administrator, educator; b. Wilkes-Barre, Pa., Mar. 4, 1942; s. I. and Clara B.; B.A., West Liberty State Coll., 1966; M.S., Eastern Ill. U., 1972; M.S. in Adminstrn., Niagara U., 1980. Dir. instrumental music Richmond, Ohio, 1966-69; music cons./specialist South Orange-Maplewood, N.J., 1969-71; music editor, staff writer-critic N.J. Music and Arts Mag. of Metro N.Y.C., 1970-72; prof. humanities, dir. fine and performing arts Medaille Coll., Buffalo, 1976—, admissions adv. counsel to pres., faculty curriculum com. for v.p. of acad. affairs, 1977-79, trustee council student affairs, 1978—, trustee com. for Non-Traditional Edn.; evaluator North Central Assn. of Schs. and Colls.; curriculum cons. Lorain County Office Edn., Ohio, since 1983—, cons. in edn. adminstrn; chmn. All-City Music, Niagara Falls, N.Y.; N.Y. State humanities resource cons. Mem. Music Critics Assn. Am., Ohio Art Educators Assn., Nat. Assn. Schs. Music, Music Educators Nat. Conf., Coll. Band Dirs., Nat. Assn., Nat. Assn. Coll. Wind and Percussion Instrs., Ohio Music Educators Assn., Assn. for Supervision and Curriculum Devel. (Citiation for Outstanding Curriculum Devel.), Jr. C. of C., Phi Delta Kappa. Contbr. articles to profl. jours.; author: N.Y. State pioneer B.S. program in arts mgmt. Home: 139 Shakespeare Ln Avon OH 44011

BABBO, JOSEPH THOMAS, rehab. counselor, social work therapist; b. Chgo., Jan. 24, 1932; s. Angelo and Anna Maria (Cereso) B.; student Loras Coll., 1956-58; Ph.B., Belmont Abbey Coll., 1963; M.S., Ill. Inst. Tech., 1973, postgrad., 1975—, Forest Inst. of Profl. Psychology, 1980-82 ; m. Mary Josephine Hamrock, Oct. 29, 1967; children—Angelo Joseph, Mary Immaculata, Martin Francis, Thomas John, Annamaria, Giovanna Carmella. Rehab. counselor Ill. Dept. Rehab. Services, Chgo., 1964—; marriage and family counselor and therapist; union rep., steward AFSCME Local 2000, 1971—, collective bargaining com., 1975—; counselor rep. Dept. Vocat. Rehab. Visitor chmn. Christian Outreach, ch. lecter, Extraordinary Minister of Holy Communion, Ch. commentator; sch. bd. mem. St. Ferdinand Elementary Sch., 1985—; mem., bd. dirs. N.W. Neighborhood Fedn. Served with USN, 1951-55; Korea. Cert. rehab. counselor; cert. social worker. Mem. Nat. Rehab. Assn., Ill. Rehab. Assn., Nat. Rehab. Counselor Assn., Ill. Rehab. Counselor Assn., Am. Psychol. Assn. (asso.), N.W. Neighborhood Fedn. Roman Catholic. Clubs: Good Counsel High Sch. Fathers', Fenwick High Sch. Fathers', Parents Assn. Loyola U. of Chgo. Home: 2910 N Meade Ave Chicago IL 60634 Office: 5015 W Lawrence Ave Chicago IL 60630

BABCOCK, DANIEL LAWRENCE, engineer, educator; b. Phila., Nov. 25, 1930; s. Lawrence Morton and Ethel (Snider) B.; m. Bettie Johann Veazey, June 14, 1980. BSChemE, Pa. State U., 1952; MSChemE, MIT, 1953; PhD in Engring., UCLA, 1970. Registered profl. engr., Mo. Chem. engr. Dow Corning Corp., Midland, Mich., 1956-59; tech. editor JHU Applied Physics Lab., Silver Spring, Md., 1959-62; supr. and project engr. space div. Rockwell Internat., Downey, Calif., 1963-69; assoc. prof. engr. U. Mo., Rolla, 1970-78, prof. engring. mgmt., 1978—. Contbr. articles to profl. jours. Served to lt. USAF, 1952-56, lt. col. Res. Mem. Engring. Mgmt. Internat. (editorial bd. 1981—), Am. Soc. Engring. Mgmt. (exec. dir. 1979—, Bernard Sarchet award 1986), Am. Soc. Engring. Edn. (chmn. engring. mgmt. div. 1973-74), Soc. Am. Mil. Engrs., Am. Soc. Quality Control (cert. quality engr.). Unitarian. Home: 1347 California St Rolla MO 65401 Office: U Mo Dept Engring Mgmt Rolla MO 65401

BABCOCK, GEORGE F., immunologist; b. Buffalo, Jan. 20, 1948; s. George F. and Iris (Dickerson) B. BS, Muskingum Coll., 1970; MS, N.D. State U., 1972; PhD, U. Nebr., Omaha, 1975. Postdoctoral research fellow U. N.C. Cancer Ctr., Chapel Hill, 1975-78; research assoc. U.N.C. Cancer Ctr., Chapel Hill, 1978-79; asst. prof. surgery, asst. immunologist M.D. Anderson Hosp., Houston, 1979-83; faculty biomed. scis. U Tex. Health Sci. Ctr., Houston, 1981-83; assoc. prof. surgery U. Cin. Med. Ctr., 1983—, adj. assoc. prof. pathology, 1983—. Contbr. articles to profl. jours. NIH fellow, 1975, 76. Mem. AAAS, Am. Assn. for Cancer Research, Am. Assn. Immunologists, Am. Soc. Microbiology, N.Y. Acad. Scis., Reticuloendothelial Soc., Soc. Analytical Cytology, Alpha Epsilon Delta, Sigma Xi. Office: U Cin Dept Surgery ML#558 231 Bethesda Ave Cincinnati OH 45267

BABCOCK, LYNDON ROSS, JR., environmental educator, administrator; b. Detroit, Apr. 8, 1934; s. Lyndon Ross and Lucille Kathryn (Miller) B.; m. Betty Irene Immonen, June 21, 1957; children—Lyndon Ross III, Sheron Lucille, Susan Elizabeth, Andrew Dag. BSChemE, Mich. Tech. U., 1956; MSChemE, U. Washington, 1958, PhD in Environ. Engring., 1970. Registered profl. engr., Calif., Ill. Chem. engr. polymers Shell Chem. Co., Calif., N.J., N.Y., 1958-67; assoc. prof. environ. engring., geography, pub. health U. Ill., Chgo., 1970-75; prof. environ. engring., geography, pub. health U. Ill.-Chgo. and Med. Ctr., 1975—, dir. environ. health scis. program Sch. Pub. Health, 1978-79, dir. environ. and occupational health scis. program Sch. Pub. Health, 1979-84, assoc. dean Sch. Pub. Health, 1984-85; co-dir. Midwest Asbestos Info. Ctr., 1986-86; cons. WHO, 1985. Mem. editorial bd. The Environ. Profl., 1979—; contbr. environ. articles to profl jours.; patentee plastics composition and processing. Co-dir. Midwest Asbestos Info. Ctr., 1986—; bd. dirs. Chgo. Lung Assn., 1981—. Fulbright lectr., Turkey and India, 1975-76, Mexico, 1986-87; fed. and state environ. research and ednl. grantee. Mem. Am. Inst. Chem. Engrs., Air Pollution Control Assn. (chmn. Lake Michigan sect. 1977-78), Am. Pub. Health Assn., Nat. Assn. Environ. Profls. (editorial bd. The Environ. Profl. 1979—), League Am. Wheelmen, Chicagoland Bicycle Fedn. (v.p. 1985-86), Ill. Assn. Environ. Profls. (bd. dirs. 1982-86), Ill. Pub. Health Assn. Home: 819 S Loomis St Chicago IL 60607 Office: U Ill Sch Pub Health PO Box 6998 Chicago IL 60680

BABCOCK, MICHAEL WARD, economics educator; b. Bloomington, Ill., Dec. 10, 1944; s. Bruce W. and Virginia (Neeson) B.; B.S. in B.A., Drake U., 1967; M.A. in Econs., U. Ill., 1971, Ph.D. in Econs., 1973; m. Virginia Lee Brooks, Aug. 4, 1973; children—John, Karen. Teaching asst. U. Ill., Urbana, 1968, 71, research asst., 1972; prof. econs. Kans. State U., Manhattan,

1972—. Served with U.S. Army, 1969-71. Fed. R.R. Adminstrn. grantee, 1976-78; U.S. Army C.E. grantee, 1978-79; U.S. Dept. Agr. grantee, 1978-79, 80-82, 84-85. Mem. Am. Assn. Agrl. Economists, Missouri Valley Econ. Assn., Mid-Continent Regional Sci. Assn., So. Regional Sci. Assn., Kans. Econ. Assn., Nat. Assn. Bus. Economists, Transp. Research Forum, Beta Gamma Sigma, Omicron Delta Epsilon. Club: Optimist. Contbr. articles to profl. jours. Home: 720 Harris St Manhattan KS 66502 Office: Kans State Univ Econs Dept Manhattan KS 66506

BABCOCK, PATRICIA ANN, nurse; b. Shelbyville, Ind., Oct. 31, 1934; d. Laurence H. and Reba D. (Conway) Underwood; B.S. in Nursing, Ball State U., Muncie, Ind., 1957, M.A., 1975, 86, Ed.D. (fellow), 1980; m. Robert A. Babcock, Mar. 30, 1958; children—Brett Alan, Richard Scott, Laura Ann. Office nurse, Muncie, 1957-60; staff nurse Porter Meml. Hosp., Valparaiso, Ind., 1961; head nurse St. Joseph Hosp., Logansport, Ind., 1963-65; sch. nurse, Gary, Ind., 1967-76; asst. prof. nursing Purdue U. North Central Campus, Westville, Ind., 1976-82, assoc. prof., 1982—, acting chmn. nursing, 1983-84, chmn. nursing, 1984—; cons. in field. Mem. AAUW (br. pres.), Am. Nurses Assn., Nat. League Nursing, Ind. League Nursing, Ind. Assn. Health Educators, AAUP (chpt. pres.), Nat. Assn. Female Execs., Concern for Dying, Ind. State Nurses Assn. (dist. pres.), Hospice of Porter County, Compassionate Friends, Eta Sigma Gamma, Sigma Theta Tau, Phi Delta Theta, Sigma Kappa. Republican. Methodist. Home: 115 Washington Ave Chesterton IN 46304 Office: Purdue U North Central Campus Westville IN 46391

BABCOCK, RICHARD DEAN, children's services executive; b. Labette City, Kans., June 9, 1942; s. Marvin Dean and Mary Conception (Yanez) B.; B.A., U. Kans., 1964; M.S., Central Mo. State U., 1971; postgrad., Columbia Pacific Univ., 1987—; m. Teresa Ann Olson, Dec. 13, 1951; children—Kelley, Dominick, Deidre, Chelsea, Luke, Patrick. Treatment program adminstr. Glenwood (Iowa) State 1976-77; social worker Parsons (Kans.) State Hosp. & Tng. Center, 1966-68; dir. Neighborhood Youth Corp. project, Ottawa, Kans., 1968; speech and lang. cons. Project Head Start, Springfield, Mo., 1969; speech therapist Mansfield (Mo.) public schs., 1970; dir. speech and hearing services Joplin (Mo.) Regional Center for Mental Retardation/Devel. Disabilities; unit dir. Marshall (Mo.) State Hosp. and Sch., 1974-75; dir. treatment programs, asst. ctr. dir. Springfield Regional Ctr. for Mental Retardation/Devel. Disabilities, 1977-80; adminstr. Springfield Children's Home, 1980—; speech and hearing cons. U.S. Med. Center for Fed. Prisoners, Springfield, 1971; mem. Child Welfare Adv. Council. Mem. Greene County (Mo.) Child Protection team, 1978-79; mem. Greene County Child Advocacy Council bd., 1979-80, 83-84, mental health rep., 1979-84, sec. exec. com. 1979-81; liaison Greene County Multidisciplinary/Child Protection team, 1979-80; mem. Greene County Assn. for Retarded Citizens, 1978-79; Spl. Olympics volunteer, 1969-84. Served with USNR, 1961-64. United Cerebral Palsy Found. grad. scholar, 1970; Mental Health Grad. fellow, 1970-71; Spl. Olympics Appreciation award, 1971-79; Certificate of Clin. Competency in Speech Pathology, Am. Speech and Hearing Assn., 1972. Mem. Mo. Tchrs. Assn. (assembly del. 1969-70), Mo. Speech and Hearing Assn., Mo. Child Care Assn. (pres.), In Child's Interest (dir., officer 1981—), Nat. Fellowship Child Care Execs., Phi Kappa Theta. Democrat. Roman Catholic. Club: Ozark Mt. Ridgerunners Running. Lodges: Kiwanis, Optimists. Contbr. articles to profl. jours. Home: Route 20 Box 2097-6 Springfield MO 65803 Office: 1212 W Lombard St Springfield MO 65806

BABCOCK, ROBERT ALLEN, construction company executive; b. Indpls., May 4, 1935; s. William Harvey and Beatrice Opal (Durst) B.; student Butler U., 1953-54; m. Virginia Ann Richardson, Sept. 2, 1955; children—Patricia Ann, Debra Sue. With William H. Babcock & Son, Indpls., 1954-70; owner Robert A. Babcock, Gen. Contractor, Indpls., 1970-77; pres. Babcock Constrn., Inc., Indpls., 1977-86; cons. 1986—; constrn, mgr. 10th Pan Am. Village, Indpls., 1986-87. Pres., Wayne Twp. Screening Caucus, 1970, pres. Danville Band Parents, 1972; trustee Danville United Methodist Ch., 1980—, dir. mission work projects Indpls. West dists., 1986—, chmn. adminstrv. council, 1983-86 . Mem. Better Bus. Bur. Republican. Methodist. Clubs: Masons, Shriners, Scottish Rite, Indpls. Country. Home: 2275 S 125 W Danville IN 46122 Office: 951 Western Dr Indianapolis IN 46241

BABINSKY, ANDREW DANIEL, manufacturing executive; b. South River, N.J., July 13, 1930; s. Andrew and Julia (Kayati) B.; m. Frances Olivia Stem, Aug. 20, 1953; 1 child, Jane Ellen. BS in Physics, Heidelberg Coll., 1952; MS in Physics, Case Western Res. U., 1962. Aeronautical research scientist Lewis Lab NASA, Cleve., 1952-55, nuclear propulsion engr., 1958-59; mgr. aircraft systems TRW, Cleve., 1959-71; dir. materials and chem. res. Diamond Shamrock, Concord, Ohio, 1971-83; pres. Mitech Corp., Willoughby, Ohio, 1983-86, chmn., 1986—. Patentee in field; contbr. articles to profl. jours. Served to lt. USNR, 1955-58. Republican. Avocations: videography, golf, woodworking, photography, bowling. Home: 54 Church St Chagrin Falls OH 44022 Office: Mitech Corp 1780 Enterprise Pkwy Twinsburg OH 44087

BABLES, MARILYN MARIE, laboratory technician; b. Kans., Nov. 21, 1954; d. Leon B.; A.A., Kansas City (Kans.) Community Coll., 1976; B.A. in Biology, Park Coll., 1978; BA Chemistry U. Mo. Kansas City. Quality control lab. technician Bayvet Labs., Shawnee Mission, Kans., 1979; microbiology lab. technician Bd. Pub. Utilities, Kansas City, Kans., 1979—; pres., founder Bables Investment Properties. Mem. Kan Valley Med. Soc., Am. Water Works Assn., Nat. Assn. Female Execs., Women in Bus. (pres. 1980—), Urban League, AAUW, Internat. Fedn. Univ. Women, Internat. Platform Assn., Smithsonian Assocs., Friends of Park Coll. Library. Republican. Mem. Christian Ch. (Disciples of Christ). Home: 1968 N 32d St Kansas City KS 66104 Office: 3601 N 12th Kansas City KS 66104

BABLITCH, WILLIAM, state supreme court justice; b. Stevens Point, Wis., Mar. 1, 1941. B.S., U. Wis., Madison, 1963, J.D., 1968. Bar: Wis. 1968. Practice law Stevens Point, Wis.; mem. Wis. Senate, 1972-85, senate majority leader, 1976-82; justice Wis. Supreme Ct., Madison, 1985—; dist. atty. Portage County, Wis., 1969-72. Mem. Nat. Conf. State Legislators (exec. com. 1979). Democrat. Office: Office of Supreme Ct Wis Madison WI 53702

BABNEAU, MELODEE ANN, accounting administrator; b. Inglewood, Calif., Apr. 21, 1960; d. Albert and Carol Lynne (Waldron) B. BBA, U. Wis., Eau Claire, 1983. CPA, Minn. Royalty acct. supr. K-Tel Internat., Inc., Mpls., 1983-84, corp. acct., 1985, corp. acctg. mgr., 1985—. Pvt. tutor Minn. Literacy Council, 1986. Mem. Am. Soc. CPA's, Minn. Soc. CPA's. Roman Catholic. Home: 11313 Crooked Lake Blvd Coon Rapids MN 55433 Office: K-Tel Internat Inc 15525 Medina Rd Plymouth MN 55447

BABU, SHISHIR CHANDRA, manufacturing company executive; b. Mysore, India, Sept. 19, 1951; came to U.S., 1975; s. Samarapuri and Shashikala (Rao) B.; m. Maru Cleoffe Baca, July 2, 1979; 1 child, Shirish Mayhew. BS in Physics and Math., U. Mysore, 1969, BSEE, 1973; MS in Indsl. Engring. and Ops. Research, U. Mich., 1976. Mktg. engr. Motwane, Ltd., Bombay, 1973-75; mgr. systems Am. Hosp. Supply Co., Waukegan, Ill., 1976-78; mgr. engring. E-Z Por Corp., Wheeling, Ill., 1978-80, mgr. mfg., 1980-82, asst. plant mgr., 1982-86; dir. mfg. E-Z Por Corp. (co. bought by Packaging Corp. Am., div. Tenneco), Wheeling, Ill., 1986—; chmn. new products div. Am. Home Products, Wheeling, 1981-82, inventory systems Am. Hosp. Supply Co., Wheeling, 1976-77; cons. plant engring. Gibbons & Green, Wheeling, 1984-85. Co-author: Financial Ratioanalysis, 1975; inventor wind-proof tab., 1984. Mem. Am. Inst. Indsl. Engrs., Am. Inst. Plant Engrs., Indian Inst. Engrs., Soc. Mfg. Engrs. Lodge: Lions (bd. dirs. 1967-70). Avocations: mountain climbing, hiking, wildlife conservation and explorations. Home: 1121 Thackeray Dr Palatine IL 60067 Office: E-Z Por Corp 1500 S Wolf Rd Wheeling IL 60090

BABUT, ROBERT BRUCE, telecommunications company executive; b. Niagara Falls, N.Y., Feb. 8, 1955; s. Henry and Emily Anne (Baccelli) B. BSBA, SUNY, Buffalo, 1982. Instr. Niagara Falls Sch. System, 1980-83; pres. Modern Communications (named changed to Mich. Communications), Ypsilanti, Mich., 1983—. Bd. dirs. Mich. Orgn. Human Rights, Detroit, 1987. Mem. Motor City Bus. Forum, ACLU. Democrat. Roman Catholic. Lodge: Moose. Avocations: bicycling, reading novels, video and audio equipment, physical fitness. Home: 1006 W Cross St Ypsilanti MI 48197-2103 Office: Modern Communications 141 Ecorse Rd Ypsilanti MI 48198-5712

BACCUS, DONALD JOSEPH, gynecologist/obstetrician; b. Laurium, Mich., Feb. 11, 1947; s. Victor P. and Mary C. (Chandonais) B.; m. Camille M. Karkoski, Jan. 28, 1977. BS in Biol. Sci., Mich. Tech. U., 1970; MD, U. Mich., 1976. Diplomate Am. Bd. Ob-Gyn. Intern St. Joseph's Hosp., Milw., 1976-77, resident in ob-gyn, 1977-80; practice medicine specializing in ob-gyn Milw., 1980—. Mem. Wisc. Polit. Action Com., 1986. Fellow Am. Coll. Ob-Gyn; mem. AMA, Wis. State Med. Soc., Am. Fertility Soc., Am. Assn. Gynecol. Laporoscopists. Republican. Roman Catholic. Home: 2738 N 117th Pl Wauwatosa WI 53222 Office: N Cen Ob-Gyn Ltd 3070 N 51st St Milwaukee WI 53210

BACH, MURIEL DUNKLEMAN, author, actress; b. Chgo., May 14, 1918; d. Gabriel and Deborah (Warshauer) Dunkleman; m. Joseph Wolfson, June 16, 1940 (div. Apr. 1962); 1 child, Susan; m. Ira J. Bach, Apr. 14, 1963 (dec. Mar. 6, 1985); stepchildren—Caroline Bach Marandos, John Lawrence; m. Josef Diamond, May 18, 1986. Student Carleton Coll., 1935-37; B.S., Northwestern U., 1939. Researcher original manuscripts for One-Woman Theatre, also costume designer, writer, set designer; actress TV commls., indsl. films, radio commls.; photog. model; tchr. platform speaking techniques to corp. execs. Active sr. citizens groups, youth groups. Recipient Career Achievement award Chgo. Area Profl. Pan Hellenic Assn., 1971. Mem. Screen Actors Guild, AFTRA, Zeta Phi Eta. Clubs: Arts, Tavern (Chgo.). Author: (plays) Two Lives, 1958; ... because of Her!, 1963; Madame, Your Influence is Showing, 1969; MS ... Haven't We Met Before?, 1973; Lady, You're Rocking the Boat!, 1976; Freud Never Said It Was Easy, 1978; Of All the Nerve, 1982; vignettes for theatre.

BACHMAN, NEAL KENYON, librarian; b. Iowa City, Aug. 10, 1950; s. Neal and Esther Elaine (Archer) B.; B.Mus. in Edn., U. Nebr., 1972, M.Ed., 1978. Tchr. instrumental and vocal music Osceola (Nebr.) Schs., 1972-73; band dir. Elkhorn (Nebr.) Public Schs., 1973-75; retail salesman Musicland, Lincoln, Nebr., 1975-76; media specialist Malcolm (Nebr.) Public Schs., 1978-83; librarian Clarinda (Iowa) High Sch., 1983-85, Eisenhower Sch., Fort Leavenworth Unified Schs., Kans., 1985—; vis. instr. U. Nebr.-Lincoln, 1982. Recipient Malcolm Parent-Tchr. Orgn. cert. of recognition, 1981. Mem. Malcolm Edn. Assn. (pres. 1980-81), Assn. for Ednl. Communications and Tech., Nebr. Alumni Band (charter), Kans. Ednl. Media Assn., Nebr. Ednl. Media Assn. (dir. 1982-83), Phi Delta Kappa. Mem. Reorganized Ch. of Jesus Christ of Latter-day Saints. Contbr. articles to profl. jours. Home: 1008 Kenton Leavenworth KS 66048 Office: Unified Sch Dist 207 Fort Leavenworth KS 66027

BACHMAN, PHILIP LAIRD, architect; b. East Chicago, Ind., June 25, 1944; s. William J. and Marjorie (Lammering) B.; m. Karen G. Bennett, Apr. 24, 1971. BArch, U. Ill., 1970, MArch, 1973. Registered architect, Ind., Ill. Architect HOK, St. Louis, 1973-77; ptnr. William J. Bachman & Ptnrs., Hammond, Ind., 1977—. Pres. bd. trustees Calumet Area YWCA, Hammond, 1985-86. Mem. AIA, Hammond C. of C. (pres. 1982-83). Lodge: Rotary. Avocation: sailing. Office: William J Bachman & Ptnrs 5116 Hohman Hammond IN 46320

BACHMAN, TIMOTHY ADAM, graphic design company executive; b. Dayton, Ohio, Apr. 13, 1947; s. Robert Dean and Gladys Lorraine (Gilbert) B.; m. Kathy Jean Hofer, May 1, 1971; children: Bronwyn Halley and Nathan Scott (twins). BFA, Ohio State U., 1969. Pres. Bachman Design, Inc., Columbus, Ohio, 1981-86; v.p. graphic group Retail Plannig Assocs., Inc., Columbus, 1986—; panel speaker Touche Ross Conf. Interactive Video in Retailing, Washington, 1987. Served with N.G., 1970-76. Recipient Best Home Improvement Store award Nat. Retail Mchts. Assn., 1985, Best Specialty Store award Chain Store Age mag., 1986. Mem. Hocking County Artist Guild (v.p. 1977), Columbus Soc. Communicating Arts (1st v.p. 1986—). Avocations: volleyball, biking, water color painting. Subject of feature in Interior Design Mag., 1986. Office: Retail Planning Assoc Graphic Group 645 S Grant Ave Columbus OH 43206

BACHMANN, JACK JOSEPH, real estate developer; b. St. Louis, July 9, 1938; s. Joseph Albert Jr. and Helen Mary (Doerer) B.; divorced; children: Joseph , James. BSBA, Wash. U., St. Louis, 1961. Pres. and chief exec. officer Kingmont Corp., St. Louis, 1979—; adv. bd. Chippewa First Fin. Bank, St. Louis, 1980—. Mem. United Ch. of Christ. Avocations: golf, music. Home: 12302 Matthews Ln Saint Louis MO 63127 Office: PO Box 8672 Saint Louis MO 63126

BACHMANN, WILLIAM VINCENT, combustion engine consultant, inventor; b. Bozen, S. Tyrol, Italy, Apr. 8, 1913; s. Johann and Franziska (Demetz) B.; student engring. Koenigliche Staatsgewerbeschule, 1929-30, pvt. study art and graphics, 1931-34; m. Diane Thomson, Jan. 3, 1977; children by former marriages—George, Francisca, Vincent. With Massey Ferguson Co., Toronto, Ont., Can., 1953-56; with Dilworth Ewbanks, cons. Can. Air Research Project, Toronto, 1956-58; body A engr. Chrysler Corp., Highland Park, Mich., 1958-70; test engr. cons. Volkswagen Mfg. Corp. Am., Warren, Mich., 1977-78; pres. Bachmann Fire Ring Engine Research Co., St. Clair Shores, Mich., 1979—. Patentee 13 U.S., numerous fgn. patents in field. Mem. Soc. Automotive Engrs., Engring. Soc. Detroit, The Inventors' Assn. of Met. Detroit. Address: 22517 Ten Mile Rd Saint Clair Shores MI 48080

BACH-Y-RITA, PAUL, neurophysiologist, rehabilitation medicine specialist; b. N.Y.C., Apr. 24, 1934; s. Pedro and Anne (Hyman) Bach-y-R.; m. Esther Wicab Gutierrez, Apr. 2, 1977; children—Jacqueline Anne, Carol Jean, Laura, Andrea. M.D., Universidad Nacional Autonoma de Mex., 1959. Diplomate: Am. Bd. Phys. Medicine and Rehab. Pub. health officer Tilzapotla, Mex., 1958-59; intern Presbyterian Hosp., San Francisco, 1960-61; resident in phys. medicine and rehab. Santa Clara Valley Med. Center, Stanford U., San Jose, Calif., 1977-79; prof. Sch. Med. Sci., U. Pacific, San Francisco, 1967-79; chief rehab. medicine service Martinez (Calif.) VA Hosp., 1979-83; prof., vice chmn. dept. phys. medicine and rehab., prof. dept. human physiology U. Calif., Davis, 1979-83; Prof., chmn. dept. U. Wis. Sch. Medicine-Madison, 1983—; assoc. dir. Smith-Kettlewell Inst. Visual Scis., San Francisco, 1967-79; dir. San Francisco Rehab. Engring. Center, 1974-78; vis. prof. U. Pisa, Italy, 1970-71, Universidad Nacional Autonoma de Mex., 1974, 86, Universidad Autonoma Metropolitana, Mex., 1975-76. Author: Brain Mechanisms in Sensory Substitution, 1972; editor 3 books; assoc. editor: Perception, 1974-78; mem. editorial adv. bd.: Internat. Jour. Neurosci, 1977—, Internat. Rehab. Medicine, 1978—, Annales Medicine Physique, 1981—, Jour. Neurol. Rehab., 1986—. Bank of Am.-Giannini fellow, 1961-62; USPHS postdoctoral fellow, 1962-63; recipient NIH research career devel. awards, 1963-73; Silver Hektoen medal AMA, 1972; Bronze Hektoen medal, 1977; Franceschetti-Liebrecht prize German Ophthal. Soc., 1974. Mem. AAAS, Internat. Rehab. Medicine Assn., Assn. for Research in Vision and Ophthalmology, Am. Physiol. Soc., Acad. Phys. Medicine and Rehab., Soc. Neurosci. Democrat. Patentee in field. Home: 3532 Blackhawk Dr Madison WI 53705 Office: 600 Highland Ave Madison WI 53705

BACK, MICHAEL DAVID, military officer; b. Middletown, Ohio, Dec. 20, 1957; s. Gerald Lee and Margaret Ann (Sloan) B.; m. Loretta Gayle Neighbors, June 15, 1979; children: Sara Ruth, Adam Jacob, David Joseph. Student, Sinclair Community Coll., 1977—, Community Coll. USAF, 1982—, NCO Prep Sch, 1985—. Enlisted USAF, 1982, staff sgt., logistician, 1982—; pub. relations rep. 2046 CG, USAF, Wright Patterson AFB, 1984—. Contbr. articles to profl. jours. Tchr. Sun. Sch. Crestview Ch. of God., Germantown, Ohio, 1985—. Recipient Air Force Achievement Medal award USAF, 1984, Airman of the Quarter, USAF, 1983, 85, Airman of Yr., 1985; Outstanding Jr. Supply Technician, USAF, 1983, 84. Republican. Avocations: woodworking, golf. Home: 3396 Pennyroyal Rd Franklin OH 45005-1013 Office: 2046 CG/LGCM Communications Rd Wright Patterson AFB OH 45433

BACK, ROBERT WYATT, institutional investment company executive; b. Omaha, Dec. 22, 1936; s. Albert Edward and Edith (Elliott) B.; m. Linaya Gail Hahn, Aug. 30, 1964; children—Christopher Frederick, Gregory Franklin. B.A., Trinity Coll., 1958; M.A., Yale U., 1960; postgrad. Northwestern U., 1958, London U., 1959-60, Harvard U., 1960-61. Head trader and security analyst Lincoln Nat. Life Ins. Co., Fort Wayne, Ind., 1964-69; sr. investment analyst Allstate Ins. Co., Northbrook, Ill., 1969-72; chmn. Consumer Analyst Group, Chgo., 1972-74; investment adv. acct. mgr. Brown Bros. Harriman & Co., Chgo., 1972-74; asst. v.p., investment analyst Harris Trust & Savs. Bank, 1974-82; v.p., instl. equity analyst Prescott Ball & Turben, 1982-83; v.p., sr. investment analyst Blunt, Ellis & Loewi, Inc., 1983-84; v.p. instl. equity sales Rodman & Renshaw, Inc., 1984—; has instructed at Purdue U., Indiana U., DePaul Univ., Mich. Tech. Univ. Contbr. numerous articles to profl. jours. Corp. mem. Scholarships for Ill. Residents, Inc., 1969—; mem. planning com. Fin. Analysts Fedn. Conv., 1984—; pres. Buffalo Grove (Ill.) Police Pension Fund, 1973—; del. Assn. Yale Alumni, 1983-85. Served to capt. USAF, 1958-64. Mem. Ill. Police Pension Fund Assn. (investment, edn. coms.). Clubs: Yale Chgo. (bd. dirs. 1983-85, chmn. grad. and profl. programs 1983—), Yale N.Y., Harvard Chgo., Harvard Grad. Soc. Home: 942 Twisted Oak Ln Buffalo Grove IL 60090 Office: Rodman & Renshaw Inc 120 S LaSalle St Chicago IL 60090

BACKE, CHRISTOPHER GEORGE, construction equipment executive; b. N.Y.C., Apr. 19, 1932; s. Christopher G. and Alice (Sweeney) B.; m. Nancy L. Horton, June 11, 1960 (div. June 1983); children: Lisa Marie, Barbara Ann, Alice Louise. Student, Fordham U., 1950, Iona Coll., 1956. Carpenter Thornberg Builders, Islip, N.Y., 1956-58; pres. Backe Constrn. Co., Islip, 1958-67; salesman Equitable Life Ins. Co., Islip, 1967-70; pres. Surfland Builders, Islip, 1970-74; regional sales mgr. Conesco Inds. Ltd., Chgo. and Little Ferry, N.J., 1974-80; v.p., owner Forming Concepts, Inc., Palatine, 1980—; Speaker World of Concrete, Atlanta, 1986. Capt. Vol. Fire Dept., Ocean Beach, N.Y., 1956-68; Rep. committeeman, Islip, 1959-60; trustee Ocean Beach Sch. Bd., 1959-60; co-founder, pres. Fire Island Small Bus. Assn., 1960-63, Robbins Rest Property Owners Assn., 1960-64. Served with USAF, 1950-54. Mem. Property Owners Assn. (pres. 1959-62), Fire Island Small Bus. Assn. (pres., founder 1961-62). Roman Catholic. Clubs: Arlington Heights Golf League (treas., sec., v.p. 1984-86, pres. 1987). Avocations: golf, sailing, fishing, hunting. Home: 755 Moore Dr Elk Grove Village IL 60007 Office: Forming Concepts Inc 632 W Colfax Palatine IL 60067

BACKER, MATTHIAS HENRY, JR., obstetrician-gynecologist; b. St. Louis, Dec. 19, 1926; s. Matthias Henry Sr. and Louise (Jokisch) B.; m. Laverne Elizabeth Knapp, June 4, 1949; children: Mary Kathryn, Matt III, Marilyn Ann Backer Parker, Mary Lou Backer Barrett, Donald, Robert, Edward, Mary Susan Backer Conklin, Mary Carol Backer Miller, Mary Patrice, Joseph, Brian, Denis. MD, St. Louis U., 1950. Diplomate Am. Bd. Ob-Gyn (examiner 1986), Nat. Bd. Med. Examiners. Intern Nat. Naval Med. Ctr., Bethesda, Md., 1950-51; resident in ob-gyn St. Louis U. Hosps., 1951-54; practice medicine specializing in ob-gyn St. Louis, 1954-85; instr. ob-gyn St. Louis U. Sch. Medicine, 1954-60, sr. instr., 1960-63, asst. clin. prof., 1963-66, assoc. clin. prof., 1966-72, clin. prof., 1972-85, prof. ob-gyn., chmn. dept., 1985—, dir. ob-gyn outpatient clinic, 1967-69, mem. com. faculty appointments and promotions, 1972-81, mem. exec. com. faculty, 1972-76, mem. faculty affairs com., 1975-78, dir. residency program, 1985—; chief ob-gyn St. Joseph's Hosp., St. Louis, 1959-62, St. Anthony's, St. Louis, Hosp., 1966-69; pres. St. Louis U. Hosps. Med. Staff, 1968-69; mem. governing bd. St. Louis U. Hosps., 1969-70; pres. med. and dental staff St. Anthony's Med. Ctr., 1984-85; lectr. Archdiocesan PreCana Council, 1955-58, Archdiocesan Sch. Commn., 1969-72; pres. Backer & Probst Inc., St. Louis, 1967-85. Contbr. numerous articles to profl. jours. Bd. dirs. St. Louis chpt. Am. Cancer Soc., 1970-76, Blue Shield Mo. Med. Service, 1970-80, St. Anthony Med. Ctr., 1984-85; lector Our Lady of Providence Ch., St. Louis, 1969—; guadrian ad litem for unborn Mo. Supremem Ct., 1971. Served to rear adm. M.C., USNR, 1944-84. Decorated Legion of Merit, Dept. Def. Superior Service medal; recipeint Backer award St. Louis U. High Sch., 1983. Fellow ACS, Am. Coll. Obstetricians & Gynecologists; mem. AMA, Mo. State Med. Assn., St. Louis Med. Soc., Am. Soc. Mil. Surgeons, Cen. Assn. Obstetricians & Gynecologists, St. Louis Gynecol. Soc. (pres. 1969-70), Naval Res. Assn. (pres. Spirit of St. Louis chpt.). Roman Catholic. Home: 101 Flamingo Dr Saint Louis MO 63123 Office: Hosp Dept Ob-Gyn 1325 S Grand Blvd Saint Louis MO 63104

BACKIS, ROBERT J., social worker. BA in Sociology, Loyola U., Chgo., 1971, M of Clin. Social Work, 1987; postgrad., Mid-Am. Inst. Cath. Charities, Chgo., 1972-73; MDiv, U. St. Mary of the Lake, Mundelein, Ill., 1975. Assoc. pastor St. Charles Lwanga Ch., Chgo., 1975-80, pastor, 1980-82; adminstr. St. Charles Lwanga Lifeline Ctr., Chgo., 1975-80; program dir. Proyecto Libre Ada S. McKinley Community Services, Chgo., 1982-83; chaplain, dir. dept. pastoral care Mercy Hosp. and Med. Ctr., Chgo., 1983-85; social worker II Ill. Dept. Children and Family Services, Chgo., 1985—; social worker Martha Washington Hosp., Chgo., 1986—. Recipient Coordinating Bd. award Assn. Chgo. Priests, 1981, Community Recognition award Robert Taylor Home Local Adv. Council, 1981. Mem. Nat. Assn. Social Workers, Nat. Assn. Cath. Chaplains, Corps Resigned priests in U.S. Home: 1225 W Chase Ave Apt E-2 Chicago IL 60626

BACKYS, DONALD JEROME, systems engineer; b. Waukegan, Ill., July 12, 1944; s. Jerome P. and Frances L. (Grobelch) B.; B.S.E.E., Mlw. Sch. Engring., 1967; M.B.A., Keller Grad. Sch. Mgmt., 1984. Registered profl. engr., Ill., Wis. Project engr. Collins Radio Co., Cedar Rapids, Iowa, 1967-69; devel. engr. Motorola, Inc., Schaumburg, Ill., 1969-72, mfg. engr., 1972-74, system design engr., 1974-77, system engring. group leader 1977—; electronics instr. Oakton Community Coll., Des Plaines, Ill., 1974-76, 80-81; cons. Hoffman Estates Zoning Bd., Ill., 1975. Mem. indsl. adv. com. Milw. Sch. Engring., 1975-81. Recipient Outstanding Alumnus award Milw. Sch. Engring., 1982. Mem. Milw. Sch. Engring. Alumni Assn. Republican. Roman Catholic. Avocations: flying; amateur radio; racquetball. Office: 1000 Mittel Dr Wood Dale IL 60191

BACON, BRETT KERMIT, lawyer; b. Perry, Iowa, Aug. 8, 1947; s. Royden S. and Aldeen A. (Zuker) B.; m. Peggy Darlene Smith, July 30, 1972; children: Jeffrey Brett, Scott Michael. BA, U. Dubuque, 1969; JD, Northwestern U., 1972. Bar: Ohio 1972, U.S. Ct. Appeals (6th cir.) 1972, U.S. Supreme Ct. 1980. Assoc., Thompson, Hine & Flory, Cleve., 1972-80, ptnr., 1980—; speaker in field. Author: Computer Law, 1982, 1984. Vice-pres. profl. sect. United Way, Cleve., 1982-86; pres. Shaker Heights Youth Ctr., Inc., Ohio, 1984-86. Mem. Bar Assn. Greater Cleve. Home: 2924 Manchester Rd Shaker Heights OH 44122 Office: Thompson Hine & Flory 1100 Nat City Bank Bldg Cleveland OH 44114

BACON, DENNIS RAY, accountant; b. Tulsa, Dec. 31, 1957; s. Johnnie Allen Bacon and Clara (Calvert) Teel; m. Michelle Marie Repchak, June 20, 1981. BBA, Harding U., 1980; MBA, No. Ill. U., 1984—. CPA, Ill., Okla. Staff auditor Deloitte, Haskins & Sells, Tulsa, 1980-81; in charge auditor Interlake, Inc., Riverdale, Ill., 1981-83; area controller Browning Ferris Industries, Melrose Park, Ill., 1983-85; sr. ops. analyst Beatrice Cos., Inc., Chgo., 1985-86; acctg. mgr. The Interlake Cos., Inc., Burr Ridge, Ill., 1986—; cons., Downers Grove, Ill., 1986—. youth dir., treas. West Suburban Ch. of Christ, Berkely, Ill., 1981-85, bd. dirs., 1982-85; participant Downers Grove (Ill.) Heritage Fest, 1983; youth dir. Naperville (Ill.) Ch. of Christ, 1986—; bd. dirs., sec., treas. Rockford (Ill.) Christian Camp, 1986—, camp counselor, 1986-87; mem. steering com., fundraiser Mich. Christian Coll., 1984-87. Mem. Am. Inst. CPA's, Am. Prodn. and Inventory Control Soc., Ill. CPA Soc. Republican. Home: 6028 Brookbank Rd Downers Grove IL 60516 Office: The Interlake Cos Inc 550 Warrenville Lisle IL 60532

BACON, GEORGE EDGAR, pediatrician, educator; b. N.Y.C., Apr. 13, 1932; s. Edgar and Margaret Priscilla (Anderson) B.; m. Grace Elizabeth Graham, June 30, 1956; children—Nancy, George, John. B.A., Wesleyan U., 1953; M.D., Duke U., 1957; M.S. in Pharmacology, U. Mich., 1967. Diplomate Am. Bd. Pediatrics, subsplty. Bd. Pediatric Endocrinology. Intern in pediatrics Duke Hosp., Durham, N.C., 1957-58; resident in pediatrics Columbia-Presbyn. Med. Ctr., N.Y.C., 1961-63; instr. U. Mich., Ann Arbor, 1963, asst. prof., 1968, assoc. prof., 1971, prof. pediatrics, 1974-86, prof. emeritus, 1986—, chief pediatric endocrinology service, dept. pediatrics, 1970-83, dir. house officer programs, dept. pediatrics, 1982-86, assoc. chmn. dept. pediatrics, 1983-86; vice chmn. dir.'s adv. council Univ. Hosp., Ann Arbor, 1981-82; prof., chmn. dept. pediatrics Tex. Tech U., Lubbock,

1986—; chief staff pediatrics Lubbock Gen. Hosp., 1986—; mem. Senate Assembly, U. Mich., 1978-80; coordinator profl. service C.S. Mott Children's Hosp., 1973-83, mem. exec. com. for clin. affairs, 1975-76, 77-79, assoc. vice chmn. med. staff, 1978-79; chmn. exec. com. C.S. Mott Children's, Women's, Holden hosps., Ann Arbor, 1973-82. Author: A Practical Approach to Pediatric Endocrinology, 1975, 2d edit., 1982. Contbr. articles to profl. jours. Served to capt. U.S. Army, 1958-61. Fellow Am. Acad. Pediatrics (treas. Mich. chpt. 1983-86, council Tex. chpt. 1986—); mem. Am. Pediatric Soc., Pediatric Endocrine Soc. Republican.

BACON, WILLIAM THOMPSON, JR., investment company executive; b. Chgo., Feb. 6, 1923; s. William Thompson and Martha (Smith) B.; grad. Phillips Acad., 1941; B.A., Yale, 1945; m. Margaret Hoyt, Apr. 18, 1942; children—William Thompson III, Catherine (Mrs. Von Stroh), Hoyt Wells, J. Knight, Christopher S. Asst. cashier First Nat. Bank of Chgo., 1946-55; partner Bacon, Whipple & Co., Chgo., 1956-82, assoc., 1982—; dir. Walbro Corp., Safecard Services, Inc., Trappers Loop, Inc.; hon. dir. Stifel Fin. Corp. Trustee Hadley Sch. for Blind, Winnetka, Ill., Fountain Valley Sch., Colorado Springs, Colo. Served with AUS, 1943-44. Mem. Elihu, Delta Kappa Epsilon. Republican. Episcopalian. Clubs: Yale (pres. 1962-63), Chicago, University (Chgo.); Onwentsia (Lake Forest, Ill.); Shoreacres (Lake Bluff, Ill.); Old Elm (Ft. Sheridan, Ill.); Indian Hill (Winnetka, Ill.); Yale (N.Y.C.); Gulfstream Golf (Delray Beach, Fla.). Home: 184 Winthrop Ln Lake Forest IL 60045 Office: 135 S LaSalle St Chicago IL 60603

BADEER, HENRY SARKIS, physician, educator; b. Mersine, Turkey, Jan. 31, 1915; came to U.S., 1965, naturalized, 1971; s. Sarkis and Persape Hagop (Koundakjian) B.; m. Mariam Mihran Kassarjian, July 12, 1948; children: Gilbert H., Daniel H. M.D., Am. U., Beirut, Lebanon, 1938. Gen. practice medicine Beirut, 1940-51; asst. instr. Am. U. Sch. Medicine, Beirut, 1938-45; adj. prof. Am. U. Sch. Medicine, 1945-51, asso. prof., 1951-62, prof. physiology, 1962-65, acting chmn. dept., 1951-56, chmn., 1956-65; research fellow Harvard U. Med. Sch., Boston, 1948-49; prof. physiology Creighton U. Med. Sch., Omaha, 1967—; acting chmn. dept. Creighton U. Med. Sch., 1971-72; vis. prof. U. Iowa, Iowa City, 1957-58, Downstate Med. Center, Bklyn., 1965-67; mem. med. com. Azounieh Sanatorium, Beirut, 1961-65; mem. research com. Nebr. Heart Assn., 1967-70, 85—. Author textbook; contbr. chpts. to books, articles to profl. jours. Recipient Golden Apple award Students of AMA, 1975; Rockefeller fellow., 1948-49; grantee med. research com. Am. U. Beirut, 1956-65. Mem. AAAS, Internat. Soc. Heart Research, Am. Physiol. Soc., Alpha Omega Alpha. Home: 2808 S 99th Ave Omaha NE 68124 Office: Creighton U Med Sch 2500 Calif St Omaha NE 68178

BADEN, ROBERT CHARLES, food products executive; b. Piqua, Ohio, Dec. 10, 1942; s. Carl A. and Lucille (Putnam) B.; m. Michele Sullivan, Mar. 20, 1971; 1 child, Bradley. BS in Acctg., Wittenberg U., 1965; MBA, Wright State U., 1972. CPA, Mich., Ohio. Auditor Ernst and Whinney, Dayton, Ohio, 1965-72; dir. budgeting Amcast, Dayton, 1972-74; asst. controller Cross and Trecker, Fraser, Mich., 1974-76; v.p., controller LaSalle Machine Tool Co., Troy, Mich., 1976-84; corp. controller Diamond Crystal Salt Co., St. Clair, Mich., 1984—. Mem. FEI, Am. Inst. CPA's, Mich. Assn. CPA's. Club: St. Clair Golf. Lodge: Rotary (treas. 1986-87). Home: 458 4th St Maryville MI 48040 Office: Diamond Crystal Salt Co 916 S Riverside Ave Saint Clair MI 48079

BADER, ALFRED ROBERT, chemist; b. Vienna, Austria, Apr. 28, 1924; came to U.S., 1947, naturalized, 1964; s. Alfred and Elizabeth Maria (Serenyi) B.; m. Isabel Overton, Jan. 26, 1982; children from previous marriage: David, Daniel. BS in Engring. Chemistry, Queens U., Can., 1945, BA in History, 1946, MS in Organic Chemistry, 1947, LLD, 1986; MA, Harvard U., 1948, PhD, 1949; DS (hon.), U. Wis.-Milw., 1980, Purdue U., 1984, U. Wis.-Madison, 1984. Research chemist, group leader charge organic research PPG Co., Milw., 1950-54; chief chemist Aldrich Chem. Co., Milw., 1954-55, pres., 1955-81, chmn., 1981—; pres. Sigma-Aldrich Corp., Milw., 1975-80; chmn. bd., chief exec. officer Sigma-Aldrich Corp., 1980-83, chmn. bd., 1983—. Author in field. Guest curator Milw. Art Ctr., 1976; trustee Queen's U., Inst. Fine Arts, N.Y. Recipient Winthrop-Sears medal Chem. Industry Assn., 1980; named Entrepreneur of Year Research Dirs. Assn., 1980. Fellow Royal Soc. Arts; mem. Am. Chem. Soc. (award Milw. sect. 1971), Chem. Soc. London, Coll. Art Assn. Jewish. Clubs: University (Milw.); Chemists (N.Y.C.). Patentee in field. Office: Sigma Aldrich Corp 940 W St Paul Ave Milwaukee WI 53233

BADER, KENNETH LEROY, association executive; b. Carroll, Ohio, May 4, 1934; s. Troy Ora and Clara Louise (Walter) B.; m. Linda Mary Silbaugh, Sept. 17, 1955; children: Bradley, Brent. B.Sc., Ohio State U., 1956, M.Sc., 1957, Ph.D., 1960. Instr. agronomy 1957-60, asst. prof., 1960-63, asso. prof., 1963-67; asst. dean Coll. Agr., 1964-67, prof., dean of students, 1968-72; vice chancellor, prof. agronomy U. Nebr., Lincoln, 1972-76; chief exec. officer Am. Soybean Assn., St. Louis, 1976—; mem. U.S. President's Export Adminstrn. Commn., 1982, U.S. Agrl. Trade Policy Com., 1981—, chmn., 1985-86. Contbr. articles on agronomy to sci. jours. Mem. exec. com. Conv. Bur., 1965-71; bd. dirs. YMCA, 1968-72, chmn., 1969-71. Recipient Nat. Agri-marketer of Yr. award, 1985, Nat. Agrl. Lender of the Yr. award Agrl. Editors, 1985; named St. Louis Agribus. Leader of Yr., 1981; Am. Council on Edn. fellow, 1967-68. Mem. Am. Soc. Agronomy (chmn. nat. commn. agrl. trade export policy 1984-86), U.S. C. of C. (food and agr. com. 1980—), Sigma Xi, Alpha Zeta (nat. agrimarketer of yr. 1985). Office: Am Soybean Assn 777 Craig Rd PO Box 27300 Saint Louis MO 63141

BADGER, CHARLES H., manufacturing company executive; b. Durant, Okla., Feb. 10, 1917; s. Charles H. and Mildred (Printz) B.; m. Rozine Fazio; children—Barbara, Bruce. B.S.E.E., U. Colo., 1938; M.B.A., Northwestern U., 1943. Student engr. Automatic Electric Co., Chgo., 1938-45; owner, pres. Relay Service Co., Chgo., 1943—. Office: Relay Service Co 1300-12 N Pulaski Rd Chicago IL 60651

BADRA, ROBERT GEORGE, educator; b. Lansing, Mich., Dec. 8, 1933; s. Razouk Anthony and Anna (Paul) B.; m. Maria Teresa Beer, Oct. 25, 1968 (div. 1973); m. 2d, Kristen Lillie Stuckey, Dec. 30, 1977; children: Rachal Jennifer, Danielle ElizabethJane. B.A., Sacred Heart Sem., 1957; M.A., Western Mich. U., 1968; M.Div., St. John's Provincial Sem., 1985. Ordained priest Roman Catholic Ch., 1961. Faculty Kalamazoo Valley Community Coll., 1968—, prof. philosophy, religion and humanities, 1968—; adj. prof. Nazareth Coll., 1985—. Bd. dirs. Kalamazoo Council for the Humanities, 1983-86. Mem. NEA, Inst. World Order. Democrat. Author: Meditations for Spiritual Misfits, 1983; columnist Western Mich. Cath., Grand Rapids, 1983—. Office: Kalamazoo Valley Community Coll 6767 West O Ave Kalamazoo MI 49009

BADRI, A. ALLEN, plastic surgeon; b. Isfahan, Iran, Mar. 1, 1929; came to U.S., 1959; m. Dorothy Helena Badri, Mar. 12, 1960; children: Susan, Cherie, Sheila. Student, Premed. Coll. of Isfahan, 1946-50; MD, U. Tehran (Iran) Med. Sch., 1959. Lic. surgeon, Va., Ill.; diplomate Am. Bd. Gen. Surgery, Am. Bd. Plastic Surgery. Intern Perth Amboy (N.J.) Gen. Hosp., 1959-60; resident in radiology Norfolk (Va.) Gen. Hosp., 1960-61; resident in surgery Newark Beth Israel Hosp., 1961-63; resident in surgery Meth. Hosp., Bklyn., 1962-63, chief resident, 1964-65; resident in surgery Meml. Hosp. for Cancer, N.Y.C., 1963-64; resident in plastic surgery St. Louis U. Group Hosp., 1965-67; plastic medicine specializing in plastic surgery, hand surgery Hinsdale, Ill., 1967—; staff mem. Gottlieb Hosp., Melrose Park, Ill., Oak Park (Ill.) Hosp., Elmhurst (Ill.) Meml. Hosp., Westlake Hosp., Melrose Park, Edward Hosp, Naperville, Ill, Den. DuPage Hosp, Winfield, Ill.; chief of Plastic Surgery Service Hines (Ill.) Vets. Adminstrn. Hosp.; asst. prof. surgery Loyola U. Med. Sch., Maywood, Ill. Fellow ACS; mem. AMA, Am. Soc. Plastic and Reconstructive Surgeons, Ill. Med.Soc., Chgo. Med. Soc., DuPage County Med. Soc., Soc. Vets. Hosp. Surgeons. Avocations: reading, travel. Office: 120 Oakbrook Ctr Mall #728 Oakbrook IL 60521 also: 7830 W North Elmwood Park IL 60635

BAEBLER, DREW CHARLES, lawyer; b. St. Louis, Feb. 11, 1960; s. Arthur G. and Iva Lea (Modde) B.; m. Laura Neri, Aug. 4, 1984. BS in Biomed. Engring. summa cum laude, Cath. U. Am., 1981; JD, Washington U., 1984. Bar: Mo. 1984, U.S. Patent Office 1984, U.S. Dist. Ct. (ea. and we. dists.) Mo. 1984, Ill. 1985. Assoc. Allegretti, Newit, Witeof & McAndrews, Chgo., 1982, Finnegan, Henderson, Farabow, Garret & Dunner, Washington, 1983, Hullverson, Hullverson & Frank, Inc., St. Louis, 1984—. Recipient Law Week award Bur. Nat. Affairs, 1984. Mem. ABA, ASME, Am. TRial Lawyers Assn., Mo. Bar Assn. (tort law com. 1985-86), Tau Beta Pi (Blue Key award 1980), Phi Delta Phi (magister). Republican. Roman Catholic. Avocations: tennis, golf, kung fu. Home: 3455 Halliday Saint Louis MO 63118 Office: Hullverson Hullverson & Frank 1010 Market Suite 1550 Saint Louis MO 63101

BAEHR, ELSA TELSER, clinical psychologist; b. Chgo., June 5, 1929; d. Philip Stein and Mildred (Mayerson) Beck; m. Eugene Telser, Aug. 24, 1947 (div.); children: Joanne, Margaret, Elizabeth; m. Rufus Baehr, June 28, 1975. BA, Roosevelt U., Chgo., 1952; MA, Roosevelt U., 1954; PhD, Northwestern U., 1971. Lic. psychologist, Ill. Sr. psychologist Cook County Hosp., Chgo., 1974-78, adminstr. Outpatient Psychol. Clinic, 1976-78; pvt. practice psychotherapy Evanston, Ill., 1971-82; clinical psychologist Baehr & Baehr, Ltd., Evanston, 1982—; cons. Milw. Psychiatric Services, 1970-74; assoc. dept. psychiatry Northwestern U. Med. Sch., 1973—; clin assoc. U. Ill, Chgo., 1981—. Mem. Am. Psychol. Assn., Ill. Psychol. Assn., Assn. for Clinical and Experimental Hypnosis, Assn. for Personality Assessment. Avocation: designing clothes. Office: 636 Church St Evanston IL 60201

BAEHR, JAMES MORSE, orthopaedic surgeon; b. Topeka, Mar. 6, 1932; s. Henry Arthur and Dorothy E. (Morse) B.; m. Mary Anne Follin, Sept. 21, 1956; children: Kenneth, Paul Russell. Student, St. Olaf Coll., 1950-52, U. Nebr., 1952-53; MD, Northwestern U., 1953-57. Diplomate Am. Bd. Orthopaedic Surgery. Orthopaedic surgeon Wichita (Kans.) Clinic, 1964-74, Greenleaf Orthopaedics, Gurnee, Ill., 1974—. Served to lt. USNR, 1959-61. Fellow ACS, Am. Acad. Orthopaedic Surgeons; mem. Clin. Orthopaedic Soc. Presbyterian. Office: Greenleaf Orthopaedics 135 Greenleaf Gurnee IL 60031

BAER, DAVID, JR., lawyer; b. Belleville, Ill., Sept. 24, 1905; s. David and Sunshine (Lieber) B.; LL.B., Washington U., 1928; m. Mary Lynne Cockrell Sweet, Apr. 18, 1938 (dec.); m. 2d, Jane Caulfield, Sept. 11, 1982. Ptnr. Lashly, Baer & Hamel, P.C., St. Louis; dir. Lindell Trust Co.; former pres., dir. Mo.-Lincoln Trust Co.; former dir. Scullin Steel Co., St. Louis. Former mem. St. Louis Boy Scout Endowment Fund Com. Served as sgt. AUS, 1943-45. Mem. Estate Planning Council St. Louis (past pres., dir.), Am., Mo., St. Louis (past chmn. group ins. com.) bar assns., Washington U. Law Alumni Assn., Jr. (life), Ill. Jr. (past pres.), U.S. Jr. Cs. of C. (senator). Clubs: Mo. Athletic, University. Lodges: Masons, De Molay (sr., Legion of Honor, past master councilor). Home: 625 S Skinker Blvd Saint Louis MO 63105 Office: 714 Locust St Saint Louis MO 63101

BAER, JOHN RICHARD FREDERICK, lawyer; b. Melrose Park, Ill., Jan. 9, 1941; s. John Richard and Zena Edith (Ostreyko) B.; m. Linda Gail Chapman, Aug. 31, 1963; children—Brett Scott, Deborah Jill. B.A., U. Ill.-Champaign, 1963, J.D., 1966. Bar: Ill. 1966, U.S. Dist. Ct. (no. dist.) Ill. 1967, U.S. Ct. Appeals (7th cir.) 1969, U.S. Ct. Appeals (D.C. cir.) 1975, U.S. Ct. Appeals (9th cir.) 1979, U.S. Supreme Ct. 1975. Assoc. Keck, Mahin & Cate, Chgo., 1966-73, ptnr., 1974—; instr. Advanced Mgmt. Inst., Lake Forest Coll., 1975-76; speaker various legal seminars, 1975, 76, 77, 80, 81; mem. adv. com. legal asst. program. Nat. Coll. Edn., 1980-83, chmn., 1982-83. Mem. Plan Commn., Village of Deerfield (Ill.), 1976-79, chmn., 1978-79, mem. Home Rule Study Commn., 1974-75, mem. home rule implementation com., 1975-76. Mem. Ill. State Bar Assn. (competition dir. region 8 Nat. Moot Ct. Competition 1974, co-chmn. nat. moot competition 1976, profl. ethics com. 1977-84, chmn. 1982-83, spl. com. on individual lawyer advt. 1981-83, profl. responsibility com. 1983-84), ABA, Fed. Bar Assn., Am. Judicature Soc., Nat. Lawyer's Club. Clubs: River (Chgo.). Editorial bd. U. Ill. Law Forum, 1964-65, asst. editor, 1965-66; contbg. editor: Commercial Liability Risk Management and Insurance, 1978. Office: 8300 Sears Tower 233 S Wacker Dr Chicago IL 60606

BAER, JOSEPH C., health care executive; b. Wauseon, Ohio, Dec. 22, 1939; s. Clarence J. and Laura A. (Crossgrove) B.; m. Joan L. Dupaski, June 25, 1960; children: Elizabeth E., Joseph C., II. BS in environ. health, Ferris State Coll., 1970; MPH, U. Mich., 1974. Registered sanatarian, Mich.; Lic. nursing home adminstr., Mich. Sr. research technician Gerber Products Co., Fremont, Mich., 1965-68; sanatarian Wayne County Health Dept., Eloise, Mich., 1970-73; adminstr. Livingston County Health Dept., Howell, Mich., 1974-75, W. Mich. Assoc. Health Dept., White Cloud, Mich., 1976-81; exec. dir. Regional Health Care, Baldwin, Mich., 1981—; adj. prof. Ferris State Coll., Big Rapids, Mich. 1986—. chmn. Dayton Township Planning Commn., Newaygo county, Mich., 1983—. Served as food specialist, U.S. Army, 1959-64. Named one of Outstanding Young Men of Am., 1976, Boss of the Yr. Nat. Secs. Assn., 1980-81, Lake County Area Jaycees, 1985. Mem. Nat. Assn. Community Health Ctrs., Mich. Primary Care Assn. (pres. 1974), Nat. Environ. Health Assn. (pres. 1984-87). Roman Catholic. Avocations: remodeling, farming, softball. Home: 4235 S Luce Fremont MI 49412 Office: Regional Health Care 4967 N Michigan Baldwin MI 49304

BAER, ROBERT J., trucking company executive; b. Oct. 25, 1937, St. Louis; s. Charles M. and Angeline Baer; m. Jo Baer, Aug. 27, 1960; children: Bob Jr., Angie, Tim, Cathy, Kristen. BA, So. Ill. U., 1962, MS, 1964. Regional supr. div. recreation City of St. Louis, 1957-64; dep. dir. Human Devel. Corp., St. Louis, 1964-70; from exec. asst. to co. exec. St. Louis County Govt, 1970-74; exec. dir. Bi-State Devel. Agy., St. Louis, 1974-77; v.p., gen. mgr. United Van Lines Inc., Fenton, Mo., 1977-80, exec. v.p., 1980-82, pres., 1982—; v.p., gen. mgr. UniGroup Inc., United Van Lines, and subs., 1977-80, exec. v.p., 1980-82, pres., chief operating officer, 1982—; adj. lectr. in bus. mgmt. Webster U., St. Louis, 1983—, Maryville Coll., St. Louis, 1984—; bd. dirs. VanLiner Ins. Co., Fenton, Merchantile Commerce Bank Bd. Pres. St. Louis Bd. Police Commn., 1984—; bd. dirs. Thomas Dunn Meml. Adult Edn. Program (bd. dirs. program coordinator), St. Louis, 1957—, KETC-9 PBS, St. Louis, 1987—. Mem. Am. Movers Conf. (bd. dirs., past chmn.), Household Goods Carriers' (vice chmn., bd. dirs.). Avocations: gardening, tennis, swimming, reading. Office: United Van Lines Inc 1 United Dr Fenton MO 63026

BAER, ZENAS, lawyer; b. Fordville, N.D., Nov. 11, 1951; s. Allan and Edna (Brubacher) B. B.A. in Polit. Sci. and German, U. Minn., 1976; J.D., Hamline U., 1980. Bar: Minn. 1980, U.S. Dist. Ct. Minn. 1980, U.S. Ct. Claims, 1985. Mng. ptnr. Wefald & Baer, Hawley, Minn., 1980—. Councilman City of Hawley, 1981—. Alt. service as conscientious objector, 1969-72. Recipient 2 awards for excellence Lawyers Coop., Bancroft-Whitney, 1979. Mem. ABA, Assn. Trial Lawyers Am., Minn. Trial Lawyers Assn., Minn. Bar Assn., Clay County Bar Assn., Hawley C. of C. Home: 420 8th St Hawley MN 56549 Office: Wefald & Baer 222 6th St Hawley MN 56549

BAERMANN, DONNA LEE ROTH, insurance analyst; b. Carroll, Iowa, Apr. 28, 1939; d. Omer H. and Awanda Lucille (Mathison) Roth; m. Edwin Ralph Baermann, Jr., July 8, 1961; children—Beth, Bryan, Cynthia. B.S., Mt. Mercy Coll., 1973; student Iowa State U.-Ames, 1957-61. Cert. profl. ins. woman; fellow Life Mgmt. Inst. Ins. agt. Lutheran Mut. Ins. Co., Cedar Rapids, Iowa, 1973; home economist Iowa-Ill. Gas & Electric Co., Cedar Rapids, Iowa, 1973-77; supr. premium collection Life Investors Ins. Co., Cedar Rapids, 1978-83, methods-procedures analyst, 1983—, supr. policy service, 1987—, mem. telecommunications study group com. 1982-83, mem. productivity task force, 1984—. Mem. Nat. Assn. Ins. Women, Nat. Mgmt. Assn. (bd. dirs. Cedar Rapids chpt.), DAR, Chi Omega. Republican. Presbyterian. Home: 361 Willshire Ct NE Cedar Rapids IA 52402 Office: Life Investors Ins Co 4333 Edgewood Rd NE Cedar Rapids IA 52499

BAETZHOLD, HOWARD GEORGE, English language educator; b. Buffalo, Jan. 1, 1923; s. Howard Kuster and Harriet Laura (Hofheins) B.; m. Nancy Millard Cheesman, Aug. 5, 1950; children: Howard King, Barbara Millard. Student, Brown U., 1940-43, MIT, 1943-44; A.B. magna cum laude, Brown U., 1944, M.A., 1948; Ph.D., U. Wis., 1953. Asst. dir. Vets. Coll., Brown U., Providence, 1947-48, dir., 1948-49, admissions officer, 1948-50; teaching asst. U. Wis.-Madison, 1950-51; asst. to assoc. dean Coll. Letters and Sci., 1951-53; asst. prof. English Butler U., Indpls., 1953-57, assoc. prof., 1957-67, prof. English, 1967—; Rebecca Clifton Reade prof. Butler U., 1981—, head dept., 1981-85; vis. prof. U. Del., summer 1963. Author: Mark Twain and John Bull: The British Connection, 1970; contbr. articles to profl. jours. Mem. Indpls. Com. Internat. Visitors, 1965—. Served to 1st lt. A.C. AUS, 1943-46. Faculty fellow Butler U., 1957-58, 69-70; grantee Am. Philos. Soc., 1958, Am. Council Learned Socs., 1967; Butler U. fellow, 1986-87. Mem. AAUP (v.p. state conf. 1955), MLA, Am. Studies Assn. (nat. council 1974-76), Midwest MLA, Gt. Lakes Am. Studies Assn. (pres. 1967-68), Ind. Coll. English Assn. (exec. bd. 1983-85), Am. Philatelic Soc., Greater Ind. Masters Swimming Assn., Art Assn. Indpls., Butler U. Odd Topics Soc., Delta Upsilon. Home: 6723 Riverview Dr Indianapolis IN 46220

BAFNA, KAILASH M., engineering educator, consultant; b. Gopalpur, Rajshahi, India, Jan. 12, 1941; came to U.S., 1965; m. Vimla Mehta, Dec. 12, 1964; children: Shamik, Shivika. BSME, Banaras (India) Hindu U., 1964; MS, U. Miss., Oxford, 1967; PhD, Purdue U., 1971. Registered profl. engr., Wis. Asst. prof. Ga. Inst. Tech., Atlanta, 1971-75; tech. dir. Coventry Spring, Nagpur, India, 1976-77; assoc. prof. U. Wis., Platteville, 1977-79; assoc. prof. Western Mich. U., Kalamazoo, 1979-83, prof. indsl. engring., 1983-86, chmn. indsl. engring., 1986—; cons. Parker Hannifin, Otsego, Mich., Kellogg Co., Battle Creek, Mich., Clark Equipment Co., Battle Creek, Flexsteel Industries, Dubuque, Iowa. Contbr. articles to profl. jours. Mem. Inst. Indsl. Engrs. (sr., chpt. pres. 1984-85, div. dir. 1985-86, dist. dir. 1986-88), Am. Soc. Engring. Edn., Coll-Industry Council on Material Handling Edn. (com. chmn. 1986—), India Assn. Kalamazoo (bd. dirs. 1980-81), Alpha Pi Mu. Hindu. Avocations: travelling, photography. Home: 1202 Northampton Kalamazoo MI 49007 Office: Western Mich U Dept Indsl Engring Kalamazoo MI 49008

BAGBY, MARVIN ORVILLE, chemist; b. Macomb, Ill., Sept. 27, 1932; s. Byron Orville and Geneva Floriene (Filbert) B.; B.S., Western Ill. U., 1957, M.S., 1957; m. Mary Jean Jennings, Aug. 31, 1957; children—Gary Lee, Gordon Eugene. With No. Regional Research Center, USDA Agrl. Research Service, Peoria, Ill., 1957—, research leader fibrous products research unit, 1974-80, mgr. No. Agrl. Energy Center, 1980-85, also research leader hydrocarbon plants and biomass research unit, 1980-82, leader oil chem. research, 1985—. Served with AUS, 1953-55. Mem. Am. Chem. Soc., AAAS, TAPPI, Am. Oil Chemists Soc., N.Y. Acad. Sci., Am. Soc. Agrl. Engrs. Methodist. Contbr. articles to profl. jours. Home: 209 S Louisiana St Morton IL 61550 Office: 1815 N University St Peoria IL 61604

BAGINSKI, GERARD HENRY, physicist, engineering analyst; b. Bialystok, Poland, Aug. 4, 1951; came to U.S., 1964; s. Julian L. and Henrietta (Kmiecik) B.; m. Yvonne Teresa Ziminski, Apr. 16, 1983; 1 child, Catherine. BS, Gannon U., 1973; MA, Kent State U., 1974, PhD, 1980. Subject matter specialist Kentron Internat., Inc., Dallas, 1979-80; physicist Sargent & Lundy Engrs., Chgo., 1980—. Contbr. articles to profl. jours. Mem. Sigma Pi Sigma. Republican. Roman Catholic. Home: 1204 Greensfield Dr Naperville IL 60540 Office: Sargent & Lundy Engrs 55 E Monroe St Chicago IL 60603

BAGLEY, CAROL ANNE, social worker; b. Milw., Aug. 21, 1926; d. William Harrison and Grace Mary (Allen) Stimson; m. Elwyn Arthur Bagley, Apr. 18, 1949; children: Anne, Patrick, Kathleen, Timothy, Daniel. BA, Carroll Coll., Waukesha, Wis., 1948; MSW, U. Wis., 1950; postgrad., U. Notre Dame, 1974-76, 85. Cert. social worker, Mich. Clin. social worker Children's Service Soc., Milw., 1950-52; clin. social worker Family and Children's Ctr., Mishawaka, Ind., 1969-71, dir. profl. services, 1971-75; clin. social worker Riverwood Community Mental Health Ctr., Niles, Mich., 1975-81, clin. team supr., 1981—; pvt. practice counseling Niles, 1973—; counselor, staff mem. Ctr. for Continuing Formation in Ministry, U. Notre Dame, 1983—; cons. Holy Cross Health System, South Bend, Ind., St. Joseph Med. Ctr., South Bend, various other orgns. Pres. Child Abuse and Neglect Task Force, Berrien County Mich., 1978-79, Suspected Child Abuse and Neglect Team, Berrien County, 1977-84; bd. dirs. Niles Community Schs. Pilot Project for Emotionally Impaired Children, 1977-78. Mem. Nat. Assn. Social Workers, Acad. Cert. Social Workers, Registry Clin. Social Workers. Presbyterian. Avocations: reading, bicycle riding, camping, family activities, music. Home: 1165 Sassafras Ln Niles MI 49120 Office: Riverwood Community Mental Health Ctr 309 N 5th St Niles MI 49120

BAGLEY, CHARLES MICHAEL, accountant, auditor; b. Memphis, Oct. 21, 1956; s. Charles Wilkes and Joyce (Gannon) B.; m. Elizabeth Ann Blakeney, June 18, 1983; 1 child, Christopher Michael. BS in Acctg. magna cum laude, David Lipscomb Coll., Nashville, 1978. CPA, Tenn., Mo. Staff acct. Price Waterhouse, Memphis, 1978-80, sr. acct., 1980-83, mgr., 1983-86; sr. mgr. Price Waterhouse, St. Louis, 1986—. Mem. Am. Inst. CPA's, Mo. Soc. CPA's, Nat. Assn. Accts. (assoc. dir. profl. devel. 1986-87, bd. dirs. 1987—), Healthcare Fin. Mgmt. Assn. Republican. Mem. Ch. of Christ. Club: Phoenix (Memphis). Avocations: golf, tennis, bicycling. Office: Price Waterhouse 1 Centerre Plaza Saint Louis MO 63101

BAGWELL, JOHN MARTIN, accountant; b. Cranford, N.J., June 27, 1949; s. Harold J. and Viola Maria (Haury) B. BA, Rutgers U., Newark, 1972, MBA, 1974. CPA, Mo. Ptnr. KMG Main Hurdman, St. Louis, 1982—. Mem. Am. Inst. CPA's, Nat. Assn. Accts., Am. Mgmt. Assn., Govt. Fin. Officers Assn., Mo. Soc. CPA's (mem. ethics com.). Clubs: Mo. Athletic, St. Louis Ambassadors. Home: 5334 Devonshire Saint Louis MO 63109 Office: 7710 Carondelet Saint Louis MO 63105

BAHDE, EUGENE JONATHAN, social worker; b. Chgo., Dec. 10, 1953; s. Robert Charles and Anna Virginia (Breicha) B. BS, George Williams Coll., 1978, MSW, 1982. Social worker Bridge Youth Services, Palatine, Ill., 1982-83; clin. social worker Chgo. Bd. Edn., 1984—; group work supr. Chicago Boys' Clubs, 1986—. Mem. South Park Ch., Park Ridge, Ill., 1979, Boys' Club Am., 1978—. Mem. Nat. Assn. Social Workers. Home: 3519 N Racine Chicago IL 60657 Office: Chgo Pub Schs Bur Social Work 1819 W Pershing Chicago IL 60657

BAHR, PATRICIA ALICE, occupational coordinator; b. Euclid, Ohio, Mar. 4, 1956; d. Joseph Edward and Alice Alberta (Skebe) Graben; m. David Lee Bahr, Sept. 8, 1978. AA in Applied Bus., Bowling Green (Ohio) State U., 1978, BS in Edn., 1978, MEd, 1985. Cert. tchr. bus. With sales and modeling depts. Halles Dept. Store, Cleve., 1974-76; sec. Citizens Fed. Savs. and Loan Co., Cleve., 1975-77; tutor, home instr. North Ridgeville City Schs. (Ohio), 1979—; shorthand instr. City of North Ridgeville Adult Edn., 1981, 83; intern English dept. Bowling Green State U., summers 1983—, coordinator Gen. Writing Studies Lab., 1985—; instr. high sch. bus. North Ridgeville City Schs., 1978-85, occupational work experience coordinator, 1985—, prin.'s adv. council, 1978, 85—, head coach girls volleyball, 1978-85, asst. athletic dir., 1983—. Judge Voice of Democracy contest VFW North Ridgeville, 1979—; active Citizens for Better Schs.; vis. mem. North Cen. Evaluation Team, 1986. Recipient Civic Commendation, City of North Ridgeville, 1983; Commendation-coaching, North Ridgeville City Schs., 1982. Mem. NEA, North Ridgeville Edn. Assn. (rec. sec. 1980—, corr. sec. 1979—), Ohio Edn. Assn., Ohio Vocat. Assn., Ohio Bus. Edn. Assn., Nat. Bus. Edn. Assn., Lorain County Guidance Assn., Occupational Experience Coordinator Assn., Chi Omega. Republican. Roman Catholic. Clubs: North Ridgeville Athletic Boosters, Slovenian Women's Union. Home: 8683 Harris Dr North Ridgeville OH 44039 Office: North Ridgeville High Sch 7000 Pitts Blvd North Ridgeville OH 44039

BAHR, ROBERT DENNIS, radiologist; b. Milw., May 21, 1928; s. Edward Valentine and Florence Fanny (Schlemberg) B.; m. Darlene Elizabeth Lueck, Mar. 2, 1955 (div. July 1979); children: Leslie, Robin, Teri, Alison; m. Patricia Jean Kerhin, Mar. 10, 1982. BS, U. Wis., 1950; MD, George Washington U., 1954. Intern USPHS Hosp., San Francisco, 1954-55; resident in radiology USPHS Hosp., Staten Island, N.Y., 1956-59; fellow Columbia-Presbyn. Hosp., N.Y.C., 1959-60; radiologist Lakeview Hosp., Danville, Ill., 1962-67, West Allis (Wis.) Meml. Hosp., 1967—. Served as surgeon USPHS, 1954-60. Mem. AMA, Am. Coll. Radiology, Radiol. Soc. N.Am. Lodge: Lions. Avocations: hunting, gardening, fishing, workshop. Home: W 269 N 1574 Meadowbrook Rd Pewaukee WI 53072 Office: West Allis Meml Hosp 8901 W Lincoln Ave Milwaukee WI 53227

BAHUGUNA, VIMAL CHAND, business strategy consultant; b. New Delhi, Apr. 7, 1952; came to U.S., 1983; s. Sita Ram and Shakuntala (Jhaldiyal) B.; m. Bulbul Toor, Nov. 18, 1977; children: Ila, Iva. MS in Engring., Friendship U., Moscow, 1975; M in Mgmt., Northwestern U., 1985. Product engr. Atlas Copco, Bombay, 1977-81; mgr. mktg. service Borosil div. Corning Glass Works, Bombay, 1981-82; pool officer Govt. of India, New Delhi, 1975-76; assoc. Booz Allen & Hamilton, Chgo., 1985—. Ministry of Edn. Exchange scholar Govt. of India, 1975. Home: 1230 Park Ave W #202 Highland Park IL 60035 Office: Booz Allen & Hamilton 3 1st National Plaza Chicago IL 60602

BAIA, ARLENE VIVIAN SKJEVELAND, nursing educator; b. Duluth, Minn., Aug. 15, 1922; d. Theodore Owen and Pearl Ruby (Thompson) Skjeveland; B.S. in Nursing Edn., U. Minn., 1945; M.S. in Edn., Iowa State U., 1973; children—Barbara Baia Thompson, Gloria Bonnie (dec.). Instr., U. Minn. Sch. Nursing, Mpls., 1945-46; asso. dir. edn. Naeve Hosp. Sch. Nursing, Albert Lea, Minn., 1954-60; instr. St. Joseph Sch. Nursing, Mason City, Iowa, 1960-62, Meth. Kahler Sch. Nursing, Rochester, Minn., 1962-68; instr. nursing North Iowa Area Community Coll., Mason City, 1968-79, chmn. health related div., 1979—. Recipient certificate for distinguished teaching in nursing Rochester C. of C., 1964; Edith Ruppert award, 1982. Mem. Am. (council advanced practitioners in med.-surg. nursing), Iowa (chmn. rev. panel for continuing edn. 1972-76) nurses assns., P.E.O., Delta Kappa Gamma. Republican. Congregationalist. Club: Order Eastern Star. Contbg. author: Child and Family: Concepts in Nursing Practice. Home: 417 S Tennessee Pl Apt 6 Mason City IA 50401 Office: 500 College Dr Mason City IA 50401

BAIGI, MARLA JEAN, state government administrator; b. Jefferson City, Mo., Sept. 13, 1959; d. Robert Louis and Dorothy Louise (Langkop) Goff; m. John H. Baigi, May 25, 1979; 1 child, Kevin Christopher. BA in Edn., Stephens Coll., 1981; MEd in Counseling and Personnel Services, U. Mo., 1983, postgrad., 1985—; EdS in Edn. Adminstrn., N.E. Mo. State U., 1985. Counselor Raleigh Hills Hosp., Jefferson City, 1983, Lincoln U., Jefferson City, 1983-84; bus. advisor Northeast Mo. State U., Kirksville, 1984; advisor career planning and placement U. Mo., Columbia, 1984-85; supr. adminstrv. services, meeting and conf. coordinator Mo. State Dept. Elem. and Secondary Edn., Jefferson City, 1985—; acting dir. alumnae Stephens Coll., 1984; attendant coordinator U. Mo. Extension, Columbia, 1984-85. Mem. Am. Psychol. Assn., Am. Assn. for Counseling and Devel., Mo. Assn. for Counseling and Devel., Nat. Assn. Female Execs., Phi Delta Kappa, Kappa Delta Pi. Republican. Avocations: reading, travel, nautilus training. Home: 3249 S Ten Mile Dr Jefferson City MO 65101

BAIKERIKAR, KAMALAKAR GHANASHYAM, chemist; b. Halge, India, Apr. 5, 1941; came to U.S., 1971, naturalized, 1975; s. Ghanashyam Ramachandra and Gulabi Dattatray (Revankar) B.; B.S., Karnatak U., 1963, M.S., 1965; Ph.D., Indian Inst. Tech., 1970; m. Vijaya Vernekar, May 25, 1970; 1 child, Kiran. Research fellow Indian Inst. Tech., Bombay, 1965-71; U.S. AEC postdoctoral fellow Ames Lab., Iowa State U., 1971-75, asst. chemist Ames Lab., U.S. Dept. Energy, 1975-80, asso. chemist, 1980—. Mem. Sigma Xi. Hindu. Contbr. articles to profl. jours. Home: 1456 Breckinridge Ames IA 50010 Office: Iowa State Univ 108 O & L Ames Lab Ames IA 50011

BAILES, RANDELL POWELL, accountant; b. Albany, Oreg., June 8, 1950; s. Virgil Theodore and Donna June (Powell) B.; m. Colene Fay Collins, Mar. 4, 1972; 1 child, Jacin. BBA, Park Coll., 1975. CPA, Kans. Personnel technician USAF, Forbes AFB, Kans., 1963-72; career adv. technician USAF, Mountain Home, Idaho, 1972-76; staff acct. City of Topeka, 1976-85, Marvin W. Maydew, CPA, Topeka, 1985—. Cubmaster Boy Scouts Am., Topeka, 1985-86. Mem. Am. Inst. CPA's, Kans. Soc. CPA's, Assn. Govtl. Accts., Air Force Assn., Air N.G. Assn. U.S. Republican. Lodges: Optimist, Moose. Home: 217 W 21st St Topeka KS 66612 Office: Marvin W Maydew CPA 820 Quincy Suite 600 Topeka KS 66612

BAILEY, ANDREW DEWEY, JR., accounting educator; b. St. Paul, Feb. 18, 1942; s. Andrew D. and Lorraine (LaBelle) B.; m. Irene S. Femrite, Mar. 22, 1964; children: Andrew D. III, Rachelle I. BS in Acctg., U. Minn., 1964, MS in Acctg., 1966; PhD in Acctg., Ohio State U., 1971. CPA, Ohio; cert. mgmt. acct., internal auditor. Assoc. prof. acctg U. Iowa, Iowa City, 1972-74; prof. mgmt. Purdue U., West Lafayette, Ind., 1974-80; prof., chmn. dept. acctg. U. Minn., Mpls., 1980-85; Arthur Young prof. acctg. Ohio State U., Columbus, 1985—; vis. prof. U. Queensland, Australia, 1978-79, U. Otago, Dunedin, New Zealand, 1986. Author: Statistical Auditing: Review, Concepts and Problems, 1981, Office Systems Technology and Organizations, 1985; contbr. numerous articles to profl. jours. and chpts. to books. Recipient Excellence in Acctg. award Haskins and Sells Found., 1963; Peat Marwich & Mitchess Research Ops. and Auditing grantee, 1979, 82, 87. Mem. Am. Acctg. Assn. (mem. mgmt. acctg. sect., auditing sect.), Am. Inst. CPAs, Am. Mgmt. Assn. (fin. div., info. systems & tech. div., research and devel. div.), Minn. Soc. CPAs, Ohio Soc. CPAs, Nat. Assn. Accts. (The Storm award 1972-74), Inst. Mgmt. Acctg., Acctg. Assn. Australia and New Zealand, Fin. Execs. Inst., Inst. Internal Auditors, Can. Acad. Acctg. Assn., The Am. Assn. Artificial Intelligence. Republican. Lutheran. Avocations: reading, travel. Office: Ohio State U Faculty Acctg College Rd Columbus OH 43210-1399

BAILEY, ANNELL DEANNE, accountant; b. Kansas City, Mo., Aug. 31, 1943; d. Ward Norman and Vida Fae (Votaw) Gibson; B.A. summa cum laude, Mo. Valley Coll., 1966; M.B.A., U. Mo., Kansas City, 1978; m. Willard Lance McGowan, May 28, 1965 (div. 1970); 1 dau., Cherlyn Deanna; m. 2d, Robert Edson Bailey, Dec. 4, 1971. Editor, Hallmark Cards, Inc., Kansas City, Mo., 1967-75; acct. Wolkow & Calys, C.P.A.s, Fairway, Kans., 1977-79, Craven Wooldridge & Dooley, C.P.A.s, Kansas City, Mo., 1979-80, Aubrey E. Richardson, C.P.A., Kansas City, Mo., 1980-82; mgr. revenue acctg. Jefferson Lines, Inc., Joplin, Mo., 1982-84, acctg. mgr., Mpls., 1984-85, Standard Aero, Inc., Edina, Minn., 1985, Aspen Med. Group, St. Paul, 1985—. Bd. dirs. Jr. Women's Philharm. Assn., 1972-79; ruling elder Knox Presbyn. Ch., Mpls., 1987.Nat. Assn. Accts., Am. Inst. CPA's, Minn. Soc. CPA's, Beta Alpha Psi. Lodge: Soroptomists. Avocations: singing, piano. Home: 5521 10th Ave S Minneapolis MN 55417 Office: Aspen Med Group PA 1295 Bandana Blvd N Suite 310 Saint Paul MN 55108

BAILEY, BRUCE STEWART, bank executive; b. Sacramento, June 2, 1936; s. Raymond Lull and Barbara Esther (Rogers) B.; m. Sandra Lee Sebrell, Dec. 20, 1959; children: Laura Lee, Valerie Catherine, Raymond Lull. BA, Denison U., 1958. Asst. v.p. City Nat. Bank, Columbus, Ohio, 1958-68; v.p., br. adminstr. City Nat. Bank, Columbus, 1975-77; pres. Farmers Savings and Trust, Mansfield, Ohio, 1968-75; pres., chief exec. officer Bank One Ravenna, Ohio, 1977-82; pres., chief exec. officer Bank One Akron, Ohio, 1982—, also bd. dirs.; pres.'s council Bank One Corp., Columbus, 1968—; tchr. banking Rutgers U., 1970-76. Campaign fund capt. Akron City Hosp.; co-chmn. Akron Quality Council; exec. bd. exec. capital drive auditor, fin. com., Great Tr. Boy Scouts Am.; v.p., exec. bd. dirs., mktg. chmn. Ohio Ballet; sr. adv. council Coll. Adminstrv. Sci. Ohio State U.; ambassador Ohio Found. Ind. Colls.; trustee, pres., bldg fund campaign chmn. Old Tr. Sch.; past pres. N. Cen. Ohio Jr. Achievement; past gen. campaign, past bd. dirs. United Way; trustee Delta Upsilon Ednl. Found., Akron Gen. Med. Ctr.; bd. dirs., pres. Akron City Club. Served with USAFR, 1961-62. Named one of 10 Outstanding Young Men, Columbus Jaycees, 1967; recipient Disting. Service award Mansfield Area Jaycees, 1971, A.Z. Baker Outstandinf Service award Rotary, 1981, 82. Mem. Am. Bankers Assn. (various coms.), Ohio Bankers Assn. (various coms.). Baptist. Avocations: golf, tennis, racquetball, photography. Office: Bank One Akron 1115 S Main St Akron OH 44301

BAILEY, CLYDE ARTHUR, JR., electrical engineer; b. Austin, Tex., Dec. 27, 1952; s. Clyde A. Sr. and Kimi H. Bailey. BSEE, U. Wis., 1979. Corp. staff engr. Econs. Labs., St. Paul, 1979-81; control systems engr. Klenzade div. Econs. Labs., South Beloit, Wis., 1981-82, sr. control systems engr. Klenzade div., 1982-87; sr. design engr. Econs. Labs., St. Paul, Minn., 1987—. Mem. Instrument Soc. Am. Club: Computer of Rockford, Ill. Avocations: bowling, telecommunications, computer games. Home: PO Box 242 Roscoe IL 61073 Office: Econs Lab PO Box 1018 South Beloit WI 53511

BAILEY, GARY LEWIS, corporate professional; b. Amarillo, Tex., Aug. 14, 1944; s. Lewis C. and Betty Louise (Giles) B.; m. Linda Jane Moore, Feb. 15, 1969; children: Tanya Lynn, Antony Brent, Lewis James. Student, U. Colo., 1966-67. Material handler IBM, Boulder, Colo., 1966-72; dispatcher IBM, Aurora, Ill., 1972-73, customer engr., 1973-80; advanced customer service rep. IBM, Oak Brook, Ill., 1980—; instr. Chgo. Edn. Ctr., 1987—. Pres. adv. bd. Elizabeth Keeler Sch., Aurora, 1973-74. Served with USN, 1963-66, Vietnam. Mem. Nat. Real Estate Bd., Ill. Real Estate Bd., Aurora Real Estate Bd., Assn. for Individual Devel. (dir. solicitations com. Aurora chpt. 1975—). Republican. Roman Catholic. Club: Italian Am. Lodge: Moose. Avocations: restoring antique guns, remodeling homes. Home: 2 Sherwick Oswego IL 60543 Office: IBM IBM Plaza Chicago IL 60600

BAILEY, JAMES (JIM BAILEY), lawyer, professional football team executive; b. Wilmington, Oreg., Aug. 21, 1946; m. Ann Bailey; children:Sarah, Jenny. Grad., Fla. State U.; J.D., U. Mich. Assoc. Guren, Merritt, Sogg & Cohen, Cleve., 1971-76, ptnr., 1976—; v.p., gen. counsel Cleve. Browns, NFL, 1978-84, exec. v.p. legal and adminstrn., 1984—. Office: Cleve Browns Tower B Cleve Stadium Cleveland OH 44114 *

BAILEY, JAMES CLYDE, plastic fabrication company executive; b. Ravenna, Ohio, Mar. 19, 1954; s. Clyde Oliver and Donna Lee (Nickol) B.; m. Deborah Jo Brugmann, May 1, 1976; 1 child, Chad James. AS, U. Cin., 1974; student, Ursline Coll., 1984. Cert. nuclear medicine technologist. Asst. chief technologist Gen. Hosp., Cuyahoga Falls, Ohio, 1974-75; dept. mgr. nuclear medicine Geauga Community Hosp., Chardon, Ohio, 1975-79, Marymount Hosp., Cleve., 1979-86; v.p., gen. mgr. Vanguard Plastics, Mantua, Ohio, 1986—. Bd. dirs. United Way, Geauga Community Hosp., 1977-78. Mem. Soc. Nuclear Medicine of No. Ohio (pres. 1981-82), United Drag Racing Assn., Internat. Hot Rod Assn., Nat. Hot Rod Assn. Republican. Methodist. Profl. race car driver. Home: 4456 Pioneer Trail Mantua OH 44255 Office: Vanguard Plastics 4466 Orchard St Mantua OH 44255

BAILEY, JAMES DAVID, former school district public relations official, writer, consultant; b. Menomonie, Wis., Sept. 3, 1922; s. Paul E. and Ruth (Chickering) B.; B.S., U. Wis., Stout, 1948; M.A., U. Denver, 1950; postgrad. U. Colo., 1962; m. Barbara Jean Swanson, Sept. 18, 1981; children by previous marriage—Dianne Bailey Zemichael, Andrea Bailey Hartwig, Jerri Pederson, Jan Rohleik, Joan Johnson, Jill White. Printing instr. Keating Jr. High Sch., Pueblo, Colo., 1948-49; instr. communications U. Denver, 1949-50; sales mgr./newscaster/announcer various radio stas., 1950-56; mgr. Northfield (Minn.) C. of C., 1956-64; free lance public relations cons., Northfield, Mpls., 1964-66; public relations/advt. asst. F&M Savings Bank, Mpls., 1966-69; owner James Bailey & Assocs., Public Relations/Advt. Agy., Mpls., 1969-72; dir. coll. relations St. Norbert Coll., Green Bay/DePere, Wis., 1972-73; public relations officer Wis. Indianhead Vocat.-Tech. Adult Edn. Dist., Shell Lake, 1973-83; freelance writer, consultant. Mem. Shell Lake planning commn., 1974-81; bd. dirs. UN of Minn., 1969-72; mem. N.G. Citizens Com., Northfield, Minn., 1963-66; safety council chmn. Red Wing, Minn., 1953-56. Recipient cert. of appreciation Shell Lake Bicentennial Com., 1976, Stout U. Found., 1975; commendation cert. Shell Lake, Wis., 1976. Mem. Public Relations Soc. Am., Wis. Newspaper Assn., Nat. Assn. Vocat. Tech. Communicators, Nat. Council for Community Relations, Shell Lake C. of C., Am. Legion (comdr. 1947-48). Republican. Clubs: Minn. Press, Lions (dist. gov. 1981-82, chmn. Wis. council govs. 1982-83), Masons Shriners. Contbr. articles to profl. jours. Newsletter editor Minn. Press Club, 1970-72, UN Assn. of Minn., 1971-72; editor Minn. Farm Bur. Tabloid, 1964-65; newspaper columnist. Home: Aleppo Ct 17201 107th Ave Sun City AZ 85351

BAILEY, JERRY LYNN, commercial bank executive; b. Robinson, Ill., Sept. 18, 1948; s. Ray Kenneth and Imogene Ilene (Roberts) B. BS, So. Ill. U., 1970. Br. mgr. CIT Credit Corp., Chgo., 1971-76; asst. v.p. Bank of Casey, Ill., 1976-78; pres., chief exec. officer Crawford County State Bank, Robinson, 1978—; instr. Lincoln Trail Coll., Robinson, 1981-85. V.p. Robinson High Sch. Acad. Found., 1985—. Republican. Baptist. Lodges: Elks, Moose. Avocations: sports, reading, public speaking. Office: Crawford County State Bank 4 N Side Sq Robinson IL 62454

BAILEY, K. RONALD, lawyer; b. Sandusky, Ohio, July 30, 1947; s. Kenneth White and Virginia (Sheddan) B.; m. Sara Ann Geary Bressler, Mar. 14, 1969 (div. May 1973); 1 child, Matthew Scott; m. Lynn Darlene Kammer, Aug. 31, 1973; children: Thomas Keith, Kenneth Richard. B in Liberal Studies, Bowling Green State U., 1979; JD, Cleveland-Marshall Law Sch., 1982. Bar: Ohio 1983, U.S. Dist. Ct. (no. dist.) Ohio 1983, U.S. Ct. Appeals (6th cir.) 1985. Tool, diemaker Gen. Motors, Sandusky, 1968-84; sole practice Huron, Ohio, 1983—; chmn. Charter Rev. Com. of Huron, 1984. Mem. Assn. Trial Lawyers Am., Nat. Assn. Criminal Def. Lawyers, Ohio State Bar Assn., Erie County Bar Assn., Trial Lawyers for Pub. Justice, Ohio Assn. Criminal Def. Lawyers. Democrat. Pentecostal. Avocations: reading, photography. Home: 513 Williams St Huron OH 44839 Office: 348 N Main St Huron OH 44839

BAILEY, KAREL LYNNE, physical education educator, coach; b. Pontiac, Mich., Nov. 14, 1952; d. Jack Thomas and Ruth Edna (Ingamells) McCulloch; m. Tony Lee Bailey, Apr. 5, 1979; 1 dau., Meghan Marie. B.S., Western Mich. U., 1974, M.A., 1982. Tchr., coach North Muskegon Pub. Schs. (Mich.), 1975—. Author paper in field, 1979. Instr. North Muskegon Recreation Dept., 1983. Named Coach of Yr. Mich. Interscholastic Track Coaches Assn., Lansing, 1980, 79, 77; Dist. Coach of Yr., Nat. High Sch. Coaches Assn., 1984; inducted into the Western Mich. U. Athletic Hall of Fame, 1987; coached track team North Muskegon to 3 state championships. Mem. Mich. Interscholastic Track Coaches Assn., Mich. High Sch. Coaches Assn. (coach of yr. 1980), Southwest Mich. Field Hockey Assn. Office: North Muskegon High Sch 1507 Mills Ave North Muskegon MI 49445

BAILEY, MARTHA JEAN, librarian; b. Beech Grove, Ind., July 24, 1929; d. Ralph Boehmer and Marie Anna (Resener) B. AB, Butler U., 1951; MS, Drexel U., 1956. Asst. librarian Eli Lilly & Co., Indpls., 1953-55, E.I. DuPont, Wilmington, Del., 1956-57; tech. librarian Union Carbide Corp., Indpls., 1957-70; physics librarian Purdue U., W. Lafayette, 1970-79, life scis. librarian, 1980—. Author: Supervisors and Middle Managers in Libraries, 1981, Special Librarian as a Supervisor or Middle Manager, 1986; contbr. articles to profl. jours. Grantee Council on Library Resources, 1975-76, 1983-85. Mem. ALA, Assn. Coll. and Research Libraries, Spl. Libraries Assn., Am. Soc. for Info. Sci. Republican. Methodist. Avocations: collecting photographs prior to 1910, writing. Office: Purdue U Life Scis Library West Lafayette IN 47907

BAILEY, MAX EDWARD, optometrist; b. Richmond, Ind., Mar. 2, 1954; s. James Earl and Joan Francis (Spalding) B.; m. Eva Lynn Tischuk, Aug. 19, 1972; children—Travis, Aaron. B.S. in Optometry, Ind. U., 1976; O.D. with honors, 1978. Gen. practice optometry Barnhart, Logan & Bailey, Richmond, Ind., 1978—. Sec. United Way of Wayne County, Richmond, 1984; v.p. Richmond Symphony Orch., 1983-84, bd. dirs., 1982-83; mem. profl. review bd., nursing div., Wayne County Health Dept., 1986—; radio disk jockey on local pub. radio sta. Recipient Irvin M. Borish award Am. Optometric Found., 1978, Bausch and Lomb Outstanding Achievement award, 1978. Mem. Whitewater Valley Optometric Soc. (pres. 1982-83), Ind. Optometric Assn., Am. Optometric Assn. Presbyterian. Avocations: running; gardening, music. Home: 316 Thornwood Ct Richmond IN 47374 Office: Drs Barnhart Logan & Bailey 2519 E Main St Richmond IN 47374

BAILEY, PAUL FREDRICK, insurance company adjuster; b. Garden City, Kans., Oct. 16, 1954; s. Paul Earnest Bailey and Pauline Elizabeth (Miller) Bailey Berend; m. Marilyn Frances Rogers, Aug. 24, 1974; children: Angela Lynn, Nathan Paul, Derrick Lee, Emily Jo. BS in Bus. Adminstrn., Kans. State U., 1977. With sales New Eng. Life, Manhattan, Kans., 1975-77; adjuster Gab Bus. Services, Colby, Kans., 1979-82, office mgr., 1982-84; adjuster Kans. Claims Services, Goodland, 1984-85; office mgr. Colby, 1985—. V.p. Sacred Heart Home and Sch. Assn., Colby, 1982-83, pres., 1983-84; bd. dirs. Sacred Heart Sch., Colby, 1983-86; asst. cub master Boy Scouts Am., Colby, 1986-87. Mem. Kans. Claims Assn., N.W. Kans. Claims Assn. (bd. dirs., v.p. 1986-87). Republican. Roman Catholic. Lodges: Kiwanis (sec. 1977-78, v.p. 1982-83, pres. 1983-84, lt. gov. elect 1987-88, lt. gov. 1988-89, Disting. Club Pres. award 1984), KC (youth dir. 1987). Avocations: bowling, hunting, fishing, boating, skiing. Home: 1380 E 8th Colby KS 67701 Office: Kans Claims Services PO Box 825 Colby KS 67701

BAILEY, PORTIA ANDREA, author, producer, photographer; b. Chgo., Aug. 5, 1945; d. A. Leon and Portia H. (Thomas) B. Student Lawrence U., 1961-64, Lake Forest Coll., 1965-66, MacMasters U., 1967-75, Peters/Long creative writing seminars, 1971-74, language, communications, dance and music tng., 1951-70, 77-78. Dir., producer Carey Temple theatrical prodns., 1958; tech. dir., producer Thomas Meml. Theatre, Chgo., 1962-65; lit. translator from and into German, 1969-75; guest lectr. German seminar, Lawrence U., 1971; lighting designer, tech. dir. touring Prosenium Players, 1971-73; guest dir., theatre prodn. cons.; developer exptl. designers research project Linguistic Cultural Communication Devel. Corp., 1972-74, music copyist, 1978; cons., demonstrator Skinner Sch. Gifted Program, 1974-78; co-producer Gil Helmsley's God Is My Lighting Designer, U.S. Inst. Theatre Tech. Midwest sect., 1978; producer, propr. Andrea Bailey Enterprises, 1979-82; producer Black Ind. Cinema, U.S.A. Film Festival, 1981. Editor Midwest Report, 1978-82. Author: (book) Christophe, One Amoung Giants; (plays) The Greatest of These, 1970, 84, (an adapted transl.) Iphigenia In Tauris, Part I, 1983, Depth of the Shadow, 1963. Author monographs including The Black Lifestyle and Period of Training, 1974, Communicators Coming into Being, 1974, Our Concept of God and Man, 1984, From Dream to Dream, 1985. Author: (TV scripts) 9 program series America—Our Ideal, Our Reality, 1983, 22 program series America—Our Ideal, Our Reality, 1984. Author of literal transls. Recipient First prize Dist. Twenty Sci. Fair, 1961. Mem. Am. Soc. Theatre Research Internat., Am. Fedn. TV and Radio Artists, U.S. Inst. Theatre Tech. (vice chmn. Midwest sect. 1981-82). Roman Catholic. Avocations: piano, gourmet cooking.

BAILEY, ROBERT ALLEN, mining company executive; b. Cleve., Feb. 2, 1951; s. Robert Lewis and Mary Elizabeth (Hosford) B.; m. Mary Kathryn Dahl, Nov. 27, 1976. BA in Polit. Sci. and Econs., Clemson U., 1974; MBA in Acctg. and Fin., U. Mich., 1978. CPA, Ohio. Legis. asst. Ho. of Reps., Washington, 1974-76; staff sr. supr. Coopers & Lybrand, Cleve., 1978-82; sr. auditor Hanna Mining Co., Cleve., 1982-84, mgr. treasury services, 1984-85, mgr. employee benefits, 1985—; cons. E.T. Horsey & Co., Euclid, Ohio, 1986—. Asst. precinct committeeman Chagrin Falls (Ohio) Rep. Ward Club, 1984—; councilman Chagrin Falls Village Council, 1985—. Mem. Am. Inst. CPA's, Nat. Assn. Accts., Ohio Soc. CPA's. Methodist. Home: 88 Locust Ln Chagrin Falls OH 44022 Office: Hanna Mining Co 100 Erieview Plaza Cleveland OH 44114

BAILEY, ROBERT SHORT, lawyer; b. Bklyn., Oct. 17, 1931; s. Cecil Graham and Mildred (Short) B.; m. Doris Furlow, Aug. 29, 1953; children—Elizabeth Jane Goldentyer, Robert F., Barbara A.-B.A., Wesleyan U., Middletown, Conn., 1953; J.D., U. Chgo., 1956. Bar: Ill. 1965, U.S. dist. ct. D.C. 1956, U.S. Supreme Ct. 1960. With U.S. Dept. Justice, 1956-61; asst. U.S. atty. No. Dist. Ill., 1961-65; ptnr. LeFevour & Bailey, Oak Park, Ill., 1965-68; sole practice, Chgo., 1968—; mem. faculty Nat. Coll. Criminal Def. Lawyers, 1975-78; panel atty. Fed. Defender Program, 1965—. Mem. Nat. Assn. Criminal Def. Lawyers (legis. chmn. 1976-78). Home: 17 Timber Trail Streamwood IL 60103 Office: 53 W Jackson Blvd Suite 1220 Chicago IL 60604

BAILEY, SUSAN CATHERINE, compensation and finance analyst; b. Medina, N.Y., June 28, 1960; s. Albert and Catherine (Copponex) Parks; m. Christopher Maurice Bailey, June 4, 1983. BA, SUNY, Fredonia, 1982; MBA, SUNY, Buffalo, 1983. Personnel asst. Carborundum Co., Niagara Falls, N.Y., 1983; compensation analyst The Sherwin-Williams Co., Cleve., 1984-85, sr. compensation analyst, 1986—. Mem. Am. Compensation Assn., Cleve. Compensation Assn. Republican. Presbyterian. Avocations: tennis, bicycling, skiing, piano. Home: 6402 Southgrove Rd Mentor OH 44060 Office: The Sherwin Williams Co 101 Prospect Ave NW Cleveland OH 44115

BAILEY, VERONICA, advertising and promotion consultant, public speaker; b. Blue River, Wis., Sept. 27, 1941; d. Raymond Joseph and Astrid (Backe) Rogers; m. Robert Arthur Bailey, July 18, 1964; children: Carol, Karl (dec.). Student, U. Conn., 1973, U. Wis., 1985-86. Founder Wis. Jazz Festival, Inc., Fond du Lac, Wis., 1982—; owner Ronny Bailey Cons. Co., Madison, Wis., 1984—. Producer, host: (local TV show) On the Town with Ronny Bailey and Friends, (jazz programs) Wisconsin Right to Life, National Right to Life, Feminist for Life. Vol. for arts; active in fundraising, membership and advt. for various civic orgns. Recipient Gov.'s award for arts, 1985. Mem. Madison Jazz Soc. (editor newsletter 1984-86), Madison Music Collective, 1984—. Avocations: jazz, public speaking, writing.

BAILEY, WENDELL, former congressman; b. Willow Springs, Mo., July 31, 1940; s. Robert Haz and Ruby (Dell) B.; m. Jane Ann Bray, Dec. 2, 1963; children: Mike, John, Jill. B.B.A., S.W. Mo. State U., 1962. Salesman Bailey Auto Co., Willow Springs, 1962-66; owner, mgr. Bailey Auto Co., 1966—; state rep. Mo. 152d Dist., 1972-80; mem. 97th Congress from 8th Mo. Dist. Councilman; mayor pro tem 97th Congress from 8th Mo. Dist. Councilman, City of Willow Springs, 1968-72; candidate for treas. State of Mo., 1984, treas., 1985—. Chmn. bd. dirs. Willow Care Nursing Home, 1978-80. Mem. Mo. Auto Dealers Assn., Nat. Auto Dealers Assn. Republican. Southern Baptist. Clubs: Willow Springs Lions, Elks. Home: 101 W 4th St Willow Springs MO 65793 Office: State Treasurer PO Box 210 Jefferson City MO 65102 *

BAILLEU, KENNETH ROSS, finance company executive, accountant, controller; b. St. Charles, Ill., Aug. 14, 1947; s. Arnold A. and Gloria M. (Anderson) B.; m. Deirdre J. Sisson, June 7, 1975; children: Laura, Scott, Adam. AB, Washington U., St. Louis, 1968; MA, U. Ill., 1973. CPA, Ill. Auditor Touche Ross & Co., Chgo., 1973-79; asst. controller Deutsche Credit Corp., Deerfield, Ill., 1979—. Pres. Lake Zurich (Ill.) Bd. Edn., 1983—. Served with U.S. Army, 1969-70. Mem. Am. Inst. CPA's (recipient Elijah Watt Sells award 1973), Ill. CPA Soc. (recipient silver medal 1973). Home: 705 Beechwood Dr Lake Zurich IL 60047 Office: Deutsche Credit Corp 2333 Waukegan Rd Deerfield IL 60015

BAILLON, AUSTIN JOHN, real estate exec.; b. Duluth, Minn., June 22, 1927; s. Austin L. and Marie M. (McDonald) B.; B.A., U. Minn., 1950; B.S., St. Paul Coll. Law, 1952, LL.B., 1954; J.D., William Mitchell Coll. Law, 1969; m. Caroline Myers, Aug. 16, 1958; children—Caroline M., Paul A., Peter M., Catherine G., Alexandra R., Frances E. Claims examiner Minn. Mut. Life Ins. Co., St. Paul, 1950-52, claims mgr., 1952-54, atty. legal dept., 1954-55; sales mgr., appraiser F. M. and E. V. Dolan, Realtors and Appraisers, St. Paul, 1955-56; pres. Baillon Co., Realtors, Real Estate Brokerage and Investment, St. Paul, 1956—; founder, pres. St. Paul Title Ins. Co. subs. St. Paul Cos., Inc., 1963-67; founder Baillon Mortgage Corp., 1964, Baillon Agy., Inc., 1963. Bd. dirs. Minn. Landmarks, 1971-74. Served with USCG, 1945-46; with U.S. Army Res., 1951-54. Mem. Soc. Real Estate Appraisers (past sec.-treas., dir.), Am., Minn. State, Ramsey County bar assns., St. Paul Bd. Realtors (past treas., dir.), St. Paul Bldg. Owners and Mgrs. Assn., Chi Psi, Delta Theta Phi. Clubs: Minn. (dir. 1970-73), Athletic (St. Paul); K.C.; Somerset Country; Biltmore Hunting. Office: 1218 Pioneer Bldg Saint Paul MN 55101

BAILLY, RICHARD CRAIG, neurologist; b. Webster, S.D., June 20, 1944; s. Charles Edward and Helen Louise (Aasen) B.; m. Margaret Jean Megorden, June 18, 1967; children: Matthew Douglas, Eric Christopher, Nathaniel Charles. BA in Music, Grinnell Coll., 1966; MD, U. Minn., 1970. Rotating intern Parkland Meml. Hosp., Dallas, 1971; resident Mayo Grad. Sch. Medicine, Rochester, Minn., 1976; neurology ptnr. The Neurologic Assocs., Fargo, N.D., 1976-85, Fargo Clinic, 1985—; vice chief of staff The Neuropsychiat. Inst. Hosp., Fargo, 1984-86; asst. clin. prof. neurology U. N.D. Med. Sch., Grand Forks, 1976-86. Mem. bd. edn. Fargo Sch. Dist., 1984—; pres. bd. dirs. Fargo-Moorhead (Minn.) Symphony, 1982-83. Served to lt. comdr. USN, 1972-74. Fellow Am. Heart Assn. (stroke council); mem. AMA, Am. Acad. Neurology, Am. Assn. Electromyography and Electrodiagnosis, Alpha Omega Alpha. Republican. Episcopalian. Lodge: Kiwanis (edn. com. chmn. Fargo club 1985-86). Avocations: marathon running, music, cooking, photography, camping. Office: The Neurologic Assocs 700 1st Ave S Fargo ND 58103

BAIN, LARRY RAY, data systems analyst; b. Cin., July 23, 1946; s. Beverly Clifton and Vera Mae (Morton) B.; m. Nancy Mary Rosenmerkel, Apr. 13, 1968; 1 child, Wendy Ann. Student, Carrol Coll., Waukesha, Wis., 1986—. Analyst Ameritech Services, Milw., 1972—. Bus. mgr. Dance Defined, Brookfield, Wis., 1982—; chmn. com. Waukesha (Wis.), Symphony Follies, 1985; bd. dirs. Miss Waukesha County, 1986—. Served with USN, 1966-72, Vietnam. Democrat. Club: Vic Tanny (Brookfield). Avocations: weight lifting, swimming. Home: 607 Crestwood Dr Waukesha WI 53188 Office: Ameritech Services 2430 10th Ave South Milwaukee WI 53172

BAINES, HAROLD DOUGLASS, professional baseball player; b. St. Michaels, Md., Mar. 15, 1959; m. Marla Henry, Oct. 29, 1983; 1 child: Antoinette. Profl. baseball player Chgo. White Sox, Am. League, 1980—. Player, Major League All-Star Game, 1985. Office: care Chgo White Sox Comiskey Park Dan Ryan at 35th St Chicago IL 60616 *

BAINTER, JACK JEFFRIES, technical institute official; b. Jennings, Kans., Sept. 20, 1931; s. Corral William and Nellie Kathleen (Randall) B.; m. Diane Flanigan, Mar. 14, 1967; children—Stephen F., Marcia Bainter Kirkpatrick, David J., Jason J., Jeffrey C. B.G.E., U. Omaha, 1964; M.S., U. So. Calif., 1968; Ed. D., Ind. U., 1974. Lic. real estate broker, Ind. Commd. U.S. Air Force, 1958, advanced through grades to maj., 1968; ret., 1971; chmn. div. gen. and tech. studies Ind. U. S.E.-New Albany, 1974-75; dean of instrn. Barton County Community Coll., Great Bend, Kans., 1975-76; program officer for acad. affairs Ind. Commn. for Higher Edn., Indpls., 1976-78; dir. instrn. Ind. Vocat. Tech. Coll., Muncie, 1978-81; v.p., dean Ind. Vocat. Tech. Coll.-S.W., Evansville, 1981-83; dir. ITT Tech. Inst., Ft. Wayne, Ind., 1983-85; nat. dir. edn. ITT Ednl. Services, Inc., Indpls., 1985—; cons. in field. Decorated Bronze Star, Meritorious Service medal, Air medal with oak leaf cluster. Mem. Ind. Vocat. Assn. (life mem.; Outstanding Service award 1982), Am. Vocat. Assn. (life), Kans. Vocat. Assn. (life), Ind. Post-Secondary Vocat. Edn. Assn. (pres. 1981-82), Ind. Council Vocat. Adminstrs. Methodist. Lodges: Elks, Masons, Order Eastern Star. Office: PO Box 68888 Indianapolis IN 46268

BAINTER, WARREN CRAIG, accountant; b. Oberlin, Kans., July 11, 1948; s. Gayle C. and Ruth M. (Carstens) B.; m. Janice A. Ryan, June 3, 1972; children: Abbie Lee, Benjamin Edward. AA, Colby (Kans.) Community Coll., 1973; BBA, Kans. State U., 1975. Staff acct. Paul M. Steele, CPA, Colby, 1976-81; ptnr. Dowling & Bainter, Chartered, Oberlin, 1981—. Sec., treas. Citizens Scholarship Found., Oberlin, 1982—; sec. Meth. Ch. Adminstrv. Council, Oberlin, 1982-86. Mem. Am. Inst. CPA's, Kans. Soc. CPA's (bd. dirs. N.W. Kans. chpt. 1985-86), Decatur Area C. of C. (pres. Oberlin chpt. 1984-85). Republican. Methodist. Lodge: Rotary (pres. Oberlin chpt. 1985-86), Kiwanis (pres. Colby chpt. 1980-81), Masons. Home: 310 S Elk Oberlin KS 67749 Office: Dowling & Bainter 187 S Penn Oberlin KS 67749

BAIRD, JAMES KENNETH, retired telephone holding company executive; b. Tanta, Egypt, Jan. 10, 1917; came to U.S., 1926; s. James Wallace and Maude Rebecca (Edgerton) B.; m. Marian Elisabeth Irish, Sept. 7, 1940 (dec.); children—J. Stacey, Bruce Wallace, Darcy Jean; m. Sally Ann Maenza, Feb. 2, 1957; children—Joan Marie, Robert K. B.A., Monmouth Coll., 1937; M.B.A., Northwestern U., 1938; J.D., 1941. Bar: Ill. 1941, Wis. 1968, Fla. 1975, U.S. Supreme Ct. 1949. Assoc., atty. U.S. Govt. Dept. of Labor, Washington, 1941-42; asst. to judge U.S. Tax Ct., 1942-43; law practice with K. Raymond Clark, Chgo., 1946-51, Baird & Lundquist, Zion, Ill., 1958-67; gen. mgr., gen. counsel Turtle Wax Auto Polish Co., Chgo., 1953-57; sr. v.p., gen. counsel Universal Telephone, Inc., Milw., 1967-87, ret., 1987. Bd. dirs. Mem. Zion Sch. Bd., 1964. Mem. ABA, Ill. Bar Assn., Wis. Bar Assn., Milw. Bar Assn., Chgo. Bar Assn., Fla. Bar Assn., Am. Corp. Counsel Assn., Am. Legion. Republican. Presbyterian. Clubs: St. Andrew's Soc., Telephone Pioneer Assn. (Milw.), Am.-Scottish Found. Lodge: Masons, Shriners, Lions.

BAIRD, JAMES NICHOLSON, JR., obstetrician-gynecologist; b. N.Y.C., Feb. 29, 1940; s. James Nicholson and Jean (Sanford) B.; B.S., Ohio State U., 1962, M.D. cum laude (Dean's award), 1966; m. Veronica De Prisco, Aug. 25, 1962; children—Lisa Nicholson, James Nicholson III. Intern, Riverside Methodist Hosp., Columbus, Ohio, 1966-67, resident in obstetrics and gynecology, 1968-71; practice medicine specializing in ob-gyn, Columbus, 1971—; mem. staff Riverside Meth. Hosp., chmn. dept. ob-gyn, 1979-81, pres. med. and dental staff, 1983-84; mem. staff Ohio State U. Hosp.; asst. clin. prof. Ohio State U. Coll. Medicine. Bd. dirs. Columbus Zoo, Franklin County Conservatory; past dir. Columbus Sch. for Girls; bd. dirs., treas. v.p. med. affairs U.S. Health Corp. Diplomate Am. Bd. Obstetrics and Gynecology. Mem. AMA (hosp. med. staff sect.), Central Assn. Ob-Gyn, Am. Coll. Ob-Gyn, Columbus Gynecol. and Obstetric Soc. (treas. 1975, sec. 1976, pres. 1978), Internat. Soc. Aquatic Medicine, Acad. Medicine of Franklin County, Ohio State Med. Assn. (alt. del.), Order of Hippocrates, Alpha Omega Alpha, Phi Gamma Delta (pres. bd. dirs. 1971-73). Republican. Roman Catholic. Clubs: Rotary (bd. dirs.). City (pres. bd. dirs.), Columbus, Scioto Country, Pres.'s of Ohio State U. Home: 4700 Old Ravine Ct Columbus OH 43220 Office: 3545 Olentangy River Rd Columbus OH 43214

BAIRD, KEITH EDWARD, industrial engineer; b. Rockwood, Tenn., Oct. 6, 1961; s. Charles Edward and Mildred Kathleen (Lowery) B.; m. Tammy Sue Hider, May 16, 1985; 1 child, Devin Tyler. Student, Kansas City Community Coll., 1981—. Indsl. engr. Champ Service Line, Edwardsville, Kans., 1979-84; mgr. ops. Swan Engring. and Supply, Kansas City, Kans., 1985-86; indsl. engring. and quality control mgr. Murphy Industries Inc., Excelsior Springs, Mo., 1986-87; corp. indsl. engr. Ristance Corp., Mishawaka, Ind., 1987—; project mgr. Hilts Inc., Kansas City, 1986, Proctor & Gamble, Kansas City, 1986. Vol. ARC, Kansas City, 1976, United Way Kansas City, 1984—, Kansas City C. of C., 1984. Mem. Inst. Indsl. Engrs. Republican. Baptist. Avocations: music, sports. Office: Ristance Products Inc PO Box 93 Argos IN 46501

BAIRD, ROBERT DAHLEN, religious scholar, educator; b. Phila., June 29, 1933; s. Jesse Dahlen and Clara (Sonntag) B.; m. Patty Jo Lutz, Dec. 18, 1954; children: Linda Sue, Stephen Robert, David Bryan, Janna Ann. BA, Houghton Coll., 1954; BD, Fuller Theol. Sem., 1957; STM, So. Meth. U., 1959; PhD, U. Iowa, 1964. Instr. philosophy and religion U. Omaha, 1962-65; fellow Asian religions Soc. for Religion in Higher Edn., 1965-66; asst. prof. religion U. Iowa, Iowa City, 1966-69, assoc. prof., 1969-74, prof., 1974—, acting dir. Sch. Religion, 1985; faculty fellow Am. Inst. Indian Studies, India, 1972; vis. prof. Grinnell Coll., 1983. Author: Category Formation and the History of Religions, 1971, (with W.R. Comstock et al) Religion and Man: An Introduction, 1971, Indian and Far Eastern Religious Traditions, 1972; editor, contbr.: Methodological Issues in Religious Studies, 1975, Religion in Modern India, 1981; book rev. editor: Jour. Am. Acad. Religion, 1979-84; contbr. articles to profl. jours. U. Iowa Faculty Devel. grantee, 1979, 86. Mem. Am. Acad. Religion, Assn. Asian Studies. Democrat. Presbyterian. Home: 3733 Rohret Rd Iowa City IA 52240 Office: Sch of Religion Univ Iowa Iowa City IA 52242

BAIRD, ROBERT LEADLEY, police chief; b. Waukesha, Wis., Aug. 15, 1929; s. Robert L. and Daisey (Beales) B.; m. Fran Ward, May 5, 1951; children—Marty Lynn, Robert L. III, Thomas W. B.A., Governors State U., 1981; grad. FBI Nat. Acad., U.S. Army Command and Gen. Staff Coll. Dep. sheriff Waukesha County Sheriff Dept., Wis., 1953-62, sgt., 1962-64, lt., 1964-65, sheriff, 1965-72; chief of police City of Elgin (Ill.), 1972—; lectr. Traffic Inst. Northwestern U., Evanston, Ill., 1967—. Pres. Greater Waukesha United Fund, 1969; bd. dirs. Greater Elgin United Way, 1984—, Greater Elgin YMCA, 1984—, Community Concern Alcohol/Drugs, 1981—. Served to lt. col. U.S. Army, 1947-75. Recipient Citation award Wis. Legislature, 1972, Meritorious Service medal. Mem. Wis. Council Criminal Justice, FBI Acad. Grads., Wis. Sheriffs Assn. (treas. 1966-67), Waukesha Dep. Sheriff Assn. (pres 1960-61), Nat. Sheriffs Assn., Ill. Chiefs Assn. (dir. 1979—), Internat. Chiefs of Police. Republican. Episcopalian. Lodge: Masons. Avocations: jogging; golf; skiing. Home: 905 Ruth Dr Elgin IL 60120 Office: Police Dept Headquarters 150 Dexter Ct Elgin IL 60120

BAISDEN, ELEANOR MARGUERITE, airline compensation executive, consultant; b. Bklyn., Nov. 7, 1935; d. Vernon McKee and Ethel Mildred (Cockle) Baisden. B.A., Hofstra U., 1970. Clk., Trans World Airlines, N.Y.C., 1953-55, sec., 1955-64, compensation analyst, 1964-75, compensation mgr., 1975-85, dir. compensation and orgn. planning, 1985—. Mem. Airline Personnel Dirs. Conf. (personnel com. 1984-85), Airline Tariff Pub. Co. (personnel com. 1978—), Nat. Fgn. Trade Council (compensation com. 1980-84), Internat. Personnel Assn. (co. rep. 1980-84), Mensa, Alpha Sigma Lambda (Scholar of Yr. 1965-66). Republican. Methodist. Club: Weatherby Lake Sailing (Mo.). Avocations: boating, swimming, piano, travel. Home: 7818 NW Scenic Dr Weatherby Lake MO 64152 Office: Trans World Airlines 11500 Ambassador Dr Kansas City MO 64153

BAJARIA, HANS J., engineering and management consultant; b. Bombay, India, June 8, 1943; came to U.S., 1965; s. Jamnadas N. and Savitri J. Bajaria; m. Niranjana H. Asher, Aug. 8, 1968; children: Seema, Sona. BSEE, Gujarat U., Surat, India, 1964, BSME, 1965; MS, N.D. State U., 1966; PhD, Mich. Tech. U., 1972. Product design engr. Ford Motor Co., Dearborn, Mich., 1972-75; qualilty and reliability engr. Rockwell Internat., Detroit, 1975-78; assoc. prof. Lawrence Tech. Coll., Southfield, Mich., 1978-81; pres. Multiface, Inc., Garden City, Mich., 1978—. Mem. NSPE, Am. Soc. Quality Control (v.p. 1980-82, Man of Yr. award 1980), Soc. Mech. Engrs., Engring. Soc. Detroit (Gold award 1982), Nat. Speaker's Bur. Home: 27206 Wilson Dearborn Heights MI 48127 Office: Multiface Inc 6721 Merriman Rd Garden City MI 48135

BAJPAI, DEEPCHAND, radiation oncologist; b. Chakadharpur, Bihar, India, July 16, 1946; came to U.S., 1975; s. Tarachand and Jyostna (Sarwan) B.; m. Kanwaljeet Kaur, May 26, 1975; children: Amar, Ankita. BS, St. Xavier's Coll., India, 1966; MBBS, Christian Med. Coll., India, 1971. Cert. Am. Coll. Radiology. Intern Hahnehman Hosp., Phila., 1975-76, resident in radiation oncology, 1976-79; practice medicine specializing in radiation oncology Ft. Wayne, Ind., 1979—. Contbr. articles to profl. jours. Fellow Am. Coll. Radiology, Am. Coll. Internat. Physicians; mem. AMA, Radiol. Soc. N.Am., Am. Soc. Therapeutic Radiology, Am. Soc. Clin. Oncology. Home: 5312 W Arlington Park Blvd Fort Wayne IN 46835 Office: 2200 Lake Ave Suite 230 Fort Wayne IN 46805

BAKER, ALFRED STANLEY, II, computer scientist; b. Hopewell, Va., Oct. 27, 1947; s. Alfred Stanley and Koma Jo (Johnson) B.; B.A. in Math., Ill. Inst. Tech., 1970; m. Janet Marie Borowski, Feb. 15, 1969; children—Jennifer, Nathan. System software designer STAT-TAB, Chgo., 1968-71; supr. system software devel. Standard Oil Co. Ind., 1971-79; v.p., programming dir. Datamension Corp. (formerly Image Producers, Inc.), Northbrook, Ill., 1979—; speaker, cons. in field. Mem. Nat. Space Inst. Baptist. Designer and author two popular spread sheet programs for IBM personal computers; author TRS-80 Programs and Applications for the Color Computer; also games for Apple, TRS-80 and Atari. Home: 2327 S Westminster St Wheaton IL 60187 Office: 615 Academy Dr Northbrook IL 60062

BAKER, BARNET, civil engineer; b. Boston, Oct. 7, 1898; s. Joseph and Sarah (Bloch) B.; B.S. in Civil Engring., Case Inst. Tech., 1922; m. Florence Kleinman, July 25, 1923; children—Saul Phillip, Melvin. Plant engr. Columbia Chem. Co., Barberton, Ohio, 1922-23; asst. civil engr. City of East Liverpool (Ohio), 1923-24; mem. engring. staff City Cleve., 1924-69, asst. civil engr., sr. asst. civil engr., civil engr., 1924-63, chief civil engr., 1963-69. Mem. social agy. com. Jewish Welfare Fedn. Cleve., 1948-57. Bd. dirs. Ind. Montefiore Shelter Home, pres., 1952-54. Zone warden, Cuyahoga County, Ohio, World War II. Registered profl. engr., surveyor, Ohio. Fellow ASCE (life); mem. Cleve. (charter, life), Ohio, Nat. socs. profl. engrs., Am. Pub. Works Assn. (life). Clubs: Masons (32 degree), Shriners (pres. sr. club 1974-75). Home: 1422 SOM Center Rd PO Box 24566 Cleveland OH 44124

BAKER, BETTY LOUISE, mathematician, educator; b. Chgo., Oct. 17, 1937; d. Russell James and Lucille Juanita (Timmons) B.: B.E., Chgo. State U., 1961, M.A., 1964; Ph.D., Northwestern U., 1971. Tchr. math. Harper High Sch., Chgo., 1961-70; tchr. math. Hubbard High Sch., Chgo., 1970-85, also chmm. dept.; tchr. Bogan High Sch., 1985—; part-time instr. Moraine Valley Community Coll., 1982-83, 84-86. Cultural arts chmn. Hubbard Parents-Tchrs.-Student Assn., 1974-76, lst v.p., program chmn., 1977-79, 82-84, pres., 1979-81; organist Hope Lutheran Ch., 1963—. Univ. fellow, 1969-70; cert. tchr. high sch. and elem. grades 3-8 math., Ill. Mem. Nat., Ill. councils tchrs. of math., Math. Assn. Am., Chgo. Tchrs. Union, Nat. Council Parents and Tchrs. (life), Sch. Sci. and Math. Assn., Assn. for Supervision and Curriculum Devel., Am. Guild of Organists, Luth. Collegiate Assn., Kappa Mu Epislon, Rho Sigma Tau, Mu Alpha Theta (sponsor), Kappa Delta Pi, Pi Lambda Theta, Phi Delta Kappa. Club: Walther League Hiking, Met. Math. Club. of Chgo.. Contbr. articles to profl. jours. Home: 3214 W 85th St Chicago IL 60652 Office: 3939 W 79th St Chicago IL 60652

BAKER, CLAUDE RUSTON, mural painter, oil company founder; b. Millersburg, Ohio, May 8, 1958; s. Leroy Andrew and Lou Henri (Feight) B.; m. Charlotte May Mosher, June 10, 1978; children: Molly, Rebecca, Andy. Student, Ohio State U., 1976-77. Supr. scheduling AM Corp., Cleve., 1978; co-founder, pntr. B&L Drilling, Killbuck, Ohio, 1979-81; founder, pres. Tidalwave Services Inc., Killbuck, 1981; v.p. Bakerwell, Killbuck, 1985—; founder, exec. dir. Hist. Mural Found., Killbuck, 1985—. Painter mural Killbuck Elem. Sch., 1986; songwriter. Mem. Mohican Investment Corp., Wooster, Ohio, 1984; pres. village council, Killbuck, 1984-86. Republican. Avocations: sports, writing, music, inventing. Home: PO Box 695 Allison Ave Killbuck OH 44637 Office: Bakerwell Hist Mural Foundation N Railroad St Allison Ave Killbuck OH 44637

BAKER, CLORA MAE, educator; b. Bedford, Ind., Jan. 21, 1948; d. Howard Perry and Bethel (Newlin) B.; B.S., Ball State U., 1970, M.A.E., 1971. Sec. to dir. human performance lab. Ball State U., Muncie, Ind., 1967-70; bus. tchr. Carmel (Ind.) High Sch., 1970-85; teaching assoc. Ohio State U., Columbus, 1985—; instr. evening div. Ind. U./Purdue U., Indpls., 1979. Mem. Internat. Word Processing Assn. (educator's adv. council 1979-81), Ind. Vocat. Assn., Am. Vocat. Assn., NEA, Ind. Tchrs. Assn., Nat. Bus. Edn. Assn., Delta Pi Epsilon (nat. council rep. 1978—), Am. Bus. Women's Assn. (named Woman of Yr., Hamilton chpt. 1980), Omicron Tau Theta, Phi Delta Kappa. Mem. Christian Ch. Home: 5138 N High St #217 Columbus OH 43214-1579 Office: Ohio State U 121 Ramseyer Hall 29 W Woodruff Ave Columbus OH 43210-1177

BAKER, DENNIS WAYNE, chemical company executive; b. Kansas City, Kans., Nov. 22, 1946; s. Abe Horace and Louise Ann (Troupe) B. BS in Bus., U. Ill., Chgo., 1973; MBA, U. Chgo., 1975. Asst. treas. CF Industries, Inc., Long Grove, Ill., 1975—; chmn. CF Industries Polit. Action Com., 1985-87. Served with USAF, 1964-68. Home: 377 Sandalwood Ln Schaumburg IL 60193 Office: CF Industries Inc Salem Lake Dr Long Grove IL 60047

BAKER, DONALD, lawyer; b. Chgo., May 28, 1929; s. Russell and Elizabeth (Wallace) B.; m. Gisela S. Carli, Oct. 6, 1960; children: Caryna, Andrew, Russell. Student, Deep Springs Coll., Calif., 1947-49; J.D.S., U. Chgo., 1954. Bar: Ill. 1955, N.Y. 1964. Ptnr. Baker & McKenzie, Chgo., 1955—; bd. dir. Trimedyne, Inc., Pharmatec, Inc., Great Pacific Holdings, Inc. Bd. dirs. exec. com. Mid-Am. Com., Chgo., 1980—; bd. dirs. Internat. Bus. Council Mid-Am., 1982-84. Mem. ABA, Ill. Bar Assn., Chgo. Bar Assn. Club: Michigan Shores (Wilmette, Ill.). Home: 544 Earlston Rd Kenilworth IL 60043 Office: Baker & McKenzie 2800 Prudential Plaza Chicago IL 60601

BAKER, DONALD EUGENE, librarian; b. Winamac, Ind., Oct. 8, 1945; s. Willard Jared and Beulah Belle (Taylor) B. AB, Ind. U., 1966, AM, 1968, MLS, 1976. Asst. editor Ind. Mag. of History, Bloomington, 1972-74; dir. Willard Library of Evansville, Ind., 1976—; adj. asst. prof. library sci. Ind. U., 1987. Picture editor: At the Bend of the River: A Pictorial History of Evansville, 1982. Former pres. Evansville Arts and Edn. Council; mem. Evansville Mus. History Com. Served with USAF, 1968-72. Mem. Tri State Geneal. Soc. (bd. dirs., ex officio), Four Rivers Area Library Services Authority (past pres.), Soc. Indiana Archivists, Midwest Archives Conf., Ind. Library Assn. (pres. dist. VII 1983-84), ALA, Adminstrs. Large Pub. Libraries in Ind. Assn. Episcopalian. Lodge: Kiwanis (sec. Evansville chpt.). Home: 219 Oak St Evansville IN 47713 Office: Willard Library 21 1st Ave Evansville IN 47710

BAKER, DOROTHY BEATRICE MAY, social services administrator; b. Albany, N.Y., July 24, 1919; d. Lawrence Beecher and Christine Agnes (Hensler) B. BA, Coll. St. Rose, 1941, D in Social Scis. (hon.), 1976; MA, N.Y. State Coll. for Tchrs., 1949; MSW, Boston Coll., 1946, LHD (hon.), 1979; postgrad., Columbia U., 1956-58; PhD in Sociology, U. Bombay, India, 1973. With Caritas, Albany, 1946-50; counselor Family Service Orgn., Worcester, Mass., 1950-56; asst. prof. Fordham U., N.Y.C., 1956-58; cons. Coll. Social Work Nirmala Niketan, Bombay, 1958, prin., 1958-82, acting prin., 1982-83, exec. sec., 1983; PhD guide U. Bombay, 1965-83, also mem. Senate, active various coms.; asst. dir. Cath. Social Services, Lincoln, Nebr., 1985—. Mem. Assn. Shcs. of Social Work in India, Internat. Assn. Schs. of Social Work, Women Grads. Union, Maharashtra State Women's Council, Catholic Charities USA Adoption Task Force, Nat. Assn. Social Workers (Nebr. sect.). Roman Catholic. Home: 3325 Sheridan Blvd Lincoln NE 68506 Office: Cath Social Service 215 Centennial Mall Suite 212 Lincoln NE 68508

BAKER, (VIRGINIA) EVE WOOD, bookstore owner; b. Elwood, Ind., Dec. 24, 1943; d. Warren Willard and Clara Bell (Johnson) Wood; m. Everett Earl Baker, June 11, 1966; 1 child, Julie Elizabeth. B.A., Purdue U., 1966. Cert. tchr., Fla. Tchr. Merritt Island Schs., Fla., 1966-67; English tchr. Satelite Beach High Sch., Fla., 1967-68; social worker Tex. Dept. Welfare, Dallas, 1970-72; ednl. dir. Happiness House, Dallas, 1972-73; owner, pres. Eve's Books, Wyoming, Mich., 1976—. Mem. 101st Airborne Assn. (life assoc. mem.), Vietnam War Newsletter Assn. (life), Nat. Rifle Assn. (endowment mem.) Ohio Gun Collectors (life), Mich. Antique Arms Assn. (life), Grand Valley Corvette Assn. (sec. 1981-83). Republican. Methodist. Avocations: reading, book collecting, needlecraft, writing. Home and Office: 10509 Brandywine Dr Fort Wayne IN 46825

BAKER, HAROLD ALBERT, federal judge; b. Mt. Kisco, N.Y., Oct. 4, 1929; s. John Shirley and Ruth (Sarmiento) B.; m. Dorothy Ida Armstrong, June 24, 1951; children: Emily, Nancy, Peter. A.B., U. Ill., 1951, J.D., 1956. Bar: Ill. bar 1956. Practiced in Champaign, Ill., 1956-78; partner firm Hatch & Baker, 1960-78; judge U.S. Dist. Ct. for Central Dist. Ill., Danville, 1978—; adj. mem. faculty Coll. Law, U. Ill., 1972-78; sr. counsel Presdl. Commn. on CIA Activities within U.S., 1975. Pres. Champaign Bd. Edn., 1967-76, pres., 1967-76. Served to lt. j.g. USN, 1951-53. Mem. ABA, Ill. Bar Assn. Democrat. Episcopalian. Office: U S Dist Ct PO Box 125 Danville IL 61832 *

BAKER, HAROLD CECIL, architect, consultant; b. Wheeling, W.Va., June 23, 1954; s. Harold Cecil Jr. and Virginia Ann (Gonot) B.; m. Amy Jean Taylor, Aug. 23, 1975; children: Nathan Taylor, Kyle Thomas. BS in Architecture, Ohio State U., 1978, MArch, 1980. Registered profl. architect, Fla., Ga., Ind., Md., Mich., Mo., N.C., Ohio, Okla., Penn., R.I., S.C., Tenn., Tex., Va. Project architect William Gilfillen Architects, Columbus, Ohio, 1977-79; v.p. Solar Design Group, Columbus, 1979-84; v.p. retail architecture Nexus Am., Columbus, 1984-86; prin. Harold C. Baker, AIA, Inc., Columbus, 1986—. Author: Town Franklin Design Guidelines, 1978. Solar Energy grantee Dept. Housing and Urban Devel., Dublin, Ohio, 1978, Silver award Inst. Bus. Designers, Nexus Corp. Hdqrs., 1985, Excellence award Columbus Inst. Bus. Designers, 1985. Mem. AIA (environ. awareness com. Columbus chpt. 1983—, critic liaison high sch. design competition 1983-84, co-chmn. hon. award com. 1983-84, chmn. 1984-85), Architects Soc. Ohio. Republican. Roman Catholic. Avocations: golf, racquetball. Office: Harold C Baker AIA Inc 673 High St Suite 204 Worthington OH 43085

BAKER, HILLIER LOCKE, JR., physician, radiologist; b. Chgo., Apr. 11, 1924; s. Hillier Locke and Marion (Cromie) B.; m. M. Jane Dyer, July 12, 1952; children: Gail D., Susan E., Hillier L. III (dec.). SB, U. Chgo., 1945, MD, 1947; MS, U. Minn., 1954. Diplomate Am. Bd. Radiology, 1953. Asst. prof. Mayo Clinic, Rochester, Minn., 1963-69; assoc. prof. Mayo Med. Sch., Rochester, Minn., 1969-73, prof., 1974, Durling prof. of radiology, 1982—. Contbr. over 105 articles to profl. jours. Served as capt. U.S. Amry, 1953-55. Mem. Radiol. Soc. Am. (pres. 1979-80, sec., treas. research and edn. fund Chgo. chpt. 1984—, Gold medal 1982), Am. Soc. Neuroradiology (pres. 1974-75), Am. Coll. Radiology, AMA, Am. Assn. Neuro Surgery. Lodge: Rotary. Avocations: gardening, travel. Home: 1122 Oakland Ct SW Rochester MN 55902 Office: Mayo Clinic 200 First St SW Rochester MN 55905

BAKER, JACK SHERMAN, architect, designer, educator; b. Champaign, Ill., Aug. 8, 1920; s. Clyde Lee and Jane Cecilia (Walker) B. BA with honors, U Ill., 1943, MS, 1949; cert., N.Y. Beaux Art Inst. Design, 1943. Aero engr., designer Boeing Aircraft, Seattle, 1943-44; assoc. Atkins, Barrow & Lasswith, Champaign, 1947-50; pvt. practice architecture Champaign, 1947—; mem. faculty U. Ill., Urbana, 1947—, prof. architecture, 1950—; former mem. exec. com. Sch. Architecture, U. Ill. Exhibitor water colors, arch. drawings, and photography; contbr. numerous jours. Mem. U. Ill. Pres. Council, U. Ill. Bronze Circle; bd. dirs. The Conservatory Cen. Ill.; adv. bd. Ruth Hindman Found.; former adv. bd. Krannert Ctr for Performing Arts, Assembly Hall U. Ill. Served with U.S. Army, 1945-46, ETO. Recipient Excellence in Teaching award U. Ill. Fellow AIA (recipient numerous honors and design excellence awards); mem. Nat. Soc. Archtl. Historians, Assn. Collegiate Schs. of Architecture, Nat. Council Architecture and Registration Bds. (cert.), Nat. Trust Hist. Preservation, Architects, Designers, Planners for Social Responsibility, Alpha Rho Chi. Clubs: Gargoyle, Scarab, Cliff Dwellers (Chgo.). Home: 71 1/2 Chester St Champaign IL 61820 Office: U Ill Sch Architecture 608 E Lorado Taft Dr Champaign IL 62820

BAKER, JAMES ALLAN, banker; b. Dayton, Ohio, Mar. 4, 1942; s. Wilbur and Lucille (Heck) B.; B.S. in Bus. Adminstrn. (Wall St. Jour. Student Achievement award 1964), Bowling Green (Ohio) State U., 1964; M.B.A., Ind. U., 1966; m. B. Lyn Wallace, Aug. 25, 1962; 3 children. With City Nat. Bank, Columbus, Ohio, 1966-75, banking officer, 1971-75; pres., chief exec. officer Bank One Mansfield (Ohio), 1975-82; pres. Bank One Eastern Ohio, Youngstown, 1982—. Chmn., Mansfield United Fund dr., 1976, chmn. allocation com., 1976-82; mem. exec. com. Youngstown United Way, 1983—, chmn. 1985 drive; mem. govt. relations com. United Way of Am.; chmn. steering com. Leadership Youngstown; mem. exec. com. Youngstown Community Corp.; trustee Mansfield Art Center, 1980, Youngstown Hosp. Assn., Youngstown Symphony Soc.; bd. dirs., pres. Richland County Growth Corp., 1975-82; bd. dirs., treas. Area Indsl. Growth, 1975-82, Mansfield Growth Corp., 1977-82; pres. Mansfield United Community Service, 1978. Named Boss of Yr., Mansfield Jr. C. of C., 1977. Mem. Am. Banking Assn., Banking Adminstrn. Inst., Young Pres. Orgn. (chmn. 1983, internat. bd. dirs., fin. com.), Ohio Bankers Assn., Ohio Citizens Council (pres. 1981-83). Republican. Episcopalian. Clubs: Youngstown Country, Youngstown. Office: 6 Federal Plaza W Youngstown OH 44503

BAKER, JAMES EDWARD SPROUL, lawyer; b. Evanston, Ill., May 23, 1912; s. John Clark and Hester (Sproul) B.; m. Eleanor Lee Dodgson, Oct. 2, 1937 (dec. Sept. 1972); children: John Lee, Edward Graham. A.B., Northwestern U., 1933, J.D., 1936. Bar: Ill. 1936, U.S. Supreme Ct. 1957. Practice in Chgo., 1936—; assoc. Sidley & Austin, and predecessors, 1936-48, ptnr., 1948-81; of counsel Sidley & Austin, 1981—; lectr. Northwestern U. Law Sch., 1951-52; Nat. chmn. Stanford U. Parents Com., 1970-75; mem. vis. com. Stanford Law Sch., 1976-79, 82-84, Northwestern U. Law Sch., 1980—, DePaul U. Law Sch., 1982-87. Served to comdr. USNR, 1941-46. Fellow Am. Coll. Trial Lawyers (regent 1974-81, sec. 1977-79, pres. 1979-80); mem. ABA, Bar Assn. 7th Fed. Circuit, Ill. State Bar Assn., Chgo. Bar Assn., Soc. Trial Lawyers Ill., Northwestern U. Law Alumni Assn. (past pres.), Order of Coif, Phi Lambda Upsilon, Sigma Nu. Republican. Methodist. Clubs: John Evans (Northwestern U.) (chmn. 1982-85); University (Chgo.); John Henry Wigmore (past pres.); Midday (Chgo.), Legal (Chgo.), Law (Chgo.) (pres. 1983-85); Westmoreland Country (Wilmette, Ill.). Home: 1300 N Lake Shore Dr Chicago IL 60610 Office: 1 First Nat Plaza Chicago IL 60603

BAKER, JAMES KENDRICK, specialty metals manufacturing company executive; b. Wabash, Ind., Dec. 21, 1931; s. Donald Dale and Edith (Swain) B.; m. Beverly Baker, Apr. 11, 1959; children—Betsy Ann, Dirk Emerson, Hugh Kendrick (dec.). A.B., DePauw U., 1953; M.B.A., Harvard U., 1958. Regional sales mgr. Arvinyl div. Arvin Industries, Inc., Columbus, Ind., 1958-60; gen. mgr. div. Arvinyl div. Arvin Industries, Inc., 1960-68, v.p., 1966-68, exec. v.p., 1968-81, pres., chief exec. officer, 1981—, also dir.; dir. Ind. Bell Telephone Co., Indpls., Ind. Nat. Corp., Pub. Service Ind., Plainfield. Bd. dirs. Associated Colls. Ind., De Pauw U.; pres. Columbus Found. for Youth, 1965, United Way of Bartholomew County, 1979; bd. dirs. Vinyl-Metal Laminators Inst. div. Soc. for Plastics Industry, 1960—, pres., 1963-64; vice chmn. Ind. Republican Conv., 1966. Served with AUS, 1953-55. Named Outstanding Boss C. of C., 1965; recipient Disting. Service award Ind. Jr. C. of C., 1966, Disting. Community Service award Columbus Area C. of C., 1983; named One of 5 Outstanding Young Men of Ind., 1966. Mem. Columbus C. of C. (bd. dirs.), Ind. C. of C. (bd. dirs.). Clubs: Rotary, DePauw University Alumni (pres. 1974), Harrison Lake Country. Home: 12044 W State Rd 46 Deer Crossing Columbus IN 47201 Office: Gen Offices Arvin Industries Inc 1531 E 13th St Columbus IN 47201

BAKER, JOHN L., data processing educator; b. Oak Park, Ill., Oct. 29, 1947; s. Elmer William and Phyllis Patricia (Tomlin) B.; m. Kathy May Rardin, Apr. 10, 1968; children: Amy, Stacia, Abigail, Jessica, Jonathan, Claire. BS in Math., U. Ill., 1969. Computer operator Montgomery Ward's, Chgo., 1968-73, edn. specialist, 1973-82, edn. adminstr., 1982—. Mem. Citizens Adv. Council, Lombard, Ill., 1983-86. Mem. Chgo. Orgn. Data Processing Educators. Home: 334 S Craig Pl Lombard IL 60148 Office: Montgomery Wards 1 Montgomery Ward Plaza Chicago IL 60671

BAKER, JOHN STEVENSON (MICHAEL DYREGROV), author, collector, donor; b. Mpls., June 18, 1931; s. Everette Barrette and Ione May (Kadletz) B.; B.A. cum laude, Pomona Coll., Claremont Colls., 1953; M.D., U. Calif. at Berkeley and San Francisco, 1957. Writer, 1958—; book cataloger Walker Art Center, Mpls., 1958-59; editor, writer neurol. research articles L.E. Phillips Psychobiol. Research Fund, Mpls., 1960-61. Recipient Disting. Service award Minn. State Hort. Soc., 1976; Cert. of Appreciation U.S. Nat. Arboretum, 1978. Mem. Nu Sigma Nu. Contbr. articles and poetry to various publs. in Eng. and U.S.; author 60 pub. poems, 17 short essays and 8 sets of aphorisms. Donor numerous varieties of native plants and seeds to Minn. Landscape Arboretum and U.S. Nat. Arboretum, papers of LeRoi Jones and Hart Crane to Yale U., Brahms recs. to Bennington Coll., many others; also contbr. various rare species of native Am. plants to the Ctr. for Plant Conservation, Arnold Arboretum, Harvard U. Office: PO Box 16007 Minneapolis MN 55416

BAKER, JOHN TERRY, banker; b. Middletown, Ohio, Feb. 22, 1947; s. John Robert and Amy Ruth (Creech) B.; student Otterbein Coll., 1966, Miami U., Middletown, 1967-69; grad. Ohio Savs. and Loan Acad., 1973; A.A.S., Sinclair Community Coll., 1977; m. Joyce Ann Evans, Feb. 26, 1966; children—Michael T., Matthew D. With Germantown Fed. Savs. Bank (Ohio), 1968—, sec.-treas., 1968-70, exec. v.p., 1970-76, pres., chief exec. officer, 1977—; pres., treas. GFS Fin. Services, Inc.; trustee Samuel Lindenmuth Trust; part-time instr. Sinclair Community Coll., Dayton, Ohio. Past chmn. Germantown Planning Commn. and Bd. of Zoning Appeals; v.p. Community Improvement Corp. of Germantown. Cert. rev. appraiser; registered mortgage underwriter; internat. cert. appraiser. Mem. Fin. Mgrs. Soc. for Savs. Instns., Inst. of Fin. Edn. (degree of distinction 1977, past dir., treas.), Nat. Assn. Rev. Appraisers, Internat. Orgn. Real Estate Appraisers, U.S. League Savs. Assns. (com. on law and regulations 1979-80, com. on fed. credit agys. 1981-83), Ohio Savs. and Loan League (past sec., v.p., pres. dist. 2 1984), Am. Assn. Mortgage Underwriters, Jaycees, Germantown C. of C. (past pres.). Lutheran. Clubs: Rotary (past pres.) (Germantown); Masons (Germantown); Odd Fellows. Home: 266 S Cherry St Germantown OH 45327 Office: Germantown Federal Savings Bank 1 N Plum St Germantown OH 45327

BAKER, JOY LILLIAN, psychologist; b. Woodstock, Ill., Nov. 14, 1943; d. David Louis and Josephine Violet (Yepsen) Davis; m. Robert Edward Groble, June 8, 1968 (div. Aug. 1972); m. Gary Gene Baker, July 31, 1975; children: John Boyd, Caryl June, Catherine Diane. BA, Augustana Coll., Rock Island, Ill., 1965; MA, U. Wis., 1969, PhD, 1971; postdoctoral clin. child psychology, Ind. U., 1974. Clin. psychologist Topeka State Hosp., 1971-72, Southeastern Ill. Mental Health Ctr., Olney, 1974-75; pvt. practice clin. psychologist, clin. child psychologist, cons. Olney, 1976—; clin. psychologist in-patient psychiat. unit Richland Meml. Hosp., Olney, 1987—; cons. psychologist Intermediate Care Facility for the Developmentally Disabled, So. Ill., 1976—; assoc. instr. Ind. U.-Purdue U., Indpls., 1973-74; part-time instr. Wabash Valley Coll., Mount Carmel, Ill., 1974, Ill. Ea. Community Coll., Fairfield, 1974-76; contact person Elisabeth Kubler-Ross Ctr., Headwaters, Va. Mem. Am. Psychol. Assn., Am. Soc. Clin. Hypnosis, Ill. Psychol. Assn., Nat. Assn. Bus. and Profl. Women. Lutheran. Home: Rural Rt 1 Box 70 Calhoun IL 62419 Office: Olney Profl Bldg 202 E Main St Olney IL 62450

BAKER, JUDY ANN, architect; b. Robinson, Ill., Nov. 9, 1953; d. George Vernon and Martha Louise (Glasscock) Hilderbrand; m. Alex Eugene Baker III, May 25, 1973. BS, Ball State U., 1976, BArch, 1977. Registered architect, Ind., Wis. Planning supr. Ball State U., Muncie, Ind., 1977-81; architect Simpson Engring., Indpls., 1982-83, Detroit Diesel Allison div. Gen. Motors, Inc., Indpls., 1984—. Tour hostess Hist. Landmarks Found., Indpls., 1986. Mem. Nat. Assn. Women in Constrn. Republican. Avocations: camping, fishing, hiking. Office: Gen Motors Inc Detroit Diesel Allison Div PO Box 894 M36 Indianapolis IN 46206

BAKER, KENNETH CARROLL, high school administrator; b. Upper Sandusky, Ohio, Oct. 25, 1955; s. Kenneth Lloyd and Frieda Faye (Carroll) B.; m. Deborah Ann Moser, July 1, 1978; children: Sarah, Eric. BS in Edn., Miami U., Oxford, Ohio, 1978; MEd, Bowling Green State U., 1982, Edn. Specialist, 1987. Cert. sch. supt.; cert. secondary sch. adminstr. English tchr. Lakota Local Schs., West Chester, Ohio, 1978-81; asst. football coach Bowling Green (Ohio) State U., 1981-82; athletic dir. Arcadia (Ohio) Local Schs., 1982-83; high sch. prin. Arlington (Ohio) Local Schs., 1983—; county coordinator Operation Prom/Graduation, Hancock, Ohio, 1983—. Author: Ednl. Jour., 1981, 84, 85. Team capt. United Way of Hancock County, Findlay, Ohio, 1983—; mem. exec. bd. Hancock County Alcoholism Council, Findlay, 1984—; mem. edn. commn., exec. bd. St. Andrew's United Meth. Ch., Findlay, 1985—. Named One of Outstanding Young Men of Am., U.S. Jaycees, 1984. Mem. Ohio Assn. Secondary Sch. Adminstrs, Ohio Football Coaches Assn., Cradle of Coaches Assn., Pi Kappa Alpha (v.p. 1976-77), Phi Delta Kappa. Republican. Methodist. Club: Tomahawk (Miami). Avocations: hunting, fishing, running, reading. Home: 1644 Queenswood Dr Findlay OH 45840 Office: Arlington Local Schs 336 S Main St Arlington OH 45814

BAKER, LARRY DALE, academic administrator; b. Shelbyville, Ind., May 25, 1838. DBA, Ind. U., 1972. Cert. profl. speaker. Prof. U. Mo., St. Louis, 1971-80; pres. Time Mgmt. Ctr., St. Louis, 1980—. Author: Time Management Profile, tape albums; pub. TimeTalk; contbr. articles to profl. jours. Recipient Spl. Achievement award Pres. of U.S., 1968. Mem. Am. Mgmt. Assn., Performax (bd. dirs. 1986—, Sammy award 1986), Acad. Mgmt., Am. Soc. Tng. and Devel., Nat. Speakers Assn. (regional advisor 1986—). Office: Time Mgmt Ctr 3855 Lucas & Hunt Rd #233 Saint Louis MO 63121

BAKER, LINDA BLOCKI, writer, public relations consultant; b. Chgo., Dec. 27, 1952; d. James Roland and Virginia (Henry) Blocki; m. William Dean Baker, June 11, 1983. BS in Radio and TV, Ill. State U., 1975; MA in Communications, U. N.Mex., 1977. Tech. editor, dir. videotape prodn. MITS, Inc., Albuquerque, 1976-78; tech. editor U. Dayton Research Inst., Albuquerque, 1979-81; nat. editor USA Singles Mag., Albuquerque, 1982-83; v.p. Jayne Whalen Assocs., Northbrook, Ill., 1985—. Editor: Computer Notes, 1978-79; contbr. over 200 articles to various publs. Pub. relations cons. ARC, North Cook County, 1986. Recipient Silver award Internat. Film Festival, N.Y., 1980. Avocations: racquetball, weightlifting, writing, cons. for artists. Home: 1610 Partridge Ct Arlington Heights IL 60004 Office: Jayne Whalen Assocs 1100 Saranac Northbrook IL 60062

BAKER, LINDA LESLIE, social services administrator, consultant; b. Eugene, Oregon, Sept. 15, 1948; d. Charles Andrew and Ashley Estelle (Durrett) M.; m. Brent Delos Cain, May 28, 1983. Lic. Social Worker. Social worker Dept. Social and Rehab. Services, Topeka, 1972-79; foster care program specialist Kans. Children's Service League, Topeka, 1979-83, adminstrv. supr., 1983—; cons. Nat. Directory Foster Care Program and Ednl. Consultant, 1985—; cons., trainer Permanency Planning Resources for Children, 1983—; field instr. U. Kans., 1986—. Active Kans. Children and Adolescent Service System Programs, Topeka, 1985-86, children's Coalition, Topeka, 1985-86; adv. bd. Family Service and Guidance Ctr., Topeka, 1985-86, Family Preservation Project, 1986—. Mem. Nat. Assn. Social Workers, Kans Assn. Social Workers, Kans Conf. Social Welfare, Topeka Assn. Human Service Agys. (exec. treas. 1983-86, exec. v.p. 1986—), Council on Children and Familes (sec. 1979—), Civitan Club, Phi Kappa Phi. Democrat. Club: YMCA. Avocations: horticulture, arts and crafts, sewing. Home: 2649 SW Ashworth Pl Topeka KS 66614 Office: Kans Children's Service League 2053 Kansas Ave Topeka KS 66605

BAKER, MICHAEL PATRICK, clinical psychologist; b. Waterloo, Iowa, Sept. 9, 1952; s. John Donovan and Shirley Margaret (Potter) B.; m. Susan E. Schmit, Dec. 15, 1973; children: Dylan, Aaron, Noah, Michele. BA, U. No. Iowa, 1977; MS, U. Miami, 1979; PhD, U. S.D., 1983. Lic. and cert. Ind. Health Service Provider, Iowa. Psychologist technician VA Med. Ctr., Miami, Fla., 1978-79; staff psychologist Cherokee (Iowa) Mental Health Inst., 1979-85; cons. psychologist Siouxland Mental Health Ctr., Sioux City, Iowa, 1984—; clin. psychologist Assocs. for Psychiat. Medicine, Sioux City, 1985-86; pvt. practice clin. and cons. psychologist Sioux City, 1986—; cons. psychologist N.W. Iowa Mental Health Ctr., Spencer, 1983-85, Family Services and Boys' and Girls' Homes, Sioux City, 1985—, Spencer Psychiatry; affiliated staff mem. St. Luke's Regional Med. Ctr., Sioux City, 1985—, Marian Health Ctr., Sioux City, 1985—, Buena Vista County Hosp., Storm Lake, Iowa, Spencer Mcpl. Hosp. Served with U.S. Army, 1971-73, Korea. Mem. Human Factors Soc., Phobia Soc. Am., Iowa Psychol. Assn., Biofeedback Soc. Am. Home: 3013 Kensington Ct Sioux City IA 51102 Office: 1025 Badgerow Bldg Sioux City IA 51101

BAKER, RICHARD E., II, banking executive; b. Newark, Ohio, June 17, 1952; s. Richard E. and Betty (Tucker) B. Student, Ohio State U., 1970-74, Am. Inst. Banking, Newark, 1976, 77; grad., Ohio Sch. Consumer Credit, 1982, Ohio Sch. Banking, 1985-86. Mgmt. trainee Park Nat. Bank, Newark, 1976-78, installment lender, 1978-82, adminstrv. asst., 1982-85, br. mgr., 1985—. Mem. Licking County Big Bros., 1982-86, loaned exec. United Way, Newark, 1982; treas. Licking County Red Cross, 1984, 85; pres. Licking County Heart Assn., 1984-86; mem. Rep. Cen. Com., Newark, 1978-80, Rep. Exec. Com., Newark, 1984-86; councilman Newark City Council, 1984-86. Mem. Newark Area Jaycees (Disting. Service award 1982, 84). Republican. Home: 481 Mount Vernon Rd Newark OH 43055 Office: Park Nat Bank 50 N Third St Newark OH 43055

BAKER, ROLAND CHARLES, insurance company executive; b. Chgo., Aug. 12, 1938; s. William T. and Ruth C. (Carrington) B.; m. Addie Joe Scott, Aug. 17, 1962; children: Scott Carrington, Stephen Christopher, Stefanie Celeste. BS, UCLA, 1961; MBA, U. So. Calif., 1962. CPA, Calif., Ill.; CLU. Analyst N.Am. Rockwell, Los Angeles, 1962-64; fin. analyst Ampex Corp., Los Angeles, 1964-65; sr. v.p. Beneficial Standard, Los Angeles, 1965-77, Colonial Penn Group, Phila., 1977-81; pres. and chief exec. officer Montgomery Ward Ins., Schaumburg, Ill., 1981-86; chmn. and chief exec. officer Signature Group, Schaumburg, 1987—; chmn., chief exec. officer CenTrust Ins. Group, Miami, Fla., 1987—, Old Am. Ins. Co., Kansas City, Mo. Bd. dirs. Chgo. Youth Ctrs., 1983—, United Way Suburban Chgo., Hinsdale, Ill., 1983—, Bus. and Profl. People for Pub. Interest, Washington, 1983—, PACE Ctr. Career Devel., Chgo., 1984—, United Way Met. Chgo., 1986—. Recipient Bus. Achievement award, Young Execs. in Politics, 1983. Fellow Life Office Mgmt. Assn. (bd. dirs. 1983-86); mem. Am. Inst. CPA's, Calif. Soc. CPA's, Am. Soc. CLU's, Fin. Execs. Inst., Am. Council Life Ins. (bd. dirs. 1985—, legis. com. 1983—), Nat. Assn. Ind. Insurers (bd. dirs. 1985—), Am. Inst. Property and Liability Underwriters (bd. dirs. 1985—), Ins. Inst. Am. (bd. dirs. 1985—), Econ. Club Chgo., Union League. Clubs: Meadow (Rolling Meadows, Ill.), Lake Barrington (Ill.) Shores Golf. Office: Signature Group 200 N Martingale Rd Schaumburg IL 60173-2096 Office: CenTrust Ins Group 101 E Flagler St Miami FL 33131

BAKER, RONALD GREGORY, city engineer; b. Owosso, Mich., July 2, 1951; s. Herbert Blanford and Joyce Marie (Nelson) B.; m. Loraine Katherine Krakosky, June 21, 1974; 1 child, Bryan Nelson. BS, Mich. State U., 1973. Registered profl. engr., Mich. Field engr. Greenfield Constrn., Livonia, Mich., 1973-78, asst. city engineer City of Albion, Mich., 1978-80; city engr. City of Owosso, 1980—; sec. City of Owosso Planning Commn., Zoning Bd. Appeals, 1980—. Mem. Am. Pub. Works Assn., Am. Water Works Assn., Mich. Concrete Paving Assn. (award of excellence, 1986). Avocations: golf, travel, bowling, skiing. Office: City of Owosso 301 W Main St Owosso MI 48867

BAKER, RONALD PHILLIP, construction company executive; b. Kansas City, Mo., Feb. 15, 1942; s. Harry and Ruth Sarah (Bornstein) B.; m. Marilyn Gitterman, Dec. 27, 1964; children: Kevin, Corey. Student, U. Okla., 1960-63; BA in Sociology and Govt., U. Mo., Kansas City, 1965, postgrad., 1965. Acct. rep. Am. House and Window Cleaning Co., Kansas City, 1965-69; dist. ops. mgr. Am. Bldg. Services, Kansas City, 1969-72; pres. BG Maintenance Mgmt., Kansas City, 1972-86; chmn. bd. dirs. BGM Industries, Kansas City, 1987—. V.p. Jewish Community Ctr., Kansas City, 1985, 86, 87; pres. Jewish Vocat. Services, Kansas City, 1979, 80, 81; bd. dirs. Beth Shalom Synagogue, Kansas City, 1985-87, Jewish Welfare Bd., 1986, 87. Mem. Bldg. Service Contractors Assn. Internat. (bd. dirs., chmn. seminars 1981, 85, speaker conv., club pres. 1981-87, mem. edn. com. 1981-87, info. cen. com. 1985, 86, 87), Bldg. Owners and Mgrs. Assn. Kansas City, Jewish Fedn. Kansas City (v.p. 1986, 87, Young Leadership award 1981), Menninger Found. (pres. club Topeka 1987), Sigma Alpha Mu, Delta Sigma Pi. Republican. Club: Meadowbrook Country. Avocations: water sports, boating, snow skiing, running, reading. Office: BGM Industries 1225 E 18th St Kansas City MO 64108

BAKER, SAUL PHILLIP, geriatrician, cardiologist, internist; b. Cleve., Dec. 7, 1924; s. Barnet and Fannie (Kleinman) B. B.S. in Physics, Case Inst. Tech., 1945; postgrad., Western Res. U., 1946-47; M.Sc. in Physiology, Ohio State U., 1949, M.D., 1953, Ph.D. in Physiology, 1957; J.D., Case Western Res. U., 1981. Intern Cleve. Met. Gen. Hosp., 1953-54; sr. asst. surgeon Gerontology Br. Nat. Heart Inst, NIH, now Gerontology Research Ctr., Nat. Inst. Aging, 1954-56; asst. vis. staff physician dept. medicine Balt. City Hosps. (now Francis Scott Key Hosp.) and Johns Hopkins Hosp., Balt., 1954-56; sr. asst. resident in internal medicine U. Chgo. Hosps., 1956-57; asst. prof. internal medicine Chgo. Med. Sch., 1957-62; assoc. prof. internal medicine Cook County Hosp. Grad. Sch. Medicine, Chgo., 1958-62; assoc. attending physician Cook County Hosp., 1957-62; practice medicine specializing in geriatrics, cardiology, internal medicine Cleve., 1962-70, 72—; head dept. geriatrics St. Vincent Charity Hosp., Cleve., 1964-67; cons. internal medicine and cardiology Bur. Disability Determination, Old-Age and Survivors Ins., Social Security Adminstrn., 1963—; cons. internal medicine City of Cleve., 1964—; medicare med. cons. Gen. Am. Life Ins. Co., St. Louis, 1970-71; cons. internal medicine and cardiology Ohio Bur. Worker's Compensation, 1964—; cons. cardiovascular disease FAA, 1973—; cons. internal medicine and cardiology State of Ohio, 1974—. Contbr. articles to profl. and sci. jours. Mem. sci. council Northeastern Ohio affiliate Am. Heart Assn.; former mem. adv. com. Sr. Adult div. Jewish Community Ctr. Cleve.; mem. vis. com. bd. overseers Case Inst. Tech.; former mem. com. older people Fedn. Community Planning Cleve. Fellow Am. Coll. Cardiology, AAAS, Gerontol. Soc. Am. (former Ohio regent), Am. Geriatrics Soc., Cleve. Med. Library Assn.; mem. Am. Physiol. Soc., AMA, Ohio Med. Assn., N.Y. Acad. Scis., Chgo. Soc. Internal Medicine, Am. Fedn. Clin. Research, Soc. Exptl. Biology and Medicine, Am. Diabetes Assn., Diabetes Assn. Greater Cleve. (profl. sect.), Am. Heart Assn. (fellow council arteriosclerosis), Nat. Assn. Disability Examiners, Nat. Rehab. Assn., Am. Pub. Health Assn., Assn. Am. Med. Colls., Acad. Medicine Cleve., Internat. Soc. Cardiology (council epidemiology and prevention), Am. Soc. Law and Medicine, Sigma Xi, Phi Delta Epsilon, Sigma Alpha Mu (past pres. Cleve. alumni club). Club: Cleve. Clinical (past sec.). Lodges: Masons (32 degree), Shriners. Mailing Address: PO Box 24246 Cleveland OH 44124

BAKER, SHAN RAY, medical educator; b. Des Moines, May 19, 1944; s. Edray Arnold and Mildred Lehman B.; widowed. BA, Drake U., 1967; MD, U. Iowa, 1971, MS, 1977. Lic. in medicine and surgery Iowa, Calif., Ill., Mich. Prof., vice chmn. U. Mich. Hosps., Ann Arbor; dir. resident edn. program U. Mich. Kosps, 1979—, Basic Sci., 1979—, Residency Tng. Program, 1982—. Served to capt., USAR, 1972-79. Mem. Am. Soc. Head and Neck Surgery, ACS, Am. Acad. Facial Plastic and Reconstructive Surgery, Am. Acad. Otolaryngology Head and Neck Surgery, Am. Triological Soc., Am. Larygologic Soc., Soc. Univ. Otolaryngologists. Home: 6485 Ford Rd Ypsilanti MI 48198 Office: U Mich Hosps Dept Otolaryngology 1500 E Medical Ctr Dr Ann Arbor MI 48109-0312

BAKER, WILBUR FRANCIS, appraiser; b. Grandview Heights, Ohio, Jan. 23, 1931; s. Edward F. and Elisabeth (Sibbald) B.; m. Jean Louise Warren, Mar. 27, 1954; children: Theresa A.F., Sandra L., Terrence A.F. BS, Ohio State U., 1959. Mortgage loan app. Panohio Mktg. Co., Columbus, Ohio, 1959-63; mortgage loan supr. Jefferson Standard Life Ins. Co., Columbus, 1963-67; comml. loan bgr. The Kissell Co., Columbus, 1967-69; chief rev. appraiser O.D.O.T., Columbus, 1969—; 1st v.p. James A. Rhodes Mortgage Co., Columbus, 1972—. Served with USN, 1948-52. John E. McCrahin scholar Ohio Assn. Real Estate Bd., 1957, 1958-59. Mem. Am. Inst. Real Estate Appraisers (chmn. legis. com. Ohio chpt. 1986—), Appraisal Inst., Disabled Am. Vets (trustee 1986), AMVETS (2d vice adj., trustee). Roman Catholic. Lodge: Elks. Avocation: woodworking. Home: 16830 Krinn Unger Keck Rd Logan OH 43138-9050 Office: Ohio Dept Transp 37 W Broad St Columbus OH 43125

BAKER, WILLIAM ROBERT, bank executive; b. Youngstown, Ohio, Jan. 13, 1945; s. William F. and Suzanne (Bulkley) B.; m. Karen Halgren, Aug. 10, 1968; children: Jennifer, Melissa. BA in Econs., Wittenberg U., 1967; MBA, Xavier U., 1974. Chartered fin. cons., Ohio. Tchr. Maysville Sch. Dist., Zanesville, Ohio, 1968-70; trust officer Huntington Nat. Bank, Columbus, Ohio, 1970-75, Bank of Okla., Tulsa, 1975-78, BancOhio Nat. Bank, Columbus, 1978—. Treas. Zanesville Devel. Corp., 1986; trustee Camp Milestone, Inc., Zanesville, 1986, Zanesville Art Ctr., 1987; pres. Good Samaritan Med. Ctr. Found., Zanesville, 1987. Mem. Am. Bankers Assn., Internat. Assn. Fin. Planners. Republican. Presbyterian. Lodges: Rotary. Avocations: tennis, jogging, reading. Home: 2847 Coldspring Rd Zanesville OH 43701 Office: BancOhio Nat Bank 11 N Fourth St Zanesville OH 43701

BAKIEROWSKI, WACLAW, political activist; b. Jekaterynburg, Russia, Dec. 9, 1915; came to U.S., 1952; naturalized, 1957; s. Kazimierz and Lidja (Popow) B.; m. Lisaweta Albrecht, Feb. 1, 1950; 1 child, Waclaw K. Law student, Poland,; D in Diplomacy (hon.). With Polish Underground, 1939-44, participant Warsaw Insurrection, 1944; POW, Germany, 1944-45; tchr., Germany, 1945-46; Polish unit transport officer, Germany, 1946-52; ins. agt. N.Y. Life Ins. Co., N.Y.C., Chgo., 1953-74; work instr. Workshop for Retarded, Dixon, Ill., 1974-76; dep. prime minister, minister fgn. affairs, minister fin. Polish Govt. in Exile, 1976-85; brig. gen. Polish Forces. Contbr. numerous articles to newspapers. Mem. Rep. Presdl. Task Force; senator Internat. Parliament for Safety and Peace. Decorated Order of White Eagle, Virtuti Mil., Great Cordon of Polonia Restituta, Cross of Valour, Golden Cross of Merit with swords, others. Roman Catholic. Lodges: Knights of Temple of Jerusalem, Sovereign Hospitaller Order of St. John, others. Address: A-6372 140th Ave Holland MI 49423

BAKKE, STANLEY OLAF WESSEL, lawyer, investment banker; b. Mpls., Nov. 10, 1939; s. Olaf Jacob Severin and Hanna Marie Borgine Wessel (Clausen) B.; m. Jeannette Sharon Anderson, July 22, 1961. BA, Wheaton (Ill.) Coll., 1961; MBA, Cornell U., 1966, JD, 1967. Bar: Minn. 1967. Assoc. Fredrikson & Byron, Mpls., 1967-71; asst. gen. counsel, asst. sec. Medtronic, Inc., Mpls., 1972-77; investment banker Dain Bosworth Inc., Mpls., 1977—; bd. dirs. Circle Rubber Co., Mpls., Portion Control Foods, Inc., Mpls. Bd. dirs. Covenant Retirement Communities of Minn., Inc., 1983—, Youth Investment Found., Mpls., 1976-79; advisor Minn. Bapt. Conf. Trust Fund Mgmt. Bd., Mpls., 1982-84; deacon, mem. various coms. 1st Bapt. Ch. White Bear Lake, Minn., 1982—. Served to 1st lt. U.S. Army, 1961-63. Mem. ABA, Minn. Bar Assn., Hennepin County Bar Assn., Nat. Assn. Indsl. and Office Parks, Minn. Indsl. Devel. Assn. Republican. Baptist. Club: Mpls. Athletic (bd. dirs. 1985—, treas. 1986-87, sec. 1987—, life mem. 1986—). Avocations: handball, nautilus, skiing. Home: 5847 Hobe Ln White Bear Lake MN 55110 Office: Dain Bosworth Inc 6th and Marquette Ave Minneapolis MN 55402

BAKKEN, BRUCE MICHAEL, software engineer; b. Milw., May 10, 1953; s. Norman Donald and Josephine Catherine (Kuzma) B.; m. Natalie Ann Rapey, Sept. 19, 1981. BS, U. Wis., Kenosha, 1975; MS, Drake U., 1977. Research programmer U. Dayton Research Inst., 1977-78; software engr. Johnson Controls, Milw., 1978-83; software mgr. Advanced Micro Systems, Milw., 1983-84; software systems engineer Kearney & Trecker, Milw., 1984—; instr. U. Wis., Milw., 1983—. Vol. Civic Music Assn., Milw., 1983—, Wis. Multiple Sclerosis Soc., 1985—; bd. dirs., bus. mgr. Knightwind Ensemble, Ltd., Milw., 1985—. Mem. IEEE, ACM. Roman Catholic. Avocations: music, snow skiing, playing washboard in a cycling circus band. Home: 4347 S 48th St Greenfield WI 53220 Office: Kearney and Trecker Corp 11000 Theodore Trecker Way Milwaukee WI 53214

BAKKEN, EARL ELMER, electrical engineer, bioengineering company executive; b. Mpls., Jan. 10, 1924; s. Osval Elmer and Florence (Hendricks) B.; m. Constance L. Olson, Sept. 11, 1948 (div. May 1979); children: Wendy, Jeff, Brad, Pam; m. Doris Jane Marshall, Oct. 21, 1982. BEE, U. Minn., 1948, postgrad. in elec. engring. Ptnr. Medtronic, Inc., Mpls., 1949-57, pres., 1957-74, chmn., chief exec. officer, 1974-76, founder, chmn., 1976-85, sr. chmn., 1985—. Contbr. articles to profl. jours.; developer first wearable, external, battery-powered heart pacemaker. Chmn. bd. dirs. Bakken Library Electricity in Life, Mpls., 1975—, Archaeus Project, Mpls., 1985—; bd. dirs. Children's Heart Fund, Mpls., 1977—. Served to staff sgt. USAAF, 1942-46. Recipient Minn. Bus. Hall of Fame award, 1978, Outstanding Achievement award U. Minn., Mpls., 1981, Med.-Tech. Outstanding Achievement award Wale Securities, 1984, Engring. for Gold award NSPE, 1984. Fellow Bakken Soc., Instrument Soc. Am., IEEE (Centennial medal 1984); mem. N.Am. Soc. Pacing and Electrophysiology (assoc., Disting. Service award 1985), Assn. Advancement Med. Instrumentation, Am. Antiquarian Soc., Minn. Med. Alley Assn. (bd. dirs. 1985—). Republican. Lutheran. Avocations: history of med. elec. tech., future studies, ballroom dancing. Office: Medtronic Inc 7000 Central Ave NE Minneapolis MN 55432

BAKKEN, JOHAN SEPTIMUS, physician, researcher; b. Drammen, Norway, Dec. 26, 1945; came to U.S., 1965; s. Johan VI and Inger Johanne (Rasmussen) B.; m. Susanne Elisabeth Povlsen, June 22, 1974; children: Johan Christian, Thomas, Bj—rn. BS in Zoology, U. Wash., 1968, MD, 1972. Diplomate Am. Bd. Internal Medicine, Am. Bd. Infectious Diseases. Intern in internal medicine UCLA Hosp., 1972-73; resident in internal medicine U. Wash. Hosp., Seattle, 1975-77; chief resident in internal medicine Lillehammer (Norway) F. Sykehus, 1978-81; fellow infectious diseases Ullevål Univ. Hosp., Oslo, 1981-85; postdoctoral fellow antibiotics Creighton U., Omaha, 1986—; scientific reviewer Antimicrobial Agts. and Chemotherapy, Washington, 1986—; speaker Omaha Schs. Council, 1987. Served as lt. Norwegian Royal Army, 1974-75. Norwegian Research Council grantee, 1985-87, Future Health Found grantee, 1985-87. Mem. Norwegian Med. Assn., Scandanavian Soc. Antibiotics, Sons of Norway (advisor 1987). Lutheran. Avocations: stamps, fishing, winter sports. Home: 6327 S 72d Ave Omaha NE 68127 Office: Creighton U Med Microbiology 2500 and California Omaha NE 68127

BAKKEN, LORI LYNN, medical technologist; b. Jackson, Mich., June 20, 1957; d. Duane Earl and Donna Jean (Schafer) Schiller; m. Michael Dwaine Bakken, June 10, 1978; children: Nicholas D., Amanda M. BS, U. Wis., 1980, postgrad., 1982. Med. technologist Stoughton (Wis.) Hosp., 1980-81, Meth. Hosp., Madison, Wis., 1981, U. Wis., Madison, 1982, U. Wis. Hosp. and Clinics, Madison, 1982; coordinator sexually transmitted diseases program Wis. State Lab. Hygiene, Madison, 1982-86; med. technologist Stoughton (Wis.) Clinic, 1986—; lectr. div. Health Family Planning, Phillips, Wis., 1985, Family Planning Wis., Milw., 1986; inservice Medic East Clinic, Madison, Grant Community Clinic, Lancaster, Wis. Mem. Am. Soc. Clin. Pathology (cert. med. technologist). Avocations: sewing, cross-stitch, dancing, figure skating. Home: 632 County Trunk N Stoughton WI 53589 Office: Stoughton Clinic 125 Church St Stoughton WI 53589

BALACEK, THOMAS VINCENT, corporation executive, engineer, management consultant; b. N.Y.C., Sept. 24, 1937; s. Theodore Vincent and Margaret Alice (Tuohy) B.; student N.Y.U. Coll. of Aeros., 1956-60; m. Joyce Eldeene Iden, Nov. 19, 1960 (dec. May 5, 1978); children—Thomas Vincent, Valerie Anne, William Theodore, Paul Frederick. Started as engr. Executone, Inc., N.Y.C., 1958-60, U.S. Testing Co., Inc., Hoboken, N.J., 1961; sales engr. Nuclear-Chgo. subs. Siemens Med. Systems, Inc., Des Plaines, Ill., 1961-65, regional mgr., 1966-67, sales mgr., 1968, advt. mgr., 1969; v.p. sales and mktg. Telemed Corp. div. Becton-Dickinson, Hoffman Estates, Ill., 1969-76; founder, pres., chief exec. officer Cardiassist Corp. div. Intermedics, Inc., Hoffman Estates, Ill., 1976-82; pres. Highview Corp., 1982—; prin. Technology Mktg. Group, Ltd., Des Plaines, Ill., 1984-85, v.p. sales, mktg., Share Health Plan of Ill., Itasca, 1985-87; v.p. mktg. Unity Health Plan, Parkridge, Ill., 1987—. Home: 506 N River Rd Fox River Grove IL 60021 Office: Unity Health Plan 444 N Northwest Hwy Park Ridge IL 60068

BALASA, RICHARD WAYNE, pathologist, educator; b. Chgo., Feb. 11, 1946; s. Frank John and Lucille Eleanor (Holsman) B.; B.A. cum laude, Yale U., 1968; M.D., St. Louis U., 1973. Research fellow pathology Rush-Presbyn.-St. Luke's Med. Center, Chgo., 1968-69; research assoc. Inst. Molecular Virology, St. Louis U. Med. Sch., 1969-72; acting intern dept. pathology Peter Bent Brigham Hosp., Boston, 1972-73; sr. asst. surgeon USPHS, resident in anatomic pathology Lab. Pathology, Nat. Cancer Inst., 1973-75; fellow surg. pathology, then resident in lab. medicine, then fellow chem. pathology, dept. lab. medicine and pathology, U. Minn. Med. Sch., Mpls., 1975-78; pathologist, dir. dept. clin. biochemistry Lutheran Gen. Hosp., Park Ridge, Ill., 1978—; clin. asst. prof. U. Ill. Coll. Medicine, Chgo., 1978—. Diplomate Nat. Bd. Med. Examiners, Am. Bd. Pathology. Mem. Am. Soc. Clin. Pathologists, Coll. Am. Pathologists, Ill. Soc. Pathologists, Chgo. Pathology Soc. Clubs: Berzelius (Yale U.); Elizabethan (New Haven); Yale (Chgo.). Home: 2959 N Mason Ave Chicago IL 60634 Office: 1775 Dempster St Park Ridge IL 60068

BALAZS, BILL (BELA) ANTAL, mechanical engineer; b. Miercurea-Ciuc, Romania, June 13, 1933; s. Andras and Emilia (Sallo) B.; came to U.S., 1957, naturalized, 1962; B.S., U. Budapest (Hungary), 1955; diploma tool die engring. Acme Tech. Inst., Cleve., 1963; A.P.M., John Carroll U., 1976; m. Vivienne Miskey, Apr. 1, 1960; 1 dau., Corrinne. Instr. tool die engring., machine design, indsl. electronics, Acme Tech. Inst., 1960-65; design engr., heating, ventilating, Morrison Product Inc., Cleve., 1963-65; project engr. Reuter-Stokes, Inc., Cleve., 1965-70, engring. project mgr., 1970-73, engring. mgr., chief engr., 1973—. Pres., Transylvania Hungarian League, 1960—. Registered profl. engr., U.S.A., Can.; cert. cost engring. engr., mfg. mgmt. engr., plant engring. engr. Mem. Am. Inst. Indsl. Engrs., Instrument Soc. Am., Soc. Mfg. Engrs., ASME, Am. Nuclear Soc., Nat., Ohio socs. profl. engrs. Designer nuclear radiation detectors and multi-sensor environ. radiation monitoring systems. Home: 7500 Woodlake Dr Walton Hills OH 44146 Office: 8499 Darrow Rd Twinsburg OH 44087

BALDACCI, LOUIS CHRISTOPHER, JR., utility company executive; b. Chgo., Aug. 4, 1925; s. Louis C. and Irene (Powell) B.; m. Geraldine Barbara Endre, June 22, 1945; children: Susan Marie Baldacci Flor, James Louis, John William, Mark Christopher. Student, Northwestern U., 1942-44, 46-47, B.S.M.E., 1947, M.B.A., 1954; student, Stanford U., 1944-45. Registered profl. engr., Ill. With Peoples Gas Light & Coke Co., Chgo., 1947—, v.p., 1971-81, exec. v.p., 1981-86, pres., chief operating officer, 1986—, also bd. dirs.; pres. Peoples Energy Corp., Chgo., chief operating officer, 1986—, also dir.; dir. North Shore Gas Co. Bd. govs. Met. Housing and Planning Council, Chgo., 1972—; bd. dirs. Greater Chgo. Safety Council, 1974—, TRUST, Inc., Chgo., 1982—. Served to sgt. U.S. Army, 1944-46. Roman Catholic. Club: University (Chgo.). Office: Peoples Gas Light & Coke Co 122 S Michigan Ave Chicago IL 60603 *

BALDWIN, ELDON DEAN, agricultural economics educator, grain marketing consultant; b. Ashley, Ohio, Sept. 23, 1939; s. John Wesley and Inez Catherine (Reeley) B.; m. Judith Carolyn Fogel, Feb. 22, 1964; children—Jeffrey, Amy. B.S., Ohio State U., 1963; M.S., U. Ill., 1967, Ph.D., 1970. Agrl. statistician Bur. Census, Washington, 1963-65; research assoc. U. Ill., Champaign, 1965-69; asst. prof. Eastern Ill. U., Charles, 1969-70, Miami U., Oxford, Ohio, 1970-74; assoc. prof. agrl. econs. Ohio State U., Columbus, 1974—; dir. electronic mktg. hog accelerated mktg. system project, 1978-81; cons. grain cos., 1976—. Webelos leader Cub Scouts Am., 1976-77, master, 1976-78, instl. rep. Boy Scouts Am., 1978-79, master, 1979-80. Anderson Grain Co. grantee, 1976, U.S. Dept. Agr. grantee, 1978-81. Mem. Am. Agrl. Econs. Assn., North Central Agrl. Econs. Assn., So. Regional Grain Mktg. Research Coms. (chmn.), Gamma Sigma Delta. Presbyterian. Contbr. articles, papers in field to profl. lit. Developer slaughter hog electronic market. Home: 4324 Hollandia Ct Westerville OH 43081 Office: Dept Agrl Econs Ohio State U 2120 Fyffe Rd Columbus OH 43210

BALDWIN, GEORGE KOEHLER, department stores company executive; b. Cedar Rapids, Iowa, Nov. 17, 1919; s. Nathan and Ada Lillian (Koehler) B. B.B.A., State U. Iowa, 1942. Office mgr., mgr. Wapsie Valley Creamery, Cedar Rapids, 1946-60; treas., head payroll, accounts payable, sales audit depts. Armstrong's, Inc., Cedar Rapids, 1960-87, also dir.; treas. Armstrong's of Dubuque (Iowa), 1982-87, also dir.; ret., 1987; also theatre organist. Mem. Cedar Rapids Performing Arts Commn.; bd. dirs. Cedar Rapids Community Concert Assn. Served with U.S. Army, 1942-46. Decorated Bronze Star medal; named hon. Ky. col.; George K. Baldwin day proclamation in his honor, Mayor of Cedar Rapids, Apr. 16, 1987. Mem. Cedar Rapids Consumer Credit Assn. (pres. 1968-69), Am. Theatre Organ Soc. (dir., treas. Cedar Rapids chpt.), Am. Legion. Methodist. Lodges: Rotary, Masons, Shriners (past pres. uniformed units). Home: 1017 F Ave NW Cedar Rapids IA 52405 Office: 3d Ave and 3d St SE Cedar Rapids IA 52401

BALDWIN, JAMES JOSEPH, orthodontist; b. Jacksonville, Ill., Sept. 26, 1925; s. Arthur K. and Louise (Murphy) B.; m. Martha Frances Wisehart, June 26, 1948; children: James David, Frank Arthur. AB, De Pauw U., 1947; MS, Yale U., 1948; DDS, Ind. U., 1954, MS in Dentistry, 1960. Diplomate Am. Bd. Orthodontics. Practice dentistry specializing in orthodontics Indpls., 1956—; from instr. to assoc. prof. Ind. U. Sch. Dentistry, Indpls., 1956—. Served with U.S. Army, 1945-46. Mem. Phi Beta Kappa, Omicron Kappa Upsilon. Unitarian. Lodge: Rotary (bd. dirs. Indpls. 1986—). Home: 6458 N Ewing St Indianapolis IN 46220

BALDWIN, JAMES PATRIC, manufacturing company executive; b. Covington, Ky., Jan. 1, 1954; s. Jon and Harriet Katherine (Knierim) B.; m. Susan Lee Olin, Sept. 15, 1979; 1 child, Christopher. BA in Bus. Admistrn., AA in Acctg., AA in Econs., Thomas More Coll., 1976; JD, U. Cin., 1979. Bar: Ohio 1979. Credit mgr. service parts div. Rockwell Internat., Florence, Ky., 1977-79, gen. acct. service parts div., 1979-81, fin. analyst service parts div., 1981-82, mgr. fin. service parts div., 1982-83; sr. div. analyst on-highway axle div. Rockwell Internat., Troy, Mich., 1983-85, mgr. fin. on-highway axle div., 1985-87, mgr. fin. on-highway products group, 1987—. Mem. ABA, Inst. Mgmt. Acctg., Am. Mgmt. Assn. Home: 2293 Kristin Troy MI 48084 Office: Rockwell Internat 2135 W Maple Rd Troy MI 48084

BALDWIN, LLOYD DEANS, management consultant, computer software company executive; b. Logan, Utah, Feb. 15, 1936; s. Kelvin Alma and Helen Ann (Deans) B.; student pub. schs., Bountiful, Utah; m. Arlene Ruth Simonis, Oct. 17, 1960; children—Rebecca Ann, Danna Lynn, David Alma, Stefanie Janine, Karina Louise, Emaline Sarah, Carl Nathaniel, Brian Lloyd. Engr., Sperry Engring Co., 1958; missionary Ch. of Jesus Christ Latter-day Saints, 1959-60; engr. IBM, 1960, tech. and mgmt. positions, San Jose, Calif., 1961-69, regional mgr., 1968-69; asst. to v.p. mktg. Info. Storage Systems, Cupertino, Calif., 1969-71; dir. ops. Cincom Systems, Cin., 1971-75; pres. Lloyd Baldwin & Assos., Cin., 1975—; v.p. Pansophic Systems Inc., Oak Brook, Ill., 1976-78; pres. SDA Products Inc., N.Y.C., 1978-80; dir. ops. Interactive Info. Systems, Inc., Cin., 1980-83, exec. dir. product and market devel. and data decisions, 1983-85; prin. LB Assocs., Cin., 1975—. Trustee, Deaconess Hosp., Cin., 1974. Served with USN, 1954-58. Mem. Software Industry Assn. (dir. 1970-77, pres. 1975-76), Computer Industry Assn., Am. Mgmt. Assn. Lodge: Rotary. Home and Office: 6790 N Clippinger Cincinnati OH 45243

BALDWIN, SUSAN OLIN, lawyer; b. Battle Creek, Mich., Sept. 1, 1954; d. Thomas Franklin and Gloria Joan (Skidmore) Olin; m. James Patric Baldwin, Sept. 15, 1979; 1 child, Christopher Mark. BA, Miami U., Ohio, 1976; JD, U. Cin., 1979. Bar: Ohio 1979, Mich. 1984. Assoc. editor Am. Legal Pub. Co., Cin., 1979-80; corp. atty. Hosp. Care Corp., Cin., 1980-84; legal counsel Peak Health Plan, Cin., 1984; assoc. Cook Pringle & Goetz, P.C., Birmingham, Mich., 1984—. Contbr. articles to profl. jours. Pres. Hunter's Green Homeowner's Assn., Independence, Ky., 1982-83; charter mem. Young Reps., Ashland, Ohio, 1972. Mem. ABA, Ohio State Bar Assn., Mich. Bar Assn., Alpha Lambda Delta, Phi Alpha Delta. Club: Am Businesswomen's Assn. (v.p. 1980-81, editor 1980). Address: 1400 N Woodward Suite 101 Birmingham MI 48011 Office: 1400 N Woodward Ave Suite 101 Birmingham MI 48011

BALDWIN, TIMOTHY WAYNE, marketing executive; b. Akron, Ohio, Mar. 14, 1946; s. Frank B. and Margaret H. (Herrington) B.; m. Kathy J. Trego, July 8, 1982; children—Veronica, Mark, Darren. B.S. in Orgn. Sci., Case Inst. Tech., 1968; postgrad. U. So. Calif., 1969, San Jose State Coll., 1972. Indsl. salesman ALCOA, Los Angeles, 1968-71; region sales mgr. Johnson & Johnson, Denver, 1971-77; zone sales mgr. Hills Bros. Coffee, San Francisco, 1977-78; sr. product mgr. Borden Inc., Columbus, Ohio, 1978-83; dir. mktg. Benco Pet Foods, Inc., Zanesville, Ohio, 1983-84; mktg. dir. Shopsmith, Inc., Dayton, Ohio, 1984—. Vice pres. English Gardens Condominiums, Westerville, Ohio, 1982-83. Republican. Methodist. Club: Toastmasters (sec. San Jose 1972-73). Avocations: tennis, golf, volleyball, racquetball, skiing. Office: Shopsmith Inc 6640 Poe Ave Dayton OH 45414

BALES, EDWARD WAGNER, manufacturing executive; b. Chgo., Jan. 30, 1939; s. Edward Joseph and Esther (Wagner) B.; m. Barbara LaVarre, Nov. 26, 1960; children: Edward Joseph, Karen Mary, Kathryn Mary, Timothy Joseph. BEE, Ill. Inst. Tech., 1960; MBA, U. Chgo., 1969. Elec. engr. Motorola, Inc., Chgo., 1963-69, sales mgr., 1969-80, mgr. mktg. and client services, 1980-85, dir. ops., 1985—. Contbr. articles to profl. jour. Pres. Park Ridge (Ill.) Sch. Bd., 1980-83. Served to lt. USN, 1960-63. Mem. Am. Soc. Tng. Devel., Nat. Soc. for Performance and Instrn. Republican. Roman Catholic. Avocations: photography, automobile repair. Office: Motorola Inc 1303 E Algonquin Rd Schaumburg IL 60196

BALES, JAMES HENRY, restaurant owner, building contractor; b. Effingham, Ill., May 18, 1940; s. Henry T. and Imogene M. (Rankin) B.; m. Melba A. Heiden, Sept. 4, 1960; children: Heidi, Scott, Jamie. BS in Edn., BA in Bus., Eastern Ill. U., 1963. Acct. Blaw-Knox Co., Mattoon, Ill., 1964-66; tchr. Sullivan (Ill.) High Sch., 1966-72; owner B&B Constrn., Sullivan, 1972—, B&W Pizza, Sullivan, 1979—. Democrat. Club: Sullivan Am. Bus. (regional project mgr. 1985). Lodge: Masons. Avocation: profl. bass fishing. Home: Rural Rt #3 Box 282 Sullivan IL 61951 Office: B&W Pizza 402 S Hamilton Sullivan IL 61951

BALESTER, VIVIAN SHELTON, law librarian, lawyer, legal research consultant; b. Pine Bluff, Ark., Dec. 10, 1931; d. Marvin W. and Mary Lena (Burke) Shelton; m. James Beverly Standerfer, Aug. 1, 1951 (dec. 1952); 1 child, Walter Eric; m. Raymond James Balester, Oct. 19, 1956; children: Carla Maria, Mark Shelton. BA cum laude, Vanderbilt U., 1955; MSLS, Case Western Res. U., 1972, JD, 1975. Bar: Ohio 1975, U.S. Dist. Ct. (no. dist.) Ohio 1975. Ind. bibliographic and legal research cons., Cleve., Washington, Nashville, 1959—; head law librarian Squire, Sanders & Dempsey, Cleve., 1975-86; Ohio del. White House Conf. Libraries/Information Services, 1979; speaker Law Librarians Nat. Conf., 1978, 80, 82; mem. adv. com. on profl. ethics Case Western Res. U., 1982-85. Lay reader St. Alban's Episc. Ch., 1978—, mem. vestry, 1977-79, 84-86, warden, 1979, 84; mem. council Diocese of Ohio, 1980-82, chmn. racial justice com., 1980-86, chmn. nominating com., 1982, del. Nat. Confs. on Faith Pub. Policy, Racism, 1982; dep. gen. Conv. of Episc. Ch. in U.S., 1985; mem. Women's Polit. Caucus, 1978—; founder and co-chmn. Greater Cleve. Ann. Martin Luther King Celebration, 1980—; convener AIDS Interfaith Coalition of Greater Cleve., 1987—; mem. County Commrs. adv. com. on handicapped, 1980-84; chmn. adolescent health coalition Fedn. Community Planning, 1979-81, mem. health concerns commn., 1981—, vice chairperson, 1986—; regional chmn. alumni edn. Vanderbilt U., 1982-83; mem. community adv. com. Cleve. Orch., 1983—; bd. dirs. Hospice Council No. Ohio, 1979-81, vol. atty., 1982-85; bd. dirs. Interch. Council Greater Cleve., 1978-84, 86—; mem. Ohio Com. Nat. Security, 1983; bd. dirs. WomenSpace, 1979-83. Recipient Outstanding Community Service award Fedn. Community Planning, 1980, Woman of Profl. Excellence award YWCA, 1983, Cleve. Mayor's award for volunteerism, 1984; NEH fellow, 1980. Mem. ABA, Cleve. Bar Assn. (Merit Service award 1979) Am. Assn. Law Libraries, Am. Soc. Info. Sci. (chmn. law sect. 1978). Democrat. Home and Office: 2460 Edgehill Rd Cleveland Heights OH 44106

BALFOUR, HENRY HALLOWELL, JR., medical educator, researcher, physician; b. Jersey City, Feb. 9, 1940; s. Henry Hallowell and Dorothy Kathryn (Dietze) B.; m. Carol Lenore Pries, Sept. 23, 1967; children: Henry Hallowell III, Anne Lenore, Caroline Dorothy. B.A., Princeton U., 1962; M.D., Columbia U., 1966. Attending pediatrician Wright-Patterson AFB, Ohio, 1968-70; asst. prof. U. Minn., Mpls., 1972-75, assoc. prof., 1975-79, prof. lab. medicine, pathology and pediatrics, 1979—, dir. div. clin. microbiology, 1974—; prin. investigator NIH grants, 1976—; NIH Nat. AIDS Treatment Evaluation Units, 1987—. Author: (with Ralph C. Heussner) Herpes Diseases and Your Health, 1984; contbr. numerous sci. articles to profl. jours. Mem. Am. Soc. Microbiology, Soc. Exptl. Biology and Medicine, Soc. Pediatric Research, Infectious Disease Soc. Am., Cen. Soc. Clin. Research. Presbyterian. Home: 6820 Harold Ave N Minneapolis MN 55427 Office: U Minn Health Sci Ctr Box 437 420 Delaware St SE Minneapolis MN 55455

BALKE, GARRETT A., real estate development and construction company executive; b. Racine, Wis., June 9, 1937; s. Arnold and Marcella (Bartz) B.; m. Joanne M. Swenson, Nov. 10, 1961; children: Gregory A., Suzanne. BA, U. Minn., 1959. Registered architect, Minn., Mo. Archtl. engr. Fegles Constrn. Co., Mpls., 1964-67; mgr. real estate and constrn. Honeywell, Inc., Mpls., 1967-70; v.p., owner Linclay Corp., St. Louis, 1970-79; owner. pres. Garrett A. Balke, Inc., St. Louis, 1979—; bd. dirs. Fin. Bancshares, St. Louis. Mem. Downtown St. Louis, Inc., 1985, Clayton (Mo.) Art Mus., 1985, Regional Commerce and Growth Assn., 1986. Served with classified counter intelligence corps U.S.Army, 1960-63. Mem. Nat. Assn. Indsl. and Office Parks, Citizens for Modern Transit. Office: 700 Saint Louis Union Station Saint Louis MO 63103

BALKE, VICTOR H., bishop; b. Meppen, Ill., Sept. 29, 1931; s. Bernard H. and Elizabeth A. (Knese) B. B.A. in Philosophy, St. Mary of Lake Sem., Mundelein, Ill., 1954, S.T.B. in Theology, 1956, M.A. in Religion, 1957, S.T.L. in Theology, 1958; M.A. in English, St. Louis U., 1964, Ph.D., 1973. Ordained priest Roman Catholic Ch., 1958; asst. pastor Springfield, Ill., 1958-62; chaplain St. Joseph Home Aged, Springfield, 1962-63; procurator, instr. Diocesan Sem., Springfield, 1963-70; rector, instr. Diocesan Sem., 1970-76; ordained, installed 6th bishop of Crookston, Minn., 1976—. Clubs: K.C., Lions. Office: Chancery Office 1200 Memorial Dr PO Box 610 Crookston MN 56716 *

BALL, BEVERLY HODGES, association executive, author; b. Meridian, Miss., Dec. 27, 1927; d. Bryant Bevil and Nola Mae (Williams) Hodges; m. Armand B. Ball, Jr., Sept. 15, 1957; children—Kathryn Lynn, Robin Armand. B.A., Blue Mountain Coll., 1948; M.R.E., Southwestern Bapt. Theol. Sem., 1957. Program dir. YMCA Camp Widjiwagan, St. Paul, 1970-74; exec. sec. Sch. Bus., Ind. U., Bloomington, 1976-77; publs. supr. Am. Camping Assn., Martinsville, Ind., 1977—, dir. instrs., outdoors living skills program. Vol. dir. tng. St. Croix Valley council Girl Scouts U.S.A., St. Paul, 1970-74, Tulip Trace council, Bloomington, 1974-76. Recipient Gold award St. Croix Valley council Girl Scouts U.S.A., 1974, cert. of appreciation Tulip Trace council, 1974-76; cons. Nat. Girl Scout Tng. Summit, 1975. Presbyterian. Co-author: Basic Camp Management, 1979. Home: 2812 Fawkes Way Bloomington IN 47401 Office: Am Camping Assn Bradford Woods Martinsville IN 46151

BALL, CHARLES THOMAS, public relations executive; b. Connersville, Ind., June 9, 1962; s. Francis Eugene and Betty Ann (Duncan) B. BA, Miami U., 1984. Mng. editor nat. hdqrs. Phi Kappa Tau, Oxford, Ohio, 1984-85, leadership cons., 1984-86, dir. devel., 1986-87, project mgr. chpt. house assn., 1986-87; v.p. Laser Communications, Indpls., 1987—. Editor: The Laurel of Phi Kappa Tau jour., 1984-85. Named one of Outstanding Young Men of Am., 1985-87. Mem. Council for Advancement and Support of Higher Edn., Coll. Fraternity Editors Assn., Soc. Archtl. Historians, Phi Alpha Theta. Republican. Methodist. Home: 619 N Guilford Ave #10 Indianapolis IN 46220 Office: Laser Communications 911 E 86th St Suite 201 Indianapolis IN 46240

BALL, CHESTER EDWIN, editor, consultant, business owner; b. Seth, W.Va., Aug. 19, 1921; s. Roman Harry and Hattie (White) B.; A.B., Marshall U., 1942; M.A., Ohio State U., 1947; m. Betty June Hively, Dec. 29, 1945; children—Beth Elaine (Mrs. John Michael Watkins), Harry Stuart, Chester Edwin. Stringer, Charleston (W.Va.) Daily Mail, 1936-40; reporter, copy editor Huntington (W.Va.) Pub. Co., 1945, 47-48; assoc. pub. Wolf Pub. Co., Cin., 1953-55; instr. journalism Marshall Coll., Huntington, W.Va., 1947-51; asst. prof. journalism Ohio State U., Columbus, 1951-56, publs. editor Engring. Expt. Sta., 1956-63; tech. editor, dir. reprographics Ohio State U. Research Found., Columbus, 1963-81, editorial cons. Ohio State U. Ednl. Resources Info. Ctr., 1981—, dept. family medicine, 1983—. Mem. Hilliard (Ohio) Charter Commn., 1958-63, vice-chmn., 1958, sec., 1960-61, 62-63; treas. Hilliard chpt. Am. Field Service, 1974-76, pres., 1976-77; mem. Scioto Darby Bd. Edn., Hilliard, 1962-78; bd. dirs. Franklin County Epilepsy Assn., 1976-82, treas., 1978-80, pres., 1980-81. Served with AUS, 1942-45; col. Res. (ret.). Decorated Silver Star, Bronze Star medal with one oak leaf cluster, Purple Heart with two oak leaf clusters. Mem. In-Plant Printing Mgmt. Assn. (pres. 1971, cert. graphics communication mgr.), Res. Officers Assn. (sec.-treas., pres. Huntington, W.Va. 1948-50), U.S. Army 5th Div. Soc. (pres. 1984-85, editor 1985—), Columbus Zoo Docent Assn. (parliamentarian 1985). Republican. Methodist (mem. bd. ushers 1956—). Club: Hilliard Kiwanis (pres. 1983-84). Home: 6174 Sunny Vale Dr Columbus OH 43228

BALL, CLIFFORD NEIL, greeting card co. exec.; b. Olathe, Kans., Jan. 20, 1928; s. Loren Gordon and Edythe Virginia (Woolery) B.; B.S. in Bus., U. Kans., 1950; m. Jo Ann Boyer, June 4, 1948; children—Neila Jo, Malissa, Twila Sue, Mark, Daniel. Merchandiser, Hallmark Card Co., Kansas City, Mo., 1950-53, mdse. control mgr., 1954-64, dir. product promotions, 1965-68, planning mgr., 1969-70, dir. product mgmt. services, 1971-72, sr. product mgr., 1973-78, group product mgr., 1978-80, corp. dir. fixture line mgmt. and visual merchandising, 1981-82, dir. retail environment, 1982-84, dir. prodn. control, 1984—. Chmn. bd. trustees, ruling elder First United Presbyn. Ch., Olathe, 1970-82; pres. Olathe Interchurch Alliance, 1971; v.p. Olathe Arts Council, 1978-79; chmn. ministerial relations crisis com. Kansas City Union Presbytery, 1979—. Served with USN, 1945-46. Recipient Family of Builders award Kans. Kiwanis Found., 1976. Democrat. Home: 605 Edgemere Dr Olathe KS 66061 Office: 25th and McGee Sts Kansas City MO 64141

BALL, DIANE ALTMAN, librarian; b. Chattanooga, Sept. 4, 1932; d. William A. and Louise (Kendrick) Altman; B.S. in Edn., Miami U., Oxford, Ohio, 1968; M.Ed., Wright State U., Dayton, Ohio, 1977; m. Richard E. Ball, Oct. 10, 1953; children—David Allen, Anne Louise. Children's librarian Miamisburg (Ohio) Public Library, 1952-53; librarian W. Carrollton (Ohio) Jr.-Sr. High Sch., 1958-60; substitute tchr. Miamisburg, W. Carrollton and Oakwood City sch. dists., 1964-68; media specialist Oakwood Jr.-Sr. High Sch., Dayton, 1968—; adj. instr. Wright State U.; mem. various assessment and evaluation teams for state and pvt. agys.; vice-chmn. Ohio Multitype Interlibrary Cooperation Com., 1975-81; co-founder Southwestern Ohio Young Adult Materials Rev. Group; Mem. Ohio Assn. Sch. Librarians (dir. Western dist. 1971-73, state pres. 1975-76), Oakwood Tchrs. Assn., Ednl. Media Council Ohio, NEA, Ohio, Western Ohio edn. assns., ALA, Am. Assn. Sch. Librarians (mem. standards com. 1976—, mem. exec. com. 1981; rep. to rev. com. Am. U. Press Services 1977—, chmn. AUPS 1982, chmn. Unit II, 1981-85; regional dir. 1978-81, rep. exec. com. 1982-83, 2nd v.p. 1984-85, chmn. policy com. 1985-87), Ohio Ednl. Library Media Assn. (1st past pres., co-chmn. consol. project, award of merit 1983), Phi Delta Kappa, Delta Kappa Gamma. Contbr. profl. publs. Home: 2410 Fairmont Ave Dayton OH 45419 Office: 1200 Far Hills Ave Dayton OH 45419

BALL, JOHN NELSON, minister; b. Mexico, Mo., Aug. 30, 1938; s. Lebbius Mac and Elizabeth Sue (Field) B.; m. Joyce Jeanne Beatty, May 31, 1959; children: John Anthony, Jeanne Alice, Jane Ann (dec.). BA in Bible Studies, Cen. Christian Coll. of Bible, 1967. Ordained to ministry, 1967. Minister Union (Iowa) Ch. Christ, 1967-68, Waterloo (Iowa) Ch. Christ, 1968-69, W. Eminence (Mo.) Christian Ch., 1969-73, S. Telegraph Christian Ch., St. Louis, 1973-74, Oak Grove (Mo.) Christian Ch., 1974-78, Callao (Mo.) Christian Ch., 1978-83, Lakeview Christian Ch., House Springs, Mo., 1983—; Co-founder, dean Iowa Sch. Missions, Liscomb, 1968-70; dean curriculum Rock Garden Christian Service Camp, Eminence, 1970-72; treas. N.E. Iowa Christian Service Camp, Bristow, 1968-69, Rock Garden Christian Service Camp, Eminence, 1971-73. Bd. dirs. Show Me Christian Youth Home, LaMonte, Mo., 1970-73, 75-79; bd. dirs. High Hill (Mo.) Christian Service Camp, 1973-74, chmn. bd. 1986—; bd. dirs. Christian Campus Fellowship, Kirksville, Mo., 1980-82, sec. 1981-82; chmn. bd. Mid-Western Camp Leaders Conf. Com., 1980-81; pres. PTA, Eminence, 1971-72; mem. Community Betterment Orgn., Callao, 1979-83. Recipient Sandy Ninanger award Mexico (Mo.) High Sch., 1956, Appreciation award Soc. Dist. High Sch. Students, Birmingham, Ala., 1977-86, Vol. award Normandy Osteo. Hosps., St. Louis, 1983—. Mem. Ministerial Alliance (v.p. Eminence chpt. 1971, pres. 1972, Oak Grove chpt. 1980-81, pres. 1982, 83). Republican. Office: Lakeview Christian Ch 3774 Hess Rd House Springs MO 63051

BALL, LINDA SUE, accountant; b. Chgo., June 6, 1955; s. Lloyd Herman and Irma Marie (Schoenfeldinger) Dewey; m. Lawrence Edward Ball, July 12, 1986. BA, North Cen. Coll., 1977; MBA with distinction, DePaul U., 1983. Asst. to v.p., research analyst Loeb Rhoades Hornblower, Chgo., 1977-78; asst. to v.p., asst. office mgr. Thomson McKinnon, Chgo., 1978-81; operational acctg. supr. MidAm. Fed., Clarendon Hills, Ill., 1983—. Mem. Nat. Mustang Assn., Beta Gamma Sigma, Delta Mu Delta. Club: Evergreen Wildlife (Lake Zurich, Ill.). Avocations: horseshow jumping, books, conservation. Home: 10406 S Moody Chicago Ridge IL 60415

BALL, LOUIS ALVIN, insurance company executive; b. Kansas City, Mo., Oct. 25, 1921; s. George Rhodom and Frances Mariam (Beals) B.; B.A. in Bus. Adminstrn., Kans. State U., 1947; m. Norma Jane Laudenberger, Jan. 17, 1947. Asst. purchasing agt. Kansas City (Mo.) br. Ford Motor Co., 1946-47; with Farm Bur. Mut. Ins. Co., Inc., Manhattan, Kans., 1947—, claims underwriting mgr., 1956-61, systems and procedures mgr., 1961—, asst. sec., 1977-81, corp. sec., 1981—. Mem. Nat. Assn. Ind. Insurers, Conf. Casualty Cos., Assn. Systems Mgmt. (Internat. Merit award 1971, Internat. Achievement award 1978, Kansas City chpt. Merit award 1970, Kansas City chpt. Diamond Merit award 1977, chmn. ann. conf. 1982). Club: Manhattan Country. Home: 1101 Pioneer Ln Manhattan KS 66502 Office: 2321 Anderson Ave Manhattan KS 66502

BALL, ROBERT ALLAN, retail jewelry executive; b. Akron, Ohio, Dec. 9, 1955; s. Walter Henry Ball and Mary Francis (Bader) Gorman; m. Patricia Ann Alandar, Sept. 19, 1981; children: Jennifer Lee, Robert Allan II, Kathryn Anne. Student, Akron U.; grad., Gemological Inst. Am. With sales dept. Henry B. Ball Co., Akron, 1974-82; mgr. Henry B. Ball Co., Canton, Ohio, 1983—. Mem. com. Hall of Fame Fashion Show, Canton, 1985. Mem. Am. Gem Soc. (registered jeweler, cert. gemologist, cert. gemologist/appraiser), Ohio Guild Am. Gem. Soc. (v.p. 1981-83, pres. 1984-86), Ohio Jewelers Assn. (bd. dirs. 1982—), Greater Canton C. of C. (ambassador 1984, 85). Republican. Roman Catholic. Avocations: golf, backgammon, sailing. Home: 124 Harcourt Akron OH 44313 Office: Henry B Ball Co 5254 Dressler Rd NW Canton OH 44718

BALL, ROBERT EDWARD, JR., data processing executive; b. Summit, N.J., Mar. 14, 1938; s. Robert E. and Mary (Glasser) B.; m. Joan H. Unterwald, Aug. 11, 1962; children: Robert M., Elizabeth E., Meredith A. BS in Math., Upsala Coll., 1962; postgrad., Stevens Inst. Tech., 1963-68. Programmer ITT, Paramus, N.J., 1962-64; sr. programmer Hess Oil and Chem., Perth Amboy, N.J., 1964-65; mgr. systems and programmer Johnson & Johnson, New Brunswick, N.J., 1965-78; dir. mgmt. info. systems Beverage Mgmt., Columbus, Ohio, 1978-83; dir. corp. info. systems Adria Labs., Dublin, Ohio, 1983—. Contbr. articles to profl. jours. Asst. scout master, com. chmn., unit commr. Boy Scouts Am., N.J. and Ohio, 1973-82, com. chmn., unit commr. Mem. Data Processing Mgmt. Assn. Club: WHCC. Avocations: tennis, fishing, boating, softball. Home: 8184 Cooperfield Dr Worthington OH 43085 Office: Adria Labs PO Box 16529 Columbus OH 43216

BALL, THOMAS JAMES, producer, director; b. Cleve., June 12, 1952; s. Gordon Bateman and Virginia (Mayfield) B.; m. Catherine Codman Eppinger, June 15, 1975; children: David Codman Turben, Nicholas Amory Turben. AB, Wooster (Ohio) Coll., 1975. Ind. producer Cleve., 1975-82; pres., founder, co-owner Telos Prodns., Cleve., 1982—. Writer, dir. (film) Vishnu's Maya, 1975, (documentary) Crawford Auto Mus., 1982, Internat. Expn. Ctr., 1984, Ohio Lottery, 1986. Recipient Golden Reel Excellence, Internat. TV Assn., 1982, 83, Silver Tower award Bus. Profl. Advt. Assn., 1984, 2 Emmy awards Nat. Acad. TV Arts and Scis., 1987, Award of Excellence, Internat. Assn. Bus. Communicators, 1987.; NEH grantee, 1975. Home: Battles Rd Gates Mills OH 44040 Office: Telos Video 67 Alpha Park Dr Cleveland OH 44143

BALL, TRAVIS, JR., ednl. adminstr.; b. Newport, Tenn., July 13, 1942; s. Travis and Ruth Annette (Duyck) B.; B.A., Carson Newman Coll., 1964; M.A., Purdue U., 1966. Instr., then asst. prof. English, Ill. Wesleyan U., Bloomington, 1966-69; vis. prof. English edn. Millikin U., 1969; asst. headmaster, chmn. English dept. Brewster Acad., Wolfeboro, N.H., 1969-72; dir. admissions, asst. to headmaster Park Tudor Sch., Indpls., 1972—; pres. Travis Ball & Assos., 1980—; mem. commn. on curriculum and grad. requirements Ind. Dept. Public Instrn., 1974-76; mem. adv. council Ednl. Records Bur. Mem. Indiana Non-Public Edn. Assn. (treas., dir., vice chmn.), Independent Schs. Assn. Central States (conf. chmn.), Nat. Council Tchrs. English, Assn. Supervision and Curriculum Devel., Council Advancement and Support Edn. (adv. com. on ind. schs.), Nat. Assn. Ind. Schs., Sigma Tau Delta, Pi Kappa Delta, Phi Delta Kappa. Baptist. Editor, Tchrs. Service Com. Newsletter for English Tchrs., 1977-82; dept. editor English Jour., 1976-82; editor/pub. Contact: Newsletter for Admissions Mgmt., 1980—. Home: 2625 N Meridian St Indianapolis IN 46208 Office: 7200 N College Ave Indianapolis IN 46240

BALL, WILLIAM JAMES, physician; b. Charleston, S.C., Apr. 16, 1910; s. Elias and Mary (Cain) B.; B.S., U. of South, 1930; M.D., Med. Coll. S.C., 1934; m. Doris Hallowell Mason, July 9, 1938. Intern, Roper Hosp., Charleston, 1934-35; resident dept. pediatrics U. Chgo. Clinics, 1935-37; instr. pediatrics Med. Coll. S.C., 1938-42; practice medicine specializing in pediatrics, Charleston, 1938-42, Northwest Clinic, Minot N.D., 1946-51, Aurora, Ill., 1951-70; physician student Health Service No. Ill. U., 1970-72; mem. staff Copley Meml., Mercy Ctr. Health Care Services; assoc. prof. Sch. Nursing, No. Ill. U., 1971-72. Mem. Bd. Health, Aurora, Ill., 1958-62; pediatrician, div. services for crippled children U. Ill., 1952-86; pediatric cons. sch. dists. 129 and 131, Aurora, 1972-85, DeKalb County Spl. Edn. Assn., 1972-81, Sch. Assn. Spl. Edn. Dupage County, 1980-83, Mooseheart, Ill., 1970-83, Northwestern Ill. Assn. Handicapped Children; chmn. adv. com. Kane County Health Dept., 1986—; pres. Kane County sub-area council Health Systems Agy., Kane, Lake, McHenry Counties, 1977-78, sec., 1978-79. Served as capt. M.C., AUS, 1942-46; col. Res., ret. Diplomate Am. Bd. Pediatrics. Fellow Royal Soc. Health, Am. Acad. Pediatrics; mem. AMA, Kane County Med. Soc. (pres. 1962), Am. Heart Assn., Am. Sch. Health Assn., Am. Cancer Soc., Juvenile Protective Assn. of Aurora and Waubonsie Child Devel. Ctr. (bd. dirs.), Phi Beta Kappa, Phi Chi, Pi Kappa Phi. Republican. Rotarian. Club: Union League (Aurora). Address: 433 S Commonwealth Ave Aurora IL 60506

BALLANTYNE, DOROTHY DUNNING, museum director, retired educator; b. Aetna, Ind., Mar. 17, 1910; d. Harry Leland and Ella L. (Larson) Dunning; m. Donald Bock Ballantyne (dec. June, 1973); children: Elin Christianson, Dorothy Eastwood, Brianne Lowery, Alexander. Student Ind U. Newspaper editor Hobart Gazette, Ind., 1929-32; clk. Home Owners Loan Fed. Govt., Hammond, Ind., 1932; dep. auditor Lake County, Crown Point, Ind., 1932-36; sub. tchr. Hobart Schs., Ind., 1954-65, spl. edn. tchr., 1965-72; vol. dir. Hobart Hist. Soc. Mus., Ind., 1970—. Contbr. articles to profl. jour. Author pamphlets Hobart Hist. Soc. Mem. adv. com. Hobart Sch. Bd., 1980—, Hobart PTA. Recipient Disting Service award West Hobart Civic Club, 1970; named one of 12 most valuable women in county Trade Winds, Lake County, Ind., 1978. Mem. Ind. Hist. Soc., Hobart Hist. Soc. (pres. 1970-76), Mensa, Hobart Jaycees (Laura Bracken Woman of yr. award 1968), LWV (pres.). Lodge: Order Eastern Star (worthy matron 1938, dist. dep. 1940). Home: 121 South Ash St Hobart IN 46342 Office: Hobart Hist Soc Mus Box 24 Hobart IN 46342

BALLARD, JOSEPH GRANT, photographer, photog. co. exec.; b. Greenville, N.C., Nov. 29, 1928; s. Charlie Edgar and Mary Velma (Keel) B.; B.S., Calif. Western U., 1976, M.B.A., 1978; grad. Woodward Sch. of Photography, 1949, Modern Sch. of Photography, N.Y.C., 1950; Ph.D. (hon.), Pacific Coll., 1976; D.D. (hon.), Christian Bible Coll., 1982, Ala. Bible Coll., 1982; H.H.D., Covington Theol. Sem., 1982; m. Sherry Rae Hall, May 2, 1961; children—Joseph Grant, Don, Patricia, Mike, Ron, Jeffrey Grant, Warren Scott, Vikki Kristine. Exec. v.p. Goldcraft Studios, Cin., 1951-61; pres. Photoland, Inc., Cleve., 1961-71, Nelson's Photography, Inc., Cleve., 1972—; cons. in mktg., promotions, budget controls and fund raising to various bus. firms and orgns., 1975—. Mem. Bicentennial Commn., Cleve., 1975; pres. Recreation Advisory Bd., North Olmsted, Ohio, 1977—; lay Baptist minister; mem. The Chapel in Berea, ordained elder, 1981, chmn. of elders, 1981; chmn. com. Child Evangelism Fellowship, Cleve., 1977-79; trustee Child Evangelism Fellowship, Warrenton, Md. Served with USAAF, 1945-47. Recipient numerous awards for portrait photography, 1953—; Joseph G. Ballard Day proclaimed in honor by mayor of Cleve., April 4, 1975. Mem. Profl. Photographers of Am. Assn., Wedding Photographers of Am. Assn., Ohio Assn. Chiefs of Police, Fraternal Order of Police, Cleveland Ad Club, Ohio Profl. Photography Assn. Home: 5612 Allandale Dr North Olmsted OH 44070 Office: 41 Colonial Arcade Cleveland OH 44115

BALLARD, LARRY COLEMAN, insurance company executive; b. Des Moines, May 31, 1935; s. Coleman Woodrow and Letitia Rebecca (Reaugh) B.; m. Rosalie Phillips, Dec. 24, 1956; children: Coleman, Tamara. B.S. in Actuarial Scis, Drake U., 1957. Asst. actuary Travelers Ins. Co., Hartford, Conn., 1957-62; v.p. Allstate Ins. Co., Northbrook, Ill., 1962-75; sr. v.p. CNA Co., Chgo., 1975-85; chmn. bd., pres., chief exec. officer Sentry Ins. Co., Stevens Point, Wis., 1985—; also dir., pres. or chmn. bd. affiliated cos., 1985—. Served with U.S. Army, 1958. Fellow Soc. Actuaries; mem. Am. Acad. Actuaries, Alliance Am. Insurers (bd. dirs.), Ins. Inst. Am. (trustee), Am. Inst. Property & Liability Underwriters (trustee). Clubs: Madison (Wis.); Milw. Athletic; Stevens Point Country. Lodge: Rotary. Office: Sentry Ins and Mut Co 1800 N Point Dr Stevens Point WI 54481

BALLENGER, HURLEY RENÉ, electrical engineer; b. Jacksonville, Ill., Nov. 26, 1946; s. Leonard Hurley and Katherine Natalie (Daniel) B.; m. Dandra Ann Rubley, Dec. 9, 1986. Student, Ill. Coll., 1964-65, 75. Technician electronics div. Hughs Aircraft, Inc., Tucson, 1973; maintenance supr. Fiatallis N.Am., Springfield, Ill., 1973-75, project engr., 1975-83, plant engr., 1983-86; tech. advisor CNC/CAM Fiatallis Europe, Springfield, Ill., 1986—. Mem. career adv. bd. Lincoln Land Community Coll., Springfield, 1983-85. Served to staff sgt. USAF, 1965-72, Vietnam. Mem. Constrn. Industry Mfrs. Assn. (mem. energy com.). Lutheran. Avocations: photography, home computing. Office: Fiat Allis NAm 701 Stevenson Dr Springfield IL 62703

BALLMER, JAMES ELIAS, research engineer; b. Pleasantville, Ohio, Dec. 22, 1925; s. Trafford David and Racel Emily (Vernon) B.; m. Doris Louise Morris, Aug. 24, 1947 (div. Feb. 1983); children: James Ballmer, Diana Upp; m. Jo Ellyn Preston, Oct. 1, 1983; children: Victor Ivers, Rebecca Colvin, Cynthia Lunt. BME, MS, Ohio State U., 1951. Registered profl. mech. engr., Ohio. Prin. engr. Battelle Meml. Labs., Columbus, Ohio, 1951-56; project leader Convair Aircraft, Ft. Worth, 1956-59; mgr. engring. Bausch and Lomb, Rochester, N.Y., 1959-65; dir. engring. Brunswick Corp., Cin., 1965-71; engring. cons. Cin., 1971-76; prin. engr. U.S. Precision Lens, Inc., Cin., 1976—; cons., Cin., 1965—. Patentee in field (20). Elder Presbyn. Ch., Rochester, 1964. Served with USAF, 1943-45. Republican. Methodist. Avocations: autos, modelbuilding, woodworking, campin. Home: 4603 Rumpke Rd Cincinnati OH 45245 Office: US Precision Lens Inc 4000 McMann Rd Cincinnati OH 45245

BALLO, BELA FRANK, radiologist; b. Budapest, Hungary, Dec. 30, 1938; s. Bela John and Luijza (Kertesz) B.; m. Patricia Ann Ragon, Mar., 1963; children: Bela Robert, Michael, Matthew, Nicole. BS, Baldwin-Wallace Coll., 1960; MD, SUNY, Buffalo, 1964. Resident in radiology Wayne State U., Detroit, 1965-68; tfellow teaching Case Western Reserve U., Cleve., 1969-71; radiologist Hill & Thomas, Cleve., 1971—; also bd. dirs. pres. Lake County Med. Assn., Painesville, Ohio, 1984. Served to capt. USAR, 1965-72. Mem. AMA, Am. Coll. Radiology, N.Am. Radiological Soc., Cleve. Radiology Soc., Ohio Radiology Soc. Clubs: Mentor Harbor Yacht, Mayfield Village Raquet. Home: 7259 Eagle Waite Hill OH 44094

BALLOU, WILLIAM EUGENE, retail executive; b. Lake Preston, S.D., Jan. 7, 1941; s. Charles Sprague and Myrtle Henrietta (Mydland) B.; m. Ila Ann Boilesen, July 16, 1948; children—Carmin Dee, Aaron Andrew, Isaac Nathan. Student Luth. Bible Sem., 1963-64, Ind. Luth. Sem., 1967-68. Dept. head Billy Graham Assn., Mpls., 1963-68; sales rep. Wm. Erdman Pub., Grand Rapids, Mich., 1968-70; office mgr. Word of Life Inc., Schroon Lake, Nebr., 1970-73; pres., mgr. The Solid Rock Inc., Kearney, Nebr., 1973—; bd. dirs. Retail Merchants Assn., Lincoln, Nebr., 1980—; bd. dirs., 2nd v.p. Christian Booksellers Assn. Internat., Colorado Springs, Colo., 1982—. Bd. dirs. Citadel Bible Coll., Ozark, Ark., 1980—; chmn. Buffalo County Republican Party, Nebr., 1980-82, Downtown Improvement Bd., Kearney, 1984—. Recipient Bookselling award Tyndale House Pub., 1979. Mem. Kearney C. of C. (bd. dirs. 1981-83). Republican. Mem. Evangelical Ch. Club: Gideon Internat. Lodge: Rotary. Avocation: yo-yoer. Office: The Solid Rock Inc 2010 Central Ave Kearney NE 68847

BALLOUN, JOSEPH LE, management educator; b. Des Moines, Mar. 26, 1941; s. Stanley Leo and Edna Ailene (Holt) B.; m. Jean Phillips, June 10, 1965 (div. 1983); m. Lois Ann Spitler, Nov. 3, 1984; 1 child, Andrew Joseph Stanley. BS, Iowa State U., 1963, MS, 1965; PhD, U. Calif., Berkeley, 1971. Lic. indsl. psychologist, Ohio. Asst. prof. U. So. Ill., Edwardsville, 1974-75, Wright State U., Dayton, Ohio, 1975-78; personnel psycholgist Wright Patterson AFB, Dayton, 1978-80; dir. mgmt. systems div. Stevens, Scheidler, Stevens and Vossler, Inc., Dayton, 1980-81; assoc. prof. mgmt. U. Dayton, 1981—; cons. in field. Contbr. numerous articles to profl. jours., chpts. to books. Mem. Acad. Mgmt., Acad. Mktg. Sci., Am. Cons. League, Am. Mktg. Assn., Becision Scis. Inst., Midwest Mktg. Assn., Soc. Indsl. and Orgnl. Psychologists, So. Mktg. Assn., Southwestern Mktg. Assn. (Best Paper award 1985), Beta Gamma Sigma, Psi Chi. Congregational. Avocations: fixing up old houses, gardening, landscaping. Home: 147 E Hadley Ave Dayton OH 45419 Office: Univ Dayton 300 College Park Ave Dayton OH 45469-0001

BALLWEG, MARY LOU, nonprofit association administrator, writer, consultant; b. Madison, Wis., Feb. 8, 1948; m. Jim Dorr; 1 child. BA in Comparative Lit. with honors, U. Wis., 1971. Staff writer Investor, Wis.' Bus. mag., Milw., 1972, mng. editor, 1973-74; scriptwriter, film dir. Moynihan Assocs., Milw., 1975; cons. communication, film making Milw., 1976-81; co-founder U.S.-Can. Endometriosis Assn., Milw., 1980-82, exec. dir., pres., 1982—. Author/editor: Overcoming Endometriosis, 1987; scriptwriter, dir.: (films) Domestic Violence: All-American Crime; contbr. articles to mags. Co-founder Margaret Sanger Community Health Clinic, Milw., 1971-72. Mem. Women in Communications (bd. dirs. southeast Wis. chpt. 1976-77, editor newsletter), Feminist Writers Guild, NOW. Office: US-Can Endometriosis Assn PO Box 92187 Milwaukee WI 53202

BALMER, ROBERT THEODORE, mechanical engineering educator, researcher; b. Chelsea, Mich., Nov. 26, 1938; s. Homer Theodore and Elsie Amelia (Horne) B.; m. Mary Anne Sorensen, Nov. 4, 1961; children—Christine Anne, Robert Lance, Theodore Austin. B.S.E. in Mech. Engring., U. Mich., 1961, M.S.E. in Mech. Engring., 1963, B.S.E. in Engring Math., 1964; Sc.D. in Mech. Engring., U. Va., 1968. Registered profl. engr., Wis. Engr. Bettis Atomic Power Lab., Pitts., 1961-62; research engr. E.I. duPont, Waynesboro, Va., 1964-68; asst. prof. U. Wis.-Milw., 1969-72, assoc. prof. mech. engring., 1972-79, prof. mech. engring., 1979—, engring. research coordinator, 1984-87; vis. prof. NATO, U. Naples, Italy, 1968-69. Contbr. articles on mech. engring. to profl. jours. Patentee chem. to mech. energy converter, 1973. Com. mem. Lakefront Festival of Arts, Milw., 1983. Recipient Teetor award Soc. Automotive Engrs., 1961, Eminent Engr. award Tau Beta Pi, 1981; numerous research grants NSF and Nat. Inst. Aging; 1970—. Mem. Am. Soc. Engring. Edn., Soc. Rheology, AAAS, Sigma Xi. Methodist. Avocation: history of Am. tech.

BALSTERS, HAROLD WALTER, real estate developer, farmer; b. Bethalto, Ill., Aug. 8, 1930; s George W. and Ella M. (Schmidt) B.; m. Peggy A. Sawyer, Apr. 18, 1953; children: Jane, Don, Amy. Grad. high sch., Bethalto, Ill. Ptnr., sec. Prairie View Farms, Bethalto, 1954—; ptnr. H & M Devel., Bethalto, 1972—; ptnr., sec. B & E Plantland, Inc., Bethalto, 1975—; ptnr., pres. Villa Rose Devel., Inc., Bethalto, 1982—; owner Re/Max Realty, Bethalto, 1985—; mem. sr. housing com. Nat. Home Builders Co., Washington, 1983—; bd. dirs. Bank of Alton, Ill., Home Builders-Madison, Edwardsville, Ill. Leader Bethalto 4-H, 1954-79; pres. sch. bd. Com. Unit #8, Bethalto, 1975—; mem. extension service U. Ill., Champaign, 1976-84. Recipient Citizenship award local bd. realtors, 1987; named State 4-H Alumni, Ill. 4-H Found., 1983. Mem. Nat. Home Builders Assn. (bd. dirs. 1984—), Nat. Bd. Realtors, State Bd. Realtors, Local Bd. Realtors. Lutheran. Home: Rt 1 Box 7 Bethalto IL 62010 Office: Re/Max Realty 64 Airport Plaza Bethalto IL 62010

BALTHASER, LINDA IRENE, university administrator; b. Kokomo, Ind., Feb. 25, 1939; d. Earl Isaac and Evelyn Pauline (Troyer) Showalter; B.S. magna cum laude, Ind. Central U., 1961; M.S., Ind. U., 1962; m. Kenneth James Balthaser, June 1, 1963. Tchr. bus. edn. Southport High Sch., Indpls., 1962-63; sec., adminstrv. sec. Office of Pres., Ind. U., Bloomington, 1963-66; with Ind. U.-Purdue U., Fort Wayne, Ind., 1969—, asst. to dean Arts and Letters, 1970-86, asst. dean art and letters, 1986—, founding co-dir. Weekend Coll., 1979-80. Bd. dirs. Associated Chs. Fort Wayne, 1980. Ind. Conf. N. Evang. United Brethren Ch. scholar, 1957-61. Mem. Fort Wayne-Allen County Hist. Assn., Embassy Theatre Found., Fort Wayne Mus. Art, Fort Wayne Zool. Soc., Nat. Assn. Women Deans, Adminstrs. and Counselors, Am. Assn. Univ. Adminstrs., Internat. Platform Assn., AAUW, Delta Pi Epsilon, Phi Alpha Epsilon, Alpha Chi, Mensa. Mem. United Ch. of Christ. Club: Univ. Women's (pres. 1967—). Home: 2917 Hazelwood Ave Fort Wayne IN 46805 Office: 2101 Coliseum Blvd E Fort Wayne IN 46805-1499

BALTHROPE, JACQUELINE MOREHEAD, educator, author, administrator, consultant; b. Phila.; d. Jack Walton and Minnie Jessie (Martin) Morehead; B.S. in Edn., Central State U., Wilberforce, Ohio, 1949; M.A. in Edn., Case Western Res. U., 1959; m. Robert Granville Balthrope, Sr.; children—Robert Granville, Yvonne Gertrude, Robin Bernice. Elem. master tchr. Cleve. Bd. Edn., 1950-65, leadership devel. tchr., 1965-69, asst. prin. elem. sch., 1969-77, prin. elem. sch., 1977-80; ednl. cons., 1980—. Recipient numerous civic, ednl. religious and social rewards. Mem. AAUW, Cleve. Council Adminstrs. and Suprs., Elem. Sch. Prins., Internat. Reading Assn., Phi Delta Kappa Frat., Delta Kappa Gamma, Alpha Kappa Mu, Zeta Sigma Pi, Pi Lambda Theta, Alpha Kappa Alpha, Phi Delta Kappa, Eta Phi Beta, Gamma Phi Delta (vol., tutor). Methodist. Clubs: Top Ladies of Distinction (local founder, past pres.), Jr. League, Zen Mer Rekh. Author: African Boy Comes to America, 1960, sequel, 1960. Contbr. articles to profl. jours., mags., newspapers. Address: 16220 Delrey Ave Cleveland OH 44128

BALTZ, SYLVIA ANN, educator; b. Mobile County, Ala., Feb. 10, 1938; d. Lawrence Monroe and Rosa Mae (Havard) Clayton; m. Howard Burl Baltz, June 23, 1967; children—Debra, Geoffrey, Jami. B.S., U. So. Miss., 1959, M.S., 1960. Instr. Tyler (Tex.) Jr. Coll., 1960-62, U. Tex., Austin, 1962-68; assoc. prof. bus. edn., coordinator dept. St. Louis Community Coll. at Forest Park, St. Louis, 1969—. Mem. Nat. Bus. Edn. Assn., North Central Bus. Edn. Assn., Mo. Bus. Edn. Assn., Am. Vocat. Assn., Mo. Vocat. Assn., St. Louis Bus. Educators Assn. (bd. dirs., sec.), Assn. Info. Systems Profls. (dir.), Profl. Secs. Internat. (assoc., exec. adv. bd.). Mem. United Ch. of Christ.

BALZANO, EDWARD C., trucking company executive; b. Cleve., Oct. 10, 1944; s. Nello and Josephine (Campana) B.; m. Linda D. Byler, April 20, 1968; children: Geoffrey, Laura. BS, Purdue U., 1968; MBA, Indiana U., 1972. Communications analyst Yellow Freight System, Inc., Overland Park, Kans., 1972-80, mgr. adminstrv. services, 1980-85, dir. adminstrv. services, 1985—. Served to 1st lt. U.S. Army, 1968-70, Vietnam. Mem. Internat. Communications Assn., Mid Am. Communications Assn. (pres. 1976-77). Republican. Roman Catholic. Office: Yellow Freight System Inc 10990 Roe Ave Overland Park KS 66207

BALZANO, LINDA MARIE, commercial finance executive; b. Carbondale, Pa., Apr. 11, 1953; d. Frank A. and Rosemarie H. Balzano. BS in Bus. Adminstrn., U. Denver, 1975; French studies, Université d'Aix Marseilles, France, 1972-73; postgrad., DePaul U., 1986—. New bus. rep. C.I.T. Corp., Chgo., 1975-76; sales mgr. Playboy Towers Hotel, Chgo., 1976-77; dist. mgr. Assocs. Comml. Corp., Assocs. Leasing, Inc., Chgo., 1977-78, from tng. mgr. to asst. dir. tng., 1979-84, mgr. tng. and orgnl. devel., 1984-87; sr. sales rep. Memorex Corp., Chgo., 1987—; mktg. sales cons. Mich. Ave. Med. Ctr., Chgo., 1985, Brooks Shoes, Chgo., 1985-86. Vol. Jr. Achievement, Chgo.; chmn. fundraising 43rd ward Rep. Orgn., Chgo., 1982, mem. exec. com., 1983; mem. campaign com. Catherine Bertini for Congress, Chgo., 1981-83; fundraiser Cystic Fibrosis Found., 1979—. Mem. Am. Soc. Tng. and Devel., Ill. Tng. and Devel. Assn. (position referral com.). Roman Catholic. Avocations: skiing, sailing, antique cars, ballet, cooking. Home: 1531 W School St Chicago IL 60657 Office: Memorex Corp 100 S Wacker Dr Chicago IL 60606

BALZER, WILLIAM KEITH, psychologist, educator; b. Queens, N.Y., Dec. 19, 1955; s. Edward Thomas and Therese Beth (Carey) B.; m. Margaret Joan Lockhart, June 1, 1985. BA in Psychology, SUNY, Stony Brook, 1978; MS in Psychology, Rensselaer Poly. Inst., 1979; PhD, NYU, 1983. Lic. psychologist, Ohio. Asst. prof. Bowling Green (Ohio) State U., 1983—; dir. Inst. Organizational Research and Devel., Bowling Green, 1984—; head indsl.-organizational psychology program Bowling Green State U., 1984—. Contbr. articles to profl. jour. Mem. Am. Psychol. Assn., Midwestern Psychol. Assn., Acad. of Mgmt. Democrat. Roman Catholic. Home: 9581 St Andrews Perrysburg OH 43551 Office: Dept Psychology Bowling Green State U Bowling Green OH 43403

BAMBERGER, DAVID, opera executive; b. Albany, N.Y., Oct. 14, 1940; s. Bernard J. and Ethel K. Bamberger; m. Carola Beral, June 8, 1965; 1 son, Steven B. B.A., Swarthmore Coll., 1962; (postgrad. U. Paris (France), 1961, Yale U., 1963. Mem. directing staff N.Y.C. Opera, 1966-70; guest dir. Nat. Opera Chile, 1970, Cin. Opera, 1968, Augusta Opera (Ga.), 1970, Pitts. Opera, 1971, 76, 81, Columbus Opera (Ohio); gen. dir. Cleve. Opera, 1976—; artistic dir. Toledo Opera Assn., 1983-85. Bd. dirs. Opera Am., Nat. Alliance Musical Theater Producers. Author Jewish history textbooks; contbr. articles to Opera News. Office: Cleveland Opera 1438 Euclid Ave Cleveland OH 44115

BAMBRICK, JAMES JOSEPH, labor economist, labor relations executive; b. N.Y.C., Apr. 26, 1917; s. James Joseph and Mae (Murphy) B.; m. Margaret Mary Donlan, June 26, 1948; children: Patricia Bambrick Benek, Thomas G., Mary Alice Bambrick Schneider, Kathleen, James Joseph Jr. BS, NYU, 1940, MBA, 1942; BS, U.S. Mcht. Marine Acad., 1946. Exec. dir. Labor Bur., N.Y.C., 1940-42; personnel dir. Allegheny Airlines, Wilmington, Del., 1942-44; mgr. labor relations research The Conf. Bd., N.Y.C., 1947-58; corp. labor economist Standard Oil Co., Cleve., 1958-81; exec. dir. Labor Econ. Inst., Cleveland Heights, Ohio, 1981—; mem. bus. adv. council U.S. Bur. Labor Stats., Washington, 1971—, chmn. wages and indsl. relations com., 1980-85; instr. NYU, 1946-53, John Carroll U., University Heights, Ohio, 1968-71; lectr. Cleve. State U., 1963-68. Author: Preparing for Collective Bargaining, 1959, Handbook of Modern Personnel Administration, 1972; contbr. chpts. to The Foreman/Supervisor's Handbook, 1984; contbr. articles to profl. jours. Chmn. Ohio Rep. Fin. Com., Cuyahoga County, Cleve., 1963—; pres. Cath. Interracial Council, Cleve., 1965-68, bd. dirs. 1969—; v.p. Navy League of U.S., Cleve., 1984—. Served to lt. USNR, 1944-46. Named Hibernian Man of the Yr. Ancient Order of Hibernians, 1974. Fellow Soc. for Advancement of Mgmt. (pres. 1955-58); mem. Am. Econ. Assn., Indsl. Relations Research Assn., U.S. Mcht. Marine Acad. Alumni Assn. (pres., bd. dirs. N.E. Ohio, 1965—). Republican. Clubs: City (Cleve.) (trustee 1972-75, v.p. Forum Found. 1981—). Lodge: K.C. Avocations: fencing, sailing, golf.

BAN, EDWARD DAVID, corporate pilot, safety manager; b. Detroit, Aug. 10, 1949; s. Steven Joseph and Rose Irene (Magyar) B. BS in Aero. Sci., Embry-Riddle U., 1973. Capt. Bristow Helicopters, Redhill, Eng., 1973-76; mng. chief pilot Allied Aggregate Transp. Co., Detroit, 1976-79; capt. Exec. Jet Aviation, Detroit, 1979-82; capt., pilot Continental Bank, Chgo., 1982—; accident prevention counselor gen. aviation dist. office 3 FAA, West Chicago, Ill., 1985. Served with U.S. Army, 1969-71, Vietnam. Mem. Soaring Soc. Am., Am. Helicopter Soc., Internat. Soc. Air Safety Investigators. Home: 2436 Forest Ave Apt #103 Bldg #2 Woodridge IL 60517 Office: Continental Ill Nat Bank 231 S LaSalle Chicago IL 60693

BANACH, ART JOHN, graphic art exec.; b. Chgo., May 22, 1931; s. Vincent and Anna (Zajac) B.; grad. Art. Inst. of Chgo., 1955; pupil painting studies Mrs. Melin, Chgo.; m. Loretta A. Nolan, Oct. 15, 1966; children: Heather Anne, Lynnea Joan. Owner, dir. Art J. Banach Studios, 1949—, cartoon syndicate for newspapers, house organs and advt. functions, 1954—, owned and operated advt. agy., 1954-56, feature news and picture syndicate, distbn. U.S. and fgn. countries. Dir. Speculators S Fund. Recipient award 1st Easter Seal contest Ill. Assn. Crippled, Inc., 1949. Chgo. Pub. Sch. Art Soc. Scholar. Mem. Artist's Guild Chgo., Am Mgmt. Assn., Chgo. Assn. of Commerce and Industry, Chgo. Federated Advt. Club, Am. Mktg. Assn., Internat. Platform Assn., Chgo. Advt. Club, Chgo. Soc. Communicating Arts. Clubs: Columbia Yacht, Advertising Executives; Art Directors (Chgo.). Home: 1076 Leahy Circle E Des Plaines IL 60016

BANASIK, ROBERT CASMER, nursing home administrator, educator; b. Detroit, Dec. 8, 1942; s. Casmer John and Lucille Nathalie (Siperek) B.; B.S. in Mech. Engring., Wayne State U., 1965; M.S. in Indsl. Engring., Tex. Tech. Coll., 1967; M.B.A., Ohio State U., 1973, Ph.D., 1974; m. Jacqueline Mae Miller, Aug. 28, 1965; (div. 1985); children—Robert John, Marcus Alan, Jason Andrew; m. Barbara Jean Willows, Oct. 12, 1985. Mgmt. systems engr. Riverside Methodist Hosp., Columbus, Ohio, 1970, 71; owner, mgmt. systems cons. Banasik Assoc., Columbus, 1972—; dir. mgmt. systems engring. Grant Hosp., Columbus, 1973-78; owner, mgr. RMJ Investment Enterprises, Columbus, 1975-85; pres. Omnilife Systems, Inc., Columbus, 1979—, RMJ Mgmt., Inc., 1983-85. Bryant Health Ctr., Inc., Ironton, Ohio, 1983—, Equity Mgmt., 1985—; owner Omnivend, 1985—; adminstr. Patterson Health Center, Columbus, 1980—, Parkview Health Ctr., Inc., Volga, S.D, 1986—, Hamilton (Ohio) Health Ctr., Inc., 1986—, Shelby Manor Helath Ctr., Inc., Shelbyville, Ky., 1986—; asst. prof. Capital U. Grad. Sch. Adminstrn., Columbus, 1973-79, assoc. prof., 1979—; dir. Asset Data Systems, Columbus. Pres. bd. dirs. United Cerebral Palsy Franklin County, 1979-80; mem. founding bd. Support Resources, Inc., 1978-85; bd. dirs. Transp. Resources, Inc., 1979-80, pres., bd. dirs. Ohio Acad. Nursing Homes, Columbus. Registered profl. engr., Ohio; lic. nursing home adminstr., Ohio. Mem. Am. Hosp. Assn., NSPE (dir. Franklin County chpt. 1976-77), Ohio Soc. Profl. Engrs., Am. Inst. Decision Scis., Am. Coll. Health Care Adminstrs., Sigma Xi, Beta Gamma Sigma, Alpha Pi Mu, Phi Kappa Phi,

Alpha Kappa Psi. Republican. Lutheran. Editor: Topics in Hospital Material Management, 1978-84; contbr. articles to profl. jours. Office: 1207 N High St Suite 300 Columbus OH 43201

BANCHET, JEAN, chef. Head chef, owner Le Francais, Wheeling, Ill. Office: Le Francais 269 S Milwaukee Ave Wheeling IL 60090 *

BANCROFT, MATTHEW BURDETTE, architect; b. Westfield, N.Y., Feb. 2, 1950; s. Burdette Richard and Joyce Ann (Aldrich) B.; m. Debra Ann Sheffer, Oct. 2, 1982. BS in Archtl. Studies, U. Wis., Milw., 1980. Registered architect, Wis. Grad. architect, designer Wright-Pierce Architects and Engrs., Topsham, Maine, 1981-82; grad. architect, draftsman Richard F. Steldt & Assocs., Inc., Butler, Wis., 1980-81; project mgr., architect Richard F. Steldt & Assocs., Inc., Milw., 1982—; freelance architect, Milw., 1982—. Active Big Bros. Wis., Sheboygan, Wis., 1979; vol. instr. U. Wis., Milw., 1982-85, La Casa de Esperanza, Waukesha, Wis., 1986. Mem. AIA (assoc.), Wis. Soc. Architects (assoc.), Experimental Aircraft Assn. Unitarian. Clubs: Japan Karate Assn. (head instr. Milw. 1978—). Avocations: motorcycling, shooting, piano. Home: 7630 W Dean Rd Milwaukee WI 53223

BANDER, THOMAS SAMUEL, dentist; b. Grand Rapids, Mich., Mar. 3, 1924; s. Samuel and Jennie (David) B.; m. DoLores Abraham, Sept. 7, 1947; children: Samuel T., Jacquelyn Marie. AS, Grand Rapids Jr. Coll., 1944; DDS, U. Mich., 1948. Pvt. practice dentistry Grand Rapids, Mich., 1948—. Pres. St. Nicholas Orthodox Ch., Grand Rapids, 1965. Served with U.S. Army, 1941-44, to capt. USAF, 1955-57. Fellow Am. Coll. Dentists, Internat. Coll. of Dentists, Acad. Gen. Dentists, ADA; mem. West Mich. Dental Soc. (pres. 1978), Mich. Dental Assn. (chmn. sci. program 1977-78), Kent County Dental Soc. (pres. 1965), Chgo. Dental Soc. Republican. Eastern Orthodox. Club: Blythefield (Belmont, Mich.) (treas. 1970-71). Lodge: Masons. Avocations: golfing, traveling, tennis. Home: 616 Manhattan Rd SE Grand Rapids MI 49506-2025 Office: 2426 Burton St SE Grand Rapids MI 49506

BANE, KEITH JAMES, electronics industry executive, lawyer; b. Chgo., May 20, 1939; s. Joseph Kenneth and Frances Carol (Wachewicz) B.; m. Kathleen Margaret Coffey, Dec. 15, 1962; children—Kimberly Ann, Kristen Marie, Karayn Lynn. B.S., Bradley U., 1961; J.D., Northwestern U.-Ill., 1968. Bar: Ill. 1968, U.S. Dist. Ct. (no. dist.) Ill. 1968. Ptnr. Kirkland & Ellis, Chgo., 1968-73; v.p. Motorola, Inc., Schaumburg, Ill., 1973—; dir. Western Acadia, Chgo., 1970-76. Mem. planning commn. City of Rolling Meadows, Ill., 1972-76; trustee Bradley U., Peoria, Ill., 1983—. Served to lt. USN, 1962-65. Decorated U.S. Navy Commendation medal, 1964. Roman Catholic.

BANE, KENNETH D., bank executive. Pres. 2d Nat. Bank Richmond, Ind. Served with USMC, 1953-55. Office: The Second Nat Bank of Richmond 8th & Promenade Richmond IN 47374 *

BANERJEE, SAMARENDRANATH, orthopaedic surgeon; b. Calcutta, India, July 12, 1932; s. Haridhone and Nihar Bala (Mukherjee) B.; m. Hima Ganguly, Mar. 1977; 1 child, Rabindranath. M.B. B.S., R.G. Kar Med. Coll., Calcutta, 1957; postgrad., U. Edinburgh, 1965-66. Intern R.G. Kar Med. Coll., Calcutta, 1956-58; resident in surgery Bklyn. Jewish Hosp. Med. Ctr., 1958-60, Brookdale Med. Ctr., Bklyn., 1960-61, Jersey City Med. Ctr., 1961-63; research fellow Hosp. for Sick Children, U. Toronto, Ont., Can., 1968-69; practice medicine specializing in orthopedics Sault Ste. Marie, Ont.; past pres. med. staff, chmn. exec. com. Gen. Hosp., Sault Ste. Marie, Ont., chief dept. surgery, mem. adv. com., 1980—; cons. orthopaedic surgeon Gen. Hosp. Plummer Meml. Hosp., Crippled Children Ctr., Ministry Nat. Health and Welfare, Dept. Vets. Adminstrn; civilian orthopaedic surgeon to 44th Div. Armed Forces Base Hosp., Kaduna, Nigeria, 1969. Trustee, Gen. Hosp., Sault Ste. Marie, 1975-76. Miss Betsy Burton Meml. fellow N.Y. U. Med. Ctr., 1963-64. Fellow Royal Coll. Surgeons Can., ACS, Royal Coll. Surgeons Edinburgh; mem. Can. Orthopaedic Assn., N.Y. Acad. Sci., Ont. Orthopaedic Assn., Can. Med. Assn. Home: 50 Alworth Pl, Sault Sainte Marie, ON Canada P6B 5W5 Office: 125-955 Queen St E, Sault Sainte Marie, ON Canada P6A 2C3

BANFIELD, WILLIAM SCOTT, II, foundation administrator; b. Kansas City, Mo., Sept. 9, 1940; s. William Scott and Libera (Williams) B.; m. Mary Carson, Aug. 11, 1962; children: Rebecca Lynn, W. Scott. AB, Mount Union Coll., 1962. Alumni sec. Mount Union Coll., Alliance, Ohio, 1964-70; dir. devel. No. Ill. U., DeKalb, 1970-73; account exec. Chas. R. Feldstein & Co., Chgo., 1973-74; dir. alumni and ann. giving Culver (Ind.) Ednl. Found., 1974-84; v.p. Knox Coll., Galesburg, Ill., 1984-86; pres. Mich. Coll. Found., Southfield, 1986—. Trustee Ind. Coll. Funds Am., Stamford, Conn., 1986—. Named one of Outstanding Young Men Am., 1968; recipient Culver Legion award, 1984. Mem. Nat. Soc. Fund Raising Execs. (chpt. officer 1985-86), Council Advancement and Support Edn. (dist. officer 1984-86), Alpha Delta Kappa. Republican. Presbyterian. Clubs: Detroit Athletic, Econ. of Detroit. Avocations: tennis, reading. Home: 250 Glengarry S Birmingham MI 48010 Office: The Mich Colls Found 26101 Northwestern Hwy Southfield MI 48076

BANIAK, SHEILA MARY, accountant; b. Chgo., Feb. 26, 1953; d. DeLoy N. and Ann (Pasko) Slade; m. Mark A. Baniak, Oct. 7, 1972; 1 child, Heather Ann. Assocs. in Acctg., Oakton Community Coll., 1986; student, Roosevelt U., 1986—. Owner, mgr. Baniak and Assocs., Park Ridge, Ill., 1984—; acct. Otto & Snyder, Park Ridge, 1984-87; spl. projects coordinator, supplemental instr. Oakton Community Coll., Des Plaines, Ill., 1986—; acctg. computer instr. Oakton Community Coll., Des Plaines, 1987—; Adv. mem. acctg. Oakton Community Coll., Des Plaines, 1986—; cons., mem. Edn. Found. Oakton Community Coll., 1986—. Author: A Small Business Collection Cycle Primer For Accountants, 1985. Ill. CPA Soc. scholar, 1984, Roosevelt U. scholar, 1986, Nat. Assn. Accts. scholar, 1985. Mem. Nat. Assn. Accts., Nat. Assn. Tax Practitioners. Home and Office: 1704 S Clifton Ave Park Ridge IL 60068

BANINA, MARY ELIZABETH, small business owner, audiologist; b. Gary, Ind., Aug. 3, 1929; d. Leon Burdette and Alpha Charolette (Williams) Walker; m. William Robert Nicoles, Apr. 30, 1950 (div. Aug. 1966); children: Christine, Jodie, Patricia; m. Jerome Albert Banina, July 31, 1977. Student, St. Mary's Mercy Sch., Gary, 1948-50. Cons. Sears Roebuck & Co., Gary, 1966-73; mgr. Sears Roebuck & Co., Merrillville, Ind., 1973-78, Beltone, Merrillville, 1978-83; owner Merrillville Hearing Unltd., 1983—; cons. Lake County Convent Home, Crown Point, Ind., 1981—. Recipient Pacesetter award Beltone, Chgo., 1980-81, Master Hearing Aid award Beltone, Chgo., 1982; named Belltone Master Cons., Chgo., 1982. Mem. Merrillville C. of C., Better Bus. Bur. Merrillville chpt., Nat. Hearing Aid Soc., Ind. Hearing Aid Specialists, Am. Bus. Women's Assn. (v.p. Hammond, Ind. chpt. 1983-84, pres. 1984-85), Parents' Club, Croation Fedn. Union (pres. 1983-85), Nat. Inst. Hearing Instruments, Bus. and Profl. Womens Assn. Methodist. Avocations: camping, music, reading. Office: Merrillville Hearing Unltd Inc 5853 Broadway Merrillville IN 46410

BANKIT, PAUL, educator; b. Milw., June 16, 1929; s. Joseph and Sally Josephine B.; student engring., U. Wis., 1946-50; B.G.E., U. Nebr., 1960; M.B.A., Mich. State U., 1966, Ph.D., 1972; m. Esther Lilly Halversen, July 8, 1950; children—Eric J., Paula A.; m. Judith Beale Watson, Aug. 9, 1980. Commd. 2d lt., U.S. Army, 1952, advanced through grades to col., 1978; armor unit comdr., Ft. Hood, Tex., 1954-57; aviation officer, Germany, 1957-59; instr. Ft. Rucker, Ala., 1959-60, test pilot, 1961-64; combat pilot, Vietnam, 1966-67; div. chief Combat Devels. Command, Ft. Eustis, Va., 1967-70; comdr. Transp. Engring. Agy., Washington, 1973-76; ret., 1978; prof. mgmt. sci. Mich. State U., East Lansing, 1978-83; chmn. bd., chief exec. officer Midwestern Airlines Inc., Lansing, Mich.; pres. Protec Research, Lansing. Decorated Legion of Merit, Bronze Star, Air Medals; named lectr. of year Army Logistics Mgmt. Center, 1974; recipient achievement award Boy Scouts Am., 1968. Mem. Ops. Research Soc. Am., Am. Mktg. Assn., Acad. Mgmt., Am. Mgmt. Assn. Republican. Lutheran. Club: Masons. Author: Logistics Systems Design, 1972; Logistics Systems Analysis, 1975. Home: 2587 Woodhill Dr Okemos MI 48864 Office: Frandor Sq Suite 105 Lansing MI 48912

BANKS, BEVERLY ANN, former restaurant executive; b. Hammond, Ind., May 26, 1933; d. Dewey Earl and Inez Irene (Clark) Rodkey; student public schs., St. Francisville, Ill.; children—Elizabeth, Gail. Co-owner St. Joe Drive In, St. Joseph, Mo., from 1965; owner, pres., gen. mgr. Henry's Restaurants, including Pyramid Drive In Inc., St. Joseph, 1971-83, Spar Investments Inc., St. Joseph, 1971-83, B.E.V. Foods, Inc., St. Joseph, 1978-83. Named Mrs. Missouri, 1965. Mem. Mo. Restaurant Assn., Nat. Restaurant Assn., St. Joseph C. of C. (diplomat). Methodist. Home and Office: 8 Dunn Dr Saint Joseph MO 64506

BANKS, GLENN LOREN, wholesale lumber company executive; b. Elkhart, Ind., Aug. 23, 1926; m. Joan E. Konrad; children: William P., John K., Stephen G., Marcia A. BS in Mktg., Ind. U., 1950. Chmn., pres. Lumber Co. Inc., Elkhart, Ind., 1957—; bd. dirs. Midwest Commerce Banking Corp. Bd. dirs. Ind. U. Found., Elkhart Gen. Hosp. Found.; mem. adv. bd. Meth. BishopState of Ind.; past pres. bd. trustees Trinity United Meth. Ch.; past pres. and bd. dirs. Elkhart County Assn. for Handicapped. Served with USN, World War II. Recipient Disting. Owner-Mgr. award U. Ind. Mem. Can. Lumbermen's Assn. (bd. dirs.), North Am. Wholesale Lumber Assn., Inc. (past pres.), Alpha Tau Omega (past pres.). Club: Elcona Country (past pres.). Home: 23268 Shorelane Elkhart IN 46514 Office: Banks Lumber Co Inc PO Box 2299 Elkhart IN 46515

BANKS, INA DUNCAN, accountant; b. St. Paul, July 4, 1946; d. Frank Howard and Bernice Alice (Schroeder) Duncan; m. Thomas Royston Banks, Sept. 16, 1967. Student Macalester Coll., 1964-66; BA, U. Minn., 1968; postgrad. in acctg. Augustana Coll., Rock Island, Ill., 1974-76. CPA, Ill. With Aetna Life & Casualty Co., Mpls., 1968; with Smith Casting Co., Mpls., 1969-74; auditor McGladrey, Hendrickson & Co., CPA's, Moline and Rock Island, Ill., 1976-80; v.p., controller Mid Continent Warehouse, Inc., Rock Island, Ill., 1980-83; owner Ina Duncan Banks, CPA, 1983—; affiliate John E. Miller & Assocs., P.C., CPA's, 1987—; officer, bd. dirs. Aspen Distbn. Inc., Salt Lake City. Treas., vol. Action Ctr. Rock Island and Scott Counties, 1980, v.p., 1981, pres., 1983; bd. dirs. unit Am. Cancer Soc.; mem. acctg. tech. adv. com. Scott Community Coll., 1983—. Mem. Am. Inst. CPA's, Am. Women's Soc. CPA's, Ill. Soc. CPA's. Lodge: Zonta (bd. dirs. Rock Island/Moline chpt. 1987—). Office: 1800 3d Ave Suite 100 Rock Island IL 61201

BANKS, JAMES DAVID, certified financial planner; b. Boonville, Mo., Sept. 22, 1951; s. Leon F. and Phyllis J. (Linsey) B.; B.S., U. Mo., 1973; postgrad. Lincoln U., 1975; m. Eileen Biesemeyer, Jan. 8, 1972; children—John David, Daleen Michelle. Asst. cashier First Nat. Bank of Callaway County, Fulton, Mo., 1973-76; securities salesman NIS Fin. Services, Kansas City, Mo., 1976—; group mgr. Ozark Nat. Life Ins. Co., Kansas City, Mo., 1977-78, dist. mgr. for Central Mo., 1979—. Fulton chmn. Jerry Lewis Telethon, 1975; bd. dirs. Trinity Luth. Child Learning Ctr., 1984-87, chmn. bd. dirs., 1986. Mem. Fulton Jr. C. of C. (treas. 1974), Nat. Assn. Life Underwriters. Lutheran. Address: 2611 Luan Ct Columbia MO 65203

BANKS, LLOYD J., insurance company executive; b. Indpls., Dec. 9, 1923; s. Estille and Bernice (Jackson) B.; m. Phyllis Ann Burns, Jan. 31, 1951; children: David Lloyd, Cheri Janeen. Student, Morehead (Ky.) State U., 1941-42, Miami U., Oxford, Ohio, 1944, 46-47, U. Mich., 1955-56. Investigator Retail Credit Co., 1947-49; with Blue Cross-Blue Shield Ind., Indpls., 1949—; group v.p., then exec. v.p. Blue Cross-Blue Shield Ind., 1974-76, pres., 1976—; chmn. bd., chief exec officer 1985—; chmn., chief exec. officer Regional Mktg. Inc.; chmn. bd. Assocs. Life Ins. Inc.; chmn. bd. Health Maintenance of Ind., Inc.; dir. Associated Ins. Cos. Inc., Ind. Nat. Bank, Internat. Fin. Services Inc. Served with USNR, 1942-46. Mem. Ind. C. of C. (bd. dirs.), Indpls. C. of C. (bd. dirs.). Clubs: Columbia, Meridian Hills Country, Wolf Run Golf. Lodges: Masons, Shriners, Rotary. Office: Associated Ins Companies Inc 120 W Market St Indianapolis IN 42604

BANN, JOHN JOSEPH, JR., engineering executive; b. Cleve., Oct. 28, 1930; s. John Joseph and Mary (Kocanik) B.; m. Joan Louise Baeckler, Nov. 21, 1953; children: Lynn, John William. BSME, Gen. Motors Inst., 1954; MS in Engring. Admnstrn., Case Inst. Tech., 1962. Sr. facilities engr. Fisher Body, Warren, Mich., 1964-65; sr. prodn. engr. Fisher Body div. Gen. Motors Corp., Tecumseh, Mich., 1965-66, plant engr., 1965-73; plant engr. Inland div. Gen. Motors Corp., Grand Rapids, Mich., 1973-78, engring. mgr., 1978—. Pres. United Fund, Lenawee County, Mich., 1971-72; mem. council City of Ferrysburg, 1975-81, mayor 1981-85. Served with USCGR, 1955-68. Republican. Dutch Reform. Avocations: fishing, hunting, travel. Home: 16057 Lake Point Dr Spring Lake MI 45456 Office: Inland Div Gen Motors Corp 2150 Alpine Hwy Grand Rapids MI 49504

BANNEN, CAROL ANN, librarian; b. St. Paul, Oct. 4, 1951; d. Virgil D. and Patricia A. (Kelly) Swanson; m. John T. Bannen, Aug. 16, 1975; children: Ryan, Kelly. BA, Coll. St. Catherine, St. Paul, 1973. Librarian Peat Marwick and Mitchell, Mpls., 1972-75; head librarian Reinhart, Boerner, Van Dueren, Norris & Rieselbach, Milw., 1975—. Mem. Law Librarians Assn. Wis. (pres. 1987—), Spl. Libraries Assn. (chmn. Ins. and E.B. div., 1986—), Library Council Met. Milw., Am. Assn. Law Libraries. Office: Reinhart Boerner Van Dueren et al 111 E Wisconsin Ave Milwaukee WI 53202

BANNES, LORENZ THEODORE, construction company executive; b. St. Louis, Oct. 24, 1935; s. Lawrence Anthony and Louise Clair (Vollet) B.; B.S. in Civil Engring., St. Louis U., 1957; m. Janet Ann Bruening, Aug. 10, 1957; children—Stephen W., Michael F., Timothy L. From project engr. to exec. v.p. Gamble Constrn. Co. Inc., St. Louis, 1960-69, pres., 1969-72; founder, pres. Bannes-Shaughnessy, Inc., St. Louis, 1972-77, chmn. bd., 1977—; dir., v.p. St. Louis Constrn. Manpower Corp., 1977—. Tchr. civil engring. dept. St. Louis U., 1969—; tchr. contracting and constrn. methods U. Mo. Extension Center, 1970—; tchr. constrn. mgmt. Grad. Engring. Center, U. Mo., St. Louis, 1968—, Sch. Architecture, Washington U., St. Louis, 1974—; lectr. So. Ill. U., Edwardsville, 1982—; tchr. estimating concrete constrn.; tchr. Nat. Assn. Women in Constrn., 1973—; mem. seminar faculty World of Concrete, 1984—; Mem. adv. com. in civil engring. Florissant Valley Community Coll.; mem. adv. com. constrn. tech. Jefferson Coll. Chmn. trustees Aspenhof, 1973; adv. bd. Little Sisters of Poor, 1975—; nat. adv. bd. Sisters St. Joseph of Carondelet, 1985—, chmn. nat. devel., 1986—; nat. bd. Living and Learning, Jesuit ednl. program for disadvantaged; mem. Human Rights Commn., Archdiocese of St. Louis, 1980—; chmn. bd. trustees Christian Bros. Coll. High Sch., St. Louis, 1980—. Served with USAF, 1957-60. Recipient Alumni Merit award St. Louis U., 1972; named Man of Yr., Exec. Club of St. Louis U., 1978; named to Hall of Fame, Christian Bros. Coll. High Sch., 1981. Mem. Nat. Soc. Profl. Engrs. (recipient Young Engr. of Year award 1971), Mo. Soc. Profl. Engrs. (chmn. Y.E. com.), Concrete Council of St. Louis (pres. 1972-73, Distinguished Service award 1973), Assoc. Gen. Contractors Am. (Nat. Build/Am. award 1973), Assoc. Gen. Contractors St. Louis (Chmn. of Year 1973), ASCE (nat. com. constrn. research 1973-74), Am. Soc. Concrete Constructors (nat. bd. dirs. 1982—, nat. v.p. 1986—), Young Presidents Orgn., Sr. Execs. Org. Engrs. Club St. Louis (dir. 1975-76, 86—, hon. mem. 1986, award of merit 1987), Nat. Assn. Women in Constrn. (hon. mem., Disting. service award 1974), Mo. Soc. Profl. Engrs. (profl. engring. in constrn. award 1987), Xe Chi Epsilon (chpt. hon. mem. 1980). Home: 1345 Cragwold Rd Kirkwood MO 63122 Office: 6767 Southwest Ave Saint Louis MO 63143

BANNWARTH, MICHAEL FRANCIS, accountant, controller; b. Sioux Falls, S.D., Aug. 12, 1959; s. Eldon Louis and Vernique Mary (Reecy) B.; m. Mary Kay McMahon, July 11, 1981; children: Justin Michael, Eric Andrew. BS in Acctg., U. S.D., 1981. CPA, S.D., Iowa. Mem. staff, sr. acct. Shull & Co., P.C., Indianola, Iowa, 1981-84; mgr. planning and budgeting Western Bank, Sioux Falls, 1984-86; controller Miktomm Mortgage Corp., Sioux Falls, 1986—. Jr. high basketball coach YMCA, Sioux Falls, 1985-86. Mem. Am. Inst. CPA's, Iowa Soc. CPA's, S.D. Soc. CPA's (long-range planning com. 1986—, Outstanding New Mem. 1986). Democrat. Roman Catholic. Avocations: skiing, racquetball. Office: Miktomm Mortgage Corp 100 N Phillips Ave Sioux Falls SD 57102

BANSE, TIMOTHY PAUL, consultant, author; b. Clinton, Iowa, Oct. 12, 1951; s. Robert Louis and Helen Leone B.; B.A. in Journalism, U. Iowa, 1981; children—Christopher Patrick, Jessica Marie. Pres., Banse and Kelso Assocs., Iowa City, 1979—; author articles in mags. including Mechanix Illustrated, Timex/Sinclair User, Personal Computer World (U.K.), MicroComputing, Boating, Pick-Up, Van; contbg. editor Motor Boating and Sailing; monthly columnist Tim Banse's Engine Room. Served with M.I., Spl. Forces, U.S. Army, 1969-72. Recipient Wilbur Petersen award U. Iowa Sch. Journalism, 1975, James W. Blackburn award, 1975. Mem. Am. Defense Preparedness Assn., Washington Ind. Writers Group, Writers Guild Am., Author's Guild, Authors League Am. Author: Home Applications and Games for Atari Computer, The Atari Book of Secrets. Home: 3512 N 2d St Clinton IA 52732 Office: PO Box 5535 Coralville IA 52241

BANSEN, GINTER DETLEF, resort owner; b. Koenigsberg, Fed. Rep. Germany, July 1, 1942; came to U.S., 1954; s. Albert and Herta E. (Gerber) B.; m. Ursela Gerda Eichorst, Mar. 20, 1971; children: Aaron Albert, Rachel Michelle. BS in Indsl. Engring., Lake Mich. Coll., 1963; BSBA, Tri-State U., 1971. Research tech. Whirlpool Corp., St. Joseph, Mich., 1966-67; indsl. engr. Walker Mfg., Racine, Wis., 1971-74; owner Benton Harbor KOA, Riverside, Mich., 1974—. Served with U.S. Army, 1964-66. Mem. Mich. Assn. Pvt. Campground Owners, Nat. Campground Owners Assn., Kampground Owners Assn., S.W. Mich. Tourist Assn., West Mich. Tourist Assn., Mich. Kampground Owners Assn. Republican. Avocations: fishing, camping, sports. Home and Office: Benton Harbor KOA 3527 Coloma Rd Riverside MI 49084-0136

BANSER, ROBERT FRANK, JR., newspaper editor; b. Chgo., Aug. 20, 1946; s. Robert Frank and Alice Rita (Proctor) B.; student Chgo. City Coll., 1965-67; B.S., No. Ill. U., 1969; M.A., 1972; m. Lucille Ann Collins, Nov. 7, 1976; children—Robert Ernest, Christopher James, Mary Louise. News reporter Paddock Publs., Arlington Heights, Ill., 1968; adminstrv. intern, City of Elgin, Ill., 1969-71; gen. assignment news reporter Star Publs. and predecessor firm Star-Tribune Publs., Chicago Hts., Ill., 1971-76, assoc. editor, 1976—. Mem. Internat. City Mgmt. Assn., Soc. Profl. Journalists, Chgo. Headline Club, Sigma Delta Chi, No. Ill. U. Alumni Club. Roman Catholic. Lodge: K.C. Home: 1346 Campbell Ave Chicago Heights IL 60411 Office: 1526 Otto Blvd Chicago Heights IL 60411

BANVILLE, EDMUND JOSEPH, III, educational administrator; b. Cleve., Mar. 28, 1948; s. Edmund Joseph and Leocadia Patricia (Dremel) B.; m. Judith Cain, Aug. 22, 1970; 1 child, Melissa Anne. B.S. in Edn., Ohio U., Athens, 1970, M.Ed., 1972. Cert. Ohio Dept. Edn. Elem. tchr. mentally retarded students Nelsonville (Ohio)-York City Schs., 1970-72; work-study coordinator mentally retarded students Whitehall (Ohio) City Schs., 1972-74; high sch. tchr. mentally retarded students Lancaster (Ohio) City Schs., 1974-75; supr. programs for educable mentally retarded Fairfield County Schs., Lancaster, 1975-78, dir. spl. projects, 1978-84, asst. county supt., 1985—; lectr. spl. edn. adminstrn. Pres. bd. trustees Fairfield Industries, Inc., 1978-85; chmn. edn. com. Fairfield Assn. Disabled Citizens, 1981-82. Recipient Exceptional Adminstr. of Yr. award Hocking Valley Council Exceptional Children, 1978. Mem. Council for Exceptional Children, Assn. for Supervision and Curriculum Devel., Internat. Platform Assn., Buckeye Assn. Sch. Adminstrs., Ohio Assn. Pupil Personnel Adminstrs., Mensa. Home: 1194 N Columbus St Lancaster OH 43130 Office: Hall of Justice 216 E Main St Lancaster OH 43130

BANWART, PATRICIA GAIL, physical education and health educator; b. Hibbing, Minn., Sept. 24, 1950; d. Jack J. and Blanche Josephine (Shubat) Laurich; m. Mark Steven Banwart, Aug. 15, 1985; 1 child, Benjamin Jacob-Ulrich. AA with honor, Hibbing Jr. Coll., 1970; BS with honor, St. Cloud State U., 1972; MEd, U. Minn., 1975. Cert. phys. edn. tchr. Elementary phys. edn. specialist Northview Sch., Eagan, Minn., 1972-82; tchr. phys. edn. and health Scott Highland Sch., Apple Valley, Minn., 1982-87; head dept. physical edn., health Scott Highlands Schs., Apple Valley, 1983-87; gymnastics coach Scott Highlands Sch., Apple Valley, 1983-86; tchr. phsy. edn. and health Rosemount (196) Sch. Dist. #196, 1972-87; choreographer Regina High Sch., Mpls., 1975-76; aerobics instr. YMCA, Mpls., 1978-82. Head marshall Twin Cities marathon, Mpls., 1984-86; publicity chairperson Nat. Pub. Parks Tennis Championships, Bloomington, Minn., 1976-78; del. Twin Cities Ski Clubs, Mpls., 1980-82. Mem. Am. Assn. Health Edn. Recreation, Minn. Assn. Phys. Edn. Health Recreation. Home: 8317 Scott Ave N Brooklyn Park MN 55443 Office: Rosemount Sch Dist 196 14445 Diamond Path Rd Rosemount MN 55068

BANZHAF, CAROL ROTTIER, civic worker; b. Beaver Dam, Mich., Sept. 16, 1923; d. John A. and Marguerite (Mueller) Rottier; student Calvin Coll., 1942-43; A.B., Kalamazoo Coll., 1946; postgrad. Long Beach State Coll., 1954; M.A., Stetson U., 1959; m. Roger A. Goodspeed, 1946; children—Linn Marie, Carol Rottier; m. 2d, Henry F. Banzhaf, Aug. 6, 1965. Service rep. Mich. Bell Telephone Co., Grand Rapids, 1946; receptionist Littles' Studio, Palm Beach, Fla., 1947; tchr. kindergarten Cosa Mesa Union Schs., Calif., 1953-55; directress St. James' Day Sch., Ormond Beach, Fla., 1955-60; dean of girls, tchr. English, Milw. U. Sch., 1960-65; tchr. adult edn. Milw. Area Tech. Coll., 1973-75. Bd. dirs. Vol. Services of Greater Milw., 1963-66, Episcopal Campus Rectory, Milw., 1964-72, Women of St. Mark's Episcopal Ch., 1967-73, St. John's Home, Milw., 1976—, Dept. of Missions, Episcopal Diocese, 1978; bd. dirs. Women of St. Simon the Fisherman, Port Washington, Wis., 1973—, chmn., 1974-76; bd. dirs. St. John's Home and Tower, 1981, v.p., 1983—; vol. Lit. Services Wis.; mem. Milw. Children's Hosp. Aux.; pres. St. John's Home Aux. and Assn. Mem. Nat. Women Deans and Counselors, Am. Personnel and Guidance Assn., Herb Soc. Am. Episcopalian. Club: Women's of Wis. Home: Rural Route 1 5236 Sandy Beach S Belgium WI 53004

BANZIGER, GEORGE JOSEPH, JR., academic dean, gerontology educator; b. Manchester, Conn., Dec. 26, 1942; s. Claire V. Bemis; m. Gwendolyn Simpson, Aug. 28, 1970; children: Dean Ralph, Bryan Eugene, Minda Renee Banziger Sia. BA, Macalester Coll., 1964; MA, Syracuse U., 1971, PhD, 1972. Assoc. prof. psychology Marietta (Ohio) Coll., 1972-86, dean continuing edn., asst. provost, 1986—; cons., researcher gerontology and personnel mgmt., Marietta, 1978—. Pres. First City Recovery Ctr., Marietta, 1979-84; pres. Washington County Mental Health Services, Marietta, 1976-78. Mem. Gerontol. Soc., Ohio Network Ednl. Cons. in Aging (v.p. 1984—). Democrat. Unitarian-Universalist. Avocations: running, coaching youth soccer. Home: 628 2d St Marietta OH 45750 Office: Marietta Coll Office Continuing Edn Marietta OH 45750

BAPTIST, ALLWYN J., health care consultant; b. India, July 10, 1943; came to U.S., 1971; s. Peter L.G. and Trescilla (Lobo) B.; m. Anita Lobo, Sept. 8, 1973; children: Alan, Andrew, Annabel. BCS, U. Calcutta, India, 1962; cert. mgmt., U. Chgo., 1978. CPA, Ill; chartered acct., India. Divisional acct. Rallis India Ltd., Bombay, 1967-71; mgr. Chgo. Blue Cross, 1972-79; sr. mgr. Price Waterhouse, Chgo., 1979-84; v.p., dir. Truman Esmond and Assocs., Barrington, Ill., 1984-86; ptnr. Laventhol and Horwath, Chgo., 1986—. Contbr. articles to profl. jours. Mem. fin. com. St. James Ch., Arlington Heigths, Ill., 1987. Mem. Healthcare Fin. Mgmt. Assn. (dir., sec. 1983—, recipient William J. Follmer award 1984), India Cath. Assn. Am. (treas. 1980, 87). Avocations: travel, reading, tennis, golf. Office: Laventhol & Horwath 300 S Riverside Plaza Chicago IL 60606

BAPTIST, ERROL CHRISTOPHER, pediatrician, educator; b. Colombo, Sri Lanka, Feb. 24, 1945; came to U.S., 1974; s. Egerton Cuthbert and Hyacinth Margaret (Colomb) B.; M.B.,B.S., Faculty of Medicine, U. Ceylon, 1969; m. Christine Rosemary Francke, Aug. 7, 1976; children—Lauren Marianne, Erik Christopher. Intern, Colombo Gen. Hosp. and Children's Hosp., Colombo, Sri Lanka, 1969-70; resident house officer Dist. Hosp., Gampola, Sri Lanka, 1970-71; resident house officer Base Hosp., Kegalle, Sri Lanka, 1971-74; family practitioner, Marawila, Sri Lanka, 1974; resident physician in pediatrics Coll. Medicine and Dentistry N.J., Newark, 1975-77; practice medicine specializing in pediatrics, Rockford, Ill., 1977—; asst. prof. pediatrics U. Ill. Coll. Medicine, Rockford, 1977—; chmn. dept. pediatrics St. Anthony Med. Ctr., Rockford, 1986—. Recipient Raymond B. Allen Instructorship award U. Ill., 1979, 80; diplomate Am. Bd. Pediatrics. Mem. Am. Acad. Pediatrics, So. Med. Assn. Roman Catholic. Home: 10696 Whispering Pines Way Rockford IL 61111 Office: Mulford Village Office Park 461 N Mulford Rd Rockford IL 61107

BAPTIST, JEREMY EDUARD, allergist; b. Chgo., Mar. 22, 1940; s. Arthur Henry and Margaret Jane (Beck) B.; m. Sylvia Evelyn Bonin, July 21, 1962; children—Sarah, Margaret, Catherine. B.S. in Physics, U. Chgo., 1960, Ph.D. in Biophysics (USPHS predoctoral fellow), 1966; M.D., U. Mo., Kansas City, 1978. Asst. prof. radiation biophysics U. Kans., 1966-73; claims authorizer Social Security Adminstrn., 1974-75; intern in medicine Northwestern U., 1978-79; allergist Speer Allergy Clinic, Shawnee Mission, Kans., 1979—, v.p., 1985—. Co-author: Handbook of Clinical Allergy, 1982; contbr. to Britannica Yearbook of Science and the Future, 1973, 74; mem. editorial bd. Topics in Allergy and Clinical Immunology, 1982-83. Brown-Hazen grantee, 1970. Mem. So. Med. Assn., AMA, Am. Coll. Allergists, Kans. Med. Soc., Johnson County Med. Soc., AAAS, N.Y. Acad. Scis., Am. Assn. Clin. Immunology and Allergy, Internat. Corr. Soc. Allergists (asst. editor Allergy Letters 1984-85, assoc. editor 1985—), Internat. Assn. Aerobiology, Sigma Xi. Mem. Reorganized Ch. of Jesus Christ of Latter-day Saints. Home: 3501 W 92d St Leawood KS 66206 Office: 5811 Outlook Dr Shawnee Mission KS 66202

BAPTIST, SYLVIA EVELYN, data service company executive, consultant; b. Chgo., Feb. 15, 1944; d. Clarence Walter and Evelyn Alphild (Fagerberg) Bonin; m. Jeremy Eduard Baptist, July 21, 1962; children—Sarah, Margaret, Catherine. Student Mich. State U., 1961-62; B.S., Roosevelt U., 1965. Instr. IBM, Chgo., 1965-66, systems engr., Topeka, Kans., 1966-67; tchr. computer sci. Lawrence High Sch., Kans., 1968; pres. Multiple Data Services, Leawood, Kans., 1983—; cons. in field. Alumni Disting. scholar Mich. State U., 1961-62, Internat. Ladies' Garment Workers Union scholar Roosevelt U, 1964-65. Lodge: Vasa (master ceremonies 1986—) . Avocations: Scandinavian dancing; cooking; writing. Office: Multiple Data Services 3501 W 92d St Leawood KS 66206

BARACH, PHILIP G., shoe company executive; b. Boston, 1930; (m); 3 children. Ed., Boston U., 1951, Harvard Grad. Sch. Bus. Adminstrn., 1955. With U.S. Shoe Corp. Cincinnati, 1960—; division head, Vaisey-Bristol div. 1961-65, Corp. v.p. (U.S. Shoe Corp.), pres. Vaisey-Bristol div.; pres., chief exec. officer U.S. Shoe Corp., Cincinnati, 1968—, Pres., chmn. bd., 1972—; dir. Fifth Third Union Trust Co. Home: 7600 Willow Brook Ln Cincinnati OH 45237 Office: U S Shoe Corp One Eastwood Dr Cincinnati OH 45227 *

BARALD, KATHARINE FRANCESCA, developmental molecular neurobiologist, biochemist; b. Greenville, S.C., May 11, 1945; d. Fred Charles and Francesca (Marion) B.; m. Douglas M. Jewett, Dec. 29, 1971; 1 child, Ethan MacNeil Barald Jewett. AB in Biology, Bryn Mawr Coll., 1967; MS in Molecular Biology, U. Wis.-Madison, 1969, PhD, 1974. NIH postdoctoral fellow U. Calif.-San Diego, La Jolla, 1975-76; Muscular Dystrophy Assn. Am. postdoctoral fellow 1976-78; NIH postdoctoral fellow Stanford (Calif.) U., 1978-80; asst. prof. anatomy and cell biology U. Mich., Ann Arbor, 1980—; cons. various indsl. and univ. hybridloma facilities, 1979—; mem. study panel NSF, Washington, 1984—. Author jour. articles and book chpts. Mem. Soc. Neurosci., Soc. Cell Biology, Soc. Devel. Biology, AAAS, Sigma Xi. Office: U Mich Dept Anatomy and Cell Biology 5740 Med Sci II Ann Arbor MI 48109

BARANOWSKI, FRANK JOHN, JR., school administrator, educator; b. Chgo. Apr. 12, 1950; s. Frank John, Sr., and Vilma Marie (Toth) B. B.A. in History and Political Sci., U. Scranton (Pa.), 1976; language cert. Jagiellonian U., Cracow, Poland, 1975; edn. cert. Madonna Coll., Livonia, Mich., 1981 state of Mich., 1981; M.A. in History, Oakland U. Rochester, Mich., 1985; M.Religious Edn., Sts. Cyril and Methodius Sem., 1984. Public relations cons., Scranton, Pa., 1973-76; agt. Equitable Life Ins. Co. Am., 1976-77; public relations cons., Arlington, Va., 1977-78; tchr. St. Michael's Sch., Tunkhannock, Pa., 1978-79; tchr. St. Mary's Preparatory Sch., Orchard Lake, Mich., 1979-82, dean, 1982-85; prin. Our Lady of Lakes High Sch., Waterford, Mich., 1985-86, Acad. of Detroit, Southfield, Mich., 1986—. Recipient Outstanding Advisor in Nation award Nat. Teen-Age Republicans, Manassas, Va., 1976, 81; Jaycees Outstanding Young Men in Am. award, 1976, 80, 81. Mem. Nat. Assn. Student Activity Advisors, Nat. Council for the Social Studies, Nat. Assn. Secondary Sch. Prins., Mich. Assn. Secondary Sch. Prins., Cath. Edn. Assn., Mich. Council for Social Studies. Republican. Roman Catholic. Author: (monographs) Lackawanna County Home Rule Charter, 1975; Casimir Pulaski, 1976; In Congress Assembled, 1982, History of the Orchard Lake Schools, 1985. Home: 14248 Glastonbury St Detroit MI 48223 Office: 18330 George Washington Southfield MI 48075

BARANY, JAMES WALTER, industrial engineering educator; b. South Bend, Ind., Aug. 24, 1930; s. Emery Peter and Rose Anne (Kovacsics) B.; m. Judith Ann Flanigan, Aug. 6, 1960 (div. 1982); 1 child, Cynthia. B.S.I.E., Notre Dame U., 1953; M.S.I.E., Purdue U., 1958, Ph.D., 1961. Prodn. worker Studebaker-Packard Corp., 1949-52; prodn. liaison engr. Bendix Aviation Corp., 1955-56; mem. faculty Sch. Indsl. Engring. Purdue U., West Lafayette, Ind., 1958—, now prof., assoc. head indsl. engring. Sch. Indsl. Engring.; cons. Taiwan Productivity Ctr., Western Electric, Gleason Gear Works, Am. Oil Co., Timken Co. Served with U.S. Army, 1954-55. Recipient best counselor award Purdue U., 1978, best engring. tchr. award, 1983; NSF and Easter Seal Found. research grantee, 1961, 63, 64, 65. Mem. Inst. Indsl. Engring. (Fellows award 1982), Am. Soc. Engring. Edn., Methods Time Measurement Research Assn., Human Factors Soc., Order of Engr., Sigma Xi, Alpha Pi Mu. Home: 101 Andrew Pl Apt 201 West Lafayette IN 47906 Office: Purdue U Dept Indsl Engring West Lafayette IN 47907

BARASH, IRA SHELDON, computer programmer, analyst; b. Uniontown, Pa., July 12, 1953; s. P. Fred and Esther (Schlein) B.; m. Jayne Greer, Sept. 1, 1984; stepchildren: John Remley, Julie Remley. BBA, U. Cin., 1976; postgrad., Wright State U., 1984—. Programmer PPG Industries, Inc., Pitts., 1976-78; acct. PPG Industries, Inc., Delaware, Ohio, 1979; programmer, analyst NCR Corp., Dayton, Ohio, 1980—. Avocations: home remodeling, running, weight lifting. Home: 27 Cameron Circle Centerville OH 45459 Office: NCR Corp 1700 Patterson Blvd WHQ-BE Dayton OH 45479

BARBER, DAVID HAROLD, municipal official; b. Cleve., Apr. 9, 1950; s. Harold Leroy and Elizabeth Ann (Fazzan) B.; m. Judy Kay Power East, Aug. 7, 1971 (div. Sept. 1979); 1 child, Bethany Lyn; m. Carol Rutkowski, Sept. 27, 1980. BSCE, Ohio U., 1972, MSCE, 1973. Registered profl. engr., Ohio. Project engr. Finkbeiner, Pettis & Strout Ltd., Toledo, 1973-80; dir. pub. works City Bowling Green, Ohio, 1980—; advisor constrn. coll. tech. Bowling Green State U., 1986-87, student co-op program, 1984—. Bd. dirs. Wood County Human Services Bd., Bowling Green, 1986—; chmn. Bowling Green Community Day, 1985—. Named one of Outstanding Young Men of Am., 1986. Mem. Am. Pub. Works Assn. (bd. dirs. 1985—), Am. Water Works Assn., Water Pollution Control Fedn., Profl. Ofcls. N.W. Ohio (sec.-treas. 1987). Roman Catholic. Lodge: Optimists. Avocation: golfing. Office: City Bowling Green Dept Pub Works 304 N Church St Bowling Green OH 43402

BARBER, DAVID RAYMOND, radio-television talk show host, motivational speaker; b. Flint, Mich., Apr. 25, 1955; s. Raymond Wallace and Catherine (Pavelich) B. A.A., Mott Coll. postgrad., Central Mich. U.; B.S., Saginaw Valley State Coll. Disc Jockey Sta. WTRX, Flint, Mich., 1973-82; talk show host Sta. WTAC, Flint, 1982—, Sta. WEYI-TV, Flint, 1984—; cons. in field. Bd. dirs. Big Brothers, Flint, 1983—. Named Salesman of Yr., Sales and Mktg. Execs., 1980, 82. Roman Catholic. Clubs: Univ., Atlas Golf. Avocations: flying; golf; entertaining. Home: 2114 Barth St Flint MI 48504 Office: Sta WTAC PO Box 600 Flint MI 48501

BARBER, DENNIS DAN, gynecologist/obstetrician; b. Hayward, Wis., Mar. 16, 1933; s. Dan Elmer and Lena Sophie (Horne) B.; m. Virginia Lou Krentz, Nov. 30, 1957; children: Michelle Rae, Kimberly Joy. B of Med. Sci., U. Wis., 1955, MD, 1958. Diplomate Am. Bd. Ob-Gyn. Commd. 2d lt. USAF, 1959, advanced through grades to col., 1973; intern St. Luke's Hosp., Denver, Colo., 1958-59; resident Baylor U. Affiliated Residency Program, Houston, 1961-64; chmn. dept. ob-gyn USAF Acad. Med. Ctr. USAF, Colorado Springs, Colo., 1970-74; chmn. dept. ob-gyn Wright-Patterson AFB Med. Ctr. USAF, Fairborn, Ohio, 1974-79; retired USAF, 1979; assoc. prof. ob-gyn Wright State U., Dayton, Ohio, 1979—. Fellow Am. Coll. Ob-Gyn; mem. AMA, Montgomery County Med. Soc., Montgomery County Ob-Gyn Soc. Avocations: golf, reading, classical music. Office: Wright State U Sch Medicine Dept Ob-Gyn 1 Wyoming St Dayton OH 45409

BARBER, KATHLEEN LUCAS, political science educator; b. Canton, Ohio, Apr. 9, 1924; d. Homer C. and Lela (Hay) Lucas; m. D. Robert Barber, June 1, 1946; children: Robert L., Ann Barber Keane, John C., Charles A. BA, Wellesley Coll., 1944; MA, Case Western Res. U., 1965, PhD, 1968. Research asst. Dem. Nat. Com., Washington, 1946-47, Nat. Edn. Assn., Washington, 1947-49; from asst. to assoc. to prof. of polit. sci. John Carroll U., Cleve., 1968—, chairperson dept. polit. sci., 1977-85. Contbr. articles to profl. jours. Mem. Shaker Heights (Ohio) City Council, 1973-79; vice Mayor City of Shaker Heights, 1979; mem. bd. overseers Case Western Res. U., 1984—; trustee George Gund Found., Cleve., 1980—, Ctr. for the Gt. Lakes, Chgo., 1983—, Ohio Envir. Council, Columbus, 1984-86, Barnett R. Brickner Meml. Found., Cleve., 1984—, Govt. Research Inst., Cleve., 1986—; chmn. bd. trustees Cleve. Pub. Radio, 1985—. Mem. Unitarian Ch. Home: 3005 Kingsley Rd Shaker Heights OH 44122 Office: John Carroll U Cleveland OH 44118

BARBER, TENA IRENE, nursing educator; b. Wichita, Kans., Aug. 16, 1944; d. Gloyd Varian and Lucy (Higgins) Vogle; m. Richard Rollin Barber, Aug. 8, 1964; children—Todd Jerard, Lea Jodene. R.N., St. Francis Sch. of Nursing, 1965; B.A., Kans. Newman Coll., 1972; M.A., Kans. State U., 1974; M. in nursing, Wichita State U., 1979. Registered nurse, Kans. Staff nurse St. Francis Hosp., Wichita, Kans., 1965-67; instr. St. Francis Sch. of Nursing, Wichita, 1967-80; nursing service educator St. Joseph Hosp., Wichita, 1980-81; asst. prof. St. Mary Plains Coll., Wichita, 1981-82, assoc. prof., coordinator Assoc. Degree Nursing program, 1982—. Mem. Am. Nurses Assn. (bd. dirs. dist. 6, 1985-86), Nat. League for Nursing. Democrat. Roman Catholic. Avocations: writing fiction; sewing; reading.

BARBER, TIMOTHY ALLEN, air force noncommissioned officer, translator; b. Framingham, Mass., June 23, 1960; s. Donald Edmund and Marjorie Louise (Johnston) B.; m. Silvania Brandao de Andrade, Sept. 14, 1985. Cert. in law enforcement City Colls. Chgo., 1980; diploma USAF Command Non-commd. Officer's Acad., 1984. Enlisted USAF, 1977, advanced through grades to staff sgt., 1982; aircraft guard, alarm response team leader Fairchild AFB, Wash., 1978-79; security response team leader Zaragoza AFB, Spain, 1979-81, security controller, 1981-83, security controller and desk sgt., 1983-84, translator Spanish and Portuguese, 1979-84; alert fire team leader, Minot AFB, N.D., 1984—, site security supr., 1985—, trainer, 1981—, dormitory council mem., 1985—, fin. mgmt. adviser, 1985—, supr. alert aircraft site security, 1986, student pilot, 1986. Youth soccer coach, honor guard, hostage negotiator, bailiff, Zaragoza AFB, 1980-84. Mem. Air Force Assn. Republican. Mem. Pentecostal Ch. Avocations: jogging, soccer, foreign languages. Home: 12 Buchanan Ave Minot AFB ND 58704

BARBOLINI, ROBERT R., chem. engr.; b. N.Y.C., May 30, 1938; s. Renato J. and Dorothy L. (Curry) B.; B.S., Mass. Inst. Tech., 1959; M.Engring., Yale U., 1962; M.B.A., U. Chgo., 1973; m. Betty M. Halford, Sept. 11, 1976. Chem. engr. Union Carbide Corp., Tonawanda, N.Y., 1959-60; project mgr. Process Plants Corp., N.Y.C., 1961-68; asst. chief engr. Met. San. Dist. Greater Chgo., 1968—. Registered profl. engr., Conn., Ill., N.Y. Mem. Water Pollution Control Fedn., Air Pollution Control Assn., Am. Pub. Works Assn. Home: 2500 Lakeview Ave Chicago IL 60614 Office: 100 E Erie St Chicago IL 60611

BARBOUR, JOHN BARTON, optometrist; b. Dexter, Mo., Aug. 18, 1940; s. Gaylord Milton and Monte Verterie (Barton) B.; m. Frances Kay Carney, Mar. 30, 1961; children: Frances Jeanyne Barbour Bartley, John Kipling. Student, U. Mo., 1958-60, Memphis State U., 1960-62; BS, OD, Southern Coll. Optometry, 1967. Practice optometry Mexico, Mo., 1967-69, Fulton, Mo., 1969. Mem. Scope Internat. (internat. seminar panel, 1981—), Heart of Am. Contact Lens Soc., Gideons Internat. (faith fund coordinator, 1978—), Travelers Protection Assn. Republican. Baptist. Home: Route 5 Box 115 Fulton MO 65251 Office: 602 Market Fulton MO 65251

BARBOUR, RICHARD NORMAN, retail shoes executive; b. Peotone, Ill., June 28, 1953; s. Malcolm Wells and Lois (Norman) B.; m. Barbara Ann Anderson, July 26, 1986; 1 child, Melissa Amanda Anderson. BA, Northwestern U., 1975; postgrad., John Marshall U., 1976. Real estate rep. J.D. Berman Corp., Hinsdale, Ill., 1977-79; broker Threshold Realty, Tomahawk, Wis., 1979-81; regional site coordinator Meineke Discount Muffler Shops, Des Plaines, Ill., 1981-84; real estate rep. Volume Shoe Corp., Mt. Prospect, Ill., 1984-86; real estate mgr. Volume Shoe Corp., Mt. Prospect, 1986—. Mem. Nat. Assn. Corp. Real Estate Execs., Internat. Council Shopping Ctrs., Lincoln County Real Estate Brokers Bd. (bd. dirs. 1979-81). Presbyterian. Home: 22370 Timberlea Ln Kildeer IL 60047 Office: Volume Shoe Corp 1500 S Elmhurst Rd Mount Prospect IL 60056

BARBU, ROBERT CORNELL, educational administrator; b. Cleve., Apr. ll, 1937; s. Cornelius Alexander and Flora Jane (Siegler) B.; B.S., Ohio State U., 1959; M.Ed., Kent State U., 1972; m. Janice Marilyn Jacobs, Nov. 28, 1960; children—Scott, Terrance, Troy. Engring. drawing instr. West Tech. High Sch., Cleve., 1960-65; instr. electronics Westlake (Ohio) High Sch., 1965-70; AV-ITV dir. Westlake City Schs., 1970-83; instr. indsl. robotics Lorain County Community Coll., 1984—; v.p. Profl. Computer Services, Inc., Avon Lake, Ohio, 1971, Guidelines, Inc., Fairview Park, Ohio, 1975. Chmn. audio-visual com. Greater Cleve. Sch. Supts. Group Purchasing Council, 1976-77, 80-81; chmn. Avon Lake Cable Adv. Com., 1982-83; recreation dir. City of Avon Lake, 1974-75. Mem. Assn. Ednl. Communication Tech., Ohio Ednl. Library Media Assn. (dist. dir. 1978-80), NEA, Ohio Edn. Assn., Northeastern Ohio Tchrs. Assn., Ohio Indsl. Arts Assn., Westlake Tchrs. Assn., Nat. Ski Patrol System, Boy Scouts Am. Writer, producer, host instrnl. TV series Choose It, 1974. Home: 32699 Carriage Ln Avon Lake OH 44012 Office: 27830 Hilliard Rd Westlake OH 44145

BARCIO, BERNARD FRANCIS, teacher; b. Cudahy, Wis., Oct. 10, 1938; s. Theodore James and Stella (Nudi) B.; m. Lillian Rose Hacker, June 11, 1967; children: Marsha, Sheryl, Karen, Cyndi, Phillip. AB, Holy Cross Sem., 1960; MA, U. Mich., 1962; LHD (hon.), Butler U., 1986. Cert. tchr., Ind. Tchr. Cen. High Sch., Bay City, Mich., 1962-64; chmn. dept., tchr. Park Sch., Indpls., 1965-70; tchr. Washington Twp., Indpls., 1970-78, Wayne Twp., Indpls., 1978-81, Carmel (Ind.) High Sch., 1981—; pres. Pompeiiana Inc., Indpls., 1974—, bd. dirs.; sec.-treas. Ind. Classical Conf., 1979—, chmn. resource ctr., 1974—; mem. learning and achievement task force Ind. State Dept. Edn., Indpls., 1985-86. Author: Catapult Construction, 1978; (movie) Catapults in Action, 1977; teaching filmstrips, 1975-84; patentee butterfly conf. table, 1966. Named Tchr. of Yr., Carmel-Clay Schs., 1985, Tchr. of Yr., Ind. State Dept. Edn., 1986; scholar Am. Council Learned Socs., 1962; fellow Fanny Burr Butler, 1962. Mem. Am. Classical League, Classical Assn. Midwest and South, Nat. Jr. Classical League, Ind. Jr. Classical League. Democrat. Roman Catholic. Avocations: character portrayals, mandolin playing, camping, hiking, swimming. Office: Carmel High Sch 520 E Main St Carmel IN 46220

BARCLAY, LAWSON EUGENE, agricultural productionist; b. Macomb, Ill., June 9, 1945; s. C. Wilson and Audrey M. (Kennedy) B.; m. Martha J. Ault, Feb. 14, 1976; children: Bradford, Austin. BA in Chemistry, USAF Acad., 1968; MBA, So. Ill. U., 1974. Commd. 2d lt. USAF, 1968, advanced through grades to maj., 1975—; prodn. engr. Midwest Control Products, Bushnell, Ill., 1974-76; instr. mktg. Western Ill. U., Macomb, 1976-77; pvt. practice agrl. productionist Macomb, 1976—; pilot Frontier Airlines, Denver, 1977-86, Piedmont Airlines, Winston-Salem, N.C., 1987—. Advisor Congressman Evans Mil. Adv. Group, Moline, Ill., 1984—. Recipient Freedom Found. Soc. award Valley Forge, Pa., 1981; named one of Outstanding Young Men of Am., 1980. Mem. N.G. Assn. Ill., N.G. Assn. U.S., Ill. Farm Bur. Republican.

BARCUS, CHAUNCEY HAROLD, architect, educator; b. Farmersville, Ill., Sept. 9, 1921; s. Chauncey Hobart and Edna Rose (Smith) B.; B.S. in Archtl. Engring., U. Ill., 1947, M.S. in Architecture, 1948; m. Georganne Coon, Dec, 28, 1946; children—Harold Lloyd, David Alan. Grad. asst. U. Ill., 1948; draftsman, archtl. supt. U. Ill. Architect's Office, Urbana, Ill., 1949; architect assoc. Small, Wertz, Barcus & Swift, Architects and Engrs., Oxford, Ohio, 1950-86, Barcus, Moore, Zwirn, Architects, 1986—; prof. architecture Miami U., Oxford, Ohio, 1949—; works include library, dining hall, dormitories for Western Coll., Oxford, city recreation bldg., swimming pool and bathhouse, fire sta., Oxford, Oxford Lane Library; mem. Oxford Bible Fellowship Ch.; Delta Zeta Nat. Hdqrs. and Mus., several comml. bldgs., chs., frat. houses and residences; cons. architect in energy-efficient bldg. design and solar heating. Served with USN, 1941-45; PTO. Registered architect, Ill., Ohio. Mem. AIA, Assn. Collegiate Schs. Architecture, Illuminating Engring. Soc., Architects Soc. Ohio, ASHRAE, Am. Solar Energy Soc. Clubs: Oxford Country; Fairfield Glade (Tenn.) Community. Home: 5176 Westgate Dr Oxford OH 45056 Office: Dept Architecture Miami U Oxford OH 45056

BARCUS, ROBERT GENE, association executive; b. Monticello, Ind., Oct. 22, 1937; s. Harold Eugene and Marjorie Irene (Dilling) B.; B.P.E. (Alumni scholar 1957), Purdue U., 1959; M.A., Ball State U., 1963; postgrad. Ind. U., summer 1966; supts. license Butler U., 1967; m. Mary Evelyn Shull, Aug. 9, 1959; children—Jennifer Sue, Debra Lynn. Tchr., coach Wabash (Ind.) Jr. High Sch., 1959-63; tchr. Wabash High Sch., 1963-64; tchr., coach North Central High Sch., Indpls., 1964-65; salary cons. Ind. Tchrs. Assn., Indpls., 1965-67, asst. dir. research, 1967-68, dir. spl. services, 1968-70, exec. asst., 1971-72, adminstrv. asst., 1972-73, asst. exec. dir. spl. services and tchr. rights, 1973-82; asst. exec. dir. adminstrn., personnel and governance, 1982-85, asst. exec. dir. labor relations and adminstrn., 1985—. Mem. NEA, Wabash City (past pres.), Washington Twp. (past pres.) tchrs. assns., Kappa Delta Pi, Pi Delta Kappa. Mem. Ch. of the Brethren (clk. 1966-74, chmn. 1979-83, 87—). Clubs: Indpls. Press, Columbia, Ind. Schoolmen's. Home: 2230 Brewster Rd Indianapolis IN 46260 Office: 150 W Market St Indianapolis IN 46204

BARD, JAMES ALAN, psychologist; b. Youngstown, Ohio, June 1, 1925; s. John Linus and Mildred Marian (Lackey) B.; divorced; children: Jennifer, Christopher. BS, U. Pitts., 1948; PhD, Western Res. U., 1953. Lic. psychologist, Ohio. Asst. dir. Children's Aid Soc., Cleve., 1951-53; prof. psychology Cleve. State U., 1953-85; mem. faculty Inst. for Rational Emotive Therapy, 1975—; bd. dirs. Cleve. Inst. for Rational Living, 1975—. Author: Rational Therapy in Practice, 1980, I Don't Like Asparagus, 1986. Served with USN, 1943-46. Mem. Cleve. Acad. Cons. Psychologists, Cleve. Psychol. Assn., Am. Psychol. Assn. Avocations: writing plays, music. Home: PO Box 24196 Cleveland OH 44124

BARD, SANDRA ANN, personnel executive; b. Chgo., Aug. 30, 1936; d. Maurie Laskin and Frances (Schneider) Wolfson; m. Gerald W. Bard, July 28, 1956; children: Loryn, Nancy, Jeffrey, Corey, Betsy. Student U. Wis., 1954-55, U. Fla., Gainesville, 1955-56; BA in Psychology, Northeastern Ill. U., 1981. Ins. asst. State Farm Ins., Deerfield, Ill., 1974-81; acct. exec. Mgmt. Recruiters, Bannockburn, Ill., 1981-82; personnel asst. MRCA, Northbrook, Ill., 1982-83, personnel administrator, 1983-84, mgr. personnel, 1984-87; dir. personnel MRCA Info. Services, Northbrook, Ill., 1987—. Mem. Deerfield (Ill.) Village Caucus, 1980. Mem. Am. Soc. Personnel Adminstrn., No. Ill. Assn. Personnel Adminstrs., LWV. Avocations: tennis, music, the arts. Office: MRCA Info Services 2215 Sanders Rd Northbrook IL 60062

BARD, SUSAN MARTHA, small business owner; b. Trenton, N.J., Apr. 4, 1954; d. Max and Miriam (Marcus) B. BA in Polit. Sci., Rutgers U., 1976; MS in Journalism, Northwestern U., 1977. Reporter, copy editor Commodity News Services, Chgo., 1977-79, asst. bur. chief, 1979; staff writer pub. relations dept. Chgo. Bd. Trade, 1979-80; local trader and broker MidAm. Commodity Exchange, Chgo., 1980-82; mgr. pub. affairs Nat. Futures Assn., Chgo., 1982-83; founder, owner Letters Etcetera, Chgo., 1983—; free-lance writer. Contbr. articles to profl. jours. Mem. Internat. Assn. for Fin. Planning, Futures Industry Assn. (mem. exec. com. Chgo. div. 1986—), Douglass Coll. Alumnae Assn. (sec. Class 1976 chpt. 1981—). Clubs: Plaza (Chgo.) (social com. 1987—); Nat. Writers (Denver). Avocations: baking, cooking. Home: 360 E Randolph St Chicago IL 60601 Office: Letters Etcetera PO Box 811280 Chicago IL 60681-1280

BARDEEN, JOHN, physicist, emeritus educator; b. Madison, Wis., May 23, 1908; s. Charles Russell and Althea (Harmer) B.; m. Jane Maxwell, July 18, 1938; children—James Maxwell, William Allen, Elizabeth Ann Bardeen Greytak. B.S., U. Wis., 1928, M.S., 1929; Ph.D., PrincetonU., 1936. Geophysicist Gulf Research & Devel. Corp., Pitts., 1930-33; mem. Soc. Fellows Harvard, 1935-38; asst. prof. physics U. Minn., 1938-41; with Naval Ordnance Lab., Washington, 1941-45; research physicist Bell Telephone Labs., Murray Hill, N.J., 1945-51; prof. physics, elec. engring. U. Ill., 1951-75, emeritus, 1975—; mem. Pres.'s Sci. Adv. Com., 1959-62. Recipient Ballantine medal Franklin Inst., 1952; John Scott medal Phila., 1955; Fritz London award, 1962; Vincent Bendix award, 1964; Nat. Medal Sci., 1966; Morley award, 1968; medal of honor IEEE, 1971; Franklin medal, 1975; co-recipient Nobel prizes in physics, 1956, 72; Presdl. medal of Freedom, 1977. Fellow Am. Phys. Soc. (Buckley prize 1954, pres. 1968-69); mem. Am. Acad. Arts and Sci., IEEE (hon.), Am. Philos. Soc., Royal Soc. Gt. Britain (fgn. mem.), Acad. Sci. USSR (fgn. mem.), Indian Nat. Sci. Acad. (fgn.), Japan Acad. (hon.), Pakistan Acad. Sci. (fgn.), Austrian Acad. Sci. (corr.), Hungarian Acad. Sci. (fgn.). Office: Dept Physics Univ of Ill Urbana IL 61801

BARDEN, KENNETH EUGENE, lawyer, educator; b. Espanola, N.Mex., Nov. 21, 1955; s. Lloyd C. and Beverly A. (Coverdale) B.; m. Janice Reece, 1986. B.A. cum laude, Ind. Central U., 1977; J.D., Ind. U., 1977; cert. Harvard U. Law Sch., 1983. Bar: Ind. 1981, U.S. Dist. Ct. (so. dist.) Ind. 1981, U.S. Tax Ct. 1983, U.S. Ct. Mil. Appeals 1983, U.S. Ct. Appeals (7th cir.) 1983, U.S. Ct. Internat. Trade 1983. Law clk. Marion County Prosecutor's Office, Ind., 1976-78, Krieg Devault Alexander & Capehart, Indpls., 1978-79; bailiff Marion County Mcpl. Ct. 7, 1979-81, commr.-judge pro tem, 1981; pub. defender criminal div. 1, Marion County Superior Ct., 1981; asst. to U.S. magistrate, U.S. Dist. Ct. (so. dist.) Ind. Indpls., 1982-84; city atty. City of Richmond, Ind., 1984—; corp. counsel Richmond Power and Light Co., 1984—; adj. prof. law Ind. Central U., Indpls., 1983. Nat. v.p. Coll. Democrats of Am., 1979-82; ward chmn. Marion County Dem. Party, 1977-81; precinct committeeman Wayne County Dem. Party, 1985—, treas. 2d dist. 1986— ; del. to NATO European Youth Leadership Conf., 1980; co-founder Hubert H. Humphrey Tng. Inst. for Campaign Politics, 1980; treas. Perry Twp. Dem. Club, 1980-83; alt. del. Dem. Nat. Conv., 1980; del. White House Forum on Domestic and Econ. Policy, 1975; del. Youth Conf. on Nat. Security and the Atlantic Alliance, Mt. Vernon Coll., Washington, 1976, Am. Council Young Polit. Leaders Fgn. Policy Conf., 1987; mem. U.S. Youth Council under Pres. Carter, 1980; mem. Ind. Gov.'s Community Corrections Com., 1973-75; mem. adv. council Friends of the Battered, 1985—; mem. personnel policies forum Bur. Nat. Affairs, 1985—. Recipient Youth In Govt. award, Optimist Club, 1972; named one of Outstanding Young Men of Am., 1986. Mem. ABA (com. on industry regulation, Young lawyers div. labor law com., lawyers and arts com., chmn. town hall com. 1987—), Fed. Bar Assn., Ind. State Bar Assn., Indpls. Bar Assn., Wayne County Bar Assn., Ind. Council on World Affairs, Phi Alpha Delta, Epsilon Sigma Alpha, Alpha Phi Omega. Methodist. Clubs: Athenaeum (Indpls.): World Trade of Ind., Kiwanis. Home: 426 S 23d St Richmond IN 47374 Office: 50 N 5th St Richmond IN 47374

BARDEN, TOM PRESTON, medical, educator; b. Chgo., Aug. 16, 1932; s. Horace George and Laura (Stauffacher) B.; m. Beverly Daoust, June 24, 1972; children: Michael, Elizabeth, Matthew. BS, Northwestern U., 1954; MD, Ind. U., 1958. Diplomate Am. Bd. Ob-Gyn. Intern Marion County Gen. Hosp., Indpls., 1958-59; resident in ob-gyn. Ind. U. Med. Ctr., Indpls., 1959-63; faculty ob-gyn. Ind. U., Indpls., 1965-68, U. Cin., 1968—. Served to capt. USAF, 1963-65. Fellow Am. Coll. Ob-Gyn.; mem. Am. Gynecol. Obstet. Soc., Cen. Assn. Ob-Gyn., Soc. Perinatal Obstetrics. Home: 1225 W Rookwood Dr Cincinnati OH 45208 Office: U Cin Dept Ob-Gyn Cincinnati OH 45267

BARDSLEY, JOHN LESTER, radiologist; b. Collinsville, Ill., July 12, 1939; s. Orville David and Katie Bertha (Wachter) B.; m. Dolores Marie Powell, Sept. 1, 1962; children: Christine Marie, Diana Lynn. BA, U. Ill., 1960; MD, U. Ill., Chgo., 1964. Diplomate Am. Bd. Radiology. Intern Barnes Hosp., St. Louis, 1964-65; resident Mallingkrodt Inst. Radiology, St.

Louis, 1965-69; chief radiol. services Ehrling Berquiest USAF Regional Hosp., Offatt AFB, Nebr., 1969-71; radiologist St. John's Mercy Med. Ctr., St. Louis, 1971—; asst. radiologist Barnes Hosp., St. Louis, 1972—; asst. prof. clinical radiology Washington U., St. Louis, 1978—; bd. dirs. Mo. Radiological Soc., St. Louis, 1979-85. Contbr. articles to profl. jours. Served as maj. USAF, 1964-71. Mem. St. Louis Met. Med. Soc., Mo. State Med. Soc., AMA, Greater St. Louis soc. Radiologists, Mo. Radiol. Soc. (bd. dirs. 1979-85), Am. Coll. Radiologists, Radiol. Soc. N.Am. Republican. Roman Catholic. Home: 12116 Carberry Pl Saint Louis MO 63131 Office: West County Radiology Group Inc 621 S New Ballas Rd Saint Louis MO 63141

BARDWELL, REBBECA, psychologist, educator; b. Appleton, Wis., Feb. 4, 1948; d. Roger Willis and Mary (Wells) B.; m. Eugene Fred Braaksma, Aug. 23, 1986. BA, U. Iowa, 1972, MA, 1973, PhD, 1977; postgrad., U. Wis., 1974. Lic. psychologist, Wis. Research scientist U. Iowa, Iowa City, 1976-78; asst. prof. Marquette U., Milw., 1978-85, dir. tchr. edn., 1979-82; pvt. practice psychology Waukesha, Wis., 1984-86; assoc. prof. Marquette U., Milw., 1985—. Contbr. articles to profl. jours. Adv. com United Cerebral Palsey, Milw., 1984-86, Wis. Pro Choice, Milw., 1983-86. Mem. Internat. Council Psychologists, Am. Psychol. Assn. (com. chmn. 1980-84), Am. Ednl. Research Assn., Midwest Psychol. Assn., Wis. Psychol. Assn. Avocations: sailing, skiing, weaving. Office: Marquette U Milwaukee WI 53233

BARECKI, RICHARD LEWIS, dentist; b. Grand Rapids, Mich., Nov. 28, 1945; s. Chester Joseph and Anne Catherine (Downer) B.; m. Bonee Sue Bartlett, May 25, 1968; children: Julia Catherine, Gregory Peter. BA, Grand Rapids Jr. Coll., 1965; DDS, U. Mich., 1970. Gen. practice dentistry Grand Rapids, 1970—; staff mem. Mary Freebed Hosp., Grand Rapids, 1974—, St. Mary's Hosp., Grand Rapids, 1974—; cons., instr. Am. Straight Wire Orthodontic Assn., Fresno, Calif., 1985; chmn. Grand Rapids Project for Dentistry for the Elderly and Nursing Home Patients, 1983—. bd. dirs. St. Jude Sch., Grand Rapids, 1976-78. Mem. ADA, Mich. Dental Assn., Nat. Found. Dentistry for the Handicapped (local coordinating unit chmn. 1976-80), Mich. Acad. of Dentistry for the Handicapped (v.p. 1980-83, pres., chmn. bd. 1983—). Roman Catholic. Avocations: skiing, reading, golf, racquetball, travel. Home: 320 Dakota NW Grand Rapids MI 49504 Office: 1323 Michigan Grand Rapids MI 49504

BARELLI, PAT ANTHONY, physician, rhinologist; b. Kansas City, Mo., Feb. 13, 1919; s. Antonio Enrico Barelli and Jennie (Montalbano) Barelli-DeSimone; m. Sarah June Paulk, Sept. 6, 1942; children: Anthony E., John P., Thomas P., Michael A., Janet Sue. AB, U. Kans., Lawrence, 1941; MD, U. Kans., Kansas City, 1944. Practice medicine specializing in rhinology Kansas City, Mo., 1950—. Served to capt. M.C., U.S. Army, 1943-47, ETO. Recipient Teaching award Truman Med. Ctr. U. Kansas City, 1980, Golden Head Mirror award, 1965. Mem. AMA, Am. Rhinologic Soc. (Golden Head Mirror award), Am. Acad. Otolaryngology (Teaching award, 1986). Avocation: photography. Home: 5609 Mission Dr Mission Hills KS 66208 Office: 2929 Baltimore Kansas City MO 64108

BAREWIN, RALPH R., chemical company executive; b. Hastings, Nebr., Nov. 19, 1915; s. Samuel Phillip and Anna Rose (Sudarsky) B.; m. Gertrude Hoffman, Dec. 3, 1939; children: Barbara Barewin Riley, Deborah Shari Barewin Mullen. BA, Roosevelt U.; M in Social Services, Jane Addams. V.p. Barcos Chem. Products, Inc., Chgo., 1932-44, Bar-Win Tool Supply Co., Inc., Chgo., 1946-47; pres. Barco Chem. Products, Inc., Chgo., 1947—. Mem. U.S. SBA, Am. Tech. Soc. Office: 327 S LaSalle St Suite 1642 Chicago IL 60604

BARFIELD, STEWART BAYNE, counseling therapist; b. Macon, Ga., May 19, 1957; s. Lee Bayne and Corinne Powers (Cole) B. BA in Psychology, Furman U., 1980; MA in Edn. Counseling, Washington, St. Louis, 1982, MSW in Family Therapy, 1984. Residence counselor Marshall I. Pickens Hosp., Greenville, S.C., 1978-81; counselor Reproductive Health Services, St. Louis, 1981-82, Luth. Family and Children's Services, St. Louis, 1983-84; hospice counselor Charter Hosp., St. Louis, 1983-85; family therapist Cen. Bapt. Family Services, St. Louis, 1984-86; med. social worker Am. Nursing Resources, St. Louis, 1985—; substance abuse counselor Magdala Found., St. Louis, 1986—; instr. Mo. Valley Coll., St. Charles, 1987—. Vol. phone counselor Life Crisis Services, St. Louis, 1984—. Named one of Outstanding Young Men of Am., 1984, 85. Methodist. Avocations: running, cycling, weight training, reading, theatre. Office: Magdala Found 4158 Lindell Blvd Saint Louis MO 63108

BARIFF, MARTIN LOUIS, accounting educator, consultant; b. Chgo., Jan. 26, 1944; s. George and Mae (Goldberg) B. BS in Acctg., U. Ill., 1966, MA in Acctg., 1967, PhD in Acctg., 1973. CPA, Chgo. Asst. prof. acctg. and decision scis. Wharton Sch., Phila., 1973-78; vis. asst. prof. acctg. U. Chgo., 1978-79; assoc. prof. acctg. and mgmt. info. decision systems Case Western Res. U., Cleve., 1979-83; Coleman-Fannie May Candies Found. assoc. prof. info. resources mgmt., dir. Ctr. for Research on the Impacts of Info. Systems, Ill. Inst. Tech., Chgo., 1983—; cons. in field, N.Y.C., Phila., Washington, 1976—; exec. v.p. EDP Auditors Found., 1979-80; program chmn. Internat. Conf. Info. Systems, Phila., 1980. Contbr. articles to profl. jours. Bd. dirs. Community Accts. Inc. of Phila., 1974-75. Mem. Am. Inst. CPA's, Am. Acctg. Assn. (chmn. acctg., behavior and orgns. sect. 1987-88), Assn. Computing Machinery (sec. 1981-85), Soc. Info. Mgmt., Inst. Mgmt. Sci. Jewish. Avocations: running, flying, photography. Office: Ill Inst Tech 10 W 31st St Chicago IL 60610

BARKAN, JOHN MARTIN, JR., architect; b. Warren, Ohio, Mar. 16, 1945; s. John Martin and Esther (Wagoner) B.; m. Darlene Rose Kast, Oct. 14, 1972; children: Leilani, John III. BArch, Kent State U., 1969. Registered architect, Ohio. Draftsman Mallalieu, Ross & Roberts, Massillon, Ohio, 1968-72, architect, 1972-76; architect capt. Lawrence, Dykes & Goodenberger, Canton, Ohio, 1977-80; project architect Wilson Archtl. Group, North Canton, Ohio, 1982-86; pvt. practice architecture North Canton, 1986—. Prin. works include Massillon City Hall, McKinley Centre, Ergun residence. Mem. AIA (sec. 1983-84). Republican. Roman Catholic. Avocations: golf, art, tennis. Home: 1237 Ridge Rd NW Canton OH 44703

BARKEMA, ALAN DEAN, economist; b. Belmond, Iowa, Oct. 11, 1951; s. Foster Donald and Evelyn Jean (Schulte) B. BS in Farm Ops., Iowa State U., 1973, MS in Agrl. Econs., 1985, PhD in Econs., 1986; MS in Plant Breeding, Cornell U., 1978. Farmer Alexander, Iowa, 1977-83; economist Fed. Reserve Bank Kansas City (Mo.), 1986—. Deacon Collegiate Presbyn. Ch., Ames, Iowa, 1985-86. Recipient Iowa State U. Research Excellence award, 1986. Mem. Am. Agrl. Econs. Assn., Phi Kappa Phi, Mu Sigma Rho, Gamma Sigma Delta. Avocations: distance running, backpacking. Office: Fed Reserve Bank Kansas City 925 Grand Ave Kansas City MO 64198

BARKER, DANIEL THOMAS, JR., manufacturing company executive; b. Appleton, Wis., Apr. 9, 1954; s. Daniel James and Nancy Louise (Stadler) B.; m. Dawn Gay Fritz, Mar. 5, 1977; children: Rachel, Adam, Ruth, James. A.A. in Metal Fabrication and Welding, Fox Valley Tech. Inst., Appleton, Wis., 1973; A.A., U. Wis.-Fox Valley, Menasha, 1978; B.S. in Econs., U. Wis., Oshkosh, 1981. Assembly supr. Pierce Mfg., Appleton, Wis., 1981-83, plant supt., 1983—. Mem. Delta Omicron Epsilon. Roman Catholic. Home: 804 Tayco St Menasha WI 54952 Office: Pierce Mfg 2600 American Dr PO Box 2017 Appleton WI 54911

BARKER, GREGSON LEARD, retired business form printing executive; b. Chgo., Jan. 19, 1918; s. Walter R. and Margaret (Gregson) B.; m. D'Arcy Timmons, Aug. 19, 1978; children by previous marriage—Margaret Louise Barker Thompson, John Leard, Eric Walter, William Jordan. With UARCO, Inc., designers, printer bus. forms, Barrington, Ill., 1937-86, pres., 1955-86; dir. LaSalle Nat. Bank, Hammond Corp., Chgo., First Nat. Bank Barrington, Chgo. Profl. Basketball Corp., Carson Pirie Scott & Co. Mem. Chgo. Crime Commn.; mem. citizens bd. U. Chgo.; bd. dirs., v.p. Jr. Achievement Chgo.; bd. dirs. Infant Welfare Soc. Chgo., Glenwood Sch. Mem. Computer and Bus. Equipment Mfrs. Assn. (dir.), Ill. Mfrs. Assn. (pres., dir.), Chgo. Assn. Commerce and Industry (dir., v.p.), Ill. State C. of C. (dir.), Employers Assn. Chgo. (dir.), Young Pres.'s Orgn., Northwestern U. Assos. Republican. Episcopalian. Clubs: Economic, Commercial, Executive, Commonwealth, Chicago, Mid-Am., Racquet, Meadow (Chgo.); Barrington Hills Country; Lyford Cay (Bahamas); Metropolitan (N.Y.C.). Home: 81 Meadow Hill Rd Barrington IL 60010

BARKER, HUGH ALTON, electric utility company executive; b. Stillwater, Minn., Nov. 26, 1925; s. George Clarence and Minerva (Register) B.; m. Janet M. Breitenbucher, Mar. 18, 1949; 1 child, Pamela J. B.B.A. with distinction, U. Minn., 1949. C.P.A., Minn. Prin. Haskins & Sells, C.P.A.s, Mpls., 1949-58; asst. to exec. v.p. Pub. Service Ind., Plainfield, Ind., 1958-60; fin. v.p. Pub. Service Ind., 1960-68, exec. v.p., 1968-74, pres., 1974-80, chief exec. officer, 1977—, chmn., 1980—, also dir.; bd. dirs. Bank One Indiana Corp, Bank One Indpls., NA, Bank One Plainfield, NA; mem. Ind. Commn. on Tax and Financing Policy, 1969-73, chmn., 1971-73. Bd. govs. Assoc. Colls. Ind.; mem. Ind. Acad., Ind. Local Govt. Property Tax Control Bd., 1973-74, Gov.'s Water Resources Study Commn., 1977-80; trustee Methodist Hosp., Indpls., 1975-81, Butler U.; bd. dirs. Edison Electric Inst., 1978-81, 83-86, Ind. Legal Found., Inst. for Nuclear Power Operation, 1982-84. Served with AUS, 1944-45, ETO. Mem. Nat. Assn. Electric Cos. (dir. 1974-78, chmn. 1978), Ind. Mfrs. Assn. (dir. 1976-81), Ind. Electric Assn. (dir., past pres.), Am. Inst. C.P.A.s, Minn. Soc. C.P.A.s, Ind. C. of C. (dir. 1978—), Sigma Alpha Epsilon, Beta Gamma Sigma. Clubs: Columbia, Indpls. Athletic; Union League (Chgo.). Office: Pub Service of Ind 1000 E Main St Plainfield IN 46168

BARKER, KEITH RENE, investment banker; b. Elkhart, Ind., July 28, 1928; s. Clifford C. and Edith (Hausmna) B.; A.B., Wabash Coll, 1950; M.B.A., Ind. U., 1952; children by previous marriage—Bruce C., Lynn K.; m. Elizabeth S. Arrington, Nov. 24, 1965; 1 dau., Jennifer Scott. Sales rep. Fulton, Reid & Co., Inc., Ft. Wayne, Ind., 1951-55, office, 1955-59, asst. v.p., 1960, v.p., 1960, dir., 1961, asst. sales mgr., 1963, sales mgr., 1964, dir. Ind. ops.; sr. v.p. Fulton, Reid & Co., 1966-75; pres., chief exec. officer Fulton, Reid & Staples, Inc., 1975-77; ptnr. William C. Roney & Co., 1977-79; exec. com. Cascade Industries, Inc.; assoc. A.G. Edwards & Sons, Inc., 1984—; dir. Fulton, Reid & Staples, Inc., Craft House Corp., Nobility Homes, Inc. Pres. Historic Ft. Wayne, Inc.; cons. to Mus. Historic Ft. Wayne; nominee, trustee Ohio Hist. Soc.; mem. Smithsonian Assocs.; bd. dirs. Ft. Wayne YMCA, 1963-64. Served to lt. USNR, 1952-55. Recipient Achievement certificate Inst. Investment Banking, U. Pa., 1959. Mem. Ft. Wayne Hist. Soc. (v.p.), Alliance Française, VFW (past comdr.), Co. Mil. Historians, Cleve. Grays, Am. Soc. Arms Collectors, 1st Cleve. Cavalry Assn., Nat. Assn. Securities Dealers (bus. conduct com.), Phi Beta Kappa. Episcopalian. Mason. Clubs: Beaver Creek Hunt, Cleve. Athletic. Home: 351 Cranston Dr Berea OH 44017 Office: 1965 E 6th St Cleveland OH 44114

BARKER, NANCY L., college official; b. Owosso, Mich., Jan. 22, 1936; d. Cecil L. and Mary Elizabeth (Stuart) Lepard; m. J. Daniel Cline, June 6, 1956 (div. 1971); m. R. William Barker, Nov. 18, 1972; children—Mary Georgia, Mark Lepard, Richard Earl, Daniel Packard, Melissa Bess, John Charles, Helen Grace, Wiley David, James Glenn. B.Sc., U. Mich., Ann Arbor, 1957. Spl. edn. instr. Univ. Hosp., U. Mich., Ann Arbor, 1958-61; vice pres. Med. Educator, Chgo., 1967-69; asst. to chmn., dir. careers for women Northwood Inst., Midland, Mich., 1970—, chmn. dept. fashion mktg., 1972-77; v.p. Northwood Inst., 1978—; cons. and lectr. in field. Author: Wendy Well Series, children's books, 1970—. Contbr. chpts. to books, articles to profl. jours. Advisor, Mich. Child Study Assn., 1972—; chmn. Matrix: Midland Festival, 1978; bd. dirs. Nat. Council of Women, 1971—, pres., 1983-85, chmn. centennial com., 1988; bd. dirs. Concerned Citizens for the Arts, Mich. Recipient Honor award Ukrainian Nat. Women's League, 1983; Disting. Woman award Northwood Inst., 1970; Outstanding Young Woman, Jr. C. of C., 1974; nominee Mich. Women's Hall of Fame, 1984, 85. Mem. The Fashion Group, Nat. Home Fashions League (pres. Mich. chpt. 1974-77), Mich. Women's Studies Assn. (founding mem.), Midland Art Council (pres. 2 terms, 25th anniversary award), Internat. Women's Forum, Women's Forum of Mich., Phi Beta Kappa, Phi Kappa Phi, Alpha Lambda Delta, Phi Lambda Theta, Phi Gamma Nu, Delta Delta Delta. Republican. Episcopalian. Clubs: Contemporary Review, Midland County Lawyer's Wives (Midland); Zonta. Home: 209 Revere Midland MI 48640 Office: Northwood Inst Midland MI 48640

BARKER, ROBERT OSBORNE, assn. exec.; b. Cleve., June 13, 1938; s. Cecil E. and Barbara O. (Osborne) B.; student Henry Ford Community Coll., 1950; B.A. in Communication Arts and Sci., Mich. State U., 1954; student LaSalle U. Law Sch., 1966-68; m. Sharon Ann; children—Debra, Stephen Robert, Dawn, Michael, Colleen. With public relations dept. Ford Motor Co., Dearborn, Mich., 1953; mgr. Kaiser Aluminum Co., Chgo., 1956-58; advt. adminstrv. mgr. Bastian Blessing Co., Chgo., 1958-59; mgr. Sun Co., Detroit, 1959-71, Goodyear Tire & Rubber Co., Detroit, 1971-72; dis. mgr., NAM, Washington and Southfield, Mich., 1972—, registered lobbyist, 1978—. Twp. trustee, Findlay, Ohio, 1962; mem. vestry Episcopal Ch., 1981; precinct del. Mich. Republican Conv.; bd. dirs. Dearborn Civic Theater, 1980-84; City Beautiful commr. emeritus, chmn. bus. com., 1970-86; res. police officer, Dearborn, 1968—. Served with USNR, 1954-56. Mem. Assn. Execs. Met. Detroit, Pub. Relations Soc. Am., Mich. State U. Alumni (past pres.). Clubs: Elks; Rotary; Masons (master); Shriners (dir. pub. relations 1984). Home: 201 N York Blvd Dearborn MI 48128 Office: 4000 Town Ctr Suite 540 Southfield MI 41406

BARKER, SARAH EVANS, judge; b. Mishawaka, Ind., June 10, 1943; d. James McCall and Sarah (Yarbrough) Evans; m. Kenneth R. Barker, Nov. 25, 1972. B.S., Ind. U., 1965; J.D., Am. U., 1969; postgrad. Coll. William and Mary, 1966-67, George Washington U. Bar: Ind., U.S. Dist. Ct. (so. dist.) Ind., U.S. Ct. Appeals (7th cir.), U.S. Supreme Ct. Legal asst. to senator U.S. Senate, 1969-71; spl. counsel to minority govt. ops. com. permanent investigations subcom., 1971-72; dir. research, scheduling and advance Senator Percy Re-election Campaign, 1972; asst. U.S. atty. So. Dist. Ind., 1972-75, 1st asst. U.S. atty., 1976-77, U.S. atty., 1981-84; judge U.S. Dist. Ct. (so. dist.) Ind., 1984—; assoc., then ptnr. Bose, McKinney & Evans, Indpls., 1977-81. Bd. dirs. New Hope of Ind. Mem. Indpls. Bar Assn. (v.p., bd. mgrs.). Republican. Methodist. Office: U S Dist Ct U S Courthouse 46 E Ohio St Room 210 Indianapolis IN 46204 *

BARKER, WALTER LEE, thoracic surgeon; b. Chgo., Sept. 9, 1928; s. Samuel Robert, M.D., and Esther (Meyerovitz) B.; m. Betty Ruth Wood, Apr. 4, 1967. A.B. cum laude, Harvard U., 1949, M.D., 1953. Diplomate Am. Bd. Surgery, Am. Bd. Thoracic Surgery. Intern, resident in gen. and thoracic surgery Cook County Hosp. and Presbyn. St. Luke's Med. Ctr. and affiliated hosps., Chgo., 1953-62; practice medicine specializing in thoracic surgery Chgo., 1962—; clin. prof. surgery U. Ill.; head sect. thoracic surgery Cook County Hosp.; chmn. dept. surgery St. Joseph Hosp., Chgo.; researcher on tuberculosis, pleural infections, lung cancer. Author: The Post Operative Chest, 1977; contbr. articles to profl. jours. Served with M.C., USNR, 1955-57. Fellow Am. Coll. Chest Physicians, ACS; mem. Am. Assn. Thoracic Surgery, AMA, Boylston Med. Soc., Chgo. Med. Soc., Ill. Med. Soc., Chest Club, Chgo. Surg. Soc., Ill. Surg. Soc., Central Surg. Soc., Inst. Medicine, Soc. Thoracic Surgeons (founding mem.), Sigma Xi. Home: 2912 N Commonwealth Ave Chicago IL 60657 Office: 2800 N Sheridan Rd Room 604 Chicago IL 60657

BARKIN, BEN, public relations consultant; b. Milw., June 4, 1915; s. Adolph and Rose Dora (Schumann) B.; m. Shirley Hinda Axel, Oct. 19, 1941; 1 child, Coleman. Student pub. schs. Nat. field dir. Jr. B'nai B'rith, 1937-41; cons. war finance dept. U.S. Treasury Dept., 1941-45; pub. relations cons. Ben Barkin & Asso., 1945-52; chmn. Barkin, Herman, Solochek & Paulsen, Inc. (and predecessor firm), Milw., N.Y.C.; pub. relations counsel Barkin, Herman, Solochek & Paulsen, Inc. (and predecessor firm), 1952—; partner Milw. Brewers Baseball Club, Inc., 1970—. Bd. dirs., v.p., mem. exec. com. Mt. Sinai Med. Center, also chmn. corp. program; pres. Mt. Sinai Med. Center Found.; chmn. bd. trustees Athletes for Youth, Inc.; corp. mem. Milw. Children's Hosp., Columbia Hosp., United Way; mem. mgmt. adv. com. Milw. Urban League, We-Milwaukeeans, Greater Milw. Com.; mem. civil rights exec. com. Anti-Defamation League; mem. Wis. exec. com. United Negro Coll. Fund, 1981. Named man yr. Milw., 1945; recipient Knight of Bohemia award Milw. Press Club, 1978, Headliner award Milw. Press Club, 1983; Disting. Service award Sales and Mktg. Execs. Milw., 1986; Benefactor of Yr. award Wis. United Negro Coll. Fund, 1986; Lamplighter award Greater Milw. Conv. and Visitors Bur., 1986; Father of Yr. award Children's Outing Assn., 1986; Community Service award Am. Legion, 1987; Charles E. Zehner, Jr. Innovation award Assn. Model Railroad Clubs, 1987; Vol. Ctr. Greater Milw., Inc. award, 1987. Mem. Pub. Relations Soc. Am. (Paul Lund award 1978), NCCJ., B'nai B'rith (nat. chmn. youth commn. 1966-68). Home: 1610 N Prospect Ave Milwaukee WI 53202 Office: Barkin Herman Solochek & Paulsen Inc 777 E Wisconsin Ave Milwaukee WI 53202

BARKMAN, G. J., provincial judge. Judge Ct. of Queen's Bench, Winnipeg, Man., Can. Office: Court of Queen's Bench, Law Courts Bldg, Winnipeg, MB Canada R3C 0V8 *

BARKSDALE, CLARENCE CAULFIELD, banker; b. St. Louis, June 4, 1932; s. Clarence M. and Elizabeth (Caulfield) B.; m. Emily Catlin Keyes, Apr. 4, 1959; children: John Keyes, Emily Shepley. A.B., Brown U., 1954; postgrad., Washington U. Law Sch., St. Louis, 1957-58, Stonier Grad. Sch. Banking, Rutgers U., 1964, Columbia U. Grad. Sch. Bus., 1968; LL.D. (hon.), Maryville Coll., St. Louis, 1976, Westminster Coll., Fulton, Mo., 1982. With Centerre Bank NA (formerly 1st Nat. Bank), St. Louis, 1958—, asst. cashier, 1960-62, asst. v.p., 1962-64, v.p., 1964, exec. v.p., 1968-70, pres., 1970-76, chief operating officer, 1974—, chmn. bd., chief exec. officer, 1976—; also dir. Centerre Bank NA, St. Louis; chmn., bd. dirs. Centerre Bancorp., Centerre Trust Co., Allied Bank Internat., Pet Inc., Wetterau Inc.; bd. dirs. Southwestern Bell Corp. Bd. dirs. Mo. Bot. Gardens, United Fund Greater St. Louis, Civic Progress Inc. Served with M.I. AUS, 1954-57. Mem. Am. Bankers Assn., Assn. Res. City Bankers, Alpha Delta Phi. Clubs: St. Louis (St. Louis), Mo. Athletic (St. Louis), St. Louis Country (St. Louis), Noonday (St. Louis), Brown University (St. Louis), Bogey (St. Louis); Links (N.Y.C.). Office: Centerre Bank NA One Centerre Plaza Saint Louis MO 63101

BARLING, BETH ALLYN, accountant; b. Bloomington, Ill., July 11, 1960; d. Fred William and June Katherine (Gardner) B. BS in Acctg. and Bus. Adminstrn., Ill. State U., 1982. CPA, Ill. Adminstrv. asst. payroll Gen. Telephone Ill., Bloomington, 1982-85, acct. product cost systems, 1985—. Mem. Am. Inst. CPA's. Avocations: tennis, skiing. Home: 302 W Bissell Bloomington IL 61701 Office: Gen Telephone Ill 1312 E Empire Bloomington IL 61701

BARLOW, JAMES CRAIG, engineer; b. Pitts., Jan. 29, 1946; s. Robert Craig and Sara Elizabeth (Lewis) B.; Bonnie Jo Swegman, Mar. 29, 1971; children: Edward, Scott, Ryan. BS in Indsl. Engring., Syracuse U., 1968, BA in Math., 1967. Field engr. Leeds and Northrup, Pitts., 1968-71; sr. controls engr. Westinghouse Australia, Sydney, 1971-74; mgr. Australia liaison Westinghouse Corp., Pitts., 1974-75; mgr. configured systems Foxboro (Mass.) Co., 1975-1984; mgr. info. systems Allen Bradley, Highland Heights, OH, 1984—. Contbr. articles to prof. jour. Coach Youth Soccer, Franklin, Mass. and Hudson, Ohio, 1979-86. sr. mem. Instrument Soc. Am. (newsletter editor 1978-81), Soc. Mfg. Engring. Republican. Episcopalian. Avocations: chess, personal computers. Home: 123 S Hayden Hudson OH 44236 Office: Allen Bradley Co 747 Alpha Dr Highland Heights OH 44143

BARLOW, JOHN LESLIE ROBERT, physician; b. Skipton, Yorkshire, Eng., May 6, 1926; came to U.S., 1966; s. John and Louise Baker (Pollok) B.; m. Janice Barlow; children—Louise Claire, Donal Patrick, Mary Teresa, Margaret Anne, Catherine Jayne Maria. B.A., Cambridge U., 1947, M.B., B.Chir., 1950. Resident in gen. medicine, gen. surgery, ob-gyn. South West Eng., 1950-56; practice medicine South West Eng., 1956-66; with internat. div. Abbott Labs., North Chicago, 1966-77, med. dir., 1974-77; dir. clin. research Merrell Dow Pharms., Cin., 1976—. Mem. Brit. Med. Assn., Drug Info. Assn. Office: Merrell Dow Pharmaceuticals 2110 Galbraith Rd Cincinnati OH 45215

BARLOW, VAL JOHN, internist; b. Salt Lake City, Sept. 5, 1947; s. Leo Joseph and Harriet Anne (Webster) B. BA in Pre-med. and Biology, Stanford U., 1971; MD, U. Colo., 1976. Diplomate Am. Bd. Internal Medicine. Resident in internal medicine St. Joseph Hosp., Denver, 1979; asst. med. dir., physician Advanced Health Systems, Denver, 1979-81; med. dir., physician Horizon Health Corp., St. Louis, 1981-86; practice internal medicine St. Louis, 1981—; mem. staff Forum Hosp., 1986—. Mem. AMA, Am. Soc. Internal Medicine, Mo. Med. Soc., St. Louis Met. Med. Soc., Mo. Soc. Internal Medicine. Avocations: computer, reading, travel, swimming, vol. work. Home and Office: 14443 Bantry Ln Suite 22 Chesterfield MO 63017

BARNARD, CARL ALVIN, health facility executive; b. Liberty Ctr, Ohio, Dec. 16, 1946; s. Howard Alvin and Olive Rebecca (Baldwin) B.; m. Judith Ann Toland, Nov. 8, 1969; children: Jon, Sarah. BS, Bowling Green (Ohio) State U., 1969. CPA, Ohio. Acct. Ernst & Whinney, Toledo, 1969-72; asst. fin. dir. Mercy Hosp. Toledo, Toledo, 1972-75, treas., chief fin. officer, 1975-86, exec. v.p., chief operating officer, 1986—, also trustee, sec. bd. trustees; vice chmn. Family Health Plan, Toledo, 1985—; treas. bd. dirs. Share Health Plan, Toledo, 1985—; trustee St. Charles Hosp., Oregon, Ohio, 1987—. Mem. facilities com. Health Planning Assn. NW Ohio, Toledo, 1981-82, Diabetes Youth Adv. Bd., Toledo, 1984-86, personnel com. Greater Toledo Area ARC, 1981-83. Mem. Am. Inst. CPA's, Fin. Execs. Inst., HealthCare Fin. Mgmt. Assn. (advanced, pres. 1979-80), Ohio Hosp. Assn., Beta Alpha Psi. Methodist. Avocations: tennis, jogging, golf. Home: 665 Kirkshire Dr Perrysburg OH 43551 Office: Mercy Hosp Toledo 2200 Jefferson Ave Toledo OH 43624

BARNARD, ELEANOR BETTY, public relations executive; b. Chgo., Aug. 16, 1912; d. Harry S. and Lona Ruth (Brill) Spivak; Ph.B., U. Chgo., 1933, postgrad., 1936; m. Morton John Barnard, Aug. 16, 1936; 1 son, James W. Pres. Elbar Assocs., public relations and advt., Winnetka, Ill., 1974—; vol., fundraiser law-related edn., 1974—; bd. dirs. Chgo. project Constnl. Rights Found.; mem. bd. sch. St. Law Project Loyola U. Law Sch., Chgo.; mem. standing com. Law-Related Edn. for Public, Ill. State Bar Assn.; mem. Ill. Commn. Edn. Law and Justice, Youth Edn. for Citizenship Adv. Commn., ABA, 1983—, steering com. Ill. Pub./Pvt. Ptnrship. Conf. on Law-Related Edn., 1984, com. in commemoration U.S. Constn. in Ill., 1986—. Recipient Citizen of Yr. award Constnl. Rights Found, 1987. Mem. LWV (asso. editor county bull. 1972-74), Am. Lawyers Aux. (bd. dirs. 1973-84, pres. 1976-77), Sigma Delta Tau. Author articles, pamphlets in field; contbg. author: Building Bridges to the Law, 1981. Home: 228 Woodlawn Ave Winnetka IL 60093

BARNARD, JOHN LOCKHART, JR., medical director, surgeon; b. St. Louis, Sept. 17, 1926; s. John Lockhart Sr. and Marion A. Barnard; m. Mary Ludlow Crooks, Sept. 2, 1950; children: Douglas A., David M., Amy L. Student, Duke U., 1944-46; AB, Washington U., St. Louis, 1947; MD, Northwestern U., 1951. Diplomate Am. Bd. Orthopaedic Surgeons. Intern Kansas City (Mo.) Gen. Hosp., 1951-52; resident surgeon Dickson-Diveley Orthopaedic Clinic, Kansas City, 1952-57, pvt. practice surgery, ptnr., 1958-85; primary staff surgeon St. Luke's Hosp., Kansas City, 1958—, chmn. orthopaedic surgery dept., 1975-79, pres. med. staff, 1983-84, dir. med. affairs, 1985—; clinical prof. surgery U. Mo., Kansas City; assoc. orthopaedics Mo. State CRippled Children's Service, Kansas City; dir. Orthopaedic Residency Tng. Program Kansas City Affiliated Hosps., 1966-81; cons. staff Childrens' Mercy Hosp., Kansas City, 1958—, chmn. dept. orthopaedic surgery, 1970-81, pres. med. staff, 1973; cons. staff Truman Med. Ctr. (formerly Gen. Hosp.), 1958—, chmn. dept. orthopaedic surgery, 1970-81, pres. med. staff, 1970-71; cons. Kansas City VA Hosp., 1958—. Served as comdr. USNR, 1952-54. Fellow Am. Acad. Orthopaedic Surgeons, Am. Coll. Surgeons (past chmn. Kansas City Com. on Trauma); mem. Mid-Central States Orthopaedic Soc., Mo. Orthopaedic Soc., Clinical Orthopaedic Soc., AMA, Mo. State Med. Assn. (del. 1965-66), Kansas City S.W. Med. Soc. (pres. 1981), Jackson County Med. Soc. (council mem. 1964-66). Republican. Episcopalian. Avocations: golf, hiking, travel, photography, gardening. Office: St Luke's Hosp 4400 Wornall Rd Kansas City MO 64111

BARNARD, JOSEPH LLOYD, IV, data processing company executive; b. Toledo, Sept. 17, 1942; s. Joseph Lloyd III and Betty L. (Myers) B.; m.

Christine S. Lashley, May 1, 1965; children: Joe, Gary. BS, Bowling Green (Ohio) State U., 1964; MS in Ednl. Adminstrn., Akron U., 1972. Tchr. pub. schs. Massillon and Maple Heights, Ohio, 1964-72; principal pub. schs. Fostoria and Malvern, Ohio, 1972-81; owner, operator Computer Fun, Marysville, Ohio, 1981—. Named Rookie of Yr., Am. Contract Bridge League, 1983. Avocations: genealogy. Ranked one of top bridge players in Am., 1983-87. Home and Office: 20560 Orchard Rd Marysville OH 43040

BARNELL, MICHAEL JAMES, business products executive; b. Syracuse, N.Y., May 23, 1956; s. Thomas M. and Katherine E. (Borrow) B.; m. Vicki Mendelson, Aug. 20, 1983. BA in Econ., Holy Cross Coll., 1978; MBA in Fin., Cornell U., 1981, JD, 1982. Atty. Exxon Co., Houston, 1982-84; v.p. Am. Loose Leaf Bus. Products, St. Louis, 1984—. Home: 15 Rio Vista Saint Louis MO 63124 Office: Am Loose Leaf Bus Products 4015 Papin St Saint Louis MO 63110

BARNES, BRUCE ERNEST, mktg. exec.; b. Lowville, N.Y., June 16, 1949; s. Earle Ernest and Marion L. (Sunderhaft) B.; B.S., Syracuse U., 1972; M.B.A., Fairleigh Dickinson U., 1974; m. Candyce A. Boutin, Oct. 25, 1980; 1 child, Stephanie Louise. Sales rep. N.Y. area Warner-Lambert Co., Morris Plains, N.J., 1972-74; mktg. staff asst. Colgate Palmolive, Internat. div., N.Y.C., 1974-75, internat. product mgr. Household Products div., 1975-78; product mgr. new products Swift & Co., Chgo., 1978-79, sales planning merchandising mgr., 1979, product mgr. C.P.D. div., 1979, v.p. Strongheart Pet Products, new products Derby Foods, 1979-81; gen. mgr. Skilcraft div. Mattel Inc., Morton Grove, Ill., 1981-85; dir. mktg. retail sales Orval Kent Food Co., Wheeling, Ill., 1985-87; cons. account mgmt. A.C. Nielsen Co., Northbrook, Ill., 1987—. Co-chmn. Syracuse U. ann. fund raising, 1975. Avocation: scuba diving. Club: Syracuse U. Alumni. Home: 2631 Sunnyside Ave Westchester IL 60153

BARNES, BRUCE FRANCIS, cons. engr.; b. Evanston, Ill., Nov. 18, 1926; s. Bruce Francis and Ruth Evelyn (Achuff) B.; B.M.E., Washington U., St. Louis, 1949; m. Gwendolyn Lou Gnaegy, Feb. 17, 1951; children—Sharon Anne Barnes Koch, Steven Bruce. With Fairbanks Morse Engine div. Colt Industries, Beloit, Wis., 1949-68, area sales mgr. St. Louis, 1960-68; asso. Warren & Van Praag, Inc., St. Louis, 1969-72; pres., gen. mgr. Barnes, Henry, Meisenheimer & Gende, Inc., St. Louis, 1972—. Mem. adminstrv. bd. Webster Hills United Meth. Ch., 1968—. Served with USAF, 1944-45. Recipient Order of the Arrow, Boy Scouts Am., 1967. Mem. Nat., Mo. socs. profl. engrs., ASME, Engrs. Club St. Louis. Clubs: Pachyderm, Mo. Athletic. Home: 1503 Azalea Dr Webster Groves MO 63119 Office: 4658 Gravois Ave Saint Louis MO 63116

BARNES, EDWARD HOLT, banking executive; b. Albany, Mo., July 21, 1933; s. J. Howard and Lorena Frances (Coffey) B.; m. Janice Lee Briggs, Aug. 13, 1955 (div. Aug. 1979); children: Lori Beth, Gregory Edward; m. Nancy Lynn Barnes, Sept. 23, 1979; 1 child, Robert Charles. BABA, U. Columbia, Mo., 1956, BS in Mktg. Sales rep. ARMCO, Inc., Kansas City (Mo.), Omaha, 1957-71; asst. v.p. United Mo. Bank, Kansas City, 1971-73; v.p. Gen. Savs., Mission, Kans., 1973-80, Franklin Savs. Assn., Ottawa, Kans., 1980—. Served to 2d lt. U.S. Army; capt. USAR, 1957-67. Mem. Fin. Instns. Mktg. Assn., 1st Nationwide Network Advt. Adv. Council. Republican. Clubs: Ottawa Country (bd. dirs. 1984—). Lodge: Optimists (pres. Mo. chpt. 1962-63). Avocations: golf, gardening, reading. Home: 5625 W 82d St Prairie Village KS 66208 Office: Franklin Savs Assn 6263 Nall Box 558 Shawnee Mission KS 66201

BARNES, FRANCIS MERRIMAN, III, state legislator, lawyer; b. St. Louis, July 19, 1918; s. Francis M. and Carlotta (Kimlin) B.; A.B., U. Mo., 1941; LL.B., Washington U., 1948; m. Mary Shore Johnson, Oct. 16, 1948; children—Elizabeth J., Francis Merriman, Barbara Anne. Admitted to Mo. bar, 1947; asst. city counselor City of St. Louis, 1948-49; atty. Southwestern Bell Telephone Co., St. Louis, 1949-51, Gaylord Container Corp., St. Louis, 1951-59; sr. v.p. Crown Zellerbach Corp., San Francisco, 1959-73; state rep. State of Mo., Jefferson City, 1977—. Mem. Gov. Reagan's Com. to Reform Tax Laws, 1968-69; bd. dirs. St. Louis YMCA, 1975—, Mercantile Library, 1986—; trustee St. Louis Art Mus., 1976-79; trustee Mo. Hist. Soc., 1978—, pres., 1983-86. Served with U.S. Army, 1941-46. Mem. St. Louis Bar Assn., Mo. Bar Assn. Republican. Presbyterian. Editor, Kirkwood (Mo.) Hist. Rev., 1980-84. Home: 217 S Woodlawn Ave Kirkwood MO 63122 Office: State Capitol Room 105 Jefferson City MO 65101

BARNES, JAMES RICHARD, county official, retired rancher; b. Reeds Spring, Mo., Nov. 2, 1921; s. George Alvis and Bessie Armenta (Blair) B.; m. Faye Margaret Norris, July 6, 1940; 1 dau., Barbara Anne Doucey. Grad. numerous law enforcement seminars. Sheriff Stone County, Galena, Mo., 1965-85; rancher, Galena, 1946-85, now ret. Mem., v.p. Law Enforcement Council, Springfield, Mo., 1970-80; mem. com. Farm and Home Orgn., Galena, 1960-64; past pres. Reeds Spring Sch. Bd.; former mem. County Sch. Bd., Galena, Galena County Rd. Commn.; chmn. Agrl. Stabilization Corp., Galena. Served with U.S. Army, 1944-46, CBI. Mem. Mo. Sheriff Orgn., Peace Officers Assn., VFW. Republican. Lodges: Lions, Masons. Avocation: ranching. Home and Office: Route 3 Box 19 Galena MO 65656

BARNES, JANEVA LEIGH, interior designer; b. Caney, Kans., July 1, 1949; d. Ernest Lee Woods and Garnett Geneva (Barnard) Thomas; m. Philip D. Morrow, Sept. 19, 1965 (div. June 1977); children: Cress Matthew, Chad Philip; m. Michael Barnes, July 9, 1977 (div. Mar. 1986). Real estate sales Little Realty, Coffeyville, Kans., 1972-77; dept. mgr. Alex R. Masson Greenhouse, Linwoods, Kans., 1977-79; cost control mgr. Gen. Services, Coffeyville, 1979-80; interior design asst. Medicalodge, Inc., Coffeyville, 1980-81, interior designer Architecture Unlimited div., 1982—; cost estimator Decker Constrn., Coffeyville, 1981-82. County chmn. March of Dimes, Montgomery County, Kans., 1973-74. Mem. Jaycee Janes (treas. Coffeyville chpt. 1970-72), Epsilon Sigma Alpha. Avocation: aerobics. Home: 1226 W 2d Coffeyville KS 67337 Office: Medicalodge Inc Architecture Unltd Div 516 W 11th Coffeyville KS 67337

BARNES, JOHN JAMES INGALLS, business executive; b. Detroit, July 4, 1936; s. Russell Curtis and Ruth Constance (Ingalls) B.; A.B. in Econs., Harvard U., 1958; 1 son, Andrew Harrison. Trainee, Ford div. Ford Motor Co., 1961-63; research analyst, copywriter J. Walter Thompson, Detroit, 1963-65; copywriter Gray & Kilgore Advt., 1965-67; sr. copywriter, creative supr. Young & Rubicam Advt., Atlanta and Detroit, 1967-70; creative dir. Detroit News, 1970-74; gen. adminstrv. asst., mgr. advt. and sales promotion, mktg. staff mgr. Mich. Bell Yellow Pages, Detroit, from 1974, later mgr. direct mktg.; mgr. new ventures Mich. and Ill. divs. Ameritech Pub.; cons. ARAMCO, Dhahran, Saudi Arabia, 1984; v.p., mktg. dir. AT&T Internat., Bangkok, Thailand, 1985-86, asst. dir. Ameritech Publ. Internat., 1986—, Troy, Mich. Mem. Friends of Modern Art, Founders Soc. of Detroit Inst. Arts. Episcopalian. Club: Cranbrook Indoor Tennis. Home: 4806 Malibu Dr Bloomfield Hills MI 48013-3237 Office: 100 E Big Beaver Troy MI 48084

BARNES, LOIS SANDVEN, government official; b. York, N.D., June 8, 1921; d. Kittle Bernhard and Elvira (Trandum) Sandven; B.A., Concordia Coll., Moorhead, Minn., 1943; M.A. in Public Adminstrn. (HEW grantee), U. Minn., 1970. Bookkeeper various cos., Washington and Rugby, N.D., 1946-56; claims rep. Social Security Adminstrn., Minot, N.D., 1956-68, claims rep., Devils Lake, N.D., 1973—; intern Ramsey County (Minn.) Dept. Welfare, 1969, Minn. State Dept. Welfare, St. Paul, 1969, aging program OEO, Washington, 1970. Mem. AAUW, Am. Acad. Polit. and Social Sci., Smithsonian Assocs., Nature Conservancy, Am. Assn. Ret. Persons, Nat. Assn. Ret. Fed. Employees, Beta Sigma Phi. Republican. Lutheran. Clubs: Sons of Norway, 400 of Concordia Coll., 1200 of N.D. Home: Box 349 Leeds ND 58346

BARNES, MARSHALL HAYES, II, personnel relations executive; b. Canton, Ohio, May 15, 1937; s. Frederick Dancy and Mary Anna (Burns) B.; m. Mary Elizabeth Watkins, Mar. 23, 1958; children: Marshall H. III, Mitchell L. BSBA, Ohio State U., Columbus, 1985. Budget analyst Columbia Gas of Ohio, Inc., Columbus, 1966-68, supr. reports unit, 1968-72, EEO coordinator, 1972-77, dir. personnel relations, 1977—. Bd. dirs. Met. YMCA, Columbus, 1983—. Mem. Adminstrv. Mgmt. Soc. (chpt. pres. 1984-85, asst. area dir. 1985—, merit award 1985), Acad. Cert. Adminstrv. Mgrs., Columbus Bar Assn. (fee arbitration com. 1984-86, ethics and profl. conduct com. 1986—). Avocations: carpentry, tennis. Office: Columbia Gas Distbn Companies 200 Civic Center Dr Columbus OH 43216-0117

BARNES, MICHAEL DENNIS, coal mining co. exec.; b. San Antonio, Tex., Jan. 26, 1948; s. William David and Mildred Boatner (Crosley) B.; B.S. in Mech. Engring., Mont. State U., 1972; A. in Mechanics and Welding, No. Mont. Coll., 1969; m. Carol Ann Faller, June 17, 1972; children—Shaina, Ian, Rachel. Mechanic, partsman, engr. Long Constrn. Co., Colstrip, Mont., 1972-77; master mechanic Arch Minerals Corp., Hanna, Wyo., 1977-78; dragline erection engr., constrn. supt. N.Am. Coal Co., Bismarck, N.D., 1978-80, shop ops. mgr., 1981-83, maintenance mgr., 1984—. Den leader, com. chmn. Big Sky council Boy Scouts Am., 1972-77; vol. fireman City of Colstrip, 1973-77; squad leader Vol. Ambulance Services, 1985—; religious edn. instr. 1985—. Mem. Assn. Emergency Care Technicians, Nat. Registry Emergency Med. Technicians. Roman Catholic. Home: 1201 Sunrise Dr Hazen ND 58545 Office: North American Coal 2200 Schaffer Dr Bismarck ND 58501

BARNES, RANDALL CURTIS, osteopath; b. Kansas City, Kans., July 9, 1953; s. Horace Wayne and Virginia Jeanne (Steidley) B.; m. Teresa Colleen Schopp, June 9, 1973; children: Tiffany, Tyson, Tisha. BS, Northeast Mo. State U., 1975; DO, Kirksville (Mo.) Coll. Osteo. Medicine, 1979. Intern Warren (Ohio) Gen. Hosp., 1979-80; physician, owner Grim Smith Hosp., Kirksville, 1982—, dir. emergency room, 1982-86, med. dir., 1986—; ptnr. Gardner-Marino-Barnes Clinic, Kirksville, 1985—; pres. Ran-TC, Inc., Kirksville, 1986—. V.p. bd. dirs. Adair County Ambulance Dist., Kirksville, 1985, 86. Mem. Am. Osteo. Assn., Am. Coll. Gen. Practitioners, Mo. Assn. Osteo. Physicians and Surgeons, Northeast Mo. Osteo. Assn., Kirksville C. of C. (bd. dirs. 1986). Republican. Baptist. Club: Kirksville Country. Avocations: golf, tennis, racquetball. Home: 2305 York Kirksville MO 63501 Office: Gardner Marino Barnes Clinic 1 Crown Dr Kirksville MO 63501

BARNES, ROSEMARY LOIS, pastor; b. Grand Rapids, Mich., Sept. 17, 1946; s. Floyd Herman and Cora Agnes (Beukema) Herms; m. Louis Herbert Adams, Feb. 22, 1969 (div. Oct. 1976); 1 child, Louis Herbert Jr.; m. Robert Jearold Barnes, Oct. 8, 1976. BA, Calvin Coll., 1968. Ordained to ministry Home Ministry Fellowship, 1980; cert. social worker. Group worker Kent County Juvenile Ct., Grand Rapids, Mich., 1966-68; tchr. Sheldon Elem. Sch., Grand Rapids, 1968-69; social worker Kent Dept. Social Services, Grand Rapids, 1969-75, 75-84; tchr., mission worker Emmanuel House, San Diego, 1975; co-pastor, founder River of Life Ministries, Grand Rapids, 1980—; tchr., founder River of Life Sch. Christian Leadership, Grand Rapids, 1981—; v.p. Aglow, Grand Rapids, 1982-83; sec., treas. Western Mich. Full Gospel Ministers Fellowship, Grand Rapids, 1984-85; mem. bd. chaplains Dunes Correctional Facility, Saugatuck, Mich., 1986—; coordinator 1988 Washington for Jesus March, One Nation Under God, Inc. Bd. dirs. Alcohol Incentive Ladder, Grand Rapids, 1979. Mem. Women in Leadership. Democrat. Mem. Ind. Charismatic Ch. Avocations: computers, trumpet, reading, swimming, Scrabble. Home and Office: 2636 Madison SE Grand Rapids MI 49507

BARNES, SANDRA S., association executive; b. Olathe, Kans., Aug. 26, 1950; d. Arthur Hamlin and Dorothy (Parsons) Harvey; m. Kenneth C. Barnes, July 1, 1976; 1 child, Barbara Joy. BA, U. Kans., 1972; postgrad., Ind. U., 1973. Passenger agt. Trans World Airlines, Kansas City, Mo., 1975-79; asst. to gen. mgr. San Francisco Auto Club, 1980-83; ops. mgr. Chgo. Auto Club, 1983—. Trustee Chgo. Dance Coalition. Mem. Am. Automobile Touring Alliance, Chgo. Pub. Relations Roundtable (past. v.p.). Club: Whitehall. Home: 537 S Butterfield Rd Libertyville IL 60048

BARNES, ZANE EDISON, communications company executive; b. Marietta, Ohio, Dec. 2, 1921; s. Emmett A. and Frances (Canfield) B.; children: Frances, Zane Edison, Shelley Barnes Donaho. B.S., Marietta Coll., 1947. With Ohio Bell Telephone Co., 1941-60; asst. v.p. operations Ohio Bell Telephone Co., Cleve., 1961-63; gen. plant mgr. Ohio Bell Telephone Co., 1963-64, v.p. personnel, 1965-67; with engring. dept. AT&T, N.Y.C., 1960-61; v.p., gen. mgr. Pacific N.W. Bell Telephone Co., Portland, 1964-65; v.p. operations Pacific N.W. Bell Telephone Co., 1967-70; pres. Pacific N.W. Bell Telephone Co., Seattle, 1970-73, Southwestern Bell Telephone Co., 1973-74; pres., chief exec. officer, dir. Southwestern Bell Telephone Co., St. Louis, 1974-86; chmn. bd., pres., chief exec. officer Southwestern Bell Corp., St. Louis, 1983—; dir. H & R Block, Inc., Centerre Bancorp., Centerre Bank, Burlington No., Inc., Gen. Am. Life Ins. Co., Reading & Bates Corp., INTERCO Inc. Bd. dirs. St. Louis Area Council Boy Scouts, St. Louis Variety Club, Barnes Hosp., St. Louis Symphony Orch., Am. Productivity Ctr., Target; trustee Washington U., Com. for Econ. Devel., Jefferson Nat. Expansion Meml. Assn., life assoc. trustee Marietta Coll. Mem. Bus. Com. for Arts, Bus. Roundtable, Conf. Bd., Ctr. for Telecommunications Mgmt., Civic Progress, Brookings Inst., Round Table, Backstoppers, Coalition of Chief Exec. Officers. Address: Southwestern Bell Corp One Bell Center Saint Louis MO 63101

BARNETT, DON BLAIR, plumbing contractor; b. Mt. Vernon, Ohio, Oct. 21, 1921; s. Homer V. and Bessie (Skeels) B.; student public schs., LaRue, Ohio; m. Virginia V. Ireland, June 24, 1943; children—James, Faye. Maintenance and supervision positions Perfection Steel Body Co., Galion, Ohio, 1942-44; owner, operator Barnett Plumbing and Hearing, Galion, 1948—. Active, Jehovah's Witness Ch., supr. installation and maintenance, nat. and internat. convs., 1950—. Mem. Galion Plumbing Contractors Assn., Christian Labor Union Assn. Home and Office: 127 Wilson Ave Galion OH 44833

BARNETT, JACOB HENRY, JR., horticulturist; b. Columbia, S.C., May 20, 1961; s. Jacob Henry and Dolly MaDella (White) B. Student, Spartanburg Meth. Coll., 1979-80, U. S.Carolina, 1980; BS in Plant Scis., Clemson U., 1984. Tech. research asst. ICI Ams., Inc., Goldsboro, N.C., 1984; application engr. food processing machinery div. FMC Corp., Hoopeston, Ill., 1984-87; sales rep. sterilizing systems Stork Food Machinery, Inc. (div. UMF Stork), Hoopeston, 1987—. Mem. Clemson U. Alumni Assn., S.C. Horticulture Soc., Ducks Unltd., Alpha Gamma Rho.

BARNETT, JAMES MONROE, JR., rector, author; b. Baton Rouge, La., Oct. 21, 1925; s. James Monroe Sr. and Egeria Overton (Brooks) B.; m. Marian Jean Scofield, Aug. 15, 1956; children: James Mark, John Michael, Thomas Overton, Paul Winston. BA, La. State U., 1946; MDiv., Seabury-Western Theol. Sem., 1951; Doctor of Ministry, U. of South, 1979. Ordained priest Episc. Ch., 1952. lectr. theol. seminaries, U.S. and Eng. Author: The Diaconate: A Full and Equal Order, 1979. Chmn. Nebr. Liturgical Commn., Omaha, 1970—; mem. exec. council Diocese of Nebr., Omaha, 1980—; mem. Commn. on Ministry, Omaha, 1982-86. Mem. N.Am. Assn. for Diaconate (v.p. 1985—, bd. trustees), Associated Parishes, Assn. of Liturgy and Music Commns. Avocations: woodworking, antique furniture restoration, swimming. Home: 1207 Norfolk Ave Norfolk NE 68701 Office: Trinity Episcopal Ch 111 S 9th St Norfolk NE 68701

BARNETT, MARCUS CARNEY, dentist; b. Springfield, Mo., Mar. 21, 1958; s. Shirley and Carolyn (Cheatum) B.; m. Kelly Burke, Nov. 10, 1984. BA in Chemistry, William Jewell Coll., Liberty, Mo., 1979; DDS, U. Mo., Kansas City, 1984. Dentist VA Hosp., Kansas City, Mo., 1984—; gen. practice dentistry Nixa, Mo., 1985—. Mem. ADA, Mo. Dental Assn., Springfield Dental Soc., acad. Gen. Dentistry. Mem. Christian Ch. Avocations: skiing. water skiing, golf. Home: Rt 3 Box 71 Nixa MO 65714 Office: PO Box 547 Nixa MO 65714

BARNETT, MARGARET EDWINA, nephrologist, researcher; b. Ft. Benning, Ga., July 28, 1949; d. Eddie Lee and Margaret Thomas (Herndon) Barnett. B.S. magna cum laude with distinction in Zoology, Ohio State U., 1969; M.D., Johns Hopkins U., 1973; Ph.D. in Anatomy, Case Western Res. U., 1984. Intern, Greater Balt. Med. Center, Towson, Md., 1973-74; med. resident Cleve. Clinic Ednl. Found., 1974-75, Univ. Hosps. Cleve., 1975-76; nephrology fellow, 1976-78, med. teaching fellow, 1978-84; nephrology rounding physician Community Dialysis Ctr., Cleve. and Mentor, Ohio, 1978-83; research assoc. Case Western Res. U., Cleve., 1978-79, 83-84; physician emergency medicine Huron Regional Urgent Care Ctrs., Inc., Cleve., 1983-84; preceptor renal correlation conf., Case Western Res. Sch. Medicine, 1980-81, lectr. anatomy and histology 1979-83; asst. prof. medicine/nephrology Milton S. Hershey Med. Ctr. Penn. State Univ., Hershey, 1984—; practice medicine specializing in nephrology Arnett Clinic, Lafayette, Ind., 1987—. Scholar Gen. Motors, Leo Yassinoff, Alpha Epsilon Delta, Beanie Drake, Am. Heart Assn., 1977; recipient NIH-Nat. Research Service award, 1979-82; Ohio div. Am. Heart Assn. grantee, 1980-81; Ohio Kidney Found. grantee, 1977-78; Pres.'s Scholarship award, 1967-69; AMA Physician Recognition award, 1984-87. Mem. John Hopkins Med. and Surg. Soc., AMA (physician research evaluation panel 1981-83), Internat. Soc. of Nephrology, Nat. Kidney Found., World Tae Kwon Do Fedn., Seoul, Korea, MENSA, Am. Film Inst., Phi Beta Kappa, Alpha Epsilon Delta, Alpha Kappa Alpha. Democrat.

BARNETT, MARILYN, advertising agency executive; b. Detroit, June 10, 1934; d. Henry and Kate (Boesky) Schiff; B.A., Wayne State U., 1953; children: Rhona, Ken. Supr. broadcast prodn. Northgate Advt. Agy., Detroit, 1968-73; founder, part-owner, pres. Mars Advt. Co., Southfield, Mich., 1973—. Named Advt. woman of Yr., Women's Club of Detroit, 1986. Mem. AFTRA (dir. 1959-67), Screen Actors Guild, Adcraft. Women's Adcraft. Creator, producer radio and TV programs, 1956-58; nat. spokesperson on TV, 196-70. Club: Economic (Ad Woman of Yr. 1986). Office: 24209 Northwestern Hwy Southfield MI 48075 Office: Mars Advt Co 7720 Sunset Blvd Los Angeles CA 90046

BARNETT, ROBERT EUGENE, physician; b. Sedalia, Mo., Feb. 10, 1957; s. Charles Owen and Mary Lorene (Renno) B.; m. Deidre Marie Moss, Nov. 19, 1983; 1 child, Brandon Christopher. BS in Chemistry magna cum laude, Washburn U., 1978; MD, Washington U., St. Louis, 1982. Diplomate Nat. Bd. Med. Examiners. Internship, residency Barnes Hosp. Washington U., St. Louis, 1982-86, adminstrv. chief resident, 1985-86; with Womens Health Ctr., Topeka, 1986—. Resident Tchr. of Yr., 1985-86. Mem. AMA, Kans. Med. Assn., County Med. Soc., Edn. Found., Am. Coll. Ob-Gyn (Jr. fellow), Phi Kappa Phi. Roman Catholic. Clubs: St. Louis Brews. Avocations: sailing, beer brewing, camping, photography, canoeing. Home: 3118 W 11th St Topeka KS 66604 Office: Med Park West 823 Mulvane Suite 280 Topeka KS 66606

BARNETT, ROBERT FULTON, JR., radiologist; b. Pitts., Feb. 7, 1929; s. Robert Fulton and Mary Elizabeth (Henry) B.; A.B., Princeton U., 1946-50; M.D., U. Pa., 1954; m. Elizabeth Sherwood McConnel, June 21, 1952; children—Katherine, Robert, William, James. Intern, Henry Ford Hoso., Detroit, 1954-55; communicable disease officer Los Angeles County (Calif.) Health Dept., 1957-58; resident in radiology U. Mich., Ann Arbor, 1958-61; practice medicine specializing in radiology, Grayling, Mich., 1961-69, Cadillac, Mich., 1961—; clin. instr. radiology, U. Mich., 1960-61; bd. dirs. NBD Cadillac Bank; cons. in field; dir. radiology, nuclear medicine Mercy Hosp., Cadillac; cons. med. arts. group, Cadillac; dir. 1st Nat. Bank of Evart (Mich.), West Mich. Fin. Corp., Cadillac State Bank. Served with M.C., USN, 1955-57. Diplomate Am. Bd. Radiology. Mem. AMA, Mich. State, Wexford-Missaukee County (sec. 1963-64, pres. 1964-65) med. secs., W. Mich., Mich. radiol. secs., Am. Coll. Radiology, F.J. Hodges Radiology Soc., Phi Beta Kappa. Republican. Presbyterian. Home: 1000 Stimson St Cadillac MI 49601 Office: Mercy Hosp Cadillac MI 49601

BARNETT, SUSANNE LA MAR, social worker; b. Princeton, Ind., Nov. 14, 1946; d. Henry Grant and Harriet Katheryn (Gwaltney) La Mar; m. John Vincent Barnett, Aug. 3, 1968; children: Jeffrey, Callane. AA, William Woods Coll., 1966; BA, Ind. U., 1968, MSW, 1978; postgrad., U. Cin. Social worker Child Guidance Clinic Ft. Wayne (Ind.) Mental Health Ctr., 1969-70; patient and family counselor Good Samaritan Hosp., Cin., 1970-75; social worker Winona Meml. Hosp., Indpls., 1975, Tri County Mental Health Clinic, Noblesville, Ind., 1978-85; pvt. practice clin. social work Indpls., 1983—; chmn. Child Abuse and Protection Team, Boone County, Ind., 1978-81; cons., instr. Ind. Resolve, Inc., 1980—. Bd. dirs. Big Sisters of Cen. Ind., 1981—, pres., 1985. Recipient Cert. of Recognition, Boone County Mental Health Assn., 1980, Cert. Recognition, Big Sisters Cen. Ind., 1986. Mem. Nat. Assn. Social Workers (diplomate clin. social work cert., clin. cert., task force on adoption Ind. chpt. 1987—), Network Women in Bus., Indy Women. Methodist. Avocations: needlework, reading. Home: 10366 Briar Creek Pl Carmel IN 46032 Office: 8060 Knue Rd Suite 230 Indianapolis IN 46250

BARNETT, THOMAS GLEN, shipping supply, marking and coding equipment company executive; b. Olney, Ill., Aug. 15, 1946; s. Burl and Florence Ann (Gant) B.; m. Diana Kay O'Dell, Jan. 27, 1968; children—Kevin Thomas, Kelli Lyn. B.S. in Acctg, Millikin U., Decatur, Ill., 1968. C.P.A., Mo., Ill. Staff acct. Arthur Young & Co. (C.P.A.'s), Chgo., 1968-70; sr. acct. Arthur Young & Co. (C.P.A.'s), 1970-73, audit mgr., 1973-75; dir. internal audit Chromalloy Am. Corp., St. Louis, 1975-76; asst. controller Chromalloy Am. Corp., 1976-78, v.p., controller, 1978-80, exec. v.p. fin., 1980-87; chief fin. officer The Marsh Co., 1987—; adv. bd. Protection Mut. Co. Mem. Fin. Execs. Inst., Am. Soc. C.P.A.'s, Mo. Soc. C.P.A.'s. Republican. Presbyterian. Office: The Marsh Co 707 E "B" St Belleville IL 62221

BARNETT, WALLACE H., music educator, composer; b. Evansville, Ind., May 23, 1916; s. Charles H. and Dorothy W. (Blair) B.; m. Mary Lois Armor, Apr. 20, 1924; children—Paul Christopher, Kerry Daniel. B.S., U. Evansville, 1946; M.A. in Music Edn., Millikin U.; postgrad. U. So. Calif., U. Maine. Tchr. instrumental music, music cons. Decatur (Ill.) Pub. Schs., 1948-72; assoc. prof. Millikin U., Decatur, 1972—, head of percussion dept., dir. univ./sch. relations Coll. Fine Arts, 1983—; cons. J.C. Deagan Inc. Bd. dirs. Decatur Mcpl. Band. Mem. Piano Technicians Guild, Am. Fedn. Musicians, ASCAP, Music Educators Nat. Conf., Phi Mu Alpha (Alpha Orpheus award for lasting contbn. to music in Am.) Presbyterian. Composer numerous works. Home: 1737 Burning Tree Dr Decatur IL 62521 Office: 1184 W Main Decatur IL 62522

BARNETTE, JOSEPH D., JR., bank holding company executive; b. 1939. BA, Wabash Coll., 1961; MBA, Ind. U., 1968; postgrad., Rutgers U., 1972. With Am. Fletcher Nat. Bank & Trust, Indpls., 1962-69, 82—, pres., chief operating officer, 1982—; sr. v.p., then pres., chief exec. officer First Nat. Bank, Evanston, Ill., 1969-76; pres., chief exec. officer Lakeview Trust and Savs. Bank, Chgo., 1976-81. Office: Am Fletcher Corp 101 Monument Circle Indianapolis IN 46277 *

BARNEY, CAROL ROSS, architect; b. Chgo., Apr. 12, 1949; d. Chester Albert and Dorothy Valeria (Dusiewicz) Ross; m. Alan Fredrick Barney, Mar. 22, 1970; children: Ross Fredrick, Adam Shafer, John Ross. BArch, U. Ill., 1971. Registered architect, Ill. Assoc. architect Holabird & Root, Chgo., 1972-79; prin. architect Orput Assoc., Inc., Wilmette, Ill., 1979-81; prin. architect, pres. Carol Ross Barney Architects, Inc., Chgo., 1981—; asst. prof. U. Ill., Chgo., 1976-78. Plan commr. Village of Wilmette, 1986—; trustee Children's Home and Aid Soc. Ill., Chgo., 1986—; mem. adv. bd. Small Bus. Ctr. for Women, Chgo., 1985—, Loop Coll., Chgo., 1986. Mem. AIA (bd. dirs. Chgo. chpt. 1978-80, v.p. 1981-82, Disting. Service award Chgo. chpt., 1978, Ill. Council 1978), Nat. Council Archtl. Registration (cert.), Chgo. Women in Architecture (founding, pres. 1978-79), Chgo. Network. Home: 601 Linden Ave Wilmette IL 60091 Office: 11 E Adams Chicago IL 60603

BARNEY, CHARLES RICHARD, transportation company executive; b. Battle Creek, Mich., June 7, 1935; s. Charles Ross and Helena Ruth (Croose) B.; m. Grace Leone Nightingale, Aug. 16, 1958; children: Richard Nolan, Patricia Lynn. B.A., Mich. State U., 1957; M.B.A., Wayne State U., 1961. Fin. analyst Ford Motor Co., Dearborn, Mich., 1958-65; gen. mgr. RentCo div. Fruehauf Corp., Detroit, 1965-72; pres. Evans Trailer Leasing, Des Plaines, Ill., 1973-77; v.p., gen. mgr. U.S. Rwy. Equipment Co., Des Plaines, 1972-77; pres. Evans Railcar div. Evans Trans. Co., 1978-84, W.H. Miner div. Miner Enterprises Inc.,, 1985—; Mem exec com. Ry. Progress Inst., 1984—. Served to 1st lt., inf. U.S. Army, 1958. Mem. Ry. Supply Assn. (dir. 1977-80). Congregationalist. Clubs: St. Charles Country (Ill.); Union

League (Chgo.). Home: 1650 Hampton Course Saint Charles IL 60174 Office: 1200 E State St Geneva IL 60134

BARNEY, DUANE LOWELL, scientist, consultant; b. Topeka, Kans., Aug. 3, 1928; s. James Earl and Irene (Franz) B.; m. Virginia Beulah Eddy, June 30, 1950; children—Linda Elizabeth, Mary Virginia. B.S. in Chemistry with honors, Kans. State U., 1950; M.S., Johns Hopkins U., 1951, Ph.D., 1953. Research chemist Gen. Electric Co., Gainesville, Fla., 1953-66, mgr. battery tech. lab., 1966-68, mgr. engring., 1968-72, battery sect., 1972-74, gen. mgr. home laundry engring. dept., 1974-78; sr. engr., assoc. dir. chem. tech. div. Argonne Nat. Lab., Ill., 1978—. DuPont fellow, 1952-53. Mem. Am. Chem. Soc., Electrochem. Soc., AAAS, Phi Kappa PHi, Sigma Xi. Presbyterian. Contbr. articles in field.

BARNEY, DUANE R., real estate company executive; b. Spanish Fork, Utah, Mar. 26, 1956; s. Doyle Duane and Wanda (Robertson) B.; m. Debra Lynne Cox, July 15, 1977; children: Niesha, Nathan Duane. Student, Ricks Coll., 1974; AS in Bus., Coll. Eastern Utah, 1979; BA in Polit. Sci., Brigham Young U., 1980. Asst. bldg. mgr. Los Angeles World Trade Ctr., 1980-81; property mgr. Atlanta div. Equitec Properties Co., 1981-82; dir. property mgmt. Equitec Properties Co., Phoenix, 1982-84; dir. mortgage aquisisitions Equitec Properties Co., Oakland, Calif., 1984, v.p. mortgage aquisisitions, 1984-85; v.p. Equitec Properties Co. div. Equitec Fin. Group Inc., Oakland and Chgo., 1985—; sr. mgmt. council Equitec Fin. Group Inc., Oakland, 1985—; bd. dirs. Chgo. Devel. Council. Author: poetry, short stories. Campaign mem., mgr. Utah Reps., Salt Lake City, 1977-81; rally leader Young Reps., Provo, Utah, 1979-81. Named Eagle Scout, Boy Scouts Am., Spanish Fork, 1969. Mem. Inst. Real Estate Mgmt., Bldg. Owners Mgrs. Assn., Phi Kappa Phi, Phi Rho Pi. Mormon. Avocations: family, camping, hunting. Home: 2 S 524 Danbury Dr Glen Ellyn IL 60137 Office: Equitec Properties Co div Equitec Fin Group Inc Montgomery Ward Plaza 12N Chicago IL 60671

BARNEY, ROBERT L., restaurant franchise executive; b. Ashland, Ky.; married. Student, U. Ky., Ohio U. With Ky. Fried Chicken Corp., 1962-70; with Arthur Treachers, 1970-71; with Wendy's Internat., Inc., Dublin, Ohio, 1971—, pres., 1971-82, chief exec. officer, 1971—, chmn., 1982—; dir. Wendy's Internat., Inc. Served with USAF, 1955-58. Office: Wendy's Internat Inc 4288 W Dublin-Granville Rd Dublin OH 43017

BARNHART, GENE, lawyer; b. Pineville, W. Va., Dec. 22, 1928; s. Forrest H. and Margaret (Harshman) B.; student W.Va. U., 1946-48; student Coll. Steubenville, 1949-50; J.D., U. Cin., 1953; m. Shirley L. Dunn, Jan. 28, 1952; children—Sheryl Lynne (Mrs. John Dickey), Deborah Lee (Mrs. Kim Orians), Taffie Elise, Pamela Carole Barnhart-Perez, Margaret Melanie. Admitted to Ohio bar, 1953; counsel clothing br. Armed Services Procurement Agy., Washington, Phila., 1953-55; assoc. Black, McCuskey, Souers & Arbaugh, L.P.A., Canton, Ohio, 1955-60, ptnr., 1961-84, pres. 1984-86, vice-chmn. 1986—; gen. counsel First Fed. Savs. and Loan Assn. of Canton; lectr. Ohio Legal Center Inst., Ohio Bar Assn., Am. Inst. Banking. Mem. Jackson Local Bd. Edn., 1966-74, pres., 1970; mem. Jackson Twp. Bd. Zoning Appeals, 1964—, chmn., 1978—; vice-chmn. Jackson Zoning Ordinance Revision Com.; past pres. Council of Chs. of Central Stark County; past pres. Family Counseling Services Central Stark County; mem. Stark County Bd. Health; com. chmn. Congressional Action Com., Greater Canton Chamber; trustee Canton Preservation Soc., Interfaith Campus Ministry Kent State-Stark Regional Campus. Served with USNR, 1948-49. Recipient Disting. Service award Jackson Twp. Jaycees, 1981; Community award Jackson-Belden C. of C., 1982. Mem. ABA, Stark County (grievance, disputed fee, voluntary pro bono coms.), Ohio State (legal edn. com., com. legal specialization), bar assns., Order of Coif, Phi Alpha Delta. Home: 2805 Coventry Ln NW Canton OH 44708 Office: 1000 United Bank Plaza Canton OH 44702

BARNUM, JAMES ALYMER, lawyer; b. St. Paul, Sept. 13, 1950; s. Alymer Russel and Constance Adele (Carlson) B. BA in Cultural Anthropology, U. Minn., 1972; JD cum laude, William Mitchell Coll. Law, 1984; postgrad. speech and communication, U. Minn., 1977-80. Bar: Minn. 1984, U.S. Dist. Ct. Minn. 1984, U.S. Ct. Appeals (8th cir.) 1984. Assoc. Meshbesher, Singer & Spence, Ltd., Mpls., 1983-84; clk. to sr. judge U.S. Dist. Ct. Minn., 1984-86; assoc. Leonard, Street and Deinard, Mpls., 1986—. Contbr. articles to law jours. Mem. ABA, Fed. Bar Assn., Minn. Bar Assn., Hennepin County Bar Assn., Assn. Trial Lawyers Am., Minn. Alumni Assn. (asst. dir. 1977-81), William Mitchell Coll. Law Alumni Assn. (bd. dirs. 1980-84), Phi Kappa Phi, Bach Soc. Minn. (bd. dirs. 1985—). Avocations: swimming, bicycling. Home: 2150 Watson Ave Saint Paul MN 55116-1146 Office: Leonard Street and Deinard 100 S 5th St Suite 1500 Minneapolis MN 55402

BARNUM, TERRY MARTIN, manufacturing company executive; b. Canandaigua, N.Y., June 4, 1948; s. Frederik Martin and Shirley (Holden) B.; B.A., Adrian Coll., 1969; M.Div., Garrett Theol. Sem., 1972; M.A.L.S., Rosary Grad. Sch. Library Sci., River Forest, Ill., 1973; Ed.D., No. Ill. U., 1979; m. Sally Carolyn Justis, June 4, 1969. Media technician/studio mgr. Oakton Community Coll., Morton Grove, Ill., 1973-74; dir. instructional media Coll. Podiatric Medicine, Chgo., 1974-76; designer edn. and tng. AM Internat., Schaumburg, Ill., 1979-81, mgr. tng. eval., 1981-82; corporate mgr. tech. tng. Container Corp. Am., Chgo., 1982-86; pres. TMB Assocs., Evanston, Ill., 1986—. Mem. Assn. Edn. Communications and Tech., Am. Soc. Tng. and Devel., Ill. Tng. and Devel. Assn., No. Ill. Media Assn. Home: 1234 Dewey Ave Evanston IL 60202 Office: TMB Assocs 1609 Sherman Ave Suite 302 Enanston IL 60201

BARNWELL, ADRIENNE KNOX, pediatric psychologist; b. Elkhart, Ind., Jan. 31, 1938; d. Everett K. and Arlyne F. (Miller) Knox; m. Franklin H. Barnwell, June 13, 1959; 1 child, Elizabeth B. BS, Northwestern U., 1959, MA, 1962, PhD, 1965. Lic. consulting psychologist, Minn. Vis. prof. Northwestern U., Evanston, Ill., 1967-70, Hamline U., St. Paul, 1971-73; dir. psychol. services dept. pediatrics St. Paul Ramsey Med. Ctr., 1971—; cons. St. Paul Rehab. Ctr., 1974-82, East Communities Family Ctr., Maplewood, Minn., 1983—. Mem. Am. Psychol. Assn., N.Y. Acad. Sci., Soc. Pediatric Psychology, Am. Soc. Clin. Hypnosis. Home: 2015 Kenwood Pkwy Minneapolis MN 55405 Office: St Paul Med Ctr Dept Pediatrics 640 Jackson St Saint Paul MN 55101

BARON, RAYMOND CHARLES, dentist; b. Mpls., Nov. 9, 1928; s. Raymond Frank and Rosallia Mary (Rutten) B.; m. Frances Mary Hynan, Nov. 16, 1958; children: Connie Ann, John Charles. Student, St. John's U., 1946-49; BS, U. Minn., 1952, DDS, 1953. Diplomate Minn. Bd. of Dentistry. Gen. practice dentistry Mpls., 1959, Wayzata, Minn., 1959-81; pres. Perident, Inc., Wayzata, 1972—, also bd. dirs.; pres. R.C. Baron, DDS, PA, Wayzata, 1981-86, also bd. dirs.; pres. Quadrant, Inc., 1972-80; ptnr. H & B Seminars, 1979-86. Served to capt. USAF, 1953-57, with Res. 1957-83. Mem. ADA, Minn. Dental Assn., Mpls. Dental Assn. Republican. Roman Catholic. Club: Baurers Trap Team (1st pl. Sundown League 1984, 2d pl. 1986). Avocations: hunting, fishing, gardening, stained glass work, painting.

BARON, SELMA ARLEEN, advertising executive; b. Ft. Worth. B.S., Northwestern U., 1947. Pres. Baron Advt. Inc., Cleve., 1973—. Mem. Cleve. Advt. Club (bd. dirs.), Bus. and Profl. Advt. Assn. (bd. dirs. Cleve. chpt.). Office: Baron Advt Inc 645 Hanna Bldg Cleveland OH 44115 Office: Baron Advt Inc 1422 Euclid Ave Room 645 Cleveland OH 44115

BAROWSKY, HARRIS WHITE, physician, educator; b. Holyoke, Mass., Mar. 6, 1949; s. Maurice and Rosalie Lenore (White) B.; m. Diane Mariann Turajlich, June 10, 1979; children by previous marriage: Robert Jr., Randall. AB, Clark U., 1971; MD, U. Chgo., 1975. Diplomate Am. Bd. Internal Medicine, Am. Bd. Endocrinology. Intern, then resident U. Pitts., 1975-78, clin. instr., 1978-79; fellow in endocrinology Michael Reese Hosp., Chgo., 1979-81; instr. medicine Rush Med. Coll., Chgo., 1981-82; dir. internal medicine resident program, dir. med. edn. South Chgo. Community Hosp., Chgo., 1982—. Mem. AMA, Ill. State Med. Soc., Chgo. Med. Soc. Republican. Jewish. Avocation: golf. Home: 1044 Evergreen Dr Olympia Fields IL 60461 Office: South Chgo Community Hosp 2320 E 93d St Chicago IL 60617

BARR, EMILY T., social services administrator; b. Danville, Ill., Sept. 13, 1953; d. Norman W. and Gwen (Clark) Taylor; m. Thomas F. Barr, Oct. 13, 1984. BS, Ill. State U., 1975; MSW, U. Ill., 1982. Cert. social worker, Ill. Case worker McLean County Ctr. for Retarded Citizens, Bloomington, Ill., 1975-78; case mgr. McLean County Ctr. for Human Services, Bloomington, 1978-82, asst. program mgr., 1982-84, program mgr., 1984—. Mem. Nat. Assn. Social Workers, Acad. Cert. Social Workers. Methodist. Avocations: gardening, tennis. Office: McLean County Ctr Human Services 108 W Market Bloomington IL 61701

BARR, GLENN RICHARD, JR., accountant; b. Cedar Rapids, Iowa, May 8, 1959; s. Glenn Richard and Marjorie Dean (Barton) B.; m. Karen G. Gutekanst, June 25, 1983. BS cum laude, DePaul U., 1984. CPA, Ill. Sr. acct. Arthur Andersen & Co., Chgo., 1984—. Mem. Am. Inst. CPA's, Ill. CPA Soc.

BARR, JOAN HARRIS, professional counselor; b. N.Y.C., July 30, 1925; d. William Eber and Rachel Augusta (Sheffield) Harris; B.A., Ohio Wesleyan U., 1947; M.Ed., Kent State U., 1976, Ed.S., 1978; m. Wayne Arthur Barr, 1949 (div. 1969); children—Jacqueline and Jeffrey (twins). Sec. to v.p. Internat. B.F. Goodrich, 1949-54; sec. to headmaster Old Trail Sch., Bath, Ohio, 1969-73; sec. to v.p. pub. affairs Kent State U., 1973-74; aftercare counselor Portage Family Counseling and Mental Health Services, Ravenna, Ohio, 1976-77; asso. Cons. for Orgnl. and Personal Effectiveness, Inc., Kent, 1976-82; pvt. practice career counseling, 1976—; psychiat. social worker, vocat. counselor Western Res. Psychiat. Habilitation Center, 1977-82; psychol. asst. Portage Psychol. Assocs., 1986— . Mem. Am. Assn. for Counseling and Devel., Ohio Assn. Counselng and Devel. (archives chmn.), Nat. Vocat. Guidance Assn., Am. Mental Health Counselors Assn., Ohio Mental Health Counselors Assn. (merbership chmn.), Chi Sigma Iota, Kappa Kappa Gamma, Gertrude Sandford Doll Club. Home and office: 3575 Darrow Rd Stow OH 44224

BARR, JOHN MONTE, lawyer; b. Mt. Clemens, Mich., Jan. 1, 1935; s. Merle James and Wilhelmina Marie (Monte) B.; student Mexico City Coll., 1955; B.A., Mich. State U., 1956; J.D., U. Mich., 1959; m. Marlene Joy Bielenberg, Dec. 17, 1954; children—John Monte, Karl Alexander, Elizabeth Marie. Admitted to Mich. bar, 1959, since practiced in Ypsilanti; mem. firm Ellis B. Freatman, Jr., 1959-61; partner, chief trial atty. Freatman, Barr, Anhut & Moir and predecessor firm, 1961-63; pres. Barr, Anhut, Sacks, P.C., 1963—; city atty. City of Ypsilanti, 1981. Lectr. bus. law Eastern Mich. U., 1968-70. Pres., Ypsilanti Family Service, 1967; mem. Ypsilanti Public Housing Com., 1980-84; sr. adviser Explorer law post Portage Trail council Boy Scouts Am., 1969-71, commr. Potawatomi dist., 1973-74, commr. Washtenong dist., 1974-75, dist. committeeman, 1984; bd. dirs. Mich. Mcpl. League Legal Def. Fund. Served with AUS, 1959-60. Mem. State Bar Mich. (grievance bd. 1969—, state rep. assembly 1977-82), Am., Ypsilanti, Washtenaw County (pres. 1975-76) bar assns., Am., Mich. trial lawyers assns., Mich. Mcpl. Attys. Assn. (bd. dirs.), U.S. (instr. piloting, seamanship, sail), Ann Arbor (comdr. 1972-73) power squadrons. Lutheran. Club: Washtenaw Country. Contbr. articles to boating mags. Home: 1200 Whittier Rd Ypsilanti MI 48197 Office: 105 Pearl St Ypsilanti MI 48197

BARR, SANFORD LEE, dentist; b. Chgo., Jan. 18, 1952; s. Mike and Bernice (Kaplan) B.; m. Randy Joyce Briskman, Dec. 24, 1973; children: Shelby Paige, Blake Jared, Taylor Ashley. BS, U. Ill., 1972; DDS, Northwestern U., 1976. Resident gen. practice VA Hosp., Chgo., 1976-77; gen. practice dentistry Chgo., 1977—; attending dentist Rush Med. Coll., Chgo., 1977—; asst. prof. Presbyn.-St. Luke's Hosp., Chgo., 1977—, Northwestern U. Sch. Dentistry, Chgo., 1977-83; cons. VA Hosp., Chgo., 1978—. Mem. adv. bd. Homehealth of Ill. Chgo., 1984—. Fellow Acad. Gen. Dentistry, Acad. Facial Aesthetics; mem. ADA, Acad. Hosp. Dentistry, Chgo. Dental Soc., Alpha Omega (treas. 1984—), Tau Delta Phi. Jewish. Lodge: B'nai Brith (v.p. Chgo. chpt. 1984—). Avocations: computers, photography, golf, baseball. Home: 632 Dauphine Ct Northbrook IL 60062 Office: 25 E Washington Chicago IL 60602

BARRE, LOREN D., manufacturing company executive; b. Benton City, Mo., Nov. 22, 1925; s. Thomas Horner and Ina (Baxter) B.; children—Anne, Lynn, Dana. B.S.E.E., U. Calif.-Berkeley, 1947; M.B.A., Stanford U., 1949. Registered profl. engr., Oreg. Sales rep. Allis Chalmers, Milwaukee, 1949-56; sales staff RTE Corp., Waukesha, Wis., 1956-57; asst. to v.p. RTE Corp., 1957-61; mktg. mgr., 1961-62, v.p. sales, 1962-65, v.p. mktg., 1965-68, sr. v.p. ops., 1968-70;, pres., chief operating officer, 1970-76, pres., chief exec. officer, 1976-83, chmn. bd., chief exec. officer, 1983—; dir. Stolper Industries, Menomonee Falls, Wis., Electronic Telecommunications, Inc., Waukesha, Wis. Bd dirs. Florentine Opera Co., Milw. Mem. IEEE. Club: Merrill Hills Country (pres. 1969-70), Bluemound Golf and Country, University. Home: 929 N Astor St Apt 808 Milwaukee WI 53202 Office: RTE Corp Brookfield Lakes Corp Ctr 175 N Patrick Blvd Brookfield WI 53005-5884

BARRERA, RUBEN, JR., state agency auditor; b. Gary, Ind., Nov. 13, 1955; s. Ruben and Gloria (Gomez) B.; m. Susan Bea Reetz, Aug. 19, 1978. BBA, Aquinas Coll., 1981. Medicare auditor Blue Cross Northwest Ohio, Toledo, 1981-82; bus. tax auditor Mich. Dept. Treasury, Ann Arbor, 1982-85; fin. ops. auditor Mich. Dept. Mgmt. and Budget, Lansing, 1985-86; internal auditor Mich. Lottery, Lansing, 1986—. Mem. Am. Inst. CPA's, Mich. Assn. CPA's. Home: 7351 Cowell Rd Brighton MI 48116 Office: Mich State Lottery 6545 Mercantile Way Lansing MI 48909

BARRETT, BARBRO ANNA-LILL, research technician; b. Gothenburg, Sweden, Feb. 21, 1939; came to U.S., 1964; d. Klaus Erik Olof and Gullan Iris (Olofson) Nilsson; m. James Thomas Barrett, July 31, 1967; children: Annika, Nina. Med tech. diploma, Laborantskola, Gothenburg, 1959. Cert. electron microscope technologist. Research technician Sahlgrenska Hosp., Gothenburg, 1959-64, Univ. Mo., Columbia, 1964-65, Nat. Jewish Hosp., Denver, 1965-67, U. Mo., Columbia, 1967-81; health/electron microscope technician Truman VA Hosp., Columbia, 1981—. Contbr. articles to profl. jours. Mem. Electron Microscopy Soc. Am., Cen. States Electron Microscopy Soc. Home: 901 Westport Dr Columbia MO 65203 Office: Truman Va Hosp Hospital Dr Columbia MO 65521-0002

BARRETT, CHARLES MARION, insurance company executive, physician; b. Cin., Mar. 10, 1913; s. Charles Francis and May (Ryan) B.; m. May Belle Finn, Apr. 27, 1942; children: Angela, Charles, John, Michael, Marian, William. AB, Xavier U., 1934, LLD (hon.), 1974; MD, U. Cin., 1938. Assoc. med. dir. Western & So. Life Ins. Co., Cin., 1942, med. dir., 1951-73, exec. v.p., 1965-73, pres., 1973-84, chmn., pres., chief exec. officer, 1984—, also bd. dirs.; prof. depts. surgery and radiology U. Cin. Coll. Medicine, after 1957, prof. emeritus, 1974—; chmn. Columbus Mut. Life Ins. Co., 1982—; bd. dirs. Eagle-Picher Industries Inc. Bd. dirs. Our Lady of Mercy Hosp., Bethesda Hosp. and Deaconess Assn.; chmn. Cin. Bus. Com., 1986—. Recipient Taft medal U. Cin., 1973, spl. award Ohio Radiol. Soc., 1974, Daniel Drake award, 1985; named Great Living Cincinnatian, 1987. Fellow Am. Coll. Radiology; mem. AMA, Life Ins. Assn. Am., Greater Cin. C. of C. (chmn. 1985-86). Office: Western & So Life Ins Co 400 Broadway Cincinnati OH 45202

BARRETT, EDWARD DUANE, dentist, microbiologist; b. Detroit, July 1, 1925; s. Thomas Joseph and Thelma Louise (Johnson) B.; m. Evelyn Thelma Trammell, Sept. 2, 1950; children: Heather, Mary Patricia, Theresa, Edward D., Margaret. Student Marquette U., 1944-45; BS, U. Detroit, 1947, MS, 1949, DDS, 1954; postgrad. Wayne State U., 1949-50. Microbiologist, Wayne State U., Detroit, 1948-50; gen. practice dentistry, Auburn Heights, Mich., 1954-84; mem. microbiology faculty U. Detroit Dental Sch., 1950-57, grad. div., 1965-70, dir. continuing edn., 1977—, clin. prof. Dept. Microbiology/biochemistry. Editor U. Detroit Sch. Dentistry Newsletter. Pres. Auburn Heights Boys Club, 1960-66; Active Pontiac (Mich.) United Fund, 1963-65. Bd. mgrs. Rochester (Mich.) YMCA, 1971-77, chmn., 1973-75; mem. State Mich. Gov's Adv. Expert Com. on AIDS, 1985-86 Served with USN, 1944-46. Fellow Internat. Coll. Dentists, Acad. Dentistry International, Acad. Gen. Dentistry (master, pres. Mich. 1976-78, nat. dir. 1979-85, v.p. 1985-86, pres. elec. 1986-87, pres. 1987-88), Am. Coll. Dentists; mem. Am. Acad. Oral Medicine, U. Detroit Dental Alumni Assn. (dir.), Oakland County Dental Soc. (pres. 1969-70), Am. Dental Assn. (ho. of dels. 1981—), Mich. Dental Assn. (trustee 1981-86, editor 1986—, exec. com. 1986), Pierre Fauchard Acad., Detroit Dental Clinic Club (sect. chmn. 1985-87, bd. govs. 1985—), Am. Assn. Dental Schs. (chmn. continuing education section 1986-87), Eastern Conf. Dental Continuing Educators (pres. 1982-83), Am. Legion, Alpha Sigma Nu, Psi Omega. Roman Catholic. K.C., Elk. Club: Auburn Heights Lions (pres. 1960-61). Author: (with Mattman, Barrett) Laboratory Experiments in Nursing Microbiology, 1952; (with Mattman, Barrett) Laboratory Experiments in Medical Microbiology, 1956; (with Mattman, Barrett, Rossmore) Exercises in Introductory Microbiology, 1958. Contbr. articles to sci. and profl. jours. Home: 220 Rochdale Dr Rochester MI 48063

BARRETT, GARRET DALE, prosthodontist; b. Detroit, Jan. 2, 1946; s. C. Dale and Virginia B.; m. Linda Louise D'Agostino, Dec. 22, 1968; children: Lora, Kelly. BS, Wayne State U., 1968; DDS, U. Detroit, 1972; MS, U. Mich., 1978. Diplomate Am. Bd. Prosthodontists. Practice dentistry specializing in prosthodontics Mt. Clemens, Mich., 1983-87, Macomb, Mich., 1987—. Patentee Surgical Guide Stents. Manitoba Master Angler award In Fisherman, 1985, 86. Fellow Acad. Gen. Dentistry, Internat. Coll. Prosthodontists, Am. Coll. Prothodontists; mem. ADA, Macomb Dental Soc. (bd. dirs. Tri County Dental Health Council), Chgo. Dental Soc. Clubs: IFGA (Fla.). Avocations: fishing, sports. Office: 42450 Garfield Mount Clemens MI 48044

BARRETT, GERALD VAN, psychologist, educator; b. Bellefontaine, Ohio, Aug. 3, 1936; s. Charles L. and Evelyn Marie (Snapp) B.; m. Colleen Patricia Gregory, Aug. 20, 1960; children: Charles, Jera, Gregory. BA, Wittenberg U., 1958; MS, PhD, Case Western Res. U., 1962; JD, Akron U., 1985. Bar: Ohio 1985; lic. psychologist, Ohio; diplomate Am. Bd. Profl. Psychologists. Instr. Cleve. State U., 1962; dir., research assoc. Goodyear Aerospace, Akron, Ohio, 1962-67; assoc. dir. U. Pitts., Ohio, 1967-68; assoc. dir., assoc. prof. U. Rochester, N.Y., 1968-73; prof., head dept. psychology U. Akron, 1973—; mng. ptnr. Orgnl. Cons. Group, Akron, 1975-85; pres. Barrett & Assocs., Akron, 1985. Author: Motivation in Industry, 1966; co-author: Man, Work and Organization, 1972, Assessment of Managers, 1979, People, Work and Organization, 1981. Fellow Am. Psychol. Assn. (psychol. tests and mgmt. com.); mem. ABA, Internat. Personnel Mgmt. Assn., Acad. Mgmt., Human Factors Soc., AAAS. Home: 3088 Highland Dr Silver Lake OH 44224 Office: U Akron Dept Psychology Akron OH 44325

BARRETT, JOHN ANTHONY, trauma surgeon; b. Cork, Ireland, Apr. 17, 1945; came to U.S., 1971; s. Richard and Rita (O'Keefe) B.; m. Kathleen M. Curzon; children—Julia, Dominic. M.B., B.Ch., B.A.O., Nat. U., Ireland, 1963-69, M.Ch., 1975. Ainsworth research fellow, Cork, 1973-74; research fellow Tulane U., New Orleans, 1973-75; attending surgeon Cook County Hosp., Chgo., 1980-82, dir. trauma unit, 1982—; asst. prof. surgery U. Ill.-Chgo., 1980—. Contbr. chpt. to book, articles to med. jours. Chmn. Ill. Coalition for Safety Belt Use, 1984; pres. Chgo. Interhosp. Trauma Conf. Fellow Royal Coll. Surgeons Ireland, ACS (sec.-treas. Chgo. com. on trauma); mem. AAAS, Assn. for Acad. Surgery, Am. Trauma Soc. (bd. govs. Ill. div.), Am. Soc. Law and Medicine. Home: 644 N Oak Park Ave Oak Park IL 60302 Office: Trauma Office M7 Cook County Hosp 1835 W Harrison St Chicago IL 60612

BARRETT, KEITH ALLEN, communications company executive; b. Kansas City, Mo., Aug. 18, 1953; s. Allen Atwell and Betty Jo (Mullins) B.; m. Susan Hays Guenther, May 23, 1980. BS in Bus., Avila Coll., 1979; MBA in Fin., U. Mo., 1982. Asst. buyer Macy's Midwest, Kansas City, 1982-83, mgr. advt. scheduling, 1983-84; founder, pres. TeleRepair, Inc., Kansas City, Kans., 1984—; small bus. cons. Small Bus. Adminstrn., U. Mo., Kansas City, 1982. Councilman City of Fairway, Kans., 1979. Republican. Avocations: racquetball, reading. Office: TeleRepair Inc 3100 S 24th St Kansas City KS 66106

BARRETT, MARGARET ANN, needlework designer, consultant; b. Concordia, Kans., Nov. 9, 1939; d. Thayne Arthur and Hilma Margaret (Larson) Coulter; m. Phillip Leroy Barrett, Dec. 29, 1958; children—Michael John, Debra Ann. Student Ariz. State U., 1957-61; U. Kans., 1984-86. Pres., designer Peggi Barrett Originals, Stilwell, Kans., 1974-83; rep. Leiter's Designer Fabrics, Kansas City, Mo., 1983-87, asst. buyer, stylist, 1986-87 ; wholesale/retail rep. Fabric Culture, Kansas City, Mo., 1986— ; pres., assoc. cons. Color Profiles, Ltd., Stilwell, 1984—; translator: Bergere de France, Bar-le-Duc, France, 1985—; model Talent Plus, Kansas City, 1986—; cons. Coe Coll., Cedar Rapids, Iowa, numerous fabric retailers and clothiers; translator knitting patterns. Mem. presdl. adv. council Coe Coll., 1980-83. Cons. Rose Brooks Ctr. for Battered Women, 1987—. Mem. Assn. Fashon andd Image Cons., Nat. Assn. Female Execs., Kans. Council Commerce and Industry, Coe Coll. Alumni Council, Ariz. State U. Alumni Assn., Chi Omega. Methodist. Avocations: cross-country skiing, backpacking. Home: 18550 Metcalf St Stilwell KS 66085

BARRETT, TOM HANS, rubber company executive; b. Topeka, Aug. 13, 1930; s. William V. and Myrtle B.; m. Marilyn Dunn, July 22, 1956; children—Susan and Sara (twins), Jennifer. Grad. Chem. Engr., Kans. State U., 1953; grad., Sloan Sch. Mgmt. MIT, 1969. With Goodyear Tire & Rubber Co., various locations, 1953—; pres., chief operating officer Goodyear Tire & Rubber Co., Akron, Ohio, 1982—; also dir. Goodyear Tire & Rubber Co.; dir. A.O. Smith Corp., Rubbermaid Corp. Served with U.S. Army, 1953-55. Decorated officer with crown Order Merite Civil et Militaire, Luxembourg, 1976; recipient Sigma Phi Epsilon citation, 1979. Home: 2135 Stockbridge Rd Akron OH 44313 Office: The Goodyear Tire & Rubber Co 1144 E Market St Akron OH 44316

BARRETT, WILLIAM A., engineer; b. St. Clair, Mich., Mar. 23, 1958; s. William A. and Helen (Hemmen) B.; m. Kim L., June 6, 1981. BSMechE, Mich. Technol. U., 1980. Registered profl. engr., Mich. Mech. engr. Daverman Assocs., Grand Rapids, Mich., 1980-83, assoc., 1983-85, sr. assoc., 1985-87; facilities engr. Steelcase, Inc., Grand Rapids, Mich., 1987—. Mem. ASHRAE, NSPE, Assn. Energy Engrs. Avocation: sports. Home: 7934 Engelhurst Dr Jenison MI 49428

BARRIE, DAVID SCOTT, lawyer; b. Cleve., Oct. 3, 1952; s. David Ray and Evelyn Agnes (Vild) B.; m. Robyn Elizabeth Voss, Sept. 7, 1985; children: Nicholas, Katherine. AB, Kenyon Coll., 1974; JD, Cornell U., 1978. Bar: Ohio 1978. Assoc. Fuller & Henry, Toledo, 1978-84; atty. Trinova Corp., Toledo, 1984—, asst. sec., 1986—. Trustee Toledo Hearing ans Speech Ctr., 1982—, Planned Parenthood N.W. Ohio, Toledo, 1984-85. Mem. ABA, Am. Soc. Corp. Secs., Ohio State Bar Assn., Toledo Bar Assn., Kenyon Alumni Assn. N.W. Ohio (pres. 1984—). Episcopalian. Avocations: photography, cooking. Home: 3745 Edgevale Rd Toledo OH 43606 Office: Trinova Corp 1705 Indian Wood Circle Maumee OH 43537

BARRIENTOS, G. OMAR, mortgage company executive; b. Santiago, Chile, Sept. 29, 1940; came to U.S., 1968; s. Hugo Teran and Fresia Gahona (Mitchell) B.; m. Isabel Luza Lenquezi, July 24, 1965; children: Omar II, Hugo III, Elizabeth. Student, Chilean Air Force Coll., Santiago, 1961; Assoc., B in Electronics, No. U., Arica, Chile, 1965. Gen. mgr. True Technicians, La Paz, Bolivia, 1966-68, Mexican Villages, Los Angeles, 1969-75; owner, mgr. Rockerville Trading, Rapid City, S.D., 1975-80; pres. Tri-Star Mortgage Banking, Rapid City, 1981—, Consolidated Systems, Rapid City, 1985—, Mex. U.S.A., Inc., Rapid City, 1986—; v.p. Tri-Star Devel., Rapid City, 1983—, also bd. dirs. Inventor electric device. Vol. Fire Dept., Arica, 1958-65. Served to brig. Chilean Air Force, 1958-61. Named one of Small Bus. Men of Am., 1980. Mem. Rapid City C. of C. Roman Catholic. Club: Archery. Avocations: sculpturing, hunting, reading. Office: Mexico USA Inc 725 Indiana Rapid City SD 57701

BARRIGER, JOHN WALKER, IV, transportation consultant, former railroad executive; b. St. Louis, Aug. 3, 1927; s. John Walker and Elizabeth Chambers (Thatcher) B.; m. Evelyn Dobson, Dec. 29, 1955; children: John Walker V, Catherine Brundige. BS, MIT, 1949; CT, Yale U., 1950. With Santa Fe Ry., 1950-68, 70-83, supt. transp., 1965-68, mgr. staff studies and planning, Chgo., 1970-77, asst. v.p. fin., 1977-79, asst. to pres., 1979-83; dir. spl. services Santa Fe So. Pacific Corp., 1983-85, prin. John W. Barriger and Assocs., Chgo., 1985-86; v.p. corp. devel. Venango River Corp., South Shore Ry., Chgo. Mo. and Western Ry.. 1987—; mgr. transp. controls div.

Sylvania Info. Systems, Waltham, Mass., 1968-70; mem. vis. com. dept. civil engring. MIT, 1972-75; chmn. MIT Mgmt. Conf., Chgo., 1984. Trustee Village of Kenilworth (Ill.), 1978-85, North Suburban Mass Transit Dist., 1985—, chmn. railrod com.; pres. John W. Barriger III R.R. Library, St. Louis; bd. dirs. St. Louis Merc. Library. Served with USN, 1946. Recipient Bronze Beaver award MIT, 1975, Employee Campaign Chmn. of Yr. award United Way/Crusade of Mercy, 1979. Mem. Am. Assn. R.R. Supts. (bd. dirs. 1958-68), Am. Ry. Engring. Assn., Ry. Planning Officers Assn. (chmn. 1971-76), Transp. Research Bd., Transp. Research Forum, Western Ry. Club (pres. 1979-80), Newcomen Soc., MIT Alumni Assn. (bd. dirs. 1968-72), Delta Kappa Epsilon. Republican. Roman Catholic. Clubs: Econ. Chgo. Exec. Chgo., MIT Chgo. (pres. 1972-73), Kenilworth, Union League Chgo. Home: 155 Melrose Ave Kenilworth IL 60043 Office: 10 N Dearborn St Chicago IL 60602

BARRINGER, FLOYD SAMUEL, neurosurgeon; b. Emden, Ill., Apr. 7, 1915; s. Bert Montrose and Lizzie Amanda (Hughes) B.; m. Winifred Lois Wain, June 2, 1945; children: Judith, Daniel, David, Douglas. AS, Lincoln (Ill.) Coll., 1934; BS in Medicine, U. Ill., Chgo., 1937, MD, 1940; HHD (hon.), Lincoln (Ill.) Coll., 1974. Prof. neurol. surgery So. Ill. U. Sch. Medicine, Springfield, 1972-82. Pres. Abraham Lincoln Assn., Springfield, 1971-84; trustee Lincoln Acad., Springfield, 1971-84. Served with British Emergency Med. Service, 1941-46. Democrat. Presbyterian. Avocations: Sangamon County)Ill.) history, studying Lincoln. Home: Rural Rt 6 Box 100 Springfield IL 62707

BARRINGER, ROBERT STEWART, architect; b. St. Louis, Sept. 3, 1952; s. Robert Gerard and Florence Marie (Deutschmann) B. BArch, U. Notre Dame, 1976. Registered architect, Mo. Project architect Smith-Entzeroth, Inc., St. Louis, 1976-84, v.p., 1984-86; assoc. Stone, Marraccini, and Patterson, St. Louis, 1986—; instr. Washington U., St. Louis, 1983-86. Office coordinator United Way, St. Louis, 1980-85; mem. St. Clement Fin./Bldg COms., St. Louis, 1983—; friend St. Louis Art Mus., 1983—. Mem. AIA (program chmn. 1985—, design honor award St. Louis chpt. 1982), Clayton C. of C. (office rep. 1979-86), Tau Sigma Delta. Roman Catholic. Clubs: Notre Dame, DeSmet Jesuit High Sch. Men's (St. Louis) (sec. 1982-83). Avocations: reading, watercolor painting. Home: 1322 Bansbach Rd Saint Louis MO 63131 Office: Stone Marraccini and Patterson 7777 Bonhomme Ave Saint Louis MO 63105

BARRINGTON-CARLSON, SHARYN MARIE, computer program developer; b. East Cleveland, Ohio, Oct. 9, 1946; d. Robert John and Violet (Pierrou) Carlson; m. Leonard F. Barry Barrington, Oct. 3, 1975. BS, Baldwin Wallace Coll., 1968; postgrad, John Hopkins U., 1968-74; cert. with honors in computer career program, DePaul U., 1983. Legis. affairs asst. Am. Mining Congress, Washington, 1973-75; program adminstr. Smithsonian Instn., Washington, 1976-79; computer programmer Office Ill. Atty. Gen., Chgo., 1984-85; computer program specialist Cognos Corp., Schaumburg, Ill., 1985—; prin. Cue Systems, Inc., Chgo., 1979—; cons. Legal Services Orgn., Washington, 1979, Centel Corp., Bethesda, Md., 1979-80, Womens Equity, Washington, 1980-81, World Future Soc., Bethesda, 1980-81. Editor (newsletter) Good News, 1980; creator (film) Scarecrow and Fairies, 1970; (workshops) Consciousness Raising Colloquium, 1974, Careers in Internat. Trade, 1985; author/adaptor (artificial intelligence program) Expert System Advisor, 1987. Campaigner Mikulski for Congress, Rockville, Md., 1976, 78, Venetoulos for Gov., Bethesda, 1978; area drive planner Jerry Brown for Pres., Washington, 1976; chmn. precinct dr. John Anderson for Pres., Washington, 1980. Fellow HEW, 1971. Mem. World Future Soc., Am. Assn. Polit. and Social Sci., Women in Internat. Trade (1st v.p.), Data Processing Mgmt. Assn., Swedish-Am. Ctr., Phi Mu (chatelaine). Democrat. Episcopalian. Home: 1021 N Dunton Ave Arlington Heights IL 60004-5558 Office: Cognos Corp 1834 Walden Office Sq Schaumburg IL 60173

BARRIS, BERNICE MARGARET, drilling company executive; b. Cleve., Mar. 29; d. Claude Thomas and Nettie Carolin (Martinek) Sebek; m. Robert Lee Barris, Feb. 22, 1941; children: Susan Lee, Robert Joel, Charles Britt. AS in Real Estate, Cuyahoga Community Coll., 1976, AA in Arts, 1977, AS in Aviation, 1978, AS in Nursing, 1979. Registered nurse, Cleve.; lic. comml. pilot, real estate agt. Pvt. practice nurse Cleve.; sec. Hupp Well & Pump, Cleve., 1956-82; pres. ABC Drilling, Willoughby, Ohio, 1982—. Pres. Child Care Assn., Cleve., 1966-86, The Ninety Nine, Clve., 1963-86; bd. mgrs. Rainey Inst., Cleve., 1978-86; mem. Civil Air Patrol, Cleve., 1983-86; vol. ARC first aid Mobil Corp. Mem. Flying Nurses Assn. Avocation: flying. Home: 5480 Highland Rd Highland Heights OH 44143 Office: ABC Drilling 4996 Campbell Rd Willoughby OH 44094

BARRON, HOWARD ROBERT, lawyer; b. Chgo., Feb. 17, 1930; s. Irwin P. and Ada (Astrahan) B.; m. Marjorie Shapira, Aug. 12, 1953; children: Ellen J., Laurie A. Ph.B., U. Chgo., 1948; B.A., Stanford U., 1950; LL.B., Yale U., 1953. Bar: Ill. 1953. Assoc. Jenner & Block, Chgo., 1957-63, ptnr., 1964—. Contbr. articles in field to profl. jours. Mem., then pres. Lake County Sch. Dist. 107 Bd. Edn., Highland Park, 1964-1971; pres. Lake County Sch. Bd. Assn., 1970-71; mem. Lake County High Sch. Dist. 113 Bd. Edn., Highland Park, 1973-77, Highland Park Zoning Bd. Appeals, 1984—. Served to lt. j.g. USNR, 1953-57. Mem. ABA (chmn. subcom. labor and employment law, com. corp. counsel litigation sect. 1983—), Ill. State Bar Assn. (chmn. antitrust sect. 1968-69), Fed. Bar Assn., Chgo. Bar Assn., Yale Law Sch. Assn. (v.p. 1978-81), Yale Law Sch. Assn. Ill. (pres. 1962). Democrat. Clubs: Standard, Cliff Dwellers (Chgo.). Home: 433 Ravine Dr Highland Park IL 60035 Office: Jenner & Block 1 IBM Plaza Chicago IL 60611

BARRON, PAMELA GURSKY, marketing specialist; b. N.Y.C., Apr. 23, 1943; d. Aaron Harry and Ruth (Bernstein) G.; student Cornell U., 1959-62; B.A., CCNY, 1963; M.A., Kent State U., 1968, postgrad., 1974; children—Matthew, Seth, Leila. Social worker Canton (Ohio) Welfare Dept., 1964-66; caseworker Info. and Referral Service, 1973-78; founder, exec. dir. Pyramid, Inc., Canton, 1976-79; dir. mktg. services ABS div. Diebold, Inc., North Canton, 1979-82, mgr. media ops., 1982-84, mktg. mgr. media, 1984-86, dir. mktg. accessory product sales, customer services group, 1986—; tchr., cons. Kickoff chmn. United Way, 1975-77; media programmer Canton City Schs., 1975-77; program adminstr. Goodwill Industries, 1974-76; bd. dirs. Canton Hometown Affirmative Action Plan, Planned Parenthood; mem. exec. com., chmn. employment com. Canton-Stark-Wayne CETA Adv. Council. Mem. Nat. Personnel and Guidance Assn., Am. Mgmt. Assn., North Central Sociol. Assn., Pi Gamma Mu. Jewish. Clubs: Hadassah (pres. 1974-76), Jr. League. Office: Diebold Inc 818 Mulberry Rd SE Canton OH 44707

BARROQUILLO, JIMMIE LEE, educational administrator; b. LaGrange County, Ind., Feb. 2, 1941; s. Servando Pedro and Jessie Pauline (Koon) B. B.S., Ind. U., 1963; M.S., 1969. Tchr., Lakeland Sch. Corp., Wolcottville, Ind., 1963; vol. U.S. Peace Corps, Brazil, 1964-65; art dir. Lance Litho Corp., Chgo., 1969-70; v.p. Kitzrow Co., Chgo., 1971-75; adminstr. Kennedy-King Coll., City Colls. Chgo., 1976—, asst. dean adult continuing edn., 1981—; sr. cons. Ednl. Mgmt. Assocs. & Cons., Inc., Park Forest, Ill., 1980—. Leader, 4H, 1974; sec., founding trustee Chgo./Cook County 4-H Found., 1976-87; mem. adv. council U. Ill./USDA Agr. Extension Service, 1974-79. 81-87; U.S. del. 4-H, Philippines, 1963; Recipient Outstanding Nat. 4-H Alumni award, 1978; recipient Merit award Youth Motivation com. Chgo. Assn. Commmerce and Industry, 1980—. Mem. Ind. U. Alumni Assn. (life), Ind. U. Found., Nat. Coll. Placement Council, Newberry Library Assocs., Nat. Geneal. Soc., Artists Guild Chgo., Smithsonian Instn. Assocs., Field Mus. Natural History, Tau Kappa Epsilon, Theta Alpha Phi, Phi Theta Kappa (hon.). Recipient Design award Champion Paper, 1975 Home: Rural Route 1 Wolcottville IN 46795

BARROS, GLORIA K., systems analyst; b. Canton, Ohio, Nov. 30, 1937, d. Herbert O. LeMunyon and Muriel J. (Newland) King; m. Paul N. Barros, Dec. 16, 1955 (div. Mar. 1984); children: Stephanie, Mary, Michael, Daniel, Melissa, Kirk, Alyse, Jennifer. Fin. analyst Perkins Diesel, Canton, Ohio, 1975-79; data processing mgr. M. Conley Co., Canton, Ohio, 1980-84; systems and procedural analyst, owner Shadbush Assocs., Canton, Ohio, 1984—. Mem. Am. Mgrs. Assn., Data Processing Mgrs. Assn. Jehovah's Witness.

BARROW, ALFRED ROBERT, clinic director, psychotherapist; b. Salem, Ohio, Apr. 14, 1952; s. Robert Souder and Donna Vean (Thompson) B.; m. June Ellen Garrett, June 7, 1980; children: Emily Jean, Nathan Garrett. AB, Grove City (Pa.) Coll., 1974; MEd, Ga. State U., 1975; doctoral studies, Ind. State U., 1983—. Psychotherapist Michael A. Campion and Assocs., Ill. and Ind., 1976-86; clinic dir.and psychotherapist Primary Mental Health Care of Ind., Indpls., 1986-87; directing assoc., therapist Michael A. Campion, PhD & Assocs., Greenwood, Ind., 1987—; psychological cons. OMS Internat., Greenwold, Ind., 1981—, Dept. Welfare, Shelbyville, Ind., 1981—, Ind. Children's Christian Home, Ladoga, 1980—. Mem. Ind. Psychol. Assn., Am. Acad. Behavioral Scis. (assoc.), Am. Assn. for Counseling and Devel., Christian Assn. for Psychol. Studies, Pi Gamma Mu, Phi Kappa Phi. Presbyterian. Avocations: piano, guitar, reading, participating and watching sports. Office: Michael A Campion PhD & Assocs 435 E Main A-3 Greenwood IN 46142

BARROW, CRAIG STEPHEN, computer company executive; b. Toledo, Oct. 27, 1951; s. Irvin Stephen and Rosemary (Gill) B.; m. Debra Suzanne Beckett, June 30, 1978; 1 child, Rebecca. BBA, U. Toledo, 1973, MBA, 1975, JD, 1979. Bar: Ohio, 1980, U.S. Dist. Ct. (no. dist.) Ohio, 1980. Various acctg., fin. positions Owens-Ill., Toledo, 1973-83; pres. Universal Material Inc., Mogadore, Ohio, 1983-85; v.p. fin. Riverside Hosp., Toledo, 1985-86; v.p. mktg. Comshare, Inc., Ann Arbor, Mich., 1986—. Mem. exec. com. Toledo Silverstreaks Wheelchair Basketball, 1986-87; com. chmn. Toledo Festival: A Celebration of the Arts, 1987; prin. Toledo Ballet Assn., 1987—. Named an Outstanding Young Man Am., Jr. C. of C., 1985. Mem. ABA, Fin. Execs. Inst., Ohio Bar Assn., Toledo Bar Assn., U. Toledo Alumni Assn. (homecoming chmn. 1980). Republican. Roman Catholic. Club: Toledo. Home: 4972 Damascus Dr Toledo OH 43615 Office: Comshare Inc 3001 S State Ann Arbor MI 48104

BARROW, THOMAS DAVIES, former oil and mining company executive; b. San Antonio, Dec. 27, 1924; s. Leonidas Theodore and Laura Editha (Thomson) B.; m. Janice Meredith Hood, Sept. 16, 1950; children—Theodore Hood, Kenneth Thomson, Barbara Loyd, Elizabeth Ann. B.S., U. Tex., 1945, M.A., 1948; Ph.D., Stanford U., 1953; grad. advanced mgmt. program, Harvard U., 1963. With Humble Oil & Refining Co., 1951-72; regional exploration mgr. Humble Oil & Refining Co., New Orleans, 1962-64, sr. v.p., 1967-70, pres., 1970-72, also dir.; exec. v.p. Esso Exploration, Inc., 1964-65; sr. v.p. Exxon Corp., N.Y.C., 1972-78, also dir.; chmn., chief exec. officer Kennecott Corp., Stamford, Conn., 1978-81; vice chmn. Standard Oil Co., 1981-85; investment cons. Houston, 1985—; mem. commn. on natural resources NRC, 1973-78, commn. on phys. sci., math. and natural resources, 1984-87, bd. on earth scis., 1982-84; dir. Tex. Commerce Bankshares, McDermott Internat. Inc., Am. Gen. Corp., GeoQuest Internat., Inc., Cameron Iron Works; trustee Woods Hole Oceanographic Instn., 20th Century Fund-Task Force on U.S. Energy Policy. Pres. Houston Grand Opera, 1985-87, chmn., 1987—; trustee Am. Mus. Natural History, Stanford U. 1980—, Baylor Coll. Medicine, Tex. Med. Ctr., 1983—, Geol. Soc. Am. Found., 1982-87. Served to ensign USNR, 1943-46. Recipient Disting. Achievement award Offshore Tech. Conf., 1973, Disting. Engring. Grad. award U. Tex., 1970, Disting. Alumnus, 1982, Disting. Geology Grad., 1985; named Chief Exec. of Yr. in Mining Industry, Fin. World, 1979. Fellow N.Y. Acad. Scis.; mem. Nat. Acad. Engring., Am. Mining Congress (bd. dirs. 1979-85, vice chmn. 1983-85), Am. Assn. Petroleum Geologists, Geol. Soc. Am., Internat. Copper Research Assn. (bd. dirs. 1979-85), Nat. Ocean Industry Assn. (bd. dirs. 1982-85), AAAS, Am. Soc. Oceanography (pres. 1970-71), Am. Geophys. Union, Am. Petroleum Inst., Am. Geog. Soc., Sigma Xi, Tau Beta Pi, Sigma Gamma Epsilon, Phi Eta Sigma, Alpha Tau Omega. Episcopalian. Clubs: Houston Country, Clove Valley, Petroleum, River Oaks Country, Ramada.

BARRY, JAMES P(OTVIN), writer, editor, association executive; b. Alton, Ill., Oct. 23, 1918; s. Paul Augustine and Elder (Potvin) B.; m. Anne Elizabeth Jackson, Apr. 16, 1966; B.A. cum laude, Ohio State U., 1940. Commd. 2d. lt. Arty., U.S. Army, 1940, advanced through grades to col., 1953; served ETO, 1944-46; adviser to Turkish Army, 1951-53; detailed Army Gen. Staff, Washington, 1953-56; ret., 1966; adminstr. Capital U., Columbus, Ohio, 1967-71; freelance writer, editor, Columbus, 1971-77; dir. Ohioana Library Assn., 1977—; editor Ohioana Quar., 1977—; sr. editor Inland Seas, 1984—; photographer, exhbn. and book illustrator, 1968—. Recipient award Am. Soc. State and Local History, 1974, nonfiction history award Soc. Midland Authors, 1982. Mem. Gt. Lakes, Marine, Ohio hist. socs., World Ship Soc., Phi Beta Kappa. Clubs: Royal Can. Yacht; Columbus Country, University (Columbus). Author: Georgian Bay: The Sixth Great Lake, 1968, rev. edit., 1978; The Battle of Lake Erie, 1970, Bloody Kansas, 1972; The Noble Experiment, 1972; The Fate of the Lakes, 1972; The Louisiana Purchase, 1973; Henry Ford and Mass Production, 1973; Ships of the Great Lakes (Dolphin Book Club selection), 1973; The Berlin Olympics, 1975; The Great Lakes: A First Book, 1976; Wrecks and Rescues of the Great Lakes (Dolphin Book Club selection), 1981; also booklet on Lake Erie for Ohio EPA, 1980; also mag. and jour. articles. Home: 353 Fairway Blvd Columbus OH 43213 Office: 65 S Front St 1105 Ohio Depts Bldg Columbus OH 43215

BARRY, THOMAS HUBERT, pub. co. exec.; b. Phillips, Wis., Mar. 18, 1918; s. John Sumner and Helen (Maloney) B.; student U. Notre Dame, 1936-38; B.A., Marquette U., 1941; m. Rosemary Klein, July 8, 1944 (dec. May 1983); children—Kathleen Barry Ingram, Patricia Barry Turriff, Mary Beth Barry O'Donnell, Julie Barry Carden. Western mgr., welding engr. McGraw Hill Pub. Co., Chgo., 1947-53; Western mgr. Iron Age, Chilton Co., Chgo., 1953-66; Western mgr. Control Engring., Tech. Pub. (a Dun and Bradstreet Co.), Chgo., 1966-69, sales mgr., N.Y.C., 1969-72, assoc. pub., Chgo., 1972-76, pub., Barrington, Ill., 1977-86; pub. Control Engring., Cahners Pub. Co., Barrington, 1986—. Bd. dirs. Boys' Hope. Served with USMC, 1941-47. Decorated Bronze Star, Purple Heart. Mem. Nat. Indsl. Advertisers Assn., Assn. Indsl. Advertisers (dir. Chgo. chpt. 1963-65), Bus.-Profl. Advt. Assn., Indsl. Mktg. Club St. Louis, Rockford Advt. Club, Marine Corps Res. Officers Assn., 1st Marine Div. Assn. (officer, dir. 1954—, pres. 1979-84). Roman Catholic. Clubs: KC, Notre Dame of Chgo., Marquette U. Chgo., Holy Name Soc. Home: 611 Carriage Hill Dr Glenview IL 60025 Office: 1301 S Grove Ave Barrington IL 60010

BARRY, WALTER RICHARD, JR., food company executive; b. Minneapolis, Apr. 24, 1933; s. Walter Richard and Geraldine (Dunne) B.; m. Jane Dickey Randall, Jan. 17, 1964; children—Walter Richard III, Randall Dunne, Stewart MacNeil. B.A., Princeton U., 1955; postgrad. advanced mgmt. Harvard U., 1973. With Gen. Mills Inc., Mpls., 1958—, group v.p., 1973-81, exec. v.p., 1981-87. Served to capt. U.S. Army, 1956-58. Roman Catholic. Club: Woodhill Country (pres. 1981-82); Princeton (N.Y.C.). Office: Gen Mills Inc 678 Northstar E 608 2d Ave St Minneapolis MN 55402 also: PO Box 1113 Minneapolis MN 55440 also: Gen Mills Inc 9200 Wayzata Blvd Minneapolis MN 55426

BARSAN, ROBERT BLAKE, dentist; b. Akron, Ohio, Apr. 7, 1948; s. Emil O. and Letitia (Dobrin) B.; m. Cheryl Lee Adams, Dec. 16, 1972; 1 child, Erin Lee. BS, U. Cin., 1970; DDS, Ohio State U., 1974. Resident U. Chgo., 1976; gen. practice dentistry Cuyahoga Falls, Ohio, 1976—. Contbr. editor Modern Dental Mag., 1984—. Fellow Acad. Gen. Dentistry; mem. Am. Dental Assn., Am. Endodontic Soc., Akron Gnathological Soc. (pres. 1986). Home: 3084 Silver Lake Blvd Silver Lake OH 44224 Office: 330 Stow Ave Cuyahoga Falls OH 44221

BARSHES, WARREN BARRY, corporate compensation official; b. Chgo., July 14, 1943; s. John and Anne (Jonases) B.; B.A. in Psychology, DePaul U., 1965, M.A. in Psychology, 1967; M.S. in Indsl. Relations, Loyola U., 1975; m. Laraine Chorvat, Aug. 10, 1969; children—David Warren, Neal Ryan, Krista Hope. With Wm. Wrigley Jr. Co., Chgo., 1969—, personnel mgr., 1977-81, corp. compensation mgr., 1981—; instr. psychology, personnel mgmt. Moraine Valley Community Coll., Palos Hills, Ill., 1974-82. Pres. Palos Gardens Civic Assn., 1985-87; bd. dirs. Nat. Hydrocephalus Found., 1983—. Served to lt. 1st, US Army, 1967-69. Mem. Am. Compensation Assn., Ill. Psychol. Assn., Indsl. Relations Assn. Chgo. (past dir., sec.), Vietnam Vets. of Am. Office: 410 N Michigan Ave Chicago IL 60611

BART, WILLIAM MARVIN, psychologist; b. Chgo., Nov. 29, 1943; s. Joseph Marvin and Madelynne Joanne (Stroik) B.; B.S., Loyola U., Chgo., 1965; A.M., U. Chgo., 1967, Ph.D., 1969. Asst. prof. ednl. psychology U. Minn., Mpls., 1969-72, asso. prof. ednl. psychology, 1972-80, prof., 1980—. Fulbright-Hays Research scholar, W. Ger., 1974-75. Mem. Am. Psychol. Assn., Am. Ednl. Research Assn., Soc. Research in Child Devel., Jean Piaget Soc. Contbr. articles to Jour. Math. Psychology, Jour. Ednl. Psychology. Home: 890 22nd Ave SE Minneapolis MN 55414 Office: 330 Burton Hall U Minn Minneapolis MN 55455

BARTA, JAMES OMER, priest, educator, academic administrator; b. Fairfax, Iowa, Oct. 22, 1931; s. Omer J. and Bertha (Brecht) B. BA, Loras Coll., 1952; Sacrae Theologiae Licentiatus, Gregorian U., Rome, 1956; PhD, Fordham U., 1962. Ordained priest Roman Cath. Ch., 1955; lic. psychologist, Iowa. Prof. psychology Loras Coll., Dubuque, Iowa, 1957—, v.p. acad. affairs, 1977—; chaplain Clarke Coll., Dubuque, 1966—. Mem. Am. Psychol. Assn., Iowa Psychol. Assn. Address: Loras Coll Dubuque IA 52004-0178

BARTEK, GORDON LUKE, radiologist; b. Valpraiso, Nebr., Dec. 27, 1925; s. Luke Victor and Sylvia (Buner) B.; m. Ruth Evelyn Rowley, Sept. 10, 1949; children—John, David, James. B.Sc., U. Nebr., 1948, M.D., 1949. Diplomate Am. Bd. Radiology. Intern Bishop Clarksen Hosp., Omaha, 1949-50; resident in medicine Henry Ford Hosp., Detroit, 1952-53, resident in radiology, 1953-56; staff radiologist Ferguson Hosp., Grand Rapids, Mich., 1956-76, Holland City Hosp., Mich., 1956-76, Logan Hosp., Utah, 1976-78, St. Lawrence Hosp., Lansing, Mich., 1978—; dir. Accord Ins. Co., Cayman Islands, 1983—. Served to lt. USN, 1949-52. Fellow Am. Coll. Radiology; mem. Mich. Radiology Practice Assn. (bd. dirs. 1984—, chmn. western Mich. sect. 1970-71), Am. Coll. Radiology (councilor 1972-76). Republican. Roman Catholic. Club: Manhattan Tennis (pres.). Avocations: flying; photography; skiing; snorkeling. Home: 1536 Stanlake Dr East Lansing MI 48823

BARTEL, DALE RONALD, teacher; b. Hustisford, Wis., Mar. 24, 1938; s. Martin Albert and Adele Anna (Bornfleth) B.; m. Mary Ellen Ferris, Aug. 12, 1967; children: Lorna Marie, Steven Shea, Jeffrey Dale. BE, U. Wis., Whitewater, 1964; MBus. Edn., U. Wis., 1967. Tchr. Wausau High Sch., Wis., 1964-68; credit mgr. Wausau Ins., Southfield, Mich., 1968-72; tchr. med. office mgmt. Northeast Wis. Tech. Inst., Green Bay, 1972—. Asst. scoutmaster Boy Scouts Am., Green Bay, 1981—; chmn. ins. com. Northeast Tech. Inst. Faculty Assn., 1984—. Served with USN, 1956-60. Lutheran. Avocations: fishing, skiing, boating, golf. Home: 506 Scott Dr Green Bay WI 54303 Office: Northeast Tech Inst 2740 W Mason St PO Box 19042 Green Bay WI 54307-9042

BARTEL, FRED FRANK, consulting engineer; b. Milw., Nov. 4, 1917; s. Fred F. and Alma O. (Koppelmeyer) B.; m. Ann E. Staudacher, Oct. 23, 1943; children—Betty Jo, Susan, Mary Jo, Robert. B.S. in Civil Engring., U. Wis., 1940; M.S., U. Md., 1942. Engring. aide Wis. Hwy. Dept., 1936-40; asst. dir. engring. Nat. Ready Mixed Concrete Assn., Silver Spring, Md., 1942-49; chief engr., sales mgr. Tews Lime and Cement Co., Milw., 1949-75, pres., chief exec. officer, 1975-83; cons. engr. on concrete and cement aggregates Milw., 1983—; trustee in bankruptcy, 4X Corp., Neenah, Wis., 1985. Contbr. to books and other tech. pubs. Served to capt. USAAF, 1942-46. Stanton Walker research fellow U. Md., 1942. Fellow ASCE; mem. ASTM, Am. Concrete Inst., Nat. Ready Mixed Concrete Assn. (chmn. bd. dirs. 1979), Wis. Ready Mixed Concrete Assn. (pres. 1969), Builders Exchange Milw. (pres. 1966-67). Republican. Roman Catholic. Lodge: Rotary. Home and Office: 5421 N Shoreland Ave Milwaukee WI 53217

BARTEL, ROGER FRANCIS, nuclear information manager; b. Chgo., Nov. 21, 1951; s. Frank Anthony and Wanda Geroldine (Restko) B.; m. JoAnn Roelands, June 26, 1975; children: Ross Daniel and Beth Alexandra. AS in Applied Sci. with honors, Daley Jr. Coll., Chgo., 1977; BS in Info. Scis., Northeastern Ill. U., 1981; M in Engring. Mgmt., Northwestern U., 1985. Engring. asst. Commonwealth Edison Co., Maywood, Ill., 1974-76; assoc. engr. Commonwealth Edison Co., Maywood, 1976-79; methods analyst Commonwealth Edison Co., Glen Ellyn, Ill., 1979-82; systems analyst Commonwealth Edison Co., Joliet, Ill., 1982-84; project staff analyst Commonwealth Edison Co., Braidwood, Ill., 1984—. Bd. dirs. Timberlake Civic Assn., Clarendon Hills, Ill., 1985—. Served with USN, 1969-73, Vietnam. Mem. Nuclear Info. and Records Mgmt. Assn. Republican. Roman Catholic. Avocation: fly fishing. Home: 8001 Tennessee Ave Clarendon Hills IL 60514 Office: Commonwealth Edison Co Braidwood Sta Rural Rt 1 Box 81 Braceville IL 60407

BARTELS, KENNETH ERVIN, educational administrator; b. Elmhurst, Ill., Aug. 24, 1948; s. Harvey Herman and Violet Clara (Mueller) B.; m. Claire Marie Zimmerman, Apr. 17, 1971; 1 child, Amy Beth. B.A., Carthage Coll., 1970. Devel. assoc. Carthage Coll., Kenosha, Wis., 1974-76; assoc. dir. devel., dir. planned giving Marquette U., Milw., 1977-81; dir. of devel. and pub. relations Elmhurst Coll., Ill., 1981—. Mem. com. Cable TV for City of Elmhurst, 1984-85. Served with USN, 1971-74. Mem. Council for the Advancement and Support of Edn., Nat. Soc. of Fund Raising Execs., Ill. Coll. Relations Council, Carthage Coll. Nat. Alumni Council Bd., Sigma Tau Delta, Phi Alpha Theta, Blue Key. Republican. Lutheran. Lodge: Rotary (dir. 1983-85). Avocations: collecting stained glass windows; creative writing. Home: 794 Linden Ave Elmhurst IL 60126 Office: Elmhurst Coll 190 Prospect Ave Elmhurst IL 60126

BARTH, DAVID KECK, business executive; b. Springfield, Ill., Dec. 7, 1943; s. David Klenk and Edna Margaret (Keck) B.; m. Dian Oldemeyer, Nov. 21, 1970; children—David, Michael, John. B.A. cum laude, Knox Coll., Galesburg, Ill., 1965; M.B.A., U. Calif., Berkeley, 1971. With data processing div. IBM Corp., Chgo., 1966; with No. Trust Co., Chgo., 1971-72; mgr. treasury ops., then treas. fin. services group Borg-Warner Corp., Chgo., 1972-79; treas. W.W. Grainger, Inc., Skokie, Ill., 1979-83, v.p., 1984—. Served to lt. USNR, 1966-69. Mem. Econ. Club Chgo., Beta Gamma Sigma, Phi Delta Theta. Lutheran. Office: 5500 W Howard St Skokie IL 60077

BARTHELMAS, NED KELTON, investment banker; b. Circleville, Ohio, Oct. 22, 1927; s. Arthur and Mary Bernice (Riffel) B.; m. Marjorie Jane Livezey, May 23, 1953; children: Brooke Ann, Richard Thomas. B.S. in Bus. Adminstrn., Ohio State U., 1950. Stockbroker Ohio Co., Columbus, 1953-58; pres. First Columbus Corp., 1958—; pres., dir. Ohio Fin. Corp., Columbus, 1960—; trustee, chmn. Am. Guardian Fin., Republic Fin.; dir. Nat. Foods, Liebert Corp., Midwest Capital Corp., Lancaster Colony Corp., Capital Equity Corp., Franklin Nat. Corp., Midwest Nat. Corp., 1st Columbus Realty Corp., Court Realty Co., all Columbus. Served with Adj. Gen.'s Dept. AUS, 1945-47. Mem. Nat. Assn. Securities Dealers (past vice chmn. dist. bd. govs.), Investment Bankers Assn. Am. (exec. com. 1973), Investment Dealers Ohio (sec., treas. 1956-72, pres. 1973), Nat. Stock Traders Assn., Young Pres.'s Orgn. (pres. 1971), Nat. Investment Bankers (pres. 1973), Columbus Jr. C. of C. (pres. 1956), Ohio Jr. C. of C. (trustee 1957-58), Columbus Area C. of C. (dir. 1956, named an Outstanding Young Man of Columbus 1962), Newcomen Soc., Phi Delta Theta. Clubs: Kiwanis, Execs., Stock and Bond, Columbus, Scioto Country (Columbus); Crystal Downs Country (Frankfort, Mich.). Home: 1000 Urlin Ave Columbus OH 43212 Summer Home: 6498 Bixler Rd Beulah MI 49617

BARTHENHEIER, KAREN ANN, interior designer; b. Racine, Wis., Feb. 19, 1959; d. Fred and Nancy Ann (Amrock) B. BS in Interior Design, U. Wis., 1981. Interior designer Devenish Assocs., Inc., Madison, 1981-82, Brust-Heike Design Assocs., Inc., Milw., 1982-83, Forrer Bus. Interiors, Milw., 1984—. Mem. Inst. Bus. Designs (v.p. membership Wis. Chpt.). Republican. Roman Catholic. Avocations: weaving, golf, tennis, skiing, biking. Office: Forrer Bus Interiors 180 N Jefferson Milwaukee WI 53202

BARTHOLD, CLEMENTINE B., judge; b. Odessa, Russia, Jan. 11, 1921; came to U.S., 1925; d. Joseph Anton and Magdalene (Richter) Schwan; m. Edward Brendel Barthold, July 5, 1941 (dec.); children—Judith Anne Barthold DeSimone, John Edward; m. 2d, Joel L. Stokes, Jr., Feb. 7, 1981. Student Aberdeen Bus. Coll., 1940; B.G.S., Ind. U. Southeast, 1978; J.D.,

Ind. U.-Indpls., 1980. Bar: Ind. 1980, U.S. Dist. Ct. (so. dist.) Ind., 1980. Sec. and asst. to mgr. Clark County C. of C. (Ind.), 1959-60; chief probation officer Clark Circuit Ct. and Superior Cts., Jeffersonville, 1960-72; research cons. Pub. Action Correctional Effort, Clark and Floyd Counties, 1972-75; instl. parole officer Ind. Women's Prison, Indpls., 1975-80; atty. State of Ind., 1980-83; judge Clark Superior Ct. No. 1, Jeffersonville, 1983—. Active in developing and implementing juvenile delinquency prevention and alternative programs, group counseling for juvenile delinquents and restitution programs; mem. Ind. Juvenile Justice Task Force. Treas. Ladies Elks Aux., Jeffersonville. Recipient Good Govt. award Jeffersonville Jaycees, 1966, also Good Citizenship award, 1967; Wonder Woman award, 1984, Robert J. Kinsey award, 1986, Sagamore of Wabash award, 1986, Outstanding Community Service award Social Concerns League, Jeffersonville, 1966, Disting. Service award, Outstanding Contbn. to Field of Correction award, Women of Achievement award, Jeff BPW Appreciation award, Juvenile Justice award, Disting. Contemporary Women in History award, Disting. Leadership award. Mem. ABA, Ind. Bar Assn., Clark County Bar Assn., Ind. Correctional Assn. (pres. 1971, Disting. Service award 1967, 85), Nat. Assn. Women Judges, Ind. Judges Assn., Ind. Juvenile and Family Ct. Judges, Jefferson County Women Lawyers Assn., Am. Bus. Women's Assn, NAACP, Jeff Preservation, Inc., Clark County C. of C., Older Women's League, Ind. U. Alumni Assn., Howard Steamboat Mus., LWV, Bus. and Profl. Women's Club. Democrat. Roman Catholic. Home: 948 E 7th St Jeffersonville IN 47130 Office: Clark Superior Ct No 1 500 E Court Ave Jeffersonville IN 47130

BARTHOLOMAY, WILLIAM C., insurance brokerage company executive, professional baseball team executive; b. Evanston, Ill., Aug. 11, 1928; s. Henry C. and Virginia (Graves) B.; m. Gail Dillingham, May 1968 (div. Apr. 1980); children—Virginia, William T., Jamie, Elizabeth, Sara. Student, Oberlin Coll., 1946-49, Northwestern U., 1949-50; B.A., Lake Forest Coll., 1955. Ptnr. Bartholomay & Clarkson, Chgo., 1951-63; v.p. Alexander & Alexander, Chgo., 1963-65; pres. Olson & Bartholomay, Chgo. and Atlanta, 1965-69; sr. v.p. Frank B. Hall & Co. Inc., N.Y.C. and Chgo., 1969-72, exec. v.p., 1972-73, pres., 1973-74, vice chmn., 1974—; chmn. bd., dir. Atlanta Braves, 1966—; bd. dirs. Turner Broadcasting System, Inc., Atlanta, Nat. Security Bank, Chgo., WMS Industries Inc., Chgo., Frank B. Hall & CO. Inc. Commr. Chgo. Park Dist., 1980—; bd. dirs. Chgo. Maternity Ctr.; bd. govs. Sarah Siddons Soc., Chgo.; former trustee Lake Forest Coll., Ill., Ogelthorpe Coll., Atlanta; trustee Marymount Manhattan Coll., N.Y. Served with USNR, 1951-54. Mem. Million Dollar Round Table (life), Chief Execs. Orgn., World Bus. Council, Chgo. Pres.'s Orgn., Nat. Assn. CLU's, Chgo. Assn. CLU's. Episcopalian. Clubs: Chicago, Racquet, Saddle and Cycle, Economic (Chgo.); Onwentsia, Shoreacres (Lake Forest); Economic, Brook, Links, Racquet & Tennis, Doubles (N.Y.C.); Piedmont Driving, Atlanta Country, Peachtree Golf, Commerce (Atlanta). Home: 180 E Pearson St Chicago IL 60611

BARTHOLOMEW, DAVID ALAN, electrical engineer; b. Clinton, Ind., Jan. 8, 1952; s. Don Wayne and Alice Irene (Hannafin) B.; m. Carol Lynn Potts, July 4, 1982 (div. Apr. 1984); children: Bobbi Jo, David Alan Jr., Shawn Kenneth, Kelly Amanda Marie, Alitia Dawn; m. Nilda M. Hertzlieb, Feb. 1, 1987; stepchildren: Norma Hertzlieb, Maria Hertzlieb, Lisa Hertzlieb. BEE, Purdue U., 1974. Elec. engr. Cen. Foundry div. Gen. Motors, Defiance, Ohio, 1976-77, maintenance foreman, 1977-78, pre-prodn. engr., 1978-79; elec. engr. No. Ind. Pub. Service Co., Hammond, Ind., 1979-83, computer engr., 1983—. Deacon Presbyn. Ch., Crown Point, Ind., 1983-85. Mem. IEEE. Club: Hammond Pub. Service. Lodge: Kiwanis. Avocations: bass guitar, volleyball, raquetball, tennis, swimming. Home: 23527 Fillmore St PO Box 36 Shelby IN 46377 Office: No Ind Pub Service Co 5265 Hohman Ave Hammond IN 46320

BARTHOLOMEW, DONALD DELKE, inventor, business executive, engineer; b. Atlanta, Aug. 2, 1929; s. Rudolph A. and Rubye C. (Delke) B.; m. Paula Hagood; children: John Marshall, Barbara Ann, Deborah Paige, Sandra Dianne. Student in Physics, Ga. Inst. Tech., 1946-48, 55-58. Owner Happy Cottons and Jalopy Jungle, Atlanta, 1946-48, Beach Hotel Supply, Miami Beach, Fla., 1949-50; engr. Sperry Microwave Electronics, Clearwater, Fla., 1958-61; v.p., owner Draft Pak, Inc., Tampa, Fla., 1961-65, Merit Plastics, Inc., East Canton, Ohio, 1966-79; pres., owner Modern Tech., Inc., Marine City, Mich., 1979—; owner, officer and dir. various internat. mfg. companies, 1981—. Patentee in field. Served to sgt. USAF, 1951-54. Mem. Soc. Automotive Engrs., Soc. Plastics Engrs. (dir. 1982), Soc. Mfg. Engrs., Holiday Isles Jr. C. of C. (founding dir.). Republican.

BARTL, GEORGE RICHARD, neurology surgeon; b. Detroit, Sept. 13, 1937; m. Carol Wiedbusch, Sept. 2, 1961; children: Betty, Catherine, Lynn. BS, Wayne State U., 1960, MD, 1964. Intern Grace Hosp., Detroit, 1964-65; resident in neurosurgery Wayne State U., Detroit, 1965-71; mem. staff Neurologic Assocs. of Waukesha (Wis.), Ltd., 1971—. Fellow ACS; mem. Congress Neurol. Surgeons, Wis. Neurol. Soc. (pres. 1983-84). Office: Neurologic Assocs Waukesha Ltd 1111 Delafield St Waukesha WI 53188

BARTLAM, RAYMOND EDWARD, mechanical engineer; b. Pitts., Aug. 3, 1943; s. Edward James and Anna Mary (Holzer) B.; m. Virginia Anne Canfield, May 25, 1968; children: Eric Raymond, Noelle Virginia. BS in Mech. Tech., U. Akron, Ohio, 1980. Quality control engr. Babcock & Wilcox, Lynchburg, Va., 1980-85; project engr. Inland div. Gen. Motors Co., Dayton, Ohio, 1985—. Served as cpl. USMC, 1961-65. Home: 7891 Manning Rd Miamisburg OH 45342 Office: Gen Motors Inland Div 2701 Home Ave Dayton OH 45401

BARTLESON, JOHN DAVID, JR., neurologist; b. Cleve., Mar. 18, 1947; m. Barbara Ellen Wrieden, Dec. 29, 1970; children: John, Jeffrey, Peter. BS, Northwestern U., 1969, MD, 1971. Diplomate Am. Bd. Psychiatry and Neurology. Intern Evanston (Ill.) Hosp., 1971-72; resident in neurology U. Mich., Ann Arbor, 1972-75; sect. head dept. neurology Mayo Clinic, Rochester, Minn., 1984—, cons. in neurology, 1977—. Contbr. articles to profl. and scholarly jours. Served to maj. U.S. Army, 1975-77. Fellow Am. Acad. Neurology, Stroke Council of Am. Heart Assn.; mem. Am. Assn. for Study of Headache, Minn. Soc. Neurol. Scis. Home: 2303 Crest Ln SW Rochester MN 55902 Office: Mayo Clinic 200 SW 1st St Rochester MN 55905

BARTLETT, BUD (BYRON ALLAN), TV executive; b. Las Vegas, Nev., Feb. 14, 1940; s. Byron Edwin and Yvonne (Lodwick) B.; B.A. in Radio-TV, Ariz. State U., 1963; M.A. in Radio-TV-Film, U. Denver, 1967. Producer Sta. KAET-TV, Phoenix, 1963-65; producer, instr. So. Ill. U. Broadcasting Service, stas. WSIU-TV, WUSI-TV, WSIU Radio, Carbondale, 1966-71; instructional TV specialist TV sect. Ill. State Bd. Edn., Springfield, 1971—; pres. Springfield Ednl. Communications Assn., 1977-78, producer, writer 41 public TV programs and ednl. films including; A Tale of Two Builders, Number Please and Sifting the Sands of Time, 1963—; co-producer: Survival in Auschwitz; author: By Wave and Wire, 1974; contbr. articles to profl. jours. Served with U.S. Army, 1963. Nevada Alexander Hamilton Bicentennial scholar, 1957. Mem. Nat. Writers Club, Nat. Assn. State Ednl. Media Profls. Home: 520 S 2d St Apt 1102 Springfield IL 62701 Office: 100 N 1st St Springfield IL 62777

BARTLETT, D. BROOK, federal judge; b. 1937. B.A., Princeton U., 1959; LL.B., Stanford U., 1962. Assoc. Stinson, Mag, Thomson, McEvers & Fizzell, 1962-67, ptnr., 1967-69; asst. atty. gen. Mo., 1969-73, 1st asst. atty. gen., 1973-77; assoc. Blackwell, Sanders, Matheny, Weary & Lombardi, 1977-78, ptnr., 1978-81; judge U.S. Dist. Ct. (we. dist.) Mo., Kansas City, 1981—. Office: U S Dist Ct US Courthouse 811 Grand Ave Room 654 Kansas City MO 64106 *

BARTLETT, DAVID E., veterinarian; b. Bloomfield, N.J., Mar. 18, 1917; s. Clarence Durand and Grace (Zeliff) B.; m. Marjorie Cooper Heiner, July 22, 1945; children: David Heiner, Paul Cooper. DVM, Colo. State U., 1940; PhD, U. Minn., 1952. Diplomate Am. Coll. Theriogenologists (pres. 1971-73). Veterinarian USDA, Beltsville, Md., 1940-48; commd. veterinary med. officer USPHS, 1948; instr. vet. medicine U. Minn., St. Paul, 1948-52; v.p. Am. Breeders Service, DeForest, Wis., 1953-78; lectr. Cen. Univ., Maracay, Venezuela, 1978; cons. Internat. Cooperation Adminstrn., Porto Alegre, Brazil, 1958, AID, Terceira, Azores, 1979, FAO, Rome, 1981. Author 75 scientific publs. Bd. mem. Oakwood Found., 1982—, Oakwood Village Retirement Apts., Madison, 1980—. Recipient Alumni award Colo. State U., 1976; David E. Bartlett Lecture Award named in his honor Am. Coll. Theriogenologists, 1984, delivered inaugural lecture. Mem. AVMA (Borden award 1970), Wis. Veterinary Med. Assn. (Meritorious Service award 1977), Nat. Assn. Animal Breeders (Disting. Service award 1980). Republican. Lutheran. Lodges: Masons, Rotary, Shriners. Home and Office: 6240 S Highlands Ave Madison WI 53705

BARTLETT, FREDERICK PAUL, JR., architect; b. Saginaw, Mich., July 29, 1959; s. Frederick Paul and Sharon Kay (Leaman) B.; m. Julie Mae Kennedy, July 7, 1979; children: Aaron Frederick, Spencer Leaman. BS in Architecture, Lawrence Inst. Tech., 1982. Archtl. draftsman Michael L. Oxman & Assocs., Reston, Va., 1982, John Keegan Assocs., Falls Church, Va., 1982, Cumberland Corp., Reston, Va., 1982-85, Dow-Howell-Gilmore Assocs., Midland, Mich., 1985-86, Wakely, Hacker Assocs., Bay City, Mich., 1986—. Mem. AIA (assoc.). Avocations: geneology, camping, fishing. Home: 187 S 6th Box 379 Freeland MI 48623 Office: Wakely Hacker Assocs Suite 202 Davidson Bldg 916 Washington Ave Bay City MI 48708

BARTLETT, JAMES T., manufacturing company executive. Pres., chief operating officer Acme-Cleve. Corp. Office: Acme-Cleveland Corp 30195 Chagrin Blvd Cleveland OH 44124 *

BARTLETT, LARRY DEAN, law educator; b. Denision, Iowa, May 26, 1942; s. Verl George and Lois Marie (Skarin) B.; m. Sally Stoll, Aug. 1, 1964 (div. Mar. 1986); children: Bradley Winston, Matthew Benjamin. BA, U. No. Iowa, 1964; JD, U. Nebr., 1974; PhD, Iowa State U., 1983. Tchr., dept. chmn. Omaha Pub. Schs., 1964-71; legal cons. Iowa Dept. Edn., Des Moines, 1971-85; asst. prof. U. Iowa, Iowa City, 1985—; state hearing officer Dept. Edn., Des Moines, 1985—, practices com. Iowa Profl. Teaching, Des Moines, 1985—. Contbr. articles to profl. jours. vice chmn. adv. com. Govs. Juvenile Justice Dept., Des Moines, 1982—. Mem. Nat. Orgn. for Legal Problems in Edn., Univ. Council for Ednl. Adminstrn. (plenary rep. 1985—). Democrat. Episcopalian. Avocations: tennis, sports, child advocacy. Office: U Iowa 210 Lindquist Ctr Iowa City IA 52242

BARTLETT, MICHAEL SHOFNER, pharmaceutical company executive consultant; b. Shelbyville, Tenn., Nov. 22, 1954; s. Ottie and Emily (Johnston Shofner) B.; m. Jan Marie Hickmott; 1 child, Emily. BS in Biology, Middle Tenn. State U., 1977, BS in Agr. and Animal Husbandry, 1977, postgrad. in Bus. Adminstrn., 1978-79. Supr. quality assurance Swan Drugs div. CMC, Inc., Smyrna, Tenn., 1978-79, asst. mgr. to mgr. quality assurance, 1979-81; supr. quality assurance Key Pharms., Inc., Miami, Fla., 1981-82, prodn. mgr., 1982-83; quality assurance dir. Labeltape-Meditect, Inc., Grand Rapids, Mich., 1983—; cons. Orgn. of Quality Assurance Depts., 1981—; owner Pharm. Cons. Co.-Pharm. Co. Mem. Am. Soc. Quality Control (regional dir. 1983, exec. com. 1982, govt. com. 1982), Nat. Rifle Assn., Kappa Alpha. Republican. Methodist. Club: Nat. Grotto. Home: PO Box 8741 Grand Rapids MI 49508 Office: Labeltape-Meditect Inc 4275 Airwest Dr Grand Rapids MI 49508

BARTLETT, PAUL D., JR., agribusiness executive; b. Kansas City, Mo., Sept. 16, 1919; s. Paul D. and Alice May (Hiestand) B.; m. Joan Jenkins, May 14, 1949; children—J. Alison Bartlett Jager, Marilyn, Paul Dana III, Frederick Jenkins. B.A., Yale U., 1941. Chmn. Bartlett and Co., Grain, Kansas City, Mo., 1961-77; pres., chmn. bd. Bartlett Agri Enterprises, Inc., Kansas City, 1977—; dir. United Mo. Bank, United Mo. Bancshares. Served to lt. USN, 1942-46. Office: Bartlett and Co 4800 Main St Suite 600 Kansas City MO 64112

BARTLETT, PETER GREENOUGH, engineering company executive; b. Manchester, N.H., Apr. 22, 1930; s. Richard Cilley and Dorothy (Pillsbury) B.; Ph.B., Northwestern U., 1955; m. Jeanne Eddes, July 8, 1954 (dec. 1980); children—Peter G., Marta, Lauren, Karla, Richard E.; m. Kathleen Organ, Aug. 25, 1984. Engr., Westinghouse Electric Co., Balt., 1955-58; mgr. mil. communications Motorola, Inc., Chgo., 1958-60; pres. Bartlett Labs., Inc., Indpls., 1960-63; assoc. prof. elec. engring. U. S.C., Columbia, 1963-64; dir. research Eagle Signal Co., Davenport, Iowa, 1964-67; div. mgr. Struthers-Dunn, Inc., Bettendorf, Iowa, 1967-74; pres. Automation Systems, Inc., Eldridge, Iowa, 1974, also dir. Mem. IEEE. Republican. Presbyterian. Patentee in field. Home: 2336 E 11th St Davenport IA 52803 Office: Lancer Park Eldridge IA 52748

BARTLETT, ROGER DANFORTH, engineering executive; b. Brentwood, Mo., Dec. 19, 1949; s. Robert Danforth and Margaret Elizabeth (Gruber) B.; m. Cynthia A. Adkins, July 1, 1978; children—Rex Danforth, Ryan Andrew, Megan Leigh. B.S. in E.E., Bradley U., Peoria, Ill., 1971. Engr., Revomat, Parkville, Mo., 1971-72; div. engr. Am. Multi-Cinema, Inc., Kansas City, Mo., 1972-75, project mgr., 1975-78, assoc. dir. corp. engring., 1978-82, dir. corp. engring., 1982-85; dir. constrn. Commonwealth Theatres, Inc., 1985—. Mem. IEEE, Constrn. Specifications Inst., Nat. Fire Protection Assn. Home: 8701 W 72d St Merriam KS 66204 Office: Commonwealth Theatres Inc 215 W 18th St Kansas City MO 64108

BARTLETT, SHIRLEY ANNE, accountant; b. Gladwin, Mich., Mar. 28, 1933; d. Dewey J. and Ruth Elizabeth (Wright) Frye; m. Charles Duane Bartlett, Aug. 16, 1952 (div. Sept. 1982); children: Jeanne, Michelle, John, Yvonne. Student, Mich. State U., 1952-53, Rutgers U., 1972-74. Auditor State of Mich., Lansing, 1951-66; cost acct. Templar Co., South River, N.J., 1968-75; staff acct. Franco Mfg. Co., Metuchen, N.J., 1975-78; controller Thomas Creative Apparel, New London, Ohio, 1978-80; mgr. gen. acctg. Ideal Electric Co., Mansfield, Ohio, 1980-85; staff acct. Logangate Homes, Inc., Girard, Ohio, 1985—; pvt. practice acctg. Youngstown, 1985—; v.p. Lang Industries, Inc., Youngstown, 1984—. Author: (play) Our Bicentennial-A Celebration, 1976. Soloist various orchestras, Mich., Va.; mem. Human Relations Commn., Franklin Township, 1971-77; treas. Heritage Found., New Brunswick, N.J., 1973-74, New London Proceeds Corp., 1979-83; commr. Huron Park Commn., Ohio, 1979-83; elected Dem. com. mem., N.J., Ohio, 1970-82. Mem. NOW (treas. Youngstown 1986—), Am. Soc. Women Accts. (bd. dirs. 1986—), Nat. Assn. Female Execs., Bus. and Profl. Women (v.p. 1980—). Democrat. Unitarian. Club: Franklin JFK (treas. 1970-72, v.p. 1973-78), Chataqua Literary, Scientific Circle (pres. 1979—). Avocations: music, knitting, needlecrafts. Home: 4793 Ardmore Ave Youngstown OH 44505-1101 Office: Logangate Homes Inc 1200 S State St Girard OH 44420

BARTLETT, VIRGIL LOUIS, emeritus teacher educator; b. Roswell, N.Mex., Mar. 20, 1916; s. Brant Louis and Elsie Mert (Allee) B.; B.A., Andrews U., 1944; M.A., Tex. Christian U., 1947; Ed.D. (fellow), Ball State U., 1970; m. Frances Irene May, July 3, 1939; children—Verlyne May, Sandra Ann. Book and Bible house mgr. Texico Conf. of Seventh Day Adventists, 1944-45; head bus. adminstrn. dept. Southwestern Jr. Coll., Keene, Tex., 1945-48; prin. Union Springs (N.Y.) Acad., 1948-51; bus. mgr. Philippine Union Coll., Manila, 1951-52; pres. Mountain View Coll., Malaybalay, Philippines, 1952-55; ordained to ministry Seventh-day Adventist Ch., 1956; ednl. supt., treas. Far Eastern Island Mission, Agana, Guam, 1955-56; prin. Sheyenne River Acad., Harvey, N.D., 1956-59; prin. Ind. Acad., Cicero, 1959-68; ch. pastor, Muncie, Ind., 1968-69; coordinator tchr. edn., dir. student tchrs. Andrews U., Berrien Springs, Mich., 1970-83, prof. emeritus, 1983—. Mem. Phi Delta Kappa. Republican. Club: Lions (pres.). Home: 2719 Willo Dr Berrien Springs MI 49103 Office: Bell Hall Andrews U Berrien Springs MI 49104

BARTLETT, WILLIAM R., II, real estate executive; b. Michigan City, Ind., July 26, 1944; s. William R. and Marjorie K. (Kubsch) B.; m. Pamela Anne Wise, Feb. 14, 1981 (div.); children: Amanda Catherine, William R. III, Jacob Ryan. BS, Western Ky. U., 1966. V.p. Bartlett Wright & Assocs., Evansville, Ind., 1973-82; pres. Bartlett & Assocs., Inc., Evansville, 1982-85; v.p. Appraisal Co., Inc., Evansville, 1985—. Named Kentucky Col. Mem. Am. Inst. Real Estate Appraisers, Soc. Real Estate Appraisers (v.p. Evansville chpt. 1986, pres. 1983), Ind. Assn. Realtors, Ky. Assn. Realtors. Episcopalian. Lodge: Elks. Avocations: boating, fishing. Office: Appraisa Co Inc 528 Main St Evansville IN 47708

BARTLETTE, DONALD LLOYD, social worker, counselor, educator, consultant, public speaker, lay minister; b. Walhalla, N.D., Dec. 17, 1939; s. Abraham Bruno and Lily Alice (Houle) B.; Ph.B., U. N.D., 1962; M.A., N.D. State U., 1966; Ph.D., C.P.U., 1981; m. Julie Gay Poer, Feb. 1, 1969; children—Lisa Maaca, Joanna Leigh, Andrea Gay, Marisa Anne, Laura Bethany, Sara Elizabeth, Seth VanAdams. Camp worker, program dir. Camp Grassick, N.D., 1957-62; Unit supr., counselor Cambridge State Sch. and Hosp., 1963-64; group worker Children's Village, Fargo, N.D., 1964-65; supr. Meth. Children's Village, Detroit, 1966-68; program dir. Mich. Children's Inst., Ann Arbor, 1968-70; exec., program dir. Madison County (Ind.) Assn. for Retarded, 1970-71; dir. program and social work services Outreach Community Center, Mpls., 1972-73; exec. dir. Minn. Epilepsy League, St. Paul, 1974-75; pvt. cons. in retardation, 1972-75; coordinator spl. services, adviser Human Rights Commn. City of Bloomington (Minn.), 1975-78; assoc. pastor, dir. social services Am. Indian Evang. Ch., Mpls., 1978-79; dir. social services Stark County (Ohio) Bd. Mental Retardation, 1979-80; field work instr. Sch. Social Work, U. Minn., Augsburg Coll., Mpls., 1972-73; off-campus tchr. in retardation and social work Anderson Coll., 1970-71; adj. faculty Univ. Without Walls, U. Minn., 1972-73. Founder Bartlette Scholarship award U. N.D., 1971-75; pres. Nat. Minority Affairs Coalition, 1977-78, sec., 1976-77; mem. Met. Developmental Disabilities Task Force, 1975; chmn. Pub. Info. Coalition Project on Developmental Disabilities, 1974-75; vol. mem. Pres.'s, Minn. Gov.'s coms. on employment handicapped; task force minority affairs Pres.'s Com. Mental Retardation. Bd. dirs. N.W. Hennepin Human Services Council, 1975-76; bd. dirs., chmn. poverty com. Anoka County Assn. for Retarded, 1974-79; bd. dirs. Family and Childrens Services of Greater Mpls., Stark County Mental Health Bd., Citizen Advocacy Program of Stork County; cons. People First of Stark County; adv. Indian children Council for Exceptional Children; patron and com. mem. Lake Center Christian Sch., Hartville, Ohio; trustee Cuyahoga Valley Christian Acad., 1985—; adv. cons. Christian Berets, Keystone Acad. and Navajo Missions; mem. adv. bd. Mentor, Inc., Ohio; speaker Assn. Christian Schs. Internat.; founder travel ministry, 1974—. Fellow Acad. Ednl. Disciplines; mem. Am. Acad. Mental Retardation, Nat. Assn. Christian Social Workers, Nat. Assn. Retarded Citizens (dir., chmn. com. on poverty and mental retardation 1973-74), Internat. Platform Assn., Assn. Am. Indian Social Workers, Soc. for Protection Unborn through Nutrition (life mem.), Reading Reform Found., Am. Coalition Citizens with Disabilities, Focus on Family, Internat. Inst. for Christian Sch. Tchrs., Christian Home Educators Ohio, Phi Delta Kappa, Kappa Delta Pi. Club: 700. Author presentation: Macaroni at Midnight; film participant Believing for the Best in You, 1985. Focus of play Macaroni at Midnight, Erie, Pa., 1986. Home: 2602 Ocelot NE North Canton OH 44721

BARTLEY, DIANA ESTHER RIVERA, educator; b. N.Y.C., May 18, 1940; d. Manuel Peláez Rivera and Lila Esther Camacho; cert. in French, U. Fribourg (Switzerland), 1960; B.A., Rosemont Coll., 1961; cert. in Italian, U. Florence, 1962; M.A., Middlebury Coll., 1963; A.M., Stanford U., 1964, Ph.D., 1970; research scholar U. Leningrad (USSR), Hertzen Pedagogical Inst., Leningrad, 1967-68, U. Moscow and First Moscow State Pedagogical Inst. Fgn. Langs., 1968, U. Helsinki, 1967; 1 son. Tchr., USIA Bi-Nat. Center, Madrid, 1961-62; tchr. French and Spanish, Fairfield (Conn.) Sch. Dist., 1963, Palo Alto (Calif.) Unified Sch. Dist., 1964-66; research asst. Ctr. R&D in Teaching, Stanford U., 1966-69; instr. dept. Spanish and Portuguese, U. Wis.-Milw., 1969-70, asst. prof. dept. curriculum and instrn., 1970-73, asso. prof., 1973-78, 80—, fed. project dir., 1970-78; vis. prof. U. Ala., Tuscaloosa, 1986, dir. summer immersion program, 1986; cons., lectr. in field; mem. nat. rev. panels U.S. Office Edn. and U.S. Dept. Edn., 1975, 77, 80, 81, 82, 83, 84, 85-87; mem. scholar diplomat seminar U.S. Dept. State, 1981. Bd. dirs. Florentine Opera Aux., Milw., 1973-76, Literacy Services of Wis., 1974-76, Centro del Nino, Inc., Milw., 1982-84; con. Mequon-Ruensville Recreation Dept., New World Montessori Sch., Fox Point; past mem. Jr. League, Milw.; mem. bd. Mequon PTA, 1981-83; other civic activities USIA visitor to Bulgaria, 1979. Fulbright Hays Sr. Fellow U. Warsaw (Poland), 1978-80, Ministry, Edn., Sofia, Bulgaria, 1980. Mem. Am. Council Teaching Fgn. Langs., Am. Assn. Tchrs. French, Am. Assn. Tchrs. Spanish and Portuguese, MLA, Nat. Assn. Bilingual Edn., Am. Ednl. Research Assn., AAUW, TESOL, Wis. TESOL Assn., Fulbright Alumni Assn. Author numerous books and monographs, including: The Latin Child Goes Forth, Bilingual Early Education Experience Based Lessons, 1975; The Adult Basic Education TESOL Handbooks, 1979; contbr. numberous articles to profl. jours. Third place Helen H. Heffernan scholar, 1966. Office: Univ Wis Sch Edn Dept Curriculum PO Box 413 Milwaukee WI 53201

BARTLING, CHARLES EDWIN, finance company executive; b. DeLand, Fla., Aug. 25, 1938; s. Edwin Phillip and Mabel Emma (Brooks) B.; m. Ann Louise Sisinger, Sept. 2, 1967; children: Hugh Edwin, Allison Brooks. BA, U. Fla., 1959; MS, Northwestern U., 1962. Fin. editor Jacksonville (Fla.) Journal, 1963-64; midwest bur. chief Am. Banker, Chgo., 1964-68; v.p. Teach 'em, Inc., Chgo., 1970-73; pres. CEBAR Communications, Inc., Evanston, Ill., 1973-78; v.p. Bank Mktg. Assn., Chgo., 1978—. Mem. Am. Soc. Assn. Execs., Am. Soc. Bus. Press Editors (hon. lifetime exec. v.p.), Pub. Relations Soc. Am., Issues Mgmt. Assn., Soc. Nat. Assn. Pubs., Chgo. Soc. Assn. Execs. Home: 2923 Lincoln St Evanston IL 60201 Office: Bank Mktg Assn 309 W Washington St Chicago IL 60606

BARTLING, KIM KEVIN, banker, accountant; b. Waterloo, Iowa, Jan. 12, 1958; s. Lynn and Margaret Edna (Ford) B.; 1 child, Stephanie Jo. BA in Acctg. with high honors, U. No. Iowa, 1982. CPA, Iowa. Staff acct., auditor McGladrey Hendrickson & Pullen CPA's, Davenport, Iowa, 1982-85; v.p., chief fin. officer First Nat. Bank, Muscatine, Iowa, 1985—. Dir. Muscatine Community workship, 1986—. Mem. Am. Inst. CPA's, Iowa Soc. CPA's. Avocations: sports, reading.

BARTMAN, HERBERT MARVIN, electrical engineer; b. Sheboygan, Wis., May 26, 1923; s. John and Lena (Frei) Pluskat; B.S. in Elec. Engring., U. Wis., 1950; postgrad. Ohio State U. 1964-72; M.S. in Engring. Mgmt., U. Dayton, 1979; m. Alma A. Glanert, Sept. 3, 1949; children—Douglas M., Debra A., Margarett L. Project scientist communications lab. Wright Patterson AFB, Ohio, 1951-61, sr. project engr. Air Force avionics lab., 1961-70, prin. electronic engr., avionics lab., 1970-79, Air Force aero. lab., 1980-85; fed. annuitant, 1985—; lectr. Sinclair Community Coll., 1985—. Asst. scoutmaster, instl. rep. Miami Valley Council Boy Scouts Am., 1962-72; mem. bd. evangelism Concordia Evang. Luth. Ch., 1980-82, chmn. Bd. Christian Edn., 1982—. Served with AUS, 1943-46, USAF, 1950-51. Mem. IEEE, Air Force Assn., Sigma Xi. Asso. editor IEEE Electromagnetic Compatibility Transactions, 1971-83. Home: 5303 Middlebury Rd Dayton OH 45432

BARTO, JOSEPH ALLAN, psychology, educator; b. Valentine, Nebr., Jan. 28, 1922; s. Joel monte and Florence Mae (Cunard) B.; m. Vivian Eileen Tiemens, June 3, 1950; 1 child, Craig Joel. BS, Nebr. State Coll., 1949; MEd, U. Nebr., 1954, DEd, 1966. Cert. psychologist, Kans. Tchr. math., sci. Valentine (Nebr.) High Sch., 1950-52, Nebr. City High Sch., 1952-56; prin. Correctionville (Iowa) High Sch., 1956-57, Ashland (Nebr.) High Sch., 1957-58; asst. prof. edn. Nebr. State Coll., Chadron, 1958-62; prof. psychology Emporia (Kans.) State U., 1964-85, prof. emeritus, cons., 1985—. Served to sgt. USAF, 1942-45, ETO. Republican. Methodist. Avocation: electronics. Address: 947 Oxford Dr Emporia KS 66801

BARTOLOMEI, MARGARET MARY, community education director, nursing consultant; b. Detroit, Nov. 28, 1933; d. Fred and Mary Dolores (Bonaudo) Colombo; m. Peter Bartolomei, Aug. 18, 1956 (div.); children—Frederick, Edward. B.S. in Nursing, Mercy Coll. Detroit, 1955; M.S. in Edn., U. Mich., 1978, Ph.D. in Edn., 1984. R.N., Mich. Mem. faculty Mercy Sch. Nursing, Detroit, 1955-57; charge nurse St. John Hosp., Detroit, 1958-64; mem. faculty St. Joseph Sch. Practical Nursing, Mt. Clemens, Mich., 1967-70; inservice coordinator Harrison Community Hosp., Mt. Clemens, 1970-73; nursing cons. Qualicare Nursing Ctr., Detroit, 1973-85; tchr., coordinator Fraser (Mich.) High Sch., 1973-85; program asst. leadership devel. program in adminstrn. of vocat. tech. edn. U. Mich., 1979-80; cert. instr. Competency Based Edn.; secondary chairperson for health occupations Macomb Occupational Articulation project; mem. task force on health occupations Mich. Vocat.-Tech. Edn. Service. Recipient John Trytten award; named Mich. Vocat. Tchr. of Yr., Mich. Vocat. Tchr. of Excellence. Mem. Am. Vocat. Assn., Am. Vocat. Edn. Personnel Devel. Assn., Council

Vocat. Edn., Macomb Oakland Coordinators Assn., Mich. Health Occupations Educators (past pres.), Mich. Occupational Edn. Assn. (sec. 1978-86), Mich. Vocat. Coordinators Assn., Mich. Vocat. Curriculum Leaders, Nat. Assn. Health Occupations Tchrs., Phi Delta Kappa, Iota Lambda Sigma. Democrat. Roman Catholic. Club: Prosperity (pres. women's aux.) (Detroit). Co-author: Tuned-in Teaching, 1977. Home: 19442 Rockport Dr Roseville MI 48066 Office: 33466 Garfield Rd Fraser MI 48026

BARTON, BENNIE CARSON, automotive parts manufacturing executive; b. Muncie, Ind., Apr. 24, 1936; s. Kenneth Carson and Pearl Bell (Morgan) B.; m. Joelene Heathery, Sept. 11, 1971. High sch. diploma, Cowan, Ind., 1954. Gen. laborer Warner Machine Products, Muncie, Ind., 1957-63, asst. product. control mgr., 1973-70; mgr. product control Essex and United Tech., Muncie, 1970-75; sales service adminstr. United Technologies, Orleans, Ind., 1975-82; product mgr. after mktg. United Technologies, Dearborn, Mich., 1982-86. Served to sgt. U.S. Army, 1959-61. Republican. Lodge: Moose. Avocations: golf, fishing, camping. Home: 9310 Decatur Detroit MI 48228 Office: United Technologies 5200 Auto Club Dr Dearborn MI 48126

BARTON, BRIAN FREDERICK, engineering and marketing executive; b. Pontiac, Mich., Nov. 8, 1951; s. Ben Frederick Barton and Norma Jean (Martin) Nicholai; children: Michael Robert, Kevin Matthew. BSEE, U. Mich., 1973, MBA, 1985. Engring. mgr. Comshare, Ann Arbor, Mich., 1973-77; engring. dir. MDSI, Ann Arbor, 1977—; engring. and mktg. dir. Applicon, Ann Arbor; cons. Ford Motor Co., Rawsonville, Mich., 1972-73. Patentee in field. Mem. Aimtech, Electrical Industry Assn. (EIA-IE31). Avocations: snow skiing, water skiing, sailing. Home: 9686 Winston Dr Pinckney MI 48169

BARTON, LARRY DAVID, headmaster; b. Searcy, Ark., Oct. 10, 1947; s. David Monroe and Ruby (Akridge) B.; m. Claudia Diane Martin, May 23, 1970; children: Karen Elise, Jason Bernard, Laura Summer, Philip Jerome. BA, Bemidji (Minn.) State U., 1979, MA, 1981, BS, 1985. Cert. secondary tchr. Instr. Bemidji State U., 1979-86; headmaster Heartland Christian Acad., Bemidji, 1986—; cons. Eagle Writing Service, Bemidji, 1980—; mem. N. Country Writing Project, 1981-86. Elder, deacon Christian Life Fellowship, Bemidji. Served with U.S. Army, 1967-71, Vietnam. Avocation: baseball. Home: 2516 Minnesota Ave Bemidji MN 56601 Office: Heartland Christian Acad 9914 Heartland Circle NW Bemidji MN 56601

BARTON, PETER RICHARD, III, communications executive; b. Washington, Apr. 6, 1950; m. Laura Perry. BA, Columbia U., 1971, MS, 1972; postgrad., Harvard U., 1979, MBA, 1982. Mem. gov's staff State of N.Y., 1975-80; sr. v.p. Tele-Communications Inc., Englewood, Colo., 1982-86; pres. Cable Value Network, Mpls., 1986—.

BARTTER, KENNETH LEE, telephone company executive; b. Toledo, Oct. 8, 1932; s. Clarence A. and Hazel D. (Watson) B.; B.A., Ohio State U., 1958, M.A., 1961; m. Loretta J. Hurst, June 27, 1953; children—Sheryl Lea Higgins, Kathleen Ann Meginness, Barbara Lee Wilson, Carolyn J. Prodn. mgr. Sta. WOSU-TV, Columbus, Ohio, 1957-60; mgmt. trainee Gen. Telephone Co. of Ohio, Marion, 1960-62, div. public relations rep., 1962-65, gen. office public relations rep., 1965-67, community relations mgr., 1967—; pres. Bartter & Assocs.; frequent public speaker; speech cons. Mem. exec. bd. Harding Area council Boy Scouts Am., 1968—; bd. dirs. Jr. Achievement of Dover-New Philadelphia, Inc., 1963-65; vice chmn. planning and steering com. for proposed Tuscarawas County Joint Vocat. Sch., 1965; vice chmn. Marion Repeater com., 1979; mem. Marion Econ. Council; trustee Ohio Council Econ. Edn., 1981—. Served with USN, 1951-55. Named Lion of the Yr., Marion Lions, 1974. Mem. Laser Inst. Am., Ind. Telephone Pioneer Assn. (dir. 1978—), Am. Radio Relay League, Nat. Soc. to Prevent Blindness, Marion Area C. of C., Alpha Epsilon Rho. Republican. Presbyterian. Clubs: Marion Amateur Radio, Marion Racquet, Central Ohio Radio, Masons, Shriners, Lions (pres. 1978-79, zone chmn.). Home: 1196 Yorkshire Dr Marion OH 43302 Office: 100 Executive Dr Marion OH 43302

BARTZ, DALE HERBERT, manufacturing executive; b. Milw., Feb. 13, 1959; s. Gene Herbert and Nancy Ruth (Clemence) B.; m. Cheryl Ann Deau, May 4, 1985. BS in Engring. Tech., U. Wis., Platville, 1981. Heat treatment technologist Rexnord Hydraulics Inc., Racine, Wis., 1982; with time study and methods dept. Rexnord Hydraulics Inc., Zanesville, Ohio, 1982; asst. mold designer Rexnord Plastics, Inc., Grafton, Wis., 1982; process engr. Rexnord Bearing, Inc., Downers Grove, Ill., 1982-84, automation project mgr., 1984-85, chief engr. design and mfg. dept., 1985—. Co-inventor ultrasonic welding of composite bearing material. Mem. SME, Naperville Jaycees. Lutheran. Avocations: golf, raquetball, water skiing, auto repair. Home: 106 S Columbia St Naperville IL 60540 Office: Rexnord Bearing Inc 2400 Curtiss Ave Downers Grove IL 60515

BARTZ, DANIEL CLARENCE, data processing executive; b. Watertown, Wis., Feb. 23, 1954; s. Clarence Edward and Phyllis Rose (Appendfeldt) B.; m. Vicki Lyn Yenser, Jan. 7, 1978; children: Joshua, Jonathan, Katrina. BBA in Mgmt. Computer Systems, U. Wis., Whitewater, 1980. Analyst programmer Oscar Mayer, Co., Madison, Wis., 1980-83; programmer Gen. Electric Med. Systems, Milw., 1984-85, sr. programmer, 1985-87, sr. systems analyst, 1987—. Served to sgt. USAF, 1972-76. Methodist. Avocations: hunting, fishing, bowling. Home: 611 S 5th Watertown WI 53094 Office: Gen Electric Med Systems 16335 W Lincoln New Berlin WI 53151

BARWINSKI, RICHARD CONRAD, chemical dependency treatment program director; b. Detroit, Mar. 5, 1951; s. Adam Frank and Jane Charlotte (Mastalerz) B.; m. Jennifer Lynn Pearson, July 12, 1986. BA, Western Mich. U., 1973; MA, U. Mich., 1979. Cert. addictions counselor. Employee counselor Kelsey-Hayes Corp., Romulus, Mich., 1980; therapist Cen. Substance Abuse Services, Warren, Mich., 1980-81; therapist, adminstrv. coordinator, program dir. Eastwood Community Clinics, Detroit, 1981—. Vol. U.S. Peace Corps, Chaiyaphum, Thailand, 1974-76. Mem. Assn. Labor Mgmt. Adminstrs. and Cons. on Alcoholism, Mich. Alcohol and Addiction Assn. (bd. dirs. 1985—). Avocations: travel, art, sports, exercise.

BASAVARAJA, HIRE MATADA, anesthesiologist; b. Bellary, India, Aug. 30, 1944; came to U.S. 1975, naturalized, 1981; s. Gurusanthiah and Nagamma (Nagamma) Hirematada; m. Ratna Basappa, Mar. 11, 1974; 1 child, Vinay. B.S. Veerasaiva Coll., Karnataka, India, 1963; M.D., Mysore Med. Coll., Karnataka, 1969. Diplomate Am. Anesthesiology Bd. Intern Fairview Gen. Hosp., Cleve., 1975-76; resident in anesthesiology Huron Rd. Hosp./Cleve. Clinic, 1976-77, Univ. Hosps. of Cleve., 1977-78; lectr. in anatomy Mysore Med. Coll., 1970-75; anesthesiologist Ball Mem. Hosp., Muncie, Ind., 1978—. Mem. Am. Soc. of Anesthesiology. AMA, Ind. State Med. Assn. Home: 4109 Squire Muncie IN 47304

BASELER, DAVID JOHN, communications executive; b. St. Louis, July 17, 1939; s. L. Lee and Louise H. (Loizeaux) B.; m. Phyllis Diane Hartley, Sept. 23, 1961; children: Katherine, Marcia, Angela. BA in Speech, Wheaton Coll., 1961. Mgr. broadcast standards Sta. WJBK, Detroit, 1965-69; counselor sales personnel Dunhill of Detroit, 1969-70; supr. communications research ctr. Eaton Corp., Southfield, Mich., 1970-78, mgr. mktg. services Brave div., 1978-79; mgr. mktg. communications Transmission div. Eaton Corp., Kalamazoo, 1979-84; v.p. mktg. services The ServiceMaster Co., L.P., Downers Grove, Ill., 1984—; pres. Azimuth Advt., Inc. (subs. The ServiceMaster Co., L.P.), Downers Grove, 1984—. Served to capt. U.S. Army, 1961-63. Avocations: photography, travel. Home: 4217 Main St Downers Grove IL 60515 Office: The ServiceMaster Co LP 2300 Warrenville Rd Downers Grove IL 60515

BASFORD, JAMES ORLANDO, container manufacturing company executive; b. Akron, Ohio, Apr. 17, 1931; s. Napoleon Orlando and Hazel Martha (Fersner) B.; m. Mary Eleanor Hagmeyer, Mar. 16, 1957; children: Jeffrey James, Gregory Robert, Lisa Jean. Student, Kent State U., 1949-51, 55-58. Asst. sales mgr. San Hygene Mfg. Co., Akron, 1958-60; gen. sales mgr. Adjusta Post Mfg., Akron, 1960-64; area sales mgr. Gaylord Container, Columbus, Ohio, 1964-74; v.p. Buckeye Container Co., Wooster, Ohio, 1974-78, pres., 1978—, also bd. dirs.; bd. dirs. Peoples Fed. Savs. Bank, Wooster, United Telephone of Ohio, Mansfield, Ohio. Dir. Boys Village, Smithville, Ohio, 1985—. Served with USAF, 1951-54, Korea. Mem. Wooster C. of C. (bd. dirs. 1977-80). Republican. Lutheran. Club: Wooster Country (pres. 1981-83). Lodge: Rotary (bd. dirs. Wooster club 1978-81). Avocations: golf, tennis, skiing. Home: 1097 Greens View Dr Wooster OH 44691 Office: Buckeye Corrugated Container 326 N Hillcrest Dr Wooster OH 44691

BASGALL, BERNARD A., JR., insurance company executive; b. Chgo., Oct. 15, 1940; s. Bernard A. and Mildred (DeJulius) B.; m. Carolyn Dorothy Austin, June 27, 1964; children: Gregory, Carrie. BA, Ill. Benedictine Coll., 1963. CPCU. Account mgr. Allstate Ins. Co., Northbrook, Ill., 1966-78; v.p. Frank B. Hall & Co., Chgo., 1978-80; mgr. mktg. Argonaut Ins. Co., Chgo., 1980-83; exec. v.p. G.A. Mavon & Co., Hinsdale, Ill., 1983-85; sr. v.p. Fred S. James & Co., Chgo., 1985—. Mem. CPCU Soc. (bd. dirs. Chgo. West Suburban chpt. 1985—). Avocations: sailing, golfing. Office: Fred S James & Co 230 W Monroe St Chicago IL 60606

BASHIAN, CHARLES, publishing executive; b. Phila., Dec. 9, 1927; s. Hagop and Esguhe (Gazoorian) Kojabashian; m. Audrey Joan Schwarzmann, Jan. 25, 1958; children: Alison Hermine, Jack Otto. BA, Kent (Ohio) State U., 1951. V.p. W.G. Holdsworth & Assocs., Cleve., 1964-70; pub. Midwest Purchasing, Cleve., 1970-82; pres. Bashian Pub., Inc., Cleve., 1978—. Served to cpl. U.S. Army, 1946-47. Mem. Bus. Profl. Advt. Assn., Assn. Purchasing Publs. (exec. dir. 1974-76, pres. 1976-82). Democrat. Baptist. Lodges: Shriners, Masons. Office: Bashian Pub Inc 1501 Euclid Ave Cleveland OH 44115

BASHORE, GREGG LEE, accountant; b. Van Wert, Ohio, Feb. 20, 1957; s. Christie Francis and Juanita Virginia (Whitmore) B.; m. Sandra Kay Hurless, Nov. 16, 1985. AA, Internat. Bus. Sch., 1977; BA, St. Francis Coll., 1979. CPA, Ohio. Sr. staff mem. Arend, Laukuf & Stoller, Van Wert, 1979—. Capt. United Way, Van Wert, 1984; bd. dirs. Jr. Achievement, Van Wert, 1986; fin. sec. Cav. Evang. Ch., Van Wert, 1983-86; bd. dirs. West Ohio Youth for Christ, 1985. Mem. Am. Inst. CPA's, Ohio Soc. CPA's. Lodge: Optimists (local pres. 1986-87). Avocations: sports, reading. Home: 1284-C Sunrise Ct Van Wert OH 45891 Office: Arend Laukhuf & Stoller 685 Fox Rd Van Wert OH 45891

BASICH, VLADIMIR WALTER, architect; b. Zagreb, Yugoslavia, Mar. 22, 1934; came to U.S., 1961; s. Juraj and Olga (Cokl) B.; m. Elena Caridad Gonzalez, Apr. 22, 1967; children: Adrian G., Anthony O., Alex M. Degree in architecture, Tech. Sch., Zagreb, 1952; student, U. Architecture, Zagreb, 1952-54. Architect Plumb, Tuckett & Hubbard, Gary, Ind., 1962-63; chief draftsman Kaitis & Summer, Chgo., 1963-65; designer A. Epstein & Sons, Inc., Chgo., 1965-67, project mgr., 1967-74, v.p., 1974—. Founding dir. Croatian Cultural Ctr. Chgo.; active Chgo. Council on Fgn. Relations. Served as cpl. C.E., Yugoslavian Army, 1954-56. Recipient 4 awards for excellence SARA Nat. Design Awards, 1975, 80, 83. Mem. Croatian Acad. Am., Smithsonian Inst. Roman Catholic. Avocations: racquetball, reading, music, chess, travel. Office: A Epstein & Sons Inc 600 W Fulton St Chicago IL 60606

BASILE, FRANK MICHEL, property management company executive; b. New Orleans, Oct. 6, 1939; s. Vincent Charles and Ursula Mary (Sendker) B.; children: Jeffrey, Jason. BBA, Tulane U., 1961. Cert. property mgr.; cert. speaking profl. With Ford Motor Co., 1963-75, gen. field mgr., Indpls., 1971-75; pres. Charisma Publs., Inc., Indpls., 1977—; v.p. Gene Glick Mgmt. Corp., Indpls., 1975—. Author: Come Fly With Me, 1978, Back to Basics with Basile, 1978, Management Company Reporting Structure, 1978, Beyond the Basics, 1980, Professional Multihousing Management, 1981, Flying to Your Success, 1983; also articles; contbg. editor mgmt. Indpls. Bus. Jour.; columnist Ind. Bus. Mag. Pres. Indpls. Free U., 1982-83; internat. bd. dirs. Parents Without Ptnrs., 1977-78; bd. dirs. Ind. Better Bus. Bur. Mem. Nat. Apt. Assn. (v.p. 1980), Nat. Assn. Home Builders, Inst. Real Estate Mgmt. (nat. faculty), Nat. Speakers Assn. (pres. Ind. chpt.), Apt. Assn. Ind. (pres. 1979), Indpls. Sales and Mktg. Execs. (pres. 1981-82), Beta Gamma Sigma. Club: Woodland Springs. Office: 8330 Woodfield Crossing Indianapolis IN 46240

BASILE, ROBERT MANLIUS, geographer, soil scientist, emeritus educator; b. Youngstown, Ohio, Mar. 12, 1916; s. Giustino G. and Minnie H. (Bailey) B.; B.S., Washington and Lee U., 1938; M.S., Mich. State U., 1940; Ph.D., Ohio State U., 1953; m. Anne Judson Webb, May 23, 1945; children—Elizabeth Anne (dec.), L. Lorraine Allison, Karen L. Nofziger. Instr., Northwestern State Coll., Alva, Okla., 1940-42; soil scientist Bur. Reclamation, Huron, S.D., 1947-48, 1950; instr. geography Ohio State Univ., Columbus, 1953-56, asst. prof., 1956-62, assoc. prof., 1962-68, prof., 1968-69; prof. geography U. Toledo, 1969-81, prof. emeritus, 1981—; vis. prof. Ohio U., summer 1952, U. Winnipeg, summer 1960, San Jose State U., summer 1966, U. S.C., summer 1967, U. Wyo., summer 1981. Served with USN, 1942-45. NATO grantee, 1966; Nat. Resources Inst. grantee, 1966-67. Mem. Assn. Ohio Pedologists, Wilderness Soc., Phi Kappa Phi, Gamma Theta Upsilon. Author: A Geography of Soils, 1972; editor: Selected Readings in the Geography of Soils, 1980; illustrator textbook Ohio: The Buckeye State; contbr. articles to profl. jours. Home: 5929 Angleview Ct Sylvania OH 43560 Office: Univ of Toledo Bancroft St Toledo OH 43606

BASKA, JAMES LOUIS, lawyer, wholesale grocery company executive; b. Kansas City, Kans., Apr. 0, 1927; s. John James and Stella Marie (Wilson) B.; m. Juanita Louise Carlson, Oct. 10, 1950; children: Steven James, Scott David. B.S. in Bus. Adminstrn, U. Kans., 1949; J.D., U. Mo., 1960. Bar: Kans. Pres., chief exec. officer Baska Laundry Co., Kansas City, Kans., 1949-62; partner firm Rice & Baska, Kansas City, 1962-76; corporate sec., gen. counsel Asso. Wholesale Grocers Inc., Kansas City, 1976-77; v.p., sec., gen. counsel Asso. Wholesale Grocers Inc., 1977-79, exec. v.p., chief fin. officer, sec., gen. counsel, 1979-84, pres., chief exec. officer, 1984—; pres., chief exec. officer Super Market Developers Inc., Super Market Investment Co. Inc., Grocers Dairy Co. Inc.; dir. United Mo. Bank of Kansas City, N.A. Served with U.S. Army, 1945-47. Mem. Am., Kans., Johnson County, Wyandotte County bar assns. Republican. Roman Catholic. Home: 17405 W 159th St Olathe KS 66061 Office: Associated Wholesale Grocers Inc 5000 Kansas Ave Kansas City KS 66106

BASLER, WILLIAM LAWRENCE, manufacturing executive; b. Highland, Ill., Oct. 19, 1944; s. Carl Henry and Bernice Mary Elizabeth (Gruenenfelder) B.; m. Margaret Louise Armbruster, June 18, 1966; children: Matthew Lawrence, Gregory Scott, Christopher Lee. Student, Lincoln (Ill.) Coll., 1962-64; BS, Hillsdale Coll., 1967. Sales asst., then prodn. control mgr. Basler Electric Co., Highland, Ill., 1967-71, mfg. mgr., 1971-76, adminstrv. asst. to exec. v.p., 1976-84, chmn. bd., chief exec. officer, 1984—; dir. 1st Nat. Bank, Highland, 1984—. Roman Catholic. Clubs: Missouri Athletic, Media (St. Louis). Lodge: K.C. Office: Basler Electric Co Rt 143 Box 269 Highland IL 62249

BASOLO, FRED, chemistry educator; b. Coello, Ill., Feb. 11, 1920; s. John and Catherine (Marino) B.; m. Mary P. Nutley, June 14, 1947; children: Mary Catherine, Freddie, Margaret-Ann, Elizabeth Rose. B.E., So. Ill. U., 1940, D.Sc. (hon.), 1984; M.S., U. Ill., 1942, Ph.D. in Inorganic Chemistry, 1943. Research chemist Rohm & Haas Chem. Co., Phila., 1943-46; mem. faculty Northwestern U., Evanston, Ill., 1946—; prof. chemistry Northwestern U., 1958—, Morrison prof. chemistry, 1980—, chmn. dept. chemistry, 1969-72; guest lectr. NSF summer insts.; chmn. bd. trustees Gordon Research Conf., 1976; pres. Inorganic Syntheses, Inc., 1979-81; mem. bd. chem. scis. and tech. NRC-Nat. Acad. Scis.; cons. in field; Riley lectr. Notre Dame U.; Welch lectr. U. Tex.; Disting. vis. lectr. U. Iowa; Arthur D. Little lectr. MIT; Zuffanti lectr. Northwestern U.; Krug lectr. U. Ill.; hon. prof. Lanzhou U., Peoples Republic of China. Author: (with R.G. Pearson) Mechanisms of Inorganic Reactions, 1958; author: (with R.C. Johnson) Coordination Chemistry, 1964; asso. editor: Chem. Revs, 1960-65, Inorganica Chemica Acta, 1967—, Inorganica Chemica Acta Letters, 1977—; editorial bd.: Jour. Inorganic and Nuclear Chemistry, 1959—, Jour. Molecular Catalysis, Chem. Revs.; mem. adv. bd. 43d-45th edits.: Who's Who in Am.; co-editor: Catalysis; Transition Metal Chemistry; editor: Inorganic Syntheses XVI; contbr. articles to profl. jours. Recipient Ballar medal, 1972, So. Ill. U. Alumni Achievement award, 1974, Dwyer medal, 1976, James Flack Norris award for Outstanding Achievement in Teaching of Chemistry, 1981, Oesper Meml. award, 1983; Guggenheim fellow, 1954-55; NSF fellow, 1961-62; NATO sr. scientist fellow Italy, 1981. Fellow Nat. Acad. Scis. U.S.A., AAAS (chmn. chemistry sect. 1979), Am. Acad. Arts and Scis.; Mem. Am. Chem. Soc. (asst. editor jour. 1961-64, chmn. div. inorganic chemistry 1970, pres. 1983, bd. dirs. 1982-84, award for research in inorganic chemistry 1964, Disting. Service award in inorganic chemistry 1975, N.E. regional award 1971), Chem. Soc. London, Italian Chem. Soc. (hon.), Sigma Xi, Phi Lambda Upsilon, Alpha Chi Sigma, Phi Kappa Phi, Kappa Delta Phi, Phi Lambda Theta (hon.). Office: Dept Chemistry Northwestern U Evanston IL 60201

BASS, CAROL SUE, bank executive; b. Hamilton, Mo., Feb. 27, 1940; d. Leo Hadley and Emma Ruth (Shipley) Mikes; m. Leonard Kenneth Bass; children: Jeff, Michelle, Stacia. Sr. v.p. Standard State Bank, Independence, Mo., 1973—. Mem adv. com. Independence Pub. Schs. Vacat. Guidance and Counseling Program, Community Assn. Arts, Vaile Mansion Soc., Bingham-Waagoner Hist. Soc.; bd. dirs. Community Founds., Independence, 1982, Hope House, Inc., Independence, 1983—, Civic and Cultural Com., Independence, 1984. Mem. Am. Inst. Banking, Am. Bankers Assn., Mo. Bankers Assn. (mktg. com. 1980-83), Bank Mktg. Assn., Independence C. of C.(bd. dirs. 1975—, chmn. elect 1987, Centurian award 1980, Disting. Service award 1986). Office: Standard State Bank 10801 E 23rd St Independence MO 64052

BASS, HAROLD EUGENE, communications company executive; b. Neosho, Mo., July 30, 1940; s. Harold Virgil and Mildred Lucille (Charelton) B. m. Virginia Lea Bass, Sept. 27, 1958; children—David Eugene, Carolyn Sue, Robert Lee, Ronald Dean. A.A., West Valley Jr. Coll., 1971. Frameman to chief equipment man Pacific Telephone Co., Santa Clara, Calif., 1968-79; switching equipment technician, supr. network services Southwestern Bell Telephone, Sedalia, Mo., 1979-84, Marshall, Mo., 1984-87, mgr. network maintenance, Sedalia, 1987—. Pres., Pettis County unit Am. Cancer Soc., 1979-83, v.p., 1984, chmn. pub. edn. com. Pettis County unit, 1981-83, dir. pub. edn. dist. 5, 1982-84, bd. dirs. Mo. div., 1983-84, chmn. div. pub. edn., exec. com. Mo. div., 1984-86; chmn. human rights commn. City of Sedalia, 1985—; bd. dirs. United Way, Jr. Achievement, ARC. Served with USN, 1958-68. Mem. Naval Enlisted Res. Assn., U.S. Naval Inst., Navy League, Telephone Pioneers Am., Naval Acad. Info. Officers. Republican. Baptist. Club: Noonday Optimist. Lodges: Rotary, Masons. Home: 1001 Douglas Ln Sedalia MO 65301 Office: 220 E 5th St Sedalia MO 65301

BASS, LARRY JUNIOR, clinical psychologist, educator; b. Granby, Mo., Aug. 2, 1944; s. Harold Virgil and Mildred Lucille (Charlton) B.; B.S., U. Mo., 1966, M.S. (NDEA fellow), 1967; Ph.D., Washington U., St. Louis, 1972; m. Meredith Aenone Copeland, Aug. 17, 1968; children—Mark, Darren, Adam. Research asst. Washington U., 1967-68, staff psychologist Child Guidance Clinic, 1970; intern Mt. Zion Med. Center, San Francisco, 1968-69; clin. psychologist Jewish Hosp., St. Louis, 1971-75; assoc. prof. Evangel Coll., Springfield, Mo., 1975-84; pvt. practice clin. psychology, Springfield, 1975-84, 87—; dir. Montclair Psychol. Ctr., Inc., 1984-87. Mem. Am. Psychol. Assn., Mo. Psychol. Assn. (chmn. com.), Mo. State Com. Psychologists (chmn. 1983-85), Phi Delta Kappa. Home: 5146 S Aleshire Ct Springfield MO 65807 Office: 1000 E Primrose Suite 430 Springfield MO 65807

BASS, MITCHELL H(IRSCH), mortgage broker; b. Chgo., May 12, 1935; s. Saul Z. and Juliet C. (Cohn) B.; m. Marlene Stein, June 30, 1957; children—Leonard E., Deborah P., Naomi R. B.S. in Fin., U. Ill., 1957; M.B.A., U. Chgo., 1972. Asst. cashier Fox Lake State Bank (Ill.), 1958—; exec. v.p. Unity Savs., Norridge, Ill., 1981—; pres. Bass Fin. Corp., Chgo., 1981—; pres., chmn. bd. Midwest Mortgage Co. Inc., Glenview, 1983—. Chmn. Chgo. Norridge Crusade of Mercy; active Weitzman Inst., Rehovot, Israel; bd. dirs. North Suburban Jewish Community Ctr., Highland Park, Ill. Jewish. Office: 950 Milwaukee Ave Glenview IL 60025

BASS, RICHARD MARTIN, otolaryngologist, head and neck surgeon; b. Chgo., May 20, 1942. BS, Loyola U., Chgo., 1964; MD, U. Ill., Chgo., 1968, MS, 1969. Diplomate Nat. Bd. Med. Examiners, Am. Bd. Otolaryngology, Head and Neck Surgery. Intern Northwestern Meml. Hosp., Chgo., 1968-69; resident in otolaryngology Northwestern U. Hosp., Chgo., 1969-74; mem. staff St. John's Hosp., Springfield, Ill., Meml. Med. Ctr., Springfield; clin. assoc. prof. surgery So. Ill. U., Springfield, 1976—; cons. staff Humana Hosp., Springfield, Lincoln (Ill.) Hosp. Contbr. numerous articles to profl. and scholarly jours.; producer ednl. films. V.p. Found. for Med. Care Cen. Ill., Springfield, 1984-87. Served to maj. M.C., U.S. Army, 1974-76. Recipient Clin. Surg. Mem. Attending Staff of Yr., So. Ill. U., 1984. Fellow ACS, Am. Acad. Otolaryngology, Am. Soc. for Head and Neck Surgery; mem. AMA, Am. Council Otolaryngology, Ill. Soc. Ophthalmology and Otolaryngology, Ill. Cancer Council, Soc. Univ. Otolaryngologists, Ill. State Med. Soc. Sangamon County Med. Soc. Office: 319 E Madison St Springfield IL 62701

BASSELL, GERARD MAURICE, anesthesiologist, educator; b. Sydney, Australia, Oct. 9, 1946; s. Gustave and Mary Thelma (Foster) B.; m. Edith Erna Bock, Feb. 3, 1976; children: Candice M., Torsten M. MB, BS, U. Sydney, Australia, 1972, MD, 1973. Diplomate Am. Bd. Anesthesiology. Asst. prof. U. Calif., Irvine, 1978-80, dir. obstetric anesthesia, 1980-83; assoc. prof. anesthesia U. Kans., Wichita, 1983-86, prof., 1986—; dir. obstetric anesthesia Wesley Women's Hosp., Wichita, 1983—. Editor: (book) Obstetric Anesthesia & Analgesia, 1980; contbg. editor Obstetric Anesthesia Digest, N.Y.C., 1981-86, co-editor, Wichita, 1986—; contbr. articles to profl. jours.. Fellow Am. Coll. Anesthesiologists, Am. Coll. Ob-Gyns (assoc.), Royal Soc. Medicine; mem. AMA, Kans. Med. Assn., Sedgwick County Med. Assn., Am. Soc. Anesthesiologists (com. perinatology 1986—), Internat. Anesthesia Research Soc. Avocations: snow skiing, tennis, swimming, theatre. Home: PO Box 8288 Wichita KS 67208-0288 Office: Mid-Continent Anesthesiology PO Box 18748 Wichita KS 67218

BASSETT, EDWARD POWERS, university dean; b. Boston, Feb. 27, 1929; s. Fraser W. and Fanny (Powers) B.; m. Karen Elizabeth Jack, Dec. 21, 1954; children: Sarah Jack Bassett Williams, Laura Powers, Lisa Wightman. AB, Washington and Lee U., 1951, LLD, 1984; MA, U. Mich., 1955; PhD, U. Iowa, 1967. Ct. reporter Louisville Courier-Jour., 1955-56; asst. editor Falmouth (Mass.) Enterprise, 1956-57; city editor Anderson (Ind.) Herald, 1957-58; editorial writer Longview (Wash.) Daily News, 1958-60; lectr. Lower Columbia Jr. Coll., 1959-60; instr., pub. U. Iowa, 1960-67; asst. prof. journalism U. Mich., 1967-70, acting chmn. dept. journalism, 1969-70; dean Sch. Journalism U. Kans., 1970-74, assoc. vice chancellor acad. affairs, 1974-75; dir. Sch. Journalism U. So. Calif., 1975-80; editor Statesman-Jour., Salem, Oreg., 1980-84; dean Medill Sch. Journalism Northwestern U., Evanston, Ill., 1984—; bd. dirs. Gannett Ctr. for Media Studies. Bd. dirs. Found. Am. Communications. Recipient citation for reporting Am. Polit. Sci. Assn., 1960. Mem. Assn. Edn. in Journalism and Mass Communication (pres. 1975-76), Am. Assn. Schs. and Depts. Journalism (pres. 1974-75), Sigma Delta Chi, Kappa Tau Alpha., Delta Tau Delta. Office: Northwestern U Medill Sch Journalism Evanston IL 60208

BASSETT, JOHN GIBBS, healthcare company executive; b. Long Branch, N.J., Mar. 4, 1948; s. John Jewett and Helen (Gibbs) B.; m. Sara Ludwig, Aug. 30, 1969; 1 child, Ian. BS in Econs., U. Pa., 1970; MBA, SUNY, Albany, 1977. V.p. Hosp. Assn. N.Y. State, Albany, 1977-80, sr. v.p. fin., 1980; v.p. Green Rd. Mgmt. Co., Ann Arbor, Mich., 1980-83; chief exec. officer Commn. on Profl. and Hosp. Activities, Ann Arbor, 1983-85, sr. v.p., 1985—; instr. Columbia Sch. Pub. Health, N.Y.C., 1978, Rensselaer Poly. Inst., Troy, N.Y., 1978-80; chmn. Nat. Health Info. Systems, Ann Arbor, 1984-85. Contbr. articles to profl. jours. Mem. campaign bd. United Way of Washington County, Mich., 1982-85; bd. dirs. ARS MUSICA, Ann Arbor, 1983-85. Named one of Outstanding Young Men of Am., 1981—. Avocations: golf, tennis, jogging, reading. Home: 815 Green Rd Ann Arbor MI 48105 Office: CPHA 1968 Green Rd Ann Arbor MI 48105

BASSETT, KEITH T., metallurgist; b. Leicester, Eng., Apr. 28, 1933; came to U.S., 1974; s. Joseph William and Lillian May (Wightman) B.; B.Sc. in Applied Sci., U. Durham (Eng.), 1954; m. Doris Nicholson, May 14, 1955; children—Martyn John, Peter Richard, Joanne Elizabeth. Metallurgist,

Fairey Aviation, Hayes, Eng., 1954-56; mgr. extraction metallurgy Henry Wiggin & Co., Hereford, Eng., 1956-60; sales metallurgist Park Gate Iron & Steel Co., Rotherham, Eng., 1960-62; vacuum degassing service metallurgist English Steel Corp., Sheffield, Eng., 1962-65; sr. service metallurgist Atlas Steels Co., Welland, Ont., Can., 1965-74; mgr. metallurgy Danly Machine Corp., Cicero, Ill., 1974-84; mgr. quality assurance Sci. Metal Treating, Des Plaines, Ill., 1984-85; midwest mgr. tech. services Uddeholm Steel Corp., Itasca, Ill., 1985-87; product mgr. tool steels, Thyssen Splty. Steels Inc., Carol Stream, Ill., 1987—; seminar lectr.; lectr. Coll. of DuPage; Metals Engring. Inst. course instr., 1969—, nat. chmn., 1981-83. Chmn. Hamilton and Dist. Cricket League, 1968-74, Ont. Cricket Assn., 1972-74; nat. rep. Can. Cricket Assn., 1973-74. Mem. Am. Welding Soc. (nat. subcom. chmn. 1975-85), Am. Soc. Metals (nat. com. 1978-83, chmn. nat. com. 1981-83, vice-chmn. 1983-84, chpt. chmn. 1982-83, nat. com. vice-chmn. 1983—; Outstanding Chpt. Mem. 1982-83). Office: Specialty Steels Inc 365 Village Dr Carol Stream IL 60188-1828

BASSI, RICHARD ANTHONY, military officer; b. N.Y.C., Dec. 6, 1947; s. A. R. (Rick) and N. Frances (Signorini) B.; m. Linda Marie Martinez, Dec. 16, 1973; children: Marie Louise, Mark Nicholas. BS, USAF Acad., 1969; MS, George Washington U., 1974. Commd. 2d lt. USAF, 1969, advanced through grades to maj., 1980; comdr. Office of Spl. Investigations USAF, Hill AFB, Utah, 1977-80; program security mgr. test and evaluation ctr. USAF, Las Vegas, 1980-81; mem. missile combat crew USAF, McConnell AFB, Kans., 1981-83, team mgr. wing exercise evaluation, 1983-84, comdr. 381 headquarters squadron, 1984-86; comdr.'s mgr. inspections and evaluations USAF, Whiteman AFB, Mo., 1986—. Contbr. articles to base newspapers. Mem. allocations com. United Way Wichita and Sedgwick County, Kans., 1985-86; mem. Sedgwick County Hist. Mus., 1982—; treas. Kans. chpt. Victorian Soc. Am., Wichita, 1983, 84, pres. 1985. Decorated Bronze Star; recipient Disting. Service award United Way of Wichita and Sedgwick County, 1985. Mem. Whiteman AFB Mil. Affairs Com., Nat. Trust for Hist. Preservation. Roman Catholic. Avocations: collecting coins, carnival glass, antiques, volleyball, bowling. Home: PO Box 555 Warrensburg MO 64093

BAST, KARIN DORATHE ANDERSON, computer consultant, educator; b. Little Falls, Minn., Oct. 17, 1945; s. Garfield Allan and Dorathe (Bergin) Anderson; m. William H. Bast, Aug. 19, 1967; children: Michael, Katherine, Kristine. BA cum laude, U. Minn., 1967; MBA, U. Wis., La Crosse, 1986. Mgr. Call-A-Computer, Mpls., 1967-69; instr. Western Wis. Tech. Inst., La Crosse, 1969-71; user relations coordinator La Crosse Area Computers in Edn., 1972-75; instr. U. Wis., La Crosse, 1975-80; pres. Automated Info. Mgmt., Inc., La Crosse, 1983—; trustee Western Wis. Tech. Inst. Found.; instr. U. Wis., La Crosse. Contbr. column to City Bus., 1985-87. Judge Excellence award, Wis. Vocat. Tech. and Adult Edn. Bd., Madison, 1986; mem. Automation Task Force La Crosse Pub. Library, 1986, Computer Activities Com. La Crosse Pub. Schs., 1986. Mem. Coulee Region Data Processing Assn., Avant, Math/Sci. Network. Home and Office: 3504 Ebner Coulee Rd La Crosse WI 54601

BAST, KENNETH GEORGE, health care executive; b. Milw., Oct. 31, 1949; s. George H. and Genevieve (Zimmel) B.; m. Patricia A. Hogan, Nov. 17, 1973. BBA, Marquette U., 1971; MBA, U. Wis., 1977. Personnel asst. St. Joseph Hosp., Warren, Ohio, 1972-74; v.p. ops. Meml. Hosp., Burlington, Wis., 1974-80; pres. No. Ill. Med. Ctr., McHenry, Ill., 1980-82; v.p. TW3 Corp., Downer's Grove, Ill., 1982-84; v.p. health services John Knox Village, Lee's Summit, Mo., 1984—; project dir. Mobile Intensive Care program Emergency Med. Services, McHenry, 1981-82; instr. Cen. Mo. State U., Kansas City, 1986—; bd. dirs. Multi Hosp. Mutual Ins., Hamilton, Bermuda. Mem. McHenry Econ. Commn., 1982, Govs. Adv. Council on Aging, Mo., 1985—. Mem. Am. Hosp. Assn., Nat. Council on aging, Am. Coll. Health Care Adminstrs., Kansas City C. of C. (Pres. Club). Roman Catholic. Avocation: photography. Office: John Knox Village 400 N Murray Lee's Summit MO 64081

BASTIAN, LAWRENCE JACOB, talent agent; b. Chgo., July 11, 1930; s. Lawrence J. and Charlotte J. (Templeton) B.; m. Dianne L. Holmberg, Jan. 16, 1965; children—Michelle, Nicolle, Danielle. Student U. Ill., 1952. Mem. staff William Morris Agy., Chgo., 1954-55, 60-67; agt. Ziv TV Co., Cin., 1956-59, M.C.A., Chgo., 1959-60; owner, mgr., agt. Larry Bastian Agy., Riverwoods, Ill. 1967—. Served with U.S. Army, 1952-54. Home and Office: 2580 Crestwood Ln Riverwoods IL 60015

BASTILLA, ROBERT FRANCIS, banker; b. Elmira, N.Y., Feb. 2, 1927; s. Francis John and Marjorie Flora (Hoag) B.; m. Shirley Jean Hug, June 7, 1947; children: Robert Michael, Nancy Ann Bastilla McCaw. Owner, operator Bastilla Egg Co., Highland, Ill., 1959-67; sales mgr., broadcaster Sta. WINU, Highland, 1967-68; newsman, broadcaster Sta. WRTH, Cottage Hills and Woodriver, Ill., 1968-69; dir. pub. relations 1st Nat. Bank of Highland, 1969-81, asst. v.p., dir. pub. relations, 1981—. Alderman City of Highland, 1957-63; mem. exec. bd. Cahokia Mound council Boy Scouts Am., 1970-75, 76—, dist. chmn., 1979-81, 84—; bus. chmn. Highland Cancer Crusade, 1980-84; pres. Madison County Fair Assn., 1973-79; mem. and sec. planning commn. City of Highland, 1979-83; exec. bd. Faith Countryside Homes, 1980-84; bd. dirs. Highland Sesquicentennial Assn., Inc. 1985-86, sec. 1985—. Served with USN, 1945-46. Recipient Outstanding Civic Leader award Highland Jaycees, 1979, award of merit Kickapoo dist. Cahokia Mound council Boy Scouts Am., 1982, Silver Beaver award, 1985. Mem. Ill./Mo. Mktg. Assn. (past pres.), Bank Mktg. Assn., Highland C. of C., Highland Pistol and Rifle Assn., Helvetia Sharpshooters Soc., VFW. Club: Toastmasters (past pres.). Lodge: Lions (past pres., zone chmn. 1981-82, 84-85, dep. dist. gov. 1982-83, Lion of Yr. 1981, Membership Growth award 1983). Home: 80 Suppiger Ln B1 Highland IL 62249 Office: 1000 Broadway PO Box 10 Highland IL 62249

BASTO, LA DONNA JOAN, business administrator; b. Mpls., July 22, 1933; d. Mayland and Irene (Bennett) Bussart; m. Ronald Martin Basto, June 5, 1952; children: Patricia Ann, Richard Martin, Judith Renee. Bookkeeper various cos., Wichita, Kans., 1964-74; office mgr. William R. Hurst Co., Inc., Wichita, 1974—. Mem. Adminstrv. Mgmt. Soc. (bus. expo chairperson 1984-86, Achievement award 1985, exec. v.p. 1985-86, pres. 1986—, cert. of Appreciation 1986, asst. area dir. 1987—, chmn. strategic planning com. 1987—). Republican. Presbyterian. Avocations: golf, bowling, spectator sports. Office: Wm F Hurst Co Inc PO Box 47488 Wichita KS 67201

BASTOKY, BRUCE MICHAEL, human resource executive; b. Cleve., June 15, 1953; s. Irving Benjamin and Esther (Naff) B.; m. Karen Kay Robinson, June 13, 1987. Student, Cuyahoga Community Coll., 1971-73, U. Akron, 1984-85. Personnel/tng. adminstr. The May Co., Cleve., 1974-77; cons. Roth Young, Cleve., 1978-80; dir. human resources The Lawson Co., Cuyahoga Falls, Ohio, 1980-86, Cardinal Industries, Columbus, Ohio, 1986—. Author: Supervisor's Guide, 1985; producer (films/videos) The Visitor, 1984, Deli Heros, 1985. Mem. Youth Motivation Task Force, Akron, Ohio, 1983—; officer Pvt. Industry Council, Akron, 1983—. Recipient Silver Quill for Scriptwriting award Internat. Assn. Bus. Communicators, 1985, Best Film/Video Series award Nat. Assn. Convenience Stores, 1985. Mem. Am. Soc. Personnel Adminstrn. (bd. dris. 1985-86), Am. Soc. Tng. and Devel., German Village Soc. Jewish. Avocations: reading, photography, film making, stained glass design. Home: 769 1/2 S 3d St Columbus OH 43206 Office: Cardinal Industries Inc 4223 Donlyn Ct Columbus OH 43232

BATCHELDER, ALICE M., federal judge; b. 1944; m. William G. Batchelder III; children: William G. IV, Elisabeth. BA, Ohio Wesleyan U., 1964; JD, Akron U., 1971. Tchr. Plain Local Sch. Dist., Franklin City, Ohio, 1965-66, Jones Jr. High Sch., 1966-67, Buckeye High Sch., Medina County, 1967-68; ptnr. Williams & Batchelder, Medina, Ohio, 1971-83; judge U.S. Bankruptcy Ct., Ohio, 1983-85, U.S. Dist. Ct. (no. dist.) Ohio, Cleve., 1985—. Mem. ABA. Office: US District Court 256 US Courthouse 201 Superior Ave NE Cleveland OH 44114 *

BATCHELDER, ANNE STUART, former publisher, political party official; b. Lake Forest, Ill., Jan. 11, 1920; d. Robert Douglas and Harriet (McClure) Stuart; student Lake Forest Coll., 1941-43; m. Clifton Brooks Batchelder, May 26, 1945; children—Edward, Anne Stuart, Mary Clifton, Lucia Brooks. Clubmobile driver ARC, Eng., Belgium, France, Holland and Germany, 1943-45; pub., editor Douglas County Gazette, 1970-75; bd. dirs. 1st Nat. Bank Omaha; dir., treas. U.S. Checkbook Com. Mem. Republican Central Com. Nebr., 1955-62, 70-83, vice chmn. Central Com., 1959-64, chmn., 1975-79, mem. fin. com., 1957-64; chmn. women's sect. Douglas County Rep. Finance Com., 1955, vice chmn. com., 1958-60; v.p. Omaha Woman's Rep. Club, 1957-58, pres., 1959-60; alternate del. Nat. Conv., 1956, 72, del., 1980, 84; mem. Rep. Nat. Com. for Nebr., 1964-70; asst. chmn. Douglas County Rep. Central Com., 1971-74; 1st v.p. Nebr. Fedn. Rep. Women, 1971-72, pres., 1972-74; chmn. Nebr. Rep. Com., 1975-79; chmn. fundraising com. Nat. Fedn. Rep. Women, 1981-85; mem. Nebr. State Bldg. Commn., 1979-83; Rep. candidate for lt. gov., 1974. Sr. v.p. Nebr. Founders Day, 1958; bd. dirs. YWCA, 1983—; past trustee Brownell Hall, Vis. Nurse Assn.; trustee Hastings Coll., Nebr. Meth. Hosp. Found.; pres. Nebr. chpt. Freedoms Found. at Valley Forge. Elected to Nebr. Rep. Hall of Fame, 1984. Mem. Mayflower Soc., Colonial Dames, P.E.O., Nat. League Pen Women. Presbyterian (elder). Clubs: Omaha Country, Omaha. Home: 6875 State St Omaha NE 68152

BATCHELLER, TOM, food products company executive. Pres. Zip Feed Mills, Inc., Sioux Falls, S.D. Office: Zip Feed Mills Inc Box 500 Sioux Falls SD 57101 *

BATE, CHARLES THOMAS, lawyer; b. Muncie, Ind., Nov. 14, 1932; s. Thomas Elwood and Vina Florence (Jackson) B.; m. Barbara Kay Dailey, June 17, 1955; children—Charles Thomas, Gregory Andrew, Jeffrey Scott. A.B., Butler U., 1955, postgrad., 1955-56; student, Christian Theol. Sem., Indpls., 1956-57; J.D., Ind. U., 1962. Bar: Ind. 1962. Staff adjuster State Automobile Ins. Assn., Indpl., 1953-57; claim supr. State Automobile Ins. Assn., 1958-59, office mgr., 1960-61, casualty claim mgr., 1961-62, atty., 1962-63; mem. firm Smith & Yarling, Indpls., 1963-67; sr. ptnr. Bate, Harrold & Meltzer, Shelbyville, Ind., 1967—; city atty. City of Shelbyville, 1981-86; dir., v.p., gen. counsel Discovery Life Ins. Co., Indpls., 1966-70. Bd. dirs. Nat. Pensions Bd. of Ch. of God, 1970-74; bd. dirs. Glendale Ch. of God Inc. 1958-80, lay speaker, 1962—, sec. nat. by-laws com. 1968-72); trustee emeritus Warner Pacific Coll., Portland, Oreg., 1984—; trustee Anderson U., Ind., 1982—. Recipient Merit award Ind. Jud. Council, 1962, Outstanding Student award Ind. U. Law Week, 1962. Fellow Ind. Bar Found.; mem. ABA, Ind. Bar Assn. (ho. of dels. 1978-80), Indpls. Bar Assn., Shelby County Bar Assn. (pres. 1979), Am. Judicature Soc., Am. Arbitration Assn. (panel arbitrators), Assn. Trial Lawyers Am., Ind. Trial Lawyers Assn. (dir. 1979—), Tex. Trial Lawyers Assn., Pa. Trial Lawyers Assn., Am. Bd. Trial Advocates. Republican. Lodge: Elks. Home: Box 26 Shelbyville IN 46176 Office: 3044 Tiffany Ct Carmel IN 46032

BATEMAN, DAVID N., business communication educator; b. Peoria, Ill., Jan. 25, 1940; s. Raymond Jennings and Dorothy (Hoffmann) B.; m. Marianne Webb, Oct. 3, 1970. BA, Parsons Coll., 1961; MA, So. Ill. U., 1962, MS, 1964, PhD, 1970. Asst. budget dir. So. Ill. U., Carbondale, 1969-72, asst fin. dir., 1972-74, prof., 1982—; pres. Productive Communication, Carbondale, 1982—. Author: Communication in Business, 1981, 85, Business Communication Concepts, 1983. Named AMOCA Great Tchr., AMOCO, Inc., Chgo., 1982, Nat. Innovative Tchr., So. Bus. Assn., New Orleans, 1984. Mem. Acad. Mgmt., Bus. and Tech. Communications (editorial bd.), Am. Bus. Communication Assn. (bd. dirs. 1978—, pres. elect 1985-86), Assn. for Bus. Communication (pres. 1986-87), Am. Guild of Organists (sec. 1985—). Republican. Episcopalian. Avocations: art collecting, organ music. Home: 1027 Briarwood Carbondale IL 62901 Office: So Ill University Mgmt Dept Carbondale IL 62901

BATEMAN, ROBERT PARKER, industrial engineer; b. Batavia, N.Y., Oct. 31, 1935; s. Parker Thomas and Sarah Meriva (Bixby) B.; m. Betty Loujean Daniels, July 3, 1959; children: Stephen P., Jeanne Anne, Sabrina S., Michelle C. BS in Mil. Engring., U.S. Mil. Acad., 1957; MS in Astronautical Engr., Air Force Inst. Tech., 1973; PhD Indsl. Engr., Texas A&M, 1980; MA in Experimental Psychology, U. Dayton, 1981. Commd. 2d lt. USAF, 1957, advanced through grades to maj., 1968, ret., 1978; scientist Systems Research Labs., Inc., Dayton, Ohio, 1978, sr. scientist, 1980-85; instr. Texas A&M, Coll. Sta., Tex., 1979-80; prin. engr. Boeing, Wichita, Kans., 1985-86; supr. crew performance tech. staff Boeing, Wichita, 1986—. Contbr. articles about human factors and the man-machine interface to profl. jours. Decorated Silver Star, Disting. Flying Cross with three oak leaf clusters, Air Medal with 15 oak leaf clusters. Mem. Human Factors Soc., Air Force Assn., Daedalians, Sigma Xi. Avocation: writing poetry. Home: 807 Morningview Derby KS 67037 Office: Boeing Co M/S K76-23 Wichita KS 67277-7730

BATES, BRUCE ALAN, dentist; b. Detroit, June 15, 1958; s. Morton Gaylord and Margurite (Davis) B.; m. Siobhan R. Gorman, Aug. 6, 1983. BS in Zoology, U. Mich., 1980, DDS, 1984. Gen. practice dentistry Manchester, Mich., 1984. Recipient Research grant U. Mich. Dental Research Inst., 1982. Mem. ADA, Mich. Dental Assn., Washtenaw Dental Assn., Detroit Dental Soc., Manchester Jaycees (v.p. 1986), Manchester C. of C. Lodge: Optimists. Avocations: music, photography, literature, travel. Home: 216 Auburn Manchester MI 48158 Office: 500 Galloway Dr Manchester MI 48158

BATES, DONNETTE MARIE, career placement counselor; b. Sleepy Eye, Minn., Nov. 27, 1949; d. Donald Arthur and Betty Jane (Eickholt) Yackel; m. Thomas William Bates, Sept. 17, 1970; children: Sarah Todd, Molly Erin. Student, St. Cloud (Minn.) State U., 1967-68. Placement counselor St. Paul Employment, 1972-73, Comml. Employment, St. Paul, 1973-77, A and B Personnel, St. Paul, 1978-80; career trainer, specialist WEST-Cap, Glenwood City, Wis., 1980-81; placement specialist Metro Rehab. Services, Mpls., 1981-83; owner, operator Bates Placement Services, St. Paul, 1983—. V.p. bd. Pre-School Playhouse, Turtle Lake, Wis., 1980-81; mem. Mahtomedi (Minn.) Sch. Parent Assn., 1986-87; asst. leader 4-H, Mahtomedi, 1986—. Mem. Nat. Assn. Rehab. Services, Am. Soc. Profl. Women. Democrat. Roman Catholic. Avocations: traveling, reading, crafts. Office: Bates Placement Services 80 W County Rd C #804 Saint Paul MN 55117

BATES, GARY DEAN, engineering corporation executive; b. Covington, Ky., May 10, 1941; s. Harold V. and Anna J. (Crupper) B.; m. Joyce Ann Wiedemer, Nov. 14, 1964; children: Cynthia Lynne, Christopher Scott. Student Anderson (Ind.) Coll., 1959-61; BSCE, U. Ky., 1964, MS, 1967; postgrad. U. Cin., 1977-79; postgrad. in real estate Cin. Tech. Coll., 1978-79. Registered profl. engr., Ohio, Ky., Ind.; lic. real estate agt., Ohio. Design engr. Ky. Dept. Highways, Lexington, 1963-67; project engr. Exxon Corp., Linden, N.J., 1967-69; project mgr. Skilken-Roslovic Design-Build, Inc., Columbus, Ohio, 1969-71; asst. ops. mgr. Miller-Valentine Constrn. Co., Dayton, Ohio, 1971-72; constrn. mgr. Jackson's Realty and Builder's, Indpls., 1972-74; v.p., dir. tech. services KZF, Inc., Cin., 1975-81; bus. mgr. indsl. cons. SDRC, Inc., Milford, Ohio, 1981-85; sr. v.p. engring. div. Belcan Corp., 1985-87; exec. v.p.. gen. mgr. McGill, Smith, Punshon, Internat., Inc., 1987— ;instr. constrn. mgmt. program U. Cin., 1975-82. Tutor minority children Urban League, Columbus, 1970-71; v.p. Woodlands Homeowners Assn., Carmel, Ind., 1973-74; mem. Leadership Cin.; mem. Anderson Twp. Planning and Zoning Commn. Mem. ASCE (exec. com. engring. mgmt. div.), Lambda Chi Alpha Alumni. Republican. Methodist. Home: 730 Birney Ln Cincinnati OH 45230 Office: 2000 Eastman Dr Milford OH 45150

BATES, JAMES EDWARD, trade association executive; b. Elkhart, Ind., Aug. 6, 1921; s. Roy Ernest and Maggie (Lynn) B.; m. Ann Finnell, Dec. 9, 1945 (div. June 1975); children—Jon Kenric, Daryl, David Scott. B.S. in Bus., North Central Coll., 1943; student Elkhart Bus. U., 1949-51; M.B.A., Harvard Bus. Sch., 1961. Cert. assn. exec., 1977. Factory supt., v.p. prodn., v.p. mktg., sales, dir. Finnell System, Inc., Elkhart, 1946-68; pvt. practice, Naperville, Ill., 1968-69; account exec. Proven Mgmt. Inc., Evanston, Ill., 1969-75; pres. JEBINC Mgmt. Services, Arlington Heights, Ill., 1975—. Bd. dirs. Nat. Safety Council, Chgo. Editor 12 Safe-Low Cost Maintenance pamphlets. Mem. Presdl. Commn. for Peace Time Use of Atomic Energy, Washington, 1951-54. Served as lt. USN, 1942-46, PTO. Recipient Ednl. award Northwood Inst., 1978; Nat. Safety Council product safety award, 1976, 78, 85; ednl. tng. award Nat. Assn. Hardware Mfrs., 1982-83, C-Flag Presdl. Citation, 1986. Mem. Inst. Assn. Mgmt. Cos., Chgo. Soc. Assn. Execs., Am. Soc. Assn. Execs., U.S. C. of C. Republican. Lodges: Masons, Shriners. Home: 1717 Crystal Ln Mount Prospect IL 60056

BATES, LYNN SHANNON, advanced technology company executive; b. Salem, Ohio, May 7, 1940; s. Harvey Delmore and Olive (Stratton) B. m. Gyll Colette Floding, Aug. 21, 1966; children: Tammy Colette, Heidi Lynne, Kerri Nicole, Mindy Suzanne. BS, Heidelberg Coll., 1962; MS, Purdue U., 1966; PhD, Kans. State U., 1972. Instr. dept. biochemistry Purdue U., West Lafayette, Ind., 1966; biochemist, head Protein Quality Lab. Maize and Wheat Improvement Ctr., Mex., 1966-68; research asst. Kans. State U., Manhattan, 1968-72, asst. prof. grain sci., 1972-81; pres. Alteca Ltd., Manhattan, Kans., 1981—; sec. Asima Corp., Independence, Kans., 1985—. Contbr. articles to profl. jours. Mem. Am. Assn. Cereal Chemists, Am. Assn. Feed Microscopists, Am. Chem. Soc., Inst. Food Technologists, Bot. Soc. Am., Phi Tau Sigma, Gamma Sigma Delta. Republican. Methodist. Home: 1814 Laramie Manhattan KS 66502 Office: Alteca Ltd 731 McCall Rd Manhattan KS 66502

BATES, MARK WELDON, university administrator; b. Bloomington, Ill., Aug. 14, 1934; s. Ralph Elbert and Margaret (Weldon) B.; student U. Ill., 1952-54; B.S. in Journalism, Northwestern U., 1956; m. Janet Alice Fjellberg, Jan. 5, 1957; children—Michael John, Scott Weldon, Anne Elizabeth. Personnel asst. Washington Nat. Ins. Co., Evanston, Ill. 1957-58; asst. dir. devel. Northwestern U., Evanston, 1958-61; dir. devel. Ill. Inst. Tech., Chgo., 1961-67, v.p. instl. devel., 1968-72, v.p. planning and devel., 1975-79, v.p., exec. sec. to bd. trustees, 1979-83; v.p. instl. advancement Coll. of St. Francis, Joliet, Ill., 1983-85; asst. vice chancellor Washington U., St. Louis, 1985—; exec. v.p. Am. Fund for Dental Health, Chgo., 1973-75; dir. PSI Inc. Trustee Union League Boys Club; governing mem. Ill. Tech. Coll.; bd. dirs. Simon Found. Served with AUS, 1957. Mem. Nat. Soc. Fund Raisers, Chgo. Soc. for Fund Raising Execs. (pres. 1972-73), Union League Club. Clubs: Economic, Chicago Press; Michigan Shores; Wilmette. Home: 54 York Dr Saint Louis MO 63144 Office: 6510 Ellenwood Saint Louis MO 63105

BATES, NORMAN JAMES, manufacturing engineer, mechanical technologies educator; b. Bay City, Mich., Jan. 28, 1952; s. Norman R. and Theresa Mary (Carbary) B. B.S.E. in Aerospace, U. Mich., 1974. Coordinator numerical control Wilson Machine, Saginaw, Mich., 1978—; instr. mech. techs. Delta Coll., University Center, Mich., 1980—; mgr. numerical control programming Am. Hoist & Derrick, Bay City, 1976-78; dir. StarPak Energy Systems, Novi, Mich., 1976—. Author: SPIDAR (Solar Powered Ion Driven Asteroid Belt Research), 1974; chpt. preface Metalworking, 1982. Sr. mem. Soc. Mfg. Engrs. Roman Catholic. Avocations: botanist; hang gliding; ultralight pilot; cross country skiing. Home: 1500 S Mackinaw Kawkawlin MI 48631 Office: Wilson Machine Div 400 Florence St Saginaw MI 48602

BATES, ROBERT EDWARD, JR., personnel director; b. St. Louis, July 13, 1947; s. Robert Edward and Ann Shaw (Liggett) B.; m. Susan Elizabeth Spear, Dec. 19, 1970 (div. Aug. 1984); children: Robert E. III, Andrew Thomas; m. Sandra Jeanette Leith, Sept. 15, 1984. BS, U. Mich., 1969, MBA, 1971. Auditor Peat, Marwick, Mitchell & Co., Albany, N.Y., 1971-72; field sales mgr. Ford Motor Co., Dearborn, Mich., 1972-81; staff asst. to pres. Cars of Concepts Inc., Brighton, Mich., 1981-84; dir. adminstrn. ADP Network Services, Ann Arbor, Mich., 1984—; instr. Dale Carnegie Assn., Southfield, Mich., 1978-83. Asst. chmn. United Way, Livingston County, Mich., 1983. Republican. Presbyterian. Avocations: World War II aircraft, sports, travel. Home: 766 Fairway Trails Dr Brighton MI 48116 Office: ADP Network Services 175 Jackson Plaza Ann Arbor MI 48106

BATES, WALTER ALAN, lawyer; b. Wadsworth, Ohio, Oct. 27, 1925; s. Edwin Clinton and Gertrude (Connor) B.; m. Aloise Grasselli O'Brien, Feb. 9, 1957; children—Charles, Aloise, Walter Alan Jr., Thomas, David. B.S. cum laude, Harvard U., 1945, LL.B., 1950. Bar: Ohio 1950, U.S. Dist. Ct. (no. dist.) Ohio, 1954, U.S. Ct. Appeals (6th cir.) 1965, U.S. Ct. Appeals (7th cir.) 1966, U.S. Dist. Ct. Conn. 1976, U.S. Dist. Ct. Minn. 1978, U.S. Ct. Appeals (2d cir. 1977), U.S. Ct. Appeals (8th cir.) 1980, U.S. Ct. Appeals (5th cir.) 1984. Assoc. McKeehan, Merrick, Arter & Stewart, Cleve., 1950-60; ptnr. Arter & Hadden, Cleve., 1960—. Chmn. bd. trustees Cleve. Inst. Music, 1980-85; assoc. v.p., chmn. new programs com. United Way Services, Cleve., 1982-85, trustee, 1985—. Served to lt. USN, 1945-46, 51-53. Mem. ABA (antitrust sect.), Ohio State Bar Assn. (bd. govs. antitrust sect.), Cleve. Bar Assn., Fed. Bar Assn. Republican. Roman Catholic. Clubs: Kirtland Country (sec., bd. dirs. 1981-86), Mentor Harbor Yachting (bd. dirs. 1980—, vice commodore), Union, Tavern, Clevelander. Avocations: sailing; traveling. Home: 18235 Shaker Blvd Shaker Heights OH 44120 Office: Arter & Hadden 1100 Huntington Bldg Cleveland OH 44115

BATHEL, DARRYL DONALD, state fisheries management administrator; b. Owatonna, Minn., Mar. 3, 1949; s. Donald E. and Pearl E. (Nipp) B.; m. Virginia M. Snarski, Sept. 16, 1978. BS in Fisheries Mgmt., U. Minn., 1971. Vol. marine resources Peace Corp, Palau, Micronesia, 1972-73; fisheries technician Minn. Dept. Natural Resources, St. Paul, 1974-75, hatchery mgr., 1975-76; asst. hatchery mgr. Minn. Dept. Natural Resources, Duluth, 1976-78, hatchery supr., 1978—. Mem. Am. Fisheries Soc. (fish culture sect., computer users sect.). Roman Catholic. Club: Apple User's, PC User's (Duluth). Avocations: camping, gardening, cross-country skiing, hunting, computers. Office: French River Coldwater Hatchery 10033 North Shore Dr Duluth MN 55804

BATHURST, LONNIE LEE, manufacturing executive; b. Belleville, Ill., July 31, 1953; s. Daris and Lola Ann (Greenwood) B.; m. Phyllis Ann Jones, Aug. 26, 1976; children: Brooke Ann, Brittany Lea. BA in Econs., Eastern Ill. U., Charleston, 1976; postgrad., So. Ill. U., Edwardsville, Ill., 1977-78. Regional sales rep. Zimmerman Equipment, Litchfield, Ill., 1976-77; regional sales rep. Zimmerman Equipment, Litchfield, 1977-81, nat. sales mgr., 1981-83, exec. v.p., 1985—, chief operating officer, 1985—; pres. Chmn. Civic Pride Redevel. Com., Litchfield, 1984-87; bd. dirs. Litchfield Indsl. Commn., 1984-86; dir. Hosp. Sisters Found. Bd., 1986—. Mem. Grain Elevator and Processing Soc., Nat. Grain and Feed Assn., Litchfield C. of C. (dir. 1981-83, v.p. 1983-84, pres. 1984-86). Republican. Mem. Christian Faith. Lodges: Rotary, Antlers, Elks. Avocations: tennis,raquetball, golf, collecting electric trains, landscaping. Home: 27 Horseshoe Ln Litchfield IL 62056 Office: Zimmerman Equipment Co 216 Sherman Litchfield IL 62056

BATT, NICK, lawyer; b. Defiance, Ohio May 6, 1952; s. Dan and Zenith (Dreher) B.; m. Jeannie Batt, May 8, BS, Purdue U., 1972; JD, U. Toledo, 1976. Bar: Ohio 1976. Asst. prosecutor Lucas County, Toledo, 1976-80, civil div. chief, 1980-83; village attorney, Village of Holland, Ohio, 1980—; law dir. City of Oregon, Ohio, 1984—; spl. counsel State of Ohio, 1983—. Mem. Maumee Valley Girl Scout Council, Toledo, 1977-80; bd. mem. Bd. Community Relations, Toledo, 1975-76; mem. Lucas County Democratic Exec. Com., 1981-83. Named One of Toledo's Outstanding Young Men, Toledo Jaycees, 1979. ABA, Ohio Bar Assn., Mem. Toledo Bar Assn., Ohio Council of Sch. Bd. Attorneys, Ohio Mcpl. Attorneys Assn. Democrat. Roman Catholic. Club: Toledo. Lodge: K.C. Office: 325 10th St Toledo OH 43624

BATTEN, MICHAEL ELLSWORTH, manufacturing executive; b. Racine, Wis., Apr. 14, 1940; s. John Henry and Katherine (Vernet) B.; m. Gloria Strickland, July 6, 1963; children—John, Elizabeth, Louise, Timothy. B.A., Yale U., 1964; M.B.A., Harvard U., 1970. Account exec. Ted Bates & Co., N.Y.C., 1964-68; asst. sec. Twin Disc, Inc., Racine, Wis., 1970-71, sec. and asst. treas., 1971-75, v.p. and sec., 1975-76, exec. v.p., 1976-83, pres. and chief exec. officer, 1983—; bd. dirs. Briggs & Stratton Corp., First Wis. Corp., Universal Foods Corp., Walker Forge, Inc., Racine. Trustee Prairie Sch., Racine, 1974—; bd. dirs. Jr. Achievement; exec. com. Pub. Expenditure Survey Wis. Mem. NAM (bd. dirs.), Machinery and Allied Products Inst., Soc. Automotive Engrs., Farm and Indsl. Equipment Inst., Racine Area Mfrs. and Commerce (dir.). Republican. Clubs: University, Milwaukee. Home: 3419 Michigan Blvd Racine WI 53402 Office: Twin Disc Inc 1328 Racine St Racine WI 53403

BATTERSBY, JR. JAMES LYONS, English educator; b. Pawtucket, R.I., Aug. 24, 1936; s. James Lyons and Hazel Irene (Deuel) B.; m. Beverly Ann McClure, Aug. 24, 1957 (div. 1980); 1 child, Julie Ann. B.S. magna cum laude, U. Vt., 1961; M.A., Cornell U., 1962, Ph.D., 1965. Asst. prof. U. Calif.-Berkeley, 1965-70; assoc. prof. English Ohio State U., Columbus, 1970-82, prof., 1982—; cons. Ohio State U. Press, U. Ky., Press, U. Calif. Press, Prentice-Hall, McGraw Hill. Author: Typical Folly: Evaluating Student Performance in Higher Education, 1973; Rational Praise and Natural Lamentation: Johnson, Lycidas and Principles of Criticism, 1980; Elder Olson: An Annotated Bibliography, 1983. Contbr. articles to profl. jours. Served with U.S. Army, 1954-57. Woodrow Wilson fellow, 1961-62, 64-65, Samuel S. Fels fellow, 1964-65, U. Calif. Summer Faculty fellow, 1966, Humanities Research fellow, 1969; recipient Kidder Medal U. Vt., 1961. Mem. MLA, Am. Soc. 18th Century Studies, Midwest Soc. 18th Century Studies, Royal Oak Found., Phi Beta Kappa, Phi Kappa Phi, Kappa Delta Pi. Democrat. Home: 472 Clinton Heights Ave Columbus OH 43202 Office: Dept English Ohio State U 164 W 17th Ave Columbus OH 43210

BATTERSBY, PATRICIA JOSEPHINE, lawyer; b. Detroit, Aug. 8, 1951; d. Christopher James Sr. and Helen Marie (Buckley) B. AB, U. of Detroit, 1976; JD, Detroit Coll. of Law, 1985. Bar: Mich. 1986, U.S. Dist. Ct. (ea. dist.) Mich. 1986. Spl. asst. pros. atty. Wayne County Pros.'s Office, Detroit, 1983-85; assoc. Zamplas, Paskin, Nagi et al, Troy, Mich., 1985—. Editor Law Jour. Adelphia, 1984. Mem. ABA, Assn. Trial Lawyers Am., Irish-Am. Lawyers Assn., Women Lawyers Assn. of Mich., Mich. Bar Assn. (bar journal adv. bd., editor). Office: Zamplas Paskin Nagi et al 1189 W Long Lake Rd Troy MI 48098

BATTEY, RICHARD HOWARD, federal judge; b. 1929; m. Shirley Ann Battey; children: David, Russell, Dianne. BA, U. S.D., 1950, JD, 1953. Atty. City of Redfield, S.D., 1956-63; state's atty. Spinti County, S.D., 1959-65, 81-85; judge U.S. Dist. Ct. S.D., Rapid City, 1985—; ptnr. Gallagher & Battey, Redfield, 1956-85. Served with AUS, 1953-55. Office: U S Dist Ct 318 Fed Bldg 515 9th St Rapid City SD 57701 *

BATTISTI, FRANK JOSEPH, federal judge; b. Youngstown, Ohio, Oct. 4, 1922; s. Eugene and Jennie (Dalesandro) B. B.A., Ohio U., 1947; LL.B., Harvard U., 1950. Bar: Ohio 1950. Asst. atty. gen. Ohio, 1950; atty. adviser C.E. U.S. Army, 1951-52; 1st asst. dir. law Youngstown, 1954-59; judge Common Pleas Ct., Mahoning County, Ohio, 1959-61; judge U.S. Dist. Ct. (no. dist.) Ohio, Cleve., 1961-69, chief judge, 1969—. Served with C.E., U.S. Army, 1943-45; ETO. Mem. ABA, Mahoning County Bar Assn., Cleve. Bar Assn., Am. Judicature Soc. Roman Catholic. Office: US District Court 302 US Courthouse Cleveland OH 44114 *

BATTLE, JOE DAVID, engineer; b. Montgomery, Ala., Apr. 11, 1958; s. Marvin Andrew and Mary Della (Reynolds) B.; m. Margaret Carol Gillum, Jan. 18, 1980; children: Chloe Christine, John Edward. BS in Civil Engring., U. Ala., 1981. Coop. engr. Harbert Internat., Birmingham, Ala., 1977-78, B. E&K Inc., Birmingham, 1979-80; estimator Campbell & Assocs., Tuscaloosa, Ala., 1980-81; project coordinator Pitts.-Desmoines Corp., Birmingham, 1981-83; staff project engr. VA, Dublin, Ga., 1983-85; asst. chief engr. VA, Indpls., 1985—. Mem. Fed. Exec. Assn. Baptist. Avocations: softball, outdoor sports. Office: VA Med Ctr 1481 W 10th St Indianapolis IN 46202

BATTON, CALVERT VORWERK, appliance co. exec.; b. Cuyahoga Falls, Ohio, June 29, 1926; s. Ramsey T. and Mildred B. (Vorwerk) B.; student Bowling Green U., 1946; B.S. in Bus. Adminstrn., Kent State U., 1950, postgrad. Grad. Bus. Sch., 1960-63; m. Edith Sayre Jones, May 18, 1957; children—Susan, Sally, Pamela. With Hoover Co., Canton, Ohio, 1951—, auditor, 1951-53, mgr. br. office, 1953-56, mgr. field accounting, 1956-58, gen. office mgr., 1958-61, asst. budget mgr., 1961-62, mgr. adminstrv. services, 1962-64, asst. v.p., 1964-65, adminstrv. v.p., 1965-75, sr. v.p., 1986—; Bd. dirs. United Way, Canton, Canton Cultural Center; bd. dirs., pres. Kent U. Found. Served with AUS, 1944-45. Mem. Adminstrv. Mgmt. Soc., Nat. Assn. Accountants, Am. Mgmt. Assn., Sigma Delta Epsilon. Republican. Presbyn. Home: 30 Auburn Ave SE North Canton OH 44709 Office: 101 E Maple North Canton OH 44720

BATTS, WARREN LEIGHTON, diversified industry executive; b. Norfolk, Va., Sept. 4, 1932; s. John Leighton and Allie Belle (Johnson) B.; m. Eloise Pitts, Dec. 24, 1957; 1 dau., Terri Allison. B.E.E., Ga. Inst. Tech., 1961; M.B.A., Harvard U., 1963. With Kendall Co., Charlotte, N.C., 1963-64; exec. v.p. Fashion Devel. Co., Santa Paula, Calif., 1964-66; dir. mfg. Olga Co., Van Nuys, Calif., 1964-66; v.p. Douglas Williams Assocs., N.Y.C., 1966-67; co-founder Triangle Corp., Orangeburg, S.C., 1967; pres., chief exec. officer Triangle Corp., 1967-71; v.p. Mead Corp., Dayton, Ohio, 1971-73; pres. Mead Corp., 1973-80, chief exec. officer, 1978-80; pres., chief operating officer Dart Industries, Inc. div. Dart & Kraft, Inc., Los Angeles, 1980-81, Dart & Kraft, Inc., Northbrook, Ill., 1981-86; chmn., chief exec. officer Premark Internat. Inc., Northbrook, 1986—. Trustee Ga. Tech. Found., 1978—, Am. Enterprise Inst., 1980—, Com. for Econ. Devel., 1981—, Art Inst. Chgo., 1983—, Children's Meml. Hosp., Chgo., 1984—, Chgo. Symphony Orch., 1986—. Office: Premark Internat Inc 1717 Deerfield Ave Deerfield IL 60015

BATULIS, LEE FRANCIS, manufacturing engineer; b. Elmira, N.Y., Jan. 5, 1950; s. Frank William and Eleanor Marie (Jankiewicz) B.; m. Ruthe Ann Stanage, Aug. 11, 1973; children: Matthew, David, Michael. AS in Engring. Sci., Broome Tech. Community College, 1970; BS in Indsl. Engring., SUNY, Buffalo, 1972; MBA, Coll. St. Thomas, 1984. Sales rep. Monroe Calculator Co., Rochester, N.Y., 1972-73; mgr. indsl. engring. Carrier Air Conditioning, Syracuse, N.Y., 1973-75, Carrier Air Conditioners, Chgo., 1975-78; facilities engring. mgr. Barry Blower, Mpls., 1978-79; prodn. engring. mgr. ADC Magnetic Controls, Mpls., 1979-82, mfg. ops. mgr., 1982-85; mgr. advanced mfg. engring. Washinton Scientific, Long Lake, Minn., 1985—; pres. Advanced Tech. Integration, Burnsville, Minn., 1986. Mem. Soc. Mfg. Engrs. (sr.). Republican. Lutheran. Club: Burnsville Athletic. Avocations: skiing, water skiing, jogging, fishing, camping. Home: 1608 W 139th St Burnsville MN 55337

BAUDER, KENNETH F., association executive; b. Chgo., Sept. 26, 1946; s. Frederick William and Myrtle Emma (Zenke) B.; B.S., So. Ill. U., 1969, M.A., 1971. Founder with E.R. Homewood, The Ontario Press, Chgo., 1971-74, dir., 1972—; dir. Lambda Books; dir. pub. relations Am. Bar Endowment, Chgo., 1974-75; freelance photographer, journalist, 1975-77; dir. publs. Shoe Service Inst. Am., Chgo., 1977-80, asst. treas., 1977-80. Tchr., Model Cities program, Chgo., 1972-74; bd. dirs. Our Children Found., Chgo., 1980-81; corp. fundraiser Ill. chpt. Nat. Kidney Found. Mem. Chgo. Soc. Assn. Execs. (vice chmn. coll. and univ. relations com. 1978-79), Am. Assn. Assn. Execs., MLA, Am. Pub. Works Assn. (dir. publs. 1980—, mem. communications com. 1982-83). Office: 1313 E 60th Chicago IL 60637 *

BAUER, BRUCE SAMUEL, pediatric plastic surgeon; b. N.Y.C., Sept. 10, 1948; s. Irving L. and Marion (Osserman) B.; m. Sally Kruglik, June 28, 1970; 1 child, Erik. BS, Hobart Coll., 1970; MD, Northwestern U., 1974. Diplomate Am. Bd. Plastic Surgery. Intern Northwestern U. Med. Sch., Northwestern Meml. Hosp., Chgo., 1974-75, resident gen. surgery, 1975-77, resident plastic surgery, 1977-79; attending plastic surgeon Children's Meml. Hosp., Chgo., 1979—, chief plastic surgery, 1986—, dir. craniofacial team, 1986—, active various coms.; asst. prof. surgery Northwestern U., Chgo., 1984—, attending plastic surgeon, 1985—; attending plastic surgeon VA Lakeside Hops., Chgo., 1983—. Contbr. numerous articles to profl. jours. Laurel M. Koennecke scholar, 1973. Fellow ACS, Am. Acad. Pediatricians; mem. Am. Cleft Palate Assn., Am. Soc. Plastic and Reconstructive Surgeons, Assn. Craniofacial Team, Midwestern Assn. Plastic Surgeons, Chgo. Soc. Plastic Surgery. Home: 4343 W Morse Ave Lincolnwood IL 60646 Office: Childrens Meml Hosp 2300 Childrens Plaza Chicago IL 60614

BAUER, CARL THOMAS, lawyer; b. Springfield, Mass., Dec. 23, 1945; s. Edmond S. and Jean L. (Benney) B.; m. Patti Jane Hawkins, Aug. 1, 1975. A.B., Colgate U., 1967; J.D., Wash. U., 1980. Bar: Mo., 1980. Counsel, St. Louis Blues Hockey Club, 1981-83; atty. Ralston Purina Co., St. Louis, 1980—; asst. gen. counsel, sec. Continental Baking Co., 1985—. Served as lt. comdr. USN, 1968-78. Decorated D.F.C., Air Medal (14), others. Mem. ABA, Mo. Bar Assn., Met. St. Louis Bar Assn., Colgate U. Alumni Club of St. Louis.

BAUER, DALE ROBERT, publisher; b. Evanston, Ill., June 10, 1928; s. Valentine H. and Lutie (Jacobsen) B.; m. Sheila Gregory, Feb. 1955 (div. Aug. 1982); children: Richard Gregory, Courtney Anne; m. Peggy Kent, June 1986. B.S. in Econs., U. Pa., 1954. Pub. Med. World News, N.Y.C., 1966-72; group pub., v.p. McGraw-Hill, Inc., N.Y.C., 1972-76; pres. Billboard Pub., N.Y.C., 1976-78, Standard Rate & Data Service, Inc., Wilmette, Ill., 1978-85; chmn. Standard Rate & Data Service, Inc., Wilmette, 1985—; group v.p. Macmillan, Inc., N.Y.C., 1981—; bd. dirs. Am. Bus. Press, N.Y.C., Analytics Communications System, Inc., Reston, Va. Served to lt. (j.g.) USNR, 1946-52, Korea. Republican. Episcopalian. Club: University (N.Y.C.). Avocation: boating. Office: Standard Rate & Data Service Inc 3004 Glenview Rd Wilmette IL 60091

BAUER, EDWARD ALPHONSE, electrical contractor; b. Waite Park, Minn., Aug. 6, 1942; s. Michael Frank and Olive Ann (Lardy) B.; grad. jr. acct. Drews Bus. Coll., St. Cloud, 1961; elec. grad. Dunwoody Indsl. Sch., Mpls., 1967; A.A., St. Cloud State Coll., 1969; m. Carol Ann Lobb, July 8, 1967; children—Steven J., Gwen Marie, John Edward. Owner, pres. Bauer Inc., elec. contractors, Waite Park, Minn., 1969—; sec., v.p. JAB, Inc., 1975-82. Chief, Waite Park Fire Dept., 1980—; scoutmaster Boy Scouts Am., 1979-84. Served with USNR, 1961-62; Res. ret. Decorated Naval Meritorious Service medal, Nat. Def. medal; others. Mem. Nat. Assn. Bus. and Ednl. Radio, U.S. C. of C., Minn. Elec. Assn., Waite Park C. of C., Am. Legion. Republican. Roman Catholic. Clubs: Boosters, Rifle (Waite Park). Lodges: Eagles, Moose. Home: 149 7th Ave N Waite Park MN 56387 Office: Bauer Inc 522 3d St N Waite Park MN 56387

BAUER, ELIZABETH HALE WORMAN, legal services agency executive; b. Mpls., Dec. 28, 1937; d. James R. and Virginia H. (Murty) Worman; B.A., Mt. Holyoke Coll., 1959; M.A., Ohio State U., 1975; postgrad. U. Minn., 1959, Wayne State U., 1978, Mich. State U., 1978; m. George Bittner Bauer, Sept. 12, 1959; children—Anna Stuart, Robert Bittner, Virginia Hale, Edward Russell. Speech therapist Morris County Easter Seal Rehab. Center, Morristown, N.J., 1959-60; travel coordinator AFS Internat., N.Y.C., 1960-63; speech therapist St. Barnabas Home, Gibsonia, Pa., 1967-71; tchr. St. Peter's Child Devel. Center, Sewickley, Pa., 1971-72; tchr. cons. spl. edn., Pontiac, Mich., 1975-78; dir. tng. Plymouth Center for Human Devel., Northville, Mich., 1978-80; adminstr. community placement Mich. Dept. Mental Health, Met. Region, 1980-81; exec. dir. Mich. Protection and Advocacy Service , Inc., Lansing, 1981—; cons. devel. disabilities tech. assistance system U. N.C., 1974-75; mem. adv. bd. Georgetown U. Child Devel. Center, 1978—. Founder, Montessori in Arlington, Upper Arlington, Ohio, 1973; bd. dirs. Franklin County (Ohio) Assn. Retarded Citizens, 1973-75, Ohio Assn. Retarded Citizens, 1975; bd. dirs. Southfield Youth Symphony Orch., pres., 1978-79; bd. dirs. Epilepsy Center Mich., Detroit, 1975-80, pres., 1978-80; bd. dirs. Mich. Acad. Dentistry for Handicapped, 1983-86; mem. adv. bd. Mich. Soc. for Autistic Citizens, 1981—, Wayne State Univ. Developmental Disabilities Inst., Detroit, 1984—; trustee St. Mark's Day Sch., Jackson Heights, N.Y., 1962-67; trustee Am. Field Service Internat./Intercultural Programs, Inc., 1971-73, bd. dirs., 1973-84, trustee, 1986—. Named Outstanding Tchr. Sch. Dist. City of Pontiac, 1978. Mem. Council for Exceptional Children, Epilepsy Found. Am., Assn. Persons with Severe Handicaps, Am. Assn. on Mental Deficiency, Nat. Assn. Protection and Advocacy Systems (bd. dirs. 1981-83, sec. bd. dirs. 1985-87, dir Kenny Rehab. 1984-87, 1st v.p. 1986), Nat. Assn. for Retarded Citizens, Mich. Assn. for Retarded Citizens, Mt. Holyoke Coll. Alumnae Assn. Episcopalian. Contbr. articles to profl. publs. Home: 1355 Lake Park Birmingham MI 48009 Office: Mich Protection and Advocacy 109 W Michigan Ave Lansing MI 48933

BAUER, EUGENE LEO, otorhinolaryngologist; b. Elmhurst, Ill., Apr. 14, 1915; s. Carl Ferdinand and Marie Louise (Von Bibra) B.; m. Lillian Margaret Weigel, July 10, 1943; children: Margaret, Joan, Carl, Cheryl, John. BS, Elmhurst Coll., 1938; MD, U. Ill., 1942. Cert. Am. Bd. Otolaryngology. Otolaryngology fellow Mayo Clinic Found., Rochester, Minn., 1943-44, 46-49; staff St. Joseph Hosp., St. Paul, 1949, Miller Hosp., St. Paul, 1949-80, United Hosp., St. Paul, 1980—. Served to maj. M.C. U.S. Army, 1944-46, ETO. Decorated Bronze Star. Mem. Am. Acad. Ophthalmology and Otolaryngology, Am. Interprofl. Inst., Minn. Acad. Otolaryngology, Minn. Med. Soc., Ramsey County Med. Soc. Club: Indian Hills Golf (Stillwater, Minn.). Avocations: golf, tennis, Finnish carpentry. Home and Office: 1563 Edgewater Ave Saint Paul MN 55112

BAUER, FREDERICK CHARLES, JR., physician, pathologist; b. Champaign, Ill., Jan. 19, 1918; s. Frederick Charles and Louise (Garrett) B.; m. Margaret Vaniman, June 21, 1941; children—Richard Charles, Peter Frederick. B.S., in Chemistry, U. Ill., 1939; M.D., Harvard U., 1943; M.S. in Pathology, U. Chgo., 1945, Ph.D. in Pathology, 1949. Diplomate Am. Bd. Pathology, Nat. Bd. Med. Examiners. Chief lab. U.S. Army and Vet. Hosp., Northport, N.Y., 1945-47; Seymour-Coman fellow in pathology U. Chgo., 1947-49, asst. prof. pathology, 1951-59; clin. assoc. prof. pathology U. Ill., Chgo., 1959—; attending med. staff St. Lukes and Presbyn. St. Lukes Hosps., Chgo., 1950-60; dir. dept. pathology Silver Cross Hosp., Joliet, Ill., 1960-79, chief of staff, 1968-69, dir. Sch. Med. Tech., 1961-79. Contbr. articles to profl. jours. Trustee Coll. St. Francis, Joliet, 1974-79; pres. Am. Cancer Soc., Joliet, 1978-79. Fellow Am. Soc. Clin. Pathologists, ACP, Inst. Medicine Chgo.; mem. Internat. Acad. Pathologists, AMA. Clubs: Chgo. Yacht; Sturgeon Bay Yacht. Lodge: Rotary. Home: PO Box 173 Sturgeon Bay WI 54235

BAUER, JEFFREY PATRICK, accountant; b. Columbus, July 8, 1949; s. Harold Richard and Agnes Elizabeth (Dunnigan) B.; m. Mary Lue Maiberger, Sept. 23, 1972; children: Bradley Joseph, Scott R., Karen E. BA, Ohio State U., 1971, M Acctg., 1977. CPA, Ohio. Audit supr. Ernst & Whinney, Columbus, Ohio, 1977-82; asst. controller JC Penney Casualty Ins. Co., Westerville, Ohio, 1982-85; acct. project mgr. Nationwide Ins. Co., Columbus, 1985-86, investment, gen. acctg. mgr., 1986—. Served to 1st lt. U.S. Army, 1972-74. Mem. Am. Inst. CPA's, Ohio Soc. CPA's, Cen. Ohio Football Officials Assn. (pres. 1986-87). Roman Catholic. Lodge: Optimist (bd. dir. 1981-83). Home: 1318 Inglis Ave Columbus OH 43212 Office: Nationwide Ins Co 1 Nationwide Plaza Columbus OH 43216

BAUER, JERRY, neurosurgeon; b. Pocking, Fed. Republic Germany, Aug. 18, 1948; s. Morris and Tema Bauer; m. Adrienne Lee Franklin, Sept. 5, 1971; children: Michelle, Hillary, Aaron. BS, U. Ill., Chgo., 1970, MD, 1974. Diplomate Am. Bd. Med. Examiners, Am. Bd. Neurol. Surgery. Intern Northwestern U., 1974-75; resident U. Ill. Hosp., 1975-79; asst. prof. neurol. surgery U. Ill. Med. Ctr., Chgo., 1979—; practice medicine specializing in neurosurgery Park Ridge, Ill., 1979—; cons. neurosurgery Martha Washington Clinic for Handicapped Children, Park Ridge, Ill., 1983—. Mem. Bd. Edn. Dist. #27, Northbrook, Ill., 1985—. Mem. AMA, ACS, Ill. Med. Soc., Chgo. Med. Soc., Chgo. Neurol. Soc., Cen. Neurol. Soc., Am. Assn. Neurol. Surgeons. Office: 1875 Dempster Park Ridge IL 60068

BAUER, JOHN FRANCIS, office service manager; b. St. Paul, Dec. 23, 1938; s. John Joseph Bauer and Loretta Matilda (Kunesh) Johnson; m. Mary Rose Mc Courtney, Apr. 24, 1966 (div. 1979); children: John Michael, William Patrick. Student, U. Minn., 1956-76. Prodn. scheduler 3M Co., St. Paul, 1959-70; asst. office service mgr. Ellerbe, Bloomington, Minn., 1970-77; office mgr. Leef Bros., Mpls., 1977-78; office service mgr. Lieberman Enterprises Inc., Bloomington, 1979—. Dir. Bavarian Musik Meisters. Served with U.S. Army, 1961-63. Mem. Wetherby Judging Assn. (pres. 1970—), Twin City Purchasing Mgrs. Assn. (chmn. office prodn. group 1980—), Am. Legion. Republican. Roman Catholic. Avocations: music, softball. Home: 636 W Larpenteur Ave Saint Paul MN 55113 Office: Lieberman Enterprises Inc 9549 Penn Ave S Bloomington MN 55431

BAUER, MICHAEL WARREN, brokerage executive; b. Mpls., June 3, 1952; s. Francis C. and Marion (Ackerman) B.; B.S., St. John's U., 1975; m. Margaret Mary Weber, Sept. 29, 1978; children—David Michael, Theresa Ann, Mark Anthony, John Benedict. Acct., Touche Ross & Co., Mpls., 1975-78; controller Juran & Moody, Inc., St. Paul, 1978-81; treas., controller, 1982-87; v.p., treas. Fin. Programming Inc., Mpls., 1981-83; chief exec. officer, treas. McClees Investments, Inc., 1987—. Chmn., Oktoberfest, Incarnation Ch., 1981, 82. C.P.A., Minn. Mem. Am. Inst. C.P.A.s, Minn. Soc. C.P.A.s. Republican. Roman Catholic. Clubs: Northwest Health, Men's. Lodge: KC. Home: 6541 Beach Rd Eden Prairie MN 55344-5231 Office: 920 2d Ave S Suite 555 Minneapolis MN 55402

BAUER, NANCY MCNAMARA, TV and radio network executive; b. Madison, Wis., Mar. 17, 1929; d. Richard Hughes and Lucy Jane (Whitaker) Marshall; B.A., U. Wis., 1950, M.S., 1963; m. J.B. McNamara, Dec. 29, 1952 (div. Mar. 1962); children—Margaret Ann, William Patrick; m. 2d, Helmut Robert Bauer, Mar. 4, 1974. Elem. tchr., Madison, 1963-66; specialist ednl. communications U. Wis., Madison, 1966-71, asst. prof., 1971-72; dir. educative services Ednl. Communications Bd., Wis. Ednl. TV and Radio Networks, Madison, 1972—; dir. Central Ednl. Network, 1973-80, 83—, exec. com., 1973-74, chmn. Instructional TV Council, 1977-79; adv. bd. Instructional TV Coop., 1972-75, exec. com., 1976-77; mem. instrnl. radio adv. com. Nat. Public Radio, 1979-82; mem. instructional TV adv. com. Public Broadcasting System, 1978-79, service com., 1980-83; mem ITV Study com. Corp. for Pub. Broadcasting, 1983-85. Ford Found. scholar, 1961-63; recipient Ohio State award, 1975, ABA Gavel award, 1975, Am. Legion Golden Mike award, 1976. Mem. Nat. Assn. Ednl. Broadcasters. Producer, writer numerous instructional series, as nationally distributed Patterns in Arithmetic and Looking Out Is In, TV, 1967, Inquiry: The Justice Thing, radio, 1973. Home: 127 Kensington Dr Madison WI 53704 Office: 3319 W Beltline Hwy Madison WI 53713

BAUER, WILLIAM GENE, diversified manufacturing executive; b. Neillsville, Wis., Aug. 20, 1951; s. Gerald William and Nancy Jane (Heinze) B.; m. Linda Susan Schroeder, June 16, 1973; children: Lance, Brooke, Luke, Courtney. AA in Acctg., Western Wis. Tech. Inst., 1971. Employee Bauer Feed Service, Wilton, Wis., 1965-76; sec., treas. Modern Insulation, Inc., Spencer, Wis., 1976—, B & B Specialties, Inc., Spencer, 1982—; pres. Spencer Transport, Inc., Spencer, 1983—; sec., treas. FACSA, Inc., Spencer, 1985—. Vol. Spencer Boy Scouts, 1981—; mem. com. United Way, 1983, PTA, Spencer, 1985—. Served to sgt. Wis. N.G., 1971-77. Named one of Outstanding Young Men Am., 1986. Mem. Holy Name Soc., Jaycees (officer 1979—, treas. 1981, 85-86, mgmt. v.p. 1982, state dir. 1983-84, local dir. 1984-85, One of Outstanding Young Wisconites 1983). Republican. Roman Catholic. Clubs: Triple Tunnel Snowmobile (Wilton, Wis.) (sec. 1974-75), Bakerville Sno-Rovers (Marshfield, Wis.) (sec. 1976-77). Lodge: K.C. (3d degree 1982). Avocations: bowling, walking, bike riding, swimming. Home: 405 Chestnut St PO Box 338 Spencer WI 54479 Office: FACSA Inc 1206 S Monroe St PO Box 157 Spencer WI 54479

BAUER, WILLIAM JOSEPH, chief judge; b. Chgo., Sept. 15, 1926; s. William Francis and Lucille (Gleason) B.; m. Mary Nicol, Jan. 28, 1950; children—Patricia, Linda. A.B., Elmhurst Coll., 1949, LL.D. (hon.), 1969; J.D., DePaul U., 1952; LL.D. (hon.), John Marshall Law Sch., 1987. Bar: Ill. bar 1951. Partner firm Erlenborn, Bauer & Hotte, Elmhurst, Ill., 1953-64; asst. state's atty. Du Page County, Ill., 1952-56; 1st asst. state's atty. 1956-58, state's atty., 1959-64; judge 18th Jud. Cir. Ct., 1964-70; U.S. dist. atty. No. Ill. Chgo., 1970-71; judge U.S. Dist. Ct. (no. dist.), Chgo., 1971-75; judge U.S. Ct. Appeals, 7th Circuit, 1975-86, chief judge, 1986—; instr. bus. law Elmhurst Coll., 1952-59; adj. prof. law DePaul U., 1978—; former mem. Ill. Supreme Ct. Com. on Pattern Criminal Jury Instrns.; chmn. Fed. Criminal Jury Instrn. Com. 7th Cir. Trustee Elmhurst Coll., 1979—, De Paul U., 1984—, DuPage Meml. Hosp.; bd. advisors Mercy Hosp. ; bd. dirs. Elmhurst YMCA. Served with AUS, 1945-47. Served with U.S. Army, 1945-47. Mem. ABA, Ill. Bar Assn., Du Page County Bar Assn. (past pres.), Chgo. Bar Assn., Fed. Bar Assn. (former bd. dirs.). Roman Catholic. Clubs: Union League, Law, Legal (Chgo.). Home: 213 Grace St Elmhurst IL 60126 Office: U S Ct of Appeals 219 S Dearborn St Chicago IL 60604

BAUGH, MARYMARGARET MAGDALEN OSADCHY, nurse; b. Minot, N.D., Aug. 1, 1928; d. Nazar and Mary (Paul) Osadchy; B.S. in Nursing, Jamestown Coll., 1971; M.S. in Edn. and Adminstrn., N.D. State U., 1979; postgrad. Minn. State U., Moorhead, 1978—; m. Donald P. Baugh, May 13, 1950; children—Deborah, Seemann, Patrick, MaryBeth, Michael. With N.D. State Hosp., Jamestown, 1961—, staff devel. dir., 1974—; nurse ARC, 1959—. Registered nurse, N.D. Mem. Am., N.D. nurses assns., Am. Soc. Health Edn. Tng. (pres. N.D. 1977-78), AAUW (treas., historian, publicity Jamestown 1975-79). Roman Catholic. Home: 1103 1st Ave N Jamestown ND 58401 Office: Staff Devel Dept ND State Hosp Jamestown ND 58401

BAUGHMAN, GEORGE WASHINGTON, III, university official, fin. cons.; b. Pitts., July 7, 1937; s. George W. and Cecile M. (Lytel) B.; m. Sandra Ann Johnson, June 21, 1987; 1 child, Lynn. B.S. in Psychology, Ohio State U., 1959, M.B.A., 1961, postgrad., 1961-63; Pres., Advanced Research Assos., Worthington, Ohio, 1960—; asst. instr. fin. Ohio State U., Columbus, 1961-63, research asso., office of controller, 1964-66, dir. data processing, 1966-68, 70-72, dir. adminstrv. research, 1966-72, asso. to acad. v.p., 1968-70, exec. dir. univ. budget, 1970-72, dir. spl. projects, office of pres., 1972—; chmn. bd. Hosp. Audiences, Inc., 1974-80. Founding bd. dirs. Coll. and U. Machine Records Conf., 1971-73; bd. dirs. Uniplan Environ. Groups, Inc., 1970-73, chmn., 1971-73; chmn. Franklin County (Ohio) Republican Demographics and Voter Analysis Com., 1975-80; bd. dirs. Cedar Hill Assocs., 1980—, Alarm Ctr. Internat., Forerunner Corp. 1984—, Inventors Council Ohio, 1984-86; Home Health Inst., 1984-86; mem. Ohio State Dental Bd., 1980-85; mem. Gov.'s Export Council, 1982-83; mem. Gov.'s Tech. Task Force, 1982-83. Am. Council on Edn. grantee, 1976-77; Nat. Assn. Coll. and Univ. Bus. Officers grantee, 1977-79; NSF grantee, 1980-86; Reisman fellow, 1962. Mem. Assn. Instl. Research, Press Club Ohio, Coll. and Univ. Systems Exchange, AAAS, Phi Alpha Kappa, Delta Tau Delta. Republican. Presbyterian. Author: (with D.H. Baker) Writing to People, 1963; (with R.W. Brady) University Program Budgeting, 1968, Administrative Data Processing, 1975; contbr. articles to profl. publs. Home: 833 Lakeshore Dr Worthington OH 43085 Office: 190 N Oval Mall Columbus OH 43210

BAUGHMAN, ROY ALLAN, peace corps recruiter, fisheries consultant; b. Okmulgee, Okla., Feb. 23, 1957; s. Jack Wesley and Shirley Evelyn (Newstrom) B.; m. Dana Lesley Hamm, Aug. 28, 1986. BS, Okla. State U., 1979. Fisheries technician Ministry of Agr., Liberia, 1981-82; fisheries extension officer Ministry of Agr., Fiji, 1982-83; fisheries extension trainer U. Okla., Norman, 1984; recruiter Peace Corps, Kansas City, Kans., 1984—. Treas. Kansas City Returned Peace Corps Vols., 1985-86. Home: 1255 S Topeka Ave Topeka KS 66612

BAUGHN, MICHAEL LYNN, educator, mayor; b. Colby, Kans., Apr. 30, 1948; s. James Leslie and Wilma Jean (Burkhead) B.; A.B., Asbury Coll., 1970; M.S., Ft. Hays Kans. State U., 1976. Tchr., Brewster (Kans.) Unified Sch. Dist., 1970-76, instr. secondary social studies, 1970-81, prin., 1976-81; curator Butterfield Trail Mus., 1966-73, elem. supr., 1973-76. Dep. sheriff Thomas County, 1970-81, 82—, capt., 1986—; dep. sheriff Logan County, 1970—; dir. Brewster Civil Def., 1971-79; city marshal, Brewster, 1970-74; mem. Brewster City Council, 1974-79, pres., 1979, mayor, 1979—; owner, operator Brewster IGA Store, 1981-85; pres., Butterfield Trail Assn., 1974—; chmn. Hi-Plains History Commn., 1971-73 86—, dir. pub. relations, 1973-79; vol. rural fireman, 1975-85; vol. city fireman, 1980-85; mem. CAP, 1981—; precinct committeeman Republican Party, 1974—; mem. Thomas County Rep. Central Com., 1974—, sec.-treas., 1980—; justice of peace, 1972-74; mem. Selective Service Local Bd. 31, 1983—; mem. adv. bd. Ret. Sr. Vol. Program, 1978-81; mem. Thomas County Council on Aging, 1979-82; mem. adult edn. adv. bd. Colby Community Coll., 1975-82; mem. adminstrv. bd. Brewster United Meth. Ch., 1976-79; treas. Thomas County Centennial Com., 1983-86; bd. dirs. Brewster Sr. Citizen Ctr., 1986—; chmn. U.S. Constn. Bicentennial Commn. Brewster. Mem. Northwestern Plains Am. Revolution Bicentennial Park Assn. (pres. 1974-77, treas. 1981—), Western Plains Arts Council (sec. 1973-74), Nat. Assn. Secondary Sch. Prins. (chpt. sec. 1981), Kans. Hist. Soc. (dir. 1979-82), Monument High Sch. Alumni Assn. (v.p. 1983-86, pres. 1986—), Phi Delta Kappa (chpt. sec.). Clubs: Masons (past master), Shriners, Lions (pres. 1975, gov. dist. 17NW 1979). Home: PO Box 216 Brewster KS 67732 Office: 225 N Court Colby KS 67701

BAULDRICK, WALTER RYLAND, SR., engineering company executive; b. Winston Salem, N.C., Oct. 10, 1946; s. Cleveland P. and Rachel (Allen)

Cheek; m. Patricia Ann White, June 8, 1968; children—Walter, Shani, Rahmad. B.S. in Civil Engring., S.C. State Coll., 1968; M.Div., McCormick Theol. Sem., 1981. Design engr. Process div. UOP, Des Plaines, Ill., 1968-72, sr. engr., 1972-79, mgr. employee relations, 1979-82, dir. employee relations, 1982-86, dir ops. 1986—. Bd. dirs. NAACP, DuPage County, Ill., 1982; mem. Maywood Human Relations Commn., Ill., 1970-76; mem. African Episcopalian Ministerial Alliance, Chgo., 1981—. Mem. Am. Soc. Personnel Adminstrn., Tech. Human Relations Mgrs. Assn., Alpha Phi Alpha. Office: Signal Research Ctr Inc 50 E Algonquin Rd Box 5016 Des Plaines IL 60017

BAUM, H. JAMES, retailing executive; b. Morris, Ill., Mar. 20, 1938; s. George Humphrey and Iona (Grey) B.; m. Carol Topping, Nov. 4, 1961. B.A., Dartmouth Coll., 1961. City planner Boston Redevel. Authority, 1961; v.p. Baum's Inc., Morris, 1963-85, pres., 1985—; dir. Grundy County Nat. Bank, Morris; pres. Grundy Nat. Bldg. Corp., 1983—. Pres. Morris Community High Sch. Bd. Edn., 1984, Morris Community Hosp., 1975-79; chmn. Morris Planning Commn., 1965-68; v.p. Rainbow council Boy Scouts Am., 1974; elder First Presbyn. Ch., Morris, 1980—. Served with U.S. Army, 1961-63. Republican. Club: Morris Country (v.p. 1973-74). Avocations: reading, outdoor landscaping, sailing. Home: 718 Briar Ln Morris IL 60450 Office: Baum's Inc 221 Liberty St Morris IL 60450

BAUM, JAMES JOSEPH, infosystems specialist; b. Chgo., May 5, 1958; s. Joseph John and Ruth Edith (Peterson) B.; m. Jamil Van Duser, Oct. 14, 1984. BA, Augustana Coll., 1980. Salesman Active Elec. Supply Co., Chgo., 1981-85; computer programmer, analyst Law Bulletin Pub. Co., Chgo., 1985—. Lutheran. Home: 903 Newport Chicago IL 60657 Office: Law Bulletin Pub Co 415 N State St Chicago IL 60614

BAUM, JEFFREY DAVID, aviation company executive; b. Milw., June 21, 1952; s. Leo Alvin and Jean Phyliss (Stern) B.; m. Krystine Marie Brown, 1986. BBA, U. Wis., Whitewater, 1974, MBA, 1975. Lic. comml. pilot. Asst. to chancellor U. Wis., Whitewater, 1975-79; various positions Watertown (Wis.) Aviation Inc., 1979-81; pres. Air Sinclair, Inc., Milledgeville, Ga., 1985—, Wis. Aviation, Inc., Watertown, 1981—; Pres. Wis. Aviation Maintenance Inc., Watertown, 1987—; lectr. U. Wis., Whitewater, 1976-83. Contbr. articles to profl. jours. Mem. Wis. Aviation Traders Assn. (bd. dirs. 1985—, Aviation Businessman of Yr. 1985). Home: 508 Oak Park Ave Watertown WI 53094 Office: Wis Aviation Inc 1741 River Dr Watertown WI 53094

BAUM, M(ARY) CAROLYN, occupational therapist; b. Chgo., Mar. 26, 1943; d. Gibson Henry and Nelle (Curry) Manville; B.S., U. Kans., 1966; M.A., Webster Coll., 1979; 1 dau., Kirstin Carol. Staff occupational therapist U. Kans. Med. Center, 1966-67; staff occupational therapist Research Med. Center, Kansas City, Mo., 1967, dir. occupational therapy, 1967-73, dir. phys. medicine and rehab., 1973-76; dir. occupational therapy, clin. services Washington U. Sch. Medicine, St. Louis, 1976—, asst. research prof. neurology; vis. prof. NYU and U. Mo., 1985—; allied health rep. AMA Health Policy Agenda for Am. People. Coordinator St. Louis Ind. Living Council, 1980-81; pres. Am. Occupational Therapy Cert. Bd.; mem. nominating com. Greater Kansas City Health Systems Agy.; vice-chmn. Village Ch. Accessibility Task Force, 1974-76. Named Employee of Yr., Research Hosp., 1974, Kans. Occupational Therapist of Year, 1975. Fellow Am. Occupational Therapy Assn. (chmn. standards and ethics commn. 1973-77, nat. v.p. 1978-82, pres. 1982-83, Eleanor Clarke Slagel Lectureship award 1980, award of Merit 1984, pres. cert. bd. 1986—); mem. Mo. Occupational Therapy Assn. (occupational therapy clinician of yr. 1985), Mo. Assn. Rehab. Facilities (past bd. dirs.), St. Louis Med. Rehab. Soc. (pres.-elect 1987). Author: Understanding the Prospective Payment System: A Business Perspective, 1986; contbg. author: Occupational Therapy, 1978, 83; contbr. articles to profl. jours. Office: Dept Occupational Therapy Washington U Sch Medicine 509 S Euclid St Saint Louis MO 63110

BAUMAN, CLARENCE, accountant, small business owner; b. Java, S.D., Feb. 18, 1923; s. Fred G. and Rosina (Fiechtner) B.; m. Marilyn J. Sauer, July 16, 1950; children: Steven, Clyde, William, Amy. BA in Acctg., No. State Tchrs. Coll., 1955. Mgr. Comml. Coll., Bismarck, N.D., 1955-60; acct. Dunaley Paint Spot, Bismarck, 1960-63; controller Holiday Inn, Bismarck, 1963-64; chief acct. Calvert Drilling, Bismarck, 1964-66; controller Kirschmann Mfg. Co., Bismarck, 1966-71; owner, acct. Drumstick Cafe, Bismarck, 1972—. Editor newsletter, 1983—. Mem. N.D. Soc. Pub. Accts. (sec.-treas. 1980-84), Germans from Russia (v.p. 1983-86). Avocations: reading, outdoor work. Home: 822 W Owens Ave Bismarck ND 58501 Office: Drumstick Cafe 307 3d St Bismarck ND 58501

BAUMANN, DANIEL E., newspaper executive; b. Milw., Apr. 10, 1937; s. Herbert F. and Agnes V. (Byrne) B.; m. Karen R. Weinkauf, Apr, 29, 1961; children: James W., Jennifer R., Colin D. BJ, U. Wis., 1958, MA in Polit. Sci., 1962, Cert. in Russian Area Studies, 1962. Reporter South Milwaukee (Wis.) Voice Jour., 1958-59, East St. Louis (Ill.) Jour., 1959-60; pub. relations rep. Credit Union Nat. Assn., Washington, 1962-64; reporter Paddock Publs., Inc., Arlington Heights, Ill., 1964-66, mng. editor, 1966-68, exec. editor, 1968-70, editor and pub. Circle newpapers, 1970-75, v.p., editor, 1975-83, sr. v.p., gen. mgr., editor, 1983-86, pres., editor, 1986—. Mem. High Tech. Corridors Council, Palatine, Ill., 1986—; bd. dirs. Greater Woodfield Conv. and Visitors Bur., Schaumburg, Ill., 1985—, Twinbrook YMCA, Roselle, Ill., 1986—. Served with USNR. Recipient William Alan White award U. Kans., 1976. Mem. Am. Newspaper Pubs. Assn., Am. Soc. Newspaper Editors, Internat. Newspaper Advt. and Mktg. Execs., Soc. Profl. Journalists, Chgo. Headline Club (Peter Lisagor award 1983), Chgo. Assn. Dir. Mktg., Sigma Delta Chi. Avocations: photography, travel. scuba diving. Office: Paddock Publs Daily Herald 217 W Campbell St PO Box 280 Arlington Heights IL 60006

BAUMANN, GARY JOSEPH, accountant; b. N.Y.C., Dec. 7, 1949; s. Gerard Joseph and Mary Cecelia (Dunn) B.; m. Rosalyn Marie Gavrilovich, Oct. 30, 1971; children: Lauren Rosemary, Michael Gerard. BS, U. Detroit, 1973, MBA, 1976. CPA, Mich. Staff acct. Ernst & Whinney, Detroit, 1974-75, sr. acct., 1975-76, supr., 1976-78, mgr., 1978-83, ptnr., 1983—; adj. lectr. grad. sch. bus. adminstrn. U. Mich., Ann Arbor, 1986—. Treas. Camp Oakland Youth Programs, Inc., Oxford, Mich., 1980—. Served to sgt. U.S. Army, 1971-73. Mem. Am. Inst. CPA's. Republican. Roman Catholic. Clubs: Detroit Athletic, Oakland Hills (Birmingham, Mich.). Avocations: golf, collecting wine. Office: Ernst & Whinney 200 Renaissance Ctr Suite 2300 Detroit MI 48243

BAUMANN, GREGORY WILLIAM, physician, consultant; b. Detroit, June 20, 1947; s. Alfred Louis Baumann and Marian (Bartholomew) Martens; m. Cynthia Rae Bruhnsen, May 18, 1986. BS, U. Mich., 1968, MD cum laude, 1972. Diplomate Am. Bd. Emergency Medicine. Intern Albert Einstein Coll. Medicine Bronx Mcpl. Dept. Neurology, 1972-73; resident in neurology U. Mich., 1973-74; staff physician Foote Hosp., Jackson, Mich., 1974—, chmn. emergency med. dept., 1979—, med. dir. emergency med. services project, 1981-86, dir. ambulatory care, 1982—; cons. emergency med. services, Jackson, 1982—; mem. adv. life support tech. com. Mich. Dept. Pub. Health, Lansing, 1985—; exec. bd. dirs. Mich. Assn. Med. Examiners, Ann Arbor, 1986—; med. dir. Mich. Internat. Speedway, Bklyn., 1986—; chief med. examiner Jackson County, 1986—. Bd. dirs. Hospice of Jackson, 1984—. Recipient Merit award March of Dimes, 1970; research grantee U. Mich. Med. Sch., 1972. Mem. AMA, Mich. Med. Soc., Jackson County Med. Soc., Am. Coll. Emergency Physicians, Nat. Assn. Med. Examiners, Am. Assn. Med. Systems and Informatics. Lutheran. Avocation: computer applications in medicine. Office: Foote Hosp Inc 205 N East Ave Jackson MI 49201

BAUMANN, PAUL ARTHUR, radiation oncologist; b. West Allis, Wis., Sept. 30, 1932; s. Erwin Harry and Lydia Emma (Steinke) B.; m. Bethel Horter Smith, May 13, 1961; children: Bethel Ann, Annette, Ruth. BS in Med. Sci., U. Wis., 1954, MD, 1957. Intern U. Pitts., 1957, resident in pathology, 1960; resident in radiology U. Minn., 1963-66; fellow U. Tex. M.D. Anderson Hosp. & Tumor Inst., Houston, 1967-68; chief dept. radiation therapy Wesley Med. Ctr., Wichita, Kans., 1968—; practice medicine specializing in radiation oncology Wichita, 1968—. Pres. Kans. Div. Am. Cancer Soc., Topeka, 1979. Served to lt. comdr. USPHS, 1962-63. Fellow Am. Coll. Radiology; mem. AMA, Radiology Soc. N.Am., Am. Radium Soc., Am. Soc. Therapeutic Radiology and Oncology, Kans. Radiol. Soc. Republican. Presbyterian. Avocations: stamp collecting, swimming, carpentry, wind surfing. Home: 6042 E 13th St Wichita KS 67208 Office: 3333 E Central Wichita KS 67208

BAUMEISTER, CARL F., retired physician; b. Dolliver, Iowa, May 15, 1907; s. Charles F. and Lida Bard (Moore) B.; B.S.; Chicago U., 1930; M.D., Iowa U., 1933; m. Eleanor Hoskins, Apr. 19, 1930; children—Richard. Physician in internal med., Ind. U. Hosps., 1933-36, Louisville U. Hosps., 1936-37, Council Bluffs Clinic, 1937-43, Berwyn (Ill.) Surburban Med. Center, from 1943; mem. staff MacNeal Meml. Hosp., Berwyn; instr. internal medicine U. Ill., 1943-50, clin. asst. prof., 1950-71, 73-82, ret., 1982; clin. asst. prof. medicine Stritch Sch. Medicine Loyola U., Maywood, Ill., 1971-73; med. staff Loyola U. Hosp., 1971-73. Fellow Inst. of Medicine Chgo.; member AMA, Am. Heart Assn., Assn. Am. Med. Colls., Am. Med. Writers Assn., Am. Diabetes Assn., S.A.R., N.Y. Acad. Sci. Mason. Contbr. articles to med. jours. Abstract editor on med. education Excerpta Medica of Amsterdam. Author: Computer Diagnosis of the Acute Surgical Abdomen. Research diagnosis and treatment new type vascular headache. Home: 120 S Delaplaine Rd Riverside IL 60546

BAUMGAERTNER, JAMES CARL, dermatologist, peace activist; b. St. Paul, Oct. 13, 1950; s. Carl Joseph and Mary Catherine (Mahoney) B.; m. Peggy Lynn Carter, Dec. 29, 1973; children: Karen Melissa, John William, Paul Joseph. BS, Calif. Polytechnic State U., 1972; MD, U. Minn., 1976. Diplomate Am. Bd. Dermatology. Intern Hennepin County Med. Ctr., Mpls., 1976-77; dermatology resident Univ. Minn. Hosps., Mpls., 1977-80; staff dermatologist Gundersen Clinic, La Crosse, Wis., 1980—. Treas. Physicians for Social Responsibility, La Crosse, 1985—; founder, coordinator Internat. Peace Lantern Exchange Project, La Crosse, 1985—. Mem. Am. Acad. Dermatology, Wis. Med. Soc., Minn. Dermatol. Soc., Wis. Dermatol. Soc., Alpha Omega Alpha. Democrat. Roman Catholic. Office: Gundersen Clinic Ltd 1836 South Ave La Crosse WI 54601

BAUMGARDNER, DAVID KEITH, printing company executive; b. Mpls., Aug. 4, 1956; s. Dwight E. and Lorraine (Sprader) B.; m. Rita O'Malley, Aug. 1, 1982; 1 child, Laura. BA, Coll. St. Thomas, 1978, MBA, 1982. CPA, Minn. Audit mgr. Taylor, McCaskill & Co., Ltd., St. Paul, 1978-86; v.p. fin. H.M. Smyth Co., Inc., St. Paul, 1986—. Mem. Am. Inst. CPA's, Minn. Soc. CPA's, Nat. Assn. Mgmt. Accts. Roman Catholic. Avocations: tennis, skiing, camping. Home: 1746 Palisade Circle Eagan MN 55123 Office: HM Smyth Co Inc PO Box 64669 Saint Paul MN 55164

BAUMGARTEN, MARION BETOR, personnel administrator; b. Washington, May 15, 1960; d. Gregory Alden and Gwendolyn Swift (Althauser) Betor; m. Jonathan David Baumgarten, Aug. 14, 1982. BA, St. John's Coll., 1982. Claims examiner U.S. R.R. Retirement Bd., Chgo., 1982-83, employee relations specialist, 1983-87; employee relations staffing specialist U.S. Dept. Labor, Chgo., 1987—. Mem. Parking and Traffic Commn., Oak Park, Ill., 1987—, Lone Tree area council personnel task force Girl Scouts U.S., Oak Park, 1986—, Ctr. for Bus. and Ethics, Chgo., 1986—. Home: PO Box 83 Oak Park IL 60303 Office: US Dept Labor-Personnel Office 230 S Dearborn 10th Floor Chicago IL 60604

BAUMGARTNER, ALDEN (FREDERICK), JR., transportation and distribution executive; b. Chgo., Nov. 29, 1930; s. Alden F. and Anne R. (Sehocke) B.; A.A., Wilson Jr. Coll., 1947-49; B.A., Roosevelt U., 1949-51; Asso., Coll. Advanced Traffic, 1956-57; m. Rosalie O'Connor, Nov. 13, 1954; children—Diane, Iris, Melissa, Kevin. Dist. mgr. Spector Freight Systems Co., St. Louis, 1961-63; regional mgr. To FC div. Fruehauf Co., Chgo., 1970-76, Acme Fast Freight, 1978-79; v.p. Transp. Cons., Chgo., 1978—; mem. faculty Coll. Advanced Traffic. Mem. com. Ind. Voters Mo. and Ill. Served with USNR, 1945-50; Transp. Corps USAR, 1955-59; flotilla comdr. USCG Aux. Mem. Am. Soc. Traffic, Delta Nu Alpha (pres. St. Louis chpt. 1969-70). Roman Catholic. Clubs: St. Louis Transp., Chgo. Transp., Masons, Shriners. Office: 18264 Prince Dr South Holland IL 60473

BAUMRUCK, SCOTT ALAN, professional association administrator; b. Berwyn, Ill., Feb. 1, 1952; s. Earl E. and Trudy M. (Greenall) B.; children: Scott Jr., Kimberly. Student, Morton Coll., 1970-71. Employment specialist Sears, Roebuck & Co., Chgo., 1971-80; employment mgr. Urban Investment, Chgo., 1980-81; mgr. corp. compliance Chgo. Title, 1981-85; mgr. mem. devel. and edn. Nat. Sporting Goods Assn., Mt. Prospect, Ill., 1986; mgr. div. and edn. services Paper Industry Mgmt. Assn., Arlington Heights, Ill., 1986—. Active Zoning Bd. Appeals, Brookfield, Ill., 1986. Mem. U.S. Jaycees (v.p. 1986, pres. Brookfield chpt. 1981-82, v.p. Ill. chpt. 1984-85, pres. 1985-86, Outstanding Local Pres. 1981-82, Outstanding Dist. Dir. 1982-83, Outstanding Regional Dir. 1983-84, Outstanding Area v.p. 1984-85, Presdl. Award of Honor 1981-85, Outstanding Local Dir. Brookfield chpt. 1980-81).

BAUMWELL, STERLING HOWARD, obstetrician, gynecologist; b. Flushing, N.Y., Aug. 6, 1950; s. Leo and Beatrice (Karman) B.; m. Kathie Sue Sawyer, Sept. 12, 1981; 1 child, Stephanie Noelle. BA, U. Rochester, 1972; MD, Washington U., 1976. Diplomate Am. Bd. Ob-Gyn. Obstetrician/gynecologist Sterling-Rock Falls (Ill.) Clinic, 1980-81; practice medicine specializing in ob-gyn. Sterling, 1981—; med. dir. family planning Whiteside County Health Dept., Morrison, Ill., 1981-85. Mem. AMA, Ill. Med. Soc., Whiteside County Med. Soc. Home: 1981 Ave G Sterling IL 61081 Office: 202 W Miller Rd Sterling IL 61081

BAUR, DALE ALAN, dentist; b. Cleve., June 13, 1954; s. Richard Daniel and Clara (Jezewski) B.; m. Nancy Marie Ivansek, Aug. 1, 1980 (div. May 1985); m. Nancy K. Dellisanti, Nov. 28, 1986. BS in Bioengring., Cleve. State U., 1976; DDS, Case Western Res. U., 1980. Lic. dentist, Ohio, Md., Ill. Gen. practice dentistry Lorain, Ohio, 1983—; cons. St. Paul Ins. Co., Cleve., 1984—; mem. faculty Case Western Res. U. Sch. Dentistry, Cleve., 1985—. Vol. dentist Free Med. and Dental Clinic, Cleve., 1985—; mem. Rep. Nat. Com., 1983—. Served to capt. U.S. Army, 1980-83, with res. Mem. Am. Acad. Dental Radiology (Outstanding Achievement award 1980), Tau Beta Pi. Republian. Roman Catholic. Avocations: boating, running. Office: 1083 Meister Rd Lorain OH 44052

BAURER, JOAN RUTH, investment company executive, certified financial planner and consultant; b. N.Y.C., July 10, 1934; d. Jack Maurice and Elsie Frank (Galkin) Lawson; B.A., Queens Coll., 1955; postgrad. Hunter Coll., 1955-57, Fresno State Coll., 1966-67; postgrad. in fin. Calif. State Coll., Bakersfield, 1973-76; m. Martin E. Baurer, Sept. 23, 1953 (div. May 1979); children—Benjamin Zachary, Valery Suzanne. Tchr. home econs., Astoria, N.Y., 1957-59, New Rochelle, N.Y., 1958-60; tchr. gen. sci., Liverpool, N.Y., 1960; account exec. Internat. Securities Co., Bakersfield, 1975-77, Blunt, Ellis & Loewi Co., Inc., Waukegan, Ill., 1977-79; with All Am. Mgmt., Des Plaines, Ill., 1979-83; br. mgr., registered rep. Integrated Resources Equity Corp., N.Y.C., 1984—; pres. Joan Baurer & Co., Inc., registered investment advisors; admitted to registry of fin. planning practictioners. Vol. dir. menu planning Guild House, restaurant for benefit Child Guidance Clinic, Bakersfield, 1964-66. Mem. Internat. Assn. Fin. Planners, Inst. Cert. Fin. Planners. Clubs: Women's Network (Crystal Lake); Ski. Office: 610 Crystal Point Dr Suite 3 Crystal Lake IL 60014

BAUSCHARD, RICHARD BACH, architect; b. N.Y.C., July 11, 1944; s. Fred George and Harriett (Durlin) B.; m. Jane M. O'Brien, July 2, 1966; 1 dau., Laura. B.A., Syracuse U., 1967, B.Arch., 1968; M.Arch., U. Pa., 1969. Project designer Van Dijk, Johnson & Partners-Architects, Cleve., 1971-75, assoc. design, 1976-78, assoc. partner, dir. mktg., 1979-81, partner, dir. mktg., 1982—; adj. lectr. Case Western Res. U., 1973-78; architecture lectr. Cleve. Area Arts Council, Cleve. State U., 1979-85. Vol. United Way campaign, 1975-79, team leader, 1980-83, group leader, 1984—; mem. nominating com. Cleve. Arts Prize, 1986-87, NOVA; mem. fine arts adv. bd. City of Cleve., 1985; mem. nat. monument adv. com. Siegel & Schuster; bd. dirs. City Cleve. Fine Arts Council, 1985. Served to lt. (j.g.) USN, 1969-71. Recipient medal N.Y. State Soc. Architects, 1968. Mem. AIA (exec. com. Cleve. chpt. 1980-86, treas. 1982-83, pres. 1984-86, vice chmn. nat. practice com. 1987, nat. compensation task force 1986—, Sch. medal 1968), Soc. Mktg. Profl. Services, Architects Soc. Ohio (bd. mem. 1980), Psi Upsilon. Clubs: Union League (Chgo.); Skating, Athletic (Cleve.). Home: 14500 Shaker Blvd Shaker Heights OH 44120 Office: 700 St Clair W Suite 400 Cleveland OH 44113

BAUX, DAVID KEVIN, computer scientist; b. Long Beach, Calif., Apr. 27, 1958; s. Paul Eugene and Anna Lorene (Martin) B. BS, U. Wis., La Crosse, 1980. Lectr. Columbia (Mo.) Coll., 1982-84; data base analyst Mayo Clinic, Rochester, Minn., 1985—; cons. Baux Computing Assocs., Waynesville, Mo., 1982-84. Served to capt. U.S. Army, 1980-84. Mem. Assn. Computing Machinery, Blue Key, Upsilon Pi Epsilon (sec. 1978-79). Democrat. Mem. Reorganized Ch. Latter Day Saints. Avocations: photography, art collecting, backpacking, music. Office: Mayo Clinic 200 1st St SW Rochester MN 55905

BAVASI, PETER, professional baseball executive. Pres., chief operating officer Cleve. Indians. Office: Cleve Indians Cleve Stadium Cleveland OH 44114

BAXTER, ELAINE, secretary of state; b. Chgo., Jan. 16, 1933; d. Clarence Arthur and Margaret (Clark) Bland; m. Harry Youngs Baxter, Oct. 2, 1954; children: Katherine, Harry, John. BA, U. Ill., 1954; teaching cert., Iowa Wesleyan Coll., 1970; MS, U. Iowa, 1978. History tchr. Burlington (Iowa) High Sch., 1972; city council mem. Burlington City Council, 1973-75; sr. liaison officer U.S. Dept. HUD, Washington, 1979-81; state rep. Iowa Ho. Reps., Des Moines, 1982-86; sec. state State of Iowa, Des. Moines, 1987—; cons. Devel. Research Co., Des Moines, 1982. Sr. advisor Mondale/Ferraro campaign, 1984; del. Dem. Midterm Conv., Kansas City, Mo., 1974; chairperson Steamboat Days, Burlington, 1976; adv. bd. mem. Found. for Iowa Children and Family Services, 1987—; appointed by Pres. Jimmy Carter to 8th Cir. Ct. Appeals nominating panel. Mem. Women's Equity Action League (bd. dirs.), Victorian Soc. of Iowa (adv. bd.), Am. Soc. of Pub. Adminstrn. (bd. dirs. Iowa chpt.). Avocation: hist. preservation. Home: 1016 N 4th St Burlington IA 52601 Office: Sec of State Statehouse Des Moines IA 50319

BAXTER, JOHN THOMAS, chemical company executive; b. Anderson, Ind., Apr. 15, 1959; s. Donald Charles and Mary Hannah (Bender) B. AA, Fla. Keys Community Coll., 1983; student, U. Fla., 1983-84, Ball State U., 1987—. V.p. Del. Chem. Corp., Daleville, Ind., 1984—. Served with USN, 1978-81, with Res. 1981-83. Mem. Blu Key. Avocations: remodeling old structures, sailing, skiing. Home: 1005 Dresser Dr Anderson IN 46011 Office: Del Chem Corp 3d and Pleasant Sts PO Box 126 Daleville IN 47334

BAXTER, JOSEPH DIEDRICH, dentist; b. New Albany, Ind., Sept. 11, 1937; s. James William, Jr. and Beatrice (Diedrich) B.; A.B., Ind. U., 1959, D.M.D., U. Louisville, 1969; m. Carroll Jane Bell, Dec. 23, 1972. Practice dentistry, New Albany, 1969—. Bd. dirs. Floyd County (Ind.) Econ. Opportunity Corp., 1971-76. Served with AUS, 1960-61. Mem. Floyd County Dental Soc. (pres. 1972-74), Am. Dental Assn., Phi Gamma Delta. Republican. Methodist. Home: 36 Bellewood Dr New Albany IN 47150 Office: Professional Arts Bldg New Albany IN 47150

BAXTER, RICHARD BRIAN, lawyer; b. Detroit, Feb. 22, 1927; s. Charles Lewis and Madelyn (Kilburtus) B.; m. Margaret Elizabeth, May 28, 1949; children—Judith Ann, Janet Carole, Richard Brian, Jr. A.B., U. Mich., 1951, J.D., 1954. Bar: Mich. 1954. ptnr. Dykema, Gossett, Spencer, Goodnow & Trigg and predecessor, Grand Rapids, 1965—, sr. ptnr., 1979—; mem. faculty, participant continuing legal edn., Advocacy Inst. Served with USAAC, 1944-46. Recipient Exceptional Performance citation Def. Research Inst., 1981. Mem. Fellow Mich. Bar Found., Am. Bar Found.; mem. Grand Rapids Bar Assn. (pres. 1977), Mich. Def. Trial Counsel (pres. 1981), Am. Coll. Trial Lawyers, Internat. Acad. Trial Lawyers (dir. 1985—), Internat. Soc. Barristers, Fedn. Ins. Counsel Internat. Assn. Ins. Counsel Am. Judicature Soc. Club: Cascade Hills Country (Grand Rapids). Author: Michigan Continuing Legal Education Defenses in Legal Malpractice, 1974; Defenses in Wrongful Death Cases, 1975; contbr. chpts. and articles to legal publs. Home: 1318 Woodcliff Dr SE East Grand Rapids MI 49506 Office: Dykema Gossett Spencer et al 200 Oldtown Riverfront Bldg 348 Louis Campau Promenade NW Grand Rapids MI 49503

BAYER, BARRY DAVID, lawyer; b. Chgo., Mar. 5, 1943; s. William Robert and Jeanne (Rosner) B.; m. Susan Irene Platt, June 21, 1964; children: William, Jonathan, Elisabeth. AB, U. Chgo., 1964; JD, U. Ill., 1969. Bar: Ill. 1969. Sole practice Homewood, Ill., 1969-83, Chgo., 1983—; bd. dirs. Internat. Apple Core, Inc. Author: Dynamics of VisiCalc, 1983; contbg. editor Computers in Acctg. mag., 1985—, Apple Orchard, 1982-84; contbr. and columnist Desktop Computer mag., 1981-83; contbr. articles to profl. jours. Hearing officer Ill. State Bd. Edn. Mem. Chgo. Bar Assn. (chmn. legis. subcom. real property law com. 1983-86), Am. Arbitration Assn. (arbitrator 1984-85), Computer Press Assn. (sec. 1984—). Avocations: music, sci. fiction, electronic computer communication. Home: 2842 Walnut Homewood IL 60430 Office: 950 W 175th St PO Box 1506 Homewood IL 60430

BAYER, MAX HENRY, stone quarry company executive; b. Manhattan, Kans., Oct. 23, 1934; s. Henry B. and Wilma (Buntis) B.; m. J. Sue Campbell, May 18, 1958; children: Steven M., Brent B., Janell L. Student, Kans. State U., 1954-56. Pres. Bayer Stone, Inc., St. Marys, Kans., 1956—; bd. dirs. Bayer Constrn. Co., Inc. Mem. Bldg. Stone Inst., St. Marys C. of C. Republican. Methodist. Avocations: community involvement, sponsoring stone symposiums for Kans. Sculptors Assn. Home: 507 Mission Saint Marys KS 66536 Office: Bayer Stone Inc 120 N 6th Saint Marys KS 66536

BAYES, STEVEN LESLIE, social services organization administrator, financial consultant; b. Dayton, Ohio, Feb. 24, 1956; s. Herbert and Dorothy Louise (Baker) B.; m. Roberta Ann Borkowski, Oct. 31, 1981 (div. Aug. 18, 1986). Cert., St. Louis U., 1969; BSBA, Capital U., 1986. Billing clk. Children's Med. Ctr., Dayton, 1975-76, accountant, 1976-79, mgr. grants, 1979-81; dir. fin. Planned Parenthood of Miami Valley, Dayton, 1981—. Mem. steering com. West YMCA/YWCA, Dayton; pres. St. Adalbert Cath. Ch., Dayton, 1984-86; bd. dirs. Big Bros./Big Sisters Orgn., Dayton; active Polish Am. Dem. Club. Named one of Outstanding Young Men Am., 1986; named speaker of month Greater Dayton Jaycees, 1986. Mem. Montgomery County Jaycees (v.p.), Gem City Dog Obedience Club. Avocations: jogging, photography, cycling, classical music, volleyball. Office: Planned Parenthood Miami Valley 224 N Wilkinson St Dayton OH 45402

BAYH, EVAN, secretary of state; b. Terre Haute, Ind., Dec. 26, 1955; s. Birch Evans Jr. and Marvella (Hern) B.; married. BS in Bus. Econs., Ind. U., 1978; JD, U. Va., 1981. Sec. of state State of Ind., Indpls., 1987—. Democrat. Office: Sec of State's Office State House Rm 201 Indianapolis IN 46204

BAYLESS, LAWRENCE GRANT, artist; machinery company executive; b. Crawfordsville, Ind., May 19, 1935; s. Lloyd Richard and Geneice (Patton) B.; B.F.A., Bradley U., 1957; m. Joyce Ann Stribling, June 23, 1957; children—Robert, Michael, John, Ann, Mark, Amy, Joe. Artist, Squires Advt. Agy., Springfield, Ill., 1957-59, Greeley Advt., Springfield, 1959-60; artist, designer Mueller Co., Decatur, Ill., 1960-65; art dir. Evan and Assoc., Springfield, 1965-70; head designer Bur. of Design, Public Hearing Services, State of Ill., Springfield, 1970; acting supr. program design, artist edn. center Fiat-Allis, Springfield, 1970-74, supr. multi-media graphics, world-wide publs., 1974—; judge Macon County Art Exhibit, 1964, 67, 71, 73, Town and Country Art Exhibit, U. Ill., 1971; tchr. Bement Art Club. Bd. dirs. Aid to Retarded Citizens, 1968-70; bd. dirs. Lincolnland Pony Baseball, 1972, 73, v.p., 1974-85, coach, 1974-85; mem. com. Boy Scouts Am., 1969-79; bd. dirs. Petersburg Jr. Baseball, 1973-85; coach Thorobred Baseball, 1978, 80-82; coach Little League, 1966-70, Flag football, 1969-71; pres. Lincolnwood Pony League, 1983-86; trustee Methodist Ch.; bd. dirs. Porta Athletic Booster Club, 1974-81, pres., 1975, 79; bd. dirs. Lake Petersburg Assn., 1981-82; field dir. Div. I North Zone Pony Baseball Inc., 1981-86. Served with U.S. Army, 1958, 61-62. Recipient art edn. award State of Ill., 1957; award of merit State of Ind. Art Award, 1953. Mem. Advt. and Pub. Relations Club Springfield, Sangamon County Referees Assn., Internat. Graphics Inc. (charter), Nat. Audio-Visual Inst., Am. Amateur Baseball

Congress, Bradley U. Alumni Assn., Sigma Phi Epsilon Alumni. Republican. Home: Rural Rt 1 424 Hemlock St Petersburg IL 62675 Office: Fiat-Allis 3000 S 6th St Springfield IL 62710

BAYLESS, STEVE ALLEN, chemical company executive; b. Pueblo, Colo., June 9, 1944; s. Billie Burton and Lois Harriett (Britton) B.; m. Judy Kay Dacus, June 4, 1966 (div. Apr. 1975); children: Tanya Lynn, Randy Allen; m. Eloise (Lou) Virginia Matthews, Oct. 14, 1978; 1 child, Leslie Brooke. BS in ChemE, Tex. Tech. U., 1962-66; MBA in Fin., Lamar U., 1968-72. Bus. ctr. mgr. Gulf Oil Corp., Houston, 1978-81, mgr. new bus. devel., 1981-83, gen. mgr. spl. chems., 1983-85; v.p. mktg. Morton Thiokol Carstab, Cin., 1985, v.p., gen. mgr., 1985—. Mem. Soc. Plastics Engrs., Comml. Devel. Assn. Republican. Avocations: skiing, tennis, reading. Home: 7920 New Brunswick Dr Cincinnati OH 45241 Office: Carstab Products Morton Thiokol 2000 West St Cincinnati OH 45215

BAYLY, MELVYN ARTHUR, JR., obstetrician-gynecologist; b. Chgo., July 1, 1945; s. Melvyn Arthur and Lila (Seneff) B.; m. Elizabeth Anne Czyl, Aug. 28, 1971; children: Leslie Anne, Andrew Philip. BS, Colgate U., 1967; MD, Northwestern U., 1971. Diplomate Am. Bd. Ob-gyn. Intern then resident in ob-gyn Parkland Hosp., Dallas, 1971-75; attending physician Northwestern Meml. Hosp., Chgo., 1978—; mem. faculty Northwestern Med. Sch., 1978—. Served to maj. U.S. Army, 1975-78. Fellow Am. Coll. Ob-Gyn; mem. AMA, Phi Beta Kappa. Home: 1900 Glen Oak Dr Glenview IL 60025 Office: Prentice Womens Hosp 333 E Superior St Chicago IL 60611

BAYMAN, ALICE OTTE, savings and loan association executive; b. Seymour, Ind., Nov. 5, 1956; d. Lawrence and Paula Delores (Dringenburg) Otte; m. Bruce Harold Bayman, Nov. 29, 1980. BA, Wittenberg U., 1978; MBA, Wright State U., 1986. CPA, Ohio; cert. mgmt. accountant; cert. internal auditor; lic. stockbroker. Auditor Peat, Marwick, Mitchell & Co., Indpls., 1978-80; sr. auditor Deloitte, Haskins & Sells, Dayton, Ohio, 1980-84; sr. fin. audit mgr. Gem Savs., Dayton, 1984—. Mem. Am. Inst. CPA's, Ohio Soc. CPA's, Nat. Assn. Accts., Inst. Mgmt. Acctg., Omicron Delta Kappa (Regional Student Leader of Yr., 1978), Alpha Xi Delta. Republican. Lutheran. Avocations: traveling, gardening, reading. Home: 1601 Hillside Dr Dayton OH 45432

BAYMILLER, LYNDA DOERN, social worker; b. Milw., July 6, 1943; d. Ronald Oliver and Marian Elizabeth (Doern) B. B.A., U. Wis., 1965, M.S.W., 1969; student U. Hawaii, 1962, Mich. State U., 1965. Peace Corps vol., Chile, 1965-67; social worker Luth. Social Services of Wis. and Upper Mich., Milw., 1969-77, contract social worker, 1978-79; dist. supr. Children's Service Soc. Wis., Kenosha, 1977-78; social work supr. Sauk County Dept. Social Services, Baraboo, Wis., 1979—. Bd. dirs. Zoo Pride, Zool. Soc. Milw. County, 1975-77, Sauk County Mental Health Assn., 1979-84; mem. Harmony chpt. Sweet Adelines, West Allis, Wis., 1970-75, pres. chpt., 1971; pres. bd. dirs. Growing Place Day Care Center, Kenosha, 1977-78; mem. Baraboo (Wis.) Centennial Com., 1982; bd. dirs. Laubach Literary Council, Baraboo, 1986—. Mem. Nat. Assn. Social Workers, Acad. Cert. Social Workers, Wis. Social Services Assn., AAUW (br. sec. 1982-84), U. Wis. Alumni Assn. (life mem.), Am. Legion Aux., DAR, Nat. Soc. Magna Charta Dames, Eddy Family Assn. (life mem.), Nat. Soc. Ancient and Hon. Arty. Co. of Mass., Morris Pratt Inst., Sauk County Hist. Soc., Internat. Crane Found. (patron), Daus. Colonial Wars, Zool. Soc. Milwaukee County (life), Am. Bus. Women's Assn., Friends of Baraboo Zoo, Alpha Xi Delta. Lodges: Order Eastern Star, Ladies Aux. of Fraternal Order Eagles. Author: (with Clara Amelia Hess) Now-Won, A Collection of Feeling (poetry and prose), 1973. Home: 332 4th Ave Baraboo WI 53913

BAYORGEON, BETTE O., sales executive; b. Hibbing, Minn., Feb. 14, 1946; s. Anthony David and Violet (Vukmir) Osojnicki. BA in Polit. Sci., Marquette U., 1968. Computer programmer A.O. Smith Corp., Milw., 1968-72; project leader Am. Appraisal, Milw., 1972-78; mktg. systems mgr. Miller Brewing Co., Milw., 1978—. Vol. Skylight Comic Opera, Milw., Am. Heart Assn., Milw. Clubs: Bookfellows. Avocations: reading, traveling, conversational French, theater, music. Office: Miller Brewing Co 3939 W Highland Blvd Milwaukee WI 53201

BAYS, KAREN LEE, school psychologist; b. Altoona, Pa., Nov. 9, 1950; d. Arthur Gerald and Iva Mae Shirley (Sommer) Stevens; m. Ivan Dean Bays, Aug. 12, 1972; children: Benjamin Dean, Brooke Elizabeth. BA, Grace Coll., Winona Lake, Ind., 1972; MEd, Wright State U., 1974. Cert. sch. psychologist, tchr. spl. exceptional children, spl. edn., ednl. adminstrn. pupil personnel, local sch. supt. Substitute tchr. Temple Christian Sch., Dayton, Ohio, 1972-73; tchr. developmentally handicapped Milton-Union Exempted Village Sch., West Milton, Ohio, 1973-74; intern sch. psychologist Miami County Schs., Troy, Ohio, 1974-75; sch. psychologist Huber Heights (Ohio) City Schs., 1975-79, Troy (Ohio) City Schs., 1979—; psychologist Christian Counseling Assn., Huber Heights, 1984—. Co-author: How to Organize Your Entire Life Into a 3-ring Binder, 1982. Mem. Nat. Assn. for Sch. Psychologists. Republican. Club: Christian Women's (Troy). Avocations: decorating, travel. Home: 2555 Marr Rd Casstown OH 45312 Office: Troy City Schs 500 N Market St Troy OH 45373

BAYS, KARL DEAN, hospital supply company executive; b. Loyall, Ky., Dec. 23, 1933; s. James K. and Myrtle (Criscillis) B.; m. Billie Joan White, June 4, 1955; children: Robert D., Karla. BS, Eastern Ky. U., 1955, LLD (hon.), 1977; MBA, Ind. U., 1958; DCS (hon.), Union Coll., Ky., 1971. With Am. Hosp. Supply Corp., Evanston, Ill., 1958-85, pres., bd. dirs., 1970, chief exec. officer, 1971-85, chmn. bd., 1974-85; chmn. bd. Baxter Travenol Labs., Deerfield, Ill., 1985-87; chmn., chief exec. officer IC Industries, Inc., Chgo., 1987—, also bd. dirs.; bd. dirs. Amoco Corp. Delta Air Lines, Inc., No. Trust Corp. Trustee emeritus Duke U., Northwestern U.; life mem. bd. dirs. Lake Forest Hosp. Served with USMCR, 1955-57. Recipient Trojan MBA Achievement award U. So. Calif., 1972, Horatio Alger award, 1979, Disting. Alumni Service award Ind. U., 1977; named Outstanding Alumnus Eastern Ky. U., 1973, Mktg. Man of Year Sales and Mktg. Execs. Assn. Chgo., 1977, Outstanding Chief Exec. Officer in hosp. and health-care supplies industry, Fin. World, 1981-82, 85, Outstanding Chief Exec. Officer in hosp. supply industry, Wall St. Transcript, 1980, 84. Mem. Health Industries Mfrs. Assn. (chmn.). Clubs: Chgo., Execs., Econ., Comml., Mid-Am. (Chgo.); Glen View; Old Elm, Onwentsia. Office: IC Industries Inc 111 E Wacker Dr Chicago IL 60601

BAZIK, EDNA FRANCES, mathematician, educator; b. Streator, Ill., Dec. 26, 1946; d. Andrew and Anna Frances (Vagasky) B.; B.S.Ed., Ill. State U, 1969; postgrad. Hamilton Coll., summer 1971, Ill. State U., 1972, Augustana Coll., summer 1973; M.Ed., U. Ill., 1972; Ph.D., So. Ill. U., 1976, gen. adminstrv. cert., 1980. Tchr. math. Northlawn Jr. High Sch., Streator, 1969-74; instr. math. edn. So. Ill. U., 1974-76; asst. prof. math. Concordia Coll., 1976-78; asst. prof. math. Ill. State U., Normal, 1978-85; assoc. prof. math. Eastern Ill. U., 1985—; inservice presentations, workshops for tchrs.; cons. to sch. dists. NSF grantee, 1980—. Mem. AAUP, Assn. Tchr. Educators, Ill. Assn. Tchr. Educators, Nat. Council Tchrs. Math., Ill. Council Tchrs. Math. (governing bd., dir. coll. and univ. level), Math. Assn. Am., Nat. Council Suprs. Math., NEA, Ill. Edn. Assn., Sch. Sci. and Math. Assn., U.S. Metric Assn., Am. Ednl. Research Assn., Assn. Supervision and Curriculum Devel., Ill. Assn. Supervision and Curriculum Devel., Assn. Childhood Edn. Internat., Council Exceptional Children, Ill. Curriculum Council, Research Council Diagnostic and Prescriptive Math., Kappa Delta Pi, Phi Delta Kappa (pres. Ill. State U. chpt. 1982-83), Pi Mu Epsilon, Delta Kappa Gamma, Phi Kappa Phi. Republican. Lutheran. Co-author: Elementary Mathematical Methods, 1978; Mind Over Math, 1980; Teaching Mathematics to Children with Special Needs, 1983; Step-by-Step: Addition, 1984; Step-by-Step: Subtraction, 1984; Step-by-Step: Multiplication, 1984; Step-by-Step: Division, 1984; (with Robert Wisner) Problem-Solving Sourcebook, 1985. Home: 202 Riss Dr Normal IL 61761 Office: Eastern Ill U Math Dept Charleston IL 61920

BEACH, OSCAR HARDING, JR., statistician; b. Cottekill, N.Y., Feb. 5, 1929; s. Oscar H. and Edna Mae (Pine) B.; B.S., Syracuse U., 1954, M.B.A., 1961; m. Mary Louise Nisbet, Sept. 1, 1951; 1 dau., Nancy Woodburn. Field rep. Travelers Ins. Co., Conn., Cleve., 1954-58, group supr., Cleve., 1958; sr. research asst. Fed. Res. Bank, Cleve., 1959-61, asst. economist, 1961-63, asso. economist, 1963, statistician, 1963-65, asst. cashier, 1965-71, asst. v.p., 1971—. Served with U.S. Army, 1946-49. Mem. Am. Statis. Assn. Office: Fed Res Bank PO Box 6387 Cleveland OH 44101

BEACHLER, KENNETH CLARKE, univ. adminstr.; b. Battle Creek, Mich., Oct. 11, 1935; s. Hubert Waldo and Nina Kathryn (Eitelbuss) B.; B.A. with high honors, Mich. State U., 1963. Profl. actor and singer, Chgo., 1955-57; radio announcer WKAR-AM/FM, East Lansing, Mich., 1959-62, WSWM-FM, East Lansing, 1962-64; music program dir. WKAR-FM, East Lansing, 1964-70; dir. lecture-concert series Mich. State U., East Lansing, 1971-81, dir. Wharton Ctr. for Performing Arts, 1981—. Host weekly radio program Arts Billboard, 1972—. Bd. dirs. Lansing Symphony Orch., 1971-73, 78-82, Okemos Barn Theatre, 1970-71, Opera Co. Greater Lansing, 1978-79, Pashami Dancers, 1976—. Served with AUS, 1957-59; to comdr. USNR. Named Best Actor, Okemos Barn Theatre, 1974, Best Dir., 1969, 71, 76, 80, 81; recipient Mich. Gov.'s Minuteman award, 1983, Thomas Jefferson Excellence in Journalism award Dept. Def., 1985; Mich. State U. Bd. Trustees tuition scholar, 1960, Hinman Broadcasting scholar, 1961-63. Mem. Internat. Soc. Performing Arts Adminstrs. (dir. 1974-77), Assn. Coll., Univ. and Community Arts Adminstrs., Naval Res. Assn. (life). Mem. United Ch. of Christ. Lodge: Rotary (bd. dirs. 1985—). Club: University of Mich. State U. (dir. 1978-82, v.p. 1980-82). Home: 1450 Hitching Post Rd East Lansing MI 48823 Office: Mich State U East Lansing MI 48824

BEADLE, BRUCE ROBERT, engineer; b. Beloit, Wis., Jan. 15, 1944; s. Robert Hugh and Bertha Margaret (Fenne) B.; m. Sandra Phyllis Goldberg, July 18, 1971; 1 child, Beth Michelle. BSME, Ill. Inst. Tech., 1966; MSME, U. Wis., 1967, PhD, 1971. Sr. mech. devel. engr. Giddings & Lewis Machine Tool Co., Fond du Lac, Wis., 1970-75; sr. elec. devel. engr. Gidding & Lewis Electronics, Fond du Lac, 1975-78, supr. systems products, 1978-80, mgr. engring., 1980-81, v.p. engring., 1981-82; v.p. engring. motion control div. Gould Inc., Racine, Wis., 1982—. Contbr. articles to profl. jours. Patentee in field. Avocations: jogging, travel, music. Home: 8392 Parkridge Ln Greendale WI 53129 Office: Gould Inc Motion Control div 2701 N Greenbay Rd Racine WI 53404

BEADOUT, DOUGLAS HOWARD, personnel search firm executive, software consultant; b. Akron, Ohio, Sept. 3, 1950; s. Howard Franklin and Bonnie Lee (Coontz) B.; m. Gayle Ann Webber, Sept. 21, 1972 (div. Oct. 1978); 1 child, David Robert; m. Debra Sue Irvin, Apr. 7, 1979. BS, U. Akron, 1972; postgrad., Pepperdine U., 1976-77. Exec. recruiter Monte Denbo Assocs., Dayton, Ohio, 1979-81; pres., owner Douglas William Assocs., Inc., Kettering, Ohio, 1981—. Served to capt. SAC USAF, 1972-79. Recipient Eagle Scout award, Boy Scouts Am., 1963. Mem. Nat. Assn. Personnel Cons. (cert.), Dayton C. of C. Republican. Avocations: personal computers, watersports, photography, audio and videophile. Home: 2247 E Whipp Rd Kettering OH 45440 Office: Douglas Williams Assocs Inc 5450 Far Hills Ave Suite 108 Kettering OH 45429

BEAL, BERT LEONARD, JR., elec. engr.; b. Birmingham, Ala., June 19, 1911; s. Bert Leonard and Catherine (Marks) B.; B.S., Washington U., St. Louis, 1934; m. Josephine Watkins, Feb. 24, 1943; 1 son, Albert G. Asst. mine mgr. So. Coal, Coke & Mining, Belleville, Ill., 1935-36; engr. Carrier Corp., Newark, 1936-37; asst. foreman, foreman tng. supr., engr., asst. gen. mech. supt. St. Joe Minerals Corp., Bonne Terre, Mo. 1937-54. gen. mech. supt., 1954-66, dir. engring., 1966-75; pres. Beal Enterprises, engring. cons. and agribus., 1975—. Active in civic affairs. Trustee Presbyterian Children's Home, bd. chmn., 1973. Served from lt. to lt. col. AUS, 1941-46. Registered profl. engr. Mem. Soc. Mining Engrs., Rivermines Engrs. Club (sec. 1951, v.p. 1952, pres. 1953), St. Francis County Hist. Soc. (pres. 1964), Am. Legion. Presbyterian (deacon, elder). Rotarian (sec. 1955, dir. 1972). Home and Office: 615 W Columbia St Farmington MO 63640

BEAL, EUGENE ALEXANDER, association executive; b. Detroit; s. Walter J. and I. Irene (Kay) B. Cert. teaching religion, Archdiocese of Detroit, 1963. Cert. social worker, Mich. Dir. display Winkelman Co., Port Huron, Mich., 1960-64; dir. news Midwest Broadcasting Co., Alpena, Mich., 1964-68; exec. dir. Boys Club Alpena, 1968—; owner, mgr. No. Design Service, Alpena, 1976—. Designer displays Alpena Mall, 1976—; critic, reviewer Thunder Bay Theater, Alpena, 1976. V.p. Alpena County Bicentennial Commn., 1975-76; pres. Alpena Sr. Citizens Council, Inc., 1979-80. Recipient Bronze Keystone award Boys Clubs Am., 1983, Community Service award VFW, 1980, Service award Alpena Sr. Citizens Ctr., 1985. Mem. Am. Horticultural Soc., Founder Soc. Jesse Besser Mus. Avocations: collection St. Nicholas/Santa Claus figures. Home: 7261 US 23 S Ossineke MI 49766 Office: Boys Club Alpena 601 River St Alpena MI 49707

BEAL, LARRY JOHN, production engineer; b. Jackson, Mich., Oct. 13, 1956; s. John Preston and Marilyn Birdell (Kendall) B.; m. Margaret Ellen Fear Apr. 22, 1978; children—Brandon John, Alison Nicole. B.S. in Mech. Engring., Rose-Hilman Inst., 1978. Registered profl. engr., Ind. Test engr. Central Ill. Pub. Service Co., Hutsonville, 1978-80; engr. Pub. Service Co. of Ind., Gibson County, 1980-82, prodn. engr., 1982—. Bd. dirs. Ind. chpt. Cystic Fibrosis Found., also county br. coordinator; mem. adminstrv. bd. United Methodist Ch. Named Varsity Golf Most Valuable Player, 1977. Mem. ASME, Nat. Soc. Profl. Engrs. Lodge: Kiwanis (bd. dirs. Fort Branch, Ind.). Avocations: golf; tennis; softball. Home: 102 E Oak St Fort Branch IN 47648 Office: Pub Service Co of Ind PO Box 1009 Mount Carmel IL 62863

BEALE, HELEN RUBY, insurance company administrative assistant; b. Michigamme, Mich., Mar. 29, 1922; d. Edwin Martin and Katherine Mae (Rahilly) Stensrud; m. Roland Earl Beale, June 19, 1944 (dec.); children—John Robert, Ann Marie Beale Trachtenberg, James Edward. Student Mich. State U., St. Catherine's Coll., U. Wis., Platteville. Cert. adminstrv. mgr. Owner Beale Funeral Home, Michigamme, 1943-60; asst. to pres. Ind. Mgmt. Cons., Madison, Wis., 1966-73; sec. Sch. Dist. Office, Oregon, Wis., 1974-76; adminstrv. asst. Modern Kitchen Supply, Madison, 1976-81; agy. adminstrv. asst. Bankers Life, Madison, 1981—. State advisor U.S. Congl. adv. bd. Am. Security Council Found., Washington, 1983; mem. Sen. Robert Dole Exploratory Com. Mem. Adminstrv. Mgmt. Soc. (pres. 1981-82), Am. Mgmt. Assn., Nat. Tax Limitations Com., Madison Deanery (v.p. 1982-84, regents 1981-85). Roman Catholic. Club: Toastmasters.

BEALL, DARYL E., publishing executive; b. Fort Dodge, Iowa, Dec. 11, 1946; s. Wayne Woodrow and Marjorie (Pence) B.; m. Jo Ann, Mar. 10, 1968; children: Lora Sue, Scott Michael, Christen Lisabeth. AA, Iowa Cen. Community Coll., Ft. Dodge, 1967; student, U. No. Iowa, 1967-68; BA, Buena Vista Coll., 1969; M in Pub. Adminstrn., Drake U., 1978. Profl. permanent teaching cert. Tchr. Urbandale (Iowa) High Sch., 1969-74; mgr. Furniture World, Ft. Dodge, 1974-84; gen. mgr. Des Moines Register Hometown, Ft. Dodge, 1984-85; pub. relations mgr. Des Moines Register, 1985-86; editor, pub. Record-Herald & Indianola Tribune, Indianola, Iowa, 1986—. columnist Ft. Dodge Messenger, 1982-84. Nat. committeeman Young Dem. Clubs Am., 1970-72; candidate for Sec. of State, Iowa, 1972; justice of the peace, Dallas County, Waukee, Iowa, 1970-73; sch. bd. mem. Ft. Dodge Community Sch. Dist., 1980-85; chmn. Philanthropy Day, Des Moines, 1986; bd. dirs. Downtown Des Moines Inc., 1985-86, Nat. Balloon Championships, Indianola, 1985—. Taft fellow Macalester Coll., St. Paul, 1971; recipient Tchr.'s medal Freedoms Found. at Valley Forge, 1973. Mem. Pub. Relations Soc. of Am., Iowa Newspaper Found., Indianola C. of C. (bd. dirs.). Democrat. Methodist. Lodges: Rotary, Kiwanis (pres. Ft. Dodge club 1978-79). Avocations: photography, travel, aviation. Home: 510 North G St Indianola IA 50125 Office: Record-Herald & Indianola Tribune Tribune PO Box 259 Indianola IA 50125

BEALL, MELISSA LOUISE CHRISTENSEN, English and speech educator, consultant; b. Pilger, Nebr., June 4, 1944; d. Emil Peter and Olga Elizabeth (Hansen) Christensen; m. Hugh Fulton Beall, Mar. 13, 1971. B.S., U. Nebr., 1967, M.A. (Ak-Sar-Ben tchr. scholar), 1971, Ph.D., 1982; fellow Northwestern U., 1978. Tchr. English, speech and drama Raymond Central pub. schs., Agnew, Nebr., 1967-71; instr. speech U. Nebr., Lincoln, 1971-74; 1981, 82 (summer); tchr. English, speech and debate Lincoln S.E. High Sch., 1974—, dir. forensics, 1979—; communication cons. U.S. V.I. Dept. Edn., 1980-81; mem. implementation team Target: Communications Skills Program, in-service team leader, 1982-83; dir. Lincoln Pub. Schs. Repertory Theatre Co., 1975-77; mem. Helping Tchr. Cadre, Lincoln Pub. Schs., 1982-83; asst. prof. U. N.D., U. Nebr.; lectr. speech communication dept. U. Nebr., Lincoln, fine arts and speech dept. Doane Coll., Lincoln. speech cons. Campaign worker Kerrey for Gov., 1982. Recipient Cooper Found. award, 1987; named Scottish Rite Tchr. of Yr., 1986. Mem. Central States Speech Assn. (sec. states adv. council), Nebr. Speech Communication Assn. (exec. sec., past pres., Outstanding Young High Sch. Tchr. Speech 1974, John Thurber Disting. Teaching award 1981), Speech Communication Assn. (chmn. edn1. policies bd. 1984—, mem. adminstrv. com. 1985-87, legis. council), Nebr. Council Tchrs. English, Nat. Council Tchrs. English, Nebr. Assn. of Gifted, Am. Forensic Assn., Nat. Forensic League (coach), Phi Delta Kappa, Delta Kappa Gamma. Democrat. Lutheran. Writer, editor communication skills curriculum guide; contbr. articles to profl. jours.; mem. numerous editorial rev. bds. Home: 3802 S 37th St Lincoln NE 68506 Office: Lincoln Southeast High Sch 2930 S 37th St Lincoln NE 68506

BEALL, WARE THOMPSON, JR. (TOM), metal processing company sales professional; b. Savannah, Ga., June 24, 1940; s. Ware Thompson and Elise (Trowell) B.; m. Inez Todd, Oct. 22, 1960; children: John Keith, Renée Denise. AA, Armstrong Coll. of Savannah, 1964; BS in Electron Physics, La. State U., 1966; MS in Engring. Mgmt. with honors, Milw. Sch. Engring., 1983. Research physicist Linde div. Union Carbide Corp., Indpls., 1966-69; sr. research physicist Linde div. Union Carbide Corp., Tarrytown, N.Y., 1969-75; regional sales engring. rep. Linde div. Union Carbide Corp., Milw., 1975-81, sales rep., 1981-84, sr. sales rep., 1984-85; sales rep. L-Tec Welding and Cutting Systems, Waukesha, Wis., 1985—; grad. lectr. Milw. Sch. Engring., 1982—. Author tech. reports; contbr. articles to scholarly jours. Elected precinct com. chmn. Indpls. Reps., 1967-69; appointed pres. Eagle Creek Rep. Club, Indpls., 1968; vice chmn. Cherry Hill Homeowners Assn., Yorktown Heights, N.Y., 1970-71; com. chmn. vol. Yorktown Heights Fire Dept. troop Boy Scouts of Am., 1971-75, asst. scoutmaster, 1974-75; speaker Wis. Assn. Vocat. and Adult Edn., Madison, 1977. Served with USN, 1959-63. Mem. Am. Soc. Engring Mgmt., Assn. MBA Execs., Am. Soc. for Metals, Am. Welding Soc. (seminar leader 1977—), Sales and Mktg. Execs. of Milw. Republican. Methodist. Club: Toastmasters (local exec. v.p. 1967-68). Avocations: fishing, golf, computers. Home: 2300 Napa Trail Waukesha WI 53188

BEALS, CLEM KIP, III, dentist; b. Springfield, Ohio, Mar. 7, 1949; s. Clem II and Betty Jane (Epley) B.; m. Mary Elizabeth Barry, June 10, 1974 (div. Feb. 1985); 1 child, Elizabeth Allison; m. Mary Margaret Ewing, June 8, 1985; 1 child, Andrew Jonathan. BS, Urbana (Ohio) Coll., 1971; DDS, Ohio State U., 1974. Resident in dentistry St Elizabeth Hosp., Youngstown, Ohio, 1975-76; gen. practice dentistry Marion, Ohio, 1976—; exec. dir. Marion County Dental Clinic, Marion, 1979—; chmn. dept. dentistry Marion Gen. Hosp., 1984—. NSF grantee, 1970. Mem. ADA, Acad. Gen. Dentistry, Cen. Ohio Dental Soc. (v.p. 1986—), Marion Acad. Dentistry (pres. 1977, sec./treas. 1979—), Marion Jaycees (bd. dirs. 1978-79). Republican. Methodist. Lodge: Kiwanis. Avocations: flying, skiing. Home: 396 E Church St Marion OH 43302 Office: 1241 E Center St Marion OH 43302

BEALS, KENNETH ALBERT, minister; b. Findlay, Ohio, Apr. 26, 1946; s. Raymond Kenneth and Mary Elizabeth (Parks) B.; m. Jaquelyn Kaye Whitaker, June 22, 1968; children: Eve Elisabeth, Kurt Andrew. BA, Wittenberg U., 1968; ThM, Boston U., 1971, ThD, 1982. Ordained to ministry United Meth. Ch., 1969. Pastor Comml. Point (Ohio) Ch., 1973-76; assoc. pastor Ch. of the Master, Westerville, Ohio, 1976-81; pastor Northridge United Meth. Ch., Springfield, Ohio, 1981—. Mem. Bethesda Sunda Com., Dist. Com. on Superintendency, Springfield, 1984-87, Dist. Com. on Ordained Ministry, Springfield, 1985; marshall United Meth. Ch. Gen. Conf., Balt., 1984; pres. bd. dirs. Metro Ministries, Springfield, 1984—. Jacob Sleeper fellow Boston U., 1971. Mem. Clark County Ministerial Fellow, Westerville (Ohio) Ministerial Assn. (pres. 1979). Democrat. Lodge: Sertoma (treas. 1980). Home: 4842 Ridgewood Rd W Springfield OH 45503 Office: Northridge United Meth Ch 4610 Derr Rd Springfield OH 45503

BEALS, KENNETH LLOYD, social worker; b. St. Louis County, Mo., Feb. 19, 1935; s. Arthur Loyd and Edna (Dollar) B.; B.S., Washington U., St. Louis, 1961, M.S.W., 1967; postgrad. S.W. Baptist Sem., 1961-62; m. Frances Kay Stricklin, Apr. 18, 1959; children—Michael Lloyd, Rebecca Kay. Ordained to Gospel ministry So. Bapt. Conv., 1963. Cartographer, negative engraver Aero Chart Plant, U.S. Air Force, St. Louis, 1954-61; caseworker Mo. Bapt. Children's Home, St. Louis, 1962-65; protective service caseworker Child and Family Service, State of Ill., East St. Louis, 1965-68; acting dir. Hoyleton (Ill.) Children's Home, 1968-69; dir. residential care Child and Family Service, Muskegon, Mich., 1969-75; exec. dir. Brookview, Inc., Fenton, Mich., 1975-79; supr. Central Bapt. Family Service, Effingham, Ill., 1979-81; adminstr. New Hope Living and Learning Center, Waterloo, Ill., 1981-83; dir. social services St. Mary's Hosp., Centralia, Ill., 1983—, adminstr., dir. psychol. services, 1983—, mem. bd. ethics com. 1985—; pvt. practice, 1981-85; mem. faculty Mich. Assn. Child Agys., 1972-74; BCMW Head Start Health Adv. Bd., 1985—. Recipient 30 Yr. Vet. Scouter award, 1974. Mem. Nat. Assn. Social Workers, Ill. Child Care Assn., Acad. Certified Social Workers, West Marion County Cancer soc.(bd. dirs. 1984—), Am. Diabeties Assn. (bd. dirs. Marion chpt. 1985—). Home: Rt 6 Box 193D Centralia IL 62801 Office: 400 Pleasant Centralia IL 62801

BEALS, VAUGHN LEROY, JR., vehicle manufacturing company executive; b. Cambridge, Mass., Jan. 2, 1928; s. Vaughn LeRoy and Pearl Uela (Wilmarth) B.; m. Eleanore May Woods, July 15, 1951; children: Susan Lynn, Laurie Jean. B.S., M.I.T., 1948, M.S., 1954. Research engr. Cornell Aero. Lab., Buffalo, 1948-52, MIT Aero Elastic and Structures Research Lab., 1952-55; dir. research and tech. N.Am. Aviation, Inc., Columbus, Ohio, 1955-65; exec. v.p. Cummins Engine Co., Columbus, Ind., 1965-70, also dir.; chmn. bd., chief exec. officer Formac Internat., Inc., Seattle, 1970-75; dep. group exec. Motorcycle Products Group, AMF Inc., Milw., 1975-77; v.p. and group exec. Motorcycle Products Group, AMF Inc., Stamford, Conn., 1977-81; chmn. chief exec. officer Harley-Davidson Motor Co., Inc., Milw., 1981—; mem. adv. bd. Traffic Inst. Northwestern U.; bd. dirs. Simplicity Mfg., Inc. Bd. dirs. Greater Milw. Com. Clubs: University, Milw. Country (Milw.). Home: 1707 E Fox Ln Milwaukee WI 53217 Office: Harley-Davidson Motor Co Inc 3700 W Juneau Ave Milwaukee WI 53201

BEAM, C. ARLEN, judge; b. Stapleton, Nebr., Jan. 14, 1930; s. Clarence Wilson and Cecile Mary (Harvey) B.; m. Betty Lou Fletcher, July 22, 1951; children—Randal, James, Thomas, Bradley, Gregory. B.S., U. Nebr., 1951, J.D., 1965. Feature writer Nebr. Farmer Mag., Lincoln, 1951; with sales dept. Steckley Seed Co., Mount Sterling, Ill., 1954-58, advt. mgr., 1958-63; ptnr. Knudsen, Berkheimer, Beam, et al, Lincoln, 1965-82; judge U.S. Dist. Ct. Nebr., Omaha, 1982-86, chief judge, 1986—; mem. com. on lawyer discipline Nebr. Supreme Ct., 1974-82; mem. Conf. Commrs. on Uniform State Laws, 1979—, chmn. Nebr. sect., 1980-82. Contbr. articles to profl. jours. Chmn., Nebr. Young Republicans, 1960-62; mem. Nebr. Rep. Central Com., 1970-78. Served to capt. U.S. Army, 1951-53, Korea. Regents scholar U. Nebr., Lincoln, 1947, Roscoe Pound scholar U. Nebr., Lincoln, 1964. Mem. ABA, Nebr. State Bar Assn. Lodges: Kiwanis, Masons. Office: US Dist Ct PO Box 1297 DTS Omaha NE 68101

BEAM, FIELD, office furniture executive; b. Canton, Ill., June 20, 1916; s. Carl R. and Elva J. (Joiner) B.; m. Marion Cardwell, May 15, 1944; children: Christopher, Elizabeth. BS in Journalism, U. Ill., 1937. With editorial and promotion staff The Chgo. Daily News, 1937-42; account exec. T.R. Bauerle Advt. Agy., Chgo., 1946-48; asst. exec. sec. Paraffined Carton Assn., Chgo., 1948-50; founder, owner, pres. Red Tiger Products, Inc., Chgo., 1950—; pvt. practice mktg. and pub. relations, Chgo., 1948; bd. dirs. David Kinley Found., Chgo. Served to lt. USN, 1942-46. Mem. Christian Scientist Ch. Home: 420 Elder Ln Winnetka IL 60093 Office: Red Tiger Products Inc 176 W Adams St Chicago IL 60603

BEAM, KAREN GRACE KLOOS, human resource consultant; b. Mercer, Pa., Mar. 12, 1942; d. John and Alice Mae (Livermore) Kloos. Student, Allegheny Coll., 1960-62; AB, Ohio U., 1964; MLS, Ind. U., 1974, EdD, 1981. Supr. library cataloging Ohio U., 1964-67; asst. catalog librarian Ind. State U., Terre Haute, 1967-68; librarian Vigo County Sch. Corp., Terre Haute, 1968-73; cons. Ind. Dept. Pub. Instrn., Indpls., 1974-76; assoc. Robbins Assoc. Mgmt. Services, Inc., Greenfield, Ind., 1978-79; owner Resource Devel. Co., Indpls., 1979—. Mem. Indpls. Mus. Art, 1974—. Mem. Am.

Soc. Tng. and Devel. (chmn. chpt. awards 1986-88), pres. Cen. Ind. chpt. 1984), Indpls. C. of C., Beta Phi Mu, Phi Delta Kappa, Pi Lambda Theta. Office: Resource Devel Co 1908 E 64th St South Dr Indianapolis IN 46220

BEAM, NORMAN LEWIS, educator; b. Golden, Miss., Sept. 18, 1939; s. Noel D. and Lovie (Humphrey) B.; m. Ima Marlin, May 18, 1963; children—John, Sally. B.S., Florence State U., 1968; M.Ed., Western Md. Coll., 1972; Ed.D., Ball State U., 1983. Foreman, Blue Bell, Inc., Greensboro, N.C., 1963-65; with Reynolds Metals Co., Listerhill, Ala., 1965-68; tchr. Franklin County Schs., Russellville, Ala., 1968-69; tchr. Ala. Sch. for the Deaf, Talladega, 1969-73; tchr. Ind. Sch. for the Deaf, Indpls., 1973-78, supervising tchr., 1978-80, curriculum projects dir., affirmative action expediter, chmn. comprehensive system of personnel devel. com., 1980—, middle sch. supervising tchr., 1983—; cons. in field; conductor workshops in field. Served to capt. Army N.G., 1962-68. Ball State U. doctoral fellow, 1977-78. Mem. Conv. of Am. Instrs. of Deaf, Conf. of Ednl. Adminstrs. Serving the Deaf, Assn. for Supervision and Curriculum Devel., Ind. Auctioneers Assn., Phi Delta Kappa. Presbyterian. Office: Itawamba County Schs 304 W Wiygul Fulton MS 38843

BEAM, WILLIAM NICHOLAS, electronics company executive; b. Chgo., Sept. 7, 1924; s. Peter Victor and Anna M. (Miller) B.; m. Dolores C. Nohr, Feb. 4, 1950; children: Carol, William Jr., Bruce, Denise, Diane, Craig, Debra, Robert. BSME, Mass. Inst. Tech., 1945; MBA, U. Chgo., 1949. Mfg. engr. Teletype Corp., Chgo., 1949-51; sales engr. Controls Co. of Am., Schiller Park, Ill., 1951-56; regional sales mgr. Automatic Timing & Controls, King of Prussia, Pa., 1956-61; nat. sales mgr. Licon div. Ill. Tool Works, Inc., Chgo., 1961-69; dir. mktg. Jefferson Electric, Bellwood, Ill., 1969-84; pres. Teledyne Big Beam, Crystal Lake, Ill., 1984—. Served with USN, 1943-46, PTO. Avocation: reading. Office: Teledyne Big Beam PO Box 518 Crystal Lake IL 60014

BEAMAN, KENNETH DALE, microbiology educator; b. Colorado Springs, Colo., Apr. 4, 1953; s. Dale Paul and Phyllis Ann (Carpenter) B.; m. Penelope Ann Lungo, Nov. 30, 1979; 1 child, James Dale. BS, Colo. State U., 1975; MS, Cleve. State U., 1977; PhD, Ohio State U., 1982. Predoctoral fellow Cleve. Clinic Found., 1976-78; project scientist Fairview Gen. Hosp., Cleve., 1978-79; research assoc. Ohio State U., Columbus, 1980-82; postdoctoral fellow Yale U., New Haven, 1982-85; prof. microbiology Chgo. Med. Sch., North Chicago, Ill., 1985—. Recipient Nat. Research Service award NIH, 1982-85. Mem. Am. Soc. Microbiology, Internat. Orgn. Mycoplasmologists, Am. Assn. Immunologists, Sigma Xi. Home: 965 Estes Gurnee IL 60031 Office: Chgo Med Sch U Health Scis 3333 Green Bay Rd North Chicago IL 60064

BEAMISH, PATRICIA MARY, counseling psychologist; b. Nashville, Feb. 19, 1952; d. Richard Joseph III and Josephine (Phelps) B. BA, U. Fla., 1973, MEd, 1975, EdS, 1975; EdD, W.Va. U., 1979. Lic. psychologist; cert. clin. mental health counselor. Dir. Gainsville (Fla.) Open House, 1974-75; drug abuse counselor Fla. Correctional Instn., Lowell, 1975-76; coll. counselor West Liberty (W.Va.) State Coll., 1976-77; counseling psychologist U. Tex., El Paso, 1979-82, Ohio U., Athens, 1982—; cons. Isleta Ind. Sch. Dist., El Paso, 1981-82, Basset House, Athens, 1985—, Personal Devel. Inst., Athens, 1985—. Editorial rev. bd. Pub. Offenders Jour., 1980-86.; contbr. articles to profl. jours. Trainer Crisis Hotline, Wheeling, W.Va., 1976-77. Profl. Service award Southeastern Regional Council on Alcoholism, Athens, 1986; recipient Mental Health Counselor of Yr. award Ohio Assn. Counseling and Devel., 1987. Mem. Am. Psychol. Assn., Am. Assn. Counseling and Devel., Am. Mental Health Counselors Assn. (chmn. continuing edn. com. 1978-82, dist. coordinator 1984-85, bd. dirs. 1985—, Profl. Service award 1981, 82, 83, 84, 86), Ohio Mental Health Counselors Assn. (exec. bd. dirs. 1984—). Democrat. Avocations: bridge, sports, travel. Home: PO Box 655 Athens OH 45701 Office: Ohio U Counseling and Psychol Services Hudsen Health Ctr Athens OH 45701

BEAN, BARRY SAMUEL, podiatrist; b. Detroit, Oct. 18, 1950; s. Herbert and Shirley Lois (Weiner) B.; m. Renee Ellen Siporin, Aug. 29, 1971; children: Marla, Emily, Julie. Student, Wayne State U., 1968-70; DPM, Ohio Coll. Podiatric Medicine, 1974. Pvt. practice podiatry Detroit, 1974—. Bd. dirs. Old Newsboys Goodfellow Fund, Detroit, 1975—. Fellow Am. Acad. Podiatric Sports Medicine, Am. Acad. Ambulatory Foot Surgery; mem. Am. Podiatric Med. Assn. Lodge: B'Nai B'rith (pres. Detroit, 1982, bd. dirs. 1975—). Avocations: golf, bowling, fundraising, softball, coin collecting. Home: 30112 Deer Run Farmington Hills MI 48018 Office: 19350 W 7 Mile Rd Detroit MI 48219

BEAN, DAVID KEITH, osteopathic physician, surgeon; b. Moberly, Mo., Jan. 22, 1948; s. Pollard and Lavônne (Conway), B.; m. Judith Ann Orlet, Apr. 24, 1976; 1 child, Emily Louise B.S., Northeast Mo. State U., 1970; D.O., Kirksville Coll. Osteo. Medicine, 1974. Cert. Am. Osteo. Bd. Gen. Practice, 1982. Intern, then resident in internal medicine Normandy Osteo. Hosps., St. Louis, 1974-77; practice medicine Ellisville Family Medicine, Inc., Mo., 1977—; chmn. dept. gen. practice, Normandy Osteo. Hosps., St. Louis, v.p., St. Louis Assn. Osteo. Physicians and Surgeons. Bd. dirs. Normandy Osteo. Med. Ctr. St. Louis and Normandy Osteo. Hosps., 1984—. Mem. Am. Osteo. Assn., Mo. Assn. Osteo. Physicians and Surgeons (chmn. pub. relations com. 1983-84, Presidents award 1983), St. Louis Assn. Osteo. Physicians and Surgeons (v.p. 1979—), West St. Louis County C. of C. Republican. Baptist. Avocations: music; piano. Home: 3751 Sawmill Rd Pacific MO 63069 Office: Ellisville Family Med Inc 53 Clarkson Rd Ellisville MO 63011

BEAN, MARVIN DAY, clergyman; b. Tampa, Fla., Sept. 8, 1921; s. Marvin Day and Lillian (Howell) B.; A.B., Fla. So. Coll., 1946, M.S. in Social Work, Vanderbilt U., 1948; postgrad. Ohio State U., 1951-52, Northwestern U., 1950; B.D., Garrett Theol. Sem., 1950; children—Bethany Louise, Thomas Holmes, Carol Sue. Ordained to ministry Methodist Ch., 1950; pastor, Lena Vista, Fla., 1946; asso. pastor San Marcos Meth. Ch., Tampa, 1947; pastor Cedar Lake (Ind.) Meth. Ch., 1948-50, Shepard Meth. Ch., Columbus, Ohio, 1951-68, Stonybrook Meth. Ch., Gahanna, Ohio, 1960-65, Obetz (Ohio) Meth. Ch., 1968-73, Neil Ave. Ch., Columbus, 1973-79, St. Andrew Ch., Columbus, 1979—. Asst. to exec. sec. Meth. Union in Ch. Extension, Columbus, 1965-74; v.p. com. info. and pub. relations Ohio Conf. Meth. Ch., 1964-68, vice chmn. health and welfare ministries, 1968-72, chmn. urban life com. Bd. Missions, 1968-70, asso. sec. Bd. Missions, 1968-72, chmn. Services to Children and Youth, 1962-72; chmn. research Ohio Area Study on Aging, Ohio area Meth. Ch., 1959-64; sec. Columbus dist. conf. Meth. Ch., 1960-68; chmn. sch. religion Columbus area Council Chs., 1953; sec. United Meth. Hist. Soc. of Ohio, 1984; trustee Meth. Retirement Ctr. Central Ohio, Columbus; trustee United Meth. Children's Home, Worthington, Ohio, 1973-74; chmn. bd. trustees Neil Ave. Found., 1973-79; sec. 2d chpt. W. Ohio Commn. Archives and History. Served with AUS, 1943-46. Recipient Wolfley Found. recognition award for inner city work, 1961. Mem. Columbus Meth. Ministerial Assn. (pres. 1960-61), Ohio Council Chs. (rep. com. strategy and planning 1965-68). Nat. Assn. Social Workers, Acad. Cert. Social Workers. Author: A Guide to United Methodist Building, 1973; You Are on the District Board, 1974; Unto the Least of These, 1981; contbr. articles to profl. jours. Home: 122 W Henderson Rd Columbus OH 43214 Office: 1033 High St Worthington OH 43085

BEAN, RICHARD ALAN, publisher; b. Lima, Ohio, Sept. 20, 1951; s. Richard James and Dorothy Louise (Gisler) B.; m. Patricia Kay Vegge, July 21, 1973; children: James, Michael. BA in History, Capital U., 1973; MA in Edn. Adminstrn., Bowling Green State U., 1976. Tchr., coach Calvert High Sch., Tiffin, Ohio, 1973-76; circulation mgr. Advertiser Tribune, Tiffin, Ohio, 1976-81, publisher, 1983—; news editor York (Pa.) Daily Record, 1982; Advisor Students in Free Enterprise, Tiffin U.; adv. com. Sentinel Vocat. Ctr. Com. mem. Pride that Shows, 1983-85, Heritage Festival, 1985-86, Mohawk House, 1984-85; v.p. Krout Sch. PTA, 1985, pres., 1986; mem. First Luth. Ch. council; trustee Tiffin Devel Corp., 1983, United Way; chmn. bd. Seneca Indsl. and Econ. Devel. Corp., 1983-84; sec. bd. YMCA, 1986. Mem. Am. Newspaper Pubs. Assn., Ohio Newspaper Assn., Tiffin C. of C. (v.p. bd. trustees, 1986, pres. 1987—). Club: Mohawk Golf (Tiffin). Lodge: Rotary. Avocations: sports, reading, lawn work. Home: 122 Sunny Ln Tiffin OH 44883 Office: Advertiser Tribune 320 Nelson St Tiffin OH 44883

BEANE, WENDELL CHARLES, educator, clergyman; b. Hamilton, Bermuda, Oct. 21, 1935; came to U.S., 1952; s. Sydney Inkle Bean and Olive Louise Ebbin; m. DeAnna Easily Banks, June 6, 1959 (div.); children: Songhai Marie, Mark Wendell. BA, Howard U., 1958, BD cum laude, 1961; MA, U. Chgo., 1966, PhD, 1971. Pastor United Meth. Ch., Arlington, Va., 1959-63; instr. Rutgers U., New Brunswick, N.J., 1969-79; assoc. prof. history of religions, phenomenology of religion U. Wis., Oshkosh, 1979—; Co-editor: Myths, Rites, Symbols: A Mircea Eliade Reader, 1976; author: Myth, Cult and Symbols in Sakta Hinduism, 1977; contbr. articles to profl. jours. U. Chgo. scholar, 1963-68. Fellow Am. Inst. Indian Studies; mem. Am. Acad. Religion, Assn. for Asian Studies, Internat. Assn. Buddhist Studies, Wis. State Human Relations Assn., Alpha Phi Alpha. Democrat. Methodist. Office: U Wis Dept Religion A&C Bldg Rm 301 800 Algoma Blvd Oshkosh WI 54901

BEAR, CAROL JANE, nursing educator; b. Columbia, Mo., Jan. 3, 1934; d. Herbert Hadley and Mary Oneeda (McMaster) Dickson; m. Ronald Stephen Miller, Dec. 21, 1956; 1 son, Stephen; m. 2d, Karl Richard Bear, Sept. 14, 1962; children—Lisa, Richard, Leslie. B.S. in Nursing, U.Mo.-Columbia, 1956, M.Ed., 1979; postgrad. So.Ill.-Edwardsville U. Registered nurse, Mo.; cert. tech. tchr., Mo. Nurse Boone County Hosp., Columbia, 1956-57, 59, Skaggs Meml. Hosp., Branson, Mo., 1957, 59, Burge Hosp., Springfield, Mo., 1957-58; office nurse, Columbia, 1960; supr. cardiac lab U.Mo., Columbia, 1960-62, charge nurse, 1960-62; night supr. Christian Hosp. N.W., Florissant, Mo., 1968-69; nurse Depaul Hosp., St. Louis, 1973-79, instr., 1962-64, 69-72; nurse Christian Old People's Home, St. Louis, 1979-80; instr. Mo. Baptist Hosp. Sch. Nursing, St. Louis, 1966; instr. Jewish Hosp. Sch. Nursing, St. Louis, 1966-67; assoc. prof. nursing St. Louis Community Coll., Florissant, 1973—; cons. and lectr. in field. Mem. Ferguson (Mo.) Citizens Com., 1976—; bd. dirs. Christian Ministry in Learning Soc., St. Louis; friend St. Louis Art Mus. Mem. Am. Nurses Assn., Mo. Perinatal Assn., Nat. Perinatal Assn., Midwest Congress on Aging, U. Mo. Alumni (rep. 1956—), Nat. Assn. Health Occupations Tchrs. (v.p. Region 3), Mo. Vocat. Assn., Am. Vocat. Assn., NEA, Am. Primrose Assn., Mo. Bot. Garden Friends Soc., Beta Sigma Phi, Phi Theta Kappa. Democrat. Presbyterian (elder 1985—). Clubs: DeMolay Mothers, St. Louis Zoo Assn. Author and developer of edn. programs in nursing. Home: 108 Fenwick Dr Saint Louis MO 63135 Office: 3400 Pershall Rd Ferguson MO 63135

BEAR, SHARON LOUISE, broadcasting company official; b. Dover, Ohio, June 28, 1946; d. Byron Williams and Dicie Edna (Willis) B.; B.A., Malone Coll., 1968; M.A., Bowling Green State U., 1970. Communication disorders cons., Akron, 1970-82; instr. mass media communications U. Akron, 1981; cons. Group Travel Sales and Incentive Travel Cons., Akron, 1977-82; promotions dir. Sta. WHLO, Susquehanna Broadcasting Co., Akron, 1982-86; local sales mgr., 1984-86, WERE, Cleve., 1986—. Mem. Women in Communication. Clubs: Cleve. Ad, Jr. League of Akron. Office: 1500 Chester Ave Cleveland OH 44114

BEAR, THOMAS WILLIAM, marketing executive; b. Dearborn, Mich., Feb. 10, 1954; s. Robert Alfred and Joyce Isabelle (Garnier) B.; m. Linda Lee Chlipala, Aug. 18, 1973; children: Brian, Shawna, Steven. Salesman General Cycle, Lincoln Park, Mich., 1973; salesman Tech-S, Inc., Livonia, Mich., 1973-81, sales mgr., 1981-83, mktg. planning mgr., 1983—. Avocation: running. Home: 7424 Rosedale Allen Park MI 48101 Office: Tech-S Inc 12997 Merriman Rd Livonia MI 48150

BEARD, BOBBY JO, petroleum geologist; b. Cushing, Okla., Feb. 1, 1958; s. Bobby Gene and JoAnn (Culp) B.; m. Kay F. Beard, Jan. 31, 1986. Student Barton County Coll., Great Bend, Kans., 1976-77; B.S. in Geology, Fort Hays State U., 1980. Summer trainee ARCO Oil and Gas Co., Covington, Okla., 1976-80, Great Bend, Kans., 1980; staff geologist Roxanna Corp., Great Bend, 1981-83; pres. Bobby J. Beard Inc., Great Bend, 1983—; chmn. bd. Blackhawk Energy Corp., 1984—; cons. petroleum geologist, Kans., Okla., Colo., 1980—. Mem. Am. Assn. Petroleum Geologists, Kans. Geol. Soc., Am. Petroleum Inst. (central Kans. chpt. 1980—), Great Bend Jaycees, Sigma Tau Gamma. Republican. Baptist. Avocation: Hunting; fishing; waterskiing; snowskiing. Home: 1324 Warner Circle Great Bend KS 67530 Office: PO Box 1910 1622 Main Great Bend KS 67530

BEARD, CYNTHIA ANN, accountant; b. Owensboro, Ky., Sept. 21, 1958; d. John Wallace and Cynthia (Herndon) B. BS in Acctg., Butler U., 1980; postgrad. in law, Ind. U., 1983—. CPA, Ind. Staff acct. Geo. S. Olive & Co., Evansville, Ind., 1980-81; auditor, sr. med. auditor Blue Cross/Blue Shield, Indpls., 1981-83, medicare appeals specialist, 1983-84, fin. analyst, 1984-86; sr. acct. Health Maintenance of Indiana Inc., Indpls., 1986-87, mgr. provider and cost acctg., 1987—. Vol. Pan Am. Games, Indpls., 1987. Mem. Am. Inst. CPA's, Ind. CPA Soc. Republican. Avocations: snow skiing, reading. Home: 1451 N Central Ave #206 Indianapolis IN 46202 Office: Health Maintenance Indiana Inc 333 Alabama Suite 300 Indianapolis IN 46204

BEARD, HAZEL MOBLEY, sales trainer; b. Opelika, Ala., Feb. 28, 1947; d. Roy G. and Bertha (Price) Mobley; m. Stanley J. Beard, Sept. 5, 1965 (div. Mar. 1986); children: Rebecca Renee, Lori Leann. BBA, Kent State U., 1980. Dist. tng. specialist Xerox Corp., Cleve., 1981—. Mem. Am. Mktg. Assn., Delta Sigma Pi (v.p. 1979-80, Pres's. award 1980). Avocations: skiing, golf. Office: Xerox Corp 1100 Superior Ave Cleveland OH 44114

BEARD, JAMES EDWARD, periodontist; b. Modesto, Calif., Dec. 9, 1950; s. Estle Faires and Edith Elizabeth (Walters) B.; m. Florentina Ramniceanu, June 6, 1982. BA, Stanford U., 1973, MA, 1974; DMD, U. Pa., 1979; MS in Periodontology, Northwestern U., 1982. Cert. in periodontics, Ill. Resident in dentistry Michael Reese Hosp., Chgo., 1979-80; gen. practice dentistry Chgo., 1980-82, practice dentistry specializing in periodontics, 1982—; staff dept. surgery Ravenswood Hosp., Chgo., 1983—. Mem. ADA, Am. Acad. Periodontology, Midwest Soc. Periodontology, Chgo. Dental Soc. Avocations: sailing, tennis, skiing. Home: 3150 N Lake Shore Dr #34-A Chicago IL 60657 Office: 620 W Webster Chicago IL 60614

BEARDSLEY, RALPH HAROLD, systems engineer; b. Defiance, Ohio, Sept. 12, 1925; s. Leroy Everett and Ethel (Runnion) B.; m. Betty Jean Rost, Nov. 22, 1951; 1 child, Lisa Jean. BSEE, Ohio No. U., 1952; postgrad., Defiance Coll., Ind. Inst. Tech., 1965-66, Purdue U., Ft. Wayne, 1967; cert. personnel mgmt., Ind. U., Ft. Wayne, 1956. Engr. Magnavox, Ft. Wayne, 1952-53; engr. ITT Corp., Ft. Wayne, 1954-64, reliabilty engr., 1964-85, sr. systems reliabilty engr., 1985—; treas. ITT Mgmt. Assn., 1980. Patentee Plasma Power Supply for ARC Discharge Device, 1969. Treas. Brentwood Community Assn., Ft. Wayne, 1978-80, Ind. Coalition Mentally Ill, Indpls., 1984-85; pres. Ft. Wayne Alliance Mentally Ill, 1983, treas. 1985. appointed by gov. mem. adv. bd. P&A Mental Illness. Served with USN, 1944-46. Mem. Armed Forces Communications and Electronics Assn. (dir. membership 1985-86). Republican. Roman Catholic. Avocations: golf, boating, fishing. Office: ITT Corp Aerospace/Optical Div 3700 E Pontiac St Fort Wayne IN 46803

BEARDSLEY, ROBERT MASON, advertising executive; b. Dayton, Ohio, May 23, 1940; s. Orville Lynne and Ethel Grace (Piggot) B.; m. Barbara Thompson Bailey, Aug. 17, 1963; children: Christine Lynne, Robert William. BBA, Western Mich. U., 1966. Div. mgr. Doubleday Bros. & Co., Kalamazoo, 1964-69; mtkg. mgr. Stryker Corp., Kalamazoo, 1969-73; account exec. Jaqua Co., Grand Rapids, Mich., 1973-75, Biggs Assocs., Kalamazoo, 1975-78; pres., chief exec. officer Beardsley and Co., Inc., Richland, Mich., 1978—. Republican. Presbyterian. Avocations: sailing, tennis. Home: 4400 E Gull Lake Dr Hickory Corners MI 49060 Office: Beardsley & Co Inc 8807 Gull Rd PO Box 347 Richland MI 49083

BEARE, GENE KERWIN, company director; b. Chester, Ill., July 14, 1915; s. Nicholas Eugene and Minnie Cole (St. Vrain) B.; m. Doris Margaret Alt, Dec. 11, 1943 (dec.); children: Gail Kathryn, Joanne St. Vrain; m. Patricia Pfau Cade, Sept. 12, 1964. B.S. in Mech. Engring, Washington U., 1937; M.B.A., Harvard, 1939. Registered profl. engr., Ill. With Automatic Electric Co., Chgo., 1939-58; successively asst. to v.p. and gen. mgr., asst. to pres., mgr. internat. affiliated cos., gen. comml. mgr. Automatic Electric Co., 1939-54, v.p. prodn., 1954-58, dir., 1956-61; pres., dir. Automatic Electric Internat., Inc., 1958-61; chmn., dir. Automatic Electric (Can.), Ltd., Automatic Electric Sales (Can.), Ltd., 1958-61; pres., dir. Sylvania Internat., 1959-60; pres. Gen. Telephone & Electronics Internat., Inc., 1960-61, dir., 1960-72; also dir. numerous subs. in Gen. Telephone & Electronics Internat., Inc., Colombia, Mex., Venezuela, Argentina, Switzerland, Panama, Brazil, Bel; dir. Am. Research and Devel. Corp., 1967-74, Canadair Ltd., 1972-75; pres. Sylvania Electric Products, Inc., 1961-69, dir., 1961-72; exec. v.p. mfg., dir. Gen. Telephone & Electronics Corp., 1969-72; exec. v.p., dir. Gen. Dynamics Corp., St. Louis, 1972-77; pres. Gen. Dynamics Comml. Products Co., 1972-77; chmn. Asbestos Corp. Ltd., 1974-77; dir. Arkwright-Boston Mut. Ins. Co., Westvaco Corp., Emerson Electric Co., St. Joe Minerals Corp., Am. Maize-Products Corp., Datapoint Corp., Nooney Realty Trust, Inc. Served to lt. USNR, 1942-45. Mem. Pan Am. Soc., Nat. Elec. Mfrs. Assn. (bd. govs. 1963-72, v.p. 1964, pres. 1965-66), Armed Forces Communications and Electronics Assn., Nat. Security Indsl. Assn. (trustee 1969-72). Clubs: Wee Burn (Darien, Conn.) (gov. 1963-68); Union League (N.Y.C.), Econ. (N.Y.C.); St. Louis (dir. 1979—); Old Warson (Ladue, Mo.) (dir. 1979—). Home: 801 S Skinker Blvd Saint Louis MO 63105 Office: Pierre Laclede Center 7701 Forsyth Blvd Suite 545 Saint Louis MO 63105

BEARON, ARTHUR HOWARD, obstetrician, gynecologist; b. Quincy, Mass., July 20, 1940; s. Israel and Muriel (Castleman) B.; m. Carole Jean Pozner, Dec. 28, 1971; children: Jeanne Catherine, David Michael. BA, Williams Coll., 1961; MD, U. Minn., 1965. Diplomate Am. Bd. Ob-Gyn. Intern D.C. Gen. Hosp., 1965-66; resident U. Minn. Hosps., Mpls., 1966-69, postgrad. fellow, 1971-73; practice medicine specializing in ob-gyn John Haugen Assocs. P.A., Mpls., 1973—. Served to maj. M.C., U.S. Army, 1969-71. Fellow Am. Coll. Ob-Gyn; mem. Am. Fertility Soc., Minn. State Ob-Gyn Soc., Mpls. Council Obstetricians and Gynecologists. Home: 4646 Sunset Ridge Minneapolis MN 55416 Office: John Haugen Assocs PA 411 Medical Arts Bldg Minneapolis MN 55402

BEARY, RODNEY PAUL, consulting company executive; b. Phila., May 9, 1944; s. Louis A. and Natalie M. (Deck) B.; m. Mary Carter Ford, Apr. 8, 1967; children—Todd, Matthew, Susannah. B.A. in Sociology, Pa. State U., 1966; M.S. with honors in Indsl. Relations, Loyola U., Chgo. 1981. Personnel rep. Radio Corp. Am., Camden, N.J., 1967-68; personnel adminstrn. rep. Fibre Industries div. Celanese Corp., Shelby, N.C., 1968-70; regional personnel mgr. Standard Brands Inc., Kensington, Ga., 197074; labor relations mgr. Weyerhaeuser Co. Inc., Chgo., 1974-80; indsl. relations mgr. North Am. Car Co., Chgo., 1980-81; sr. cons. John Sheridan Assocs., Chgo., 1981-83; owner, operator The Beary Consulting Group, Naperville, Ill., 1983—; dir. Paper Ind. Mgmt. Assn. Tng.-Inst.; chmn. bd. Amerchee Investment Corp., 1974; instr. George Williams Coll., Downers Grove, Ill., also Inst. Indsl. Relations, Loyola U., Chgo. Chmn. Opportunities Industrialization Ctr. for Eastern N.C., 1975; active Republican Nat. Com. Mem. Am. Soc. Personnel Adminstrs. Club: Penn State Alumni. Nat. quadruple skulls champion, 1964-65. Address: 903 River Oak Dr Naperville IL 60565

BEATH, PATRICIA JEAN, nurse anesthetist; b. Des Moines, Iowa, Sept. 17, 1942; d. John Neil and Harriet Millicent (Pike) Chicken; m. Arnold Ray Beath, Aug. 9, 1964 (div. 1984); children: Scott Ray, Jeffrey Neil. Diploma, Iowa Meth. Sch. Nursing, 1963; diploma in anesthesia, Ravenswood Sch. of Anesthesia, 1977; BS in Health Arts, Coll. of St. Francis, 1982. Staff nurse Iowa Meth. Hosp., Des Moines, 1963, U. Iowa VA Hosp., Iowa City, 1964-65; staff nurse Meml. Hosp., Manhattan, Kans., 1968-69, supr. evenings, 1969-72, supr. operating room, 1972-74; staff anesthetist St. Mary of Nazareth, Chgo., 1977-79; chief anesthetist Greene County Med. Ctr., Jefferson, Iowa, 1979-81; anesthetist Beath CRNA Services P.C., Jefferson, 1981—; mem. nurse adv. com. Sen. Harkin, Des Moines, 1985—; mem. task force on prescription drugs Iowa Nursing Bd., 1983. Mem. Am. Assn. Nurse Anesthetists, Am. Assn. Nurses, Am. Soc. Regional Anesthesia, Iowa Assn. Nurse Anesthetists (v.p. 1984-85, pres. 1985-86, dist. dir. 1983-85, dir. continuing edn. 1985—), Iowa Assn. Nurses (bd. dirs. 1984-85). Republican. Methodist. Lodge: PEO Sisterhood. Avocations: cross-stitch, snow skiing, sailing, biking. Home and Office: 505 W Russell Jefferson IA 50129

BEATON, IAN WILSON, advertising agency executive; b. Sydney, N.S., Can., Mar. 10, 1924; s. William Murray and Margaret (MacKenzie) B.; came to U.S., 1924, naturalized, 1945; B.S., Northwestern U., 1950; m. Carol Jean Lindner, Dec. 30, 1950; children—Lynda (Mrs. David Bence), Scot. Merchandising mgr. AC Spark Plug Div., Gen. Motors Corp., 1950-56; copywriter Leo Burnett Co. Mich. Inc. (formerly D. P. Brother & Co.), 1956-58, account exec., 1958-61, v.p., gen. account exec., 1961-66, v.p., adminstrn., personnel, 1966-70, v.p., account supr., 1970-74; v.p., sr. account supr. Campbell-Ewald Co., Detroit, from 1975, now sr. v.p., group mgmt. supr., Warren, Mich. Served with AUS, 1943-45; PTO. Mem. Detroit Advt. Assn., Pi Kappa Alpha. Presbyterian. Clubs: Detroit Adcraft, Great Oaks Country, Recess. Home: 1200 Oakwood Ct Rochester MI 48063 Office: Campbell Ewald Bldg Warren MI 48093

BEATTY, ALAN EDWIN, metal processing executive; b. Custar, Ohio, Oct. 12, 1933; s. Rowland Daniel and Agnes Norma (Jones) B.; m. Constance Jane MacCartney, Apr. 3, 1956; children: Lorne, Gary, Heather. BBA, Bowling Green State U., 1958. CPA, Mich. Acct. Coopers & Lybrand, Detroit, 1958-60; controller Mich. Chem., Chgo., 1961-69; v.p. Victor Comptometer, Chgo., 1970-76; pres., owner Meyers Industries, Tecumseh, Mich., 1977—; Pres., bd. dirs. Beatty Industries, Tecumseh, 1985-86, Mich. Craft Corp., Tecumseh, 1985-86. Commnr. Lenawee County Bd. Commerce, Adrian, Mich., 1985-86; trustee Tecumseh Bd. Edn., 1980-85. Served with USN, 1952-54, Korea. Mem. Nat. Marine Mfg. Assn., Mich. Boating Industry Assn., Nat. Contract Mgmt. Assn., Am. Inst. CPA's, Mich. Inst. CPA's. Republican. Methodist. Lodge: Kiwanis, Masons. Avocations: boating, canoeing, tennis. Office: Meyers Industries Inc PO Box 188 Tecumseh MI 49286

BEATTY, DAVID LEROY, podiatrist; b. Paulding, Ohio, Aug. 11, 1951; s. Albert L. and Louise M. (Ringger) B. BA, Miami U., Oxford, Ohio, 1973; D Podiatric Medicine, Ill. Coll. Podiatric Medicine, 1979. Diplomate Nat. Bd. Podiatric Examiners. Resident in podiatrics VA Hosp., Marion, Ind., 1979-80; assoc. Riverside Podiatry, Marion, 1984-86, AAL Footcare Ctrs., Lima, Ohio, 1986—. Served to capt. U.S. Army, 1981-84. Named one of Outstanding Young Men Am., Chgo. Jaycees, 1979. Mem. Am. Podiatric Med. Assn. Republican. Presbyterian. Lodge: Rotary. Avocations: films, books, fishing, bowling, trivia. Home: 2453 Heathway Ln Lima OH 45801 Office: AAL Footcare Ctrs 658 W Market St Suite 217 Lima OH 45801

BEATTY, MARION LEE, lawyer; b. Vinton, Iowa, Apr. 24, 1953; s. Charles Edward and Marcella Ann (Robbins) B.; m. Peggy Jo Hall, Apr. 15, 1976; children: Benjamin Wade, Laura Ann, Jeffrey Michael. BA, Luther Coll., 1975; JD, U. Iowa, 1977. Bar: Iowa, Minn., U.S. Dist. Ct. (no. and so. dists.) Iowa. Practiced in Decorah, Iowa; ptnr. firm Miller, Pearson, Gloe, Burns, Beatty & Cowie, P.C., Decorah. Bd. dirs. Porter House Mus., Decorah, 1978-84; mem. ch. council Decorah Luth. Ch., 1980-82; mem. Decorah Republican Central Com.; Winneshiek County chmn. for re-election Congressman Tom Tauke, 2 terms, for re-election Congressman Cooper Evans, 1982-84; past pres. Winneshiek County Hist. Soc., Decorah; mem. Congressman Tauke's Acad. Selection com. 2d dist. Iowa, 4 yrs.; gen. gifts chmn. Fund for Luther, Luther Coll., Decorah, 1983-84; mem. legal adv. bd. Area Agy. on Aging, N.E. Iowa Tech. Inst., 1982-84. Recipient Regional Key Man award Iowa Jaycees, 1981, runnerup Outstanding Young Iowan award, 1986. Mem. Iowa Bar Assn., Winneshiek County Bar Assn. (pres. 1979), Decorah C. of C. (sec.-treas. 1981, v.p. 1982, pres. 1983), Decorah Jaycees (dir. 1980, Outstanding Dir. award 1978), Young Lawyers Assn. Iowa (various coms. 1977—), Winneshiek County Hosp. Found. (pres. bd. dirs. 1984-87). Republican. Lutheran. Club: Silvercrest Golf and Country (v.p. 1982, pres. 1983). Lodge: Elks. Home: 1303 Panorama Dr Decorah IA 52101 Office: Miller Pearson Gloe Burns et al 301 W Broadway Box 28 Decorah IA 52101

BEATTY, MARK W., researcher dental materials; b. Peoria, Ill., Nov. 1, 1953; s. E.W. and Peggy L. (Peavler) B.; m. Mona Sue McCormack, June 20, 1981; 1 child, Alesha. BS, Purdue U., 1974; DDS, U. Iowa, 1981; student, Purdue U. Research asst. U. Iowa, Iowa City, 1975-77; staff dentist Community Health Care Ctr., Davenport, Iowa, 1981-83; asst. scientist INd. U., Indpls., 1985—. Recipient Dentist Scientist award Nat. Inst. Health, 1985.

Mem. Internat. Assn. for Dental Research, Am. Soc. for Metals, Am. Dental Assn., Am. Assn. Dental Schs. Office: Ind Univ Sch Dentistry 1121 W Michigan St Indianapolis IN 46202

BEATTY, ROBERT ALFRED, surgeon; b. Colchester, Vt., May 7, 1936; s. George Lewis and Leila Margaret (Ebright) B.; B.A., U. Oreg., 1959, B.S., 1960, M.D., 1961; m. Frances Calomeni, Aug. 24, 1963; children—Bradford, Roxanna. Intern, U. Ill. Research and Edn. Hosp., Chgo., 1961-62; resident neurosurgery U. Ill., 1962-66; practice neurosurgery, Hinsdale, Ill., 1967—; mem. staff Hinsdale Hosp., Community Meml. Hosp., LaGrange, Ill., Meml. Hosp., Elmhurst, Ill., U. Ill. Hosp., Chgo., Good Samaritan Hosp., Downers Grove, Ill.; clin. assoc. prof. neurosurgery U. Ill., 1967—; adviser Marion Joy Rehab. Center, Wheaton, Ill., 1969-72. Served to capt. M.C., AUS, 1968. Research fellow St. George's Med. Sch., London, 1966-67. Diplomate Am. Bd. Neurol. Surgery. Mem. AMA, Ill. Med. Soc., Dupage County Med. Soc., Am. Assn. Neurol. Surgeons, A.C.S., Congress Neurol. Surgeons, Soc. Brit. Neurol. Surgeons, Internat. Microsurg. Soc., English Speaking Union, SAR, Phi Beta Kappa, Phi Beta Pi, Phi Kappa Psi. Republican. Clubs: Les Nomades, Butterfield Country. Contbr. articles to profl. jours.; research on intracranial aneurysms, lumbar discs. Office: 333 Chestnut St Hinsdale IL 60521

BEATTY, WILLIAM LOUIS, federal judge; b. Mendota, Ill., Sept. 4, 1925; s. Raphael H. and Teresa A. (Collins) B.; m. Dorothy Jeanne Starnes, June 12, 1948; children: William S., Steven M., Thomas D., Mary C. Student, Washington U., St. Louis, 1945-47; LL.B., St. Louis U., 1950. Bar: Ill. 1950. Gen. practice law Granite City, 1950-68; circuit judge 3d Jud. Circuit Ill., 1968-79; U.S. dist. judge So. Dist. Ill., 1979—. Served with AUS, 1943-45. Mem. Am. Bar Assn., Ill. Bar Assn., Madison County Bar Assn., Tri-City Bar Assn. Roman Catholic. Office: U S Dist Ct 501 Belle St Alton IL 62002 *

BEATY, BRETT JOSEPH, advertising executive; b. Toledo, Feb. 25, 1958; s. David Robert and Caroline Nancy (DeBenedetto) B. AA, Edison State Coll., 1979; BS, Ohio U., 1981, MA, 1982. Account exec. Lancelot Advt., Piqua, Ohio, 1982-83, Willis Case Harwood, Dayton, Ohio, 1983—; instr. Edison State Coll., Piqua, 1982-84, retreat counselor 1983—; instr. Ohio U. 1981-82, Sinclair Community Coll., Dayton, 1984—. Parade Marshall Kettering Holiday at Home Staff, 1984. Mem. Am. Soc. for Tng. and Devel., Dayton Advt. Club. Roman Catholic. Avocations: teaching, basketball, bicycling, reading, hiking. Office: Willis Case Harwood Inc 3411 Office Park Dr Dayton OH 45439

BEATY, JAMES RALPH, clergyman; b. Evansville, Ind., May 16, 1929; s. James Clifford and Amanda Ann (Apgar) B.; m. Emma Jean Galloway, June 13, 1950; children—Ralph Norman, James Robert, Ann Lynn, Jerri Elizabeth, William Clifford. B.A., Franklin Coll. Ind., 1951, D.D., 1979. M.Div., So. Bapt. Theol. Sem., 1954; D.D., Judson Coll., 1970. Ordained to ministry Am. Baptist Chs. U.S.A., 1952. Asst. to pastor 1st Bapt. Ch., Evansville, 1948; pastor Exeter Ave. Bapt. Ch., Indpls., 1949-52, Veale Creek Bapt. Ch., Washington, Ind., 1952-54, 1st Bapt. Ch., Salem, Ind., 1954-57; field counselor Div. World Mission Support, Am. Bapt. Conv., 1958-66; exec. minister Indpls. Bapt. Assn., 1966-67; regional minister Am. Bapt. Chs. of the Great Rivers Region, 1977—. Mem. alumni council Franklin Coll., 1960-70; mem. Ch. Fedn. Greater Indpls., 1966-67; mem. Ill. Conf. Chs., 1977—, Mo. Council of Chs., 1977—; bd. dirs. Shurtleff Fund, 1977—; trustee No. Bapt. Theol. Sem., 1977—, Franklin Coll., 1982—, Judson Coll., 1971; mem. Midwest commn. on ministry Am. Bapt. Conv., 1966—, mem. Regional Exec. Ministers Council, 1966—, mem. Gen. Staff Council, 1972—. Recipient citations Christian Higher Edn. Challenge, Am. Bapt. Conv., 1960, Franklin Coll. Alumni Council, 1971, Ch. Fedn. Greater Indpls., 1975, Ind. Bapt. Conv., 1976, Indpls. Bapt. Assn., 1977; Alumni of Yr. citation So. Bapt. Theol. Sem., 1981; Certificate of Appreciation, World Mission Campaign of Am. Bapt. Conv., 1968. Mem. Lambda Chi Alpha. Address: Am Bapt Chs in the USA Gt Rivers Region Box 3786 Springfield IL 62708 *

BEATY, THOMAS KIM, military officer; b. Whitecastle, La., June 8, 1951; s. Albert Carrol and Edna Elise (Briehn) B.; m. Cynthia Elayne Allen, Feb. 19, 1971; children: Apryl Michelle, Ethan Thomas, Alexander Charles. BA in Sociology, N. Tex. State U., 1973. Commd. 2d lt. U.S. Army, 1975, advanced through grades to capt.; exec. officer U.S. Army, Federal Republic of Germany, 1981-82, flight ops. officer, 1982-83, aerial reconniassance officer, 1983-84; comdr. U.S. Army, Ft. Harrison, Ind., 1984-85, exec. officer, 1985—. Councilman Ft. Huachuca (Ariz.) Community Chapel, 1983-84; coach Little League Baseball, Ft. Huachuca, 1984; com. chmn. Men for Missions Internat., Greenwood, Ind., 1985; project leader Cooper's Homw Owners Assn., Greenwood, 1986. Named one of Outsatanding Young Men of Am., Jr. C. of C., 1985, 86, recipient Meritorius Medal for Outstanding Achievement, 1986; recipient Cert. of Appreciation, Girl Scouts U.S., 1984, Kiwanis, Indpls., 1986. Mem. Army Aviation Assn. Am. (v.p. 1985—), Assn. of U.S. Army, Army Speakers Bur., Good News Club (bd. dirs. county chpt. 1983-84). Republican. Avocations: public speaking, fishing, sports, family. Home: 1199 Pilgrim Rd Greenwood IN 46142 Office: HQ 1230 Arcom Fort Harrison IN 46216

BEAUBIEN, ELAINE ESTERVIG, business educator, human relations consultant; b. Madison, Wis., Oct. 27, 1949; d. Raymond Knute and Hazel (Shultis) Estervig; m. Kenneth Charles Beaubien, Aug. 2, 1975. B.S., Wis. State U.-Platteville, 1971; M.B.A., U. Wis., 1975. Dept. mgr. J.C. Penney Co., Madison, 1971-74; instr., chmn. dept. econs. Detroit Coll. Bus., 1975-76; instr. bus., econs. Mercy Coll. of Detroit, 1976-78; lectr. mgmt. dept. U. Wis.-Whitewater, 1978-81; assoc. prof., chmn. dept. bus. Edgewood Coll., Madison, 1981—; cons. in human relations, 1978—; tng. coordinator, owner Mgmt. Tng. Seminars, 1980—; speaker, seminar leader on women in mgmt., 1980—. Mgmt. mem. Adv. Com. for Cert. Profl. Secs. Cert., 1982—. Recipient Outstanding Alumnus award Wis. State U.-Platteville, 1973, Appreciation cert. Madison Met. Distributive Edn. Assn., 1973; named An Outstanding Young Woman of Am., Gen. Fedn. Women's Clubs, 1982. Evjue scholar, 1970. Mem. Wis. Profl. Speakers Assn., Internat. Bus. Assn., Nat. Assn. Female Execs., Am. Mgmt. Assn., Am. Mktg. Assn., Nat. Speakers Bur. Methodist. Lodge: Order Eastern Star (trustee 1979-82). Home: Route 1 Box 66-E Waterloo WI 53594 Office: Edgewood Coll 855 Woodrow St Madison WI 53711

BEAUCHAMP, DON WENDELL, petroleum geologist; b. Guide Rock, Nebr., Oct. 10, 1936; s. Howard Scott and Erma Lorene (Miner) B.; m. Billy Ray Brown, May 15, 1959 (div. 1975); children: Toni R., Jeffrey S., Brian Craig; m. Linda Sue Peterson, July 24, 1976; stepchildren: Troy Bailey, Brenda Bailey. BS in Geology, Wichita State U., 1959. Exploration geologist Walters Drilling Co., Wichita, Kans., 1959-71; v.p. Berexco Inc., Wichita, 1971-86, exploration mgr. Beren Corp., Wichita, 1971-86, exploration mgr. Okmar Oil Co., Wichita, 1971-86; owner Beauchamp Oil and Royalty Co., 1986—. Mem. Am. Assn. Petroleum Geologists (alt. del. midwestern sect.) Kans. Geol. Soc. (bd. dirs. 1970-72, pres. 1985—), Nat. Red Setter Field Trial Assn. (pres. 1978-80), Kans. Red Setter Field Trial Assn. (pres. 1976-79), Kans. Field Trial Assn. (pres. 1982-84). Republican. Methodist. Club: Petroleum of Wichita (1st v.p. 1978-79). Avocations: hunting, field trailing, skiing, tennis, golf. Home: RR 1 Box 118 Cheny KS 67025

BEAUCHAMP, E(DWARD) WILLIAM, priest, lawyer, management educator, university administrator; b. Detroit, May 16, 1942; s. Edward F. and Marion K. Beauchamp. BS in Acctg., U. Detroit, 1964, MBA, 1966; postgrad., Mich. State U., 1966-71; JD, U. Notre Dame, 1975, MDiv, 1981. Bar: Mich. 1975; ordained priest Roman Cath. Ch., 1982. Tchr., assoc. dir. admissions Alma (Mich.) Coll., 1966-71; ptnr. Goggin, Baker and Beauchamp, Alma, 1975-77; asst. prof. mgmt., adminstrv. asst. to exec. v.p. U. Notre Dame, South Bend, Ind., 1980-84, exec. asst. to pres., 1984-87, exec. v.p., 1987—. Recipient Wall St. Jour. award, 1964, Bernstein, Bernstein, Wile and Gordon award, 1963. Office: U Notre Dame Office of Exec VP Notre Dame IN 46556

BEAUCHAMP, RAYMOND EDMOND, transportation company executive; b. Ironwood, Mich., Mar. 20, 1946; s. Leo J. and Clara M. (Clement) B.; m. Kathleen J. De Gabriele, July 18, 1970. BSBA, Mich. Tech. U., 1968; MBA, U. Wis., Oshkosh, 1985. CPA, Ill. Acct. Coopers & Lybrand, Rockford, Ill., 1968-78; controller Leicht Transfer & Storage Co., Green Bay, Wis., 1978—; v.p. fin. Leicht Industries Inc., Green Bay, 1984—; sec. Pioneer Credit Union, Green Bay, 1986-87, treas., 1987—. Served to 1st lt. U.S. Army, 1969-71. Mem. Am. Inst. CPA's, Ill. Soc. CPA's, Am. Trucking Assn. (fin. council). Avocations: bowling, tennis, gardening, photography. Home: 834 Basel St DePere WI 54115 Office: Leicht Industries Inc PO Box 2161 Green Bay WI 54306

BEAUDETTE, JAMES STANLEY, publishing executive, consultant; b. Windsor, Ont., Can., June 4, 1945; s. Cyril James and Helen Dorothy (Garrod) B.; m. Patricia Ann Sylvester, June 25, 1966 (div. Sept. 1980); children: Daryl, Brian, Rachelle; m. Donna Mary Kay, Oct. 3, 1980; 1 child, Heather. BSc, U. Windsor, 1967; MBA, U. Detroit, 1973. Refinery auditor Shell Can., Sarnia, Ont., 1970-72; operation auditor Parke Davis & Co., Detroit, 1972-73; fin. mgr. J.L. Hudson Co., Detroit, 1973-75; fin. officer, dir. personnel PVS Chem. Inc., Detroit, 1975-81; operational analyst, budget dir. and adv. mgr. Detroit Free Press, 1981—. Treas. Westland (Mich.) Jaycees, 1973-74; pres. Hampton Hills Homeowners' Assn., Bloomfield Hills, Mich., 1976-77. Chrysler Can. Ltd. scholar, 1964. Mem. Fin. Execs. Inst. (membership com., acad. relations com.), Adcraft Club Detroit. Avocations: reading, sailing, golf, tennis. Home: 35050 Renfrew Mount Clemens MI 48045 Office: Detroit Free Press 321 W Lafayette Detroit MI 48013

BEAUDETTE, ROBERT LEE, transportation and packaging executive; b. White City, Kans., May 28, 1943; s. Axle John and Beatrice A. (Beaudette) Olson; m. Beverly Ann Robell, May 14, 1971; children: Jason M., Sara Ann. A in Commerce, Henry Ford U., 1975; postgrad., U. Mich., 1986. Traffic mgr. Detroit Stoker Co., Monroe, Mich., 1981-83; chief exec. officer Timely Air Freight, Romulus, Mich., 1985, v.p. spl. projects, 1986—; cons. Multiplex Systems, Wyandotte, Mich., 1985—. Served to sgt. U.S. Army, 1960-66. Mem. The Packaging Inst. (profl.), Am. Legion, Fraternal Assn. of Police (sec.), Vietnam Vets. Am., Delta Nu Alpha. Republican. Roman Catholic. Lodge: KC. Avocations: woodworking, golf, coaching soccer. Home: 2050 22d St Wyandotte MI 48192 Office: Timely Air Freight PO Box 364 Taylor MI 48180

BEAUDIS, MICHAEL VINCENT, JR., project engineer; b. Youngstown, Ohio, Dec. 11, 1946; s. Michael Vincent Beaudis and Florence L. (Walsh) McMasters; m. Marguerite Rose Bokesch, Sept. 21, 1968; children: Craig, Tricia. BEE, Youngstown State U., 1975. Registered profl. engr., Ohio, Tex. Project engr. Mosure & Syrakis Co., Youngstown, 1970-78, Comml. Shearing, Inc., Youngstown, 1978—. Served with USN, 1966-68. Mem. ASCE (pres. Youngstown br. 1981-82). Democrat. Roman Catholic. Avocation: coaching youth soccer. Home: 2604 Barrington Ct Youngstown OH 44515 Office: Comml Shearing Inc 1775 Logan Ave Youngstown OH 44501

BEAUDOIN, ROBERT LAWRENCE, small business owner; b. Newberry, Mich., Nov. 22, 1933; s. Leo Joseph and Edith Wilhelmina (Graunstadt) B.; m. Margaret Cecelia Linck, June 20, 1953; children: Eugene Robert, Kathleen Therese, Annette Marie, Suzanne Margaret. Student, Marquette U., 1952-53. With Fisher plant Gen. Motors, 1953; dock hand State of Mich., St. Ignace, 1953; sch. bus driver Engadine (Mich.) Consol. Schs., 1957; owner, operator Beaudoin's Texaco, Beaudoin's Cafe, Naubinway, Mich., 1956-82, Beaudoin's Cafe and Marathon, Naubinway, 1982-83, Beaudoin's Cafe, Naubinway, 1956—; bd. dirs. Naubinway Mchts. Inc., 1985—. Mem. Naubinway July 4th Com., 1954—; vol. fireman Garfield Twp. Fire Dept., Naubinway, 1980—; mem. recreation com. Garfield Twp. Bd., Engadine, 1983; support fellow N.G. and Res., support mem. U.S. Army Recruiting Main Sta., Detroit. Recipient Cert. of Appreciation, U.S. Army Recruiting Main Sta., Detroit, 1971, Statement of Support, N.G. and Res., 1976. Mem. West Mackinac C. of C., Nat. Fedn. Ind. Bus. (mem. adv. bd. 1971—, 20 yr. award 1985). Roman Catholic. Club: Hiawatha Sportsmans (mem. bd. govs. Engadine 1965-67). Lodges: KC (grand knight 1979-83, Mich. State Council mem., program dir. East Marquette diocese 1984—), Lions (3d v.p. Engadine club 1970-71). Avocations: hunting, fishing. Home: PO Box 143 E Main St Naubinway MI 49762 Office: Beaudoins Cafe PO Box 143 W US2 Naubinway MI 49762

BEAULIEU, RONALD PATRICK, educator; b. Indpls., Mar. 15, 1949; s. Peter Calice and Charlotte Genevieve Beaulieu; B.S., Purdue U., 1972; M.B.A., Ind. U., 1975, D.B.A., 1976; m. Kathleen Michele; children, Allison Kathleen, Elliott. Asso. instr., Ind. U., Bloomington, 1973-76; asst. prof. mgmt. U. Notre Dame (Ind.), 1976-79. Central Mich. U., Mt. Pleasant, 1979—. Mem. Am. Psychol. Assn., Acad. Mgmt., Am. Soc. Personnel Adminstrn., Beta Gamma Sigma, Sigma Iota Epsilon. Home: 515 N Kinney Mount Pleasant MI 48858 Office: Central Michigan U Sch Bus Mount Pleasant MI 48859

BEAVES, GREGORY ALAN, engineer; b. Dubuque, Iowa, July 21, 1959; s. George William and Dorothy Muriel (Zakoscielny) B.; m. Heidi Jayne Peterson, June 19, 1982 (div. July 1984). BSEM, USAF Acad., 1981. Commd. 2d lt. USMC, Quantico, Va., 1981; advanced through grades to 1st lt. USMC; served with arty. unit USMC, various location; advanced to 1st lt. USMC, 1983, resigned, 1985; applications engr. Union Carbide Corp., Cleve., 1985—. Com. mem. United Way, Cleve., 1986; mem. Choral Arts Performing Soc. Recipient Comdg. Gen. Cert. of Commendation award Marine Corps Devel. and Edn. Comd., Quantico, 1983. Mem. Soc. Automotive Engrs., Am. Ceramic Soc. Republican. Roman Catholic. Avocations: ice hockey, running, singing. Home: 4110 Parkside Dr Brooklyn OH 44144 Office: PO Box 94637 Cleveland OH 44101

BEBKO, WILLIAM MATTHEW, corporate safety and standards engineer; b. Pittsfield, Mass., June 12, 1937; s. Matthew F. and Martha (Orbanek) B.; m. Mary Ann Tudbury, Apr. 4, 1959; children: Anne, Sara, Benjamin, Mark. BS, Antioch Coll., 1959. Supr. Vernay Labs., Yellow Springs, Ohio, 1961-70, prodn. mgr., 1970-78, plant mgr., 1978-83, facilities mgr., 1983-85, dir. corp. safety and plant services, 1985—. Avocations: flying, outdoor activities. Office: Vernay Labs ES College St Yellow Springs OH 45387

BECHER, MARILYN JUDITH, medical consultation services executive; b. Appleton, Wis., May 28, 1941; d. Alvin O. and Ethel M. (Braun) Adrian; Diploma Madison (Wis.) Gen. Hosp. Sch. Nursing, 1962; student U. Wis.-Madison, 1962-63; B.S. in Nursing, Alverno Coll., 1980; postgrad. Cardinal Stritch Coll., Milw. R.N., Wis. Staff nurse Univ. Hosps., Madison, 1962-63; staff nurse Theda Clark Regional Med. Ctr., Neenah, Wis., 1963-65, asst head nurse ob-gyn, 1965-68, head nurse orthopedic, neurology unit, 1968-70, head nurse med.-surg., pediatrics, 1970-71, head nurse psychiatry, 1971-80, dir. nurses, 1980-81, v.p. nursing adminstr., 1981-85; program mgr. rehab. program; lectr. in field. Bd. dirs. Rehab. House, Neenah, 1973-76; v.p. Winnebago County Health Resource Bd., 1978-81, pres., 1981-82; mem. Alverno Coll. Pres. Task Force, 1980; bd. dirs. Rynderson Foster Home, Appleton, Wis., 1983; mem. Nursing Interaction Group, Winnebago County, 1981—. Mem. Am. Nurses Assn. (cert. nursing adminstr.), Wis. Nurses Assn., Appleton Dist. Nurses Assn., Wis. League Nursing, Nat. League Nursing, Am. Orthopsychiat. Assn., Wis. Assn. Nursing Adminstrs., Am. Assn. Rehab. Nurses, Alverno Coll. Alumni Assn. Home: 824 Zemlock Ave Neenah WI 54956 Office: Med Cons Services 824 Zemlode Ave Neenah WI 54956

BECHERER, HANS WALTER, agricultural equipment manufacturing executive; b. Detroit, Apr. 19, 1935; s. Max and Mariele (Specht) B.; m. Michele Beigbeder, Nov. 28, 1959; children: Maxime, Vanessa. B.A., Trinity Coll., Hartford, Conn., 1957; student, Munich U., Germany, 1958; M.B.A., Harvard U., 1962. Exec. asst. office of chmn. Deere & Co., Moline, Ill., 1966-69; gen. mgr. John Deere Export, Manheim, Germany, 1969-73; dir. export mktg. Deere & Co., Moline, Ill., 1973-77; v.p. Deer & Co., Moline, Ill., 1977-83; sr v.p. Deere & Co., Moline, Ill., 1983-86, exec. v.p., 1986-87, pres., chief operating officer, 1987—; dir. U.S.-Yugoslav Econ. Council, Deere & Co.; mem. industry sector adv. com. U.S. Dept. Commerce, 1975-81. Vice pres., trustee St. Katharine's-St. Mark's Sch., Bettendorf, Iowa, 1983. Served to 1st lt. USAF, 1958-60. Mem. Farm and Indsl. Equipment Inst. (bd. dirs. 1987—). Republican. Roman Catholic. Clubs: Rock Island Arsenal Golf (Ill.); Davenport (Iowa). Home: 788 25th Ave Ct Moline IL 61265 Office: Deere & Co John Deere Rd Moline IL 61265

BECHTEL, PETER JOHN, biology educator; b. Mpls., Apr. 9, 1943; s. Martin John and Audrey (Jensen) B.; m. Edith Jane Rietfors, 1964; children: Christian, Matthew. BS, Parsons Coll., 1966; PhD, Mich. State U., 1971. Chemist Quaker Oats Co., Chgo., 1966-67; biologist Agrl. Research Service, USDA, Bettsville, Md., 1970-71; research fellow U. Calif., Davis, 1971-75; research expert NIH NCI Mol. Biol., Bethesda, Md., 1976-77; asst. prof. biology Iowa State U., Ames, 1977-80; assoc. prof. biology U. Ill., Urbana, 1980-86, prof. biology, 1986—. Editor: Muscle as Food, 1986. Fellow USPHS, Muscular Dystrophy Assn. Am. Mem. Am. Inst. Nutrition, Inst. Food Technologist, Am. Meat Sci. Assn., Am. Soc. Animal Sci. Home: 405 McHenry Urbana IL 61801 Office: U Ill Muscle Biology Lab 1503 Maryland Dr Urbana IL 61801

BECHTOL, LAUREN LEONHARDT, JR., jewelry company executive; b. Bryan, Ohio, Apr. 15, 1951; s. Lauren Leonhardt and Ann Margaret (Schuck) B.; m. Christine Ann King, Sept. 10, 1977; children: Jeremy Lauren, Kaitlyn Christine. BS in Geology, Kent State U., 1973; cert. diamond grader, cert. colored stones identifier Gemological Inst. Am., 1980, 84, gemologist diploma, 1987; cert. advanced goldsmithing, repair Queen City Seminars, E.J. Swigart Co., Cin., 1981. Jewelry clk., buyer Schuck Jewelers, Bryan, 1973-76, jeweler, goldsmith, 1976—, diamond appraiser, 1980—, co-owner, 1983—, gemstone appraiser, 1984—; appraiser local ins. cos., 1980—. Bd. dirs., bd. pub. affairs, city utilities Bryan, 1973-83, chmn., 1976, 79, 82. Colored Gemstone Identification scholar Gemological Inst. Am., 1981, Diamond Grading scholar Gemological Inst. Am. and Ohio Jewelers Assn., 1986, Ohio Retail Jewelers Assn. scholar, 1987. Mem. Gemological Assn. Gt. Britain, Alumni Assn. of Kent State U., Ohio Jewelers Assn. (scholarship winner 1986), Gemmological Inst. Am., Wilderness Soc., Sierra Club. Republican. Roman Catholic. Avocations: gemstone research, jewelry design, camping, bicycle touring. Office: Schuck Jewelers 120 S Lynn St Bryan OH 43506

BECK, BARBARA LEA, publishing executive; b. Havre, Mont., Feb. 5, 1954; d. Harold D. and Ramona M. (Trulson) B. BS, Eastern Mont. Coll., 1976. Coop. adminstr. corp. advt. Coast to Coast Stores, Mpls., 1976-80; dist. mgr. and coop. regional mgr. Standard Rate and Data Service, Wilmette, Ill., 1980-84; dir. field services Am. Assn. Yellow Pages Pubs., Chesterfield, Mo., 1984—. Mem. Nat. Assn. Coop. Advt. Profls. (mem. chmn. 1986), Chgo. Coop. Advt. Assn., Chgo. Advt. Club. Office: Am Assn Yellow Pages Pubs 500 Chesterfield Ctr Chesterfield MO 63017

BECK, DANIEL JAMES, information systems manager; b. Cin., Aug. 5, 1948; s. William Albert and Mary Theresa (Moriarty) B.; m. Sandra Sue Wilson; 1 child, Hillary. BA in Polit. Sci., U. Cin., 1970; MA in Polit. Sci., Ohio State U., 1972, M in Pub. Adminstrn., 1978. Sr. mgmt. analyst Ohio Dept. Mental Health and Menatl Retardation, Columbus, 1978-80; mgr. adminstrn. systems Ohio Dept. Mental Retardation, Columbus, 1980—. Mem. Am. Soc. for Pub. Adminstrn. Democrat. Avocations: personal computers, science fiction, writing. Office: Ohio Dept Mental Retardation 30 E Broad St Room 1240J Columbus OH 43215

BECK, DAVID ALLAN, lawyer; b. Cleve., Nov. 29, 1944; s. Henry Louis and Miriam Doris (Lockwood) B. BS, Ohio State U., 1970; MA, U Iowa, 1971; JD, Cleve. Marshall Law Sch., 1981. Bar: Ohio 1982, U.S. Ct. Appeals (6th cir.) 1982, U.S. Dist. Ct. (no. dist.) Ohio 1982. Asst. prof. history Kirkwood Community Coll., Cedar Rapids, Iowa, 1971-74; chief steward AFSCME, Iowa City, 1976-78; sole practice law, Cleve., 1982—; instr. Creative Learning Inst., Cleve., 1984—. Editor: Cleve. Law Rev., 1980-81. Mem. ABA, Assn. Trial Lawyers Am., Ohio Bar Assn., Bar Assn. Greater Cleve., Cuyahoga County Bar Assn., Citizens League Greater Cleve., Ohio State Alumni Assn. Lodge: Lions. Home: 106 Manning Dr Berea OH 44017 Office: 1034 Standard Bldg Cleveland OH 44113

BECK, DONALD STEVEN, architect; b. Indpls., July 17, 1949; s. David C. and Beverly Edith (Barker) B. B in Community Planning, U. Cin., 1972, BS in Architecture, 1985. Designer Woodie Garber, Cin., 1972-73; urban designer Vogt, Sage & Pflum, Cin., 1974-77; pres. Interform, Inc., Cin., 1978—; bd. dirs. Miami Purchase Revolving Loan Fund, Cin., Hillside Trust, Cin. Mem. AIA (assoc.). Republican. Home: 550 Liberty Hill Cincinnati OH 45210 Office: Interform Inc 550 Liberty Hill Cincinnati OH 45210

BECK, HELEN (LIELAND), social worker; b. Indpls., Oct. 14, 1933; d. John Edward and Mary Stella (Weber) Lieland; m. George Joseph Beck, May 13, 1961; children: Jennifer, Nancy, Betsy, Jan. BA, Marian Coll., 1955; postgrad., Ind. U., 1956-59, U. Ill., 1985—. Registered social worker, Ill. Caseworker Cath. Charities, Indpls., 1955-60, Waukegan, Ill., 1982—; probation officer Marion County Juvenile Ct., Indpls., 1960-62. Active Archdiocese Commn. on Human Rights, Omaha, 1969-74, Social Settlement of Omaha, 1969-74; bd. dirs. Bowman Jr. High Sch., Plano, Tex., 1978-79, Greater Libertyville (Ill.) Soccer Assn., 1979-80, Girl Scout Service Team, Libertyville, 1980-82, Youth Adv. council, Libertyville, 1981-83; field aide Lake View Girl Scouts, Waukegan, 1979-82. Democrat. Roman Catholic. Avocations: tennis, soccer, bridge, theater. Home: 820 Crestfield Ave Libertyville IL 60048 Office: Cath Charities 1 N Genesee St Waukegan IL 60085

BECK, J(AMES) FRED(ERICK), finance executive; b. Lockport, N.Y., Dec. 23, 1924; s. Frederick George and Felicia Lamanda (McGrath) B.; m. Audrey Helen Zebold, Aug. 27, 1949. Student, U. Buffalo, 1947-59; BS, Rollins Coll., 1963, MBA, 1968. Dir. Addressograph Multigraph, Cleve., 1976-78; pvt. cons. Buffalo, 1978-79; project mgr. Blue Cross of West N.Y., Buffalo, 1979-81; sr. systems analyst Moore Bus. Forms, Niagara Falls, N.Y., 1981-85; dir. EDP ops. ITT Consumer Fin. Corp., Mpls., 1985-87, dir. field support, 1987—. Patentee poncho disposable raincoat. Served with USNR. Republican. Roman Catholic. Lodge: Elks. Avocations: golf, tennis. Home: 4237 Goldenrod Ln N Plymouth MN 55442 Office: Itt Consumer Fin Corp 400 South County Rd 18 Suite 800 Minneapolis MN 55440

BECK, JOHN LEROY, university program administrator; b. New Brunswick, N.J., May 29, 1947; s. Frank Victor and Pluma Victoria (Overholser) B.; m. Mary Lee Schneider, Aug. 2, 1980; 1 child, Erin Kristine. BS in Chemistry, Stanford U., 1969; MS in Computer Sci., U. Wis., 1973. Programmer/analyst Control Data Corp., Sunnyvale, Calif., 1969-71; coordinator U. Wis., Madison, 1974-79; engr. software design Tektronix, Wilsonville, Oreg., 1979-80; mgr. software U. Wis., Eau Claire, 1980-84; asst. dir. U. Wis., La Crosse, 1984-86, acting dir., 1986—. Mem. Assn. Computing Mfgrs. Avocations: hockey officiating, aikido. Office: U Wis 1725 State St La Crosse WI 54601

BECK, JOHN MATTHEW, educator; b. Rogoznig, Austria, Apr. 10, 1913; s. Matthias and Antoinette (Bukowski) B.; came to U.S., 1914, naturalized, 1942; B.S., Ind. State Coll. (Pa.), 1936; M.A., U. Chgo., 1947, Ph.D., 1953; m. Frances Josephine Mottey, Aug. 23, 1941. Tchr., Clymer (Pa.) High Sch., 1937-41; instr. history and philosophy of edn. De Paul U., 1948-53; instr. Chgo. State College, 1953-56, chmn. dept. edn., 1959-60, asst. dean, prof. edn., 1960-66, dean coll., 1966-67; dir. Chgo. Tchr. Corps, 1967—; exec. dir. Chgo. Consortium Colls. and Univs., 1968—; prof. urban tchr. edn. Govs. State U., 1972—; cons. U.S. Office of Edn., 1968—. Mem. Ill. State Advisory Com. on Guidance, 1963—, Citizens Schs. Com., Chgo., 1953—; chmn. curriculum adv. com. Ednl. Facilities Center, Chgo., 1971—; exec. bd. Cook County OEO, 1971—; adv. com. interstate interinstnl. cooperation Ill. Bd. Higher Edn., 1972—; mem. Chgo. Mayor's Adv. Commn. Sch. Bd. Nominations, 1975, Mayor's Adv. Council on Aging, 1976—, Exec. Service Corps. of Chgo., 1983—, Mayor Washington's Task Force on Edn., 1983. Bd. govs. Chgo. City Club, 1961—, v.p., 1962-63, 64-65; mem. Exec. Service Corps of Chgo., 1983—. Served with AUS, 1941-46. Decorated Bronze Star. Recipient W. Germany grant, 1972. Fellow AAAS, Philosophy of Edn. Soc.; mem. Am. Hist. Assn., Am. Edn. Research Assn., Ill. Edn. Assn. (pres. Chgo. div. 1960-62). Co-author: Extending Reading Skills, 1976. Editor: Chgo. Sch. Jour., 1964-65; co-editor: Teaching the Culturally Disadvantaged Child, 1966; contbr. articles to profl. jours. and encys. Home: 5832 Stony Island Ave Chicago IL 60637 Office: 95th and King Dr Suite 204 Chicago IL 60628

BECK, JOHN ROBERT, accountant; b. Omaha, Feb. 28, 1954; s. Donald W. Beck and Peggy A. (Raapke) Ederer; m. Terri A. Mattern, May 16, 1975; children: Kelly, Jeffrey. BBA, Creighton U., 1975. CPA, Nebr. Auditor Peat-Marwick-Mitchell, Omaha, 1975-77; acctg. supr. Lozier Corp., Omaha, 1977-78; controller Bishop Bldg. Services, Omaha, 1978-84, Pepsi Cola Bottling Co., Omaha, 1984—. Mem. Nebr. Soc. CPA's. Republican. Roman Catholic. Lodge: Optimist (treas. 1984—). Avocations: basketball, running, golf, spectator sports. Home: 8249 Keystone Dr Omaha NE 68134 Office: Pepsi Cola Bottling Co 4603 S 72d St Omaha NE 68127

BECK, M. FRANK, JR., dentist; b. Youngstown, Ohio, Apr. 11, 1956; s. M. Frank and Mary Louise (McGovern) B.; m. Jennifer Boyle, June 5, 1981; 1 child, Lauren Elizabeth. BChemE magna cum laude, John Carroll U., 1978; DDS, Ohio State U., 1981. Resident in dentistry St. Elizabeth Hosp. Med. Ctr., Youngstown, 1981-82, chief dental resident, 1982-83, instr. in dentistry, 1983—, mem. resident selection com., 1985—, coordinator geriatric dental program, 1986; cons. Windsor Nursing Homes, Youngstown, 1983—, Mil Creek Child Care Ctr, Youngstown, 1983—. Editor: Jeghers Med. Index Library, 1982. Mem. ADA, Ohio Dental Assn., Corydon-Palmer Dental Soc., Acad Gen. Dentistry, Am. Assn. Hosp. Dentists, Am. Equilibration Soc., Am. Soc. Geriatric Dentistry. Roman Catholic. Avocations: tennis, woodworking. Home: 25 Brookline Ave Youngstown OH 44505 Office: 3711 Starrs Centre Dr Canfield OH 44406

BECK, ROBERT KNOWLTON, retired newspaper publisher; b. Centerville, Iowa, July 17, 1915; s. Jesse McFall and Edna (Needham) B.; B.A., Iowa Wesleyan Coll., 1937, LL.D. (hon.), 1977; m. Charlotte V. Allen, June 24, 1939; children—Thomas Allen, Barbara (Mrs. Phil Climie), Martha Hoch. Editor-pub. Daily Iowegian and Citizen, Centerville, Iowa, 1943-83; asso. pub. Weekly Corydon Times-Republican, 1967-78; partner Daily Blade-Tribune, Oceanside, Calif., 1943-54, asso. pub. semi-weekly newspaper Glendora, Charter Oak, Azusa, 1958-65; chmn. bd. dirs. Centerville Nat. Bank, 1968-76; pres. Centerville Broadcasting Co., 1948-54; dir. Hawkeye Bancorp. Mem. Iowa Ho. of Reps., 1953-54; mem. Iowa Hwy. Commn., 1955-59; commr. Iowa Devel. Commn., 1969-77. Bd. trustees Iowa Wesleyan Coll., 1962-81; trustee Hoover Library Assn., 1975—. Recipient 1st place in Iowa for editorial writing excellence, 1954; newspaper classed 1st in Ia. cities 12000 population or less, 1951, 53, 60, 2d place, 55, 57, 58; recipient Des Moines Press and Radio Bent Cane award, 1960; Ia. Master-Editor Pub. award, 1963, Iowa Daily Press Community Service award, 1963, 83. Mem. Iowa Press Assn. (past pres.), C. of C. (past pres.), Iowa Good Roads Assn. (pres. 1963-65, chmn. bd. 1966-74), Sigma Delta Chi. Methodist (del. jurisdictional conf. 1952 and 1964). Mason, Elk, Lion (past pres.). Clubs: Centerville Country (past pres.); Rathbun Lake Assn. (pres.); Lincoln of Iowa (pres. 1979-81). Home: Golfview Addition R3 Centerville IA 52544 Office: 105-7 N Main St Centerville IA 52544

BECK, VEARL J., chemical engineer; b. American Fork, Utah, Oct. 9, 1955; s. Dewain J. and Beverly Lois (Hicks) B.; m. Holly Susan McClendon, Apr. 24, 1978; children: Adele, Lois Kae. BSChE, MSChE, Brigham Young U., 1980. Process engr. E.I. DuPont Co., Parkersburg, W.Va., 1980-86; chief engr. Do-It Corp., South Haven, Mich., 1986—. Mem. Tau Beta Pi (asst.), Sigma Xi (asst.). Mormon. Avocation: computers. Home: 1327 Monroe Blvd South Haven MI 49090 Office: Do-It Corp PO Box 592 South Haven MI 49090

BECKELHIMER, WILLIAM FRANKLIN, accountant; b. Arkansas City, Kans., Apr. 25, 1961; s. George Thomas Beckelhimer and Doloreta Virginia (Wilson) Judd. BS in Acctg., Kans. State U., 1983. CPA, Kans. Sr. acct. Grant Thornton, Wichita, Kans., 1983-85; acct. Restaurant Mgmt. Co., Wichita, 1985—. Am. Inst. CPA's, Kans. Soc. CPA's. Methodist. Avocations: golf, snowskiing, backpacking. Home: 8131 E Harry #305 Wichita KS 67207 Office: Restaurant Mgmt Co 555 N Woodlawn Suite 3102 Wichita KS 67208

BECKER, BENJAMIN MAX, lawyer; b. Chgo., Feb. 3, 1909; s. Max and Etta Becker; J.D., DePaul U., 1933; m. Jean Merin, Dec. 25, 1930; children—David M., Merle Lynn. Admitted to Ill. bar, 1935; since practiced in Chgo.; partner firm Warden & Becker, 1935-42; asso. mem. firm Levinson Becker Peebles & Swiren, 1942-47; sr. partner firm Becker & Savin, 1947-72; counsel firm Antonow & Fink, Chgo., 1973-83; writer and bus. cons. to various firms, 1983—. Dir. DePaul Inst. Fed. Taxation, 1952, 53. Mem. Chgo. City Council, 1947-55. Bd. dirs. Chgo. chpt. UN Assn. Recipient distinguished service award Chgo. Life Ins. Underwriters Assn., 1970, several civic awards. Mem. Am., Ill., Chgo. bar assns., Internat. Soc. Law, Decalogue Soc. Co-author: (with Edward Warden) Illinois Lawyer's Manual (2 vols.) 1939, (with Bernard Savin, David M. Becker and David Gibberman), ann. supplements, 1948—, legal checklists (2 vols.), Ann. Supp. 1963, (with David M. Becker) Simplified Estate Planning, 1965, (with Ben Poth) rev. edit., 1982, (with Bernard Savin and David M. Becker) Legal Checklists (3 vols.), 1966, ann. supplements, 1986, Is the United Nations Dead, 1969, (with Fred A. Tillman) The Family Owned Business, 1975, 2d edit., 1978, (with David Gibberman) On Trial Law, 1987, Lawyers and Judicial System; contbr. over 60 articles to profl. jours. on law, ethics, United Nations, arms control, disarmament. Home: 1771 W Mission Hills Rd Northbrook IL 60062

BECKER, BETTIE GERALDINE, artist; b. Peoria, Ill., Sept. 22, 1918; d. Harry Seymour and Magdalene Matilda (Hiller) Becker; B.F.A. cum laude, U. Ill., Urbana, 1940; postgrad. Art Inst. Chgo., 1942-45, Art Student's League, 1946, Ill. Inst. tech., 1948; m. Lionel William Wathall, Nov. 10, 1945; children—Heather Lynn (dec.), Jeffrey Lee. Dept. artist Liberty Mut. Ins. Co., Chgo., 1941-43; with Palenskie-Young Studio, 1943-46; free lance illustrator N.Y. Times, Chgo. Tribune, Saturday Rev. Lit., 1948-50; co-owner, operator Pangaea Gallery/Studio, Fish Creek, Wis.; pvt. tutor, tchr. studio classes. Exhibited one-man show Crossroads Gallery, Art Inst. Chgo., 1973; exhibited group shows including Critics' Choice show Art Rental Sales Gallery Art Inst. Chgo., 1972, Evanston-North Shore exhbns., 1964, 65, Chgo. Soc. Artists, 1967, 71, Union League, 1967, 72, Women in Art, Appleton (Wis.) Gallery Art; represented in permanent collection Witte Meml. Mus., San Antonio; executed mural (with F. Wiater) Talbot Lab. U. Ill., Urbana, 1940. Active Campfire Girls, Chgo., 1968, 70; art chmn., mem. exec. bd. local PTA, 1959-60; active various art festivals, 1967—. Recipient Newcomb award U. Ill., 1940. Mem. Chgo. Soc. Artists (rec. sec. 1968-77), Internat. Platform Assn., Accademia d' Europa, Soc. Illustrators, Wis. Arts Council, Northeast Wis. Arts Council (dir.), Alumni Assn. Art Inst. Chgo., Accademia d'Europa, Internat. Platform Assn. Republican. Mem. Unity Ch. Contbr. articles, illustrations to mags. and newspapers. Home: 3992 Juddville Rd Fish Creek WI 54212

BECKER, BRUCE CARL, II, medical educator, family physician; b. Chgo., Sept. 8, 1948; s. Carl Max and Lillian (Podzamsky) B. B.S. in Aero. and Astron. Engring., U. Ill., 1970; M.S.M.E., Colo. State U., 1972; postgrad. Wright State U., 1973-74; M.D., Chgo. Med. Sch., 1978; M.S. in Health Services Adminstrn., Coll. St. Francis, Joliet, Ill., 1984. Diplomate Am. Bd. Family Practice. Resident in surgery U. N.C.-Chapel Hill, 1978-79, in family practice St. Mary of Nazareth Hosp. Ctr., Chgo., 1979-81, chmn., program dir. dept. family practice, 1985—; clin. instr. Chgo. Med. Sch., 1982, affiliate instr., 1982-83, asst. prof., vice chmn. dept. family medicine, 1983—; asst. dir. med. edn. St. Mary of Nazareth Hosp. Ctr., Chgo., 1981-82, dir. family practice residency, 1983—, chief Family Practice Ctr., 1983-85, chmn. dept. family practice, 1985—, med. dir. Home Health Service, 1985—, med. dir. HMO-Ill., 1985—, mem. fin. com. governing bd., 1987—. Contbr. articles to profl. jours. Served to capt., USAF, 1970-75. Recipient Literary Key award St. Mary of Nazareth Hosp. Ctr., 1981, 85. Fellow Am. Acad. Family Physicians; mem. Ill. Acad. Family Physicians (commn. on internal affairs 1986, commn. pub. and govt. policy 1987), Soc. Tchrs. of Family Medicine, Assn. Am. Med. Colls., Alliance Continuing Med. Edn., Am. Coll. Health Care Execs., AMA, Chgo. Med. Soc. (councilor for Chgo. Med. Sch. 1986—), Ill. State Med. Soc. (mem. council on edn. and manpower 1986—, chmn. subcom. physican placement and practice issues 1986—), Phi Delta Epsilon. Lutheran.

BECKER, DAVID BRUCE, data processing company executive; b. Indpls., Nov. 8, 1953; s. Alton Arthur and Minnie Ann (Pierce) B.; m. Bonita Ann Linxwiler, May 30, 1980 (div. Oct. 1983); 1 son, Jason Edward. BA, DePauw U., 1975. Br. mgr. Gen. Electric, Indpls., 1975-76, Credit Corp., South Bend, Ind., 1976-78; sr. cons. Ind. Credit Union League, Indpls., 1979-81; pres., founder ReMember Data processing, Indpls., 1981—; pres., bd. dirs. Compass, Inc., Indpls., 1982—, Becker & Assocs., Inc., Indpls., 1982—, Checks, Inc., Indpls., 1983—; bd. dirs. L. Scott Corp., Indpls., Muskies Inc. Mem. Indpls. C. of C. Home: 9030 Mud Creek Rd Indianapolis IN 46256 Office: ReMember Data Processing Services Inc 8455 Keystone Crossing Indianapolis IN 46240

BECKER, DAVID NORBERT, insurance company executive; b. St. Louis, July 18, 1945; s. William Paul and Estelle Katherine (Meyer) B.; B.S. cum laude, St. Louis U., 1967, Ph.D. (fellow), 1973; M.A. (fellow) Washington U., St. Louis, 1969, A.S.A., 1977, F.S.A., 1979; m. JoAnn Elizabeth Clark, June 7, 1969. Instr. John Burroughs Sch., Ladue, Mo., 1969-70; instr. math. St. Louis U., 1970-73; asst. prof. math St. Francis Coll., Fort Wayne, Ind., 1973-75; actuarial cons. Lincoln Nat. Life Ins. Co., Ft. Wayne, 1975-79, asst. actuary, 1979-80, dir. group/ind. products, 1980-81; asst. v.p., dir. fin. planning and analysis, reins. div. Lincoln Nat. Corp., 1982-83, asst. v.p., individual life actuary individual products div., 1983-85, 2d v.p., 1985—. Fellow Soc. Actuaries; mem. Am. Math. Soc., Math. Assn. Am., Pi Mu Epsilon. Contbr. articles to profl. jours. Home: 2208 Forest Glade Fort Wayne IN 46825

BECKER, ELIZABETH SCHUTZ, financial analyst; b. Madison, Wis., Mar. 8, 1958; d. John George and Betty Lou (Bank) Schutz; m. Daniel Edward Becker, Oct. 5, 1985. BA, Carleton Coll., 1979; MBA, U. Wis., 1983. CPA, Minn. Gift shop mgr. Sheraton Gift Shop, Madison, 1979-80; sr. auditor Coopers & Lybrand, Mpls., 1983-86; sr. fin. analyst MSI Ins., Arden Hills, Minn., 1986—. W.K. Kellogg grantee, 1982. Mem. Am. Inst. CPA's, Minn. Soc. CPA's. Presbyterian. Avocations: golf, tennis, piano. Office: MSI Ins 2 Pine Tree Dr Arden Hills MN 55112

BECKER, GARY LEIGH, dentist, real estate broker; b. Dayton, Ohio; s. Donald R. Becker and Faye B. (Bowman) McElwee; m. Sandra Lee Schneider, June 30, 1973; children: Brett, Erin. BS, Ohio U., 1973; DDS, Ohio State U., 1976. Pvt. practice dentistry Dayton, 1976—; real estate broker, 1973—; cons. dental mktg., mgmt., 1976—. Mem. ADA, Ohio Dental Assn., Dayton Dental Soc. Methodist. Clubs: Dayton Bicycle; Sycamore Creek Country (Springboro, Ohio). Avocations: golf, tennis, racquetball, woodworking. Home: 1530 Lindenhurst Dayton OH 45459 Office: 7809 N Dixie Dayton OH 45414

BECKER, GARY MICHAEL, controller; b. Waterloo, Iowa, July 27, 1958; s. Daniel Bernard and Patricia Kay (Mitchell) B.; m. Michelle Marie Haase, Oct. 1, 1983; 1 child, Abby Marie. BA in Bus., U. No. Iowa, 1980. CPA, Iowa. Acct. McGladry Hendrickson, Dubuque, Iowa, 1981-82, FDL Foods, Inc., Dubuque, 1982-84; controller, treas. Riverside Tractor/Trailer, Dubuque, 1984-86; controller Dubuque Savs. and Loan, Dubuque, 1986—. Advisor Jr. Achievement, Dubuque, 1981-82, tchr., 1987—, bd. dirs. tri-state chpt., 1986—. Iowa State scholar, 1976. Mem. Am. Inst. CPA's, Nat. Assn. Accts. (v.p. membership tri-state chpt. 1986—), Iowa Soc. CPA's (program dir. northeast Iowa chpt. 1985—), Fin. Mgrs. Soc. Republican. Roman Catholic. Avocations: softball, racquetball, bowling, golf. Home: 2640 Autumn Dubuque IA 52001 Office: Dubuque Savs & Loan Assn 2560 Dodge Dubuque IA 52001

BECKER, GERALD ARTHUR, publisher; b. Elyria, Ohio, Sept. 29, 1941; s. Louis A. and Eleanor (Phillipson) B.; m. Ryna L. Trope, Nov. 27, 1965; children: David, Adam. BS in Journalism, Ohio U., 1963. Asst. to pub. Penton/IPC, Cleve., 1964-69; editorial dir. CRC Press, Cleve., 1969-77; v.p., assoc. pub. Oster Communications, Chgo., 1977-84; pub. Commodity Perspective div. Knight Ridder, Inc., Chgo., 1984—, Commodity Research Bur. div. Knight Ridder, Inc., N.Y.C., 1984—; sr. v.p. Commodity News Services, Inc., Chgo. Served with USCGR, 1963-69. Mem. Futures Industry Assn. Avocations: tennis, bowling, reading. Home: 2930 Huntington Dr Arlington Heights IL 60004 Office: Commodity Perspective div Knight Ridder Inc 30 S Wacker Dr Room 1820 Chicago IL 60606

BECKER, GORDON M., psychologist, educator; b. N.Y.C., Mar. 8, 1924; s. Bernard Fred and Viola (Borgas) B.; m. Ellen Ferris, Feb. 3, 1949 (div. Jan. 1, 1965); children: Mark Halliday, Karin Stuart, Jonathan Stuart; m. Micki Rose, June 1, 1965 (Aug. 1, 1969); m. Andrea Lee Binkley, Jan. 12, 1976; 1 child, Andrew Lee. BS, U. Conn., 1948; MA, Columbia U. Tchrs. Coll., 1949; PhD, U. Pitts., 1956. Lic. psychologist, Nebr., Conn. Research assoc. Yale U., New Haven, Conn., 1960-61, U. Calif. at Los Angeles, 1961-62; long range planning staff Gen Electric, N.Y.C., 1962-64; assoc. prof. Ferkauf Grad. Sch., N.Y.C., 1964-66, Howard U., Washington, 1966-69; prof. U. Nebr., Omaha, 1970—; pres. Nebr. Zen Med. Ctr., Omaha, 1985—; mem. adv. bd. Am. Indian Alcohol Program, Omaha, 1979-85; bd. dirs. Unkiyep Alcohol Program, Omaha, 1985—, MARR, Omaha, 1982-85;. Editor: (newsletter) Zen Monkey, 1982-83; contbr. articles to profl. jours. town council Electorate Waterford Conn., 1959. Served to lt. USNR, 1942-45. Mem. Boston Computer Soc., Nat. Council Health Service Providers in Psychology. Republican. Buddhist. Avocation: camping. Home: 816 S 67th St Omaha NE 68106 Office: U Nebr at Omaha Dodge St Omaha NE 68182

BECKER, JAMES MURDOCH, surgeon, educator; b. Cleve., Jan. 7, 1949; s. Norman O. and Mildred Edith (Murdoch) B.; m. Christine Louise Lohmann, Dec. 30, 1972; children: Alexander, Selby, Catherine, Anne. BA in Biology, Yale U., 1971; MD, Case Western Res. U., 1975. Diplomate Nat. Bd. Med. Examiners, Am. Bd. Surgery; lic. surgeon, Minn., Utah, Mo. Intern in surgery U. Utah Hosps., Salt Lake City, 1975-76, resident in gen. surgery, 1976-79, chief resident in surgery, 1976-79; research fellow in surgery U. Utah Sch. Medicine, 1977-78, asst. prof. surgery, 1982-86; mem. surg. staff VA Hosp., Salt Lake City, 1982-86, chief green service, 1983-86, head nutritional support team, 1983-86; mem. cons. staff Intermountain Unit Shriners Hosps. for Crippled Children, Salt Lake City, 1984-86; assoc. prof. surgery, dir. gastrointestinal surgery Washington U. Sch. Medicine, 1986—. Contbr. articles to profl. jours., chpts. to books. NIH fellow, Mayo Clinic, 1980-82; grantee Johnson & Johnson Products, Inc., 1985, NIH, 1985—, Sandeoz Corp., 1985—, Ethicon, Inc., 1985-86. Mem. ACS, AMA, Am. Gastroenterol. Assn., Am. Motility Soc., Am. Pancreatic Assn., Assn. Acad. Surgery (issues com. 1984-86), Utah State Med. Assn., Salt Lake County Med. Assn., Am. Soc. Parenteral and Enteral Nutrition, Utah Profl. Standards Rev. Orgn., Salt Lake Surg. Soc., Internat. Biliary Assn., Collegium Internat. Chirurgiae Digestivae (Grassi prize 8th World Congress 1984), Soc. for Surgery Alimentary Tract, Soc. Univ. Surgeons, Salt Lake City Chpt. United Ostomy Assn., Inc. (bd. med. advisors 1984—), Yale U. Alumni Assn., Alpha Omega Alpha. Office: Washington U Sch Medicine Dept Surgery Suite 6108 4948 Barnes Hosp Plaza Saint Louis MO 63110

BECKER, JILL B., neuroscience and psychobiology educator; b. Redwood City, Calif., July 25, 1952; d. Wesley Clemence Becker and Barbara Ann (Beckel) Eriksen; m. Terrance Earl Robinson, Aug. 26, 1980. BA, U. Kans., 1973, MA, 1976; PhD, U. Ill., 1980. Post-doctoral fellow U. Mich., Ann Arbor, 1980-83, asst. research scientist, 1983-87, asst. prof., 1987—. Contbr. articles to profl. jours. Recipient numerous research grants. Mem. AAAS, Soc. for Neurosci., Mich. Soc. for Neurosci. Club: Jazz Dance Theatre (pres. 1986—) (Ann Arbor). Avocation: contemporary dance. Home: 919 Pomona Rd Ann Arbor MI 48103 Office: Univ Mich 1103 E Huron Ann Arbor MI 48104-1687

BECKER, JOHN ALPHONSIS, banker; b. Kenosha, Wis., Jan. 26, 1942; s. Paul Joseph and Hedwig (Hammacke) B.; m. Bonny J. Anderson, July 4, 1963; children: Danial, Todd, Kathryn, Erik. B.S., Marquette U., 1963, M.B.A., 1965. Asst. v.p. 1st Wis. Nat. Bank of Milw., 1970-73, v.p., 1973-76, 1st v.p., 1976-79; pres. 1st Wis. Nat. Bank of Madison, 1979-86; exec. v.p. 1st Wis. Nat. Bank of Milw., 1986—. Div. chmn. United Way, Madison, 1984; trustee Edgewood Coll., Madison, 1980—; mem. fin. com. Madison Republican Com. Served to 1st lt. U.S. Army, 1965-67. Mem. Wis. Bankers Assn. (exec. com.), Greater madison C. of C. (chmn. bd. 1983). Roman Catholic. Clubs: Madison, Maple Bluff Country. Office: 1st Wis Nat Bank of Milw 777 E Wisconsin Ave Milwaukee WI 53202 *

BECKER, KENNETH MELVIN, accountant; b. Portland, Oreg., Apr. 13, 1948; s. Melvin P. and Martha M. (Pfaff) B.; m. Gail Diane Dawson, June 14, 1970; 1 child, Arthur. BA in Econs. and Bus. Adminstrn., Seattle Pacific U., 1970; MBA, U. Wyo., 1975. CPA, Minn.; cert. mgmt. acct. Cost acct. FMC Corp., Portland, 1976-77; mgmt. acct. ESCO Corp., Portland, 1977-79; controller, office mgr. Miller Pub. Co., Mpls., 1979-83; v.p., chief fin. officer Rockwood Research Co., St. Paul, 1984—. Planning commnr. New Brighton, Minn., 1985—. Served with USAF, 1971-75. Mem. Nat. Assn. Accts. (local pres. 1986-87, bd. mem. of yr. 1984-85), Minn. Soc. CPA's, Am. Inst. CPA's. Club: Trails of Oreg. (Portland)(treas. 1977-79). Home: 1445 NW 16th St New Brighton MN 55112-5559 Office: Rockwood Research Corp 1751 W County Rd B Saint Paul MN 55113-4037

BECKER, LANSON, engineering executive; b. Kalamazoo, Mich., Feb. 10, 1941; s. Ellis and Elizabeth May (Coville) B.; m. Linda Diane Schuyler, June 1, 1963; children: Timothy Ray, Matthew Jay, Lanson Tyler. BS, Western Mich. U., 1963, MBA in Fin., 1978. Layout draftsman Argonne Nat. Labs., Lemont, Ill., 1963, Hydreco Co. div. Gen. Signal Corp., Kalamazoo, Mich., 1963-65; from asst. project engr. to v.p. engring. Hydreco Co. div. Gen. Signal Corp., Kalamazoo, 1965—. Patentee in field (6). Chmn. Cub Scouts Am., Galesburg, Mich., 1975-83; mem., then chmn. Galesburg City Planning Commn., 1965-75. Mem. Soc. Mfg. Engrs., Soc. Automotive Engrs. (remote controls and steering subcom. 1966—), Nat. Fluid Power Assn. (T3.5 valve sect., 1967—, Standards Devel. award 1986). Methodist. Avocations: automobile restoration, stained glass, racquetball. Home: 12505 Fort Custer Dr Galesburg MI 49053 Office: Hydreco 9000 E Michigan Ave Kalamazoo MI 49003

BECKER, NORMAN OTTO, surgeon; b. Fond du Lac, Wis., Jan. 16, 1918; s. John H. and Ottilie A. (Graf) B.; m. Mildred Murdoch, June 20, 1943; children—Mary Gail, James Murdoch, Julia Brown, Constance Marjorie. B.A., U. Wis., 1940, M.D., 1943. Diplomate Am. Bd. Surgery. Intern, resident, chief resident in surgery Cleve. Met. Hosp., 1943-49; asst. clin. prof. surgery U. Wis.; surgeon Assoc. Physicians, Fond du Lac, Wis., 1949—; dir. 1st Wis. Nat. Bank, Fond du Lac. Bd. dirs. Med. Coll. Wis.; chmn. bd. dirs., mem. exec. com. U. Wis. Found., 1983—; pres. Citizens Council of U. Wis. Ctr. Served with USNR, 1944-46, PTO. Fellow ACS (bd. govs.); mem. Wis. Med. Soc., Fond du Lac County Med. Soc., AMA, U. Wis. Alumni Assn. (past pres., Disting. Service award 1976), Wis. Surg. Soc. (past pres.). Lutheran. Lodge: Fond du Lac Rotary (past pres., Paul Harris fellow). Home: 1022 Mary Hill Park Fond du Lac WI 54935 Office: Assoc Physicians 505 E Division St Fond du Lac WI 54935

BECKER, RALPH LEONARD, psychologist; b. Cin., July 15, 1927; s. Morris and Sarah Ruth B.; m. Evelyn Zeifman, Aug. 15, 1976. BA in Sci., Ohio State U., 1958, BS in Edn., 1960, MA in Psychology, 1961, PhD in Psychology, 1979. Lic. psychologist, Ohio; cert. counselor, Ohio. Spl. tchr. Columbus (Ohio) City Schs., 1962-64; staff psychologist Ohio Dept. Mental Retardation/Devel. Disabilities, Columbus, 1964-68, research scientist, 1968-72, research assoc., 1972-82; research dir. Elbern Pubs., Columbus, 1982—. Author: Reading-Free Vocational Interest Inventory, 1981; Occupational Title List, 1984; also articles. Grantee State of Ohio, 1966, 67, U.S. Office of Edn., 1968. Fellow Am. Assn. on Mental Deficiency; mem. Council for Exciptional Children, Ohio Psychol. Assn., Ohio State Alumni Assn. Avocations: carpentry, elec. wiring, gardening, woodcraft. Office: Elbern Publications PO Box 09497 Columbus OH 43209

BECKER, RICHARD HARMAN, wholesale hardware executive; b. Evansville, Ind., July 26, 1940; s. Richard Fenneman and Daisy Elizabeth (Harman) B.; m. Sally Ann Newhouse, Aug. 4, 1974 (div.); children: Ann Sweeny, John Harman. BES in Indls. Engring., Johns Hopkins U., 1962. With Ohio Valley Hardware Co., Inc., Evansville, 1965-77, pres., 1977—, also bd. dirs.; chmn. bd. Davidson-Amos, Inc., Evansville, 1979-86; bd. dirs. Complete Lumber Ky., Inc. Dir. Evansville Assn. for the Blind, 1974—; mem. exec. com. Buffalo Trail Council, Boy Scouts Am., 1978—. Served to capt. AUS, 1963-64. Mem. Soc. Am. Mil. Engrs., Evansville C. of C. Mem. Christian Ch. (Disciples of Christ). Club: Evansville Country. Lodge: Rotary. Home: 10920 Browning Rd Evansville IN 47711 Office: Ohio Valley Hardware Co Inc PO Box 747 Evansville IN 47705

BECKER, ROBERT JEROME, allergist, health care consultant; b. Milw., May 29, 1922; s. Jacob and Sarah (Saxe) B.; m. June Granof, June 25, 1950; children: Scott M., Jill Becker Wilson, Jon G. BS, U. Wis., Milw., 1943; MD, Med. Coll. Wis., 1949. Intern Michael Reese Hosp., Chgo., 1949-50; resident in internal medicine VA Hosp., Wood, Wis., 1950-53; resident in allergy Roosevelt Hosp., N.Y.C., 1955-56; practice medicine specializing in allergy Joliet, Ill., 1956-82; founder, chmn. HealthCare COMPARE, cons. health care cost mgmt., 1982—; med. dir. Quad River Found. Med. Care, 1976-84; pres. Am. Assn. Profl. Standards Rev. Orgns., 1980-82; exec. v.p. Joint Council Allergy and Immunology., 1978-86; mem. adv. council Nat. Inst. Environ. Health Scis. Author articles in field. Pres. bd. edn. Joliet Twp. High Sch. Dist. 204, 1969-70, 75-76. Recipient Clemens von Pirquet award George U. Internat. Interdisciplinary Center Immunology, 1978. Fellow ACP, Am. Acad. Allergy, Am. Coll. Allergists (pres. 1987), Am. Coll. Chest Physicians; mem. Ill. Soc. Internal Medicine (pres. 1984-86), Asthma and Allergy Assn. Am. (bd. dirs. 1987—), Alpha Omega Alpha, Alpha Sigma Nu. Office: 730 Springer Dr Lombard IL 60148

BECKER, STEPHEN PHILIP, oncologist; b. Aurora, Ill., Jan. 9, 1943. BS, U. Ill., Chgo., 1968, MD, 1968. Diplomate Am. Bd. Otolaryngology. Intern Cook County Hosp., Chgo., 1968; resident Norhtwestern U., Chgo., 1974; fellow Northwestern U. McGaw Med. Ctr., Chgo., 1975; attending staff Northwestern Meml. Hosp., Chgo., 1975—, Childrens Mel. Hosp., Chgo., 1975—, Skokie (Ill.) Valley Hosp., 1976—, Holy Family Hosp., Des Plaines, Ill., 1981—; asst. prof. Northwestern U. Med. Sch., Chgo., 1976—. Author: Carcinoma of the Paranasai Sinuses and Cranial Facial Resection, Head and Neck Cancer, 1976, Tumors of the Major Salivary Glands, Laryngoscope, 1977, Total Larygectomy and Reconstruction of Pseugodlottis, 1978. Fellow ACS; mem. AMA, Am. Acad. Opthamology and Otolaryngology, Ill. State Med. Soc., Chgo. Med. Soc. Office: Otolaryngology Assoc SC 64 Old Orchard Suite 634 Skokie IL 60077

BECKER, TIMOTHY MICHAEL, engineer; b. Cin., July 15, 1955; s. Charles Fredrich and Rosemary Marie (Frisby) B.; m. Mary Elizabeth Norman, May 6, 1978; children: Timothy Michael Jr., Amanda Michel. Student, Miami U., 1973-75; BS MechE, Ohio State U., 1977; MS in Bus. Adminstrn., Ind. U., 1983. Registered profl. engr., Ind. Process engr. Allen Bradley, Lafayette, Ind., 1977-80; prodn. engr. Magnavox, Ft. Wayne, Ind., 1980-82, lead engr., 1982-83, tool engr., 1983-84, staff engr., 1984—. Mem. Magnavox Mgmt. Club. Republican. Roman Catholic. Avocations: chess, woodworking, home repair. Home: 925 Wolverton Dr Fort Wayne IN 46825 Office: Magnavox 1313 Production Way Fort Wayne IN 46808

BECKER, TIMOTHY TODD, lawyer; b. Cresco, Iowa, Oct. 19, 1953; s. Herbert Barton and Elizabeth Jane (Liewer) B.; m. Mary Jane Koehn, June 1, 1975; children—Lisa Ann, Justin Todd. B.A. with high distinction, U. Iowa, 1976, J.D. with honors, 1980. Bar: Iowa 1980, U.S. Dist. Ct. (no. and so. dists.) Iowa 1980, U.S. Ct. Appeals (8th cir.) 1980, U.S. Dist. Ct. (cen. dist.) Ill. 1984; diplomate Ct. Practice Inst. Mem. Tom Riley Law Firm, P.C., Cedar Rapids, Iowa, 1980—. Fellow Iowa Acad. Trial Lawyers; mem. Iowa State Bar Assn., Assn. Trial Lawyers Am., Linn County Bar Assn., Phi Beta Kappa. Lutheran. Home: 430 Fairway Terr SE Cedar Rapids IA 52403 Office: Tom Riley Law Firm PC 4040 First Ave NE Cedar Rapids IA 52402

BECKER, WILLIAM DENNIS, health administrator; b. St. Louis County, Mo., Oct. 23, 1931; s. Robert James and Virginia Hazel (Windmoeller) B.; B.S., U. Mo., 1953; postgrad. So. Ill. U., Edwardsville, 1974—; m. Mary Ann Hanson, Sept. 27, 1952; children—Katherine Ann, William David. Mdse. mgr., asst. mgr. sales Brown Shoe Co., St. Louis, 1953-68; adminstrv. mgr. contract service A.S. Aloe Co., St. Louis, 1968-69; adminstrv. officer health planning Alliance for Regional Community Health, Inc., St. Louis, 1969-73, dep. dir., 1973-76; exec. dir. Mo. Area V Health Systems Agency, Poplar Bluff, 1976-82; exec. dir. Community Health Ctr., Hillsboro, Mo., 1982-84; adminstr. Olsten Health Care, Clayton, Mo., 1985 ; pres., chief exec. officer Sr. Services Unltd., 1986— ; pres. B&D Gun Shop, Inc., owner

The Shoe Box. Pres. Clayton (Mo.) Brownbilt Credit Union, 1964-68; bd. dirs. greater St. Louis Family Planning Council; active YMCA. Served as officer USAF, 1953-55; Korea. Mem. Am. Health Planning Assn., Mo. Public Health Assn. Mem. United Ch. Christ. Lion. Home: 36 Lake Wood Dr Hillsboro MO 63050 Office: 7930 Clayton Rd Clayton MO 63117

BECKER, WILLIAM DOUGLAS, marketing executive; b. Chgo., Oct. 29, 1947; s. William Louis and Helen H. (Stevenson) B.; m. Susan Lynn Heinz, Oct. 15, 1977. Student, Lincoln Coll., 1965-67; BS, Bowling Green State U., 1970; postgrad., John Marshall Law Sch., 1971-72. Regional mgr. Hazeltine Corp., Oak Brook, Ill., 1970-72; v.p. mktg. DJC Corp., Chgo., 1972-79; account exec. Bus. Incentives, Mpls., 1979-84; pres., founder W.D. Becker Assocs. Ltd., Chgo., 1984—; cons. mktg. Odyssey, Inc., Chgo., 1986—; keynote speaker SITE U., Miami, Fla., 1985; mem. faculty SITE U., San Diego, 1986; bd. dirs. Benchmark Communications Corp., Chgo., 1979—. Author: Incentive Marketing...How it Really Works, 1985; contbr. articles to profl. jours.; inventor infra red audio communications. Chmn. bd. dirs. 4200 Marine Dr. Condominium Assn., Chgo., 1979-81; sponser/educator Lincoln Park Zool. Soc., Chgo., 1978-86; sponsor The Neediest Children Fund, Chgo., 1980-86. Served to capt. U.S. Army, 1967-72. Mem. Soc. Incentive Travel Execs. (educator 1984—), Mktg. Communication Execs. Internat., Meeting Planners Internat., Sales and Mktg. Execs. (chmn. edn. com. 1978-85), Nat. Premium Execs. Inc. Clubs: East Bank, Chgo. Walkers (pres. 1985) (Chgo.). Avocations: racewalking, tennis, golfing, reading. Home: 4200 Marine Dr Chicago IL 60613 Office: WD Becker Assocs Ltd 414 N Orleans Plaza Chicago IL 60610

BECKER, WILLIAM HENRY, judge; b. Brookhaven, Miss., Aug. 26, 1909; s. William Henry and Verna (Lilly) B.; m. Geneva Moreton, June 9, 1932; children—Frances Becker Mills, Patricia Becker Hawkins, Nancy Becker Hewes, Geneva Becker Jacks, William Henry III. Student, La. State U., 1927-28; LL.B., U. Mo., 1932. Bar: Miss. 1930, Mo. 1932, U.S. Supreme Ct. 1937. Assoc. firm Clark & Becker, Columbia, Mo., 1932-36; mem. firm Clark & Becker, 1936-44, 46-61; judge U.S. Dist. Ct. Western Dist. Mo., 1961—, chief judge, 1965-77, sr. judge, 1977—; judge U.S. Temp. Emergency Ct. Appeals, 1977—; spl. master Supreme Ct. of U.S., 1979-83; counsel to Gov. Lloyd Stark; counsel to Gov. Lloyd Stark in Kansas City Criminal Investigation, 1938-39; spl. asst. to dir. econ. stblzn. Office of War Mobilization and Reconversion, Washington, 1945-46; spl. commr. Mo. Supreme Ct., 1954-58; spl. counsel Mo. Ins. Dept., 1936-44; chmn. Mo. Supreme Ct. Com. to Draft Rules of Civil Procedure for Mo., 1952-59, mem. coordinating com. for multiple litigation, 1962-68, vice chmn., 1967-68; chmn. subcom. drafting Jury Selection and Service Act, 1968; mem. jud. panel on multidist. litigation Jud. Conf. U.S., 1968-77, mem. com. on operation of jury system, 1966-68; faculty Fed. Jud. Center seminars and workshops for U.S. Dist. judges, 1968—; chmn. subcom. drafting Jury Selection and Service Act of 1968. Bd. editors Manual for Complex Litigation, 1968—; chmn., 1977-81. Served with USN, 1944-45, PTO; with Res. 1944-52. Decorated Phillipines Liberation Ribbon with Bronze Star. Fellow Am. Bar Found., Am. Coll. Trial Lawyers, Am. Coll. Probate Counsel; mem. ABA, Am. Judicature Soc., Fed. Bar Assn. (award 1977), Mo. Bar Assn., Kansas City Bar Assn. (spl. award 1977), Lawyers Assn. Kansas City (Charles Evans Whittaker award 1977). Office: US Courthouse 811 Grand Ave Kansas City MO 64106

BECKER, WILLIAM KOHL, engr.; b. St. Louis, June 13, 1927; s. William C. and Bessie (Kohl) B.; m. Lois Matthews, Feb. 4, 1951; 1 dau., Joan. B.S., Washington U., 1949; M.S., U. Ill., 1951. Registered profl. engr., Iowa, Mo., Minn., Nebr., Ohio, Pa., Tex., and others. Structural engr. Convair Aircraft Inc., Ft. Worth, 1953-55, William C. E. Becker, St. Louis, 1955-70; pres. Becker, Becker and Pannell, Inc., St. Louis, 1970—. Bd. govs. Washington U., 1975—, chmn. alumni annual giving fund Sch. of Engring. and Applied Sci., 1975—. Mem. ASCE, Am. Concrete Inst., Nat., Mo. socs. profl. engrs., Am. Consulting Engrs. Council, Mo. Athletic Club, Rotary, William Greenleaf Eliot Soc., Theta Xi, Sigma Xi. Office: 411 N 7th St Saint Louis MO 63101

BECKETT, GRACE, economics educator emerita; b. Smithfield, Ohio, Oct. 7, 1912; d. Roy Martin and Mary (Hammond) Beckett. AB, Oberlin Coll., 1934, AM, 1935; PhD, Ohio State U., 1939. Music supr. Pub. Schs., Kelleys Island, Ohio, 1935-36; grad asst. econs. Ohio State U., 1936-39; assoc. prof. econs. and music Ind. Central Coll., 1939-41: with U. Ill., Champaign-Urbana, 1941—, asst. prof. econs., 1945-51, assoc. prof. econs., 1951-73, assoc. prof. emerita Coll. Commerce and Bus. Adminstrn., 1973—. Author: Reciprocal Trade Agreements Program, 1941, 72; contbr. profl. pubs. Mem. Am. Econ. Assn., Music Educators Nat. Conf., Ill. Music Educators Assn., Econ. History Assn., Am. Finance Assn., Am. Hist. Assn., AAAS, N.Y. Acad. Scis., Ohio Acad. History, Winchester-Frederick County (Va.) Hist. Soc., Ill. Music Tchrs. Assn., Music Tchrs. Nat Assn., Interlochen Alumni Assn. (life), Friends of Art of the Allen Meml. Art Mus. at Oberlin Coll., Nat. Sch. Orch. Assn., Krannert Art Mus. Assos. (U. Ill.), Ohio State U. Alumni Assn., Nat. Honor Soc., Mary Ball Washington Mus. and Library, Met. Mus. Art (N.Y.C.) (nat. asso.), Oberlin Coll. Alumni Assn., Alpha Lambda Delta (hon.), Phi Beta Kappa, Pi Lambda Theta, Phi Chi Theta (hon.). Methodist. Club: Women's at the University of Ill., Oberlin Coll. Half-Century. Address: PO Box 386 Urbana IL 61801

BECKETT, ROBERT DUDLEY, language professional, educator; b. Detroit, July 16, 1934; s. Ernest L. and Corine J. (Fehner) B.; m. Muriel M. Freidhoff, Sept. 15, 1956; children: Amy, Julia, Timothy, Daniel, Peter, Jonathan, Laura, Gregory. BA, U. Mich., 1957, MA, 1961; PhD, U. Colo., 1967. Tchr. Walled Lake (Mich.) Pub. Sch., 1957-61; instr. S.W. Mo. State U., Springfield, 1963-67, asst. prof., 1967-70, assoc. prof., 1970-74, prof., 1974—, chmn. faculty senate, 1981-83; mem. exec. sec. Programs and Services State Master Planning, Mo., 1976. Del. Nat. Dem. Conv., Kansas City, 1974; mem. Greene City Dem. Cen. Com., Springfield, 1968-84. Served with U.S. Army, 1953-55. Regents Alumni scholar, U. Mich., 1951; Univ. fellow U. Colo., 1961. Mem. MLA, Am. Assn. Colls. Tchrs. Edu., Nat. Council Tchrs. English, Midwest Modern Lang. Assn., Assn. Can. Studies U.S., Midwest Assn. Can. Studies. Democrat. Roman Catholic. Avocations: racquetball, jogging, political activities. Home: 1310 E Meadowmere Springfield MO 65804 Office: Dept English Southwest Mo State U 901 S National Springfield MO 65804

BECKETT, THEODORE CORNWALL, lawyer; b. Heidelberg, Fed. Republic of Germany, Nov. 21, 1952 (parents Am. Citizens); s. Theodore Charles and Daysie Margaret (Cornwall) B.; m. Patricia Anne McKelvy, June 18, 1983; children: Anna, Kathleen. B.A., U. Mo., 1975, J.D., 1978. Bar: Mo. 1978, U.S. Dist. Ct. (we. dist.) Mo. 1978. Ptnr. Beckett & Steinkamp, Kansas City, Mo., 1978—. Bd. dirs. Kans. Spl. Olympics, 1979-84. Mem. ABA, Mo. Bar Assn., Kansas City Bar Assn., Mo. Assn. Trial Attys., Assn. Trial Lawyers Am., Beta Theta Pi. Democrat. Presbyterian. Clubs: Kansas City, Carriage. Office: Beckett & Steinkamp 600 Commerce Bank Bldg PO Box 13425 Kansas City MO 64199

BECKWITH, ROBERT JOHN, engineer; b. Ashland, Wis., Sept. 24, 1932; s. John Joseph and Marguerite Ester (Tobin) B.; m. Gretta Joyce Beckwith, Apr. 1, 1957; children: Joy, Judy, Robert Jr. Mktg. Butler Bin, Waukesha, Wis., 1962-66; project engr. Alloy Products, Waukesha, 1966-71, Rexnord-Envirex, Waukesha, 1971-86; pres. Great Lakes Water Inc., Waukesha, 1987—. Baseball, softball umpire, southeastern Wis. area, 1958-86; mgr. Little League, Waukesha, 1958-60. Served with USN, 1951-53. Mem. Tech. Assn. of the Pulp and Paper Industry (steam and power com., deaerator com. 1983-86), Nat. Assn. Corrosion Engrs. Republican. Roman Catholic. Avocation: sausage making, baseball. Home: 127 Felix St PO Box 175 Wales WI 53183 Office: Great Lakes Water Inc 1116B Adams St Waukesha WI 53186

BEDELL, BERKLEY WARREN, congressman; b. Spirit Lake, Iowa, Mar. 5, 1921; s. Walter Berkley and Virginia (Price) B.; m. Elinor Healy, Aug. 29, 1943; children: Kenneth, Thomas, Joanne. Student, Iowa State U. Founder, chmn. bd. Berkley and Co. (fishing tackle mfrs.), Spirit Lake, 1921—; mem. 94th-99th congresses from 6th Dist. Iowa. Served with USAAF, 1943-45. Named 1st U.S. Small Businessman of Year SBA, 1964. Democrat. Methodist. Home: Spirit Lake IA 51360

BEDI, ASHOK RAMPRAKASH, psychiatrist; b. Feb. 10, 1948; m. Usha Bedi, July 26, 1972; children: Ami Sian, Siddhartha. BSC, Gujarat U., India, 1966, MD, 1970. Diplomate Royal Coll. Psychiatrists. Intern B.J. Med. Coll. and affiliated Hosps., Gujarat, India, 1970-72; resident Gujarat U., India, 1972; clinical asst. in surgery Ballochmyle Hosp., Scotland; resident in psychiatry No. Wales Psychiat. Hosp., Denbigh, 1972-73; surgeon Maelor Gen. Hosp., No. Wales, Britain; registrar in psychiatry St. Crispin Hosp., Northampton, Eng., 1974-76, sr. registrar, 1976; sr. fellow in community psychiatry Med. Coll. Wis., 1976-77; staff psychiatrist Milw. County Mental Health Cen., 1977-79; catchment area dir. Westside Community Mental Health Cen., Milw., 1979-80; asst. prof. in psychiatry and mental health scis. Med. Coll. Wis., 1977-80, asst. clinical prof., 1980-82; attending psychiatrist Milw. Psychiat. Hosp., 1980—; assoc. clin. prof. Med. Coll. Wis., 1982—; clin. dir. Milw. Psychiat. Hosp., 1984—. Contbr. numerous articles to profl. jours. Mem. Gen. Med. Council, Royal Coll. Psychiatrists, Royal Coll. Physicians and Surgeons, Am. Group Psychotherapy Assn, Am. Psychiat. Assn., Wis. Psychiat. Assn., AMA, Am. Med. Soc. on Alcololism and Other Drug Abuse Dependencies, Inc. Office: Milw Psychiat Hosp 1220 Dewey Ave Wauwatosa WI 53213

BEDNAR, CAROLYN DIANE, dentist; b. Akron, Ohio, Oct. 7, 1953; d. William Adolph and Marilyn Minns (Hadfield) B.; m. Steven Kent Good, Sept. 25, 1982. BA in Chemistry, De Pauw U., 1975; DDS, Ohio State U., 1978. Gen. practice dentistry Columbus, 1978—; mem. staff Southwest Community Health Ctr., Columbus, Ohio, 1979-82. Vol. pub. oral cancer screenings and dental edn., Am. Cancer Soc., Columbus; vol. speaker dentistry Columbus Pub. Schs., 1982-85; vol. fundraiser Multiple Sclerosis Soc., Columbus, 1986-87. Mem. ADA, Ohio Dental Assn., Columbus Dental Assn., Profl. Women's Forum (sec. 1982-84), Ohio State U. Alumni Assn., Alpha Phi. Republican. Avocations: oil painting, macramé, doll collecting, traveling, Czech language. Home: 8862 Easton Dr Pickerington OH 43147 Office: 1600 Brice Rd Reynoldsburg OH 43068

BEDNAR-ERNST, BETH ANN, television news director and anchor person; b. Glencoe, Minn., July 6, 1953; d. Florence M. (Weier) Bednar; m. James J. Ernst, May 29, 1982; children: Britton, Alex. Student, U. Minn., 1974, Brown Inst., Mpls., 1975. Reporter Sta. KAAL-TV, Austin, Minn., 1977-79, producer, 1979-82, exec. producer, 1982-85, news dir., 1985—; instr. journalism Austin Community Coll., 1980-81. Mem. Muscular Dystrophy Assn. Named Young Career Woman of Yr., Bus. and Profl. Women Assn. Minn., 1980. Mem. Radio and TV News Dir.'s Assn., Minn. News Council. Avocations: reading, needle-art travel. Office: Sta KAAL-TV PO Box 577 Austin MN 55912

BEDWELL, TOMMY JOE, mechanical engineer; b. Linton, Ind., June 17, 1939; s. Harry Clifford and Mary Teressa (White) B.; m. Freda Faye Speedy, June 16, 1961; 1 child, Cathy Lynne. BME, Rose Poly. Inst., 1961. Registered profl. engr., Ind. Engr. Ind. Pub. Service Co., summer 1960; test engr. truck div. Internat. Harvester, Ft. Wayne, Ind., 1961-64, rotational trainee, 1964-65, devel. engr. research div., 1965-68, sr. devel. engr., 1968-75; staff engr. piston design and devel. Bohn Aluminum and Brass Co. div. Wickes Mfg. Co. (formerly Gulf and Western Industries, Inc.), South Haven, Mich., 1975—, asst. chief engr. piston design and devel., 1979-80, chief engr. piston design and devel., 1980-82, chief engr. and v.p. research and engring. ctr., engine and foundry div., 1982—. Patentee in field. Mem. ASME, Soc. Automotive Engrs., Am. Soc. for Metals. Republican. Mem. Christian Ch. (Disciples of Christ. Lodge: Masons. Home: 739 Seawatch Rd Holland MI 49424 Office: Wickes Mfg Co Engine and Foundry Div 1310 Kalamazoo St South Haven MI 49090

BEE, KENNETH JAMES, manufacturing company executive; b. Big Spring, Tex., Sept. 12, 1943; s. William Richard and Pauline Florence (Wileman) B.; m. Carolyn Louise Faucett, Mar. 20, 1970; children: Carl James, Adam Kenneth. BBA, Youngstown U., 1966; MPM, Ind. No. U., 1979; Exec. Devel. degree, Ohio State U., 1983. Product mgr. Diebold, Inc., Canton, Ohio, 1969-81; dir. mktg. Diebold, Inc., Canton, 1979-81; mgr. mktg. and sales Stark Ceramics, Canton, 1981-85, dir. mktg. and sales, 1985—. Rep. precinct capt., Canton, 1982-86. Served to capt. U.S. Army, 1966-69, Vietnam, Res. 1969—. Decorated disting. flying cross, bronze star. Methodist. Avocations: flying, camping, boating, sailing. Home: 566 N Orchard Bolivar OH 44612 Office: Stark Ceramics PO Box 8880 Canton OH 44711

BEECHER, REXINE ELLEN, civic worker; b. Eldora, Iowa, Aug. 16, 1915; d. Vernon Richard and Gladys Metha (Bateson) Wardman; student U. No. Iowa, 1936-37; B.A., State U. of Iowa, 1939; m. Loyd Giff Beecher, June 15, 1939; 1 dau., Ellen Beth Beecher Feldick. Legal sec. Bateson & Ryan, attys., Eldora, Iowa, 1932, 33-35; asst. bus. mgr. College Eye Newspaper, Cedar Falls, Iowa, 1936-37; sec. econs. dept. Iowa State U., Ames, 1961-62; tchr. English, Union (Iowa) Sch., 1962-63; librarian Union Pub. Library, 1967-69; nat. promoter Children Am. Revolution. Mem. DAR (50 yr., state registrar 1976-78), DAR State Officers Club, Daus. Colonial Wars, Farm Bur., Iowa Lassies (25-yr. mem. honoree 1981). Republican. Author hist. brochures, books and genealogies. Home: PO Box 362 Union IA 50258

BEECHER, W. LOUIS, bank executive. Chmn. Iowa Nat. Bankshares Corp., Waterloo, Iowa. Office: Iowa Nat Bankshares Corp 100 E Park Ave Waterloo IA 50703 *

BEECKMAN, RICHARD LEE, insurance executive, consultant, educator; b. San Francisco, June 29, 1943; s. Albert Oscar and Virginia Lee (Paul) B.; m. Phyllis Ann Chandler, Apr. 19, 1974; children—Megan Elizabeth, Michael Albert, Brian George, Carol Ann, James Paul. Student Wayne State U., 1967-72, U. Mich. 1978-79. Assoc. in Risk Mgmt., Ins. Inst., Malvern, 1976; C.P.C.U., Am. Inst., Malvern, Pa., 1977. With Variable Annuity Life Co., Detroit, 1966-70; mktg., claims, EDP, mgmt. positions State Mut. Ins. Co. and subs. Citizens Ins. Co., various cities, 1970-80; prin., owner, v.p. Blanchet, Weadock & Co., Saginaw, Mich., 1980—; part-time faculty Wayne State U./U. Mich., 1978-81, Delta Coll., Saginaw, 1981—, coordinator ins. studies, 1981—; part-time faculty Lawrence Inst., Southfield, Mich., 1984—; seminar instr. Mich. Assn. C.P.A.s, 1979—, Ind. Assn. C.P.A.s, 1984—, Lawrence Inst., 1984, 85; seminar leader Mich. State U. Mgmt. Cons. Program, 1983—. Author: How to Read Financial Statements for the Producer, other seminar instrn. material. Bd. dirs. Saginaw YMCA, 1984—, bus. chmn., 1982-83, gen. chmn., 1984-85. Served with USNR, 1963-65. Mem. Am. Soc. C.P.C.U.s (sec. Northeastern Mich. chpt. 1982-83, v.p., 1983-84, pres. 1984-85, ednl. chmn. 1982—), Mich. Assn. Cons. Avocations: reading; chess; running; triathlon bicycling; karate. Home: 4865 Cactus Dr Saginaw MI 48603 Office: RL Beeckman & Co 1523 Court St PO Box 6205 Saginaw MI 48608

BEECY, ROBERT E., JR., marketing executive; b. Waltham, Mass., Dec. 16, 1950; s. Robert Ernest and Emily Alice (Buckley) B.; m. Mary Margret Goldsmith, Nov. 28, 1975; children: Brenden, Kristen. BS, U. Mass., 1972; MBA, Wright St. U., 1981. Asst. mgr. Macke Co., Springfield, Ohio, 1976-77; inventory supr. Robbins & Myers, Springfield, 1977-79, prod. control supr., 1979-81, materials mgr., 1981-84, mktg. mgr., 1984—; adv. com. Witt Univ. Bus. Sch., Springfield, 1986—. Loaned exec. Springfield United Way, 1979-80; mem. exec. adv. com. Springfield Jr. Achievement, 1982. Mem. Am. Prodn. and Inventory Control Soc. (pres. 1986-87, cert.), Nat. Assn. Purchasing Mgrs. (cert. 1984), Phi Kappa Phi, Beta Gamma Sigma. Lutheran. Lodge: Lions (pres. 1982). Avocations: sports, furniture refinishing. Home: 1827 Fairway Dr Springfield OH 45504 Office: Robbins & Myers Inc 326 S Thompsen St Springfield OH 45506

BEEM, JOHN KELLY, mathematician, educator; b. Detroit, Jan. 24, 1942; s. William Richard and June Ellen (Kelly) B.; m. Eloise Masako Yamamoto, Mar. 24, 1964; 1 child, Thomas Kelly. A.B. in Math., U. So. Calif., 1963, M.A. in Math., 1965, Ph.D. in Math., 1968. Asst. prof. math. U. Mo., Columbia, 1968-71, assoc. prof., 1971-79, prof., 1979—. Co-author: (with P. Y. Woo) Doubly Timelike Surfaces, 1969, (with P. E. Ehrlich) Global Lorentzian Geometry, 1981; condr. research in differential geometry and gen. relativity. NSF fellow, 1965, 68. Mem. Math. Assn. Am., Am. Math. Soc., Phi Beta Kappa. Home: 1906 Garden Dr Columbia MO 65202

BEEMSTER, JOSEPH ROBERT, manufacturing company executive; b. Chgo., Nov. 11, 1941; s. Joseph Z. and Emily (Dehaus) B.; B.A., DePaul U., 1962; postgrad. Ill. Inst. Tech., 1976, 77, U. Minn., 1979, 80; m. Judith L. Scheffers, Sept. 7, 1963; children—David, Susan. Mfg. mgr. Johnson & Johnson, Chgo., 1967-71, mgr. safety and security, 1971-78; corporate dir. safety and health GNB, Inc., St. Paul, 1978—. Author: Safe Work Practices for Workers Exposed to Lead; producer videotapes on health and safety tng. Chmn., Bolingbrook (Ill.) Human Relations Commn., 1971-77. Mem. Am. Soc. Safety Engrs., Am. Indsl. Hygiene Assn. Home: 8280 Kingslee Rd PO Box 64100 Bloomington MN 55438 Office: PO Box 64100 Saint Paul MN 55164

BEER, BARRETT LYNN, historian, educator; b. Goshen, Ind., July 4, 1936; s. Peter J. and Mabel M. Beer; m. Jill Parker, July 31, 1965; children—Peter, Caroline. B.A., DePauw U., 1958; M.A., U. Cin., 1959; Ph.D., Northwestern U., 1965. Instr. history Kent State U., Ohio, 1962-65; assoc. prof. Kent State U., 1968-76, prof., 1976—; asst. prof. U. N.Mex., Albuquerque, 1965-68; asst. dean Coll. Arts and Scis. U. N.Mex., 1966-68; Fulbright prof. U. Tromso, Norway, 1983. Author: Northumberland: The Political Career of John Dudley, Earl of Warwick and Duke of Northumberland, 1973; Rebellion and Riot: Popular Disorder in England during the Reign of Edward VI, 1982; editor: (with S.M. Jack) The Letters of William, Lord Paget of Beaudesert, 1547-1563, 1974. Am. Philos. Soc. grantee, 1966; Am. Council Learned Socs. grantee, 1973. Mem. Am. Hist. Assn., Conf. on Brit. Studies, Ohio Acad. History, Phi Beta Kappa. Episcopalian. Home: 445 Dansel St Kent OH 44240 Office: Kent State U Dept History Kent OH 44242

BEER, RICHARD LAMBERT, law librarian, educator; b. Detroit, Sept. 14, 1930; s. William John and Dora (Lambert) B.; m. Jean O., June 29, 1957; 1 dau., Laurie Ann. B.A., U. Mich., 1957; M.L.S., Wayne State U., 1971. Dir., Adams-Pratt Oakland County Law Library, Pontiac, Mich., 1960—; mem. faculty legal asst. program Oakland U., Rochester, Mich., 1973—; exec. dir. Oakland Law Library Found., Pontiac, 1981—; law library cons., 1968—; mem. budget and fin. com. Mich. Library Consortium, 1984—. Author: Michigan Legal Literature, 1973; Access to American, 1976; (with M.S. Merzon) Legal Research and Writing, 1979. Chmn., Twp. Planning Commn., Lake Orion, Mich., 1964-78; sr. warden St. Mary's Episcopal Ch. vestry, Lake Orion, 1970, lay reader, 1973—; bd. dirs. Pontiac-Oakland Symphony Orch., Pontiac, 1982—. Named Lion of Yr., Lions Club, Lake Orion, Mich., 1962; recipient Meritorious Service award Waterford Orgn. Retarded Children, 1966; Outstanding Service award Oakland County Bar Assn., 1977. Mem. Am. Assn. Law Libraries (treas. 1983-86), Ohio Regional Assn. Law Libraries (pres. 1977-78), Mich. Assn. Law Libraries (exec. bd. 1980-81), Mich. Library Assn. Episcopalian. Office: Oakland County Library Bd Adams-Pratt Law Library Div 1200 N Telegraph Rd Pontiac MI 48053

BEERBOHM, CYNTHIA JENNIFER, advertising executive, actress; b. Detroit, Sept. 6, 1940; d. Marvin and Regina Cynthia (Barfknecht) B; m. James V. Ficco, Aug. 19, 1975 (div. Feb. 1977). BA in Speech and Theater, U. Mich., 1962; postgrad., Yale Sch. Drama, 1963-64. Sr. media buyer Young & Rubicam, 1968-73; media buyer Marschalk Advt., Cleve., 1973-75; account exec. KDKA-TV, Pitts., 1975-76; v.p., assoc. media dir. Griswold, Inc., Cleve., 1976-83; media supr. Campbell-Ewald, Inc., Warren, Mich., 1983-85; sr. media supr. McCann-Erickson, Inc., Troy, Mich., 1985—. vol. Reach-to-Recovery program Am. Cancer Soc., Southfield, Mich., 1985—; mem. St. Dunstan's Guild, Bloomfield Hills, Mich. Mem. Am Fedn. TV/Radio Artists, Actors Equity, Pentwater (Mich.) Hist. Soc. Avocations: theater, traveling, reading, restoring old homes. Office: McCann-Erickson Inc 755 W Big Beaver Rd Troy MI 48084

BEERING, STEVEN CLAUS, university president, medical educator; b. Berlin, Germany, Aug. 20, 1932; came to U.S., 1948, naturalized, 1953; s. Steven and Alice (Friedrichs) B.; m. Catherine Jane Pickering, Dec. 27, 1956; children: Peter, David, John. B.S. summa cum laude, U. Pitts., 1954; M.D., 1958. Intern Walter Reed Gen. Hosp., Washington, 1958-59; resident Wilford Hall Med. Center, San Antonio, Tex., 1959-62; chief internal medicine, edn. coordinator Wilford Hall Med. Center, 1962-69; prof. medicine Ind. U. Sch. Medicine, Indpls., 1969—; asst. dean Ind. U. Sch. Medicine, 1969-70, assoc. dean, dir. postgrad. edn., 1970-74, dir. statewide med. edn. system, from 1970, dean, 1974-83; chief exec. officer Ind. U. Med. Center, 1974-83; pres. Purdue U. and Purdue U. Research Found., West Lafayette, Ind., 1983—; dir. Eli Lilly and Co., Arvin Industries; cons. Indpls. VA Hosp., St. Vincent Hosp., Eli Lilly & Co.; chmn. Ind. Commn. Med. Edn., 1972—, Med. Edn. Bd. Ind., 1974-83, Liaison Com. on Med. Edn., 1976-80. Contbr. articles to sci. jours. Sec. Ind. Atty. Gen.'s Trust., 1974-83. Served to lt. col. M.C. USAF, 1957-69. Fellow A.C.P.; mem. Am. Fedn. Clin. Research, Am. Diabetes Assn., Endocrine Soc., Assn. Am. Med. Colls. (chmn. 1982-83), Council Med. Deans (chmn. 1981-82), AMA (chmn. sect. on med. schs. 1976-78), Nat. Acad. Sci. Inst. of Medicine, Phi Beta Kappa, Sigma Xi, Alpha Omega Alpha, Phi Rho Sigma (U.S. v.p. 1976—). Presbyn. (elder). Clubs: Indpls. Athletic, Columbia, Skyline, Woodstock, Meridian Hills, University. Home: 575 McCormick Rd West Lafayette IN 47906 Office: Purdue Univ Office of Pres West Lafayette IN 47907

BEERMANN, ALLEN JAY, state official; b. Sioux City, Iowa, Jan. 14, 1940; s. Albert and Amanda (Schoenrock) B.; m. Linda R. Dierking, May 23, 1971; children: Matthew Allen, John William. B.A., Midland Lutheran Coll., Fremont, Nebr., 1962; J.D., Creighton U., Omaha, 1965. Bar: Nebr. 1965. Legal counsel, adminstrv. asst. to sec. state of Nebr., 1965-67, dep. sec. state, 1967-71; sec. of state 1971—; Bd. dirs. NEBRASKAland Found. Bd. dirs. Immanuel Med. Ctr., Omaha; exec. bd. Cornhusker council Boy Scouts Am. Served to lt. col. USAR. Recipient Distinguished Service plaque Omaha Legal Aid Soc., 1964, Silver Beaver award Boy Scouts Am., 1979; named Outstanding Young Man Lincoln Jaycees, 1975, Outstanding Young Man Nebr. Jaycees, 1975. Mem. Nat. Assn. Secs. State (pres. 1976-77), Am., Nebr. bar assns., Nebr. Press Assn., Am. Legion, Pi Kappa Delta, Phi Alpha Delta. Lutheran. Club: Elks. Address: Office Sec State State Capitol Lincoln NE 68509

BEERUP, ROBERT DALE, accountant, auditor; b. Jacksonville, Ill., Mar. 27, 1949; s. Dale Philip and Mary Wallace (Miller) B.; m. Darla Jean Lovin, Aug. 10, 1968; children: Heather, Mariah, Matthew. BS, So. Ill. U., 1971. CPA. Jr. auditor to audit mgr. Ill. Agrl. Auditing Assn., Mt. Vernon, Jacksonville, Bloomington, Ill., 1971—; lectr., discussion leader Ill. CPA Found., other state CPA socs., 1983—; planning task force mem., speaker for ednl. programs Chgo. Bd. Trade, 1984; lectr. Bookkeeper and Mgr.'s Sch. Grain and Feed Assn. Ill., Springfield, 1986; CPA-in-Residence Western Ill. U., Macomb, 1985. Contbr. articles to profl. pubs. Vol. Spl. Olympics, Bloomington, 1984—; bd. dirs., asst. treas., exec. com. Home Sweet Home Mission, Bloomington, 1987. Mem. Am. Inst. CPA's, Ill. Soc. CPA's (chmn. and/or mem. planning task forces for continuing profl. edn. confs. 1983—, agribus. com. 1983—, chmn. elevator subcom. 1985—), Nat. Soc. Accts. for Coops. (lectr. nat. and regional chpts. 1981—, leader, instr. various acctg., taxation tng. courses 1984). Lodge: Kiwanis. Home: 306 Garden Rd Normal IL 61761 Office: Ill Agrl Auditing Assn 1701 Towanda Ave PO Box 2901 Bloomington IL 61701

BEERY, KENNETH EUGENE, food scientist; b. Lancaster, Ohio, Apr. 30, 1943; s. Robert David and Lucille Ester (Scholl) B.; B.S., Ohio State U., 1965; Ph.D., Pa. State U., 1970; m. Marci Annear, Aug. 22, 1965; children—Kevin, Kendra, Kelli, Kyle. With U.S. Dept. Agr., Berkeley, Calif., 1972-75, Union Carbide Corp., Chgo., 1975-76; dir. research Archer Daniels Midland Co., Decatur, Ill., 1976-84, Central Soya Co., Ft. Wayne, Ind., 1984—. Served with U.S. Army, 1970-72. Recipient Honored Grad. Student award Am. Oil Chemists Soc., 1969. Mem. Inst. Food Technologists (chmn. Iowa sect. 1978-79), AAAS, Am. Meat Sci. Assn., Am. Soc. Animal Sci., Am. Mgmt. Assn., Am. Assn. Cereal Chemists, Research Soc. Am., Sigma Xi, Alpha Gamma Sigma, Gamma Sigma Delta, Alpha Zeta, Phi Tau Sigma. Editorial adv. bd. Food Tech. mag., 1975-78; contbr. articles profl. jours. Office: PO Box 1400 Fort Wayne IN 46801

BEESLEY, BRUCE ALLYN, savings and loan association executive, educator; b. Vincennes, Ind., May 28, 1954; s. Richard V. and Naomi R. (Rehwald) B.; m. Janice L. Stephen, Sept. 26, 1981; 1 child, Christopher S. AB, Ind. U., 1975; student, Grad. Sch. Savs. and Loan; grad., U. Ga.

Sch. Exec. Devel., 1983. Sr. v.p. Home Bldg. Savs. and Loan, Washington, Ind., 1975—; instr. Vincennes U., 1985—. Mem. Inst. Fin. Edn. (degree 1980). Lodge: Rotary (pres. Washington, Ind. club 1986). Avocations: reading, automobiles, traveling. Home: 18 Lynwood Dr Washington IN 47501 Office: 200 E Van Trees St PO Box 518 Washington IN 47501

BEESON, WILLIAM HAROLD, facial plastic surgeon; b. Knox, Ind., May 21, 1951. BA, Ind. U., 1973, MD, 1976. Diplomate Am. Bd. Otolaryngology. Intern Meth. Hosp., Indpls., 1976-77, surgery resident, 1977-78; otolaryngology resident Ind. U. Med. Ctr., Indpls., 1978-81; practice medicine specializing in facial plastic and reconstructive surgery Indpls., 1982—; vis. clin. prof. surgery div. otorhinolaryngology U. Ala. Sch. Medicine, Birmingham, 1981—, clin. assoc. prof. dept. otolaryngology Ind. U. Sch. Medicine, 1982—; accreditation surveyor Accreditation Assn. for Ambulatory Health Care, Inc.; med. adv. bd. Pan Am. Games XIII; bd. dirs. Head and Neck Cancer Rehab. Inst. Author: (book) Aesthetic Surgery of the Aging Face, 1986; editor (book) Developing a Practice in Facial Plastic Surgery, 1986; contbr. articles to profl. jours. Adv. bd. State Ind. on Juvenile Justice and Delinquency Prevention, 1976-80. Fellow ACS, Am. Acad. Facial Plastic and Reconstructive Surgery (chmn. pub. info. forum 1986—, various coms.), Am. Acad. Cosmetic Surgeons, Am. Acad. Otolaryngology and Head and Neck Surgery, Inc.; mem. AMA, Marion County Med. Soc. (bd. dirs., pres. 1987, membership service com.), Ind. State Med. Assn. (trustee 1984—, sports medicine com., med. affairs com.), Soc. Office Based Surgery, Freestanding Ambulatory Surgery Assn., Ind. U. Sch. Medicine Alumni Assn. (past pres., mem. exec. council), Indpls. Entrepreneurship Acad. (bd. dirs.), Ind. C. of C., Indpls. C. of C., Sigma Alpha Epsilon. Methodist. Lodges: Masons, Shriners. Office: Beeson Facial Surgery 8803 N Meridian St Indianapolis IN 46260

BEETS, F. LEE, insurance company executive; b. Paola, Kans., Apr. 2, 1922; s. William Francis and Nellie (Bryan) B.; B.B.A., Tulane U., 1945; postgrad. Harvard U., 1945, evening sch. U. Kansas City, Rockhurst Coll.; m. Dorothy Loraine Shelton, June 20, 1945; children—Randall Lee, Pamela Lee. Sr. accountant Lunsford Barnes & Co., Kansas City, Mo., 1946-49; v.p., gen. mgr. Viking Refrigerators, 1949-53; v.p., sec.-treas. Equipment Finance Co., 1949-53; exec. v.p., treas., gen. mgr. T.H. Mastin & Co., Consol. Underwriters, Mo. Gen. Ins. Co., Plan-O-Pay, Inc., Mid-Am. Data Co., B O L Assos., Inc., 1953-69; founder, chmn. bd., chief exec. officer Fin. Guardian Group, Inc., and subs., 1969-84; chmn. Consolidated Ins. Service, Inc. Served with USNR, 1942-45. C.P.A., Mo. Mem. Am. Inst. C.P.A.'s, Soc. C.P.C.U.'s, Pi Kappa Alpha, Sigma Tau Gamma, Phi Mu Alpha Sinfonia. Home: 16 Le Mans Ct Prairie Village KS 66208

BEHLING, CHARLES FREDERICK, psychology educator; b. St. George, S.C., Sept. 8, 1940; s. John Henry and Floy (Owings) B.; 1 son, John Charles. BA, U. S.C., 1962, MA, 1964; MA, Vanderbilt U., 1966, PhD, 1969. Asst. dean of students U. S.C., Columbia, 1962-63; asst. state news editor The State Newspaper, Columbia, 1963-64; asst. prof. psychology Lake Forest (Ill.) Coll., 1968-74; assoc. prof. Lake Forest Coll., 1974-77, prof., 1977—, chmn. dept., 1977-84; pvt. practice psychotherapy Lake Bluff, Ill., 1970—. Contbr. articles to profl. jours. Bd. dirs. Nat. Abortion Rights Action League; mem. long-range planning com. Lake Bluff Bd. Edn. Named Outstanding Prof., Underground Guide to Colls., Outstanding Tchr., Lake Forest Coll., 1981; NASA fellow. Mem. Am. Psychol. Assn., Soc. Psychol. Study of Social Issues, Assn. Humanistic Psychology, AAUP, Univ. S.C. Alumni Assn., Psi Chi, Sigma Delta Chi. Democrat. Home: 116 E Prospect St Lake Bluff IL 60044 Office: Lake Forest College Dept Psychology Lake Forest IL 60045

BEHLING, JAMES EUGENE, restaurant owner; b. New Philadelphia, Ohio, June 19, 1932; s. Herman E. and Mildred (Rodd) B.; m. Barbara Brickley; children: John Thomas, David Matthew, Karen Theresa, James Christopher. BS in Bus. Adminstrn., Kent State U., 1960. Group controller Glidden Co., Cleve., 1966-74; dir. adminstrn. SCM, Cleve., 1974-78; pres., chief exec. officer Dolphin Seafoods Inc., Parma, Ohio, 1978-80; pvt. practice bus. analysis Twinsburg, Ohio, 1980-82; owner, operator Christopher's Restaurant, Northfield, Ohio, 1982—. Author: Automation Implication on Education; participant (film) Guide to ParentsOf Drug Users. Fin. advisor Twinsburg Bd. Edn.; troop chmn. Boy Scouts Am., Twinsburg; chmn. Meth. Ch., Twinsburg; sect. leader United Fund, Cleve. Served with USN, 1952-56. Mem. Nordonia Hills (Ohio) C. of C. Home: 9677 Darrow Rd Twinsburg OH 44087 Office: Christopher's 9750 Olde Eight Rd Sagamore Hills OH 44067

BEHNKE, BRUCE IVAN, manufacturing company executive; b. Grand Rapids, Mich., Dec. 6, 1944; s. Walter Dale and Marjorie Elizabeth (Fonger) B; m. Linda Diane Powell, Oct. 12, 1974; children: Derek, Ethan. BA, U. Mich., 1967; MBA, Mich. State U. Mktg. mgr. Multi Elmac, Novi, Mich., 1976-79, pres., gen. mgr., 1982-83; v.p. mktg. Stanley Magic Door, Farmington, Conn., 1979-82; pres., gen. mgr. Stanley Door Systems div. The Stanley Works, Troy, Mich., 1983—. Served to 1st lt. USMC, 1967-71, Vietnam. Republican. Lutheran. Avocations: golf, stock market. Home: 12030 Glenview Dr Plymouth MI 48170 Office: Stanley Door Systems 1225 E Maple Rd Troy MI 48084

BEHNKE, WILLIAM DAVID, biochemistry educator; b. Pasadena, Calif., Jan. 15, 1941; s. William and Elizabeth (Williamson) B.; m. Carolyn Goodwin, Aug. 25, 1962. A.B., U. Calif.-Berkeley, 1963; Ph.D., U. Wash., 1968. Postdoctoral, fellow Harvard Med. Sch., Boston, Mass., 1968-71, research assoc., 1971-72; asst. prof. chemistry U. S.C., 1972-74; asst. prof. biol. chemistry U. Cin., 1974-79, assoc. prof., 1979—, dir. biophysics lab., 1974—. NIH grantee, 1979—; recipient award Phi Beta Kappa, 1963. Mem. Am. Soc. Biol. Chemists, Biophys. Soc., N.Y. Acad. Sci. Democrat. Episcopalian. Club: Literary. Contbr. articles to profl. jours. Home: 2821 Digby Ave Cincinnati OH 45220 Office: 231 Bethesda Ave Room 3259 Cincinnati OH 45267

BEHREND, FRANK LUDWIG, obstetrician-gynecologist; b. Berlin, Germany, July 1, 1938; came to U.S., 1947; m. Carole Triska; children: Robbie, Nichole. BA, Augustana Coll., 1961; MD, U. Ill., 1965. Diplomate Am. Bd. Ob-Gyn. Intern Cook County Hosp., Chgo., 1965-67, resident, 1967-70; practice medicine specilizing in ob-gyn. Valparaiso, Ind., 1970—. Mem. ACS, AMA, Am. Fertility Soc., Am. Soc. for Colposcopy and Cervical Pathology, Am. Assn. Gynecologic Laparoscopists, Am. Coll. Ob-Gyn., Calif. Med. Assn., Ind. Med. Assn. Porter County Med. Soc. Home: 2208 Wynnewood Valparaiso IN 46383 Office: Obstetrical & Gynecological Assocs Inc 1101 E Glendale Blvd Valparaiso IN 46383

BEHREND, JACK, film producer, director; b. Evanston, Ill., Apr. 2, 1929; s. Bill and Jean Good (Polson) B.; m. Dorothy Jane Lutter, Mar. 12, 1952 (div. Sept. 1980); children: Susan, Thomas, June, Carol, William, Joan; m. May Pietz Ball, Sept. 29, 1984. BSMechE, Ill. Inst. Tech., 1951. Pres. Behrend's, Inc., Chgo., 1951—; sales mgr. BHP, Inc., Chgo., 1983-86; bd. dirs. Chgo. Filmmakers, 1982—. Contbg. editor Tech. Photography Mag., N.Y.C., 1981—; author column for Video/Film Scene, 1981-86; producer/dir. over 100 indsl. and adventure films, 1972—; contbr. articles to SMPTE Jour., 1958—. Served with U.S. Army, 1951-53. Fellow Soc. Motion Picture and TV Engrs. (past chmn.); mem. Dirs. Guild Am. (Chgo. coordinating com. 1984—), Chgo. Film Council (bd. dirs., program chmn. 1985—). Club: Columbia Yacht (Chgo.). Avocations: cruising, chess, astronomy, making telescopes. Home: 5555 Sheridan Rd Chicago IL 60640 Office: Behrend's Inc 219 N Carpenter Chicago IL 60607

BEHRENDT, DAVID FROGNER, journalist; b. Stevens Point, Wis., May 25, 1935; s. Allen Charles and Vivian (Frogner) B.; m. Mary Ann Weber, Feb. 4, 1961; children: Lynne, Liza, Sarah. BS, U. Wis., 1957, MS, 1960. Reporter Decatur (Ill.) Review, 1957-58; reporter Milw. Jour., 1960-70, copy editor, 1970-71, editorial writer, 1971-84, editorial page editor, 1984—. Home: 1928 Hillside Ct Delafield WI 53018 Office: PO Box 661 Milwaukee WI 53201

BEHRENS, JAN, insurance executive; b. Arlington Heights, Ill.; s. Carl M. and Selma (Heiman) B.; m. Ellen Catherwood, May 28, 1965 (div. Apr. 1973); m. Barbara J. Stendal, Sep. 28, 1978; children: Tammy, John, Trevor, Jan, Kim, Julie. V.p., treas. Homfinders Realtors, Arlington Heights, Ill., 1960-70; pres. Behrens Ins. Agy, Arlington Heights, Ill., 1965-86; v.p., sec. ERA, Behrens & Zion, Palatine, Ill., 1970-80; sec. M.A.P. Multiple Listing Service, Palatine, 1975. Deacon Willow Creek Community Ch., South Barrington, Ill, 1976-86. Mem. Chgo. Bd. Ind. Ins. Agts. Lodge: Rotary (Arlington Heights). Avocations: sailing, tennis. Home: 303 Tall Trees Ln Palatine IL 60067 Office: CFM Behrens Insurance Agency 300 E Northwest Hwy Arlington Heights IL 60004

BEHRENS, KENNETH CHARLES, wholesale importing and distributing company executive; b. St. Louis, Mar. 19, 1942; s. Miller Louis and Theresa Mary Behrens; m. Patricia Ann Edkstrnad, 1965; children: Cheryl Ann, Brian Charles. BS, S.E. Mo. State U., 1967. CPA, Mo. Acct. Coopers & Lybrand, St. Louis, 1967-70, Alexander Grant & Co., 1975; chief fin. officer Tacony Corp., 1975—, sr. v.p. fin., 1976-86, sr. v.p. fin. and adminstrn., 1986—. Trustee Employees Pension Plan and Employees Profit Sharing Plan, 1975—; corp. bd. dirs., 1984—. Served with U.S. Army, 1961. Recipient Most Outstanding Performance award Alexander Grant & Co., 1974, Service award Tacony Corp., 1985. Mem. Nat. Assn. Accts., Am. Inst. CPA's, Mo. Soc. CPA's, Sigma Chi. Home: 9569 Banyon Tree Ct Saint Louis MO 63126 Office: Tacony Corp 1760 Ginsinn Ln Fenton MO 63116

BEHRINGER, SAMUEL JOSEPH, JR., lawyer; b. Detroit, Oct. 6, 1948; s. Samuel Joseph and Evania Theresa (Cherry) B.; m. Linda Suzanne Gross, Sept. 7, 1979; 1 child, Kathryn Elizabeth. B.S. in Labor and Indsl. Relations, Mich. State U., 1970; J.D., U. Detroit, 1973. Bar: Mich. 1974, U.S. Dist. Ct. (eastern dist.) Mich. 1974, U.S. Ct. Claims 1975, U.S. Tax Ct. 1975, U.S. Ct. Appeals (6th circuit) 1974, U.S. Supreme Ct. 1980. Asst. U.S. atty. Ea. Dist. Mich., Detroit, 1974-80; group v.p., gen. counsel Mich. Nat. Bank Detroit, 1980-83; sole practice, Birmingham, 1983—; chmn. young lawyers sect. 6th cir. admission ceremony State Bar Mich., 1975-83. Recipient Merit commendations U.S. Dept. Justice, 1977, 78; Spl. Commendation Outstanding Service U.S. Atty. Gen., 1979. Mem. ABA, Fed. Bar Assn. (chmn. chpt. host com. of nat. conv. Detroit, 1985, mem. exec. bd. Detroit chpt. 1979-81), Detroit Bar Assn., Comml. Law League Am., Am. Corp. Counsel Assn., Assn. Trial Lawyers Am., Nat. Rifle Assn., Phi Kappa Tau, Gamma Eta Gamma. Contbr. legal articles to profl. publs. Home: 333 McKinley Ave Grosse Pointe Farms MI 48236 Office: Simpson & Moran 5th Floor North 555 S Woodward Birmingham MI 48011

BEHRINGER, SCOTT MARTIN, dentist; b. Two Rivers, Wis., July 10, 1952; s. Robert John and Joan Rene (Greenwood) B.; m. Julie Rae Lewin, Mar. 27, 1982. DDS, Marquette U., 1977. Gen. practice dentistry Mishicot (Wis.) Clinic, 1977—. Mem. ADA, Am. Endodontic Assn. Republican. Lutheran. Club: Branch River Country (Manitowoc, Wis. golf chmn.). Avocations: photography, tennis, golf. Home: 1667 Skyline Dr Manitowoc WI 54220 Office: Mishicot Clinic 511 E Main St Mishicot WI 54228

BEHRMAN, HARRY MICHAEL, academic administrator; b. N.Y.C., Mar. 17, 1954; s. George Nathaniel Behrman and Susan (Gelman) Cohen; m. Barbara Marge Gassner, June 4, 1977 (div. 1987); 1 child, Michael Abraham Gassner Behrman. BS, U. Wis., 1976, MS, 1980. cert. secondary tchr. Educator Mass. Dept. Pub. Health, Amherst, 1977-78; human relations program coordinator Sch. Edn. U. Wis., Madison, 1981-84; lectr. ednl. policy U. Wis., Madison, 1983-84, 87; asst. dean residential life Dartmouth Coll., Hanover, N.H., 1984-85; program dir. Wis. Union, Madison, 1985—. Contbr. articles on tutoring and conflict resolution to profl. jours. Bd. dirs. Bernie's Place Day Care Ctr., Madison, 1985—; mem. Ctr. for Conflict Resolution, Madison, 1981-84. Mem. Wis. Coll. Personnel Assn., Vol. Adminstrs. Dane County (bd. dirs. 1986—). Jewish. Avocations: film, music, baseball, baseball cards, African studies. Home: 612 S Mills St Madison WI 53715 Office: Wis Union 303 Union S 227 N Randall Ave Madison WI 53715

BEIDEMAN, RONALD PAUL, chiropractor, college dean; b. Norristown, Pa., Mar. 22, 1926; s. Jonas Paul and Bertha May (Cane) B.; student Temple U., 1948; D. Chiropractic, Nat. Coll. Chiropractic, Chgo., 1952; postgrad. Wheaton Coll.; B.A., Lewis U., 1976; m. Lorraine Marian Barrett, Aug. 19, 1950 (dec.); children—Ronald Paul, J. Kirk; m. 2d, Peggy Ann Bartlett, May 31, 1980. Dir. dept. diagnosis Nat. Coll. Chiropractic, Chgo., 1952-66, registrar, 1966-78, dean admissions and records, 1973—, ofcl. coll. historian, 1987—; exam. physician Chgo. Gen. Health Service, 1954-65; lectr. in field; pvt. practice chiropractic Chgo., 1954—; mem. nat. profl. standards rev. council, Health Care Financing Adminstrn., HHS, 1982; prof. Nat.-Lincoln Sch. Postgrad. Edn., 1964—; accrediting evaluator Council on Chiropractic Edn., 1978—, mem. task force panels on admissions Commn. on Accreditation, 1980, 84-86; accrediting evaluator Western Assn. Schs. and Colls., 1985. Served with USAAF, 1944-46. Fellow Internat. Coll. Chiropractors (faculty); mem. Nat. Coll. Chiropractic (corp. sec. 1972—), Nat. Bd. Chiropractic Examiners (chmn. test com. 1967-69), Ill., Chgo. chiropractic socs., Am. Chiropractic Assn. (vet. affairs com. 1979-81), Am. Legion (post comdr. 1957-58), Am., Ill. assns. Collegiate Registrars and Admissions Officers, Ill. Assn. Student Financial Aid Adminstrs., Nat. Assn. Coll. Admissions Counselors, Sigma Phi Kappa, Lambda Phi Delta. Contbr. articles to profl. publs. Office: 200 E Roosevelt Rd Lombard IL 60148

BEIERLE, PHILIP JOHN, diversified company executive, systems analyst; b. Milw., Oct. 23, 1947; s. Clarence Berthold and Ethel Mae (Madison) B.; m. Linda Julia Hausenflock, Sept. 15, 1978; 1 child, Philip John. BA, Wis. State U., Milw., 1969; PhD, U. Wis., 1975. Chmn. service mdse. Payless Stores, Kansas City, Mo., 1976-78; v.p. Nat. Systems, Inc., Kansas City, 1977—; pres., chief exec. officer Magic Systems, Inc., Kansas City, 1979—. Author: A Dictionary of Sales, 1978, The Application of Social Psychology, 1980. Research planner Mo. Planning Commn., Kansas City, 1977. Recipient Disting. Community Service award, Kansas City, 1980, cert. appreciation, Liberty Assn., 1980; named to Sales Hall of Fame Nat. Housewares, Inc., 1981. Mem. Nat Housewares Assn. (Master Diamond award 1970), Internat. Brotherhood Magicians. Lutheran. Club: Houdini (Milw.). Avocations: golf, magic.

BEIERSDORF, GERALD LEE, bank holding company executive; b. Sheboygan, Wis., Sept. 18, 1942; S. Francis Elroy and Arlene Clara (Rieck) B.; m. Patricia Elaine Clarke, Nov. 23, 1963; children: Joey David, Jay Lee. BBA in Acctg., U. Wis., Milw., 1973. Dir. labor relations LCL Transit Co., Green Bay, Wis., 1973-76; treas. Citizens Bancorporation, Sheboygan, 1976-77; gen. mgr. Alpha Distbrs., Madison, Wis., 1977-79; asst. treas. Kohler (Wis.) Co., 1979-82; exec. v.p. First Interstate Corp. Wis., Sheboygan, 1982—; pres. First Interstate Mgmt. Services Corp., 1982—; bd. dirs. First Interstate Bank Milw.; pres. Wis. Automated Clearing House; assoc. adj. prof. Lakeland Coll., Sheboygan, 1980-82. Author: A CPA Exam Review: Auditing, 1975. Served with USMC, 1959-63. Mem. Fin. Execs. Inst. (bd. dirs. Milw. chpt. 1986—). Republican. Lutheran. Avocation: running. Home: 519 Church St Kohler WI 53044 Office: First Interstate Corp Wis 636 Wisconsin Ave Sheboygan WI 53044

BEIGL, WILLIAM, naturopath, hypnotist, consultant; b. Chgo., July 9, 1950; s. William C. Beigl and Mary Tomlinson; m. Mavis Johnson, Aug. 5, 1977. BA in Elem. Edn., U. S. Fla., 1971; D of Natural Medicine, Acad. Sci. of Man, Sussex, Eng., 1979. Pvt. practice hypnotherapy Chgo., 1977—, pvt. practice naturopathic medicine, 1979—; mem. research team Donsbach U., 1980; chief researcher disease prevention B.P.H. Corp.; bd. dirs. Mid-West Hypnosis Conv., 1983; cons. in field. Editor, pub. Portage Park News, 1980; originator of the Paramedic System, 1968 (honored by Pres. Johnson 1968, Pres. Nixon, 1969); contbr. articles on natural healing and hypnosis to newspapers and mags.; patentee in field. Assoc. bd. mgrs. Robert R. McCormick chpt. Chgo. Boy's Club, 1975. Served to capt. U.S. Army, Vietnam. Recipient award Congressman Sidney Yates, 1971, Disease Prevention award Beter Positive Health Found., 1979; named Chicagoan of Yr., Mayor Richard J. Daley, 1968, Chgo. Cath. of Yr., Cardinal John Cody, 1968, Illinoisan of Yr., Gov. Richard B. Ogilvie, 1968, one of Ten Outstanding Young Citizens, Chgo. Jaycees, 1980, Citizen of Week, Sta. WBBM, 1984; nominee for Nobel Prize, 1984. Mem. Internat. Naturopathic Assn. (cert., named Naturopathic Physician Yr. 1985), Nat. Assn. Naturopathic Physicians (cert.), Assn. Advance Ethical Hypnosis (cert., past v.p., past sec. Ill. chpt., bd. dirs. 1986), Minn. Assn. Naturopathic Physicians (cert.), Hemlock Soc., Chgo. Meml. Assn., Boy's Clubs Am. (life, named Nat. Boy of Yr. 1968). Lodge: Moose. Office: 2521 W Montrose Chicago IL 60618

BEILMAN, MARK EMIL, architect; b. Nebraska City, Nebr., Feb. 23, 1935; s. Ewald A. and Rose (Sand) B.; B.Arch., U. Nebr., 1966; m. Marlene Maria Freeman, May 11, 1957; children—Eric M., Kurt W., Mark E. Draftsman, Walter, Dorwin, Teague & Assos., Denver, 1957-58; estimator M.W. Anderson Constrn. Co., Lincoln, Nebr., 1966-67; draftsman John J. Flad & Assos., Madison, Wis., 1967-68; designer Daverman & Assos., Madison, Wis., 1968-69; asst. project mgr. State of Wis., Madison, 1970-77, roofing specialist, 1977-81; propr. Mark E. Beilman, Architect, Roofing Cons., 1981—. Served with USAF, 1954-57. Mem. Badger Bonsai Soc. Republican. Roman Catholic. Clubs: Waunona Way Assn., Lake Monona Sailing. Inventor Adjus-to-Fit bicycle handlebar adjuster. Home and office: 2702 Waunona Way Madison WI 53713

BEIS, SARA JANE, laboratory executive, pharmacist; b. Akron, Ohio, Aug. 25, 1954; d. George Andrew and Buena Marie (Greer) B. B.S. in Pharmacy, U. Mich., 1977. Registered pharmacist, Ohio. Pharmacy intern Akron Gen. Med. Ctr., 1973-76; staff pharmacist Ohio State U., Columbus, 1977-80; clin. pharmacist VA, Columbus and Columbia, S.C., 1980-82; mgmt. cons. Hosp. Pharmacy, 1982—; sales rep. Smith Kline & French Labs., Phila., 1983-87; pharmacist Barberton (Ohio) Citizens Hosp., 1987—; clin. instr. Coll. Pharmacy, Ohio State U., 1978-81, U. S.C., Columbia, 1981-82. Patentee pill packaging. Vol. Children's Hosp., Columbus, 1983. Recipient dist. achievement award Smith Kline & French Labs., Inc., 1985. Fellow Am. Soc. Cons. Pharmacists; mem. Am. Soc. Hosp. Pharmacists, Akron Area Soc. Hosp. Pharmacists, U. Mich. Alumni Assn. (life), Nat. Assn. Female Execs., Pi Beta Phi (v.p. Akron area chpt. 1987—). Republican. Roman Catholic. C-lub: Akron Alumni (v.p.). Home: 2556 Durand Rd Akron OH 44313

BEITO, GEORGE ANTHONY, banker; b. Thief River Falls, Minn., Jan. 11, 1933; s. George A. and Anne J. (Strande) B.; B.A., St. Olaf Coll., Northfield, Minn., 1955; grad. Rural Banking Sch., 1968; m. Gretchen Urnes, June 29, 1957; children—David A., Kathryn A., Laura E. Asst. cashier No. State Bank, Gonvick, Minn., 1958-60, pres., chmn. bd., 1965—, v.p., No. State Bank, Thief River Falls, 1960-65, pres., chmn. bd., 1965—; pres., chmn. bd. Security State Bank, Oklee, Minn., 1st Nat. Bank, McIntosh, Minn., Marshall County State Bank, Newfolden, Minn.; treas. Valley Home, Thief River Falls, Jobs Inc., Thief River Falls; v.p. Hartz Found. Served to 1st lt. USNR, 1955-58. Named outstanding young man of Thief River Falls, 1962. Mem. Am. Bankers Assn. (governing council 1978-79; EDP council 1983-86), Minn. Bankers Assn. (mem. council 1970-73, pres. 1977-78), Thief River Falls C. of C. (pres. 1963). Clubs: Rotary, Elks, Eagles. Home: 2211 Nelson Dr Thief River Falls MN 56701 Office: 201 E 3d St Thief River Falls MN 56701

BEKINS, JOHN MELVIN, moving company executive; b. Omaha, July 3, 1957; s. Frederick Melvin and Sally Jane (Grainger) B.; m. Angela Marie Foran, Apr. 11, 1986. BS in Psychology, Westminster Coll., 1980. Warehouse asst. Bekins Van & Storage Corp., Omaha, 1980-81, records mgr., 1981-85, sales mgr., 1985—; membership dir. Met. Omaha chpt. Am. Records Mgrs. Assn., 1982-84. Membership dir. Omaha Jaycees, 1981-82. Named one of Outstanding Young Men Am. U.S. Jaycees, 1984. Mem. Nebr. Bus. Assn. (bd. dirs. 1981-84), Omaha Execs. Assn. Republican. Presbyterian. Lodges: Masons, Shriners. Avocations: tennis, golf, bicycling, music. Home: 10842 Seward St Omaha NE 68154

BEKKEDAHL, BRAD DOUGLAS, dentist; b. Williston, N.D., Nov. 23, 1957; s. Oliver Lawrence Jr. and Gudrun Joan (Sundby) B. BA, Jamestown (N.D.) Coll., 1979; BS, U. Minn., 1982, DDS, 1984. Gen. practice dentistry Williston, 1984—; dental staff Mercy Med. Ctr. Scoutmaster Boy Scouts Am., Williston, 1984-86; pastoral com. Gloria Dei Luth. Ch., Williston, 1986—; pres. Am. Legion Drum and Bugle Corps, Williston, 1986—; bd. dirs. Basin Empire United Way, Williston, 1986. Mem. ADA, N.D. Dental Assn., N.W. Dist. Dental Assn. Republican. Club: Williston Hockey (bd. dirs. 1986—). Lodge: Elks. Avocations: youth coaching, camping, woodworking, sports. Home: 2501 13th Ave W Williston ND 58801 Office: 115 2d Ave W PO Box 2443 Williston ND 58801

BEKKUM, OWEN D., gas company executive; b. Westby, Wis., Mar. 2, 1924; s. Alfred T. and Huldah (Storbakken) B.; m. Dorothy A. Jobs, Aug. 26, 1950. B.B.A., U. Wis., 1950; postgrad., Northwestern U. C.P.A. With Arthur Andersen & Co., 1951-57, Hertz Corp., 1957-62; with No. Ill. Gas Co., Aurora, 1963—; asst. comptroller No. Ill. Gas Co., 1966-68, comptroller, 1968-70, adminstrv. v.p., 1970-73, exec. v.p., 1973-76, pres., 1976—, chief exec. officer, 1981—, also dir.; dir. NICOR Inc., New Eng. Energy Co. Bd. dirs. Jr. Achievement, Chgo., 1975-79, vice chmn., 1976-79; bd. dirs. Protestant Found. Greater Chgo., 1975—, pres., 1985—, Pace Inst., 1977-83, Andrew Corp., 1980—. Served with AUS, 1943-46. Mem. Am. Mgmt. Assn., Am. Gas Assn. (dir. 1978-82, 83—), Inst. Gas Tech. (dir. 1978-82), Gas Research Inst. (dir. 1982—). Clubs: Economic, Comml., Mid-Day (Chgo.). Home: 46 Royal Vale Dr Oak Brook IL 60521 Office: No Ill Gas Co PO Box 190 Aurora IL 60507

BELASCO, KENT STEPHEN, bank executive; b. Chgo., Mar. 1, 1951; s. Eugene Peter and Geraldine (Langan) B.; m. Carol Witte, Dec. 20, 1980. AA, Lake County Coll., 1973; BA, Lake Forest Coll., 1975; MBA, Lake Forest Grad. Sch. Mgmt., 1982; postgrad. in acctg., De Paul U., 1983-84. CPA, Ill. Collection mgr. GoldBlatt Bros., Inc., Chgo., 1976-79, Citicorp Credit Service, Rosemont, Ill., 1979-80; v.p. Exchange Nat. Bank, Chgo., 1985-86; dir. bank ops. First Midwest Bancorp, Inc., Naperville, Ill., 1986—. Mem. Am. Inst. CPA's, Ill. CPA Soc., Soc. Cert. Consumer Credit Execs. Republican. Roman Catholic. Avocation: free lance artist. Home: 1004 Providence Ln Buffalo Grove IL 60089 Office: First Midwest Bancorp Inc 1230 E Diehl Rd Suite 302 Naperville IL 60566

BELCHAK, FRANK ROBERT, computer technologist; b. Chgo., June 21, 1943; s. Paul and Marion (Vrba) B. BS, Roosevelt U., 1969. Computer tech. capacity planner, systems developer Navistar Internat., Oakbrook Terrace, Ill., 1969—; mem. Navistar ISS Council of Future employee recognition program. Mem. Computer Measurement Group, Assn. Individual Investors, Art Inst. Chgo., Chgo. Zool. Soc., Edward J. Sparling Soc. Roman Catholic. Office: Navistar Internat Corp 1901 S Meyers Rd Oakbrook Terrace IL 60148

BELCHER, PAUL C., insurance company executive; b. Peoria, Ill., Nov. 23, 1957; s. George Delbert Jr. and Julia Dee (Wilson) B.; m. Barbara Marie Snick, June 23, 1979; children: Courtney Elizabeth, Caitlyn Joy. BA in Econs., Wheaton COll., 1979. Service supr. State Farm Ins. Co., Bloomington, Ill., 1979-81; agt. State Farm Ins. Co., Eagle River, Wis., 1981—. Deacon Three Lakes (Wis.) Evangelical Free Ch., 1985; chmn. fin. com. Eagle River Meml. Hosp., 1987—. Mem. Omicron Delta Epsilon. Republican. Avocations: sailing, downhill skiing, tennis, racquetball, reading. Home: 7900 Birchwood Dr Saint Germain WI 54558 Office: State Farm Ins Co 4941 Hwy 70 W Eagle River WI 54521

BELDING, ESER UZUN, management educator; b. Sivas, Turkey, Mar. 23, 1951; came to U.S., 1975; d. Irfan and Hayriye Uzun; BA, U. Istanbul (Turkey), 1974; MA, U. Mich., 1977, PhD in Organizational Psychology, 1980. Lectr., mem. research staff dept. psychology and Sch. Bus. Adminstrn., U. Istanbul, 1973-75; teaching asst., coordinator dept. psychology U. Mich., Ann Arbor, 1975-77, research assoc. Inst. for Social Research, 1976-79; health services research scientist VA Med. Ctr., Ann Arbor, 1979-80; research investigator Inst. Social Research; 1980-81; adj. prof. organizational scis. Wayne State U., Detroit, 1982; asst. prof. mgmt. U. Mich., Flint, 1982—. Mem. Acad. Mgmt. Assn., Am. Mgmt. Assn., Acad. Internat. Bus., Soc. Gen. Systems Research, Internat. Assn. Applied Psychology., Decision Sci. Inst. Contbr. articles to profl. jours. Home: 7270 Parkwood Dr Fenton MI 48430 Office: U Mich Sch Mgmt Flint MI 48502

BELDING, MERIC WINTHROP, construction company executive; b. West Chicago, Nov. 21, 1922; s. Harlow Hartley and Ferne (Chaffe) B.; m. Shirley Eleanor Saville; children: Jeffrey Saville, Richard Allen, Pamela Sue. BS, Northwestern U., 1944. Ops. supr. Belding Corp., West Chicago,

1946-50, sec., treas., 1950-60, pres., 1960-75, chmn. bd. dirs., chief exec. officer, 1975—; pres., chmn. bd. dirs. Modern Hydraulics, West Chicago, 1950-62. Mem. fin. com. West Chicago Econ. Devel., 1986-87; bd. dirs. Jr. Achievement DuPage County, 1986-87. Served to sgt. U.S. Army, 1943-46. Decorated Purple Heart. Mem. Nat. Constrn. Employers Council (vice chmn.1987—), Specialized Carriers and Rigging Assn. (pres. 1980-81, bd. dirs. 1981-82), Nat. Council Erectors, Fabricators and Riggers (chmn. bd. dirs. 1977-78), Heavy Specialized Carriers Council (chmn. labor com. 1975-77), Crane and Rigging Group (chmn. bd. dirs. 1972-73), Steel Erectors Assn. (chmn. bd. dirs. 1968-70), Ironworkers Negotiating Council, Specialized Carriers and Rigging Assn. (sec., treas. Millwright group 1980—). Republican. Club: St. Charles Country. Lodges: Rotary (charter), Elks, Masons, Amity. Avocations: flying, woodworking, gardening, reading. Office: Belding Corp 130 W Grand Lake Blvd West Chicago IL 60185

BELDING, THOMAS KIRBY, data processing company executive; b. Cleve., June 29, 1951; s. John Albert and Doris (Kirby) B.; m. Eser Uzun, July 5, 1980; children: Orhan Kirby, Arman Albert. BA in Zoology, Math., U. Maine, 1973; student, Johns Hopkins U., 1973-74; MS in Human Genetics, U. Mich., 1976, MA in Applied Econs., 1977, MHSA in Pub. Health, 1977. Research asst. Harvard Inst. Internat. Devel., Cambridge, Mass., 1978; cons. Am. Pub. Health Assn., Washington, 1978-79; product mgr. Automatic Data Processing, Ann Arbor, Mich., 1979-81, ops. and devel. mgr., 1981-83, mktg. mgr., 1983-86, nat. sales mgr., 1986—; guest lect. U. Mich. Sch. Bus., Ann Arbor, 1985, Istanbul (Turkey) U., 1985. Contbr. articles to profl. jours. N.Y. State Regents scholar, 1969, U. Maine Pulp and Paper Found. Scholar, 1969-71; recipient Corporate Excellence award Automatic Data Processing, 1985; traineeship NIH, 1974-76. Mem. Info. Ind. Assn., Dale Carnegie Assn. (class pres. 1984). Club: Friends Co-op (Ann Arbor) (pres. 1974-75). Avocations: piano, harmonica, intercultural exchange, langs., reading. Home: 7270 Parkwood Dr Fenton MI 48430 Office: Automatic Data Processing 175 Jackson Plaza Ann Arbor MI 48106

BELEW, JOE EDWARD, obstetrician, gynecologist; b. Lonedell, Mo., Aug. 27, 1931; s. Robert David and Effie Mary (Ueltzen) B.; m. Mary Jane Ash, Aug. 28, 1955; children: Taina Rae, Cynthia Jo, Mark Edward. BS, Cen. Coll., Fayette, Mo., 1953; MD, St. Louis U., 1957. Diplomate Am. Bd. Ob-Gyn. Asst. resident in ob-gyn. St. Louis Maternity Hosp., 1958-59; intern St. Luke's Hosp., 1957-58, asst. resident in ob-gyn., 1958-59, chief resident in ob-gyn., 1960-61, intern coms., 1964-69, mem. various coms., 1966-83, pres. med. staff, 1987—; asst. chief ob-gyn. Mo. Baptist Hosp., 1981-85, mem. various coms., 1970-83, pres. med. staff, 1985-86; pratice medicine specializing in ob-gyn. St. Louis, 1985—; mem. pharmacy com. St. Joseph Hosp. Kirkwood, 1969-70; clin. instr. Washington U. Sch. Medicine. Contbr. articles to profl. jours. Mem. admintrv. bd. Kirkwood Meth. Ch. Served to capt. U.S. Army, 1961-64. Fellow Am. Acad. Ob-Gyn (vice chmn. Mo.); mem. AMA, St. Louis Med. Soc., Mo. Ob-Gyn Soc., Mo. Gynecol. Soc., St. Louis Gynecol. Soc. (treas. 1971-74, sec. 1975-76, pres. 1979-80, maternal welfare com. 1964-73, sec. 1974-75), Cen. Assn. Ob-Gyn, Maternity Hosp. Soc., Continetal Gynecol. Soc. Republican. Lodge: Shriners. Home: 14011 Baywood Villages Dr Chesterfield MO 63017

BELFER, MARK HARRIS, physician; b. Grand Rapids, Mich., Oct. 7, 1952; s. Gerald Charles and Sylvia Mae (Shinwell) B.; m. Nancy Lynn Sharp, June 9, 1974; children: Rachel, Aaron, Bret. BS, Mich. State U., 1974; DO, Coll. Osteo. Med. and Surgery, Des Moines, 1977. Diplomate Nat. Bd. Osteo. Med. Examiners, Am. Bd. Family Practice. Commd. U.S. Army, 1978, advanced through grades to maj., resigned, 1986; brigade surgeon U.S. Army, Bamberg, Fed. Republic Germany, 1978-80; gen. med. officer U.S. Army Health Clinic, Bamberg, 1980-81; family practice resident U.S. Army, Ft. Benning, Ga., 1981-83; dir. family practice ctr. Tripler Army Med. Ctr., Honolulu, 1983-86; pvt. practice family medicine Warren, Ohio, 1986—; asst. clinical prof. U. Hawaii, Honolulu, 1983-86; with staff Trumbull Meml. Hosp., Warren, 1986—, St. Joseph/Riverside Hosp., 1986—. Advisor Med. Explorers Boy Scouts Am., Warren, 1986. Fellow Am. Acad. Family Physicians; mem. Sigma Alpha Mu. Republican. Jewish. Lodge: B'nai Brith. Avocations: golf, photographing nature. Home: 9181 Briarbrook Dr NE Warren OH 44484 Office: 311 Niles-Cortland Rd Warren OH 44484

BELFORT, ANNE ELLEN, marketing instructor; b. N.Y.C., Apr. 6, 1954; d. Alan Michael and Anne Dorothy Belfort. Student, Georgetown U., 1972, U. Pa., 1975; BA, Hollins Coll., 1975; MS in Mgmt., Purdue U., 1976. Mgmt. services industry specialist, Info. Services Bus. div. Gen. Electric Co., Rockville, Md., 1978-79; assoc. mktg. rep., Data Processing div. IBM Corp., Chgo., 1979-80, mktg. rep., Processing div., 1980-81, account mktg. rep., Nat. Accounts div., 1982-85; adv. instr., Southwest Mktg. div. IBM Corp., Irving, Tex., 1985—. Editor corp. news mag. The Bottom Line, 1978. Bd. dirs. Vanderbilt U. Model UN Econ. and Social Council, 1974; rep. Hollins (Va.) Coll. Student Govt., 1972-75; sec. gen. Hollins Coll. Model UN, 1975; mem. Purdue U. Pres.'s Council, 1977—, Purdue U./Krannert Sch. Dean's Adv. Council, 1985—, Purdue U./Krannert Grad. Sch. Alumnae Bd., 1980-82. Named One of Outstanding Young Women of Am., 1979; recipient Leadership award YWCA, Chgo., 1980, Voltaire medal Ecole Champlain, Paris, 1970. Mem. Assn. MBA Execs., AAAS. Republican. Club: Alliance Francaise.

BELIZARIO, FRANCISCO, otolaryngologist; b. Manila, Sept. 27, 1946; came to U.S., 1973; s. Vicente and Waltdetrudes (Ylanan) B.; m. Evangelina Mendoza, May 5, 1973; children: Vicente, Aileen. BS, Ateneo de Manila U., 1966; MD, U. Philippines, 1971. Diplomate Am. Bd. Otolaryngology. Rotating intern St. Michael's Hosp., Milw., 1973-74; gen. surgery residency Buffalo Gen. Hosp., 1974-75; resident in otolaryngology U. Ill. Hosps., Chgo., 1975-78; practice medicine specializing in otolaryngology Elmwood Park, Ill., 1978—; attending specialist St. Anne's Hosp., Chgo., Gottlieb Meml. Hosp., Melrose Park, Ill., Oak Park (Ill.) Hosp., Westlake Hosp. & Med. Ctr., Melrose Park, Good Samaritan Hosp., Downers Grove, Ill. Mem. AMA. Office: 7518 W North Ave Elmwood Park IL 60635

BELKIN, HOWARD ROBERT, lawyer, dentist; b. Detroit, Dec. 7, 1955; s. Jack Eugene and Anne (Brownstein) B.; m. Kathy Susan Berman, Dec. 26, 1982. BS, U. Mich., 1976, DDS, 1980; JD, Detroit Coll. Law, 1985. Bar: Mich. 1985. Dentist Warren (Mich.) Dental Assocs., P.C., 1983—; assoc. Gittleman, Paskel, Tashman & Blumburg, Southfield, Mich., 1985—; malpractice and injury cons., 1982—. Contbr. articles to profl. jours. Recipient Am. Acad. Periodontology award, 1980, Charles H. King award Detroit Coll. Law, 1985, Sybil M. Lyon award, 1985. Mem. ABA, Detroit Coll. Law Alumni Assn., U. Mich. Sch. Dentistry Heritage Soc. Office: Gittleman Paskel et al 24472 Northwestern Hwy Southfield MI 48075

BELKNAP, ELMER CLINTON, retired medical social worker; b. Gordon, Nebr., Dec. 24, 1905; s. Elmer Curtis and Kitty Luella (Moss) B.; B.A., Simpson Coll., 1929; M.A., U. Chgo., 1937; m. Mildred Pearl Breniman, May 23, 1932 (dec. June 1978); children—Rowan Curtis, Dean Edward; m. 2d, Mildred Shook Robson, June 7, 1979. Asso. boys' work sec. YMCA, Sioux City, Iowa, 1930-31; jr. boys clubs and handicraft dir. U. Chgo. Settlement House, 1932-33; sr. case worker Cook County Bur. Pub. Welfare, Chgo., 1933-34; dir. Hall County Emergency Relief and Pub. Assistance Adminstrn., Grand Island, Nebr., 1934-44; Nebr. field rep. Nat. Found. Infantile Paralysis, N.Y.C. and Lincoln, Nebr., 1944-65; with Nebr. State Dept. Pub. Welfare, Lincoln, 1965—, dir., 1967-68, med. social work cons., 1969-76; mem. Nebr. Crippled Children Adv. Com., Lincoln, 1947-55, Nebr. Health Planning Com., 1947-52, Nebr. Comprehensive Health Planning Adv. Council, 1967-69. Bd. dirs. Lancaster County chpt. Nat. Found.-March of Dimes, 1965-69. Recipient Distinguished Service citation Nat. Found.-March of Dimes, N.Y.C., 1964. Mem. Am. (nat. bd. dirs. 1968-69), Nebr. (pres. 1937-38) pub. welfare assns., Nebr. Pub. Health Assn. (state sec. 1955-56), Nat. Rehab. Assn. (state dir. 1961-64), Nebr. State Hist. Soc., New Eng. Historic and Geneal. Soc., Pi Kappa Delta. Methodist (chmn. com. edn. 1955-56). Author: A Belknap Genealogy, 1974; A Moss Genealogy, 1977; Nebraska and the Fight Against Polio, 1944-1965, 1982. Home: 2019 Harwood St Lincoln NE 68502

BELL, CARL COMPTON, psychiatrist, researcher, consultant, martial artist; b. Chgo., Oct. 28, 1947; s. William Yancy and Pearl Louise (Debnam) B.; m. Joanne Scott, Jan. 1, 1969 (div. Apr. 1971); 1 child, Cristin Carol; m. Dora Dixie, Dec. 1984; children: Erin Nickole, Audrey. B.S. in Biology, U. Ill.-Chgo., 1967; M.D., Meharry Med. Coll., 1971. Diplomate Am. Bd. Psychiatry and Neurology (examiner). Intern, Ill. State Psychiat. Inst., Chgo., 1971-72, resident, 1972-74, pvt. practice medicine specializing in psychiatry, Chgo., 1974—; dir. psychiat. emergency services Jackson Park Hosp., Chgo., 1976-77, assoc. dir. div. behavioral and psychodynamic medicine, 1979-82, mem. staff, 1972—; staff psychiatrist Human Correctional and Services Inst., Chgo., 1977-78, Chgo. Bd. Edn., 1977-79, Chatham Avalon Mental Health Ctr., Chgo., 1977-79; staff psychiatrist Community Mental Health Council, Chgo., 1977-79, med. dir., 1983-87, exec. dir. 1987—; assoc. prof. clin. psychiatry U. Ill., 1983—; lectr. U. Chgo., 1986-87; cons. in field. Mem. profl. adv. panel Mental Health Assn. Greater Chgo., 1983—; bd. dirs. Nat. Commn. on Correctional Health Care, 1983—; lectr. U. Chgo., 1986; tchr. martial arts, 1973—. Producer, creator animation Book Worm, 1984; contbr. chpts., numerous articles to profl. publs. Served to lt. comdr. USN, 1974-76. Recipient plaque in recognition and appreciation Chatham-Avalon Mental Health Ctr., 1979, plaque in gratitude and appreciation Div. Behavioral Medicine, 1982, Scholastic Achievement award Chgo. chpt. Nat. Assn. Black Social Workers, 1980, Ellen Quinn Meml. award, 1986, Monarch award Alpha Kappa Alpha, 1986; Goldberger fellow, 1969, Dr. Martin Luther King, Jr. fellow, 1970-71. Am. Psychiat. Assn. (Falk fellow 1972-73, fellow 1985, task force-delivery psychiat. services to poverty areas 1972-73), Nat. Med. Assn. (local chmn. sect. on neurology and psychiatry 1983 conv., nat. chmn. sect. on psychiatry and behavioral scis. 1985-86), Black Psychiatrists Am. (editor Bottom Line newsletter 1977-82, v.p. 1980-82), Cook County Physicians Assn., Prairie State Physicians, Ill. Psychiat. Soc., Am. Assn. Community Mental Health Ctr. Psychiatrists (bd. dirs. 1985—), Nat. Council Community Health Ctrs. (sec. bd. dirs. 1986—, sec., treas. 1987), Underwater Explorers Soc., Shorei Goju Karate Soc. (5th degree Black Belt), Martial Arts Karate Assn., Alpha Omega Alpha. Office: Jackson Park Hosp 8704 S Constance Chicago IL 60617 Office: Community Mental Health Council 1001 E 87th St Chicago IL 60619

BELL, CHARLES EDWARD, psychologist; b. Galveston, Tex., Feb. 7, 1936; s. Ben Franklin and Johnnie Odet (Rush) B.; m. Marvell Marie Mossom, Dec. 20, 1968; children—Charles Butler, Beverly Ann, Laurie Marvell. B.S., U. Houston, 1962, M.A., 1965; Ed.D., N. Tex. U., 1977. Asst. prof. Ouachita Bapt. U., Arkadelphia, Ark., 1967-69; staff psychologist Benton (Ark.) State Hosp., 1968-71, Vernon (Tex.) Project for Drug Dependent Youth, 1973-74, S.E. Kans. Mental Health Center, Humboldt, 1974-78; dir. S.E. Kans. Mental Health Assos., Chanute, 1978-82; staff psychologist Ozark Ctr., Neosho, Mo., 1982—; vis. prof. Vernon Regional Jr. Coll., 1974, Henderson State Coll., 1967-68; teaching fellow U. Houston, 1963-67, N. Tex. State U., 1972-73. Author: Transactional Analysis for Classroom Teachers, 1977; A Comparison of Three Techniques for Teaching Oral Hygiene, 1978. Chmn. bd. dirs. Circle B Boys Ranch, Inc.; mem. council, mayor pro tem, Neosho. Mem. AAUP, Am., Southwestern psychol. assns., Phi Chi, Phi Delta Kappa. Republican. Mem. Assembly of God Ch. Clubs: Rotary, Kiwanis, Elks. Home: 1510 Oakridge Dr Neosho MO 64850 Office: 214 N Washington Neosho MO 64850

BELL, CHARLES EUGENE, JR., industrial engineer; b. N.Y.C., Dec. 13, 1932; s. Charles Edward and Constance Elizabeth (Verbelia) B.; B. Engring., Johns Hopkins U., 1954, M.S. in Engring., 1959; m. Doris R. Clifton, Jan. 14, 1967; 1 son, Scott Charles Bell. Indsl. engr. Signode Corp., Balt., 1957-61, asst. to plant mgr., 1961-63, plant engr., 1963-64, div. indsl. engr., Glenview, Ill., 1964-69, asst. to div. mgr., 1969-76, engring. mgr., 1976—; host committeeman Internat. Indsl. Engring. Conf., Chgo., 1984. Served with U.S. Army, 1955-57. Registered profl. engr., Calif. Mem. Am. Inst. Indsl. Engrs. (pres. 1981), Indsl. Mgmt. Club Central Md. (pres. 1964), Nat. Soc. Profl. Engrs., Ill. Soc. Profl. Engrs. Republican. Roman Catholic. Home: 1021 W Old Mill Rd Lake Forest IL 60045 Office: Signode Corp 3650 W Lake Ave Glenview IL 60025

BELL, DAVID, physician; b. N.Y.C., Jan. 16, 1940; s. Henry Benjamin and Leah Pearl (Rabinowitz) B.; m. Anne Key, Mar. 31, 1972; children: Paul Henry, Sarah Leah, Rachel Shana. BA, CCNY, 1960; PhD, Brown U., 1965; MD, Tulane U., 1976. Cert. Am. Bd. Radiology. Instr. U. Calif., Berkeley, 1967; asst. prof. math. Rice U., Houston, 1967-71; assoc. prof. math. La. State U., New Orleans, 1971-72; intern Charity Hosp., New Orleans, 1976-77; resident M.D. Anderson Hosp., Houston, 1977-81; radiation therapist Regional Hosp., Terre Haute, Ind., 1982—. Mem. AMA, Radiol. Soc. N.Am., Am. Soc. Therapeutic Radiologists, Am. Coll. Radiology. Democrat. Jewish. Avocations: Jewish history, weight lifting. Office: Regional Hosp 601 Hospital Ln Terre Haute IN 47802

BELL, DAVID CHAMBERS, dentist; b. Lake Forest, Ill., Aug. 21, 1957; s. David Chambers and Jean (Cary) B. BA in History and Econs., Vanderbilt U., 1979; DDS, Ohio State U., 1983. Mem. Up Down-Towners, Cin., 1983—, Fundraisers of Cin., 1986—. Mem. ADA, Ohio Dental Soc., Cin. Dental Soc., Phi Beta Kappa, Phi Eta Sigma, Ohio State U. Alumni Assn. (v.p. Cin. 1986, scholarship coordinator 1986—). Republican. Methodist. Avocations: triathalon, backpacking, canoeing, tennis, golf. Office: 2767 Ene Ave Cincinnati OH 45208

BELL, DAVID CURTIS, manufacturing company executive; b. St. Paul, Nov. 5, 1953; s. Dwain Curtis and Aurel Lorna (Waknitz) B.; m. Lee Ellen Wandersee, Feb. 12, 1982; B.A. summa cum laude with honors, Concordia Coll., 1975; postgrad. Am. U., 1973. Prodn. asst. Pako Photo, Mpls., 1975; sales rep. Pako Corp., Chgo. and eastern Wis., 1976-79; venture plant sales mgr. Pako Corp., Mpls., 1979-83; mktg. dir. system sales Multi-Arc (div. of Andal Corp.), St. Paul, 1983—; dir. Bell Mfg. & Services, Inc., Mpls. Mem. Internat. Machine Tool Assn. (selected speaker 1986), North Side Jaycees (officer 1976-78), New Hope Jaycees (pres. 1981-82). Republican. Lutheran. Club: C-400, Kiwanis (Mpls.). Office: 261 E 5th St Saint Paul MN 55101

BELL, DENNIS ARTHUR, lawyer; b. Chgo., July 5, 1934; s. Samuel Arthur and Frances (Gordon) B.; m. Judith Gail Young, Nov. 6, 1977. B.S. in Accountancy, U. Ill., 1955; J.D., DePaul U., 1961. Bar: Ill. 1961, U.S. Supreme Ct., 1964. C.P.A., Ill., 1956. C.P.A. Peat, Marwick Mitchell, Chgo., 1957-62; staff acct., atty. SEC, Washington, 1957-62; capital devel. officer U.S. AID, Ankara, Turkey, 1966-68; pvt. cons., Chgo., 1968-70; group controller Nat. Student Mktg. Corp., Chgo., 1970-72; dir. corp. fin. dept. and house counsel Rothschild Securities Corp., Chgo., 1973-74; corp. sec., assoc. gen. counsel Midwest Stock Exchange, 1974-79; pres. Dennis A. Bell & Assocs. Ltd., Chgo., 1979—; dir., sec., treas. Joy Internat. Corp., 1977—, Lyric Internat. Corp., Chgo. and Hong Kong, 1983—. Bd. dirs. Mental Health Assn., Chgo. Clarence Darrow Community Ctr. Served with USAR, 1957-62. Mem. ABA, Fed. Bar Assn., Ill. Bar Assn., Ill. C.P.A. Soc., Am. Soc. Corp. Secs. Democrat. Jewish. Club: Attic (Chgo.); International (Chgo.). Home: 1325 N State Pkwy 10F Chicago IL 60610 Office: 140 S Dearborn St Suite 800 Chicago IL 60603

BELL, DONNA STEVENS, teacher; b. Evansville, Ind., Apr. 20, 1950; d. Paul Richard and Vivian Earline (Crum) Hill; m. Bruce Allen Bell, June 2, 1973; children: Matthew, Connor, Alissa. BA, U. Louisville, 1971. Cert. elem. tchr., Ky., Colo., Wis. Sec., receptionist U. Louisville, 1967-71; tchr. Jefferson County Schs., Louisville, 1971-73; sec. to dir. U. Northern Colo., Greeley, 1973-74; tchr. Loveland (Colo.) R2-J Sch. Dist., 1974-77; designer Collector's Gallery, Oshkosh, Wis., 1982-84; acct. cons. Robert's Group, Waukesha, Wis., 1985-86; tchr. Hartford Joint 1 Sch. Dist., 1986—; freelance graphic designer, Oshkosh, Hartford, Wis., 1978—. Chmn. UNICEF folk fair First Presbyn. Ch., Oshkosh, 1981, benefit dinner, auction Hartford (Wis.) Meml. Hosp. Aux., 1985, auction chmn., 1986; judge Fox River Valley needlework competition, Neenah, Wis., 1982, 84; team dir. Sideliners Soccer League, Hartford, 1985-86. Recipient 1st Pl. award Fox River Valley Needlework Competition, 1985. Avocations: reading, knitting design, needlework design, sewing, sailing, camping, gardening. Home: 1070 Kings Rd Hartford WI 53027

BELL, EDWARD FRANCIS, telecommunications company executive; b. Evanston, Ill., 1930. BSEE, U. Ill., 1951; MBA, Northwestern U., 1960. Engr. AT&T Co., 1962-64; with Ill. Bell Telephone Co., 1952-62, 64-75, former asst. v.p. corp. planning; with Ohio Bell Tel. Co., Cleve., 1976—; v.p. engring. & corp. planning Ohio Bell Tel. Co., 1976-78, exec. v.p., 1978-83, chief operating officer, from 1978, pres., 1983—, now also chief exec. officer, dir.; dir. Leaseway Transp. Corp. Served with U.S. Army, 1951-53. Office: Ohio Bell Telephone Co 45 Erieview Plaza Cleveland OH 44114 *

BELL, JEFFREY GEORGE, gynecologic oncologist; b. Canton, Ohio, June 20, 1950; s. George Edwin and Evelyn M. (Adams) B.; Brenda Lynn Backus, Dec. 22, 1972; children: Heather, Holly. BA magna cum laude, Wittenberg U., 1972; MD cum laude, Ohio State U., 1975. Diplomate Am. Bd. Ob-Gyn. Intern Nat. Naval Med. Ctr., Bethesda, Md., 1975-76, resident in ob-gyn, 1976-79; staff physician USNR, Jacksonville, Fla., 1979-81; fellow in ob-gyn U. Miami, Fla., 1981-84; dir. gynecol. oncology Riverside Hosp., Columbus, Ohio, 1984—; mem. staff Riverside Meth. Hosp., Columbus, Grant Hosp., Columbus, Ohio State U. Hosp., Columbus; clin. asst. prof. dept. ob-gyn Ohio State U., Columbus, 1984—. Contbr. articles to profl. jours. Served to lt. comdr. USNR, 1973-81. Fellow Am. Coll. Obstetricians and Gynecologists; mem. AMA, Ohio State Med. Soc., Columbus Ob-Gyn Soc., Acad. Medicine Columbus and Franklin County, Cen. Ohio Soc. Clin. Oncologists, Soc. Gynecol. Oncology. Avocation: tennis. Office: 3555 Olentangy River Rd Columbus OH 43214

BELL, JOHN RICHARD, dentist; b. Peoria, Ill., May 18, 1922; s. Ross G. and Frances A. (Seiler) B.; D.D.S., Washington U., St. Louis, 1946; m. Norma Jean Oltmann, June 1979. Gen. practice dentistry, Peoria, Ill., 1946-86; mem. hosp. staff St. Francis Hosp., Peoria, Ill. 1953—. Dental cons. Aetna Life & Casualty Co. Bd. dirs., past treas. Peoria County chpt. Am. Cancer Soc. Served to lt. comdr. USNR, 1954-56. Mem. Am. Dental Assn., Ill., Peoria Dist. (treas. 1963-65, pres. 1965-66) dental socs., Sigma Chi, Delta Sigma Delta. Republican. Roman Catholic. Home: 25 Oriole Ln Pekin IL 61554

BELL, LARRY PRENTICE, physician, researcher; b. Port Arthur, Tex., Dec. 15, 1950; s. Harry Prentice and Bernice (Street) B.; m. Robin Lynn Saltzman, July 7, 1984. BS, Lamar U., 1973; MD, U. Tex. Med. Br., Galveston, 1978. Diplomate Am. Bd. Internal Medicine. Intern U. Tex. Affiliated Hosps., Houston, U. Tex., 1978-79; resident U. Calif., Davis; pvt. practice specializing in internal medicine Doctors Hosp., Pinole, Calif., 1981-84; resident U. Calif., Davis, 1978-81; fellow clin. nutrition U. Minn., Mpls., 1984-86; sr. research fellow Lipid Research Clinic, Mpls., 1986—; asst. dir., asst. prof. heart disease prevention clinic U. Minn., 1987—; cons. Optifast Clinics, Mpls., 1986—. Mem. AMA, Hennepin County Med. Soc., Am. Soc. Parenteral and Enteral Nutrition, Beta Beta Beta, Kappa Kappa Kappa. Club: Gopher Wheelman (Mpls.). Avocations: reading, hiking, biking. Office: U Minn UCHH 501 East River Rd Box 192 Minneapolis MN 55455

BELL, MARK GERALD, physician, surgeon; b. Winfield, Kans., Dec. 29, 1950; s. Gene LeRoy and Erma Lorraine (Marshall) B.; m. Joyce Linda Rumsey, Jan. 9, 1971 (div. Feb. 1980); 1 child, Tara Kimberly; m. Joy Elaine Bermel, June 22, 1980 children: Tamera Michelle, Tia Joanna. BA in Biology, Kans. State U., 1972; MD, U. Kans. Med. Sch., 1975. Cert. Am. Bd. Otolaryngology. Resident gen. surgery St. Luke's Hosp., Kansas City, Mo., 1975-77; resident otolaryngology Kans. U. Med. Ctr., Kansas City, 1977-80; chief dept. otolaryngology U.S. Naval Regional Med. Ctr., Okinawa, Japan, 1980-83; mem. staff St. John's-Asbury Hosps., Salina, Kans., 1983—; chmn. emergency room-intensive care unit com. U.S. Naval Regional Med. Ctr., Okinawa, 1981-83; chmn. emergency room com. St. John's-Asbury Hosps., Salina, 1984-85. Mem. Horizon Fifty Cultural Patrons, Salina, 1986—; officer bd. edn. First Christian Ch., Salina, 1986-87. Served to lt. comdr. USN, 1980-83. Recipient Resident Teaching award St. Luke's Hosp., Kansas City, Mo., 1977, Service Commendation award U.S. Naval Regional Med. Ctr., Okinawa, 1983. Mem. AMA, Am. Bd. Otolaryngology, Kans. Med. Soc. (resolution reference com. 1986, sec.-treas. ear nose throat subdiv. 1986—), Salina County Med. Soc. (del. Kans. Med. Soc. 1984—). Republican. Avocations: gun collecting, photography, tennis, flying. Home: 7 Crestview Salina KS 67401 Office: Cen Kans ENT Assocs PA 909 E Wayne Salina KS 67401

BELL, ROBERT ALAN, architect; b. Cleve., June 29, 1938; s. George Robert and Irene Ethyl (Cole) B.; m. Carolyn Vassar Westerman, June 18, 1960 (div. 1982); children: Peter, Karen, James, Julie, Sarah; m. Ellen J. Alldredge, Nov. 20, 1982; 1 stepchild, Michelle. BA, Cornell U., 1961. Registered architect, Ill., Wis., Ind. Architect Mittelbusher & Tourtelot, Chgo., 1961-64, Harry Weese & Assocs., Chgo., 1964-70; v.p. Sturr Young Assocs., Ltd., Oak Park, Ill., 1971-76; pres. Robert A. Bell Architects, Ltd., Oak Park, 1976—; instr. archtl. tech. Triton Coll., River Grove, Ill., 1974-76, 83-86. Prin. works include day care facility Resurrection Hosp., restoration of Frank Lloyd Wright's Unity Temple, banking facilities St. Paul Fed. Bank. Chmn. Oak Park Landmarks Commn., 1971-76, Park Dist., Oak Park, 1969-72; mem. Human Rights Housing Com., Oak Park, 1963-68. Mem. AIA (Honor award 1987), Nat. Council Archtl. Registration Bd., Landmarks Preservation Council, Chi Phi. Clubs: Oak Park Runners, Cornell U. of Chgo. Avocations: running, racquetball, golf. Home: 811 S Kenilworth Ave Oak Park IL 60304 Office: 115 N Marion St Oak Park IL 60301

BELL, ROBERT PAUL, former university president; b. Charlottesville, Ind., Sept. 28, 1918; s. Paul H. and Emma Adaline (Overman) B.; m. Margaret Cora Strattan, Apr. 3, 1942; children: Paul Strattan, Barbara Ann. B.S. Ball State Tchrs. Coll, Muncie, Ind., 1940; M.C.S., Ind. U., 1942, Ed.D., 1952. Tchr. bus. Pendleton High Sch., Ind., 1940-41; grad. asst. Sch. Bus., Ind. U., 1941-42; instr. U.S. Naval Tng. Sch., 1942-44, Lab. Sch., Sch. Edn., Ind. U., 1944-47; mem. faculty Ball State U., Muncie, 1947—; prof. head dept. bus. Ball State U., 1954-61, prof. bus. edn., dean div. fine and applied arts, 1961-65; dean Coll. Bus., 1964-73, v.p. bus. affairs, treas., 1972-81, univ. pres., from 1981, now ret.; dir. Muncie Fed. Savs. & Loan Assn. Author: Instructional Materials in Accounting, 1948, Instructional Materials in Typewriting, 1963, 2d edit., 1972; also articles.; editor: Ball State Commerce Jour, 1954—. Div. chmn. Muncie United Fund, 1962-63; bd. dirs. Delaware County Soc. Crippled, 1963—, United Way, 1973—, Community Found. of Muncie and Delaware County, Ball Meml. Hosp., 1982-84 (and 4 subs., 1984—), The Community Found. of Muncie and Del. County, Inc. Mem. Nat. Bus. Tchrs. Assn. (1st v.p. 1960), N. Central Bus. Edn. Assn. (pres. 1963), Nat. Bus. Edn. Assn. (bd. dirs. 1963), Future Bus. Leaders Am. (Ind. adviser 1954-61), NEA, Ind. Tchrs. Assn., Nat. Thrift Com., Blue Key, Delta Pi Epsilon, Pi Omega Pi, Sigma Tau Gamma., Beta Gamma Sigma, Sigma Iota Epsilon. Clubs: Exchange (pres. Muncie 1962-63), Rotary (hon.). Home: 3200 W Beechwood Muncie IN 47304

BELL, ROGER EUGENE, marketing representative, educator; b. Kansas City, Mo., July 12, 1939; s. Ivan Morris and Evelyn Flora (Kresin) B.; m. Patricia Louise Francis, June 11, 1961; children—Michael Eugene, Michelle Annette. B.A. in Bus. Adminstrn., Park Coll., Parkville, Mo., 1978; M.A. in Bus. Mgmt., Central Mich. U., 1979. With Burroughs Corp., 1962-75; mktg. rep. Sycor Inc., Kansas City, Mo., 1975-78; br. mgr. Anderson Jacobson Inc., Kansas City, Mo., 1978-80; mktg. rep. NCR Comten, Kansas City, Mo., 1980—. Prof. bus. adminstrn., mgmt. Park Coll., 1980. Mem. Park Bd. City of Lenexa (Kans.), 1983, damage assessment supr. Office of Emergency Preparedness, 1967. Served with USAF, 1957-62. Mem. Data Processing Mgmt. Assn., Sigma Iota Epsilon, Osborne Computer Users Group. Republican. Baptist. Home: 8914 Rene St Lenexa KS 66215 Office: 3100 Broadway Suite 330 Kansas City MO 64111

BELL, SAMUEL H., federal judge; b. Rochester, N.Y., Dec. 31, 1925; s. Samuel H. and Marie C. (Williams) B.; m. Joyce Elaine Shaw, 1948 (dec.): children—Henry W., Steven D.; m. Jennie Lee McCall, 1983. B.A., Coll. Wooster, 1947; J.D., U. Akron, 1952. Practice law Cuyahoga Falls, Ohio, 1956-68; asst. pros. atty. Summit County, Ohio, 1956-58; judge Cuyahoga Falls Mcpl. Ct., Ohio, 1968-73, Ct. of Common Pleas, Akron, Ohio, 1973-77, Ohio Ct. Appeals, 9th Jud. Dist., Akron, 1977-82, U.S. Dist. Ct. (no. dist.) Ohio, Akron, 1982—; mem. adv. bd. U. Akron Sch. Law, trustee Dean's Club. Recipient Disting. Alumni award U. Akron, 1983, St. Thomas More award, 1987. Mem. ABA, Fed. Bar Assn., Akron Bar Assn., Ohio Bar Assn., Akron U. Sch. Law Alumni Assn. (disting. alumni award 1983), Phi Alpha Delta. Republican. Presbyterian. Club: Akron City. Lodge: Masons. Office: US Courthouse 2 S Main St Akron OH 44308

BELL, THOMAS MICHAEL, home building corporation executive, realty executive; b. Marietta, Ohio, Sept. 5, 1954; s. Grosvenor Story and Louise

(Crew) B. Student Ohio U., Ohio State U. Owner, mgr. Bell Properties, Columbus, Ohio, 1975—; pres. Bell Homes, Inc., Columbus, 1976—; dir. Bel-Per Properties, 1981—, Olentangy Builders, Columbus, 1979—, Columbus First Realty, 1981—; guest lectr. Coll. Bus. Adminstrn., Miami U., Ohio, various profl. groups. Mem. Building Industry Assn. Central Ohio, Columbus Bd. Realtors. Republican. Presbyterian. Home: 7691 Southwick Dr Dublin OH 43017 Office: Bell Homes Inc 1050 Freeway Dr N Suite 301 Columbus OH 43229

BELLA, DANTINA CARMEN QUARTAROLI, consultant; b. Providence, May 11, 1922; d. Bernardo and Jennie (Zinno) Quartaroli; B.A., Bryant Coll.; M.A., Alfred U., 1952, M.S. in Adminstrn., U. Notre Dame, 1973; postgrad. U. Mich., 1977; m. Salvatore J. Bella, Dec. 30, 1946; children—Theresa, Joseph, Jennifer. Rehab. counselor R.I. Dept. Edn., 1942-46; admissions counselor Coll. Bus. Adminstrn., Boston U., 1946-49; asst. to dean Coll. of Ceramics, Alfred (N.Y.) U., 1949-53; dir. pupil personnel services, asst. prin. Marian High Sch., Mishawaka, Ind., 1968-74; registrar, admissions officer Ind. Vocat. Tech. Coll., South Bend, 1974-76; resident counselor, dir. Forever Learning Inst., Harvest House, South Bend, 1977-84; pres., owner Potentials for Greying Ams., Notre Dame, Ind., 1984—; exec. dir. Battell Sr. Workers, Inc., Mishawaka, 1985—; textbook cons. South Bend Community Sch. Corp., 1974-77; lectr., workshop coordinator, 1974-80. Bd. dirs. Cath. Social Service Center, 1968—, Women Career Center, 1974; pres. South Bend Commn. on Status of Women, 1975-78. Mem. Am. Assn. Counseling Devel., AAUW, Beta Gamma Sigma. Democrat. Roman Catholic. Author, also producer TV series Pub. Broadcasting System; Better Understanding of Self Through Literature, 1978; Mothers of the Depression, 1979. Home: 1029 Clermont Dr South Bend IN 46617 Office: Battell Sr Workers Inc 120 E Battell St Mishawaka IN 46544

BELLAMKONDA, RAMESH, physician; b. Bangalore, India, Sept. 1, 1952; came to U.S., 1975; s. Betaiah Setty Ramakrishnaiah and Sundaralaxmi (Chindaluru) B.; m. Pancharathna K. Athmaram, June 19, 1978. MB, B in Surgery, All India Inst. Med. Scis., New Delhi, 1974. Diplomate Am. Bd. Internal Medicine. Intern in internal medicine N.J. Med. Sch., Newark, 1976-77, resident in internal medicine, 1977-79; fellow Stanford (Calif.) U., 1979-80, U. S.C., Columbia, 1980-81; practice medicine specializing in gastro-enterology Morris County, N.J., 1981-84, Mansfield, Ohio, 1984—. Mem. AMA, Ohio State Med. Assn., Richland County Med. Assn. Hindu. Office: 661 Park Ave E Mansfield OH 44905

BELLAMY, EDWARD JOHN, marketing executive; b. St. Louis, Feb. 26, 1946; s. Samuel Walter and Clara Alma (Overmann) B.; m. Karen Jean Rocchio, June 22, 1968; children: Edward Samuel, Todd Eric, Gina Maria. BA, U. Mo., St. Louis, 1968. Account exec. Top Value Enterprises, St. Louis, 1968-70; asst. dir. sales CurLee Clothing, St. Louis, 1970-75; exec. v.p. sales Modern Jacket Co., St. Louis, 1975-85; pres. In Gear Mktg., St. Louis, 1985—. Served to sgt. USAR, 1968-74. Republican. Roman Catholic. Avocations: baseball cards, reading. Home and Office: In Gear Mktg 4560 Zamora Saint Louis MO 63128

BELLANTE, DONALD J., metal processing company executive, financial consultant; b. Cleve., July 29, 1945; s. Zopito Anthony and Susan Catherine (Cirino) B.; m. Antonette Cirino, Feb. 4, 1967; children: Jacqueline, Catherine, Anita, Susanne, Alicia. BBA, Case Western Res. U., 1967; postgrad., John Marshall Law Sch., 1973-75. CPA, Ohio. Sr. auditor Arthur Andersen & Co., Columbus, Ohio, 1967-71; mgr. auditing Bick Fredman, CPA, Cleve., 1971-73; v.p. fin. Roth Steel Products Co., Cleve., 1973—; cons. Donald J. Bellante, CPA, Mentor, Ohio, 1987—. Mem. fin. com. St. Bede Parish, Mentor, 1978-80; arbitrator Better Bus. Bur., Cleve., 1986—. Mem. Am. Inst. CPA's, Ohio Soc. CPA's (industry com. 1986—). Republican. Roman Catholic. Home: 8821 Arrowood Ct Mentor OH 44060

BELLAR, WILLIS FRANKLIN, bakery products company executive; b. Eldorado, Ariz., Mar. 3, 1933; s. Curtis E. and Hattie M. (Willis) B.; m. Dennis L. Clesi, Aug. 22, 1955; children: Kirk, Kent, Jennifer. BS in Baking Sci. and Mgmt., Florida State U., 1955. Baking specialist Gen. Foods Corp., Terry Town, N.Y., 1961-71; gen. mgr. Spudnuts, Salt Lake City, 1972-74; pres., gen. mgr. Wetterau Bakery Products, St. Louis, 1974—. Served to 1st lt. USMC, 1956-59. mem. Am. Soc. Bakery Engrs., Internat. Deli Bakery Assn. (chmn. edn. com. 1982-83), Retail Bakers Am., Nat. Restaurant Assn. Avocations: antiques, gardening. Home: 3339 Town & Country Saint Charles MO 63301 Office: Wetterau Bakery Products 8840 Pershall Rd Hazelwood MO 63042

BELLAS, ROBERT CALDWELL, JR., venture capitalist; b. Miami, Fla., Mar. 23, 1942; s. Robert Caldwell and Audrey (Conner) B.; BS, U.S. Naval Acad., 1966; MBA, Stanford U., 1973; m. Terrye Lynn Armstrong, July 1, 1967; children: Tamsinn, Erika. Vice pres. mktg. EMI Therapy Systems, Inc., Sunnyvale, Calif., 1973-78; dir. mktg. Acurex Corp., Mountain View, Calif., 1978-80; gen. mgr. Crystal and Electronic Products div. Harshaw/Gulf Oil Co., Solon, Ohio, 1980-83; gen. ptnr. Morgenthaler Venture Ptnrs., Cleve., 1984—. Served to lt. USN, 1966-71, Vietnam. Mem. Stanford U. Alumni Assn., U.S. Naval Acad. Alumni Assn. Republican. Club: Cleve. Athletic. Home: Woodstock Rd Gates Mills OH 44040 Office: 700 Nat City Bank Bldg Cleveland OH 44114

BELLIS, KENNETH ELMER, manufacturing company executive; b. Cleve., Dec. 1, 1928; s. Andrew and Carrie (Fligel) B.; m. Delores Eleanor Faehnrich, Aug. 19, 1950; children: Diane, Gregory, Kim. Student, Ohio State U., 1948-49; AAS in Tool and Die Design, Cleve. Engring. Inst., 1957. Asst. foreman B.L. Marble Co., Bedford, Ohio, 1949-52, 54-55; foundry design engr. Grabler Mfg. Co., Cleve., 1955-61; operations mgr.Shalco Systems div. Roberts Corp., Cleve. and Detroit, 1961—; expert witness foundry equipment Acme Cleve, Corp., 1970—. Patentee in field. Served as cpl. U.S. Army, 1952-54. Mem. Am. Foundrymen's Soc. (bd. dirs. Cleve. chpt. 1978-81). Roman Catholic. Avocation: photography. Home: 388 Huntington Ct Rochester MI 48063 Office: Roberts Corp Shalco Systems div 18100 Cross Ln Fraser MI 48026

BELLMAN, JOSEPH A., draftsman; b. Lima, Ohio, Dec. 19, 1951; s. Norman L. and Ruth E. (Balbaugh) B.; m. Martha L. DuBry, Dec. 1 1973, children: Brian P., Angela M. AS, ITT Tech. Inst., Dayton, Ohio, 1972. Draftsman Daub Builders, Ottawa, Ohio, 1973-74, Triplett Corp., Bluffton, Ohio, 1974-75, Marathon Oil Co., Findlay, Ohio, 1975—. Mem. St. Michael's Parish Improvement Com., Findlay, 1985—; pres. Liberty Benton Midget Football, Findlay, 1986—; coach Liberty Benton Softball, Findlay, 1986—. Republican. Roman Catholic. Avocations: volleyball, softball, football, camping, fishing. Home: 429 California Ave Findlay OH 45840 Home: Marathon Oil Co 539 S Main Findlay OH 45840

BELLON, ERROL MANFRED, radiologist, educator, researcher; b. Beaufort West, South Africa, May 13, 1938; s. Michael and Roslyn (Sklaar) B.; m. Eveline Morgenstern, Apr. 5, 1962; children—Steven F., Richard J., Jennifer R. M.D., U. Cape Town (South Africa), 1961. Diplomate Am. Bd. Radiology. Intern Groote Schuur Hosp., Cape Town, 1962; resident in radiology Mpilo Central Hosp., Bulawayo, Rhodesia, 1963; resident in radiology Univ. Hosps. Cleve., 1964-67, asst. radiologist, 1967—; chief radiology service VA Hosp., Cleve., 1968-73; assoc. dir. dept. radiology Cuyahoga County Hosp., Cleve., 1973-76, dir. dept. radiology, 1976—; asst. prof. radiology Case Western Res. U., Cleve., 1968-73, assoc. prof., 1973-82, prof., 1982—; surveyor AMA Joint Rev. Com. on Edn. in Radiologic Tech., 1975—. James Picker Found. scholar, 1967-69. Fellow Am. Coll. Radiology; mem. Radiol. Soc. N.Am., Soc. Photo-Optical Instrumentation Engrs., Assn. Univ. Radiologists, Am. Roentgen Ray Soc., Am. Acad. Med. Dirs. Author: Radiologic Interpretation of ERCP: A Clinical Atlas, 1983 also sci. papers. Office: Dept Radiology 3395 Scranton Rd Cleveland OH 44109

BELLOW, SAUL, writer; b. Lachine, Quebec, Can., June 10, 1915; s. Abraham and Liza (Gordon) B.; children: Gregory, Adam, Daniel. Student, U. Chgo., 1933-35; B.S., Northwestern U., 1937, Litt.D., 1962; Litt.D., Bard Coll., 1962, Harvard U., 1972, Yale U., 1972, McGill U., 1973, Brandeis U., 1974, Hebrew Union Coll.-Jewish Inst. Religion, 1976, Trinity Coll., Dublin, Ireland, 1976. Tchr. Pestalozzi-Froebel Tchrs. Coll., Chgo., 1938-42; faculty Princeton, N.Y. U., U. Minn.; faculty English dept. U. Chgo., 1963—, mem. com. on social thought, 1963—, chmn. com. on social thought, 1970-76, now Raymond W. and Martha Hilpert Gruiner Distinguished Services prof.; Tanner lectr. Oxford U. Author: Dangling Man, 1944, The Victim, 1947, The Adventures of Augie March, 1953 (Nat. Book award 1953), Seize the Day, 1956, Henderson the Rain King, 1959, Dessins, 1960, Herzog, 1964 (James L. Dow award 1964, Internat. Lit. prize 1965, Nat book award 1965, Soc. Midland Authors Fiction award 1976), (play) The Last Analysis, 1964, Mosby's Memoirs and Other Stories, 1968, Mr. Sammler's Planet, 1969 (Nat. Book award 1970), The Future of the Moon, 1970, Technology and the Frontiers of Knowledge, 1974, Humboldt's Gift, 1975 (Pulitzer prize 1976), To Jerusalem and Back, 1976, The Dean's December, 1982; short stories Him With His Foot in His Mouth, 1984; contbr.: fiction to Esquire and lit. quarterlies; criticisms appear in New Leader, others; short story to Atlantic's 125th Anniversary Edit., 1982. Decorated Croix de Chevalier des Arts et Lettres France, Comdr. Legion of Honor France; recipient Nat. Inst. Arts and Letters award, 1952; Friends of Lit. Fiction award, 1960; Communicator of Yr. award U. Chgo. Alumni Assn., 1971; Nobel prize for lit., 1976; Medal of Honor for lit. Nat. Arts Club, 1978; O. Henry prize for short story A Silver Dish, 1980; Malaparte Lit. award, 1984; Guggenheim fellow, 1955-56; Ford Found. grantee, 1959-61. Mem. Am. Acad. Arts and Scis. Address: care Com Social Thought Univ of Chicago 1126 E 59th St Chicago IL 60637

BELLOWS, GLEN LEE, consulting engineer; b. Spencer, Iowa, Jan. 9, 1937; s. Glen LeVern and Virginia Irene (Adams) B.; B.S. in M.E., U. Ill., 1959; m. Sylvia Ruth Dean, June 11, 1959; children—Alice, Ann (dec.), Kevin, Peter. Mech. engr. Brown, Manthei, Davis & Mullins, Champaign, Ill., 1959-65; prin., pres. Buchanan, Bellows & Assocs., Ltd., Bloomington, Ill., 1966—; tchr. seminar Am. Mgmt. Assn., 1974. Bd. dirs. McLean County Occupational Devel. Center, 1969-78, treas., 1972-73, 75-78; vice chmn. Bloomington Bldg. Code Rev. Bd., 1972-76; mem. Bloomington Heating and Cooling Bd., 1969-73, Normal (Ill.) Heating and Cooling Bd., 1973—, chmn., 1979—; mem. Nat. Engring. Bd. Cons. First counselor Peoria (Ill.) Stake Mission Presidency, 1987—. Registered profl. engr., Ill, Ind. Mem. ASHRAE, NSPE, Constrn. Specifications Inst. (nat. SPECTEXT com. 1986—), Ill. Soc. Profl. Engrs., Ill. C. of C., Nat. Fire Protection Assn., Delta Sigma Omicron (Harold Sharper service award 1959). Republican. Mormon (ward bishop 1977-84, welfare services region agt. 1984—). Home: 210 Foster Dr Normal IL 61761 Office: 1509 N Clinton Blvd Bloomington IL 61701

BELLOWS, RANDALL TRUEBLOOD, ophthalmologist, educator; b. Chgo., June 1, 1946; s. John D. and Mary Frances (Trueblood) B. B.S., Northwestern U., 1968, M.D., 1971. Intern Los Angeles County-U. So. Calif., 1972; resident U. Fla., Gainesville, 1972-75; practice medicine specializing in eye surgery and diseases Chgo., 1975—; assoc. dir. Am. Soc. Contemporary Medicine, Surgery and Ophthalmology, 1975—; chmn., head dept. surgery Henrotin Hosp., 1981-83. Editor: Glaucoma Jour, Annals of Ophthalmology, Jour. Ocular Therapy and Surgery, Comprehensive Therapy; contbr. chpts. to textbooks, articles to profl. jours. Recipient cert. of competence in ophthalmic practice. Mem. AMA (recognition awards 1981-85), Am. Soc. Contemporary Ophthalmology, Am. Soc. Contemporary Medicine and Surgery, AAAS, Am. Acad. Ophthalmology, Am. Intraocular Implant Soc., Chgo. Med. Soc., Ill. Med. Soc., Chgo. Inst. Medicine, Chgo. Ophthmol. Soc., Pan-Am. Assn. Ophthalmology, Internat. Glaucoma Congress, Internat. Assn. Ocular Surgeons. Office: 233 E Erie #710 Chicago IL 60611

BELLOWS-BLAKELY, DAVID SEWELL, psychiatrist; b. Topeka, Aug. 13, 1951; s. Charles Graham and Audrey Marie (Smith) B.; m. Karen Faye Bellows, July 5, 1976; 1 child, Benjamin Taylor. AB with distinction, Stanford U., 1973; postgrad., U. Kans., 1973-74; MD, U. Kans., Kansas City and Wichita, 1977. Diplomate Am. Bd. Psychiatry and Neurology. Intern, resident then chief resident Stanford (Calif.) U. Dept. Psychiatry, 1977-81; fellow then adv. fellow Austen Riggs Ctr., Stockbridge, Mass., 1981-85; psychiatrist Santa Clara Valley Med. Ctr., San Jose, Calif., 1980-81, Santa Clara County Jail, San Jose, 1981, Berkshire Med. Ctr., Pittsfield, Mass., 1981-85; pvt. practice psychiatry Stockbridge, Mass., 1981-85; mem. psychiat. staff Prarie View, Inc., Newton, Kans., 1985—; cons. psychiatrist Westfield (Mass.) Mental Health Ctr., 1981-82, Westfield Community Support, Mass. Soc. Prevention of Cruelty to Children, 1984-85; cons. staff Axtell Christian Hosp., 1985—, Bethel Deaconess Hosp., 1985—. Mem. AAAS, AMA, Am. Psychiat. Assn., Kans. Psychiat. Soc., N.Y. Acad. Scis., Harvey County Med. Soc. (sec.-treas. 1987—), Audubon Soc., Alpha Sigma Phi (bd. dirs. Tau chpt. 1979-81). Republican. Congregationalist. Avocations: various outdoor and team sports. Home: 1027 E Broadway Newton KS 67114 Office: Prairie View Inc 1901 E First PO Box 467 Newton KS 67114

BELSARE, JAYANT VISHNU, physician; b. Sinnar, India, Dec. 19, 1938; s. Vishnu Govind and Triveni Vishnu (Khaladkar) B.; came to U.S., 1967; M.B., B.S., U. Poona, 1963; M.S., 1966; children—Shubhada, Geeta Nandini. Intern, CPR Hosp., Kolhapur, India, 1962; resident in gen. surgery Sassoon Hosps., Poona, 1963-64, in anesthesia, 1964-65, in orthopedics, 1965; jr. lectr. B.J. Med. Coll., Poona, 1965-66; hon. surgeon Talegaon Gen. Hosp. (India), 1966-67; resident surgery Watts Hosp., Durham, N.C., 1967-69, Johnston Willis Hosp., Richmond, Va., 1969-71; preceptee surgery Surg. Asso., Mason City, Iowa, 1971-72; pvt. practice surgery, Clarinda, Iowa, 1972-73, Mt. Pleasant, Iowa, 1973—; mem. staff Henry County Health Center, Mt. Pleasant, Burlington (Iowa) Med. Center; med. adviser Henry County Cancer Soc. Diplomate Am. Bd. Surgery. Fellow Royal Coll. Surgeons Can.; mem. ACS, Iowa, Henry County med. socs., AMA, Iowa Acad. Surgery, Mt. Pleasant C. of C. Home: 612 N Lincoln Mount Pleasant IA 52641 Office: 114 E Monroe St Mount Pleasant IA 52641

BELSHO, EDWARD, business equipment executive; b. Orange, Ohio, Sept. 27, 1925; s. Vincent and Margaret (Orban) B.; m. Virginia C. Belsho, Mar. 31, 1961. BS in Journalism, Ohio U., 1950. Dir. pub. relations, asst. to pres. Royal-McBee Corp., N.Y.C., 1959-65; gen. mgr. automatic typing div. Litton ind., N.Y.C., 1965-66, v.p. and asst. to office communication equipment group exec., 1966-73; v.p. European ops. Royal Imperial, Leicester, Eng., 1973-75; pres. McBee Binders, Springfield, Mo., 1976—. Served with USN, 1944-46, PTO. Home: 1528 S Forrest Heights Springfield MO 65804 Office: McBee Looseleaf Binders 424 N Cedarbrook Springfield MO 65802

BELTAIRE, BEVERLY ANN, public relations and marketing executive; b. Detroit, Aug. 21, 1926; d. Charles H. and Henrietta (Lucker) Strauss; m. Mark A. Beltaire, Nov. 7, 1947; children: Mark, Jeffrey, Barbara, Suzanne. Student, Highland Community Coll., Highland Park, Mich., 1944-45, Wayne State U., 1946-47. Writer Detroit Free Press, 1945-47; pub. The Skyline mag., Detroit, 1947-55; v.p. Gille Beltaire, Inc., Detroit, 1956-59; women's editor Sta. WXYZ-TV, Detroit, 1956-59; pres. Beltaire, Vincent & Hull, Detroit, 1959-61; pres. and chief exec. officer PR Assocs., Inc., Detroit, 1961—. Mem. Pvt. Industry Council, Gov.'s Commn. Future for Higher Edn.; sec. Mich. Devel. Found., Detroit, Com. of 200; chmn. Leadership Detroit; bd. govs. Greater Mich. Found., Lansing; bd. dirs. Econ. Alliance for Mich., Detroit, Met. Detroit Conv. and Visitors Bur., Detroit Econ. Growth Corp. Named Advt. Woman of Yr., Women's Ad Club, 1978, Mich. Woman of Yr., Am. Lung Assn. Southeastern Mich., 1985; recipient Nat. Clarion award Women in Communications, Inc., 1978. Mem. Pub. Relations Soc. Am. (Silver Anvil award 1972, 83), Women in Communications (Headliner award 1982), Greater Detroit C. of C. (chmn. bd. dirs. 1982-83). Clubs: Adcraft Detroit, Econ. Detroit (exec. bd. dirs.), Detroit, Renaissance; Hunt (Grosse Pointe, Mich.). Home: 1227 Yorkshire Grosse Pointe MI 48230 Office: PR Assocs Inc 1600 Penobscot Bldg Detroit MI 48226

BELTER, EDGAR WILLIAM, clergyman, addiction clinic administrator; b. Guttenberg, Iowa, Jan. 6, 1929; s. Robert Rudolf and Erna Dora (Teegan) B.; B.A., Carthage Coll., 1948, D.D., 1969; M.Div., N.W. Lutheran Theol. Sem., 1951: m. Deloris Ann Koenig, July 10, 1954; children—Timothy William, Christine Ann. Ordained to ministry Lutheran Ch., 1951; pastor Peace Luth. Ch., Steelville, Ill., 1951-57; asst. to pres. Wartburg Synod, United Luth. Ch. in Am., 1958, 59; sr. pastor Emmanuel Luth. Ch., Racine, Wis., 1959-69; pres., exec. dir. A-Center, Racine, 1969—; pres. Good Shepherd Health Systems, 1984—; bd. dirs. Carthage Addiction Inst., 1969-80, Addiction Found., 1984—; chmn. legis. com. Alcohol/Drug Problems Assn. N.Am., 1972—, bd. dirs., chmn. bd. mgrs., council of agys., 1977—; chmn. Gov.'s Task Force Alcohol-Drug Ins., 1970-76, Nat. Invitational Policy Forum on Alcohol/Drugs, 1982—; cons. Nat. Inst. Drug Abuse, S.C. Commn. on Alcohol and Drugs, Wis. Bur. Alcohol and Other Drug Abuse; mem. program rev. com. S.E. Wis. Health Systems Agy.; mem. alcohol/drug adv. com. Mission in N. Am. div. Luth. Ch. Am., 1977-78; dir. Wis.-Upper Mich. Synod, Luth. Ch. Am., Strength for Mission Campaign, 1977-78. Pres. Racine County Mental Health Assn., 1969-72; v.p. Wis. Mental Health Assn., 1972-74. Mem. Alcohol/Drug Problems Assn. N. Am. (treas. 1980—, bd. dirs. 1978-81), Wis. Alcohol Drug Treatment Providers Assn. (pres. 1982-84), Racine Mfg. and Employers Assn. (dir.). Home: 6520 Hoods Creek Rd Franksville WI 53126 Office: Good Shephard Health Systems 2000 Domanik Dr Racine WI 53404

BELTON, JOHN THOMAS, lawyer; b. Yonkers, N.Y., Feb. 24, 1947; s. Harry James and Anne Marie (Kupko) B.; m. Linda Susanne Cheugh, Jan. 6, 1973; 1 child, Joseph Timothy. B.A., Ohio State U., 1972; postgrad. in bus. adminstrn. 1972-73; J.D., Ohio No. U., 1976. Bar: Ohio 1977. Sole practice, Columbus, Ohio, 1976-83; ptnr. Belton, Wherry, Dougherty, Golowin & Cheugh and predecessor firm Belton, Goldwin & Cheugh, Columbus, 1983—; arbitrator Franklin County Ct. Common Pleas, 1983—; dir. Weeks-Finneran Inc. Republican precinct chmn., 1983; v.p. Far Northwest Coalition, 1984; mem. ch. council St. Peter's Parish, 1984—; pres. Dublin youth Athletics, 1985—. Served with USAF, 1968-71. Mem. Dublin Jr. C. of C., ABA, Columbus Bar Assn. (com. chmn. 1976—), U.S. Dist. Ct. Fed. Bar, Ohio Bar Assn., Assn. Trial Lawyers Am., Order of Barristers, Omicron Delta Kappa, Phi Alpha Delta (justice 1975). Clubs: The Pres., Ohio State Alumni, Republican Glee. Republican. Roman Catholic. Lodge: K.C. Avocations: reading; chess; golf; racquetball; recreational activities. Home: 2510 Slateshire Dr Dublin OH 43017 Office: Belton Wherry Dougherty et al 2066 W Henderson Rd Columbus OH 43220

BELTRAN, VIOLETA CENTENO, gynecologist; b. Manila, Philippines, Oct. 18, 1930; came to U.S., 1966; d. Julian D. and Josifina (Domantay) Centeno; widowed; children: Josifina, Pascual, Marcelo, Alberto. AA, U. St. Tomas, Manila, 1949, MD, 1954. Practice medicine specializing in ob-gyn Chgo., 1958—; chmn. dept. ob-gyn Ravenswood Hosp., Chgo. 1986—. Author: Look, I'm Fine Again, 1985. Recipient Annual Pub. Service award Chgo. Med. Soc., 1985. Office: 2256 W Lawrence Ave Chicago IL 60625

BELTT, BRUCE MARSHALL, psychologist; b. Cloquet, Minn., Mar. 24, 1942; s. Rudolph M. and Elsie E. (Penttila) B.; m. Laura Louise Genier, July 14, 1973. BA, U. Chgo., 1964; MA, U. Wis., 1966, PhD, 1970. Lic. psychologist, Minn. Asst. prof. psychology Rensselaer Poly. Inst., Troy, N.Y., 1969-75; chief psychologist Minn. Security Hosp., St. Peter, 1975—; forensic psychologist Minn. Ct. System, 1975—; chmn. instl. research rev. bd. St. Peter Regional Treatment Ctr., 1975—. Mem. Am. Psychol. Assn., Midwestern Psychol. Assn. Avocations: horticulture, mycology, photography, woodworking, contract bridge. Office: Minn Security Hosp Sheppard Dr Saint Peter MN 56082

BELTZ, CHARLES ROBERT, engineer; b. Pitts., Feb. 23, 1913; s. Charles Fred and Ester (Johnston) B.; m. Amy Margaret Ferguson, Oct. 23, 1935; children: Charles R., Mra. A.N. Bonnie Hatch, Homer F., William T., Mrs. Carol E. Marks, Mrs. M. Joy O'Keefe. Student, Greenbrier Mil. Sch., 1930-33; MSE, Cornell U., 1934; MS in Aero. Engring., U. Pitts., 1937. Engr. Crane Co., 1937-39; design engr. Stout Skycraft Corp., 1939-43; project engr. Cycle-Weld Labs., 1943-44; project engr., mgr. Fairchild E&A Corp., Roosevelt Field, 1944-46; corp. engr. Chrysler Corp., 1946-47; pres. Charles R. Beltz & Co., Detroit, 1947-85, Beltz Engring., 1950—, Beltemp, Inc., 1969-81. Author: Ice Skating, Skating Weather or Not, ABC's Air-conditioning, Roatable Aircraft. Mem. English-Speaking Union, Air Force Found., Toledo Zool. Soc., Detroit Sci. Ctr. Mem. Nat. Aero. Assn. (pres.), Air Conditioning Inst. (pres.), Inst. Aero. Scis. (vice chmn.), ASHRAE (contbg. author), Engring. Soc. Detroit, Air Force Assn., Grosse Pointe Hist. Soc. Clubs: Aero (bd. dirs.), Economic, Curling (Detroit); Grosse Pointe Yacht, Grosse Pointe Hunt (Mich.); Lost Lake Woods. Address: 500 Lakeland Ave Grosse Pointe MI 48230

BELZER, FOLKERT OENE, surgeon; b. Soerabaja, Indonesia, Oct. 5, 1930; came to U.S., 1951, naturalized, 1956; s. Peter and Jacoba H. (Gorter) B.; Aug. 4, 1956; children—Ingrid J., John B., G. Eric, Paul O. A.B., Colby Coll., Waterville, Maine, 1953; M.A., Boston U., 1954, M.D., 1958. Diplomate: Am. Bd. Surgery. Intern Grace-New Haven Hosp., 1958-59; asst. resident 1960-62; chief resident U. Oreg. Med. Sch., 1962-63, instr. surgery, 1963-64; asst. research surgeon U. Calif. Med. Center, San Francisco, 1964; asst. prof. surgery U. Calif. Med. Center, 1966-69, asst. prof. ambulatory and community medicine, 1966-69; asst. chief Transplant Service, 1967-69, co-chief, 1969-72, chief, 1972-74, asso. prof. surgery, 1969-72, asso. prof. ambulatory and community medicine, 1969-72, prof. surgery, 1972-74; dir. Exptl. Surgery Labs., 1973-74; sr. lectr. Guys Hosp., London, Eng., 1964-66; prof., chmn. dept. surgery U. Wis., Madison, 1974—. Contbr. articles to med. jours. Recipient Samuel Harvey award as outstanding resident, 1960. Mem. A.C.S., Am., Calif. med. assns., Am. Soc. Transplant Surgeons (pres. 1975), Calif. Soc. Transplant Surgeons (pres. 1970-72), Am., Central surg. assns., Calif. Acad. Medicine, Halsted Soc., C. Naffziger Surg. Soc., Madison Surg. Soc., Pacific Coast Surg. Soc., San Francisco Surg. Soc. (chmn. program com. 1973-74), Wis. surg. socs), Nat. Kidney Found. (vice chmn. com. on dialysis and transplantation 1974-76), Société Internationale de Chirurgie, Soc. Vascular Surgery, Soc. Surg. Chairmen, Soc. U. Surgeons, Surg. Biology Club III, Transplantation Soc., Whipple Soc. Republican. Developed method and machine for human kidney preservation. Home: 6105 S Highlands Dr Madison WI 53705 Office: U Wis Center for Health Scis 600 N Highland Ave Madison WI 53792

BELZER, JEFFREY A., lawyer, automobile dealer and developer; b. Mpls., Sept. 8, 1941; s. Meyer S. and Kathleen (Bardin) B.; B.A., St. Cloud State U., 1963; J.D., Drake U., 1968; children—Steven, Michael, Anna, Jeffrey. Admitted to Minn. bar, 1968, U.S. Dist. Ct. bar., 1969; mem. firm Henretta, Muirhead, McGinty, Ltd., Mpls., 1968-71; pres., sr. atty. Belzer & Brenner Ltd., Mpls., 1971-80; pres., dir. Walesch Devel. Co., Mpls., 1969—, Walsch Estates, Inc., Mpls., 1971—, Jeff Belzer's Todd Chevrolet Inc., Lakeville, Minn., 1980—. Mem. Am., Hennepin County, Minn. bar assns., Phi Alpha Delta. Staff: Drake Law Rev., 1966-67. Office: PO Box 965 Hwy 50 and Cedar Ave Lakeville MN 55044

BEMILLER, JAMES NOBLE, biochemist, educator; b. Evansville, Ind., Apr. 7, 1933; s. LaMar N. and Mabel (Gruber) BeM.; m. Paraskevi Mavridis, Aug. 6, 1960; children: Byron N., Philip J. BS, Purdue U., 1954, MS, 1956, PhD, 1959. Asst. prof. biochemistry Purdue U., 1959-61; asst. prof. biochemistry dept. chemistry and biochemistry So. Ill. U., Carbondale, 1961-65; assoc. prof. So. Ill. U., 1965-68, prof., 1968-85, acting chmn. dept. chemistry and biochemistry, 1966-67; prof. biochemistry So. Ill. U. Sch. Medicine, 1971-85; asst. dean curriculum Sch. Medicine So. Ill. U., 1977-79, dean Coll. Sci., 1976-77, chmn. dept. med. biochemistry, 1980-83; prof. dept. food sci. Purdue U., West Lafayette, Ind., 1986—; dir. Whistler Ctr. for Carbohydrate Research Purdue U., 1986—; Pres. U.S. adv. com. Internat. Carbohydrate Symposia, 1982—. Editor: Industrial Gums, 1959, 73, Methods in Carbohydrate Chemistry, 1-8, 1962—, Starch: Chemistry and Technology, Vols. 1 and 2, 1965, 67, 84; Mem. adv. bd.: Carbohydrate Research, 1971—, Jour. Carbohydrate Chemistry, 1984—, Food Hydrocolloids, 1985—; assoc. editor: Cereal Chemistry, 1975-78. Mem. exec. bd. Egyptian council Boy Scouts Am., 1982-85, pres., 1985; bd. dirs. Luth. Sch. Theology, Chgo., 1967-73, sec., 1971-73; bd. dirs. ACS group ins. trust, 1974-76; bd. dirs. Christ Sem., 1976-79, mem. devel. com., 1979-86; exec. bd. Ill. Synod Luth. Ch. Am., 1978-85. Mem. Am. Chem. Soc. (councilor 1967—), Am. Soc. Biol. Chemists, Am. Assn. Cereal Chemists, AAAS, Soc. for Complex Carbohydrates, Internat. Carbohydrate Orgn. (U.S. rep. 1978—, pres. 1986—), Am. Inst. Chemists (dir. 1982-84, sec. 1985, pres. elect 1986—), Inst. Food Technologists, AAUP, Ill., N.Y. acads sci., TAPPI, Sigma Xi, Alpha Chi Sigma, Alpha Tau Omega. Home: 400 N River Rd Apt 1008 West Lafayette IN 47906 Office: Dept Food Sci Purdue U Smith Hall West Lafayette IN 47907

BEMMANN, KATHRYN CHIZEK, psychiatrist; b. Cato, Wis., Oct. 29, 1931; d. Frank and Celia (Cigler) Chizek; m. Irving Stewart Bemmann, May

3, 1958. BS in Medicine, Marquette U., 1953, MD, 1956. Diplomate Am. Bd. Psychiatry and Neurology. Intern St. Joseph Hosp., Milw., 1956-57; resident Assoc. Tng. Program of Milw., 1958-61; staff physician Milwaukee County Hosp. for Mental Diseases, 1957-58; staff psychiatrist Milw. Psychiat. Hosp., 1961-62; practice medicine specializing in psychiatry, victimology Waukesha, Wis., 1962—; founder, med. dir. Women & Families Clinic, Waukesha, 1978-86; mem. courtesy staff Waukesha Meml. Hosp., 1962—, med. dir. psychiat. unit, 1967-70; asst. clin. prof. Med. Coll. Wis. (formerly Marquette U. Sch. Medicine), Milw., 1964—. Mem. Wis. State Commn. on Status of Women, 1977-78, Women's Ctr., Inc., 1977-81, now mem. adv. bd.; mem. adv. bd. Sexual Assault Treatment Ctr., Family Hosp., Milw., 1976-78, Planned Parenthood of Wis., Waukesha, 1983-86; mem., organizer Victim Services Coordinating Council, Waukesha, 1978-80; chair steering com. Women Students Loan Fund, Med. Coll. Wis., 1986—. Named Outstanding Woman, Coalition of Waukesha County Women's Groups, 1978; recipient Founder's award, U. Wis. Friends and Alumni, Waukesha, 1981. Fellow Am. Psychiat. Assn. (mem. subcom. on edn. of psychiatrists on ethical issues); mem. AMA, Am. Med. Women Assn. (pres. state group Women in Medicine in Wis. 1977-80, bylaws com. chmn. 1986-87), Wis. Psychiat. Assn. (chpt. pres. 1976-77, chmn. com. on women 1977—, chmn. ad hoc work group on edn. of psychiatrists on sexual exploitation of profls. 1985-87), State Med. Soc. of Wis. (founder Com. on Women Physicians 1980-83), Waukesha County Med. Soc., Alpha Sigma Nu. Democrat. Home: 412 N West Ave Waukesha WI 53186 Office: 251 W Broadway Waukesha WI 53186

BENCE, RICHARD, endodontist; b. Milw., July 26, 1943; s. Jerome Anthony and Blanche Theresa (Skroud) B.; m. Dawn Rodman, Dec. 3, 1977; children: Sherri L., Michele, Diana. DDS, Marquette U., 1968; MS, Loyola U., Maywood, 1972. Endodontist Drs. Meyers, Bence and Knoff, S.C., Milw., 1972—; assoc. clin. prof. Marquette U. Sch. Dentistry, Milw., 1972—. Author: Handbook Clinical Endodontics, 1976; contbr. articles to profl. jours. Served to capt. USAF, 1968-70. Mem. ADA, Am. Assn. Endodontists, Wis. Dental Assn., Greater Milw. Dental Assn., Wis. Assn. Endodontists (pres. 1984). Republican. Avocation: pvt. piloting. Home: W325 N 7086 Clearwater Dr Hartland WI 53029 Office: 2600 N Mayfair Rd Milwaukee WI 53226

BENCHIK, EDWARD JOHN (JACK), engineer, geologist, columnist; b. Logansport, Ind., May 25, 1938; s. Edward Andre and Betty Jane (Bowen) B.; m. Rosemary Cecelia Boughal, July 4, 1964; children—Edward Patrick, Jacquelyn Rosemary, Marilyn Cecelia. B.S. in Geology, U. Notre Dame, 1959, postgrad. in law, 1972-73; M.S. in Engring., L.I. U., 1971. Registered instr. Nat. Safety Council. Geologist, NASA Apollo Project, Grumman Aerospace Corp., 1968-71; engring. mgr. Facilities Devel. Corp., 1971-72; mem. staff U. Notre Dame, South Bend, Ind., 1972-73; safety engr. Travelers Ins. Co., Cleve., 1973-77; cons. Safety Engring. Resources, Inc., South Bend, 1977-82; safety dir., risk mgr. City of South Bend (Ind.), 1980—; philatelic writer Cleve. Press, 1975-80. Treas. Mayor's Citizen Traffic Commn. Served with C.E., U.S. Army, 1960-68; maj. Res. and N.G. Recipient Zone Chmn. award Greater Cleve. council Boy Scouts Am., 1976; Apollo Achievement award NASA, 1969; named hon. Ky. Col. Mem. Am. Soc. Safety Engrs. (past pres. Michiana sect.), U. Notre Dame Band Alumni Assn. (pres.), South Bend C. of C. (chmn. safety sect. 1977-79, Nat. Eagle Scout Assn.). Clubs: Elks, Collectors. Editor: The Czechoslovak Specialist, 1969-71. Home: 2104 Rockne Dr South Bend IN 46617 Office: City of South Bend County City Bldg South Bend IN 46601

BENDA, GEORGE JOSEPH, utilities executive; b. Berwyn, Ill., Oct. 12, 1953; s. George Joseph and Jarmilla (Domansky) B.; m. Patricia Lynne Turner, May 16, 1976. BS, Rockford Coll., 1975; MA, U. Chgo., 1977. Asst. to dir. Ill. Dept. of Energy and Natural Resources, Chgo., 1975-79, mgr. coal bond fund program, 1979-81, dir. energy programs, 1981-83; pres. Chelsea Group, Springfield, Ill., 1983-86; regional dir. HEC Energy Corp., Palos Heights, Ill., 1986—; also cons. HEC Energy Corp., Boston; cons. Am. Hosp. Assn., Chgo., 1984-86, Inst. Gas Tech., Chgo. Author: Cost Containment Through Energy Management, 1984, Hospital Energy Management Procedures, 1985, Bar Code Applications In Health Care, 1986. Mem. Am. Mgmt. Assn., Assn. Energy Engrs., Am. Soc. Hosp. Engrs. Avocations: canoeing, camping, building harpsichords, study, writing. Home: 11556 Highwood Dr Palos Park IL 60464 Office: HEC Energy Corp 7330 College Dr Palos Heights IL 60463

BENDA, THOMAS JAMES, otolaryngologist; b. Dubuque, Iowa, Sept. 24, 1926; s. Frank Michael and Elizabeth M. (Sullivan) B.; m. Margaret Ann Connell, Sept. 6, 1952; children: Dennis, John, Anne, Therese, Thomas Jr., Margaret M., Martha, Jane. BS, Loras Coll., 1950; MD, U. Iowa, 1953. Resident U. Iowa, Iowa City, 1957; pres. Dubuque Otolaryngology Head & Neck Surgery, 1957—; clin. assoc. prof. otolaryngology U. Iowa Hosp. Served with USN, 1944-46, PTO. Fellow ACS (councilor 1985—), Am. Neurol. Soc., Am. Acad. Otolaryngology, Am. Laryngol., Otol. and Rhinol. Soc. Republican. Roman Catholic. Avocation: gardening. Home: 1160 S Grandview Ave Dubuque IA 52001 Office: 310 N Grandview Ave Dubuque IA 52001

BENDEL, WILLIAM LOUIS, JR., retired physician; b. Monroe, La., Mar. 1, 1921; s. William Louis and Marie (Gariepy) B.; B.S., Tulane U., 1941, M.D., 1944; Ph.D. in microbiology, Baylor U., 1966; m. Margaret Rose Butler, Feb. 18, 1944 (dec. Jan. 1970); children—Susan Marie, Jan Ann; m. 2d, Kathleen Doris Mabley, Apr. 16, 1971. Intern, Charity Hosp., New Orleans, 1944, resident gen. surgery, 1949-52, resident thoracic surgery, 1952; resident gen. surgery Mt. Carmel Mercy Hosp., Detroit, 1947-48; surgery teaching fellow Tulane U., New Orleans, 1948-49; gen. practice medicine, Monroe, 1953-58; resident pathology Baylor U. Med. Center, Dallas, 1959-63; dir. labs. Unity Hosp., Mpls. Served from 1st lt. to capt., M.C., AUS, 1945-46. Diplomate in anatomic pathology and clin. pathology Am. Bd. Pathology, Am. Bd. Med. Microbiology. Mem. AMA, Minn., Hennepin County med. assns., Holy Name Soc., Alpha Kappa Kappa, Kappa Sigma. Republican. Roman Catholic. Club: K.C. (4 deg.). Contbr. numerous articles to med. jours. Home: 14601 Atrium Way Apt 311 Minnetonka MN 55345

BENDER, BURWYN BOYNE, truck manufacturer; b. Columbus, Ohio, Oct. 2, 1929; s. Alfred Carl and Ethel May (Ryan) B.; m. Evelyn Juanita Roden, May 14, 1955; children: Kathy, Michael, Gregory. BSME, Case Inst. Tech., 1951; MS in Automotive Engring., Chrysler Inst. Tech., 1953; grad. advanced mgmt. program, Harvard U., 1978. Registered profl. engr., Mich. Mgr. advance prodn. planning missile div. Chrysler Corp., Sterling Heights, Mich., 1960-62; mgr., mfg. engr. space div. Chrysler Corp., New Orleans, 1962-68; ops. mgr. missile div. Chrysler Corp., Sterling Heights, 1968-70; v.p., gen. mgr. Cooper Bessemer div. Cooper Industries, Mt. Vernon, Ohio, 1970-80; group v.p. Gulf & Western Mfg. Co., Southfield, Mich., 1980-83; owner, chief exec. officer Ottawa (Kans.) Truck Corp., 1983—. Served with U.S. Army, 1954-56. Mem. Soc. Automotive Engrs. (New Orleans sect. chmn. 1963-65), Computer-Aided Systems Assn. of Soc. Automotive Engrs. (bd. dirs. 1978-80), Machine and Allied Products Inst. (mem. mktg. council 1986—), Soc. Mfg. Engrs. (bd. dirs. 1978-80). Republican. Lodge: Masons. Office: Ottawa Truck Corp 415 E Dundee Ottawa KS 66067

BENDER, CLIFFORD EARL, civil engineer, geotechnical consultant; b. Jamestown, N.Y., May 23, 1935; s. Clifford Lewis and Florence Adeline (Stanton) B.; student Allegheny Coll., 1953-55; B.C.E., Syracuse U., 1962; m. Hildegarde Elsa Groseclose, Aug. 21, 1955; children—William Stanton, Clifford Earl, Jennifer Smiley, Amy Lynette. Project engr. Linde div. Union Carbide Corp., Tonawanda, N.Y., 1963-64, design engr., 1964-66, estimator and cost control, 1966-69; estimator, design engr. Turzillo Contracting Co., Richfield, Ohio, 1969-77, chief engr., chief estimator, 1977-83; geotech. cons., 1983—; assoc. Bender Assocs., P.C.; instr. math. Erie County Tech. Inst.; soils cons. Registered profl. engr., N.Y., Ohio, Minn., Ga., Tex., Fla. Mem. ASCE, Nat. Soc. Profl. Engrs., Ohio Soc. Profl. Engrs. Episcopalian. Home and Office: 1378 Wilbur Rd Medina OH 44256

BENDER, DIANE LOUISE WOLF, lawyer; b. Evansville, Ind, Oct. 21, 1955; d. Thomas Joseph and Margaret Gertrude (Horn) Wolf; m. John Frederick Bender, June 15, 1985. BBA with highest honors, U. Notre Dame, 1977, JD cum laude, 1980. Bar: Ind. 1980. Ptnr. Kahn, Dees, Donovan & Kahn, Evansville, Ind., 1980—. Bd. dirs. Vis. Nurses Assn. of Southwestern Ind., Inc., 1983—, United Way of Southwestern Ind., Inc., 1984—, Health Skills, Inc., Evansville, 1984—, Cath. Press of Evansville, Inc., 1985—. Mem. ABA, Ind. Bar Assn., Evansville Bar Assn., Am. Inst. CPA's, Ill. CPA Soc. Home: PO Box 9164 Evansville IN 47710 Office: Kahn Dees Donovan & Kahn PO Box 3646 Evansville IN 47735-3646

BENDER, ROBERT EDWARD, educator; b. Marion, Ohio, Nov. 7, 1952; s. Walter John and Leona Lucille (Slob) B.; m. Sue Ann Stahr, Dec. 18, 1982. B.S., Ohio State U., 1974, M.S., 1981. With Quality Farm & Fleet, Inc., Marion, Ohio, 1974-76; former Walter J. Bender Farm, Prospect, Ohio, 1974—; sales agt. Bender Ins. Agy., Prospect, 1973—; instr. agrl. edn. River Valley High Sch., Marion, Ohio, 1976—; condr. workshops in field. Adminstrv. bd. Prospect St. United Meth. Ch., 1974—; adviser Future Farmers Am., 1976—. Named Dist. 6 Outstanding Young Vocat.-Agrl. Tchr., 1980-81, Outstanding Tchr. Dist. 3, 1982, Outstanding Young Vocat.-Agr. Tchr., State of Ohio, 1982, others. Mem. Ohio Vocat. Agr. Tchrs. Assn., Nat. Vocat. Agr. Tchrs. Assn., Ohio Vocat. Assn., Am. Vocat. Assn., River Valley Tchrs. Assn., Central Ohio Tchrs. Assn., Marion County Edn. Assn., Ohio Pork Improvement Assn., Marion County Pork Improvement Assn., Farm Bur., Prodn. Credit Assn., Prospect Farmer's Exchange, Am. Soybean Assn., Ohio State U. Alumni Assn., Ohio State U. AES Alumni Assn. Clubs: Ohio Yorkshire, Am. Yorkshire, Moose. Office: 1267 Columbus-Sandusky Rd Marion OH 43302

BENDER, WILLIAM RICHARD, architect; b. Schenectady, N.Y., Dec. 7, 1954; s. John Hughes and Patricia Eloise (Sheppard) B.; m. Mary Gertrude Merdian, Oct. 13, 1979; 1 child, Andrew Jacob. BArch., U. Ill., 1977. Draftsman Young Architects, Bloomington, Ill., 1977-80, Forrest, Capps & Assocs., Jefferson City, Mo., 1980-81, Darrough & Co., Columbia, Mo., 1981; draftsman, project mgr. Melotte-Morse, Springfield, Ill., 1981-86; project mgr. Steckel-Parker, Springfield, 1986. Youth sponser St. Joseph's Cath. Youth Orgn., Chatham, Ill., 1981—; religious edn. tchr. St. Joseph's Cath. Ch., Chatham, 1983-84, 86. Mem. AIA. Avocation: stamp collecting. Office: Steckel-Parker Architects Inc 711 S 5th St Springfield IL 62703

BENEDEK, ELISSA LEAH, psychiatrist; b. Detroit, Sept. 28, 1936; m. Richard S. Benedek; children: David, Joel, Sarah, Dina. Student, U. Mich., 1954-56, MD, 1960. Diplomate Am. Bd. Psychiatry and Nuerology, Am. Bd. Psychiatry and Neurology, Child Psychiatry, Am. Bd. Forensic Psychiatry, Nat. Bd. Med. Examiners. Intern Sinai Hosp., Detroit, 1960-61; resident in gen. psychiatry U. Mich. Neuropsychiat. Inst., Ann Arbor, 1961-63; adminstr. York Woods Ctr., Ypsilanti, Mich., 1966-70, assoc. dir., 1970-73; tng. dir. Forensic Ctr., Ann Arbor, 1974-80, dir. tng., 1980—; clin. prof. psychiatry U. Mich., Ann Arbor, 1979—. Author: Secret Worry, 1984, Child Psychiatry and the Law, 1985; editorial bd. Contemporary Psychaitry. Fellow Am. Psychiat. Assn. (v.p. 1984-85, sec. 1985—, editorial bd. jour. 1980); mem. AMA, Am. Acad. Child Psychiatry, Group for Advancement Psychiatry. Home: 3607 Chatham Way Ann Arbor MI 48105 Office: Ctr Forensic Psychiatry 3501 Willis Ypsilanti MI 48106

BENEDEK, WILLIAM CLARK, utilities executive; b. New Castle, Pa., Mar. 2, 1957; s. Joseph and Virginia Elanor (Murphy) B. BS, Geneva Coll., 1979, BSBA, 1979. Analyst Wis. Bell, Inc., Milw., 1979-84, computer staff analyst, 1984-86, staff analyst end user computing, 1986-87, staff mgr. Info. Ctr., 1987—. Mem. missions com. Elmbrook Ch., Waukesha, Wis., 1986. Republican. Evangelical. Avocations: philately, missions work. Home: 4241 N 67th St Milwaukee WI 53216 Office: Wis Bell Inc ASC-2 733 N Van Buren St Milwaukee WI 53202

BENEDICT, GARY CLARENCE, educational administrator; b. Valley City, N.D., Oct. 22, 1938; s. Clarence Augustus and Mary Rae (Spink) B.; m. Carmen Jean Schreiner, May 29, 1965; children—Andrew Scott, Anne Kathleen. B.E., Wis. State U., 1964; M.S., U. Wis., 1968; Ed.D., Marquette U., 1978. Tchr., New Berlin (Wis.) Pub. Schs., 1960-67; supt. Merton (Wis.) Joint Sch. Dist. 9, 1967-75; dir. curriculum and instrn. Mukwonago (Wis.) Sch. Dist., 1975-84; adminstrv. asst. curriculum Shorewood Sch. Dist., 1984-87; supt. St. Louis Affton Sch. Dist., 1987—; adj. instr. Lakeland Coll., Sheboygan, Wis., 19-. Mem. state adminstrv. com. Democratic Party, 1983; active Mental Health Assn. Waukesha County. Charles F. Kettering Found. fellow, 1981-86. Mem. Am. Assn. Sch. Adminstrs., Nat. Assn. Supervision and Curriculum Devel., Wis. Sch. Pub. Relations Assn. (sec.), Wis. Assn. Supervision and Curriculum Devel., Wis. Assn. Tchr. Educators, Phi Delta Kappa. Contbr. articles in field to profl. jours. Home: 7549 Terri Lynn Dr Saint Louis MO 63123 Office: 8701 MacKenzie Rd Saint Louis MO 63123

BENEDICT, JOSEPH WILLIAM, real estate developer; b. Corning, Ohio, Dec. 28, 1930; s. Joseph and Pauline Caroline (Marolt) B.; m. Myrna Leigh Hester, Oct. 11, 1972; children: Christina, Joseph, Jeffrey. BS, Ohio State U., 1952; MBA, Mich. State U., 1963. Commd. 2d lt. USN, 1952, advanced through grades to comdr., 1966, ret., 1973; pvt. practice real estate broker, developer Columbus, Ohio, 1975—. Mem. Gahanna (Ohio) Community Improvement Corp., 1975—, past pres. Mem. Jefferson Twp. Bus. Assn. Republican. Avocation: farming. Home: 4055 N Waggoner Rd Blacklick OH 43004 Office: PO Box 30846 Gahanna OH 43230

BENEKE, MILDRED (MILLIE) STONG, civic worker, city ofcl., author; b. Prairie City, Iowa; d. Rueben Ira and Lillian (Garber) Stong; student Wash. U., 1942-43; off-campus student U. Minn., Mankato State Coll., 1951-67; m. Arnold W. Beneke, Aug. 10, 1939; children—Bruce Arnold, Paula Rae, Bradford Kent, Cynthia Jane, Lisa Patrice. Exec. sec. chmn. Vol. Services, ARC, St. Paul, 1940-41; v.p. Pi House, St. Paul, 1972—; founder, bd. dirs. chmn. Project Interaction Boutique, Minn. Correctional Instn. for Women, Shakopee, 1971—, supervising vol., 1970—. Bd. dirs. Mpls. Children's Theatre Co. Republican chairwoman McLeod County (Minn.), 1969-73; mem. Rep. Minn. Platform com., 1970; bd. dirs. Buffalo Creek Players, 1975—, v.p., 1980-82; mem. Rep. Feminist Caucus; alderman Glencoe City Council, 1974-80. Glencoe elderly housing named Millie Beneke Manor, 1977. Mem. Dramatists Guild, Glencoe Bus. and Profl. Women (Woman of Yr. 1975). Lutheran. Author: (play) The Garage Sale, 1978; Politics Unusual, 1979; (play) The Househusband and the Working Wife, 1982. Home: 330 Scout Hill Dr Glenview Woods Glencoe MN 55336

BENES, CHARLES JAMES, banker; b. Cleve., May 22, 1904; s. James and Mary (Poskecil) B.; m. Rose AnnaBelle Jankovsky, July 20, 1950; 1 child, Charles J. Student Dyke Coll. Bus., 1919-20. Sec., treas. First Fed. Savs. & Loan Assn., Cleve., 1933-78; bd. dirs. First Fin. Services and Devel. Corp., Cleve., 1st Fed. Savs. Bank. Commr. zoning and planning City of Pepper Pike, Ohio, 1956-69. Mem. Am. Savs. and Loan Inst. (pres. Northeast Ohio chpt. 1951-52). Clubs: Mentor (Ohio) Yachting; Shaker Heights (Ohio) Country. Lodges: Masons (32 degree), Shriners. Home: 29026 Gates Mills Blvd Pepper Pike OH 44124 Office: Park Centre 1255 Superior St Cleveland OH 44114

BENES, SUSAN CARLETON, neuro-ophthalmologist; b. Cleve., Jan. 2, 1948; d. Edward Fulton and Rita Elyse (True) Carleton; m. James David Benes, Dec. 27, 1969; children—Jennifer, David, Olivia. B.S., U. Mich., 1970, cert. tchr., 1969; M.D., Med. Coll. Pa., 1975. Diplomate Am. Bd. Ophthalmology. Resident in internal medicine Lankenau Hosp., Phila., 1975-76; resident in ophthalmology Wills Eye Hosp., Phila., 1976-79, fellow in neuro-ophthalmology, 1979-80, staff physician Wills Eye and Grad. Hosp., 1980-81; lectr. in neuro-ophthalmology Kenyatta U., Nairobi, Kenya, 1980; asst. prof. neuro-ophthalmology Ohio State U., Columbus, 1981—; practice medicine specializing in neuro-ophthalmology, Columbus, 1981—; cons., sugeon Quito, Ecuador, 1985; advisor to undergrads. Ohio State U., 1984-86. Contbr. chpts. to books, articles to profl. jours. Mem. mission council First Community Ch., Columbus, 1982-85; chmn. Youth Council, 1984-87; leader Camp Fire Girls, Columbus, 1983—. Recipient Wakian Service award Camp Fire, Inc., 1986; Outstanding Grad. award Upjohn Co., 1975, diploma Lay Inst. Youth Ministry, 1985-86; grantee NIH, 1984-87. Fellow Am. Acad. Ophthalmology; mem. AMA, Ohio State Med. Assn., Franklin County Med. Soc., Alpha Omega Alpha, Kappa Kappa Gamma.

BENEZRA, E. ELIOT, psychiatrist; b. Istanbul, Turkey, Sept. 3, 1922; came to U.S., 1944; s. Isak and Rachel (Eskenazi) B.; m. Elizabeth Howe, Sept. 15, 1946 (div. 1972); children: Philip, Elizabeth, Thomas; m. Barbara DeBellis, Sept. 2, 1984. BA, Robert Coll., Istanbul, Turkey, 1943; post-grad., Carleton Coll., 1944-45; MD, Northwestern U., 1949. Cert. Am. Bd. Med. Examiners, Am. Bd. Psychiatry. Intern Wesley Meml. Hosp., Chgo., 1949-50; resident psychiatry Menninger Sch. Psychology, Topeka, 1950-51, U. Rochester, N.Y., 1951-53; sr. psychiatrist VA West Side Hosp., Chgo., 1957; chief psychiatrist VA Mental Hygiene Clinic, Chgo., 1958-59; practice medicine specializing psychiatry Elmhurst and Oakbrook, Ill., 1959—; chmn. dept. psychiatry Elmhurst Hosp., 1982-84, co-chmn., 1986, chmn. dept. psychiatry Hinsdale Hosp., 1986—; cons. med. adv. bd. York High Sch., Elmhurst, 1974—. Served to capt. USAF, 1955-57. Fellow Am. Psychiat. Assn. (life); mem. AMA, Dupage Med. Soc., DuPage Mental Health Soc. (pres. 1962-63). Club: Oakbrook Bath and Tennis. Avocations: tennis, swimming, antiques, clocks, African sculpture. Home: 35 Windsor Dr Oakbrook IL 60521 Office: 120 Oakbrook Ctr Oakbrook IL 60521

BENFER, ROBERT ALFRED, JR., anthropologist, educator; b. 1939; married; 1 child. BA in Psychology and Anthropology, U. Tex., 1963, MA in Anthropology and Stats., 1964, PhD in Anthropology, 1968. Asst. prof. anthropology U. Wis., Milw., 1967-69; asst. prof. U. Mo., Columbia, 1969-71, assoc. prof., 1971-77, chmn. dept. anthropology, 1971-75, prof., 1977—, co-dir. human skeletal identification lab., 1980-84; mem. NSF dissertation improvement fellowship com., 1979, chmn. 1980. Contbr. numerous articles to profl. jours. Grantee U. Mo. Research Council, 1970-87, NSF, 1972-74, 76-79, 81-83, Wentworth Found., 1986. Fellow AAAS, Am. Anthrop. Assn.; mem. Cen. States Anthrop. Soc. (exec. bd. 1972-75), Am. Assn. Physical Anthropologists, Soc. Am. Archaeology, Am. Ethnological Soc., Human Biology Council, Sigma Xi, Phi Kappa Phi. Home: 634 Huntridge Columbia MO 65201 Office: U Mo Dept Anthropology Columbia MO 65211

BENFORD, ARTHUR EUGENE, plastics engr.; b. Benton Harbor, Mich., July 21, 1931; s. George Everet and Gladys Irene (Hendrix) B.; student Lake Mich. Coll., 1951, U. Mich., 1952; B.S. in Polymer Chemistry, Western Mich. U., 1957; m. Bernice Irene Kowerdlick, June 29, 1952; children—Lauri Beth, Brice Allen, Blair Ashley. Research materials engr. Whirlpool Research Labs., St. Joseph, Mich., 1956-60, mgr. materials research dept., 1960-72; mgr. plastics research and applications Whirlpool Refrigeration Group, Evansville, Ind., 1972-74, sr. product engr., 1974—. Chmn. Parks Dept., St. Joseph Twp., Mich., 1965-72; mem. Rep. County Commn., 1965-72. Served with U.S. Army, 1952-55. Elected Plastics Pioneer, Plastics Valley Expo, 1987; recipient Elisha Gray award Whirlpool Research Labs. Mem. Research Soc. Am., Soc. Plastics Engrs., Sigma Xi. Lutheran. Patentee, contbr. articles to various publs. Home: Rural Route 7 Box 216B Evansville IN 47712 Office: US 41 North Evansville IN 47727

BENGHIAT, RUSSELL ALAN, advertising agency exective; b. N.Y.C., July 10, 1948; s. Isaac and Pearl (Feld) B.; 1 child, Joshua Laurence. BA in English Lit., Swarthmore Coll., 1970; MS in Advt., U. Ill., 1972. Copywriter Kight, Cowman, Abram, Columbus, Ohio, 1972-73; assoc. creative dir. Johnson & Dean, Grand Rapids, Mich., 1973-76; mktg. analyst FTC, Cleve., 1976-81; v.p. Nicholes & Benghiat Advt., Cleve., 1981-83; pres. Benghiat Advt. and Mktg., Inc., Chesterland, Ohio, 1983-86. Pres. bd. dirs. Cleve. Dancers, 1983; del. Dem. Nat. Convention, San Francisco, 1984. Recipient Nat. Addy award Am. Advt. Fedn., 1974. Democrat. Home and Office: 11284 Caves Rd Kew Farm Chesterland OH 44026

BENJAMIN, HARRISON RUSSELL, computer engineer; b. Hastings, Minn., July 7, 1934; s. Harry Murtice and Florence Elizabeth (Severson) B.; m. Patti Cox, July 16, 1960; children—David, Lisa. BS in Engring. with distinction, U. Minn., 1956, postgrad., 1958. Instr., U. Minn. Inst. Tech., 1957-58; electromech. engr. Gen. Mills electronics div., Mpls., 1958-61; engr. mgr. Control Data Corp., Mpls., 1961-68, dir. engring., 1969-71, gen. mgr. terminal devel. div., 1972-75, gen. mgr. small computer devel. div., 1976, gen. mgr. data systems devel., 1977-80, gen. mgr. microcomputer services, 1981-85; gen. mgr. Tax Filing Services, 1985—; bd. dirs. Elbit Inc., Haifa, 1975-80; Elbit Inc. U.S.A., N.Y.C., 1975-83, Connectype, Mpls., 1982-85. Mem. Com. for Effective Crime Control. Recipient Honor Student award U. Minn. Mem. Territorial Pioneers Assn. Minn., Hort. Soc. (Minn.), Internat. Wood Collectors Soc., Nat. Rifle Assn., Model T Collectors Assn., Minn. Hist. Soc., Dakota County Hist. Soc., Sci. Mus. Minn., Aircraft Owners and Pilots Assn., Minn. Conservation Fedn., Tau Beta Pi. Home: 4805 Eriks Blvd Eagan MN 55122 Office: 8100 34th Ave S Minneapolis MN 55440

BENJAMIN, JAMES COVER, controller, manufacturing company executive; b. Peoria, Ill., Oct. 25, 1952; s. Kenneth Edward and Jane (Cover) B.; m. Catherine Louise Guthrie, June 8, 1974; children: Jennifer, Sara, Eric. BS, U. Ill., 1974. CPA, Wis. Audit sr. mgr. Price Waterhouse, Peoria, Ill., Milw. and London, 1974-86; controller, v.p. Harnischfeger Industries, Brookfield, Wis., 1986—. Mem. Am. Inst. CPA's, Wis. Inst. CPA's, Ill. Inst. CPA's, Financing Exec. Inst. Office: Harnischfeger Industries Inc PO Box 554 Milwaukee WI 53201

BENJAMIN, NEAL B. H., civil engineer; b. Santa Cruz, Calif., Oct. 24, 1934; s. Charles Hugh and Mildred Emily (Neal) B.; m. Mary Louise Schroeder, July 6, 1963; children: Charles Edward, Julia Anne, Kathryn Mary. B.S., U.S. Coast Guard Acad., 1956; B.C.E., Rensselaer Poly. Inst., 1962; M.S.C.E., Stanford U., 1967, Ph.D., 1969. Registered profl. engr., Mo.; registered football official, 1981—. Research asst. Stanford U., 1967-69; asst. prof. civil engring. U. Mo., Columbia, 1969-72; asso. prof. U. Mo., 1972-75, prof., 1975—, Black & Veatch Prof. Engring., 1986—; coordinator Grad. Program in Constrn. Engring. and Mgmt. Contbr. articles to profl. jours. Served in U.S. Coast Guard, 1956-66. Fellow ASCE (exec. com. constrn. div. 1978-82), Nat. Soc. Profl. Engrs., Mo. Soc. Profl. Engrs, Project Mgmt. Inst., Panel Constrn. Arbitrators, Am. Arbitration Assn., Columbia Football Officials Assn. Roman Catholic. Lodge: K.C. Home: 1108 S Glenwood Ave Columbia MO 65203 Office: 1039 Engineering Bldg U Mo Columbia MO 65211

BENJAMIN, ROBERT PAUL, accounting educator; b. Montpelier, Ohio, Dec. 2, 1939; s. Herbert Ray and Velma Irene (Shade) B.; m. Marcia Ann Delong, June 16, 1963; children: Beth, David, John. BBA, Bowling Green State U., 1962; MBA, U. Mich., 1964; M in Acctg., Fla. State U., Tallahassee, 1974. CPA. Staff acct. Arthur Young & Co., Toledo, 1962-63; asst. to div. controller TRW, Inc., Lafayette, Ind., 1964-67; prof. acctg. Catawba Coll., Salisbury, N.C., 1967-77, Marion (Ind.) Coll., 1977-79, Taylor U., Upland, Ind., 1979—. Treas. Jefferson Twp. Baseball Bd. Mem. Am. Inst. CPA's, Nat. Assn. Accts., The Gideons Internat. (sec. N.C. 1970-73, treas. 1974-77, camp. pres. Hartford City 1986-87). Republican. Baptist. Avocations: fishing, miniature golfing. Home: 1301 S 2nd St Upland IN 46989 Office: Taylor U Upland IN 46989

BENJAMINS, DAVID, child neurologist; b. Hart, Mich., July 7, 1941; s. James and Elizabeth (Krum) B.; m. Joyce Ann Livak, Dec. 27, 1964; children: Laura Jane, Mary Elizabeth. BA, Albion Coll., 1958-61; MD, Wayne State U., 1961-65. Diplomate Am. Bd. Psychiatry and Neurology. Asst. prof. pediatrics and neurology Wayne State U., Detroit, 1975-82; med. dir. Detroit Inst. Children, 1985—. Fellow Am. Acad Pediatrics; mem. Am. Acad. Neurology, Child Neurology Soc., Internat. Neuropsychol. Soc., Am. Acad. Cerebral Palsy and Devel. Medicine. Home: 1310 S Oxford Grosse Pointe Woods MI 48236

BENKIN, RICHARD LEE, writer, corporate communications specialist; b. Phila., Oct. 25, 1951; s. Gilbert Joseph and Nancy Marilyn (Ignatin) B.; m. Toby Jane Zallman, May 23, 1976 (div. Dec. 1981); m. Barbara Marie Budnick, May 5, 1984; 1 child, Sarah Elizabeth. BA, MA in Sociology, U. Pa., 1973, PhD in Sociology, 1976. Asst. prof. DePaul U., Chgo., 1975-78; freelance writer Chgo., 1978-80; mental health specialist Ill. Dept. Mental Health, Chgo., 1980-82; long term care cons. Chgo., 1982-83; dir. planning and resident services Calif. Gardens Nursing Ctr., Chgo., 1983-84; v.p. planning and devel. Comp Care Services, Ltd., Lincolnwood, Ill., 1985-87; cons. corp. communications Chgo., 1987—; cons. editor, writer various orgns. Author: Sociology: A Way of Seeing, 1981, Overcoming Powerlessness: The Jews of Eastern Europe, 1985; (play) Love is Not Enough, several film scripts; contbr. articles to profl. jours. Mem. adv. com. State of Ill. on Alzheimer's Disease. Democrat.

BENNER, RICHARD EDWARD, JR., investment consultant; b. Jersey City, Dec. 7, 1932; s. Richard E. and Dorothy (Linstead) B.; children: Linda, Richard III, Christopher. BS, Lehigh U., 1954; postgrad., NYU, 1959-63. Sales exec. IBM Corp, Norwalk, Conn., 1955-58; with Avon Products, Inc., N.Y.C., 1959-78, group v.p. mktg. and internat., 1976-78; exec. v.p. The Fuller Brush Co., Kansas City, Mo., 1979-86; investment cons. Kansas City, Mo., 1987—; bd. dirs. Game Hill, Inc., Westin, Mo. Active Boy Scouts Am., Bergan County, N.J., 1967, Eccumedia, 1987—; maj. corp. com. chmn. United Way, N.Y.C., 1976; Rep. committeeman, Bergan County, 1973. Served with U.S. Army, 1955-57. Mem. Direct Selling Assn. Edn. Found. (bd. dirs. 1982-84). Lutheran. Club: Beaverkill Trout (Livingston Manor, N.Y.) (bd. dirs. 1975-78); Old Pike Country (bd. dirs. 1987). Lodge: Rotary. Avocations: fly fishing, hunting, investing, gardening, piano. Home and office: 4404 NW Normandy Ln Kansas City MO 64116

BENNETT, BLAKE DREW, manufacturers agent, sales executive; b. Kansas City, Kans., Mar. 11, 1960; s. Charles F. and Carol Ann (Troutz) B.; m. Barbara Janel Parent, May 25, 1985; children: Ann Kathleen, Taylor Charles. BS, Fort Hays (Kans.) State U., 1982. Crew material chief Mann Fence Co., Olathe, Kans., 1982-83; salesman Bennett Group, Inc., Overland Park, Kans., 1983—; pres. Imperial Church Interiors, Overland Park, 1983—; salesman Fence Builders Wholesale, Olathe, 1984-85. Mem. Nat. Assn. for Self-Employed, Mfrs. Agents Nat. Assn. Avocations: woodworking, model building. Office: Imperial Church Interiors PO Box 4219 Overland Park KS 66204

BENNETT, BRUCE W., construction company executive, civil engineer; b. St. Joseph, Mo., Dec. 24, 1930; s. Bruce W. and Laura Louella (Clark) B.; m. Barbara Gail Haase, July 26, 1957; children: Stacy Suzanne, Bruce W. B.S. in Civil Engring., U. So. Calif., 1954. Project mgr. George A. Fuller & Co., Chgo., 1956-61; contract mgr. Huber, Hunt & Nichols, Indpls., 1961-70, v.p., 1970-82, exec. v.p., 1982-84, pres., 1984—; dir. Hunt Corp., Indpls. Served to capt. USAF, 1954-57. Mem. Archimedes Circle, David Wilson Assocs., Newcomen Soc. Republican. Clubs: Indpls. Athletic, Skyline (Indpls.). Avocations: tennis; golf. Office: Huber Hunt and Nichols Inc 2450 S Tibbs St Indianapolis IN 46206

BENNETT, DANIEL S(IDNEY), dentist; b. Indpls., Aug. 23, 1949; s. Bertie L. and Mary Jane (Frank) B.; m. Pamela Kay Humble, June 27, 1970; children: Matthew Brandon, Blake Michael. B in Indsl. Engring., Gen. Motors Inst., 1972; DDS, Ind. U., 1978. Indsl. engr. Delco-Remy div. Gen. Motors, Anderson, Ind., 1972-73; gen. practice dentistry Pendleton, Ind., 1978—; dental rep. Madison County AIDS Adv. Task Force, Anderson, 1986—. Lay leader Pendleton First United Meth. Ch., 1986—. Fellow Acad. Gen. Dentistry; mem. ADA, Ind. Dental Assn., Madison County Dental Soc. (pres. 1986—), Am. Soc. Dentistry for Children. Lodge: Optimists (pres. 1986). Avocations: golf, reading, bldg. custom furniture and golf clubs, collecting antiques. Home: R R4 Box 199 Anderson IN 46011 Office: PO Box 213 Pendleton IN 46064

BENNETT, DAVID JOEL, architect, educator; b. N.Y.C., Aug. 25, 1935; s. Jacob and Rose (Rothstein) B.; m. Judith Deutsch, Sept. 8, 1957; 1 child, Sarah Ariel. Student, Cooper Union, 1954-57; B.Arch., U. Minn., 1959. Registered architect, Ariz., Colo., Iowa, Minn., Nebr., Wis., Wyo. Project architect Hammel Green & Abrahamson, Mpls., 1963-65; prin. Myers Anonsen & Bennett, Mpls., 1965-68, Myers & Bennett Architects, Mpls., 1968-73, Bennett-Ringrose-Wolsfeld-Jarvis-Gardner, Inc. (BRW, Inc.), Mpls., 1973—; prof. Sch. Architecture U. Minn., Mpls., 1968—; speaker profl. confs., U.S., Germany, Can. Prin. architect earth sheltered bldgs. Williamson Hall; prin.: earth sheltered bldgs. USAF Visitors Ctr., C-ME Bldg., Walker Library, Ft. Snelling Visitor Ctr.; co-author: Making the Scene, 1970; co-inventor passive solar lighting system; patentee. Rep. Gov.'s Commn. Employment of Handicapped, 1962-63; mem. Minn. High Tech. Council. Recipient award for excellence Design and Environ., 1975; merit award Minn. chpt. Am. Soc. Landscape Architects, 1975, nat. merit award, 1975, award 1977; award Progressive Architecture, 1975, Com. on Urban Design, 1977; nat. award Concrete Reinforcing Steel Inst., 1977, 83; Energy Conservation award Owens-Corning Fiberglass Co., 1980, 82; nat. award Prestressed Concrete Inst., 1982; 1st honor award for concept Design award U.S. Air Force, 1982, Outstanding Civil Engring. Achievement award ASCE, 1983; regional award of merit Twin Cities sect. Illuminating Engring. Soc. N.Am., 1983, lighting design honor award, 1984; renovation of yr. award Nat. Assn. Indsl. and Office Parks, 1985. Fellow AIA (P.A. design award Minn. Soc. 1975, merit award 1975, hon. award 1983). Home: 5715 Clinton Ave S Minneapolis MN 55419 Office: BRW Inc 700 3d St S Minneapolis MN 55415

BENNETT, DAVID SPENCER, publishing executive; b. Chgo., Nov. 17, 1935; s. David Spencer and Edna Virginia (Hewling) B.; m. Charlotte Ann Nalley, Sept. 14, 1957 (div. Mar. 1979); children: Tucker David, Charles Roy, Ward Ross, Spencer Hill; m. Donna Mae Boeser, Feb. 8, 1981. Exec. v.p. Bennett Advt., Harlingen, Tex., 1958-63; account exec. Leo Burnett Advt., Chgo., 1963-65; editor, pub. M-G Publs., Inc., Chgo., 1965-66; exec. dir. mem. services Am. Bus. Press, N.Y.C., 1966-69; mgr. mktg. services Miller Pub. Co., Mpls., 1969-81; gen. mgr. Doane Pub., Control Data Corp., St. Louis, 1981—; bd. dirs. Finan Pub. Co. Co-author: New Heights for Journalism, 1969, A Guide to New Profit Opportunites, 1970; author: The Publication Marketing Plan, 1981. Chmn. Am. Agr. Day, 1973, 1974, 1977; bd. dirs. Kirkwood (mo.) Library. Served to capt, USAFR, 1957-65. Mem. Nat. Agrimarketing Assn. (Dir. 1982-83), Agr. Day Found. (pres. 1979-80), St. Louis Agr. Bus. Club., Sales and Mktg. Execs. (bd. dirs. 1987—). Lodge: Rotary (bd. dir. Webster Groves 1986-87). Avocations: pub. speaking, writing, photography, antiques.

BENNETT, DEANN AUMAN, accountant; b. Baxter Springs, Kans., Dec. 27, 1959; d. Harold Dean and Elizabeth Ann (Dickson) Auman; m. Ross Lee Bennett, Dec. 12, 1981. BBA, Pittsburg State U., 1980. CPA, Kans. Staff acct. Cusack, Mense, Brown & Co., CPA's, Joplin, Mo., 1980-82, Jimmie D. Allen, CPA, Baxter Springs, 1982-85; pvt. practice acctg. Baxter Springs, 1985—. Mem. budget com., bd. dirs. Baxter Springs United Fund, 1987—; mem. Baxter Springs Hist. Soc., 1987. Mem. Am. Inst. CPA's, Kans. Soc. CPA's (pub. relations com. 1986-87), Baxter Springs C. of C. (bd. dirs., treas. 1987). Republican. Avocations: gardening, sewing, swimming, aerobics, exercise. Office: 1004 Military Suite 2 Baxter Springs KS 66713

BENNETT, FOSTER CLYDE, die casting consultant; b. Wilmette, Ill., Oct. 14, 1914; s. Stacy Clyde and Laurine T. (Foster) B.; m. Mary Lou MacPhail, Jan. 12, 1940; children—Donald, William, Tom, Jim, George, Elizabeth, Karen. B.S. in Engring. Physics, U. Ill., 1936; M.S., Calif. Inst. Tech., 1937. Research engr. to assoc. scientist Dow Chem. Co., 1937-72; sr. researcher Battelle Meml. Inst., 1972-81; pres. Die Casting Cons., Inc., Columbus, Ohio, 1981—. Recipient Doehler award Am. Die Casting Inst., 1964; Soc. of Die Casting Engrs. Disting. Life Membership award, 1979; Award of Merit, Am. Foundrymen's Soc., 1962. Mem. Soc. Die Casting Engrs. Republican. Patentee in field; contbr. articles to profl. jours.

BENNETT, JAMES WALTER, veterinarian; b. Glenwood, Minn., Aug. 27, 1956; s. Chester William and Marianne Carolyn (Svec) B. BA in Natural Sci., St. John's U., 1977; BS in Vet. Sci., U. Minn., 1979, DVM, 1981. Staff vet. No. Valley Animal Clinic, Rochester, Minn., 1981—. Mem. Am. Assn. Bovine Practioners, AVMA, Minn. Vet. Med. Assn. (com.), Southeastern Minn. Vet. Med. Assn. (pres. 1983-85), Soc. for Theriogonology. Mem. Democratic Farm Labor Party. Roman Catholic. Club: Nordic Nomads Ski (trails dir. 1986—). Lodge: Lions (sec. Elgin 1986). Avocations: cross country skiing, canoeing, bicycling, backpacking, sports. Home: 205 1st St NW Box 507 Elgin MN 55932 Office: No Valley Animal Clinic 1201 33 St NE Rochester MN 55904

BENNETT, MARGARET ETHEL BOOKER, psychotherapist; b. Spartanburg, S.C., June 15, 1923; d. Paschal and Ovie (Grey) Booker. B.S., N.C. A&T State U., 1944; M.S.W., U. Mich., 1947; Ph.D., Wayne State U., 1980. Caseworker, field instr. Family Services Soc. Met. Detroit, 1947-52; caseworker, field instr., casework supr. Wayne County Cons. Center, 1952-60, Psychiat. Social Service, Wayne County Gen. Hosp., 1960-62; psychotherapist, field instr., asst. dir. Wayne County Mental Health Clinic, 1962-76; asst. dir. psychiat. social service Wayne County Psychiat. Hosp., 1976-77; dir. med. social service Wayne County Gen. Hosp., 1977-78; treatment cons. Project Paradigm; pvt. practice psychotherapy, Detroit, 1965—; psychotherapist, pres. Booker Bennett & Assocs., 1980—; founder Consultation Center of Ecorse, Mich., 1961; instr. Immanuel Luth. Coll., 1944-45; lectr. U. Mich., 1975-76. Bd. dirs. Crossroads, 1980—; exec. council Episcopal Diocese of Mich., 1974-77, 80—, exec. com. 1982—; governing bd. Cathedral Ch. of St. Paul, Detroit, 1971-74, 76-77, 79-82, v.p. governing bd., 1977; bd. dirs. Cathedral Terrace, 1981—, U. Mich. Women, 1982—, Wayne State U. Sch. Social Work Alumni Assn., 1981—. Cert. marriage counselor, cert. social worker, Mich.; cert. Acad. Cert. Social Workers. Fellow Am. Orthopsychiat. Assn.; mem. Mich. Assn. Marriage and Family Therapy, Am. Assn. Marriage and Family Therapy, Mich. Assn. Clin. Social Worker's Nat. Assn. Social Workers, Phi Delta Kappa, Alpha Kappa Alpha. Democrat. Episcopalian. Co-author: The Handbook of Psychodynamic Therapy; contbr. articles to profl. jours. Home and Office: 1971 Glynn Ct Detroit MI 48206

BENNETT, OTES, JR., coal company executive; b. Barbour County, W.Va., July 30, 1921; s. Otes and Bertha (Cozad) B.; m. Naomi Ruth Queen, May 5, 1941; children: Barbara (Mrs. Charles R. Hertzler), Rebecca (Mrs. A.J. Beal), Jeffrey. B.S. in Mining Engring, W.Va. U., 1955. Registered profl. engr., W.Va., Ohio, Pa. With N. Am. Coal Co., Cleve., 1955—, v.p., 1961-65, pres., 1965-70, pres., chief exec. officer, 1970-83, chmn., chief exec. officer, dir., 1983—; chmn. NACCO Industries, Inc., Cleve. Served with USAAF, 1942-45, ETO. Decorated Air medal with 4 oak leaf clusters. Mem. Nat. Coal assn. (dir.). Office: N Am Coal Corp 12800 Shaker Blvd Cleveland OH 44120 *

BENNETT, RICHARD CARL, social worker; b. Eau Claire, Wis., July 25, 1933; s. Ira Anthony and Marion Rhoda (Johnson) B.; B.A., Hamline U., St. Paul, 1955; M.S., George Williams Coll., 1957; M.S. (Lou Hougttellian fellow, Am. Lutheran Ch. fellow), U. Chgo., 1962; postgrad. Loyola U., Chgo., Roosevelt U., Chgo., Forest Inst., Chgo., Alfred Adler Inst., Chgo., Coll. Fin. Planning, Denver; grad. in computer sci. Nat. Radio Inst.,1985; m. Patricia Ann Work, Oct. 27, 1972; children—Matthew, Elizabeth, Kimberly, Timothy. Caseworker, Rock County Welfare Dept., Janesville, Wis., 1957-61; area dir. Luth. Family Service Oreg., Eugene, 1962-67; exec. dir. Family Service Travelers Aid, Fort Worth, 1967-70; mgr. agy. ops. Tarrant County United Way, Fort Worth, 1970-73; mile coordinator Hands Accorss Am., 1986, coordinator Porter County Share Food, 1986—; exec. dir. Luth. Family Service N.W. Ind., Merrillville, 1973-80; exec. v.p. Listening Inc., 1979—; exec. dir. Family Service Assn. Porter County, 1982—; host TV show Life's Dimensions; cons. internat. bd. Parents without Partners; cons. numerous social agys. Served with U.S. Army, 1958-62. Mem. Nat. Assn. Social Workers (dir. Ind. chpt.), Acad. Cert. Social Workers (diplomate in clin. social work), Assn. Marriage and Family Therapists. Author divorce mgmt. materials and newspaper column, profl. manuals; pub. Step Parent News, 1979—; editor: The Business of Social Work, 1983-84. Home and office: 8716 Pine St Gary IN 46403

BENNETT, RICHARD DOUGLAS, electrical engineer; b. St. Louis, Jan. 30, 1948; s. Robert Meyer and Dolores Marie (Wahl) B.; m. Shirley Rae Edwards, May 31, 1969; 1 child, Andrew Douglas. BEE, U. Mo., 1970, MEE, 1979. Registered profl. engr., Mo. Project elec. engr. Burns & McDonnell, Kansas City, Mo., 1974-79; dir. credit union Burns & McDonnell, Kansas City, 1977-79; engr. Lutz, Daily & Brain, Shawnee Mission, Kans., 1979—. Adv. South East High Sch. Explore Post, Kansas City, 1978. Served to lt. USN, 1970-74. Mem. NSPE, IEEE (sr.), Mo. Soc. Profl. Engrs. (sr.), Power Engring Soc. (sec., treas. 1984, vice chmn. 1985, chmn. 1986), U. Mo. Alumni Assn. (life). Avocations: photography, camping, sailing. Home: 206 Landings Circle Lees Summit MO 64064 Office: Lutz Daily & Brain 6400 Glenwood Overland Park KS 66201

BENNETT, ROBERT THOMAS, lawyer, accountant; b. Columbus, Ohio, Feb. 8, 1939; s. Francis Edmund and Mary Catherine (Weiland) B.; B.S., Ohio State U., 1960; J.D., Cleve. Marshall Law Sch., 1967; m. Ruth Ann Dooley, May 30, 1959; children—Robert Thomas, Rose Marie. Admitted to Ohio bar, 1967; C.P.A., Ernst and Ernst, Cleve., 1960-63; with tax assessing dept. Cuyahoga County (Ohio) Auditor's Office, Cleve., 1963-70; mem. firm Bartunek, Bennett, Garofoli and Hill, Cleve., 1975-79; mem. firm Bennett & Klonowski, Cleve., 1979-83; mem. firm Bennett & Harbarger, Cleve., 1983—; mem. bd. Cuyahoga County Port Authority, 1974-80. Exec. vice chmn. Cuyahoga County Rep. orgn. Republican. Roman Catholic. Clubs: Cleve. Athletic, Clevelander, Citizens League; Capitol Hill (Washington). Contbr. articles to profl. publs. Home: 4800 Valley Pkwy Fairview Park OH 44126 Office: 800 Standard Bldg 1370 Ontario St Cleveland OH 44113

BENNETT, WILLIAM EDWARD, service company executive; b. Dayton, Ohio, Apr. 25, 1946; s. Wilbur Marion and Hester E. (Thompson) B.; m. Virginia Louise Pfeifer, Feb. 7, 1970; children: Paul Thomas, William Michael, John Matthew. BA in Bus. Administrn., Coll. St. Thomas, 1968; JD, U. Denver, 1971. Bar: Minn. 1971, Colo. 1971; CPA, Minn. Sole practice Denver, 1971-72; tax specialist, mgr. exec. offices Deloitte Haskins Sells, Mpls., 1972-78; mgr. U.S. tax practice in Europe Deloitte Haskins Sells, London, 1978-81; tax mgr. McGladrey Hendrickson, St. Paul, 1981-82; ptnr. KMG Main Hurdman, Mpls., 1982-85; gen. counsel, treas. I. C. System, Inc., St. Paul, 1985—; pvt. practice tax law and cons. White Bear Lake, Minn., 1985—; instr. acctg. Coll. St. Thomas, St. Paul, 1975-78; bd. dirs. Atrix Tool Co., Burnsville, Minn. Contbr. articles on tax issues to profl. jours. Chmn. fin. com. St. Pius X Cath. Ch., White Bear Lake, 1985—; mem. Founders Club for Senator Dave Durenberger, Mpls., 1986—. Served with USN, 1969. Recipient Conf. Speaker of Yr. U.K. Chartered Accts., 1980. Mem. ABA, Am. Inst. CPA's, Minn. CPA Soc. (chmn. com. 1983-84). Republican. Office: I C System Inc 444 E Hwy 96 Vadnais Heights MN 55110

BENNETT-KASTOR, TINA, linguist; b. La Mesa, Calif., Feb. 8, 1954; d. Clayton Leon and Patricia Jean (Howard) Bennett; B.F.A., Calif. Inst. Arts, 1973; M.A., U. So. Calif., 1976, Ph.D., 1978; m. Frank Sullivan Kastor, Oct. 28, 1979; children—Kristina Rebecca, Patrick Bennett. Teaching asst. linguistics dept. U. So. Calif., 1975-78, research asst., 1975-76; research asso., co-dir. research John Tracy Clinic, Los Angeles, 1977; research cons. R. M. Lencione, U. Calif. Rehab. Center, Los Angeles, 1977; asst. prof. English and linguistics Wichita (Kans.) State U., 1978-87, assoc. prof. 1987. Recipient Wichita State U. research award, 1979-80, 81-82, 85-86. Mem. AAAS, Linguistic Soc. Am., MLA, Am. Speech-Lang.-Hearing Assn., N.Y. Acad. Scis., Children's Audio Service (humanitites advisor 1984—). Episcopalian. Author books; contbr. articles to profl. publs. Home: 115 N Fountain Wichita KS 67208 Office: Dept English Wichita State Univ Wichita KS 67208

BENNINGTON, DONALD LEE, general contractor; b. Martin's Ferry, Ohio, Nov. 26, 1942; s. Wesley Alonzo and Loucille Marjorie (Brown) B.; m. Brenda Sharon Parrish, Mar. 7, 1964; children: Brian Lee, Tawny Lynn. Student, Kent State U., 1961-64. Prin. Donald L. Bennington Contractors, Massillion, Ohio. Democrat. Presbyterian. Lodge: Masons. Avocation: flying. Home: 1047 Brook Ave NW Massillon OH 44646 Office: 3701 Lincoln Way E Massillon OH 44646

BENNINGTON, MARCY MARIE, former school psychologist; b. South Bend, Ind., Feb. 1, 1949; d. John William, Jr. and Constance Dorothy (Weingartner) Truemper; A.B., Ind. U., Bloomington, 1971; M.Ed., U. Mo., St. Louis, 1976; Ph.D. (teaching asst./instr.), St. Louis U., 1981; m. Mark Ian Bennington, Sept. 7, 1968. Adminstrv. asst. Psychol. Service Center, St. Louis, 1974-75; personnel asst. Orchard Corp. Am., St. Louis, 1975-77; sch. psychology intern Pattonville Schs., Maryland Heights, Mo., 1978-79; diagnostician, eval. coordinator Wentzville Schs., Mo., 1979-80, dir. spl. edn., 1980-85. Speaker to community groups. Phi Beta Kappa scholar. Mem. Am. Psychol. Assn., Nat. Assn. Sch. Psychologists, Am. Assn. Counseling and Devel., Council Exceptional Children.

BENNINK, DUANE EARL, association executive; b. Guthrie County, Iowa, July 21, 1935; s. Lawrence D. and Cora M. Bennink; B.S., Iowa State U., 1959; m. Marlene V. Clark, Aug. 24, 1958; children—Karen C., Kathleen J., David D. Vocat. agr. instr. Marathon (Iowa) Consol. Schs., 1959-63; asst. dir. Iowa Soil Conservation Com., Des Moines, 1963-68; cons. N.W. Iowa Farm Bus. Assn., Sheldon, 1968-79; state coordinator Iowa Farm Bus. Assns., Ames, 1979—. Mem. Iowa Soc. Farm Mgrs. and Rural Appraisers, Am. Soc. Farm Mgrs. and Rural Appraisers, Iowa Consultants Assn. (pres. 1975-77), Nat. Assn. Farm Bus. Analysis Specialists (pres. 1979-80), Iowa State U. Alumni Assn. Methodist. Home: 126 Britson Circle Roland IA 50236 Office: Iowa Farm Bus Assns 226 SE 16th St Ames IA 50010

BENO, CAROLYN ELIZABETH, pharmacist, marketing professional; b. Council Bluffs, Iowa, Sept. 2, 1953; d. Adolph Frank Jr. and Gertrude Marie Sophie (Spetman) B. BA, U. Nebr., 1975, BS in Pharmacy, 1976; MS, U. Iowa, 1978; postgrad., U. S.C., 1980—. Asst. prof. pharmacy Temple U., Phila., 1978-80; pharmacist Kroger and Springwood Lake Pharmacies, Columbia, S.C., 1982-84; sr. analyst U.S. pharm. and nutrition group Bristol Myers, Evansville, Ind., 1985—; chmn. drug edn. com. coll. pharmacy U. Nebr., Lincoln, 1973-74; vol. cons. Chem. Dependency Agy. S. W. Iowa, Council Bluffs, 1975-77; vol. pharmacist Iowa City (Iowa) Free Med. Clinic, 1977-78. Contbr. articles to profl. jours. Mem. Am. Pharm. Assn., Alpha Mu Alpha, Kappa Epsilon (co-advisor 1983-84), Phi Lambda Sigma. Republican. Lutheran. Avocations: reading, softball, volleyball, racquetball. Home: 3211 Bellemeade Ave Evansville IN 47715 Office: Bristol Myers US Pharm and Nutrition Group 2404 W Pennsylvania Evansville IN 47721

BENO, THOMAS JOHN, physician; b. Green Bay, Wis., July 17, 1921; s. John Joseph and Dorothy A. (Lurquin) B; m. Louvain Ann Menard, July 9, 1945; children: Barbara, Becky, Thomas, Christopher. BA, St. Norbert Coll., De Pere, Wis., 1943; MD, U. Wis., 1946. Diplomate Am. Bd. Surgery. Intern St. Joseph's Hosp., Marshfield, Wis., 1946-47; resident in gen. surgery Aultman Hosp., Canton, Ohio, 1947-49; resident in gen. and thoracic surgery VA Hosp. and Marquette Med. Coll. Wis., Milw., 1949-52; surgeon Muncie (Ind.) Clinic, 1954-57; surgeon Deckner Clinic, Green Bay, 1957-87, ret., 1987, pres., 1986—. Contbr. articles to profl. jours. Med. dir. civil def. Emergency Govt., Green Bay, 1960—; mem. bd. edn., Green Bay, 1968-74, pres. 1973-74; trustee St. Norbert Coll., 1986—. Served as capt. U.S. Army, 1952-54, Korea. Recipient Vietnam Service Appreciation cert. USAID, 1967, Appreciation cert. Republic of Vietnam, 1967, Appreciation cert. AMA, 1967, Alma Mater award St. Norbert Coll., 1968, Disting. Alumnus award U. Wis. Med. Sch., 1986. Fellow ACS; mem. Wis. Surg. Soc. (pres. 1982-83). Republican. Roman Catholic. Home: 140 St Mary's Blvd Green Bay WI 54301 Office: Deckner Clinic 1751 Deckner Ave Green Bay WI 54302

BENOIT, DONALD ANTHONY, agronomist; b. Beaverville, Ill., May 3, 1936; s. Donald O'Neil and Edith Maude (Giasson) B; m. Susanne Elisabeth Haller, Nov. 9, 1957 (div. Oct. 1975); children: Jeanette M., Jacqueline T., James P., Christine A., John A., Derryl A. (dec.); m. Linda Ruth Grundy, Nov. 3, 1978 (div. Feb. 1984); 1 child, Lorrie. Gen. equivalency diploma, USAF Inst. (Europe), U.S. Army, 1960. Commd. U.S. Army, 1954, advanced through grades to sgt.; communications specialist U.S. Army, Europe, 1954-65; resigned U.S. Army, 1965; fin. cons. Vega & Assocs., Rainy River, Ont., Can., 1965-66; communications specialist Uniroyal, Inc., Joliet, Ill., 1966-68; chmn., chief exec. officer Rainy River L&C, Ltd., 1972-84; chmn, chief exec. officer, investment cons. Agbank, Inc., Baudette, Minn., 1984—. Decorated Army Occupation medal U.S. Army, Germany, 1954, Nat. Def. Service medal, U.S. Army, Europe, 1954, Good Conduct medal, U.S. Army, Continental U.S., 1965. Mem. DAV, Am. Legion. Roman Catholic. Avocations: travel, fishing, wildlife and environmental conservation. Home and Office: AGBANK Inc Box 429 R R #1 Baudette MN 56623-0429

BENSCHNEIDER, DONALD, agricultural products company executive. Pres. Landmark, Inc., Columbus, Ohio. Office: Countrymark Inc 35 E Chestnut St Box 479 Columbus OH 43216 *

BENSHOFF, DIXIE LEE, psychologist; b. Ravenna, Ohio, Apr. 11, 1950; d. Roy Orrison and Pauline (Gatewood) B.; B.A., Hiram Coll., 1972; postgrad. Cambridge (Eng.) U., 1970, 73; M.Ed., Kent State U., 1973, Ph.D., 1977. Counselor, Hiram (Ohio) Coll., 1973; counselor, counseling and group resources center Kent (Ohio) State U., 1973-74, asst. to sch. counseling program for counseling and personnel services edn. dept., 1974-75; asst. dir. Portage County Mental Health Bd., Kent, 1975-78; psychologist, outpatient dir. Kevin Coleman Mental Health Center, Kent, 1978-81; instr. clin. psychology/family medicine Coll. Medicine, Northeastern Ohio U., 1979—; pres. Portage County Council Health and Social Agys., 1980; dir. aftercare and transitional services Western Res. Human Services, Akron, Ohio, 1981—; allied health profl. Akron City Hosp. Diplomate in profl. psychotherapy Internat. Acad. Profl. Counseling and Psychotherapy; lic. psychologist, Ohio. Mem. Am. Psychol. Assn., Ohio Psychol. Assn., Am. Assn. Marriage and Family Therapists (clin.), Kappa Delta Pi. Contbr. articles in field to profl. jours. Home: 1928 Middleton Rd Hudson OH 44236 Office: 1640 Franklin Ave Suite 200-7 Kent OH 44240

BENSON, BARBARA ANN, elementary school teacher; b. Wooster, Ohio, Aug. 22, 1943; d. Eldin Lavon and Rose Isabelle (McBane) Bennett; m. Daryl Gene deNeui, Aug. 14, 1965 (dec. July 1975); children: Michael Robert deNeui, Laura Jeanne deNeui; m. Donald Leroy Benson, June 30, 1979. BA, Sterling Coll., 1965. Cer. tchr.; lic. real estate agent. Tchr. Dubuque (Iowa) Community Sch., 1965-68, Clarksville (Iowa) Community Sch., 1968-69; sec. to bank teller First Nat. Bank, Waverly, Iowa, 1977-86; tchr. Waverly-Shell Rock (Iowa) Schs., 1978—; real estate agent Perpetual Ptnrs., Cedar Falls, Iowa, 1986. Head ednl. div. United Way, Waverly, 1983-84. Mem. NEA, AAUW, Iowa State Edn. Assn., Waverly-Shell Rock Ednl. Assn. (v.p. 1983-84, pres. 1984-85), United Meth. Women. Republican. Methodist. Avocations: reading, traveling, piano. Home: 1512 Hickory Heights Waverly IA 50677 Office: Waverly-Shell Rock Schs 6th St SW Waverly IA 50677

BENSON, BRUCE LEE, protective services official; b. St. Joseph, Mich., June 17, 1947; s. Orval Lee and Viola Clara (Kolberg) B.; m. Margaret Catherine Eads, June 9, 1968 (div. June 1983); children: Rebecca, Daniel; m. Melinda Jo Castleman, Mar. 3, 1984; stepchildren: Shayne Kelley, Gregory Kelley. BS in Police Adminstrn., Mich. State U., 1969, MS in Criminal Justice, 1971; PhD in Adminstrn. and Supervision, U. Mich., 1980. Patrolman Flint (Mich.) Police Dept., 1969-74, police sgt., 1974-77, police lt., 1977-81, dep. chief of police, 1981-86; dir. pub. safety Mich. State U., East Lansing, 1986—; cons. in field; mem. faculty Mich. State U., Saginaw Valley State Coll.; mem. faculty, mem. criminal justice adv. bd. C.S. Mott Community Coll., Flint; mem. adv. bd. Detroit Coll. Bus. Recipient Flint Human Relations award City of Flint, 1979, Spl. Tribute, State Senate of Mich., 1986. Mem. FBI Nat. Acad. Assocs., Mich. Assn. Chiefs Police, Am. Soc. Indsl. Security, Mich. State U. Criminal Justice Alumni Assn. (nat. pres. 1985-86), Crime Prevention Assn. of General County. Lutheran. Lodge: Arrowhead (pres. 1976-77). Avocations: family, travel, reading, basketball, wallyball. Home: 5450 Maple Ridge Dr Haslett MI 48840 Office: Mich State U Dept Public Safety 87 Red Cedar Rd East Lansing MI 48824-1219

BENSON, BYRON OBIE, social worker, educator, entrepreneur; b. Mitchell, S.D., May 20, 1944; s. Bruce LeRoy and Francis May (Hunt) B.; m. Jeanne Claire Earl, Apr. 7, 1966; 1 child, Angela Ann; m. Valorie Jean Dains, Apr. 15, 1983; 1 child, Benjamin Luke. BA, Dakota Wesleyan U., Mitchell, 1966; MSW, U. Nebr., 1973. Lic. social worker, Kans. Tchr. Chamberlain High Sch., S.D., 1967-69; social worker S.D. Dept. Social Services, Rapid City, Mitchell, 1969-74; asst. prof. social work, program dir. Dakota Wesleyan U., Mitchell, 1974-76; family living tchr. Boys Town, Nebr., 1976-79; chief of social services Kans. Social and Rehab. Services, Pratt, 1980-84; dir. Bob Johnson Youth Shelter, Hutchinson, 1985-86; owner RFD Photography; tchr. psychology Pratt Community Coll., Kans., 1981-84, instr. foster parenting Social and Rehab. Services, Kans., 1983-86. V.P. Mental Health Assn., Mitchell, 1973-74, pres., 1974-75. Named one of Outstanding Young Men of Am., 1975. Mem. Child Care Workers Assn., Kans. Foster Parent Assn. Democrat. Lutheran. Club: Ercoup Owners. Avocations: photography, flying, skiing, reading, swimming. Home: 2920 Homestead Rd Hutchinson KS 67502

BENSON, DENNIS KEITH, research consultant b. Dayton, Ohio, Dec. 20, 1946; s. Charles Prue and Virginia Elizabeth (Zindorf) B.; BA, Miami U., 1969; MA (fellow), Ohio State U., 1972, PhD (fellow), 1976; m. Rose Anne Fredericks, Aug. 30, 1969 (div. July, 1986); 1 child, Kristopher Elliott.

Simulation dir. behavioral scis. lab., Ohio State U., Columbus, 1969-73, survey research dir., 1972-73, dep. dir., 1971-73, project dir. Coll. Social Work, 1977; assoc. dir. Benchmark program Acad. for Contemporary Problems, Columbus, 1973-74, dir., 1974-75; v.p., treas. C. C. DeJon, Ltd., Columbus, 1976-78; project dir. Capital U., Columbus, 1977-78; pres., chmn. bd. dirs. Appropriate Solutions, Inc., 1978—; conf. evaluator Am. Soc. Pub. Adminstrn., 1980-81; speaker, cons. in field. Trustees, corr. sec. N.W. Civic Assn., 1972-73; trustee Bus. Council Homebound Disabled Persons; state issues coordinator Ohio Carter Campaign Staff, 1976; mem., chmn. com. Central Ohio Bicentennial Commn., 1975-76. Fellow, Acad. for Contemporary Problems, 1974-75, Nat. Security Edn. Seminar, 1972. Mem. Am. Assn. for Pub. Opinion Research, U.S. Capital Hist. Soc., Columbus Bus. Devel. Club (past pres.), Columbus Area C. of C. (edn. and tng. com. 1981-82). Republican. Mem. Am. Bapt. Ch. Author: Social Area Analysis and State Social Policy Management, 1976; A Needs Assessment Survival Kit, 1978; Voluntary Service: A Study of Potential, 1979. Contbg. author: Simulation and Games, 1972, 73; pub. The Columbus Report, TECHnology NETwork; contbr. articles to profl. jours. Home: 511 Garden Dr Worthington OH 43085-3820 Office: Appropriate Solutions Inc 1357 W Lane Ave Suite 207 Columbus OH 43221-3590

BENSON, GEORGE LEONARD, telecommunications corporation executive; b. Seattle, Sept. 20, 1934; s. George and Gertrude (Rolph) B.; m. Kyleen Susan Gordon, Sept. 22, 1962; children—William, Barbara, Stephen, Kristin, Shanon, Pamela. B.A. in Bus., U. Wash., 1959. Sales rep. Bus. Systems, Inc., Los Angeles, 1959-64, sales mgr., 1964-66; mgr. Pacific div. NCR, San Francisco, Calif., 1966-69; br. mgr., Rochester, Minn., 1969-74, dist. dir., Milw., 1974-78; pres. Telecom North, Inc., Little Chute, Wis., 1979—. Served to sgt. U.S. Army, 1953-55. Mem. No. Wis. Telecom Assn. Republican. Methodist. Avocations: sports; reading; travel. Lodge: Rotary. Home: 6786 Pheasant Run Rd Hartford WI 53027 Office: Telecom N Inc 2301 Kelbe Dr Little Chute WI 54140

BENSON, HARRY C., bank executive. Chmn., chief exec. officer Norwest Bank, Des Moines. Office: Norwest Bank Des Moines NA 7th & Walnut Sts Des Moines IA 50304 *

BENSON, JERRY SANFORD, JR., computer industry executive; b. Syracuse, N.Y., Oct. 8, 1956; s. Jerry Sanford Sr. and Nancy (Burns) B.; m. Stephanie Mizutowicz, Feb. 20, 1982; 1 child, Bethany Rae. BA in Pyschology cum laude, Duke U., 1979. With sales dept. Atlantic RIchfield Oil Co., Waterbury, Conn., 1980-82; executive mktg. and sales Amdek Corp., Chgo., 1982-86; v.p. mktg. NEC Corp., Wood Dale, Ill., 1987—; lectr. Internat. Laser Disc. conf., 1987. Robert L. Flowers scholar Duke U., 1976. Republican. Roman Catholic. Avocations: computer music, painting with watercolors. Home: 35 W Hattendorf Ave Roselle IL 60172 Office: NEC Corp 1255 Michael Dr Wood Dale IL 60191

BENSON, KATHERINE ALICE, psychology educator; b. Mpls., June 12, 1949; d. Gerald Philip and Gladys Irene (Berg) B.; m. James Lyman Staebler, Aug. 8, 1981 (div. Sept. 1986); 1 child, David James. B.S. summa cum laude, U. Minn., 1972; M.S., U. Mass.-Amherst, 1976, Ph.D., 1979. Instr. psychology U. Mass., Amherst, 1977-78; asst. prof. U. Minn., Morris, 1978—. Precinct chmn. Ward 1 Stevens County Democratic-Farmer-Labor Party, 1982-85, dir., 1986—. Grantee Council on Liberal Edn., 1980, U. Minn. Grad. Sch., 1981-83; U. Minn. Grad. Sch. fellow, 1983; Bush Found. sabbatical fellow, 1985-86. Mem. Minn. Commn. on Martin Luther King, Jr., Holiday. Mem. Minn. Women Psychologists, AAAS, Am. Psychol. Assn., Soc. Research in Child Devel., Nat. Women's Studies Assn., NOW (Minn. chpt. adv. bd. 1983-84), Bus. & Profl. Women. Unitarian-Universalist. Contbr. articles to profl. jours. Office: Div Social Sci Univ Minn Morris MN 56267

BENSON, LAWRENCE EDWARD, retired insurance company executive; b. Mpls., July 31, 1916; s. Linus Edward and Hilma Agnita (Olausson) B.; m. Phyllis Elaine Newman, Aug. 23, 1941; children: Laurel, Natalie, Lois, Philip, Kjersti. Student Bethel Coll., 1936-37; BS, U. Minn., 1939. Underwriter, Employers of Wausau, Mpls., 1940-48; underwriting mgr. Federated Mut. Ins. Co., Owatonna, Minn., 1948-50; underwriting mgr. Mut. Service Ins. Co., St. Paul, 1950-56, dir. underwriting, 1956-61, dir. casualty actuarial dept., 1961-72, v.p. personnel, 1972-76, v.p. casualty, 1976-81; dir., chmn. Minn. Ins. Guaranty Fund, Minn. FAIR Plan. Bd. mgmt. YMCA, Mpls., 1955-72, chmn., 1964-66; bd. regents Bethel Coll. and Sem., St. Paul, 1959-64, treas., 1960-62, vice chmn., 1962-64, mem. bd. President's Assos., 1967-83; mem. Minn. Cen.Republican Com., 1966-69; bd. dirs. Minn. Soc. Prevention Blindness, 1973—, United Way, St. Paul, 1973-80. Served with U.S. Army, 1942-46. Recipient service award YMCA, 1963, Bethel Coll. and Sem., 1965, Minn. Central Rep. Com., 1966, also various PTA's; cert. Life Office Mgmt. Assn. Mem. Soc. C.P.C.U.'s (cert.), Am. Acad. Actuaries (cert.), Am. Swedish Inst. Republican. Baptist. Club: Midland Hills Country. Contbr. to ins. publs.

BENSON, RODNEY FREDRICK, chamber of commerce executive; b. Sheldon, Iowa, Jan. 3, 1938; s. Fredrick William and Myrtle (Steen) B.; m. Kay Harlean Halden, Oct. 26, 1963 (div. 1982); children—Darcy, Lisa, Heather, Tricia; m. Carol Roberts, Mar. 5, 1983. B.A., U. Colo., 1961. Cert. chamber exec. Exec. v.p. S. St. Paul C. of C., 1966-67; dist. mgr. U.S. C. of C., Jacksonville, Fla., 1968-69; pres. Kalamazoo County C. of C., Mich., 1970-74, pres. Boulder C. of C., Colo., 1975-80; project mgr. City Venture Corp., Mpls., 1980-81; pres. Ann Arbor Area C. of C., Mich., 1982—; dir. Mich. Tech. Council, Ann Arbor, Mich., 1982—; dir., treas. Tech. Internat. Council, Ann Arbor, 1983—, Washenaw Devel. Council, Ann Arbor, 1983—. Trustee Kalamazoo Valley Community Coll., Mich., 1971-74; regent U.S. C. of C. Insts., Washington, 1973-78; dir. Ann Arbor Summer Festival, 1984-86 . Served with U.S. Army, 1960-61. Mem. Am. C. of C. Execs., Colo. C. of C. Execs. (pres. 1978), Mich. C. of C. Execs. (pres. 1973-74, bd. dir. 1984—). Republican. Avocations: boating; cooking. Office: Ann Arbor Area Chamber Commerce 211 E Huron Suite 1 Ann Arbor MI 48104

BENSON, VERNE HOWARD, insurance executive; b. Lancaster, Ohio, Aug. 4, 1940; s. Starling Edward and Esther Marie (Beck) B.; m. Wanda M. Mahaffey, Aug. 10, 1963 (div. 1987); children: Teresa, Verne Jr., Tonda. BS in Bus. Adminstrn., Ohio State U., 1962. Claims service mgr. E&E Ins., Columbus, Ohio, 1970-72; facilities planning mgr. JC Penney Casualty Ins. Co., Westerville, Ohio, 1972—; instr. gen. ins. Ins. Inst. Am., 1971-80. Served to capt. USAF, 1963-70, Vietnam. Mem. Work Place Environment Group (bd. dirs. 1986—), Office Landscape Users Group (speaker 1979-86). Avocations: walking, swimming, study of comparative religions and philosophies. Home: 28 King Arthur Blvd Westerville OH 43081 Office: JC Penney Casualty Ins Co 800 Brooksedge Blvd Westerville OH 43081

BENT, ALAN EDWARD, political science educator, administrator; b. Shanghai, China, June 22, 1939; s. Walter J. and Tamara (Rocklin) B.; m. Dawn Bickler, Aug. 13, 1977; 1 son by previous marriage, Ronald Geoffrey. B.S., San. Francisco State U., 1963; M.A., U. So. Calif., 1968, Claremont Grad. Sch., 1970; Ph.D., Claremont Grad. Sch., 1971; M.B.A., Xavier U., 1985. Instr. polit. sci. Chapman Coll., Orange, Calif., 1969-70; research assoc. Mcpl. Systems Research, Claremont Grad. Sch., 1970-71; asst. prof. polit. sci., assoc. dir. Inst. Govtl. Studies and Research Memphis State U., 1971-74; assoc. prof., chmn. dept. pub. adminstrn. Calif. State U., Dominguez Hills, 1974-77; prof. polit. sci. U. Cin., 1977-81, 82—, head dept. polit. sci., 1977-81; dean Coll. Arts and Scis. U. No. Colo., Greeley, 1981-82, prof. polit. sci., 1981-82; cons. police agys., govtl. and pvt. instns. Author Escape from Anarchy: A Strategy for Urban Survival, 1972; The Politics of Law Enforcement: Conflict and Power in Urban Communities, 1974, 2d edit., 1976; co-author: Police, Criminal Justice and the Community, 1976, Collective Bargaining in the Public Sector: Labor-Management Relations and Public Policy, 1978; co-editor, contbr. Urban Administration: Management, Politics and Change, 1976, 2d edit. 1977; contbr. articles to profl. jours.; bd. editors: Rev. Pub. Personnel Adminstrn., 1980—, Spectrum, A Jour. of Comparative Politics and Devel., New Delhi, 1984—. Served to capt. USAF, 1964-69. NASPAA fellow, 1981-82. Mem. AAUP. Office: U Cin Dept Polit Sci ML 375 Cincinnati OH 45221

BENTELE, RAYMOND F., corporate executive; b. 1936; (married). B.S., N.E. Mo. State Coll., 1960. Accountant S.D. Leidesdorf & Co., 1960-65; treas., controller Germania Savs. and Loan Assn., 1965-67; with Mallinckrodt, Inc. (became wholly-owned subs. Internat. Mineral and Chem. Corp. 1986), St. Louis, 1967—, asst. controller, 1969-71, controller, 1971-74, v.p., 1974-76, v.p. fin. and adminstrn., 1976-77, v.p. internat. group, 1977-78, sr. v.p., group exec., 1978-79, pres., chief exec. officer, 1979-86; sr. v.p. Internat. Minerals & Chem. Corp., 1986—. Office: care Mallinckrodt Inc 675 MCDonnell Blvd Saint Louis MO 63134

BENTLEY, JAMES HERBERT, electrical engineer; b. Portland, Oreg., May 23, 1935; s. Robert Athy and Helen Louise (Niles) B.; B.S. in Elec. Engring., Mich. Tech. U., 1957; M.S. in Elec. Engring. (Hughes Fellow), U. So. Calif., 1959; m. Elizabeth Anne Willard, Aug. 19, 1958; children—Mary Katherine, John Robert. Elec. engr. Hughes Aircraft Co., Los Angeles, 1957-59, Philco Corp., Palo Alto, Calif., 1960-64, Bendix Corp., Washington, 1964-65, Univac, St. Paul, 1965-68, Honeywell, Inc., Mpls., 1968-76, 3M Co., St. Paul, 1976-79, Magnetic Peripherals, Inc., Mpls., 1979; dir. Ecology Enterprises, Inc.; adj. prof. elec. engring. U. Minn., Mpls. Mem. Edina Planning Commn.; past chmn. Edina Environ. Quality Commn., 1975-76. Recipient Mayor's commendation award City of Edina, 1976; registered profl. engr., Minn. Mem. Nat., Minn. socs. profl. engrs., Tau Beta Pi, Eta Kappa Nu. Presbyterian. Home: 5120 Grove St Edina MN 55436 Office: 5850 Clearwater Dr Minnetonka MN 55343

BENTLEY, JANICE BABB, librarian, retired; b. Phila., Jan. 13, 1933; d. John William and Janice (Whittier) Babb; A.B., U. Ill., 1954, M.S., 1956; Dir. dept. information Nat. Assn. of Real Estate Bds., Chgo., 1956-63; librarian CNA Financial Corp., Chgo., 1963-76, firm Mayer, Brown & Platt, Chgo., 1976-85. Mem. Am. Assn. Law Librarians, Chgo. Assn. Law Libraries (pres. 1978-79), Spl. Libraries Assn. (chmn. housing bldg. and planning sect. 1962-63, chmn. social sci. div. 1965-66, pres. Ill. chpt. 1967-68, chmn. ins. div. 1974-75). Illiniweks (chmn. Chgo. 1959). Author: (with Beverly F. Dordick) Real Estate Information Sources, 1963, Real Estate Appraisal Bibliography, 1965. Home: 405 N Wabash Ave Chicago IL 60611

BENTLEY, THOMAS HORTON, III, construction company executive; b. Milw., Aug. 3, 1946; s. Thomas Horton and Virginia M. (Zivney) B.; B.S. in Bus. Adminstrn., Bucknell U., 1969; m. Sally Lynne Ross, Oct. 9, 1971; children—Todd, Lauren, Kimberly. Sec.-treas. Bentley & Son, Inc., Milw., 1970-83, pres., 1983—, also dir., export mgr., export boxing div., 1969—; pres., owner Bentley Corp. Wis., 1983—; bd. dirs., chmn. legis. com. Associated Gen. Contractors, Milw. chpt., 1972—, Allied Constrn. Employers Asso., 1974—; chmn. Nat. A.G.C. Legis. Network, Wis., 1974—; vice chmn. City of Milw. Bd. of Standards and Appeals. Bd. dirs. Bel Canto Chorus Milw., 1983-84. Mem. Builders Exchange, Asso. Gen. Contractors, Milw. World Trade Assn. (membership chmn. 1987-88), Allied Constrn. Employers Assn. Lutheran. Clubs: Town Tennis, Wis. (bd. dirs. 1985—), Sons of Bosses Internat. (pres. Milw. chpt. 1979-81), Milw. World Trade, Milw. North Shore Racquet. Lodge: Rotary (chmn. Milw. club 1987-88). Office: Mundelein Coll 6363 Sheridan Rd Chicago IL 60660

BENTON, JULIE ANN, hospital administrator; b. Detroit, Dec. 17, 1952; d. George R. and Florence Ella (Evans) B. BS, U. Detroit, 1980; MS, Meharry Med. Coll., 1982. Asst. adminstr. Detroit Receiving Hosp. and U. Health Ctr., 1983-84, 1984—. Com. mem. New Detroit, Inc., 1985—; vol. Presdl. Classroom for Young Ams., Washington, 1985—. Mem. Am. Coll. Healthcare Execs., Nat. Assn. Health Services Execs. (chair nat. membership com. 1984—, treas. Detroit chpt. 1986—), S.E. Mich. Healthcare Execs. Forum, Jr. League of Detroit. Avocations: racquetball, reading, swimming. Office: Detroit Receiving Hosp & U Health Ctr 4201 Saint Antoine Detroit MI 48201

BENTON, PHILIP EGLIN, JR., automobile company executive; b. Charlottesville, Va., Dec. 31, 1928; s. Philip Eglin and Orient (Nichols) B.; m. Mary Ann Zadosko, May 23, 1974; children: Katherine Benton Harris, Deborah A., Cynthia Benton Nelson, Philip Eglin, III, Paula R. AB in Econs. and Math. magna cum laude, Dartmouth Coll., 1952; MBA in Fin. with highest distinction, Amos Tuck Sch., 1953. With Ford Motor Co., 1953—; v.p. truck ops. Ford of Europe Detroit, 1977-79; v.p. N.Am. Auto Ops., Detroit, 1979-81, v.p. sales ops., 1981-85; exec. v.p. diversified products N.Am. Auto Ops., Dearborn, Mich., 1985-86; exec. v.p. Ford Internat. Automotive Ops. Ford Motor Co., Dearborn, Mich., 1986—. Trustee Tabor Acad., Marion, Mass., Mich. Opera Theatre; bd. dirs. United Found.; mem. Pres.'s Soc., The Edison Inst., Founders Soc., Detroit Inst. Arts; bd. overseers Amos Tuck Sch. Bus. Adminstrn.; exec. com./. vice chmn. Meadow Brook. Served with USMCR, 1946-48. Mem. Am. Inst. for Contemporary German Studies (bd. dirs.), Detroit Hist. Soc. (trustee), Detroit Zool. Soc. Clubs: Bloomfield Hills (Mich.) Country; Grosse Pointe (Mich.); Dartmouth (Detroit). Office: Ford Motor Company The American Rd Dearborn MI 48121

BENTON, TIMOTHY THOMAS, cattle rancher; b. Kansas City, Mo., Oct. 25, 1948; s. Thomas R. and Arlene (Marcum) B. BAgr, Kans. State U., Manhattan, 1970. Registered cattle breeder. Owner Hillhouse Angus Ranch, Garnett, Kans., 1971—; cons. profl. farm mgmt. Farm Mgmt. Assn., Kans City, 1986—; judge numerous county and regional beef cattle exhibitions, 1971—. Beef cattle supt. Anderson County Fair, Garnett, 1980—; chmn. Anderson County Dave Owen for Gov. Commn., 1982. Served with Kans. Army N.G., 1971-77. Mem. Nat. Cattleman's Assn., Am. Angus Assn., Kans. Angus Assn. (bd. dirs. 1983-85), Kans. Livestock Assn. (bd. dirs. 1976-80), Anderson County Farm Bur. (pres. 1981-82). Repbulican. Mem. Independent Full Gospel. Avocations: softball, basketball, gospel music. Home: Rt 2 Garnett KS 66032 Office: Farm Mgmt Assocs 1009 Baltimore Kansas City MO 64105

BENTROTT, ELENOR JANE, teacher; b. Baldwin, Iowa, Apr. 1, 1934; d. Christian F. and Julia Dorothea (Schroeder) B.; m. Dwane Henry Bentrott, Dec. 27, 1952; Children: Diane, Randy, Brent, Terri. Student, Clinton Community Coll., 1967-69; Ba, Marycrest Coll., Davenport, Iowa, 1972; postgrad., U. Iowa. Cert. tchr. Tchr. math. Wheatland (Iowa) Community Sch., 1972—. Mem. NEA, ISEA, Wheatland Edn. Assn. (pres.), Nat. Council Tchrs. of Math, Iowa Council tchrs. of Math (pres. 1986, Presdl. award 1984). Republican. Lutheran. Avocations: reading, swimming, biking, golfing, travel. Home: Box 186 Lost Nation IA 52254 Office: Calamus-Wheatland High Sch Dept Math Box 278 Wheatland IA 52777

BENTZEL, CHARLES HOWARD, business executive; b. Balt., July 30, 1928; s. Reece Emory and Idel Burton; m. Wandalee Baer, July 27, 1947; children: Brent, Alan, Leslie. B.A., U. Balt., 1952, B.S., 1962; D.Comml. Sci., London Inst. Applied Research, 1973; Vice pres., chief fin. officer Roblin Industries, Inc., N.Y.C., 1968-69; v.p., dir. fin., controller ITT and subs., N.Y.C. and abroad, 1969-76; v.p., chief fin. officer Trane Co., Wis., 1976-79, Iscott, Trinidad, 1980-82; pres., chief exec. officer Serverance Ref. Lab., San Antonio, 1982-84, also dir.; pres., chief exec. officer Foam Cutting Engrs., Inc., Addison, Ill., 1984—; also bd. dirs.; dir. Data Terminals Corp. Contbg. author : The Modern Accountants Handbook, 1973. Bd. dirs. YMCA, Wis., 1976-79. Mem. Internat. Assn. Fin. Execs. Insts. (bd. dirs.), Brazilian Fin. Execs. Inst. (hon., life mem.), Fin. Execs. Inst., Am. Acctg. Assn., Nat. Assn. Accts., Internat. Treas. Assn. Republican. Clubs: N.Y. Athletic, Marco Polo, Fair Oaks Golf and Country, Plaza, Ariel House. Lodge: Masons (Md., Argentina, Brazil). Home: 25632 Drake Rd Barrington IL 60010

BENZ, JOHN DOUGLAS, architect; b. Sheffield, Iowa, May 7, 1937; s. Lester G. and Marguerite (Held) B.; m. Diana J. Baker, Dec. 21, 1958; children: Philip Andrew, Mary Elizabeth. BArch, Iowa State U., 1962. Registered architect, Iowa, Colo., Calif., Nebr., N.Mex., Fla., Ala., Wis., N.J., Conn., Md. Architect Durrant Group, Dubuque, Iowa, 1961-66; prin., v.p. Hansen Lind Meyer, Iowa City, 1966—. Archtl. works include: Iowa City Pub. Library, 1982, Green Hills, Ames, Iowa, 1985, Harrogate Community, Lakewood, N.J., 1984, Rose Med. Ctr., Denver, 1985, North Oaks Community, Balt., 1985, Essex (Conn.) Meadows, 1986. Mem. AIA, Soc. of Mktg. Profl. Services, Am. Assn. Homes for Aged, Soc. Am. Mil. Engrs., Constrn. Specialization Inst. (mem. forum for healthcare planning). Republican. Methodist. Clubs: Order of Knoll (Ames); Univ. Iowa Presidents, Univ. Athletic (Iowa City). Lodge: Rotary. Home: Rt 6 Iowa City IA 52240 Office: Hansen Lind Meyer Drawer 310 Iowa City IA 52244

BENZ, JON, data processing executive; b. Milw., Mar. 11, 1939; s. Erwin and Marie (Fritsche) B.; m. Yvonne Ann Mansavage, May 14, 1966; children: Dawn Elizabeth, Victoria Jean. BS in Mgmt., Cardinal Stritch U., 1984. Various tech. positions Wis. Telephone Co., Milw., 1957-67, programmer, analyst, 1967-77, dir. record mgr., 1977-80; mgr. data peocessing edn. Bucyrus-Eric, South Milwaukee, Wis., 1980-83; sr. systems analyst First Wis. Nat. Bank, Milw., 1983—; cons. Personal Devel. Systems, Menomonee Falls, Wis., 1976—. treas. Milw. Marriage Encounter, 1980-82; trustee Village Bd. Menomonee Falls, 1980-84; active Menomonee Falls Zoning Bd. Appeals, Housing Authority. Served with U.S. Army, 1959-62. Mem. Data Processing Assn., Am. Banking Exec. Republican. Roman Catholic. Avocations: public speaking, writing, reading, photography. Home: N87 W 17728 Shepherd Dr Menomonee Falls WI 53051 Office: First Wis Nat Bank 777 E Wisconsin Ave Milwaukee WI 53202

BENZ, LINDA LOU, academic adminstrator; b. Carbondale, Ill., Sept. 9, 1957; d. Homer A. and Marguerite (Stief) B. BS, So. Ill. U., 1979, MS, 1984. Office mgr. Coll. Edn. So. Ill. U., 1979-81, office mgr. Research Inst., 1981—. Sec., team capt. United Way, Carbondale, Ill., 1985—. Named one of Outstanding Young Women Am., 1982, 83, 84. Mem. Bus. and Profl. Women's Orgn. (v.p., networking chmn. 1986—), So. Ill. U. Alumni Assn. (sec. Jackson County 1984—), Delta Pi Epsilon (sec. corresponding 1985—). Avocations: reading, travel, exercising. Home: 1433 E Walnut 9C Carbondale IL 62901 Office: So Ill U Instl Research Studies Faner Hall 2179 Carbondale IL 62901

BENZ, THOMAS E., federal agency administrator; b. Kampsville, Ill., Oct. 21, 1943; s. Arthur J. Benz; m. Mary Joan Stelbrink, July 3, 1965; children: Sherri, Cindy, Laura. BS, So. Ill. U., 1966. Asst. county supr. Farmers Home Adminstrn., Carlinville, Ill., 1966-68; county supr. Farmers Home Adminstrn., Carrollton, Ill., 1968—. Mem. Carrollton Community Sch. Dist. Bd., 1981-85, adv. bd. St. Johns Cath. Ch., Carrollton, 1983-85, adv. com. Lewis and Clark Jr. Coll., Godfrey, Ill., 1985—. Mem. County Suprs. Assn., Ducks Unltd. (treas. Twin Rivers chpt. 1982-85, pres. 1985). Lodge: KC. Home: Rural Rt #1 Kane IL 62054 Office: Farmers Home Adminstrn Rural Rt #3 Box 129B Carrollton IL 62016

BENZON, HONORIO TABAL, anesthesiologist; b. Ilocos Sur, Philippines, Sept. 12, 1946; came to U.S., 1972, s. Alejo Gonzales and Concepcion Tacto (Tabal) B.; B.S., Far Eastern U., Manila, 1966, M.D., 1971; m. Julieta Palpal-latoc, May 30, 1970; children—Barbara Hazel, Hubert Anthony. Intern, Overlook Hosp., Summit, N.J., 1972-73; resident in anesthesia U. Cin. Med. Center, 1973-75, Northwestern U. affiliated hosps., 1975-76; practice medicine specializing in anesthesiology, Chgo., 1976—; assoc. prof. dept. anesthesia Northwestern U. Med. Sch., 1985—, asst. prof., 1980-85 ; assoc. staff Northwestern Meml. Hosp., 1976-82, attending staff, 1982—; attending staff VA Lakeside Hosp., 1976—; attending staff Brigham and Women's Hosp., 1985-86;instr. dept. anesthesia Harvard Med. Sch., 1985-86; cons. staff Rehab. Inst. Chgo. Diplomate Am. Bd. Anesthesiology. Fellow Am. Coll. Anesthesiologists; mem. AMA, Am. Soc. Anesthesiologists, Internat. Anesthesia Research Soc., Am. Soc. Regional Anesthesia. Roman Catholic. Contbr. numerous articles to med. jours., chpts. to books. Home: 1150 White Mountain Dr Northbrook IL 60062 Office: 303 E Chicago Ave Chicago IL 60611

BERCAW, BEVERLY ANN, bank executive; b. Pontiac, Mich.; d. Owen Mitchell and Luanna (Spaller) Jones; m. Allan McLain Bercaw, July 30, 1976; children: Walter Mitchell, Laurie Anne. AS in Computer Sci., Lawrence Inst. Tech., 1978; BS in Mgmt., Oakland U., Rochester, Mich., 1980. Systems analyst Chrysler Corp., Highland Park, Mich., 1963-80; sr. systems analyst RAMS Coop., Madison Heights, Mich., 1980-83; project mgr. Mfgs. Nat. Bank, Detroit, 1983—; instr., lectr. Lawrence Inst. Tech., Southfield, 1981—. Mem. Data Processing Mgmt. Assn., Tau Iota. Home: 4437 Yanich Dr Troy MI 48098 Office: Mfrs Nat Bank 17177 N Laurel Park Dr Suite 390 Livonia MI 41852-2659

BERDAHL, CLARENCE ARTHUR, educator; b. Baltic, S.D., June 14, 1890; s. Anders J. and Karen (Otterness) B.; A.B., St. Olaf Coll. 1914, LL.D., 1958; A.M., U. S.D., 1917, LL.D., 1961; Ph.D. (fellow), U. Ill., 1917-20; m. Evelyn Tripp, June 9, 1926. Clk. archives div. War Dept., Washington, 1914-15; asst. in periodicals div. Library of Congress, 1916; instr. polit. sci. U. Ill., 1920-22, asso., 1922-25, asst. prof., 1925-29, asso. prof., 1929-30, prof., 1930-61, prof. emeritus dept. polit sci., 1961—, chmn. div. social scis., 1935-39, chmn. dept. polit. sci., 1942-48; tchr. summers U. Tex., 1920, Tulane U., 1921, Ohio State U., 1923, U. Colo., 1928, Syracuse U., 1929, Columbia U., 1934, Stanford U., 1950; lectr. L'Institut Universitaire de Hautes Etudes Internationales, Geneva, 1932; vis. prof. govt. So. Ill. U., 1958-67; vis. prof. polit. sci. U. Del., 1965; chmn. bd. editors Ill. Studies in Social Scis., 1941-52; cons. U.S. Dept. State 1942-45; on London staff Office Strategic Services, 1944; mem. Internat. Secretariat, UN Conf., San Francisco, 1945; adv. com. on fgn. relations Dept. State, 1957-64, chmn., 1963-64, cons. hist. office, summer 1961; mem. exec. com. Commn. To Study Orgn. of Peace, 1953—; mem. European Conf. Tchrs. Internat. Law and Relations, Carnegie Endowment for Internat. Peace, summer 1926. Served in inf. U.S. Army, 1918. Social Sci. Research Council grantee for study abroad, 1931-32. Mem. Am. Polit. Sci. Assn. (exec. council 1932-35, 3d v.p. 1939, 2d v.p. 1944), Norwegian-Am. Hist. Assn., Am. Soc. Pub. Adminstrn. (council 1944-47), Ill. Hist. Soc., Midwest Polit. Sci. Assn. (pres. 1957-58), Am. Soc. Internat. Law (exec. council 1939-42, 43-46, 52-54), Fgn. Policy Assn., Soc. Advancement of Scandinavian Study, Geneva Research Center (adv. com. 1932-36), Conf. Tchrs. Internat. Law and Related Subjects (exec. com. 1933-42, 47-50), Internat. Studies Assn. (adv. com. 1965-69), Phi Beta Kappa (book award com. Ralph Waldo Emerson award 1966-68). Clubs: Univ., Cosmos (Washington). Author or co-author books including: War Powers of the Executive in the United States, 1921; The Policy of the United States with Respect to the League of Nations, 1932; Aspects of American Government, 1950; Toward a More Responsible Two-Party System, 1950; Presidential Nominating Politics, 1952; also articles. Home: Clark-Lindsey Village 101 W Windsor Rd Apt 4105 Urbana IL 61801

BERDASCO, JACK ALAN, chemical executive; b. San Juan, P.R., Oct. 3, 1958; s. Jack and Gloria Maria (Alvarez) B.; m. Nancy Anne McMichael, May 21, 1982. BS, U. Tampa, 1979; PhD, N.C. State U., 1983. Technician Caribbean Refrescos Inc., San Juan, 1976-77; sr. research chemist Dow Chem. Co., Midland, Mich., 1983-86, project leader, 1986—. Fellow NSF, 1979-82. Mem. Am. Chem. Soc., Sigma Xi, Phi Kappa Phi, Phi Lampa Upsilon. Avocations: cross country skiing, bowling, photography. Office: Dow Chem Co Polymeric Materials Research Ctr 574 Bldg Midland MI 48667

BERENBERG, DANNY BOB, restaurateur; b. Mpls., Sept. 10, 1944; s. Morris and Theresa Clara B.; m. Christina Ann Thompson, Sept. 10, 1977; children—Jake Robert, Jena Thompson. B.A., U. Minn., 1966; J.D., 1970. Bar: Minn. 1970, U.S. Supreme Ct. 1976. Mem. firm Schermer, Schwappach, Borkon & Ramstead, Mpls., 1970-75; mgr. Lincoln Dels Restaurants, Bloomington, Minn., 1975-77, sr. exec., 1981—; vice chmn. Lincoln Baking Co., 1981—, Lincoln Dels Inc., 1981—. Founder Kaiser Roll Found. and Kaiser Roll, wheelcair and able-bodied race; bd. dirs. Bloomington Hospitality Assn.; founder S.W. Hospitality Assn.; founder, pres., bd. dirs. 494 Ministry, 1982—; mem. Minn. Conv. Facility Comm., 1984—, Minn. Internat. Trade Commn., 1984—. Served to 1st lt. AUS, 1968. Named Bloomington Man of Yr., Bloomington mag. 1982, Small Bus. of Yr. award, 1982; recipient Teamsters Law Enforcement Recognition award, 1982, merit award Minn. N.G., 1982; Omar Bonderud-Human Rights award City of Bloomington, 1983, Minn. Human Rights award, 1985, Good Neighbor award WCCO, 1986, Disting. Community Citizen award March of Dimes, 1986. Mem. Conv. Bur. (dir.), Minn. Restaurant Assn., Hennepin County Bar Assn., Minn. Bar Assn., Norwegian Home Guard Friends (founder). Jewish.

BERENDT, WILLIAM EDWARD, manufacturing company executive; b. Chgo., June 18, 1943; s. Alex and Ethel (Tryon) B.; m. Marilynn Carita Hess, Apr. 15, 1965; children: Marc Alexander, Lisa Marie. BS in Acctg., No. Ill. U., 1966, MBA, 1985. Acctg. mgr. GTE, Automatic Electric, Northlake, Ill., 1966-72; controller Beloit Passavant, Birmingham, Ala., 1972-73; div. controller Control Data Corp., Mpls., 1973-74; exec. v.p. Atlantic India Rubber, Chgo., 1974-78; owner, pres. Web Assocs., Arlington

Heights, Ill., 1979-81; chief operating officer Triple-A-Specialty Co., Chgo., 1981—, also bd. dirs.; ptnr. Kalman Investments, Chgo., 1986—. Chmn. bd. dirs. northwest suburbs Am. Cancer Soc., 1986-87. Avocations: woodworking, radio control airplanes, golf. Home: 1157 S Chestnut Arlington Heights IL 60005

BERENS, EUGENE JOHN, accounting executive; b. Dubuque, Iowa, May 24, 1946; s. Eugene John and Marcella Grace (Saville) B.; m. Barbara Ann Kiely, Aug. 2, 1975. BA, Loras Coll., 1968; MBA, Loyola U., Chgo., 1979; MS in Taxation, De Paul U., 1986. CPA, Ill. Sr. auditor Arthur Andersen & Co., Chgo., 1968-76; corp. controller Anadite, Inc., Chgo., 1976-82; asst. controller Sun-Diamond Growers, Stockton, Calif., 1982-83; treas. Cashco Oil Co., Chgo., 1983—. Served with U.S. Army, 1968-70, Vietnam. Mem. Am. Inst. CPA's, Ill. CPA Soc. Avocations: tennis, skiing, travel. Home: 651 W Sheridan 6D Chicago IL 60613 Office: Cashco Oil Co 141 W Jackson Suite 3900 Chicago IL 60613

BERENT, STANLEY, psychologist, educator; b. Norfolk, Va., Mar. 10, 1941; s. David and Esther (Laibstain) B.; m. V. Joy McKeever; children: Melissa Virginia, Alison Renée, Rachel Irene. BS, Old Dominion U., 1966; MS, Va. Commonwealth U., 1967; PhD, Rutgers U., 1972. Diplomate Am. Bd. Profl. Psychology. Prof. U. Va., Charlottesville, 1972-79, U. Mich., Ann Arbor, 1979—; chief of psychology, VA Med. Ctr., Ann Arbor, 1979-85. Contbr. over 50 articles to profl. jours. Bd. dirs. Arbor Hills Assn., 1986—. Served with USMC, 1959-63. Fellow Am. Psychol. Assn.; mem. Assn. Advancement Sci., Neurosci. Soc., Am. Epilepsy Soc. Office: U Mich Hosps Box 0840 Med Inn Bldg Suite 480 Ann Arbor MI 48109

BERES, MICHAEL JOHN, plant facilities engineer; b. Gary, Ind., June 26, 1950; s. Edward Kenneth and Joan Marie (Petrovich) B.; m. Susan Eileen Heminger, Oct. 26, 1973; children: Amanda Eileen, Matthew James. AAS, Purdue U., 1972, BS, 1973. Registered profl. engr., Ill. Estimator, field engr. J.M. Foster, Inc., Gary, 1973-74; civil engr. Brown & Root, Inc., Oakbrook, Ill., 1974-76; field piping engr. Dedelow, Inc., Gary, 1977; plant facilities engr. Reynolds Metals Co., McCook, Ill., 1977—. Team leader Dupage County Pub. Action to Deliver Shelter, Downers Grove, Ill., 1985-86. Roman Catholic. Club: Reynolds Golf League (McCook) (pres.). Avocation: golf. Achievements: Pioneered the use of "Thermiser Energy System Dampers" in radiant tube furnaces in the aluminum industry. Furnaces can be adjusted to reduce load cycle time up to 27% or reduce fuel consumption by 20%. Home: 4210 Highland Ave Downers Grove IL 60515 Office: Reynolds Metals Co 1st Ave and 47th St McCook IL 60525

BEREUTER, DOUGLAS KENT, congressman; b. York, Nebr., Oct. 6, 1939; s. Rupert Wesley and Evelyn Gladys (Tonn) B.; m. Louise Meyer, June 1, 1962; children: Eric David, Kirk Daniel. BA, U. Nebr., 1961; M. in City Planning, Harvard U., 1966, M.P.A., 1973; postgrad., Eagleton Inst. Politics, 1975. Urban planner HUD, San Francisco, 1965-66; dir. div. state and urban affairs Dept. Econ. Devel., 1967-68, state planning dir., 1968-69; dir., coordinator fed.-state relations Nebr. State Govt., 1969-71, urban planning cons., 1971-78; assoc. prof. U. Nebr., Kans. State U., 1973-78; mem. Nebr. Legislature, 1975-78; mem. 96th-100th congresses from 1st Nebr. Dist., 1979—, mem. com. on fgn. affairs, com. on banking, fin. and urban affairs com., select com. on hunger, Nat. Agrl. Export Commn., 1984-85; chmn. standing com. on urban devel. Nat. Conf. State Legislatures, 1976-78; mem. Nebr. State Crime Commn., 1969-71. Served as officer U.S. Army, 1963-65. Mem. Am. Planning Assn., Phi Beta Kappa, Sigma Xi. Republican. Lutheran. Office: 2446 Rayburn House Office Bldg Washington DC 20515

BERG, B(LAINE) RICHARD, association executive; b. Los Angeles, Dec. 21, 1932; s. Henry Clemenson and Winifred Chisholm (Carr) B.; m. Jean Stewart, Apr. 7, 1956; children—Scott Richard, Gregory Stewart. B.A., Calif. State U.-Fresno, 1954; M.S., Boston U., 1957; Ph.D., St. Louis U., 1972. Newspaper reporter Bakersfield Californian and Fresno (Calif.) Bee, 1953-54; dir. pub. relations Crippled Children's Soc. Los Angeles County, 1957-60; dir. pub. info. Occidental Coll., Los Angeles, 1960-63; dir. pub. relations George Washington U., Washington, 1963-65; dir. pub. info. Smithsonian Instn., Washington, 1965-67; v.p. Lindenwood Coll., St. Charles, Mo., 1967-78, Brilliant Builders, Inc., Brentwood, Mo., 1978-80; sr. v.p. communications United Way of Greater St. Louis, 1980—. Bd. dirs. UN Assn. Greater St. Louis, Indsl. Devel. Corp., St. Charles County; mem. coordinating council Presbytery of Giddings-Lovejoy; chmn. Arts and Letters Commn. University City (Mo.). Served with U.S. Army, 1954-56. Mem. Pub. Relations Soc. Am. (v.p. St. Louis chpt.). Club: Nat. Press (Washington). Home: 7103 Waterman Ave University City MO 63130 Office: United Way Greater St Louis 915 Olive St Saint Louis MO 63101

BERG, DOUGLAS JAMES, teacher; b. Wichita Falls, Tex., Mar. 26, 1943; s. James W. and Norma V. (Williams) B.; m. Marlene M. Malkush, Oct. 18, 1968; 1 child, Charles Russell. BS, St. Cloud (Minn.) State U., 1965, MA in English, 1973. Cert. tchr. (life), Minn., vocat. tchr., Minn. Tchr., coordinator Minnetonka (Minn.) High Sch., 1965—; bd. dirs. Nexus, Inc., Eden Prairie, Minn.; cons. Boy Scouts Am., Minnetonka, 1985—. Recipient Service award Nexus, Inc., 1983. Mem. NEA, Minn. Edn. Assn., Minnetonka Edn. Assn., Sierra Club, Exptl. Edn. Assn., Minn. Assn. of Alternative Programs. Avocations: cross-country skiing, canoeing, backpacking, bicycling, running. Home: 4230 Jefferson St Excelsior MN 55331 Office: Minnetonka High Sch Mini-Sch Program 18301 Hwy #7 Minnetonka MN 55345

BERG, EVELYNNE MARIE, geography educator; b. Chgo.; d. Clarence Martin and Mildred (Strnad) B.; B.S. with honors, U. Ill., 1954; M.A., Northwestern U., 1959. Geography editor Am. Peoples Ency., Chgo., 1955-57; social studies tchr. Hammond (Ind.) Tech.-Vocat. High Sch., 1958-59; geography tchr. Carl Schurz High Sch., Chgo., 1960-66; faculty geography Morton Coll., Cicero, Ill., 1966—. Asst. leader Cicero council Girl Scouts U.S.A., 1951-53; mem. Greater Chgo. Citizenship Council. Fulbright scholar, Brazil, 1964; NSF scholar, 1963, 65, 71-72; NDEA fellow, 1968-69; fellow Faculty Inst. S. and S.E. Asia, 1980; NEH scholar DePaul U., 1984; recipient award Ill. Geog. Soc., 1977. Fellow Nat. Council Geog. Edn. (state coordinator 1973-74, exec. bd. 1973-77); mem. Nat., Ill. (sec.-treas. 1968-69, sec. 1969-70, v.p. 1970-71, pres. 1971-72), De Paul U., Chgo. (exec. bd. 1980-84, sec. 1984—) geog. socs., Am. Overseas Educators (sec. Ill. chpt. 1974-76, v.p. chpt. 1977-78), AAUW (Chgo. br. rec. sec. 1963-65), Assn. Am. Geographers, Ill., Chgo. acads. sci., AAAS (scholar 1973-74), Nat. Assn. Geology Tchrs., Ill. Council Social Studies, Geol. Socl. Am., Ill. Community Coll. Faculty Assn. (v.p. membership and del. affairs 1982-84), Sierra Club, Sigma Xi, Gamma Theta Upsilon, Delta Kappa Gamma. Clubs: Order Eastern Star, Bus. and Profl. Women's (acting pres. 1980-81). Contbr. to profl. jours. Home: 3924 N Pioneer Ave Chicago IL 60634 Office: Morton Coll 3801 S Central Ave Cicero IL 60650

BERG, JAMES BRUCE, accountant; b. Ontario, Wis., May 1, 1946; m. Kathryn Berg, June 3, 1967; children: Melissa, Michael. BA, U. Wis., LaCrosse, 1968; MBA, U. Wis., Madison, 1972. CPA, Wis. Acct. McGladrey, Janesville, Wis., 1973-76; med. mgr. Janesville Ortho, 1976-83, Hampton RDS Ortho, Newport News, Va., 1983-84; med. auditor Blue Cross-Minn., St. Paul, 1985—. Served to sgt. U.S. Army, 1968-71, Vietnam. Mem. Am. Inst. CPA's, Wis. Inst. CPA's. Baptist.

BERG, JOHN PAUL, container manufacturing company executive; b. Grasston, Minn., Apr. 16, 1920; s. Alf F. and Mary Berg; student U. Minn., 1946-50; m. Helen Berg, June 19, 1941; children—Barbara, Roxanne. Chief indsl. engr. Kickernick Inc., Mpls., 1946-57; indsl. engr. Greif Bros., St. Paul, 1957-62, mgr. mfg., 1962-70, v.p., div. gen. mgr., 1970-79, pres., 1979—. Served to capt. AUS, 1942-46. Mem. Paper Shipping Sack Assn. (past pres.). Roman Catholic. Rotarian. Office: Greif Bros Corp 621 Pennsylvania Ave Delaware OH 43015 *

BERG, KENNY ROBERT, agricultural products company executive; b. Livingston, Wis., Sept. 10, 1935; s. Lelan O. and Kathryn Grace (Coombs) B.; m. Jeanne L. Matousek, June 16, 1956; children: Kelly, Tony, Julie, Lisa, Cory, Kim. Grad., Cobb High Sch., 1953. Dist. mgr. Wis. Liquid Feed Inc., Dodgeville, 1958-65, exec. v.p., 1965-77; pres. Quality Liquid Feed Inc., Dodgeville, 1977—. Served with U.S. Army, 1954-56, with Res. Mem. Am. Feed Industry Assn. (bd. dirs. liquid feed div.), Dodgeville C. of C. Office: Quality Liquid Feeds Inc Hwy 23 N Box 44 Dodgeville WI 53533

BERG, MICHAEL CLEMENS, printing company executive; b. Mannheim, Fed. Republic Germany, Oct. 9, 1935; came to U.S., 1939; s. Kurt N. and Marie H. (Hirsch) B.; m. Patricia D. Wetherald, Nov. 28, 1953 (div. Oct. 1984); children: Cathrine M., Debborah A., Michael C., Jr., William K. Student, Hamline U., 1953-54, U. Minn., 1955-59. Service work Shell Oil Co., St. Paul, 1952-61; with art and direct mail Honeywell, Inc., 1954-63; v.p. sales Tech. Pub., Inc., Mpls., 1963-68; pres. Michael C. Berg Assoc., Mpls., 1968—, Hoppe Printing Co., Mpls., 1971—; chmn. bd. Swenko Research, Mpls., 1961-81; bd. dirs. Intran Corp., Mpls. Contbr. articles to tech. jours. Active Rep. Presdl. Task Force, Washington, 1982-86; Ellis Island Found., Inc., N.Y.C., 1985-86. Mem. Chgo. Art Inst., Crossings Condominium Assn. (chmn. bd. 1982—), Port Superior Marina Assn. (chmn. bd. 1984-85). Lutheran. Lodges: Joppa, Zuhrah Shrine Temple. Avocations: fishing, hunting, boating, flying, travel, hotels. Home: 121 Washington Ave S Minneapolis MN 55401 Office: Berg Industries 108 Washington Minneapolis MN 55401

BERG, NORBERT R., computer company executive; b. 1932. BA, St. John's U., 1955; MA, U. Minn., 1957. Asst. to pres. Esso Research and Engrng. Co., 1957-59; with Control Data Corp., Mpls., 1959—, supr., 1959-62, dir. adminstrn. computer group, 1962-65, corp. dir. adminstrv. personnel, 1965-67, v.p. adminstrv. personnel, 1967-70, chmn. bd. dirs., 1970—. Served to lt. AUS, 1951-53. Office: Control Data Corp 8100 34th Ave S Minneapolis MN 55440 *

BERG, REBECCA ANNE, accountant; b. Marshalltown, Iowa, June 21, 1957; d. Charles Robert and Maxine Eloise (Tuffree) B. AA in Acctg., Marshalltown Area Community Coll., 1977; BA in Acctg., U. No. Iowa, 1982. CPA, Iowa. Acct. research and devel. div. Chamberlain Mfg. Corp., Waterloo, Iowa, 1981-82; sr. tax acct. Duchossois Industries, Elmhurst, Ill., 1982-84; with tax staff McGladrey, Hendrickson & Pullen, Mason City, Iowa, 1984-87; controller Omega Cabinets (Bertch Wood Specialties), Waterloo, Iowa, 1987—. Mem. Am. Inst. CPA's, Nat. Assn. Accts., Inst. Mgmt. Accts., Iowa Soc. CPA's. Home: 640 Lunar Ln Waterloo IA 50701 Office: Omega Cabinets 1205 Peters Dr WAterloo IA 50703

BERG, ROBERT STURE, data base administrator; b. Chgo., May 15, 1948; s. Sture John and Josephine Marie (Pitrowski) B.; student U. Ill., Chgo., 1966-68; B.S., U. Ky., 1970. Programmer, U.S. Air Force, Wright Patterson AFB, Ohio, 1970-73, computer specialist, 1973-75; computer specialist VA Hosp., Hines, Ill., 1976; systems analyst Ill. Bell Tel. Co., Chgo., 1976-79; sr. analyst/cons. Gould Inc., Rolling Meadows, Ill., 1979-80; data base adminstr., staff analyst/software support Ill. Bell Telephone Co., Chgo., 1980-85; mgr. data base Northwestern Meml. Hosp., 1985-87, W.W. Grainger, Niles, Ill., 1987—. Mem. William Ferris Chorale, Chgo., 1982-85, Grant Park Symphony, Chgo., 1983. Home: 4455 N Malden Apt 2 Chicago IL 60640 Office: W W Grainger 7300 N Melvina Niles IL 60648

BERG, STANTON ONEAL, firearms and ballistics cons.; b. Barron, Wis., June 14, 1928; s. Thomas C. and Ellen Florence (Nedland) Silbaugh; student U. Wis., 1949-50; LL.B., LaSalle Extension U., 1951; postgrad. U. Minn., 1960-69; qualified as ct. expert witness in ballistics various cts.; m. June K. Rolstad, Aug. 16, 1952; children—David M., Daniel L., Susan E., Julie L. Claim rep. State Farm Ins. Co., Mpls., Hibbing and Duluth, Minn., 1952-57, claim supt., 1957-66, divisional claim supt., 1966-70; firearms cons., Mpls., 1961—; regional mgr. State Farm Fire and Casualty Co., St. Paul, 1970-84; bd. dirs. Am. Bd. Forensic Firearm and Tool Mark Examiners, 1980—; instr. home firearms safety, Mpls.; cons. to Sporting Arms and Ammunition Mfrs. Inst.; internat. lectr. on forensic ballistics. Adv. bd. Milton Helpern Internat. Center for Forensic Scis., 1975—; mem. bd. cons. Inst. Applied Sci., Chgo.; cons. for re-exam. of ballistics evidence in Sirhan case Superior Ct. Los Angeles, 1975; mem. Nat. Forensic Ctr., 1979, internat. study group in forensic scis., 1985; chmn. internat. symposiums on forensic ballistics, Edinburgh, Scotland, 1972, Zurich, 1975, Bergen, Norway, 1981. Served with CIC, AUS, 1948-52. Fellow Am. Acad. Forensic Sci.; mem. Assn. of Firearm and Tool Mark Examiners (exec. council 1970-71, Distinguished Mem. and Key Man award 1972, exam. and standards com., spl. honors award 1976, nat. peer group on cert. of firearms examiners 1978—), Forensic Sci. Soc., Soc., Internat. Assn. Forensic Scis., Internat. Assn. Forensic Scis., Internat. Assn. for Identification (mem. firearms subcom. of sci. and practice com. 1961-74, chmn. firearm subcom. 1964-66, 69-70), Firearms Western Conf. Criminal and Civil Problems (sci. adv. com.), Am. Ordinance Assn., Nat. Rifle Assn., Minn. Weapons, Internat. Cartridge collectors assns. Contbg. editor Am. Rifleman mag., 1973-84; mem. editorial bd. Internat. Microform Jour. Legal Medicine and Forensic Sciences, 1979—, Jour. Forensic Medicine and Pathology, 1979—; contbr. articles on firearms and forensic ballistics to profl. publs. Address: 6025 Gardena Ln NE Minneapolis MN 55432

BERGAN, JOSEPH ANTHONY, surgeon; b. South Bend, Ind., Mar. 30, 1920; s. William N. and Ellen (Hagerty) B.; m. Marvada Ann French, May 16, 1953; children—Bridget, Joseph, Patrick, Mary, Susan, Thomas, James, George, Peter. B.S., U. Notre Dame, 1942; M.D., Loyola U., 1945. Diplomate Am. Bd. Surgery. Chief surgery St. Anthony Hosp., Michigan City, Ind., 1967-69, 1974-76, pres. staff, 1969-70; practice medicine specializing in surgery Michigan City, 1949—. Served to capt. U.S. Army, M.C., 1946-48. Fellow Internat. Coll. Surgeons, Pan Pacific Surg. Assn., Am. Geriatric Soc.; mem. AMA, Ind. State Med. Assn. Roman Catholic. Clubs: Serra (pres. 1959-60), Notre Dame (pres. 1957-58) (Michigan City). Home: 422 Marquette Trail Michigan City IN 46360 Office: 217 W Homer St Michigan City IN 46360

BERGE, ROBERT ALLEN, fashion apparel company executive, marketing consultant; b. Detroit, Apr. 28, 1952; s. Joseph Andrew and Marion Rose (Wilfinger) B. BS, Eastern Mich. U., 1974; MA, U. Detroit, 1980. Sales rep. Prentice-Hall, Inc., Englewood Cliffs, N.J., 1974-75, Amoco Oil Co., Chgo., 1975-76, 3M Co., St. Paul, 1976-81, Compugraphic Corp., Wilmington, Mass., 1983-86; pres., chief exec. officer Bergé Ltd., Southfield, Mich., 1985—; mktg. cons. Delta Concepts Unltd., Inc., Southfield, 1979—. Editor/pub. (profl. newsletter) Image and Style, 1986. Republican. Roman Catholic. Avocations: physical fitness, photography, reading trade and professional publications. Home: 19827 W 12 Mile Rd #240 Southfield MI 48076 Office: 4000 Town Ctr Suite 675 Southfield MI 48075

BERGEN, M(ARCELENE) BETSY, sociology and family relations educator; b. Carbondale, Kans., May 12, 1928; d. Walter Thomas and Aleatha Mae (Tyner) Clark; m. D.E. Moberly, Aug. 30, 1947 (div. 1966); children: Joe, Alan; m. Gerald Roy Bergen, June 30, 1967. BA, Ottawa U., 1949; MS, Kans. State U., 1964, PhD, 1972. Tchr. human sexuality and family relationships Kanopolis (Kans.) Pub. Schs., 1949-56, St. John (Kans.) Pub. Schs., 1956-65; faculty Kans. State U., Manhattan, 1965—; pvt. practice counseling and therapy, Topeka, 1972—. Author: A Century of Family Living, 1976. Named Outstanding Instr., Kans. State U., 1969. Mem. Nat. Council Family Relations, Soc. for Sci. Study Sex, Am. Assn. Sex Edn., Counseling and Therapy (cert.), Kans. Counseling Family Relations (pres. 1983-84), Assn. Couples for Marriage Enrichment (leader), Delta Kappa Gamma (pres. 1976-80, Internat. scholarship 1971). Republican. Methodist. Avocation: quilting. Home: 5732 SW 33d Topeka KS 66614 Office: Kans State U 309 Justin Hall Manhattan KS 66506

BERGEN, MICHAEL WILLIAM, teacher; b. Fond du Lac, Wis., Oct. 26, 1942; s. William Francis Bergen and Jeannette Frances (Kostuch) Jagdfeld. BA in Philosophy, St. Joseph Coll., 1965; MA in Theology, St. Anthony Seminary, 1967; cert. English, Colo. Coll., 1977. Instr. St. Mary Springs Acad., Fond du lac, Wis., 1966-68, Xavier High Sch., Appleton, Wis., 1968-73, Roosevelt Jr. High Sch., Appleton, 1973-74, Appleton High Sch. East, 1975—; film instr. Lawrence U., Appleton, 1976, co-op tchr. 1969-86; co-op tchr. U. Wis., Oshkosh, 1980. Mem. Wis. High Sch. Forensic Assn., Nat. Council Teachers English, Nat. Forensic League, VFW (adv. voice of democracy 1975—). Democrat. Roman Catholic. Avocations: acting, directing local theater groups. Home: 1625 S Telulah Ave Appleton WI 54915 Office: Appleton High Sch 2121 Emmers Dr Appleton WI 54915

BERGEN, THOMAS JOSEPH, lawyer, nursing home executive, association executive; b. Prairie du Chien, Wis., Feb. 7, 1913; s. Thomas Joseph and Emma Marilla (Grelle) B.; m. Jean Loraine Bowler, May 29, 1941 (dec. Aug. 1972); children—Kathleen Bergen McElwee, Eileen Bergen Bednarz, Patricia Bergen Buss, Thomas Joseph, Patrick Joseph, John Joseph. Student, U. Wis., 1930-32; J.D., Marquette U., 1937, postgrad., 1937-38. Bar: Wis. 1937, U.S. Supreme Ct. 1972. Practice law Milw., 1937—; exec. sec. Wis. Assn. Nursing Homes, 1957-71; legal counsel, exec. dir. Am. Coll. Nursing Home Adminstrs., Milw., 1967-68; sec., dir. Bayside Nursing Home, Milw., 1967—; pres., dir. N.W. Med. Ctrs., Inc., Milw., 1968—, Northland Med. Ctrs., Inc., Milw., 1968—; treas., exec. dir. Nat. Geriatrics Soc., Milw., 1971—; pres. Sen. Joseph R. McCarthy Found., Inc., 1983, pres. bd. dirs., 1979—; mem. program planning com. Nat. Conf. on Aging, del. to conf., 1974; panel speaker Nat. Justice Found. Conv., 1974. Editor: Silver Threads, Wis. Assn. Nursing Homes publ., 1963-71, News Letter, Am. Coll. Nursing Home Adminstrs., 1967-68; Views and News, Nat. Geriatrics Soc., 1971—; mem. editorial bd. Educational Gerontology, 1973-85; contbr. articles to nursing home publs. Bd. dirs., treas. Nat. Geriatrics Ednl. Soc., 1971—; bd. dirs., pres. Wis. Justice Found., 1971—. Served with AUS, 1943, 44. Recipient Merit award Wis. Assn. Nursing Homes, 1962, Outstanding Leadership award Nat. Geriatrics Soc., 1976. Mem. ABA, Wis. Bar Assn., Milw. Bar Assn. (pres., exec. dir.), Real Estate Profls. Assn. (pres. 1974—), Am. Med. Writers Assn., Delta Theta Phi, Delta Sigma Rho. Roman Catholic. Home: 10324 W Vienna Ave Wauwatosa WI 53222 Office: 212 W Wisconsin Ave Milwaukee WI 53203

BERGER, CYNTHIA MARIE, financial analyst; b. El Campo, Tex., Aug. 5, 1958; d. Leon J. Berger and Clara C. (Leopold) Bruemmer. AAS, Wharton (Tex.) County Jr. Coll., 1978; BBA, U. Houston, 1980; MBA, N.Mex. State U., 1985. CPA, Tex., Minn. Acct. The El Paso Co., Houston, 1981-83; sr. acct. El Paso (Tex.) Exploration Co., 1984; fin. analyst Burlington No. R.R. Co., St. Paul, 1986—. Mem. Am. Inst. CPA's, Minn. Soc. CPA's (continuing profl. edn. com. 1987, mems. in industry com.), Women in Mgmt. Avocations: cooking, piano, organ, hiking. Home: 767 Blair Saint Paul MN 55104 Office: Burlington No RR Co PO Box 64957 Saint Paul MN 55164-0957

BERGER, GREGORY ALAN, dentist; b. Jasper, Ind., Jan. 4, 1954; s. Daniel Jacob and Roberta Jacqueline (Stewart) B.; m. Monica Marie Buechlein, Jan. 12, 1986. BA, Ind. U., 1976, DDS, 1979. Gen. practice dentistry Jasper, 1979—; mem. staff Meml. Hosp. and Health Care Ctr. Active parish council Holy Family Cath. Ch., Jasper, 1980-84, Jasper Boys Basketball Booster Club, Jasper Football Booster Club; bd. dirs. Dubois County Am. Cancer Soc., Jasper, 1982—. Mem. ADA, Acad. Gen. Dentistry, Ind. Dental Assn., First Dist. Dental Soc., Am. Soc. Dentistry for Children (Cert. of Merit 1979), Jasper C. of C., Jasper Jaycees (Disting. Service award 1983), Serra Club. Lodges: Optimists (various offices Jasper chpt., Pres. Service award 1983, Pres. Honor Club 1982, Disting. Dist. Club Sec. 1983), KC (squires scholarship fund drive 1985-86), Fraternal Order of Police. Avocations: golf, softball, gardening, community activities for youths. Home: 1019 Hochgesang Ave Jasper IN 47546 Office: 721 W 13th St Jasper IN 47546

BERGER, KENNETH WALTER, audiologist; b. Evansville, Ind., Mar. 22, 1924; s. Walter P. and Ida (Block) B.; m. Barbara Jane Steadman, Aug. 31, 1946; children—Robert W., Kenna J., Laura M., Karen S. B.A., U. Evansville, 1948; M.A., Ind. State U., 1949; M.S., S. Ill. U., Carbondale, 1960, Ph.D., 1962. Speech and hearing therapist pub. schs. Carmi, Ill., 1955-61; dir. audiology Kent State U., Ohio, 1962—; prof. Kent State U., 1967—; curator hearing aid museum. Author: Speechreading Principles and Methods, 1971, The Hearing Aid: Its Operation and Development, 1974, also monographs; Contbr. articles to profl. jours. Served to capt. U.S. Army, 1943-46; Served to capt. USAF, 1951-55. Fellow Am. Speech and Hearing Assn., Am. Audiology Soc., Acoustical Soc. Am. Home: 647 Longmere Dr Kent OH 44240 Office: Speech and Hearing Clinic Kent State Univ Kent OH 44242

BERGER, KURT WILHELM, fin. counselor; b. Frankfurt, Germany, Mar. 10, 1912; came to U.S., 1937, naturalized, 1943; s. Walter W. and Bea (Wendel) B.; Ph.D. in Econs., U. Frankfurt, 1936; m. Gudrun M. Wolf, Aug. 24, 1959; 1 dau., Gisela P. Market analyst Merck, Darmstadt & N.J., 1936-37; treas. Express Freight Lines, Inc., Milw., 1943-67; v.p., treas. E.F.L. Motors, Inc., Milw., 1945-67, Transport Services, Inc., Milw., 1945-67; exec. v.p. Nat. Life Ins. Co., Frankfurt, 1968-70; pvt. practice counseling internat. fin. and investments, Koenigstein, W.Ger., 1969-70; ind. mgmt. cons., fin. counselor, 1970—. Mem. Wis. N.G., 1947-49. Mem. Nat. Acctg. and Fin. Council (past v.p., pres., chmn.), Am. Trucking Assn., Motor Carrier Accts. Soc. (past pres.), Personnel Evaluation Inst. (past pres.). Unitarian. Contbr. articles to profl. jours. Home: 4540 N Ardmore Ave Shorewood WI 53211

BERGER, MICHAEL ERLING, psychologist; b. West Fargo, N.D., Mar. 17, 1941; s. Leif Erling and Dorothy (Adelle) B.; 1 child, Joshua Ian. BA, Concordia Coll., 1964; MA, U. N. Iowa, 1968; PhD, U. Minn., 1982. Psychologist Hopkins (Minn.) Schs., 1968-78; pvt. practice psychology Mpls., 1978—; instr. psychology St. Thomas Coll., St. Paul, 1969-1972; instr. counseling psychology U. Minn., Mpls., 1973; cons. Minn. Dept. Human Relations, Dept. Edn., 1975, Chem. Dependency Treatment Ctr., Mpls., 1976—. Co-Author: (tng. manual) Family Communication Systems. V.p. bd. dirs., mem. adv. bd. St. Mary's Treatment Ctr., 1981—. Fellow Soc. Clin. Hypnosis; mem. Mpls. Psychologist Assn., Am. Psychol. Assn., Mpls. Soc. Clin. Hypnosis. Lutheran. Avocations: reading, fishing, sporting activities, scuba diving. Home: 12000 Doug Lynn Dr Minnetonka MN 55345 Office: 4725 Excelsior Blvd #500 Saint Louis Park MN 55416

BERGER, RONALD, real estate investor; b. Chgo., June 30, 1933; s. Albert Erwin and Dorothy (Ginsberg) B.; m. Meta Schwartz; children: Jan Ellen, Louis Alan, Jonathan David. BBA, U. Miami, 1955. V.p. Mid-Am. Appraisal, Chgo., 1959-63; pres. Callner Corp., Chgo., 1963-70, Berger Fin. Services, Chgo., 1970—; bd. dirs. Mid Town Bank, Chgo., Columbia Nat. Bank, Chgo. Mem. Lambda Alpha. Clubs: Standard (Chgo.); Bryn Mawr Country (Lincolnwood, Ill.). Home: 1501 N State Pkwy Chicago IL 60610 Office: Berger Fin Services 180 N LaSalle St Chicago IL 60601

BERGERE, CARLETON MALLORY, contractor; b. Brookline, Mass., Apr. 4, 1919; s. Jason J. and Anna Lillian B.; student Burdett Bus. Coll., 1938, Babsons Sch. Bus., 1940; m. Jean J. Pach, Oct. 1, 1950. Self-employed contractor, Chgo., 1949-57; pres. Permanent Bldg. Supply Co., Inc., Chgo., 1957-62, Gt. No. Bldg. Products, Inc., Chgo., 1962-67, C.M. Bergere Co., Inc., Chgo., 1967—. Served with USN, 1944. Named Man of Yr., Profl. Remodelers Assn. Greater Chgo., 1978. Mem. Profl. Remodelers Assn. (dir., past treas., v.p., sec.; pres. greater Chicagoland chpt.), Nat. Assn. Remodeling Industry (also mem. NARI of Greater Chgoland.), Chgo. Assn. Commerce and Industry (indsl. devel. com.), Better Bus. Bur. Met. Chgo., Industry Trade Practice Com. on Home Improvement (chmn.), Nat. Panel Consumer Arbitrators. Club: Exec. (Chgo.). Address: 175 E Delaware Pl Chicago IL 60611

BERGERSON, DAVID RAYMOND, lawyer, manufacturing company executive; b. Mpls., Nov. 23, 1939; s. Raymond Kenneth and Katherine Cecille (Langworthy) B.; m. Nancy Anne Heeter, Dec. 22, 1962; children—W. Thomas C., Kirsten Finch, David Raymond. B.A., Yale U., 1961; J.D., U. Minn., 1964. Bar: Minn. 1964. Assoc. Fredrikson Law Firm, Mpls., 1964-67; atty. Honeywell Inc., Mpls., 1967-74, asst. gen. counsel, 1974-82, v.p., asst. gen. counsel, 1983-84, v.p., gen. counsel, 1984—; bd. dirs. Honeywell Fin. Inc., Mpls.; bd. dirs. Am. Corp. Counsel Assn. Minn. Chpt., 1986—, officer, 1986-87. Bd. dirs. Pillsbury United Neighborhood Services, Inc., Mpls., 1983—, officer, 1984—. Mem. ABA, Minn. State Bar Assn., Hennepin County Bar Assn., Am. Corp. Counsel Assn. (officer Minn. chpt. 1986, bd. dirs. Minn. chpt. 1987). Republican. Club: Minneapolis. Avocations: tennis; bird-hunting. Home: 2303 Huntington Point Rd E Wayzata MN 55391 Office: Honeywell Inc Honeywell Plaza Minneapolis MN 55408

BERGESCH, LOUIS WILLIAM (BILL), professional sports team executive; b. St. Louis, June 17, 1927; s. Louis Woestman and Rose (Schiermeier) B.; m. Virginia Else Kammerer, Mar. 8, 1948; children: Robert, Susan. B.S. in Bus. Adminstrn., Washington U., St. Louis, 1948. Gen. mgr. minor leagues St. Louis Cardinals, 1948-60; asst. gen. mgr. Kansas City Athletics, Mo., 1961; pres. Pioneer Capital, N.Y.C., 1962-77; v.p. New York Yankees, Bronx, 1978-84; exec. v.p., gen. mgr. Cin. Reds, 1984—. Mem. N.Y. Housing Authority, Mamaroneck, 1969—; mem. Westchester County Republican Com., N.Y. Methodist. Office: Cincinnati Reds 100 Riverfront Stadium Cincinnati OH 45202 *

BERGGREN, RONALD BERNARD, surgeon, emeritus professor; b. S.I., N.Y., June 13, 1931; s. Bernard and Florence (Schmidt) B.; m. Mary Beth Griffith, Nov. 25, 1954; children: Karen Ann, Eric Griffith. BA, Johns Hopkins U., 1953; MD, U. Pa., 1957. Diplomate Am. Bd. Surgery, Nat. Bd. Med. Examiners, Am. Bd. Plastic Surgery (bd. dirs. 1982—, chmn. 1987—). Asst. instr. surgery U. Pa., 1958-62, instr., 1962-65; gen. surg. resident Hosp. U. Pa., 1958-62, resident plastic surgery, 1963-64, chief resident plastic surgery, 1964-65; sr. resident surgery Phila. Gen. Hosp., 1962-63; asst. prof. surgery Ohio State U. Sch. Medicine, 1965-68, dir. div. plastic surgery, 1965-85, assoc. prof. surgery, 1968-73, prof. surgery, 1973-86, emeritus prof. surgery, 1986—; attending staff Ohio State U. Hosps., chief of staff, 1983-85, hon. staff, 1986—; attending staff, dir. div. plastic surgery Children's Hosp., Columbus, Ohio; v.p. Plastic Surgery Ednl. Found., 1984-85, pres.-elect, 1985-86, pres., 1986-87; sec. Plastic Surgery Tng. Program Dirs., 1981-83, chmn., 1983-85; mem. med. adv. bd. Ohio Bur. Crippled Children's Services, 1974—. Trustee Mid Ohio Health Planning Fedn., 1979-82, 84, PSRO, 1980-84, Scioto Valley Health Systems Agy., 1985-87. Fellow ACS; mem. Central, Columbus surg. socs., Am. Soc. Plastic and Reconstructive Surgeons, Ohio Valley Plastic Surg. Soc., Am. Cleft Palate Assn., AMA, Am. Assn. Plastic Surgeons (treas. 1982-85), Franklin County Med. Soc. (pres.-elect 1982-83, pres. 1983-84), Soc. Cryosurgery, Plastic Surg. Research Council Ohio, Soc. Cryobiology, N.Y. Acad. Scis., Am. Assn. Surgery Trauma, Assn. Acad. Surgery, Am. Burn Assn., Am. Trauma Soc., Am. Soc. Aesthetic Plastic Surgery, Am. Soc. Maxillofacial Surgery, Am. Bd. Plastic Surgery (chmn. 1987—, resident rev. com. for plastic surgery 1983—), Accreditation Council for Grads. Med. Edn., Council Med. Specialty Socs. (chmn. 1978-79), Sigma Xi, Phi Kappa Psi, Alpha Kappa Kappa. Home: 1960 Hampshire Rd Columbus OH 43221 Office: 410 W 10th Ave Columbus OH 43210

BERGIA, ROGER MERLE, educational administrator; b. Peoria, Ill., Nov. 26, 1937; s. Merle Frederick and Doris Ann (Markham) B.; B.A., Eureka Coll., 1960; M.A., Bradley U., 1967, postgrad., 1968—; m. Valerie Jean Lane, Oct. 16, 1960; children—Lori, Amy, Beth. Tchr., coach Jr. High Sch., Peoria Heights Sch., 1960-65; prin., Kelly Ave. Grade Sch., Peoria Heights, Ill, 1965-74; supt. Peoria Heights Schs., 1974—. Mem. exec. com. W.D. Boyce council Boy Scouts Am. Named Sch. Adminstr. of Yr., Ill. Bd. Edn., 1981-82. Mem. Phi Delta Kappa, Lambda Chi Alpha. Republican. Presbyterian. Home: 6723 N Gem Ct Peoria IL 61614 Office: 1316 E Kelly Ave Peoria Heights IL 61614

BERGLUND, ROBERTA LEOLA, educator; b. Freeport, Ill., May 20, 1944; d. Ralph LeRoy and Maxine (Lynch) Hanson; B.S., Ill. State U., 1965; M.S. Ed., No. Ill. U., 1978, EdD, 1985 ; m. David Lee Berglund, June 18, 1966. Tchr. elem. sch. Flanagan, Ill., 1965-69; reading specialist Dixon (Ill.) Public Schs., 1969-84, dir. Title I program, 1977-84; instr. Northern Ill. Univ., 1984-85; Asst. prof. U. Wis., Whitewater, 1985—. Recipient Excellence in Edn. award Ill. State Bd. Edn., 1985. Mem. Ill. Reading Council (dir. 1977-78, 81-83, 84-87, chmn. parents and reading 1982-83, corr. sec. 1981-82, chmn. publs. 1984-87, assoc. editor Jour. 1984—), Sauk Valley Reading Council (pres. 1977-78), Internat. Reading Assn. (Outstanding Contbns. award 1978, Achievement award 1986), No. Ill. Reading Council, South Kettle Moraine Reading Council, Nat. Reading Conf., Nat. Council Tchrs. English, Lang. Experience Approach Spl. Interest Council (v.p. 1983-84, pres. 1984-85), PEO, Am. Ednl. Research Assn., Nat. Sci. Tchrs. Assn., Coll. Reading Assn., Wis. State Reading Assn. (dir. student membership), Delta Kappa Gamma. Unitarian. Editor, Reading Unlimited newsletter, 1980-82, Ill. Reading Communicator, 1981-82; contbr. articles to profl. jours. Home: 880 Riverside Dr White Oak Estates Dixon IL 61021 Office: Univ Wisc 3032 Winther Hall Whitewater WI 53190

BERGLUND, RONALD GARY, healthcare administrator; b. Milw., Mar. 7, 1943; s. Gunnar E. and Margaret (Neilsen) B.; m. Mary L. Garvey, Sept. 27, 1969; children: Ronald Keith, Timothy Patrick. BA in Econs., Psychology, Wayne State U., 1972; MPH, U. Mich., 1980. Mgr. Mich. Dept. Social Services, Detroit, 1978-84; mgmt. system mgr. Wayne County Exec., Detroit, 1984-86; dir. planning and mktg. Saratoga Community Hosp., Detroit, 1986—; dir. health and substance abuse New Detroit, Inc., 1982—; tech. advisor Health Care Aces Project, Lansing, Mich., 1986—; bd. dirs. SHAR-Found., Detroit, 1984—. Mem. parish council St. John Neuman Parish, Canton, 1985—; advisor health Canton Oakwood Ctr., 1985—; coach Canton Soccer Club, 1978—; mem. pub. relations com. Am. Cancer Soc. Mem. Health Care Fin. Mgmt. Assn., Nat. Council on Aging, Nat. Forum for Health Care Planning. Republican. Roman Catholic. Club: Swedish, Colony Swim (Plymouth). Avocations: golf, soccer, travel. Home: 9632 Red Pine Dr Plymouth MI 48170 Office: Saratoga Community Hosp 15000 Gratiot Detroit MI 48205

BERGMAN, CLAUDIA LYNN, accountant; b. Kokomo, Ind., Mar. 12, 1952; d. Richard Kerby and Alice Mae (Lovelace) Ortman; m. John Joseph Bergman, June 2, 1973; children: Brett Richard, Zane Joseph. BS, Ball State U., 1973. CPA, Ind. Staff acct. Bergstrom & Bergstrom, Kokomo, 1973-83; practice acctg. Russiaville, Ind., 1983—; instr. Ind. Vocat. Tech. Coll., Kokomo, 1982. Mem. Am. Soc. Women Accts. (pres. chpt. 1985—), Ind. CPA's Soc., Am. Inst. CPA's.

BERGMAN, GREG ALAN, social worker; b. Lorain, Ohio, Feb. 12, 1951; s. Ivan Russell and Marjorie Ann (Yalman) B.; B.A., Ohio State U., Columbus, 1973; M.S.W., U. Nebr., 1975; m. Katherine Holaday, June 24, 1979. Asst. dir., acting dir. social services Dr. Sher Nursing Home, Omaha, 1975-77; social service worker Richard Young Hosp., Omaha, 1974-75; program dir. Social Settlement Assn. Omaha, 1978-80; social service worker Harry S. Truman Meml. Vets. Hosp., Columbia, Mo., 1980—. Mem. Columbia Community Band, 1982-84, No One in Particular Comedy Troupe, 1983-84, Catfish Night Club Band, 1983-84, stage band Maplewood Barn Community Theatre, Columbia, 1985—; mem. Columbia Diamond Council, 1982—, v.p., 1984-85, treas. 1986-87. Lic. nursing home adminstr., Nebr., Mo. Mem. Acad. Cert. Social Workers, Nat. Assn. Social Workers (state dir. 1978-79, regional chmn. 1978-79), Nebr. Welfare Assn. (regional dir. 1979-80). Author statistics textbook. Home: 2513 Willowbrook Ct Columbia MO 65202 Office: 800 Stadium Rd Columbia MO 65201

BERGMAN, JANET LOUISE, flutist, educator; b. St. Louis, June 15, 1920; d. Isadore and Rose (Seidenberg) Marx; student pub. schs., St. Louis; student John F. Kiburz, Laurent Torno; m. Albert Solomon Bergman, June 15, 1947; children—Shelley, Gary Evan, Dana Lynn. Mem. St. Louis Woman's Symphony, 1937-38, St. Louis Opera Co., 1942, St. Louis Symphony, 1943-47; first flutist St. Louis Little Symphony, 1943-47, soloist, 1943-47; flutist Oklahoma City Symphony, 1944-45, soloist, 1944-45; flutist New Orleans Symphony and Opera Co., 1945-47, Chgo. Women's Sinfonietta, 1948, Civic Orch. of Chgo., 1948, Chgo. Park Band Concerts, 1947—, Chgo. Chamber Orch., 1954-58, Lyric Opera Orch., Chgo., 1964-71; 1st flutist, soloist City Symphony Chgo., 1963—, Aoelian Woodwind Ensemble, Chgo., 1965—; prof. flute Chgo. Conservatory Coll., 1968-78, Northeastern Ill. U., Chgo., 1978—, Am. Conservaory of Music, Chgo., 1978-81; conductor Chgo. Park Band Concert, 1984—; soloist City Symphony of Chgo., 1987; mem. music faculty Niles E. and Niles W. high schs., 1964—, New Trier E. and W. high schs., 1977—; founder, condr. Flute Sinfonietta, 1975—; condr. Chgo. Flute Ensemble, 1980—; soloist Artist Assocs., 1976-77; adjudicator Ill. High Sch. Solo Assn., 1973-79, Flute Concourse, U. Que., Montreal, 1974, 77, 84. Recipient music award Chgo. Pub. Library Cultural Ctr., 1980; 20 Yr. Service award City Symphony Chgo., 1983. Mem. Chgo., St. Louis fedns. musicians, Nat. Flute Assn., Soloist Artists Assn. Chgo., Nat. Health Fedn. (sec. Chgo. chpt. 1975-76, speaker 1976-77, sec. 1978—, sec., treas. 1985—), Chgo. Flute Soc. (founder, pres. 1977—), Soc. Am. Musicians. Author: Do's and Don'ts of Flute Playing, 1967. Home: 1817 G W Hood St Chicago IL 60660

BERGMAN, ROBERT SCRIBNER, toy manufacturing executive; b. Aurora, Ill., Nov. 23, 1934; s. Ross M. and Mary O. (Ochsenschlager) B.; B.S., Ill. Inst. Tech., 1956; postgrad., Stanford U., 1956-58; m. Patricia LeBaron, June 10, 1956; children—David C., Lynne M., Joseph R. With Hughes Aircraft Co., Culver City, Calif., 1956, Gen. Electric Co., Palo Alto, Calif., 1957, Sylvania, Mountain View, Calif., 1958-61; with Processed Plastic, Montgomery, Ill., 1961—, pres., 1969—; treas. Intertoy, Montgomery, 1977—, Graphic Label Co., Montgomery, Ill., 1977—; bd. dirs. Brunsport, Montgomery; chmn. bd. Lektro-Vend, Aurora, Ill.; chmn. bd., treas. Berkir Sales, Montgomery, 1986. Mem. Am. Phys. Soc., Toy Mfrs. Am. (dir. 1981-85). Republican. Mem. United Ch. of Christ. Club: Elks. Home: 1330 Monona Ave Aurora IL 60506 Office: 1001 Aucutt Rd Montgomery IL 60538

BERGMAN, ROY THOMAS, surgeon; b. Cassopolis, Mich., Dec. 20, 1935; s. Roy Edwin and Lois (Townsend) B.; m. Sally Jo Proshwitz, June 28, 1958; children: Roy T., Amy Lynn, Samara Edlyn. BS with high honors, Mich. State U., 1957, DVM with high honors, 1959; MD, Northwestern U., 1964. Diplomate Am. Bd. Surgery. Rotating intern Evanston (Ill.) Hosp. Assn., 1964-65, resident in gen. surgery, 1967-71; Am. Cancer Soc. clin. fellow in oncological surgery Northwestern U., Chgo., 1970-71; practice medicine specializing in gen. surgery and oncology, Escanaba, Mich., 1972; mem. staff St. Francis Hosp., Escanaba, 1972—, chmn. tumor bd., 1972—, also chief of staff, chief of surgery; instr. surgery U. So. Calif. Med. Ctr., Los Angeles, 1972-73; assoc. prof. surgery Mich. State U. Coll. Human Medicine, East Lansing, 1974—, also surg. coordinator Upper Peninsula med. edn. program; attending physician Nat. Sports Festival, Colorado Springs, 1978-79, Syracuse, N.Y., 1981, U.S. Olymic Com., Pan Am. Games, P.R., 1979, Summer Games, Russia, 1980, Summer Games, Los Angeles, 1984; head physician U.S. Olympic Com., Caracas, Venezuela, 1983; polyclinic U.S. Olympic Com. Winter Games, Lake Placid, N.Y., 1980; attending physician U.S. Olympic Men's Rowing Team, Germany, 1981; mem. Council on Sports Medicine, U.S. Olympic Com., 1985—. Served to capt. M.C., U.S. Army, 1965-67. Recipient Disting. Citizen award No. Mich. U., 1987; named to Mich. Upper Peninsula Sports Hall of Fame. Fellow ACS (local chmn. com. trauma, chmn. com. on applicants Mich. Dist. 4), Alpha Omega Alpha. Office: Doctors Park Escanaba MI 49829

BERGMAN, SIGRID ELIZABETH, hosp. services adminstr.; b. Lafayette, Ind., June 20, 1940; d. Philip A. and Josephine Elizabeth (Miller) Henderson; B.A., U. Nebr., 1963, M.A., 1970; m. Edward T. Bergman, June 9, 1962; children—Kimberly Kay, Lucinda Sue. Pediatric counselor Nat. Jewish Hosp., Denver, 1962-63; home services rep. Cengas, Lincoln, Nebr., 1963-65; guidance counselor St. Elizabeth Sch. Nursing, Lincoln, 1966-70; dir. social services St. Elizabeth Community Health Center, Lincoln, 1970—; guest lectr. social work and vocat. rehab. U. Nebr. Bd. dirs. Lancaster County Unit Am. Cancer Soc., 1975-78; mem. adv. bd. Tabitha Home Health Care, 1975-81, sec. 1975-76; mem. Cath. Social Services Bd., 1977-79; mem. adv. bd. Lincoln Youth Symphony, 1977-82, projects chmn., 1978-79, sec., 1979-80, pres., 1980-81. Mem. Soc. for Hosp. Social Work Dirs. of Am. Hosp. Assn., Nebr. Soc. Hosp. Social Work Dirs. (pres. 1981-82, treas. 1985-86), Zeta Tau Alpha. Democrat. Presbyterian. Club: Alpha Chi Omega Mothers (co-chmn. 1981-82). Home: 1109 Lancaster Ln Lincoln NE 68505 Office: St Elizabeth Community Center 555 S 70th St Lincoln NE 68510

BERGMAN, WILLIAM ALLEN, civil engineer; b. New Orleans, Mar. 25, 1947; s. Samuel Bergman and June (Gordon) Feldman; m. Jo Anne Hannula, June 14, 1968; children: David Robert, Elisabeth Ann. BSChemE, U. Minn., 1970; MS in Environ. Engring., Ill. Inst. Tech., 1981. Registered profl. engr., Ill., Wis., Fla. Asst. civil engr. Met. Sanitary Dist., Chgo., 1972—, now prin. civil engr. Contbr. articles to profl. jours. PTA rep. Chgo. Sch. Council, 1974; com. chmn. Cub Scouts Am., Chgo., 1979, asst. scoutmaster, Boy Scouts Am., 1982. Named Winston Churchill fellow English Speaking Union, 1985. Mem. ASCE (chmn. environ. div. Ill. sect. 1986—), Am. Inst. Chem. Engrs. (com. awards sect. Chgo. 1978-79), Ill. Soc. Profl. Engrs. (bd. dirs. 1985-86), Mpls. Indsl. Edn. Soc. (Pres. award 1965), Chgo. Guitar Soc. Avocations: playing and building classical guitar, butterfly collecting and life history research. Home: 6237 N Hermitage Chicago IL 60660 Office: Met Sanitary Dist 111 E Erie Chicago IL 60611

BERGQUIST, BARRY DARRIL, importing company executive; b. Cloquet, Minn., Oct. 18, 1945; s. Richard Emil and Margaret (Bengston) B.; B.A. in Bus. Adminstrn., U. Minn., Duluth, 1968; m. Vivian Elizabeth Cook, Nov. 30, 1974. Salesman, mgr. Cades Ltd., Elk Grove, Ill., 1971; dist. mgr. Mass. food equipment div. McGraw Edison Co., 1973; sales mgr., then v.p. Bergquist Imports, Inc., Cloquet, 1977—, pres., owner, 1980—; dir. Cloquet Devel. Corp., 1983—, ex-officio mem., 1986—. Vice chmn., chmn. fin. com. 8th Congl. Dist. Republican Party, 1979-81, dist. chmn., 1981-83; chmn. Carlton County Rep. Party, 1976-81; trustee Cloquet Library Bd., 1979—; bd. dirs. Cloquet chpt. Am. Cancer Soc., 1980—; regional rep. bd. Minn. Assn. Commerce and Industry, 1986—. Served with USAR, 1968-70. Club: Cloquet Kiwanis (pres.). Home: 318 Ave D Cloquet MN 55720 Office: 1412 Hwy 33 S Cloquet MN 55720

BERGSETH, ROBERT REID, military officer; b. Clarksville, Tenn., Feb. 20, 1945; s. Robert Andrew and Elsie D. (Dommer) B.; m. Paula C. Bissell, June 17, 1967 (div. Mar. 1979); m. Mary Jane Oscielowski, Aug. 28, 1982; children: Heather A., Amy D. (twins). BS, Va. Polytechnic Inst., 1968; MBA, So. Ill. U., 1973. Commd. USAF, 1968, advanced through grades to maj.; tng. support mgr. Electronic Systems Div., Hanscom AFB, Mass., 1974-77, contracts evaluation mgr., 1977-79, bus. mgr., 1980-81; ops. research analyst Def. Intelligence Agy., Washington, 1981-82; asst. prof., adminstrv. officer Rensselaer Polytechnic Inst., Troy, N.Y., 1982-85; spl. asst. for tng. Tng. and Devel. div., Wright-Patterson AFB, Ohio, 1985—; adj. prof. mgmt. Wright State U., Dayton, Ohio, 1986—. Mem. Am. Soc. for Tng. and Devel., Assn. for Psychol. Type, Am. Def. Preparedness Assn. Club: Toastmaster (v.p. 1984-85, competent toastmaster 1985). Avocations: psychology, photography, astronomy, model railroading, hiking. Home: 2791 Woodmont Dr Xenia OH 45385 Office: Aeronautical Systems Div Employee Devel and Tng div Wright-Patterson AFB OH 45433

BERGSETH, THOMAS LYLE, architect; b. Mpls., Mar. 1, 1944; s. Lyle Dayton and Edna (Walker) B.; m. Wendy Ann Martin, Sept. 17, 1966; children: Amy, Ross. BArch, U. Minn., 1966. Registered architect. Architect Cerny Assocs., Mpls., 1966-72; project architect Bentz-Thompson, Mpls., 1972-74; dir. architecture Setter-Leach & Lindstrom, Mpls., 1974-76; corp. architect Dayton-Hudon Corp., Mpls., 1976-82; dir. facilities planning and design Walgreen Co., Deerfield, Ill., 1982—. Chmn. Appearance Code Commn., Deerfield, 1986—, staff, parish bd. Christ United Meth. Ch., Deerfield, 1986—; v.p. adv. com. Deerfield, Highland Park High Sch. Orchestra, 1984-87. Served to sgt. USAR, 1966-72. Mem. AIA, Nat. Fire Protecton Assn., Am. Concrete Inst., Internat. Council Shopping Ctrs., Constrn. Specifications Inst. Avocations: travel, piano. Home: 865 Warwick Rd Deerfield IL 60015 Office: Walgreen Co 200 Wilmot Rd Deerfield IL 60015

BERGSTRESSER, MELVIN HUBERT, retail executive; b. Frobischer, Sask., Can., June 16, 1932; s. Waldemar and Selma (Kolke) B.; student in Bus. Mgmt., U. Man., 1967-70; student in Theology, N. Am. Bapt. Coll., Edmonton, 1950-52; m. Doreen Laura, June 26, 1954; children—Wayne, Arden, Heather, Kevin. With Gambles Can., Winnipeg, Man., 1956-82, buyer major appliances, sporting goods, asst. mgr. sales promotion and advt., group mgr. sporting goods div., 1979-82; pres., owner Creative Family Living Assn., 1969—, Parking Lot Marking Services, 1975—, Distinctive Products, 1975—, Melberg Enterprises Ltd., 1982—, Barbecues Parts and Service Village Ltd., 1983—; lectr. family living seminars. Bd. dirs. N.Am. Bapt. Coll., 1967-79; chmn. Man. Bapt. Assn., 1975-78; moderator Grant Park Bapt. Ch., 1972-78, Sunday Sch. tchr., 1959—, capt. Christian Service Brigade Boys, 1964-82. Home: 16 Glengarry Dr, Winnipeg, MB Canada R3T 2J6

BERGSTROM, BETTY HOWARD, association executive; b. Chgo., Mar. 15, 1931; d. Seward Haise and Agnes Eleanor (Uek) Guinter; B.S. in Speech, Northwestern U., 1952, postgrad., 1983; postgrad U. Nev., Reno, 1974; m. Robert William Bergstrom, Apr. 21, 1979; children—Bryan Scott, Cheryl Lee, Jeffrey Alan, Mark Robert, Philip Alan. Dir. sales promotion and pub. relations WLS-AM, Chgo., 1952-56; account exec. E.H. Brown Advt. Agy., Chgo., 1956-59; v.p. Richard Crabb Assocs., Chgo., 1959-61; pres., owner Howard Assocs., Calif. and Chgo., 1961-76; v.p. Chgo. Hort. Soc., 1976—. Del., Ill. Constl. Conv., 1969-70, mem. com. legis. reform, 1973-74, cts. and justice com., 1971-74; apptd. mem. Ill. Hist. Library Bd., 1970, Ill. Bd. Edn., 1971-74. AAUW fellowship grant named in her honor; recipient Communicator of Yr. award Women in Communication, 1983. Mem. Nat. Soc. Fund Raising Execs. (cert. fund raising executive, bd. dirs. 1983-87, sec. 1986), Am. Assn. of Museums, Am. Assn. Bot. Garden and Arboreta, Garden Writers Am., AAUW, Northwestern U. Alumni, U. So. Calif. Alumni Assn., LWV. Mem. Glenview Community Ch. Editorial bd. Garden Mag., 1977—; editor Garden Talk, 1976-86; contbr. articles on fund devel., horticulture, edn. advt. and agr. to profl. jours.; editor Ill. AAUW Jour., 1966-67. Office: PO Box 400 Glencoe IL 60022

BERGSTROM, GEORGE FREDERICK, association executive; b. Chgo., July 9, 1950; s. Clarence George and Emily (Kawacin) B.; m. Karen Susan Faber, Oct. 8, 1978; children: Scott Mitchell, Christopher John. BA, Grinnell Coll., 1972; MA, U. Iowa, 1974. Staff assoc. Am. Hosp. Assn., Chgo., 1974-75, staff specialist, 1975-77, asst. regional dir., 1978-81, asst. div. dir., 1981-85, dir. div. allied assn. and regional office services, 1985—; adminstrv. resident North Meml. Med. Ctr., Mpls., 1973. Compiler: Provision and Legislative Intent of Public Law 93-641, 1975. Bd. dirs. Edgebrook Community Assn., Chgo., 1986—. Mem. Am. Coll. Healthcare Execs., Chgo. Health Execs. Forum. Republican. Methodist. Avocation: gardening. Home: 6620 N Loron Ave Chicago IL 60646 Office: Am Hosp Assn 840 N Lake Shore Dr Chicago IL 60646

BERGSTROM, JOHN JACOB, manufacturing and research executive; b. Waterloo, Iowa, Nov. 29, 1925; s. Daniel Everett and Johanna Elizebeth (Hansen) B.; m. Jo Ann Straight, July 21, 1946; children: Becky Ann Forsberg, Lori Jo Ruhlman. BA, U. No. Iowa, 1949; postgrad., State U. Iowa, 1951-52. Mathematician Chamberlain Mfg. Corp., Waterloo, Iowa, 1954-55, project leader, 1955-58, engring. supr., 1958-66, asst. gen. mgr., 1966-70, gen. mgr., 1970-73; group v.p. Chamberlain Mfg. Corp., Elmhurst, Ill., 1973-79, exec. v.p., 1979-85, pres., 1985—, also bd. dirs.; bd. dirs. Mason Chamberlain Inc., Picayune, Miss., Mfg. Scis. Corp., Oakridge, Tenn., Saco (Maine) Def. Inc. Patentee in field; contbr. articles to profl. jours. Served with USN, 1943-46, PTO. Mem. Am. Def. Preparedness Assn. (bd. dirs. 1987—, Tech. Leadership award 1973, Firepower award 1986). Unitarian. Avocations: chess, fishing, cycling. Home: 1124 Perry Dr Palatine IL 60067 Office: Chamberlain Mfg Corp 845 Larch Ave Elmhurst IL 60126

BERGSTROM, RICHARD NORMAN, civil engineer; b. Chgo., Dec. 11, 1921; s. Carl William and Ellen Amanda Victoria (Anderson) B.; m. Patricia Ann Chessman, Apr. 19, 1947; children: George Norman, James Donald, Laura Ann, Martha Jean. B.S. in Civil Enging, Ill. Inst. Tech., 1942, M.S., 1952. Registered profl. engr., Ill., 17 other states. Design engr. Carnegie-Ill. Steel Corp., Gary, Ind., 1942; with Sargent & Lundy (engrs.), Chgo., 1946-82; partner Sargent & Lundy (engrs.), 1966-81, mgr. tech. services dept., 1977-81; mem. nuclear standards mgmt. bd. Am. Nat. Standards Inst., 1975-80. Contbr. to profl. publs. Stated clk. Presbyn. Ch., Barrington, Ill.; bd. dirs. Presbyn. Home, Evanston, Ill.; mem. council emeritus advisers. Bus. Coll. of Ariz. State U.; dir. Foothills Community Found., Ariz. Served to lt. USNR, 1942-46. Decorated Purple Heart. Fellow ASCE, Am. Cons. Engrs. Council; mem. ASME, Am. Nuclear Soc., Am. Concrete Inst., Am. Inst. Steel Constrn., Western Soc. Engrs., Ill. Cons. Engrs. Council (dir.), Tau Beta Pi, Chi Epsilon. Clubs: Union League (Chgo.); Barrington Hills (Ill.) Country; Desert Forest Golf, Meadow, Golf at Desert Mountain, Econ. (Phoenix). Home: 274 Leeds Dr Barrington Hills IL 60010

BERGSTROM, ROBERT CARLTON, geologist; b. Highland Park, Ill., Aug. 20, 1925; s. Carl Hilding and Ethel Rose (Hill) B.; B.S., Northwestern U., 1950, M.S., 1954; postgrad. U. Chgo., 1960-61, 67-69; m. Virginia Mae Jensen, June 7, 1952; children—Gary Carlton, Bradley James, Neil Reid. Tchr., Morton High Sch., Cicero, Ill., 1950-53; instr. Morton Coll., Cicero, 1953-63, asso. dean for admissions and records, 1964-74, prof. geology and geography, 1974-84, prof. emeritus, 1984—. Active, Boys Scouts Am. Served with U.S. Army, 1944-46. NSF fellow, 1960-61. Mem. Ill. State Acad. Sci., Nat. Assn. Geology Tchrs., Soc. Vertebrate Paleontology, Great Lakes Planetarium Assn., Sigma Xi. Luthern.

BERGSTROM, ROBERT WILLIAM, lawyer; b. Chgo., Nov. 8, 1918; s. C. William and Ellen (Anderson) B.; m. Betty Howard; children: Mark Robert, Philip Alan, Bryan Scott, Cheryl Lee, Jeffrey Alan. M.B.A., U. Chgo., 1947; LL.B., Ill. Inst. Tech.-Chgo. Kent Coll. Law, 1940, J.D., 1970. Bar: Ill. 1940, U.S. Supreme Ct. 1950. Ptnr. Bergstrom, Davis & Teeple (and predecessors), 1951—; founder Ill. Statewide Com. on Cts. and Justice, 1971—; bd. dirs. Ill. Com. for Constl. Conv., 1969, Ill. Constl. Research Group, 1970; spl. counsel Ill. Joint Legislative Com. to Investigate Met. San. Dist. of Cook County, 1967, Ill. Senate Mcpl. Corp. Com., 1970. Co-author: The Law of Competition in Illinois, 1962, Antitrust Developments, 1955-68, Antitrust Advisor, 1985; author Marxism, Senator Sherman, and Our Economic System, 1968, and numerous articles on antitrust, constl. law, and econs.; Editor: Chgo. Bar Record, 1971-72. Served to lt. USNR, 1941-46. Named Chicagoan of Yr. in Law and Judiciary Chgo. Jaycees, 1969; recipient medal Ill. Constl. Conv., 1970, Disting. Pub. Service award Union League Club, 1981. Mem. ABA, Ill. Bar Assn., Chgo. Bar Assn. (sec. 1969-71). Club: Union League (pres. 1971-72). As chmn. Com. for Legis. Reform, drafted constl. amendment enacted 1980, reducing Ill. Ho. of Reps. by 1/3 and abolishing cumulative voting. Office: Bergstrom Davis & Teeple 39 S LaSalle St Suite 800 Chicago IL 60603

BERGT, GREGORY PAUL, chemist, consultant; b. West Point, Nebr., Nov. 20, 1948; s. Lowell Duane and Elaine Angela (Schula) B.; m. Diann Helen Stigge, May 6, 1972; children—Matthew, Lisa, Troy, Ross. B.S., Nebr. Wesleyan U., 1971; postgrad. U. Minn., 1974. Chemist, Wendt Labs., Belle Plaine, Minn., 1971-77, dir. sci. and regulatory affairs, 1978-87; v.p. Eudaemonic Corp., Omaha, 1987—; cons. VA Hosp., Mpls., 1977. Patentee in field. Pres., St. John's Lutheran Ch., Belle Plaine, Minn., 1981; sponsoring liason Boy Scouts Am., Belle Plaine, 1980-84; county del. Republican party, Scott County, Minn., 1982. Recipient award Chemistry Tng. Program, NSF, 1967. Mem. Animal Health Inst., Parenteral Drug Assn., Am. Dairy Sci. Assn., Am. Chem. Soc., Am. Inst. Chemists, Am. Fedn. Ind. Pharm. Mfrs. (sec.-treas., dir. 1979—), Council Agrl. and Sci. Tech. Republican. Lutheran. Clubs: Tiger Booster (pres. 1973-75), Rotary (pres. 1984-85) (Belle Plaine, Minn.). Home: 200 Oakwood Circle Belle Plaine MN 56011 Office: Eudaemonic Corp 7031 N 16th St Omaha NE 68112

BERINGER, ROBERT MCGINNIS, education institute program director; b. Akron, Ohio, Sept. 6, 1957; s. Charles A. and Rita (McGinnis) B. BA in Communications, John Carroll U., 1980; MBA, Cleve. State U., 1987. Tech. mgr. Cleve. Bus. Cons., 1980-83; placement dir. Bryant & Stratton Bus. Inst., North Olmsted, Ohio, 1983—. Mem. Am. Soc. Personnel Adminstrn. Club: North Coast Catamaran Assn. (Rocky River, Ohio). Office: Bryant & Stratton Bus Inst 26700 Brookpark Rd North Olmsted OH 44070

BERK, BURTON BENJAMIN, optometrist; b. Cleve., Jan. 31, 1930; s. Benjamin C. and Ruth S. (Hirsohn) B.; B.S. in Optometry, Ohio State U., 1953, O.D., 1977; m. Margery A. Rocco, June 17, 1951; children—Deborah L., Bruce C., Michael S., Lawrence R. Practice optometry, Columbus, Ohio, 1953—. Instr. optometry Ohio State U., 1967—. Dir. Corporate Futures, Rochester, N.Y.; sec. Ohio Profl. Investment Corp., 1968; pres. Quality Vision Plan Inc., Columbus, 1984—, Viscare Mgmt. Inc., Canton, 1986—; Exec. dir. Viscare Plans Inc., Bexley, Ohio, 1986—. Pres. Ohio State Bd. Optometry, 1972—. Mem. Nat. Eye Research Found., Optometric Extension Found., Inc., Ohio Vision Service, Better Vision Inst., Vision League of Ohio. Fellow Am. Acad. Optometry; mem. Central Ohio, Ohio, Am. optometric assns., Internat. Orthokeratology Assn., Am. Optometric Found., Phi Sigma Delta. Republican. Clubs: B'nai B'rith, Whitehall Lions, Presidents of Ohio State U. Home: 2775 Brentwood Rd Columbus OH 43209 Office: 5180 E Main St Columbus OH 43213

BERK, LEON MAURICE, accountant; b. Joliet, Ill., July 13, 1925; s. Abraham and Miriam (Podorov) B.; m. Miriam Chusit, Aug. 5, 1949 (div. 1977); m. Natalie Burk, Dec. 25, 1980; children: Paula, Martha, Jeffrey, Daniel, Edward, Amy, Jody. BA, U. Wis., 1946. Pres. Berk's Stores Inc.,

Green Bay, Wis., 1951-77, BBB Inc., Mantowoc, Wis., 1977-79, Berk & Berk Bus. Services Inc., Green Bay, 1979-86; treas. Nat. Assn. Tax Practitioners, Kaukauna, Wis., 1981—; also bd. dirs. NATP, Kaukaeune, Wis.; treas. Start Plastics, Green Bay, 1986—; enrolled agt. IRS, Green Bay, 1982—; accredited acct. NSPA, Alexandria, Va., 1983—. Office: care Start Plastics Inc PO Box 12434 Green Bay WI 54307

BERKENES, JOYCE MARIE POORE, family counselor; b. Des Moines, Aug. 29, 1953; d. Donald Roy and Thelma Beatrice (Hart) Poore; m. Robert Elliott Berkenes,Jan. 3, 1976; children: Tiffany Noelle, Cory Matthew. BA in Social Work and Biology, Simpson Coll., Indianola, Iowa., 1975. Resident counselor and group home mgr. Chaddock Boys Home, Quincy, Ill., 1976-78; social service dir. N. Adams Nursing Home, Mendon, Ill., 1978; home tchr. Head Start, Camp Point, Ill., 1978-79, home tchr. supr./edn. and parent involvement coordinator, 1979-82; family counselor Iowa Children's and Family Services, Des Moines, 1982-85; family counselor and vol. coordinator Luth. Social Services, Des Moines, 1985—; cons. in field, 1975-76. Mem. Iowa Soc. Autistic Children, Home Based Family Service Assn. (sec. 1984—), Nat. Assn. Social Workers. Democrat. Methodist. Avocations: collecting antiques, reading, playing piano, ballet, church work. Home: 2901 NE 80th St Altoona IA 50009 Office: Luth Social Services 2525 E Euclid Suite 110 Des Moines IA 50317

BERKEY, VERNON ATKESON, radiologist; b. Fortuna, Mo., Feb. 1, 1918; s. Joseph M. and Stella Mae (Atkeson) B.; m. Suzanne Anderson, Mar. 2, 1954; children: Elizabeth, Carolyn, Joseph A., Kristin Mae. AB, Kans. U., 1940, MD, 1943. Diplomate Am. Bd. Radiology. Radiologist Neosno Meml. Hosp., Chanute, Kans., 1954-72, Mercy Hosp., Fort Scott, Kans., 1955-73, Mount. Carmel Hosp. Med. Ctr., Pitts., 1957—; med. dir. Centennial Life Inc. Co., Pitts., 1963-74. Served to capt. USMC, 1945-47. Fellow Am. Coll. Radiology; mem. Crawford County Med. Soc., Kans. Med. Soc., AMA, Radiol. Soc. N.Am. Republican. Presbyterian. Club: Crestwood Country (Pitts.). Lodge: Elks. Avocations: sports, fishing, music.

BERKLEY, EUGENE BERTRAM (BERT), envelope company executive; b. Kansas City, Mo., May 8, 1923; s. Eugene Bertram (Bert) Berkowitz and Caroline Newman (Newburger) B.; m. Joan Meinrath, Sept. 1, 1948; children—Janet Lynn Berkley Moody, William Spencer, Jane Ellen Berkley Levitt. B.A., Duke U., 1948; M.B.A., Harvard U., 1950. Pres., Tension Envelope Corp., Kansas City, Mo., 1962—, pres., chmn. bd., chief exec. officer, 1966—; dir. Bookstop, Inc. Patentee in field. Trustee, chmn. U. Mo.-Kansas City, 1983-85 , vice chmn., 1981-83, North Campus Devel. com., policy bd., charter mem. Univ. Assocs.; chmn. Kansas City minority suppliers devel. council; vice chmn. Ctr. for Bus. Innovation; bd. dirs. human resources com. Heart of Am. United Campaign, 1983, chmn. Comprehensive Needs and Service Survey Com., 1971; pres. Civic Council of Greater Kansas City, 1981-82, bd. dirs. 1982-83; pres. C. of C. of Greater Kansas City, 1968-69; bd. dirs., planning policy com. Menorah Med. Ctr., 1981—; trustee Midwest Research Inst., exec. com., 1969-72; bd. dirs. Kansas City Area Health Planning Council, Inc., 1982-83, Mid-Am. Coalition on Health Care; chmn. bd. dirs. Human Services Testing and Retng. Council, 1983—; active Eddie Jacobson Meml. Found.; mem. exec. com. Ctr. for Mgmt. Assistance, 1980-83; mem. Mayor's Prayer Breakfast Com., 1964—; mem. exec. com., met. chmn. Nat. Alliance of Businessmen of Met. Kansas City, 1973; bd. govs. Am. Royal Assn.; chmn. bd. dirs. Johnson Country Library, 1979-80; mem. exec. com. Voluntary Action Info. Ctr.; mem. exec. council Am. Jewish Com., 1979—, bd. dirs. Kansas City chpt., chmn., 1958-61; vice chmn. Jewish Fedn. and Council of Greater Kansas City, 1964, gen. chmn., 1961. Served to 1st lt. AUS, 1943-46; PTO 1950-52, Korea. Decorated Bronze Star; recipient numerous awards, including Mr. Kansas City award C. of C. of Greater Kansas City, 1972; Disting. Service award Johnson County Friends of the Library (Johnson County, Kans.), 1982. Mem. NCCJ (sec.; adv. com. to bd. dirs. 1981—, chmn. 1972 citation dinner, bd. dirs. 1956-74, 1968 Brotherhood award) (Kansas City chpt.), Nat. Fire Protection Assn. (envelope industry rep.), Envelope Mfrs. Assn. of Am. (exec. com. 1977-79, vice chmn. exec. com. 1981-83, v.p. 1981-83, pres. 1983-85), Nat. Parks and Conservation Assn. (adv.). Republican. Clubs: Oakwood Country, Homestead Country; Kansas City Racquet. Office: Tension Envelope Corp 819 E 19th St Kansas City MO 64108

BERKLEY, RICHARD L., mayor. Grad., Harvard U. Sec., treas. Tension Envelope Corp., Kansas City, Mo.; mem. City Council Kansas City, Mo.; mayor City of Kansas City, 1979—; chmn. Jackson County (Mo.) Republican Com. Office: Office of Mayor City Hall 414 E 12th Kansas City MO 64106 *

BERKMAN, ARNOLD STEPHEN, clin. psychologist; b. N.Y.C., Sept. 2, 1942; s. Henry and Marion (Lampert) B.; A.B., Oberlin Coll., 1964; M.S., U. Pitts., 1966, Ph.D., 1969; m. Claire Fleet, Apr. 27, 1975; children—Eric, Joshua, Janna. Fellow in clin. psychology U. Chgo. Pritzker Sch. Medicine, Chgo., 1968-69; asst. prof. Counseling Center, Mich. State U., East Lansing, 1969-73, asso. prof., 1973-74; asso. prof. dept. psychiatry, 1974-87. UPSHS trainee, 1964-67. Mem. Mich. Psychol. Assn. (v.p. profl. affairs 1978-79, pres. elect 1981, pres. 1982), Am. Psychol. Assn. Jewish. Home: 4780 Arapaho Trail Okemos MI 48864 Office: 1812 Mich Nat Tower Lansing MI 48933

BERKMAN, CLAIRE FLEET, psychologist; b. New Orleans, Dec. 5, 1942; d. Joel and Margaret Grace (Fishler) Fleet; m. Arnold Stephen Berkman, Apr. 27, 1975; children: Janna Samantha, Micah Seth Siegel. BA, Boston U., 1964; MEd, Harvard U., 1966; EdD, Boston U., 1970. Asst. prof. Counseling Ctr., Mich. State U., East Lansing, 1971-75, assoc. prof., 1975-78, assoc. prof. dept. psychiatry, 1975-82, clin. assoc. prof., 1986-87; pvt. clin. practice, 1975—; cons. Cath. Family Social Service, Lansing, 1979-83. V.p. Kehillat Israel Synagogue, 1975-76; bd. dirs. Jewish Welfare Fedn., Lansing, 1974-75, 84-87. NDEA fellow, 1968-70. Mem. Am. Psychol. Assn., Mich. Psychol. Assn., Am. Mental Health Assn. of Israel, Mich. Soc. Forensic Psychologists. Office: 1812 Michigan National Tower Lansing MI 48933

BERKOVICH, GARY A., architect; b. Kharkov, USSR, May 26, 1935; came to U.S., 1977; s. Aron M. and Maria Y. (Schnider) B.; m. Marina S. Guz, May 17, 1962; children: Lana, Stan. A in Architecture, Kharkov Bldg. Tech. Sch., 1953; MArch, Moscow Inst. Architecture, 1964; PhD in Architecture, R&D Inst. Housing Design, Moscow, 1973. Registered architect, Ill. Architect, group leader State Design Firms, Moscow, 1953-54, chief architect, 1961-76; architect Skidmore, Owings & Merrill, Chgo., 1977-79, sr. architect, 1981-83; project architect Perkins & Will, Chgo., 1979-81; designer, project architect A.J. Greenberg & Assocs., Chgo., 1984—. Patentee in field; contbr. articles to profl. jours. Recipient Outstanding New Citizen award Citizenship Council Met. Chgo., 1984, various archtl. awards and distinctions. Mem. Am. Inst. CPA's (chmn. housing com. Chgo. chpt.). Office: AJ Greenberg & Assocs 3 E Huron Chicago IL 60611

BERKOWER, LARY RONALD, psychiatrist; b. Detroit, Sept. 10, 1937; s. Saul and Alice (Rothstein) B.; m. Janice Helene Bard, Feb. 5, 1967; children: Tamara Lee, Sarah Beth, David Louis. BA, Wayne State U., 1959, MD, 1962. Diplomate Am. Bd. Psychiatry and Neurology, 1972. Practice medicine specializing psychiatry Southfield, Mich., 1968—; asst. prof. psychiatry Wayne State U., Detroit, 1968—; staff Kingswood Hosp., Ferndale, Mich., 1969—, Detroit Psychiat. Inst., 1968—. Contbr. articles to profl. jours. Served to capt. USAF, 1963-65. Recipient Magic Flute award Salzburg Mozarteum, 1986. Mem. AMA, Am. Psychiat. Assn., Wayne County Med. Soc., Mich. Psychiat. Soc., Assn. Orthodox Jewish Scientists, Pro-Mozart Soc. (bd. dirs. 1982—). Republican. Avocations: classical music, table tennis. Home: 17030 Cedarcroft Southfield MI 48076 Office: 15901 W 9 Mile Suite 312 Southfield MI 48075

BERKOWITZ, DAVID VICTOR, psychiatrist; b. N.Y.C., Oct. 6, 1943; s. Abrahm Benjamin and Esther (Yellin) B.; m. Julie Diane Erpelding, Dec. 20, 1968; children: Susan, Mark, Steven, Joshua. BA, Northwestern U., 1965; MD, U. Cin., 1970. Diplomate Am. Bd. Psychiatry and Neurology. Intern then resident in psychiatry U. Cin. Med. Ctr., 1970-73; instr. psychiatry U. Cin. Coll. Medicine, 1975-77; practice medicine specializing in psychiatry Cin., 1977—; cons. Sleep Disorder Clinic of Greater Cin., 1986—, Mental Health Services of N. Cen. Cin., 1986—. Served to maj. U.S. Army, 1973-75. Mem. AMA, Ohio Med. Assn., Am. Psychiat. Assn., Ohio Psychiat. Assn., Acad. of Medicine of Cin. Home: 3155 Veazey Ave Cincinnati OH 45238 Office: 3310 Ruther Ave Cincinnati OH 45220

BERLAND, THEODORE, author; b. Chgo., Mar. 26, 1929; s. Samuel and Lena (Siegel) B.; B.S. in Journalism, U. Ill., 1950; A.M. in Sociology, U. Chgo., 1972; postgrad. Bowling Green (Ohio) State U., Northwestern U.; m. Cynthia Rich, Dec. 23, 1956; children—Leslie Myra, Elizabeth Ann, David Rueben. Gen. assignment reporter, wire editor Champaign-Urbana (Ill.) Courier, 1950-51; sci. writer Michael Reese Hosp., Chgo., 1955-56, 66-84, 87—, Rush-Presbyn.-St. Luke's Med. Ctr., Chgo., 1984-87 ; sci. writer, editor Research Reports, U. Chgo. public relations office, 1956-59; free lance writer, Chgo., 1959—; fgn. corr. Chgo.'s American, Algiers, 1962, Chgo. Daily News, Antarctica, 1963, AMA News, Rotarian Mag., Caribbean, 1965; cons. EPA, 1971-73; instr. sci. writing Medill Sch. Journalism, Northwestern U., 1973, 75; instr. nutrition Columbia Coll., Chgo., 1977-80, chmn. dept. journalism, 1980-82; vis. asst. prof. journalism Bowling Green State U., 1979-80; lectr. in mass. communication U. Wis., Milw., 1980-81; assoc. prof. communications Grand Valley State Coll., Allendale, Mich., 1982—. Pres., North Town Community Council, 1970-73, also Citizens Against Noise; pres. dist. 2 edn. council Chgo. Bd. Edn., 1972-73; v.p. Bernard Horwich Jewish Community Center, 1970-75, pres., 1975-77; pres. Jewish Community Council West Rogers Park, 1975-76; bd. dirs. Ind. Voters Ill., 1974-75, Citizens Schs. Com., 1974-75. Served to 1st lt. USAF, 1951-55. Recipient Journalism award Am. Osteo. Assn., 1963; certificate of Recognition med. journalism awards contests AMA, 1964, 66; 8th prize U.S. sect. Internat. Honeywell/Asahi Pentax Photo Contest, 1965; Med. Journalism award Ill. Med. Soc., 1967; Sci. Writers award ADA, 1968, 69; Distinguished Service in Journalism award Am. Optometric Assn., 1973; Distinguished Achievement in Med. Writing award Chgo. chpt. Am. Med. Writers Assn., 1973; Beth Fonda award for excellence in Med. feature writing, 1975, 78. Fellow Am. Med. Writers Assn. (pres. 1981-82); mem. Headline Club Chgo. (treas. 1972-73), Authors Guild, Nat. Assn. Sci. Writers (life mem.), Soc. Midland Authors (pres. 1975-78, treas. 1978-79), Soc. Profl. Journalists. Author: The Scientific Life, 1962; (with Alfred E. Seyler) Your Children's Teeth, 1968; The Fight for Quiet, 1970; (with Mitchell Spellberg) Living with Your Ulcer, 1971; (with Robert Addison) Living with Your Bad Back, 1972; (with Gordon Snider) Living with Your Bronchitis and Emphysema, 1972; (with Richard Perritt) Living with Your Eye Operation, 1973; Rating the Diets, 1974, rev. edits., 1975-86; (with Leslie Sandlow and Richard Shapiro) Living with Your Colitis and Hemorrhoids and Related Disorders, 1976; (with Frank Z. Warren) Acupuncture Diet, 1976; The Fitness Fact Book, 1980, 81; (with Henry A. Jordan) After the Diet . . . Then What?, 1980, The Doctor's Calories-Plus Diet, 1981; (with L. Fischer-Pap) Living With Your Allergies and Asthma, 1983; The Dieter's Almanac, 1984; Fitness for Life, 1986; contbg. author: Stimulus, 1960; Perspectives on Living, 1962; Compact Handbook of College Composition (Maynard J. Brennan), 1964; A Treasury of Tips for Writers, 1965; Great Ideas Today, 1966; World Book Year Book, 1970; Crisis of Survival, 1970; Writing the Magazine Article, 1971; Readings in Health, 1972; The Endangered Environment (Ashley Montagu), 1974; Current Thinking and Writing, 1976; Together, 1977; The Complete Diet Guide for Runners and Other Athletes, 1978; TV Today, 1981; editor: The Medical Importance of Wine; contbr. over 200 articles to major mags. and jours.; author column The Thin Man, Chgo. Sun-Times, 1978-80, also numerous newspapers through Field News Service, United Feature Syndicate and Enterprise Sci. Service; author documentary movies. Office: PO Box 597602 Chicago IL 60659-7602

BERLIN, LEONARD, radiologist, surgeon; b. Chgo., May 5, 1935; s. Irving and Beatrice (Barth) B.; m. Phyllis Panitch, June 24, 1956; children: Steven, Paul, Robert, Jonathan. BS, U. Ill., Chgo., 1957, MD, 1959. Diplomate Am. Bd. Radiology. Intern St. Francis Hosp., Evanston, Ill., 1959-60; resident U. Ill., 1960-63; assoc. radiologist Skokie Valley Hosp., Skokie, Ill., 1966-77, dir. radiology, 1977—, also chmn. bd. trustees. Contbr. articles to profl. jours. Served to capt. USAF, 1963-65. Fellow Am. Coll. Radiology; mem. AMA, Am. Coll. Nuclear Med., Am. Coll. Legal Med., Radiol. Soc. N. Am. Home: 518 Meadow Dr W Wilmette IL 60091 Office: Skokie Valley Hosp 9600 Gross Point Rd Skokie IL 60076

BERMAN, HERBERT MARTIN, lawyer, arbitrator, mediator; b. Louisville, Mar. 22, 1936; s. Robert J. and Freda (Baer) B.; B.A., Ind. U., 1958; LL.B., U. Louisville, 1961; m. Sondra Ann Ignatow, Dec. 21, 1958; children—Michael, Frances, Jennifer. Admitted to Ky. bar, 1961, Ill. bar, 1971; asso. firm Shaikun & Helmann, Louisville, 1961-62; field atty. NLRB, Cin., 1962-63; asst. gen. counsel Internat. Brewery Workers Union, Cin., 1963-68; labor relations counselor Brunswick Corp., Chgo., 1968-70; asso. firm Lederer, Fox & Grove, Chgo., 1970-73; partner firm Arnold & Kadjan, Chgo., 1973-76; pres., partner firm Berman & Landrum Ltd., Chgo., 1976-79; prin. firm Herbert M. Berman & Assos., Ltd., Chgo., 1979—; mem. panel labor arbitrators Fed. Mediation and Conciliation Service. Mem. Am. Arbitration Assn. (panel), ABA, Soc. Profls. in Dispute Resolution. Home: 244 Willow Ave Deerfield IL 60015 Office: PO Box 350 Deerfield IL 60015

BERMAN, JAY MICHAEL, obstetrician-gynecologist; b. Bronx, Apr. 25, 1952; s. Edward and Jeanette (Goodman) B.; m. Nancy Beth Rubenstein, Dec. 19, 1976; children: Jeremy Paul, Daniel Aaron. BA in Biology cum laude, CUNY, Flushing, 1973; MD, Wayne State U., 1977. Diplomate Am. Bd. Ob-Gyn. Resident in ob-gyn Sinai Hosp., Detroit, 1977-81; practice medicine specializing in ob-gyn Southfield, Mich., 1981—; clin. instr. ob-gyn Wayne State U., Detroit, 1983—; instr. laser surgery Sinai Hosp., Detroit, 1986. Fellow Am. Coll. Obstetricians and Gynecologists; mem. Am. Fertility Soc. Jewish. Avocations: tennis, ham radio, photography, computers. Office: 29275 Northwest Hwy Southfield MI 48034

BERMAN, RONALD CHARLES, accountant; b. Chgo., July 7, 1949; s. Joseph and Helen (Neiderman) BBS with highest honors, U. Ill., 1971, JD with honors, 1974. Bar: Ill. 1974, Wis. 1976; CPA, Wis. Tax staff Grant Thornton, Chgo., 1974-76, tax supr., Madison, Wis., 1976-78, tax mgr., 1978-81; ptnr. tax dept. Grant Thornton, Madison, 1981—. Mem. editorial adv. bd. Physician's Tax Advisor Newsletter, 1986—; Scoutmaster Boy Scouts Am., Middleton, Wis., 1978—; fin. chmn. Mohawk Dist. Four Lakes council Boy Scouts Am., Madison, 1981-85, endowment fund chmn., 1984—, exec. bd., 1982—; bd. dirs. Scouts on Stamps Soc. Internat., 1986—, Madison Pension Council, 1986—. Recipient Bronze Tablet, U. Ill., 1971, Silver Beaver Boy Scouts Am., 1981. Mem. ABA (employee benefits com. taxation sect), Am. Inst. CPA's (Sells award Hon. mention 1971), Wis. Soc. CPA's, State Bar of Wis., Ill. Bar Assn., Order of Coif, Alpha Phi Omega, Phi Kappa Phi, Phi Alpha Delta. Lodge: Optimist. Avocations: photography, philately, camping. Home: 3906 Rolling Hill Dr Middleton WI 53562 Office: Grant Thornton 2 E Gilman PO Box 8100 Madison WI 53708

BERNACCHI, JEFFERY MICHAEL, commodity futures trader; b. LaPorte, Ind., Apr. 5, 1958; s. Peter James and Patricia Jean (Wysocki) B.; m. Mary Lynn Scovill, May 30, 1981. BA in Econs., DePauw U., 1979; MBA, U. Chgo., 1982. Self-employed commodities futures trader Chgo., 1979—; v.p. Kor-It Sales, Inc., La Porte, Ind. Mem. Chgo. Mercantile Exchange (equity indices com.), Singapore Internat. Monetary Exchange. Roman Catholic. Avocations: international travel, skiing, sailing, windsurfing. Home: 128 Briar Pl Barrington IL 60010 Office: Chgo Mercantile Exchange 30 S Wacker Dr Chicago IL 60606

BERNARD, DAVID JOHN, controller; b. Canton, Ohio, Feb. 5, 1954; s. John Joseph and Lucy (Ziccardi) B.; m. Linda Sue Yutzy, June 3, 1978; children: Christina Marie, Anthony David. BA in Acctg., Walsh Coll., 1976. CPA, Ohio. Staff auditor Sorkin, Thayer and Co., Akron, Ohio, 1975-77, sr. auditor, 1977-78, audit mgr., 1978-81, auditing ptnr., acctg. ptnr., v.p., 1981-83, also bd. dirs.; controller Biskind Devel. Co., North Olmsted, Ohio, 1983—; acctg. instr. Walsh Coll., Canton, 1979. Bd. trustees Akron Hoban High Sch., 1982-83. Mem. Am. Inst. CPA's, Ohio Soc. Cert. CPA's. Republican. Roman Catholic. Club: Walsh Coll. Bus. (treas. 1975-76). Avocations: tennis, racquetball, softball, reading, music. Home: 7506 Cheryl Ln NW Massillon OH 44646 Office: Biskind Devel Co 4970 Great Northern Mall North Olmsted OH 44070

BERNARD, DEBORAH LYNN, construction company executive; b. Detroit, Feb. 2, 1954; d. Ernest B. and Ilene Evelyn (Jones) B. BS, Mich. State U., 1976. Inventory control Mich. Products, Lansing, 1977-78; expeditor VanDervoort's, Lansing, 1978-80; office mgr. MACA Constrn. Co., Wooster, Ohio, 1980-83, sec.-treas., 1983-85, pres., 1985—. Roman Catholic. Avocations: gardening, needlecraft. Office: MACA Constrn Co Inc 2380-E Cardinal Ct Wooster OH 44691

BERNARD, JAMES HARVEY, JR., lawyer; b. Kansas City, Mo., June 8, 1951; s. James and Marjorie Ann (Kirts) K.; m. Sara Faye Dickerson, Oct. 25, 1979; 1 child, James Harvey III. BA, U. Kans., 1973; JD, Creighton U., 1976. With Slagle & Bernard, Kans. City, Mo., 1976—, ptnr., 1981—. Pres. bd. Historic Kans. City Found., 1986—; sec. bd. Genesis Sch., Inc., Kans. City, 1985—; elder Second Presbyn. Ch., Kans. City, 1985—. Mem. ABA, Kans. City Bar Assn., Mo. Bar Assn., Lawyers Assn. Kans. City. Avocations: travel, amateur radio, stamp collecting. Office: Slagle & Bernard 127 W 10th Suite 500 Kansas City MO 64105

BERNARDI, JAMES EDWARD, retail liquor merchant, real estate investor; b. Highland Park, Ill., July 26, 1946; s. Irving D. and Nell D. (Dimmitt) B.; m. Michelle DiCarlo, June 12, 1976; children—Jamie Elizabeth, Michael James. B.A., North Park Coll., 1969. Tchr., coach Carmel High Sch., Mundelein, Ill., 1969-75; gen. mgr. and officer Foremost Liquors, Mundelein, 1976—; Mem. Com. Bus. Devel. Commn., Mundelein, ARC, Mundelein. Mem. Ill. High Sch. Assn. (ofcl. 1969—), No. Ofcls. Assn. (past pres., bd. dirs.). Roman Catholic. Officiated Ill. High Sch. Basketball Championship Series for past 12 yrs. Avocations: golf, officiating football and basketball. Home: 849 Braemar Mundelein IL 60060 Office: Foremost Liquors 425 Townline Rd Mundelein IL 60060

BERNARDIN, CARDINAL JOSEPH LOUIS, archbishop; b. Columbia, S.C., Apr. 2, 1928; s. Joseph and Maria M. (Simion) B. A.B. in Philosophy, St. Mary's Sem., Balt., 1948; M.Ed., Cath. U. Am., 1952. Ordained priest Roman Catholic Ch., 1952; asst. pastor Diocese of Charleston, S.C., 1952-54; vice chancellor Diocese of Charleston, 1954-56, chancellor, 1956-66, vicar gen., 1962-66, diocesan consultor, 1962-66, adminstr., 1964-65; aux. bishop Atlanta, 1966-68; pastor Christ the King Cathedral, 1966-68; sec., mem. exec. com. Nat. Conf. Cath. Bishops-U.S. Cath. Conf., gen. sec., 1968-72, pres., 1974-77; archbishop of Cin. 1972-82, of Chgo., 1982—; mem. Sacred Congregation Bishops, 1973-78; del., mem. permanent council World Synod of Bishops, 1974, 77—; mem. Pontifical Commn. Social Communications, Rome, 1970-72, Sacred Coll. Cardinals, 1983—. Mem. adv. council Am. Revolution Bicentennial, 1975, Pres.'s Adv. Com. Refugees, 1975. Mem. Nat. Cath. Edn. Assn. (chmn. bd. 1978-79). Address: Archdiocese of Chgo 1555 N State Pkwy Chicago IL 60610 *

BERNAU, SIMON JOHN, mathematics educator; b. Wanganui, N.Z., June 12, 1937; came to U.S., 1969; s. Earnest Lovell and Ella Mary (Mason) B.; m. Lynley Joyce Turner, Aug. 11, 1959; children: Nicola Ann, Sally Jane. B.Sc., U. Canterbury, Christchurch, N.Z., 1958, M.Sc., 1959; B.A., Cambridge (Eng.) U., 1961, Ph.D., 1964. Lectr. U. Canterbury, 1964-65, sr. lectr., 1965-66; prof. math. U. Otago, Dunedin, N.Z., 1966-69; assoc. prof. U. Tex., Austin, 1969-76, prof., 1976-85; prof., head math. dept. Southwest Mo. State U., Springfield, 1986—. Researcher numerous publs. in field, 1964—; referee profl. jours., 1965—. Gulbenkian jr. research fellow Churchill Coll., Cambridge U., 1963-64. Mem. Am. Math. Soc. (reviewer 1965—), Math. Assn. Am., London Math. Soc. Home: 3887 E Linwood Springfield MO 65804 Office: Dept Math Southwest Mo State U Springfield MO 65804

BERNAUER, CAROL CANDICE, advertising executive; b. Cleve., Nov. 12, 1956; s. Nelson Clarence and Lois Carol (Calmer) B. BFA, Cleve. Inst. Art, 1979; MBA, Baldwin Wallace Coll., 1987. Advt. coordinator Ferro Corp., Cleve., 1980—. Author 2 poetry chpt. books, 1984, over 30 published poems. J. Huntington Found. scholar Cleve. Inst. Art, 1977-78. Home: 1304 W 105 St Cleveland OH 44102 Office: Ferro Corp One Erieview Plaza Cleveland OH 44114

BERNAUER, NORMAN LANG, advertising executive; b. Pitts., Apr. 19, 1926; s. Norman Leo and Frieda Dorothy (Allmendinger) B.; m. Barbara Jean Hands, Sept. 26, 1953; children: Allise Jean, Richard Martin. AA, Graceland Coll., 1949; BA, U. Wis., Madison, 1951; cert. TV prodn., Sch. Radio and TV Technic, N.Y.C., 1952. Ordained to ministry Reorganized Ch. of Jesus Christ of Latter-day Saints, 1954. With Ford Found., Sta. WOI-TV, Ames, Iowa, 1952; with Sta. WDAF-TV, Kansas City, Mo., 1952-66; pres. Ber-Raye Prodns. Co., Kansas City, 1966-68; v.p. Raveill Farley Advt., Independence, Mo., 1968-74; exec. v.p. Everett, Brandt & Bernauer, Inc., Independence, 1974—. Mem. Kansas City Mayor's Task Force on Airport Commn., 1977-82; chmn. Citizens Com. for Eastern Jackson County Airport, 1978-86; bd. dirs. Restoration Trail Found. Mem. Stake High Council, 1963—; pastor Reorganized Ch. of Jesus Christ of Latter-day Saints, 1954-61, 82. Served with U.S. Army, 1944-46. Mem. Kansas City Advt. Fin. Club, Advt. Agys. for Action, FIMA (mem. pub. relations and pub. affairs com. 1981-82). Lodge: Kiwanis (pres. inter-city club 1986-87). Home: 427 W 70th St Kansas City MO 64113 Office: 1805 Grand Ave Suite 200 Kansas City MO 64108

BERNDT, CYNTHIA JEAN, auditor; b. Parkston, S.D., Oct. 10, 1957; d. Arthur Jr. and Elaine Delores (Pepplitsch) B. BA in Acctg. and Econs. summa cum laude, Dakota Wesleyan U., 1979. CPA, S.D. Analyst cost separations Martin & Assocs. Inc., Mitchell, S.D., 1979-82; internal auditor Comml. Trust & Savs. Bank, Mitchell, 1982-87, cashier, ops. officer, 1987—; instr. acctg. and auditing Dakota Wesleyan U., Mitchell, 1981, 83. Smith-Shoemaker scholar Dakota Wesleyan U., 1977. Mem. Am. Inst. CPA's, Phi Kappa Phi, Phi Gamma Mu, Alpha Lamda Delta. Home: PO Box 72 Mitchell SD 57301 Office: Comml Trust & Savs Bank 201 E 3d Mitchell SD 57301

BERNDT, DAVID JOHN, psychologist; b. Elgin, Ill., July 14, 1950; s. Melvin John and Edith W. B.; B.S. summa cum laude, Coll. of Charleston, 1977; M.A., Loyola U., Chgo., 1979, Ph.D. (NIMH fellow, Doyle fellow), 1981; m. Sheila MacDonald, Mar. 7, 1978. Mental health asst. Charleston (S.C.) County Hosp., 1976-77; intern Michael Reese Hosp. and Med. Center, Chgo., 1979-80, staff psychologist, 1981—, asst. dir. psychology, 1984—; exec. dir. Affect, Behavior and Cognition; mem. faculty Ctr. Psychoanalytic Study. asst. prof. dept. psychiatry U. Chgo. Mem. Assn. Advancement Psychology, Eastern Psychol. Assn., Am. Psychol. Assn., Soc. Personality Assessment. Contbr. articles to profl. jours., chpts., books. Home: 212 Burlington Riverside IL 60546

BERNDT, JOAN GASSAWAY, music educator; b. Toledo, May 4, 1936; d. Henry Griffith and Florence Louise (Schwyn) Gassaway; m. William C. Berndt, Aug. 18, 1962; 1 son, Ronald W. MusB, U. Mich., 1958, MusM, 1962. Dir. orch. Birmingham (Mich.) pub. schs., 1958-64; instrumental music tchr. Rochester (Mich.) Community Schs., 1972-73; dir. orch. Ferndale (Mich.) City Schs., 1979-80, 83—; lectr. music dept. Oakland U., Rochester, Mich., 1973-79; condr. Troy (Mich.) Community Orch., 1982—; pvt. music tchr.; clinician; performer. Author: Preliminary Tone Studies for the Beginning Oboist, 1981, Sneaky Sight-Reading Studies, 1981, The Oboist's Fullrange Scales, 1981. Recipient Oreon E. Scott Humanities award U. Mich., 1958; James Babcock scholar, 1958. Mem. Music Educators Nat. Conf., Nat. Sch. Orch. Assn., Mich. Sch. Band and Orch. Assn. (adjudicator), Phi Beta Kappa, Sigma Alpha Iota, Phi Kappa Phi, Pi Kappa Lambda. Republican. Lutheran. Club: Birmingham Musicale.

BERNDT, KIM L., product manager; b. Sioux Falls, S.D., Mar. 28, 1956; d. Clinton L. and Verna M. (Helm) B.; m. Michelle L. Allen, Aug. 17, 1985. BS in Elec. Engring., S.D. Sch. Mines and Technol., 1978; MBA, Kans. State U., 1981. Direct salesman The Southwestern Co., Nashville, Tenn., 1975-81; teaching asst. Kans. State U., Manhattan, 1979-81; product mgr. The Trane Co., LaCrosse, Wis., 1982-84, Tennant Co., Mpls., 1984—. Home: 7356 116th Pl N Champlin MN 55316 Office: Tennant Co 701 N Lilac Dr Minneapolis MN 55422

BERNEIS, KENNETH STANLEY, physician, educator; b. Bloomington, Ind., Dec. 25, 1951; s. Hans Ludwig and Regina (Fischhoff) B.; m. Karen Lou Sachs, Nov. 23, 1975; children—Erica, Erin, Ellen, Elaina. B.S., U.

Mich., 1973, M.D., 1977. Diplomate Am. Bd. Family Practice. Intern-resident Bronson Hosp., and Borgess Med. Ctr., 1977-80; practice family medicine, Ostego, Mich., 1980—; pres., owner Ostego Family Physicians, P.C., 1981—; clin. instr. Mich. State U., 1980—; preceptor Southwestern Mich. Area Health Edn. Ctr., 1980—; chief of staff Pipp Community Hosp., 1982-85, vice-chief of staff, 1985-86, chief of staff, 1986—, chief ob-gyn, 1985—, chief pharmacy and therapeutics, 1984—; chief quality assurance Mirnet Research Network, 1981—, mem. steering com., 1982—. Mem. Am. Acad. Family Physicians, AMA, Nat. Rifle Assn. Home: 131 N Sunset St Plainwell MI 49080 Office: 900 Dix St Otsego MI 49078 also: 1576 Main St Martin MI 49070

BERNER, JANE FAITH, academic administrator; b. Hancock, Mich., Dec. 10, 1941; d. Raymond Matti and Fannie Alma (Kohtala) Eilola; m. James Walter Berner, July 31, 1965; 1 child, Jay Charles. BA, Mich. State U., 1964; MSBA, Mich. Tech. U., 1976. Coordinator continuing edn. Mich. Tech. U., Houghton, 1971-84, dir. women in engring., 1972-84, mgr. office systems and tng., 1984—. Lutheran. Avocations: reading, camping, sports. Home: 1415 Roberts Hancock MI 49930 Office: Mich Tech U Houghton MI 49931

BERNET, J. J., transportation company executive. Pres. U.S. Truck Lines Inc. Del., Cleve. Office: U S Truck Lines Inc of Del 785 Huntington Bldg Cleveland OH 44115 *

BERNET, WILLIAM G., transportation company executive. Chmn., chief exec. officer U.S. Truck Lines Inc. Del., Cleve. Office: U S Truck Lines Inc of Del 785 Huntington Bldg Cleveland OH 44115 *

BERNETT, THEODORE BYRON, educator, management consultant; b. Chgo., Aug. 30, 1924; s. Joseph and Julia (Gorski) B.; B.S. in M.E., U. Ill., 1950; student bus. adminstrn., U. Wis., Milw., 1953-54; m. Helen Brower, Apr. 23, 1949; children—Richard, Michael, James. Julie, Amy. founder T.B. Bernett & Assos., Kenosha, Wis., 1980—. Served with USNR, 1943-46. Home: 6622 59th Ave Kenosha WI 53142-2931

BERNEY, JOSEPH HENRY, appliance manufacturing company executive; b. Balt., May 7, 1932; s. Eugene Philip and Blanche (Ney) B.; m. Phyllis Pearlove, Jan. 18, 1956; children: Richard, Philip, Julia, David. B.S., U. Pa., 1953; M.S., Columbia U., 1954. C.P.A., Va., Wis. Staff accountant Touche, Niven, Bailey & Smart, C.P.A.s, N.Y.C., 1954, A.M. Pullen & Co., C.P.A.s, Richmond, Va., 1954-56; vice chmn. Nat. Presto Industries, Inc., Eau Claire, Wis., 1956—, also bd. dirs.; officer, dir. Nat. Holding Investment Co., Canton Mfg. Corp., Jackson Sale & Storage, Presto Mfg. Co., Presto Internat. Ltd., Nat. Pipeline Co. Bd. dirs. Outward Bound, Inc., United Fund Eau Claire, U. Wis.-Eau Claire Found., Eau Claire YMCA, Minn. Outward Bound Sch.; past pres. Chippewa Valley council Boy Scouts Am. Mem. Am. Inst. C.P.A.s, Va., Wis. socs. accountants, Beta Gamma Sigma, Delta Sigma Rho. Home: 104 Skyline Dr Eau Claire WI 54703 Office: care Nat Presto Industries Inc Eau Claire WI 54703

BERNHARD, BRIAN AHRENS, civil engineering consultant; b. Parkston, S.D., Oct. 30, 1946; s. Harry Theodore and Joan P. (Ahrens) B.; m. Marlys Joyce Struck, June 29, 1968; children: Angela, Travis, Daniel, Marisa. BSCE, S.D. Sch. of Mines and Tech., 1970. Registered profl. engr., S.D., Nebr., Iowa; registered land surveyor, S.D., Nebr. Engr. Wash. Hwy. Dept., Vancouver, 1970-71, S.P.N. & Assocs., Mitchell, S.D., 1973-76; owner, engr. B & E Engring., Inc., Yankton, S.D., 1976—. Active Boy Scouts Am. Served to 1st lt. C.E., U.S. Army, 1971-73. Mem. ASCE, Am. Waterworks Assn., NSPE, Prof. Land Surveyors Assn. of Nebr., S.D. Profl. Land Surveyors Assn. Republican. Lutheran. Lodges: Sertoma (bd. dirs Yankton 1983-86), Rotary, Masons. Avocation: music. Home: 613 W 10th St Yankton SD 57078 Office: B & E Engring Rt 1 Box 256 Yankton SD 57078

BERNHARDT, DANIEL JOSEPH, architect; b. Quincy, Ill., Nov. 19, 1954; s. Carl G. and Margie A. (Venver-Hoh) B. BArch, Iowa State U., 1976, MArch, 1981. Registered architect, Iowa, Mo. Architect Meyer and Peter Architects, Quincy, 1982-83, Peckham and Wright Architects, Columbia, Mo., 1983-84; project mgr. State of Mo., Jefferson City, Mo., 1984—. Mem. AIA. Home: R3 1208 Autumn Ridge Dr Holts Summit MO 65043 Office: State Mo Div Design & Constrn PO Box 809 Jefferson City MO 65102

BERNHARDT, GREGORY RALPH, psychologist, academic administrator, educator; b. Denver, May 25, 1948; s. Rienhardt Ralph and Eileen Margaret (Schmidt) B.; m. Susan Gray Praeger, Aug. 10, 1974; children: Sarah, Christopher. BA, Colo. State U., 1971; MS, Kans. State Tchrs. Coll., 1973; EdD, U. No. Colo., 1979. Lic. psychologist; cert. nat. counselor. Assoc. prof. edn. and human services Wright State U., Dayton, Ohio, 1979—, dir. div. human services, 1985—; bd. dirs. Suicide Prevention Ctr., Dayton, 1980—; rep. Ohio Network Ednl. Cons. in Aging, Columbus, Ohio, 1984—. Contbr. articles to profl. jours. Recipient Teaching Excellence award Wright State U. Alumni Assn., 1984-85. Mem. Am. Assn. Counseling and Devel., Assn. Counselor Educators and Suprs., Am. Psychol. Assn. (div. counseling psychology). Democrat. Roman Catholic. Avocations: skiing, scuba diving, running. Home: 690 Omar Circle Yellow Springs OH 45387 Office: Wright State U Coll Edn and Human Services Dayton OH 45435

BERNIE, BRUCE JEREMY, obstetrician, gynecologist; b. Dayton, Ohio, Dec. 8, 1948; s. David L. and Helen (Kuhr) B.; m. Vicki Lynn Fisher, Sept. 16, 1978; children: Andrew, Emily, Aaron. BA summa cum laude, Miami U., Oxford, Ohio, 1969; MD, Med. Coll. Va., 1971. Resident in ob-gyn Med. Coll. Va., Richmond, 1971-74; fellow in maternal and fetal medicine Dept. Ob-Gyn U. Minn., Mpls., 1974-75; practice medicine specializing in ob-gyn Davue Ob-Gyn Assocs., Inc., Dayton, 1975—; asst. clin. prof. dept. ob-gyn Wright State U. Med. Sch, Dayton, 1976—. Fellow Am. Coll Ob-Gyn, Am. Fertility Soc.; mem. AMA, Am. Soc. Gyn Laparosocopists, Ohio State Med. Assn., Montgomery County Med. Soc., Dayton Ob-Gyn Soc. Avocations: golf, fishing. Office: Davue Ob-Gyn Assocs Inc 2200 Philadelphia Dr #447 Dayton OH 45406

BERNING, PAUL EDGAR, financial specialist; b. Cin., Apr. 30, 1934; s. Edgar Joseph and Irene M. (Bennett) B.; m. Dolores Clare Prell, June 2, 1956; children: Mary Ann, Joseph, Diane, Thomas. Assoc., Xavier U., Cin., 1958. CPA, Ohio. Mgr. Boyd Roebuck & Co., CPA's, Cin., 1958-65; chief fin. officer Friés & Friés Inc., Cin., 1965-76; pvt. practice acctg. Cin., 1976—; seminar author and condr., 1986. Leader Boy Scouts Am., Cin., 1958-85, Order of Arrow, Cin., 1960-86. Recipient Scouters Key for Commrs. Boy Scouts Am.,1961, Vigil Hon. Order of Arrow, 1965, Scouters Key for Unit Leaders Boy Scouts Am., 1968, 71, 78, St. George award Cath. Com. Scouting, 1970. Mem. Am. Inst. CPA's, Internat. Assn. Fin. Planning, Am. Assn. Personal Fin. Planners, Ohio Soc. CPA's, The Planning Forum, Real Estate Investors Assn. (auditor 1980-84). Republican. Roman Catholic. Lodge: KC (treas. Madonna Council 1959-60). Avocation: hiking.

BERNSTEIN, CHARLES BERNARD, lawyer; b. Chgo., June 24, 1941; s. Norman and Adele (Shore) B.; A.B., U. Chgo., 1962; J.D., DePaul U., 1965; m. Roberta Luba Lesner, Aug. 7, 1968; children—Edward Charles, Louis Charles, Henry Jacob. Admitted to Ill. bar, 1965, U.S. Supreme Ct. bar, 1972; asso. firm Axelrod, Goodman & Steiner, Chgo., 1966-67, Max & Herman Chill, Chgo., 1967-74, Bellows & Assos., Chgo., 1974-81, Marvin Sacks Ltd., Chgo., 1981; individual practice law, 1981—; basketball press dir. U. Chgo., 1967-74. Vice pres. Congregation Rodfei Zedek, 1979, bd. dirs., 1978—. Recipient Am. Jurisprudence award, 1963; citation meritorious service Dist. Grand Lodge 6 B'nai B'rith, 1969; My Brothers Keeper award Am. Jewish Congress, 1977. Mem. Chgo. Bar Assn., Ill. State Bar Assn., Chgo. Jewish Hist. Soc. (treas. 1977-79, v.p. 1979-82, dir. 1977—), Chgo. Pops Orch. Assn. (treas., exec. com. 1975-81), Am. Jewish Hist. Soc., Art Inst. of Chgo., Chgo. Hist. Soc., Jewish Geneal. Soc. (dir. 1977—), Nu Beta Epsilon. Club: B'nai B'rith. Author: (with Stuart L. Cohen) Torah and Technology: The History and Genealogy of the Anixter Family, 1986; contbr. articles to mags., profl. jours. Home: 5400 S Hyde Park Blvd Apt 10-C Chicago IL 60615 Office: 120 W Madison St Chicago IL 60602

BERNSTEIN, CHARLES MARC, oil company scientist; b. Buffalo, July 19, 1952; s. M. Robert and Ethel-Rita Beverly (Rocklin) B. Tech. support supr. Bowling Green (Ohio) State U., 1972-79; sr. system programmer TRW, Cleve., 1979-80, Gould Ocean Systems, Cleve., 1980-82; systems cons. Systemation, Cleve., 1982-85; project engr. research and devel. Standard Oil Co., Cleve., 1985—; tech. advisor Cleve. Planetarium, 1979-82. Mem. Digital Equipment Computer Users Soc. Avocations: reading, magic. Home: 19955 Rockside Rd Apt 1503 Bedford OH 44146 Office: Standard Oil Research And Devel 4440 Warrensville Ctr Cleveland OH 44128

BERNSTEIN, DAVID ISAAC, allergist; b. Cin., Dec. 9, 1951; s. I. Leonard and Miriam (Goldman) B.; m. Cheryl Koff, May 29, 1977; children: Daniel Albert, William Zev. BA, U. Cin., 1973, MD, 1977. Diplomate Am. Bd. Internal Medicine, Am. Bd. Allergy and Immunology. Intern then resident Cleve. Clinic Hosp., 1977-80; research fellow Northwestern U., Chgo., 1980-82; practice medicine specializing in internal medicine and allergy Cin., 1982—; mem. staff Univ. Hosp., Cin., 1982—, VA Hosp., Cin., 1982—, Deaconess Hosp., Cin., 1982—; asst. prof. medicine U. Cin., 1982—, co-dir. allergy research lab., 1982—. Contbr. articles to profl. jours. Mem. ACP, Am. Acad. Allergy and Immunology. Jewish. Office: 8464 Winton Rd Cincinnati OH 45231

BERNSTEIN, HARVEY JAY, computer specialist; b. Detroit, Apr. 16, 1945; s. Morris and Bernice (Rothman) B.; student U. Toledo, 1963-65: AS, Cuyahoga Community Coll., 1974; BS magna cum laude, Dyke Coll., 1977; MBA, Case Western Res. U., 1984; Sec. of Navy Fin. Mgmt. fellow Weatherhead Sch. Mgmt., Case Western Res. U., 1980-83; m. Irene Harriet Hoffman, Jan. 21, 1968; children: Bradley J., Matthew A. Fiscal acctg. asst. Navy Fin. Ctr., Cleve., 1971-72, fiscal acct. officer, 1972-73, mil. pay regulation specialist, 1973-79, fin. systems specialist, 1979-82, computer programmer analyst, 1982-84, supervisory computer specialist, dir. resource allocation and evaluation Consol. Data Ctr., 1984—; instr. John Carroll U., 1978-82, Cuyahoga Community Coll., 1977—, Dyke Coll., 1984-85. Served with USN, 1965-71. Recipient Career Service award Cleve. Fed. Exec. Bd., 1978; lic. real estate broker. Mem. Am. Soc. Mil. Comptrollers (pres. Cleve. chpt. 1976-77), Cleve. Area Bd. Realtors, Am. Contract Bridge League (life master), Mensa. Jewish. Office: US Navy Finance Center Cleveland OH 44199

BERNSTEIN, IRVING C., psychiatrist; b. Chgo., Apr. 15, 1918; s. David and Tillie (Bucky) B.; m. Dorothy Milzer, June 27, 1948; children: Mark, Gail, Paul. BS with distinction, U. Minn., 1940, MB, 1942, MD, 1943; MS, U. Colo., 1952. Diplomate Am. Bd. Psychiatry and Neurology. Practice psychiatry Mpls., 1951—; clin. prof. ob-gyn and psychiatry, U. Minn. Med. Sch., Mpls., 1951—; clin. prof. psychiatry U. Calif., San Diego; cons. Health Care Financing Adminstrn., Washington, 1978—. Contbr. 40 articles on psychiat. aspects of ob-gyn. Served to capt. USMC, 1943-46, ETO. Recipient Pres.'s award Minn. State Med. Assn., 1979. Fellow Am. Psychiat. Assn. (life). Democrat. Jewish. Avocation: skiing. Home: 1235 Yale Pl #1102 Minneapolis MN 55403 Office: 511 11th Ave S Minneapolis MN 55415

BERNSTEIN, JENNIFER FINE, nurse; b. Evanston, Ill., Dec. 6, 1956; d. Bernard and Yvonne Ruth (Borde) Fine; m. Louis David Bernstein, Aug. 15, 1982. BA in Chemistry, Goucher Coll., 1979; BS in Nursing, Columbia U., 1982. RN, N.Y., Ill. Sales rep. Stauffer Chem. Co., Westport, Conn., 1979-80; staff RN North Shore U. Hosp., Manhasset, N.Y., 1982-85; utilization rev. coordinator Crescent Counties Found. for Med. Care, Chgo., 1986, reconsideration coordinator, 1986—. Mem. Am. Nurses Assn., Ill. Assn. Quality Assurance Profls. Avocation: marathon running. Home: 1625 Sheridan Rd Wilmette IL 60091 Office: Crescent Counties Found Med Care 10 S Riverside Plaza Suite 1968 Chicago IL 60606

BERNSTEIN, JESSE AARON, human resource executive; b. Bklyn., Apr. 17, 1948; s. Morris David and Norma Mildred (Sprung) B.; m. Lenore Harriet Orenstein; children—Zachary Jacob, Mara Devorah. B.A., SUNY-New Paltz, 1968; M.S.W., U. Mich., 1970. Social worker Washtenaw County, Ann Arbor, Mich., 1970-73; pres. Western Wayne Counseling Assocs., Mich., 1973-80, Employee Assistance Assocs., Ann Arbor, Mich., 1981—. Pres. Westland C. of C., 1977-78; founding mem. Employee Assistance Cert. Commn., 1986; mem. Blue Cross-Blue Shield Mental Health Adv. Com., 1977—. Mem. Assn. Labor Mgmt. Adminstrs. and Cons. on Alcoholism (pres. Greater Detroit chpt. 1985-86, mem. orgn. rev. com. 1986), Nat. Assn. Social Workers, U. Mich. Sch. Social Work Alumni Assn. (bd. dirs. 1983—). Jewish. Home: 3552 Frederick Ann Arbor MI 48105 Office: Employee Assistance Assocs 1250 Eisenhower Pl Ann Arbor MI 48104

BERNSTEIN, MALCOLM ALBERT, ins. agt.; b. Cin., Feb. 18, 1933; s. Herbert B. and Mildred (Abrohams) B.; B.S., U. Pa., 1954; m. Ann Maxine Berkman, Nov. 24, 1960; children—Sarah Elizabeth, Alexander Isaac Joshua. With Isaacs & Bernstein Inc., Cin., 1954-69; v.p. Frederick Rauh & Co., Cin., 1969-82; owner M.A. Bernstein & Co., Cin., 1982—; pub. Music & Matter mag., 1958-59; pres. Dimension Cin. mag., 1963-65. Bd. dirs. Cin. Jewish Community Relations Council, 1958—, pres., 1980-82; bd. dirs. Jewish Family Service, 1965-79, Assn. Home Care Agencies, 1976-79; bd. dirs. Easy Riders, 1975—, pres., 1977-79. CPCU. Mem. Queen City Assn. (dir. 1968-69), Soc. CPCU. Jewish. Club: Losantiville Country. Home: 59 Oliver Rd Cincinnati OH 45215 Office: 1055 Saint Paul Pl Cincinnati OH 45202

BERNSTEIN, MURRAY M., social worker; b. Milw., July 3, 1938; s. Louis and Rae (Kurzer) B.; B.S., U. Wis., Milw., 1966, M.S.W., 1970; Ph.D., Eastern Nebr. Christian Coll., 1973; m. Nancy Siegel, Jan. 26, 1964; children—David J., Sarah Lynn. Program dir. Milw. Boys Club, 1964-68; social work psychologist VA Hosp., Woods, Wis., 1974—; asst. prof. dept. psychiatry Med. Coll. Wis.; pvt. cons.; lectr. in field; dir. Inst. Directive Therapy; cons. therapist Assn. Research and Enlightenment (Edgar Cayce Found.) del., lectr. People to People program, China, 1982. Contbr. articles on traumatic stress disorder on Am. ex-prisoners of war to profl. jours.; developer directive therapy method of psycho-social approach to psychotherapy. Pres. Temple Anshe Emeth, Milw., 1979-80. Served with USAF, 1956-60; to capt. M.C., U.S. Army, 1970-74. Cert. Acad. Cert. Social Workers. Mem. Am. Psychiat. Assn. (peer reviewer), Am. Group Psychotherapy Assn., Nat. Assn. Social Workers, Internat. Transactional Analysis Assn. Home: 8615 W Petersik St Milwaukee WI 53224 Office: Woods VA Hospital Woods WI 53193

BERNSTEIN, RICHARD A., publishing company executive; b. N.Y.C., June 28, 1946; s. Sidney and Ethel Helen (Shankman) B.; m. Amelia Fishman, Nov. 21, 1944; children: Bradley Ross, Jennifer Ann. BA in Econs., NYU, 1968. V.p. Pease & Ellman Inc., N.Y.C., 1968-73; pres. P&E Properties Inc., N.Y.C., 1973—; chmn. Western Pub. Co. Inc., N.Y.C., 1984—; chmn., pres., chief exec. officer Western Pub. Group Inc., N.Y.C., 1986—; chmn. Gen. Med. Corp., Richmond, Va., 1987—, Western Pub. Co., Racine, Wis.; bd. dirs. Hosp. for Joint Diseases, N.Y.C., N.Y. State Employee Retirement System, N.Y.C. Trustee Police Athletic League, N.Y.C., 1982—; chmn. N.Y. State Commn. on Regulation of Lobbying, Albany, 1982-86; candidate for comptroller City of N.Y., 1981. Served with U.S. Army, 1969. Fellow Yeshiva U., N.Y.C., 1986. Republican. Jewish. Home: Pilgrim Rd Rye NY 10580 Office: Western Pub Co 444 Madison Ave New York NY 10022 also: Western Pub Co 1220 Mound Ave Racine WI 53404

BERNSTEIN, ROBERT LEE, dentist; b. Massillon, Ohio, Feb. 11, 1933; s. Theodore and Dorothy Marie (Huff) B.; m. Ruth Anne Baker, Dec. 19, 1957; children—Jeffrey Kent, Bradley James. B.A., Case Western Res. U., 1956, D.D.S., 1961. Pvt. practice dentistry, Massillon, 1961—. Fellow Acad. Gen. Dentistry, Am. Soc. Dentistry for Children, Acad. Dentistry Internat.; mem. ADA, Stark County Dental Soc. (peer rev. com. 1981), Massillon Dental Soc. (pres. 1975-77). Republican. Episcopalian. Avocations: pottery; woodworking; electronics; boating; swimming. Office: 215 Erie St N Massillon OH 44646

BERNSTEIN, SUSAN POWELL, development and fundraising executive; b. Chgo., May 17, 1938; d. Herman and Frances (Dobkin) Powell; m. Phillip Bernstein, Sept. 4, 1957; children: Kenneth, Robert, Michael. BA in Human Services, Northeastern Ill. U., Chgo., 1978. Real estate assoc. Martin-Marbry, Inc., Skokie, Ill., 1971—; exec. dir. B'nai B'rith Women, Land of Lakes Region, Skokie, 1978-83; dir. resource devel. Travelers and Immigrants Aid, Chgo., 1984—; cons. Durban, South Africa, Community Arts Workshop. Founder, exec. dir., pres. Nat. Forum for Women, Woodstock, Ill., dir., 1980-83; mem. planning com., Chgo. hon. bd. Jane Addams Conf. for Peace in Nuclear Age. Named Citizen of Yr., Lerner Life newspapers, Chgo., 1980. Mem. Nat. Soc. Fundraising Execs. (Chgo. chpt.), Women in Devel. Professions, NOW. Democrat. Jewish. Home: 1501 Maple Ave #801 Evanston IL 60201

BERNSTINE, RICHARD LEE, obstetrician/gynecologist, educator; b. Phila., Jan. 8, 1925; s. J. Bernard and Rena (Berkowitz) B.; m. Joyce Tully, June 1, 1971. Student, St. Joseph's Coll., 1942-43, Villanova U., 1943-44; MD, Jefferson Med. Coll., 1948. Diplomate Am. Bd. Obstetrics & Gynecology. Intern Jefferson Med. Coll., Phila., 1948-50, instr. dept. obstetrics and gynecology, 1952-56, fellow in obstetrics and gynecology, 1954-56; enlisted USN, 1948, advanced through grades to capt., 1968; resident in obstetrics and gynecology U.S Naval Hosp., L.I., N.Y., 1956-59; with obstetrics and gynecology staff U.S Naval Hosp., Portsmouth, Va., 1959-62; sr. med. officer U.S. Naval Support Activity, London, 1962-65; force med. officer CINCUSNAVEUR, London, 1964-65; with clin. investigation dept. staff U.S. Naval Med. Research Inst. Nat. Med. Ctr., Bethesda, Md., 1965-70; with obstetrics and gynecology staff U.S. Naval Hosp., Bethesda, Md., 1966-70; retired USN, 1970; sr. research scientist Dept. Chemistry Am. U., Washington, 1970-73; head clin. specialties br. Research div. Bur. Medicine and Surgery USN, Washington, 1970-73; research scientist Health Care Study Ctr. Batelle Human Affairs Research Ctrs., Seattle, 1973-76; prof. obstetrics and genecology The Northeastern Ohio Univs. Coll. of Medicine, Rootstown, Ohio, 1976—; dir. edn. St. Elizabeth Hosp. Med. Ctr., Youngstown, Ohio, 1976—. Author: (with others) Clinical Ultrasound in Obstetrics and Gynecology, 1978, Principles and Practice of Obstetrics and Perinatology, 1981, Ultrasound in Medicine and Biology, 1982, Operative Perinatology, Invasive Obstetric Techniques, 1984, Obstetrics/Gynecology: A Problem-Oriented Approach, 1985; contbg. editor Jour. of Clin. Ultrasound and scientific exhibits. Recipient Certificate of Merit AMA, 1956, 59, Bronze award AMA, Am. Acad. Pediatrics, 1971, Prize award Am. Coll. Obstetricians and Gynecologists, 1972. Mem. Am. Coll. Obstetrics and Gynecology (Prize award 1970), ACS, Am. Inst. Ultrasound in Medicine, Ohio State Med. Assn., Mahoning County Med. Soc., Nat. Bd. Med. Examiners. Home: 232 N Cadilla Dr Youngstown OH 44512 Office: St Elizabeth Hosp Med Ctr 1044 Belmont Ave Youngstown OH 44501

BERNZEN, AVRIL MARIE CLARK, microbiologist; b. Quincy, Ill., Jan. 26, 1924; d. Wallace Edward and Marie A. (Recker) Heberling; B.S., Quincy Coll., 1945; voice grad. Quincy Conservatory Music; piano grad. Notre Dame Conservatory Music; student St. John Hosp. Sch. of Med. Tech., 1946-47; m. George W. Bernzen; 1 dau., Joan Marie Clark English. Microbiologist, St. John's Mercy Hosp., St. Louis, 1948-52; med. technologist St. Frances Hosp. Lab., Peoria, Ill., 1956-58; lectr. in microbiology Quincy Coll., 1966-70; adminstrv. technologist, ednl. dir. St. Mary Hosp., Quincy, 1959-78, program/ednl. dir., 1978—. Pres. Altrusa Club, 1974-76; bd. govs. for Dogwood Festival, C. of C., 1975-77; bd. dirs. Quincy Soc. Fine Arts, United Way, 1978—, v.p. planning, 1983-87, sec., 1984-85, also chmn. pub. relations; chair adv. bd. Helpline, 1986-87 ; bd. dirs. Quincy Community Little Theatre, Quincy Art Club, ESA World Center Found., Am. Cancer Soc.; bd. dirs. Quincy Mus. Natural History and Art, pres., 1983-85, dir. publicity, chair grants, 1985—. Named Outstanding Woman of Ill., ESA Orgn., 1968; Outstanding Woman of Quincy, 1970; Outstanding Alumnus, Biology Dept. of Quincy Coll., 1980. Mem. Am. Soc. Med. Tech.; Am. Soc. Clinical Pathologists, Internat. Platform Assn., Midwest Assn. for Ednl. Resource Sharing (pres. 1981-83). Epsilon Sigma Alpha (Outstanding Mem. award 1977). Republican. Roman Catholic. Clubs: Elks Aux., Spring Lake Country, Altrusa (Outstanding Mem. 1978-79). Home: 2236 Vermont St Quincy IL 62301 Office: 1415 Vermont St Quincy IL 62301

BEROLZHEIMER, KARL, lawyer; b. Chgo., Mar. 31, 1932; s. Leon J. and Rae Gloss (Lowenthal) B.; m. Diane Glick, July 10, 1954; children: Alan, Eric, Paul, Lisa. BA, U. Ill., 1953; JD, Harvard U., 1958. Bar: Ill. 1958, U.S. Ct. Appeals (7th cir.) 1964, U.S. Ct. Appeals (9th cir.) 1969, U.S. Supreme Ct. 1976. Assoc. Ross & Hardies, Chgo., 1958 66, ptnr., 1966-76; v.p. legal Centel Corp., Chgo., 1976-77, v.p., gen. counsel, 1977-82, sr. v.p., gen. counsel, 1982—; bd. dirs. Will County Water Co., Chgo., Milton Industries, Chgo., Devon Bank, Chgo.; cons. Mt. Pulaski Telephone and Electric Co., Lincoln, Ill., 1981—; sec., gen. counsel Consol. Water Co., Chgo., 1968-72. Bd. dirs. NCCJ, Chgo., 1977—; trustee, sec. Beth Emet Synagogue, Evanston, Ill., 1985-87. Served to 1st lt. U.S. Army, 1953-55. Mem. ABA (chmn. telecommunications com of corp., banking and bus. law sect. 1982-98, chmn. dispute resolution com. of corp., banking and bus. law sect. 1986—), Ill. State Bar Assn., Chgo. Bar Assn., Chgo. Council Lawyers. Democrat. Clubs: Univ., Legal (Chgo.). Home: 414 Ashland Ave Evanston IL 60202 Office: Centel Corp 8725 Higgins Rd Chicago IL 60631

BERON, GAIL LASKEY, real estate analyst, consultant, appraiser; b. Detroit, Nov. 13, 1943; d. Charles Jack Laskey and Florence B. (Rosenthal) Eisenberg; divorced; children: Monty Charles, Bryan David. Cert. real estate analyst, Mich. Chief/staff appraiser Ft. Wayne Mortgage Co., Birmingham, Mich., 1973-75; pvt. practice fee appraiser S.C., Iowa, Mich., 1976-80; pres. The Beron Co., Southfield, Mich., 1980—; cons. ptnr. Real Estate Counseling Group Conn., Storrs, 1983—, Real Estate Counseling Group Am., affiliated prin., 1984—; lectr. real estate confs. Recipient M. William Donnally award Mortgage Bankers Assn. Am., 1975. Mem. Soc. Real Estate Appraisers (bd. dirs. Detroit chpt. 1980-82, nat. faculty mem. 1983—), Am. Inst. Real Estate Appraisers (bd. dirs. Detroit chpt. 1982-86, nat. faculty mem. 1984—), Nat. Assn. Realtors, Detroit Bd. Realtors, Southfield Bd. Realtors, Women Brokers Assn. (treas. Southfield chpt. 1981-83), Young Mortgage Bankers (bd. dirs. 1974-75). Lodge: B'nai Brith. Avocations: art, music, piano, dancing. Home: 7008 Bridge Way West Bloomfield MI 48033 Office: Beron Co 17228 W Hampton Rd Southfield MI 48075

BERREAU, ALFRED JAMES, architect; b. Brewster, Minn., Aug. 25, 1932; m. Rosemary Elizabeth Forrette, Sept. 1, 1956; children: Linda, Shaun, Nicholas, A. Justin, Misha. BArch, U. Minn., 1961. Architect Carl Graffunder, Mpls., 1958-60, 1963-65, 1960-63, 1965-71; pres., owner A.J. Berreau & Assocs., Inc., Mpls., 1972—. Mem. AIA, Minn. Soc. Architects, Mpls. Soc. AIA. Home: 204 Meander Rd Golden Valley MN 55422 Office: A J Berreau & Assocs Inc 1220 Glenwood Ave Minneapolis MN 55405

BERREY, ROBERT WILSON, III, lawyer, judge; b. Kansas City, Mo., Dec. 6, 1929; s. Robert Wilson and Elizabeth (Hudson) B.; A.B., William Jewell Coll., 1950; M.A., U. S.D., 1952; LL.B., Kansas City U., 1955; LL.M., U. Mo. at Kansas City, 1972; grad. Trial Judges Coll., U. Nev., 1972; m. Katharine Rollins Wilcoxson, Sept. 5, 1950; children—Robert Wilson IV, Mary Jane, John Lind. Admitted to Mo. bar, 1955, Kans. bar, 1955, since practiced in Kansas City; asso. mem. firm Shugert and Thomson, 1955-56, Clark, Krings & Bredehoft, 1957-61, Terry and Welton, 1961-62; judge 4th Dist. Magistrate Ct., Jackson County, Mo., 1962-79; asso. cir. judge 16th Jud. Cir. Ct., Jackson County, Mo., 1979-81, cir. judge, 1981-83, mem. mgmt.-exec. com., 1979-83; judge Mo. Ct. Appeals-Western Dist., Kansas City, 1983—; mem. Supreme Ct. Com. to Draft Rules and Procedures for Mo.'s Small Claims Ct., 1976-86. Vol. legal cons. Psychiat. Receiving Center. Del. Atlantic Council Young Polit. Leaders, Oxford, Eng., 1965; Kansas City rep. to President's National Conference on Crime Control; del.-at-large White House Conf. Aging, 1972; former pack chmn. Cub Scouts Am.; counselor, com. mem. Boy Scouts Am., sponsor Eagle Scouts; vice chmn. water fowl com. Mo. Conservation Fedn., 1968-69, chmn. water fowl com., 1971-73; v.p. Cook PTA, 1967-68; mem. cts. and judiciary com. Mo. bar, 1969-73; mem. Midwest region adv. com. Nat. Park Service, 1973-78, chmn., 1973-78; mem. Mo. State Judicial Planning Commn., 1977; bd. dirs., founder Kansas City Open Space Found., 1976. Regional dir. Young Rep. Nat. Fedn., 1957-59, gen. counsel, 1959-61, nat. vice-chmn.; chmn. Mo.

Young Rep. Fedn., 1960, nat. committeeman, 1959-60, 61-64; Mo. alternate at large Republican Nat. Conv., 1960, asst. gen. counsel, 1964, del. state and dist. convs., 1960, 64, 68. Bd. dirs. Naturalization Council, Kansas City, pres., 1973—; trustee Kansas City Mus., 1972-73, Hyman Brand Hebrew Acad., 1983—; hon. life dir. Rockhurst Coll. Mem. Mo. Bar (Disting. Service award 1973, agr. law com., com. council 1980-81), Kansas City Bar Assn., Urban League (exec. com., dir.), S.A.R., Kansas City Mus. Natural Sci. Soc. (charter), Tex. Longhorn Breeders Assn. (life), Am. Royal (bd. of govs. 1986), Mo. Longhorn Breeders Assn. (life), Alpha Phi Omega, Delta Theta Phi, Pi Gamma Mu, Tau Kappa Epsilon. Mem. Christian Ch. Mason, mem. DeMolay Legion Honor. Clubs: Kansas City; Waldo Optimist (v.p. 1967-68); Capitol Hill (Washington); Ducks Unltd. (state com. 1981—, nat. trustee 1986—), The Explorers. Home: Rural Rt 2 Box 1078 Excelsior Springs MO 64024 Home (summer): Route 2 Battle Lake MN 56515 Office: Mo Ct Appeals Bldg 1300 Oak St Kansas City MO 64106

BERRY, BRYAN HATHORN, editor, writer; b. Nyack, N.Y., June 24, 1952; s. Sidney Bryan and Anne Florine (Hayes) B.; m. Jill Adrienne McCree, Oct. 15, 1982; children: Adrienne, Joanna. Student, U. Sheffield, Eng., 1972-73; BA in English, Columbia U., 1974. Asst. editor Popular Sci. mag. Times-Mirror Corp., N.Y.C., 1975-78; freelance editor Random House, Prentice-Hall, N.Y.C., 1979-80; Detroit editor Iron Age mag./Metalworking News newspaper Fairchild Publs. div. Capital Cities/ABC, Troy, Mich., 1981—. Contbr. articles to profl. jours. Recipient Bus. Journalism citation U. Mo. Sch. Journalism, 1982, Journalism award Aviation/Space Writers Assn., 1984, Journalism award Detroit Press Club Found., 1986, 87. Mem. Detroit Auto Writers Group (treas. 1985, pres. 1986). Lutheran. Home: 1904 McIntyre Ann Arbor MI 48105 Office: Fairchild Publs 755 W Big Beaver Rd Troy MI 48084

BERRY, ILONA MAE, lawyer; b. Berwyn, Ill., June 27, 1956; d. Donald J. and Helen Jeanne (Zeleznik) B.; m. John Augustine Krivicich, July 28, 1984. BA, Bradley U., 1977; JD, U. Ill., 1980. Bar: Ill. 1980, U.S. Dist. Ct. (no. dist.) Ill. 1980, U.S. Ct. Appeals (7th cir.) 1981. Lawyer 1st Nat. Bank Chgo., 1980-82, atty., 1982-84, sr. atty., 1984—. Mem. ABA, Ill. State Bar Assn., Chgo. Bar Assn. Roman Catholic. Office: First National Bank of Chicago One First National Plaza Chicago IL 60670-0292

BERRY, JANET PATRICIA, educator; b. Columbus, Ohio, Feb. 12, 1923; d. Maurice Denver and Mary (Funk) B.; B.S., Ohio State U., 1944, post-grad., 1945, 60, 73-76; postgrad. Otterbein Coll., 1960-61; M.A., Ohio State U., 1978; m. Escalus E. Elliott, Jr., Apr. 1944 (div. May 1962); 1 son, Escalus E. III; m. Edward J. Hannon, Jan. 7, 1966 (div. June 1980). Instr. dept. fine arts Ohio State U., 1945-46; art supr., tchr. Gahanna (Ohio) Public Schs., 1960-61; mem. art guide com. Franklin County Bd. Edn., 1960-61; exec. sec. Columbus Town Meeting Assn., producer-dir. Columbus Town Meeting Forum, 1963-72; promotions, personnel devel. and field services div. Nat. Center for Research in Vocat. Edn., Ohio State U., 1972-77, 80—. Pres. bd. trustees West Side and Ohio Av. Day Care Centers Assn., 1958-60; gen. chmn. Twigs of Children's Hosp., 1955-57. Recipient cert. of merit Franklin County Bd. Edn., 1961. Mem. Pi Lambda Theta, Delta Phi Delta, Kappa Kappa Gamma. Home: 4355 Latin Ln Columbus OH 43220 Office: 1960 Kenny Rd Columbus OH 43210

BERRY, JOHN WILLIAM, telephone directory advertising company executive; b. Dayton, Ohio, July 8, 1922; s. Loren Murphy and Lucille (Kneipple) B.; m. Marjorie Louise Wendel, Mar. 5, 1944 (div. Jan. 5, 1959); children: George W., John W., David L., Charles D.; m. Mardell Smith, Mar. 1, 1962 (div. Jan. 1984); 1 son, Richard L.; m. Marilynn St. John, July 1986. B.A., Dartmouth Coll., 1944; postgrad., La. State U., 1943-44. With L.M. Berry & Co., Dayton, 1940—, mng. dir., 1960-63, pres., 1963-73, chmn., chief exec. officer, 1973-86, vice chmn., 1986—; chmn., dir. Society Bank Na, Dayton, 1972—; dir. ITT World Directories, N.Y.C., Super Food Services, Inc., Dayton, Krug Internat. Corp., Dayton. Trustee U. Dayton, 1980—; trustee Ohio State U., 1981—; mem. exec. com. Ohio Republican Fin. Com., Columbus. Served in U.S. Army, 1943-46. Recipient hon. recognition Newcomen Soc. N.Am., 1971; recipient Spirit of Life award City of Hope, 1977. Mem. Ind. Telephone Pioneers Am., Bell Telephone Pioneers Am. Episcopalian. Clubs: Moraine Country (Dayton); Bohemian (San Francisco). Lodges: Masons, Shriners. Office: LM Berry And Co 3170 Kettering Blvd PO Box 6000 Dayton OH 45401

BERRY, PAMELA LYNN, physician; b. Detroit, June 26, 1954; d. Harold White and Molean Antoinette (Mole) B.; m. Van Calvin Momon, Jr., May 19, 1979. BS in Physiology, Ea. Mich. U., 1975; MD, Wayne State U., 1979. Diplomate Nat. Bd. Med. Examiners. Intern Henry Ford Hosp., Detroit, 1979-80, resident in pediatrics, 1980-82, chief resident in pediatrics, 1982; physician fellow in adolescent medicine Children's Hosp., Cin., 1982-83; staff physician Children's Med. Ctr., Dayton, Ohio, 1983-86; asst. clin. prof. Wright State U. Sch. Medicine, 1985-86; adolescent medicine specialist St. John's Hosp., Detroit, 1987—. Fellow Am. Acad. Pediatrics; mem. Soc. Adolescent Medicine, Western Ohio Med. Soc., Am. Profl. Practice Assn. Democrat. Lutheran. Home: 28541 Eldorado Pl Lathrup Village MI 48076 Office: St John's Hosp Dept Pediatrics 22101 Moross Detroit MI 48236

BERRY, ROBERT NEIL, engineering executive; b. Iowa City, Mar. 21, 1933; s. Harlen Neil and Lila Ann (Dow) B.; m. Brenda V. Harberts, June 14, 1969; children: Renee, Randy, Robert, Richard, Tracy, Rhonda, Neil. Cert. in electronic, Devrey Inst. Tech., Chgo., 1954; mech. cert., Allied Inst., 1956. Registered engr., Iowa. Foreman Processive Tool, Waterloo, Iowa, 1949-51; pres. Berry Tool & Die Co., Cedar Falls, Iowa, 1956-79, Berry Industries, Cedar Falls, 1979—; cons. Berry and Assocs., Cedar Falls, 1981—; bd. dirs. Am. Fedn. Bus., Chgo., 1985-86. developer, patentee in field. Served to cpl. U.S. Army, 1951-53. Mem. Fabricating Mfrs. Assn. Republican. Methodist. Club: N.E. Iowa Businessman's. Lodge: Rotary (bd. dirs. 1983, chmn. bd. 1986), Masons, Shriners.

BERRY, THOMAS ERNEST, mechanical engineer; b. West Branch, Mich., Mar. 30, 1947; s. Thomas and Evelyn (Yost) B.; m. Sheila Ann Williams, Oct. 4, 1975; children: David Alan, Mark Thomas, Thomas Dennis. Journeyman toolmaker, Buick Motor Co., 1971; A in Mech. Tech., Mott Community Coll., 1972; BS in Mech. Tech., Cen. Mich. U., 1980. Toolmaker Gen. Motors-Buick Motor Co., Flint, Mich., 1967-80; instrument repairman hydramatic div. Gen. Motors, Three Rivers, Mich., 1980-81, gage engr. hydramatic div., 1981-82, quality control supr. hydramatic div., 1982-84, process engr. hydramatic div., 1984—; resource counselor Glen Oaks Community Coll., Centreville, Mich., 1986—. community liason 4th dist. U.S. Congress, Mich., 1983—. Republican. Soc. of Friends. Home: 180 Plum St Constantine MI 49042 Office: Gen Motors Hydramatic Div One Hydramatic Dr Three Rivers MI 49042

BERTELS, WILLIAM CHARLES, adolescent counselor; b. Lakefield, Minn., May 1, 1951; s. Floyd William and Lorna Harriet (Wartenburg) B.; divorced. BA, S.W. State U., Minn., 1975; postgrad., N.D. State U., 1977, Jamestown Coll., 1977-78. Adolescent counselor N.D. State Hosp., Jamestown, 1977-79; counselor adolescent treatment unit Willmar (Minn.) Regional Treatment Ctr., 1979—. Republican. Lutheran. Avocations: fishing, hunting, travel, philatelist, numismatist.

BERTHELSEN, JOHN ROBERT, printing company executive; b. Albert Lea, Minn., July 23, 1954; s. Robert Eugene and Erna Catherine (Petersen) B.; m. Debra Denise Peterson, June 29, 1974; children—Angela Marie, Derek John. Student public schs. Albert Lea, Minn. Prodn. worker Arrow Printing Co., Albert Lea, 1972-73; journeyman Munson Printing Co., Red Wing, Minn., 1973-75; prep. foreman O'Connor Printing Co., Sioux Falls, S.D., 1975-76; preparation supr. Modern Press Inc., Sioux Falls, 1976-79; gen. mgr. Suttle Press, Inc., Waunakee, Wis., 1979-82, pres., 1982—. Recipient 1st place Nat. Skill Olympics (printing), Vocat. Indsl. Clubs Am., 1972, Gold award best managed printing co. Nat. Assn. Printers and Lithographers, 1983, 87, Silver award Mgmt. Plus Program Nat. Assn. Printers and Lithographers, 1986. Mem. Madison Craftsmen (pres. 1983-85), Internat. Assn. Printing House Craftsmen (gov. 6th dist. 1985-87, internat. treas. 1987—). Home: 6318 Sleepy Hollow Circle Middleton WI 53562 Office: Suttle Press Inc 806 S Division St PO Box 370 Waunakee WI 53597

BERTOG, EUGENE TRACY, educator; b. Chgo., Nov. 29, 1930; s. Frank Carl and Grayce (Tracy) B.; B.S., Loyola U., Chgo., 1952, M.Ed., 1973; m. Elaine Kohl, June 25, 1955; children—Eugene, Elaine, Joseph, Steven, Robert. Dir. edn. and tng. Continental Casualty Co., Chgo., 1955-69; dir. cdnl. services CNA Fin. Corp., Chgo., 1969-72; gen. mgr. Lake Shore Club Chgo., 1972-74; prof., chmn. dept. hotel mgmt. Oakton Community Coll., Des Plaines, 1974—. Mem. deans adv. council Loyola U., 1976—, also mem. citizens bd.; pres. PTA, 1971-73. Served as lt. AUS, 1953-55; Korea. Named Alumnus of Yr., Loyola U., 1967; mem. Loyola U. Athletic Hall of Fame; recipient service to youth through athletics awards, Teaching Effectiveness award Oakton Community Coll., Tchr. Yr. award Council Vocat. Edn. Mem. Hotel Sales Mktg. Assn. (dir.), Soc. Ins. Tng. Edn., Am. Acad. Polit. and Social Sci., Am. Soc. Tng. and Devel., U.S. Olympic Soc., Loyola U. Alumni Assn. (pres. 1969-72), Ill. Tng. Dirs. Assn., U.S. Navy League, Blue Key, Alpha Kappa Psi, Beta Gamma Sigma, Tau Kappa Epsilon. Clubs: North Shore Country; Lake Shore (pres. dir.), Executives (Chgo.); Internat. (Chgo.). Home: 2314 Sussex Ln Northbrook IL 60062 Office: 1600 E Golf Des Plaines IL 60016

BERTONCIN, THOMAS MICHAEL, advertising executive; b. Kansas City, Mo., June 7, 1951; s. Bert Edward Sr. and Charlotte Marie (Thomas) B.; m. Elizabeth Ann Campbell, Mar. 8, 1975 (div. 1978). Student, Rockhurst Coll., 1969-71; BA in Psychology, U. Mo., 1973, MA, 1975. Mgr. advt. Lee's Summit (Mo.) Jour., 1975-77; mgr. prodn. Lane & Leslie Advt. Agy., Hutchinson, Kans., 1977-79; account exec. Lane & Leslie Advt. Agy., Wichita, Kans., 1979-80, account supr., 1980-83; account supr. Lida Advt. Co., Wichita, 1983—; bd. dirs. Wichita Festvals, Inc. Co-chmn. campaign communications United Way of Wichita and Sedgwick County, 1986, mktg. commn. 1986-87. Mem. Am. Advt. Fedn. Democrat. Roman Catholic. Club: Advertising (Wichita) (treas. 1982-83, 2d v.p. 1983-84). Avocations: sailing, aerobics. Office: Lida Advt Co 393 N McLean Blvd Wichita KS 67203

BERTRAM, JEFF NICKOLAS, farmer, state legislator; b. Paynesville, Minn., Jan. 24, 1960; s. Clarence Arnold and Viola (Gruber) B. AA, St. Cloud State U., 1985. Farmer Paynesville, Minn., 1960—; mem. Minn. Ho. Reps., 1986—. Contbr. articles to profl. jours. Campaign mgr. Joe Bertram for Minn. State Senate Dist. 16, 1980-84; mem. Minn. Citizens Concerned for Life. Named one of Outstanding Young Men of Am., 1985. Mem. Nat. Fedn. Ind. Bus. (guardian), Nat. Rifle Assn., Minn. Jaycees (past offices, C. William Brownfield award 1979). Democrat. Roman Catholic. Lodge: KC. Avocations: snowmobiling, walking, reading, traveling. Home: 662 Spruce St Paynesville MN 56362 Office: Bertram Farm Rural Rt 1 Box 88 Paynesville MN 56362

BERTSCH, ROBERT JOSEPH, research chemist; b. Phila., May 6, 1948; s. Robert James Joseph and Mildred Frances (Hennik) B; m. Pamela Patricia Smith, June 20, 1970; children: Denise Nicole, Kirsten Elizabeth. BS in Cemistry, Drexel U., 1970; PhD in Chemistry, Ohio State U., 1975. Assoc. research and devel. BF Goodrich, Brecksville, OH, 1975—. Cntbr. articles to profl. jours.; patentee in field. Mem. Am. Chem. Soc. United Methodist. Avocations: photography, tennis, gardening, history studies. Home: 10241 Log Cabin Ct Brecksville OH 44141 Office: BF Goodrich 9921 Brecksville Rd Brecksville OH 44141

BERTUCA, DANIEL ANTHONY, sales representative; b. Chgo., Apr. 26, 1948; s. Anthony Francis and Angeline Geraldine (Serritella) B. AA, Wenatchee (Wash.) Coll., 1971; BA, Northeastern Ill. U., 1977, MA, 1981; PhD, Western Pacific U., 1985. Coordinator Neighborhood Housing Devel Services, Chgo., 1978-79; counselor Dept. of Justice, Chgo., 1978-80; sales rep. Player Sports, Chgo., 1979—. Pres., founder Louie's People Community Youth Orgn. and Action Group. Served with USMC, 1965-66. Home: 1501 Glenlake Chicago IL 60660

BERUBE, MICHAEL DAVID, systems engineer; b. Lafayette, Ind., Mar. 21, 1962; s. Milton Albert and Mary Ann (Marco) B.; m. Glenda Jane Schell, July 20, 1985. BSChemE, Pa. State U., 1984. Sales engr. Edwards High Vacuum, Grand Island, N.Y., 1984-86; systems engr. Electronic Data Systems Corp., Lordstown, Ohio, 1986—. Roman Catholic. Avocations: softball, racquetball, weightlifting, baseball card collecting, auto repair. Home: 78 LeMans Dr #4 Boardman OH 44512 Office: Electronic Data Systems Corp 2300 Hallock Young Rd Warren OH 44482

BERUTTI, JAMES WILLIAM, retail executive; b. Detroit, Oct. 12, 1942; s. Valentine William and Amelia Linda Berutti; m. Carole Emma Jolliffe, Dec. 28, 1968; children: William Samuel, Margaret Lynn. BS in Mktg., Mich. State U., 1964; postgrad., Lazarus Mgmt. Inst., 1985. Assoc. buyer furniture Lazarus Dept. Store, Columbus, Ohio, 1965-67, buyer sheets and towels, 1967-71, merchandise mgr. intimate apparel and accessories, 1971-75, merchandise mgr. textiles and draperies, 1975-80, merchandise v.p. textiles, tabletop and housewares, 1980-86, merchandise v.p. textiles and draperies, 1986—; bd. dirs. Federated Steering Com., N.Y.C.; advisor Home Textiles Today Bd., N.Y.C., 1984-86. Republican. Roman Catholic. Clubs: Columbus Country, Athletic, City (Columbus). Avocations: swimming, tennis, golfing. Office: Lazarus Dept Store 7th and Race St Cincinnati OH 45243

BERZINS, VALDIS, dentist; b. Riga, Latvia, Aug. 20, 1940; came to U.S., 1951; s. Verners and Erna (Meilands) B.; m. Maija Heinsons, Feb. 26, 1967 (div. Aug. 1973); children: Marina, Raymond; m. Vladislava Stephanik, Sept. 20, 1975; 1 child, Aurelius Prochazka. BS, Baldwin Wallace Coll., 1963; postgrad., Kent (Ohio) State U., 1964; DDS, Case Western Res. U., 1968. Gen. practice dentistry Parma, Ohio, 1970—. Served to capt. USAF, 1968-70. Mem. ADA, Acad. Gen. Dentistry, Ohio State Dental Assn., Cleve. Dental Soc. Lutheran. Avocations: skiing, swimming, kung fu. Home: 8224 Valley Ln Parma OH 44130 Office: Parmatown Med Bldg S 6688 Ridge Rd Suite 1410 Parma OH 44129

BESCHLOSS, MORRIS RICHARD, valve manufacturing exec.; b. Berlin, Mar. 7, 1929; s. Otto and Manya (Levine) B.; B.S., U. Ill., 1952; m. Ruth Greenwald, Nov. 13, 1954; children—Michael, Steven. Advt. mgr. Hammond Valve Corp. (Ind.), 1956-58, asst. sales mgr., 1958-61, field sales mgr., 1961-62, v.p. sales, 1962-63, pres., 1963-68, chmn. bd., 1968—, also dir.; pres. Condec Flow Control 1968-84; v.p., dir. Condec Corp.; pres. Plumbing-Heating-Cooling Info. Bur., 1971-72, chmn. bd., 1973-80. Sec.-treas. Flossmoor-Homewood (Ill.) Area Sch. Bd., 1969-73. Served from 2d lt. to capt. AUS, 1952-54. Recipient Distinguished Eagle award Boy Scouts Am., 1974. Mem. Valve Mfrs. Assn. (dir. 1971—, pres. 1971-73), Assn. Industry Mfrs. (charter pres.), World Bus. Council, Tau Delta Phi, Sigma Delta Chi, Alpha Phi Omega. Clubs: Execs., Econ. (Chgo.). Office: 840 N Michigan Ave Chicago IL 60611

BESPOLE, DOUGLAS ROBERT, food products executive; b. Elmhurst, Ill., Aug. 9, 1956; s. Walter William and Florence Evelyn (Fischer) B.; m. Victoria Bespole. Student, DePauw U., 1974-75, North Cen. Coll., Naperville, Ill., 1976-77. V.p. Gt. Lakes Milk Products, Franklin Park, Ill., 1972—. Republican. Presbyterian. Clubs: Chgo. Yacht, Oak Park Country (Ill.). Lodge: Shriners. Avocation: golf profl. Home: 7213 Division St River Forest IL 60305 Office: Great Lakes Milk Products Inc 9109 Belden Ave Franklin Park IL 60131

BESS, TIMOTHY ALAN, school psychologist; b. Clarksville, Ark., Mar. 30, 1950; s. George William and Angie (Allen) B.; B.A. in Psychology, Butler U., Indpls., 1974, M.S. in Counseling, 1977; M.S. Ed., U. Wis.-River Falls, 1983; m. Nancy Helen Jaracz, Mar. 11, 1977; children—Jonathan, Jeffrey. Assoc. instr. communication and cognitive devel. Marion County Assn. Retarded Citizens, Indpls., 1975, employment specialist, 1975-76; coordinator psychol. services and spl. edn. Plainfield (Ind.) Community Sch. Corp., 1977-78; coordinator 3-R program emotionally disturbed/behavioral problems students Ind. Sch. Dist. 834, Stillwater, Minn., 1978-79; sch. psychologist Ind. Sch. Dist. 191, Burnsville, Minn., 1979-80, Ind. Sch. Dist. 833, Cottage Grove, Minn., 1980—; coordinator Alternative Learning Ctr. Ind. Sch. Dist. 833, Cottage Grove. Mem. Nat. Assn. Sch. Psychologists, Assn. Specialists Group Work, Butler U. Alumni Assn., Phi Delta Kappa. Home: 7781 Inskip Trail Cottage Grove MN 55016 Office: Park Sr High Sch 8040 80th St S Cottage Grove MN 55016

BESSER, HOWARD RUSSELL, lawyer; b. Cleve., Sept. 12, 1941; s. Morris Milton and Florence Helen (Sandler) B.; m. Barbara Kaye, Sept. 3, 1972; 1 child, Matthew Emerson Doublas. B.A., Ohio State U., 1963, J.D., 1966. Bar: Ohio 1966, U.S. Dist. Ct. (no. dist.) Ohio 1967, U.S. Ct. Appeals (6th cir.) 1975, U.S. Supreme Ct. 1977. Assoc. Griff, Weiner & Orkin, Cleve., 1966-68; asst. dir. law, counsel to mayor City of Cleve., 1968-71; U.S. dist. counsel EEOC, 1971-76; trial atty. Ohio Bell Telephone Co., 1976—; lectr. law Cleve. State U., 1971-85, adj. prof., 1985—. Contbr. articles to profl. jours. State pres. ACLU, 1973-75, 83—, v.p., 1982-83, 70-73, bd. dirs., 1968-77, 80—; mem. adv. council Mus. Arts Assn., 1983—; vice-chmn. New Democratic Coalition Cuyahoga County, 1969-71; trustee No. Ohio Unit Am. Jewish Congress, 1983—. Recipient Outstanding Civil Libertarian of Yr. award ACLU, 1975. Mem. ABA, Ohio Bar Assn. (chmn. civil rights com. 1980—), Cuyahoga County Bar Assn. (trustee 1983—), Cleve. Bar Assn., Sphinx, Tau Epsilon Rho. Home: 3554 Stoer Rd Shaker Heights OH 44122 Office: Ohio Bell Telephone Co 45 Erieview Plaza Room 1448 Cleveland OH 44114

BESSIRE, HOWARD DEAN, foundation executive, consultant; b. Missouri Valley, Iowa, Mar. 1921; s. Howard Dean and Etta Blanche (Pound) B. B.S. in Bus. Adminstrn., U. Neb., 1948; grad. Organization Mgmt. Inst., Economic Devel. Inst., Sec. C. of C., Colby, Kans., 1948-49, exec. dir., Clinton, Iowa, 1949-53, El Paso County Texas Ind. Devel. Corp., 1962-66, Cofco Indsl. Found., Council Bluffs, Iowa, 1953-57; economic developer, chief operating officer Walla Walla County Port Dist., Washington, 1957-59; exec. v.p. Idaho East Oreg. Economic Devel. Council, Boise, 1959-62, Indsl. Devel., Inc., Wichita Falls, Tex., 1966-70; exec. dir., chief operating officer Indsl. Found., Inc., South Bend, Ind., 1973; sec. H & S Cons., Inc., South Bend, 1969—; also dir.; dir. Am. Economic Devel. Council, Chgo.; chmn. Ind. Area Devel. Council, Indpls., 1979; v.p. Pacific Northwest Industrial Devel. Council, 1961. Author: Techniques of Industrial Development, 1964, Practice of Industrial Development, 1970, A Handbook for the 80s Industrial Development, 1981. Served as 1st sgt. U.S. Army, 1940-45, ETO. Fellow Am. Economic Devel. Council (bd. dirs. 1981—); mem. Ind. Area Devel. Council (chmn. 1979), Mid-Am. Econ. Devel. Council. Democrat. Lodges: Masons, Shriners. Avocations: writing; indsl. park and building designer. Office: Industrial Found Inc PO Box 4216 South Bend IN 46634

BESTEHORN, UTE WILTRUD, librarian; b. Cologne, Fed. Rep. of Germany, Nov. 6, 1930; came to U.S., 1930; d. Henry Hugo and Wiltrud Lucie (Vincentz) B. BA, U. Cin., 1954, BEd, 1955, MEd, 1958; MS in Library Sci., Western Res. U. (now Case-Western Res. U.), 1961. Tchr. Cutter Jr. High Sch., Cin., 1955-57; tchr., supr. library Felicity (Ohio) Franklin Sr. High Sch., 1959-60; librarian sci. dept. Pub. Library Cin. and Hamilton County, 1961-78, librarian info. desk, 1978—; textbook selection com., Felicity-Franklin Sr. High Sch., 1959-60; supr. Health Alcove Sci. Dept. and annual health lectures, Cin. Pub. Library, 1972-77. Book reviewer Library Jour., 1972-77; author and inventor Rainbow 40 marble game, 1971, Condominium game, 1976; patentee indexed packaging and stacking device, 1973, mobile packaging and stacking device, 1974. Recipient Cert. of Merit and Appreciation Pub. Library of Cin., 1986. Mem. Ohio Library Assn., Cin. Chpt. Spl. Libraries Assn. (archivist 1964-64, editor Queen City Gazette bull. 1964-69), Pub. Library Staff Assn. (exec. bd., activities com. 1965, welfare com. 1966, recipient Golden Book 25 yr. service pin, 1986), Friends of the Library, Greater Cin. Calligraphers Guild (reviewer New Letters pub. 1986—), Delta Phi Alpha. Republican. Mem. United Ch. of Christ. Avocations: calligraphy, painting and sketching, writing, photography, violin. Home: 3330 Morrison Ave Cincinnati OH 45220 Office: Pub Library Cin 800 Vine St Cincinnati OH 45202

BESTLER, GERALD MILTON, electronics company executive; b. Berywn, Ill., Sept. 6, 1929; s. Thomas Andrew and Grace Maude (Carey) B.; m. Myrtle Caroline Bloom, June 16, 1951 (dec.); 1 son, David; m. Shirley Mae Pohl, July 19, 1969; children—Cheryl, Rick, Chris, Carol, Jon Hailey. B.A. in Chemistry, Carleton Coll., 1950; grad. Minn. Exec. Program, U. Minn., 1980. Mgr. Semiconductor div. Honeywell, Mpls., 1953-60; dir. computer graphics UNIVAC, St. Paul, 1960-68; pres. Fabri-Tek Circuits, Baldwin, Wis., 1968-71; v.p. internat. ops. MTS Systems Corp., Mpls., 1971-82; corp v.p., pres. spl. products group BMC Industries, St. Paul, 1982—. Served to sgt. U.S. Army, 1950-53. Republican. Lutheran. Clubs: St. Paul Athletic, New Richmond Golf.

BETHUREM, JAMES DWIGHT, banker; b. Lebanon, Mo., Oct. 17, 1947; s. George R. and Myrl (Hayes) B.; m. Linda J. Johnson, June 3, 1968; children: Jeff, Stacie. BS, U. Mo., 1970. Beef cattle technician U. Mo., Columbia, 1969-70; supr. FmHA, Columbia, 1970-74, farmer project specialist, 1974-81; v.p. Commerce Bank of Lebanon, 1981—; Rep. Fed. Crop Ins., Columbia, 1984-85. Mem. Lake of Ozarks Council Local Govts. Econ. Devel. Com., Camdenton, Mo., 1986; bd. dirs. Lebanon Found., 1984—, Laclede County Fair, 1983—. Mem. Lebanon Area C. of C. (chmn. agrl. com. 1984—, bd. dirs. 1986—, sec.). Republican. Methodist. Lodge: Kiwanis (treas. Lebanon club 1982-84). Avocation: farming.

BETSCHMAN, RICHARD FRANK, locksmith, hardware executive; b. Norwalk, Ohio, May 25, 1932; s. Cyrillus N. and Martha (Egle) B.; m. Dolores Catherine Seifker, Aug. 25, 1951; children—David Paul, Ronald Gerard, Sharon Marie, Kathy Ann, Diane Marie. Foreman outboard finishing line Lyman Boats Co., Sandusky, Ohio, 1953-57; shipping clk. Rotary Printing Co., Norwalk, Ohio, 1957-63; service mgr. appliance repairs P & R Electric Co., Norwalk, 1963-67; owner, operator Hess Hardware Co., Monroeville, Ohio, 1970—; lectr. security. Pres. Monroeville Hist. Soc., 1974—; sec. Mayor's Area Devel. Com., Monroeville, Ohio, 1975-76; chmn. Town Meeting Monroeville, 1977; organizer, gen. chmn. Community Picnic Day, 1979-84; v.p. Monroeville Community Affairs Com., 1983-85; treas. Firelands Council Hist. Socs., 1985—; mem. Firelands Tourism task force, 1986—. Mem. Asso. Locksmiths Am., Pa.-Ohio Locksmiths Assn., Am., Ohio hardware assns., Am. Hardware Probe Panel, Sentry Hardware Dealer Probe, Huron County (Ohio) Am. Heritage Com. Democrat. Roman Catholic. Clubs: Lockmasters Tru-Center, Kiwanis (sec.-treas. Monroeville 1973-77). Home: 20 Horseshoe Dr Monroeville OH 44857 Office: 2 N Main St Monroeville OH 44847

BETTAN, ANITA ESTHER, public relations specialist, writer; b. Cin., Nov. 30, 1928; d. Israel and Ida Judith (Goldstein) B. B.A., U. Cin., 1950; M.A., Columbia U., 1951. Copywriter, Shillito's, Cin., 1953-55; continuity dir. Sta. WSAI, Cin., 1955-57; copywriter, jr. account exec. William F. Holland Agy., Cin., 1957-61; account coordinator Stockton-West-Burkhart, Inc., Cin., 1962-67; asst. to info. officer U. Cin. Coll-Conservatory of Music, 1967-71; info. services writer U. Cin., 1971—, mem. com. on aging, 1981-84. Contbr. articles to mags. Dep. foreman Hamilton County Grand Jury, Cin., 1979, foreman petit jury, 1980; pres. career div. Council Jewish Women, Cin., 1962-64; vol. Jewish Hosp., Cin., 1954-59; mem. Sr. Olympics Com., Cin., 1981-84. Mem. Women in Communications. Home: 2101 Grandin Rd Cincinnati OH 45208 Office: U Cin Mail Location No 65 Cincinnati OH 45221

BETTASSO, KATHRYN ANN, lawyer; b. Oak Park, Ill., July 4, 1958; d. Robert Francis and Dorothy Catherine (Kaiser) B. BA cum laude, St. Mary's Coll., 1980; JD, Loyola U., 1983. Bar: Ill. 1983, U.S. Dist. Ct. (no. dist.) Ill. 1983. Assoc. Hayes & Power, Chgo., 1983-85, Patricia C. Bobb & Assocs., Chgo., 1985—. Mem. ABA, Ill. Bar Assn. (council 1985—), Chgo. Bar Assn., Assn. Trial Lawyers Am., Ill. Trial Lawyers Assn., Women's Bar Assn. Ill. Roman Catholic. Avocations: music, theater, travel. Home: 1450 Astor St Chicago IL 60610 Office: Patricia C Bobb & Assocs 3 First Nat Plaza Chicago IL 60602

BETTEN, PAUL ROBERT, engineer; b. Pitts., Oct. 31, 1946; s. Peter Paul and Julia Ann (Kerstukus) B.; m. Gayle Dorothy Solier, Jan. 2, 1982. BS, Carnegie-Inst. Tech., 1969, MS, 1970; PhD in Mech. Engring., Carnegie-Mellon U., 1973. Registered profl. engr., Ill. Sr. engr. Combustion Enging. Inc., Windsor, Conn., 1973-77; mech. engr. Argonne (Ill.) Nat. Lab., 1977—. Patentee in field; contbr. articles to profl. jours. NDEA fellow U.S. Fellow, 1970-71; recipient Pacesetter award Argonne Nat. Lab., 1985. Mem. ASME (rev., 1974—, nuclear heat exchanger, 1978—), Shotokan Karate Club (founder 1977—). Republican. Roman Catholic. Avocations: karate, scuba. Home: 10 S 537 Whittington Ln Naperville IL 60565 Office: Argonne Nat Lab 9700 S Cass Ave Argonne IL 60439-4820

BETTENDORF, JAMES BERNARD, clergyman, church association administrator; b. Jackson, Mich., Oct. 22, 1933; s. Bernard Anthony and Kathryn Marie (Vaughan) B. B.A., Sacred Heart Sem., 1955; postgrad. U. Detroit, 1956, U. Notre Dame, 1957, Cath. U. of Am., 1958; S.T.B., St. John Sem., 1959; M.A., Western Mich. U., 1970; postgrad. St. Mary Coll., 1981—. Assoc. pastor Holy Trinity Ch., Fowler, Mich., 1959-60, St. Phillip Ch., Battle Creek, Mich., 1960-63, Sacred Heart Ch., Flint, 1963-66; dir. Flint Newman Ctr., Flint Cath. Info. Ctr., Mich., 1966—; pastor Good Shepherd Ch., Montrose, Mich., 1983—. Mem. exec. bd. dirs. Genesse-Lapeer-Shiawasee Health Planning Commn., Flint, 1966-86, Urban Coalition, Flint, 1968—; mem. Tall Pine council Boy Scouts of Am.; trustee C.S. Mott Community Coll., 1987—; vice chmn. Flint Neighborhood Improvement and Preservation Project. Mem. Lansing Cath. Campus Ministry Assn. (diocesan bd. dirs. 1971—), Mich. Cath Campus Ministry Assn., Nat. Assn. Diocesan Dirs. Campus Ministry (mem. exec. bd.), Cath. Campus Ministry Assn. (recipient Charles Forsyth award 1983). Home: 1802 E Court St Flint MI 48503 Office: Flint Newman Ctr 609 E Fifth Ave Flint MI 48503

BETTI, JOHN A., automobile manufacturing company executive; b. Ottawa, Ill., Jan. 6, 1931; s. Louis and Ida (Dallari) B.; m. Joan Doyle, Aug. 22, 1953; children: Diane Marie, Denise Marie, Donna Marie, Joan Marie. B.S. in Mech. Engring, Ill. Inst. Tech., 1952; M.S. in Engring, Chrysler Inst. Engring., 1954; postgrad., U. Detroit, 1963. Registered profl. engr., Mich. Student engr. to asst. chief engr. Chrysler Corp., 1952-62; with Ford Motor Co., 1962—, chief light truck engr., chief engine engr., chief car planning mgr., chief car engr., then v.p., gen. mgr. truck ops., 1975-76; v.p. product devel. Ford of Europe, Inc., Warley, Essex, Eng., 1976-79, also dir.; v.p. powertrain and chassis ops. Ford N.Am. Ford Motor Co. automotive ops., Dearborn, Mich., 1979-84, exec. v.p. tech. affairs, 1984-85; exec. v.p. tech. affairs and operating staffs Ford Motor Co., Dearborn, Mich., 1985—, dir., 1985—; chmn. bd. Ford Motor Co. Caribbean Inc., 1979-84, Ensite Ltd., Can., 1979-84; dir. Ford of Germany, 1978, Ford of Mex., 1984-85; past instr. Lawrence Inst. Engring., Wayne State U., Detroit; bd. dirs. Truck Hist. Mus., 1975-76; mem. exec. com. Western Hwy. Inst.; trustee GMI Engring. and Mgmt. Inst., 1985—. Bd. dirs. Mich. Opera Theatre, 1984—; chmn. bd. govs. Marian High Sch., Detroit; trustee Detroit Inst. for Children, 1985—; mem. nat. adv. com. U. Mich., 1985—. Recipient Alumni Profl. Achievement award Ill. Inst. Tech., 1980; John Morse Meml. scholar. Mem. Soc. Automotive Engrs. (fin. com.), Tau Beta Pi, Pi Tau Sigma, Alpha Sigma Phi. Clubs: Bloomfield Hills (Mich.) Country; Renaissance (Detroit). Office: Ford Motor Co The American Rd Dearborn MI 48121

BETZ, EUGENE WILLIAM, architect; b. Dayton, Ohio, Jan. 12, 1921; s. Jesse Earl and Elizabeth Freda (Meyer) B.; m. Marjorie Lois Frank, Oct. 30, 1948; children—Douglas William, Gregory Vincent. B.S., U. Cin., 1944. Pres. Eugene W. Betz, Architects, Inc., Dayton, 1956—; Chmn. Bd. Building Standards and Appeals, 1960-63, Kettering Planning Commn., 1957-61. Served with AUS, 1944. Recipient Honor award Architects Soc. Ohio, 1967, 71; Award of Merit, 1968, 77, 78; Nation's Sch. Month award Nat. Council Schoolhouse Constrn., 1967; Nat. Citation Am. Assn. Sch. Adminstrs., 1967, 71; Masonry award of excellence, 1976, 78; Outstanding Health Care Facility award UCLA/Columbia U./Archtl. Record, 1980. Mem. AIA (nat. com. architecture for health), Am. Hosp. Assn., Am. Assn. Hosp. Planning. Clubs: Masons, Rotary. Home: 5561 Lotusdale Dr Dayton OH 45429 Office: 2223 S Dixie Ave Dayton OH 45409

BETZ, RONALD PHILIP, pharmacist; b. Chgo., Nov. 26, 1933; s. David Robert and Olga Marie (Martinson) B.; BS, U. Ill., 1955; MPA, Roosevelt U., 1987; m. Rose Marie Marella, May 18, 1963; children—David Christian, Christopher Peter. Asst. dir. of pharmacy U. Ill., Chgo., 1959-62; dir. pharmacy Mt. Sinai Hosp., Chgo., 1962—; pres. Pharmacy Systems, Inc., 1982—; teaching assoc. Coll. of Pharmacy, U. Ill., Chgo., 1977—; pres. Pharmacy Service and Systems, 1972-81; dir. Ill. Coop. Health Data Systems, 1976-80. Bd. dirs. Howard/Paulina Redevel. Corp., 1983—. Served with U.S. Army, 1956-58. Mem. Am. Pharm. Assn., Am. Soc. Hosp. Pharmacists, Ill. Pharm. Assn. (pres. 1975), Ill. Acad. Preceptors in Pharmacy (pres. 1972), No. Ill. Soc. Hosp. Pharmacists (pres. 1966), Kappa Psi. Democrat. Lutheran. Contbr. articles in field to profl. jours. Home: 7505 N Sheridan Rd Chicago IL 60626 Office: 2750 W 15th Pl Chicago IL 60608

BEUC, RUDOLPH, JR., architect, real estate broker; b. St. Louis, Nov. 7, 1931; s. Rudolph M. and Lillian Ann (Rethemeyer) B.; B.Arch., Washington U., St. Louis, 1955; m. Mildred Hild, Jan. 25, 1968; children—Rudolph III, Ralph M. Archtl. draftsman Bank Bldg. & Equipment Corp. Am., St. Louis, 1950, Hammond & Gorlock, architects, St. Louis, 1957-58; designer Schwarz & Van Hoefen, architects, St. Louis, 1958; architect George E. Berg Architects, St. Louis, 1958-60; architect R. Beuc, Architects, Inc., St. Louis, 1960—, pres., 1960—, also dir.; pres., dir. Hilterdevco, Inc., St. Louis, 1964—; Dir. pub. works Peerless Park, 1967—; deacon Webster Groves Presbyn. Ch. Served with AUS, 1955-57. Mem. AIA, Soc. Am. Registered Architects, Mo. Council Architects, Mo. Assn. Bldg. Ofcls. and Inspectors, Bldg. Ofcls. Council Am., Webster Groves C. of C., Am. Legion (past comdr.). Clubs: Mason, Lion (past pres.); Order Eastern Star, DeMolay, High Twelve (past state pres.), Scottish Rite, Washington University, Westborough Country. Home: 138 W Glendale Rd St Louis MO 63119 Office: 142 W Glendale Rd Saint Louis MO 63119

BEUCHEL, PATRICK THOMAS, mechanical engineer; b. New Haven, Ind., Jan. 7, 1959; s. Robert Joseph and Marcella Joanne (Nix) B. BSME, Purdue U., 1981. Jr. engr. Magnavox, Ft. Wayne, Ind., 1981-82, design engr., 1983—. Treas. Young Cath. Adults, Ft. Wayne, 1985-86. Mem. ASME (assoc.). Club: Mgmt. of Ind. Home: 7225 Lakeridge Fort Wayne IN 46819 Office: Magnavox 1010 Production Rd Fort Wayne IN 46808

BEUGEN, JOAN BETH, communications company executive; b. Chgo., Mar. 9, 1943; d. Leslie and Janet (Glick) Caplan; B.S. in Speech, Northwestern U., 1965; m. Sheldon Howard Beugen, July 16, 1967. Founder, prin., pres. The Creative Establishment, Inc., Chgo., N.Y.C., San Francisco and Los Angeles, 1969—; speaker on entrepreneurship for women. Del., White House Conf. on Small Bus., 1979; vice-chmn. Ill. Del. to White House Conf., 1979; trustee Mt. Sinai Hosp. Med. Ctr.; bd. dirs. Chgo. Network; bd. dirs. Chgoland. Enterprise Ctr. Recipient YWCA Leadership award, 1985; named Entrepreneur of Yr., Women in Bus. Mem. Nat. Assn. Women Bus. Owners (pres. Chgo. chpt. 1979), Ill. Women's Agenda, Chgo. Assn. Commerce and Industry, Chgo. Audio-Visual Producers Assn., Chgo. Film Council, Women in Film, Com. of 200, Nat. Women's Forum, Overseas Edn. Fund Women in Bus. Com. Contbr. articles in field to profl. jours. Office: 1421 N Wells St Chicago IL 60610

BEUKELMAN, DOUGLAS DONN, accountant; b. Sioux City, Iowa, Jan. 4, 1955; s. Didrich Donald and Eloyce Ruth (Wicken) B.; m. Janelle Kay Mulder, Aug. 9, 1974; children: Sara, Ryan, Justin. BA, U. No. Iowa, 1977. CPA, Iowa. Staff acct. Peat, Marwick, Mitchell & Co., Des Moines, 1977-79; acct., mgr. Dethmers Mfg. Co., Boyden, Iowa, 1979—; bd. dirs. Security State Bank, Sheldon, Iowa. Bd. dirs. Crime Stoppers of Sioux County, Orange City, Iowa, 1985-87, NW Iowa Town Health Ctr., Sheldon, 1984-87. Mem. Am. Inst. CPA's. Republican. Baptist. Club: Community (v.p. 1987, pres. 1988). Avocations: softball, golf. Home: 1009 Pleasant St Boyden IA 51234 Office: Dethmers Mfg Co Hwy 18 East Boyden IA 51234

BEUMER, ORIAN FRANKLIN, personnel executive; b. Holland, Ind., Nov. 14, 1926; s. Frank Emil and Lydia Clara (Linstrot) B.; student Butler U., 1947-48; BA in English, U. Evansville, 1952, MA in Continuing Studies, 1982; children—Toni Lynn, Steven Laune. Pub. relations aide Internat. Harvester Co., Evansville, Ind., 1952-55; employee communications editor Mead Johnson & Co., Evansville, 1955-58, supr. profl. employment, 1958, mgr. new product scheduling and coordination, 1958-66; franchised distbr. Vanda Cosmetics, Evansville, 1966-67; personnel dir. St. Mary's Med. Center, Evansville, 1967—; tchr. nursing home adminstrn. Lockyear Bus. Coll.; pres. bd. dirs. Youth Emergency Service, Inc., Evansville, 1977-80; bd. dirs. Conrad Baker Found., 1986—, pres. 1987—. Served with USN, 1944-46. Mem. Am. Soc. Personnel Adminstrn. (dist. dir. 1980-85, v.p. region 11, 1986, accredited exec. in personnel 1976), Ind. Health Careers Inc. (dir. 1972-79), Ind. Soc. Hosp. Personnel Adminstrn. (pres. 1969-70, editor newsletter 1971-73), Am. Soc. Hosp. Personnel Adminstrn., Am. Hosp. Assn., Ind. Personnel Assn. (dir. 1981-82, pres. 1985), Evansville Personnel Assn. (pres. 1976-77), Vis. Nurse Assn. Southwestern Ind. (dir. 1976-79, v.p. 1983-84, pres. 1981-85), Am. Soc. Healthcare Human Resource Adminstrn., Profl. Secs. Internat. (mem. exec. adv. bd. Ind. div., Exec. of Yr. 1982), Ind. State C. of C. (personnel and indsl. relations com. 1981-84). Home: 1566 Old Plank Rd Newburgh IN 47630 Office: St Mary's Med Ctr 3700 Washington Ave Evansville IN 47750

BEUSE, DONALD LEE, foundry executive; b. Davenport, Iowa, July 2, 1933; s. William Alfred and Helen (Hartog) B.; m. Beverly June Burkamper, Dec. 21, 1956. Grad. high sch., Davenport; apprentice in pattern making, 1950-53, 1955-67. Owner, pres. Beuse's Pattern Works, Inc., Le Claire, Iowa, 1967—. Vol. tchr. Quad Cities Pattern Making Apprentice Program, Moline, Ill. 1964-67; comdr., pres. Vol. Fire Dept., Le Claire, 1968; Dem. committeeman, Davenport, 1958-60. Served to cpl. U.S. Army, 1953-55. Mem. Am. Foundrymens Assn., Le Claire Businessmen's Assn., Am. Legion (vice comdr. 1962). Club: Clinton Engrs. Lodges: Moose, Masons, Shriners. Home: Rural Rte 1 Box 296 Le Claire IA 52753 Office: Beuses Pattern Works Inc 304 S Cody Rd Le Claire IA 52753

BEUTEL, ERNEST WILLIAM, thoracic surgeon, lawyer; b. Chgo., Feb. 14, 1946; s. Ernest and Hazel Augusta (Zachow) B.; B.S. magna cum laude, Loyola U., Chgo., 1967, M.D., 1971, J.D., 1985; m. Anita Paulie Harrison, June 11, 1976; children—Ernest Wiley, William Andrew Harrison. Intern, St. Joseph Hosp., Chgo., 1971-72, resident in surgery, 1972-76; resident in thoracic surgery Cook County Hosp., 1976-78; staff thoracic surgeon Naval Regional Med. Center, Great Lakes, 1978-80 ; attending thoracic surgeon Resurrection Hosp. and St. Joseph Hosp., Chgo.; surgical assoc. Northwestern U. Med. Sch.; adv. bd. Loyola U. Health Law Inst. Of Counsel Querrey, Harrow, Gulanick and Kennedy, Ltd., Chgo. Diplomate Am. Bd. Surgery and Am. Bd. Thoracic Surgery. Fellow ACS, Am. Coll. Chest Physicians; assoc. fellow Am. Coll. Cardiology, Phi Sigma Tau, Phi Beta Pi; mem. AMA, Def. Research Inst., Chgo. Surgical Soc., Ill. Bar Assn., Am. Coll. Legal Medicine, Chgo. Bar Assn. Medical Office: PO Box 31130 Chicago IL 60631-0130 Legal Office: Querrey Harrow Gulanick and Kennedy 135 S LaSalle St Chicago IL 60603

BEUTLER, ARTHUR JULIUS, manufacturing company executive; b. LaCrosse, Wis., Sept. 2, 1924; s. Arthur Julius and Augusta Henrietta (Dobe) B.; m. Carolee Yvonne Crawford, Dec. 28, 1952; 1 child, Karen Elizabeth. BSEE, U. Wis., 1948, Grad. in EE, 1968. Registered profl. engr., Wis. Trainee inventor program Gen. Electric Co., Schenectady, N.Y., 1948-51; devel. engr. Gen. Electric Co., Milw., 1951-59, project engr., 1959-61, sr. engr., 1961-64; chief engr. Dings Magnetic Separator Co., Milw., 1964-67; pres., owner Creative Engring. Assocs., Inc., Greendale, Wis., 1967-72; v.p. mfg. Gettys Mfg. Co., Racine, Wis., 1972-79, v.p. internat., 1979-81; v.p. tech. planning div. motion control div. Gould, Inc. (formerly Gettys Mfg. Co.), Racine, 1981—. Patentee elec. controls. Served with U.S. Army, 1943-46, PTO. Mem. IEEE (sr., chpt. chmn. 1969-72), NSPE, Soc. Mfg. Engrs. (cert.), Tau Beta Pi, Eta Kappa Nu. Office: Gould Inc 2701 N Green Bay Rd Racine WI 53404

BEUTLER, STEPHEN ALBERT, minister; b. Mishawaka, Ind., Aug. 30, 1952; s. Albert Jacob and Barbara Jean (Heeter) B.; m. Jayna Diane Ringer, Aug. 14, 1976; children: Jason Richard, Sara Jayne, Stephanie Janae. BA, Bethel Coll., Mishawaka, 1974; postgrad. , Inst. Holy Land Studies, Jerusalem, 1974-75; M in Div., Asbury Theol. Sem., 1978. Ordained deacon United Meth. Ch., 1981, elder, 1983. Pastor Faith Missionary Ch., Flint, Mich., 1978-79, First United Meth. Ch., Mishawaka, 1979-83, Fairmount (Ind.) United Meth. Ch., 1983-85, Upland (Ind.) United Meth. Ch., 1985—; registrar Bd. Ordained Ministry, Ind. Conf., 1985—; gen. chmn. Good News Nat. Convocaiton, Wilmore, Ky., 1986—; mem. dist. bd. ministry, Marion, Ind., 1985—; dir. youth South Bend (Ind.) Dist. United Meth. Ch., 1982-83. Sec., chmn. Grant County ARC, 1986-87;, Marion, Ind.; chmn. St. Joseph County Am. Cancer Soc., South Bend, 1982-83; bd. dirs. Am. Cancer Soc. Recipient Barrett Merit scholarshipfor acad. achievement Asbury Theol. Sem., 1976-79. Mem. Ministerial Assn. (v.p. 1984-85). Avocations: magic tricks (TOPS award for Magician of the Month presentation 1967), music, stamp collecting, travel. Home and Office: 214 Grant St Box 11 Upland IN 46989

BEVACQUA, RONALD ANTHONY, food products executive; b. Jersey City, Dec. 14, 1945; s. Guido Ferrar and Anna (Lostumbo) B.; m. Joan Marie Stanley, May 25, 1968; children: Dawn Nicole, Stefanie Michele. BS, NYU, 1967. CPA, N.J. Plant mgr. Pepperidge Farm Inc. Campbell Soup Co., Downingtown, Pa., 1980-82; v.p., controller Mrs. Paul's Kitchens Campbell Soup Co., Phila., 1982-84, Campbell Soup U.S.A., Camden, N.J., 1984-85; exec. v.p., chief fin. officer Interstate Bakeries, Kansas City, Mo., 1985—. Mem. Am. Inst. CPA's, N.J. Soc. CPA's, Nat. Assn. Accts. Avocations: chess, stained glass, exercise fitness. Home: 3612 W 122 Terrace Leawood KS 66209 Office: Interstate Bakeries Corp 12 E Armour Blvd Kansas City MO 64141

BEVER, TIMOTHY MICHAEL, software systems engineer; b. Eaton Rapids, Mich., Nov. 10, 1953; s. Harry S. and Jean A. (Cramer) B.; m. Dorothy J. Farrell, Apr. 22, 1977; 1 child, Sharon E. BBA with honors, Saginaw Valley State Coll., 1981. Computer programmer Saginaw (Mich.) Steering Gear, 1981-83, systems analyst, 1983-84; systems engr. Electronic Data Systems, Saginaw, 1984-86, software systems engr., 1986—. Sustaining mem. Rep. Nat. Com., Washington, 1985. Served with USN, 1971-76. Republican. Home: 4440 Lynndale St Saginaw MI 48603 Office: Electronic Data Systems 5225 Exchange Dr Flint MI 48507

BEVERLY, URIAS HARRISON, minister; b. Indpls., Nov. 20, 1941; s. Roy Winston and Rosa Miller (Robinson) B.; m. Diana Marie Beverly, Dec. 30, 1966 (div. Dec. 1977); 1 adopted child, Dycus; m. Gladys Elizabeth Johnson, Apr. 6, 1985. BA in Psychology, Ind. Cen. Coll. (now U. Indpls.), 1973; MS in Edn., Butler U., 1974; MDiv., Christian Theol. Sem., Indpls., 1978; postgrad., Ind. U., Indpls., 1980-84. Pastor Trinity Bapt. Ch., Indpls., 1967-69; asst. pastor Unity Bapt. Ch., Indpls., 1970-73; co-pastor Zion Unity Ch., Indpls., 1973-76; pastoral care resident Ind. U. Hosp., Indpls., 1976-77; asst. pastor Mt. Zion Bapt. Ch., Indpls., 1976-87; staff chaplain Meth. Hosp., Indpls., 1987—; Pastoral counselor Buchanan Counseling Ctr., Indpls., 1978—; field edn. cons. Christian Theol. Sem., 1985—; parish counseling educator Congress of Nat. Black Chs., Washington, 1986—. Copyright music and poems; contbr. articles to profl. jours. Midwest community workshop leader, 1976—; mem. steering com. Staying Healthy After 50 chpt. ARC; chmn. bd. Mt. Zion Geriatric Ctr., 1984—, One-to-One Prison Visitation Program, 1984—. Served with U.S. Army, 1959-62. Fellow Coll. Chaplains (council mem. 1983-86), Am. Protestant Hosp. Assn.; mem. NAACP (life), Urban League (supporting), AGAPE Soc. (founder, bd. dirs. 1978—), Am. Assn. Pastoral Counselors, Assn. Clin. Pastoral Edn. (full supr., chairperson East cen. region 1984—), Christian Theol. Sem. Alumni Assn. (bd. dirs. 1986—). Democrat. Avocations: music, piano, organ, tennis, long distance running. Home: 4260 Springwood Trail Indianapolis IN 46208 Office: Meth Hosp of Ind Inc 1701 N Senate Boulevard Indianapolis IN 46202

BE VIER, WILLIAM A., teacher educator; b. Springfield, Mo., July 31, 1927; s. Charles and Erma G. (Ritter) BeV.; B.A., Drury Coll., 1950; Th.M., Dallas Theol. Sem., 1955, Th.D., 1958; M.A., So. Meth. U., 1960; Ed.D., A.B.D., Wayne State U., 1968; m. Jo Ann King, Aug. 11, 1949; children—Cynthia, Shirley. With Frisco Ry., 1943-45, 46-51, John E. Mitchell Co., Dallas, 1952-60; instr. Dallas Theol. Sem., 1958-59; teaching fellow So. Meth. U., Dallas, 1959-60; prof. Detroit Bible Coll., 1960-74, registrar, 1962-66, dean, 1964-73, exec. v.p., 1967-74, acting pres., 1967-68; prof., dean edn., v.p. for acad. affairs Northwestern Coll., Roseville, Minn., 1974-80, prof., 1980—. Bd. drs. Religious Analysis Service, Mpls., 1979—. Served with USMC, 1945-46, 50-51; ret. col. Army Res. Mem. Res. Officers Assn., Ind. Fund Chs. of Am., Huguenot Hist. Soc., Bevier-Elting Family Assn., Phi Alpha Theta. Office: Northwestern Coll Roseville MN 55113

BEVINGTON, ROBERT CHARLES, optometrist; b. Akron, Ohio, Mar. 2, 1956; s. Robert Ray and Viola (Sansonetti) B.; m. Rita Ann Groves, Sept. 29, 1980; 1 child, David Lawrence. Student in pre-optometry, Ohio State U., 1974-76, OD, 1980. Lic. optometrist, Ohio, N.Y., Colo. Optometrist Visioncare Assocs., Akron, 1980—; Advisor phys. edn. dept. U. Akron, 1981—, Cuyahoga Falls (Ohio) High Sch. Athletic Dept., 1981—, tchr. inservice program Akron Pub. Schs., 1981—; cons. Ohio Youth Commn., 1980—, Northeast Ohio Devel. Commn., 1980—, Sports Medicine Ctr. Akron, 1982—. Contbr. articles to profl. jours. Mem. Rep. Nat. Com., 1983—, Northeast Ohio Jazz Soc., 1983—, Akron Zool. Soc., 1983—; trustee Young Life, Akron, 1981—. Mem. Am. Optometric Assn., Summit County Optometric Soc. (pres. 1983), Ohio State U. Alumni Assn., Epsilon Psi Epsilon, Beta Sigma Kappa. Club: Commerce of Akron. Lodge: Lions. Avocations: writing, hiking, photography, art, softball. Home: 92 Melbourne Ave Akron OH 44313 Office: Visioncare Assocs 1234 Weathervane Akron OH 44313

BEVIS, JAMES WAYNE, manufacturing company executive; b. Quincy, Fla., Sept. 29, 1934; s. Harold Wayne and Maude (Kelley) B.; m. Bettye Jane Johns, Aug. 29, 1954; children—Harold, Graydon, Tina. B.S. in Indsl. Engring., U. Fla., 1959. With Gen. Electric, 1959-69; v.p. Rupp Industries, Mansfield, Ohio, 1969-73; v.p. ops. Rolscreen Co., Pella, Iowa, 1973-80, pres., 1980—. Republican. Home: Rural Route 3 Pella IA 50219 Office: Rolscreen Co 102 Main St Pella IA 50219 *

BEXTERMILLER, THERESA MARIE, architect; b. St. Charles, Mo., Feb. 9, 1960; d. Charles Frederick and Loretta Joan (Unterreiner) B. BArch, Kans. State U., 1978-83; postgrad., Wash. U., St. louis, 1985, Pratt Inst., 1988. Architect Fleming Corp., St. Louis, 1984-85; architect, prototype mgr. Casco Corp., St. Louis, 1985-87, HBE Corp., St. Louis, 1987—. Mem. AIA. Roman Catholic. Avocations: biking, photography, painting. Home: 1813 Kenilworth Saint Louis MO 63144 Office: HBE Corp 11330 Olive St Rd Saint Louis MO 63141

BEYER, BRUCE KEMP, research teratologist; b. Buffalo, Feb. 11, 1953; s. Donald Kemp and Sally Mason (St. John) B.; m. Valerie Constance Crawford, June 16, 1984. BA in Biology, Gettysburg Coll., 1975; MS in Human Physiology, Fairleigh Dickinson U., 1979; PhD in Pharmacology, Med. Coll. Ga., 1984. Sr. research fellow U. Wash., Seattle, 1984-86; scientist Warner-Lambert/Parke-Davis, Ann Arbor, Mich., 1986—. Mem. Am. Soc. Pharmacol. and Exptl. Therapeutics, Soc. Toxicology, Teratology Soc., Midwest Teratology Soc., Mich. Soc. Toxicology, N.Y. Acad. Scis., Sigma Xi, Alpha Phi Omega, Beta Beta Beta, Sigma Nu. Episcopalian. Avocations: reading, music, jogging, sports. Office: Warner-Lambert/Parke-Davis Dept Pathology/Exptl Toxicology 2800 Plymouth Rd Ann Arbor MI 48105

BEYER, EMIL E., JR., state legislator; b. Omaha, May 20, 1929; m. Barbara; children—Linda, Diane, Randall, Vicki. Real estate exec.; mem. Nebr. Legislature, 1980—; mem. state officeholder for safety com. U.S. Dept. Transp. Bd. dirs. Gretna Parent-Tchr. Orgn.; chmn. Gretna Planning Bd.; pres. Gretna Civic Orng. Mem. Nebr. Motor Carriers Assn. (bd. dirs.). Club: Optimists (dir.).

BEYER, KAREN ANN, social worker; b. Cleve., Jan. 30, 1942; d. William Pryor and Evelyn Ann Haynes; B.A., Ohio State U., 1965; M.S.W., Loyola U., Chgo., 1969; postgrad. Family Inst., Northwestern U., 1979; 1 dau., Jennifer. with Cuyahoga County Div. Child Welfare, Cleve., 1965, Dallas County Child Welfare Unit, Dallas, 1966; with Lutheran Welfare Services Ill., Chgo., 1967-73; pvt. practice psychotherapy, family mediation, Schaumburg, Ill., 1975—; therapist Family Service Assn. Greater Elgin (Ill.), 1973-77, dir. profl. services, 1977-83; dir. HHS Village of Hoffman Estates, Ill., 1983—; fieldwork social work instr. for Loyola U., U. Ill., 1977-80. Bd. dirs. Talkline, 1982-85; mem. mental health adv. bd. Elgin Community Coll. Mem. Nat. Assn. Social Workers, Acad. Cert. Social Workers (clin. and approved supr.), Am. Assn. Marriage and Family Therapy, Am. Orthopsychiat. Assn. Unitarian. Home: 824 Brendon Dr Schaumburg IL 60194

BEYER, WAYNE HERMAN, parks and recreation director; b. Breckenridge, Minn., Aug. 30, 1956; s. Herman John and Helen Elizabeth (Ficenec) B.; m. Joan Marie Henke, Apr. 20, 1985. AS, N.D. Sci. Sch., 1976; BS, Moorhead (Minn.) State U., 1979. Dir. recreation Wahpeton (N.D.) Park Dist., 1980-82, dir. parks and recreation, 1982—; area coordinator Spl. Olympics, Wahpeton, 1980—; commnr. N.D. Amateur Softball Assn., Wahpeton, 1982—; sports chmn. Boy Scouts Am., Wahpeton, 1983—; sec. Urban Forestry Commn., Wahpeton, 1985. Sec. Chahinkapa Zoo Assn., Wahpeton, 1981—; bd. dirs. Head of the Red United Way, Wahpeton, 1982; sec.-treas. Kinship Program, Wahpeton, 1983. Recipient Extra Mile award Wahpeton C. of C., 1986; named one of Outstanding Young Men Am., 1985. Mem. N.D. Recreation and Parks Assn. (newsletter editor), N.D. High Sch. Coaches Assn., Wahpeton Jaycees (Disting. Service award 1983). LOdge: Optimists. Home: 426 N 1st Wahpeton ND 58075 Office: Wahpeton Park Dist 120 N 4th St Wahpeton ND 58075

BEYERS, JAMES DALEY, hospital executive; b. Marquette, Mich., Feb. 8, 1939; s. Foster John and Lila Mary (Daley) B.; m. Margaret Kathleen O'Neill, June 29, 1968; children: Patricia Colleen, Foster John II. BS in Econs., Western Mich. U., 1961; MHA, U. Mich., 1970. Labor economist U.S. Dept. of Labor, Chgo., 1961-66; economist Upper Peninsula Com. for Area Progress, Escanaba, Mich., 1966-67; asst. dir. Presby.-U. Pa. Med. Ctr., Phila., 1969-73; assoc. dir. Champlain Valley Physicians' Hosp. Med. Ctr., Plattsburgh, N.Y., 1973-76; v.p. N. Mich. Hosp., Petoskey, Mich., 1976-82; pres. St. Clare Hosp., Monroe, Wis., 1982—. Councilman Petoskey City Council, 1980-82; chmn. Monroe United Way, 1985; bd. dirs. Petoskey Library, 1978-80. Served to capt. USAF, 1962-66. Mem. Am. Coll. Healthcare Execs,, Wis. Hosp. Assn. (bd. dirs 1983—), Cath. Health Assn. of Wis. (chmn. 1985—), Monroe C. of C. (bd. dirs. 1984—). Club: Monroe Country. Avocations: reading, racquetball, tennis, World War II history. Home: 2615 Golfview Ct Monroe WI 53566 Office: St Clare Hosp 515 22d Ave Monroe WI 53566

BEYNEN, GIJSBERTUS KOOLEMANS, bibliographer, educator; b. Surabaya, Indonesia, June 12, 1935; s. G.J.W. and Froukje (de Jong) Koolemans Beijnen; Jur. Cand., Leiden (Netherlands) U., 1957, Lit. Slav. Cand., 1959; PhD, Stanford U., 1967; MLS, SUNY, Geneseo, 1974; m. Patricia Joan McBride; children: Johanna, Margaret, Axel, Sophia, Andrew, Elisabeth Blake Warner. Asst. prof. Russian, Emporia State U., 1963-66; asst. prof. Fordham U., N.Y.C., 1966-69; asst. prof. U. Rochester (N.Y.), 1969-73; assoc. prof. Ohio State U. Libraries, Columbus, 1974—; vis. asst. prof. Kent (Ohio) State U., 1983-85; part-time lectr. in Russian, Ohio Wesleyan U., 1985; chmn. Slavic and East European sect. Assn. Coll. and Research Libraries, 1983-84. Contbr. articles to profl jours. Recipient 1300 Yrs. Bulgaria medal, 1982; Internat. Research and Exchanges Bd. fellow Moscow State U., 1970-71; Nat. Endowment Humanities translation grantee 1981-82; Midwest Universities Consortium for Internat. Activities exchange fellow Moscow State U., 1981-82; NDEA Title VI fellow, 1962-63. Mennonite. Home and Office: 609 Woodsfield Dr Columbus OH 43214-1331

BEZAZIAN, PAUL D., advertising agency executive; b. Providence, Mar. 29, 1906; s. John B. and Daisy (Babasinian) B.; m. Florence Irene Bell, Sept. 9, 1933; children: John P., Paulette F., Harold A. BA, Oberlin Coll., 1927. Salesman Meyer Connor & Co., Chgo., 1927-31; sales mgr. Credit Firm, Chgo., 1931-36; ptnr. Bezazian & Sutherland, Niles Center, Ill., 1936-37; mgr., ptnr. Bezazian Bros., Chgo., 1937-40; mng. ptnr., treas. Burton Browne Advt., Chgo., 1941—. Club: Gaslight (chmn. bd. dirs., chmn. exec. com. 1975-76). Home: 5555 N Sheridan Rd Apt 1002 Chicago IL 60640

BEZKOROVAINY, ANATOLY, medical educator, biochemist; b. Riga, Latvia, Feb. 11, 1935; s. Ignatius and Olga (Solovey) B.; m. Marilyn Grib, June 14, 1964; children—Gregory, Alexander. B.S., U. Chgo., 1956; Ph.D., U. Ill., 1960; J.D., Ill. Inst. Tech., 1977. Bar: Ill. 1977. Research assoc. Oak Ridge Nat. Lab., Tenn., 1960-61; chemist U.S. Dept. Agriculture, Ames, Iowa, 1961-62; mem. faculty Rush-Presby. St. Lukes' Med. Center, Chgo., 1962—, asst. prof., 1962-67, assoc. prof., 1967-73, prof. biochemistry, 1973—, assoc. chmn., dir. ednl. programs biochemistry dept., 1980—. Author: Basic Protein Chemistry, 1970; Biochemistry of Nonheme Iron,

1980; (with Rafelson and Hayashi) Basic Biochemistry, 1980. Contbr. articles to profl. jours. Grantee numerous NSF, NIH, Am. Heart Assn., 1973-80. Fellow Nat. Acad. Clin. Biochemistry (bd. dirs. 1984-86); mem. Am. Soc. Biol. Chemists, Am. Chem. Soc., Am. Inst. Nutrition. Eastern Orthodox. Home: 6801 Kilpatrick Ave Lincolnwood IL 60646 Office: Rush-Presbyn-St Luke's Med Center Biochemistry Dept 1753 W Congress Chicago IL 60612

BEZOUSEK, ROBERT JOSEPH, meat processing company executive; b. Omaha, Nebr., Oct. 9, 1953; s. Louis Edward and Irene Frances (Victor) B.; m. Deborah Ann Milani, Aug. 3, 1974; children: Robert Jr., Joseph, Michael. BS in Bus. Adminstrn., U. Nebr., Omaha, 1975. Plant mgr. Omaha Steaks Internat., 1976-84, dir. operations, 1984—. Pres. Home and Sch. Assn. Mary Our Queen Sch., Omaha, 1984-85, mem. sch. bd., 1986—. Named one of Outstanding Young Men Am., U.S. Jaycees, 1984. Omaha Softball Assn. Democrat. Roman Catholic. Lodge: Rotary (Millard Nebr. sgt. at arms 1986-87). Avocations: coaching youth baseball and soccer. Home: 13114 Jefferson Circle Omaha NE 68137 Office: Omaha Steaks Internat 4400 S 96th St Omaha NE 68127

BHAKUNI, ROSA INÉS, English educator; b. San Juan, P.R., July 12, 1941; d. Federico A. and Celeste (Alfonzo) Collazo; m. Roop S. Bhakuni, June 27, 1965; children: Nila, Tara, Sarita, Pravin. BA, U. P.R., 1962; MA, U. Akron, 1964, postgrad. Cert. tchr., Ohio. Teaching asst. U. Akron, Ohio, 1962-64, mem. faculty, 1975—; prof. English U. P.R., Rio Piedras, 1964-65; coordinator writing ctr., cons. Kenmore High Sch., Akron, 1985—. Bd. dirs. Internat. Inst., Akron, 1980—. Recipient English Edn. Merit award Dept. Secondary Edn., Coll. Edn. U. Akron, 1986. Mem. Greater Akron Tchrs. of English, Schs. for the Future (lang. arts com. 1986—), Internat. Reading Assn., Nat. Council Tchrs. of English, Pi Lambda Theta. Avocations: sewing, needlework, travel, reading. Office: Univ Akron English Dept 337 Olin Hall E Buchtel Ave Akron OH 44313

BHARANI, SAKINA NITINCHANDRA, allergist, immunologist; b. Calcutta, India, Dec. 10, 1942; s. Nooraddin Ebrahim and Ateka (Galely) Chinwalla; m. Nitinchandra Kalyanji, Apr. 18, 1971; children: Sunita, Nootan, Sujata. Premed. degree, St. Xaviers Coll., 1962; MBBS, Grant Med. Sch., 1967. Diplomate Am. Bd. Pediatrics, Am. Bd. Allergy and Immunology. Intern J.J Hosp., Bombay, 1967-68, resident in pediatrics, 1968-71; intern in pediatrics Cook-County Hosp., Chgo., 1971-72; resident in pediatrics Rush Med. Ctr., Chgo., 1972-73, fellow in allergy and immunology, 1973-75; practice medicine specializing in allergy and immunology Downers Grove, Ill., 1975—. Contbr. articles to profl. jours. Fellow Am. Acad. Allergy, Am. Coll. Allergy, Ill. Soc. Allergy; mem. Allergy and Asthma Found. of Am. (dir. sub chpt., 1985—). Office: 3825 Highland Downers Grove IL 60515

BHATIA, SUBHASH CHANDAR, psychiatry educator; b. Hanuman, India, May 9, 1945; came to U.S., 1974; s. Nand Lal and Ishwar Devi Bhatia; m. Shashi K. Bhatia, Mar. 4, 1972; children: Shivani, Sameer, Supriya. MBBS, Govt. Med. Coll. Rohtak, Haryana, India, 1968; MD, Inst. Med. Edn. and Research, Chandigarh, India, 1973. Diplomate Am. Bd. Psychiatry and Neurology. Instr. in psychiatry Creighton U. Sch. Medicine, Omaha, 1977-80, asst. prof. in psychiatry, 1980—, dir. jr. clerkship, 1979-81, dir. residency tng., 1981—. Pres. St. Joseph Ctr. Mental Health, Omaha, 1986. Fellow India Psychiat. Soc., Am. Psychiat. Assn.; mem. India Assn. Nebr. (pres. 1985), Acad. Med. Scis. Democrat. Hindu. Avocations: tennis, jogging. Office: Creighton U Dept Psychiatry 2205 S 16th St Omaha NE 68108

BHATNAGAR, DHARMVIR KRISHAN, civil engineer; b. Patiala, Punjab, India, Dec. 16, 1943; came to U.S., 1980; s. Balbir Krishan and Shanti Bhatnagar; m. Renuka Akhaury, May 17, 1971; children: Tanmaya, Ritu. Student, K.R. Intermediate Coll., Mathura, India, 1960; BS, AGRA U., Nainital, India, 1962; BSCE, U. Roorkee, India, 1966; M of Hydraulics, U. Iowa, 1984. Registered profl. engr., Iowa. Officer grad. sect. Post & Telegraph dept. Govt. India, New Delhi, 1967-68; asst. engr. United Provinces Irrigation Dept., Lucknow, India, 1968-80; research asst. U. Iowa, Iowa City, 1981-84; natural resource engr. soil conservation div. Iowa Dept. Agriculture and Land Stewardship, Des Moines, 1984—. Mem. ASCE, Indo Am. Assn. Iowa (sec. 1987—). Club: Toastmasters Internat. (CTM award 1984). Avocations: tennis, reading, chess, writing. Office: Div Soil Conservation 900 E Grand Des Moines IA 50319

BHATTACHARYYA, BENOYENDU, gynecologist, obstetrician; b. Rajnarayanpur, India, Feb. 2, 1936; came to U.S., 1963; s. Birendra Krishna and Nivedita (Lahiri) B.; m. Bani Mitra, Apr. 25, 1964; children: Neiloyendu, Timothy. BS, U. Calcutta, India, 1956, MB, BS, 1963. Diplomate Am. Bd. Ob-Gyn. Rotating internship St. Luke's Hosp., Milw., 1962-63; resident in gen. surgery Royal Alexandra Hosp., Edmonton, Alb., Can., 1967-68; resident in ob-gyn McGill U. Hosps., Montreal, Que., Can., 1968-71; practice medicine specializing in ob-gyn Clinic Ob-Gyn S.C., Aurora, Ill., 1971—. Fellow Am. Coll Ob-Gyn, Am. Coll. Surgeons, Internat. Coll. Surgeons, Royal Coll. Surgeons Can.; mem. Soc. Perinatal Obstetricians. Office: Clinic Ob-Gyn SC 853 N Highland Ave Aurora IL 60506

BHIMANI, MOHAMEDRAZA HUSSEIN, dentist; b. Bukoba, Tanzania, Nov. 7, 1950; came to U.S., 1977; s. Hussein Rajabali and Fatmabai Hussein Bhimani; m. Tahera Mahamedraza Kanji, Dec., 1976. Student, K.C. Coll., Bombay, 1970; BDS, Govt. Dental Coll., Bombay, 1974; DMD, Tufts U., 1980. Gen. practice dentistry Kaplan Med. Ctr., Chgo., 1980—; cons. Belmont Nursing Home, Uptown Shelter Care, Lakeside Nursing Home, Ill. Found. Dentistry for Homebound, all in Chgo., 1981—. Mem. ADA, Ill. State Dental Soc., Chgo. Dental Soc. Home: 15245 Coventry Ct Orland Park IL 60462 Office: Kaplan Med Ctr 3527 W Roosevelt Rd Chicago IL 60624

BIAGINI, ESTHER PIER, interior designer, retailer; b. Chgo.; d. Silvio and Ilia (Paganelli) Nannini; m. Giulio J. Biagini, Oct. 5, 1952; children: Marc, Nannette, Lisa. Student, U. Ill., 1951-52; grad. Harrington Inst. Interior Design. Graphoanalyst; personal cons. in field; pub. relations cons. Bevmar Co., 1976; pres. Design Factory, Inc.; mgr. Fenco Galleries, Imports. Active PTA; pres. Brookfield (Ill.) Library Bd., 1969-70, 72-73, treas., 1970-71, sec., 1967-68, 73-74. Recipient Am. Legion award, 1950. Mem. ALA, Ill. Library Assn., Ill. Dirs. Library Assn., Am. Soc. Interior Designers, Brookfield Woman's Club. Home: 116 Princeton Rd Hinsdale IL 60521

BIANCHINI, MASSIMO, architect; b. Lucca, Tuscany, Italy, May 20, 1952; came to U.S., 1955; s. Alessandro G. and Adriana (Fambrini) B.; m. Kathleen Ann Ladik, Oct. 13, 1973; 1 child, Ginevra Ladik. BArch Design, U. Ill., Chgo., 1978. Licensed architect, Ill., Wis. Project architect Med. Architectonics/Interior Environments, Chgo., 1978-81; prin. Archtl. Resource Assocs., Chgo., 1981; corp. architect AMOCO Corp., Chgo., 1981-85; pres. Archtl. Resource Corp., Oak Forest, Ill., 1985—; cons. Columbus-Cungo-Cabrini Med. Ctr., Chgo., 1978—. Prin. works include Passive Solar Homes. Active Econ. Devel. Corp. Southwest Suburbs, Palos Heights, Ill., 1985—, Historic Preservation Commn. Orland Park, Ill., 1986—; mem. com. Morraine Valley Community Coll. Fine and Performing Arts Profl. Review. Mem. AIA, Nat. Council Archtl. Registration Bds. Roman Catholic. Lodge: Rotary. Avocations: jogging, cycling, golf. Office: Archtl Resource Corp 15020 S Cicero Ave Oak Forest IL 60452

BIANCO, CHRISTINA MARIE, librarian; b. Joliet, Ill., Oct. 3, 1962; d. Edward Robert and Florine Lee (De Angelis) Kovalcik; m. Thomas Bianco, May 9, 1987. Cert.in Library Tech. Asst., Coll. St. Francis, Joliet, 1983. Page Crest Hill (Ill.) Library, 1978-79, part-time clk., 1979-81, clk., 1981-83, library tech. asst., 1983-84, asst. librarian, 1984—. Mem. Friends of Crest Hill Library, 1982—, treas., 1987—. Avocations: aerobics, bowling, softball, music. Office: Crest Hill Pub Library Theodore & Willowbridge Rd Crest Hill IL 60435

BIANCO, RICHARD PETER, maxillofacial surgeon; b. Gary, Inc., Sept. 4, 1939; s. Richard John and Martha Evelyn (Mitchl) B.; m. Lucy Lovell Steel, Aug. 13, 1966 (div. Sept. 1976); m. Kimberly Ann Barrus, Nov. 7, 1985; children: Richard John II, Tamara Ann. AB, Hanover Coll., 1963; DDS, Ind. U., 1967. Oral-maxillofacial surgeon Christie Clinic Assoc., Champaign, Ill., 1972—; clin. instr. U. Ill. Sch. Medicine, Urbana, 1974—. Served to lt. USN, 1967-69. Fellow Am. Assn. Oral-Maxillofacial Surgery, Internat. Assn. Oral-Maxillofacial Surgeons, Am. Coll. Oral-Maxillofacial Surgeons, Am. Coll. Oral Implantology; mem. ADA, Am. Dental Soc. Anesthesiology. Republican. Episcopal. Avocations: golf, tennis, fishing. Home: 504 W Oak St Mahomet IL 61853

BIBB, MARY HOYT, psychiatrist; b. Indpls., June 3, 1944; d. Lester Harold and Esther (Harding) Hoyt; m. Richard E. Bibb, Mar. 30, 1985; 1 child, Matthew H. May. BS, Purdue U., 1966; MD, U. Ill., Chgo., 1969. Diplomate Am. Bd. Psychiatry and Neurology. Intern Christ Hosp., Cin., Emerson A. North Hosp., Cin.; resident U. Ky. Med. Ctr., Lexington, 1969-71; staff psychiatrist Bluegrass Comprehensive Care Ctr., Lexington, 1971-72, Georgetown, Ky., 1975-77; practice medicine specializing in psychiatry Georgetown, 1975-77; resident U. Cin. Med. Ctr., 1977-78; practice medicine specializing in psychiatry Twenty-Six Hundred Euclid, Inc., Cin., 1978—; bd. dirs. Help Ctr., Inc., Georgetown, 1972-73; cons. Bluegrass Comprehensive Care, Paris, Ky., 1980-82. Cons. Ky. Task Force on Children with Emotional Problems., 1975. Mem. Am. Psychiat. Assn., Ohio Psychiat. Assn. Cin. Psychiat. Soc. Office: Twenty Six Hundred Euclid Inc 2600 Euclid Ave Cincinnati OH 45219

BIBBO, MARLUCE, physician, educator; b. Sao Paulo, Brazil, July 14, 1939; d. Domingos and Yolanda (Ranciaro) B. M.D, U. Sao Paulo, 1963, Sc.D., 1968. Intern Hosps. das Clinicas, U. Sao Paulo, 1963; resident in ob-gyn 1964-66; instr. dept. morphology and ob-gyn U. Sao Paulo, 1966-68, asst. prof., 1968-69; asst. prof. sect. cytology dept. ob-gyn U. Chgo., 1969-73, asso. prof., 1973-77, asso. prof. pathology, 1974-77, prof. ob-gyn and pathology, 1978—; asso. dir. Cytology Lab., Approved Sch. Cytotech and Cytocybernetics, AMA-Am. Soc. Clin. Pathologists, 1970—; Mem. research com. Ill. div. Am. Cancer Soc., 1976—. Contbr. numerous articles to profl. jours. Fellow Internat. Acad. Cytology (v.p. 1987, dep. editor Acta Cytologica); mem. Am. Soc. Cytology (exec. com., pres. 1982-83). Home: 400 E Randolph St Apt 2009 Chicago IL 60601 Office: 5841 S Maryland Ave Chicago IL 60637

BIBBY, JAMES JOHN, mental health agency administrator; b. Milw., Oct. 3, 1947; s. James Elias and Marion (Herrmann) B.; m. Kathleen Denise (Jones), Nov. 8, 1980. B.A., Marquette U., 1969; M.S., Purdue U., 1972. Psychology trainee Marion VA Hosp. (Ind.), 1971-73; therapist Child and Adult Mental Health Center, Youngstown, Ohio, 1973-74, emergency mgr., 1974-75; with Four County Comprehensive Mental Health Center Inc., Logansport, Ind., 1975—, adminstr., 1978-79, exec. dir., 1979—. Bd. dirs. United Way of Cass County (Ind.), 1980-84, pres., 1982-83. Mem. Am. Psychol. Assn. Republican. Roman Catholic. Clubs: Logansport Jaycees, Rotary, Elks. Office: Four County Counseling Ctr 1015 Michigan Ave Logansport IN 46947

BIBLE, RICHARD LEE, business executive; b. Bryan, Ohio, Mar. 15, 1947; s. Earl Leroy and Lillian Marie (Weber) B.; m. Sandra Sue Johnston, Apr. 12, 1969; children—Christopher, Suzette. Student, Lain Tech. Inst., Indpls., 1966, Tri State Coll., Angola, Ind., 1967. Design draftsman The Aro Corp., Bryan, Ohio, 1967-71, tech. mktg. supr., 1971-74, dist. sales mgr., Chgo., 1974-77; nat. sales mgr. Indsl. Pumping & Petroleum Systems Products., Bryan, 1977-83; v.p. mktg. Reelcraft Industries, Inc., Columbia City, Ind., 1984—. Mem. Petroleum Equipment Inst. (bd. dirs.), Am. Supply & Machinery Mfrs. Assn. Inc., Mem. United Methodist Ch. Club: Orchard Ridge Country. Home: Oak Borough of Coventry 2925 Smugglers Cove Fort Wayne IN 46804

BIBLE, ROY HENDERSON, JR., industrial research chemist; b. Roanoke, Va., May 31, 1926; s. Roy Henderson and Susie Mae (Robertson) B.; m. Harriett Virginia Bertoglio, June 10, 1951; 1 child, Keith Christopher. BS, Va. Tech. U., 1948; MS, U. Ill., 1949, PhD, 1951. Research investigator G.D. Searle & Co., Skokie, Ill., 1951-66, head physical methodology, 1966-74, asst. dir. analytical resources and methodology, 1974-79, research fellow, dir. physical methodology, 1979—. Author: Interpretation of NMR Spectra: An Empirical Approach, 1967, A Guide to NMR Interpretation Spectra, 1978; patentee in field; contbr. articles to profl. jours. Judge sci. fair Ill. Jr. Academy Sci., 1972—; pres. Nat. Chem. Exposition, 1976-78, bd. dirs., 1968—. Recipient Merit award Chgo. Tech. Soc. Council, 1973. Mem. Am. Chem. Soc. (com. on coms., 1976-81, com. on nominations and elections 1982—, joint bd. and council com. econs. status, councilor 1964—), Chgo. sect. Am. Chem. Soc. (chmn. 1967-68, treas. 1964-65, Disting. Service award 1985), Soc. Applied Spectroscopy, Alpha Chi Sigma, Sigma Xi, Phi Lambda Upsilon. Club: Chgo. Chemists' (pres. 1962-63, treas. 1958-60). Avocations: photography, hiking, technical rock climbing, electronics. Home: 9012 Mango Ave Morton Grove IL 60053 Office: GD Searle & Co 4901 Searle Pkwy Skokie IL 60077

BICK, DAVID GREER, health care marketing; b. Toledo, June 29, 1953; s. James D. and Carol Jean (Hermann) B.; m. Laurie Kay Cuprys, Nov. 8, 1975; children: Jennifer Kelly, Jesse Quinn, Matthew Adam, Wylie Christine. BE, U. Toledo, 1975; cert. health cons. Purdue U., 1981. Dist. mgr. Blue Cross Northwest Ohio, Tiffin, 1977-79, regional mgr., Sandusky, 1979-81, dir. sales, Toledo, 1981-82; v.p. mktg. Blue Cross/Blue Shield Central N.Y., Syracuse, 1983; exec. dir. Preview-Health Benefits Mgmt. of Ohio, Toledo, 1984—, chief mktg. exec. Medchoice/Dentachoice HMO Blue Cross and Blue Shield of Ohio, 1984—. Author: Paupers and Profiteers (poetry). Mem. Toledo Found. for Life, PTA, People's Med. Soc., The Park Ridge Ctr. Inst. for the Study of Health, Faith & Ethics, Toledo Zoological Soc., Toledo Mus. Art. Mem. Am. Coll. Utilization Rev. Physicians, Hastings Ctr./Inst. & Soc. of Ethics and Life, Am. Hosp. Assn., Toledo C. of C. Roman Catholic. Lodge: Rotary. Avocations: photography, golf, basketball, skiing, tennis. Home: 1658 Kalida Toledo OH 43612 Office: 3737 Sylvania Ave PO Box 887 Toledo OH 43623

BICKEL, ERMALINDA, real estate broker; b. Casole Bruzio Provincia di Cosenza, Italy, Nov. 8, 1919; d. Saverio and Emilia (Fortino) Fortino; came to U.S., 1927, naturalized, 1927; student pub. schs., Italy, Elkhart, Ind.; Grad. Real Estate Inst., Purdue U.; m. William E. Bickel, Aug. 10, 1946; 1 dau., Patricia Ann Heiser. Office clk. Gen. Telephone, Elkhart, 1939-41; sec. to pres. Ames Co. div. Miles Labs., Inc., Elkhart, 1941-52, tech. sec. pharmacy research dept., 1962-82; freelance legal sec., 1956-61; owner, founder Blue Chip Realty, Inc., Elkhart, 1968-86. Mem. Nat., Ind., Elkhart real estate bds., Delta Theta Tau, Elkhart C. of C. Roman Catholic. Lodge: Zonta, Moose Women. Office: 26258 Cottage Ave Elkhart IN 46514

BICKEL, FLOYD GILBERT, III, investment counselor; b. St. Louis, Jan. 10, 1944; s. Floyd Gilbert II and Mary Mildred (Welch) B.; B.S. in Bus. Adminstrn., Washington U., St. Louis, 1966; M.S. in Commerce, St. Louis U., 1968; m. Martha Wohler, June 11, 1966; children—Christine Carleton, Susan Marie, Katherine Anne, Jennifer Anne, Laura Elizabeth, Andrew Barrett (dec.). With research dept. Yates, Woods & Co., St. Louis, 1966-67; asst. br. mgr. E.F. Hutton & Co., Inc., St. Louis, 1967-70; asst. v.p., resident mgr. Bache & Co., Inc., St. Louis, 1970-72; pres. Donelan-Phelps Investment Advisors, Inc., St. Louis, 1972-80; first v.p., dir. consulting services E.F. Hutton & Co., Inc., St. Louis, 1980—; pres., dir. Drew Petroleum, Inc. Biclan, Inc.; pres. Biomel, Inc.; chmn., dir. Data Research Assos., Inc., St. John's Bancshares, Inc., Maverick Tube Co. Mem. City of Des Peres (Mo.) Planning and Zoning Commn., 1975-76; chmn. St. Louis County Bd. Equalization, 1976-79; pub. safety commr. City of Des Peres, 1977-80, mem. audit and fin. com., 1980-86; mem. Gov.'s Crime Commn., 1981—; bd. dirs. Villa Duchesne Sch. Mem. Internat. Soc. Cert. Employee Benefit Specialists, Internat. Found. Employee Benefit Plan, St. Louis Soc. Fin. Analysts. Republican. Presbyterian. Clubs: Bellerive Country (bd. dirs.); St. Louis; John's Island; Commanderie de Bordeaux. Contbr. bus. articles to mags. Home: 30 Huntleigh Woods Saint Louis MO 63131 Office: 100 S Brentwood Blvd Saint Louis MO 63105

BICKFORD, KENT WALTER, controller; b. Chgo., Feb. 2, 1958; s. Willard W. and Norma (Seekamp) B.; m. Julie Kathryn Baum, July 9, 1983. BS in Acctg., U. Ill., 1980. CPA, Ill. Asst. payroll mgr. Eisner Food Stores, Champaign, Ill., 1980-81; controller, treas. Clyde's Delicious Donuts, Chgo., 1981—. Mem. Am. Inst. CPA's, Ill. CPA Soc. Republican. Lutheran. Club: Medinah (Ill.) Country. Avocations: golf, reading, music, winter sports. Office: Clyde's Delicious Donuts 2500 W Chicago Ave Chicago IL 60622

BICKFORD, THOMAS EDWARD, civil engr.; b. Newton, Mass., May 22, 1929; s. Edward Milton and Mabel Etta (Eldridge) B.; B.S. in Civil Engring., Northeastern U., 1957; postgrad. Ohio State U., 1960-72; m. Edna Harriett Thompson, Oct. 22, 1955 (div. 1979); m. Carol Schar Shay, May 24, 1981; children—Douglas Thomas, Linda Kathryn. Civil engr. Columbia Gas System Service Corp., Columbus, Ohio, 1957-60, Scioto Conservancy Dist., Columbus, 1962-64; civil engr. Burgess & Niple, Ltd., Columbus, 1961-62, 64-70, asst. personnel dir., 1966-70, human resources dir., 1971—. Vice-pres. PTA, Columbus, 1969-70, pres., 1971-72; chmn. engrs. group, profl. div. United Way, 1969-70; trustee Forest Park Civic Assn. Registered profl. engr., Ohio, Fla. Mem. ASCE, Personnel Assn. Cen. Ohio (v.p. 1972, treas. 1977), Am. Soc. Personnel Adminstrn. Independent Republican. Home: 7029 Muirfield Dr Dublin OH 43017 Office: 5085 Reed Rd Columbus OH 43220

BICKLEY, JOHN HOWARD, JR., lawyer; b. Chgo., May 12, 1929; s. John H. and Letta (McGraw) B.; student Evanston Twp. Community Coll., 1948; J.D., Chgo. Kent Coll. Law, 1951; children—John H., III, Lisa F., Kathryn M. Admitted to Ill. bar, 1952; partner Peterson, Bogucki & Bickley, Attys., Chgo., 1957-67, individual practice, Chgo., 1968—; mem. firm Bickley & Bickley; spl. asst. atty. gen. Ill., 1968-69; chief environ. control div. Ill. Atty. Gen.'s Office, 1970-71; asst. U.S. atty. No. Dist. Ill., 1955-57; trial atty. Forest Preserve Dist. Cook County; spl. prosecutor Chgo. Police Burglar Scandal, 1961; mem. lecture forum MidWest U.S. Attys. Conf., 1963; apptd. to dist. performance assistance com. U.S. Dist. Ct. for No. Dist. Ill. to determine qualifications of applicants for admission to trial bar of ct. Mem. dist. council SBA, 1971-72; legal cons. Ill. State Bd. Elections. Trustee, Village of Mount Prospect (Ill.), 1961-63, 1st v.p. Regular Republican Orgn., Elk Grove Twp., 1961-62; candidate for state's atty. Cook County, 1964. Served with USMCR, now lt. col. (ret.). Named one of Chgo.'s 10 Outstanding Young Men, Chgo. Jaycees, 1964; One of Outstanding Young Men U.S., 1965; named to alumni honor council Chgo. Kent Coll. Law, 1978. Mem. Internat. Acad. Law and Sci., Ill., Chgo., Fed. (pres. Chgo. chpt. 1972-73, nat. v.p. 1973-74) bar assns., Am. Arbitration Assn. (nat. panel arbitrators), Am., Ill. (pres. 1971-72), trial lawyers assns., Trial Lawyers Club Chgo., Soc. Trial Lawyers, Law Club Chgo., Legal Club Chgo., Globe and Anchor Soc. Ill. (past pres.), Chgo. Kent Coll. Law Alumni Assn. (dir.), Am. Legion. Episcopalian. Clubs: Masons (32 deg., Shriner), Tavern, Plaza (Chgo.). Secured conviction of syndicate crime leader Paul (The Waiter) Ricca, 1957. Office: 230 N Michigan Ave Chicago IL 60601

BICKNELL, BRIAN KEITH, dentist; b. Orlando, Fla., Mar. 8, 1957; s. Keith Arthur and Mary Lou (Papish) B. BS, U. Notre Dame, 1979, U. Ill., Chgo., 1981; DDS, U. Ill., Chgo., 1983. Practice gen. dentistry Batavia, Ill., 1984—. Mem. ADA, Ill. State Dental Soc., Fox River Valley Dental Soc., Acad. Gen. Dentistry. Roman Catholic. Home: 1024 Lorlyn Circle 3C Batavia IL 60510 Office: 109 E Wilson Batavia IL 60510

BICZAK, ALAN JOSEPH, osteopath; b. Passaic, N.J., Aug. 26, 1932; s. Geza John and Margaret (Tomescko) B.; m. Marilyn Winifred Bush, Sept. 6, 1983; children: Sharon, Cathy, Joyce, Alan, Nancy, Laura, Mary Alice, David. AB, Drew U., 1954; MS, Stevens Inst. Tech., Hoboken, N.J., 1960; DO, Phila. Coll. Osteo. Medicine, 1969. With Colgate-Palmolive, 1954-65; mgr. personnel Playtex Internat., Dover, Del., 1965; intern Phila. Coll. Osteo. Medicine, 1969; practice osteo. medicine Muskegon, Mich., 1970—; fellow staff Muskegon Gen. Hosp.; chmn. Dept. Gen. Practice, Muskegon, Dept. Ethics and Grievances, Muskegon. Director various med. videos. Republican.. Roman Catholic. Lodges: Moose, Elks. Avocations: photography, golf. Office: 420 S Wolf Lake Rd Muskegon MI 49442

BIDDINGER, JOHN WESLEY, financial exec.; b. Indpls., May 5, 1940; s. Noble L. and Eleanor Jane (Lynch) B.; B.S., Ind. U., 1963; m. Margaret Jo Hunt, Sept. 1, 1962; children—Karen Elizabeth, Katherine Jane. With City Securities Corp., Indpls., 1963—, salesman, 1963-67, v.p., 1967-69, exec. v.p., dir., 1969-79, pres., dir., 1979-80; pres. Biddinger Investment Capital Corp., Global Tech., Inc., Access Tech., Inc., Retrieval Systems, Inc., Capital Corp., Ind. Ventures, Inc., Internat. Transaction System Inc., U.S.A. Vault Corp.; chmn. bd. Crime Control Inc., Diamond Electronics, Inc., M.P.D. Inc.; dir. Asbury Mgmt. & Fin. Corp. Crime Control, Inc., Media Omaha, Inc., Starlight Musicals; treas., chmn. exec. com. SunGroup Inc. Bd. dirs. Found. Assos. Hon. Ky. col., col. a.d.c. Tenn.; cert. gen. agt., life ins. agt. Mem. Confrerie des Chevaliers du Tastevin, Internat. Wine and Food Soc., Confrerie de la Chaine des Rotisseurs, Indpls. Bond Club, Nat. (nominating com., affiliate liaison com., bd. govs. 1978—, chmn. publ. com.), Indpls. (inaugural pres.) security traders assns., Indpls. Jaycees, Well House Soc., Second Century Club of Indpls. Mus. Art, Cousteau Soc., Oceanic Soc., Ind. U. Sch. Bus. Alumni Assn., Ind. U. Alumni Assn. (bd. mgrs., chmn. nominating com., mem. dues, ins. and outdoor edn. coms.), Dean's Assos. Ind. U. Bus. Sch., Ind. U. Varsity Club, Ind. U. Hoosier 100, Sigma Chi. Clubs: Pacesetters, Pointe Golf and Tennis, Meridian Hills Country, Manor House, Andre's. Lodge: Masons. Home: 9121 Spring Hollow Dr Indianapolis IN 46260 Office: 9102 N Meridian St Indianapolis IN 46260

BIDDISON, JACK MICHAEL, oil company executive, geologist, engineer; b. Columbus, Ohio, Feb. 27, 1954; s. Jack Carpenter and Betty Yvonne (Mollette) B; m. Qiang Zhang, Oct. 25, 1986. B.S. in Geology and Mineralogy, Ohio State U., 1977; M.B.A., Kent State U., 1985. Cert. profl. geol. scientist. Geologist, Inland Drilling Co., Ravenna, Ohio, 1978-81; geol. engr. Gasearch, Inc., Girard, Ohio, 1981; geotech. engr. CER Corp., Las Vegas, Nev., 1981-82; mgr. petroleum engring. and geol. services Energy Devel. Ops., Gen. Electric Co., Kent, Ohio, 1982-87; chief div. oil and gas Ohio Dept. Natural Resources, Columbus, 1987—. Mem. Am. Inst. Profl. Geologists, Am. Assn. Petroleum Geologists, Soc. Petroleum Engrs., Ohio Geol. Soc., Beta Gamma Sigma. Methodist. Avocations: Basketball; rock collecting; cross country skiing. Home: 6035 Hampstead Dr W Columbus OH 43229 Office: Gen Electric Co Energy Devel Operation 2007 State Rte59 Kent OH 04113

BIDDIX, RANDALL DUANE, accountant, manufacturing executive, educator; b. Hudson, Mich., Aug. 14, 1954; s. Raymond Duane Biddix and Anna Lou (Sallows) Lantz; m. Edna May McLaughlin, Oct. 22, 1977; children: Casey Ann, Chad Andrew. BA, Siena Heights Coll., 1980. CPA, Mich. Acctg. clk. Markowski & Co., CPA's, Jackson, Mich., 1977, staff auditor, 1977-79, sr. auditor, 1979-84; controller Ann Arbor (Mich.) Machine, 1984—; inst. acctg. Jackson Community Coll., 1984—. Served with U.S. Army, 1972-75. Am. Inst. CPA's, Mich. Assn. CPA's. Republican. Methodist. Avocations: softball, bowling, golf. Home: 2922 S Sandston Jackson MI 49201 Office: Ann Arbor Machine Co PO Box 1206 Ann Arbor MI 49286

BIDEAU, EDWIN HALE, III, lawyer; b. Chanute, Kans., Oct. 1, 1950; s. Edwin H. and Beverly Maxine (Semon) B.; m. Margaret E. Fritton, June 30, 1973; children: Scott E., Sarah M., Jenny E. AA, Neosho Community Coll., 1970; BBA, Washburn U., 1972, JD, 1975. Bar: Kans. 1975, U.S. Dist. Ct. Kans. 1975, U.S. Dist. Ct. Okla. 1984. Law clk., atty. Kans. Ins. Commn., Topeka, 1973-75; asst. county atty. Neosho County Atty.'s Office, Chanute, Kans., 1975-76, county atty., 1976-85; sole practice, Chanute, 1975-83, sr. ptnr., Bideau Law Offices, 1983—; adj. instr. Washburn U., Topeka, 1974-75, Neosho Community Coll., Chanute, 1975-83; pres. Profl. Software Assocs., Inc., Chanute; state rep. Kans. Legis. 5th Dist., 1985—. Mem. adv. com. bus. dept. Neosho Community Coll., Chanute, 1984—; Rep. precinct committeeman Neosho County, 1984; mem. adv. com. Social and Rehab. Services, 1980; bd. dirs. Chanute Pub. Library, 1980; mem. Neosho County Law Library Com., 1978-83; mem. Kans. Legislature from 5th dist., 1985—; chmn. House Jud. and Legis. Appointment com., 1987—; deacon First Presbyn. Ch., Chanute. Named Outstanding Young Man, Chanute Jaycees, 1978, 83. Mem. ABA, Assn. Trial Lawyers Am., Nat. Dist. Atty.'s Assn., Kans. Dist. Atty.'s Assn., Kans. Bar Assn., Southeast Kans. Bar Assn., Neosho County Bar Assn. (pres. 1978-79), Kans. Trial Lawyers Assn., Neosho Valley Hist. Soc. (pres. 1980), Neosho River Muzzle Loaders, Sigma Phi Epsilon (bd. dirs. Kans. Delta chpt. 1972-78). Lodge: Elks. Home: 14 S Rutter St Chanute KS 66720 Office: 18 N Forest Chanute KS 66720

BIDINGER, LAWRENCE PAUL, information systems manager; b. Cin., Dec. 16, 1946; S. George Vincent and Viola Lorine (Etienne) B.; m. Vivian Michaud, Feb. 7, 1970; 1 child, Jaimy. AB in English, Dartmouth Coll., Hanover, N.H., 1968. Supr. Task Force, Inc., San Francisco, 1968-69; systems supr. Province Data Ctr., Cin., 1969-74; sr. systems analyst Great Am. Ins., Cin., 1974-79; info. systems mgr. Gen. Electric Co., Cin., 1979—. Home: Box 245B Rt 5 Brookville IN 47012 Office: Gen Electric Aviation Comp Svc Ctr 333 W Seymour St Cincinnati OH 45216

BIDWILL, WILLIAM V., football executive; s. Charles W. and Violet B. Mng. gen. partner, now chmn. St. Louis Cardinals Football Team. Office: St Louis Cardinals Busch Stadium 200 Stadium Plaza Saint Louis MO 63102 *

BIEBEL, CURT FRED, JR., dentist; b. St. Louis, Dec. 7, 1947; s. Curt F. and Jewell (Frank) B.; m. Linda Doreen Shepard; children: Betheny Doreen, Brendon Matthew. AB in Psychology, U. Mo., Columbia, 1970; DDS, U. Mo., Kansas City, 1974. Assoc. dentist Louis R. Nolan, Inc., St. Louis, 1976-79; gen. practice dentistry Chesterfield, Mo., 1979—. Served to capt. (dental officer) USAF, 1974-76. Mem. ADA, Greater St. Louis Dental Soc., Chgo. Dental Soc., Internat. Congress Oral Implantologists. Club: Cherry Hills Country, Forest Park Handball Assn. Home: 12370 Oak Hollow Creve Coeur MO 63141 Office: 14378 Woodlake Dr Chesterfield MO 63017

BIEBER, OWEN F., labor union official; b. North Dorr, Mich., Dec. 28, 1929; s. Albert F. and Minnie (Schwartz) B.; m. Shirley M. Van Woerkom, Nov. 25, 1950; children: Kenneth, Linda, Michael, Ronald, Joan. H.H.D., Grand Valley Coll., 1983. Rep. Internat. Union UAW, Grand Rapids, Mich., 1961-72, asst. regional dir. Region ID, 1972-74, regional dir Region ID, 1974-80; v.p. Internat. Union UAW, Detroit, 1980-83, pres., 1983—. Chmn. Kent County Dem. Com., Wyoming, Mich., 1964-66, mem. exec. bd., 1966-80; del. Nat. Dem. Convs., 1968, 76, 80. Named Labor Man of Yr., Kent County AFL-CIO, 1965. Mem. NAACP (life), Grand Rapids Urban League. Roman Catholic. Club: Economic of Detroit. Office: Internat Union UAW 8000 E Jefferson Ave Detroit MI 48214

BIEBERSTEIN, HEINZ GÜNTHER, industrial engineering executive; b. Aschaffenburg, Fed. Republic Germany, Sept. 28, 1930; s. Hans Jakob and Margaret (Schuster) B.; m. Christine E. Roggendorf, Feb. 21, 1969; 1 child, Karen K. BBA, Municifa Bus. Community Coll., 1950; grad., Indsl. Engring Coll., Chgo., 1960. Indsl. engr. Chgo. Printed String Co., 1959-64; sr. indsl. engr. Hawley Products Co., St. Charles, Ill., 1964-65; indsl. engr. Joanna Western Mills, Co., Chgo., 1965-66, prodn. planning mgr., 66-71, chief indsl. engr., 1971-75; mgr. indsl. engring. Joanna Western Mills Co., St. Charles, 1975-79, mgr. mfg. adminstrv. services and indsl. engring., 1979—; instr. Indsl. Engring. Coll., 1960-65. Mem. Inst. Indsl. Engrs. (sr., pres. local chpt. 1982-83, bd. dirs. 1983—, Newsletter Nat. Silver award 1985), Indsl. Mgmt. Soc. (pres. Chgo. chpt. 1981-82). Roman Catholic. Home: 1217 Heatherfield Glenview IL 60025 Office: Joanna Div CHF Inc 2141 S Jefferson St Chicago IL 60616

BIEDRON, THEODORE JOHN, newspaper advertising executive; b. Evergreen Park, Ill., Nov. 30, 1946; s. Theodore John and Ione Margaret B.; B.A. in Polit. Sci., U. Ill., 1968; m. Gloria Anne DeAngelo, Nov. 7, 1970; children—Jessica Ann, Lauren. Recruitment advt. mgr. Chgo. Sun-Times, 1968-74; classified advt. mgr. Pioneer Press, Wilmette, Ill., 1974-76; classified mgr., v.p. Lerner Newspapers, Chgo., 1976-79, assoc. pub., 1980-82, advt. dir., 1982—. Bd. dirs. Northeastern Ill. Univ. Found. Mem. Assn. Newspaper Classified Advt. Mgrs. (past bd. advisors), Suburban Newspapers of Am. (award for best classified advt. sect. 1975, cert. of excellence 1979), Ill. Press Assn., Nat. Newspaper Assn. Home: 1130 Lake St Wilmette IL 60091 Office: 7519 N Ashland St Chicago IL 60626

BIEGELSEN, ELAINE LANDER, accountant; b. St. Louis, Feb. 8, 1939; d. Louis and Edna (Schramm) Lander; m. Paul Simeon Biegelsen, June 29, 1961; children: Elizabeth, Rebecca, Annie. BS, Washington U., St. Louis, 1961; MS, Purdue U., 1964; MBA, Xavier U., 1984. CPA, Ohio. Tchr. phys. edn. Fairborn (Ohio) City Schs., 1961-62; with payroll, personnel depts. Glen Manor Home, Cin., 1980-81; acct. Clayton Scroggins & Assocs., Cin., 1981-86, Wm. Lammert, CPA, Cin., 1986—. Mem. Am. Inst. CPA's, Ohio Soc. CPA's, Am. Soc. Women Accts. Avocation: athletics.

BIEHLE, JAMES TOWNSEND, architect; b. N.Y.C., Feb. 9, 1944; s. Judson Townsend and Reba Carolyn (Strickland) B.; m. Cynthia Ellen Ferguson, Aug. 20, 1966; children: Sean Jason, Drew Ferguson, Craig Townsend, Megan Patricia. BA, Williams Coll., 1966; MArch, U. Pa., 1969. Registered architect, Tex., Fla., Mo. Edn. officer asst. CUNY, N.Y.C., 1971-73; ops. mgr. CM Inc., Houston, 1973-77; pres. KBA Constrn. Mgrs., Inc., St. Louis, 1977-83; pres. Facilities Resources, Inc., St. Louis, 1983—, also bd. dirs.; v.p. Inside-Out Architecture, Inc., St. Louis, 1984—, also bd. dirs.; v.p. Westerfield Devel. Corp., St. Louis, 1985—, also bd. dirs. Contbr. articles to profl. jours. Asst. scoutmaster Boy Scouts Am., St. Louis, 1985-87. Mem. Am. Inst. Architects (treas. St. Louis chpt. 1982-83, bd. dirs. 1985-86). Avocations: hiking, canoeing, fishing, tennis, golf. Office: Facilities Resources, Inc. 130 S Bemiston Suite 705 Saint Louis MO 63011

BIEL, ERNEST LEONARD, dentist; b. Dickinson, N.D., May 25, 1940; s. Ernest Paul and Kathryn Rosemand (Haich) B.; m. Sharon Elizabeth Hanrahan, Apr. 20, 1963; children: Rick, Steven, Anthony. BS, BA, Dickinson (N.D.) State Coll., 1961; MS, St. Mary's Coll., Winona, Minn., 1969; DDS, Marquette U., 1980. Tchr. LaCrescent (Minn.) High Sch., 1965-69; chemist Oconomowoc (Wis.) Electroplating, 1969-71; tchr. U. Lake Sch., Hartland, Wis., 1971-76; gen. practice dentistry Oconomowoc, 1980—. Served to 1st lt. USAF, 1962-65. Mem. ADA, Wis. Dental Assn., Waukesha County Dental Assn. (editor newsletter 1983—). Roman Catholic. Lodge: KC (grand knight Oconomowoc 1974-75). Avocations: stained glass, woodworking, cross country skiing, gardening.

BIELIAUSKAS, LINAS AUGUSTINE, clinical psychologist; b. Munich, Federal Republic of Germany, July 22, 1948; s. Vytautas J. and Danute G. (Širvydas) B.; m. Britt Andersen, July 30, 1972; children: Nina, Anton. BS, Xavier U., Cin., 1970; MS, Ohio U., 1973, PhD, 1976. Diplomate Am. Bd. Profl. Psychology. Asst. prof. psychology Rush-Presby. St. Luke's Med. Ctr., Chgo., 1976-82, assoc. prof., 1982—; dir. clin. tng. dept. psychology Rush-Presby. St. Luke's Med. Ctr., 1978—. Author: Stress and Its Relationship to Health and Illness, 1982, The Influence of Individual Differences in Health and Illness, 1983; contbr. articles to profl. jours. Judge behavioral scis. Chgo. Pub. Sch. Sci. Fair, 1978—. Served to maj. USAR, 1970-86. Mem. Am. Psychol. Assn. (div. exec. com. 1984—), Internat. Neuropsychol. Soc. (bd. govs. 1986—), Am. Psychosomatic Soc., Soc. Behavioral Medicine, AAAS, Sigma Xi. Republican. Roman Catholic. Avocation: piano. Office: Rush-Presbyterian St Luke's Med Ctr 1753 W Congress Pkwy Chicago IL 60612

BIELKE, PATRICIA ANNE, psychologist; b. Bay Shore, N.Y., May 11, 1949; d. Lawrence Curtis and Marcella Elizabeth (Maize) Widdoes; m. Stephen Roy Bielke, July 10, 1971; children: Eric, Christine. BA, Carleton Coll., 1971; PhD, U. Minn., 1979. Lic. psychologist, Wis. Research asst. Nat. Inst. Mental Health, Washington, 1972-74; sch. psychologist Roseville Pub. Schs., St. Paul, 1978-79; psychologist Southeastern Wis. Med. and Social Services, Milw., 1979—, Brief Family Therapy Ctr., Milw., 1981—; staff psychologist Elmbrook Meml. Hosp., 1986—; supr., cons. Catalyst Counseling Ctr., Wauwatosa, Wis., 1981—; cons. psychologist Family Health Plan, Brookfield, Wis., 1985—. Bd. dirs. League of Women Voters, Brookfield, 1984—. Mem. Am. Assn. Marriage and Family Therapists. Home: 17455 Bedford Dr Brookfield WI 53005 Office: Southeastern Wis Med & Social 10721 W Capitol Dr Wauwatosa WI 53222

BIELSKI, DONALD JOSEPH, lawyer; b. Houston, Mar. 25, 1959; s. Walter Thomas and Carol Elizabeth (Nauman) B. BA with distinction, U. Wis., 1981, JD cum laude, 1984. Bar: Wis. 1984, U.S. Dist. Ct. (we. dist.) Wis. 1984. Trial atty. State Pub. Defender, Kenosha, Wis., 1984—; legal asst. U. Wis. Sch. Edn., Madison, 1979-81. Dist. commr. Boy Scouts Am., Racine, Kenosha, Wis., 1986; mem. steering com. Garvey for Senate, Kenosha City, Wis., 1986. Mem. ABA, ACLU, Am. Trial Lawyers Assn., Amnesty Internat., Wis. Bar Assn., Kenosha Bar Assn., Tau Kappa Epsilon. Democrat. Roman Catholic. Avocations: golf, swimming, music, lit. Home: 1073 Sheridan Rd 206 Kenosha WI 53140 Office: State Pub Defenders Office 604 57th St Kenosha WI 53140

BIEN, STANLEY DANIEL, accountant, systems manager; b. Gary, Ind., Nov. 13, 1954; s. Stanley E. and Lillian Bien; B.S., Ferris State Coll., 1977; M.P.A., Western Mich. U., 1982; m. Jean Ann Lotoszinski, Oct. 13, 1979; children—Nicholas James, Katie Marie. Program accountant fin. mgmt. sect. Dep. Dir.'s Office, Mich. Dept. Public Health, Lansing, 1977-82, chief system and procedures for acctg., 1982-85; chief mgmt. systems sect. Mich. Dept. Pub. Health Bur. Community Services, 1985—. Recipient Hoosier State Scholarship award, 1973-74. Mem. Nat. Assn. Accts., State Govtl. Accts. Assn. Mich., Mich. State Employees Assn., Assn. Govt. Accts., State Assn. Accts. Auditors and Bus. Adminstrs., Fellowship Christian Athletes, Delta Sigma Pi. Clubs: Canoe, Accounting. Home: 1085 Craig St Lansing MI 48906 Office: Mich Dept Pub Health Bur Community Services 3500 N Logan Lansing MI 48909

BIENENFELD, DAVID GERALD, physician; b. Canton, Ohio, Mar. 9, 1953; s. Joseph and Freda (Weber) B.; m. Jill Ann Armentrout, Mar. 8, 1981; 1 child, Allison Rachel. BA in Cellular and Molecular Biology, U. Pa., 1974; MD, U. Cin., 1978. Diplomate Am. Bd. Psychiatry and Neurology, Am. Bd. Med. Examiners. Resident in psychiatry U. Cin., 1978-81, fellow in geriatric psychiatry, 1981-82; physician P.W. Lewis Ctr., Cin., 1981—; asst. prof. psychiatry U. Cin., 1983—; dir. Ctr. Adult Devel., U. Cin. , 1984—, dir. geriatric psychiatry, 1985—. Contbr. articles to profl. jours. Exec. bd. Cin. Area Sr. Services, 1984-87. Recipient Maurice Levine Essay award U. Cin., 1982; NIMH grantee, 1985—; fellow Vanderbilt U., Nashville, 1975. Mem. Am. Psychiat. Assn., Am. Geriatrics Soc., Gerontol. Soc. Am., Am. Group Psychotherapy Assn., Am. Assn. Geriatric Psychiatry, Assn. Acad. Psychiatry. Democrat. Jewish. Avocations: photography, cycling, cooking. Home: 4004 Beechwood Ave Cincinnati OH 45229-1410 Office: U Cin Dept Psychiatry ML #559 Cincinnati OH 45267-0559

BIENENSTEIN, KATHLEEN LINDA, engineering company executive; b. Detroit, June 20, 1951; d. Charles August and Emily Linda (Tomolillo) B.; m. Alfred Reginal Trainer, III, Sept. 11, 1970 (div. 1972). BA Oakland U., Mich., 1973; AA in Bus., Kellogg Community Coll., Battle Creek, 1980. Owner retail store, Livonia, Mich., 1973-75; designer Criterion Design, Royal Oak, Mich., 1975-77; designer Eaton Corp., Galesburg, Mich., 1977-81; v.p. engring. services Charles S. Davis & Assoc. Inc., Pontiac, Mich., 1981-87, gen. mgr., 1984-85; engring. group mgr. Ruecker Engring Ltd., 1987—. Patentee camshaft bushing. Sponsor, Star Theatre, Flint, Mich., 1983-86. Mem. Soc. Automotive engrs., Soc. Body Engrs., NOW, Nat. Assn. Female Execs. Democrat. Office: Ruecker Engring Ltd 30800 Van Dyke Warren MI 48093

BIERBOWER, JEFFREY SHANNON, financial company executive; b. Belpre, Ohio, Oct. 21, 1958; s. Hugh Shannon and Lois Ann (Hellein) B.; m. Kim Ann Gentry, Aug. 20, 1983; 1 child, Matthew Shannon. BS in Prodn. and Ops. Mgmt., Ohio State U., 1981. Engr. I ITT, Delaware, Ohio, 1981-82; v.p. Fin. Devel. Co., Inc., Columbus, Ohio, 1982-86; account coordinator Transam. Fin. Systems and Concepts, Columbus, 1986—; cons. in field. Mem. Block Watch, Gahanna, Ohio, 1986. Republican. Lutheran. Club: KAB Investment (Columbus) (bd. dirs. 1985—). Office: Transam Fin Systems and Concepts 7100 Huntley Rd Columbus OH 43229

BIERY, JOHN CARL, Physician; b. Columbus, Ohio, Nov. 10, 1944; s. Richard J. and Evelyn Joy (Bowman) B.; m. Kathleen Ford, June 1, 1968; children—John Carl Jr., Allison Kathleen. B.S., Northeast Mo. State U., 1972; D.O., Kirksville Coll. Osteo. Medicine, 1974. Team physician Bowling Green State U., 1976-77; ptnr. Ottawa Med. Ctr., Ohio, 1975-85; founder The Sports Med. Clinic, 1986—; emergency room physician Fostoria City Hosp., Ohio, 1982-85, St. Rita's Med. Ctr., Lima, Ohio, 1975—; mem. Putnam County Bd. Health, 1976—, pres. 1986-87. Served with USAF, 1964-68. Fellow Am. Coll. Sports Medicine; mem. Ohio Osteo. Assn. (pres. Acad. Dist. II 1982-87), Am. Osteo. Assn., Am. Coll. Family Practice, VFW. Avocations: swimming, golf, reading. Home: 9086 Cherokee Pl Ottawa OH 45875 Office: 110 Selhorst Dr Box 326 Ottawa OH 45875

BIESTEK, JOHN PAUL, lawyer; b. Chgo., May 28, 1935; s. John P. and Selma (Glick) B.; m. Elizabeth Mary Frer, Dec. 31, 1956; children—Scott, Becky. B.S., Loyola U., Chgo., 1957, J.D., 1964. Bar: Ill. 1964, U.S. dist ct. (no. dist.) Ill. 1964. Sr. ptnr. Biestek & Facchini, Chgo., 1965-74; founding ptnr. Biestek & Assocs., Arlington Heights, Ill., 1974—. Atty. Wheeling Twp. Republican. Orgn., 1978, fin. chmn., 1982-84; founder, chmn. Arlington Heights Econ. Devel. Commn., 1983-84. Mem. NW Suburban Bar Assn. (pres. 1977-78), Arlington Heights C. of C. (pres. 1982-84, dir. and atty., 1972-86, award Extraordinary Commitment and Leadership 1984), Bridgeview C. of C. (pres. 1969). Roman Catholic. Clubs: Rolling Green Country (sec. 1978-81, atty. 1980-84). Lodge: Rotary (sec. Arlington Heights chpt. 1987—). Home: 805 S Salem Ave Arlington Heights IL 60005 Office: John P Biestek & Assocs Ltd 115 N Arlington Heights Rd Arlington Heights IL 60004

BIETILA, JACOB ANSELM, dentist; b. Ishpeming, Mich., Apr. 28, 1935; s. Jacob Anselm and Selma Johanna (Abramson) B.; m. Fay Diane Storhok, June 27, 1964; children: Jay, Jaclyn, Bret, Betsy. DDS, U. Mich., 1959. Gen. practice dentistry Ishpeming, 1959—. Pres. Ishpeming Diplomats, 1968. Mem. ADA, Mich. Dental Assn., Superior Dist. Dental Soc. (sec. 1964-65). Apostolic Lutheran. Club: Ishpeming Ski (pres. 1960-72). Lodge: Kiwanis (pres. Ishpeming 1965). Avocations: hunting, fishing, dog training, travel, painting. Home: Rt 1 Box 20 Ishpeming MI 49849 Office: 117 S First St Ishpeming MI 49849

BIGELOW, WALLACE W., chief executive officer; b. Claremont, Minn., Jan. 30, 1943. BA, Mankato State, 1965; MS, U. Wis., Menomonie, 1970. Prodn. control IBM, Rochester, Minn., 1965-67; psychometrist State of Minn., Cambridge, 1967-68; adminstrn. Goodwill Industries Vocat. Enterprises, Duluth, Minn., 1970-74; chief exec. officer Ability Bldg. Ctr. Inc., Rochester, 1974—. Office: Ability Bldg Ctr Inc B 6938 Rochester MN 55903

BIGGAR, JAMES MCCREA, food company executive; b. Cleve., Dec. 5, 1928; s. Hamilton Fisk and Ruth Carolyn (McCrea) B.; m. Margery Dean Stouffer, Dec. 29, 1950; children: Elizabeth, James, William, David. B.S. in Mech. Engring. and Engring. Adminstrn., Case Inst. Tech., 1950. With Reliance Electric Co., Cleve., 1950-60; mgr. alternating current products Reliance Electric Co., 1955-60; with frozen foods div. Stouffer Corp., Cleve., 1960-70; mktg. v.p. Stouffer Corp., 1960-66, v.p., gen. mgr., 1966-68, pres., 1968-70; v.p. food service group Litton Industries, Solon, Ohio, 1970-72; pres., chmn. bd., dir. Stouffer Corp., Solon, Ohio, from 1972; pres., chief exec. officer Nestle Enterprises, Inc., Solon, Ohio, 1983—, also dir.; pres., chief exec. officer, dir. Nestle Holdings Inc., Wilmington, Del., 1985—; dir. Nat. City Bank of Cleve. Pres. Orange Local Sch. Bd., Pepper Pike, Ohio, 1967-68; v.p. Vocat. Guidances and Rehab. Services, Cleve., 1970-76; bd. dirs. Cleve. Clinic, Cleve. Tomorrow, Greater Cleve. Growth Assn.; trustee Univ. Sch., 1981-83. Mem. Am. Frozen Food Inst. (past chmn., dir.), Grocery Mfrs. Am. (dir.), Phi Kappa Psi, Theta Tau, Beta Gamma Sigma. Presbyterian. Clubs: Cleve. Country, Clevelander, Pepper Pike Country, Rolling Rock. Home: 31600 Fairmount Blvd Pepper Pike OH 44124

BIGGS, NANCY ANN, system software specialist; b. Springfield, Ill., Feb. 27, 1941; d. Ralph Calvin and Grace Florence (Stephens) Buecker; m. John David Biggs, June 3, 1960; 1 child, Kent Edward. M.A. in Computer Sci., Sangamon State U., 1982. Computer programmer Ill. Dept. Revenue, Springfield, 1982-83, Ill. Community Coll. Bd., Springfield, 1983-84; computer programmer/analyst Horace Mann Ins. Cos., Springfield, 1984-85; systems software specialist strategic planning and policy analysis Ill. Office Comptroller, Springfield, 1985—. Mem. Assn. Systems Mgmt. (treas. 1983-85), Assn. Computing Machinery. Democrat. Avocations: antiques; traveling; computer graphics; sewing. Home: 308 Natchez Trace Springfield IL 62702 Office: Ill State Office Comptroller 320 W Washington St 5th Floor Springfield IL 62706

BIGHAM, DARREL EUGENE, history educator; b. Harrisburg, Pa., Aug. 12, 1942; s. Paul D. and Ethel B.; BA, Messiah Coll., 1964; postgrad. Harvard Div. Sch., 1964-65; PhD, U. Kans., 1970; m. Mary Elizabeth Hitchcock, Sept. 23, 1965; children: Matthew, Elizabeth. Asst. prof. history U. So. Ind., Evansville, 1970-75, assoc. prof., 1975-81, prof., 1981—. Exec. dir. Leadership Evansville, 1976-79; dir. archives div. Conrad Baker Found., 1971-85; chmn. Evansville Bicentennial Council, 1974-77; bd. dirs. Evansville Mus., 1972—, sec., 1977-78, pres., 1979-81; trustee Evansville Vanderburgh County Pub. Library, 1971-80; bd. dirs. Met. Evansville Progress Commn., 1981—, chmn., 1983-85; bd. dirs. Evansville Arts and Edn. Council, 1982—, chmn. 1983-85, pres., 1984-85; pres. Vol. Action Ctr., 1983-85; bd. dirs. Conrad Baker Found., 1971-85, Planned Parenthood S.W. Ind., 1978-79; chmn. 175th Anniversary Com. City of Evansville, 1985-87. Rockefeller Bros. Theol. fellow, 1964-65; NDEA fellow, 1965-68. Mem. Soc. Ind. Archivists (dir. 1972-75, pres. 1977-79), Am. Hist. Assn., Orgn. Am. Historians, Ind. Hist. Soc., So. Hist. Assn., Vanderburgh County Hist. Soc. (pres. 1981-84). Mem. United Ch. of Christ. Clubs: Rotary, Petroleum, Oak Meadow Country. Author: We Only a Fair Trial, 1987; contbr. articles to scholarly jours. Home: 8215 Kuebler Rd Evansville IN 47712 Office: Dept History Univ So Ind Evansville IN 47712

BIGLER, BERNARD HENRY, commercial writer; b. Mesler, Mo., Feb. 19, 1923; s. Joseph Frank and Josephine Helen (Schumacher) B.; m. Lola Mary Schell, June 21, 1952; children: Anne Leslie Bigler Lindgren, Mark Joseph, Lisa Mary Bigler Kohlrus. BA in Journalism, Ohio State U., 1949. Reporter Zanesville (Ohio) News, 1949-50; wire editor Ohio State Jour., Columbus, 1950-51; account exec. Jay H. Maish Co., Marion, Ohio, 1951-59, Western Advt. Agy., Racine, Wis., 1959-62; copy writer Potts-Woodbury & Success, Kansas City, Mo., 1962-81, Bryant Lahey & Barnes, Kansas City, 1981—. Served with USN, 1942-45. Republican. Roman Catholic. Avocations: vol. work with Agrl. Hall of Fame. Home: 8028 Fontana Prairie Village KS 66208 Office: Bryant Lahey & Barnes Inc 4200 Pennsylvania Kansas City MO 64111

BIGNALL, ALAN FREDERICK, information systems executive; b. Nottingham, Eng., May 31, 1951; came to U.S., 1979; s. Frederick and Hilda (Cowley) B.; m. Susan Jane Wooltorton, Sept. 1, 1971 (div. Dec. 1978); m. Marcia Kay Pinkston, Mar. 1, 1979; children: Jason Paul, Ian Alan, Drew Alexander. MBA, Coll. of St. Thomas, 1985. Programmer, analyst Rolls Royce Ltd., Derby, Eng., 1969-72; systems devel. mgr. Fodens Trucks Ltd., Sandbach, Eng., 1972-76; sales support specialist ITT Bus. Systems, Brighton, Eng., 1976-77; project mgr. Royal Bank of Can., Montreal, Que., 1977-79; v.p. corp. systems IDS Fin. Services Inc., Mpls., 1979—. Office: IDS Fin Services Inc IDS Tower Minneapolis MN 55474

BIHLER, FREDERICK HENRY, electronics company executive; b. N.Y.C., Sept. 8, 1926; s. Frederick H. and Isabelle A. (Ziegler) B.; m. Ruth M. Hinck, Sept. 18, 1948 (dec. July 1973); children: Barbara Bihler Schmidt, Douglas, Carol Bihler De Loriea, Susan Bihler Bandman; m. Nancy E. Woodruff, Feb. 22, 1975. BSEE, NYU, 1950. Nat. sales mgr. Furnas Electric Co., Batavia, Ill., 1962-69; v.p. sales and mktg. Clare div. Gen. Instrument Corp., Chgo., 1969-76; sr. v.p. Fujitsu Am. Inc., San Jose, Calif., 1976-85; pres. Advantest Am., Inc., Lincolnshire, Ill., 1985—; mgmt. cons., Lake Forest, Ill., 1976, 85. Inventor dairy automation control system, 1960. Served with USN, 1944-46, PTO. Mem. IEEE. Avocations: horseback riding, photography, philately, sailing. Home: 435 E Illinois Rd Lake Forest IL 60045 Office: Advantest Am Inc 300 Knightsbridge Pkwy Lincolnshire IL 60069

BIHUN, THOMAS A., management information services executive; b. Detroit, Mar. 23, 1943; s. Fred and Olga (Misthal) B.; m. Nora Jane McGuire, Apr. 29, 1967; children: Lisa Marie, Jason Allen. BA in Bus. and Mktg., Northeastern Ill. U., 1981. Pres. Am. Prodn. & Inventory Control Soc., Detroithurch, 1978-79, Chgo., 1983-84; pres. Ill. 38 User Group, Chgo., 1984-85; dir. mgmt. info. services Internat. Jensen, Schiller Park, Ill., 1985—. Author: Capacity Management Certification Review Course; contbr. articles to profl. jours. Served to sgt. USMCR, 1966-70. Home: 3412 Maple Leaf Dr Glenview IL 60025 Office: Internat Jensen 4136 N United Pkwy Schiller Park IL 60176

BILAND, ALAN THOMAS, computer integrated manufacturing executive; b. Pontiac, Mich., Sept. 13, 1958; s. Alfred T. and Janice J. (Bortreger) B.; m. Martha R. Wegner, Sept. 15, 1979; children: Benjamin A., Elizabeth L. BA in Biology and Psychology, Kalamazoo Coll., 1980; postgrad., U. Wis., 1986—. Computer aided design/computer aided mfg. Ronningen Research, Vicksburg, Mich., 1980-81; sr. industry cons. Computervision, Bedford, Mass., 1981-85; mgr. CAD/CAM N.Am. J.I. Case Co., Racine, Wis., 1985—. Mem. Computer and Automated Systems Assn., Soc. Mfg. Engrs. Republican. Lutheran. Avocations: fishing, travel, studying German. Office: JI Case Co 24th & Mead Racine WI 53403

BILD, FRANK, state senator; b. Romania, Sept. 30, 1911; s. Anton and Katerina (Schiebel) B.; came to U.S., 1913, naturalized, 1937; B.S. in Edn., Ind. U., 1934; J.D., St. Louis U., 1942; m. Flora Huss, Sept. 18, 1937; children—Brian Alan, Karen Ann, Norman Anton, Kathleen Ann. Dir. athletics Southside St. Louis YMCA, 1936-42; admitted to Mo. bar, 1946, since practiced in St. Louis. Republican committeeman Concord (Mo.) Twp., 1956-66; mem. Mo. Ho. of Reps. from 47th Dist., 1963-64, 67-72; mem. Mo. Senate from 15th Dist., 1973—; mem. Mo. Atomic Energy Commn. Served to capt. AUS, 1942-46. Recipient Meritorious award St. Louis Globe Democrat. Lutheran. Club: Concord Village Lions. Office: 11648 Gravois Rd Saint Louis MO 63126

BILKEY, PETER C., biotechnology company executive; b. Willamantic, Conn., May 26, 1954; s. Warren J. and Angelica (Romero) B. BS in Horticulture, U. Wis., 1976, MS in Horticulture, 1978; PhD in Botany, U. Nottingham, Eng., 1981. Research scientist Internat. Plant Research Inst., Inc., San Carlos, Calif., 1982; research cons. Pillsbury Co., Mpls., 1983; bus. devel. mgr. George J. Ball, Inc., West Chicago, Ill., 1984-85; pres. Advanced Botanics Corp., Middleton, Wis., 1986—. Contbr. articles to profl. jours. Avocations: antique collecting, ice skating, diving. Office: Advanced Botanics Corp 3103 Laura Ln Unit C Middleton WI 53562

BILKEY, WILLIAM WALTER, JR., industrial engineer; b. St. Louis, Sept. 21, 1943; s. William W. and Romona (Foosey) B.; student S.E. Mo. State U., 1962, Jefferson Coll., 1967-75; B.S. in Indsl. Mgmt. and Psychology, Washington U., St. Louis, 1983. With Carter Automotive subs. Fed. Mogul (formerly Carter Carburetor div. A.C.F. Industries), St. Louis, 1963—, gen. foreman carburetor assembly, 1976-78, mgr. tooling and indsl. engring., 1978-82, mgr. statis. mfg. analysis, 1982, dir. quality assurance and statis. programs, 1982-85, v.p. ops., 1985-86, gen. mgr., 1986—. Mem. Am. Inst. Indsl. Engrs., Am. Soc. Quality Control. Club: Moo do Kwan.

BILLAK, RICHARD JOHN, psychologist; b. Sharon, Pa., Dec. 9, 1947; s. Andrew A. and Paula R. (Capson) B.; m. Arlene J. Izenas, Aug. 16, 1969; 1 child, Damian A. BA, Gannon U., 1969; PhD, Kent State U., 1976. Lic. psychologist, Ohio. Exec. dir. Community Corrections Assn., Inc., Youngstown, Ohio, 1973—; mem. adj. faculty Youngstown State U., 1974—, Kent (Ohio) State U., 1975—; cons. commn. on accreditation for corrections, Rockville, Md., 1984—. Coordinator Mondale-Ferraro Campaign 17th dist. Ohio, 1984, Sec. State Brown campaign, Mahoning County, 1986; mem. Leadership Youngstown, 1985. Recipient Outstanding Contrn. award Market St. Mchts. Assn., Youngstown 1986. Mem. Am. Correctional Assn., Acad. Criminal Justice Scis., Am. Assn. Counseling and Devel., Ohio Psychol. Assn., Ohio Halfway House Assn. (pres. 1978-79). Roman Catholic. Office: Community Corrections Assn Inc 1608 Market St Youngstown OH 44507

BILLE, DONALD ALLEN, nurse, educator; b. Waupun, Wis., Feb. 10, 1943; s. Arthur and Ada (Wellhouse) B.; grad. St. Luke's Hosp. Sch. Nursing, 1964; B.S.N., U. Wis., Madison, 1966, Ph.D., 1975; M.S.N., Marquette U., 1971. Mem. faculty Coll. Nursing, Marquette U., Milw., 1970-72;

coordinator intensive care unit VA Med. Center, Wood, Wis., 1973-74; dir. nursing edn. Mercy Hosp., Chgo., 1975-77; asst. prof. U. Ill. Med. Center, Chgo., 1978-79; asso. prof. nursing DePaul U., Chgo., 1979-84, prof., 1984—, chmn. grad. program, 1980-81. Served with Nurse Corps, U.S. Army, 1966-70. Mem. Ill. League Nursing (chmn. program com., dir.), Nat. League Nursing, Chgo. Council Fgn. Relations (patron), Assn. Supervision and Curriculum Devel., Am. Soc. Health Edn. and Tng., Phi Delta Kappa, Sigma Theta Tau (Zeta Sigma chpt.) Congregationalist. Author: Staff Development: A Systems Approach, 1982. Editor: Practical Approaches to Patient Teaching, 1981. Mem. editorial bd. Quality Rev. Bull., Jour. Nursing Edn., Nursing Adminstrn. Quar.; editorial bd., book rev. editor Today's OR Nurse; contbr. numerous articles to profl. jours. Home: 3749 N Wilton Ave Chicago IL 60613 Office: DePaul U 2323 N Seminary Ave Chicago IL 60614

BILLER, CARMEN GEORGE, manufacturing executive; b. Newark, Jan. 12, 1953; s. Edward and Carmella Veronica (Iula) B.; m. Ann Louise Nenno, June 14, 1975; children: Eric Edward, Mark Evan. BEE, N.J. Inst. Tech., 1975. Product design engr. Westinghouse Electric Co., Buffalo, 1975-78; sr. elec. engr. Electric Apparatus Co., Howell, Mich., 1978-79, chief elec. engr., 1979-82, pres., 1982—. Mem. IEEE. Home: PO Box 346 Pinckney MI 48169 Office: Electric Apparatus Co PO Box 227 Howell MI 48844

BILLIG, THOMAS CLIFFORD, magazine publisher; b. Pitts., Aug. 20, 1930; s. Thomas Clifford and Melba Helen S. B.; m. Helen Page Hine, May 14, 1951; children: Thomas Clifford, James Frederick. BSBA summa cum laude, Northwestern U., 1956. Ins. mgr., asst. dir. personnel, asst. to chmn. Butler Bros. (now City Products Corp.), Chgo., 1954-59; market research mgr. R.R. Donnelley & Sons, Chgo., 1959-61; pres., dir. Indsl. Fiber Glass Products Corp., Scottville and Ludington, Mich., 1962-69; cons. mass mktg. mgr. Mpls., 1969-71; v.p. Mail Mktg. Systems and Services, St. Paul and Bloomington, Minn., 1971-74; pres. Billig and Assocs., Mpls., 1979—, also bd. dirs.; pres. NIARS Corp., Mpls., 1974—, also bd. dirs.; pres. Fins and Feathers Pub. Co., Mpls., 1977—, also bd. dirs. Served with USNR, 1948-56. Recipient Samuel Dresner Plotkin award Northwestern U., 1956. Mem. Delta Mu Delta, Beta Gamma Sigma. Office: 318 W Franklin Ave Minneapolis MN 55404 also: Fins & Feathers Fins & Feathers Publishing Co 401 N 3rd St Minneapolis MN 55401

BILLIMORIA, F. BILL, financial planning executive; b. Bombay, India, Aug. 13, 1943; came to U.S., 1966; s. Manchershaw N. and Meher Billimoria; m. Huty F. Kelawala, Dec. 22, 1974; children: Jimmy, Eric. BSME, Victoria Jubilee Tech. Inst., Bombay, 1965; BS in Indsl. Engring., Ill. Inst. Tech., 1967, MS in Indsl. Engring., 1970; MBA in Fin., U. Chgo., 1973. CPA, Ill.; cert. fin. planner. Systems analyst/programmer J. T. Ryerson & Son Inc., Chgo., 1967-71; sr. systems analyst Washington Nat. Ins. Co., Evanston, Ill., 1971-74; mgmt. cons. Ernst & Whinney, Chgo., 1974-78; sr. mgmt. cons. A.T. Kearney, Inc., Chgo., 1978-82; pres. Integrated Fin., Inc., Arlington Heights, Ill., 1982—. Mem. Internat. Assn. for Fin. Planning Inc. (treas. greater O'Hare chpt. 1983-84, exec. v.p. 1984-85, pres. 1985-87), Inst. for Cert. Fin. Planners. Republican. Zoroastrian. Lodge: Rotary Internat. (program chmn. Arlington Heights 1986-87). Avocations: travel, reading, crosswords. Home: 1081 King Charles Ct Palatine IL 60067 Office: Integrated Fins Inc 605 E Algonquin Rd #400 Arlington Heights IL 60005

BILLING, DAVID RICHARD, obstetrician, gynecologist; b. Sidney, Ohio, Apr. 25, 1943; s. Richard Edgar and Evelyn Louise (Stein) B.; m. Evangeline Ruth Erny, June 3, 1965; children: Marcy, Richard, Stacey. AB, Asbury Coll., 1965; MS, Ohio State U., 1967; MD, Univ. Autonomo de Guadalajara, Mex., 1972. Practice medicine specializing in ob-gyn Springfield, Ohio, 1976—. Trustee Asbury Coll., Wilmore, Ky., 1981—. Fellow Am. Coll. Ob-Gyn, ACS, Am. Fertility Soc., Am. Soc. Colposcopy. Republican. Baptist. Avocations: tennis, skiing. Home: 738 Linmuth Ct Springfield OH 45503 Office: Physicians & Surgeons for Women Inc 1821 E High St Springfield OH 45505

BILLINGHAM, DAVID RALPH, social service administrator; b. Rockford, Ill., Apr. 10, 1949; s. Ralph B. and Elfrieda K. (Muehleisen) B.; B.S. in Psychology, Rockford Coll., 1971; M.S.W., U. Ill., Chgo., 1975; m. Jean Caughey, June 2, 1973; 1 son, Matthew David. Social worker Ill. Dept. Children and Family Services, 1971-73; lead social worker Mental Health Advocacy Project, Chgo., 1975-76; forensic psychiatry program social worker Ill. State Psychiat. Inst., Chgo., 1977-80; grant specialist Region II, Ill. Dept. Mental Health, 1980-81; dir. residential services Victor C. Neumann Assn., Chgo., 1981—; chmn. human rights com. W.A. Howe Center for Developmentally Disabled, 1982-84. Cert. social worker, Ill. Mem. Acad. Cert. Social Workers, Alt. Living Mgrs. Assn., Am. Orthopsychiat. Assn., Nat. Assn. Social Workers, Am. Assn. Mental Deficiency, Ill. Assn. Retarded Citizens, Ill. Assn. Rehab. Facilities (residential com. 1986—). Office: 2354 N Milwaukee Ave Chicago IL 60647

BILLINGS, CHARLES HARRY, lawyer; b. St. Louis, Sept. 17, 1952; s. Charles Patrick and Mary Eileen (Hixson) B.; m. Kathleen Ann Bruntrager, July 30, 1976; children—Charles, Daniel, Anne. B.A., St. Louis U., 1975; J.D., St. Mary's U., San Antonio, 1978. Bars: Mo. 1978, U.S. Dist. Ct. (ea. and we. dists.) Mo. 1978, U.S. Supreme Ct. 1982. Prosecutor, St. Louis Circuit Atty., 1978-80; assoc. Bruntrager & Billings, St. Louis, 1980-82, ptnr., 1982—. Judge, City of Pine Lawn, Mo., 1979—, City of Des Peres, 1985—, City of Lakeshire, 1986—. Mem. Assn. Trial Lawyers Am., ABA, Mo. Bar Assn., St. Louis Bar Assn., Phi Kappa Psi. Roman Catholic. Home: 13025 Winding Trail Saint Louis MO 63131 Office: Bruntrager Bruntrager & Billings PC 1015 Locust St Suite 1140 St Louis MO 63101

BILLINGS, DOUGLAS GLEN, corporate executive; b. Creston, Iowa, Mar. 9, 1942; s. Glen Dale and Nancy Jane (Wilhelm) B.; m. Annette Louise Sellergren, June 21, 1969; children—Melissa Smith, Abigail Fleming. B.A., Parsons Coll., 1963. Assoc. instr. Parsons Coll., Fairfield, Iowa, 1965-66; retail operator Men's Wear, Red Oak, Iowa, 1967-71; innkeeper Holiday Inn, Red Oak, 1971-80; pres. Red Coach Enterprises Inc., Red Oak, 1980-82, chmn., pres., 1982—; pres. Acorn Devel. Co., Red Oak, 1981—; chmn. Internat. Assn. Holiday Inns Inc. Polit. Action Com., Memphis, 1982-84. Mem. Iowa Devel. Commn., 1976-80; chmn. Housing Agy. of Red Oak, 1981-84; mem. fin. com. Iowa Democratic Com., 1982—, chmn. bus. council, 1983—; dist. chmn. Mid.-Am. council Boy Scouts Am., 1983—. Served with U.S. Army, 1967-72. Recipient Outstanding Achievement award Internat. Assn. Holiday Inns Inc., 1979-82. Mem. Internat. Assn. Holiday Inns Inc. (com., bd. dirs. 1984—), Am. Hotel and Motel Assn., Iowa Hotel-Motel Assn. (past dir.), Iowa Restaurant Assn., Sigma Phi Epsilon. Episcopalian. Club: Embassy (Des Moines). Lodge: Elks. Home: 802 8th St Red Oak IA 51566 Office: Red Coach Enterprises Inc US Hwy 34 Red Oak IA 51566

BILLINGS, ROBERT, engineer; b. Portland, Maine, Jan. 18, 1949; s. Richard and Elaine Wilma (Smith) B.; m. Barbara Ann Baughman, July 17, 1971; children: Amy Elaine, Cari Nicole, Ryan Joseph. BS in Engring. Mechanics, USAF Acad., 1971; MA in Indsl. Mgmt., Cen. Mich. U., 1978. Commd. 2d lt. USAF, 1971, advanced throught grades to capt., 1975; mech. engr. armament div. USAF, Eglin AFB, Fla., 1971-74; mech. engr. life support office USAF, Wright-Patterson AFB, Ohio, 1974-82; resigned USAF, 1978; with USAFR, 1978—; advanced through grades maj. USAF, 1985; lead engr. life support office USAF, Wright-Patterson AFB, Ohio, 1985, chief engr. life support office, 1985-87; chief support systems engr. Advanced Tactical Fighter Office, Wright-Patterson AFB, 1987—; mech. engr. F-16 office USAF, Wright-Patterson AFB, 1982-84; cons. NASA, Johnson Space Ctr., Houston, 1986—. Coach youth soccer, Tipp City, Ohio, 1982-84. Mem. Safety and Flight Equipment (v.p. local chpt. 1986—), Assn. Grads. U.S. Air Force Acad. (pres. local chpt. 1987—). Avocation: gardening. Office: Advanced Tactical Fighter Office ASD/TASE Wright-Patterson AFB OH 45433

BILLINGS, STEVEN PAUL, orthodontist; b. Wichita, Kans., Nov. 8, 1950; s. Raymond Riley and Edythe Leticia (Gilmore) B.; m. Debora Kay Renft, Aug. 31, 1985. BA, U. Kans., 1972; DDS, U. Mo., Kansas City, 1977. Emergency room technician Wesley Med. Ctr., Wichita, 1968-72, respiratory therapist, 1972-73; respiratory therapist Menorah Med. Ctr., Kansas City, 1973-75; pvt. practice gen. dentistry Independence, Mo., 1977-79; pvt. practice orthodontics Parkville, Mo., 1979—. Pres. Hidden Lakes Home Assn., Kansas City, 1985-86. Mem. ADA, Mo. Dental Assn., Am. Soc. of Dentistry for Children (sec. 1985-86), Greater Kansas City Dental Soc. (del. to state assn. 1984-86, various coms.), Clay-Platte Dental Soc., Am. Assn. Orthodontics, Am. Soc. for Functional Orthodontics, Midwestern Soc. Orthodontics, U. Mo. at Kansas City Alumni Assn. (pres. 1985-86), Jaycees. Republican. Presbyterian. Clubs: Tweed Study, Westport Study (Kansas City). Avocations: boating, fishing, sports. Home: 7117 NW Belleview Kansas City MO 64118 Office: 8600 NW 64th St Suite 204 Parkville MO 64152

BILLINGS, WILLIAM HOWARD, chief justice; b. Kennett, Mo., Aug. 21, 1921; s. James. v. and Leora (Sapp) B. Student naval aviator program, U. Iowa, 1942-43; LL.B., U. Mo., 1952. Bar: Mo., U.S. Dist. Ct. (ea. dist.) Mo., U.S. Supreme Ct. Ptnr. McHaney, Billings & Welman, Kennett, 1952-66; judge 35th jud. cir., Kennett, 1966-73, so. dist. Mo. Ct. Appeals, Springfield, 1973-82, Mo. Supreme Ct., Jefferson City, 1982—; lectr. Mo. State Hwy. Patrol, 1971-72. Pres., v.p. bd. curators U. Mo., Columbia, 1965-74. Served to capt. USMCR, 1942-45. Mem. ABA, Mo. Bar. Assn., Dunklin County (Mo.) Bar Assn., Am. Legion, VFW, Amvets, Order of Coif, Phi Delta Phi, Pi Kappa Alpha. Methodist. Lodge: Masons. Home: 1500 Rosewood Jefferson City MO 65101 Office: Supreme Ct Mo Supreme Ct Bldg Jefferson City MO 65101

BILLMAN, DEAN ARTHUR, electronics company executive; b. Sacramento, Nov. 13, 1954; s. Neil Elton and Eunice Marie (Potter) B.; m. Margaret Ann Miller, June 11, 1983. BSBA, Bowling Green (Ohio) State U., 1976; postgrad., W.Va. Coll. Grad. Studies, 1981-82; MBA, Xavier U., 1986. Retail mgr. Tandy Corp., Cin., 1976-80; sales engr. Gen. Electric Co., Charleston, W.Va., 1980-82; sales engr. Gen. Electric Co., Blue Ash, Ohio, 1983-86, account mgr., 1986—. Mem. Pulp and Paper Sect.of IEEE, Tech. Assn. Pulp and Paper Industry. Republican. Episcopalian. Avocations: traveling, writing, outdoor activities. Home: 8557 Island Pines Dr Maineville OH 45039 Office: Gen Electric Co 11311 Cornell Park Dr Blue Ash OH 45242

BILLMAN, FRED LEO, mfg. co. exec.; b. Hebron, Nebr., June 19, 1941; s. Elsworth Leo and Ruth Marie (Livergood) B.; student Omaha U., 1958-59; B.S. in Chemistry and Math., Fla. State U., 1963; M.S., Wayne State U., 1965, Ph.D., 1969; m. Mary Renee Hagarty, Aug. 7, 1971; children—Thomas Lloyd, Aaron Donald, Ellen Marie. Research asst. Wayne State U., 1963-69; research chemist basic organic research Johnsons Wax, Racine, Wis., 1969-74, sr. research chemist Johnson Wax Internat., 1974-77, research and devel. dir., Mex., 1977-80, Chile, 1980-81, internat. research and devel. mgr., 1981—. Mem. Coledonia Twp. (Wis.) Planning Bd., 1975-76. Mem. Am. Chem. Soc., Mexican Aerosol Soc. Patentee fabric softening agts. Home: 4840 Three Mile Rd Racine WI 53406 Office: 1525 Howe St Racine WI 53403

BILLQUIST, JOSEPH RONALD, systems specialist; b. Joliet, Ill., June 29, 1961; s. Ronald Joseph and Mary Dianne (Kochalka) B.; m. Merla Sue Hansel, Dec. 17, 1983. BS in Computer Sci., Fin., No. Ill. U., 1983; MBA, De Paul U., 1986. Programmer, analyst Trailer Train Co., Chgo., 1983-85, sr. programmer, analyst, 1985-86, systems analyst, 1986—. Mem. Soc. for Preservation and Encouragement of Barber Shop Quartet Singing in Am. Lutheran. Club: Toastmasters. Home: 735 Liberty Ave Saint Charles IL 60174 Office: Trailer Train Co 101 N Wacker Dr Chicago IL 60606

BILLS, EDWIN LYNN, training specialist; b. Delaware, Ohio, Dec. 20, 1942; s. Harold Lynn and Lucille (Sharp) B.; B.S. in Edn., U. Cin., 1973, M.Ed., 1975; Ohio Vocat. Edn. Adminstrn. intern, Kent State U., 1977-78; m. Shirlee Costello, June 9, 1972; children—Amylynn, Nathan. Computer ops. shift supr. U.S. Shoe Corp., Cin., 1970-73; communications electronics instr. Great Oaks Joint Vocat. Sch. Dist., Cin., 1973-77, trade and indsl. edn. supr., 1977-80; assoc. dir. Scarlet Oaks Career Devel. Center, Cin., 1980-82; mgr. internal tng. Cin. Milacron Electronic Systems, 1982-85, tng. mgr., 1985—. Bd. dirs. Ripley County Ind. ARC, 1978-83, Public Service award, 1978, Cath. Charities, Indpls., 1984-86; rep. Ripley County Disaster Council; bd. dirs. Catholic Charities, Indpls. Served with USN, 1962-69. Mem. Am. Radio Relay League (Public Service award), Nat. Alumni Assn. Coll. Edn. U. Cin. (v.p., mem. exec. bd.). Roman Catholic. Clubs: Laughery Valley Amateur Radio (past pres.), U. Cin. Vets. (charter, past sec.). Home: Rt 1 Box 195A Sunman IN 47041 Office: Rt 48 and Mason Rd Lebanon OH 45036

BILSEL, YILMAZ CELIK, physician; b. Istanbul, Turkey, May 17, 1927; s. Huseyin Sabri and Makbule (Ahmet) B.; m. Zeliha Tanriover, Oct. 29, 1960; children—Deniz, Kurt. M.D., U. Istanbul, 1949. Physician, R.R. Co., Adana, Turkey, 1951-53; resident in internal medicine Eskisehir, Turkey, 1953-56; internist, R.R. Hosp., Izmir and Istanbul, Turkey, 1956-58; resident, Homer G. Phillips Hosp., St. Louis, 1958-61; fellow in hematology, Med. Coll. Ga., Augusta, 1961-63; practice medicine, Kirklareli, Turkey, 1963-66; supr. City Hosp., 1966-70; practice medicine specializing in internal medicine, East St. Louis, Ill., 1970—; bd. mem. St. Mary's Hosp., East St. Louis; pres. staff Centreville Twp. Hosp. (Ill.). Served to lt. M.C. Turkish Army, 1949-50. Mem. AMA, Ill. State Med. Soc., Mo. Med. Soc., Clair County Med. Soc., So. Ill. Med. Soc. Co-author: Angiotensin II and Erythropoiesis, 1963. Home: 25 Huntleigh Woods Saint Louis MO 63131 Office: 4601 State St East Saint Louis IL 62205

BILSKY, EARL, textile/apparel company executive; b. Fall River, Mass., Sept. 26, 1928; s. David and Rose (Nulman) B.; B.S., S.E. Mass. U., 1952; M.S. (research fellow), Inst. of Textile Tech., 1954; m. Betty Ann Funk, Dec. 5, 1954; children—Edward Scott, Karen Lee, Matthew Kolman. Engr. specialist Goodyear Aerospace Corp., Akron, Ohio, 1960-62; merchandise mgr. apparel and indsl. Am. Cyanamid Co., N.Y.C. and Wayne, N.J., 1962-71; exec. v.p. Aileen, Inc., N.Y.C. and Abilene, Tex., 1971-76, also dir.; pres. Eagle Knitting Mills, Milw., 1976—. Bd. dirs. United Way, Abilene, 1975-76, YMCA, Abilene, 1973-76, Abilene Art Mus., 1974-75, Milw. Council on Drug Abuse, 1981-83. planning/zoning commr. City of Abilene, 1975-76. Served with USMC, 1946-48. Patentee in field. Office: Eagle Knitting Mills 507 13 S 2d St Milwaukee WI 53204

BILZING, GLENN ALFRED, real estate corporation officer; b. St. Louis, Sept. 3, 1935; s. A.O. Walter and Hortense (Budke) B.; m. Patricia Ann Dobyns, Nov. 5, 1960 (div. May 1974); children: Nancy Anna, Derick Glenn, Denise Kay. BS in Bus., Tarkio Coll. Leasing agt. I.T. Cook Co., St. Louis, 1957-60; regional v.p. G.W. Warnecke Corp., St. Louis, 1960-78; regional leasing mgr. Equitable Life Ins. Co., St. Louis, 1978-80; sr. mktg. officer Clayton Towers Devel., St. Louis, 1980-81; pres. Glennmor, Ltd., St. Louis, 1981—. Mem. Jr. Chamber Internat. Senators, St. Louis, 1972. Mem. Bldg. Owners Mgrs. Inst. Internat. (cert., bd. dirs. 1972-75, pres. 1974), St. Louis Advt. Club. Republican. Mem. United Ch. Christ. Clubs: Euclid 505, Mo. Athletic (bd. govs. 1980-83, sec. 1983) (St. Louis). Lodges: Masons, Shriners. Avocations: golfing, floating. Office: Glennmor Ltd PO Box 18697 Saint Louis MO 63118

BINDER, MARTIN RANDALL, manufacturing company executive; b. Chgo., Dec. 20, 1918; s. Jack Henry Binder and Anna Moses; m. Marjorie Schorr, June 23, 1940; 1 child, Richard. LLB, DePaul U., 1940. Chmn. Abbott-Interfast Corp., Wheeling, Ill., 1945—; chmn. bd. Bank of Bellwood, Ill., 1985—; chmn. exec. com. 1st Nat. Bank Lincolnshire, 1983—. Chmn. Ill. State Toll Hwy. Authority, 1972; mem. adv. bd. Chgo. Council of Fine Arts, 1986, Ill. Arts Council, 1986. Lodge: Masons. Office: Abbott Interfast Corp 190 Abbott Dr Wheeling IL 60090

BINDLEY, WILLIAM EDWARD, pharmaceutical executive; b. Terre Haute, Ind., Oct. 6, 1940; s. William F. and Gertrude (Lynch) B.; m. Martha Leinenbach, June 10, 1961; children: William Franklin, Blair Scott, Sally Ann. B.S., Purdue U., 1961; grad. wholesale mgmt. program, Stanford U. Sch. Bus., 1966. Asst. treas. Controls Co. Am., Melrose Park, Ill., 1962-65; vice-chmn. E.H. Bindley & Co., Terre Haute, 1965-68; chmn. bd., chief exec. officer Bindley Western Industries, Inc., Indpls., 1968—; Scholl Scholarship guest lectr. Loyola U., Chgo., 1982; guest lectr. Young Pres. Orgn., Palm Springs, Calif. and Dallas, 1981, 82, 84; guest instr. Ctr. for Entrepreneurs, Indpls., 1983; bd. dirs. Ameri Trust Ind. Corp. State dir. Bus. for Reagan-Bush, Washington and Indpls., 1980; trustee Indpls. Civic Theatre, St. Vincent Hosp., Indpls.; bd. dirs. Nat. Entrepreneurship Found.; mem. pres.'s council Purdue U., West Lafayette, Ind.; hon. sec. of state State of Ind. Named hon. Ky. Col., 1980. Mem. Young Pres. Orgn. (area dir., chmn. 1982; award 1983), Nat. Wholesale Druggists Assn. (dir. 1981-84; Service award 1984), Purdue U. Alumni Assn. (life). Republican. Roman Catholic. Clubs: Woodstock, Meridian Hills Country (Indpls.). Avocations: skiing; tennis; golf; boating. Office: Bindley Western Industries Inc 4212 W 71st St Indianapolis IN 46268

BINGHAM, MARJORIE JEAN WALL, educator; b. St. Paul, Nebr., May 27, 1936; d. George Richard and Fay Maugerite Wall; B.A., Grinnell Coll., 1958; M.A., U. Minn., 1959, Ph.D., 1969; m. Thomas Egan, Feb. 28, 1975. Tchr. public schs., Davenport, Iowa, 1959-62, St. Louis Park, Minn., 1963-77; dir. women in world area studies St. Louis Park and Robbinsdale (Minn.) Schs., 1977—. Mem. Minn. Humanities Commn., 1983—, chair, 1986-87. Woodrow Wilson fellow, 1958-59; recipient Minn. Bus. award for excellence in edn. Mem. Women Historians of Midwest (pres. 1980—, mem. exec. bd. 1978—), Minn. Hist. Soc. (mem. edn. bd. 1979—), Minn. Council of Social Studies (mem. exec. bd. 1977—), Am. Hist. Assn. (teaching div.), Phi Beta Kappa. Co-author: Women in the U.S.S.R., 1980; Women in Islam, 1980; Women in Israel, 1980; Women in China, 1980; Women in India, 1980; Women in Africa, 1982; Women in Ancient Greece and Rome, 1983; Women in Medieval and Renaissance Europe, 1984; Women in Latin America, 1985, Women in Japan, 1986; mem. editorial bd. The History Tchr., Orgn. Am. Historians (OAH) Mag. of History. Home: 5732 Lake Rose Dr Minnetonka MN 55343 Office: 6425 W 33d St Saint Louis Park MN 55426

BINNING, WILLIAM CHARLES, political scientist, educator; b. Boston, Mar. 8, 1944; s. Kenneth William and Josephine Agnes (Crotty) B.; B.A. in Politics, St. Anselm's Coll., 1966; Ph.D. in Govt. and Internat. Relations (NDEA fellow), U. Notre Dame, 1970; m. Maureen G. Fannon, Nov. 26, 1966; children: Patrick, Catherine. Asst. prof. polit. sci. Youngstown (Ohio) State U., 1970-77, asso. prof., chmn. polit. sci., 1977-84, prof., 1984—; project dir. NSF, 1978-79, grant evaluator, 1979. Trustee Internat. Inst., Youngstown, 1972—, Children and Family Services Bd., Mahoning County, 1977—; vice chmn. Mahoning County Republican Central Com., 1973-74, chmn., 1980—; del. Rep. Nat. Com., 1984; chmn. Mahoning County Rep. Exec. Com., 1980—; mem. Mahoning County Bd. Elections, 1980—. Mem. Am. Polit. Sci. Assn., Internat. Studies Assn., Latin Am. Studies Assn., Midwest Polit. Sci. Assn., AAU. Home: 2893 Algonquin Dr Poland OH 44514 Office: Dept Polit Sci Youngstown State U Youngstown OH 44555

BINOTTI, DAVID ALLEN, orthodontist; b. Chgo., Apr. 8, 1943; s. Evo Joseph and Anne (DiVita) B.; D.D.S., Loyola U. (Chgo.), 1967, M.S. in Oral Biology, 1969, Certificate Specialty Orthodontics, 1969; m. Barbara J. Rizzo, June 24, 1967; children—Eric David, Nicholas Allen. Practice orthodontics, Oak Lawn, Ill., 1969—, Lombard, Ill., 1971—; asso. with Dr. Ernest Panos, Chgo., 1969-74; clin. instr. dept. orthodontics Sch. Dentistry, Loyola U., 1969-72. Mem. ADA, Chgo. Dental Soc., Am. Assn. Orthodontists, Ill. Soc. Orthodontists. Roman Catholic. Office: 5208 W 95th St Oak Lawn IL 60453 also: 805 S Main St Suite 2 Lombard IL 60148

BINSFELD, CONNIE BERUBE, state senator; b. Munising, Mich., Apr. 18, 1924; d. Omer J. and Elsie (Constance) Berube; B.S., Siena Heights Coll., 1945, D.H.L. (hon.), 1977; postgrad. Wayne State U., 1966-67; m. John E. Binsfeld, July 19, 1947; children—John T., Gregory, Susan, Paul, Michael. County commr., Leelanau County, Mich., 1970-74; mem. Mich. Ho. of Reps., 1974-82; mem. Mich. Senate, 1982—, asst. majority leader. Del., Republican Nat. Conv., 1980. Named Mich. Mother of Year, Mich. Mothers Com., 1977; Northwestern Mich. Coll. fellow. Mem. Nat. Council State Legislators, LWV, Siena Heights Coll. Alumnae Assn. Republican. Roman Catholic. Home: 8944 County Rd 675 Maple City MI 49664 Office: Mich Senate State Capitol Lansing MI 48909 *

BIRCH, ROBERT WILLIAM, psychologist; b. Pitts., Nov. 24, 1935; s. Harold Boyd and Helen Margaret (Fulton) B.; m. Judith Ann Hawkins, Sept. 1, 1960 (div. May 1982); children: Joel Tyler, Bradley Jay, Rebecca Boyd; m. Susan Ambs, June 1, 1985. BA, Muskingum Coll., 1960; MA, Ohio U., 1962; PhD, U. Wis., 1967. Diplomate Am. Bd. Family Psychology; lic. psychologist, Ohio; cert. Am. Coll. Sexologists. Sch. psychologist Dane County Pub. Schs., Madison, Wis., 1964-66; clin. psychologist Tri-County Comprehensive Mental Health Ctr., Baraboo, Wis., 1966-68; chief psychologist Muskingum Comprehensive Mental Health Ctr., Zanesville, Ohio, 1968-70, clin. services dir., 1970-73; pvt. practice psychology Columbus, Ohio, 1973—; cons. Cerebral Palsy Clinic, U. Wis. Med. Ctr., Madison, 1964-66, Cooperative Ednl. Service Agy., Portage, Wis., 1967-68, Ohio Bur. Vocat. Rehab., St. Clairsville, 1972-76, Muskingum Area Forensic Psychiatry Ctr., 1974-76, Riverside Meth. Hosp. Dept. Ob-Gyn, Columbus, Ohio, 1977—, others; adj. faculty dept. psychology Ohio U., Athens, 1968-70; bd. dirs. Profl. Edn. Cons., Columbus. Contbr. articles to profl. and popular jours. Mem. mental health tech. adv. com. Muskingum Area Tech. Coll., 1970-78; mem. adv. com. Parents Without Partners, Cambridge, Ohio, 1974-76; bd. examiners Am. Bd. Family Psychology, Waco, Tex., 1982-85; mem. adv. com. Ohio State U. Dept. Family Relations, Columbus, 1984—; mem. Central Ohio AIDS Taskforce, Columbus, 1985—; bd. dirs. Muskingum Alcoholism Council, 1973-74, Muskingum Mental Health Assn., 1974-75. Served to sgt. U.S. Army, 1955-58. Fellow Am. Assn. Marriage and Family Therapy (bd. dirs. 1980-82, cert. of award 1981, cert. of appreciation 1982); mem. Am. Psychol. Assn., Ohio Psychol. Assn. (cert. of recognition 1972), Cen. Ohio Psychol. Assn., Ohio Assn. for Marriage and Family Therapy (pres. 1977-79, recognition plaque 1979, award of Honor 1985), Am. Assn. Sex Educators, Counselors and Therapists (cert., sec. 1982-84, bd. dirs. 1984—, cert. of appreciation 1984), Ohio Assn. Sex Educators, Counselors and Therapists (pres. 1979-81, Appreciation plaque 1981), Soc. for Sci. Study of Sex (treas. midcontinent region 1984-85), Sex Info. and Edn. Council of U.S. Democrat. Home: 183 Richards Rd Columbus OH 43214 Office: 3230 Northwest Blvd Columbus OH 43221

BIRCKHEAD, OLIVER W., bank executive; b. 1922. Student, Nichols Coll. With Cen. Bancorp, Inc., Cin., 1968—, pres., chief exec. officer, 1969—. Served with USAAF, 1942-46. Office: Cen Bancorporation Inc 5th & Main Central Trust Center Cincinnati OH 45202 *

BIRD, DANIEL FRANCIS, fertilizer and grain manufacturing executive; b. Oakland, Calif., July 8, 1943; s. George Herbert and Frances Agnes (Lishman) B.; m. Neila Rutkoskey, Jan. 1, 1982; children: Patrick, Mara, Ryan. BA, Hope Coll., 1972; MSW, MA, U. Mich., 1973, postgrad., 1977—. Cert. social worker, Mich.; lic. social worker, Fla. Dir. substance abuse South County Mental Health Ctr., Delray Beach, Fla., 1975-77; pvt. practice psychology Boca Raton, Fla., 1977-78; prof. social work La. State U., New Orleans, 1978-79; pvt. practice cons. psychotherapist Rockford, Mich. and Boca Raton, 1979—; pres., chief exec. officer Bird Fertilizer & Grain Services, Greenville, Ionia and Edmore, Mich., 1979—; mem. tng.-ednl. com. Mich. Grain and Agrl. Dealers, Lansing, 1984-85. Served with U.S. Army, 1961-67. Mem. Nat. Assn. Social Workers (diplomate), Porsche Club Am., Mercedes Benz Club U.S.A., Phi Delta Kappa, Psi Chi. Avocations: antiques, classic automobiles, boating, travelling, running. Home: 6359 Buena Vista Ct Rockford MI 49341 Office: Bird Fertilizer & Grain Services Inc 1100 N Irving St Greenville MI 48838

BIRD, HARRIE WALDO, JR., psychiatrist, educator; b. Detroit, Sept. 21, 1917; s. Harrie Waldo and Ann Josephine (Tossy) B.; m. Della Mae Clemmer, Jan. 4, 1943; children: Harrie Waldo, Kathleen Bird Steinhour, Deborah Bird Hall, Mark Henry, Matthew Alexius, Liza George-Aidan. A.B., Yale U., 1939; postgrad., U. Mich. Med. Sch., 1939-41; M.D., Harvard U., 1943. Intern Phila. Gen. Hosp., 1943-44; resident Menninger Sch. Psychiatry, Topeka, 1946-48; chief infirmary sect. Winter VA Hosp., Topeka, 1946; psychiatrist Adult Psychiat. Clinic, Detroit, 1949; acting dir. Adult Psychiat. Clinic, 1950; psychiat. cons. Mich. Epilepsy Center, Detroit, 1950-55; clin. instr. psychiatry Wayne State U., Detroit, 1952-55; asso. prof. psychiatry U. Chgo., 1955-56, U. Mich., Ann Arbor, 1956-63; asst. dean Med Sch., 1959-61; prof. psychiatry, asso. dean St. Louis U. Sch. Medicine, 1965-68, clin. prof., 1970—; dir. Family Psychicenter Inc., St. Louis, 1972—; lectr., cons. in field. Bd. dirs. Mich. Epilepsy Ctr., 1956-63, Wayne County Mental Health Soc., 1956-63, Mich. Epilepsy Assn., 1956-63, El Paso Mental Health Assn., 1969-70, Cranbrook Sch., 1961-63. Served with M.C. AUS,

1944-46. Recipient Mental Health Inst. award St. John's U., 1966. Fellow Am. Psychiat. Assn. (life); mem. Am. Family Therapy Assn. (charter), AMA, Group for Advancement Psychiatry, Am. Psychosomatic Soc., Am. Psychopath. Assn., Mo., Med. Soc., St. Louis Met. Med. Soc., Eastern Mo. Psychiat. Soc., Phi Beta Kappa. Home and Office: Family Psychicenter 62 Conway Ln Saint Louis MO 63124

BIRD, MERLE KENDALL, steel processing company executive; b. Mt. Pleasant, Iowa, July 1, 1927; s. Eugene Clifford and Freida Fern (Kerr) B.; m. Helen Marie Hohn, June 16, 1951; children—Stephen Kent, Cynthia June, David Kurt, Kim Marie, Kevin Lee, Rebbecca Susan. Student, U. Minn., 1945-46; B.S. in Edn., Western Ill. U., 1949; M.S. in Edn., No. Ill. U., 1956. Basketball ofcl. Ill. High Sch. Assn., Colusa and Crystal Lake, Ill., 1949-67, football ofcl., 1952-67; tchr., coach, athletic dir. Sch. Dist. 311, Colusa, 1949-52, Sch. Dist. 47, Crystal Lake, 1952-57; prodn. mgr. TC Industries, Inc., Crystal Lake, 1957-65, personnel mgr., 1965-74, dir. employee and pub. relations, 1974—, dir. employee relations TC Industries Can., TC Industries Europe Ltd., 1985—. Pres. McHenry County Tuberculosis Assn., 1962-65, St. Thomas Sch. Bd., 1967-68, DuPage-McHenry Lung Assn., 1968-71, Crystal Lake Park Dist., 1970, 73, Four Colonies Townhouse Assn., 1981-83; marshall 4th of July Parade, Crystal Lake; campaign exec. United Way; cubmaster Blackhawk Area council Boy Scouts Am., 1964-66; sec. McHenry Hosp. Bd., 1974-79; v.p. Am. Lung Assn. Ill., 1980, 83, 87. Served with USN, 1945-46. Mem. McHenry County Mfg. Assn. (pres. 1961), McHenry County Personnel Mgrs., Crystal Lake Jr. C. of C. (pres. 1960-61, awards 1959, 62), Am. Legion. Republican. Roman Catholic. Club: Lions. Editor, Terra Cotta Newsletter, 1966—. Home: 601 Cress Creek Crystal Lake IL 60014 Office: TC Industries Inc PO Box 477 Crystal Lake IL 60014

BIRD, MILFORD GILBERT, mechanical engineer; b. Algona, Iowa, Jan. 21, 1917; s. Henry Francis and Verona May (Gilbert) B.; student Chgo. Tech. Coll., 1938-41, U. Minn., 1949-53; m. Bernice Laura Stoeckel, Sept. 9, 1944; children—Ronald Gilbert, Bonnie Laura. With CCC, Grand Rapids, Minn., 1934; asst. to ednl. adviser Roberts-Hamilton Co., Mpls., 1935-38; draftsman Tri-City Roofing & Sheet Metal Works, Whiting, Ind, 1938-41; office mgr. Honeywell, Inc., Mpls., 1944-45; field research engr. Reese Assos., Mpls., 1945-49; v.p. Bird, Bird & Assos., Mpls., 1949-73; sr. mech. engr., pres. U.S. Postal Service Design & Constrn., St. Paul, 1973—. Served with U.S. Army, 1941-44. Mem. Minn. Assn. Cons. Engrs. (pres. 1966-67), Am. Cons. Engrs. Council (nat. dir. 1970-72), Nat., Minn. socs. profl. engrs., Profl. Engrs. In Govt., Assn. Energy Engrs. Republican. Lutheran. Home: 3200 46th Ave N Robbinsdale MN 55422 Office: 180 E Kellogg Blvd Saint Paul MN 55169

BIRD, PHILLIP CRAIG, mortgage company executive; b. Harlan, Iowa, Feb. 22, 1947; s. Victor T. and Dorothy Ann (Book) B.; m. Jane Ann Wilwerding, Aug. 1, 1970; children: Andrea, Sheri, Kelley. Student, U. Nebr., Omaha, 1969-72, Ottawa U., Kansas City, Mo., 1981-82. Lic. real estate broker, Mo. Asst. sec. Iowa Securities, Omaha, 1971-72; asst. v.p. Banco Mortgage Co., Omaha, 1974-75; v.p., br. mgr. Banco Mortgage Co., Denver, 1975-76; v.p. Banco Mortgage Co., Overland Park, Kans., 1976-79; v.p., br. mgr. Norwest Mortgage, Overland Park, 1979-84; pres. Newport Fin., Kansas City and Overland Park, 1984—. Served with U.S. Army, 1966-68. Mem. Nat. Assn. of Indsl. and Office Parks (v.p., sec. 1982-83, bd. dirs. 1984-85, newsletter editor 1982), Comml. Investment div. Johnson County Bd. Realtors (bd. dirs. 1985—). Republican. Roman Catholic. Club: Kansas City Breakfast. Avocations. golf, indoor soccer, bowling. Office: Newport Fin Services Inc 6405 Metcalf Suite 317 Overland Park KS 66202

BIRDSALL, ARTHUR ANTHONY, chemical executive; b. Oneonta, N.Y., Feb. 28, 1947; s. Charles Albert and Mary (Danzi) B.; m. Jane Elaine Fink, Jan. 28, 1967; children: Robert, Thomas, William. AAS in Chemistry, Erie County Tech. Inst., 1966; BS in Chemistry, Saginaw Valley Coll., 1969. Applications engr. Dow Corning Corp., Midland, Mich., 1966-70; product devel. chemist Dow Corning Corp., Elizabethtown, Ky., 1970-71, quality reliability engr., 1971-73; quality assurance supr. Dow Corning Corp., Chgo., 1973-75; product devel. specialist Dow Corning Corp., Midland, Mich., 1975-77; pilot plant mgr. Dow Corning Corp., Freeland, Mich., 1977-80; quality mgr., govt. relations coordinator Dow Corning Ophthalmics, Inc. div. Dow Corning Corp., Cosa Mesa, Calif., 1980; quality mgr., govt. relations coordinator Dow Corning Ophthalmics, Inc. div. Dow Corning Corp., Midland, 1980-82, mgr. quality/regulatory affairs, 1982-85; corp. mgr. product stewardship Dow Corning Corp., Midland, Mich., 1985—; cons. ophthalmic device regulations Dow Corning Corp., Midland, 1985; bd. dirs. Contact Lens Inst., also vice-chmn. bd., 1983-84, treas., 1984-85; chmn. pro-tem ophthalmic device com. Health Industry Mfrs. Assn., Washington, 1982-84, mem. Product Safety Mgmt. Forum. Co-inventor silicone resins for optical devices, 1977; contbr. articles to profl. jours.; patentee in field. Chmn. Cub Scout Pack com., Midland, 1979, treas. local Parent Tchr. Orgn., Midland, 1977, v.p., 1978, pres., 1979; tchr. Cath. Youth Council, Midland, 1985; bd. dirs. Blessed Sacrament Sch., 1986-87, mem. edn. commn., 1986—. Contbr. recipient I.R. 100 award silicone contact lens devel., 1982. Mem. Am. Soc. Quality Control, Regulatory Affairs Profl. Soc. Republican. Roman Catholic. Avocations: reading, writing prose and poetry, sailing, gardening. Home: 2311 Dilloway Dr Midland MI 48640

BIRDSALL, WESTON DONALD, utilities company official; b. Cleve., Dec. 28, 1920; s. Albert Barton and Mary Helen (McCreery) B.; m. Anne Marie Wodder, May 29, 1943; children—Susanne, Sonne, Scott, Shan, Steven. B.S. in Edn., Ohio State U., 1942; B.S.M.E., U. Nebr., 1949. Engr., Phillips Petroleum Co., 1949-53; gen. mgr., ptnr. Davidson Gas & Electric Co., 1953-66; v.p. Mgmt. Computer Network, 1966-72; gen. mgr. Osage Mcpl. Utilities (Iowa), 1972—; dir. Home Trust & Savs. Bank. Co-chmn. indsl. devel. bd. Community Chest. Served with AUS, 1944-47; ETO. Recipient Pres.'s award for energy efficiency, 1980; Energy Innovators award Am. Pub. Power Assn., 1981; Community citation Iowa VFW, 1981; award for excellence in energy conservation Gov. of Iowa, 1982; Seven Hats award Am. Pub. Power Assn., 1982, nat. award for energy innovation Dept. Energy, 1984. Mem. Iowa Assn. Mcpl. Utilities (pres. 1979-81), VFW, Am. Legion. Republican. Lutheran. Club: Rotary. Contbr. articles to Pub. Power Mag., various newspapers. Home: Route 2 Osage IA 50461 Office: 720 Chestnut St Box 207 Osage IA 50461

BIRELEY, MARLENE KAY, educator, psychologist, consultant; b. Edgerton, Ohio, Mar. 11, 1936; d. Forest William and Pauline May (Faber) Bergman; m. Michael Ewing Bireley, Nov. 21, 1959 (div. Feb. 1981); children: Laura Jo Weaver, Christina. BS in Elem. Edn., Bowling Green State U., 1957; MA in Spl. Edn., The Ohio State U., 1961, PhD in Psychology of Exceptional Children, 1966. Lic. psychologist, Ohio. Elem. and learning disabilities tchr. Worthington (Ohio) Pub. Schs., 1957-60; spl. edn. tchr. Columbus (Ohio) Pub. Schs., 1960-61; instr., then assist. prof. The Ohio State U., Columbus, 1962-63, 68-69; shc. psychologist Franklin County Schs., Columbus, 1963-68; assoc. prof., assoc. dean. Wright State U., Dayton, Ohio, 1969-76, 78-82, prof. coll. edn. and human services, 1976—; psychologist, pvt. cons., State of Ohio, 1974—. Co-producer: I Can Learn; contbr. articles to profl. jours. Mem. Ohio Assn. for Learning Disabilities (Talisman award 1976), Nat. Assn. Sch. Psychologists (charter, sec. 1971-72), Ohio Sch. Psychologists Assn. (Clyde Bartlett award 1983), Ohio Assn. Gifted Children (disting. service award 1986). Avocations: travel, theater. Office: Wright State U 373 Millett Hall Dayton OH 45435

BIRG, LAURA DARNELL, sociologist, educator; b. Milw., May 11, 1939; d. Shapley B. and Margaret (Austin) Darnell; m. Herwart G. Birg, Apr. 9, 1963; children: Carter Frederick, Erika Clarke. BS, Northwestern U., 1961; MS in Sociology with honors, Roosevelt U., Chgo., 1977; PhD, U. Ill., Chgo., 1981. Promotion mgr. Northwestern U. Press, Evanston, Ill., 1960-61; editor Fact-index Compton's Ency., Chgo., 1961-64, 72-73; freelance writer Marquis Who's Who, Inc., Chgo., 1964-86, writer, editor, 1968-86; asst. prof. St. Xavier Coll., Chgo., 1980-84, assoc. prof., 1984—, chmn. dept. sociology and anthropology, 1982-85, co-dir. Family Studies Inst., 1986-87, dir., 1987—; dir. Gerontology Inst., 1986—: cons. editor New Standard Ency., Chgo., 1966—; cons. Ency. Brit., Chgo., 1982-83; lectr. U. Ill., Chgo., Barat Coll., Roosevelt U., Northeastern Ill. U., others. Author: Support Systems of Female Felons, 1981; editor: Midwest Feminist Papers V, 1984-85; mem. editorial bd. Assn. Humanist Sociology, 1986—; also articles. Active PTA, Elmhurst, Ill., 1970-76, pres. local chpt., Elmhurst, 1975-76; active Girl Scouts U.S., Boy Scouts Am., LWV. Grantee NIMH, 1978-80, Small Projects grantee St. Xavier Coll., 1982—, Retirement Research Found. grantee, 1986—. Mem. Am. Sociol. Assn., Ill. Sociol. Assn. (treas. 1983-85, bd. dirs. 1986—), Midwest Sociol. Assn. (com. status of women 1983-86), Sociologists for Women in Soc. (chairperson 1983-84), Mid-Am. Congress on Aging, Soc. Applied Sociologist, others. Democrat. Home: 217 Geneva Ave Elmhurst IL 60126 Office: St Xavier Coll Dept Sociology and Anthropology 3700 W 103d St Chicago IL 60655

BIRK, TIMOTHY EDWARD, computer information scientist; b. Akron, Ohio, July 19, 1951; s. John Calvin Birk and Stella Louise (Cooper) Clapper; m. Nancy Brown, June 10, 1973; 1 child, Joshua Scott. BS in Applied Sci., Miami U., 1973. Programmer Goodyear Tire and Rubber, Akron, 1973-76, programmer/analyst, 1976-80; programmer/analyst Diebold, Inc., Canton, Ohio, 1980-83; database adminstr. Diebold, Inc., North Canton, Ohio, 1983-85, systems programmer, 1985—. Singer Men of Praise, Akron, 1975—; trustee Clarence E. Josephson Edn. Trust, 1978—, Fox Run Condominium Assn., 1980-84. Mem. Nat. Systems Programmers Assn. Republican. Club: Am. Contract Bridge League (Canton). Avocations: duplicate bridge, personal computers, bicycling. Home: 1364 Athena Dr Kent OH 44240 Office: Diebold Inc 5995 Mayfair Rd North Canton OH 44720

BIRKELAND, ARTHUR CLARENCE, farmer; b. Pierpont, S.D., Aug. 7, 1904; s. Christian Hans and Anna Marie (Askevoll) B.; m. Verna Dorothy Thompson, Feb. 19, 1949. BS in Edn., No. State Tchrs. Coll., Aberdeen, S.D., 1930. Grade sch. tchr., high sch. coach New Effington, S.D., 1925-26; prin. Tromald (Minn.) Pub. Sch., 1927-28; tchr., asst. coach Merrill (Wis.) High Sch., 1930-42; v.p., legis. rep. Day County Farm Bur., Webster, S.D.; farmer Bristol, S.D.; Gov. appointee State of S.D. Wheat Commn., 1982-85. Rep. chmn. Day County, S.D., 1958-70, nat. del. 1964. Mem. S.D. Wheat Producers. Lutheran. Lodge: Masons, Shriners. Home: Box 475 Bristol SD 57219

BIRKHOLZ, GABRIELLA SONJA, communication agency executive; b. Chgo., Apr. 11, 1938; d. Ladislav E. and Sonja (Kosner) Becvar. BA in Communications and Bus. Mgmt., Alverno Coll., 1983. Editor, owner Fox Lake (Wis.) Rep., 1962-65, McFarland (Wis.) Community Life and Monona Community Herald, 1966-69; bur. reporter Waukesha (Wis.) Daily Freeman, 1969-71; community relations staff Waukesha County Tech. Inst., Pewaukee, Wis., 1971-73; pub. relations specialist JI Case Co., Racine, Wis., 1973-75, corp. publs. editor, 1975-80; v.p., bd. dirs. publs. Image Mgmt., Valley View Ctr., Milw., 1980-82; pres. Communication Concepts, Unltd., Racine, 1983—; guest lectr. Alverno Coll., U. Wis.; adj. faculty U. Wis.-Parkside. Contbr. articles to profl. jours. Bd. dirs. Big Bros./Big Sisters Racine County; mem. Downtown Racine Devel. Corp., Downtown Racine Assn.; mem. community adv. bd. Sta. WGTD-FM. Recipient awards Wis. Press Assn., Nat. Fedn. Press Women; named Wis. Woman Entrepreneur of Yr., 1985. Mem. Internat. Assn. Bus. Communicators (accredited mem.; bd. dirs. 1982-85, various awards), Wis. Women Entrepreneurs, Nat. Assn. Female Execs., Alverno Alumnae Assn. (governing bd.), Ad Club of Racine (bd. dirs.), Sigma Delta Chi. Home: 901 Kingston Ave Racine WI 53402 Office: 312 Main St Racine WI 53403

BIRLA, SUSHIL KUMAR, automotive manufacturing executive; b. Sirsa, Haryana State, India, Oct. 1, 1943; came to U.S., 1969, naturalized, 1978; s. Mahabir Prasad and Lalita Devi (Mohunta) B.; B.S.M.E., Birla Inst. Tech. and Sci., Pilani, India, 1965; M.S.E.E., Wayne State U., 1971; m. Pramila Kela, Dec. 14, 1972; children—Jyoti, Asheesh, Preeti. Mng. partner Madhu Woodcraft Industries, Jaipur, India, 1965-66; supt. prodn. planning and control Hindustan Motors, Uttarpara, India, 1966-69; proposal, controls engr. Cross Co., Fraser, Mich., 1969-73; design engr. Excello Machine Tool Products, Detroit, 1973-76; staff devel. engr. Gen. Motors Advanced Engring. Staff, GM Tech. Center, Warren, Mich., 1976—; mem. Machine Tool Task Force for U.S. Air Force Materials Lab., Dept. Def., 1978-80. Vol. probation aide Macomb County, Mich., 1976-77; vol. probation counselor Sterling Heights, Mich., 1979-81; pres. Macomb County (Mich.) chpt. Mothers Against Drunk Drivers, 1983. Recipient Outstanding Contbn. award Dept. Def.; cert. mfg. engr. Mem. Soc. Mfg. Engrs., IEEE (sr.), ASME. Club: Toastmasters (pres. chpt. 676 1982). Home: 42380 Buckingham Dr Sterling Heights MI 48078 Office: Gen Motors Advanced Engring Staff GM Tech Center 30300 Mound Rd Mail Code A/MD-15 Warren MI 48090-9040

BIRMELE, RAYMOND ELSWORTH, small business owner; b. Watervliet, Mich., Oct. 16, 1948; s. Marvin E. and Mary Ann (Bodine) B.; m. DiAnn M. Birmele, June 7, 1970; children: Andrea, Candace. AAS, Ferris State Coll., 1968. Gen. foreman Auto Specialties Mfg., Hartford, Mich., 1979-80, prodn. supt., 1980-81; owner, pres. Pro Slot Mfg., Hartford, 1981-85, Fantom Racing Enterprises, Hartford, 1980—; desing engring. cons. Race Car Research Co., Hartford, 1968-75, N.Am. Oil Co., Schaumburg, 1973-74; cons. Racer Products, Inc., Livermore, Calif., 1984-87. Served with USN, 1968-70, Vietnam. Mem. Nat. Fedn. Small Bus. Methodist. Avocations: model car racing, watching nascar racing. Home: 101 Washington St Hartford MI 49057 Office: Fantom Racing Enterprises 209 N Haver St Hartford MI 49057

BIRMINGHAM, WILLIAM JOSEPH, lawyer; b. Lynbrook, N.Y., Aug. 7, 1923; s. Daniel Joseph and Mary Elizabeth (Tighe) B.; m. Helen Elizabeth Roche, July 23, 1955; children—Deirdre, Patrick, Maureen, Kathleen, Brian. M.E., Stevens Inst. Tech., 1944; M.B.A., Harvard U., 1948; J.D., DePaul U., 1953. Bar: Ill. 1953, U.S. Patent and Trademark Office, 1953, U.S. Dist. Ct. (no. dist.) Ill. 1960, U.S. Supreme Ct. 1961, U.S. Ct. Appeals (7th cir.) 1962, U.S. Ct. Appeals (3d cir.) 1968, U.S. Ct. Appeals (D.C. cir.) 1973, U.S. Ct. Mil. Appeals 1973, U.S. Ct. Appeals (fed. cir.) 1982, U.S. Ct. Claims 1986. Chem. engr. Standard Oil Co. (Ind.), Chgo., 1948-53, patent atty., 1953-59; assoc. Neuman, Williams, Anderson & Olson, Chgo., 1959-60, ptnr., 1961—. Served to capt. USNR, 1942-75. Mem. ABA, Ill. Bar Assn., Chgo. Bar Assn., Bar Assn. Seventh Fed. Cir., Fed. Cir. Bar Assn. Am. Intellectual Property Law Assn., Patent Law Assn. Chgo. (bd. mgrs. 1976-77), Internat. Patent and Trademark Assn., Licensing Execs. Soc. Club: Mid-Day (Chgo.). Registered profl. engr., Ill., Ind. Home: 233 Pine St Deerfield IL 60015 Office: Neuman Williams Anderson & Olson 77 W Washington St Chicago IL 60602

BIRNBERG, HOWARD GENE, publisher, management consultant, architect; b. N.Y.C., Aug. 26, 1950; Alexander and Harriet (Fox) B.; m. Diane Mix, Apr. 24, 1982. BArch, Ohio State U., 1972; MBA, Washington U., 1974. Mktg. dir. Saunders-Thalden Assn., St. Louis, 1973-74; corp. comptroller Metz, Train, Olson, Youngren, Chgo., 1974-76; pres. Birnberg & Assocs., Chgo., 1976—; prin. Birnberg/Robin Assocs., Chgo., 1979—; adj. asst. prof. U. Ill., Chgo., 1981-83. Author: Small Design Firm Marketing Manual, 1983, Financial Management for Small Design Firms, 1984, Project Management for Small Design Firms, 1986; (with others) Building Products Marketing Manual, 1979; columnist Bldg. Design & Constrn. mag., Chgo., 1982-83. City chmn. Washington U. Alumni Assn., Chgo., 1977, mem. alumni bd. govs., St. Louis, 1977; mem. Chgo. Real Estate Bd., 1978. Mem. AIA (chmn. various coms. Chgo. chpt., 1975—, former bd. dirs.), Am. Arbitration Assn. Club: Cliffdwellers (Chgo.). Home and Office: 1227 W Wrightwood St Chicago IL 60614

BIRNEY, MARGARET LINDA HAMILTON, nursing educator; b. Springfield, Pa., Nov. 13, 1954; s. Leo Francis and Margaret Frances (Smiley) Hamilton; m. Rudolph Nelson Birney, May 20, 1978. BS in Nursing magna cum laude, West Chester U., 1976; MS in Nursing, U. Del., 1978; postgrad., Wayne State U. RN, Pa., Del., Mich. Staff nurse Crozer Chester (Pa.) Med. Ctr., 1976-78; staff nurse St. Francis Hosp., Wilmington, Del., 1978-81, from staff educator to instr. nursing, summer 1981; from instr. to asst. prof. U. Del., Newark, 1978-84; lectr. Wayne State U., Detroit, 1984-86; asst. prof. Oakland U., Rochester, Minn., 1987—; cons. Del. Bd. Dover, 1983—, BlueCross/Blue Shield, Wilmington, 1982-83; past mem. numerous coms. U. Del., Wayne State U. Author: Pathophysiology, 1987; contbr. articles to profl. jours., chpts. to books. Active Adams West Civic Assn., 1984—. Mem. Am. Nurses Assn., Mich. Nurses Assn., Mich. Nursing Diagnosis Assn., Am. Assn. Critical Care Nurses, Sigma Theta Tau, Alpha Lambda Delta. Avocations: jogging, aerobics, reading, cross country skiing, sailing. Office: Oakland U 415 O'Dowd Hall Rochester MI 48063

BIRR, DANIEL HOWARD, interior architect; b. Coffeyville, Kans., Nov. 22, 1951; s. Daniel Harry and Olive Jean (Perkins) B.; m. Christina M. Carden. B. in Interior Architecture, Kans. State U., 1974. Registered architect. Designer, G Interiors, Rapid City, S.D., 1974-76; space planner/designer Alpha Techne, Rapid City, 1976-80; project designer Comml. Builders of Kans., Wichita, 1980-81; sr. project architect Pizza Hut Inc., Wichita, 1981—. Mem. AIA. Episcopalian. Home: 3607 N Clarence Wichita KS 67204 Office: Pizza Hut Inc 9111 E Douglas Wichita KS 67207

BIRRELL, NANCY KAY, business systems executive; b. Mpls., Feb. 25, 1957; d. Robert Harry and Esther Alta (Neumann) Peterson; m. Andrew Stuart Birrell, Dec. 27, 1981; 1 child, James Andrew. BA in Sociology and Urban Studies, St. Olaf Coll., 1979; postgrad., Antioch Sch. Law, 1980; MBA in Mgmt. Info. Systems, U. Minn., 1985. Info. ctr. cons. Land O' Lakes Inc., Arden Hills, Minn., 1983-84, bus. systems mgr., sr. applications cons., 1984-86; circulation systems mgr. Mpls. Star and Tribune, 1986—. Mem. AAUW, Assn. Systems Mgmt. Democrat. Avocation: jogging. Home: 2620 Inglewood Ave S Saint Louis Park MN 55416 Office: Mpls Star and Tribune 425 Portland Ave S Minneapolis MN 55488

BIRT, DIANE FEICKERT, nutrition educator, researcher; b. Petaluma, Calif., Oct. 12, 1949; d. Joseph Ernst and Dorothy Beatrice (Cunningham) Feickert; m. Kenneth Allen Birt, June 10, 1973; children: Arlene Lydia, Michelle Dorothy. BA in Chemistry and Home Econs., Whittier Coll., 1972; PhD in Nutrition, Purdue U., 1975. Asst. prof. nutrition Iowa State U., Ames, 1975-76; asst. prof. Eppley Inst. for Research in Cancer U. Nebr. Med. Ctr., Omaha, 1976-82, assoc. prof., 1982—; assoc. prof. dept. Pharm. Scis. U. Nebr., 1982—, assoc. prof. biochemistry, 1985—; mem. faculty senate U. Nebr., 1983-86, v.p., 1984-86; mem. acad. computing adv. com. U. Nebr. Med. Ctr., 1980—, chmn. 1982-85, mem. search com. 1981-82, chancellor's task force on computing, 1983-84, campus task force on nutrition, 1984, campus computing steering com., 1984-85, faculty hand book com., 1985, faculty senate com. on role, mission and goals, 1985; mem. animal care com. Eppley Inst., 1977—, chmn. 1983—, mem. legis. com., 1980-81; cons. NIH, Washington, 1984—. Contbr. numerous articles to profl. jours. and chpts. to books; mem. editorial bd. Drug Nutrient Interactions. Gen. Foods fellow, 1974-75; NIH grantee, 1979-82, 83-86, 84-87, 86-89. Mem. Am. Inst. Nutrition, Am. Assn. for Cancer Research, Am. Cancer Soc. (profl. edn. com. Douglas and Sarpy County chpts. 1982—), Am. Home Econs. Assn., Phi Kappa Phi, Sigma Xi. Democrat. Avocations: hiking, bicycling, skiing, backpacking, gardening. Home: 2539 Country Club Ave Omaha NE 68104 Office: U Nebr Med Ctr Eppley Inst Research in Cancer 42d & Dewey Ave Omaha NE 68105-1065

BISCHOF, MILTON J., JR., architect; b. St. Louis, Aug. 17, 1929; s. Milton and Catherine (Kersting) B.; m. Evelyn M. Bright, June 28, 1952; children—Deborah Ann, Lauri Ann, Mark Richard. B.Arch., Washington U., 1952; Energy Auditor, U. Mo., 1978. Registered architect, Mo. Architect, Bernard Bloom, St. Louis, 1954-57; architect, ptnr. Manske-Dieckmann & Ptnrs., St. Louis, 1957-70; architect, v.p. mktg. Hellmuth, Obata & Kassabaum, St. Louis, 1970-79; architect, dir. mktg. The GCE Internat. Inc., Cons. Engrs., St. Louis, 1979-83; exec. v.p. Russell & Axon, Engring-Architects-Planners, Inc., 1983—. dir. Home Fed. Savs. & Loan. Chmn., Met. St. Louis Sewer Dist., 1978—; mem. St. Louis County Council, 1968-76; pres. St. Louis County Grand Jury Assn.; co-chmn. City-County Bi-centennial Commn., 1976; mem. adv. bd. St. Louis Council YWCA; mem. Regional Commerce & Growth Assn. Served with U.S. Army, 1952-54. Recipient various awards C. of C., 1975, 77, Am. Revolution Bi-centennial Adminstrn., 1977, Conv. and Visitors Bur. Greater St. Louis, 1977. Mem. AIA, Mo. Council Architects, St. Louis AIA, Engrs. Club St. Louis, Soc. Mktg. Profl. Services, Soc. Am. Mil. Engrs. Republican. Roman Catholic. Clubs: Media, Mo. Athletic, St. Louis Advt., St. Louis Ambassadors. Contbr. articles to profl. jours. Home: 6 Elmcrest Acres Saint Louis MO 63138 Office: 319 N 4th St Saint Louis MO 63102

BISCIGLIA, ANTHONY FRANK, junior high school administrator; b. Kenosha, Wis., May 28, 1938; s. Joseph Thomas and Marie (Bruno) B.; m. Rita Frances Savaglio, Aug. 22, 1964; children—Anthony J., Susan M., Linda A. B.S. in History, U. Wis.-Madison, 1960; M.S. in Guidance, Marquette U., 1968, doctoral student in Sch. Adminstrn., 1980—. Elem. tchr. Milw. Pub. Schs., Wis., 1962-68, elem. sch. guidance counselor, 1968-69; elem. sch. principal Kenosha Unified Sch. Dist., Wis., 1969-75, jr. high sch. prin., 1975—; bd. mem. Wis. Dept. Pub. Insts. State Superintendents Adv. Com. on the Deaf, 1984—; sch. chmn. Effective Schs. Research Lance Jr. High Sch., Kenosha, 1984—; co-chmn. Modern Tech. Conf. for Educators, U. Wis., 1983. Bd. dirs. Kenosha United Way, 1972-79, pres., 1975-76, campaign chmn., 1974-75; campaign chmn. Archbishop's Funds Appeal, Kenosha, 1970-71; mem. commonwealth parent com. Carthage Coll., 1984, co-chmn. devel. campaign, 1987-88; v.p. pub. relations Kenosha Civic Vet.'s Parade com., 1984, v.p., 1985, 87; chmn. Kenosha Plus Task Force, 1985. Recipient Distng. Service award Girl Scouts of U.S., Kenosha, 1974. Mem. Kenosha Schs. Administrn Assn. (pres. 1976), Kenosha Industrial Task Force (bd. mem. 1984—), Kenosha Econ. Devel. Commn., Nat. Soc. Study Edn., Wis. Assn. Middle Level Educators, U. Wis. Alumni Club (pres. 1977), Rotary West Found. (bd. dirs. 1981-86), Marquette U. Alumni Assn. (rep. for Kenosha, 1982), Phi Delta Kappa, Delta Sigma Phi. Roman Catholic. Lodge: Rotary (pres. 1982, Paul Harris award 1983, bd. mem. 1973—, rep. SE Wis. in New South Wales, Australia 1972). Home: 4470 Harrison Rd Kenosha WI 53142 Office: Bullen Jr High Sch 2804 39th Ave Kenosha WI 53142

BISEK, STEVE FRANCIS, insurance company executive; b. New Prague, Minn., Nov. 8, 1955; s. John F. and Dorothy C. (Zika) B.; m. Lynn R. Brandenburg, June 25, 1983. BS in Teaching, Mankato (Minn.) State U., 1978. Sci. tchr. East Chain (Minn.) High Sch., 1978-79; exec. sec. Cath. Workmen, New Prague, Minn., 1980—; also bd. dirs. Cath. Workman, New Prague, Minn.; trustee Cath. Workman Br. 1, New Prague, 1985—. Mem. New Prague Jaycees (pres. 1981), Nat. Fraternal Congress Am., Minn. Fraternal Congress (exec. officer 1984—, exec. com., legis. com.). Roman Catholic. Avocations: hunting, fishing, softball. Office: Cath Workman 111 W Main New Prague MN 56071

BISEL, HARRY FERREE, oncologist; b. Manor, Pa., June 17, 1918; s. George Culbertson and Mary Stotler (Ferree) B.; m. Sara Louise Clark, Oct. 30, 1954; children: Jane, Clark, Harold. B.S., U. Pitts., 1939, M.D., 1942. Intern U. Pitts. Med. Center, 1942-43; resident U. Pa., 1948-49, Harvard U. Boston City Hosp., 1949-50; resident physician Meml. Sloan Kettering Cancer Center, 1951-53; cancer coordinator medicine U. Pitts., 1953-63; chmn. div. med. oncology Mayo Clinic, Rochester, Minn., 1963-72; sr. cons. div. med. oncology Mayo Clinic, 1972—; prof. oncology Mayo Med. Sch., 1967—; cons. Nat. Cancer Inst. Served to capt. M.C. USNR, 1943-47. Recipient Philip S. Hench Disting. Alumnus award U. Pitts. Sch. Medicine, 1972. Mem. Am. Soc. Clin. Oncology (past pres.), Soc. Surg. Oncology, Am. Assn. Cancer Edn., Am. Assn. Cancer Research. Presbyterian. Club: Rotary. Home: 1223 Skyline Dr Rochester MN 55902 Office: Mayo Clinic Rochester MN 55905

BISH, MILAN DAVID, consultant; b. Harvard, Nebr., July 1, 1929; s. Charles and Mabel E. (Williams) B.; m. Allene Rae Miller, Mar. 17, 1951; children: Cindy, Linda, Charles. BA, Hastings Coll., 1951. Pres. Bish Machinery Co., 1951-72, Mid-Continent Enterprises, 1974-81; ptnr. Grand Island, Nebr., 1979—; hwy. commr. State of Nebr., Grand Island, 1979-81; U.S. ambassador to Antigua and Barabados, Bridgetown, 1981-84; also ambassador to Commonwealth of Dominica, St. Lucia, St. Vincent and the Grenadines; spl. rep. to St. Christopher and Nevis; pres. Bish, Inc., 1984—; vice chmn. Overland Nat. Bank, Grand Island, Nebr., 1986—. Mem. Statue of Liberty Ellis Island Commn., 1986—; chmn. Nebr. Rep. Party, 1971-72; del., chmn. Rep. Nat. Conv., Kansas City, 1976; regional polit. dir. Reagan-Bush Campaign, 1980, mem. Presdl. Transition Team, 1980-81. Recipient Outstanding Alumni award Hastings Coll., 1986, CIA medallion award, 1984, award for excellence Grand Island Area C. of C., 1984, Superior Honor Group award State Dept, 1983. Mem. Council of Am. Ambassadors,

Delta Phi Sigma. Presbyterian. Lodges: Rotary (dist. gov. 1970); Masons; Shriners; Elks; Eagles. Office: PO Box 2156 Grand Island NE 68802

BISHARA, SAMIR EDWARD, orthodontist; b. Cairo, Oct. 31, 1935; s. Edward Constantin and Georgette Ibrahim (Kelela) B.; children: Dina Marie, Dorine Gabrielle, Cherine Noelle. B. Dental Surgery, Alexandria U., Egypt, 1957; diploma in orthodontics, 1967; M.S., U. Iowa, 1970, cert. in orthodontics, 1970, D.D.S., 1972. Diplomate Am. Bd. Orthodontics. Practice gen. dentistry Alexandria, 1957-66; specializing in orthodontics Iowa City, Iowa, 1970—; fellow in clin. pedontics Guggenheim Dental Clinic, N.Y.C., 1959-60; resident in oral surgery Moassat Hosp., Alexandria, 1960-61; mem. staff Moassat Hosp., 1961-68; asst. prof. dentistry U. Iowa, 1970-73, asso. prof., 1973-76, prof., 1976—; vis. prof. Alexandria U., 1974-75. Contbr. articles profl. jours., chpts. in books. Fellow Am. Coll. Dentists, Internat. Coll. Dentists; mem. ADA, AAAS, Iowa Dental Assn., Midwestern Soc. Orthodontists, Am. Assn. Orthodontics, Internat. Dental Fedn., Internat. Assn. Dental Research, Am. Cleft Palate Assn., Assn. Egyptian Am. Scholars, Omicron Kappa Upsilon, Sigma Xi. Home: 1014 Penkridge Dr Iowa City IA 52240 Office: Orthodontic Dept College of Dentistry University of Iowa Iowa City IA 52242

BISHOP, ALLEN JOHN, savs. and loan assn. exec.; b. Berwyn, Ill., Feb. 17, 1948; s. John Edward and Mildred Alice (Chovancek) B.; B.S., Eastern Ill. U., 1971, M.B.A., 1972. With Clyde Fed. Savs. and Loan Assn., North Riverside, Ill., 1973—, dir. mktg., 1975-76, asst. v.p., dir. mktg., 1976-80, v.p., dir. mktg., 1980—; instr. Inst. Fin. Edn., Morton Coll., 1973-74. Mem. Savs. Assn. Council (dir.), Savs. Instns. Mktg. Soc. Am. (dir. chpt. 1, v.p. 1981, pres. 1982 Mktg. award 1976), Eastern Ill. U. Alumni Assn. Chgo. Fin. Advertisers, Delta Chi, Delta Mu Delta. Roman Catholic. Home: 2428 Danbury Dr Woodridge IL 60517 Office: Clyde Savs & Loan Assn 7222 W Cermak Rd North Riverside IL 60546

BISHOP, ELIZABETH SHREVE, psychologist; b. Ann Arbor, Mich., Nov. 18, 1951; d. William Warner Jr. and Mary Fairfax (Shreve) B. AB, U. Mich., 1972; MA, Ohio State U., 1973, PhD, 1976. Lic. psychologist, Mich., Minn. Psychologist Franklin County Program for the Mentally Retarded, Columbus, Ohio, 1974, WC Mental Health, Willmar, Minn., 1977-83; chief psychologist Battle Creek (Mich.) Child Guidance Ctr., 1981; dir. psychometrics Meridian Profl. Psychology Cons., East Lansing, Mich., 1983—. Troop leader Girl Scouts U.S., Minn., Mich. and Ohio, 1971—; v.p. Willmar LWV, 1980-81. Assoc. fellow Univ. London Inst. Edn., 1976. Fellow Am. Orthopsychiat. Assn.; mem. Am. Psychol. Assn., Mich. Psychol. Assn., Council for Exceptional Children (local pres. 1977-78), Internat. Council Psychologists, Internat. Sch. Psychology Assn. Avocations: reading, traveling, birdwatching, photography, music. Home: 5652 DeVille Ct East Lansing MI 48823 Office: Meridian Profl Psychology Cons 5031 Park Lake Rd East Lansing MI 48823

BISHOP, GEORGE FRANKLIN, political social psychologist, educator; b. New Haven, July 26, 1942; s. George Elwood and Mary Bridget (Trant) B.; m. Lucille C. Minervini, Aug. 14, 1971; 1 child, Kristina. B.S. in Psychology, Mich. State U., 1966, M.A., 1969, Ph.D., 1973. Instr. Multidisciplinary Social Sci. program Mich. State U., East Lansing, 1972-73; asst. prof. dept. sociology and anthropology U. Notre Dame, Ind., 1973-75; research assoc. behavioral sci. lab U. Cin., 1975-77, sr. research assoc., 1977—, co-dir. Greater Cin. Survey, 1978-81, dir. Greater Cin. Survey, 1981—, assoc. prof. polit. sci., 1982-87, prof., 1987—; assoc. dir. Ohio Poll, 1981—; guest prof. Zentrum für Umfragen, Methoden und Analysen, Mannheim, Fed. Republic Germany, Aug.-Oct., 1985. Sr. editor The Presdl. Debates: Media, Electoral and Policy Perspectives, 1978; sr. author various articles in profl. jours.; editorial bd. mem. Pub. Opinion Quar., 1987—. Served with U.S. Army N.G., 1960-63. NSF grantee, 1977-84. Mem. Midwest Assn. Pub. Opinion Research (pres. 1977-78), Am. Assn. Pub. Opinion Research, Am. Polit. Sci. Assn., Soc. Advancement of Social Psychology, World Assn. Pub. Opinion Research (treas. 1983-85). Home: 459 Karenlaw Ln Cincinnati OH 45231 Office: ML132 Univ Cin Cincinnati OH 45221

BISHOP, JACK LAWSON, JR., management consultant; b. Rockville Centre, N.Y., Dec. 3, 1939; s. Jack Lawson and Elizabeth Janet (Blee) B.; B.S. in Chem. Engring., U. Colo., 1961; Ph.D., U. Ill., 1972; m. Donna Norine Leavens, June 24, 1962; children—Elizabeth Anona, Jack Lawson, Kathleen Anne, Caroline Donna Van Alstine. Product devel. engr., mgmt. scis. specialist Dow Corning Corp., Midland, Mich., 1961-72; instr. Central Mich. U., Mt. Pleasant, 1969-70; mgr. mgmt. scis. Ky. Fried Chicken, Louisville, 1972-73; mgr. econ. and gen. research May Dept. Stores Inc., St. Louis, 1973-76; mgr. strategic and econ. planning Brunswick Corp., Skokie, Ill., 1976-83; prin. Bishop Assocs., Evanston, Ill., 1983—; dir. tech. commercialization ctr. Northwestern U., Evanston, 1985—, dir. tech. innovation ctr., 1986—; bd. dirs. Evanston Bus. Investment Corp., 1986—; adv. Purchasing Mgmt. Assn. Chgo.; producer monthly TV programs. Mem. exec. com., community relations com. Midwest regional office Am. Friends Service Com., 1978-83; exec. bd. dirs., treas. Midwest Friends Housing Corp., 1980-82; mem. policy com. Friends Com. on Nat. Legislation, 1981-86. Mem. Ops. Research Soc. Am., Chgo. Council Fgn. Relations, Inst. Mgmt. Sci., Am. Econ. Assn., Am. Statis. Assn., Nat. Assn. Bus. Economists, Am. Inst. Decision Scis. Author: Insect, Disease and Weed Control, 1972; Practical Emulsions, 1968. Home: 2000 Sherman Ave Suite 202 Evanston IL 60201 Office: Northwestern U Tech Innovation Ctr 906 University Pl Evanston IL 60201

BISHOP, JOYCE ANN, financial consultant; b. West Mansfield, Ohio, June 16, 1935; d. Frederic J. and Marjorie Vere (Stephens) Armentrout; A.B., Albion Coll., 1956; M.A., Western Mich. U., 1969, postgrad., 1972-87; children—Belinda Lee, Thomas James. Tchr. phys. edn., health and cheerleading Walled Lake (Mich.) Jr. High Sch., 1956-58; instr. slimnastics adult edn. Milw. Pub. Schs., 1959-65; demonstrator, co. rep. Polaroid Corp., Cambridge, Mass., 1960-81; research asst. fetal electrocardiography Marquette U., Milw., 1962-64; tchr. phys. edn., health and cheerleading Brown Deer (Wis.) High Sch., 1963-65; instr. slimnastics adult edn., instr. volleyball Lakeview High Sch., Battle Creek, Mich., 1966—; dir. student activities, counselor, asst. prof. Kellogg Community Coll., Battle Creek, 1971—, transfer counselor; asst. prof. Olivet (Mich.) Coll., 1969-71. Sec. adult bd. Teens, Inc., 1965-68; bd. dirs. Battle Creek Day Care Ctrs., sec., 1984, pres., 1984-86; team capt. United Way Awareness Week, 1984. United Arts Fund Dr., 1985, chmn., 1986. Cert. social worker. Recipient Master Teaching award Lakeview Schs., 1969, 87; mem. Battle Creek Leadership Acad. Mem. Mich. Assn. Collegiate Registrars and Admissions Officers (pres. 1979-80, historian 1984-87), Am. Assn. Collegiate Registrars and Admissions Officers (mem. com. 1984-87), Am. Personnel and Guidance Assn., Am. Coll. Personnel Assn., Mich. Personnel and Guidance Assn., Mich. Coll. Personnel Assn., Mich. Assn. Women Deans, Adminstrs. and Counselors, Mich. Assn. Coll. Admissions Counselors, AAUW, Alpha Chi Omega, Beta Beta Beta. Clubs: Battle Creek Road Runners (v.p. 1983-85), Battle Creek Altrusa. Home: 721 Eastfield Dr Battle Creek MI 49015 Office: Richard M Groff Assocs Inc 5320 Holiday Terr Kalamazoo MI 49009

BISHOP, MARGARET WEBBER, accountant; b. Plymouth, Mich., Mar. 20, 1958; s. Robert F. and Elizabeth (Glenn) Webber; m. Joseph R. Bishop, May 31, 1980; 1 child, Angela. BBA, U. Mich., 1980. CPA, Mich. Mgr. Beene Garter & Co., Grand Rapids, Mich., 1980—. Pres. Quota Club Grand Rapids, 1986—, v.p., treas., 1984-86; mem. South Kent Mental Health Bd., Grand Rapids, 1986—. Mem. Am. Inst. CPA's, Mich. Assn. CPA's (program dir.). Avocations: golf, water skiing, travel. Home: 3969 Honeyvale Ct SW Grandville MI 49418 Office: Beene Garter & Co 50 Monroe Ave Suite 600 Grand Rapids MI 49503

BISHOP, MARSHALL EDWARD, academic administrator; b. Amsterdam, N.Y., Aug. 3, 1942; s. Raymond Murle and Muriel Katherine (Johnson) B.; B.A., Oakland U., 1964, M.S., 1967; Ph.D., SUNY, 1975; m. Jacqueline Ann Winter, July 13, 1968; children—Eric Alan, Kathryn Ann. Exptl. spectroscopist Gen. Motors Corp., Pontiac, Mich., 1964-66, 67-69; instr. chemistry Oakland U., Rochester, Mich., 1968; research fellow SUNY, Albany, 1969-75; instr. chemistry, spl. projects cons. to pres. Southwestern Mich. Coll., Dowagiac, 1975—, coordinator chem. tech. program; dean coll. arts and scis., 1986-87, v.p. for instrn., 1987—; instr. continuing edn. Oakland U., 1968-69. Mem. adv. com. Southwestern Mich. Coll. Mus.; mem. sci. cons. com. Sci. for Citizens, Western Mich. U. Named Student of Distinction, Oakland U., 1961, 62, 64; NDEA Title IV grad. fellow, 1970-73; cert. profl. chemist Am. Inst. Chemists. Mem. Am. Chem. Soc., Chem. Soc. London, Mich. Coll. Chemistry Tchrs. Assn., Mich. Assn. Computer Users in Learning, Mich. Hist. Soc., Cass County Hist. Soc., Dowagiac Hist. Soc., Am. Canal Soc., Sigma Xi. Republican. Methodist. Club: Grange. Contbr. articles to profl. jours. Home: 54255 Twin Lakes Rd Dowagiac MI 49047 Office: Southwestern Mich Coll V P for Instrn Cherry Grove Rd Dowagiac MI 49047

BISHOP, ROBERT DEANE, nuclear engineer; b. Emporia, Kans., June 23, 1946; s. Clarence Dwight and Cora Frances (Foley) B.; m. Sheila Roberts, Dec. 18, 1976; B.S., Kans. State U., 1969; M.B.A., U. Chgo., 1977. Engr. in tng. State of Kans., 1969; nuclear engr. Commonwealth Edison Co., Dresden sta., 1971-75, tech. staff supr. LaSalle County sta., 1975-80, asst. supt. sta., 1980-85, services supt., 1985—. Served to 1st lt., inf. U.S. Army, 1970-71. Decorated Bronze Star medal; licensed nuclear reactor operator. Mem. Am. Nuclear Soc. Home: 907 Lynwood Ct Shorewood IL 60436 Office: LaSalle County Station Box 240 Marseilles IL 61341

BISHOP, ROBERT LEWIS, pianist-vocalist, songwriter, publisher; b. Peoria, Ill., Nov. 8, 1955; s. Thomas James and Mary Ellen Grant. Grad. Spalding Inst., Peoria, 1973. Founder, pres. LeVec Pub. Co., Peoria, 1976—; rec. artist Permian Records, 1985, AIR Records, 1986—; mem. cons. faculty Ill. State U., pianist/vocalist, 1975; rec. artist, 1977—; composer numerous songs, 1974—, including If I Can't Hold You in My Arms, 1975; Lady in My Corner, 1976; Stay, 1977; Middle of the Night, 1980; albums include Good Groove; appeared as opening act for Phyllis Diller, 1985, Milton Berle, 1985, Henny Youngman, 1985. Winner numerous music competitions as pianist and singer, Midwest, N.Y., Calif.; Coll. Performing Arts grantee Harvard U., 1973. Mem. Am. Fedn. Musicians, ASCAP. Roman Catholic.

BISHOP, STEVEN EUGENE, structural engineer; b. Bloomington, Ill., July 25, 1949; s. J. Reid and Gladys A. (Anderson) B.; m. Marie D. Simon, Nov. 4, 1979. BArch with honors, U. Ill., 1973, MS, 1974. Registered architect, Ill., structural engr., Ill. Design engr. Ralph Hahn & Assocs., Springfield, Ill., 1974-76; designer LZT Assocs., Inc., Peoria, Ill., 1976-77; design engr. Perkins & Will, Chgo., 1977-79; assoc. Phillips Swager Assocs., Peoria, 1979-86; sr. structural engr. Randolph & Assocs., Inc., Peoria, 1986—. Author: (with others) (data survey for archtl. history book) Peoria Two, 1977. Mem. AIA (treas. Peoria chpt. 1982, sec. 1983, chmn. 1984), ASCE (treas. 1984-85), Am. Concrete Inst., Structural Engrs. Assn. of Ill. Home: 325 W Ivy Ln Peoria IL 61614 Office: Randolph & Assocs Inc 8901 N Industrial Rd Peoria IL 61615

BISHOP, WARNER BADER, business executive; b. Lakewood, Ohio, Dec. 13, 1918; s. Warner Brown and Gladys (Bader) B.; m. Katherine Sue White, Dec. 15, 1944; children: Susan, Judith, Katharine, Jennifer; m. Barrie Osborn, Feb. 4, 1967 (div. Dec. 1980); children: Wilder, Brooks.; m. Susan Bragg Howard, June 3, 1982. A.B., Dartmouth, 1941; M.B.A., Amos Tuck Grad. Sch., 1942; grad. Advanced Mgmt. Program, Harvard U., 1955. With Archer-Daniels-Midland Co., Cleve., 1946-59; successively sales rep., export mgr., sales mgr., divisional gen. mgr., asst. v.p. Archer-Daniels-Midland Co., 1946-56, v.p., 1956-59; pres. Fed. Foundry Supply Co., 1957-59, Wyodak Clay & Chem. Co., 1957-59, Basic, Inc., until 1963, Union Fin. Corp., Cleve., 1963-74; pres. Union Savs. Assn., 1963-74, chmn., 1970—; chmn., pres. Transohio Financial Corp., Cleve., 1974-85; dir. Blue Cross-Blue Shield Ohio, Med. Cons. Imaging Co.; trustee Med. Cleve. Mut.; dir. Med. Life Ins. Co. Sec. Foundry Ednl. Found., 1956-60. Contbr. articles to trade jours. Gen. campaign mgr. Cleve. Area Heart Soc., bd. chmn., 1960-61; mem. corp. Fenn Coll.; Bd. dirs. Ohio Heart Soc.; chmn. Highland Redevel. Corp., 1963-68; pres. Council High Blood Pressure, 1964-69. Served to lt. USNR, 1942-45; comdg. officer escort vessels. Clubs: Indian House, Union (N.Y.C.); Meadow (Southampton, N.Y.); Chagrin Valley Hunt, Union, Kirtland Country, Tavern (Cleve.); Bath and Tennis, Everglades (Palm Beach, Fla.). Home: 300 S Ocean Blvd Penthouse B Palm Beach FL 33480 also: Two Bratenahl Pl Apt 14D Bratenahl OH 44108

BISHOP TIMOTHY (MICHAEL NEGREPONTIS), bishop; b. Athens, Greece, June 7, 1924; s. Anastasios and Maria Negrepontis. Sacred Theology, U. Thessalonika, Greece; M.Div., Holy Cross Greek Orthodox Theol. Sch., Boston; B.A. with honors, Hellenic Coll. Ordained deacon Greek Orthodox Ch., 1950, ordained priest, 1952. Pastor St. Nicholas Ch., Bethlehem, Pa., 1955-61, Parish of Sts. Constantine and Helen, Middletown, Ohio, 1961-62; pastor Holy Trinity Ch., London, Ont., Can., 1962-67, Harrisburg, Pa., St.; pastor Dionysios Ch., Kansas City, Kans., St. Barbara; dean Holy Trinity Archdiocesan Cathedral, N.Y.C., until 1969; spl. asst. to chancellor and personnel dir. archdiocesan staff Archdiocesan Hdqrs., N.Y.C., from 1969; pastor St. Anargyroi Ch., Marlboro, Mass., until 1973, Ch. Holy Ascension, Fairview, N.J.; elevated to Titular Bishop of Pamphilos, 1973, consecrated bishop, 1974; bishop Greek Orthodox Diocese in S.Am., 1974-79; aux. bishop to the Archbishop 7th Archdiocesan Dist. Detroit, now Greek Orthodox Diocese of Detroit, 1979; bishop of Greek Orthodox Diocese of Detroit, 1979—; apptd. pastor Greek Orthodox Communities of Republic of Panama. Decorated Grand Master of Order of Vasco Nuñez de Balboa, Republic of Panama, Grand Taxiarch, Order Orthodox Crusaders of Holy Sepulcher. Address: 19405 Renfrew Rd Detroit MI 48221

BISKIND, EDWARD IAN, real estate development executive; b. Cleve., July 13, 1952; s. Saul and Rosalind (Ackerman) B.; m. Janine Marie Reynolds, Sept. 25, 1983. BA, Case Western Res. U., 1979. V.p. Biskind Devel. Co., North Olmsted, Ohio, 1979—. Author: (with others) Fashion Image, Psychographics, and Shopping Center Patronage, 1981; contbr. articles to profl. jours. Trustee North Olmsted Community Improvement Corp., 1983—, WCPN Pub. Radio, Cleve., 1986—; mem. adv. bd. SPACES, Cleve., 1986—. Mem. Internat. Assn. Corp. Real Estate Execs., Internat. Council Shopping Ctrs. (designated cert. shopping ctr. mgr.), Nat. Assn. Indsl. and Office Parks, Northeastern Ohio Areawide Coordinating Agy. Avocations: music, visual arts, films, wine. Office: Biskind Devel Co 4970 Great Northern Mall North Olmsted OH 44070

BISSEL, KENNETH CHARLES, accountant, tax administrator, real estate broker; b. Fargo, N.D., July 16, 1939; s. Charles William and LaVerne Evangeline (Davis) B.; m. Shirley Ann Ibach, Aug.24, 1968; children: Ryan, Gregory. B of Univ. Studies with honors, N.D. State U., 1974; postgrad., Moorhead (Minn.) State U., 1975-76. CPA, N.D.; lic. real estate broker, N.D. Bookkeeper, credit mgr. Peavey Co., Fargo, 1966-68; office mgr. Cummins Diesel, Fargo, 1968-71; real estate broker Sun Realty, Fargo, 1968—; tax adminstr. Am. Crystal Sugar Co., Moorhead, 1974—. Mem. fin. com. Holy Spirit Cath. Ch., Fargo, 1984-86. Served with U.S. Army, 1962-64; N.D. Air N.G., 1971-75. Mem. Am. Inst.CPA's, Nat. Assn. Accts. (dir. community affairs Fargo chpt. 1980), N.D. State Soc. CPA's, Fargo-Moorhead Chpt. CPA's, Am. Legion, Phi Kappa Phi. Republican. Avocations: outdoors, physical conditioning, home projects, gardening, computers. Home: 313 N 21st Ave Fargo ND 58102 Office: Am Crystal Sugar Co 101 N 3d Moorhead MN 56560

BISSELL, BRENT JOHN, marketing professional; b. Dearborn, Mich., July 10, 1950; s. Ernest Ross and Virginia Jane (Pete) B.; m. Libby Schulak, Dec. 4, 1971; children: John, Sarah, Elizabeth. BA, U. Toledo, 1971. Pres. Bissell Advt., Inc., Toledo, 1975-78; v.p. Communications Concepts, Toledo, 1978-79; creative dir. Stark Bros. Nurseries & Orchards Co., Louisiana, Mo., 1979-80; divisional gen. mgr. Consumer Pub. Co., Canton, Ohio, 1980-82; mng. dir. D'Arcy, MacManus, Massius Direct Mktg., Bloomfield Hills, Mich., 1982-85; v.p., mng. dir. Bozell, Jacobs, Kenyon & Eckhardt Direct Mktg., Chgo., 1985-87; dir. mktg. communications Nat. Bus. Systems, Ft. Wayne, Ind., 1987—. Musician, author, speaker. Nat. pub. relations dir. Nat. Assn. Congl. Chs., 1979. Mem. SAR, Mayflower Descendants. Club: Toledo. Lodge: Masons. Home: 5820 Weybridge Pl Fort Wayne IN 46815 Office: Nat Bus Systems 1530 Progress Rd Fort Wayne IN 46808

BISSEN, GREGORY JOHN, utilities company media producer; b. Austin, Minn., Mar. 10, 1953; s. Benno and Mary (Bergstrom) B.; m. Joan Marie Stadtherr, Dec. 28, 1974; children: Patrick, Kathleen. BS, U. Minn., 1977. Dir. TV Osseo (Minn.) Area Schs., 1976-81; media producer No. States Power, Mpls., 1981—; video cons. Target Stores, Mpls., 1978-81, Medium Well Done, Mpls., 1983—. communications cons. Mpls. Mgmt. Asst. Program, 1982—. Recipient Silver Plaque Chgo. Internat. Film Festival, 1982, Best Show award Edison Elec. Inst., Washington, 1983, Gold Medal award Internat. Film and TV Festival N.Y., 1985. Mem. Internat. TV Assn., (Golden Reel award 1980), Assn. Visual Communicators (Silver award 1985, Bronze 1986). Roman Catholic. Avocation: music. Home: 304 Little John Dr Circle Pines MN 55014 Office: Northern States Power 414 Nicollet Mall Minneapolis MN 55401

BISSETT, BARBARA ANNE, steel distribution company executive; b. Cleve., Sept. 27, 1950; d. George Jr. and Helen (Kirkwood) B.; m. Kerry Mark Kitchen, Oct. 6, 1979; m. Mark Jeffrey, Lauren Brooke. BFA, U. Denver, 1974. Inside sales rep. Bissett Steel Co., Cleve., 1977-78, inside sales mgr., 1978-80, v.p., 1980—; mentor strategic planning course Greater Cleve. Growth Assn., 1987—. Mem. Am. Soc. Metals, Steel Service Ctr. Inst. (com. mem. Young Execs. Forum 1987—), Council Smaller Enterprises, Assn. Women in Metals Industries. Republican. Presbyterian. Club: Cleve. Yacht. Home: 1994 Coe's Post Run Westlake OH 44145 Office: The Bissett Steel Co 9005 Bank St Valley View OH 44125

BISSEY, LEE R., health care executive; b. Clay City, Feb. 9, 1945; s. Russell G. and Evelyn M. (Staley) B.; m. Mary Elizabeth Harris, Aug. 16, 1969; children: Laura Caroline, Jason Alexander. BA, U. Ill., 1968, MBA, 1983. Group v.p. Americana Healthcare Corp., Monticello, Ill., 1973-82; dir. ops. St. Joseph's Med. Ctr., Bloomington, Ill., 1982-84; v.p. ops. The Carle Found. Hosp., Urbana, Ill., 1984-86; v.p. healthcare services The Carle Found., Urbana, 1986—. vice chmn. bd. dirs. ARC, Champaign, Ill., 1984—. Served to capt. USAF, 1968-73, Vietnam. Mem. Chi Psi. Republican. Presbyterian. Home: 209 W Delaware Ave Urbana IL 61801 Office: The Carle Found 611 W Park St Urbana IL 61801

BISSEY, WILLIAM KARL, international economic research executive; b. Columbus, Ind., Aug. 18, 1940; s. Harry Carl and Mary M. (Fleming) B.; B.S. (Ford fellow), Ind. U., 1962, M.B.A., 1964. Purchasing agt. Arvin Industries, Inc., Columbus, 1964-68; instr. Ohio No. U., Ada, 1968-73; credit analyst Mchts. Nat. Bank, Indpls., 1974-78; v.p. internat. econ. research Bank One, Indpls., 1978—. Served with U.S. Army, 1963-64. Mem. Alpha Kappa Psi, Delta Sigma Phi, Beta Gamma Sigma, Omicron Delta Epsilon. Presbyterian. Home: 8305 Sobax Dr Indianapolis IN 46268 Office: 111 Monument Circle Indianapolis IN 46277

BISSING, AL MARCUS, former dentist; b. Hays, Kans., Mar. 1, 1902; s. Jacob and Kathrine (Depperschmit) B.; m. Beatrice Gertrude Habiger, Oct. 1, 1941; 1 child, Patricia. DDS, U. Mo., 1926. Gen. practice dentistry Dodge City, Kans., 1926-40, Wichita, Kans., 1946-85; mem. Govs. Task Force, Topeka, 1986. Author: Feeding, Breeding, Training Greyhounds, 1948. Served to maj. U.S. Army, 1940-46, ETO. Mem. ADA, DAV, VFW, Wichita Dental Soc., Nat. Greyhound Assn. (Hall of Fame 1984, Man of Yr. 1985). Democrat. Roman Catholic. Lodge: Lions. Home: 141 N. Yale Wichita KS 67208

BISSMAN, JOHN PETER, audio visual specialist; b. Mansfield, Ohio, Dec. 29, 1939; s. John Foltz and Elizabeth (Weinert) B.; m. Marlis Knoll, Aug. 5, 1966; children: Michael D., Annette E., J. Martin, Andrew. BFA, U. Cin., 1963. 1st class lic., FCC. Engr. Sta. WCPO-TV, Cin., 1962-63; engr. and editor Sta. WKRC-TV, Cin., 1968—. Served with U.S. Army, 1963-66. Mem. Soc. Broadcast Engrs. Republican. Presbyterian. Avocation: photography. Home: 457 Pintail Dr Loveland OH 45140 Office: Sta WKRC TV 1906 Highland Ave Cincinnati OH 45219

BISSONNETTE, KARWYN MARY, psychologist; b. St. Paul, May 6, 1931; d. William James and Alvina Cecilia (Young) St. Onge; m. Howard Louis Bissonnette, June 23, 1956; children: Daniel, Lee Anne, Suzanne. BS, U. Minn., 1953, MA, 1957. Lic. psychologist, Minn. Instr., counselor N.D. State U., Fargo, 1962-68; instr. Lakewood Community Coll., White Bear Lake, Minn., 1974-81; pvt. practice psychology Mpls. and Golden Valley, Minn., 1981—. Avocation: lapidary arts. Office: Prinsen Counseling Ctr 2960 Winnetka St Golden Valley MN 55427

BITELER, CORNELIUS ROYAL, electronic co. exec.; b. Flint, Mich., Oct. 20, 1931; s. Royal Cornelius and Maude Melvia B.; B.S. in Mech. Engring., Purdue U., 1956; grad. Gen. Electric Mfg. Tng. Program, 1959; m. Jean Elaine Moyer, Sept. 27, 1958; children—Mark Christian, Dawn Christina. Mfg. engr., Gen. Electric, 1956-62, Bohn Aluminum, 1962-66; gen. foreman All Steel Equipment, 1966-69; asst. plant mgr. North Electric, Kenton, Ohio, 1969-75; v.p. Gleason Assos., Chgo., 1975-77; ops. analyst GTE Automatic Electric, Northlake, Ill., 1977-78, mgr. mfg. ops. analysis, 1978-80, productivity mgr., 1980—. Active Yokefellows Internat. Home: 141 Joyce Chicago Heights IL 60411 Office: 400 N Wolf Northlake IL 60164

BITKER, MARJORIE MARKS (MRS. BRUNO VOLTAIRE BITKER), writer, editor; b. N.Y.C., Feb. 9, 1901; d. Cecil Alexander and Rachel (Fox) Marks; A.B. magna cum laude (Caroline Duror Meml. fellow), Barnard Coll., 1921; M.A., Columbia U., 1922; m. James C. Jacobson, 1922 (div. 1942); children—Emilie J. Jacobi, Margaret J. Strange, Elizabeth J. Reiss; m. 2d, John C. Mayer, Oct. 24, 1942 (dec. June 1945); m. 3d, Bruno Voltaire Bitker, Oct. 10, 1957 (dec. 1984). Free lance writer, 1922—; editor Farrar Straus, N.Y.C., 1946-47, G.P. Putnam's Sons, N.Y.C., 1947-53, David McKay Co., N.Y.C., 1953-55; now editorial cons., book reviewer, feature writer. Lectr., Hunter Coll., Coll. City N.Y., 1949-53; Women's Chair for Humanistic Studies, Marquette U., 1972-73. Mem. pres.'s council Alverno Coll., 1975-77; bd. visitors U. Wis., 1962-68; alumnae trustee Barnard Coll., 1964-68, Barnard-in-Milw.; co-founder, past pres., hon. bd. dirs. in perpetuity Bookfellows: Friends Wis. Libraries. Recipient Barnard Alumnae Recognition award, 1978. Mem. AAUW, Women's Nat. Book Assn., Bookfellows Milw. (pres. 1971-73, dir.), Phi Beta Kappa. Author: (novels) Gold of Evening, 1975, A Different Flame, 1976; contbr. articles, and book revs. to mags. and newspapers. Address: 2330 E Back Bay Milwaukee WI 53202

BITTERMANN, ROBERT JOHN, data processing executive; b. Joliet, Ill., Dec. 23, 1943; s. Russell J. and Kathryn L. (Neth) B.; m. Patricia Ann Bittermann, Oct. 12, 1968; children: Andrew J., Bradley J. BSBA, Western Ill. U., 1966; MBA in Mgmt. Info. Systems, Am. U., 1969. CPCU. Analyst data processor State Farm Ins. Co., Bloomington, Ill., 1969-70, sr. analyst data processor, 1970-72, mgr. data processing, 1972-76, asst. dir. data processing, 1976-83, dir. data processing, 1983—. Commr. Housing bd. City of Bloomington, 1985—. Served with U.S. Army, 1966-68. Mem. Data Processing Mgmt. Assn. Avocations: golf, travel. Office: State Farm Mutual Ins #1 State Farm Plaza A-4 Bloomington IL 61702

BITTING, PHYLLIS DIANE, real estate broker; b. Kosciusko County, Ind., Oct. 11, 1935; d. Earl Vance and Edna Ruth (Powers) Davis; student Ind. U., 1971, 75-77; m. James Duane Bitting, June 26, 1953; 1 son, Andrew Vance. Real estate broker Center Realty, Warsaw, Ind., 1973—; operator real estate appraisal service, 1980—; sec., treas. Kosciusko Bd. Realtors, Warsaw, 1975-76, v.p., 1977-78, pres., dir., 1978—; state sec. by law com. Ind. Assn. Realtors, Indpls., 1977—. Trustee, Walnut Creek United Methodist Ch., Warsaw, 1977—. Mem. Nat. Bd. Realtors, Ind. Realtors Assn. (state dir. 1979-82, state public relations and communications com. 1981—, mem. honor soc.), DAR (regent Anthony Nigo chpt. 1974-75). Home and Office: Rt 2 Box 88 Warsaw IN 46580

BJORK, KENNETH O., ret. educator, editor; b. Enderlin, N.D., July 19, 1909; s. Theodore S. and Martha (Arneson) B.; B.A., St. Olaf Coll., 1930; M.A., U. Wis., 1931, Ph.D., 1935; Ph.D. (hon.), U. Oslo, 1976; m. Thora Lie, Apr. 1, 1960; children—Kenneth T., Arnold L.; children by previous marriage—Herum P., Mark P.; stepchildren—Ellen, Jon T. Asst. prof. history U. Mont., Havre, 1935-37; asst. prof. St. Olaf Coll., Northfield, Minn., 1937-39, asso. prof., 1939-44, prof., 1944-74, prof. emeritus, 1974—, chmn. dept. history, 1960-65; vis. asso. prof. U. Nebr., Lincoln, summers 1938, 40, U. Mich., Ann Arbor, 1940-41, U. Wis., Madison, 1943-44; Rockefeller Found. rep., prof. U. East Africa, 1965-67; editor Norwegian-Am. Hist. Assn., Northfield, 1960-80, editor emeritus, 1980—, pres., 1973-75. Chmn. Gov.'s Com. on Refugee Relief, State of Minn., 1955-58. Decorated knight

1st class Order St. Olav (Norway). Social Sci. Research Council fellow, 1947-48, 51-52; Fulbright scholar, 1959-60. Democrat. Lutheran. Author: Saga in Steel and Concrete, 1947; West of the Great Divide, 1958; editor books; contbr. articles to profl. jours. Address: 500 W Woodley Apt 302 Northfield MN 55057

BLAAUW, RUSSELL WAYNE, legislative liaison; b. Chgo., July 20, 1944; s. John Joseph and Bernice (Rabusch) B.; m. M. Bernadette Lynch, June 20, 1981. B.A. So. Ill. U., 1968, M.S., 1974. Legis. budget analyst Ill. Ho. of Reps., Springfield, 1972-77; legis. fiscal analyst La. Legis. Fiscal Office, Baton Rouge, 1977-78; exec. dir. Commn. on Welfare Law Revision, Springfield, 1978-80; assoc. dir. Washington office, Ill. Legislature, 1980-81; legis liaison Dept. Mental Health Devel. Disabilities, Springfield, 1981-87, bur. chief, 1987—; cons. Ill. Council on Nutrition, Springfield, 1980, Legis. Adv. Commn. on Welfare, Springfield, 1975-77; speaker-panelist Nat. Legal Services Corp., Kansas City, Mo., 1977. Vol. Big Brother/Big Sister of Sangamon County, Springfield, 1979-78, bd. dirs. 1979-80; vol. Family Court East Baton Rouge Parish, 1978-79; co-dir. Elem. Ed. Tutoring Program, Springfield, 1976-77. Avocations: traveling; photography; skiing; canoeing; running. Home: 1778 Old Chatham Rd Springfield IL 62704 Office: Ill Dept of Mental Health & Developmental Disabilities 401 Spring St Springfield IL 62706

BLACHFORD, WILLIAM WARREN, accountant, corporate financial consultant; b. Detroit, July 11, 1943; s. Herbert Ewing and Margaret Mary (Warren) B.; m. Patricia Ann Kulesa, July 20, 1968; children: Ann Jeré, William Rand. BBA, Detroit Inst. Tech., 1965. CPA, Mich. Sr. Coopers & Lybrand, Detroit, 1968-74; pvt. practice acctg. Farmington Hills, Mich., 1974-81; mgr. acctg. Baditoi Segroves & Co., Southfield, Mich., 1981-85; controller Moti Enterprises Internat., Inc., Sterling Heights, Mich., 1985-86; chief fin. cons. A.R. Brasch Advt. Co., Southfield, 1986—. Served with U.S. Army, 1966-68. Mem. Mich. Assn. CPA's (mgmt. cons. services com. 1981-86), Am. Inst. CPA's. Republican. Roman Catholic. Lodges: Toastmasters, Elks. Avocations: bowling, golf, sailing, travel. Home: 4707 Fairmont Troy MI 48098 Office: A R Brasch Advt Inc 24567 Northwestern Hwy Southfield MI 48098

BLACK, ALBERT VINCENT, school system administrator; b. Dayton, Ohio, July 6, 1942; s. Albert Vincent and Enid Ruth (Martin) B.; m. Mary Jo Stuckman, Dec. 16, 1978; children: Katherine Elizabeth, Margaret Anne. BS in Edn., Ohio State U., 1965, MA, 1977; postgrad., Ashland (Ohio) Coll., 1982—. Cert. secondary tchr., prin., Ohio. Tchr. Mansfield (Ohio) City Schs., 1966-78, administr., 1978—; cons. Niagara Falls (N.Y.) Sch. Dist., 1986. Mem. Nat. Assn. Secondary Sch. Prins., Ohio Assn. Secondary Sch. Administrs., Richland Alt. Program, Inc. (pres. 1984—), Phi Delta Kappa (sec. 1980-84). Congregationalist. Club: University (Mansfield). Avocations: reading, photography. Home: Rt #10 Garver Rd Mansfield OH 44903 Office: Mansfield Sr High Sch 145 W Park Blvd Mansfield OH 44906

BLACK, CHARLES ALLEN, soil scientist, educator; b. Lone Tree, Iowa, Jan. 22, 1916; s. Guy Cameron and Katharine Lavina (Loehr) B.; m. Marjorie Anderson, June 11, 1939; children: Carol Anne, Richard Allen, Marilyn Jean. B.S. in Chemistry and Agronomy, Colo. State U., 1937; M.S. in Soil Fertility, Iowa State U., 1938, Ph.D., 1942. Mem. faculty Iowa State U., 1939—, prof. soils, 1949-79, disting. prof., 1967-79, adj. prof., 1979-85, emeritus prof., 1985—; vis. prof. Cornell U., 1955; sr. postdoctoral fellow NSF, 1964-65; research asso. Kearney Found., U. Calif., 1964, U. Calif., 1965. Author: Soil-Plant Relationships, 1957, 2d edit., 1968; Editor-in-chief: Methods of Soil Analysis, 1965; Am. editor: Soils Derived from Volcanic Ash in Japan, 1977. Served with USNR, 1945-46. Recipient award of Merit Gamma Sigma Delta, 1976; Dir.'s award Midwest Agrl. Chems. Assn., 1979; Disting. Service award Am. Agrl. Editors Assn., 1979; Henry A. Wallace award Iowa State U., 1980; Recipient Nat. Award for Agrl. Excellence Nat. Agri-Mktg. Assn., 1983; named honor alumnus Coll. Agrl. Scis., Colo. State U., 1983. Fellow AAAS, Am. Soc. Agronomy (hon. mem., exec. com. 1961-63, Soil Sci. award 1957, nat. pres. 1970-71, Edward W. Browning Achievement award 1976, Agronomic Service award 1986), Am. Inst. Chemists, Soil Sci. Soc. Am. (hon. mem., chmn. div. 2 1954, nat. pres. 1962, Bouyoucos Soil Sci. Disting. Career award 1981); mem. Council Agrl. Sci. and Tech. (chmn. bd. 1972, nat. pres. 1973, exec. v.p. 1974-85, exec. chmn. bd. 1985—, Charles A. Black award), Internat. Soc. Soil Sci. (sec. commn. 2 1960), Am. Soc. Agrl. Engrs. (hon.). Address: 137 Lynn Ave Ames IA 50010

BLACK, CHARLES WILLIAM, JR., labor union administrator; b. Georgetown, Ohio, Oct. 28, 1938; s. Charles William Sr. and Ethel Luella (Jones) B.; m. Joyce Marie Feck, Jan. 17, 1959 (div. Sept. 1972); children: Sandra, Charles III, Jeffrey, Jason, Jeremy; m. Carolyn Sue Hull, Feb. 22, 1974; 1 child, Melissa. Student, I.C.S., 1979, Ohio State U., 1981, U. Ky., 1980-81, U. Colo., 1982. Area rep. Communications Workers Am., Cin., 1978-84, v.p., 1984—; editor Local 4400 Communications Workers Am., 1981—. Mem. fin. com. Clermont County Mental Health Bd., Batavia, Ohio, 1984—; pres. bd. trustees 1st United Meth. Ch., Batavia, 1985-86; bd. dirs. eastern div. United Appeal, Batavia, 1985—. Served as cpl. U.S. Army, 1957-59. Named Ky. Col., State of Ky., 1987. Mem. Internat. Assn. Quality Circles (speaker 1987—), Ohio AFL-CIO (del. 1978—), Cin. AFL-CIO (cen. labor council 1978—), Telephone Pioneers Am. Democrat. Methodist. Lodge: Masons (master 1985-86). Avocations: travel, tennis, bowling. Home: 755 Shelley Dr Batavia OH 45103 Office: Communications Workers Am 2562 W North Bend Rd Cincinnati OH 45239

BLACK, CURTIS DOERSAM, pharmacy educator; b. Toledo, Mar. 23, 1951; s. Arthur Herman and Virginia Ruth (Girkins) B.; m. Marilyn Couch, Aug. 24, 1974; 1 child, Andrew Curtis. BS in Pharmacy, U. Toledo, 1974; MS in Clin. Pharmacy, Purdue U., 1976, PhD, 1978. Licensed pharmacist, Ohio, Ind. Staff pharmacist Flower Hosp., Toledo, 1974; resident in pharmacy Bronson Hosp., Kalamazoo, Mich., 1975-76; grad. asst. Purdue U., West Lafayette, Ind., 1976-78, asst. prof., 1978-84, assoc. prof. pharmacy, 1984—, assoc. dept. head, 1986—; cons. edn. Searle Labs., Skokie, Ill., 1983—. Contbr. numerous articles to pharm. and med. jours; mem. editorial bd. Drug Intelligence, Cin., 1982—; reviewer Am. Jour. Hosp. Pharmacists, 1986—. V.p., mem. Ind. Nutritional Council, Indpls., 1982—. Fellow Am. Found. Pharm. Edn., 1976-78. Mem. Am. Coll. Clin. Pharmacy, Am. Soc. Parenteral and Enteral Nutrition, Ind. Soc. Hosp. Pharmacists, Sigma Xi (pres., v.p. 1985—), Rho Chi (mem. exec. council 1985—). Mem. United Church of Christ. Avocations: bowling, photography. Home: 16 Oriole Dr Lafayette IN 47905 Office: Purdue U Dept Pharmacy Practice West Lafayette IN 47907

BLACK, DANIEL ALBERT OLEISKY, industrial engineer; b. Mpls., Jan. 17, 1954; s. Albert Samuel and Shirley Jean (Peterson) Oleisky B.; B.Math. with distinction, U. Minn., 1975, M.S. with honors, 1976; m. Vicki Ann Reed, Dec. 18, 1976. Loan collector First Nat. Bank Mpls., 1975-76; quality control engr. Graco Inc., Mpls., 1976-79; quality assurance mgr. Webster Electric Co. div. Sta-Rite Industries, Inc., Racine, Wis., 1979-80, mgr. planning and prodn. control, 1980-81; mfg. supt. Fairbanks Morse Engine div. Colt Industries, Beloit, Wis., 1981-82, prodn. and inventory control mgr., 1982-84; mgr. materials Rockwell Internat, Automotive, Troy, Mich., 1984-86; dir. ops. Autocall div. Fed. Signal Corp., Shelby, Ohio, 1986—. Advisor, Jr. Achievement, Mpls., 1977-79; mem. ARC Safety Services, Mpls., 1968-75; trustee Minn. Phi Gamma Delta Ednl. Found., 1975-80; bd. dirs. Phi Gamma Delta House Corp., 1975-80. Named Minn. Young Engr. of Yr., 1978; recipient U. Minn. Outstanding Student Leadership award, 1975; Phi Gamma Delta Weum and Devaney awards, 1975; cert. quality engr., cert. reliability engr., cert. prodn. and inventory mgmt. Mem. Am. Soc. Quality Control, Am. Inst. Indsl. Engrs., Am. Prodn. and Inventory Control Soc., Automotive Industry Action Group. Home: 35 Otterbein Lexington OH 44904 Office: 41 E Tucker Shelby OH 44875-0496

BLACK, DAVID RANDALL, psychology educator; b. Watsonville, Calif., Mar. 24, 1947; s. Charles Alexander and Helen Louise (Dahna) B.; m. Judy Kay Edson, Aug. 30, 1969; children: Brian Alexander, Diane Margaret. BA, Calif. State U., Fresno, 1969; MA, Stanford U., 1971, PhD, 1978. Staff psychologist Dinuba (Calif.) Community Counseling Ctr., 1972-73; sch. psychologist Fresno County Schs. Office, Fresno, Calif., 1973-74; teaching asst. Stanford U., 1977-78, research assoc., 1978-80; asst. prof. U. Nebr. Med. Ctr., Omaha, 1980-84; assoc. prof. Purdue U., West Lafayette, Ind., 1984—. Contbr. articles to profl. jours. Served to maj. USAR, 1969—. Grantee U. Nebr. Med. Ctr., Omaha, 1981, Purdue U., 1985. Mem. AAAS, Am. Psychol. Assn., Am. Pub. Health Assn., Assn. for Advancement of Behavior Therapy, Am. Assn. Colls. of Pharmacy. Home: 616 Dodge St West Lafayette IN 47906 Office: Purdue U 106b Lambert West Lafayette IN 47907

BLACK, DENISE LOUISE, educator; b. Ft. Sill, Okla., Apr. 16, 1950; d. Nelson Arthur and Virginia Mary (Smith) Taber; A.A., Community Coll. of Allegheny County, Boyce campus, 1970; B.S., Slippery Rock State Coll., 1972; M.A., Eastern Mich. U., 1978; m. Robert Paul Black, Aug. 12, 1972; children—Paula Ann, Jennifer Lea. Adult edn. tchr. ecology and physiology Huron Valley Schs., Milford, Mich., 1973-74; tchr. gen. biology and earth sci. Howell (Mich.) Public Schs., 1974-75; adult edn. tchr. life sci. Holly (Mich.) Area Schs., 1978-80, Hartland (Mich.) Consol. Schs., 1978-86; tchr. biology Walled Lake (Mich.) Consol. Schs., 1980—. Coach, Milford Youth Athletic Assn., 1973-85. Cert. guidance and counselor. Mem. Nat. Assn. Biology Tchrs., Mich. Assn. Biology Tchrs., Mich. Sci. Tchrs. Assn., Beta Beta Beta, Phi Kappa Phi, Phi Theta Kappa. Methodist. Home: 2576 Shady Ln Milford MI 48042

BLACK, JACINTH BAUBLITZ, clinical social worker; b. Corpus Christi, Tex., Feb. 17, 1944; m. Donald James Baublitz, Oct. 26, 1968 (div. June 1979); children: Jessica Ruth, Stefanie Elizabeth; m. Robert Drummond Black, Mar. 14, 1987. BA, Sam Houston U., 1965; MSW, Boston Coll., 1972; postgrad., Am. Assn. Sex Educators, Counselors and Therapists, Washington, 1976-77; advanced studies with Maxie Maultsby Jr., U. Ky., 1980. Diplomate Nat. Assn. Social Workers, cert. social worker. Tchr. English and Spanish Brazosport Schs., Freeport, Tex., 1965-67; caseworker Harris County Child Welfare Unit, Houston, 1967-69; vocat. counselor Mass. Employment Security, Lowell, 1969-70; family therapist Cath. Family Service, Saginaw, Mich., 1973-75; pvt. practice clin. social work Midland, Mich., 1975—; cons., lectr., speaker various profl. and lay orgns. Author: Relationshift, 1983, A Singles Guide to Tight Spots and Tricky Situations, 1986; newspaper advice columnist, 1985—. Bd. dirs. Big Sisters Am., Inc., Midland, 1978-80. Mem. Nat. Assn. Social Workers, Nat. Assn. Counseling and Devel., Mich. Personnel and Guidance Assn., Mich. Mental Health Counselors Assn. Episcopalian. Home: 4553 S Saginaw Rd Midland MI 48640 Office: PO Box 2227 Midland MI 48641-2227

BLACK, JAMES ROBERT, industrial engineer; b. Davenport, Iowa, Feb. 17, 1948; s. Robert James and Anne Louise (Johnson) B.; B.S. in Indsl. Engring. (Fisher Governor scholar 1968-69, Maytag scholar 1969-70), Iowa State U., 1970, M.S., 1971; M.B.A., U. Chgo., 1976; m. Mary Ann O'Malley, June 5, 1971; 1 son, Robert Joseph. Indsl. engr. Inland Steel Co., East Chicago, Ind., 1971-76, sr. indsl. engr., 1976-77; indsl. engring. supr. Clark Equipment Co., Jackson, Mich., 1977-78; indsl. engring. mgr. Harrison Plant, Graphic Systems div. Rockwell Internat., Rockford, Ill., 1978-83; corp. supr. adminstrv. work mgmt. Kohler Co. (Wis.), 1983—; co-leader, guest lectr. Am. Mgmt. Assn., 1979-80. Cons. Project Business div. Jr. Achievement, 1980; pack com. chmn. Cub Scouts, Boy Scouts Am., 1980-83; Webelos leader, 1982-83, asst. scoutmaster, 1983-84, scoutmaster, 1984—. Wood Badge trained, 1984, dist. vice chmn. 1984-86, dist. chmn., 1986—; asst. soccer coach, 1981-83, coach, 1984-85. Mem. Am. Inst. Indsl. Engrs. (sr. mem.; treas. 1979-80, pres. 1980-81, past pres. 1981-82, seminar speaker 1984, 86), Kohler Engring. and Tech. Orgn. (program chmn. 1986-87, chmn. 1987—). Contbr. articles to profl. jours. Home: 4500 Prairie View Rd Sheboygan WI 53081 Office: Kohler Co 44 Highland Dr Kohler WI 53081

BLACK, JOHN BUNYAN, civil engineer; b. Kansas City, Mo., Dec. 25, 1927; s. Ernest Bateman and Faye Irene (Bunyan) B.; B.S., U. Kans., 1949; m. Marilyn McConnell, Feb. 2, 1957; children—Katherine Faye, Helen Winslow, Robert Winslow II. Diplomate Am. Acad. Environ. Engrs. Asst. resident engr. Black & Veatch, cons. engrs., Los Alamos, 1949-50; engr. Alvord, Burdick & Howson, engrs., Chgo., 1953-65; project mgr. Greeley & Hansen, engrs., 1966-67, asso., 1968-74; owner John B. Black Cons. Engrs., 1975—. Served with AUS, 1951-52. Registered profl. engr., Calif., Colo., Iowa, Ill., Mich., Mo., Man., N.Y., Ind., Wis., Va. Fellow ASCE (com. water laws 1977—; dir. Ill. sect. 1977-78, sec. 1979-80, pres. 1982-83); mem. Am. Water Works Assn. (life), Central States Water Pollution Control Assn., Man. Assn. Profl. Engrs., Sigma Alpha Epsilon. Republican. Episcopalian. Club: Colo. Mountain (Boulder). Contbr. articles to profl. publs. Home: 595 Washington Ave Glencoe IL 60022 Office: 2 N Riverside Plaza Chicago IL 60606

BLACK, KENNETH WALLACE, lawyer; b. Peoria, Ill., Dec. 10, 1912; s. Wallace John and Margaret B. (Robinson) B.; m. Edith Adele Lowry, Aug. 10, 1938 (dec.); children: Barbara Black Brown, Kenneth Lowry, Bruce Wallace; m. Dorothy W. Powell, May 12, 1978. BS, Bradley U., 1934; JD, U. Chgo., 1937. Sole practice Washington, Ill., 1937-75; atty. City of Washington, 1941-53, 57-77; ptnr. Black & Black, Washington, 1975—. Vice chmn. Rep. Cen. Com. Tazewell County, Ill., 1956—; alt. del. Rep. Nat. Conv., 1968; trustee Bradley U., 1947—, chmn. bd. trustees, 1970-76. Mem. ABA, Ill. Bar Assn., Peoria County Bar Assn., Tazewell County Bar Assn. (past pres.), Am. Judicature Soc., SAR, Phi Alpha Delta, Sigma Chi. Lutheran. Clubs: Peoria Country, Creve Coeur. Lodges: Masons (consistery), Shriners, Jesters.

BLACK, LARRY D., library director. Exec. dir. Pub. Library of Columbus, Ohio. Office: Pub Library of Columbus & Franklin County 28 S Hamilton Rd Columbus OH 43213 *

BLACK, LEO ALLEN, dentist; b. Owensboro, Ky., Aug. 25, 1954; s. Leo Allen and Carolyn Bell (Barnes) B. BS, Georgetown U., 1976; DMD, U. Ky., 1981. Gen. practice dentistry Cin., 1982—; cons. Procter & Gamble, Cin., 1982. Sunday sch. tchr., Cin. Mem. East Side Dental Study Club. Republican. Club: Eastern Hills Exchange (bd. dirs. 1985-86, pub. relations chmn. 1986). Avocations: choir singing, piano. Home: 1732 E McMillan St Cincinnati OH 45206

BLACK, MARY ELLEN STEWART, jewelry store executive, buyer, bookkeeper; b. Ind., Sept. 21, 1903; d. George Thomas and Sarah Victoria (Demaree) Stewart; m. E.J. Black, July 7, 1928; children—George H., Vincent L. Student Central Bus. Coll., 1922. Stenographer, J.C. Hume Fuel Saver Corp., Indpls., 1921-22; receptionist funeral home, Osgood, Ind., 1928-47; stenographer, bookkeeper Prudential Ins. Co., Madison, Ind., 1922-28; mgr. Black's Jewelry Store, Lawrenceville, Ill., 1947-85. Recipient Retailer of Yr. award Lawrence County C. of C., 1983-84. Mem. Lawrence County Bus. and Profl. Women's Club (named Woman of Yr. 1983-84), D.A.R. Republican. Methodist. Lodge: Order Eastern Star. Avocation: reading.

BLACK, MAUREEN TARA SIMS, psychologist; b. Chester, Pa., Oct. 31, 1948; d. Maurice Russell Sims and Jean Theresa (Gibson) Park; m. Robert Nathaniel Black Jr., Sept. 8, 1972; children: Robert Nathaniel III, Zakiya Theresa, Austin Nathaniel. BS in Psychology, Morgan State U., 1969; MA in Psychology, MA in Edn., U. Mich., 1972, PhD in Edn. and Psychology, 1974. Lic. psychologist. Psychology intern North Cen. Willson's Children's Ctr., Columbus, Ohio, 1974-76; staff psychologist Cen. Ohio Psychiat. Hosp., Columbus, 1978-86; dir. psychology dept. Orient (Ohio) Correctional Inst., 1986—; adj. instr. Ohio State U., Columbus, 1975-76; instr. psychology Capital U., Cloumbus, 1978; cons. Gentle Care Adoption Services, Columbus, 1985—, bd. dirs. 1985-86. Mem. policy council Columbus Met. Area Community Action Orgn. Head Start Ctrs., Columbus, 1975, 76; mem. community adv. council Office of Minority Affairs Ohio State U., 1983-85. Mem. Nat. Assn. Black Psychologists, Ohio Psychol. Assn., Links Inc. (sec. 1984—), Jack and Jill of Am. Inc. (v.p. 1986—), Alpha Kappa Alpha, Phi Delta Kappa. Presbyterian. Home: 361 Indian Mound Rd Columbus OH 43213

BLACK, ROBERT GREENOUGH, language educator; b. Roswell, N.Mex., Dec. 17, 1944; s. Wilbur Eugene and Cynthia Frances (Greenough) B.; m. Anne Elisabeth LaRiviere, Mar. 17, 1968; 1 child, Matthew Robert. AB in Spanish, U. Calif., Berkeley, 1969, MA in Spanish, 1973, PhD in Romance Langs. and Lit., 1977. Vol. Peace Corps, Venezuela, 1964-66; teaching assoc. U. Calif., Berkeley, 1976-77; asst. prof. Beloit (Wis.) Coll., 1977-83, assoc. prof., 1983—; cons., lexicographer Seminary of Spanish Medieval Studies, Madison, Wis., 1985—. Contbr. articles to profl. jours. V.p. bd. dirs. YMCA, Beloit, 1985—. Fulbright fellow, 1975-76, NEH Summer Seminar fellow, 1979; named Tchr. Yr. Beloit Coll., 1983. Mem. Mediaeval Soc. Am., Modern Lang. Assn., Midwest Modern Lang. Assn., Am. Assn. Tchrs. Spanish and Portuguese. Democrat. Presbyterian. Clubs: El Cerrito Tennis (pres. 1972-74) (Calif.); Beloit Tennis (bd. dirs. 1985—). Avocations: tennis, travel. Home: 2184 W Collingswood Dr Beloit WI 53511 Office: Beloit College Beloit WI 53511

BLACK, ROBERT MICHAEL, lawyer; b. Trenton, N.J., July 28, 1958; s. Walter Lee and Merl Jeanne (Markham) B.; m. Joyce Marie Brewer, Aug. 7, 1982. AA, Three Rivers Community Coll., 1978; BA, U. Mo., 1980; JD, Memphis State U., 1983. Bar: Tenn. 1984, Mo. 1985, U.S. Dist. Ct. (ea. dist.) Mo. 1985. Spl. agent FBI, 1984; assoc. Law Firm of Jack Hoskins, Cape Girardeau, Mo., 1985; sole practice Poplar Bluff, Mo., 1985—. Office: 212 S Main Poplar Bluff MO 63901

BLACK, ROBERT STITT, public utility executive; b. Newport News, Va., Oct. 31, 1951; s. William Holmes and Catherine Louise (Stitt) B.; B.A. cum laude in Econs., Kenyon Coll., 1973; M.B.A. in Fin., U. Mich., 1975; m. Christine Carr, Aug. 17, 1974; children—Robert Stitt II, Michael Todd. Regulatory affairs analyst El Paso Natural Gas Co. (Tex.), 1975-76; asst. to pres. Waterville Gas and Oil Co. (Ohio), 1976-77, pres., 1977—; spokesman for gas cos. at legis. and regulatory agy. hearings, 1978—. Mem. Ohio Gas Assn. (trustee 1981—, v.p. 1983-84, pres. 1984-85), Waterville C. of C. (dir. 1977-78, pres. 1983). Republican. Episcopalian. Clubs: Toledo, Waterville Rotary (bd. dirs. 1981-84, pres. 1985-86), Belmont Country, Masons. Home: 26623 W River Rd Perrysburg OH 43551 Office: PO Box 259 Waterville OH 43566

BLACK, SAMUEL PAUL WEST, neurosurgery educator; b. Barbourville, Ky., Dec. 19, 1916; s. Read Postlethwaite and Louise (West) B.; m. Betty Lohman, Dec. 23, 1944; children—Susan Postlethwaite, John Sheldon, Nancy Read, Samuel Paul West. B.S., Yale U., 1940; M.D., Johns Hopkins U., 1943. House officer gen. surgery New Haven Hosp., 1944-47; resident neurol. surgery Yale U., New Haven, 1948-50; instr. neurosurgery Yale U., 1950-52, asst. prof., 1952-55; prof. neurosurgery U. Mo., Columbia, 1955-82, prof. emeritus, 1982—; dir. intracranial aneurysm study dept. pathology U. Mo., 1982—. Contbr. articles to profl. jours. Served with USNR, 1944-46. George H. Knight fellow Yale U., 1947-48. Mem. New Eng. Neurosurg. Soc. (exec. com. 1953-55), Am. Assn. Neurol. Surgeons, A.C.S., Assn. Research in Nervous and Mental Disease, So. Neurosurgical Soc., Mo. Med. Soc., Mo. Neurosurg. Soc. (pres. 1980-81), Sigma Xi. Clubs: Austrian Mountain, Pithotomy; Rotary (Columbia) (pres. 1981-82). Home: 300 S Glenwood St Columbia MO 65201 Office: 807 Stadium Rd Columbia MO 65201

BLACK, STEVEN BITTERS, plastic surgeon; b. Rochester, Minn., June 4, 1946; s. Albert Seward and Madge Marie (Bitters) B.; BS, U. Nebr., Lincoln, 1969, MD, Omaha, 1972; 1 child, Michelle Marie; m. Joyce Marie Graupmann, July 14, 1979; children: Jonathan Steven, Kathryn Joyce, Patricia Bitters. Diplomate Am. Bd. Plastic Surgery, Am. Bd. Surgery. Intern, Mayo Clinic, Rochester, Minn., 1972-73; surg. resident Mayo Grad. Sch. Medicine, Rochester, 1973-77, plastic surgery resident, 1977-79; practice medicine specializing in plastic surgery, Omaha, 1979— ; instr. U. Nebr. Coll. Medicine; mem. staff Bishop Clarkson Meml., Nebr. Meth., Immanuel, Children's hosps. (all Omaha), U. Nebr. Hosps. and Clinics. Fellow ACS; mem. AMA, Nebr. Med. Assn., Met. Omaha Med. Soc., Am. Soc. Plastic and Reconstructive Surgeons. Contbr. articles to med. jours. Home: 1306 S 218th St Elkhorn NE 68022 Office: Suite 219 Doctors Bldg 44th and Farnam Sts Omaha NE 68131

BLACK, THOMAS ALEXANDER, JR., dentist; b. Pitts., Jan. 10, 1943; s. Thomas Alexander and Griselda (Best) B.; BS, Purdue U., 1965; DMD, Washington U., St. Louis, 1975, MBA, 1975; m. Sandra Jean Gredys, May 10, 1969. Prodn. supr. Proctor & Gamble, St. Louis, 1968-69; with Mallinckrodt Chem. Works, St. Louis, 1969-71; gen. practice dentistry, Marlborough, Mo., 1976—; clin. instr. dentistry Washington U., St. Louis, 1976-78, asst. prof., 1978-82; staff dentist Bethesda Dilworth Meml. Home. Deacon, mem. choir Webster Groves (Mo.) Presbyn. Ch.; pres. York Village Assn. Served to capt. C.E., AUS, 1965-68. Mem. ADA, Mo. Dental Assn., Am. Soc. Geriatric Dentistry, Greater St. Louis Dental Soc., Am. Philat. Soc., Soc. Am. Mil. Engrs., Am. Revenue Assn., Nat. Eagle Scout Assn., Xi Psi Phi, Alpha Phi Omega. Club: Rotary (dir.). Home: 70 York Dr Brentwood MO 63144 Office: 8460 Watson Rd Suite 112 Marlborough MO 63119

BLACK, WALTER KERRIGAN, lawyer; b. Birmingham, Ala., Jan. 27, 1915; s. Timuel Dixon and Mattie (McConner) B.; m. Dorothy E. Wickliffe, July 2, 1950 (dec. Apr. 1982). A.B., U. Ill., 1939; LL.B., John Marshall Law Sch., 1952. Bar: Ill. 1952, U.S. Dist. Ct. (dist.) Ill. 1956 U.S. Supreme Ct. 1967. Ptnr. McCoy & Black, Chgo., 1952-59, McCoy, Ming & Leighton, Chgo., 1959-64, McCoy, Ming & Black, Chgo., 1965-77; prin. Mitchell & Black, Chgo., 1977-86; sr. counsel Mitchell Williams Holland & Rux, 1986-87, Caldwell & Black, 1987—; village atty., Robbins, Ill., 1952-69, 81-85, East Chicago Heights, Ill., 1954-69, 77-85; hearing examiner Ill. Fair Practices Commn.; dir., gen. counsel Fuller Products Co., LaCade Products Co., Lawndale Packaging Corp.; spl. counsel R.W. Borrowdale Co. Inc. Mem. governing bd. Cook County Legal Assistance Found., Inc.; atty., trustee emeritus African Methodist Episcopal Ch.; spl. co-counsel for Richard Hatcher, Mayor of Gary, Ind., 1967, 71. Served with AUS, 1942-46. Mem. Ill. Bar Assn., Cook County Bar Assn., Chgo. Bar Assn., Am. Arbitration Assn. (arbitrator 1971—), Kappa Alpha Psi. Home: 2231 E 67th St Chicago IL 60649 Office: 180 W Washington St Suite 300 Chicago IL 60602

BLACK, WILLIAM A., electric utility company executive; b. Blackenridge, Pa., 1924; married. B.S., MIT, 1949, M.S. in Elec. Engring., 1950, M.S. in Indsl. Mgmt., 1962. With Ohio Power Co., 1950-78; exec. v.p. Ind. & Mich. Electric Co., Ft. Wayne, Ind., 1978-80, pres., chief operating officer, dir., 1980—; dir. Am. Elec. Power Service Corp., Inc.-Ky. Elec. Corp., Lincoln Nat. Bank, Lincoln Fin. Corp.; v.p., dir. various subs Am. Elec. Power Co. Inc. Served with USMCR, 1943-45. Office: Ind & Mich Electric Co Inc PO Box 60 Fort Wayne IN 46801

BLACK, WILLIAM G., clergyman. Bishop So. Ohio region Episcopal Ch., Cin. Office: Episc Ch 412 Sycamore St Cincinnati OH 45202 *

BLACKBURN, CATHERINE ELAINE, lawyer, pharmacist; b. Columbus, Ohio, Nov. 5, 1953; d. Robert Jerome and Patricia Ann (Buchman) B. B.S. in Pharmacy with high honors, U. Ky., 1978; J.D. with honors, Ohio State U., 1982. Bars: Ohio 1982, U.S. Dist. Ct. (so. dist.) Ohio 1983. Chief pharmacist Louisa Community Hosp., Ky., 1978; pharmacist Riverside Meth. Hosp., Columbus, Ohio, 1978-82; law clk. Michael F. Colley Co., L.P.A., Columbus, 1980-82, assoc., 1982-87; asst. prof. law U. Louisville Sch. Law, Ky., 1987—; workshop leader Ohio Drug Studies Inst., Columbus, 1982, 83, 14th Nat. Conf. on Women and the Law, Washington, D.C., 1983, Nat. Assn. for Rights, Protection and Advocacy , 1986, 15th Nat. Conf., 1985; lectr./speaker Iowa Trial Lawyers Assn., Iowa City, 1984; speaker Nat. Assn. for Rights Protection and Advocacy, Nat. Conf., Boston, 1986; lectr. legal writing Coll. Law Ohio State U., 1986. Contbr. article to profl. jour. Staff writer, editor Ohio State U. Law Jour., 1980-82. Trustee Women's Outreach for Women, Columbus, 1982-85, Amethyst, Inc., 1985—; incorporator Columbus Career Women Inc., 1986-87, treas., 1986—. Fellow Am. Soc. Pharmacy Law; mem. Assn. Trial Lawyers Am. (lectr./speaker 1982—), Ohio Acad. Trial Lawyers, Columbus Bar Assn., Ohio Bar Assn. Columbus Career Women, Inc. (trustee, treas. 1986-87), Order of Coif, Phi Beta Kappa, Rho Chi Soc. Democrat.

BLACKBURN, HAROLD DENNIS, wholesale company finance executive; b. Chgo., Oct. 20, 1954; s. Harold Edward and Martha (Descorcy) B.; m. Claudia Mary Kuckla, Apr. 15, 1983. BA in Acctg. and Bus. Mgmt., Northeastern Ill. U., 1977. CPA, Ill. Staff auditor Field & Field's CPA's,

Chgo., 1977-79; sr. auditor Alexander Grant & Co., Chgo., 1979-80; audit supr. Bernstein & Bank, Ltd., Chgo., 1980-82; audit and acctg. ptnr. William E. Huml & Co., Ltd., Lincolnshire, Ill., 1982-85; v.p. fin., controller Recycled Paper Products, Inc., Chgo., 1985—; acct., Ill. Dept. Registration and Edn., Springfield, 1984—. Mem. Am. Inst. CPA's, Ill. CPA Soc. Republican. Avocations: reading, jogging, weight lifting. Office: Recycled Paper Products Inc 3636 N Broadway Chicago IL 60613

BLACKBURN, HAROLD LEE, JR., state agency administrator; b. Edgemont, S.D., Dec. 14, 1927; s. Harold Lee Sr. and Neva Beatrice (Pratt) B.; m. Donna Jean Spotts, Dec. 26, 1961; children: Lee, Laurie. BS, Kans. State U., 1950; MEd, Phillips U., Enid, Okla., 1953; EdD, U. Kans., 1961. Assoc. supt. Topeka Pub. Schs., 1961-67; dir. edn. programs U.S. Dept. Edn., Kansas City, Mo., 1967-80, sec., regional rep., 1980-82; asst. commr. edn. Kans. State Dept. Edn., Topeka, 1982-83, commr. edn., 1983—; mem. Kans. Council Econ. Edn., Manhattan, 1985—; bd. dirs. Mid-Continent Regional Edn. Lab., Kansas City, 1983—. Served to capt. U.S. Army, 1950-56. Mem. United Sch. Adminstrs., Kans. Educators Club, Phi Delta Kappa. Club: Knife and Fork. Lodge: Rotary. Home: 9543 Connell Dr Overland Park KS 66212 Office: Kans State Dept Edn 120 E 10th Topeka KS 66612

BLACKETT, THOMAS EUGENE, publishing company executive; b. Lincoln, Nebr., Feb. 3, 1951; s. Alfred Lee and Arvid LaJune (Larson) B. BA in Journalism, Drake U., 1975, postgrad., 1984. Pub. affairs dir. Am. Chiropractic Assn., Des Moines, 1976-81; pub. info. dir. Iowa Devel. Commn., 1981-83; mktg. dir. Bus. Publs. Corp., Des Moines, 1984—; cons. mktg. Iowa Title Co., Des Moines, 1984—. Mem. Pub. Relations Soc. Am. (profl. devel. com. 1986, inst. com. 1987), Advt. Profls. Des Moines, Greater Des Moines C. of C. Fedn. (bur. econ. devel. com. 1985-87). Home: 2512 46th St Des Moines IA 50310-3113 Office: Bus Publs Corp The Depot at Fourth 100 4th St Des Moines IA 50309-4742

BLACKLEDGE, DAVID NOEL, manufacturing company executive; b. Ft. Polk, La., Dec. 7, 1953; s. David William and Diana Marjorie (Wiley) B.; m. Linda Ann Aguanno, June 7, 1975; children: Heidi Lynn, Danielle Marie, Noel Christine. BS in Engring., U.S. Mil. Acad., 1975; MBA, U. Wis., 1987. Commd. 1st lt. U.S. Army, 1976; fire direction officer U.S. Army, Gelnhausen, Fed. Republic Germany, 1976-77; exec. officer U.S. Army, Hanau, Fed. Republic Germany, 1977-79; advanced through grades to capt. U.S. Army, 1979; battery commdr. U.S. Army, Ft. Campbell, Ky., 1979-81; resigned U.S. Army, 1981; team mgr. Procter and Gamble, Green Bay, Wis., 1981-83, mech. mgr., 1983-85, dept. mgr. paper products, 1985—. Solicitor United Way of Brown County, Green Bay, 1981-83; coach Soccer Assn. for Youth, Green Bay, 1984-86. Named one of Outstanding Young Men of Am., 1984. Mem. Assn. Grads. U.S. Mil. Acad., Res. Officers Assn. Avocations: cross country skiing, triathlons, music. Home: 2638 Hilly Haven Rd Green Bay WI 54301 Office: Procter and Gamble Paper Products Co PO Box 8020 Green Bay WI 54302-8020

BLACKMAN, HOWARD PHILIP, educational association executive; b. N.Y.C., July 6, 1944; s. Max and Ethel (Weinstein) B.; m. Marsha Anne Novak, Feb. 16, 1980. BA, Jersey City State Coll., 1966, MA, 1967; EdD, Syracuse U., 1980. Cert. elem. and spl. ed. tchr., Ill., N.J., N.Y., Mass. Tchr. Ridgewood (N.J.) Pub. Schs., 1967-71; state program dir. N.J. Assn. Children with Learning Disabilities, Convent Station, 1971-75; legis. advocate Ctr. on Human Policy, Syracuse, N.Y., 1975-77; research assoc. Syracuse Research Corp., 1977-79; adminstr. Westchester County Bd. Childrens and Ednl. Services, White Plains, N.Y., 1979-80; exec. dir. LaGrange (Ill.) Area Dept. Spl. Edn., 1980—; adj. prof. U. Ill., Chgo., 1985—; mem. Chgo. Area Sch. Efficiency Council, 1986—; mem. faculty adv. com. Northern Ill. U., DeKalb, 1985—; field editor Council Exceptional Children, Reston, Va., 1986—; chmn. No. Ill. Spl. Edn. Dir.'s Roundtable, 1984—; mem. Pres.'s Com. on Mental Retardation, 1987—. Author: Effective Child Advocacy, 1980. Mem. adv. council 9th Congl. Dist. Edn., Hinsdale, Ill., 1985—, Pres.'s Com. on Mental Retardation, 1987—; chmn. Inter-Agy. Council for Handicapped, N.J., 1972-74, Community Support Services, LaGrange, 1980-82. Recipient Disting. Service award Inter-Agy. Council for Handicapped, N.J., 1974, Community Support Services, LaGrange, 1981. Mem. Council for Exceptional Children (field editor 1986—), Ill. Assn. Spl. Edn. Administrs. (bd. dirs. 1983—), Ill. Assn. Severely Handicapped (bd. dirs. 1986—). Jewish. Lodges: B'nai Brith (pres. local chpt. 1972-74), Kiwanis (bd. dirs. local club 1974-75). Home: 4941 Central Ave Western Springs IL 60558 Office: 1301 W Cossitt Ave LaGrange IL 60525

BLACKMAR, CHARLES BLAKEY, state justice; b. Kansas City, Mo., Apr. 19, 1922; s. Charles Maxwell and Eleanor (Blakey) B.; m. Ellen Day Bonnifield, July 18, 1943 (dec. 1983); children: Charles A., Thomas J., Lucy E. Blackmar Alpaugh, Elizabeth S., George B.; m. Jeanne Stephens Lee, Oct. 5, 1984. A.B. summa cum laude, Princeton U., 1942; J.D., U. Mich., 1948. Bar: Mo. bar 1948. Practiced in Kansas City; mem. firm Swanson, Midgley, Jones, Blackmar & Eager, and predecessors, 1952-66; professorial lectr. U. Mo. at Kansas City, 1949-58; prof. law St. Louis U., 1966-82, prof. emeritus; judge Supreme Ct. Mo., 1982—; spl. asst. atty. gen. Mo. 1969-77, labor arbitrator.; Chmn. Fair Pub. Accommodations Commn. Kansas City, Mo., 1964-66; mem. Commn. Human Relations Kansas City, 1965-66. Author: (with Volz and others) Missouri Practice, 1953, West's Federal practice Manual, 1957, 71, (with Devitt) Federal Jury Practice and Instructions, 1970, 3d edit., 1977; contbr. (with Devitt) numerous articles on probate law to profl. publs. Mem. Jackson County Republican Com., 1952-58; mem. Mo. Rep. Com., 1956-58. Served to 1st lt., inf. AUS, 1943-46. Decorated Silver Star, Purple Heart. Mem. Am. Law Inst., Nat. Acad. Arbitrators, Mo. Bar (spl. lectr. insts.), Disciples Peace Fellowship, Scribes (pres. 1986-87), Order of Coif, Phi Beta Kappa. Mem. Disciples of Christ Ch. Home: 612 Hobbs Rd Jefferson City MO 65101 Office: Mo Supreme Ct Supreme Ct Bldg Jefferson City MO 65102

BLACKMORE, CAROL LYNN, sign printing company executive; b. St. Louis, Oct. 18, 1949; d. John Frederick and Mary Louise (Cunningham) Albrecht; m. Luther Frederick Blackmore, Oct. 21, 1980; children: Victoria Louise, Alexander Welles. BS in Elem. Edn., S.E. Mo. State U., 1973; MBA, Washington U., St. Louis, 1985. Cert. tchr., Mo. Adminstrv. asst. Washington U., St. Louis, 1978-83, acct., 1983-85; installation coordinator United Van Lines, St. Louis, 1985-86; proprieter Banners & Signs PDQ, St. Louis, 1986—. Treas. Gethsemane Luth. Ch., St. Louis, 1984-86. Mem. Am. Soc. Women Accts. (bd. dirs. 1985—, membership chmn. 1985—), Bus. and Profl. Women's Club of St. Louis. Republican. Avocations: personal computer software studies, gourmet cooking, camping, canoeing. Home: 31 Sylvester Ave Saint Louis MO 63119 Office: Banners & Signs PDQ 105 Concord Plaza Suite 211 Saint Louis MO 63128

BLACKORBY, EDWARD CONVERSE, historian, educator; b. Hansboro, N.D., May 30, 1911; s. Charles Edward and Clara Ellen (Converse) B.; B.S., Mayville State Tchrs. Coll., 1930; Ph.D., U. N.D., 1958; postgrad. Am. U.; m. Jewel Catherine Barenscheer, Nov. 24, 1937; 1 son, Charles Edward. Tchr. public schs., Russell, Niagara, Pembina and New Rockford, N.D., 1930-49; prof. history Dickinson (N.D.) State Tchrs. Coll., 1949-59; prof. history U. Wis., Eau Claire, 1959-81, prof. emeritus, 1981—. Pres. N.D. Edn. Assn., 1948-49; mem. City Council Eau Claire, 1966-68, chmn. Cable TV Adv. Com., 1975-82; mem. Park Bd.; clk. Sch. Dist. Named Tchr. of Yr., U. Wis., Eau Claire, 1968; Edward C. Blackorby award for excellence in history named in his honor, 1982. Mem. Orgn. Am. Historians, Am. Hist. Assn., State Hist. Soc. Wis., N.D. Hist. Soc., Western History Assn., Agrl. History Assn., Nat. Council Social Studies, AAUP, Wis. Council Social Studies, NEA, SAR, Phi Alpha Theta, Phi Delta Kappa, Phi Kappa Phi, Phi Eta Sigma (hon.). Democrat. Congregationalist. Club: Masons. Author: Prairie Rebel: The Public Life of William Lemke; George B. Winship: Progressive Journalist of the Middle Border; contbr. to Ency. Americana, Dictionary of Am. Biography, profl. jours. Home: 1004 Village Sq Altoona WI 54720 Office: Dept History HHH 729 U Wis Eau Claire WI 54701

BLACKWELL, DAN LOWELL, orthodontist; b. Polo, Mo., Feb. 4, 1938; s. Arnold Bernard and Floyde Evelyn (McNary) B.; m. Nancy Elizabeth Browning, Apr. 10, 1966; children: Deborah Elizabeth, Molly McNary. BA, U. Mo., 1960; DDS, U. Mo., Kansas City, 1968, grad. specializing in Orthodontics, 1972. Cert. orthodontist. Sales rep. IBM Corp., Kans., 1961-64; practice dentistry specializing in orthodontics Lee's Summit, Mo., 1972—. Chmn. Kansas City Children's Dental Health Week, 1975; pres. Mo. State Bd Edn., 1985-86, Lee's Summit Hosp. Found., 1985-86; v.p. Lee's Summit Indsl. Devel. Authority, 1985-86. Served to lt comdr. USN, 1968-70. Mem. ADA, Am. Assn. Orthodontists, Mo. Soc. Orthodontists (pres. 1980-81), Midwest Soc. Orthodontists (chmn. 1986), Greater Kansas City Dental Soc. (trustee 1973-76), Omicron Delta Kappa. Lodge: Rotary. Home: 211 Hillcrest Ln Lee's Summit MO 64063 Office: Blackwell & Osborne DDS PC 200 S Douglas Lee's Summit MO 64063

BLACKWELL, KENNETH EMERSON, chem. engr.; b. Clendenin, W.Va., Dec. 13, 1930; s. John Ervin and Ava (Strickland) B.; student N.C. State Coll., 1950-51, Tri-State Coll., 1959-60; B.S., Fla. State Christian Coll., 1972; M.S., Tenn. Christian U., 1977, Ph.D., 1978; m. Harriet Pauline Anderson, Feb. 10, 1953; children—Vicky Jo, Yma Yvonne. Chem. processing supr. Am. Viscose Corp., Nitro, W.Va., 1953-59; chem. processing supr. Purex Corp., St. Louis, 1960-67, sr. project engr., 1967-80, sr. field engr., 1980-81, regional project engr., 1981-85, mgr. tech. info., The Dial Corp., St. Louis, 1985—. Served with USAF, 1948-52. Mem. Inst. for Cert. of Engring. Technicians. Mem. United Ch. Christ. Home: 12040 Larimore Rd Saint Louis MO 63138 Office: Purex Corp 6506 N Broadway Saint Louis MO 63147

BLACKWELL, ROBERT WALLINGFORD, printing company executive; b. Oak Park, Ill., Oct. 28, 1952; s. Clifford Earl and Abigail (Gunderson) B.; m. Laurie Ann Munoz, Dec. 30, 1975; children—Jennifer Ross, Christopher Miles. B.A., Coe Coll., 1974. Research analyst Rocliff Assocs., Delavan, Wis., 1975; customer service rep. Deluxe Check Printers, Milw., 1976, sales rep., 1977-80, asst. plant mgr., 1980-82, methods and procedures mgr., St. Paul, 1982-84, nat. dir. customer service, 1984—; cons. Jr. Achievement, St. Paul, 1984. Bd. dirs. Delavan Lake Improvement Assn., Delavan, 1980-82. Mem. Internat. Customer Service Assn., Soc. Consumer Affairs Profls. in Bus. Republican. Lutheran. Clubs: Delavan Lake Yacht (vice chmn. 1980-82), Delavan Lake Sailing Sch. (sec. 1980-82). Avocations: competitive sailing, golf, tennis, skiing. Home: 1149 Amble Dr Arden Hills MN 55112 Office: Deluxe Check Printers 1080 West County Rd F Shoreview MN 55112

BLACKWOOD, R(OBERT) ROSS, metallurgical co. exec.; b. Windsor, Ont., Can., Sept. 12, 1928; came to U.S., 1929; s. Robert Alexander and Annie (Beecroft) B.; B.S. in Metall. Engring. U. Wis., 1953; m. Beverly Joy Svenson, June 21, 1953; children—Kari Lynn, Scott Andrew. Metall. engr. A.C. Spark Plug Co., Flint, Mich., 1953-54; mgr. T. H. Cochrane Labs., Milw., 1954-60, pres., owner, 1960-74; pres. Tenaxol Inc., Milw., 1965—, chmn. bd., 1967—. Served with U.S. Army, 1946-48; Japan. Recipient Outstanding Engring. award U. Wis., 1977; registered profl. engr., Wis. Mem. Am. Soc. Metals, AIME (chmn. Wis. chpt. 1962-63), Soc. Automotive Engrs., Soc. Mfg. Engrs., Nat. Soc. Profl. Engrs. Republican. Presbyterian. Clubs: Lions, (Wauwatosa, Wis.); Masons, Shriners. Patentee metal quenching medium. Home: 2877 N 122d St Wauwatosa WI 53222 Office: 5801 W National Ave Milwaukee WI 53214

BLADDY, CHARLEN LECRONE, special educator; b. Tiffin, Ohio, Dec. 4, 1943; d. Charles Relna and Luella Adeline (McCracken) LeCrone; m. Jerome Stanley Bladdy, Feb. 17, 1968. B.A., Heidelberg Coll., 1965; M.S. Edn., No. Ill. U., 1974. English, Spanish tchr. Columbian high sch., Tiffin, Ohio, 1965-67; stewardess United Airlines, Chgo., 1967; exec. sec. Frederick Chusid, Chgo., 1968; tchr. hearing impaired Chgo. Bd. Edn., 1968—. Mem. Delta Kappa Gamma (membership chmn. 1982-83). Home: 1233 Colgate Wilmette IL 60091 Office: Jamieson Sch 5650 N Mozart Chicago IL 60659

BLAGDEN, CAROLYN MARGARET, editorial executive, writer; b. Summit, N.J., Apr. 19, 1944; d. Raymond and Margaret Ida (Noll) Hunt; m. Robert B. Blagden, June 25, 1966 (div. Jan. 1984); children: Kathryn E., Michael G. BA in German, English, Grove City (Pa.) Coll., 1966; MS in Communicative Disorders, San Francisco State U., 1981. lic. speech pathologist, Calif., Iowa. Speech, lang. clinician Scottish Rite Clinic, San Francisco, 1980-83, Alameda Unified Sch. Dist., 1983-84; editorial mgr. LinguiSystems, Inc., Moline, Ill., 1984—. Author: (with others) (books) UnTherapy for Thinking Skills, 1985, RAPP: Resource of Activities for Peer Pragmatics, 1986; (test) Interpersonal Language Skills Assessment, 1983, 84, Teaching Voabulary Worksheets, 1987, Good Thinking!, 1987, Thinking to Go, 1987; (pictures) PPICS: Picture Program for Interpersonal Communicative Skills, 1986, Blooming Recipes, 1987. Mem. Am. Speech., Lang. and Hearing Assn. (cert. clin. competence), Iowa State Speech. Lang. and Hearing Assn., Quad Cities Speech, Lang. and Hearing Assn. (pub. awareness chairperson, 1986-87). Republican. Avocations: cooking, entertaining, sewing, traveling, music. Home: 4545 Aspen Hills Circle Bettendorf IA 52722 Office: LinguiSystems Inc 716 17th St Moline IL 61265

BLAHA, DAVID DAVENPORT, dentist; b. Whitten, Iowa, Feb. 8, 1917; s. George Andrew and Helen Barnes (Davenport) B.; m. Mary Kathryn Bell, Sept. 18, 1940; children: David D., Catharine Blaha Courtnage, Robert B. BA, U. Iowa, 1940, DDS, 1942; postgrad. Gen. practice dentistry Marshalltown, Iowa, 1946—. Past pres., chmn. bldg. com., bd. dirs. YMCA; treas. and sr. warden vestry St. Paul's Episcopal Ch.; mem. health council Boy Scouts Am. Served to capt. U.S. Army, 1943-46, PTO. Fellow Acad. Gen. Dentistry, Internat. Coll. Dentistry, Am. Coll. Dentistry; mem. ADA (del.), Iowa Dental Assn. (pres., treas.,task force to Title XIX, membership council, ins. council, jour. policy com., chmn. journalism com., trustee), Pierre Fauchard Acad., Marshall County Dental Soc., Waterloo Dist. Dental Soc., Marshall County Dental Study Club, Cen. Iowa Art Assn., U. Iowa Alumni Assn. (life, exec. com., nat. com. Iowa Endowment 2000, Iowa Dental Alumnus of Yr. 1984), U. Iowa Parent Assn. (life), Am. Legion. Republican. Episcopalian. Clubs: U. Iowa Dental Centennial, U. Iowa Found. Pres.'s. Lodge: Elks, Masons, Shriners. Office: 6 1/2 E Main St Marshalltown IA 50158

BLAIN, ALEXANDER, III, surgeon, educator; b. Detroit, Mar. 9, 1918; s. Alexander William and Ruby (Johnson) B.; m. Josephine Woodbury Bowen, May 3, 1941; children—Helen Bowen, Alexander IV, Bruce Scott Murray, Josephine Johnson; m. Mary E. Mains, 1968. B.A., Wayne U., 1940, M.D., 1943; M.S. in Surgery, U. Mich., 1948. Diplomate Am. Bd. Surgery. House officer, Halsted fellow in surgery Johns Hopkins U., 1943-46; resident surgeon U. Hosp., Ann Arbor, Mich., 1946-50; instr. surgery U. Mich., 1950-57; chief surgeon 14th Field Hosp., Bad Kreuznach, Fed. Republic Germany; clin. asst. prof. surgery Wayne State U., 1962—; surgeon-in-chief Alexander Blain Hosp., Detroit, 1953-78; cons. surgeon Highland Park Gen. Hosp, St. Josephs's Hosp., Detroit Riverview Hosp., Blain Clinic, Ostego Meml. Hosp., Gaylord, Mich.; med. dir. The Budd Co., 1977-82; Pres. Met. Detroit Family Service Assn., 1962-63, Detroit Mus. Soc., 1961-62; staff Harper Hosp., Detroit, Crittenton Hosp., Rochester, Mich., Detroit Deaconess Hosp.; surgeon Detroit Urban Indian Health Ctr., 1982—. Author: (with F.A. Coller) Indications For and Results of Splenectomy, 1950, Prismatic Papers and an Ode, 1968, Prismatic Haiku Poems (Remembered Voices), 1973, (poems) Shu Shu Ga, 2d edit., 1983, Clackshant, 1982; contbr. numerous articles to surg. jours.; editorial bd. Rev. Surgery, 1959-79. Mem. Detroit Zool. Park Commn., 1974-82, pres., 1978-82; trustee Alexander Blain Hosp., 1942-67, Ostego Meml. Hosp. Found., Gaylord, Mich., 1976—; bd. dirs. Detroit Zool. Soc., 1972-75, 82—; pres. W.J. Stapleton Found. Health Edn., 1978-84. Served as lt. M.C., AUS, 1942-44, maj., 1955-57. Recipient Wayne State U. Med. Alumni award, 1968. Fellow ACS, N.Y. Acad. Scis.; mem. Internat. Cardiovascular Soc., F.A. Coller Surg. Soc., Am. Fedn. for Clin. Research, Cranbrook Inst. Sci., Soc. Vascular Surgery, Am. Thyroid Assn., Societe Internationale de Chirugie, Mich. Med. Soc. (chmn. surg. sect. 1963), Assn. Clin. Surgery, Pan-Pacific Surg. Assn., Acad. Am. Poets, Am. Poetry Assn., Mich. Poetry Soc., Acad. of Surgery of Detroit, Council of The Wayne County Med. Soc., Nu Sigma Nu, Phi Gamma Delta. Clubs: Grosse Pointe (fleet surgeon 1986—), Otsego, Prismatic (pres. 1967), Detroit, Detroit Racquet (pres. 1976-80), Cardio-Vascular Surgeons (pres. 1961-62), Acanthus, Waweatonong (pres. 1978), Circumnavigators. Home: 8 Stratford Pl Grosse Pointe MI 48230

BLAIN, CHARLOTTE MARIE, physician; b. Meadeville, Pa., July 18, 1941; d. Frank Andrew and Valerie Marie (Serafin) B.; student Coll. St. Francis, 1958-60, DePaul U., 1960-61; M.D., U. Ill., 1965; m. John G. Hamby, June 12, 1971 (dec. May 1976); 1 son, Charles J. Hamby. Intern, resident U. Ill. Hosps., Chgo., 1967-70; practice medicine specializing in internal medicine, Elmhurst, Ill., 1969—; instr. medicine U. Ill. Hosp., 1969-70; asst. prof. medicine Loyola U., 1970-71; mem. staff Elmhurst Meml. Hosp., 1970—; clin. asst. prof. Chgo. Med. Sch., 1978—. U. Ill. fellow in infectious diseases, 1968-69. Bd. dirs. Classical Symphony. Diplomate Am. Bd. Family Practice, Am. Bd. Internal Medicine. Fellow A.C.P., Am. Acad. Family Practice; mem. AMA, Am. Med. Women's Assn., Am. Soc. Internal Medicine, Am. Fedn. Clin. Research, Am. Profl. Practice Assn., AAAS, Royal Soc. Medicine, DuPage Med. Soc. Roman Catholic. Club: Univ. (Chgo.). Contbr. articles and chpts. to med. jours. and texts. Home: 320 Cottage Hill Elmhurst IL 60126 Office: 135 Cottage Hill Elmhurst IL 60126

BLAIN, DONALD GRAY, physician; b. Detroit, Feb. 27, 1924; s. Alexander and Ruby (Johnson) B.; ed. Princeton, 1946; M.D., Wayne State U., 1950; m. Grace Carpenter, June, 1954; children—Elizabeth, Ian, Patricia. Intern, Union Meml. Hosp., Balt., 1950-51; gen. surg. resident Ch. Home Hosp., Balt., 1953-55, Henry Ford Hosp., Detroit, 1955-56, Alexander Blain Hosp., Detroit, 1956-58; staff Blain Hosp.; resident urology N.C. Bapt. Hosp. and instr. urology Bowman Gray Sch. Medicine, Winston-Salem, 1962-65; pvt. practice urology, Mount Clemens, Mich., 1965—; pres. Oakland Macomb Profl. Standards Rev. Orgn., 1973-79. Mem. Gov.'s Conf. on Health Manpower, 1973; bd. dirs. Mich. MDPAC. Served to capt. USAF, 1951-53. Diplomate Am. Bd. Urology. Fellow A.C.S.; mem. Macomb County Med. Soc. (past pres.), Am. Assn. Clin. Urologists, Am. Urologic Assn., Societe Internationale d'Urologie, Detroit Surg. Soc. (council), St. Andrews Soc. Republican. Presbyterian. Clubs: Country of Detroit, Metamora Hunt, Sedgefield Hunt. Home: 34136 E Jefferson St Saint Clair Shores MI 48082

BLAINE, WILLIAM MCKINLEY, JR., sales executive; b. Chgo., Apr. 9, 1931; s. William McKinley and Edith Alvina (Charbonnier) B.; A.B. in Sociology/Anthropology, U. Ill., 1954; M.A. in Edn., U. Chgo., 1955; postgrad. U. Wis., 1962-63; M.B.A., Northwestern U., 1980; m. Tokiko Tanabe, Mar. 24, 1956; children—William McKinley III, James. Elem. tchr. Dept. Public Instrn., Territory Hawaii, 1955-56; area mgr. World Book Childcraft Internat., Inc., 1957-58, dist. mgr., 1958-59, div. mgr., 1959-62, div. mgr., Hayward, Calif., 1962-76, asso. sales tng., Chgo., 1976-80, dir. mktg. services/ins. projects, 1980-83; nat. sales dir. Nationwide Legal Services, Inc., 1984-85, v.p. bus. devel., 1985-86, pres. Profl. Mktg. Group, Inc., 1986—; guest lectr. Chabot Community Coll., Hayward, 1973. Sec., Oahu Democratic County Com., 1959-60; mem. Sch. Adv. Com., Hayward, 1972; bd. dirs. East Bay Youth Symphony, Hayward, 1973-76; neighborhood commr. Boy Scouts Am., Hayward, 1964-66; pres. Woodland Estates Community Assn., 1973; bd. dirs. Mt. Prospect Public Library, 1979—. Mem. ALA (mem. library trustee div.), C. of C. Democrat. Methodist. Clubs: Des Plaines Yacht, Rotary. Home: 119 N Emerson St Mount Prospect IL 60056 Office: 20 N Wacker Chicago IL 60606

BLAIR, BENJAMIN RALPH, tax consultant; b. Lafayette, Ind., July 26, 1958; s. Frank A. and Doris (Keffer) B.; m. Cynthia A. Kalberer, May 17, 1980; 1 child, Benjamin A. BS, Ind. U., 1980, MBA, 1981. CPA, Ind. Mgr. Crowe, Chizek & Co., South Bend, Ind., 1981—. Contbr. articles to profl. jours. Mem. Am. Inst. CPA's, Ind. CPA Soc. (mem. various coms.). Home: 5011 N State Rd 39 LaPorte IN 46350 Office: Crowe Chizek & Co 330 E Jefferson Blvd South Bend IN 46624

BLAIR, JOSEPH SKILES, JR., educator; b. Niles, Ohio, Dec. 16, 1919; s. Joseph Skiles and Elizabeth Leo (Higgins) B.; B.S., Kent State U., 1942; M.A., Columbia U., 1948; Ph.D. (Danforth Found. fellow), Ohio State U., 1962; m. Marjorie Ella Jacot, June 15, 1946; children—Brenda Ruth, Lawrence Paul. Exec. dir. City Coll. N.Y. YM-YWCA and N.Y. U. Med. Students Club, 1948-52; coll. exec. Ohio-W.Va. area YMCA, 1952-59; ednl. services mgr. Nationwide Ins. Co., 1962-68; prof. Franklin U., Columbus, Ohio, 1968-83, prof. emeritus, 1983—; mgmt. cons., 1983—; owner, mgr. Brookside Conf. Center; pres. Vicinia, Inc. Home: 254 E Torrence Rd Columbus OH 43214

BLAIR, LACHLAN FERGUSON, urban planner, educator; b. Lakewood, Ohio, Sept. 6, 1919; s. Neil Ferguson and Rebecca Henderson (Gunn) B.; m. Mary Anne Novotny, Dec. 12, 1942; children: Douglas MacLachlan, Marilyn Ruth. Student, Cleve. Sch. Arch., Western Res. U., 1936-40; B. City Planning, MIT, 1949. Archtl. designer various firms Cleve., 1940-43; sr. planner Providence City Plan Commn., 1949-51; chief state planning div. R.I. Devel. Council, 1952-56; pres. Blair Assocs., Planning Cons., Providence, Syracuse, N.Y. and; Washington, 1957-66; assoc. prof. urban planning U. Ill., Urbana, 1966-70; prof. urban and regional planning U. Ill., 1970—; pres. Urbana Group Inc., planning cons., 1986—; Mem. Ill. Hist. Sites Adv. Council, 1969-77, 1984-86; chmn. Urbana Plan Commn., 1973-80; mem. Champaign County Regional Planning Comm., 1974-86. Editor: Cape Cod 1980, 1962, College Hill: A Demonstration of Historic Area Renewal, 1959, 67, The Distinctive Architecture of Willemstad, 1961. Served with C.E. AUS, 1943-46. EPA Public adminstrn. fellow, 1972-73. Mem. Am. Inst. Cert. Planners (past pres. New Eng. and Ill. chpts.; gov.), Am. Planning Assn., Partners for Livable Places, Nat. Trust Hist. Preservation, Preservation Action, Tau Beta Pi. Democrat. Unitarian. Home: 506 W Illinois St Urbana IL 61801 Office: 1003 W Nevada St Urbana IL 61801

BLAIR, PHILIP JOSEPH, lawyer; b. Dugway, Utah, Feb. 7, 1955; s. Philip T. and Mary Jo (Zurfluh) B.; m. Marilaine Sue Lister, Oct. 19, 1985. BA with Honors, U. Wis., 1976, JD, 1979. Bar: Wis.; cert. title ins. licensee, Wis., real estate broker, Wis. V.p. Shorewood Realty, Inc., Madison, 1978-81; assoc. Armstrong Law Offices, Ltd., Madison, 1981-82; atty., title officer Badger Abstract & Title Corp., Madison, 1982—; lectr. in field. Alderman City of Madison, 1981-83, mem. plan commn., 1981-83, alcohol license com., 1986—; mem. govtl. affairs com. Greater Madison Bd. Realtors, 1986—. Mem. Wis. Bar Assn., Dane County Bar Assn., U. Wis. Alumni Assn. (life award 1976). Roman Catholic. Lodge: KC (grand knight U. Wis. campus 1979-80). Avocations: world travel, golf. Home: 4153 Iroquois Dr Madison WI 53711 Office: Badger Abstract and Title Corp 900 John Nolen Dr #200 Madison WI 53713

BLAIR, VIRGINIA ANN, public relations executive; b. Kansas City, Mo., Dec. 20, 1925; d. Paul Lowe and Lou Etta (Cooley) Smith; m. James Leon Grant, Sept. 3, 1943 (dec. July 1944); m. 2d, Warden Tannahill Blair, Jr., Nov. 7, 1947; children—Janet, Warden Tannahill, III. B.S. in Speech, Northwestern U., 1948. Free-lance writer, Chgo., 1959-69; writer, editor Smith, Bucklin & Assocs., Inc., Chgo., 1969-72, account mgr., 1972-79, account supr., 1979-80, dir. pub. relations, 1980-85; pres. GB Pub. Relations, 1985—; judge U.S. Indsl. Film Festival, 1974, 75; instr. Writer's Workshop, Evanston, Ill., 1978; dir. Northwestern U. Library Council, 1978—. Emmy nominee Nat. Acad. TV Arts & Scis., 1963; recipient Service award Northwestern U., 1978, Creative Excellence award U.S. Indsl. Film Festival, 1976, Gold Leaf merit cert. Family Circle mag. and Food Council Am., 1977. Mem. Pub. Relations Soc. Am. (counselors acad.), Women's Advt. Club Chgo. (pres.), Publicity Club Chgo., Nat. Acad. TV Arts & Scis., Zeta Phi Eta (Service award 1978), Alpha Gamma Delta. Author dramas (produced on CBS): Jeanne D'Arc: The Trial, 1961; Cordon of Fear, 1961; Reflection, 1961; If I Should Die, 1963; 3-act children's play: Children of Courage, 1967. Home and Office: 463 Highcrest Dr Wilmette IL 60091

BLAIR, WILLIAM TRAVIS (BUD BLAIR), organization executive; b. Canton, Ohio, Dec. 17, 1925; s. George Neely and Helen Irene (Travis) B.; m. Eleanor I. Reid, Mar. 16, 1954; children: Carol Blair Oliver, Timothy R., Anne T. Blair Sisson, Linda S. B.A., Ohio Wesleyan U., 1950; grad., Advance Mgmt. Inst. for Assn. Execs., Mich. State U., 1964. Assoc. dir. legis. affairs Ohio C. of C., Columbus, 1958-61; dir. indsl. devel. Ohio C. of C., 1961-77, dir. social legislation, 1963-77, dir. legis. affairs, 1973-77, exec. v.p., 1977-80, pres., 1980—; sec., mem. exec. com. Ohio Med. Indemnity, Inc., Worthington, 1966-79. Chmn. bd. mgmt. Central YMCA, Columbus, 1974; bd. trustees Center of Sci. and Industry, 1962—. Served with USCG, 1943-46. Mem. Ohio Commodores, Am. C. of C. Execs., C. of C. U.S., Am. Soc. Assn. Execs., Newcomen Soc. N. Am., Council State C. of C. (sec. treas. 1978, vice chmn. 1979, mem. exec. com., chmn. 1980-82), Ohio Trade Assn. Execs. (dir. 1979—), SAR, C. of C. Execs. of Ohio (dir. 1978), Ohio Wesleyan U. Alumni Assn. (v.p.), Phi Mu Alpha, Phi Kappa Psi. Presbyterian. Clubs: University (dir. 1980-83, v.p. 1982-83), Columbus Athletic, York

Temple Country. Lodges: Rotary, Masons. Home: 138 W Cooke Rd Columbus OH 43214 Office: 35 E Gay St Columbus OH 43215

BLAKE, DARLENE EVELYN, political worker, consultant, educator; b. Rockford, Iowa, Feb. 26, 1947; d. Forest Kenneth and Violet Evelyn (Fisher) Kuhlemeier, m. Joel Franklin Blake, May 1, 1975; 1 child, Alexander Joel. AA, N. Iowa Area Community Coll., Mason City, 1967; BS, Mankato (Minn.) State Coll., 1969; MS, Mankato (Minn.) State U., 1975. Cert. profl. tchr., Iowa; registered art therapist. Tchr. Bishop Whipple Sch., Faribault, Minn., 1970-72; art therapist C.B. Wilson Ctr., Faribault, 1972-76, Sedgwick County Dept. Mental Health, Wichita, Kans., 1976-79; cons. Batten, Batten, Hudson & Swab, Des Moines, 1979-81; pres. Blake Seminars, Des Moines, 1984—; polit. cons. to Alexander Haig for Pres., 1987—. Exhibited in one-woman show at local library, 1970. Chmn. U.S. Selective Service Bd. #27, Polk County, Iowa, 1981—; sustaining mem. Rep. Nat. Com.; Rep. candidate Polk County Treas., Des Moines, 1982; chmn. Polk County Rep. Party, 1985—; commr. Des Moines Commn. Human Rights and Job Discrimination, 1984—; mem. Martin Luther King Scholarship Com., 1986; mem. Iowa State Bd. Psychology Examiners, 1983-87. Mem. Am. Art Therapy Assn., (cert., standards com. 1986—), Am. Soc. Tng. Devel., Iowa Art Therapy Assn. (pres. elect. 1984-85, founder), Iowa Assn. Counseling and Devel., Iowa Mental Health Counselors Assn. Lutheran. Clubs: Des Moines Garden (pres. 1984-85), Saylorville Yacht (Des Moines) (social chair 1983), Polk County Rep. Women (pres. elect 1983-85). Avocations: sewing, gardening, fine arts, music, reading. Home: 2802 SW Caulder Des Moines IA 50321 Office: Polk County Reps 1124 Grand Ave Des Moines IA 50309

BLAKE, FAYE SIDES, physical education educator; b. Dora, Ala., Dec. 26, 1935; d. Victor Hugo and Clara Lucy (King) Sides; m. Thomas Edison Blake, Feb. 3, 1956; children—Thomas Craig, Victor Bruce, David Alan. B.S., Jacksonville State U., 1957; M.A., George Peabody Coll. for Tchrs., 1962. Tchr. math. Wildwood (Fla.) Pub. Schs., 1957-58; tchr. phys. edn. Bethany (Ill.) Pub. Schs., 1958-60, Matteson (Ill.) Pub. Schs., 1960-68; tchr. Homewood Flossmoor (Ill.) High Sch., 1968—, coach basketball, tennis and golf, 1970-80, athletic equipment mgr., 1983-86; chmn. North Central Evaluation Com., Homewood Flossmoor, 1983-84. Author: Shaping Your Child into an Athlete, 1978; co-author phys. edn. curriculum guide. Mem. NEA (life), Women's South Inter-Conf. Assn. (pres. 1967-68), Ill. Edn. Assn., Homewood Flossmoor Athletic Assn. Democrat. Baptist. Home: 3534 W 218th St Matteson IL 60443 Office: Homewood Flossmoor High Sch 999 Kedzie Ave Flossmoor IL 60422

BLAKE, FRANK BURGAY, medical record librarian; b. N.Y.C., Feb. 10, 1924; s. Francis Gilman and Marguerite (Burgay) B.; B.S., U. Minn., 1947; B.S. in Med. Record Library Sci., St. Louis U., 1948; M.S., N.Y. U., 1951; diploma Air U., 1960; m. Filomena Yolanda Ciaccio, Dec. 15, 1962; children—Anthony Francis, Robert Burgay. Staff U.S. Army Hosp., Ft. Ord, Calif., 1964-65; med. record librarian County of Tulare, Visalia, Calif., 1966-69, Winnebago (Wis.) Mental Health Inst., 1970-81; preceptor U. Minn. ind. study program in mental health adminstrn., 1977; exec. dir. Medica, Inc., Tulare, Calif., 1968-70. 1968-70; cons. Brown County Mental Health Center, Green Bay, Wis., 1971-76; cons. Med. record program evaluation Herzing Insts., Inc., Milw., 1971-73, mem. bd. advisers med. stenographer program, 1971-72; bd. advisers med. record technician program Moraine Park Tech. Inst., Fond du Lac, Wis., 1974—. Mem. Northeastern Assn. Med. Record Librarians (v.p. 1970-71). Author: Medical Terminology Source Book, 1983; An Instruction Manual for the Problem Oriented Medical Record in Correctional Institutions, 1984. Contbr. artices to profl. jours. Home: 1446 W New York Ave Oshkosh WI 54901-2703 Office: Box 1581 Oshkosh WI 54902-1581

BLAKE, GEORGE ROWELL, newspaper editor, journalist; b. Chgo., Dec. 4, 1945; s. Robert John and June (Grace) B.; m. Mary Catherine Softcheck, Dec. 27, 1969. BS in Econs., Wheeling Coll., 1967. Reporter Herald News, Joliet, Ill., 1967-73; copy editor Times-Union, Rochester, N.Y., 1973; mng. editor Pacific Daily News, Agana, Guam, 1973-76; corr. Gannett News Service, Washington, 1977; exec. editor News-Press, Fort Myers, Fla., 1977-80; editor, v.p. Cin. Enquirer, 1980—. Bd. dirs. Neediest Kids of All, Cin., Free Store Food Bank, Cin., 1986—; mem. Task Force on Minorities in Newspaper Bus. Recipient Disting. Alumni award Wheeling Coll., 1981. Mem. AP Mng. Editors Assn. (bd. dirs. 1980-86), Am. Soc. Newspaper Editors (vice chmn. minorities com. 1983—). Roman Catholic. Clubs: Coldstream Country, Banker's, Cincinnati. Avocations: golf; darts. Home: 7056 Goldengate Dr Cincinnati OH 45244 Office: The Cin Enquirer Inc 617 Vine St Cincinnati OH 45201

BLAKE, HAYWARD ROBERT, graphic design consultant; b. West Haven, Conn., Aug. 29, 1925; s. Floyd Brewer and Marie Clara (Kuehl) B.; m. Simone Louise Roussy, July 21, 1948; children—Paul Andre, Christophe Henri, Yvonne Elizabeth. Degree in Visual Design, Ill. Inst. Tech., 1958. Staff designer Container Corp. Am., Chgo., 1952-53, Raymond Loewy Assoc., Chgo., 1953-54, Sears Roebuck & Co., Chgo., 1954-55; design dir. Ekco-Alcoa Containers, Wheeling, Ill., 1955-60; v.p. design Low's Inc., Chgo., 1961-63; pres. Hayward Blake & Co., Evanston, Ill., 1964—; mem. 27 Chgo. Designers, 1961—; lectr. Am. Press Inst., Reston, Va., 1978-81, U. Ill., Chgo., 1981-84; exhbn. judge Chgo. Book Clinic, 1980-81. Designer: (graphic neon) Color-Ed, Whitney Mus., 1974; (sculpture) No Right Turn, Ryder Gallery, 1976; (book) Discoveries from Kurdish Looms, Chgo. Book Clinic, 1984. Bd. dirs. Evanston Art Ctr., 1976, Design/Evanston, 1981, Evanston Library Friends, 1985. Served to sgt. U.S. Army, 1943-46; ETO. Recipient Disting. award Am. Inst. Graphic Arts, N.Y.C., 1976; Merit award N.Y. Type Dirs. Club, 1980; Award of Excellence, Art Mus. Assn., San Francisco, 1984. Fellow Soc. Typographic Arts (pres. 1959-60, dir. 1970-75, ex-officio 1980-85, cert. excellence 1982). Club: Caxton (Chgo.) (council 1981-84). Home: 1440 Sheridan Rd #506 Wilmette IL 60091-1857

BLAKE, JOSEPH ALFRED, sociology and social psychology educator, researcher, consultant; b. Ware, Mass., Nov. 24, 1938; s. Joseph Maxim and Dorothy Lillian (Decoteau) B.; m. Dorothy Louise Nixon, Feb. 23, 1963; children—Adrienne Dorothy, Joseph Ervin. A.S., Jr. Coll. Broward County, 1965; B.A., Fla. Atlantic U., 1967; M.A., Northwestern U., 1969, Ph.D., 1973. Asst. prof. U. N.Mex., Albuquerque, 1971-73; asst. prof. Va. Poly. Inst. and State U., Blacksburg, 1973-78; vis. asst. prof. Wright State U., Dayton, Ohio, 1979; asst. prof. sociology and social psychology Ind. U.-East, Richmond, 1980-83, assoc. prof., 1984—; dir., project mgr. Ind. Area IX Agy. on Aging Needs Assessment Project; CD cons. on human response to disaster. Mem. Ind. Area IX Agy. on Aging Policy Bd.; mem. Miami Valley (Ohio) Gerontology Council. Served with U.S. Army, 1958-60. Mem. Inter-Univ. Seminar on Armed Forces and Soc., Am. Sociol. Assn., Ind. Acad. Social Scis., Soc. Sci. Exploration. Contbr. articles on collective behavior, war and mil., organizational behavior and sociology of knowledge to profl. jours. Home: 6835 Hubbard Dr Dayton OH 45424 Office: Ind U-East Richmond IN 47374

BLAKE, MICHAEL JAMES, computer product executive; b. Chgo., Apr. 11, 1956; s. James Richard and Sharon Marie (Schreiber) B.; m. Janice Lynn Grady, Oct. 9, 1982. BA in Acctg., Lewis U., 1983, MBA, 1985; grad. exec. program, De Paul U., 1987. Mgr. Silverman's Mens Wear at Woodfield, Schaumburg, Ill., 1976-80; product mgr. AT&T Co., Lisle, Ill., 1980-87; pres. Games By James, Plymouth, Minn., 1987—, also bd. dirs.; cons. Found. Window Systems, Park Forest, Ill., 1984—; mem. adv. bd. Lewis U. MBA Program, Romeoville, Ill., 1983-85. Dir. Operation Santa Charity Run, Lisle, 1985, 86, 87; mem. adv. bd. MBA programLewis U., Romeoville, Ill., 1983-85. Republican. Roman Catholic. Clubs: We Ski (Lisle) (pres. 1982—), Sunjoy Triathlon (Wheaton, Ill.). Avocations: skiing, triathlons, track, softball. Office: Games by James Store 2495 Xenium Ln Plymouth MN 55441

BLAKE, NORMAN PERKINS, JR., financial services company executive; b. N.Y.C., Nov. 8, 1941; s. Norman Perkins and Eleanor (Adams) B.; m. Karen Cromwell, Sept. 12, 1965; children: Kellie, Kimberly, Adam. BA, Purdue U., 1965, MA, 1966; postgrad., Washington U., St. Louis, 1966-67, 71. With Gen. Electric Co., 1967-74, 76—; mgr. strategic planning ops., plastics bus. div. Gen. Electric Co., Pittsfield, Mass., 1976-78, mgr. bus. devel. consumer products and services sector, 1978-79; staff exec. Gen. Electric Co., Fairfield, Conn., 1979; v.p., gen. mgr. comml. and indsl. fin. div. Gen. Elec. Credit Corp., Stamford, Conn., 1979-81, exec. v.p. financing ops., 1981-84; chmn. and chief exec. officer Heller Internat. Corp., Chgo., 1984—; with Top, Inc., Troy, Mich., 1974-76, pres., 1976. Office: Heller Fin Inc 200 N LaSalle St Chicago IL 60601

BLAKE, ROBERT, minister; b. Milan, Ohio, Nov. 10, 1949; s. Dean Orville and Helen Ann (Gehring) B.; m. Rebecca May Keys, June 22, 1974; children: Elizabeth, Bonnie, Brittany. Diploma, Moody Bible Inst., 1975; BA, Trinity Coll., 1976; MDiv, Earlham Sch. Religion, 1983. Ordained recorded friends pastor, Aug. 1983. Pastor Arba Friends Meeting, Lynn, Ind., 1976-83, Spiceland (Ind.) Friends Meeting, 1983—; mem. denominationl bd. Ind. Ministry and Membership Commn., 1980—. Republican. Lodge: Lions. Avocation: auto mechanic, woodworking, genealogy. Home: 437 W Main St Spiceland IN 47385 Office: Spiceland Friends Meeting 401 W Main St Spiceland IN 47385

BLAKE, RUTH RICHARDS, real estate developer; b. Kansas City, Mo., Jan. 11, 1926; d. Alva Kenneth and Anna Jane Richards; m. Russell Storr Blake, Jan. 19, 1946; children—Rhayma Ann, Roger Thomas, Brian Richard. B.A., U. Mo., Columbia, 1945, M.A., Kansas City, 1954. Pres., Blake Devel. Co., Kansas City, Mo., 1968—; part owner, dir. RMI Media Prodns., Inc., Kansas City, Mo., 1967-83; mem. consumer adv. planning group Kansas City Power & Light Co., 1984—. Bd. dirs. Susan B. Anthony Found., 1980-82, Mo. Corp. Sci. and Tech., 1983—, CORO Found., 1983—; chmn. Jackson County Econ. Devel. Commn., 1980-83, mem., 1977-83.; chmn. alumni support group Mo. Council Pub. Higher Edn., 1979-81; chmn. bd. dirs. Kansas City Civic Orch., 1971-75; bd. dirs., founding mem. Dimensions Unltd., 1973-79; mem. adminstrv. bd. Central United Meth. Ch.; trustee Kansas City Mus., 1986—. Recipient Community Service award U. Mo. Kansas City, 1974, Alumni Achievement award 1963. Mem. U. Mo. Alumni Alliance (chmn. 1980-82), Greater Kansas City C. of C. (dir. 1977-80, chmn. govt. relations council 1978-80, chmn. state affairs com. 1977), Nat. Assn. Women Bus. Owners (v.p. Mid-Am. chpt. 1979), U. Mo. Kansas City Alumni Assn. (pres. 1968), Kansas City Met. Jr. Coll. Found., 1985—, Women's C. of C. Greater Kansas City (v.p. 1971), Music Tchrs. Nat. Assn., Sigma Alpha Iota. Methodist. Office: Blake Devel Co 12632 Baltimore Ct Kansas City MO 64145

BLAKE, WILLIAM HENRY, credit and public relations consultant; b. Jasonville, Ind., Feb. 18, 1913; s. Straude and Cora (Pope) B.; m. Helen Elizabeth Platt, Jan. 2, 1937; children—William Henry, Allen Howard. Student, Knox Coll., 1932-35; B.S., U. Ill., 1936, M.S., 1941, postgrad., 1946; student, N.Y. U., 1950-51, Am. U., 1955-56, 1958; grad., Columbia U. Grad. Sch. Consumer Credit, 1956, Northeastern Inst., Yale U., 1957. Tchr. Champaign (Ill.) Pub. Schs., 1936-41; exec. sec. Ill. Soc. C.P.A.s, Chgo., 1941-44; dean men, assoc. prof. bus. adminstrn. Catawba Coll., 1947-51; dir. research Nat. Consumer Fin. Assn., Washington, 1954-59; exec. v.p. Internat. Consumer Credit Assn., St. Louis, 1959-78; pres. Consumer Trends Inc., also Blake Enterprises, cons., 1978—; cons. Decatur Consumer Credit Assn., 1979—; adminstr. Soc. Cert. Consumer Credit Execs., 1961-78. Author: Good Things of Life on Credit, 1960, rev., 1975, How to Use Consumer Credit Wisely, 1963, rev., 1975, Home Study Courses in Credit and Collections, 1968, Human Relations, 1969, Communications, 1970, Retail Credit and Collections, rev., 1974, Adminstrative Office Management, 1972, Consumer Credit Management, 1974; pub.: Consumer Trends Newsletter. Mem. pres.'s adv. cabinet Southeastern U.; adviser Office Edn. Assn.; chmn. public relations com. Ill. Heart Assn., 1979—; bd. dirs. Salvation Army, Decatur, 1979—; mem. fund raising com. Sch. Edn., U. Ill., 1979—; chmn. bd. trustees Alta Deana div. University City, 1970-73, congressional liaison, 1959-78; trustee Internat. Consumer Credit Assn. Ins. Trust and Retirement Program, 1960-78. Served to lt. USNR, 1944-47; lt. comdr. 1951-54. Named Man of Year Mo. Consumer Credit Assn., 1977. Mem. Credit Grantors Assn. Can. (dir. 1959-72), U.S. C. of C. (banking and currency com. 1968-71, trade assn. com. 1964-67), Am. Soc. Assn. Execs. (dir. 1965-68), Public Relations Soc. Am. (chpt. treas. 1979—), Press Club St. Louis, Internat. Platform Assn., Am. Soc. Assn. Execs., Washington Trade Assn. Execs., Am. Public Relations Assn. (chpt. pres. 1958-59), U. Ill. Alumni Assn., Phi Sigma Kappa. Republican. Presbyterian. Clubs: Capitol Hill (Washington), Exchequer (Washington). Lodge: Rotary (pres. Decatur 1985-86). Home and Office: 5 Edgewood Ct Decatur IL 62522

BLAKELY, GIVEN OBED, data processing executive; b. Evansville, Ind., Nov. 3, 1935; s. Fred Orville and Rubye W. (Burnham) B.; m. Adanna LeDean Matias, Mar. 17, 1956 (dec. Jan. 1979); children: Pamela, Michelle, Rochelle, Michael, Leah, Mark; m. June Ellen Raymond, June 16, 1980; children: Adah, Benjamin, Jonathan, Eva. BA, Lincoln (Ill.) Christian Sem., 1956; postgrad., Ind. U., 1960, Purdue U., 1964. Cost acct. Simmons Co., Munster, Ind., 1958-60; fin. acct. Lever Bros. Co., Hammond, Ind., 1960-71, supr. maintenance, 1971-73, supr. payroll, data processing, 1973-78, dir. mgmt. info. systems, 1978—. Editor The Word of Truth, Cedar Lake, Ind., 1957—. Minister Pilgrim Tabernacle, Merrillville, Ind., 1960—. Mem. Am. Mgmt. Assn. Avocation: photography. Home: 10701 W 124th Ave Cedar Lake IN 46303

BLAKEMORE, WILLIAM ROSS, communications company executive; b. San Antonio, July 27, 1944; s. James Edward and Margaret Elizabeth (Wylie) B.; m. Shirley Ilene Johns, Mar. 20, 1971; children—William Scott, Bethany Brooke. B.B.A. in Personnel Mgmt., North Tex. State U., 1966. Sales rep. Word Inc., Waco, Tex., 1970-71; owner, mgr. Agape Booksellers, Jackson, Mich., 1971-84; dist. sales mgr. Thomas Nelson Publishers, Nashville, Tenn., 1984—. Treas., Christian Bus. Men's Com., Jackson, Mich., 1977, South Central Youth for Christ, Jackson, 1982-86. Served with USN, 1967-68. Republican. Free Methodist. Avocations: sailing, reading, tennis. Home: 6110 Browns Lake Rd Jackson MI 49203

BLAKESLEY, WAYNE LAVERE, JR., production engineer; b. Goshen, Ind., Mar. 26, 1926; s. Wayne L. Blakesley Sr. and Thelma (Brown) Cobb. Test engr. Bendix Missile Div., Mishawaka, Ind., 1952-53, engring. tech., 1955-59; field engr. RCA Service Co., Camden, N.J., 1953-55; design engr. Crown Internat., Elkhart, Ind., 1959-72, prodn. engr., 1979—; pres. Blakesley Electronics, Syracuse, Ind., 1972-78. Inventor, designer automated system for radio stas., printed circuit bd. prototyping system, printed circuit bd. multilayer overlay; designer multi-unit electronic learning lab. Mem. So. Mfg. Engrs. (sr. mem. Robotics Internat. div.), Mensa, Intertel. Avocation: public speaking. Home: PO Box 53 Syracuse IN 46567 Office: Crown Internat 1718 Mishawaka Rd Elkhart IN 46517

BLAKSLEE, GEORGE WARREN, retired geologist; b. Llanerch, Pa., July 12, 1921; s. Leigh Wallace and Grace Belle (Lamb) B., Sr.; m. Kathleen Jeanette Peterson, Sept. 16, 1948; children—Warren Leigh, Sharon Lee Blakslee Curtis. B.A., Pa. State U., 1943; postgrad. U. Pa., 1946, Pa. State U., 1951. Geologist, ARAMCO, Dhahran, Saudi Arabia, 1946-51; subsurface geologist Tidewater Assoc. Oil, Regina, Sask., Can., 1952-57, Ankara, Turkey, 1957-60, Tidewater Oil Co., Madrid, 1960, chief geologist, Karachi, Pakistan, 1960-62, gen. mgr., 1962-63; liaison rep. Getty Oil Co., Tehran, Iran, 1963-65, chief geologist, 1965-67, mgr. dir., 1967-70; mng. dir. Getty Petroleum Co., Algiers, Algeria, 1970-73; chief geologist internat. div., Los Angeles, 1973-77; dir. Bank of Brodhead, Wis. Contbg. Author: Jurassic and Carboniferous of Western Canada, 1958. Trustee Greenwood Cemetery, Brodhead, 1980—; town bd. supr.. Decatur Twp., Green County, Wis., 1980-85. Served to 2d lt. USAAF, 1943-46. Fellow Royal Geog. Soc.; mem. Pa. State Alumni Assn., Nat. Holstein-Friesian Assn., Wis. Holstein-Friesian Assn., Am. Assn. Petroleum Geologists, Wis. Farm Bur., Am. Legion (comdr. Gehr post 1984), Phi Kappa Sigma. Republican. Episcopalian. Clubs: Karachi Yacht (Pakistan) (life); Decatur Lake Country (Brodhead)(v.p., bd. dirs.). Lodge: Lions (Pakistan) (charter) (Brodhead) (v.p., bd. dirs. 1978-84). Avocations: golf; photography; history; travel; painting. Home: N 3976 Park Rd Brodhead WI 53520

BLAKUT, MITCHELL ANTHONY, manufacturing company executive; b. Chgo., Feb. 15, 1921; s. Anthony and Anna (Ducal) B.; student North Park Coll., 1950; m. May 1, 1943; children—Mary Ann, Charles Mitchell. Process and mfg. engring. Pioneer Tool Co., Chgo., 1958-61; sr. process engr. Pyle Nat. Co., Chgo., 1961-64; quality control supr. Bell & Howell Co., Chgo., from 1964; then with Memorex-Bell & Howell Home Video, Northbrook, Ill; now cons. in field. Served with Inf., AUS, 1944-46. Asst. scoutmaster, commr. Chgo. Area council Boy Scouts Am. Mem. Soc. Mfg. Engrs. (v.p., cert. mfg. engr.), Am. Soc. Quality Control, Internat. Biog. Assn. Democrat. Roman Catholic. Registered profl. engr., Calif. Home: 5725 N Marmora St Chicago IL 60646 Office: 3055 MacArthur Blvd Northbrook IL 60062

BLAMEY, RICHARD LYLE, accountant; b. Fond du Lac, Wis., Dec. 13, 1941; s. Lyle Donald and Lucille Hazel (Immel) B.; B.B.A., U. Wis., 1964; m. Ann-Elizabeth McCallum, Aug. 14, 1976; children—Richard Scott, Heather Lynn, Jennifer Ann. CPA, Wis. Staff acct. Ronald Mattox & Assos., Madison, Wis., 1965-71, audit mgr., Fond du Lac, 1971-74, ptnr., 1974-75; ptnr. Alexander Grant & Co., Fond du Lac, 1975-85, v.p. K.W. Muth Co., 1985—; treas. Am. Woodstock Co., 1987—; v.p., treas. Ledgeview Devel. Corp., Fond du Lac, 1971-77, pres., 1977—; ptnr. Mt. Calvary Assos., 1979—. Mem. Fond du Lac Civic Center Com., 1972—; adviser Jr. Achievement, 1974-75; chmn. accts. div. Dane County United Fund drive, 1970-71; first reader First Ch. of Christ Scientist, Fond du Lac, 1975-78, second reader, 1987, chmn. bd., 1980-81; bd. dirs., treas. Student Cen. Found., Madison, 1969-71. Mem. Nat. Assn. Accts. (pres. Sheboyan Lakeshore chpt. 1977-78), Wis. Inst. C.P.A.s, (chmn. practice mgmt. com. and seminar 1972), Fond du Lac Jaycees (v.p. 1974-75), U. Wis. Alumni Assn. (pres. 1977-78). Republican. Clubs: Pinn Hills Country (treas. 1978-81), Wis. Region Classic Car, Antique Auto Club Am. Home: Route 4 Ledgeview Springs Fond du Lac WI 54935 Office: Box 909 Sheboygan WI 53081

BLAN, KENNITH WILLIAM, JR., lawyer; b. Detroit, Dec. 15, 1946; s. Kennith William and Sarah Shirley (Shane) B.; m. Rebbeca Jo McCraken, Mar. 6, 1981; 1 son, Noah Winton. B.S., U. Ill., 1968, J.D., 1971. Bar: Ill. 1972, U.S. Supreme Ct. 1978. With Office State's Atty., Vermilion County, Ill., 1971-72; atty. Chgo. Title & Trust Co., 1972; asso. firm Graham, Meyer, Young, Welsch & Maton, Chgo., Springfield and Danville, Ill., 1972-74; individual practice law, Danville, 1975—; spl. asst. atty. gen. Ill., 1974-76; atty. City of Georgetown, Ill., 1985— . Chmn. Vermilion County Young Republican Club, 1975-77; founding sponsor Civil Justice Found.; capt. CAP. Mem. ABA, Ill. Bar Assn., Vermilion County Bar Assn., Lawyer-Pilots Bar Assn., Assn. Trial Lawyers Am., Ill. Trial Lawyers Assn., Ind. Trial Lawyers Assn., Am. Soc. Law and Medicine. Republican. Mem. Ch. of Christ. Club: Danville Country. Lodge: Elks. Office: Towne Ctr Suite 206 2 E Main St Danville IL 61832

BLANCHARD, JAMES J., governor; b. Detroit, Aug. 8, 1942; m. Paula Parker; 1 son, Jay. B.A., M.B.A., Mich. State U., Lansing; J.D., U. Minn. Bar: Mich. 1968. Legal aid elections bur. Office Sec. State, State of Mich., 1968-69; asst. atty. gen. State of Mich., 1969-74, adminstrv. asst. to atty. gen., 1970-71, asst. dep. atty. gen., 1971-72; mem. 94th-96th Congresses from 18th Mich. Dist.; gov. State of Mich., 1983—; mem. Pres.'s Commn. on Holocaust. Mem. Oakland County exec. club Mich. State U. Mem. Assn. Asst. Attys. Gen., Ferndale Jaycees, State Bar Mich., Am. Bar Assn., LWV, U. Minn. Law Sch. Alumni Club, U. Detroit Titan Club. Democrat. Office: Office of the Governor State Capitol Lansing MI 48933 *

BLANCHARD, THOMAS EARLE, business owner, consultant; b. Schenectady, Mar. 14, 1943; s. Edward W. and Elanor A. (Butler) B.; m. Janet Lee Marsh, Oct. 10, 1946; children: Marcy Lee, Michael Thomas. AAS, Paul Smith's Coll., 1964. Regional credit ctr. mgr. W.T. Grant Co., Albany, N.Y., 1964-72, store mgr., 1972-75; distbn. mgr. Central Warehouse Corp., Albany, 1975-80; gen. mgr. Toledo Cold Storage Inc., 1980-81; chmn., pres. Great Lakes Cold Storage Inc., Toledo, 1981—, Blanchard Oil Co., 1984—, Jiffy Mart Inc., 1983—, cons. Served with Air N.G., 1964-70. Mem. Internat. Assn. Refrigerated Warehouses, Toledo Chamber of Commerce, Maumee Valley Petroleum Dealers Assn., Ohio Petroleum Mktg. Assn., Toledo Area Small Bus. Assn. Home: 2383 Hubbard Rd Monroe MI 48161 Office: 355 Morris St Toledo OH 43602

BLANCHETTE, THOMAS LAROUX, marketing and sales executive; b. Oneida, N.Y., Aug. 28, 1950; s. Napoleon Joseph and Ruth (Hiller) B.; m. Cathy Marie Riva, Oct. 2, 1976. Student, Wabash Coll., 1969-71; BA, St. Lawrence U., 1973; MBA, U. Conn., 1976. Sales rep. Shaw Walker, Hartford, Conn., 1974-79; mktg. mgr. Shaw Walker, Muskegon, Mich., 1979-83; dir. product devel. and mktg. communication Domore, Elkhart, Ind., 1983-84; dir. sales and mktg. Montisa Office Furniture, Greenville, Mich., 1984—. Recipient Creativity Eighty Distinction award Art Dir. mag., 1980, Bronze Product Design award Inst. Bus. designers and Contract mag., 1985. Mem. Nat. Office Products Assn. Republican. Roman Catholic. Club: Western Mich. Brittany (pres. 1985—). Avocation: raising and training bird dogs. Home: 7190 Camino Del Rey Rockford MI 49341 Office: Montisa Office Furniture 701 Ranney Dr Greenville MI 48838

BLANCHLEY, BONNIE L., television producer; b. Washington, Aug. 23, 1958; d. Joseph Hugh and Aleta Romain (Troutman) B. BA, U. Wis., Milw., 1980. Entertainment reporter news focus Sta. WVTV-TV, Milw., 1979-81, newscaster, 1981-82, morning show host, producer, 1982-85, producer, host 18 Video St., 1984—; movie critic, show host Take Two Carmichael Communications, Chgo., 1983-84. Methodist. Avocations: golf, running, sculpting. Home: 7440 N Granville Rd #8 Milwaukee WI 53224 Office: Sta WVTV-TV 4041 N 35th St Milwaukee WI 53201

BLAND, ROBERT DANIEL, educator; b. Terre Haute, Ind., Aug. 23, 1937; s. William Frank and Pearl Averil (Morgan) B.; B.S., Ball State U., 1960, M.S., 1964; Ph.D., U. Minn., 1971; m. Mary Ellen Anderson, July 28, 1968; children—Cynthia, Stephanie. Coordinator gen. biol. program U. Minn., Mpls., 1970-74; faculty dept. biology Coll. St. Thomas, St. Paul, 1974—. Author: General Biology Laboratory Guide, 1973; Freshwater Biology, 1974; Dissertation Abstracts, 1971; contbr. articles to profl. jours. Home: 1639 Ridgewood Ln Saint Paul MN 55113 Office: Dept Biology Coll of St Thomas Saint Paul MN 55105

BLANEY, DENNIS JOSEPH, priest; b. East Chicago, Ind., Aug. 26, 1932; s. Joseph and Esther (Krieger) B. Student, Our Lady of the Lake Coll., Wawasee, Ind.; BA in Philosophy, Mt. St. Mary's of the West, Cin., 1954. Ordained priest Roman Cath. Ch., 1958. Parish priest, high sch. tchr. Hammond, Ind., 1958-64; parish priest St. Patrick's Ch., Chesterton, Ind., 1964-67, St. Thomas Ch., Munster, Ind., 1967-70; parish priest, pastor Sacred Heart Ch., Michigan City, Ind., 1970—; coordinator Apostolate for Handicapped, Gary, Ind. Diocese, 1970—, Friends Club, 1978—, Respite Care, 1980—, Share Found., 1982—. Named Humanitarian of Yr. Mich. City, Ind., 1986; recipient State Gov. Profl.-in-Service with Handicapped award, 1986, St. Joseph the Worker award Bd. Dirs. Calumet Coll. of St. Joseph, 1987. Mem. Nat. Cath. Edn. Assn., Ind. Coordinating Council, Ind. State Assn. Cerebral Palsy, Nat. Assn. Retarded Citizens, Nat. Apostolate Mentally Retarded, Assn. Deaf in Vocat. Rehab. (state adv. bd.), Ind. Assn. Retarded Citizens (bd. dirs.). Home and Office: 1001 W 8th St Michigan City IN 46360

BLANK, RICHARD JOHN, radiologist; b. Wausau, Wis., Jan. 5, 1938; s. Eylward Russel and Vivian Delores (Salscheider) B.; m. Patricia Kathryn Paul, Sept. 7, 1963; children: Lisa, John, Michael, Matthew. BS, U. Wis., 1960; MD, Marquette U., 1964. Diplomate Am. Bd. Radiology, Am. Bd. Nuclear Medicine. Asst. prof. U. Wis., Madison, 1970-71; staff radiologist Sacred Heart Hosp., Eau Claire, Wis., 1971-72; staff radiologist Grand Forks (N.D.) Clinic, 1973—, chmn. radiology, 1975—, also bd. dirs.; mem. staff United Hosp., chmn. radiology, 1974-80, 1982—. Served to capt. USAF, 1965-67. Fellow Am. Coll. Radiology (pres. N.D. 1985—, councilor 1980-85); mem. AMA, Radiol. Soc. N.Am., N.D. Med. Assn. Roman Catholic. Lodge: Elks. Avocation: fishing. Home: 3207 Walnut St Grand Forks ND 58201 Office: Grand Forks Clinic 1000 S Columbia Grand Forks ND 58201

BLANK, WALLACE JAMES, manufacturing executive; b. Neenah, Wis., Apr. 16, 1929; s. Julius August and Caroline Ann (Werner) B.; B.S. in Mech. Engring., U. Wis., 1952; m. Margaret Mary Schultz, June 7, 1958. Registered profl. engr., Wis. Staff engr. Fairbanks Morse & Co., Beloit, Wis., 1952-59; sr. engr. Thiokol Chem. Co., 1960, N. Am. Aviation Atomics, internat. div., 1961; dir. mil. engring. FWD Corp., Clintonville, Wis., 1962-68; tech. dir. Oshkosh Truck Corp. (Wis.), 1968-74, v.p. engring., 1974—. Patentee in field of truck suspensions and transmissions. Mem. Soc. Auto Engrs., Am. Def.

Preparedness Assn., Assn. U.S. Army, Air Force Assn. Roman Catholic. Home: 5352 Iahmaytah Rd Oshkosh WI 54901 Office: 2300 Oregon St Oshkosh WI 54903

BLANKENBAKER, RONALD GAIL, physician; b. Rensselaer, Ind., Dec. 1, 1941; s. Lloyd L. and Lovina (Anderson) B. B.S. in Biology, Purdue U., 1963; M.D., Ind U., 1968, M.S. in Pharmacology, 1970. Diplomate: Am. Bd. Family Practice. Intern Meth. Hosp. Grad. Med. Center, Indpls., 1968-69; resident in family practice Meth. Hosp. Grad. Med. Center, 1969-71; med. dir. Indpls. Home for Aged, 1971-77, Am. Mid-Town Nursing Center, Indpls., 1974-77, Home Assn., Tampa, Fla., 1977-79; asst. prof. family practice Ind. U., Indpls., 1973-77, clin. prof., 1980—, clin. prof. sch. nursing, 1986—; asst. dean for St. Vincent Hosp., Ind. U., Indpls., 1985—; v.p. med. affairs St. Vincent Hosp. and Health Care Ctr., 1984—; prof. dept. family medicine U. South Fla., Tampa, 1977-79, chmn. dept., 1977-79; health commr. State of Ind.; sec. Ind. State Bd. Health, Indpls., 1979-84; dir. family practice edn. Meth. Hosp. Grad. Med. Center, 1971-77; family practice editor Reference and Index Services, Inc., Indpls., 1976-77, sr. editor, 1977-79; legis. lobbyist Ind. Acad. Family Physicians, 1973-77; med. advisor New Hope Found. Am., Inc., 1974-79. Bd. dirs. Meals on Wheels, Inc., Peoples Health Center Indpls., Marion County Cancer Soc., Ind. Sports Corp.; mem. Ind. Gov.'s Council Phys. Fitness and Sports Medicine, Nat. Com. on Vital and Health Stats., 1984—, chmn., 1986—, Marion County Heart Assn.; mem. med. commn. Pan Am. Sports Orgn., 1985—; pres., bd. dirs. Hoosier Safety Council, 1985—, Hoosiers for Safety Belts, 1986—; med. coordinator Nat. Sports Festival IV, 1983; chief drug control team U.S. Olympic Com., 1986—; co-chmn. med. services Pan Am. Games X, 1987. Served to col. USAFR, 1971—. Recipient Disting. Service award Ind. Pub. Health Assn., 1984; Decorated Meritorious Service medal; recipient Service to Mankind award Sertoma Club, 1975, Outstanding Alumnus award Mt. Ayr (Ind.) High Sch., 1976, Sen. Lugar's Health Excellence award, 1983, Pub. Health excellence award Marion County Health Dept., 1984; named a Sagamore of the Wabash by Gov. of Ind., 1980, 84. Fellow Am. Acad. Family Physicians, Am. Coll. Preventive Medicine, Soc. Prospective Medicine (pres., dir.); mem. AMA, Ind. State Med. Assn., Marion County Med. Soc. (bd. dirs.), Ind. Acad. Family Physicians (v.p. 1977, bd. dirs., pres. 1987—), Ind. Allied Health Assn. (pres. 1973-74), Ind. Acad. Sci., Ind. Pub. Health Assn., Soc. Tchrs. Family Medicine, Ind. Assn. Pub. Health Physicians, Ind. Arthritis Found. (bd. dirs.), Orgn. Am. States, World Med. Assn., Aerospace Med. Assn., Ptnrs. for the Ams., Ind. Lung Assn. (bd. dirs.), Assn. Am. Med. Colls., Assn. Depts. Family Medicine, Fla. Acad. Family Physicians (bd. dirs.). Republican. Office: St Vincent Hosp 2001 W 86th St PO Box 40970 Indianapolis IN 46240-0970

BLANKENSHIP, RICHARD EUGENE, marketing representative; b. Steubenville, Ohio, July 20, 1948; s. Alonzo Willard and Virginia Cornelia (Sczcepkowski) B.; m. Teresa Lee Lowry, Mar. 17, 1978 (div. June 1981). BS in Aerospace Engring., W.Va. U., 1971; student, U. Mo., 1972-73; MBA, San Diego State U., 1978; student, U. Kans., 1980. Civil engr. Starvaggi Industries, Inc., Wierton, W.Va., 1971-72; commd. U.S. Army, 1975-81, advanced through grades to capt., 1976; analysis officer Combined Arms Ctr., U.S. Army, Ft. Leavenworth, Kans., 1981-83, program mgr., 1981-83; resigned U.S. Army, 1983; prin. mktg. rep. Honeywell Ind., Mpls., 1983—; cons. Mead Resources Inc., Mpls. Author: Heavy Divisions, 1982. Vol. Spl. Olympics, Minnetonka, Minn., 1984, 1985. Decorated Oak Leaf Cluster. Mem. Am. Def. Preparedness Assn., Assn. U.S. Army, Minn. Orchestral Assn. (fund raiser 1985-87). Republican. Roman Catholic. Avocations: photography, music, basketball, golf. Home: 21 Luverne Ave S Minneapolis MN 55419 Office: Honeywell Inc 5640 Smetana Dr Minnetonka MN 55343

BLANKENSHIP, SAMMY DELANO, computer specialist, educator; b. Chattanooga, Mar. 25, 1936; s. William Doyle and Daisy Irene (Alford) B.; B.S., Murray State U., 1960, M.S. 1968; postgrad. (Bus. Research fellow) Ind. U., 1976-77, Miss. State U., 1978; m. Shirley Elaine Morlock, Sept. 10, 1955; children—Susan Elaine, James Kelley. Systems engr. IBM, Evansville, Ind., 1968-69; tchr. Evansville-Vanderburgh Sch. Corp., 1969-70; systems rep. Honeywell Info. Systems, Evansville, 1970: asst. prof. in bus. Ind. State U., Evansville, 1970-81; sr. applications specialist Gen. Electric Co., 1981-84; chmn. info. systems dept. IVTC Region 13 1984-85; pres. SBCS, Inc., 1985—; info. systems cons. to bus., govt. and edn. Precinct committeeman Democratic Party, Vanderburgh County, 1978—; mem. Vanderburgh County Election Bd., 1978-79; candidate Ind. Legislature, 1972. Methodist. Lodges: Masons, Elks, Lions. Contbr. articles to newspapers and Midwest Bus. Adminstrn. Assn. Home: Rural Route 1 Box 351C Evansville IN 47712 Office: 2401 McDowell Rd Evansville IN 47712

BLANKENSHIP, VIRGINIA RADER, psychology educator; b. Washington, Ind., Jan. 2, 1945; d. Owen Richard and Kathleen Virginia (Eads) Rader; m. Timothy Sims, Feb. 8, 1963; 1 son, Mark Alan; m. 2d, Bruce Blankenship, May 25, 1974. B.S., Ind. State U., 1974, Ph.D., U. Mich., 1979. Asst. prof. sch. edn. Ind. U., Bloomington, 1979-81; asst. prof. psychology, coordinator women's studies program Oakland U., Rochester, Mich., 1981—. Recipient Spencer Found. award, 1980. Mem. Am. Psychol. Assn., Am. Ednl. Research Assn., Internat. Soc. for Study Behavioral Devel., Sigma Xi. Democrat. Contbr. articles to profl. jours. Home: 30701 Stellamar St Birmingham MI 48010 Office: Dept Psychology Oakland U Rochester MI 48309-4401

BLANKSHAIN, JEFFREY RICHARD, dentist; b. Elmhurst, Ill., Oct. 10, 1954; s. Richard Harvey and Ruth Anna (Boyer) B.; m. Diane Frances Zwinn, Nov. 14, 1982; 1 child, Christopher Jeffrey. BA, Emory U., 1976; DDS, U. Ill., 1980. Gen. practice dentistry Oak Park, Ill., 1980—; staff dentist Oak Park-River Forest Infant Welfare Soc., Oak Park, 1984—. Bd. dirs. Oak Park-River Forest (Ill.) C. of C., 1982-83, Oak Park-River Forest unit Am. Cancer Soc. Mem. Chgo. Dental Soc., Ill. State Dental Soc., ADA. Home: 1604 S Brophy Park Ridge IL 60068 Office: 1 Erie Ct Suite 6160 Oak Park IL 60302

BLANTON, HELEN IRENE, nurse; b. Maryville, Tenn., Jan. 12, 1946; d. William Justian and Emily Irene (Hendry) B. Diploma, St. Mary's Sch. Nursing, Knoxville, 1967; B.S., U. Md., 1977; M.S., U. So. Calif., 1979; M.A., Webster Coll., 1981; M.A., Webster U., 1984. Staff nurse operating room U. Tenn. Hosp., 1967-68; from staff nurse to supr. hosps. U.S. Army, U.S., Vietnam, W.Ger., 1968-80; asst. chief nursing service Hines (Ill.) VA Hosp., 1981-83, utilization rev. mgr., 1983—; adj. prof. Surgical Tech. Program, Triton Coll. Res. dep. sheriff Lake County, Ill. Served to capt. U.S. Army, 1968-80, to maj. Res. Decorated Bronze Star, Vietnam Cross Gallantry, Vietnam Civic Action medal. Mem. Assn. Operating Room Nurses (cert.), Assn. Advancement Med. Instrumentation, Am. Nurses Assn. (cert.), Nat. Assn. Quality Assurance Profls. (cert.), Ill. Assn. Quality Assurance Profls., Res. Officers Assn. (life). Contbr. articles to profl. jours. Home: PO Box 351 Mundelein IL 60060 Office: 00A3 Hines VA Hosp Hines IL 60141

BLANTON, LEONARD FRANKLIN, educational consultant; b. Long Beach, Calif., May 16, 1944; s. Alvin Hamilton and Helen (Scrivner) B.; m. Chrystal Conant, Apr. 26, 1975; children: Paul Hamilton, Troy Franklin. BS Indsl. Tech., Berea Coll., 1967; M in Pub. Adminstrn., Ohio State U., 1974; MBA, Capital U., 1981. Supr. Ohio Employment and Tng., Columbus, 1976-78, dir. planning, 1978-80, state dir., 1980-83; cons. LFB & Assocs., Worthington, Ohio, 1983—; researcher Nat. Ctr. for Research, Columbus, 1985-86; ednl. cons. OHio Dept. of Edn., Columbus, 1986—; dir. Ohio Mgmt. and Tng. Assn., Columbus, 1980-83. Pres. Colonial Hills Civic Assn., Worthington, 1978-82; bd. dirs. Worthington Christian Ch., 1985—. Served with USAF, 1968-72. Recipient Columbus Area Leadership award, 1981; named one of Outstanding Young Men Am., 1979, 80. Mem. Am. Vocat. Assn., Ohio Vocat. Assn., Am. Soc. of Pub. Adminstrn., Ohio Manpower Assn. (bd. dirs. 1981-83), Columbus Area Leadership Alumni. Republican. Club: 356 Registry (Columbus). Home: 541 Meadoway Park Worthington OH 43085 Office: State Dept of Edn 65 S Front St Columbus OH 43215

BLASCHKE, RICHARD CRAIG, manufacturing executive; b. Milw., July 18, 1951; s. Richard Franklin and Joan Mae (Satek) B.; m. Barbara Jean Marnocha, Aug. 13, 1973 (div. Aug. 1978); 1 child, Matthew James; m. Helen Linda Noggle, Nov. 29, 1982; 1 child, Melissa Susan. Student, Ind. U., South Bend, 1969-70, 73-74, 77, 86—. Dir. mfg. engring. DePuy div. Boehringer Mannheim Corp., Warsaw, Ind., 1968-78; adv. bd. CAD/CAM Inst., Ft. Wayne, Ind., 1985—; bd. advisors Project Start, Ft. Wayne, 1985—. Roman Catholic. Home: Rural Rt 2 Box 159A Claypool IN 46510 Office: DePuy div Boehringer Mannheim Corp PO Box 988 Warsaw IN 46580

BLASCO, ALFRED JOSEPH, business and financial Consultant; b. Kansas City, Mo., Oct. 9, 1904; s. Joseph and Mary (Bevacqua) B.; m. Kathryn Oleno, June 28, 1926; children: Barbara Blasco Lowry, Phyllis Blasco O'Connor. Student, Kansas City Sch. Accountancy, 1921-25, Am. Inst. Banking, 1926-30; Ph.D. (hon.), Avila Coll., 1969. From office boy to asst. controller Commerce Trust Co., Kansas City, Mo., 1921-35; controller Interstate Securities Co., Kansas City, 1935-45; v.p. Interstate Securities Co., 1945-53, pres., 1953—, chmn. bd., 1961-68; sr. v.p. ISC Fin. Corp., 1968-69, hon. chmn. bd., 1970-77, pres., 1979—; chmn. bd. Red Bridge Bank, 1966-72; Mark Plaza State Bank, Overland Park, Kans., 1973-77; spl. lectr. consumer credit Columbia U., N.Y.C., 1956, U. Kans., Lawrence, 1963-64. Contbr. articles to profl. jours. Pres. Cath. Community Library, 1955-56; Mem. Fair Public Accomodations Com., Kansas City, Mo., 1964-68; ward committeeman, 1972-76; pres., hon. bd. dirs. Baptist Meml. Hosp., 1970-74; chmn. bd. dirs. St. Anthony's Home, 1965-69; chmn. bd. trustees Avila Coll., 1969—. Decorated papal knight Equestrian Order Holy Sepulchre of Jerusalem, 1957, knight comdr., 1964, knight grand cross, 1966, knight of collar, 1982, lt. No. Lieutenancy U.S., 1970-77, vice gov.-gen., 1977-82, Knight of Collar; named Bus. Man of Yr. State of Mo., 1957, Man of Yr. City of Hope, 1973; recipient Community Service award Rockne Club Notre Dame, 1959, wisdom award of honor, 1979; Brotherhood award NCCJ, 1979. Mem. Soc. St. Vincent de Paul (pres. 1959-67), Am. Indsl. Bankers Assn. (pres. 1956-57), Am. Inst. Banking (chpt. pres. 1932-33), Bank Auditors and Controllers Assn., Fin. Execs. Inst. (chpt. pres. 1928-29), Nat. Assn. Accts., Kansas City C. of C. Clubs: Rotary, Kansas City, Hillcrest Country, Serra (pres. 1959-60). Office: 8080 Ward Pkwy Kansas City MO 64114

BLASDEL, JEFF ERVIN, pharmacist; b. Cin., July 11, 1956; s. John Edgar and Clara Wilma (Fondong) B.; m. Michelle Elaine Wiedeman, June 27, 1981; children—Carey, Jacob. B.S., Purdue U., 1979; postgrad. Ball State U., 1983-84. Registered pharmacist, Ind. Pharmacist, asst. mgr. Hook Drugs, Inc., Brookville, Ind., 1979-81, pharmacist, mgr., Connerville, Ind., 1981—. Treas., bd. dirs. Regenstrief Boys Club, Connersville, 1984—; chmn. bus. div., bd. dirs. Fayette County United Way, Connersville, 1983—; chmn. council on ministries First United Methodist Ch., Connersville, 1984—. Recipient Eli Lilly Achievement award, 1979, Silver Knight award Hook Drugs, Inc., 1983, 84, Gold Key award, 1983, 84, President's award, 1983-84. Mem. Ind. Pharmacists Assn. (employer-employee relations com. 1982—), Purdue U. Alumni Assn. (life mem.), Connersville C. of C. (diplomat 1984—), Rho Chi (award 1978). Republican. Lodge: Kiwanis (v.p. 1984—). Avocations: tennis, golf, photography, basketball, community service. Home: 1201 S Cherokee Ln Connersville IN 47331 Office: Hook Drugs Inc 309 Central Ave Connersville IN 47331

BLASINGAME, DAVID THOMAS, academic administrator; b. Dermott, Ark., July 7, 1947; s. Ruel Esker and Novella (Mhoon) B.; widowed; 1 child, Joshua Scott. AB, Washington U., 1969, MBA, 1971. Mgmt. assoc. U.S. Postal Service, Washington, 1971; assoc. dir. alumni relations Washington U., St. Louis, 1974-76, dir. devel. sch. bus., 1976-85, exec. dir. alumni and devel. programs, 1985, asst. vice chancellor, 1985-87, assoc. vice chancellor, 1987—; cons. Mercantile Library, St. Louis, 1983-84; cons. in field. Coach Mancester Athletic Assn., St. Louis, 1976-85; bd. dirs. Gifted Resource Council, St. Louis, 1985—. Served to 1st lt. U.S. Army, 1971-73. Mem. Council Advancement of Secondary Edn., William Greenleaf Eliot Soc., Kappa Sigma Alumni Assn. Republican. Avocation: golf. Home: 824 Parkfield Saint Louis MO 63021 Office: Washington U One Brookings Dr Box 1210 Saint Louis MO 63130

BLASIUS, DONALD CHARLES, appliance company executive; b. Oak Park, Ill., June 10, 1929; s. Ervin A. and Frances C. (Critchfield) B.; m. Carle Ann Forslew, Oct. 11, 1952; children: Douglas Charles, Ann Louise. BSBA, Northwestern U., 1951. Various exec. positions McCulloch Corp., 1953-68; various exec. positions J.I. Case Co., 1968-74, v.p., gen. mgr. div., 1970-72, sr. v.p., gen. mgr. div., 1972-74; exec. v.p., chief operating officer Tappan Co., Mansfield, Ohio, 1974-76, pres., chief exec. officer, 1976-84, chmn. bd., chief exec. officer, 1984-86; chmn., chief. exec. officer home products group White Consol. Industries, Inc., Columbus, Ohio, 1986-87, sr. exec. v.p., 1987—; group v.p. Dometic, Inc., Cleve.; bd. dirs. Nat. Edison Co., Akron. Served with Spl. Services, AUS. Home: 5790 St Anns Ct Dublin OH 43017 Office: White Consol Industries Home Products Group Hdqtrs 300 Phillipi Rd Columbus OH 43218

BLASS, MARCUS GABRIEL, physician; b. St. Paul, Mar. 5, 1950; s. Gerhard Alois and Barbara Leanora (Siegert) B.; m. Carol Lynn Mersman, June 29, 1979; children: Janice RenÉe, Jonathan David. BS, U. Detroit, 1971; MD, U. Mich., 1975. Diplomate Am. Bd. Surgery. Intern, resident in gen. surgery Blodgett Meml. Med. Ctr., Grand Rapids, Mich., 1975-79; physician, surgeon Morris (Minn.) Med. Ctr., 1979-81; practice medicine specializing in surgery Ionia, Mich., 1981—; bd. dirs. Am. Cancer Soc., Ionia, 1982—; med. advisor Ionia Area Hospice, Ionia, 1983—. Acting pres. Ionia area Right to Life, 1985-86, v.p., 1986—. Fellow ACS,; mem. Mich. Soc. Gen. Surgeons, Midwest Surg. Assn., Ionia C. of C. Mem. Christian Reformed Ch. Avocations: woodworking. Home: 340 E Main St Ionia MI 48846 Office: 302 E Main St Ionia MI 48846

BLASZKIEWICZ, CYNTHIA BERNADETTE, insurance company analyst; b. Detroit, Sept. 23, 1949; d. Albert Joseph and Alma Rose (Miller) Allen; m. Daniel Alexander Blaszkiewicz, June 6, 1976 (div. 1984). Counter clk. Gil's Cleaners, Detroit, 1965-66; coop. student Mich. Blue Cross, Detroit, 1966-67; sec. Blue Cross Blue Shield Mich., Detroit, 1967-77, analyst, 1977—; cosmetologist, 1974—. Mem. Women's Econ. Club of Detroit, Nat. Mgmt. Assn. (charter Blue Cross/Blue Shield Mgmt. Assn. Mich.), Nat. Assn. Female Execs. Health and People Pac. Avocations: snow skiing; bowling; tennis; racquet ball; swimming; needlecraft. Office: Blue Cross Blue Shield Mich 600 Lafayette E Detroit MI 48226

BLATT, SIDNEY ISRAEL, chemical company executive, container company executive; b. Columbus, Ohio, June 5, 1921; s. Rudolph S. and Clara (Mattlin) B.; m. Selma Mae Kantor, July 11, 1943; children—Meredith Gail, Cynthia Blatt Paine, Laura Jo Blatt Paul. BBA, Ohio State U., 1946. V.p. Columbus Barrell Cooperage Co., 1947-50, pres., 1950-55; pres. Columbus Steel Drum Co. div. Franklin Steel Co., 1955—, Surface Research Corp., Columbus, 1959—. Bd. dirs., mem. exec. com. Columbus Jewish Fedn., 1966—, v.p., 1968-74, pres., 1974-76; bd. dirs. Big Bros. Assn., Columbus, 1967-70, Heritage House, Columbus, Jewish Ctr., Columbus; chmn. Jewish Community Relations Com., Columbus, 1969-73; v.p. Temple Israel Found., Columbus, 1970-72, pres. temple, 1977-78; mem. campaign cabinet United Way Franklin County, 1978. Served with inf. AUS, 1943-45. Recipient plaque for outstanding leadership State of Israel Bonds, 1968, Centennial Man of Yr. award ORT, 1980; named Ohio Small Bus. Man of Yr., Columbus C. of C., 1970, Temple Man of Yr., Temple Israel Brotherhood, 1979, co-honoree New Mem. Class, Temple Israel, 1980. Mem. Nat. Barrel and Drum Assn. (dir., treas., exec. com., chmn. bd. dirs. 1984-85), Pres.'s Assn., Nat. Assn. Indsl. and Office Parks. Clubs: Winding Hollow Country (pres. 1973-75), Firestone Country, Jockey, Capital (founding mem.). Address: 330 Stanberry Ave Columbus OH 43209 Office: Franklin Steel Co 1385 Blatt Blvd Blacklick OH 43004

BLAUVELT, BRIAN MOURRIE, chemical company executive; b. Tehran, Central, Iran, July 16, 1956; s. Donald Mourrie and Norma Jean (Klebesadel) B. BS in Civil and Environl. Engring., Cornell U., 1978; MBA, U. Mich., 1980. Supply analyst Exxon Chem. Americas, Houston, 1980-81, sr. mkt. planner, 1985-86; tech. sales rep. Mpls., 1981-83; sr. tech. sales rep. Seattle, 1983-85; v.p., corp. sec., sr. acct. exec. Exxon Chem. Fertilizer Co., Mpls., 1986—. Mem. Nat. Rifle Assn. (life), U.S. Yacht Racing Union, Chi Epsilon. Clubs: Corinthian Yacht (Seattle); Soaring Soc. Am. Avocations: ski racing, sailboat racing, scuba diving, hunting, fishing. Home: 11071 Oregon Circle Bloomington MN 55438 Office: Exxon Chem Fertilizer Co 5001 W 80th St Suite 670 Bloomington MN 55437

BLAZEK, JOHN MICHAEL, health care association executive, business administration educator; b. Omaha, Dec. 14, 1954; s. George R. and Mary I. (Schramek) B.; m. Michaela Ann Finnigan, Mar. 10, 1978; children: Sara Ann, Megan Elizabeth. BS in Pharmacy, Creighton U., 1977, MBA, 1986. Registered pharmacist, Nebr. Community pharmacist Kohll's Pharmacy, Omaha, 1979-82; pharmacist Clarkson Hosp., Omaha, 1978-86; v.p. Total Home Care, Inc., Omaha, 1982—; prof. mtkg. U. Nebr., Omaha, 1986—. Mem. Alumni Council Creighton U., Omaha, 1985—. Mem. Grad. Bus. Assocs., Council Bluffs Pharmacists Assn. Republican. Roman Catholic. Club: Regency Lake and Tennis (Omaha), Omaha Press. Avocations: teaching, jogging, music. Home: 16112 Ontario Circle Omaha NE 68130 Office: Total Home Care Inc 11329 P St #23 Omaha NE 68137

BLECHMAN, GERALD AARON, psychologist; b. Detroit, Jan. 11, 1941; s. Morris and Clara (Taub) B.; children: Mari Suzanne, James Michael, Jonathan Miles; m. 2nd Doris Knoche, Sept. 4, 1983. BA, Wayne State U., 1963; MA, Northwestern U., 1965, PhD, 1968. Staff psychologist Children's Meml. Hosp., Chgo., 1967-72; dir. outpatient psychology services Northwestern U. Med. Sch., Evanston, Ill., 1971-72; dir. psychol. services Project Head Start, City of Chgo., 1972-76; pvt. practice clin. psychology, Skokie, Ill., 1975—; dir. outpatient dept. Old Orchard Hosp., Skokie, Ill., 1984—; cons. Northwestern U. Speech and Lang. Clinic, 1976-81. Mem. Am. Psychol. Assn., Ill. Psychol. Assn. Office: 9700 Kenton Ave Skokie IL 60076

BLECK, THOMAS FRANK, architect; b. Waukegan, Ill., Aug. 13, 1929; s. Henry Bernard and Edna (Kilbert) B.; m. Virginia Eleanore Pavlik, June 16, 1951; children: Thomas G., James H., Catherine Bleck Muschler, Marilynn Bleck Cobbs, Robert F., Susan M., Linda M., John W., Charles D. BS in Archtl. Engring., U. Ill., 1951. Lic. architect, Ill., Wis., N.J., Tex., Mass. Architect Ganster & Hennighausen, Waukegan, 1956; pvt. practice architecture Waukegan, 1956—. Mem. AIA, Nat. Council Archtl. Registration Bds. Republican. Roman Catholic. Avocations: skiing, fishing, traveling, hiking. Home: 10330 W Yorkhouse Rd Waukegan IL 60087 Office: 1321 Glen Roak Ave Waukegan IL 60085

BLECK, VIRGINIA ELEANORE, illustrator; b. Waukegan, Ill., Dec. 22, 1929; s. George William and Eugenia (Van Honder) Pavlik; m. Thomas Frank Bleck, June 16, 1951; children: Thomas G., James H., Catherine Bleck-Muschler, Marilynn Bleck-Cobbs, Robert F., Susan M., Linda M., John W., Charles D. Student, U. Ill., 1947-48, Art Inst. Chgo., 1948-50. Free lance artist Waukegan, Ill., 1950-86; artist Merrill-Chase Galleries, Chgo., 1972-77, Hallmark Cards Inc., Kansas City, Mo., 1977—. Republican. Roman Catholic. Avocations: motherhood, conservation, hiking, travel, forestry. Home and Office: 10330 W Yorkhouse Rd Waukegan IL 60087

BLESCH, CHRISTOPHER JOHN, systems engineer; b. Whittier, Calif., Jan. 9, 1958; s. William Robert and Beverly Jean (Schurman) B.; m. Melinda Catherine Lewis, Aug. 25, 1979. B.S. in Mech. Engring., Ohio State U., 1979, M.S. in Mech. Engring., 1981, M.B.A., 1985. Registered profl. engr., Mich. Engr. Owens-Corning Fiberglas, Granville, Ohio, 1980-85; systems engr. Electronic Data Systems, Dallas, 1985—. Mem. ASME, ASHRAE. Republican. Methodist. Avocations: reading; photography; bicycling. Home: 2411 Seville Dr Okemos MI 48864 Office: Electronic Data Systems 905 Southland Lansing MI 48910

BLESS, ROBERT, securities company executive; b. Chgo., May 22, 1962; s. Anton and Susanne (Rebel) B.; m. Karol Jean Runge, Feb. 22, 1986; 1 child, Jennifer Jean. BS in Mgmt., Northeastern Ill. U., 1984, BS in Acctg., 1987. Acct. exec. McCarthy & Assocs., Chgo., 1984—; sales assoc. Century 21/ Peters & Fulk Realty, Arlington Heights, Ill., 1986—. Home: PO Box 401 Palatine IL 60078 Office: McCarthy & Assocs 6748 W Belmont Ave Chicago IL 60634

BLESSING, ROLAND WARREN, hospital executive; b. Elizabeth City, Va., Apr. 19, 1944; s. Roland F. and Margaret P. (Cook) B.; m. Diana M. Deeter, Dec. 13, 1962 (widowed Nov. 1980); m. Dora E. Knight, June 13, 1981; children: Ann, Aaron. AS in Acctg., Sinclair Coll., 1964; BS in Fin., Baldwin-Wallace, 1977; MBA in Gen. Mgmt., Ashland Coll., 1987. Cert. systems profl. Mgr. product acctg. Sherwin-Williams, Cleve., 1978-80, mgr. real acctg., 1980-81, project mgr., 1982-84; systems cons. Blessing Assocs., Strongsville, Ohio, 1984-85; project leader Aultman Hosp., Canton, Ohio, 1985—; systems cons. Blessing Assocs., Wadsworth, 1985—. Bd. dirs., treas. Westside Christian Sch., Cleve., 1983-85. Mem. Assn. MBA Execs., Assn. for Systems Mgmt. Republican. Avocation: personal computing. Home: 7211 State Rd Wadsworth OH 44281-9702 Office: Aultman Hosp 2600 6th St SW Canton OH 44710

BLESSING, TRISHA, corporate communications specialist; b. Ft. Wayne, Ind., Apr. 18, 1950; d. Howard Carl and Edith Elizabeth (Feltz) Neuhaus; m. Terrence Elwood Dougherty, June 27, 1970 (div. Oct. 1981); children: Monica Lee, Jeanne Therese; m. Thomas Dale Blessing, Sept. 9, 1983. BS, Ind. U., 1972; grad., Ind. Economic Devel. Acad. TV producer, moderator Sta. WPTA-TV, Ft. Wayne, 1978-80; pub. relations rep. Northeastern Ind. Regional Coordinating Council, Ft. Wayne, 1978-82, planning supr., 1982-85; dir. client relations The Turnbell Group, Ft. Wayne, 1985—. Contbg. editor numerous profl. jours. Mem. tech. adv. com. Ind. Dept. Commerce, 1982-85. Vol. U.S. Peace Corps, Afghanistan, 1972-75; mem. Ind. Planning Assn., Ind. Assn. of Counties, Am. Pub. Works Assn., Ind. Economic Devel. Acad., League of Women Voters (pub. relations chmn. 1977, environ. chmn. 1978-79, TV media chmn. 1978-80, del. nat. conv. Washington 1980), Ft. Wayne C. of C. (chmn. bus. retention com. 1986), Ind. U. Alumni Club. Avocations: writing, travel, gardening, politics. Office: The Turnbell Group 519 Tennessee Ave Fort Wayne IN 46805

BLESSINGER, THOMAS LEON, process development engineer; b. Evansville, Ind., Apr. 2, 1947; s. Leon Albert and Alma Anna (Rashe) B.; m. Deanna Kay Deason, Jan. 6, 1968; children: David Wayne, Christopher Scott, Terra Dawn, Chad Michael. Draftsman Jasper (Ind.) Electronics, 1965-66, electronics draftsman, 1970-75; drafting mgr. Kimball Electronics, Jasper, 1975-82, process devel. engr., 1983—. Served with USN, 1966-70. Mem. Internat. Soc. Hybrid Microelectronics. Lodge: Optomists.

BLETTNER, EDWARD FREDERICK, banker; b. Chgo., Dec. 9, 1907; s. Edward Frederick and Mary (Klaner) B.; m. Margaret Maw, Mar. 19, 1943 (dec. July 1982); children: Margaret Jean Blettner Angell, Elizabeth Mary; m. Beverly Dowls, Dec. 30, 1983. AB, Harvard U., 1928, MBA, 1930; JD, John Marshall Law Sch., 1935. Various positions First Nat. Bank of Chgo., 1930-62, exec. v.p., 1962-67, pres., 1968-69, vice chmn. bd., 1969-73, hon. dir., 1973-78. Life mem. bd. dirs. Lyric Opera of Chgo.; life trustee Newberry Library, Chgo.; life trustee Rush-Presbyn. St. Luke's Med. Ctr., Chgo.; governing mem. Art Inst. of Chgo. Served to lt. col. AUS, 1942-45. Congregationalist. Clubs: Chgo., Comml. (Chgo.), Old Elm (Lake Forest, Ill.). Home: 1448 Lake Shore Dr Chicago IL 60610

BLETTNER, JAMES DONALD, engineering company executive; b. Indpls., May 8, 1924; s. Joseph Anthony Blettner and Dorothea C. (Daum) Linville; m. Margaret P. Falkenroth, Aug. 22, 1948; 1 child, Dale Thomas. BEE, Purdue U., 1949. Registered profl. engr., Ind. Prodn. engr. Brown Rubber Co., Lafayette, Ind., 1949-52; tooling engr. Brown Rubber Co., Lafayette, 1952-55, head research div., 1955-58; supt. job shop Leaman Machines, Lafayette, 1958-60; pres. Blettner Engring. Co., Fairland, Ind., 1961—. Patentee in field. Elder St. James Luth. Ch., Lafayette, 1983-85. Served with USAF, 1943-46. Republican. Club: Power Squadron Stuart (Fla.). Avocations: sailing, fishing, swimming, golf. Home: 121 Main St Buck Creek IN 47924

BLINN, CARLA KAY, information systems analyst; b. Dayton, June 29, 1945; d. Carl Foster and Amy Louise (De Motte) Hoke; m. Robert D. Blinn, Dec. 14, 1985. BA, Miami U., Oxford, Ohio, 1967; M in Teaching of Scis., Coll. William and Mary, 1972; cert. reading specialist, Akron (Ohio) U., 1977; postgrad., Bowling Green U., 1980-82. Cert. elem. and high sch. tchr.,

Ohio. Tchr. math., German Berea (Ohio) Schs., 1967-75; dir. devel. ctr. Polaris Jr. Vocat. Sch., Middleburg Heights, Ohio, 1975-79; dir. Reading Acad. Bowling Green (Ohio) State U., 1979-80; dir. devel. learning ctr. Bowling Green State U., 1980-82; manpower specialist Owens-Corning Fiberglas, Toledo, 1982-85, sr. systems analyst, 1985—; cons. various sch. systems, Ohio, 1975—, Ohio Bd. Edn., Columbus, 1975—, Delmar Pubs., Albany, N.Y., 1977—. Author: Vocational Reading Tests, 1978-79, (with others) Manual for Junior Vocational School Reading, 1981. Council chairperson Puritas Luth. Ch., Cleve., 1969-75; pres. adv. bd. A.B.L.E., Bowling Green, 1980; chairperson Bloodmobile, Food Basket programs, St. Mark's Luth. Ch., Bowling Green, 1984-86. Nat. Sci. Found. scholar, 1969-71. Mem. Delta Kappa Gamma, Phi Delta Kappa. Democrat. Avocations: crafts, reading, sewing, gardening. Home: 425 Wallace Bowling Green OH 43402 Office: Owens-Corning Fiberglas Fiberglas Tower Toledo OH 43659

BLINZLER, ALAN PATRICK, lawyer; b. Bartlesville, Okla., June 26, 1954; s. Glenn Frederick and Jane (Kirkpatrick) B.; m. Kelly Lynn Connelley, Dec. 31, 1977; children—Adam Frederick, Erin Lynn. B.A. cum laude in History, Southwestern Coll., 1976; M.B.A., J.D., U. Kans., 1979. Bars: Kans. 1979, U.S. Dist. Ct. Kans. 1979, Mo. 1980, U.S. Dist. Ct. (we. dist.) Mo. 1980, U.S. Ct. Appeals (10th cir.) 1982. Assoc. Blackwell, Sanders, Matheny, Weary & Lombardi, Overland Park, Kans., 1980—. Asst. scoutmaster Heart of Am. council Boy Scouts Am., 1977-80, scoutmaster, 1980-83; Rep. precinct committeeman, Prairie Village, Kans., 1980-86; mem. Rep. Cen. Com., Johnson County, Kans., 1980-86; treas. Johnson County Fire Dist. No. 2, Prairie Village, 1981-82; chmn. Prairie Village Rep. Party, 1982-84, Johnson County Rep. Policy Com., 1982-84; mem. Kansas City Consensus, Mo., 1983-84, Johnson County Rep. Exec. Com., 1983-84, Internat. Relations Council, Kansas City, Mo., 1983-86; del. to Rep. State Cen. Com. of Kans., 1983-86, 3d Congl. Dist. Rep. Central Com., 1983-87; com. mem. Explorer Post, Boy Scouts Am., Olathe, Kans., 1984-87; com. mem. Kansas City Mayor's Commn. on Union Sta., 1987. Named Eagle Scout Boy Scouts Am., 1969; recipient Best Brief in Nation award ABA Appellate Advocacy Contest, 1978. Mem. ABA (com. on discovery reform 1983-84), Kans. Bar Assn., Mo. Bar Assn., Kansas City Bar Assn., Johnson County Bar Assn. Mem. Disciples of Christ. Lodge: Lions (v.p. 1984, pres. 1986), Rotary. Home: 12326 Walmer Overland Park KS 66209 Office: Blackwell Sanders Matheny Weary & Lombardi 9401 Indian Creek Pkwy Overland Park KS 66225

BLISS, DAVID C., retail executive; b. Muskegon, Mich., Apr. 27, 1937; s. Percy R. and Alada (Christopher) B.; m. Sandra Rakoski, June 16, 1962; children: Roger S., Stever C. BBA, Western Mich. U., 1960. Various fin. positions Brunswick Corp., various cities, 1961-67; v.p. fin. Ott Chemical, Muskegon, Mich., 1967-70, Charlotte, N.C., 1970-71; treas. Story Chemical, Charlotte, 1972-74; pres. Quality Stores, Muskegon, 1974—. Bd. dirs. Jr. Achievement, Muskegon, 1980—, YFCA of Muskegon, 1986—; trustee North Muskegon Pub. Schs., 1981-85. Club: Muskegon Country Club (bd. dirs. 1973-79). Home: 501 Ruddiman Dr North Muskegon MI 49445 Office: Quality Stores Inc 1460 Whitehall Rd Muskegon MI 49445

BLIWAS, PHILIP R., insurance executive, tax and financial planner; b. Milw., June 28, 1920; s. Rubin and Caroline B.; student U. Wis., 1937-40, U. Ind., 1946-47; LLB, Marquette U., 1947; postgrad. Columbia U., 1942, Ind. U. Law Sch., 1946-47, Purdue U. Ins. Inst., 1980-81. Cert. farm estate planning U. Minn., 1977; cert. Keypact Inst. Advanced Studies, 1979; m. Joyce Shirley Strauss; children: James Charles, Janice M. Sec., Charles Strauss Shoes, Milw., 1947-51; pres., gen. mgr., chief exec. officer Korbe Shoe, Inc., Mpls., 1951-74; field underwriter N.Y. Life Ins. Co., 1975-79; gen. agt., owner Philip Bliwas Agy., Chaska, Minn., 1978—; founder, chief exec. officer Janus Fin. Mktg. Corp., 1980-84, Von Hertzen Fin. Services, Inc., 1978-86. Del. to county and state convs. Minn. Dem. Farm Labor Party, 1972, 76, 80; vol. work Carver County Family Services. Served to lt. USN, 1941-46; PTO. Recipient Life Ins. Nat. Sales Achievement ann. award Nat. Assn. Life Underwriters, 1978-82, Nat. Quality award, 1977, 78, 81; named Top Life Ins. Producer of 1981, Nat. Travelers Life Co. Mem. Nat. Assn. Life Underwriters, Million Dollar Round Table (life, qualifying, Top of Table 1982). Home: 110922 Von Hertzen Circle Chaska MN 55318 Office: Hopkins MN 55343

BLIX, SUSANNE, psychiatrist; b. Crawfordsville, Ind., Oct. 29, 1949; d. Fred Mayor and Marjorie Marie (Durst) B.; m. William Charles McGraw, June 20, 1971; children: Annmarie Blix McGraw, Annalisa Ruth McGraw. BA, DePauw U., 71; MD, Ind. U., 1975. Diplomate Am. Bd. Psychiatry and Neurology. Intern internal medicine Ind. U. Med. Sch., Indpls., 1975-76, resident psychiatry, 1977-79, fellow child psychiatry, 1979-81, asst. prof. psychiatry, 1981—, asst. dir. psychiat. services Riley Children's Hosp., 1981-85, dir. psychiat. services, 1985—; cons. Ind. Pastoral Counselling Ctr., Indpls., 1978-79; cons. Cummins Mental Health Ctr., Danville, Ind., 1981-84, Midtown Mental Health Ctr., Indpls., 1984-85. Contbr. articles to profl. jours. Mem. Ind. Psychiat. Soc. (membership sec. 1983-84), Am. Psychiat. Assn., Am. Acad. Child Psychiatry, Marian County Med. Soc., Ind. State Med. Assn., Ind. Council Child and Adolescent Psychiatry (treas. 1985-86, pres. 1986-87), Kappa Alpha Theta, Phi Beta Kappa. Mem. Disciples of Christ Ch.

BLIXT, ROY ELOF, retired judge; b. Etna, Nebr., Apr. 12, 1915; s. Elof E. and Alice D. (Oman) B. AB, U. Nebr., 1940, JD, 1941. Bar: Nebr. 1940, U.S. Dist. Ct. Nebr. 1946, U.S. Supreme Ct. 1962. County atty. Blaine County, Brewster, Nebr., 1941-50; dep. county atty Custer County, Nebr., 1965-74; judge County Ct., Ord, Nebr., 1976-87. Mem. Nebr. Rep. State Com., 1957; city treas., Arnold, Nebr., 1951-73. Served with U.S. Army, 1943-46. Mem. ABA. Presbyterian. Club: Rotary. Lodges: Moose, Masons, Shriners, K.T., Elks. Home: 1514 1/2 L St Ord NE 68822

BLIZMAN, PAUL J., lawyer, social worker; b. Wyandotte, Mich., June 4, 1940; s. Paul J. and Olga G. (Rudenko) B.; student U. Mich., 1958-62; A.B., Wayne State U., 1966, M.S.W., 1969; J.D., Detroit Coll. Law, 1980; m. Leah Snyder, Sept. 3, 1967; 1 dau., Alexis. Counselor, Reception Center W.J. Maxey Sch., Whitmore Lake, Mich., 1969-71, dir., 1972-74, social work supr., 1971-72; licensing cons. Mich. Dept. Social Services, 1974-78; clin. social worker Health Care Inst., Detroit, 1979-80, Detroit Receiving Hosp., Univ. Health Center, 1980-82; sole practice, 1981-83, 86—; ptnr. Melamed & Blizman, P.C., 1983-84, Melamed Blizman & Dailey, P.C., 1984-86 ; pvt. practice social work, Birmingham, Mich., 1975—; field instr. social work Wayne State U., 1979-82. Mem. Farmington Hills Energy Commn., 1984-86. Mem. ABA, Mich. State Bar, Oakland County Bar Assn., Southfield Bar Assn., Farmington Hills Historic Dist. Commn., Delta Theta Phi. Home: 28700 Herndonwood Dr Farmington Hills MI 48018 Office: 24901 Northwestern Hwy Suite 314B Southfield MI 48075

BLOBAUM, COLLEEN ANN, child and family therapist; b. Lincoln, Nebr., Jan. 14, 1950; d. Duane Henry William and Aleta Verleda (Feyerherm) B.; divorced. BA, Valparaiso U., 1972; MEd, U. Ill., 1977. Registered social worker, Ill. Coordinator, tchr. Dewey Family Daycare, Evanston, Ill., 1972-75; research asst. U. Ill., Chgo., 1975, child devel. specialist, 1975-79; supr., ednl. therapist Jewish Family & Community Service, Chgo., 1979-86; pvt. practice child and family therapy Urbana, Ill., 1986—; cons. Winthrop Day Care Ctr., Chgo., 1981-84, U. Ill. Med. Ctr., Chgo., 1981; instr. psychology Parkland Coll., Champaign, Ill., 1987—. Assoc. Rainbow Adventures, Inc., Evanston, 1982—. Mem. Am. Orthopsychiat. Assn., Nat. Assn. Social Workers, Nat. Assn. for Edn. Young Children. Avocations: leading wilderness trips for women, bicycling, hiking, photography. Office: 123 W Main St Suite 220 A Urbana IL 61801

BLOCH, HENRY WOLLMAN, tax preparation company executive; b. Kansas City, Mo., July 30, 1922; s. Leon Edwin and Hortense Bienenstok; m. Marion Ruth Helzberg, June 16, 1951; children: Robert, Thomas M., Mary Jo, Elizabeth Ann. B.S., U. Mich., 1943; D.B.A. (hon.), Avila Coll., Kansas City, Mo., 1977; LL.D. (hon.), N.H. Coll., 1983. Partner United Bus. Co., 1946-55; pres., chief exec. officer H & R Block, Inc., Kansas City, 1955—, also dir.; dir. Commerce Bank Kansas City, Southwestern Bell Corp. Bd. dirs., vice chmn. Kansas City Art Inst.; past trustee Clearinghouse for Midcontinent Founds.; past bd. dirs. Menorah Med. Ctr.; bd. dirs., past pres. Menorah Med. Ctr. Found.; former mem. president's adv. council Kansas City Philharmonic Assn.; pres. H & R Block Found.; trustee U. Mo. at Kansas City, Nelson-Atkins Mus. Art; former trustee Am. Mus. Assn.; bd. dirs. Jewish Fedn. and Council Greater Kansas City; dir., past pres. Civic Council Greater Kansas City; gen. chmn. United Negro Colls. Fund, 1986; bd. dirs. St. Luke's Hosp.; former mem. bd. dirs. Council of Fellows of Nelson Gallery Found., Am. Jewish Com.; former mem. bd. govs. Kansas City Mus. History and Sci.; bd. dirs. Midwest Research Inst., Kansas City Symphony, Greater Kansas City Community Found.; gen. chmn. Heart of Am. United Way Exec. Com., 1978; past met. chmn. Nat. Alliance Businessmen; former mem. bd. regents Rockhurst Coll.; former mem. bd. chancellor's assocs. U. Kans. at Lawrence; former mem. bd. dirs. Harry S. Truman Good Neighbor Award Found.; bd. dirs. Internat. Relations Council; bd. dirs., v.p. Kansas City Area Health Planning Council; past pres. Found. for a Greater Kansas City. Served to 1st lt. USAAF, 1943-45. Decorated Air medal with 3 oak leaf clusters; named Mktg. Man of Yr. Sales and Mktg. Execs. Club, 1971, Chief Exec. Officer of Yr. for service industry Fin. World, 1976; recipient Disting. Exec. award Boy Scouts Am., 1977, Salesman of Yr. Kansas City Advt. Club, 1978, Civic Service award Hyman Brand Hebrew Acad., 1980, Chancellor's medal U. Mo.-Kansas City, 1980, President's trophy Kansas City Jaycees, 1980, W.F. Yates medal for disting. service in civic affairs William Jewell Coll., 1981, bronze award for service industry Wall Street Transcript, 1981, Disting. Missourian award NCCJ, 1982, Lester A. Milgram Humanitarian award, 1983, Hall of Fame award Internat. Franchise Assn., 1983; named to Bus. Leader Hall of Fame Jr. Achievement, 1980; Chief Exec. of Yr. Service Industry, Fin. World. Mem. Assn. Trusts and Founds., Greater Kansas City C. of C. (past pres.), C. of C. Greater Kansas City (Mr. Kansas City award 1978). Jewish. Clubs: Oakwood Country, River, Carriage (Kansas City), Kansas City Racquet. Office: H&R Block Inc 4410 Main St Kansas City MO 64111

BLOCHOWSKI, THOMAS KENNETH, manufacturing engineer; b. Toledo, Oct. 27, 1942; s. Edmund Eugene and Helen Alice (Sobieralski) B.; Asso. Mfg. Tech., U. Toledo, 1965; m. Judith Ann Gasiorowski, Aug. 24, 1963; children—Kenneth Robert, Cynthia Ann, Kevin Michael. Sales mgr. Block Indsl. Service, Toledo, 1964-69; chief tool engr. Mather Co., Milan, Mich., 1969-71; mfg. engr. machine shop M-S/Tillotson Co., Toledo, 1971-74; sr. lead process engr. Harley Davidson Motor Co., Milw., 1974-75; mfg. engr. corp. staff Prestolite Co., Toledo, 1975-81; pres. Bisel Mfg. Inc., screw machine plant, Toledo, 1981—; mem. faculty Monroe County (Mich.) Community Coll. Bd. dirs. Goodwill Industries, Toledo, cons. sheltered workshop program. Registered profl. mfg. engr., Calif. Mem. Soc. Mfg. Engrs. (sr. mem., chmn. Toledo chpt. 1971-72), St. Francis De Sales Alumni Assn. Roman Catholic. Clubs: Tamaron Country, The Racquet. Home: 6014 Tetherwood Dr Toledo OH 43613 Office: 1121 Hazelwood St Toledo OH 43605

BLOCK, ALLAN MARTIN, accountant; b. Kansas City, Mo., Sept. 13, 1942; s. Joseph Abraham and Freda (Frank) B.; m. Susan Feinberg, May 21, 1982. BS in Acctg., U. Ill., 1964; MBA in Mgmt., U. So. Calif., Los Angeles, 1971; cert. in mgmt., Harvard U., 1979. CPA, Mo., Kans. Sr. staff acct. Peat, Marwick, Mitchell & Co., Kansas City, 1964-67; sr. internal auditor Trans World Airlines, Kansas City, 1967-69; mgr. reports, budgets Universal Pictures, Universal City, Calif., 1969-72; pvt. practice in acctg. Kansas City, 1972—; instr. CPA review course, Kansas City, 1974-84. Treas. Nat. Kidney Found., Kans., Western Mo., 1987—; bd. dirs. Friends of The Symphony, Kansas City; mem. citizen's review bd. Heart of Am. United Way, Kansas City; del., chaplain USSR and China People to People Internat. CPA trip, Kansas City, 1985. Mem. Mo. Soc. CPA's (pres., bd. dirs. Kansas City chpt. 1982-83, chmn. practice mgmt. com. 1977-78, benefits com. 1985—), Am. Inst. CPA's (vice chmn. hospitality com. 1985-86), Am. Assn. Ind. Investors (treas. 1987), Greater Kansas City C. of C. (centurion leadership program 1986—, treas. 1987—). Jewish. Clubs: Kansas City (hospitality com. 1987), Kansas City Chiefs (v.p., treas., bd. dirs. 1983—). Avocations: classical music, racquetball, gourmet cooking, travel, piano. Home: 1900 W 63d St Mission Hills KS 66208 Office: 2300 Commerce Tower 911 Main St Kansas City MO 64105

BLOCK, CORY ANDREW, advertising executive; b. Watertown, Wis., Oct. 15, 1956; s. Lee Arthur and Virginia S. (Soper) B. BS in Communication, U. Wis., Stevens Point, 1975-79; MS in Advt., U. Ill., 1980. Asst. account rep. J. Walter Thompson, Chgo., 1981-83; account exec. Cramer-Krasselt Co., Milw., 1983—. vis. lectr. U. Ill.-Urbana, 1981. Mem. Am. Advt. Fed. Club: Milw. Advt. Home: 1342 E Randolph Ct C Milwaukee WI 53212 Office: Cramer-Krasselt Co 733 N Van Buren St Milwaukee WI 53202

BLOCK, JOHN ROBINSON, newspaper editor; b. Toledo, Oct. 1, 1954; s. Paul Jr. and Marjorie Jane (McNab) B. BA, Yale U., 1977. Reporter AP, Miami, Fla., 1977-78, N.Y.C., 1978-80; Washington corr. The Toledo Blade, 1980-82; European corr. The Toledo Blade, London, 1982—; asst. mng. editor The Toledo Blad, 1982—; v.p., bd. dirs. P.G. Pub. Co., Pitts., Monterey (Calif.) Peninsula Herald Co.; bd. dirs. Blade Communications, Inc., Toledo. Chmn. City Mgr.'s Hist. Preservation Com., Toledo, 1983-85. Mem. Am. Soc. Newspaper Editors, Soc. Profl. Journalists. Clubs: Yale (N.Y.C.); Belmont Country (Perrysburg, Ohio). Home: 5502 Citation Rd N Toledo OH 43615 Office: Blade Communications Inc 541 Superior St Toledo OH 43660

BLOCK, MARTIN STEPHEN, retail executive; b. Chgo., July 5, 1951; s. Melvin and Rita Doris (Youngerman) B. BS in Edn., No. Ill. U., 1973. Cert. diamondtologist; cert. tchr. Tchr. Niles (Ill.) Pub. Schs., 1973-75; corp. officer Mistigull Jewelers Co., Skokie, Ill., 1975-78; mgr. Rogers Jewelers, Chgo., 1978-79; supr. Elayne Jewelers Inc., Chgo., 1979-81; sales exec. Citizen Watch Co., Indpls., 1981—. Mem. Jewelers Assn. Traveling Salesmen (v.p. 1984—). Avocations: reading, jazz, golf, volleyball, softball.

BLOCK, MICHAEL ROBERT, real estate executive; b. Kansas City, Mo., Feb. 10, 1957; s. Allen Jacob and Gloria (LeSuer) B.; m. Phyllis Ann Walsh, Oct. 20, 1984; 1 child, Leslie Gail. BS, U. Kans., 1979. Cert. property mgr. V.p. Block and Co., Inc., Kansas City, 1979—. Pres. Avidus, Kans. City, 1985. Mem. Nat. Assn. Realtors, Mo. Assn. Realtors (life, Million Dollar Club), Inst. Real Estate Mgmt. (chmn. 1983-85), Met. Bd. Realtors (Million Dollar Club). Republican. Jewish. Avocations: tennis, golf, swimming. Home: 5521 Roe Roeland Park KS 66205 Office: Block and Co Inc 605 W 47th St Kansas City MO 64112

BLOCK, PHILIP DEE, III, former steel company executive; b. Chgo., Feb. 14, 1937; married; 2 children. BS in Indsl. Adminstrn. with high honors, Yale U., 1958. Trainee and engr. Inland Steel Co., Chgo., 1958-60, raw materials coordinator, 1961-65, gen. mgr. purchases, 1966-72, gen. mgr. corp. planning, 1973-76; v.p. materials and services Inland Steel Container, Chgo., 1977-79, v.p. purchases, 1980-85; v.p. Capital Guardian Trust Co., Chgo., 1986—; Mem. vis. com. to phys. scis. div. U. Chgo.; mem. nat. strategic materials and minerals program adv. com. Sec. of Interior; bd. dirs. Rand-McNally & Co., Skokie, Ill. Bd. dirs. Barker Welfare Found., Children's Meml. Hosp.; trustee Chgo. Hist. Soc. Served with USAR, 1959-64. Home: 1430 Lake Shore Dr Chicago IL 60610 Office: Guardian Trust Co One 1st Nat Plaza Suite 2544 Chicago IL 60603

BLOCK, ROBERT MICHAEL, endodontist, educator, reseacher; b. Ann Arbor, Mich., Oct. 15, 1947; s. Walter David and Thelma Violet (Levine) B.; m. Anne Powell Marshall, Sept. 4, 1977. B.A., DePauw U., 1969; D.D.S., U. Mich.-Ann Arbor, 1974; cert. in endodontics, Va. Commonwealth U., 1977; M.S. in Pathology, Va. Commonwealth U., 1978. Diplomate Am. Bd. Endodontics. Clin. instr. Va. Commonwealth U., 1975-77, instr. pathology, 1977-78; research assoc. endodontics U. Conn.-Farmington, 1975—; vis. sr. scientist Nat. Med. Research Inst., Bethesda, Md., 1976-78; research assoc. McGuire Vets. Hosp., Richmond, Va., 1975-78; vis. research scientist U. Conn.-Farmington, 1978—; lectr. endodontics Flint Community Schs. Contbr. articles profl. jours., chpt. in book. Exec. mem. campaign com. candidate for U. Mich. Bd. Regents, 1980; candidate for Mich. State Bd. Edn., 1982. HEW and NIH summer research fellow, 1970-71; research grantee McGuire Vets. Hosp., 1976-78. Mem. Internat. Assn. Dental Research (Edward P. Hatton award 1977), Am. Assn. Dental Research, Am. Assn. Endodontists (Meml. Research award 1977), Lapeer Dental Study Club (treas. 1978-82), ADA (Preventive Dentistry award 1973). Club: Bourben Barrell Hunt (Imlay City, Mich.). Office: G 3163 Flushing Rd Suite 212 Flint MI 48504

BLOCK, ROBERT RAYMOND, city administrator; b. Joliet, Ill., Aug. 14, 1948; s. Robert Raymond Sr. and Radgene T. (Schulz) B.; m. Mary Jo Ann Carpenter, Jan. 20, 1973; children: Kristen, Angela, Jeffery. BS in Urban Planning, Iowa State U., 1970; MA in Pub. Adminstrn., Oakland U., 1981. Asst. planner C. Gardner & Assocs., Chgo., 1970-71; asst. planner City of Southfield, Mich., 1972-76, dep. city planner, 1976-78, asst. to city adminstr., 1978-82, asst. city adminstr., 1985—. Mem. Southfield Non-Profit Housing Commn., 1985—, Southfield Bldg. Authority, 1985—. Mem. Internat. City Mgmt. Assn., Mich. City Mgmt. Assn., Am. Soc. Pub. Adminstrn., Am. Planners Assn. Avocations: sailing, golf. Office: City of Southfield 26000 Evergreen Rd Southfield MI 48076

BLOCK, SANFORD LEE, oral surgeon; b. Chgo., Aug. 30, 1943; s. Harry Leo and Sophie (Dombek) B.; m. Noal S. Blender, May 30, 1966; children—Jared Gavin, Darren Randall, Nicole Suzanne. Student U. Ill., 1964; D.D.S., Loyola U., Chgo., 1969; LL.B., Blackstone Law Sch., 1973. Cert. Am. Bd. Dental Examiners. Asst. prof. oral surgery U. Ill. Coll. Dentistry, Chgo., 1972—, clinic coordinator Temporomandibular Joint and Facial Pain Research Ctr., 1974-84; dir. dentistry/oral surgery Swedish Covenant Hosp., Chgo., 1976—; cons. Office of Med. Examiner Cook County, Chgo., 1980—. Co-author: The Temporomandibular Joint, 1980. Contbr. articles to profl. jours. C.V. Mosby scholar, 1969; Marcus Levy scholar Chgo. Jewish Fedn., 1967-68; Alpha Omega scholar, 1969. Fellow Acad. Implants and Transplants; mem. ADA, Ill. Dental Soc., Chgo. Dental Soc., Am. Assn. Dental Research, Internat. Assn. Study of Pain, Blue Key. Avocations: archeology; computers; guitar. Office: Swedish Covenant Hosp 5145 N California Ave Chicago IL 60625

BLOCK, SHAUN CUDAHY, food manufacturing executive; b. Chgo., Aug. 28, 1941; s. Michael and Annie May (Henry) C.; m. Andrew Keith Block, Jan. 4, 1964; children—Andrew Keith, Christopher P., Shauna B. B.A., Northwestern U., 1964. Vice pres. Top Hat, Chgo., 1982—; v.p., dir. Open Lands Project, Chgo., 1975—. Mem. Ill. Commn. on State Banks & Trusts, 1980-84; exec. com. Women's Bd. U. Chgo., 1983-84. Roman Catholic. Avocations: reading, golf, skiing.

BLOCK, WILLIAM, newspaper publisher; b. N.Y.C., Sept. 20, 1915; s. Paul and Dina (Wallach) B.; m. Maxine Horton, Mar. 23, 1944; children: William, Karen Block Ayars, Barbara Block Burney, Donald. A.B., Yale U., 1936. With circulation, other depts. Toledo Blade, 1937-39, asst. to gen. mgr., 1939-41; co-pub. Pitts. Post-Gazette and Toledo Blade, 1941—; pres. Post-Gazette; v.p. Toledo Blade. Bd. dirs. Pitts. Communications Found., Pitts. Symphony Soc., Pitts. Ctr. for the Arts, Gateway to Music Inc.; trustee Am. Assembly; sponsor Allegheny Conf. on Community Devel. Served to capt. AUS, 1941-46; served in mil. govt. in 1945-46, Korea. Mem. Internat. Press Inst., Am. Soc. Newspaper Editors., Soc. Profl. Journalists, Hist. Soc. Western Pa. (bd. dirs.). Office: The Blade 541 Superior St Toledo OH 43660

BLOCKER, CECIL ARLO, JR., manufacturing executive; b. Columbus, Ohio, Feb. 15, 1931; s. Cecil Arlo and Elizabeth Agusta (Davis) B.; B in Mining Engring., B in Petroleum Engring., Ohio State U., 1956, M.B.A., 1964; M in Bus.Mgmt., Frostburg State Coll., 1978; m. Virginia Travis Wakeman, Sept. 2, 1978; children by previous marriage—Debra, Victoria, Craig, Jacqueline. Refinery lab head, petroleum engr. Standard Oil of N.J., Sumatra, Indonesia, 1958-63; mgr. quality assurance Cummins Engine Co., Columbus, Ind., 1965-68; dir. quality assurance Levinson-Hayes, Pitts., 1968-70; plant mgr. Levinson-Levco, Pitts., 1970-73; dir. quality assurance Pullman Trailmobile, Chgo., 1973-75; dir. quality control Pullman-Standard, Chgo., 1975-76; operations mgr., prodn. control mgr., quality control mgr. Frick Co., Waynesboro, Pa., 1976-78, dir. ops. Frick Forest Products, Waynesboro, Pa., 1978; dir., v.p. quality assurance Campbell-Hausfeld Group of Scott Fetzer Co., Harrison, Ohio, 1978-82, corp. dir. quality improvement Scott Fetzer Co., 1982—; pres. Ultramax Corp., 1982—; cons. high tech. Served with USAF, 1956-58. Registered profl. engr., Ohio. Mem. Am. Soc. Quality Control (Cin. chmn. 1979-81, Pitts. chmn. 1972, mem. Chgo. bd. 1974-75). Republican. Unitarian. Club: Elks. Home and Office: 6245 Twinwillow Ln Cincinnati OH 45247

BLOCKER, JOHN DANIEL, financial analyst; b. Houston, Jan. 2, 1950; s. Daniel James Jr. and Helen Vance (McCrary) B.; m. Valerie Julia Forro, June 28, 1975. BA, Williams Coll., 1973. CLU, CPCU. Fin. analyst Aetna Life and Casualty, Hartford, Conn., 1973—; v.p. Surety Assn. Iowa, Des Moines, 1985-86, pres., 1986—. V.p. Syracuse (N.Y.) Jaycees, 1976-77. Mem. Pa. Soc. CPCU, CLU Soc. Republican. Presbyterian. Avocations: golf, Woodworking. Home: 3517 Tripoli Ct SE Grand Rapids MI 49506

BLOCKI, JAMES R., advertising executive; b. Chgo., July 6, 1925; s. Gale and Lucile V. (Laughlin) B.; m. Virginia Henry, June 16, 1951; children: Linda J., William G., Richard S. BS, Northwestern U., 1948. Advt., pub. relations Toni Co. div. Gillette, Chgo., 1949-50; salesman Toni Co. div. Gillette, Tex., N.Mex., Okla., 1950-51; asst. advtg. and sales promotions mgr. Nesco, Inc., Chgo., 1951-52; asst. prodns. advtg. mgr. Kraft, Inc., Chgo., 1951-55, v.p., dir. advtg. and mktg. services, 1983-85, v.p. spl. projects, 1986—. Pres., founder Westgate Community Assn., 1954-56; Rep. block capt.; bd. dirs. U. Ill. Sch. Advt. and Bus., 1982—; mem. Sch. Bd. Selection Com., 1958, N.W. Community Hosp. Served with USN, 1943-46, PTO. Mem. Assn. Nat. Advts. (bd. dirs. 1983-85), Promotional Mktg. Assn. Am. (bd. dirs. 1985-87), Am. Advt. Fedn. (bd. dirs. 1985-86, vice-chmn. 1986), Nat. Captioning Inst. (adv. bd. advt. council). Presbyterian. Avocations: family, sports, gardening, photography, running. Home: 527 S Dwyer Ave Arlington Heights IL 60005

BLODGETT, FRANK CALEB, food company executive; b. Janesville, Wis., Apr. 22, 1927; s. Frank Caleb Pickard and Dorothy (Korst) B.; m. Jean Ellen Fountain, June 23, 1951; children: Caleb J., Barbara F., David K. Grad., Beloit Coll., 1950; postgrad., Advanced Mgmt. Program, Harvard U., 1969. First v.p., dir. Frank H. Blodgett Inc., Janesville, 1947-61, pres., dir., 1961-62; with Gen. Mills Inc., Mpls., 1961—, v.p., dir. mktg., 1967-69, gen. mgr., v.p., 1969-73, group v.p., 1973-76, exec. v.p., 1976-80, vice chmn., 1981—, chief fin. and adminstrv. officer, 1985—; dir. Gen. Mills Inc., 1980—; dir. Medtronics, Inc., Northwestern Nat. Life Ins. Co.; bd. dirs. Cereal Inst., 1970-76, chmn., 1973-74; trustee Nutrition Found., 1980-84, Gen. Mills Found., 1980—. Trustee Washburn Child Guidance Center, 1972-75, Beloit Coll., 1976—. Served with U.S. Navy, 1944-46, PTO. Mem. Millers Nat. Fedn., Young Millers Orgn. (past pres.), U.S. C. of C. (dir.), Greater Mpls. C. of C. (dir. 1975-76), Phi Kappa Psi (trustee alumni bd. Beloit 1961-62), Phi Eta Sigma. Home: 688 Hillside Dr Wayzata MN 55391 Office: Gen Mills Inc 9200 Wayzata Blvd Minneapolis MN 55440

BLODGETT, HARRIET ELEANOR, child psychologist, school administrator; b. Lyndonville, Vt., Sept. 28, 1919; d. Floyd Kidder and Clara Inez (Goss) B. BS, Tufts U., 1940; MA, U. Minn., 1943, PhD, 1953. Diplomate Am. Bd. Profl. Psychology; lic. cons. psychologist. State psychologist State Minn., St. Paul, 1943-46; instr. psychologist U. Minn., 1946-53, asst. prof., 1953-54; clinical psychologist Rochester (Minn.) State Hosp., 1954-55; program dir. Sheltering Arms Sch., Mpls., 1955-83. Author (with G. Warfield) Understanding Mentally Retarded Children, 1959, Mentally Retarded Children: What Parents and Others Should Know, 1971. Recipient Merit award Minn. Assn. for Retarded Citizens, 1963, Disting. Service award Minn. Psychological Assn., 1982. Fellow Am. Assn. Mental Deficiency; mem. Am. Psychological Assn. Avocations: music, reading, writing, editing. Home: 2401 34th Ave S Minneapolis MN 55406

BLODGETT, VIRGINIA JUNE BALLARD (MRS. RALPH WESLEY BLODGETT), ednl. adminstr.; b. Detroit; d. William King and Marie (Crossley) Ballard; A.B., Asbury Coll., 1935; M.S., Butler U., 1962; postgrad. U. Louisville, Ind. State U., Ball State U., Ohio State U., San Francisco State U.; Ph.D. (hon.), Colo. State Christian Coll.; m. Ralph Wesley Blodgett, Sept. 25, 1935; children—Vivian Sue Shields, Rebecca June Downing, Judith Elaine (Mrs. David Purvis). Tchr. Dependent Schs., Europe, 1951-54, English various high schs., Ind., Va., Fla., 1942—, chmn. English dept. Woodview Sch., Indpls., 1961—, dean girls, 1964—; instr. evening div. Ind. Central Coll., Indpls., 1964-69, adult counselor, 1965—. Active various community drives. Gen. Electric Co. fellow, 1967. Mem. Am., Ind. (sec. 1969) assns. women deans and counselors, NEA, Ind. State Tchrs. Assn., Warren Twp. Classroom Tchrs., Central Ind., Ind. personnel and guidance assns., Alpha Delta Kappa. Methodist (tchr. ch. schs. 1935—). Office: 901 N Post Rd Indianapolis IN 46219

BLOEMER, JOHN WILLIAM, mechanical engineer; b. Indpls., June 5, 1935; s. Frank William and Bonnie Grace (Smith) B.; B.S. in Mech. Engring., Purdue U., 1957; M.S. in Mech. Engring., Ohio State U., 1963: M.S. in Mgmt., Case Western Res. U., 1971; m. Sandra A. Updike, Sept. 1, 1956; children—Sherrie, Jennifer, John, Joseph, Kristen. Research engr. Battelle Meml. Inst., Columbus, Ohio, 1957-65; prin. engr. Eaton Corp., Willoughby Hills, Ohio, 1965—. Served with C.E., U.S. Army, 1960. Registered profl. engr., Ohio, Fla.; cert. master hazardous materials mgr. Mem. ASME, Inst. Noise Control Engrs. Mem. Church of Christ. Home: 8217 Yorkshire Dr Mentor OH 44060 Office: Eaton Corp 32500 Chardon Rd Willoughby Hills OH 44094

BLOMQUIST, ROGER VINCENT, environment engineering company executive; b. Iron Mountain, Mich., Feb. 11, 1944; s. William Thure and Ellen Dagmar (Johnson) B.; B.S. with honors, Mich. State U., 1966; Ph.D., U. Wis., 1971; Exec. Devel. Program, Cornell U., 1976; grad. Mgmt. Inst. U. Minn., 1985; m. Patricia Ann Beaty, Sept. 6, 1969; children—Jason, Matthew. Agronomist, Internat. Minerals and Chem. Co., Libertyville, Ill., 1966; research assoc. U. Wis., Madison, 1966-70; postdoctoral research fellow U. Guelph (Ont., Can.), 1971; v.p., treas., dir. Nat. Biocentric Inc., St. Paul, 1971-79; br. mgr. Environ. Research Group, St. Paul, 1979-82; v.p., gen. mgr. Braun Environ. Labs., 1982—; mem. adv. com. Rice Creek Watershed Dist.; mem. Ramsey County Engring. and Environ. Adv. Com. Precinct vice chmn. Democratic Farm Labor Party, 1976-78, del., dist. conv., 1972, 74, 76, del. county conv., 1972; mem. New Brighton City Council, 1978-85, acting mayor, 1978-85; pres. Ramsey County League of Local Govts., 1984-85; mem. Park Bd., 1977-79, Planning Commn., 1986—. Named one of Ten Outstanding Young Minnesotans, 1978. Bush Found. fellow, 1976; Wis. Alumni Research Found. fellow, 1967-70; Louis Ware scholar, 1966; 4-H scholar, 1962-66. Mem. Nat. Assn. Environ. Profls., Minn. Assn. Environ. Profls., Water Pollution Control Fedn., Air Pollution Control Assn., Izaak Walton League, Am. Soc. Agronomy, Sales and Mktg. Execs., New Brighton Jaycees (v.p. 1973), Sigma Xi, Alpha Zeta. Lutheran. Home: 2023 Pleasant View Dr New Brighton MN 55112

BLOMSTEDT, ERIK RAGNAR, library administrator; b. Lulea, Sweden, May 10, 1947; came to U.S., 1956, naturalized, 1965; s. Ragnar Johan and Anna Viktoria (Sundkvist) B.; m. Lily Anna Yakich, May 18, 1974; children—James, Jennifer. B.A., Northeastern Ill. U., 1969; M.S., U. Ill., 1973; M.P.A., Roosevelt U., 1976; student Universidad de las Americas, 1967. Reference librarian Chgo. Pub. Library, 1973-75; dir. Cook County Corrections Library Program, Chgo., 1975-77; dir. Three Rivers Pub. Library Dist., Channahon, Ill., 1977—. Contbr. articles on folk music to profl. jours. Mem. exec. bd. Sunny Ridge Family Ctr., Wheaton, Ill., 1982—, Midwest Baptist Conf., Park Ridge, Ill., 1981—. Served with U.S. Army, 1969-72; Vietnam. Decorated Bronze Star. Ill. State Library scholar, 1972. Mem. Am. Library Assn., Ill. Library Assn. (treas. DLRT 1978-79), Beta Phi Mu, Psi Chi. Home: 1111 C Gael Dr Joliet IL 60410 Office: Three Rivers Pub Library Dist 210 Channon Dr Channahon IL 60410

BLOOM, BRYAN SCOTT, accountant; b. Chgo., Mar. 29, 1955; s. John Edward and Jacqueline (Bechtel) B.; m. Pamela Lynn Ray, Feb. 20, 1982; 1 child, Callie Lynn. AA in Bus., Harper Coll., 1974; BS in Accountancy, U. Ill., 1976. Acct. State Univ. Retirement System Ill., Champaign, 1977-80, chief acct., 1980-87, dep. dir. fin., 1987—. Treas. Twin City Bible Ch., Urbana, 1983-86. Mem. Am. Inst. CPA's. Republican. Avocations: golf, reading. Home: 1805 Galena Urbana IL 61801 Office: State Univ Retirement System Ill 50 Gerty Dr Champaign IL 61820

BLOOM, STEPHEN I., banker; b. Bklyn., July 15, 1945; s. David H. and Estelle (Braunstein) B.; m. Rochelle Malkin, June 11, 1967; children—Alisa, Stacy, Jaime. B.B.A., Ohio State U., 1967; postgrad. in econs. and fin., Cleve. State U., 1972. Pres. U.S. Mortgage Co., Inc., Cleve., 1975—, Capcom, Inc., Cleve., 1977—; gen. ptnr. Hampton Hills Assn., Newark, 1982—, U.S. Ventures, Ltd., Cleve., 1984-85, Boca Raton, Fla., 1985—, pres. 1986—; chmn. Instasign, Boca Raton, 1986—. Chmn. Adopt-a-Sch., Cleve. Jewish Fedn., 1983-84, U.S. Com. Sports for Israel, Phila., 1984—, Housing Our Citizens, Cleve., 1984—; pres. Menorah Fed. Credit Union, 1977-78; chmn. U.S. Fast Pitch Softball Team of U.S. Com. Sports for Israel, 1984—, Mass Care Palm Beach County ARC, 1986—; mem. Gov.'s Task Force Seed Capital Financing, 1986, mass care chmn. ARC Palm Beach, Fla., 1986—; v.p. Fla. Innovation Found., 1986—. Served to 2d lt. U.S. Army, 1967-68. Mem. Mortgage Bankers Assn. Am., Nat. Assn. Review Appraisers and Underwriters, Internat. Inst. Valuers, Nat. Assn. Home Builders, Urban Land Inst., Internat. Council Shopping Ctrs., Venture Capital Seed Fund Assn. Fla. (co-founding), Gold Coast Venture Capital Club (dir. 1986—). Clubs: Univ. (pres. 1974-75). Lodge: B'nai B'rith (interlodge council pres. 1977-78, Label Katz Young Leadership award 1978, Univ. Lodge Man Yr. 1980). Avocations: marathon running; boating; public speaking.

BLOOM, STEPHEN JOEL, distribution company executive; b. Chgo., Feb. 27, 1936; s. Max Samuel and Carolyn (Gumbiner) B.; m. Nancy Lee Gillan, Aug. 24, 1957; children: Anne, Bradley, Thomas, Carolyn. B.B.A., U. Mich., 1958. Salesman, then gen. mgr. Cigarette Service Co., Countryside, Ill., 1957-65, pres., chief exec. officer, 1965—; exec. v.p., chief exec. officer S. Bloom, Inc., Countryside; pres., dir. Intercontinental Cons. Corp., Balt., chmn. bd., 1978—; bd. dirs. Horizon Bancorp, LaGrange, Ill., N.W. Drug Co., Seattle. Bd. dirs. Clarendon Hills United Fund, Ill., 1975—; fin. chmn. DuPage County Republican Com., 1976; mem. Chgo. Crime Commn. Named Man of Yr. Chgo. Tobacco Table, 1972; named to Tobacco Industry Hall of Fame, 1985. Mem. Nat. Automatic Mdsg. Assn. (Minuteman award 1974), Nat. Assn. Tobacco Distbrs. (chmn. nat. legis. com. Young Exec. of Yr. award, dir. 1978), Ill. Assn. Tobacco Distbrs., Young Pres. Orgn. Lodge: Rotary. Home: 3 Hamill Ln Clarendon Hills IL 60514 Office: 7512 S County Line Rd Burr Ridge IL 60521

BLOOM, VICTOR, psychiatrist; b. N.Y.C., Aug. 17, 1931; s. Hyman and Anna (Victor) B.; m. Shirley Dobie, June 30, 1973; children—Dorcas D., Claire B., Gordon D., David B., Elizabeth D. B.S. U. Mich., 1953, M.D., 1957. Diplomate Am. Bd. Psychiatry and Neurology. Intern Sinai Hosp. of Detroit, 1958; psychiat. resident Lafayette Clinic, Detroit, 1959-61, chief adult inpat. service, 1968-72; clin. assoc. prof. Wayne State U., Detroit, 1972—; pvt. practice psychiatry, Detroit, 1961-85, Grosse Pointe Park, Mich., 1973—. Mem. AMA, Am. Psychiat. Assn., Mich. State Med. Soc., Wayne County Med. Soc., Mich. Psychiat. Soc., Friends of Mich. Psychoanalytic Soc. Contbr. articles on psychotherapy, group psychotherapy, bioenergetic analysis, liaison psychiatry, death and dying, prevention of suicide, psychotherapy of schizophrenia to profl. jours. Home and Office: 1007 Three Mile Dr Grosse Pointe Park MI 48230

BLOOMFIELD, CATHERINE SANDRA, psychologist; b. Louisville, Oct. 24, 1950; s. Coleman and Shirley (Rosenbaum) B.; m. Brock Martin Siegel, Dec. 19, 1978; children: Justin Siegel, Aaron Siegel, Rachael Siegel. BA, U. Minn., 1972, MA, 1977. Lic. psychologist, Minn. Instr. U. Minn. Extension, Mpls., 1976—; psychologist, counselor Coll. St. Catherine, St. Paul, 1977-84; psychologist Psychol. Assocs., St. Paul, 1984—. Mem. Am. Psychol. Assn., Minn. Psychol. Assn., Minn. Lic. Psychologists, Minn. Women Psychologists (mem. steering com., treas. 1979-80). Avocations: sailing, pottery, bicycling.

BLOOMFIELD, COLEMAN, insurance company executive; b. Winnipeg, Man., Can., July 2, 1926; came to U.S., 1952, naturalized, 1958; s. Samuel and Bessie (Staniloff) B.; m. Shirley Rosenbaum, Nov. 4, 1948; children: Catherine, Laura, Leon, Diane, Richard. B.Commerce, U. Man., 1948. With Commonwealth Life Ins. Co., Louisville, 1948-51; actuary, sr. v.p. Minn. Mut. Life Ins. Co., St. Paul, 1952-70; exec. v.p. Minn. Mut. Life Ins. Co., 1970-71, pres., chief exec. officer, 1971—, chmn. bd., 1977—; dir. Northwestern Bell Telephone Co., 1st Nat. Bank St. Paul. Bd. dirs. Minn. Orch. Assn.; bd. dirs. St. Paul United Way. Fellow Soc. Actuaries; mem. St. Paul C. of C., Am. Council Life Ins. (dir.). Office: Minn Mut Life Ins Co 400 N Robert St Saint Paul MN 55101 *

BLOOMFIELD, RANDALL CHARLES, marketing executive; b. Lakewood, Ohio, Feb. 27, 1948; s. Joseph Earl and Charlotte (Ackermann) B.; m. Cheryl Lynn Schudel, June 24, 1972; children: Michael, Jeffrey. BSBA, Bowling Green U., 1970; MBA, Cleve. State U., 1972. Mktg. and fin. analyst Cleve. Elect. Illum Co., 1970-74; sr. market analyst Republic Steel, Cleve., 1974-79, asst. to gen. mgr. tubular products, 1979-84; mgr. planning anlysis LTV Steel, Cleve., 1984-85; v.p. mktg. Comtype Bus Services, Fairview Park, Ohio, 1985-86; mktg. and account mgr. Bekaert Steel Wire, Akron, Ohio, 1986—. Mem. Nat. Assn. Bus. Economists, Automotive Industry Action Group. Republican. Club: Cleve. Bus. Econ. Home: 4781 W 228th St Fairview Park OH 44126

BLOOMFIELD, SAUL SOLOMON, academic physician, clinical investigator, clinical pharmacologist; b. Montreal, Can., June 30, 1925; came to U.S., 1965, permanent resident; s. Oscar H. and Tillie S. (Schoilovitch) B.; m. Ellen S Steinberg, Jan. 9, 1949; children—Laurence, Patricia, Matthew. B.S., McGill U., Montreal, 1946, M.S., 1948; M.D., U. Geneva, 1953; M.S., U. Montreal, 1965. Intern Montreal Gen. Hosp., 1953-54; resident in internal medicine Queen Mary Vets. Hosp., Montreal, 1954-55; gen. practice medicine, Montreal, 1955-63; instr. pharmacology U. Montreal, 1963-65; from asst. to assoc. prof. U. Cin., 1965-77, prof. medicine and pharmacology, 1977—; vis. scientist Merrell Internat., Strasbourg, France, 1972-73; acting dir. div. clin. pharmacology U. Cin., 1979-81; vis. prof. Oxford U., 1980. Contbr. articles to profl. jours. Mem. Com. Human Research, Cin., 1969-77; del. U.S. Pharmacopeia Conv., Cin., 1972-80; pres. U. Cin. Coll. Medicine Faculty Forum, 1985-87, pres., 1985-87. NIH research grantee, 1968-72; research fellow Can. Found. Advancement Therapeutics, 1964-65, NIH, 1966-68. Mem. Am. Soc. Clin. Pharmacology and Therapeutics, Am. Soc. Pharmacology and Exptl. Therapeutics, Am. Fedn. Clin. Research, Am. Pain Soc., Internat. Assn. Study of Pain, Cin. Soc. Internal Medicine. Club: Faculty. Home: 57 Carpenter's Ridge Cincinnati OH 45241 Office: U Cincinnati Med Ctr 5502 Med Scis Bldg Cincinnati OH 45267-0578

BLOOMQUIST, ALDRICH CARL, sugar company executive; b. Willmar, Minn., Mar. 20, 1921; s. Aldrich Albin Carl and Leola Hannah (France) B.; m. Meredith May Scheid, Dec. 24, 1943. BA, Gustavus Adolphus Coll., 1943. Editorial staff Mankato (Minn.) Free Press, 1946-49; sales staff Jostens, Owatonna, Minn., 1949-52, Brings Press, Mpls., 1952-55; regional mgr. Western Beet Sugar Producers, Mpls., 1962-72; v.p. pub. affairs Am. Crystal Sugar Co., Moorhead, Minn., 1972—. Served with USN, 1943-45. Named Sugar Man of Yr., 1977; recipient Alumni Achievement award Gustavus Adolphus Coll., 1978. Lutheran. Avocations: collecting stamps. Home: 516 S 7th St Moorhead MN 56560

BLOOMQUIST, JOHN HAYES, special education teacher, horse breeder; b. Ashland, Wis., July 30, 1946; s. John Joel and Elizabeth Amanda (Wheelock) B.; m. Sue Ann Peterson, July, 1969 (div. 1974). BS in Edn., Northland Coll., 1969; M in Spl. Edn., U. Minn., 1986. Tchr. mentally retarded Ashland (Wis.) Schs., 1968-75; dir. ski patrol Powderhorn/Indianhead Mountain, Bessemer, Mich., 1975-79; tchr. emotionally disturbed/behaviorally disabled Ashland Schs., 1981—; instr. advanced first aid Northland Coll., Ashland, 1974—; co-founder Taquis Toys, Inc., Ashland, 1987—. Contbr. articles to profl. jours. Mem., advisor Pilot Parents, Ashland, 1981—; mem. Chequamegon Theatre Assn., Ashland, 1978—; instr. first aid ARC, 1974—; scout leader Boy Scouts Am., Ashland, 1968-74. Recipient Wood Badge award, Boy Scouts Am., 1973; named one of Outstanding Profl. Patrolmen Nat. Ski Patrol, 1975. Mem. Upper Midwest Endurance and Competitive Riding Assn., Jaycees. Republican. Methodist. Club: EZ Riders (Ashland) (top sr. gamer 1976-79, 84-86, top sr. gamer riders informed 1986, pres., dir. 1983, 85-86). Avocations: canoeing, camping, snow skiing, scuba diving, hunting. Home: Rt 1 Box 204 Ashland WI 54806

BLOSER, DIETER, radiologist; b. Yugoslavia, Aug. 17, 1944; came to U.S., 1947, naturalized, 1954; s. Peter and Eva Helen B.; A.B., Princeton U., 1966; M.D., Case Western Res. U., 1970; m. Deborah Pierce Forbes, Nov. 25, 1967; children—Peter Forbes, Timothy Philip. Intern dept. medicine U. Hosps. of Cleve., 1970-71, resident in radiology, 1971-72, 74-76, chief resident, 1975-76; practice medicine specializing in radiology, Parma, Ohio, 1976—; mem. staff Parma Community Gen. Hosp., 1976—, chief nuclear medicine, 1977—, chief radiology, 1984—; mem. staff U. Hosps. of Cleve., Cleve. Met. Gen. Hosp. Bd. dirs. Cleve. chpt. Juvenile Diabetes Found., 1986—; active Am. Diabetes Assn., 1985—; trustee Case Western Reserve U. Sch. Med Alumni Assn., 1985—. Served to lt. comdr. USN, 1972-74. Diplomate Am. Bd. Radiology. Mem. Am. Coll. Radiology, Radiol. Soc. N. Am., Ohio Radiol. Soc., Cleve. Radiol. Soc. (pres.-elect 1986-87, pres. 1987-88), Am. Inst. Ultrasound in Medicine, Cleve. Acad. Medicine, AMA, Ohio Med. Assn., Princeton Alumni Assn. No. Ohio, Phi Beta Kappa, Alpha Omega Alpha. Lutheran. Home: 1251 Oakridge Dr Cleveland Heights OH 44121 Office: 7007 Power Blvd Parma OH 44129

BLOSSOM, JOHN SEIBERT, consulting engineer; b. Detroit, Aug. 10, 1917; s. John and Catherine (Seibert) B.; m. Enid Foege, May 13, 1940 (dec. Aug. 1973); 1 child, John Albert; m. Harriet Snowdon, July 28, 1974. Student in mech. engring. Lawrence Inst. Tech., 1942, 46-47. Registered profl. engr., Mich., Ohio, Ind., Ky., Md., N.Y., D.C., Pa., W.Va., S.C. Chief instr. Thermal Inst., Detroit, 1937-39; chief engr., sec. Mech. Heat & Cold, Inc., 1939-44, 46-57; ptnr. Ziel-Blossom & Assoc., Cin., 1957-71; pres. ZBA, Inc. and Ziel-Blossom & Assocs., Inc., 1971-84; v.p., treas. ZBA, Inc., Cin., 1984-86, mgmt. cons. 1986—. Contbr. articles to profl. jours. Mem. ad hoc com. on solid wastes Nat. Acad. Scis.-Bldg. Research Adv. Bd., Washington, 1967-74; trustee Shadybrook House of Laymen's Movement, Cleve., 1964-71, arbitrator Am. Arbitration Assn., Cin., 1968—. Served with USNR, 1944-46. Fellow ASHRAE (chmn. handbook, pub., research and tech. coms. 1960-84, Wolverine Diamond Key award 1959, tech. council 1985—); mem. Nat. Soc. Profl. Engrs., Mich. Soc. Profl. Engrs. (chmn. bldg. code com. 1953-56). Presbyterian. Avocations: squash racquets; tennis. Home: 7351 S Mingo Ln Madeira OH 45243 Office: 35 E 7th St Cincinnati OH 45202

BLOSSOM, TIFANIE THEYLON, minister; b. Toledo, Dec. 6, 1947; d. Jerome Harvey and Ruth Marie (Adcock) Rollins; m. Thomas Alva Downey, Jan. 28, 1967 (div. June 1975); children: Heath Thomas, Nathan Michael; m. Jon Raulph Blossom, Nov. 15, 1978. Acctg. student, Owens Tech. Sch., Toledo, 1970-73; student psychology, theology, U. Toledo, 1973-76; grad., Religious Sci. Internat. Ministerial Sch., Chgo., 1984. Lic. Religious Sci. practitioner. Mgr. Elaine Powers Figure Salon, Toledo, 1974-75; asst. comptroller, sec. Huss Enterprises, Toledo, 1975-77; cooking instr. Amana Corp., Toledo, 1977-78; med. rep. Gerber Products, Inc., Fremont, Mich., 1978-79; owner, operator Tifanie's Kitchen, Toledo, 1979-81; pres. Blossom Health Ctr., Toledo, 1981—; substitute minister North Shore Ch. Religious Sci., Evanston, Ill., First Ch. Religious Sci., Chgo.; interim minister New Beginning Ch. of Religious Sci., Toledo; lectr. various orgns., seminars on nutrition, lifestyle, self awareness, transactional analysis. Author: Breadmakers' Handbook, 1982. Bd. dirs. March of Dimes, Toledo, 1987—, mem. Gourmet Gala food com.; bd. dirs. East Toledo Community Mental Health, 1976-78; vol. St. Vincent's Hosp., Little Sisters of Poor. Mem. Internat. New Thought Alliance, Internat. Transactional Analysis Orgn. Avocations: gardening, swimming, aerobics, skiing, reading. Office: Blossom Health Ctr 5900 Southwyck Blvd Toledo OH 43614

BLOUCH, SUSAN ELIZABETH, training specialist; b. Cleve., Aug. 23, 1947; d. Robert William and Dorothy Belle (Herig) B. BS, Miami U., Oxford, Ohio, 1969. Social worker Adult Service Ctr., Detroit, 1976-81, supr. mental health, 1977-81, dir. sr. citizens' programs devel., 1981-84; seminar leader Hosp. Learning Ctr., Los Angeles, 1984-85; tng. specialist The Taubman Co., Bloomfield Hills, Mich., 1985—; instr. Wayne County Community Coll., Detroit, 1977-82; cons. in field. Creator human relations programs. Assoc. cons. CHANGE, H.R.D., Detroit, 1981-85; bd. dirs. YWCA and YMCA, Detroit, 1983-84. Mem. Am. Soc. Tng. and Devel., Nat. Speakers Assn., Internat. Customer Service Assn. Avocations: marathon swimmer, reader, travel. Home: 3575 Karen Pkwy 203 Waterford MI 48054 Office: The Taubman Co 200 E Long Lake Rd Bloomfield Hills MI 48303

BLOUIN, FRANCIS XAVIER, JR., archivist; b. Belmont, Mass., July 29, 1946; s. Francis X. and Margaret (Cronin) B. AB, U. Notre Dame, 1967; MA, U. Minn., 1969, PhD, 1978. Asst. dir. Bentley Library U. Mich., Ann Arbor, 1974-75, assoc. archivist Bentley Library, 1975-81, dir. Bentley Library, 1981—, asst. prof. history and library sci., 1979-83, assoc. prof., 1983—. Author: The Boston Region..., 1980; editor Intellectual Life on Michigan Frontier, 1985, Archival Implications Machine..., 1980. Trustee Mich. Student Found., 1986—; dir. Am. Friends of Vatican Library, 1981—. Fellow Soc. Am. Archivist (mem. governing council 1985-88); mem. Orgn. Am. Historians, Hist. Soc. Mich. (trustee 1982-88, pres. 1987-88), Assn. Records Mgrs. and Adminstrs., Internat. Council on Archives. Lodge: Rotary. Office: Univ Mich Bentley Hist Library 1150 Beal Ave Ann Arbor MI 48109

BLOUNT, MICHAEL EUGENE, lawyer; b. Camden, N.J., July 9, 1949; s. Floyd Eugene and Dorothy Alice (Geyer) Durham; m. Janice Lynn Brown, Aug. 22, 1969; children—Kirsten Marie, Gretchen Elizabeth. B.A., U. Tex., 1971; J.D., U. Houston, 1974. Bar: Tex. 1974, Ill. 1980, D.C. 1981, U.S. Ct. Appeals (D.C. cir.) 1978, U.S. Ct. Mil. Appeals 1975, U.S. Supreme Ct. 1977. Atty. advisor Office of Gen. Counsel SEC, Washington, 1977-78, legal asst. to chmn., 1978-79; assoc. Gardner, Carton & Douglas, Chgo., 1980-84; ptnr. Arnstein, Gluck, Lehr, Barron & Milligan, Chgo., 1984-86, Seyfarth, Shaw, Fairweather & Geraldson, Chgo., 1987—. Served as lt. JAGC, USN, 1974-77. Mem. ABA (fed. regulation of securities com.), Chgo. Bar Assn., Order of Barons, Phi Alpha Delta (chpt. treas. 1973.) Club: Univ. of Chgo. Home: 1432 S Highland Ave Arlington Heights IL 60005 Office: Seyfarth Shaw Fairweather & Geraldson 55 E Monroe Chicago IL 60603

BLUE, ROBERT LEE, educator; b. Columbiaville, Mich., Apr. 23, 1920; s. Arthur Floyd and Elma (Ellis) B.; B.A., Mich. State U., 1941; M.A., U. Mich., 1952; m. Dorothy L. Seward, July 15, 1961. Tchr., Chesaning (Mich.) High Sch., 1941-42, 45-57; prin. Ricker Jr. High Sch., Saginaw, Mich., 1957-59, Buena Vista High Sch., Saginaw, 1960-69; asst. prof. secondary edn. Central Mich. U., Mt. Pleasant, 1969—. Bd. dirs. Hartley Edn. Nature Camp, 1957-69. Served with U.S. Army, 1942-45. Decorated Bronze Star. Mem. NEA (life), Mich. Edn. Assn., Assn. Tchr. Educators, Mich. Assn. Tchr. Educators, Nat. Assn. Secondary Sch. Prins., Mich. Assn. Secondary Sch. Prins., Mich. PTA (hon. life), Am. Legion, Mich. Hist. Soc., Saginaw County Hist. Soc., Lapeer County Hist. Soc., Phi Delta Kappa. Republican. Methodist. Clubs: Optimist, Knife and Fork, Pit and Balcony, Masons. Author: Footsteps Into The Past, A History of Columbiaville, 1979, also articles. Home: 4584 Colonial Dr Saginaw MI 48603 Office: 115 W Genesee Saginaw MI 48602

BLUESTEIN, BERNARD R., research administrator, chemist; b. Phila., Oct. 7, 1925; s. Joseph and Minnie Bluestein; m. Claire Kraiman, June 22, 1947; children: Rhona C., Sherrie L., Hazel M., Carol J. BS in Chemistry, U. Pa., 1946; MS, U. Ill., 1947, PhD in Organic Chemistry, 1949; MBA, Fairleigh Dickinson U., 1967. Research assoc. Rutgers U., New Brunswick, N.J., 1949-51; instr. Purdue U., West Lafayette, Ind., 1951-52; asst. prof. chemistry Coe Coll., Cedar Rapids, Iowa, 1952-55; dir. research, asst. supt. mfg. Sonneborn Chem. & Refining Corp., Petrolia, Pa., 1955-62; asst. dir. research & devel. Witco Chem. Corp., Oakland, N.J., 1962-76, dir. research & devel., 1976-83; v.p. research & devel. Allied-Kelite div. Witco Chem. Corp., New Hudson, Mich., 18936; continuing edn. prof. Pa. State U., Butler, 1957-61. Editor, author: Amphoteric Surfactants, 1982. Fellow Royal Soc. Chemistry; mem. Am. Chem. Soc. (chmn. N.J. com. 1977), Am. Inst. Chemistry (N.J. council), Am. Oil Chemists Soc., Assn. Research Dirs. Office: Witco Corp 29111 Milford Rd New Hudson MI 48165

BLUESTEIN, JUDITH ANN, rabbi, educator diversified industry executive; b. Cin., Apr. 2, 1948; d. Paul Harold and Joan Ruth (Straus) Bluestein; B.A., U. Pa., 1969; postgrad. Am. Sch. Classical Studies, Athens, Greece, 1968, Vergilian Soc., 1970, 76, 77, 78, Hebrew Union Coll., Jewish Inst. Religion, Jerusalem, 1971, 1979-80, Am. Acad. in Rome, 1975; M.A. in Religion, Case Western Res. U., 1973, M.A. in Latin, 1973; M.Ed., Xavier U., 1984; M.A.H.L., Hebrew Union Coll.-Jewish Inst. Religion, Cin., 1983. Ordained rabbi, 1984. Sec., Paul H. Bluestein & Co., Cin., 1964—; v.p. Panel Machine Co., 1966—, Blujay Corp., 1966—, Ermet Products Corp., 1966—; partner Companhia Engenheiros Industrial Bluestein do Brasil, Cin., 1971—; tchr. Latin, Cin. Public Schs., 1973-79; rabbi Temple Israel, Marion, Ohio, 1980-84, Temple Sholom, Galesburg, Ill., 1985-86; co-chmn. Interfaith Plea for Soviet Jews, 1986; lectr. Hebrew Union Coll.-Jewish Inst. Religion, 1986; vis. lectr./Jewish chaplain Denison U., 1987. bd. dirs. Cin. Council for Soviet Jews, 1982-84, 85—, sec. 1985—. Fellow Case Western Reserve U., 1973, Hebrew Union Coll.-Jewish Inst. Religion, 1985—; Revson fellow Jewish Theol Sem. Am., 1984-85; Hausmon Meml. fellow Hebrew Union Coll. Jewish Inst. Religion, 1985—. Mem. Archeol. Inst. Am., Assn. Jewish Studies, Am. Acad. Religion, Classical Assn. Middle West and South (v.p. Ohio 1976-79), Central Conf. Am. Rabbis, Am. Classical League, Ohio Classical Conf. (council 1976-79), Vergilian Soc., Soc. Bibl. Lit., Cin. Assn. Tchrs. Classics (pres. 1976-78), Am. Philol. Assn. Address: 3420 Section Rd Cincinnati OH 45237

BLUESTEIN, PAUL HAROLD, management engineer; b. Cin., June 14, 1923; s. Norman and Eunice D. (Schullman) B.; m. Joan Ruth Straus, May 17, 1943; children: Alice Sue Bluestein Greenbaum, Judith Ann. B.S., Carnegie Inst. Tech., 1946, B.Engring. in Mgmt. Engring., 1946; M.B.A., Xavier U., 1973. Registered profl. engr., Ohio. Time study engr. Lodge & Shipley Co., 1946-47; adminstrv. engr. Randall Co., 1947-52; partner Paul H. Bluestein & Co. (mgmt. cons.), 1952—, Seinsheimer-Bluestein Mgmt. Services, 1964-70; gen. mgr. Baker Refrigeration Co., 1953-56; pres., dir. Tabor Mfg. Co., 1953-54, Bluejay Corp., 1954—, Blatt & Ludwig Corp., 1954-57, Jason Industries, Inc., 1954-57, Hamilton-York Corp., 1954-57, Earle Hardware Mfg. Co., 1955-57, Hermas Machine Co., 1956—, Panel Machine Co., Ermet Products Corp., 1957-86, Tyco Labs., Inc., 1968-69, All-Tech Industries, 1968; gen. mgr. Hafleigh & Co., 1959-60; sr. v.p., gen. mgr. McCauley Ind. Corp., 1959-60; gen. mgr. Am. Art Works div. Rapid-Am. Corp., 1960-63; sec.-treas., dir. Liberty Baking Co., 1964-65; pres. Duguesne Baking Co., 1964-65, Goddard Bakers, Inc., 1964-65; pub. Merger and Acquisition Digest, 1962-69; partner Companhia Engenheiros Indsl. Bluestein Do Brasil, 1970-84; v.p., gen. mgr. Famco Machine div. Worden-Allen Co., 1974-75; exec. v.p., gen. mgr. Peck, Stow & Wilcox Co., Inc., 1976-77; mem. Joint Engring. Mgmt. Conf. Com., 1971-78. Served with AUS, 1943-46. Mem. ASME, Internat. Inst. Indsl. Engrs., Am. Soc. Engring. Mgmt., N.Am. Mgmt. Council; C.I.O.S.-World Council Mgmt. (dir.). Home and Office: 3420 Section Rd Amberley Village Cincinnati OH 45237

BLUETT, THOMAS BYRON, SR., child psychologist; b. Milw., May 29, 1931; s. Byron Walter and Ida Mae (Mineau) B.; m. Daina Lauretta Kubilius, Sept. 21, 1974; children: Thomas Jr., Elizabeth, William, Martha, Dorothea (dec.), Byron. BS, U. Wis., 1953, MS, 1955, PhD, 1971. Counselor Appleton (Wis.) Pub. Schs., 1955-57; psychologist Green Bay (Wis.) Pub. Schs., 1957-65; exec. dir. United Cerebral Palsy, Green Bay, 1965-68; dir. pupil services Cooperative Edn. Service Agy., Wis., 1968-71; child psychologist Pediatrics Beaumont Clin., Green Bay, 1972—; sec., treas. Tri-State Testing Service, Inc., DePere, Wis., 1958—; child psychologist Sta. WTMJ-TV and Radio, Milw., 1981—, Sta. WOAI, San Antonio, 1986—; lectr. child devel., U. Wis., Green Bay, 1968-73. Author, presenter (TV series) In-Charge Parenting, 1982, (book, audio tapes) In-Charge Parenting Kit, 1983; author: Conquering Low Impulse Control, 1984; co-author: Youth Tutoring Youth, 1970. Bd. dirs. United Cerebral Palsy, N.Y.C., 1957-65; mem. Wis. Day Care Adv. Bd., Wis., 1960-65; exec. dir. Nat. Early Childhood Edn. Fund., Wis., 1971-80. Served to corp. U.S. Army, 1953-55, Korea. Grantee Rural Pupil Services, HEW, Washington, D.C., 1969, Early Childhood Edn. , ESEA, Madison, 1970. Fellow Am. Assn. Mental Deficiency, Nat. Assn. Mental Deficiency; charter mem. Wis. Soc. Clin. Cons. Psychologists (co-chmn. publicity 1986—), Nat. Assn. Sch. Psychologists (charter), Brown County Clin. Cons. Psychologists (treas. 1985-87), Phi Delta Kappa (pres. 1958-60). Episcopalian. Club: Packer Monday Night Quarterback. Lodges: Elks (handicapped children's chmn. 1958-68), Optimist (youth chmn. 1957-68). Avocations: fishing, hunting, playing banjo. Home: 503 Fulton St DePere WI 54115 Office: Beaumont Clinic Ltd 1821 S Webster Ave Green Bay WI 54301

BLUM, DANIEL JOHN, physician, otolaryngologist; b. Earling, Iowa, Aug. 11, 1948; s. LaVerne Francis and Lucille Philamena (Wilwerding) B.; m. Linda Marie Hillabrand, Nov. 5, 1968; children: Lisa, David, Christina, Melissa, Anthony, Katherine. BS in Pharmacy, Creighton U., 1972, MD,

1978. Diplomate Am. Bd. Otolaryngology, Nat. Bd. Med. Examiners of Am. Staff pharmacist Bergan Mercy Hosp., Omaha, 1972-80; intern St. Joseph Affiliated Hosp., Omaha, 1978-79; staff emergency physician Lincoln (Nebr.) Gen. Hosp., 1979-80, Midlands Hosp., Papillion, Nebr., 1979-80; resident Mayo Clinic, Rochester, Minn., 1980-84; ear, nose and throat-head and neck surgeon Wolfe Clinic, Marshalltown, Iowa, 1984—; chief of surgery Marshalltown Med. and Surg. Ctr., 1986—. Contbr. articles to profl. jours. Cub Scout leader Boy Scouts Am., Rochester, 1983. Recipient Resident Research Essay award (1st place) Am. Bronchoesophagologic Assn., Palm Beach, Fla., 1984. Fellow: Am. Acad. Otolaryngology-Head and Neck Surgeons; mem. AMA, Iowa Med. Soc., Marshall County Med. Soc. Avocations: auto racing and constrn., woodworking, hunting, fishing, scuba diving. Home: 605 Westwood Dr Marshalltown IA 50158 Office: Wolfe Clinic 309 E Church St Marshalltown IA 50158

BLUM, STEVEN B., clinical psychologist; b. Mineola, N.Y., Nov. 5, 1951; s. Lowell Blum and Selma (Blumenfeld) Sonne; m. Pamela A. Davy, Feb. 14, 1982; 1 child, Amy. BA, SUNY, Albany, 1973; PhD, U. Nebr., 1980. Cert. clin. psychologist. Program dir. Valley Hope Alcoholism Treatment Ctr., Lincoln, Nebr., 1980-86; staff psychologist Health Am., Lincoln, 1986—; pvt. practice psychology Lincoln, 1986—; cons. in field. Am. Psychol. Assn., Nebr. Fellowship Christian Counselors. Messianic Jew. Office: 3701 O St Suite B-3 Lincoln NE 68510

BLUME, HERBERT EDWARD, accountant; b. Tripoli, Iowa, Sept. 20, 1917; s. William C. and Hulda D. (Hagenow) B.; student LaSalle Extension U., 1943-44; m. Elvera E. Kelling, Sept. 25, 1938; children—Carol (Mrs. Merlin H. Franzen), Marjorie (Mrs. Arthur F. Maynard), Marilyn (Mrs. Robert F. Seefeld). Farmer, nr. Tripoli, 1938-40; pvt. tax practice, Tripoli, 1944—; pvt. practice accounting, 1945—; treas. Tripoli Devel. Corp., 1959—; pres. Aids for Handicaps, Inc., 1958—; pub. Farm Record. Sec. Bremer County Zoning Commn., 1963-80; presdl. elector 3d Dist. Iowa, 1980, 84. Accounting practitioner, 1975—. Sec. finance Iowa dist. east Lutheran Ch.-Mo. Synod, 1960-66; chmn. St. John Luth. Ch., Denver, Iowa, 1980. Mem. Nat. Soc. Pub. Accountants (accredited), Accts. Assn. Iowa (pres. 1970-71), Nat. Assn. Tax Practitioners, Iowa Soc. Acctg. Practitioners, Luth. Laymen's League, Farm Bur. Republican. Patentee stairwalking crutches, 1945. Address: Tripoli IA 50676

BLUMENBERG, RICHARD MITCHELL, cinema and photography educator; b. Gloversville, N.Y., May 26, 1935; s. Ella Olga Sesonski; m. Julia Porcher Wickham Porter, Mar. 1970 (div. Aug. 1982); m. Irena Lane Grant, June 22, 1984; 1 child, Robert John. BA, U. Iowa, 1959, MFA, 1963; PhD, Ohio U., 1969. Asst. prof. Slippery Rock (Pa.) State U., 1969-70; prof. cinema and photography So. Ill. U., Carbondale, 1970—; assoc. producer Optos Ltd., 1969—; pres. Windmill Prodns., Inc., 1985—. Assoc. producer, writer (film) America First, 1972 (Edinburgh Film Festival award 1972); author: Critical Focus, 1975, (poems) Mentor Midwest Poets, 1966; contbr. articles to profl. jours. Bd. trustees Univ. Film and Video Found., 1984—. Served with U.S. Army, 1954-57. Ohio U. Italian fellow, 1968, Earl Siegfred Arts scholar, 1969; ICA grantee, 1979; recipient travel award British Council, 1982. Mem. Soc. for Cinema Studies, Univ. Film and Video Assn. (pres. 1984-86). Democrat. Jewish. Avocations: swimming, classical guitar. Office: So Ill U Dept Cinema and Photography Carbondale IL 62901

BLUMENSHINE, MAHLON, banker; b. Washington, Ill., May 11, 1928; s. Mahlon and Mabel Mae (Schick) B.; m. Carolyn Sue Longden, June 26, 1960; children: J. Wesley, Bradley Ward, Blake Alan. Standard Banking degree, So. Ill. U., 1967; Grad. Banking degree, U. Wis., 1974. V.p. Community Bank, East Peoria, Ill., 1956-75; pres., trust officer Sunnyland Bank, Washington, Ill., 1975—; also bd. dirs. Sunnyland Bank. Alderman City of Washington, Ill., 1979-83; treas. Dist. 50 Schs., Washington, 1983-87; past chmn. Easter Seal Drive, Heart Fund Drive, Cancer Fund Drive. Served as cpl. U.S. Army, 1950-52. Mem. Am. Inst. Banking (pres. cen. Ill. chpt. 1957-58), Washington C. of C., Am. Legion, VFW. Republican. Methodist. Lodge: Kiwanis. Avocations: stamp and coin collecting, gardening, golf. Home: 910 N Hampton Rd Washington IL 61571 Office: Sunnyland Bank Box 99 Washington IL 61571

BLUMENTHAL, DAVID LIONEL, psychoanalyst; b. Chgo., Apr. 22, 1926; s. Sol and Ida (Schniederman) B.; B.S. in Mech. Engring., Purdue U., 1948; M.S.W., U. Chgo., 1949, postgrad., 1950; M.A., Butler U., Indpls., 1959; postgrad. Nat. Psychol. Assn. for Psychoanalysis, N.Y.C., 1955-70; M.A., Christian Theol. Sem., 1982; Sc.D. (hon.), Lincoln Coll., Indpls., 1962; Rel.D., Ind. Christian U., 1984; m. Patricia Louise Wright, Apr. 19, 1968; 1 dau., Jill Ann. Psychiat. caseworker Ind. U. Med. Center, 1950-51; caseworker, supr., adminstrv. asst. Family Service Assn. Indpls., 1951-54; pvt. practice psychotherapy and psychoanalysis, Indpls., 1954—; psychotherapist, dir. Shelby County Mental Health Center, Shelbyville, Ind., 1955-58; mem. faculty Ind. U., Purdue U., Butler U., Lincoln Coll., 1954-74. Served with USNR, 1944-46. Recipient Public Relations award Family Service Assn. Indpls., 1952, 54. Mem. Acad. Cert. Social Workers, Nat. Assn. Social Workers (charter), Am. Acad. Psychotherapists, Am. Group Psychotherapy Assn., Am. Soc. Group Psychotherapy and Psychodrama, Ind. Soc. Clin. Social Workers, NAACP. Jewish. Author articles in field. Address: 8100 Sargent Rd Indianapolis IN 46256

BLUMENTHAL, KENNETH WAYNE, osteopathic physician and surgeon; b. Chgo., Sept. 17, 1952; s. Alfred Rolland and Florence (Crane) B.; m. Jeanne Ellaine Beers, June 9, 1978; children: Robert Scott, David Edward. BS, Duke U., 1974; DO, Chgo. Coll. Osteo. Medicine, 1978. Physician, pres. Blumenthal Med. Corp., Portage, Ind., 1981—; sec. med. staff Porter Meml Hosp. Valparaiso, Ind. 1983. Bd. dirs. Porter County Assn. Retarded Citizens, 1981, Vis. Nurses Porter County, 1982—. Mem. Am. Osteo. Assn., Am. Osteo. Assn. Allergy and Immunology, Ind. Med. Assn., Porter County Med. Soc. (sec.-treas. 1985, pres. 1987). Jewish. Avocations: jazz, saxophone, sculpture. Home: 1122 N 475 E Chesterton IN 46304 Office: Blumenthal Med Corp 3110 Willowcreek Rd Portage IN 46368

BLUMENTHAL, W. MICHAEL, manufacturing company executive, former secretary Treasury; b. 1926. BS, U. Calif., Berkeley, 1951; MA, MPA, Princeton U., 1953, PhD, 1956. Research assoc. Princeton U., 1954-57; v.p., also bd. dirs. Crown Cork Internat. Corp., 1957-61; dep. asst. sec. for econ. affairs Dept. State, 1961; apptd. Pres.'s dep. spl. rep. for trade negotiations with rank of ambassador 1963-67; pres. Bendix Internat., 1967-70; also bd. dirs. Bendix Corp., 1967-77, vice chmn., 1970-71, pres., chief operating officer, 1971-72, chmn., pres., chief exec. officer, 1972-77; sec. of Treasury Washington, 1977-79; also bd. dirs. UNISYS Corp. (formerly Burroughs Corp.), Detroit, 1979—; vice chmn., chief exec. officer Unisys Corp. (formerly Burroughs Corp.), 1980-81, chmn., chief exec. officer, 1981—; bd. dirs. Tenneco, Inc., Pillsbury Co., Chem. N.Y. Corp. and subs. Chem. Bank. Bd. dirs. Detroit Renaissance, New Detroit, Detroit Symphony Orch.; v.p., bd. dirs. Detroit Area council Boy Scouts Am.; v.p., bd. dirs., mem. exec. com. United Found. Detroit. Mem. Bus. Council, Bus. Roundtable, Am. Econ. Assn., Rockefeller Found. (trustee). Club: Economic of Detroit (bd. dirs.). Office: Unisys Corp PO Box 418 Detroit MI 48232 also: Burroughs Corp Burroughs Pl Detroit MI 48232

BLUMER, ABRAHAM, gynecologist, obstetrician; b. Detroit, Dec. 15, 1923; s. Raphael and Sarah (Rothenberg) B.; m. Joyce Dashow, Nov. 28, 1946; children: Mark Edward, Gary Ross, Robin Allen. Student, Detroit Inst. Tech., Wayne State U., Newark Coll. Engring., Amherst Coll.; MD, Cornell U., 1949. Diplomate Am. Bd. Ob-Gyn. Intern Grace Hosp., Detroit, 1949-50, resident, 1950-54; practice medicine specializing in ob-gyn Detroit, 1955-63; group practice Woodland Med. Group, Detroit, 1963-83, 12 Mile Ob-Gyn, Lathrup Village, Mich., 1983—. Served to lt. U.S. Army, 1951-52. Fellow Am. Coll. Ob-Gyn, ACS; mem. Mich. Soc. Ob-Gyn. Avocations: woodturning, amateur radio. Office: 12 Mile Ob-Gyn 18211 W 12 Mile Rd Lathrup Village MI 48076

BLUMER, THOMAS WILLIAM, accountant; b. Chicago Heights, Ill., Oct. 27, 1954; s. Thomas Edward and Grace (Peters) B.; m. Becki Lynn Holt, Aug. 1, 1981; 1 child, Sarah Jane. BS in Acctg., Miami U., Ohio, 1975, MBA in Fin., 1976. CPA, Ohio. Staff acct. Bramel & Ackley, Cin., 1978-79; audit sr. Arthur Young, Cin., 1979-85; audit edn. resident Arthur Young, Reston, Va., 1985-86; mgr. entrepreneurial services group Arthur Young, Cin., 1986—. Author, editor instuctive manuals. Mem. Am. Inst. CPA's, Ohio Soc. CPA's, Greater Cin. Venture Assn. Home: 7827 Carraway Ct Maineville OH 45039 Office: Arthur Young Cen Trust Ctr Suite 2200 Cincinnati OH 45202

BLUNT, ROY D., state official; b. Niangua, Mo., Jan. 10, 1950; s. Leroy and Neva (Letterman) B.; m. E. Roseann Ray; children—Matthew Roy, Amy Roseann, Andrew Benjamin. B.A., S.W. Baptist U., 1970; M.A., S.W. Mo. State U., 1972. Tchr. Marshfield High Sch., Mo., 1970-73; instr. Drury Coll., Springfield, Mo., 1973-82; county clk. Greene County, Springfield, 1973-85; sec. of state State of Mo., Jefferson City, 1985—. Author: (with others) Missouri Election Procedures: A Layman's Guide, 1977; Voting Rights Guide for the Handicapped. Chmn. Mo. Housing Devel. Commn., Kansas City, 1981, Republican State Conv., Springfield, 1980; Rep. candidate for lt. gov. of Mo., 1980; U.S. observer, del. NATO, Rome, 1983; active local ARC, Muscular Dystrophy Assn., others. Named One of 10 Outstanding Young Americans, U.S. Jaycees, 1986, Springfield's Outstanding Young Man, Jaycees, 1980, Mo.'s Outstanding Young Civic Leader, 1981. Mem. Nat. Assn. Secs. of State. Baptist. Lodges: Kiwanis, Masons. Office: Sec of State State Capitol Bldg Jefferson City MO 65102

BLUSCHKE, JAMES BRIAN, quality engineer; b. St. Joseph, Mich., July 20, 1954; s. Stanley Otto and Eleanor Mae (Grieser) B. AS in Pre-Engring., Lake Mich. Coll., 1975; BS in Indsl. Mgmt., Cen. Mich. U., 1979. Indsl. engr. Leco Corp., St. Joseph, 1975-79; quality systems engr. Whirlpool Corp., St. Joseph, 1979-76, gen. supr. quality, resident engr., 1986—. Mem. Am. Soc. Quality Control (sec. 1986—, bd. birs., edn. chmn. 1982-86). Avocations: woodworking, fishing, bowling, outdoor activities. Home: 3175 Ravine Ave Saint Joseph MI 49085 Office: Whirlpool Corp Saint Joseph Div Upton Dr Saint Joseph MI 49085

BLUTZA, STEVEN JAY, marketing executive; b. N.Y.C., Oct. 4, 1945; s. Charles and Anne (Rosenberg) B. B.A., CCNY, 1966; M.A., U. Calif.-Berkeley, 1967, Ph.D., 1978. Instr. polit. sci. U. Ill., Urbana, 1972-75; pres. Consumer Services Orgn., Chgo., 1978-81, Profl. Services Mktg. Corp., Chgo., 1982—. Mem. Am. Prepaid Legal Services Inst., Nat. Resource Ctr. for Consumers of Legal Services, Phi Beta Kappa. Home: 5020 S Lake Shore Dr Apt 3415 Chicago IL 60615 Office: 1 Quincy Ct Suite 1622 Chicago IL 60604

BLYTHE, EVELYN BARBARA, insurance company executive, consultant; b. Bury, Lancashire, Eng., Aug. 29, 1934; came to U.S., 1968; d. Thomas and Pearl (Seddon) Park; m. Philip A. Blythe, Aug. 24, 1957; children: Elaine and Stephen (twins), Donna. BA summa cum laude, Ohio Dominican Coll., 1985. RN, Ohio, Calif.; state cert. midwife, state registered nurse, Eng. Supr. utilization rev. Nationwide Ins. Co., Columbus, Ohio, 1969-72, sr. cost containment analyst, 1986—; supr. bur. Ohio Dept. Human Services, Columbus, 1972-74, program planner, 1974-80, chief bur., 1980-84, cons. health care, 1984-87. Organist Victory Bapt. Ch., Etna, Ohio. Recipient Silver Medal Bury Hosp. Assn. Club: Franklin Internat. Training in Communication (Columbus) (treas. 1987-88). Avocation: crafts. Home: 1312 Epworth Ave Reynoldsburg OH 43068 Office: Nationwide Ins Co 1 Nationwide Plaza Columbus OH 43216

BLYTHE, MARGUERITE MARYANNA ELIZABETH, psychiatrist; b. Manhattan, Kans., Feb. 17, 1947; d. Benjamin George and Rhea (Krehbiel) B. BA, Barnard Coll., 1971; MA, Tchrs. Coll. Columbia U., 1973; BS in Nursing, Cornell U., 1978; MD, U. Cin., 1985. Diplomate Am. Bd. Med. Examiners. With nursing dept. VA, Long Beach, Calif., 1979-81; with U. Cin., Ohio, 1981-85, U. Cin. dept. psychiatry, 1985—; assoc. dir. Way Enterprises, Cin., 1980—; attending psychiatrist Lewis Ctr., Cin., 1986—. Fellow Am. Orthopsychiat. Assn.; mem. Acad. Medicine Cin. (steering com. Women in Medicine), ACLU, AMA, Am. Psychiat. Assn. Democrat. Office: U Cin ML 559 Dept of Psychiatry 231 Bethesda Cincinnati OH 45267

BOADEN, LUCILLE ANN, editor, English educator; b. Moline, Ill., Nov. 27, 1945; d. Rhys Bartlett and Evelyn Euseba (Nowers) B. AB, Augustana Coll., 1967; AM, U. Chgo., 1968, PhD, 1976. Instr. English Augustana Coll., Rock Island, Ill., 1970-79, asst. prof. English, 1979—; editor Augustana Coll. mag., Rock Island, 1979—. Author: (with Youngberg) The Mystery of the Singing Mermaid, 1987; contbr. articles and short stories to various publs. Pres. Augustana Hist. Soc., Rock Island, 1983-86, editor newsletter 1983—, bd. dirs. 1980—. Ford Found. fellow, 1968. Mem. Phi Beta Kappa. Lutheran. Avocations: music, walking, needlepoint, reading detective novels. Office: Augustana Coll Rock Island IL 61201

BOAL, MARCIA ANNE RILEY, clinical social worker; b. Carthage, Mo., Sept. 29, 1944; d. William Joseph and Thelma P. (Simpson) Riley; m. David W. Boal, Aug. 12, 1967; children: Adam J. W., Aaron D. Boal. BA, U. Kans., 1966, MSW, 1981. Lic. clin. social worker. Child therapist Gillis Home for Children, Kansas City, Mo., 1981; social worker Leavenworth (Kans.) County Spl. Edn. Cooperative, 1981-84; sch. social worker, dir. health services Kans. State Sch. for Visually Handicapped, Kansas City, Kans., 1984—; pvt. practice counseling and workshops, 1981—. Author: Surviving Kids, 1983. Nat. networking chmn. Jr. League Kansas City, 1977-81; bd. dirs. Wyandotte House Ind, 1973-81, Kans. Action For Children, Topeka, 1981, Gov.'s Commn. on Parent Edn., Topeka, 1984—. Mem. Council Exceptional Children, Nat. Assn. Social Workers, Kans. Assn. Sch. Social Workers, Am. Orthopsychiat. Assn., Phi Kappa Phi. Home: Lake of the Forest Bonner Springs KS 66012 Office: Kans State Sch the Visually Handicapped 1100 State Ave Kansas City KS 66102

BOAND, CHARLES WILBUR, lawyer; b. Bates County, Mo., Aug. 19, 1908; s. Albert and Edith Nadine (Pipes) B.; m. Phoebe Bard, Aug. 2, 1980; children: Bard, Barbara. AA, Jr. Coll. Kansas City; JD summa cum laude, U. Mo., Kansas City; MBA, LLB cum laude, U. Chgo. Bar: Mo. 1931, D.C. 1936, Ill. 1937, U.S. Supreme Ct. 1935, U.S. Ct. Appeals (1st, 2d, 5th, 7th, 9th, 10th, 11th and D.C. Cirs.), trial bar of U.S. Dist. Ct. (no. dist.) Ill. Assoc. Moore & Fitch, St. Louis, 1933; atty. Gen. Counsel's Office, U.S. Treasury Dept., 1933-36; assoc. Wilson & McIlvaine, 1937-42, ptnr., 1945—, chmn. exec. com., 1974-86, sr. ptnr., 1982—; mem. Nat. Conf. Lawyers and CPA's, 1976-82. Mem. grad. sch. bus. council U. Chgo., 1961-68, citizens bd., vis. com. to libraries, 1985—; trustee Muskingum Coll., 1965-79; stated clk. Presbyn. Ch. Barrington, 1962-65. Served as officer USNR, 1942-45, lt. comdr. Res. (ret.). Mem. ABA, Ill. Bar Assn. (chmn. exec. com. corp. securities law sect. 1954-56), Chgo. Bar Assn. (chmn. com. corp. law 1963-64), Fed. Bar Assn., 7th Circuit Bar Assn., U. Chgo. Alumni Assn. (pres. 1975-80, alumni cabinet 1964-70, 72-80, v.p. 1973-74, 1st Alumni Disting. Service award 1981), U. Chgo. Law Sch. Alumni Assn. (pres. 1968-70, bd. dirs. 1950-72), Order of Coif, Beta Gamma Sigma, Sigma Chi, Phi Alpha Delta. Clubs: Chgo., Mid-Am., Met., Law, Legal (Chgo.); Barrington Hills (Ill.) Country (bd. dirs. 1947-55); Los Caballeros Golf (Ariz.). Home: 250 W County Line Rd PO Box 567 Barrington Hills IL 60011 Office: 135 S LaSalle St Chicago IL 60603

BOARDMAN, RICHARD LAWRENCE, school counselor, psychologist; b. Stanley, Wis., May 13, 1949; s. Lawrence and Ethel Emma (Hoff) B.; m. Lucianne Mae Beckman, May 29, 1976; children: Dathan Jared, Tria Nicole, Jevin Reid. BS, U. Wis., Eau Claire, 1971; MS in Edn., U. Wis., Menomonie, 1975. Cert. sch. counselor, Wis; cert. sch. psychologist, Wis. Tchr. pub. schs. Menomonee Falls, Wis., 1971-74; psychologist pub. schs. Port Edwards, Wis., 1975-77, Prescott, Wis., 1977-78, Eau Claire, Wis., 1978-80; counselor elementary schs. Eau Claire, 1981-85, pvt. practice sch. psychology, 1979—; pres. Kids In Progress, Inc., Eau Claire, 1983—. Fellow Wis. Assn. for Counseling and Devel., Wis. Sch. Psychologists Assn.; mem. Wis. Sch. Counselors Assn. (elem. v.p. 1986—). Democrat. Lutheran. Avocations: fishing, canoeing, camping, sailing. Home: 2749 3d St Eau Claire WI 54703

BOATMAN, PAUL ERNEST, educator, pastoral counselor; b. Wichita, Kans., July 21, 1944; s. Russell E. and Lutie I. (Kenney) B.; m. Mary E. Kinney, June 11, 1966; children: Angela, Rachelle. BA, St. Louis Christian Coll., 1966; M of Divinity, Lincoln Christian Sem., 1974; D of Ministry, Eden Theol. Sem., 1977. Minister Christian Ch., Sailor Springs, Ill., 1966-69, W. Ln. Christian Ch., Indpls., 1969-73; dir. His Place, Inc., St. Louis, 1973-78; prof., assist. dean Lincoln (Ill.) Christian Sem., 1978—; bd. dirs. Ill. Pastoral Services Inst., Bloomington, Ill.; counselor Christian Counseling Ctr., Champaign, Ill., 1978—. Mem. Am. Assn. Pastoral Counselors. Republican. Avocations: photography, canoeing, backpacking. Home: Rt. 1 Lincoln IL 62656 Office: Lincoln Christian Sem Box 178 Lincoln IL 62656

BOATRIGHT, ANN LONG, music educator, dancer, choreographer, pianist; b. Louisville, Jan. 11, 1947; d. William Frazier and Mary Madolin (Hagan) Long; m. Ned Collins Boatright Jr., June 15, 1968; 1 child, Elizabeth. Student, Jordan Coll. Music, 1960-65, Butler U., 1965-68; BA, SUNY, Plattsburgh, 1970; M of Music, Ithaca Coll., 1974. Cert. tchr. N.Y., Ohio. Music tchr. pub. schs., Plattsburgh, Ithaca, and Rochester, N.Y., 1970-76; head dance program Columbus (Ohio) Sch. for Girls, 1977-82; cert. instr. Suzuki piano Capital U., 1982-85, instr. eurythmics, 1982—; tchr. Suzuki and traditional piano Columbus, 1985—; past tchr. eurythmics, music, movement Lake Forest Coll., Wittenberg U., Ohio State U., Eastern Mich. U., Denison U., Utah State U. Ballet soloist with Jordan Coll. Music Co., Butler U., Ithaca Ballet Co.; dancer with Indpls. Civic Ballet Co., Columbus Theatre Ballet Co.; pianist with Butler U. String Trio. Mem. Arts For Peace-Unify Ohio, 1986; mem. women's service bd. Grant Med. Ctr., Franklin Park Conservatory, St. Mark's Episcopal Ch.; mem. jr. council Columbus Museum Art, Zephyrus League. Mem. Music Tchrs. Nat. Assn. (nat. cert.), Ohio Music Tchrs. Assn. (conductor various workshops), Nat. Guild Piano Tchrs., Am. Coll. Musicians (faculty), Suzuki Assn. Ams., Suzuki Assn. Ohio. Republican. Avocations: skiing, bicycling, travel, gardening. Home: 4000 Newhall Rd Columbus OH 43220

BOBB, JUDITH KAY, educator; b. Seymour, Ind., Jan. 27, 1941; d. Albert Carl and Grace Ione (Persinger) Judd; m. Louis Earl Bobb, July 23, 1961; children—Douglas Allen, Julia Ann. B.A. in Elem. Edn., Purdue U., 1964, postgrad. in Spl. End. for Gifted Children, 1979-81; M.S., Ind. U., 1970. Cert. elem. tchr., Ind. Second grade tchr. Brownstown (Ind.) Elem. Sch., 1964-84; 4th grade tchr. 1984—; second grade tchr. Brownstown Elem. Sch., 1964 ; organizer activities for gifted pupils. Mem. NEA, Ind. State Tchrs. Assn., Brownstown Classroom Tchrs. Assn., Assn. for Supervision and Curriculum Devel., Ind. Assn. for Supervision and Curriculum Devel., Delta Kappa Gamma. Lutheran. Club: Tri Kappa, Seymour, Ind. Home: RR 3 Seymour IN 47274

BOBBITT, JOHN FRANKLIN, education educator; b. Galax, Va., June 27, 1940; s. John Edward and Jessie Elizabeth (Isom) B.; m. Norma Lee smith, Sept. 1, 1961; 1 child, Michael Franklin. BS, Va. Poly. Inst., 1962, MS, 1964; EdD, U. Ill., 1969. Tchr. Wythe County Schs., Wytheville, Va., 1963-66, U. Ill., Urbana, 1966-69; prof. edn. Mich. State U., East Lansing, 1969—; cons. U.S. Agy. Internat. Devel., Maseru, Lesotho,1982, Kingston, Jamaica, 1984, Roseau, Dominica, 1985, govt. of Trinidad, Port of Spain, 1983. Contbr. articles to profl. jours. Chmn. Mich. State Agr. Labor Commn., Lansing, 1978-82. Named Outstanding Educator, Wytheville Jaycees, 1965. Mem. Am. Assn. Tchr. Educators, Am. Vocat. Assn., Mich. Occupational Tchr. Edn. Assn. (pres. 1978-79), Assn. Internat. Agrl. Edn. (program chmn. 1985), Phi Delta Kappa. Methodist. Avocations: hunting, fishing. Home: 1442 Oscoda Rd Okemos MI 48864 Office: Mich State U 410 Agriculture Hall East Lansing MI 48824-1039

BOBCO, WILLIAM DAVID, JR., consulting engineering company executive; b. Chgo., Aug. 11, 1946; s. William David and Eleanor Josephine (Dvojack) B.; m. Donna Domenica DiFrancesca, Sept. 13, 1969. BS in Engring., U. Ill., Chgo., 1969; MBA in Prodn. Mgmt., U. Chgo., 1983. Prodn. mgr. Am. Can Co., Maywood, Ill., 1972-73; with Footlik & Assocs., Evanston, Ill., 1973—; exec. v.p. Footlik & Assocs., Evanston, 1986—. Served to capt. U.S. Army, 1969-72, Vietnam. Mem. ASME (bd. dirs. 1984—), Engring. Alumni Assn. U. Ill. Chgo. (pres. 1984—, bd. dirs. 1975—), U. Ill. Alumni Assn. (bd. dirs. 1985—). Roman Catholic. Avocations: travelling, home repairs, music. Office: Footlik & Assocs 2521 Gross Point Rd Evanston IL 60201

BOBER, MARY LOU, manufacturing consultant; b. East Chicago, Ind., July 13, 1955; d. Joseph F. and Myrtle (Bessler) B.; A.B., Ind. U., 1977, M.B.A., 1979. Staff cons. Inland Steel Co., East Chicago, Ind., 1979-85, assoc. mgmt. cons. div. The Austin Co., Rosemont, Ill., 1985—. Office: Austin Co Cons Div 9801 W Higgins #720 Rosemont IL 60018

BOBZIEN, H. J., transportation company executive; b. 1935. BA, Bellarmine Coll., 1956. With Am. Comml. Lines Inc., Jeffersonville, Ind., 1958—, now pres., also bd. dirs. Office: Am Comml Lines Inc 1701 E Market St Jeffersonville IN 47130 *

BOCHNOWSKI, FRANK JOSEPH, lawyer; b. Hammond, Ind., June 9, 1938; s. Joseph Stanley and Estelle Katherine (Gajda) B. BS, U.S. Mil. Acad., 1960; MBA, Fairleigh Dickinson U., 1973; JD, St. John's U., 1981. Commd. U.S. Army, 1960, advanced through grades to lt. col., served in Vietnam, ret., 1981; v.p., gen. counsel, trust officer People's Fed. Savs. and Loan Assn., Munster, Ind., 1984—. Home: 5497 W 86th Terr Crown Point IN 46307 Office: Peoples Fed Savs and Loan Assn 9204 Columbia Ave Munster IN 46321

BOCK, DONALD CARLTON, small businessman; b. Charles City, Iowa, Feb. 10, 1927; s. Carl Fred and Margaret Elizabeth (Ladwig) B.; m. Jessie Lavon Bishop, July 19, 1949 (div. May 1967); children: Larry Wayne, Ronald Carl, Sandra Kaye. Student, Walsh Inst. Acctg., 1947. Mem. assembly line Fall Spring and Wire Co., Warren, Mich., 1945-51; foreman Cole Carbide, Warren, 1951-65, Valeron Corp., Oak Park, Mich., 1965-66; ptnr. Keyn Tool Co., Hazel Park, Mich., 1966-70, Stanhope Tool and Gage, Madison Heights, Mich., 1970-79; owner, operator Don. B. Tool Co., Warren, 1979—. Served with USCG, 1944-45, PTO. Lutheran. Avocations: victanny, weightlifting, golfing. Office: 22806 Dequindre Warren MI 48091

BOCKELMAN, JOHN RICHARD, lawyer; b. Chgo., Aug. 8, 1925; s. Carl August and Mary (Ritchie) B. Student, U. Wis., 1943-44, Northwestern U., 1944-45, Harvard U., 1945, U. Hawaii, 1946; B.S. in Bus. Adminstrn, Northwestern U., 1946; M.A. in Econs, U. Chgo., 1949, J.D., 1951. Bar: Ill. 1951. Atty.-advisor Chgo. ops. office AEC, 1951-52; asso. firm Schradzke, Gould & Ratner, Chgo., 1952-57, Brown, Dashow & Langeluttig, Chgo., 1957-59, Antonow & Weissbourd, Chgo., 1959-61; partner firm Burton, Isaacs, Bockelman & Miller, Chgo., 1961-69; individual practice law Chgo., 1970—; prof. bus. law Ill. Inst. Tech., Chgo., 1950-82; lectr. econs. DePaul U., Chgo., 1952-53; dir., v.p., sec. Secretaries, Inc., Beale Travel Service, Inc; dir., sec. Arlington Engring. Co.; dir., v.p. Universal Distbrs., Inc. Pres. 1212 Lake Shore Dr. Condo Assn. Served with USNR, 1943-46. Mem. Am. Bar Assn., Ill. Bar Assn., Chgo. Bar Assn., Cath. Lawyers Guild Chgo., Phi Delta Theta. Clubs: Lake Point Tower (Chgo.), Barclay Ltd. (Chgo.), Whitehall (Chgo.), Internat. (Chgo.); Anvil (East Dundee, Ill.). Home: 1212 Lake Shore Dr Chicago IL 60610 Office: Suite 808 104 South Michigan Ave Chicago IL 60603

BOCKSTIEGEL, DOUGLAS WARREN, financial executive; b. Cin., June 5, 1949; s. Robert Henry Bockstiegel and Jean Alvina (Rullman) Gulden; m. Mary Kathleen Becker, Sept. 21, 1974; children: Gwen Marie, Keri Lynn. BBA cum laude, U. Cin., 1972. CPA, Ohio. Staff acct. Arthur Andersen & Co., Cin., 1972-75; asst. to v.p., controller Miller Brewing Co., Milw., 1983-84, mgr. corp. tax and banking, 1984—, supr. brewery budget, 1975-77; mgr. brewery acctg. Miller Brewing Co., Eden, N.C., 1977-80; controller brewery Miller Brewing Co., Irwindale, Calif., 1980-82; controller brewing dept. Miller Brewing Co., Trenton, Ohio, 1982-83; trustee Citizens Govt. Research Bur., 1987—. Com. long range planning Cross of Life Luth. Ch., Brookfield, Wis., 1986; trustee Citizens Govt. Research Bur., Milw., 1987. Avocations: cross country skiing, cycling, hiking.

BODENSTEIN, IRA, lawyer; b. Atlantic City, Nov. 9, 1954; s. William and Beverly (Grossman) B. Student, Tel Aviv U., 1974-75; BA in Govt., Franklin & Marshall Coll., 1977; JD in Econs., U. Miami, 1980. Bar: Ill. 1980, U.S. Dist Ct. (no. dist.) Ill. 1980, U.S. Ct. Appeals (7th cir.) 1982, Fla. 1983. Assoc. James S. Gordon Ltd., Chgo., 1980-85, mem., 1985—. Mem. Lawyers for Mayor Byrne, Chgo. 1983. Named one of Outstanding Young Men Am., 1986. Mem. ABA (antitrust com., rep. young lawyers div. dist.

15 1986-87), Chgo. Bar Assn. (bd. dirs. young lawyers sect. 1985-87, chmn.-elect 1987—, antitrust com., chmn. athletics com. 1984-85, Cert. of Appreciation 1984), Trial Lawyers Assn. Democratic. Jewish. Home: 2820 N Racine Chicago IL 60657

BODENSTEINER, ROBERT THEODORE, trucking industry executive; b. Decorah, Iowa, May 14, 1933; s. Cyril Mathew and Acquin Marie (Kilcoin) B.; B.S., Iowa State U., 1955; postgrad. Iowa U., 1957; postgrad. N.Y. City Coll., 1958; m. Amalia Frances Valenti, Nov. 28, 1959; children—Theodore Girard, David Neil, Susan Frances. Internal auditor N.Y. Life Ins. Co., N.Y.C., 1957-59; adminstrv. asst. Ft. Dodge (Iowa) By-Products Co., 1960-63; spl sales agent Lincoln Nat. Life Ins. Co., Ft. Dodge, 1963-67; stock and commodity broker Lamson Bros. and Co., Ft. Dodge, 1967-73, pres., gen. mgr. Center Line, Inc., Ft. Dodge, 1973—; chmn. bd. Internat. Mining and Devel., Inc., Ft. Dodge By-Products Co., Webster Rendering Co., Hot Line, Inc., Bowlerama, Inc., Air Lanes, Inc., Center Line, Inc. Pres., Sertoma Club of Ft. Dodge, 1967, gov. West Iowa dist. Sertoma Internat., 1970-72; bd. dirs., treas. Lakota Council Girl Scouts U.S.A., 6 yrs. Served to lt. (j.g.) USN, 1955-57. Recipient various sales awards, Lincoln Nat. Life Ins. Co. and Lamson Bros. & Co. Mem. Ft. Dodge C. of C., Nat. C. of C. Republican. Roman Catholic. Club: Barbershoppers (div. v.p.). Home: 2222 22d Ave N Fort Dodge IA 50501 Office: Box 1275 Fort Dodge IA 50501

BODIFORD, CHARLENE, teacher; b. Saginaw, Mich., Sept. 26, 1953; d. Ralph and Olean (McGhee) B.; 1 child, Charlotte. BA, Saginaw Valley Coll., 1974, MA, 1976. Tchr. pre-kindergarten Buena Vista Schs., Saginaw, 1974-80; dispatcher Saginaw County Govt., 1980-81; day care dir. Mid-Mich. Kinder-Kare, Saginaw, 1981-82; tchr. Saginaw City Schs., 1982—. Home: 3341 Livingston Dr Saginaw MI 48601 Office: 3025 Davenport Saginaw MI 48601

BODMAN, GERALD RICHARD, consulting engineer; b. Catawissa, Pa., May 22, 1944; s. Gerald Frederick and Betty Mae (Stevenson) B.; B.S., Pa. State U., 1966, M.S., 1968; m. Mary Ellen Ahler, July 21, 1973; children—Lee, Melanie, Julian. Self-employed as irrigation system designer, Catawissa, Pa., 1964-67; instr. Pa. State U., University Park, 1966-68; engr./constrn. supr. New Eng. Pole Builders, Inc., Ludlow, Mass., 1968-70: self-employed in home bldg. and remodeling, Ludlow, Mass., 1970-71; extension agrl. engr., asst. prof. Pa. State U., University Park, 1971-78; pvt. practice cons. agrl. and structural engring. Space Preceptors Assocs., State College, Pa., Ludlow, Mass., Lincoln, Nebr., 1970—; specialist on farmstead engring., livestock housing, milking systems and procedures, grain drying, solar energy for livestock housing, extraneous voltage; assoc. prof., extension agrl. engr. U. Nebr., Lincoln, 1978—; vis. prof. dept. home econs. Ind. U., Bloomington, 1972. Mem. bd. deacons State College Presbyn. Ch., 1974-78, chmn., 1978; deacon Eastridge Presbyn. Ch., Lincoln, 1981-83, trustee 1987—. Recipient Excellence in Extension Programming award for Solar livestock housing U. Nebr., 1983, Walnut Grove Livestock Service award, 1986. Registered profl. engr., Pa. N.Y., Mass., Ind., Calif., Maine, N.H., Vt., Md., Colo., Iowa, Kans., Tenn., Del., Conn., Ill., Mo., Minn., Nebr., Ohio, N.J., Va., R.I., W.Va., S.D., Tex., Oreg., Wis., Mich.; lic. land surveyor, Pa. Mem. Am. Soc. Agrl. Engrs. (mem. exec. com. North Atlantic region 1975-78, 1st vice-chmn. program 1977-78, chmn.-elect Pa. sect. 1977-78, Blue Ribbon awards in Ednl. Aids Competition, 1975, 77, 78, 79, 80, 81, 82, 83, 84, 87, Young Extension Engr. of Yr. 1982-86, chmn. ad hoc applications publ. com. 1982—, profl. devel. dept. 1983-84, cons. guidelines subcom., milk handling equipment com. 1985-86, meetings com. 1985-86), Profl. Engrs. in Pvt. Practice, Nat., Nebr. socs. profl. engrs., AAAS, N.E. Dairy Practices Council (chmn. practical plumbing for milking centers subcom.), Nebr. Dairymen's Assn. (bd. dirs. 1983—), Am. Dairy Sci. Assn., Internat. Assn. Electrical Insps. ASHRAE. Republican. Contbr. 250 articles to profl. jours. and popular publs. Lic. pvt. pilot. Home and Office: 5911 Sunrise Rd Lincoln NE 68510-4052

BODNARIK, MICHAEL THOMAS, food company executive; b. Vancouver, B.C., Can., Aug. 4, 1953; came to U.S., 1972; s. Michael Anthony and Elizabeth Mary (Nevakchenoff) B.; m. Barbara Ellen Michalski, June 21, 1975; 1 child, Anthony. AABA, Douglas Coll., Richmond, Can., 1972. Cert. medical technician. Sales rep. Standard Brands, Milw., 1977-79, key account mgr., 1979-81; market devel. mgr. Nabisco Inc., Chgo., 1981-83, asst. regional mgr., 1983-85; asst. div. mgr. Nabisco Inc. div. R.J. Reynolds, Chgo., 1985-86, region merchandising mgr., 1986—. Active Rep. Re-election Campaign, Milw., 1974. Mem. Chgo. Tobacco Table, Grocery Mfrs. Sales Execs., United Schutzhund Clubs Am. (exec. bd. 1985—, working dog judge), Verein Für Deutsche Schäferhund. Hoem: 32876 Atkinson Rd Grayslake IL 60030 Office: Nabisco Brands 1700 Higgins Rd Des Plaines IL 60018

BODNER, BRUCE ALAN, real estate developer; b. Indpls., Oct. 31, 1951; s. Robert Stewart and Elizabeth (Wolf) B. BS in Bus., Ind. U., 1972; JD, Cumberland Law Sch., 1975. Bar: Ind. 1975, Ariz. 1976, U.S. Dist. Ct. (so. dist.) Ind. 1975, U.S. Dist. Ct. Ariz. 1976. Owner Bodner Cos., Indpls., 1977—. Mem. Ind. Bar Assn., Ariz. Bar Assn. Jewish. Avocations: swimming, golf, flying, walking. Office: Bodner Cos 10455 N College Ave Indianapolis IN 46280

BODON, HAROLD WOLFGANG, foreign language educator; b. Stuttgart, Fed. Republic of Germany, May 19, 1936; came to U.S., 1952; s. Heinrch and Lina (Bullerdieck) B.; m. Sonja Nelly Zbinden, Aug. 23, 1957; children: Peter, Michael. BA, U. Utah, 1959; MS, Calif. State U., Hayward, 1966; PhD, Brigham Young U., 1978. Instr. German and French Clearfield (Utah) High Sch., 1961-62, Newark (Calif.) High Sch., 1962-69; instr. French Brigham Young U., Provo, Utah, 1969-71; instr. German and French Mo. So. State Coll., Joplin, 1971—, prof. German and French, 1987—; cons. in field. Contbr. articles to profl. jours. Soccer coach Joplin Boy Scouts Am. Mem. Modern Lang. Assn., Mo. State Teachers Assn., Pi Delta Phi, Delta Phi Alpha, Nat. Assn. Soccer Coaches (sec. 1981). Republican. Mormon. Office: Mo Southern Coll Joplin MO 64801

BOECHE, MARK RICHARD, dentist; b. Chgo., Feb. 20, 1952; d. Richard Clement and Dorothy Ruth (Snyder) B.; m. Sheila Josephine Martin, Mar. 20, 1976 (div. Feb. 1980); m. Stephanie Kaye Miller, Apr. 9, 1983; 1 child, Niles Richard. BS with honors, U. Ill., Chgo., 1973, BS in Dentistry, 1976, DDS, 1978. Pvt. practice dentistry Springfield, Mo., 1978-84, Janesville, Wis., 1984—; dental cons. Maramoths Village, Springfield, 1982-84. Bd. of Stewardship St. Paul Luth. Ch., Janesville, 1985—, also Sunday sch. tchr. Recipient Alumni Leadership award U. Ill. Alumni Assn., 1978. Mem. ADA, Acad. Gen. Dentistry. Lodge: Kiwanis (sec., treas., 1985—). Avocation: woodworking, sailing. Home: 1103 Columbus Circle Janesville WI 53545

BOECK, LAVERNE DWAINE, fermentation microbiologist; b. Johnson, Nebr., May 16, 1930; s. Otto Bernhard and Alma Marie (Stutheit) B.; student U. Nebr., 1947-49, Wartburg Coll., 1949-50; B.S. in Biology, Butler U., 1958, M.S. in Microbiology, 1963; m. Fredia Mae Jarrett, Oct. 25, 1953; children—Deborah, Kirk, Bruce, Eric, Gregg, Craig. Clerical engring. analyst Allison div. Gen. Motors Corp., Indpls., 1953-57; asso. microbiologist Eli Lilly & Co., Indpls., 1958-63, microbiologist, 1963-65, asst. sr. microbiologist, 1965-67, asso. sr. microbiologist, 1967-72, sr. microbiologist, 1972—. Served to lt., Anti-aircraft Arty., U.S. Army, 1951-53. Mem. Am. Soc. Microbiology, Soc. Indsl. Microbiology, Am. Chem. Soc., Sigma Xi. Republican. Lutheran. Contbr. articles to profl. jours.; patentee in field. Home: 741 Chapel Hill West Dr Indianapolis IN 46214 Office: Eli Lilly Research Labs Indianapolis IN 46285

BOEDDEKER, TIMOTHY MARK, postal executive; b. St. Louis, Aug. 16, 1948; s. Clyde and Constance Faye (McCollum) B.; m. Margaret Mary Botts, May 15, 1971; children—Abigail Faye, Timothy Mark. Student, William Jennings Bryan Coll., 1967-70; B.A., Webster Coll., 1976, M.A., 1981. Supr. mails U.S. Postal Service, St. Louis, 1977-80, mgmt. trainee, 1980, mgr. Creve Coeur br., 1981-85, mgr. Wheeler Sta., 1985—. Deacon, West County Christian Ch., 1979-85; trustee Internat. Soc. Christian Endeavor, 1979—; 2d v.p. Traditional Sch., Pattonville Sch. Dist. PTA, 1983-85, pres., 1985-86. Served with USCG, 1970-74, USCGR, 1974—. Mem. Nat. Assn. Postal Suprs., Res. Officers Assn. Republican. Home: 11115 Morrow Dr Saint Ann MO 63074

BOEHM, MARGARET STITT, accountant; b. Detroit, Sept. 29, 1944; d. Ralph Frank and Ella (Marks) Stitt; m. Edward W. Harris III, June 11, 1966 (div. June 1974); children: Deborah DePerez Harris, David Edward Harris; m. Theodore R. Boehm, Jan. 27, 1985. BA, Mt. Holyoke Coll., 1966. CPA, Ind. Owner Peggy Harris, CPA, Indpls., 1976-81; commr. Pub. Service Commn. of Ind., Indpls., 1981-85; head dept. fin. Meth. Hosp., Indpls., 1985-86; dep. dir. State Budget Agy., Indpls., 1986—. Treas. Meridain Kessler Neighborhood Assn., Indpls., 1977. Mem. Am. Inst. CPA's, Ind. CPA Soc., Govt. Fin. Officers Assn. Democrat. Home: 123 E 44th St Indianapolis IN 46205-1707 Office: State Budget Agy 212 State House Indianapolis IN 46204

BOEHMER, DANIEL PATRICK, mental health facility administrator; b. St. Louis, June 8, 1949; s. Todd and Dorothy (Nugent) B.; m. Cheryl L. Miller, Nov. 9, 1974; children: Laura, Lisa. BS, Southeast Mo. State, 1971, MA, 1976. Registered social worker, Ill. Mental health specialist Ill. Dept. Mental Health, Cairo, Ill., 1971-73, Pulaski-Alexander Mental Health Ctr., Cairo, 1973-76; exec. dir. Cumberland County Mental Health Ctr., Toledo, Ill., 1976-84, Dewitt County Human Resources Ctr., Clinton, Ill., 1984—; christian counselor, Greenup, Ill., 1984-86; tchr. Lakeland Coll., Mattoon, Ill., 1984-85. Bd. dirs. East Cen. Ill. Area Agy. on Aging, Bloomington, 1976—, Life Ctr. Sr. Ctr., Toledo, 1983-84, Maroa (Ill.) Bible Ctr. Ch., 1986. Mem. Ill. Alcohol and Drug Dependency Assn. Lodge: Rotary. Avocations: hunting, fishing. Home: 818 West Woodlawn Clinton IL 61727 Office: DeWitt County Human Resource Ctr 1150 Rt 54 W Clinton IL 61727

BOEKA, MICHAEL PAUL, tax specialist; b. Fairbury, Nebr., May 2, 1949; s. Paul Gustav and Donna Lee (Mussman) B.; m. Sarah Jane Woods, Oct. 12, 1974; children: Amanda Marie, Adam Michael. BSBA, U. Nebr., 1973. Staff acct. Buckley & Mockett, Lincoln, Nebr., 1973-74; sr. acct. Williams & Co. CPAs, Onawa, Iowa, 1974-77; tax analyst No. Natural Gas, Omaha, Nebr., 1977-79; asst. tax mgr. Peter Kiewet & Sons, Omaha, 1979-80; tax mgr. Valmont Ind. Inc., Valley, Nebr., 1980-85; mgr. tax Upland Industries Corp., Omaha, 1985—. Mem. Am. Inst. CPAs, Nebr. Soc. CPAs, Nebr. Tax Council, U. Nebr. Alumni Assn. Republican. Methodist. Club: Blair Country. Avocations: reading, hunting, fishing, music, golf. Home: 636 N 10th Ave Blair NE 68008 Office: Upland Industries Corp 302 S 36th St Omaha NE 68131

BOELENS, THEODORE MARTIN, hotel maintenance engineering executive; b. Groningen, Netherlands, Oct. 13, 1943; came to U.S., 1947; s. Martin and Tena (Spaak) B.; m. Agnes DeGraaf, June 22, 1968; children: Scott Alan, Erik Martin, Kelly Anne. Diploma, Franklin Inst., Boston, 1968; A in Civil Tech., N.Y. State Tech. Coll., 1970. Cert. engring. ops. exec. Engring tech. Engrs. Inc. Vt., South Burlington, Vt., 1970-76; chief engr. Radisson Hotel, Burlington, Vt., 1976-80, Radisson Muehlebach Hotel, Kansas City, Mo., 1980-81; dir. engring. Doubletree Hotel, Overland Park, Kans., 1981-84, Amway Grand Plaza Hotel Corp., Grand Rapids, 1984—; guest lectr. Mich. State U., East Lansing, 1984-85, Grand Valley State Coll., Allendale, Mich., 1986. Served to sgt. USAF, 1961-65. Mem. ASHRAE (affiliate), Nat. Assn. Power Engr., Am. Hotel and Motel Assn. (exec. engrs. com.). Mem. Christian Reformed Ch. Avocation: golf. Home: 8756 Rivercrest Dr Jenison MI 49428 Office: Amway Grand Plaza Hotel Pearl at Monroe Grand Rapids MI 47503

BOELZ, THOMAS LEONARD, furniture restorer, antique dealer; b. St. Cloud, Minn., Sept. 15, 1935; s. Lawrence John and Priscilla Angeline (Jackson) B. Grad. high sch., St. Cloud, Minn., 1953. Driver Concrete Industry, St. Cloud, Minn., 1953-77; owner Thomas Park Antiques, Clear Lake, Minn., 1977—. mem. Clear Lake City Council, 1979— Clear Lake Planning Commn., 1980—; del. Sherburne County High Task Force, Becker, Minn., 1985—; bd. dirs. Sherburne County Hist. Soc., Becker, 1980-86. Served to sgt. Minn. N.G., 1956-64. Mem. Am. Legion, Carriage Assn. Am., Whip Wheels Carriage and Driving Soc. Republican. Roman Catholic. Clubs: Horn'N Hame Horse (Sauk Rapids, Minn.), No. Minn. Draft Horse (St. Francis, Minn.). Avocations: Clydesdale horses, antique horse wagons, collecting. Home: Rural Rt 2 Clear Lake MN 55319

BOEMI, A. ANDREW, banker; b. N.Y.C., Mar. 3, 1915; s. S. and Marietta (Boemi) B.; B.C.E., Coll. City N.Y., 1936, M.C.E., 1938; m. Flora Dorothy DeMuro, Apr. 26, 1941; children—Andrew A., Marcia Rosamond Buchanan. Engr., Gibb & Hill, Cons. Engrs., N.Y.C., 1937; city planner N.Y. Planning Comm., 1938-41; cons. U.S. Bur. Budget, Exec. Office of President, Washington, 1942; asst. loan officer, planning cons., asst. v.p., v.p. First Fed. Savs. & Loan, Chgo., 1946-57; pres., chief exec. officer Madison Bank & Trust Co., Chgo., 1957-84, chmn. bd., 1974—; pres., chmn. bd. Madison Fin. Corp., Chgo., 1974-84, chmn. bd., chief exec. officer, 1985—; chmn. bd. Madison Nat. Bank of Niles (Ill.), 1976—, 1st Nat. Bank of Wheeling (Ill.), 1978—, MFC Mortgage Co., 1983—. Mem. exec. com. Archdiocesan Commn. Human Relations and Ecumenism, 1969-72; mem. Mayor's Commn. Landmarks Preservation Council, 1972-75. Bd. dirs. Met. Housing and Planning Council, 1950—, pres., 1975-76; mem. Elem. Sch. Bd., Park Ridge, Ill., 1953-59, pres., 1956-59; citizens bd. Loyola U., Chgo.; chmn. Joint Action Com. Civic Assns. for location Chgo. campus U. Ill., 1960-61; chmn. Gateway Com., Chgo., 1958-63; bd. dirs. Duncan YMCA, 1964-77. Served to lt. comdr. USNR, 1942-46. Recipient commendation ribbon from sec. navy, World War II; decorated Knight Order Holy Sepulchre of Jerusalem. Mem. Am. Bankers Assn., Ill. Bankers Assn. (fed. legis. and regulation com.), ASCE, Am. Inst. Planners, Navy League U.S., Newcomen Soc. N.Am., Am. Legion, Lambda Alpha, Alpha Beta Gamma. Republican. Roman Catholic. Clubs: Economic, Bankers, University (Chgo.); Park Ridge Country. Lodge: Knights of Malta (decorated). Home: 1110 N Lake Shore Dr Apt 7-S Chicago IL 60611 Office: 400 W Madison St Chicago IL 60606

BOERGER, THEODORE GEORGE, manufacturing plant manager; b. Piqua, Ohio, Dec. 22, 1951; s. George William and Dorothy Emma (Kalkoff) B.; m. Susan Kay Amspaugh, Aug. 7, 1971; children: Jeremy L., William P., Amanda K. BS in Engring., Gen. Motors Inst., 1975; MBA, U. Dayton, 1979. Supr. Delco Air div. Gen. Motors Corp., Dayton, Ohio, 1975-79; engring. mgr. Fram Corp., Nevada, Mo., 1980-83; plant mgr.aftermarket div. Allied Corp., Nevada, 1983—; mem. Nevada Area Econ. Devel. Commn., 1984-87. Bd. dirs. United Community Funds of Vernon County, Nevada, 1985—. Recipient Gold Award United Way, 1985. Mem. Inst. Indsl. Engrs. (sec. 1973-74), Soc. Mfg. Engrs., Theta Xi. Republican. Roman Catholic. Clubs: Three Rivers Amatuer Radio (Butler, Mo.), Orleans Trail Yacht (Stockton, Mo.). Lodges: Rotary, KC (v.p. local chpt. 1985-86). Avocations: sailing, ham radio, golf, computing. Office: Allied Aftermarket Div 1200 E Highland Nevada MO 64772

BOERGER, WILLIAM GEORGE, oral and maxillofacial surgeon; b. St. Cloud, Minn., May 30, 1941; s. Milton Carl and Geneva Marie (Spaniol) B.; m. Hiroko Hamada, Nov. 16, 1968 (div. 1978); 1 child, Jeffrey; m. Theresa M. Wagner, Nov. 3, 1978; children: Megan, John. Student Crosier Sem., Onamia, Minn., 1959-61, St. Cloud State Coll., 1961-63; BS, U. Minn., 1965, DDS, 1967. Resident in oral surgery U. Minn., Mpls., 1969-72; practice oral surgery, Wayzata, Minn., 1972—, also Edina and Burnsville, Minn.; mem. staffs Meth. Hosp., St. Louis Park, Minn., Fairview Southdale Hosp., Edina, Fairview Ridges Hosp., Burnsville, Waconia Ridgeview Hosp., also Children's Health Ctr., Mpls. Served with USNR, 1967-69. Fellow Am. Dental Soc. Anesthesiology, Am. Assn. Oral and Maxillofacial Surgeons; mem. ADA, Minn. Dist. Dental Soc., Mpls. Dist. Dental Soc., Mpls. Soc. Oral and Maxillofacial Surgeons, Minn. Soc. Oral and Ma xillofacial Surgeon, Minnetonka Dental Study Club, Bloomington Dental Study Club, Southdale Dental Soc., Omicron Kappa Upsilon. Office: 250 N Central Ave #209 Wayzata MN 55391

BOESCHENSTEIN, WILLIAM WADE, glass products manufacturing executive; b. Chgo., Sept. 7, 1925; s. Harold and Elizabeth (Wade) B.; m. Josephine H. Moll, Nov. 28, 1953; children: William Wade, Michael M., Peter H., Stephen S. Student, Phillips Acad., 1944; B.S., Yale, 1950. With Owens-Corning Fiberglas Corp., 1950—; br. mgr. Owens-Corning Fiberglas Corp., Detroit, 1955-59; v.p. central region Owens-Corning Fiberglas Corp., 1959-61; v.p. sales br. operations Owens-Corning Fiberglas Corp., Toledo, 1961-63; v.p. marketing Owens-Corning Fiberglas Corp., 1963-67, exec. v.p., 1967-71, pres., 1971—, chief exec. officer, 1972—, chmn., 1981—, dir., 1967—; dir. Prudential Ins. Co. Am., FMC Corp., Chgo., M. A. Hanna Co., Cleve. Trustee Toledo Mus. Art, Phillips Acad., Andover, Mass., Edison Inst.; mem. nat. bd. Smithsonian Assocs. Mem. The Bus. Council, The Conf. Bd. Clubs: Links (N.Y.C.), Econ. (N.Y.C.), Toledo (Toledo), Inverness (Toledo), Belmont Country (Perrysburg, Ohio), Augusta (Ga.), Nat. Home: 3 Locust St Perrysburg OH 43659 Office: Owens-Corning Fiberglas Corp Fiberglas Tower Toledo OH 43659

BOESE, ROBERT FRANK, JR., insurance company executive; b. Galveston, Tex., Mar. 29, 1939; s. Robert F. Sr. and Elizabeth (Olsen) B.; m. Joyce L. Lewis, July 29, 1961; children: Robert, David, Michael, Barbara. BBA, Tex. A&M U., 1961. Various positions Allstate Ins. Co., Dallas, Houston and Atlanta, 1963-75; dir. field ops. Great Am. Ins. Co., Cin., 1975-76; dir. corp. ops. CNA Ins. Co., Chgo., 1976-78, v.p. group claims, adminstrn., 1978-84; v.p. group claims, adminstrv. services Mut. of Omaha, 1984—. Served to capt. U.S. Army, 1961-63. Mem. Health Ins. Assn. Am., Am. Mgmt. Assn., Internat. Claims Assn. (chmn. group issues com.), Tex. A&M Former Student Assn. Republican. Roman Catholic. Avocations: football, tennis, golf, swimming, camping. Home: 12767 Hamilton St Omaha NE 68154 Office: Mut of Omaha Mut of Omaha Plaza Omaha NE 68175

BOESE, VIRGINIA ELLEN, curator; b. Troy, Ohio, July 16, 1907; d. William Harry and Virginia Grace (Meeker) Gilbert; student Western Coll. for Women, Oxford, Ohio, 1924-26; B.A., Ohio Wesleyan U., Delaware, 1928; m. Carl Wimmler Boese, Aug. 5, 1929. Tchr. Latin and English, Concord Twp. Sch., Miami County, Ohio, 1928-29; legal sec. to William Harry Gilbert, Troy, 1931-45; dir. Troy Hist. Soc., 1965-76, archivist-librarian, 1966-76, genealogist, 1966—, dir. hist. room, 1966-76, asst. archivist-librarian, 1976—; dir., curator Overfield Log Tavern Mus., 1966-75, asst. curator, 1975—. Pres., violinist Troy Music Club, 1932-33; pres. Troy Altrurian Club, 1933-34, Current Events Club, 1954-55. Co-recipient (with husband) Community Service award Troy Jaycees, 1972, 85. Mem. DAR, Colonial Dames XVII Century, LWV, Daus. of Founders and Patriots Am., Phi Mu, Kappa Delta Pi. Republican. Presbyn. (deacon). Author: Overfield Genealogy Research Notes, 1968, rev., 1970; Revolutionary Soldiers of Miami County, Ohio, 1976, rev., 1979; Meeker Genealogy, 1975; Genealogy of Knoop Family of Miami County, Ohio, 1981; Ball Family of England and America, 1982; Thomas Family of St. Mary's County, Md. Compiler, Index to Beers 1880 History, of Miami County, Ohio, 1973. Home: 106 S Plum St Troy OH 45373 Office: 201 E Water St Troy OH 45373

BOESEL, MILTON CHARLES, JR., lawyer, business exec.; b. Toledo, July 12, 1928; s. Milton Charles and Florence (Fitzgerald) B.; m. Lucy Laughlin Mather, Mar. 25, 1961; children—Elizabeth Parks, Charles Mather, Andrew Fitzgerald. B.A., Yale, 1950; LL.B., Harvard, 1953. Bar: Ohio bar 1953, Mich. bar 1953. Of counsel firm Ritter, Boesel, Robinson & Marsh, Toledo, 1956—; pres., dir. Michabo, Inc.; dir. 1st Nat. Bank of Toledo. Served to lt. USNR, 1953-56. Episcopalian. Clubs: Toledo, Toledo Country; Leland Country (Mich.). Home: 2268 Innisbrook Rd Toledo OH 43606 Office: 240 Huron St Toledo OH 43604

BOFF, KENNETH RICHARD, engineering research psychologist; b. N.Y.C., Aug. 17, 1947; s. Victor and Ann (Yunko) B.; m. Judith Marion Schoer, Aug. 2, 1969; children: Cory Asher, Kyra Melissa. BA, CUNY, 1969, MA, 1972; MPhil, Columbia U., 1975, PhD, 1978. Research scientist Human Resources Lab., Wright Patterson AFB, Ohio, 1977-80; sr. scientist Armstrong Aerospace Med. Research Lab., Wright Patterson AFB, Ohio, 1980—, dir. design tech., 1980—; project custodian Internat. Air. Standard Coordination Com., Washington, 1984; chmn. com. Tri-Service Human Factors Tech. Adv. Group, Washington, 1984—. Editor: Handbook of Perception and Human Performance, 1986, Human Engineering Data Compendium, 1987, System Design: Behavioral Perspectives on Designers, Tools and Organizations, 1987; contbr. articles to profl. jours. Travel grantee Rank Prize Found., Cambridge, Eng., 1984. Mem. IEEE, Human Factors Soc., Am. Psychol. Assn. (div. 21 engring. psychology). Avocations: computers, photography. Home: 3114 Village Ct Dayton OH 45432 Office: Armstrong Aerospace Med Research Lab Wright-Patterson AFB OH 45433

BOGART, KEITH CHARLES, neurologist; b. Lorain, Ohio, Apr. 12, 1936; s. Lloyd William and Evelyn (Overmyer) B.; m. B. Diane Seigel, June 8, 1967; children: Keith Charles Jr., Catherine Michelle; m. Alice Craib, July 21, 1976; 1 child, Matthew William. BA, Ohio State U., 1958, MD, 1961. Diplomate Am. Bd. Psychiatry and Neurology, Am. Bd. Qualification in EEG. Asst. prof. neurology U. Wis., Madison, 1968-69, Creighton U., Omaha, Nebr., 1975-78; chmn. neurology Gunderson Clinic, Lacrosse, Wis., 1969-75; clin. neurologist Mansfield (Ohio) Neurology, Inc., 1978—; cons. neurology VA Hosp., Omaha, 1977-78. Mem. christian edn. com. First Congl. Ch., Mansfield, 1986; bd. dirs. Boy Scouts Am., Mansfield, 1986. Served to lt. comdr. USPHS, 1963-65. Fellow Am. Acad. Neurology, Am. EEG Soc. (mem. lab. accreditation bd. 1984—); mem. AMA (Physician's Recognition award 1969, 72, 77, 82), Cen. Assn. EEGers (pres. 1977-78), Nebr. Epilepsy League (pres. 1976-78), Wis. Med. Soc. (chmn. neurology sect. 1975), Wis. Neurol. Soc. (pres. 1973), Richland County Med. Soc. (sec.-treas. 1986—), Knights of Magic (pres. 1986—, Magician of Yr. 1984, 85), Internat. Brotherhood Magicians (v.p. ter. 1986—). Lodge: Rotary. Avocations: professional magician, travel, golf, reading. Home: 730 Woodhill Mansfield OH 44907 Office: Mansfield Neurology Inc 222 Marion Ave Mansfield OH 44903

BOGDON, CHRISTOPHER ROBERT, retail company executive; b. Orlando, Fla., June 13, 1961; s. William M. Bogdon and Margaret Ann (Smith) Hoogerheide. Student, U. Denver, 1979-80; BSBA, Drake U., 1983. Exec. trainee Venture Stores, O'Fallon, Mo., 1984; asst. buyer Venture Stores, O'Fallon, 1984-85, impulse sales coordinator, 1985—; cons. Caldor Stores, Norwalk, Conn., 1987—. Roman Catholic. Avocations: camping, snow and water skiing, bicycling, lacrosse, golf. Home: 326 S Hanley Apt 2S Clayton MO 63105 Office: Venture Stores Inc 2001 E Terra Ln O'Fallon MO 63366

BOGDON, GLENDON JOSEPH, orthodontist; b. Green Bay, Wis., Sept. 23, 1935; s. Joseph Frank and Anne Marie (Jacklin) B.; m. Susanne Ellen Daley, Aug. 8, 1959; 1 child, Amy Sue. BS, St. Norbert Coll., DePere, Wis., 1957; DDS, Marquette U., 1971, MS in Clin. Dentistry, 1973. Officer IRS, Chgo., 1958; social worker Cath. Welfare Bur., Milw., 1958-59; tchr. secondary sch. So. Door County Schs., Brussels, Wis., 1959-67; practice dentistry specializing in orthodontics Milw., 1973—; pres. So. Orthodontic Services, Milw., 1986—. Contbr. articles to profl. jours. Served with U.S. Army, 1957-58. Mem. Greater Milw. Dental Assn. (Continuing Edn. award 1971-73), Wis. Dental Assn. (Continuing Edn. award 1971-74, 79-81), ADA (Continuing Edn. award 1976-78), Royal Soc. Health, Wis. Soc. Orthodontists, Midwestern Soc. Orthodontists, Am. Assn. Orthodontists. Democrat. Roman Catholic. Avocations: bread baking, jogging. Office: 3044 S 92d St West Allis WI 53227

BOGEL, HENRY GLENN, engineer; b. New Orleans, La., Nov. 20, 1931; s. Henry and Rebecca Ernestine (Dickey) B.; m. Patricia June Ramsey, Sept. 15, 1956; children: Elizabeth Ann, Steven Henry. BS in Electronics, John Brown U., 1953. Component engr. ITT Fed. Labs., Ft. Wayne, Ind., 1953-63; engr. transformer design Ballastran Corp., Ft. Wayne, 1963-68; component engr., staff engr. Magnavox Govt. and Indsl. Electronics Co., Ft. Wayne, 1968—. Methodist. Avocations: amateur radio, photography, woodworking. Home: 8427 Sakaden Pkwy Fort Wayne IN 46825 Office: Magnavox Govt and Indsl Electronic 1010 Production Rd Fort Wayne IN 46808

BOGGINS, SALLY LOUISE, advertising executive; b. Cleve., Sept. 28, 1952; d. John and Barbara Jean (Evans) Harvey; m. Michael Edward Boggins, Jan. 18, 1980. BS, Bowling Green State U., 1974. Tchr. Brecksville (Ohio) High Sch., 1974-78; freelancer Beckwith & Assocs., Cleve., 1974-80; v.p., media dir. Mills Hall Walborn Advt., Cleve., 1978—; bd. dirs., officer Cleve. Assn. Broadcasters, 1984-87; speaker Advt. Women of Cleve. Seminars, 1985-86. Mem. cleve. Media Group. Home: 34550 Bainbridge Rd Solon OH 44139 Office: Mills Hall Walborn 29125 Chagrin Blvd Cleveland OH 44139

BOGIN, HARVEY MICHAEL, dentist; b. Bronx, N.Y., July 9, 1949; s. Norman and Marilyn (Fishkin) B.; m. Pamela Slusher, Aug. 25, 1973. BA, U. Vt., 1971; DDS, Northwestern U., 1975. Gen. practice dentistry Winfield, Ill., 1975. Served to lt. USN, 1975-77. Fellow Acad. Gen. Dentistry; mem. ADA, Ill. Dental Soc., Chgo. Dental Soc. Republican. Avocations: reading, weightlifting. Home: 27 W 414 Fischer Ln Winfield IL 60190 Office: 0S165 Church St Winfield IL 60190

BOGINA, AUGUST, JR., state senator; b. Girard, Kans., Sept. 13, 1927; s. August and Mary (Blazic) B.; B.S., Engring., Kans. State U., 1950; m. Velma M. Rank, 1949; children—Kathleen A., August III, Michael E., Mark A. Owner, Bogina & Assocs., Lenexa, Kans., 1962-70; pres. Bogina Cons. Engrs., 1970—; partner Bogina Petroleum Engineers, 1983—; mem. Kans. Ho. of Reps., 1974-80, Kans. Senate, 1980—. Precinct committeeman Kans. Republican party, 1970-74, chmn. city com., 1972-74. Served with U.S. Army, 1946-48. Registered profl. engr., Kans., Mo., Colo., Okla. Mem. Nat., Mo. socs. profl. engrs., Kans. Engring. Soc., Kans. Soc. Land Surveyors, Mo. Registered Land Surveyors. Roman Catholic. Office: 9020 Rosehill Rd Lenexa KS 66215

BOGLE, DAVID MASSON, infosystems specialist; b. Detroit, Aug. 29, 1929; s. Henry Charles and Mathilde (Masson) B.; m. Janet Van Osdol, Jan. 25, 1962 (dec. Nov. 1981); children: Henry, Mary; 1 stepchild, Thomas H. Keating; m. Helen Livingstone, Dec. 29, 1982. AB, Kenyon Coll., 1951; BSChemE, BSMetE, U. Mich., 1953. Materials mgr. Ford Motor Co., Dearborn, Mich., 1966-72; v.p. Gemini Corp., Mt. Clemens, Mich., 1972-74; dir. mfg. Burroughs Corp, Detroit, 1974-79, gen. mgr. fabrication, 1979-81, dir. mfg. control, 1981-85; dir. product definition Unisys Corp, Detroit, 1985—. Patentee impact tool. Active Detroit Hist. Mus., 1987. Republican. Episcopalian. Clubs: Grosse Pointe (commodore 1980-81, chmn. 1986-87), Yondotega. Avocations: tennis, golf, sailing, skiing. Home: 93 Merriweather Rd Grosse Pointe Farms MI 48236 Office: Unisys Corp Burroughs Place Detroit MI 48232

BOGOLIN, KATHLEEN MARGARET, banker; b. Oelwein, Iowa, May 21, 1953; d. Joseph Jerome and Judy Margaret (Harr) Murray; m. William F. Bogolin, Nov. 13, 1976. BA, Coll. St. Teresa, 1975; M Mgmt., Northwestern U., 1987. CPA, Ill. Audit supr. First Chgo., 1975-78, credit trainee, 1978-79, officer comml. lending, 1979-83; asst. v.p. Mfrs. Hanvoer Trust Co., Chgo., 1983-85, v.p., 1985—. Mem. Am. Inst. CPA's. Home: 104 W Ridge Prospect Heights IL 60070 Office: Mfrs Hanover Trust Co 10 S LaSalle St Chicago IL 60603

BOGOMOLNY, RICHARD JOSEPH, retail food chain executive. Chmn., chief exec. officer First Nat. Supermarkets Inc., Maple Heights, Ohio, also dir. Office: First Nat Supermarkets Inc 17000 Rockside Rd Cleveland OH 44137 *

BOGUSKY, RACHEL M., physician, counseling psychologist; b. Throop, Pa., Mar. 10, 1939; d. John Paul and Veronica (Farkas) Bogusky; student pvt. schs.; B.S., So. Conn. State Coll.; M.A., U. Conn.; Ed.S., Columbia U., Ed.D.; M.D., Universidad Autonoma de Ciudad Juarez, Mex. Tchr. East Haven (Conn.) Bd. Edn., 1961-62; dir. program for gifted, coordinator sci., master tchr. Greenwich (Conn.) Bd. Edn., 1962-69, 71-72; counseling therapist Psychol. Consultation Center, Columbia U., N.Y.C., 1970-71, instr. applied human devel., 1970-71; asst. prof. edn. U. Mich., Ann Arbor, 1973-76; behavior therapist, assertive tng. cons. Inst. for Behavior Change, Ann Arbor, 1975-76; ednl. psychologist, ednl. mgr. Med. Corp., Ann Arbor, 1976-77; pvt. cons. and counseling practice, Ann Arbor, 1975—. Recipient certificate recognition for ednl. contbns. Greenwich C. of C., 1969. Mem. Am. Psychol. Assn., Am. Personnel and Guidance Assn., Council for Exceptional Children (pres. chpt. 359, Fairfield County 1968-69), Assn. Advancement Behavior Therapy, Am. Soc. Tng. and Devel., Kappa Delta Pi. Author books, monographs and articles. Home and Office: 1 Haverhill Ct Ann Arbor MI 48105

BOHARDT, THOMAS FREDERICK, industrial executive; b. Dayton, Ohio, Jan. 22, 1947; s. Edwin Frederick and Betty Jean (Nigh) B.; m. Judith Jane Deem, June 5, 1967; children: Emily Ann, Amanda Deem. BBA, Bowling Green State U., 1969; MBA, U. Dayton, 1974. Indsl. engr. NCR, Dayton, 1969-72; indsl. engring. mgr. Reliance Electric Co., Madison, Ind., 1972-77; prodn. mgr. Reliance Electric Co., Ft. Worth, 1977-79; plant mgr. Reliance Electric Co., Cleve., 1979-84, group customer service mgr., 1984-86, nat. service mgr., 1986—; mem. steering com. United Techs. Ctr., Cleve., 1984—. Fund raiser Explorer Scouts, Lake County, Ohio, 1985. Republican. Roman Catholic. Avocation: golf. Office: Reliance Electric Co 24703 Euclid Ave Cleveland OH 44117

BOHL, ROBERT DANIEL, urologist; b. Louisville, July 23, 1948; s. Robert William and Marjorie (Rernert) B.; m. Jennifer Myerberg, Oct. 22, 1951; children: Casey, David. BA, Denison U., 1970; MD, Case Western Res. U., 1974. Resident in surgery U. Cin., 1974-77, resident in urology, 1977-80; urologist Urological Assocs., Inc., Columbus, Ohio, 1980—; mem. staff Mt. Carmel Hosp., Riverside Hosp. Mem. AMA, Am. Urol. Assn., Ohio Urol. Assn., Cen. Ohio Urol. Assn. Office: Urologists Assocs Inc Columbus OH 43222

BOHLE, DANIEL JAMES, obstetrician and gynecologist; b. Sumner, Iowa, Apr. 3, 1946; s. Arnold Henry and Marie Louise (Zell) B.; m. Anne Maureen Herbst, Mar. 4, 1978; children: Erin Kristine, Crista Noelle, Nicholas David, William Kenneth. BS, U. Iowa, 1968, MD, 1972. Diplomate Am. Bd. Ob-Gyn. Intern St. Paul-Ramsey County Hosp., 1972-73; emergency room physician Mercy Hosp., Cedar Rapids, Iowa, 1973-75, Finley Hosp., Dubuque, Iowa, 1975-80; resident West Va. U., Morgantown, 1980-83; practice ob-gyn. Dubuque, 1983—; chmn. ob-gyn. dept. Finley Hosp., Dubuque, 1984-85. Jr. fellow Am. Coll. Ob-Gyns; mem. Dubuque County Med. Soc. Republican. Lutheran. Avocations: classical music, church organ, piano, racquetball. Home: 3075 Olde Country Ln Dubuque IA 52001 Office: 777 Mazzuchelli Dubuque IA 52001

BOHLIM, RICHARD CHARLES, civil engineer; b. Michigan City, Ind., Sept. 5, 1952; s. George A. and Margaret (Elias) B.; B.S.C.E., Ind. Inst. Tech., 1974. Registered profl. engr., Kans.; lic. pvt. pilot. Service engr. Combustion Engring., Martins Creek, Pa., 1974, Boston, 1974-75, St. Louis, 1975-76, lead service engr. for combustion engring., Lawrence, Kans., 1976-78, resident service engr., Overland Park, Kans., 1978-80, resident supr. tech. services Kansas City Dist., 1980—, dist. mgr. tech. services, Kansas City, 1981—. Mem. ASCE (citation award 1974), Alpha Sigma Phi. Roman Catholic. Club: Moose. Home: 11521 Mastin Overland Park KS 66210 Office: 6362 College Blvd Overland Park KS 66211

BOHLKE, CATHERINE ANN O'BRIEN, accountant; b. Manchester, Iowa, Oct. 17, 1959; d. James Thomas and Rose Marie (Doyle) O'Brien; m. David James Bohlke, June 12, 1982; 1 child, Kristin Mary. BA in Acctg., U. No. Iowa, 1982. CPA, Iowa. Acct. Gosling & Co. P.C. (formerly Dee, Gosling & Co.), Manchester, 1982—. Recipient McGladrey Hendrickson Accountancy award, 1981-82. Mem. Am. Inst. CPA's, Iowa Soc. CPA's. Democrat. Roman Catholic. Home: 720 Tanglewood Dr Manchester IA 52057 Office: Gosling & Co PC 217 N Franklin St Manchester IA 52057

BOHLMANN, RALPH ARTHUR, clergyman, church official; b. Palisade, Nebr., Feb. 20, 1932; s. Arthur Erwin and Anne Fredericka (Weeke) B.; m. Patricia Anne McCleary, Apr. 19, 1959; children: Paul, Lynn. Student, St. Johns Coll., Winfield, Kans.; B.A., Concordia Sem., 1953; M.Div., 1956, S.T.M., 1966; Fulbright scholar, U. Heidelberg, 1956-57; Ph.D., Yale U., 1968. Ordained to ministry Lutheran Ch. (Mo. Synod), 1958; instr. history and religion Concordia Coll., 1957-58; pastor Mt. Olive Luth. Ch., Des Moines, 1958-60; prof. systematic theology Concordia Sem., St. Louis, 1960-71, acting pres., 1974-75, pres., 1975-81; pres. Luth. Ch.-Mo. Synod, 1981—; exec. sec. Commn. Theology and Ch. Relations Luth. Ch. Mo. Synod, St. Louis, 1971-74; mem. Faith and Order Commn. Nat. Council Chs., 1973-76. Author: Principles of Biblical Interpretation in the Lutheran Confessions, 1968. Office: 1333 S Kirkwood Rd Saint Louis MO 63122

BOHM, ARTHUR CECIL, manufacturing executive; b. N.Y.C., Aug. 27, 1903; s. Rudolph and Carrie (Worms) B.; widowed; children: Robert P., James E., Edith C. Bohm Johnson. Apprentice knitter Phoenix Hosiery Co., Milw., 1919-20; purchasing agent & sec. Monarch Mfg. Co., Milw., 1920-55; exec. v.p., gen. mgr. Monarch Inc., Milw., 1955-57; coordinator, purchasing agt. Brill Bros. Inc., Milw., 1957—. Jewish. Avocations: swimming, biking. Home: 2610 E Capitol Dr Shorewood WI 53211 Office: Brill Bros Inc PO Box 641 2102 W Pierce St Milwaukee WI 53201

BOHM, MILFORD MILES, consumer services company executive; b. Sharon, Pa., Oct. 29, 1921; s. Joseph and Irene Golda B.; m. Leona Cytron, June 15, 1952; children—Miriam G., Vicki L., David R., Robert D. Student U. Pa., U. Paris. Chmn. emeritus, founder, dir. CPI Corp., St. Louis, 1942—; dir. Mark Twain State Bank, St. Louis, 1968—; chmn., chief exec. officer Cencit Inc., St. Louis, 1983—; mem. adv. bd. Early Stages Co., San Francisco, 1985—. Chmn., Jewish Fedn. Council Lif Mems., St. Louis, 1984; dir. St. Louis Metro RCGA,; trustee Transp. Mus. Assn.; trustee Internat. Bd. Govs. for Technion U., Haifa, Israel, Recipient Prime Minister's award State of Israel; Appreciation award Better Bus. Bur., 1979, Albert Einstein award Am. Soc. for Tech., 1987; CPI Corp. Founders scholar, 1982. Mem. Profl. Photographers Assn. Am., Master Photo Finishers and Dealers Assn., Met. Assn. Philanthropy (St. Louis). Jewish. Clubs: Creve Coeur Racquet, Washington U., B'nai B'rith (St. Louis). Avocations: tennis; swimming; jogging; boating; reading. Office: CPI Corp 1706 Washington Ave Saint Louis MO 63103

BOHN, MELVIN MICHAEL, information sciences educator; b. Manhattan, Kans., Nov. 2, 1942; s. Fred Andrew and Margaret M. (Mason) B.; m. Vicki S. Johnson, July 3, 1969; children: Eric Christopher, Adam Anthony. BA, Calif. State U., Long Beach, 1968, MA, 1970; MLS, Emporia State U., 1976; PhD, U. Nebr., Lincoln, 1986. Instr. info. sci. U. Nebr., Omaha, 1977-81, asst. prof., 1981-86, assoc. prof., 1986—; pres. Alyeska Pub. Co., Inc., 1987—; cons. Bellevue (Nebr.) Coll., 1985. Author: Mostly California Poems, 1978; editor: Annex 22, 1981; contbr. book revs. to Choice mag., 1982—. Mem. exec. bd. Friends of Internat. Students and Scholars, Omaha, 1986—. Mem. ALA, Nebr. Library Assn., Nebr. Ednl. Tech. Assn. Republican. Episcopal. Club: German-American Soc. Avocations: travel, photography. Home: 11105 X St Omaha NE 68137 Office: Univ Nebr Library Omaha NE 68182-0237

BOHON, ELLIS G(RAY), accountant, management and tax consultant; b. LaBelle, Mo., Sept. 1, 1902; s. Frank W. and Lee (Ellis) B.; m. Joyce L. Finlayson, Apr. 15, 1939; children: Walter Duncan, Ellis Gray II (dec.). Student Westminster Coll., Fulton, Mo., 1920-21; BS cum laude, Knox Coll., Galesburg, Ill., 1924; postgrad. Walton Sch. Commerce, 1927-29, Northwestern U., 1930-33, 1935, 1965-66, YMCA Community Coll., 1963-71, Chgo. Bd. Trade Grain Inst., 1955-56 (all Chgo.); CPA, U. Ill., 1935. Enrolled as atty. Tax Ct. U.S.A.; CPA, Ill., Ky., Iowa, Mo. Staff accountant Ernst & Ernst, CPA's, Chgo., 1927-30; partner R. L. Pearce & Co., CPAs', 1930-36; propr. E. G. Bohon & Co., CPA's, 1936—; former lectr. Am. Inst. Banking, Walton Sch. Commerce, Ill. Inst. Tech., Chgo., Lake Forest (Ill.) Coll. Author papers. Former advisor, treas. Lakes chpt. Order DeMolay, bus. men's adv. council Jones Comml. High Sch. (Chgo.). Member Am. Inst. CPA's, Am. Accounting Assn., Ill. (past chmn. tech. com.), Ia. socs. CPA's, Nat. Assn. Accountants, Am. Arbitration Assn., Accounting Research Assn., Am. Inst. Laundering, Ky. Hist. Soc., Midwest Bus. Adminstrn. Assn., Phi Delta Theta. Presbyterian. Clubs: Masons, Shriners (treas. club 1978), Union League, Univ. of Evanston. Home: 523 E North Ave Lake Bluff IL 60044 Office: 53 W Jackson Blvd Room 824 Chicago IL 60604

BOHRA, SHARAD KUMAR, mechanical engineer; b. Udaipur, Rajasthan, India, Sept. 8, 1954; came to U.S., 1978; s. Onkar Lal and Jatan Devi Bohra; m. Sangeeta Bhandari, Jan. 24, 1981; 1 child, Sumit. B of Tech. in Mech. Engring., Banaras Hindu U., Varanasi, India, 1976; MBA, U. Wis., Milw., 1982. Engring. mgr. Thurner Heat Treating Corp., Milw., 1978-83; devel. engr. Gen. Electric Med. Systems Group, Waukesha, Wis., 1984—. Mem. Assn. MBA Execs., India Cultural Soc. Milw. (bd. dirs. 1986—). Jain. Avocations: tennis, travel, photography. Home: 2734 Turnberry Ct Waukesha WI 53188 Office: Gen Electric Co Med Systems Group 3000 Grandview Blvd Waukesha WI 53188

BOILEAU, OLIVER CLARK, JR., aerospace company executive; b. Camden, N.J., Mar. 31, 1927; s. Oliver Clark and Florence Mary (Smith) B.; m. Nan Eleze Hallen, Sept. 15, 1951; children: Clark Edward, Adrienne Lee, Nanette Erika, Jay Marshall. B.S. in Elec. Engring., U. Pa., 1951, M.S., 1953; SM in Indsl. Mgmt., MIT, 1964. With Boeing Aerospace Co., 1953-79, mgr. Minuteman, v.p., 1968, pres., 1973-79; pres. Gen. Dynamics Corp., 1980—, also bd. dirs.; bd. dirs. Centerre Bank; mem. vis. com. aeronautics and astronautics MIT, Lincoln Lab. Adv. Bd.; trustee Conf. Bd. Mem. corp. Lawrence Inst. Tech.; trustee Ranken Tech. Inst.; v.p. exec. bd. St. Louis Area council Boy Scouts Am.; bd. overseers U. Pa.; trustee St. Louis U. Served with USN, 1944-46. Sloan fellow, MIT, 1963-64. Mem. AIAA, Navy League, Air Force Assn., Am. Def. Preparedness Assn., Assn. U.S. Army, Nat. Aeros. Assn., Nat. Space Club, Naval War Coll. Found., Nat. Acad. Engring. Office: Gen Dynamics Corp Pierre Laclede Ctr Saint Louis MO 63105

BOIMAN, DONNA RAE, art academy executive; b. Columbus, Ohio, Jan. 13, 1946; d. George Brandle and Donna Rae (Rockwell) Hall; m. David Charles Boiman, Dec. 8, 1973. BS in Pharmacy, Ohio State U., 1969; student, Columbus Coll. Art & Design, 1979-83. Registered pharmacist, Ohio. Pharmacist, mgr. various retail stores, Cleve., 1970-73, Columbus, 1973-77; owner L'Artiste, Reynoldsburg, Ohio, 1977-81; pres. Cen. Ohio Art Acad., Reynoldsburg, 1981—; cons. to Mayor City of Reynoldsburg, 1986-87. Represented in permanent collections including Collector's Gallery Columbus Mus. Art, Gallery 200, Columbus, Art Exchange, Columbus, The Huntington Collection, Dean Witter Reynolds Collection, Zanesville Art Ctr. Mem. Pa. Soc. Watercolorists, Nat. Soc. Layerists in Multimedia, Columbus Art League, Cen. Ohio Watercolor Soc. (pres. 1983-84), Am. Quarter Horse Assn., Ohio Quarter Horse Assn. Avocations: showing horses, skiing, white water river running, judging figure skating. Office: Cen Ohio Art Acad 7297 E Main St Reynoldsburg OH 43068

BOKEMPER, RICHARD KEITH, dentist; b. Wakefield, Nebr., Mar. 22, 1956; s. Duane Edward and Doris Marie (Fischer) B.; m. Theresa Marie Grovijohn, Sept. 18, 1982. BS in Dental Sci., U. Nebr., 1978, DDS, 1981. Pvt. practice dentistry Scribner, Nebr., 1984, Sergeant Bluff, Iowa, 1984—. Mem. City of Scribner Fire Dept., 1981-84. Mem. ADA, Iowa Dental Assn., Northwest Iowa Dist. Dental Soc., Sioux City Dental Society, Jaycees (New Jaycee of the Quarter 1986, Chmn. of Month). Democrat. Lutheran. Avocations: softball, golf, Civil War Studies. Home: 2714 Ivanhoe Sergeant Bluff IA 51054 Office: 703 First St Sergent Bluff IA 51054

BOLAM-JENKINS, NANCY JANE, psychologist; b. Cleve., Oct. 11, 1936; s. Howard Walter and Jane Harriet (Carter) Leonhart; m. Darrell Winston Bolam (dec. Feb. 1983); children: Marlene, Vicki, Darrell, Kathy, Alan; m. Don Raymond Jenkins, Aug. 3, 1984; 1 stepson, David. AA, U. Cin., 1959, BA, 1967, MEd, 1970. Cert. sch. psychologist, Ohio; lic. psychologist, Ohio. Accounts payable clk. and expediator Proctor & Gamble, Cin., 1955-65; tchr. Cin. Bd. Edn., 1965-72; supportive reading coordinator, sch. psychologist Sycamore Bd. Edn., Cin., 1973-80, sch. psychologist, 1973—; pvt. practice psychology Cin., 1977—; Cons. Aring Inst., Cin., 1985-86. Booth chmn. Beech Acres, Cin., 1963-. Mem. Nat. Assn. Sch. Psychologists, Ohio Sch. Psychologist Assn. (bd. dirs 1983-86), Southwestern Ohio Sch. Psychologist Assn. (pres. 1981-83), Am. Bus. Women (v.p. 1975, Woman of the Yr. 1979), Phi Kappa Epsilon (pres. 1964-65). Episcopalian. Club: Cin. Turners (cultural chmn. 1959—). Avocation: sewing. Home: 11865 Mill Rd Cincinatti OH 45240 Office: Sycamore Bd Edn Cooper Rd Cincinatti OH 45242

BOLAND, ROBERT KENT, dentist; b. Des Moines, May 23, 1953; s. Donald Edward and Elizabeth Jean (Thompson) B.; married, 1984. BA, U. Mo., 1975; DDS, U. Mo., Kansas City, 1980. Dental technician Hansen Dental Labs., Shawnee, Kans., 1975; with hematology-urology dept. Truman Med. Ctr., Kansas City, Mo., 1978-80; gen. practice dentistry Clinton, Mo., 1980-83; dentist Peculiar (Mo.) Dental, 1983, Kansas City Denture Clinic, Gladstone, Mo., 1984—; vol. dentist Westport Free Health Clinic, Kansas City, 1978-80, Macy Indian Reservation, Nebr., 1979. Vol. Mothers Against Drunk Drivers, Kansas City, 1986. Mem. Gladstone C. of C. Club: Bicycle (Peculiar) (pres. 1983). Avocations: sports, photography, nature study. Office: K C Denture Clinic 200 A NW 72d St Gladstone MO 64118

BOLDRY, JOSEPH STUART, JR., bank executive; b. Pitts., July 15, 1956; s. Joseph Stuart and Miriam Brown (Anderson) B.; m. Jennifer Paula Zittnan, Apr. 26, 1986. BA in Econs., Boston Coll., 1978; MBA, U. Chgo., 1982. Supr. bankcard ops. Harris Trust & Savs. Bank, Chgo., 1979-80, human resource coordinator, 1980-82, remittance processing mgr., 1982-84, systems project mgr., 1984-85, check processing mgr., 1985—; cons. job-search workshop North Park Coll., Chgo., 1981-86; pres., organizer ABLE Burroughs user group, 1985-86. Mem. Boston Coll. Alumni Assn., U. Chgo. Alumni Assn. Republican. Roman Catholic. Club: Univ. (Chgo.). Lodge: Order of the Cross and Crown. Avocations: reading, golf, travel, cooking.

BOLEN, CHARLES WARREN, univ. dean; b. West Frankfort, Ill., Sept. 27, 1923; s. William and Iva (Phillips) B.; m. Maxine Sheffler, Aug. 1, 1948; children—Ann, Jayne. B. Mus. Edn., Northwestern U., 1948; M.Mus., Eastman Sch. Music, 1950; Ph.D., Ind. U., 1954. Instr. music Eastern Ill. U., 1950-51; chmn. music dept. Ripon (Wis.) Coll., 1954-62; instr. flute Nat. Music Camp, summers 1954-62; dean Sch. Fine Arts, U. Mont., Missoula, 1962-70, Coll. Fine Arts, Ill. State U., Normal, 1970—. Contbr. articles to profl. jours. Chmn. Mont. Arts Council, 1965-70; mem. Pres.' Adv. Council to Arts, Pres.'s Adv. Council to J.F. Kennedy Center for Performing Arts, 1970; cons. Chancellor's Panel on Univ. Purposes, State U. N.Y., 1970, Ednl. Mgmt. Services; pres. Central Ill. Cultural Affairs Consortium, 1975-76. Mem. Music Tchrs. Nat. Assn. (pres. East central div. 1961-62, nat. v.p. states and divs. 1962-65), Music Educators Nat. Conf., Am. Musicol. Soc., Internat. Council Fine Arts Deans (chmn. 1969-70), Fedn. Rocky Mountain States (arts and humanities com. 1966-70), Assn. Western Univs. Home: 1007 Barton Dr Normal IL 61761

BOLENDER, TODD, choreographer; b. Canton, Ohio, 1919. Student, Hanya Holm, N.Y.C.; enrolled, Sch. American Ballet, N.Y.C., 1936. Joined Lincoln Kirstein's Ballet Caravan, 1937; formed Am. Concert Ballet; choreographed 1st ballet, 1943; also danced with Ballet Theatre, 1944 and Ballet Russe de Monte Carlo, 1945, joined Ballet Soc., 1946; prin. dancer N.Y.C. Ballet, 1948-61; dir. ballet cos. of opera houses of Cologne and Frankfurt; numerous nat. and internat. freelance choreography assignments, 1952-80; artistic dir. State Ballet of Mo., Kansas City, 1981—. Recipient Mo. Arts Council Arts award, 1987. Offices: Kansas City Ballet State Ballet of Mo 706 W 42d St Kansas City MO 64108

BOLES, CHRIS A., columnist; b. Purdy, Mo., Feb. 4, 1944; d. Alvin J. and Wilma Agnes (Parrigan) Ceselski; m. James Hugh Boles, July 6, 1963; children—Tammy Jo, Rana Dawn, Russell James. Student Wichita Bus. Coll., Crowder Coll. With Farm and Ranch World, Tulsa, 1971-81; stringer Country World, Tulsa, Joplin Globe, 1972-82; columnist Calif. Horse Rev., Fla. Horse Country, Tex. and So. Quarter Horse Jour., Horses Unltd., Valley Horse News, Continental Horseman; contbr. over 1200 articles to horse mags.; advt. cons.; press sec. Mo. Parimutuel Horse Racing, 1983—; pub. relations chairperson Quarter Horse Racing Assn. Mo., 1981—; regional dir. Quarter Horse Racing Owners Am., Ft. Worth. Home: PO Box 225 Stark City MO 64866 Office: Hook Up Communications PO Box 161 Fairview MO 64842

BOLGER, T(HOMAS) MICHAEL, lawyer; b. Minocqua, Wis., Dec. 23, 1939; s. Patrick Edward and Mary Frances (McConville) B.; B.A., Marquette U., 1961; M.A., St. Louis U., 1966, Ph.L., 1966; J.D., Northwestern U., 1971; m. Virginia Kay Empey, Aug. 24, 1968; children—John, Jennifer. Admitted to Wis. bar, 1971; mem. firm Quarles & Brady, Milw., 1971—, partner, 1978—; instr. philosophy Marquette U., Milw., 1967-68. Vice chmn. United Performing Arts Fund drive, 1976-77; bd. dirs. Kearney Negro Welfare Found., 1974—, Milw. Repertory Theatre, 1977—, Milw. Ballet Found., Inc., 1981—, Permanent Diaconate Program of Milw. Archdiocese, 1977—; pres. Artreach, Inc., 1979—, Milw. Repertory Theater, 1980—; pres. bd. trustees Highland Community Sch., 1976—; trustee, sec.). U. Wis.-Milw. Found., 1976—; pres. bd. dirs. Hickory Hollow, 1978—. Mem. Am. Bar Assn., Milw. Bar Assn., Wis. Bar Assn., Fed. Bar Assn., Marquette U Alumni Assn. (pres. 1982-84), Alpha Sigma Nu, Phi Sigma Tau. Clubs: Univ., The Town. Contbr. articles in field to profl. jours.; editor Northwestern Jour. of Criminal Law, 1970-71. Home: 137 E White Oak Way Mequon WI 53092 Office: 780 N Water St Milwaukee WI 53202

BOLINSKE, ROBERT EDWARD, physician, allergist; b. Appleton, Wis., Oct. 6, 1924; s. Edward Joseph and Hyacinth (Krautkramer) B.; m. Anne Kramolowsky, Oct. 20, 1986; children: Mary Jane Bolinske Driscoll, Kathryn A. Bolinske Carroll, Janet L., Ellen, Robert Jr. MD, Marquette U., 1948. Diplomate Am. Bd. Pediatrics, Am. Bd. Allergy and Immunology. Pvt. practice allergy and immunology Creve Coeur, Mo., 1958—; asst. prof. St. Louis U., 1958-85, assoc. prof., 1985—. Served to capt. USAF, 1954-56. Fellow Am. Acad. Allergy (ethics com. 1983-86), Am. Coll. Allergists, Assn. Clinical Allergy and Immunology. Home: 56 Portland Dr Frontenac MO 63131 Office: 11722 Studt Ave Creve Coeur MO 63141

BOLLENBACHER, HERBERT KENNETH, steel company official; b. Wilkinsburg, Pa., Apr. 16, 1933; s. Curtis W. and Ebba M. (Frendberg) B.; m. Nancy Jane Cercena, June 29, 1957; children—Mary E., Kenneth E. A.B., U. Pitts., 1960, M.Ed., 1963. Cert. safety profl. Staff asst. tng. J & L Steel Co., Pitts., 1963-66; mgr. tng., devel. and accident prevention Textron Corp., Pitts., 1966-72; supr. safety Copperweld Steel Co., Warren, Ohio, 1972-75, mgr. safety, security, 1975-78, mgr. human resources conservation, 1978—; mem. adj. faculty Pa. State U. Served with U.S. Army, 1954-56. Mem. Am. Soc. Safety Engrs. (past pres. Ohio-Pa. chpt., Ohio Safety Profl. of Yr. 1983-84), Ohio Soc. Safety Engrs. (past pres.), Am. Iron and Steel Inst. (chmn. safety task force), Mfrs. Assn. Eastern Ohio and Western Pa. (safety chmn. 12 yrs.; safety profl. of yr. award 1984, coordinator Ohio seat belt coalition 1986, Gov.'s spl. recognition award), Trumbull Camp Gideons Internat. (past pres.), Ohio Gideons (area coordinator, membership cabinet). Presbyterian (elder). Lodge: Rotary. Author suprs. monthly discussion guide, article for tech. publ. Avocations: softball; volleyball; reading.

BOLLI, ROBERT EDWIN, insurance agent; b. Columbia, Mo., Mar. 26, 1943; s. Jacob and Iva Duval (Hudnell) B.; m. Mary Ann Alborn; children: Jana Marie, Kara Jane, Jade Leanne, Jonathan Drew. Student, Cen. Meth. Coll., Rockhurst Coll. Lic. comml. pilot. Assembler Douglas Aircraft Co., Tulsa, 1964-65; gen. mgr. Hart Aviation, Inc., Columbia, Mo., 1965-66; mgr. office services M.F.A. Oil Co., Columbia, 1966-72; comptroller Skyway Aviation, Inc., Ft. Leonard Wood, Mo., 1972-73; v.p. United Mo. Bank of Kansas City, 1973-86; agt. Am. Family Ins. Co., Hamilton, Mo., 1986—. Pres. Hamilton Recreation Com., 1985. Served with U.S. Army. Mem. Am. Inst. Banking (counsel 1973—.). Republican. Methodist. Avocations: gardening, photography, sailing. Home: Rt 2 Box 264D Hamilton MO 64644 Office: Am Family Ins Co 100 N Ardinger Hamilton MO 64644

BOLLINGER, ROBERT OTTO, hospital information systems executive; b. Detroit, June 15, 1939; s. Robert R. and Velma (Gire) B.; m. Ruth Margaret Collins, June 16, 1962; children: Christopher, Susan. BS, Wayne State U., 1962, MS, 1965, PhD, 1972. Asst. prof. Eastern Ill. U., Charleston, Ill., 1969-71, Wayne State U., Detroit, 1976—; research assoc. Child Research Ctr. Mich., Detroit, 1971-81; dir. med. info. ctr. Children's Hosp. Mich., Detroit, 1981—; cons. Health Info. Analysts, Detroit, 1981—; medicine informatics curriculum coordinator Wayne State U., 1985—; mem. adv. bd. Metro Ctr. High Tech., Detroit, 1986—. Contbr. articles to profl. jours. Served with USAR, 1957-63. NDEA fellow, 1962-65. Mem. Am. Assn. Med. Systems and Informatics, Biomed Soc. of IEEE. Office: Children's Hosp Mich 3901 Beaubien Blvd Detroit MI 48201

BOLLMEIER, EMIL WAYNE, manufacturing company executive; b. Hurst, Ill., Jan. 16, 1925; s. Emil Philip and Flossie Louise (Swain) B.; m. Nancy Lee Mercier, Feb. 9, 1972; children—David Wayne, Ann Louise, Paul Wesley. B.S. in Chem. Engring, U. Nebr., 1947; postgrad., U. Minn., 1949-51. With 3M Co., St. Paul, 1947-82; div. v.p. electro products div. 3M Co.,

1965-72, group v.p. elec. products group, 1973-83, mem. 3M ops. com.; chief exec. officer, gen. ptnr. C-TEK Ltd. Partnership, 1983—; pres. Dynex Research, Inc., 1983—; chmn. bd., pres. Global Thermoelectric Power Systems Ltd., 1985-86. Mem. Planning Commn., Mendota Heights, Minn., 1960-65; chmn. Republican Party, Dakota County, Minn., 1965-68. Served with USNR, 1945-46. Fellow IEEE; mem. Nat. Elec. Mfrs. Assn. (bd. govs.), Sigma Xi, Sigma Tau. Presbyterian. Patentee in field. Home: 265 Burlington Rd Saint Paul MN 55119 Office: 3615 29th Ave NE Minneapolis MN 55418

BOLT, ROLF JAMES, periodontist; b. Grand Rapids, Mich., Nov. 26, 1948; s. Ralph John and Nell Theresa (Flietstra) B.; m. Meribeth Bloomfield Bolt, Apr. 22, 1979. BS, Calvin Coll., Grand Rapids, 1970; DDS, U. Mich., Ann Arbor, 1974, MS in Periodontics, 1979. Clinical instr. U. Mich. Dental Sch., Ann Arbor, 1976-79; pvt. practice Grand Rapids, 1979—. Served to capt. USAF, 1974-76. Mem. Am. Acad. Periodontology, ADA, West Mich. Dental Assn., Kent County Dental Assn. Mem. Reformed Ch. Am. Avocations: running, tennis, golf, skiing (alpine and cross country), reading. Home: 2410 Thornapple Road Dr Grand Rapids MI 49506 Office: 2000 Burton St SE Grand Rapids MI 49506

BOLTRES, H. WILLIAM, merger and acquisition consultant, corporate executive; b. Canton, Ohio, Apr. 7, 1936; s. Henry W. and Sarah A. Boltres; student Malone Coll., Ohio State U.; m. Doris Jean Kaufman, Aug. 9, 1958; children: Martin W., Christine A. With Addressograph-Multigraph Corp., Cleve., 1957-63, H.W. Boltres & Assos., Canton, 1963-65, Ohio Dept. Natural Resources, Columbus, 1965-75; pres. The Boltres Co., Columbus, 1975—; pres. The Am. Wick Co., Inc., 1983-85, Indsl. Steam Coals Inc., 1977-79, Driveseal Inc., 1985—; cons. Mem. fin. com. Licking County Republican party, 1978-80. Served with USMC, 1953-54, U.S. Army, 1954-56. Mem. Nat. Rifle Assn., Ducks Unltd. Methodist. Clubs: Columbus Touchdown, Big Red Touchdown, Capital. Home: 57 Donald Ross Dr Granville OH 43023 Office: 2720 Westbelt Dr Columbus OH 43228

BOLWELL, HARRY JAMES, manufacturing company executive; b. Bloomfield, N.J., May 17, 1925; s. Harry George and Ann Lillian (Seymour) B.; m. Suzanne Ruth Poljacik, Sept. 24, 1949 (dec. 1984); children: Brian, Suzanne. B.S., U. Vt., 1949; M.S., Stevens Inst. Tech., 1952. Gen. mgr. Combustion Engring., Inc., Chattanooga, 1959-61; v.p., gen. mgr. Surface Combustion div. Midland-Ross Corp., Toledo, 1961-65; group v.p. corp. Midland-Ross Corp., 1965-69, pres., 1969-77; chief exec. officer Midland-Ross Corp., Cleve., 1969—; chmn. Midland-Ross Corp., 1977—; dir. Nat. City Corp., Cleve., Cleve. Cliffs Iron Co., Leaseway Transp. Corp., Provident Life and Accident Ins. Co. Trustee Boys Club Cleve., Cleve. Scholarship Programs, Inc., Laurel Sch. for Girls, NCCJ, Cleve. Council World Affairs. Served to 1st lt. USAAF, 1942-45. Decorated D.F.C., Air Medal. Mem. Ohio, Cleve. chambers commerce, Sigma Alpha Epsilon. Episcopalian (vestryman). Clubs: The Clevelander, The Country, Cleve. Racquet, Pepper Pike, Union. Office: Midland-Ross Corp 20600 Chagrin Blvd Cleveland OH 44122 *

BOLYARD, CHARLES WESLEY, psychologist; b. Ft. Wayne, Ind., May 28, 1937; s. Charles Wesley and Virginia Maxine Bolyard; BBA, Ind. Central U. (now U. Indpls.), 1960; MA, Ball State U., 1962; PhD, Purdue U., 1971; m. Martha E. Hudson, Aug. 14, 1960; children—Mark Gregory, Todd Andrew. Sch. counselor MSD Perry Twp., Indpls., 1963-68; univ. adminstr. Purdue U., 1968-70; prof., univ. adminstr. Ind.-Purdue U., Ft. Wayne, 1970-77, instr. bus. and supervision, 1979—; behavioral sci. cons. Lincoln Nat. Life Ins., Ft. Wayne, Ind., 1977—; cons. William C. Weber and Assocs., 1979—; instr. bus. and supervision St. Francis Coll., 1979—. Pres. exec. bd. Allen County Mental Health Assn., 1983-84; mem. adv. bd. Jr. League of Ft. Wayne, 1977—; adminstrv. bd., sec.-treas. Parent Club, Homestead High Sch., 1977-79; mem. area com. Internat. Yr. of Disabled Persons; mem. adv. com. Ind. Vocat. Services; mem. adv. bd. Nat. Spinal Cord Injury Found.; bd. dirs. ARC, Am. Cancer Soc.; mem. Ft. Wayne Area Council on Employment of Handicapped; mem. Ind. State Exec. Fellows Program Adv. Com.; bd. dirs. United Way Allen County, 1983-84; mem. edn. com. McMillen Health Ctr. NDEA fellow, 1964, community adv. bd. Sta. WBNI pub. radio; alumni bd. dirs. U. Indpls. Mem. Organizational Devel. Network, Am. Soc. Personnel Adminstrn., Am. Psychol. Assn., Personnel Assn. Ft. Wayne. Methodist. Club: Optimists (v.p.). Author: (with Robert S. Barkhaus) Threads: A Tapestry of Self and Career Exploration, 1980; Career Development in the 1980's: Theory and Practice, 1981; contbr. chpt. to book, articles to profl. jours. Home: 5010 Pinebrook Dr Fort Wayne IN 46804 Office: 1300 S Clinton St Fort Wayne IN 46801

BOMBYK, GEORGE, professional safety consultant; b. Caro, Mich., Feb. 2, 1928; s. Martin Bombyk and Marie Schuberta; m. Violet Marjorie Hendra, Nov. 10, 1951; children: David, Kathleen, Marjorie, Robert. BSE, Ea. Mich. U., 1955. Conf. leader Ford Motor Co., Wayne, Mich., 1955-56; safety adminstr. Chrysler Corp., Highland Park, Mich., 1956-75; dir. safety Kelsey-Hayes Corp., Phila., 1977-78; safety tech. specialist Nat. Safety Council, Chgo., 1978-80; indsl. and product safety cons., speaker, trainer safety seminars McCarthy Robinson, Assocs., Grand Blanc, Mich., 1981—. Served with U.S. Army, 1946-49. Mem. Nat. Safety Council, Am. Soc. Safety Engrs., System Safety Soc., World Safety Orgn. (cert., affiliate), Am. Soc. Agrl. Engrs. (affiliate). Republican. Avocations: bowling, boating, canoeing. Home: 28561 Leona St Garden City MI 48135 Office: Mc Carthy-Robinson Assocs 9309 N Holly Rd Grand Blanc MI 48439

BOMMARITO, VINCENT JOSEPH, restaurateur; b. St. Louis, Oct. 17, 1930; s. Anthony and Lucille (Randazzo); m. Martha Beasley, Apr. 28, 1956; children: Lucy Ann, Anthony, Vincent, James, Dianna. Pres., chief exec. officer Tony's, St. Louis, 1949—; bd. dirs. Landmark Bank, St. Louis. past bd. dirs. Campbell House Found., St. Louis Zoo, St. Louis Ambassadors, Boy's Club St. Louis; mem. president's adv. council St. Louis Community Coll.; chmn. bd. dirs. St. Louis Conv. Ctr. Commn., Downtown Taxing Dist.; bd. dirs. chmn. beautification com. Downtown St. Louis, Inc.; bd. dirs. First St. Forum; vice chmn. Operation Brightside. Recipient Man of Yr. award Unico, 1981, City of Hope award, 1982, Hiram W. Neuwnehner award Better Bus. Bur. and Advt. Club of Greater St. Louis, 1982, Toast of the Town award Cystic Fibrosis, 1985, 5 Star awards Mobil, Travel/Holiday awards, Ivy award; mem. Nat. Hall of Fame, Mo. Hall of Fame. Mem. Chain des Rotisseure Commandrie de Bordeaux Societies, Regional Commerce and Growth Assn. Office: Tony's Inc 826 N Broadway Saint Louis MO 63102

BONA, RICHARD ADAM, dentist, educator; b. Hammond, Ind., Mar. 31, 1953; s. Richard Adam Sr. and Frances Helen (Wislocki) B.; m. Mary Patricia Curran, July 1, 1978; children: Kathleen, Andrew, Maureen. DDS, U. Ill., 1978; spl. cert., Marquette U., 1984. Assoc. dentist Dr. R. Bona Sr., Calumet City, 1978-81; adj. instr. Marquette U., 1981-84; gen. practice dentistry Lansing, Ill., 1984—; asst. prof. U. Ill., Chgo., 1984—; prosthodontic cons. Olympia Fields (Ill.) Hosp., 1985—, TMJ Clinic, Olympia Fields, 1985—. Mem. ADA, Ill. State Dental Soc., Chgo. Dental Soc. (membership com. 1980-81). Roman Catholic. Avocations: baseball, kite flying, hiking. Office: 19111 Burnham Ave Lansing IL 60438

BONAFIGLIA, JOSEPH C., plastics company executive; b. Phila., Dec. 6, 1938; s. Ralph and Theresa (Severino) B.; m. Dolores Jean Niccoletti, Mar. 7, 1973; children—Maria Kristine, Ruppert, Jeffrey, Scott. B.A. in Math., Temple U., 1979. Research lab. mgr. Rohm & Haas Co., Bristol, Pa., 1974-77, salesman, N.Y.C., 1977-78, Mich., 1978-80; mktg. mgr. CertainTeed Corp., Troy, Mich., 1980-81, regional sales mgr., 1981—. Patentee in field. Vol. Project Concern-Walk for Mankind, Troy, 1980-84. Mem. Soc. Plastics Industry (chmn. Houston conf. 1983-84, Expo II 1985—), Soc. for Advancement of Materials and Process Engring. (chmn. 1984, bd. dirs. 1985), Soc. Plastics Engrs., MENSA, Troy C. of C. Roman Catholic. Avocations: sketching; oil and acrylic painting; woodworking; electronics; reading. Home: 1500 Brentwood Dr Troy MI 48098 Office: CertainTeed Corp 1450 Souter Troy MI 48083

BONAHOOM, MEG TASSIE, financial investment executive; b. Toledo, Dec. 4, 1946; s. Glennon Bloomfield and Frances (Garza) Tassie; m. John Robert Bonahoom, Jan. 25, 1971 (div. Oct. 1975); 1 child, Tobie Elias. BA in Human Relations, U. Ky., 1970; MBA, U. Toledo, 1983. Counselor Pikes Peak YMCA, Colorado Springs, Colo., 1975-76; retail sales rep. Lasalle's, Toledo, 1976-78; mgr. Arby's Inc., Toledo, 1978-81; research analyst Seagate Capital Mgmt., Toledo, 1983-85; mgr. investment portfolio Toledo Trust Co., Toledo, 1985—. Active Toledo YWCA; mem. allocations com. Lucas County Mental Health Bd., Toledo, Women Involved in Toledo. Mem. Fin. Analysts Toledo. Avocations: needlework, travel. Home: 5119 Secor Rd #8 Toledo OH 43623 Office: Toledo Trust Co Three Seagate Toledo OH 43603

BONARETTI, EDWARD WAYNE, human resources director; b. Kenosha, Wis., May 3, 1934; s. Amedeo G. and Angeline L. (Forgianni) B.; m. Janice Marie Rasmussen, Feb. 24, 1962; children: Jeanne Marie, Julie Ann. BBA in Acctg., Spencerian Coll., 1959. Lic. real estate broker, Wis.; notary pub. Office adminstr. Snap-on Tools Corp., Kenosha, Wis., 1965-80; sales rep. ERA/OAK Realty, Kenosha, 1980-81; office mgr., controller Protecon, Inc., Kenosha, 1981-84; mgr. human resources Vista Internat. Packaging, Kenosha, 1984—. Served with U.S. Army, 1954-55. Mem. Kenosha Mfg. Employers Assn. Roman Catholic. Lodge: Elks. Home: 2543 Buchanan Rd Kenosha WI 53140 Office: Vista Internat Packaging Co 1126 88th Pl Kenosha WI 53140

BONAVENTURA, LEO MARK, gynecologist, educator; b. East Chicago, Ill., Aug. 1, 1945; s. Angelo Peter and Wanda D. (Kelleher) B.; student Marquette U., 1963-66; M.D., Ind. U., 1970; married; children—Leo Mark, Dena Anne, Angela Lorena, Nicole Palmira, Leah Michelle, Adam Xavier. Intern in surgery, Cook County Hosp., Chgo., 1970-71; resident in ob-gyn., Ind. U. Hosps., 1973-76, fellow in reproductive endocrinology and infertility, 1976-78; asst. prof. ob-gyn., Ind. U., 1976—, asst. head sect. reproductive endocrinology and infertility, 1978-80, head sect., 1980-81. Served with USN attached to USMC, 1971-73. Named Intern of Yr., Cook County Hosp., 1971. Diplomate Am. Bd. Obstetrics and Gynecology, Am. Bd. Reproductive Endocrinology and Infertility. Mem. Central Assn. Ob-Gyn., Am. Coll. Obstetricians and Gynecologists, Am. Fertility Soc., Can. Fertility Soc., Soc. Reproductive Endocrinologists, Soc. Reproductive Surgeons. Roman Catholic. Contbr. articles to profl. jours. Office: 8091 Townshipline Rd Indianapolis IN 46260

BOND, CHRISTOPHER SAMUEL, U.S. senator, lawyer; b. St. Louis, Mar. 6, 1939; s. Arthur D. and Elizabeth (Green) B.; m. Carolyn Reid, May 13, 1967; 1 child, Samuel Reid. B.A. with honors, Princeton U., 1960; LL.B., U. Va., 1963. Bar: Mo. bar 1963, U.S. Supreme Ct. bar 1967. Law clk. to chief judge U.S. Ct. of Appeals, 5th Dist., Atlanta, 1963-64; assoc. firm Covington & Burling, Washington, 1965-67; practice law Mexico, Mo., 1968; asst. atty. gen., chief counsel consumer protection div. State of Mo., 1969-70; auditor 1971-73; gov. State of Mo., 1973-77, 81-85; ptnr. law firm Gage & Tucker, Kansas City and St. Louis, 1985-87; U.S. senator from Mo., 1987—; pres. Gt. Plains Legal Found., Kansas City, Mo., 1978-81; chmn. Republican Govs. Assn.; chmn. Midwestern Govs. Assn.; exec. com. Nat. Govs. Conf., chmn. com. on econ. and community devel., 1981-83, chmn. com. on energy and environment, 1983-84. Republican. Presbyterian. Office: Room 321 Hart Senate Bldg Washington DC 20510 *

BOND, EPPERSON ELLIS, chemist; b. Nashville, Apr. 5, 1923; s. Epperson Porter and Margaret (Reed) B.; m. Marian Ruth Philips, June 9, 1950; 1 child, Michael Ellis. B.A., Fisk U., 1944, postgrad., 1945; postgrad., DePaul U., 1946. Research assoc. Glidden Co., Chgo., 1946-47; research assoc. Med. Sch., U. Ill., Chgo., 1947-50, Northwestern U., Chgo., 1950-53; chemist VA Hosp., Hines, Ill., 1953—, now research chemist; Chmn. credit com. Hines Fed. Credit Union, 1963-73, pres., 1973—; chmn. EEO com. Hines Hosp.; chmn. EEO program council Med. Dist. 17. Bd. dirs., pres. Roseland Heights Community Assn.; mem. community adv. council Chgo. State U., 1984—. Fellow Am. Inst. Chemists; mem. Am. Assn. Clin. Chemists (bd. dirs.), Am. Chem. Soc., Ill. Kidney Found., Alpha Phi Alpha. Methodist (vice chmn. bd. stewards). Club: Men's (Chgo.). Home: 9835 Forest Ave Chicago IL 60628 Office: PO Box 41 Hines IL 60141

BOND, MORRIS LINDSAY, banker; b. Columbia, S.C., Sept. 30, 1936; s. Lindsay Johnson and Lossie Mae (Johnson) B.; B.S., Clemson U., 1958; M.B.A., St. Louis U., 1967; postgrad. Southwestern Grad. Sch. Banking, So. Meth. U., 1980; m. Patricia Jeanne Hunter, June 14, 1962; children—Stephanie Jane, Michael Morris. Research technologist Corp. Research and Devel. Center, Pet, Inc., Greenville, Ill., 1959-61, supr. project control, 1961-66, sect. chief, 1966-68, mgr. adminstrv. services, 1968-73; ops. improvement officer Centerre Bank N.A., St. Louis, 1974-76, asst. v.p., 1976-78, v.p. account services div., 1978-81, v.p. info. systems devel., 1981-83, v.p. account services div., 1983—; pres. bd. dirs. Women's Self Help Ctr., 1986—; instr. bus. mgmt. Greenville Coll., 1977—, Am. Assn. Indsl. Mgmt., St. Louis, 1977-83. Mem. Am. Inst. Indsl. Engrs., Am. Inst. Banking. Methodist. Clubs: Masons, Shriners. Home: Springwood Estates Route 2 Box 145C Greenville IL 62246 Office: One Centerre Plaza St Louis MO 63101

BOND, ROBERT LANCE, rehabilitation center executive, vocational consultant; b. Franklin, Ind., Feb. 4, 1954; s. Allen Dale and Lois Jean (Chitwood) B.; m. Kathy Lynn Moberly, Sept. 8, 1973; 1 child, Robert Ryan. B.S. in Edn., Auburn U., 1976, M.Ed., 1977; Ed.D., Ball State U. Vocat. cons., Fort Wayne, 1979—; vocat. expert Social Security Adminstrn., Washington, 1982—, U.S. R.R. Retirement Bd., 1985—; pres. Vocat. Counsulting Network, Inc., Fort Wayne, 1985—; dir. rehab. services Anthony Wayne Rehab. Ctr., Fort Wayne, 1977-85. Mem. adv. bd. Purdue U. Mental Health Tech. Program, Fort Wayne, 1980—; exec. bd. Fort Wayne Area Adv. Council for Employment Handicapped, 1984. Named Disting. Hoosier, Gov. Ind., 1972. Mem. Nat. Rehab. Assn., Vocat. Evaluation and Work Adjustment Assn., Ind. Vocat. Evaluation and Work Adjustment Assn. (pres. Indpls. 1983-85), Ind. Assn. Rehab. Facilities (chmn. rehab. services div. 1983-85), Rho Sigma Epsilon. Avocations: coin collecting; sports. Home and Office: Vocat Counseling Network Inc 1105 W Oakdale Fort Wayne IN 46807

BOND, RONALD RICHARD, accountant; b. Madison, Wis., Aug. 13, 1958; s. Richard Clayton and Joyce Marilyn (Schallert) B.; m. Debra Ann Hamilton, Aug. 16, 1980; 1 child, Courtney Marie. BBA in Acctg. and Fin., U. Iowa, 1981. CPA, Iowa, Ill. Staff acct. Ernst & Whinney, Chgo., 1981-83, sr. acct., 1983-85, mgr., 1985—. Recipient Citizens award VA, 1976. Mem. Am. Inst. CPA's, Iowa Soc. Pub. Accts. Republican. Methodist. Avocations: carpentry, cabinetry, snow and water skiing. Office: Ernst & Whinney 150 S Wacker Dr Chicago IL 60606

BOND, SHARON ANNE, bank executive; b. Belleville, Ill., July 1, 1947; d. Melvin Charles and Pearl Gertrude (Luetzelschwab) Schuchardt; m. William Charles Bond, Mar. 18, 1972. BS, Cornell U., 1969; M in Urban Planning, Mich. State U., 1972. Assoc. planner City of East Lansing, Mich., 1970-72; asst. mgr. mgmt. div. Mich. State Housing Devel. Authority, Lansing, 1972-75; gen. mgr. Prudential Ins. Co., Detroit, 1975-79; v.p., mgr. urban properties trust dept. Continental Bank, Chgo., 1979-84, v.p., asst. mgr. properties services, 1984—. Mem. Chgo. Council of Fgn. Relations, Art Inst. of Chgo. Mem. Nat. Assn. of Banking Women, Urban Land Inst., Inst. Real Estate Mgmt. (cert. prop. mgr.), Nat. for Trust Historic Preservation, Ill. Historic Preservation Agy. Avocations: fine art, antiques, classical music. Home: 9437 Hamlin Ave Evanston IL 60203 Office: Continental Bank 231 S LaSalle St Chicago IL 60697

BONDAR, ANDREW ARTHUR, dentist; b. Manchester, N.H., Oct. 23, 1914; s. Arthur George and Anna (Greneshen) B.; student U. N.H., 1932-34; D.M.D., Tufts U., 1938; diploma U.S. Army Med. Field Service Sch., 1969; cert. Command and Gen. Staff Coll., 1972; m. Ellen Ferguson Stewart, July 24, 1953; 1 dau., Billie Arlene. Pvt. practice dentistry, Manchester, 1939-42, 46-49; dentist VA Hosp./Dental Service, 1949-82. Lectr., clinician dist. and local dental socs. in N.H., N.Y., Que., Can. Asst. coach Jr. Am. Legion Baseball Team, Manchester, 1947-49; nat. chmn. Nat. German Prisoner of War Meml. Service, Ft. Custer, Mich., 1973-75. Served to capt. AUS, 1942-46, now col. Res. ret. Fellow Am. Acad. Gen. Dentistry, Midwest Acad. Prosthodontics; mem. ADA, New Eng. Dental Soc., Northeastern Dental Soc., Assn. U.S. Army, Tufts Coll., U. N.H. alumni assns., Assn. Mil. Surgeons U.S., Am. Soc. Geriatric Dentistry (nat. treas. 1975-81), Am. Legion, VFW, DAV, United War Vets. (judge-advocate council greater Battle Creek, Mich., cert. commendation, 1979), Mil. Order of World Wars, Vets. of Battle of the Bulge, Res. Officers Assn. U.S. (brigade of vols., past pres. chpt.; dental surgeon Mich. dept. 1973-77, 79—), 40 and 8. Lodges: Elks, Eagles. Home: 519 Alvena Ave Battle Creek MI 49017

BONDIMAN, ROBERT ANTHONY, data processing executive; b. Chgo., June 3, 1951; s. Ernest and Marie (Tavernaro) B.; m. Janice Ann Kilar, June 15, 1974; 1 child, Robert Michael. AA in Data Processing, Thornton Community Coll., 1971; BS in Acctg., No. Ill. U., 1973; MBA, Northwestern U., 1981. CPA, Ill. Sr. auditor Altschuler, Melvoin & Glasser, Chgo., 1973-76; internal auditor Gen. Telephone and Electric, Stamford, Conn., 1976-77; EDP auditor Kraft Inc., Glenview, Ill., 1977-79; sr. cons., auditor Esmark Inc., Chgo., 1979-84; mgr. EDP audit Combined Internat., Chgo., 1984—. Mem. EDP Auditors Assn. (sec. Chgo. chpt. 1986—), Am. Inst. CPA's, Internal Auditors Assn. Avocations: jogging, weight tng., golfing. Home: 1479 Fourth Ave Des Plaines IL 60018

BONE, CHARLES HUGH, architect; b. Gary, Ind., Aug. 27, 1937; s. David Alexander and Charlotte (Fonken) B.; m. Carolyn Joyce Dawson, Oct. 8, 1960; children: Jeffrey Charles, Sherri Lynn, Jill Ann. BS in Architect, U. Cin., 1961. Registered architect, Ind. Draftsman, designer Wildermuth & Wildermuth, Gary, 1956-62, R.L. Wildermuth, Gary, 1962-63; architect, ptnr. Wildermuth & Bone, Gary and Portage, Ind., 1963-71, Design Orgn., Valparaiso, Ind., 1971—. Bd. dirs. Porter/Starke Services, Inc., Valparaiso, 1977—, Valepark Pyschiat. Hosp., 1983—, Ind. Council Mental Health Ctrs., Indpls., 1982-84; bd. dirs., pres. Valparaiso YMCA, 1985-87. Mem. AIA (Ind. Design award 1976, 83). Presbyterian. Avocations: golf, tennis, racketball, woodworking, travel.

BONEBURG, ANITA STROETZ, educator; b. Hammond, Ind., Feb. 23, 1920; d. Earl S. and Gertrude M. (Willarson) Stroetz; B.S. in Home Econs., Milw. Downer U. (now Lawrence U.), 1942; M.S. in Edn., Cleve. State U., 1978; postgrad. John Carroll U., 1970-75; Kent State U., 1979; m. Chester J. Boneburg, Aug. 25, 1942; children—Katharine D. Karawas, Thomas J., Peter K. With Gallup-Robinson Opinion Surveys, Cleve. and Princeton, N.J., 1957-59; U.S. census taker U.S. Dept. Commerce, Washington, 1960; with Cleve. Public Schs., 1960-85, substitute tchr., 1960-63, tchr. Blossom Hill Correctional Facility, 1963-68, tchr. home econs. dept. Lincoln-West High Sch., 1968—, newspaper advisor, 1984-85; mem. textbook com. Greater Cleve.; participant Martha H. Jennings Econ. Edn. Interface Program, 1981-82; mem. facilitators team High Schs. for the Future, 1984-85; cons., documentor Lincoln-West High Schs. for the Future Team, 1985—. Mem. Future Homemakers Am. Task Force, 1980-83, Ohio regional com. Juvenile protection chmn. PTA, 1964; active West Shore Rep. Club, 1959-64; mem. World Hunger Com., 1979-80; adv. ARC and Human Relations Clubs, 1970-78, Welcome Club, 1980-81, Swords to Plowshares Com.; mem. Urban League Aux., 1983-84, Cleve. Playhouse Women's Com., 1985—; patron Quintessance Celebrity Series Playhouse. Recipient Martha Holden Jennings tchr. leadership award, 1972; scholar award, 1966; ARC service award, 1975, 80; Quincy Washington Reading award; Sohio Tchrs. award, 1981-82; Am. Assn. Christians and Jews human relations grantee, 1970. Mem. Am. Vocat. Assn. (public relations com., legis. com. nat. network), Am. Home Econs. Assn., Ohio Vocat. Assn., Greater Cleve. Home Econs. Assn., Cleve. Council on Human Relations, Ohio Ret. Tchrs., Cleve. Econ. Council, Cleve. Teachers Union (conf. com., del. assembly rep., 1970-75), Lawrence U. Alumni Assn., Cleve. State U. Alumni Assn. Episcopalian. Clubs: Pinehurst Country (Pinehurst, N.C.), Coll. Club West. Active curriculum devel., task forces, research coms. in field; fund raising, Lawrence U., 1973—. Home: 18429 Sloane Lakewood OH 44107

BONÉE, JOHN RAOUL, retired information technologies company executive; b. New Orleans, Nov. 11, 1923; s. John Raoul and Lucille Evelyn (Schwarzenbach) B.: student Loyola U., New Orleans, 1940-42; M.A., Aquinas Inst., 1946, 50; Ph.D., U. Fribourg (Switzerland), 1953; m. Mavis Long Heyl, Dec. 22, 1967; children—Mavis Heyl McClung, Larrye Heyl Steldt. Joined Dominican Order, Roman Catholic Ch., 1942, ordained priest, 1949, laicized, 1967; prof. modern and contemporary philosophy Aquinas Inst., River Forest, Ill., 1953-61; prof. communications and homiletics St. Rose Priory, Dubuque, Iowa, 1961-67; mgr. Ill. Bell Tel. Co., Chgo., 1967-83, mgr. corp. communications, 1970-83; pub. relations mgr. exec. support Ameritech, 1983-85; lectr. DePaul U., 1968-82; adj. assoc. prof. communications Rosary Coll., River Forest, Ill., 1984-86, mgr. pub. relations planning, Ill. Bell, 1985-86; cons. VISCAM, Cameroon, Africa, 1980-82. Mem. Community Relations Commn. Oak Park (Ill.), 1973-74. Mem. Public Relations Soc. Am., Chgo. Pub. Relations Clinic, Chgo. Press Club. Roman Catholic. Office: 30 S Wacker Dr Chicago IL 60606

BONGERS, JAMES KEVIN, dentist; b. Omaha, Jan. 28, 1955; s. Leo Vincent and Margaret Mary (Stanosheck) B. BA in Biology, Benedictine Coll., 1977; DDS, Creighton U., 1980. Gen. practice dentistry Junction City, Kans., 1980—; advisor Valley View Profl. Care Ctr., Junction City, 1980—, Valley Vista Profl. Care Ctr., Junction City, 1980—. Bd. govs. Benedictine Coll., Atchison, Kans., 1985—. Mem. ADA, Am. Assn. Functional Orthodontics, Midwest Soc. Orthodontics for Gen. Practitioners, Geary County Dental Soc. (pres. 1981—), Pierre Fauchard Acad., Junction City C. of C. Roman Catholic. Club: Woodbury Study. Lodges: Rotary, KC (state youth chmn. 1986—), Jaycees, Optimists. Home: 926 S Jefferson Junction City KS 66441 Office: Junction City Family Dentistry 112 N Eisenhower Junction City KS 66441

BONGIORNO, JOHN ANTHONY, sales manager; b. Chgo., Sept. 29, 1951; s. John Anthony and Stephanie Marie (DiTusa) B.; A.S. in Accounting and Bus. Adminstrn., Triton Coll., 1971; student in Mktg., U. Ill., Chgo., 1969-73; m. Sharon Louise Bernath, July 12, 1975. Sales rep. electronic data processing Chgo. office Reynolds & Reynolds Co., Elk Grove Village, 1973-75, sales rep. automotive forms, 1975-81, Eastern div. sales mgr. automotive forms, Dayton, Ohio, 1981-83, N.E. regional sales mgr. bus. forms and systems div., 1983—. Named to 300 Club for sales excellence Reynolds and Reynolds Co., 1975-77, 79-80, President's Club for Sales Mgmt. Excellence and Number 1 Region Honors, 1986. Mem. Dayton Sales and Mktg. Club (bd. dirs. 1984-86, v.p. growth 1985-86). Roman Catholic. Home: 7540 Pelway Dr Dayton OH 45459 Office: 3555 Kettering Blvd PO Box 2237 Dayton OH 45401

BONHAUS, LAURENCE ALLEN, lawyer, urban planner; b. Cin., May 27, 1949; s. Alphonse Lawrence and Mary Kathryn (Muchmore) B.; divorced; 1 child, Andrew Laurence. B.S. in Architecture cum laude, U. Cin., 1973, J.D., 1976. Bar: Ohio 1976, U.S. Supreme Ct. 1982. Draftsman, designer Arend & Arend Architects, Cin., 1969-72; designer Kral, Zepf, Frietag and Assos., Architects & Engrs., Cin., 1972-73; designer, OSHA specialist offices Robert Harter Snyder, Cin., 1973-76; OSHA and bldg. code specialist, Project Designer AEDES Assos., Inc., 1973-76; individual practice archtl. and planning law, Cin., 1976—; v.p., urban planner Citysystems, Inc., Cin., 1976—; arbitrator Am. Arbitration Assn.; sec. P.D.A., Inc. Co-chmn. Ohio Confederation, 1970-72, lobbyist for state and state affiliated univs.; mem. Gradison Campaign com., N.Avondale Neighborhood Assn.; past pres., treas., trustee NAPA; v.p. Fairview/Clifton Heights housing devel. corp.; v.p. Asbury property mgmt. non-profit housing corp.; mem. Greater Cin. Beautiful Com., Contemporary Arts Center; condr., music dir. The Cin. Civic Orch., concert master emeritus; mus. dir., condr. Gilbert and Sullivan Soc., Cin., also bd. dirs.; condr. Cin. Young Peoples Theater; co-chmn., treas., bd. dirs., exec. com. Ohio Solar Resources Adv. Panel; v.p. Cin. Archtl. Found.; keynote speaker State Solar Design competition, 1986; sustaining mem. Republican Nat. Com. Mem. AIA (co-chmn. nat. conv. com. 1980, nat. codes and standards com., Henry Adams cert., 1973, chmn. Cin. chpt. speakers bur., by-laws com.), ABA, Cin. Bar Assn. (chmn. OSHA com., mem. constrn. and engring. law com., real property law com., mus. dir. for ann. meeting), Architects Soc. Ohio, Lawyers Club of Cin., Southwest Ohio Alt. Energy Assn. (founding mem., dir., exec. com.), Ohio Solar Energy Assn. (pres. dir.), Nat. Passive Solar Conf. Planning Com., Cin. Energy Network (co-founder), Cin. Engrs. Club (bd. dirs.), SCARAB (v.p., 1970-71), Greater Cin. C. of C. (energy com.), Phi Alpha Delta (alumni justice Cin. chpt., dep. internat. justice, Outstanding Service cert. 1980, 82). Methodist (mem. adminstrv. bd.). Clubs: Cin. CINgles (dirs., dir. devel.), Updowntowners (Oktoberfest planning com.), Cincinnatus, Metro. Works include interior design and execution of mosaic panel Forest Chapel United

Meth. Ch., 1969, restoration Fleischman mansion, 1974-76, Conroy mansion, 1977-79; new zoning code and land use plan Union Twp., Clermont County, Ohio, 1977-78; handicapped accessibility study Montgomery County, Ohio, 1979-81; urban renewal study Newark, Ohio, 1977-78; ind. living facility Total Living Concepts, Inc., Cin., 1980-81, solar zoning ordinances, 1982-83. Home: 948 Dana Ave Cincinnati OH 45229

BONIFACE, KENNETH JOSEPH, JR., emergency physician; b. Charleston, S.C., June 26, 1948; s. Kenneth Joseph and Mary Elizabeth (Morris) B.; m. Elizabeth Hampton Lesesne, Sept. 28, 1974; children: Sarah Hampton, Elizabeth Harleston. AB in History, Spring Hill Coll., Mobile, Ala., 1971; MD, Med. U. S.C., 1975. Diplomate Am. Bd. Emergency Medicine. Intern Providence Med. Ctr., Seattle, 1975-76; resident U. Chgo., 1976-78; asst. prof. emergency medicine U. Cin., 1978-81; med. dir. dept. emergency medicine St. Francis and St. George Hosps., Cin., 1981—. Fellow Am. Coll. Emergency Physicians; mem. Soc. Tchrs. Emergency Medicine (sec. 1980-81), U. Assn. Emergency Medicine. Avocation: golf. Home: 1885 Madison Rd Cincinnati OH 45206 Office: 3131 Queen City Ave Cincinnati OH 45238

BONIOR, DAVID EDWARD, congressman; b. Detroit, June 6, 1945; s. Edward John and Irene (Gaverluk) B.; children: Julie, Andy. B.A., U. Iowa, 1967; M.A. in History, Chapman Coll., Calif., 1972. Mem. Mich. Ho. of Reps., 1973-77; mem. 95th-100th congresses from 12th Mich. Dist., 1977—, dep. majority whip, mem. com. on rules. Author: The Vietnam Veteran: A History of Neglect, 1984. Served in USAF, 1968-72. Democrat. Roman Catholic. Office: US House of Representatives 2242 Rayburn House Office Bldg Washington DC 20515 *

BONK, EUGENE THEODORE, market development executive; b. Chgo., July 8, 1918; s. Leopold and Katherine (Jurczak) B.; m. Gisela Julie Zimmermann, June 25, 1954; children: Carolyn, Ralph, Shirley. BBA, Northwestern U., 1947, MBA, 1971. Sales promotion mgr. Humphryes Mfg. Co., Mansfield, Ohio, 1948-50; market devel. mgr. Bruning div. AM Internat., Mt. Prospect, Ill., 1955-65, Motorola Communicatons, Schaumburg, Ill., 1965-85; pres. Market Intelligence Internat., Arlington Heights, Ill., 1986—. Mem. Chgo. Council Foreign Relations, 1986; mem. coordinating com. on internat. bus. Ill. Dept. Commerce and Community affairs. Served with USAF, 1941-45, 50-54, lt. col. Res. ret. Mem. Internat. Council for Small Bus. (sr. v.p. 1982-86, chmn. 1980-81, Wilford White fellow 1981), Sales and Mktg. Execs. Chgo. (pres. 1979-80), Sales and Mktg. Execs. Internat. (area rep.), Armed Forces Communications and Electronics Assn. (v.p. membership), Assn. Old Crows, Pi Sigma Epsilon (v.p. 1975-77). Republican. Roman Catholic. Club: Northwestern U. Mgmt. Avocations: photography, art appreciation, military strategy history, golf. Home and Office: 534 S Pine Ave Arlington Heights IL 60005

BONKOWSKI, RONALD L., mayor; b. Detroit, June 6, 1938; s. Estelle (Nowakowski) B.; m. Christine Bonkowski; children: Robert, Lori, Mark, Lisa. Student, Walsh Inst. Acctg., 1957-58; BBA, U. Detroit, 1969. Acct. Gen. Motors Corp., 1960-66; budget analyst, indsl. engr. Chrysler Corp., 1966-69; indsl. engr. LTV Aerospace, 1969-70; dist. sales mgr. Sales Follow Up Corp., 1970-71; fin. officer Macomb County Pub. Works, Mich., 1971-85; mayor City of Warren, Mich., 1985—. Councilman City of Warren, 1969-70, 79-85; commr. Macomb County Commn., 1971; mem. Gov.'s task force on welfare reform, Gov.'s Commn. on Job Tng. Partnership Adminstrn.; past sec., past chmn. Warren Bd. Appeals; past chmn. Warren Bldg. Com.; active with St. Dorothy's Ch.; trustee Macomb Community Coll., treas., 1977-79. Served with U.S. Army, 1958-60. Mem. VFW (Polish Legion), Am. Polish Citizens Macomb County. Club: Am. Polish Century. Lodge: KC. Home: 29220 Scarborough Warren MI 48093 Office: Office of the Mayor 29500 Van Dyke Ave Warren MI 48903

BONNER, ANTHONY CARL, credit analyst; b. Flint, Mich., May 3, 1958; s. Auborn Carl and Louise (Relerford) B.; m. Dorla Elaine Coleman, June 21, 1986. BBA, U. Mich., Flint, 1983; postgrad., Cen. Mich. U., 1987—. Loan adjustor Citizen's Bank, Flint, 1975-79, check analyst, 1979-84, credit assoc., 1984-86, credit analyst, 1986—; salesperson Ornamental Security Doors, Flint, 1980-84. Tchr. youth Sunday Sch. Faith Temple Ch. of God in Christ, 1977—, pres., v.p. youth dept., 1977-81; mem. allocations panel United Way of Genesee and Lapeer Counties, 1985—, loaned exec. for corp. fundraising, 1984-85; candidate for Flint Community Devel. Corp., 1986—; mem. fin. planning com., econ. com. Urban Coalition of Greater Flint, 1986—. Recipient Cert. Recognition, Leadership Flint, Inc., 1985, Cert. Recognition, United Way of Genesee and Lapeer Counties, 1984, 85; named one of Outstanding Young Men of Am., 1985. Mem. Greater Flint Jaycees (v.p. community devel., 1985—, dir., editor newsletter, 1984-85, Flint Jaycee of Month award 1984, Outstanding Dir. Flint Jaycees award 1985), U. Mich.-Flint Alumni Soc. (Black alumni subcom.). Club: Toastmasters. Lodge: Optimists (bd. dirs. Cen. Flint club 1987—). Avocations: swimming, weight lifting, collecting Afro-Am. literature and artifacts, pub. speaking. Home: G-4606 Beecher Rd Flint MI 48504 Office: Citizens Bank Credit Dept 1 Citizens Banking Ctr Flint MI 48502

BONNER, THOMAS NEVILLE, history and higher education educator; b. Rochester, N.Y., May 28, 1923; s. John Neville and Mary (McGowan) B.; children by previous marriage: Phillip Lynn, Diana Joan; m. Sylvia M. Firnhaber, Dec. 28, 1984. A.B., U. Rochester, 1947, M.A., 1948; Ph.D., Northwestern U., 1952; LL.D., U. N.H., 1974, U. Mich., 1979. Acad. dean William Woods Coll., 1951-54; prof. history, chmn. dept. social sci. U. Omaha, 1955-62; Fulbright lectr. U. Mainz, Germany, 1954-55; prof., head history dept. U. of Cin., 1963-68, v.p. acad. affairs, provost, 1967-71; pres. U. N.H., Durham, 1971-74, Union Coll.; chancellor Union U., Schenectady, 1974-78; pres. Wayne State U., Detroit, 1978-82, disting. prof. history and higher edn., 1983—; vis. prof. U. Freiburg, W.Ger., 1982-83. Author: Medicine in Chicago, 1957, The Kansas Doctor, 1959, (with others) The Contemporary World, 1960, Our Recent Past, 1963, American Doctors and German Universities, 1963; Editor, translator: (Jacob Schiel) Journey Through the Rocky Mountains, 1959. Democratic candidate for Congress, 1962; legis. aide to Senator McGovern, 1962-63. Served with Radio Intelligence Corps AUS, 1942-46, ETO. Guggenheim fellow, 1958-59, 64-65. Mem. Am. Hist. Assn., Orgn. Am. Historians, Am. Assn. for History Medicine, Phi Beta Kappa, Pi Gamma Mu, Phi Alpha Theta. Home: 408 Hillboro Birmingham MI 48010

BONNEVIER, SUSAN GRETHER, elementary teacher, preschool administrator; b. Dayton, Apr. 8, 1940; d. Stanley Edward and Jane Louise (Scholl) Grether; m. Gerald Louis Bonnevier, Apr. 13, 1968; children—Perry Stewart, Jeffrey James. B.S. in Edn., Ohio U., 1962; postgrad. Nat. Coll. Edn. Tchr., Green County Sch. System, Xenia, Ohio, 1961-64, Sch. Dist. 102, LaGrange, Ill., 1964-69, Sch. Dist. 101, Western Springs, Ill., 1969-72; co-creator pre-sch. Western Spring Village Ch., 1975-82, dir., 1982-86 ; elem. tchr. LaGrange Sch. Dist., 1986—; mem. ad hoc sub group chmn. LaGrange Park Pub. Library, Ill., 1984—; docent Nettie McKinnon Art Gallery, LaGrange, 1985. Vol. Women's Aux. Community Meml. Gen. Hosp., 1965-71, Am. Cancer Soc., Easter Seal Soc. Mem. Chgo. Assn. Edn. Young Children, Nat. Assn. Edn. Young Children, Parent and Childbirth Edn. Soc. Avocations: skiing; gardening; aerobics; artist; tennis. Home: 742 N Kensington St LaGrange Park IL 60525 Office: Western Springs Village Ch PO Box 265 45th and Wolf Rd Western Springs IL 60558

BONSETT, CHARLES ALLEN, physician, educator; b. Indpls., Mar. 22, 1921; s. John Allen and Edith Marie (Wilt) B.; m. Olga Monica Koenig; 1 child, Tom C. BS, Butler U., 1949; MD, Ind. U., 1952. Diplomate Am. Bd. Psychiatry and Neurology. Intern Indpls. Meth. Hosp., 1952-53; resident in neurology Ind. U. Med. Ctr., 1953-56; practice medicine specializing in neurology Indpls., 1956—; prof. clin. neurology Ind. U. Sch. Medicine, Indpls., 1980—, prof. med. humanities, 1986—; dir. Ind. U. Muscular Dystrophy Clinic, 1956-86, Ind. Neuromuscular REsearch Lab., 1959—. Author: Studies of Pseudohypertrophic Muscular Dystrophy, 1969; editor Ind. Med. History Quar.; assoc. editor Ind. Medicine; contbr. numerous articles to profl. jours. Chmn. com. to save Old Pathology Bldg., Indpls., 1969-75, com. to place Bldg on Nat. Register, com. to devel. INd. Med. Mus. Served with air corps U.S. Army, 1942-45. Recipient Hansen Anderson medal Arsenal Tech. High Sch., 1975, Butler medal Butler U., 1984. Fellow Am. Acad. Neurology; mem. AMA, Ind. Neurol. Soc. (pres.), Ind. Hist. Soc. (bd. dirs. 1974—), Alpha Omega Alpha. Republican. Avocation: gardening. Home: 6133 E 54th Pl Indianapolis IN 46226

BONSETT, GLEN LEO, former educator, organization official; b. Scott County, Ind., July 29, 1924; s. Leo and Glen Anna (Mahan) B.; student Hanover Coll., 1942-43, Berea Coll., 1943-44; B.S., Ind. U., 1948, M.S., 1949, P.E.D., 1957; postgrad. Mich. State U., 1966-67, U. Calif-Santa Barbara, 1978; m. Melba June Mace, Feb. 21, 1980; children by previous marriage—Sandra Marie, Andrea Lee, Candace Lynn. Tchr., coach Ind. U. Lab. Sch., 1948-53; mem. faculty Hanover (Ind.) Coll., 1953-61, prof., 1955-61, coach intercollegiate athletics, 1953-61, student personnel adminstr., dean of men, 1961-75, v.p. for devel., 1975-81; with Goettler Assocs., Columbus, Ohio, 1981-83; spl. asst. to chief exec. officer estate preservations trusts and endowment ARC, 1984—; vis. lectr. Ind. U., 1954-60. Served with USNR, 1943-46; to comdr. Res. Mem. Council Advancement and Support Edn., Ind. Coll. Personnel Assn. (pres. 1971), Nat. Assn. Student Personnel Adminstrn., Ind. Personnel Guidance Assn., Nat. Soc. of Fund Raising Execs., Fund Raising Execs. of Metro Louisville, Ind. High Sch. Athletic Assn., AAHPER, Ind. Assn. Health, Phys. Edn. and Recreation (chmn. research sect.), Health, Phys. Edn. and Recreation Alumni Assn. Ind. U. (pres.), Ind. U. Alumni Assn. (dir.), Phi Epsilon Kappa, Lambda Chi Alpha, Phi Delta Kappa, Sigma Pi Sigma, Alpha Phi Omega. Republican. Methodist. Lodges: Masons, Elks, Moose, Shriners.

BONSIB, RICHARD EUGENE, advertising agency executive; b. Ft. Wayne, Ind., Nov. 8, 1931; s. Louis William and Marietta Anna (Jacobs) B., Sr.; B.S. in Mktg., Ind. U., 1953; postgrad course Am. Mgmt. Assn., 1966; m. Gretchen Allen, Aug. 23, 1958; children—Gregory Allen, Stephen Richard. Owner, pres. The Century Press, Ft. Wayne, 1948-53; with Bonsib Inc., Ft. Wayne and Indpls., 1953—, pres., chmn., 1975-85, chmn., chief exec. officer, 1985—; v.p., dir. L.W. Bonsib Found., Inc., Ft. Wayne, 1961-74; v.p. Prodn. Concepts Ltd., Creative Concepts, 1980-81; treas. HPL, Inc., Ft. Wayne, 1965-66; pres. Leemark Tours, Inc., Chgo., 1968-70. Founding dir. Ft. Wayne Horizons Econ. Devel. Council; past v.p., dir. Allen County-Ft. Wayne YMCA; former v.p., dir. fathers bd. Culver (Ind.) Mil. Acad.; former pres. Allen County-Ft. Wayne Hist. Soc.; v.p., bd. dirs. United Way Allen County; mem. steering com., past chmn. Leadership Prayer Breakfast; past chmn., founding dir. Summit Tech. and Research Transfer, Inc.; v.p., bd. dirs. Harold W. McMillen Ctr. for Health Edn.; chmn. fin. com., v.p., bd. trustees First Presbyn. Ch. of Fort Wayne. Served with U.S. Army, 1955-57; Korea. Mem. Ft. Wayne Advt. Club (pres. 1963), Am. Assn. Advt. Agys. (mem. gov. relations com.), Ind. Fedn. Advt. Agencies (pres.), Greater Ft. Wayne C. of C. (dir.), Phi Gamma Delta. Republican. Home: 2815 Covington Lake Dr Fort Wayne IN 46804-2507 Office: Bonsib Bldg 927 S Harrison St Fort Wayne IN 46802-2154 also: 9100 Keystone Crossing Suite 700 Indianapolis IN 46240

BONSKY, JACK ALAN, chemical exec., lawyer; b. Canton, Ohio, Mar. 12, 1938; s. Jack H. and Pearl E. Bonsky; A.B., Ohio U., 1960; J.D., Ohio State U., 1964; m. Carol Ann Portmann, Sept. 2, 1960; children—Jack Raymond, Cynthia Lynn. Bar: Ohio 1964, U.S. Dist. Ct. (so. dist.) Ohio 1969. With Metcalf, Thomas & Bonsky, Marietta, Ohio, 1964-69, Addison, Fisher & Bonsky, Marietta, 1969-70; asst. counsel GenCorp., Inc. (formerly Gen. Tire & Rubber Co.), Akron, Ohio, 1970-75, assoc. gen. counsel, 1975-86, asst. sec., 1977-86, v.p. and sec., 1986; v.p.. sec., gen. counsel DiversiTech Gen., Inc., 1986—; solicitor City of Marietta, Ohio, 1966-67; legal advisor City of Marietta Bd. of Edn., 1966-67; police prosecutor, Belpre, Ohio, 1969-70; comml. law instr. Am. Inst. Banking, 1969; dir. Frontier Holdings, Inc., Denver, Frontier Airlines, Denver, 1985 (merged with People Express Airlines, 1985). Mem. Marietta Income Tax Bd. of Rev., 1966-67; mem. Traffic Commn., 1966-69, chmn., 1967; mem. Civil Service Commn., 1969; trustee Urban League, 1978-81, pres., 1980-81; trustee Akron Community Service Ctr., 1978-81, United Way of Summit County, 1982—; bd. dirs. Washington County Soc. for Crippled Children, 1964-70; bd. dirs. S.E. Ohio unit Arthritis Found., 1967-70, chmn., 1968-70; mem. Washington County Health Planning Com., 1968-70; mem. ho. of dels. Ohio Easter Seal Soc., 1968-70. Recipient Akron Community Service Ctr. and Urban League Leadership award, 1981. Mem. Ohio Bar Assn. Home: 4234 Idlebrook Dr Akron OH 44313 Office: GenCorp Inc 1 General St Akron OH 44329

BOODEN, JOHN MORRIS, pharmaceutical company official; b. Kalamazoo, July 25, 1939; s. Marinus and Anna (Brunsting) B.; m. Carol M. Werner; children—Scott Alan, Michael John; stepchildren: Margaret, Susan, Stacy. B.B.A., Western Mich. U., 1963. Salesman, NCR, Kalamazoo, 1963-65; European fin. analyst Upjohn Internat., Kalamazoo, 1965-72, controller R&D, 1972-80, mgr. corp. budgeting, 1980-83, mgr. corp. fin. planning, 1983-84, dir. corp. fin. planning and analysis, 1985—. Mem. Kalamazoo Hist. Commn., 1980-83; bd. dirs. Kalamazoo Child Guidance Clinic, 1983-85, Kalamazoo Consultation Ctr., 1986—. Served with U.S. Army, 1957-58. Recipient W.E. Upjohn award, 1986. Mem. Planning Forum, Am. Mgmt. Assn. Republican.

BOODY, CHARLES G(EORGE), analyst/programmer, music consultant; b. Dawson, Minn., Nov. 8, 1939; s. George Boody and Violet Marie (Haeusler) Gaylord; m. Nancy Lee Hayden, Dec. 31, 1955; children: Sandra Jean, Tamara Lynn. BA in Music, Macalester Coll., 1961; MA in Musicology, U. Minn., 1968, PhD in Musicology, 1975. Instr. music various high schs., Minn., 1961-64; research fellow, teaching assoc. U. Minn., Mpls., 1965-70; asst. prof. Austin Coll., Sherman, Tex., 1970-78; choral dir. Belle Plaine (Minn.) High Sch., 1978-80; analyst/programmer Ind. Sch. Dist. 270, Hopkins, Minn., 1980—; cons. music. Author: (computer software) Music Tutor, 1979, 83, Houghton Computer Mgmt. System, 1985, (choral composition) Freedom Trail, 1970, What Tidings Bringest Thou Messenger, 1971, 3 Medieval carols, 1972; editor: (book revs.) Choral Jour., 1968-73, (yr. book) Assn. for Tech. in Music Instrn., 1977-85; contbr. articles to profl. jours. Mem. Nat. Consortium for Computer Based Music Instrn. (yr. book editor 1977-85), Am. Choral Dirs. Assn., Music Educators Nat. Conf., Coll. Music Soc., Assn. for Tech. in Music Instrn. (pres. 1985—), Mini'App'les (sec. 1978—), Pi Kappa Delta, Kappa Delta Pi, Pi Kappa Lambda. Avocations: recorder playing, hammer dulcimer playing, photography. Home: 121 Harrison Ave S Hopkins MN 55343 Office: Ind Sch Dist 270 Evaluation Ctr 1001 Hwy 7 Hopkins MN 55343

BOOE, JAMES MARVIN, chemical engineer; b. Austin, Ind., Nov. 12, 1906; s. James Ross and Grace (Hesler) B.; B.S., Butler U., 1928; m. Dortha Maud Weaver, July 30, 1938; children—James Marvin, Ann Marie, John Weaver. Chemist, Indpls. Plating Co., 1929; chief chemist P. R. Mallory & Co., 1929-45, dir. electrochem. research, 1945-51, exec. chem. engr., 1951-53, dir. chem. and metall. research corp. labs., 1953-63; dir. chem. labs. Mallory Capacitor Co., Indpls., 1963-72, cons., 1972—. Advisory bd. Am. Security Council; bd. dirs. Irvington Benton House Assn.; pres., bd. dirs. Irvington Hist. Landmarks Found. Accredited profl. chemist Am. Inst. Chemists. Recipient Army-Navy E civilian award, Naval Ordnance Devel. award. Fellow Am. Inst. Chemists; mem. Am. Chem. Soc., Electrochem. Soc., Irvington Hist. Soc., Am. Def. Preparedness Assn., Indpls. Scientech Soc. (bd. dirs.), Smithsonian Instn. (asso.), Indpls. Mus. Art, Goodwill Industries, Ransburg YMCA, Presbyterian (elder, trustee). Lodge: Kiwanis. Patentee in field (38). Research on electrolytic capacitors, batteries, resistors, semiconductors. Home: 548 N Audubon Rd Indianapolis IN 46219 Office: 3029 E Washington St Indianapolis IN 46201

BOOHER, CATHERINE ELIZABETH, accountant; b. Dayton, Ohio, Mar. 23, 1956; d. Albert Eugene and Margaret June (Deem) Gantner; m. Gary Dean Booher Jr., Dec. 6, 1974 (dec. Apr. 1976). BSBA, U. Dayton, 1977. CPA, Ohio. Staff acct. Kentner, Sellers, Hines & Steinke, Vandalia, Ohio, 1977-80, supr., 1981-85, mgr., 1985—. Mem. Am. Inst. CPA's, Ohio Soc. CPA's, Am. Women's Soc. CPA's. Mormon. Home: 4146 E Idle Hour Circle Dayton OH 45415 Office: Kentner Sellers Hines & Steinke 705 S Brown School Rd Vandalia OH 45377

BOOKER, DEBORAH SHANNON, educator; b. Washington, Apr. 6, 1937; d. Angus R. and Barbara (Stratton) Shannon; B.A., U. Mo., 1959; m. Paul Booker, Nov. 26, 1960; children—Margaret, Sarah, Charles. Psychol. technician U. Mo., Columbia, 1959-61; owner, mgr. The Horse Fair, Columbia, 1965—; asst. prof. equestrian sci. William Woods Coll., Fulton, Mo., 1972-85, assoc. prof. 1985-86; acting dir. riding Stephens Coll., Columbia, 1986—; nat. examiner, mem. instrn. council U.S. Pony Clubs, Inc., 1978—. Mem. Am. Horse Shows Assn. (tech. del. for combined tng. and dressage, registered steward), U.S. Combined Tng. Assn., U.S. Pony Clubs, Inc. Episcopalian. Home: Route 9 Columbia MO 65202 Office: Stephens Coll Stables Box 2071 Columbia MO 65215

BOOKER, EUGENE M., diversified manufacturing company executive. B.A., U. Minn., 1954. Product supt. Booker & Wallestad, 1954-58; pres. Thermotech Plastics, Inc., 1958-70, ITT Thermotech, 1970-77; v.p. ops., pres. Roper Plastics subs. Plant Industries, 1977-79; v.p. corp. planning McQuay-Perfex, Inc., 1979-81, sr. v.p., group exec., 1981-82, exec. v.p., 1982-83; pres., chief operating officer McQuay-Perfex, Inc. (now known as McQuay Inc.), 1983—; also dir. McQuay, Inc. *

BOOKOUT, JOHN G., insurance company executive. Pres. Woodmen of World Life Ins. Soc., Omaha. Office: Woodmen of the World Life Ins Soc 1700 Farnam St Omaha NE 68102 *

BOOM, GEORGE, funeral services executive; b. Lennox, S.D., Dec. 16, 1925; s. George Albert and Ella Mae (Otten) B.; m. Faye Elaine Anderson, July 9, 1950; 1 child, David George. BS in Mortuary, U. Minn., 1948. Lic. funeral service dir., Minn., S.D. Funeral dir., embalmer Gedstad Funeral Home, New Ulm, Minn., 1949-51, Miller Funeral Home, Sioux Falls, S.D., 1951-54; ptnr., funeral dir., embalmer Banton Funeral Home, Sioux Falls, 1954-56; owner, funeral dir., embalmer George Boom Funeral Home (formerly Banton Funeral Home), Sioux Falls, 1956-83; chief exec. officer, pres., sec. Pioneer Enterprises, Inc., Sioux Falls, 1983—; sec. Otten Mgmt. subs. of Care Group, Inc., George Boom Funeral Home, Sioux Falls, Miller Funeral Home, Sioux Falls, Rudes Funeral Home , Brookings, S.D., Geise Funeral Home, Estelline, S.D., Wass Funeral Home, Beresford, S.D., Schroeder Funeral Home, Akron, Iowa; coroner Minnehaha County, Sioux Falls, 1964-68; various offices S.D. Bd. Funeral Services, 1968-72. Precinct com. man Minnehaha County, 1954-64. Served with USN, 1944-46, PTO. Mem. S.D. Funeral Dirs. Assn., (various offices 1972-80), Internat. Order of Golden Rule (state chmn. 1970—), Rep. Govs. Club. Lodges: Odd Fellows, Masons, Shriners. Avocations: walnut tree lumbering and woodworking, hunting, fishing. Home: 3408 E 10th St Sioux Falls SD 57103 Office: Pioneer Enterprises Inc 515 South Dakota Ave Sioux Falls SD 57102

BOONE, ELLEN CHRISTINA, psychologist; b. Washington, Sept. 23, 1941. Student, Wake Forest U., 1959-61; BS, U. Wis., 1963, MS, 1967; postgrad., U. Toledo, 1967-68. Lic. clin. psychologist, Ohio. Instr. Madison (Wis.) Jr. Coll., 1965-66; clin. psychologist Moundbuilders Guidance Ctr., Newark, Ohio, 1969-71, Toledo Mental Health Ctr., 1973—. Conbtr. articles to profl. jours. Mem. Am. Psychology Assoc., State Assoc. Psychologists (treas. 1981—), 1199 Health Care Union (exec. bd.). Office: Toledo Mental Health Ctr Caller No 10002 Toledo OH 43699

BOONE, ROBERT LEE, data processing executive; b. Morrison, Ill., Apr. 18, 1950; s. Robert Louis and Barbara Ann (Johnson) B. AA in Sci., Sauk Valley Jr. Coll., 1970. Dir. data processing County of Whiteside, Morrison, 1981—. Served as sgt. USAF, 1970-73. Mem. Midwest Honeywell Users Group. Roman Catholic. Avocations: lap swimming, bicycling. Home: 500 Locust St Prophetstown IL 61277 Office: Whiteside County Courthouse 200 E Knox St Morrison IL 61270

BOOR, KENNETH STEVEN, marketing executive; b. Chgo., June 20, 1945; s. Steven and Irene (Holiga) B.; m. Maureen Margaret Lauer, Apr. 14, 1973; children: Matthew, Ann. AA, Mayfair-Amundsen Coll., 1968; BSBA, Roosevelt U., 1970, MBA, 1983. Salesman Morand Bros., Chgo., 1970-72; sales mgr. High Strength Adhesives, Chgo., 1972-76; mktg. mgr. United States Gypsum Co., Chgo., 1976-85; v.p. mktg. Aqua-Flo Corp., Carol Stream, Ill., 1985—; pvt. cons., Western Springs, Ill., 1985. Treas. Ridgewood Civic Assn., Western Springs, 1985—. Served with U.S. Army, 1963-66, Korea. Mem. Plumbing Mfrs., Inst., Mech. Contractors Assn. Am. Avocations: sailing, woodworking. Home: 1140 Longmeadow Ln Western Springs IL 60558 Office: Aqua Flo Corp 373 Randy Rd Carol Stream IL 60188

BOOR, MYRON VERNON, psychologist, educator; b. Wadena, Minn., Dec. 21, 1942; s. Vernon LeRoy and Rosella Katharine (Eckhoff) B. BS, U. Iowa, 1965; MA, So. Ill. U., 1967, PhD, 1970; MS in Hygiene, U. Pitts., 1981. Lic. psychologist, Kans., Ky., R.I. Research psychologist Milw. County Mental Health Ctr., 1970-72; asst. prof. clin. psychologist Ft. Hays State U., Hays, Kans., 1972-76; assoc. prof. Ft. Hays State U., Hays, 1979-81; NIMH postdoctoral fellow in psychiat. epidemiology U. Pitts., Western Psychiat. Inst. and Clinic, 1976-79; research psychologist R.I. Hosp. and Butler Hosp., Providence, 1981-84; clin. psychologist Newman Meml. County Hosp., Emporia, Kans., 1985—; clin. psychologist Ft. Hays State U., 1972-79; asst. prof. psychiatry and human behavior Brown U., Providence, 1981-84; adj. faculty Emporia State U., 1985—. Contbr. articles to profl. jours. U.S. Pub. Health Service fellow, 1965-67, NIMH fellow 1979-81. Mem. Am. Psychol. Assn., Soc. for Psychol. Study of Social Issues, Internat. Soc. for Study of Multiple Personalities (charter). Home: 2225 Prairie Emporia KS 66801 Office: Newman Meml County Hosp 12th & Chestnut Emporia KS 66801

BOOS, FREDERICK CARPENTER, hotelier, tourism consultant; b. Mpls., Aug. 2, 1933; s. George W. and Elizabeth (Carpenter) B.; m. Mary Cote, June 10, 1960; children—Julia, Carolyn, Cynthia. B.A., Colgate U., 1955. Sales rep. Foote Lumber, Mpls., 1958-63; sales rep. Grand View Lodge, Brainerd, Minn., 1963-65, asst. mgr., 1965-70, gen. mgr., owner, 1970—; Chmn. Minn. Assn. of Commerce and Industry, St. Paul, 1984—; pres. Minn. Heartland Assn., 1978-80. Served to sgt. U.S. Army, 1956-58, Korea. Named Tourism Man of Yr., Minn. Dept. Tourism. 1984. Mem. Minn. Resort Assn. (pres. 1971-73, Man of Yr. 1982), Upper Midwest Hospitality Assn. (chmn. 1982—), Minn. Hotel Assn. (bd. dirs. 1980—). Avocations: reading; tennis; fishing; skiing. Home: 4618 Edgebrook Pl Edina MN 55424 Office: Grand View Lodge Route 6 Box 22 Brainerd MN 56401

BOOSALIS, ELSIE, real estate management executive; b. Cedar Rapids, Iowa, Dec. 1, 1913; adopted dau. of Peter and Rose (Halleck) B.; student Phoenix Bus. Coll., 1943-44, Northwestern U., 1952-53, U. Minn. Property mgr. Peter Boosalis Bldg. Trust, Mpls., 1953—, trustee, 1960—. Bd. dirs. Greater Lake St. Council; sustaining mem. council Girl Scouts U.S.A.; bus. mem. Powderhorn Devel. Corp.; donor Guthrie Theater; active ARC, YWCA, WAMSO. Mem. Mpls. Soc. Fine Arts, Minn., Hennepin County hist. socs., Mpls. C. of C., Minn. Orch. Assn. (guarantor, chmn.), English Speaking Union, Am. Swedish Inst. Home: 4551 Dupont Ave S Minneapolis MN 55409 Office: 2951 Chicago Ave Minneapolis MN 55407

BOOTH, GEORGE D., business, marketing and merchandising services executive, publisher; b. Highland Park, Mich., Jan. 4, 1927; s. George H. and Gladys L. (Rich) B.; m. Marie Newberry, July 17, 1948; children—Glenn A., Rick L. Student, Graceland Coll., 1947, Drake U., 1948. Owner, operator Booth Dept. Stores, Garden City, Mich., 1948-50, Booth Motor Sales, Monroe, Mich., 1950-56; merchandising exec. Chrysler Corp., Highland Park, 1956-77; pres. Merchandising Bus. Services, Inc., Southfield, Mich., 1978—, Nat. Bus. Opportunities Ctrs., Inc., 1980-84, Nat. Print & Copy Marts, Inc., 1980—, Channel 1 Video Prodns., 1981—; editor, pub. The Mini Shopper, Internat., 1969-77, Idea-Motives, 1977-78, The Am. Merchandising Report, 1983—; mktg. cons., speaker. Served with USAF, 1945-47. Mem. sales Promotion Execs. Assn. (past pres. Detroit chpt., Sales Promotion Exec. of Yr. 1967). Lodge: Kiwanis. Author materials on motivation, careers. Home: 1570 Forest Ln Birmingham MI 48010 Office: Merchandising Bus Services 24611 Greenfield Rd Southfield MI 48075

BOOTH, HEATHER TOBIS, social action organization executive; b. Brookhaven, Miss., Dec. 15, 1945; d. Jerome Sanford and Hazel (Weisband) Tobis; s. Paul R. Booth, July 2, 1967; children: Eugene Victor, Daniel Gerrison. BA, U. Chgo., 1967, MA, 1970. Dir. Midwest Acad., Chgo., 1972-78, Citizen Labor Energy Coalition, Chgo., 1977-80, State and Local Leadership Project, Chgo., 1980-83, Citizen Leadership Found., Chgo., 1983-85; co-dir. Citizen Action, Chgo., 1983—; pres. Midwest Acad., Citizen Leadership Found. Author: Citizen Action and the New American

Populism, 1986; contbr. articles to profl. jours. Commr. Chgo. Women's Commn. Avocations: cooking, theater, reading, dance, travel. Office: Citizen Action 600 W Fullerton Chicago IL 60614

BOOTH, JAMES ALBERT, engineer; b. Salem, Ohio, Dec. 14, 1946; s. Kenneth Bishop and Helen Elizabeth (Kelly) B.; m. Anita Jean Willford, Aug. 10, 1974; children: Jennifer Lynn, Stephen Andrew. BS, Bowling Green (Ohio) State U., 1968, MS in Physics, 1973; MS in Nuclear Engring., Ohio State U., 1974; MS in Engring. Mgmt., U. Dayton, Ohio, 1983. Registered profl. engr., Ohio. Sr. research engr. Monsanto Research Corp., Dayton, 1974-81, mgr. engring. design, 1981-84; group leader non-destructive testing Miamisburg, Ohio, 1984-86; group leader quality engring. 1986—. Served as sgt. U.S. Army, 1969-71, Vietnam. Mem. Am. Soc. for Non-Destructive Testing (treas. Miami Valley sect. 1985-86), ASME, Am. Soc. for Quality Control (cert. quality engr.). Methodist. Avocations: reading, astronomy, computers. Home: 3141 Westview Dr Xenia OH 45385 Office: Monsanto Research Corp Miamisburg OH 45342

BOOTHE, JACQUELINE ANN, nursing educational administrator; b. Terre Haute, Ind., May 5, 1931. Student Maryville Coll. of Sacred Heart, 1948-50, Washington U., St. Louis, 1950-51; B.S. in Nursing, diploma, Johns Hopkins U., 1954, M.Ed., 1970. Assoc. dir. nursing edn. Deaconess Hosp. Sch. Nursing, St. Louis, 1954-66; adminstrv. asst. Johns Hopkins Hosp. Sch. Nursing, Balt., 1966-70; dir. Good Samaritan Hosp. Sch. Nursing, Cin., 1970—; regional group on nursing Ohio Commn.'s Study on Nursing Needs and Resources, 1979-82; mem. Ohio Commn. on Nursing, 1984—. Mem. ednl. com. Am. Cancer Soc., 1984-86; mem. Ohio Council on Nursing, 1986—; bd. dirs. Cin. Cancer Control Council; mem. adv. com. Council on Aging; mem. adv. com. Cin. Continuing Edn. Com.; mem. women's com. Cin. Symphony Orch., 1970—. Mem. Nat. League for Nursing (program com. 1975-81, accreditation team 1976-78, chmn. nominating com. 1981-83), Ohio League for Nursing (dir. 1975-79), Assembly of Hosp. Schs. of Nursing, Cin. Dirs. Conf. Group of Nursing Leadership, Ohio Council Diploma Nurse Educators (chmn. 1984-86), Buckeye State Nurses Orgn. (co-founder), Am. Assn. for Higher Edn., AAAS, Assn. for Supervision and Curriculum Devel., Cin. Symphony Assn., Friends of Cin. Parks. Presbyterian (pres. bd. trustees Cin. Presbytery). Home: 2380 Madison Rd Cincinnati OH 45208 Office: Good Samaritan Hosp Sch Nursing Cincinnati OH 45220

BOOTY, M. D., food company executive. Pres. Westfair Foods Ltd., Winnipeg. Office: Westfair Foods Ltd, 101 Weston St, Winnipeg, MB Canada R3E 2T4 *

BOOZ, GRETCHEN ARLENE, marketing executive; b. Boone, Iowa, Nov. 24, 1933; d. David Gerald and Katherine Bevridge (Hardie) Berg; m. Donald Rollett Booz, Sept. 3, 1960; children: Kendra Sue (dec.), Joseph David, Katherine Sue. AA, Graceland Coll., 1955. Mktg. services mgr. Herald Pub. House, Independence, Mo., 1975—. Author: (book) Kendra, 1979. Mem. Citizens Adv. Bd., Blue Springs, Mo., 1979—; trustee Graceland Coll., Lamoni, Iowa, 1984—. Mem. Independence C. of C. (diplomat). Republican. Mem. Reorganized Ch. Jesus Christ Latter Day Saints. Avocation: writing and presenting monologues of hist. women. Home: 1200 Crestview Dr Blue Springs MO 64015 Office: Herald Pub House 3225 S Noland Rd Independence MO 64055

BOOZELL, MARK ELDON, state legislative affairs executive; b. Mason City, Iowa, Mar. 4, 1955; s. Eldon Dwayne Boozell and Betty Jean (Gordon) Kruger; m. Susan Elizabeth Abelt, Nov. 26, 1977; children: Kari Elizabeth, Lindsay Patricia. BA, Augustana Coll., 1977. Budget analyst rep. staff Ill. Ho. of Reps., Springfield, 1977-78, dep. dir. rep. staff, 1978-80; legis. liaison Ill. Dept. Transp., Springfield, 1980-83; dir. legis. affairs Ill. Sec. State, Springfield, 1983—. Named one of Outstanding Young Men Am., 1980. Republican. Lutheran. Home: 78 Stony Creek Chatham IL 62629 Office: Dept Legis Affairs Sec of States 476 Centennial Bldg Springfield IL 62756

BORAM, CLIFFORD WAYNE, JR., small business owner; b. Chgo., Dec. 24, 1933; s. Clifford Wayne Sr. and Catherine Elizabeth (Logan) B. BA, Columbia U., 1955; MEd, Harvard U., 1967; MA, New Sch for Social Research, N.Y.C., 1972. Tchr. Peace Corps, Gaoual, Guinea, 1964-66, Bur. of Indian Affairs, Birch Creek, Alaska, 1967-69, Divanap Community Sch., Oksapmin, Papua New Guinea, 1973-76, Heart Butte (Mont.) Schs., 1978-79; owner Autonomy House Publs., Monticello, Ind., 1981—, Antique Stove Info. Clearing House, Monticello, 1981—; advisor Schroeder's Antiques Price Guide, Covington, Ind., 1985—. Author: Oksapmin Children, 1980, How to Get Parts Cast for Your Antique Stove, 1982. Served with U.S. Army, 1955-57. Mem. Antique Stove Assn. (founder, sec. 1984—, editor). Home and Office: 417 N Main St Monticello IN 47960

BORANYAK, MARK, brewing company executive; b. Topeka, Kans., Jan. 6, 1950; s. Rudolph and Atha M. (Rounkles) B.; m. Sharon Rae Etzel, Apr. 20, 1974. Student Washburn U., 1968-69; B.S., Kans. State U., 1972. Cert. assn. exec. Mgr. pub. and govtl. affairs Topeka C. of C., 1972-75; exec. dir. Kans. Beer Wholesalers Assn., Topeka, 1975-83; mgr. industry and govt. programs Anheuser Busch Cos., St. Louis, 1983, mgr. state affairs, 1984-86, dir. state affairs, 1986—; speaker Leadership Manhattan (Kans.), 1982. Officer, Nat. Council on Alcoholism, Topeka, 1983, bd. dirs., 1982-83; mem. Topeka-Shawnee County Litter Control Commn., 1977; mem. Topeka Friends of the Zoo, 1980-83; team capt. United Way of Greater Topeka, 1979; mem. Topeka Assn. for Retarded Citizens, 1980-83; vol. fundraiser Boys Club of Topeka, 1977; mem. Topeka Jaycees, 1972-73; bd. dirs. Jr. Achievement of Northeast Kans., Topeka, 1973-75; mem. Shawnee County Manpower Commn., Topeka, 1974. Mem. Wholesale Beer Assn. Execs. (officer 1981-82), Kans. Soc. Assn. Execs. (chmn. com. 1980, speaker 1982), Am. Soc. Assn. Execs. (cert. 1983), Pub. Relations Soc. Topeka, Kans. Assn. Commerce and Industry (Leadership Kans. 1982), Kans. State U. Alumni Assn. Republican. Roman Catholic. Club: St. Louis 3d Friday (co-chmn. 1986—). Home: 5808 Mango Dr St Louis MO 63129 Office: Anheuser Busch Cos One Busch Pl Saint Louis MO 63118

BORANYAK, SHARON ETZEL (MRS. MARK BORANYAK), writer, editor; b. Topeka, Kans., May 2, 1951; d. Raymond Francis and Julia Elizabeth (Porubsky) Etzel; BS, Kans. State U., 1973; m. Mark Boranyak, Apr. 20, 1974. Assoc. editor Capper's Weekly, Topeka, Kans., 1973-76; pub. info. specialist Stormont-Vail Hosp., Topeka, 1976; informational writer Water Quality Mgmt. sect. Kans. Dept. Health and Environment, Topeka, 1976-77, pub. relations dir. div. environment, 1977-79; editor Kans. Legis. Div. of Post-Audit, 1979-83; sr. tech. editor McDonnell Douglas Corp., St. Louis, 1983—; cons. Topeka Broadcast Council. Mem. Women in Communications (treas. Topeka chpt. 1975-79), Nat. Fedn. Press Women (v.p. Topeka chpt. 1978-79, pres. 1980—), Topeka Home Econs. Assn., People to People. Republican. Roman Catholic. Contbr. articles to profl. jours. Home: 5808 Mango Dr Saint Louis MO 63129

BORATYN, GEORGE MICHAEL, JR., lawyer, banker, Doberman Pinscher breeder and trainer; b. Chgo., Feb. 24, 1947; s. George Michael and Joane Mary (Sterczek) B.; m. Judith F. Gawlik, June 22, 1975. Grad. Loyola U., 1970; J.D., Lewis U., 1979; J.D., No. Ill. U., 1981; postgrad. Northwestern U. Tchr., St. Thecla Elem. Sch., Chgo., 1969; with comml. loan div. Colonial Bank & Trust Co. of Chgo., 1973-78; asst. v.p. comml. loan div. First Nat. Bank & Trust Co. of Barrington (Ill.), 1979-80; v.p., comml. loan officer Mt. Prospect State Bank (Ill.), 1981-83; sr. loan workout specialist F.D.I.C., Knoxville, Tenn., 1984; v.p. comml. loan div. Bank of Ravenswood, Chgo., 1986—; pres. Juris Canis Inc.; cons. to contbg. editor Dog World, Dog Sports, others. Served with U.S. Army, 1969-75. Recipient letters of accomodation. Mem. Midwest Credit Conf., Robert Morris Assos., Am. Kennel Club, Can. Kennel Club, Doberman Pinscher Club Am. and Breeders Assn., Owner-Handlers' Assn., Tau Kappa Epsilon, (past pres.), Tau Epsilon Rho. Roman Catholic. Designer, distbr. Guard Dog Sign; contbr. articles to publs. including Barrington Courier Rev., Crain's Chgo. Bus., Nat. Inquirer, Dog World, Doberman Quar., Doberman Monthly, Belmont-Central Leader, Barrington Leader Publs., Paddock Publs.; author case study for NIMH, HEW.

BORCHARDT, PHYLLIS HENDERSON, optometrist; b. Moose Lake, Minn., May 19, 1928; d. Robert and Gertrude Ingebord (Schoen) Henderson; m. Fred C. Borchardt, Nov. 29, 1952; children: Janet, Frederick, David, Ralph, Carl. OD, No. Ill. Coll. Optometry, 1949. Pvt. practice optometry Moose Lake, 1950-57, Willow River, Minn., 1957—; cons. in field, 1968-82. Sunday sch. tchr., Moose Lake, 1944-46, Willow River 1956-61; mem. Pine County (Minn.) Devel., 1958-60; clk. Willow River Sch. Bd., 1966-78; leader 4-H, Whispering Pines, Minn., 1967-72. Lutheran. Avocations: children and grandchildren, dairy farming. Home and Office: 2699 County Rd 41 Willow River MN 55795

BORCHERT, ROGER NORMAN, geologist; b. Faribault, Minn., Jan. 10, 1947; s. August Fredrick and Winoma Shirley (Kirkman) B.; m. Nancy Ann Kotlarz, Dec. 20, 1969; children—Heather Leigh, Shelley Christine. B.S., Winona State Coll., 1969. Tchr. Sch. Dist. No. 1, Schaumberg, Ill., 1970; tchr., head sci. dept. Sch. Dist. No. 1, Hulett, Wyo., 1970-73; chemist, applications engr. Pesek Engring Co., Golden Valley, Minn., 1973-75; petroleum engr. II, N.D. Geol. Survey, Grand Forks, N.D., 1975-80; geologist Harris, Brown & Klemer, Bismarck, N.D., 1980-83, v.p., 1983—. Mem. Am. Inst. Mining Engrs., Am. Assn. Petroleum Geologists (del. Rocky Mountain sect. 1986-87, chmn. 1986—), Am. Inst. Profl. Geologists, N.D. Geol. Soc. (v.p. 1986-87, chmn. Williston Basin Symp. 1987), N.D. Archeol. Assn. Lutheran. Club: Dakota Petroleum (bd. dirs. 1985—). Lodges: Elks, Masons (32d degree). Avocations: hunting, fishing, camping, fossil and Indian artifact collecting, trap shooting. Home: 826 N 5th St Bismarck ND 58501 Office: Harris Brown & Klemer Inc PO Box 5006 Bismarck ND 58502

BORCHERT, STEVEN JOHN, chemist; b. Madison, Wis., Jan. 20, 1950; s. Willard W. and Beatrice N. Borchert; B.A., U. Wis., 1972; A.M. (NSF fellow 1972-74, Standard Oil Co. Calif. scholar 1971), Harvard U., 1973, Ph.D., 1977. Research chemist Upjohn Co., Kalamazoo, 1977—. Mem. Am. Chem. Soc., Parenteral Drug Assn. Home: 1706 Whitby Ave Portage MI 49002 Office: Upjohn Co 7000 Portage Rd Kalamazoo MI 49001

BORDEN, DANIEL JAMES, small business executive; b. Mpls., Sept. 13, 1957; s. Richard James and Gloria Lavonne (Knutson) B. Student, U. Wis., 1976-77, U. Minn., 1977-80. Programmer Circuit Sci., Inc., Mpls., 1972-76; auditor Multaplex Corp., Mpls., 1976-79; pres. Programming Enterprises, Mpls., 1977-78, Sandwich Factory, Inc., Mpls., 1979—. Avocations: music, soccer, running, biking, tennis, hockey. Home: 606 E Minnehaha Pkwy Minneapolis MN 55417 Office: Sandwich Factory Inc 7300 Metro Blvd Edina MN 55435

BORDER, NICHOLAS JOE, union representative; b. Zanesville, Ohio, Sept. 9, 1948; s. William Wilbur and Mildred Alice (Leffler) B.; m. Linda Irene Bradfield, July 5, 1969; children: Sandra Nicole, Joseph Daniel. Student, Ohio State U., 1975, Kenyon Coll., 1976, Kent (Ohio) U., 1980. With Packard Electric of Gen. Motors, Warren, Ohio, 1971—; ins. and supplemental benefit rep. Union Local 717, Warren, Ohio; also exec. bd. dirs. Union Local 717. Pres. Trumbull County Memorial Day Assn., 1985—; active Ohio Veterans Home, other orgns for disabled veterans and the handicapped. Decorated Bronze Star with silver oak leaf cluster, Purple Heart, Air medal, Cross of Gallantry (Vietnam); named one of Outstanding Young Ams., 1985; recipient Volunteer Work award Ohio Veterans Home, 1985, 86, Resolution, Ohio Senate, 1985. Mem. Internat. Union Elect., Radio and Machine Workers (rep. 1976—, chmn. veterans com. 1985—), Disabled Am. Veterans (membership com., chmn. prisoner of war/missing in action com.) Am. Legion, VFW, Trumball County Vietnam Veterans, Vietnam Veterans Am. Democrat. Avocations: fishing, hiking, camping, hunting, bowling. Home: 7306 Kinsman Nickerson Rd Kinsman OH 44428

BORDLEY, ROBERT FRANCIS, automotive company researcher; b. Columbus, Ohio, Aug. 15, 1955; s. Robert Guy and Ann Mary Bordley. B.S. in Physics, Mich. State U., 1975, B.A. in Pub. Policy, 1976, M.S. in Systems Sci., 1976; M.S. in Ops. Research, U. Calif.-Berkeley, 1977, M.B.A., 1979, Ph.D. in Ops. Research, 1979. Intern Coop. League, Washington, 1975; assoc. sr. research Gen. Motors Research Labs., Warren, Mich., 1978-80, sr. researcher, 1980-82, staff researcher, 1982-86, sr. staff researcher, 1986—; supr. mission analysis group GM trilby design project, 1985—, supr. decision support systems group, 1986—, mgr. decision support sect., 1987—, mem. decision analysis council, 1987—; adj. prof. U. Mich.-Dearborn, 1980. Recipient Wildlife Conservation award Va. Game Commn. Assn., 1973, speaking awards Am. Legion, 1971, 73; Nat. Merit scholar, 1973-76; Mich. State U. alumni disting. scholar, 1973-76; NSF fellow, 1976-79. Mem. Ops. Research Soc. Am., Am. Inst. Indsl. Engrs., Pub. Choice Soc., Inst. Mgmt. Scis., Am. Econ. Assn., Soc. for Promotion Econ. Theory, Soc. Risk Analysis, AAAS, James Madison Coll. Alumni Assn. (dir. 1982-84, pres. 1984—), Cosmos Soc., Phi Beta Kappa, Sigma Xi, Phi Kappa Phi. Contbr. articles to profl. publs. Home: 803 W 4th St Royal Oak MI 48067 Office: Dept Operating Scis Gen Motors Research Labs Warren MI 48090

BOREN, ARTHUR RODNEY, JR., investment services executive; b. Dayton, Ohio, June 25, 1946; s. A. Rodney and D. Charlotte (Polk) B.; m. Susan Stansfield; children: Justin S., Celia C. B.A., Washington and Lee U., 1968; M.I.M., Am. Grad. Sch., Phoenix, 1973. Tchr. Miami Valley Sch., Dayton, 1968-70; adminstr. 1970-71; internat. banker Norwest Bank Mpls., N.A., 1974-78, nat. banker, 1978-81, v.p. nat. dept., 1980, v.p. treasury div., 1981-83, sr. v.p. security sales dept., 1983-86; pres. Norwest Investment Svcs., Inc., 1983-86. Mem. Am. Inst. Banking. Republican. Episcopalian. Clubs: Miami Valley Hunt and Polo (Dayton); Minneapolis (Mpls.). Office: Norwest Investment Services Inc 222 S 9th St Minneapolis MN 55479

BORENSTINE, ALVIN JEROME, search company executive; b. Kansas City, Mo., Dec. 14, 1933; s. Samuel and Ella C. (Berman) B.; m. Roula Alakiotou, Dec. 31, 1976; Ella Marie and Sami (twins). B.S. in Econs., U. Kans., 1956; M.B.A., U. Pa., 1960. Analyst, Johnson & Johnson, New Brunswick, N.J., 1961-62; systems mgr. Levitt & Sons, Levittown, N.J., 1962-66; dir. mgmt. info. services Warren Brothers Co., Cambridge, Mass., 1966-71; mgr. fin. and adminstrv. systems Esmark, Inc., Chgo., 1971-72; pres. Synergistics Assocs. Ltd., Chgo., 1972—; mem. bus. adv. council, Program Able Hellenic Dimensions. Mem. bus. adv. council St. Xavier U., Project Able, Hellenic Dimensions. Mem. Assn. for Systems Mgmt. (pres. Boston chpt. 1969, Disting. Service award 1970), Soc. Info. Mgmt. Systems and Procedures Assn. research fellow, 1959-60; Eddie Jacobson Found. scholar, 1958-60. Club: Carlton. Lodge: B'nai B'rith. Home: 6033 N Sheridan Chicago IL 60660 Office: 320 N Michigan Ave Suite 1803 Chicago IL 60601

BORGER, FREDERICK HOWARD, manufacturing company executive; b. Jamaica, N.Y., Apr. 2, 1946; s. Howard Francis and Irene Albie (Koucky) B.; B.B.A., St. John's U., 1967; M.B.A., N.Y. U., 1970; m. Joan A. Manning, June 24, 1967; children—Kristin, James. Orgn. devel. cons. Western Electric Co., N.Y.C., 1968-72; v.p., cons. Cin. Comml. Cons., Cin., 1972-73; mgr. corp. staffing Borden Inc., Columbus, 1973-78; dir. human resources O.M. Scott & Sons, Marysville, Ohio, 1978-87; sr. v.p. Diversified Community Services, Columbus, 1987—. Vice pres. Homeowners Assn., Norwich, 1974-75; trustee Homeowners Assn., Columbus, Ohio, 1974-76, sec.-treas. Grandview Hts. Youth Athletic Assn., 1983, v.p., then pres., 1983-85. Mem. Am. Soc. Tng. and Devel., Am. Soc. Personnel Adminstrn., Central Ohio Personnel Assn., Orgn. Devel. Inst. Republican. Roman Catholic. Home: 1149 Ashland Ave Columbus OH 43212 Office: Diversified Community Services 1651 E Main St Columbus OH 43205

BORGERT, JAMES HAROLD, accountant; b. St. Henry, Ohio, Nov. 1, 1956; s. Wilmer Bernard and Rita Marie (Stahl) B.; m. Nancy Ann Reier, Oct. 3, 1981. BS, Wright State U., 1980. CPA. Tax acct. Peat, Marwick and Mitchell, Cin., 1979; staff auditor Touche, Ross and Co., Dayton, Ohio, 1980-82; supr. Stroh, Borgert and Co., Wapakoneta, Ohio, 1982-84, ptnr., 1984—. Mem. Am. Inst. CPA's, Ohio Soc. CPA's, Wapakoneta C. of C. (treas. 1986). Club: Country (Wapakoneta). Lodges: Kiwanis, Elks. Avocations: golf, tennis, reading. Home: 221 Penn St Wapakoneta OH 45895 Office: Stroh Borgert and Co 105 S Blackhoof Wapakoneta OH 45895

BORGIC, ROSEMARY AURORA, chemical dependency consultant; b. Grand Rapids, Mich., July 24, 1927; d. Marcel Raphael and Antoinette (Caron) Despres; m. Richard P. Strzyz, June 10, 1950 (dec. July 1979); children: Jeanne M., Paul R., Jon R., Thom C., Anne C., Lynne M., Luke G.; m. George W. Borgic, Jan. 1, 1985. AA, Grand Rapids Jr. Coll., 1947; BS, Grand Valley State Coll., Allendale, Mich., 1975; postgrad., Western Mich. U., Kalamazoo, 1986—. Counselor Alcohol Out-Patient, Inc., Grand Rapids, 1975-80; program developer, coordinator Project Rehab. Shiloh Family, Grand Rapids, 1980—; mem. exec. bd., workshop presenter Western Mich. Workers for Women Alcoholics, Grand Rapids, 1978—. Mem. Mich. Assn. Children's Agys. Roman Catholic. Avocations: hiking, camping, traveling, swimming, reading.

BORGWARDT, ROBERT G., pastor, TV preacher; b. Milw., Aug. 7, 1922; s. Erwin R. and Hilda M. (Meier) B.; m. Ruth Fossum, June 14, 1947 (dec. 1963); children—Kathryn, John, Stephen; m. Joan Renee Gullickson, Sept. 25, 1964; children—Anne, Eric. B.A., St. Olaf Coll., Minn., 1944; M.T., Luther Sem., St. Paul, 1947; D.D. (hon.), Carthage Coll., Wis., 1975. Ordained: Minister, Am. Lutheran Ch. Sr. pastor Trinity Lutheran Ch., Madison, Wis., 1947-53; assoc. pastor Central Lutheran, Mpls., 1953-55; sr. pastor First Lutheran Ch., Sioux Falls, S.D., 1955-63, Bethel Lutheran Ch., Madison, 1963—; pub. relations com. Lutheran Council, U.S.A., 1964-67; pres. Madison Area Council Chs., 1969-70; active div. coll. and univ. services Am. Luth Ch., 1974—; bd. regents Wartburg Coll., Waverly, Iowa, 1972-77; cert. visit Bethel Bible Series, Japan, Korea, 1975. Author: Men Who Knew Jesus, 1958; Kind and Heavenly Father, 1967; Don't Blow Out The Candle, 1969; I am Hurting...Please Help Me. Mem. Wis. State Bd. Ethics, 1980-85. Recipient Young Man of Yr. award C. of C., Sioux Falls, 1958; Disting. Alumni award St. Olaf Coll., Minn., 1985; British Fgn. Office Conf. Participant, Wilton Park, Sussex, Eng., 1974, 84. Club: Rotary (bd. dirs. Madison 1964-66). Avocations: cycling; golf; tennis; travel. Office: Bethel Lutheran Ch 312 Wisconsin Ave Madison WI 53703

BORIS, WALTER R., retired utility company executive, financial consultant; b. Amsterdam, N.Y., 1921; married. Student, St. Lawrence U., 1948; B.S. in Aero. Engring., U. Mich., 1948, J.D., 1950. Bar: N.Y. 1981, Mich. 1981. Title examiner Consumers Power Co., Jackson, Mich., 1950-52, atty. legal dept., 1952-53, exec. staff asst., 1953-56, sec., 1956-68, v.p. fin., 1968-75, exec. v.p., dir., 1975-86; fin. cons. Consumers Power Co., Jackson, 1986—; dir. Camp Internat., Nat. Bank of Jackson. Office: Consumers Power Co Inc 145 S Jackson St Jackson MI 49201

BORKGREN, JOHN ANDREW, architect; b. Geneseo, Ill., Sept. 12, 1952; s. Raymond Irwin and Janet Elaine (Johnson) B.; m. Gayle Lynn Altenbern, Aug. 9, 1975 (div. Apr. 1977). A Archtl. Tech., S. Ill. U., 1976, B Archtl. Communication, 1976. Registered architect, Ill. Design architect Sargent & Lundy Engrs., Chgo., 1976-78, W.E. Nelson & Assocs., Geneva, Ill., 1978-80, Norman A. White & Assocs., Hinsdale, Ill., 1980-81; project architect Opus Corp., Mt. Prospect, Ill., 1981—. Designer solar panel collector. Mem. AIA (corp.), Fellowship Christian Athletes. Republican. Avocations: golf, hockey, softball, cooking, woodworking. Home: 728 E Golf Des Plaines IL 60016 Office: Opus Corp 411 N Bus Ctr Dr Mount Prospect IL 60056

BORKHOLDER, FREEMON, construction executive, developer; b. Bremen, Ind., Oct. 11, 1932; s. Daniel J. and Emma (Coblentz) B.; student pub. schs.; m. Margaret Hershberger, Apr. 26, 1956; children: Lorene Kaye, Suetta, Dwayne Alan, Jonathan Jay, Cheryl Elaine. With Coppes Inc., Nappanee, Ind., 1955-62; owner, pres. F.D. Borkholder Co., Nappanee, 1960—; v.p. Borkholder Bldgs., Nunica, Mich., 1967—; sec.-treas. Newmar Industries, Nappanee, 1968—; pres., founder Amish Crafted Am. Vintage Furniture, 1982—; developer indsl. parks, 1967—. Bd. dirs. No. Youth Programs, Hope Rescue Mission, South Bend, Ind. Mem. Nat. Frame Builders Assn. (pres. 1971-72, dir., pres. Ind. chpt. 1979), Internat. Platform Assn. Mennonite. Home: RD 1 Bremen IN 46506 Office: PO Box 32 Nappanee IN 46550

BORLAND, BRUCE HENNINGER, transportation equipment management and leasing company executive; b. Butler, Pa., Dec. 28, 1929; s. Bruce Sylvester and Mary Elizabeth (Henninger) B.; m. Beatrice Anne Buckler, Nov. 25, 1952; children—Cheryl Borland McClure, Bruce David. B.S., Northwestern U., 1951. Sales promotion staff Bell & Howell, Chgo., 1952-53; mgr. Hotpoint Co., Chgo., 1956-58; sales rep. GATX Corp., Chgo., 1958-60, dist. mgr., 1960-79, sales mgr., 1979-80; pres., chmn., chief exec. officer Temco Corp., Lake Bluff, Ill., 1981—; dir. Omnicard Internat., Wheeling, Ill.; mem. Shippers Adv. Bd. Mem. U.S. Congl. Adv. Bd. Served with JAGC, U.S. Army, 1952-54. Mem. Am. Petroleum Inst., Chgo. Traffic Club, Covered Hopper Car Shippers Assn., Fertilizer Inst., Traffic Clubs Internat., Internat. Platform Assn., Am. Mgmt. Assn., Am. Legion, R.R. Progress Inst. Republican. Clubs: Forge; Evanston (Ill.) Golf; Union League (Chgo.), Post and Paddock, Market; Stonebridge. Home: 2801 Orange Brace Rd Riverwoods IL 60015 Office: Temco Corp 100 E Scranton Lake Bluff IL 60044

BORLAUG, DAVID P., newspaper publisher; b. Turtle Lake, N.D., Sept. 8, 1956; s. Oliver Sanford and Judith Meneva (Riskedahl) B.; m. Ruth Marie Rockenbach, July 30, 1983. Advt. mgr. Washburn (N.D.) Leader, 1975-79; pres. Borlaug Pub. Co., Washburn, 1979-85; pres., pub. Guide Pub. Co., Bismarck, N.D., 1980—. Pres. Washburn Civic Club, 1978; commr. Washburn Park Bd., 1977-80. Mem. Nat. Agrl. Marketers, N.D. Agrl. Assn., Council Agrl. Sci. and Tech., Dakota Zool. Soc. (bd. dirs. 1985—), Bismarck C. of C., Fargo C. of C. Republican. Lutheran. Lodge: Optimists. Avocations: reading, music, lawn and garden. Home: 232 Coulee Dr Washburn ND 58577 Office: Guide Pub Co 4023 N State St Bismarck ND 58501

BORLEIS, HERBERT WILLIAM, pharmaceutical company executive; b. Balt., Sept. 5, 1937; s. Herbert Henry and Elmyra Elizabeth (Feuchter) B.; m. Patricia Ann Allen, Mar. 28, 1964; children: Robyn, David, H. William. AB, Transylvania U., 1960. Asst. v.p. personnel and pub. relations Chevron Oil, Perth Amboy, N.J., 1960-66; sales analyst Squibb Corp., N.Y.C., 1966-68; market research analyst Winthrop Labs, N.Y.C., 1968-69; sr. market analyst Beecham, Bristol, Tenn., 1969-73; mgr. mktg. research Bristol-Myers, Syracuse, N.Y., 1973-81; v.p., gen. mgr., dir. strategic planning Rorer Group div. Kremers-Urban Co., Inc., Port Washington, Wis., 1981-86; pres. Kremers-Urban Co., Milw., 1986—, also bd. dirs. Patentee spl. drug delivery applicator, 1985. Active United Way, Syracuse, 1978, Milw., 1983-85, Nat. Ileitis and Colitus Found., Milw., 1984-85; elder Elmbrook Ch., Brookfield, Wis. Served with U.S. Army, 1961-63. Recipient Progress award Milw. United Way, 1983, Commendation award Nat. Ileitis and Colitis Found., 1984, 85, Wis. Gov.'s New Product award, 1987. Mem. Pharm. Mktg. Research Assn., Pharm. Mfg. Assn., Pharm. Research Group, Nat. Wholesale Druggist Assn., World Trade Info. Bur., Wis. Mfrs. and Commerce Assn. (mem. com. for gov. cost control), Milw. C. of C. Office: Kremers-Urban Co Inc 5600 W County Line Rd Mequon WI 53092

BORMAN, PAUL, retail chain company executive; b. Detroit, 1932; s. Abraham B.; married. Grad., Mich. State U., 1954. With Borman's Inc., Detroit, 1959—, gen. mgr., 1959-60, v.p., 1960-65, pres., chief exec. officer, dir., 1965—, also dir.; dir. First Fed. of Mich. Office: Borman's Inc PO Box 446 Detroit MI 48232 *

BORMAN, WILLIAM J., dentist, gerodontist, educator; b. Indpls., Aug. 13, 1920; s. Harry and Sarah Borman; m. Harriet Elaine Levy, Apr. 17, 1944; children: Lewis, Richard, Robert, James. DDS, Ind. U., Indpls., 1942. Intern Eastman Clinic, Rochester, N.Y., 1943; gen. practice dentistry Indpls., 1946—; asst. prof. oral medicine Ind. U. Sch. Dentistry, Indpls.; gov.'s conf. on aging, 1977; bd.dirs. Hooverwood Nursing Home. Contbr. articles to profl. jours. Advisor Boy Scouts Am., Indpls., Explorer Scouts Am., Indpls.; mem. Ind. Hist. Soc., chmn. Ind. Multiple Sclerosis Com.; bd. dirs. Indpls. Hebrew Congregation Ind. U. Ctr. on Aging and Aged Program Devel. Served with U.S. Army, 1943-46. Mem. ADA, Acad. Gen. Dentistry, Indpls. Dist. Dental Soc. (bd. dirs. 1984-85, sec. 1985), Am. Children's Dental Soc., Am. Prosthetic Soc., Am. Soc. Geriatric Dentistry (pres.), Am. Gerontology Soc., Orgn. Tchrs. Oral Diagnosis, Ind. U. Alumni Assn., Alpha Omega, Omicron Kappa Upsilon. Home: 8770 Washington Blvd W Dr Indianapolis IN 46240 Office: 4647 W 30th Georgetown Sq Indianapolis IN 46222

BORNHOEFT, JACK HARRY, construction company executive; b. Chgo., July 16, 1923; s. Elmer J. and Lilliam M. (Matthias) B.; B.S., Northwestern U., 1947; m. Sept. 6, 1947; children—Nancy, Susan, Gregg. With Gerhardt F. Meyne Co., Chgo., 1945—, chmn., 1978—. Bd. dirs. Chgo. Bldg. Congress, 1978—. Served with USAAF, 1942-45, USAF, 1950-51. Decorated Air medal. Mem. Western Soc. Engrs. Republican. Presbyterian. Clubs: Tower, Rotary, East Bank; Park Ridge Country. Office: Gerhardt F Meyne Co 345 N Canal St Chicago IL 60606

BORNHOEFT, JOHN WILLIAM, III, microbiologist; b. Lakewood, Ohio, Apr. 24, 1943; s. John William and Billie Louise (Parshall) B.; B.A., Beloit Coll., 1965; M.S., Chgo. Med. Sch., 1972; Ph.D. (fellow), Loyola U., 1980; m. Margaret Teresa, June 13, 1971 (dec. 1981); 1 son, John William IV. Research asst. U. Ill. Med. Ctr., Chgo., 1967-69, Chgo. Med. Sch., 1970-71; clin. instr. Loyola U. Dental Sch., 1974-75; research asst. Loyola U., Chgo., 1976-79, research assoc., 1979-81; applied microbiologist, mgr. Am. Convertors Co., Evanston, Ill., 1981-85; pres. J.W.B. Assocs., cons. to healthcare industry, 1985—; cons. Rapid Med. Services, 1976-77; mem. faculty Mundelein Coll. Chgo., part time 1980; clin. microbiologist Loyola Student Health Services, 1976-81. Mem. Am. Soc. Microbiology, Am. Inst. Biol. Scis., N.Y. Acad. Scis., Sigma Xi. Club: Alfa Romeo Owners.

BORNS, ROBERT AARON, real estate developer; b. Gary, Ind., Oct. 24, 1935; s. Irving Jonah and Sylvia (Mackoff) B.; m. Sandra Solotkin Mar. 30, 1958; children—Stephanie, Elizabeth, Emily. BS, Ind. U., 1957. Account exec. Reynolds & Co., Chgo., 1957-59, Francis I. duPont Co., Indpls., 1960; owner, operator Borns & Co., Indpls., 1960-63; chmn. Borns Mgmt. Corp., Indpls., 1963—; bd. dirs. Heritage Venture Group, Inc., Indpls. Power and Light Co. Bd. dirs. Indpls. Mus. of Art-Life, Children's Mus. of Indpls., Indpls. Conv. and Visitors Bur., Corp. Community Council; trustee Marion Coll., Indpls. Symphony Orch.; bd. dirs., mem. exec. com. St. Vincent's Hosp. Found.; mem. bd. visitors Jewish Studies Program, Ind. U. Recipient Enterprise award Indpls. Bus. Jour., 1982. Jewish. Clubs: Economic (bd. dirs.), Univ. Office: 200 S Meridian St Indianapolis IN 46225

BORNSTEIN, HOWARD RUSSELL, tax accountant; b. Cleve., Mar. 11, 1955; s. Jerome Irving and Elaine Jean (Lish) B.; m. Judith B. Russell, June 17, 1978; 1 child, Cameron. BBA, U. Wis., 1978. CPA, Wis. Ptnr. Peat Marwick Main & Co., Milw., 1978—. Bd. dirs. Edn. Found. Elderly, Milw., 1985—, Congregation Shalom, Milw., 1987—. Mem. Wis. Inst. CPA's, Am. Inst. CPA's, Ins., Accts. and Systems Assn. Lodge: Kiwanis. Avocations: skiing, reading, tennis. Office: Peat Marwick Main & Co 777 E Wisconsin Ave Milwaukee WI 53202

BORNSTEIN, PHILIPP EMANUEL, psychiatrist; b. St. Louis, Jan. 14, 1941; s. Frederick Philipp and Clara (Lowenstein) B.; m. Barbara Bayer, Jan. 20, 1968; children: Andrea, P. Eric. BS, Tex. Western Coll., 1962; MD, Washington U., St. Louis, 1967. Diplomate Am. Bd. Psychiatry and Neurology. Intern in medicine U. Rochester, N.Y., 1967-68; resident in psychiatry Washington U. Barnes Hosp., St. Louis, 1968-69, 71-73; ptnr. Vine St. Clinic, Springfield, Ill., 1973—; chmn. dept. psychiatry St. Johns Hosp., Springfield, 1981—; clin. asst. prof. So. Ill. U. Sch. Medicine, Springfield, 1981—; examiner part II Am. Bd. Psychiatry and Neurology. Contbr. articles to profl. jours. Served to maj. U.S. Army, 1969-71. Mem. Am. Psychiat. Assn., Am. Acad. Clin. Psychiatrists (pres. 1978-80), Am. Acad. Forensic Scis., Royal Coll. Psychiatrists (London, overseas affiliate), Am. Acad. Psychiatry and Law. Club: Springfield Med. (pres. 1985-86). Avocations: running, tennis, trekking, photography, sailing. Office: Vine St Clinic at 6th and Madison 301 N 6th St Springfield IL 62701-1098

BOROFF, EUGENE ALLEN, postmaster; b. Kearney, Nebr., Feb. 25, 1942; s. Frank Eugene Boroff and Nancy Elizabeth (Fread) Harris; m. Paula Jean Christensen, Oct. 22, 1977; children: Robert, Vickie. Student, U. Nebr., 1984. Postal clk., carrier U.S. Postal Service, Fremont, Nebr., 1966-69, career clk., 1969-72, civil service examiner, 1970-72; postmaster U.S. Postal Service, Herman, Nebr., 1972-78, Valley, Nebr., 1978-85; assoc. office coordinator U.S. Postal Service, Omaha, 1982-85; postmaster U.S. Postal Service, Glenwood, Iowa, 1985-86, Plattsmouth, Nebr., 1986—. Scoutmaster Boy Scouts Am., 1974-78. Served with U.S. Army, 1959-62. Recipient Community Service award City of Valley, 1985, Merit award Boy Scouts Am., 1973. Mem. Nat. League of Postmasters (pres. Nebr. br. 1981-83, v.p. Nebr. br. 1978-81, Postmaster of Yr. 1985), Am. Legion, Glenwood C. of C. (v.p. 1986), C. of C. Valley Nebr. (pres. 1984-85). Democrat. Methodist. Lodge: Rotary, Masons (master 1977-78). Avocations: cat breeding, fishing, hunting, travel. Home: 208 10th St Glenwood IA 51534-1149 Office: US Postal Service 802 Ave B Plattsmouth NE 68048-9998

BOROWY, RICHARD, sales executive; b. Chgo., July 21, 1952; s. Edwin R. and Gloria P. (McDade) B. BA in Communications, U. Minn., 1984; BA, So. Ill. U., 1985. Salesman various cos., Chgo., 1974-76; asst. sales mgr. Screen, Inc., Chgo., 1976-80; asst. mgr. McDade Sales Co., Mpls., 1980-82; gen. mgr. Katz, Inc., Mpls., 1982—. Author: The One To Watch, 1982. Mem. Nat. Sales Mktg. Assn., Video Software Dealers Assn. Avocations: dancing, bicycling, golf, auto racing. Office: Box 14647 Minneapolis MN 55414

BORR, ERNEST BERNARD, university administrator; b. Strasburg, N.D., Aug. 20, 1934; s. Ernest O. and Kathryn (Schafer) B.; m. Donna Mae Hall, Sept. 21, 1957; children: David, Thomas, Richard, Karen, Michael. BA, Jamestown Coll., 1956; MA, U. No. Colo., 1962. Music tchr., dir. bands Napoleon (N.D.) Pub. Schs., 1956-57, Mandan (N.D.) Pub. Schs., 1958-72; music tchr., dir. bands U. Mary, Bismarck, N.D., 1972-76, v.p. for pub. affairs, 1976—; bd. dirs. St. Alexius Med. Ctr., Bismarck, 1985—, First S.W. Bank, Mandan, 1985—. Rep. dist. chmn., Mandan, 1979-86. Served with U.S. Army, 1957-58. Outstanding Alumni Achievement award Strasburg High Sch., 1966. Mem. Nat. Soc. Fund Raising Execs. (cert., pres. N.D. chpt. 1986), Nat. Band Assn. (Citation of Excellence 1967), Mandan Jaycees (Disting. Service award 1964). Roman Catholic. Lodge: Elks (Exalted Ruler Mandan 1975-76, Elk of the Yr. 1982), KC (Grand Knight). Home: 708 Custer Dr Mandan ND 58554 Office: U Mary 7500 University Dr Bismarck ND 58501

BORRA, P. C., health care company executive. Pres. Health Care and Retirement Corp. Am., Lima, Ohio. Office: Health Care & Retirement Corp of Am 1885 McCullough St Lima OH 45802 *

BORROR, D. A., construction company executive. Chmn., chief exec. officer Borror Corp., Columbus, Ohio. Office: Borror Corp 1225 Dublin Rd Columbus OH 43215 *

BORSELLINO, CHARLES CLIFFORD, psychology educator; b. Hamilton, Ont., Can., June 29, 1952; came to U.S., 1972; s. Angelo E. and Mary (Dowdy) B.; m. Jennifer DeEtte Price, July 26, 1978. BS, Evangel Coll., 1976; MS, SW Mo. State U., 1978; PhD, N. Tex. State U., 1982. Prof. psychology Evangel Coll., Springfield, Mo., 1982—, dir. counseling and health ctrs., 1984—; pvt. practice psychology Montclair Psychol. Assn., Springfield, 1984—. Single adults pastor Evangel Temple, Springfield, 1984—. Named one of Outstanding Young Men Am., U.S. Jaycees, 1982. Mem. Am. Psychol. Assn., Am. Assn. for Marriage and Family Therapy, Am. Bd. Med. Psychotherapists, Nat. Mental Health Assn., Am. Anorexic-Bulimic Assn. Mem. Assembly of God Ch. Home: 1905 E Vincent Springfield MO 65804 Office: Evangel Coll Dept Psychology 1111 N Glenstone Springfield MO 65802

BORST, WILLIAM PAUL, data processing executive; b. Flushing, N.Y., Jan. 18, 1949; s. William Henry and Mary Gertrude (Foffa) B.; m. NamJu Lee, Nov. 22, 1975; children: Andrew Lee, Jennifer Lee. BS in Math., Norwich U., 1970. Programmer Met. Life Ins. Co., N.Y.C., 1972-73; programmer, analyst Securities Industry Automation Corp., N.Y.C., 1973-75; systems mgr. FMC Corp., Chgo., 1975-79; project mgr. Northern Trust Co., Chgo., 1979—. Served to 1st lt. U.S. Army, 1970-72, Vietnam. Republican. Presbyterian. Avocations: investing, baseball, chess, reading, music. Home: 2169 Menomoni Ln Wheaton IL 60187 Office: Northern Trust Co N-15 125 S Wacker Dr Chicago IL 60675

BORTEL, ROBERT WILLIAM, director student publications; b. Toledo, Nov. 23, 1954; s. Robert Charles and Dortha Helen (Bach) B.; m. Ann Cashin Arvidson, Nov. 19, 1983. BS in Journalism, Bowling Green (Ohio) State U., 1977, MBA, 1983. Editor sports Franklin (Ohio) Chronicle, 1977-78, mng. editor, 1979-80; grad. teaching asst. Bowling Green (Ohio) State U., 1980-82, dir. student pubs., 1982—; adviser Soc. Profl. Journalists, Bowling Green, 1986. Mem. NW Ohio Writers Forum (v.p., treas. 1984—). Methodist. Avocations: running, reading, chess, outdoor recreation. Office: Bowling Green State U Bowling Green News 214 W Hall Bowling Green OH 43403

BORTH, ROBERT JOHN, accountant; b. Sheboygan, Wis., Aug. 18, 1953; s. Raymond Arthur and Bernice Alma (Riemer) B. BBA, U. Wis., 1975. Acctg. sr. Arthur Young & Co., Milw., 1975-78, Ritz Holman & Co., Milw., 1978-79; mgr. fin. reporting Wis. Gas Co., Milw., 1980—. Mem. Wis. Entomol. Soc. (treas. 1987). Lutheran. Avocations: entomology, tennis, tropical research. Office: Wis Gas Co 626 E Wisconsin Ave Milwaukee WI 53217

BORUCKI, WALTER C., distribution company executive; b. Detroit, June 11, 1916; s. Adam J. and Agata (Hardy) B.; student U. Poznan (Poland), 1937-39; m. Helen Jeza, Jan. 6, 1954; children—Judith Ellen, Mary Elizabeth. Prof. chemistry St. Mary's Coll., Orchard Lake, Mich., 1944-46; pres. Vets. Supply & Distbg. Co., Hamtramck, Mich., 1946—. Served with M.C., U.S. Army, 1941. Clubs: Polish Nat. Alliance, Polish Falcons, Alliance Poles, Polish-Am. Century, Amvets, Am. Legion. Author: Historia Stanow Zjednoczonych Ameryki Polnocnej, 1955, The First Complete History of U.S.A. in Polish Language. Home: 26420 Saint Josaphat Dr Warren MI 48091 Office: 3225 Caniff St Hamtramck MI 48212

BORUFF, DONALD VICTOR, mfg. co. exec.; b. Greene County, Ind.; s. Harvey Victor and Perla Clara (Wonder) B.; student Ind. Central U., Ind. U.; m. Berniece Hagaman, 1934; children—Donna Carpenter, Roma Carrick. Personnel dir. Mitts & Merrill, Saginaw, Mich., 1951-65, Am. Hoist Co., Bay City, Mich., 1966-68, KC Engring. & Machine Co., Saginaw, 1969-81; personnel mgmt. cons., Bay City, Mich., 1981—; lectr. in field. Active YMCA; bd. dirs. Saginaw City Rescue Mission; leader fund drives Saginaw United Way; mem. steering com. Saginaw Intermediate Sch. Dist.; leader vol. programs Bay City Pubs. Schs.; tchr. Bible Sch. Mem. Am. Soc. Personnel Adminstrn. (accredited exec. in personnel, cert. in A.E.P., Superior Merit award 1978), Valley Soc. Personnel Adminstrs. (pres. 1977—), Saginaw Employment Mgrs. Club (officer). Clubs: Ind. Execs. (bd. dirs.). Lodge: Masons. Address: 3358 Nottingham Dr Bay City MI 48706

BORUFF, JOHN DAVID, government official; b. Lakewood, Ohio, July 8, 1930; s. Glenn Tourner and Edith (Weybright) B.; m. Martha Lois Myers, June 12, 1953; children: Martha Yvonne Boruff Wyatt, Audrey Elaine, David Paul, Kenneth Edward. AB in Biology, Ind. U., 1953, MS in Health and Safety Edn., 1965. Sanitarian Ind. State Bd. Health, 1957-60, tng. officer food and drugs div., 1960-63, health edn. cons. div. health edn., 1963-65, statistician div. pub. health records, coordinator health data unit pub. health stats., 1969-83, health planner, statistician office health planning and policy devel., 1983-86, statistician div. pub. health stats., 1986—; health-housing coordinator Associated Migrant Opportunity Services, Inc., Indpls., 1965-66; extension health edn. specialist Purdue U., 1966-69; former state data mgr. Nat. Public Health Program Reporting System, Assn. State and Territorial Health Ofcls. Author: Health Trends in Indiana 1900-1973, Indiana Health Profile 1968-80; contbr. Ind. State Bd. Health Bull. Served as hosp. corpsman USCGR, 1953-57, former sr. asst. health service officer USPHS Res. Mem. No. Nut Growers Assn., Ind. Nut Growers Assn. (editor bull.), Theta Xi. Presbyterian. Clubs: Indpls. Valley Scottish Rite Orch., Athenaeum Turners Orch. Lodge: Masons (32 deg.). Home: RR 1 Box 128 Roachdale IN 46172 Office: 1330 W Michigan St Indianapolis IN 46206

BORUSZKOWSKI, LILLY ANN, film educator; b. Elizabeth, N.J., Jan. 8, 1955; d. Stanley Anthony and Lillian (Morofsky) B. BS in Speech, Northwestern U., 1976, MFA in Film, 1980. Filmmaker Dept. Edn., New Brunswick, N.J., 1980-81, Audio-Visual Aids Commn., New Brunswick, 1981; asst. prof. Northwestern U., Evanston, Ill., 1981-82, Southern Ill. U., Carbondale, 1982—; vis. lectr. U. Ill., Chgo., 1981-82; negative matcher My Sister's Cutting Room, Chgo., 1977; videographer, editor Norlin Music Co., Lincolnwood, Ill., 1979; asst. dir., Projected Backgrounds Prodns., N.Y.C., 1980; dir. photography Displaced Homemakers, Carbondale, 1984. Producer, writer, dir. films: Zurke, 1980 (Sinking Creek Film Celebration award, Greenville, Tenn. 1980), Stash (on Photography), 1980 (Sinking Creek Film Celebration award, 1980), Distant Music, 1982 (Ill. Filmmakers award 1983), One For Every Month, 1986 (Golden Athena award 1986). Mem. Univ. Film and Video Assn. (bd. dirs. 1986—), Am. Film Inst., Soc. for Cinema Studies, Modern Lang. Assn. Democrat. Roman Catholic. Avocations: travel, hiking, canoeing. Home: 315 N Westridge Dr Carbondale IL 62901 Office: So Ill Univ Dept Cinema and Photography Carbondale IL 62901

BORYC, NICHOLAS MICHAEL, transportation company executive; b. Waukegan, Ill., Oct. 30, 1952; s. Louis J. and Cecile D. B.; B. Applied Scis. with honors, Western Ill. U., 1975; m. Mary C. Rushforth, Nov. 12, 1977; 1 child, Sarah Anne Agnes. Sales rep. Roadway Express Inc., Chgo., 1976-78, mgr. terminal, 1979-82; pres., account mgr. Consol. Freightways, McCook, Ill., 1982-87; sales mgr. Consol. Freightways Truckload Services, Des Plaines, Ill., 1987—. Active Boy Scouts Am. Mem. Better Govt. Assn. Home: 112 Woodstock St Clarendon Hills IL 60514 Office: Consol Freightways Truckload Services 2340 Des Plaines Ave Des Plaines IL 60016

BORYSEWICZ, MARY LOUISE, editor; b. Chgo.; d. Thomas J. and Mabel E. (Zeien) O'Farrell; B.A., Mundelein Coll., 1970; postgrad. in English lit. U. Ill, 1970-71; grad. exec. program U. Chgo., 1982; m. Daniel S. Borysewicz, June 11, 1955; children—Mary Adele, Stephen Francis, Paul Barnabas. Tchr. advanced level English for fgn.-speaking adults Evanston Twp. (Ill.) High Sch., 1969-71; editor sci. publs. AMA, Chgo., 1971-73; exec. mng. editor Am. Jour. Ophthalmology, Chgo., 1973—; asst. sec., treas Ophthalmic Pub. Co., 1985—; guest lectr. U. Chgo. Med. Sch., 1979, Harvard U. Med. Sch., 1978, Northwestern U. Med. Sch., 1979, Am. Acad. Ophthalmology, 1976, 81. Mem. Am. Soc. Profl. and Exec. Women, Council Biology Editors (fin. com. 1985—), Internat. Fedn. Sci. Editors Assns. Contbr. articles to sci. publs.; editor: Ophthalmology Principles and Concepts, 6th edit., 1986. Home: 4415 N California Ave Chicago IL 60625 Office: 435 N Michigan Ave Chicago IL 60611

BOS, CAROLE DIANNE, lawyer; b. Grand Rapids, Mich., May 31, 1949; d. James and Alberdean (Kooiker) Berkenpas; m. James Edwin Bos, Apr. 3, 1969; B.A. with high honors, Grand Valley State Coll., 1977; J.D. cum laude, T.M. Cooley Law Sch., Lansing, Mich., 1981. Bar: Mich. 1981. Asst. mgr. Army & Air Force Base Exchange, Soesterberg, Netherlands, 1969-73; mgmt. asst. Selfridge Air Nat. Guard Base, Mt. Clemens, Mich., 1973-74; legal asst. John Boyles, Grand Rapids, 1974-77; law clk. Cholette, Perkins & Buchanan, Grand Rapids, 1977-82; trial atty. Hecht, Buchanan & Cheney, Grand Rapids, 1982-84; ptnr. Buchanan & Bos, Grand Rapids, 1984—; mem. adv. bd. Grand Valley State Coll., 1981—. Co-author: Video Techniques in Trial and Pretrial, 1983, Video Technology: Its Use and Application in Law, 1984, How to Use Video in Litigation, 1986, (contbg. author) Women Trial Lawyers: How They Succeed in Practice and in the Courtroom, 1986; contbr. articles to profl. jours. Bd. dirs. Jellema Ho., Grand Rapids; trustee Grand Valley State Coll. Found. Breen scholar, 1977. Mem. Grand Rapids Bar Assn. (library com. 1983—), Mich. State Bar Assn. (communications com. 1983—), ABA, Fed. Bar Assn. (regional dir. 1984—), Am. Trial Lawyers Assn. Office: Buchanan & Bos 6th Floor Frey Bldg Grand Rapids MI 49503

BOSCH, ANN ENGEL, county extension agent; b. Mpls., Dec. 1, 1938; d. Fred James and Hazel Anjie (Slough) Engel; m. Evan R. Bosch, Nov. 24, 1963 (dec. 1980); 1 child, Mark Lee. BS, U. Minn., 1960, MEd, 1987. County extension agt. Agrl. Extension Service, Willmar, Minn., 1962-84, dist. program cons., 1984-85; county extension agt. Minn. Extension Service, Willmar, 1986—. Recipient Disting. Faculty award U. Minn., 1983. Mem. Am. Home Econ. Assn. (dist. pres. Minn. chpt. 1974), Nat. Assn. Extension Home Economists (sec. Minn. chpt. 1978, pres. Minn. chpt. 1982), Minn. Hort. Soc., Epsilon Sigma Phi (pres. Pi chpt. 1987). Methodist. Avocations: raising cats, reading, traveling. Home: Rt 1 Box 116 Atwater MN 56209 Office: County Extension Service Box 977 Willmar MN 56201

BOSCH, JOHN ALBERT, manufacturing executive, consultant; b. Buffalo, Mar. 14, 1929; s. Carl Edwin and Elizabeth (Babson) B.; m. Marna Eline Kunstmann, July 10, 1954; children: Corinne Ida, Carl Martin, Kenneth Paul, Christopher John. BS in Agrl. Engring., Pa. State U., 1951. Dir. engring., gen. mgr. Gen. Electric, Lynn, Mass. and Binghamton, N.Y., 1953-82; v.p., gen. mgr. Sheffield Measurement, Dayton, Ohio, 1982—; chmn. Nat. Research Council Panel for Evaluation of Nat. Bur. of Standard Programs; chmn., chief exec. officer Commander Aero Inc., Xenia, Ohio, 1985—. Editor 66 Centuries of Measurement, 1984. Group chmn. United Way, Dayton, 1986; vice chmn. Joint Labor Mgmt. Council, 1986. Served to 1st lt. USAF, 1951-53. Fellow Am. Soc. Aerospace Engring. (assoc.); mem. IEEE (sr.), Soc. Automotive Engrs. (sr.), Soc. Mfg. Engrs. (sr.). Lodge: Rotary. Avocation: piloting.

BOSCHWITZ, RUDY, U.S. senator; b. Berlin, 1930; m. Ellen; children: Gerry, Ken, Dan, Tom. Student, Johns Hopkins U., 1947-49; B.S. in Bus, N.Y. U., 1950, LL.B., 1953. Bar: N.Y. State bar 1954, Wis. bar 1959. Founder, owner, operator Plywood Minnesota (do-it-yourself bldg. materials chain), 1963—; mem. U.S. Senate from Minn., 1979—; Del. Minn. Republican Conv., 1968-78, Republican Nat. Conv., 1972-76. State chmn. Am. Cancer Soc.; state chmn. Minn. Mental Health Assn., Minn. Kidney Found., Lubavitch House, St. Paul. Served with Signal Corps U.S. Army, 1954-55. Office: 506 Hart Senate Bldg Washington DC 20510 *

BOSCIA, JON ANDREW, financial services company executive; b. Pitts., Apr. 15, 1952; s. Louis C. and Stella (Weryha) B.; m. Donna M. Lowar, Aug. 18, 1973; children: Nicole Marie, Brandon Jon. BA, Point Park Coll., 1973; MBA, Duquesne U., 1979. Corp. planner Consolidated Nat. Gas, Pitts., 1974-79; fin. sales rep. Westinghouse, Pitts., 1979-80; asst. v.p. Mellon Bank, Pitts., 1980-83; sr. v.p. Lincoln Nat. Pension, Ft. Wayne, Ind., 1983—; sr. v.p. Lincoln Nat. Life, Ft. Wayne, 1984—; bd. dirs. Lincoln Nat. Investment Mgmt. Co., Ft. Wayne, 1985—. Contbr. articles to profl. jours. Mem. coms. Pitts. Bd. Edn., 1974-79; chmn. coms. Arlington Park, Ft. Wayne, 1983-86; mem. START program Ft. Wayne Community Schs., 1985. PPC Found. scholar, 1973. Mem. Nat. Assn. Bus. Economists, Planning Forum. Democrat. Methodist. Avocations: jogging, racquetball, playing drums, swimming, reading. Home: 5005 Litchfield Rd Fort Wayne IN 46835 Office: Lincoln Nat Pension Ins Co 1300 S Clinton PO Box 1110 Fort Wayne IN 46801

BOSCO, ANTHONY FRANK, sales executive, consultant; b. Bay City, Mich., July 17, 1943; s. Frank Carl and Jeanette Elizabeth (Frontiera) B.; m. Connie Jo Marie Billow, Apr. 22, 1967; children: Lisa Marie, Amy Sue, Toni Anne. Assoc. in Bus., Delta Coll., 1967; BBA, Western Mich. U., 1969; postgrad., Saginaw Valley Coll., 1979, Murray State U., 1980. Security officer USAF, Pope AFB, N.C., 1962-66; mgr. Wickes Lumber, Saginaw, Mich., 1966-83; nat. sales mgr. Wolohan Lumber, Saginaw, 1983—; mem. exec. com. Component Mfg., St. Louis, 1976-80. Author: Trusses Make Sense, 1978, Take 5, 1979. Dem. precinct del., Saginaw, Mich., 1979; pilot CAP, Selfredge AFB, Mich., 1972-74. Served to sgt. USAF, 1962-66. Named one of Outstanding Young Men of Am., U.S. Jaycees, 1980-81, Jaycess Internat. Senator, U.S. Jaycees, 1980. Roman Catholic. Lodge: Sons of Italy. Avocations: golfing, tennis, jogging, raising horses, private piloting. Home: 12068 Sanders Dr Freeland MI 48623 Office: Wolohan Lumber 1740 Midland Rd Saginaw MI 48603

BOSCO, JAY WILLIAM, optometrist; b. Bay City, Mich., May 6, 1951; s. Frank Carl and Jeanette (Frontiera) B.; m. Mary Lou Roth, Jan. 22, 1972; children: Angela, Jason, Andrea. BS, Saginaw Valley State Coll., 1977; OD, Ill. Coll. Optometry, 1982. Pvt. practice optometry Bay City, Mich., 1982-83; dir. vision care services Group Health Service of Mich., Saginaw, 1983—. Served with USAF, 1969-73. Mem. Am. Optometric Assn., Mich. Optometric Assn., Beta Sigma Kappa. Roman Catholic. Lodge: Lions (chmn. Site-Mobile, Bay City, 1984—). Home: 1382 N Wagner Rd Essexville MI 48732 Office: Group Health Service 4200 Fashion Sq Blvd Saginaw MI 48603

BOSCO, JOSEPH ANTHONY, lawyer; b. River Forest, Ill., Nov. 26, 1957; s. Anthony J. Bosco; m. Ileana M. Guardia. BA, U. Notre Dame, 1979; JD, U. Loyola, Chgo., 1982; LLM, McGill U., Montreal, Que., Can., 1986. Bar: Ill. 1983. Assoc. John J. Kennelly & Assocs., Chgo., 1983—. Contbr. articles to profl. jours. Mem. ABA, Ill. State Bar Assn., Chgo. Bar Assn., Assn. Trial Lawyers Am., Inst. Air & Space Law Assn. Home: 1019 Bonnie Brae River Forest IL 60305 Office: John J Kennelly & Assocs 111 W Washington St Suite 1449 Chicago IL 60602

BOSEKER, BARBARA JEAN, educator; b. Milw., Dec. 2, 1944; d. Edward Herbert and Alice Margaret (Maas) B.; student U. Nigeria, Nsukka, 1966; B.S. (hon.) in Secondary Edn. (Elks Nat. and State Youth scholar), U. Wis., Milw., 1968; M.A. in Anthropology (Ford Found. fellow 1968-69, NDEA fellow 1970-71), U. Wis., Madison, 1971, Ph.D. in Edn. (NDEA fellow), 1978; m. Dale Leslie Sutcliffe, Aug. 8, 1975. Chemistry lab. technician Allen-Bradley Corp., Milw., 1963; coordinator Neighborhood Youth Corps, Madison, 1970; program devel. specialist Tchr. Corps, Madison, 1976-77; asst. prof. edn. Occidental Coll., 1978-80, Moorhead State U., 1980-86, assoc. prof., 1986—; cons. Inst. Latin Am. Studies, U. Tex., Austin, 1980. Grant writer Fargo-Moorhead (N.D.) Indian Center, 1980. Cert. intermediate and secondary English tchr., Wis. Mem. NEA, Minn. Edn. Assn., Am. Assn. Colls. Tchr. Edn., Mortar Bd., Phi Kappa Phi, Pi Lambda Theta, Kappa Delta Pi, Sigma Tau Delta, Sigma Epsilon Sigma. Democrat. Christian Scientist. Contbr. articles to profl. jours. Home: 809 19th Ave S Fargo ND 58103 Office: Moorhead State U Moorhead MN 56560

BOSHINSKI, DEBRA LYNNE, optometrist; b. Lansing, Mich., May 13, 1958; s. Gordon L. and Charlene Anne (Jaques) Shelts; m. William E. Boshinski, Aug. 27, 1983; 1 child, Joseph William. OD, Ohio State U., 1983. Pvt. practice optometry Reynoldsburg, Ohio, 1983-84; optometrist Boshinski & Boshinski, Dayton, Ohio, 1984-86; clin. assoc. Ohio State U. Coll. Optometry, Columbus, 1983-84; vision cons. Miami Valley Child Devel. Ctrs., Northmont Twp. and Harrison Twp. Lions' Clubs, 1984—. Tchr. Catholic Religious Edn., Englewood, Ohio, 1985-86. Mem. Am. Optometric Assn., Ohio Optometric Assn. (asst. zone gov. 1986—). Home: 506 Rohr Ln Englewood OH 45322 Office: 8141 N Main St Dayton OH 45415

BOSILJEVAC, JOSEPH EDWARD, surgeon; b. Omaha, Oct. 21, 1951; s. Joseph Edward Sr. and Dolores Mary (Duracinski) B.; m. Cheryl Lucille Black, May 25, 1975; children: Corbin Joseph, Tyler John, Kristin Lee. BS, Emporia (Kans.) U., 1972; MD, U. Kans., Kansas City, 1975. Diplomate Am. Bd. Gen. Surgery; cert. Nat. Bd. Med. Examiners. Intern Charity Hosp., New Orleans, 1975-76; resident in gen. surgery Wesley Med. Ctr., Wichita, Kans. 1976-81; gen. and vascular surgeon St. Mary's Hosp. and Newman Meml. County Hosp., Emproia, 1981—; chmn. exec. com. St. Mary's Hosp. and Newman Meml. County Hosp., 1983, also mem. various hosp. coms.; sec., treas. Newman Meml. County Hosp., 1986. Contbr. numerous articles to profl. jours. v.p. Flint Hills chpt. Am. Hearth Assn., 1982, pres., 1983-86; dep. coroner Lyon County, Emporia, 1984—. Fellow ACS (field liaison cancer commn.); mem. AMA, Flint Hills Med. Soc., Kans. State Med. Soc., Emporia C. of C., Alpha Omega Alpha. Republican. Roman Catholic. Avocations: astronomy, traveling. Home: 1530 Berkeley Emporia KS 66801 Office: 2522 W 15th Emporia KS 66801

BOSLAUGH, LESLIE, judge; b. Hastings, Nebr., Sept. 4, 1917; s. Paul E. and Ann (Herzog) B.; m. Elizabeth F. Meyer, Aug. 10, 1943; children: Marguerite Ann, Sarah Elizabeth, Paul Robert. B.B.A., U. Nebr., 1939, LL.B., 1941. Bar: Nebr. bar 1941. Mem. staff Nebr. Statute Revision Commn., 1941-43; pvt. practice law Hastings, 1946-47; asst. atty. gen. Nebr., 1947-48; mem. firm Stiner & Boslaugh, Hastings, 1949-60; judge Nebr. Supreme Ct., Lincoln, 1961—. Served to lt. AUS, 1943-46. Mem. Nebr. Bar Assn., Am. Judicature Soc., Inst. Jud. Adminstrn., Appellate Judges Conf., Order of Coif. Office: Supreme Court Box 4638 Lincoln NE 68509 *

BOSS, PAULINE GROSSENBACHER, family social science educator, researcher; b. New Glarus, Wis., July 11, 1934; children: David, Ann Marie. BS, U. Wis., 1956, MS, 1971, PhD, 1975. Pvt. practice family therapy New Glarus, Madison and St. Paul, 1976—; asst. prof. U. Wis., Madison, 1975-80, assoc. prof., 1980-81; assoc. prof. U. Minn., St. Paul, 1981-85, prof., 1986—; lectr., key note speaker, numerous colls. and orgns., 1978—; adj. prof. Family Study Ctr., Mpls., 1982—; cons. on family stress U.S. Army, 1982—. Author various book reviews; editor: (with others) The Father's Role in Family Systems: An Annotated Bibliography, 1976, Family Stress, 1980, Family Stress Management Sage, 1987; assoc. editor numerous profl. jours.; contbr. numerous articles to profl. jours. Mem. priorities com. United Way, Mpls. and St. Paul, 1981-82; mem. com. on Use of Human Subjects in Research, U. Minn., 1981—, chmn. behavioral research com., 1982—; chmn. bd. Ctr. Early Edn. and Devel., U. Minn., 1984—. Recipient numerous grants for family sociology research, 1974—. Fellow Am. Assn. Marriage and Family Therapists (chair research com. 1981-82, supr. 1984), Am. Orthopsychiat. Assn.; mem. Internat. Sociol. Assn. (family research com.), Nat. Council Family Relations (chair various coms. 1976-84, bd. dirs 1979-81, program chair 1984—), Groves Conf. Marriage and the Family (bd. dirs. 1981-84, nat. pres. 1984—), Am. Sociol. Assn., Am. Home Econs. Assn., Am. Family Therapy Assn. (charter), Minn. Assn. Marital and Family Therapists, Minn. Council on Family Relations, Minn. Home Econs. Assn., Wis. Home Econs. Assn. (Disting. Alumna award 1979), Phi Upsilon Omicron, Omicron Nu. Home: 1586 Burton Saint Paul MN 55108 Office: U Minn Family Social Sci 290 McNeal Hall 1985 Burford Saint Paul MN 55108

BOSSE, JOSEPH BERNARD, insurance company executive, real estate developer; b. St. Louis, Jan. 6, 1950; s. Joseph F. and Lucille (Falbe) B.; m. Sandra N. Maloney, Apr. 27, 1974; children: Joseph J., John J. BA in Personnel Mgmt., Northwestern Mo. State U., 1972; MBA in Fin., St. Louis U., 1975. Rep. mktg. Royal Ins. Co., St. Louis, 1972-76; pres. Noonan East-Cen. Ins. Agy., Pacific, Mo., 1976—; v.p. Kingsley Devel. Co., St. Clair, Mo., 1987—. Roman Catholic. Home: 9838 Sunset Green Saint Louis MO 63127 Office: Noonan East Cen Ins Agy PO Box 478 Saint Louis MO 63069

BOSSE, PETER ALAN, food service executive; b. Muskegon, Mich., Oct. 30, 1960; s. Albert Henry and Lorraine (Cowles) B.; m. Jeanne E. Ainslie, Oct. 2, 1982; 1 child, Robert Andrew. BA, Mich. State U., 1984; MBA, U. Mich., 1986. Asst. mktg. mgr. Pizza Hut, Inc., Wichita, Kans., 1986—. Served with U.S. Army, 1980-82, 1stlt. Res. Mem. Res. Officers Assn. Republican. Home: 320 N Rutan Wichita KS 67208 Office: Pizza Hut Inc 9111 E Douglas Wichita KS 67201

BOSSIO, ALAN JOHN, accountant, consultant; b. Dearborn, Mich., Aug. 12, 1956; s. Patrick and Ida (Provenzano) B. BBA, U. Mich., 1978; MST, Walsh Coll., 1982. CPA, Mich. Pvt. practice acctg. Farmington Hills, Mich., 1982—; cons. in field. Home: 6687 Lakeview Blvd Apt 6311 Westland MI 48185 Office: 31807 Middlebelt Rd Suite 103 Farmington Hills MI 48018

BOSTIAN, HARRY EDWARD, chemical engineer; b. Lewisburg, Pa., Jan. 16, 1933; s. Harry Edward Sr. and Florence Anne (Musser) B.; m. Marion E. Maurer, July 30, 1955. BS, Bucknell U., 1954; M in Chem. Engring., Rensselaer Poly. Inst., 1956; PhD, Iowa State U., 1959. Registered profl. engr., N.J. Asst. prof. U. N.H., Durham, 1959-61; engr. Exxon Research, Baton Rouge and Florham Park, N.J., 1961-65; assoc. prof. U. Miss., Oxford, 1965-70; chem. engr., research program mgr. U.S. EPA, Cin., 1970—. Contbr. articles to profl. jours. NSF grantee, 1969-70, U.S. Dept. Agr. grantee, 1969-70. Mem. Am. Inst. Chem. Engrs., AAAS, Water Pollution Control Fedn., Sigma Xi, Tau Beta Pi, Alpha Chi Sigma. Home: 6001 Bagdad Dr Cincinnati OH 45230 Office: US EPA Cincinnati OH 45268

BOSTICK, TRUDY ANN, mathematics and computer science educator, consultant; b. Portsmouth, Ohio, Oct. 3, 1951; d. Floyd Kenneth and Mary Alice (Jackson) B. BS in Math. and Computers cum laude, Ohio U., 1972; postgrad., Ohio State U., 1977; MS in Math. and Computers cum laude, Wright State U., Dayton, Ohio, 1977; postgrad., Ohio U., 1982-83; postgrad. in computer sci. edn., Nova U., Ft. Lauderdale, Fla., 1983—. Cert. elem. and secondary tchr., Ohio. Math. instr. Northwest Local Schs., Lucasville, Ohio, 1972-82; math. instr. for blind and handicapped Wright State U., 1976-77; math. and data processing instr. Shawnee State U., Portsmouth, Ohio, 1977—; math., computer sci. and math edn. instr. Ohio U., 1983—; computer sci. instr. for the gifted Continuing Edn., Shawnee State U., 1981—; software critical advisor various orgns., 1982—; pres., chief programmer, statis. cons. Scioto Software Systems, Inc., South Webster, Ohio, 1983—; computer sci. educator Community Action Orgn., Portsmouth, 1983—. Author: (novel) The Oval Mirror, 1982; (computer programs) The Inventory Wizard, 1983, The Questionnaire, 1985; contbr. articles on math. and computers to mags. Mem., jr. leader Scioto County 4-H Club, 1959-69, leader, mem. bd., officer, 1969—. Recipient numerous Ednl. Excellence awards Gov. of Ohio, 1977, Automobile Assn. Am. of So. Ohio, 1973-83, Ohio Ho. of Reps., 1981, 82, U.S. Congress, 1982. Mem. NEA, Ohio Edn. Assn., Scioto County Edn. Assn., Nat. Council Tchrs. Math., Ohio Council Tchrs. Math., Am. Math. Assn., Math. Assn. Am., Ednl. Computer Consortium of Ohio, Ohio's Women's Caucus, AAUW, Bus. and Profl. Women, Bloom Local Alumni Assn. (electronic media sec. 1969—). Democrat. Methodist. Avocations: writing, graphic art, literature, gourmet cooking, playing Jeopardy. Home: 12 W Main St South Webster OH 45682-0165 Office: Shawnee State U 904 Second St Portsmouth OH 45662

BOSTON, DONALD STEPHEN, JR., chemical company executive; b. Chgo., Feb. 26, 1943; s. Donald S. and Beverly (Hasbrook) B.; m. Lynn P. Assenheimer, Sept. 7, 1969; children: Cynthia L., Lori A., Marc W. BSBA in Acctg., Eastern Ill. U., 1964; MBA in Fin., Mich. State U., 1971. CPA, Ohio. Staff acct. Price Waterhouse & Co., Chgo., 1964-68; internal audit mgr. Blount, Inc., Montgomery, Ala., 1971-74; controller Ashland (Ky.) Coal, Inc., 1974-78; asst. controller Ashland Oil, Inc., 1978-83; adminstv. v.p. Ashland Chem. Co., Columbus, Ohio, 1983—; bd. dirs. Dublin (Ohio) Fund, 1983—. Served to cpl. USMC, 1969-70. Mem. Am. Inst. CPA's, Ohio Soc. CPA's, Fin. Execs. Inst. Republican. Methodist. Club: Muirfield Country. Home: 8573 Crail Ct Dublin OH 43017 Office: Ashland Chem Co PO Box 2219 Columbus OH 43216

BOSWELL, HENRY OLIVER, oil company executive; b. Corsicana, Tex., June 13, 1929; s. Henry Oliver and Opal B.; m. Jean Sylvia Wirtz, Sept. 4, 1954; children: Henry Oliver, Laura Jean Boswell Schulze, Diane Elizabeth Boswell McGowen, Mary Gail. B.S. in Petroleum Engring., U. Houston, 1954; grad. advanced mgmt. program, U. Western Ont. Sch. Bus., Can., 1969. Engr. Stanolind Oil & Gas Co., Houston and Lake Charles, La., 1953-57; engring. supr. Pan Am. Petroleum Corp., New Orleans, Tulsa, Houston and Beaumont,, Tex., 1957-70; v.p.-prodn. Amoco Can., Calgary, Alta., 1970-73, pres., 1973-75; v.p.-prodn. Amoco Internat. Oil Co., Chgo., 1975-78; v.p.-Africa and Middle East Amoco Internat. Oil Co., Houston, 1978-79, exec. v.p., 1979-81; pres.-internat. Amoco Prodn. Co., Chgo., 1981-83, pres., 1983—; dir. Amoco Corp.; bd. dirs. ServiceMaster Industries, Inc. Bd. dirs. Central DuPage Hosp., Naperville, 1983; trustee Am. U. in Cairo, 1985—. Served as 2d lt. U.S. Army, 1946-48. Mem. Am. Petroleum Inst., Soc. Petroleum Engrs., Nat. Ocean Industries Assn. (dir. 1984—), 25-Yr. Club Petroleum Industry. Republican. Baptist. Clubs: Mid-America, Chicago (Chgo.); Petroleum (Houston). Office: Amoco Prodn Co 200 E Randolph Dr Chicago IL 60601 *

BOSWELL, JOHN ANDREW, programmer; b. Manitowoc, Jan. 13, 1954; s. John Andrew and June Ann (Reibe) B.; m. Cathy Anderson, May 21, 1977 (div. Dec. 1983); 1 child, Jason Allen; m. Lynne Susan Emard-Boswell, June 23, 1985. Grad., Milw. Bus. Tng. Inst., 1973. Data processing mgr. Checker Express Trucking, Milw., 1973-77; programmer analyst Bordens Inc., Milw., 1977-78, Milw. Valve Co., Milw., 1978-82; lead programmer Am. Soc. Quality Control, Milw., 1982—. Mem. Systems 38 Users Group. Club: Wis. Jaguars Ltd. (Milw.) (treas. 1985—, bd. dirs. 1986—). Home: 3957 S Lake Dr Saint Francis WI 53207 Office: Am Soc Quality Control 310 W Wisconsin Ave Milwaukee WI 53203

BOSWELL, MICHAEL DEAN, industrial systems executive; b. Auburn, Ind., Mar. 17, 1956; s. Willis Eugene and Loretta Jean (Watkins) B.; m. Joyce Ann Vanderpool, Sept. 11, 1982; children: Erik Christopher, Jaime Meredith. BS in Bus. Mgmt., Ind U., 1978. Sales rep. Hefner Chevrolet, Ft. Wayne, Ind., 1978, Mid-City Typewriter, Auburn, 1978-79; gen. mgr. Mid-City Office Systems, Auburn, 1979-82, pres., 1982—. Bus. cons. Project Bus., Ft. Wayne, 1985-87; treas. Auburn Park Bd., 1987. Mem. Nat. Office Machine Dealers Assn. (bd. dirs. 1984-86), Ind. Office Machine Dealers Assn. (pres. 1984-85), Auburn C. of C. (dir. 1985—). Republican. Club: Ind. U. Alumni. Lodges: Lions, Elks. Home: 1004 Nicholas St Auburn IN 46706 Office: Mid City Office Systems Inc 138 E 7th St Auburn IN 46706

BOSWELL, NATHALIE SPENCE, speech pathologist; b. Cleve., May 9, 1924; d. Harrison Morton and Nathalie Muriel (Clem) Spence; student Skidmore Coll, 1941-42; Mus.B. in Edn., Northwestern U., 1945; M.A., Western Res. U., 1961; m. June 15, 1946; children—Louis Keith, Donna Spence, Deborah Anne. Speech therapist Highland View Hosp., Cleve., 1961-64; speech pathologist Cleve. VA Hosp., 1964—; chmn. Equal Employment Opportunity Counselors, 1969-74, Fed. Women Speakers Bur., 1968—, Fed. Career Info. Program, 1970-72, Fed. Coll. Relations Council, 1970-74, Fed. Exec. Bd., 1972-73; adj. instr. Case Western Res. U., 1982—; mem. adv. council sch. electromedicine scis., City U. Los Angeles, 1985; mem. adv. bd. Nat. Inst. Electromedicine Info., 1985. Mem. Cleve. Orch. Chorus, 1969-82; vol. Seamen's Service, 1976—; patron Police Athletic League. Endowed Tuba Chair, Cleve. Orch., 1983. Recipient Performance award Equal Employment Opportunities, 1973; Quality Increase award, 1980; others; lic. speech pathologist, Ohio. Mem. Am. Speech and Hearing Assn. (cert. clin. competence), Ohio Speech and Hearing Assn., Aphasiology Assn. Ohio, Chi Omega Alumni Assn., Musical Arts Assn., Western Res. Hist. Soc., Cleve. Mus. Natural History, Cleve. Mus. Art, Smithsonian Assos., Nat. Wildlife Fedn., Audubon Soc., Nat. Trust Hist. Preservation, Am. Heritage Soc. Mem. Ch. Reorganized Latter-Day Saints. Author: Guidelines for EEO Counselors in their Training Program, 1973; prin. author: Laryngectomy-Orientation for Patients and Families, 1981; asst. editor: Am. Jour. Electromedicine, 1984. Home: 2946 Berkshire Rd Cleveland Heights OH 44118 Office: 10701 East Blvd Cleveland OH 44106

BOSWELL, ROBERT BOWEN, automobile company executive; b. Washington, Feb. 14, 1920; s. Roscoe Conkling and Ida Blanche (Fowler) B.; B.S. in Metall. Engring., U. Mich., 1942; m. Ruth Ione Capron, Aug. 16, 1942; children—Robert Capron, James Russell, John Richard. Research metallurgist Chrysler Corp., Highland Park, Mich., 1946-50, chief metallurgist Tank Engine div., New Orleans, 1951-54, chief engr. Forge and Foundry div., Highland Park, 1955-60, mgr. product engring. various mfg. divs., Detroit, 1961-75, mgr. material cost analysis, Highland Park, 1975-80, mgr. chassis cost analysis, 1980-82, program mgr. Mich. div. Barnes & Reinecke, Inc., Madison Heights, 1982-86; tech. writer Chrysler Corp., Highland Park, 1986—; evening sch. instr. Wayne State U., 1948-51. Served to lt. Ordnance, USNR, 1942-45. Mem. Am. Soc. Metals (chmn. Detroit chpt. 1961-62), Soc. Automotive Engrs. (governing bd. Detroit sect. 1964-66). Republican. Presbyterian. Club: C.I.T. (Detroit) Contbr. articles trade jours. Patentee in field. Home: 2743 Woodward Ave Apt A Bloomfield Hills MI 48013 Office: Chrysler Corp PO Box 1118 Detroit MI 48288

BOSWORTH, JEFFREY WILLSON, insurance company executive, computer systems specialist; b. Sayre, Pa., Dec. 5, 1948; s. Joseph Reinhart and Jean Margaret (Willson) B.; m. Anne Marie Bollinger, May 29, 1982. Student, Pa. State U., 1966-68; AA in Communications, Harrisburg Area Community Coll., 1973; BS in Pub. Communications, Syracuse U., 1975. Mktg. rep. Ins. Co. N.Am., Lemoyne, Pa., 1978-80; comml. underwriter Nationwide Ins. Co., Syracuse, N.Y., 1975-78; systems analyst Nationwide Ins. Co., Columbus, Ohio, 1980-83, office mgr., fin. analyst, 1983-84, spl. projects analyst, 1984-85, systems programming mgr., 1985—; cons. computer programming, Columbus, 1983—. Author: (software product) PCSecure, 1986. Mem. Civic Action Program, Columbus, 1980—. Served with USN, 1968-72. Mem. Columbus Astron. Assn., Am. Mgmt. Soc., Planetary Soc., Phi Kappa Phi. Republican. Avocations: sailing, computers, astronomy. Office: Nationwide Ins Co 1 Nationwide Plaza Columbus OH 43216

BOSWORTH, MICHAEL FRANCIS, physician, osteopath, educator; b. Scranton, Pa., Oct. 31, 1950; s. Frank M. and Rosemary (Garvey) B.; m. June Tigue, June 23, 1973. BS, U. Scranton, 1972; DO, Coll. Osteo. Medicine and Surgery, 1975. Intern then resident Wright AFB Hosp, Ohio, 1975-78, mem. faculty, 1978-79; dir. dept. osteo. Wright Patt AFB Hosp, Ohio, 1978-79; assoc. dir. dept. family practice St. Eliz Hosp., Dayton, Ohio, 1979-80; dir. family practice residency program Good Samaritan Hosp., Dayton, 1985—; asst. prof. dept. family practice Wright State U. Sch. Medicine, Dayton, 1981—. Contbr. articles to profl. jours. Served to maj. USAF, 1975-80. Fellow Am. Acad. Family Practice; mem. Am. Osteo. Assn., Soc. Tchrs. Family Medicine, Ohio Acad. Family Practice. Roman Catholic. Avocations: reading, golf. Home: 1339 Woodland Greens Springboro OH 45066 Office: Family Practice Program Good Samaritan Hosp 2157 Benson Dr Dayton OH 45406

BOSWORTH, PAUL RAYMOND, health care company executive; b. Phila., June 22, 1937; s. Harry J. and Edith E. (Moore) B.; m. Maria M. Cozanitis, Sept. 2, 1960; children: P. Craig, Scott C., Timothy A., Michael A. BSEE, U. Pa., 1960; MS in Ops. Analysis, Navy Postgrad. Sch., 1974. Commd. USN, 1960, advanced through grades to comdr.; dir. ops. naval supply system command USN, Arlington, Va., 1974-77; dir. planning mil. transp. mgmt. command USN, Alexandria, Va., 1977-79; comdg. officer regional fin. ctr. USN, Great Lakes, Ill., 1979-80; ret. USN, 1980; dep. controller ops. City of Chgo., 1980-81; mgr. corp. fin. ops. Baxter Travenol Labs., Deerfield, Ill., 1982-87. Dir. Lake County Marathon, Highland Park, Ill., 1984-87, Simek Meml. Counseling Ctr., Techny, Ill., 1986-87; pres. Greater Libertyville Soccer Assn., 1985-87. Republican. Roman Catholic. Avocation: soccer referee. Home: 919 Warwick Ln Libertyville IL 60048 Office: Baxter Travenol Labs Inc One Baxter Pkwy Deerfield IL 60015

BOTANA, PHILIP CHARLES, aviation service company executive; b. West Hartford, Conn., Mar. 8, 1945; s. Philip Gordon and Florence A. (McKenna) B.; m. Roberta Lee Bellis; children: Philip Aaron, Josh Michael. BSBA, Bryant Coll., Providence, 1968. V.p., gen. mgr. Internat. Aviation Services, White Plains, N.Y., 1973-78, Burlington Northern Airmotive, Mpls., 1978-82; v.p. airport services Van Dusen Air, Mpls., 1982-86; exec. v.p., chief operating officer Exec. Jet Aviation, Columbus, Ohio, 1986—. Served to sgt. USMCR, 1970-76. Mem. Nat. Air Transp. Assn. (bd. dirs. 1981-84, chmn. bd. dirs. 1983), Aircraft Owners and Pilots Assn., Minn. Bus. Pilots Assn. Avocations: skiing, tennis, home improvement, family fun. Office: Exec Jet Aviation PO Box 19707 Columbus OH 43219

BOTHUN, DONALD DEAN, controller; b. Spring Grove, Minn., June 19, 1947; s. Erdman Everett and Marian Eleanor (Wangen) B.; m. Cynthia Jo Hegge, Sept. 2, 1972; children: Kelly Jo, Sara Jo. BA in Acctg., Winona (Minn.) State U., 1976; MBA in Mgmt., Coll. St. Thomas, 1984. CPA, Iowa. Plant acct. Wallace Computer Services, Osage, Iowa, 1976-79; controller Desaulniers & Co, Moline, Ill., 1979-81; asst. controller St. Paul Pioneer Press Dispatch, 1981-84, controller, 1985—. Served with U.S. Army, 1967-69. Mem. Am. Inst. CPA's. Avocations: reading, golf, racquetball, weightlifting. Home: 9020 79th St S Cottage Grove MN 55016 Office: St Paul Pioneer Press Dispatch 345 Cedar St Saint Paul MN 55101

BOTKIN, KERMIT MALCOLM, real estate executive; b. Marion, Ind., Mar. 20, 1950; s. Kermit Abraham and Dorothy Elizabeth (Tyler) B.; m. Deborah Jo Ann Botkin, June 5, 1970 (div. Feb. 1987); children: Kermit Thomas, Greta Elizabeth Ann. Student, Ind. U., 1968-69, Taylor U., 1969-71. Emergency med. technician Marion Gen. Hosp., 1971-73; apprentice embalmer Devine Colonial Mortuary, Marion, 1971-73; property mgr. FCH Services, Inc., Indpls., 1973-78; v.p., ptnr. Triangle Assocs., Inc., Indpls., 1979-87; v.p., dir. property mgmt. Hanover Group, Inc., Indpls., 1987—; trustee Triangle and Assocs. Benefit Trust, Indpls., 1983—. Named to Hon. Order of Ky. Colonels; named one of Outstanding Young Men of Am., 1980. Mem. Nat. Assn. Housing Coops., Midwest Assn. Housing Coops. (speaker), Ind. Council of Coop. Housing, Inst. Real Estate Mgmt., Met. Indpls. Bd. Realtors, Apt. Assn. Ind. (govt. housing subcom.), Fraternal Order of Police. Republican. Presbyterian. Clubs: Big Red. Lodge: Masons. Avocations: swimming, raising small animals. Home: 8750 Royal Meadow Dr Indianapolis IN 46217 Office: Triangle Assocs Inc 8320 Craig St Suite 196 Indianapolis IN 46250

BOTSAS, ELEFTHERIOS NICHOLAS, economics educator; b. Achladine, Greece, Apr. 6, 1931; came to U.S., 1956, naturalized, 1971; s. Nicholas Themistokles and Helen J. (Karabetsos) B.; B.S., U. Detroit, 1960; Ph.D. (grad. fellow 1960-64, Mendelson research fellow 1962, 64), Wayne State U., 1965; m. Chrysoula G. Kyriakou, Dec. 26, 1965; children—Helena G., Nicholas George. Asst. prof. Lafayette Coll., Easton, Pa., 1964-66; asst. prof. Oakland U., Rochester, Mich., 1966-70, assoc. prof., 1970-76, chmn. econs. dept., 1972-78, prof. econs. and mgmt., 1976—; mem. Council of Econ. Advisors Oakland County, Mich., 1966-68. Exec. bd. Am. Hellenic Congress, 1974—, chmn. exec. bd., 1979-80; mem. Diocesan Council, Greek Orthodox Ch. N.Am. and S.Am. Served with Greek Army, 1953-55. Recipient Teaching Excellence award Gold Key Soc., 1981. Mem. Am. Econ. Assn., AAAS, Am. Assn. S.E. European Studies, Mich. Acad. Arts, Letters and Scis., AAUP, Modern Greek Studies Assn., Am. Hellenic Ednl. Progressive Assn. Contbr. writings in field to publs. Home: 2539 Yorkshire Ln Bloomfield Hills MI 48013 Office: Sch Econs and Mgmt Oakland Univ Rochester MI 48063

BOTTARINI, ROBERT THOMAS, accountant; b. San Francisco, Oct. 4, 1945; s. Ambrose Thomas and Catherine Mary (Brady) B.; m. Lois Eileen Kelly, Aug. 14, 1971; children: Anna, Eileen, Elise. BS in Bus., U. Steubenville, 1967; MBA, Ohio U., 1968. Planning specialist Anchor Hocking Corp., Lancaster, Ohio, 1968-70; internal auditor U.S. Shoe Corp., Cin., 1970-71; acct. Chem. Abstract Service, Columbus, Ohio, 1971-76, costs adminstr., 1976-82, cost mgr., 1982-87, mgr. costs and budgets, 1987—. V.p. Southeast Ohio council Camp Fire, Inc., Lancaster, 1985—. Mem. Nat. Assn. Accts. (assoc., dir. membership com. 1982—), Lambda Chi Alpha. Republican. Roman Catholic. Lodge: KC. Avocations: golf, swimming. Home: 8210 W Bowling Green Ln Lancaster OH 43130 Office: Chem Abstracts Service 2540 Olentangy River Rd Columbus OH 43210

BOTTICELLI, MARIE JOHNSON, computing management executive; b. DeKalb County, Ind., July 29, 1940; d. Edward R. Johnson and Emogene (Emrick) Johnson Sowle; m. Stanley Alger, Aug. 1960 (div. 1968); m. James T. Botticelli, Jan. 1971 (div. 1976); 1 child, Jessica Marie. BS, Manchester Coll., 1962; MS, U. Wis.-Milw., 1976. Programmer, tng. coordinator Blue Cross/Blue Shield, Milw., 1967-71; customer support Burroughs Corp., Milw., 1976-81, systems specialist, 1981-84, dist. mktg. support mgr., 1982-84; mgr. tech. services Milw. Pub. Schs., 1984—. Recipient Exemplary Action award Burroughs Corp., 1983-84. Mem. Data Processing Mgmt. Assn., Am. Mgmt. Assn., NOW, Nat. Women's Polit. Caucus, Adminstrv. Women's Assn., Women's Coalition Home: 6107 W Calumet Rd Milwaukee WI 53223 Office: Milwaukee Pub Schs Drawer 10K Milwaukee WI 53210-8210

BOTTKE, DAVID PAUL, dentist; b. Iowa City, Feb. 6, 1956; s. Karl Andrew and LaVerne Eva (Baer) B.; m. Rhonda Jean Ball, Aug. 5, 1978; children: Benjamin David, Brooke Elizabeth. BS, U. Iowa, 1978, DDS, 1982. Gen. practice dentistry Cedar Falls, Iowa, 1982—; cons. Black Hawk County Health Dept. Child Health Clinic, Waterloo, Iowa, 1985—. Recipient Outstanding Achievement award Bd. Oral and Maxillofacial Surgeons, 1982, Wesley Collins Darby award U. Iowa Coll. Dentistry, 1982, 1st Pl., Iowa Press Assn. Mem. ADA, Acad. Gen. Dentistry, Soc. Dentistry for Children, Acad. Sports Dentistry, Sports Car Club Am. Republican. Lutheran. Avocations: jazz drumming, painting, sports car racing. Home: 4025 S Lawn Rd Cedar Falls IA 50613 Office: 3411 Midway Dr Cedar Falls IA 50613

BOTTOM, DALE COYLE, association executive; b. Columbus, Ind., June 25, 1932; s. James Robert and Sarah Lou (Coyle) B.; m. Frances Audrey Wilson, June 6, 1954 (div.); children: Jane Ellen, Steven Dale, Sharon Lynn, Carol Ann. BS, Ball State U., Muncie, Ind., 1954. Admissions counselor Stephens Coll., Columbia, Mo., 1958-61; exec. asst., then staff v.p. Inst. Fin. Edn., Chgo., 1961-67; pres. Inst. Fin. Edn., 1967—; exec. v.p., chief fin. officer U.S. League Savs. Instns., 1985—; chmn., dir. SAF-Systems & Forms Co.; bd. dirs. USL Savs. Instn. Ins. Group, Ltd.; dir., chief fin. officer USL Savs. Ins. Group, Ltd. Chmn. bd. Barrington (Ill.) United Meth. Ch., 1981. Served as officer USAF, 1955-58; to comdr. USNR, 1967-78. Mem. Fin. Mgrs. Soc. (dir.), Savs. Instns. Mktg. Soc. Am., Navy League, Ind. Soc. Chgo. Republican. Clubs: Tavern, Medinah Country, East Bank (Chgo.). Home: 50 E Bellevue Pl #2303 Chicago IL 60611 Office: 111 E Wacker Dr Chicago IL 60601

BOTTUM, CURTIS EDWARD, JR., contractor; b. Ann Arbor, Mich., June 29, 1927; s. Curtis Edward and Gladys Elizabeth (Jarvis) B.; m. Olivia Graye Boyd, Aug. 8, 1953; children: Olivia Lynn, Carolyn Lee. Student, Iowa State Coll., 1944-46; B.S., U. Mich., 1948, M.S., 1949. Registered profl. engr., Mich., Ohio, Utah. Field engr. Townsend & Bottum, Inc., Pa. and Ohio, 1949-52; Ohio Dist. mgr. Townsend & Bottum, Inc., Lorain, 1954-59; v.p. Townsend & Bottum, Inc., Ann Arbor, 1959-67; pres. Townsend & Bottum, Inc., 1968-86, chmn. bd., 1986—; chmn. commn. on creative strategies Eastern Mich. U. Served with USN, 1944-46, 52-54. Recipient Outstanding Alumni Achievement award U. Mich. Coll. Engring., 1984. Mem. Nat. Soc. Profl. Engrs., ASCE, Tau Beta Pi, Phi Kappa Phi. Republican. Congregationalist. Club: Rotary. Home: 1620 Covington Dr Ann Arbor MI 48103 Office: Townsend & Bottum Inc 2245 S State St Ann Arbor MI 48106

BOUCEK, GEORGE WASHINGTON, lawyer; b. Berwyn, Ill., Jan. 11, 1912; s. Frank and Hattie (Horacek) B.; m. Blanche Korecek, Dec. 2, 1942; 1 child, Melinda Kathy. Paralegal cert., Morton Jr. Coll., 1930; LLB, LLD, Chgo. Kent Coll. Law, 1930-33; LHD (hon.), Carroll Coll., 1978. Bar: Ill. 1934, U.S. Dist. Ct. (no. dist.) Ill. 1936. Law clk. to Robert F. Bradburn, Chgo., 1930-33; assoc. Bradburn & Dammann, 1934-37; ptnr. Bradburn, Dammann & Boucek, 1938-59, Bradburn & Boucek, 1960-67; sole practice, Berwyn, Ill., 1967—. Nat. dir. CSA Frat. Life, Berwyn, Ill., 1942-46, 77—; treas. Berwyn Pub. Health Dist., 1958-77; active Boy Scouts Am., 1924—; twp. assessor Berwyn Twp., 1958-77; cemetery care adv. bd. Comptroller of Ill., 1972—. Served as 1st lt. U.S. Army, 1944-46, ETO. Recipient Commendation Ribbon for war crimes duty, London, 1945. Mem. Am. Legion (nat. fin. commn. 1978—, vice chmn. 1983-86, chmn. 1986—), Ill. dept. judge advocate 1979—), Ill. Bar Assn., West Suburban Bar Assn., Bohemian Lawyers Assn., Chgo. Law Inst., Judge Advocates Assn., Twp. Ofcls. Ill. (assoc.), 40 and 8, VFW, Am. Czechoslovak Legion, Sokol Tabor Gymnastic Assn., Bohemian Nat. Cemetery Assn. (gen. counsel 1935—), Unity of Czech Ladies and Men (gen. counsel 1963-77), Czechoslovak Soc. Am. (pres. T.A. Edison chpt. 1942-44, trustee 1944—). Democrat. Lodge: Elks. Home: 1938 Maple Ave Berwyn IL 60402 Office: 6915 W Cermak Rd Berwyn IL 60402

BOUCHARD, THOMAS JOSEPH, JR., psychology educator, researcher; b. Manchester, N.H., Oct. 3, 1937; s. Thomas and Florence (Charest) B.; m. Pauline Marina Proulx, Aug. 13, 1960; children: Elizabeth, Mark. BA, U. Calif., Berkeley, 1963, U. Calif., Berkeley, 1963; PhD, U. Calif., Berkeley, 1966. Asst. prof. U. Calif., Santa Barbara, 1966-69; asst. prof. U. Minn., Mpls., 1969-70, assoc. prof., 1970-73, prof., 1973—, chmn. dept. psychology, 1985—; dir. Minn. Ctr. Twin and Adoption Research, U. Minn., Mpls., 1980—. Assoc. editor Jour. Applied Psychology, 1977-80, Behavior Genetics, 1982-86; contbr. over 60 articles to profl. jours. Served with USAF, 1955-58. Fellow AAAS, Am. Psychol. Assn.; mem. Phi Delta Kappa, Sigma Xi. Home: 901 Dartmouth Pl Minneapolis MN 55414 Office: Univ of Minn Dept of Psychology 75 E River Rd Minneapolis MN 55455

BOUDOULAS, HARISIOS, physician; b. Velvendo-Kozani, Greece, Nov. 3, 1935; married; 2 children. MD, U. Salonica, Greece, 1959. Resident in medicine Red Cross Hosp., Athens, Greece, 1960-61; resident in medicine U. Salonica First Med. Clinic, 1962-64, resident in internal medicine, 1964-66, resident in cardiology, 1967-69, lectr., 1969-70; postgrad. fellow, instr. div. cardiology Ohio State U. Coll. Medicine, Columbus, 1970-73, 75, asst. prof. medicine, 1975-78, assoc. prof., 1978-80, dir. cardiac non-invasive lab., 1978-80, prof. medicine div. cardiology, 1983—, prof. pharmacy, 1984—, dir. cardiovascular research div., 1983-85; prof. medicine div. cardiology Wayne

State U., Detroit, 1980-82, chief clin. cardiovascular research, 1980-82, acting dir. div. cardiology, 1982; chief cardiovascular diagnostic and tng. center VA Med. Ctr., Allen Park, Mich., 1980-83; acting chief sect. cardiology Harper-Grace Hosps., Detroit, 1982; co-dir. Overstreet Teaching and Research Labs. Contbr. numerous articles to med. jours. Named Disting. Research Investigator, Cen. Ohio chpt. Am. Heart Assn., Columbus, 1983. Fellow ACP, Am. Coll. Angiology, Am. Coll. Clin. Pharmacology, Council Clin. Cardiology, Am. Coll. Cardiology; mem. Am. Heart Assn., Greek Heart Assn., Greek Com. Against Hypertension, Central Soc. Clin. Research, Am. Fedn. Clin. Research. Office: Ohio State U Div Cardiology 1655 Upham Dr Columbus OH 43210

BOUDREAU, EDWARD DAVID, JR., physician; b. Hartford, Conn., Nov. 21, 1951; s. Edward David Sr. and Margaret (Murphy) B.; m. Susan Kathleen Giblin, Sept. 17, 1978; children—Kristen, Michael. B.S. in Chemistry, Bates Coll., 1973; D.O., Mich. State U., 1977. Diplomate Am. Bd. Emergency Medicine. Intern Doctors Hosp., Columbus, Ohio; staff physician emergency dept. Point Pleasant Hosp., N.J., 1981-82; dir. emergency dept. Doctors Hosp., Columbus, 1982—, chmn. dept. emergency medicine, 1984-85; chmn. dept. emergency medicine St. Ann's Hosp., Westerville, Ohio, 1986—; asst. clin. prof. preventive medicine Ohio State U., Columbus, 1986. Served to capt. U.S. Army, 1978-81. Dana scholar Bates Coll., 1970. Fellow Am. Coll. Emergency Physicians; mem. Phi Beta Kappa. Roman Catholic. Avocation: sailing catamaran. Home: 5205 Ashford Rd Dublin OH 43017 Office: St Ann's Hosp Emergency Medical 500 Cleveland Ave Westerville OH 43281

BOULANGER, RODNEY EDMUND, energy company executive; b. Detroit, Apr. 4, 1940; m. Nancy Ann Ewigleben, Dec. 29, 1962; children: Brent, Karla, Melissa. BS, Ferris State Coll., Big Rapids, Mich., 1963; MBA, U. Detroit, 1967. Various fin. planning and econ. positions Am. Nat. Resources Co., 1963-78; v.p. system econs. and diversification Am. Natural Service Co., Detroit, 1978-80; v.p. fin. adminstrn ANG Coal Gasification Co., Detroit, 1980-82, v.p., fin. sec., 1983-84; treas., chief fin. officer Gt. Plains Gasification Assocs., Detroit, 1982-84; exec. v.p., chief fin. and adminstrv. officer ANR Pipeline Co., Detroit, 1984-86; pres., chief exec. officer ANG Coal Gasification Co., Bismarck, N.D., 1986—. Mem. Beta Gamma Sigma. Clubs: Detroit Athletic; Duck Lake Country (Albion, Mich.); Apple Creek Country (Bismarck). Office: ANG Coal Gasification Co 401 E Broadway Bismarck ND 58501

BOULGER, WILLIAM CHARLES, lawyer; b. Columbus, Ohio, Apr. 2, 1924; s. James Ignatius and Rebecca (Laughlin) B.; m. Ruth J. Schachtele, Dec. 29, 1954; children—Brigid Carolyn, Ruth Mary. A.B., Harvard Coll., 1948; LL.B., Law Sch. Cin., 1951. Bar: Ohio, 1951, U.S. Dist. Ct. (so. dist.) Ohio 1952, U.S. Supreme Ct. 1957. Ptnr. with Thomas A. Boulger, Chillicothe, Ohio, 1951-73; sole propr. Law Offices of William C. Boulger, Chillicothe, 1974—. Pres. Ross County Welfare Assn., Chillicothe, 1954-60; mem. Chillicothe. ARC, 1958-84, chmn., 1959-63, 1985—; mem. Democratic Exec. Com., Chillicothe, 1950s. Served as pfc. U.S. Army, 1943-45, ETO. Mem. Ross County Bar Assn. (pres. 1971), Ohio Bar Assn., ABA. Roman Catholic. Clubs: Sunset, Symposiarchs (pres.). Avocations: tennis, golf. Home: 31 Club Dr Chillicothe OH 45601 Office: 10-14 Foulke Block Chillicothe OH 45601

BOULIER, RITA MARIE, civic worker; b. Grosse Pointe, Mich., Aug. 9, 1949; d. Henry Joseph and Rita Louise (Ketcheson) Mularski; m. William Arthur Boulier, May 4, 1968; children: William Michael, Michael Thomas. Tax preparer H&R Block, Algonac, Mich., 1977-78, owner, 1978-86; organize community events Algonac, 1986—; speaker in filed; instr. in filed. Chmn. Muscular Dystrophy Assn., 1969-76, vol. Mo. Telethon, 1969-85, organizer mail room. Fellow Lupus Found.; mem. St. Clair County Flood Control (chmn., block capt.),. Roman Catholic. Avocations: helping others, boating. Home: 7225 Flamingo Algonac MI 48001

BOULOS, RIDA WAHBA, obstetrician-gynecologist; b. Sannouris, Egypt, Apr. 29, 1941; came to U.S., 1966; s. Wahba and Labiba (Boctor) B.; m. Barbara Ann Wossidlo, Oct. 9, 1971; children: Jeffery Alexander, Deborah Ann. MB, BCh, Cairo U., 1964; MPH, Johns Hopkins U., 1967. Diplomate Am. Bd. Ob-Gyn; cert. specialist ob-gyn, Que., Can. Rotating intern Cairo U. Sch. Medicine, 1963-64; sr. house officer and registrar various hosps., Eng., 1967-68; rotating intern Reddy Meml. Hosp., Montreal, Can., 1968-69; resident ob-gyn Royal Victoria Hosp. McGill U., Montreal, Que., Can., 1968-72; resident in gen. surgery Ottawa (Ont., Can.) Gen. Hosp., 1972-73; clin. fellow in perinatology Kingston (Ont.) U., 1973-74; practice medicine specializing in ob-gyn, dir. perinatology St. Mary's Hosp., Montreal, 1974-77; practice medicine specializing in ob-gyn North Peoria (Ill.) Ob-Gyn Assocs, 1977—; lectr. McGill U., Royal Victoria Hosp., 1974-77; clin. asst. prof. ob-gyn Peoria Sch. Medicine, U. Ill., 1980—; chmn. dept. ob-gyn Proctor Community Hosp., 1981-85. Fellow Am. Coll. Ob-Gyn; mem. AMA, Can. Med. Assn., Que. Med. Assn., Mich. Med. Assn., Ill. Med. Assn., Peoria Ob-Gyn Soc. (pres. 1986—). Avocations: tennis, travelling, reading, photography. Office: North Peoria Ob-Gyn Assn 5401 N Knoxville #207 Peoria IL 61614

BOULTON, EDWIN CHARLES, bishop; b. St. Joseph, Mo., Apr. 15, 1928; s. Glen Elwood and Elsa Adina Elizabeth (Person) B.; m. Betty Ann Fisher, July 17, 1949; children—Ann Lisa, Charles Mitchell, James Clay, Melanie Beth. A.B., William Jewell Coll., 1950; M.Div., Duke U., 1953; D.Div., Iowa Wesleyan Coll., 1974, Rust Coll., 1982; D.H.L., Simpson Coll., 1980, Westmar Coll. Ordained to ministry Methodist. Ch., 1953; pastor chs., West End-Vass, N.C., 1953, Republic Community, Iowa, 1954-57, Pocahontas, Iowa, 1957-64, Bettendorf, Iowa, 1964-70; dist. supt., Dubuque, Iowa, 1970-73; adminstrv. asst. to bishop, Des Moines, 1973-80, bishop of Dakotas Area, Mitchell, S.D., 1980—; bd. dirs. World Meth. Council. Named Disting. Alumnus, Duke U. Divinity Sch., 1980. Office: 2410 12th St N Fargo ND 58102-1807 Office: PO Box 460 Mitchell SD 57301 *

BOUMA, GERALD DALE, educator; b. Orange City, Iowa, Oct. 8, 1944; s. Ralph and Jenny Marjory (Reinsma) B.; student Dordt Coll., 1962-65; A.B., Northwestern Coll., 1967; M.Mus., Ariz. State U., 1969, Ed.D., 1982; m. Donna Mae Duistermars, July 14, 1966; children—Tonya Nicole, Caron Leigh. Ch. choir dir. Calvary Christian Ref. Ch., Orange City, 1962-66, 72-75; music instr. Unity Christian High Sch., Orange City, 1964-68; prof. music Dordt Coll., Sioux Center, Iowa, 1969-85, condr. of bands, 1974-85; prof. music Westmont Coll., Santa Barbara, Calif., 1985—. Mem. fin. bd. Orange City Christian Sch., 1969-72; bd. dirs. Sioux County Concert Series, 1969-72; dir. musicals Sioux County Arts Council, 1976, Orange City Community Prodns., 1968-79. Mem. Music Educators Nat. Conf., Nat. Band Assn., Iowa Bandmasters Assn. Republican. Christian Ref. Ch. Composer: Sonnet for Brass Choir, 1969; March Mae, 1971; Sketch for Euphonium and Band, 1969. Office: Dordt Coll Sioux Center IA 51250

BOUNDS, NANCY, modeling and talent company executive; b. Rodney, Ark.; d. William Thomas and Mary Jane (Fields) Southard; m. Robert S. Bounds, 1960 (div. 1965); 1 child, Ronnie Jean; m. Mark Curtis Sconce, Nov. 28, 1972. Student Northwestern U., 1950. Exec. dir. Internat. Fashion/Modeling Assn., N.Y.C., 1978; founding pres. Internat. Talent and Model Schs. Assn., N.Y.C., 1979-80; pres. Nancy Bounds Internat., Omaha, 1959—. Contbr. articles to profl. jours. Producer TV Heart Fund Auction, 1965; chairperson Douglas/Sarpy County Heart Assn., Omaha, 1966, 73-74. Recipient Nat. Tchr.'s award MiLady Pub. Co., 1965, Outstanding Service award Mayor of Omaha, 1984, Uta Halee Girls Village, 1983-87. Mem. Internat. Models and Talent Assn. Unitarian. Avocations: reading, painting, travel, golf, tournament bridge. Home and office: 4803 Davenport Omaha NE 68132

BOURDELAIS, GILLIAN MARY, hospital administrator, nurse; b. Lawrence, Mass., Sept. 14, 1945; d. Charles Matthew and Dorothy (Sheperd) Crane; m. Robert Jeffery Bourdelais, Oct. 30, 1965; children: Heather Anne, Robert Michael, Andrew Patrick. Diploma in Nursing, Melrose-Wakefield Hosp. Sch. Nursing, 1966. RN, Wis., Mass. Asst. clin. instr. Melrose (Mass.)-Wakefield Hosp., 1966; RN Marinette (Wis.) Gen. Hosp., 1966-67; charge RN pediatrics St. Vincent Hosp., Green Bay, Wis., 1967-75, Brown Count Mental Health Ctr., Green Bay, 1975-76; RN, sect. leader mgr., asst. v.p. to v.p. Bellin Meml. Hosp., Green Bay, 1976—; advisor operating room tech. program N.W. Tech. Inst., Green Bay, 1985—, advisor respiratory therapy program, 1986—. Mem. campaign Youth for Kennedy, North Reading, Mass., 1959, Lakeland chpt. ARC, Green Bay, 1980—, Mothers Against Drunk Driving, 1985—; chmn. teen com. Brown County Heart Assn., Green Bay, 1979; active Brown County United Way, 1981, 83. Mem. Am. Assn. Med. Adminstrs., Am. Assn. Cardiology Adminstrs., Northeast Wis. Orgn. Nurse Execs. Democrat. Avocations: golf, crafts, reading, sports, collecting. Office: Bellin Meml Hosp 744 S Webster Ave Green Bay WI 54301

BOURKE, MARY ANNE, retail executive; b. Chgo., Apr. 6, 1956; d. Stephen J. and Georgene Helen (Tarnowski) DiNanno; m. Kevin James Bourke, May 1, 1982. BA in French summa cum laude, Ariz. State U., 1978. Sales asst. Merrill Lynch, Chgo., 1978-79; stockbroker E F Hutton, Chgo., 1979-85; pres., owner The Postal Exchange Inc., Palos Hills, Ill., 1985—. Mem. Assn. Comml. Mail Receiving Agys., Phi Beta Kappa, Palos Hills C. of C. Club: Hickory Hills Women's (Ill.). Home: 10521 S Prospect Ave Chicago IL 60643 Office: The Postal Exchange Inc 10705 S Roberts Rd Palos Hills IL 60465

BOURLAND, JAMES LYNN, dentist; b. Butler, Mo., Aug. 23, 1950; s. Milan Grover and Vera Lorene (Reasoner) B.; m. Joann Bourland, June 4, 1969; children: Cammie Lynette, Andrea Jolynn. BA, Cen. Mo. U., 1972; DDS, U. Mo., 1978. Gen. practice dentistry Clinton, Mo., 1978—. Bd. dirs. Am. Cancer Soc., Henry County, Mo., 1981-86, Henry County United Way, 1983-85; Clinton Pub. Sch., 1986—. Mem. ADA, Mo. Dental Assn. Lodge: Optimists. Home: 2200 Arcadia Clinton MO 64735 Office: 9th and Ohio Clinton MO 64735

BOURNE, ROBERT THOMAS, transportation executive; b. Yonkers, N.Y., May 5, 1949; s. Thomas Goodwin and Anne Katherine (Szymanski) B.; m. Joan Marie Grabenstetter, sept. 2, 1972; children: Emily, Katherine. BSME, Northwestern U., 1972, MS in Civil Engring., 1976. Ptnr. OTR Transp. Con., Wilmette, Ill., 1972-74; asst. gen. mgr. Nortran, Des Plaines, Ill., 1975-78; dir. suburban bus ops. Regional Transit Authority, Chgo., 1978-81; dir. transp. Ames (Iowa) Transit Agy., 1981—; instr. Iowa State U., Ames, 1983-86. mediator Com. Criminal Justice, Ames, 1985—, bd. dirs. 1985—. Mem. Transp. Research Bd. Democrat. Roman Catholic. Avocations: hockey, railroads. Office: Cy-Ride 1700 W 6th St Ames IA 50010

BOUSEMAN, JOHN KEITH, entomologist, naturalist; b. Clinton, Iowa, Aug. 11, 1936; s. Thomas Elmer and Kathryn Teresa (Van Buer) B.; m. Barbara Ann Busby, Aug. 21, 1956; children—Karen, David, Thomas, Lynn, Paul; m. 2d, Tamara Faye Moore, Oct. 15, 1977; 1 child, William. B.S. in Entomology, U. Ill., 1960, M.S. in Entomology, 1962. Registered profl. entomologist, Ill. Expdn. entomologist Am. Mus. Natural History, Uruguayan Expdn., 1963, Bolivian Expdn., 1964, 65; instr. U. Ill., Urbana, 1965-66; asst. entomologist agrl. entomology Ill. Agrl. Expt. Sta., Urbana, 1972—; asst. entomologist Ill. Natural History Survey, Champaign, 1972-84, assoc. entomologist, 1984—; entomol. expdns. to Bolivia, Brazil, Paraguay, Zambia, Uruguay, Venezuela, W.I., Mex.; cons. Zambia Ministry Agr. and Water Devel., 1984; mem. tech. adv. com. on mgmt. Ill. Nature Preserves Commn., 1985—. Sci. Research Soc. Am. grantee, 1961; NSF grantee, 1982. Mem. Am. Entomol. Soc., Coleopterists Soc., N.Y. Entomol. Soc., Internat. Soc. Hymenopterists, Mich. Entomol. Soc., Torrey Bot. Club, Entomol. Soc. Washington, Kans. Entomol. Soc., Sigma Xi. Club: Ill. Field Entomologists (Champaign). Contbr. numerous publ. to profl. jours. Office: Ill Natural History Survey 607 E Peabody Champaign IL 61820

BOUTWELL, ROSWELL KNIGHT, oncology educator; b. Madison, Wis., Nov. 24, 1917; s. Paul Winslow and Clara Gertrude (Brinkhoff) B.; m. Luella Mae Fairchild, Sept. 25, 1943; children—Paul F., Philip H., David K. B.S. in Chemistry, Beloit Coll., 1939; M.S. in Biochemistry, U. Wis., 1941, Ph.D., 1944. Instr. U. Wis., 1945-49, asst. prof., 1949-54, assoc. prof., 1954-67; prof. oncology med. ctr. U. Wis., Madison, 1967—; vis. lectr. Inst. for Environ. Medicine, NYU, summer 1966; mem. cancer study group Wis. Regional Med. Program, 1967-70; mem. adv. com. on inst. research grants Am. Cancer Soc., 1967-74, chmn., 1972-74; mem. food protection com. NRC, 1971-75; mem. lung cancer segment Nat. Cancer Inst., 1971-75; mem. adv. com. on pathogenesis of cancer Am. Cancer Soc., 1960-63; mem. Nat. Cancer Adv. Bd., 1983-90; chief research Radiation Effects Research Found., Hiroshima, Japan, 1984-86. Mem. editorial adv. bd. Cancer Research, 1959-64, assoc. editor, 1973-83. Mem. Monona Grove Sch. Bd., 1952-54; bd. dirs. Madison Gen. Hosp. Found. Fellow AAAS, Am. Assn. Cancer Research (dir.), Am. Soc. Biol. Chemists. Office: U Wis Dept Oncology Madison WI 53706

BOUWKAMP, GERALD RAYMOND, manufacturing company executive; b. Lamont, Mich., Feb. 22, 1925; s. William Harm and Beatrice Mae (Harmsen) B.; m. Phyllis E. Hammond, May 31, 1947; children—James William, Mary Beth Brink, Thomas Gerald, Carol Jane Monger. B.S.A.E., U. Mich., 1945; M.B.A., U. Chgo., 1967. Sr. project engr. Gen. Motors Corp., Grand Rapids, Mich., 1946-53; factory mgr. Stanadyne, Inc., Windsor, Conn., 1962-67, v.p. ops., 1967-69, group v.p., 1969-75, exec. v.p., 1975-83, pres., chief exec. officer, dir., 1983—; dir. Desoto Inc., Chgo. Vice chmn. Greater Hartford chpt. ARC, Conn., 1984—; bd. dirs. St. Francis Hosp., Hartford, 1985—, Hartford Grad. Ctr., 1981—; trustee United Way, 1984—. Served to lt. (j.g.), USN, 1943-46. Mem. Soc. Automotive Engrs. Republican. Methodist.

BOUZEK, ROBERT EDWARD, communications executive; b. Prairie du Chien, Wis., Sept. 24, 1933; s. Edward James and Emma Regina (White) B.; B.S.J., U. Wis.-Madison, 1962; m. Mary Elizabeth Scott, Dec. 20, 1960; children—Michaelle, Elizabeth Mary, Lisa Diane, Jane Ann. Editor, Courier-Press, Prairie du Chien, 1957-58; govtl./bus. reporter Waukesha (Wis.) Freeman, 1958-59; reporter, copy editor Wis. State Jour., Madison, 1959-63; copy editor supr. Milw. Jour., 1963-67; pub. relations specialist Am. Mut. Ins. Alliance, Chgo., 1967-68; pub. relations counsel Carl Byoir & Assos. Inc., Chgo., 1968-70; account supr. Harshe-Rotman & Druck Inc., Chgo., 1970-77, v.p., 1977-79; mgr. media relations Ill. Bell Telephone Co., Chgo., 1979-81, mgr. advt., 1981-83; v.p. Bernard E. Ury Assocs., Inc., 1983—. Home: 69 E Quincy St Riverside IL 60546 Office: 307 N Michigan Ave Chicago IL 60601

BOVEE, EUGENE CLEVELAND, protozoologist, emeritus educator; b. Sioux City, Iowa, Apr. 1, 1915; s. Earl Eugene and Martha Nora (Johnson) B.; m. Maezene B. Wamsley, May 18, 1942; m. Elizabeth A. Moss, May 9, 1968; children—Frances, Gregory, Matthew; stepchildren—Lynne, Lisa. B.A., U. No. Iowa, 1939; M.S., U. Iowa, 1948; Ph.D., UCLA, 1950. Instr. zoology Iowa U., 1940-41; biology tchr. Greene High Sch., Iowa, 1941-42; instr. biology U. No. Iowa, 1946-48; instr. zoology UCLA, 1948-50, research zoologist, 1962-68; asst. prof. biology Calif. Poly. U., 1950-52; assoc. prof. zoology, dept. chmn. N.D. State U., 1952-53; asst. prof. biology U. Houston, 1953-55; assoc. prof. U. Fla., 1955-62; prof. physiology and cell biology U. Kans., Lawrence, 1968-85; emeritus U. Kans., 1985—; cons. Am. Type Culture Collection, 1980-82, W.C. Brown, Pub., 1978-82. Editor Kans. Sci. Bull., 1974-79; co-editor: An Illustrated Guide to the Protozoa, 1985; co-author: How to Know the Protozoa, 2d edit., 1979; contbr. chpts. to books, articles to jours. Served to 1st lt. U.S. Army, World War II. Research grantee NIH, 1957-62, NSF, 1970-74, NIH, NSF and ONR, 1962-68, Kans. Fed. Water Resources Inst. and U. Kans., 1968-81; recipient Disting. Alumni award U. No. Iowa, 1980. Mem. Soc. Protozoology (pres. 1979-80, v.p. 1970-71, treas. 1972-78, exec. com. 1970-81), Am. Inst. Biol. Sci., Am. Microscop Soc. (mem.-at-large exec. com. 1959-62), Western Soc. Naturalists, Iowa Acad. Sci., Kans. Acad. Sci. (life mem., pres. 1979-80, exec. com. 1975-81), Kans. Authors Club, Lawrence Art Guild, Sigma Xi. Home: 808 Mississippi St Lawrence KS 66044

BOVEE, JOAN GUILDENBECHER, home economist, educator; b. Muncie, Ind., May 8, 1946; d. Robert and Kathryn E. (Bullock) Guildenbecher; B.S., Purdue U., 1968; M.S., St. Francis Coll., 1972; postgrad. Ind. U., 1979-80; m. Norman Alan Bovee, Dec. 28, 1967. Jr. fashion merchandizing cons. Montgomery Wards, Fort Wayne, Ind., 1963-67; clothing and textile lab. technician Purdue U., w. Lafayette, Ind., 1966-67; vocat. home econs. tchr. Prairie Heights Community High Sch., LaGrange, Ind., 1968—; Ind. Secondary Sch. Adminstr., 1986—; also dir. student activities, 1972—; cons. for local 4-H workshops, 1968—; mem. staff Student Leadership Inst., Ind. U., Bloomington, 1983—, advisor workshop coordinator, 1984—; staff mem., tchr. Wood Youth Ctr. for Population Edn. Project. Mem. adv. com. Prairie Heights Outdoor Community Edn. Center, 1979—, Sol D. Wood Ctr., 1984—; mem. planning com. Prairie Heights Ann. Fall Farm Festival, 1972—. Mem. Nat. Assn. Vocat. Home Econs. Tchrs. (state contact person 1980, sec. candidate 1983), Nat. Assn. Student Council Advisors (workshop presenter 1984), Am. Home Econs. Assn. (mem. ho. of dels. 1978-79), Am. Vocat. Assn. (mem. ho. of dels. 1978-80), Ind. Vocat. Assn. (mem. awards com. 1981), Ind. Vocat. Home Econs. Assn. (pres. 1979-80, dist. pres. 1978), Ind. Home Econs. Assn. (mem. public relations com. 1979—, liaison com. with Ind. Vocat. Home Econs. Assn. 1982—, dist. 2 newsletter editor and nominating com. 1983—, state nominating com. 1984—), Ind. Assn. Student Council (exec. bd. dirs., newsletter editor 1986—), NEA, Ind. State Tchrs. Assn., Prairie Heights Edn. Assn., Nat. Council of Family Relations, Ind. Council of Family Relations, LaGrange County Mental Health Assn., Kappa Delta Pi, Omicron Nu. Mem. Apostolic Christian Ch. Contbg. author: Indiana State Interpersonal Relations Curriculum Guide, 1977, Indiana State Human Development Curriculum Guide, 1979. Home: Rural Rt 1 PO Box 320 Wolcottville IN 46795

BOWDEN, DAVID LLOYD, television photojournalist, producer; b. Phila., Jan. 28, 1958; s. Frank J. Jr. and Marjorie F. (Thomson) B.; m. Greta Anne Hesse, Aug. 31, 1985. Diploma art/design, Bournemouth & Poole Coll. Art, Eng., 1979; BFA, Mpls. Coll. Art & Design, 1980. Freelance still photographer Mpls., 1973—; TV photojournalist, editor Sta. WCCO-TV, Mpls., 1980—; free-lance still photographer, 1973—, TV photojournalist, editor, Mpls., 1980—. Producer, photographer various art videos; TV documentaries include A Time to Weep, 1985 (Nat. Press Photographers Assn. first place award 1985), AIDS: Fabian's Story, 1985, Sudden Death, 1986, Where There's Smoke, 1987. Mem. Nat. Press Photographers Assn. Club: Union League (Phila.). Avocations: photography, art, reading, outdoor and sporting pursuits. Office: WCCO TV Pub Affairs Unit 90 S 11th St Minneapolis MN 55403

BOWDEN, JOHN LAWRENCE, manufacturing executive; b. Bay City, Mich., Sept. 14, 1946; s. William Edward and Corrine Goldie (Hall) B.; m. Mona Marise Shark, Apr. 21, 1972; children: Elizabeth Marise, Patrick John. BS, Saginaw Valley State U., 1970. Gen. foreman Chevrolet Motor div. Gen. Motors, Flint, Mich., 1969-74; sr. mfg. engr. Wescon Products Co., Wichita, Kans., 1974-75; mgr. indsl. engring. White Motor Co., Ogden, Utah, 1975-78; mgr. mfg. engring. Clark Equipment Co., Battle Creek, Mich., 1978-84; mgr. indsl. engring. Cooper Industries, Houston, 1984-85; dir. mfg. Durametallic Corp., Kalamazoo, 1985—. Chmn. bldg. com. Gull Lake United Meth. Ch., Richland, Mich., 1986. Served with USN, 1971. Mem. Soc. Mfg. Engrs. (sr.). Avocations: shooting sports, flying, golf. Home: 8746 Merrimac Richland MI 49083 Office: Durametallic Corp 2104 Factory St Kalamazoo MI 49001

BOWDEN, OTIS HEARNE, II, management consulting firm executive; b. Stuttgart, Ark., Jan. 2, 1928; s. Otis Hearne and Donna (Trice) B.; B.S. in Bus. Adminstrn., Washington U., 1950, M.B.A., 1953; m. Helen Carol Lamar, June 25, 1949. Financial analyst St. Louis Union Trust Co., St. Louis, 1950-53; dist. mgr. TRW, Inc., Cleve., 1953-63; dir. Mass Transit Center, B.F. Goodrich Co., Akron, Ohio, 1963-67; v.p. E.A. Butler Assocs., Inc., Cleve., 1967-71; pres. Bowden & Co., Inc., Cleve., 1972—; guest lectr. Akron U., 1972—. Nat. promotion dir. Laymen's Hour Radio Broadcast, 1959-63; chmn. commerce and industry div. United Fund of Greater Cleve., 1962; pres. Am. Baptist Men of Ohio, 1962-63; trustee Alderson-Broaddus Coll., Philippi, W.Va., 1965-76; vice chmn. bd. dirs. Eastern Coll., Phila.; alumni bd. govs. Washington U., St. Louis; bd. dirs. Am. Bapt. Fgn. Mission Soc., 1962-71; regional dir. Project Winsome Internationale; vice chmn. adv. bd. Salvation Army of Greater Cleve., 1979—, also chmn. program com. Served with USMCR, 1951. Mem. Am. Mgmt. Assn., Ohio Cons. Assn. (pres. 1982), Am. Mktg. Assn. Club: Red Apple Country. Lodge: Rotary (trustee 1975-77, Paul Harris fellow 1978), Union. Office: 5000 Rockside Rd Cleveland OH 44131

BOWDLE, FREDERICK CHARLES, obstetrician, gynecologist; b. Napoleon, Ohio, Mar. 31, 1934; s. Charles P. and Reta Belle (Stuempel) B.; student U. Mich., 1952-55, M.D., 1959; m. Sandra Kay Lowe, June 22, 1963; children—Brian Frederick, Julie Rochelle. Intern, St. Vincent Med. Center, Toledo, 1959-60, resident, 1962-65, now mem. staff, chmn. dept. obstetrics and gynecology, 1971-75, practice medicine specializing in obstetrics and gynecology, Toledo, 1965—; mem. staffs Toledo Hosp., Med. Coll. Ohio; clin. asst. prof. ob-gyn Med. Coll. Ohio, Toledo, 1972-84, clin. assoc. prof., 1984—; mem. profl. edn. com. Lucas County (Ohio) unit Am. Cancer Soc., 1971. Served as capt. M.C. USAF, 1960-62. Diplomate Am. Bd. Obstetrics and Gynecology. Fellow Am. Coll. Obstetrics and Gynecology, A.C.S.; mem. Acad. Medicine of Toledo and Lucas County, Toledo, Mich. socs. obstetrics-gynecology, Central Assn. Obstetrics-Gynecology, AMA, N. Am. Gynecol. Soc., Am. Assn. Gynecologic Laparoscopists, Am. Fertility Soc., U. Mich. Alumni Assn., Ohio State Alumni Assn. Republican. Methodist. Clubs: Royal Order Jesters, Masons, Shriners (potentate 1979). Home: 4629 Beaconsfield Ct Toledo OH 43623 Office: Sunforest Med Bldg 3900 Sunforest Ct Toledo OH 43623

BOWDOIN, DENNIS L., video rental franchiser; b. Brighton, Mich., Dec. 31, 1946; s. Donald and Tessa (Priestley) B.; m. Joan Cook (div.); m. Martha Battle; 1 child, Charles. Student, Ferris State Coll., Big Rapids, Mich. Former policeman Mich.; now pres., chief exec. officer, franchise owner Movieland, Inc., South Lyon. Mem. Video Software Dealers Assn. (bd. dirs.). Mormon. Office: Movieland Inc 228 Lafayette South Lyon MI 48178

BOWEN, CARL ALLEN, engineer; b. Indpls., Jan. 5, 1944; s. Fred Jasper and Kathleen Marie (Hinshaw) B.; m. Trena Kay Massey, June 12, 1968; children: Shane Michael, Emma Goldie. BS in Gen. Engring., U.S. Mil. Acad., 1967. Commd. 2d lt. U.S. Army, 1967, advanced through grades to capt., 1969, artillory officer, 1967-71, resigned, 1971; employment supr. Johns-Manville Corp., Alexandria, Ind., 1971-73; process engr. Guide div Gen. Motors, Anderson, Ind., 1973—. Pres. Anderson Christian Sch., 1978. Decorated Bronze Star. Republican. Mem. Church of Christ. Office: Fisher Guide div Gen Motors 2915 Pendleton Ave Anderson IN 46018

BOWEN, GILBERT WILLARD, minister; b. Muskegon, Mich., Dec. 30, 1931; s. Bruce Oliver and Beatrice Lillian (Sibley) B.; m. Marlene Mary Michell, July 31, 1954; children: Kathryn Leigh, Mark Kevin, Stephen James. BA, Wheaton Coll., 1955; MDiv, McCormick Theol. Sem., 1957, PhD in Ministry, 1976; cert., Ctr. for Religion and Psychotherapy, 1976; DLL (hon.), Nat. Coll. Edn., 1987. Ordained to ministry Presbyn. Ch., 1956. Minister 1st United Presbyn. Ch., Blue Earth, Minn., 1956-63, Faith United Presbyn. Ch., Tinley Park, Ill., 1963-65, Community Presbyn. Ch., Mt. Prospect, Ill., 1965-70, Kenilworth (Ill.) Union Ch., 1970—; exchange minister Johanneskirche, Neuwied, Fed. Republic Germany, 1961-62; pres. bd. Ctr. for Religion and Psychotherapy; bd. dirs. McCormick Theol. Sem., Chgo., Anatolia Coll., Thessaloniki, Greece, Presbyn. Home, Evanston. Mem. adv. com. North Shore Sr. Ctr., Winnetka, Ill.; bd. dirs. Hospice of North Shore, Wilmette, Ill., Shelter for Battered Women, Evanston; chmn. Instl. Rev. Bd., Evanston. Mem. Am. Assn. Pastoral Counselors, Acad. Parish Clergy, Am. Waldensian Aid Soc. Republican. Club: Indian Hill. Avocations: tennis, golf, vocal music. Home: 417 Warwick Rd Kenilworth IL 60043 Office: Kenilworth Union Ch 211 Kenilworth Ave Kenilworth IL 60043

BOWEN, JUDITH MARGARETE, psychiatrist; b. Nashville, Mar. 1, 1955; d. Jess Sewell Jr. and Margarete Gladney (Chesnut) B.; m. Stephen Frank Kowalski, Sept. 13, 1986. BA in Biology, Zoology, U. Tenn., 1977; MD, East Tenn. State U., 1982. Resident in psychiatry Karl Menninger Sch. Psychiatry, Topeka, 1982-86; staff psychiatrist The Menninger Found., Topeka, 1986—; instr. Karl Menninger Sch. Psychiatry, Topeka, 1986—; Mem. utilization rev. com., operating principles rev. com. C. F. Menninger Hosp., Topeka, 1986—. Bd. dirs. Topeka Symphony Orch., 1987—. Seeley fellow, 1985-86. Mem. AMA, Am. Psychiat. Assn., Am. Med. Women's Assn., Kans. Med. Soc., Kans. Psychiat. Soc. (chmn. residents' com. 1984-86), Chi Omega Alumnae. Avocations: water sports, music, travel, entertaining, cooking. Home: 1417 SW MacVicar Ave Topeka KS 66604 Office: The Menninger Found PO Box 829 Topeka KS 66601

BOWEN, TERRELL LEE, controller; b. Poplar Bluff, Mo., Feb. 7, 1958; s. Terrell Adrian Bowen and Hattie Lee (Brannum) Weitzel; m. Jerilyn Kay Newton, Mar. 20, 1982. BS, S.W. Mo. State U., 1979. CPA, Mo. Tex. Staff acct. Baird, Kurtz & Dobson, CPA's, Springfield, Mo., 1980-81; div. controller Leggett & Platt, Inc., Ennis, Tex., 1981-84; staff controller Leggett & Platt, Inc., Carthage, Mo., 1984—. Mem. Am. Inst. CPA's, S.W. Mo. State U. Alumni Assn., Bass Anglers Sportsman's Soc.(life), Ducks Unlimited. Republican. Club: S.W. Mo. State U. Bears. Avocations: fishing, hunting. Home: Rt 6 Box 283 Neosho MO 64850 Office: Leggett & Platt Inc 1 Leggett Rd Carthage MO 64836

BOWEN, WILLIAM JOSEPH, management consultant; b. N.Y.C., May 13, 1934; s. Edward F. and Mary Alice (Droney) B.; m. Betsy Bass, Oct. 31, 1983; children—William J., Timothy M., Priscilla A., Robert B. B.S., Fordham U., 1956; M.B.A. NYU, 1963. Trainee Smith, Barney, N.Y.C., 1959-61; asst. v.p. Citicorp, N.Y.C., 1961-67; v.p. Hayden, Stone, N.Y.C., 1967-69; 1st v.p. Shearson Hammill, N.Y.C., 1969-73; vice chmn. Heidrick & Struggles, N.Y.C., Chgo., 1973—. Served to capt. USAF, 1956-59. Republican. Roman Catholic. Clubs: Chgo.; Onwentsia (Lake Forest, Ill.); N.Y., Marco Polo, Union League (N.Y.C.). Office: Heidrick & Struggles Inc 125 S Wacker Dr 2800 Chicago IL 60606

BOWER, EVA ROSE, freelance writer, photographer; b. Galien, Mich., Jan. 5, 1913; d. Frank and Herriett (Collins) Grow; m. Lawrence P. Bower, Aug. 27, 1933 (dec. Nov. 1982); children: Joy Mae Bower Rorick, Donald Lawrence. BA, Western Mich. U., 1966. Cert. secondary tchr. Tchr. English and Library Mich. Pub. Schs., 1966-71; news correspondent Herald Palladiam, St. Joseph, Mich., 1977-87; columnist Daily News, Dowagiac, Mich., 1983-86; freelance writer Dowagiac, 1986-87, Kalamazoo, 1987—. Mem. Nat. Press Women, Bus. and Profl. Woman. Home and Office: 433 Den Adel Ct Kalamazoo MI 49001

BOWER, GLEN L., lawyer; b. Highland, Ill., Jan. 16, 1949; s. Ray Landis and Evelyn Ferne (Ragland) B. BA, So. Ill. U., 1971; JD with honors, Ill. Inst. Tech., 1974. Bar: Ill. 1974, U.S. Ct. Mil. Appeals 1975, U.S. Ct. Appeals (7th cir.) 1976, U.S. Dist. Ct. (so. dist.) Ill. 1977, U.S. Supreme Ct. 1978, U.S. Tax Ct. 1984, U.S. Ct. Claims 1986. Sole practice Effingham, Ill., 1974-83; prosecutor Effingham County, Ill., 1976-79; mem. Ill. House of Reps., Springfield, 1979-83; asst. dir., gen. counsel Ill. Dept. Revenue, Springfield, Ill., 1983—; mem. U.S. Dept. Justice Nat. Adv. Com., Washington, 1976-80, U.S. Econ. Adv. Bd., Washington, 1982-85, Ill. Gen. Assembly State Adv. Com. on Cir. Ct. Fin., Springfield, 1984, Revenue Bd. Appeals, Chgo., 1985—, chmn., 1986—; mem. com. of 50 on Ill. Constn., 1987—. Alt. del. Rep. Nat. Conv., Miami Beach., Fla., 1972; vice chmn. Effingham County Rep. Cen. Com., Illinois, 1976—. Served as maj. USAFR, 1974—. Recipient Outstanding Legislator award Ill. Conservative Union, 1980, Cert. of Appreciation, Ill. Fedn. for Right to Life, 1980, 82, Outstanding Freshman Legislator award Ill. Edn. Assn., 1980, Legis. of Yr., Ill. Assn. Rehab. Facilities, 1981, 82, cert. of Appreciation Ill. chpt. Prevention of Child Abuse, 1981, Recognition and Appreciation award Ill. Sheriff's Assn., 1981, Presdl. Citation, Ill. Environ. Health Assn., 1981, Cert. of Appreciation for extraordinary service Ill. Pharmacist Assn., 1981, Outstanding Legislator award Ill. Pub. Health Assn., 1982, Dist. Service award Ill. Assn. Homes for the Aging, 1984, Dist. Service award Ill. Petroleum Marketers Assn., 1984. Mem. ABA (adminstrv. practice com. of taxation sect.), Ill. State Bar Assn. (state taxation sect. council, labor law sec. council, sec. 1987), Effingham County Bar Assn. (sec. 1976-77, pres. 1983-84), Chgo. Bar Assn., Nat. Assn. Tax Adminstrs. (vice chmn. attys. sect. 1985-86, chmn. 1986—), Effingham County Old Settlers Assn. (pres., bd. dirs. 1983-86), Ill. State Hist. Soc. (v.p. 1979-81, bd. dirs. exec. com. 1983-86), Effingham Regional Hist. Soc., SBA Adv. council (bd. dirs. 1973-77), Effingham County Mental Health Assn. (bd. dirs. 1975-77), Effingham County Operation Drug Alert Council (bd. dirs. 1975-77), Effingham County C. of C. (chmn. legis. com. 1976-78), Ill. Mental Health Assn. (pub. affairs com. 1977-78), U.S. Capitol Hist. Soc. (charter), So. Ill. Univ. Alumni Assn. (life), Am. Legion, Ill. Farm Bur. Methodist. Lodges: Shriners, Kiwanis (pres. 1977-78), Elks, SAR, Fraternal Order Police. Home: PO Box 1106 Effingham IL 62401 Office: Ill Dept Revenue 101 W Jefferson 6 SW Springfield IL 62794

BOWER, MARVIN D., insurance company executive; b. Stanford, Ill., July 20, 1924; s. Charles Howard and Marjorie Dale (Garst) B.; m. Mari Morrissey, June 1, 1946 (dec. 1981); children: Stacie (Mrs. John Killian), Jim, Pete, Molly (Mrs. Christopher Miller), Tom, John.; m. Carolyn Paine Newland, Apr. 24, 1983; stepchildren: Linda (Mrs. Bradley Gleason), Lori (Mrs. Paul Lorenz), Leslie, William, David. Ph.B., Ill. Wesleyan U., 1948. C.L.U. Agt. Northwestern Mut. Life, Bloomington, Ill., 1949-52; with State Farm Life Ins. Co., 1952—; sec. for Can. State Farm Life Ins. Co., Toronto, 1955-58; exec. v.p., sec. State Farm Life and Accident Assurance Co., 1961—, also bd. dirs.; v.p. health State Farm Mut. Auto Ins. Co., 1968—; exec. v.p. State Farm Life Ins. Co., Bloomington, Ill., 1973—, chmn. bd., 1985—, also dir. Served to capt. AUS, 1943-46. Fellow Life Office Mgmt. Inst.; mem. Phi Gamma Delta. Home: 49 Country Club Pl Bloomington IL 61701 Office: State Farm Life Ins Co One State Farm Plaza Bloomington IL 61710

BOWER, ROBERT HEWITT, surgeon, surgical educator, researcher; b. Omaha, Aug. 20, 1949; s. John Walter and Dorothy May (Sibert) B.; m. Debra Lea Goettsche, July 4, 1980; children—Timothy Conrad, Michael Harvey. B.A., Grinnell Coll., 1971; M.D., U. Nebr., 1975. Diplomate Nat. Bd. Med. Examiners, Am. Bd. Surgery. Intern, U. Nebr., 1975-76, resident in surgery, 1976-80, chief resident, 1979-80; clin. and research fellow U. Cin., 1980-81; asst. prof. surgery, dir. nutritional support service U. Cin., 1981—, assoc. prof. surgery, 1985—, dir. surg. residency, 1986—. Fellow ACS; mem. AMA, Cen. Surg. Assn., Am. Coll. Nutrition, Soc. Am. Gastrointestinal Endoscopic Surgeons, Assn. Acad. Surgery, Am. Soc. Gastrointestinal Endoscopic Surgeons, Am. Soc. Parenteral and Enteral Nutrition, Ohio Med. Assn., Acad. Medicine Cin., Cin. Surg. Soc. Presbyterian. Contbr. articles to profl. jours., chpts. to books. Office: U Cin Med Ctr Dept Surgery Cincinnati OH 45267-0558

BOWER, SHIRLEY MAE (MRS. JAY R. BOWER), Realtor; b. Marshfield, Mo., Apr. 2, 1935; d. James Oliver and Ruth Irene (Hyde) Day; B.A. in Speech and Dramatics cum laude, Culver-Stockton Coll., 1957; grad. Ill. Inst. Real Estate Brokers, 1972; m. Jay R. Bower, Aug. 5, 1956; 1 dau., Lisa Lynne. Tchr. speech, drama and English Quincy (Ill.) Jr. High Sch., 1951-58; tchr. speech and drama Central High Sch., Camp Point, Ill., 1958-60, 65—; real estate broker, 1976-78; relocation dir. and co-owner Bower Realtors, ERA, Quincy, Camp Point, Ill., 1967—; pres. Quincy Bd. Realtors, 1987. Co-dir. Quincy Jr. Theater, 1957-58, bd. dirs.; bd. dirs. Family Service Agy., Quincy, 1967-68, Quincy Jr. High Sch. PTA, 1973; alumni bd. dirs. Culver-Stockton Coll., 1967—, pres., 1965-66. Mem. Quincy Bd. Realtors, Nat. Assn. Real Estate Brokers, Nat. Inst. Real Estate Brokers, Quincy Service League. Chi Omega. Presbyterian. Home: 2828 Southfield Dr Quincy IL 62301 Office: 503 Maine St Quincy IL 62301

BOWER, WILLIAM WALTER, aeronautical engineer; b. Hammond, Ind., Jan. 9, 1945; s. William Walter and Frances Anita (Good) B. B.S. in M.E., Purdue U., 1967, M.S., 1969, Ph.D., 1971. Sr. engr. Propulsion dept. McDonnell Aircraft Co., St. Louis, 1971-74, sr. scientist flight scis. dept. Research Labs., 1974—; grad. instr. mech. engring. Purdue U., 1970-71. Contbr. articles to tech. jours. NDEA Title IV fellow, 1967-70. Assoc. fellow AIAA (Meritorious Tech. Contbn. award St. Louis Sect. 1977); mem. ASME (fluid mechanics com.). Presbyterian. Club: McDonnell Douglas Corp. St. Louis Mgmt. Home: 847 Woodpoint Dr Apt A Chesterfield MO 63017 Office: McDonnell Douglas Corp PO Box 516 Saint Louis MO 63166

BOWERS, FRAME JOHN, III, aviation executive; b. Washington, Feb. 8, 1947; s. Frame John Jr. and Nancy (Rawls) B.; m. Judy Wiggins, Dec. 18, 1971; children: Jennifer Elise, David Frame. BS, U.S. Mil. Acad., 1969; MS in Aeronautical Engring., Princeton U., 1976; MBA, Xavier U., 1983. Commd. U.S. Army, 1970, advanced through ranks, resigned, 1980; product support engr. GE AEBG, Cin., 1980-83, mgr. tech. pub., 1983—. Served to maj. USAR, 1969—. Daedalian Soc. fellow, 1974. Mem. Army Aviation Assn., Armor Assn. Republican. Episcopal. Avocations: soccer, jogging, computers. Home: 106 Fieldstone Dr Terrace Park OH 45174 Office: CPSD Rm 133 111 Merchant St Cincinnati OH 45246

BOWERS, MAYNARD CLAIRE, botanist; b. Battle Creek, Mich., Nov. 5, 1930; s. Frederick Claire and Elnora Alice (Hard) B.; A.B., Albion Coll., 1956; M.Ed., U. Va., 1960; Ph.D., U. Colo., 1966; m. Leenamari Kangas, Aug. 16, 1970; children—Maynard Claire, Janet Louise, Piiamari Riikka, Eerik Maynard Johannes. Tchr., Whittier Jr. High Sch., Flint, Mich., 1956-57, Meadowlawn Jr. High Sch., St. Petersburg, Fla., 1957-59; asst. prof. Towson (Md.) State Coll., 1960-62, Catonsville (Md.) Community Coll., 1961-62; prof. botany No. Mich. U., Marquette, 1966—; seasonal naturalist Nat. Park Service, Shenandoah Nat. Park, 1956, Glacier Nat. Park, 1957-66. Served with USAF, 1951-52. U. Colo. scholar, 1965-66; Peter White scholar North Mich. U., 1986-87; NSF grantee, 1959-60. Mem. Am. Bryological and Lichenological Soc., Internat. Assn. Bryologists, Internat. Assn. Plant Taxonomists, Internat. Orgn. Plant Biosystematists, Mich. Bot. Club, Nordic Bryoloigal Soc., Sigma Xi. Clubs: Am. Legion, Masons. Contbr. articles to profl. jours. Home: 2 Northwoods Ln Marquette MI 49855 Office: Dept Biology No Mich U Marquette MI 49855

BOWERSOX, BERNARD RICHARD, perfusionist; b. Ashtabula, Ohio, Jan. 15, 1950; s. Richard A. and Bernice (Wagoner) B.; m. Janice Rose, June 24, 1972; children: Elizabeth Ruth, Brian Charles. BS in Allied Med. Professions, Ohio State U., 1972. Cert. Am. Bd. Cardiovascular Perfusion, Internat. Bd. Clin. Technologies. Staff perfusionist Ind. U. Med. Ctr., Indpls., 1972-74, chief perfusionist, 1974-79; dist. agt. Prudential of USA, Gallipolis, Ohio, 1979-84; staff perfusionist Hans Zwart MD, Inc., Dayton, Ohio, 1984-85; pres. Dayton Perfusionists Assoc., Inc., Dayton, 1985—; chmn. continuing edn. AmSect, Reg. V, Ohio, 1978-79. Mem. Am. Soc. for Extracorporeal Tech. Republican. Baptist. Home and Office: Dayton Perfusion Assocs Inc 6311 Millbank Dr Centerville OH 45459

BOWIE, DAVID BERNARD, pastor; b. Jamaica, N.Y., Mar. 30, 1954; s. Matthew Bowie and Vanzetta Lorigné (Moore) Whittaker; m. Angela Baughman, Nov. 27, 1976; children: Courtney Alyce, Brooke Marie. BA, Talladega Coll., 1974; MDiv., Interdenominational Theological Ctr., 1983. Ordained to ministry Presbyn. Ch., 1983. Asst. braille tchr. Erasmus Hall High Sch., Bklyn., 1975-77; employment counselor Woodward High Sch., Cin., 1978-79; student asst. pastor Westhills Presbyn. Ch., Atlanta, 1980-82; asst. pastor 1st Presbyn. Ch. of East Cleve., Ohio, 1983-84, assoc. pastor, 1984—; mem. nominating com. Presbytery of the Western Res., Cleve., 1985—, moderator, 1987; mem. at-large mission council, 1984-85, mem. ex-oficio, 1987—; participant study excursion Synod of Covenant Columbus, Ohio to Cuernavaca, Mex., 1986, alternate commr., 1987; mem. Ch. Devel./Redevel., Cleve., 1984-85; seminary adv. del. Gen. Assembly United Presbyn. Ch., Houston, 1981. Mem. Interdenominational Ministerial Alliance; clergy/counselor Career Beginnings program Shaw High Sch. Mem. East Cleve. Ministerial Assn., Alban Inst., Kappa Alpha Psi. Lodge: Kiwanis. Home: 848 Montford Rd Cleveland Heights OH 44121 Office: 1st Presbyn Ch East Cleve 16200 Euclid Ave East Cleveland OH 44112

BOWLBY, RICHARD ERIC, computer systems analyst; b. Detroit, Aug. 17, 1939; s. Garner Milton and Florence Marie (Russell) B.; m. Gwendoline Joyce Coldwell, Apr. 29, 1967. B.A., Wayne State U., 1962. With Ford Motor Co., Detroit, 1962-65, 66—, now computer systems analyst; pres. 1300 Lafayette East-Coop., Inc., 1981-82. Mem. Antiquaries, Friends Detroit Pub. Library, Friends Orch. Hall. Club: Founders Soc. (Detroit). Office: Ford Motor Co 300 Renaissance Ctr Suite 3000 Box 43314 Detroit MI 48243

BOWLDS, THOMAS RAYMOND, controller; b. Evergreen Park, Ill., June 8, 1957; s. Raymond T. and Ann (Pluta) B.; m. Noreen Sullivan; children: Thomas R., Jennifer L. BS in Acctg., Lewis U., Romeoville, Ill., 1979. CPA, Ill. Staff acct. Selden, Fox & Assocs., Oak Brook, Ill., 1979-80; asst. controller CEF Industries, Inc., Addison, Ill., 1980-81; div. controller CEF Industries, Inc., Haines City, Fla., 1981-83, gen. mgr., 1983-85; corp. controller CEF Industries, Inc., Addison, 1985-86, Walterscheid, Inc., Burr Ridge, Ill., 1986—, Walterscheid Agmaster, St. Thomas, Ont., Can., 1986—. Mem. Am. Inst. CPA's, Nat. Assn. Accts., Ill. CPA's Soc. Republican. Roman Catholic. Office: Waltersheid Inc 16 W 030 83d St Burr Ridge IL 60521

BOWLES, EVELYN M., county government official; b. Worden, Ill., Apr. 22, 1921; d. Ira Milton and Anna (Augustine) B. AA, Ill. State U., 1941; student, Greenville Coll., 1947, Southwest Photo Arts Inst., Dallas, 1945-46, Lewis & Clark Community Coll., 1984. Tchr. Livingston Elementary Sch., 1941-43, 46-50; chief dep. County Clks. Office, Edwardsville, Ill., 1951-74; county clk. Madison County, Edwardsville, 1974—. Mem. Madison County Welfare Com., 1980—; meml. chmn. Cancer Soc., Edwardsville, Ill., 1980—; bd. dirs. Madison County Hospice, Granite City, sec., 1983-84; pres. adv. bd. Rape and Sexual Abuse Care Ctr., 1984-86; mem. voting systems som. Ill. Bd. Elections; pres. parish council St. Mary's Ch., mem. lector sec. Served with USMC, 1943-45, USCG. Recipient Alice Paul award Metro-East NOW, 1979. Mem. Ill. Assn. Clks., Recorders, Election Officials and Treas., Ill. Assn. County Officials, Ill. Fedn. Bus. and Profl. Women (Outstanding Working Women of Ill. 1986), Collinsville Bus. and Profl. Women (Boss of Yr. 1976), Edwardsville Bus. Profl. Women (pres. 1957-58, Woman of Achievement award 1978), Metro-East Women's Assn., Am. Legion. Avocations: reading, yard work, fishing. Home: 322 Thomas Terrace Edwardsville IL 62025 Office: Madison County Clk 155 N Main St Edwardsville IL 62025

BOWLES, MYRON A., manufacturing project engineer; b. Rocky Mountain, Va., Aug. 10, 1943; s. Frank Edward and Irene Asline (Alexander) B.; m. Linda Jo Moore, Apr. 1965 (div. May 1975); m. Susan L. Rick, June 23, 1981; children: Rhonda Lee, John Michael. Tool and die maker Bourns CAI, Barrington, Ill., 1966-71; model maker Cheshire Xerox, Mundelein, Ill., 1971-78; pres., owner Waukegan (Ill.) Cycle, 1971-80; owner M.B. Tool and Die Co., Waukegan, 1975-78; model and mold maker Zenith Corp., Glenview, Ill., 1980-82; project engr. Bell & Howell, Evanston, Ill., 1982—; cons. Automatic Feeder, Elk Grove Village, Ill., 1980—. Co-inventor mail insertion machine, 1982; sole inventor infeed outfeed sheet feeder, 1984. Home: 2859 Darrow Ln Waukegan IL 60085

BOWLEY, NEWELL LYNN, accountant; b. Lexington, Nebr., Oct. 7, 1958; d. John William and Frances Kay (Leibhart) B. BS, Kearney State Coll., 1981. CPA, Nebr.; cert. mgmt. acct., Nebr. Staff auditor Touche Ross & Co., Lincoln, Nebr., 1981-82, sr. auditor, 1982-84; sr. fin. analyst Mut. of Omaha Ins. Co., Omaha, 1984-86, corp. cost acctg. supr., 1986—. Mem. Am. Inst. CPA's, Nebr. Soc. CPA's (mem. com.). Home: 7718 Howard St Apt #1 Omaha NE 68114 Office: Mutual of Omaha Ins Co Mutual of Omaha Plaza Omaha NE 68175

BOWLING, DAVID SAMUEL, geophysicist; b. Bennett, Ky., July 10, 1929; s. Reece Madison and Nancy Elizabeth (Knipp) B.; B.A., Berea Coll., 1956; m. Anna Louise Ogle, Dec. 22, 1955; children—Marla Lucille, Theresa Anne, David Reece, John Anthony. Computer trainee Geophys. Service Inc., Dallas, 1956-56, 2d computer, 1956-57, 1st computer, 1957-59, seismologist, 1959-60, party chief, 1960-62; cons. geophysicist Bowling, Roberson and Ward Seismic Assos., Norman, Okla., 1962-63; area supr. explosives product group Monsanto Co., St. Louis, 1963-68; project engr. G.W. Murphy Industries Inc., Houston, 1968-70, ops. mgr., 1970; ptnr. White Engring. Assos. Inc., Joplin, Mo., 1970—, pres., 1972—; pres., prin. owner White Indsl. Seismology, Inc., 1983—. Served to sgt., U.S. Army, 1948-52. Registered geophysicist, Calif.; certified geologist Maine; certified profl. geol. scientist Am. Inst. Profl. Geologists. Mem. Soc. Exploration Geophysicists, AAAS, ASTM, Soc. Mining Engrs. of AIME, Soc. Am. Mil. Engrs., Seismol. Soc. Am., Am. Assn. Petroleum Geologists (assoc., founding mem. energy minerals div.). Methodist. Clubs: Masons, K.T, Rotary. Patentee in field. Home: Rte 7 Box 186 Joplin MO 64801 Office: PO Box 1256 Joplin MO 68402

BOWLING, JOHN ROBERT, osteopathic physician, educator; b. Columbus, Ohio, Feb. 18, 1943; s. Ardyce Saul and Wilma Garcia (Snider) B.; m. Janet Lou Bowman, July 10, 1965; children: Jack Robert, James Richard, Jason Russell. BS, Ohio U., 1965; DO, Kirksville (Mo.) Coll. Osteopathic Medicine, 1969. Cert. Am. Osteopathic Bd. Gen Practice. Rotating intern Drs. Hosp., Columbus, 1969-70; gen. practice osteo. medicine Lancaster, Ohio, 1970—; clin. assoc. prof. Ohio U. Coll. Osteo. Medicine, Athens, 1977—; med. dir. Lancaster Health Care Ctr., 1980—; co-dir. Family Practice Residency Program Drs. Hosp., 1979, acting dir. 1980, sr. attending staff 1970-86; chmn. dept medicine Lancaster Fairfield Community Hosp. 1975, sec. med. staff 1982-83, pres. 1985; team physician Bloom Carroll Sch., Carroll, Ohio, 1973-86. Med. adv. Drug Abuse Bd., Lancaster; pres. bd. sirs. Montessori Presch., Lancaster, 1975; chmn. Youth Basketball Com. YMCA, Lancaster, 1980-84; Youth coordinator, tchr., mem. adminstrv. bd. United Meth. Ch.; coach Little League Baseball, Lancaster. Mem. Am. Osteo. Assn., Ohio Osteo. Assn., Am. Coll. Gen. Practitioners in Osteo. Medicine and Surgery, Acad. Applied Osteopathy, Columbus Acad. Osteo. Med. (at large exec. com., membership chmn. 1978), Ohio Soc. Am. Coll. Gen. Practioners. Republican. Methodist. Avocations: tennis, golf, photography. Home: 545 Orchard Hill Dr Lancaster OH 43130 Office: 1981 Granville Pike Lancaster OH 43130

BOWMAN, ARDEN LEROY, insurance brokerage company executive; b. Hagerstown, Ind., July 4, 1937; s. Charles Elmer and Neva LuFreda (Nicholson) B.; m. Josette M. Reynolds, Dec. 6, 1959 (div. Apr. 1983); children: Bradley R., Amy Jo; m. Silvia M. Helmsing, Oct. 29, 1983; stepchildren: Trent D. Davis, Angela L. Davis. Grad. high sch., Hagerstown. Br. mgr. Household Fin., Indpls., 1961-62; agy. mgr. Commonwealth Ins., Richmond, Ind. and Indpls., 1962-70; dist. agt. Indpls. Life, Cambridge City, Ind., 1970-75; chief ops. officer Am. Communications Network, Knightstown, Ind., 1975-77; chief exec. officer Wasson-Bowman-Thalls & Assocs., Inc., Hagerstown, 1977—; pres. Eagle Mgmt. Corp., Hagerstown, 1984—. Contbr. articles to profl. jours. V.p. Nettle Creek Players, Inc., Hagerstown, 1984—; active Life Underwriters Polit. Action, Washington, 1962—, 2d Amendment Found., Washington, 1980—. Served with USCG, 1957-61. Fellow Life Underwriter Tng. Council; mem. Nat. Rifle Assn. (cert. pistol instr.), Am. Found. Musicians (local v.p. 1985—), Western Wayne C. of C. (past bd. dirs.), Jaycees (pres. 1969-70). Republican. Mem. Ch. Brethren. Lodges: Masons, Kiwanis (local pres. 1983-84). Avocations: tuba playing, electric bass playing, golf, fishing, hiking. Home: 199 S. Washington Hagerstown IN 47346 Office: Wasson-Bowman-Thalls & Assocs 12 E Main Hagerstown IN 47346

BOWMAN, BRUCE EDWARD, automotive company production executive; b. Marengo, Ind., Feb. 19, 1942; s. Robert Hutslar and Mary Dorothy (Totten) B.; m. Judy Gail Wilkerson, Nov. 6, 1964; children: Bruce Jr., Kellie, Christopher. BS, Western Ky. U., 1964. Quality systems engr. Ford Motor Co., Dearborn, Mich., 1980-82, vehicle evaluation mgr., 1982-83, quality assurance mgr., 1983-84, prodn. supt., 1984-85, prodn. mgr., 1985—. Avocations: golf, fishing, tennis. Home: 42279 Old Bedford Northville MI 48167 Office: Ford Motor Co Wixom Assembly Plant 5000 Wixom Rd Wixom MI 48096

BOWMAN, CARL PRESTON, finance executive; b. York, Nebr., Dec. 12, 1949; s. Al Preston and Virginia I. (Burney) B.; children: Carrie, Anthony. ASBA, Cen. Community Coll., Hastings, Nebr., 1970; student, Kearney (Nebr.) State Coll., 1979-81. Credit mgr. Meml. Hosp., Aurora, Nebr., 1970-72; office supr. Mary Lanning Meml. Hosp., Hastings, 1972-75; controller York Gen. Hosp., 1975-77; v.p. fin. St. Francis Med. Ctr., Grand Island, Nebr., 1977—; mem. data processing adv. bd. Cen. Community Coll., 1979. Treas. 1st United Meth. Ch., Grand Island, 1986-88. Named one of Outstanding Young Men Am., 1985. Mem. Am. Guild Patients Accounts Mgr., Healthcare Fin. Mgmt., (sec., v.p., pres. Ak-Sar-Ben chpt. 1980—, pres. 1986—), Step Family Assn. Am. (treas. Grand Island chpt. 1985—). Republican. Lodge: Kiwanis (pres. 1986—). Avocations: waterskiing, boating, fishing, bowling, golf. Home: 3111 W College #72 Grand Island NE 68803 Office: St Francis Med Ctr 2620 W Faidley Grand Island NE 68802

BOWMAN, DOUGLAS SCOTT, social services executive; b. Larned, Kans., May 17, 1956; s. Robert Hugh and Mary Lou (Robertson) B.; m. Sandra Kay DeKock, Oct. 23, 1982; children: Benjamin, Robert. BA, U. Kans., 1978; MS, Purdue U., 1980. Instr. Barton County (Kans.) Community Coll., Great Bend, 1978-79; youth advisor Shawnee County Youth Ctr., Topeka, 1982-83, program, tng. specialist, 1983-85; exec. dir. Big Bros. and Big Sisters Corp., Topeka, 1985—. Vol. instr. ARC, Topeka, 1985-86; co-founder Big. Bros. and Big Sisters of Cen. Kans., 1979. Mem. Topeka Assn. Human Service Agy. Execs. Avocations: nature, gardening, fishing.

BOWMAN, HOWARD JOSEPH, human resources consultant; b. Bklyn., Oct. 3, 1935; s. Ernest Solon and Mary Ann (Flaherty) B.; m. Natalie Jean, July 4, 1959; children: Jill, Gail, Jeanne, Ellen. BS, St. John's U., 1957; MA, Fordham U., 1960. Chmn. English dept. NYC Bd. Edn., 1957-69; dir. tng. and devel. Interstate Stores, N.Y.C., 1969-75; dir. assessment ctr. Philip Morris, Inc., Richmond, Va., 1975-78; v.p. human resources Mfrs. Bank, Detroit, 1978-81; pvt. practice human resources cons. Detroit, 1981—; nat. accts. exec. Development Dimensions Internat., Pitts., 1986—; faculty Wayne State U., 1985—. Supernuminary Mich. Opera Theater. Mem. Am. Soc. for Tng. Devel. (program chmn.), Nat. Soc. for Performance and Instrn., Am. Soc. Quality Control. Republican. Roman Catholic. Avocation: golf. Home and Office: 2075 S Hammond Lake Rd West Bloomfield MI 48033

BOWMAN, MARK DOUGLAS, structural engineer; b. Logansport, Ind., Aug. 9, 1952; s. John Robert and Mabel Louise (Nelson) B.; B.S.C.E. (Elks scholar), Purdue U., 1974, M.S.C.E. (Nellie Munson award), 1975; Ph.D. (C.P. Siess award), U. Ill., 1981; m. Barbara Baerwald, Aug. 6, 1977; children—Katherine Elaine, Benjamin Robert. Civil engr. Chgo. Bridge & Iron Co., Oakbrook, Ill., summer 1974; teaching and lab. asst. Purdue U., West Lafayette, Ind., 1974-75; structural design engr. Precast/Schokbeton Inc., Kalamazoo, 1975-77; assoc. prof. civil engring. Purdue U., 1981—. Recipient Harold Munson award 1984, Ross J. Buck award, 1986. Mem. ASCE (chmn. com. fatigue and fracture of steel structures), Am. Concrete Inst. (com. fatigue concrete structures), Am. Railway Engring. Assn. (com. 15 steel structures), Am. Soc. Engring. Edn., Nat. Geog. Soc., Soc. Exptl. Mechanics, Sigma Xi, Phi Kappa Phi, Chi Epsilon, Tau Beta Pi, Triangle Frat. (chpt. advisor 1982—). Lutheran. Asst. editor Mich. Civil Engr., 1976-77. Contbr. articles to profl. jours. Home: 16 N 20 St Lafayette IN 47904 Office: Purdue U Civil Engring Bldg West Lafayette IN 47907

BOWMAN, MONROE BENGT, architect; b. Chgo., Aug. 28, 1901; s. Henry William and Ellen Mercedes (Bjork) B.; m. Louise Kohnmann, Nov. 1944; 1 son, Kenneth Monroe; B.Arch., Ill. Inst. Tech., 1924. Registered architect, Ill., Wis., Ind., Ohio, Colo. Asso., Benjamin H. Marshall, Chgo., 1926; exhibited models and photographs of Bowman Bros. comtemporary designs at Mus. Modern Art, N.Y.C., 1931; pvt. practice architecture, Chgo., 1941-44; asso. Monroe Bowman Assos., Chgo., 1945—; cons. Chgo. Dept. City Planning, City of Sparta (Wis.), Alfred Shaw, Architect. Mem. Navy League U.S. Important works include Boeing Aircraft bldgs., Wichita, Kans., Emerson Electric bldgs., St. Louis, Maytag Co., Newton, Iowa, Douglas Aircraft bldgs., Park Ridge, Ill., Shwayder Bros. bldgs., Denver, Clark Equipment Co., Buchannon, Mich., Radio-TV Sta. WHO, Des Moines, Foote, Cone & Belding offices, Chgo., Burridge Devel., Hinsdale, Ill., Yacht Club and recreational facilities, Lake Bemiji, Minn., United Airlines offices downtown Chgo., Automatic Sprinkler Corp., Chgo., King Machine Tool div. Am. Steel Foundries, Cin., Marine Terr. Apts., Chgo., Dorchester Park Apts., Chgo., Manteno (Ill.) State Hosp., No. Ill. Gas Co. bldgs., LaGrange, Joliet, Streator and Morris, 1340 Astor St. Apt. Bldg., Burnham Center, Chgo., NSF, Green Bank, W.Va., Naval Radio Research Sta., Sugar Grove, W.Va., Columbus Boy Choir Sch., Princeton, N.J., office bldg. and hotel, Charleston, W.Va. Home: 730 Ridge Ave Evanston IL 60201

BOWMAN, NORMAN DENNIS, agricultural consultant; b. Carlinville, Ill., Oct. 6, 1957; s. Norman Bauer and Donna Faye (McCawley) B.; m. Gayle Maureen Simpson, June 18, 1983. AS, Lewis and Clark Community Coll., 1980; BS, Western Ill. U., 1981. Cons. Maxi-Yield Cons. Service, Carlinville, 1980-81; agrl. advisor county extension U. Ill. Coop. Extension

Service, Urbana, 1981—. Bd. dirs. Western Ill. 4-H Camp, Jacksonville, 1982-85; bd. dirs., vice chmn. St. Catherine's Cemetery Bd., Hagamon, Ill., 1985—. Mem. Nat. Assn.. County Agrl. Agts. (dist. bd. dirs. 1984-85, Action award, 1985). Republican. Roman Catholic. Avocations: reading, computers, skiing. Home: Rural Rt 1 Box 262 Clinton IL 61727 Office: DeWitt County Extension Office Box 347 803 W Leander Clinton IL 61727

BOWMAN, PASCO MIDDLETON, II, judge; b. Timberville, Va., Dec. 20, 1933; s. Pasco Middleton and Katherine (Lohr) B.; m. Ruth Elaine Bowman, July 12, 1958; children: Ann Katherine, Helen Middleton, Benjamin Garber. B.A., Bridgewater Coll., 1955; J.D., NYU, 1958; LLM, U. Va., 1986. Bar: N.Y. 1958, Ga. 1965, Mo. 1980. Assoc. firm Cravath, Swaine & Moore, N.Y.C., 1958-61, 62-64; asst. prof. law U. Ga., 1964-65, assoc. prof., 1965-69, prof., 1969-70; prof. Wake Forest U., 1970-78, dean, 1970-78; vis. prof. U. Va., 1978-79; prof., dean U. Mo., Kansas City, 1979-83; judge U.S. Ct. Appeals (8th cir.), Kansas City, MO., 1983—. Mng. editor: NYU Law Rev, 1957-58; Reporter, chief draftsman: Georgia Corporation Code, 1965-68. Served to col. USAR, 1959-84. Fulbright scholar London Sch. Econs. and Polit. Sci., 1961-62, Root-Tilden scholar, 1958. Mem. N.Y. Bar, Ga. Bar, Mo. Bar. Home: 11109 Blue River Rd Kansas City MO 64131 Office: US Courthouse Rm 819 811 Grand Ave Kansas City MO 64106

BOWMAN, ROBERT ALLOTT, state official; b. Evanston, Ill., Apr. 12, 1955; s. John Benjamin and Constance (Judkins) B. B.A., Harvard U., 1977; M. in Bus. Adminstrn., The Wharton Sch., U. Pa., 1979. Spl. asst. domestic fin. U.S. Treasury Dept., Washington, 1979-81; assoc. mcpl. fin. Goldman, Sachs & Co., N.Y.C., 1981-83; state treas. State of Mich., Lansing, 1983—. Democrat. Methodist. Home: 161 Rampart Way Apt 301 East Lansing MI 48823 Office: Mich Dept Treasury PO Box 11097 Lansing MI 48901 *

BOWMAN, ROGER MANWARING, service executive; b. Duluth, Minn., Dec. 3, 1916; s. Lawrence Fredrick and Gladys (Manwaring) B.; m. Judith Claypool, Apr. 10, 1942; Ann, David, Mary Bowman Johnson, Lawrence II. Student, U. Mich., 1934-36, Wayne State U., 1937. Pres. N. Star Airways, Duluth, 1946-50, Lawrence F. Bowman Co., Duluth, 1950-70, Gen. Cleaning Corp., Duluth, 1954—, Bowman Corp., Duluth, 1970-83, Bowman Properties, Duluth, 1983—; chmn. Deltona Corp., Miami, Fla., 1985—; cons. Topeka Group, Duluth, 1985—; bd. dirs. Parish Corp., Minn. Power, Norwest Bank. Chmn. St. Louis County Welfare, Duluth, 1964-69, chmn. Govs. Real Estate Adv. Commn., 1968-1970; pres. Duluth Devel. Corp., 1960-68; trustee Ordean Found., Duluth, 1968—; active Duluth Bd. Realtors; pres. Duluth Bldg. Owners and Mgrs. Assn. Internat., 1963-65. Served to lt. col. USMCR, 1940-45. Recipient Silver Beaver award Boy Scouts Am., 1959, Mayor's Commendation, City of Duluth, 1976. Mem. Duluth Steam Coop. (bd. dirs. 1970-86), Duluth Bldg. Owners and Mgrs. Internat., Duluth Bd. Realtors, Real Property Adminstrs. (founder). Republican. Episcopalian. Club: Kitchi Gammi (dir. 1974-78). Avocation: cooking. Home: 3800 London Rd Duluth MN 55804 Office: 700 First Bank Pl Duluth MN 55802

BOWMAN-DALTON, BURDENE KATHRYN, educator, computer consultant; b. Magnolia, Ohio, July 13, 1937; d. Ernest Mowles and Mary Kathryn (Long) Bowman; B.M.E., Capital U., 1959; M.A. in Edn., Akron U., 1967, postgrad. 1976—; m. Louis W. Dalton, Mar. 13, 1979. Profl. vocalist, various clubs in the East, 1959-60; music tchr. East Liverpool (Ohio) City Schs., 1959-62; music tchr. Revere Local Schs., Akron, Ohio, 1962-75, elem. tchr., 1975-80, elem. team leader/computer cons., 1979-85, tchr. middle sch. math., gift-talented, computer literacy, 1981-86, dist. computer specialist, 1987—; local and regional dir., Olympics of the Mind, also World Problem Captain for computer problem, 1984-86; cons., workshop presenter State of Ohio, 1987—. Mem. Citizen Com., Akron, 1975-76; profl. rep. Bath Assn. to Help, 1978-80; mem. Revere Levy Com. 1986; audit com. BATH, 1977-79; volunteer chmn. Antique Car Show, Akron, 1972-81. Martha Holden Jennings Found. grantee, 1977-78; Title IV ESEA grantee, 1977-81. Mem. Assn. for Devel. of Computer-Based Instructional Systems, Assn. Supervision and Curriculum Devel., Ohio Assn. for Gifted Children, Phi Beta. Republican. Lutheran. Home: 353 Retreat Dr Akron OH 44313 Office: 3195 Spring Valley Rd Bath OH 44210

BOXWELL, GEORGE FREDERICK, osteopathic physician; b. Detroit, July 20, 1951; s. Norman Lloyd and Rebecca (Manning) B.; m. Grace L. Hoerauf, June 23, 1973; children—Jennifer Ann, Daniel F., Katherine P. B.A., Olivet Coll., 1973; D.O., Kirksville Coll. Osteo. Medicine, 1976. Diplomate Nat. Bd. Examiners; cert. in gen. practice. Intern Art Centre Hosp., Detroit, 1976-77; pvt. practice medicine St. Helen Med. Ctr., Mich., 1979—; dir. continuing med. edn. Tolfree Hosp., West Branch, Mich., 1980—, v.p. med. staff, 1983-85, pres. med. staff, 1985-86; gen. practice medicine St. Helen, 1986—. Served with USPHS, 1977-79. Mem. Am. Osteo. Assn., Am. Coll. Gen. Practice, Mich. Assn. Osteo. Physicians and Surgeons, Osteo. Gen. Practitioners Mich. Avocations: Landscaping, cross country skiing, golf, camping. Home: 9272 Tippedy St Saint Helen MI 48656 Office: Saint Helen Med Ctr 1360 N St Helen Rd Saint Helen MI 48656

BOYARSKY, ROSE EISMAN, psychologist; b. Jersey City, Mar. 16, 1924; d. Isadore and Clara (Klingenstein) Eisman; m. Saul Boyarsky, June 17, 1946; children: Myer William, Terry Linda, Hannah Gail. BS in Chemistry, U. Vt., 1944; MA, Columbia U., 1946; PhD, Duke U., 1969. Psychologist Durham (N.C.) County Mental Health Clinic, 1969-70; counselor U. Mo. Counseling Center, St. Louis, 1971-72; research assoc. Masters and Johnson Inst., St. Louis, 1972-75; pvt. practice psychology, Boyhill Center, St. Louis, 1975—; research assoc. depts. surgery and urology Washington U. Med. Ctr., St. Louis, 1977—; mem. assoc. staff Jewish Hosp. of St. Louis, 1971—; dir. Archway Community for Drug Rehab., 1973—; mem. Ea. Mo. Regional Adv. Council for Psychiat. Services, 1975-81; apptd. mem. Mo. State Com. Psychologists, 1983—, chmn., 1986—. Contbr. articles in field to profl. jours.; mem. editorial bd. Profl. Psychology, 1979—, Psychology and Pvt. Practice, 1983—, Young Couples Internat., 1983—; editor SCOP Newsletter, 1984. Trustee Judea Reform Congregation of Durham-Chapel Hill, N.C., 1967-69, Portland Place Assn., 1980-83; mem. adv. bd. Victim Service Council, 1985—. Mem. Psychologists in Pvt. Practice, Mo. Psychol. Assn. (pres. 1977-78), Am. Psychol. Assn., AAAS, Am. Women in Psychology, Soc. of Columbia Chemists, Phi Beta Kappa, Iota Sigma Pi. Home: 45 Portland Pl Saint Louis MO 63108 Office: 4625 Lindell Blvd Saint Louis MO 63108

BOYCE, DARON E., meteorologist; b. Wellsville, N.Y., Sept. 2, 1943; s. Donald S. and Gwen K. (Morse) B. BS, Pa. State U., 1965. Meteorologist Nat. Weather Service, Cleve., 1966-71, 72—, Buffalo, 1971-72. Contbr. articles to profl. jours. Pres. bd. mgrs. Condominium Assn., Olmsted Falls, Ohio, 1982—; bus. mgr. Stony Glen Camp, Madison, Ohio, 1980—, trustee, 1985—. Recipient Outstanding Pub. Service award U.S. Coast Guard, Washington, 1980. Mem. Am. Meteorol. Soc. Republican. Baptist. Avocation: camping. Home: 26735 Lake of Fall Blvd Cleveland OH 44138

BOYD, CARL RITTER, radiologist; b. Paoli, Ind., July 14, 1943; s. Carl McKinley and Rosemary (Ritter) B.; m. Cherylynn Anne Morazewski, July 11, 1970; children: Michael, James. BS in Aeronautical Engring., Purdue U., 1965; MD, Ind. U., 1969. Diplomate Am. Bd. Radiology. Intern Wilford Hall USAF Med. Ctr., San Antonio, 1969-70, resident, 1972-75; staff radiologist Scott USAF Med. Ctr., Scott AFB, Ill., 1975-76; ptnr. Assoc. Radiologists, Inc., Logansport, Ind., 1976—. Served to lt. col. USAF, 1969-76, res. 1976—. Mem. AMA, Am. Coll. Radiology, Radiologic Soc. N. Am., Soc. Nuclear Medicine, Tau Beta Pi. Presbyterian. Lodge: Elks. Home: 431 Greenlawn Dr Logansport IN 46947 Office: Assoc Radiologists Inc 800 Fulton Suite 81 Logansport IN 46947

BOYD, CAROL ANNE, public relations executive; b. N.Y.C., Apr. 1, 1953; d. Felix Richard and Muriel B.; m. Aelred William Sheldon, Oct. 19, 1984. BA, Vassar Coll., 1975. Salesperson Procter & Gamble, N.Y.C., 1975-77; dist. field rep. Procter & Gamble, N.Y.C. and Buffalo, 1978-79; unit mgr.-sales Procter & Gamble, Buffalo, 1979-82; pub. relations mgr. Procter & Gamble, Cin., 1983—. Pub. chmn. Arthritis Found., Cin., 1983; v.p. bd. dirs. Better Housing League, Cin., 1984-86; div. coordinator United Appeal, Cin., 1985, mem. council advisors, 1986—. Roman Catholic. Avocation: travel. Home: 735 Riddle Rd Cincinnati OH 45220 Office: Procter & Gamble Co One Procter Plaza Cincinnati OH 45220

BOYD, DOROTHY RUTH, musician, educator; b. Atlantic City, Oct. 20, 1907; d. Herbert C. and Alice Frambes (Boice) Doughty; pvt. student of music, 1923-25; student Progressive Series Piano Inst., Jenkintown, Pa., 1924, Muskingum Coll., summers 1926-30; m. Merton Greer Boyd, June 24, 1930; children—Alys J. Boyd Carpenter, Merilyn J. Boyd Drumm, Merton Greer, Mildred K. Boyd Hibbard. Propr. pvt. music studios in N.J. and Ohio, 1924—, Mansfield, Ohio, bgng. 1957, now in Lexington, Ohio; adjudicator, condr. music workshops; pres. Coshocton (Ohio) Music Club, 1944-45; organist, choir dir. Cambridge (Ohio) First Baptist Ch., 1930-37; organist Newcomerstown (Ohio) Methodist Ch., 1938-41, Coshocton Evang. and Reformed Ch., 1942-46, St. Paul Lutheran Ch., Mansfield, 1958-80, South Side Christian Ch., Mansfield, 1983—; choir dir. Bucyrus (Ohio) First Meth. Ch., 1947-57. Active local Camp Fire Girls, Girl Scouts, 4-H Club; mem. bd. Mansfield YWCA, 1960-62, 74-76; mem. women's com. Mansfield Symphony Soc. Mem. Nat. Guild Piano Tchrs., Nat. Organ and Piano Guild, Nat. Guild Auditions (chmn. Mansfield area 1978—), Music Tchrs. Nat. Assn., Ohio Music Tchrs. Assn. (county chmn. 1957-60, vice chmn. N. Central dist. 1976—, chmn. 1961-67), Richland County Music Tchrs. Assn. (sec.-treas. 1980-82 83-84), Nat. Fedn. Music Clubs, Independent Music Tchrs. Forum (state chmn. 1977-80), Am. Coll. Musicians, Mansfield Music Study Club (sec. 1972-77). Republican. Mem. Christian Ch. Club: Order Eastern Star. Address: 30 Darby Dr Lexington OH 44904

BOYD, GLENDA LORENE, home economics educator; b. Evansville, Ind., Feb. 14, 1937; d. James Glendale and Helen Marie (Johnson) Riney; m. Gerald David Boyd, Aug. 30, 1968. BA, U. Evansville, 1971, MA, 1975. Cert. home economist. With Mead Johnson & Co., 1957-68, lab. asst. pharm. product devel. Research Center, 1961-68; educator vocat. day care and child devel. classes, vocat. class Cen. High Sch., Evansville, 1971—. Mem. Am. Home Econs. Assn., Nat. Tchrs. Assn., Ind. Home Econs. Assn. (dist. pub. relations chmn.), Ind. Tchrs. Assn., Evansville Home Econs. Assn., Evansville Tchrs. Assn., Nat. Soc. Tole and Decorative Painters, Inc. Home: 13201 Woodland Ln Evansville IN 47711 Office: 5400 1st Ave Evansville IN 47710

BOYD, GREGORY ALLAN, information systems company executive; b. Detroit, Aug. 21, 1951; s. John L. and Frieda R. Boyd; B.S. in Bus. Adminstrn., Wayne State U., Detroit, 1973; M.B.A. in Fin., U. Detroit, 1978. Asst. credit mgr. Hughes & Hatcher, Inc., Detroit, 1973-76; acct. Cadillac div. Gen. Motors Corp., Detroit, 1976-78; credit supr. Fed.-Mogul Corp., Southfield, Mich., 1978-79, credit mgr., 1979-82; group credit and collection mgr., Burroughs Corp., 1982-85; mgr. regional ops. Burroughs Fin. Corp., 1985—. Membership recruiter Jr. Achievement Southeastern Mich., 1978; treas. Balmoral Club Condominium Assn., 1986—; trustee, chairperson bldg. com. St. James Missionary Baptist Ch., Southfield, Mich. Mem. Am. Mgmt. Assn., Nat. Assn. Credit Mgmt., Nat. Black M.B.A. Assn. (pres. Detroit chpt. 1986—), Assn. M.B.A. Execs., Omega Psi Phi. Home: 30200 Southfield Rd Apt 208 Southfield MI 48076 Office: Unisys Corp One Unisys Place Detroit MI 48232

BOYD, JANET SCOTT, nursing school administrator, nursing education and nursing research consultant; b. Haverstraw, N.Y., July 21, 1921; d. Russel Thomas and Nora (Burke) S.; m. Robert David Boyd, Mar. 21, 1953; children—Robert Jr., Bruce Scott, Keith Ian. B.S.N., Case-Western Res., 1948; M.A., U. Chgo., 1952; Ph.D., U. Wis., 1976. Asst. prof. U. Wis., Madison, 1961-65, dept. head nursing, 1965-69; asst. exec. adminstr. Wis. Nurses Assn., Madison, 1972-75; dir. nursing sch. Eastern Mich. U., Ypsilanti, 1976—; bd. dirs. Midwest Alliance Nursing, Indpls., 1982-84; pres. Mich. Colls. Nursing, 1978-82; v.p. Mich. League Nursing, Detroit, 1978-84; chmn. legis. com. Mich. Nurses Assn., East Lansing, 1977-83. Office: Ea Mich Univ Dept Nursing Baccalaureat Ypsilanti MI 48197

BOYD, JOHN KENT, advt. exec.; b. Portsmouth, Ohio, Oct. 17, 1910; s. Lambert Thomas and Faery Ann (Ritter) B.; student Tulane U., New Orleans, 1927-29; m. Jeanne Marie Dunlap, Dec. 26, 1935; children—John Kent, Barbara Ann. Mem. staff advt. dept. Am. Rolling Mill Co., Middletown, Ohio, 1929-31; advt. mgr. Pitts. and Midway Coal Mining Co., Kansas City, Mo., 1932-35; v.p. Ferry-Hanly Co., 1935-44; partner Bruce B. Brewer & Co., Kansas City and Mpls., 1944-66; pres., chief exec. officer Bruce B. Brewer Co., Inc., 1967-72, chmn. bd., chief exec. officer, 1972-75; dir. Marco Mfg. Co.; past pres., dir. Quivira, Inc.; pres. Kaybee, Inc. Cochmn. United Funds publicity com., 1953; dir. United Cerebral Palsy Assn. of Kansas City; active Boy Scouts Am.; bd. govs. Starlight Theatre Assn., YMCA, Quiet Birdmen; bd. dirs. Kansas City Crime Commn. Control adv. com. FAA Kansas City Air Traffic. Named Man of Yr. in Gen. Aviation, 1969; recipient silver medal Am. Advt. Fedn., 1972. Mem. AIM, Nat. Aero. Assn., Am. Legion, Kansas City Sr. Golf Assn., Kansas City Promotion Com., Airplane Owners and Pilots Assn. (nat.). Am. Mktg. Assn. (dir. Kansas City chpt.), Am. Royal Assn. (gov.), C. of C., Snipe Class Internat. Racing Assn., Nat. Pilots Assn. (dir.) Am. Bonanza Soc., Air Force Assn., Silver Wings. Clubs: Kansas City, Advt., Sales Execs., Quivira Country, Mission Hills Country, Aero of Kansas City, OX5 of Am.; Capital Hill (Washington); Quivira Sailing (past commodore); Diamondhead Yacht and Country; Bay-Waveland Yacht. Author: Jerry Dalrymple, 1931, Crowded Skies, 1969. Home: 3400 Yacht Club Circle Bay Saint Louis MS 39520 Office: 6512 Maple Dr Mission KS 66202

BOYD, MARGUERITE ELIZABETH, vocational educator; b. Carlsbad, N.Mex., Sept. 7, 1946; d. Hiley Thompson and Bernice Marguerite (Fanning) B.; 1 child, Brian Allan Croxdale. B.S., S.W. Mo. State U., 1968; M.S., Pittsburg State U., 1977, prin. cert., 1979; Ph.D., U. Mo.-Columbia, 1983. Secondary lang. arts and social studies tchr., Springfield, Dallas, Webb City, and Joplin, Mo., 1968-76; lang. arts and math. assessment coordinator Joplin R-VIII Sch. Dist. (Mo.), 1977-80, alternative sch. dir., 1978-80; research asst. U. Mo.-Columbia, 1980-81, coordinator vocat. equity project, 1981-83; unit dir. vocat. edn. curriculum St. Louis Pub. Schs., 1983-86; dir. continuing edn. Lewis and Clark Community Coll., Godfrey, Ill., 1986—; tech. writer Columbia Pub. Schs., 1981. Peabody scholar, U. Mo.-Columbia, 1982. Mem. AAUW, Am. Vocat. Assn., Am. Soc. Tng. and Devel., Nat. Employment and Tng. Assn., Ill. Vocat. Assn., Phi Delta Kappa. Democrat. Author: (with John W. Schell) Missouri Skill Center Evaluation Instrument, 1981; (with Kathy M. Shaffer) Employing Nontraditional Students, 1982. Office: Lewis and Clark Community Coll Godfrey IL 62035

BOYD, W(ILLIAM) FLETCHER, JR., restauranteur, consultant; b. Indpls., Mar. 11, 1950; s. William Fletcher Sr. and Patricia Jean (Henning) B.; m. Gloria Ann Janzen, July 1, 1972; children: Graham Fletcher, Jared Janzen. Cert., U. Freiburg, Fed. Republic Germany, 1970-71; BS, Wabash Coll., 1972; postgrad., Ind. U. Sch. Law, 1972-74, Ind. U.-Purdue U. at Indpls., 1975-76. Legis. asst. Ind. Ho. of Reps., Indpls., 1972-74; legis. liaison Ind. Dept. Edn., Indpls., 1974-77; mgr. Harrison's Restaurant, Indpls., 1977-79; gen. mgr. Mon Reve Restaurant, Indpls., 1979-84; restauranteur, owner Fletcher's Am. Grill & Cafe, Indpls., 1984—; cons. Culinary Prodns., Indpls., 1979—. Bd. dirs. Circlefest, Indpls., 1986; campaign mgr. Jean Merritt for State Auditor, Indpls., 1974. Recipient Best New Restaurant award Indpls. Monthly, 1985. Mem. Downtown Indpls. Restaurant Assn. (v.p. 1985-86, pres.), Chaine De Rotisseurs (maitre d' Table). Avocation: magic. Home: 5879 N Compton Dr Indianapolis IN 46220 Office: Fletcher's Am Grill & Cafe 107 S Pennsylvania St Indianapolis IN 46204

BOYER, ALAN BRUCE, marketing professional; b. Chgo., Sept. 12, 1947; s. Sol and Dora (Feldman) B. BS, U. Ill., Chgo., 1970. Adminstr. direct mail Ency. Brit., Chgo., 1971-74, mgr. direct mail, 1974-81, dir. direct mail, 1981-83, exec. dir. nat. advt. and direct mail, 1983—. Mem. Direct Mktg. Assn. (achievement award 1985), Chgo. Assn. Direct Mktg., Die-Hard Chgo. Cubs Fan Club. Jewish. Avocations: sports, theater, museums, zoos. Office: Ency Brit 310 S Michigan Ave Chicago IL 60604

BOYER, DANIEL BRUCE, dentistry educator; b. Esterville, Iowa, Apr. 21, 1944; s. Bruce D. and Shirley L. (Yager) B.; m. E. Marcia Hazelett, June 13, 1970; 1 child, Daniel F. B.A., U. Iowa, 1966, D.D.S., 1970; Ph.D., Poly. Inst. N.Y., 1975. Asst. prof. U. Iowa, Iowa City, 1974-78, assoc. prof. dentistry, 1978—; cons. Council Dental Edn., Council Dental Therapeutics Am. Dental Assn., 1983—. Contbr. articles to profl. jours. U. Iowa scholar 1967-69. Fellow Acad. Dental Materials; mem. Internat. Assn. Dental Research (pres. Iowa sect. 1985—), Am. Dental Assn., Iowa Dental Assn., Univ. Dist. Dental Soc., Johnson County Dental Soc., Dental Materials Group Am. Assn. Dental Research, Sigma Xi, Psi Omega, Omicron Kappa Upsilon. Democrat. Avocations: micro computer programming; travel; reading; fishing. Home: 1004 Penkridge Dr Iowa City IA 52240 Office: Coll Dentistry U Iowa Iowa City IA 52242

BOYER, JOHN JOSEPH, computer company executive; b. Wadena, Minn., July 25, 1936; s. John Henry and Mathilde (Ament) B.; m. Hazel Mendenhall, Mar. 10, 1973 (dec.); 1 adopted child, Robert. BA, Coll. St. Thomas, 1961; MS, U. Wis., 1982. Research asst. U. Cin., 1965; computer programmer Medcomp Research, Cin., 1965-69, Willoughby Sch. Dist., Cleve., 1970-72, U. Wis., Parkside, 1972-78; founder, pres. Computers to Help People, Inc., Madison, Wis., 1981-84, dir. research and devel., 1984-86, exec. dir., 1986—. Mem. Am. Assn. Artificial Intelligence. Democrat. Roman Catholic. Lodge: KC. Home and Office: 1221 W Johnson St Madison WI 53715

BOYER, TIMOTHY ANDERSON, data processing executive; b. Norfolk, Va., Feb. 24, 1956; s. Carl Ellsworth and Rebecca Ann (Price) B.; m. Heather Sharman Garvin, Sept. 21, 1980; 1 child, Phillip C. AS in Computer Sci., Kent (Ohio) State U., 1981; postgrad., Hiram Coll., 1983—. Cert. data processor. Mgr. EDP Denman Rubber Mfg. Co., Warren, Ohio, 1975—; pres. Champion (Ohio) Computer Systems, 1986—; cons. DACO Computer, Warren, 1984. Contbg. editor FOCUS mag.; contbr. monthly article to Inside ICOBOL mag. Mem. N.Am. Data Gen. User's Assn. (mem. editorial adv. bd. 1986—, meetings com. 1986—), N. Ohio Data Gen. User's Assn., MENSA. Democrat. Presbyterian. Avocations: music, sci. fiction, computers. Home: 433 Stewart St Warren OH 44483 Office: Denman Rubber Mfg Co PO Box 951 Warren OH 44482

BOYERS, MATTHEW ERIN, program director; b. Wauseon, Ohio, Mar. 11, 1959; s. Jerry Lee and Janeth Marie (Slagle) B.; m. Lanita Jean King, May 18, 1979; children: Luke Brandon, Nicholas Michael. BS, Purdue U., 1981; M in Religious Edn., Trinity Sem. Lay youth advisor West Lafayette, Ind., 1980-81, youth dir., 1983—; lay youth advisor Wauseon, 1981-83. Contbr. articles to profl. jours. Republican. Avocations: golf, woodworking, sports, reading. Home: 408 Evergreen St West Lafayette IN 47906 Office: Covenant Presbyn Ch 211 Knox Dr West Lafayette IN 47906

BOYETT, ALON BROCKWAY, construction executive; b. San Antonio, June 9, 1955; s. James Barney and Joann (Worthing) B.; m. Lisa Ann Ridgeway, June 26, 1982; 1 child, Austyn Leigh. BS in Environ. Design, U. Okla., 1977. Draftsman McDonald's Corp., Washington, 1977, archtl. coordinator, 1977-78, constrn. engr., 1978-82, sr. constrn. engr., 1982-84; asst. constrn. mgr. McDonald's Corp., Houston, 1984-85; regional constrn. mgr. McDonald's Corp., Overland Park, Kans., 1985—. constrn. advisor Ronald McDonald House, Kansas City, Mo., 1986. Named Outstanding Sr. Constrn. Engr. McDonald's Corp., Oak Brook, Ill., 1983. Avocations: running, golf, stamp and coin collecting, model railroading. Home: 14520 W 94th St Lenexa KS 66215 Office: McDonalds Corp 11880 College Blvd Overland Park KS 66210

BOYKE, BRUCE CARL, contractor, concrete and masonry; b. Chgo., May 12, 1930; s. Carl and Elsie Marie (La Ffin) B.; student public schs., Zion, Ill.; m. Kathleen J. McManaman, Sept. 16, 1950;children—Laura, Karen, Bruce, Blair, Kerry. Founder, pres. Bruce Concrete Constrn., Inc., Skokie, Ill., 1959—; formed Bruce Boyke Masonry Corp., Skokie, 1963—. Bruce Boyke Imperial Manor, Waukegan, 1964 (pres.); founder Bruce Boyke's Imperial Towers, Waukegan, 1968—. Spl. mem. Boy Scouts America. Republican committeeman Waukegan, 1951-53; pres. Village of Green Oaks, 1977-81. Served with AUS, 1947-51. Mem. Chgo. Assn. Commerce and Industry (indsl. devel. com.), Lake County Contractors Assn., Zion Benton C. of C., Waukegan-North Chicago C. of C. Office: 805 Baldwin Waukegan IL 60085

BOYKIN, NANCY MERRITT, school administrator; b. Washington, Mar. 20; d. Matthew and Mary Gertrude (White) Merritt; m. Ulysses Wilhelm Boykin, Apr. 17, 1965; 1 dau. by previous marriage—Taunya Lovell Banks. B.S., D.C. Tchrs. Coll.; M.A., Howard U., M.S.W., 1965; Ph.D., U. Mich., 1976. Employee relations counselor Office Chief of Fin., U.S. Army, Washington; adminstrv. asst. to Civilian Aide to Sec. of Def., Washington; policewoman Met. Police Dept., Washington; social worker Dept. Pub. Welfare, Washington; adminstrv. asst. to dir. Active Community Teams, Inc., Detroit, 1965-66; dir. continuing edn. for girls program Detroit Pub. Schs., 1966—; cons. U.S. Dept. Edn., 1982; presdl. appointee Nat. Adv. Council on Extension and Continuing Edn., 1973-80. Mem. Mich. Bd. Examiners of Social Workers, 1978-83; mem. Mich. Republican Com., 1975-80, 83—; presdl. appointee to nat. adv. bd. Community Coll. of Air Force, 1984—; gov.'s appointee Mich. Youth Adv. Com., 1984-87; sec. 1st Rep. Dist., 1973-77; mem. Nat. Black Republicans., 1972—. Named Educator of Yr., Nat. Black Women's Polit. Leadership Caucus, 1981, Hon. Lt. Col. Aide De Camp in Ala. Militia, Gov. Wallace, 1986; recipient disting. contbn. plaque Pres.'s Nat. Adv. Com., 1973-80, Spirit of Detroit award, 1979, Meritorious Service plaque, Air Force Bd. Vis., 1986, Superior Service to USAF Enlisted Personnel plaque, Air Force Bd. Vis., 1986, others. Mem. Profl. Women's Network, Nat. Assn. Supervision and Curriculum Devel., Detroit Orgn. of Sch. Adminstrs., Nat. Assn. Black Sch. Educators, Detroit Assn. Univ. Mich. Women, Sch. Edn. Alumni Assn. Wayne State U. (bd. govs.), U. Mich. Alumnae Assn., Mich. Assn. Concerned with Sch. Age Parents (Recognition award, 1986), Phi Delta Kappa. Contbr. articles to profl. jours. Home: 17224 Fairfield Ave Detroit MI 48221 Office: 2200 Ewald Circle Detroit MI 48238

BOYLAN, BRIAN RICHARD, author, theatre director, photographer; b. Chgo., Dec. 11, 1936, s. Francis Thomas and Mary Catherine (Kane) B.; student Loyola U., 1954-58; children—Rebecca, Gregory, Ingrid. Editor, Jour. AMA, Med. World News, The Statesman, 1956-64; author, 1965—; works include: The New Heart, 1969; Infidelity, 1971; Benedict Arnold: The Dark Eagle, 1973; A Hack in a Hurry, 1980; Final Trace, 1983; works include 12 books, 3 plays, 2 screenplays; photographer, 1966—; theatre dir., 1970—; works include 31 plays, videotapes and films. Home: 1530 S 6th St Minneapolis MN 55454

BOYLAN, PATRICK J., financial relations counselor; b. Chgo., Apr. 13, 1957; s. Arthur G. and Catherine M. (Kissane) B.; m. Annabel R. Yackle, Aug. 18, 1979. BA, Eastern Ill. U., 1978; MBA, U. Colo., 1986. Account exec. Hill & Knowlton, Denver, 1981, Adam Smith, Inc., Denver, 1982; pub. relations dir. Promotech, Inc., Denver, 1982; owner Investor Communications, Inc., Denver, 1982-86; office mgr. Investor Communication Systems, Denver, 1985; sr. assoc. The Investor Relations Co., Northbrook, Ill., 1986—; cons. Citizens Coalition for Shelter, Denver, 1982-83. County coordinator John Anderson for Pres., Jefferson County , Colo., 1980; vice chmn. cen. com. House Dist. 23, Lakewood, Colo., 1981-82; treas. Friends for David O'Boyle, Lakewood, 1984-85; chmn. cen. com. Senate Dist. 14, Wheatridge, Colo., 1985-86. Mem. Pub. Relations Soc. Am., Nat. Investor Relations Inst., Nat. Assn. Over-the-Counter Cos. Democrat. Avocation: board games. Home: 307 Fairview Dr Champaign IL 61820 Office: The Investor Relations Co 601 Skokie Blvd Northbrook IL 60062

BOYLAN, TIMOTHY VIRGIL, college registrar; b. Elyria, Ohio, July 30, 1938; s. Theodore Virgil and Kathleen (Ryan) B.; m. Kathryn Carnes, June 10, 1961; children: John T., Mary Frances, Anne V. BS, Xavier U., 1960; MA, John Carroll U., 1965. Social worker Lorain County Children Services, Elyria, 1960-61; tchr. St. Mary's Sch., Elyria, 1961-62; dir. guidance Elyria Cath. High Sch., 1962-66; dir. Lakewood Ctr. Cleve. State U., 1966-67; dir., registrar admissions Lorain County Community Coll., Elyria, 1967—. Bd. dirs., pres. Neighborhood House Assn. Lorain County, 1984-86; bd. dirs., chmn. Elyria Sports Hall of Fame, 1985, 86, 87. Mem. Ohio Assn. Collegiate Registrars (pres. 1977-78). Democrat. Roman Catholic. Home: 239 Eastern Heights Blvd Elyria OH 44035 Office: Lorain County Community Coll 1005 N Abbe Rd Elyria OH 44035

BOYLE, BRYAN DOUGLAS, computer system engineer; b. Fall River, Mass., June 11, 1956; s. Edwin Clayton and Lucille Annemarie (Gouin) B.; m. Paula DeAngelis, Jan. 19, 1980 (div. Mar. 1983). B.A. in Communications, Fordham U., 1978. Computer designer ABC, N.Y.C., 1978-85; system engr. IMR Systems, Leavenworth, Kans., 1985-86; sr. engr. Data Gen. Corp, 1986—; editor Globecom Pub., Prairie Village, Kans., 1981-85 ; pres. Beta Processing, Bronx, 1981-87; computer cons. Soc. Broadcast Engrs., Indpls., 1983-86, Roncom Broadcast Design, Fairfield, N.J., 1984—. Software author Bi-Tech Enterprises, Bohemia, N.Y., 1980-83; computer editor Broadcast Communication, 1981-84; contbg. editor Broadcast Mgmt./Engring. Mag., 1984—; editor Broadcast Communications mag., 1981-83. Decorated Order of St. John, Knight of Malta. Mem. Soc. Broadcast Engrs. (sec. 1977-80, 85—, award 1983). Republican. Roman Catholic. Avocations: automobile restoration and racing.

BOYLE, JOHN LAWRENCE, II, management consultant; b. Duluth, Minn., Sept. 5, 1945; s. John Laurence and Betty Marie (Melander) B.; m. Kathleen Rebecca Moore, July 2, 1966; children: Kristopher Edward, Jason Michael, Karen Marie. BBA, Ga. State U., 1967, MBA, 1969; MS, U. Pa., 1971. With Ford Motor Co., Dearborn, Mich., 1971-78; v.p. fin., chief fin. officer Gallup-Silkworth, Ann Arbor, Mich., 1978-81; exec. v.p. ops. Am. Home Video, Denver, 1981; ptnr. Alsan Internat., Dearborn, Mich., 1982—; mng. ptnr. J.L. Boyle & Co., Ann Arbor, 1982—; chmn., chief exec. officer Adtech Inc., Jackson, Mich., 1983—; bd. dirs. New Directions Internat., Southfield, Mich.; cons. Backos Engring., Wayne, Mich., 1986—, Meta Systems Inc., Ann Arbor, 1986—, Health Services Group, Altanta, 1986—. Mem. Blue Key Soc., Alpha Kappa Psi (awardee 1966), Omicron Delta Kappa. Republican. Club: Detroit Athletic. Avocations: jogging, weight-lifting, downhill skiing, flying, bicycling. Home: 3285 Miller Rd Ann Arbor MI 48103 Office: Adtech Inc 2100 Brooklyn Rd Jackson MI 49204

BOYLE, KAMMER, management psychologist; b. New Orleans, June 17, 1946; d. Benjamin Franklin and Ethel Clair (Kammer) B.; m. Edward Turner Barfield, July 23, 1966 (div. 1975); children—Darren Barfield, Meloe Barfield. B.S. in Mgmt., magna cum laude, U. West Fla., 1976; Ph.D. in Indsl./Organizational Psychology, U. Tenn., 1982. Lic. psychologist, Ohio, Tenn. Pvt. practice mgmt. psychology, Knoxville, 1978-81; teaching and research asst. U. Tenn., Knoxville, 1977-81; mgmt. trainer U.S. State Dept., Washington, 1978; cons. PRADCO, Cleve., 1982-83; pres., cons. Mgmt. and Assessment Services, Inc., Cleve., 1983—; author and presenter ann. Conf. Am. Psychol. Assn., 1980, Southeastern Psychol. Conf., 1979, ann. Conf. Soc. Indsl./Organizational Psychologists, 1987. Mem. Jr. League Am., Pensacola, Fla., 1970-75; treas. Bar Aux., Pensacola, 1971. Recipient Capital Gifts Stipend, U. Tenn., 1976-80; Walter Bonham fellow, 1980-81. Mem. Cleve. Psychol. Assn., Orgn. Devel. Inst., Am. Psychol. Assn., Acad. of Mgmt., Soc. of Advancement of Mgmt. (pres. 1974-75), Am. Soc. Tng. and Devel. (chpt. rep. career devel. 1984-86), Cleve. Psychol. Assn. (bd. dirs. 1987—), Mensa. Office: Mgmt & Assessment Services Inc 4 Commerce Park Sq Suite 600 23200 Chagrin Blvd Cleveland OH 44122-5403

BOYLE, LYNNETTE ZELLNER, lawyer; b. Sandusky, Ohio, July 9, 1952; d. Berlin C. Zellner and Betty May Grube; m. James Edward Boyle Sr., Oct. 7, 1972; children: James E. Jr., Matthew C.; guardian of: Cheryl Purvis, Elizabeth Purvis. AA, Palm Beach Jr. Coll., 1972; BS in Nursing, Vanderbilt U., 1974; MS, Kans. State U., 1977; JD, U. Nebr., 1985. Certified flight instr., instrument; bar: Nebr. 1985, U.S. Dist. Ct. Nebr. 1985. Flight instr. Werner Aviation, Omaha, 1982-84; nurse VA Med. Ctr., Omaha, 1978-85; assoc. Tate and Alden, Lincoln, Nebr., 1985-86; ptnr. Tretjen, Simon & Boyle, Omaha, 1986—. Author: (book chpt.) Living Wills and the Right of the Terminally Ill Patient to Terminate Treatment, 1986; guest editor Elderlaw Rev., 1986. Mem. Com. on Delivery of Legal Service to the Elderly, 1985—. Served to capt. USAR, 1972-79, with Res., 1987—. Named one of Outstanding Young Women Am., 1983, 85. Mem. ABA, Nebr. State Bar Assn. Democrat. Methodist. Avocations: aviation, photography, reading, Taekwan Do, coaching soccer. Home: 13922 Washington Cir Omaha NE 68137 Office: Tietjen Simon & Boyle 3528 Dodge St Omaha NE 68131

BOYLE, PATRICIA JEAN, judge. Student, U. Mich., 1955-57; B.A., Wayne State U., 1963, J.D., 1963. Bar: Mich. Practice law with Kenneth Davies, Detroit, 1963; law clk. to U.S. Dist. judge, 1963-64; asst. U.S. atty., Detroit, 1964-68; asst. pros. atty. Wayne County; dir. research, tng. and appeals Wayne County, Detroit, 1969-74; Recorders Ct. judge City of Detroit, 1976-78; U.S. dist. judge Eastern Dist. Mich., Detroit, 1978-83; justice Mich. Supreme Ct., Detroit, 1983—. Active Women's Rape Crisis Task Force, Vols. of Am. Named Feminist of Year Detroit chpt. NOW, 1978; recipient Outstanding Achievement award Pros. Attys. Assn. Mich., 1978; Spirit of Detroit award Detroit City Council, 1978. Mem. Women Lawyers Assn. Mich., Fed. Bar Assn., Mich. Bar Assn., Detroit Bar Assn., Wayne State U. Law Alumni Assn. (Disting. Alumni award 1979). Office: Mich Supreme Ct 1425 Lafayette Bldg Detroit MI 48226 *

BOYLE, WILLIAM DEAN, JR., periodontist; b. Salt Lake City, Dec. 11, 1934; s. W. Dean Boyle; m. Alice Ruth, Apr. 19, 1963; children: Rebecca Lynn, Adam Dean. Student, U. Oreg., 1953-56; DDS, Northwestern U., 1960; MS, U. N.C., 1971. Commd. 1st lt. USAF, 1960, advanced through grades to col., 1980, retired, 1982; practice dentistry specializing in periodintics Minot, N.D., 1982. Mem. Minot Dental Soc. (pres. 1985-86), Am. Acad. Periodontology, ADA, N.D. Dental Assn. Lodge: Rotory Club. Office: 600 22d Ave NW Minot ND 58701

BOYLES, CHARLES MCKINLEY, JR., engineer; b. St. Louis, July 30, 1943; s. Charles M. and Virginia A. (Hannefin) B.; m. Susan Laidlaw, Feb. 11, 1967; children: Thomas G., Kate. BS in Indsl. Engring., U. Ill., 1976. Gen. mgr. Cabinetmakers, Champaign, Ill., 1971-73; test engr. Inland Steel, East Chicago, Ind, 1977-78; chief engr., mgr. plant engring., mgr. environ. affairs Amco Engring., Schiller Park, Ill., 1978—. Den leader Boy Scouts Am., Glenview, Ill., 1985. Served to lt. U.S. Army, 1966-68, Vietnam. Mem. Am. Inst. Plant Engrs. (pres. chpt. 43 1987—), Nat. Archery Assn. Avocations: wilderness camping, hunting. Home: 1000 Meadowlark Glenview IL 60025 Office: Amco Engring 3801 N Rose Schiller Park IL 60176

BOYNTON, LYNN WILLIAM, orthopaedist; b. Chgo., Sept. 21, 1935; s. Ben Lynn and Elizabeth (Katterjohn) B.; m. Jacqueline Duncan, June 9, 1958; children: Melbourne D., Rebecca D., Jennifer D., Charles D. BS, Beloit Coll., 1958; MD, Northwestern U., 1962. Diplomate Am. Bd. Orthopaedic Surgery. Intern Chgo. Wesley Meml. Hosp., 1962-63; resident in orthopaedic surgery Northwestern U., Chgo., 1966-71; clin. assoc. prof. orthopaedic surgery Med. Coll. of Ohio, Toledo, 1972—; pres. Drs. Boynton, Shiple & Hartwig, Inc., Sylvania, Ohio, 1976—; chief orthopaedic surgery Toledo Hosp., 1986—; bd. dirs. Physicians Ins. Co. Mut.; team cons. U. Toledo, 1984—; dir. med. edn. orthopaedic surgery Toledo, 1985—; presenter numerous papers to profl. socs. Leader United Meth. Ch., Toledo; bd. dirs. March of Dimes Orgn., Toledo, 1975—; vol. U.S. Olympic Com., Colorado Springs, Colo., Lake Placid, N.Y. and Ohio, 1984—. Served to capt. USAF, 1963-69. Fellow Am Acad. Orthopaedic Surgeons, Ohio Orthopaedic Soc.; mem. Arthroscopic Assn. N.Am., Internat. Arthroscopic Assn., AMA, Am. Med. Athletic Assn. Republican. Clubs: Inverness Country, Toledo Road Runners, Rolls Royce Owners. Qualifier Boston Marathon, 1980, 81. Avocations: restoring antique cars, jogging. Home: 3805 Sulphur Spring Rd Toledo OH 43606 Office: Drs Boynton Shiple & Hartwig Inc 4747 Holland-Sylvania Rd Sylvania OH 43560

BOYSEN, THOMAS J., podiatrist; b. Chgo., Feb. 25, 1946; s. Vernon L. and Irene B.; B.S., No. Ill. U., 1968; D. Podiatric Medicine, Ill. Coll. Podiatric Medicine, 1972; m. Stephanie Hutter, Oct. 9, 1970; 1 dau., Wendi. Resident in surgery St. Bernard Hosp., Chgo., 1972-73; practice podiatry Oak Forest, Ill., 1974—, mem. staff St. Anne's Hosp. West, Northlake, Ill., Northwest Surgicare, Arlington Heights, Ill., St. Anne's Hosp., Chgo., Mercy Health Center, Justice, Ill. Diplomate Am. Bd. Podiatric Surgery. Mem. Ill. Podiatry Soc., Am. Podiatric Med. Assn., Am. Coll. Foot Surgeons (assoc.), Am. Public Health Assn., Ill. Podiatric Med. Assn. (past pres. Zone 11, 2d v.p., del. to bd., sec.). Office: 5601 W Victoria Dr Oak Forest IL 60452 also: 3235 W 111th St Chicago IL 60655 also: 2210 Dean St Saint Charles IL 60174

BOZARTH, RONALD L., insurance underwriter; b. Topeka, Jan. 12, 1947; s. Edwin Leslie and Nina Mae (Mueller) B.; m. Cheryl E. Crowder, July 27, 1967 (div. July 1979); children: Ronald Jr., Michelle; stepchildren: Robin Truhe, Patrick Truhe; m. Lois Jean Yocum, May 4, 1985. BA in Polit. Sci., Washburn U., 1969. Comml. casualty underwriter supr. Northwestern Nat., Topeka, 1970-86; comml. sr. underwriter The St. Paul Cos., Overland Park, Kans., 1986—. Mem. Cert. Ins. Counselors, Topeka Underwriters Assn. (bd. dirs.). Home: 10935 Reeder Overland Park KS 66210

BOZSA, DEBORAH ANN, advertising company associate media director; b. Belleville, Ill., Aug. 8, 1953; d. James Andrew and Clara Elizabeth (Buescher) B.; m. Charles Alan Mecum, Jan. 18, 1975. BA, So. Ill. U., 1974, MS, 1978. Mgmt. info. specialist Office of Manpower Devel., Edwardsville, Ill., 1976-78; territorial advt. mgr. CPI Corp., St. Louis, 1979-81; media mgr. D'Arcy, Masius, Benton & Bowles, St. Louis, 1981-87; instr. Belleville (Ill.) Area Coll., 1978-81; cons. McKendree Coll., Lebanon, Ill., 1979. V.p., bd. dirs. Madison County Info. Line, Edwardsville, 1975-76; bd. dirs., dir. project rev. com. St. Louis Health Systems Agy., 1978-82. Fellow So. Ill. U., 1975-76. Mem. Bus. Profl. Advt. Assn. Office: D'Arcy Masius Benton & Bowles 1 Memorial Dr Saint Louis MO 63102

BOZUNG, DAVID ALLEN, television executive; b. Lansing, Mich., Jan. 8, 1948; s. Allen Leo and Dora Ellen (U'Ren) B.; m. Lauraine Ann Hayes, Mar. 3, 1973; children: Paula, Pamela, Lorrie, Corrie. BA, Sioux Falls Coll., 1986. Pres. U.S. Indsl. inc., Southfield, Mich., 1971-73; owner, operator Carcusel Cleaners, Detroit, 1973-74; operations mgr. ServiceMaster Inc., Sioux Falls, S.D., 1974-84; bldg. maintenance engr. ServiceMaster Inc., Redwing, Minn., 1977-78; regional ops mgr. ServiceMaster Inc., Sioux Falls, 1978-82; survey engr. ServiceMaster, Inc., Sioux Falls, S.D., 1982-84; pres. Team T.V. Inc., Sioux Falls, 1984—; cons. ERS Bldg. Co., Southfield, 1976. Served with USN, 1966-70. Republican. Mem. Assembly of God. Avocations: piloting, golfing, power walking. Office: Team TV Inc 1000 E 41st St Sioux Falls SD 57105

BRAAFHART, JAMES LEE, manufacturing company executive; b. Pella, Iowa, Jan. 14, 1948; s. Nick and Catherine (Menniga) B.; m. Barbara Kay Kuiper, Sept. 4, 1970; children: Scott James, Matthew Lee, Jeffrey Jay. BS, Cen. Coll., Pella, Iowa, 1973, student, 1967-68. Accounts supr. Vermeer Mfg. Co., Pella, 1973-78, office mgr., 1979—. Democrat. Lodge: Kiwanis (dir. Pella chpt. 1983-85). Avocation: running. Office: Vermeer Mfg Co Box 200 New Sharon Rd Pella IA 50219

BRAATEN, KATHLEEN ANN, nurse, educator, administrator; b. South Milwaukee, Wis., Sept. 1, 1945; d. Edward S. and Alice F. Weinstock; student Edgewood Coll., Madison, Wis., 1963-64; R.N., St. Marys Sch. Nursing, Madison, 1966; lic. nursing home adminstr., U. Wis., 1976; B.S. (Nursing scholar), Coll. of St. Francis, Joliet, Ill., 1977; M.S., U. Wis., 1983; m. Lyle D. Braaten, Aug. 6, 1966; children—Todd Allen, Jennifer Lynn, Sara Ann. Staff nurse, supr., dir. nurses, asst. adminstr. Mt. Carmel Nursing Home, Greenfield, Wis., 1966-79; instr. nursing Milw. Tech. Coll., 1979-84; program mgr. allied health Waukesha Tech. Inst., Pewaukee, Wis., 1985—; operating room nurse St. Marys Hosp., Manhattan, Kans., 1966; staff nurse Irwin Army Hosp., Ft. Riley, Kans., 1967-68; dir. nursing Woodstock N.W. Health Center, 1971-73. Mem. Nat. League for Nursing, Wis. Soc. Allied Health Professions (pres.-elect), Am. Soc. Allied Health Professions, Wis. Assns. for Adult and Continuing Edn., Am. Assn. of Med. Transcription, Wis. League for Nursing. Roman Catholic. Home: W332 N5543 Linden Circle W Nashotah WI 53058 Office: 800 Main St Pewaukee WI 53072

BRABER, JUDITH ANN, social worker; b. Bay City, Mich., Sept. 19, 1935; d. Stanley J. and Mary Edith (Radigan) B. BA, Aquinas Coll., Grand Rapids, Mich., 1959; MA in Edn., U. Mich., Ann Arbor, 1968; MA in Clinical Psychology, Western Mich. U., Kalamazoo, 1983. Cert. social worker, psychologist. Tchr. Grand Rapids Cath. Schs., 1960-62; registrar, admissions officer Aquinas Coll., Grand Rapids, 1968-71; adminstr. Marywood Dominican Sisters Motherhouse, Grand Rapids, 1972-77; youth care social worker, supr. Salvation Army Booth Services, Grand Rapids, 1980-82, program coordinator, 1983—. Recipient Achievement award Nat. Assn. Counties, 1985, Am. Pub. Welfare Assn., 1985. Mem. Nat. Assn. Social Workers, Am. Psychol. Assn., Mich. Assn. Infant Mental Health. Roman Catholic. Home: 2025 E Fulton Grand Rapids MI 49503 Office: Salvation Army Booth Services 1215 E Fulton Grand Rapids MI 49503

BRABSON, HOWARD VICTOR, social worker, educator; b. Knoxville, Tenn., Sept. 18, 1925; s. Alfred L. and Fannie Ruby Brabson; BS in Social Scis., Coll. of Ozarks, 1956; MSW Cath. U. Am., 1962, D in Social Work (fellow), 1975; m. Rudienne Houston, Sept. 13, 1952. Asst. supt. Cedar Knoll Schs., Laurel, Md., 1958-61; supt. vocat. edn. Boys Indsl. Sch., Lancaster, Ohio, 1962-63; dep. commr. Ohio Youth Commn., Columbus, 1963-65; area supr. Vista, Washington, 1965-67, program mgr., Great Lakes region, Chgo., 1967-69; asso. prof. social work U. Mich., Ann Arbor, 1969—; cons. to various community orgns. and schs., 1969—; mem. planning com. Internat. Conf. Social Welfare, 1978. Mem. mayor's Com. for Community Revitalization, Ann Arbor, 1975-76; bd. dirs. Octagon House, 1976-77, chmn., 1977-78. Served to capt. inf., U.S. Army, 1946-58; PTO. Recipient Man of Yr. award Willow Run Adversary Club, 1978; Faculty Recognition award U. Mich., 1981. Mem. Acad. Cert. Social Workers, Mich. Assn. Black Social Workers (Outstanding Service award 1978), Assn. Voluntary Action Scholars (dir. 1976-78), Nat. Assn. Black Social Workers (nat. pres. 1978-82, mem. steering com. 1971—, founder 1968), Huron Valley Assn. Black Social Workers (pres. 1973—), Zeta Chi Beta. Roman Catholic. Contbr. articles to social work jours. Home: 1325 S Maple St Apt 301 Ann Arbor MI 48103 Office: Univ Mich Sch of Social Work 1065 Frieze Bldg Ann Arbor MI 48109

BRACEY, MICHAEL ALAN, electronics distribution company executive; b. Jackson, Mich., Nov. 13, 1954; s. Thomas L. and Dolores V. (Lacinski) B. AA with honors, Jackson Community Coll., 1974; BA, BBA, Eastern Mich. U., 1979. CPA, Mich. Pub. acct. Hungerford Cooper Luxon, Taylor, Mich., 1978-82; fin. mgr. Dobson The Mover Co., Bay City, Mich., 1982-85; pres., prin., chief exec. officer, fin. cons. Olson Anderson CO., Bay City, 1985—; prin. N.Am. Devel. Co., Bay City, 1983—. Bd. dirs. citizens console Washtenaw Community Bd. Mental Health, Ann Arbor, Mich., 1976-78. Mem. Am. INst. CPA, Bay Area C. of C. Avocations: play writing, music, running, micro-computers.

BRACEY, WILLIE EARL, lawyer, university program director; b. Jackson, Miss., Dec. 21, 1950; s. Dudley and Alvaretta (King) B. AA, Wright Jr. Coll., 1971; BS, Mt. Senario Coll., 1974; MS, Eastern Ill. U., 1976; JD, So. Ill. U., 1979. Bar: Ill. 1979. Dir. student legal services Western Ill. U., Macomb, 1979-86, adj. prof., 1981-84, asst. v.p. student affairs, spl. services, 1986—; asst. pub. defender McDonough County, Macomb, 1983-84. Mem. Ill. Com. on Concern of Blacks in Higher Edn., 1984—, Chgo. Com. on Fgn. Realtions, 1986—, McDonough/Fulton County Youth Service Bd., Macomb, 1985-86. Mem. ABA, Ill. Bar Assn., McDonough County Bar Assn., Assn. Trial Lawyers Am., Nat. Legal Aid and Defender Assn., Ill. Student Atty. Assn., (v.p. 1984—), Nat. Assn. Student Personnel Adminstrs., NAACP. Avocations: chess, cooking. Home: 1006 Derry Ln Macomb IL 61455 Office: Western Ill U Student Legal Services Sherman Circle Macomb IL 61455

BRACK, MARY JANE, accountant; b. Jefferson City, Mo., Mar. 22, 1957; s. Eugene Edwin and Mary Amanda (Dunlap) Wilson; m. Ronald Keith Brack, June 7, 1986. BSBA, U. Mo., 1979; MS in Acctg., U. Ark., 1982. CPA, Mo. Staff acct. Worsham Profl. Assn., Fayetteville, Ark., 1980-82, Dale E. Brown, CPA, Fayetteville, 1982; sr. staff acct. Magazine Lerner & Co., Kansas City, Mo., 1982—. Mem. Am. Inst. CPA's, Mo. Soc. CPA's, Alpha Kappa Psi. Baptist. Avocations: sewing, cooking, bicycling, teaching Sunday sch., singing in ch. choir.

BRACKEN, RICHARD H., osteopath, vascular surgeon; b. Ashland, Ohio, June 5, 1940; s. Stanley and Elizabeth Katherine (Shag) B.; m. Beverly Ann Walker, Dec. 19, 1965 (div. Feb. 1981); children: Christopher, Kathleen, Todd; m. Sheila Ann Moloney, Sept. 9, 1983. BS, Kent State U., 1962; DO, Kirksville (Mo.) Coll. Osteo. Medicine, 1968. Intern Doctor's Hosp., Columbus, Ohio, 1968-69, resident in surgery, 1969-73; practice medicine specializing in vascular surgery Columbus, 1973—; dir. resident program Doctor's Hosp., 1980-84, chmn. dept. surgery, 1982-84, pres. staff, 1987—. Fellow Am. Coll. Osteo. Surgeons; mem. Am. Osteo. Assn., Ohio Osteo. Assn. Republican. Lutheran. Club: Worthington Hills Country (Worthington, Ohio). Avocation: surgery.

BRACKEN, WILLIAM TERRY, police officer; b. Saginaw, Mich., Dec. 13, 1955; s. Everett L. and Wilma L. (Porter) B.; m. Joanne Lee, Sept. 9, 1978; children: William Terry II. Degree, Delta Coll., 1983. Cert. arson investigator, criminal investigator. Dep. Saginaw County, Mich., 1980-84; patrolman Dallas Police Dept., 1984-86, Conrail Police Dept., Detroit, 1986—; law advisor Saginaw Bd. Edn., 1978-80. Pres. Jr. Achievement, 1971-74, Saginaw; leader Law Explorers, Saginaw, 1975-80. Recipient Malcom X award Delta Coll., 1974. Mem. Teamsters, Saginaw Divers Assn., Police League. Democrat. Methodist. Lodge: Masons. Avocations: tennis, swimming, bowling. Home: 2326 Stark Saginaw MI 48602

BRACKETT, EDWARD BOONE, III, orthopedic surgeon; b. Fort Worth, Jan. 5, 1936; s. Edward Boone and Bessie Lee (Hudgins) B.; student Tex. Tech. Coll., 1957; M.D., Baylor U., 1961; m. Jean Elliott, July 11, 1959; children—Bess E., Geoffrey, Elliott Mencken, Edward Boone IV, Anneke Gail. Intern, Cook County Hosp., Chgo., 1961-62; resident Northwestern U., Chgo., 1962-66; practice medicine specializing in orthopedic surgery, Oak Park, Ill., 1966—, Westgate Orthopaedics Ltd., Oak Park, 1969—; mem. staff Loyola U., Oak Park Hosp., Loretto Hosp., Rush Med. Sch.; chmn. dept. orthopedics West Suburban Hosp., pres. med. staff, 1982-84 ; clin. assoc. prof. orthopedics Loyola U.; chmn. bd. Chgo. Loop Mediclinic, 1973-75; cons. orthopedic surgery City Service Oil Co., 1970. Guarantor, Lyric Opera Chgo., 1971-84; guest condr. Chgo. Symphony Orch., 1979, Chgo. Chamber Orch., 1980; mem. humanities adv. council Triton Coll., 1983-84; charter mem. vis. com. Northwestern U. Sch. Music, 1982—. Served as lt. comdr. USNR, 1967-69; Vietnam. Recipient Outstanding Tchr. award Dept. Orthopedic Surgery, West Suburban Hosp., 1978, 79. Diplomate Am. Orthopedic Bd. Surgery, Am. Bd. Neurol. Orthopedic Surgeons. Fellow A.C.S., Am. Acad. Orthopedic Surgeons, Inst. of Medicine of Chgo., Am. Acad. Neurol. and Orthopedic Surgeons, Am. Assn. for Hand Surgery, Internat. Coll. Surgeons; mem. Am. Trauma Soc. (founder), Royal Soc. Medicine, Ill. Orthopedic Soc., Chgo. Orthopedic Soc., AMA, Chgo. Med. Soc. (alt. councilor), Clin. Orthopedic Soc., Internat. Platform Assn., Civil War Round Table, Friends Chgo. Symphony Orch., Chgo. Chamber Orch. Assn. (dir.), Symphonia Musicale (dir.), Sigma Alpha Epsilon, Phi Eta Sigma, Phi Chi, Alpha Epsilon Delta. Cons. orthopedic editor Jour. Indsl. Medicine, 1966-67. Cert. instrument flight instr., FAA. Home: 1407 Ashland Ave River Forest IL 60305 Office: 1125 Westgate St Oak Park IL 60301

BRACKETT, TRACEY SMITH, banker; b. Trenton, N.J., Sept. 1, 1961; d. Herbert Harris and Doris Claire (Burgess) Smith; m. David Millard Brackett, June 30, 1984. BSBA summa cum laude, U. Denver, 1982; M in Mgmt., Northwestern U., 1984. CPA, Ill. Auditor Peat, Marwick, Mitchell and Co., Denver, 1984-85; with 1st Insterstate Bank of Denver, 1985-86; assoc. Security Pacific Merchant Bank, Chgo., 1986—. BaL F. Swan scholar U. Denver, 1981-82. Presbyterian. Avocations: sailing, tennis. Office: Security Pacific Merchant Bank 55 W Monroe Suite 3600 Chicago IL 60603

BRADBURN, THOMAS LYLE, safety engineer; b. Detroit, Jan. 6, 1942; s. James Lyle and Lucile Irene (Cushing) B.; m. Sandra Caroline Stover, July 27, 1963; 1 son, Travis Lyle. B.S. in Indsl. Mgmt., Lawrence Inst. Tech., 1977. Cert. Bd. Cert. Safety Profls. Service coordinator Dennison Copier div. Dennison Mfg. Co., Orlando, Fla., 1966-68; jr. engr. Truck and Coach div. Gen. Motors Corp., Pontiac, Mich., 1968-76, safety rep. truck and bus mfg. div., 1976—. Asst. scoutmaster troop 134 Boy Scouts Am., 1979-82. Served with USAF, 1962-66. Mem. Am. Soc. Safety Engrs. (profl.), Inst. Indsl. Engrs., Soc. Mfg. Engrs., Engring. Soc. Detroit, Mich. Indsl. Hygiene Assn. Baptist.

BRADBURY, DANIEL J., library administrator; b. Kansas City, Kans., Dec. 7, 1945; m. Mary F. Callaghan, May 10, 1967 (div. 1987); children—Patricia, Tracy, Amanda, Anthony, Sean. B.A. in English, U. Mo., Kansas City, 1971; M.L.S., Emporia State U., 1972. Assoc. dir. extension service Waco-McLennan Library, Tex., 1972-74; library dir. Rolling Hills Consol. Library, St. Joseph, Mo., 1974-77, Janesville Pub. Library, Wis., 1977-83; dir. leisure services City of Janesville, 1982-83; library dir. Kansas City Pub. Library, Mo., 1983—; interim exec. dir. Kansas City Sch. Dist., Mo., 1985; faculty Baylor U., Waco, 1973-74; participant Gov.'s Conf. on Library and Info. Sci., Wis., 1979; mem. council Kansas City Metro Library Network, 1984—, pres., 1987, mem. coordinating bd. for higher edn. library adv. com., 1984—, chmn., 1986-87. Bd. dirs. Arrowhead Library System, Janesville, 1978-83, Mid-Town Troost Assn., Kansas City, St. John's Sch., Janesville, 1980-83. Mem. ALA (various offices 1972—), Mo. Library Assn. (legis. chmn. 1984-85), Library Adminstrn. and Mgmt. Assn. (sec. 1983-85), Wis. Library Assn. (pres. 1982). Roman Catholic. Lodge: Rotary. Home: 4328 Summit Kansas City MO 64111 Office: Kansas City Pub Library 311 E 12th St Kansas City MO 64106

BRADEN, BERWYN BARTOW, lawyer; b. Pana, Ill., Jan. 10, 1928; s. George Clark and Florence Lucille (Bartow) B.; m. Betty J.; children—Scott, Mark, Mathew, Sue, Ralph, Ladd, Brad. Student, Carthage Coll., 1946-48, U. Wis., 1948-49; J.D., U. Wis., 1959. Bar: Wis. 1959, U.S. Supreme Ct. 1965. Ptnr. Genoar & Braden, Lake Geneva, Wis., 1959-63; individual practice law Lake Geneva, Wis., 1963-68, 72-74; ptnr. Braden & English, Lake Geneva, Wis., 1968-72, Braden & Olson, Lake Geneva, Wis., 1974-86, Braden, Olson & Olm, Lake Geneva, 1986—; counsel Citizens Nat. Bank, 1959—; city atty. City of Lake Geneva, 1962-64; tchr. Law Sch., U. Wis., 1977. Bd. dirs. Lake Geneva YMCA. Mem. Walworth County Bar Assn. (pres. 1962-63), ABA, State Bar Wis. (chmn. conv. and entertainment com. 1979-81, chmn. adminstrn. Justice and Judiciary com., 1986—, mem. exec. com. Wis. Bicentennial Com. on Constn.), Wis. Acad. Trial Lawyers (sec. 1975, treas. 1976, dir. 1977-79), Assn. Trial Lawyers Am., Phi Alpha Delta. Home: 101 Broad St Lake Geneva WI 53147 Office: 716 Wisconsin St Lake Geneva WI 53147 also: PO Box 512 Lake Geneva WI 53147

BRADFIELD, ROBERT JOHN, obstetrician; b. Ann Arbor, Mich., Mar. 18, 1933; s. Robert John and Margaret (Jewell) B.; m. Ruth Janet Cohen, Nov. 23, 1955; children: Janet Ann, Robert John, William Kimball. Student, Kenyon Coll., 1951-52; AB in Spanish, U. Mich., 1956; MD, Wayne State U., 1952. Cert. Am. Coll. Ob-Gyn. Customer research div. Gen. Motors, Detroit, 1956-1958; intern St. Joseph Mercy Hosp., Ann Arbor, Mich., 1962-63, resident, 1963-66; practice medicine specializing in ob-gyn. Grosse Point, Mich., 1966—; clin. instr. Bon Secours Hosp., Grosse Pointe, 1975—. Fellow Am. Coll. Ob-Gyns.; mem. AMA, Mich. Med. Soc., Wayne County Med. Soc., Delta Kappa Epsilon. Republican. Episcopalian. Avocations: antique automobiles, wild animal rescue and welfare, environ. protection activities. Office: 18120 Mack Ave Grosse Pointe MI 48224

BRADFORD, CHRISTINE ELLEN, computer software sales executive; b. Boston, Apr. 28, 1955; d. Robert Staunton and Irene (Nyeste) B. BA in Psychology, Northwestern U., 1977; postgrad., U. Calif., Berkeley, 1977-79. Research asst. Ednl. Testing Service, Evanston, Ill., 1980-81; mktg. rep. Service Bureau Co. div. Control Data Corp., Chgo., 1981-84; sr. mktg. rep. SIR Inc., Skokie, Ill., 1984-86; account mgr. Uccel Corp., Chgo., 1986—. Mem. Jr. League, Evanston. Mem. AAAS, Nat. Network Women in Sales, Chgo. High Tech. Assn., ACLU, Amnesty Internat., LWV, Chgo. Council Fgn. Relations, U.S.-China Peoples Friendship Assn., Mensa. Avocations: reading Chinese philosophy, jazz, swimming, hiking, horseback riding. Office: Uccel Corp 10 S Riverside Plaza Chicago IL 60606

BRADFORD, KIMERLEE JAY, mechanical engineer; b. Putnam, Conn., Mar. 22, 1932; s. H. Jay and Dorothy Gertrude (Martin) B.; B.S., U. N.H., 1965; postgrad. U. Ariz., 1970-73; m. Shigeko Shikuma, June 18, 1955; children—Jon Chandler, Karyl Ann, William Jay, Charles Martin. Enlisted USAF, 1950, advanced through grades to maj., 1965; missile ops. officer, N.Mex., W.Ger., 1957-60; missile maintenance officer, W.Ger., 1960-62; program mgmt. specialist, Los Angeles, 1965-70; ret., 1970; reliability engr. Control Data Corp., St. Paul, 1973-81; mgr. receiving insp. No. Telecom Inc.-EOS, 1981-82, mgr. in-process quality engring., 1982-83, sr. engr. reliability assurance, 1983-87, engr. product safety, 1987—. Committeeman,

Boy Scouts Am., 1972-73. Recipient Tech. Excellence award Control Data Corp., 1977. Mem. ASME, Am. Soc. Quality Control, Ret. Officers Assn., USCG Aux. (flotilla staff officer pub. edn. 1986). Home: 310 107th St W Bloomington MN 55420 Office: 245 E 6 St Saint Paul MN 55101

BRADFORD, ORCELIA SYLVIA, info systems specialist; b. Kansas City, Mo., Apr. 28, 1953; d. Thomas Wayne and Sylvia (Fueston)Ryan; m. Stanley Lynn, Sept. 26, 1975; children: Richard Lee, April Orcelia. Grad., Belleville Area Coll., 1979. Operator Fin. Data Systems, St. Louis, 1979-81; operator Community Fed. Savs. and Loan, St. Louis, 1981-82, scheduler, 1982-84; prodn. control scheduler Citicorp Person-to-Person, Inc., St. Louis, 1984-87; tech. cons. Cap Gemini Am., Overland Park, Kans., 1987—. Republican. Baptist. Avocations: writing, golfing, canoeing, reading, movies. Home: 8075 Colony Ln Lenexa KS 66214 Office: Cap Gemini America 7101 College Blvd Overland Park KS 66215

BRADFORD, TED C., insurance executive; b. Arthur, Ill., June 1, 1927; s. Orie Oland and Gladys (Robinson) B.; m. Rose Mary Hill, May 5, 1950; children: Shelly Rose Bradford Brown, Stephen Ray. BA, James Millikin U., Decatur, Ill., 1950. Claims examiner Motors Ins. Corp., Decatur, 1950-51; underwriter, supr., office mgr., purchasing officer Fed. Kemper Ins. Co., Decatur, 1951—. Pres. Decatur Mcpl. Band, 1962—. Served with USNR, 1945-46. Republican. Methodist. Avocations: music, woodworking. Home: 18 Green Ridge Dr Decatur IL 62526 Office: 2001 E Mound Rd Decatur IL 62526

BRADLEY, BETTY HUNT, psychologist; b. Oelwein, Iowa, Dec. 17, 1932; s. Hollis Nelson and Mildred (Wilkins) Hunt; m. Ray P. Bradley, Apr. 21, 1962; 1 child, Teresa Bradley Taylor. BA, Coe Coll., 1954; MA, Ohio State U., 1955. Licensed psychologist, Ohio. Psychologist Columbus (Ohio) Devel. Ctr., 1954—. Co-author Teaching Moderately and Severely Retarded Children, 1971; contbr. articles to profl. jours. Mem. Cat Welfare Soc., Columbus, Columbus Zoo. Mem. Phi Kappa Phi, Phi Beta Kappa. Methodist. Avocation: collecting postcards. Home: 90 E Henderson Rd Columbus OH 43214 Office: Columbus Devel Ctr 1601 W Broad St Columbus OH 43223

BRADLEY, DANNY, educator; b. Atlanta, Nov. 26, 1945; s. Robert and Gloria (Milner) B.; B.A., Clark Coll., 1967; M.A.T., Northeastern Ill. U., 1976; postgrad. Loop Coll., 1982—. Tchr., Atlanta Bd. Edn., 1973-75; tchr. Chgo. Bd. Edn., 1967-73, 1975—, now mathematics/computer programming tchr. Percy L. Julian High Sch., Wells High Sch., Schurz High Sch.; cons. Profl. Computer Applications, Inc., summer 1982; GED, math instr. City Colls. Chgo., S. Shore Evening High Sch., 1982—, Calumet Evening Sch., 1975-77, Dunbar Evening Sch., 1977-80, others. Mem. Assn. for Supervision and Curriculum Devel., Nat. Council Tchrs. Math., Ill. Council Tchrs. Math., Ill. Assn. for Supervision and Curriculum Devel., Assn. for Ednl. Data Systems, Minn. Ednl. Computer Consortium, Assn. Math. Advanced Placement Tchrs., World Future Soc., Am. Voc. Assn., Phi Delta Kappa, Omega Psi Phi. Democrat. Baptist. Contbr. articles to profl. jours. Home: 1515 W Morse #410 Chicago IL 60626 Office: Percy Julian Sch 10330 S Elizabeth Chicago IL 60643

BRADLEY, LEON CHARLES, music educator; b. Battle Creek, Mich., Sept. 8, 1938; s. Leon Harvey and Sigrid Pearl (Anderson) B.; B.A., Mich. State U., 1961, M.M. Brass Specialist, 1967; postgrad. U. Okla., summer 1974, U. Wis., summer 1975; m. Mary Elizabeth Bradley, Dec. 23, 1968; children—Kyle Newman, Shannon Sigrid, Karl Norman, Charles Nathan. Band dir. Owosso-St. Paul, Mich., 1958-61, Hopkins (Mich.) Public Schs., 1961-62, Cedar Springs (Mich.) Public Schs., 1962-65; grad. asst. music theory-aural harmony Mich. State U., East Lansing, 1965-67; asst. prof. asst. dir. bands Minot (N.D.) State Coll., 1967-69; asso. prof. instrumental music & music edn., dir. bands Sch. of the Ozarks, Point Lookout, Mo., 1969—, dept. chmn., 1987—; clinician low brass instruments Selmer, Inc., 1979—. Active, Springfield Symphony Orch., 1969-72, 81—, Springfield Regional Opera Orch., 1981—; dir. Abou Ben Adhem Shrine Band, 1978-80. Mem. Coll. Band Dir.'s Nat. Assn. (nat. chmn. Sacred Wind Music commn.), Music Educators Nat. Conf., Nat. Assn. Jazz Educators, Nat. Assn. Wind & Percussion Instrs. (new music reviewer, assn. jour. 1968-71), Mo. Music Edn. Assn., Mo. Bandmasters Assn., Percussive Arts Soc., Music Tchrs. Nat. Assn., Mo. Music Tchrs. Assn., Branson Arts Council, Am. Fedn. Musicians (local 150), Ducks Unltd. (mem. com. 1978-81, chmn., 1981), Phi Mu Alpha (life). Episcopalian. Lodges: Masons, Lions (pres. 1983-84), Scottish Rite. Contbr. articles in field to profl. jours. Home: 119 South Dr Branson MO 65616 Office: Sch of the Ozarks Music Dept Point Lookout MO 65726

BRADLEY, RONALD HOWARD, neuro-anatomist; b. Detroit, Aug. 21, 1950; s. Clarence Edward and Lorraine Day (Moyers) B.; B.A., Wayne State U., 1973, M.S., 1978; Ph.D., Mich. State U., 1983, D.O., 1984. Chef, Hotel St. Regis. Detroit, 1968-70; chief lab. mgr. Mich. Cancer Found. Electron Microscopy Lab., 1973-76; sr. research asst. anatomy Wayne State U., 1976-80; with neurosci. program Mich. State U., 1980-84, intern, 1984-85; resident U. Mich., 1985—; Mem. Am. Assn. Cell Biologists, Electron Microscopy Soc. Am., N.Y. Acad. Sci., AAAS, Am. Osteo. Assn., Am. Assn. Anatomists, Sigma Xi, Sigma Sigma Phi, Methodist. Mason. Home: 14580 Stofer Ct Chelsea MI 48118 Office: Mich State U Fee Hall 5th Floor East Lansing MI 48824

BRADLEY, WILLIAM ARTHUR, civil engineering educator; b. Lansing, Mich., Nov. 11, 1921; s. Arthur and Amy F. (Barringer) B.; m. Elizabeth G. Ewing, June 29, 1949; children—David, Nancy, Susan. B.S.C.E., Mich. State U., 1943; M.S., U. Ill., 1947; Ph.D., U. Mich., 1956. Engr. Douglas Aircraft, El Segundo, Calif., 1943-44; engr. G.M. Foster (Bridge Cons.), Lansing, 1945-46; mem. faculty Mich. State U., East Lansing, 1947—; prof. mechanics and civil engring. Mich. State U., 1961—; cons. Dow Chem. Corp., 1959-61. Recipient Disting. Faculty award Mich. State U., 1963, Western Elec. Fund award, 1966. Mem. ASCE, Am. Concrete Inst., Internat. Assn. Bridge and Structural Engrs., Am. Soc. Engring. Edn., Sigma Xi, Phi Kappa Phi, Tau Beta Pi, Chi Epsilon. Home: 1919 W Kalamazoo St Lansing MI 48915 Office: Coll Engring Mich State U East Lansing MI 48824

BRADLYN, KARL, financial cons., planner; b. N.Y.C., June 26, 1932; s. Morris and Rose (Rehm) B.; widowed, 1978; children: Linda K., Glen L. Student, Los Angeles State U., 1955-56, Cerritos (Calif.) Community Coll., 1958-59. Cert. fin. planner. Sales rep. Los Angeles Times, 1955-64; pres. Forney Mfg. Co., Evansville, Ind., 1964-66; sales engr. Donnelon McCarthy, Indpls., 1966-67; fin. cons. Shearson Lehman Bros. Inc., Indpls., 1967—; v.p. Shearson Ins., Indpls., 1975—; cons. Auto Tire Inc., Indpls., 1983—. Trustee Sertoma Found., Kansas City, Mo., 1981—. Served with USN, 1950-54. Lodges: Elks, Sertoma (pres. Greenwood, Ind. 1973-74, state dir. Ind. 1978-80, local, dist., state, and regional Sertoman of Yr. 1984). Home: 2256 Hanover Dr Indianapolis IN 46227 Office: Shearson Lehman Bros Inc 101 W Washington St Indianapolis IN 46204

BRADNA, JOANNE JUSTICE, medical laboratory science educator; b. Evergreen Park, Ill., May 1, 1952; d. John George and Virginia Dorothy (Breault) J.; m. William Charles Bradna, Aug. 20, 1972; children: Trevor William, Cameron Jon. Student, North Cen. Coll., Naperville, Ill., 1970-72; BS, NorthwesternU., 1974; MS, U. Ill., Chgo., 1981. Med. technologist Northwestern U. Med. Sch., Chgo., 1974-76, Good Samaritan Hosp., Downers Grove, Ill., 1977-78; instr. med. lab. scis. U. Ill., Chgo., 1976-81, asst. prof., 1984—, clin. coordinator, 1984—; tech. sales rep. Analytab Products, Plainview, N.Y., 1981-84; ednl. cons. Hinsdale (Ill.) Hosp., 1979-80; mem. adv. com. Moraine Valley Community Coll., Palos Hills, Ill., 1982—. Contbr. articles and abstracts to profl. jours. Mem. St. Isaac Jogues Ch. Youth Commn., Hinsdale, 1986—; treas. Hinsdale Jr. Woman's Club, 1983-85, pres. 1985-86; 3d v.p. Ill. Fedn. Women's Clubs, 1986—. Recipient Cert. Recognition, Ill. Med. Technologists Assn., 1978, 79; named Outstanding Mem., Hinsdale Jr. Woman's Club, 1981, 82. Mem. Am. Soc. Clin. Pathologists, Am. Soc. Med. Tech. (Cert. Appreciation, 1977), Chgo. Soc. Med. Tech. (bd. dirs. 1977-80, Cert. Recognition, 1978, 79, 80), Am. Soc. Microbiology, Ill. Soc. Microbiology (sec. 1981-83, bd. dirs. 1985), South Cen. Assn. Clin. Microbiology, Ill. Fedn. Woman's Club. Roman Catholic. Avocations: children and family, sports. Office: U Ill Dept Med Lab Scis 808 S Wood St Room 690 CME Chicago IL 60612

BRADSHAW, LAWRENCE JAMES, artist, educator; b. St. Paul, Kans., Sept. 21, 1945; s. James Lawrence and Pauline Marie (Nunnink) B.; B.F.A., Pittsburg (Kans.) State U., 1967, M.A., 1971; M.F.A., Ohio U., Athens, 1973. Designer, Union Oil Co., Honolulu, summer 1967; proofreader, typist CBS-TV, Hollywood, Calif., 1967-69; prodn. artist Writers Service, Hollywood, 1969; advt. mgr. J.C. Penney Co., Pittsburg, 1970-71; teaching asst. Pittsburg State U., 1970-71, Ohio U., 1971-73; instr. Akron (Ohio) Art Inst., summer 1973; assoc. prof. art U. Nebr., Omaha, 1973—, dir. univ. galleries, 1974-76; visual arts rep., designer Met. Arts Council, Omaha, 1976; art dir. Akron City Scholarship Program, 1973; juror various art exhbns., 1974—; one-man exhbns. include U. Nebr., 1974, Pitts. State U., 1974, 77, Barton County Community Coll., Great Bend, Kans., 1987, Peru (Nebr.) State Coll., 1987; group exhbns. include Museo Nazionale dell' Accademia Italia, 1983, Centre Internat. D'Art Contemporian, Paris, 1985, Manhatten Coll., Riverdale, N.Y., 1986, Esta Robinson Gallery, N.Y.C., 1982, others. Recipient Spl. award Internat. Platform Assn., 1981; Sardinian Regional prize Internat. Inviational Biennial, Calgari, Italy, 1984; named Outstanding Young Alumnus Pitts. State U., 1982; recipient Gold medal for artistic merit Internat. Parliament, Salsamaggiore, Italy, 1983. NDEA fellow, 1967; Nebr. Arts Council grantee 1976. Mem. Accademia Italia, Nat. and Mid-Am. Coll. Art Assn., Accademia Europea, Visual Individualists United (trustee), Visual Artists and Galleries Assn. Office: U Nebr 391 A Arts & Scis Omaha NE 68182-0011

BRADSHAW, MICHAEL G., sales executive; b. Rochester, N.Y., Apr. 9, 1948; s. Gardiner Darby and Marilyn (Williams) B.; m. Nancy Jean Davis, Nov. 14, 1970; children: Jennifer Dawn, Kristin Michelle, Jason Michael. BArch, U. Tex., 1975. Engring. mgr. Hussmann Insulation Panel Co., Dallas, 1976-81; gen. mgr. Granco div. Nat. Steel Products, Houston, 1981-83; v.p. mktg. Deraspan Corp., Dayton, Ohio, 1983-86, pres., chief exec. officer, 1986—, also bd. dirs.; pres., chief exec. officer D-Span Holding Co., Dayton, 1986—, also bd. dirs. Served to sgt. USAF, 1967-71. Mem. Internat. Assn. Refrigerated Warehouses (assoc.), Nat. Assn. Cold Storage Conractors. Avocation: fishing.

BRADT, DONA MARY SONTAG, corporate information center manager; b. Hastings, Minn., Oct. 17, 1930; d. Edwin Gervase and Maude Marie (Hatten) S.; student Mt. St. Marys Coll., 1948, Library Sch. U. Minn., 1968-70; B.A., Met. State U., 1975; Mt. m. Arnold L. Bradt (div.); children—Michael Edwin, Robert Dana, Jeffrey Arnold, Peter Matthew, Andrew Hatten. librarian Econ Lab., Inc., St. Paul, 1965—, head librarian, 1979-80, mgr. corp. info. center, 1980—. Mem. Am. Soc. Info. Sci., Spl. Libraries Assn., ALA, Minn. Library Assn., AAAS. Republican. Roman Catholic. Home: 7981 115th St S Cottage Grove MN 55016 Office: Econ Lab Inc 840 Sibley Meml Hwy Saint Paul MN 55118

BRADY, DARLENE ANN, artist, designer; b. Ft. Hood, Tex., Aug. 4, 1951; d. Egbert Leo, Jr. and Eleanor Rose Marie (Wollenhaupt) B.; m. Mark M. English, 1984. B.F.A. summa cum laude, Ohio U., 1976; M.L.S. summa cum laude, U. Pitts, 1978, M.F.A. summa cum laude, 1980; MS in Architecture summa cum laude, U. Cin., 1986. Painter stained glass artist, 1976—; ptnr. Archi-Textures, Cin., 1984—; vis. asst. prof. design U. Cin., 1984-85; grad. and teaching asst. U. Pitts., 1977-80; fine arts bibliographer Tulane U., 1981-83; guest curator of stained glass from Mellon Collection, U. Pitts., 1979, intern Frick Library, 1978; instr. Ohio U., winter 1976, curator B.F.A. Grad. Exhibit, 1976, asst. curator fine arts slide library, 1973-77. Group exhbns. include Fest for All '81, Broussard Galleries, Baton Rouge, 1981, Assocs. Exhibit, Stained Glass Assn. Am., 1980-84, Glass on Holiday, Gazebo Gallery, Gatlinburg, Tenn., 1981, Ark.-La.-Tex. Glass Invitational, La. Tech. U. Art Gallery, 1981, Nat. Exhbn., Royal Ont. Mus., Toronto (best use of antique glass award), 1985, "Vitraux des U.S.A," Micheline Loire Gallery, Chartres, France, 1985; commns. include stained glass panel Athens Humane Soc., 1976, Athens Landscape painting for McDonald's Restaurant, 1976, Transitions stained glass windows Tompson residence, Athens, 1977. La. Cypress stained glass panels entrance door Hainesworth residence, Ruston, La., 1979, stained glass triptych Marybell Holstead residence, Ruston, 1981, solar room with 7 stained glass panels wollenhaupt residence, Lima, Ohio, 1984, others. Author: Stained Glass Index, 1906-77, 1979; Stained Glass: A Guide to Information Sources, 1980; Le Corbusier: An Annotated Bibliography, 1985. Contbr. articles to profl. jours. Scholar Phi Kappa Phi, 1977, J.W. Morgan, 1977, Deans fall 1978, Provost, 1978. Mem. Coll. Art Assn., Glass Arts Soc., Stained Glass Assn. Am. (assoc., rep. 1980-81), Beta Phi Mu, Phi Kappa Phi. Home: 1665 Pullan Ave Cincinnati OH 45223

BRADY, MARK EDWARD, insurance business executive; b. Minneola, N.Y., Dec. 25, 1931; s. Edward Patrick and Vivian Evelyn (Vizard) B.; B.A., A.A., Passionist Fathers Sem., 1954; postgrad. Yale U., 1956, Hudson Coll., 1957-58, Suffolk U. Sch. Law, 1959; m. Anne M. Sughrue, Feb. 11, 1956; children—Pamela, Kent, Joy, Sean. Mgmt. trainee State St. Trust Co., Boston, 1954-55; with Universal C.I.T., Inc., N.Y.C., 1959-65, br. mgr., 1961-63, dist. mgr., 1963-65; dist. mgr. Yegen Assocs., Teaneck, N.J., and Pitts., 1965-67, div. head, 1967-72, v.p., 1972; founder, chmn. Columbus Assocs., Inc. (Ohio), 1972—, Brady Ins. Co. (Ohio), 1972—, Nat. Crown Life Ins. Co., 1974—; dir. Britannia Ins. Co. Ltd. (B.W.I.); chmn. Brady Cons. Assocs. Inc., N.Y. State, Mass., CAI Acceptance Corp., Tara Cons., Tara Fin. Services. Mem. Pres.'s Council, Georgetown U.; mem. parents com. Middlebury Coll. Served with USAF, 1955-58. Recipient Freedoms Found Bronze George Washington medal, 1958. Mem. Ohio Mobile Home Assn., U.S. Savs. and Loan League, Ohio Savs. and Loan League, Am. Bankers Assn., Ohio Bankers Assn. Republican. Clubs: Columbus Acad., Pillars, Buckeye, Ohio State U. Pres. Home: Top O' The Mornin' Pataskala OH 43062 Office: 1303 S High St Columbus OH 43206

BRADY, MICHAEL WADE, manufacturing executive; b. Lincoln, Nebr., July 11, 1948; s. Richard G. and Marjorie A. (Remington) B.; m. Velda K. Friesen, Mar. 27, 1971; children: Ryan C., Nathan M. Student, U. Nebr., 1981-86. Cert. mfg. engr. Draftsman Bruning Hydraulics, Lincoln, 1966-71, chief draftsman, 1971-73, tooling engr., 1973-76, mfg. engr., 1976-81, mgr. mfg. engr., 1981—; mem. mfg. engring. adv. bd., Southeast Community Coll., Lincoln, 1979-84, mem. drafting adv. bd. Southeast Community Coll., Milford, Nebr., 1982-84. Asst. scout master Boy Scouts Am., Lincoln, 1966, asst. cub master, 1984. Served with U.S. Army, 1968-69, Vietnam. Mem. Soc. Mfg. Engrs. (chmn. 1980-81), Mensa. Republican. Baptist. Avocations: photography, 3-D collecting, stamp and coin collecting. Office: Bruning Hydraulics PO Box 81247 Lincoln NE 68501

BRADY, WILLIAM ARTHUR, speech pathologist; b. Titusville, Pa., May 13, 1942; s. Walter Robert and Alma Cecelia B.; B.S. in Speech and Speech Correction, Clarion State Coll., 1966; M.Ed. in Speech Pathology (Office Edn. fellow), Pa. State U., 1967; Ph.D. in Speech Pathology, Kent State U., 1978. Speech therapist Lawrence County (Pa.) Pub. Schs., 1966-68, Titusville (Pa.) Area Schs., summer 1966, Ellwood City (Pa.) Area Schs., 1968; instr. speech pathology dept. Edinboro State Coll., summer 1968, Clarion State Coll., 1968-69, Ill. State U., 1969-70, Allegheny Coll., 1970-71; teaching fellow in speech pathology Kent State U., 1971-74, adj. asso. prof. speech pathology, 1976-77; dir. speech pathology St. Elizabeth Hosp. Med. Center, Youngstown, Ohio, 1974-86; practice medicine specializing in neurocommunication services, Youngstown, 1986—. Mem. Am. (certified in clin. comptence in speech pathology), Ohio (chmn. com. clin. and hosp. affairs 1976-77), Mahoning Valley (v.p. 1976-77) speech and hearing assns., Aphasiology Assn. Ohio. Contbr. articles to profl. jours. Home: 4521 Washington Sq Apt 2 Youngstown OH 44515 Office: 755 Boardman-Canfield Rd Bldg C-1 Youngstown OH 44512

BRAGAW, RICHARD SHERMAN, public relations counselor, writer; b. Evanston, Ill., Aug. 7, 1940; s. James Berry and Sylvia Elizabeth (Callender) B.; m. Lenore Kathleen Gonzales, May 6, 1972; children—Richard Ernest, Kevin Patrick, Daniel Berry. B.A., Dartmouth Coll., 1962, M.A. in Eng. Lit., U. Minn., 1964; postgrad. Wayne State U., 1968-69. Reporter Detroit Free Press, 1964-67; pub. relations mgr. Chrysler Corp., Detroit, N.Y.C. and Los Angeles, 1967-70; reporter, bur. chief Dayton Daily News, Dayton and Columbus, Ohio, 1971-74; campaign press sec., research dir., U.S. Sen. John H. Glenn, 1974; v.p. Food Mktg. Inst., Chgo., Washington, 1974-78; pub. affairs dir. Cereal Inst. Inc., Schaumburg, Ill., 1978-81; prin. Bragaw Pub. Relations Services, Palatine, Ill., 1981—; teaching asst. U. Minn., 1962-64; dir. Inner City Bus. Improvement Forum, Detroit, 1967-69. Vestry, St. Hilary's Episcopal Ch., 1982-85. Recipient Perkins prize Dartmouth Coll., 1962; awards Ohio AP, Outdoor Writers of Ohio, 1972; shared Pulitzer Prize, Detroit Free Press, 1967. Mem. Pub. Relations Soc. Am., Publicity Club Chgo., Arlington Heights Centennial Commn. Contbr. numerous articles to profl. jours.

BRAGG, MICHAEL ELLIS, lawyer; b. Holdrege, Nebr., Oct. 6, 1947; s. Lionel C. and Frances E. (Klinginsmith) B.; m. Nancy Jo Aabel, Jan. 19, 1980; children: Brian Michael, Kyle Christopher. B.A., U. Nebr., 1971, J.D., 1975. Bar: Alaska 1976, U.S. Dist. Ct. Alaska 1976, Nebr. 1976, U.S. Dist. Ct. Nebr. 1976. Assoc. White & Jones Anchorage, 1976-77; field rep. State Farm Ins., Anchorage, 1977-79, atty. corp. law dept., Bloomington, Ill., 1979-81, sr. atty., 1981-84, asst. counsel, 1984-86, counsel, 1986—. Contbr. articles to profl. jours. Bd. dirs. Friends of Arts, Bloomington, 1984-85, lectr., contbr. legal seminars. Served with USNG, 1970-76. Mem. ABA (vice chmn. property ins. com., corp. counsel and antitrust coms., arrangements chmn. torts and ins. practices sect. 1987), Am. Corp. Counsel Assn., Internat. Platform Assn. Republican. Mem. Unitarian Ch. Club: Crestwicke Country. Office: State Farm Ins Cos 1 State Farm Plaza Suite E-6 Bloomington IL 61710

BRAGUE, NORMAN EVERETT, lawyer; b. Marietta, Ohio, Oct. 16, 1946; s. Clive Levi and Kate (Bircher) B. B.B.A. cum laude, Ohio U., 1968; J.D., Ohio State U., 1971. Bar: Ohio. Assoc. Parker & Parker, Akron, Ohio, 1971-72; pvt. practice, Wadsworth, Ohio, 1972-76; asst. city solicitor City of Wadsworth, 1973-75, city solicitor, 1976-77, dir. law, 1977—; trustee Community Improvement Corp., Wadsworth, 1976—. Active Medina County Republican Central Com., 1974—. Mem. ABA, Ohio State Bar Assn., Medina County Bar Assn., Phi Alpha Delta, Pi Kappa Alpha. Republican. Episcopalian. Clubs: University (Akron), Rotary (Wadsworth), SAR. Lodges: Masons, Elks. Avocation: History. Home: 324 Portage St Wadsworth OH 44281 Office: City of Wadsworth 145 High St Wadsworth OH 44281

BRAHAM, DELPHINE DORIS, government accountant; b. L'Anse, Mich., Mar. 16, 1946; d. Richard Andrew and Viola Mary (Niemi) Aho; m. John Emerson Braham, Sept. 23, 1967; children: Tammy, Debra, John Jr. BS summa cum laude, Drury Coll., 1983; M in Mgmt., Webster U., St. Louis, 1986. Bookkeeper, Community Mental Health Ctr., Marquette, Mich., 1966-68; credit clk. Remington Rand, Marietta, Ohio, 1971-72; acctg. technician St. Joseph's Hosp., Parkersburg, W.Va., 1972-74; material mgr. U.S. Dept. Army, Ft. Leonard Wood, Mo., 1982-86, accountant, 1986—; instr. acctg., adj. faculty Tarkio (Mo.) Coll., 1987—. Leader Girls Scouts U.S., Williamstown, W.Va., 1972-74, Hanau, W.Ger., 1977-79. Mem. AAUW (treas. Waynesville br. 1986—, sec Fed. Women's program com. 1986—), Nat. Assn. Female Execs., Fed. Women's Program Com. (chmn. recruitment subcom., sec. 1986—), Am. Soc. Mil. Comptrollers, Alpha Sigma Lambda. Lutheran. Home: 76 Sheppard Fort Leonard Wood MO 65473

BRAHE, NEIL BENTON, dentist; b. Appleton, Wis., June 21, 1926; s. Ralph Bertrand and Mary Jesse (O'Brien) B.; children by previous marriage: Alison Ann, David Carlton, Bruce Benton; m. Barbara Hughes, May 28, 1983 (div.); m. Sally Neville, Aug. 29, 1987. Student Ripon Coll., 1946-49; DDS, Loyola U., Chgo., 1953. Mem. faculty Marquette U., Milw., 1961—, asst. prof. dental practice adminstrn., 1961-65; gen. practice dentistry, Appleton, 1953—; founder, pres. Project D, Appleton, 1961—. Author: Dental Assistants' Self Training Program, 1967, Executive Dynamics in Dental Practice, 1969, We Like These Ideas, 1970, Wonderful World of Modern Dentistry, 1971, Great Ideas for Dental Practice, 1972, Marketing/Public Relations Letters for the Dental Practice; (with Alison A. Brahe) Dental Letter Book, 1975. Mem. ADA, Greater Milw. Dental Assn., Wis. State Dental Soc., Chgo. Dental Soc. (assoc.), Outagamie Dental Soc., A.V. Purinton Acad., Am. Legion, Appleton C. of C. Clubs: Northside Bus., Appleton Yacht; Oshkosh (Wis.) Power Boat. Lodges: Rotary, Elks, Masons. Office: 335 E Wisconsin St Appleton WI 54911

BRAINERD, GERTRUDE PERKINS, educator; b. Canton, Ill., Feb. 19, 1924; d. Keith Carey and Eva C. (Eggert) Perkins; B.S., Western Ill. U., 1945, M.S., 1955; postgrad. Bradley U., 1950, 62-63, Washington U., 1964, Ind. U., 1965-68; m. Robert W. Brainerd, May 22, 1968. Tchr. Augusta Community High Sch., 1945-47, Canton (Ill.) Jr. and Sr. High Sch., 1948-63, Belleville Twp. High Sch. W., 1963-65; instr. Belleville (Ill.) Area Coll., 1963-66, instr. English, 1970-82, chmn. dept., 1977-79; teaching assoc. Ind. U., 1966-68. Pres. bd. dirs. YWCA, Canton. Mem. AAUW (Ill. div. dir. 1974-77, 2d v.p. pub. info. 1975-77, corr. sec. 1977, project dir. 1979), AAUP (br. v.p. 1974), Pi Lambda Theta. Home: 1411 Princeton Dr O'Fallon IL 62269

BRAM, ISABELLE MARY RICKEY MCDONOUGH (MRS. JOHN BRAM), clubwoman; b. Oskaloosa, Ia., Apr. 4; d. Lindsey Vinton and Heddy (Lundee) Rickey; B.A. in Govt., George Washington U., 1947, postgrad., 1947-49; m. Dayle C. McDonough, Jan. 20, 1949; m. 2d, John G. Bram, Nov. 24, 1980. Dep. tax assessor and collector Aransas Pass Ind. Sch. Dist., 1939-41; sec. to city atty., Aransas Pass, Tex., 1939-41; info. specialist U.S. Dept. State, Washington, 1942-48. Treas. Mo. Fedn. Women's Clubs, Inc., 1964-66, 2d v.p., 1966-68, 1st v.p., 1968-70, pres., 1970-72; bd. dirs. Gen. Fedn. Women's Clubs. Mem. steering com. Citizens Com. for Conservation; mem. exec. com. Missourians for Clean Water. Pres., DeKalb County Women's Democratic Club, 1964. Bd. dirs. DeKalb County Pub. Library, pres., 1966; bd. dirs. Mo. Girls Town Found. Mem. AAUW, Nat. League Am. Pen Women, DeKalb County Hist. Soc., Internat. Platform Assn., Law Soc. U. Mo., Zeta Tau Alpha, Phi Delta Delta, Phi Delta Gamma. Democrat. Episcopalian. Mem. Order Eastern Star. Clubs: Tri Arts, Shakespeare, Wimodausis, Gavel, Ledgers, Jefferson. Editor: Mo. Clubwoman mag. Home: Sloan and Cherry Sts Box 156 Maysville MO 64469

BRAMA, RICHARD LEROY, construction company executive; b. Mpls., Mar. 23, 1935; s. August and Flora (DeGidio) B.; m. Angela Ann Walrod, July 8, 1977; children—Cheryl Ann, Robert LeRoy, Thomas Anthony, Lisa Michelle, Kathleen Marie, Christy Ann, Flora Angela, Gina Maria, Richard LeRoy II. Student U. Minn., 1952-54. With mgmt. staff, salesman Boutells-Leaders, Mpls., 1951-60; salesman, investor Petruzza Realty, Mpls., 1960-62; owner Brama Constrn., Mpls., 1962—. Bd. dirs. St. John's Prep. Sch., Collegeville, Minn., 1975—. Mem. Italian Am. Club (treas. 1959-69). Republican. Roman Catholic. Avocations: softball; boating; hunting; volleyball; fishing. Office: Brama Constrn Suite 1 800 W County Rd D New Brighton MN 55112

BRAMAN, DONALD WILLIAM, public relations consultant; b. Mpls., June 19, 1917; s. Maurice I. and Ida (Garber) B.; B.A. cum laude, U. Minn., 1937; m. Sally Davidson, June 16, 1946; children—Stuart, Sandra, Richard. With Mpls. Star, 1937-41; dir. public relations Manson-Gold Advt. Agy., Mpls., 1946-47; public relations staff, publs. editor Toni Co., St. Paul, 1947-49; assoc. dir. public relations Olmsted & Foley, Mpls., 1950-58; co-founder, pres. Don Braman & Assos., Inc., Mpls., 1958-77; v.p. Doremus & Co., N.Y.C. 1977-82; pub. relations cons., 1982—; cons. Internat. Exec. Service Corps., Service Corps Retired Execs.; teaching asst., lectr. Sch. Journalism U. Minn.; dir. Minn. Advt. Fedn. Chmn. Mayor's Com. for Employment of Handicapped, 1950's; chmn. Mpls. Symphony Orchestra Guaranty Fund Campaign, 1960's; fin. com. Mpls. LWV, 1970's; dir. Am.-Israel Chamber of Commerce & Industry of Minn., 1980's. Served with USMC, 1941-45. Mem. Public Relations Soc. Am. (dir., pres. Minn. chpt., mem. exec. com. counselors acad., Disting. Service award 1973, accredited), Nat. Investor Relations Inst. (dir., pres. Minn. chpt.), Mpls. Area C. of C. (chmn. coms. various dates), Marine Corps Combat Correspondents Assn., U. Minn. Alumni Assn., Nat. Audubon Soc., Ariz. Archeol. Soc., Sigma Delta Chi, Zeta Beta Tau. Clubs: Minn. Press, Masons, Scottish Rite, Shrine. Contbr. articles in field to profl. publs., travel articles to popular publs.

BRAMHALL, ROBERT RICHARD, financial consultant; b. Ft. Smith, Ark., Oct. 30, 1927; s. Richard Marion and Ima Lucille (Stovall) B.; A.B., Harvard U., 1951, M.B.A., 1960; m. Mary Margaret Bundy, Aug. 10, 1957; children—Robert Richard Jr., Laura Louise. With Gen. Electric Co.,

N.Y.C., 1954-66, Philco-Ford subs. Ford Motor Co., Phila., 1966-68, Warwick Electronics subs. Whirlpool Corp., Niles, Ill., 1968-70; prin. Bramhall Assocs., Lake Forest, Ill., 1970—; cons. to Rockwell Internat., Bunker-Ramo Corp., Dan River Inc., Molex, Spartan Mills, Rollins, Inc., Lubrizol Corp., Sears (Can.) Ltd., Northrop Corp. Pres. Chgo. Tennis Patrons, Inc., 1974-75. Served with U.S. Army, 1946-48. Republican. Presbyterian. Club: Harvard of Chgo. Home: 855 Buena Rd Lake Forest IL 60045 Office: 222 Wisconsin Bldg Lake Forest IL 60045

BRAMLETT, DERALD LEE, executive management consultant, seminar speaker; b. Omaha, Jan. 9, 1938; s. William S. and Alma D. (Evans) B.; m. Paula Mae Carlson, June 14, 1958; children—Terri, Carol, David, Karen. B.S.B.A., U. Minn., 1960; M.B.A., U. Nebr., 1968. Sales rep. Jello div. Gen. Foods Corp., Omaha, 1964-66; dir. personnel Bishop Clarkson Meml. Hosp., Omaha, 1966-68; cons. A.T. Kearney & Co., Chgo., 1968-71; exec. v.p. Monarch Printing Co., Chgo., 1971-74; pres., owner Lamson/Griffiths Assocs., Chgo., 1974—; exec. and profl. recruiter and cons. Served to capt., USAF, 1961-64. Mem. Chgo. Exec. Club. Republican. Baptist. Contbr. articles profl. jours. Home: 1 Cedar Glen Rd Rolling Meadows IL 60008

BRANCH, RAYMOND LEE, nursing home administrator; b. Balt., Aug. 3, 1928; s. Augustus Lee Branch and Irene Frances (Colbert) Branch Gilmore; B.S. in Health Care Adminstrn., Wichita State U., 1980; m. Idaline Clark, Dec. 27, 1963; children—Joan L. Branch Roberts, Pamela L. Branch Gilyard, Pamela J. Branch Whitaker, Bonnie F. Branch Marshall. Served as enlisted man U.S. Air Force, 1947-74, advanced through grades to master sgt., 1971; various supervisory positions in personnel and records, U.S., Korea, Eng. and Vietnam, 1951-72; personnel supt., chief customer service center 81st Combat Support Group RAF Bentwaters, Eng., 1972-74; ret., 1974; data intern Health Systems Agy. S.E. Kans., Wichita, 1978-79; asst. adminstr. Stafford Homes, Wichita, Kans., 1980-81; nursing home adminstr. Medicalodg South of Kansas City (Kans.), 1981-82, Spl. Care Devel. Ctr., Haven, Kans., 1982-83, Heartland Care Ctr., Belleville, Kans., 1983-84, Directions Unltd., Winfield, Kans., 1985, Hill Haven of Wichita, 1985-86, Medicalodge of Goddard, Kans., 1987—. Decorated Bronze Star medal, Meritorious Service medal, Air Force Commendation medal with oak leaf cluster. Democrat. Baptist. Club: Am. Legion. Home: 615 E Maywood Wichita KS 67216 Office: 501 Easy St Goddard KS 67052

BRANCH, THOMAS ERIC, financial officer; b. Detroit, Sept. 17, 1957; s. Thomas Martin and Edith Lenore (Kranich) B.; m. Catherine F. Attwater, June 1, 1979. BS in Acctg., Walsh Coll., 1981. CPA, Mich. Staff acct. Follmer Rudzewicz, CPA, Southfield, Mich., 1978-81, Joel Winograd, CPA, Houston, 1981-82; sr. acct. Carter Hamilton CPA, Grand Rapids, Mich., 1982-84; sr. auditor Mich. Nat. Bank, Grand Rapids, 1984-86; v.p. fin. Daverman Assocs., Grand Rapids, 1986—. Treas. Family Park Project, Grand Rapids, 1986; vol. Sta. WGVC Pub. TV., Grand Rapids, 1986. Mem. Am. Inst. CPA's, Mich. Assn. CPA's, Jaycees, Grand Rapids C. of C. Republican. Avocations: reading, off-road motorcycling, photography, travel, Mich. football. Office: Daverman Assoc Inc 82 Ionia NW Grand Rapids MI 49503

BRANCHAW, BERNADINE PATRICIA, English educator; b. Joliet, Ill., Jan. 23, 1933; d. Louis and Catherine (Svircek) B. AB, Coll. St. Francis, 1964; MS in Edn., No. Ill. U., 1970, EdD, 1972. Prof. bus. communication Western Mich. U., Kalamazoo, 1971—; cons. in field; mem. adv. bd. Ctr. for Women's Services Western Mich. U. Co-author: Business Report Writing, 1984, SRA Reference Manual, 1986, Business Communication, 1987; author: English Made Easy, 2d edit., 1986. Recipient Governing Bds. award Mich. Assn. Governing Bds., 1987. Mem. Assn. for Bus. Communication (bd. dirs. 1986, Francis Week's award 1982). Republican. Roman Catholic. Lodge: Zonta (past pres. Kalamazoo chpt. 1976). Home: 809 Weaver Ave Kalamazoo MI 49007 Office: Western Mich U Kalamazoo MI 49008

BRAND, DAVID BRIAN, accountant; b. Bridgeport, Conn., Nov. 10, 1956; s. Raymond Lester Brand and Martha Ann (Norton) Brand-Greenblatt; m. Rosalie Estelle Lugibihl, Sept. 11, 1982; 1 child, Naomi Eliza. AA in Social Service, Wright Jr. Coll., 1976; BS in Acctg., Roosevelt U., 1980. CPA, Ill. Acct. Harry F. Shea & Co., Chgo., 1980-85, Shepard, Schwartz & Harris, Chgo., 1985-86, Mittenthal, Goldman & Co., Skokie, Ill., 1986—; tax cons. Chgo. area, 1980—. Mem. Am. Inst. CPA's, Ill. Soc. CPA's. Jewish. Office: Mittenthal Goldman & Co 5214 W Main Skokie IL 60077

BRAND, GROVER JUNIOR, state agricultural official; b. Stark City, Mo., July 5, 1930; s. Grover Cleveland and Ada Neomi (Evans) B.; m. Juanita Sue Warden, Aug. 30, 1952 (div. Oct. 1968); children: Ellen E., Teresa L., Lisa S. B Liberal Studies, U. Okla., 1970. Cert. profl. purchasing agent. Mgr. Crest Drive-In Commonwealth Theatres, Joplin, Mo., 1952-58; buyer Eagle-Picher Ind., Joplin, 1958-65, purchasing mgr., 1965-73; project coordinator Atlas Industries, Oswego, Kans., 1973-78; warehouse examiner Kans. State Grain Inspection, Topeka, 1979—. Mem. Nat. Assn. Purchasing Mgrs. (chmn. value techniques com. 1972-73). Avocation: stock investing. Home: PO Box 207 Oswego KS 67356

BRAND, STEVE AARON, lawyer; b. St. Paul, Sept. 5, 1948; s. Allen A. and Shirley Mae (Mintz) B.; m. Gail Idele Greenspoon, Oct. 9, 1977. BA, U. Minn., 1970; JD, U. Chgo., 1973. Bar: Minn. Supreme Ct. 1973, U.S. Dist. Ct. Minn. 1974, U.S. Supreme Ct. 1977. Assoc. Briggs & Morgan, St. Paul, 1973-78. Pres., Jewish Vocat. Service, 1981-84; pres. Mt. Zion Hebrew Congregation, 1985-87. Mem. ABA, Minn. Bar Assn. (chmn. probate and trust law sect. 1984-85), Am. Coll. Probate Counsel, Phi Beta Kappa. Democrat. Club: Minnesota. Lodge: B'nai B'rith. Home: 1907 Hampshire Ave Saint Paul MN 55116 Office: Briggs & Morgan 2200 1st Nat Bank Bldg Saint Paul MN 55101

BRANDENBURG, JEFFREY A., accountant; b. Ft. Atkinson, Wis., Nov. 22, 1959; s. Alfons R. and Elaine B. (Wittman) B.; m. Maureen Lynn Cloute, May 21, 1983. BBA, U. Wis., Whitewater, 1982. CPA, Wis. Staff acct. Hill, Christensen & Co., CPA's, Columbus, Wis., 1982-83; sr. asst. Hill, Christensen & Co., CPA's, Columbus, 1983-84, sr. acct., 1984-87, supr., 1987—. Mem. Am. Inst. CPA's, Wis. Inst. CPA's (com. mem. 1987), Nat. Soc. of Accts. for Coops. Democrat. Lutheran. Avocations: racquetball, softball, basketball, sports. Office: Hill Christensen & Co 1130A Park Ave Columbus WI 53925

BRANDES, ANNETTE THERRIEN, educator, consulting psychologist; b. Cokato, Minn., Nov. 6, 1940; d. Frederick George and Geneva Orcella (Therrien) B.; B.S., U. Minn., 1962, M.A., 1967; postgrad. Ariz. State U., 1969; Ph.D., U. Chgo., 1981. Lic. cons. psychologist. Tchr. phys. edn. Meml. High Sch., Eau Claire, Wis., 1962-64; phys. edn. specialist Stillwater (Minn.) Schs., 1964-66; counselor Centennial High Sch., Circle Pines, Minn., 1966-68, St. Louis Park (Minn.) Schs., 1968-69; dir. counseling Rhein-Main Am. Schs., Frankfurt, West Germany, 1969-71; asst. dean students (dean of women) Westminster Coll., Salt Lake City, 1971-72; head counselor, instr. dept. psychology St. Scholastica Coll., Duluth, Minn., 1972-74; research cons. dept. research and evaluation Chgo. Bd. Edn., 1978-79; asst. to v.p. acad. affairs U. Minn., 1981-84; pvt. practice mgmt./ednl. cons., Mpls., 1981—; owner, clin. dir. Brandes Stepfamily Services; cons. edn. and human relations, Duluth. Leader, Girl Scouts U.S.A., Duluth, 1972-74. Laverne Noyes Found. scholar, 1974-75. Recipient Arrowhead Leadership award U. Minn., Duluth, 1961. Mem. Am. Psychol. Assn., Minn. Psychol. Assn., Minn. Psychologists in Pvt. Practice, Minn. Womens Psychol. Assn., Pi Lambda Theta. Author novels under pseudonym. Home: 826 Main St NE Minneapolis MN 55413

BRANDES, NORMAN SCOTT, psychiatrist; b. N.Y.C., Dec. 19, 1923; s. Frederic Emile and Claire (Grodin) B.; children—Roger Neil, Fred Emile, Deborah Ann. B.A., NYU, 1947; M.D., U. Tenn., 1950. Diplomate Am. Bd. Psychiatry and Neurology; cert. in psychoanalysis Nat. Accreditation Assn. for Psychoanalysis. Intern N.Y. Polyclinic Postgrad. Med. Sch. and Hosp., N.Y.C., 1950-51; resident Brooke Army Hosp., San Antonio, 1952-53, Ft. Campbell Hosp., Ky., 1953-54, Bridgeport Gen. Hosp., Conn., 1954-55, Ohio State U. Hosp., 1955-57; practice medicine specializing in psychiatry Columbus, Ohio, 1957—; cons. Starling-Loving Mental Health Clinic, Ohio State U., Columbus, 1957-60; asst. dir. Columbus Children's Psychiat. Hosp., 1957-58, dir., 1958-60; cons. adolescent psychiatry Columbus State Hosp., 1961-66; asst. clin. prof. psychiatry Ohio State U., Columbus, 1966-69, assoc. clin. prof. psychiatry, 1969-80; sr. faculty Columbus Inst. for Tng. in Group Psychotherapy, 1968-72; mem. staff Riverside Meth. Hosp., 1958—, Children's Hosp., 1958—, Ohio State U. Hosp., 1958—. Editor, chief contbg. author: Group Therapy for the Adolescent, 1973; (audio tape) Para-analytic Treatment Approaches for the Adolescent Group Psychotherapy, 1974; author, producer: (audio tape cassette book) From The Therapy Bag of An Adolescent Group Therapist, 1976; contbg. author More Columbus Unforgettables, 1986; columnist It's Your Mind, Suburban News Publ. 1986—; contbr. articles to profl. jours. Served to capt. M.C., AUS, 1951-58. Fellow Am. Psychiat. Assn., Am. Assn. Psychoanalytic Physicians, Am. Group Psychotherapy Assn. (bd. dirs. 1970-75, teaching award 1971); mem. AMA (physician's recognition award 1969, 72, 79, 82, 85, 86), Columbus Acad. Medicine, Tri-State Group Psychotherapy Assn. (pres. 1966-67, recognition plaque 1972), Ohio Psychiat. Assn., Soc. for Adolescent Psychiatry. Clubs: Athletic of Columbus, Columbus Indoor Tennis. Office: 6230 Busch Blvd Suite 310 Columbus OH 43229

BRANDHORST, LARRY DALE, architect; b. Wash., Mo., July 17, 1950; s. Herbert Henry and Thelma (Schroff) B.; m. Pamela Jill Tennal, Aug. 19, 1972 (div.); children: Wesley Aaron, D'Arcy Michelle. Student, Lincoln U.e U., 1968-70; BArch, Kans. State U., 1974. Registered architect, Mo. Architect intern Lewis-Eaton Partnership, Jackson, Miss., 1973; architect The Architects Alliance, Inc., Jefferson City, Mo., 1974—. Profl. chmn. Jefferson City Area United Way Campaign, 1985; scouting coordinator Boy Scouts Am. Council, Jefferson City, 1984-85. Mem. AIA (sec.-treas. 1985, bd. dirs. 1982-83), Jefferson City Area C. of C., Jaycees (gen. chmn. Cole County chpt. 1983-84, v.p. Jefferson City chpt. 1982-83, treas. 1984—, chmn. Cole County Fair, 1983-84, Outstanding Man of Yr. 1984). Republican. Methodist. Avocations: softball, basketball, bowling, snow skiing. Office: The Architects Alliance Inc 1431 Southwest Blvd Jefferson City MO 65101

BRANDIN, DONALD NELSON, bank holding company executive; b. N.Y.C., Dec. 28, 1921; s. Nils F. and Dorothy May (Mead) B.; m. Mary Elliott Keyes, Jan. 1, 1982; children: Robert N., Patricia Brandin Barnes, Douglas M.; 1 stepdau., Elizabeth E. White. A.B., Princeton U., 1944. With Bankers Trust Co., N.Y.C., 1946-56; with Boatmen's Nat. Bank, St. Louis, 1956—; chmn. exec. com. Boatmen's Nat. Bank, 1968-70, pres., chief operating officer, 1971-72, chmn. bd., pres., chief exec. officer, 1973-78, chmn. bd., chief exec. officer, 1978-84, chmn. bd., 1984-85, also dir.; exec. v.p. Boatmen's Bancshares, Inc., St. Louis, 1969-72; chmn. bd., chief exec. officer Boatmen's Bancshares, Inc., 1973—, also dir.; dir. Boatmen's Mortgage Co., Petrolite Corp., Wm. S. Barnickel & Co., Sigma-Aldrich Corp., Laclede Gas Co., all St. Louis, Boatmen's Life Ins. Co., Phoenix, Boatmen's 1st Nat. Bank of Kansas City, Mo., Conv. Plaza Redevel. Corp., St. Louis. Bd. dirs. Arts and Edn. Council Greater St. Louis, St. Louis Symphony Soc., Washington U.; trustee Midwest Research Inst. Served to capt. AUS, 1943-46. Mem. Assn. Bank Holding Cos., Assn. Res. City Bankers, Am. Banking Assn., Mo. Bankers Assn., Bank Adminstrn. Inst., Robert Morris Assocs., Internat. Fin. Conf. (bd. dirs.). Clubs: Blind Brook (Purchase, N.Y.); St. Louis, Old Warson Country, Bogey, Stadium (St. Louis); Metropolitan (Chgo.); Garden of Gods (Colorado Springs, Colo.); Kansas City (Mo.). Office: Boatmen's Bancshares Inc 100 N Broadway PO Box 236 Saint Louis MO 63166

BRANDON, EDWARD BERMETZ, banker; b. Davenport, Iowa, Sept. 15, 1931; s. William McKinley and Mary Elizabeth (Bermetz) B.; m. Phyllis Anne Probeck, Aug. 7, 1954; children: William M., Robert P., Beverly A., Beth A., E. Matthew. B.S., Northwestern U., 1953; M.B.A., Wharton Sch. Banking & Fin., 1956. Mgmt. trainee Nat. City Bank, Cleve., 1956-61, sr. v.p., corp. banking head, 1978-79, exec. v.p. corp. banking group, 1979-82, vice chmn., 1982-83, pres., 1984—, chief exec. officer, 1985—; exec. v.p. Nat. City Corp., 1982-83, pres., dir., 1986—; chmn., chief exec. officer Nat. City Bank, 1987—; bd. dirs. Standard Products Co. Trustee, exec. com. Greater Cleve. Growth Assn.; trustee John Carroll U., St. Vincent Charity Hosp., NCCJ, Leadership Cleve., United Way Services, Greater Cleve. Roundtable; vice chmn. bd., exec. com. Greater Cleve. YMCA; bd. advisors, exec. com. Notre Dame Coll. of Ohio; chmn. individual gifts campaign Playhouse Sq. Found. Served to lt. USN, 1953-55. Mem. Am. Bankers Assn., Ohio Bankers Assn., Assn. Res. City Bankers. Republican. Methodist. Clubs: Union (Cleve.); Shaker Heights (Ohio) Country; Firestone Country; Pepper Pike; 50 Club; Tavern. Office: Nat City Bank 1900 E 9th St Cleveland OH 44114

BRANDSTATTER, RICHARD PAUL, real estate executive; b. Chgo., Feb. 7, 1956; s. Walter J. and Bertha F. (Niklaus) B. BBS, Loyola U., Chgo., 1978. CPA, Ill. Tax intern Peat, Marwick, Mitchell& Co., Chgo., 1975-78, auditor, 1978-81; controller Paschen Contractors, Chgo., 1981-86; prin. Brandon-Endicott Group, Chgo., 1986—; pres. Streeterville Ctr. Condominium Assn., Chgo., 1984—. Mem. Ill. Assn. CPA's, Am. Inst. CPA's, Constrn. Fin. Mgmt. Assn. (com. mem.). Office: The Brandon-Endicott Group 111 E Wacker Dr Chicago IL 60601

BRANDSTETTER, DAVID ALBERT, telephone product sales cos. exec.; b. St. Louis, Apr. 7, 1937; s. Edward Otto and Jeannette Eleanor (Leitner) B.; B.S.B.A., Washington U., St. Louis, 1958; m. Holly Nylander, Dec. 28, 1975; children—Sheri, Scott, Kevin, Jason, Troy. Sales rep. S.G. Adams Printing & Stationery, St. Louis, 1958-61; regional mgr. Allied Carbon and Ribbon Mfg. Co., N.Y.C., 1961-65; founder, pres. Electronic Communications Ltd., St. Louis, 1965-85, Phone World, St. Louis, 1978-85, Arch Communications, Inc., 1985—. Recipient Dictaphone Achievement awards, 1975-82. Mem. Adminstrv. Mgmt. Soc., St. Louis Jaycees, Sales and Mktg. Execs., Regional Commerce and Growth Assn. Contbr. articles to Progressive Mgmt. mag., 1979, 80, 81. Home: 1652 Foxleigh Ct Saint Louis MO 63131 Office: 1327 Hampton Ave Saint Louis MO 63139-3113

BRANDT, DAVID DEAN, accountant, financial planner; b. Estherville, Iowa, Feb. 4, 1947; s. Floyd August and Evelyn Ruth (Littell) B.; m. Ruth Dorothea Adams, Aug. 25, 1968; children: Lesley Marie, Jonathan Dean. BA, U. No. Iowa, 1969. CPA, S.D., Iowa; cert. fin. planner, S.D. Staff acct. McGladrey, Hansen, Dunn & Co., Clinton, Iowa, 1969-73, supr., mgr., 1973-75; ptnr. Wohlenberg, Gage and Co., Sioux Falls, S.D., 1975-80; mng. ptnr. La Follette, Jansa, Brandt & Co., Sioux Falls, 1980—. Mem. Sioux Falls Pub. Sch. Dist. Sch. Bd., 1977-82; treas. Asbury United Meth. Ch., Sioux Falls, 1982—; bd. dirs. Sioux Falls Vol. and Info. Ctr., 1982—, Sioux Falls Area Jr. Achievement, 1984—, Sioux Falls Literacy Council, 1986—. Mem. Am. Inst. CPA's, S.D. Soc. CPA's (bd. dirs. 1982-84, pres. elect 1986—, pres. 1987—), Iowa Soc. CPA's, Nat. Assn. Accts. (pres. Sioux Falls chpt. 1981-82), Internat. Bd. Standards and Practices for Cert. Fin. Planners, Continental Assn. CPA Firms (acctg. and auditing com. 1978-80). Republican. Methodist. Avocation: woodworking. Home: 4209 Glenview Rd Sioux Falls SD 57103 Office: LaFollette Jansa Brandt & Co 622 S Minnisota Ave Sioux Falls SD 57104

BRANDT, JERRY, entrepreneur; b. La Grange, Ill., Apr. 16, 1944; s. Wilbert G. and Martha Elizabeth (West) B.; m. Mary Linda Kiefer, Oct. 26, 1963; children: Scott K., Jeffery Todd, Tamara Leann. BBA, Gem City Coll., Quincy, Ill., 1969. Pres. Brandt Enterprises, Inc., La Grange; owner, mgr. La Grange Satellite Systems. Patentee antenna feed support, 1985; designer parabolic antenna, 1986. Mayor City of La Grange, 1979-83; pres. La Grange PTA, 1975-79. Mem. Soc. Pvt. and Comml. EArth Stations, Satellite Antenna Specialists Assn., La Grange C. of C. (pres. 1984). Republican. Baptist. Lodge: Lions. Home: 204 Bates St La Grange MO 63448

BRANDT, WILLIAM ARTHUR, JR., consulting executive; b. Chgo., Sept. 5, 1949; s. William Arthur and Joan Virginia (Ashworth) B.; B.A. with honors, St. Louis U., 1971; M.A., U. Chgo., 1972, postgrad., 1972—; m. Patrice Bugelas, Jan. 19, 1980; children: Katherine Ashworth, William George. Asst. to pres. Pyro Mining Co., Chgo., 1972-76; commentator on bus. and polit. affairs Sta. WBBM-AM, Chgo., 1977; with Melaniphy & Assocs., Inc., Chgo., 1976-78; pres., cons. Devel. Specialists, Inc., Chgo., 1978—; dir. Lafayette Coal Co., Pyro Mining Co., Black Tam Mining Co., Harper Sq. Housing Corp., C-Way Industries, Inc., Nu-Door, Inc., Smith Tool Co., Central Transfer Corp., Ashworth Interiors, Ltd. Mem. adv. bd. Sociological Abstracts, Inc., San Diego, 1979—. LaVerne Noyes scholar, 1971-74. Mem. Am. Sociol. Assn., Am. Coll. Real Estate Cons., Internat. Sociol. Assn., Nat. Assn. Housing and Redevel. Ofcls., Nat. Assn. Real Estate Counsellors, Brit. Sociol. Assn., Chgo. Council Fgn. Relations, Ill. Sociol. Assn., Midwest Sociol. Soc., Soc. Social Research, UN Assn., Aircraft Owners and Pilots Assn. Democrat. Roman Catholic. Clubs: Petroleum (Evansville, Ind.); Amelia Island (Fla.) Plantation. Contbr. articles to profl. jours. Office: 53 W Jackson Blvd Suite 1122 Chicago IL 60604

BRANDYS, ROBERT, home furnishings store executive, pharmacist; b. Hammond, Ind., Dec. 10, 1938; s. Frank Edward and Ann (Smolen) B.; m. Lynn Diane Poplawski, June 30, 1962; children—Robert F., Todd A. B.S. in Pharmacy, Purdue U., 1960. Registered pharmacist, Ill., Ind. Pharmacist Hotz Drugs, Lansing, Ill., 1960-61, Ford Hopkins Drug Co., Melrose Park, Ill., 1961-71, Johnson Drug Co., Batavia, Ill., 1969-71; owner, operator Potpourri, Calumet City, Ill., 1971-85; v.p. , dir. store ops.L. Brandys, Inc., Naperville and Oakbrook, Ill., 1983—. Served to capt. U.S. Army, 1962-65. Decorated Army Commendation medal. Mem. Phi Eta Sigma, Rho Chi. Roman Catholic. Avocations: playing piano, fishing. Office: L Brandys Inc 1010 Fullerton Ave Suite D Addison IL 60101

BRANN, EDWARD R(OMMEL), editor; b. Rostock, Mecklenburg, Germany, May 20, 1920; s. Guenther O.R. and Lilli (Appel) B.; came to U.S., 1938, naturalized, 1966; BA, Berea Coll., 1945; MA, U. Chgo., 1946; postgrad. U. Wis., 1948-56; m. Helen Louise Sweet, Dec. 9, 1948; children: Johannes Weidler, Paul George. Asst. membership sec. central YMCA, Chgo., 1946-48; asst. editor Credit Union Mag., Madison, Wis., 1955-65; dir. hist. projects, asst. dir. publs. CUNA Internat., Inc., Madison, 1965-70, staff historian, 1958-65; asst. dir. publs. Credit Union Nat. Assn., Inc., Madison, 1970-72, 83-84, asst. dir. communications, 1973-83, sr. editor Credit Union mag., 1973-84, coordinator Innovative Ideas Center, 1980-84; contbg. editor Credit Union Exec. mag., 1982-84; dir. hist. projects World Council of Credit Unions, Inc., 1970-79, dir. European relations, 1972-83. Active ARC, various coms. Dane County chpt., vol. cons., 1984—. Recipient Christo et Ecclesiae award Concordia Coll., Milw., 1968, Distinguished Alumnus award Berea Coll., 1977, Risser award Dane County chpt. ARC, 1983; named Ky. col. Mem. Am. Hist. Assn., NEA, Assn. Higher Edn., Luth. Laymen's League, Wis. Hist. Soc., Delta Phi Alpha, Pi Gamma Mu. Lutheran. Contbr. articles to profl. jours. Home: PO Box 383 Madison WI 53701 Office: PO Box 5905 Madison WI 53705

BRANN, LESTER WILLIAM, JR., association executive; b. Madison, Wis., Mar. 24, 1925; s. Lester William and Esther (Jacobsen) B.; m. Lois Winter, Sept. 4, 1948; children—Lester William III, Thomas Edwin. Student, Los Angeles City Coll., 1944; J.D., U. Wis., 1950. Bar: Wis. bar 1950. Practiced in Racine, 1950-57; with Milw. Assn. Commerce, 1957-67, exec. v.p., dir., 1960-67; exec. v.p., dir. Credit Bur. Milw., Inc., 1960-67; exec. v.p. Ill. C. of C., 1967-70, pres., 1970—. Alderman, Racine, 1953-55 Served with AUS, 1943-46. Decorated Purple Heart. Mem. Am., Wis. bar assns., Am. C. of C. Execs. (dir. 1967-71, v.p. 1971-73, chmn. elect 1973-74, chmn. 1974-75), Wis. Alumni Assn., Wis. Law Alumni Assn., Kappa Sigma, Phi Alpha Delta. Clubs: Union League (Chgo.), Economic (Chgo.), Executives (Chgo.), Tower (Chgo.). Home: 337 Forest Rd Hinsdale IL 60521 Office: Ill State C of C 20 N Wacker Dr Chicago IL 60606

BRANNAN, HAROLD DAVID, psychologist, management consultant; b. Bartesville, Okla., Dec. 21, 1949; s. Harold Arnold and May (Lindsey) B.; m. Sydney Lang, May 27, 1984. BS, U. Mo., Columbia, 1971, MEd, 1972; EdS, U. Mo., Kansas City, 1975, PhD, 1978. Lic. psychologist, Mo. Tng. coordinator UMKC, Kansas City, Mo., 1978; dir. tng. Opportunities Industrialization Ctr., Kansas City, 1978-81; coordinator adult outpatient services Community Mental Health Ctr. South, Kansas City, 1981-84, mgr. bus. and industry dept., 1984-86; sr. v.p. EFL Assocs., Kansas City, 1986—. Served as 1st lt. U.S. Army, 1973-75. Mem. Am. Soc. Tng. and Devel., Greater Kansas City Psychological Assn., Personnel Mgmt. Assn. Lodge: Masons. Avocations: scuba diving, golf, reading. Home: 8631 Lamar Overland Park KS 66207 Office: EFL Assocs Corporate Woods 14 Suite 650 8717 W 110th St Overland Park KS 66210

BRANNEN, MALCOLM ERSKINE, violinist, educator; b. Lawrence, Mass., Oct. 12, 1946; s. Weston Louis and Mabel Elizabeth (Robbins) B.; m. Marilyn Sue Bulgarella, Dec. 27, 1985. MusB, Fla. State U., 1968; MusM, Cath. U. Am., 1972; B in Music Edn., Aquinas Coll., 1974. Cert. music edn. tchr., Mich. Tchr. violin Grand Rapids, Mich., 1973—, Grand Rapids Pub. Schs., 1974—, Grand Rapids Jr. Coll., 1980—; concertmaster Kent Philharmonic Orch., Grand Rapids, 1984—. Served with USN, 1968-72. Mem. Am. Fedn. Musicians. Mem. Christian Reformed Ch. Avocations: skiing, sailing, running, sports cars. Office: Grand Rapids Jr Coll 143 Bostwick NE Grand Rapids MI 49508

BRANNON, VICTOR DEWITT, retired research inst. exec.; b. Des Moines, Aug. 26, 1909; s. Ralph William and Carrie Pearl (Hamblin) B.; A.B., U. Ariz., 1931, A.M., 1932; student U. Wis., 1935-36; Ph.D., U. Mo., 1938; m. Dorothy Ellen Webb, Aug. 20, 1933; children—Vicki Rae, Richard Carlyle. Instr. polit. sci. U. Ariz., summers 1931, 33; tchr. social scis. San Simon High Sch., 1933-34; research asst. N.Y. Bd. Regents Inquiry into the cost and character of pub. edn., 1936-37; researcher and statistician Mo. State Hwy. Dept. and Mo. State Planning Bd., 1938-39; asst. dir. St. Louis Govtl. Research Inst., 1939-46, dir., 1947-83; research cons. St. Louis, St. Louis County Bd. Freeholders, 1954, bd. trustees Met. St. Louis Sewer Dist., 1955, St. Louis Charter Bd. Freeholders, 1956-57; research cons. St. Louis Police Dept., 1947-49, 1957-65; sec. Constl. Revision Study Com., 1962; research cons. Com. on Municipalities and Services in St. Louis County, 1958, St. Louis County Charter Com., 1979. Adv. council U. Mo. Sch. Bus. and Pub. Adminstrn., 1965-66. Mem. Govtl. Research Assn. (trustee 1950, 51, pres. 1961-62), Phi Kappa Phi, Phi Delta Kappa. Author articles on polit. sci. Home: 7 Hillard Rd Glendale MO 63122

BRANOFF, DENNIS KOSTA, franchise owner; b. Flint, Mich., Apr. 4, 1953; s. Kosta Vasil Branoff and Sophia Zaccaria (Lambo) Freiberg; m. Alexis Georgette Menoutes, Feb. 22, 1975; children: Andrew Kosta, Jonathan George. Student, U. Mich., 1971, 73, Internat. U. Santader, Spain, 1972. Tng. dir. Weight Watchers, Lansing, Mich., 1969-70, v.p. ops., 1971-72, v.p., dir., 1973—, co-owner, 1978—, chief operating officer, 1984—; bd. dirs. Alona Advt. Agy., Inc., Lansing, United Exporting Services, Inc., Flint; cons. Psychol. Health Services, Inc., Lansing, 1986—. Editor-in-chief- bimonthly newspaper Sophia's Slender Reflections, 1974, Dimagrire Sorridendo, 1984, Ta Nea Mas, 1984. Founding mem. Mich. Statewide Nutrition Coalition, Lansing, 1976; state commr. Mich. Nutrition Commn., Lansing, 1978; dir. Lansing Twp. Devel. Authority, 1980-83; mem. Mich. Bicentennial Commn., Lansing, 1975. Mem. Weight Watchers Franchise Assn., Inc., Phi Eta Sigma. Republican. Greek Orthodox. Clubs: Mich. State U. Pres., Mich. State U. Hon. Coaches. Avocations: playing guitar and piano, golfing, snow skiing. Office: Weight Watchers Omni Bldg 500 N Homer Suite 101 Lansing MI 48912

BRANSDORFER, STEPHEN CHRISTIE, lawyer; b. Lansing, Mich., Sept. 18, 1929; s. Henry and Sadie (Kohane) B.; m. Peggy Ruth Deisig, May 24, 1952; children: Mark, David, Amy, Jill. A.B. with honors, Mich. State U., 1951; J.D. with distinction, U. Mich., 1956; LL.M., Georgetown U., 1958. Bar: Mich. 1956, U.S. Supreme Ct. 1959. Trial atty. Dept. Justice, Washington, 1956-58; atty., editor Office of Public Info., Office of Atty. Gen., 1958-59; spl. asst. U.S. Atty. for D.C., 1958-59; assoc. firm Miller, Johnson, Snell & Cummiskey, Grand Rapids, Mich., 1959-63; partner Miller, Johnson, Snell & Cummiskey, 1963—; pres. State Bar of Mich., 1974-75, commr., 1968-75; chmn. Mich. Civil Service Commn., 1977-78, mem., 1975-78; adv. com. 6th Circuit Jud. Conf., 1984—. Asst. editor: U. Mich. Law Rev, 1956. Pres. Grand Rapids Child Guidance Clinic, 1969-71; chmn. Kent County Coms., Griffin for Senator, 1972, Lenore Romney for Senator, 1966; mem. council legal advisers Rep. Nat. Com., 1981—; Rep. candidate for atty. gen., Mich., 1978; trustee, v.p. Mich. State Bar Found., 1985—; chmn. Mich. State Bd. Canvassers, 1985-87. Served with U.S. Army, 1951-53. Fellow Am. Bar Found.; mem. 6th Cir. Jud. Conf. (life), ABA, Grand Rapids Bar Assn., Fed. Bar Assn. (pres. West Mich. chpt. 1984), Phi Kappa Phi. Presbyterian. Clubs: Grand Rapids Athletic, Cascade Hills Country. Lodge: Rotary.

Home: 7250 Bradfield Rd SE Ada MI 49301 Office: 800 Calder Plaza Bldg Grand Rapids MI 49503

BRANSON, JAMES R., bank official; b. Springfield, Mo., Sept. 18, 1940; s. Ivan Roland Diao and Freida Elizabeth (Baker) B.; student MacMurray Coll., Abilene, Tex., 1961-62; B.A. in Psychology, Drury Coll., 1966; m. Mary Diane Kempker, Nov. 7, 1964; children—Andrew Franklin, Susan Marie. With outing products div. Coleman Co., Wichita, Kans., 1966-67; with ammunition plant Nat. Gypsum Co., Parsons, Kans., 1967-69; dir. personnel Boatmens Nat. Bank, Springfield, Mo., 1969—; personnel cons. 7-11 Corp.; instr. Am. Inst. Banking. Exec. advisor Jr. Achievement, 1979-80; chmn. March of Dimes, 1971-77; adv. bd. Bridgway Program, St. John's Hosp., 1983—; chmn. personnel adv. bd. ARC, 1982—; commr. Ozark council Boy Scouts Am., 1969-71, scoutmaster, 1980-82, adv. Order of Arrow, 1982-84; mem. personnel com. YMCA, 1984—; mem. guidance and counseling bd. Springfield Pub. Schs., 1984-87; mem. Mid Continent Bank Video Edn. Bd., 1984—, Springfield Personnel Bd., 1984-87. Served with USAF; 1959-63. Mem. Springfield C. of C. (loaned exec. program dir. 1982-83), Am. Soc. Personnel Adminstrs., Nat. Audubon Soc., Sierra Club. Republican. Home: 2218 E Cardinal St Springfield MO 65804 Office: PO Box 1157 Southside Station Springfield MO 65807

BRANSTAD, TERRY EDWARD, governor of Iowa, lawyer; b. Leland, Iowa, Nov. 17, 1946; s. Edward Arnold and Rita (Garl) B.; m. Christine Ann Johnson, June 17, 1972; children: Eric, Allison, Marcus. BA, U. Iowa, 1969; JD, Drake U., 1974. Bar: Iowa. Sr. ptnr. firm Branstad-Schwarm, Lake Mills, Iowa, until 1982; farmer Lake Mills; mem. Iowa Ho. of Reps., 1973-78; lt. gov. Iowa 1979-82; gov. State of Iowa, 1983—; Bd. dirs. Am. Legion of Iowa Found. Served in U.S. Army, 1969. Mem. Nat. Govs. Assn. (chmn. agrl. com.), Midwestern Govs. Assn. (chmn.), Am. Legion, Farm Bur. Republican. Roman Catholic. Lodges: Lions, KC. Office: Office Gov Statehouse Des Moines IA 50319

BRANT, JOHN S., petroleum products company executive; b. Toronto, Ont., Can., May 29, 1939; s. Theodore Jack and Ruth Gladys (Spall) B.; m. Frances Patricia Zayette, May 14, 1960; children: David (dec.), Paul, Tina. BA, U. Toronto. Zone mgr. U.S. Elevator Co., 1969-71; asst. to pres. Dover Corp. Ltd., 1971-72; v.p., gen. mgr. Can. Elevator Corp., 1972-76; pres. Dover Corp., 1976-81; pres., chief exec. officer Emco Ltd., London, Ont., 1984—. Office: Emco Limited, 1108 Dundas St E, London, ON Canada N6A 4N7 *

BRANT, MARJORIE HASSELBACK, lawyer; b. Pitts., July 27, 1947; d. George and Jean Gwendolyn (Wible) Hasselback; m. John Wesley Brant, July 20, 1974; children: Douglas, John, Laura. BA, Ind. U. Pa., 1969; MA, Purdue U., 1971; MLS, U. Pitts., 1973; JD, Ohio State U., 1983. Bar: Ohio, 1983, U.S. Dist. Ct. (so. dist.) Ohio, 1983. Librarian Columbia Gas Systems Service Corp., Columbus, Ohio, 1973-80; lawyer Columbia Gas Dist. Cos., Columbus, Ohio, 1983—. Contbr. articles to profl. jours. Recipient Medal of Excellence Moot Ct. Am. Coll. Trial Lawyers. Mem. ABA, Ohio Bar Assn., Columbus Bar Assn., Women Lawyers Franklin County, Beta Phi Mu. Home: 2605 Bryan Circle Grove City OH 43123 Office: Columbia Gas Dist Cos 200 Civic Ctr Dr Columbus OH 43216

BRANT, RICHARD ROSS, manufacturing company official; Cin., Sept. 29, 1934; s. Albert Herman and Alice (Gard) B.; m. Helen Baukin, Sept. 4, 1954; children—Kristen, Mark, Eric. B.A., DePauw U., 1956; M.B.A., Western Mich. U., 1967. Mgr., Comfast Ill. Tool Works, Des Plaines, Ill., 1977—. Active Boy Scouts Am. Served to capt. USAF, 1957-60. Mem. Soc. Cable TV Engrs., U.S. Ind. Telephone Assn., Am. Mgmt. Assn. Republican. Lutheran. Club: Rotary (Elgin, Ill.).

BRANTLEY, JAMES MORRIS, quality engineer; b. Sturgis, Ky., Sept. 11, 1943; s. Morris Alonzo and Pearl (Ritchie) B.; m. Silveriana C. Saya-Ang, Aug. 18, 1966; children: James, Richard, Charles. BS in Liberal Arts, SUNY, Albany, 1985. Enlisted USAF, 1964, advanced through grades to msgt., 1982; mem. aircrew USAF, Vietnam, 1965-72; aircraft maintenance mgr. USAF, 1972-76, metrologist, 1976-82; quality assurance mgr. USAF, Tullahoma, Tenn., 1982-84; ret. USAF, 1984; sr. quality engr. Midland-Ross Corp., Urbana, Ohio, 1985—. Decorated Gallantry Cross (Republic of Vietnam); recipient Meritorious Service award, 1984. Mem. USAF Assn., Am. Soc. Quality Control. Methodist. Avocations: genealogy, hist. research, writing hist. fiction. Home: 555 Lewis Dr Fairborn OH 45324 Office: Midland-Ross Corp Grimes Div Aerospace Group 550 Rt 55 Urbana OH 43078

BRASS, RICHARD JOHN, management and training consultant; b. Greeley, Colo., Oct. 20, 1942; s. Earlyon F. and Matilda E. (Harnisch) B.; divorced; children: Clinton T., Laura R. BA, Valparaiso (Ind.) U., 1965, postgrad., 1971; MA, U. Iowa, 1973; postgrad., U. Calif., San Diego, 1981. Nat. youth work dir. Japan Luth. Ch., Tokyo, 1965-70; exec. dir. Internat. Assistance and Understanding Program, Tokyo, 1966-70; dir. elderly and handicapped transp. Kirkwood Community Coll., Cedar Rapids, Iowa, 1973-75; co-founder, dir. services Pub. Resources Council, Swisher, Iowa, 1975-76; assoc. dir., office of community coll. affairs U. Iowa, Iowa City, 1976-81; pres. Brass, Richie & Betts, Iowa City, 1981—; instr. Hokusei Sr. Coll., Sapporo, Japan, 1965-67; founder Tokyo Free U., 1969-70; cons. fgn. culture adaption Luth. Ch. Miss. Synod, St. Louis, 1972; cons. rural trans. U.S. Adminstrn on Aging, Kansas City, 1974-75. Editor: Kernels, 1978-80; author: Community Colleges the Future and SPOD, 1984 (merit award Soc. Tech. Communication, 1985); publ.: Toki No Ba, 1968-70. Mem. Am. Soc. Tng. and Devel. (author tng. film bibliography, HRD Excellence award 1985), Profl. and Orgnl. Devel. Network in Higher Edn., Nat. Council for Staff, Program and Orgnl. Devel. (charter, John Fry Individual Merit award 1980-81), Iowa Council for Staff, Program and Orgnl. Devel. (charter, pres. 1979-80). Office: Brass Richie & Betts Inc 1232 E Burlington Iowa City IA 52240

BRASTED, KENNETH PARKER, II, bank executive; b. Wichita, Kans., Aug. 15, 1935; s. Kenneth Parker and Lulu (Humphrey) B.; m. Sherrie Grayston, Oct. 19, 1963; children: Kenneth P. III, Amy Doreen. BA, Dartmouth Coll.; MBA, U. Pa. Asst. treas. Star-Kist Foods, Inc., Terminal Island, Calif., 1962-63; asst. to sr. v.p. fin. H.J. Heinz Corp., Pitts., 1963-64; pres. Mid-Kansas Fed. Savs. and Loan Assn., Wichita, 1964—, also bd. dirs.; Mem. adv. com. Fed. Home Loan Mortgage Corp., Washington, 1984-86; bd. dirs. Fed. Home Loan Bank Topeka, Midwest Heart Inst. Trustee Wichita State U. Endowment Assn., 1978—, Wichita Art Assn., 1982—; treas. Wesley Hosp. Endowment Assn., Wichita, 1980—; bd. dirs. Music Theater Wichita, 1980—, Greater Wichita Community Found. Served to 1st lt. U.S. Army, 1957-59. Mem. Kans. League of Savs. Assns. (chmn. 1983), Kans. Assn. Commerce and Industry (chmn. 1986—). Republican. Congregationalist. Home: 620 Stratford Wichita KS 67226 Office: Mid Kans Fed Savs and Loan Assn 230 S Market Wichita KS 67202

BRASUNAS, ELLEN LYDIA, psychotherapist; b. Columbus, Ohio, Nov. 16, 1924; d. Arthur Theodore and Norma Caroline (Wagner) W.; m. Anton deSales Brasunas, Nov. 16, 1946; children: James Anton, Kay Ellen, Anne Elizabeth. BS in Nursing, Ohio State U., 1946; MA in Counseling, Webster U., 1978. RN. Pub. health nurse St. Louis County, 1971-75; pub. sch. nurse Normandy Sch. Dist., St. Louis, 1975-79; psychotherapist Christian Psychol. and Family Services, St. Louis, 1979-83, Creve Coeur Counseling, St. Louis, 1983—; vol. Nat. Council on Alcoholism, St. Louis, 1983—. Recipient Outstanding Vol. award Nat. Council on Alcoholism, St. Louis, 1984. Mem. Am. Assn. Marriage and Family Therapy (clin.), Ethical Soc. St. Louis. Democrat. Club: Dulcimer (St. Louis). Avocations: dulcimer, tennis, swimming, needlepoint. Home: 8030 Daytona Dr Saint Louis MO 63105

BRATHWAITE, DOLLIE MAE, nurse, consultant; b. Woodstock, Ala., Apr. 12, 1941; d. Oscar L. and Kinny D. (Mitchell) Bryant; divorced; children: Amaryllis Johnson, April Johnson. AA, Highland Park Community Coll., 1971; BS, Wayne State U., 1974, MS, 1976, postgrad., 1976—. Staff nurse Hutzel Hosp., Detroit, 1965-74; supr. Model Neighborhood, Detroit, 1974-75; nursing instr. Highland Park (Mich.) Community Coll., 1975-80; dir. Health and Education Profls., Detroit, 1979—; Instr. Wayne County Community Coll., 1976—, Madonna Coll., Livonia, Mich., 1983—; cons. Detroit Dept. Health, 1983—, CareerWorks, Inc., Detroit, 1982, Universal Variable, Detroit, 1982-84, North Detroit Gen. Hosp., Detroit, 1986. Treas. local sch. adv. bd., Detroit, 1975; vice chmn. Mich. Health Occupation Council, Lansing, 1983. Fellow Am. Nurses Assn.; mem. Am. Pub. Health Assn., Nat. Black Nurses Assn., Detroit Black Nurses Assn. (pres. 1980-84), Better Care Coalition (vice chmn. 1985), NAACP (life). Avocations: walking, aerobics, reading, traveling. Home: 16688 Turner Detroit MI 48221 Office: Health and Edn Profls 16875 James Couzens Detroit MI 48235

BRAU, KATHLEEN A., reading educator; b. Milw., Feb. 8, 1948; d. Edmund Ralph and Emily Josephine (Sadowski) Janowiak; m. Anthony Joseph Brau, Oct. 12, 1970. BS, U. Wis., 1971, MS, 1974. Tchr. Milw. Pub. Schs., 1971-74, tchr. reading, 1974-77, reading specialist, 1977—; instr. Milw. Area Tech. Coll., 1985—; reading cons. Gareth Stevens, Milw., 1986—. Mem. Internat. Reading Assn., Wis. Reading Assn., Milw. Area Council Reading, Phi Delta Kappa. Avocations: reading, bicycling, running, Eskimo art and depression glass collecting. Home: 2906A S 14th St Milwaukee WI 53215

BRAU, RAY FRANCIS, insurance company executive; b. Arlington, Minn., July 31, 1961; s. Leonard C. and Marion E. (Rutherford) B. BS in Biology and Bus., St. John's U., Collegeville, Minn., 1983. Physiologist Health and Wellness Clinic, Bloomington, Minn., 1983-84; pres. Take Care, Inc., Eden Prairie, Minn., 1984—; acct. exec. Sentry Ins., Mpls., 1986—. Mem. Minn. Assn. Life Underwriters. Home: 7470 Chanhassen Rd Chanhassen MN 55317

BRAUCHT, DAVID WILLIAM, architect; b. Jacksonville, Fla., May 9, 1954; s. William Chester and Miriam Lenore (Keilman) B.; m. Becky Jo Brugger, Mar. 22, 1975; children: Jason, Joshua, Lacey. BArch, U. Minn., 1976. Registered architect, Wis., Minn., Mich., Ill., Ind., Iowa. Mgr. design Marshall Erdman & Assocs., Inc., Madison, Wis., 1976—. Deacon Westminster Presbyn. Ch., Madison, 1983-85. Mem. AIA. Avocations: computers, fishing. Home: 1402 Club Circle Middleton WI 53562 Office: Marshall Erdman & Assocs Inc 5117 University Ave Madison WI 53705

BRAUDE, MICHAEL, board of trade executive; b. Chgo., Mar. 6, 1936; s. Sheldon and Nan B.; m. Linda Rae Miller, Aug. 20, 1961; children—Peter, Adam. B.S., U. Mo., 1957; M.S., Columbia U., 1958. Vice pres. Commerce Bank, Kansas City, Mo., 1960-73; vice pres. Mercantile Bank, Kansas City, Mo., 1966-73; exec. v.p. Am. Bank, Kansas City, Mo., 1973-84; pres., chief exec. officer Kansas City Bd. Trade, Mo., 1984—; dir. Overland Park Savs. & Loan, Kans. Author: Managing Your Money, 1975, also 12 childrens books. Pres. Metr. Community Coll. Found., Kansas City, Mo., 1982-84; mayor City of Mission Woods, Kans., 1982-84. Mem. Futures Industry Assn., Nat. Futures Assn., U. Mo. Alumni Assn (bd. dirs. 1985—). Jewish. Club: Homestead Country (Prairie Village, Kans.). Avocations: running; public speaking. Home: 5319 Mission Woods Terr Shawnee Mission KS 66205 Office: Kansas City Bd Trade 4800 Main St #303 Kansas City MO 64112

BRAUDE, THEODORE R., psychotherapist, musician, social activist; b. Detroit, Mar. 11, 1952; s. Daniel and Leonore Harriet (Leff) B.; m. Victoria Marie Yelletz, July 28, 1985. BA magna cum laude, Oakland U., Rochester, Mich., 1974; MA, Merrill-Palmer Inst., 1981. Lic. psychologist (ltd.), Mich.; cert. social worker, Mich. Cons. Sunshine Assocs., Livonia, Mich., 1975; psychotherapist Alternative Lifestyles, Pontiac, Mich., 1977; tchr. Friends Sch. in Detroit, 1977-80; psychotherapist Ind. and Group Psychol. Services, Rochester, 1981-83, St. Joseph Ctr. for Family Counseling, Mt. Clemens, Mich., 1982-85, New Beginnings Counseling Ctr., Royal Oak, Mich., 1983—; workshop presenter, 1982-86; core-facilitator The Day Before Project, Detroit, 1983; mem. Nat. Council Interhelp, Inc., Northampton, Mass., 1985-86. Composer several songs, 1979-81; producer The Atomic Comics, Detroit, 1985-86; editorial columnist Daily Tribune, 1986-87; contbr. articles to mags., 1984-86. Coordinator, mem. steering com. South Oakland Region of Detroit Area Nuclear Freeze, 1982-84; coordinator Citizen's Network, Detroit, 1985. Recipient Creative Music Art Prodn. award The Detroit News, 1970. Jewish. Avocations: reading, swimming, outdoor activities, woodworking, guitar making. Office: New Beginnings Counseling Ctr 123 S Main St Royal Oak MI 48067

BRAUER, FRED GÜNTHER, mathematics educator; b. Königsberg, Germany, Feb. 3, 1932; came to U.S., 1960; s. Richard D. and Ilse (Karger) B.; m. Esther Luterman, June 22, 1958; children: David, Deborah, Michael. B.A., U. Toronto, 1952; S.M., Mass. Inst. Tech., 1953, Ph.D., 1956. Instr. U. Chgo., 1956-58; lectr., then asst. prof. U. B.C., 1958-60; mem. faculty U. Wis., Madison, 1960—; prof. math. U. Wis., 1966—. Author: (with J.A. Nohel) Ordinary Differential Equations: A First Course, 1967, 2d edit., 1973, Elementary Differential Equations; Principles, Problems, Solutions, 1968, Problems and Solutions in Ordinary Differential Equations, 1968, Qualitative Theory of Ordinary Differential Equations, 1969, (with J.A. Nohel and H. Schneider) Linear Mathematics, 1970, Introduction to Differential Equations with Applications, 1986. Mem. Am. Math. Soc. (asso. editor Proc. 1971-74), Math. Assn. Am., Canadian Math. Congress, Soc. Indsl. and Applied Math., Sigma Xi. Home: 5113 Coney Weston Pl Madison WI 53711

BRAUN, BRIAN ALAN, lawyer; b. Chgo., Jan. 21, 1947; s. Jerome and Lillian (Schuster) B.; m. Terre J. Tibbles, Dec. 18, 1980; children: David Joshua, Aaron Jonathan. BS, U. Ill., 1969; JD, DePaul U., 1975. Bar: Ill. 1975, U.S. Dist. Ct. (cen. and so. dists.) Ill. 1983. Gen. counsel Ill. Assn. Sch. Bds., Springfield, 1977-82; ptnr. Miller, Tracy, Braun & Wilson, Ltd., Monticello, Ill., 1982—. Author: Teacher Salaries and Fringe Benefits, 1980; contbr. numerous articles to profl. jours. Mem. Ill. Bar Assn., Platt County Bar Assn. Home: 6 Eton Ct Champaign IL 61820 Office: Miller Tracy Braun & Wilson Ltd PO Box 227 Monticello IL 61856

BRAUN, BRUCE BIDWELL, government executive; b. Albany, N.Y., Dec. 15, 1942; s. Carl Frederick and Ruth Alice (Cooley) B.; m. Nancy Jane Ostrander, Aug. 26, 1965; children: Deborah Ann, Bonnie Lynn. B in Forestry, SUNY Coll. of Forestry, Syracuse, 1964; MPA, Maxwell Sch. Pub. Affairs, Syracuse, 1965. State budget officer Wis. Dept. Adminstrn., Madison, 1965-72, property planning chief, 1972-78; planning div. adminstr. Wis. Dept. Natural Resources, Madison, 1978-82, dep. sec., 1982—; from vice chmn. to chmn. Wis. Lab. of Hygiene Bd., Madison, 1980—; mem. Wis. Coastal Mgmt. Council, Madison, 1980-85. treas. Citizens to Elect Bill Lunney, Dane County, Wis., 1972; treas., vice chmn., chmn. Greenfield Neighborhood Assn., Fitchburg, Wis., 1978-80; worker Com. to elect Tony Earl Gov., Dane County, 1982, 86. Recipient Exceptional Performance awards Dept. Sec. 1976, 77 78, 80, Gov.'s Spl award, 1978, Cert. Appreciation State Bldg. Commn. and Legis., 1978. Avocations: sports, travel, reading, music, photography. Home: 2277 Gold Dr Rt 4 Madison WI 53711 Office: Dept Nat Resources 101 S Webster St GEF II Madison WI 53707

BRAUN, GERRY COLE, oil company executive; b. Washington, Aug. 12, 1948; s. John Walter and Lary Hall (Dalton) B.; m. Christy Lynn Andersen, July 7, 1979; children: Scott, Paul, Brittany. BS, U. Tenn. Cost acct. Star-Kist, Terminal Island, 1973-75; mgr. mfg. acctg. Federated Dept. Stores, Los Angeles, 1975-77; chief acct. Santa Fe Internat., Orange, Calif., 1977-80; dir. planning and control Anaconda Advanced Technology div. Arco, Dublin, Ohio, 1980—. Served to sgt. U.S. Army, 1971-73. Mem. Los Angeles Nat. Acctg. Assn., Strategic Planning Forum, Kappa Sigma. Democrat. Presbyterian. Club: Civic (treas. Va. chpt. 1966). Avocations: photography, sports. Home: 2294 Starleaf Ln Worthington OH 43085 Office: Anaconda Advanced Technology 5160 Blazer Memorial Pkwy Dublin OH 43017

BRAUN, RICHARD EDWARD, entrepreneur, educator, consultant; b. Duluth, Minn., Aug. 21, 1942; s. Edward Walter Braun and Eleanor Leone (Radig) Burns; m. Nancy Nyquist, Dec. 31, 1968; children: Victoria Dawn, Nichole Anissa, Shanda Anneke. Diploma advanced acctg., bus. adminstrn., Duluth Bus. U.; BBA, U. Minn., 1975; cert. in systems analysis, U. Wis. Owner Avis Rent A Car, Duluth, 1963-65; computer supr. Jeno's Inc., Duluth, 1967-79; data processing mgr. Paulucci Enterprises, Duluth, 1979-82; computer coordinator, dir. entrpreneurship program Coll. St. Scholastica, Duluth, 1982—; owner Seagull Enterprises, Duluth, 1976—; bd. dirs. Minn. Ednl. Computing Corp., Elem., Secondary, Vocat. Computer Council, U. Minn. Duluth Bus. and Econs. Alumni Assn. Editor: (monthly community newsletter) The Breeze of Park Point, 1972—. Councilor, City of Duluth, 1986—; dir., treas., chmn. bus. and fin. com. Duluth Sch. Bd., 1978-85; Episc. lay leader, chalice bearer St. Andrews by the Lake Ch. Mem. Data Processing Mgmt. Assn. (individual performance silver award). Club: Duluth Rowing. Lodge: Kiwanis. Avocations: cross country skiing and running, stamp and coin collecting, Tae Kwon Do, swimming, sailing. Home: 3422 Minnesota Duluth MN 55802 Office: Coll St Scholastica 1200 Kenwood Ave Duluth MN 55811

BRAUN, ROBERT ALEXANDER, psychiatrist; b. Chemnitz, Germany, Dec. 14, 1910; s. Leo and Bertha (Eisenschiml) B.; came to U.S., 1939, naturalized, 1946; M.D., U. Vienna (Austria), 1937; m. Gertrud E. Mittler, Jan. 6, 1946; children—Eleanor, Ronald. Intern, William McKinley Meml. Hosp., Trenton, N.J., 1940-41; resident in psychiatry Rochester (Minn.) State Hosp., 1950-51, staff psychiatrist, 1951-56; resident in psychiatry Lafayette Clinic, Detroit, 1956-58, staff psychiatrist, clin. dir. Clinton Valley Center (formerly Pontiac State Hosp.), Pontiac, Mich., 1958-60, dir. Oakland Div., 1963-80; pvt. practice psychiatry, 1980—; Diplomate Am. Bd. Psychiatry. Life fellow Am. Psychiat. Assn. Office: 25882 Orchard Lake Rd Suite 203 Farmington Hills MI 48018

BRAUN, ROBERT CLARE, association and advertising executive; b. Indpls., July 18, 1928; s. Ewald Elsworth and Lila (Inman) B.; B.S. in Journalism-Advt., Butler U., 1950; postgrad. Ind. U., 1957, 66. Reporter, Northside Topics Newspaper, Indpls., 1949, advt. mgr., 1950; asst. mgr. Clarence E. Crippen Printing Co., Indpls., 1951; corp. sec. Auto-Imports, Ltd., Indpls., 1952-53; pres. O. R. Brown Paper Co., Indpls., 1953-69; pres., chief exec. officer Robert C. Braun Advt. Agy., 1959-70, Zimmer Engraving Inc., Indpls., 1964-69; former chmn. bd. O. R. Brown Paper Co., Zimmer Engraving, Inc.; advt. cons. Rolls-Royce Motor Cars, 1957-59; exec. dir., chief exec. officer Historic Landmarks Found., Ind., 1969-73; exec. v.p., Purchasing Mgmt. Assn. Indpls., 1974-85; cen. dist. coordinator Ind. Regional Minority Supplier Devel. Council, 1985—; pres. A.P.S. Industries, Inc., 1979—; nat. v.p. Associated Purchasing Publs., 1981-85; gen. mgr. Midwest Indsl. Show, 1974-85, Midwest Office Systems and Equipment Show, 1974-85, Grand Valley Indsl. Show, 1974-85, Evansville Indsl. Show, 1982-85, Ind. Bus. Opportunity Fair, 1985—. Chmn., Citizens' Adv. Com. to Marion County Met. Planning Dept., 1963; pres. museum com. Indpls. Fire Dept., 1966—; mem. adv. com. Historic Preservation Commn. Marion County, 1967-73; Midwestern artifacts cons. to curator of White House, Washington, 1971-73; mem., chmn. Mayor's Contract Compliance Adv. Bd., 1977—; mem. Mayor's Subcom. for Indpls. Stadium, 1981—; adv. bd., exec. com. Inpls. Office Equal Opportunity 1982—; mem. Ind. Minority Bus. Opportunity Council, 1985—; mem. Met. Mus. Art, Indpls. Mus. Art. Bd. dirs. Historic Landmarks Found. Ind., 1960-69; dir., sec. Ind. Arthritis and Rheumatism Found., 1960-67, pres., 1969, dir., 1970—, dir. Asso. Patient Services, 1976—; pres. Amanda Wasson Meml. Found., 1961-72, Huggler-Ault Meml. Trust, 1961-72. Recipient Meritorious Service award St. Jude's Police League, 1961; citation for meritorious service Am. Legion Police Post 56, 1962; Tafflinger-Holiday Park appreciation award, 1973; Nat. Vol. Service Citation, Arthritis Found., 1979; Margaret Egan Meml. award Ind. Arthritis Found., 1980; Indpls. Profl. Fire Fighters meritorious service award, 1982. Mem. Marion County Hist. Soc. (dir. 1964—, pres. 1965-69, 74-76, 1st v.p. 1979), Am. Guild Organists (mem. Indpls. chpt., charter mem. Franklin Coll. br.), Indpls. Humane Soc., Ind. Museum Soc. (treas., dir. 1967-74), Internat. Fire Buff Assos., Indpls. Second Alarm Fire Buffs (sec.-treas. 1967, pres. 1969), Ind. Hist. Soc., Nat. Hist. Soc., Nat. Trust Historic Preservation, Smithsonian Assn., Soc. Archtl. Historians, Am. Heritage Soc., N.A.P.M. Editors Group (nat. sec. 1979-81, nat. chmn./pres. 1981—), Am. Assn. State and Local History, Decorative Arts Soc. Indpls., Ind. Soc. Assn. Execs., Nat. Assn. Purchasing Mgmt. (W.L. Beckham internat. pub. relations award 1983), Purchasing Mgmt. Assn. Indpls. (dir. 1974—), Victorian Soc. Am. (nat. sec. 1971-74), Lambda Chi Alpha, Alpha Delta Sigma, Sigma Delta Chi, Tau Kappa Alpha. Club: Indpls. Press, Rolls-Royce Owners. Author: The Mr. Eli Lilly that I Knew, 1977. Editor: Historic Landmarks News, 1969-74; Hoosier Purchasor mag., 1974-85, I.R.M.S.D.C. News, 1985—. Contbr. articles to profl. jours. Home: 1415 W 52d St Indianapolis IN 46208 Office: 300 E Fall Creek Pkwy ND Suite 403 Indianapolis IN 46205

BRAUN, VICKI ANN COSTAN, public relations specialist, public speaker; b. Cleve., Aug. 31, 1949; d. Lewis Costan and Victoria (Borza) C.; m. Raymond Richard Braun, Jan. 8, 1972. B.S., U. Dayton, 1970; postgrad. U. Hawaii, 1972, Wright State U., 1982. Coordinator Sta. KTHI-TV, Grand Forks, N.D., 1973-74; continuity asst. Avco Broadcasting Co./Grinnell Broadcasting Co., Dayton, Ohio, 1974 76, continuity dir., 1976-78; devel. project mgr. Greater Dayton Pub. TV, 1978-79, membership dir., 1980-81; devel./pub. relations coordinator Hearing and Speech Ctr., Dayton, 1981-84; asst. dir. hosp. communications Children's Med. Ctr., Dayton, 1984-86; communications cons., 1986—; speaker United Way Speaker's Bur. Mem. adv. council Community Services for Deaf; mem. communications adv. council United Way Greater Dayton. Recipient Golden Mike award, 1978; Ohio Ednl. Broadcasting Commn. award, 1981, Golden Quill award for feature writing, 1985, Ohio State Hosp. Pub. Relations Soc. award, 1986. Mem. Nat. Acad. TV Arts and Scis. (dir., officer), Women in Communications. Home: 128 Oak Knoll Dr Dayton OH 45419

BRAUN, VICTOR F., plumbing parts manufacturing company executive. Chmn., chief exec. officer Ladish Corp., Cudahy, Wis. Office: Ladish Co 5481 S Packard Ave Cudahy WI 53110 *

BRAUNSDORF, JAMES ALLEN, physics educator; b. South Bend, Ind., Apr. 13, 1938; s. Walter Louis and Ruth Harriet (Tuttle) B.; m. Donna Lou Munson, June 10, 1960; children: Kevin Scott, Allen Keith, Walter James. AB in Physics, De Pauw U., 1960; MS in Math., Purdue U., 1965. Cert. secondary tchr., Ind. Tchr. physics Greencastle Schs., 1960-62, Mishawaka (Ind.) Sch., 1962—; tax preparer, Mishawaka, 1967—; adj. lectr. Ind. U., South Bend, 1981—. Pres. Beiger Heritage Corp., Mishawaka, 1981-86. Mem. NEA, Ind. State Tchrs. Assn., Am. Assn. Physics Tchrs. (Ind. Disting. Physics Tchr. 1984), Nat. Sci. Tchrs. Assn., Mishawaka Edn. Assn. (pres. 1970-74), Phi Beta Kappa. Methodist. Avocations: computing, plate collecting. Home: 449 Edgewater Dr Mishawaka IN 46545

BRAUNSTEIN, ETHAN MALCOLM, skeletal radiologist; b. Chgo., June 16, 1945. BA, Dartmouth Coll., 1967; MD, Northwestern U., Chgo., 1970. Instr. radiology U. Mich., Ann Arbor, 1976-81, assoc. prof., 1983-87; asst. prof. radiology Harvard U., Cambridge, Mass., 1981-83; prof. Ind. U., Indpls., 1987—. Contbr. numerous articles to profl. jours. and chpts. to books. Trustee Kelsey Museum of Archeaology, Ann Arbor, 1983—. Served to maj. USAF, 1973-75. Mem. Internat. Skeletal Soc., Am. Assn. Physical Anthropologists, Radiologic Soc. N.Am., Assn. Univ. Radiologists. Office: Ind U Hosps Dept Radiology Indianapolis IN 46223

BRAVERMAN, BRUCE JOEL, controller; b. Chgo., Feb. 2, 1958; s. Casper Roy and Rochelle Ethel (Kaufman) B.; m. Carolyn Ann Chakiris; 1 child, Samuel Philip. BS in Fin., U. Ill., 1980. Registered commodity rep. Fin. analyst Chgo. Bd. Trade, 1980-81; controller Dorman Trading Co., Inc., Chgo., 1981-85, Goldenberg, Hehmeyer & Co., Chgo., 1985—; ind. commodity trader, Chgo., 1984—. Mem. Chgo. Bd. Trade, Pi Lambda Phi, Tau DElta Phi, Phi Lambda Alumni Corp. Jewish. Office: Goldenberg Hehmeyer & Co 141 W Jackson Blvd #1701A Chicago IL 60604

BRAVOS, THOMAS WILLIAM, data processing executive, accountant; b. Chgo., Feb. 4, 1947; s. William John and Violet (Kachiroubas) B.; m. Mary Louise Soboleski, Sept. 13, 1969; children—Christina, Stephanie, Carolyn, William (dec.), Joanna. B.A., McConmar Coll., 1969; postgrad. Lewis U., 1971, DePaul U., 1972. C.P.A., Ill. Staff acct. Arthur Greenman & Co., C.P.A.s, Chgo., 1968-71; mgr. audit Philip Rosenstrock & Co., C.P.A.s, Chgo., 1971-75; mgr. audit/MAS, Coleman, Epstein, Berlin & Co., C.P.A.s, Chgo., 1975-77; mgr. audit Schwartz, Frumm & Millman, C.P.A.s, Chgo., 1981; v.p., asst. corp. sec., dir. data processing Mercury Metal Products, Inc., Schaumburg, Ill., 1981-84; audit mgr. Schwartz, Frumm & Millman, C.P.A.s, 1984—; fin. and tax cons. Mem. Am. Inst. C.P.A.s, Ill. C.P.A. Soc.

Home: 153 Braintree Dr Bloomingdale IL 60108 Office: Schwartz Frumm & Millman CPAs 6 N Michigan Ave Chicago IL 60612

BRAWLEY, REX ALFRED, resort owner; b. Litchfield, Ill., Aug. 2, 1924; s. Theodore Fuller and Alice (Smith) B.; m. Bebe June Hogsett; 1 child, Wendy. Ptnr. Brawley Bros. Wholesale Distbg. Co., Litchfield, 1946-71; owner Rainmaker Resort, Litchfield, 1967—. Pres. region 16 Assoc. Beer Dist., Litchfield, 1968-71, exec. sec., 1971-86. Served to staff sgt. USAF, 1942-45, ETO. Republican. Avocation: world travelling. Home and Office: PO Box 219 Litchfield IL 62056

BRAY, ANDREW MICHAEL, graphics company executive; b. Norway, Mich., July 31, 1938; s. Andrew John and Ethel Mary (Cronick) B.; B.S.M.E., Mich. Tech. U., 1960; postgrad. U. Wis., Milw., 1961-63; registered profl. engr.; children—Susan Mary, Mark Andrew. Engr., AC Electronics Co., 1960-63; engr. research and devel. Paper Converting Machine Co., Green Bay, Wis., 1963-67; chief engr. Magna-Print Co., Green Bay, 1967-68; sales engr. J.M. Grimstad Inc., Green Bay, 1968-74; pres. OEM Devel. Corp., Oconto Falls, Wis., 1974-77; pres. Tech Draulics Ltd., Oconto Falls, 1975-84; ABAH Sports, Ltd.; mgr. research Magna-Graphics Corp.; pres. Abah Sports, Ltd.; instr. mech. engring. U. Wis., Green Bay, 1964-69; coach Howard-Suamico High Sch. Hockey. Town chmn. Town of Suamico (Wis.), 1974-81; sec. Suamico San. Dist., 1972-84; bd. dirs. Brown County Youth Hockey Bd.; pres. Howard-Suamico Youth Hockey Assn.; active Big Bros./Big Sisters of Brown County. Mem. Fluid Power Soc. Roman Catholic. Clubs: K.C., Elks, Optimists. Contbr. articles to profl. publs. Inventor in field. Home: 3244 Maple Grove Ln Suamico WI 54141 Office: Magna-Graphics Corp 220 Van Buren Oconto Falls WI 54154

BRAY, MICHAEL JOHN, telecommunications executive; b. Kansas City, Mo., Mar. 23, 1956; s. John Bray and Julia Marie (Graham) Mansour; m. Mary Anne Hansen, Sept. 11, 1982; children: Christopher, Nicholas. BSBA, Rockhurst Coll., 1978. CPA, Kans. Acct. Deloite, Haskins & Sells, Kansas City, 1978-81; mgr. Tymshare, San Jose, Calif., 1981-83, United Telecom, Kansas City, 1983-84; controller United Telecom Communications, Kansas City, 1984-85; dir. fin. U.S. Telecom, Kansas City, 1985-86; dir. network planning U.S. Sprint, Kansas City, 1986—; chmn. acctg. com. Comptel, Washington, 1985-86. Mem. Am. Inst. CPA's, Kans. Soc. CPA's, Acctg. Research Assn. Republican. Roman Catholic. Home: 9517 W 116 Terr Overland Park KS 66210 Office: US Sprint 9300 Metcalf Overland Park KS 66212

BRAY, PIERCE, consultant; b. Chgo., Jan. 16, 1924; s. Harold A. and Margaret (Maclennan) B.; m. Maud Dorothy Minto, May 14, 1955; children—Margaret Dorothy, William Harold, Andrew Pierce. B.A., U. Chgo., 1948, M.B.A., 1949. Fin. analyst Ford Motor Co., Dearborn, Mich., 1949-55; cons. Booz, Allen & Hamilton, Chgo. and Manila, Phillipines, 1955-58; mgr. pricing, then corp. controller Cummins Engine Co., Columbus, Ind., 1958-66; v.p. fin. Weatherhead Co., Cleve., 1966-67; v.p. Mid-Continent Telephone Corp. (name now ALLTELL Corp.), Hudson, Ohio, 1967-70, treas., 1967-77, v.p. fin., 1970-81, exec. v.p., chief fin. officer, 1981-85, dir., 1976-85, chmn. various subs.; dir. Cardinal Fund, 1969—; trustee Cardinal Govt. Securities Trust, 1980—; instr. fin. and econs. U. Detroit, 1952-54; chmn. investor relations com. U.S. Ind. Telephone Assn., 1974-85; chmn. exec. com. Inst. Public Utilities, 1981-83. Mem. alumni council U. Chgo. Sch. Bus., 1967; Trustee Beech Brook Children's Home, Pepper Pike, Ohio, 1972—, treas., 1976-79, pres., 1979-81. Served with AUS, 1943-46. Mem. Fin. Execs. Inst., Cleve. Treasurers Club, Delta Upsilon. Presbyterian. Clubs: Union (Cleve.), Midday (Cleve.); Downtown Athletic (N.Y.C.); Walloon Yacht (chmn. bd. 1980-81, 1985-86, commodore 1981-82), Walloon Lake Country. Home: 31173 Northwood Dr Pepper Pike OH 44124 Office: 100 Executive Pkwy Hudson OH 44236

BRAY, SYLVIA CECILE, tax practitioner, bookkeeper, insurance agent; b. Sidney, Ohio, Dec. 10, 1929; d. Joseph Carter and Emma Faye (Barlow) Bedford; m. Robert Bray, Aug. 17, 1946; children—James Ray, Linda Faye Dubois. Cert. proficiency Southwestern Acad., 1967. Owner, pres. Bray's Income Tax Service, Sidney, 1964—; auditor Copeland Corp., Sidney, 1969-73; ins. agt. Rumbaugh & Assocs., Lima, Ohio, 1977—; rep., mem. adv. com. Women Bus. Owners; cons. in tax savs. field. Recipient Millionaires Club award Am. Bankers Life Ins. Co., 1980-81, Women of Yr. award, 1979; one of three women bus. owners present at presdl. signing of exec. order establishing adv. com. on women's bus. ownership. Buckeye Mem. Nat. Assn. Income Tax Practitioners (cert., pres. Ohio chpt.), Nat. Fedn. Ind. Bus. Mem. Ch. of God. Club: Altrusa Internat. (Sidney). Home and office: 1359 S Main Ave Sidney OH 45365

BREADON, GEORGE EDWARD, otolaryngologist, surgeon; b. Dublin, Ireland, Oct. 6, 1943; came to U.S., 1970; s. Joseph Herbert and Mary Jane (Kenny) B.; m. Gabrielle Ethel O'Sullivan, Apr. 5, 1972; children: Gavin E., Eoin J., Enda O., Desmond M. B in Surgery, MB, Nat. U. Ireland, Dublin, 1968; MS, U. Minn., 1978. Diplomate Am. Bd. Otolaryngology. Tutor in anatomy Nat. U. Ireland, 1969-70; resident in gen. surgery Mater Miseri Cordie Hosp., Dublin, 1971-72; resident in gen. surgery Mayo Clinic, Rochester, Minn., 1972-73, resident in ORL, 1973-77; cons. otolaryngology The Monroe (Wis.) Clinic, 1977—, head ORL dept., 1979—; attending surgeon St. Clare Hosp., Monroe, 1977—; attending surgeon ORL St. Clare Hosp., 1977—, sec. med. staff, chmn. credential com., 1981-85, chmn. surgery dept., 1986-87. Fellow ACS, Am. Acad. Otolaryngology Head and Neck Surgery, Internat. Coll. Surgeons, Am. Acad. Facial Plastic and Reconstructive Surgery (Benjamin Schuster award 1977); mem. AMA, Wis. Otolaryngology Soc., Wis. State Med. Soc. Roman Catholic. Lodge: Optomists (exec. bd. Monroe 1978-80). Avocations: tennis, photography, reading. Home: 2021 11th St Monroe WI 53566 Office: The Monroe Clinic 1515 10th St Monroe WI 53566

BREAKSTONE, JERRY, architect; b. Battlecreek, Mich., June 16, 1940; s. Robert and Sylvia B.; m. Lynne Turner, Jan. 28, 1967; children: Collin, Aaron. BArch, Washington U., St. Louis, 1962, MArch, 1966; M in Urban Studies, U. Chgo., 1970. Registered architect, Calif., Ill. Designer Harry Weese, Chgo., 1966-68, SOM, Chgo., 1968-69; urban designer Perkins & Will, Chgo., 1969-70; sr. v.p. HOK, St. Louis, 1972-85; v.p. SMP, St. Louis, 1985—; asst. prof. Calif. State Poly., San Luis Obispo, Calif., 1970-72; cons. Park Forest South, Chgo., 1970; lectr. Washington U., 1980, Tex. A&M, College Sta., 1984, U. Mo., Columbia, 1984. Contbr. articles to profl. jours. Advisor First St. Forum Gallery, St. Louis, 1986; com. mem. Mo. Bot. Gardens, St. Louis, 1986; design advisor Univ. City High Sch., St. Louis, 1986. Recipient Cert. of Appreciation Detroit Bd Realtors, 1982. Mem. Am. Assn. Hospital Planning, AIA, Am. Planning Assn., Urban Land Inst., Am. Inst. Cert. Planners. Club: Les Amis du Vin (Los Angeles). Avocations: cooking, wine collecting, European travel. Home: 7220 Princeton Saint Louis MO 63130 Office: SMP 7777 Bonhomme Saint Louis MO 63105

BRECHMACHER, CHARLES WILLIAM, savings and loan institution executive; b. Washington, Dec. 21, 1954; s. Richard Frederick Jr. and Charlotte Rebecca (Call) B.; m. Retha Fay Speirs, Dec. 4, 1976; children: Scott Adam, Traci Elaine, Aaron Lee. BS in Acctg., U. Akron, 1976. CPA, Oreg., Ohio. Staff auditor Arthur Andersen & Co., Cleve., 1977-78; sr. auditor J.W. Callahan & Co., Eugene, Oreg., 1978-80; internal auditor, asst. controller Dealership Services, Eugene, 1980-82; chief fin. officer Am. Fed. Savs. and Loan, Anderson, Ind., 1982—; treas. Ind. chpt. personal computer users group Fed. Home Loan Bank Indpls., 1985—. Mem. Am. Inst. CPA's, Fin. Mgrs. Soc. Republican. Mem. Ch. of God. Avocations: camping, bowling, jogging. Home: HCR #3 Box 215 Edgar Springs MO 65462 Office: Am Fed Savs and Loan 1100 Broadway Anderson IN 46012

BRECKENRIDGE, DONALD EDGAR, hotel company executive; b. St. Louis, Dec. 27, 1931; s. Frank E. and Rachel O. (McKean) B.; m. Diane Smith, divorced; children: Karen, Linda, Jennifer; m. Diane Emmenegger, May 15, 1970; children: Brick, Holly, Donnie. BBA, U. Ariz., 1953. Salesman Brach Candy Company, St. Louis, 1956-58; pres. Breckenridge-Smith Developers, St. Louis, 1958-75, Breckenridge Hotels, St. Louis, 1963—. Mem. Arts and Edn. Council, St. John's Mercy Med. Ctr. Bd.; pres. Convention and Visitors Bur. (com. on tourism); trustee Maryville Coll.; bd. dirs. Boy Scouts Am., St. Louis, 1986, Muscular Dystrophy Assn. Am., 1985. Mem. Sr. Execs. Orgn. Club: St. Louis Variety (pres. 1987). Office: Breckenridge Hotels Corp 45 Progress Pkwy Maryland Heights MO 63043

BRECKON, DONALD JOHN, educator; b. Port Huron, Mich., June 11, 1939; s. Robert Joseph and Margaret Elizabeth (Wade) B.; A.A., Port Huron Community Coll., 1959; B.S., Central Mich. U., 1962, M.A., 1963; M.P.H. (USPHS trainee), U. Mich., 1968; Ph.D., Mich. State U., 1977; postgrad. U. Wis., 1965-66, Western Mich. U., 1968; m. Sandra Kay Biehn, Sept. 4, 1959; children—Lori E., LeeAnne M., Lisa C., Lynanne W. Instr. health edn. Central Mich. U., Mt. Pleasant, 1963-68, asst. prof., 1968-72, assoc. prof., 1972-81, prof. health edn., 1978-81, asst. dean health, phys. edn. and recreation, 1981-82, assoc. dean edn., health and human services and dean grad. studies/assoc. provost for research 1982-87; pres. Park Coll., Parkville, Mo., 1987—; mem. governing council Health Systems Agy., Region 6, Mich., 1976-79; bd. dirs. Am. Cancer Soc., 1977-79, Community Council on Drug Misuse, 1976-78. Recipient Central Mich. U. Teaching Effectiveness award, 1975; Disting. Service award Mich. Alcoholism and Addiction Assn., 1977; Mich. Dept. Edn. scholar, 1971; Yale U. Drug Dependence Inst. scholar, 1973; Midwest Inst. Alcohol Studies, Mich. Dept. Public Health scholar, 1974; Am. Council on Edn. Leadership Devel. program fellow, 1979. Mem. Mich. Public Health Assn. (pres. 1976-77), Am. Public Health Assn., Soc. Public Health Edn. (pres. 1978-79), Internat. Soc. Pub. Health Edn., Coalition of Mich. Health Edn. Orgns., Mich. Alcohol and Addiction Assn., Am. Alliance for Health and Phys. Edn. Contbr. articles to profl. jours.; author: Hospital Health Education: A Guide to Program Development, 1982; Community Health Education: Setting, Roles and Skills, 1985, Microcomputer Applications to Health Education and Health Science, 1986. Home: 1413 Crosslanes St Mount Pleasant MI 48858 Office: Park Coll Office of Pres Parkville MO 64152

BRECKON, PATRICK WILLARD, real estate executive, investment consultant; b. Whitewater, Wis., Dec. 13, 1944; s. Fred S. and Dorothy M. (Vivian) B.; m. Mary Alice Edge, Apr. 1, 1972; children—Sean, Mark. B.S. in Anthropology, U. Wis., 1976. Lic. realtor, Wis. Salesperson, Parkwood Realty, Madison, Wis., 1977-78, Casey, Carney & White, Madison, 1978-80, First Realty, Madison, 1980-81; owner, pres. Real Estate Clearinghouse, Madison, 1981—; with Prudential Fin. Services, 1983-86; prin. Patrick W. Breckon & Assocs., 1986—. Developed real estate brokerage system for residential sales. Served in USAF, 1965-69. Named Airman of Yr., Edwards AFB, 1967. Mem. Greater Madison Bd. Realtors, Wis. Realtors Assn., Nat. Assn. Realtors.

BREDENKAMP, NORMAN LOUIS, elec. engr.; b. Peoria, Ill., Jan. 2, 1944; s. John Louis and Dagmar (Soyring) B.; student DeVry Tech. Inst., 1962-64. Self-employed radio technician, Browns, Ill., 1958-62, radio and TV technician, Browns, 1964-65; elec. engr. Pacific Press & Shear, Mount Carmel, Ill., 1967-70; computer analyst RCA, Palm Beach Gardens, Fla., 1967-70; self-employed radio and TV technician, Palm Beach Gardens, 1970-72; radio announcer, program dir. WVMC-WSAB, Mt. Carmel, Ill., 1972-73; self-employed trouble shooter, Grayville, Ill., 1973—. Mem. Grayville Days Com.; vol. Fire Dept.; active Civil Defense. Mem. IEEE, Instrument Soc. Am., C. of C., Am. Sunbathing Assn. Clubs: CB Radio; Traveliers (Lake Geneva, Wis.). Home: Route 1 Grayville IL 62844 Office: Alexander Ln Grayville IL 62844

BREECE, ROBERT WILLIAM, JR., lawyer; b. Blackwell, Okla., Feb. 5, 1942; s. Robert William Breece Sr. and Helen Elaine (Maddox) Breece Robinson; m. Elaine Marie Keller, Sept. 7, 1968; children—Bryan, Justin, Lauren. B.S.B.A., Northwestern U., 1964; J.D., U. Okla., 1967; LL.M., Washington U., St. Louis, 1970. Ptnr. Mazur, Raben, Breece, Frankel, Kaiser & Jones, St. Louis, 1968—. Mem. Internat. Bar Assn., ABA, Mo. Bar Assn., Okla. Bar Assn., Phi Alpha Delta, Beta Theta Pi. Clubs: University, Forest Hills Country (pres. 1978). Office: #35 Crown Manor Dr Saint Louis MO 63017

BREED, EILEEN JUDITH, educator; b. Chgo., Sept. 18, 1945; d. John Joseph and Helen Agatha (Hoy) Kennedy; B.A., Northeastern Ill. U., 1966, M.A., 1976, postgrad., 1980-81; postgrad. Nat. Coll. Edn., 1981, 83, No. Ill. U., 1987—; m. Harvey Breed, Feb. 3, 1973; 1 dau., Diana Marie Parks. Tchr., Canty Elem. Sch., Chgo., 1967-76; tchr. St. Raymond's Sch., Mt. Prospect, Ill., 1976-78; pvt. practice diagnosis and remediation learning disabilities, cons. spl. edn., Des Plaines, Ill., 1976-78; prin. Angel Town Pvt. Sch., Des Plaines, 1978-79; tutoring, coop. work tng. coordinator Nipper Sch., spl. edn. facility, Des Plaines, 1979-86; tchr. acad. resources Oak Terr. Sch., Highwood, Ill., 1986-87; tchr. life skills program Lake Pk. High Sch., Sch. Assn. Spl. Edn. DuPage County, Roselle, Ill., 1987—; tchr. parent-edn. classes; cons. pvt. schs. Mem. Council Exceptional Children, Council on Understanding Learning Disabilities, Nat. Assn. Retarded Citizens. Initiated various spl. edn. programs. Home: 1011 W Grant Dr Des Plaines IL 60016 Office: Oak Terr Sch 240 Prairie Ave Highwood IL 60040

BREED, STERLING LARUE, college educator, counselor; b. Paw Paw, Mich., Oct. 9, 1928; s. LaRue H. and Eda L. (Ayars) B.; m. Betty Hansen, June 17, 1953; 1 child, Thomas Sterling. B.S., Western Mich. U., 1955; M.A., 1958; postgrad. Mich. State U., 1960-65, U. Mich., 1974-81. Trooper, Mich. State Police, Traverse City, 1950-53; tchr. Paw Paw Jr. High Sch., 1955-56; asst. dean of men Western Mich. U., Kalamazoo, 1956-60, counselor, coordinator acad. advising, 1960-73, dir. counseling ctr., 1973-76, counselor, prof., 1976—. Served with U.S. Army, 1946-48; ETO. Recipient Meritorious Service award Mich. State Police, 1952, Disting. Service award Western Mich. U., 1985. Mem. Mich. Coll. Personnel Assn. (Outstanding Service award 1978, pres. 1971-72, 86-87, bd. dirs. 1979-85), Am. Coll. Personnel Assn. (state membership chmn. 1966-77), Mich. Personnel and Guidance Assn. (bd. dirs. 1984-85), Kalamazoo County Personnel and Guidance Assn. (exec. bd. 1976-77), Am. Assn. Counseling and Devel., Nat. Vocat. Guidance Assn., Mich. Vocat. Guidance Assn., Mich. League Nursing (pres. 1979-81, Outstanding Service award 1981), Nat. League Nursing (region vice-chmn. 1981-83, nat. bd. dirs. 1983—), AAUP, Assn. Humanistic Edn. and Devel., Phi Delta Kappa, Sigma Tau Gamma (pres. 1964-66), Western Mich. U. Alumni Assn. (pres. 1980-82). Republican. Episcopalian. Avocations: tennis; travel; photography. Home: 867 Dobbin Dr Kalamazoo MI 49007 Office: Western Mich U Counseling Ctr Kalamazoo MI 49008

BREEDEN, CHRIS DAVID, accountant; b. Ft. Wayne, Ind., May 7, 1955; s. William Harrison and Rose (Geroff) B. BBA, Valparaiso U., 1977. CPA, Ind. Sr. staff acct. Coopers & Lybrand, Ft. Wayne, 1977-82; sr. auditor Gen. Telephone, Ft. Wayne, 1982; acct. Ron Hertenstein, CPA, Ft. Wayne, 1982-83; ptnr. Breeden & Lewis, CPA's, Ft. Wayne, 1983-86; pvt. practice acctg. Ft. Wayne, 1986—. Coach Harding Sr. Little League, Ft. Wayne, 1979—; v.p. Peace Luth. Ch., Ft. Wayne, 1983—. Mem. Am. Inst. CPA's, Ind. CPA Soc. (pub. relations com. 1986—0, Ft. Wayne C. of C. (small bus. council 1983-84), OMNI Bus. Group (treas. 1983-84). Republican. Avocations: reading, music, sports, coaching baseball. Home: 6325 Hillsboro Ln Fort Wayne IN 46835 Office: 6066 E State Fort Wayne IN 46815

BREEDEN, REX EARL, real estate developer; b. French Lick, Ind., Oct. 19, 1920; s. Charles Henry and Ella Zoe (Lashbrooks) B.; m. Joy Rosalie Conley, Apr. 19, 1941 (div. 1961); children: Rebecca S. Cseszko, Jeanne Kay Matson, Diane Louise Lee; m. Barbara Ann Horst, Aug. 4, 1965. BS, Ind. State U., 1942. High sch. tchr. Clinton (Ind.) Pub. Schs., 1942-43; designer Gulf Shipbuilding Corp., Chickasaw, Ala., 1943; founder, pres. Brex Corp., Columbus, Ind., 1946-84; founder, chmn. Breeden, Inc. Realtors and Developers, Columbus, 1952—, Blairex Labs., Inc., Evansville, Ind., 1976—; founder Columbus Bank & Trust Co., 1976—, also bd. dirs.; pres. Jarex Corp., Columbus, 1985—. Inventor water treatment container, 1983. Dir. Heritage Fund, Columbus, 1979-80; dir. William R. Laws Scholarship Found., Columbus, 1963-67; past pres., mem. Ind. State U. Bd. Trustees, Terre Haute, Ind. Served to lt. j.g. USN, 1943-46, PTO. Mem. Soc. Indsl. Realtors (pres. Ind. chpt. 1982-83), Columbus Area C. of C. (past pres., Community Service award 1977), Ind. Real Estate Commn. (commr. 1965-73), Beta Gamma Sigma. Republican. Presbyterian. Clubs: Harrison Lake (pres. 1971-72), Card Sound Golf, Anglers, Columbia, Meridian Hills, Skyline, Ind. Soc. Home: 3671 Shoshone Dr Columbus IN 47203 Office: Breeden Inc Realtors Developers 1427 Washington St Columbus IN 47201

BREEDEN-CSESZKO, REBECCA SUE, property manager; b. Terre Haute, Ind., July 10, 1943; d. Rex Earl and Joy Rosalie (Conley) Breeden; m. M. Thomas Hopkins, June 30, 1962 (div. 1967); children: Jeffery Thomas, Kimberly Allyson; m. Robert James Cseszko, Nov. 23, 1974; children: Christian Robert, Emily Rebecca, Rachel Elisabeth. Student, Ind. U., 1961, 62; cert., Johnson Inst., Mpls., 1982, Tri-County Alcoholism Ctr., Columbus, Ohio, 1982. Copywriter Virginian Pilot/Ledger Star, Norfolk, 1962-64; v.p. Custom-Brushed, Inc., Columbus, Ind., 1975—; ptnr. Imagination II Advt., Columbus, 1977-81; owner Trilogy Mgmt. Co., Columbus, 1983—; counselor Pleasant Grove Hosp., Louisville, 1982, Bartholomew Consol. Sch. Corp., Columbus, 1986—; bd. dirs., sec. Brex Corp. 1966-83. Mem. Bartholomew County Hosp. Auxiliary, Columbus, 1968-73, Columbus Arts Guild, 1970-74, Columbus Area Alcohol and Drugs Council, 1982—, Bartholomew Assn. Gifted Edn., Columbus, 1986—, Driftwood Valley Arts Council, Columbus Art League; bd. dirs., treas. Columbus Gymnastics Ctr., 1986—; publicity chmn. United Way Fund Drive, Columbus, 1980, 82; chmn. Spl. Olympics, Columbus, 1972; facilitator Family Hope Recovery Program, Columbus, 1981-85; mem. Columbus Peace Fellowship. Mem. Pi Beta Psi. Avocations: collecting antiques and Indian artifacts, gourmet and ethnic cooking, English history, music, art.

BREEN, JOHN ALOYSIUS, III, advertising executive; b. Evanston, Ill., Apr. 25, 1942; s. John Aloysius and Jane Mary (Molyneaux) B.; m. Mary Helen McCarthy, June 22, 1968; children: Molly, Marnie E., John A. IV. BA, John Carroll U., 1964. Account exec. Tatham-Laird & Kudner, Chgo., 1967-74; sr. v.p., mgmt. supr. D'Arcy Masius Benton & Bowles, Chgo., 1974—; cons. ProgramAble, Chgo., 1986—. Bd. dirs. Chgo. Boys and Girls Club, 1986; Northbrook (Ill.) Hockey League, 1986—. Served to capt. U.S. Army, 1964-67. Roman Catholic. Clubs: Chgo. Advt.; North Shore Country (Glenview, Ill.). Avocations: fishing, golf, woodwork, power boating, sky diving. Office: D'Arcy Masius Benton & Bowles 200 E Randolph St Chicago IL 60601

BREEN, JOHN GERALD, manufacturing company executive; b. Cleve., July 21, 1934; s. Hugh Gerald and Margaret Cecelia (Bonner) B.; m. Mary Jane Brubach, Apr. 12, 1958; children: Kathleen Anne, John Patrick, James Phillip, David Hugh, Anne Margaret. B.S., John Carroll U., 1956; M.B.A., Case Western Res. U., 1961. With Clevite Corp., Cleve., 1957-73, gen. mgr. foil div., 1969-73, gen. mgr. engine parts div., 1973-74; group v.p. indsl. group Gould Inc., Rolling Meadows, Ill., 1974-77, exec. v.p., 1977-79; pres. Sherwin Williams Co., Cleve., 1979-86, chief exec. officer, 1979—, chmn., 1980—, also dir.; dir. Parker Hannifin Corp., Cleve., Nat. City Bank, Cleve. Served with U.S. Army, 1956-57. Clubs: Pepper Pike, Union, Cleve. Skating. Home: 2727 Cranlyn Rd Shaker Heights OH 44122 Office: Sherwin-Williams Co 101 Prospect Ave NW Cleveland OH 44115 *

BREEN, KATHERINE ANNE, speech and language pathologist; b. Chgo., Oct. 31, 1948; d. Robert Stephen and Gertrude Catherine (Bader) Breen; B.S., Northwestern U., 1970; M.A. (U.S. Rehab. Services trainee), U. Mo., Columbia, 1971. Speech/lang. pathologist Fulton (Mo.) pub. schs., 1971-73; co-dir. Easter Seal Speech Clinic, Jefferson City, Mo., summers 1972, 73; speech/lang. pathologist Shawnee Mission (Kans.) pub. schs., 1973—; staff St. Joseph's Hosp., Kansas City, Mo., 1978-81, Midwest Rehab. Ctr., Kansas City, 1985—; pvt. practice speech therapy; cons. East Central Mo. Mental Health Center; guest lectr. Fontbonne Coll., St. Louis. Clin. certification in speech pathology. Mem. Am., Kans. speech and hearing assns., NEA, Mo. State Tchrs. Assn., Kansas City Alumni Assn. of Northwestern U. (dir. alumni admissions council, Outstanding Leadership award for work on alumni admissions council 1981), Friends of Art Nelson/Atkins Art Gallery and Museum (vol.), Nat. Trust Hist. Preservation, Kansas City Hist. Found., Zeta Phi Eta. Methodist. Home: 6865 W 51st Terr Apt 1C Shawnee Mission KS 66202 Office: 7235 Antioch Shawnee Mission KS 66204

BREGAR, ROBERT J., architect; b. Cleve., Dec. 17, 1927; s. Joseph and Amelia C. (Bucar) B.; m. Barbara E. Rushworth, May 10, 1952; children: Catherine, Robert D., Mark, Laura, Kim Marie. BArch, Ohio U., 1950. Registered architect, Ohio. Draftsman Ward & Conrad, Cleve., 1950-52; project architect Ward, Conrad, Schneider, Szabo, Cleve., 1952-56; assoc. Ward, Conrad, Schneider, Cleve., 1956-61; assoc. ptnr. Ward & Schneider, Cleve., 1961-69; prin. Robert J. Bregar Assoc., Inc., Chagrin Falls, Ohio, 1969—; chmn. Dial Industries, Inc., Cleve., 1981—; arbitrator Am. Arbitrators Assn., Cleve., 1979—; tech. analyst Ohio Dept. of Energy, Cleve.; cons. architect Temp. Profl. Services, Inc. Mem. Cuyahoga Community Coll. and Bldg. Tech., Cleve., 1969—; chmn. Max Hayes High Sch. Archtl. Drafting Course, Cleve., 1972—; commn. mem., sec. Villa Angela High Sch. Edn. Community, Cleve., 1977—; trustee Mt. Pleasant Youth Activities Ctr., Cleve., 1984—, Fed. Cath. Community Services, Cleve., 1983—; pres. Cath. Soc. Services of Cuyahoga County, Cleve., 1983—; vol. United Way Services M.D.P. Program, Cleve., 1984—. Served with U.S. Army, 1945-46. Recipient Award for Excellence Aftercare Resource Ctr., Cleve., 1982. Mem. AIA, Architects Soc. of Ohio (bd. trustees 1977-78, state sec. 1978). Roman Catholic. Home: 110 Sterncrest Dr Moreland Hills OH 44022 Office: 110 Sterncrest Dr Chagrin Falls OH 44022

BREGMAN, BARBARA JEAN, advertising executive; b. Chicago Heights, Ill., Aug. 3, 1956; d. Jacob Israel and Mona Gladys Madan. BS in Speech, Northwestern U., 1978. Media estimator Clinton E. Frank, Advt., Chgo., 1978-79, media planner, 1979-81; media planner Cunningham & Walsh, Chgo., 1981-83; media planner Bozell, Jacobs, Kenyon & Eckhardt, Inc., Chgo., 1984, media supr., 1984-86, assoc. media dir., 1986—. Dem. election judge, Chgo. 1984; co-chmn. jr. bd. dirs. Lawrence Hall Sch. for Boys, Chgo., 1984-86, activities chmn. 1985. Mem. Nat. Agri-Mktg. Assn. (membership chmn. 1986—). Jewish. Club: Lakeshore Ctr. Bridge (Chgo.). Avocations: tennis, travel, bridge. Home: 1825 N Lincoln Plaza #1005 Chicago IL 60614 Office: Bozell Jacobs et al 625 N Michigan Ave Chicago IL 60611

BREGMANN, MARK JOSEPH, marketing administrator; b. Mpls., June 5, 1956; s. Eugene Joseph and Charlotte Ann (O'Heron) B. BA, U. Minn., 1978; postgrad., Met. State U., 1985—. Prodn. coordinator Honeywell-Avionics, St. Louis Park, Minn., 1979-83; lead prodn. coordinator Honeywell- Comml. Aviation, St. Louis Park, 1983-85; sr. forecast adminstr. Honeywell-Comml. div., Mpls., 1985—. Dir. U. Minn. Coll. Liberal Arts Alumni Constituent Soc., 1984-87, sec.-treas., 1987—. Republican. Roman Catholic. Avocations: sports, history. Home: 9708 Russell Ave S Bloomington MN 55431 Office: Honeywell Comml Div Honeywell Plaza 27-6246 Minneapolis MN 55408

BREGSTEIN, RICHARD FREDRIC, marketing executive; b. N.Y.C., Apr. 25, 1936; s. Samuel Joseph and Muriel (Rubine) B.; B.A., U. Vt., 1957; m. Jane Bell Henning, Dec. 18, 1968; children—Alison Ruth, Jared Joseph. Mgr. community relations Prudential Ins. Co., Newark, 1960-71; mgr. public info. Coll. of Medicine and Dentistry of N.J., Newark, 1971-73; pres. Aspen Group, Inc., Newark, 1973-74; dir. community relations and health info. Martland Med. Center, 1974-76; dir. pub. affairs Ill. Hosp. Assn., Oak Brook, 1976-79; dir. public and profl. relations Joint Commn. on Accreditation of Hosps., Chgo., 1979-82; regional dir. Planco, 1982-86, v.p., regional sales mgr. Am. Capital Mktg., 1986—; pres. Chippewa Grap, Inc., 1985-86; lectr. on mktg., public relations governing bds. and fin. planning. Pres. bd. New Well Narcotic Rehab. Center, 1971-72; bd. dirs. Urban League Essex County, 1973-76; bd. dirs. Interracial Council for Bus. Opportunity of N.J., 1965-68; bd. dirs. Am. Lung Assn. of N.J., 1975-76; mem. City of Newark Narcotic Adv. Council, 1971-76; bd. dirs. Newark dist. ARC, 1973-76. Mem. Am. Mktg. Assn., Chgo. Mktg. Assn., N.Y. Acad. Scis., Acad. Hosp. Public Relations. Home and Office: 606 Chippewa Ln Darien IL 60559

BREHANY, RONALD LANG, chiropractor; b. Mossel Bay, Cape Province, Republic of South Africa, May 6, 1935; came to U.S., 1976; s. Clarence and Clara Francis (Cobbing) B.; m. Katriana Louisa Le Roux, July 17, 1956; children: Shaun Earle, Rodney Clarence. Diploma, Witwatersrand Tech.,

Johannesburg, Republic of South Africa, 1961; D of Chiropractic, Sherman Coll., Spartanburg, S.C., 1979. Communications technician South African Railways, Port Elizabeth, 1953-65; personnel mgr. British United, Port Elizabeth, 1965-66; indsl. engr. Ford Motor Co., Port Elizabeth, 1966-69; personnel mgr. Bus Bodies-S.A. Ltd., Port Elizabeth, 1970-76; chiropractor Brehany Chiropractic Ctr., Warsaw, Ind., 1979—. Mem. bd. regents Sherman Coll. Mem. Internat. Chiropractic Assn., Fedn. of Straight Chiropractic, Fellowship for Advancement of Chiropractic, Greater Warsaw C. of C., Sherman Coll. Alumni Assn. Republican. Baptist. Avocations: fishing, exercise. Home: 1318 E Island View Dr Warsaw IN 46580 Office: Brehany Chiropractic Ctr Inc 600 E Winona Ave Warsaw IN 46580

BREHENEY, BERNARD JAMES, sales professional; b. Jersey City, Oct. 9, 1954; s. Bernard Luke and Maryann (Brown) B.; m. Mary Fern, Aug. 8, 1981; children: Jane, Jesse. BA, St. Francis Coll., 1976; MA, Emerson Coll., 1986. Cert. paralegal, N.Y. Account mgr. McGraw-Hill, Boston, 1980-83; account exec. Colony Communications, Boston, 1983-85; sales mgr. Colony Communications, Peoria, Ill., 1985-87, Grand Rapids, Mich., 1987—. Mem. Am. Mktg. Assn., Peoria Ad Club, Peoria C. of C. (exec. roundtable). Democrat. Roman Catholic. Avocations: running, basketball. Home: 1525 W Sunnyview Dr Peoria IL 61614 Office: Colony Communications 6147 28th St SE Grand Rapids MI 49506

BREHM, WILLIAM ALLEN, JR., urban planner; b. Neenah, Wis., Jan. 18, 1945; s. William Allen and Katharine (Gilbert) B.; B.A., Lawrence U., 1967; M.U.P. (Richard King Mellon fellow 1967-68), Mich. State U., 1973; m. Patricia Lee Kelley, Dec. 30, 1967; children—Laura Kelley, William Hunt, Katharine Ann. Dir. planning Charter Twp. of Meridian (Mich.), 1969-72; v.p., treas. Planning Cons. Services, Inc., Lansing, Mich., 1972-76; dir. planning Manson, Jackson, Kane, Architects, Inc., Lansing, 1974-76; dir. planning and devel. City of Appleton (Wis.), 1976—, exec. dir. Redevel. Authority, 1979—; mem. Appleton Devel. Council, Inc., 1977—, Wis. State Hist. Soc., 1978—, Outagamie Hist. Soc., 1980—, steering com. Outagamie Mus., 1985—; dir. Appleton Gallery of Arts, 1984-85. Trustee, Charter Twp. of Meridan, 1972-74, supr., 1974-76; dist. chmn. Boy Scouts Am., 1979-81; bd. dirs. Pub. Art Found., 1985—. Lic. profl. community planner, Mich. Mem. Am. Inst. Cert. Planners, Am. Planning Assn., Urban Land Inst., Nat. Trust Historic Preservation, Council Urban Econ. Devel., Mid-Am. Econ. Devel. Council, Assn. Wis. Planners (treas. 1977-79, pres. 1981-82), Wis. Econ. Devel. Assn., Houdini Club Wis., Internat. Brotherhood Magicians, Delta Tau Delta. Mem. United Ch. of Christ. Club: Rotary. Home: 716 S Fidelis Dr Appleton WI 54915 Office: 200 N Appleton St Appleton WI 54911

BREHMER, STEVEN LESTER, educator, consultant; b. Owattana, Minn., Mar. 30, 1952; s. H.L. and Ruth Ann (Lindblom) B.; m. Linda Marie Yeager, Dec. 27, 1975; children: Sarah Marie, David William. BS, Mankato State U., 1974. Cert. tchr. Tchr. Swea City (Iowa) High Sch., 1974, Wanamingo (Minn.) High Sch., 1976—; cons. computer MECC, Mpls., 1982, Kenyon (Minn.) Pub. Sch., 1984-86; space ambassador NASA, Washington, 1985—. Community edn. dir. Wanamingo Pub. Sch., 1982—; edn. intern Congressman Penny, Washington, 1984, Wanamingo City Council, 1985—. Mem. Wanamingo Edn. Assn. (pres., negotiator 1978—), Minn. Edn. Assn., Nat. Edn. Assn., Minn. Sci. Tchrs. Assn., Nat. Sci. Tchrs. Assn., Minn. Sci. Mus., Traveler's Soc. (Soviet seminar 1986). Democrat. Home: Box 122 Wanamingo MN 55983 Office: Wanamingo Pub Sch Box 75 Wanamingo MN 55983

BREIDENBACH, DON HOWARD, data processing executive; b. St. Louis, May 9, 1947; s. Irvin Alloys and Mildred (Loos) B.; m. Cheryl Elizabeth LaFlam, July 5, 1969; 1 child, Christina Elizabeth. BA, So. Ill. U., 1969; MS, U. So. Calif., 1976. Systems engr. Electronic Data Systems, Mpls., 1976-80; tech. support mgr. Midwest Fed. Savs. and Loan, Mpls., 1980—. Coach Prior Lake (Minn.) Athletics Assn. Served to maj. USAF, 1970-75, USNG, 1976—. Delyte Morris scholar So. Ill. U., 1965; recipient Lavina Micjen Meml. award So. Ill. U., 1966. Mem. Assn. for Systems Mgmt., Data Processing Mgmt. Assn., NG Assn., Prior Lake Jaycees. Lutheran. Avocations: classical piano, jogging. Home: 5450 W 150th St Prior Lake MN 55372 Office: Midwest Fed Savs and Loan 801 Nicollet Mall Minneapolis MN 55493

BREIDERT, KATHLEEN MILLER, state agency administrator; b. Chgo., July 13, 1943; d. Forrest Tillman Miller and Ruth DeLatour) Thomas; m. robert Bruce Breidert, June 10, 1967 (div. 1985); 1 child, Matthew. BA in Communications, U. Ill., 1965. Clk. City of Park Ridge, Ill., 1977-81; exec. asst. cong. John Parker, Northbrook, Ill., 1980-82; asst. to minority leader Ill. Ho. of Reps., Springfield, 1983-86; campaign mgr. Lt. Gov. George Ryan, Ill., 1986; asst. dir. Ill. Dept. Pub. Aid, Chgo., 1987—; cons. to Lt. Gov. George Ryan, Springfield, 1986—. Chmn. Com. to Retain Home Rule, 1976; mgr. campaign Homeowners Party, Park Ridge, 1981, 83; mem. Chgo. area Pub. Affairs Group. Mem. Chgo. Women in Govt. Relations. Republican. Office: Ill Dept Pub Aid 624 S Michigan Suite 1300 Chicago IL 60605

BREIHAN, CARL WILLIAM, JR., electrical engineer, supply company executive; b. St. Louis, Sept. 9, 1949; s. Carl William, Sr. and Ethel (Venarde) B.; m. Maeme Yee, July 23, 1973; children—Eric, Marc, Tara. B.S. in Elec. Engring., Mich. State U.; M.A. in Thermal and Fluid Dynamics, U. Del. Registered profl. elec. engr. Sales mgr. Ogden Mfg. co., Chgo., 1973-78; ptnr. Tac, Inc., Greenwood, Ind., 1980—; pres., ARC, Inc., Greenwood, 1982—, CEM Electric, Inc., Greenwood, 1978—; chmn. bd. and chief exec. officer CEMCO Enterprises, Greenwood, 1982—. Served to USN, 1968-73. Mem. Soc. of Plastics Engrs., Soc. of Plastic Industry. Republican. Roman Catholic. Club: St. Louis Water Safety (pres. 1963-68). Lodges: Elks, Moose. Avocations: scuba diving; boating; race car building and driving. Home: 1802 Davis Dr Franklin IN 46131 Office: CEM Electric Co Inc 1747 Industrial Dr Greenwood IN 46142

BREIHAN, EDNA MARIA THIES, retired educator; b. Flossmoor, Ill., Jan. 22, 1911; d. Henry Frederick and Anna (Cohrs) Thies; student Valparaiso U., 1928-30; A.B., Coll. of St. Francis, 1953; M.Ed., De Paul U., 1957; certificate advanced study in reading U. Chgo., 1966; m. Armin Henry Breihan, June 26, 1937; children—Joanne, James. Tchr., Lutheran Parochial Schs., Detroit, Chgo., 1930-37; pvt. tchr. remedial reading, Homewood, Ill., Flossmoor, 1945-51; tchr. Culbertson Sch., Joliet, Ill., 1953-57, Central Sch., Lockport, Ill., 1955-58; reading cons. Lockport Twp. High Sch. 1958-66; reading coordinator Lockport Twp. Sch. Dist. 205, 1966-71, chmn. reading dept., 1971-75. Mem. Lockport Woman's Club (hon.), NEA, Nat. Soc. for Study Edn., Internat. Reading Assn. (past pres. Will County council), Ill. Edn. Assn., Internat. Platform Assn., Lockport Bus. and Profl. Women's Assn., Assn. Supervision and Curriculum Devel., Am. Inst. Mgmt. (exec. council), AAUW, Delta Kappa Gamma, Chi Sigma Xi. Lutheran. Home: 1512 Briggs St Box 344 Lockport IL 60441

BREIHAN, STEVEN M., bank officer; b. St. Louis, Apr. 14, 1961; s. Erwin R. and Antoinette (Corcoran) B. BS, Lake Forest (Ill.) Coll., 1983. Asst. to dean admissions Lake Forest Coll., 1983-84; mgmt. trainee Mercantile Bank N.A., St. Louis, 1984-85, sr. credit analyst, 1985-86, bank officer corp. real estate, 1986-87; sales rep. Wallace McNeill Co., Clayton, Mo., 1987—. Mem. Clayton Jaycees, St. Louis C. of C. Republican. Roman Catholic. Club: Mo. Athletic. Avocations: swimming, waterpolo, tennis, squash, golf. Home: 4605 Lindell #1003 Saint Louis MO 63108 Office: Wallace McNeill Co 120 S Central Clayton MO 63105

BREIMAYER, JOSEPH FREDERICK, patent lawyer; b. Belding, Mich., May 4, 1942; s. Ronald and Crystal Helen (Reeves) B.; m. Margaret Anne Murphy, Aug. 26, 1967; children: Kathleen A., Deborah L., Elizabeth L. BEE, U. Detroit, 1965; JD, George Washington U., 1969. Cooperative engr. Honeywell Inc, Mpls., 1962-65; patent examiner U.S. Patent and Trademark Office, Washington, 1965-70; patent atty. Eastman Kodak Co., Rochester, N.Y., 1970-73; sr. patent counsel Medtronic Inc., Mpls., 1973. pres. Good Shepherd Home and Sch. Assn., 1984; precinct chmn. DFL, 1980-82. Mem. Minn. Intellectual Property Law Assn. (treas. 1986). Avocations: boating, skiing, travel. Home: 4700 Circle Downs Golden Valley MN 55416 Office: Medtronic Inc 7000 Central Ave Minneapolis MN 55432

BREINER, SANDER JAMES, psychiatry educator, psychoanalyst; b. Fiume, Italy, July 12, 1925; (parents Am. citizens); s. Alfred and Margaret (Steiner) B.; m. Beatrice Marsha Oboler, Mar. 18, 1951; children: Linda Marie, Myles Steven, Robert Ethan. BS, U. Ill., 1948; MB, MD, Chgo. Med. Sch., 1953. Diplomate Nat. Bd. Med. Examiners, Am. Bd. Psychiatry and Neurology. Asst. prof. psychology Wayne State U., Detroit, 1957—; assoc. prof. Mich. State U., East Lansing, 1970—; attending chief psychiatry dept. Harper Grace Hosp., Detroit, 1960—, William Beaumont Hosp., Birmingham, Mich., 1968—, Pontiac (Mich.) Gen. Hosp., 1980—; cons. depts. ob-gyn, surgery and medicine Harper Grace Hosp., 1960—; cons. Oak City Mental Health Clinic, Pontiac, 1971—; cons. dept. family med. Pontiac Gen. Hosp., 1980—; cons. dept. ob-gyn William Beaumont Hosp., 1982—. Contbr. numerous articles to profl. jours. Cons. Detroit Commn. on Children and Youth, 1957-62; cons. bd. edn. Detroit, Garden City and Bloomfield Hill, 1957—. Served with inf. U.S. Army, 1943-45, ETO. Fellow Am. Psychiat. Assn., Am. Soc. Psychoanalytic Physicians; mem. AMA, Am. Assn. Forensic Sci. Psychosomatic Medicine, AAAS, N.Y. Acad. Sci. Democrat. Avocations: gardening, mountain hiking, psychohistory. Home and Office: 7410 Franklin Rd Birmingham MI 48010

BREIPOHL, WALTER EUGENE, real estate broker; b. Ottawa, Ill., Mar. 24, 1953; s. Eugene E. and Margaret L. (Hughes) B. BS, Loyola U., Chgo., 1974. Real estate broker and devel. Breipohl Co., Ottawa, 1975—; bd. dirs. No. Ill. Devel. Corp. Bd. dirs. Greater Ottawa, Inc., 1984—; chmn. Econ. Devel. Commn., Ottawa, 1985—; trustee Community Hosp. Ottawa, 1986—. Mem. Illini Valley Bd. Realtors (sec.-treas. 1983-85, Pres. award 1985), Ill. Assn. Realtors, Nat. Assn. Realtors, Nat. Assn. Real Estate Appraisers, Nat. Assn. Home Builders, Ottawa Area C. of C. and Industry (chmn.-elect 1987). Republican. Roman Catholic. Club: Boat (Ottawa). Lodges: Elks, KC. Home and Office: PO Box 1039 Ottawa IL 61350

BREITBARTH, STEVEN ELDOR, clergyman, family therapist; b. Truman, Minn., Sept. 28, 1949; s. Eldor and Lois Minnie (Olhoft) B.; m. Janelle Kay Young, Oct. 14, 1972; children: Jonathan, Timothy, Marcus. AA, Bethany Jr. Coll., Mankato, Minn., 1969; BS, Mankato State U., 1978; M in Div., Concordia Sem., Ft. Wayne, Ind., 1980; postgrad., U. Wis., Superior, 1981. Ordained to ministry, 1980. Pastor Grace Luth. Ch., Chisholm, Minn., 1977—; therapist Luth. Social Service, Hibbing, 1983-86; vol. Family Program Cen. Mesabi Treatment Ctr., Hibbing, 1980—; adv., speaker Aid to Victims of Sexual Assault, Virginia, Minn., 1981—; advisor Luth. Youth Group, No. Minn., 1984—; cons., bd. dirs. Northstar Hospice, Hibbing. v.p. PTA, Chisholm, 1981. Mem. Am. Assn. Marriage and Family Therapy (clin.). Clubs: Chisholm Skating (bd. dirs 1981-84, pres. 1984-86), Blueline (Chisholm) (bd. dirs. 1983—). Home: 313 NW 4th St Chisholm MN 55719 Office: Grace Luth Ch 508 NW 9th St Chisholm MN 55719

BREITENBECK, JOSEPH M., bishop; b. Detroit, Aug. 3, 1914; s. Matthew J. and Mary A. (Quinlan) B. Student, U. Detroit, 1932-35; B.A., Sacred Heart Sem., Detroit, 1938; postgrad., Gregorian U., Rome, Italy, 1938-40; S.T.L., Catholic U., Washington; J.C.L., Lateran U., Rome, 1949. Ordained priest Roman Catholic Ch., 1942; asst. at St. Margaret Mary Parish, Detroit, 1942-44; sec. to Cardinal Mooney, 1944-58, Cardinal Dearden, 1959; pastor Assumption Grotto, 1959-67; consecrated bishop 1965, ordained titular bishop of Tepelta and aux. bishop of Detroit, 1965-69; bishop of Grand Rapids, Mich., 1969—; Episcopal adviser Nat. Cath. Laymens Retreat Conf. Mem. Nat. Conf. Cath. Bishops (com. chmn.). Home and Office: Chancery Office 660 Burton St SE Grand Rapids MI 49507 *

BREMER, JOHN PAUL, actuary; b. Anderson, Ind., Oct. 17, 1941; s. George Franklin and Barbara Esther (Jones) B. BS in Journalism, Northwestern U., 1966, MBA, 1968. CPA, Mich. Ops. research scientist Kimberly-Clark Corp., Neenah, Wis., 1968-69; analyst Continental Casualty Co., Chgo., 1969-70; mem. staff Coopers & Lybrand, Chgo., 1971-75; sr. cons. Coopers & Lybrand, Detroit, 1980—; asst. actuary Calif. West States Life Ins. Co., Sacramento, 1975-80. Treas., bd. dirs. Opportunities for the Handicapped Inc., Sacramento, 1977-80. Served with U.S. Army 1964-66. Fellow Soc. Actuaries; mem. AAAS, Am. Acad. Acturies, Am. Inst. CPA's, Mich. Assn. CPA's, Acctg. Aid Soc. (membership com. 1985-86). Club: Chgo. Mountaineering. Avocations: golf, skiing, mountaineering. Home: 300 Riverfront Park Detroit MI 48226 Office: Coopers & Lybrand 400 Renaissance Ctr Detroit MI 48243

BREMS, HANS JULIUS, economist, educator; b. Viborg, Denmark, Oct. 16, 1915; s. Holger and Andrea (Golditz) B.; m. Ulla Constance Simoni, May 20, 1944; children: Lisa, Marianne, Karen Joyce. Cand. polit., U. Copenhagen, 1941, dr.polit., 1950; Hedersdoktor (hon.), Svenska Handelshögskolan, Helsinki, Finland, 1970. Asst. prof. U. Copenhagen, 1943-51; lectr. U. Calif., Berkeley, 1951-54; mem. faculty U. Ill., Champaign-Urbana, 1954-86; prof. U. Ill., 1955-86; vis. prof. U. Calif., Berkeley, 1959, Harvard U., 1960, U. Kiel, (W.Ger.), 1961, U. Colo., 1963, U. Göttingen, (W.Ger.), 1964, U. Hamburg, (W.Ger.), 1967, U. Uppsala, (Sweden), 1968, U. Stockholm, 1980, U. Zurich, 1983, others. Author: Product Equilibrium under Monopolistic Competition, 1951, Output, Employment, Capital, and Growth, 1959, 2d edit., 1973, Quantitative Economic Theory, 1968, Labor, Capital, and Growth, 1973, Inflation, Interest, and Growth—A Synthesis, 1980, Dynamische Makrotheorie—Inflation, Zins und Wachstum, 1980, Fiscal Theory Government, Inflation and Growth, 1983, Pioneering Economic Theory, 1630-1980, 1986; contbr.: articles to profl. jours. and Ency. Americana. Rockefeller fellow, 1946-47; Fulbright prof., 1961, 64. Mem. Am. Econ. Assn., Royal Econ. Soc., Danish Acad. Scis. and Letters (fgn.). Home: 1103 S Douglas Ave Urbana IL 61801 Office: Box 99 Commerce West 1206 S 6th St Champaign IL 61820

BRENEMAN, JAMES RICHARD, architect; b. Kansas City, Mo., Feb. 9, 1941; s. D. Earl and Jessie Irene (Dean) B.; m. Susan Marie Oke, Jan. 29, 1966; children: Laura M., David E. BArch, Kans. State U., 1964, M. in Regional Planning, 1966. Registered architect, Kans., Mo. Architect Northern & Hamlin, Kansas City, 1970-73; v.p. Hamlin-Walker-Breneman, Kansas City, 1973-76; sr. assoc. Monroe & Lefebvre, Kansas City, 1976—. Prin. works include New Mark Jr. High Sch., 1971 (recognition award Am. Assn. Sch. Adminstrs. 1972). Cubmaster Boy Scouts Am., 1982-84; coach youth basketball and soccer, 1976-87; mem. community standards com. City of Prarie Village, Kans., 1984; elder Countryside Christian Ch., Mission, Kans., 1981-84, youth group sponsor, 1970-72. Served to capt. USAF, 1966-70. Named one of Outstanding Young Men in Am., U.S. Jaycees, 1968. Mem. AIA, Mo. Council Architects, Am. Arbitration Assn. (constrn. panel 1980—). Republican. Avocations: photography, reading, sports, travel. Home: 5327 W 69th St Prairie Village KS 66208 Office: Monroe & Lefebvre 1021 Pennsylvania Kansas City MO 64105

BRENIZER, NED WICKLIFFE, management information specialist; b. Ft. Wayne, Ind., Oct. 20, 1930; s. Leo Cletus and Hazel Elizabeth (Wickliffe) B.; student Drake U., 1948-50; m. Adeline P. Sylvia, July 15, 1978; children—(by previous marriage) Scott R., Beth A.; stepchildren—Christine, Michael, James. With Capehart-Farnsworth Materials Mgmt., Ft. Wayne, 1951-57; PERT specialist ITT Fed. Div., Ft. Wayne, 1957-65; with Tokheim Corp., Ft. Wayne, Ind., 1965—, mgr. info. systems, mgr. sales adminstrn., 1978—; lectr., cons. in field. Recipient Assn. Systems Mgmt. Merit award, 1974, Achievement award, 1979, Disting. Service award, 1983; Am. Prodn. and Inventory Control Soc. Best Jour. Article of Year award, 1978; winner essay contest Adminstrv. Mgmt. Assn. and IAM of London, 1985; cert. systems profl. Mem. Assn. Systems Mgmt., Internat. Customer Service Assn. Presbyterian. Contbr. articles to profl. jours. Home: 6312 Dumont Dr Fort Wayne IN 46815 Office: 1602 Wabash Ave Fort Wayne IN 46802

BRENNAN, BERNARD FRANCIS, retail chain store executive; b. Chgo., 1938; married. B.A., Coll. St. Thomas, 1964. With Sears, Roebuck & Co., Chgo., 1964-76; with Sav-A-Stop, Inc., 1976-82, group v.p.-service mdse. group, 1976-78, pres., chief operating officer, 1978-79, pres., chief exec. officer, 1979-82, chmn., 1982; exec. v.p. Montgomery Ward & Co., Inc., Chgo., 1982-83, pres., chief exec. officer, 1985—; pres. Household Merchandising Inc., Des Plaines, Ill., 1983-85. Served with U.S. Army, 1958-60, 62. Office: Montgomery Ward & Co Inc Montgomery Ward Plaza Chicago IL 60671 *

BRENNAN, CORINNE PATRICIA, nurse; b. St. Louis, June 23, 1954; d. Thomas Patrick and Audrey Sybil (Bryce) Sullivan. RN, Barnes Hosp., 1974. Staff nurse Barnes Hosp., St. Louis, 1974-76; charge nurse orthopedics St. Louis City Hosp., 1977-81, charge nurse CCU, 1983-85; charge nurse, acting dir. nursing Mo. Ea. Corrections Ctr., Pacific, 1981-83, Jewish Hosp., 1985—. Mem. Am. Assn. Critical Care Nurses, St. Louis Assn. Critical Care Nurses. Republican. Roman Catholic. Home: 8169 Rockledge Trail Saint Louis MO 63123

BRENNAN, DANIEL JOSEPH, plastic surgeon; b. St. Louis, Mo., June 17, 1942; s. Patrick Louis and Louise Martini (Schranz) B.; m. Carole Frances Gaylo, Apr. 21, 1944; children: Kathleen Louise, Daniel J. II. Student, St. Louis U., 1963, MD, 1967. Diplomate Am. Bd. Surgery, Am. Bd. Plastic and Reconstructive Surgery. Pres., physician Plastic Surgery Affiliates Inc., St. Louis, 1974—; instr. plastic surgery St. Louis U., 1974—. Fellow ACS; mem. Am. Soc. Plastic and Reconstructive Surgery, Am. Cleft Palate Assn., St. Louis Met. Med. Soc., St. Louis Plastic Surgery Soc., Am. Assn. Surgery Hand. Avocation: sports. Home: 13614 Peacock Farm Rd Saint Louis MO 63131 Office: Plastic Surgery Affiliates Inc 621 S New Ballas Rd Saint Louis MO 63141

BRENNAN, EDWARD A., retail executive, financial services executive; b. Chgo., Jan. 16, 1934; s. Edward and Margaret (Bourget) B.; m. Lois Lyon, June 11, 1955; children: Edward J., Cynthia Walls, Sharon Lisnow, Donald A., John L., Linda. BA, Marquette U., Milw., 1955. With Sears, Roebuck and Co., 1956—; exec. v.p. So. terr. Sears, Roebuck and Co., Atlanta, 1978-80; pres., chief operating officer for merchandising Sears, Roebuck and Co., Chgo., 1980-81, chmn. bd., chief exec. officer mdse. group, 1981-84, pres., chief operating officer, 1984-86, chmn., chief exec. officer, 1986—, also bd. dirs.; bd. dirs. Minn. Mining & Mfg. Co., Chgo. Council Fgn. Relations; mem. bd. trustees Savs. and Profit Sharing Fund of Sears Employees. Trustee, Marquette U., De Paul U.; mem. Chgo. Urban League, 1980—, Chgo. Mus. Sci. and Industry, The Sears Roebuck Found.; bd. govs. United Way Am. Mem. Pres.' Export Council, Bus. Roundtable, Conf. Bd. Clubs: Econ., Comml. Address: Sears Roebuck and Co Sears Tower Chicago IL 60684

BRENNAN, EMMET JAMES, III, personnel consultant; b. St. Louis, Oct. 4, 1945; s. Emmet James Jr. and Rita Katherine (Perkinson) B.; student St. Louis U., 1963-65, Washington U., St. Louis, 1965-70, U. Mo., St. Louis, 1975; B.A. with honors in Mgmt., Webster U., 1978; m. Elizabeth Jane Webb, Mar. 7, 1970. Personnel specialist Otto Faerber & Assos., St. Louis, 1965-70; indsl. relations personnel mgr. Rexall Drug Co., St. Louis, 1970-71; compensation analyst Dart Industries, Los Angeles, 1971-74; corp. wage and salary adminstr., personnel devel. assoc. Mallinckrodt, Inc., St. Louis, 1974-78; dir. St. Louis office Sullivan, Eisemann & Thomsen, St. Louis, 1978-80; pres. Brennan, Thomsen Assocs., Inc., Chesterfield, Mo., 1980—; asst. dir. Compensation Inst., 1981-82; guest lectr. various univs. and profl. socs. Lector, Incarnate Word Roman Cath. Parish. Served with U.S. Army, 1966-68. Mem. Am. Compensation Assn., Am. Soc. for Personnel Adminstrn., Adminstrv. Mgmt. Soc. (bd. dirs.), Nat. Com. on Pay Equity (job evaluation task force), Chesterfield C. of C., St. Louis Writers Guild, Phi Kappa Theta. Author: Geographic Salary and Cost of Living Differentials, 1980; The Compensation Audit, 1981; Payout, 1987; contbg. editor, founding mem. bd. editorial advisors Personnel Jour., 1984—; St. Louis mgr. Today's Mgr., 1985—; contbr. articles to profl. jours. Office: Brennan Thomsen Assocs Inc 106 Four Seasons Ctr Chesterfield MO 63017

BRENNAN, JAMES KEVIN, food service executive; b. Binghamton, N.Y., Dec. 26, 1947; s. John James and Dorothy Mary (Garvey) B.; m. Beverly Marie Sisson, Apr. 15, 1979; 1 child, Dorothy Grace. AS in Hotel and Restaurant Mgmt., Paul Smith's Coll., 1968; student, U. Denver, 1970-72. Mgr. Top's Restaurant, Wheatridge, Colo., 1974; sous chef Marriott Hotel, Denver, 1974-75; mgr. Cottage Inn Restaurant, Lakewood, Colo., 1976-78; dir. food services Saga Food Service, Franklin, Ind., 1978-83; owner, operator Brennan Food Service, Franklin, 1984-86; dir. food services Marriott Corp., Trinity Coll., Trinity Evang. Div. Sch., Deerfield, Ill., 1986—. Ice sculpture spl. segment Channel 8 News, 1982, Channel 10 News, 1983. Presenter Jr. Achievement awards banquet, Johnson County. Recipient Service award Kiwanis, 1983, Photo Contest award Indpls. Star, 1985, Spl. Recognition award Milton Coll., 1980. Mem/ Nat. Restaurant Assn., Franklin C. of C. Republican. Roman Catholic. Lodge: Rotary (speaker 1985). Avocations: photography, golf.

BRENNAN, MARY THERESE, city ofcl.; b. St. Louis, Apr. 12, 1951; d. Francis Charles and Beulah Mary (Tornatore) B.; student parochial schs., St. Louis. Stenographer, Council on Human Relations, City of St. Louis, 1969-71, sec. Mcpl. Bus. Devel. Commn., 1971-73, exec. sec. to dir. Community Devel. Agy., 1973-80, exec. sec., adminstrv. asst. to mayor's exec. asst. Mayor's Office, 1980—. Home: 3410 McCausland Ave Saint Louis MO 63139 Office: City Hall Mayor's Office Market and Tucker Sts Room 200 Saint Louis MO 63103

BRENNAN, MICHAEL JAMES, consultant; b. Evergreen Park, Ill., Aug. 31, 1961; s. Frank Robert and Catherine Ellen (Muldowney) B. AA, Harper Coll., 1982; BA, Western Ill. U., 1984. CPA, Ill. Pub. acct. Thomas Havey & Co., Chgo., 1984-85; computer and acctg. cons. Horizon Fed. Savings Bank, Glenview, Ill., 1985-87; pvt. practice micro computer cons. Arlington Heights, Ill., 1987—; corp. sec. Brookridge Devel., Inc., Glenview, 1987—; treas. Berndorf ICB Internat. Conveyor Belts Inc., Schaumburg, Ill., 1987—. Mem. Am. Inst. CPA's, Ill. Inst. CPA's. Roman Catholic. Avocations: scuba diving, skiing, sports. Home: 1415 W Miner St Arlington Heights IL 60005 Office: PO Box 486 Arlington Heights IL 60006-0486

BRENNAN, ROBERT LAWRENCE, psychometrician; b. Hartford, Conn., May 31, 1944; s. Robert and Irene Veronica (Connors) B.; B.A., Salem State Coll., 1967; M.A.T., Harvard U., 1968, Ed.D., 1970. Research assoc., lectr. Grad. Sch. Edn., Harvard U., Cambridge, Mass., 1970-71; asst. prof. edn. SUNY-Stony Brook, 1971-76; sr. research psychologist Am. Coll. Testing Program, Iowa City, 1976-79, dir. measurement research dept., 1979-84, asst. v.p. for measurement research, 1984—; adj. faculty Sch. Edn. U. Iowa, 1979—; cons. Office Child Devel., HEW, 1975-79. Harvard prize fellow, 1967. Mem. Am. Ednl. Research Assn. (Div. D award 1980), Midwestern Ednl. Research Assn. (pres.-elect 1987—), Am. Statis. Assn., Am. Psychol. Assn., Nat. Council Measurement Edn., Psychometric Soc. Assoc. editor Jour. Ednl. Measurement, 1978-83, Applied Psychological Measurement, 1982—; contbr. articles to profl. jours. Home: 218 N Friendship Iowa City IA 52240 Office: The Am Coll Testing Program Hwy 1-I 80 PO Box 168 Iowa City IA 52243

BRENNAN, ROBERT WALTER, assn. exec.; s. Walter R. and Grace A. (Mason) B.; m. Mary J. Engler, June 15, 1962; children: Barbara, Susan (twins). BS, U. Wis., 1957. Tchr., coach Waukesha (Wis.) High Sch., 1960-63; track coach U. Wis., Madison, 1963-71; exec. asst. to mayor City of Madison, 1971-73; pres. C. of C., Madison, 1973—. Mem. adv. council U. Wis.-Madison Sch. Edn., 1984—; mem. Madison Urban League, 1971—; bd. dirs. Cherokee Park, Inc., Wis. Nordic Sports Found., Very Spl. Arts, Wis. Named Madison's Favorite Son, 1971. Mem. Wis. Alumni Assn. (pres. 1985-86, chmn. bd. 1986-87), "W" Club (life, cert. of merit), Theta Delta Chi. Home: 5514 Comanche Way Madison WI 53704 Office: PO Box 71 Madison WI 53701

BRENNAN, T. CASEY, writer; b. Port Huron, Mich., Aug. 11, 1948; s. William James and Mildred Alice (Goodrich) B. Free-lance writer Avoca, Mich., 1969—. Leader of campaign to ban smoking portrayals in comic books and other children's pubs. Subject hon. resolution Mich. State Legislature, 1987. Democrat. Home: 4238 Bricker Rd Avoca MI 48006-9615 Office: care Neil Staebler 202 E Washington #308 Ann Arbor MI 48104-2121

BRENNAN, THOMAS EMMETT, JR., lawyer, judge; b. Detroit, Mar. 20, 1952; s. Thomas Emmett and Pauline Mary (Weinberger) B.; m. Julie Schafer, Apr. 23, 1977; children—Thomas Emmett III, Patrick Joseph. B.S., Mich. State U., 1974; J.D., Thomas M. Cooley Law Sch., 1978. Bar: Mich. 1978. Assoc. McGinty, Brown & Jakubiak, P.C., East Lansing, Mich., 1978-

79; ptnr. Klug & Brennan, P.C., East Lansing, 1979-81; dist. judge 55th Dist. Ct., Mason, Mich., 1981—; 9th Dist. commr. Ingham County Bd., Mason, 1979-81; bd. dirs. Thomas M. Cooley Law Sch. Lansing, 1980—, adj. prof., 1983—; adj. prof. Mich. State U., 1983—. Mem. Ingham County Bar Assn., ABA, Am. Judges Assn., Ingham County Trial Judges Assn., Mich. Dist. Judges Assn., Thomas M. Cooley Law Sch. Alumni Assn. (Disting. Alumnus award 1983). Clubs: Mich. State U., Downtown Coaches (Lansing) (bd. dirs.). Lodge: Rotary (East Lansing). Office: 55th Dist Ct 700 Buhl Mason MI 48854

BRENNAN, TIMOTHY S., lawyer; b. South Bend, Ind., July 17, 1958; s. Patrick and Ruth E. (Gaudig) B.; m. Geneva M. Chamberlin, Sept. 15, 1984. BS, Ind. U., 1980; JD, Ohio No. U., 1983. Bar: Ind. 1973, U.S. Dist. Ct. (no. and so. dists.) Ind. 1983. Ptnr. Brennan & Brennan, South Bend, Ind., 1984—. Bd. dirs. Park Ave. Neighborhood Assn., South Bend, 1984—. Mem. ABA, Ind. Bar Assn., Assn. Trial Lawyers Am., Delta Theta Phi. Democrat. Roman Catholic. Lodges: KC, Optomists. Avocations: bicycling, golf, fishing, woodworking. Home: 534 W 8th St Mishiwaka IN 46544 Office: 215 W Marion St South Bend IN 46601

BRENNEMAN, HUGH WARREN, JR., federal magistrate; b. Lansing, Mich., July 4, 1945; s. Hugh Warren and Irma June (Redman) B.; m. Katrina Cup Kindel, Apr. 30, 1977; children: Justin Scott, Ross Edward. B.A., Alma Coll., 1967; J.D., U. Mich., 1970. Bar: Mich. 1970, D.C. 1975, U.S. Dist. Ct. (we. dist.) Mich. 1974, U.S. Dist. Ct. Md. 1973, U.S. Ct. Mil. Appeals 1971, U.S. Ct. Appeals (6th cir.) 1976, U.S. Ct. Appeals (D.C. cir.) 1981, U.S. Supreme Ct. 1980. Law clk. Mich. 30th Jud. Cir., Lansing, 1970-71; asst. U.S. atty. Dept. Justice, Grand Rapids, Mich., 1974-77; assoc. Bergstrom, Slykhouse & Shaw, P.C., Grand Rapids, 1977-80; U.S. magistrate U.S. Dist. Ct. (we. dist.) Mich., Grand Rapids, 1980—. Mem. exec. bd. West Michigan Shores council Boy Scouts Am., 1984-87, adv. council, 1987—. Served to capt. JAGC, U.S. Army, 1971-74. Mem. State Bar Mich. (rep. assembly 1984—), D.C. Bar, Fed. Bar Assn. (pres. Western Mich. chpt. 1979-80, nat. del. 1980-84), Grand Rapids Bar Assn. (chmn. U.S. Constn. Bicentennial com.), Nat. Council U.S. Magistrates, ABA, Phi Delta Phi, Omicron Delta Kappa. Congregationalist. Clubs: Peninsular, Rotary (dir., pres.), Econ. of Grand Rapids (past dir.). Office: 240 Fed Bldg Grand Rapids MI 49503

BRENNEMAN, MARY BETH, language professional; b. Youngstown, Ohio, Nov. 8, 1950; d. Stanley Earle and Jane M. (Samuel) Babcock; m. Carl S. Brenneman, May 26, 1979; children: Jeffrey Scott, Lisa Marie; 2 stepchildren. BA summa cum laude, Miami U., Oxford, Ohio, 1973; MA, U. Mich., 1975; student, Inst. d'Etudes Francaises, Tours, France. Cert. tchr., Mich. Teaching fellow U. Mich., Ann Arbor, 1973-75; French tchr. Sturgis Public Schs., Mich., 1975—; chaperone for student trips to Wiesloch, West Germany, 1977-79; co-ordinator Sturgis-Wiesloch Student Exchange Program. Mem. Sister Cities Affiliation Bd., 1985—. Mem. Sturgis Edn. Assn., Mich. Edn. Assn., Nat. Edn. Assn., Alpha Lambda Delta, Phi Kappa Phi, Phi Beta Kappa. Methodist. Avocations: flutist in concert band. Home: 408 Maplecrest Sturgis MI 49091 Office: Sturgis Public High Schs 216 Vinewood Sturgis MI 49091

BRENNEN, WILLIAM ELBERT, management consultant; b. Mo., Sept. 30, 1930; s. William E. and Frances (Andrew) B.; m. Natalia Summers, Nov. 14, 1958 (div. 1979); children: William, Natalia Jane, Elizabeth; m. Sharon Russell, Aug. 8, 1987. BS, U.S. Mcht. Marine Acad., 1952; MBA, U. Chgo., 1964. Ship's officer, traffic and ops. mgr. States Marine Lines Inc., Korea and Japan, 1952-61; with Case & Co./Stevenson Jordan & Harrison, Inc. Mgmt. Cons., Chgo. and N.Y.C., 1961-68; dir. internat. materials mgmt. Internat. Minerals & Chems., Skokie, Ill., 1968-71, Abbott Labs., North Chicago, Ill., 1971-73; pres. W.E. Brennen Cons., Inc. (name changed to Brennen Cons. Inc. 1987), 1987—. Mgmt. Cons., Evanston, Ill., 1973—; v.p., mng. prin. Fry Cons., 1982—. Served to lt. USNR, 1953-55. Mem. Am. Mktg. Assn. (pres. Chgo. chpt. 1982-83), Bus. Mktg. Council, Inst. Mgmt. Cons., Nat. Council Logistics Mgmt. Episcopalian. Office: 500 Davis Center Evanston IL 60201

BRENNER, MICHAEL JOHN, accountant; b. Detroit, Nov. 9, 1945; s. Frederick William and Marian (Dailey) B.; m. Margaret Skown, Aug. 12, 1967; children: Renee, Michele, William. BS, U. Detroit, 1967; MBA, U. Mich., 1968. CPA, Mich. Mgr., staff acct. Coopers & Lybrand, Detroit, 1967-77, ptnr., 1977—; chmn. nat. real estate industry services group Coopers & Lybrand, 1985—. Contbr. articles to profl. jours. Chmn. Detroit Urban League, 1982-84; trustee Bus./Edn. Alliance, Detroit, 1978-85; bd. dirs. Jr. Achievement of Southeast Mich., Detroit, 1977-85. Mem. Am. Inst. CPA's, Mich. Assn. CPA's, Nat. Assn. Real Estate Investment Trusts (acctg. com.), Nat. Assn. Real Estate Comp. (advisor to fin. acctg. standards com.). Republican. Roman Catholic. Clubs: Orchard Lake Country (Mich.) (chmn. fin. com. 1981-84, bd. govs. 1987—); Detroit Athletic. Office: Coopers & Lybrand 400 Renaissance Ctr Detroit MI 48243

BRENT, IRA MARTIN, psychiatrist; b. N.Y.C., Nov. 1, 1944; m. Terry Suffet. BS, L.I. U., 1966; MD, Chgo. Med. Sch., 1970. Diplomate Am. Bd. Psychiatry and Neurology. Intern U. Calif. at Irvine Orange County Med. Ctr., Orange, 1970-71; dir. dept psychiatry St. Mary's Hosp., Decatur, Ill., 1971—; asst. clin. prof. psychiatry So. Ill. U. Sch. Medicine, Springfield; clin. faculty So. Ill. U. Sch. Medicine, Springfield. Served to capt. USAF, 1971-73. Mem. AMA, Ill. Med. Soc., Am. Phychiat. Assn., Ill. Psychiat. Soc., Macon County Med. Soc., Am. Assn., Psychoanalytic Physicians. Address: 1900 E Lakeshore Dr Decatur IL 62521

BRENT, RUTH STUMPE, design educator; b. Washington, Mo., Sept. 11, 1951; d. Clarence Frank and Dorothy May (Horstick) Stumpe; m. Edward Everett Brent, May 14, 1972; children: Jessica Elizabeth, Jonathan Edward. BS cum laude, U. Mo., 1972; MA, U. Minn., 1974, PhD, 1978. Postdoctoral fellow in socio-clin. geriatrics NIMH, 1978-79; asst. prof. U. Mo., Columbia, 1981-86, assoc. prof. design, 1986—, acting dept. chair, 1984-85, chair housing and interior design dept., 1985—; project dir. Adminstrn. on Aging Grant, 1979-81; cons. Idea Works, Inc., Columbia, 1981—; reviewer of standards Am. Nat. Standard, 1985. Contbr. articles to profl. jours.; editorial bd. Home Econs. Research Jour., Washington, 1982-85. Active Mayor's Task Force, Columbia Low-Income Housing, 1982-83; dist. chair United Way, Columbia, 1981, 85; mem. adv. bd. Pub. Housing Authority, Columbia, 1984—; vol. Dem. Party, Columbia, 1986, Nuclear Freeze Campaign, Columbia, 1986. Grantee Adminstrn. on Aging, 1979-81, VA, 1981, Am. Home Econs. Assn., 1981-82, Joel Polsky Found. Interior Design Research, 1985-86. Mem. Am. Home Econs. Assn. (chmn. art and design sect. 1984-87, New Achievers award 1987), Interior Design Educators Council, Am. Assn. Housing Educators, Environ. Design Research Assn., Gerontol. Assn., Omicron Nu, Phi Upsilon Omicron. Club: Columbia Area Stock Holders. Home: 100 W Briarwood Columbia MO 65203 Office: Dept Housing and Interior Design 137 Stanley Hall Columbia MO 65211

BRESLIN, THOMAS RAYMOND, manufacturing executive; b. St. Paul, May 13, 1944; s. Raymond Edward and Marion Evelyn (Thomas) B.; m. Frances Lee Preiner, June 6, 1964; children: Sean Edward, Heather Maire. BA, Coll. St. Thomas, 1968. Asst. to pres. Richard Mfg. Co., Mpls., 1959-69; sales engr. Mid Continental Engring., Mpls., 1969-72; v.p. K.Y., Inc., Mpls., 1972-74; cons., gen. mgr. Metals Engring., St. Paul, 1974-76; v.p. Richard Mfg. Co., Eden Prairie, Minn., 1976—; bd. dirs. Gallery Photo, New Brighton, Minn.; pres. 120 Creative Corner, Mpls., 1971-77. Pres. Pike Lake PTA, New Brighton, 1974; chmn. Pike Lake Library Com., New Brighton, 1975. Mem. Photo Mktg. Assn. Republican. Roman Catholic. Avocations: boating, photography. Home: 1246 North Court New Brighton MN 55101

BRESLOW, IAN HAROLD, technical writer, communications specialist; b. Leeds, Eng., Dec. 10, 1940; came to U.S., 1949; s. Milton and Fay (Weinman) B.; m. Shirley Christine Rodgers, July 18, 1963; children: Anne Leslie, Alan William. Assoc. in Gen. Studies, U. Nebr., 1979. Chief clerk So. Pacific Co., Los Angeles, 1960-65; writer online system procedures So. Pacific Co., San Francisco, 1965-69; mgr. tech. publs. Firemen's Fund Am. Ins. Cos., San Francisco, 1969-71; written communications specialist and supr. Union Pacific R.R. Co., Omaha, 1971—; lectr. on written communications, Omaha, 1973-75.

BRESSACK, MITCHELL LESLIE, dermatologist; b. Bklyn., May 8, 1953; s. Irwin and Irene Sally (Kramer) B.; m. Diane H. Schaar, Mar. 8, 1980; children: Seth Mason, Rachel Mara. BS, SUNY, Stoney Brook, 1973; MD, SUNY, Bklyn., 1978. Diplomate Am. Bd. Dermatology. Intern Cook County Hosp., Chgo., 1978-79, resident, 1979-82; practice medicine specializing in dermatology Dermatology Ctr., Merrillville, Ind., 1982—. Mem. Citizen's Utility Bd., Chgo., 1985—. Mem. Am. Acad. Dermatology, Ind. State Med. Soc., Lake County Med. Soc. Jewish. Office: Dermatology Ctr PC 1000 E 80th Pl Merrillville IN 46410

BRESSAN, CAROL ANN, university administrator; b. Springfield, Ill., Apr. 22, 1941; d. Gino John and Clarice (Bourgasser) B. Student, Lincoln Land Community Coll., 1969-71; BA, Sangamon State U., 1975, M Pub. Adminstrn., 1980. Sec. State of Ill. Dept. Mental Health and Dept. Revenue, Springfield, 1960-70; adminstrv. sec. Sch. Medicine So. Ill. U., Springfield, 1970-73, asst. to dean, 1973-82, asst. provost, 1982—. Bd. dirs. Assn. Retarded Citizens, Springfield, 1981—; 1st v.p., 1987. Mem. Assn. Am. Med. Colls. (groups on bus. affairs and instnl. planning 1975—), Harbinger Soc., Am. Assn. Univ. Adminstrs., Am. Soc. Profl. and Exec. Women, Planetary Soc., Sierra Club. Avocations: photography, reading, traveling. Home: 2512 Sherborn Springfield IL 62702 Office: So Ill U Sch Medicine 801 N Rutledge PO Box 3926 Springfield IL 62708

BRESSMAN, ROBERT ALLEN, periodontist; b. Chgo., June 13, 1952; s. Melvin Jerome and Elfrieda (Frischman) B.; m. Ariel Shaewitz, Aug. 10, 1974; children: Shauna Meredith, Ilana Brooke. BS, U. Ill., 1974; DDS, Northwestern U., 1978, MS, 1981. Cert. periodontist, Ill. Practice dentistry specializing in periodontics Chgo., 1978—; asst. prof. periodontics Northwestern U., Chgo., 1978-83; chmn. periodontics sect. gen. practice residency Ill. Masonic, Chgo., 1983-87. Mem. Skokie (Ill.) Bd. Health, 1986—. Mem. Am. Acad. Periodontics (ann. student award 1978), ADA, Ill. Dental Soc., Ill. Soc. Periodontists, Chgo. Dental Soc. (dir. edn1. TV 1980-87, columnist rev. 1985—, mem. pub. relations commn. 1985—, chmn. speakers bur. 1985—). Jewish. Lodge: Rotary (editor Skokie 1985-87). Avocations: motorcycles, photography, tv prodn., computers. Office: 9631 Gross Point Rd Skokie IL 60076

BREST VAN KEMPEN, GUSTAAF F., architect; b. Jakarta, Indonesia, Apr. 11, 1939; came to U.S., 1954; s. Carel Pieter and Maria Herbertina (Jakobs) Brest van K.; m. Helen Dorothy Burn, Dec. 26, 1969; children: Gillian Ann Charlotte, Katherine Elisabeth. BArch, U. Pa., 1964. Registered architect, Ill. Architect U.S. Peace Corps, Tunis, Tunisia, 1964-66; from asst. to assoc. prof. architecture U. Utah, Salt Lake City, 1966-70, 71-75; resident project mgr. Skidmore, Owings and Merrill, Algiers, Algeria, 1976-78; project mgr., assoc. Skidmore, Owings and Merrill, Chgo., 1978-83; architect, prin. Evanston, 1983—; design cons., Salt Lake City, 1966-75; visiting prof. architecture U. Tunis, 1970-71; cons. Perkins & Will Internat., Chgo., 1983; cons. The World Bank, Jamaica & Morocco, North Yemen, Tunisia, 1985—. Chief editor Utah Architect, 1973-75. JGB adv. council Chgo. Symphony Orchestra, 1980—. NEA grantee, 1986-87; Council for Internat. Exchange of Scholars Fulbright Research grantee, 1985-86. Mem. AIA. Avocations: violin, tennis, violinist with Evanston Symphony Orchestra.

BRETHEN, ROBERT HERSCHELL, building components manufacturing company executive; b. Rochester, N.Y., June 29, 1926; s. Milton R. and Ethyl H. (Herschell) B.; m. Alma Hommel; children: Karen E., David M. B.S., Syracuse U., 1949. Regional sales mgr. Delco Appliance div. Gen. Motors Corp., Rochester, 1949-62; v.p., gen. mgr. Kitchen Machine div. Toledo Scale Corp., Rochester, 1963-68; group v.p. Fuqua Industries, Atlanta, 1968-71, Nat. Service Industries, Atlanta, 1971-73; pres. Philips Industries, Inc., Dayton, Ohio, 1973—, chief exec. officer, 1986—, also bd. dirs.; bd. dirs. Hobart Bros. Mfg. Co., 1st Nat. Bank. Trustee Miami Valley Hosp.; bd. dirs. Jr. Achievement of Dayton and Miami Valley, Planned Parenthood Assn. Miami Valley, Inc. Mem. Dayton C. of C. (solicitations rev. com.), LWV (adv. bd. greater Dayton area), Sigma Phi Epsilon. Republican. Home: 2445 Ridgeway Rd Dayton OH 45419 Office: Philips Industries Inc 4801 Springfield St PO Box 943 Dayton OH 45401

BRETT, GEORGE HOWARD, professional baseball player; b. Moundsville, W.Va., May 15, 1953; s. Jack Francis and Ethel (Hansen) B. Student, El Camino Jr. Coll., Torrance, Calif. Third baseman Kansas City (Mo.) Royals Profl. Baseball Team, 1974—. Named Am. League batting champion, 1976, Am. League Most Valuable Player, 1980. Mem. Am. League All Star Team, 1976-85. Address: care Kansas City Royals PO Box 1969 Kansas City MO 64141 *

BRETT, JOSEPH MILLER, optometrist; b. Joliet, Ill., Jan. 19, 1944; s. Glen Allen and Ruby (Qually) B. BA, U. Ill., 1967; OD, Ill. Coll. Optometry, 1971. Pvt. practice optometry Chesterton, Ind., 1982—. Republican. Lutheran. Avocations: reading, landscaping, talking. Home: 8716 Carolina St Highland IN 46322 Office: 209 S Calumet Chesterton IN 46304

BRETT, RANDALL PHILIP, mgmt. cons.; b. Balt., June 14, 1950; s. Herbert Saul and Muriel (Berns) B.; B.A., U. Ill., 1972; M.Mgmt., Northwestern U., 1977; m. Deborah L. Lieber, May 20, 1973. Personnel mgr. Interstate Service Corp., Chgo., 1972-74; personnel mgr. Motorola, Inc., Schaumburg, Ill., 1974-77, 79; sr. cons. assoc. Drake-Beam & Assos., Inc., Des Plaines, Ill., 1977-79; prin. Employee Relations Assos., Chgo., 1979-82; v.p. Drake Beam Moran, Inc., 1982—. Mem. Soc. Human Resources Profls., Am. Soc. Profl. Cons., Am. Soc. Personnel Adminstrn., Am. Soc. Tng. and Devel. Democrat. Mem. editorial rev. com. Am. Soc. Personnel Adminstrn. Contbr. articles to profl. jours.

BRETT, RICHARD JOHN, speech pathologist; b. Chgo., Sept. 5, 1921; s. Richard J. and Emily (Salter) B.; B.Ed., No. Ill. State Tchrs. Coll., 1943; M.S., U. Ill., 1947; student U. Amsterdam (Holland), 1949, U. Chgo., 1948-49, 62, 66-67, Northwestern U., 1967. Speech supr. Summer Residential Clinic, U. Ill., Urbana, 1948, 50, 52; speech pathologist Waukegan (Ill.) High Schs., 1946—; chmn. Chgo. Regional Interviewing Com. for Exchange of Tchrs., U.S. Info. Agy., 1962-86; del. to Internat. Fedn. of Free Tchr. Unions, Switzerland. 1953. Founder, Pub. Sch. Caucus, Chgo., 1973, chmn., 1973-76. Served with U.S. Army, 1943-45. Fellow Am. Speech-Lang.-Hearing Assn. (membership com. 1975-77, conv. program com. 1974, 77, internat. affairs com. 1987—); mem. Ill. Speech and Hearing Assn. (chmn. legis. com. 1964-65, treas. 1977-78, v.p. bus. affairs 1978-79), Internat. Council Exceptional Children (pres. Chgo. suburban chpt. 1949-50), Am. (co-chmn. internat. relations com. 1952-63), Ill. (chmn. profl. standards com. 1952-57), Lake County (pres. 1949-51, 64-67) fedns. tchrs., U.S.-China Peoples Friendship Assn. (v.p. Chgo. chpt. 1987—), UN Assn., Mus. Contemporary Art, ACLU, Common Cause, Art Inst. Chgo., Chgo. Symphony Soc. Club: National Travel. Compiler: World Study and Travel for Teachers, 1952-85; editor Five-O-Format, 1951-56, 66-69. Home: 616 4th St Waukegan IL 60085 Office: Waukegan East High Sch 1101 Washington St Waukegan IL 60085

BRETZ, RONALD JAMES, lawyer; b. Detroit, Nov. 11, 1951; s. James Louis and Nancy Kathleen (Murphy) B.; m. Leslie Jane Lucas, June 13, 1973; children: Jeffrey, Elissa, Sarah. BA, Mich. State U., 1973; JD, Wayne (Mich.) State U., 1976. Bar: Mich. 1976, U.S. Supreme Ct 1985. Asst. defender Appellate Defender Office Sate of Mich., Lansing, 1977—; lectr. Mich. Appellate Assigned Counsel System, Lansing, 1985, Cooley Law Sch., Lansing, 1985-86. Mem adv. com. Community Alternatives Program, Lansing, 1984-85. Mem. Nat. Lawyers Guild (pres. Lansing chpt. 1985-86, sec. 1986-87), U.S. Supreme Ct. Bar Assn., State Bar Assn. Mich., Criminal Def. Attys. Mich. (lectr. 1982, Outstanding Criminal Def. Work award 1986). Avocations: reading, playing guitar, cycling, movies, sports. Office: State Appellate Defender Office 340 Bus and Trade Ctr 200 Washington Sq N Lansing MI 48913

BRETZKE, WILLIAM FREDRICK, administrative services executive, consultant; b. Mpls., Dec. 9, 1951; s. Robert Milton and Eileen Catherine (Crummey) B.; m. Kathleen Ann Bukkila, Nov. 26, 1976; children: Timothy, John. BS in Bus., U. Minn., 1976. Personnel asst. Deaconess Hosp., Mpls., 1976-77; work mgmt. analyst MSI Ins., St. Paul, 1977-80, work mgmt. mgr., 1980-84, personal lines analyst, 1984-85, dir. bldg. services, 1985—; instr. Mpls. Pub. Schs., Mpls., 1984—; v.p., bd. dirs. Co-op. Printing Assn., Mpls., 1985—. V.p. Lake Hiawatha Recreation Council, Mpls., 1986. Mem. Nat. Assn. Fleet Adminstrs. Roman Catholic. Club: Toastmasters (Mpls.) (v.p. 1981-83). Avocations: fishing, sailing. Home: 4055 S 24th Ave Minneapolis MN 55406 Office: MSI Insurance 2 Pine Tree Dr Arden Hills MN 55112 Mailing Address: Box 64035 Saint Paul MN 55164

BREU, GEORGE, accountant; b. Milw., May 8, 1954; s. George and Grace (Rossmaier) B.; m. Nancy Lee Roblee, June 6, 1987. BBA in Acctg. cum laude, U. Wis., Milw., 1976. CPA, Wis. Audit staff Reilly, Penner & Benton, Milw., 1976-78; tax mgr. Radke, Schlesner & Wernecke, S.C., Milw., 1978—. Treas. Elmbrook Hist. Soc., Brookfield, Wis., 1981-83. Mem. Am. Inst. CPA's (tax div.), Wis. Inst. CPA's, U. Wis. Milw. Tax Assn., Germany Philatelic Soc. (treas. Milw. chpt. 1978—), U. Wis. Milw. Philatelic Soc. (founder, treas. 1972-81), Milw. Philatelic Soc. Inc. (corp. registered agt. 1986—), U. Wis. Alumni Assn. Republican. Roman Catholic. Avocations: stamp collecting, reading history, traveling. Home: 15840 Fieldbrook Dr Brookfield WI 53005 Office: Radke Schlesner & Wernecke SC 2949 N Mayfair Rd Milwaukee WI 53222

BREUER, COY LEBURN, civil engr.; b. Phelps County, Mo., Apr. 3, 1924; s. Thomas Franklin and Minnie Mae (Agee) B.; B.S. in Civil Engring., U. Mo., Rolla, 1949; m. Ruby Irene Wycoff, Jan. 19, 1946; children—Rhonda Jean, Randal Coy, Rodney Kent. With Mo. Hwy. and Transp. Dept., and predecessor, 1949—, sr. engr., 1964-69, asst. div. engr., Jefferson City, 1969—. Bd. dirs. Meml. Community Hosp., Jefferson City, Mo., 1979. Served with AUS, 1943-45. Registered profl. engr., Mo. Mem. Acad. Civil Engrs., ASCE, Nat. Soc. Profl. Engrs., Hwy. Engrs. Assn. Mo., Mo. Soc. Profl. Engrs. Office: State Hwy Bldg Jefferson City MO 65102

BREUER, LINDA HARPER, business educator; b. Prairie du Chien, Wis., Jan. 20, 1940; s. Walter D. and V. Grace (Taylor) Harper; m. Adam A. Breuer, July 1, 1975. BS in Edn., U. Wis., Whitewater, 1961; MS in Edn., No. Ill. U., 1965. Tchr. Ela-Vernon High Sch., Lake Zurich, Ill., 1961-62, Hinsdale (Ill.) Cen. High Sch., 1962-65; instr. bus. Triton Coll., River Grove, Ill., 1965—, dept. chairperson, 1970-87. Mem. Nat. Bus. Edn. Assn., Ill. Bus. Edn. Assn., Delta Pi Epsilon. Avocations: architecture, travel, golf, aerobics, bridge. Home: 830 Camden Ln Northfield IL 60093 Office: Triton Coll 2000 5th Ave River Grove IL 60171

BREUHAUS, ROBERT CHARLES, accountant; b. Chgo., Mar. 23, 1940; s. Herbert C. and Helen Dorothy (Griffith) B.; m. Barbara Louise Bollinger, Feb. 11, 1967; 1 child, Debra. BS in Acctg., Bradley U., 1966. CPA, Ill. Staff acct. Krieger, Greiner & Allovid, Peoria, Ill., 1965-71, McGladrey, Hansen Dunn & Co., Peoria, 1971-74; sr. acct. Alexander Grant & Co., Bloomington, Ill., 1974-76; cashier, v.p. Heights Bank, Peoria, 1977-78; pvt. practice acctg. Peoria, 1978—; auditor Peoria Ambucs, 1965—. Served to staff sgt. U.S. Army, 1959-62. Mem. Am. Inst. CPA's, Nat. Assn. Accts., Ill. CPA Soc., Am. Bus. Club, Christian Bus. Mens Club. Republican. Presbyterian. Avocations: puzzles, gardening. Home and Office: 3321 W Capitol Dr Peoria IL 61614-2310

BREWER, ANNIE M(ULLER), editor; b. Rahway, N.J., Mar. 31, 1925; d. Raymond William and Annie Whitefoord (Hill) Muller; m. Donald Edward Brewer, Aug. 12, 1943; children: Donald Christopher, Richard Whitefoord, David Scott. BA, U. Mich., 1966, MLS, 1968. With Gale Research Co., Detroit, 1969—, sr. editor, librarian, 1980—. Editor: Publishers Directory, 1978, Biography Almanac, 1981, Dictionaries, Encyclopedias and Other Word-Related Books, 4th edit., 1987. Mem. ALA, Spl. Libraries Assn. (chmn. pub. div. 1986-87). Avocation: gardening. Home: 24245 Fairmount Dr Dearborn MI 48124 Office: Gale Research Co 835 Penobscot Bldg Detroit MI 48226

BREWER, DANA, lawyer, educator; b. Concordia, Kans., Jan. 25, 1952; s. Dean Decker and Irma Elaine (Ames) B. B.S. cum laude, Kans. State U., 1974; J.D., Washburn U., 1976. Bar: Kans. 1977, U.S. Dist. Ct. Kans. 1977. Assoc. Baldwin, Paulsen & Buechel, Chartered, Concordia, 1977-82; ptnr. Paulsen, Buechel, Swenson, Uri & Brewer, Chartered, Concordia, 1982—; educator Cloud County Community Coll., Concordia, 1979—. Chmn. United Lutheran Ministries, N. Central Kans., 1981-83; commr. Indsl. Devel. Adv. Commn., Concordia, 1982—; bd. dirs. Pan-Am. Hwy. Assn., 1984—. Mem. Cloud County Bar Assn. (sec. 1977-79), Kans. Bar Assn. (com. on legal issues affecting elderly 1985—), ABA (probate and trust div., com. post-mortem tax problems and fed. death tax problems of estates and trusts), Kans. Sch. Attys. Assn. (bd. dirs. 1984—), Concordia C. of C. (bd. dirs. 1984—, chmn. 1986—), Jaycees (community devel. v.p. 1983-84). Republican. Lutheran. Lodges: Moose, Lions. Home: RR 2 Concordia KS 66901 Office: Paulsen Buechel Swenson Uri & Brewer 613 Washington St PO Box 327 Concordia KS 66901

BREWER, DAVID KEITH, diagnostic radiologist; b. Kansas City, Mo., Feb. 28, 1952; s. Jerome and Pearl (Schere) B.; m. Hannah Susan Gurin, June 3, 1979; children: Valerie, Russell. BS, BA, U. Kans., Lawrence, 1974; MD, U. Kans., Kansas City, 1977. Diplomate Am. Bd. Radiology. Resident in radiology U. Kans., Kansas City, 1978-80, Rhode Island Hosp., Brown U., Providence, 1980-82; diagnostic radiologist Marian Health Ctr., Sioux City, Iowa, 1982—. Mem. AMA, Am. Coll. Radiology, Radiol. Soc. N.Am., Phi Beta Kappa, Phi Lamba Upsilon. Avocations: amatuer radio. Office: Marian Health Ctr 801 5th St Sioux City IA 51101

BREWER, DEBRA CATHERINE, sales executive; b. Ft. Smith, Ariz., Sept. 5, 1957; d. Melvin William and Bernette Ann (Ellenbecker) Gruber; m. John Alza Brewer Jr, Apr. 27, 1985. BBA in Mkgt., U. Wis., Whitewater, 1979. Sales rep. Wallce Bus. Forms, Milw., 1979-81, Simplex Time Recorder, Greenbay, Wis., 1981-82, Accurate Bus Controls, Appleton, Wis., 1982-83; bus. systems analyst Thilmany Pulp and Paper, Kaukauna, Wiss., 1984-85; supr. telemktg. Rayovac Corp., Madison, Wis., 1985-86, mgr. telemktg., 1986—. Mem. Wis. Telemktg. Mgrs. Assn., Am. Telemktg. Assn. Roman Catholic. Avocation: snow skiing. Home: 6829 Putnam Rd Madison WI 53719 Office: Rayovac Corp 601 Rayovac Dr Madison WI 53711

BREWER, EDWARD EUGENE, tire and rubber company executive; b. Findlay, Ohio, July 19, 1925; s. William B. and Edna (Hurrel) B.; m. Joyce K. Josephsen, Feb. 7, 1948; children: Stephen, Rebecca, Mary, Sara, Debra. B.S. in Mech. Engring., Purdue U., 1949. With Cooper Tire & Rubber Co., Findlay, 1949-56; v.p. Cooper Tire & Rubber Co., 1956-70, exec. v.p., 1970-77, pres., chmn. bd., 1977-82, chmn. bd., chief exec. officer, 1982—. Home: 857 S Main St Findlay OH 45840 Office: Cooper Tire & Rubber Co Lima & Western Aves Findlay OH 45840 *

BREWER, GEORGE EUGENE FRANCIS, chemical consultant; b. Vienna, Austria, Jan. 23, 1909; came to U.S., 1940, naturalized, 1945; s. Ernest and Sophia (Segalla) B.; m. Frances Joan Werner, June 29, 1933 (dec. Nov. 1965); m. Maxine R. Levin, Mar. 4, 1967 (dec. Mar. 1985). A.B., State Coll. Vienna, 1928; M.Sc., U. Vienna, 1930, Ph.D. in Chemistry, 1932. Cert. cons. chemist, profl. chemist, mfg. engr. Asst. lectr. U. Vienna, 1933-36; tech. mgr. S. Wolf & Co. Textile Refining Mill, Erlach, Austria, 1936-38; lectr. Inst. de l'Industrie Textile de Brabant, Brussels, 1939; prof. Rosary Coll., River Forest, Ill., 1940-43; biochemist NRC project Elgin State Hosp., Ill., 1943-44; prof. chemistry, head dept. Marygrove Coll., Detroit, 1944-67; cons. Ford Motor Co., Detroit, 1957-67; staff scientist Mfg. Devel. Ctr. Ford Motor Co., Dearborn, Mich., 1968-72; affiliated with Coating Research Inst. Eastern Mich. U., Ypsilanti, 1986—; Matiello Meml. lectr. Fedn. Socs. Paint Tech., 1973; mem. NRC com. ciphers, codes and punched card techniques, Washington, 1957-59; abstractor Chem. Abstracts, 1948-63. Contbr. articles to profl. jours.; patentee electrophoretic deposition organic coatings. Recipient Midgley medal Detroit sect. Am. Chem. Soc., 1969, Doolittle award div. organic coatings and plastics chemistry, 1969. Fellow Am. Inst. Chemists (chmn. Mich. inst. 1969, pres. 1977-81, Chem. Pioneer award 1978), Engring. Soc. Detroit (Engr.'s Week Gold award 1981); mem. Am. Chem. Soc. (councilor 1951-83; chmn. Detroit sect. 1960; sec. div. organic coatings and plastics chemistry 1971, chmn. 1974), Met. Detroit Sci. Club (bd. dirs. 1948), N.Y. Acad. Sci., Nat. Sci. Tchrs. Assn., Chem. Coaters

Assn. (program chmn. 1971-73, bd. dirs. 1974-77, pres. 1976), Assn. Analytical Chemists (pres. 1959), Mich. Coll. Chemistry Tchrs. Assn. (pres. 1954), Assn. Cons. Chemists and Chem. Engrs. Home and Office: 6135 Wing Lake Rd Birmingham MI 48010

BREWER, JOHN ISAAC, obstetrician, gynecologist; b. Milford, Ill., Oct. 9, 1903; s. John H. and Edna (Ishler) B.; widowed, Jan. 1985, ; m. Ruth Russell, June 2, 1928; 1 child, John Vernon. BS, U. Chgo., 1925, MD, 1928, PhD, 1935; student, Bradley U., 1921-24. Diplomate Am. Bd. Ob-Gyn. Instr. to assoc. prof. ob-gyn Northwestern U., Chgo., 1930-48, prof. ob-gyn, 1948-74, prof. emeritus and dept. chmn. ob-gyn, 1974-76; investigator cancer Northwestern U. Sch. Medicine, 1935—; mem. Joint Commn. on Accreditation of Hosps., Chgo., 1959-74, chmn. bd. 1963. Author: Textbook of Gynecology 4th edit., 1967; editor-in-chief Am. Jour. Ob-Gyn, 1959—. Served to lt. col. USAF, 1942-45. Decorated Legion of Merit; named to Sr. Citizen Hall of Fame City of Chgo., Bradley U. Fellow Royal Coll. Obstetricians and Gynecologists; mem. AMA, ACS, Ill. Med. Soc., Chgo. Med. Soc., Am. Bd. Ob-Gyn (bd. dirs. 1974—), Ill. Cancer Soc. (trustee, 1959-74, pres. 1963), Am. Coll. Obstetricians and Gynecologists (pres. 1959), Am. Gynecol. Soc. (pres. 1965), Am. Assn. Obstetricians and Gynecologists (pres. 1969), Am. Gynecol. Club (pres. 1971), Cen. Assn. Obstetrician and Gynecologists (pres. 1952), Chgo. Gynecol. Soc. (past pres., regent Am. Coll. Surgeons 1962-71, Am. Anatomists Assn., Chgo. Pathology Soc., Soc. Pelvic Surgeons, Sigma Xi. Republican. Congregationalist. Club: Flossmoor (Ill.) Country. Avocation: sports. Home: 860 N Lake Shore Dr Chicago IL 60611 Office: Northwestern U Cancer Ctr 710 N Fairbanks Ct Chicago IL 60611

BREWER, MARK WAYNE, food products executive; b. Denver, May 2, 1949; s. Cecil Earl and Alice Marie (Schwartz) B.; m. Jan Louise Bowhay, July 26, 1975; 1 child, Jeffrey. BA, U. Kans., 1971. Research assoc. Stanford Sch. Psychiatry, Palo Alto, Calif., 1974; intake specialist Cen. Plains Drug Treatment, Topeka, Kans., 1974-76; dir. treatment State of Kans., Topeka, 1976-79; dep. dir. N.E. Kans. Health Systems, Topeka, 1979; dir. devel. United Meth. Homes, Topeka, 1979-80; exec. v.p. Falley's, Inc., Topeka, 1980—, also bd. dirs.; exec. sec., bd. dirs. Food 4 Less Nat. Adv. Bd., Topeka; cons. Tchr. Corps, Yakima, Wash., 1973, Vista Corps, Kansas City, Kans., 1974, City of Lawrence, Kans., 1971, Lawrence High Sch., 1972. Vice chmn. United Way, Topeka, 1986. Avocations: golf, reading. Home: 1554 SW Belle Topeka KS 66604 Office: Falley's Inc 3120 S Kansas Ave Topeka KS 66611

BREWER, NELSON SHELBY, internist; b. Cape Girardeau, Mo., June 20, 1940; s. Benjamin Grinstead and Frances (Shelby) B.; m. Karol Anne Kuersteiner, Nov. 8, 1968; children: Heather, Shelby, Boone, Kirsten. Ba, Vanderbilt U., Nashville, 1962; MD, Tulane U., 1966. Diplomate Am. Bd. Internal Medicine. Intern Tulane Hosp., New Orleans, 1966-67, resident in internal medicine, 1967-68; resident in internal medicine Mayo Clinic, 1970-72, fellow in infectious deseases, 1972-74, cons., 1974-80; asst. prof. Mayo Med. Sch., Rochester, Minn., 1974-80; practice medicine specializing in infectious diseases Columbia, 1980—; asst. clin. prof. U. Mo., 1980-86; chmn.infectious control com. St. Francis Med. Ctr., Cape Girardeau, Mo., Southeast Hosp., Cape Girardeau; bd. dirs. Chateau Girardeau Nursing Ctr. Contbr. jour. articles and book chpts. Served to capt. USAF, 1968-70. Fellow ACP (adv. council, chmn. com. of credentials 1984); mem. Mo. Soc. Internal Medicine (adv. council 1985). Republican. Presbyterian. Home: 648 Sylvan Ln Cape Girardeau MO 63701 Office: 60 Doctors' Park Cape Girardeau MO 63701

BREWER, ROBERT NEAL, motel company executive; b. Herrin, Ill., June 13, 1924; s. Denver and Effie M. (Row) B.; divorced; children: Robert D., Danny N. Grad. high sch., Herrin, Ill., 1942. Owner, operator Brewer Distbg. Co., Herrin, 1946-70; owner, operator, pres. Family Fun, Inc., Herrin, 1968-76; ptnr., operator Brewer/O'Neal Partnership, Herrin, 1964-81; pres. Am.'s Best Inns, Inc., Marion, Ill., 1981—, Brewer Mgmt. Co., Marion, 1981—; bd. dirs. Best Am. Health Care, Inc., Chattanooga, First Fed. Savs. and Loan, Herrin, Herrin Security Bank. Pres., chmn. Herrin United Way, 1960-61. Named 1984 So. Ill. Citizen of Yr., So. Ill., Inc. Mem. Nat. Assn. Small Bus., Herrin Jaycees (pres. 1955-56, Jaycee Outstanding Ill. Local Pres. 1955-56), Herrin C. of C. (bd. dirs. 1959—). Lodges: Elks, Rotary (pres. Herrin chpt. 1967-68). Home: Rt 2 Box 154 Apt 3B Carterville IL 62918 Office: Am's Best Inns Inc 1205 Skyline Dr Box 1719 Marion IL 62959

BREWER, THELMA MAE, nurse; b. Ohiopyle, Pa., Jan. 31, 1921; d. Binger Addison and Ada (Burnworth) Show; m. Forest Salyer, Dec. 15, 1952; 1 son, James Allen; m. 2d, Kenneth Wilson Brewer, Jan. 19, 1955; children—Geoffrey Lynn, Mary Elizabeth. Grad. Massillon City Hosp. Sch. Nursing, 1942; postgrad. St. John's Hosp., Springfield, Ill., 1949, Mary Manse Coll., 1970. R.N., Ohio, Mo. Gen. duty nurse Massillon (Ohio) City Hosp., 1942-44, asst. operating room supr., 1950-53; operating room supr. Burge Meth. Hosp., Springfield, Mo., 1944-46; operating room supr. Riverside Hosp., Toledo, Ohio, 1950-53, head nurse, recovery room, 1957-77, dir. central supply dept., 1977-85; central supply dept. supr. St. Charles Hosp., Oregon, Ohio, 1953-56. Mem. Massillon Community Hosp. Alumnae Assn.

BREWSTER, DONALD ELLIOTT, association executive; b. Paterson, N.J., Jan. 29, 1924; s. Benjamin John and Sarah Neille (Elliott) B.; student U. Ill., 1942; B.S., Bradley U., 1950; postgrad. Ind. U., 1968, Washington U., St. Louis, 1971; m. Jerre Owens, Nov. 1958; children—Stephanie, Barbara Jean, Dawn. With Am. Cancer Soc., 1960-87, exec. v.p. Mich. div., Lansing, 1970—; asso. dir. Ketchum, Inc., Pitts., 1956-60. Chmn. fund raising campaign St. Paul Episcopal Ch., 1976, sr. warden vestry, 1978. Served with USN, 1943-46. Mem. Nat. Soc. Fund Raising Execs., Am. Soc. Assn. Execs., Mich. Soc. Assn. Execs., U.S. Power Squadron, U.S. Coast Guard Aux. Republican. Clubs: University, Muskegon Yacht, Lansing Racquet. Office: Am Cancer Soc 1205 E Saginaw St Lansing MI 48906

BREYFOGLE, PETER HOWARD, informations systems specialist; b. Maseana, N.Y., July 19, 1958; s. Darrell Bernard and Martha Ann (Kornabettor) B.; m. Nancy Ann Poser, Aug. 11, 1984. BA in Maths.magna cum laude, Southwest State U., Marshall, Minn., 1980; postgrad., St. Thomas U., St. Paul, 1984-86. Assoc. programmer Hormel Corp., Austin, Minn., 1980-81; systems programmer Hormel Corp., Austin, 1981-84; sr. systems programmer St. Paul Cos., 1984-85, supr. dist. planning, 1985—; chief exec. officer Corner Cafe, Taunton, Minn., 1982-86. Mem. Phi Kappa Delta. Avocations: bike touring, tennis, raquetball, reading. Home: 4089 Brogadoon Dr Shoreview MN 55126 Office: St Paul Cos 385 Washington St Saint Paul MN 55102

BREZINA, VALORIE JANE, real estate broker; b. Harlan, Iowa, Mar. 24, 1953; d. Lynn Gerald and Vadene Althea (Wiggins) Craig; m. Dorrance Leonard Brezina, Sept. 4, 1982. Real estate broker Iowa Realty Co., West Des Moines, Iowa; founder Zina 2000 Co. Home: 1532 42d St Des Moines IA 50311 Office: Zina 2000 Co PO Box 65892 West Des Moines IA 50265

BRICE, L. RIDER, architect; b. Toledo, Ohio, Dec. 9, 1943; s. Leonard Rider Brice and Peggy Jean (Neale) Hall; student Principia Coll., 1961-63; B.F.A., Ohio State U., 1968, B.Arch., 1975; m. Kristine Kay Artopoeus, Sept. 21, 1968; children—Trey, Colin, Tina. Design expeditor Richardson/Smith Inc., Worthington, Ohio, 1965-67, design service salesman, 1967-68; project designer Artolier Lighting & Sound div. Emerson Electric Co., Garfield, N.J., 1968-72; div. sales mgr. Electrolux div. Consol. Foods Corp., Fairfield, N.J., 1971-73, cons. designer, 1971-73; salesman Kenco Security Systems, Columbus, Ohio, 1974-76; archtl. designer Gene Swartz & Assocs., Chillicothe, Ohio, 1976-77, C. Curtiss Inscho & Assocs., Columbus, 1978-83, Noverre Musson Assocs., 1983-85 ; prin. L. Rider Brice Architects, 1985—; v.p. Delta Tau Delta House Corp., 1973—; cons. residential design, 1976—. Mem. AIA, Interfaith Forum Religion, Art, Architecture. Christian Scientist. Home: 2164 Fairfax Rd Upper Arlington OH 43221 Office: 3135 Trabue Rd Columbus OH 43204

BRICHFORD, MAYNARD JAY, archivist; b. Madison, Ohio, Aug. 6, 1926; s. Merton Jay and Evelyn Louise (Graves) B.; m. Jane Adair Hamilton, Sept. 15, 1951; children—Charles Hamilton, Ann Adair Brichford Martin, Matthew Jay, Sarah Lourena. B.A., Hiram Coll., 1950; M.S., U. Wis., 1951. Asst. archivist State Hist. Soc. Wis., 1952-56; methods and procedures analyst Ill. State Archives, 1956-59; records and space mgmt. supr. Dept. Adminstrn. State of Wis., Madison, 1959-63; archivist U. Ill., Urbana, 1963—; asso. prof. U. Ill., 1963-70, prof., 1970—. Contbr. articles in field. Served with U.S. Navy, 1944-46. Council on Library Resources grantee, 1966-69, 70-71; Nat. Endowment for the Humanities grantee, 1976-79; Fulbright grantee, 1985. Fellow Soc. Am. Archivists (pres. 1979-80); mem. Ill. Archives Adv. Bd. (chmn. 1979-84). Republican. Methodist. Home: 409 Eliot Dr Urbana IL 61801 Office: 19 Library 1408 W Gregory Dr Urbana IL 61801

BRICKLEY, JAMES H., judge; b. Flint, Mich., Nov. 15, 1928; s. J. Harry and Marie E. (Fischer) B.; 6 children. B.A., U. Detroit, 1951, LL.B., 1954, Ph.D. (hon.), 1977; LL.M., NYU, 1957; Ph.D. (hon.), Spring Arbor Coll., 1975, Detroit Coll. Bus., 1975, Ferris State Coll., Big Rapids, Mich., 1980, Saginaw Valley State Coll., University Center, Mich., 1980, Detroit Coll. Law, 1981. Bar: Mich. 1954. Spl. agent FBI, Washington, 1954-58; sole practice law Detroit, 1959-62; mem. Detroit City Council, 1962-67, pres. pro tem, 1966-67; chief asst. prosecutor Wayne County, Detroit, 1967-69; U.S. atty. U.S. Dist. Ct. (ea. dist.), Detroit, 1969-70; lt. gov. State of Mich., Lansing, 1971-74, 79-82; justice Supreme Ct. of Mich., Lansing, 1982—; pres. Eastern Mich. U., Ypsilanti, 1975-78; lectr., adj. prof. U. Detroit, Wayne State U., U. Mich., Ann Arbor, Cooley Law Sch., 1958-73. Mem. Mich. Bar Assn., ABA, Inst. Jud. Adminstrn. Republican. Roman Catholic. Office: Mich Supreme Ct PO Box 30052 Lansing MI 48909

BRICKMAN, ROBERT OTTO, landscape company executive; b. Chgo., Jan. 22, 1938; s. Theodore William and Amy Edith (Kitzelman) B.; B.A. in Bus. Adminstrn., Lake Forest Coll., 1960; m. Gail Field Walkemeyer, Aug. 29, 1959; children—Jill, Barbara, Cynthia. Sales rep. UARCO, Inc., Chgo., 1960-61; landscape supr. Theodore Brickman Co., Long Grove, Ill., 1961-63, sales mgr., 1964-67, v.p., sec., 1967—; dir. Mid. Am. Hort. Trade Show, 1983—. Mem. exec. bd. N.W. Council Boy Scouts Am., 1976-77; trustee Immanuel Ch. New Jerusalem, Glenview, 1971—; bd. dirs. Buehler YMCA. Recipient distinguished service award Countryside Center Handicapped. Mem. Asso. Landscape Contractors Am., Ill. Nurserymen's Assn. (treas., v.p.). Republican. Club: Rotary (sec. 1963-65, pres. 1973-74, dist. gov.'s rep. 1974-77 dist. gov. 1981-82, chmn. internat. youth activities com. 1983-84). Home: 1025 Gladish Ln Glenview IL 60025 Office: Long Grove Rd Long Grove IL 60047

BRICKNER, GERALD BERNARD, highway construction company executive; b. Minot, N.D., Dec. 6, 1938; s. Harry Jerome and Cathern Elizabeth (Doyle) B.; divorced; 1 child, Derek. BSCE, S.D. Sch. Mines and Tech., 1961. With Everetts & Assocs. Inc., Jamestown, N.D., 1958-65, owner, engr., 1965—. Served with U.S. Army, 1962-64. Mem. Associated Gen. Contractors. Republican. Roman Catholic. Lodge: Eagles. Avocations: flying, horticulture. Home: 408 Holiday Park Jamestown ND 58401 Office: Everetts & Assocs Inc West End 5th St NW Jamestown ND 58402

BRIDGER, GLENN WILLIAM, transportation agency administrator; b. Boise, Idaho, July 19, 1944; s. Clyde Arthur and Florence Helen (Maw) B.; m. Karen Elizabeth Hays, June 12, 1966; children: Alison, Valerie. Student, Blackburn Coll., 1961-63, U. N.C., 1963; BA, Whitman Coll., 1965. Realty specialist U.S. Bur. Pub. Rds., Olympia, Wash., 1965-66, Baton Rouge, 1966, Harrisburg, Pa., 1967; realty specialist Fed. Hwy. Adminstrn., Trenton, N.J., 1967-73, Washington, 1973-76; div. right-of-way officer Fed. Hwy. Adminstrn., Madison, Wis., 1976—. Columnist The Valuer's Line mag., 1977-78. Bd. dirs. Student Ctr. Found., Madison, 1983—. Recipient Sec.'s award U.S. Dept. Transp., 1984, Sec.'s award Wis. Dept. Transp., 1986. Mem. Internat. Right-of-Way Assn., Am. Soc. Appraisers (sr. mem.), Assn. Fed. Appraisers (pres. 1977-78). Mem. Ch. of Christ, Scientist. Club: Toastmasters. Office: Fed Hwy Adminstrn 4502 Vernon Blvd Madison WI 53705

BRIDGEWATER, BERNARD ADOLPHUS, JR., apparel and fabric manufacturing company executive; b. Tulsa, Mar. 13, 1934; s. Bernard Adolphus and Mary Alethea (Burton) B.; m. Barbara Paton, July 2, 1960; children: Barrie, Elizabeth, Bonnie. A.B., Westminster Coll., Fulton, Mo., 1955; LL.B., U. Okla., 1958; M.B.A., Harvard, 1964. Bar: Okla. 1958, U.S. Supreme Ct. 1958, U.S. Ct. of Claims 1958. Asst. county atty. Tulsa, 1962; assoc. McKinsey & Co.; mgmt. cons. McKinsey & Co., Chgo., 1964-68, prin., 1968-72, dir., 1972-73, 75; assoc. dir. nat. security and internat. affairs Office Mgmt. and Budget, Exec. Office Pres., Washington, 1973-74; exec. v.p. Baxter Travenol Labs., Inc., Chgo. and Deerfield, Ill., 1975-79, dir., 1975-85; pres. Brown Group, Inc., Clayton, Mo., 1979—, chief exec. officer, 1982—, chmn., 1985—, also dir.; dir. FMC Corp., Chgo., Celanese Corp., N.Y.C., Centerre Bancorp., St. Louis, Centerre Nat. Bank, St. Louis, McDonnell Douglas Corp., St. Louis; cons. Office Mgmt. and Budget, 1973, 75. Author: (with others) Better Management of Business Giving, 1965. Trustee Rush-Presbyn.-St. Luke's Med. Center, 1974-84, Washington U., St. Louis, 1983—. Served to lt. USNR, 1958-62. Recipient Rayonier Found. award Harvard U., 1963; George F. Baker scholar, 1964. Mem. Beta Theta Pi, Omicron Delta Kappa, Phi Alpha Delta. Clubs: Chgo., Econ. (Chgo.); River (N.Y.C.); St. Louis Country, Log Cabin (St. Louis); Indian Hill Country (Winnetka, Ill.). Office: Brown Group Inc 8400 Maryland Ave Clayton MO 63105 *

BRIDGEWATER, WALTER CLEVELAND, educator, guidance consultant; b. Scottsburg, Ind., Mar. 11, 1938; s. Walter Scott and Mabel Clarice (White) B. BA, Wabash Coll., 1960; MA, Ind. U., 1961; postgrad., Purdue U., 1969. Cert. English tchr., reading specialist, sch. counselor. Reading specialist Ind. U. Ctr. for Child Study, Bloomington, 1960-61; English tchr. Crawfordville (Ind.) Community Schs., 1961-68, reading specialist, 1969-77; instr. English Purdue U., West Lafayette, Ind., 1968-69; reading specialist Indpls. Pub. Schs., 1977-78; fed. programs dir. Scott County Schs. Dist. 2, Scottsburg, 1978—, dir. gifted, talented edn. program, 1983-85, in-service dir., 1983—; vol. admissions cons. for 7 colls. and 2 prep schs.; liaison Nat. Inst. Edn. Contbr. articles to edn. jours. Active Boy Scouts Am., Crawfordville and Scottsburg, 1961—; cert. lay speaker United Meth. Ch., So. Ind. Conf., 1973—. Hon. fellow Truman Library Inst. Internat. Affairs, Independence, Mo., 1968; recipient Dist. Award of Merit, Boy Scouts Am., New Albany, Ind., 1982. Mem. Nat. Edn. Assn. (life), Internat. Reading Assn., Scottsburg Classroom Tchrs. Assn., Ind. State Tchrs. Assn., Phi Delta Kappa (life, 2d v.p. 1982-83). Lodges: Optimists, Masons (chaplain local club 1968-69). Avocations: reading, models, camping, bicycling, travel. Home: RR 6 Crawfordsville IN 47933-9806 Office: Scott County Sch Dist 2 375 E McClain Ave Scottsburg IN 47170-1798

BRIDWELL, BERNICE WAYNETTE, nurse; b. Zanesville, Ohio, Feb. 21, 1943; d. Wayne Everett and Marjorie Elsie (Monteith) Fitz; student Wittenberg U., 1960-61; dipl., Springfield City Hosp. Sch. Nursing, 1965; student Ohio State U., 1972; B.S.N., Ohio U., 1979; m. John Robert Bridwell, Jan. 8, 1966; children—Sherry Lu, Robert John. Staff nurse surg. intensive care unit Ohio State U. Hosps., Columbus, 1965; pediatric staff nurse Bethesda Hosp., Zanesville, Ohio, 1966, asst. clin. instr. Sch. Nursing, Zanesville, 1966-67, adult practical nursing instr., 1967-69, instr. pharmacology, 1970-77, jr. instr. high sch. practical nursing, 1972-74, sr. instr. practical nursing Mideast Ohio Vocat. Sch. Dist., 1979—. Sec., mgr. Girl's Youth Slowpitch Softball League, Zanesville, 1973; tchr. Sun. sch. St. John Luth. Ch., Zanesville, 1967-68, 74-77, planner area Bible Sch., 1977, pres. St. John Luth. Ch. Women, 1973-75, altar chmn., 1977-79, circle leader, 1969-70. Mem. Muskingum Valley Dist. Nurses Assn., Ohio Nurses Assn., Am. Nurses Assn., Mideast Edn. Assn., Ohio Edn. Assn., NEA, Ohio Vocat. Assn., Am. Vocat. Assn., Ohio Orgn. Practical Nurse Educators. Clubs: Vocat. Indsl. Clubs of Am. (asst. advisor Muskingum Area chpt. 1980-81), Nat. Vocat. Clubs of Am., Ohio Vocat. Indsl. Clubs of Am. Home: 5585 Kenny Dr Zanesville OH 43701 Office: 400 Richards Rd Zanesville OH 43701

BRIEF, NEIL, rabbi; b. Bklyn., Oct. 10, 1934; s. Hyman and Bella (Saltzman) B.; m. Erica Greenbaum, June 16, 1957; children: Dena Brief Wald, David Chaim, Debra Pearl. BS, NYU, 1955; B of Hebrew Letters, Hebrew Union Coll. Jewish Inst. Religion, N.Y.C., 1957, M of Hebrew Letters, 1960; DD (hon.), Hebrew Union Coll. Jewish Inst. Religion, Cin., 1985; MA, Bklyn. Coll., 1958. Ordained rabbi, 1960. Post Jewish chaplain U.S. Army, Ft. Huachuca, Ariz., 1960-62; rabbi Ventura County Jewish Council, Ventura, Calif., 1962-71, Niles Twp. Jewish Congregation, Skokie, Ill., 1971—. Author: What Helped Me When My Loved One Died, 1980. Chmn. Human Relations Adv. Council, Ventura, 1963-69; mem. Skokie Human Resources Commn., 1984—; bd. dirs. Mayer Kaplan-Bernard Horwich Jewish Community Ctr. Served to capt. U.S. Army, 1960-62. Recipient Outstanding Leadership award Jewish Reconstructionist Found., N.Y.C., 1980. Mem. Cen. Conf. Am. Rabbis, Rabbinical Assembly, Chgo. Bd. Rabbis (mem. exec. com.), Clergy Forum of Niles Twp. (chmn.). Home: 4214 Suffield Ct Skokie IL 60076 Office: Niles Twp Jewish Congregation 4500 Dempster St Skokie IL 60076

BRIEN, RONALD ERNEST, accountant; b. Fond du Lac, Wis., Feb. 15, 1953; s. Ernest c. and Gertrude A. (Puro), B.; m. Glenda Lee Gaulke, June 28, 1975; children: Rebecca Laura. BBA, U. Wis., Whitewater, 1975. Staff acct. Conley, McDonald, Sprague and Co., Milw., 1975-77; sr. acct. Alexander Grant and Co., La Crosse, Wis., 1978-80, Smith and Gesteland, Madison, Wis., 1980-81; pvt. practice accctg. Fond Du Lac, Wis., 1981-83; pres. Wallschlaeger and Brien, S.C., Fond Du Lac, 1983—. Mem. Am. Inst. CPA's, Wis. Inst. CPA's. Lutheran. Lodge: Optimists (dist. sec./treas., 1987—, lt. gov. zone 2 1985-86, pres. Fond Du Lac chpt. 1982-83). Avocations: golf, bowling. Home: 327 Illinois Ave North Fond Du Lac WI 54935 Office: Wallschlaeger & Brien SC 7 Sheboygan St Fond Du Lac WI 54935

BRIER, JACK HAROLD, state official; b. Kansas City, Mo., June 25, 1946; s. Marshall W. and M. Pearl (Munden) B. Student, U. Kans., 1964-67, 77—; B.B.A., Washburn U., 1970. Dep. asst. sec. of state for legis. matters State of Kans., Topeka, 1969-70; asst. sec. of state State of Kans., 1970-78, sec. of state, 1978-87. Hon. state bd. advisors, hon. chmn. Kans. Cavalry, Close Up Found.; nat. v.p. Muscular Dystrophy Assn.; trustee Kans. Jaycee Found.; hon. bd. advisers Close Up Kans.; adv. bd. for Greater Univ. Fund, U. Kans.; hon. bd. dirs. Police Athletic League; bd. dirs. Leadership Kans.; bd. dirs. Met. Topeka Airport Authority. Named Outstanding Young Topekan, 1979, Outstanding Young Kansan, 1979; recipient internat. communications and leadership award Toastmasters Internat., DeMolay Legion of Honor. Mem. Nat. Assn. Secs. of State (past pres.), Kans. State Hist. Soc. (bd. dirs., nominating com.), Shawnee County Hist. Soc., Am. Council Young Polit. Leaders (council), Fraternal Order Police (assoc.), Blue Key (hon.), Sagamore Nat. Honor Frat. (hon.), Washburn U. Alumni Assn. (bd. dirs.). Republican.

BRIERTON, DAVID LAWRENCE, housing developer; b. Milw., Sept. 25, 1942; s. Bernard Lawrence and Ruth Margaret (Conway) B.; B.B.A., Wis. State U., Whitewater, 1969; M.S. (HUD fellow), U. Wis., 1970; m. Judith Ann Ruch, Aug. 20, 1966; children—Kristin, Kerry, Kevin, Keely, Kolin, Korey. Project mgr. Gene B. Glick Co., Indpls., 1970-72; pres. Dominion Group Inc., Mpls., 1972—; mem. adv. bd. Ann. Nat. Apt. Builders and Developers Conf. and Exposition, Atlanta, 1978. Served with USAF, 1962-65. Mem. Nat. Leased Housing Assn. (dir. 1979—), Minn. Multi-Housing Assn. (dir. 1979—), Wis. Assn. Housing Authorities. Roman Catholic. Clubs: Rolling Green Country, Calhoun Beach. Home: 3020 Jewel Ln Plymouth MN 55391

BRIGGS, DENNIS HERBERT, orthodontist; b. Cedar Rapids, Iowa, Feb. 17, 1942; s. Carroll T. and Virginia (Mohler) B.; m. Carol Ann Starrett, July 3, 1965; children—Sean Colin, Chad Michael. B.A., U. Iowa, 1964, D.D.S., 1969, M.S. in Orthodontics, 1973. Practice dentistry specializing in orthodontics, Neenah, Wis., 1973—; owner Carden Quarter Horses, Neenah, 1979—. Mem. Neenah Planning Commn., 1983—. Served to capt. USAF, 1968-70. Kinnick Athletic scholar U. Iowa, 1960-64. Mem. Wis. Dental Assn., Winnebago County Dental Assn., Neenah-Menasha Dental Assn., Am. Assn. Orthodontists, Wis. Soc. Orthodontists, Am. Quarter Horse Assn., Wis. Quarter Horse Assn., N.E. Wis. Quarter Horse Assn. Club: Optimists. Home: 1330 Woodenshoe Rd Neenah WI 54956 Office: 151 E Forest Ave Neenah WI 54956

BRIGGS, LESLIE RAY, mechanical engineer; b. Knoxville, Iowa, Dec. 18, 1944; s. Raymond Edward and Doris Geraldine (Wallace) B.; m. Donna Lou VanDyke, July 1, 1967; children: Douglas William, Rebecca Lynn. AS in Mech. Tech., Iowa State Tech. Inst., Ames, 1966; BSME cum laude, U. Evansville, 1986. Registered profl. engr., Iowa. Engring asst. Alcoa, Davenport, Iowa, 1966-79; tech. asst. Alcoa, Newburgh, Ind., 1979-85, tech. specialist, 1985-86, mech. engr., 1986—. Mem. NSPE, Phi Beta Chi. Republican. Baptist. Lodge: Masons. Avocation: classic automobiles. Home: 5477 Lakeside Dr Newburgh IN 47630-1918 Office: Alcoa Warrick Ops PO Box 10 Newburgh IN 47630-0010

BRIGGS, ROBERT HENRY, infosystems specialist; b. Elk River, Minn., Apr. 25, 1937; s. Archie Elwin and Charlotte Lorette (Rand) B.; m. Jacqueline Hascoet, Apr. 20, 1963; children: Thomas Henry, Terence Gregory. BA in Bus., U. Wash., 1960. Indsl. engr. Boeing Co., Seattle, 1962-66; with 3M, St. Paul, 1966—, catalog analyst, 1966-68, sr. file control coordinator, 1968-74, advanced analyst, 1974-80, sr. analyst, 1980-85, lead analyst, 1985—. Mem. Community Edn. Adv. Council South Washington County (Minn.) Schs., 1979—, chmn. 1981-82; chmn. Gottage Grove (Minn.) Parks and Recreation Commn., 1980; mem. Internat. Inst. Minn., St. Paul, 1982—. Served with U.S. Army, 1960-62. Mem. Data Adminstrn. Mgmt. Assn., Cottage Grove Jaycees (bd. dirs. 1972-73). Lutheran. Avocations: coaching, photography, golf. Home: 8369 80th St S Cottage Grove MN 55016 Office: 3M 3M Ctr Saint Paul MN 55144-1000

BRIGGS, RODNEY ARTHUR, agronomist, consultant; b. Madison, Wis., Mar. 18, 1923; s. George McSpadden and Mary Etta (McNelly) B.; m. Helen Kathleen Ryall, June 1, 1944; children: Carolyn, Kathleen, David, Andrew, Amy. Student, Oshkosh (Wis.) State Coll., 1941-42; B.S. in Agronomy, U. Wis., 1948; Ph.D. in Field Crops, Rutgers U., 1953. Extension asso. farm crops Rutgers U., New Brunswick, N.J., 1949-50, 52-53; mem. faculty U. Minn., 1953-73; supt. West Central Sch. and Expt. Sta., Morris, Minn., 1959-60; prof. agronomy, dean U. Minn.; administrv. head, provost U. Minn. (Morris Campus), 1960-69, sec. bd. regents, 1971-72, exec. asst. to pres., 1971-73; on leave of absence Ford Found. as asso. dir., dir. research Internat. Inst. Tropical Agr., Ibadan, Nigeria, 1969-71; pres. Eastern Oreg. State Coll., La Grande, 1973-83; exec. v.p. Am. Soc. Agronomy/Crop Sci. Soc. Am./Soil Sci. Soc. Am., Madison, Wis., 1982-85; ind. cons. 1985—; chmn. Nat. Silage Evaluation Com., 1957; sec. Minn. Corp Improvement Assn., 1954-57; columnist crops and soils Minn. Farmer mag., 1954-59; judge grain and forage Minn. State Fair, 1954-61; mem. ednl. mission to Taiwan, Am. Assn. State Colls. and Univs., 1978, chmn. ednl. mission to Colombia, 1982, state rep., 1974-76, mem. spl. task force of pres.'s on intercollegiate athletics, 1976-77, mem. nat. com. on agr., renewable resources and rural devel., 1978-82, nat. sec.-treas., 1980-82; mem. com. on govt. relations Am. Council Edn. Com., 1981; mem. Gov.'s Commn. on Fgn. Lang. and Internat. Studies, State Oreg., 1980-83; Mem. Gov.'s Commn. Law Enforcement, 1967-69; adv. com. State Planning Agy., 1968-69, Minn. Interinstnl. TV, 1967-69. Bd. dirs. Rural Banking Sch., 1967-69; bd. dirs. Channel 10 ETV, Appleton, Minn., Grande Ronde Hosp., 1980-83; chmn. policy adv. com. Oreg. Dept. Environ. Quality, 1979-81. Served with inf. AUS, 1942-46, 50-52. Recipient Staff award U. Minn., 1959, spl. award U. Minn. at Morris, 1961; commendation Soil Conservation Soc. Am., 1965; Rodney A. Briggs Library named in his honor U. Minn., Morris, 1974. Fellow AAAS, Soil Conservation Soc. Am.; mem. Am. Soc. Agronomy, Crop Sci. Soc. Am., AAAS, Wis. Acad. Sci. and Arts, Am. Assn. State Colls. and Univs., Am. Forage and Grassland Council, Am. Inst. Biol. Scis. (dir. 1982-83), ACLU, Sigma Xi, Alpha Gamma Rho. Congregationalist. Home: 1109 Gilbert Rd Madison WI 53711

BRIGGS, WALTER OWEN, IV, accountant; b. Detroit, Nov. 14, 1956; s. Walter Owen III and Gwen (Luce) B.; m. Andrea Gilles, Sept. 2, 1984; 1 child, Walter Owen V. BA in Math., Duke U., 1979; postgrad., Mich. State U., 1980-82. CPA, Mich. Tchr. math. Canterbury Sch., New Milford, Conn., 1979-80; asst. lacrosse coach Mich. State U., East Lansing, 1980-82; staff acct. Ernst & Whinney, Detroit, 1982-83, advance staff, 1983-85, sr. cons., 1985—. Mgmt. advisor WDET Pub. Radio, Detroit, 1983—. Mem. Am. Inst. CPA's, Mich. Assn. Pub. Accts., Assn. for Systems Mgmt. Avocations: tennis, lacrosse, backpacking, climbing, skiing. Office: Ernst & Whinney 200 Renaissance Ctr Detroit MI 48243

BRIGGS, WILLIAM BENAJAH, aeronautical engineer; b. Okmulgee, Okla., Dec. 13, 1922; s. Eugene Stephen and Mary Bettie (Gentry) B.; m. Lorraine Hood, June 6, 1944; children—Eugene Stephen II, Cynthia Anne, Julia Louise, Spencer Gentry. B.A. in Physics, Phillips U., 1943, D.Sc. (hon.), 1977; M.S. in Mech. Engring., Ga. Inst. Tech., 1947. Aero. scientist NACA, Cleve., 1948-52; propulsion engr. Chance Vought Aircraft/LTV, Dallas, 1952-64; mgr. advanced planning McDonnell Douglas Co., St. Louis, 1964-80, dir. program devel. fusion energy, 1980-87; mem. planetary quarantine adv. panel NASA. Contbr. articles on aero. engring. and energy to profl. jours.; patentee in field. Chmn. bd. Christian Bd. Publs., St. Louis, 1974—; chmn. Disciples Council Greater St. Louis, 1969-73. Served with USN, 1943-46. Assoc. fellow AIAA (dir. region 5 1974-77, v.p. mem. services 1978-79); mem. Am. Nuclear Soc. Mem. Disciples of Christ Ch. Lodge: Masons. Home: 1819 Bradburn Dr Saint Louis MO 63131

BRIGHAM, JAMES REMMERS, JR., manufacturing executive; b. St. Louis, Oct. 11, 1945; s. James and Barbara (Ramsay) B.; m. Holland Vose, May 5, 1979; children: Carlisle Vose, James Watson Holland. B.A., Duke U., 1967; M.B.A., U. Chgo., 1969. Vice pres. Morgan Guaranty Trust Co., N.Y.C., 1969-78; spl. counselor to dep. mayor for fin. City N.Y., 1976-77; budget dir. City of N.Y., 1978-81; chmn. N.Y.C. Pub. Devel. Corp., 1981-85; pres. Diagraph Corp., St. Louis, 1981—; cons., dir. strategic planning Marsh & McLennan Cos., Inc., N.Y.C., 1981-83; dir. Menasha Corp., Neenah, Wis., 1982-86; N.Y. Shakespeare Festival, N.Y. Bot. Garden; vice chmn., treas. Gracie Mansion Conservancy, 1982—. Republican. Episcopalian. Clubs: Union League, The Links. Office: Diagraph Corp 13789 Rider Trail N Saint Louis MO 63045

BRIGHT, MYRON H., senior judge; b. Eveleth, Minn., Mar. 5, 1919; s. Morris and Lena A. (Levine) B.; m. Frances Louise Reisler, Dec. 26, 1947; children: Dinah Ann, Joshua Robert. B.S.L., U. Minn., 1941, J.D., 1947. Bar: N.D. and Minn. Assoc. firm Wattam, Vogel, Vogel & Bright, Fargo, N.D., 1947-48; ptnr. Wattam, Vogel, Vogel & Bright, 1949-68; judge 8th U.S. Circuit Ct. Appeals, Fargo, 1968-85, sr. judge, 1985—; disting. prof. law St. Louis U., 1985—. Served to capt. AUS, 1942-46, CBI. Mem. ABA N.D. Bar Assn., Jud. Conf. U.S. (com. on adminstrn. of probation system 1977-83). Office: U S Ct of Appeals Fed Bldg US Post Office PO Box 2707 Fargo ND 58108

BRILL, ALAN RICHARD, corp. exec.; b. Evansville, Ind., July 5, 1942; s. Gregory and Bernice Lucille (Froman) B.; A.B., DePauw U., 1964; M.B.A., Harvard U., 1968; m. Bonnie Faye Phillips, May 26, 1973; children—Jennifer Leigh, Katherine Anne, Alison Elizabeth. Mgmt. cons. Peace Corps, Ecuador, 1964-66; sr. acct., cons. Arthur Young & Co., N.Y.C., 1968-71; v.p. ops. Charter Med. Mgmt. Co., Inc. and v.p.-controller Hosp. Investors, Atlanta, 1972-73; v.p., treas., dir. Worrell Newspapers, Inc., and Worrell Broadcasting Inc., Charlottesville, Va., 1973-79; pres. Brill Assos., Evansville, Ind., 1979—, Brill Media Co., Inc., Evansville, 1980—. Mem. Am. Inst. C.P.A.s, N.Y. State Soc. C.P.A.s, Inst. Newspaper Controllers and Fin. Officers. Republican. Methodist. Clubs: Farmington Country (Charlottesville); Safari Internat. Home: 211 E Jennings Newburgh IN 47630 Office: PO Box 3353 Evansville IN 47732

BRILLER, MARGARET JOAN, public relations executive; b. Cleve., June 8, 1949; d. Edward F. and Helen T. (Droba) Polewka; m. David D. Briller, Mar. 29, 1980; 1 child, William David. AA, Cuyahoga Community Coll., Cleve., 1969; BA, Kent State U., 1971. Copy writer Griswold-Eshelman, Cleve., 1971; asst. to dir. of student union Kent (Ohio) State U., 1971-74; copy writer Hesselbart & Mitten, Fairlawn, Ohio, 1976-77; pub. relations specialist Cuyahoga Community Coll., Parma, Ohio, 1977-80; account exec. Jaeger Advt., 1980-84; pub. relations mgr. Sonnhalter & Assocs., 1984—; cons. in field. Grantee No. Ohio Indsl. Editors Assn., 1970. Mem. Pub. Relations Soc. Am., Kent State U. Alumni Assn. Roman Catholic. Avocations: flying, boating, travel. Home: 9806 Huntington Park Dr Strongsville OH 44136 Office: Sonnhalter/PDA 633 W Bagley Rd Berea OH 44017

BRILLHART, JAMES RICHARD, gynecological surgeon; b. Indpls., Mar. 28, 1929; s. Claud Ischmael and Velma Lorraine (Roberts) B.; m. Jean Iris Sawyer, June 3, 1948 (div. Mar. 1969); children: J.H., Richard Mark, David Michael, Susan Kay; m. Kathryn Norann Dowden, Mar. 8, 1980. BS, Butler U., 1949; MD, Loma Linda U., 1955. Diplomate Am. Bd. Ob-Gyn. Resident Ind. U. Med. Ctr., Indpls., 1956-60; practice medicine specializing in gynecol. surgery Indpls., 1960—; asst. clin. prof. dept. family practice Ind. U. Sch. Medicine, Indpls., 1975-84, asst. clin. prof. dept. ob-gyn, 1985—; bd. dirs. Ind. Asphalt Paving Co., Indpls., Med. Scis., Indpls.; dir. ob-gyn tng. Community Hosp., Indpls., 1975-84; med. advisor Planned Parenthood, Indpls., 1986—. Judge Am. Kennel Club, N.Y.C., 1968—; sec.-treas. Indpls. Womens Ctr., 1975-86. Fellow Am. Coll. Ob-Gyn; mem. AMA, Ind. State Med. Assn., Marion County Med. Soc., Am. Fertility Soc., Brit. Royal Soc. Medicine, Am. Inst. Ultrasound in Medicine, Siberian Husky Club Am. Democrat. Adventist. Club: Pointe Country. Avocations: sports cars, dogs, diving. Home: 4500 E 75th St Indianapolis IN 46250 Office: Indpls Ob-Gyn Inc 4956 E 56th St #7 Indianapolis IN 46220

BRILLION, STEVEN MATTHEW, accountant; b. Waukegan, Ill., Aug. 15, 1959; s. Robert Emery and Donna Marie (Floyd) B.; m. Debra Ann Ward, Aug. 14, 1982. AS in Acctg., Coll. of Lake City, 1979; BS in Acctg., No. Ill. U., 1981. CPA, Ill. Sr. staff acct. Laventhol & Horwath, Chgo., 1981-83; supr. Grant Thornton Internat., Chgo., 1983-84; mgr. Wm. Huml & Co., CPA's, Lincolnshire, Ill., 1984-86; ptnr. Wm. Huml & Co., CPA's, Lincolnshire, 1986—. Mem. Am. Inst. CPA's, Ill. CPA's Soc. Republican. Roman Catholic. Avocation: landscape design and architecture.

BRINCK, ROBERT WILLIAM, comptroller; b. Chgo., May 23, 1949; s. Edward Michael and Mary Catherine (Sheridan) B.; m. Evajean Conroy, Aug. 10, 1980; children: Nicole, Jonathan. BA in Fin., U. Ill., 1972; postgrad. in bus., De Paul U., 1977-80, 85—. CPA, Ill. Customer service rep. Gen. Foods Corp., Northlake, Ill., 1973-80; supr. data processing system Arlington Fed. Savs. and Loan, Arlington Heights, Ill., 1980-85; comptroller Home Fed. Savs. and Loan of Lake City, Waukegan, Ill., 1985-87, First Family Mortgage Co., Lisle, Ill., 1987—. Served as cpl. USMCR, 1969-75. Mem. Am. Inst. CPA's, Ill. CPA Soc., Mortgage Banker's Assn. Republican. Roman Catholic. Avocations: reading, tennis, golf. Office: First Family Mortgage Co Inc 2900 Ogden Ave Lisle IL 60532

BRINGE, BERNARD GLENN, airline exec.; b. Northwood, Iowa, Feb. 11, 1934; s. Melvin Theodore and Gladys Joy (Pangburn) B.; B.S., U. Wis., Whitewater, 1961; M.B.A., Roosevelt U., Chgo., 1968; m. Erna Lynne Tripp, May 29, 1965. Tchr. high sch. bus., Slinger and Salem, Wis., 1961-65; with United Airlines, 1966—, mgr. passenger revenue systems, Chgo., 1978—. Served with U.S. Army, 1955-57. Mem. NEA, Nat. Bus. Edn. Assn., Chgo. Mgmt. Club, Pi Omega Pi. Republican. Presbyterian. Home: 1588 Clover Dr Inverness IL 60067 Office: United Airlines EXOKA PO Box 66100 Chicago IL 60666

BRINGHAM, WILLIAM TALBERT, fraternal organization executive; b. Normal, Ill., Dec. 16, 1924; s. Russell Wilson and Sarah E. (Talbert) B.; m. Ruth Irene Jaeger, Jan. 10, 1947; 1 son, William Talbert. Ph.B., Ill. Wesleyan U., 1948; J.D., Vanderbilt U., 1951; grad. trust devel. sch., Northwestern U. Sch. Commerce, 1953. Spl. agt. FBI, 1951-52; exec. v.p. Sigma Chi frat., Wilmette, Ill., 1954—; v.p. Sigma Chi Found., 1956—, also sec.; sec. bd. grand trustees Sigma Chi; exec. v.p., sec., exec. com., sec. grand council Sigma Chi Corp.; bd. dirs., v.p. Nat. Interfrat. Found.; bd. dirs. Found. ASAE. Author booklet on alumni relations Sigma Chi; chmn. editorial com. Visitation Manuel for College Fraternities. Del. Ill. Republican Conv.; former mem. Cook County Rep. Cen. Com.; committeeman Northfield Twp. Rep. Com.; del. Sch. Bd. Caucus; past chmn. Fire and Police Commn., Wilmette.; mem. corp. Kendall Coll., past trustee, City of Wilmette. Served with USNR, 1942-46. Recipient Significant Sig and Order of Constantine awards Sigma Chi, 1975. Mem. Am. Personnel and Guidance Assn., Am. Soc. Assn. Execs. (cert., Key award 1973, mem. and v.p. awards com.; dir. Found.), Chgo. Soc. Assn. Execs. (past pres.), Nat. Assn. Student Personnel Adminstrs., pres. 1984-85), Wilmette Hist. Soc., Evanston Hist. Soc., Travelers Protective Assn., Nat. Assn. Student Personnel Adminstrs., U.S. C. of C., Am. Legion, Frat. Execs. Assn. (pres., exec. com.), Evanston C. of C. (past dir.), SAR, Soc. Golden Key, Omicron Delta Kappa, Phi Delta Phi. Clubs: Univ. (Evanston) (pres.); Westmoreland Country (Wilmette). Lodges: Masons (33 deg.), Shriners, KT, Kiwanis (past pres.), Royal Order of Scotland; Red Cross of Constantine. Address: 4020 Bunker Ln Wilmette IL 60091

BRINGS, LAWRENCE MARTIN, publisher; b. St. Paul, Sept. 29, 1897; s. Lee Brings and Bertha (Haugen) B.; m. Ethel Mattson, Aug. 26, 1921 (dec.); 1 son, Keith; m. Nettie A. Johnson, Jan. 9, 1961. A.B., Gustavus Adolphus Coll., 1920, A.M., 1925. High sch. tchr. 1920- 21; head dept. speech No. State Tchrs. Coll., Aberdeen, S.D., 1921- 23; instr. speech U. Minn., 1923-26; pres., dir. dept. oratory Mpls. Sch. Music, Oratory and Dramatic Art, 1923-25; prof. speech Luther Theol. Sem., St. Paul, 1923-46, Northwestern Theol. Sem., Mpls., 1925-49; founder, pres. Northwestern Coll. Speech Arts, Mpls., 1926-51, Northwestern Press, 1926—, T.S. Denison & Co., 1944—, Brings Press, 1951-77, Denison Yearbook Co., 1952-76; dir. Graphic Arts Cons. Service, 1977—; lectr., dramatic reader. Compiler, editor: numerous books, most recent being Minnesota Heritage, 1960, One-Act Dramas and Contest Plays, 1962, Rehearsal-less Skits and Plays, 1963, Gay Nineties Melodramas, 1963, Golden Book of Christmas Plays, 1963, What God Hath Wrought, 1969. Pres. Minn. Protestant Found., Central Luth. Ch. Found.; pres. Golden Valley Coll. Found.; regent emeritus Golden Valley Luth. Coll., Count Folke Bernadotte Meml. Found. Served in U.S. Army, World War I. Mem. USCG League, Internat. Platform Assn., Nat. Assn. Tchrs. Speech, Nat. Thespian Dramatic Soc. (hon.), Am. Legion, Phi Kappa Delta, Phi Beta (hon.). Republican. Lutheran. Clubs: Mason (32 deg., Shriner), Rotary, Mpls. Auto, Minnetonka Country. Home: 4350 Brookside Ct Minneapolis MN 55436 also: 961 Antigua Ave Bay Indies Park Venice FL 33595 Office: 9601 Newton Ave S Minneapolis MN 54431

BRINK, JOSEPH JOHN, data processing executive; b. Cin., Mar. 9, 1957; s. John Albert and Irene (Cowen) B.; m. Nancy Esther Peña, July 26, 1986; children: James, Marco, Julie. Student, John Carroll U., 1975-77; BS, Inst. Computer Mgmt. Sch. Bus., 1977. Supr. programming Revco Drug Stores, Inc., Twinsburg, Ohio, 1980-81, sr. systems software programmer, 1981-84, mgr. tech. support, 1984—. Archbishop Hoban scholar John Carroll U., 1975. Mem. Cleve. S/38 User Group, Akron S/38 User Group, COMMON. Avocations: rock music, soccer. Home: 17516 Dartmouth Ave Cleveland OH 44111 Office: Revco Drug Stores 1925 Enterprise Pkwy Twinsburg OH 44087

BRINKER, DAVID GEORGE, structural engineer; b. Toledo, Oct. 21, 1953; s. George Calvin and Donna Lou (Rollins) B.; m. Leslie Montgomery, May 30, 1981; children: Brian David, Clayton George, Spencer Thomas. BCE, Ohio No. U., 1975. Registered profl. engr., structural engr. Structural engr. Sargent & Lundy, Chgo., 1975-80; structural dept. head Assoc. Engrs., Peoria, Ill., 1981-84; dir. engring. UNR-Rohn, Peoria, 1984—. Mem. ASCE, Am. Concrete Inst. Home: 25 Sky View Dr East Peoria IL 61611 Office: UNR Rohn 6718 W Plank Rd PO Box 2000 Peoria IL 61656

BRINKER, KENNETH CHRIS, lawyer, corporation executive; b. Melrose Park, Ill., July 23, 1953; s. Charles Francis and LaVera Ann (Koller) B.; m. Sharon Frances Vincolese, Apr. 20, 1980. BA, Elmhurst Coll., 1975; MBA, Northwestern U., 1977; JD, De Paul U., 1982. Bar: Ill. 1983; CPA, Ill. Tax mgr. Arthur Andersen & Co., Chgo., 1977-83; sec., counsel Fairmont Homes, Inc., Nappanee, Ind., 1983—. Mem. ABA, Am. Inst. CPA's, Ill. Bar Assn., Ill. CPA Soc., Ill. Manufactured Housing Assn. (bd. dirs. 1983-87), Mich. Manufactured Housing Assn. (bd. dirs. 1985-87). Avocation: tennis. Office: Fairmont Homes Inc 502 S Oakland PO Box 27 Nappanee IN 46550

BRINKERHOFF, TOM J., accountant; b. Decatur, Ill., July 18, 1939; s. Lee Allen and Dorothy Mae (Jones) B.; m. Linda Lou Craig, June 19, 1960; children: Christine Gail, J. Douglas. BS of Accountancy, U. Ill., 1960, M of Acctg. Sci., 1961. CPA, Ill., Ind., Minn. Staff acct. Filbey, Andrews & Filbey, Champaign, Ill., 1960-61; mgr. Ernst & Whinney, Chgo., Indpls., 1961-73; tax officer The St. Paul Co.'s, Inc., 1973-74; sr. mgr. Arthur Andersen & Co., Indpls., 1974-76; founding ptnr. Brinkerhoff, Franklin & Co., Inc., Indpls., 1976-84; mng. ptnr. Ford, Brinkerhoff & Koehler, Indpls., 1984—; treas. NYE Metals, Inc., Indpls., 1973-74. Bd. dirs. Indpls chpt. March of Dimes, 1971-73, Indpls. chpt. Jaycees, 1969-72; chmn. elders East 91st St. Christian Ch., 1986-87, also vice-chmn., bd. dirs. chmn. fin. and stewardship; bd. dirs. Hope for Am., 1984—. Recipient Disting. Service award Indpls. Jaycees, 1969. Mem. Am. Inst. CPA's, Ind. Soc. CPA's (various com. chmnships), Internat. Assn. Fin. Planning (bd. dirs. 1981-82). Republican. Club: Meridian Hills Country. Home: 6910 N Pennsylvania St Indianapolis IN 46220 Office: Ford Brinkerhoff & Koehler 9000 Keystone Crossing #600 Indianapolis IN 46240

BRINKLEY, GEORGE ARNOLD, JR., educator; b. Wilmington, N.C., Apr. 20, 1931; s. George Arnold and Ida Bell (West) B.; A.B., Davidson Coll., 1953; M.A., Columbia U., 1955, Ph.D., 1964; m. Ann Mae Kreps, Aug. 9, 1959; 1 dau., Heidi Ann. Instr. polit. sci. Columbia U., N.Y.C., 1957-58; with dept. govt. U. Notre Dame, 1958—, prof., 1970—, dir. Program of Soviet & East European Studies, 1969—, chmn. dept., 1969-77, dir. Inst. Internat. Studies, 1975-78. Ford Found. fellow, 1954-57; Internat. Affairs fellow Council on Fgn. Relations, 1968-69. Mem. Am. Assn. Advancement of Slavic Studies (chmn. membership com. 1978-81); Midwest Slavic Assn. (chmn. exec. com. 1979-81), Phi Beta Kappa. Methodist. Author: The Volunteer Army and Allied Intervention in South Russia, 1917-1921, 1966. Office: U Notre Dame Dept Govt Notre Dame IN 46556

BRINKLEY, WILLIAM JOHN, educator; b. Shawneetown, Ill., Dec. 8, 1925; s. William Henry and Frances (Leath) B.; B.S., U. Ill., 1945. Tchr. high sch., McLeansboro, Ill., 1945—, high sch. coordinator vocations, 1968—; owner Brinkley Interiors and Galleries, antique porcelain, McLeansboro. Mem. adv. bd. Ill. Edn. Council, 1967—; mem. Pres.'s Com. 100, 1968; mem. Hamilton County Bicentennial Com.; chmn. rehab. com. McCoy Meml. Library and Hamilton County Hist. Soc. Bldg.; mem. Friends of Mus., Mitchell Mus., Mt. Vernon, Ill., 1978-84; mem. Hamilton County Republican Com., 1950-68. Recipient Tchr. of Year award U. Ill. Edn. Dept., 1963; Merit award Gov. Ill. 1964; Disting. Service award Future Farmers Am., 1967; George Washington medal honor Freedoms Found. Am., 1966, 69; Outstanding Vocat. Edn. award Ill. State Vocat. Edn. Service, 1981; Presbyn. Service award, 1984. Mem. NEA, Ill. Edn. Assn., Hamilton County (pres. 1970), Gallatin County hist. socs., Nat., Ill. (Tchr. of Tchrs.) assns. vocat. agr. tchrs., Rend Lake Symphony Soc., Arts and Humanities Soc., SAR (bd. govs. Ill., state chmn. constructive citizenship com.), Hereditary Register of U.S., Phi Beta Kappa, Delta Sigma Phi. Presbyterian. Lodges: Masons, Kiwanis, Elks, Lions, Rotary (charter mem., bd, dirs. 1986). Home: 401 Washington St S McLeansboro IL 62859 Office: 200 S Pearl St McLeansboro IL 62859 Office: 401 S Washington Ave McLeansboro IL 62859

BRINKMAN, MARILYN THERESA SALZL, historian, writer; b. St. Martin, Minn., May 9, 1943; d. Henry Gerhard and Cecelia (Moonen) Salzl; m. Harold Joseph Brinkman, June 23, 1962; children: Nancy, Brian, Karen. BA Am. Studies, St. Cloud (Minn.) State U., 1984. Farmer Brinkman Farms, Albany, Minn., 1962—; free-lance writer The Land mag., Litchfield, Minn., 1983—; editor Minn. Holstein Assn., St. Cloud, Minn., 1984; research historian Wright County (Minn.) Hist. Soc., Buffalo, 1985; researcher, historian Stearns Coop. Elec. Assn., Melrose, Minn., 1986; cons. Stearns County (Minn.) Hist. Soc., St. Cloud, 1986—, researcher, historian, 1987—. Author: Current and Kilowatts, 1986, The Harvest of Milk, 1987; (with others) Centennial- St. Catherine's Parish and Twp., 1979, Light From The Hearth, 1983. Officer St. Catherine's Parish, 1966—. Minn. Humanities Commn. grantee, 1982, 86. Mem. Cen. Minn. Writer's Club, Minn. Hist. Soc., Stearns County Hist. Soc., Wright County Hist. Soc. Roman Catholic. Avocations: quilting, poetry, softball, bowling, golf. Home and Office: Rt #1 PO Box 249 Albany MN 56307

BRINKMAN, RICHARD J., financial services company executive; b. 1930. BS, U. Iowa, 1951, JD, 1954. With Norwest Fin. Inc., Des Moines, 1959—, asst. counsel, 1959-65, dir. legal dept. and adminstrn., 1965-67, asst. v.p., 1967-69, v.p., 1969-72, v.p., gen. counsel, 1972-78, sr. v.p., gen. counsel, 1978-79, chief operating officer, exec. v.p., 1979-81, pres., chief operating officer, 1981-83, pres., chief exec. officer, 1983—, also bd. dirs. Served with AUS, 1954-58. Office: Norwest Fin Inc 206 8th St Des Moines IA 50307 •

BRINKMAN, RICHARD JOSEPH, pharmacist; b. Amarillo, Tex., Feb. 4, 1955; s. Edward Herman and Caroline Eliza (Huseman) B.; m. Kathy Marie Schumaker, July 23, 1977; children: Heather Dawn, Kristopor Aaron. BS, U. Kans., 1983, postgrad. in toxicology, 1986—. Licensed pharmacist, Kans., Mo. Sr. pharmacy technician Wesley Med. Ctr., Wichita, Kans., 1980-81; intern in pharmacy Lawrence (Kans.) Meml. Hosp., 1981-83; chief pharmacist Dept. Corrections, Lansing, Kans., 1983-85; poison specialist Mid-Am. Poison Ctr. U. Kans. Med. Ctr., Kansas City, 1985—, lectr. OUtreach Program; cons. in field, Lawrence, 1985—; lectr. Young Astronaut Program, Lawrence, 1986—. Editor Poison-Gram newsletter, 1985—. Den leader Cub Scouts Am., Lawrence, 1986. Mem. Am. Assn. Clin. Toxicology, Am. Assn. Poison Control Ctrs. (scientific com.), Am. Soc. Hosp. Pharmacists, Fedn. Internat. Pharmacetique, Kans. Pharmacists Assn. (profl. affairs com. 1986—), Kans. Soc. Hosp. Pharmacists, Rock Island Technician Soc., Ark. Hist. Railroad Soc., U. Kans. Alumni Assn. Republican. Roman Catholic. Avocations: model railroading, photography, snow skiing, writing. Home: 1502 W Third Lawrence KS 66044 Office: Mid-Am Poison Ctr U Kans Med Ctr 3900 Rainbow Kansas City KS 66103

BRINKMEYER, LOREN JAY, data processor, college administrator; b. Udall, Kans., Apr. 21, 1925; s. William Frederick and Verna Christina (Mead) B.; student U. Kans., 1943, 50-51, U. Wis., 1943-44; D. Mus. Dramatics, U. Heidelberg (Germany), 1954; D. Internat. Comml. Law, U. Poitiers (France), 1964; B.S.B. with honors, Emporia State U., 1972, M.S.B. with honors, 1978; Ph.D. in Computer Info. Systems, Loyola U., Paris, 1983; also student numerous data processing and computer sci. courses; m. Helen Josephine Walkemeyer, Mar. 10, 1946; 1 son, Karl Phillip. Served as enlisted man U.S. Army, 1943-45, commd. 2d lt., 1945, advanced through grades to lt. col., 1962; data processing supr., Hawaii, 1945-51, W. Ger., 1951-54, U.S., 1955, 60-61, Alaska, 1956-59, France, 1962-64, ret., 1964; dir. data processing Butler County Community Coll., El Dorado, Kans., 1964—; cons. data processing. Pres. El Dorado Mcpl. Bd., 1971-83; mem. choir United Methodist Ch., El Dorado, 1964—; mem. Kans. U. Alumni Band, 1972—. Decorated Army Commendation medal, Bronze Star with two oak leaf clusters, Purple Heart. Mem. NEA, Kans. Higher Edn. Assn., Am. Vocat. Assn., Kans. Vocat. Assn., Kans. Bus. Occupations Assn., Kans. Bus. Edn. Assn., Kans. Bus. Computerized Student Follow-up (adv. bd.), Data Processing Edn. Kans., Assn. Ednl. Data Systems, Data Processing Mgmt. Assn. (cert.), Assn. Computing Machinery, Soc. Data Educators, Internat. Assn. Computer Programmers, Ret. Enlisted Assn., Ret. Officers Assn., 96th Inf. Div. Assn., Nat. Assn. Uniformed Services, Am. Legion, VFW. Independent Republican. Author: Electrical Accounting Machines, 2d edit., 1964; Automated Inventory and Financial Systems, edit., 1976; Punched Card Business Data Processing, 3d edit., 1974. Office: Butler County Community Coll Data Ctr Haverhill and Towanda Dorado KS 67042

BRINKMEYER, WILLIS ROBERT, farm corp. exec.; b. Beatrice, Nebr., Jan. 4, 1931; s. Henry and Amelia Marie (Helmke) B.; graduate Bus. Adminstrn., Lincoln (Nebr.) Sch. Commerce; m. Shirley Louis Mitchell, Jan. 1, 1961; children—Renee, Mae Marie. Pres. Brinkmeyer Farms, Inc., Cortland, Nebr., 1972-80. Mem. 18th Dist. Jud. Nominating Commn., 1973—. Mem. Top Farmers of Am. Republican. Lutheran. Home: Route 1 Cortland NE 68331

BRISCOE, KEITH G., college president; b. Adams, Wis., Oct. 16, 1933; m. Carmen Irene Schweinler, Aug 15, 1956; 1 dau., Susan Ann. B.S., Wis. State U., La Crosse, 1960; M.Ed., U. N.H., 1968; postgrad., Case Western Res. U., Iowa State U., Okla. State U.; LL.D. (hon.), Coll. Idaho, 1977; L.H.D., Buena Vista Coll., 1979. Asst. dir. Coll. Union, Wis. State U., Stevens Point, 1960-62, U. N.H., 1962-64; dir. Coll. Union; dir. student activities, asst. prof. student life Baldwin Wallace Coll., Berea, Ohio, 1964-70; v.p. Coll. Steubenville, Ohio, 1970-74; pres. Buena Vista Coll., Storm Lake, Iowa, 1974—; higher edn. cons. Cuyahoga Community Coll., Coll. Wooster; v.p., treas. Ednl. Task, Inc., Berea, 1967-69; mem. nat. adv. bd. Coll. Transition Program, Berea, 1967-69; bd. dirs., chmn. Council Ind. Colls., 1981-83; mem. exec. com., bd. dirs., vice chmn. Presbyn. Coll. Union, 1981—; bd. dirs. mem. exec. com. us. Iowa Coll. Found.; bd. dirs. Coll. and Univ. Partnership Program, Am. Council on Edn., mem. coordinating council, 1981; co-chmn. Sino-Am. Inst. Higher Edn., Republic of China, 1981; bd. dirs., officer Coll. of Mid-Am.; past chmn. exec. com. Assn. Ind. Colls. and Univs.; past chmn. Iowa Coll. Pres.'s. Author: Directory of College Unions, 1963, An Annotated Bibliography of the College Union, 1967, A Study of Alternatives to Financing Private Higher Education, 1973; contbr. articles to profl. jours. Mem. Iowa Sister State Friendship Com., 1985-87, Iowa Product Devel. Com., 1986-87. Served with U.S. Army, 1956-58. Mem. Assn. Coll. and Univ. Concert Mgrs. (trustee), UN Assn., Nat. Meth. Found., Phi Kappa Epsilon, Phi Delta Kappa. Republican. Methodist. Clubs: Masons, Des Moines, Order of Arch, Rotary. Address: Office of Pres Buena Vista Coll Storm Lake IA 50588

BRITT, RONALD LEROY, mechanical engineer; b. Abilene, Kans., Mar. 1, 1935; s. Elvin Elbert and Lona Helen (Conn) B.; B.S.M.E., Wichita State U., 1963; m. Judith Ann Salter, June 29, 1957; children—Brett Gavin, Mark Damon, Melissa Ann. Product engr. to product planner Hotpoint div. Gen. Electric Co., Chgo., 1963-68; product planner Norge Co., Chgo., 1968; product mgr., asst. dir. engring. Leigh Products Inc., Coopersville, Mich., 1968-74; mgr. research and devel. MiamiCarey div. Jim Walter Corp., Monroe, Ohio, 1974-84; v.p. engring. div. SICO, Belvedere Co., Belvidere, Ill., 1984—; industry rep. for electric fans Underwriters Labs. Active, Boy Scouts Am., 1970-73, PTA, 1973—; exec. adviser Jr. Achievement, 1984-85, Boone County chmn., 1986—. Served with U.S. Army, 1958-60. Recipient Inventor's award Gen. Electric Co., 1967. Mem. ASME, Home Ventilation Inst. (engring. com. 1975-84), Belvidere C. of C. (bd..dirs. 1986—). Republican. Congregationalist. Clubs: Free Blown Glassblowing, Carnival and Art Glass Collectors. Lodge: Rotary. Patentee in field. Home: 11858 Limetree Ln Belvidere IL 61008 Office: 725 Columbia Ave Belvidere IL 61008

BRITTEN, WILLIAM HARRY, editor, publisher; b. Zearing, Iowa, Aug. 25, 1921; s. Harry William and Gertrude Alice (Lehman) B. B.A., Western Union Coll., 1943; student Iowa State Coll., summer 1942; M.A., State U. Iowa, 1948. Reporter, Worcester (Mass.) Telegram, 1948-55; landscaper John F. Keenen, Leicester, Mass., 1956; sales dept. clk. Reed & Prince Mfg. Co., Worcester, 1957-63, inventory control clk., 1964, chief expeditor, 1965; state editor Marshalltown (Ia.) Times-Republican, 1965-66, staff writer, 1966-67; news editor Denison (Ia.) Bull. and Rev., 1967-68; city editor Boone News Republican, 1968; editor, pub., owner The Tri-County News, Zearing, 1968—; editor, pub. Hubbard (Iowa) Rev., 1969-72; Sec., Young Men's Republican Club, Worcester, 1957; corr. sec. Young People's Rep. Club, 1958; mem. Ward 8 Rep. Com., Worcester, 1960-65; Rep. candidate Mass. state legislature, 1960; ward chmn. to elect Edward W. Brooke atty. gen. Mass., 1962, 64; bd. dirs. Story County Cancer Soc., 1976-81. Served with AUS, 1943-45. Mem. Iowa Newspaper Assn., Nat. Newspaper Assn., Am. Fedn. Arts, Am. Legion (post comdr. 1982-83), Westmar Coll., U. Iowa alumni assns. Mem. Ch. of Christ. Home: 416 S Pearl St Zearing IA 50278 Office: Main St Zearing IA 50278

BRITTON, KENNETH RAY, osteopath; b. Walla Walla, Wash.; s. William Edward and Betty Lou (Eccles) B.; m. Rita Marie Schell; children—Abigail, Benjamin, Elizabeth, Sarah, David. B. in Biology, U. No. Iowa, 1976; DO, Coll. Osteo. Medicine and Surgery, 1979. Rotating intern Des Moines Gen. Hosp., 1979-80; gen. practice osteo. medicine, Albia, Iowa, 1980-82, 82—; chmn. ob-gyn dept. Monroe County Health Care Ctr., Albia, also chmn. nutritional support team and mem. utilization rev. com. Community medicine preceptor for Coll. of Osteo. Medicine and Surgery. Served with USPHS, 1980-82. Mem. Iowa Osteo. Med. Assn. (trustee), Am. Osteo. Assn., Iowa Soc. Osteo. Physicians and Surgeons. Home: 515 E Benton Ave Albia IA 52531 Office: 15 N Main St Albia IA 52531

BRIXIUS, FRANK JOSEPH, lawyer; b. St. Cloud, Minn., May 23, 1938; s. Albert J. and Mary Kathryn (Thiesen) B.; B.S. (William scholar), U. Minn., 1961; J.D., William Mitchell Coll. Law, 1966; m. Suzanne DeLong, July 14, 1962; children—Elizabeth Ann, Mary Alanah, Frank Joseph. With First Nat. Bank Mpls., 1962-66; admitted to Minn. bar, 1966; assoc. Hvass, Weisman & King, Mpls., 1966-69, ptnr., 1969—, v.p., chief fin. officer, 1984—. Mem. Greenwood (Minn.) City Council, 1970-71, 71-83, chmn. adv. com., 1970, council rep. to Hennepin County League Municipalities and Met. League Municipalities, 1972-76; mayor, Greenwood, 1973-83; co-chmn. Hennepin County Criminal Justice Council, 1974-75. Dir. Suburban Rate Authority; dir., mem. exec. com. Suburban League Municipalities, 1974-75, also chmn. pub. safety dept. 1974-75, 77-78, 80-82. Trustee Alpha Nu Trust Fund, 1974—. Recipient West Publishing Outstanding Law Student award, 1965. Fellow Internat. Soc. Barristers; mem. Am., Minn., Hennepin County bar assns., Am., Minn. trial lawyers assns., Assn. Met. Municipalities (dir., exec. com. 1974-75), Am. Judicature Soc., Chi Psi. Home: 21720 Fairview Greenwood MN 55331 Office: 100 S 5th St Suite 2100 Minneapolis MN 55402

BRO, KENNETH ARTHUR, plastic manufacturing company executive; b. Tsingdao, Shandung, China, Aug. 28, 1921 (parents Am. citizens); s. Albin Carl and Margueritte (Harmon) B.; m. Patricia Welch, May 6, 1944; children—William, Peter, Kenneth M., Patricia, Elizabeth, A. Charles. B.S., Northwestern U., 1949. Purchasing agent Welch Mfg. Co., Chgo., 1950-56; v.p. Welch Sci. Co., Chgo., 1957-64; v.p., co-owner Webb Plastic Co., Northbrook, Ill., 1965—. Chmn. bd. trustees Northland Coll., Ashland, Wis., 1957, 70-74; pres. bd. dirs. Chgo. Commons Assn., 1962, 70-74; dist. chmn. bd. dirs. Jr. Achievement, Chgo., 1970, 72-74; pres. Found. for Sci. Relaxation, 1965—. Served to pvt. 1st class U.S. Army, 1944-46, ETO. Decorated Bronze Star, Purple Heart. Mem. Am. Vaccum Soc., Am. Assn. Physics Tchrs. Republican. Congregationalist. Clubs: Indian Hill (Winnetka, Ill.); University, Chgo. Yacht, Economic, Executive (Chgo.). Avocations: sailing; flying; travel. Home: 375 Sheridan Rd Winnetka IL 60093 Office: Webb Plastic Inc 2820 Old Willow Rd Northbrook IL 60062

BROACH, ALGNER EUGENE ADOLOPHUS, III, podiatrist; b. Cin., June 2, 1933; s. Algner Eugene Adolophus II and Susie Belle Broach (Lindsey) B.; B.S., Central State U., 1958; D.P.M., Ohio Coll. Podiatric Medicine, 1966; m. Lillie Mae Morton, Aug. 15, 1959; children—Connie M., Charisse M., Cheryl A., Cynthia L., Algner E. A.IV. Practice podiatry, Cin., 1967—; mem. staff, dept. med. dir. Walnut Hills-Evanston Med. Center, 1975-78; mem. staff West End Health Center, 1975—; mem. Cin. Health Dept. Task Force; pres. bd. dirs. Walnut Hills-Evanston Med. Center. Mem. Walnut Hills Community Council, 1980-81. Served with M.C., USAF, 1951-53, U.S. Army Res., 1978—. Diplomate Nat. Bd. Podiatry Examiners. Fellow Am. Acad. Podiatric Laser Surgery, Am. Assn. Hosp. Podiatrists; mem. Am. Podiatry Assn., Ohio Podiatry Assn., So. Ohio Acad. Podiatry, Jewish Hosp. Assn., Assn. Mil. Surgeons, Nat. Podiatry Assn., Res. Officers Assn., Greater Cin. Minority Bus. and Profl. Assn., Alpha Phi Alpha, Phi Alpha Pi. Clubs: Masons. Home: 1139 Cheyenne Dr Cincinnati OH 45216 Office: 2916 Gilbert Ave Ideal Medical Bldg Cincinnati OH 45206

BROAD, EDWARD R., JR., pharmaceutical company executive, industrial engineer; b. Mineola, N.Y., Jan. 3, 1938; s. Edward R. and Elizabeth L. (DeLano) B.; m. Dorothy Ann Graham, Feb. 4, 1961; children: Donald K., E. Richard, Jonathan M., Pamela A., Kimberly S. BS in Engring., U. Mich., 1961, MBA, 1964. Project engr. Eli Lilly & Co., Indpls., 1964-69, fin. planning, 1965-73, dept. head ind. engring., 1973-81, dept. head equipment devel., 1981—. Active Carmel (Ind.) Jaycees, 1964-73; elder Orchard Park Presbyn. Ch., Indpls., 1965—; commr. First Bapt. 6-8 Baseball Program, Indpls., 1970-77; program dir. Jordan YMCA, Indpls., 1971-85. Republican. Club: Greyhound Boosters (Carmel, Ind.) (patron chmn. 1985—). Home: 10132 Marwood Trail E Dr Indianapolis IN 46280 Office: Eli Lilly & Co Lilly Corp Ctr Indianapolis IN 46285

BROADBENT, ROBERT R., retail company executive; b. Lisbon, Ohio, May 25, 1921; s. Raymond and Ruth Edna (Schoonover) B.; m. Mary; 1 son, William Stuart. B.S., U. Akron, Ohio, 1946. Personal asst. to Cyrus S. Eaton, Cleve., 1946-49; various positions in retailing 1949-58; exec. v.p., dir. Higbee Co., Cleve., 1958-73; pres., vice chmn. bd. Higbee Co., 1979-84, chmn. bd., chief exec. officer, 1984—; also dir.; chmn. bd., chief exec. officer Gimbel's, N.Y.C., 1973-76; pres., chief exec. officer Liberty House-Mainland, San Francisco, 1976-79; dir. Huntington Bank of N.E. Ohio. Bd. dirs., exec. com. Greater Cleve. Growth Assn.; bd. dirs. Kent State Found., Cleve. Tomorrow, Cleve. 500 Found.; trustee Kent State U. Served with USAAF, 1943-45, ETO. Decorated D.F.C., Air medal with 4 oak leaf clusters. Mem. Am. Retail Fedn. (bd. dirs.). Clubs: Cleve. Racquet (Cleve.), Cleve. Country (Cleve.), Union (Cleve.); Union League (N.Y.C.). Address: Higbee Co 100 Public Sq Cleveland OH 44113

BROCCO, KAREN JEAN, psychiatrist; b. Cleve., Feb. 28, 1948; d. John L. and Eleanor J. (Cocker) B.; m. Frank D. Kish, Oct. 7, 1978; 1 child, Justin D. Kish. BA, Case Western Res. U., 1970; MD, Med. Coll. Pa., 1974. Staff psychiatrist Cleve. Met. Gen. Hosp., 1978—; asst. prof. psychiatry Case Western Res. U., Cleve., 1980—; cons. psychiatrist Cuyhoga County Probate Ct., Cleve., 1981—, North Coast Guidance, Cleve., 1985—; mem. med. records com. Cleve. Met. Gen. Hosp., 1982-85. Mem. Cleve. Psychiat. Soc., Cleve. Acad. Medicine, Ohio State Med. Soc. Avocations: nutrition, exercise, dogs, cats. Office: Cleve Met Gen Hosp 3395 Scranton Rd Cleveland OH 44109

BROCK, CHARLES MARQUIS, lawyer; b. Watseka, Ill., Oct. 8, 1941; s. Glen Westgate and Muriel Lucile (Bubeck) B.; m. Elizabeth Bonilla, Dec. 17, 1966; children—Henry Christopher, Anna Melissa. A.B. cum laude, Princeton U., 1963; J.D., Georgetown U., 1968; M.B.A., U. Chgo., 1974. Bar: Ill. 1969, U.S. Dist. Ct. (no. dist.) Ill. 1969. Asst. trust counsel Continental Ill. Nat. Bank, Chgo., 1968-74; regional counsel Latin Am., Can. Abbott Labs., Abbott Park, Ill., 1974-77, regional counsel, Europe, Africa and Middle East, 1977-81, div. counsel, 1981—; sec. mgmt. com. TAP Pharms., 1985—. Served with Inter-Am. Def. Coll., U.S. Army, 1964-66. Mem. ABA, Chgo. Bar Assn., Phi Beta Kappa. Republican. Clubs: Princeton (Chgo.); Princeton (N.Y.C.), Mich. Shores (Wilmette, Ill.) Home: 1473 Asbury Ave Winnetka IL 60093 Office: Abbott Labs Abbott Park IL 60064

BROCK, JUDITH ANNE, magazine editor, marketing consultant; b. McAlester, Okla., July 8, 1950; s. Eddie W. and Irene Laverne (Hicks) Lee; m. James Lavern Hodge, Jan. 30, 1970 (div. Dec. 1977); 1 child, Joshua Lee; m. Paul Edward Brock, May 31, 1980. AA in Bus., Crowder Coll., 1972. Pres. J.L.I., Neosho, Mo., 1981—; v.p., mktg. Brock Corp., Neosho, 1982—; editor In..Joplin (Mo.) Mag., 1984—; dir. mktg. TechMark, Ltd.; entrepreneur, mktg. cons. Neosho, 1980—. inventor card game Josh, 1982. Pres. Neosho PTA, 1982-84. Named Woman of Yr., Beta Sigma Phi, Neosho, 1983-84; recipient Bringing Out Your Best award Budweiser Light, 1983. Mem. Am. Mktg. Assn. (exec.), Neosho C. of C. (retail dir. 1983-84), Gifted Assn. (pres. 1985—), Mensa. Lodge: Soroptimist (treas. 1984-85). Avocations: hot air ballooning, running, cycling, internat. traveling. Office: Brock Corp 317 Fairground Rd Neosho MO 64850

BROCKERT, KENNETH LEE, hosp. lab. adminstr., med. technologist; b. Springfield, Mo., June 15, 1932; s. Thomas Edward and Lula Rachel (Love) B.; clin. lab. technician certificate U.S. Navy, 1952; A.A. in Liberal Arts, Kent State U., 1973; m. Marilyn Lois Noll, Sept. 29, 1956; children—Ann Marie, Mark Alan, Matthew Lee, Nina Jane. Histology technician U.S. Naval Hosp., North Chicago, Ill., 1956; adminstrv. technologist Timken Mercy Hosp. Lab., Canton, Ohio, 1956-72; lab. dir. Alliance (Ohio) City Hosp., 1972-87; asst. lab. mgr. Alliance Community Hosp., 1987—; mem. nat. lab. panel Market Potential Corp. Bd. dirs. Alliance chpt. ARC, 1972-77; mem. St. Michael's Men's Choir, 1977—; lay dir. Canton Cursillo Center, 1978-80; mem. adv. bd., med. lab. technologists program Stark Tech. Coll., 1980—; treas. Irish Oaks Homeowners Assn., 1981—. Served with USN, 1950-56. Mem. Am. Soc. Clin. Pathologists (certified histology technician), Registry Med. Technologists, Am. Heart Assn. (certified in basic cardiac life support), Am. Soc. Med. Technologists, Ohio Soc. Med. Technologists (treas. dist. 1, 1983-87), Citizens Hosp. Assn. Alliance. Democrat. Roman Catholic. Clubs: St. Michaels Men's (sec.); Kiwanis (dir. local club 1974-77, pres. 1977-78, div. chmn. spiritual aims 1982-83) (Alliance). Participant in designing lab. for Alliance Community Hosp. Home: 5055 Tralee Circle NW Canton OH 44720 Office: 264 E Rice St Alliance OH 44601

BROCKMAN, TERRY JAMES, lawyer; b. Wisconsin Rapids, Wis., July 10, 1955; s. Wilbert Francis and Angeline Catherine (Huser) B.; m. Mary Jane Amdor, Oct. 2, 1982; children: John, Kristen. BBA, Creighton U., 1977, JD, 1980. Bar: Nebr. 1981, U.S. Dist. Ct. Nebr. 1981, U.S. Tax Ct. 1981. Tax cons. Touche Ross, Omaha, Nebr., 1980-83, tax supr., 1983-85; tax mgr. Grant Thornton, Omaha, 1985-86; sr. tax mgr. Peat Marwick Main, Omaha, 1986—. Mem. ABA, Nebr. Bar Assn., Omaha Bar Assn., Am. Inst. CPA's, Nebr. Soc. CPA's. Republican. Roman Catholic. Lodge: Rotary. Home: 1010 S 36th St Omaha NE 68105 Office: Peat Marwick Main 600 Kiewit Plaza Omaha NE 68131

BROD, DONALD FREDERICK, journalism educator, magazine editor, professional association executive; b. St. Charles, Mo., May 10, 1932; s. Theodore Frank and Caroline (Hammer) B.; m. Nancy Lee Schelker, Sept. 28, 1957 (div. 1983); children—Andrew, Stephen. B.A., Southeast Mo. State Coll., 1954; M.A., U. Mo., 1958; Ph.D., U. Minn., 1968. Reporter, editor Montezuma Valley Jour., Cortez, Colo., 1958-60; mem. journalism faculty U. Wis., River Falls, 1960-69, No. Ill. U., DeKalb, 1969—, chmn. dept., 1976-81, 87—; editor Grassroots Editor, DeKalb, 1981—; exec. sec. Internat. Soc. Weekly Newspaper Editors, DeKalb, 1981—; tchr. journalism classes, Britain, China, Ger., 1982-85. Contbr. numerous articles to profl. jours. Served to cpl. U.S. Army, 1955-57. Recipient 1st place photojournalism award Colo. Press Assn., 1960, Excellence in Teaching award No. Ill. U., 1987. Mem. Assn. for Edn. in Journalism and Mass Communication, Soc. Profl. Journalists, Internat. Soc. Weekly Newspaper Editors. Home: 43 White Oak Circle Saint Charles IL 60174 Office: Dept Journalism Northern Ill Univ DeKalb IL 60115

BRODBECK, SHARON KAY, data methods specialist; b. Covington, Ky., Feb. 11, 1956; d. John A. and Ruth Catherine (Robbins) McGinnis; m. Robert Thomas Brodbeck, July 23, 1983. BS in Math., No. Ky. U., 1978; BA in Astronomy, Lycoming Coll., 1981. Planetarium program specialist Cin. Mus. Nat. History, 1982-84; engring. asst. Gen. Electric Co., Cin., 1984-86, data method specialist, 1986—. Mem. Optical Soc. Am. Avocations: astronomy, photography. Home: 3310 Lambert Pl Cincinnati OH 45208 Office: Gen Electric Co AEBG 1 Neumann Way MDJ185 Cincinnati OH 45215

BRODBECK, WILLIAM JAN, retail executive; b. Platteville, Wis., Feb. 14, 1944; s. Richard William and Helen (Stoneman) B.; m. Janet Piwonka, Feb. 4, 1967; children: Allison S., Courtney K., Stephanie L. BA in Econs., Hillsdale (Mich.) Coll., 1966. Asst. to v.p. Hillsdale Coll., 1966-68; mgr. advt. Brodbeck Enterprises, Inc., Platteville, 1968-72, v.p., 1972-79, pres., chief exec. officer, 1980—; gov. Uniform Product Code Council, Dayton, Ohio, 1977-86; chmn. First Nat. Bank, Platteville, 1986—. Contbr. articles to profl. jours. Chmn. Third Congl. Dist. Reagan Campaign, 1976; pres. Platteville Area Indsl. Devel., 1976-79; bd. dirs. Thursday's Child, Madison, Wis., 1983—, Wis. Shakespeare Festival, Platteville, 1986—. Mem. Nat. Grocers Assn. (bd. dirs. 1977-85), Food Mktg. Inst. (bd. dirs. 1982—), U. Wis. Platteville Found. (pres. 1980-81), Hillsdale Coll. Alumni Forum, Platteville C. of C. (pres. 1972-73), Omicron Delta Kappa (chpt. v.p. 1966). Office: Brodbeck Enterprises Inc 255 McGregor Plaza Platteville WI 53818

BRODERICK, WILLIAM DANIEL, accountant; b. Chgo., Aug. 6, 1939; s. William John and Veronica (O'Brien) B.; m. Kathleen Kiley, Nov. 5, 1966; children: Kathleen, Anne, William. BBA, U. Notre Dame, 1961; MBA, U. Chgo., 1965. CPA, Ill. Fin. analyst Ford Motor Co., Dearborn, Mich., 1966-68; sr. cons. Alexander Grant & Co., Chgo., 1968-70; asst. adminstr. Loretto Hosp., Chgo., 1970-73; v.p. fin., controller Evangelical Hosp. Assn., Oak Brook, Ill., 1973-78; treas. Patten Industries, Elmhurst, Ill., 1978-79; gen. mgr. Centel Communcations Co., Chgo., 1980—. Bd. dirs. St. John of the Cross, Western Springs, Ill., 1974-76, Nazareth Acad., LaGrange Park, Ill., 1983-85. Served to lt. USN, 1961-63. Fellow Healthcare Fin. Mgmt. Assn. (bd. dirs. 1977-78).; mem. Am. Inst. CPA's, Ill. Soc. CPA's, Am. Assn. Equipment Lessors. Roman Catholic. Club: Over 21 (v.p. 1964-65). Avocations: golf, tennis, travel. Home: 3928 Clausen Western Springs IL 60558 Office: Centel Communications Co 8735 Higgens Chicago IL 60631

BRODEUR, ARMAND EDWARD, pediatric radiologist; b. Penacook, N.H., Jan. 8, 1922; s. Felix and Patronyne Antoinette (Lavoie) B.; m. Gloria Marie Thompson, June 4, 1947; children: Armand Paul, Garrett Michael, Mark Stephen, Mariette Therese, Michelle Bernadette, Paul Francis. A.B., St. Anselm Coll., 1945, M.D., 1947, M.Rd., 1952; LL.D. (hon.), Anselm's Coll., 1974. Intern St. Louis U. Hosps., 1947-48, resident in pediatrics, 1948-49, resident in radiology, 1949-52; instr. St. Louis U. Sch. Medicine, 1952-60, sr. instr., 1960-62, asst. prof., 1962-65, assoc. prof., 1965-70, prof. radiology, 1970—, chmn. dept. radiology, 1975-78, vice chmn. dept., 1978—, prof. pediatrics, 1979—, prof. juvenile law, 1979—; pvt. practice medicine specializing in pediatric radiology St. Louis, 1954-56; radiologist-in-chief Cardinal Glennon Meml. Hosp. for Children, St. Louis, 1956—; bd. dirs. Mark Twain Bank; lectr. and cons. in field. Radio show host Doctor to Doctor, Sta. KMOX-C.B.S., St. Louis, also host daily show To Your Health; Author: Radiologic Diagnosis in Infants and Children, 1965, Radiology of the Pediatric Elbow, 1980, Radiologic Pathology for Allied Health Professions, 1980; author monographs; contbr. articles to profl. jours., numerous teaching tapes. Bd. dirs. ARC, Tb Soc., others. Served with U.S. Army, 1942-46, with USPHS, 1952-54. Recipient Pillar of Univ. award St. Louis U., 1973; knighted Equestrian order Holy Sepulchre Jerusaleum, 1985. Fellow Am. Coll. Radiology, Am. Acad. Pediatrics; mem. AMA (Bronze medal), Soc. Pediatric Radiology, Radiol. Soc. N.Am., Nat. Assn. Physician Broadcasters (charter, 1st pres. 1987), Sigma Xi, Alpha Omega Alpha, Alpha Sigma Nu, Rho Kappa Sigma. Roman Catholic. Home: 400 Bambury Way Saint Louis MO 63131 Office: 1465 S Grand Blvd Saint Louis MO 63104

BRODHUN, ANDREW R., banker; b. 1940; married. B.A., Mich. State U., 1965. Pres. Mich. Nat. Bank-West Metro, 1974-80; v.p. Mich. Nat. Corp., 1980-85, sr. v.p., dir., 1985—; group v.p. Mich. Nat. Bank of Detroit Inc., Troy, 1965-74, pres., 1981—. Served with USN, 1962-64. Office: Mich Nat Bank of Detroit 22595 W 8 Mile Rd Detroit MI 48219 *

BRODKEY, JERALD STEVEN, neurosurgeon; b. Omaha, Jan. 20, 1934; s. Fred Donald and Sylvia (Adler) B.; m. Arielle Kozloff, May 11, 1974; children: Jason, Daniel. AB magna cum laude, Harvard U., 1955; MS, U. Nebr., 1959, MD cum laude, 1960. Diplomate Am. Bd. Neurol. Surgery. Intern Barnes Hosp., St. Louis, 1960-61, resident, 1961-62; resident Mass. Gen. Hosp., Boston, 1962-67; asst. attending neurosurgeon Presbyn.-St. Lukes Hosp., Chgo., 1967-69; attending neurosurgeon Hines VA Hosp., Chgo., 1967-69; chief neurol. surgeon VA Hosp., Cleve., 1969-83; med. dir. pain unit St. Luke's Hosp., Cleve., 1983—, chief nuerosurgery, 1984—; asst. neurosurgeon Univ. Hosp., Cleve., 1969-71, assoc. neurosurgeon, 1971-73; asst neurosurgeon Met. Gen. Hosp., Cleve., 1971-73; clin. prof. neurosurgery Case Western Res. U., Cleve., 1983—. Fellow ACS; mem. Neurosurgical Soc. Am., IEEE, Soc. for Neuroscience, Am. Acad. Neurol. Surgery. Avocations: photography, fishing, music. Office: 247555 Chagrin Blvd Beachwood OH 44122

BRODSKY, EASTON EVERETT, dentist; b. Detroit, Sept. 12, 1930; s. Isadore and Rosalie (Rosen) B.; m. Linda Kay Victor, Aug. 14, 1961; children: Dennis, Eric, Ronda, Burton, Amy. DDS, U. Detroit, 1959. Diplomate Am. Acad. Electrosurgery (pres. 1971). Gen. practice dentistry Southfield, Mich., 1959—. BCLS instr. Am. Heart Assn., Southfield, 1984—. Served as cpl. Mich. Air N. G., 1948-51, U.S. Army, 1951-53. Fellow Am. Acad. Gen. Dentistry (master 1978); mem. Detroit Dist. Dental Soc. (editor 1980-83). Home: 6117 Northfield West Bloomfield MI 48033 Office: 29201 Telegraph #603 Southfield MI 48034

BRODSKY, IRA STEWART, marketing professional; b. Chgo., Dec. 4, 1953; s. Michael and Mae (Weiner) B.; m. Maureen G. Movshin, May 1, 1983; 1 child, Sarah M. BA in Philosophy, Northwestern U., 1975. Sales engr. Gandalf Data, Wheeling, Ill., 1979-83; data communications specialist Tektronix, Rolling Meadows, Ill., 1984-86; product mktg. mgr. US Robotics, Skokie, Ill., 1986—. Editor The Holographer, 1986. Bd. dirs. Fine Arts REsearch and Holographic Ctrs., Sch. of Holography. Club: Toastmasters (Skokie) (v.p. adminstrn. 1987). Avocations: amateur radio, holography. Office: USRobotics Inc 8100 N McCormick Blvd Skokie IL 60076

BRODSKY, ROBERT JAY, wholesale executive; b. Chgo., June 1, 1939; s. Victor Robert and Anille (Evans) B.; m. Anna-Marie H. Miller, June 21, 1969; children: Paul, David. AB, U. Chgo., 1961, MBA, 1962. With J.J. Brodsky & Sons, Inc., Chgo., 1962—, pres., 1986—. Served to 1st lt. C.E., Mil. Police, Ill. Army Reserve N.G., 1962-68. Mem. Nat. Candy Wholesalers Assn., Ill. Assn. Tobacco and Candy Distbrs. (bd. dirs. 1987). Republican. Jewish. Avocation: photography. Office: J J Brodsky & Sons Inc PO Box 19700 7300 S Kimbark Ave Chicago IL 60619

BRODY, FREDERICK S., advertising company executive; b. Chgo., Apr. 4, 1930; s. Max Steven and Estelle (Norton) B.; m. Grace Catherine Meixner, Apr. 27, 1955; children: Matthew, Lydia Brody Oppen. BS, Northwestern U., 1950; cert. in pyschol. warfare, foreign service sch., Georgetown U., 1952. V.p. Schram Advt., Chgo., 1956-68, Manobach & Simms, Chgo., 1968-70, Martin J. Simmons Advt., Chgo., 1970-77, Christenson, Barclay & Shaw, Chgo., 1977-78; acct. dir. Ableson-Frankel, Chgo., 1978-80; pvt. practice advt. agy Northbrook, Ill., 1980—. Served to 1st lt. USAF, 1951-54. Home: 2754 Arlington Highland Park IL 60035 Office: 666 Dundee Rd Northbrook IL 60062

BRODY, ROBERT, dermatologist; b. Cleve., June 15, 1948; s. Melvin and Nancy Elizabeth Brody; A.B. with distinction, Stanford U., 1970; M.D., U. Mich., 1974. Intern in internal medicine, Cleve. Clinic, 1974-75, resident in dermatology, 1975-78; practice medicine specializing in dermatology, Cleve., 1978—; staff physician Kaiser-Permanente Med. Center, 1978-82, mem. profl. edn. com., 1978-82, chmn., 1980-82, also sec. exec. com., 1980; pvt. practice, 1982—; asst. clin. prof. Case Western Res. U. Med. Sch., 1978-80, 83—, clin. instr., 1980-83, dermatology dept. rep. to gen. faculty, 1980-82; asst. physician Univ. Hosps. Cleve., 1979—. Sec., Cleve. Play House Men's Com., 1979-82; mem. ann. fund com. Stanford U., 1978—, regional co-chmn., 1981-82. Diplomate Am. Bd. Dermatology. Mem. Am. Acad. Dermatology, Cleve. Acad. Medicine. Contbr. articles to med. jours. Club: Cleve. Skating. Home: 13415 Shaker Blvd Cleveland OH 44120 Office: 3461 Warrensville Ctr Rd Shaker Heights OH 44122

BROEHL, DAVID ROBERT, management consultant; b. Chgo., Sept. 4, 1947; s. Wayne G. and Jean K. Broehl; m. Margo E. Broehl, Aug. 24, 1969; children: Nathan, Julia, Daniel. BA in Sociology, Coll. of Wooster, 1969; MA in Urban Studies, Occidental Coll., 1977. Dir. Neighborhood Youth Corps, Wooster, Ohio, 1969-72; ombudsman City of Wooster, 1972-76; asst. dir. Area Agy. in Aging, Akron, Ohio, 1977-80; mgmt. cons. David Broehl & Assocs., Wooster, 1980—. Chmn. long range planning Wooster United Way, 1978-81, Citizens' Adv. Bd. Apple Creek Devel. Ctr., Ohio, 1985—; pres. Wayne Head Start, Wooster, Ohio, 1986—. Nat. Urban fellow, 1976-77. Mem. Wooster Jaycees (bd. dirs. 1976-78, v.p. adminstrn. 1978-79). Avocations: antiques, golf, tennis, soccer, reading. Home: 900 Quinby Ave Wooster OH 44691 Office: David Broehl and Assocs 105 W Pine St Wooster OH 44691

BROENE, G(ILBERT) RICHARD, religious organization administrator; b. Grand Rapids, Mich., May 19, 1948; s. Gilbert James and Annette (Star) B.; m. Mary Jo Katerberg, July 20, 1973; children: Richard James, Jeffrey Robert, Pamela Jo. BA, Calvin Coll., 1970. Pres. Calvinist Cadet Corps, Grand Rapids, 1977-83, exec. dir., 1983—; sec. Gideon Camp, Grand Rapids, 1982-85, v.p. 1985. Republican. Avocation: youth religious activities. Home: 6962 Buchanan SW Grand Rapids MI 49508 Office: Calvinist Cadet Corps 1333 Alger SE Grand Rapids MI 49507

BROEREN, STUART WAYNE, construction company executive; b. Champaign, Ill., June 9, 1955; s. Wayne Henry and Cecile Marie (Creath) B.; m. Sally Ann McConkey, Nov. 11, 1978; children: Michael, Allyson, Gregory. AA, Parkland Coll., Champaign, 1975; BS in Fin., U. Ill., 1978. Chief exec. officer S.W. Broeren, Inc., Champaign, 1978—; guest lectr. U. Ill., Champaign, 1983. Republican. Roman Catholic. Office: SW Broeren Inc 602 Country Fair Dr Champaign IL 61821

BROFFMAN, MORTON HOWARD, management and media consultant; b. N.Y.C., Aug. 17, 1920; s. Samuel L. and Fannie B. (Mack) B.; B.A. cum laude, CCNY, 1940; M.A., N.Y. U., 1943; M.A. (teaching fellow 1949-50), Harvard U., 1950, M.P.A., 1951, Ph.D., 1953; m. Louise Hargrove, Dec. 24, 1969; children—Trudy, Jane, Michael. Vice pres., dir. mfg. and engring. Rayco Co., 1953-56, sr. v.p., dir. mktg. and retail stores, 1956-61; exec. v.p., gen. mgr. L.A. Darling Co., 1961-63; exec. v.p., chief operating officer United Brands Corp., 1964-70; pres., chief exec. officer John Morrell & Co., 1968-71; pres. Am. Biltrite, Inc., Boston, 1970-74; pres., chief exec. officer Combined Mgmt. Services Corp., N.Y.C., 1975-80, Public Media Inc., Wilmette, Ill., 1980—; pres. Sound Video Unlimited Inc., Niles, Ill., 1985—; dir. Sterndent Corp., Films, Inc., Public Media Corp., Bldg. Materials Distbrs. Co.; mem. faculty Northeastern U., Boston, 1950-51, Rutgers U., 1955-56. Bd. dirs. Save the Children Fedn., 1978—. Served with USN, 1944-46. Mem. Am. Mgmt. Assn., Conf. Bd., Am. Mktg. Assn., Inst. Indsl. Engrs. Clubs: Harvard (Boston and N.Y.C.); Manhattan, Drug and Chem., Internat., Whitehall, Touhy Tennis. Author, cons. editor profl. publs. Home: 1410 Sheridan Rd Wilmette IL 60091 Office: Sound Video Unlimited Inc 7000 N Austin Ave Niles IL 60648

BROGLA, MARTHA LEONE, accountant; b. Taylorsville, Ill., Oct. 31, 1955; d. Richard Wayne and Susan Bernadine (Adermann) Lamb; m. Vernon Gerard Brogla, May 20, 1978; children: Lucinda, Cynthia, Garrett. B in Acctg., Ill. State U., 1981. CPA, Ill.; CLU, Ill.; cert. mgmt. acct. Tax acct. State Farm Ins., Bloomington, Ill., 1982—. Fellow Life Office Mgmt. Assn.; mem. Am. Inst. CPA's, Ill. CPA Soc., Soc. Chartered Life Underwriters, Inst. Mgmt. Accts. Roman Catholic. Club: Toastmasters (competent Toastmaster). Avocation: waterskiing. Home: 2002 Woodfield Rd Bloomington IL 61701 Office: State Farm Ins One State Farm Plaza Bloomington IL 61710-0001

BROIHAHN, MICHAEL ALLEN, computer company executive; b. Cuba City, Wis., June 2, 1948; s. Lester E. and Shirley L. (Bendorf) B.; m. Cynthia Barbara Andreas, May 29, 1982; children: David Michael, Matthew Allen. BS, U. Wis., 1972; MBA, U. Wis., Milw., 1973, MS, 1976. CPA, Wis.; cert. mgmt. acct.; cert. fin. planner. Auditor Price Waterhouse & Co., Milw., 1976-78; portfolio controller Fox & Carskadon Fin. Corp., San Mateo, Calif., 1979-82; corp. controller Computerland Corp., Hayward, Calif., 1982-84; v.p. fin. Computers Unltd./Computer Bay, Milw., 1985—; lectr. U. Wis., Milw., 1977-78, Keller Grad. Sch., Mgmt., Milw., 1986—. Fellow Wis. Inst. CPA's; mem. Am. Inst. CPA's, Nat. Assn. Accts. (bd. dirs., 1981-85), Inst. Cert. Mgmt. Accts., U. Wis. Alumni Assn., Kappa Sigma. Republican. Lutheran. Avocations: gemology, numismatics, travel, sports, reading. Home: 5567 N Hollywood Ave Whitefish Bay WI 53217 Office: Computers Unltd/Computer Bay 9055 D N 51st St Milwaukee WI 53223

BROKENS, GARY EDWARD, computer systems manager; b. Monticello, Iowa, Mar. 18, 1949; s. Edward and Velda (Rickles) B.; m. Lucinda Nell Carlson, July 31, 1976; children: Lindsay, Ashley, Jonathan. AAS in Constrn. Technol., Iowa State U., 1970. Cert. engring. technician. Design draftsman Cuckler div. Lear Siegler Inc., Monticello, 1970-72, structural engr., 1972-76, programmer, analyst, 1976-82; dir. ops. The Gazette Co., Cedar Rapids, Iowa, 1982-85; computer services mgr. Star Mfg. Co. (formerly Cuckler div. Lear Siegler Inc.), Monticello, 1985-86; informational services mgr. Thomas Proestler Co., Davenport, Iowa, 1986—. Mem. Data Processing Mgmt. Assn. (program chmn. Cedar Rapids chpt. 1983-84, bd. dirs. 1985). Lutheran. Home: RR 1 PO Box 99 Scotch Grove IA 52331-9744 Office: Star Mfg Co 102 W South St Monticello IA 52310

BROM, ROBERT H., bishop; b. Arcadia, Wis., Sept. 18, 1938. Ed., St. Mary's Coll., Winona, Minn., Gregorian U., Rome. Ordained priest Roman Catholic Ch., 1963, consecrated bishop, 1983. Bishop of Duluth Minn., 1983 . Home and Office: Chancery Office 215 W 4th St Duluth MN 55806 *

BROMELKAMP, MICHAEL LOUIS, controller; b. Ft. Dodge, Iowa, Feb. 27, 1953; s. Henry James and Elaine Theresa (Kuhl) B.; m. Patricia Marie Dietsch, June 11, 1977; children: Brian Michael, Scott Joseph. BA in Acctg., St. John's U., Collegeville, Minn., 1975; MBA, U. Minn., 1985.

CPA, Minn. Sr. acct. Arthur Andersen and Co., St. Paul, 1975-79; asst. controller Conwed Corp., St. Paul, 1979-83; controller I.C. System, Inc., Vadnais Heights, Minn., 1983—. Bd. dirs. Vadnais Heights Econ. Devel. Corp., 1985—. Mem. Am. Inst. CPA's, Minn. Soc. CPA's (mem. industry com. 1981—), Am. Philatelic Soc. Roman Catholic. Avocations: basketball, tennis, golf, softball, stamp collecting. Home: 4518 Oakhurst Ave Vadnais Heights MN 55110 Office: IC System Inc 444 E Hwy 96 Vadnais Heights MN 55127

BRONIATOWSKI, MICHAEL, otolaryngologist; b. Maidstone, Eng., Dec. 25, 1944; s. Andre C. and Irmgard (Fruchtzweig) B.; m. Sharon F. Grundfest, June 18, 1978; children: Daniel C., David A. MD, Faculty of Medicine, Paris, 1969. Diplomate Am. Bd. Otolaryngology. Practice medicine specializing in otorhinolaryngology Paris, 1975-76; resident Case Western Res. U. Hosps., Cleve., 1977-80; fellow head and neck surgery Cleve. Clinic, 1983-84; dir. otolaryngology St. Vincent Charity Hosp., Cleve.; instr. Case Western Res. U. 1980-83, asst. prof. 1984-86, asst. clin. prof. 1986—; adj. staff dept. artificial organs Cleve. Clinic Found. Fellow Am. Coll. Surgeons, Am. Acad. Otolaryngology, Head and Neck Surgery; mem. Assn. for Research in Otolaryngology, Am. Acad. Facial Plastic Reconstructive Surgery (assoc.). Avocations: piano, photography. Office: St Vincent Charity Hosp 2351 E 22d St Cleveland OH 44115

BRONN, DONALD GEORGE, radiation oncologist, medical researcher; b. Karlsruhe, W.Ger., Oct. 12, 1948; s. Count Jakov Ivanovich and Agnes (Pervak) Broschnovsky; came to U.S., 1950; m. Leslie Joan Boyle, Aug. 21, 1973; children—Jacob Alexander, Natasha Nisa. B.A., Ohio State U., 1972, M.S., 1976, Ph.D. in Cell Physiology, 1979, M.D., 1982. Grad. research assoc. in surgery Ohio State U., 1975-79, research coordinator Lab for Breast Cancer Research, Ohio State U. Hosps., 1977-85, research assoc. ultrasound and nuclear medicine divs., dept. radiology, 1980-82; asst. prof. radiation oncology Wayne State U., 1986-87; asst. prof. radiation therapy Med. Coll. Ohio; attending radiation oncologist Children's Hosp. Mich., Hutzel Hosp., Detroit Med. Ctr., Med. Coll. Ohio Hosps., ToledoSamuel J. Roessler Found. Med. Research fellow, 1980-82; Cancer Soc. fellow in clin. oncology, 1985-86; clin. instr. div. of radiation oncology, dept. radiology Ohio State U., 1982-85. Named to Landacre Soc. Ohio State U. Coll. Med., 1979, Outstanding Research Presentation, 1979; pres., 1981-82; grantee Am. Cancer Soc., Elsa U. Pardee Found., Bremer Found., 1975-85; recipient Nat. Student Research Forum 1st prize, 1979; Mead Johnson Excellence of Research award, 1979; Surgery award Ohio State U. Coll. Medicine, 1982, Robert M. Zollinger Research award, 1982; Am. Radium Soc. young oncologist travel grantee, 1985. Fellow Royal Micros. Soc.; mem. AAAS, AMA, Am. Soc. for Cell Biology, N.Y. Acad. Scis., Am. Coll. Radiology, Radiol. Soc. N. Am., Soc. for Magnetic Resonance Imaging, Am. Soc. Clin. Oncology, Radiation Research Soc., Am. Soc. Therapeutic Radiology and Oncology, Mich. State Med. Soc., Mich. Soc. Therapeutic Radiologists, Wayne County Med. Soc., Sigma Xi. Author: The Hormonal Characterization of Breast Cancer By Oxygen Consumption Levels, 1979; contbr. articles on cancer biology and medicine to profl. publs.; inventor Bronn intraoperative treatment unit for Microtron generated long distance electron beam radiation in the operative suite. Home: 4901 Susans Way Bloomfield Hills MI 48013 Office: Gershenson Radiation Oncology Ctr 3990 John R St Detroit MI 48201

BRONN, LESLIE JOAN BOYLE, radiologist; b. White Plains, N.Y., Aug. 23, 1948; d. Myles Joseph and Harriet Geib (Warburton) Boyle; m. Donald George Bronn, Aug. 21, 1973; children: Jacob Alexander, Natasha Nisa. BS, Ohio State U., 1970, MD, 1976. Diplomate Am. Bd. Radiology. Intern internal medicine Ohio State U. Hosp., Columbus, 1976-77, resident internal medicine, 1977-78, resident diagnostic radiology, 1978-81; chief radiology service VA Outpatient Clinic, Columbus, 1981-86; chief radiology service, diagnostic radiology and nuclear medicine services Allen Park (Mich.) VA Hosp. Med. Ctr., 1986—; clin. asst. prof. radiology Ohio State U. Coll. Medicine, 1981-86, Wayne State U. Sch. Medicine, 1986—. mem. Am. Coll. Radiology, Radiol. Soc. N.Am., Assn. VA Chiefs of Radiology, Am. Assn. Women Radiologists, Phi Beta Kappa, Alpha Lambda Delta. Office: VA Med Ctr Chief Radiology Service Outer Dr and Southfield Rd Allen Park MI 48101

BRONTON, ARNE WIGGO, designer; b. Esbjerg, Denmark, July 31, 1930; came to U.S., 1952, naturalized, 1957; s. Soren Peter and Camilla (Jensen) B.; degree in architecture, Tech. Coll., Esbjerg, 1949; postgrad. U. Chgo., spl. courses; m. Elsa Louise Drenning, Sept. 17, 1960; children—Christian, Allen. Founder, Crown Custom Designs, Inc., Barrington Hills, Ill., 1952-87, pres., chief exec. officer, chmn. bd., 1975-87; pres., chief exec. officer Crown Investments Ltd., 1986—; pres. Bank Bldg. Cons.; cons. fin. instns. Past pres., chmn. Danish Nat. Com.; bd. dirs. Royal Danish Guards, Danish Lang. Found., Sovereign Order St. John. Served to 2d lt. Royal Danish Guards, 1950-51. Decorated Knight of Malta, Yugoslav Commemorative War Cross, Knight Order Dannebrog (Denmark), Ordre de la Liberation (France), Badge of Ravna Gora, Royal Order White Eagle III, (Serbia); recipient bronze and gold medal in design, 1949-50. Mem. Pres.'s Assn., Am. Mgmt. Assn., AIA, Am. Soc. Interior Designers, Internat. Assn. Fin. Planners (bd. dirs.), Constrn. Specifications Inst., Exec. Club Chgo., Internat. Assn. Architects. Republican. Lutheran. Club: Quail Creek Country (Naples, Fla.). Lodges: Masons, Sertoma (life), Shriners, Rotary. Office: Crown Custom Design Inc 409 W County Line Rd Barrington Hills IL 60010

BROOK, GARY FRED, accountant; b. Chicago, Nov. 9, 1961; s. Marvin A. and Jeanne A. (Suhring) B.; m. Jeanette Marie Heniff, Oct. 12, 1985; 1 child, Sarah. CPA, Ill. Mem. staff Touche Ross & Co., Chgo., 1985—. Mem. Am. Inst. CPA's, Ill. CPA Soc. Avocations: microcomputers, photography, swimming. Office: Touche Ross & Co 111 E Wacker Dr Chicago IL 60601

BROOK, SUSAN G., state agency administrator; b. N.Y.C., Dec. 7, 1949; d. Alvin Ira and Sally (Behar) Greenberg. BA, Northwestern U., 1971; MA in Child Devel. and Pub. Adminstrn., Mich. State U., 1975. Community rep. Office Child Devel. HEW, Chgo., 1971-72; program asst. office of pres. OEO, Chgo., 1972-73; exec. coordinator Mich. 4-C Council Mich. Dept. Mgmt. and Budget, Lansing, 1973-80; adminstr. office interagy. transp. coordination Mich. Dept. Transp., Lansing, 1980-83; adminstr. freight div. Bur. Urban and Pub. Transp., Mich. Dept. Transp., Lansing, 1983—; chairperson legis. com. Mich. Council Family Relations, Lansing, 1976-77; mem. coalition on children and youth, Lansing, 1976-80; co-chairperson Mich. White House Conf. on Families, Lansing, 1979-80, gov's liaison Internat. Yr of the Child, Lansing, 1978-79; guest lectr. Mich. State U., East Lansing, 1976; inst. Lansing Community Coll., 1978; mem. curriculum devel. adv. com. Lansing community coll., 1979-80. Advisor neighborhood health clinic, Chgo., 1969; youth group advisor Shaare Tikvah Congregation, Chgo., 1967-71; campaign treas. city council candidate, East Lansing, Mich., 1981. Mem. Nat. Assn. Edn. Young Children, Mich. Assn. Edn. Young Children (hon.), Nat. Assn. State Dirs. Child Devel. (gubernatorial appointee), Soc. Women Transp., Women in State Gov., Nat. Assn. Female Execs., Nat. Conf. State Railway Ofcl., Mich. League Human Services, Animal Protection Inst., Am. Soc. Prevention of Cruelty to Animals, Ingham County Humane Soc., Greenpeace, Calif. Marine Mammal Ctr, 1985—. Avocations: horseback riding, cross country skiing, jogging, walking. Office: Mich Dept Transp 425 W Ottawa St Lansing MI 48909

BROOKE, DOLORES ANN, teacher, municipal government official; b. Livingston, Ill., July 27, 1937; d. Joseph Francis and Tillie (Pelko) DallaRiva; m. Eddie Wayne Brooke, Dec. 22, 1956; children: Todd Wayne, Tari Jo Brooke Cerentano. BS in Elem. Edn. with honors, So. Ill. U., Edwardsville, 1971; MS in Spl. Edn., So. Ill. U., 1975. Tchr. learning disabled Edwardsville Dist. 7, 1971-73, 3d grade tchr., 1973-74, 2d grade tchr., 1974—. Pres. Village of Livingston, 1985—; mem. PTA, PTO. Mem. NEA, Ill. Edn. Assn., Edwardsville Edn. Assn., Delta Kappa Pi. Democrat. Lutheran. Avocations: swimming, reading, bike riding, traveling, walking. Home: Box 82 442 S 3d Livingston IL 62058 Office: Village of Livingston Box 388 Livingston Ave Livingston IL 62058

BROOKE, PATRICK TEAL, controller; b. Ft. Worth, Tex., Jan. 22, 1953; s. Vinus Ray and Lela Mae (Teal) B.; m. Mary Kay Kirkendall, Jan. 26, 1977; children: Emily Elizabeth, Jeffrey Kirk. BBA, U. Tex., Arlington, 1979. CPA, Ill. Operator programmer Can.-Am. Resources Fund, Inc., Ft. Worth, 1973-74; programmer Shop-Rite Foods, Inc., Grand Prairie, Tex., 1974-76; systems analyst Tandy Corp., Ft. Worth, 1976-78; controller Golden Bros. Inc., Galesburg, Ill., 1979-82; pub. acct. Hofner & Hofner CPA's, Wheaton, Ill., 1982-84; controller Wheaton Coll., 1984—; cons. in field, Wheaton, 1984—. Bd. dirs. Marklund Children's Home, Bloomingdale, Ill., 1985—. Mem. Am. Inst. CPA's, Ill. CPA Soc. Republican. Avocations: tennis, cycling, reading. Home: 2102 Paddock Ln Wheaton IL 60187 Office: Wheaton Coll 501 E Seminary Ave Wheaton IL 60187

BROOKER, THOMAS KIMBALL, investment banker; b. Los Angeles, Oct. 1, 1939; s.Robert Elton and Sally Burton Harrison (Smith) B.; m. Nancy Belle Neumann, 1966; children: Thomas Kimball Jr., Isobel, Vanessa. BA in French Lit., Yale U., 1961; MBA, Harvard U., 1968. Assoc. in corp. fin. Morgan Stanley & Co., Inc., N.Y.C., 1968-73, v.p., 1973-75, mng. dir., 1976—; head Chgo. office Morgan Stanley & Co., Inc., 1978—; bd. dirs. Barbara Oil Co.; gov. Midwest Stock Exchange, 1980, vice chmn., 1986—. Mem. vis. com. Library at U. Chgo., Yale U. Pres. Council, 1980-84; assoc. fellow Saybrook Coll. Yale U.; bd. dirs. Lyric Opera Chgo., Ctr. for Am. Archeology, 1980-84, Alliance Francaise-Maison Francaise de Chgo., Chgo. Council Fgn. Relations; vice chmn., trustee Newberry Library; chmn. Yale U. Com. on Library, 1980-84; trustee Yale Library Assocs., chmn. 1976-79. Served as lt. USN, 1962-66. Mem. Securities Industry Assn. (exec. com. cen. states dist.), Conseil d' Administrn. Assn. Internationale de Bibliophilie. Home: 1500 N Lake Shore Drive Chicago IL 60610 Office: Morgan Stanley & Co Inc One Financial Pl 440 S LaSalle St Chicago IL 60605

BROOKS, CATHERINE MARIE, nurse, anesthetist; b. Harrison, Mich., Apr. 11, 1954; d. James Neil Brooks and Barbara Louise (Bies) Fogel. AS, Henry Ford Community Coll., 1975; student, Wayne State U., 1979—. Staff anesthetist Harper Grace Hosp., Detroit, 1972—; staff anesthetist, clin. instr. Detroit Receiving Hosp., 1984—. Mem. Am. Assn. Nurse Anesthetists. Democrat. Avocations: historic preservation, photography, sports. Office: Harper-Grace Hosps 18700 Meyers Detroit MI 48235

BROOKS, CHARLES JOSEPH, broadcasting executive; b. Youngstown, Ohio, Nov. 23, 1952; s. Charles Michael and Loretta Frances (Donnelly) B.; m. Leanne Baresch, Sept. 29, 1979; children: Matthew, Amanda, Charles. BBA, Youngstown U., 1976. Account exec. Sta. KXOL, Ft. Worth, 1976-77, Sta. KESS, Ft. Worth, 1977-78, Sta. WFAA, Dallas, 1978-80; gen. sales mgr. Sta. KLAT, Houston, 1980-85; v.p., gen. mgr. Sta. WIND, Chgo., 1985—. Mem. Radio Broadcasters of Chgo. Republican. Roman Catholic. Home: 119 N Main St Lombard IL 60148 Office: Sta WIND 625 N Michigan Ave Chicago IL 60611

BROOKS, CHRISTOPHER ALLEN, architect; b. Niles, Mich., July 5, 1952; s. Allen B. and Barbara J. (Smith) B.; m. Elizabeth K. Lockwood, May 24, 1975. BS, U. Mich., 1974, MArch, 1976. Registered architect, Mich. Jr. engineer, draftsman R.W. Petrie & Assoc., Benton Harbor, Mich., 1976-78; architect, draftsman Pearson Constrn., Benton Harbor, 1978-82; architect Sternaman Assocs., Watervliet, Mich., 1982-83; owner, architect Brooks Archtl., Benton Harbor, 1983—. Mem. Andrews U. Archtl. Com., Berrien Springs, Mich., 1986—, Downtown Devel. Authority, Benton Harbor, 1986. Mem. AIA (pres. Western Mich. chpt. 1986). Avocation: golf. Home: 235 Robbins Ave Benton Harbor MI 49022 Office: Brooks Archtl 204 W Main PO Box 215 Benton Harbor MI 49022

BROOKS, CYNTHIA PHYLLIS, clinical psychologist; b. N.Y.C., June 21, 1934; d. Abram and Bernice (Tunis) Shorr; m. Rodney A. Brooks, June 7, 1957 (div. Dec. 1981); children: David, Mark. AB, Bklyn. Coll., 1954; AM, Boston U., 1956; PhD, Marquette U., 1983. Lic. clin. psychologist, Wis. Research asst. Mass. Dept. Mental Health, Boston, 1956-58; mental health coordinator Met. State Hosp., Waltham, Mass., 1958-60; therapeutic tutor Boston, 1960-66; prin. psychologist Solomon Mental Health Ctr., Lowell, Mass., 1968-70; sr. psychologist Milw. Pub. Schs., 1970—; clin. psychologist Milw., 1983—. Mem. Am. Psychol. Assn., Wis. Psychol. Assn., Psychol. Assn. Milw. Pub. Schs., Phi Delta Kappa. Home and Office: 8460 N Fielding Rd Milwaukee WI 53217

BROOKS, EDWARD DAVID, engineering services manager; b. Duluth, Minn., May 28, 1942; s. Henry Oliver and Dorothy Carol (Molitor) B.; m. Cheryle Lynn Rebro, Aug. 31, 1968; children: Christopher David, Matthew Allyn. Diploma, Inst. Tech., Duluth, 1968; student, U. Minn., 1969-79. Drafter Horton Mfg., Mpls., 1968-70, designer, 1970-74, sr. designer, 1974-80, engring. services mgr., 1980—. Contbr. articles to Power Transmission Design mag., 1984, 1986. Patentee combination clutch-brake. Inventor robot brake. Mem. Soc. Automotive Engrs. (assoc.), Soc. Mfg. Engrs. (assoc.), Sports Car Club of Am. Lutheran. Home: 6506 Hickory St NE Fridley MN 55432 Office: Horton Mfg Co Inc PO Box 9455 Minneapolis MN 55440

BROOKS, EVANS BARTLETT, retired graphic arts company executive; b. New Albany, Ind., Jan. 28, 1900; s. William Wilson and Bertha (Evans) B.; m. Margaret Marby, Mar. 6, 1926; children: Marcia Jayne Brooks Browne, Sandra Lee Brooks Jordan. Student bus. adminstrn., Louisville YMCA Extension and Ind. U. Extension. Vice pres. Del. Engraving Co., Muncie, Ind., 1926-30, Ditzel-Brooks Co., Dayton, Ohio, 1931-32; v.p.-sec. Wayne Colorplate Co. Ohio, Dayton, 1932-37; pres., treas. Wayne Colorplate Co. Ohio, 1937-84; v.p., treas. Brooks Investment Co., Dayton, 1953-84; emeritus chmn. bd. Third Nat. Bank & Trust Co., Dayton. Charter mem. Dayton Area Progress Council, 1961; chmn. Montgomery County Bldg. Commn.; founder, mem. 1st pres. All- Dayton Com., 1945-47; past chmn. Montgomery County chpt. ARC; past pres. Dayton Philharmonic Assn.; mem., past chmn. Bd. Mental Retardation; trustee, exec. com. Air Force Mus.; trustee Dayton and Montgomery County Pub. Library (past pres.); pres. Dayton Art Inst., 1951-53; emeritus trustee U. Dayton. Mem. Am. Photoengravers Assn. (past pres.), Photo-Engravers Research Inst. (dir., past pres.), Dayton Printing Industry Assn. (past pres.), Dayton C. of C. (past pres.), Research and Engring. Council Graphic Arts (dir.), Newcomen Soc. Presbyterian (past pres. Ohio Bd. Home Missions; ch. elder). Clubs: Moraine Country, Engineers. Lodges: Masons, Rotary (past pres.). Home: 4365 Delco Dell Rd Dayton OH 45429 Office: 40 E 1st St Dayton OH 45402

BROOKS, FRANK MARSHALL, petroleum geologist; b. Wichita, Kans., Oct. 7, 1912; s. Herman O. and Stella M. (Thompson) B.; m. Carolyne Ann, Feb. 26, 1938 (dec. Feb. 1958); children—Stephanie Ann, Rodger Alan; m. Lena Mae Downs, Mar. 27, 1976. B.A., U. Wichita, 1934; postgrad. U. Iowa, 1936-37. Geologist, Gulf Oil Corp., Wichita, 1934-39, Indpls., 1939-43, Bridgeport Oil Co., Wichita, 1943-46; geologist El Dorado Refining Co., Kans., 1946-56, v.p., 1948-56; v.p., geologist Sterling Drilling Co., Hutchinson, Kans., 1956-58; ind. geologist, Wichita, 1958—. Mem. Wichita State U. Alumni Assn. (bd. dirs. 1980-86 , v.p. 1981-83), Kans. Geol. Soc. (pres. 1950), Soc. Ind. Profl. Earth Scientists (chpt. pres. 1974), Am. Inst. Profl. Geologists (chpt. pres. 1980), Shocker Alumni and Faculty Club (bd. dirs. 1981-84, sec. 1983-84), Wichita Petroleum Club (bd. dirs. and v.p. 1949-51). Republican. Congregationalist. Lodge: Masons (Wichita). Avocations: golfing; travel. Office: 1735 KSB Bldg Wichita KS 67202

BROOKS, GENE EDWARD, federal judge; b. Griffin, Ind., June 21, 1931; s. Claude Romelia and Martha Margaret (Crawford) B.;divorced; children: Marc, Gregory, Penny; m. Jan D. Gibson, Oct. 16, 1982; 1 child, Gene E. Jr. Bar: Ind. Pros. atty. Posey County, Ind., 1959-68; bankruptcy judge So. Dist. Ind., 1968-79, U.S. dist. judge, 1979-87, chief judge, 1987—; mem. faculty Fed. Jud. Ctr., apptd. to bankruptcy edn. com., 1987—; pres. Nat. Conf. Bankruptcy Judges. Contbr. articles to legal jours. Served with USMCR, 1953-55. Recipient Disting. Alumni award Ind. State U., Disting. Service cert. Fed. Bar Assn., Outstanding Service award Nat. Conf. Bankruptcy Judges. Mem. Ind. Bar Assn., Posey County Bar Assn., Vanderburgh County Bar Assn., VFW, Am. Legion. Democrat. Episcopalian. Clubs: Elks, Kiwanis. Office: U S Dist Ct 310 Federal Bldg 101 NW 7th St Evansville IN 47708

BROOKS, GLADYS SINCLAIR, public affairs consultant; b. Mpls.; d. John Franklin and Gladys (Phillips) Sinclair; student U. Geneva, Switzerland, 1935; B.A., U. Minn., 1936; LL.D., Hamline U., 1966; m. Wright W. Brooks, Apr. 17, 1941; children—Diane (Mrs. Roger Montgomery), John, Pamela (Mrs. Jean Marc Perraud). Dir. Farmer's and Mechanics Bank, 1973-82; mem. Met. Council, 1975-83; lectr. world affairs, 1939—; mem. Mpls. City Council, 1967-73; mem. Met. Airports Commn., 1971-74; pres. World Affairs Ctr. U. Minn., 1976-83; instr. continuing edn. for women U. Minn.; lectr. on world tours as Am. specialist U.S. Dept. State, 1959-60; pres. Brooks/Ridder & Assocs. Mem. Mpls. Charter Commn., 1948-51; pres. YWCA, 1953-57, mem. nat. bd., del. world meeting, Denmark; pres. Minn. Internat. Ctr., 1953-63; chmn. Minn. Women's Com. for Civil Rights, 1961-64; mem. U.S. Com. for UNICEF, 1959-68; mem. Gov.'s Adv. Com. Children and Youth, 1953-58, Minn. Adv. Com. Employment and Security, 1948-50; Midwest adv. com. Inst. Internat. Edn.; mem. nat. com. White House Conf. Children and Youth, 1960; chmn. Gov.'s Human Rights Commn., 1961-65; dir. Citizens Com. Delinquency and Crime, 1969-81; chmn. Mpls. Adv. Com. on Tourism, 1976-82, Ctr. Women in Govt.; vice chmn. Nat. Community Partnerships Seminars, 1977-82; mem. Midwest Selection Panel, White House Fellows, 1981. Del. Rep. Nat. Conv., 1952; state chmn. Citizens for Eisenhower, 1956; founder, pres. Rep. Workshop; co-chmn. Mpls. Bicentennial Commn., 1974-76; pres. Internat. Center for Fgn. Students; dir. Minn. Alumni Assn.; trustee United Theol. Sem., YWCA, Met. State U.; bd. dirs. Hamline U., Midwest China Ctr., Walker Health Services; mem. pres.'s adv. council St. Catherine's Coll. Recipient Centennial Women of Minn. award Hamline U., 1954; Woman of Distinction award AAUW, Mpls. 1956; Woman of Yr. award YWCA, 1973; Brotherhood award NCCJ, 1975; Service to Freedom award Minn. State Bar Assn., 1976; Community Leadership award YWCA, 1981. Mem. World Affairs Council (pres. 1942-44), Minn. LWV (dir. 1940-45), Mpls. Council Ch. Women (pres. 1946-48), Nat. Council of Chs. (mem. gen. bd., v.p. 1961-69), Minn. Council of Chs. (1st woman pres. 1961-64, Christian service award 1967), Mpls. Council of Chs. (v.p. 1946-48), United Ch. Women (bd. mgrs.), Minn. UN Assn. (dir.), Nat. League Cities (human resources steering com. 1972-73), Am. Acad. Polit. Sci., Mpls. C. of C., Minn. Women's Polit. Caucus, Minn. Women's Econ. Roundtable, AAUW, Women's Symphony Assn., Delta Kappa Gamma (hon.). Presbyn. Clubs: Horizon 100, Women's, Lafayette (Mpls.). Home: 5056 Garfield Ave S Minneapolis MN 55419

BROOKS, GWENDOLYN, author; b. Topeka, June 7, 1917; d. David Anderson and Keziah Corinne (Wims) B.; m. Henry L. Blakely, Sept. 17, 1939; children: Henry L., Nora. Grad., Wilson Jr. Coll., Chgo., 1936; L.H.D., Columbia Coll., 1964. Instr. poetry Columbia Coll., Chgo., Northeastern Ill. State Coll., Chgo.; mem. Ill. Arts Council; cons. in poetry Library of Congress, 1985-86. Author: poetry A Street in Bronzeville, 1945, Annie Allen, 1949, Maud Martha; novel, 1953, Bronzeville Boys and Girls; for children, 1956, The Bean Eaters; poetry, 1960, Selected Poems, 1963, In the Mecca, 1968, Riot, 1969, Family Pictures, 1970, Aloneness, 1971, To Disembark, 1981; autobiography Report From Part One, 1972, The Tiger Who Wore White Gloves, 1974, Beckonings, 1975, Primer for Blacks, 1980, Young Poets' Primer, 1981, Very Young Poets, 1983, The Near-Johannesburg Boy, 1986, Blacks, 1987. Named One of 10 Women of Year Mademoiselle mag., 1945; recipient award for creative writing Am. Acad. Arts and Letters, 1946; Guggenheim fellow for creative writing, 1946, 47; Pulitzer prize for poetry, 1950; Anisfield-Wolf award, 1969; named Poet Laureate of Ill., 1968. Mem. Soc. Midland Authors. Home: 7428 S Evans Ave Chicago IL 60619

BROOKS, HERBERT PAUL, hockey coach; b. St. Paul, Aug. 5, 1937; s. Herbert David and Pauline E. (Johnson) B.; m. Patricia Diane Brooks, Sept. 27, 1965; children: Daniel, Kelly. BA, U. Minn., 1962. Coach U. Minn., Mpls., 1972-79, U.S. Olympic Team, 1979-80, N.Y. Rangers-NHL, N.Y.C., 1981-85, St. Cloud (Minn.) State U., 1986-87, Minn. North Stars-NHL, Mpls., 1987—; salesman Jostens, Mpls., 1985-86. Home: 5423 Carlson Rd Shoreview MN 55126 Office: Minnesota North Stars 7901 Cedar Ave South Bloomington MN 55420

BROOKS, MICHAEL LYNN, advertising agency executive; b. Lafayette, Ind., Feb. 9, 1943; s. Ray Daniel and Velda Deane (Smith) B.; B.S., Ind. State U., 1965; postgrad. Ind. U., 1966. Spl. assignment writer Indpls. News, 1965-68; advt. dir. Eastern Express, Inc., Terre Haute, Ind., 1968-72; pres. CRE, Inc., Indpls., 1972-87, chmn. bd., 1972—, chief exec. officer, 1987—. Bd. dirs. Katherine Hamilton Mental Health Center, Inc., Terre Haute, 1980-84. Ford Found. grantee, 1966. Mem. Nat. Agri-Mktg. Assn., Ind. Fedn. Advt. Agys. (past dir.), Bank Mktg. Assn., Advt. Club Indpls. Clubs: Indpls. Press, Columbia, Skyline. Office: CRE Inc 400 Victoria Centre 22 E Washington Indianapolis IN 46204

BROOKS, NANCY TOFT, psychotherapist, hospital department administrator; b. Beloit, Wis., Sept. 13, 1945; d. George Andrew and Marilyn Vogel (Grulke) Toft; m. Charles Anthony Brooks, Nov. 1, 1968. BA, U. Wis., 1967; MSW, U. Ill., Chgo., 1975. Supr. Ill. Dept. Pub. Aid, Chgo., 1968-75; social worker Holy Cross Hosp., Chgo., 1975-79, dir. social work, 1979—; pvt. practice psychotherapy Chgo., 1980—; pres., bd. dirs. Southwest Adult Day Care, Evergreen Park, Ill., 1983—. Mem. Am. Hosp. Assn. (sec. 1986—), Nat. Assn. Social Workers, Soc. for Hosp. Social Work Dirs., Am. Continuity of Care, Ill. Continuity of Care (treas. 1984-86). Lutheran. Avocation: travel. Home: 3860 W 178 Pl Country Club Hills IL 60477 Office: Holy Cross Hosp 2701 W 68 St Chicago IL 60629

BROOKS, RICHARD EDGAR, JR., engineering consultant, educator; b. Chattanooga, Dec. 2, 1943; s. Richard E. and Phyllis (McCoy) B.; m. Karen J. Rasmussen, Dec. 27, 1969; children: Robin, Jon, James. BSME, Mich. State U., 1966; MSME, Mich. Tech. U., 1968. Registered profl. engr., Wis.; lic. profl. engr., Mich. Instr. Mich. Tech. U., Houghton, 1967-72; research engr. White Pine (Mich.) Copper, 1972-73; project engr. Rapidex Inc., Gloucester, Mass., 1973-78; sr. design engr. Harnischfeger Co., Escanaba, Mich., 1979-80; chief engr. Defiance Co., Calumet, Mich., 1980-81; proprietor Brooks Snyder Assn., Chassell, Mich., 1981—; pres. Brooks Sales and Engring., Inc.; tchr. pre-engring. Suomi Coll., Hancock, Mich. Mem. ASME, Nat. Soc. Profl. Engrs. (past pres., sec-treas. local chpt.), Soc. Mining Engrs., Am. Soc. Heating Refrigeration and Air-conditioning Engrs., Nat. Acad. Forensic Engrs. Lutheran. Club: Onigaming Yacht. Lodge: Kiwanis (v.p. 1985—, pres. 1986—). Home and Office: Paradise Rd Rt 1 Box 263 Chassell MI 49916

BROOKS, ROBERT ALEXANDER, oil company executive; b. Ft. Knox, Ky., Sept. 12, 1944; s. Robert and Meredith (Boller) B.; m. Carol Mateer, Aug. 13, 1966; children—Alison, Joy, Robert, Deborah. B.S., U. Ill., 1966; M.S., La. State U., 1969, Ph.D., 1970. Assoc. La. Water Resources Research Inst., Baton Rouge, 1966-70; scientist Conoco, Ponca City, Okla., 1970-74; team leader uranium exploration U.S. Geol. Survey, Denver, 1974-77; v.p. minerals Energy Res. Group, Wichita, Kans., 1977-82, BHP Petroleum (Americas), v.p. oil exploration, 1982-86; pres. Resource Masters Assocs., Wichita, 1986—; chief exec. officer Rio Gold Mining Ltd., 1987—; rep. uranium resource com. UN, Rome, 1976. Contbr. articles to profl. jours. Mem. Am. Assn. Petroleum Geologists, Soc. Econ. Geologists, Denver Regional Exploration Geologists (pres. 1977-80), Kans. Geol. Soc. Republican. Presbyterian. Clubs: Wichita Country, Wichita; Hiwan (Evergreen, Colo.). Avocations: skiing, tennis, swimming, scuba. Home: 646 Edgewater St Wichita KS 67230 Office: Resource Masters Assocs 646 Edgewater Suite 100 Wichita KS 67230

BROOKS, ROGER ALAN, political scientist; b. Ann Arbor, Mich., Aug. 9, 1944; s. Warren Wilfred and Sylvia May (Burrell) B.; B.A., U. Mich., 1966; postgrad. U. Strathclyde, Glasgow, Scotland, 1969-70; Ph.D. (NDEA fellow), Mich. State U., 1973; m. Ronnie Lee Durchlag, May 8, 1966; children—Kirsten, Russell. Instr. polit. sci. U. Fla., Gainesville, 1970-71; asst. prof. polit. sci. Macalester Coll., St. Paul, 1971-78; adj. prof. polit. sci. U. Minn., Mpls., 1978-82, Augsburg Coll., Mpls., 1979-82; prin. program evaluator Minn. Office of Legis. Auditor, St. Paul, 1978-84, dep. legis. auditor, 1984—. Mem. St. Paul Cable Communications Bd., 1979-81, St. Paul Heritage Preservation Commn., 1986—; trustee Actors Theatre, St. Paul, 1986—. Woodrow Wilson fellow, 1969-70; European Parliamentary fellow, 1977-78; William Warner Bishop prize U. Mich., 1965. Mem. Am. Polit. Sci. Assn., Minn. Polit. Sci. Assn. (mem. exec. com. 1978-80), Am. Soc. for Public Adminstrn., Am. Evaluation Assn., Citizens League, Sierra Club (vice chmn. Northstar chpt. 1979-81). Home: 1671 Pinehurst Ave Saint Paul MN 55116 Office: 122 Veterans Service Bldg Saint Paul MN 55155

BROOKS, ROGER KAY, insurance company executive; b. Clarion, Iowa, Apr. 30, 1937; s. Edgar Sherman and Hazel (Whipple) B.; m. Marcia Rae

Ramsay, Nov. 19, 1955; children—Michael, Jeffrey, David. B.A. magna cum laude, U. Iowa, 1959. With Central Life Assurance Co., Des Moines, 1964—; asst. sec. Central Life Assurance Co., 1964-68, v.p., 1968-70, exec. v.p., 1970-72, pres., 1972—; bd. dirs. Interstate Assurance Co. Bd. dirs. Iowa Meth. Med. Ctr., Drake U., Des Moines, Des Moines Art Ctr. Fellow Soc. Actuaries; mem. Greater Des Moines C. of C. (1st vice chmn.), Actuaries Club of Des Moines (past pres.), Phi Beta Kappa. Presbyterian (elder). Club: Des Moines (past pres.). Home: 300 Walnut Des Moines IA 50309 Office: 611 5th St Des Moines IA 50309

BROOKS, STEPHEN EDWARD, financial planner; b. Kansas City, Mo., Mar. 31, 1952; s. John R. and Blanche S. (Page) B.; m. Linda Marie Regan, Oct. 11, 1980. BS in Edn., U. Mo., 1975. Energy info. coordinator utilities City of Springfield, Mo., 1977-84; employee involvement facilitator Lily Tulip, Inc., Springfield, 1985-86; fin. planner First Fin. Planners, Inc., Springfield, 1986—. Cons. Mayor's Energy Task Force, Springfield, 1983-84, mem. traffic adv. bd., Springfield, 1987—. Democrat. Club: Ozark Mountain Ridgerunners (treas., bd. dirs. 1984—). Avocations: running, traveling, reading. Home: 901 E University Springfield MO 65807 Office: First Fin Planners Inc 1300B E Sunshine Springfield MO 65804

BROOKS, WILLIAM EMMETT, JR., editor, publisher; b. Mobile, Ala., Jan. 1, 1922; s. W. Emmett and Catherine (Ryan) B.; m. Edward Archibald, Nov. 18, 1944; children: William E., Priscilla, Rebecca, Jordan E. BA, U. Ala., 1943. Mng. editor Brewton (Ala.) Standard, 1946-58; editorial writer Indpls. Star, 1958-64; exec. editor Vincennes (Ind.) Sun-Comml., 1964-78, editor, pub., 1978—. Trustee Good Samaritan Hosp., Vincennes, 1987—, U. So. Ind., Evansville, 1985—. Served to comdr. USNR, 1941-46. Mem. Am. Soc. Newspaper Editors, Am. Newspaper Pubs. Assn., Ala. Press Assn. (pres. 1953), Hoosier State Press Assn. (pres. 1976), Vincennes Antique and Hist. Soc. (pres. 1976), Ind. AP Mng. Editors (pres. 1974). Methodist. Club: Indpls. Press (pres. 1963). Lodge: Rotary (dist. gov. Ind. 1981, pres. Vinciennes 1979). Avocations: music, history, naval affairs. Office: Vincennes Sun-Comml 702 Main St Vincennes IN 47591

BROOMES, EDWARD LOUIS, physician and surgeon; b. Morahwhanna, Guyana, Nov. 17, 1913; came to U.S., 1935; s. Charles Thomas Wesley and Sarah Rebecca (Hamilton) B.; m. Anna Leatha Brown, Dec. 4, 1946; children: Claude, Crystal. BS, Howard U., 1939, MD, 1942; LLD (hon.), Loyola, Chgo., 1981, Calumet Coll., Whiting, Ind., 1986. Intern Homer G. Phillips Hosp., St. Louis; resident St. Mary's Infirmity Hosp., St. Louis; practice gen. medicine East Chicago, Ind., 1945—; physician Lakeside Med. Clinic, East Chicago, 1957—; dep. coroner Lake County, Ind., 1968-76; mem. staff St. Catherin's Hosp.; mem. East Chicago Bd. Health, 1951-72, past pres., organizer 1st multi-zonal system of immunization, 1963; mem. East Chicago Bd. Safety, 1973-77, pres. 1975-77, pres. Northwest Ind. Naval Adv. Council, 1968. Patentee snoring prevention device. Scout master Boy Scouts Am., East Chicago, 1948-56; organizer East Chicago Jr. Police Patrol, 1968; founder No. Ind, Polit. Action Alliance, 1968, pres., 1968—; bd. dirs. Lake Area United Way, various other community orgns.; organizer East Chicago Combined Health Orgn., 1976. Numerous awards for service including Prince Hall Freedom award for Jurisdiction of Ind., 1973, Humanitatian award East Chicago Women's Club, 1974, Golden Arrow Achievement award Gov. of Guyana, 1979. Fellow Internat. Coll. Surgeons; mem. NAACP, Am. West Indian Assn. (pres. 1950-60), Frontiers Club (pres. 1960, organizer 1st overseas chpt. Guyana), Alpha Phi Alpha. Lodges: Masons (3d degree), Shriners, Consistory (32 degree). Pioneer in civil rights movement. Home: 2301 Lituanica East Chicago IN 46312 Office: Lakeside Med Clinic 2402 Broadway East Chicago IN 46312

BROOMFIELD, TYREE SIMS, police chief, consultant, lecturer; b. Feb. 11, 1938; s. Tyree Sims and Emma (Anderson) B.; m. Geraldine Jackson, July 2, 1966; 1 child, Tyree Sims, III. B.A., Central State U., 1973; H.H.D. (hon.), Wilberforce U., 1983. Intergroup relations specialist human relations dept., City of Dayton, Ohio, 1969-70; adminstrv. asst. to police chief Dept. of Police, City of Dayton, 1970-72, dir. conflict mgmt., 1970, supt., 1972-76, dep. dir., 1976-83, dir., chief of police, 1983—; cons. U.S. Dept. Justice, Washington, 1969—; bd. dirs. Nat. Orgn. Human Rights Workers, 1969-74; mem. Nat. Minority Council on Criminal Justice, Washington, 1976-80; charter bd. mem. Nat. Orgn. Police/Community Relations Officers. Contbr.: Police and the Behavioral Sciences, 1974; Police Community Relations, 1974; The Inequality of Justice, 1982. 2d v.p. ARC, Dayton, 1976—; chmn. personnel com. Dayton Art Inst., 1979—; bd. dirs. Montgomery County Council on Aging, 1980-83; bd. trustees Dayton Soc. Natural History, 1984—. Named One of Top Ten Outstanding Young Men, Greater Dayton Area Jaycees, 1969, Outstanding Young Man, 1969; Exec. of Yr., Dayton Area Exec. Club, 1983; recipient Brotherhood award Frontier's Internat., 1972. Mem. Am. Arbitration Assn. (panelist 1972-75), Internat. Assn. Chief of Police, Ohio Assn. Chiefs of Police, Nat. Orgn. Black Law Enforcement Execs. (charter). Democrat. Mem. African Methodist Episcopal Ch. Club: Boule. Lodge: Rotary. Home: 4501 Greenleaf Dr Dayton OH 45417 Office: Dept Police City of Dayton 335 W 3d St Dayton OH 45402

BROOMFIELD, WILLIAM S., congressman; b. Birmingham, Mich., Apr. 28, 1922; s. S.C. and Fern (Taylor) B.; m. Jane Thompson, 1951; children: Susan, Nancy, Barbara. Student, Mich. State U. Mem. Mich. Ho. of Reps., 1948, 50, 52, Mich. State Senate, 1954, 85th to 100th congresses from 19th Dist. Mich., Washington, 1957—; Congl. adviser to U.S. delegation to Geneva Disarmament Conf., 1970, 71, 73; vice chmn. com. fgn. affairs; mem. small bus. com.; mem. select com. to investigate the Iran/Contra Arms Sales; mem. commn. on the Ukrainian Famine; apptd. by pres. U.S. Ambassador U.N. 22d Gen. Assembly. 1967, congl. advisor Nat. Bipartisan Commn. on Cen. Am., 1983, mem. comm. on security and econ. assistance, 1983, congl. advisor U.S. Delegation 2d Spl. Session U.S. Gen. Assembly on Disarmament, 1982, Counicl Ministers Orgn. for Econ. Cooperation and Devel., 1979; presl. commn. mem. orgn. govt. on the conduct fgn. policy, 1975; congl. advisor U.S. delegation 2d Internat. Conf. Assistance to refugees in Africa., 1985; del. Strategic Arms Limitations Talks, 1977-80, NATO, 1955, 60, 73-80, 82, 85—, alt. del., 1984, U.N. Law Sea Adv. Com., 1976-77, 78-82, Interparliamentary Union Conf., 1980-82, U.S. Conf. on Sci. and Tech. for Devel., 1979, U.N. Pleding Session on Cambodian Relief, 1979, U.S. Nat. Commn. for the U.N. Edn., Scientific and Cultural Orgn., 1961-62; mem. Can.-U.S. Interparliamentary Conf., 1961-64, 67-70, 72, 78-80, 83-84, 86—, Mex.-U.S. Interparliamentary Conf., 1973-74, Korea-U.S. Interparliamentary Group. 1967-74, U.K.-U.S. Interparliamentary Conf., 1962. Mem. Mich. Ho. of Reps., 1948-54, Mich. Senate, 1954-56. Mem. Am. Legion, Oakland County C. of C. (life). Presbyterian. Clubs: Republican. Capitol Hill (pres. 1970-74). Lodges: Mason, Odd Fellow, Optimist, Lion, Shriners. Home: 5750 Whethersfield Ln Birmingham MI 48010 Office: US House of Reps 2306 Rayburn House Office Bldg Washington DC 20515

BRORSEN, B(ARTON) WADE, agricultural economist, educator; b. Perry, Okla., July 6, 1957; s. Bart Williams and Lanora Ann (Lowry) B.; m. Emily Kathleen Davidson, July 17, 1982; children: Kurt Ryan, Russell Charles. BS, Okla. State U., 1979, MS, 1980; PhD, Tex. A&M U., 1983. Research asst. Okla. State U., Stillwater, 1979-80, Tex. A&M U., College Sta., 1980-83; asst. prof. Purdue U., West Lafayette, Ind., 1983—. Contbr. articles to profl. jours. Ctr. for the Study Futures Markets grantee 1983, Chgo. Bd. Trade grantee 1984. Mem. Am. Assn. Agrl. Economists, Econometric Soc., Am. Statistical Assn., So. Assn. Agrl. Economists, Am. Fin. Assn., Phi Kappa Phi. Baptist. Home: 10 Wake Robin Ct West Lafayette IN 47906 Office: Purdue U Dept Agrl Econs West Lafayette IN 47907

BROSE, JOHN ADOLPH, medical educator; b. Teaneck, N.J., Oct. 6, 1950; s. Adolph Dahlke and Mary Wilhelmina (Quattlebaum) B.; m. Linda Diane Way, Aug. 20, 1972; children: Steven William, Christine Marie. DO, Tex. Coll. Osteo. Medicine, 1976; postdoc. fellow, Ohio State U., 1985-86. Diplomate Am. Bd. Family Practice. Resident Scott (AFB Ill.) Med. Ctr., 1979, resident faculty, 1979-82; assoc. prof. Ohio U., Athens, 1982—, head academic tng. program, dir. family medicine fellowship program, 1983—; clin. asst. prof. coll. medicine Ohio State U., 1985—. Served to maj. USAF, 1976-82. Named Outstanding Instr. Am. Med. Women's Assn., 1984, Family Medicine Club, 1984, Sigma Sigma Phi Honor Soc., 1983, 86. Fellow Am. Acad. Family Physicians; mem. Am. Osteo. Assn., Am. Coll. Gen. Practice (mem. undergrad. com. 1982—), Ohio Acad. Family Physicians (pres. Hocking Valley chpt.). Home: 925 Beechwood Dr Athens OH 45701 Office: Ohio U Coll Osteo Medicine Athens OH 45701

BROSE, MERLE LEVERNE, physician; b. Cedar Falls, Iowa, Aug. 23, 1922; s. Robert Lisle and Amy Belle (Shedd) B.; B.S., U. Wis., 1943; M.D., 1946; m. Phyllis Marie Magill, Jan. 10, 1948; children—Linda (Mrs. Steven Kleinsteiber), Cheryl (Mrs. William Zieman), Pamela (Mrs. Thomas Zembal), Sandra (Mrs. Gerald Jackson), William. Intern, Columbia Hosp., Wilkinsburg, Pa., 1946-47, resident in surgery, 1947-48; gen. practice medicine, Irwin, Pa., 1950-63; med. dir. Nat. Union Ins. Co., Pitts., 1962-63; gen. practice medicine, Menomonee Falls, Wis., 1963-65; physician Health Service, U. Wis., Madison, 1965—; mem. faculty U. Wis. Med. Sch., 1965—. Served to capt. USAF, 1948-50. Mem. U.S. Power Squadrons (Madison squadron sec. 1969, treas. 1970, adminstrv. officer 1971, exec. officer, 1972, dist. adminstrv. officer 1972, comdr. 1973, grade Navigator 1970, dist. exec. officer 1974, dist. comdr, 1975). Club: Four Lakes Yacht (commodore 1978) (Madison). Lodges: Masons, Shriners (pres. Shrine Concert Band). Home: 4517 Gregg Rd Madison WI 53705 Office: 1552 University Ave Madison WI 53705

BROSE, PHYLLIS MARIE, nurse; b. Stewartsville, Pa., Sept. 20, 1925; d. George Allan and Roberta Fern (Lintner) Magill; R.N., Columbia Hosp. Sch. Nursing, Wilkinsburg, Pa., 1946; certificate Sch. Anesthesia St. Francis Hosp., Pitts., 1948; m. Merle LaVerne Brose, Jan. 10, 1948; children—Linda Brose Kleinsteiber, Cheryl Brose Zieman, Pamela Brose Zembal, Sandra Brose Jackson, William. Nurse, Columbia Hosp., 1946-47, anesthetist, 1948, staff nurse, 1949-50; nursing supr., coordinator dialysis U. Wis. Hosp., Madison, 1966—. Mem. med. and sci. bd. Kidney Found. Wis., 1970—; mem. adv. council Nat. Center Health Care Tech.; bd. dirs. S. Central chpt. Wis. Kidney Found., 1980-81; mem. Network 13 Coordinating Council End-Stage Renal Disease, Inc. Recipient Exceptional Performance award in nursing U. Wis., 1977. Mem. Am. Assn. Nephrology Nurses and Technicians (pres. Wis. chpt. 1978-79), Am. nephrology Nurses Assn. (exec. bd. network 13 1985-86). Club: Four Lakes Yacht. Home: 4517 Gregg Rd Madison WI 53705 Office: 600 Highland Ave Madison WI 53706

BROSHEARS, KEITH MACER, dentist; b. Terre Haute, Ind., Dec. 14, 1948; s, Kenneth P. and Geraldine (Maler) B.; m. Donnette Jean Yenne, Dec. 10, 1982; children: Shelly L'Dee, James Lee, Robert Evan, Brian Keith. BA, DePauw U., 1971; DDS, Ind. U., 1976. Dentist Linton (Ind.) Dental Clinic, 1976—; prin. Linton Dental Lab., 1979—; medical staff Greene County Gen. Hosp., Linton, 1976—; dental cons. PSC, Inc., Madison, Wis., 1983—. Author: How Tibbar Learned to Fly, 1971 (Lit. Excellance award 1971). Councilman Greene County, Bloomfield, 1978-82. DePauw U. scholar, 1967-71; State of Ind. Hoosier scholar, 1967-71; Robert Woods Johnson fellow, 1971-76. Mem. ADA, Internat. Coll. Oral Implantology, Ind. Dental Assn., Greene Dist. Dental Soc. Republican. Lodge: Rotary, Elks, Moose. Avocations: electronics, piloting, scuba diving. Home: PO Box 144 Linton IN 47441 Office: Linton Dental Clinic 290 A St SE PO Box 675 Linton IN 47441-0675

BROST, EILEEN MARIE, pastoral minister; b. Medford, Wis., July 18, 1909; d. Peter and Pauline (Rudolph) B. BA, Loyola U., 1939, MEd, 1970; MA, St. Xavier U., 1954; postgrad. Alverno Coll., Milw. State Tchrs. Coll., DePaul U., Lewis U., Marquette U., Alfred Adler Inst., Chgo., Marylhurst Coll., Oreg. Cert. tchr., Ill., Wis. Joined Sch. Sisters of St. Francis, Roman Cath. Ch., 1925; tchr. various locations, Ill., Oreg. and Wis., 1927-68; religious edn. coordinator St. Anne's Parish, Barrington, Ill., 1968-72; guidance counselor, various schs., Chgo. Pub. Sch. System and Chgo. Archdiocese, 1972-85; parish minister, 1982—. Active parish orgns. Roman Catholic. Home and Office: 8000 S Linder Burbank IL 60459-2064

BROTBECK, GEORGE NATHAN, software company executive; b. Chattanooga, July 30, 1946; s. Charles Bourbon and Eva Mae (Watkins) B.; m. Mary Emeline Wise, Feb. 1, 1969 (div. Sept. 1974); m. Mary Jane Adams, Feb. 27, 1978; children: Rebekah Kelly, Sarah Elizabeth. BA in Math., U. Chattanooga, 1969; MA in Math., U. N.Mex., 1973, postgrad., 1975. Staff mem. Los Alamos (N.Mex.) Nat. Lab, 1969-76; sr. programmer analyst Edison Community Coll., Ft. Myers, Fla., 1976-78; supr. engring. software Gen. Dynamics, Pomona, Calif., 1978-80; mgr. mktg. and customer support Harris Computer Systems div., Ft. Lauderdale, Fla., 1980-81; group software mgr. Digital Equipment Corp., Atlanta, Ga., 1981-85; v.p. info. systems Colwell Systems Inc., Champaign, Ill., 1985-87; dir. systems and ops. Addamax Corp., Champaign, 1987—; instr. Calif. Poly. Inst., Pomona, 1979. Mem. Am. Mgmt. Assn., Am. Prod. and Inventory Control Soc., Data Processing Mgmt. Assn., Assn. for Systems Mgmt. Democrat. Methodist. Lodge: Rosicrucians. Avocations: golf, tennis, reading science fiction novels, home computing, singing. Home: 406 Arbours Dr Savoy IL 61874 Office: Addamax Corp 2009 Foxlane Champaign IL 61820

BROTHERS, DELORES MAY, controller; b. Evansville, Ind., June 12, 1926; d. Joseph Gilbert and Loretta Katherine (Heinz) Cook; m. Damian Louis Brothers, July 24; children—Jerry, Ronald, Nancy. A.A., Lockyears Bus. Coll., 1965; B.S., U. Evansville, 1972. Tax acct. Al Umbach C.P.A. Co., Evansville, 1967-69, Klein Acctg. Co., Evansville, 1969-72; with Evana Tool & Engring., Inc., Evansville, 1972—, controller, 1983—; tchr. cost acctg. Ind. State U., Evansville; cons. to small bus. firms. Active Freedom Festival, YWCA fund raising, ARC blood bank drive. Named Jr. Achievement Leader, 1981. Mem. Am. Soc. Women Accts. (mem. yr. award 1983), Am. Inst. Corp. Controllers, Nat. Assn. Accts. Roman Catholic. Clubs: Altrusa Internat. Bus. Profl. Women's (Evansville). Office: 5825 Old Boonville Hwy Evansville IN 47715

BROTHERTON, WILLIAM JAMES, optometrist; b. Keokuk, Iowa, Nov. 22, 1947; s. Walter Boley and Marline Margaret (Horn) B.; m. Rita Lynn Shapiro, Jan. 1, 1972; children: Amy Rachel, James Matthew. BA, Culver-Stockton Coll., Canton, Mo., 1969; postgrad., N.E. Mo. State U., 1970; BS, Ind. U., 1972, OD, 1974. Pvt. practice optometry Nashville, Ind., 1974-80; optometrist, dept. head Hamilton (Mo.) Med. Ctr., 1981—. Mem. Am. Optometric Assn., N.W. Mo. Optometric Soc. Lodge: Lions. Avocations: music, antique collecting. Home: PO Box 205 501 E Dudley St Hamilton MO 64644 Office: Hamilton Med Ctr PO Box 246 Cross St Hamilton MO 64644

BROTINE, BERT ALLEN, sales executive; b. Chgo., Nov. 18, 1934; s. Samuel and Gertrude Ida (Barr) B.; m. Nanette Barbara Firk, May 29, 1960; children: Howard, Jill. BS in Bus. Mgmt., Chgo. City Coll., 1959; diploma, Dale Carnegie, Chgo., 1960. Salesman Northwestern Supplies, Chgo., 1963-65; gen. mgr. Vibrant Products Corp., Chgo., 1965-79; sales mgr. Prestype Corp., South Orange, N.J., 1979-82; regional sales mgr. Morilla Corp. div. Ampad, Holyoke, Mass., 1982-84; nat. sales mgr. Ill. Bronze Paint Co., Lake Zurich, 1984—. Bd. dirs. Leukemia Research Found., Morton Grove, Ill., 1966—. Served as sgt. U.S. Army, 1952-58. Mem. Nat. Art Materials Trade Assn., Associated Creative Craft Industries. Democrat. Jewish. Lodge: B'nai Brith (pres. Northbrook chpt. 1980-82). Avocations: bowling, fishing, car racing. Home: 1035 Longaker Rd Northbrook IL 60062 Office: Ill Bronze Paint Co 300 E Main St Lake Zurich IL 60047

BROUGHTON, KATHY ANN, tax service executive; b. Scott AFB, Ill., July 27, 1959; d. Walter Merritt and Jeanette Marie (Boatwright) Wooters; m. Ronnie Ray Broughton, July 16, 1977 (div. Nov. 1982); children: Amy Michelle, Bethany Ann. Cert. tax practitioner. Machine operator Primo Pants, Inc., Versailles, Mo., 1983-84; owner, operator Tax Service, Versailles, 1984—; clk., Morgan County Assessor's Office, 1986-87, sec., 1987—; client asst. Mo. Ozarks Econ. Opportunity Corp., Richland, Mo., 1985. Vice pres. Head Start program, 1984-85, pres., 1985-86. Mem. United Pentecostal Ch. Avocations: sewing, notary public. Office: Kathy Broughton's Tax Service 503 W DeKalb Versailles MO 65084

BROUK, J. JOHN, bldg. and insulation material mfg. co. exec.; b. St. Louis, Apr. 30, 1917; s. Joseph John and Marie (Hilgert) B.; B.S. in Ceramic Engring., U. Ill., 1938: m. Ruthe Garman, Nov. 1, 1946; children—Joseph John, Joanne Marie. Refractory researcher metallurgy dept. Naval Research Lab., Washington, 1943-46; pres. Precast Slab & Tile Co., St. Louis, 1951-54, Perlite Insulation Co., St. Louis, 1951-54; v.p. Fed. Cement Tile Co., Chgo., 1954-57; pres. Brouk Co., St. Louis, 1957—; pres. Perlite Inst., 1950-52; nat. sales agt. perlite ore Great Lakes Carbon Co., 1952-72, Grefco, Inc., 1966-72. Bd. dirs. Mt. St. Rose Hosp., St. Louis Conservatory and Sch. for Arts, Multiple Sclerosis Soc.; mem. nat. bd. Young Audiences. Mem. Internat. Vermiculite Assn. (pres. 1976-80), Young Presidents Orgn. (pres. St. Louis chpt. 1959, lectr. mgmt. seminars). Contbr. numerous articles on perlite insulation to profl. and trade jours.; patentee perlite brick veneer wall panel; developer combined perlite and vermiculite concrete and corrugated metal roof-deck system. Office: Brouk Co 1367 S Kings Hwy Saint Louis MO 63110

BROWER, KENT EVERETT, religious educator; b. Calgary, Alta., Can., Sept. 4, 1946; s. Barry Howard and Jean Agnes (Dixon) B.; m. Francine Louise Taylor, Aug. 25, 1967; children: Deirdre René, Derek Leigh. B Sacred Lit., Can. Nazarene Coll., 1967; MA, Eastern Nazarene Coll., 1969; PhD, U. Manchester, Eng., 1978. Lectr., bursar Brit. Isles Nazarene Coll., Manchester, Eng., 1974-79; assoc. prof. bibl. language and lit. Can. Nazarene Coll., Winnipeg, Man., 1979—; com. mem. Ch. of the Nazarene, Kansas City, Mo., 1982—; lectr. U. Winnipeg, 1980-81, U. Man., 1983—; vis. prof. Africa Nazarene Theol. Coll., Johannesburg, Republic of South Africa, 1983, Nazarene Theol. Seminary, Kansas City, 1984. Pres. Constituency Orgn. Polit. Party, Wainwright, Alta., 1972-73. Mem. Soc. Bibl. Lit., Can. Soc. Bibl. Study, Tyndale Fellowship, Wesleyan Theol. Soc. Home: 47 Quincy Bay, Winnipeg, MB Canada R3T 4K2 Office: Can Nazarene Coll, 1301 Lee Blvd, Winnipeg, MB Canada R3T 2P7

BROWN, ALAIN B., account manager; b. Tehran, Iran, May 10, 1955; s. Donald Spencer and Micheline (Charbonnel) B.; m. Marilyn Simpson, Aug. 16, 1980. BA in Internat. Relations, U. Colo., Boulder, 1978; M in Internat. Mgmt., Am. Graduate Sch. Internat. Mgmt., Glendale, Ariz., 1981. Bus. analyst Allis Chalmers Corp., Milw., 1981-83; planning analyst Amcast Indsl. Corp., Dayton, Ohio, 1983-84, corp. mgr. mktg. planning and analysis, 1984-86, account mgr., 1986—; asst. to chmn. transp. com. Area Progress Council, Dayton, 1985—. Mem. N. Am. Soc. for Corp. Planners, Soc. Am. Engrs.. Office: Amcast Indsl Corp 3931 S Dixie Ave Kettering OH 45439

BROWN, ANDREA KAYE, psychotherapist, consultant; b. Chgo., Jan. 3, 1951; d. William Samuel and Rudelle (Edmonds) Anderson; divorced; 1 child, Adam Leyland Brown. BS, U. Wis., 1972; MEd, U. Ill., 1978; MA, Columbia Coll., 1986. Registered social worker, Ill.; registered dance movement therapist. Tchr. Visitation High Sch., Chgo., 1972-79; clin. coordinator West Side Orgn., Chgo., 1979-81; clin. therapist Englewood Health Services, Chgo., 1981—; cons. Emerson Payne Assocs., Chgo., 1985—, Catholic Charities, Chgo., 1986, Columbia Coll., Chgo., 1987. Mem. Am. Dance Therapy Assn. (program chmn. nat. conv. 1986), Phi Kappa Phi, Alpha Kappa Alpha. Avocations: jewelry making, modern dance.

BROWN, ANDREW, JR., mechanical and chemical engineer; b. Tuscaloosa, Ala., June 21, 1949; s. Andrew Lee and Willie Mae (Williams) B.; m. Malaney L. Gilliard, Apr. 2, 1972. BS in ChemE, Wayne State U., 1971, MBA in Fin. and Mktg., 1975; MS in Mech. Engring., U. Detroit, 1978. Registered profl. engr., Mich. Engring. supr. energy mgmt. and plant engring. tech. ctr. Gen. Motors Corp., Warren, Mich., 1975-80, mgr. adminstrv. projects and spl. programs mfg. staff, 1980-81, plant estimating and investment tax credit analyst, dept. head, 1981-84, mgr. staff orgnl. studies, 1984-85, mgr. Saturn Car Facilities, 1985-87, mgr. advanced facilities engring. and planning, 1987—; adj. instr. profl. devel. in engring., U. Mich., Dearborn, 1978-82; mem., past chmn. State of Mich. Bd. Registration for Profl Engrs., Lansing, 1978-85; bd. dirs. Urban Cons., Inc., Detroit, 1978—. Contbr. articles to profl. jours.; patentee in field. Promoter Blair Gravity Wall System, 1969-71; mem. Wayne State U. Presdl. Selection Adv. Com., 1970-71; coordinator HUD Model City Program, 1969-71; cons. Mayor's Com. on Human Resources, 1969-71; campaign mgr. C. Martin for County Freeholder State of N.J., 1971; past pres. Tutorial Commn., 1968-71. Mem. NSPE, Mich. Soc. Profl. Engrs. (sec. 1986—), Engring. Soc. Detroit (Young Engr. of Yr. award 1982), Soc. Engrs. and Applied Scientists (founder, past pres., Leadership and Dedication award 1983), Nat. Council Engring. Examiners (Contribution and Achievement award 1984), Soc. Mfg. Engrs., Wayne State U. Engring. Alumni Assn. (past pres.), Tau Beta Pi. Avocations: fishing, racquetball, basketball, baseball, golf. Home: 37534 Colonial Dr S Westland MI 48185

BROWN, ANTHONY LEMAR, revenue rate analyst, accountant; b. St. Louis, July 26, 1957; s. Pennington and Doris Marie (Robinson) B. BS, Morehouse Coll., 1982. CPA, Mo. Sr. auditor Ernst & Whinney, St. Louis, 1982-85; supervising sr. auditor KMG Main Hurdman, St. Louis, 1985-86; revenue rate analyst Contel, St. Louis, 1986—. Asst. fin. sec. Washington Tabernacle Bapt. Ch., St. Louis, 1986; vol. ARC. Named one of Outstanding Young Men Am., 1985, 86, 87. Mem. Nat. Assn. Black Accts. (fin. co-chmn. 1986, treas. 1987—). Lodge: Masons. Avocations: softball, volleyball, bowling, reading. Home: 5938 Enright Ave Saint Louis MO 63112 Office: CONTEL 680 Mason Ridge Ctr Dr Saint Louis MO 63141

BROWN, ARVILL BUELL, civil engineer; b. Wetonka, S.D., Aug. 5, 1923; s. Arvill Clay and Anna (Gunderson) B.; B.S., Tri-State U., Angola, Ind., 1946; certificate small homes council course U. Ill., 1954; m. June Strong, Oct. 13, 1944; children—Duane Arvill, LuReign Anne, Anita June. Asst. project engr. Ind. State Hwy. Dept., 1946-47; project engr. Tri-State Coll., Angola, Ind., 1947-48; field engr. James Stewart Corp., Chgo., 1948-50; chief engr., gen. field supt. and estimator Fisher-Stoune, Inc., Decatur, Ill., 1950-60; chief engr. aluminum bldg. products div. Maco Corp., Huntington, Ind., 1960-64; partner B & K Engring. Company, Huntington, 1963-64, v.p., 1964-65, pres. B & K Engring., Inc., Kendallville, Ind., 1966-77, also dir.; pres. Brown Cons. Engrs., Inc., Kendallville, 1977—; owner Arvill B. Brown, profl. engr., Kendallville, 1971—; constrn. mgr., engr. Great Lakes Bible Coll., Lansing, 1971-76; pres. Noble County (Ind.) Plan Commn., 1967-71; hwy. engr. Noble County, 1965-71, surveyor, 1967-71; mem. Noble County Drainage Bd., 1967-71. Active Boy Scouts, Cub Scouts; trustee, sec., forwarding agt. Christian Edn. Assn. of Orient, Inc., 1965—; mem. exec. com. New Chs. Christ Evangelism, 1965—; dir. Lake James Christian Assembly, Angola, Ind., 1970-75; nat. alumni dir. Tri-State Coll., Angola, Ind., 1971-75; trustee Gt. Lakes Bible Coll., Lansing, 1982—. Served with USNR, 1944-46. Registered profl. engr., Ill., Ind., Ohio, Mich., Ky., Ga.; profl. land surveyor, Ind.; certified fallout shelter analyst U.S. Dept. Def.; certificates on energy-comml. and residential bldgs., Wis. Mem. Decatur Contractors Assn. (past sec.-treas.). Mem. Ch. of Christ (elder). Patentee in field. Home: PO Box 725 357 N Main St Kendallville IN 46755 Office: PO Box 546 212 S Main St Kendallville IN 46755

BROWN, B. ALEX, physicist; b. Columbus, Ohio, Sept. 25, 1948; s. Frank L. and E. Catherine (Chenoweth) B.; m. Mary J. Hohenstein, July 21, 1984. BA in Physics, Ohio State U., 1970; MS in Physics, SUNY, Stony Brook, 1971, PhD in Physics, 1974. Research fellow Japan Soc. for the Promotion of Sci., Tokyo, 1974-75; research assoc. Mich. State U., East Lansing, 1975-78; research officer Oxford U., Eng., 1978-82; assoc. prof. physics Mich. State U., East Lansing, 1982—. Contbr. over 100 articles to physics jours., 1970—. Mem. The Am. Phys. Soc. Avocations: piano, squash. Office: Mich State U Cyclotron Lab East Lansing MI 48823

BROWN, BAIRD, ret. ins. co. exec.; b. Chgo., Aug. 8, 1922; s. George Frederic and Irene (Larmon) B.; A.B., Washington and Lee U., 1949; student U. Chgo., 1946-48. Vice pres. Geo. F. Brown & Sons, Inc. Chgo., 1948-52, dir., sec., 1952-70, v.p., 1957-70; exec. v.p., dir. Interstate Nat. Corp., 1970-74; pres. Internat. Visitors Center, 1964-65, Lyric Opera Guild, 1958-59; mem. Ill. Arts Council, 1966-67; mem. Joseph Jefferson Awards Com., 1971-79, 81-85, Com. for the Acad., 1985—. Bd. dirs. Friends of Parks, 1986—. Served with USAAF, 1943-45. Mem. UN Assn. (dir. Chgo. br. 1967-73), Sigma Chi. Club: Arts. Home: 2440 N Lakeview Ave Chicago IL 60614

BROWN, BETTY ANN, university administrator; b. What Cheer, Iowa; d. William F. and Anna (Kelley) Tinsley; B.A., Iowa Wesleyan Coll., 1943; M.A., Ill. State U., 1971, postgrad., 1971—; m. Forrest Edwin "Dick" Brown, Nov. 19, 1943; children—Joanne Kelley, Thomas Edwin, Kenneth Scott (dec.), Richard Scott (dec.). Placement counselor Ill. State U. Placement Service, Normal, 1966-67; employment interviewer Ill. State Employment Service, 1967-68; fin. aid adv. Ill. State U., Normal, 1968—. Bd. dirs. Family Services of McLean County, 1979—; mem. Ill. N.G. Scholarship Bd., 1979—; mem. Ill. State U. Adult Learners Scholarship Com., 1985-86. Mem. Nat. Assn. Student Employment Adminstrs. (historian 1983-84), Midwest Assn. Student Employment Adminstrs. (service award 1980, sec. 1982-84), Ill. Guidance and Personnel Assn. (treas. 1976-77), Am. Coll. Personnel Assn., Nat. Assn. Women Deans, Adminstrs. and Counselors, Nat. Assn. Work and the Coll. Student, Ill. Assn. Fin. Aid Adminstrs., Ill. State Univ. Adminstrs. Club, Kappa Delta Pi (pres. Mu chpt. 1979-81). Presbyterian. Club: Altrusa (chpt. pres. 1979). Home: 1907 Owens Dr Bloomington IL 61701 Office: Hovey 211 Ill State Univ Normal IL 61761

BROWN, BLASE PATRICK, dentist; b. Chgo., Jan. 5, 1953; s. Robert Milner and Joan Catherine (Waters) B.; m. Nancy Elizabeth French, Aug. 2, 1981; children: Blair Marie, Bridget Mary. AB History, Loyola U., Chgo., 1975, MS Biology, 1978, DDS, 1981. Lic. dentist, Ill., Mich. Assoc. dentist Dr. G.P. Scanlon, Chgo., 1984—; gen. practice dentistry Lyons, Ill., 1985—; dental dir. Primary Care Initiative, Detroit, 1981-84, mem. quality control com., 1982-84; mem. med. staff Samaritan Health Ctr., Detroit, 1981-84, assoc. mem. dept. surgery, 1981-85, dental cons. 1982-84. vol. Muscular Dystrophy Assn., Allen Park, Mich., 1982; recreation asst. Handicapped Skating Program, Troy, 1982. Served to lt. USPHS, 1981-84. Mem. ADA (1st place Research award 1980), Ill. Dental Soc., Chgo. Dental Soc. (vol. speakers bur., 1984-86), Acad. Gen. Dentistry, Chgo. Odontographic Soc. (award 1981), Lyons C. of C., Loyola Alumni Assn. (area coordinator admissions team 1986, exec. com. 1986), Alpha Sigma Nu, Omicron Kappa Upsilon (Harry A. Sicher award 1981). Roman Catholic. Avocations: camping, backpacking, bicycling, tennis, skiing. Office: 4212 S Joliet Ave Lyons IL 60534

BROWN, BRADLEY DAVID, computer information scientist; b. Carbondale, Ill., Dec. 30, 1961; s. Joseph Birney and Julia Louis (Miles) B.; m. Kristen Lynn Haas, June 4, 1983. BS in Applied Computer Sci., Ill. State U., Normal, 1983. System mgr. Pioneer Hi-Bred Internat., Princeton, Ill., 1983-85; programmer analyst I Midwest Stock Exchange, Chgo., 1985-86, sr. programmer analyst II, 1986—; cons. in field. Mem. U.S. Jaycees (chmn. 1984-85), Sigma Tau Gamma. Republican. Presbyterian. Avocations: sports, woodworking, computers. Home: 2272 Briarhill Dr Naperville IL 60565 Office: Midwest Stock Exchange 440 S LaSalle Chicago IL 60565

BROWN, CHARLES ALTON, obstetrician-gynecologist; b. Mt. Gilead, Ohio, Feb. 16, 1943; s. Richard Alton and Marjorie (Alspach) B.; m. Rebecca Ann McPeek, Mar. 20, 1965; children: Nicholas Alton, Douglas Wilson. BS in Pharmacy, Ohio No. U., 1970; MD, Ohio State U., 1974. Diplomate Am. Bd. Ob-Gyn. Practice medicine specializing in ob-gyn Wooster (Ohio) Clinic, 1976—. Served to maj. USAF, 1974-76. Mem. Am. Coll. Ob-Gyn, Ohio State U., Wayne County Med. Soc., Internat. Jugglers Assn. Republican. Avocations: tennis, juggling. Office: Wooster Clinic 1740 Cleveland Rd Wooster OH 44691

BROWN, CHARLES ASA, lawyer; b. Woodsfield, Ohio, Oct. 17, 1912; s. Charles A. and Anna Miriam (Hayes) B.; A.B. Va. Mil. Inst., 1931-35; student U. Mich., 1937; J.D., Western Res. U., 1938 children—Charles A. III, Ridgley. Bar: Ohio, 1938. Pvt. practice Portsmouth, 1938—; asst. atty. gen. State of Ohio, 1963; owner Raven Rock Farm and Feurt Farm, Scioto River Farm Tract, Winters Farm. Lectr. Indian lore. Active Boy Scouts Am., 1946—, serving as merit badge counsellor, exec. bds. Scioto Area council, Portsmouth dist. commr., scout master troop 12, 1966-80; developer, adviser Indian dance team Portsmouth dist., 1964-78, v.p. Scioto Area council, 1967-68, nat. rep. Nat. council, 1967-68; adv. council Girl Scouts of Am., 1947-48; adv. Indian Tribes, 1961-63; councilman Western Black Elk Keetowah, Cherokee Nation, 1964—; mem. Cedar River Tulsa Muskogee Band. Bd. dirs. Portsmouth Little League Baseball Assn., 1957-58, Scioto County unit Am. Cancer Soc., 1973-80; adv. bd. Practical Nurses Assn., 1960-61; sr. warden Episcopal Ch., lay reader, 1950-76; lay reader Anglican Orthodox Ch., 1976-77, Anglican Ch. N. Am., 1977-81. Served from 1st lt. to capt. U.S. Army, 1941-46; lt. col. Res. (ret.). Decorated Bronze Star with oak leaf cluster, Purple Heart, Am. Defense medal, Victory medal, Occupational medal, European theatre ribbon, 3 battle stars; named Ky. Col.; recipient Silver Beaver award Boy Scouts Am., 1968, Vigil Order of Arrow, 1971. Mem. Am. Indian Bar Assn., Ohio Bar Assn., Portsmouth Bar Assn. (trustee 1966-71), Am. Legion, VFW, DAV, Nat. Rifle Assn., Ohio Farm Bur., various Am. Indian orgns. Club: Daniel Boone Muzzle Loading Rifle. Lodges: Odd Fellow, Mason (32 deg., master of lodge 1965, past sovereign master, Allied Masonic degrees); Shriner (past comdr., trustee lodge 1966-71, excellent high priest chpt. 1976-77, illustrious master council 1978-79, pres. 5th dist. Royal Arch Masons 1979, arch adjutant 6th arch council 1979-81, dist. dep. grand high priest 1980-83, anointed high priest RAM, recipient silver trowel), Royal Order Scotland, Knight Masons Ireland, Nat. Sojourners, Order of Corks, Tall Cedars Lebanon, York Cross of Honour, K.T. (priest), Knight Masons of USA, Order of the Bath, K.P. (grand tribune Ohio 1961, past chancellor comdr.), Red Br. of Erie, Ohio Masonic Vets., Philalethes Soc., Elk, Eagle, Fraternal Order of Police, Order Eastern Star (patron 1966, trustee 1967-70), White Shrine of Jerusalem. Designer flood wall, Portsmouth, Ohio, 1936. Office: 721 Washington St Portsmouth OH 45662

BROWN, CHARLES ERIC, biochemistry educator, analytical instrumentation consultant; b. Spangler, Pa., Nov. 23, 1946; s. Charles E. and Dorothy R. (Riddle) B.; m. Kathy Louise Houck, July 24, 1971; 1 son, Eric Nathaniel. B.A. in Chemistry, SUNY-Buffalo, 1968, Ph.D. in Biochemistry, Northwestern U., 1973. Instr., postdoctoral fellow depts. chemistry, biochemistry and molecular biology Northwestern U., Evanston, Ill., 1973-75; research fellow Roche Inst. Molecular Biology, Nutley, N.J., 1975-77; asst. prof. biochemistry Med. Coll. Wis. Milw., 1977-83, assoc. prof., 1983—; cons. Nicolet Instrument Corp., Metriflow, Inc., 1984—. NIH predoctoral fellow, 1968-72; Cottrell Research grantee, 1979-82; Arthritis Found. grantee, 1984. Mem. Soc. Neurosci., Am. Chem. Soc., AAAS, Internat. Soc. Magnetic Resonance, Am. Soc. Pharmacology and Exptl. Therapeutics, Am. Soc. for Mass Spectrometry, Sigma Xi, Phi Lambda Upsilon. Contbr. articles in field to profl. jours., chpts. to books; developer biomedical equipment and techniques; patentee in field. Office: Med Coll Wis Dept Biochemistry 8701 Watertown Plank Rd Milwaukee WI 53226

BROWN, CHARLES EUGENE, retired electronics company executive; b. Huntingburg, Ind., Oct. 31, 1921; s. Lemuel C. and Bertha (McCormack) B.; m. Elizabeth Sherman McAllister, Aug. 16, 1952; children—Deborah, Judith, Robert, Sarah. B.S., Ind. U., 1948, M.B.A., 1950. Corp. staff Glidden Co., Cleve., 1949-59; dir. indsl. relations Cleve. Pneumatic Tool Co., 1959-62; dir. indsl. relations Honeywell, Inc., Mpls., 1962-73, v.p. employee relations, 1973-80, v.p. exec. human resources, 1980-85, sr. staff v.p., 1985-86. Bd. dirs. Abbot-Northwestern Hosp., Mpls., Family and Children's Services, Mpls., Minn. Opera, Ordway Music Theater. Served with U.S. Army, 1942-45, ETO. Decorated Purple Heart. Clubs: Minneapolis, Interlachen Country. Home: 5029 Bruce Pl Edina MN 55424 Office: Honeywell Cons Ltd 801 Nicollet Mall Suite 1930 Minneapolis MN 55402

BROWN, CLIFFORD F., state supreme ct. justice; b. Bronson Twp. Norwalk, Ohio, Jan. 21, 1916; s. Ignatius A. B.; m. Katherine Brown; adopted children: Charles, Margaret (Mrs. David Kramb), Sheila, Ann (Mrs. Leonard Playko, Jr.). A.B. magna cum laude, U. Notre Dame, 1936, LL.B. cum laude, 1938. Bar: Ohio bar 1938, Mich. bar 1938. Practice law Norwalk, Ohio, 1938-64; judge Huron County Ct., 1958-65, Ohio Ct. Appeals, 1965-81; asso. justice Ohio State Supreme Ct., Columbus, 1981-87. Served with U.S. Army, World War II. Mem. Am. Bar Assn., Ohio State Bar Assn., Lucas County Bar Assn. Democrat. Clubs: Kiwanis, KC, Torch. Home: 135 State Rt 61 E Norwalk OH 44857

BROWN, DANIEL, company executive, art critic, artists' model; b. Cin., Nov. 4, 1946; s. Sidney H. and Genevieve Florence (Elbaum) B.; m. Ellen Neveloff, May 24, 1970; m. 2d, Jane Felson, Sept. 14, 1980; stepchildren—Christopher Minton, Scott Minton. A.B. cum laude, Middlebury Coll., 1968; A.M., U. Mich., 1970; postgrad. Princeton U., 1971-72. Dir. cultural events U. Cin., 1972, spl. asst. to pres., 1973; v.p., corp. sec. Brockton Shoe Trimming Co., Cin., 1974—; prin. Daniel Brown, Inc.; art critic Cin. Mag., 1980-83, Cin. Art Acad. Newsletter; art reviewer Dialogue Mag., 1983—; art commentator Sta. WKRC-TV, Cin., art and movie critic Sta. WCPO-TV, Cin., 1986; frequent guest lectr. on arts; corr. editor: Dialog Mag., 1986. Recipient The Critic's Purse award, Dialogue mag., 1985. Mem. exhbns. com. Contemporary Arts Ctr.; mem. membership com. Cin. Art Mus.; sec., bd. dirs. Mercantile Library, 1985—, treas. 1986, chmn. programs com., 1987—; trustee Contemporary Arts Ctr. 1984—, Vocal Arts Ensemble, 1984, Enjoy the Arts, 1985—, v.p. 1986; mem. bd. advisors Cin. Artists Group Effort, 1986—; guest curator Carnegie Arts Ctr., Covington, Ky., 1986—; juror art competitions Cin. and Columbus, Ohio, 1986-87. Mem. Shoe and Leather Club, Two-Ten Nat. Found., Internat. Platform Assn. Club: University (Cin.). Home: 3900 Rose Hill Ave Apt 401B Cincinnati OH 45229 Office: Brockton Shoe Trimming Co 212 E 8th St Cincinnati OH 45202

BROWN, DARMAE JUDD, librarian; b. Jefferson City, Mo., Sept. 14, 1952; d. William Robert and Dorothy Judd (Curtis) B. BA, W.Va. Wesleyan Coll., 1974; MA, U. Denver, 1975; postgrad. Odessa Coll., 1982-84, U. No. Ia., 1984—. Searching assoc. Bibliog. Ctr. for Research, Denver, 1975-76; librarian N.E. Colo. Regional Library, Wray, 1976-81; head tech. services Ector County Library, Odessa, Tex., 1981-84, Waterloo (Iowa) Pub. Library, 1984—. Organist numerous chs. in Md., W.Va., Colo., Tex., 1969-84, St. Barnabas Episc. Chapel, Odessa, 1981-84. Mem. ALA, Iowa OCLC Users Group (pres. 1986-87), Iowa Library Assn., Library and Info. Tech. Assn., Beta Phi Mu, Sigma Alpha Iota. Home: 1143 Lantern Sq #12 Waterloo IA 50701

BROWN, DAVID EDWARD, architect; b. Grand Rapids, Mich., Oct. 17, 1945; s. Raymond Francis and Thelma Ruth (Nichols) B.; m. Judy Ann Osborn, Aug. 8, 1970; children: Debra, Cindy. AS, Ferris State Coll., 1965; BArch, U. Mich., 1967, MArch, 1971. Registered architect, Mich. Hwy. tech. Mich. Dept. State Hwys, Lansing, 1963-65; draftsman Daverman Assocs., Grand Rapids, 1971-74, job capt., 1974-77; chief architect Newhof and Winer, Inc., Grand Rapids, 1977-81, dir. architecture, 1981-85; owner, sec., treas. The Design Forum Inc., Grand Rapids, 1985—; expert witness bldg. constrn. Newhof and Winer, 1979—. Designer Marina Club Bldg., Anchorage Marina Corp, 1983. Mem. AIA, Mich. Soc. Architects, Bldg. Ofls. and Code Adminstrs. Internat., Council Ednl. Facility Planners Internat. Republican. Roman Catholic. Avocations: travel, swimming, camping. Home: 1400 Mount Mercy Dr NW Grand Rapids MI 49504 Office: The Design Forum Inc 124 E Fulton Suite 402 Grand Rapids MI 49503

BROWN, DAVID HILL, food products company executive, consultant; b. Elkins, W.Va., May 30, 1940; s. Henry William and Mary Margaret (Hill) B.; m. Virginia Elaine Russ, June 23, 1962; children: Pamela, David S., Robert, Jeffrey. BS in Dairy Tech., Ohio State U., 1962. Leader research group Ross Labs, Columbus, Ohio, 1968-69; v.p. mktg. Dairyland Food Labs, Waukesha, Wis., 1969-78; tech. sales dir. Frigo Cheese Corp., Lena, Wis., 1978-79; pres. Brown & Assocs., Worthington, Ohio, 1979—, Dairy Specialties, Inc., Worthington, 1979—. Mem. Am. Assn. Cereal Chemists, Am. Dairy Sci. Assn., Inst. Food Technologists. Republican. Methodist. Lodge: Masons (jr. deacon Pilgrim lodge 1968-69). Avocations: reading, world travel, computers. Home: 466 Delegate Dr Worthington OH 43085 Office: Dairy Specialties Inc PO Box 594 Worthington OH 43085

BROWN, DAVID ROBERT, engineering company executive; b. Columbus, Ohio, June 4, 1923; s. David Earl and Helen Martha (Neubeck) B.; m. Helen Jeanne O'Connor, Apr. 3, 1945; children: Barbara, Patricia, Carol, Charles, James, Mary, Kathleen, William, Michael, Elaine, Edward. Student, Notre Dame U., 1941-42, U. Ill., 1943-44. Ordained deacon. Foreman Harbison Walker, East Chicago, Ind., 1945-54; sales mgr. East Chicago Machine Tool Corp., 1954-58, Lake Engrng. Corp., Hammond, Ind., 1958-62; v.p. Maren Engrng Corp., South Holland, Ill., 1962-73, pres., 1973—. Roman Catholic. Office: Maren Engrng Corp PO Box 278 South Holland IL 60473

BROWN, DAVID RUPERT, engineering executive; b. Chgo., Sept. 11, 1934; s. Hugh Stewart and Sara (Daniels) B.; m. Mary Heaton Nicolaus, Sept. 6, 1958; children: David R. Jr., Robert N., Sara D. BSME, Purdue U., 1956; MBA, U. Akron, 1968. V.p. engrng. Diamond Power Specialty Co., Lancaster, Ohio, 1974-77, v.p. ops., 1977-80, pres., 1980-82; sr. v.p., group exec. Babcock & Wilcox, Lancaster, 1982-85, Barberton, Ohio, 1985-87; v.p., gen. mgr. Babcock & Wilcox, Barberton, 1987—; bd. dirs. Diamond Power Speciality Ltd, Dumbarton, Scotland, Great No. Savs., Barberton, 1986—. Served with U.S. Army, 1957-58. Mem. Am. Soc. Mech. Engrs., Pi Tau Sigma, Tau Beta Pi. Clubs: Fairlawn Country (Akron, Ohio); Lancaster Country. Home: 1833 Breezewood Dr Akron OH 44313

BROWN, DAVID WAYNE, financial representative; b. Evansville, Ind., July 24, 1955; s. Norman R. and Phyllis Jane (Carraway) B.; m. Jane Ann Harris, June 24, 1978; children: Emily Jane, Justin David. BS in Indsl. Engrng., Purdue U., 1977; MBA, Coll. St. Thomas, 1986. Engr. indsl. abrasives div. 3M Co., Ames, Iowa, 1978-81; staff process engr. 3M Co., St. Paul, 1981-83, quality gen. supr., 1983-86, fin. rep. treas. div., 1986—. Sunday sch. tchr. White Bear Lake United Meth. Ch., Minn., 1983—. Avocations: golf, tennis, music, reading. Office: 3M Co 3M Ctr Saint Paul MN 55144

BROWN, DEAN E., social services administrator; b. Lansing, Mich.; m. Ann R. Brown, Mar. 7, 1975; 1 child, Lisa M. BA, Concordia Coll., 1975. Cert. profl. scouter Boy Scouts Am. Minister of evangelism Luth. Ch. Miss. Synod., 1974-80; bd. missions Luth. Ch. Miss. Synod., Ann Arbor, Mich., 1977-79, instr. Gospel Communication Clinic, 1977-80; fin. dir. Lake Huron Area council Boy Scouts Am., Auburn, Mich., 1980—. Mem. Evangelism com. St. John Luth. Ch., Midland, 1984-85; active Midland County Rep. Party, 1985. Mem. Saginaw Valley IBM-PC Users Group (treas. 1985). Lodge: Rotary (youth dir. Cass City, 1983-84). Avocations: tennis, golf, computers. Office: Boy Scouts Am Lake Huron Council 5001 S Eleven Mile Auburn MI 48611

BROWN, DENSIL ALLEN, real estate company executive; b. Warsaw, Ind., June 25, 1933; s. Dean Lamont and Ilean Alta (Clase) B.; m. Peggy Marie Williams, Nov. 29, 1952; children: Cynthia Kay, Deborah Sue, David Allen, Matthew Dean. Degree med. tech., Gradwohl Sch. Tech., 1952; BS, Butler U., 1956. Med. tech. Dr. Williams Lab., St. Louis, 1951-52; lab. supr. Meth. Hosp., Indpls., 1952-56; lab. dir. Prospect Clin. Lab., Prospect Heights, Ill., 1956-70; pres. midwest div. Med. Analytics Reference Lab., Mt. Prospect, 1970-73; health officer City of Mt. Prospect, Ill., 1971-75; pres., lab. dir. Brown Clin. Labs., Inc., Palatine, Ill., 1973-82; health officer City of Prospect Heights, 1975—; asst. to pres., lab. dir. Metpath, Inc., Des Plaines, Ill., 1982—; pres., bd. dirs. Brown Mgmt. Corp., D.A. Brown and Co., Mt. Prospect; v.p., bd. dirs. Case Works of Chgo.; pres., med. dir. Analytical Labs., Mt. Prospect, 1983—. Mem. Gov. Thompson Adv. Bd. to Pub. Health, Springfield, Ill., 1980—; deacon Arlington Heights (Ill.) Evangelical Ch., 1985—. Mem. Am. Assn. Clin. Chemists, Am. Assn. Bioanalysts (chmn. govtl. relations com. Ill. sect.), Am. Soc. Microbiologists, Am. Assn. Med. Techs., Ill. Assn. Clin. Labs., Ill. Assn. Registered Sanitarians, Nat. Assn. Registered Sanitarians. Republican. Club: Meadow (Rolling Meadows, Ill.). Avocations: auto mechanics, woodworking, golf, gardening, music. Home: 201 N Schoenbeck Rd Prospect Heights IL 60070 Office: DA Brown & Co 709 N Main St Mount Prospect IL 60056

BROWN, DONALD ALAN, psychology educator; b. Detroit, Sept. 22, 1927; s. Sidney Lee and Edith Irma (Broese) B.; m. Roberta Engstrom, July 22, 1972; children: Mary, Laura. AB, U. Mich., 1954, MA, 1959, PhD, 1973. Lic. psychologist; cert. sex therapists. Counselor Northville (Mich.) High Sch., 1960-67; housing adminstr. Eastern Mich. U., Ypsilanti, 1970-71; dir. counseling U. Mich., Dearborn, 1971—; pvt. practice psychology Dearborn, 1978—; asst. prof. human sexuality U. Mich., Dearborn, 1981—; cons. Mich. Edn. Assn., Lansing, 1976-77. Author, editor: (book) Sexuality in America, 1981; contbr. articles to profl. jours. Pres. Northville Edn. Assn., 1963-65. Served to 2d lt. U.S. Army, 1946-49. Mem. Am. Psychol. Assn., Am. Assn. Sex Educators, Counselors, Therapists, Am. Assn. Counseling and Devel., Mich. Psychol. Assn., Assn. Scientific Study. Club: Fairlane. Lodge: Optimist. Home: 1349 Rainer Canton MI 48187 Office: U Mich Dearborn MI 48128

BROWN, DONALD RAY, psychologist, university administrator; b. Evansville, Ind., Jan. 7, 1935; m. Shirley M. Miller, July 12, 1985; children: Danielle, Melissa, Scott, Linda, Angela. BS, Purdue U., 1957, MS, 1959, PhD, 1961. Asst. prof. Ohio State U., Columbus, 1961-62, prof., 1962-78, assoc. provost, 1978-81; v.p., dean Purdue U., West Lafayette, Ind., 1981—; chmn. Ind. Curriculum Adv. Bd., 1984-86, Ednl. Policy Com., 1986. Contbr. articles to profl. jours. Served to lt. U.S. Army, 1959. Mem. Phi Beta Kappa, Sigma Xi. Home: 30 N 575W West Lafayette IN 49706 Office: Purdue U West Lafayette IN 49706

BROWN, DONALD RICHARD, capacitor engineer, consultant; b. Milw., Sept. 25, 1925; s. Edwin Frances and Loretta Ethlyn (Howard) B.; m. Dorothy Jane (Carey), Sept. 5, 1947; children: Donald R. Jr., Kenneth Allen. BS in Physics and Math., Monmouth (Ill.) Coll., 1950. Dept. chief engrng. Western Electric, Cicero, Ill., 1951-85; pres. D.R.B. Tech. Services, Ltd., Downers Grove, Ill., 1985—. Patentee in field. Pres. Bruce Lake Home Owners Assn., 1960, Downer's Grove PTA, 1962. Served with USAF, 1944-45. Named one of top 100 technologists in western world by Tech. Mag., 1981. Avocations: fishing, personal computers, gardening, tennis, sports.

BROWN, DONALD ROBERT, psychology educator; b. Albany, N.Y., Mar. 5, 1925; s. J. Edward and Natile (Roseberg) B.; m. June Gole, Aug. 14, 1945; children: Peter Douglas, Thomas Matthew, Jacob Noah. A.B., Harvard U., 1948, M.A., U. Calif.-Berkeley, 1951, Ph.D., 1951. Mem. faculty Bryn Mawr Coll., 1951—, prof. psychology, 1963—; sr. research cons. Mellon Found., Vassar Coll., 1953-63; part-time vis. prof. Swarthmore Coll., U. Pa., also U. Calif.-Berkeley, 1953-63; fellow Center Advanced Study Behavioral Scis., 1960-61; prof. psychology, sr. research scientist, dir. Center Research Learning and Teaching, U. Mich., 1964—; cons. Peace Corps, 1965-71; hon. research fellow Univ. Coll., London, 1970-71; Fulbright sr. research fellow Max Planck Inst., Berlin, 1982; Netherlands Basic Sci. fellow, Leyden, 1983. Author articles, chpts. in books; editor: Changing Role and Status of Soviet Women, 1967, Frontiers of Motivational Psychology, 1986; co-editor: Frontiers of Motivational Psychology. Served with AUS, 1943-46, ETO. Fellow Am. Psychol. Assn.; mem. Soc. Psychol. Study of Social Issues, AAAS, AAUP, Sigma Xi, Psi Chi. Home: 2511 Hawthorn Ann Arbor MI 48104

BROWN, DOROTHY A., accountant; b. Minden, La., Sept. 4, 1953; d. David and Dinkie (Hampton) Rabb; m. Frankie Carl Brown, July 20, 1974; 1 child, Detris Damaris. BS in Acctg., So. U., Baton Rouge, 1975; MBA in Fin., DePaul U., 1981. CPA, Ill. Staff acct. Commonwealth Edison, Chgo., 1975-77; staff auditor Arthur Andersen & Co., Chgo., 1977-80; sr. auditor First Nat. Bank Chgo., 1981-84; mgr. Odell Hicks & Co., Chgo., 1984—. Mem. Ill. Soc. CPA's, Am. Inst. CPA's, Nat. Assn. Black Accts. (dir. Student Affairs 1982-83, pres. 1984-85) (Nat. Pub. Relations award 1985). Democrat. Mem. Ch. of God in Christ. Avocations: sewing, sports. Office: Odell Hicks & Co 19 S LaSalle Chicago IL 60603

BROWN, DOUGLAS DELAFIELD, neurologist; b. Moffat, Scotland, Mar. 21, 1920; s. Edward Delafield and MAry Symonds (Tait) B.; m. Sonia Frances, July 2, 1949; children: Sharon Mary, Fiona Madeleine. MB, BS, U. Newcastle on Tyne, England, 1952. Diplomate Am. Bd. Neurology, Am. Bd. Psychiatry. Intern St. Vincent's Hosp., Erie, Pa., 1952-53; resident in neurology U. Hosps. Cleve., 1960-63, fellow in neuropathology, 1966-68, child psychiatrist, 1970-71; resident in psychiatry Fairhill Psychiat. Hosp., Cleve., 1968-70; med. dir. Cuyahoga Valley Mental Health Ctr., Cuyohoga Falls, Ohio, 1980—. Served to lt. British Army, 1939-46. Fellow Am. Acad. Neurology. Democrat. Club: Cleve. Skating, Link. Home: 21439 Claythorne Rd Shaker Heights OH 44122 Office: Cuyahoga Valley Mental Health Ctr 1931 Bailey Rd Cuyahoga Falls OH 44221

BROWN, DRENDA KAY, psychologist; b. Carrollton, Mo., Jan. 15, 1952; d. Ethan Lyle Pracht and Wilma Estelene (Henderson) Lucas; m. David Kent Brown, June 23, 1973; 1 child, Matthew Kent. BA in Psychology, William Jewell Coll., 1974; MS in Clinical Psychology, Cen. Mo. State U., 1976; PhD in Psychology, Fielding Inst., Santa Barbara, Calif., 1987. Lic. psychologist, Minn. Therapist Briscoe Carr Cons., Kansas City, Mo., 1978-79; psychologist Crittenton Ctr., Kansas City, 1979-81, Cen. Minn. Mental Health Ctr., St. Cloud, 1981-85, St. Cloud Hosp., 1985-87; gen. practice psychology St. Cloud, 1985—; cons. St. Benedicts Ctr., St. Cloud, 1984—, St. Cloud Manor, 1986—. Mem. Cen. Minn. Child Abuse Team, St. Cloud, 1981-85; bd. dirs. Cen. Minn. Child Care Assn., St. Cloud, 1982-83. Mem. Cen. Minn. Psychological Assn. (pres. 1984-85), Minn. Licensed Psychologists, Minn. Psychol. Assn., Mo. Psych. Assn., Alpha Delta Pi Alumni Assn. Presbyterian. Avocations: piano, needlework, reading, arts and crafts. Office: 600 S 25th Ave Suite 105 Saint Cloud MN 56301

BROWN, EDITH, community development agency administrator; b. Milw., Nov. 25, 1935; d. Anton J. and Elizabeth K. (Kribitsch) Volk; m. Edward S. Brown. B.S., U. Wis., 1958, M.S. in Social Work, 1964; M.S. in Mgmt., Cardinal Stritch Coll., Milw., 1985. Hosp. admissions worker, 1958-60; welfare worker, 1960-62; with Kiwanis Children's Ctr. and Children's Hosp. Psychiat. Clinic, Milw., 1962-64; social worker Lutheran Social Services, Milw., 1964-67; foster care supr. Milwaukee County Dept. Social Services, 1967-71, social services adminstr. child protection and parent services, comprehensive emergency services and a coordinated community edn. and support services, 1971-79; assoc. dir. Community Devel. Agy., City of Milw., 1979—; tech. advisor for child abuse, neglect, women abuse, domestic violence; grantswriter, tchr., cons. in field. Mem. Summerfest Adv. Council, Mayor's Beautification Com.; chmn. Summerfest Planting, 1972—; chmn. Milwaukee County Child Abuse and Neglect Task force, 1976-78; chmn. adv. council Milw. Boy's Club, 1981-84; vice chmn. Internat. Yr. for Disabled Persons, 1982; liaison Nat. Yr. for Disabled Persons, City of Milw., 1982-83; asst. chairperson City of Milw. United Way Campaign, 1983; mem. Mayor's Youth Initiatives Task Force, 1984-85; mem. adv. panel M.P.A. degree program U. Wis., 1984—. Office of Vocat. Rehab. scholar, 1962-64; Successful Women in Mgmt. award J. Wis., 1977; award Community Tchrs. Corps, 1977; Changemaker award Wis. Fed. Jr. Women's Clubs, 1978; Outstanding Community Services award Milwaukee County, 1979, Outstanding Services award, 1979, Exemplary Service award, 1982; Woman of Yr. award Mcpl. Women's Assn., 1981. Mem. Acad. Cert. Social Workers, Nat. Assn. Social Workers, Internat. Council on Social Welfare, Internat. Fedn. Social Welfare, Am. Soc. for Pub. Adminstrn. (pres. Milw. chpt., Outstanding Service and Dedication award 1984-85), Research Clearinghouse, Am. Bus. Women's Assn. (Woman of Yr. award 1975), Internat. Graphoanalysis Soc. (pres. Wis. chpt.). Club: Variety of Wis. Tech. contbr. to profl., community, resource documents, 1971—; author print and broadcast programs. Office: Community Devel Agy 200 E Wells St Milwaukee WI 53202

BROWN, EDWARD LINUS, patent agent, civil engineer; b. Erie, Pa., July 30, 1906; s. William George and Anna Josephine (Metz) B.; B.S. in Civil Engring., Case Inst. Tech., 1928; m. Doris Anne Maloy, Apr. 11, 1931; children—Anne Brown Manning, Edward Linus, Constance Brown Guild. With Pa. R.R., 1926-35; various position in sales, product design and devel., constrn. Armco Steel Corp., Middletown, Ohio, also Denver, 1936-71; cons. engr., 1971-75; admitted to practice U.S. Patent Office, 1975; patent agt., Middletown, Ohio, 1975—. Chmn. traffic com. Middletown Area Safety Council, 1952; chmn. advancement com. Boy Scouts Am., 1952-60; pres. Friends of Library, 1979-80. Fellow ASCE; mem. Nat. Soc. Profl. Engrs. (life), Ohio Soc. Profl. Engrs. (life, Outstanding Service award 1951, 75), Engrs. Found. Ohio, Sigma Alpha Epsilon. Roman Catholic. Patentee in field of steel products. Home and Office: 3011 Central Ave Middletown OH 45044

BROWN, EDWIN LEWIS, JR., lawyer; b. Parker, S.D., Mar. 15, 1903; s. Edwin Lewis and Lucy Elizabeth (Lowenberg) B.; m. Faye Hulbert, May 8, 1926; children—Betty Lou Brown Trainer, Lewis Charles. J.D., U. Nebr., 1926. Bar: Nebr. bar 1926, Ill. bar 1933, U.S. Supreme Ct. bar 1960. Practiced in Chgo., 1933-85; partner firm Brown, Cook, Hanson, 1950-85; Mem. Nat. Conf. Lawyers and Collection Agys., 1964-74. Mem. wills and bequests com. Shriners Crippled Children's Hosp., Chgo.; pres. H.P. & S. Crowell Found. Named Time mag.-NADRA Man of Year, 1974. Mem. ABA, Ill. Bar Assn. (sr. counsellor 1976), Chgo. Bar Assn., Am. Judicature Soc., Comml. Law League Am. (pres. 1963-64), Comml. Law Found. (treas.

1969-74), Nat. Conf. Bar Presidents, Phi Alpha Delta. Republican. Presbyterian. Lodges: Masons (32 deg.), K.T, Shriners. Clubs: Union League (Chgo.); Westmoreland Country (Wilmette, Ill.); Lighthouse Point (Fla.) Yacht and Racquet. Home: 2617 Hurd Ave Evanston IL 60201 Office: 135 S LaSalle St Chicago IL 60603 Office: 2530 Crawford Ave Evanston IL 60201

BROWN, EMMA JEAN MITCHELL, educator; b. Marshall, Tex., June 1, 1939; d. Johnnie D. and Elvia L. Mitchell Nickerson. BS, Bishop Coll., 1961; MS, Boston State Coll., 1967; postgrad. Boston U., 1963, 66, Howard U., 1974, U. Dayton, 1979, 80, 81, Miami U., Oxford, Ohio, 1980, Wright State U. Tchr. English, N.E. Jr. High Sch., Kansas City, Kans., 1961-62; info.-mail clk. Boston U., 1962-63; service rep. New Eng. Tel. & Tel., Boston, 1963-65; tchr. Harvard Elem. Sch., Boston, 1965-66, Carter Avery Elem. Sch., Needham, Mass., 1966-67; instr. Sinclair Community Coll., 1971-73, Wright State U., 1971-75; vis. lectr. U. Ibadan (Nigeria), 1975-76; tng. coordinator Dayton (Ohio) Job Corps., 1979; reading specialist Colonel White High Sch., Dayton, 1979-81, Int. Alt. Sch., 1981-82, Martyrs Cath. Sch., 1983-84, Patterson Co-Op High Sch., 1984-86; supr. commn. arts, Dayton Pub. Schs., 1986—; also newsletter editor, 1986—. Third v.p. Dayton Urban League Guild, 1977. Recipient medallion City of Dayton, 1981. Mem. Internat. Reading Assn., Nat. Council Tchrs. of English, Dayton Adminstrn. Assn., Dayton Mgmt. and Supr.'s Assn., Ohio Edn. Assn., NEA, Miami Valley African Assn., City Folk, Miami Valley Literacy Assn., Ch. Women United, Zeta Phi Beta. Methodist. Author: Come Sit at My Table: A Mini African Cookbook, 1980; (poetry) Network Africa, 1984 contbr. articles to profl. jours. Home: 473 Marathon Dayton OH 45406 Office: 4280 N Western Ave Dayton OH 45406

BROWN, ERNEST EDMOND, poultry company executive; b. Wayne City, Ill., June 7, 1921; s. George Havard and Dorothy Marie (Smith) B.; m. Ella Corinne Wolverton, July 28, 1946; children: Mark, Marsha, Danny, Corinne. Student, Ref. Sch., Florence, Italy. Exec. v.p. Corn Belt Hatcheries, Gibson City, Ill., 1951-78; v.p., gen. mgr. Loda (Ill.) Poultry Co., 1983—; retired 1987. Sec. Gibson City Hosp. Bd., 1958-84; pres. Arrowhead council Boy Scouts Am., 1964-67, chmn. trust fund, 1980-84; mem. U. Ill. adv. bd. to Dean Agriculture, 1964-68; advisor to Animal Sci. Dept. U. Ill., 1964-68, State of Ill. on agriculture environ. problems, 1968-69; pres. parent's council Milliken U., 1969-73; chmn. Nutritional Research Com. Am. Egg Bd., 1974; trustee MacMurray Coll., Jacksonville, Ill., 1981-85; mem. fin. com. Council of Ministries and Bd. Mgrs. East Bay Camp, 1980—; past chmn. bd. United Meth. Ch.; served on various egg bds. and coms. Served as sgt. U.S. Army, ETO, 1942-45. Recipient Silver Beaver award Boy Scouts Am., Champaign, Ill., 1967, Gamma Sigma Delta award U. Ill., Urbana, 1971; named Outstanding Citizen Gibson City C. of C., 1970. Mem. Am. Poultry and Hatchery Fedn. (dir. Ill. chpt. 1960-70), Ill. Hatchery and Poultry Fedn. (pres. 1961), Ill. Poultry Industry Council (pres. 1963). Republican. Lodges: Lions, Masons. Home: 205 W 18th St Gibson City IL 60936 Office: Loda Poultry Co Inc 1st and Oak St Loda IL 60948

BROWN, FRANK MUSTARD, chaplain, educator; b. Bland, Va., Dec. 8, 1931; s. Otis Calhoun and Lela Seagle (Mustard) B.; m. Louise Landrum, Aug. 20, 1954 (div. 1978); children: Virginia, Mark; m. Doloris Aho, Sept. 4, 1982. BA, King Coll., 1954; MDiv, Columbia Theol. Sem., 1957; STM, Dubuque Theol. Sem., 1975, D Ministry, 1978. Dir. chaplaincy services Research Med. Ctr., Kansas City, Mo., 1980. Mem. Am. Assn. Pastoral Counselors (counselor Rochester, Minn. chpt. 1973-80, counselor Kansas City chpt. 1980-86), Assn. Clin. Pastoral Edn. Presbyterian. Office: Research Med Ctr 2316 E Meyer Blvd Kansas City MO 64132

BROWN, FREDERICK DOUGLAS, physiologist, educator; b. Springfield, Ohio, June 3, 1929; s. Charles David and Ruth Noami B.; m. Joyce Louise Burton, June 11, 1955; children—Fred, Sharon, Michael Regina, Stephan, Monica. B.S., U. Dayton, 1956; M.S., Miami U., Ohio, 1958; postgrad. Case Western Res. U., 1963-66; Ed.D., Nova U., 1981. Researcher artificial organs and exptl. heart surgery Cleve. Clinic, 1958-63; predoctoral fellow Case Western Res. U., Cleve., 1963-66; instr. sci. Cleve. Bd. Edn., 1966-69; asst. prof. St. John's Coll., Cleve., 1969-73; instr. Sch. Anesthesia Cleve. Clinic, 1973-74; prof. anatomy and physiology Cuyahoga Community Coll., Warrensville, Ohio, 1973—. Pres., Bd. Catholic Edn., Diocese of Cleve., 1972-73; chmn. CSC Warrensville Heights (Ohio), 1970-72; councilman Warrensville Heights, 1982-85. Served to 2d lt. U.S. Army, 1952-54. NIH fellow, 1963-66. Mem. AAUP, N.Y. Acad. Scis., Nat. Assn. Advisors of Sci., Ohio Coll. Biology Tchrs. Assn., Alpha Phi Alpha. Democrat. Contbr. articles to profl. jours.

BROWN, FREDERICK LEE, health care executive; b. Clarksburg, W.Va., Oct. 22, 1940; s. Claude Raymond and Anne Elizabeth (Kiddy) B.; m. Mary Ruth Price, Aug. 22, 1964; children—Gregory Lee, Michael Owen-Price. B.A. in Psychology, Northwestern U., 1962; M.B.A. in Health Care Adminstrn., George Washington U., 1966. Vocat. counselor Cook County Dept. Pub. Aid, Chgo., 1962-64; adminstrv. resident Meth. Hosp. Ind., Inc., Indpls., 1965-66, adminstrv. asst., 1966, asst. adminstr., 1966-71, assoc. adminstr., 1971-72, v.p. ops., 1972-74; exec. v.p., chief operating officer Meml. Hosp. DuPage County, Elmhurst, Ill., 1974-82, Meml. Health Services, Elmhurst, 1980-82; pres., chief exec. officer Christian Hosp. NE-NW, St. Louis, 1982—, Christian Health Care Systems, Inc., St. Louis, 1983—, CH Allied Services, Inc., St. Louis, 1983-85, Christian Health Services, St. Louis, 1986—; adj. instr. Washington U. Sch. of Medicine, St. Louis, 1982—; dir. Health Link, Inc., mem. exec. com. 1986; pres., chief exec. officer Village North, Inc., 1986—; bd. dirs. Am. Healthcare Systems, Inc., chmn. shareholder communications com. 1985—, Commerce Bank St. Louis. Contbr. articles to profl. jours. Co-chmn. hosp. div. United Way Greater St. Louis, 1983, chmn. health services div., 1984, chmn., 1985—, bd. dirs., 1986; bd. dirs. Kammergild Chamber Orch., 1984—, v.p., 1985—; trustee, mem. adminstrv. bd. United Methodist Ch. Wentzville, Mo., 1984—; chmn. emergency room services task force St. Louis Regional Med. Ctr., 1985. Fellow Am. Coll. Healthcare Execs. (chmn. credentials com. 1978, mem. Gold Medal award com. 1985, chmn. task force on governance and constituencies 1986-87); mem. Am. Acad. Med. Adminstrs. (life), Internat. Health Econ. and Mgmt. Inst., Hosp. Pres.'s Assn., Advt. Club Greater St. Louis, Am. Hosp. Assn. (council on mgmt. 1986), Am. Pub. Health Assn., George Washington U. Alumni Assn. for Health Services Adminstrn. (pres. 1979-80, Alumnus of Yr. award 1981), Hosp. Assn. Met. St. Louis (bd. dirs. 1984—, sec. 1985-86, treas. 1987—, chmn. council on pub. affairs and communications 1985, vice chmn. 1987—, various coms.), Mo. Hosp. Assn. (mem. council on research and policy devel. 1983, chmn. council on multi-instnl. hosps. 1986, chmn. dist. council pres.'s 1986), Central Eastern Mo. Profl. Rev. Orgn. (bd. dirs. 1982-85, various coms.). Republican. Clubs: Norwood Hills Country, Arena, Stadium (St. Louis). Lodge: Rotary. Home: 115 Mason Wevster Groves MO 63119 Office: Christian Health Services 11155 Dunn Rd Saint Louis MO 63136

BROWN, FREEZELL, JR., diaconal minister; b. Indpls., Aug. 19, 1957; s. Freezell Brown and Alice Samuel. BA in Religion, Carroll Coll., Waukesha, Wis., 1979; MA in Religious Edn., Christian Theol. Sem., Indpls., 1984. Consecrated diaconal minister United Methodist Ch., 1985. Youth dir. YMCA, Waukesha, 1980-81; minister with youth N. United Meth. Ch., Indpls., 1983, minister with youth and community, 1984-87; mem. com. Religionand Race, So. Ind. Conf. United Meth. Ch., alt. com. investigation; adv. bd. Metro Adv. Ministry, Butler U. Campus Ministry, Indpls. Profl. adv. bd. Buchanan Counseling Ctr.; adv. bd. Coll. Ave. Youth Behavior Acad.; mem. Christian Educators Fellowship of United Meth. Ch. Democrat. Avocations: painting, music composition and performance, drama, reading. Home: 2121 Sheridan Rd Evanston IL 60201

BROWN, GARY LARUE, law enforcement officer; b. Tipton, Ind., Aug. 21, 1955; s. Omer L. and Joanna M. (Powell) B.; m. Vicki L. Baker, Feb. 9, 1979. Cert., Ind. Law Enforcement Acad., Plainfield, 1978. With Hamilton County Hwy. Dept., Noblesville, Ind., 1974-77; officer Cicero (Ind.) Police Dept., 1977; dep., rd. sgt. Hamilton County Sheriff Dept., Noblesville, 1977—. Mem. Ind. Sheriff's Assn., Hamilton County Fraternal Order Police. Avocations: vol. work for ch., 4-H, and community endeavors, farming, scuba diving. Home: 208 N John St Arcadia IN 46030 Office: Hamilton County Sheriff Dept 18100 Cumberland Rd Noblesville IN 46060

BROWN, GARY RONALD, advertising executive; b. Columbus, Ohio, Nov. 20, 1947; s. Lawrence C. and Geraldine (Dixon) B.; m. Sandra Lynn Barney, Nov. 24, 1966 (div. July 1969). Grad. high sch., Worthington, Ohio, 1965. Owner, operator MDI Mktg. & Audio-Visual, Columbus, 1978-85, Bisco Auto Parts, Inc., Columbus, 1975-80, Contact Audio Visual, Columbus, 1972-78; founder, pres., chief exec. officer, chmn. bd. Card-Bds. Am., Inc., Columbus, 1985—. Author: (sales book) Creative Advertising and Marketing Techniques for Small Businesses, 1986. Served with U.S. Army, 1967-70, Vietnam. Mem. Am. Mktg. Assn., Internat. Franchising Assn., Columbus C. of C. Republican. Presbyterian. Avocations: snow skiing, inventor, antique collector. Home: 122 E Stafford Ave Worthington OH 43085 Office: Card Bds of Am Inc 6330 Proprietors Rd Columbus OH 43085

BROWN, GERALD EUGENE, minister; b. Garden City, Kans., July 16, 1949; s. Alva E. and Louise I. (Newcomb) B.; m. Susan L. McConnell, Nov. 14, 1970; children: Patricia, Mark Thomas, Robert. BA cum laude, S.W. Mo. State U., 1972; M Div. cum laude, Midwestern Bapt. Theol. Sem., 1975. Ordained to ministry Christian Ch., 1974. Pastor Ludlow (Mo.) Bapt. Ch., 1973-75; dir. Christian ministries Tabernacle Bapt. Ch., Kansas City, Mo., 1975-79; minister Longview Chapel Christian Ch., Lee's Summit, Mo., 1980-87, Antioch Community Ch., Kansas City, Mo., 1987—; bd. dirs. The Together Ctr., Kansas City; asst. chaplain Lee's Summit Community Hosp., 1986-87; organizing dir. The Shepherd's Ctr. of Lee's Summit, 1985-87. Sec. Flood Relief Task Force, Kansas City, 1977-78; exec. dir. Emergency Assistance Coalition, Inc., Kansas City, 1980-84; mem. Mayor's Task Force on Energy, Kansas City, 1983-84. Democrat. Home: 613 NE 44th St Kansas City MO 64116 Office: Antioch Community Church 4805 NE Antioch Rd Kansas City MO 64119

BROWN, GLADYS SADDLER, educator; b. Memphis, Jan. 27, 1923; s. Henry Rutherford and Edith Estee (Hawkins) Saddler Mahone; m. Joseph L. Brown, Nov. 10, 1950; children—Lorelle Joan, Karen Renee. B.S. in Edn., Central State U., 1947; M.S. in Counseling, Chgo. State U., 1968. Asst. to library film advisor ALA, Chgo., 1947-53; sec. to sec. Musicians Union Local 208, Chgo., 1953-60; tchr. Chgo. Bd. Edn., 1960-68; asst. prof. Chgo. City Coll., 1968—, mem. adv. council Olive-Harvey campus, 1978-82; sr. sponsor Hyde Park High Sch., Chgo., 1964-68, coordinator coop. edn., 1967-68. Mem. Chgo. Bus. Tchrs. Assn., Ill. Edn. Assn., Am. Fedn. Tchrs., Phi Beta Lambda, Alpha Kappa Alpha. Democrat. Episcopalian. Club: Merry Eight Bridge. Office: Olive Harvey Coll 10001 S Woodlawn Chicago IL 60628

BROWN, GORDON MARSHALL, research engineer; b. Detroit, Feb. 17, 1934; s. Everett J. and Agnes (Craig) B.; student Greenville Coll., 1952-54; B.M.E., Gen. Motors Inst., 1958; M.S., U. Mich., 1959; m. Sharla A. Smith, Aug. 16, 1958; children—Gordon C., Julie Marie. Tooling project engr. Fisher Body div. Gen. Motors Corp., Pontiac, Mich., 1954-58; grad. asst. nuclear engring. U. Mich., 1960-61; project engr. nuclear scis. Bendix Aerospace Systems, Ann Arbor, Mich., 1961-67; dir. engring., mgr. mfg. GCO, Inc., Ann Arbor, 1967-73; prin. research engr., mem. research staff Ford Motor Co., Dearborn, Mich., 1973—; optical systems cons. Recipient Gen. Motors Grad. fellowships in nuclear engring., 1960-61. Mem. Am. Soc. Non-Destructive Testing (Achievement award 1970), Soc. Photo-Optical Instrumentation, Soc. Automotive Engrs., Optical Soc. Am. Contbr. to Holographic Nondestructive Testing, 1975. Patentee holographic method for testing tires, 1971. Home: 181 Woodcrest Dr Dearborn MI 48124 Office: Ford Motor Co Room S-1023 SRL PO Box 2053 Dearborn MI 48121

BROWN, GREGORY DAVID, infosystems specialist; b. Rochester, N.Y., Sept. 16, 1947; s. Thomas Blackburn and Marilyn Ernestine (Frost) B.; m. Diane Elizabeth Rodgers, July 4, 1974 (div. July 1976); m. Pamela Gay Beal, July 12, 1986. BA, St. Lawrence U., Canton, N.Y., 1969. Asst. prodn. conrtol mgr. Ritter div. Sybron, Rochester, 1974-76; bus. systems analyst Lapp Ins. div. Interpace, LeRoy, N.Y., 1976-77; security supr. Doyle Detective Bur., Rochester, 1977-79; security officer St. Elizabeth Med. Ctr., Granite City, Ill., 1979-82, staff asst., research, 1982-84, dir. mgmt. info. systems, 1984—; cons. Fraternal Order of Eagles, Granite City, 1984-85, Trinity Tabernacle, Granite City, 1986—, Novotny Chevrolet, Granite City, 1986. Author: (software) Home Health Reporting System, 1984, DRG Reporting System, 1985. Served with U.S. Army, 1969-72. Republican. Avocations: ornithology, statistical simulations, golf, chess, microcomputers. Home: 2230 Lee Ave Granite City IL 62040

BROWN, HERBERT CHARLES, chemistry educator; b. London, May 22, 1912; came to U.S., 1914; s. Charles and Pearl (Gorinstein) B.; m. Sarah Baylen, Feb. 6, 1937; 1 son, Charles Allan. A.S., Wright Jr. Coll., Chgo., 1935; B.S., U. Chgo., 1936, Ph.D., 1938, D.Sc., 1968, hon. doctorates, 1968; hon. doctorates, Wayne State U., 1980, Lebanon Valley Coll., 1980, L.I. U., 1980, Hebrew U. Jerusalem, 1980, Pontificia Universidad de Chile, 1980, Purdue U., 1980, U. Wales, 1981. Asst. chemistry U. Chgo., 1936-38; Eli Lilly post-doctorate research fellow 1938-39, instr., 1939-43; asst. prof. chemistry Wayne U., 1943- 46, asso. prof., 1946-47; prof. inorganic chemistry Purdue U., 1947-59, Richard B. Wetherill prof. chemistry, 1959, Richard B. Wetherill research prof., 1960-78, emeritus, 1978—; vis. prof. U. Calif. at Los Angeles, 1951, Ohio State U., 1952, U. Mexico, 1954, U. Calif. at Berkeley, 1957, U. Colo., 1958, U. Heidelberg, 1963, State U. N.Y. at Stonybrook, 1966, U. Calif. at Santa Barbara, 1967, Hebrew U., Jerusalem, 1969, U. Wales, Swansea, 1973, U. Cape Town, S. Africa, 1974, U. Calif., San Diego, 1979; Harrison Howe lectr., 1953, Friend E. Clark lectr., 1953, Freud-McCormack lectr., 1954, Centenary lectr., Eng., 1955, Thomas W. Talley lectr., 1956, Falk-Plaut lectr., 1957, Julius Stieglitz lectr., 1958, Max Tishler lectr., 1958, Kekule-Couper Centenary lectr., 1958, E. C. Franklin lectr., 1960, Ira Remsen lectr., 1961, Edgar Fahs Smith lectr., 1962, Seydel-Wooley lectr., 1966, Baker lectr., 1969, Benjamin Rush lectr., 1971, Chem. Soc. lectr., Australia, 1972, Armes lectr., 1973, Henry Gilman lectr., 1975, others; chem. cons. to indsl. corps. Author: Hydroboration, 1962, Boranes in Organic Chemistry, 1972, Organic Synthesis via Boranes, 1975, The Nonclassical Ion Problem, 1977; Contbr. articles to chem. jours. Bd. govs. Hebrew U., 1969—. Served as co-dir. war research projects U. Chgo. for U.S. Army, Nat. Def. Research Com., Manhattan Project, 1940-43. Recipient Purdue Sigma Xi research award, 1951; Nichols medal, 1959; award Am. Chem. Soc., 1960; S.O.C.M.A. medal, 1960; H.N. McCoy award, 1965; Linus Pauling medal, 1968; Nat. Medal of Sci., 1969; Roger Adams medal, 1971; Charles Frederick Chandler medal, 1973; Chem. Pioneer award, 1975; C.U.N.Y. medal for sci. achievement, 1976; Elliott Cresson medal, 1978; C.K. Ingold medal, 1978; Nobel prize in chemistry, 1979; Priestley medal, 1981; Perkin medal, 1982; Nat. Acad. Scis. Award in Chem. Scis., 1987. Fellow Royal Soc. Chemistry (hon.), AAAS, Indian Nat. Sci. Acad. (fgn.); mem. Am. Acad. Arts and Scis., Nat. Acad. Scis., Chem. Soc. Japan (hon.), Pharm. Soc. Japan (hon.), Am. Chem. Soc. (chmn. Purdue sect. 1955-56), Ind. Acad. Sci., Phi Beta Kappa, Sigma Xi, Alpha Chi Sigma, Phi Lambda Upsilon (hon.). Research in phys., organic, inorganic chemistry relating chem. behavior to molecular structure; selective reductions; hydroboration; chemistry of organoboranes Research in phys., organic, inorganic chemistry relating chem. behavior to molecular structure; selective reductions; hydroboration; chemistry of organoboranes. Office: Purdue Univ Dept of Chemistry West Lafayette IN 47907

BROWN, HERBERT RUSSELL, justice, lawyer; b. Columbus, Ohio, Sept. 27, 1931; s. Thomas Newton and Irene (Hankinson) B.; m. Beverly Ann Jenkins, Dec. 2, 1967; children: David Herbert, Andrew Jenkins. BA, Denison U., 1953; JD, U. Mich., 1956. Assoc. Vorys, Sater, Seymour and Pease, Columbus, Ohio, 1956, 60-64, ptnr., 1965-82; treas. Sunday Creek Coal Co., Columbus, 1970-86; assoc. justice Ohio Supreme Ct., Columbus, 1987—; examiner Ohio Bar, 1967-72, Multi-State Bar, 1971-76, Dist. Ct. Bar, 1968-71; commnr. Fed. Lands, Columbus, 1967-68, Lake Lands, Columbus, 1981. Mem. editorial bd. U. Mich. Law Rev., 1955-56. bd. dirs. Cen. Community House Columbus, 1967-75; deacon, mem. governing bd. 1st Community Ch., 1966-80; candidate Ohio State Legis., 1966. Served to capt. JAGC, U.S. Army, 1956-57. Fellow Am. Coll. Trial Lawyers; mem. Ohio Bar Assn., Columbus Bar Assn. Democrat. Office: Ohio Supreme Ct 30 E Broad St Columbus OH 43215

BROWN, HORACE LUDWIG, civil engineer, land surveyor; b. Newark, Ohio, Dec. 20, 1906; s. Horace Randolph and Mary Anna (Steubs) B.; m. Ruth Elizabeth Anne, Nov. 28, 1936. Registered profl. engr., Ohio; profl. land surveyor. Rodman Chmn. City of Newark, 1928-41, engr. surveyor, 1945—, design engr., 1950—; surveyor Indsl. Gas Corp., Newark, 1941-45; pvt. practice engring.-surveying, Licking County, Ohio, 1944-75. Poet, writer and composer vocal, piano and symphonic music. Contbr. Devel. Fund, Ohio State U., Columbus; mem. N.Y. Philharmonic Soc., Friends of N.Y. Philharmonic, Met. Opera Guild of N.Y. Mem. Am. Congress Surveying-Mapping (life). Republican. Avocations: microscopy; astronomy; photography; electricity; electronics. Home: 135 N 21st St Newark OH 43055 Office: City of Newark 40 W Main St Newark OH 43055

BROWN, HOWARD EARL, community college president; b. Springfield, Ill., June 22, 1922; s. Lorenza Dee and Zona (Sharp) B.; m. Helen Rebecca Bundy, Apr. 10, 1944; children—Bill Wayne, Becky Louise Flora, Sally Elizabeth Schepper. B.S., Ill. State U.-Normal, 1948; M.S., Colo. State U., 1953; Specialist Edn., Eastern Ill. U., 1971; postgrad. Columbia U., 1967, U. Ill., 1976. High sch. coach, tchr., Blue Mound, Ill., 1948-55, prin., 1957-59, sch. supt., 1959-65; county supt. Macon County Ednl. Service Region, Decatur, Ill., 1965-80, regional supt., 1980-85; pres. Richland Community Coll., 1985—; tchr. Richland Community Coll., 1979-82, pres., 1985—; prof. Millikin U., 1976-78; mem. Ill. State Tchr. Certification Bd., 1970-74; chmn. Ill. Task Force-Study of Declining Enrollment, 1975-76. Pres., Mental Health Assn. Macon County; pres. Decatur Area Arts Council; mem. United Fund Bd.; chmn. Farm Bur. Rural/Urban Com. Youth Program; bd. dirs. Salvation Army, Decatur Macon County United Way; chmn. High Risk Infant Screening Com. Macon County; chmn. Billy Graham Golden Prairie Crusade for Christ, Decatur, 1967. Served with U.S. Army, 1942-45. Decorated Bronze Star medal; recipient Voice of Democracy Service award VFW, 1968-69, 79-80, 81-82, Nat. Schoolman's award Freedoms Found., 1971, Disting. Service award Macon County Council Exceptional Children, 1975. Mem. Am. Assn. Sch. Adminstrs., Ill. Assn. Sch. Adminstrs., Ill. Assn. Regional Supts. Schs. (past pres.), Ill. Assn. County Ofcls., VFW, Am. Legion, Macon County Hist. Soc. Methodist. Lodges Rotary (pres. 1971; pub. speaking award) (Decatur), Masons (32 deg.), Shriners. Home: 1989 W Macon St Decatur IL 62522 Office: 2425 Federal Ct Decatur IL 62526

BROWN, JACK MCCARTNEY, chemical company executive; b. San Juan, P.R., Nov. 13, 1940; m. Bonnie Lila Blackstock, June 23, 1962; children: Michele, Bryan. BS, U.S. Naval Acad., 1962; MBA in Production, Mich. State U., 1968. Commd. ensign USN, 1962, advanced through grades to lt., 1965, resigned, 1967; supr. communications Dow Chem. Co., Midland, Mich., 1972-74, project specialist basic ops., 1974-77, supt. power control, 1977-79, project mgr. project sunray, 1979-82, sect. mgr. energy and utilities, 1982—. Mem. Energy Adv. Com., Midland, 1984—. Mem. Mich. Mfg. Assn. (chmn. energy adv. com. 1985), Assn. Bus. Advocating Tariff Equity (vice chmn. 1984, rep.). Republican. Methodist. Avocations: skiing, boating, tennis. Home: 5523 WhiteHall Midland MI 48640 Office: Dow Chem Co 1101 Building Midland MI 48667

BROWN, JAMES LEHMON, chem. co. exec.; b. Detroit, Nov. 20, 1929; s. Abram Lehmon and Donnabelle (Chenoweth) B.; A.B., U. Mich., 1951, M.B.A., 1952; m. Judith Marsh Sinclair, June 28, 1952; children—Kirk, Scott, Kim, Carrie, Elizabeth. Propr. constrn. firm, Ann Arbor, Mich., 1955-58; sales mgr. Sinclair Mfg. Co., Toledo, 1958-64, pres., 1964—, also chmn. bd.; chmn. bd. Sinclair Mfg. Assos., WGTE-TV-FM, 1980-84 ; bd. dirs. 1st Nat. Bank of Toledo, Craft House Corp., Hunt Chem., Inc., St. Paul. Mem. Toledo Citizens Com. for Effective Govt., 1971-72; pres. Toledo Area Govtl. Research Assn., 1974-75; trustee Toledo Area council Boy Scouts Am., 1971—, exec. bd., 1970—, pres., 1975—; trustee U. Toledo Corp., 1975—, Toledo chpt. ARC, 1977-79. Served with AUS, 1952-55. Mem. Phi Eta Sigma, Theta Delta Chi, Sigma Delta Chi. Club: Toledo. Home: 30 Meadow Ln Toledo OH 43623 Office: 2650 N Reynolds Rd Toledo OH 43615

BROWN, JAMES MARTIN, railroad executive; b. Lancaster, N.Y., Apr. 10, 1945; s. David and Christine (Anzie) B.; m. Patricia Ann Willison, Nov. 4, 1967; 1 son, Michael Todd. Student pub. schs., Depew, N.Y. Dispatching foreman Penn Central, Selkirk, N.Y., 1970-75, gen. foreman, New Haven, Conn., 1975-76; gen. foreman Nat. R.R. Passenger Corp., New Haven, 1976, gen. supr. N.E. corridor, 1976-79, supt. locomotives, 1979-80, facility mgr., Chgo., 1980-84; plant mgr. Chrome Locomotive, Silvis, Ill., 1984-86, v.p. ops., 1986 . Cubmaster Quinnipiac council Boy Scouts Am., 1978, scoutmaster, 1979; mem. Bethany Baptist Ch., Moline, Ill., 1984—. Served with USN, 1963-66. Recipient Order of Arrow, Boy Scouts Am., 1980. Mem. Locomotive Maintenance Officers Assn. Democrat. Lodge: Masons. Home: 3525 56th Street Ct Moline IL 61265 Office: Chrome Locomotive PO Box 197 Silvis IL 61282

BROWN, JANET WILLIS, human resources executive; b. Sikeston, Mo., Sept. 17, 1950; d. Jess Hahn Willis and Neva Lucille (Little) Long; m. Robert Lewis Brown, June 15, 1984. BS in English and Theater, Ill. State U., 1972. Dir. community ctr. Recreation Commn., Cin., 1974-78; edn. dir. Great Rivers Girl Scout Council, Cin., 1978-82; dir. fund devel. Buckeye Trails Girls Scout Council, Dayton, Ohio, 1984-85; human resource devel. specialist Automatic Data Processing, Cin., 1982-84; mgmt. skills trainer Automatic Data Processing, Indpls., 1985—; cons. Cin. Zoo, 1980-81, Interaction Inc., Dayton, 1981-82; trainer Kellogg Found., Cin. bd. dirs., trainer Kellogg Found., Cin., 1979-81, United Way, Dayton, 1984-85. Mem. Am. Soc. Tng. and Devel. Republican. Baptist. Avocations: wildlife activism, thoroughbred horses. Home: 1402 Shawnee Rd Indianapolis IN 46260 Office: Automatic Data Processing 3665 Priority Way South Dr Indianapolis IN 46280-0419

BROWN, JERRY DUANE, accountant; b. Jefferson, Iowa, Dec. 28, 1958; s. Wayne Eldon and Phyllis Lorraine (Jacobson) B.; m. Kristie Ann Naeve, Aug. 14, 1982. BA, U. No. Iowa, 1981. CPA, Iowa. Supr., acct. Erpelding Voigt & Co., Algona, Iowa, 1981—. Bd. dirs. United Way, Algona, 1983. Mem. Am. Inst. CPA's, Iowa Soc. CPA's. Republican. Lutheran. Lodge: Lions (pres. Algona 1986-87). Avocations: golf, tennis, piano. Home: Rural Rt 1 Box 249 Algona IA 50511 Office: Erpelding Voigt & Co 307 E Call Algona IA 50511

BROWN, JOAN LEE, social worker, nurse clinical specialist; b. Jackson, Mich., Oct. 13, 1945; d. Jack Winton and Alma Florence (Gibbard) Brown; m. Thomas H. Shultz, Dec. 22, 1975; children—Jennifer Lee, Sandra Joan, Kristin Lynn. B.S. in Nursing, Spalding U., Louisville, 1968; M.S. in Nursing, U. N.C., 1972. Nurse intensive-care units various instns.; instr. med. surg. nursing U. N.C., Chapel Hill, 1972-73; evening supr. Addison (Mich.) Community Hosp., 1973-74; clin. specialist in psychiatry Chelsea (Mich.) Community Hosp., 1976-82; mental health specialist St. Joseph's Mercy Hosp., Ann Arbor, Mich., 1982—; practice psychotherapy, 1977—;lectr. in field. Lic. cert. social worker. Mem. U. N.C. Alumni Assn., Spalding Coll. Alumni Assn., Sigma Theta Tau. Methodist. Home: 3978 Scio Church Rd Ann Arbor MI 48103

BROWN, JOHN CAREY, data processing executive; b. Kansas City, Mo., Jan. 21, 1948; s. Donald M. and Ruth Emma (Beaumont) B.; m. Jana Kay Kesterson, Apr. 21, 1973; children: David Michael, Elizabeth Anne. BA, Wichita (Kans.) State U., 1971; M of Pub. Adminstrn., Kans. State U., 1980. Adminstrn. officer Kans. Bur. Investigation, Topeka, 1978-82; sr. policy analyst Div. Info. Systems and Communications State of Kans., Topeka, 1982-84, spl. projects asst., 1984-86, asst. to dir., 1986—. Bd. dirs. ct.-appointed spl. advs. of Shawnee County, 1987—. Mem. Assn. Computing Machinery (Wichita chpt. pres. 1972), Assn. Pub. Safety Commn. Officers (hon. life), Assn. Landlords of Kans. (v.p. 1986—), Shawnee County Landlords Assn. (editor 1984—). Republican. Presbyterian. Office: State of Kans Div Info Systems and Communications Landon State Office Bldg Topeka KS 66612-1275

BROWN, JOHN J., church financing company executive; b. Vinita, Okla., May 10, 1946; s. Johny H. and Mary Jo (Reece) B.; m. Donna J. Hayward, Mar. 11, 1966; children: Soncee, John H. Student, S.W. Mo. State U., 1964, Drury Coll., 1964-67, Cen. Bible Coll., 1977. Mktg. dir. HQ Corp., Springfield, Mo., 1977-80; v.p. ICBM, Springfield, 1980-82; pres. No. Capital Resource, Springfield, 1982—; cons. John Brown Assocs., Springfield, 1980-87. Author: Church Financing for the '80s, 1985. Mem. Paul Harris Fellows, Southeast Springfield, Mo., 1984, E.C. Council, Springfield, 1984-

87, Nat. Rep. Com. (sustaining), 1985-87. Recipient Outstanding Achievement award Alyeska Service Orgn., 1975, 76, Outstanding Contribution award Royal Heritage Soc., 1983. Mem. Am. Mgmt. Assn., Chief Exec. Officers Assn., Assn. Church Financing Profls. (pres. 1987—). Mem. Assemblies of God. Lodge: Rotary. Avocations: hunting, fishing, skiing, reading. Home: 5949 S Thetford Rd Springfield MO 65804 Office: Northern Capital Resource Corp One Corporate Ctr Suite 110 Springfield MO 65804

BROWN, JOHN L., state legislator, farmer, rancher; b. Rapid City, S.D., July 22, 1952; s. Lawrence M. and Helen D. (Davis) B.; m. Roberta Jean Haskell, Aug. 11, 1979; children—Erin Susanne, Colin Elliot. B.S. in Animal Sci., S.D. State U., 1974. Sec.-treas. Cave Hills Cattle Co., Buffalo, S.D., 1974—; mem. S.D. Legislature, 1978-80, mem. S.D. Senate, 1980—. Bd. dirs. Sky Ranch for Boys, 1985—; chmn. Harding County Rep. Party, S.D., 1974-78; alt. del. Rep. Nat. Conv., 1976. Lutheran. Lodge: Lions (pres. Buffalo 1977-78).

BROWN, JOHN QUINCY, orthopedic surgeon; b. Oakland, Calif., Mar. 19, 1910; s. John Quincy and Helen (Gager) B.; married, 1938; children: John Q. Jr., Marjorie M., Julia G., Ann C. Brown. BA, Ohio State U., 1931, MD, 1936. Diplomate Am Bd. Orthopedic Surgery, Ohio State Med. Bd. Practice medicine specializing in orthopedic surgery Columbus, Ohio, 1938—; instr. orthopedics Ohio State U., Columbus, 1938-52. Served to capt. Med. Service Corps, AUS, 1942-46, PTO. Mem. Am. Acad. Orthpedic Surgery, Mid-Am. Orthopedic Soc., Am. Med. Soc., Ohio State Med. Soc., Ohio Orthopedic Soc. (pres. 1962), Columbus Orthopedic Soc. (pres. 1959). Lodges: Rotary, Masons (33 degree). Avocations: bowling, spectator sports, masonry. Office: Columbus Orthopedic Clinic 3555 Olentangy River Rd Columbus OH 43214

BROWN, JOHN SEBASTION, JR., manufacturing engineer; b. Durant, Miss., Dec. 16, 1945; s. John S. and Lucinda E. (Love) B.; children: Mona, John III, Valerie, Charles, Ashley, Ayron. BS, Youngstown State U., 1976. Engr. Wean-United, Youngstown, Ohio, 1967-70, Gen. Motors, Lordstown, Ohio, 1970-71, E.W. Bliss Co., Salem, Ohio, 1971-76, U.S.I. Clearing, Chgo., 1976-78, Gen. Electric Co., Cleve., 1978-85; plant engr. Pattin Mfg. div. Eastern Co., Marion, Ill., 1985-87. Patentee mine bolt anchor system, 1986. Vol. tutor math. and sci., Youngstown, 1965-78; vol. Adult Basic Edn., Income Tax Service for Poor, Youngstown, 1967-77. Recipient Vol. Service award Youngstown Action Council, 1970, 71, 72, 73. Mem. Soc. Mfg. Engrs. (sr.). Baptist. Avocations: ping pong, writing, reading, auto restoration. Office: Pattin Mfg div Eastern Co 809 Skyline Dr Marion IL 62959

BROWN, JONATHAN T., accountant; b. Ellwood City, Pa., Jan. 14, 1960; s. Floyd E. and Mary Brown; m. Brenda Lakin, Oct. 26, 1985. BS in Acctg., Stockton State Coll., 1982. Staff acct. Coopers & Lybrand, Akron, Ohio, 1984, Ernst & Whinney, Akron, 1985; dept. mgr. Lomax & Soful, CPAs, Akron, 1986; sr. acct. Meaden & Moore, Wooster, Ohio, 1986. Republican. Clubs: Akron Astronomy, Tiretown Corvettes. Home: 4580 Max Rd North Canton OH 44720 Office: Meaden & Moore CPAs Buckeye and Liberty Wooster OH 44691

BROWN, JOSEPH ANDREW, JR., transportation consultant; b. Bristol, Conn., July 28, 1915; s. Joseph Andrew and Emma Virginia (Robey) B.; student Morse Coll., 1934-35; m. Edythe E. Hill, May 2, 1942 (div.); children—Michael R., Peter D., Stephen J., Kathleen V., Julie Ann, Anthony R. Freight service mgr. Eastern Express Inc., Terre Haute, Ind., 1947-56; v.p. ops., mem. exec. com. Mchts. Motor Freight, Inc., St. Paul, 1957-60; dir. freight claim prevention Spector Freight System, Inc., Chgo., 1960-63; salesman Callner Corp. and Ken-Di Realty Co., Chgo., 1964-70; search cons. Cadillac Assos., Inc., Chgo., 1971-84. Mem. transp. adv. com. Richard J. Daley Coll., Chgo., 1979-84. Served to lt. col. inf. OSS, AUS, 1941-46. Decorated Legion of Merit; recipient cert. of meritorious service Am. Trucking Assn. Mem. Am. Soc. Traffic and Transp. (a founder, emeritus), Nat. Council Physical Distbn. Mgmt. Patentee cargo cart conveyor. Home: 445 W Barry St Apt 524 Chicago IL 60657

BROWN, KAREN KAY, microbiologist, corporate executive; b. Manhattan, Kans., July 25, 1944; s. Clarence Christian and Edna Dorothy (Spiecker) Kilker; m. Harold G. Brown, June 18, 1966. BS, Washburn U., 1966; PhD, Okla. State U., 1972. Quality assurance microbiologist Haver-Lockhart, Shawnee, Kans., 1972; research scientist Cutter-Haver-Lockhart, Shawnee, 1972-80; prin. scientist Bayvet div. Miles Labs., Merriam, Kans., 1981-84; mgr. biol. research Mobay Animal Health, Merriam, 1984—; pres. Pair O' Docs Investments, Kansas City, Mo., 1984—; biohazards officer Mobay Animal Health, 1975—; mem. USDA/DNA task force, Washington, 1985—. Contbr. articles to profl. jours.; patentee in field. CPR instr. Am. Heart Assn., Kansas City, 1985—; mem. Emergency Med. Services Team, Kansas City, 1985—. Recipient Miles Sci. and Tech. award, 1984, Mobay Sci. and Tech award, 1985-86; USPHS fellow. Mem. AAAS, Am. Assn. Lab. Animal Scientists (examining bd., 1983—), Am. Soc. Microbiology, N.Y. Acad. Sci. Avocations: sailing, sailboarding, fishing, tennis, skiing. Home and Office: 5501 NW Foxhill Rd Parkville MO 64152

BROWN, KELLY GENE, firefighter, program developer; b. Rapid City, S.D., May 24, 1955; s. Ted Eugene and Phyllis Kay (Levy) B.; m. Becky Marie Rick, May 21, 1977 (div. Feb. 1983); 1 child, Jared Russell; m. Hazel Judy Souza, Apr. 14, 1984; 1 child, Justin Henry. Grad. high sch., Rapid City, 1973. Contractor Brown Constrn., Rapid City, 1974-75, 77-80; mgr. Belanger & Co., Rapid City, 1975-77; firefighter Rapid City Fire Dept., 1980-84; program developer S.D. Fire Marshal, Pierre, 1984-87, dir. tng., 1987—; emergency med. technician Pierre Fire Dept., 1980; field instr. Nat. Fire Acad., Emmitsburg, Md., 1986; tng. officer Pierre Fire Dept., 1985—. Named one of Outstanding Young Men of Am., T.J. Sanborn, 1985-86. Mem. Internat. Soc. Fire Service Instrs. (state rep. 1984), Nat. Fire Protection Assn., S.D. Fire Fighters Assn., S.D. Fire Chiefs Assn., S.D. Fire Dept. Instrs. Assn. Republican. Club: Black Hills 4-Wheelers (Rapid City) (sec. 1983-84). Avocations: stock car driving, off-road touring. Home: 914 N Euclid #32 Pierre SD 57501 Office: SD Fire Marshall's Office 118 W Capitol Pierre SD 57501

BROWN, KENT LOUIS, hospital adminstrator, educator; b. Springfield, Ill., June 19, 1952; s. Paul Louis and Mary Lou (Pickett) B.; m. Patricia Lee Wallace, Feb. 17, 1973; 1 child, Keith Louis. AS in Chemistry, Black Hawk Coll.ž, 1979; BS in Pharmacy, U. Ill., Chgo., 1982; MBA, U. Iowa, 1986. Registered pharmacist, Ill. Staff pharmacist Illini Hosp., Silvis, 1982-83; dir. pharmacy Mercer County Hosp., Aledo, Ill., 1983-84, Jane Lamb Health Ctr., Clinton, Iowa, 1984-86; cons. pharmacist Gateway Long-term Care, Clinton, 1984-86; mem. Whiteside County Bd. Pub. Health. Author: Pharmacology 210, 1985; editor newsletter Pharmacy Bulletin, 1982—. Coach Youth Soccer Club, East Moline, Ill., 1986—. Served with USN, 1971-77. Recipient Kirshner award Jane Lamb Health Ctr., Clinton, 1985, 86. Fellow Am. Soc. Cons. Pharmacists; mem. Am. Soc. Hosp. Pharmacists, Am. Pharm. Assn., Ill. Pharmacists Assn., Am. Coll. Healthcare Execs., Morrison C. of C., Rho Pi Phi (fraternity chancellor 1980-81). Lodge: Rotary. Avocations: boating, sailing, bicycling, photography. Home: 302 Scenic Dr Morrison IL 61270 Office: Morrison Community Hosp Morrison IL 61270

BROWN, LARRY THOMAS, automobile dealer; b. Inkster, Mich., Apr. 21, 1947; s. Nander and Mattie Lou (Lewis) B.; m. Angelina Dolores Caldwell, Aug. 28, 1971. AA, Wayne Community Coll., Detroit, 1971; BA, Wayne State U., 1973; MA, Cen. Mich. U., Mt. Pleasant, 1979. With Ford Motor Co., Dearborn, Mich., 1969-79; market mgr. Dealer Computer Services Ford Motor Co., Chgo., 1979-84; pres., gen. mgr. Ottawa (Ill.) Ford-Lincoln Mercury, Inc., 1984—; pres. CIRCON, Inc., Detroit, 1979. Bd. dirs. Awareness, Inc., Detroit, 1976, YMCA, Detroit, 1975, Lake Hinsdale Vill. Condo, Willowbrook, Ill., 1981. Served as sgt. USAF, 1965-69. Mem. Ottawa C. of C., Black Ford-Lincoln Mercury Dealers Assn., Nat. Assn. Minority Auto Dealers, Wayne State U. Alumni Assn. Baptist. Lodge: Rotary. Home: 410 E Pearl St Ottawa IL 61350 Office: Ottawa Ford LM Inc 1800 E Norris Dr Ottawa IL 61350

BROWN, LAWRENCE HAAS, banker; b. Evanston, Ill, July 29, 1934; s. Robert C. and Alice (Haas) B.; m. Ann Ferguson, June 23, 1956; children—Michael, Kenneth, Russell. Student, Cornell U., Ithaca, N.Y., 1952-54; B.B.A., U. Mich., 1956. Sr. v.p. No. Trust Co., Chgo., 1958—; chmn., Pub. Securities Assn., N.Y.C., 1980; vice chmn. Mcpl. Securities Rulemaking Bd., Washington, 1982. Served to lt. USN, 1956-58. Republican. Presbyterian. Clubs: Exmoor Country (Highland Park, Ill.) (pres. 1984-85); Municipal Bond (pres. 1977), Union League (Chgo.). Avocations: tennis; curling; golf. Home: 201 Michigan Ave Highwood IL 60040 Office: No Trust Co 50 S La Salle St Chicago IL 60675

BROWN, LEE JORGENSEN, retailer; b. Cadillac, Mich., Jan. 17, 1940; s. Thaddeus James and Marian Katherine (Jorgensen) B.; m. Pamela Sue Cochran, Feb. 25, 1967 (div.); 1 dau., Susannah Jane; m. Roberta Ann Preston, Apr. 7, 1984; stepchildren—Jane Marie, Jacqueline Lee. B.A., Augustana Coll., 1962; M.A., Western Mich. U., 1966, M.A., 1967. Head dept. English, Loy Norrix High Sch., Kalamazoo, 1963-72; pres. Brown's Men's Wear, Inc., Cadillac, Mich., 1972—; dir. NBD Evart Bank, Mich., Pantree Restaurants. Lutheran. Home: 408 E Harris St Cadillac MI 49601 Office: 109 N Mitchell St Cadillac MI 49601

BROWN, MABEL ESTLE, retired educator; b. Muscatine County, Iowa, Oct. 6, 1907; d. Chester Millar and Mayme (Bell) Estle; m. Robert G. Brown, Dec. 30, 1931; children—Patricia Jane Brown Hoback, Linnaeus Estle. B.A., U. Iowa, 1929; M.S., Iowa State U., 1953. Cert. secondary tchr., guidance counselor, sch. librarian, Iowa. High sch. tchr., Conesville, Iowa, 1930-32, 42-48, Nichols, Iowa, 1949-50; grad. asst. journalism Iowa State U., Ames, 1950-53; tchr., librarian Lone Tree High Sch., (Iowa), 1953-60, guidance counselor, 1960-70; chmn. Carrie Stanley Scholarship Com., Lone Tree, 1962-70. Author: The Fork of the Rivers: History Is People, 1978. Chmn., Muscatine County Farm Bur. Women, Muscatine, Iowa, 1938-42; judge, clk. Twp. Election Com., Conesville, 1970-84. Mem. NEA (life), Iowa Edn. Soc. (life), ALA, Iowa Acad. Sci., Theta Sigma Phi. Republican. Home: Rural Route Conesville IA 52739

BROWN, MARK ALAN, customer service administrator; b. Davenport, Iowa, Jan. 21, 1956; s. Richard Leroy and Albena K. (Pauletti) B. BBA in Econs., U. Iowa, 1980; MBA, St. Ambrose Coll., 1983. Collection mgr. Cox Cable Communications, Moline, Ill., 1981-84; asst. customer service rep. Ford Motor Credit Co., Davenport, 1984-85; customer service rep. Ford Motor Credit Co., Kansas City, Mo., 1985-86; customer service supr. Ford Motor Credit Co., Kansas City, 1986—. Fellow Assn. MBA Execs.; mem. St. Ambrose Grad. Alumni Assn., U. Iowa Alumni Assn. Democrat. Roman Catholic. Avocations: tennis, running, basketball, softball, racquetball. Home: 12830 W 88th St Circle Apt #74 Lenexa KS 66215 Office: Ford Motor Credit Co 4400 W 109th Suite 300 Overland Park KS 66211

BROWN, MARK GRAHAM, human resource specialist, consultant; b. Detroit, Apr. 9, 1955; s. Donald Graham and Joan T. (Malese) B. BA in Psychology, Western Mich. U., 1977, MA in Applied Behavior Analysis, 1979. Bus. and conv. coordinator Assn. Behavior Analysis, Kalamazoo, Mich., 1978-79; program developer Creative Universal, Inc., Southfield, Mich., 1979-81, dir. planning, 1981-84, group mgr. tnr. and performance improvement, 1984; assoc. R.A. Svenson & Assocs., Wheaton, Ill., 1984—. Contbr. articles to profl. pubs. Mem. Nat. Soc. Performance and Instrn., Chgo. Soc. Performance and Instrn., Mich. Soc. Instrnl. Tech. (pres. 1983-84), Orgnl. Behavior Mgmt. Network. Home: 1224 N Dearborn Apt 2-R Chicago IL 60610 Office: R A Svenson & Assocs 2100 Manchester Rd Suite 103 Wheaton IL 60187

BROWN, MARVIN, advertising executive; b. Boston, Mar. 17, 1926; s. Frank A. and Frances (Caplan) B.; student Cornell U., 1943-44, U. Mo., 1946-49; B.J., N.Y. U., 1955; m. Constance Ruth Kaminsky, Sept. 5, 1948; children—Valerie Kay, Mark Kenneth, Randall Craig. Reporter, asst. city editor Shreveport (La.) Times, 1949-53; pub. relations mgr. Glenn Mason Advt., Shreveport, 1953-54; advt. and pub. relations dir. Radio-TV Tng. Assn., N.Y.C., 1954-57; creative services mgr. Nationwide Ins. Cos., Columbus, Ohio, 1957-64; pub. Key Mag., Columbus, 1959—; pres. Marbro Advt., Inc., Columbus, 1965—; pub. Columbus Scene Mag., 1981—, Columbus Bride and Groom Mag., 1985—. Pres., Columbus Quincentennial Expn., 1970—; bd. dirs. Columbus Conv. and Visitors Bur., 1981—. Served with U.S. Army, 1944-46. Mem. Columbus Advt. Fedn. (pres. 1972-73), Columbus Area C. of C. (dir. 1972-73). Clubs: Columbus Athletic, Winding Hollow Country. Home: 180 S Harding Rd Columbus OH 43209 Office: 303 E Livingston Ave Columbus OH 43215

BROWN, MARY JO, nurse educator; b. Bellevue, Iowa, Aug. 12, 1958; d. Lorin J. and Cecilia M. (Kueter) Hager; m. David A. Brown, May 19, 1979. A in Nursing, Area One Vocat.-Tech. Sch., Dubuque, Iowa, 1978; BS in Nursing magna cum laude, U. Dubuque, 1979; postgrad., Drake U., 1980—. RN, Ill., Iowa; cert. critical care nurse. Staff and charge nurse Mercy Health Ctr., Dubuque, 1978-81; charge nurse Meml. Med. Ctr., Springfield, Ill., 1981-82, Iowa Luth. Hosp., Des Moines, 1982-85; nursing instr. Iowa Meth. Sch. Nursing, Des Moines, 1985—, continuing edn. instr., 1986—; proposal reviewer W.B. Saunders Co., 1986—. Basic life provider Am. Heart Assn., 1978—. Mem. Am. Assn. Critical Care Nurses (editor 1984—), Faculty Assn. Continuing Edn., U. Dubuque Nursing Honor Soc. (charter mem.). Avocations: golf, cross-stich. Home: 1726 56th St Des Moines IA 50310 Office: Iowa Meth Sch Nursing 1117 Pleasant Des Moines IA 50309

BROWN, MELVIN FLOYD, minister, educator; b. Chgo., Oct. 13, 1943; m. Floyd Friedrich and Mamie Leona (Boling) B.; m. Barbara Mae Carlson, June 5, 1965; children: Lori, Cheryl, Tim. BTh, Bapt. Bible Coll., 1967; BA, Evangel Coll., 1968; MS, Western Ill. U., 1977; DD, Japan Bapt. Coll., Tokyo, 1985; EdD, No. Ill. U., 1986. Cert. marriage and family therapist, Ill.; ordained Bapt. Ch., 1963. Sr. pastor Edgewood Baptist Ch., Rock Island, Ill., 1968—; pvt. practice marriage and family therapy Rock Island, Ill., 1975—; spl. instr. Moody Bible Inst., Chgo., 1978—; cons. East Moline (Ill.) Christian Sch., 1980-; coordinator Moody Bible Inst., Chgo., 1984—; pres. Marriage and Family Counseling Ctr., Rock Island, Ill. Mem. Am. Assn. for Marriage and Family Therapy, Phi Kappa Phi, Pi Kappa Delta, Delta Psi Omega. Avocation: golf, skiing, reading. Home: 3109 29th St Moline IL 61265 Office: Edgewood Baptist Ch 2704 38th St Rock Island IL 61201

BROWN, MICHAEL RICHARD, reverend; b. Columbus, Ohio, Mar. 2, 1959; s. Cornelius Paul Brown and Pearl Elizabeth (Baker) Buck; m. Christine Elaine Stanley, Aug. 23, 1980; 1 child, Stephanie Nicole. BA in Bible and Religion, Huntington Coll., 1981, MMinistry, 1983, postgrad., 1984. Ordained Christian Ministry. Minister Monroe (Ind.) United Brethren Ch., 1982—. co. dir. Adams County Soccer Clinic, Decatur, Ind., 1984-85; chmn. Adams County Child Protection Team, Decatur, 1985; v.p. Adams County Energy Assistance Inc., 1986. Named one of Outstanding Young Men of Am., 1985. Republican. Lodge: Optimists. Avocations: soccer coach, running. Home: 202 S Adams St Monroe IN 46772 Office: Monroe United Brethren Ch 305 S Adams St Monroe IN 46772

BROWN, NORMAN WESLEY, advertising agency executive; b. Columbus, Ohio, Jan. 27, 1931; s. Leonard and Alvena (Folker) B.; m. Blanche; children—Pamela, Kendall; m. Lynn Godfrey, Jan. 3, 1980; children—Justin Godfrey, Brendan Godfrey. B.A., Ohio State U., 1953; M.B.A., Harvard U., 1958. Account exec. Foote, Cone & Belding, Los Angeles, 1959-63, account supt., 1963-73, gen. mgr., 1973-79; gen. mgr. Foote, Cone & Belding, Chgo., 1979-81, pres., 1981—, chief exec. officer, 1982—; chmn. bd., chief exec. officer, dir. Foote, Cone & Belding Communications Inc., Chgo. Mem. bus. adv. council Chgo. Urban League, 1983—; bd. govs. Sch. Art Inst. Chgo., 1983—; dir. Chgo. Council on Fgn. Relations. Served to 1st lt. USAF, 1954-56. Mem. Am. Assn. Advt. Agys. (gov. at large 1983—). Republican. Clubs: Tavern, East Bank (Chgo.), Saddle and Cycle. Avocation: mountainclimbing. Home: 209 E Lake Shore Dr Chicago IL 60611 Office: Foote Cone & Belding Communications Inc 101 E Erie St Chicago IL 60611

BROWN, PATRICIA LEROI, accountant, educator; b. Lake Forest, Ill., Sept. 25, 1932; d. William Paul and Florence (Edgar) LeRoi; m. William Brown, July 31, 1957 (div. Aug. 1987). AB, Wellesley Coll., 1954; EdM, Harvard U., 1957; postgrad., Northern Ill. U., 1974-77. CPA, Ill. Elementary sch. tchr. Stamford, Conn., 1956-57; nursery sch. tchr. Bogota, N.J., 1961-63; acct. Arthur J. Krupp, CPA, DeKalb, Ill., 1974-77, Robert E. Clausen, CPA, DeKalb, 1977-80; pvt. practice accounting DeKalb, 1980—; part-time instr. Waubonsee Community Coll., Sugar Grove, Ill., 1980—. Chairperson DeKalb Sch. Citizens Adv. Com., 1983-85; bd. DeKalb Community Unit Sch. Dist. 428, 1985—, sec., 1986—. Mem. Am. Inst. CPA's, Ill. CPA Soc., Am. Womens' Soc. CPA's, DeKalb County Estate Planning Council (bd. dirs. 1986-88), Altrusa Internat. (fin. com. chmn. DeKalb-Sycamore, Ill. chpt. 1986-87). Avocations: cross-country skiing, hiking, sailing, gardening. Home: 125 Terrace Dr DeKalb IL 60115 Office: 147 N 2d St Suite 4 DeKalb IL 60115

BROWN, PATRICIA LYNN, information scientist, laboratory executive; b. Lafayette, La., Oct. 1, 1928; d. William Madison and Maude Juanita (Thomas) Brown; B.S. in Chem. Engring., U. Southwestern La., 1947; M.A. in Chemistry, U. Tex., 1949. Instr. analytical chemistry Smith Coll., Northampton, Mass., 1949-50; chemist R&M Labs., Peabody, Mass., 1950; research asso. indsl. toxicology Albany (N.Y.) Med. Coll., 1950-51; mem. info. services staff Ethyl Corp., Ferndale, Mich., 1951-55; sr. tech. writer, editor, staff engr. Westinghouse Atomic Power Div., Pitts., 1955-57; supr., then mgr. info. services, tech. info. cons. Tex. Instruments, Dallas, 1957-66; sr. info. scientist, sr. researcher Battelle Columbus (Ohio) Labs., 1966-76; mgr. sci. services, assoc. dir., info. counselor Travenol Labs., Morton Grove, Ill., 1976-86 ; mgr. tech. info. seminars, Stepan Co., Northfield, Ill., 1987—. Loaned exec. United Way Campaign, 1972, 73. Bd. dirs. Engring. Socs. Library, 1961-63, 66-71. Mem. Soc. Women Engrs. (pres. 1961-63), Am. Chem. Soc., Spl. Libraries Assn., Am. Soc. Info. Sci., Soc. Tech. Communication. Author publs. in field. Home: 1109 Skylark Dr Palatine IL 60067 Office: Stepan Co 22 W Frontage Rd Northfield IL 60093

BROWN, PAUL, football exec.; b. Norwalk, Ohio, July 9, 1908. Ed., Ohio State U., Miami U., Ohio. Coach Severn (Md.) Prep. Sch., 1930-32; coach football and basketball Massillon (Ohio) High Sch., 1932-41; coach Ohio State U., Columbus, 1941-43, Great Lakes Coll., 1944-45; coach profl. football team Cleve. Browns, 1946-62; coach profl. football team Cin. Bengals, 1968-76, v.p., gen. mgr., 1976—. Office: care Cin Bengals 200 Riverfront Stadium Cincinnati OH 45202 *

BROWN, PAUL ALAN, accountant; b. Detroit, May 23, 1938; s. Kenneth Harvey and Marian June (Cooley) B.; m. Gail Kristin Ruth, Sept. 5, 1959 (div. June 1974); children: Kristin, Randall, Stephanie; m. Margaret Lindsay Clark, July 21, 1974. BS, Northwestern U., 1960. CPA, Ill. Sr. ptnr. Brown, Coleman & Co., Evanston, Ill., 1962—. Bd. dirs. Evanston Pub. Library, 1968-74, pres. 1972-74; treas. Evanston Rep. Orgn., 1974-86; mem. Bus. Dist. Redevel. Commn., Evanston, 1977-81. Mem. Am. Inst. CPA's (Elijah Watt Sells cert. 1965), Ill. CPA Soc. (Silver Medal award 1965). Republican. Presbyterian. Lodge: Rotary (treas. Evanston 1985-87). Avocations: skiing, boating, water skiing. Home: 1114 Lake Shore Blvd Evanston IL 60202 Office: Brown Coleman & Co 1800 Sherman Ave Suite 500 Evanston IL 60201

BROWN, PAUL EDWIN, JR., dentist; b. Muncie, Ind., Jan. 27, 1951; s. Paul Edwin Sr. and Lestelle (Lyon) B.; m. Carolyn Anne Patterson Brown, Nov. 4, 1978. BS, Ball State U., 1973; DDS, Ohio State U., 1976. Assoc. B. Newbauer, DDS, Marion, Ind., 1976-78; gen. practice dentistry Marion, 1978—. Mem. ADA, Ind. Dental Assn., Wabash Valley Dental Soc. (v.p. 1985-86, pres. 1986-87), Acad. Gen. Dentistry. Lodge: Rotary. Home: 1511 Ironwood Dr Marion IN 46952 Office: 211 S D St Marion IN 46952

BROWN, PAUL LEROY, academic administrator; b. Ft. Wayne, Ind., Apr. 3, 1933; s. James Thomas and Mathilda Vivian (Horney) B.; m. Yvonne Elaine Martin, June 17, 1960; children: Jill, Tracy, Gregory, Douglas. BA, U. Minn., 1956, M in Pub. Adminstrn., 1958. Adminstrv. analyst Minn. Hwy. Dept., St. Paul, 1958-60, budget officer, 1960-67; budget dir. State of Wis., Madison, 1967-70; adminstr. Wis. Dept. Adminstrn., Madison, 1970-85; v.p. U. Wis., Madison, 1985—; bd. dirs. Wis. Health Facility Authority, Madison. Bd. dirs. Big Bros./Big Sisters of Dane County, Madison, 1980-85. Served with USAR. Roman Catholic. Avocations: fishing, reading. Home: 129 Nautilus Dr Madison WI 53705

BROWN, PHILIP KIMBLE, business executive; b. Lorain, Ohio, Nov. 27, 1937; s. Harold August and Hildred Opal (Jones) B.; m. Deborah Ann Manning, Sept. 7, 1976; 1 child, Derek Nolan; children by previous marriage: Philip Kimble Dane, Stuart Kipling Zane. AB in Sociology, Coll. of Wooster, Ohio, 1957; postgrad. U. Mich., 1962, Nat. Rural Devel. Leaders Sch., Cin., 1976. Mgmt. trainee United Parcel Service, Cleve., 1957-59; mgr. Montgomery Ward, Cin., 1959-61; case worker Lucas County (Ohio) Child Welfare Bd., Toledo, 1961-63; owner, operator farm, Warsaw, Ohio, 1963—; owner, operator Warsaw (Ohio) Milling Co., 1967-75; manpower adminstr. Kno-Ho-Co, Warsaw, 1969-75, exec. dir., 1975—; pres. Muskingum Coach Co., 1981—; pres. Insulation Supply Co., Mt. Vernon, Ohio, 1983—; founder, pres. Chief Petty Paper Co., 1986; founder, chief exec. officer Arrowhead Printing Co., Fredricktown, Ohio, 1986—; chief exec. officer Eagle Rock Tours, 1986—. Bd. dirs. Corp. for Ohio Appalachian Devel., Area Six Health Planning Systems Agy., Marietta, Ohio, 1977, Fed. Emergency Mgmt. Agy., 1986—. Recipient Govs. award for community action, 1975; USDA scholar. Mem. Nat. Assn. Transp. Disadvantaged, Ohio Assn. Community Action Agys. (trustee 1975—), Nat. Assn. R.R. Passengers, Am. Motorcycle Assn. Home: 53192 TR 170 Fresno OH 43824 Office: 300 Bridge St Nellie Warsaw OH 43844

BROWN, RAYMOND MARTIN, accountant; b. Gunnison, Utah, Dec. 31, 1946; s. Guy Martin and Roberta (Peterson) B.; m. N. Sue Ramsey, Dec. 18, 1970; children: Jeffrey, Rebecca. BS cum laude, U. Utah, 1974; M in acctg., Brigham Young U., 1980. CPA, Utah. Acct. Alta (Utah) Peruvian Lodge, 1974-75, Robison, Hill & Co., Salt Lake City, 1975-79; tax supr. Touche Ross & Co., Dayton, Ohio, 1980-86; tax mgr. Dayton Walther Corp., 1986—. Served to sgt. USMC, 1966-70, Vietnam. Mem. Am. Inst. CPA's, Ohio Soc. CPA's (mem. tax com. 1985—), Dayton Soc. CPA's (bd. dirs. 1986—), Tax Exec. Inst. Republican. Mormon. Avocations: woodworking, camping, hunting. Home: 9542 Copper Creek Ct Miamisburg OH 45342 Office: Dayton Walther Corp 2800 E River Rd Dayton OH 45439

BROWN, RICHARD EUGENE, accounting educator, consultant; b. Little Falls, N.Y., June 30, 1937; s. Edward Stanislaus Brown and Mary Elizabeth (Metz) Brown Lynch; A.B. (Coll. scholar), Hope Coll., 1959; M.P.A. (Mich. Fellow), U. Mich., 1960; D.P.A. (Littauer Fellow), Harvard U., 1968; m. Beverly Ann Shaffer, Feb. 25, 1961; children—Kelly Christine, Christopher Richard, Kirsten Marie. With TVA, Knoxville, 1961-69, asst. to gen. mgr., 1967-69; dir. audit ops. Legis. Commn. on Expenditure Rev., Albany, N.Y., 1970-75; state auditor Kans. Legislature, Topeka, 1975-83; prof. non-profit acctg. Kent State U., 1983—; ptnr. Shaffer, Brown & Assocs., 1985—; spl. cons. Price Waterhouse, 1983—; acad. research. con. Govtl. Acctg. Standards Bd., 1987—; prof. or adj. prof. fin. and adminstrn. William and Mary Coll., U. Kans., U. Tenn., Kans. State U., SUNY, Albany; cons. GAO, various state legislatures. Scoutmaster, Boy Scouts Am. Mem. Am. Soc. Public Adminstrn. (chmn. mgmt. sci. sect.), Nat. Conf. State Legislatures (exec. com.), Public Adminstrn. Soc. (pres. Topeka), Am. Inst. C.P.A.s (task force on operational auditing). Author: The GAO; Untapped Source of Congl. Power, 1970; editor: The Effectiveness of Legislative Program Review, 1979; co-author: Auditing the Performance of Government; contbr. articles to profl. jours.; editorial bd. Govt. Accts. Jour., 1983—, Public Adminstrn. Rev., 1980-83; co-editor Public Budgeting and Finance. Home: 2373 Glenn Echo Dr Hudson OH 44236 Office: Coll Bus Adminstrn Kent State U Kent OH 44242

BROWN, RICHARD OSBORNE, physician; b. Detroit, May 20, 1930; s. Richard Wells and Flossie Eva (Osborne) B.; B.A., Wayne State U., 1953; M.D., Howard U., 1959; m. Dolores Debro, Jan. 23, 1954; children—Richard Debro, Kevin Michael; m. 2d, Martha Evelyn McGregor, Oct. 6, 1973; children—Vincent, Tiffany Diane. Intern, Wayne County Gen. Hosp., 1959-60; resident ophthalmology Homer G. Phillips Hosp., St. Louis, 1962-65; staff ophthalmologist CHA-Met. Hosp., Detroit, 1965-67; practice medicine specializing in ophthalmology, Detroit, 1967—; chief med. staff Kirwood Gen. Hosp., 1974-76, now trustee, Cons., Met., SW Detroit, Lakeside, Kirwood, St. Joseph hosps. Mem. Draft Bd., 1971-76. Served with

AUS, 1953-55. Mem. Am. Assn. Ophthalmology, Nat. Med. Assn. (2d v.p. 1981-83, 1st v.p. 1983-85, trustee 1985—), AMA, Wayne County, Detroit (treas. 1972-78, pres. 1978-80), Mich. State med. socs., Detroit C. of C., Am. Profl. Practice Assn., Council Med. Staffs Mich. (dir. 1971—). Episcopalian. Home: 22854 Newport Southfield MI 48075 Office: 3800 Woodward St Detroit MI 48201

BROWN, ROBERT MARTIN, veterinarian; b. Jacksonville, Ill., Sept. 8, 1940; s. James Robert Daggett and A. Ruth (Martin) B.; m. Judy Ann Jensen, July 3, 1964; children: Kevin, Laura. BS, N. D. State U., 1962; DVM, Kans. State U., 1966. Vet. Westonka Animal Hosp., Mound, Minn., 1969-70, Butler (Wis.) Animal Hosp., 1970-83, Jackson (Wis.) Area Pet Hosp., 1983—. Author: The Doberman Owner's Medical Manual, 1987. Served to capt. U.S. Army, 1966-69, Vietnam. Mem. AVMA, Am. Animal Hosp. Assn. Republican. Methodist. Avocations: showing, breeding, judging dogs. Home: 3360 Jackson Dr Jackson WI 53037 Office: Jackson Area Pet Hosp 3370 Jackson Dr Jackson WI 53037

BROWN, ROBERT VENTON, government official; b. Oklahoma City, June 10, 1936; s. David L. and Grace A. B.; B.A. in Bus., U. Md., 1969; M.B.A., U. Utah, 1971; grad. Air Command and Staff Coll., 1972; sr. exec. fellow, Harvard U., 1980; student U. Okla., 1957-63; m. Barbara Lee Garrett, Sept. 1, 1957; children—Lee-Anita, Jennifer Lynne, Yvonne Kathleen, Denise Ladele. With maintenance and materiel mgmt. Air Force Logistics Command, Okla. and Calif., 1959-66; logistics staff U.S. Air Force Europe, Germany, 1966-71; chief tech. support sect. Inventory Mgmt. Div., Tex., 1972-77; chief product performance evaluation div. Air Force Acquisition Logistics div. Air Force Logistics Command, Wright-Patterson AFB, Ohio, 1977-78, dir. acquisition control Air Force dep. for avionics control, 1978-81, asst. to comdr., 1981-86; former mem. Fed. Sr. Exec. Service; instr. logistics Our Lady of the Lake U., San Antonio, 1973-77; part-time faculty local colls. Safety com. PTA; adv. bd. Order of Rainbow for Girls; booster High Sch. Math. and Sci. Club; advisor 4-H Clubs Am. Served with USN, 1954-57. Mem. Soc. Logistics Engrs. (ednl. chmn. Tex. 1975-76), Am. Def. Preparedness Assn., Air Force Assn., Assn. of Grads. Air Force Inst. Tech. (charter). Clubs: VFW, Masons, Scottish Rite, Shrine. Contbr. papers to profl. seminars and symposia. Office: HQ AFALC/CA Wright-Patterson AFB OH 45433

BROWN, ROGER WILLIAM, manufacturers representative, real estate developer; b. Lansing, Mich., Feb. 25, 1940; s. Gustave Adolph and Beulah Alice (Bates) B.; m. Janet Rose Neiman, Apr. 16, 1977. BA, Denison U., 1961; commerce diploma, U. Birmingham, Eng., 1962; MBA, U. Chgo., 1966. Instr. Dept. Econs. Denison U., Granville, Ohio, 1966-67; lectr. Dept. Econs. Ohio State U., Columbus, 1966-67; cons. Boston Cons. Group, Boston and London, 1967-69; mgr. mktg. services Graflex div. Singer Co., Rochester, N.Y., 1969-70; v.p. Gustave Brown and Assoc., Inc., Oak Brook, Ill., 1970-87; pres. Roger Brown and Assoc., Inc., Elburn, Ill., 1987—. Author: Study to Learn, 1965; contbr. articles on USAF programmed instrn., econs, corp. strategy. Mem. land use com. Campton Twp., Kane County, Ill., 1978-81. Served to 1st lt. USAF, 1962-65. Mem. Omicron Delta Epsilon, Rho Beta Chi, Omicron Delta Kappa. Republican. Methodist. Clubs: Upton Country (Jamaica), Runaway Bay Country (Jamaica). Avocation: grain and cattle farmer. Home: 4N654 Anderson Rd Elburn IL 60119 also: Tranquillity PO Box 224, Ochos Rios Jamaica Office: PO Box 420 Elburn IL 60119

BROWN, RONALD WAYNE, fire chief; b. Marion, Ind., Sept. 18, 1946; s. James Pershing and Elizabeth Ann (Langer) B.; m. Marsha Pollos, June 9, 1964; children: Shane W., Rachelle A., Jason J. AAS, Purdue U., Ft. Wayne, Ind., 1981. Firefighter Ft. Wayne Fire Dept., 1970-76, capt., 1976-78, platoon capt., 1978-81, dist. chief, 1981-82, asst. chief, 1982-84, chief, 1984—; instr. Nat. Fire Acad., Emmitsburg, Md., 1982—. Bd. dirs. Ind. Vocat. Tech. Coll. Served to sgt. USAF, 1964-68. Mem. Nat. Fire Protection Assn., Internat. Assn. Fire Chiefs, Ind. Fire Instrs. Assn. (bd. dirs. 1982—), Allen County Fire Chiefs Assn. (pres. 1986—). Office: Office of the Fire Chief City County Bldg 3d floor Fort Wayne IN 46802

BROWN, RONALD WESLEY, endodontist; b. Middlesboro, Ky., Feb. 22, 1942; s. Ben and Dorothy (Euster) B. DDS, Ohio State U., 1967, Cert. in Endodontics, 1974. Gen. practice dentistry Miami, Fla., 1969-72; practice dentistry specializing in endodontics Cin., 1975—. Patentee in field. Served to capt. U.S. Army, 1967-69. Mem. ADA, Am. Assn. Endodontists, Alpha Omega. Office: 8060 Montgomery Rd Cincinnati OH 45236

BROWN, SHERROD CAMPBELL, state official; b. Mansfield, Ohio, Nov. 9, 1952; s. Charles G. and Emily (Campbell) B.; m. Larke Ummel, Aug. 25, 1979; children: Emily, Elizabeth. B.A., Yale U., 1974; M.A. in Edn., Ohio State U., 1979, M.A. in Pub. Adminstrn., 1981. Mem. Ohio Ho. of Reps., Mansfield, 1975-82; Sec. of State State of Ohio, Columbus, 1983—; instr. Ohio State U., Mansfield, 1978-79; sec. Commrs. Sinking fund, Columbus, 1983—. Mem. State Democratic Exec. Com., Columbus, 1976-83; mem. Ohio Pub. Facility Commn., 1983—, United Way Allocation Com., 1983—. Recipient Pro Deo et Patria Boy Scouts Am., 1966; recipient Friend of Edn. award, 1978. Mem. Nat. Assn. Secs. State. Democrat. Lutheran. Office: State of Ohio 30 E Broad St 14th Floor Columbus OH 43266 •

BROWN, SOLON AUTRY, psychology educator, clergyman; b. Watson, Okla., May 1, 1924; s. Solon Lemley and Bessie Jane (Wilhelm) B.; m. Opal Irene Landers, Sept.5, 1942; children: Juanice, Rebecca, Steven, Deborah. BA, Eastern N.M. U., 1950; M of Div., New Orleans Bapt. Theol. Sem., 1955, MRE, 1956, EdD, 1968; postgrad., Colo. State U., 1970, Southwest Mo. State U., 1985. Ordained to ministry Bapt. Ch., 1942. Pastor Bookcliff Bapt. Ch., Grand Junction, Colo., 1957-61, Carrollton Ave. Bapt. Ch., New Orleans, 1962-64, Immanuel Bapt. Ch., Ft. Collins, Colo., 1964-72; asst. prof. psychology Mo. Bapt. U., St. Louis, 1972-74; asst. prof. psychology Southwest Bapt. U., Bolivar, Mo., 1974-76, prof. psychology, 1978—, dir. counseling services, 1978—; cons. family ministry Colo. Bapt. Gen. Conv., Denver, 1976-78. Author: Church Family Life Conference Guidebook, 1973; contbr. books, profl. jour. Recipient Spl. Services award Bd. Trustees New Orleans Bapt. Theol. Sem., 1972. Mem. Am. Assn. Marriage and Family Therapy, Mo. Assn. Marriage and Family Therapy (Spl. Service award 1984, treas. state exec. bd. 1979-83), Ozark Assn. Marriage and Family Therapy (pres. 1985-86), Mo. Assn. Counseling and Devel., Fellows Menniger Found. Lodge: Optimists (Community Service award 1972). Avocation: collecting antique barbed wire. Home: 1223 Woodland Cir Bolivar MO 65613 Office: Southwest Bapt U Bolivar MO 65613

BROWN, SORREL (MARTHA), agronomist; b. Frankfurt, Germany, Nov. 5, 1949; parents U.S. citizens; d. Arthur William and Luisa Margarita (Badaracco) B.; student Tex. Christian U., 1967-69, U. Tex., Austin, 1969-70; B.S. in Psychology, Ariz. State U., 1972, M.S. in Soil Sci., 1977. Plant pathologist Ariz. Public Service Utilities Co., Phoenix, 1976, 77; field agronomist Chevron Chem. Co., Des Moines, 1977-80; crop prodn. specialist Iowa State U. Extension, Des Moines, 1980—; speaker in field. Mem. Iowa Sister-State Friendship Com.; chmn. fundraising Iowa-Yucatan Ptnrs. of Am. Recipient McVickar Agronomy Achievement award Chevron Chem. Co., 1978; Sarah Tyson Bradley Meml. fellow, 1973-74; Laura M. Bohem Found. scholar, 1974-75. Mem. Am. Soc. Agronomy, Soil Sci. Soc. Am., Nat. Assn. County Agrl. Agts. (Career Guidance award 1981), Alpha Zeta. Home: 2806 Adams Des Moines IA 50310 Office: 109 W Winds 1454 30th St West Des Moines IA 50265

BROWN, SPENCER HUNTER, historian; b. Knoxville, Tenn., June 10, 1928; s. John Orville and Edith Frances (Hunter) B.; m. Doris Lucille Craig, Aug. 4, 1951; 1 dau., Rebecca Lee. B.A. in Teaching Social Studies magna cum laude, U. Ill., 1954, M.A. in History; fellow, 1955; Ph.D. in History (African Studies fellow), Northwestern U., 1964. Tchr., chmn. social scis. dept. Carl Sandburg High Sch., Orland Park, Ill., 1955-59; mem. faculty Western Ill. U., Macomb, 1962—; prof. history Western Ill. U., 1971—, chmn. dept., 1976-84. Gen. editor: Jour. Developing Areas, 1965-76; bus. mgr., 1976—, assoc. editor, 1984—. Served with USNR, 1945-47. Ford Found. fellow, 1961-62. Mem. African Studies Assn., Am. Hist. Assn., Phi Beta Kappa. Home: Box 47 Tennessee IL 62374 Office: Dept of History Western Illinois University Macomb IL 61455

BROWN, STEPHEN MICHAEL, air force officer; b. Jackson, Mich., June 25, 1952. A.A., Jackson County Community Coll., 1975; B.A. in Psychology, Siena Heights Coll., 1976; M.A. in Counseling, Cen. Mich. U. 1981; Airman USAF, 1971, advanced through grades to capt., 1982; personnel specialist McConnell AFB, Kans., 1971-72, psychiat. technician USAF Hosp., 1972-74; youth specialist Adrian (Mich.) Tng. Sch., 1976-77; computer systems devel. officer/systems analyst Wright-Patterson AFB, Ohio, 1979-81, air force logistics command spl. projects mgr., 1981; test psychologist Randolph AFB, Tex., 1981-84; systems analysis officer Def. Logistics Service Ctr., Battle Creek, Mich., 1984—; drug and alcohol counselor; grad. teaching asst. Cen. Mich. U., 1977. Methodist. Office: Def Logistics Service Ctr 74 N. Washington Battle Creek MI 49017-3084

BROWN, STEPHEN ROBERT, manufacturing executive; b. London, England, Apr. 22, 1939; arrived in U.S., 1980; s. Henry Robert and Anne (Platten) B.; m. Lesley Maunsell, Apr. 16, 1966; children: Hilary, Christopher, Michael, Rebecca. MA, Oxford U., England, 1962; MBA, U. Western Ont., 1970. Acct. Shell Internat. Petroleum Co. Ltd., Genoa, Italy, Oman, 1963-68; fin. mgr. Alcan Can. Products Ltd., Toronto, 1970-72; mfg. mgr. Alcan Extrusions, Kingston, Ont., 1972-74, Alcan Rolled Products, Kingston, Ont., 1975-78; gen. mgr. cen. region Alcan Bldg. Products, Toronto, 1978-80; v.p. planning Alcan Aluminum Corp., Cleve., 1980-82, exec. v.p., 1982—; pres. Alcan Bldg. Products Co., Warren, Ohio, 1980-82, Alcan Rolled Products Co., Cleve., Toronto, 1985—; exec. v.p. Alcan Aluminum Corp., Cleve., 1985—, also bd. dirs.; v.p. Aluminum Co. of Can., Ltd., Montreal, 1985—; bd. dirs. Logan Aluminum Inc., Russellville, Ky., Alcan Smelters and Chems. Ltd., Montreal. Active United Way, Cleve., 1987. Mem. The Aluminum Assn. Anglican. Clubs: Country, Cleve. Racquet (Pepper Pike, Ohio); York, Toronto Lawn Tenis (Tornonto). Avocations: tennis, squash, golf. Office: Alcan Aluminium Corp 100 Erieview Plaza Cleveland OH 44114

BROWN, STEVEN DOUGLAS, psychologist; b. Troy, Ohio, Feb. 17, 1947; s. Irvin Russell and Elma Mae (Lamka) B.; m. Linda Heath, 1985. B.A., Muskingum Coll., 1969; M.A., U. Va., 1972; Ph.D., U. Calif., Santa Barbara, 1977. Psychologist, Central State Hosp., Petersburg, Va., 1971-73; mental health cons. San Mateo County (Calif.) Mental Health Services, San Mateo, 1973-74; cons. drug abuse program Fed. Correctional Instn., Lompoc, Calif., 1976-77; fellow dept. psychiatry U. Wis., Madison, 1977-78; dir. counseling psychology clinic, counseling psychology program U. Calif., Santa Barbara, 1978-79; asst. prof. psychology U. Minn., Mpls., 1979-84; assoc. prof. counseling and ednl. psychology Loyola U. Chgo., 1984—; cons. in field. Cora I. Orr fellow, 1968-69. Mem. Am. Psychol. Assn., Am. Assn. Counseling and Devel., Assn. for Advancement of Behavior Therapy, Sigma Xi, Psi Chi, Phi Sigma, Kappa Delta Pi. Home: 1415 Lincoln St Evanston IL 60626 Office: Dept Counseling and Ednl Psychology Loyola U 820 N Michigan Ave Chicago IL 60611

BROWN, STEVEN MICHAEL, acoustician, physicist; b. N.Y.C., Dec. 3, 1944; s. Raphael and Olga (Sacharoff) B.; m. Carol Lynn Swanson, 1969; children: Alycia, Daniel. BA, Johns Hopkins U., 1966, MA, 1969, PhD, 1972. Physicist U.S. Naval Research Lab., Washington, 1966-70; research assoc., instr. physics Johns Hopkins U., Balt., 1966-72; research resident and sci. sec. Ctr. Theoretical Studies, U. Miami, Fla., 1972-73; dir. quality control AMSCO, Inc., Warren, Pa., 1973; sr. research scientist Armstrong World Industries, Lancaster, Pa., 1973-86; sr. research engr. Steelcase, Grand Rapids, Mich., 1986—. Sci. sec., co-editor: Fundamental Interactions in Physics, 1973; contbr. articles to profl. jours. Active local sch. dist., 1979—. NSF fellow, 1966, NASA fellow, 1966-69. Fellow Acoustical Soc. Am. (tech. com. archtl. acoustics 1979—, TCAA fellowship subcom. 1985—); mem. Am. Phys. Soc., ASTM (sec. 1980—, coms.), Inst. Noise Control Engring. (affiliate), Am. Assn. Physics Tchrs., Phi Beta Kappa, Sigma Xi, Omicron Delta Kappa. Home: 599 Rookway SE Grand Rapids MI 49506 Office: Steelcase Inc Grand Rapids MI 49501

BROWN, SUZANNE WILEY, musuem executive; b. Cheyenne, Wyo., Aug. 28, 1938; d. Robert James and Catharine Helen (Schroeder) Wiley; B.S. with honors, U. Wyo., 1960, M.S., 1964; postgrad. U. Cin. Med. Sch., 1965-66, U. Ill., 1969-72; m. Ralph E. Brown, July 19, 1968; 1 dau., Nina M. Research asst. Harvard Med. Sch., 1962-63; research asst. U. Cin. Med. Sch., 1964-65; sr. lab. asst. U. Chgo., 1966-67; research assoc. U. Colo. Med. Sch., 1968; teaching asst. U. Ill., 1971-73; exec. asst. Chgo. Acad. Scis., 1974-82, asst. dir., 1982-84, assoc. dir., 1984—. NDEA fellow, 1960-62. Mem. Mus. Educators of Greater Chgo., Am. Assn. Museums, Internat. Council Museums, Brookfield Zool. Soc. (bd. govs.), Pub. Relations in Service to Musuems, Midwest Mus. Conf., Phi Beta Kappa, Sigma Xi, Phi Kappa Phi. Office: 2001 N Clark St Chicago IL 60614

BROWN, TERRY RAY, obstetrician, gynecologist; b. Jasper, Ind., Sept. 11, 1951; s. Clarence Ray and Betty Jean (Peak) B.; m. Betty Ann Brang; children: Krista Linn, Jonathan Evan-Hunter, Kathleen Marie. BA, Ind. U., 1973, MD, 1977. Intern, then resident in ob-gyn Ind. U. Hosps., Indpls., 1977-81; practice medicine specializing in ob-gyn Jasper, 1981—; sec. med. staff Meml. Hosp., Jasper, 1986. Contbr. articles to med. jours. Mem. found. bd. Vincennes U., Jasper Ctr., 1986. Fellow Am. Coll. Obstetricians and Gynecologists; mem. AMA, Ind. State Med. Assn. Avocation: photography. Office: 939 Meml Dr PO Box 723 Jasper IN 47546

BROWN, THANE ROSS, engineering manager; b. Merrill, Wis., Feb. 8, 1939; s. Thane Edwin and Gretchen Elizabeth (Kellogg) B.; m. Nancy Jean Sonntag, Aug. 12, 1965; children: Stephanie J.; Thane E. BSChemE, Oreg. State U., 1961. Registered profl. engr., Ohio. Dept. mgr. mfg. Procter & Gamble Co., Long Beach, Calif., 1961-67; engr. Procter & Gamble Co., Cin., 1967-68, group leader engring., 1968-72, section head engring., 1972-76, assoc. dir. engring., 1976-84, dir. engring., 1984—. Contbr. articles to Chem. Engring. Mag. Coach Soccer Assn. for Youth, Cin., 1974-81; cub scout leader Boy Scout Am., 1979-80. Served as 1st lt. U.S. Army, 1961-63. Republican. Presbyterian. Avocations: hunting, fishing, travelling. Home: 7945 Nieman Dr Cincinnati OH 45224 Office: Winton Hill Tech Ctr 6250 Center Hill Rd Cincinnati OH 45224

BROWN, THOMAS NEIL, pharmacist; b. Saginaw, Mich., June 14, 1951; s. Donald Arthur and Shirley (Welzel) B.; m. Marilyn Sarafian, Feb. 22, 1981; children: Michael Thomas, Maegan Lynn. BS in Phamacy, U. Mich., 1974, PharmD, 1977. Pharmacist Henry Ford Hosp., Detroit, 1974-75; asst. chief resident Univ. Hosp., Ann Arbor, Mich., 1976-77; adj. asst. prof. pharmacy Coll. Pharmacy and Allied Health Professions Wayne State U., Detroit, 1979—; asst. dir. pharmacy Harper Hosp., Detroit, 1979-84; asst. corp. dir. pharmacy Harper-Grace Hosps., Detroit, 1984—. Recipient Share Our Savings spl. award Mich. Hosp. Assn., 1981. Mem. Am. Pharm. Assn., Am. Soc. Hosp. Pharmacists, Mich. Pharmacists Assn., Southeastern Mich. Soc. Hosp. Pharmacists (sec. 1980-82, pres. 1983-84), Mich. Soc. Hosp. Pharmacists (exec. sec. 1986—). Lutheran. Home: 2691 Stonebury Dr Rochester MI 48063

BROWN, VIRGINIA MARY, insurance agent; b. Smith Creek, Mich., Mar. 5, 1938; d. John Milford and Mary Elizabeth (Pratt) Rockstroh; m. Thomas Wesley Brown, Mar. 1, 1969; 1 child, Sue Ann. Student, Port Huron Jr. Coll., 1957-58; grad., Eastern Mich. Coll. Commerce, 1959; student in ins., Mich. State U. Lic. real estate agt. Agt. Brown Ins. Agy., Inc., Birch Run, Mich. Mem. Birch Run Sesquicentenial. Mem. Profl. Ins. Agts. (membership com. 1987—), Ind. Agts. Mich., Ind. Agts. Genesee County, Birch Run C. of C. (bd. dirs.), Birch Run Businessmen's Assn. Lodge: Order Eastern Star. Home: 7784 Main St PO Box 117 Birch Run MI 48415

BROWN, VIVIAN KEYS, administrative services executive; b. Wisner, La., Nov. 24, 1946; d. Eugene and Ethel (Neal) Keys; m. Willie Brown, Sept. 4, 1982. B.S., Grambling State U., 1968; M.A., Central Mich. U., 1975; student U. Mich., 1980. Tchr., Franklin Parish Schs., Winnsboro, La., 1968-72; tchr. Buena Vista Pub. Schs., Saginaw, Mich., 1972-77, sch. adminstr., 1977—, dir. spl. programs, student personnel, 1977—. Mem. NAACP, Mich. Assn. State and Fed. Program Specialists, Assn. for Supervision and Curriculum Devel., Mich. Reading Assn., Buena Vista Adminstrs. Assn. (v.p.), Delta Sigma Theta. Home: 4672 S Gregory Pl Saginaw MI 48601 Office: 705 N Towerline Rd Saginaw MI 48601

BROWN, WAYNE LEE, kitchen and bath design executive; b. Fairmont, W.Va., Oct. 16, 1946; s. Paul Wayne and Pansy Virginia (Shaver) B.; m. Nancy Ann Rundle, Dec. 16, 1966; children: Michele Lee, Lora Ann. BA, Fairmont State U., 1969; A in Bus. Supervisory Skills, Parkersburg (W.Va.) Community Coll., 1980. Driller's asst. Sprague & Henwood, Fairmont, 1965; machinist T&T Machine Shop, Fairmont, 1971-72; machine operator Alcan Aluminum, Fairmont, 1971-72; kitchen designer Bauer Home Ctr., Parkersburg, 1973-85; mgr. Bauer Kitchen & Bath Ctr., Marietta, Ohio, 1985—. Pres. Wood County Spl. Olympics., Parkersburg, W.Va., 1986-87. Served to capt. U.S. Army, 1969-71, Vietnam. Named one of Outstanding Young Men. of Am., 1983. Mem. Washington County Home Builders. Democrat. Methodist. Lodge: Civitan (lt. gov. W.Va. chpt. 1982-83, bd. dirs. 1983-84, club pres. 1986-87, Disting. Lt Gov. 1983, Civitan of Yr. 1984), Masons, Moose. Avocations: hunting, fishing, golf. Home: 107 36th St Vienna WV 26105 Office: Bauer Kitchen and Bath Ctr 109 Pike St Marietta OH 45750

BROWN, (ROBERT) WENDELL, lawyer; b. Mpls., Feb. 26, 1902; s. Robert and Jane Amanda (Anderson) B.; m. Barbara Ann Fisher, Oct. 20, 1934; children: Barbara Ann (Mrs. Neil Maurice Travis), Mary Alice (Mrs. Alfred Lee Fletcher). A.B., U. Hawaii, 1924; J.D., U. Mich., 1926. Bar: Mich. 1926, U.S. Supreme Ct 1934, U.S. Ct. Appeals (6th cir.) 1952, U.S. Dist. Ct (ea. dist.) Mich. 1927, U.S. Dist. Ct. (we. dist.) Mich. 1931, U.S. Bd. Immigration Appeals 1944, U.S. Tax Ct 1973. Lawyer firm Routier, Nichols & Fildew, Detroit, 1926, Nichols & Fildew, 1927-28, Frank C. Sibley, 1929, Ferguson & Ferguson, 1929-31; asst. atty. gen. Mich., 1931-32; with legal dept. Union Guardian Trust Co., Detroit, 1933-34; sole practice law Detroit, 1934-81, Farmington Hills, Mich., 1981—; Legal adviser Wayne County (Mich.) Graft Grand Jury, 1939-40; asst. pros. atty. civil matters Wayne County, 1940; spl. asst. city atty. to investigate Police Dept. Highland Park, Mich., 1951-52. Chmn. citizens com. to form Oakland County (Mich.) Community Coll., 1962-63; Pres. Farmington (Mich.) Sch. Bd., 1952-56; chmn. Oakland County Republican County Conv., 1952; trustee Farmington Twp., Oakland County, 1957-61; pres. Oakland County Lincoln Rep. Club, 1958; Treas., bd. dirs. Friends of Detroit Library, 1943-44; bd. dirs. Farmington Friends of Library, Inc., 1952-58, pres., 1956-57; Hon. mem. Farmington Hist. Soc., 1966, St. Anthonys Guild, Franciscan Friars, 1975. Mem. Am. Bar Assn., State Bar Mich. (chmn. or mem. various coms. 1935-52, 77-80), Oakland County Bar Assn., Detroit Bar Assn. (bd. dirs. 1939-49, pres. 1948-49). Presbyn. (elder). Home: 29921 Ardmore St Farmington Hills MI 48018 Office: Quakertown Plaza 32969 Hamilton Ct Suite 115 Farmington Hills MI 48018

BROWN, WESLEY ERNEST, U.S. judge; b. Hutchinson, Kans., June 22, 1907; s. Morrison H.H. and Julia (Wesley) B.; m. Mary A. Miller, Nov. 30, 1934; children: Wesley Miller, Loy B. (Mrs. John K. Wiley). Student, Kans. U., 1925-28; LL.B., Kansas City Law Sch., 1933. Bar: Kans. 1933, Mo. 1933. Practiced in Hutchinson, 1933-58; county atty. Reno County, Kans., 1935-39; referee in bankruptcy U.S. Dist. Ct. Kans., 1958-62, judge, 1962-79, sr. judge, 1979—; chief judge, 1971-77; appointee Temporary Emergency Ct. of Appeals of U.S., 1980—; Dir. Nat. Assn. Referees in Bankruptcy, 1959-62; mem. bankruptcy div. Jud. Conf., 1963-70; mem. Jud. Conf., U.S., 1976-79. Served with USNR, 1944-46. Mem. ABA, Kans. Bar Assn. (exec. council 1950-62, pres. 1964-65), Reno County Bar Assn. (pres. 1947), Wichita Bar Assn., S.W. Bar Kan., Delta Theta Phi. Office: U S Dist Ct 423 U S Courthouse 401 N Market St Wichita KS 67202

BROWN, WILLIAM BOYD, tax firm executive, educator; b. Sioux Falls, S.D., June 19, 1939; s. Leo and Florence (Mullen) B.; m. Annette McDonald, June 18, 1966; children—Brenda, Bridget, Elizabeth. B.S.B.A., State U. S.D., 1961; J.D., U. Minn., 1966. Bar: Minn. With Deloitte Haskins & Sells, N.Y.C., 1966-69, Mpls., 1969—, now ptnr. in charge taxes Minn. offices; mem. faculty U. Minn. Served to 1st lt. U.S. Army, 1961-63. Mem. Minn. Soc. C.P.A.s (tax com.), Am. Inst. C.P.A.s, ABA, Minn. Bar Assn., Internat. Fiscal Assn., Minn. C. of C. and Industry, Assn. Gen. Contractors, C.P.A. Tax Roundtable (former chmn.), Mpls. Aquatennial Assn., Citizens League, Hennepin County Bar Assn., Sigma Alpha Epsilon, Delta Theta Phi. Independent Republican. Clubs: Libbs Bay Boat (commodore); Mpls. Athletic, Interlachen Country; Excelsior Bay Yacht. Office: Deloitte Haskins and Sells 625 4th Ave S Suite 1000 Minneapolis MN 55415

BROWN, WILLIAM DARREL, mechanical engineer; b. Portland, Oreg., June 2, 1939; s. Charles Frank Lafollette and Mildred Caroline (Bredenbeck) B.; B.S. in M.E., Oreg. State U., 1961; M.S., U. Wash., 1970; m. Sharon Lee Hawley, July 14, 1961; children—Shannon, Ross, Robby. Project engr., Esco Inc., Portland, Oreg., 1961-62; prin. engr. Silver Eagle Co., Portland, 1963-64; design engr. Omark Industries Inc., Portland, 1965-66; mech. engr. Sandwell Intrnat., Inc., Portland, 1967-68; mech. engr. Pacific Rim Inc., Tacoma, Wash., part time 1968-70; mech. engr. Sargent & Lundy, Chgo., 1970-73; sr. nuclear engr. Fluor Pioneer Inc., Chgo., 1973-78; sr. mech. engr. Laramore Douglass and Popham, Cons. Engrs., Chgo., 1978-79; assoc. M.W. Brown & Assocs., Chgo., 1979-82; propr. Darrel Brown, Profl. Engr., 1983—; cons. Inst. Cultural Affairs. Mem. Village of Oak Park Econ. Devel. Com., 1973; co-founder Beye Neighborhood Council, Oak Park, 1973—; mem. Townmeeting Task Force, 1975-76. Mem. ASME, Am. Nuclear Soc. Democrat. Mem. First Ch. of Religious Science. Home: Box 893 Oak Park IL 60303

BROWN, WILLIAM EVERETT, food packaging consultant, chemical engineer; b. Auburn, N.Y., Nov. 9, 1927; s. Everett Lawton and Helen May (Rasmussen) B.; B.S., Syracuse U., 1951; m. Natalie Smith, Oct. 3, 1953; children—Matthew, Kevin, Paul, Lorraine, Rebecca. With Dow Chem. Co., Midland, Mich., 1951-85, head testing sect., 1956-62, head performance and design, 1962-66, sr. sect. head automotive sect., 1967, new applications devel., 1967-70, tech. mgr. new ventures research and devel., 1970-74, research mgr. Saran and Converted Products research, 1974-80, sr. research mgr., 1980-83, sr. research mgr. plastics dept., 1983-85, cons. 1986—. Chmn. planning com. Bay-Midland OEO, 1970-72; pres. Men of Music, Midland, 1979-80. Served with U.S. Army, 1946-47. Mem. ASTM, Am. Assn. Cereal Chemists., Inst. Food Technologists, Research and Devel. Assocs., Sigma Xi. Contbr. articles to profl. jours. Editor: Testing of Polymers, book series, 1965-70. Home: 4950 Grandview Circle Midland MI 48640 Office: PO Box 2006 Midland MI 48641

BROWN, WILLIAM MARSHALL, columnist, teacher, small business owner; b. Huntingburg, Ind., May 25, 1954; s. Robert Carl and Grace (Marshall) B.; m. Elaine Marie Becher, May 10, 1975; 1 child, Marissa Liane. BS, Ind. U., 1976. Tchr. Forest Park High Sch., Ferdinand, Ind., 1976-79; columnist The Jour. and Dem. Newspaper, Rockport, Ind., 1978—, Pizza Today and Catering Today mags., Santa Claus, Ind., 1983—; co-owner Brown Bros. Lumber Co. Inc., Dale, Ind., 1979—; seminar leader Pizza Today mag., Orlando, Fla. and Las Vegas, 1984, 85, Nat. Restaurant Assn., New Orleans, 1986; tchr. computer classes The Sound of Music Store, Jasper, Ind., 1982-85. Author (book) Personal Computers: A Handbook for Beginners, 1984; contbr. articles to computer mags. Mem. Jaycees (v.p. 1978-79). Republican. Lodge: Kiwanis (v.p. Dale chpt. 1986—). Avocations: reading, photography, running, sailing. Home: Rural Rt 3 Box 254 Ferdinand IN 47532 Office: Brown Bros Lumber Co Inc Medcalf & Main Dale IN 47523

BROWNE, ALDIS JEROME, JR., real estate broker; b. Chgo., Mar. 21, 1912; s. Aldis J. and Elizabeth (Cunningham) B.; B.A., Yale U., 1935; m. Bertha Erminger, Oct. 22, 1938; children—Aldis J. III, Howell E., John Kenneth. Vice pres., dir. Browne & Storch Inc., and predecessors, Chgo., 1935-81, dir., 1961-81; with Quinlan & Tyson, Evanston, Ill., 1981-84, L.J. Sheridan Co., 1985—. Bd. dirs. English Speaking Union, Civic Fedn., Mil. Order World Wars; chmn. Bldg. Rev. Bd. Lake Forest; vestryman, St. James Episcopalian Ch., 1947-60; trustee, Old People's Home, Chgo.; bd. dirs. Key West Art and Hist. Soc. Served to capt. USNR. Mem. Chgo. (dir.), Ill., N. Side Chgo. real estate bds., Nat. Realtors Assn., Order Founders and Patriots (gov. Ill. chpt.), Soc. Colonial Wars (gov. Ill. chpt.), Order St. Lazarus, Mil. Order World Wars (past comdr. Chgo. br.), Mil. Order Loyal Legion, Chgo. Art Inst. (governing life), Navy League (past dir.). Republican. Clubs: Chgo., Tavern, Army Navy Washington, Masons. Office: LJ Sheridan & Co 30 N LaSalle St Chicago IL 60602

BROWNE, EDMUND JOHN PHILLIP, oil company executive; b. Hamburg, Fed. Republic Germany, Feb. 20, 1948; came to U.S., 1986; s. Edmund and Paula Browne. MA in Physics, Cambridge U., Eng., 1969; MS in Bus., Stanford (Calif.) U., 1981. Registered profl. engr., United Kingdom. Petroleum engr. Brit. Petroleum Co., N.Y., Calif. and Alaska, 1969-79; regional petroleum engr. Brit. Petroleum Co., London, 1979-80, comml. mgr.., 1981-83, group treas., 1984-86; mgr. forties Brit. Petroleum Co., Aberdeen, Scotland, 1983-84; exec. v.p., chief fin. officer Standard Oil Co. of Ohio, Cleve., 1986—, also bd. dirs.; adv. bd. mem. Weatherhead Sch. Mgmt., Cleve., 1986—; bus. adv. council Carnegie-Mellon U., Pitts., 1986—. Bd. dirs. Cleve. Ballet. Trevelyan open scholar. Fellow Inst. Mining and Metallurgy. Clubs: Athenaeum (London); Union (Cleve.). Avocations: ballet, opera, tennis, photography. Office: Standard Oil Co 200 Public Sq Cleveland OH 44114

BROWNE, JOHN PATRICK, legal educator; b. East Cleveland, Ohio, Dec. 17, 1935; s. Patrick Joseph and Margaret Anne (O'Grady) B. BS in Social Sci., John Carroll U., 1957; JD, U. Detroit, 1960; MLS, Case Western Res. U., 1965. Bar: Ohio 1960, Mich. 1960, U.S. Dist. Ct. (no. dist.) Ohio 1966, U.S. Dist. Ct. (ea. dist.) Mich. 1966. Assoc. Gallagher, Sharp, Fulton & Norman, Cleve., 1965-69; prof. law Cleve.-Marshall Coll. Law, 1969—. Contbr. articles to profl. jours. Served to capt. JAGC, U.S. Army, 1960-64. Mem. ABA, Ohio Bar Assn., Mich. Bar Assn., Cleve. Bar Assn., Def. Research Assn., Delta Theta Phi. Democrat. Roman Catholic. Home: 17200 Clifton Blvd Lakewood OH 44107-2364 Office: Cleve U Marshall Coll Law 1801 Euclid Ave Cleveland OH 44115

BROWNE, MELODEE JOHNSON, small business owner; b. Chgo., Dec. 17, 1954; 1 child, Jomel Bobbitt. BSin Elem. Edn., Chgo. State U., 1975. Various positions fed. govt., 1973—; pres. Profl. Enterprises Inc., Chgo., 1984—. Mem. HALT, Am. Soc. Notaries, Internat. Credit Assn., Women Employed, Am. Cons. League, Nat. Taxpayers Union. Home: 6954 N Greenview Ave Chicago IL 60626 Office: Profl Enterprises Inc 8 S Michigan Ave Chicago IL 60603

BROWNE, MICHAEL JOSEPH, automotive executive; b. St. Louis, Oct. 18, 1941; s. Basil Campbell and Evelyn Beatrice (Biver) B.; m. Billie Francine Geders, Apr. 11, 1964; children: Michelle, Michael Jr. BSME, U. Mo., Rolla, 1967; MBA, Wright State U., 1981. Registered profl. engr., Ohio. Staff sales engr. Inland div. Gen. Motors Corp., Dayton, Ohio, 1969-78, sr. sales engr., 1978-85, adminstr. sales, 1984-85, adminstr. strategic planning, 1985-86, adminstr. bus. and tech. processes, 1986—. Mem. Ohio Hist. Soc., Columbus, 1978. Mem. Soc. Automotive Engrs. (assoc.), U. Mo.-Rolla Alumni Assn. (pres. Ohio chpt. 1967-70), Ohio Gun Collectors Assn, Nat. Rifle Assn. (life). Congregationalist. Avocations: hunting, fishing, firearms, history. Home: 7150 Keeneland Dr Dayton OH 45414 Office: Inland div Gen Motors Corp 2701 Home Ave Dayton OH 45417

BROWNE, ROBERT W., healthcare company executive. Chmn., pres. Care Corp., Grand Rapids, Mich. Office: Care Corp 200 Trust Bldg Grand Rapids MI 49503 *

BROWNE, WILLIAM ALBERT, JR., architectural firm executive; b. Indpls., Oct. 25, 1955; s. William Albert Sr. and Jane (Thundere) B.; m. Vicki Lynn Lamanna, Dec. 14, 1985. BS in Architecture, U. Ill., 1977; diploma, Preservation Inst., Nantucket, Mass., 1977; MA in Architecture, U. Fla., 1979. Registered architect, Ind., Fla., N.C. Grad. architect Ehrenkrantz Group, Washington, 1979-80, Pappas Assocs., Jacksonville, Fla., 1980; assoc. architect Browning Day Pollack Mullins Inc., Indpls., 1980-82; prin. HDG Architects Inc., Indpls., 1982-85, pres., 1985—; preservation officer Soc. Archtl. History, Indpls., 1982-87. Mem. AIA. Republican. Presbyterian. Lodge: Optimists. Avocations: choir, intramural sports. Office: HDG Architects Inc 260 Century Bldg 36 S Pennsylvania St Indianapolis IN 46204

BROWNELL, MELVIN RUSSELL, retail druggist, pharmacist, mayor; b. Grand Meadow, Minn., Sept. 1, 1925; s. Howard Russell and Helen Frances (Doten) B.; m. Ann Linden, Nov. 10, 1952; children—Thomas, James, John, Richard, Mary, Christopher, Paul. B.S. in Pharmacy, U. Minn., 1950. Registered pharmacist. Pharmacist, mgr. Ted Maier Drug, Inc., Winona, Minn., 1950-55; pres., pharmacist Brownell Drug, Inc., St. Charles, Minn., 1955—. Alderman, City of St. Charles, 1965-77, mayor, 1977—; vice chmn. Winona County Planning and Zoning Commn., 1976—; chmn. Dover, Eyota, St. Charles Sanitary Dist., 1968—; mem. Minn. Peace Officers Standards and Tng. Bd., 1982-84, Milti-County Housing-Rehab. Authority, Wabasha, Minn., 1982—. Served with USN, 1944-46. Recipient C. C. Ludwig award Minn. League Cities, 1985. Mem. Nat. Assn. Retail Druggists, Minn. State Pharm. Assn. (chmn. dist. 1 1979), U. Minn. Century Mortar Club, St. Charles C. of C. (pres. 1958), Am. Legion, Phi Delta Chi. Republican. Roman Catholic. Club: Lions (pres. St. Charles 1960). Lodge: Moose. Avocation: Photography. Home: 161 W 5th St Saint Charles MN 55972 Office: Brownell Drug Inc 925 Whitewater Ave Saint Charles MN 55972

BROWNING, D. DEAN, banker; b. Christopher, Ill., July 24, 1951; s. Frank S. and D. Lucille (Sileven) B.; m. Vicki L. Lance, Mar. 13, 1971; children: Kristi L., Kyle L. AAS in Acctg., Logan Coll., 1971. Teller Bank of Benton, Ill., 1972-74; asst. v.p. First Bank of Johnston City, Ill., 1974-77, exec. v.p., 1977-84, pres., 1984—, also bd. dirs.; bd. dirs. First Bank of Carbondale, Ill. Republican. Baptist. Lodge: Lions (pres. Johnston City 1980-81). Avocations: chess, golf. Home: PO Box 104 Johnston City IL 62951 Office: First Bank Johnston City PO Box H Johnston City IL 62951

BROWNING, EARL DEAN, sch. adminstr.; b. Annawan, Ill., Jan. 21, 1926; s. Earl F. and Velma L. Browning; B.S., Western Ill. U., 1951; M.A., U. Ill., 1957; advanced cert. of specialist Sc. Ill. U., 1968; m. Ardythe A. Machesney, June 23, 1951; 1 dau., Lexa Linn. Indsl. arts tchr. Alton (Ill.) Community Sch. Dist., 1951-57, dir. adult edn., 1957-67, adminstrv. asst. vocat. edn., 1967—. Served with U.S. Army, 1944-46. Decorated Bronze Star; recipient Those Who Excel award Ill. Bd. Edn., 1976; named Outstanding Vocat. Adminstr. of Yr., Ill. Council Local Adminstrs., 1981. Mem. Am. Vocat. Assn., Ill. Vocat. Assn., Ill. Indsl. Arts Assn., Nat. Council Local Adminstrs., NEA. Methodist. Home: 5502 Ladue St Godfrey IL 62035 Office: Alton Community School Dist 1854 E Broadway Alton IL 62002

BROWNING, ROBERT DOYLE, construction company executive; b. Daviess County, Ind., Sept. 30, 1917; s. Ray and Pearl (Browning) B.; grad. high sch.; student Internat. Corr. Sch.; m. Betty Overton, Sept. 2, 1942; children—Sondra Chapman, Larry, Gerald. Farmer, Washington, Ind., 1936-41; asst. engr. roads Ind. State Hwy., 1945-50; with Thompson Constrn. Co., Inc., Indpls., 1950—, field engr., 1961, office engr., estimator, 1961-70, exec. v.p., 1970—, also dir. Bd. dirs. Patton Park. Treas. Young Republicans, Daviess County, Ind., 1946-50; trustee Camby (Ind.) Community Ch. Served to master sgt. USAF, 1941-45. Decorated Bronze Star. Mem. V.F.W., Ind. Constructors Inc. (sec.-treas. 1978-79), Am. Legion. Clubs: Masons, K.P. Home: 8641 Camby Rd Camby IN 46116 Office: 3840 Prospect St Indianapolis IN 46203

BROWNING, ROBERT LYNN, educator, clergyman; b. Gallatin, Mo., June 19, 1924; s. Robert W. and Nell J. (Trotter) B.; B.A., Mo. Valley Coll., 1945; M.Div., Union Theol. Sem., 1948; Ph.D., Ohio State U., 1960; postgrad. Columbia U., 1951-53, Oxford (Eng.) U., 1978-79, 84-85; m. Jean Beatty, Dec. 27, 1947 (dec. 1977); children—Gregory, David, Peter, Lisa; m. 2d. Jackie L. Rogers, Aug. 26, 1979. Ordained to ministry Disciples of Christ Ch., 1949, transferred to United Meth. Ch., 1950; minister edn. Old Stone Ch., Meadville, Pa., 1946-51, Community Ch. at the Circle, Mt. Vernon, N.Y., 1951-53, North Broadway United Meth. Ch., Columbus, Ohio, 1953-59; prof. Christian edn. Meth. Theol. Sch., Delaware, Ohio, 1959-72, William A. Chryst prof. Christian edn., 1972—; pres. Meth. Conf. on Christian edn., 1967-69; exec. dir. Commn. on Role of the Professions in Soc., 1974-76, cons., 1976—. Bd. dirs. Southside Settlement, Columbus, 1968-74, Tray-Lee Center, Columbus, 1955-59, Ohio State U. Wesley Found., 1960-78, vice chmn. 1976-78; bd. ministry Ohio West Conf. United Meth. Ch., 1982—. Served with USN, 1942-45. Recipient Paul Hinkhouse award Religious Public Relations Council Am., 1971. Mem. Assn. for Profl. Edn. for Ministry (editor proc. 1980—), Religious Edn. Assn., Assn. of Profs. and Researchers in Religious Edn., Meth. Univ. Profs. Christian Edn. Author: Communication with Junior Highs, 1968; Guidelines for Youth Ministry, 1970; What on Earth Are You Doing, 1966; (audiotape) (with Charles Foster) Communicating the Faith with Children, 1971; Ways the Bible Comes Alive, 1975; Ways Persons Become Christian, 1976; (with Charles Foster, Everett Tilson) Looking at Leadership with the Eyes of Biblical Faith, 1978; (with Roy Reed) the Sacraments in Religious Education and Liturgy: An Ecumenical Model, 1985; contbg. author: Preventing Adolescent Alienation: An Interprofessional Approach, 1983, Children, Parents and Change, 1984, Interprofessional Education, 1987; editor: Integration: Objective Studies and Practical Theology, Proc. Assn. Profl. Edn. for Ministry, 1981; contbr. articles on religious edn. to profl. jours. Home: 6613 Hawthorne St Worthington OH 43085 Office: 3081 Columbus Pike Delaware OH 43015

BROWNING, ROY STANLEY, manufacturers representative, sales and marketing executive; b. Dayton, Ohio, Feb. 12, 1936; s. Roy S. and Eileen (Turner) B.; m. Norma Jean Sowder, June 10, 1965 (div. Mar. 1970); m. Marilyn Jean Neal, Apr. 12, 1971; children: Kimberly, Nicole. BA, U. Dayton, 1961. Mil. liaison rep. Clifton Precision, Dayton, Ohio, 1961-66; sales engr. Kollsman Instrument, Dayton, Ohio, 1966-69; dist. mgr. Winchester Electric Co., Dayton, Ohio, 1969-70; pres. Compass Assocs., Dayton, Ohio, 1971-76; v.p. sales Imtech, Inc., Dayton, Ohio, 1976-84; owner Tech. Devices, Dayton, Ohio, 1984—. Lodge: Optimists. Home: 7540 Glenhurst Dr Dayton OH 45414 Office: Tech Devices 8435 N Dixie Dr Dayton OH 45414

BROWNING, STERLING EDWIN, II, chemist; b. Ardmore, Okla., Aug. 27, 1933; s. Sterling Edwin and Viola Mae (Jones) B.; student Okla. A&M U., 1951-56, Tulsa U., 1961-62; B.A., Okla. State U., 1967; m. Merlene Fox, Sept. 29, 1962; children—Melissa Anne, Sterling Edwin III, Jonathan Brian. Lab. helper Pan Am. Oil Corp., Tulsa, 1956-57; partner Browning's Carpet Co., Tulsa, 1957-61; research asst. chemistry Dowell div. Dow Chem. Co., Tulsa, 1961-63; tech. corr. Fisher Sci. Co., St. Louis, 1963-65; lab. technician Okla. State U., Stillwater, 1965-67; analytic chemist Sci. Assocs., St. Louis, 1967-68; chief chemist Sherwood Med. Industries, St. Louis, 1968-74; sr. analytical chemist, spectroscopist Sigma Chem. Co., St. Louis, 1974—; staff Applied Sci. Cons., St. Louis, 1972—. Trustee Greenmar Subdiv., Mo., 1972-73; active Boy Scouts Am., Girl Scouts U.S.A., 1975—. Mem. Am. Chem. Soc. (treas. gen. topics group St. Louis sect. 1981-82), Am. Inst. Chemist, St. Louis Soc. Analysts, Soc. for Applied Spectroscopy, Coblentz Soc., St. Louis Chromatography Discussion Group, Sigma Study Group, Sigma Alpha Epsilon. Republican. Presbyterian.

BROXTON, GARY LEE, mechanical engineer; b. Pana, Ill., Sept. 2, 1947; s. Gordon Ross and Georgette E. (Pastor) B.; m. Janet Charlene Beverly, Feb. 23, 1968 (div. Dec. 1980); 1 child, Nolan Matthew; m. Amy Ellen Benjamin, May 1, 1982; 1 child, Lee Ross. BS in Aero. Engring., St. Louis U., 1970. Registered aero. and mech. engr., Ind. Engring. planner McDonnell-Douglas, St. Louis, 1970; mech. engr. Naval Weapons Support Ctr., Crane, Ind., 1970—. Mem. Am. Def. Preparedness Assn. (dir. Rogers Lewis Clark chpt. 1983—), Alpha Chi (Ill. Gamma chpt.). Avocations: skiing, fishing, racketball, golf, travel. Home: 5860 W Gifford Rd Bloomington IN 47401 Office: Naval Weapons Support Ctr Code 5062 Crane IN 47522

BROYHILL, CRAIG GARY, industrial and agricultural manufacturing executive; b. Sioux City, Iowa, Oct. 20, 1948; s. Roy Franklin and Arline W. (Stewart) B.; m. Jean Marie Messenger, Feb. 8, 1974; children: Ann Marie, Sara Louise, Adam Gary. BS in Bus. and Econs., U. Nebr., 1970. Purchasing agt. The Broyhill Co., Dakota City, Nebr., 1970-74, sales mgr., 1974-83, chief operating officer, 1983-85, pres., 1985—; pres. The Broyhill Investment Co., Dakota City, Nebr., 1979—; bd. dirs. Star Printing and Publ., South Sioux City; mem. NACI, Sioux City; pres. Freedom Aerolights, Dakota City, 1981-86. Contbr. articles to profl. jours. Pres. Dakota City Bus. Orgns., Dakota City, 1979-82; councilman City of Dakota City, 1978—. Mem. Farm Equipment Mfg. Assn., Aircraft Owners and Pilots Assn. (regional ultralight examiner 1983-85). Republican. Presbyterian. Club: Boatclub (Sioux City). Avocations: skiing, golf, reading. Office: The Broyhill Co North Market Sq Box 475 Dakota City NE 68731

BROYHILL, ROY FRANKLIN, indsl. turf and agrl. equipment mfg. exec.; b. Sioux City, Iowa, June 20, 1919; s. George Franklin and Effie (Motes) B.; B.B.A., U. Nebr., 1940; m. Arline W. Stewart, Jan. 30, 1943; children—Lynn Diann (dec.), Craig G., Kent Bryan, Bryce Alan. Trainee mgr. Montgomery Ward Co., 1940; semi-sr. acct. L. H. Keightley, 1941-42; chief accountant Army Exchange Service, Sioux City, 1942-46; pres. Broyhill Co., 1946-86, chmn., 1946—; pres., dir. Star Printing & Pub. Co., South Sioux City, 1949—; pres. Broyhill Corp., 1953-86, chmn., 1953—; v.p. Broyhill Mfg. Co., 1978-87, pres., 1987—; pres., chmn. bd. Broyhill Inc.; dir. 1st Nat. Bank, Sioux City. Mem. U.S.A. Exec. Res.; mem. Nebr. dist. adv. council SBA, 1971—. Mayor of Dakota City, 1951-53; mem. Nebr. Republican Central Com., 1954-56. Past mem. local sch. bd. Trustee U. Nebr., U. Nebr. Found. Served with AUS, 1940-41. Mem. Nitrogen Solutions Assn. (dir. 1956-60), Farm Equipment Mfrs. Assn. (dir., pres. 1971-72), Atokad Racing Assn. (past dir.), N.A.M., U.S., South Sioux City chambers commerce, Nebr. Assn. Commerce and Industry (dir. 1972-73), Alumni Assn. U. Nebr. (past dir.), Am. Legion (life), Beta Theta Pi, Alpha Kappa Psi. Presbyn. (elder). Club: U. Nebr. Chancellor's. Lodges: Masons (Shrine), Kiwanis. Home: 1610 Broadway Dakota City NE 68731 also (winters): 2185 Ibis Isle Rd Palm Beach FL 33480 Office: Broyhill Co N Market Sq Dakota City NE 68731

BROYLES, LAURA JANE, accountant; b. Topeka, Kans., Dec. 23, 1958; d. John Kenneth and Ermyl Mae (Reeder) B. BBA, Washburn U., 1980; M in Acctg., Kans. State U., 1981. CPA, Kans. Staff acct. Fox & Co., CPA's, Topeka, 1982-83, Dean Lemmon and Co., CPA's, Topeka, 1983-85, Lemmon, Yadon and Vaught, CPA's, Topeka, 1985-86; audit supr. Lemmon, Summers, Yadon and Vaught, CPA's, Topeka, 1986-87, Summers, Yadon and Vaught, CPA's, Topeka, 1987—. Mem. Am. Inst. CPA's, Am. Women Soc. CPA's, Am. Soc. Women Accts. (v.p. 1986-87, pres. 1987—), Am. Bus. Women's Assn., Kans. SOc. CPA's (treas. N.E. Kans. chpt. 1986-87). Republican. Methodist. Home: 3001 Maupin Ln #5 Topeka KS 66614 Office: Summers Yadon & Vaught Chartered 5825 SW 29th Suite 202 Topeka KS 66614

BROYLES, PATRICK JAMES, government official; b. Columbus, Ohio, July 5, 1950; s. Nick and Elzetta Pearl (Presson) B.; m. Phyllis Caughman, July 5, 1981; 1 child, Brenda Gail Caughman. BS, Okla. State U., 1975; MS, 1978. Cert. profl. soil erosion and sediment control specialist. Grad. asst. Okla. State U., Stillwater, 1975-77; range conservationist Soil Conservationist Service, U.S. Dept. Agr., Pawhuska, Okla., 1977-80, Cheyenne, Okla., 1980-81, dist. conservationist, Columbus, Kans., 1981-85, Cottonwood Falls, Kans., 1985—. Deacon First Christian Ch., 1978-80. Served with M.I., U.S. Army, 1970-73. Mem. Soc. for Range Mgmt. (life; sec.-treas. 1978, chmn. producer affairs com. Kans.-Okla. sect. 1980-82, chmn. pub. affairs com. 1985—), Nat. Wildlife Fedn. (life), Council for Agrl. Sci. and Tech., Kans. Livestock Assn. (natural resources com.), Soil Conservation Soc. Am. (Bluestem chpt. pres. 1985—), Orgn. of Profl. Employees Dept. Agr., Nat. Assn. Conservation Dists., Kans. Assn. Conservation Dists., Am. Legion, Nat. Rifle Assn. (life). Republican. Lodge: Lions (pres. Pawhuska 1979-80). Home: Rt 1 PO Box 67A Strong City KS 66869 Office: Box F 336 Broadway Cottonwood Falls KS 66845

BROZMAN, J. L., day care centers executive. Pres., treas. La Petite Acad. Inc., Kansas City, Mo. Office: La Petite Acad Inc PO Box 26610 Kansas City MO 64196 *

BROZMAN, R. F., day care centers executive. Chmn. La Petite Acad. Inc., Kansas City, Mo. Office: La Petite Acad Inc PO Box 26610 Kansas City MO 64196 *

BROZOVIC, RICHARD, mfg. co. exec.; b. Briar Hill, Pa., Apr. 2, 1932; s. Albert Elmer and Emily Louise (Yelinek) B.; student pub. schs., Jefferson, Pa.; m. Jean E. Heverling, Apr. 18, 1953; 1 son, Robert A. Served from pvt. to 1st sgt. U.S. Army, 1947-71, ret., 1971; pres., gen. mgr. Geyer Bros. Brewing Co., Frankenmuth, Mich., 1975—. Decorated Bronze Star medals (2), Purple Heart. Mem. Am. Legion. Roman Catholic. Clubs: Frankenmuth Conservation, Men's of Blessed Trinity Cath. Ch. Home: 448 Sunburst Dr Frankenmuth MI 48734 Office: 425 S Main St Frankenmuth MI 48734

BRUBAKER, CHARLES WILLIAM, architect; b. South Bend, Ind., Sept. 28, 1926; s. Ralph and Mary (Holderman) B.; m. Elizabeth Allen Rogers, June 25, 1955; children: William Rogers, Elizabeth Allen, Robert Andrew. Student, Purdue U., 1945; B.Arch., U. Tex., 1950. Architect, designer, partner Perkins & Will, Architects, Chgo., 1950-69; exec. v.p. Perkins & Will, Architects, Chgo., Washington and N.Y.C., 1970-84; chmn. bd., pres. Perkins & Will, Architects, 1985—; Pres. Council of Ednl. Facilities Planners; bd. govs. Met. Planning Council; v.p. Chgo. Architecture Found. Prin. works include Richland Coll., Dallas, First Nat. Bank Chgo. Served with USNR, 1945-46. Fellow AIA; mem. Chgo. Assn. Commerce and Industry, Phi Gamma Delta, Lambda Alpha (pres. Ely chpt.). Clubs: Chicago Yacht (Chgo.), Mid-Day (Chgo.); Cosmos (Washington). Home: 82 Essex Rd Winnetka IL 60093 Office: Perkins & Will 2 N LaSalle St Chicago IL 60602

BRUBAKER, JAMES CLARK, construction executive; b. Normal, Ill., Mar. 22, 1947; s. Walter Clark and Vernie Helen (Rubenaker) B.; m. Celeste Renee Rohling, Jan. 16, 1971; children: Elizabeth, Andrew. BS in Communications, U. Ill., 1969. Sales mgr. Proctor & Gamble, Chgo., 1969-71, Johnson & Johnson, St. Louis, 1971-74; v.p. sales Omega Sports, St. Louis, 1976-79; exec. v.p. Thomas Constrn., St. Louis, 1982—; pres. JB Ventures, St. Louis. Dir. Grace Ch. of Mid Mo., St. Louis. Recipient Eagle Scout award, 1961. Mem. St. Louis Remodelers Guild. Republican. Fundamentalist. Avocations: reading, bible study, physical fitness, softball, running. Home: 3411 Erman Bridgeton MO 63044 Office: Thomas Constrn 10855 Metro Ct Saint Louis MO 63043

BRUBAKER, KAREN SUE, tire manufacturing company executive; b. Ashland, Ohio, Feb. 5, 1953; d. Robert Eugene and Dora Louise (Camp) B. BSBA, Ashland Coll., 1975; MBA, Bowling Green State U., 1976. Supr. tire ctr. ops. B.F. Goodrich Co., Akron, Ohio, 1976-77, supr. tire acctg., 1977-79, asst. product mgr. radial passenger tires, 1979-80, product mgr. broadline passenger tires, 1980-81, group product mgr. broadline passenger and light truck tires, 1981-83, mktg. mgr. T/A high tech radials, 1983-86; product mgr. B.F. Goodrich T/A radials, The Uniroyal Goodrich Tire Co., Akron, 1986—. Sect. chmn. indsl. div. United Way, Akron, 1983-86. Recipient Alumni Distinguished Service award Ashland Coll., 1986; Alpha Phi Clara Bradley Burdette scholar, 1975. Mem. Am. Mktg. Assn. (pres. Akron/Canton chpt. 1982-83, Highest Honors award 1983, v.p. bus. mktg. to nat. bd. dirs. 1984-86, v.p. profl. chpts. 1987—), Susan B. Anthony Soc. of Akron Women's Network, Nat. Assn. Female Execs., Beta Gamma Sigma, Omicron Delta Epsilon. Lodge: Zonta Internat. Home: 1862 Indian Hills Trail Akron OH 44313 Office: The Uniroyal Goodrich Tire Co 600 S Main St Akron OH 44318

BRUBECK, ANNE ELIZABETH DENTON, artist; b. Beardstown, Ill., Mar. 5, 1918; d. Harry B. and Helen Jean (Gibbs) Denton; student Christian Coll., 1935-36; B.Design, Newcomb Coll., Tulane U., 1939; postgrad. Art Inst. Chgo., 1939-40; A.A. (hon.), Wabash Valley Coll., 1981; m. William E. Brubeck, Dec. 14, 1940; children—Jean Brubeck Stayman, William E. Instr. painting Wabash Valley Coll., Mt. Carmel, Ill., 1962-67; painter; one-man shows include N.Y.C., 1961, 63-67, Evansville, Ind., 1963-69; retrospective, Wabash Valley Coll., 1980; juried exhbns. include: Evansville Mus., 1963, 64, 65, Swopes Gallery, Terre Haute, Ind., 1964, 68, Nashville, 1967. Trustee, Mt. Carmel Pub. Library, 1954—, chmn., 1975-6; mem. cultural events com. Wabash Valley Coll., 1976-80. Brubeck Art Center named in her and her husband's honor, 1976; named to Mt. Carmel High Sch. Centennial Hall of Fame, 1982. Mem. Ill. Library Assn., Nat. League Am. Penwomen, PEO. Methodist. Club: Reviewers Matinee. Home and Office: 729 Cherry St Mount Carmel IL 62863

BRUCE, CAROLYN CORRINGTON, nurse; b. North Vernon, Ind., Apr. 28, 1936; d. Ottis C. and Ruth E. (Davis) Corya; m. Reginald A. Bruce, July 16, 1976; children by previous marriage: Douglas Corrington, Judith Scrivner, Carla Corrington. RN, Meth. Hosp., Indpls., 1956; BS in Health Edn., Ind. U., 1975, postgrad., 1976; spl. course in respiratory therapy U. Chgo., 1973. Charge nurse metabolic unit Meth. Hosp., Indpls., 1956-59, head nurse metabolic unit, 1959-63, head nurse ICU, 1968-69, head nurse med. unit, 1969-70, dir. respiratory therapy, 1970-75, asst. dir. nursing, 1975-76; dir. nursing Paris (Ill.) Hosp., 1976-77, Crawford Meml. Hosp., Robinson, Ill., 1978-79; adminstr. Lincolnland Vis. Nurse Assn., 1980—; 1982-84; pres. Jennings Vis. Nurse Assn., Inc., 1983—, Home Health Care Inc.; vol. ARC, Am. Cancer Soc. Mem. Am. Nurses Assn. (cert. nursing adminstr.), Ill. Nurses Assn . Presbyterian. Home: 15 Doral Ct Route 3 Mattoon IL 61938

BRUCE, DAVID RAE, manufacturing company executive; b. Syracuse, N.Y., May 11, 1925; s. John Rae and Florence (Nicholson) B.; m. Mary Jayne Watson, Sept. 13, 1947 (div. Mar. 1966); children: Bonnie Bruce, Lane W.; m. ELeanor Royer, Dec. 29, 1966; 1 child, Whitney R. Grad., Northwestern U., 1949. Salesman, nat. account mgr. Tousey Varnish Co., Chgo., 1952-71; nat. sales mgr. Protectseal Co., Bensenville, Ill., 1971-82; v.p. sales Justrite Mfg. Co., Des Plaines, Ill., 1982—; corp. officer Justrite Mfg. Co., 1984—. Mem. Northfield (Ill.) Civic Bd., 1975; vestry St. James Episcopal Ch., Northfield, 1982-84. Served to corp. U.S. Army, 1943-45, CBI. Decorated D.F.C., Air medal. Mem. Aux. to Farm Indsl. Equipment (various offices, pres.), Nat. Fire Prevention Assn. Republican. Episcopalian. Club: Sunset Ridge Country (Northbrook, Ill.). Office: Justrite Mfg Co 2454 Dempster St Des Plaines IL 60016

BRUCE, HARRY JAMES, transportation company executive; b. Newark, July 2, 1931; s. John William and Anna Margaret (Ackerman) B.; m. Vivienne Ruth Jennings, Sept. 10, 1955; children: Robert, Stacy, Bethann. B.S., Kent State U., 1957; M.S., U. Tenn., 1959; cert. Advanced Mgmt. Program, Harvard U., 1979. Diplomate: cert. Am. Soc. Transp. and Logistics; 1960. Transp. research asst. U.S. Steel Co., Pitts., 1959-64; dir. market devel. Spector Freight Co., Chgo., 1964-67, v.p. mktg., 1967-69; dir. distbn. Joseph Schlitz Brewing Co., Milw., 1969-71, asst. v.p. plant ops., 1971-72; v.p. mktg. Western Pacific R.R., San Francisco, 1972-75; sr. v.p. mktg. Ill. Central Gulf R.R., Chgo., 1975-83, chmn., chief exec. officer, 1983—, also dir.; bd. dirs. Lake View Trust and Savings Bank. Author: How to Apply Statistics to Physical Distribution, 1967, Distribution and Transportation Handbook, 1971; inventor vari-deck, 1970. Bd. dirs. Glenwood Sch. for Boys, Ill.; mem. adv. bd. U. Tenn.; bus. adv. com. Northwestern U. Served to 1st lt. U.S. Army, 952-55, ETO. Mem. Newcomen Soc., Nat. Council Phys. Distbn., Nat. Freight Transp. Assn., Nat. Def. Transp. Assn., Northwestern U. Assocs. Republican. Presbyterian. Clubs: Glenview (Ill.); Chicago, Mid-Am. (dir.) (Chgo.); Metropolitan (N.Y.C.). Home: 88 Woodley Rd Winnetka IL 60093 Office: Ill Cen Gulf RR 233 N Michigan Ave Chicago IL 60601

BRUCE, ROBERT KEADY, librarian; b. Laramie, Wyo., May 12, 1935; s. Robert Hall and Huldah (Means) B.; m. Lin McLaughlin, Aug. 23, 1958; children: Robert McLaughlin, MaryLin, David Murray, Scott Michael. BA, U. Wyo., 1957, MA, 1959; MLS, Rutgers U., 1960, postgrad., 1960-63. Library adv. USAID of U. Wyo., Kabul, Afghanistan, 1966-68; head librarian Gorham (Maine) St. Coll., 1968-69; coll. librarian Carleton Coll., Northfield, Minn., 1969-75; acting head librarian U. Alaska, Juneau, 1975-77; head history dept. Mpls. Pub. Library and Info. Ctr., 1977—, acting head spl. collections, 1986; mem. adv. com. Library Devel. and Systems, St. Paul, Minn., 1983—, A-V Inst., Mankato (Minn.) State U., 1979-80; cons. election news Mpls. Star and Tribune, 1979-80. contbr. book reviews to profl. jours. Deacon, 1st United Ch. of Christ, Northfield, 1982-85, chmn. religous edn., 1977-80. Fellow Council Library Resources, 1974-75. Mem. ALA (various sects., coms.), Minn. Library Assn. (chair continuing library, info. and media edn. com. 1983—, chair pub. library div. 1980-81, chair academic library div. 1983-84), Nat. Library Devel. Ctr., Phi Alpha Theta, Beta Phi Mu, Omicron Delta Kappa, Sigma Nu. Congregationalist. Avocations: biking, walking, community theatre. Home: 411 Winona St Northfield MN 55057 Office: Mpls Pub Library & Info Ctr 300 Nicollet Mall Minneapolis MN 55401

BRUCE, TERRY L., congressman; b. Olney, Ill.; m. Charlotte Roberts; children: Emily Anne, Ellen Catherine. J.D., U. Ill., 1969. Mem. farm labor staff Dept. Labor, Washington; then mem. staff Congressman George Shipley and Ill. Senator Philip Benefiel legis. intern, 1969-70; mem. Ill. Senate, Springfield, 1970-85, asst. majority leader, 1975-85; mem. 99th-100th Congress from 19th Ill. dist., Washington, 1985—. Named Outstanding Legislator of Yr., Ill. Edn. Assn., 1973; winner Right to Know award Ill. Press Assn., 1975; recipient Ill. Community Coll. Trustees Assn. award. Democrat. Office: Ho of Reps Office House Members Washington DC 20515 *

BRUCHS, GREGORY JAMES, optometrist; b. Mpls., Sept. 4, 1955; s. Richard James and Dwan Marilyn (Stoekmann) B.; m. Mary Beth Neatherton, Dec. 17, 1977; children: Brian, Hallisy, John. BS, Miami U., Oxford, Ohio, 1976; OD, Ohio State U., 1979. Assoc. optometrist John D. Bullock, MD, Inc., Dayton, 1981—, Plumwood Ophthalmics Inc., Dayton, 1981—; cons. computer vision Plumwood Ophthalmics Inc., 1985—. Bausch and Lomb Contact Lens Scholar, 1979; Nikon Scholar, 1976. Mem. Am. Optometric Assn. Democrat. Roman Catholic. Lodge: Kiwanis. Avocations: sports, art, landscaping. Home: 315 Winding Trail Xenia OH 45385 Office: 1520 S Main St Suite 230 Dayton OH 45401

BRUCKER, WILBER MARION, III, lawyer; b. Detroit, Aug. 31, 1956; s. Wilber Marion Jr. and Doris Ann (Shover) B.; m. Renée Janush Brucker, Sept. 21, 1986. Student, U. Utah, 1974-75; BS in Psychology, Mich. State U., 1979; JD, Detroit Coll. Law, 1983. Bar: Mich. 1983, U.S. Dist. Ct. (so. dist.) Mich. 1983, D.C. 1985. Assoc. McInally, Brucker, Newcombe, Wilke, and DeBona, P.C., Dearborn, Mich., 1983—. Rep. precinct del., Grosse Pointe, Mich., 1978—; chmn. polit. action com. Detroit Young Reps., 1980-83; bd. dirs. 14th Congl. Rep. Com., 1985—. Mem. ABA, Am. Trial Lawyers Assn., Mich. Bar Assn., D.C. Bar Assn., Detroit Bar Assn. Presbyterian. Club: Detroit Athletic. Office: McInally Brucker Newcombe Wilke & DeBona PC 23400 Michigan Ave Suite 1200 Dearborn MI 48124

BRUCKNER, LUANNE FROSCH, paralegal; b. Savanna, Ill., July 29, 1949; d. Cecil W. Frosch and Bette Jane (Lewis) Meakins; m. Howard F. Henneman, Nov. 25, 1967 (div. June 1980); children: Matthew, Amie, Heidilu; m. Lawrence L. Bruckner, June 28, 1981. Student, Ill. State U., 1967-68, LaSalle U., 1970-73, Sauk Valley Coll., 1980-83. Owner Rolling H Western Wear, Thomson, Ill. and Clinton, Iowa, 1971-78; ptnr. F/L Enterprises, Thomson, 1974-80; paralegal Law Offices of Lawrence L. Bruckner, Savanna and Dixon, Ill., 1981—. Author: (booklet) How to Budget Your Way Out of Debt, 1981. Trustee Village of Thomson, 1985—. Named one of Outstanding Young Women of Am., 1979, 80, 85, 86. Mem. DAR (vice chmn., 1985—, state treas., 1978-80, hon. sr. state pres. Ill. Children Am. Revolution), Thomson Melon Days Assn. (chmn. 1984—). Republican. Methodist. Club: Thomson Women's (chpt. chmn.). Lodge: Dames of the Ct. of Honor. Avocations: genealogy, sports. Home: 1003 Locust Box 428 Thomson IL 61285

BRUENING, WILLIAM PAUL, controls co. exec.; b. St. Louis, Mar. 8, 1935; s. Francis Joseph and Crystal Verda (Baumgartner) B.; B.E.E., U. Dayton, 1957. Sales engr. Cutler-Hammer Inc., St. Louis, 1957-63, O'Brien Equipment Co., St. Louis, 1963-69; v.p., sec. Central Controls Co., Inc., St. Louis, 1969-76; pres. Process Controls Co., Inc., St. Louis, 1976-86; chief exec. officer A.D. Michel Co., Inc. (formerly Process Controls Co. Inc.), St. Louis, 1986—; dir. Bannes-Sheughnessy Inc. Served with U.S. Army, 1957-63. Mem. Instrument Soc. Am. (sr.), Confrerie des Chevaliers du Tastevin, Newcomen Soc. N.Am., Mercedes-Benz Club Am., Commanderie de Bordeaux. Republican. Roman Catholic. Clubs: St. Louis, Mo. Athletic. Home: 6813 Aliceton Ave Saint Louis MO 63123 Office: 2505 Metro Blvd Maryland Heights MO 63043

BRUETT, TILL ARTHUR, bank executive; b. Milw., Mar. 15, 1938; s. Till A. and Marion (Langman) B.; m. Alice Ann Heinen, Oct. 16, 1982; Karen E. Lynn, T. Andrew, Chris J., Kris A. BS in Acctg., Marquette U., 1960; BS in Fin., Marquette (Wis.) U., 1960; grad. degree in banking, U. Wis., 1965. V.p. Security 1st Nat. Bank, Sheyboygan, Wis., 1960-72; exec. v.p. 1st Nat. Bank, Racine, Wis., 1972-78; v.p. Marine Bank, Milw., 1978-80; pres. Elkin Co., Milw., 1980-84; v.p. 1st Wis. Nat. Bank, Milw., 1984—; pres., owner First Fed. Fin. Services, 1976-86; bd. dirs. Family Social and Psychol. Services, Milw., 1978—, Automated Processes, Milw., 1982—. Bd. dirs., chmn. Racine Area United Way, Racine, 1974-78; bd. dirs. A-Ctr., Racine, 1974-78, St. Luke's Hosp., Racine, 1975-78. Served with U.S. Army, 1960-62. Named one of Five Outstanding Young Men, State of Wis., 1968. Mem. Sheboygan C. of C. (bd. dirs., treas. 1968-72). Republican. Roman Catholic. CLubs: Oconomowoc Country, Wauwatosa Curling (pres. elect 1986). Lodge: Rotary. Avocations: golf, curling, reading. Home: 2885 N Pilgram Rd Brookfield WI 53005 Office: First Wis Nat Bank 777 E Wisconsin Ave Milwaukee WI 53202

BRUGLER, RICHARD KENNETH, steel and iron mfg. co. exec.; b. Warren, Ohio, Oct. 28, 1928; s. Herman Kenneth and Mildred Marrietta (Fell) B.; B.S. in Mech. Engring., Case Inst. Tech., 1952, B.S. in Elec. Engring., 1954; m. Jean Elizabeth Brooks, Dec. 22, 1951; children—David Kenneth, Diane Jean, Eric Paul, Kurt Ernst. Draftsman, Perfection Stove Co., Cleve., 1951-52; lab. machinist Thompson Products Co., Cleve., 1952-54; with Heltzel Co., Warren, 1954—, chief engr., 1962-65, v.p. engring., 1965-78, v.p. ops., 1978-80, exec. v.p., 1980-83, pres., 1983—; chmn. Concrete Plant Mfrs. Bur., 1975-78. Served with USNR, 1946-48. Mem. Nat. Readymix Assn. (dir.), Nat., Trumbull County (sec. 1976-78, pres. 1979) socs. profl. engrs., IEEE (sr.), Nat. Scalemens Assn., Antique Wireless Assn., Palatine Soc. Methodist. Club: Masons. Patentee in field. Home: 1359 Beechcrest St Warren OH 44485 Office: 1750 Thomas Rd Warren OH 44484

BRUGMANN, DONALD FRANCIS, missionary administrator; b. Denver, Apr. 19, 1928; s. Frank James and Hazel Ina (Parks) B.; m. Mary Elizabeth Sullivan; children: Sharon, Stephen, Sheree. BA, Roosevelt U., 1958; BD, No. Bapt. Sem., 1959; D of Missiology, Trinity Evang. Divinity Sch., 1984. Candidate sec. Greater Europe Mission, Wheaton, Ill., 1960-73, exec. dir., 1973-87. Served with U.S. Army, 1946-49. Mem. Bible Ch. Home: 423 E Grand Lake West Chicago IL 60185 Office: Greater Europe Mission PO Box 668 Wheaton IL 60189

BRUHNKE, PAUL EDWARD, appliance mfg. co. exec.; b. Chgo., June 11, 1946; s. Edward G. and Viola Ellen (Krueger) B.; B.S. in Mktg., U. Ill., 1969; M.B.A., DePaul U., Chgo., 1970; m. Joan Mary Murphy, Aug. 29, 1970. Sales rep. Dun & Bradstreet, Inc., 1972-73; account exec. GR Co. div. Kelvinator, Inc., Grand Rapids, Mich., 1973-74; nat. accounts mgr. Kelvinator Appliance Co., Grand Rapids, 1974-75, div. sales mgr., 1975—. Served with U.S. Army, 1970-72. Decorated Army Commendation medal. Office: 300 Phillipi Rd Columbus OH 43228

BRUINS, ELTON JOHN, college dean, religion educator; b. Fairwater, Wis., July 29, 1927; s. Clarence Raymond and Angeline Theodora (Kemink) B.; m. Elaine Ann Redeker, June 24, 1954; children—Mary Elaine Bruins Plasman, David Lewis. B.A., Hope Coll., 1950; B.D., Western Theol. Sem., 1953; S.T.M., Union Theol. Sem., 1957; Ph.D., NYU, 1962. Ordained to ministry Reformed Ch., 1954. Pastor, Reformed Ch., Elmsford, N.Y., 1955-61, Flushing, N.Y., 1961-66; prof. religion Hope Coll., Holland, Mich., 1966—, chmn. religion dept., 1977-84, dean arts and humanities, 1984—; archivist Western Theol. Sem., Holland, 1967-78, Netherlands Mus., Holland, 1968—, also v.p., 1980—. Author: The Americanization of a Congregation, 1970. Contbr. articles to profl. jours. Chmn. Hist./Cultural Commn., Holland, 1978-82. Served with USNR, 1945-46. Named to Evert J. and Hattie E. Blekkink Chair of Religion, Hope Coll., 1980. Mem. Assn. for Advancement Dutch-Am. Studies (pres. 1983), Am. Soc. Ch. History, Presbyn. Hist. Soc., Midwest Archives Conf., State Hist. Soc. Wis. Democrat. Mem. Reformed Ch. Home: 191 W 15th St Holland MI 49423 Office: Hope Coll Holland MI 49423

BRULL, HANS FRANK, social worker; b. Berlin, Germany, May 17, 1921; s. Victor and Ellen (Berendsen) B.; came to U.S., 1933, naturalized, 1943; B.A., CCNY, 1949; M.S.W., U. Pa., 1951; postgrad. U. Chgo., 1962, HHD with honors, Mary Crest Coll., 1986; m. Rose Weiss, May 3, 1953 (div.); children—Ellen Sandra Brull Lavie, Steven Victor; m. 2d, Olive Rue, Dec. 20, 1969. Caseworker Childrens Ct. Clinic, Melbourne, Australia, 1951, Jewish Family and Childrens Service, Mpls., 1951-53, Jewish Children's Bur., Chgo., 1953-56; head sch. social work dept. New Trier High Sch.-West, Northfield, 1963-75, ret. 1975—, clin. asst. prof. Sch. Social Work, Smith Coll., Northampton, Mass., 1975. Pvt. practice as clin. social worker, Winnetka. Mem. citizens adv. com. Youth Employment Service, 1965—; pres. Glenview Human Relations Com., 1963-64; mem. bd. Gates House Inc., 1970-73; mem. New Trier Twp. Com. on Youth, 1980-84. Served with M.I., AUS, 1943-46. Mem. Nat. Assn. Social Workers (mem. state bd. 1976-77, del. nat. assembly 1977), Ill. Soc. Clin. Social Work (ethics com.). Contbr. articles to profl. publs. Home: 1416 Edgewood Ln Winnetka IL 60093 Office: 525 Winnetka Ave Winnetka IL 60093

BRULLO, RAYMOND WILLIAM, podiatrist; b. Chgo., Aug. 19, 1957; s. Ralph V. and Vicky M. (Santapa) B. BS in Biology, Loyola U., Chgo., 1979; D in Podiatric Medicine, Ill. Coll. Podiatric Medicine, 1983. Intern in foot surgery Marshalltown (Iowa) Hosp., 1983-84; pvt. practice podiatry Chgo., 1984—; cons. Regency Home Health Service, Niles, Ill., 1984—; staff Regency Nursing Ctr. Mem. Norwood Park C. of C. (bus.). Roman Catholic. Avocations: music, classical guitar, cross country skiing. Home: 5028 N Newland Chicago IL 60656 Office: 6426 N NW Hwy Chicago IL 60631

BRULLO, ROBERT ANGELO, marketing executive; b. Chgo., Aug. 20, 1948; s. Ralph V. and Vicky M. (Santapa) B.; m. Susan Doris Posedy, June 20, 1970; children: Jennifer, Dawn. BSChemE, Ill. Inst. Tech., 1970; MBA, Coll. St. Thomas, 1976. Sr. analyst corp. mktg. 3M Co., St. Paul, 1977-78, supr. market devel. comml. chems. div., 1978-80; sr. account rep. comml. chems. div. 3M Co., Detroit, 1980-82; mgr. market devel. comml. chems. div. 3M Co., St. Paul, 1982-86, global mktg. mg. indsl. chem. products div., 1986—. Patentee in field. Mem. Soc. Automotive Engrs., Am. Chem Soc. (rubber div. area bd. dirs. 1986—), Twin Cities Rubber Group (sec. 1979-80). Methodist. Home: 1387 Belmont Dr Woodbury MN 55125 Office: 3M Co ICDP Bldg 223-6S-04 3M Ctr Saint Paul MN 55144

BRUMBACK, CHARLES TIEDTKE, newspaper executive; b. Toledo, Sept. 27, 1928; s. John Sanford and Frances Hannah (Tiedtke) B.; m. Mary Louise Howe, July 7, 1951; children: Charles Tiedtke, Anne V., Wesley W., Ellen P. B.A., Princeton U., 1950; postgrad., U. Toledo, 1953-54. C.P.A., Ohio, Fla. With Arthur Young & Co., C.P.A.s, 1950-57; bus. mgr., v.p., treas., pres., chief exec. officer, dir. Sentinel Star Co., Orlando, Fla., 1957-81; pres., chief exec. officer Chgo. Tribune Co., 1981—. Trustee Robert R. McCormick Charitable Trust, Northwestern U., Culver Ednl. Found., Chgo. Symphony Orch. Northwestern Meml. Hosp.; bd. dirs. United Way of Chgo. Served to 1st lt. U.S. Army, 1951-53. Decorated Bronze star. Mem. Am. Inst. C.P.A.s, Ohio, Fla. socs., C.P.A.s, Fla. Press Assn. (treas. 1969-76, pres. 1980, bd. dirs.), Am. Newspaper Pubs. Assn. (bd. dirs.). Home: 1500 N Lake Shore Dr Chicago IL 60610 Office: Chgo Tribune Co 435 N Michigan Ave Chicago IL 60611

BRUMBAUGH, WILLIAM JAY, coal and hard rock minerals company executive; b. Pittsburg, Kans., Aug. 21, 1930; s. John A. and Leona Geneva (Finley) B.; m. Geraldine Ponchur, June 18, 1953; children—Teri L. Forsythe, Curtis A., W. Kent, John V. B.S. in Edn., Pittsburg State U., 1951; postgrad. Okla. State U., 1974. Mathematician engring. dept. McNally Pittsburg Inc., Kans., 1951-52, chief process engr., 1954-71, asst. to pres., 1971-73, v.p., gen. mgr., 1973-80, corp. mgr. tech. services, 1980-82, corp. v.p. tech. services, 1982—, v.p. sales, 1987— ; bd. dirs. McNally Australia Proprietary Ltd., North Ryde, New South Wales, 1982—; chmn. bd. dirs. Kans. div. McNally Pittsburg Inc., 1973-80. Mem. Am. Mining Congress Export Council, 1982—, coal preparation com. Am. Mining Congress, 1986—; bd. dirs. Pittsburg United Way, 1978-84, v.p., 1983; active Jr. C. of C., Pittsburg, 1955-65, v.p., 1962, pres. 1963. Served to lt. comdr. USNR, 1949-72. Mem. Nat. Coal Council Clean Coal Tech. Work Group, Pittsburg State U. Alumni Assn. (bd. dirs. 1960-62, pres. 1962, trustee, 1976-79), Soc. Mining Engring. of AIME, Rocky Mountain Coal Mining Inst., Nat. Assn. Mfrs., Pittsburg C. of C. Republican. Avocations: tennis; golf; bowling; hunting; waterskiing. Home: Drawer D 307 W 3d St Pittsburg KS 66762 Office: McNally Pittsburg Inc PO Box 651 100 N Pine St Pittsburg KS 66762

BRUMLIK, JOEL, neurologist; b. Chgo., Jan. 5, 1933; s. Charles and Esther (Rothschild) B.; m. Stephanie Ann Holmquist, Sept. 5, 1981; children: Marc David, Rachel Vanessa. B.S., Northwestern U., 1953, M.D., 1956, M.S., 1959, Ph.D., 1961. Diplomate: Am. Bd. Neurology. Intern Chgo. Wesley Meml. Hosp., 1956-57; resident in neurology Northwestern U. Med. Sch. hosps., 1957-60; instr., then assoc. prof. neurology; mem. faculty Stritch Sch. Medicine, Loyola U., Maywood, Ill., chmn. dept. neurology, 1970-82; now prof. Stritch Sch. Medicine, Loyola U. Author articles, revs. in field. Recipient S. Wier Mitchell award, 1962. Mem. AMA, Am. Neurol. Assn., Am. Assn. Neurologists, Ill. Med. Soc., Chgo. Med. Soc. Jewish.

BRUMM, BRIAN ALLEN, accountant; b. Osage, Iowa, Oct. 6, 1954; s. Othmar Cornelius and Elizabeth Ann (Blake) B.; m. Joanne Leigh Toney, June 16, 1979; children: Emily Lynne, Allison Leigh. AA, North Iowa Area Community Coll., 1974; BA in Acctg., U. No. Iowa, 1976. CPA, Iowa. Staff acct. Augustine & Co. CPA's, Des Moines, 1976-79; sr. acct. Weber, Hein & Co. CPA's, Des Moines, 1979-80; controller Roto-Rooter Corp., West Des Moines, Iowa, 1981-83; chief fin. officer, v.p., treas. Roto-Rooter, Inc., Cin., 1983—, also bd. dirs. Mem. Am. Inst. CPA's, Iowa Soc. CPA's. Avocations: exercise, spectator sports, family. Office: Roto-Rooter Inc 511 Walnut St Suite 1400 Cincinnati OH 45202

BRUMM, BRUCE HAROLD, ophthalmologist; b. West Point, Nebr., Nov. 11, 1949; s. Harold and Kay B.; m. Patricia Grosserode, 1973; children: Matthew, Kristen. BS with Honors, U. Nebr., 1972, MD, 1975. Diplomate Am. Bd. Ophthalmology, Nat. Bd. Med. Examiners. Anesthesia intern U. Wis., Madison, 1975; resident in opthalmology U. Nebr. Med. Ctr., Omaha, 1976-79; practice medicine specializing in ophthalmology Omaha, 1979—; staff Immanuel Med. Ctr., Clarkson Hosp., Vets. Hosp., Nebr. Meth. Hosp., Omaha. U. Nebr. Regents Scholar, 1968. Fellow Am. Acad. Opthalmology; mem. AMA, Douglas County Med. Soc., Nebr. Med. Assn., Omaha Ophthalmological Soc., Met. Omaha Med. Soc., Nebr. Ophthalmological Soc., Phi Eta Sigma, Phi Beta Kappa. Home: 13611 Seward St Omaha NE 68154 Office: Immanuel Profl Plaza 6801 N 72d St Omaha NE 68122

BRUMMEL, MARK JOSEPH, magazine editor; b. Chgo., Oct. 28, 1933; s. Anthony William and Mary (Helmreich) B. B.A., Cath. U. Am., 1956, S.T.L., 1961, M.S. in L.S, 1964. Joined Order of Caretians, Roman Cath. Ch., 1952, ordained priest, 1960; librarian, tchr. St. Jude Sem., Momence, Ill., 1961-70; asso. editor U.S. Cath. mag., Chgo., 1971-72; editor U.S. Cath. mag., 1972—; dir. Claretian Publs., Chgo., 1972—; bd. dirs. Eastern Province Claretians, 1973-86; pres. bd. dirs. Claretian Med. Center, 1980—; bd. dirs. 8th Day Center, 1980—. Editor Today mag., 1970-71. Home: 3200 E 91st St Chicago IL 60617 Office: US Cath Mag 205 W Monroe St Chicago IL 60606

BRUNDAGE, MARJORIE UNDERWOOD, computer executive; b. Bellefontaine, Ohio, Feb. 5, 1940; d. James Madison and Mary Louise (Mustaine) Underwood; m. Richard Keith Brundage, Dec. 20, 1967; children: Jennie Lee, Judith Lynn. BS, Bowling Green State U., 1962. Systems trainee IBM, Toledo, 1962-63; systems analyst Kaiser Jeep Corp., Toledo, 1963-64, Lazarus Dept. Store, Columbus, Ohio, 1964-66; research assoc. Ohio State U., Columbus, 1966-67, supr. computer dept., 1967-79, dir. computer dept., 1979—; cons. U.S. Post Office, Columbus, 1972, labor reseach service, Columbus, 1971-79, local bank, Columbus, 1978-79. Contbr. articles to profl. jours. Trustee and violinist Met. Chamber Orch., Columbus, 1979—; elder and tchr. Cen. Presbyn. Ch., Columbus, 1966—; com. mem. Scioto Valley Presbytery, Columbus, 1985—; mem. Columbus Landmarks Nat. Trust, 1980—. Mem. Assn. Computer Machinery, Assn. Female Execs. Republican. Avocations: music, swimming, reading. Home: 328 Glenmont Ave Columbus OH 43214 Office: Ohio State U Coll Bus 1775 College Rd Columbus OH 43210

BRUNE, LINDA RUTH, educator; b. DuQuoin, Ill., Aug. 13, 1947; d. Louis John and Martha Frieda (Zinke) B. BS in Edn., So. Ill. U., 1969, MS in Edn., 1987. Tchr. Community Consol. Dist. 204, Pinckneyville, Ill., 1969—. Active Epilepsy Found. Am.; mem. ladies' aid soc., layman's league, LWML, fellowship club Trinity Luth. Ch., tchr. Sunday sch. Mem. NEA, Ill. Edn. Assn. Home: Rural Route 3 Box 25 Nashville IL 62263 Office: Community Consol 204 Sch Pinckneyville IL 62274

BRUNER, JOHN JUSTIN, accountant; b. Warsaw, Ind., Oct. 22, 1941; s. George Wesley and Helen (Hall) B.; m. Barbara Jean Runyan. June 10, 1968 (dec. 1975); children: Bruce, Kelley; m. Cassandra Anne Palkowski, Oct. 31, 1975; children: Todd, Peter. A in Bus., Internat. Coll., Ft. Wayne, Ind., 1963. Staff acct. Sanford, Myers & Dewald, Ft. Wayne, 1963-64, New Idea Farm Equipment, Coldwater, Ohio, 1964-65; project acct. Dalton Foundries, Inc., Warsaw, 1965-69, gen. acct., 1969-75, supr. acctg., 1975-85, mgr. acctg., 1985—. Bd. dirs. Marriage Encounter, Warsaw, 1983—. Served to staff sgt. USAF, 1963-69. Republican. Roman Catholic. Avocation: boating. Home: Rural Rt 8 Box 70 Warsaw IN 46580 Office: Dalton Foundries Inc PO Box 1388 Warsaw IN 46580

BRUNER, PHILIP LANE, lawyer; b. Chgo., Sept. 26, 1939; s. Henry Pfeiffer and Marjorie (Williamson) B.; A.B., Princeton U., 1961; J.D., U. Mich., 1964; M.B.A., Syracuse U., 1967; m. Ellen Carole Germann, Mar. 21, 1964; children—Philip Richard, Stephen Reed, Carolyn Anne. Admitted to Wis. bar, 1964, Minn. bar, 1968. Mem. Briggs and Morgan P.A., Mpls., St. Paul, 1967-83; sr. ptnr. Hart, Bruner, O'Brien & Thorton, P.A., Mpls., 1983— ; adj. prof. William Mitchell Coll. Law, St. Paul, 1970-78, 81; lectr. law seminars univs.; bar assns. and industry. Mem. Bd. Edn., Mahtomedi Ind. Sch. Dist. 832, 1978-86. Served to capt. USAF, 1964-67. Recipient Disting. Service award St. Paul Jaycees, 1974; named One of Ten Outstanding Young Minnesotans, Minn. Jaycees, 1975. Fellow Nat. Contract Mgmt. Assn.; mem. Internat. Am., Fed., Minn., Wis., Ramsey, Hennepin bar assns., Internat. Assn. Ins. Counsel, Am. Arbitration Assn. (nat. panel arbitrators). Club: Mpls. Athletic. Contbr. articles to profl. jours. Home: 8432 80th St N Stillwater MN 55082 Office: 1221 Nicollet Mall Minneapolis MN 55403

BRUNER, WILLIAM EVANS, II, ophthalmologist, educator, researcher; b. Cleve., Oct. 10, 1949; s. Clark Evans and Pauline (Schrenk) B.; m. Susan Lee Fraser, June 7, 1975; children—Amanda Lee, Andrew Evans. B.A., Wesleyan U., 1971; M.D., Case Western Res. U., 1975. Diplomate Am. Bd. Ophthalmology. Intern in surgery Univ. Hosps., Cleve., 1975-76; resident in ophthalmology, 1976-79; fellow in cornea and anterior segment surgery Johns Hopkins Hosp., Balt., 1979-81; asst. prof. ophthalmology Case Western Res. U., Cleve., 1981—. Sr. editor: Manual of Corneal Surgery, 1987; contbr. chpts. to med. textbooks and articles to profl. jours. Recipient Alfred S. Maschke award Case Western Res. U. Sch. Medicine, 1975. Fellow Am. Acad. Ophthalmology; mem. AMA, Assn. Research in Vision and Ophthalmology, Wilmer Residents Assn., Cleve. Acad. Medicine, Alpha Omega Alpha. Republican. Clubs: Cleve. Skating, The Kirtland. Avocations: snow skiing; tennis; golfing; music; art. Home: 2906 Weybridge Rd Shaker Heights OH 44120 Office: Univ Suburban Health Ctr 1611 S Green Rd Cleveland OH 44121

BRUNETTE, BRUCE JONATHAN, electronics company executive; b. Superior, Wis., Aug. 13, 1946; s. William Alexander and Veronica Genevieve (Herrick) B.; m. CarolJane Cziok, Oct. 17, 1970; children: David, Peter. BSME, U. Wis., 1969; MBA in Mktg., U. Minn., 1973. Prodn. engr. Honeywell, Inc., Mpls., 1969-71; product planning mgr. Medtronic, Inc., Mpls., 1973-81; mktg. mgr. Wagner, Inc., Mpls., 1981-83; dir. mktg. Ciprico, Inc., Mpls., 1983-85; pres. Introl Corp., St. Paul, 1985—; mem. adv. bd. Tech. Forums, Inc., San Jose, Calif., 1986. Coach basketball and soccer Armatage Recreational Ctr., Mpls., 1984-86; active Minn. Transp. Mus., Mpls., 1980-86; fin. dir. local polit. party, Mpls., 1978-82. Home: 5132 Oliver Ave S Minneapolis MN 55419 Office: Introl Corp 2675 Patton Rd Saint Paul MN 55419

BRUNGS, ROBERT ANTHONY, theology educator, institute director; b. Cin., July 7, 1931; s. Adolph and Helen (Klosterman) B. AB, Bellarmine Coll., Plattsburgh, N.Y., 1955; Licentiate in Philosophy, Fordham U., 1956; PhD in Physics, St. Louis U., 1962; Sacred Theology Licentiae, Woodstock (Md.) Coll., 1965. Asst. prof. physics St. Louis U., 1970-75, assoc. prof. physics, 1975-83; dir. Inst. for Theol. Encounter with Sci. and Tech., St. Louis, 1968—; cons. Vatican, Rome, 1973-84, Council Cath. Bishops, Washington, 1973—; mem. adv. bd. Zygon Mag., Chgo., 1975—. Exec. producer video program Lights Breaking, 1985; author: Building the City, 1967, A Priestly People, 1968; contbr. 60 articles to mags., newspapers, profl. jours. Mem. AAAS, Am. Phys. Soc., Sigma Xi, Phi Beta Kappa. Office: Inst for Theol Encounter with Sci & Tech 221 N Grand Blvd Saint Louis MO 63103

BRUNING, JAMES LEON, university official; b. Bruning, Nebr., Apr. 1, 1938; s. Leon G. and Delma Dorothy (Middendorf) B.; m. E. Marlene Schaff, Aug. 24, 1958; children: Michael, Stephen, Kathleen. B.A., Doane Coll., 1959; M.A., U. Iowa, 1961, Ph.D., 1962. Lic. psychologist, Ohio. Chmn. dept psychology Ohio U., Athens, 1972-76, acting dean arts and scis., 1976-77, assoc. dean, 1977-78, vice provost, 1978-81, provost, 1981—; planning cons. NCHEMS, Boulder, Colo., 1979-80. Author: Computational Handbook of Statistics, 1968, Research in Psychology, 1970; contbr. articles to profl. jours. Grantee Esso., 1963-64; grantee NIMH, 1963-66, EPDA, 1974-75. Mem. Am. Psychol. Assn., Midwestern Psychol. Assn., AAAS, Sigma Xi. Democrat. Lutheran. Home: 86 Melnor Dr Athens OH 45701 Office: Ohio Univ Cutler Hall Athens OH 45701

BRUNING, WALTER H., computer components company executive. Pres. (United Sch. Services Am., Inc.) Control Data Corp., Mpls. Office: Control Data Corp 8100 34th Ave S Minneapolis MN 55440 *

BRUNK, SAMUEL FREDERICK, medical oncologist; b. Harrisonburg, Va., Dec. 21, 1932; s. Harry Anthony and Lena Gertrude (Burkholder) B.; m. Mary Priscilla Bauman, June 24, 1976; children—Samuel, Jill, Geoffrey, Heather, Kirsten, Paul, Barbara. B.S., Eastern Mennonite Coll., 1955; M.D., U. Va., 1959; M.S. in Pharmacology, U. Iowa, 1967. Diplomate Am. Bd. Internal Medicine, Am. Bd. Internal Medicine in Med. Oncology. Straight med. intern U. Va., Charlottesville, 1959-60; resident in chest diseases Blue Ridge Sanatorium, Charlottesville, 1960-61; resident in internal medicine U. Iowa, Iowa City, 1962-64, fellow in clin. pharmacology (oncology), 1964-65, 66, asst. prof. internat. medicine, 1972-76; fellow in medicine (oncology) Johns Hopkins U., Balt., 1965-66; vis. physician bone marrow transplantation unit Fred Hutchinson Cancer Treatment Ctr., U. Wash., Seattle, 1975; practice medicine specializing in med. oncology Des Moines, 1976—; attending physician Iowa Luth. Hosp., 1976—, Iowa Meth. Med. Ctr., 1976—, Charter Hosp., 1976—, Mercy Hosp. Med. Ctr., 1976—; cons. physician Des Moines Gen. Osteo. Hosp., 1976—; prin. investigator Iowa Oncology Research Assn. in assn. with N. Central Cancer Treatment Group and Eastern Coop. Oncology Group, 1978-83. Contbr. articles to profl. jours. Bd. dirs. Iowa div. Am. Cancer Soc., 1971—, Johnson County chpt., 1968-72. Mosby scholar, U. Va., 1959. Fellow ACP, Am. Coll. Clin. Pharmacology; mem. AMA, Iowa Med. Soc., Polk County Med. Soc., Iowa Thoracic Soc., Am. Thoracic Soc., Iowa Clin. Med. Soc., Am. Fedn. Clin. Research, Iowa Heart Assn., Am. Assn. Cancer Edn., Am. Soc. Hematology, Am. Soc. Clin. Pharmacology and Therapeutics, Cen. Soc. Clin. Research, Raven Soc., Alpha Omega Alpha. Roman Catholic. Home: 3940 Grand Ave W West Des Moines IA 50265

BRUNNER, GEORGE EDWARD, III, architect; b. Akron, Ohio, Jan. 5, 1956; s. George Edward Jr. and Margaret Cossitt (McPherson) B.; m. Gayle Lee Wiley. B. Environ. Design, Ball State U., 1980, BArch, 1981. Registered architect Ill., Ind. Project architect Cole Assoc., Inc., Indpls., 1980-82, Boyd/Sobieray Assoc., Inc., Indpls., 1982-83, Toth, Garriss, Assoc., Indpls., 1983-84, Beaman, Guyer, Assoc., Indpls., 1984; pvt. practice architecture Shelbyville, Ind., 1984—. Mem. AIA, Ind. Soc. Architects, Associated Builders and Contractors, Indpls. Chpt. AIA, Ind. Metal Building Assn. (charter), Nat. Trust for Hist. Preservation, Hist. Landmarks Found. Ind., Shelbyville Hist. Soc. Republican. Presbyterian. Avocations: drawing, music, camping, photography. Home: 14 Mildred St Shelbyville IN 46176 Office: 26 Public Sq Suite 300 Shelbyville IN 46176

BRUNNER, JERI LYNN MARION, Spanish educator, artist; b. Milw., Mar. 17, 1947; d. Clyde Robert Bodenbach and Marie Mrytle (Bohn) Winter; m. Gerald Olen Brooks, Feb. 22, 1969 (div. Nov. 1970); m. Thomas Joseph Brunner, June 17, 1978; children: Charles, Sandra, James. BS in Edn., No. Ariz. U., 1969; postgrad., Ariz. State U., 1970-71. Instr. art No. Ariz. U., Flagstaff, 1967; tchr. art Phoenix Pub. Schs., 1972; instr. art and Spanish NE Wis. Tech Inst., Shawano, 1975-86; tchr. Spanish Shawano-Gresham (Wis.) Sch. Dist., 1985—; substitute tchr. Shawano-Gresham Sch. Dist., 1975-76; tchr. Spanish Bonduel (Wis.) Sch. Dist., 1976; free-lance artist, 1964—. Author: Art Edn. Curriculum Guide, 1976. Mem. Shawano Civic Players, set. dir., assoc. dir., 1975-79; co-founder, ptnr. Gold Star Prodns., 1980—, assoc. dir.; pres. Am. Cancer Soc., Shawano, 1985—. Mem. AAUW, Am. Assn. Univ. Women. Avocations: reading, travel, theatre, exercise, movies. Home: Rt 3 Box 256A Shawano WI 54166 Office: Gresham High Sch Rt 1 Gresham WI 54128

BRUNNER, KAY LORRAINE, sr. human resource planning specialist; b. Columbus, Ohio, July 17, 1949; d. Clarence Edward and Virginia Belle Yahn; m. David W. Brunner Jr., June 24, 1972. BS, Bowling Green (Ohio) State U., 1970, MEd, 1976; postgrad. U. Toledo, 1977—. Elem. tchr. public schs., Sylvania, Ohio, 1971-75; adminstrv. masters intern, grad. asst., acad. counselor U. Toledo, 1976-78; asst. employment mgr. Ohio Citizens Trust Co., Toledo, 1978-79, personnel devel. mgr., 1979-81; cons. Career Devel., Inc., 1982-85; human resource planning specialist Blue Cross/Blue Shield Mich., Detroit, 1985-86, sr. human resource planning specialist, 1986—. Mem. Internat. Assn. Personnel Women, Am. Soc. Tng. and Devel. (pres. Toledo chpt. 1986, career devel. exec. com. 1987—), Bowling Green State U. Alumni Assn., Phi Delta Kappa, Gamma Phi Beta, Pi Lambda Theta, Sigma Alpha Iota, Phi Kappa Phi. Methodist.

BRUNNER, ROBERT H., lawyer, arbitrator; b. Brazil, Ind., Oct. 7, 1932; s. Louis E. and Erna (Fischel) B.; m. Caroline Perkins Wilbur, Oct. 23, 1954; children: Claire C., Daniel T. BS, Purdue U.; JD, Ind. U. Bar: Ind. 1981, U.S. Dist. Ct. (so. dist.) Ind. 1981. With Brulin and Co., Inc., Indpls., 1954-84; atty., arbitrator Ross Brunner and Strahm, Indpls., 1984—; mem. panel Ind. Edn. Employment Relations Bd. Pres. bd. trustees Indpls. Unitarian-Universalist Ch., 1975-77, 84-85. Mem. ABA, Indpls. Bar Assn., Ind. State Bar Assn., Am. Arbitration Assn. (labor and comml. panels), Nat. Panel of Consumer Arbitrators, Nat. Mediation Bd. (arbitrator panel), Purdue Assn. of Indpls. (pres. 1973-74). Office: Ross Brunner and Strahm 300 Morrison Opera Pl 47 S Meridian St Indianapolis IN 46204-3527

BRUNO, OSBERT LEWIS, sales and marketing executive; b. Trinidad, Oct. 1, 1947; came to U.S., 1965; s. Crispin Adolphus and Sylvia (Bruno) Lewis; m. Margaret Patricia Goveia, Nov. 29, 1980; 1 child, Sheldon Jason. AAS, Acad. Aeronautics, N.Y.C., 1974; BT in Ops. Mgmt., N.Y. Inst. Tech., 1975, MBA in Mktg. and Mgmt., 1975. Mgr. network sales proposals cen. div. ABC Network TV, N.Y.C., 1973-85; dir. sales and mktg. Johnson Publ. Co., Chgo., 1985—. Mem. Am. Mgmt. Assn., Broadcast Ad Club Chgo. Avocations: music, photography, swimming, tennis. Office: Johnson Publ Co Inc 820 S Michigan Chicago IL 60605

BRUNO, THOMAS ANTHONY, lawyer; b. Berwyn, Ill., Feb. 8, 1954; s. Alexander Nicholas and Mildred Mary (Biciste) B.; m. Elizabeth Ann Matthias, June 12, 1976; children: Anthony Alexander, Evan Stanley. B.A., U. Ill. 1976, J.D., 1979. Bars: Ill. 1980, U.S. Dist. Ct. (cen. dist.) Ill. 1980, U.S. Supreme Ct. 1985. Prin. Thomas A. Bruno and Assocs., Urbana, Ill., 1980—; lectr. U. Ill. Law Sch., Urbana, 1981—; host TV show "Legal-Ease." Author (newspaper column) Honest Lawyer, 1983. Bd. dirs. Devel. Services Ctr., Champaign, Ill., 1979-82; vice chmn. bd. Disabled Citizens Found., Champaign, 1982—; mem. Humane Soc. Champaign County, 1984, Chgo. Zool. Soc. Ill. Legis. scholar, 1972-76. Mem. ABA, Ill. Bar Assn., Champaign County Bar Assn., Assn. Trial Lawyers Am., Champaign County Assn. Criminal Defense Lawyers (past pres. Champaign chpt. 1982—), Nat. Assn. for Prevention Child Abuse (v.p. Champaign county chpt.), Phi Eta Sigma. Democrat. Roman Catholic. Clubs: U. Ill. Quarterback, U. Ill. Rebounder. Lodges: K.P., Kiwanis. Home: 1109 W Park Ave Champaign IL 61821 Office: Thomas A Bruno and Assocs 303 W Green St Urbana IL 61801

BRUNO, THOMAS RALPH, orthopedic surgeon; b. Chgo., Oct. 7, 1939; s. Albert and Ann (Broccolo) B.; m. Sharon Marie Kelly, June 13, 1964; children—Maria, Thomas Jr., Anna, Leah, Michael, Caroline, Matthew. Student Loyola U.-Chgo., 1957-70, M.D., 1964. Diplomate Am. Bd. Orthopedic Surgery. Intern Cook County Hosp., Chgo., 1964-65; resident in orthopedic surgery, Northwestern U., Chgo., 1965-70, fellow hand surgery, 1970-71; staff orthopedic surgeon, hand cons. N.W. Community Hosp., Arlington Heights, Ill., 1972—; cons. hand surgery, orthopedic surgery O'Hare Ind. Clinic, Elk Grove Village, Ill., 1973—; asst. prof. orthopedic surgery Rush Presbyn. St. Luke's Med. Ctr., Chgo., 1973—. Contbr. articles to profl. jours. v.p. Inverness Soccer Assn. (Ill.), 1982—; bd. dirs. The Elgin (Ill.) Acad., 1987—. Served to maj USAF, 1970-72. U.S. Govt. fellow, 1969-70. Fellow Am. Acad. Orthopedic Surgeons; mem. AMA, Christian Med. Soc., Orthopedic Soc., Midwest Orthopedic Soc., ACS (com. trauma 1977—). Roman Catholic. Clubs: Inverness Golf; Right Tennis (Shaumburg, Ill.). Avocations: tennis; aerobic conditioning, art. Office: Orthopedic Assocs SC 2010 S Arlington Heights Rd Arlington Heights IL 60005

BRUNOW, EDWIN EDWARD, metall. cons.; b. Milw., July 28, 1912; s. John Johann and Anna Henrietta (Radmann) B.; student U. Wis., Milw., 1931-38, Marquette U., 1933-36; m. Grace Gladys Alma De Sham, June 27, 1942; children—Barry W., Nancy G. Brunow Hornsby. Plant metallurgist Sivyer Steel Co., Milw., 1938-59, metall. engr., 1959-63, tech. dir., 1963-69; metall. engr. Ervin Industries, Adrian, Mich., 1969-74, tech. dir., 1974-77; metall. cons., 1977—. Vice-chmn. Potawatomi council Boy Scouts Am.; mem. local sch. bds., 1953-58. Mem. Am. Foundrymen's Soc., Am. Soc. Metals, ASTM, Steel Founders Soc. Am. Research included cast armor plate, early warning system, minuteman silos, nuclear reactors; developed 450 and 250 micron size steel balls for xerography. Home: 1343 Feeman Ct Adrian MI 49221

BRUNS, BILLY LEE, consulting electrical engineer; b. St. Louis, Nov. 21, 1925; s. Henry Lee and Violet Jean (Williams) B.; B.A., Washington U., St. Louis, 1949, postgrad. Sch. Engring., 1959-62; m. Lillian Colleen Mobley, Sept. 6, 1947; children—Holly Rene, Kerry Alan, Barry Lee, Terrence William. Supt., engr., estimator Schneider Electric Co., St. Louis, 1950-54, Ledbetter Electric Co., 1954-57; tchr. indsl. electricity St. Louis Bd. Edn., 1957-71; pres. B.L. Bruns & Assos., cons. engrs., St. Louis, 1963-72; v.p., chief engr. Hosp. Bldg. & Equipment Co., St. Louis, 1972-76; pres., prin. B.L. Bruns & Assos. cons. engrs., St. Louis, 1976—; tchr. elec. engring. U. Mo. St. Louis extension, 1975-76. Mem. Mo. Adv. Council on Vocat. Edn., 1969-76, chmn., 1975-76; leader Explorer post Boy Scouts Am., 1950-57. Served with AUS, 1944-46: PTO, Okinawa. Decorated Purple Heart. Registered profl. engr., Mo., Ill., Wash., Fla., La., Wis., Minn., N.Y., Iowa, Pa., Miss., Ind., Ala., N.C. Mem. Nat., Mo. socs. profl. engrs., Profl. Engrs. in Pvt. Practice, Am. Soc. Heating, Refrigeration and Air Conditioning Engrs., Illuminating Engrs. Soc., Am. Mgmt. Assn. Baptist. Club: Masons. Tech. editor The National Electrical Code and Blueprint Reading, Am. Tech. Soc., 1959-65. Home: 1243 Hobson Dr Ferguson MO 63135 Office: 10 Adams Suite 111 Ferguson MO 63135

BRUNS, DENNIS VIRGIL, accountant; b. Sedalia, Mo., Aug. 26, 1951; s. Leo Frederick Bruns and Shirley Ann (Ragar) Bergmann; m. Deborah Jameson Pelham, Aug. 18, 1973; children: Sarah, Douglas, David. BBA, U. Mo., 1973. CPA, Mo. Mem. cons. staff Touche Ross & Co., St. Louis, 1975-84, ptnr., dir. mgmt. cons., 1984—, nat. dir. long-term care services, 1985—. Contbr. articles to various publs. Mem. West St. Louis Jaycees, 1976-78, treas., 1977. Mem. Nat. Assn. Sr. Living Industries, Inst. Mgmt. Cons. (local sec. 1987—), Am. Inst. CPA's, St. Louis Friends of the Zoo Assn. Republican. Lutheran. Club: Media (St. Louis). Office: Touche Ross & Co 2100 Railway Exchange Bldg Saint Louis MO 63101

BRUNS, EDWARD ALBERT, osteopath; b. St. Louis, Feb. 8, 1941; s. Edward F. and Thelma A. (Siekerman) B.; m. Mary Lou Kelley, Oct. 7, 1961; children: Cynthia K., Catherine L., Chris M. BS, N.E. Mo. U., 1964; DO, Kirksville Coll. Osteo. Medicine, 1968. Diplomate Am. Osteo. Bd. Internal Medicine. Asst. prof. medicine Kirksville Coll. Osteo. Medicine, 1968-72; attending physician Buenger Clinic, Memphis, Mo., 1972-74, Med. Specialists, St. Louis, 1974—. Fellow Am. Coll. Utilization Rev. Physicians; mem. Am. Osteo. Assn., Am. Coll. Osteo. Internists. Methodist. Avocation: photography. Home: 12928 Briar Fork Ct Saint Louis MO 63131 Office: Med Specialists Inc 456 N New Ballas Rd Saint Louis MO 63141

BRUNSDALE, JOHN EDWARD, farmer; b. Fargo, N.D., Apr. 22, 1931; s. Karl H. and Mary Elizabeth (Swanston) B.; m. Mitzi Louisa Mallarian, Dec. 2, 1961; children: Margaret Louisa, Jean Ellen and Maureen Lois(twins). BS, N.D. State U., 1955; postgrad., U. Minn., 1956-57, Colo. State U., 1958. Farmer Steele, Traill, Cass Counties, N.D., 1950—; postal facility contractor U.S. Postal Services, various states, 1969—; pres. Red River Valley Coop., 1972-75; bd. dirs. chmn. bd., v.p. 1st and Farmers Bank, Portland, N.D.. Rep. precinct committeeman 20th Dist., Traill County, 1966—; bd. dirs. No. Lights Council Boy Scouts Am., Fargo, 1974-79; mem. Mayville-Portland Sch. Bd., 1980-83. Served to staff sgt. USAF, 1950-53. Recipient Excellence in Life award Red River Valley Hist. Soc., 1975, N.D. Sci. and Industry award Greater N.D. Assn., 1975. Mem. N.D. Ind. Bankers Assn., Mayville-Portland Jaycees (v.p. 1963-66), Red River Valley Sugar Mktg. Assn. (bd. dirs. 1969-71, v.p. 1973-75). Roman Catholic. Lodges: Masons (worshipful master 1983-84), Elks, Shriners, Grand Lodge of N.D. (fin. com. 1985—). Home and Office: Rural Rt 1 Box 9 Mayville ND 58257

BRUNSDALE, MITZI LOUISA MALLARIAN, English language educator, book critic; b. Fargo, N.D., May 16, 1939; d. Gregory Starn and Phyllis (Grobe) Mallarian; B.S. with honors (Nat. Merit scholar), N.D. State U., 1959, M.S., 1961; postgrad. Ind. U., 1959-60; Ph.D. (Danforth fellow), U. N.D., 1976; m. John Edward Brunsdale, Dec. 2, 1961; children—Margaret Louisa, Jean Ellen and Maureen Lois (twins). Departmental tchr. N.D. State U., 1958-59, grad. asst., 1960-61, instr. English and French, 1961; grad. asst. Ind. U., 1959-60; book critic Houston Post, 1971—; book reviewer Chgo. Tribune, 1987—; instr. English, Mayville (N.D.) State Coll., 1975-76, asst. prof., 1976-78, assoc. prof., 1978-83, prof., 1983—. Sec., 20th Dist. N.D. Republican Party, 1963-70; chmn. N.D. Humanities Council, 1980, 81-82; grant rev. panelist Nat. Endowment for Humanities. Mem. MLA, Rocky Mountain MLA, D.H. Lawrence Soc. Am., AAUP, Fgn. Lang. Assn. Red River, Linguistic Circle Man. and N.D., P.E.O., Phi Kappa Phi, Sigma Alpha Iota, Kappa Alpha Theta. Republican. Contbr. articles to profl. jours. and reference encys. Home: Rural Route 1 Box 9 Mayville ND 58257 Office: Dept English Mayville State Coll Mayville ND 58257

BRUSH, JOHN BURKE, retired chemical company executive, inventor, researcher; b. N.Y.C., Nov. 25, 1912; s. Frederick Louis and Florence Ann (Bullen) B.; m. Lois Jane Pogue, Mar. 22, 1941 (dec.); children: Deborah Gay, Jay Philip, Burke Frederick, Randal Moorman, Gary Stoddard; m. Marian Elise Natorp, May 13, 1971. BSME, Cornell U., 1934. Registered profl. engr., Ohio. Engr. Procter & Gamble, Cin., 1934-41, assoc. chief engr., 1945-55, mgr. airplane ops., 1950-60, mgr. research and devel., 1960-76; chief engr. Philippine Mfg. CO., Manila, 1941-45; owner, pres. Brush Autoboat Co., Cin., 1958-86. Patentee in field. Mem. ASME, Soc. Automotive Engrs., Engring. Soc. Cin. Republican. Avocation: flying. Home and Office: Brush Autoboat Co 2 Beech Knoll Dr Cincinnati OH 45224

BRUSIUS, BETTY LORRAINE, religious and educational organization administrator; b. Didsbury, Alta., Can., Sept. 2, 1935; s. Alexander and Mathilda (Schuhart) Weitz; m. Ronald William Brusius, June 17, 1953; children—Cathy Merrill, Ronda Carlson, Paula Brusius Owens, Krista. Student Concordia Tchrs. Coll., Seward, Nebr., 1968-72. Exec. dir. Nat. Lutheran Parent-Tchr. League, St. Louis, 1979; co-developer Mo. Synod Luth Ch. marriage, family enrichment experiences; nat. trainer leader couples marriage enrichment; leader couple, marriage communications labs., effective tng., stress mgmt. Mem. Council Affiliated Marriage Enrichment Orgns., Assn. Couples Marriage Enrichment; program leader Active Parenting. Cons. Concordia Sex Edn. series; contbr. articles to religious publs.; producer videotape parenting program. Office: 123 W Clinton Pl Room 102 Saint Louis MO 63122

BRUSKI, PAUL STEVEN, public relations executive; b. Kansas City, Mo., Mar. 10, 1949; s. Paul and Elizabeth Ann (Cravens) B.; m. Mary Margaret Williams, May 5, 1980. BS in Journalism, U. Berlin, Fed. Republic Germany, 1972. With engring. mgmt. Storage Tech. Corp., Louisville, 1973-77; dir. IMC, Denver, 1977-79; ptnr. Flack and Bruski Advt., Denver, 1979-81; dir. tech. Services D. J. Moore Advt., Guilderland, N.Y., 1983; dir. mktg. The Software Group, Ballston Lake, N.Y., 1984-86; dir. corp. communications Innovative Software, Inc., Lenexa, Kans., 1986—; cons. publ. Brodock Press Inc., Utica, N.Y., 1983-86; computer cons. and free-lance journalist, 1974—. Author: Collected Works, 1977. Served with U.S. Army, 1968-72. Accredited mem. Pub. Relations Soc. Am. Avocations: race car designer, ski racing. Office: Innovative Software Inc 9875 Widmer Rd Lenexa KS 66215

BRUSS, CAROL LOUISE, educator, actress; b. Milw., May 30; d. Walter Julius and Erna Caroline (Pieplow) Bruss. B.A., Carthage Coll., 1951; postgrad. Alverno Coll.-Milw., 1971-72. Life cert. secondary tchr., Wis. Personnel clk. Sears & Roebuck Co., 1951-55; mgr. Security Nat. Ins. Agy., Milw., 1955-60; student, dir., producer Sta. WMUS, Milw. Area Tech. Coll., 1960-65; office mgr. Stat Tab Corp., Milw., 1965-71; career specialist Milw. Pub. Schs., 1971—; theatre career specialist, 1977-84; tchr. English and speech Bay View High Sch., 1984—; actress, dir. Milw. community theatres; soprano soloist Lake Park Ch., Milw. Active South Div. Civic Assn., Milw.; mem. Marquis Library N.Y Soc.; life mem. (hon.) Lutheran Ch. Women. Recipient producer's award for best program Channel 10 Milw. Area Tech. Coll., 1962; Best Artistic award Act One Theatre Co., Milw. Pub. Schs., 1981. Mem. Wis. Theatre Assn., Impresarios-Milw. Performing Arts Ctr., AAUW, South Div. Civic Assn., Milw. Zool. Soc., Phi Lambda Omega, Alpha Mu Gamma, Alpha Psi Omega. Club: Coll. Women's. Home: 2216 S 28th St Milwaukee WI 53215

BRUST, DAVID PETER, architect; b. Fond Du Lac, Wis., Feb. 16, 1941; s. John Joseph and Majorie Helen (Twohig) B.; m. Sara Sue Collins, July 11, 1970; children: John James, Christopher David. BArch, Cath. U. Am., 1964; MBA, Marquette U., 1968. registered architect, real estate agt., Wis. Exec. v.p. Brust-Zimmerman Inc., Milw., 1964-77, Brust-Heike/Design Assocs., Milw., 1977-84; V.P. SBF Mgmt., Milw., 1984-86; sole proprietor Brust/Design Assocs., Milw., 1986—. Designer/architect Milw. Cath. Home, 1974 (AIA Wis. Merit award 1975), restoration Tivoli Palm Garden Bldg., 1979 (AIA Wis. Merit award 1980). Recipient Henry Adams award Henry Adams Fund, 1964. Mem. AIA (various offices Southeast Wis. chpt.), Nat. Council Archtl. Registration Bds., Wis. Soc. Architects. Roman Catholic. Lodge: Kiwanis (trustee 1975-78). Avocations: hunting, running, philately, reading. Home and Office: 4400 N Lake Dr Shorewood WI 53211

BRUTSMAN, MELVIN EZEKIEL, restaurant owner; b. Harnell, N.Y., Dec. 7, 1947; s. Ronald Glee and Marjorie Mary (Ross) B.; m. Grace Ann Thomas, June 12, 1971; children: Helene, Thomas, Margaret, Mary Allyce. AA, Erie Community Coll., 1969; BA, Stout State U., 1971. Food supr.residence halls, catering mgr. meml. union Purdue U., West Lafayette, Ind., 1971-80; pres. Sarge Oak on Main, Inc., Lafayette, Ind., 1980—. Deacon Cen. Presbyn. Ch., 1977-80, trustee, 1987—; mem. Tippecanoe County Hist. Assn., Friends of Downtown, Lafayette, v.p. 1985, pres. 1986. Served with NG, 1971-78. Mem. Ind. Restaurant Assn., Greater Lafayette Restaurant Assn. (exec. bd. 1985-87). Avocations: reading, fishing, bldg. restoration. Home: 321 S 7th Lafayette IN 47901 Office: Sarge Oak on Main Inc 721 Main St Lafayette IN 47901

BRUURSEMA, LESLIE RICHARD, metaphysical educator; b. San Bernadino, Calif., July 8, 1956; s. Albert and Mary Lou (Hirschler) B.; m. Sheila Marie Wade, Nov. 26, 1982; 1 child, Anna Michelle. Student, U. Nebr., 1974-78; BA in Metaphysics, Sch. Metaphysics. Br. dir. Sch. Metaphysics, Topeka, 1979-80, Kansas City, Mo., 1980-82; owner, dir. New Life Research, Roeland Park, Kans., 1983—; founder, pres. New Life Ctr., Kansas City, 1985—. Contbr. articles to profl. jours. Bd. dirs. Clean Up Am. project, Topeka, 1979-80, Food for Life project, Kansas City, 1987. Mem. Phi Eta Sigma. Mem. New Age Metaphysical Ch. Avocation: sculpting. Home: 5321 Buena Vista Roeland Park KS 66205 Office: New Life Ctr 4550 Main St Suite 202 Kansas City MO 64111

BRYAN, HENRY C(LARK), JR., lawyer; b. St. Louis, Dec. 8, 1930; s. Henry Clark and Faith (Young) B.; m. Sarah Ann McCarthy, July 28, 1956; children—Mark Pendleton, Thomas Clark, Sarah Christy. A.B., Washington U., St. Louis, 1952, LL.B., 1956. Bar: Mo. 1956. Law clk. to fed. judge 1956; assoc. McDonald & Wright, St. Louis, 1956-60; ptnr. McDonald, Bernard, Wright & Timm, St. Louis, 1961-64, McDonald, Wright & Bryan, St. Louis, 1964-81, Wright, Bryan & Walsh, St. Louis, 1981-84; v.p., dir. Harbor Point Boat & Dock Co., St. Charles, Mo., 1966-80, Merrell Inst. Agy., 1966-80; dir. Stanley Hanks Painting Co., 1983-84. Served to 1st lt. AUS, 1952-54. Mem. ABA, Mo. Bar Assn., St. Louis Bar Assn. (past chmn. probate and trust sect., marriage and divorce law com.), Kappa Sigma, Phi Delta Phi. Republican. Episcopalian. Lodge: Elks. Home: 41 Ladue Terr Ladue MO 63124 Office: 11 S Meramec Ave Saint Louis MO 63105

BRYAN, JERRY LYNN, public relations professional; b. Poplar Bluff, Mo., Oct. 17, 1939; s. Chester Lee and Bernita Louise (Henson) B.; m. Melva Pauline Tate, June 28, 1959; children: Jeffrey Lynn, Bernita Ruth, Jay Matthew. B in Journalism, U. Mo., 1961. News dir. Sta. KLIK, Jefferson City, Mo., 1962-67; pres. sec. Gov. Mo., Jefferson City, 1967-73; v.p. Wright & Manning, Inc., St. Louis, 1973-77; dir. communications Consol. Aluminum, St. Louis, 1977-78; mgr. bus. devel. Sverdrup Corp., St. Louis, 1978-81, dir. corp. communications, 1981—. Nat. adv. bd. U. Mo. Sch. Journalism, 1984—; chmn. strategic planning council Parkway Sch. Dist., St. Louis, 1985-87; world trade council Regional Commerce and Growth Assn., St. Louis, 1985—; bd. dirs. Press Club Met. St. Louis, 1985—, St. Louis Mental Health Assn., 1987—, St. Louis Journalism Found., 1987, Confluence St. Louis, exec. com., 1987—. Mem. Pub. Relations Soc. Am. (exec. com. corp. sect. 1986—, vice chmn. 1987, bd. dirs. St. Louis chpt. 1987—), Internat. Assn. Bus. Communicators (pres. St. Louis chpt. 1987, chmn. internat. awareness 1986, dist. IV Communicator of Yr. 1985), Bus. Profl. Advt. Assn. (pres. St. Louis chpt. 1985-86, internat. v.p. 1986-87, treas. 1987—; Chpt. of Yr. Leadership award 1986). Democrat. Baptist. Club: Mo. Athletic. Avocation: photography. Home: 1411 Silverleaf Ln Saint Louis MO 63146 Office: Sverdrup Corp 801 N 11th Saint Louis MO 63101

BRYAN, JOHN HENRY, JR., food and consumer products company executive; b. West Point, Miss., 1936. B.A. in Econs. and Bus. Adminstrn, Rhodes Coll., Memphis, 1958. With Sara Lee Corp. (formerly known as consol food corp.), Chgo., 1960—, exec. v.p. ops., 1974-75, pres., chief exec. officer, 1975-76, chmn. bd., chief exec. officer, 1976—; also dir. Sara Lee Corp. (formerly known as consol food corp.); dir. Amoco Corp., First Chgo. Office: Sara Lee Corp 3 1st National Plaza Chicago IL 60602-4260 *

BRYAN, NORMAN E., dentist; b. South Bend, Ind., Jan. 20, 1947; s. Norman E. and Frances (Kuhn) B.; m. Constance C. Cook, Feb. 23, 1984 (div. Apr. 1985); m. Linda Markley, Dec. 31, 1986; 1 child, Noelle. AB, Ind. U., 1969; DDS, Ind. U. Purdue U., Indpls., 1973. Sr. dentist Bryan-Benifier, Elkhart, Ind., 1975—. Author: Canine Endodontics, 1982. Mem. ADA, Ind. Dental Assn., Elkhart Dental Assn. (pres. 1976-77, 84-86). Republican. Club: Great Lakes Cruising (Chgo.). Avocations: sailor, photography, painter. Office: 505 Vistula Elkhart IN 46516

BRYAN, ORPEN W., public school system administrator; b. Chgo., Mar. 17, 1931; s. Roland and Alberta (Davis) B.; m. Mary L. Washington, Aug. 21, 1967. A.A., Wilson Jr. Coll., 1950; B.Ed., Chgo. Tchrs. Coll., 1952; B.E., Loyola U., Chgo., 1959, M.Ed., 1963; Ed.D., Nova U., 1975. Cert. tchr. and prin., Ill. Elem. tchr., Chgo. Bd. Edn., 1954-61, counselor, asst. prin., 1961-65, prin., 1965-73, dist. supt., 1973-81, dep. supt., 1981-85, asst. supt., 1985—; mem. State of Ill. Edn. Adv. Council, 1976-81. Pres. Joint Negro Appeal; bd. dirs. Beatrice Caffrey Youth Services, Inc., Abraham Lincoln Ctr. Served with U.S. Army, 1952-54. Recipient Outstanding Service award State of Ill. Commn. on Delinquency, 1979. Mem. Am. Assn. Sch. Adminstrs., Assn. Curriculum and Supervision Devel., Nat. Assn. Black Sch. Educators, Urban League, NAACP, Am. Legion, Phi Delta Kappa. Methodist. Club: City (Chgo.). Office: 1819 W Pershing Rd Chicago IL 60609

BRYANT, ARTHUR LEE, insurance company executive; b. Corydon, Iowa, Oct. 25, 1934; s. Everett Harold Bryant and Helen Pauline (Rowland) Alcorn; m. Carol Fay Shanahan, Aug. 20, 1955; children: Lynn Ann Bryant Still, Janice Lee Bryant Gravelle, Michael Arthur. BA, DePauw U., 1956. With State Life Ins. Co., Indpls., 1956—, asst. v.p., sec., 1968-70, v.p., sec., 1970-80, sr. v.p. mktg., 1980-83, pres., chief operating officer, 1983-85, chmn. bd. dirs., pres., 1985—. Fellow Soc. Actuaries. Republican. Methodist. Clubs: Columbia, Highland Country (Indpls.). Avocation: golf. Home: 6852 Alnwick Ct Indianapolis IN 46220 Office: State Life Ins Co 141 E Washington St Indianapolis IN 46204

BRYANT, ARTHUR WILLIAM, prosthodontist, army officer; b. Murfreesboro, Tenn., May 14, 1950; s. Arthur Elbert and Nell (Keith) B.; m. Rebecca May Clanin, Mar. 22, 1972 (div. Mar. 1985); 1 child, Jennifer; m. Barbara Ann Berberich, Apr. 20, 1985; children: Kevin, Joseph. BS, Wright State U., 1972; DMD, U. Ky., 1976. Commd. capt. U.S. Army, 1976, advanced through grades to lt. col., 1987; resident in gen. dentistry DENTAC, U.S. Army, El Paso, Tex., 1976-77; gen. dentist DENTAC, U.S. Army, Ft. Sill, Okla., 1977-80; officer in charge of clinic DENTAC, U.S. Army, Stuttgart, Fed. Republic of Germany, 1980-83; resident in prosthodontics DENTAC, U.S. Army, Ft. Sam Houston, Tex., 1983-85; chief removable prosthodontics DENTAC, U.S. Army, Ft. Leonard Wood, Mo., 1985—. Fellow Acad. Gen Dentistry; mem. Am. Coll. Prosthodonists. Methodist.

BRYANT, BETTY JANE, shopping center exec.; b. Camden, Ind., June 19, 1926; d. Claude Raymond and Louise (Eckert) Wickard; B.S., Purdue U., 1947; m. Harry R. Bryant, Aug. 21, 1949; children—Susan, Patricia. Retail mgmt. and advt. L.S. Ayres, Indpls., 1947-49, Burdine's, Miami, Fla., 1950-51, Joske's, San Antonio, 1968, Dillard's, San Antonio, 1968-70; with Sterling Advt. Agy., N.Y.C., 1949; mktg. dir. Mary Ann Fabrics and Designer's Fabrics By Mail, Evanston, Ill., 1971-75; instr. Ray-Vogue Sch., Chgo., 1976; mktg. dir. Woodfield Shopping Center, Schaumburg, Ill., 1977—. Mem. council Fashion Group of Chgo. Bd. dirs. Northwest Area council Girl Scouts Am., 1982-83, Greater Woodfield Conv. and Visitors Bur., 1984-85, sec., 1986—. Mem. N.W. Suburban Assn. (dir.), Commerce and Industry (v.p. 1981-82), Chgo. Area Shopping Center Mktg. Dirs.'s Assn., Women in Mgmt., Mortar Board, Kappa Kappa Gamma. Home: 2008 Bayberry Ln Hoffman Estates IL 60195 Office: Woodfield Merchants Assn 5 Woodfield Mall Schaumburg IL 60195

BRYANT, DOROTHY TAYLOR, educator; b. Indpls., Mar. 22, 1931; d. George E. and Lalla Marie (Bass) Taylor; m. Alvin Jones, Dec. 6, 1958; 1 dau., Pamela M.; m. 2d, William J. Bryant, June 27, 1974. B.S. in Edn., Ind. U., 1953; M.A., Northeastern Ill. U., 1968; Ed.D., Vanderbilt U., 1982. Tchr. pub. schs., Gary, Ind., 1953; tchr. elem. sch. Chgo. Bd. Edn., 1954-68, 80-83, evaluator ECIA Chpt. 1 programs, 1984-86, math. sci. instrn. coordinator, 1986—, lang. arts cons., 1968-75, instrn. coordinator Dists. 11, 23, 1976-80. Founding mem. Profl. Women's Aux. Provident Hosp.; bd. dirs. Beatrice Coffery Youth Services. Recipient 20 yr. service award Profl. Women's Aux. Provident Hosp. Mem. Assn. Supervision and Curriculum Devel. (trustee), Chgo. Assn. for Supervision and Curriculum Devel. (founder), AAUW, Neal Marshall Alumni of Ind. U., Phi Delta Kappa, Delta Sigma Theta. Mem. United Ch. of Christ. Home: 2246 W 91st St Chicago IL 60620

BRYANT, KRAIG DAVID, bank executive; b. Oconto Falls, Wis., Sept. 12, 1959; s. John Raleigh and Faith (Kendall) B. BS in Bus. Adminstrn., U. Wis., 1981; diploma retail banking, Am. Inst. Banking, 1984; degree, Grad. Sch. Banking, 1986. Lic. stockbroker and life ins. agt. Retail loan officer Heritage Bank & Trust, Racine, Wis., 1982-83, asst. v.p., 1983—. Small bus. acct. rep., reviewing mem. ann. budgets Racine Area United Way, 1982—. Named one of Outstanding Young Men of Am., 1985. Mem. Assembly of God Ch. Lodge: Optimists (v.p. Racine Wednesday 1986—, v.p. 1986, pres.

1987). Avocations: tennis, racquetball, golf, waterskiing, writing. Home: 326 Mertens Ave Racine WI 53405 Office: Heritage Bank and Trust 5901 Durand Ave Racine WI 53405

BRYANT, NORMAN FRANCIS, real estate executive; b. Rushville, Ind., Jan. 26, 1925; s. William McKinley and Freda Lucille (Comestock) B.; m. Barbara Ann Tucker, July 10, 1954 (div. 1976); m. Janise Carol Folkening, Sept., 1979; children: Jeffrey, Suzan, Douglas, Gregory, Andrea. BA, Butler U., 1950. V.p. Am. Nat. Bank, Indpls., 1954-57; exec. v.p. Carriage Co., Indpls., 1958-68; pres., chmn. The Bryant Co., Indpls., 1968—; past state dir. Independent Ins. Agents Ind., Inc.; bd. dirs. Ind. Ins. Edn. Found.; mem. Met. Indpls. Bd. Realtors, bd. dirs. comml. indsl. div. Past dir. Family Service Assn., Meridan Meth. Ch., Indpls.; past pres. Marion County Heart Assn., Lawrence Cen. High Sch. Bd. Dirs.; past trustee Ind. Safety Council, Inc.; past bd. dirs., v.p. Cen. Ind. council Boy Scouts Am. Served with USAF, 1943-45, CBI. Recipient Exceptional Service award Am. Heritage Found. Mem. Nat. Inst. Real Estate Brokers, Inst. Real Estate Mgmt., Nat. Assn. real Estate Bds., real Estate Securities and Syndication Inst. (profl. standards com., edn. com.), Nat. Assn. Ins. Agents, Indpls. Jaycees (past pres., Disting. Service award), Alpha Delta Sigma. Republican. Clubs: Indpls. Gyro, Columbia Indpls., Hillcrest Golf and Country, Civitan. Lodge: Optimists. Avocations: squash, tennis, hiking, hunting, fishing. Home: 15018 Shoreway E S Dr Carmel IN 46032 Office: The Bryant Co 8500 Keystone Crossing Indianapolis IN 46240

BRYANT, RHYS, chemical company executive; b. Swansea, Wales, Nov. 28, 1936; s. Sydney Rees and Margaret (Jones) B.; m. Jayne Louise Morgan, Sept. 5, 1960; children: Louise Mary, Timothy Richard Morgan, Daniel Rees. BS summa cum laude, U. Wales, 1957, PhD, 1960. Research fellow Yale U., New Haven, 1960-61; fellow Mellon Inst., Pitts., 1961; research chemist Unilever Research Labs., Bedford, Eng., 1962-63; asst. lectr. U. Manchester, Eng., 1963-65; group leader Mead Johnson and Co., Evansville, Ind., 1965-67, sect. leader, 1967-68, dir. pharm. quality control, 1968-76; v.p. quality control Plough div. Schering-Plough Corp., Memphis, 1976-78; group dir. quality assurance G.D. Searle & Co., Skokie, Ill., 1978-86, dir. tech. transfer, 1987—, including spl. assignments as v.p. quality assurance U.S., 1979-81. Author The Pharm. Quality Control Handbook; contbr. articles to profl. jours. Fulbright scholar, 1960-61. Fellow Chem. Soc. (London); mem. Royal Inst. Chemistry (London), Soc. Genealogists (London), Am. Chem. Soc., Research Soc. Am. Methodist. Office: PO Box 5110 Chicago IL 60680

BRYANT, RICK H., protective services official, small business owner; b. Keokuk, Iowa, Feb. 9, 1957; s. Richard Gene and Barbara Ann (Reeves) B.; m. Tamara Lyn Rouse, Aug. 2, 1980. Cert. emergency med. tech., Southeastern Community Coll., 1984. Salesman Life Investors, Cedar Rapids, Iowa, 1980-84; paramedic Lee County Ambulance, Montrose, Iowa, 1981—; police officer City of West Point, Iowa, 1983—; owner, mgr. Keokuk Ambulances, Inc., 1984—; owner Keokuk Kab, Inc., 1985—; instr. Southeastern Community Coll., 1985, Profl. Diving Inst., 1986. Instr. Am. Heart Assn., Keokuk, 1982—; auctioneer Bryant Auction, Keokuk, 1970—. Mem. Nat. Assn. Emergency Mgrs., Profl. Diving Instrs. Assn., Ducks Unlimited. Democrat. Methodist. Clubs: Fortunaires, Keokuk Yacht. Avocations: diving, flying. Home: 3036 Sunset Terr Keokuk IA 52632

BRYANT, TERRY LYNN, counselor; b. Parsons, Kans., Mar. 26, 1952; s. Earl Morris and Neva L. (Sissel) B.; m. Debra Kay Brown, June 14, 1980; children: Kyle David, Andrew Michael. AA, Labette Com. Jr. Coll., 1972; BS, Kans. State Coll., 1974, MS, 1975; EdS, Pittsburg (Kans.) State U., 1981. Counselor, Kans. State Dept. Human Resources, Pittsburg, 1975—, handicapped applicant specialist, 1983—; manpower generalist State of Kans., 1976-77. Mem. Am. Personnel and Guidance Assn., Kans. Assn. Pub. Employees, Assn. Specialists in Group Work, Internat. Assn. Personnel in Employment Security, S.E. Kans. Assn. Personnel in Employment Security, Phi Theta Kappa. Baptist. Home: PO Box 457 Arma KS 66712 Office: 104 S Pine St Pittsburg KS 66762

BRYANT, WILLIAM H., assn. exec.; b. Albany, N.Y., June 21, 1933; s. James W. and Olma A. (Bryant) B.; m. Nancy McClurg, Aug. 26, 1972; children: Dana, Alethea, Jeff. B.S. in Bus. Adminstrn, Akron U., 1960. Trainee Mohawk Tire, Akron, Ohio, 1954; dir. research Tri County Planning Assn., Akron, 1957-63, Ohio Dept. Devel., Columbus, 1963-69; with Greater Cleve. Growth Assn., 1969—, pres., 1980—; Bd. dirs. Conv. and Visitors Bur., 1980—, Cleve. Area Devel. Corp., 1980—. Served with USAF, 1952-56. Mem. U.S. C. of C. (bd. dirs.), Ohio C. of C. Home: 4720 West Point Dr Fairview Park OH 44126 Office: Greater Cleve Growth Assn 690 Union Commerce Bldg Cleveland OH 44115 *

BRYANT, WILLIAM ROBERT, JR., attorney; b. Detroit, May 4, 1938; s. William Robert and Mary Frances (Fisk) B.; m. Lois Anne Rupp, Sept. 21, 1963; children: Jennifer, Andrew. AB, Princeton U., 1960; LLB, U. Mich., 1963. Bar: Mich. 1964. Lawyer Watson, Lott & Wunsch, Detroit, 1963-70; mem. Ho. of Reps., Lansing, Mich., 1971—, rep. floor leader, 1975-78, rep. leader, 1979-82, rep. leader emeritus, 1983—; mem. Wayne County Bd. Commissions, Mich., 1969-70. Avocations: tennis, badminton, hiking. Home: 331 Mt Vernon Grosse Pointe Farms MI 48236 Office: Ho of Reps State Capitol Lansing MI 48909

BRYCE, GARY LYNN, educator; b. Detroit, Mar. 28, 1941; s. David and Ingrid (Saastomian) B.; B.S., U. Mich., 1963, M.A., 1975, labor relations certificate, 1975; children—Amy Lynn, David Vincent. Faculty, U. Pitts., 1963-64; tchr. St. Williams Sch., Walled Lake, Mich., 1964-65, Clawson (Mich.) pub. schs., 1965-67; tchr., coach Royal Oak (Mich.) pub. schs., 1967-85; mem. faculty, coach women's basketball and softball Wayne State U., Detroit, 1985—; clinic organizer Mich. Softball Coaches, 1979. U. Pitts. fellow, 1963-64; named Mich. High Sch. Softball Coach of the Yr., 1979; Wayne State U. Softball Coach of Yr., Gt. Lakes Interscholastic Conf., 1982. Mem. Mich. High Sch. Softball Assn. (dir. 1981—), Nat. High Sch. Coaches Assn., Nat. Softball Assn., Nat. Women's Basketball Assn., Mich. High Sch. Coaches Assn., Mich. Softball Assn., NEA, Mich. Edn. Assn., Internat. Platform Assn., Am. Security Council, Am. Def. Preparedness Assn. Democrat. Unitarian. Address: 101 Matthae Wayne State U Detroit MI 48202

BRZEZINSKI, I(GNATIUS) FRANK, dentist; b. Chgo., Nov. 15, 1919; s. Frank Anthony and Mary (Orlowski) B.; D.D.S., Loyola U. (Chgo.), 1944; m. Therese Victoria Istok, Nov. 23, 1950; children—Paul Frank, Daniel Steven, Carol Ann. Practice gen. dentistry, Chgo., 1947—; asso. clin. prof. emeritus operative dentistry Sch. Dentistry Loyola U., 1970—; mem. Chgo. Council on Fgn. Relations. Served to lt. Dental Corps, USNR, 1944-46. Fellow Am. Coll. Dentists, Acad. Gen. Dentistry, Internat. Coll. Dentists; mem. Chgo. Dental Soc. (dir., past pres. N.W. br., bd. dirs.), Dental Arts Club Chgo., Am. Prosthodontic Soc. (exec. council), Pierre Fauchard Acad., Odontographic Soc., Omicron Kappa Upsilon. Club: Polish Am. Comml. Home: 5440 N Panama St Chicago IL 60656 Office: 5301 W Fullerton St Chicago IL 60639

BRZOSKA, MICHAEL JEROME, corporation executive; b. Detroit, Oct. 5, 1940; s. William Michael and Stella (Bardyga) B.; m. Nancy Brzoska, Aug. 8, 1959; childen: Michael, Shelley, Kathleen. B in Indsl. Engr. and Mgmt., Detroit Coll. Applied Sci., 1967. Mgr. prodn. Clipper Industries, Roseville, Mich., 1963-72; v.p. BJR, Madison Heights, Mich., 1973-78; pres. Bachan, Windsor, Ont., 1978-83, ACR Industries, Roseville, Mich., 1983—. Mem. Soc. Mech. Engring. Office: ACR Industries Inc 29200 Calahan Roseville MI 48066

BUA, NICHOLAS JOHN, judge; b. Chgo., Feb. 9, 1925; s. Frank and Lena (Marino) B.; m. Camille F. Scordato, Nov. 20, 1943; 1 dau., Lisa Annette. J.D., DePaul U., 1953. Bar: Ill. 1953. Trial atty. Chgo., 1953-63; judge Village Ct., Melrose Park, Ill., 1963-64; asso. judge Circuit Ct. Cook County, Chgo., 1964-71; circuit judge Circuit Ct. Cook County, 1971-76; justice Appellate Ct. Ill., 1st Dist., 1976-77; judge U.S. Dist. Ct., Chgo., 1977—; Mem. exec. com. Jud. Conf. Ill., also mem. supreme ct. rules com., 1970-77; lectr. DePaul U.; mem. faculty Def. Tactics Seminar, Ill. Def. Counsel Seminar, 1971; Fellow Nat. Coll. State Trial Judges, U. Nev., 1966. Contbr. articles to legal publs. Bd. govs. Gottlieb Meml. Hosp., 1978—; trustee Schwab Rehab. Hosp., 1977—. Served with AUS, World War II. Named Man of Yr. Justinian Soc. Lawyers, 1977; recipient Alumni award DePaul U., 1977. Mem. Am. Justinian Soc. Jurists (pres. 1978). Clubs: Nat. Lawyers (Chgo.), Legal (Chgo.), Union League (Chgo.), Lex Legio DePaul U. (Chgo.). Office: US Dist Ct 219 S Dearborn St Chicago IL 60604

BUBY, DAVID GRANT, osteopath, oncologist; b. Columbiaville, Mich., Jan. 12, 1938; s. Winston Enold and Dorothy Rose (Nicholson) B.; m. JoAnn Elizabeth Latta, June 30, 1962 (div. July 1985); children: Cynthia Rene, Daniel Gerald. AS, Flint (Mich.) Jr. Coll., 1958; student, U. Mich., Flint, 1958-59; DO, Kirksville (Mo.) Coll. Osteo. Medicine, 1964. Intern South Bend (Ind.) Osteo. Hosp., 1964-65, dir. med. edn., 1966-72; resident in internal medicine Flint Osteo. Hosp., 1972-74, clin. oncologist, 1976-78, chief of oncology, 1978—; fellow in med. oncology Wayne State U., Detroit, 1974-76; practice osteo. medicine specializing in oncology Flint, 1978—; clin. asst. prof. Mich. State U., East Lansing, 1981—, Coll. Osteo. Medicine, Des Moines, 1980—; chief of staff Flint Osteo. Hosp., 1984—; chmn. bd. dirs. Community Hosp. Oncology Program. Pres. Mich. div. Am. Cancer Soc., 1984-85; nat. del. Am. Cancer Soc., N.Y.C., 1985—. Mem. Am. Osteo. Assn., Mich. Assn. Osteo. Physicians and Surgeons, Ind. Assn. Osteo. Phusicians and Surgeons (v.p. 1971), Genesee County Osteo. Assn. (pres. 1981-82). Republican. Methodist. Avocations: scuba diving, sailing, fishing. Home: G- 13210 Charter Oaks Davison MI 48423

BUCAR, ALBERT ANTHONY, optometrist; b. LaSalle, Ill., Jan. 20, 1931; s. Louis and Angela (Spolar) B.; m. Linda Carol Stahl, Oct. 17, 1981; children: Albert B., James F., Albert A. BS, Ill. Coll. Optometry, 1953, OD, 1955, DOS, 1985. Practice medicine specializing in optometry St. Louis, 1955—. Contbr. articles to profl. jours. Bd. dirs. Antioch Community High Sch.; chmn. St. Peters Grade Sch. Bd.; vice chmn. Antioch Bicentennial Commn., 1975-76. Fellow Am. Acad. Optometry; mem. Am. Optometric Assn. (trustee 1978-80, sec./treas. 1980-82, v.p. 1982-83, pres. elect 1983-84, pres. 1984-85), Nat. Eye Research Found., Lake County Comprehensive Health Planning (bd. dirs.), Lake, Kane, McHenry HSA Health Service Agy. (bd. dirs.), Ill. Vision Services (chmn. bd. dirs., Outstanding Service award 1984), Lake/McHenry Optometry Soc. (pres. 1963-65), Ill. Optometric Assn. (pres. 1968-69, Optometrist of Yr. 1970), Am. Optometric Assn. (pres. 1984-85). Office: 395 Orchard St Antioch IL 60002

BUCCI, HENRY ARNOLD, utilities company executive; b. New Castle, Pa., May 23, 1948; s. Henry D. and Mary Ann (Fazzone) B.; m. Andrea Lynne Pecano; children: Roger A., Gregory A. BSBA, Youngstown State U., 1979. CPA, Ill. Fin. and acctg. analyst Dayton (Ohio) Power and Light, 1979-82; property acct. Platte River Power Authority, Ft. Collins, Colo., 1982-85; mgr. acctg. So. Minn. Mcpl. Power Agy., Rochester, 1985, dir. fin., 1985—. Served with U.S. Army, 1968-71. Mem. Am. Mgmt. Assn., Am. Pub. Power Assn. (rep. 1986). Avocations: golf, hunting. Office: So Minn Mcpl Power Agy 500-1st Ave SW Rochester MN 55902

BUCEY, JERI KAY, architect; b. Colorado Springs, Colo., May 5, 1945; d. Clyde Herman and Martha Jean (Watson) Kepke; m. Wesley Joseph, Feb. 23, 1968; children: Lisa Kay, Wendy Jean. BS, U. Wis., 1967; BArch, U. Ill., Chgo., 1981. Architect Skidmore, Owing & Merrill, Chgo., 1981-82; designer Sargent & Lundy, Chgo., 1982-83; architect Walgreen Co., Deerfield, Ill., 1983-84, O'Donnell, Wicklund, Pigozzi and Peterson, Deerfield, Ill., 1985—. Contbr. profl. newsletter. Leader long-range palling com. Glen Ellyn (Ill.) Park Dist., 1986-87; tour guide Glen Ellyn Hist. Soc., 1982. Mem. AIA (legis. minutemen 1984-86, microcomputers users group). Republican. Avocations: computer programming, swimming, tennis, aerobics, archtl. history. Office: O'Donnell Wicklund Pigozzi & Peterson Architects Inc 570 Lake Cook Rd Deerfield IL 60015

BUCH, RAYMOND H., clinical social worker, psychotherapist; b. Detroit, July 8, 1948; s. Allen L. and Elizabeth Rebbecca (Blau) B.; m. Esther R. Broad, Aug. 25, 1973; children: Elana D., Daniel I. BA, Oakland U., 1970; postgrad., Wayne State U., 1971; MSW, U. Mich., 1975; postgrad., U. Detroit, 1986. Cert. social worker. Social worker Washtenaw Day Treatment, Ann Arbor, Mich., 1971-73, Downriver Day Treatment, Allen Park, Mich., 1975-76, Oakland County Child Clinic and Day Treatment, 1976—; psychotherapist Ctr. for Psychology, Birmingham, Mich., 1984—; counselor Oakland Family Services, Pontiac, Mich., 1984-86; speaker Mich. Sch. Social Workers, Boyne, Mich., 1984. Author, dir. video presentation One More Day, 1985. Mem. Mich. Assn. for Emotionally Disturbed Children, Mt. Clemens Lapidary Soc. Avocations: swimming, canoeing, gem cutting, reading. Office: Oak Park Children's Day Treatment Ctr 22180 Parklawn Oak Park MI 48237

BUCHANAN, ARTHUR DON, farmer; b. Wayne, Ill., Oct. 28, 1949; s. Art Buchanan and Joy Yvonne (Smith) Ervin; m. Bobbi Lynn Talbert, Apr. 16, 1974 (div. 1978); 1 child, Robert Eric; m. Karen Joyce Simpson, Aug. 24, 1979; 1 child, Arthur Aaron. BS, U. Ill., 1972. Farmer Buchanan Farms, Keenes, Ill., 1972—; with oil production Buchanan Oil, Keenes, 1976—. Avocation: flying. Home: Rural Rt 1 Box 12 Keenes IL 62851

BUCHANAN, GLENN CARL, obstetrician, gynecologist; b. Algona, Iowa, June 3, 1945; s. Allen Knowles and Noma (Wiuff) B.; m. Eunice Elizabeth Jayne (Aug. 16, 1969); children: Chad Allen, Erin Jayne. Grad., U. Iowa, 1966, MD, 1970. Intern Grady Meml. Hosp., Atlanta, 1970-71; resident in ob-gyn USN, Milton, Fla. and Boston, 1972-75; gen. med. officer USN, Milton, Fla., 1971-72; endocrinology fellow USN, Oakland, Calif., 1975-78; dir. infertility clinics USN, Portsmouth, Va., 1977-78; practice medicine specializing in ob-gyn Willmar, Minn., 1978—; chief of staff Rice Meml. Hosp., Willmar, 1980; clin. faculty U. Minn., Mpls., 1980—. Contbr. articles to profl. jours. Trustee Willmar Med. Ctr., 1981-84. Served with USN, 1971-77. Fellow Am. Coll. Ob-Gyn (Ortho award 1976); mem. Am. Fertility Soc., AMA, Minn. Med. Assn. Republican. Avocation: woodworking. Home: 7514 Long Lake Rd Willmar MN 56201 Office: Willmar Med Clinic 101 Willmar Ave Willmar MN 56201

BUCHANAN, JAMES RODGER, building manager; b. Onawa, Iowa, July 29, 1945; s. Leo James and Hazel Magdelyn (Rodgers) B.; m. Dorthea Lynn Marsh, Sept. 18, 1971; children: James Marshall, Kristen Lynn. Student, U.S. Naval Acad., 1963-64; BSBA, U. S.D., 1967; postgrad., U. Nebr., 1968. Lic. real estate salesperson. Grain merchandiser Pillsbury, Springfield, Ill., 1968-69; adminstrv. asst. Peter Kiewit Sons Co., Omaha, 1969-72, personnel mgr., 1972-76, mgr. Plaza Bldg Co. sub., 1976—. Mem. Bldg. Owners and Mgrs. Assn. of Omaha (bd. dirs. 1978-87), Omaha C. of C. (chmn. 1972, Masters award 1972). Republican. Roman Catholic. Clubs: Toastmaster (pres. 1971-72). Avocations: golf, hunting, University of Nebraska football. Home: 9818 O Circle Omaha NE 68127 Office: Plaza Bldg Co 101 Kiewit Plaza Omaha NE 68131

BUCHANAN, LARRY DEE, advertising agency executive; b. Atlantic, Iowa, Aug. 13, 1937; s. William Howard and Harriet Elizabeth (Simpson) B.; student So. Meth. U., 1958; B.A., N.Tex. State U., 1960; m. Frankie L. Henderson, Mar., 1961 (div.); 1 dau., Lauri Dee; m. 2d Karen P. Daniels, July, 1975 (div.); m. 3d, Joan C. Gidney; 1 son, Jason M. Writer graphic services dept. Collins Radio Co., Cedar Rapids, Iowa, 1961-63, writer, public relations dept., 1964; co-founder, sec., treas., dir. writer-producer Three Arts, Inc., Cedar Rapids, 1964-70, sr. v.p., dir., creative dir., 1970—. Mem. Cedar Rapids Symphony Orch. Assn., 1967-74, 81—, pres., 1970-71; search and rescue pilot CAP, 1969-71. Served with USMCR, 1955-61. cert. airline transport pilot. Mem. Advt. Fedn. of Cedar Rapids (charter, pres., 1971, named to Hall of Fame 1986), Nat. Agri-Mktg. Assn., A&S Order of Quiet Birdmen, Hawkeye Area Hangar (charter, pres. 1987—), Sigma Delta Chi, Phi Mu Alpha Sinfonia. Republican. Office: 425 2d SE 11th Floor Cedar Rapids IA 52401

BUCHANAN, MARY ELLA, nurse, army officer; b. Hot Springs, Ark., July 19, 1950; d. Robert Glynn and Georgia Catherine (Dobson) B.; B.S. in Nursing, Vanderbilt U., 1972; M.S., U. Tenn., 1974. Staff nurse Met. Health Dept., Nashville, 1972-73; commd. lt. Nurse Corps, U.S. Army, 1973, advanced through grades to maj., 1983; ambulatory care nurse clinician Family Practice Clinic, Ft. Belvoir, Va., 1974-76, Robinson Barracks Army Health Clinic, Stuttgart, Germany, 1976-77, 5th Gen. Hosp., 1977-79, Acad. Health Scis., Ft. Sam Houston, Tex., 1979-80; ambulatory care nurse clinician Walter Reed Army Med. Center, Washington, 1980-81, nurse researcher Nursing Research Service, 1980-82, Nurse Ward 72, 1982-84; head nurse Ward 4A Irwin Army Community Hosp., Ft. Riley, Kans., 1984-86, coordinator infection control, quality assurance, 1986—. Mem. Am. Nurses Assn. (cert. family nurse clinician, div. community health), Am. Pub. Health Assn., Council Primary Health Care Nurse Practitioners, Nurse Practitioner Assn. D.C. (pres.), Sigma Theta Tau. Methodist. Clubs: Smithsonian Assos., Franklin Mint Collectors Soc., Internationale Volkssportverband c.V. Home: 1601 Leavenworth Manhattan KS 66502 Office: Irwin Army Community Hosp Dept Nursing Fort Riley KS 66442

BUCHANAN, RELVA CHESTER, engineering educator; b. Port Antonio, Portland, Jamaica, Apr. 10, 1936; came to U.S., 1958; s. Stephen Eleazor and Imogene (Reid) B.; m. Nira Bernice Jonathan, Jan. 11, 1957 (div. 1967); 1 child, Annette Lorraine. BS, Alfred (N.Y.) U., 1961; PhD, MIT, 1965. Mgr. Glan Scientific Co. Indsl. Dev. Corp., Kingston, Jamaica, 1956-58; adv. research engr. IBM Corp., Poughkeepsie, N.Y., 1964-74; prof. engring. U. Ill., Urbana, 1974—. Author, editor Electronic Ceramic Applications, 1986. Fellow Am. Ceramic Soc. (chmn. electronics div. 1981-82), mem. Electrochem. Soc., Materials Research Soc. Home: 1723 Henry St Champaign IL 61821 Office: U Ill Dept Materials Sci and Engraving 105 S Goodwin Urbana IL 61801

BUCHER, OTTO NORMAN, clergyman, educator; b. Milw., June 3, 1933; s. Otto A. and Ida (Smazal) B.; B.A., Capuchin Sem. of St. Felix, Huntington, Ind., 1956; postgrad. Capuchin Sem. of St. Anthony, Marathon, Wis., 1956-60; S.T.L., Catholic U. Am., 1963; S.S.L., Pontifical Bibl. Inst., Rome, 1965. Joined Capuchin Franciscan Order, 1952; ordained priest Roman Catholic Ch., 1959; lector in scripture Capuchin Sem. of St. Anthony, Marathon, 1966-70; asso. prof. Bibl. studies St. Francis Sem., Sch. Pastoral Ministry, Milw., 1970-73; asso. prof. Bibl. studies Sacred Heart Sch. of Theology, Hales Corners, Wis., 1973—, acad. dean, 1979-85, vice rector, 1984-86, dir. field edn., 1986—; mem. exec. com. Midwestern Assn. Theology Schs., 1973-74. Mem. Cath. Bibl. Assn. Am., Soc. Bibl. Lit. Democrat. Home: St Conrad House 3138 N 2d St Milwaukee WI 53212 Office: Sacred Heart Sch Theology 7335 S Lovers Lane Rd PO Box 429 Hales Corners WI 53130

BUCHHOLZ, DAVID LOUIS, accountant; b. Wisconsin Rapids, Wis., Aug. 13, 1936; s. Lawrence Frank and Edna Ella (Benz) B.; m. Arlene Jean Benke, June 6, 1959 (div. 1982); children: Lisa Lynn Shuttleworth, Shawn Leslie Skidmore, Dana Gaye; m. Vera Rose Wombwell, June 2, 1984. Student, Wis. State Coll., 1953-54; BBA, U. Wis., 1958. CPA, Ill., Iowa, La., Mich. Head Chgo. tax div. Arthur Andersen & Co., Chgo., 1975-79, tax practice dir., 1978-79, mng. dir. tax practice, 1979-80, mng. dir. tax policies & procedures, 1980-81, mng. ptnr. tax practice, 1981—. Campaign chmn. Am. Cancer Soc., Chgo. area, 1973, Cook county area, 1974, State of Ill., 1975; bd. dirs. NCCJ, Chgo., 1979—; com. mem. U. Chgo. Fed. Tax Planning Com., Chgo., 1979—; bd. visitors U. Wis. Sch. Bus., Madison. Mem. Am. Inst. CPA's (various tax coms.), Ill. Soc. CPA's, Econ. Club Chgo., Internat. Fiscal Assn., Ill. Inst. Continuing Legal Edn., Bascom Hill Soc. of U. Wis. Clubs: Univ., Mid-Am. Avocations: photography, fishing, tennis. Office: Arthur Andersen & Co 69 W Washington St Suite 3500 Chicago IL 60602

BUCHHOLZ, DONNA MARIE, immunologist; b. Chgo., May 27, 1950; s. Arthur George and Doris Hedwig (Lewis) B. BS in Biol. Sci., Quincy Coll., 1972; Assoc. in Law (hon.), Loyola U., Chgo., 1974; MS in Microbiology and Immunology, U. Ill. Med. Ctr., 1975, PhD in Microbiology and Immunology, 1978. Post-doctoral researcher Argonne (Ill.) Nat. Labs., 1978-80; research info. scientist Abbott Labs., Abbott Park, Ill., 1980-82, project mgr., 1982-85, sr. project mgr., 1985-87, ops. mgr. thrombolytics venture, 1987—; faculty Northeastern Ill. U., Chgo., 1984—. Editor: Developments in Industrial Microbiology, 1983, 84; contbr. articles to profl. jours. Mem. nat. sci. and engring. com. Exploring Div. Boy Scouts Am., 1983—, Citizens Adv. Com. Du Page Airport, West Chicago, Ill., 1984—, West Chicago Energy Commn., 1985. Recipient award Am. Assn. Immunology, 1980—, Woman of Achievement award YWCA, 1987, Abbott Labs. Presdl. award, 1984. Fellow Am. Acad. Microbiology; mem. Am. Soc. Microbiology, Soc. for Indsl. Microbiology, Ill. Soc. for Microbiology (councilor), Sigma Xi (pres. 1984, mem. program initiatives com. 1985—, mem. regional nominating com. 1985—, mem. nat. nominating com. 1985—, head centennial planning com. 1986, mem. membership at large com., research award 1972). Roman Catholic. Avocations: oil and watercolor painting, calligraphy, horses. Home: 451 Highland Ave West Chicago IL 60185 Office: Abbott Labs D-461 AP-9 Abbott Park IL 60064

BUCHHOLZ, JEFFREY CARL, electronics executive, researcher; b. Sheboygan, Wis., June 10, 1947; s. Carl L. and Alice B. (Tyborski) B.; m. Janis D. Fleischmann, June 10, 1970 (div. Oct. 1981). BS in Physics, U. Wis., Eau Claire, 1969; MS in Phsyics, U. Wis., Madison, 1971; MS in Matls. Sci., U. Wis., 1973, PhD in Matls. Sci., 1974. Research assoc. U. Calif., Berkeley, 1974-76; sr. staff research scientist Gen. Motors Research Labs., Warren, Mich., 1976-86; pres. Micro-OpticsTechnologies, Inc., Middleton, Wis., 1986—; Contbr. over 18 articles to profl. jours.; holder five patents. Mem. Am. Phys. Soc., Am. Vacuum Soc., Optical Soc. of Am., Matls. Research Soc., Internat. Soc. for Optical Engring. Office: Micro-Optics Technologies Inc 8608 University Green #5 Middleton WI 53562

BUCHHOLZ, LLOYD ARTON, industrial relations specialist; b. Chgo., Mar. 22, 1939; s. Grinnell William and Elvera Carlina (Arton) B.; m. Virginia Jean Salzman, July 11, 1959; children: Jamie Lynn Heier, Dana Marie Parrault, Michelle Lee. Data processing mgr. Imperial-Eastman, Niles, Ill., 1964-67, A.B. Dick Co., Niles, 1967-77; mng. dir. Applied Info. Devel., Oakbrook, Ill., 1977-84; salesman Software Internat., Itasca, Ill., 1984-85, McCormack & Dodge, Schaumburg, Ill., 1985-86; owner, operator Ican Cons., Glenview, Ill., 1986—. Mem. Am. Prodn. and Inventory Control Soc. (cert. practitioner inventory mgmt., mem. cert. com. 1981). Republican. Methodist. Avocations: fishing, racquetball, photography. Office: Ican Cons PO Box 2132 Glenview IL 60025

BUCHHOLZ, RONALD LEWIS, architect; b. Milw., Jan. 14, 1951; s. Raymond LeRoy and Della (Krause) B.; B.S. in Architecture, U. Wis., Milw., 1973; m. Mary Lou Stockhausen, May 20, 1972; children—Lauren Robert, Geoffrey Alan. Archtl. appraiser Am. Appraisal Co., Milw., 1973; plan examiner, bur. bldgs. and structures, div. safety and bldgs. Wis. Dept. Industry, Labor and Human Relations, Madison, 1973-76, staff architect, 1976, architect, adminstrv. code cons., bur. code devel., 1976-80, dep. dir., 1980-83, asst. dir., 1983—; instr. U. Wis., Madison Ext., also state certification courses for bldg. and dwelling insps.; mem. Wis. Bldg. Code Adv. Rev. Bd., 1976—, Fire Prevention Council, 1978—, adv. com. Alternative Energy Tax Credits, 1978, 80, Dept. Devel. Permit Ctr., 1984—; mem. Interagy. Com. on Spills of Hazardous Materials, 1981-82, Flood Hazard Interagy. Coordinating Council, 1985—; mem. adv. com. Wis. Electric Supply, 1984—. Vol. leader Boy Scouts Am. Served with Army N.G., 1970-76. Registered architect, Wis. Mem. Resdl. Facilities Council (exec. sec. 1976-78), Bldg. Ofcls. and Code Adminstrs. Internat. Inc., Nat. Eagle Scout Assn. Roman Catholic. Lodge: KC. Author tech. reports. Home: 4925 Knox Ln Madison WI 53711 Office: 201 E Washington Ave Room 103 Madison WI 53702

BUCHOLZ, RICHARD DONALD, neurosurgeon; b. Omaha, July 11, 1952; s. Donald John and Frances (Seiler) B.; m. Kathleen Mary Keenan, May 17, 1975; children: Elizabeth Kathleen, Eleanor Ingrid. BS, Yale U., 1973, MD, 1977. Diplomate Am. Bd. Neurol. Surgery. Clin. instr. sch. medicine Yale U., New Haven, 1982-83; asst. prof.sch. medicine St. Louis U., 1983—. Mem. AMA, Congress Neurol. Surgeons, Am. Assn. Neurol. Surgeons. Republican. Avocations: personal computing, gardening, classical music. Home: 3 Kingsbury Pl Saint Louis MO 63112 Office: St Louis U 1325 S Grand Blvd Saint Louis MO 63104

BUCHSIEB, WALTER CHARLES, orthodontist; b. Columbus, Ohio, Aug. 30, 1929; s. Walter William and Emma Marie (Held) B.; B.A., Ohio State U., 1951, D.D.S., 1955, M.S., 1960; m. Betty Lou Risch, June 19, 1955; children—Walter Charles II, Christine Ann. Pvt. practice dentistry specializing in orthodontics, Dayton, Ohio, 1959—; cons. orthodontist Miami Valley Hosp., Childrens Med. Center, Dayton; asst. prof. dept. orthodontics Ohio State U. Coll. Dentistry, 1984—. Mem. fin. and program com. United Health Found., 1971-73; mem. dean's adv. com. Ohio State U. Coll. Dentistry; bd. dirs. Hearing and Speech Center, 1968-82, 2d v.p., 1976-78, pres., 1978-79; orthodontic advisor Ohio Dept. Health Bur. Crippled Children's Services, 1983-84. Served to capt. AUS, 1955-58. Mem. ADA (alt. del. 1968—, council on internat. relations 1984—), Ohio Dental Assn. (sec. council legislation 1969-78, v.p. 1978-79, pres.-elect 1979-80, pres. 1980-81, polit. action com. 1987—), Am. Coll. Dentists, Am. Dental Soc. (pres. 1970-71), Am. Bd. Orthodontics (exec. com. 1986—), Great Lakes Soc. Orthodontists (sec.-treas. 1972-75, pres. 1977-78), Internat. Coll. Dentists, Am. Assn. Orthodontists (chmn. council legislation 1976, speaker of house 1982-85), Pierre Fauchard Acad., Ohio State U. Alumni Assn., Delta Upsilon, Psi Omega. Republican. Lutheran (elder 1965-68, v.p. 1974). Clubs: Masons, Rotary (pres. 1973-74, Paul Harris fellow). Home: 1520 Brittany Hills Dr Dayton OH 45459 Office: 5335 Far Hills Ave Dayton OH 45429

BUCHTEL, FORREST LAWRENCE, college dean, musician, composer; b. St. Edward, Nebr., Dec. 9, 1899; s. Charles Stanton and Frances Marian (Stephens) B.; A.B., Simpson Coll., 1921; M.S. in Edn. (scholar), Northwestern U., 1931; B.Mus.Ed., VanderCook Coll. Music, Chgo., 1932, M.Mus.Ed., 1933; D.F.A., Simpson Coll., 1983; m. Jessie Helene Macdonald, June 6, 1925; children—Bonnie Buchtel Cataldo, Helene Buchtel Adams, Beverly Buchtel Platt, Forrest Lawrence. Tchr., South High Sch., Grand Rapids, Mich., 1921-25, Emporia (Kans.) State U., 1925-30, Lane Tech. High Sch., Chgo., 1930-34, Amundsen High Sch., Chgo., 1935-54; tchr. VanderCook Coll. Music, Chgo., 1931-81, dean of students, 1960; composer, works include: 30 sets of bandbooks, 800 solos and ensembles for sch. bands, 30 marches, 30 overtures. Served with S.A.T.C., 1918. Recipient Alumni award Simpson Coll., 1961, VanderCook Coll., 1965. Mem. Am. Bandmasters Assn., ASCAP, Bandmasters Hall of Fame, Phi Beta Mu, Phi Mu Alpha Sinfonia, Kappa Kappa Psi, Delta Upsilon. Methodist. Club: Univ. (Chgo.). Home: 1116 Cleveland St Evanston IL 60202 Office: 3209 S Michigan Ave Chicago IL 60616

BUCK, ALAN CARL, insurance executive; b. Lafayette, Ind., Jan. 20, 1947; s. Carl L. and Mary A. Buck; m. Sally Lou Stephans, Aug. 2, 1969; children: Julia Suzanne, Ryan Alan. BS, Ball State U., 1969, MA in Edn., 1972. Tchr., coach Met. Sch. Dist. Decatur Twp., Indpls., 1969-70, Indpls. Pub. Schs., 1970-71, New Albany (Ind.) Sch. Corp., 1971-78, Met. Sch. Dist. Warren Twp., Indpls., 1978-81; agt., agy. mgr. Franklin Life Ins. Co., Indpls., 1981—. Named Hoosier Hills Conf. Basketball Coach of Yr., 1978. Mem. Nat. Assn. Life Underwriters (Sales Achievement, Quality awards 1984, 85), Indpls. Assn. Life Underwriters, Nat. Assn. of Million Dollar Round Table. Republican. Methodist. Lodge: Masons. Home: Rt 1 PO Box SW-241 New Palestine IN 46163 Office: Franklin Life Ins Co P1720 E Washington St Indianapolis IN 46229

BUCK, BERNESTINE BRADFORD, school counselor; b. Altheimer, Ark., July 24, 1924; d. Henry Walker and Dora Lois Bradford; B.A., Stowe Tchrs. Coll., 1950; M.Ed., U. Mo., 1973; m. Joseph Wellington Buck, Oct. 1, 1950; children—Stanley W., Linda Carol, Debra Lois. Tchr. pub. schs., St. Louis, 1950-73, sch. counselor, 1973—. Mem. U. Mo. scholarship com., 1974-84, Antioch Bapt. Ch. scholarship com., 1980-86. Mem. Am., Mo. personnel and guidance assns., St. Louis Guidance Assn. (pres. 1979-80), Mo. Guidance Assn. (exec. council 1980-81, v.p. elem. sect.). Baptist.

BUCK, EARL CHRIS, clinical laboratory administrator; b. Duluth, Minn., Sept. 6, 1947; s. Earl Chris and Mabel Alice (Frame) B.; m. Teresa Ann Lindholm, Apr. 6, 1968; children—Sharie, Nichole, Earl. B.A., U. Minn.-Duluth, 1973; postgrad. U. No. Iowa. Vice pres., treas. Consol. Regional Labs., Inc., Waterloo, Iowa, 1978—. Mem. council Ch. of Christ, 1985-88. Served to lt. comdr. USNR, 1970-78. Mem. Clin. Lab. Mgmt. Assn. (pres. Iowa chpt., nat. bd. dirs. 1983-84, 86-89, treas. 1983-85), Am. Soc. Clin. Pathologists (assoc.), Am. Legion (past bingo treas., chaplain, pres. bldg. com.). Club: Willow Run Country (Denver, Iowa). Home: Box 609 Denver IA 50622 Office: 618 Allen St Waterloo IA 50702

BUCK, EARL WAYNE, insurance investigator; b. La Porte City, Iowa, Jan. 15, 1939; s. Edwin Earl and Uleta Pearl (Purdy) B.; m. Maxine E. Parker, Oct. 19, 1969; children: Brian, Douglas. LLB, La Salle U., 1969. Pvt. detective Sioux City, Iowa, 1968-74; asst. mgr. Chgo. br. Atwell, Vogel & Sterling, Scarsdale, N.Y., 1965-70, mgr. Milw. br., 1970; sr. auditor Comml. Union Ins. Co., Chgo., 1970-74; police chief McHenry Shores (Ill.) Police Dept., 1973-79; self-employed ins. investigator McHenry, Ill., 1980—; liquor liability investigator for various ins. cos., 1980—. Chmn. McHenry Shores (Ill.) Zoning Commn., 1972. Served with U.S. Army, 1957-61. Recipient Police Meritorius Service award Vill. of McHenry Shores, 1979. Mem. Midwest Ins. Auditors Assn., McHenry County Police Chief's Assn. Republican. Lutheran. Lodge: Moose. Avocations: flying, amateur archaelogy, photography, fishing. Office: PO Box 494 McHenry IL 60050

BUCK, HENRY WILLIAM, JR., obstetrician-gynecologist; b. Kansas City, June 4, 1934; s. Henry William Sr. and Nina Irene (Krebs) B.; m. Barbara Laviece Mallory, Sept. 6, 1963; children: Mallory Renee, Andrew William. BA, U. Kans., 1956, MD, 1960. Cert. Am. Bd. Ob.-Gyn. Gynecologist Student Health Service U. Kans., Lawrence, 1967—; pres. bd. dirs. Douglas County Citizens' Com. on Alcoholism, Lawrence, 1983—. Served to capt. USAF, 1965-67. Fellow ACS, Am. Coll. Ob-Gyns.; mem. AMA, Kans. Med. Soc., Kans. Ob-Gyn. Soc. (pres. 1980-81). Republican. Lutheran. Avocations: photography, sailing, writing. Home: 306 Homestead Dr Lawrence KS 66044 Office: U Kans Watkins Meml Hosp Lawrence KS 66044-8830

BUCK, JAMES ROY, engineering educator, consultant; b. Big Rapids, Mich., Feb. 22, 1930; s. John Robert and Lois Jenieve (Lane) B.; m. Marie Neola Gilbertson, Aug. 26, 1962; children—Carolyn Marie, John Gilbert, James Roy II. B.S., Mich. Technol. U., 1952, M.S. in Civil Engring., 1953; Ph.D., U. Mich., 1964. Materials engr. U.S. Naval Civil Engrs. Research Lab., Port Hueneme, Calif., 1952-53; structural engr. Austin Engrs. Ltd., Midland, Mich., 1956-57; field engr. Calumet Flexicore Corp., Kalamazoo, 1957-58; instr. Ferris State Coll., Big Rapids, 1958-59; research asst. U. Mich., Ann Arbor, 1959-62; asst. prof. U. Mich., Dearborn, 1962-65; assoc. prof. Purdue U., Lafayette, Ind., 1965-79, prof., 1979-81; prof. indsl. and mgmt. engring., chmn. dept. indsl. and mgmt. engring. U. Iowa, Iowa City, 1981—; cons. in field. Contbr. chpts. to books, articles to profl. jours. Served to lt. (j.g.) Civil Engring. Corps, USNR, 1953-56. Recipient Eugene Grant award Am. Soc. Engring. Edn., 1979, 86, Best Tchr. award Sch. Indsl. Engring., Purdue U., 1979. Mem. Inst. Indsl. Engrs., Human Factors Soc., Inst. Mgmt. Sci. Lutheran. Lodges: Elks, Rotary. Home: 2353 Cae Dr Iowa City IA 52240 Office: U Iowa Systems Div Room 4132 EB Iowa City IA 52242

BUCK, MAYNARD ARDEEN, JR., printing and publishing executive; b. Warren, Ohio, May 21, 1929; s. Maynard Ardeen and Gertrude Wilhelmina (Reuss) B.; m. Anne Williams, Aug. 27, 1950; 1 child, Maynard Ardeen III. B.Sc., Kent State U., 1953, M.A., 1954. Pres. Freeport Press, Ohio, 1957—, Carrollton Graphics, Inc., Ohio, 1975-83, chmn., 1983—; pub. Harrison News-Herald, Cadiz, Ohio, 1968—, Free Press standard, Carrollton, 1975—. Bd. dirs. Muskingum Watershed Conservancy Dist., Ohio, 1978—; sch. bd. mem. Cadiz Local Schs., 1971-76; trustee Harrison Community Hosp., Ohio, 1969-81. Served to lt. USAF, 1954-56. Mem. Ohio Newspaper Assn. (pres. 1982-83, chmn. bd. 1983-84). Presbyterian. Lodge: Masons. Office: Carrollton Graphics Inc 707 Canton Rd Carrollton OH 44615

BUCK, ROBERT O'NEIL, construction company executive; b. Ames, Iowa, Jan. 12, 1932; s. Harold B. and Margaret (Mason) B.; m. Anne Knuths, Aug. 24, 1951; children: Bruce, Steven, Lisa. BS, Iowa State U., 1956. Foreman Bliss Constrn., Ames, Iowa, 1956-61; ores. Buck Constrn. Co., Inc., Ames, 1961—. Bd. dirs. Ames Library, Coll. Prebyn. Ch. Mem. Ames Homebuilders Assn. (officer 1963-69), Ames Jaycees (v.p.), Ames C. of C. Republican. Presbyterian. Home: 217 22d Ames IA 50010

BUCK, SCOTT FARLEY, utility company executive; b. Bloomington, Ill., Aug. 1, 1950; s. Robert Dan and Sara Jane (Farley) B.; m. Mary Kathleen Briggs, Dec. 21, 1974; children: Susan Marie, Matthew Scott. Student, Eastern Ill. U., Charleston, 1968-70; BS in Oceanography, BA in Zoology, U. Wash., 1976; postgrad., Ill. State U., Normal, 1986—. Enlisted USN, 1970, commd. ensign, advanced through grades to lt. commdr., resigned, 1981; with Res., 1981—; quality control inspector Baldwin Assocs., Clinton, Ill., 1981-82; quality control inspector Ill. Power Co., Clinton, 1982-84, quality assurance engr., 1984-87, licensing and safety specialist, 1987—. Den leader Boy Scouts Am.; Pre-Hosp. Care Providers of Ill. Mem. Internat. Oceanographic Found., Naval Res. Assn., Am. Legion. Republican. Methodist. Avocations: home renovation, horseback riding, scuba diving. Home: Rural Rt #1 Box 27 McLean IL 61754 Office: Ill Power Co PO Box 678 V-215 Clinton IL 61727

BUCKINGHAM, FRANK ELWOOD, writer; b. Fairfield, Iowa, Dec. 12, 1932; s. Joseph James and Laura Agnes (Fritz) B.; m. Nancy Lee Martin, Feb. 22, 1956; children: Jaclyn, Clark, Laura, Carl, Lois. BS in Agrl. Engring., Iowa State U., 1959; postgrad., Drake U., 1970. Editor agrl. engring. Implement and Tractor mag., Kansas City, Mo., 1959-63; product specialist Massey-Fergusen Inc., Indpls., 1963-66; creative supr. Massey-Fergusen Inc., Des Moines, 1966-70; mgr. advt. Clay Equipment Corp., Cedar Falls, Iowa, 1971-73; freelance writer, equipment cons. Agri-Bus. Writing, Cedar Falls, Iowa and Springfield, Mo., 1973—; industry tech. rep. U.S. Dept. Commerce Royal Agrl. Show, Kenilworth, Eng., 1977; cons. in lawn and garden equipment. Author: Fundamentals of Machine Operations, Tillage, 1974, Machinery Maintenance, 1981, Compact Equipment Power Trains, 1983; contbr. numerous articles to profl. jours. Served as U.S. Army, 1953-54, Korea. Mem. Am. Soc. Agrl. Engrs. (dir. pubs. 1980-82). Methodist. Avocations: gardening, woodworking, reading. Home and Office: 6451 E Skyline Dr R9 Springfield MO 65804

BUCKINGHAM, RICHARD ALBERT, otolaryngologist; b. Chgo., Dec. 27, 1922; s. Brice Albert and Mary Eugenia (Ahern) B.; m. Mary Grace Carney, Sec. 28, 1946: children: Rosamond, Richard, John, Marita, Barbara, Lawrence, Roberta, Donald, Celeste, Elisabeth. Student, Loyola U., Chgo., 1941-42; MD, U. Ill., 1946, postgrad., 1949-50. Diplomate Am. Bd. Otolaryngolgy. Intern Cook County Hosp., Chgo., 1946-47, resident, 1949, 50-52; practice medicine specializing in otolaryngology Chgo., 1952—; staff Resurrection Hosp., St. Luke's Hosp., Hines VA Hosp.; clin. prof. otolaryngology U. Ill. Coll. Medicine, Chgo. Author: (with others) Atlas of Otorhinolaryngolgy and Brochoesophagology, 1969, Tomography and Cross Sections of the Ear, 1975, Radiology of the Ear, Nose and Throat, 1984. Served to lt. (j.g.) USNR, 1947-49. Decorated comdr. Order del Condor de los Andes (Bolivia). Mem. AMA, Pan Am. Med. Assn., Am. Acad. Opthamology and Otolaryngology, Am. Triological Soc., Chgo. Med. Soc., Chgo. Laryngol. and Otological Soc., Ill. Med. Soc., Am. Otological Soc., Sigma Xi. Home: 434 Willow Rd Winnetka IL 60093 Office: 145 S Northwest Hwy Park Ridge IL 60068

BUCKINGHAM, WILLIAM BRICE, physician; b. Chgo., July 25, 1924; s. Brice Albert and Mary (Ahern) B.; student John Carroll U., Cleve., 1942-44; M.D., U. Ill., 1947, B.S., 1956; m. Margery L. Cross, Sept. 16, 1950; children—Cathlin, Megan, Gillian, William Brice, Peter, Michael, John, Maura, Mark, David, Dierdre. Intern, Cook County Hosp., Chgo., 1947-49, resident, 1950-52; fellow Northwestern U., 1951-52. Diplomate Am. Bd. Internal Medicine. Practice medicine, specializing in internal medicine, Chgo., 1952—; attending physician Oak Park Hosp., 1952-85, cons. physician 1985—; attending physician Augustana Hosp., Chgo., 1954-66; staff physician Oak Forest Tb. Hosp. 1952-55; assoc. attending pulmonary disease sect. Cook County Hosp., 1952-56, attending physician, 1956-64, chief pulmonary sect., 1963-64, attending physician dept. medicine, 1964-66; cons. DeKalb County Tb. Hosp. and Clinic, 1954-60; attending physician St. Elizabeth's Hosp., Chgo., 1954-65, chmn. dept. medicine 1959-64; attending physician St. Josephs Hosp., Chgo., 1964-68; attending physician VA Research Hosp., Chgo., 1960-70, cons. pulmonary diseases, 1970; attending physician Northwestern Meml. Hosp., 1966—, dir. pulmonary lab., 1968-75, mem. med. records and quality assurance com. 1974—; clin. asst. Northwestern U. Med. Sch., 1952-56, instr., 1956-59, assoc. in medicine, 1959-68, asst. prof., 1968-70, assoc. prof., 1970—, chief, sect. gen. medicine, 1975-78; mem. sci. adv. com. Mcpl. Tb. Sanitarium, 1968-72, course dir. introduction clin. diagnosis 1966-67; chmn. Gov.'s Adv. Com. Tb., 1978—; cons. in tb. Ill. Dept. Pub. Health, 1973—; tb. control officer Chgo. Bd. Health, 1974-84; vis. prof. medicine Universidad Autonoma de Guadalajara Med. Sch., 1975, 80; cons. med. editor Quality Rev. Bull., Joint Commn. on Accreditation of Hosps., 1975. Fellow A.C.P., Am. Coll. Chest Physicians (pres. Ill. chpt. 1966-67, gen. chmn. First Fall Sci. Assembly, Chgo. 1969), Inst. of Medicine Chgo.; mem. AMA, Am. Soc. Internal Medicine, Ill. Soc. Internal Medicine (chmn. underwriting adv. com. 1986—, exec. council 1965-85, pres. 1973-75), Chgo. Soc. Internal Medicine (pres. 1977-78), Am. Thoracic Soc., Ill., Chgo. med. socs., Chgo. Tb. Inst. (dir.), Am. Assn. Inhaalation Therapists (bd. med. advisers 1969-72), Riverside Golf Club. Contbr. articles to profl. jours. Home: 319 Linden Ave Oak Park IL 60302 Office: 233 E Erle St Chicago IL 60611

BUCKLASCHUK, JOHN MICHAEL, province government official; b. Rossburn, Man., Can., July 18, 1939; s. Mike and Agnes (Woycheshin) B.; m. Colleen Christena Hagan, July 5, 1968; children: Tara, Tyler. BE, U. Man., 1968; BA, Brandon (Man.) U., 1970. Tchr. high sch. 1959-75; spl. asst. to atty gen. Province of Man., Winnipeg, 1975-77, minister of coop. devel., consumer and corp. affairs, 1982—, minister responsible for pub. ins. corp. affairs, 1982—, minister of housing, 1983-86, minister mcpl. affairs, 1986—; dir. orgn. Man. New Dems., Winnipeg, 1977-81. Home: PO Box 1588, Gimli, MB Canada R0C 1B0 Office: Ministry of Mcpl Affairs, Legis Bldg Room 330, Winnipeg, MB Canada R3C 0V8

BUCKLEY, GREGORY MICHAEL, manufacturing executive; b. Saginaw, Mich., Dec. 25, 1953; s. James Claire and Mary Loretta (Ryan) B.; m. Susan Jane Moulton, Apr. 25, 1975; children: Kara, Krista, Marissa. BSME, U. Mich., 1976; MBA, Harvard U., 1979. With engring. Gen. Motors Corp., Saginaw, 1973-79; with Ford Motor Co., Dearborn, Mich., 1979-81; mfg. mgr. Libbey-Owens-Ford Co., Laurinburg, N.C., 1981-83, gen. facility mgr., 1983-85; dir. planning Libbey-Owens-Ford Co., Toledo, 1985—. Home: 5019 Larkhaven Toledo OH 43623 Office: Libbey-Owens-Ford Co 811 Madison Ave Toledo OH 43624

BUCKLEY, JOHN JOSEPH, obstetrician, gynecologist; b. Youngstown, Ohio, Jan. 21, 1930; s. John Joseph and Rosalie Catherine (Singler) B.; m. Anne Theresa Finnerty, Apr. 24, 1954; children: John, Joy, Colleen, Mollie. BS in Biology cum laude, Holy Cross Coll., 1952; MD, Ohio State U., 1959. Staff St. Elizabeth Med. Ctr., Youngstown, Ohio, 1963—, chief ob-gyn., 1977-80, chief of staff, 1986—; practice medicine specializing in ob-gyn. Youngstown, Ohio, 1963—; asst. prof. Northeastern Ohio Coll. Medicine, Rootstown, 1980—. co-founder Right to Life, Youngstown, 1970. Served to lt. USN, 1952-55, with res. MC, 1959-63. Fellow Am. Coll. Ob-Gyn; mem. AMA, Ohio Med. Assn., Mahoning County Med. Assn., Youngstown Soc. Ob-Gyns., Alpha Omega Alpha. Democrat. Roman Catholic. Clubs: Youngstown Country, Cotillion. Avocations: skiing, water sports, stamps, travel. Home: 1337 Stonington Dr Youngstown OH 44505 Office: 975 Boardman Canfield Rd Youngstown OH 44512

BUCKLEY, STEPHEN PHILIP, engineering administrator; b. Kansas City, Mo., Dec. 6, 1943; s. Charles Michael and Virginia Marie (Mayer) B.; m. Marilee Kimberly Strand, June 19, 1965; children: Christine Marie, Carl Kristian, Eric Joseph. Assoc. in Engring., Jr. Coll. of Kansas City, Mo., 1964; BSME, U. Mo., Rolla, 1966, MSME, 1968; ž. Registered profl. engr., Mo., Ohio. Engr. proving grounds Gen. Motors Corp., Milford, Mich., 1966; asst. instr. U. Mo., Rolla, 1966-68; engr. Design and Devel., Inc. subs. Booz, Allen & Hamilton Inc., Cleve., 1968-71; sr. project engr. Hallmark Card Corp., Kansas City, Mo., 1971-74, program leader, 1974-81, equipment devel. mgr., 1981—; adj. prof. mech. engring. U. Mo., Columbia. Patentee in field. Mem. NSPE, Soc. Mfg. Engrs., Project Mgmt. Inst., Mo. Soc. Profl. Engrs., Pi Tau Sigma, Tau Beta Pi, Phi Kappa Phi. Republican. Roman Catholic. Avocations: reading, jogging, soccer, computers. Home: 11904 Summit Kansas City MO 64145 Office: Hallmark Card Corp Advanced Tech Research PO Box 419580 Kansas City MO 64141-6580

BUCKLIN, LEONARD HERBERT, lawyer; b. Mpls., Apr. 17, 1933; s. Leonard A. and Lilah B. (Nordland) B.; m. Charla Lee Bucklin; children—Karen, Anne, David, Douglas, Lea, Gregory. B.S. in Law, U. Minn., 1955, J.D., 1957. Bar: Minn. 1957, N.D. 1960, U.S. Dist. Ct. Minn., U.S. Dist. Ct. N.D., U.S. Ct. Appeals (8th cir.), U.S. Supreme Ct. Ptnr. Larson, Loevinger, Lindquist, Freeman & Fraser, Mpls., 1957-60, Zuger & Bucklin, Bismarck, N.D., 1960—; lectr. on product liability to various groups; mem. Joint Trial Procedure Com. N.D. Jud. Council, 1977—; mem. N.D. Supreme Ct. Camera in Courtroom Com., 1980—. Elder First Presbyterian Ch., 1974—; mem. Dakota West Arts Council. Mem. ABA (litigation sect.), Burleigh County Bar Assn. (pres. 1973), 4th Jud. Dist. Bar Assn., N.D. Bar Assn. , Assn. Trial Lawyers Am., Internat. Acad. Trial Lawyers, Am. Council on Transplantation (membership com. 1986—), Order of Coif, Phi Delta Phi, Delta Sigma Rho. Author: Civil Practice of North Dakota, 1975, Products Litigation, Dakota, 1987. Home: 225 Juniper Dr Bismarck ND 58501 Office: PO Box 7276 Bismarck ND 58501

BUCKMAN, CHARLES EDWARD, JR., information systems executive; b. Kansas City, Mo., Sept. 27, 1943; s. Charles Edward and Geraldine Clara (Herold) B.; student Ill. State U., 1961-64; B.S., Quincy Coll., 1966; postgrad. U. Ill., 1967-68; m. Judith Brosi, Nov. 19, 1966; children—Christina Elaine, Erin Noel, Brian Charles. Juvenile parole agent Ill. Youth Commn., 1966-67, regional supr., Springfield, 1967-68; account salesman Ill. Bell Telephone, Moline, 1967-70, communications cons., 1970-72, data communications specialist, 1972-74, account mgr., 1974-76, mgr. data tech. support, Chgo., 1976-77, product mgr., 1977-80, industry mgr., 1980-82; nat. account mgr. Am. Bell, Inc., 1983; pres. Blythe-Nelson Midwest, Inc., 1983-86; regional dir. Luma Telecom, Inc., 1986-87; v.p. Richard Thomas Assocs., 1987—; adj. prof. Ill. Inst. Tech., 1986—. Treas. Christian Family Movement, 1975-76; lectr. MBA program Ill. Inst. Tech. Stuart Sch., 1986—; Mem. religious edn. bd. Sacred Heart Ch., Moline, 1975-76; mem. curriculum adv. com. Black Hawk Coll., Moline, 1973-76; mem. exec. bd. DuPage Area council Boy Scouts Am.; pres. Hobson Village Assn. Mem. Data Processing Mgmt. Assn., Am. Mgmt. Assn., Nat. Eagle Scouts Assn. Roman Catholic. Lodge: Kiwanis. Home: 1081 Challdon Ct Naperville IL 60540 Office: Luma Telecom Inc 800 Biermann Ct Mount Prospect IL 60056-2173

BUCKMAN, REPHA JOAN, artist, educator; b. St. Paul, Kans., Aug. 18, 1942; d. Francis Albert and Leona Myrtle (Aronholdt) Glenn; m. Larry Dean Buckman, Jan. 15, 1961 (div. Jan. 1978); children: Eric Dean, Alan Glenn, Martin Lance. Student, Washburn U., 1960-61; BA, Southwestern Coll., Winfield, Kans., 1970; postgrad., Wichita (Kans.) State U., 1974-75; MA, Ft. Hays (Kans.) State U., 1978. Cert. secondary tchr., Kans. Tchr. Burrton (Kans.) Schs., 1970-74, Sterling (Kans.) Schs., 1974-79; bus. mgr. Hutchinson (Kans.) Repertory Theatre, 1980-81; artist-in-edn. Kans. Art Commn., Wichita, Western Plains, 1982-86, Hogoton, 1986-87, Wichita, 1987—; artistic dir., pres., bd. dirs. Tri-Crown Family Theatre, Sterling, 1983—; artistic dir. Recreation Services for Handicapped, Inc., Hutchinson, 1985; tech. dir., tchr. Hutchinson Community Coll., 1985-86. Author: Repha, 1986. Child care worker Bob Johnson Youth Shelter, Hutchinson, 1985-86; project dir. Kans. Com. for Humanities, 1981; bd. dirs. Kans. Pub. Braodcasting Sta., Wichita, 1982-86, Hutchinson Theatre Guild, 1983-85, Bob Woodley Found. Drama Edn., Topeka, 1986—. Mem. Sterling Tchrs. Assn. (polit. action com. 1975-79), Assn. Kans. Theatres, Kans. Writers Assn. (bd. dirs.), Kans. State Poetry Soc., Friends of Kans. Com. for Humanities, Kans. Authors Club. Democrat. Avocations: reading, mask making, crewel. Office: Tri-Crown Enterprizes Inc 210 S Broadway Sterling KS 67579

BUCKNER BRIGHT, ROSE L., psychologist; b. Dallas, Feb. 4, 1945; d. William Oliver and Juanita Odell (Reeves) Laminack; divorced; children: Rod Laminack Buckner, Beth Rosalyn; m. James E. Bright. BS, North Tex. State U., 1967, MS, 1972; postgrad., S.W. Mo. State U., 1979-82; EdD, U. Ark., 1985. Lic. psychologist, Mo. Dir. occupational, recreational and group therapy Ft. Worth Neuropsychiat. Hosp., 1968-70; instr. psychology S.W. Mo. State U., Springfield, 1970-78; pvt. practice clin. psychologist Springfield, 1972—; diagnostic cons. Willard (Mo.) Pub. Schs., 1979-80; with grants and contracts div. Mo. Div. Family Service, Fed. VA Grant for Vets. and Greene County Juvenile Ct., Springfield, 1980-85; instr. abnormal psychology S.W. Mo. State U., Springfield, 1984, psychology, 1970-78, mem. dean's external adv. com., 1984-86; staff privileges St. John's Hosp. Marion Ctr., Springfield, 19856; cons. CASA & Willard Pub. Schs., 1985-86; mem. com. for excellence Sunshine Elem. Sch., Springfield, 1984-86; mem. Child Advocacy Council and Child Protection Team, Springfield. Mem. Am. Assn. Counseling and Devel., Ozark Area Psychol. Assn., Mo. Psychol. Assn., Springfield Jr. League, Ark. Alumni Assn. Avocations: piano, jogging. Home: 1235 S Pickwick Springfield MO 65804 Office: 1111 S Glenstone Suite 2-101 Springfield MO 65804

BUCUR, NICHOLAS ANTHONY, III, data processing executive; b. Managua, Nicaragua, Oct. 11, 1950; (parents Am. citizens); s. Nicholas A. and Jacoba (Galo) B. Student, Cuyahoga Community Coll., 1969-71. Cert. computer profl. Propr. Infinity Co., Cleve., 1968—, data processing cons., 1973-82; editorialist Sta. WZAK, Cleve., 1969-73, dir. pub. affairs, 1975-82, moderator, announcer People's Voice program, 1973—; pub. Cleve. Feminist mag., 1973; systems mgr. Systems Info. Services, Cleve., 1976-78; sr. systems analyst Picker Corp., Cleve., 1978-85; prin. engr. Keithley Instruments, Inc., 1986—; instr. data processing Cuyahoga Community Coll. V.p. Greater Cleve. Young Rep. Club, 1971; mem. human relations com. Fedn. for Community Planning, 1973. Mem. Nat. Mgmt. Assn., Mensa. Club: Cleve. City. Home: 10206 Clifton St Cleveland OH 44102 Office: 28775 Aurora Rd Cleveland OH 44139

BUCZAK, DOUGLAS CHESTER, financial advisor, lawyer; b. Detroit, Feb. 6, 1949; s. Chester and Rose Marie (Czech) B. BA in English, U. Mich., 1971; JD, U. Detroit, 1975. Bar: Mich. 1975. Sole practice Lansing, Mich., 1976-78; mgmt. cons. Creative Interiors, East Lansing, Mich., 1978-80; bus. cons. Dynamic Learning Systems, Farmington Hills, Mich., 1981-82; fin. planner Pacific Fin. Cos., Farmington Hills, 1982-86, Pacific Fin. Group, Birmingham, 1986—. Mem. Mich. Bar Assn., Internat. Assn. Fin. Planning, Sigma Phi Epsilon (pres. alumni bd., Ann Arbor, Mich. 1983—). Lodge: Optimists (pres. Farmington Hills 1984-85, sec. Farmington Hills 1985-87). Home: 24749 W Woodside Farmington Hills MI 48018 Office: Pacific Fin Group 30400 Telegraph Rd Birmingham MI 48010

BUCZYNSKI, TIMOTHY JOHN, accountant; b. South Bend, Ind., Mar. 27, 1960; s. Daniel Richard and Elizabeth Catherine (Trimboli) B.; m. Sharon Kay Scott, Aug. 20, 1983. BBA, U. Notre Dame, 1982, MBA, 1983. CPA, Ohio. Sr. cons. Deloitte, Haskins & Sells, Cleve., 1983—. Mem. Am. Inst. CPA's, Ohio Soc. CPA's. Democrat. Roman Catholic. Avocations: jogging, travelling. Home: 2927 Hereford Dr Parma OH 44134 Office: Deloitte Haskins and Sells 1717 E Ninth St Cleveland OH 44114

BUDDE, RICHARD BERNARD, neurosurgeon; b. Covington, Ky., July 30, 1929; s. Bernard P. and Clara M. (Heringhaus) B.; m. Leah Barbara Hehl, June 18, 1955; children: Richard B. Jr., Elizabeth Ann, Frank Edward, Mark David. BS, Xavier U., 1951; MD, St. Louis U., 1955. Diplomate Am. Bd. Neurol. Surgery. Intern Good Samaritan Hosp., Cin., 1955-56, resident in neurosurgery, 1956-61; neurosurgeon Mayfield Neurol. Inst., Cin., 1961—. Contbr. articles to profl. jours. Community adv. bd. Sta. WCET-TV, 1979; trustee Coll. Mount Saint Joseph, Ohio, 1978-84, Med. Found. Cin., 1979, chmn. bd. trustees, 1983—; pres. bd. trustees Mayfield Edn. Research Fund, 1977—; tech. adv. com. CORVA, 1979, Acute Care Study Task Force, 1979. Mem. Acad. Medicine (treas. 1974-75, trustee 1975-78, pres. elect 1978-79, pres. 1979-80, Greater Cin. distbn. com. 1985—), Am. Assn. Neurol. Surgeons, Am. Heart Assn., Cin. Soc. Neurology and Neurosurgery, Med. Dental Hosp. Bur., Inc. (bd. dirs. 1979—), Ohio State Med. Assn., Ohio State Neurosurgical Assn. Home: 1270 Balmoral Dr Cincinnati OH 45238 Office: Mayfield Neurol Inst 506 Oak St Cincinnati OH 45219

BUDEV, HARI, obstetrician/gynecologist; b. Sabasaba, Kenya, May 1, 1937; came to U.S., 1963; s. Nathalal Dharamshi and Dudhiben N. (Madlani) Buddhdev; m. Rekha Amritlal Shah, June 23, 1964; children: Ashish, Sapna. B in Medicine, BS, B.J. Med. Coll., Ahmedabad, India, 1961. Lic. ob-gyn, Ohio. Intern Little Co. of Mary Hosp., Evergreen Park,

Ill., 1963-64; resident Wayne State U., Detroit, 1964-68; practice medicine specializing in ob-gyn Nairobi, Kenya, 1969-73, Cin., 1975-76; obstetrician/gynecologist HMO Group Health Assocs., Inc., Cin., 1977—, mem. exec. com., 1985—. Fellow Am. Coll. Ob-Gyn, Am. Assn. Physicians from India (regional dir. 1985-86, sec., treas. 1986-87, v.p. 1987—), Assn. Indian Physicians (sec., treas. 1979-80, mem. exec. com. 1980-81). Hindu. Club: Ankur (mem. exec. com. 1983-85). Lodge: Lions (charter mem. 1974-75, mem. Nairobi exec. com. 1971-73). Avocations: stock market, finance, traveling. Home: 8725 Bridgewater Ln Cincinnati OH 45243 Office: Group Health Assocs Inc 8245 N Creek Dr Cincinnati OH 45236

BUDIG, GENE ARTHUR, university chancellor; b. McCook, Nebr., May 25, 1939; s. Arthur G. and Angela (Schaaf) B.; m. Gretchen VanBloom, Nov. 30, 1963; children: Christopher, Mary Frances, Kathryn Angela. B.S., U. Nebr., 1962, M.Ed., 1963, Ed.D., 1967. Exec. asst. to gov. Nebr., Lincoln, 1964-67; adminstrv. asst. to chancellor, asst. prof. ednl. adminstrn. U. Nebr., Lincoln, 1967-70; asst. vice chancellor acad. affairs, prof. ednl. adminstrn. U. Nebr., 1970, asst. v.p., dir. pub. affairs, 1971; v.p., dean univ. Ill. State U., Normal, 1972; pres. Ill. State U., 1973-77, W.Va. U., Morgantown, 1977-81; chancellor U. Kans., Lawrence, 1981—. Author: (with Dr. Stanley G. Rives) Academic Quicksand: Expectations of the Administrator, 1973; Editor, contbr.: chpts. Perceptions in Public Higher Education, 1970, Dollars and Sense: Budgeting for Today's Campus, 1972, Higher Education—Surviving the 1980s, 1981; editorial cons.: chpts. Phi Delta Kappan, 1976—; Contbr. articles to profl. jours. Mem. Intergovtl. Council on Edn., 1980-84; trustee Nelson-Atkins Mus. Art, Kansas City, Mo.; bd dirs. Truman Library Inst.; bd. dirs. Midwest Research Inst., University Field Staff Internat. Serving as maj. gen. Air N.G., asst. to comdr. Air Tng. Command USAF, 1985—. Named one of ten outstanding young persons Ill. Jaycees, 1975; one of top 100 leaders in Am. higher edn. Change mag. and Am. Council on Edn., 1979; one of 75 outstanding young men and women educators of Am. Phi Delta Kappa, 1981. Home: 1532 Lilac Ln Lawrence KS 66044 Office: Univ of Kans Cen Office Office of the Chancellor Lawrence KS 66045

BUDNY, JAMES CHARLES, federal tax executive; b. Dearborn, Mich., Aug. 11, 1948; s. William B. and Marion Catherine (Jazdzewski) B.; m. Maureen Anne Taylor, July 9, 1970; 1 child, Andrea. BBA, Ea. Mich. U., 1970; JD, Detroit Coll. Law, 1981. Revenue agent IRS, Dearborn, 1972-75; employee plans specialist IRS, Detroit, 1975-79, appeals officer, 1979-87, assoc. chief, 1987—; sec. Cass Plaza Corp., Grosse Ile, Mich., 1980—; v.p. Cass Plaza Corp., Dearborn, 1983—; also bd. dirs. Sec. Indsl. Park Promotion Com., Grosse Ile, Mich., 1986—. Mem. Nat. Assn. Accts., Delta Theta Phi. Roman Catholic. Avocations: racquetball, hiking, hunting, hockey, baseball. Office: IRS Appeals Office 477 Michigan Ave Room 470 Detroit MI 48226 also: Cass Plaza Corp PO Box 412 Grosse Ile MI 48138

BUDNY, SANDRA MARIE, personnel consultant; b. Milw., Jan. 18, 1952; d. James Thomas and Mary Margaret (Piccoli) B. BS, U. Wis., Milw., 1973; MS, Cardinal Stritch Coll., 1983. Personnel asst. Sacred Heart Rehab. Hosp., Milw., 1971-76; mgr. personnel Gimbels Corp., Milw., 1976-78; cons. Pieroth Bros., Milw., 1978-79; personnel officer exec. office ECM Resource Devel., Milw., 1980-83; outplacement coordinator Greater Milw. Re-Employment Corp., 1983-85; prin., cons. Personnel Resource Services, New Berlin, Wis., 1985—; adj. faculty mem. Cardinal Stritch Coll., 1984—. Vol. Citizen's Com. to Re-elect County Exec. O'Donnell, Milw., 1980. Mem. Personnel and Indsl. Assn., Links. Democrat. Roman Catholic. Avocations: tennis, skiing, racquetball, chess.

BUDZAK, KATHRYN SUE (MRS. ARTHUR BUDZAK), physician; b. Racine, Wis., May 6, 1940; d. Raymond Philip and Emma Kathryn (Sorensen) Myer; student Stephens Coll., 1957-58, Luther Coll., 1958-59; BS with honors, U. Wis. at Milw., 1962; MD, U. Wis., 1969; m. Arthur Budzak, Dec. 21, 1961; children: Ann Elizabeth, Lynn Marie. Intern, Madison (Wis.) Gen. Hosp., 1969-70; emergency physician, emergency suite St. Mary's Hosp., Madison, 1971-75; urgent care physician Dean Clinic, Madison, 1975—. Recipient Disting. Alumnae award Stephens Coll., 1979; named to Washington Park High Sch. Hall of Fame, 1985. Mem. Am. Coll. Emergency Physicians, Am. Coll. of Sports Medicine, AMA, Am. Acad. Family Physicians, Wis. Acad. Family Physicians (pres. south cen. chpt. 1979-81), Wis. Med. Soc., Dane County Med. Soc., Am. Med. Women's Assn. (sponser U. Wis. student br.), Women in Medicine in Wis., Wis. Med. Alumni Assn. (dir. 1979-82, pres. 1983-84), Sigma Sigma Sigma. Presbyterian. Mem. editorial bd., asst. editor Wis. Med. Alumni Quar. Home: 6110 Davenport Dr Madison WI 53711 Office: 1313 Fish Hatchery Rd Madison WI 53715

BUDZYNSKI, JOHN WALTER, accountant; b. Chgo., July 18, 1950; s. Walter and EVelyn (Kolziek) B.; m. Antoinette M. Kasprzak, Sept. 28, 1974; children: Brian W., Lindsay A. AS in Bus. Adminstrn., Robert Morris, Carthage, Ill., 1970; BS in Acctg., U. Ill., Chgo., 1973. CPA, Ill. Acct. Chgo. Bridge and Iron, 1973-77, acctg. supr., 1977-80; asst. to controller Northbrook (Ill.) Metals, 1980-82; acctg. mgr. First Family of Travel, Oak Brook, Ill., 1982-85, dir. corp. acctg. and tax, 1985—, corp. controller, 1986—. Mem. Ill. Soc. CPA's, Am. Inst. CPA's. Roman Catholic. Avocations: golf, stamp collecting. Home: 285 Wesley Dr Addison IL 60101 Office: First Family of Travel Ltd 2809 Butterfield Rd Oak Brook IL 60521

BUECHE, WENDELL FRANCIS, manufacturing company executive; b. Flushing, Mich., Nov. 7, 1930; s. Paul D. and Catherine (McGraw) B.; m. Virginia M. Smith, June 14, 1952; children: Denise, Barbara, Daniel, Brian. B.S.M.E., U. Notre Dame, 1952. With Allis-Chalmers Corp., 1952—; dist. mgr. Allis-Chalmers Corp., Detroit, 1961-64, sales and mktg. mgr., 1964-69; group exec. v.p. Allis-Chalmers Corp., West Allis, Wis., 1973-76, exec. v.p. elec. groups, 1976-77, exec. v.p., chief adminstrv. and fin. officer, 1977-80, chief adminstrv. officer, 1977-80, exec. v.p., head solids process equipment sector and fluids processing group, chief fin. officer, 1980-81, pres., chief operating officer, dir., 1981-83, pres., chief exec. officer, dir., 1984—, chmn., 1986—, also chmn. exec. com.; dir. Fiat-Allis, Siemens-Allis, Svenska Fluid carbon A.B., M&I Marshall Illsley Bank., M&I Corp., Wis. Gas Corp., WICOR, Inc. Mem. The Chgo. Com., 1981—, Greater Milw. Com., 1981—; mem. council Med. Coll. Wis., 1983—. Mem. IEEE, ASME, AIME, Machinery and Allied Products Inst., Nat. Sand and Gravel Assn. (dir.), Nat. Elec. Mfrs. Assn. (gov.). Clubs: Milwaukee Country, Westmoor Country. Office: Allis-Chalmers Corp P O Box 512 Milwaukee WI 53201 *

BUECHNER, JACK W., congressman, lawyer; b. St. Louis, June 4, 1940; s. John Edw. and Gertrude Emily (Richardson) B.; m. Marietta Rose Coon, Aug. 7, 1965; children: Patrick John, Terrance J. BA, Benedictine Coll., 1962; JD, St. Louis U., 1965. Bar: Mo. 1965, U.S. Dist. Ct. (ea. dist.) Mo. 1965, U.S. Ct. Appeals (8th cir.) 1965. Ptnr. Buechner, McCarthy, Leonard, Kaemmerer, Owen & Laderman, Manchester, Mo., 1965—; mem. 100th Congress from 2d Mo. dist., 1987—; state rep. 94th dist., Mo. Gen. Assembly, 1972-82. Mem. Mo. Tourism Commn., 1976, 82, 85. Recipient Meritorious Service award St. Louis Globe-Democrat, 1973, Legis. Achievement award St. Louis Police Officers, 1982, Pub. Service award Women's Polit., Mo., Distinguished Service award Cardinal Glennon Hosp., Mo., 1982. Mem. ABA, Mo. Bar Assn., Met. Bar Assn. Republican. Roman Catholic. Club: John Marshall (Outstanding Atty. 1986). Lodge: Lions. Avocations: softball, reading, travel. Home: 14 Ponca Tr Saint Louis MO 63122 Office: Room 502 Cannon House Office Bldg Washington DC 20515 *

BUEHLER, ALBERT CARL, III, health care consultant, accountant; b. Chgo., July 27, 1956; s. Albert C. Jr. and Patricia H. (Holmes) B.; m. Nancy L. Pollock, June 21, 1980; 1 child, Katherine Stormont. BA, DePauw U., 1978; M Mgmt., Northwestern U., 1980. CPA, Ill. Cons. Ernst & Whinney, Chgo., 1980-83; mgr. Alexian Bros. Health System, Elk Grove Village, Ill., 1983-84; mgr. fin. Ill. Hosp. Assn., Naperville, 1984-85; v.p. The Sachs Group, Chgo., 1985-86; cons. A.C. Buehler Health Care Services, Northbrook, Ill., 1986—. Firefighter Northbrook Fire Dept.; vice chmn. selection com. Northbrook Caucus; trustee Hull House Assn., Chgo., 1986—. Fellow The Wacker Inst.; mem. Healthcare Fin. Mgmt. Assn., Am. Coll. Healthcare Execs., Am. Inst. CPA's, Ill. CPA Soc. (hosps. com.).

BUEHLER, PAUL RICHARD, television videographer/editor; b. Youngstown, Ohio, Nov. 25, 1955; s. Paul Richard and Evelyn Marie (Peters) B.; m. Holly Jean Slanaker, Aug., 1987. BS in Communication cum laude, Ohio U., 1978. Studio mgr. Sta. KPLC-TV, Lake Charles, La., 1978-79; videographer Sta. WBNS-TV, Columbus, Ohio, 1979-81, Angeli Film & Video, Wilmington, Del., 1981-84; freelance videographer various cities, 1984-85; videographer Sta. WJBK-TV, Detroit, 1985—; videographer Diamond P Sports, Woodland Hills, Calif., 1979—. Videographer (documentary) My Mother, My Daughter, Myself, 1984, TV news mag. Sunday Times, 1985-86 (Emmy award 1985). Recipient Emmy award Nat. Acad. TV Arts and Scis., 1980, 81; Addy award Advt. Club Wilmington, 1984. Mem. AFTRA, Am. Film Inst., Nat. Assn. Broadcast Employees and Technicians. Avocations: photography, camping, swimming, rafting. Home: 3610 Karen Pkwy #302 Pontiac MI 48054

BUEHLMAN, KENNETH WAYNE, pediatrician; b. Woodriver, Ill., July 28, 1950; s. Joseph Walter and Catherine Edna (Geisen) B.; m. Christina Marie Kjar, Mar. 31, 1978; children: Jay, Andrea. BS, Loyola U., Chgo., 1972, MD, 1975. Fellow Am. Acad. Pediatrics. Resident in pediatrics Loyola U., Chgo., 1975-76, St. Louis U., 1976-78; practice medicine specializing in pediatrics Vincennes, Ind., 1978—; chmn. pediatrics dept. Good Samaritan Hosp., Vincennes, 1983-85. Pres. Knox County (Ind.) United Fund, Vincennes, 1985. Mem. Am. Acad. Pediatrics, Ind. State Med. Soc., Knox County Med. Soc. Republican. Methodist. Lodge: Elks. Avocations: snow skiing, scuba diving, racquetball, reading. Home: 1400 Forest Hill Vincennes IN 47591 Office: Pediatrics of Vincennes 514 S Ninth Vincennes IN 47591

BUEHNER, DONALD FRANCIS, family physician; b. Mt. Vernon, Ind., Sept. 11, 1918; s. Sylvester Henry and Anna (Engelhart) B.; m. Lucille Margaret Kollker, Dec. 31, 1941 (dec. May 1973); children: Donald C., Timothy K, Rebecca Buehner Conley, Lucinda Buehner Barkley, Nicholas J.; m. Jeanne McPherson Knight, Nov. 12, 1976. AB, Wabash Coll., 1941; MD, St. Louis U., 1950. Diplomate Am. Bd. Family Physicians. Intern Protestant Deaconess Hosp., Evansville, Ind., 1950-51; practice family medicine Evansville, 1951—; mem. staff St. Mary's Med. Ctr., pres. staff, 1959; pres. Med. Arts Bldg., Inc., Evansville. Served with AUS, 1942-45. Fellow Am. Acad. Family Physicians; mem. AMA (Physicians Recognition award), Ind. Med. Assn., Ind. Acad. Family Physicians (1st dist. pres. 1968), Beta Theta Pi. Roman Catholic. Club: Rolling Hills Country (Newburgh, Ind.). Avocation: golf. Home: 600 Cullen Ave Evansville IN 47715 Office: 3700 Belle Meade Ave Evansville IN 47715

BUERGER, TODD MARK, architect; b. Cleve., Nov. 3, 1959; s. Theodore Alphonse and Jeanne Marie (Hertz) B. B in Environ. Design, Miami U., Oxford, Ohio, 1982; MArch, U. Ill., 1984. Researcher U.S. Army C.E., Champaign, Ill., 1983-84; architect Everett I. Brown Co., Indpls., 1984—. Mem. AIA. Republican. Presbyterian. Office: Everett I Brown Co 941 N Meridian St Indianapolis IN 46204

BUERLING, SIEGFRIED FRIEDEL, historic village official; b. Essen, Germany, Jan. 29, 1932; s. Friedrich and Bertha Wilhelmiene (Wackermann) B.; came to U.S., 1959, naturalized, 1968; grad. trade sch.; m. Heidi Elisabeth Heid, Aug. 31, 1957; children—Peter Johannes, Curt Tracy. With Buerling Cabinet Shop, Essen, 1945-56; furniture restorer Canadiana Antiques, Montreal, Que., Can., 1956-59; preparator Western Reserve Hist. Soc., Cleve., 1959-62, supr. ops., 1962-66, mgr. ops., 1966-70, mgr. properties, 1970-74, dir. Hale Farm and Village, Bath, Ohio, 1975—, dir. dept. properties and preservation, 1977—; v.p. ops. Cuyahoga Valley Preservation and Scenic R.R. Assn.; restoration cons. Bd. dirs. Hower House Found., Akron, Ohio, 1974—. Recipient Woodrow Wilson award Woodlawn Conf., Nat. Trust for Historic Preservation, 1971; Outstanding Citizen award Nationality Services Center Greater Cleve., 1975. Home: 2743 Oak Hill Rd Bath OH 44210 Office: 2686 Oak Hill Rd Bath OH 44210

BUESSER, ANTHONY CARPENTER, lawyer; b. Detroit, Oct. 15, 1929; s. Frederick Gustavis and Lela (Carpenter) B.; m. Carolyn Sue Pickle, Mar. 13, 1954, 1 child, Andrew Clayton; children: Kent Anderson, Anthony Carpenter, Andrew Clayton; m. Bettina Rieveschl, Dec. 14, 1973. B.A. in English with honors, U. Mich., 1952, M.A., 1953, J.D., 1960. Bar: Mich. 1961. Assoc. Chase, Goodenough & Buesser, Detroit, 1961-66; ptnr. Buesser, Buesser, Snyder & Blank, Detroit and Bloomfield Hills, Mich., 1966-81; sole practice Birmingham, Mich., 1981—. Trustee, chmn. bd. Detroit Country Day Sch., Birmingham, Mich., 1970-82, 84-87; mem. exec. com., chmn. nominating com., 1987. Served with AUS, 1953-55. Recipient Avery Hopwood award major fiction U. Mich., 1953. Mem. ABA, Mich. Bar Assn., Detroit Bar Assn. (pres. 1976-77), Oakland County Bar Assn., Am. Judicature Soc., Am. Arbitration Assn. (arbitrator), Alpha Delta Phi, Phi Delta Phi. Clubs: Detroit, Thomas M. Cooley (Detroit). Home and Office: 32908 Outland Trail PO Box 090159 Birmingham MI 48009 Office: 32908 Outland Trail Birmingham MI 48010

BUESSER, FREDERICK GUSTAVUS, III, lawyer; b. Detroit, Apr. 30, 1941; s. Frederick Gustavus and Betty A. (Ronal) B.; B.A., U. Mich., 1964, J.D., 1966; m. Julia Forsyth Guest, June 28, 1963; children—Jennifer, Katherine, Frederick. Admitted to Mich. bar, 1966; asso. firm Buesser, Buesser, Snyder & Blank, Detroit, Bloomfield Hills, 1966, partner, 1967—; lectr. and mem. faculty legal seminars. Fellow Am. Bar Found.; mem. Am. Bar Assn., State Bar of Mich., Am. Judicature Soc., Sigma Chi, Phi Delta Phi. Episcopalian. Home: 242 N Glengarry St Birmingham MI 48009 Office: 4190 Telegraph St Bloomfield Hills MI 48013

BUETER, THOMAS LEONARD, electronics company engineering executive; b. Ft. Wayne, June 1, 1931; s. Leonard Henry and Grace Josephine (Parisot) B.; m. Mary Phyllis Osweiler, June 4, 1955; children: Anne Patrice, Ellen Maria, Marcia Elizabeth, Timothy Alexander, Elizabeth Caroline. BS in Chemistry cum laude, Xavier U., 1953. Lab. asst., process chemist Gen. Electric, Ft. Wayne, 1955-64, materials and processes specialist, 1964-66, materials engr., 1966-78, materials and processes engr., 1978-85, sr. devel. engr., 1985—. Mem. Soc. Plastics Engrs. (sr., sec., treas., past pres., nat. councilman), IEEE, Internat. Coil Winding Assn., NSPE, Ft. Wayne Engrs. Club. Roman Catholic. Club: Gen. Electric Suprs. (bd. dirs. 1970-76). Lodge: KC (Grand Knight 1964-65). Office: Gen Electric 2000 Taylor St Fort Wayne IN 46804

BUFFA, ANDREW RUSSELL, municipal purchasing agent; b. Chgo., Mar. 29, 1948; s. Andrew and Antoinette (Di Liberti) B.; m. Diane Celeste O'Brien, July 3, 1983. Buyer Jewel Food Stores, Melrose Park, Ill., 1973-81; purchasing agt. Village of Glendale Heights, Ill., 1981-84, Village of Niles, Ill., 1984—. Served with USAF, 1967-71, Vietnam. Mem. Nat. Inst. Govt. Purchasing, Chicagoland Suburban Communities Purchasing Assn. (pres. 1987—), Holy Name Soc. Office: Village of Niles 7601 N Milwaukee Ave Niles IL 60648

BUFFETT, WARREN EDWARD, corporate executive; b. Omaha, Aug. 30, 1930; s. Howard Homan and Leila (Stahl) B.; m. Susan Thompson, Apr. 19, 1952; children: Susan, Howard, Peter. Student, U. Pa., 1947-49; B.S., U. Nebr., 1950; M.S., Columbia, 1951. Investment salesman Buffett-Falk & Co., Omaha, 1951-54; security analyst Graham-Newman Corp., N.Y.C., 1954-56; gen. partner Buffett Partnership, Ltd., Omaha, 1956-69; chmn. bd. Berkshire, Hathaway, Inc., Nat. Indemnity Co., Nat. Fire & Marine Ins. Co., Asso. Retail Stores, Inc., See's Candy Shops, Inc., Columbia Ins. Co., Buffalo Evening News; bd. dirs. Capital Cities/ABC. Bd. govs. Boys Clubs Omaha, 1962—; life trustee Grinnell Coll., 1968—; trustee Urban Inst. Office: Berkshire Hathaway Inc 1440 Kiewit Plaza Omaha NE 68131 *

BUFORD, ROBERT JOHN, real estate investment company executive, lawyer; b. Chgo., Oct. 13, 1948; s. John Robert and Dorothy Myrtle (Eckstrom) B. BS Indsl. Engring., U. Ill., 1971; MBA, U. Chgo., 1975; JD, DePaul U., 1979. CPA, Ill. Dist. mgr. Pfizer Medical, Inc., Chgo., 1975-79, regional mgr., 1979-81; gen. mgr. Omnimedical, Inc., Chgo., 1981; exec. v.p. Planned Equities, Inc., Chgo., 1981-85, pres., 1985—, also bd. dirs.; exec. v.p. Planned Partnerships, Inc., Chgo., 1981-85, pres., 1985—, also bd. dirs. Rep. precinct capt., Chgo., 1976—. Mem. Chgo. Bar Assn., Ill. Inst. CPA's, Real Estate Securities and Syndication Inst. Lutheran. Club: Olympia Fields (Ill.) Country; East Bank (Chgo.). Avocations: long distance running, golf. Home: 1 East Schiller #9D Chicago IL 60610 Office: Planned Equities Inc 414 North Orleans Suite 408 Chicago IL 60610

BUGAR, RONALD JOHN, mechanical engineer; b. Chgo., Jan. 22, 1963; s. Rudolf and Katharina (Lenz) B. Mech. engring. degree, Ill. Inst. Tech., 1985. With sales and repair Jefferson Park Cyclery, Chgo., 1977-81; structural detailer R.J. Erhardt & Co., Chgo., 1981-85; design engr. United COnveyor COrp., Deerfield, Ill., 1985—. Republican. Roman Catholic. Home: 5130 N Kolmar Chicago IL 60630 Office: United Conveyor Corp 300 Wilmot Dr Deerfield IL 60015

BUHL, ROBERT CARL, manufacturing executive; b. Detroit, Nov. 27, 1931; s. Carl F. and Louise C. (Horning) B.; m. Jane Ferris Johnston, Dec. 1, 1972; children—Deborah, Carrie Robyn. B.S. in Engring. and Mgmt., U. Mich., 1956. With Bower Roller Bearing div. Fed. Mogul Corp., Detroit, 1955-67; plant mgr. Formsprag Co., Mt. Pleasant, Mich., 1967-70, v.p. ops., 1970-78; dir. mfg. Ind. div. Dana Corp., Warren, Mich., 1978—; cons. in field. Vice-pres. S.E. Park Assn., Grosse Pointe Park Civic Assn.; mem. planning commn. City of Grosse Pointe Park, 1984—; dir. fin. St. James Lutheran Ch., 1981-83. Served with U.S. Army, 1953-55. Mem. Soc. Mfg. Engrs., Engring. Soc. Detroit. Club: Lakeslands Golf & Country (Brighton, Mich.).

BUILTA, HOWARD CLAIRE, real estate development company executive; b. Lawton, Okla., Apr. 29, 1943; s. Howard Phillip and Alice Ann (Stimpert) B.; m. Claudia Lynn Mastalio, Sept. 3, 1966; children—Jeffrey B., Lindsey M. B.S., U. Ill., 1965; M.B.A., No. Ill. U., 1967. Project adminstr. Seay & Thomas, Chgo., 1969-71; v.p. Rauch & Co., Chgo., 1971-77; v.p., gen. mgr. The Whiston Group, Chgo., 1977-79; v.p. Marathon U.S. Realties, Chgo., 1979—. Mem. adv. council Lutheran Social Services, Chgo., 1976-81, Salvation Army Community Counseling Service, Chgo., 1982-86; trustee Palatine Twp. Govt., Ill., 1979-81; bd. dirs. Palatine Twp. Republican Orgn., 1979-81. Served to 1st lt. U.S. Army, 1967-69, Vietnam. Decorated Bronze Star, Army Commendation medal. Mem. Inst. Real Estate Mgmt. (cert. property mgr.), Bldg. Owners and Mgrs. Assn. Internat. (real property adminstr., pres. Suburban Chgo., Des Plaines, 1977-79, pres. North Central region 1984), Urban Land Inst., Chgo. Real Estate Bd. (pres. 1987-88), Ill. Assn. Realtors (bd. dirs. 1985, dist. v.p. 1987—), Lambda Alpha (pres. Ely chpt. 1984), Am. Legion. Club: Attic (Chgo.). Lodge: Masons. Avocations: reading; fishing. Home: 2316 Sunset Rd Palatine IL 60074 Office: Marathon US Realties 3 1st National Plaza Suite 5700 Chicago IL 60602

BUIVIDAS, THOMAS ANTHONY, podiatrist; b. Chgo., Apr. 4, 1954; s. Alex John and Jean Marie (Rauen) B.; m. Paula Jean Bresnik, Nov. 5, 1977; children: Andrea Lynn, Thomas Paul, Sarah Jean. AA, Southwest Coll., Chgo., 1973; D in Podiatric Medicine, Ill. Coll. Podiatric Medicine, Chgo., 1977. Diplomate Am. Bd. Podiatric Surgery, Am. Bd. Podiatric Orthopedics. Resident Thorek Hosp., Chgo., 1977-78; with staff Loretto Hosp., Chgo., 1978—. Fellow Am. Coll. Foot Surgeons, Am. Coll. Foot Orthopedists; mem. Ill. Podiatric Med. Assn., Am. Podiatric Med. Assn.

BUJALSKI, JUNE MARIE, accountant; b. Erie, Pa., May 27, 1957; d. Henry Anthony and Dorothy Barbara (Yurkovic) B. BS, Pa. State U., 1979. CPA, Houston, Cleve. Internal auditor Great So. Life Ins., Houston, 1979-80; staff acct. El Paso Liquefied Nat. Gas Co., Houston, 1981; oil, gas acct. Seagull Energy Corp., Houston, 1982-84; staff acct. E. Ohio Gas Co., Cleve., 1985-86, supr. accounts payable/material and supplies, 1985-86. Mem. Am. Inst. CPA's, Ohio Soc. CPA's, Nat. Assn. Accts. Home: 20948 Eastwood Ave Fairview Park OH 44126 Office: E Ohio Gas Co 1717 E 9th St Room 518 Cleveland OH 44114

BUKAR, MARGARET WITTY, accountant, civic leader; b. Evanston, Ill., June 21, 1950; d. LeRoy and Catherine Ann (Conrad) Witty; m. Gregory Bryce Bukar, June 5, 1971; children—Michael Bryce, Caroline Nicole. B.S., DePaul U., 1972, M.B.A., 1981. Staff med. technologist The Evanston (Ill.) Hosp., 1972-75, immunopathology lab. supr., 1975-77, lab. mgr., 1977-84, dir. lab. adminstrn., 1984-85; bookkeeper Ronald Knox Montessori Sch., Wilmette, Ill., 1986—. Den leader Cub Scouts, Boy Scouts Am., Wilmette, 1985—; active PTA of St. Francis Xavier Sch., 1985—, mem. sch. bd., 1986-87. Recipient Emily Withrow Stebbins award Evanston Hosp., 1985. Mem. Nat. Assn. Female Execs., Am. Soc. Clin. Pathologists, Wilmette Hist. Soc. Avocations: knitting, restoring old homes, interior design. Home: 1611 Greenwood Ave Wilmette IL 60091

BUKATY, MICHAEL EDWARD, manufacturing company executive; b. Kansas City, Mo., Aug. 2, 1936; s. Nicholas Martin and Anna Marie (Walsh) B.; m. Dale Patricia, Aug. 13, 1960; children: Lynne, Jill, Brad. BS in Engring., U. Kans., 1961; MBA, U. Mo., 1965. Design engr. Vendo Co., Kansas City, 1961-65, sales mgmt., 1965-74, v.p. sales, 1975-78; v.p. mktg. Conchemco, Inc. (formerly Wescon Products Co.), Wichita, Kans., 1978-82, pres., 1982—. Avocations: golf, tennis, reading. Home: 1202 N Shefford Wichita KS 67212 Office: Conchemco Inc PO Box 7710 Wichita KS 67277-7710

BUKOVINK, JOHN ANTON, plastic surgeon; b. Cleve., May 15, 1930; s. John and Antonie Kmet; B.; m. Nancy Lee Rentschler, May 18, 1963; children: John A. Jr., Carole Anne, Elizabeth Susan, Kathryn Jean. BA, Amherst (Mass.) Coll., 1952; MD, Case Western Res. U., 1956. Plastic surgeon Lake Plastic and Reconstructive Surgeons, Willoughby, OH, 1964—; pres. med. staff Lake County Meml. Hosp., Willoughby, 1971-73; dir. Western Rs. Health Plan, Painesville, 1983—. Mem. ACS, AMA, Ohio State Med. Assn. Cleve. Surgical Soc., Am. Soc. Plastic and Reconstructive Surgery, Am. Soc Aesthetic Plastic Surgery, Northeast Ohio Soc. Plastice and Reconstructive Surgeons (pres.). Office: Lake Plastic and Reconstructive Surgeons Inc 36100 Euclid Ave Willoughby OH 44094

BUKOWSKY, JAMES THEODORE, electronics manufacturing company executive; b. St. Louis, Apr. 18, 1954; s. Theodore J. and Mary Margaret (Burns) B.; m. Tara Waddell, Oct. 20, 1978. BBA, St. Louis U., 1976, MBA, 1981. Buyer and dept. mgr. Famous-Barr Co., St. Louis, 1976-78; sales rep. Gen. Electric Co., Cleve., 1978-81; sales mgr. Sierracin Corp. (formerly C&S Services), Sylmar, Calif., 1981-85; dist. mgr. Molex, Inc., Lisle, Ill., 1985—; mem. St. Louis Elect. Bd. Trade, 1978—, Electronics Bd. Trade, St. Louis, 1985—. Mem. Big Bros. Cen. Mo., 1985; bd. dirs. St. Peter's (Mo.) Planning and Zoning Commn., 1983, St. Peter's Park and Recreation Commn., 1984. Mem. Nat. Assn. Mktg. Execs., Nat. Assn. Sales Execs., Mo. Sheep Producers Assn., Mo. Livestock Producers Assn. Republican. Roman Catholic. Home: Rt 1 PO Box 200 Jonesburg MO 63351 Office: Molex Inc PO Box 160 Jonesburg MO 63351

BULANDR, PETER J., engineering consulting firm executive; b. Berwyn, Ill., Sept. 7, 1960; s. Jerry and Doris (Williams) B.; m. Lauralyn Pawelczyk, Aug. 4, 1984. BA in Econs., Lake Forest (Ill.) Coll., 1982; MBA in Fin., U. Chgo., 1987. Asst. v.p. Blvd. Bank NA, Chgo., 1982-87; v.p. fin. STS Cons., Ltd., Northbrook, Ill., 1987—. Republican. Avocations: racquetball, fishing, skiing, stamp collecting, classic cars.

BULL, C(HRISTOPHER) NEIL, sociology educator; b. Blackpool, Lancs, Eng., Aug. 21, 1940; came to U.S., 1968; s. Leslie Richard and Dorothy (Hulley) B.; m. Sheelagh G. Hope, Sept. 12, 1974; children: Catriona H., Hillary A. BA, U. B.C., 1965, MA, 1968; PhD, U. Oreg., 1971. Instr. U. Oreg., Eugene, 1970-71; prof. sociology U. Mo., Kansas City, 1971—; chmn. dept. sociology U. Mo., Kansas City, 1978-83; co-dir. Ctr. for Extension Gerontology, 1987—. Contbr. articles to profl. jours. and chpts. to books. Recipient MacKenzie King Travelling Scholarship U. Oreg., 1967-68; postdoct. fellow Can Council, 1969-71, Midwest Council for Social Research in Aging, 1974-76. Mem. Internat. Sociol. Assn., Am. Sociol. Assn., Midwest Sociol. Assn., Gerontological Assn. Office: U Mo Dept Sociology 5101 Rockhill Rd Kansas City MO 64113

BULL, LAWRENCE MYLES, engineer; b. Aliquippa, Pa., Feb. 20, 1931; s. Thomas Leslie and Gertrude Margaret (Miller) B.; B.S.E.E., Ind. Inst. Tech., 1955; m. Emily Jane Antal, June 7, 1958; children—L. Michael, Louis A., Laura A., James C. Transmission corrosion engr. Manufactures Light &

Heat Co., Pitts., 1955-64; corrosion engr. Columbia Gas System-Pitts. Group Co., Pitts., 1964-68; project engr. Columbia Gas Systems Service Corp., Marble Cliff, Ohio, 1968-73; mgr. corrosion and leakage control Columbia Gas Distbn. Cos., Columbus, Ohio, 1973—. Served with U.S. Navy, 1948-52. Mem. ASME, ASTM, Nat. Assn. Corrosion Engrs., Nat., Ohio socs. profl. engrs. Republican. Roman Catholic. Club: Northington Athletic Assn. Home: 829 Pipestone Dr Worthington OH 43085 Office: 200 Civic Center Dr Columbus OH 43215

BULL, ROBERT KEITH, soil scientist; b. Eckert, Colo., Mar. 10, 1927; s. Ernest Atwood and Dorothy (Nelson) B.; B.S. in Agronomy, Colo. State U., 1951, postgrad. in soil sci., 1960; M.S. in Agrl. Econs., N.Mex. State U., 1971; m. Fern Eileen Quiggle, July 21, 1962; children—Karin Elisabeth, Gretchen Louise, Lisa Irene. Soil scientist Soil Conservation Service, U.S., 1951-53; with Morrison Knudsen, Afghanistan, 1953-56, Tams, Iraq, 1956-58; soil scientist Bur. Reclamation, Dept. Interior, 1960-62, Internat. Engring. Co., Bangladesh, 1962-65, Ralph M. Parsons, Saudi Arabia, 1965-67, Internat. Engring. Co., Peru, 1967-69; with Harza Engring. Co., 1971—, Guatemala, Jamaica, Dominican Republic, Haiti, Guyana, Venezuela, Colombia, Honduras, Iran, Thailand, Senegal, Pakistan, Saudi Arabia. Served with U.S. Army, 1945-47. Mem. Am. Soc. Agronomy, Soil Sci. Soc. Am. Home: 1325 E Sanborn Dr Palatine IL 60067 Office: Harza Engring Co 150 S Wacker Dr Chicago IL 60606

BULLARD, ROCKWOOD WILDE, III, lawyer; b. Chgo., May 20, 1944; s. Rockwood Wilde, Jr. and Maryetta Moylen (Fitts) B.; m. Donna Rae Boles, Oct. 29, 1983; children—Elizabeth Ryan, Cathleen Stickney. B.A., Wayne State U., 1971; J.D., New Eng. Sch. Law, 1974. Bar: D.C. 1974, Mich. 1976, U.S. Dist. Ct. (ea. dist.) Mich. 1976, U.S. Dist. Ct. (we. dist.) Mich. 1977, U.S. Ct. Appeals (6th cir.) 1978, U.S. Supreme Ct. 1979. Atty. advisor HUD, Washington, 1974-76; assoc. Patterson & Patterson, Bloomfield Hills, Mich., 1976-82, Goodenough, Smith, Bloomfield Hills, 1982-84; ptnr. Lyon C. & Bullard, Rochester, Mich., 1984—; panel chmn. Atty. Discipline Bd. State Bar Mich., 1984—; dir. Water St. Bridge Corp., Pontiac, Mich., 1984—. Mem. instl. rev. com. Pontiac Gen. Hosp., 1976-83; chmn. attys.' div. United Way Oakland, Pontiac, 1983. Served as spl. agt. M.I., U.S. Army, 1967-69. Recipient Amos L. Taylor award New Eng. Law Sch., 1974. Mem. Oakland County C. of C. (bd. dirs. 1984-87), Oakland County Bar Assn., D.C. Bar Assn., Nat. Lawyers Club, Fed. Bar Assn. Republican. Episcopalian. Club: Otsego (Gaylord, Mich.). Office: Lyon Colbert & Bullard 431 6th St Rochester MI 48063

BULLARD, THOMAS ROBERT, retail book executive; b. Chgo., May 6, 1944; s. Henry M. and Ethel (Munday) B.; B.S., Ill. Inst. Tech., 1966; M.A., Northwestern U., 1968; Ph.D., U. Ill., Chgo., 1973. Teaching asst. history U. Ill. at Chgo. Circle, 1969-73; head nautical dept. Owen Davies, bookseller, Chgo., 1973-80, owner, Oak Park, Ill., 1980—; instr. history Sch. Art Inst. Chgo., 1975-77; cons. in field. Nat. Merit scholar, 1961-62, Hon. Ill. State scholar, 1962. Mem. U.S. Naval Inst., Internat. Naval Research Orgn., Navy Records Soc. (U.K.), Central Electric Railfans Assn., Electric Railroaders Assn., Nat. Ry. Hist. Soc., Ry. and Locomotive Hist. Soc. (dir. Chgo. chpt.). Mem. United Ch. Christ. Author: Street, Interurban and Rapid Transit Railways of the United States: A Selective Historical Bibliography, 1984, Illinois Rail Transit: A Basic History, 1986, Imperial Japanese Navy: A Bibliography of Books, 1987; Contbg. author: Biographical Dictionary of American Mayors, 1981. Home: 228 N Lombard Ave Oak Park IL 60302 Office: Owen Davies Bookseller 200 W Harrison St Oak Park IL 60304

BULLARD, WADE ARTHUR, JR., corp. exec.; b. Wilmington, N.C., Jan. 23, 1931; s. Wade Arthur and Mildred (Anderson) B.; student Columbus U. (Washington), 1949-51; B.B.A., U. Mich., 1957; m. Genie Bassage; children—Linda Kay, Cynthia Ann. Pres. gen. mgr. Patterson's, Sturgis, Mich., 1957-87, also dir.; v.p., dir. Clark Plastic Engring. Co., Sturgis, 1967-73; pres. dir. Plastek Co., 1968—, Colonial Motor Inn, Inc., 1964-76, Wade Bullard, Inc. chmn. bd. Aronco Plastics, Inc., 1974-75. (all Sturgis), 1969-77; Mem. Sturgis Bd. Zoning Appeals, 1967-77; Sturgis city commr., 1975-77; dir. Bd. Pub. Works, St. Joseph County, 1976-77; pres. Klinger Lake Assn., Sturgis, 1969-71; pres., dir. Sturgis Improvement Assn., 1966—, Sturgis Econ. Devel. Corp., 1978—. Served with CIC, AUS, 1951-54; Korea. Decorated Bronze Star medal, UN Service medal, Nat. Def. Service medal. Episcopalian. Club: Klinger Lake Country (Sturgis). Lodge: Elks. Home: Klinger Lake Sturgis MI 49091 Office: 104 N Monroe St PO Box H Sturgis MI 49091

BULLMER, KENNETH, psychologist, educator; b. St. Louis, Sept. 14, 1923; s. George and Mildred Bullmer; m. Carole Marie Hartnett, Jan. 1, 1975; children: Casey, Victoria, Elizabeth, Christina. BSBA, Washington U., St. Louis, 1949; AM, U. Mich., 1967; EdD, Ind. U., 1970. Lic. psychologist. Dir. admissions Montecello Coll., Godfrey, Ill., 1960-62, Franklin (Ind.) Coll., 1962-64; admissions officer Flint Coll., U. Mich., 1964-67; participant NDEA Inst., Ind. U., 1967-68, counselor counseling and psychol. services, 1968-69, research assoc. Inst. Sex Research, 1969-70; assoc. prof. psychology Western Mich. U., Kalamazoo, 1970—; pvt. practice psychol. counseling, 1970—; dir. Portage Community Outreach Center, 1978-84. Served with AUS, 1943-46; PTO. Decorated Bronze Star. Mem. Am. Psychol. Assn., Am. Assn. Sex Educators, Counselors and Therapists (cert. sex therapist), Mich. Psychol. Assn., Western Mich. Psychol. Assn. Author: The Art of Empathy, 1975, Empathie, 1978. Home: 6738 Rothbury St Portage MI 49002 Office: Western Mich U 3102 Sangren Hall Kalamazoo MI 49008

BULLOCK, JOHN DAVID, ophthalmic surgeon; b. Cin., July 31, 1943; s. Joseph Craven and Emilie Helen (Woide) B.; m. Gretchen Hageman, June 25, 1966; children: John David Jr., Katherine Ann, Richard Joseph. AB, Dartmouth Coll., 1965, BMS, 1966; MD, Harvard U., 1968; postgrad. Armed Forces Inst. Pathology, 1970; MS in Microbiology and Immunology, Wright State U., 1982. Diplomate Am. Bd. Ophthalmology. Intern, asst. in medicine Washington U., St. Louis, 1968-69; resident in ophthalmology and plastic surgery Yale U., 1971-74, clin. instr. ophthalmology, 1974; Heed fellow U. Calif., San Francisco, 1974-75; Orbital fellow Mayo Clinic, Rochester, Minn., 1975; clin. instr. ophthalmology Stanford (Calif.) U., 1974-75, U. Cin. Coll. Medicine, 1976-79; assoc. prof. plastic surgery, microbiology and immunology, Wright State U. Sch. Medicine, 1975-84, prof. ophthalmology and plastic surgery, 1986—, chmn. dept. ophthalmology, 1984—; asst. clin. prof. ophthalmology Ohio State U. Sch. Medicine, 1981-85; lectr. law and medicine U. Dayton Law Sch., 1981—; practice medicine specializing in ophthalmic surgery, Dayton, Ohio; mem. staff Miami Valley Hosp., Children's Med. Ctr., Kettering Med. Ctr., St. Elizabeth Hosp., Good Samaritan Hosp., Sycamore Med. Ctr. Mem. editorial bd. Jour. Ophthalmic Plastic & Reconstructive Surgery; also articles. Trustee Children's Med. Ctr., Dayton, 1977-80; bd. dirs. Lions Eye Bank W. Cen. Ohio, 1982—. Served to lt. M.C., USNR, 1969-71. Recipient numerous profl. awards. Fellow Am. Acad. Facial Plastic and Reconstructive Surgery; mem. Am. Assn. Ophthalmology, Am. Acad. Ophthalmology, ACS, AMA, Am. Coll. Cryosurgery, Am. Soc. Ophthalmic Plastic and Reconstructive Surgery, Am. Assn. Pediatric Ophthalmology and Strabismus, Assn. for Research Vision and Ophthalmology, Keratorefractive Soc., Am. Soc. Ophthalmic Ultrasound, Am. Intraocular Implant Soc., Orbit Soc., Internat. Soc. Orbital Disorders, Internat. Corneal Soc., Internat. Neuro-Ophthalmology Soc., Castroviejo Soc., Frank Walsh Soc., Soc. Heed Fellows, Ocular Microbiology and Immunology Group, Soc. of Geriatric Ophthalmology, Internat. Oculoplastic Soc., Am. Soc. Microbiology, Am. Soc. Laser Medicine and Surgery, Am. Ophthal. Soc., Soc. Eye Surgeons, Soc. Cosmetic Surgeons, Am. Soc. Law and Medicine, Am. Assn. Ophthalmic Pathologists, Theobald Soc., Sigma Xi. Clubs: Dayton Country, Dayton Racquet, Miami Valley Hunt and Polo. Home: 1155 Ridgeway Rd Dayton OH 45419

BULLOCK, RICHARD LAYNE, tax accountant; b. Smithville, Ohio, Mar. 9, 1955; s. Robert Dwayne and Betty Jean (Norris) B. BS, Southwest Mo. State U., 1978. CPA, Mo. Tax mgr. Ernst and Whinney, Kansas City, Mo., 1979-85, Laventhol and Horwath, Kansas City, 1985—. Mem. Am. Inst. CPA's, Mo. Soc. CPA's (taxation com.), Nat. Health Lawyers Assn., Health Care Fin. Mgrs. Assn. Methodist. Club: Kansas City. Home: 5100 Foxridge Mission KS 66202 Office: Laventhol and Horwath 920 Main Kansas City MO 64105

BULMAHN, FREDRICK WAYNE, accounting executive; b. Decatur, Ind., Sept. 10, 1940; s. Herman Carl and Martha Louise (Schroeder) B.; m. Jeannie L. Karshick, Jan. 27, 1963; children: Wayne, Erik, Lora. BA, Valparaiso U., 1962. CPA, Ill., Va., D.C. Internal revenue agt. IRS, Washington and South Bend, Ind., 1962-67; tax mgr. Stoy, Malone & Co., Bethesda, Md., 1967-70; mgr. corp. ops. Telco Leasing Co., Chgo., 1970-72; mng. ptnr. Bulmahn, Ulbrich & Corbett, Arlington Heights, Ill., 1972—; sponsor, speaker tax seminars 1979—. v.p. fin. St. Paul Luth. Ch., Mt. Prospect, Ill., 1979-80, chmn. 1981-82. Mem. Am. Inst. CPA's, Ill. Soc. CPA's. Republican. Lutheran. Club: Meadow (Rolling Meadows, Ill.). Avocations: tennis, gardening, boating, fishing. Office: Bulmahn Ulbrich & Corbett PC 515 E Golf Rd #103 Arlington Heights IL 60056

BULMASH, JACK MARTIN, internist; b. Chgo., May 31, 1946; s. Louis and Beatrice (Cohen) B. Student, U. Ill., Chgo., 1963-66, MD, 1970. Diplomate Am. Bd. Med. Examiners. Intern U. Ill. Hosp., Chgo., 1970-71, resident in internal medicine, 1972-75, attending physician, 1975-78; asst. prof. internal medicine Rush Med. Coll., Chgo., 1978—; asst. to assoc. attending physician internal medicine Rush-Presbyn. St. Luke's Med. Ctr., Chgo., 1978-86, sr. attending physician internal medicine, 1986—; asst. in internal medicine U. Ill. Coll. Medicine, 1970-71, instr. internal medicine, 1973-74; mem. infections com. U. Ill. Hosp., com. on student appraisal, com. student progress, chmn. JRB med. records com., asst. chmn. med. care evaluation com.; lectr. Ctr. Applied Gerontology, 1985, Cook County Grad. Sch. Medicine;asst. med. dir. Johnston R. Bowman Ctr., 1978-82, assoc. med. dir., 1982—. Contbr. articles to profl. jours. Served to capt. U.S. Army, 1971-73, Vietnam. Recipient Upjohn award, 1970. Fellow ACP; mem. Am. Geriatric Soc., Chgo. Geriatric Soc. (founding), Chgo. Soc. Internal Medicine, Gerontol. Soc. Am., Met. Coalition on Aging (steering com.). Office: Rush Presbyn St Lukes Med Ctr 1725 W Harrison Chicago IL 60610

BULTEMA, HARRY J. R., minister; b. Grand Rapids, Mich., Feb. 29, 1936; s. Harry and Magdalena (Potter) B.; m. Janice Bernice Ebels, Aug. 7, 1959; children: Deborah Faith, Timothy James, Stephen John. BA, Grace Bible Coll., Grand Rapids, 1961; M of Div., Covenant Theol. Sem., St. Louis, 1974. Ordained to ministry Bible Ch., 1963, Grace Gospel Fellowship. Pastor Berean Bible Ch., Cadillac, Mich., 1962-66, Alton, Ill., 1966-74; pastor Highland Hills Bible Ch., Lombard, Ill., 1974-76, Community Bible Ch., Grandville, Mich., 1977—; bd. dirs. Grace Ministries, Internat., Grand Rapids, 1968—, Grace Youth Camp, Mears, Mich., 1985—. Served with USN, 1955-57. Republican. Home: 7552 Astronaut St Jenison MI 49428 Office: Community Bible Ch PO Box 52 Grandville MI 49418

BUMAGIN, VICTORIA EDITH WEROSUB, social services executive; b. Free City of Danzig, June 20, 1923; d. Isaac A. and Zinaida (Towbin) Werosub; came to U.S., 1938, naturalized, 1941; B.A., City U. N.Y., 1945; M.S. Social Work, Columbia U., 1969; postgrad. U. Chgo., 1974—; m. Victor I. Bumagin, Mar. 16, 1946; children—Louisa, Susan, Elizabeth, Deborah, Jennifer. Caseworker to intake supr. to case supr. N.J. Bur. Children's Services, 1962-69; sr. social worker Dept. Social Services, Berkshire, Eng., 1970-73; dir. social services Council for Jewish Elderly, Chgo., 1974—; dir. Ctr. Applied Gerontology; assoc. prof. Loyola U., Chgo.; instr. Summer Inst., U. Chgo., univ. sr. clin. assoc.; cons. on aging issues; pvt. practice adult counseling and psychotherapy; mem. Task Force on Age Discrimination, Ill. State Task Force on Older Women; manifesto for Brit. Nat. Conf. on Aging, 1971-73; mem. tech. adv. com. Protective Service to Aged, 1977—; spl. advisor White House Conf. on Aging, 1981. Bd. dirs. ctr. for Applied Gerontology; pres. Children's Mus. Met. Chgo. Fellow Gerontol. Soc. Am.; mem. Soc. for Life Cycle Psychology, Nat., Brit. (sec., v.p.) assns. social workers, Columbia U. Sch. Social Work Alumni Assn. (dir.), Acad. Certified Social Workers, Registry Clin. Social Workers. Author: The Appliance Cookbook, 1971; co-author: Aging Is a Family Affair, 1979; also articles in profl. jours. Home: 1224 North Branch Dr Wilmette IL 60091 Office: 1015 W Howard St Evanston IL 60202

BUMB, JAMES FREDERICK, reliability engineer; b. Evansville, Ind., May 18, 1954; s. John Louis and Betty May (Roeder) B. BME, Purdue U., 1976; MBA, Ind. U., Indpls., 1981. Registered profl. engr., Ind. Mfg. engr. Ford Motor Co., Indpls., 1977-81; reliablility engr. Detroit Diesel Allison, Indpls., 1981—. Mem. Soc. Mfg. Engrs. Avocations: running, triathlons. Office: Detroit Diesel Allison PO Box 894 M44A Indianapolis IN 46206

BUMBLAUSKAS, PAUL DANIEL, controller; b. Chgo., June 8, 1957; s. Joseph J. and Alberta R. (Gosnell) B.; m. Denise L. Kitching, Jan. 19, 1979; children: Daniel, Lisa, Michael. AA, Moraine Valley Coll., Palos Hills, Ill., 1976; BS in Acctg., U. Ill., Chgo., 1981. CPA, Ill.; lic. pub. acct., Ill. Staff auditor Arthur Andersen & Co., Chgo., 1981-82, 1982-83; sr. acct. Edward Hines Lumber Co., Chgo., 1983, mgr. corp. acctg., 1984-85, controller, 1985—, trustee retirement trust, hourly employees' pension plan, salaried pension plan, 1985—; mem. profit sharing trust com. Kindt Corp., Chgo., 1986—. Supporting mem. Chgo. Zool. Soc., 1984—; bd. dirs. The Ehlco Found., Chgo. 1985—. Cert. Achievement award Nat. Alliance Bus., 1981. Mem. Am. Inst. CPA's, Nat. Assn. Accts., Inst. Cert. Mgmt. Accts. (cert.). Republican. Roman Catholic. Avocations: biking, travel, computers. Home: 14445 S Brentwood Orland Park IL 60462 Office: Edward Hines Lumber Co 200 S Michigan Chicago IL 60604

BUMGARDNER, RENA JEWELL, psychotherapist; b. Athens, Tex., Nov. 28, 1940; d. Willie and Eula Ellen (Bass) Jewell; m. Thomas Arthur Bumgardner, Aug. 25, 1962; children—Melody, Susan, Judy. Student Tex. Woman's U., 1959-62; B.S. with honors, U. Minn., 1964, M.S.W., 1966. Instr. sociology, social work U. Wis.-Superior, 1966-67; family therapist Duluth (Minn.) Family Services, 1967-68; clin. social worker Human Resource Center of Douglas County, Superior, 1970-82, exec. dir., 1982-87, psychotherapist Dept. Psychiatry Duluth (Minn.) Clinic, 1987—. Chmn. bd. dirs. Children's Corner Day Care, Superior, 1975-77; bd. dirs. Spectra, Inc., Duluth, 1983-85; mem. Superior Community Housing Resource Bd., 1985-87. Mem. Nat. Assn. Social Workers, Acad. Cert. Social Workers, Am. Bus. Women's Assn. (charter chpt. woman of yr. 1984), Nat. Assn. Female Execs., Mental Health Assn. (dir. 1982—). Democrat.

BUMGARNER, DANIEL HARRY, fish and wildlife administrator; b. Grand Rapids, Minn., Oct. 21, 1939; s. Cecil J. and Viola E. (Walsh) B.; m. Barbara A. Daigle, Sept. 3, 1960; children: Marc D., Susan A., Lisa M. BS in Zoology, Hamline U., 1961; postgrad. in fisheries, U. Minn., 1960-61. Fisheries service tng. Marion, Ala., 1963-64; hatchery mgr. U.S. Fish & Wildlife Service, Wytheville, Va., 1966-68; asst. region supv. U.S. Fish & Wildlife Service, Atlanta, 1968-73; chief br. prodn. and distbn. U.S. Fish & Wildlife Service, Washington, 1973-74; program analyst U.S. Fish & Wildlife Service, Denver, 1974-76; asst. area mgr. U.S. Fish & Wildlife Service, East Lansing, Mich., 1976-78; asst. region dir. U.S. Fish & Wildlife Service, Twin Cities, Minn., 1978-80, dep. asst. region dir., 1980—. Mem. Am. Fisheries Soc. (pres. so. div. trout com. 1974-75). Roman Catholic. Club: Valley Athletic Assn. Lodge: Ruritan (pres. Max Meadows, Va. chpt. 1967-68). Avocations: fishing, soccer coaching, racquetball, Christmas tree farming, hunting. Home: 1201 Echo Dr Burnsville MN 55337 Office: US Fish & Wildlife Service Fed Bldg Ft Snelling Saint Paul MN 55111

BUMGARNER, KATHLEEN ANN MILLER, telephone company director; b. Ottumwa, Iowa, Aug. 23, 1948; s. Harold Leroy and Beverly Laverne (Weems) Miller; m. Timothy Neal Hyde, Sept. 10, 1966 (div. Feb. 1978); 1 child, Kimberly Ann; m. Marvin Dean Bumgarner, Nov. 7, 1980. BA, U. Iowa, 1972. Sales supr. Northwestern Bell, Des Moines, 1976-82, staff supr., 1982-84, market supr., 1984-85; prodn. mgr. Northwestern Bell, Mpls., 1985—. Mem. NOW, Telephone Pioneers Am. (Community Service award 1985), Speakers Bur., U.S. West Women. Democrat. Office: Northwestern Bell 733 Marquette Room 515 Minneapolis MN 55402

BUMGAURDNER, LARRY THOMAS, osteopath; b. Ft. Worth, Tex., Aug. 28, 1954; s. George Thomas and Jennie Louis (Ramsey) B.; m. Darlene Katherine Altwies, July 26, 1975 (div. Sept. 1985); children: Heather Marie, Erik Scott, Kent Joseph. AA, Weatherford Jr. Coll., 1974; BS, U. Tex., Arlington, 1976; DO, Tex. Coll. Osteo. Medicine, 1981. Intern Riverside Hosp., Wichita, Kans., 1981-82; gen. practice osteo. medicine Wichita, 1982—; med. dir. New Horizons, Valley Ctr., Kans., 1981—. Fellow Am. Osteo. Medicine, Soc. for Creative Anachronism (Kings Champion 1986). Avocations: medieval combat, metal working, woodworking. Home: 4526 W 12th St Wichita KS 67212 Office: NW Gen Practice 759 N West St Wichita KS 67203

BUMP, WILBUR NEIL, lawyer; b. Peoria, Ill., July 12, 1929; s. Wilbur Earl and Mae (Nelson) B.; m. Elaine Bonneval, Nov. 24, 1951; children—William Earl, Jeffrey Neil, Steven Bonneval. B.S., State U. Iowa, 1951, J.D., 1958. Bar: Iowa 1958. Solicitor gen. Iowa Atty. Gen.'s Office, Des Moines, 1961-64; practice in Des Moines, 1964—; gen. counsel Iowa Luth. Hosp. Served with USAF, 1951-54. Mem. ABA, Iowa Bar Assn. (bd. govs. 1976-81, chmn. agrl. law com. 1982—), Polk County Bar Assn. (pres. 1976-77). Presbyterian. Club: Kiwanis (pres. 1974-75). Home: Route 2 Winterset IA 50273 Office: 2829 Westown Pkwy Suite 100 West Des Moines IA 50265

BUNCH, RICHARD ADDISON, clergyman; b. Springfield, Mo., Oct. 28, 1940; s. Clyde A. and Elsie Fern (Bird) B.; m. Kay Ann Burtch, Sept. 12, 1962; children: Kerby, Amy. AB, Graceland Coll., 1962; MS, Ind. U., 1965, D of Recreation, 1971; postgrad., St. Paul's Sem., 1979-80. Ordained high priest Reorganized Ch. Jesus Christ Latter Day Sts. Dist. youth leader Reorganized Ch. Jesus Christ Latter Day Sts., Chgo., 1966-69, Nauvoo, Ill., 1969-71; tech. advisor Reorganized Ch. Jesus Christ Latter Day Sts., Papeete, French Polynesia, 1971-73; regional youth commr. Reorganized Ch. Jesus Christ Latter Day Sts., Macomb, Ill., 1974-79; chaplain Graceland Coll., Lamoni, Iowa, 1980—; bd. dirs. Midwest Coll. Retreat, Stewartsville, Mo., 1981—; mem. camping task force Reorganized Ch. Jesus Christ of Latter Day Sts., Independence, Mo., 1982—. Contbr. articles to profl. jours. Mem. Lamoni Park Bd., 1981—; mem. bd. Community Counseling Service, Lamoni, 1982—. Mem. Nat. Assn. Coll. and Univ. Chaplains, Nat. Rccreation and Park Assn. (chmn. Recreation and Religion Com. 1974-79), Soc. Park and Recreation Educators (bd. dirs. 1977). Lodge: Lions. Avocations: tennis, golf, adventure programming, camping, canoeing. Office: Graceland Coll PO Box 1493 Lamoni IA 50140

BUNDY, BLAKELY FETRIDGE, educator, writer; b. Chgo., Aug. 31, 1944; d. William Harrison and Bonnie Jean (Clark) Fetridge; m. Harvey Hollister Bundy III, Aug. 20, 1966; children—H. Hollister IV, Clark Harrison, Elizabeth Lowell, Reed Fetridge. B.A. cum laude, Wheaton Coll., Mass., 1966; M.Ed., Nat. Coll. Edn., 1985. Tchr. Norwich (Vt.) Kindergarten, 1966-67, WillowWood Pre-Sch., Winnetka, Ill., 1983—, bd. dirs., 1972-81, adv. bd., 1981-83; bd. dirs. North Ave. Day Nursery, Chgo., 1970-76; accreditation system validator Nat. Acad. Early Childhood Programs, 1986—. Author pamphlets: What an Executive Should Know About Industry Sponsored Day Care, 1984, What an Executive Should Know About Child Care Services, 1985; contbr. articles to Chgo. Tribune, Redbook, Glamour mags., Dartnell Inst. Bus. Research Jour., other publs. Mem. United Rep. Fund, Chgo., 1968—; active N.E. Ill. council Boy Scouts Am., 1976-80, 85—, Ill. Shore council Girl Scouts U.S.A., 1981—, Friends of Our Cabaña Com., Cuernavaca, Mexico, 1986—. Mem. World Assn. Girl Guides and Girl Scouts, Olive Baden-Powell Soc., Chgo. Assn. Edn. Young Children (steering com. Near North Suburban div. 1986—). Episcopalian. Clubs: Indian Hill (Winnetka); Stevensville (Mich.) Yacht. Avocations: golf, sailing. Office: Willow Wood Pre-School 1255 Willow Rd Winnetka IL 60093

BUNGE, JOHN ARTHUR, market research co. exec.; b. Elgin, Ill., Mar. 14, 1941; s. Arthur August and Gracia Vinina (Webster) B.; B.S. in Mktg. Mgmt., Northwestern U., 1963; m. Barbara Jean Nall, Aug. 28, 1972; 1 son, Jason Todd. Research analyst Ben Franklin div. City Products Corp., Des Plaines, Ill., 1965-68; mgr. mktg. services Cargill, Wilson & Acree, Richmond, Va., 1968-70; dir. mktg. services Glenn Advt., Dallas, 1970-72; v.p. Message Factors, Inc., Dallas, 1972-74, Atlanta, 1974-75; sr. project dir. Britt and Frerichs, Inc., Chgo., 1975-76, br. mgr. and sr. project dir., Denver, 1976, gen. mgr., Chgo., 1977-78; partner Britt Mktg., Evanston, Ill., 1978-79; pres. Legal Mktg. Research, Inc., Evanston, 1979—; speaker at assn. meetings, seminars. Served with USN, 1963-65. Mem. Am. Mktg. Assn., Mktg. Research Assn., Council Am. Survey Research Orgns., United Comml. Travelers Am. Home and office: 1606 Central St Evanston IL 60201

BUNGE, ROBERT PIERCE, language educator; b. Oak Park, Ill., Sept. 24, 1930; s. George Herbert and Caroline Elizabeth (Pierce) B.; M.A., Roosevelt U., 1973; Ph.D., DePaul U., 1982; m. Muriel Perlman, Mar. 17, 1956; stepchildren—Harmon Berns, Hilary Berns. Tchr. adult evening sch. Maine Twp., Park Ridge, Ill., 1962-74; with Bunge Movers, Evanston, Ill., 1968-72; lectr. Roosevelt U., Chgo., 1971, 73, 75, 77, DePaul U., Chgo., 1974-79; prof. Lakota (Sioux Indian lang.), U. S.D., Vermillion, 1979—; cons. in Russian lang. and Indian culture States of S.D., Iowa and Nebr.; ct. interpreter for Lakota lang. Lectr., women's groups, bus. groups; commencement speaker North Shore Country Day Sch., Winnetka, Ill., 1974; convocation speaker Morningside Coll., 1984. Served with AUS, 1952-54; PTO. Mem. Internat. Platform Assn., Am. Philos. Assn., Theosophical Soc., Siouan and Caddoan Linguistic Soc., Rocky Mountain Lang. Soc. Author: Sioux Language Phrase Book, 1976; An American Urphilosophie, 1983; contbg. author: Sioux Collections, 1982, Dakota Children's Dictionary and Coloring Book, 1987; contbr. articles to profl. jours. Home: 6 Cherrywood Ct Vermillion SD 57069 Office: Dept Modern Langs U SD Vermillion SD 57069

BUNGER, GARY MICHAEL, dentist; b. Chgo. Heights, Ill., Oct. 16, 1954; s. Charles Henry and Jane Ann (Haight) B.; m. Carole Agnes Sieracki, Nov. 27, 1976 (div. Nov. 1979). BA, St. Mary's Coll., Winona, Minn., 1976; DMD, So. Ill. U., Edwardsville, 1980. Resident gen. dentistry U. Chgo., 1980-81; gen. practice dentistry Collinsville, Ill., 1981—; asst. prof. dentistry So. Ill. U., Alton, 1981-85. Mem. ADA, Ill. State Dental Assn., Madison Dist. Dental Soc., Acad. Gen. Dentistry, So. Ill. U. at Edwardsville Dental Alumni Assn. (pres. 1986—). Roman Catholic. Club: Harbor Point Yacht (St. Louis). Avocations: sailing, flying. Home: 2 Mamie Alton IL 62002-6023 Office: 109 E Clay Collinsville IL 62234

BUNGERT, MICHAEL G., reinsurance executive, broker; b. Chgo., Feb. 23, 1955; s. Gerard J. and Doriene (Sesterhenn) B.; m. Patricia M. Koziol, July 28, 1979; children: Michael G. Bungert Jr., Casandra M. Grad., Ill. State U., Normal, 1977. Underwriting trainee CNA Ins. Cos., Chgo., 1977-79; reins. underwriter CNA Ins. Cos., London, 1979-81; reins. mgr. CNA Ins. Cos., Chgo., 1981-84; v.p. reins. broker Thomas A. Greene Inc., Chgo., 1984-86, sr. v.p. reins. broker, 1986—. Republican. Roman Catholic. Avocations: golf, collecting port wines. Home: 234 Surrey Ln Lake Forest IL 60045 Office: Thomas A Greene Inc 440 South La Salle St Suite 2600 Chicago IL 60605

BUNGUM, JOHN LEWIS, economist, educator; b. Kasson, Minn., Dec. 17, 1942; s. Gustav Norman and Elsie Charlotte (Throndson) B.; m. Lorna Jean Thiesen, Aug. 13, 1977; children: John Lewis II, Bethany Lorna. BA, Luther Coll., Decorah, Iowa, 1963; MA, U. Iowa, 1969; PhD, U. Nebr., 1977. From instr. to assoc. prof. econs. U. Wis., Platteville, 1969-79; assoc. prof. econs. Gustavus Adolphus Coll., St. Peter, Minn., 1979—, chmn. dept. econs. and mgmt., 1984—, chmn. faculty senate, 1983-85; instr. U. Wis. Liberal Arts Center, Copenhagen, 1973. Contbr. articles to profl. jours. Served with USAR, 1964-67, Vietnam. Govt. of Norway scholar, summer 1963, U. Iowa scholar, 1968-69; U. Nebr. fellow, 1974-76, Inst. European Studies fellow, 1983, Bush Found. Leadership fellow, 1986, Inst. for Ednl. Mgmt. fellow, Harvard U., 1986. Mem. Am. Econ. Assn., AAUP, Midwest Econ. Assn., Western Econ. Assn., Atlantic Econ. Assn., Assn. Am. Colls., Minn. Econ. Assn. Lutheran. Home: 841 Church St Saint Peter MN 56082 Office: Gustavus Adolphus Coll Dept Econs Saint Peter MN 56082

BUNKER, DOUGLAS A., insurance sales executive; b. South Bend, Ind., Oct. 24, 1962; s. Donald Louis and Josephine Helen (Ferguson) B. Salesman United Am. Ins. Co., Otsego, Mich., 1982—, Mutual Protective Ins. Co., Otsego, Mich., 1982—. Office: 540 S Farmer St Otsego MI 49078

BUNNELL, SANDRA JEAN, public relations executive; b. Detroit, Mar. 1, 1945; d. David Victor and Renee (Choate) Addy; m. Richard Bunnell, Oct. 5, 1968 (div. Aug. 1972). Diploma, Centros Europeos de Lenguas y Cultura, Barcelona, Spain, 1966; BA, Wayne State U., 1967. Columnist Detroit Free Press, 1973-77; writer Anthony M. Franco, Detroit, 1976-77, copy dir., account exec., 1978-80; v.p. consumer accounts PR Assocs., Detroit, 1980-83; v.p. pub. relations Berline Group, Birmingham, Mich., 1983-84; pres. Bunnell & Co., Farmington Hills, Mich., 1984-87; pvt. practice communications cons. Detroit, 1987—, designer, jeweler, 1987—. Assoc. editor Contemporary Authors, 1972-73. Active Leadership Detroit, 1982-83; trustee Franklin Wright Settlements, Detroit, 1983—, 2d v.p., 1987—; mem. small bus. adv. council Congressman Sander Levin, 1986. Recipient commendation Community Relations Report, 1980. Mem. Pub. Relations Soc. Am., Women In Communications (pres. Detroit chpt. 1985-86, chmn. nat. pay equity com. 1986—). Club: University (Detroit). Avocations: fashion design, yoga, metaphysics.

BUNTING, NANCY ANN, psychologist; b. San Antonio, Tex., July 10, 1952; d. Bruce Brown Bunting and Floy Louise (Myers) Kroeplin; m. Elmer Thomas Sisk, Apr., 1975 (div. May 1978); m. Daniel Roth Hansen, Jr., Oct. 31, 1981; 1 child, Coreane Louise Hansen. Student, Rice U., 1970-72; BA with honors, U. N.C., 1975; MA, U. Ill., Chgo., 1980, PhD, 1983. Lic. psychologist, Wis., Ill. Intern Hines VA Hosp., 1979-80, Rush-Presbyn. St. Luke's Hosp., Chgo., 1981-82; instr. Northeastern Ill. U., Chgo., 1982; researcher dept. med. oncology Rush-Presbyn. St. Luke's Hosp., Chgo., 1983-84; pvt. practice Walworth, Wis., 1983—; psychologist Lake County Dept. Health, Waukegan, Ill., 1984-85, Meml. Hosp. for McHenry County, Woodstock, Ill., 1987—. Mem. Ill. Psychol. Assn., Am. Psychol. Assn., Phi Beta Kappa, Psi Chi, Pi Delta Phi. Office: Walworth Family Med Ctr Walworth WI 53184

BUNTON, THOMAS RICHARD, dentist; b. Colorado Springs, Colo., June 8, 1944; s. Richard Lee and Martha Maxine (Lindley) B.; m. Anne DeArmond, Aug. 24, 1968; children: David Richard, Christopher Drew. AB, U. Mo., 1966; DDS, U. Mo., Kansas City, 1970. Gen. practice dentistry Nevada, Mo., 1973—; staff dentist Moore-Few Nursing Home, Nevada, 1975—, Nevada (Mo.) Manor, 1975—. Mem. bd. edn., Nevada, 1975-86; mem. Community Council for Performing Arts, Nevada, 1978. Served to capt. U.S. Army, 1970-73. Mem. ADA, Mo. Dental Assn., Southwest Dist. Dental Soc. (bd. dirs. 1978-83), Nevada C. of C. (bd. dirs. 1976-79). Methodist. Lodge: Rotary. Avocations: bridge, hunting, fishing, choral singing. Home: Rt 3 Nevada MO 64772 Office: 425 E Walnut PO Box 575 Nevada MO 64772

BUNTROCK, DEAN LEWIS, waste management company executive. Chmn., chief exec. officer, dir. Waste Mgmt., Inc., Oak Brook, Ill. Office: Waste Mgmt Inc 3003 Butterfield Rd Oak Brook IL 60521§

BUNTZ, ROBERT ARTHUR, JR., real estate development, publishing companies executive; b. Kingston, Pa., Jan. 13, 1952; s. Robert Arthur and Helen (Catanzaro) B. Student Franklin & Marshall Coll., 1970-71, Harvard U., 1972; B.A., Grinnell Coll., 1974. Admissions officer MacAlester Coll., St. Paul, 1974-76; pres. Buntz Devel. Co., St. Paul, 1976-81, River Basin Pub. Co., St. Paul, 1979—; gen. ptnr. Rysdahl, Buntz & Assocs., St. Paul, 1981—; pres. Bluefin Resorts, Inc., Tofte, Minn., 1983—; cons. Boisclair Corp., Mpls., 1984—. Contbr. articles to newspapers. Mem. Dist. 8 St. Paul Planning Council, 1980-82, 86—, Ramsey Hill Assn., St. Paul, 1978—; bd. dirs. St. Paul YMCA, 1987—; cons. Cook County Bd. Commns., Grand Marais, Minn., 1984; bd. dirs. YMCA, St. Paul, 1987—. Mem. Nat. Homebuilders Assn., St. Paul Area Bd. Realtors, Minn. C. of C., Aircraft Owners and Pilots Assn. Avocations: flying; running; cross-country skiing; biking. Office: Rysdahl Buntz & Assocs Suite 300 198 Western Ave N Saint Paul MN 55102

BURANDT, RAYMOND WESTLEIGH, manufacturing engineer; b. Lake Forest, Ill., Feb. 11, 1951; s. Raymond Emil and Jane Augusta (Carlseen) B.; m. Sandra Niemann, May 26, 1973; children: Jason Niemann, Hilde Sue, Chelsae Lynn. BA, Carthage Coll., 1976. Cert. mfg. engr. Indsl. engr. Eaton Corp., Kenosha, Wis., 1977-79; process engr. JI Case/A Tenneco Co., Racine, Wis., 1980-81, advance planning engr., 1981-85; mfg. engr. JI Case/Antenneco Co., Racine, Wis., 1986, mfg. supr., 1986; program mgr. Briggs & Stratton Corp., Milw., 1987—. Mem. Robotics Internat., Soc. Mfg. Engrs., Machine Vision Assn. Lutheran. Avocations: golf, fishing.

BURCH, FREDERICK GENE, engineering executive; b. Rockford, Mich., Nov. 5, 1927; s. Paul Frederick and Sadie Ann (Smith) B; m. Jane Wilmot Raimer, Jan. 8, 1932; children: Sandra, Jennifer, David, Thomas. BME, Mich. State U., East Lansing, 1952. Plant layout engr. Kelvinator, Grand Rapids, Mich., 1955-58; cons. engring. Williams & Works, Grand Rapids, 1958-59; v.p. engring. Wolverine World Wide Inc., Rockford, Mich., 1959—. Mem. Water Resources Commn., State of Mich., 1980-83; active Plainfield Township Planning Commn., Belmont, Mich., 1962; Kent County Solid Waste Study Com., Grand Rapids, 1984. Served to lt. USN, 1953-55. Mem. ASHRAE, ASTM, Am. Water Works Assn., Am. Soc. Plant Engrs., Water Pollution Control Fedn. Republican. Avocations: model boat bldg., sailing, walking, wood working. Home: 2511 Rockhill Dr NE Grand Rapids MI 49505 Office: Wolverine World Wide Inc 9341 Courtland Dr NE Rockford MI 49351

BURCH, HAROLD DEE, educator; b. Vernon County, Mo., Sept. 9, 1928; s. Harry A. and Florence L. (Coonrod) B.; student Fort Scott (Kans.) Jr. Coll., 1947; B.Music Edn., Pittsburg (Kans.) State U., 1950; M.Music Edn., U. Kans., 1964, Ed.D., 1974; m. Dolores Elaine Reilley, Dec. 20, 1958; children—Stephanie Dee, Angela Kay. Music dir. elem. and secondary pub. schs., Kans., 1950-66; instr. dept. fine arts Kellogg Community Coll., Battle Creek, Mich., 1966-68; mem. faculty curriculum and instrn. dept. Mankato (Minn.) State U., 1969—, prof., 1979—, chairperson dept. curriculum and instrn., 1982-87, co-dir. Center for Personal Devel. in Teaching, 1978-83; mem. Minn. State Univ. Bd. Task Force Tchr. Edn., 19^4—. Bd. dirs. United Christian Campus Ctr., Mankato State U., 1982—; mem. adminstrv. bd. Centenary United Meth. Ch. Faculty research grantee, Mankato U., 1972, 78, 82. Asst. dir., Project HEED (U.S. Office Edn. grant project), 1974-77. Mem. Assn. of Tchr. Educators, Assn. for Supervision and Curriculum Devel., Minn. Council on Quality Edn., Minn. Assn. Tchr. Educators (past pres.), Phi Delta Kappa, Phi Mu Alpha Sinfonia. Contbg. author: (curriculum handbook) Humanizing Environment and Educational Development, 1975; mem. editorial bd. coll. edn. jour.; contbr. articles on edn. to profl. publs. Home: 120 Rita Rd Mankato MN 56001 Office: Mankato State Univ PO Box 52 Mankato MN 56001

BURCH, STEPHEN KENNETH, financial services company executive, real estate investor; b. Fairmont, W.Va., Feb. 1, 1945; s. Kenneth Edward and Gloria Lorraine (Wilson) B.; m. Juliana Yuan Yuan, June 17, 1972 (div. Feb. 1985); children: Emily, Adrien. AB in Econs., Washington U., St. Louis, 1969. V.p. TSI Mgmt., Los Angeles, 1970-71; pres. Investors Choice Cattle Co., Los Angeles, 1972-76; v.p. Clayton Brokerage Co., St. Louis, 1976-84; pres. Yuan Med. Lab., St. Louis, 1976-78; v.p. Restaurant Assocs., St. Louis, 1982-83, Am. Capital Equities, St. Louis, 1984—; pres., owner Burch Properties, Inc., St. Louis, 1984—; owner Clayton-Hanley, Inc., St. Louis, 1987—; mng. ptnr. 600 S. Ptnrs., St. Louis, 1976—, Midvale Ptnrs., St. Louis, 1979—. Mem. Sigma Phi Epsilon (pres. alumni bd. 1981—). Avocation: wine. Office: Am Capital Equities 111 W Port Plaza Saint Louis MO 63146

BURCHELL, EDWARD V., manufacturing company executive; b. Chgo., Dec. 26, 1939; s. Edward O. and Marjorie F. (Hathaway) B.; B.A., Hamline U., 1961; m. Mary G. Cossack, Dec. 2, 1961; children—Laurie Ann, Edward R., Susan M. Marketing specialist 3M Co., St. Paul, Minn., 1961-63, sales rep., Louisville, 1963-66, sales rep. converter trades-new products, Cin., 1966-68; mktg./sales specialist Conwed Corp., St. Paul, Minn., 1968-75, sales mgr., 1975-79, mktg. mgr., 1979-81; v.p. Internet, Inc., Mpls., 1981—. Basketball and baseball coach Community Youth Program, 1972-77. Named Outstanding Converter-New Product Salesman, 3M Co., 1967, Outstanding Salesman plastics div. Conwed Corp., 1973, Outstanding Mktg. Contbr., Conwed Corp., 1976. Republican. Methodist. Patentee in field. Office: 2730 Nevada Ave N Minneapolis MN 55427

BURCHETT, JAMES CLARK, minister; b. New Boston, Ohio, Apr. 25, 1932; s. James Harvey and Goldie Blanch (May) B.; m. Carolyn Jeanette Carmichael; children: Cynthia, Michael, Darla, Scott. BA, Anderson (Ind.) Coll., 1955; M of Div., Internat. Sem., 1983, DD, 1985. Ordained to ministry, 1955. Assoc. pastor Second Ch. of God, Springfield, Ohio, 1955-56; pastor First Ch. of God, Concord, N.C., 1956-63, Trinity Ch. of God, Huntington, W.Va., 1963-71, Dayspring Ch. of God, Cin., 1971—; mem. bus. com., exec. council Nat. Office of Ch. of God, 1981—. Author: A Biblical Trace of God's People, 1983, Lessons From a Bird, 1985; bd. pub. Warner Press, 1970-80. Active Cabell County (W.Va.) Bd. Edn., 1968-71; chmn. Conv. Program, Ind., 1965-66; trustee Mid Am. Bible Coll., Okla., 1978-83; vice-chmn. Citizens Concerned for Community Values, Cin., 1986—. Lodge: Kiwanis. Avocations: flying, reading. Office: Dayspring Ch of God 12010 Winston Rd Cincinnati OH 45240

BURCHFIELD, BRUCE ALLEN, bank executive; b. Ft. Dodge, Iowa, Apr. 3, 1947; s. Stanley H. and Bertha (Sampson) B.; m. Mary Ellen Porter, Dec. 15, 1971; children: Shawn, Stewart, Jennifer. BS in Engring., Iowa State U., 1970; MBA, Loyola U., Chgo., 1973. Engr. Reynolds Aluminum, Brookfield, Ill., 1970-73; v.p. First Nat. Bank Chgo., 1973-82; pres. CIRRUS System, Inc., Downers Grove, Ill., 1982—. Mem. Zoning Bd. Appeals, City of Naperville, Ill., 1978—. Mem. Electronic Funds Transfer Assn. (chmn. 1986—). Republican. Methodist. Clubs: Medinah (Ill.) Country; Union League (Chgo.). Avocations: golf, skiing. Home: 320 East Chicago Ave Naperville IL 60540 Office: CIRRUS System Inc 1333 Butterfield Rd Suite 385 Downers Grove IL 60515

BURCHFIELD, JAMES RALPH, lawyer; b. Vincennes, Ind., Feb. 6, 1924; s. James R. and Doris (Marchal) B.; m. Dorothey Alice Underwood, July 31, 1949; children—Susan Burchfield Holliday, J. Randolph, Stephanie D. B.A., Ohio State U., 1947, J.D., 1949. Bar: Ohio 1949, U.S. Supreme Ct. 1960. Sole practice, Columbus, Ohio, 1949-77; ptnr. Burchfield & Burchfield, Columbus, 1978—; pres. Ohio Bar Liability Ins. Co., 1978—, also dir. Exec. dir. Franklin County Eisenhower Orgn., Ohio, 1952; mem. Mayor's Spl. Com. on Transit, Columbus, 1955-58; trustee Columbus Goodwill, 1970; mem. Ohio Soc. Colonial Wars, 1972. Served with USAF, 1943-45. Recipient Outstanding Young Man award Columbus Jaycees, 1956, Mil. Hon. award, Scabbard & Blade, 1948. Mem. Bexley Am. Legion (post comdr. 1954), Columbus Bar Assn., Am. Arbitrator's Assn., ABA, Ohio State Bar Assn. (chmn. 1970—), Am. Jud. Assn., Eastside Bus. Assn. (pres. 1955); fellow Ohio State Bar Found.; mem. Phi Alpha Theta. Republican. Clubs: Sertoma Internat. (pres. 1967), Sertoma Found. (pres. 1977-79). Lodges: Masons (treas. 1952—), Shriners. Avocations: world travel; hiking; fishing; reading. Home: 42 Park Dr Columbus OH 43209 Office: Burchfield & Burchfield 1313 E Broad St Columbus OH 43205

BURDAKIN, JOHN HOWARD, railroad executive; b. Milton, Mass., Aug. 11, 1922; s. L. Richard and M. and Gertrude (Rogers) B.; m. Jean Campbell Moulton, Oct. 2, 1948; children: John Howard, David Campbell, Dan Edward. B.C.E., Mass. Inst. Tech., 1947. Mgr. r.r. div. Panama Canal Co., 1960-61; with Pa. R.R., 1947-68, asst. gen. mgr., 1965-68; with Penn Central R.R., 1968-71, v.p., gen. mgr.; v.p. ops., exec. v.p., then pres. Grand Trunk Western R.R., 1974-85, vice chmn., 1985—; pres. Central Vt. Ry., 1976-85, vice chmn., 1985—; pres. Duluth, Winnipeg & Pacific R.R., 1976-85, vice chmn., 1985—; pres. Grand Trunk Corp., 1976-85, vice chmn., 1985—. Served to 1st lt. C.E. AUS, World War II. Mem. Mich. C. of C. (dir.). Republican. Presbyterian. Clubs: Bloomfield Hills Country, Detroit Athletic, Masons. Office: Grand Trunk Corp 131 W Lafayette Blvd Detroit MI 48226 *

BURDGE, RABEL JAMES, sociology educator; b. Columbus, Ohio, Dec. 14, 1937; s. Alonzo Marshall and Mariam Francis (Prentice) B.; m. Sharon Sue Payne, June 30, 1962 (dec. June 1975); children—Stephanie, Amy, Jill; m. Joyce Loretta Piggush, Aug. 2, 1977. B.S., Ohio State U., 1959, M.S., 1961; Ph.D., Pa. State U., 1965. Asst. prof. sociology U.S. Air Force Acad., Colo., 1966-68; lectr. U. Colo., Colorado Springs, 1966-68; asst. prof. sociology U. Ky., Lexington, 1968-72; assoc. prof. U. Ky., 1972-76; assoc. prof. environ. sociology, rural sociology and leisure study; dept. agrl. econs. and leisure studies U. Ill. Inst. Environ. Studies, Urbana, 1976-80; prof. U. Ill. Inst. Environ. Studies, 1980—; vis. scholar Australian Sch. Environ. Studies, Griffith U., Brisbane, 1983. Author books, including: Social Change in Rural Societies; A Rural Sociology Textbook, 3d edit., 1987; (with E.M. Rogers) Leisure and Recreation Places, 1976; (with Paul Opryszek) Coping with Change: An Interdisciplinary Assessment of the Lake Shelbyville Reservoir, 1981; contbr. numerous articles to profl. publs.; editor Jour. Leisure Research, 1971-74; co-editor, founder Leisure Scis.; an Interdisciplinary Jour., 1977-82, Society and Nat. Resources: An Internat. Social Sci. Jour. Served to capt. arty. U.S. Army, 1965-68. Mem. Am. Sociol. Assn., Rural Sociol. Soc., Midwest Sociol. Assn., Nat. Recreation and Park Assn. (Theodore/Franklin D. Roosevelt award for outstanding research 1982), Internat. Impact Assessment Assn., AAAS, Acad. Leisure Scis. Democrat. Methodist. Home: 2007 Lake Side Ct Champaign IL 61821 Office: 408 S Goodwin Ave Urbana IL 61801

BURDGE, ROBERT EUGENE, savings and loan executive, advertising executive; b. Omaha, Feb. 4, 1942; s. Lloyd Richard and Betty Trier (Rettenmayer) B.; m. Cheryl Lynn Beckman, June 26, 1971; 1 dau., Christina Lynn. B.A. in Speech, U. Nebr.-Omaha, 1964. Mgr. sales promotion dept. Mut. of Omaha, 1969-80; asst. v.p., advt. pub. relations mgr. Comml. Fed. Savs. & Loan, Omaha, 1980—. Served to capt. USAF, 1965-69; lt. col. Nebr. Air N.G. Recipient Commendation award Nat. Premium Sales Execs., Inc., 1982. Mem. Savs. Instn. Mktg. Soc. Am., Pub. Relations Soc. Am. Republican. Presbyterian. Home: 11435 Taylor St Omaha NE 68164 Office: 2120 S 72d St Omaha NE 68124

BURDICK, LOU BRUM, public relations executive; b. Bloomer, Wis., Nov. 4, 1943; d. Francis Albert and Lucille May (Gorton) Peil; m. Allan L. Burdick, Feb. 12, 1981; 1 child, Matthew Francis. Adminstr. Bozell & Jacobs, Mpls., 1965-67; pub. relations mgr. Apache Corp., Mpls., 1967-76; v.p., dir. fin. relations Edwin Neuger & Assocs., Mpls., 1976-78; chmn. bd., chief exec. officer Brum & Anderson Pub. Relations, Inc., Mpls., 1978-86; pres. Padilla, Speer, Burdick & Beardsley, Inc., Mpls., 1987—; bd. dirs. Mpls. Community Bus. Employment Alliance, Spring Hill Ctr., Mpls., Minn. Racetrack, Inc., Mpls. Recipient Outstanding Achievement award for Entrepreneurship, Mpls. YWCA, 1985. Mem. Minn. Women's Econ. Round Table, Nat. Assn. Women Bus. Owners, Pub. Relations Soc. Am. (counselors acad., Pub. Relations Recognition award 1985), Minn. Press Club., Gt. Mpls. C. of C. (bd. dirs.). Republican. Club: Minnekahda Country. Home: 6609 Sally Ln Minneapolis MN 55435 Office: Padilla Speer Burdick & Beardsley Inc 425 Lumber Exch Bldg 10 S 5th St Minneapolis MN 55402

BURDICK, MARY LUELLA, hospital executive; b. Olean, N.Y., Sept. 22, 1929; d. Leone Leslie and Ida Florence (Tompkins) Sturtevant; student public schs.; m. Kenneth Gerald Burdick, Aug. 31, 1946; children—Ronald Leone, Anna Marie, Gerald Ralph. Bookkeeper, cashier Things Shoe Store, Lockport, N.Y., 1954-55; mgr. trainee Joanlee Dress Shop, Lockport, 1958; supr. Syncro Corp., Hicksville, Ohio, 1960-67; various positions Tribune Printing Co., Hicksville, 1969-77; seamstress, Hicksville, 1976-79; mgr. forms, mgmt. Parkview Meml. Hosp., Fort Wayne, Ind., 1979—. Treas., Hicksville Missionary Ch., 1970-80, 82—, past dir. children's group; mem. Nat. Assn. FemalE Execs., Am. Business Women's Assn. Home: 04512 State Route 18 Hicksville OH 43526 Office: Parkview Meml Hosp 2200 Randallia Dr Fort Wayne IN 46805

BURDICK, QUENTIN NORTHROP, U.S. senator; b. Munich, N.D., June 19, 1908; s. Usher Lloyd and Emma (Robertson) B.; m. Marietta Janecky, Mar. 18, 1933 (dec. Mar. 1958); children: Jonathan, Jan, Mary, Jennifer, Jessica; m. Jocelyn Birch Peterson; 1 son, Gage; stepchildren: Leslie, Birch. B.A., U. Minn., 1931, LL.B., 1932. Bar: N.D. 1932. Practiced in Fargo, 1932-58; mem. 86th-100th Congresses, N.D. at large; U.S. senator from N.D. 86th-100th Congresses, 1960—, chmn. Senate environ. and pub. works commn.; candidate for lt. gov., 1942, for gov., 1946, for U.S. senator, 1956. Mem. Sons of Norway, Sigma Nu. Democrat. Congregationalist. Clubs: Mason, Elk, Eagle, Moose. Office: 511 Hart Senate Bldg Washington DC 20510

BURDICK, ROBERT WILLIAM, transportation company executive; b. Cleve., Jan. 25, 1943; s. Joseph Burns and Virginia (Payne) B.; m. Jeanne B. Bolds, Apr. 16, 1967 (div. June 1982); children: Kathy, Karen; m. Sandra Rodgers, June 3, 1983. BS, Northwestern U., 1965; MBA, Ind. U., 1967. Sr. dir. pricing and econs. Ea. Cen. Motor Carriers Assn., Akron, Ohio, 1967-80; sr. v.p. mktg. Yellow Freight System, Inc., Overland Park, Kans., 1980—. Mem. Middlewest Motor Freight Bur. (bd. dirs. 1984—), Regular Common Carrier Conf. (bd. govs. 1984—), Am. Mktg. Assn., Council Logistics Mgmt., Am. Soc. Transp. and Logistics. Republican. Presbyterian. Home: 8911 Catalina Prairie Village KS 66207

BURDITT, NEIL ALAN, manufacturing company executive; b. Newark, Nov. 1, 1940; s. Carleton Meacham and Florence (McCormick) B.; m. Sandra Martine McNeill, July 24, 1970; children: Coleman James, Jennifer Leigh. BS, Pa. State U., 1962; postgrad., U. Mich., 1962-64; PhD, Oxford (Eng.) U., 1967. Assoc. prof. Knoxville (Tenn.) Coll., 1967-68; lab. mgr. Ciba-Geigy Corp., Ardsley, N.Y., 1968-76; tech. mgr. Customcolor, Cumberland, R.I., 1976-77; group leader plastics applications Ferro Corp., Independence, Ohio, 1977—. Mem. Schs. Utilization Com., Shaker Heights, Ohio, 1984-85, Epic Project Selection Com., Akron, Ohio, 1986. Mem. Am. Chem. Soc. Avocations: badminton, golf, bridge, canoeing, birding. Home: 3289 Kenmore Rd Shaker Heights OH 44122 Office: Ferro Corp 7500 E Pleasant Valley Rd Independence OH 44141

BURDON, WILLIAM FONTAINE, advertising executive; b. Ware, Mass., Dec. 21, 1926; s. Paul P. and Dorothy S. (Schaninger) B.; Assoc. B.A., Curry Coll., Boston, 1951; m. Leonora Foronda, Sept. 10, 1954; children—Susan Lee, Linda Marie. With NBC, 1952-54; exec. v.p., creative dir. Marvin Hult & Assos., advt., Peoria, Ill., 1955-61; pres. Burdon Advt., Inc., Peoria, 1962-82; pres. Burdon/Oakley, Inc., Peoria, 1982—. Mem. adv. bd. YWCA. Landmarks Found. Served with U.S. Army, 1945-47. Author published poetry. Home: 1827 W Sunnyview Dr Peoria IL 61614 Office: 2523 W Reservoir Blvd Peoria IL 61615

BURESH, THOMAS GORDON, financial services executive; b. Green Bay, Wis., Oct. 7, 1951; s. Norbert E. and Dorothy M. (Kreilkamp) B.; m. Suzan Lee Rickbeil, Mar. 21, 1980. BBA, U. Wis., 1973. CPA, Wis.; cert. fin. planner. Staff acct. Ernst & Whinney, Milw., 1973-75; sr. acct. Ernst & Whinney, Chgo., 1975-77; ptnr., v.p. Suby, Von Haden & Assocs., Madison, 1977—. Gen. mem. United Way Dane County, Madison, 1984-87; bd. dirs. Arthritis Found., Milw., 1986-87, so. dist. chmn., 1986—. Mem. Am. Inst. CPA's, Wis. Inst. CPA's, Internat. Assn. Fin. Planning, Inst. Cert. Fin. Planners. Roman Catholic. Avocations: reading, sports cars, gardening, woodworking. Home: 7865 E Oakbrook Circle Madison WI 53717 Office: Suby Von Haden & Assocs SC 901 Whitney Way Madison WI 53711

BURESH-REIST, DIANE KAY, pharmacist; b. Cedar Rapids, Iowa, Mar. 21, 1958; d. Edwin Wesley and Martha Mary (Blazek) B.; m. Jeffrey Clark Reist, Mar. 30, 1985. B.S. in Pharmacy, U. Iowa, 1981. Registered pharmacist, Iowa. Sec. Best Plumbing and Heating, Cedar Rapids, 1976-80; staff pharmacist Mercy Hosp., Cedar Rapids, 1980—; relief pharmacist Claxton Pharmacy, Cedar Rapids, 1984-86; staff pharmacist Rockwell Internat., 1986—; pharmacy-nursing liaison Mercy Hosp., Cedar Rapids, 1980-87, pharmacy supr. 1987—. Linn County Speakers Bur. rep., 1982—. Mem. Iowa Pharmacists Assn. (dist. rep. to Ho. of Dels, patient edn. com.), Iowa Soc. of Hosp. Pharmacists. Republican. Presbyterian. Club: Chandon. Avocations: gourmet cooking, skiing, bowling, travel. Home: 1620 Seminole Ave NW #8 Cedar Rapids IA 52405 Office: Mercy Hospital Pharmacy 701 10th St SE Cedar Rapids IA 52403

BURFORD, MARY ANNE, medical technologist; b. Paris, Ark., Aug. 24, 1939; d. Anthony John and Julia Elizabeth (Hoffman) Elsken; B.S. in Biology, Benedictine Coll., 1961; grad. in med. tech. St. Mary's Sch. Med. Tech., 1962; m. Joseph Paul Burford, May 11, 1968 (div. Feb. 1983); children—Sarah Elizabeth, Shawn Anthony, Joseph Paul, Daniel Aaron. Evening supr. St. Vincent's Infirmary, Little Rock, 1962-65; med. technologist Holt-Krock Clinic, Ft. Smith, Ark., 1966-68, Ball Meml. Hosp., Muncie, Ind., 1971-72, Pathologist Assoc., Muncie, 1972-73; chief technologist Ob-Gyn Inc., Muncie, 1975—; instr. microbiology St. Vincent's Infirmary, 1962-65, Sparks Med. Ctr., Ft. Smith, 1966-68. Chmn. liturgical life, St. Mary's Catholic Ch., 1979-86; treas Met. Football League, 1983-85. Mem. Am. Soc. Clin. Pathologists (affiliate mem., registered med. technologist), Am. Assn. Clin. Chemists, Am. Soc. for Microbiology. Club: Muncie Altrusa (chmn. materials and records com., constn. and by-laws com. 1985-86, chmn. community service 1984-85, recording sec. 1986-87, chmn. budget com. 1986-87, bd. liaison to youth services, bylaws, materials and records 1986-87, ways and means com.). Home: 1509 W Buckingham Dr Muncie IN 47302 Office: 2501 W Jackson St Muncie IN 47302

BURG, JAMES ALLEN, state agency administrator, farmer; b. Mitchell, S.D., Apr. 22, 1941; s. Albert Leo and Pearl Margaret (Linafelter) B.; m. Bernice Marie Kaiser, July 22, 1967; children: Jeff, Cory, Casey, Julie, Lisa. BS, S.D. State U., 1963. Fieldman Fed. Land Bank, Yanktown, S.D., 1964-67; farmer Wessington Springs, S.D., 1967—; mem. S.D. Ho. Reps., Pierre, 1975-83, S.D. State Senate, Pierre, 1984-86; pub. utility commr. State of S.D., Pierre, 1987—. Served to maj. USNG, 1963—. Mem. S.D. Retailers Assn. (bd. dirs. 1983—), Jaycees (pres. Wessington Springs chpt.), S.D. C. of C. (bd. dirs. 1983-84), Gamma Sigma Delta. Democrat. Roman Catholic. Lodge: KC. Home and Office: Rt 1 Box X Wessington Springs SD 57382

BURGBACHER, ROBERT JOSEPH, social services adminstrator; b. Hancock, Mich., May 4, 1939; s. Carl Frederick Burgbacher and Helen Mae (Larson) Sower. m. Linda Lou Wilson, May 27, 1962 (div. Mar. 1980); children: Mark Allen, Jon Paul. BS, Ind. State U., 1961, MS, 1968; LHD, Mt. Sinai U., Cin., 1972; MDiv, Christian Theol. Sch., 1965; PhD, Wesley Coll., 1975; D of Ministry, Ind. Christian, 1978. Ordained to ministry Bapt. Ch. Sr. pastor vari(is chs., Indpls., 1960-80; dean Ind. Christian, Indpls., 1978-87; exec. dir. Mary Rigg Neighborhood Ctr., Indpls., 1980—. Mem. Nat. Assn. Social Workers, N.Am Assn. Christian Counselors. Democrat. Baptist. Avocations: reading, traveling, public speaking. Home: 221 E 13th St Indianapolis IN 46202 Office: PO Box 21023 Indianapolis IN 46221-0023

BURGE, DAVID EDWARD, computer scientist; b. South Haven, Mich., Mar. 21, 1944; s. F. Leon and Luedda Imogene Burge; m. Sandra Ann. Krol, Oct. 15, 1966; children: Brian D., Katherine M. AS in Engring., Benton Harbor Jr. Coll., 1964; student, Western Mich. U., 1964-66, 82—. Specialized clk. Gen. Motors Corp., Kalamazoo, 1970-76, supr. inspection, 1976-79, programmer, 1980—. Contbr. photographs to various publs. Served with U.S. Army, 1966-69. Avocations: photography, tennis, computer games, volley ball, water skiing. Home: 6128 Enola Dr Kalamazoo MI 49004 Office: BOC div Gen Motors Corp 5200 E Cork St Kalamazoo MI 49001

BURGE, JOHN LARRY, executive staffing and personnel consultant; b. Mayfield, Ky., June 18, 1918; s. Edwin and Laura (Staten) B.; B.S., U. Kans., 1941; M.A., Villanova U., 1959; postgrad. in mgmt. Stanford U., 1962, U. Mich., 1977; m. Melva I. Grant, 1938; children—Sharon Burge Womack, Penny Burge Johansen. Dir. personnel, public relations and safety Lucky Lager Brewing Co., San Francisco, 1962-66; corp. personnel mgr., dir. pub. relations and safety MJB Coffe Corp., San Francisco, 1966-69; co-owner Ulrich Personnel Agy., Palo Alto, Calif., 1969-70; personnel mgr., area public relations dir. Bechtel Power Corp., Ann Arbor, Mich., 1970-80; exec. staffing cons. Fluor Corp., Irvine, Calif., 1981—, Procon Corp., Des Plaines, Ill., Soil Testing Services, Chgo., Domino's Pizza Corp. Ann Arbor, Mich., Ditty-Lynch & Assocs., Inc., Royal Oak, Mich., 1982—; prof. naval sci. Villanova U., 1956-59; mem. faculty St. Louis Community Coll., 1981—. Airport commr., Ann Arbor, Mich., 1975-77; mem. President's Com. on Handicapped, 1970—; coordinator Explorer Post, Boy Scouts Am. Served to comdr. USN, 1941-62. Decorated Air medal with six oak leaf clusters. Mem. Am. Soc. Personnel Adminstrn., Ann Arbor Personnel Assn. (pres. 1979-80), Navy League, C. of C. (edn. com.). Republican. Baptist. Clubs: Quiet Birdmen, K, Exchange. Middle weight Golden Gloves champion, 1937. Office: 14722 Greenleaf Valley Dr Chesterfield MO 63017

BURGE, JOHN WESLEY, JR., electric manufacturing company executive; b. Mobile, Ala., Sept. 11, 1932; s. John Wesley and Mary Jo (Guest) B.; m. Shirley Paulette Roberts, Mar. 29, 1958; children: John, Delene, Eric, Kurt, Karen. Student, Centenary Coll., San Antonio Coll., UCLA. Various engring. and mgmt. positions ITT Gilfillan, 1954-69; pres., gen. mgr. Rantec, Calabasas, Calif., 1969-71; chmn. bd. Rantec, 1971—; pres., gen. mgr. electronics and space div. Emerson Electric Co., St. Louis, 1971-80; corp. group v.p. govt., def. Emerson Electric Co., 1977—; cons. crisis mgmt., fin. planning for execs., 1975—. Dir. Progressive Youth Center, Presbyterian Ch., 1975—. Served with USAF, 1950-54. Decorated Grand Cordon of Order Al-Istiqlal Jordan). Mem. U.S. Navy League, Air Force Assn., Def. Preparedness Assn., Am. Mgmt. Assn., Air Force Communication and Electronics Assn., Internat. Security Assn. Office: Emerson Electric Co 8100 W Florissant St Saint Louis MO 63136

BURGELIN, JOHN GEORGE, chemical company executive, consultant; b. Phila., Aug. 29, 1944; s. John George and Mary Elizabeth (Little) B.; m. Joanna Faye DuBois, Dec. 28, 1965; children: Jeffrey Todd, Michael Alan, Christopher Scott. Student, Palm Beach Jr. Coll., 1962-64, U. Va., 1968-69. Supr. field Am.-DuBois, Lake Worth, Fla., 1969-72; mgr. territory Winston Industries, Noel, Mo., 1972-74; tech. rep. Nat. Chemsearch, Dallas, 1974-79; owner, operator Tech-Reps, Joplin, Mo., 1979—. Pres. com. for Better Schs., Carl Junction, Mo., 1980. Served as staff sgt. USMC, 1965-69, Vietnam. Republican. Presbyterian. Lodge: Rotary. Avocations: tennis, golf. Home: Rt 3 Box 701 Joplin MO 64801 Office: Tech-Reps N Main St Rt 3 Box 835 Joplin MO 64801

BURGER, HARRY DALLY, dentist; b. Akron, Ohio, Dec. 26, 1928; s. Marvin B. Burger and Thelma V. (Dally) Condell; m. Janet C. Dunbar, Oct. 3, 1953; children: Edith (dec.), Alice, Nancy, Eric. BA, Willenberg U., 1951; DDS, Ohio State U., 1955. Gen. practice dentistry Fremont, Ohio, 1959—. Served to capt. U.S. Army, 1955-57. Mem. N. Cen. Ohio Dental Assn., Chgo. Dental Assn., Toledo Dental Assn. Republican. Episcopalian. Club: Fremont Yacht. Home and Office: 600 3d Ave Fremont OH 43420

BURGER, HENRY G., anthropologist, educator, publisher; b. N.Y.C., June 27, 1923; s. B. William and Terese R. (Felleman) B. B.A. with honors (Pulitzer scholar), Columbia Coll., 1947; M.A., Columbia U., 1965, Ph.D. in Cultural Anthropology (State Doctoral fellow), 1967. Indsl. engr. various orgns. 1947-51, Midwest mfrs. rep., 1952-55; social sci. cons. Chgo. and N.Y.C., 1956-67; anthropologist Southwestern Coop. Ednl. Lab., Albuquerque, 1967-69; assoc. prof. anthropology and edn. U. Mo., Kansas City, 1969-73; prof. U. Mo., 1973—, founding mem. univ.wide doctoral faculty, 1974—; lectr. CUNY, 1957-65; Adj. prof. ednl. anthropology U. N.Mex., 1969; anthrop. cons. U.S. VA Hosp., Kansas City, 1971-72. Author: Ethno-Pedagogy, 1968, 2d edit., 1968; compiler, pub.: The Wordtree, a Transitive Cladistic for Solving Physical and Social Problems, 1984; contbr. to anthologies, articles to profl. jours., cassettes to tape libraries. Mem. editorial bd. Council on Anthropology and Edn., 1975-80. Served to capt. AUS, 1943-46. NSF Inst. grantee, 1970. Fellow AAAS, Internat. Union Anthrop. and Ethnol. Scis., World Acad. Art and Sci., Am. Anthrop. Assn. (life), Royal Anthrop. Inst. Gt. Britain (life); mem. Am. Dialect Soc., Soc. for Linguistic Anthropology, European Assn. for Lexicography, Assn. for Computational Linguistics, Cosmep, Dictionary Soc. N.Am. (life mem.; terminology com.), Assn. internationale de terminologie, Académie européenne des sciences, arts et lettres (corr. mem.), Soc. Conceptual and Content Analysis by Computer, Phi Beta Kappa. Office: The Wordtree 10876 Bradshaw Overland Park KS 66210-1148 Office: U Mo Kansas City MO 64110

BURGER, MARJORIE, financial executive, educator; b. Cleve., Sept. 22, 1951; d. Joseph F. and Elizabeth Alice (Kosmac) Smole; m. Andrew C. Burger, July 19, 1971; children: Rebekah, Ruth. BA, John Carroll U., 1972; MBA, Kent State U., 1980. Bookkeeper Bowman Distbn., Cleve., 1976-79; acct. Gunton Corp., Bedford Heights, Ohio, 1980-83; v.p. fin. Cleve. Hone and Mfg. Co., Eastlake, Ohio, 1983—; instr. Lake Erie Coll., Painesville, Ohio, 1985—. Mem. Am. Soc. Metals. Republican. Episcopalian. Avocation: photography. Office: Cleve Hone & Mfg Co 34560 Lakeland Blvd Eastlake OH 44094

BURGER, MARY LOUISE, psychologist, educator; b. Chgo.; d. Robert Stanley and Margaret Agnes (Brennan) Hirsh; m. William Bronson Burger, Mar. 16, 1968. B.A., Mundelein Coll.; M.Ed., Loyola U.; Ed.D., No. Ill. U., 1972. Tchr. Chgo. Bd. Edn., 1954-68; mem. faculty DePaul U., 1960-61, Roosevelt U., 1967-70; cons. psychologist Worthington-Hurst & Assos., Headstart Program, Chgo., 1972-74; prof. curriculum, instruction dept. early childhood edn. Northeastern Ill. U., 1968—, chmn., 1970-80, coordinator early childhood programs, 1985—; chmn. faculty assembly Coll. Edn; chmn. subcom. Chgo. region White House Conf. on Children, 1979-81; ednl. dir., owner Childhood Edn. Nursery and Day Care Center, Evanston, Ill., 1974-85; cons. Chgo Mayor's Office Child Care Services; ednl. psychologist, counselor Burger Cons., Ltd. Editor: bull. and pamphlets Assn. Childhood Edn. Internat, 1975-77. Chmn. bd. dirs. Univ. Community Care Center. Mem. Assn. Childhood Edn. Internat. (pres. Ill. and Chgo. brs., chmn. nominating com. 1980, tchr. edn. com. 1981—, v.p. exec. bd. 1983-86), Nat. Assn. Edn. Young Children, Assn. Higher Edn., N.W. Assn. Nursery Schs., AAUP, Phi Delta Kappa, Delta Kappa Gamma, Kappa Gamma Int. (alpha chpt. pres. 1974-76). Club: Zonta Internat. (pres. Chgo. Loop 1986—). Home: Fairfax Village 1 Kittery on Auburn Rolling Meadows IL 60008 Office: Northeastern Ill 5500 N St Louis Ave Chicago IL 60025 : Burger Cons Ltd 1699 W Woodfield Rd Schaumburg IL 60195

BURGESS, JAMES EDWARD, newspaper publisher, executive; b. LaCrosse, Wis., Apr. 5, 1936; s. William Thomas and Margaret (Forseth) B.; m. Catherine Eleanor, Dec. 20, 1958; children—Karen E. Burgess Hardy, J. Peter, Sydney Ann, R. Curtis. Student, Wayland Acad.; B.S., U. Wis.-Madison. Pub. Ind. Record, Helena, Mont., 1969-71; pub. Tribune, LaCrosse, Wisc., 1971-74; v.p. newspapers Lee Enterprises, Davenport, Iowa, 1974-81; exec. v.p. Lee Enterprises, 1981-84, dir., 1984-85; dir. Madison Newspapers, Inc., 1975—, pres., 1984—; pub. Wis. State Jour., Madison, 1984—; dir. AP, WNA, Meriter Health Services. Trustee Edgewood Coll., Madison, 1984—. Mem. Inland Daily Press Assn. (pres., chmn. 1982-84), Madison C. of C. (dir. 1985—). Home: 7410 Cedar Creek Trail Madison WI 53717 Office: Wis State Jour 1901 Fish Hatchery Rd Madison WI 53717

BURGESS, JANET HELEN, interior designer; b. Moline, Ill., Jan. 22, 1933; d. John Joseph and Helen Elizabeth (Johnson) B.; student Augustana Coll., Rock Island, Ill., 1950-51, U. Utah, Logan, 1951-52, Marycrest Coll., 1959-60; m. Richard Everett Guth, Aug. 25, 1951; children—John Joseph, Marshall Claude, Linnea Ann Guth Layman Sinclair; m. Milan Andrew Vodick, Feb. 16, 1980. One-person shows: El Pao, Bolivar, Venezuela, 1952-62; represented in pvt. collections, U.S., Europe, S.Am.; producer, designer Playcrafters Barn Theatre, Moline, Ill., 1963-65; designer, gen. mgr. Grilk Interiors, Davenport, Iowa, 1963-87 ; dir. Fine Arts Gallery, Davenport, 1978-84; chmn. bd. Product Handling, Inc., Davenport, 1981—; owner mail order bus. Amazon Vinegar & Pickling Works Drygoods, Davenport. Contbr. articles to profl. jours.; design work featured in Gift & Decorative Accessories mag., 1969, 80, Decor mag., 1979. Bd. dirs. Rock Island Art Guild, 1974—, Quad Cities Arts Council, 1980-84 ; bd. dirs. Village of East Davenport (Iowa) Assn., 1973-84 , pres., 1981; bd. dirs. Neighborhood Housing Services, Davenport, Davenport Area Conv. and Tourism Bur., 1981; mem. adv. bd. interior design dept. Scott Community Coll., 1975—; mem. Mayor's Com. Historic Preservation, Davenport, Iowa, 1976-77, 85—; bd. dirs. retail com. Operation Clean Davenport, 1981; mem. 16th Iowa Civil War Re-enactment Union. Mem. Gift and Decorative Accessories Assn. (nat. merit award 1969), Am. Soc. Interior Designers (asso.), Davenport C. of C., Nat. Trust Historic Preservation, Preservation Group, State Iowa Hist. Soc. Home: 2801 34th Ave Ct Rock Island IL 61201 Office: 2218 E 11th St Davenport IA 52803

BURGESS-CASSLER, ANTHONY, biochemist; b. Manila, Philippines, July 2, 1954; s. Bruce D. and Beverly E. Cassler; m. Karen C. Burgess, Mar. 13, 1976; two children. BA in Chemistry, Valparaiso U., 1975; PhD in Biochemistry, U. Ill., 1983. Research assoc. U. Wis., Madison, 1983—. Contbr. articles to scientific jours. Fellow NIH, 1984-86. Fellow Am. Heart Assn.; mem. Bread for the World. Lutheran. Avocations: photography, stamp collecting. Office: U Wis Dept Molecular Biology 1525 Linden Dr Madison WI 53706

BURGETTE, JAMES MILTON, dentist; b. Toledo, Aug. 18, 1937; s. James Martin and Louise (Milton) B.; A.B., Lincoln U., 1959; D.D.S., Howard U., 1964; m. Carolyn Harris, Aug. 24, 1963; children—Stephanie, James, Ngina. Practice dentistry, Detroit, 1967—. Sec. Wolverine Polit. Action Com., Detroit, 1971—. Mem. Detroit Pub. Sch. Health Council. Bd. dirs. Comprehensive Neighborhood Health Services; mem. coordinating council Black Christian Nationalist Ch.; mem. exec. bd. Congl. Dist., Democratic Party Orgn.; mem. deacon bd. Shrine of Black Madonna; trustee Comprehensive Health Planning Council Southeastern Mich. Served to lt. Dental Corps, USNR, 1964-67. Mem. Nat. Dental Assn. (mem. ho. of dels., parliamentarian 1977), Wolverine Dental Soc. Mich. (editor news jour. 1971; recipient meritorious service award 1972, pres. 1976), Acad. Gen. Dentistry, Am. Profl. Practice Com., Orgn. Black Scientists (v.p. 1979), Howard Alumni Assn. (sec. 1969-70), Am. Legion (exec. bd. Post 77), Chi Delta Mu, Omega Psi Phi. Club: Masons. Home: 1660 Lincolnshire Dr Detroit MI 48203 Office: 23077 Greenfield Rd Southfield MI 48204

BURGGRAAF, LESLIE WAYNE, restaurant owner; b. Sioux Center, Iowa, Mar. 20, 1961; s. William Peter and Geneva (Statema) B.; m. Kimberly Dee Ten Haken, June 20, 1984. AA, Northwest Iowa Tech. Coll., 1981. Asst. mgr. Towne House Restaurant, Rock Valley, Iowa, 1979-82, owner/mgr., 1983—; adv. com. mktg. mgmt. program Northwest Iowa Tech. Coll., 1985—; adv. com. NW Iowa Tech. Coll. Mem. Iowa Restaurant Assn., C. of C., Jaycees (treas. Rock Valley chpt. 1984-86), Rock Valley C. of C. Republican. Lodge: Lions. Home: Rural Rt 2 Box 42 Rock Valley IA 51247 Office: Towne House Restaurant 1523 14th St Rock Valley IA 51247

BURGHER, LOUIS WILLIAM, physician, educator; b. Centerville, Iowa, Oct. 31, 1944; s. Wendell and Dorothy (Probasco) B.; B.S., U. Nebr., 1966, M.D. with honors, 1970, M.Med. Sci., 1972, Ph.D. in Med. Sci., 1978; m. Susan Stephens, May 20, 1979; children—Tanya Jo, Tara Lynn, Lucas William, Rachel Elizabeth. Intern, U. Nebr. Coll. Medicine, 1970-71, resident in internal medicine, 1971-72; practice medicine specializing in pulmonary medicine, Omaha, 1974—; NIH fellow in pulmonary diseases Mayo Grad. Sch. of Medicine, Rochester, Minn., 1972-74, assoc. prof., 1981—, chief sect. pulmonary medicine, 1980-84; clin. research assoc. in pulmonary disease U. Nebr. Coll. of Medicine, 1969-72; med. dir. pulmonary medicine Bishop Clarkson Meml. Hosp., Omaha, 1974—; mem. pulmonary-allergy drugs adv. FDA, 1984-86; Tb cons. to Nebr. Dept. Health, 1972—. Med. dir. Nebr. Opportunity for Vols. in ACTION, 1971-72; trustee Nebr. Found., 1982—. Recipient Upjohn award Nebr. Coll. Medicine, 1970. Diplomate Am. Bd. Internal Medicine, Am. Bd. Pulmonary Medicine. Fellow Am. Coll. Chest Physicians; mem. AMA (council on med. edn. 1973-78, mem. liaison com. on med. edn. 1974-79), Nebr. Med. Assn., Am. Thoracic Soc., Zumbro Valley Med. Soc. (exec. com. 1973-74), Univ. Med. Center House Officers Assn. (pres. 1971-72), Nat. Assn. Med. Dirs. Respiratory Care (pres. 1985-87), Mayo Fellows Assn. (pres. 1973-74), Nat. Acad. Scis. (mem. task force study Inst. Medicine), Nebr. Thoracic Soc. (pres. 1980-81), U. Nebr. Med. Ctr. Alumni Assn. (pres. 1986-88), Alpha Omega Alpha. Contbr. articles on pulmonary disease to profl. jours. Home: Rt 1 Box 273 Fort Calhoun NE 68023 Office: Bishop Clarkson Meml Hosp Dewey Ave and 44th St PO Box 3328 Omaha NE 68103

BURHANS, CHARLES LEONARD, sales professional; b. Appleton, Wis., Apr. 13, 1946; s. Leonard Charles and Ruth Beatrice (Gaffaney) B.; m. Linda Jo Buntrock, June 22, 1968; children: Leah Marie, Emily Jean. BBA, U. Wis., 1968. Regional mgr. Speed Queen, Ripon, Wis., 1968-80; sales mgr. Arkla Industries, Evansville, Ind., 1980-83; nat. sales mgr. Neptune div. Elkay Mfg., Oak Brook, Ill., 1983-86; dir. sales and mktg. Aquaflo div. Elkay Mfg., Oak Brook, 1987—. Active Prince of Peace Luth. Ch., Addison, Ill. Republican. Avocations: restoration of antique cars, handball, camping, fishing. Home: 1733 Stone Ave Addison IL 60101 Office: Elkay Mfg Co 2222 Camden Ct Oak Brook IL 60521

BURICK, JOSEPH PETER, physician; b. Youngstown, Ohio, June 28, 1951; s. Joseph and Carole (Vlasic) B.; m. Jacquelyn Elaine Edgar, June 26, 1980; children—Joseph Timothy, Christina Nicole, Nichole Marie. A.B., Youngstown State U., 1969; D.O., Chgo. Coll. Osteo. Medicine, 1973. Resident in family practice St. Thomas Family Practice Center, Akron, 1977-80, dir. alcohol detoxification unit, 1980-82, chmn. family medicine, 1985—; dir. Summit County Drug Bd., 1982—; emergency rm. physician St. Thomas Hosp. Med. Ctr., Akron, Robinson Meml. Hosp., Ravenna, Ohio, part-time 1980—; mem. staff St. Thomas Hosp., Akron Gen. Med. Ctr., Children's Hosp. Med. Ctr., Akron, Akron City Hosp.; clin. instr. Northeastern Ohio Univs. Coll. Medicine, 1982—; clin. preceptor Kent State U. Coll. Nursing, 1982—; cons. alcoholism and drug abuse Edwin Shaw Hosp. Rehab. Ctr., 1982—. Mem. AMA, Am. Acad. Family Physicians, Summit County Med. Soc., Sigma Sigma Phi. Office: 578 N Main St Akron OH 44310

BURK, DAVID CHARLES, architect; b. Burlington, Iowa, Aug. 14, 1948; s. Charles Patterson and Catherine Ita Burk; m. Deborah Joan Zimmerman; children: Breanne, Caitlyne. BA, Iowa State U., 1971. Registered architect, Kans. Architect T.H.A.M., Wichita, Kans., 1976-79; project architect Law Kingdon, Wichita, 1979-82; ptnr. Breidenthal Burk Ehnen, Wichita, 1982—. Active Big Bros., Big Sisters, Wichita, 1976-79; chmn. Old Town Assn., Wichita, 1984—; chmn. Hist. Landmark Preservation Bd., Wichita, 1983—; mem. State Sites Rev. Bd. Kans., Topeka, 1985—, bd. dirs. YMCA Metro, Wichita, 1982—. Recipient Wichita Leadership 2000, Wichita C. of C., 1986, Hist. Preservation awards Historic Landmark Preservation Com., Wichita, 1983, Preservation award Kans. Preservation Alliance, Topeka, 1983. Mem. AIA (pres. local chpt. 1982, Merit award Topeka chpt. 1984). Republican. Presbyterian. Club: Y's Men, Wichita St. Railway Soc. Home: 431 S Roosevelt Wichita KS 67218

BURK, EDWARD CHARLES, JR., environmental scientist, geologist; b. Ravenna, Ohio, Oct. 9, 1958; s. Edward Charles and Bertha Pearl (Myers) B.; m. Anne Louise Rayner, Nov. 24, 1984. BS in Biology, Bowling Green State U., 1981, MS in Geology, 1983. Cert. chem. waste mgr. Animal behaviorist Sea World Ohio, Aurora, 1984; environ. scientist Jacobs Engring., Rocky River, Ohio, 1984-86; coordinator EPA, Grosse Ile, Mich., 1986—. Mem. Am. Assn. Petroleum Geologists, Delta Tau Delta (v.p. 1979-80). Democrat. Luterhan. Avocations: photography, racquetball, handball, scuba diving. Home: 9326 Whitall Grosse Ile Heights MI 48138 Office: US EPA 9311 Groh Rd Grosse Ile MI 48138

BURK, KEITH EUGENE, management consultant; b. Albion, Mich., May 31, 1941; s. Wilson Eugene and Ruth Elizabeth (Chamberlain) B.; B.S., Western Mich. U., 1969; m. Darlene Carole Nelson, Feb. 2, 1963; children—Linnea Ruth, Eric Eugene. Lab. technician U.S. Plywood (name now Champion Internat.), 1965-67, mgr. tech. engring., 1967-69, tech. service mgr., 1969-70; engring. mgr. Dover Corp., Portage, Mich., 1970-71; engr. A.B. Cassedy & Assos., Ridgefield, Conn., 1971-73, group engr., 1973-74, asst. chief, 1974-76, chief, 1976-80; co-founder KAMACO, Inc., v.p. ops., 1981—. Mem. Kalamazoo Civic Theater, 1973—; cubmaster Boy Scouts Am., 1982—. Served with U.S. Army, 1961-63. Mem. Am. Mgmt. Assn., AIAA, Am. Inst. Indsl. Engrs., Nat. Assn. Profl. Consultants, Am. Security Council. Republican. Christian Scientist. Club: Coterie Dance. Lodge: Rotary. Patentee in field.

BURK, NORMAN, oral surgeon; b. Dallas, Sept. 28, 1937; s. Rubin and Lena (Shodnisky) B.; m. Beverly Rae Hyken, Aug. 27, 1961; children: Ronald S., Steven J. BS, U. Okla., 1959; DDS, U. Mo., Kansas City, 1962. Diplomate Am. Bd. Oral and Maxillofacial Surgery. Resident in oral surgery Kansas City (Mo.) Gen. Hosp., 1965; practice dentistry specializing in oral surgery Kansas City, Mo., 1965—; mem. staff Truman Med. Ctr., Independence Sanitarium and Hosp., St. Joseph Hosp.; chief staff Baptist Meml. Hsop., 1976-77, Menorah Med. Ctr., 1975-85; clin. assoc. prof. U. Mo., Kansas City, 1965-85. Contbr. articles to profl. jours. Bd. dirs. Kehilath Israel Synagogue. Fellow Am. Coll. Oral and Maxillofacial Surgeons, Am. Assn. Oral and Maxillofacial Surgeons; mem. Kansas City Soc. Oral Surgeons (pres. 1974), Mo. Soc. Oral Surgeons (pres. 1979), ADA, Midwestern Mo. and Kansas City Soc. Oral and Maxillofacial Surgeons, Delta Sigma Delta (advisor 1966-74). Club: University Study (pres. 1970). Lodge: B'nai Brith. Avocations: cycling, photography, travel. Home: 8400 Delmar Ln Prairie Village KS 66207 Office: Burk Ennis Wendelburg & Allen 1010 Carondelet Dr Kansas City MO 64114

BURKART, ARNOLD EMIL, music educator; b. Medicine Hat, Alberta, Can., Dec. 23, 1927; Came to U.S., 1945; s. John and Anna Marie (Dressler) B.; m. Dorothy Lucile Conn, Aug. 13, 1950 (div. 1979); children: Connie Arleen Burkart Lively, Bradley Kevin; m. Rebecca Louise Sears, June 12, 1980; 1 child, Laurel Elisabeth. AB, Calif. State U., Fresno, 1951, MA, 1954; EdD, Ind. U., 1973. Music tchr. Fresno County Schs., 1949-61; music cons. Tulare County Supt. of Schs., Visalia, Calif., 1961-63, San Benito Supt. of Schs., Hollister, Calif., 1961-63; supr. music Madera (Calif.) County Supt. of Schs., 1963-67; prof. music edn. Ball State U., Muncie, Ind., 1967—; cons. Ind. State Dept. Edn., Indpls., 1971-72; pres. pubs. Keeping Up With Music Edn., Muncie, 1973—, tour dir., 1977—; bd. dirs. Internat. Gesellschaft Für Musik Pädagogische Fortbildung, Bad Berleburg, Germany, 1978—. Editor jours. Keeping Up With Exptl. Music, 1973-75, Keeping Up With Orff-Schulwerk, 1973-83; contbr. numerous articles to profl. jours. Served to cpl M.I. Corps, U.S. Army, 1949-51. Mem. Music Educators Nat. Conf., Ind. Music Educators Assn. (state bd. dirs. 1980-82), Ind. Elem. Music Educators (pres. 1976-77), Emily Kimbrough Chamber Music Assn. (founder, pres. 1983—), Am. Orff Schulwerk Assn. (pres. 1964-66, hon. mem.), So. Africa Orff Soc. (hon.). Democrat. United Methodist. Avocations: outdoors, reading. Home: 704 E Washington St Muncie IN 47305 Office: Ball State U Muncie IN 47306

BURKE, CHARLES RICHARD, accountant; b. Chgo., June 21, 1949; s. Victor Lark and Virginia Cleta (O'Neil) B.; m. Judith Lynn Wolsic, June 27, 1970; children: Christopher, David, Amanda, Gregory, Laura. BS in Bus. Adminstrn., Marquette U., 1971. CPA, Ill. Staff supr. Robert W. Baird & Co., Milw., 1971-72; staff acct. Miedema, Lemna CPA's, Kankakee, Ill., 1972-77; ptnr. Lemna Burke & Downing, Kankakee, 1977-86; pvt. practice acctg. Kankakee, 1986—. Mem. Ill. CPA Soc., Am. Inst. CPA's, Nat. Assn. Accts. (pres. Kankakee Valley chpt. 1985-86, 86, 87-88, Mem. Achievement award 1986). Home: 61 Briarcliff Ln Bourbonnais IL 60914 Office: Charles R Burke CPA Suite 515 One Dearborn Sq Kankakee IL 60901

BURKE, ELIZABETH H. FERGUSON, speech pathologist; b. Denver, Mar. 19, 1950; d. Herbert Hambright and Helen Evelyn (Myatt) Ferguson; m. James D. Burke, Oct. 20, 1973; children: Jonathan, Benjamin. BS, U. Wis., 1972, MS, 1973. Cert. speech-lang. pathologist. Speech pathologist Easter Seal Metro. Chgo., Oak Park, Ill., 1973-77, East Dubuque (Ill.) Pub. Schs., 1979-86, Mercy Hosp., Dubuque, Iowa, 1986—. Vol. Hospice Dubuque, 1984-86. Mem. Am. Speech Lang. Hearing Assn., Iowa Speech & Hearing Assn., Neurodevel. Treatment Assn. Avocations: needlework, art, reading, swimming, bicycling. Home: 410 N Booth Dubuque IA 52001 Office: Mercy Hosp St Josephs Unit Mercy Dr Dubuque IA 52001

BURKE, EMMETT CHARLES, educator; b. Montgomery, Ala., Jan. 30, 1920; s. William J. and Ethel (Scott) B.; A.B., B.S., Roosevelt U., 1945; M.A., Loyola U., 1953; M.Ed., DePaul U., 1954; O.D., Ill. Coll. Optometry, 1947; m. Sarah Scott, Aug. 14, 1949. Sr. caseworker Ill. Pub. Aid Commn., Chgo., 1948-56; asst. prin. Wm. Carter Pub. Sch., Chgo., 1957—; asst. prof. Nat. Coll. of Edn., Chgo., 1969-85; dir. Washington Pk. YMCA, Afro-Am. Family and Community Services. Active Nat. Urban League, NAACP. Served with USAAF, 1942-45. Certified social worker, Ill. Mem. Nat. Assn. of Black Profs. (dir.), Chgo. African-Am. Tchrs. Assn. (dir.), Chgo. Asst. Prins. Assn. (dir.), Chgo. Council for Exceptional Children (dir.), AAUP, NEA, Phi Delta Kappa, Alpha Phi Alpha. Home: 601 E 32nd St Chicago IL 60616 Office: 5740 S Michigan Ave Chicago IL 60637

BURKE, JOE, professional baseball executive. m. Mary B. Burke; children: Joe, Mary Ann, Jimmy, John, Alice, Bobby, Vincent. From ticket mgr. to bus. mgr. to gen mgr. Louisville Colonels, 1948-60; from asst. gen. mgr. to bus. mgr. to treas. to v.p. Washington Senators (now Tex. Rangers), 1961-73; v.p. bus. Kansas City (Mo.) Royals, 1973-74, exec. v.p., gen. mgr., 1974-81, pres., 1981—; chmn. com. ondivisional play, mem. com. on expansion, schedule, div. of receipts, player relations Am. League. Named Major League Exec. of Yr. Sporting News, 1976; recipient Mr. Baseball award 7th Ann. Kansas City Baseball Award Dinner, 1978. Office: Kansas City Royals Box 1969 Kansas City MO 64141 *

BURKE, JOHN EDWARD, communications educator; b. Huntington, W.Va., Aug. 10, 1942; s. Charles Joseph and Eloise Marie (Sang) B.; B.A., Marshall U., 1965; M.F.A., Ohio U., 1966, Ph.D., Ohio State U., 1971; children—John Lindsey, Elizabeth Ann. Intern, U.S. Ho. Reps., 1960-61; news writer, editor Sta. WSAZ-TV, Huntington, 1962-65; instr. Kent State U., 1966-69; dir. TV Arts dept. Cleve. Summer Sch. for Arts, 1967-68; asst. to dir. Ohio State U. Telecommunications Center, 1969-71; project dir. Ohio Valley Med. Microwave TV System, Columbus, 1971-73; dir., asso. prof. biomed. communications Ohio State U. Coll. Medicine, asso. prof. communications Coll. Social and Behavioral Scis., 1972-84; assoc. dean acad. affairs, prof. U. Ill. Coll. Associated Health Professions, Chgo., 1984—; cons. univs., bus., industry, including U. Tenn., Nat. Med. Audio-Visual Center, Upjohn Co., N. Central Assn. Colls. and Univs., WHO, AMA. USPHS grantee, 1972-77. Fellow Am. Soc. Allied Health Professions; mem. Health Scis. Communications Assn., Council of Biology Editors, Am. Med. Writers Assn., Alpha Psi Omega, Alpha Epislon Rho. Democrat. Roman Catholic. Author: History of Public Broadcasting Act of 1967, 1979; contbr. articles to profl. jours.; editor Jour. Allied Health, 1978—. Home: 567 Maple St Winnetka IL 60093 Office: 808 S Wood St Chicago IL 60612

BURKE, JOHN JOSEPH, JR., real estate developer; b. Milw., Oct. 10, 1941; s. John J. and Marnie (Katholing) B.; m. Kathryn Murphy, Aug. 20, 1966; children: Wendy, John, Molly, Patrick, Rory. BS, Spring Hill Coll., 1963; postgrad. Marquette U., 1963-65. Pres. Burke Assocs., Milw., 1966—; chmn. bd., chief exec. officer Midwest Ctr. Housing Mgmt., 1976—, Nat. Ctr. for Housing Mgmt., Washington, 1980—; ptnr. The Beer Baron's, Milw., 1983—, 18 Ltd. Partnerships, Milw., 1970—; mem. lay adv. bd. St. Mary's Hosp., Milw., 1986—. Mem. Planning Commn., Village of Fox Point, Wis., 1980—. Fellow Nat. Ctr. Housing Mgmt. Republican. Roman Catholic. Clubs: Ozaukee Country, Milw. Athletic. Avocations: skiing; golf; sailing. Office: N81 W12920 Leon Rd Menomonee Falls WI 53051

BURKE, KENNETH ANDREW, advertising agency executive; b. Cleve., Sept. 9, 1941; s. Frank F. and Margret M. (Tome) B.; B.S. in B.A., Bowling Green State U., 1965; m. Karen Lee Burley, July 1, 1968; children—Allison Leigh, Aric Jason. Account exec. Lang, Fisher, Stashower, Cleve., 1967-69; account supr. Tracy Locke, Dallas, 1969-72, Grey Advt., N.Y.C., 1972-76; v.p. Griswold Eshleman, Cleve., 1976-79; v.p., gen. mgr. Simpson Mktg. Communications Agy., Columbus, Ohio, 1979-81; pres., chief exec. officer, chmn. bd. Martcom, Inc., Columbus, 1981—; dir. Berkshire Product Inc., Cleve., 1979—. Adv. bd. Am. Cancer Soc., Columbus, 1980—. Recipient Navy Achievement in Advt. award, 1975; Cleve. Advt. Club award, 1968. Mem. Am. Mktg. Assn., Columbus Advt. Fedn., Columbus C. of C., Theta Chi. Roman Catholic. Clubs: Rotary, Cleve. Advt., Brookside Country, Agonis Athletic Found., Shamrock, Ducks Unltd. Author: Children's Stories, 1970. Home: 1753 Bedford Rd Upper Arlington OH 43212 Office: 2000 W Henderson Rd Columbus OH 43220

BURKE, MARY JOSEPHINE, management consulting firm executive; b. Pierre, S.D., Feb. 3, 1953; d. Charles Henry and Mary Margaret (Reardon) B. BSBA, Creighton U., 1975; MBA, St. Thomas U., 1979. CPA, Minn., Colo. Auditor McGladrey Hendrickson, St. Paul, 1976-79, Breitman, Orenstien & Schweitzer, Mpls., 1979-80; instr. U. Minn., Duluth, 1980-81; audit supr. Cen. BanCorp., Denver, 1981-83; sr. auditor Boulay, Heutmaker & Zibell, Mpls., 1984-86; pres. Baker and Burke, Mpls., 1986—, also chmn. bd.; instr. U. Minn., Mpls., 1984—; pvt. practice cons., Mpls., 1986—. Recruiter Admissions Dept. Creighton U., Mpls. 1984-86. Mem. Minn. Soc. CPA's (com. vice chmn. 1986-87, com. chmn. 1987-88), Entrepreneurs Network. Republican. Roman Catholic. Avocations: sailing, swimming, sports, reading, travel. Home and Office: 5804 Pompano Minnetonka MN 55343

BURKE, MICHAEL EDWARD, treasurer; b. Cin., Jan. 9, 1948; s. Joseph D. and Mary Jane (Zeiser) B.; m. Linda L. Litosky, Jan. 19, 1980; children: Michael S., Brianne M., Brendan M. BA, Thomas More Coll., 1971; MM, Northwestern U., 1983. Group controller Clow Corp., Glen Ellyn, Ill., 1977-79; mgr. adminstrn. and services Clow Corp., Melrose Park, Ill., 1979-84; corp. controller Carpenter Body Works, Inc., Mitchell, Ind., 1984, v.p.

fin., 1984-86, corp. sec., treas., 1986. Roman catholic. Avocation: golf. Home: 15 Meadow Moor Way Mitchell IN 47446 Office: Carpenter Body Works Inc 1500 W Main St Mitchell IN 47446

BURKE, MICHAEL RICHARD, hydrogeologist; b. Hudson Falls, N.Y., May 6, 1949; s. Thomas Edward and Marguerite Frances (Lalonde) B.; m. Kathy Rose Irvine, Aug. 22, 1971; children: Shannon Lynn, Christopher Peter. AA, Adirondack Community Coll., 1969; BA, SUNY, Potsdam, 1971; MS, U. Toledo, 1973. Cert. profl. geologist. Ground water geologist Leggette, Brashears & Graham, Inc., Wilton, Conn., 1974-78, sr. hydrogeologist, 1979-80, assoc., 1981-83, assoc., mgr., 1983-84, v.p., dir., 1985—. Mem. Am. Inst. Profl. Geologists, Geol. Soc. Am., Assn. Ground Water Scientists and Engrs., Minn. Ground Water Assn. Democrat. Episcopalian. Office: Leggette Brashears & Graham Inc 1210 W County Rd E Suite A1211 Saint Paul MN 55112

BURKE, PAUL E., JR., state senator, investment banking executive; b. Kansas City, Mo., Jan. 4, 1934; s. Paul E. and Virginia (Moling) B.; children—Anne Elizabeth, Kelly Patricia, A. Catherine, Jennifer Marie. B.S. in Bus. Adminstrn., U. Kans., 1956. V.p. Ranson & Co. Inc., Shawnee Mission, Kans., 1959—; dir., mem. internal audit com. Anchor Savs. Assn., Leawood, Kans.; dir., officer MidAm. Packing and Seals, Inc.; mem. Kans. Ho. of Reps., 1972-74; mem. Kans. State Senate, 1975—, majority leader, 1985—; vice chmn. Kans. Inc., 1986—; mem. exec. com., chmn. adv. com. on fiscal affairs Nat. Conf. State Legislators. Councilman, City of Prairie Village (Kans.), 1959-63; mem. Kans. Turnpike Authority, 1965-69, chmn., 1969; mem. adv. bd. Sec. of Corrections, 1973-78. Served to capt. USAF, 1956-59; capt. USNR, 1963—. Mem. Kans. Assn. Commerce and Industry. Republican. Episcopalian. Lodges: Masons, Shriners, Rotary. Home and Office: PO Box 6867 Leawood KS 66206 Office: Box 1268 Kansas City MO 64141

BURKE, PAUL STANLEY, JR., ins. co. exec.; b. St. Paul, Aug. 5, 1926; s. Paul Stanley and Loretta Josephine (Bertrang) B.; B.B.A., U. Minn., 1956; m. Irene Marie Wagner, Apr. 22, 1950; children—John, Steven, Nancy, Lawrence, Linda, James, Thomas. Regional mgr. Minn. Mutual Life Ins. Co., Los Angeles, 1950-61; pres. Paul Burke & Assos., Inc., ins. consultants and adminstrs., Mpls., 1961-73, Trust Life Ins. Co. Am., Scottsdale, Ariz., 1968-73, Purchase & Discount Buying Service Corp., 1977-80, Am. Reliance Corp., 1967-85, Fingertip Facts, 1987—; chmn. bd. Larson & Burke Inc., 1980—. dir. Lindbom & Assos., Inc., St. Paul. Pres., Boys Clubs of Mpls., 1974-76. Served with USAAF, 1944-47. Mem. Pilots Internat. Assn. (pres. 1966-73). Republican. Roman Catholic. Clubs: Interlachen Country, N. Am. Hunting (chmn. bd. dirs. 1978—). Home: 27 Circle W Edina MN 55436

BURKE, ROBERT HARRY, surgeon, educator; b. Cambridge, Mass., Dec. 22, 1945; s. Harry Clearfield and Joan Rosalyn (Spire) B.; m. Margaret Cauldwell Fisher, May 4, 1968; children: Christopher David, Catherine Cauldwell. Student, U. Mich. Coll. Pharmacy, 1964-67; DDS, U. Mich., 1971, MS, 1973; MD, Mich. State U., 1980. Diplomate Am. Bd. Oral and Maxillofacial Surgery. Practice medicine and dentistry specializing in oral and maxillofacial surgery Ann Arbor, Mich., 1976—; house officer oral and maxillofacial surgery U. Mich. Sch. Dentistry, U. Mich. Hosp., Ann Arbor, 1973-76; clin. asst. prof. dept. oral surgery U. Detroit Sch. Dentistry, 1976-77; adj. asst. research scientist Ctr. Human Growth and Devel. U. Mich., 1976-77, adj. research investigator, 1982-85; clin. asst. prof. Mich. State U., East Lansing, 1978-80; house officer surg. emphasis St. Joseph Mercy Hosp., Ann Arbor, 1978-80; adj. research investigator dept. anatomy U. Mich. Med. Sch., 1982-85; clin. asst. prof. oral and maxillofacial surgery U. Mich., 1984-86; lectr. U. Detroit Sch. Dentistry, 1986, assoc. clin. prof. oral and maxillofacial surgery; cons., lectr. dept. occlusion U. Mich. Sch. Dentistry, 1986; head sect. dentistry and oral surgery dept. gen. surgery St. Joseph Mercy Hosp., 1984—, mem. exec. com. dept. gen. surgery, 1984—; chmn. com. emergency care rev. Beyer Meml. Hosp., Ypsilanti, Mich., 1986, also courtesy staff; active staff St. Joseph Meml. Hosp.; courtesy staff Saline (Mich.) Community Hosp., 1978—; Chelsea (Mich.) Med. Ctr., 1978—, McPherson Community Hosp., Howell, Mich., 1984-87. Mem. editorial bd. Topics in Pain Mgmt., 1985-86. Campaign chmn. med. and dental sects. United Way Washtenaw County, Ann Arbor, 1982, dental sect. 1983; profl. adv. com. March of Dimes Genesee County Valley Chpt., Flint, 1979. Fellow Internat. Coll. Surgeons (U.S. Sect.), Am. Assn. Oral and Maxillofacial Surgeons, Mich. Soc. Oral and Maxillofacial Surgeons, Am. Coll. Oral and Maxillofacial Surgeons (v.p. 1987); mem. ADA, AMA, Chalmers Lyons Acad. Oral Surgery, European Soc. Oral and Maxillofacial Surgeons, Southeastern Mich. Surg. Soc., Great Lakes Soc. Oral and Maxillofacial Surgeons, Mich. Dental Assn. (cons., legis. com.), Washtenaw County Med. Soc. (exec. com., del. to Mich. Med. Soc., alternate del. to Mich. State Soc., sec. 1987), Mich. Med. Soc., Washtenaw County Dental Soc. (chmn. publications com., chmn. hosp. com., delta dental rep., liaison to Mich. dental polit. action com.), Inst. Study Profl. Risk (bd. dirs. 1985—), Omicron Kappa Upsilon. Republican. Congregationalist. Clubs: Barton Hills Country, Ann Arbor Racquet, Victor's, Pres.'. Avocations: golf, triathlon, music, piano. Home: 3575 Stanton Ct Ann Arbor MI 48105 Office: 2260 Huron Pkwy Ann Arbor MI 48104

BURKE, SUSAN GEORGIA, social work educator, psychotherapist; b. Chgo., Feb. 22, 1943; d. Walter James and Irene Georgia (Johnson) B.; 1 child, Meredith Burke Nash. BA, U. Ill., 1964, MSW, 1969. Psychotherapist Proviso Mental Health Ctr., Melrose Park, Ill., 1969-74, Cath. Family Cons. Service, Chgo., 1974-78; practice psychotherapy Chgo., 1970—; adj. prof. social work Loyola U., Chgo., 1979—. Mem. Nat. Assn. Social Workers, Ill. Clin. Soc. Social Work, Council on Social Work Edn., Acad. Cert. Social Workers, Lincoln Cen. Assn. Presbyterian. Home: 2024 N Howe Chicago IL 60614 Office: Loyola Univ 820 N Michigan Ave Chicago IL 60611

BURKE, THOMAS JOSEPH, civil engineer; b. Grosse Pointe Park, Mich., Sept. 1, 1927; s. Cyril Joseph and Marie Estelle (Sullivan) B.; B.C.E., Villanova U., 1949; m. Elaine Kiefer, Nov. 10, 1951; children—Judy Lee Burke Brooks, Kathleen Marie Harness, Maureen Elaine, Thomas P. Pres., Burke Rental Service, Sterling Heights, Mich., 1949—, Cyril J. Burke, Inc., Sterling Heights, Mich., 1949—. Trustee Villanova U., 1980—. Served to lt. USAF, Korea. Mem. ASCE, Detroit Builders Exchange (v.p. 1976-78, dir. 1975-78), Associated Equipment Distbrs. (dir. 1955-58, 75-78), Associated Underground Contractors (dir. 1965-68), Mich. Ready Mix Concrete Assn. (dir. 1960-65), Villanova U. Alumni Assn. (nat. v.p. 1978-79, nat. pres. 1980), Detroit Engring. Soc. Roman Catholic. Clubs: Grosse Pointe Yacht, Otsego Ski, Ocean Reef, Detroit Athletic, Villanova U. of Detroit (pres. 1955-65). Home: 578 Shelden Rd Grosse Pointe Shores MI 48236 Home: 688 N Lake Shore Rd Port Sanilac MI 48469 Office: 36000 Mound Rd Sterling Heights MI 48077

BURKE, THOMAS RICHARD, community college administrator; b. St. Louis, Oct. 2, 1944; s. Lloyd Richard and Frances Elizabeth (Yelton) B.; m. Sara Lou Jones, July 3, 1969; 1 child, Kimberly Ayre. B.A., U. Miss., 1970, M.A., 1972, Ph.D., 1981. Instr., Mountain Empire Community Coll., Big Stone Gap, Va., 1972-74, asst. prof., 1974-77, assoc. prof. history, 1977-80, acting pres., 1977, dean instrn., 1976-80; v.p. Three Rivers Community Coll., Poplar Bluff, Mo., 1980-86; pres. Independence Community Coll., 1986—. Chmn. City of Poplar Bluff Hist. Commn. Served with USAF, 1965-69. Edn. Professions Devel. Act fellow, 1970-72. Mem. Am. Assn. Community and Jr. Colls., Am. Vocat. Assn., Mo. Assn. Community and Jr. Colls. (chmn. 1984-85), Kans. Assn. Community Colls. (chmn.), S.E. Kans. Consortium Colls. and Univs., Mo. Hist. Assn., Phi Delta Kappa. Methodist. Lodges: Scottish Rite, Masons, Shriners. Home: 418 W Laurel Independence KS 67301 Office: College Ave and Brookside Dr Independence KS 67301

BURKET, GAIL BROOK, author; b. Stronghurst, Ill., Nov. 1, 1905; d. John Cecil and Maud (Simonson) Brook; A.B., U. Ill., 1926; M.A. in English Lit., Northwestern U., 1929; m. Walter Cleveland Burket, June 22, 1929; children—Elaine (Mrs. William L. Harwood), Anne, Margaret (Mrs. James Boyce). Pres. woman's aux. Internat. Coll. Surgeons, 1950-54, now bd. dirs. Mus.; nat. vice chmn. Am. Heritage of DAR, 1971-74; pres. Northwestern U. Guild, 1976-78; sec. Evanston women's bd. Northwestern U. Settlement, 1979-81, pres., 1984-86; mem. cen. com., 1986—. Recipient Robert Ferguson Meml. award Friends of Lit., 1973. Mem. Nat. League Am. Pen Women (Ill. state pres. 1952-54, nat. v.p. 1958-60), Soc. Midland Authors, Poetry Soc. Am., Women in Communications, AAUW (pres. N. Shore br. 1961-63), Ill. Opera Guild (bd. dirs. 1982—, 1st v.p. 1986—), Daus. Am. Colonists (state v.p. 1973-76), Colonial Dames Am. (chpt. regent 1974-80), Phi Beta Kappa, Delta Zeta. Author: Courage Beloved, 1949; Manners Please, 1949; Blueprint for Peace, 1951; Let's Be Popular, 1951; You Can Write a Poem, 1954; Far Meadows, 1955; This is My Country, 1960; From the Prairies, 1968. Contbr. articles, poems to lit. publs. Address: 1020 Lake Shore Dr Evanston IL 60202

BURKET, RICHARD EDWARD, agriprocessing executive; b. Sandusky, Ohio, Apr. 25, 1928; s. Firm C. and Marie (Bock) B.; m. Carolyn Anne McMillen, Feb. 22, 1951 (div. 1979); children: Leslie, Buffie, Lynn Murphy Burket. B.A., Oberlin Coll., 1950. Tech. sales mgr. Rhoades Equipment Co., Ft. Wayne, Ind., 1954-55; with Chemurgy div. Central Soya Co., Ft. Wayne, Ind., 1955-69; dir. mktg. Chemurgy div. Central Soya Co., Chgo., 1966-69; v.p. protein specialties Archer Daniel Midland Co., Decatur, Ill., 1969-74, v.p., asst. to pres., 1974-80; v.p., asst. to chmn. Archer Daniel Midland Co., Decatur, 1980—. Bd. dirs. Decatur Area Arts Council, 1972—; bd. dirs. Macon County United Way, 1974-77, Boys Club, Decatur, 1979—, Decatur Metro C. of C., 1982—. Served to 1st lt. U.S. Army, 1974-77. Mem. Sales and Mktg. Execs., Inst. Food Technologists, Am. Mgmt. Assn., Soy Protein Council (chmn. 1974-76). Clubs: Decatur, Decatur Country. Home: Route 1 Box 84A Blue Mound IL 62513 Office: Archer Daniels Midland Co 4666 Faries Pkwy Decatur IL 62525

BURKETT, DAVID FRANKLIN, social worker; b. Kansas City, Mo., July 31, 1949; s. Donald William and Helen Elizabeth (Houston) B.; m. Iley Louise Harrison, Oct. 19, 1973; children: David Kyle, Curtis William, Phillip Andrew. BA, U. Kans., 1971, MSW, 1979. Lic. clin. social worker, Kans. Pub. asst. worker Jackson County Dept. Welfare, Kansas City, 1972; caseworker Big Bros. and Sisters, Kansas City, 1973-80; sr. social worker Truman Med. Ctr. East, Kansas City, 1980—; social work cons. Outreach Rehab. Services, Kansas City, 1979-85, Medialodge Nursing Homes, Kansas City, 1982—; instr. practicum U. Kans., 1982—; social worker Norrel Home Health, Overland Park, Kans., 1985—. Editor Brother Power newsletter, 1974-75. Vol. Big Bros. and Sisters, Kansas City, 1972-77, George McGovern Presdl. Campaign, Kans., Mo., Nebr., Calif., 1972; coach Johnson County (Kans.) Soccer team, 1981-85; mgr. Yeawhos Softball team, Johnson County, 1981-85; mem. Friends of the Swope Park Zoo, Kansas City, 1986; deacon Southminster Presbyn. Ch., Prairie Village, Kans., 1983-85. Mem. Nat. Assn. Social Workers. Democrat. Home: 9700 Outlook Dr Overland Park KS 66207 Office: Truman Med Ctr East 7900 Lees Summit Rd Kansas City MO 64139

BURKETT, GLORIA ANN, small business owner; b. Centreville, Mich., Apr. 8, 1934; d. Isaac Chester and Florence (Hamann) Long; m. Chas E. Burkett, Mar. 22, 1952 (dec.1985); children: Chas Timothy, Bruce, Kelly, Karen, Janice, Thomas. Grad., Dowagiac High Sch., 1952. V.p. Burkett Sawmill, Decatur, Mich., 1972-85, pres., 1985—. Del. Rep. Conv., Cass County, Mich., 1986; mem. exec. com. Rep. Party Cass County; mem. Cass County Right to Life, 1986. Mem. U.S. Trotting Assn., Mich. Harness Horseman's Assn., Mich. Standardbred Breeder's Assn., Christian Harness Horseman's Assn. Baptist. Avocation: deer hunting. Home: 21810 Graham St Dowagiac MI 49047 Office: Burkett Sawmill 404 Harrison Decatur MI 49045

BURKETT, RANDY JAMES, lighting designer; b. DuBois, Pa., Nov. 12, 1955; s. Lloyd John and Helen Louis (North) B.; m. Carol Jeanne Collins, Aug. 22, 1981; 1 child, Meredith. B in Archtl. Engring., Pa. State U., 1978. Application engr. Johns-Manville, Denver, 1978-80; lighting designer HOK, St. Louis, 1980-82, assoc., 1982-85, v.p., 1986—. Contbr. articles to profl. jours. Mem. Illuminating Engring. Soc. (chmn. com., Internat. Illumination Design award of Merit 1986). Home: 5308 Tholozan Saint Louis MO 63109 Office: HOK 100 N Broadway Saint Louis MO 63102

BURKEY, LEE MELVILLE, lawyer; b. Beach, N.D., Mar. 21, 1914; s. Levi Melville and Mina Lou (Horner) B.; m. Lorraine Lillian Burghardt, June 11, 1938; 1 child, Lee Melville, III. B.A., U. Ill., 1936, M.A., 1938; J.D. with honor, John Marshall Law Sch., 1943. Bar: Ill., 1944, U.S. Dist. Ct., 1947, U.S. Ct. Appeals, 1954, U.S. Supreme Ct.; 1983; cert. secondary tchr., Ill. Tchr. Princeton Twp. Sch., Princeton, Ill., 1937-38; tchr. Thornton Twp. High Sch., Harvey, Ill., 1938-43; atty. Office of Solicitor, U.S. Dept. Labor, Chgo., 1944-51; ptnr. Asher, Gubbins & Segall and successor firms, Chgo., 1951—; lectr. bus. law Roosevelt Coll., 1949-52. Contbr. numerous articles on lie detector evidence. Trustee, Village of La Grange, Ill., 1962-68, mayor, 1968-73, village atty., 1973-87; commr., pres. Northeastern Ill. Planning Commn., Chgo., 1969-73; mem. bd. dirs. United Ch. Christ, Bd. of Homeland Ministries, 1981-87. Served to 2d lt. Ill. N.G., 1932. Recipient Disting. Alumnus award John Marshall Law Sch., 1973, Good Citizenship medal S.A.R., 1973, Patriot medal S.A.R., 1977, meritorious Service award Am. Legion Post 1941, 1974, Honor award LaGrange Area Hist. Soc., 1987. Mem. Chgo. Bar Assn. (substaining mem.), Ill. State Bar Assn., ABA (mem. council, sect. labor and employment law 1982-87, governance officer 1987—), SAR (state pres. 1977), S.R. Democrat. Mem. United Ch. of Christ. Club: La Grange Country Lodge: Masons, Order of John Marshall. Office: Asher Pavalon Gittler and Greenfield Ltd 2 N La Salle St Chicago IL 60602

BURKHARD, MARIANNE, language professional; b. Zurich, Switzerland, Feb. 1, 1939; came to U.S., 1968; d. Paul Hermann and Fridi (Auer) B. PhD, U. Zurich, 1965. Cultural editor Zürichsee-Zeitung Daily, Stäfa, Switzerland, 1965-68; asst. prof. German U. Ill., Urbana, 1968-76, assoc. prof., 1976—; vis. assoc. prof. U. Notre Dame, Ind., 1984. Author: Meyer und antike Mythologie, 1966, C. F. Meyer, 1978; editor: Women in German Lit., 1980, (series) Women in German Yearbook, 1985; contbr. articles to profl. jours. Mem. Modern Lang. Assn., Am. Assn. Tchrs. German, Swiss Am. Hist. Soc. (pres. 1980-86), Internat. Assn. Germanic Studies (exec. council 1985—). Roman Catholic. Avocations: music, travel. Office: Univ Ill German Dept 3072 Fgn Langs Bldg 707 S Mathews Urbana IL 61801

BURKHARDT, EDWARD ARNOLD, transportation executive; b. N.Y.C., July 23, 1938; s. Edward Arnold Burkhardt Sr. and Kathryn C. (Pfister) Dow; m. Sandra Kay Schwaegel, June, 9, 1967; 1 child, Cynthia Kay. BS Indsl. Adminstrn., Yale U., 1960. Asst. to v.p. Norfolk and Western Ry., St. Louis, 1960-67; asst. gen. mgr. Chgo. Northwestern Transp. Co., 1967-68, gen. supt. transp., 1968-70, asst. v.p. transp., 1970-76, v.p. mktg., 1976-79, v.p. transp., 1979-87; pres. Wis. Cen., Ltd., Chgo., 1987—. Trustee Village of Kenilworth, Ill., 1984—. Mem. Am. Assn. R.R. Supt., Union League. Republican. Episcopalian. Club: Kenilworth, Western Ry. (Chgo.) (pres. 1985-86). Home: 573 Earlston Rd Kenilworth IL 60043 Office: Wis Cen Ltd 54 W Hubbard St Chicago IL 60610

BURKHARDT, JUDITH CAROL, manager non-exempt staffing; b. Highland Park, Mich., Aug. 1, 1940; d. Edward Anthony and Angela Margarita (Gebell) B.; 1 dau., Barbara. B.A., Marygrove Coll., 1963; postgrad. Mich. Technol. U., 1968, U. Detroit, 1974; M.Ed., Wayne State U., 1974. Tchr., Holy Redeemer Sch., Detroit, 1964-67, St. Bede Sch., Southfield, Mich., 1967-69, St. Hugo Sch., Bloomfield Hills, Mich., 1969-73; children's supr. Oakland County Childrens Village, Pontiac, Mich., 1974; youth advisor Pontiac (Mich.) Police Dept., 1974-85; in employee relations Blue Cross-Blue Shield of Mich., 1985-86, in personnel, 1986—. Pres. Bloomfield Youth Guidance, Bloomfield Hills, 1971-73; sec. Cath. Social Services, Royal Oak, Mich., 1969-73; mem. community adv. bd. Woodland Hills Ctr., Troy, Mich.; founding mem. Bloomfield-Birmingham Ctr. for Human Devel., Bloomfield Hills, 1971; mem. Women's Polit. Caucus, Washington, 1983—. Mem. AAUW, Am. Assn. Female Execs., Nat. Mgmt. Assn., Almaca. Democrat. Roman Catholic. Office: Blue Cross Blue Shield Mich 600 Lafayette E Detroit MI 48226

BURKHART, DAMA MARTIN, educator; b. Woodsfield, Ohio, Mar. 16, 1926; d. Wilbert Earl and Carrie Mildred (Doan) Martin; B.S. cum laude, Taylor U., Upland, Ind., 1950; M.S., Butler U., Indpls., 1965; Ph.D. (grad. fellow), Purdue U., 1968; m. George F. Burkhart, Apr. 11, 1981; children by previous marriage—Paige Elizabeth Cofield, Malvin Scott Cofield. Mem. pub. relations dept. Taylor U., 1950-51; tchr., curriculum cons. Howard County (Ind.) Council Chs., 1955-65; staff counselor, psychol. services Purdue U., 1965-68, vis. prof. edn., 1969-70, human devel. specialist, dept. child devel. and family life, 1970-74, staff and program devel. specialist Sch. Home Econs. and Coop. Extension Service, 1974—, asst. dir. Coop. Extension Service, also assoc. dean Sch. Consumer and Family Scis.; adult edn. supr. Asso. Migrant Opportunities Services, 1967; v.p. Ind. Council Family Relations, 1972-74, pres., 1980—, bd. dirs., 1975-77; mem. Task Force on Career Devel. for Women, 1975-76; condr. workshops, cons. in field. Recipient Ecumenical citation Howard County, 1965. Council Chs. grantee. Mem. Nat. Council Family Relations, Am. Home Econs. Assn. Democrat. Presbyterian. Author articles, bulls. Home: 222 N Main St Woodsfield OH 43793

BURKHART, DEBORAH A., architect; b. San Diego, Dec. 9, 1956; d. James Donald and Delora Ann (Venable) B. BS in Environ. Design, BArch, Ball State U., 1980; MBA, MArch, U. Ill., 1987. Registered architect, Ind. Graphic designer Ind. Dept. Natural Resources, Indpls., 1977-78; project designer Schmidt & Claffey Architects, Indpls., 1979-80; project architect Woollen Molzan & Ptnrs., Indpls., 1980-85; tchr. architecture U. Ill., Champaign, 1985—; mgmt. cons. Shepley, Bulfinch, Richardson & Abbott, Boston, 1986. Dir. Midsummer Mime Theater, Indpls., 1985; stage mgr. Phoenix Theater, Indpls., 1984. Mem. Indpls. chpt. AIA (nat. women's task force east states regional dir. 1984-85, bd. dirs. 1984, chmn. design concepts lecture 1983-85, chmn. design award banquet 1983-84, bd. dirs. 1984-85), Mortar Bd., Gargoyle Soc., Alpha Omicron Pi. Avocations: travelling, theater, softball. Home: 308 N Prairie Apt 203 Champaign IL 61820

BURKHART, HELEN LOUISE, mathematics instructor; b. Carrollton, Ill., Feb. 3, 1944; d. William Vernon and Barbara Ella (Garrett) Wear; m. Charles James Burkhart; 1 child, Jeffrey David. MS in Math., Western Ill. U., 1966. Math. instr. Dixon (Calif.) Unified Sch., 1966-67, Carl Sandburg Coll., 1967-72, Coll. of Virgin Islands, 1973-76, Western Ill. U., 1978-81, Rend Lake Coll., Ina, Ill., 1982—. Mem. Sigma Zeta, Kappa Delta Pi. Baptist. Clubs: IUCF (Rend Lake Coll.), Womans Auxiliary (Ina). Home: PO Box 124 Ina IL 62846 Office: Rend Lake Coll Ina IL 62846

BURKHOLDER, JODY SETH, computer systems analyst; b. Kearney, Nebr., Nov. 26, 1960; s. David Verne and Karen Sue (Koski) B.; m. Connie Lynn Meyers, Aug. 16, 1980. BS in Computer Sci., Iowa State U., 1983. Programmer 3M Corp., Ames, Iowa, 1981-83; programmer analyst Gen. Mills, Inc., Mpls., 1983-86, computer systems analyst, 1986—. Active Big Bros. and Big Sister of Greater Mpls., 1985—. Republican. Methodist. Avocations: woodworking, swimming, volleyball. Home: 7523 Louisiana Ave N Brooklyn Park MN 55428

BURKHOLDER, JOSEPH MARK, electrical equipment executive; b. Honolulu, Mar. 16, 1956; s. Joe Powell and Gladys Marie (de Cordova) B.; m. Trina Russanne Latimer, Sept. 22, 1984. BS in Chemistry, Harvey Mudd Coll., 1978; BA in Lit., Claremont Mens Coll., 1978; BA in Art, Pitzer Coll., 1978. Artist Claremont, 1976-78; internat. sales engr. Westinghouse Electric, Athens, Ga., 1978, Bloomington, Ind., 1979-83; mfrs. rep. Cunningham Corp., Rosemead, Calif., 1984; internat. mktg. rep. Westinghouse Electric, Bloomington, Ind., 1985—. Mem. Bloomington Mixed Bowling League (pres. 1986—), Mensa. Republican. Episcopalian. Avocations: woodworking, gardening, glassblowing, auto repair. Office: Westinghouse Electric Corp 300 N Curry Pike Bloomington IN 47401

BURKSTRAND, C. CLAYTON, retail discount company executive; b. Kimball, Minn., Mar. 11, 1934; s. Clarence and Evelyn Ida B.; m. Linda Kay Hardas, Nov. 15, 1974; children: David, Jeff, Steve, Beth. Student, U. Minn., 1952-54, U. Alaska. Trainee, ops. mgr. Target, Mpls., 1962-64, mdse. mgr., 1964-65, store mgr., 1965-68, dist. mgr., sr. dist. mgr. then regional mgr., 1968-74; v.p. ops. Globe div. Walgreen Drug Co., Inc., Houston, 1975, pres. Globe div. and v.p. parent co., 1975-78; pres., chief operating officer Pamida, Inc., Omaha, 1978-81, chmn., pres., chief exec. officer, 1981—, also bd. dirs. Past mem. bd. advisors Discount Store News. Mem. fin. com. Hal Daub Senatorial campaign, 1987; active Nebr. Rep. Party; participant local membership drive Ak-Sar-Ben. Served with AUS, 1954-56. Named Man of Yr. Boys and Young Men's Apparel Lodge B'nai B'rith, 1982. Mem. Nat. Mass Retailing Inst. (bd. dirs. 1986). Lutheran. Avocations: hunting, fishing, boating. Office: Pamida Inc 8800 F St Omaha NE 68127

BURLEIGH, BRUCE DANIEL, JR., biochemist, endocrinologist; b. Augusta, Ga., June 23, 1942; s. Bruce Daniel and Billie Ann (Carter) B.; m. Dorothy Jean Roskos, Sept. 4, 1962 (div. 1981); 1 son, Michael Eugene. B.S., Carnegie-Mellon U., 1964; M.S., U. Mich., 1967, Ph.D., 1970. With MRC Lab, Cambridge, Eng., 1970-73; asst. prof. biochemistry M.D. Anderson Hosp., U. Tex. Cancer Ctr., Houston, 1973-79, assoc. biochemist, 1979-81; research scientist Internat. Mineral & Chem. Corp., Terre Haute, Ind., 1981-82, sr. research scientist, 1983—. NIH fellow, 1968-70; Am. Cancer Soc. fellow, 1970-72; Robert A. Welch grantee, 1979-81. Mem. Am. Chem. Soc., Am. Soc. of Biol. Chemists, Endocrine Soc., AAAS, N.Y. Acad. of Sci., Sigma Xi, Tau Beta Pi, Phi Lambda Upsilon. Episcopalian. Contbr. articles to profl. jours. Home: 075 Oak Ave Oak Terr Div Mundelein IL 60060 Office: Internat Minerals & Chem Corp R & D Div Biochem Sect 1810 Frontage Rd Northbrook IL 60062

BURLESON, BRANT RANEY, communications educator; b. Boise, Dec. 9, 1952; s. Robert Bruce and Ethel Clair (Raney) B.; m. Katherine Ellen RowAN, May 21, 1979. BA, U. Colo., 1975; MA, U. Ill., 1977, PhD, 1982. Asst. prof., lectr. SUNY, Albany, 1979-81; asst. prof. communications Purdue U., West Lafayette, Ind., 1981-85, assoc. prof. communications, 1985—. Contbr. articles to profl. jours. Fellow NEH, 1981; research grantee David Ross Found., 1984—. Mem. Speech Communication Assn. (div. chmn., 1986—, Top Paper award 1985), Internat. Communication Assn. (div. sec. 1984-86, Top Paper award 1986), Soc. for Research in Child Devel., Am. Forensic Assn. (best article 1981), Cen. States Speech Assn. Democrat. Avocations: cooking, reading, astronomy. Home: 2410 Trace #24 West Lafayette IN 47906 Office: Purdue U Dept Communications West Lafayette IN 47907

BURLESON, BYRON ELLIOT, sales executive; b. Kensal, N.D., Sept. 16, 1938; s. Glenn and Ruby Alvida (Zimmerman) B.; m. Evelyn Joanne Agler, July 24, 1965 (div.); children: Aaron Laine, Nathan Leigh; m. Linda Lee Spindler, Aug. 8, 1980. BA, Valley City State Coll., 1960; MEd, No. Tex. State U., 1966. High sch. choir, band dir. N.D., Kans. and Ill., 1960-78; sales mgr. Princeton (Ind.) Industries Co., 1978—. Mem. Rep. Nat. Com., Washington, 1975—, Princeton Industries Corp. Pres.'s Inner Circle Club. Mem. Am. Legion. Methodist. Lodge: Elks. Avocations: music, hunting, fishing, cycling, flying. Home: 1040 Jackson Pl Dyer IN 46311

BURLEY, ALAN JOHN, dentist; b. Columbus, Ohio, June 20, 1956; s. John Donald and Donna Rose (Murphy) B.; m. Cynthia Ann Schneidler, May 23, 1981; 1 child, Adam Craig. BA, Ohio State U., 1979, DDS, 1979. Ptnr. John & Alan Burley DDS Inc., Trenton, Ohio, 1979—. Bd. dirs. Middletown (Ohio) chpt. ARC, 1982-85; chmn. Indian Summer Heritage Festival, Trenton, 1982—, Butler County Bd. Health, Hamilton, Ohio, 1983—. Mem. ADA, Ohio Dental Soc., Keely Dental Soc., Trenton Area C. of C. (treas. 1982—). Republican. Presbyterian. Lodge: Lions (bd. dirs. Trenton 1983-85). Office: 604 W State St Trenton OH 45067

BURLING, IRVING R., insurance company executive. Pres., chief exec. officer Century Life Am., Waverly, Iowa. Office: Century Life of America Heritage Way Waverly IA 50677 *

BURLINGHAM, CHARLES SANFORD, III, manufacturing executive; b. Pitts., May 9, 1921; s. Charles S. Jr. and Ethel (Cooper) B.; m. Arlene R. McMurray, July 16, 1949; children: Douglas A., Alan G., Robert C. BSME, Pa. State U., 1942. Service engring. supt. Sperry Gyroscope Co., Great Neck, N.Y., 1942-55; service mgr. Gyro Mechanisms Inc., Halesite, N.Y., 1956; engring. dept. mgr. Lear Siegler, Inc., Grand Rapids, Mich., 1957-84; pres. Mich. Instruments Inc., Grand Rapids, 1985—, also bd. dirs. Patentee in field. Trustee Cascade Charter Township, Mich., 1974—; various offices Westminster Presbyn. Ch., Grand Rapids, 1960—. Republican. Presbyterian. Avocations: computers, gardening, skiing. Home: 7228 Thornapple

Park SE Grand Rapids MI 49506 Office: Mich Instruments Inc 6300 28th St SE Grand Rapids MI 49506

BURNELL, MARILYN KAY, jewelry designer; b. Lamar, Colo., Sept. 15, 1947; d. A.W. and Kathryn (Rose) W.; m. Jerry Ray Burnell, Apr. 23, 1968; children: Brandon Lee, Christy Lynn. BA in Edn. and Speech Pathology, Wichita State U., 1969, MA in Speech Pathology, 1970, postgrad. Speech pathologist Inst. of Logopedics, Wichita, Kans., 1970-72; coordinator Presch. Perdoncini Program, Wichita, 1972-75; ind. jeweler and designer various art shows, 1974-79; v.p., co-owner, operator Burnell's Creative Gold, Inc., Wichita, 1979—. Mem. Am. Speech and Hearing Assn., Jewelers of Am., Kans. Jewelers Assn., Nat. Assn. Women Bus. Owners (chmn. hospitality 1984-85, v.p. 1985-86, pres. 1986-87), Gemological Inst. Am. Republican. Methodist. Avocations: biking, jogging, stitchery. Office: Burnell Creative Gold Inc 550 N Rock Rd Wichita KS 67206

BURNETT, HENRY BRUCE, banker; b. Raleigh, Ill., May 25, 1912; s. Rex Corwin and Fayette (Wesley) B.; student U. Ill., 1930-32, U. Wis., 1950-52; m. Virginia Stinson, June 6, 1931; 1 son, Hal Bruce; m. 2d, Joan Stroub, Aug. 23, 1963. Chevrolet dealer, Eldorado, Ill., 1941-58; registered rep. Newhard, Cook & Co., St. Louis, 1960-61; chmn. Norris City State Bank (Ill.), 1962-86, bd. dirs. 1986—; pres. C.P. Burnett & Sons, Bankers, Eldorado, Ill., 1969-75, dir., 1950-78; chmn. Egyptian State Bank, Carrier Mills, Ill., 1968-72; chmn. Gallatin County State Bank, Ridgway, Ill., 1975-86, bd. dirs. 1986—; dir. So. Ill., Inc., Banterra Corp., Eldorado. Mayor, Eldorado, 1943-47; former trustee Shrutleff Coll., Alton, Ill.; bd. dirs., Ferrell Hosp., Eldorado; chmn. Ill. Indsl. Devel. Authority, Marion, 1974-79; chmn. bd. deacons Calvary Baptist Ch., 1957-58, bd. trustees, 1950-60; bd. dirs. So. Ill. U. Found., 1979—. Served with inf. AUS, 1944-46; ETO. Mem. Eldorado C. of C. (pres. 1957-59). Lodges: Rotary (pres. Eldorado 1950-51), Lions (pres. Eldorado 1939-40). Home: 1201 Pine St Eldorado IL 62930

BURNETT, JAMES RUFUS, management information systems specialist; b. Lynchburg, Va., Nov. 7, 1949; s. Joseph Rush and Ruth McCauley (Whitmore) B.; m. Shirley Ann Predragovich, Dec. 21, 1973; 1 child, William Scott. AAS in Data Processing, Cen. Va. Community Coll., 1974; BA in Bus. Mgmt., Kent (Ohio) State U., 1986. Computer operator Babcock & Wilcox, Lynchburg, Va., 1970-74; computer programmer Babcock & Wilcox, Barberton, Ohio, 1974-78, systems analyst, 1978-80, mgr. material systems, 1980-82, mgr. mgmt. info. services, 1982-84, mgr. info. ctr. and automation support, 1984-87, mgr. distributed processing support, 1987—; advisor PC Week, 1985—. Served to sgt. NG, 1969-75. Mem. Am. Prodn. and Inventory Control Soc. (treas. Akron chpt. 1980-82, seminar chmn. 1982-83, v.p. 1983-84), Akron/Canton Info. Ctr. Mgrs. (founder). Avocations: hunting, fishing, swimming, golf. Home: 4427 King Arthur Dr Uniontown OH 44685 Office: Babcock & Wilcox 20 S Van Buren Ave Barberton OH 44203

BURNETT, JEAN BULLARD (MRS. JAMES R. BURNETT), biochemist; b. Flint, Mich., Feb. 19, 1924; d. Chester M. and Katheryn (Krasser) Bullard; B.S., Mich. State U., 1944, M.S., 1945, Ph.D. (Council fellow), 1952; m. James R. Burnett, June 8, 1947. Research assoc. dept. zoology Mich. State U., East Lansing, 1954-59, dept. biochemistry, 1959-61, acting dir. research biochem. genetics, dept. biochemistry, 1961-62, assoc. prof., asst. chmn. dept. biomechanics, 1973-82, prof. dept. anatomy, 1982-84, prof. dept. zoology, Coll. Natural Sci. and Coll. Osteo. Medicine, 1984—; assoc. biochemist Mass. Gen. Hosp., Boston, 1964-73; prin. research assoc. dermatology Harvard, 1962-73, faculty medicine, 1964-73, also spl. lectr., cons., tutor Med. Sch.; vis. prof. dept. biology U. Ariz., 1979-80. USPHS, NIH grantee, 1965-68; Gen. Research Support grantee Mass. Gen. Hosp., 1968-72; Ford Found. travel grantee, 1973; Am. Cancer Soc. grantee, 1971-73; Internat. Pigment Cell Conf. travel grantee, 1980; recipient Med. Found. award, 1970. Mem. AAAS, Am. Chem. Soc., Am. Inst. Biol. Sci., Genetics Soc. Am., Soc. Investigative Dermatology, N.Y. Acad. Scis., Sigma Xi (Research award 1971), Pi Kappa Delta, Kappa Delta Pi, Pi Mu Epsilon, Sigma Delta Epsilon. Home: PO Box 308 Okemos MI 48864 Office: Dept Zoology Natural Sci Bldg Mich State U East Lansing MI 48824

BURNETT, PATRICIA HILL, artist, lecturer; b. Bklyn., Sept. 5, 1920; d. William Burr and Mimi (Uline) Hill; student U. Toledo, 1937-38, Goucher Coll., 1939-40; student Master's program Inst. D'Allende, Mexico, 1967, Wayne State U., 1972; student of John Carroll, Detroit, 1941-44, Sarkis Sarkisian, Detroit, 1956-60, Wallace Bassford, Provincetown, Mass., 1968-72, Walter Midener, Detroit, 1960-63; m. Harry Albert Burnett, Oct. 9, 1948; children—William Hill Lange, Harry Burnett III, Terrill Hill, Hillary Hill. Actress, Lone Ranger program Radio Blue Network, 1941-45; tchr. of painting and sculpture U. Mich. Extension, Ann Arbor, 1965—; lectr. N.Y. Speakers Bur., 1971—; propr. Burnett Studios, Detroit, 1962—, mgr., 1962—. Numerous one-woman shows of paintings and sculpture include: Scarab Club, Detroit, 1971, Midland (Mich.) Art Center, Wayne State U., Detroit, The Gallery, Ft. Lauderdale, Fla., Agra Gallery, Washington, Salon des Artes, Paris; numerous group shows including: Palazzo Pruili Gallery, Venice, Italy, 1971, Detroit Inst. of Arts, 1967, Butler Mus., N.Cleve., 1972, Windsor (Ont., Can.) Art Center, 1973, Weisbaden (Germany) Gallery, 1976; represented in permanent collections: Detroit Inst. of Arts, Wayne State U., Detroit, Wooster (Ohio) Coll., Ford Motor Co., Detroit, Bloomfield Art Assn., Bloomfield Hills, Mich., also private collections; numerous portrait paintings including portraits of Indira Ghandi, Benson Ford, Joyce Carol Oates, Mrs. Edsel Ford, Betty Ford, Roman Gribbs, Princess Olga Mrivani, Lord John Mackintosh, Marlo Thomas, Viveca Lindfois, Betty Freidan, Gloria Steinem, Congresswoman Martha Griffiths, Margaret Papandreou, Valentina Tereshkova. Chairwoman of Mich. Women's Commn., 1972—; pres. Detroit House of Correction Commn., 1975—; treas. Republican Dist. 1 of Mich., 1973—; mem. Issues Com., Republican State Central Com., 1975-76; sec. Republican State Ways and Means Com., 1975—; mem. Mich. State Adv. Council Vocat. Edn.; mem. Mich. Arts in Edn. Council, 1978—; mem. New Detroit Arts Com., 1979—; chmn. World Feminist Commn., 1974—. Recipient Silver Salute award Mich. State U., 1976, Most Popular award San Diego Sculpture Show, 1971, First prize award Cape Cod Artists Show, 1968; named Distinguished Woman of Mich., Bus. and Profl. Women's Orgn., 1974, Distinguished Woman Northwood Inst., 1977. Mem. Detroit Inst. Arts (dir. membership com. 1958—), Nat. Assn. of Commns. for Women (sec., dir. 1976-78), Mich. Acad. of the Arts, Detroit Soc. of Women Painters and Sculptors, Women in the Arts, Scarab Club (dir. 1962-63), Ibex Club (pres. 1951), NOW (nat. bd. 1971-75, del. UN conf., Mex., 1975), Women's Econ. Club, N.Y. Portrait Club (nat. com. 1978—), French Am. C. of C. (v.p.), Alpha Phi. Episcopalian. Clubs: Zonta Internat., Detroit (bd. dirs.). Contbr. articles to art jours. Home: 18261 Hamilton Rd Detroit MI 48203 Office: 217 Farnsworth Detroit MI 48202

BURNETT, ROBERT A., publisher; b. Joplin, Mo., June 4, 1927; s. Lee Worth and Gladys (Plummer) B.; m. Gloria M. Cowden, Dec. 25, 1948; children: Robert A., Stephen, Gregory, Douglas, David, Penelope. A.B., U. Mo., 1948. Salesman Cowden Motor Co., Guthrie Center, Iowa; then Equitable Life Assurance Soc., Joplin, Mo.; now pres., chief exec. officer Meredith Corp.; dir. Whirlpool Corp., Norwest Bank Des Moines, ITT, Iowa Resources, Dayton Hudson Corp. Past chmn. Discover Am. Travel Orgns.; bd. dirs. Grinnell Coll. Served with AUS, 1945-46. Mem. NAM (dir.), Phi Delta Theta. Congregationalist. Home: 3131 Fleur Dr Apt 905 Des Moines IA 50321 Meredith Corp: 1716 Locust St Des Moines IA 50336

BURNETT-DIXON, MARILOU, social worker, educator; b. Oklahoma City, Apr. 2, 1929; d. Irvin William and Edna Anita (Jackson) Huddleston; m. Noah M. Dixon. BA, Okla. State U., 1951; MSW, U. Ill., 1966; PhD, Union Grad. Sch., Cleve., 1976. Cert. social worker, Tex., Ill.; lic. psychologist, Tex., Ill. Child welfare worker State of Tex. Dept. Childwelfare, Amarillo, 1951-59; family service clinician Dept. Family Services, Springfield, Ill., 1960-64; clinician Inst. Juvenile Research, Springfield, 1964-66, McFarland Zone Ctr., Springfield, 1966-68; instr. Lincolnland Community Coll., Springfield, 1968-70; prof. social work Sangamon State U., Springfield, 1971—; pres. Kwen Inst., Springfield, 1970-86. Mem. Am. Acad. Psychotherapists, Am. Assn. Marriage and Family Therapists, Am. Human Psychology Assn., Avanta Network. Home: 1801 Illini Rd Springfield IL 62701 Office: Sangamon State U Toronto Rd Springfield IL 62708

BURNEY, WILLARD TRAVIS, lawyer; b. Sioux City, Iowa, Apr. 9, 1943; s. Willard Wales and Virginia E. (Travis) B.; m. Arlis Ann Bottolfsen, June 12, 1965; children: Willard Chad, Audrey Ann. Student, U. Nebr., 1960-61, JD, 1974; BS, USAF Acad., 1965. Bar: U.S. Dist. Ct. Nebr. 1975, U.S. Ct. Appeals (8th cir.) 1977. Commd. 2d lt. USAF, 1965, advanced through grades to capt., 1968, resigned, 1972; assoc. Floyd A. Sterns, Lincoln, Nebr., 1975; sole practice Lincoln, 1975—; pres. TACA Enterprises, Lincoln, 1975—. Mem. Citizens Choice, Washington, 1978—, Nat. Tax-Limitation Com., Washington, 1979—, Rep. Nat. Com., Washington, 1981-85. Decorated DFC, Bronze Star, Air medal with 12 oak leaf clusters. Mem. Nebr. State Bar Assn., Western Lancaster County Jaycees (v.p. bd. dirs. 1975-78). Lutheran. Club: Lincoln Track. Home and Office: Rural Rt 5 Lincoln NE 68531

BURNHAM, NORMAN JAMES, healthcare administrator; b. Salt Lake City, Mar. 22, 1951; s. Preston James and Patricia (McClanahan) B.; m. Susan Nelwyn Williams, Aug. 20, 1985; 1 child, Eduardo Alberto. BS in Med. Tech., U. Utah, 1974, MBA, 1978. Clin. supr. Wasatch Pathologic Labs., Salt Lake City, 1974-76, gen. mgr., 1978-83; chief med. tech. Utah Biomed. Test Lab., Salt Lake City, 1976-78; healthcare cons. Hosp. Corp. Am., Riyadh, Saudi Arabia, 1983, John Short & Assocs., Salt Lake City, 1983-85; healthcare adminstr. Med. Care Internat., Dallas, 1985-86; asst. dir. Advanced Treatment and Bionics Inst. Mt. Carmel Health, Columbus, Ohio, 1986—. Bd. dirs. U. Utah Coll. of Pharmacy, Salt Lake City, 1979-81. Mem. Am. Soc. Clin. Pathologists, Am. Coll. Hosp. Adminstrs. Episcopalian. Lodge: Masons. Avocations: skiing, sailing, hiking. Home: PO Box 20195 Columbus OH 43220 Office: Mt Carmel Health 793 W State St Columbus OH 43222

BURNISTON, KAREN SUE, nurse; b. Hammond, Ind., May 20, 1939; d. George Hubbard and Bette Ruth (Ambler) B.; R.N., Parkview Methodist Hosp., Ft. Wayne, Ind., 1961; B.S. in Nursing, Purdue U., 1974; M.S., No. Ill. U., DeKalb, 1976. Staff nurse Parkview Meml. Hosp., 1961-63, 71-73; physician office and operating room nurse, 1963-67; nurse N.W. Ind. Home Health Services, 1974; mem. faculty Michael Reese Hosp. Sch. Nursing, Chgo., 1977-79; asst. dir. nursing Mt. Sinai Hosp. Med. Center, Chgo., 1977-79; asst. adminstr. patient services St. Margaret Hosp., Hammond, 1980-85; asst. adminstr. patient services St. Catherine Hosp., East Chicago, Ind., 1985-86, chief operating officer, 1986— . adj. faculty Purdue U. Sch. Nursing, Ind. U. Sch. Nursing. Bd. dirs. South Lake Ctr. Mental Health. Served with Nurse Corps, USAF, 1967-71. Mem. Am. Nurses Assn., Am. Orgn. Nurse Execs., N.W. Ind. Council Nursing Service Adminstrs., Ind. Nurses Assn., Lake County Mental Health Assn. (bd. dirs.), Ind. Orgn. Nurse Execs., Sigma Theta Tau. Mem. Christian Ch. (Disciples of Christ). Club: Altrusa. Home: 1601 Anna St Schererville IN 46375 Office: St Catherine Hosp 3421 Fir St East Chicago IN 46312

BURNS, ARTHUR LEE, architect; b. Indpls., July 5, 1924; s. Charles Raymond and Dorothy Frances (Young) B.; m. Dorothy Maxine Kingsland, Oct. 26, 1946; children—Stephen Robert (dec.), Melody Lee. B.S. in Architecture, U. Cin., 1949. Archtl. draftsman Foster Engring. Co., Ltd., Indpls., 1941-42; archtl. draftsman Albert V. Walters (Architect), Cin., 1946-48; chief draftsman Arend & Arend (Architects), Cin., 1948-49; architect The McGuire & Shook Corp., Indpls., 1949-84; v.p. The McGuire & Shook Corp., 1964-71, sec.-treas., 1972-73, pres., 1974-75, exec. v.p., 1976-77, v.p., 1978-79, sec.-treas., 1980-84; archtl. cons. 1984—. Served with USAAF, 1943-46. Fellow AIA (sec. treas. Indpls. chpt. 1965-66, v.p. 1967, pres. 1968, mem. documents bd. 1973-85, chmn. 1978-79); mem. Ind., Soc. Architects (dir. 1968-69, v.p. 1971, pres. 1972, Edward D. Pierre Meml. medal 1972), Constrn. Specifications Inst. (Indpls. chpt. v.p. 1966-67, pres. 1967-68). Republican. Methodist. Club: Broad Ripple Sertoma Indpls. (v.p. 1973-74, pres. 1974-75, Gold Honor Club pres.). Home and Office: 7130 Wexford Dr Indianapolis IN 46250

BURNS, BETTY X., music educator; b. St. Louis, Sept. 16, 1926; d. James Arnest and Elizabeth Levina (Allen) Delvas; m. Douglas Corzine Burns, Sept. 8, 1945 (dec. 1974); children: Cynthia Burns Benavides, Stephen, Clark, Nathan. Student, Washington U., St. Louis, 1951, Sherwood Conservatory of Music, Chgo., 1960; studies with Carl Benseik, St. Louis, 1940-56; studies with Harold Zabrack, N.Y.C., 1970-73; student, U. Mo., St. Louis, 1979. Dir. New Music Acad., St. Louis, Mo., 1968—; clinician Nat. Piano Found., St. Louis, 1962-73; mem. faculty Webster Coll., St. Louis, 1969-73; adjudicator profl. assns.; dir. workshops Kjos Pub., San Diego, 1972-75; specialist jazz improvization and group teaching, 1968—. Author: (with others) You Do It Books, 1972-75; contbr. articles to mags. Mem. Piano Tchrs. Forum (pres.), Nat. Music Tchrs. Assn., Mo. Music Tchrs. Assn. (judge), Piano Tchrs. Guild (chmn.). Avocations: trading stock market, psychic healing. Home and Office: 21 Cardigan Dr Saint Louis MO 63135

BURNS, BRUCE PALMER, psychologist; b. Jamestown, N.Y., Mar. 5, 1922; s. Harold Fletcher and Genevieve Margaret (Erickson) B.; B.A., Coll. Wooster, 1965; M.A., Mich. State U., 1967, Ph.D., 1972. Gen. mgr. Burns Case Goods Corp., Jamestown, 1949-54, 59-64; pres., owner Show Off Inc., Jamestown, 1954-59; asst. program dir. Detroit Substance Abuse Treatment Program, 1972-78; pvt. practice clin. psychology, Detroit, 1976-86, Troy, Mich., 1981—; dir. Renaissance Psychol. Services, 1978-86; vis. lectr. Eastern Mich. U., Ypsilanti, 1971-72; cons. Methadone Clinic, 1975-78. Served to lt. (j.g.) USNR, 1943-46. Cert. health service provider in psychology; lic. psychologist, Mich. Mem. Am., Canadian, Mich. psychol. assns., Am. Rehab. Counselors Assn., Am. Soc. Clin. Hypnosis, Mich. Personnel and Guidance Assn., Soc. Clin. and Exptl. Hypnosis, Mich. Soc. Lic. Psychologists, Mich. Assn. Marriage Counselors, Nat. Registry Health Service Providers in Psychology, SAR, Beta Theta Pi. Club: Renaissance. Office: 755 W Big Beaver Suite 416 Troy MI 48084

BURNS, C(HARLES) PATRICK, hematologist-oncologist; b. Kansas City, Mo., Oct. 8, 1937; s. Charles Edgar and Ruth (Eastham) B.; m. Janet Sue Walsh, June 15, 1968; children—Charles Geoffrey, Scott Patrick. B.A., U. Kans., 1959, M.D., 1963. Diplomate Am. Bd. Internal Medicine, subsplty. bds. hematology, med. oncology. Intern Cleve. Met. Gen. Hosp., 1963-64; asst. resident in internal medicine Univ. Hosps., Cleve., 1966-68, sr. resident in hematology, 1968-69; instr. medicine Case Western Res. U., Cleve., 1970-71; asst. chief hematology Cleve. VA Hosp., 1970-71; asst. prof. medicine U. Iowa Hosps., Iowa City, 1971-75, assoc. prof. medicine, 1975-80, prof., 1980—, dir. sect. on med. oncology, co-dir. div. hematology-oncology, dir. div. hematology-oncology, 1985—; vis. scientist Imperial Cancer Research Fund Labs., London, 1983; cons. U.S. VA Hosp.; mem. study sect. on exptl. therapeutics NIH, support rev. com. Nat. Cancer Inst. Cancer Ctr., VA Med. Research Service Career Devel. Com. Research and publs. on hematologic malignancies, tumor lipid biochemistry, leukemia and oncology. Served to capt. M.C., AUS, 1964-66. Am. Cancer Soc. fellow in hematology-oncology, 1968-69, USPHS fellow in medicine, 1969-70; USPHS career awardee, 1978. Fellow ACP; mem. Am. Soc. Hematology, Am. Assn. Cancer Research, Internat. Soc. Hematology, Central Soc. Clin. Research, Am. Soc. Clin. Oncology, Soc. Exptl. Biology and Medicine, AAAS, Royal Soc. Medicine, Am. Fedn. Clin. Research, Royal Soc. Medicine, Lambda Chi Alpha, Phi Beta Pi, Alpha Omega Alpha. Home: 2046 Rochester Ct Iowa City IA 52240 Office: U Iowa Univ Hosps Dept Medicine Iowa City IA 52242

BURNS, ELIZABETH MURPHY, media executive; b. Superior, Wis., Dec. 4, 1945; d. Morgan and Elizabeth (Beck) Murphy; m. Richard Ramsey Burns, June 24, 1984. Student U. Ariz., 1963-67. Promotion and programming sec. Sta. KGUN-TV, Tucson, 1967-68; programming and traffic sec. Sta. KFMB-TV, San Diego, 1968-69; owner, operator Sta. KKAR, Pomona, Calif., 1970-73; co-owner Evening Telegram Co. (parent co. Murphy Stas.); pres. Morgan Murphy Stas., Madison, Wis., 1976—; dir. Nat. Guardian Life Ins. Co., various media stas. and corps. Mem. adv. bd. Wis. Chamber Orch., Madison, 1983—; bd. dirs. Duluth/Superior Symphony, Minn., 1985, TV Bur. of Advt.; bd. dirs. N.E. Midwest Inst., 1984—, now chmn. bd. dirs. Mem. Nat. Assn. Broadcasters, Wis. Broadcasters Assn. Republican. Roman Catholic. Clubs: Madison, Nakoma Country; Northland Country (Duluth). Avocations: golf, tennis, travel. Home: 180 Paine Farm Rd Duluth MN 55804 Office: Sta WISC-TV 7025 Raymond Rd Madison WI 53711

BURNS, GLENN RICHARD, dentist; b. Marietta, Ohio, Mar. 23, 1951; s. Alphas Gale Burns and Elma June (Sayres) George; m. Linda Edith Bailey, June 10, 1978; children: Geoffrey William, Katherine May. BS in Zoology, Ohio U., 1973; DDS, Ohio State U., 1980. Gen. practice dentistry Lancaster, Ohio, 1980—. Bd. dirs. Lancaster Fairfield YMCA, 1985-86. Served to sgt. U.S. Army, 1973-77. Mem. ADA, Ohio Dental Assn., Hocking Valley Dental Soc. (chmn. children's dental health month 1983-86), Acad. Gen. Dentistry, Xi Psi Phi (v.p. 1984—), Doctors With A Heart. Republican. Presbyterian. Lodge: Kiwanis. Avocations: golf, reading, fishing. Home: 3931 Mudhouse Rd NE Lancaster OH 43130 Office: 204 N Columbus St Lancaster OH 43130

BURNS, GRANT FRANCIS, librarian, editor; b. Owosso, Mich., June 18, 1947; s. Francis M. and Marie A. (Olsen) B.; m. Stephanie Winston Voight, Feb. 4, 1972; children: Andrea, Steven. BA in Sociolgy, Mich. State U., 1969; AM in English, U. Mich., 1973, MLS, 1976. Reference librarian U. Mich., Flint, 1977—. Author: The Atomic Papers, 1984, The Sports Pages, 1987; editor New Pages: News and Reviews of the Progressive Book Trade, 1981—; contbr. articles to profl. jours. Avocations: reading, furniture bldg., piano. Home: 2427 Nebraska Ave Flint MI 48506 Office: U Mich Flint Library Flint MI 48502

BURNS, JAMES WILLIAM, insurance company executive; b. Winnipeg, Man., Can., Dec. 27, 1929; s. Charles William and Helen Gladys (Mackay) B.; m. Barbara Mary Copeland, Aug. 12, 1953; children: James F.C., Martha J., Alan W. B.Comm., U. Man., 1951; M.B.A., Harvard U., 1953. With Great-West Life Assurance Co., 1953—, exec. v.p., 1970, pres., dir., 1971-79, chmn., dir., 1979—; dep. chmn. Power Corp. Can.; chmn., chief exec. officer Power Fin. Corp.; chmn. exec. com. Investors Group, Montreal Trustco Inc.; dir. Bathurst Paper Ltd., Consol.-Bathurst Inc., CB Pak Inc., IBM Can. Ltd. Bd. dirs. Montreal Gen. Hosp. Found.; chmn. Adv. Group on Exec. Compensation in Pub. Service; past. chmn. Conf. Bd. Can. hon. lt. col. Queen's Own Cameron Highlanders of Can. Clubs: St. Charles Country (Winnipeg), Man. (Winnipeg); Albany (Toronto): Toronto; Mount-Royal (Montreal), Mount-Bruno Country (Montreal).

BURNS, JERRY, professional football coach; b. Detroit, Jan. 24, 1927; m. Marilyn Burns; children: Michael, Erin, Kelly, Kathy, Kerry. BS, U. Mich., 1951. Backfield coach U. Hawaii, Honolulu, 1951, Whittier (Calif.) Coll., 1952; head coach St. Mary's of Redford High Sch., 1953; coach U. Iowa, Iowa City, 1954-61, head coach, 1961-65; coach Green Bay (Wis.) Packers (NFL), 1966-67; with Minn. Vikings (NFL), 1968—, offensive coordinator, 1968-85, head coach, 1986—. Office: Minn Vikings 9520 Viking Dr Eden Prairie MN 55344 *

BURNS, JERRY FRANK, educator; b. Clio, Iowa, Aug. 11, 1934; s. John William and Maxine Hazel (Rogers) B.; student N.E. Mo. State U., William Jewell Coll., Grandview Coll.; B.S. in Edn., S.W. Mo. State U., 1959; M.Ed., U. Mo., 1962; postgrad. U. Nebr., Eastern Mont. Coll., U. S.D.; m. Phyllis Idell Petty, Feb. 28, 1954. Tchr., asst. prin. Des Moines Pub. Schs., 1959-67; sch. psychologist Warren and Marion County Bd. Edn., Indianola, Iowa, 1967-75; coordinator spl. edn. Heartland Edn. Agy., Johnston, Iowa, 1975-78, asst. dir. spl. edn., 1978—. Former sec.-treas., bd. trustees, bd. deacons Assembly of God Ch. Lic. psychologist, Iowa. Mem. NEA (life), Nat. Assn. Sch. Psychologists (charter), Iowa Sch. Psychologists Assn. (charter), Council Exceptional Children, Des Moines Radio Amateur Assn. Republican. Club: Greater Des Moines FM. Home: 3842 Brinkwood Rd Des Moines IA 50310 Office: 6500 Corporate Dr Johnston IA 50131

BURNS, KAREN RUTH, educator; b. Rockford, Ill., June 10, 1951; d. Edward Chellis and Ruth Ann (Pritchard) Holden; m. Thomas Samuel Burns, July 28, 1972; 1 child, Andys T. BS, Western Mich. U., 1973, MA, 1975. Cert. elem. tchr., Mich. Tchr. Gull Lake Schs., Richland, Mich., 1973—, tchr. adult edn. for community edn., 1976—. Appointed spl. advocate Kalamazoo Ct., 1984—; foster parent Allegan (Mich.) County Dept. Social Service, 1984—, dog tng. leader Allegan County 4-H, 1983—; mem. consortium com. Gull Lake Schs., 1985—, mini grant com., 1985—. Grantee Kodak Corp., 1983, Gull Lake Found., 1986. Mem. NEA, Mich. Edn. Assn., Gull Lake Edn. Assn. (sec. 1984-86). Democrat. Methodist. Avocations: stenciling, dog tng., sewing, clowning. Office: Richland Elem Sch East M-89 Richland MI 49083

BURNS, KEITH R., auditor; b. Owosso, Mich., May 10, 1956; s. Richard George and Wanda Lee (Phelps) B.; m. Marcia Jane Bowles, Sept. 11, 1976; children: Michelle Nicole, Michael David. BA, Mich. State U., 1978. CPA, Mich. Staff Ernst & Whinney, Saginaw, Mich., 1978-80, sr. staff, 1980-82, mgr., 1982-84, sr. mgr., 1984-87; sr. mgr. Ernst & Whinney, Cin., 1987—. Bd. dirs. Voluntary Action Ctr., Saginaw, 1984-87. Mem. Am. Inst. CPA's, Mich. Assn. CPA's, Healthcare Fin. Mgmt. Assn. (pres. N. Cen. Mich. chpt. 1985-86). Clubs: Saginaw, Germania. Lodge: Rotary. Avocations: golf, fishing. Office: Ernst & Whinney 250 E 5th St Suite 1300 Cincinnati OH 45202

BURNS, LAWRENCE ALOYSIUS, JR., data processing executive, accountant; b. Cin., Aug. 5, 1949; s. Lawrence Aloysius and Marjorie Mary (Wiegele) Burns; m. Peggy Louise Watkins , June 16, 1979; 1 child, Eric; stepchildren: Amy Steers, Mikal Steers. BS, U. Cin., 1971, M in Bus., 1977, postgrad., 1978-79. Staff acct. Arthur Andersen & Co., Cin., 1979-81; programmer, analyst Applied Solutions, Inc., Cin., 1981-84, dir. of proprietary software, 1984—; vis. lectr. U. Cin., 1978-79; ind. tax cons., Cin., 1977—. Asst. coach Coll. Hill Knothole, Cin., 1980-84; mem. Cin. Updowntowners, 1977-79. Served with U.S. Army, 1971-73. Mem. Am. Inst. CPA's, Mensa, Phi Beta Kappa, Beta Gamma Sigma. Roman Catholic. Avocations: electronics, tennis. Home: 6661 Plantation Way Cincinnati OH 45224 Office: Applied Solutions Inc Suite 300 531 N Wayne Ave Cincinnati OH 45215

BURNS, MICHAEL J., architect; b. Minot, N.D., Jan. 28, 1952; s. Eugene Ellsworth and Joan Elizabeth (Mackley) B.; m. Pamela Colleen Andrist, June 3, 1973; children: Aaron, Jennifer, Elizabeth, Chelsea. BArch, N.D. State U., 1977, BA in Archtl. Studies, 1976. Registered architects, N.D., Minn. Designer K.R. Johnson, Architect, Fargo, N.D., 1977-80; project architect Koehnlien, Lightowler, Johnson, Fargo, N.D., 1980-83; prin. Michael J. Burns, Architects, Fargo, 1983—. Trustee 1st Presbyn. Ch., Fargo, 1981-84; mem. Nat. Trust Historic Preservation. Served with U.S. Army, 1970-72. Mem. AIA, F-M Architects (bd. dirs. 1984—), Tau Beta Pi, Tau Sigma Delta. Republican. Presbyterian. Lodge: Kiwanis. Avocations: racquetball, singing. Home: 60 32d Ave NE Fargo ND 58102 Office: 2315 N University Dr Box 8247 Fargo ND 58109-8247

BURNS, RICHARD HOWARD, lawn and garden equipment manufacturing company executive; b. Ridgewood, N.J., Sept. 26, 1930; s. Robert Orr and Opal May (Shirreffs) B.; B.S. in Applied Art (Indsl. Design), Auburn U., 1953; m. Beverly Duncan Ritchie, Sept. 9, 1953; children—Richard Howard, Laura Elizabeth Burns Scarff. Mgr. indsl. design Hobart Corp., Troy, Ohio, 1955-57, project engr., 1957-66, mgr. indsl. design, 1966-86; mgr. indsl. design Kitchenaid, Inc., 1986-87; owner, pres. Richard H. Burns' Assocs., indsl. design and engring. cons., 1985—. Mem. Miami County Planning Commn., Troy City Council, 1978-85; precinct committeeman local Rep. Orgn. Served with U.S. Army, 1953-55, capt. Res. ret. Mem. Indsl. Designers Soc. Am., Troy C. of C., Am. Def. Preparedness Assn., Boca Internat. Republican. Presbyterian (elder). Lodge: Kiwanis. Patentee in field. Home and Office: 662 Clarendon Rd Troy OH 45373

BURNS, ROBERT EDWARD, editor, publisher; b. Chgo., May 14, 1919; s. William Joseph and Sara (Foy) B.; m. Brenda Coleman, May 15, 1948; children: Maddy F., Martin J. Student, De Paul U., 1937-39; Ph.B., Loyola U., Chgo., 1941. Pub. relations dir. Cath. Youth Orgn., Chgo., 1943-45, 47-49; exec. dir. No. Ind. region Nat. Conf. Christians and Jews, 1946; exec. editor U.S. Cath. mag.; gen. mgr. Claretian Publs., Chgo., 1949-84. Author: The Examined Life, 1980, Catholics on the Cutting Edge, 1983. Bd. dirs. Thomas More Assn. Home: Route 2 Box 277 #J Montello WI 53949-9802

BURNS, ROBERT MICHAEL, marketing executive; b. Monmouth, Ill., Dec. 8, 1938; s. Robert McNamera and Kathryn (Lutrell) B.; m. Shirley Ann Meyer, May 21, 1963; children: Robin, Robert, Tammy, Amy, Julie, Mark. Student, Knox Coll., 1956, U. Ark., 1957-58; BA, Mo. State U., 1965; postgrad., U. Md., 1973. Pvt. practice gen. agt. 1968-72; v.p. Swift & Co. Ins. Group, Chgo., 1972-77; regional dir. Realty World Corp., Washington, 1977-78; exec. v.p. Ptnrs. Internat., Washington, 1978-80; pres. Breakthru Mktg., Inc., Milw., 1980—; cons. Red Carpet/Guild, San Diego, 1986—; cons., supplier Century 21 Internat., Irvine, Calif., Coldwell Banker, Irvine; bd. dirs. Ptnrs. Internat., Cedar Rapids, Iowa, 1979-81. Author: The Sales Process, 1986; co-author The Psychology of Winning, 1983; inventor computer closed-loop mgmt. system. Served with U.S. Army, 1963-65. Recipient numerous awards for Outstanding Sales, Mktg. and Mgmt. ins., real estate and franchising. Republican. Methodist. Avocation: working with youth and schs. on "psychology of winning.". Home: 16560 W Nancy Ln Brookfield WI 53005 Office: Breakthru Mktg Services Inc 21675 Doral Rd Waukesha WI 53186

BURNS, THOMAS OLIVER, orthodontist; b. Lafayette, Ind., May 31, 1954; s. William Oliver and Aenita Pearl (Needham) B.; m. Mary Ann Glockner, July 30, 1977; 1 child, Allison Sarah. AB in Biol. Scis., Ind. U., Bloomington, 1976; DDS, Ind. U., 1979; cert., Ind. U. Sch. Orthodontia, 1981. Practice dentistry specializing orthodontics Lafayette, Ind., 1981—. Mem. ADA, Ind. Dental Assn., W. Cen. Dental Soc. (bd. dirs. 1985-88), Am. Assn. Orthodontist, Hoosier Orthodontic Forum (pres. 1984-85). Avocations: Water skiing, cross country bike riding, woodwork. Home: 1343 Lockwood Dr Lafayette IN 47905 Office: 1209 Winthrop Ave Lafayette IN 47905

BURNS, TIMOTHY CLOYCE, television producer; b. Kansas City, Mo., Nov. 22, 1946; s. Gerald Floyd and Alma Louise (Poteet) B.; m. Susan Hobbit, May 21, 1983. BS in Edn., U. Mo., 1974, MA in Communications, 1979. Cert. tchr. Photographer La Beté, Kansas City, Mo., 1974-76; mgr. Craftsmen of Chelsea Ct., Kansas City, 1976-78; media specialist VA Med. Ctr., Kansas City, 1978-79; TV dir. Haskel Indian Coll., Lawrence, Kans., 1979-81; producer, dir. No. Ill. U., DeKalb, 1981—; cons. Timothy Burns Prodns., DeKalb, 1981—; producer, dir. Graphic Arts Tech. Found., Pitts., 1985—. One man shows include Finest Photography, 1982-83; prin. works include (video) Personal Archeology, 1984, One More Kiss Dear, 1985, In Memorium, 1987. Served to sgt. USAF, 1966-70, Vietnam. Grantee FAA, 1979, Dept. Health, Edn. and Welfare, 1980-81. Mem. Am. Film Inst., Internat. TV Assn., Soc. for Creative Anachronism, Interactive Video Assn., Ill. News Broadcasters Assn. Avocation: back packing. Home: 2529 N 1st St DeKalb IL 60115 Office: No Ill U Media Services 305 Altgeld DeKalb IL 60115

BURNS, WILLIAM GRADY, lawyer; b. Ashdown, Ark., Apr. 16, 1907; s. William Franklin and Ida (Graham) B.; m. Margaret McDonald, Nov. 28, 1934; children: Margaret Ann, Susan, Catherine, Graham William, David John. Ph.B., U. Chgo., 1929, J.D., 1931. Bar: Ill. 1931. Since practiced in Chgo.; mem. firm Bell, Boyd & Lloyd (and predecessors), 1943-81. Mem. Joseph Sears Bd. Edn., Kenilworth, 1956-62, pres. bd., 1960, trustee, Village of Kenilworth, 1965-69; chmn., vice chmn. rev. coms. Community Fund Chgo., 1965-70; mem. citizens bd. U. Chgo.; mem. nat. panel Am. Arbitration Assn., 1965-76; life dir. Exec. Service Corps Chgo. Mem. Am., Ill., Chgo. bar assns., Law Club Chgo., Legal Club Chgo., U. Chgo. Law Sch. Alumni Assn. (pres., dir. 1970-72), Phi Beta Kappa, Order of Coif, Delta Tau Delta, Phi Delta Phi. Republican. Baptist. Clubs: University, Economic, Commercial (exec. com. 1976-78), Attic (pres. 1978-80) (Chgo.): Kenilworth (Ill.) (pres. 1965-66); Westmoreland Country (Wilmette, Ill.) (sec., dir. 1974-76). Home: 320 Cumberland Ave Kenilworth IL 60043 Office: 3200 Three 1st Nat Plaza 70 W Madison St Chicago IL 60602

BURNSIDE, JULIAN BERNARD, electrical safety specialist; b. Tampa, Fla., Jan. 8, 1924; s. Edgar G. and Clara L. (Justen) B.; m. Ailene M. McIver, Mar. 8, 1953 (div.); children—Julian, Lorretta Gale, Ronald P.; m. 2d, Lidia Maria Myslinska, Mar. 19, 1976; 1 stepson, Mark Stys. Student in elec. engring., Auburn U., 1943-44. From meter reader to field engr. Tampa Electric Light and Power Co., 1941-57, insp., 1957-58, engr. relay tester, 1958-61; chief electric insp., city elec. engr., City of Tampa, 1961-71; code specialist, coordinator UL/inspection authority relations Underwriters Labs., Inc., Northbrook, Ill., 1971—. Served with U.S. Army, 1943-45. Mem. Internat. Assn. Elec. Insps. (cert. electric safety engr. 1965), Am. Soc. Safety Engrs., DAV, Am. Legion. Republican. Roman Catholic. Home: 8321 N Elmore St Niles IL 60648 Office: Underwriters Labs 333 Pfingsten Rd Northbrook IL 60062

BURNSIDE, WILLIAM CHARLES, investment company executive; b. Edear County, Ill., Oct. 23, 1936; s. William D. and Juanita W. (Greeson) B.; B.S., Eastern Ill. U., 1959; postgrad. N.Y. Inst. Fin., 1965; m. Lola LaFern Trovillion, Oct. 10, 1975; children—Bilinda Cheryl, William Benton, Tyler Thomas; stepchildren—Mitzi Lynn Trovillion, Scott W. Trovillion. With Millikin Nat. Bank, Decatur, Ill., 1959-63, Nat. Cash Register, Decatur, 1963-65, Mid Am Corp., Paris, Ill., 1965-70, Leowi & Co., Decatur, 1970-73; fin. prin., chief exec. officer William C. Burnside & Co. Inc., Danville, Ill., 1973—; dir. Mid-States Railcar, Inc., State Banks and Trust Co. Ill., 1978-85. Pres. Edear County Heart Assn., 1971-72; vice chmn. Ill. Heart Assn., 1969; treas. United Meth. Ch., Paris, 1966-68; vice chmn. Christian Bus. Men's Com., 1979-82, bd. dirs., 1979—; legis. asst. to state senator Max E. Coffey, 1976-82, campaign coordinator Vermillion County, 1976; mem. Eastern Ill. U. Found., 1981—; elected White House Conf. Small Bus., 1985-86; chmn. Greater Danville Plan Commn., 1986—. Served with U.S. Army, 1955-63. Named one of Outstanding Young Men Am., 1971-72. Mem. Nat. Assn. Securities Dealers, Nat. Futures Assn., Commodity Futures Trading Commn., Security Investors Protection Corp., Paris C. of C. (pres. 1970-71, bd. dirs. 1967-69), Christian Businessmen's Com. (vice chmn. 1987—), Jaycees. Home: 322 Fletcher Danville IL 61832 Office: 111 N Vermilion Danville IL 61832

BURNSTEIN, HAROLD ROBERT, lawyer; b. Chgo., May 28, 1919; s. Samuel and Fay (Fine) B.; B.S.C., Northwestern U., 1940; J.D., DePaul U., 1950; m. Harriet Kahn, May 25, 1946; children—Clifford Nolan, Joan Ellen. Pub. accountant Katz, Wagner & Co., Chgo., 1940-41; tax accountant Consol. Vultee Aircraft Corp., San Diego, 1941-45; tax accountant Hughes and Hughes, Chgo., 1946-50, counsel, 1950-79; of counsel firm Schwartz and Freeman; admitted to Ill. bar, 1950, since practiced in Chgo. Past chmn. Highland Park Voters Assn.; mem. Dist. 108 Sch. Bd., Highland Park, 1967-73, pres., 1972-73; mem. Highland Park Library Bd., 1974-80; bd. dirs. North Suburban Library System, 1976-79, Lay Response Council, 1979-81; bd. dirs. Jewish Children's Bur., 1978—, v.p., 1982—. Mem. Am., Chgo. (com. fed. taxation, past chmn.) bar assns., Ill. Soc. C.P.A.'s, Am. Inst. C.P.A.'s, DePaul Bd. Assos., Chgo. Council on Fgn. Relations, Beta Alpha Psi. Jewish. Clubs: Birchwood (past pres.) (Highland Park); Standard, Economic (Chgo.). Contbr. articles on fed. taxation to profl. jours. Home: 510 Ravine Dr Highland Park IL 60035 Office: 401 N Michigan Ave Chicago IL 60611

BURNSTEIN, MICHAEL HARRISON, child psychiatrist; b. Detroit, Sept. 5, 1947. BS, Wayne State U., 1969; MD, U. Mich., 1973. Diplomate Am. Bd. Psychiatry and Neurology. Resident in psychiatry McGill U., Montreal, Can., 1973-75; fellow in child and adolescent psychiatry U. Mich., Ann Arbor, 1976-78, lectr. psychiatry, 1978-80, clin. asst. prof., 1981—; clin. dir. Livingston County Community Mental Health Services, Howell, Mich., 1979-83; child psychiatrist Hawthorn Ctr., Northville, Mich., 1983—; examiner Am. Bd. Psychiatry and Neurology, Chgo., 1982, 84, 86. Contbr. articles on child psychiatry in nat. profl. jours. Recipient Psychiatric Research award Mcgill U. and Geigy Pharmacerticals, 1976. Fellow Royal Coll. Physicians and Surgeons of Can.; mem. Am. Psychiatric Assn., Mich. Council of Child Psychiatry. Avocations: clarinetist, swimming. Office: Hawthorn Ctr 18471 Haggerty Rd Northville MI 48167

BURPULIS, EUGENIA G., telephone company executive; b. Salem, N.J., Nov. 21, 1942; s. George S. and Thelma (Pirovolos) B.; student Kent State U., 1961-62, Cuyahoga Community Coll., 1977. With Ohio Bell Tel. Co., Cleve., 1961—, Supr., 1964-71, asst. mgr. multi-media, 1971-75, asst. mgr. course devel., 1975-78, mgr. course devel., 1978—. Mem. women's com., task force Great Lakes Theatre Festival, 1986—; trustee, exec. bd. St. Demetrios Greek Orthodox Ch., 1986—. Mem. Am. Soc. Tng. and Devel., Nat. Soc. Performance and Instrn., Am. Bus. Woman's Assn. (editor bull., newsletter editor 1982—, edn. chmn. 1982; Woman of Year), Ohio Bell Pioneers (editor newsletter 1980-81), St. Demetrios Philoptochos Soc., Nat. Chios Soc. (cmv. sec.). Club: Women's City (Cleve.). Greek Orthodox (mem. choir, past pres., treas.). Home: 35270 Drake Rd North Ridgeville OH 44039 Office: Ohio Bell Telephone Co 45 Erieview Pl Rm 704 Cleveland OH 44114

BURR, DAVID ALEXANDER, mayor, accountant; b. Windsor, Ont., Can., July 15, 1944; s. Frederick Arthur Burr and Dorothy Gladys Young; m. Ruth Anita Delang; children: Daniel, Laura, Cheryl, Colleen. Chartered Acct., Queen's U., Kingston, Ont., 1968. Pub. acct. Clark & Menzies & Co., New Zealand, 1969-70; controller G.G. McKeough, Windsor, 1971-72; tax auditor Revenue Service of Can., Windsor, 1972-73; pvt. practice acctg. Windsor, 1973-85; mayor City of Windsor, 1985—. alderman City of Windsor, 1971-85; vice chmn. Transit Windsor Bd., 1979-85; chmn. Great Lakes Mayor's Com., Mcpl. Mgmt. Devel. Bd. Mem. Inst. Chartered Accts. of Ont., Assn. Municipalities (bd. dirs. Ont. chpt. 1983-86). New Democrat. Lodge: Optimist. Avocation: golf. Office: Office of the Mayor, City Hall PO Box 1607, Windsor, ON Canada N9A 6S1

BURR, JAMES EDWARD, hotel executive; b. Utica, N.Y., July 20, 1941; s. James I. and Virginia Ellen (Davidson) B. B.S., Cornell U., 1963. Asst. budget control dir. Plaza Hotel, N.Y.C., 1963-65; asst. mgr. Danbury Motor Inn (Conn.), 1965-66; cons. to mgr. Harris, Kerr, Forster, Chgo., 1966-75, prin., Miami, Fla., 1975-77; dist. dir. Holiday Inns, Inc., Miami, 1978-79, dir. franchise relations, Toronto, Ont., Can., 1980, dist. dir., Chgo., 1981-83, gen. mgr. Holiday Inn Lake Shore Dr., Chgo., 1983-86, dist. dir. Chgo. CMI Hotels, 1986—. Cons. editor tng. manual. Neighborhood campaign ctr. chmn. Percy for Senator, Chgo., 1966; v.p. Chgo. Hospitality Council for City of Hope, 1982-83; hon. mem. Ye Hosts Hon., Ithaca, N.Y., 1962. Mem. Cornell Soc. Hotelmen (dir. 1971-72), Greater Chgo. Hotel and Motel Assn. (bd. dirs. 1985-86), Confrerie de la Chaine des Rotisseurs., MENSA. Republican. Presbyterian. Club: Canadian of Chgo. Home: 910 N Hemlock Ln Mount Prospect IL 60056 Office: 8430 W Bryn Mawr Suite 600 Chicago IL 60631

BURRELL, JAY ROBERT, retail buying executive; b. Oak Park, Ill., Oct. 31, 1956; s. Robert Earl and Margaret Irene (Wachdorf) B.; m. Barbara Frances Rajkowski, June 13, 1981. BA in Psychology, Northeastern Ill. U., 1984; postgrad. bus. adminstrn., Loyola U., Chgo., 1984—. Mgr. Saxon Paint & Home Care, Chgo., 1978-80; buyer Aldens, Chgo., 1980-82, Warshawsky & Co., Chgo., 1984—. Served to sgt. USAF, 1974-78. Mem. Soc. MBA Execs., Psi Chi, Phi Theta Kappa. Democrat. Roman Catholic. Club: Babco Ptnrs. (pres. 1984—) (Chgo.). Avocations: judo, chess, bowling, computers, music, theater. Office: Warshawsky & Co 1104 S Wabash Chicago IL 60605

BURRIS, BARBARA ANN, social worker; b. Des Moines, May 18, 1943; d. Richard Edward and Leora Grace (French) B.; m. Ronald D. Halstead, Dec. 23, 1966. BA, Wayne State U., 1979. Cert. secondary sch. tchr. Tchr. Wayne County Community Coll., Detroit, 1972-73; social worker State of Mich., Madison Heights, 1973—. Author: (play) The Daughter (Detroit film council award 1972); editor, co-publisher (newsletter) Women/Body Talk, 1986—, Health Update Press, 1986—; contbr. articles to profl. jours. Avocations: gardening, music.

BURRIS, BRADFORD, corporate publications executive; b. Redlands, Calif., July 6, 1932; s. H. Cleo and Rebecca Cook (Davis) B.; m. Carolee Cornelius, Dec. 20, 1960; children: Matthew, John. BS, U. Calif., Berkeley, 1957. Asst. dir. DeWitt Reading Clinic, San Rafael, Calif., 1958-62; test cons. Houghton Mifflin Co., Palo Alto, Calif., 1963-68; project dir. Nat. Computer Systems, Mpls., 1969-76; v.p. editorial Scott, Foresman & Co., Glenview, Ill., 1976-81; exec. v.p. Runzheimer Internat., Northbrook, Ill., 1981—, travel mgmt. cons., 1984—. Contbr. articles to profl. jours. Commr. Lake Bluff (Ill.) Park Dist., 1985; bd. dirs. multicultural com. Palo Alto, 1968. Served with U.S. Army, 1954-56. Mem. Assn. Edn. Data Systems (pres. 1976-77, editor newsletter 1970-74, Aid award 1977), Newsletter Assn., Nat. Council for Measurement in Edn., Internat. Reading Assn., Nat. Passenger Traffic Assn., Inst. Mgmt. Cons. (elected cert. mgmt. cons. 1986). Democrat. Methodist. Club: Lake Bluff Yacht (treas. 1980). Avocations: sailing, biking, wines. Office: Runzheimer Internat Publs Div 555 Skokie Blvd Northbrook IL 60062

BURROW, PETER NOEL HUNTINGTON, management consultant; b. New Haven, Aug. 2, 1959; s. Gerard Noel and Ann (Rademacher) B. AB, Brown U., 1981; MBA, Harvard U., 1985. Lic. stock broker. Mktg. analyst Merrill Lynch, N.Y.C., 1981-83; asst. to econ. sec. U.S. Embassy, Niger, West Africa, 1985; mgmt. cons. Booz, Allen & Hamilton, Chgo., 1985—. Mem Harvard Bus. Sch. Alumni Assn. (class fund agt.). Republican. Episcopalian. Club: Harvard. Avocations: writing, inventing, numismatics, eurocurrency market. Home: 211 E Ohio Suite 1922 Chicago IL 60611 Office: Booz Allen & Hamilton Three First Nat Plaza Chicago IL 60602

BURROWS, CECIL J., lawyer, judge; b. Schuyler County, Ill., Mar. 21, 1922; s. Amos R. and Florence M. (Krohe) B.; m. Virginia Pearson, June 27, 1949; children—Sandra, Carol, Deborah. B.S., Western Mich. U., 1944; J.D., Northwestern U., 1952. Bar: Ill. 1952. City atty. Pittsfield, Ill., 1957-64; state's atty. Pike County, Ill., 1964-70; sole practice, Pittsfield, to 1970; cir. judge 8th cir. Ill., 1970—. Served as officer USMC, 1943-46. Mem. ABA, Ill. State Bar Assn., Pike County Bar Assn. Clubs: Masons, Shriners. Home: 437 W Washington Pittsfield IL 62363 Office: Pike County Courthouse Pittsfield IL 62363

BURROWS, FRANK LOWELL, pharmacist, pharmaceutical sales; b. Waterloo, Iowa, May 25, 1932; s. Francis Lowell and Eva R. (Roberts) B.; m. Vesta Jean Donahue, June 3, 1953; children—Kay, John, Joan, Mary Margaret, Jane. B.S. in Pharmacy, Drake U., 1956. Registered pharmacist Iowa. Pharmacist Montross Pharmacy, Winterset, Iowa, 1956-59, Bauder Pharmacy, Des Moines, Iowa, 1959-74; med. rep. Merrell-Dow, Cin., 1974—; speaker on drug abuse, Iowa; lectr. Drake U.; tchr. drug abuse Des Moines Adult Edn. Adv. council Gov. Council Drug Abuse, Iowa, 1974; bd. dirs. Mid Iowa Drug Abuse Council, chmn. edn. com., med. com.; pres. Byron Rich Sch. PTA, 1973, 74. Recipient Pres. award Merrell-Dow Pharms. 1975, Pace Setter award Merrell-Dow Pharms., 1976. HEW Grant 1972.. Mem. Am. Pharm. Assn., Iowa Pharm. Assn. Republican. Presbyterian. Lodge: Masons. Avocations: furniture making; woodworking; fishing. Home and Office: 4305 Ashby Ave Des Moines IA 50310

BURROWS, HAROLD HENRY, financial consultant; b. Mpls., Oct. 18, 1942; s. Harold Henry and Emily (Sirotiak) B.; B.S. in Math. and Physics, Iowa State U., 1964; M.S. in Physics, U. Minn., 1967, M.B.A., 1972; m. Renée Ruth Marko, Dec. 18, 1965; children—Jason, Sonja, Suzanne. Research physicist Honeywell Inc., Mpls., 1967-69; account exec. Merrill Lynch Inc., Mpls., 1969-76; fin. cons. Shearson Lehman Bros. (formerly Shearson/Am. Express), Mpls., 1976—, v.p. investments, 1981-83, 1st v.p. investments, 1983—. Lutheran. Home: 5135 Fern Dr Loretto MN 55357 Office: 625 4th Ave S Suite 1125 Minneapolis MN 55415

BURSON, RONALD PAUL, real estate executive; b. Athens, Ohio, Dec. 19, 1951; s. Herbert Shields and Pauline Frances (McDaniel) B.; m. Nancy Sue Underwood, Sept. 6, 1986. BS in Bus. Administrn., Bowling Green (Ohio) State U., 1973. CPA, Ohio. Acct. Coopers & Lybrand, Columbus, 1973-79; v.p., treas. Fairfield Houses, Inc., Lancaster, Ohio, 1979—. Chmn. bd. ARC, Lancaster, 1979-85. Mem. Am. Inst. CPA's, Ohio Soc. CPA's. Republican. Presbyterian. Avocations: reading, golf, softball, basketball. Home: 614 Sycamore Mill Dr Gahanna OH 43230 Office: Fairfield Homes Inc 603 W Wheeling St Lancaster OH 43130

BURT, ROBERT EUGENE, civic organization administrator; b. Bussey, Iowa, June 5, 1926; s. Francis Earl and Grace (Hauenstein) B.; m. Mary Emma Bates, May 5, 1946; children: Kenneth, Roberta, Carl, Rodney, Lori. BA in Human Relations, Mo. Valley Coll., 1953. Exec. dir. USDA, Madera, Calif., 1946-51; dist. exec. Boy Scouts Am., Jefferson City, Mo., 1953-57; dist. exec. Boy Scouts Am., Mpls., 1957-61, dir. camping, 1961-68; scout exec. Boy Scouts Am., Duluth, Minn., 1968-71; dir. of program North Cen. Region Boy Scouts Am., Overland Park, Kans., 1971-86; chmn. Eagle Scout scholarship program SAR, Louisville, 1980-87. Author, editor: Camping in Minnesota, 1970. Served as cpl. USAF, 1944-46. Recipient Disting. Service award Nat. Order of Arrow, Duluth, 1986, Medal of Honor, DAR, 1985. Mem. SAR (pres. Kans. soc. 1984, Minuteman award 1987), Kans. Huguenot Soc. (pres. 1984-85), Dahlia Soc. (pres. 1979-81), Soc. Descendants Washington's Army at Valley Forge (Mo. Brigade Comdr. 1985-89), Welcome Soc. Democrat. Methodist. Clubs: Mens Garden (pres.) (Kansas City, Mo.). Lodges: Rotary, Kiwanis, Masons. Avocations: gardening, flower showing, genealogy, golf, fishing. Home: 9708 NW 75th St Kansas City MO 64152

BURTON, BETTY JUNE, minister, pastor; b. Muskegon, Mich., June 11, 1923; d. Bernard J. and Louise Ella (Weaver) Mulder; mem. Harold Ver Berkmoes, June 4, 1943 (div. 1966); children: Suzanne, James, Michael, William, Judith, David (dec.); m. Eldon Franklin Burton, June 27, 1971. Student of music and psychology, Hope Coll., 1941-45; student, Garrett Evang. Theol. Sem., 1984-85. Ordained to ministry United Meth. Ch., 1986. Librarian Vassar Hosp. Sch. Nursing, Poughkeepsie, N.Y., 1958-60, Hackley Pub. Library, Muskegon, 1960-64, Boyne City (Mich.) Pub. Library, 1972-74; reporter Ludington (Mich.) Daily News, 1975-81; caseworker Aid to Dependent Children Mich. Dept. Social Services, Hart, 1974-78; pastor various Meth. Chs., Norwood, Barnard and Charlevoix, Mich., 1981-83, Mears (Mich.) United Meth. Ch., 1985, 86; assoc. pastor United Meth. Centenary, Pentwater, Mich., 1986—; assoc. realtor Shaw Real Estate, Pentwater, 1975-81, Real Estate One, Traverse City, Mich., 1981-82, Century 21 Williams Real Estate, Pentwater, 1986—. Sec. Pentwater Planning Commn., 1985. Mem. Kappa Beta Phi (pres. 1943), Xi Gamma Beta (sec. 1970). Republican. Clubs: Women's of Pentwater (v.p. 1986—), Garden of Pentwater (pres. 1986—). Avocations: writing, fishing, gardening, birding, traveling. Home and Office: 270 Lake St PO Box 860 Pentwater MI 49449

BURTON, CHARLES VICTOR, physician, surgeon, inventor; b. N.Y.C., Jan. 2, 1935; s. Norman Howard and Ruth Esther (Putziger) B.; divorced; children—Matthew, Timothy, Andrew. Student, Johns Hopkins U., Balt., 1952-56; M.D., N.Y. Med. Coll., 1960. Diplomate Am. Bd. Neurol. Surgery, Nat. Bd. Med. Examiners. Intern surgery Yale U. Med. Ctr., 1961-62; asst. resident neurol. surgery Johns Hopkins Hosp., Balt., 1962-66, chief resident, 1966-67; assoc. chief surgery, chief neurosurgery USPHS Hosp., Seattle, 1967-69; vis. research affiliate Primate Ctr., U. Wash., 1967-69; asst. prof. neurosurgery Temple U. Health Scis. Ctr., Phila., 1970-73, assoc. prof., 1973-74; neurol. research coordinator Temple U. Health Scis. Ctr., 1970-74; dir. dept. neuroaugmentive surgery Sister Kenny Inst., Mpls., 1974-81, med. dir. Low Back Clinic, 1978—; med. dir. Inst. for Low Back Care, Mpls., 1981—, Low Back Club Internat., Mpls., 1986—; co-chmn. Joint Neurosurg. Com. on Devices and Drugs, 1973-77; chmn. FDA adv. panel on neurologic devices, 1974-77, Internat. Standards Orgn., 1974-76; mem. U.S. Biomed. Instrumentation Del. to Soviet Union, 1974. Patentee surgical devices, operating room fiberophic headlights, clin. therapy systems and techniques. Research fellow Nat. Polio Found., 1956, HEW, 1958; neurosurg. fellow Johns Hopkins Hosp., 1960-61, 62-67, 69-70. Fellow ACS; mem. Congress Neurol. Surgeons (chmn. com. materials and devices 1972-79), Am. Assn. Neurol. Surgeons, Minn. Neurosurg. Soc., AAAS, ASTM (chmn. com. materials 1973-78), Internat. Soc. Study of Lumbar Spine, Am. Nat. Standards Inst. (med. device tech. adv. bd. 1973-78), Philadelphia County Med. Soc. (med.-legal com. 1970-74), Minn. Med. Assn. (Gold medal award for best sci. presentation at 1975 meeting, subcom. on med. testimony 1978—), Hennepin County Med. Soc. (med-legal com. 1975—), Mpls. Acad. Medicine, Cor et Manus Soc. Profl. Assn. Diving Instrs. (underwater photography splty. diver), Alpha Epsilon Delta. Home: 148 W Lake St Excelsior MN 55331 Office: Inst Low Back Care 2737 Chicago Ave Minneapolis MN 55407

BURTON, COURTNEY, mining and shipping company executive; b. Cleve., Oct. 29, 1912; s. Courtney and Sarita (Oglebay) B.; m. Marguerite Rankin, Sept. 7, 1933 (dec. Apr. 1976); children: Sarita Ann Burton Frith, Marguerite Rankin Burton Humphrey; m. Margaret Butler Leitch, Dec. 20, 1978. Student, Mich. Coll. Mining and Tech., 1933-34, B.S., 1956. Dir. E.W. Oglebay Co., Cleve., 1934-57; pres. E.W. Oglebay Co., 1947-57; v.p. Ferro Engring. Co., Cleve., 1950-57; pres. Fortuna Lake Mining Co., Cleve., 1950-57; treas., dir. Columbia Transp. Co., Cleve., 1950-57; v.p. Montreal Mining Co., Cleve., 1950-57; pres. North Shore Land Co., Cleve., 1950-57; v.p., dir. Brule Smokeless Coal Co., Cleve., 1950-57; chmn. bd., chmn. exec. com. Oglebay Norton Co., Cleve., 1957—; 1dir. Nat. Bank W.Va., 1951-59, Central Nat. Bank Cleve., 1941-42, Cleve. Trust Co., 1950-76. Dir. Ohio Civilian Def. and Rationing, 1941-42; exec. asst. Office Coordinator Inter-Am. Affairs, 1942-44; mayor Village of Gates Mills, Ohio, 1948-61; mem. Cleve. Met. Park Bd., 1969-74; chmn. Ohio Republican Finance Com., 1954-61, Rep. Nat. Finance Com., 1961-64; former trustee, founder, mem. adminstrv. bd. Nat. Recreation and Park Assn.; bd. dirs. Nat. Park Found.; trustee Bethany Coll.; hon. trustee Univ. Hosp., Cleve., Oglebay Inst., Wheeling, W.Va.; pres. America's Future Trees Found. Served to lt. USNR, 1944-46. Mem. Am. Iron and Steel Inst., Nat. Coal Assn., Cleve. Zool. Soc. (pres. 1968-76). Episcopalian. Clubs: Chagrin Valley Hunt (Gates Mills) (master of hounds 1946-54); Tavern, Union (Cleve.); Rolling Rock (Ligonier, Pa.); Fort Henry, Wheeling Country (W.Va.); Kirtland (Willoughby, Ohio). Office: Oglebay Norton Co 1100 Superior Ave Cleveland OH 44114

BURTON, DANNY LEE, congressman; b. Indpls., June 21, 1938; m. Barbara Jean Logan, 1959; children—Kelly, Danielle Lee, Danny Lee II. Businessman, ins. and real estate firm owner 1968—; mem. Ind. Ho. Reps., Indpls., 1967-68, 77-80, Ind. State Senate, Indpls., 1969-70, 81-82, 98th-100th Congresses from 6th Dist. Ind., 1983—. Pres. Vols. of Am.; pres. Ind. Christian Benevolent Assn., Com. for Constl. Govt., Family Support Ctr.; mem. Ind. Ho. of Reps., 1967-68, 77-80, Ind. State Senate, 1969-70, 81-82. Served with U.S. Army, 1957-58. Republican. Office: US Ho Reps 120 Cannon House Office Bldg Washington DC 20515 *

BURTON, DARRELL IRVIN, engineering executive; b. Ashtabula, Ohio, Sept. 21, 1926; s. George Irvin and Barbara Elizabeth (Streyle) B.; B.S. in Radio Engring., Chgo. Tech. Coll., 1954; m. Lois Carol Warkentien, Apr. 14, 1951; children—Linda Jean Burton Clinton, Lisa Ann Burton Watts, Lori Elizabeth. Research and devel. engr. Motorola, Inc., Chgo., 1951-60; devel. engr. Hallicrafters, Chgo., 1960-62; chief engr. TRW, Inc., Des Plaines, Ill., 1962-65; devel. engr. Warwick, Niles, Ill., 1965-68; systems mgr. Admiral Corp., Chgo., 1968-76; elec.-electronics lab. mgr. Montgomery Ward & Co., Chgo., 1976-82; staff engr. Wells-Gardner Electronics Corp., Chgo., 1982-85; sr. engr., Zenith Electronics Corp., 1985—; tchr. electronics and math. Pres. Addison Homeowners Assn., 1958-60, v.p., 1960-62; mem. Addison Plan Commn., 1960-63; mem. Bd. Edn. Immanuel Luth. Sch., 1985—. Served with USNR, 1944. Mem. IEEE, ASTM. Club: York Amateur Radio (pres. 1984-86, bd. dirs. 1986—). Republican. Lutheran. Patentee in field. Home: 112 Lawndale Ave Elmhurst IL 60126

BURTON, DOROTHY HOPE, educator; b. Norwood, Ohio, Apr. 7, 1928; d. Osber Franklin and Ina Belle (Sears) Zachary; student Olivet Nazarene Coll., 1945-49; B.S. in Edn., Ball State U., 1960, M.A. in Edn., 1967; M.A. in Edn., Ohio State U., 1984; m. Roy Dean Burton, Nov. 28, 1947 (div.); children—Jennifer D. Burton Dooley, Sally Jo Jackson. Classroom tchr. Aroma Park (Ill.) Sch., 1954-56, Bradley (Ill.) Schs., Crawfordsville (Ind.) City Schs., 1957-58, Muncie (Ind.) City Schs., 1960-77; field placement coordinator, asst. prof. edn. Mt. Vernon (Ohio) Nazarene Coll., 1977—. Mem. Assn. Supervision and Curriculum Devel., Ohio Assn. Gifted Children, Ind. Ret. Tchrs. Assn., Am. Assn. Colls. Tchr. Educators, Assn. Tchr. Educators, Nazarene Assn. Colls. Tchr. Edn., Ohio Assn. Tchr. Educators, Kappa Delta Pi. Republican. Nazarene. Home: 9 Claypool Dr Mount Vernon OH 43050 Office: 800 Martinsburg Rd Mount Vernon OH 43050

BURTON, RAYMOND CHARLES, JR., trailer train company executive; b. Phila., Aug. 29, 1938; s. Raymond Charles and Phyllis (Clifford) B. B.A., Cornell U., 1960; M.B.A., U. Pa., 1963. Various operating positions Santa Fe Ry. Co., 1963-68, asst. controller, 1968-69; asst. treas. Santa Fe Industries, Chgo., 1969-74; asst. v.p. planning, treas. Burlington No., Inc., 1974-79; v.p. and treas. Burlington No., Inc., St. Paul and Seattle, 1979-82; v.p.

planning Internat. Harvester Co., Chgo., 1982; pres., chief exec. officer Trailer Train Co., Chgo., 1982—, Railbox Co., Railgon Co., Chgo., 1982—. Served to 1st lt. U.S. Army, 1960-61. Republican. Presbyterian. Clubs: Metropolitan, Chicago (Chgo.); Sea Island (Ga.). Office: Trailer Train Co 101 N Wacker Dr Chicago IL 60606

BURTON, WALTER ERVIN, writer; b. McMechen, W.Va., Nov. 18, 1903; s. David William and Mary Lucinda (Yoho) B.; student U. Akron, 1922-23, Johns Hopkins, 1923-24, 27-28. Editorial staffs Evening Times, Times-Press, Herald Pub. Co., Akron, 1922-23, 24-27. Mem. Nat. Assn. Home and Workshop Writers. Club: Portage Camera (Akron). Contbr. numerous articles to mags. including Popular Mechanics, Popular Sci., others. Author: Home-Built Photo Equipment, 1947; The Story of Tire Beads and Tires, 1954, others. Editor: Engineering with Rubber, 1949. Patentee in field. Address: 1032 Florida Ave Akron OH 44314

BURZYNSKI, PETER RAYMOND, psychology educator; b. Watertown, Wis., May 7, 1948; s. Eugene Edward and Helen Louise (Krieger) B.; m. M. Sue Case, July 14, 1979; 1 child, Myka Danielle. BA, Lawrence U., 1970; MS, Ind. State U., 1971, EdS, 1972, PhD, 1981. Cert. sch. psychologist, Ind. Psychologist Laporte (Ind.) Community Schs., 1972-74; asst. prof. Vincennes (Ind.) U., 1976-79, assoc. prof., 1979-83, chmn. psychology dept., 1983-86, prof., 1984—. Author: Archeus and I, 1971, Days of..., 1977, To Be a Child, 1979. Recipient research award Blumberg Found., 1975. Mem. Am. Psychol. Assn. (teaching award 1985), Internat. Sch. Psychology Assn., Nat. Assn. Sch. Psychologists, Midwestern Psychol. Assn., Ind. Psychol. Assn., Phi Delta Kappa (research award 1975). Lodge: Rotary (bd. dirs. Vincennes 1984—). Avocations: travel, photography. Home: 3116 Walnut Dr Vincennes IN 47591 Office: Vincennes U 1002 N 1st St Vincennes IN 47591

BUS, ROGER JAY, lawyer; b. Kalamazoo, Mich., Oct. 15, 1953; s. Charles J. and Sena (Wolthuis) B.; m. Lida Margaret Sell, Aug. 27, 1977; 1 child, Emily Lynn. Student, Calvin Coll., Grand Rapids, Mich., 1971-73; BA, U. Mich., 1975; JD, U. Toledo, 1979. Bar: Mich. 1979, U.S. Dist. Ct. (we. dist.) Mich. 1979. Law clk. to presiding justice Kalamazoo Cir. Ct., 1978; intern Toledo Legal Aid, 1979; staff attorney Legal Air Bur. Southwest Mich., Kalamazoo, 1979-81; assoc. Stanley, Davidoff & Gray, Kalamazoo, 1981-83; owner, attorney Debt Relief Law Ctr., Kalamazoo, 1983—. Deacon Reformed Bapt. Ch., Kalamazoo, 1983-85; precinct del. Kalamazoo County Reps., 1986—; bd. dirs., attorney Kalamazoo Gospel Mission, 1983-86; mem. Calvary Bible Ch., Kalamazoo, Mich. Mem. Mich. Bar Assn., Kalamazoo County Bar Assn., Christian Legal Soc., Fellowship of Christian Magicians, Nat. Assn. Chpt. 13 Trustees. Avocations: golf, reading, religious book collecting. Home: 5073 N Riverview Dr Parchment MI 49004 Office: Debt Relief Law Ctr 903 E Cork St Kalamazoo MI 49001

BUSBY, JOHN EDWARD, dentist; b. Madison, Wis., Aug. 31, 1954; s. Edward Oliver and Lois Elizabeth (Tehan) B.; m. Theresa Marie O'Rourke; children: Katherine, Laura, Jennifer. BS, U. Wis., Platteville, 1974; DDS, Marquette U., 1978. Exec. v.p. Affiliated Dentists, Madison, 1983—. Served to maj. U.S. Army, 1978-83, with Res. 1983—. Fellow Acad. Gen. Dentistry; mem. ADA, Wis. Dental Assn., Dane County Dental Assn., U. Wis. Platteville Alumni Assn. (bd. dirs. 1983—), Sigma Tau Gamma, Omicron Kappa Upsilon. Lodges: Kiwanis, KC. Office: Affiliated Dentists 202 N Midvale Madison WI 53705

BUSCH, AUGUST A., JR., brewing executive; b. St. Louis, Mar. 28, 1899; s. August A. and Alice (Zisemann) B.; m. Margaret Snyder, Mar. 11, 1981. Ed., Smith Acad.; LL.D. (hon.), St. Louis U., 1969. With Mfrs. Ry. Co., Lafayette South Side Bank & Trust Co.; gen. supt. Anheuser-Busch, Inc., 1924-26, 6th v.p., gen. mgr., 1926-31, 2d v.p., gen. mgr., 1931-34, 1st v.p., gen. mgr., 1934-41, pres., 1946-72, chmn. bd., 1956-77; hon. chmn. bd. Anheuser-Busch Cos., Inc., 1977—, chief exec. officer, 1971-75; pres., chmn. bd., chief exec. officer St. Louis Cardinals, 1953—; chmn. Mfrs. Ry. Co., St. Louis Refrigerator Car Co.; dir. Centerre Trust Co., Gen. Am. Life Ins. Co., Centerre Bank, St. Louis; mem. brewing industry adv. com. WPB, 1942. Chmn. pub. relations com. United Fund St. Louis, from 1964; chmn. bd. Civic Progress, Inc., 13 years, St. Louis U. Devel. Fund drive; bd. dirs. St. Louis Municipal Opera; chmn. St. Louis Bicentennial Celebration Com. Served as col. Ordnance Dept. AUS, 1942-45. Recipient Fleur-de-Lis award St. Louis U., 1960; named Man of Year St. Louis Globe-Democrat, 1961; Man and Boy award nat. bd. Boys' Clubs Am., 1966; Citizen No. 1 award Press Club Met. St. Louis, 1967; Man of Year award So. Calif. Retail Liquor Dealers Assn., 1971; hon. commodore USCG Aux., 1972. Clubs: St. Louis Country (St. Louis), Racquet (St. Louis), Old Warson (St. Louis), Log Cabin (St. Louis), Bridlespur Hunt (St. Louis); Rolling Rock (Ligonier, Pa.). Office: Anheuser-Busch Cos Inc 1 Busch Pl Saint Louis MO 63118

BUSCH, AUGUST ADOLPHUS, III, brewery executive; b. St. Louis, June 16, 1937; s. August Adolphus and Elizabeth (Overton) B.; m. Virginia L. Wiley, Dec. 28, 1974; children: Steven August, Virginia Marie; children by previous marriage: August Adolphus IV, Susan Marie II. Student, U. Ariz., 1957-58, Siebel Inst. Tech., 1960-61. With Anheuser-Busch, Inc., St. Louis, 1957—, sales mgr., 1962-64, v.p. mktg. ops., 1964-65, v.p., gen. mgr., 1965-74, pres., 1975-79, chief exec. officer, 1975—, chmn. bd., 1977—; chmn., pres. Anheuser Busch Cos., Inc., St. Louis, 1979—, also bd. dirs.; v.p. Busch Properties, Inc., St. Louis; bd. dirs. St. Louis Nat. Baseball Club, Mfg. RW Co., Norfolk So. Ry., Southwestern Bell Corp., Gen. Am. Life Ins. Co., Emerson Electric Co.; trustee St. Louis Refrigerator Car Co. Mem. adv. bd. St. John Mercy Med. Ctr.; trustee Washington U.; bd. dirs. United Way Greater St. Louis, St. Louis Symphony Soc.; bd. overseers Wharton Sch., U. Pa.; mem. exec. bd. Boy Scouts Am. Clubs: St. Louis, Frontenac Racquet, St. Louis Country, Racquet (St. Louis); Noonday, Log Cabin, Stadium. Office: Anheuser-Busch Cos Inc One Busch Pl Saint Louis MO 63118

BUSCH, MARGERET S., food products company executive; b. 1916. Student, Washington U., St. Louis. With Anheuser Busch, Inc., St. Louis, 1942-79, sec. indsl. products, adminstrv. asst., v.p. corp. promotions; v.p. corp. promotions Anheuser-Busch Cos., Inc., St. Louis, 1979—; now v.p. St. Louis Cardinals. Office: Anheuser-Busch Cos Inc 1 Busch Pl Saint Louis MO 63118 *

BUSCH, ROBERT MICHAEL, insurance company executive; b. Rice Lake, Wis., Nov. 3, 1950; s. Leonard Albert and Rosalie Susan (Schutz) B.; B.S., U. Wis., Eau Claire, 1974, B.S. in Environ. and Public Health, 1976; M.S., U. Wis., Stout, 1978; postgrad in public health U. Minn., 1978-80; m. Leah Ellan Masterson, Dec. 13, 1980; 1 child, Alyssa Lauren. With Wausau Ins. Cos., Mpls., 1980, loss control specialist, Oshkosh, Wis., 1981-82, Green Bay, 1982-83, sr. safety cons., 1982—. Mem. Am. Soc. Safety Engrs. (cert. safety profl., chpt. v.p. 1986-87), Am. Indsl. Hygiene Assn., Green Bay (Wis.) C. of C. (chmn. safety and health com., mem. exec. com.), Phi Kappa Phi. Club: Green Bay Golf League. Office: PO Box 19030 Green Bay WI 54307

BUSCH, STEVEN ALBERT, human resources executive; b. Grand Rapids, Mich., July 7, 1961; s. William Albert and Mary (Bentley) B.; m. Libbie Louise Johnson, Aug. 18, 1985. BS in Mgmt., Jacksonville U., Fla., 1984. Dir. human resource Haven-Busch Co., Grand Rapids, 1984—. Vol. United Way, Kent County, Mich., 1985—. Mem. Grand Rapids Employee Assn., Vested Benefits Grand Rapids. Congregationalist. Avocations: hiking, sailing, skiing. Office: Haven-Busch Co 3445 Chicago Dr SW Grandville MI 49418

BUSCH, THEODORE NORMAN, shooting range design consultant; b. Cleve., Dec. 29, 1919; s. Theodore S. and Norma B.; student pub. schs. Cleve.; m. 2d, Sené Rosene, June 30, 1961; 1 dau. by previous marriage, Kathy. Dir. tech. communications DoAll Co., Des Plaines, Ill., 1952-62; v.p. Shooting Equipment, Inc., Chgo., 1962-69; v.p. Caswell Equipment Co., Inc., Mpls., 1969-83; v.p., profl. cons. Seneb, Inc. Mpls., 1976—. Served with USAAF, World War II. Mem. Am. Soc. Quality Control, Soc. Mfg. Engrs., Internat. Assn. Law Enforcement Firearm Instrs., Internat. Soc. Law Enforcement and Criminal Justice Instrs., Soc. Am. Mil. Engrs., Internat. Assn. Chiefs of Police, Am. Def. Preparedness Assn., Tactical Response Assn., Nat. Forensic Ctr. Author: Fundamentals of Dimensional Metrology, 1963; Guidelines for Police Shooting Ranges, 1977; Guidelines for Commercial Shooting Ranges, 1979. Contbr. articles to profl. jours. Patentee in field. Office: 910 Mt Curve Ave Minneapolis MN 55403

BUSCHBACH, THOMAS CHARLES, geologist, consultant; b. Cicero, Ill., May 12, 1923; s. Thomas Dominick and Vivian (Smiley) B.; m. Mildred Merle Fletcher, Nov. 26, 1947; children—Thomas Richard, Susan Kay, Deborah Lynn. B.S., U. Ill., 1950, M.S., 1951, Ph.D., 1959. Geologist structural geology, stratigraphy, underground storage of natural gas Ill. Geol. Survey, 1951-78; coordinator New Madrid Seismotectonic Study, U.S. Nuclear Regulatory Commn., 1976-85; research prof. geology St. Louis U., 1978-85; geologic cons. Champaign, Ill., 1985—. Served to lt. comdr. USNR, 1942-47. Fellow Geol. Soc. Am.; mem. Am. Assn. Petroleum Geologists (chmn. stratigraphic correlations com. 1970-73), Assn. Engring. Geologists, Am. Geophys. Union. Home: 604 Park Ln Champaign IL 61820 Office: PO Box 1620 Champaign IL 61820

BUSCHE, EUGENE MARVIN, insurance company executive; b. Decatur, Ind., July 2, 1926; s. Louis Martin and Ruby (Smith) B.; m. Barbara Ann Sherow, Aug. 1, 1954; children: David Alan, Sara Lynn. B.S., Ind. U., 1950. C.L.U. Agt., Am. United Life Ins. Co., Lafayette, Ind., 1950-55; asst. gen. agt. State Mut. Life Assurance Co., Indpls., 1955-56; field supr. Indpls. Life Ins. Co., 1956-63, ednl. dir., 1963-70, adminstrv. v.p., dir., 1970-72, pres., chief exec. officer, 1972—; dir. Ind. Nat. Bank. Bd. dirs. Meth. Hosp. Found., Children's Mus., Hist. Landmarks Found. Ind.; trustee U. Indpls., Christian Theol. Sem., chmn. Jr. Achievement; trustee Meth. Hosp.; trustee Arthur Jordan Found., Benjamin Harrison Found.; bd. dirs. Greater Indpls. Progress Commn., United Way Cen. Ind. Served with USNR, 1944-46. Fellow Life Mgmt. Inst.; mem. Indpls. Soc. C.L.U. s, Indpls. Assn. Life Underwriters, Assn. Ind. Life Ins. Cos., Am. Council Life Ins. (bd. dirs.), Ind. State C. of C. (bd. dirs.), Delta Tau Delta. United Methodist. Clubs: Rotary (Indpls.), Economic (Indpls.) (dir.). Home: 12635 Royce Ct Carmel IN 46032 Office: Indpls Life Ins Co 2960 N Meridian St Indianapolis IN 46208

BUSCHER, J. MARGO, teacher; b. Langdon, Kans., Feb. 7, 1947; d. Jesse L. and Sara Emily (Hobbs) Hughes; married; children: Sarah Rachel, Charla Shawnta, Charles Bradly. BS, Emporia (Kans.) State U., 1970; MS, Wichita (Kans.) State U., 1986. Cert. elem. tchr., cert. tchr. for emotionally disturbed, Kans. Tchr. Unified Sch. Dist. 308, Hutchinson, Kans., 1970-80, Unified Sch. Dist. 418, McPherson, Kans., 1980—; instr. McPherson Coll., Bethany Coll.; cons. various orgns., 1978—; pub. speaker. Author: Effort Equals Success, 1986. Republican. Home: 110 Cherry Hills Hesston KS 67062

BUSH, F. DONALD, sales manager; b. Columbus, Ohio, May 31, 1946; s. Frederick and Mary (Shoaf) B.; m. Nancy Hidlay, Sept. 4, 1976. Student, Ohio State U., 1964-69, Franklin U., 1969-71. Supr. Kroger Co., Columbus, 1964-70, mgr., 1970-75; salesman Dictaphone Corp., Columbus, 1975-79; sales mgr. Dictaphone Corp., Rye, N.Y., 1979-85; region mgr. Dictaphone Corp., Worthington, Ohio and Chgo., 1985—. Served with Ohio Army N.G., 1968-74. Mem. Assn. Pub. Communications Officers, Ohio Assn. Chiefs of Police, Ohio Assn. Fire Chiefs, Nat. Sheriffs Assn. Avocations: art, literature, outdoors, fishing. Office: Dictaphone Corp 870 High St Worthington OH 43085 Office: Dictaphone Corp 230 Michigan Chicago IL 60601

BUSH, GARY STEVEN, manufacturing company executive; b. Cleve., Feb. 8, 1958; s. Walter J. and Eileen R. (Hronek) B.; m. Cathy Ann Gorse, Mar. 29, 1980; children: Amy Marie, Megan Elizabeth, Evan William. BBA, Kent State U., 1981. Cert. PIM. Prodn. control analyst Curtis Industries, Eastlake, Ohio, 1981-84, inventory control mgr., 1984-85; ops. analyst materials and distbn. Roll Materials div. Fasson, Painesville, Ohio, 1985—. Named one of Outstanding Young Men of Am., 1985. Mem, Am. Inventory Prodn. and Control Soc., Lake Cath. Alumni Assn. (founder), Kent State U. Alumni Assn. Roman Catholic. Club: Lakeland Exchange (Mentor, Ohio). Home: 386 Clarmont Willowick OH 44094 Office: Fasson Roll Materials div Auburn Rd Concord OH 44077

BUSH, IRVING M., urological surgeon; b. N.Y.C., Jan. 19, 1934; s. Arthur M. and Mirra (Guttman) B.; m. Jan Lanners, Jan. 27, 1956; children: Alan Michael, Steven Douglas, Aaron Phillip. BA, NYU, 1954; MD, Chgo. Med. Sch., 1958. Rotating intern, asst. resident in surgery, resident in urology Beth Isreal Hosp., N.Y.C., 1959-63; asst. clinician Sloan Kettering Inst., 1965-66; clin. research trainee Meml. Hosp., N.Y.C., 1963-65, clin. asst. surgeon, 1965-66; clin. asst. surgeon James Ewing Hosp., N.Y.C., 1965-66; sr. attending urologist Cook County Hosp., Chgo., 1966—, chmn. dept., 1966-76; asst. prof. urology Northwestern U. Med. Sch., 1966-68; clin. prof., chief div. urology Chgo. Med. Sch., 1968-79; attending urologist, chief div. Mt. Sinai Hosp., Chgo., 1968-76, mem. staff; cons. Oak Forest Hosp., 1968; mem. sci. adv. panel FDA, 1975-76; mem. staff Sycamore Mcpl. Hosp., Ill., Suburban Med. Ctr., Hoffman Estates, Ill., St. Joseph's Hosp., Elgin, Ill., Sherman Hosp., Delnor Hosp., St. Charles, Ill, Geneva Hosp., Ill.; sr. cons. Ctr. for Study GU Diseases Ltd. Editor in chief Chgo. Med. Sch. Quar., 1958; cons. editor urology Jour. Student AMA, 1966; urology editor Geriatrics Digest, 1968, Med. Portfolio, 1983. Valentine fellow N.Y. Acad. Medicine, 1964; Mosley scholar, 1958; recipient Valuable Service citation Chgo. Med. Sch., 1958. Mem. AMA (John B. Morrisey award 1965, Hektoen medal for research 1970), Am. Urol. Assn. (1st prize 1964, grand prize 1965, 1st lab. research 1968, Wirt R. Dankin hist. award 1968, 69, 72, 1st prize lab. research 1970, 1st new techniques 1979), Ill. Med. Soc., North Cen. Urol. Soc., James Soc., Internat. Soc. Nephrology, Soc. Univ. Urologists, Assn. Acad. Surgery, Assn. Clin. Urologists. Home: Burlington IL 60109 Office: Bos 365 Burlington IL 60109

BUSH, JOHN ARNOLD, rancher; b. Valentine, Nebr., Sept. 2, 1947; s. Charles Oliver and Ardath Irene (Arnold) B.; m. Marilyn Louise Stanton, Oct. 28, 1967; children: Geraldine Ardath, Jessica Lynn, Cody John Charles. Student, U. Nebr., 1965-66; BBA in Econ., Chadron State Coll., 1971. Sales rep. Cen. Bank and Trust, Lander, Wyo., 1971-74; office mgr. United Securities Inc., Casper, Wyo., 1974-77; field mgr. Vigortone Products, Fremont, Nebr., 1977-79; sales rep. Nebr. Harvestore, Norfolk, 1979-81; rancher Bush Land and Cattle Co., Valentine, 1976—; del. United Farmer Rancher Congress, St. Louis, 1986-87; spokesman, sec./treas. Prodn. Credit Assn. Stockholders of North Cen. Nebr., Valentine, 1974—. Testified at U.S. Congress hearing on farm credit system, Washington, 1985. Served with U.S. Army, 1967-69, Vietnam. Fellow Nebr. Lead Found.; mem. Sandhills Cattle Assn., Vietnam Vets of Am. (bd. dirs. 1966-67), Jaycees (past. pres., bd. dirs. state officer), Am. Legion, DVA. Republican. Presbyterian. Avocations: singing, blues and country music, politics, fishing, hunting. Home and Office: HC 32 Box 19 Valentine NE 69201

BUSH, JOSEPH LLEWELLYN, professional society administrator, accountant; b. Arlington, Va., July 10, 1953; s. Joseph Llewellyn Sr. and Mary Elizabeth (Cook) B.; m. Connie I. Mullins, July 12, 1974. A in Applied Sci., Va. Western Community Coll., 1979; BS in Acctg., Radford (Va.) U., 1980, MS in Bus., 1982. CPA. Sr. acct. Francisco Assoc. CPA's, Roanoke, Va., 1981-82; instr. acctg. Radford U., 1982-84; exec. dir. Soc. for Advancement of Mgmt., Inc., Cin., 1984—; Sec., treas. Radford U. Mgmt. Ctr., 1982-84. Mem. Nat. Assn. Accts., Soc. for Advancement of Mgmt. (hon., judge nat. mgmt. case competition 1986), Ohio Soc. CPA's, Radford U. Alumni Assn. (co-chmn. Nat. Phoneathon 1984), Phi Kappa Phi, Delta Mu Delta, Phi Theta Kappa. Republican. Methodist. Home: 102-11 Anderson Ferry Rd Cincinnati OH 45238 Office: Soc for Advancement of Mgmt Inc 2331 Victory Pkwy Cincinnati OH 45206

BUSH, SARGENT, JR., English educator; b. Flemington, N.J., Sept. 22, 1937; s. Sargent and Marion Louise (Roberts) B.; m. Cynthia Bird Greig, June 18, 1960; children: Charles Sargent, James Jonathan. AB, Princeton U., 1959; MA, U. Iowa, 1964, PhD, 1967. Asst. prof. English Washington and Lee U., Lexington, Va., 1967-71; asst. prof. English U. Wis., Madison, 1971-73, assoc. prof., 1973-79, prof., 1979—, chmn. dept. English, 1980-83; vis. prof. U. Warwick, Coventry, Eng., 1983-84. Author: (with George H. Williams, Norman Pettit and Winfried Herget) Thomas Hooker: Writings in England and Holland, 1626-1632, 1975; The Writings of Thomas Hooker: Spiritual Adventure in Two Worlds, 1980; (with Carl J. Rasmussen) The Library of Emmanuel College, Cambridge, 1584-1637, 1986; contbr. articles on lit. to profl. jours. Served with U.S. Army, 1959-62. Fellow Coop. Program in Humanities, 1969-70, Am. Council Learned Socs., 1974, Inst. for Research in Humanities, 1978; grantee NEH, summer, 1969, 86, Am. Philos. Soc., 1979. Mem. MLA, Nathaniel Hawthorne Soc., Cambridge Bibliog. Soc., Assn. Documentary Editing. Presbyterian. Home: 4146 Manitou Way Madison WI 53711 Office: Univ Wis Helen C White Hall Madison WI 53706

BUSHEY, MICHAEL EDMOND, oral and maxillofacial surgeon; b. St. Albans, Vt., Jan. 31, 1949; s. Edmond Andre and June Elizabeth (Solomon) B.; m. Martha Louise Calabrase, JUly 3, 1972; children: Jennifer Lynn, Michael Edmond Jr., Andrew W. Student, San Diego State U., 1966-69; DDS, Case Western Res. U., 1973; cert. in anesthesia and oral- maxillofacial surgery, Cleve. Met. Hosp. Case Western Res. U., 1977. Diplomate Am. Bd. Oral and Maxillofacial Surgery. Practice dentistry specializing in oral and maxillofacial surgery Boardman, Ohio, 1977—. Mem. com. Youngstown (Ohio) Symphony Guild, 1982—. Fellow Am. Bd. Oral and Maxillofacial Surgery, Great Lakes Soc. Oral and Maxillofacial Surgeons, Ohio Soc. Oral and Maxillofacial Surgeons; mem. ADA, Ohio Dental Soc., Coryton Palmer Dental Soc. Republican. Roman Catholic. Clubs: Youngstown Country, Seven Oaks Country (Beaver, Pa.). Avocations: golf, collecting coins, computer programming. Home: 6614 Ronjoy Pl Boardman OH 44512 Office: 7081 W Boulevard Suite 1 Boardman OH 44512

BUSHING, WILLIAM HENRY, acquisitions and mergers consulting co. exec.; b. Oak Park, Ill., Apr. 12, 1925; s. William G. and Rose (Hilgendorf) B.; student Mont. Sch. Mines, 1943-44; B.S. in Bus. Adminstrn., Northwestern U., 1946; postgrad. Harvard U., 1946; m. Barbara Gallond, Mar. 2, 1946; children—William Walter, Barbara Lee, Judith Ann, Nancy Jean. With A.B. Dick Co., Chgo., 1946-62; nat. sales mgr. Allstate Ins. Co., Northbrook, Ill., 1964-70; pres. W.H. Bushing & Co., Inc., Barrington, Ill., 1970—. Served with U.S. Navy, 1943-46. Office: PO Box 1950 Barrington IL 60011

BUSICK, DENZEL REX, lawyer; b. Council Bluffs, Iowa, Oct. 16, 1945; s. Guy Henry and Selma Ardith (Woods) B.; m. Cheryl Ann Callahan, June 17, 1967; children—Elizabeth Colleen, Guy William. B.S. in Bus. Adminstrn., U. Nebr.-Omaha, 1969; J.D., Creighton U., 1971. Bar: Nebr. 1971, U.S. Dist. Ct. Nebr. 1971, U.S. Ct. Apls. (8th cir.) 1975, U.S. Sup. Ct. 1974; civil diplomate Nat. Bd. Trial Advocacy. Law clk., U.S. Dist. Ct. Nebr., 1970-72; mem. Fraser, Stryker, Veach, Vaughn, Meusey, Olsen & Boyer, Omaha, 1972-78; assoc. Kay & Satterfield, North Platte, Nebr., 1979-80; ptnr. Luebs, Dowding, Beltzer, Leininger, Smith & Busick, Grand Island, Nebr., 1980—. Mem. ABA, Assn. Trial Lawyers Am., Nat. Inst. Trial Advocacy, Am. Judicature Soc., Nebr. State Bar Assn., Nebr. Assn. Trial Attys., Mensa, Phi Alpha Delta. Republican. Club: Kiwanis (Grand Island). Contbr. to publs. in field. Home: 3027 Brentwood Pl Grand Island NE 68801 Office: Wheeler at First St PO Box 790 Grand Island NE 68802

BUSKIRK, PHYLLIS RICHARDSON, economist; b. Queens, N.Y., July 19, 1930; d. William Edward and Amy A. Richardson; m. Allen V. Buskirk, Sept. 13, 1950; children: Leslie Ann, William Allen, Carol Amy, Janet Helen. AB cum laude, William Smith coll., 1951. Research asst. W.E. Upjohn Inst. for Employment Research, Kalamazoo, 1970-75, research assoc., 1976-83, sr. staff economist, 1983-87. Co-editor Bus. Conditions in the Kalamazoo Area, Quar. Rev., 1979-84, asst. editor Bus. for Western Mich., 1984-87. Mem. Civil Service Bd. City of Kalamazoo, 1977—, chmn., 1981—; trustee First Presbyn. Ch., Kalamazoo, 1984-87, chmn., 1985, 86, mgr. adminstrn. and fin., 1987—; trustee Sr. Citizens Fund, Kalamazoo, 1984—, corp. restructuring com. 1985-86. exec. bd. 1986—. Mem. Am. Statis. Assn., Indsl. Relations Research Assn., Nat. Assn. Bus. Economists. Clubs: P.E.O., Kalamazoo Network. Office: 321 W South St Kalamazoo MI 49007

BUSSE, LEONARD WAYNE, banker; b. Chgo., June 29, 1938; s. Edwald William and Elsie Helen (Weidner) B.; m. Gretchen Gnuam Beal, Sept. 7, 1963; children—Whitney Lee, Carter Douglas. B.S., Purdue U., 1960; postgrad., Northwestern U., 1964-67. C.P.A. With Continental Ill. Corp., Chgo., 1963—, v.p., 1973-81, sr. v.p., 1981—, controller, 1984—, head internat. banking dept., 1985; exec. v.p. Continental Bank, Chgo., 1985—. Bd. dirs., treas. McGraw Wildlife Found., Elgin, Ill., 1982—. Mem. Robert Morris Assn., Am. Inst. C.P.A.s. Republican. Lutheran. Club: Chicago. Avocations: skiing; hunting; fishing.

BUSSEY, RONALD JOSEPH, real estate consultant; b. Lake Leelanau, Mich., Aug. 10, 1933; s. Urban John and Cecelia Agnes (Hahnenberg) B.; m. Linda Coyle, Jan. 7, 1961; children—Brian Keith, Kevin Scott, Scott Christopher, Eric Gregory. B.S. in Gen. Bus., U. Detroit, 1957; M.Retailing, U. Pitts., 1959. Cert. counselor of real estate. Retail market analyst Flannery & Assocs., Pitts., 1959-61; v.p., office mgr. Larry Smith & Co., Inc., Chgo., 1961-74; sr. v.p. Urban Projects, Inc., Los Angeles, 1974-77; pres., owner Metro-Econs., Inc., Northbrook, Ill., 1977-79; v.p. and dir. real estate counseling Arthur Rubloff & Co., Chgo., 1979-82; sr. v.p., dir. Landauer Assocs., Inc., Chgo., 1982-84; owner, pres. Metro-Econs., Inc., Chgo., 1984—; real estate broker. Bd. dirs. Greater State Street Council, 1983—. Mem. Am. Soc. Real Estate Counselors (bd. govs.), Urban Land Inst., Internat. Council Shopping Centers, Chgo. Real Estate Bd., Nat. Assn. Realtors, Ill. Assn. Realtors, Lambda Alpha (pres. Ely chpt.). Republican. Roman Catholic. Clubs: Mid-Day, Realty (Chgo.). Home: 845 Greenwood Ave Glencoe IL 60022 Office: 123 W Madison St Suite 300 Chicago IL 60602

BUSSIAN, TODD GILBERT, optometrist; b. Freeport, Ill., Jan. 6, 1958; s. Robert George and Leveta Marie (Miller) B. BS, U. Dubuque, 1980; OD, Ill. Coll. Optometry, 1984. Optometrist Freeport (Ill.) Optometric Ctr., 1984—. Mem. Vol. Optometric Services to Humanity. Mem. Am. Optometric Assn. (sports vision sect.), Ill. Optometric Assn., Dubuque U. Alumni Bd., Le-Win Jaycees (sec. 1986), Nat. Acad. Sports Vision, Beta Sigma Kappa. Avocation: sports. Office: Freeport Optometric Ctr 451 W South St Freeport IL 61032

BUSSIERE, WILLIAM A., broadcaster; b. Chgo., July 15, 1948; s. Bert Joseph and Anna (Vanko) B. Student, Columbia Coll., 1970-74. Announcer Sta. KHJ, Los Angeles, 1972-73, Sta. WCFL, Chgo., 1973-77, CBS, Chgo., 1977-79, NBC, Chgo., 1979-83, Satellite Music Network, Mokena, Ill., 1983—; owner Furthermore, Enterprises, Mokena. Canvasser, organizer Citizens for Pucinski, Chgo., 1977; sec. Citizens for Becker, 39th ward, Chgo., 1979. Mem. Am. Fedn. Radio and TV Artists. Presbyterian. Lodge: Masons (jr. warden 1986-87). Avocations: films, music, history, investments. Office: Furthermore Enterprises PO Box 405 Mokena IL 60448

BUSTER, WILLIAM FRANK, business equipment manufacturing company executive; b. Oak Creek, Colo., Nov. 20, 1927; s. Frank Lafayette and Francis (Lamb) B.; m. Evelyn Marie Johnson, Sept. 15, 1951; children—Barbara Anne, Patricia Johanna. B.S.E.E., Milw. Sch. Engring., 1953. With NCR Corp., 1971—, gen. mgr., San Diego, 1974-76, v.p., 1976-77, v.p., Dayton, Ohio, 1977-80, sr. v.p., 1980-83, exec. v.p., 1983—; Served with USAF, 1946-49. Office: NCR Corp 1700 S Patterson Blvd Dayton OH 45479

BUSWELL, D. H., utilities company executive; b. 1921. BS, Mont. State Coll., 1947. Acct. Ulteig Engring. Corp., 1948-51; rate analyst Bonneville Power Adminstrn., 1951-55; with Interstate Power Co., Dubuque, Iowa, 1955—, rate engr., 1955-62, mgr. rate dept., 1962-69, mgr. dist. activities, 1969-71, v.p., 1971-78, exec. v.p., 1978-79, pres., 1979-81, pres., chief exec. officer, 1981-82, chmn. bd., pres., chief exec. officer, 1982—. Served with USNR, 1942-46. Office: Interstate Power Co 1000 Main St Dubuque IA 52001 *

BUTIN, JAMES WALKER, physician; b. Fredonia, Kans., July 13, 1923; s. James A. and Berenice Marie (Walker) B.; A.B., U. Kans., 1944, M.D., 1947; M.S. in Medicine, U. Minn., 1952; m. Betty Belle Launder, June 29, 1949 (dec. Oct. 1981); children—Richard Edward, Philip Walker, Lucy Elizabeth, John Murray; m. Patricia Lanning Guinan, June 10, 1984. Intern, U. Kans. Med. Center, 1947-48; resident in pathology, 1948; fellow in internal medicine Mayo Found., 1949-52; practice medicine specializing in internal medicine and gastroenterology, Wichita, Kans., 1952—; mem. staff Wichita

Clinic, St. Francis Hosp., Wesley Med. Ctr.; assoc. prof. Kans. U. Sch. Medicine, Wichita. Summerfield scholar, 1940-44. Diplomate Am. Bd. Internal Medicine (gastroenterology). Fellow ACP; mem. AMA, Am. Gastroenterol. Assn., Am. Assn. History Medicine, Kans. Med. Soc., Sedgwick County Med. Soc. (past pres.) Christian Med. Soc., Wichita Med. Edn. Assn. (chmn. 1973-74), Mayo Alumni Assn., Wichita Audubon Soc. (past pres.), Kans. Ornithol. Soc. (past pres.), Phi Beta Kappa, Alpha Omega Alpha, Nu Sigma Nu, Beta Theta Pi. Republican. Episcopalian. Contbr. articles to med. jours. Home: 38 Mission Rd Wichita KS 67206 Office: 3311 E Murdock Ave Wichita KS 67208

BUTIN, JUDIE T., probation officer; b. Iowa, July 15, 1941; d. Joseph and Hazel (Berkenbosch) Tomlonovic; m. Robert Earnest Butin, Jan. 14, 1972; children: Robert Earl, Joseph Blaine, Lesa Renae Udelhoven, Victoria Kathleen. Adminstrv. asst. Newtown Sch. System, Iowa, 1970-76; probation officer Fifth Jud. Dist. Dept. Correctional Services, Newton, Iowa, 1976—. V.P. Newton Community Sch. Bd., 1982-84; bd. dirs. Cen. Iowa Found. for Alcoholism and Drug Abuse, Newton, 1984-86, Your First Step, Inc., Newton, 1984-86, Iowa Children's and Family Services, Des Moines, 1986. Mem. Newton C. of C. Substance Abuse Com., Iowa Corrections Assn. (bd. dirs. 1983-85, pres. 1986—), Am. Corrections Assn., Am. Probation and Parole Assn. (co-chmn. spring symposium 1986). Democrat. Avocations: gardening, glass etching, cooking. Office: Dept Correctional Services P O Box 761 Newton IA 50208

BUTLER, BRINTON LEE, systems analyst; b. St. Clair, Mich., Jan. 23, 1953; s. Ralph O. and Alice M. (Rankin) B.; m. Rosalyn D. Sampeer, Dec. 30, 1978. BS, Mich. State U., 1975; MA, U. Iowa, 1978. Cert. data processing. Programmer Farm Bur. Ins. Group of Mich., Lansing, 1978-80; sr. programmer, analyst Lansing Police Dept., 1980-83, systems analysis mgr., 1983—. Mem. Assn. for Inst. for Cert. Computer Profls., Internat. Assn. HP Users. Avocation: sports officiating. Home: 212 Raritan Rd Lansing MI 48911 Office: Lansing Police Dept 124 W Michigan Ave Lansing MI 48933

BUTLER, GEOFFREY HARDIN, architect; b. Springfield, Mo., Jan. 28, 1953; s. Everett Eugene and Patsy Jane (Pulis) B.; m. Brenda Layne Buff, June 10, 1972; children: Nicole Buff, Samuel Gene. B in Environ. Design, U. Kans., 1975, BArch., 1978. Registered architect, Mo., Kans., Ark., Tex., Okla. Architect in tng. Peters Williams Kubota, Lawrence, Kans., 1975-77; architect, owner Geoffrey Butler AIA, Springfield, Mo., 1977-84; ptnr. Butler Group AIA, Springfield, 1985—. Campaign treas. Bob Holden for State Rep., Springfield, 1986; vice chmn. Bd. of Housing and Bldg. Appeals, Springfield, 1986. Mem. AIA (treas. Springfield chpt. 1978-81, pres. 1982-83, merit design award 1984, 86), Mo. Council Architects (bd. mem. 1982-87, pres. 1986). Avocations: downhill skiing, tennis, golf. Home: 2320 E Rosebrier Springfield MO 65804 Office: Butler Group AIA 1550-B E Battlefield Springfield MO 65804

BUTLER, GERALDINE HEISKELL (GERRI), designer, artist; b. Detroit, Sept. 6, 1930; d. Artist Kavassel and Geraldine Gentle (Heiskell) B.; student Wright Jr. Coll., 1946; B.E., Chgo. U., 1948; B.A. in Edn. (Delta Sigma Theta Scholar), Chgo. Art Inst., 1949, M.A. in Edn., 1950; postgrad. Harvard U., 1962-64. Tchr. pub. elementary schs., Chgo., 1949-52; tchr. art Chgo. pub. high schs., 1953-61; supr. art Chgo. Bd. Edn., 1962-75; graphic art and media coordinator, dept. instrn. Chgo. Bd. Edn., 1976-77; founder, prin. Gehebu-AK, design cons. services, Chgo., 1976—; founder, prin. Butler Studios, creative designer, Chgo., 1977—; one-man shows include: Saxon Gallery, Chgo., Roosevelt Hotel, N.Y.C., Henri IV Restaurant, Cambridge, Mass., Hilton Trinidad, B.W.I., Goldstein Gallery, Chgo.; group shows include: Triangle Gallery, Chgo., McCormick Pl., Chgo., Hyde Park Art Center, Chgo., Ill. State Fair, Peninsula Exhbts., Door County, Wis.; represented in permanent collections: rental gallery Art Inst. Chgo., Huntington Hartford Collection, N.Y.C.; judge numerous exhbts. and competitions; art cons. and designer. Mem. Ill. wing CAP, 1963—. Huntington Hartford fellow, 1956-58. Mem. Internat., Ill., Nat. art edn. assns., Western Arts Assn., Am. Craftsmen Assn., Alumni Chgo. Art Inst., Soc. Typog. Arts, Artists Guild Chgo., Chgo. Soc. Artists, N. Shore Art League, Hyde Park Art Center, Evanston Art Center, USAF Art Corps, Triangle-Lincoln Park Art Center, Am. Youth Hostels, Delta Kappa Gamma, Delta Sigma Theta. Episcopalian. Office: PO Box 11360 Chicago IL 60611

BUTLER, JAMES MARTIN, educator; b. Freeport, Ill., Apr. 20, 1948; s. Martin Harvey and Elizabeth Ann (Hillebrecht) B.; B.S., U. Ill., 1970; M.S., Northeastern Ill. U., 1978; M.A., Chgo. State U., 1982; m. Ruth Ann Dratwa, Dec. 17, 1972; children—Dawn Marie, Christine Ann, Kimberly Ann, James Martin, Jennifer Lynn. Tchr. sci., chmn. dept. Thornton Fractional North High Sch., Calumet City, Ill., 1979—. Vice pres. Holy Name Soc., St. Andrew Ch., 1979-81, pres., 1982-83. Mem. Nat. Assn. Biology Tchrs., Am. Assn. Physics Tchrs., Assn. Supervision and Curriculum Devel., Ill. Assn. Biology Tchrs., Ill. Chess Assn., U.S. Chess Fedn., U. Ill. Alumni Assn. (life), Northeastern Ill. U. Alumni Assn., Chgo. State U. Alumni Assn. Club: KC (4 deg.). Home: 426 155th St Calumet City IL 60409 Office: 755 Pulaski Rd Calumet City IL 60409

BUTLER, LOUIS ALLEN, sales, marketing manager grain trade company; b. Independence, Ky., June 6, 1935; s. Allen Woodrow and Catherine (Brown) B.; m. Muriel Ann Shepherd, Jan. 25, 1964; children—Douglas , Scott, David. B.S. in Agrl. Engring., U. Ky., 1962; M.S. in Econs., N.C. State U., 1976. Test engr. Internat. Harvester, Hinsdale, Ill., 1962-65; v.p., mgr. Culligan Soft Water, Zeeland, Mich., 1965-71; plant mgr., chief engr. Maes, Inc., Holland, Mich., 1971-72; sales engr. Aeroglide Corp., Raleigh, N.C., 1972-77; sales and mktg. mgr. Dickey-john Corp., Auburn, Ill., 1977—; pres. Grain Equipment Mfgs. Assn., Kansas City, 1984-86. Contbr. articles to profl. jours. Vestryman St. Perers Episcopal Ch., Bettendorf, Iowa, 1979-81, Christ Episcopal Ch., Springfield, Iowa, 1983—; soccer ofcl. YMCA, Bettendorf, 1978-80, YMCA, Springfield, 1981-83; mem. Springfield Art Assn., 1981—, Vachel Linsey Assn., Springfield, 1981—. Served with U.S. Army, 1959-61. Named Hon. Order of Ky. Cols. Mem. Internat. Water Conditioning Assn. (bd. dirs. 1968-70), Am. Soc. Agrl. Engring., Am. Assn. Cereal Chemists, Grain Elevator and Processing Soc., Am. Feed Industries Assn. (bd. dirs. 1984—), Farm Implement Equipment Inst. (bd. dirs. 1985—), Cereal Chemistry Mktg. Internat. (bd. dirs. 1985—), Assn. Operating Millers. Avocations: travel, oil and geology work, reading. Home: 1936 Noble Ave Springfield IL 62704 Office: Dickey-John Corp PO Box 10 Auburn IL 62615

BUTLER, MARGARET KAMPSCHAEFER, computer scientist; b. Evansville, Ind., Mar. 7, 1924; s. Otto Louis and Lou Etta (Rehsteiner) Kampschaefer; m. James W. Butler, Sept. 30, 1951; 1 child, Jay. A.B., Ind. U., 1944; postgrad., U.S. Dept. Agr. Grad. Sch., 1945, U. Chgo., 1949, U. Minn., 1950. Statistician U.S. Bur. Labor Statistics, Washington, 1945-46, U.S. Air Forces in Europe, Erlangen and Wiesbaden, Germany, 1946-48; statistician U.S. Bur. Labor Statistics, St. Paul, 1949-51; mathematician Argonne (Ill.) Nat. Lab., 1948-49, 51-80, sr. computer scientist, 1980—; dir. Nat. Energy Software Center, Dept. Energy Computer Program Exchange, 1960—; cons. AMF Corp., 1956-57, OECD, 1964, Poole Bros., 1967. Editor: Computer Physics Communications, 1969-80; Contbr.: chpt. to The Application of Digital Computers to Problems in Reactor Physics, 1968, Advances in Nuclear Science and Technology, 1976; also articles to profl. publs. Treas. Timberlake Civic Assn., 1958; rep. mem. nominating com. Hinsdale (Ill.) Caucus, 1961-62; coordinator 6th dist. Equal Rights Amendment, 1973-80; del. Republican Nat. Conv.; bd. dirs. YWCA west suburban area; mem. data processing adv. com. College of DuPage, 1987—. Fellow Am. Nuclear Soc. (mem. publs. com. 1965-71, chmn. math and computation div. 1966-67, dir. 1976-79, exec. com. 1977-78, chmn. bylaws and rules com. 1979-82, reviewer for publs.); mem. Assn. Computing Machinery (exec. com., sec. Chgo. chpt. 1963-65, publs. chmn. nat. conf. 1968, reviewer for publs.), Assn. Women in Sci. (pres. Chgo. area chpt. 1982, exec. bd. 1985-86, exec. com. 1985-86), Nat. Computer Conf. (chmn. Pioneer Day com. 1985, tech. program chmn. 1987). Home: 17W139 Hillside Ln Hinsdale IL 60521 Office: 9700 S Cass Ave Argonne IL 60439

BUTLER, M(ELFORD) DANIEL, infosystems specialist; b. Pitts., Oct. 30, 1940; s. Melford Preston and Ruth Lilie (Haslam) B.; m. Carol Jean Hoffman, May 29, 1965; children: Rebecca Marie, Brian Charles, Jason William. BS in Math., Pittsburg (Kans.) State U.; grad., U. Mo., Kansas City. Computer systems specialist Western Electric Co., Lee's Summit, Mo., 1965-68; project mgr. Electronic Data Systems, Dallas, 1968-74, mgr. mktg. and sales, 1974-79; account mgr. Electronic Data Systems, Denver, 1979-82; area mgr. Electronic Data Systems, Dallas, 1982-84; div. mgr. Electronic Data Systems, Detroit, 1984—. Mem. council Resurrection Luth. Ch., Plano, Tex., 1983, Luth. Ch. of Master, Troy, Mich, 1986; chmn. com. Boy Scouts Am., Plano, 1983, Boy Scouts Am., Troy, 1986. Served to 1st lt. U.S. Army, 1963-65. Democrat. Avocations: photography, running, camping, cycling. Home: 4855 Deepwood Troy MI 48098 Office: Electronic Data Systems 1400 N Woodward Bloomfield MI 48013

BUTLER, OWEN BRADFORD, securities advisor; b. Lynchburg, Va., Nov. 11, 1923; s. James Herbert and Ida Virginia (Garbee) B.; m. Erna Bernice Dalton, Mar. 7, 1945; children: Nancy Butler Brown, James. A.B., Dartmouth Coll., 1947. With Procter & Gamble Co., Cin., 1945-86; v.p. sales Procter & Gamble Co., 1968-70, v.p., group exec., 1970-73, exec. v.p., 1973-74, vice chmn. bd., 1974-81, chmn. bd., 1981-86; sr. advisor Daiwa Securities Am., 1986—; chmn. Cin. br. Fed. Res. Bank Cleve.; bd. dirs. No. Telecom, Ltd., Hosp. Corp. Am., Deere & Co., Equicor. Served with USNR, 1941-45, 50-51. Mem. Com. Econ. Devel. (vice chmn., research and policy com.), Phi Beta Kappa. Republican. Clubs: Queen City (Cin.); Metropolitan (Washington). Office: Procter & Gamble Co 1500 Columbia Plaza Cincinnati OH 45202

BUTLER, PAUL THURMAN, college administrator; b. Springfield, Mo., Nov. 17, 1928; s. Willard Drew and Verna Lois (Thurman) B.; Th.B., Ozark Bible Coll., 1961, M.Bibl. Lit., 1973; m. Gale Jynne Kinnard, Nov. 20, 1948; children—Sherry Lynne, Mark Stephen. Non-commd. officer U.S. Navy, 1946-56, mem. staff Amphibious Forces, Pacific, 1947-51, guided missile unit 41, Point Mugu, Calif., 1951-56; ret., 1956; ordained to ministry Christian Ch., 1958; minister Washington Christian Ch., Lebanon, Mo., 1958-60; dean admissions Ozark Christian Coll., Joplin, Mo., 1960—, prof. Bible and philosophy, 1960—. Mem. Am. Legion, SAR (sec. Mo. Soc. chpt., pres. Sgt. Ariel Nims chpt.), Mo. Territorial Pioneers, Mo. State Geneal. Soc., Tenn. State Geneal. Soc., Tenn. Pioneer Ancestors. Republican. Author: The Gospel of John, 1961; The Minor Prophets, 1968; Daniel, 1976; Isaiah, 3 vols., 1978; Esther, 1979; The Gospel of Luke, 1981 (trans. into Korean, French, Portuguese, East Indian-Tamil); Revelation, 1982; I Corinthians, 1984; II Corinthians, 1986. Home: 2502 Utica St Joplin MO 64801 Office: 1111 N Main St Joplin MO 64801

BUTLER, ROBERT ANDREWS, clinical psychologist; b. Lancaster, Calif., June 19, 1955; s. Robert Andrews and Ines Gertrude (Ottaviano) B.; m. Nadine Suzanne Pastor, Dec. 27, 1975; 1 child, Alex Robert. BA, Long Beach (Calif.) State U., 1977; MA, Dominguez Hills State U., 1979; PhD, Washington State U., 1983. Lic. psychologist, Wis. Dir. psychology Brown County Mental Health, Green Bay, Wis., 1983—; pvt. practice psychology Green Bay, 1985—; adj. prof. psychology U. Wis., Green Bay, 1983—; cons. Family Violence Ctr., Green Bay, 1984, Whitman County (Wash.) Mental Health, 1981. Contbr. articles to profl. jours. Cons. Green Bay Police Dept., 1986, Brown County Juvenile Ctrs., 1986. Fulbright fellow. Mem. Am. Psychol. Assn., Wis. Psychol. Assn., Assn. for Advancement of Behavior Therapy, Syndicat Nat. Des Psychologues Francais (hon.). Avocations: skiing, tae kwon do, skin diving. Home: 3740 Libal St Green Bay WI 54301 Office: Brown County Mental Health 2900 Saint Anthony Dr Green Bay WI 54301

BUTLER, ROBIN ERWIN, vocational technical educator; b. St. Louis, May 16, 1929; s. Erwin and Florence Catherine Butler; m. Marie Day, Aug. 22, 1947; children: Lawrence Robin, Nicki Ruth. BA, Alma Coll., 1960; MDiv., U. Dubuque, 1964; postgrad., U. Wis., 1981—, Pacific Western U., Los Angeles, 1986—. Cert. vocat., tech. and adult edn. tchr. Printer, journalist various corps., Ohio, Ky., Ind., Iowa, 1945-64; asst. pastor presby. Ch., Manitowoc, Wis., 1964-67; program dir. YMCA, Manitowoc, 1968-69; owner operator Butler & Son Contractors, Manitowoc, 1969-72; supr. Mirro Corp., Manitowoc, 1972-81; adult educator Lakeshore Tech. Inst., Cleve., 1981—, lead instr. mgmt. tech., 1985-86; adj. mgmt. prof. Cardinal STritch Coll., Milw., 1985—. Author: Andragogical Guidelines, 1985; columnist: The Midwest Flyer, 1981-85. Mem. Gov.'s Task Force on Aero. Revenues, Madison, 1981. Served to sgt. U.S. Army, 1948-49. Mem. Lakeshore Edn. Assn., Am. Mgmt. Assn., Nat. Mgmt. Assn. (mem. various coms. 1973-81). Democrat. Presbyterian. Clubs: Toastmaster (Kiel, Wis.) (pres. 1984-85); Experimental Aircraft Assn. (Cleve.) (pres. 1982-84, EAA Aviation award 1980). Home: PO Box 35 108 Parkway Cleveland WI 53015 Office: Lakeshore Tech Inst 1290 N Ave Cleveland WI 50315

BUTLER, VIRGINIA ANN, social worker; b. Salina, Kans., Aug. 14, 1948. BA, Washburn U., 1971; MSW, U. Kans., 1980. Lic. social worker,. Social worker State Dept. Social Rehab. Services, 1971-78; social service supr. State Dept. Social Rehab. Services, Osawatomie, Kans., 1980—; social worker St. Vincents Children Home, Topeka, 1978-79; social service cons. to nursing homes various cities, Kans., 1985-86; chmn. Gov.'s Conf. Prevention of Child Abuse, Kans., 1981-86. Scout leader Girl Scouts USA, Hutchinson, Kans. and Topeka, 1964-73; workshop presenter United Meth. Ch. Camps, Am. Camping Assn., Okla., Kans., Mo., 1984-86; advisor Miami County Child Youth Protection Team, 1980—, Kans. Com. for Prevention of Child Abuse, 1976—. Mem. Nat. Assn. Social Workers, Beta Sigma Phi (pres. 1968-73). Avocations: camping, flowers, antiques, crafts. Office: Osawatomie Social Rehab Service Box 1000 Osawatomie KS 66071

BUTLER, WILLIAM JOSEPH, JR., insurance broker; b. Chgo., Feb. 24, 1942; s. William Joseph and Emily Jane (Mockenhaupt) B.; B.S., Coll. of the Holy Cross, Worcester, Mass., 1964; M.B.A., St. Louis U., 1969; m. Helen Katherine O'Malley, Aug. 28, 1965 (div. 1976); children—Charlotte Anne, Emily Jane. Mgmt. trainee Clinton E. Frank Inc., Chgo., 1969-70; dist. agt. Prudential Ins. Co., Evanston, Ill., 1970-74, spl. agt., Skokie, Ill., 1974—. Mem. fin. com. St. Mary's Ch., Lake Forest, Ill., 1980-81. Served to capt. USAF, 1964-68. C.L.U. Mem. Chgo. Assn. Life Underwriters. Republican. Roman Catholic. Home: 570 N Sheridan Rd Lake Forest IL 60045 Office: Prudential Insurance Co 5150 Golf Rd Skokie IL 60077

BUTT, JIMMY LEE, association executive; b. Tippo, Miss., Oct. 13, 1921; s. H.W. and Jimmie O. (Davis) B.; m. Jane F. Williams, June 23, 1943; children—Janie Lake, Melanie Maryanne, Jimmy Lee. B.S., Auburn U., 1943, M.S., 1949. Registered profl. engr., Ala. Grad. asst. agrl. engring. dept. Auburn U., 1947-48, asst., 1948-50, asso. agrl. engr., 1950-56; exec. v.p. Am. Soc. Agrl. Engrs., 1956-86. Mem. research adv. council Auburn U., 1985—. Served as capt. F.A. AUS, 1943-46. Decorated Bronze Star; recipient Ordre du Merite Agricole (France). Fellow Am. Soc. Agrl. Engrs. (pres.-elect 1986-87, pres. 1987-88), mem. Nat. Soc. Profl. Engrs., Council Engring. and Sci. Soc. Execs. (pres. 1977-78), Am. Assn. Engring. Socs. (past dir.), Sigma Xi, Tau Beta Pi, Phi Kappa Phi, Gamma Sigma Delta, Alpha Zeta, Omicron Delta Kappa. Club: Economic. Lodge: Lions. Home: 2572 Stratford Dr Saint Joseph MI 49085

BUTTEL, THEODORE LYLE, science educator; b. Centerville, Iowa, May 26, 1939; s. Peter George and Matida Maxine (Green) B.; m. Jacqueline Kay Thompson; B.A., U. Iowa, 1966; M.A., N.E. Mo. State U., 1970; Ph.D., Walden U., 1979; children—Lisa Michele, Patricia Ann, Denise Kathleen. Tchr. sci., math. English Valley's Schs., North English, Iowa, 1960-67; tchr. sci., chmn. dept. sci. Washington Sch., Ottumwa (Iowa) Public Schs., 1967-72, tchr. sci., interdisciplinary team leader Walsh Sch., 1972-75, tchr. sci., chmn. dept. sci., 1975—, tchr. sci. Ottumwa High Sch., 1982-87; mem. Iowa Instructional and Profl. Devel. Com., 1972-74; trainer for Performance Learning Systems, 1975—; human relations cons. and tchr. Area Edn. Agy. #15, 1977-81, vice chmn. staff devel. com., 1977-80; county chmn. and mem. Iowa Bd. Polit. Action for Edn., 1966-81; dir. Washington Ednl. Field Trips for Walsh Students, 1972-81; cons., trainer in field; adj. prof. Drake U.; staff devel. instr. Ottumwa Sch. Performance Learning Systems 1000 Club. Mem. Nat. TEACH Cadre (charter), U Iowa Alumni Assn. (life), N.E. Mo. State U. Alumni Assn. (life), Ottumwa Edn. Assn. (pres. 1971-72), Iowa State Edn. Assn. (chmn. bd. State Unit 9 Ednl. Div. 1973-75), NEA (life), Nat. Sci. Tchrs. Assn., Iowa Assn. Supervision and Curriculum Devel., Iowa Acad. of Sci., Walden U. Alumni Assn., Assn. Supervision and Curriculum Devel., Assn. Tchr. Educators, Phi Delta Kappa. Democrat. Roman Catholic. Home: 122 E Alta Vista Ottumwa IA 52501 Office: 549 E 4th St Ottumwa IA 52501

BUTTERFIELD, CRAIG IRWIN, psychotherapist; b. Ft. Dodge, Iowa, June 10, 1947; s. Irwin Usher and Helen Marie (Kirkhart) B.; m. Shirley Joan Fisher, Aug. 16, 1970; children: Lindsay, Brandon. BS, Nebr. Wesleyan U., 1969; M in Div., Iliff Sch. Theology, 1972; cert., Neuro-Linguistics Inst., 1986. Cert. psychotherapist, hypnotherapist, Iowa. Adj. prof. Des Moines Area Community Coll., Ankeny, Iowa, 1973-80, Granview Coll., Des Moines, 1980-84; cons. Butterfield Mgmt. Cons. Services, West Des Moines, 1973—; pvt. practice psychotherapist Butterfield Marriage and Family Services, West Des Moines, 1973—. Named one of Outstanding Young Men of Am., 1979. Mem. Iowa Assn. Marriage and Family Therapy (pub. relations com. 1980-84, bd. dirs. 1984—), Iowa Psychol. Assn., Am. Assn. Marriage and Family Therapy, Assn. Clin. Pastoral Edn. Republican. Methodist. Avocations: jogging, outdoor activities, photography. Office: Butterfield Marriage and Family Counseling Butterfield Mgmt Cons 921 12th St West Des Moines IA 50265

BUTTERFIELD, JANET MARIE OLDT, accountant; b. Mt. Pleasant, Iowa, July 3, 1952. Acct. Davis Butterfield & Co., East Moline, Ill.

BUTTERFIELD, WILLIAM HENRY, social work and psychology educator; b. Worland, Wyo., Nov. 11, 1935; s. William Harley Butterfield and Velma Irene (Enlow) Walker; m. Mary Bolner (div.); m. Dorothy Mack, July 1, 1972; children: Christina, Heather, Lydia. BS in Spl. Edn., U. Nebr., 1960; M in Social Work, U. Mich., 1968, PhD, 1970. Lic. psychologist, Mo., Wis. From probation officer to dir. ednl. services Maricopa County (Ariz.) Juvenile Probation Dept., Phoenix, 1960-67; asst. prof., dir. family health counseling U. Wis., Madison, 1970-73; asst. dean for adminstrn. George Brown Sch. Social Work, Washington U., St. Louis, 1973-77, assoc. dean, 1977-81, chmn. PhD program, 1978-83, assoc. prof., 1983—; cons., lectr. U. Mich., Ann Arbor, 1969-70; numerous research projects, 1964—. Contbr. chpts. to psychological books; also book reviews, articles to profl. jours.; served on numerous edit. bds.; patentee (with others) behavior signal system. 5-year grantee Nat. Insts. Mental Health for tng. rural social workers; recipient Leon Levitz Annual award for Contbg. to Juvenile Delinquency Treatment, 1966. Mem. Nat. Assn. Social Workers (various coms.; pres. Mo. chpt. 1985-87), Am. Psychol. Assn., Assn. for Advancement of Behavior Therapy, Behavior Therapy and Research Soc., Council on Social Work Edn., Social Work Group for Study of Behavioral Methods, Sigma Xi. Home: 8120 Glen Echo Dr Bel-Nor MO 63121 Office: Washington U Brown Sch Social Work PO Box 1196 Saint Louis MO 63130

BUTTERICK, MERLE WALDRON, fast food company executive; b. Princeton, Ind., Oct. 17, 1946; s. Keith Horton and Iva Laurine (Waldron) B.; m. Coleen Marie Dee, June 15, 1974. AS, Wabash Valley Coll., 1971; BA, Transylvania U., Lexington, Ky., 1977. Real estate brooker Ben Moore & Assocs., Lexington, 1977-80; mgr. Domino's Pizza, Lexington, 1980-81; franchisee Domino's Pizza, Janesville, Wis., 1981—. Mem. State Wis. Steering Com. Job Service, 1984-85; bd. dirs. St. Mary's Parish, Janesville, 1986. Served with USAF, 1965-69, Vietnam. Named Restaurateur of Yr., Blackhawk chpt. Wis. Restaurant Assn., 1985; recipient commendation State of Wis. Dept. Industry, Labor, Human Relations, 1984, 85. Roman Catholic. Avocations: sailing, flying, model building, skiing. Office: Rock River Corp 109 S Jackson Janesville WI 53545

BUTTERWORTH, ALICE MATILDA BOYDEN, dentist; b. Elwood, Ind., Dec. 22, 1936; d. Frederick L. and Ethel May (Dudley) Boyden; m. Johnny Baden, May 6, 1954 (div. June 1964); 1 child, Michael; m. Frank Linton Butterworth Jr., Oct. 24, 1964; children: Deborah, Barbara, Frank L. III. BS in Bus. summa cum laude, Ball State U., 1973; DDS, Ind. U., 1977. Cert. specialist in pediatric dentistry. Gen. practice pediatric dentistry Marion, Ind., 1980—; staff Marion Gen. Hosp., 1984—. bd. dirs. East-Cen. Ind. Planned Parenthood, 1984-85. Mem. ADA, Am. Acad. Pediatric Dentistry, Internat. Assn. Orthodontics, Ind. Dental Assn., Ind. Assn. Pediatric Dentists, Grant County Dental Assn. (pres. 1982). Democrat. Episcopalian. Lodges: Order of Eastern Star, Order of Amaranth. Avocations: travel, organ, piano, snowmobiling. Home: 1208 Overlook Rd Marion IN 46952 Office: 803 Gardner Dr Marion IN 46952

BUTTERY, JANET LOUISE, movie theatre co. exec.; b. Columbus, Ohio, May 19, 1953; d. Thomas William and Pauline Adelaide (Burgess) B.; B.A., U. Kans., 1975, M.B.A., 1978; Troisième Degré, Université de Bordeaux (France), 1975. Real estate devel. Am. Multi Cinema, Kansas City, Mo., 1978—. Home: 5409 Foxridge Dr Apt 203 Mission KS 66202 Office: 106 W 14th St Suite 1700 Kansas City MO 64105

BUTTORF, HARRY WILLIAM, accountant; b. Highland Park, Mich., Apr. 10, 1952; s. Harry Trevette and Bernice Eileen (Jones) B.; m. Marta Carol Vannatter, July 26, 1975; children: Jason William, Kathryn Ann. BSBA, Wayne State U., 1975. CPA, Mich. Mem. audit staff Plante & Moran CPA's, Southfield, Mich., 1975-77; mem. tax staff Plante & Moran CPA's, Southfield, 1977-80, tax mgr., 1980-82, fin. planning mgr., 1982-87, fin. planning ptnr., 1987—. V.p. bd. dirs. City of Brighton (Mich.) Econ. Devel. Corp. Mem. Am. Inst. CPA's, Mich. Assn. CPA's, Inst. Cert. Fin. Planners. Republican. Episcopalian. Club: Investment (Detroit) (sec. 1985—). Avocations: fishing, sailing. Office: Plante & Moran CPA's 27400 Northwestern Hwy Southfield MI 48037

BUTTREY, DONALD WAYNE, lawyer; b. Terre Haute, Ind., Feb. 6, 1935; s. William Edgar and Nellie Madaline (Vaughn) B.; m. Karen Lake; children—Greg, Alan, Jason. B.S., Ind. State U., 1956; J.D., Ind. U., 1961. Bar: Ind. 1961. Law clk. to chief judge U.S. Dist. Ct. So. Dist. Ind., 1961-63; ptnr. McHale, Cook & Welch, P.C., Indpls., 1963—, pres., 1986—; chmn. central region IRS-Bar Liaison Com., 1983-84. Editor Ind. Law Jour., 1960-61. Chmn. Marion County Democratic Fin. Com., 1984-86. Served with AUS, 1956-58. Mem. ABA (taxation sect., real property, probate, trust coms. to 1986), Ind. Bar Assn. (chmn. taxation sect. 1982-83), Indpls. Bar Assn. (v.p. 1987—, mem. long-range planning com. 1985-86), 7th Cir. Bar Assn., Ind. Soc. Chgo. Phi Delta Phi, Theta Chi. Presbyterian. Clubs: Indpls. Athletic (bd. dirs. 1982—), University, Highland Country. Home: 9299 Spring Forest Dr Indianapolis IN 46260 Office: 1100 Chamber of Commerce Bldg 320 N Meridian St Indianapolis IN 46204

BUTTS, CHARLES LEWIS, state senator; b. Oberlin, Ohio, Feb. 16, 1942; m. Alice Gould; children: John, Paul, Joanna, Helen. BA in Govt., Oberlin Coll., 1967. Mem. Ohio Senate, Columbus, 1974—, minority whip, 1980-86, asst. pres. pro tem, 1982-84. Chmn. Cleve. Waterfront Coordinating Task Force, 1986—. Named Legislator of Yr., Conf. Ins. Legislators, 1982. Democrat. Avocations: sailing, racquetball. Home: 4514 Franklin Blvd Cleveland OH 44102 Office: Ohio Senate Statehouse Columbus OH 43216

BUTTS, GEORGE FRANCIS, automobile manufacturing company executive; b. Carbondale, Pa., July 16, 1923; s. George and Ethel Butts; m. Geraldine Stephania Sebek, Sept. 1, 1957; children: Teresa G., Nancy J. BS, Drexel Inst. Tech., 1949; MSME, Chrysler Inst. Engring., Detroit, 1951. Chief engr. truck div. Chrysler Corp., Detroit, 1967-72, gen. mgr. truck ops., 1972-73, v.p. product planning and devel., 1973-77, v.p. stamping and assembly div., 1977-78, v.p. vehicle quality and reliability, 1978-80, v.p. quality and productivity, 1980—. Mem. Soc. Automotive Engrs., Am. Soc. for Quality Control. Roman Catholic. Clubs: Orchard Lake Country (Detroit); Jupiter Hills Country (Fla.). Home: 3134 Myddleton Troy MI 48084 Office: Chrysler Motors 12000 Chrysler Dr Highland Park MI 48288-1919

BUTZ, BEVERLY GRAHAM, financial executive; b. Chgo., Nov. 10, 1948; d. William Otto and Catherine (Graham) B.; student Hollins Coll., 1966-68; B.A., U. Mich., 1970; M.B.A. program, U. Chgo., 1975-78. Programmer trainee No. Trust Co., Chgo., 1970-72; analyst/programmer Zurich Ins. Co., Chgo., 1972-74; programmer/analyst First Nat. Bank of Chgo., 1974-76, lead programmer/analyst, 1976-79, project mgr., 1979-82, internat. product devel. officer, 1982-86, officer of corp., 1981-84, asst. v.p., 1984-86; v.p. cash mgmt. product devel. Exchange Nat. Bank, Chgo., 1986—. Sec. bd. Counseling Ctr. Lakeview, 1986—; active Jr. League of Chgo., 1970-79; vol. Presbyn. St. Luke's Hosp., Chgo., 1970-72, Planned Parenthood, 1980; vol.

Una Puerta Abierta, 1972-74, treas. cookbook com., 1975-76; mem. Jr. Bd. of Youth Guidance, 1977-79. Mem. Nat. Assn. Female Execs. Congregationalist. Club: Midtown Tennis.

BUXTON, JEFFREY TUDOR, sales executive; b. Bristol, Pa., June 23, 1956; s. Robert Stevens and Dorothy Louise (Miller) B.; m. Julie Meister, Mar. 6, 1982; children: Casey Meister, Cale Tudor. BSEE, Pa. State U., 1978; MBA, U. Cinn., 1986. Terr. mgr. Parker Hannifin Corp., Cleve., 1978-81; sales engr. S. Himmestein & Co., Hoffman Estates, Ill., 1981—; dist. mgr. S. Himmestein & Co., Hoffman Estates, 1984—. Mem. Instrument Soc. Am., Beta Gamma Sigma, Delta Mu Delta. Republican. Home: 2911 Maureen Ct Loveland OH 45140 Office: S Himmelstein & Co 2490 Pembroke Ave Hoffman Estates IL 60195

BUYCK, BONNIE LOU, accountant; b. Gaylord, Minn., Oct. 23, 1954; d. Marvin Adrian and Geraldine (Schuette) Peterson; m. William Joseph Buyck, Aug. 2, 1980. BA in Acctg. summa cum laude, Gustavus Adolphus Coll., 1977; postgrad. in bus. adminstrn., U. Minn., 1978-79, 84-85. CPA, Minn.; cert. info. systems. auditor. EDP auditor Land O'Lakes, Mpls., 1977-79; EDP audit specialist Arthur Young & Co., Mpls., 1979-81; EDP audit sr., supr. Dayton's Dept. Store, Mpls., 1981-82; computer audit cons., mgmt. info. systems mgr. McQuay Inc., Mpls., 1982-85; computer audit mgr. Coopers & Lybrand, Mpls., 1985-86, Twin City Fed., Mpls., 1987—. Recipient Leadership award YWCA, Mpls., 1984. Mem. Am. Inst. CPA's, Minn. Soc. CPA's (mgmt. adv. services com. 1979-80, mems. in industry com. 1984-86), EDP Auditors Assn. (pubs. dirs. 1981-82, pre-meeting dir. 1982-83), Iota Delta Gamma. Lutheran. Avocations: reading, bicycling, racquetball. Home: 12916 Taylor St NE Blaine MN 55434 Office: Twin City Federal 801 Marquette Ave Minneapolis MN 55402

BUYER, DIANE M., dentist, educator; b. Indpls., July 1, 1955; d. John J. and Jean (Martschink) B. BA, Ind. U., 1978, DDS, 1982. Instr. operative dentistry Ind. U., Indpls., 1982—; pvt. practice dentistry Indpls., 1983—. Mem. ADA, Chgo. Dental Soc., Indpls. Dist. Dental Soc. (asst. editor), Ind. Dental Assn. (chmn. council on dental auxs.), Ind. Assn. Women Dentists (pres. 1984-85), Am. Assn. Women Dentists (chairperson dist. 7), Am. Bus. Women's Assn. (Boss of the Yr. award 1986). Mem. Society of Friends. Home and Office: 126 E 86th St Indianapolis IN 46240

BUZBEE, HERBERT HARRY, county coroner; b. Joliet, Ill., May 29, 1943; s. Orville F. Buzbee and Florence E. Stoner; m. Eleanor Kay Lindgren, July 31, 1971 (dec. Feb. 1985). Student, Bradley U., 1961. Asst. funeral dir. Clunsten Meml., Peoria, Ill., 1957-61, Wright Salmon Mortuary, Peoria, 1960-68, Leroy Schmidt Meml., East Peoria, Ill., 1968-72; dep. coroner Peoria County Coroner's Office, 1972-75, coroner, 1975—; cons. ABT Assn., Washington, 1984—; co-chmn. FBI Tng., Quantico, Va., 1985. Author: (with others) Suicide Criteria Classification, 1985. Co-chmn. Heart Fund, Peoria, 1983; pres. Goodwill Industries, Peoria, 1985-87. Served with U.S. Army, 1964-66, Vietnam. Mem. Internat. Assn. Coroners and Med. Examiners (exec. sec.-treas. 1982—), Bradley U. Towne and Gown Club (pres. 1980-83). Republican. Roman Catholic. Lodge: Kiwanis (pres. Peoria 1983). Avocations: golf, swimming. Home: 123 SW Jefferson #E-5 Peoria IL 61602 Office: Peoria County Coroner 6913 W Plank Rd Peoria IL 61604

BUZOGANY, WILLIAM MICHAEL, psychiatrist; b. Alliance, Ohio, Nov. 21, 1932; s. Michael and Irene (Fodor) B.; m. Phyllis Map Oakleaf, May 17, 1959; children: Bonnie, William Alan, Robert Michael. BS, Mt. Union COll., 1954; MD, U. Rochester, 1958. Intern Presbyn.-St. Lukes Hosp., Chgo., 1958-59; psychiatrist U. Wis., Madison, 1959-62; asst. clin. dir. Mendota Mental Health Inst., Madison, 1962-72; asst. dir. bur. mental health Dept. Health and Social Services, Madison, 1976-82; dir. child/adolescent program Mendota Mental Health Inst., Madison, 1982—; clin. asst. prof. psychiatry U. Wis., 1962—; psychiat. cons. Lad Lake Inc., Dousman, Wis., 1965—, NIMH, Washington, 1980—, Office of Juvenile Justice and Delinquency Prevention, Washington, 1982—. Contbr. various books, 1977—. Chmn. State mental health rep. for children and youth, 1976-78. Served to maj. Wis. N.G. Fellow Am. Psychiat. Assn. (pres. Wis. chpt. 1966); mem. Nat. Consortium for Child Mental Health Services (chmn. 1982-84), Am. Acad. Child Psychiatry, Am. Soc. Adolesent Psychiatry. Presbyterian. Avocations: grow trees, photography. Home: 4721 Regent St Madison WI 53705 Office: Mendota Mental Health Inst 301 Troy Dr Madison WI 53704

BUZZELLI, LAURENCE FRANCIS, lawyer; b. Cleve., Jan. 24, 1943; s. Frank Vincent and Viola J. (Piccolino) B.; m. Judith Louise Shope, July 16, 1966; children: Christopher L., Lauren M. BE in Edn., Ohio U., 1965; JD, Cleve. State U., 1973. Bar: Ohio, 1973; cert. secondary tchr., Ohio. Claims supr., regional analyst Allstate Ins. Co., Cleve. and Hudson, Ohio, 1969-74; atty., mng. atty. Continental Ins. Co./Buckeye Union Ins. Co., Cleve. and Cin., 1977—; arbitrator Cuyahoga County Common Pleas Ct., Cleve., 1974, Hamilton and Clermont County Pleas Ct., Cin. and Batavia, Ohio, 1978-83. Served to capt. U.S. Army, 1965-68, Vietnam. Mem. Def. Research Inst., Ohio Bar Assn., Bar Assn. Greater Cleve., Ohio Assn. Civil Trial Attys., Am. Arbitration Assn. (arbitrator), DAV (life). Office: Continental Ins Cos 55 Public Sq #1806 Cleveland OH 44113

BYARS, ANNIE MARIE, educator; b. Decatur, Ala., Nov. 19, 1944; d. Alphonso and Mary Ann (Bevels) B.; B.S., Ala. Agrl. and Mech. U., 1967; M.A., U. Detroit, 1975; postgrad. Wayne State U., 1972-73, Mich. State U., 1982-84. Vol., U.S. Peace Corps, Jamaica, West Indies, 1967-69; tchr. Lewis Bus. Coll., Detroit, 1970; life ins. sales agt. Franklin Life Ins. Co., Detroit, 1978-81; tchr. bus. edn. Detroit Pub. Schs., 1970—. Mem. Am. Vocational Assn.

BYER, CHARLES WILLIAM, JR., lawyer; b. Anderson, Ind., Jan. 28, 1956; s. William and Dorothy (Elsea) B.; m. Judith Ann, Aug. 21, 1982. BEE, Ind. U., 1978; JD, Cooley Law School, Lansing, Mich., 1984. Bar: Ind. 1984, U.S. Dist. Ct. (no. and so. dist.) Ind. 1984. Assoc. Byer & Gaus, Anderson, Ind., 1984—. Mem. Ind. Bar Assn., Madison County Bar Assn., Assn. Trial Lawyers Am. Republican. Methodist. Avocation: sports. Home: 1202 Maryland Dr Anderson IN 46011 Office: Byer & Gaus 6 W 8th St Anderson IN 46016

BYER, JOHN ALPERT, medical educator, neurologist; b. Los Angeles, May 29, 1941; s. Ted Arthur and Hilda Caroline (Augspurger) B.; m. Martha Louise Russell, Aug. 1, 1964; children: Elizabeth Carole, Anne Louise, Joan Christine. BA, Ariz. State U., 1962; MD, Baylor U., 1966. Cert. Am. Bd. Psychiatry and Neurology. Intern Med. Univ. S.C., Charleston, 1966-67; resident in neurology U. Mich., Ann Arbor, 1967-70; practice medicine specializing in neurology Columbia, Mo., 1970-71; assoc. prof. neurology U. Mo., Columbia, 1971—. Vestryman Calvary Episcopal Ch., Columbia, 1974-77. Fellow ACP, Am. Acad. Neurology, Am. Heart Assn. (stroke council). Republican. Presbyterian. Lodge: Masons. Singer U. Mo. Choral Union, Columbia, 1982—. Avocation: photography. Office: U Mo Dept Neurology One Hosp Dr Columbia MO 65212

BYERLY, DEAN LYLE, mechanics instructor; b. Fayette, Iowa, Aug. 4, 1936; s. William Henry and Vesta Lucille (Meyer) B.; m. Phyllis Maye Follmer, Aug. 4, 1962; 1 son, Robert Dean. B.S., Upper Iowa U., 1966; postgrad. U. No. Iowa, 1982, Iowa State U., 1972. Service instr. Allis-Chalmers Mfg. Co., Des Moines, 1966-67; shop mgr. Brubaker Co., Prairie City, Iowa, 1967-68; instr. Northeast Iowa Tech. Inst., Calmar, Iowa, 1968—. Bd. dirs. Ft. Atkinson Library, 1976—; mem. ann. observance com. Friends Ft. Atkinson Hist., 1976—. Served with USAF, 1956-60. Recipient Disting. Service award Iowa Future Farmers Assn., 1982; Disting. Service award Northeast Iowa Dist. Future Farmers Am., 1975, Hon. Am. Farmer Degree, Nat. Assn. Future Farmers Am., 1986. Mem. Assn. Diesel Specialists, Am. Vocat. Assn., Nat. Vocat. Agr. Tchrs. Assn., Iowa Vocat. Assn., Iowa Vocat. Agr. Tchrs. Assn. Methodist. Home: Route 2 Fort Atkinson IA 52144 Office: Northeast Iowa Tech Inst Calmar IA 52132

BYERS, DAVID EARL, construction materials executive; b. Sheridan, Mich., Aug. 13, 1951; s. David Lewis and Mary Lou (Dell) B.; m. Connie Lynn Wilson, May 22, 1971; children: Nicole Kristen, Ryan David. BS in Mktg., Ferris State U., 1973; MBA, U. Kans., 1980. With Midwest market devel. Simpson Timber, Seattle, 1974-81; dist. sales mgr. Caradco Corp., Rantoul, Ill., 1981-84; with fabricator devel. Wolverine Technologies Inc., Lincoln Park, Mich., 1984—. Active Big Rapids (Mich.) Bus. Adv. Council, 1972-73; coach S.W. United Soccer League, Overland Park, Kans., 1982—; coach Little League, Overland Park, 1986—. Presbyterian. Avocations: coaching sports, woodworking, guitar. Home and Office: 10403 Century Ln Overland Park KS 66215

BYERS, WALTER, athletic assn. exec.; b. Kansas City, Mo., Mar. 13, 1922; s. Ward and Lucille (Hebard) B.; children—Ward, Ellen, Frederick. Student, Rice U., 1939-40, U. Iowa at Iowa City, 1940-43. News reporter United Press Assn. (now U.P.I.), St. Louis, 1944; sports editor U.P.I., Madison, Wis., 1945, Chgo., 1945; asst. sports editor U.P.I., N.Y.C., 1946-47; also fgn. sports editor; dir. Big Ten Conf. Service Bur., Chgo., 1947-51; exec. asst. Nat. Collegiate Athletic Assn., Chgo., 1947-51, exec. dir., 1951-52; exec. dir. Nat. Collegiate Athletic Assn., Kansas City, Mo., 1952-73, Shawnee Mission, Kans., 1973—; Pres. Byers Seven Cross Ranch, Inc., Emmett, Kans., 1974—. Served with M.C. AUS, 1944. Home: Box 1525 Mission KS 66222 Office: Box 1906 Shawnee Mission KS 66222

BYINGTON, RICHARD PRICE, surgical supply company executive; b. Grand Rapids, Mich., July 24, 1940; s. Stanley J. and Constance Y. (Des Noyer) B.; B.S. in Pharmacy, Ferris State Coll., 1962; m. Margaret Ellen Evert, Aug. 26, 1961; children—James, Michael, Connie. Pub. relations rep. Mich. State Pharm. Assn., Lansing, 1962; pharmacist White & White Pharmacy Inc., Grand Rapids, 1962-63; sales rep. White & White Surg. Supply Inc., Grand Rapids, 1963-67, sales mgr., 1967-70, exec. v.p., 1970-74, pres., 1974—; sec.-treas. Progressive Distbn. Services Inc., Grand Rapids, Mich. Chmn. bd. trustees Mary Free Bed. Hosp., Grand Rapids; mem. Nursing Home Adminstrs. Licensure Bd., 1970-86 . Mem. Health Industries Distbrs. Assn. (bd. dirs., sr. v.p., chmn.), Am., Mich., Kent County pharm. assns., Nat. Assn. Wholesalers, Am. Mgmt. Assn. Roman Catholic. Clubs: Lions, Peninsular. Home: 3341 Ashton Rd SE Grand Rapids MI 49506 Office: 19 La Grave Ave SE Grand Rapids MI 49503

BYKOWSKI, RONALD MITCHELL, real estate investor, broker; b. Chgo., Apr. 1, 1945; s. Mitchell Andrew and Lottie Bykowski; m. Linda Francis, Apr. 23, 1983; 1 child, Amanda. Grad. high sch., Woodstock, Ill. Founder, pres. Tones Inc., McHenry, Ill., 1964-83; founder, ptnr. D&R Investment, McHenry, 1972—, Heritage Investment, McHenry, 1976—, Tower View Ltd., McHenry, 1979—; founder, pres. Trey Corp., McHenry, 1981—, Century 21 Care Real Estate, McHenry, 1977—; bd. dirs. McHenry County Bd. Realtors, Woodstock, 1981-85, Century 21 Investment, Rosemont, Ill., 1980-82. Contbr. articles on real estate and computers. Bd. dirs. Econ. Devel. Commn., McHenry, 1984—, No. Ill. Med. Enterprises & Devel. Corp. of No. Ill. Med. Ctr., McHenry, 1984—. Served as sgt. USAF, Ill. Air Nat. Guard, 1965-75. Mem. Nat. Assn. Realtors, Ill. Assn. Realtors, Lake County Bd. Realtors, McHenry County Bd. Realtors, Am. Fedn. Musicians (bd. dirs. 1972-76), Am. Legion (vice comdr. local post), Polish Legion Am. Vets. (comdr. Post 188 1982), Aircraft Owners and Pilots Assn. Republican. Roman Catholic. Lodges: Rotary (pres. McHenry club), KC (advocate 1984). Avocations: flying, music, boating, antique cars. Office: Century 21 Care Real Estate Inc 3717 W Elm St McHenry IL 60050

BYRD, JACKIE DARLENE, food service executive; b. Tipton, Ind., July 29, 1954; d. Jessie Newton and Lula Mae (Gipson) Davis; widowed; 1 child, Michelle Lynn. Grad., High Sch., Tipton, 1972. V.p. corp. services Cassidy Restaurants, Inc., Tipton, 1973—. Mem. Tipton C. of C., Tri Kappa. Republican. Avocation: reading. Home: 423 W Washington St Tipton IN 46072 Office: Cassidy Restaurants Inc PO Box 378 Tipton IN 46072

BYRD, MANFORD, JR., school system superintendent. Supt. Chgo. Pub. Schs. Office: City of Chgo Sch Dist 299 Office of the Superintendent 1819 W Pershing Rd Chicago IL 60609 *

BYRNE, DIANE MARIE, statistical specialist; b. Detroit, Nov. 11, 1952; d. Romeo Fredrick and Patricia Ann (Murphy) Bernard; m. Larry Eugene Byrne, Aug. 20, 1971; children—Jennifer Leigh, Ryan Michael. B.S., U. Mich-Dearborn, 1981. Research assoc. laser technologist Sinia Hosp., Detroit, 1979-80; coordinator math. Nat. Inst. Tech., Livonia, Mich., 1981-83; cons., trainer Schoolcraft Coll., Livonia, 1983—, Argyle Assocs., Inc., New Canaan, Conn., 1983-85; specialist in Taguchi Methods Eaton Corp., 1985—. Mem. Am. Soc. Quality Control (regional counselor automotive div. 1985—), Am. Statis. Assn., Math. Assn. Am., Schoolcraft Coll. Found. Roman Catholic. Home: 10948 Edington St Livonia MI 48150

BYRNE, MICHAEL JOSEPH, business executive; b. Chgo., Apr. 3, 1928; s. Michael Joseph and Edith (Lueken) B.; B.Sc. in Mktg., Loyola U., Chgo., 1952; m. Eileen Kelly, June 27, 1953; children—Michael Joseph, Nancy, James, Thomas, Patrick, Terrence. Sales engr. Emery Industries, Inc., Cin., 1952-59; with Pennsalt Chem. Corp., Phila., 1959-60; with Oakton Cleaners, Inc., Skokie, Ill., 1960-70, pres., 1960-70; pres. Datatax Inc., Skokie, 1970-74, Midwest Synthetic Lubrication Products, 1978—, Pure Water Systems, 1984—, Superior Tax Service, 1984—. Served with ordnance U.S. Army, 1946-48. Mem. A.I.M., VFW, Alpha Kappa Psi. Club: Toastmasters Internat. Home: 600 Grego Ct PO Box 916 Prospect Heights IL 60070

BYRNE, THOMAS JOHN, manufacturing executive; b. Claymont, Del., Mar. 23, 1934; s. Thomas John and Martina Catherine (Green) B.; m. Patricia Anne Shumard, Feb. 8, 1958; children: Thomas, Joseph, Mary, John. BS in Chemistry, U. Dayton, 1964. Mfg. process devel. mgr. Gen. Electric, Evendale, Ohio, 1965-70, shop ops. mgr., 1970-78, mfg. systems mgr., 1978-82, mfg. program mgr., 1982-83, tech. mgr., 1983—, mgmt. practices instr., 1985—. Patentee reentry vehicle, insulation material. Mem. Planning-Zoning Commn., Franklin, Ohio, 1960-61; pres. Franklin Sch. bd., 1972-80; mem. St. Mary's Parish Council. Served to 1st lt. U.S. Army, 1956-60. Home: 4575 Todd Rd Franklin OH 45005 Office: Gen Electric 1 Nuemann Way Evendale OH 45215

BYRNE, WILLIAM MADISON, JR., aerospace engineer; b. Memphis, Nov. 5, 1938; s. William Madison and Janelle (Sudlow) B.; m. Mary Constance Lamb, Dec. 17, 1960; children: Bonnie Sue Byrne Hoover, Paul William. BS, U. Mo., Rolla, 1960, PhD, 1970, hon. degree in aerospace engrng., 1986; MS, UCLA, 1964. Propulsion researcher Naval Weapons Ctr., China Lake, Calif., 1960-64; tech. engr. Beech Missile Systems, Wichita, Kans., 1964-70, project engr., 1970-80, chief tech. engr., 1980-84; mgr. missile systems Beech Aircraft Corp., Wichita, 1984—. Contbr. articles to profl. jours. Served to 1st lt. U.S. Army, 1960. Avocations: home computers, skiing, sailing, flying. Home: 2 Cypress Dr Wichita KS 67206 Office: Beech Aircraft Corp 9709 E Central Ave Wichita KS 67201

BYRNES, MICHAEL FRANCIS, podiatrist; b. Chgo., Aug. 11, 1957; s. Edward and Dorothy Franchi; m. Debra Michelle Moody, July, 31, 1982. BA, Loyola U., Chgo., 1979; D in Podiatry Medicine, Ill. Coll. Podiatry Med., 1984. Practice medicine specializing in podiatrics Ridgeland Foot Clinic., Chgo., 1984—; surgeon Mercy Surgical Ctr., Justice, Ill., 1984—, Cen. Community, Chgo., 1984—, Holy Cross Hosp., 1987—; cons., physician Ridgeland Living Ctr., Palos Heights, Ill., 1984—. Contbr. case reports to Jour. Foot Surgery, 1985. Precinct capt. 49th Dem. Ward., Chgo., 1976-80. Winner state skating championship, 1980. Mem. Am. Podiatric Med. Assn., Ill. Podiatric Med. Assn. (co-chmn. legis. com. 1985-86), Am. Acad. Podiatric Sports Medicine. Roman Catholic. Avocation: skating. Home: 213 W Wisconsin St Chicago IL 60614 Office: 19921 Southwest Hwy Oak Lawn IL 60453

BYRNS, TIMOTHY CHESTER, educator; b. Cleve., Nov. 13, 1947; s. Chester A. and Evelyn S. (Grodzynski) B.A. and B.S.Ed., Bowling Green (Ohio) State U., 1970; A.A. and A.A.B., Cuyahoga Community Coll., 1978, M.B.A. candidate in Internat. Mgmt., Baldwin-Wallace Coll.; student Touraine Inst., France, U. Salzburg, Austria, Spanish Cultural Inst., Spain. Cert. tchr., Ohio. Instr. fgn. langs. Parma (Ohio) City Schs., 1975—. Creator, producer career exploration ednl. TV series, 1983. Named Tennis Coach of Yr., New Lake Erie League, 1977. Mem. Parma Edn. Assn., Ohio Edn. Assn., NEA. Roman Catholic. Home: 454 Georgia Ave Elyria OH 44035 Office: Parma Sr High Sch W 54th St Parma OH 44129

BYRON, MARY MORRISSY, court reporter; b. Chgo., June 15, 1952; d. Eugene Vincent Morrissy and Margaret Mary (Lucitt) Leonard; m. Jeffrey Byron, July 23, 1978; children—Matthew Jason, Daniel Scott. Student MacCormac Jr. Coll., 1973, Chgo. Coll. Commerce, 1974, Daley Jr. Coll., 1972, Southwest Sch. Bus., 1971. Cert. shorthand reporter; registered profl. reporter. Court reporter Central Reporters, Chgo., 1973-74; co-owner Morrissy & McGuire, Chgo., 1974-78; owner Morrissy & Others, Chgo., 1978-83; pres. Morrissy & Others, Ltd., Chgo., 1982—. Sec., Del Mar Woods Improvement Assn., Deerfield, Ill., 1980-82. Mem. Nat. Shorthand Reporters Assn., Ill. Shorthand Reporters Assn. Home: 2620 Wildwood Ln Deerfield IL 60015 Office: Morrissy & Others Ltd 189 W Madison Chicago IL 60602

BYRON, RITA ELLEN COONEY, travel executive, publisher, real estate agent; b. Cleve.; d. Harry James and Marie (Hakey) Cooney; m. Carl James Byron Jr., Nov. 27, 1954 (dec.); children—Carey Lewis, Carl James, Bradford William. Student Cleve. Coll., 1954, Western Res. U., 1955, John Carroll U., 1956; Ph.D. (hon.), Colo. State Christian Coll., 1972. Mgr. European Immigration dept. U.S. Steamship Lines, Cleve., 1956; real estate agt. W.I. White Realtor Inc., Shaker Heights, Ohio, 1965-67, J.P. Malone Realtors Inc., Shaker Heights, 1967-70, Thomas Murray & Assocs., 1971-76, Mary Anderson Realty, Shaker Heights, 1978-79, Barth Brad & Andrews Realtors Inc., Shaker Heights, 1979—, Heights Realty, 1986—; v.p., co-owner Your Connection To Travel, Kent, Ohio, 1980—; v.p., gen. mgr. World Class Travel Agy., 1985—; dir. Travel One div. Quaker Sq., Akron, Travel Trends for Singles, 1985, Playhouse Sq. Travel, 1985, World Class Internat., 1986. Mem. U.S. Figure Skating Assn., 1960—, Wightman Cup Women's Com., 1965—; mem. women's com. Cleve. Mus. of Art, 1969—, Friendship Force Ohio, 1986 ; co-chmn. Cleve. Invitational Figure Skating Competition, 1972—; chmn. Gold Rush Rush, U.S. Ski Team, 1982, Cleve. benefit U.S. Olympic Teams, chmn. Midas Touch, 1983, Gran Apres-Ski Prix, 1981; patron Cleve. 500, 1983; originator Benefits Unltd., Exceptional Single Person's, Connections Unltd., 1983; founder, coordinator Singled Out Club, 1983; co-ptnr., adv. bd. The Service Service, 1984; benefit chmn., patroness various balls and fund-raising events; vol. Foster Parents Inc., 1983; vol. Council on World Affairs, 1983, Bellefaire Home for Spl. Children, 1983, Big Sisters Greater Cleve., 1983, Camp Cheerful, 1983, Chisholm Ctr., 1983, Children's Diabetic Camp Ho Mita Koda, 1984, Young Audiences, 1985; adv. trustee Friends of Fairmount Theatre of the Deaf, 1983; mem. Greater Cleve. Growth Assn., 1983. Mem. Western Res. Hist. Soc., Garden Ctr. Greater Cleve., Friends Cleve. Pub. Library, UN Assn. of U.S., Cleve. Council World Affairs, U.S. Ski Ednl. Fund (chmn. benefits), English Speaking Union (jr. bd.), Travel Age Exchange, Globetrotters Internat. Fedn. Women's Travel Orgns., North Coast Exec. Women's Network, Growth Assn., Council on Small Enterprises. Cleve. Real Estate Bd. Clubs: Cleve. Skating, Broadmoor World Arena Figure Skating, Colony Beach and Racquet, Suburban Ski, Cleve. Advertising, Communicator's, Towne Hall, Women's City, Gilmour Acad. Women's, Mid-Day, Cleve. Wellesley, Arctic Circle, Intrepid Traveler, Tibet, Mongolia and Cina Explorers', Himalaya Yeti (1987 Nepal Expdn.). Co-pub., exec. editor The Single Register, other publs.; featured in numerous publs. Home: 18126 Lomond Blvd Shaker Heights OH 44122 Office: Travels Unltd Rt 82 Macedonia OH 44115 Also Office: Es Turo Edificio, Kontiki, Majorica Balearic Islands Spain

BYRUM, ROBERT LANG, dentist; b. Davenport, Iowa, Mar. 10, 1953; s. Robert Jordan and Helen Mary (Lang) B.; m. Bonnie May Kleinmeyer-Hamilton, June 25, 1983; children: Jeff Kleinmeyer, Monte Kleinmeyer. BA, Wartburg Coll., 1975; DDS, U. Iowa, 1984. Gen. practice dentistry Bettendorf, Iowa, 1984—. Mem. ADA, Iowa Dental Assn., Scott County Dental Soc., Davenport Dist. Dental Soc., Acad. Gen. Dentistry, Chgo. Dental Soc., Miss. Restorative Acad. Club: Davenport, Illowa Study (v.p. 1986—). Avocations: reading, woodcarving, jewelry, dogtraining, gardening. Office: 1530 State St Bettendorf IA 52722

BYWATER, JOHN THOMAS, county official, criminal justice educator, consultant; b. Cin., Oct. 20, 1937; s. Thomas Joseph and Marie Mary (Marischen) B.; m. Suzanne Mary Tracy, July 8, 1961; children: Tracy M., Kimberly A., Kristin L., Brian J., Mara L., Kara S. BS, U. Cin., 1974; MEd summa cum laude, Xavier U., 1977; EdD, U. Cin., 1984. Mechanics helper Tom's Auto Service, Cin., 1954-56; floor mgr. Stas. WCPO-TV, WKRC-TV, Cin., 1957-58; new car salesman Tom's Chrysler Plymouth, Cin., 1958-60, salesman to gen mgr., 1962-70; from officer to adminstr. Hamilton County Sheriff's Office, Cin., 1971—; cons. criminal justice and security, CIn., 1979—; owner Source Cons., 1979—; adj. prof. criminal justice, security and psychology Thomas MoreColl., Crescent Springs, Ky., 1979—; program advisor Cin. Tech. Coll., 1980—; lectr. in field. V.p. Hamilton County Rep. 26th Ward, Cin., 1980. Recipient Police Officer of Yr. award Greater Cin. C. of C., 1976, State of Ohio U. grad. scholar, 1978-80. Mem. Internat. Assn. Chiefs of Police, Am. Corrections Assn. (profl.), Am. Soc. for Indsl. Security (bd. dirs. 1981-84), Ohio Crime Prevention Assn. (charter, state treas. 1974-75). Roman Catholic. Lodges: Police, Eagles. Avocations: golfing, swimming, scuba diving, shooting. Home: 2939 Eggers Pl Cincinnati OH 45211 Office: Hamilton County Sheriff's Office 1000 Main St Room 563 Cincinnati OH 45202

CABANISS, CHARLES WILLIAM, psychiatric therapist; b. Shelby, N.C., Mar. 5, 1933; s. Joseph Turner Sr. and Gertrude Mae (Beam) C.; m. Sarah Margaret Hull, Dec. 26, 1958; children: Jane Ellen, Charles Douglas. MusB, Okla. Bapt. U., 1961; M in Music and Edn., U. Okla., 1962; MSW, U. Ill., 1971, PhD in Psychology of Aging, 1972. Cert. social worker, Ill. Minister in music edn. 1st Bapt. Ch., Cushing, Okla., 1961—; pvt. practice psychiat. therapy Marion, Ill., 1971—; bd. dirs. various nursing homes, Ill.; cons. Christian Homes Inc., Lincoln, Ill., 1974—, Care Mgmt., Inc., Bloomington, Ill., 1972-83; participant White House Conf. on Aging, 1971; speaker in field. Served with U.S. Army, 1954-56. Named Outstanding Soldier of Yr. for liason work between army post and communities, 1955. Republican. Baptist. Avocations: music arranger, dir. choral groups. Home and Office: 1801 Westminister Rd Marion IL 62959

CABBABE, EDMOND BECHIR, plastic and hand surgeon; b. Aleppo, Syria, Feb. 21, 1947; Came to U.S., 1973; s. Bechir Wahid and Samia (Hamoui) C.; m. Rima Gorab, Apr. 22, 1973; children: Nabil, Samer, Monica. BS in Physics, Chemistry Biology, Damascus U. Sch. Scis., 1967, MD, 1972. Cert. Am. Bd. Surgery, Am. Bd. Plastic Surgery. Surg. intern St. Mary of Nazareth Hosp., Chgo., 1973-74; surg. resident U. Tenn., Chattanooga, 1974-78; resident in plastic surgery St. Louis U., 1978-80, asst. prof., 1980-86; practice medicine specializing in plastic surgery Plastic Surgery Cons., St. Louis, 1986—; chief plastic surgery John Cochran VA Hosp., St. Louis, 1981-86; bd. dirs. cleft palate clinic Cardinal Glennon Children's Hosp., St. Louis, 1984-86. Contbr. articles to profl. jours. Mem. Arab Am. Anti Discrimination Com., Washington, 1982—, World Affairs Council, St. Louis, 1986—. Fellow ACS, Internat. Coll. Surgeons; mem. Am. Soc. Plastic and Reconstructive Surgeons, Am. Assn. Hand Surgery Research (Research and Workmens Compensation Com.), Arab Am. Medical Assn. (pres. 1985-86), Nat. Assn. Arab Ams. (v.p. 1985, bd. dirs. 1984—). Roman Catholic. Club: Concord Tennis and Swim. Avocations: swimming, tennis, politics, photography. Home: 1249 Takara Ct Saint Louis MO 63131 Office: Plastics Surgery Cons Ltd 10004 Kennerly Rd Suite 200 Saint Louis MO 63128

CABLE, DON ARTHUR, dentist; b. Kirksville, Mo., June 23, 1946; s. Arthur Martin and Mary Irene (Scott) C.; m. Ellen Kaye Cromley, July 11, 1981; children: Cami, Brian, Chad, Kena, Keri, Brandon. BS in Gen. Sci., N.E. Mo. State U., 1968; DDS, U. Mo., Kansas City, 1973. Tchr. gen. sci. Kirksville Sch. Dist., 1968-69; gen. practice dentistry Sedalia, Mo., 1975—. Served to capt. USAF, 1973-75. Mem. ADA, Mo. Dental Assn. (del. 1980-84), Cen. Dist. Dental Assn. (pres. 1982-83), Sedalia Dental Soc. (pres. 1977-79). Avocations: golf, hunting, computers. Home: Rt 7 Box 36 Sedalia MO 65301 Office: 403 W Broadway Sedalia MO 65301

CABLE, STEPHEN JAMES, investment executive; b. Canton, Ohio, May 7, 1924; s. Davis Arthur and Gail (Watson) C.; B.S. in Chem. Engring., Case-Western Res. U., 1950; advanced mgmt. tng. Emory U., 1966-67; m. Jane Irwin Purdy, June 24, 1948; children—Nancy Jane, Davis James. Plant engr. Sparta Ceramic Co., 1950-54, plant mgr., 1954-56; successively mgr., sec., group v.p. Spartek, Inc. (formerly U.S. Ceramic Tile Co.), Canton, 1956-82, also dir.; chmn. bd., chief exec. officer Polywood Corp., North

Canton, 1982—; pres., chief. exec. officer; SPR Fund, Inc.; v.p., dir. Joseph A. Locker Co., Canton. Trustee Canton YMCA. Served to 2d lt. Transp. Corps, AUS, 1943-46. Mem. Sigma Xi, Tau Beta Pi, Alpha Chi Sigma. Clubs: Canton (trustee), Congress Lake (Hartville, Ohio). Contbr. articles trade jours. Patentee in field. Home: 558 N Prospect St Hartville OH 44632

CABOT, JOSEPH, pedodontist; b. Detroit, Oct. 15, 1921; s. Benjamin and Ethel (Gutkovsky) C.; B.S., Wayne State U., 1942; D.D.S., U. Mich., 1945, M.S., 1947; m. Ruth Weiner, Aug. 19, 1945; children—Bonnie Cabot Kaufman, Gary Michael, Elizabeth Ann Cabot Stenvig, Jon Elliott. Mott fellow U. Mich., 1945-46; pedontic fellow Hurley Hosp., Flint, Mich., 1946-47; individual practice pedontics, Detroit, 1947-55, Lathrup Village, Mich., 1969—. Mem. bd. Delta Dental Plan Mich., 1959—, pres., 1963-66; pres., Detroit Dental Aid, 1952-55. Local bd. chmn. Selective Service, 1959-67, appeal bd. chmn., 1969—, dental adviser to state dir., 1968—; assemblyman United Community Services, 1971-77; pres. Nat. Found. Dentistry for the Handicapped. Served to maj. Dental Corps, AUS, 1955-57. Fellow Internat. Coll. Dentists, Am. Coll. Dentists, Am. Acad. Pedodontics; mem. ADA (ho. of dels. 1965-76, trustee 1977-83, 1st v.p. 1983-84), Mich. Dental Assn. (pres. 1975-76), Mich. Soc. Dentistry for Children (pres. 1953-54), Detroit Dist. Dental Soc. (Merit award 1964, pres. 1966-67), Kenneth A. Easlick Grad. Soc. (pres. 1973-75), Pierre Fauchard Acad., Omicron Kappa Upsilon, Alpha Omega. Lion. Home: 3199 Interlaken Rd Orchard Lake MI 48033 Office: 7459 Middlebelt Rd West Bloomfield MI 48033

CABRAL, ALLEN MANUEL, accountant, educator, lawyer; b. Fall River, Mass., Sept. 18, 1944; s. Manuel and Bella (Souza) C.; m. Rita Nevers, Dec. 2, 1966; children: Aaron, Avery. Diploma in acctg., Hartford (Conn.) Inst. Acctg., 1964; BSBA, Am. Internat. Coll., 1968; MS in Acctg., Kent (Ohio) State U., 1969; JD, U. Akron, 1975; LLM, Cleve. State U., 1985. Bar: Ohio 1975; CPA, Ohio. Cost acct. L.L. LeMay, Manchester, Conn., 1964-66; acct. Rhodes, Rice and Co., Hartford, 1966-68, Ernst and Whinney, Canton, Ohio, 1968-71; prof. of acctg. Walsh Coll., Canton, 1971-72, U. Akron, Ohio, 1972—; bd. dirs. All In 1 Inc., Canton; pres. A.M. Cabral Assocs., Canton, 1980. Mem. Am. Inst. CPA's, Am. Assn. Hispanic CPA's, Ohio Soc. CPA's, Divorce Mediation Council. Home: 5944 Huckleberry NW North Canton OH 44720

CABRAL, GALILEU, internist; b. Minas, Brazil, Feb. 19, 1941; came to U.S., 1969, naturalized, 1976; s. Joaquim Azevedo and Alice Tasca (Sartori) C.; M.D., Univ. Juiz de Fora, Brazil, 1964; postgrad. cert. U. Mo., Columbia, 1973; m. Kathleen Ann Fries, May 10, 1974; children—Anthony Eugene, William Lee. Intern, Mo. Bapt. Hosp., St. Louis County, 1969, resident, 1970-73, chief med. resident, 1973, mem. active staff, 1974—, asso. chief med. staff, 1980—; pres. St. Francois Med. Center, Florissant, Mo., 1979-80; mem. continuing edn. com. Christian Hosp. N.E., 1978—. Served to lt. Brazilian Navy, 1965-68. Diplomate Am. Bd. Internal Medicine. Mem. AMA (Physician Recognition award 1972—), A.C.P., Mo. State Med. Assn., Met. St. Louis Med. Soc., Midwest Internists (v.p.). Roman Catholic. Home: 15244 Lochcrest Ct Ballwin MO 63011 Office: 14377 Woodlake Dr Suite 109 Chesterfield MO 63017

CACCIARELLI, ALEXANDER ANTHONY, pediatric radiologist; b. Newark, Feb. 28, 1940; s. Anthony Rocco and Julia (Sayna) C.; m. JoAnn Matraxia, June 12, 1965; children: Anthony, Guy, Alexander. MD, New Jersey Coll. Medicine, 1966. Diplomate Med. Coll. Radiology. Practice medicine specializing in pediatrics Royal Oak, Mich., 1969—; pediatric radiologist William Beaumont Hosp., Royal Oak, 1975—. Served to capt. USAF, 1969-71. Fellow Am. Acad. Pediatrics; mem. Soc. Pediatric Radiology, Midwest Pediatric Radiology Soc., Soaring Soc. Am., Phi Beta Kappa. Home: 3542 Ridgeland Ct West Bloomfield MI 48033 Office: William Beaumont Hosp 13 Mile Rd Royal Oak MI 48072

CACIOPPO, BENJAMIN FRANK, psychotherapist; b. Omaha, Mar. 10, 1944; s. Sam George Cacioppo and Elsie Elizabeth (Grabowski) Wichert; m. Carol Ann Petersen, Dec. 21, 1968; children: Karen Elizabeth, Stephen Benjamin, Christina Ann. BA, Christian Bros. Coll., 1966; MSW, U. Nebr., 1972, PhD, 1983. Diplomate social work. Jr., sr. high sch. tchr. Omaha Cath. Schs., 1966-70; social worker Douglas County Social Services, Omaha, 1970-74; med. social worker U. Nebr. Med. Ctr., Omaha, 1974-78, psychiat. clin. social worker, asst. prof., 1978—; chmn. practicum com. U. Nebr. Sch. Social Work, Omaha, 1984-86. Mem. Nat. Assn. Social Workers (Exemplar award 1978), Registry of Clin. Social Workers. Democrat. Roman Catholic. Avocations: hunting, gardening, woodworking, camping, reading. Home: 16112 Spring St Omaha NE 68130

CACIOPPO, JOHN TERRANCE, psychology educator, researcher; b. Marshall, Tex., June 12, 1951; s. Cyrus Joseph and Mary Katherine (Kazimour) C.; m. Barbara Lee Andersen, May 17, 1981; 1 child, Christina Elizabeth. B.S. in Econs., U. Mo.-Columbia, 1973; M.A. in Psychology, Ohio State U., 1975, Ph.D., in Psychology, 1977. Asst. prof. psychology U. Notre Dame (Ind.), 1977-79; asst. prof. psychology U. Iowa, Iowa City, 1979-81, assoc. prof. psychology, 1981-85, prof. psychology, 1985—; assoc. and cons. editor various profl. jours. Yale U. fellow, 1986; NSF grantee, 1979—. Fellow Am. Psychol. Assn., Acad. Behavioral Medicine Research; mem. Soc. Exptl. Social Psychology, Soc. Psychophysiol. Research, Soc. Advancement Social Psychology, Midwestern Psychol. Assn., AAAS, Sigma Xi. Author, editor 4 books. Contbr. over 100 articles to profl. jours.

CADE, CYNTHIA TODD, financial planner; b. Plainfield, N.J., Sept. 18, 1959; d. William Harley and Ethel Shirley (Todd) Cline; m. Philip Nicholas Kadinsky-Cade, Dec. 15, 1984; 1 child, Nicholas William. BA in Econs., Polit. Sci., Duke U., 1981; MBA in Fin., U. Chgo., 1985. CPA, Ill. Cash mgmt. cons. No. Trust Co., Chgo., 1981-84; sr. fin. cons. Arthur Andersen, Chgo., 1985-87; corp. fin. planner Kraft Inc., Glenview, Ill., 1987—; cons. in field. Contbr. articles to profl. jours. Mem. Am. Inst. CPA's, Ill. CPA Soc. Republican. Presbyterian. Office: Kraft Inc 3N Kraft Ct Glenview IL 60025

CADE, VICTOR ROSCOE, osteopathic surgeon; b. Larned, Kans., Apr. 7, 1911; s. Albert Benton and Minnie H. (Goodman) C.; m. Helen G. Shore, 1933; children—Sonya Marie Cade Steiner, Steven Ray Cade. D.O., U. Health Scis., Kansas City, Mo., 1934; diploma Am. Inst. Hypnosis, 1977; Postgrad. in surgery U. Vienna, Diplomate Am. Osteo. Bd. Surgery, Kans. State Bd. Healing Arts. Gen. practice osteo. medicine, Larned, 1934—, also Corpus Christi, Tex.; mem. staff St. Joseph Meml. Hosp., Larned, Corpus Christi Osteo. Hosp.; mem. faculty U. Health Scis. Mem. Coll. Osteo. Surgeons, ACS, Kans. Assn. Osteo. Medicine (hon. life mem.), Am. Osteopathy Assn., Am. Med. Soc. Vienna. Lodge: Masons. Office: Cade Bldg 820 Broadway Larned KS 67550

CADIEUX, EUGENE ROGERS, insurance company executive; b. Detroit, Feb. 14, 1923; s. Harold S. and Nadia (Rogers) C.; student U. Detroit Coll. Commerce and Finance, 1941-42, Sch. Law, 1952; m. Leontine R. Keane, May 10, 1975. With bond dept. Standard Accident Ins. Co., Detroit, 1951-54; bond mgr. Am. Ins. Co., Detroit, 1954-65, Fireman's Fund, Cin., 1965-66, Md. Casualty Co., Detroit, 1966-75, Zervos Agency, Inc., 1975; cons. to contractors, 1957—. Asst. dir. boys work Internat Assn. Y's Mens Clubs, 1953; committeeman YMCA, Detroit; mem. citizens council Internat. Inst., 1977—; trustee Joint Meml. Day Assn. Served with AUS, World War II. Mem. Surety Assn. Mich. (sec. 1958), Am. Assn. State and Local History, Mich., Detroit (sec. 1970—, trustee), Cin. (com. on library and acquisitions), Grosse Pointe (pres. 1980-82) hist. socs., SAR (pres. Mich. soc. 1961-62, bd. mgrs., nat. Americanism com.), Friends Pub. Library Cin., Friends Pub. Library Grosse Pointe (hist. com.), Delta Sigma Pi, Gamma Eta Gamma. Clubs: Country (Detroit), Algonquin, Grosse Pointe Ski. Home: 208 Ridgemont Rd Grosse Pointe Farms MI 48236 Office: 24724 Farmbrook St Southfield MI 48034

CADIEUX, ROBERT D., chemical company executive; b. 1937; married. B.S. in Econs. and Acctg., Ill. Inst. Tech., 1959; M.B.A., U. Chgo., 1969. Mgr. adminstrv. ctr. Amoco Oil Co., Chgo., 1972-74; mgr. budgets and control reports Amoco Corp. (formerly Standard Oil Co. of Ind.), Chgo., 1971-74, div. controller petroleum ops., from 1974; with Amoco Chems. Co., Chgo., 1959—, v.p. adminstrn. and planning, 1975-81, exec. v.p., dir., 1981-83; pres. Amoco Chems. Co., 1983—. Served with USAR, 1957-61. Office: Amoco Chems Co 200 E Randolph Dr Chicago IL 60601 *

CADMAN, WILSON KENNEDY, utility company executive; b. Wichita, Sept. 7, 1927; s. Wilson K. and Ethel Louise (Wheeler) C.; m. Mary Roslyn Rowley, Nov. 22, 1950; children: Elizabeth Louise, Robert Wilson. AB, Wichita State U., 1951, postgrad., 1953; postgrad., Okla. State U., 1965. With Kans. Gas & Electric Co., Wichita, 1951—, mgr. Witchita div., 1967-70, v.p., 1970-79, pres., 1979—, chief exec. officer, 1981—, also chmn. bd. dirs.; bd. dirs. Fourth Fin. Corp., Fourth Nat. Bank & Trust Co., Electric Power Research Inst. Bd. govs. Wichita State U. Endowment Assn.; bd. dirs. St. Frances Hosp., United Way, Music Theatre, Wichita State U. Athletic Scholarship Orgn.; mem. Gov.'s Task Force on High Tech. Devel., Mayor's Econ. Adv. Council, Kans. Water Resources Council. Served with USN, 1945-46. Mem. Mo. Valley Electric Assn. (chmn. gen. mgmt. com.), Edison Electric Inst., Atomic Indsl. Forum (bd. dirs.), Wichita Area Devel. (exec. com.), Missouri Valley Electric Assn., Wichita State U. Endowment Assn., Phi Lambda Phi. Clubs: Wichita, Wichita Country. Lodge: Kiwanis. Home: 6512 Aberdeen St Wichita KS 67206 Office: 201 N Market St Wichita KS 67202

CADOGAN, EDWARD JOHN PATRICK, mfg. co. mktg. exec.; b. London, Dec. 22, 1939; came to U.S., 1959, naturalized, 1964; B.S. in Mktg., L.I. U., 1971; M.B.A., U. Dayton, 1977; m. Wanda Maxine Evans, Dec. 30, 1975. Sr. field engr. Fairchild Camera & Instrument Corp., Syosset, N.Y., in Vietnam and Okinawa, 1964-69; mgr. Honeywell Mut. Alarm Corp., N.Y.C., 1971-72; sales engr. CAI/div. Recon-Optical, Barrington, Ill., 1972-75; mktg. engr. Cin. Electronics Corp., 1977-78; mktg. mgr. electro-optics Electronic Warfare Centre, Systems Research Labs., Dayton, Ohio, 1978-82; regional mgr. Fairchild Weston Systems, Inc., Dayton, 1982—. Mem. Republican Nat. Com. Served with USAF, 1959-63. Mem. Assn. M.B.A. Execs., Assn. Old Crows, Tech. Mktg. Soc. Am., Am. Def. Preparedness Assn., Air Force Assn., Assn. Unmanned Vehicle Systems, Nat. Contract Mgmt. Assn. Home: 5420 Pentland Circle Huber Heights OH 45424 Office: 4032 Linden Ave Dayton OH 45432

CADWELL, JAMES BURTON, information systems management executive; b. Berwyn, Ill., Oct. 3, 1942; s. Charles Stewart and Louise (Beilby) C.; m. Kathleen Anne Holland, Feb. 22, 1969; children—Kathleen M., Megan M., James P. B.A., St. Mary's Coll., 1968. Mem. mktg. staff GTE Automatic Electric, Northlake, Ill., 1968-72; ops. analyst Cook Electric Co., Morton Grove, Ill., 1972-76; systems analyst Kitchens of Sara Lee, Deerfield, Ill., 1976-79; project mgr. Walgreen Co., Deerfield, 1979-82; project leader Culligan Water Treatment div. Beatrice Foods, Northbrook, 1982-86; mgr. A.T. Kearney, Chgo., 1986—. Bd. dirs. Youth Services, Glenview, Ill., 1976; mem. fin. com. Sam Young for U.S. Ho. of Reps., Glenview, 1979. Served with U.S. Army, 1963-66. Republican. Roman Catholic. Clubs: Olph Mens; St. Mary's Veterans (Winona, Minn.) (pres. 1967-68). Lodges: Optimists, Kiwanis. Home: 1939 Palmgren St Glenview IL 60025 Office: AT Kearney Co 222 S Riverside Plaza 24th Floor Chicago IL 60606

CADY, DARREL ROBERT, historian, educator; b. Waterloo, Iowa, Apr. 17, 1933; s. Harold Frank and Rosalie Pearl (Shobe) C.; m. LaVonne Marilyn Gross, June 11, 1955; children—Shawn, Sarah. B.A., U. No. Iowa, 1958; M.A., U. Ill., 1962; Ph.D., U. Kans., 1974. Tchr. history Tipton High Sch. (Iowa), 1958-60; tchr. history, head dept. Roseburg High Sch. (Oreg.), 1962-63; tchr. history Clinton High Sch. (Iowa), 1963-65; assoc. prof. history Western Ill. U., 1969—. Served with USNR, 1953-56. Harry S. Truman Library Inst. grantee, 1967; Merchant scholar, 1966-67; NDEA fellow, Kans., 1968-69. Mem. Orgn. Am. Historians, Univ. Profls. of Ill. Office: 445 Morgan Hall Western Ill Univ Macomb IL 61455

CAFFREY, RONALD JANSS, marketing and advertising executive; b. N.Y.C., Mar. 16, 1928; s. John Parker and Mildred (Janss) C.; m. Suzanne Westermann, Apr. 2, 1949 (div. 1976); children: Carol Lyn Buchta, Karen Sue Johnson; m. Kathleen Jean Jakubiak, Dec. 7, 1977; 1 child, Ronald J. II. BS in Indsl. Engring., BBA, Yale U., 1949. Commd. USNG, 1948, advanced through grades to capt., 1953, resigned, 1959; br. mgr. N.Y. Johnson Controls Inc., N.Y.C., 1960-66; regional mgr. S.W. Johnson Controls Inc., Dallas, 1966-69; regional mgr. Midwest Johnson Controls Inc., Chgo., 1969-73; v.p. mktg. Johnson Controls Inc., Milw., 1973—; pres. Exec. Communicators, Milw., 1980—. Contbr. articles to profl. publs. Pres. Port Washington (N.Y.) Estates Assn., 1960-63, Lake Glen Assn., Milw., 1982—. Mem. Intelligent Bldgs. Inst. (pres. 1986—), ASHRAE (dir. 1970-73, Disting. Service award 1972), Bldg. Owners Mgrs. Assn., Am. Soc. Energy Engrs. Club: Milw. Yacht. Avocations: sailing, tennis, model R.R. Home: 6900 N Glen Shore Dr Glendale WI 53209 Office: Johnson Controls Inc 507 E Michigan St Milwaukee WI 53201

CAGAS, COSME RALOTA, pediatrician, endocrinologist; b. Jimenez, Philippines, Jan. 17, 1936; came to U.S., 1973; s. Cosme Leopoldo Cagas and Salud Almendras Ralota; m. Linda San Diego; children: Elcee, Chess, Georgina, Chester. BA in Medicine, U. Philippines, Quezon City, 1955; MD, U. Philippines, Manila, 1960. Diplomate Am. Bd. Pediatrics, Am. Bd. Pediatric Endocrinology. Intern Philippine Gen. Hosp., Manila, 1960, Menorah Med. Ctr., 1961; resident in pediatrics Children's Mercy Hosp., Kansas City, Mo., 1962, Kans. U. Med. Ctr., 1963; fellow in pediatrics, endocrinology and metabolism U. Okla., Okla. City, 1964-66; asst. prof. U. Philippines, Manila, 1966-73, U. Okla., Oklahoma City, 1973-76; from clin. asst. prof. to assoc. prof. St. Louis U., 1976—; practice medicine specializing in pediatrics Bellville, Ill., 1976—; from clin. asst. prof. to prof. So. Ill. U., Springfield, 1979—; cons. genetic screening program State of Ill., Springfield, 1978—. Editor: Philippine Am. Med. Bull., 1981—; literary columnist Phlippine Am. Med. Bull., 1979—; numerous articles to sci. jour. Recipient 1st Prize Speech award. elow: Am. Acad. Pediatrics; mem. Lawson Wilkins Pediatric Endoctrine Soc., St. Clair County Med. Soc. (sec. 1986—), Assn. Filipino Physicians So. Ill (founder, Disting. Service award 1984), U. Philippines Med. Alumni Soc. Am. (founder, pres. 1980—, Most Disting. Alumnus Overseas award 1986, Most Outstanding Physician 1978, 81), Philippine Econ. and Cultural Endowment (founder, pres. 1986—), Philippine Physicians in Am. (speaker ho. of dels., 1980-83). Club: Toastmasters. Avocations: tennis, journalism, poetry, public speaking. Home: 1 Bunkum Woods Fairview Heights IL 62208 Office: 6024 W Main Belleville IL 62223

CAGLE, ALBERT WAYNE, retired engineering consultant; b. High Point, N.C., May 25, 1924; s. Grady Carson and Mary (Davis) C.; B.S., High Point Coll., 1948; M.S., U. Louisville, 1950; m. Bessie Valeria Kivett, Sept. 16, 1949; children—Albert Wayne, Lynne, Deborah, Mark. Research chemist Cone Mills Research, Greensboro, N.C., 1950; with AT&T Tech. Inc., Lee's Summit, Mo., 1951-85, sr. staff engr., 1970-85; lectr. Pittsburg (Kans.) State U., 1985—. Served with U.S. Army, 1943-46. Decorated Bronze Star. Fellow Am. Soc. for Metals; mem. Am. Chem. Soc., Soc. Plastics Engrs., Soc. Mfg. Engrs. Methodist. Clubs: Masons, Shriners. Home: 622 Englewood Raytown MO 64133 Office: AT & T Tech Inc 777 N Blue Hills Pkwy Summit MO 64063

CAGLE, WESLEY JACKSON, management consultant; b. Turkey, Tex., June 12, 1930; s. Robert Nathan and Clara Mabel (Land) C.; m. Sammie Jo Pittman, Aug. 31, 1958; children: Wesley Morris, Bradley Alan. BS Agrl. Engring., Tex. Tech U., 1958; cert., U. Okla., 1951. V.p. engring. John Blue Co., Huntsville, Ala., 1971-78; v.p. mktg. and sales John Blue Co., Huntsville, 1978-80; pvt. practice cons. Huntsville, 1980-82; gen. mgr. Century Engring., Cedar Rapids, Iowa, 1982-86; pvt. practice cons. Cedar Rapids, 1986-87; v.p., gen. mgr. David Mfg. Co., Mason City, Iowa, 1987—; cons. Westeel Rosco, Toronto, Ont., Can., 1980-81. Contbr. articles to profl. jours.; patentee farm equipment. Served to sgt. USAF, 1951-53, Korea. Mem. Am. Soc. Agrl. Engrs., Soc. Automotive Engrs., Farm and Indsl. Equipment Inst., Nat. Fertilizer Solutions Assn., Farm Equipment Mfg. Assn. Republican. Lodges: Masons (chmn. 1964, 67), Shriners. Avocations: inventing, gardening, woodshop, dancing, reading. Home: 5 Country Club Pl Clear Lake IA 50428 Office: Davd Mfg Co 1600 12th St NE Mason City IA 50401

CAHALEN, SHIRLEY LEANORE, educator; b. LaHarpe, Kans., Aug. 20, 1933; d. Hugh E. and Irma Eunonia (Russell) Pearman; m. Keith E. Cahalen, Sept. 2, 1953; 1 child, Keith P. Student Iola Jr. Coll., 1951-52, McPherson Coll., 1952-53, Pratt Community Coll., 1963-64; BS, Northwestern State U., Alva, Okla., 1966; MS, Kans. State U., 1981; postgrad. Emporia State U., summer 1982. With Kans. Power & Light Co., McPherson, 1952-53, State Farm Ins. Co., Jacksonville, Fla., 1957-59, Kans. Fish and Game Commn., Pratt, 1960-62; home econs. tchr. Kirby-Smith Jr. High Sch., Jacksonville, Fla., 1966-67, Unified Sch. Dist. 254, Medicine Lodge, Kans., 1968-71, Sch. Dist. 259, Wichita East, Wichita, Kans., 1971-73, Dist. 490 El Dorado, Kans., 1975-82; tchr. spl. edn. Augusta (Kans.) Sr. High Sch., 1982—. Mem. edn. com. First United Meth. Ch., 1981-87. Mem. Walnut Valley Edn. Assn., Kans. Edn. Assn. (state rep.), NEA, Butler County Spl. Edn. Assn., AAUW (pres. 1979-81), Kappa Delta Pi, Am. Legion Aux. Methodist. Home: 318 School Rd El Dorado KS 67042 Office: Augusta Sr High Sch Augusta KS 67010

CAHILL, CHARLES ADAMS, psychiatrist; b. Milw., Mar. 2, 1930; s. Charles Adams and Beatrice Cahill. BA, Harvard U., 1951, MD, 1955. Diplomate Am. Bd. Psychiatry and Neurology. Intern U. N.C. Med. Ctr., Chapel Hill, 1955-56; resident in psychiatry Menninger Found., Topeka, 1956-58, Bellevue Hosp., N.Y.C., 1960-61; cons. psychiatrist fed., state and local govtl. agys., Southeastern Wis., 1961—; mem. legis. council mental health subcom. Wis. State Legislature, Madison, 1966-69; examiner Am. Bd. Psychiatry and Neurology, midwestern U.S., 1982—. Contbr. to book TM, 1972 (Gambrinus award 1974); contbr. articles to profl. jours. Served as lt. USNR, 1958-60, lt. col. USAR, 1983-87. Fellow Am. Psychiat. Assn.; mem. Wis. Psychiat. Ass. (councilor 1978-79). Republican. Congregationalist. Club: Harvard (Milw.). Avocations: performing arts, local hist. socs. Home: 4901 N Santa Monica Blvd Milwaukee WI 53217 Office: Counseling Ctr 339 Reed Ave Manitowoc WI 54220

CAHILL, CLYDE S., U.S. judge; b. St. Louis, Apr. 9, 1923; s. Clyde and Effie (Taylor) C.; m. Thelma Newsom, Apr. 29, 1951; children: Linda Diggs, Marina, Valerian, Randall, Kevin, Myron. B.S., St. Louis U., 1949, J.D., 1951. Bar: Mo. Sole practice 1951-56; asst. circuit atty. City of St. Louis, 1956-64; regional atty. OEO, Kansas City, 1966-68; gen. mgr. Human Devel. Corp., 1968-72; gen. counsel, exec. dir. Legal Aid Soc., St. Louis, 1972-75; circuit judge State of Mo., 1975-80; U.S. dist. judge Eastern Dist. Mo., 1980—; lectr. St. Louis U. Law Sch., 1974-79; counsel to Mo. NAACP, 1958-65. Bd. dirs. St. Louis Urban League, 1974, Met. YMCA, St. Louis, 1975—, Comprehensive Health Center, 1975, Cardinal Ritter High Sch., 1978. Served with USAAF, World War II. Recipient NAACP Disting. Service award, St. Louis Argus award. Mem. Am. Bar Assn., Nat. Bar Assn., Am. Judicature Soc., Mo. Bar Assn., Met. St. Louis Bar Assn., St. Louis Lawyers Assn., Mound City Bar Assn. Office: U S Dist Ct US Court and Custom House 1114 Market St Saint Louis MO 63101

CAHILL, LORINE, psychologist; b. Alliance, Ohio, Aug. 19, 1932; d. William Arnold and Catherine (Roberts) Roesti; m. Philip Thomas Cahill, Apr. 21, 1951; children: Jerri Nielsen, Scott, Eric. BA in Psychology, Kent (Ohio) State U., 1967; MA in Psychology, U. Akron, 1969. Lic. psychologist, Ohio. Staff developer Woodside Receiving Hosp., Youngstown, Ohio, 1971-72, chief psychologist, 1972-75, clin. programs dir., 1982—; dir. psychiat. outpatient services Eastern Mental Health Ctr., Struthers, Ohio, 1975-77, clin. dir., 1977-82; cons. psychologist Eastern Mental Health Ctr., 1982—. Bd. dirs. State Mental Health Assn., Mahoning County Mental Health Assn. Mem. Mental Health Adminstrs. Assn., Ohio Psychology Dirs. Assn., Ohio Counselors Assn. Unitarian. Avocations: writing poetry, making feathered masks. Home: 8609 Western Reserve Rd Canfield OH 44406 Office: Woodside Receiving Hosp 800 E Indianola Youngstown OH 44502

CAHILL, MARY FRAN, journalist; b. Milw.; d. Morgan Joseph and Claire Catherine (Warnimont) C.; B.A., M.A., Marquette U. Photojournalist Cedarburg (Wis.) News Graphic, 1965-67; photojournalist Milw. Jour., 1967-76, feature writer, 1976-83, food writer, 1983—; mem. unit holders council Jour. Co., 1977-79. Hon. mem. Milw. Fire Dept. Recipient Disting. Service award Milw. Fire Dept., 1972, 74, 75, 77, 78, 79, 80; cert. of appreciation USCGR, 1975, 77. Mem. Nat. Press Photographers Assn., Wis. News Photographers Assn. (sec. 1973-75), Women in Communications, Milw. Press Club, Zool. Soc. Milwaukee County, Wis. Emergency Med. Technicians Assn. (Woman of Yr. award 1975), Nat. Assn. Emergency Med. Technicians, Milw. Fire Hist. Soc. (dir. 1982-86, treas. 1982-83, sec. 1983-86), Am. Culinary Fedn., Milw. Profl. Cooks and Chefs Assn., Sigma Delta Chi, Phi Mu, Phi Alpha Theta, Pi Gamma Mu. Office: 333 W State St Milwaukee WI 53201 Home: 6609 N Lake Dr Fox Point WI 53217

CAHILL, RICHARD JOHN, advertising executive; b. Mpls., Dec. 30, 1938; s. Edward Leroy and Marjorie Marie (Dolbec) C.; m. Elda Theresa Zachman, May 3, 1969; children—Kimberly Ann, Brian Edward. A.A., U. Minn., 1958, B.A., 1960. Cert. advt. specialist, Minn. Sales corr. Shedd-Brown, Mpls., 1964-68, asst. gen. sales mgr., 1968-79, v.p., gen. mgr. Shedd-Brown, Trend Devel. Corp. Subs., 1979-82, exec v.p. Shedd-Brown, 1982-84, pres., 1984-85; pres. AdSource One, Mpls., 1986—. Served to 1st lt. U.S. Army, 1961-63. Recipient Merit award Specialty Advt. Assn., 1981, 1982, Most Beneficial Sales and Mgmt. Aids award Specialty Advt. Assn., 1980, Best Catalog award Specialty Advt. Assn., 1981, First Pl. in Offset Printing award Specialty Advt. Assn., 1982, Sales Talk Championship award Dale Carnegie & Assoc., Inc., 1968. Roman Catholic. Lodge: Lions Home: 7209 Shannon Dr Edina MN 55435 Office: Shedd-Brown 13911 Ridgedale Dr Minnetonka MN 55343

CAIN, CAROL LISA, reporter, columnist; b. Detroit, Feb. 5; d. Charles Cornelius and Ruth (Edstrom) C. BA in Communication, Mich. State U., 1981. Reporter, editor UPI, Detroit, 1981-84; reporter, columnist Detroit News, 1984—; nationally syndicated columnist 1986—. Mem. Sigma Delta Chi. Roman Catholic. Clubs: Detroit Press Club, Adcraft Club Detroit. Home: 1358 Bedford Grosse Pointe Park MI 48230 Office: Detroit News 615 Lafayette Blvd Detroit MI 48226

CAIN, CLIFFORD CHALMERS, chaplain, educator; b. Zanesville, Ohio, Feb. 15, 1950; s. Clifford Chalmers Sr. and Ethel Virginia (Bokelman) C.; m. Louise E. Lueckel, June 7, 1975; children: Rachel Mariël, Zachary Matheüs. BA, Muskingum Coll., 1972; M Div., Princeton Theol. Seminary, 1975; postgrad., Rijksuniversiteit te Leiden, The Netherlands, 1975-78; D in Ministry, Vanderbilt U., 1981. Ordained to ministry Am. Bapt. Ch., 1975. Assoc. pastor The Am. Protestant Ch., The Netherlands, 1975-78; chaplain Muskingum Coll., New Concord, Ohio, 1978-81; chaplain, assoc. prof. Franklin (Ind.) Coll., 1981—; pres. Met. Indpls. Campus Ministry, 1984-85, Ind. Office for Campus Ministries, 1985—. Contbr. articles to profl. jour. and book revs.; contbg. editor: The Intersection of Mind and Spirit, 1985. V.p. The Am. Community Council, The Hague, The Netherlands, 1977-78; bd. dirs. Evergreen Village, New concord, Ohio, 1980-81. Mem. Am. Acad. Religion, Soc. Biblical Lit., N.Am. Bapt. Peace Fellowship, Nat. Assn. Coll. and U. Chaplains (bd. dirs., v.p.). Avocations: photography, music, traveling, sports, archaeology. Home: 300 W Jefferson St Franklin IN 46131 Office: Franklin Coll East Monroe St Franklin IN 46131

CAIN, DEBRA LYNN, social service administrator; b. El Paso, Tex., Apr. 23, 1954; d. George William Cain and Patricia Carole Freeman; m. Luther Blue Jr., Dec. 21, 1979; 1 child, Matthew Luther Blue. BS in Psychology, Iowa State U., 1977; postgrad., Cen. Mich. U., 1977—. Program dir. Haven YWCA, Pontiac, Mich., 1977-82, exec. dir., 1982—; treas. Mich. Coalition Against Domestic Violence, 1979—; chmn. Tri-County Coalition Against Domestic Violence, 1981-84; bd. dirs. S.E. Mich. Anti-Rape Network, Oakland County Council for Children at Risk. Mem. Mich. Interdisciplinary Profl. Assn., NOW, Altrusa. Home: 2107 Devonshire Bloomfield Hills MI 48013 Office: Haven 92 Whittemore Pontiac MI 48058

CAIN, ROBERT BARR, computer graphics company executive; b. Detroit, July 19, 1941; s. Alexander and Bernadine (Kaiser) C.; m. Mary Elaine Kendall, Apr. 2, 1960; children—Robert A., Gary R., Sandra D. B.A. in Indsl. Mgmt., Lawrence Inst. Tech., 1967. Tech. engr. Xerox Corp., Detroit, 1965-69; pub. relations dir. Bendix Corp., Southfield, Mich., 1970-73; creative dir. Maritz Inc., St. Louis, 1973-75; pres., founder Symtec Inc., Farmington, Mich., 1974-86, Mich. Sci. Systems, Inc., Farmington, 1984—; cons. Sandy Corp., Troy, Mich., 1975-86. Author: Numerical Control Handbook, 1967. Publ. newsletter: Numerical Control Newsletter, 1967-69. Patentee flash activated laser. Served with USAF, 1959-64. Recipient Product of Yr. award Gov. State Mich., 1983. Mem. Numerical Control Soc. (Outstanding Contribution award 1964), Soc. Mfg. Engrs. (Instr. Yr. award 1970). Republican. Presbyterian. Avocations: art; travel; computer graphics design; computer programming. Home: 20009 Parkside Saint Clair Shores MI 48080 Office: Mich Sci Systems Inc 2529 Orleans Detroit MI 48207

CAIN, STANLEY ROBERT, architect; b. Peoria, Ill., Nov. 18, 1954; s. Donald Edvin and Faye Margaret (Bryan) C.; m. Susan Jane Van Klavern, Mar. 15, 1980; children: Dustin Alan. BArch, U. Ill., 1976, MArch, 1978. Registered architect, Wis., Ill. Project mgr. Continental Bank, Chgo., 1979-83; prin. Cain & Assocs., Naperville, Ill., 1983-85; officer Continental Bank, Chgo., 1985—. Mem. Naperville Mcpl. Bd., 1980—, Community Brass, Naperville, 1981—, Trombone Choir, Naperville, 1984—, Nat. Trust for Historic Preservation. Mem. AIA,. Methodist. Avocations: trombone, bicycling, modelmaking. Home: 140 N Loomis St Naperville IL 60540 Office: Continental Bank 231 S LaSalle St Chicago IL 60697

CAIN, TIM J., lawyer; b. Angola, Ind., July 12, 1958; s. Nancy J. (Nichols) C.; m. Debra J. VanWagner, Feb. 28, 1976; children: Christine M., Stephanie L., Katherine S. AB in Polit. Sci. with honors, Ind. U., 1980; JD, Valparaiso U., 1984. Bar: Ind. 1984, U.S. Dist. Ct. (no. and so. dists.) Ind. 1984. Assoc. Hartz & Eberhard, LaGrange, Ind., 1984-85; pub. defender LaGrange Cir. Ct., 1985-86; sr. assoc. Eberhard & Assocs., LaGrange, 1985-86; chief dep. to Pros. Atty.'s Office, LaGrange, 1986—; ptnr. Eberhard & Cain, LaGrange, 1986—; asst. atty. LaGrange County, LaGrange, 1984—; atty. Town of Shipshewana, Ind., 1985—. Coach Orland (Ind.) Little League, 1977-79, Prairie Heights Baseball, LaGrange, 1986—. Mem. ABA, Assn. Trial Lawyers Am., Ind. Bar Assn., LaGrange County Bar Assn. (sec.-treas. 1986—). Republican. Club: Exchange. Home: Rt 1 Box 288 Orland IN 46776 Office: Eberhard & Cain 115 S Detroit St LaGrange IN 46761

CAINE, CLIFFORD JAMES, educational administrator, consultant; b. Watertown, S.D., May 28, 1933; s. Louis Vernon and Elizabeth Matilda (Holland) C. B.A., Macalester Coll., 1955; J.D., U. Minn., 1958, Ph.D., 1975; postgrad. Harvard U., 1976. Bar: Minn. 1958. Dir. men's residence halls and student union Macalester Coll., 1959-63, dir. adminstrv. policies study, 1969-70; lectr. U. Minn., 1966-68, also coordinator Neighborhood Seminar program; asst. headmaster St. Paul Acad. and Summit Sch., St. Paul, 1970-85; dir. student services Breck Sch., Mpls., 1985-86; dir. student affairs Breck Sch., Mpls., 1986—. Author: (book) How To Get Into College, 1985; contbr. articles to profl. jours. Bd. dirs. Hallie Q. Brown Community Center, 1972-73, Family Service of St. Paul, 1973-79; ruling elder United Presbyn. Ch., 1962—; clk. of session House of Hope Presbyn. Ch., 1983-84. Mem. Am. Acad. Polit. and Social Sci., Am. Studies Assn., Nat. Assn. Coll. Admissions Counselors, Minn. Bar Assn., U.S. Profl. Tennis Assn., Minn. Assn. Secondary Sch. and Coll. Admissions Officers (pres. 1978-79). Club: Univ. (St. Paul). Home: 456 Summit Ave Saint Paul MN 55102 Office: 123 Ottawa Ave N Minneapolis MN 55422

CAJTHAML, MICHAEL JOSEPH, insurance company sales executive; b. Woodstock, Ill., Dec. 26, 1955; s. ALbert Anton and Ethel Virginia (Nykl) C.; m. Deborah Anne Pintozzi, June 2, 1979; 1 child, Michael Joseph Jr. Grad., High Sch., McHenry, Ill., 1974. Owner, operator Cyscorp, McHenry, 1972-86; registered rep. Transamerica Fin. Resources, McHenry and Oak Brook, Ill., 1986—; owner Mike Cajthaml Ins. and Investments, McHenry, 1986—. Chmn. Fiesta Days Festival, McHenry, 1984. Crimes-toppers, McHenry, 1983-85. Named one of Outstanding Young Men Am., U.S. Jaycees, 1984. Mem. Life Underwriters Tng. Council, Nat. Assn. Life Underwriters, McHenry County Assn. Life Underwriters, McHenry Area C. of C. (chmn. pub. relations 1983, bd. dirs. 1983-85). Republican. Roman Catholic. Club: Toastmasters. Avocations: painting, boating, bicycling, walking, basketball. Home: 4416 Mayfair Dr McHenry IL 60050 Office: Transamerica Fin Resources 2021 Spring Rd Suite 210 Oak Brook IL 60521

CALABRESE, CARMEN, manufacturing company executive; b. Sept. 9, 1939; s. Joseph and Rose (Locante) C.; children: Joseph W., Carmen V. BS in Engring., Drexel U., Phila., 1968; PhD in Engring., U. Pa., 1972; MBA in Mktg., Eastern Mich. U., 1983. Registered profl. engr., Pa. Mgr. mktg. Midland Ross, Toledo, 1978-80, mgr. materials, 1980-82; gen. mgr. Midland Ross, Detroit, 1982-83, mgr. mktg. and sales, 1983-84; v.p. mktg. Weldun Automation Products, Buchanan, Mich., 1984—. Contbr. articles to profl. jours. Served with USAF, 1958-62. Nat. Sci. fellow, 1972. Mem. Am. Mgmt. Assn., Am. Mktg. Assn., Am. Soc. Metals., Phi Kappa Phi. Office: Weldun Automation Products 816 E 3d St Buchanan MI 49107

CALAMARI, ARTHUR PHILIP, advertising executive; b. Chgo., June 8, 1951; s. John Philip and Rose T. (Murphy) C. BA, So. Ill. U., 1974. Art dir. Dan Pipkin Advt., Danville, Ill., 1974-80; creative dir. Creative Slides and Advt., Bloomington, Ill., 1980-85, v.p., creative dir., 1986—. Advisor Scott Ctr., Bloomington, 1986. Recipient Best of Show award Champaign Ad Club, 1986, 10 first place awards, 1985, 86. Mem. Bloomington, No. Ill. Mktg. Assn., Nat. Assn. Am. Bus. Clubs. Republican. Roman Catholic. Club: Champaign (Ill.) Ad; Crestwick Country (Bloomington).. Avocations: tennis, skiing, volleyball, golf. Home: 1913 Tracy Bloomington IL 61701 Office: Creative Slides and Advt 207 Cannmark Dr Normal IL 61761

CALAUTTI, VICTOR NICHOLAS, real estate executive; b. Mercer, Pa., Dec. 6, 1925; s. Julio and Josephine C.; m. Patricia Sterling, Aug. 23, 1963; children: Susan Lynn, Victor Louis. Enlisted U.S. Army C.E., 1944, advanced through grades to 1st sgt.; ret. U.S. Army Corps Engrs., ETO, Korea, 1952; pres., chmn. bd. Nat. Builders Corp., Youngstown, Ohio, 1954—; pres. Real Estate Maintenance, Inc., Youngstown, Ohio, 1978—; cons. Youngstown Osteopathic Hosp. Assn., 1970—. Roman Catholic. Avocations: rare coins, artwork. Office: Nat Builders Corp 833 Wick Ave Youngstown OH 44505

CALDARELLI, DAVID DONALD, otolaryngologist; b. Chgo., Nov. 7, 1941; s. David D. and Violet (Angus) C.; m. Janna Sue Nowak, Apr. 1, 1967; children: Leslie Ann, Adam David. Student, U. Wis., 1961; M.D., U. Ill., 1965, M.S., 1965. Diplomate: Am. Bd. Otolaryngology. Intern Presbyn. St. Luke's Hosp., Chgo., 1965-66; resident in surgery Presbyn. St. Luke's Hosp., 1966-67; resident in otolaryngology U. Ill. Eye and Ear Infirmary and Research and Edn. Hosps., Chgo., 1967-70; practice medicine specializing in otolaryngology Chgo., 1974—; sr. attending physician, chmn. dept. otolaryngology and bronchoesophagology Rush Med. Coll., Rush-Presbyn.-St. Luke's Med. Center, Chgo., 1974—; attending otolaryngologist U. Ill. Research and Edn. Hosps., Chgo., 1970—, St. Francis Hosp., Evanston, Ill., 1974—; otolaryngologist Center for Craniofacial Anomalies, U. Ill., Chgo., 1970—; asst. otolaryngology Coll. Medicine, U. Ill., Chgo., 1967-70, instr. otolaryngology, 1970—; prof., chmn. dept. otolaryngology and bronchoesophagology Rush Med. Coll., Chgo., 1974—; cons. otolaryngologist Chgo. Contagious Disease Hosp., 1975—. Contbr. articles to profl. jours. and textbooks. Recipient Bordan Found. Undergrad. research award in medicine, 1965; Nat. Inst. Nervous Diseases and Blindness Research trainee, 1967-70; Ford Found. fellow, 1965; NIH grantee, 1963, 65. Fellow ACS; mem. AMA, Am. Acad. Ophthalmology and Otolaryngology, Am. Council Otolaryngology, Am. Cleft Palate Soc., Chgo. Laryngol. and Otol. Soc. (pres. 1985-86), Pan Am. Assn. Oto-Rhino-Laryngology and Broncho-Esophagology, Soc. Acad. Chmn. Otolaryngology, Soc. Univ. Otolaryngologists, Am. Broncho-Esophagological Assn., Triological Soc., Am. Soc. Head and Neck Surgery, Soc. Ears, Nose and Throat Advances in Children, Am. Cancer Soc. (unit dir. 1972-75), AAUP. Home: 101 Greenleaf Evanston IL 60202 Office: Rush-Presbyn-St Luke's Med Ctr 1753 W Congress Pkwy Chicago IL 60612

CALDER, GEORGE ALEXANDER, educator; b. Detroit, Oct. 1, 1937; s. Alexander and Janette (Wolcott) C. B.A., Wayne State U., 1959, M.Ed., 1960. Cert. tchr., Mich. Math. tchr. Emerson Jr. High Sch., Livonia, Mich., 1960-79; tchr. Franklin High Sch., Livonia, 1979—, chmn. math. dept., 1980—. Recipient Outstanding Service award Livonia Edn. Assn., 1965, 1976, 1978; Outstanding Young Educator award Livonia Jaycees, 1969. Mem. NEA, Livonia Edn. Assn., Mich. Edn. Assn., Nat. Council Tchrs. Math., Detroit Council Tchrs. Math., Mich. Council Tchrs. Math., Hist. Soc. Livonia, Detroit Soc. for Geneal. Research, SAR (membership chmn. Detroit 1976-83, Nat. Membership award 1979, 81, 82). Methodist. Author: (with others) Discoveries in Modern Mathematics, Courses 1, 2, 1968, 1972; Daily Thoughts for the Classroom, 1974. Office: Franklin High Sch 31000 Joy Rd Livonia MI 48150

CALDERON, EDUARDO FIEGEHEN, neurologist; b. Santiago, Chile, May 14, 1932; came to U.S., 1974, naturalized, 1980; s. Pedro N. and Teresa F. Calderon; B.Sc., Catholic U. Chile; M.D., U. Chile, 1958; m. Yolanda Urrejola, Nov. 27, 1958; children—Eduardo Tomas, John Paul, M. Alexandra, M. Pauline, Francisco. Intern, Cath. U. Clin. Hosp., Santiago, 1958; gen. practice medicine, Chile, 1958-63; trainee, then instr. in neurology U. Chile, 1963-68, asst. prof. neurology, 1971-74; postdoctoral fellow Stanford U. Med. Sch., 1968-71; practice medicine specializing in neurology, Toledo, 1974—; mem. staff St. Luke's Hosp., Mercy Hosp.; clin. asso. prof. Med. Coll. Ohio, Toledo; bd. dirs. Multiple Sclerosis Soc. N.W. Ohio, Toledo, 1974—. Diplomate Am. Bd. Psychiatry and Neurology, Am. Bd. EEG Qualification. Mem. Am. Acad. Neurology, Am. EEG Soc., Ohio Med. Assn., Lucas County Acad. Medicine. Roman Catholic. Home: 5815 Swan Creek Dr Toledo OH 43614 Office: 3949 Sun Forest Ct Toledo OH 43623

CALDERONE, ANTHONY S., social worker; b. Albion, Mich., Apr. 22, 1930; s. Victor and Elvira (Cacciatore) C.; divorced; children: Lisa, Paul, Mary Lyn. BBA, Western Mich. U., 1966. Pvt. practice social work Battle Creek, Mich., 1966—. Bd. dirs. South Cen. Mich. Commn. on Aging, Kalamazoo, 1980-84, Calhoun County Commn. on Aging, Marshall, Mich., 1982-84, Easter House, Battle Creek, 1982-84, Pegasus, Battle Creek, 1982-84. Roman Catholic. Avocations: hunting, bicycling, walking, music, golf. Home and Office: 74 Rambling Ln Battle Creek MI 49015

CALDWELL, ARTHUR BRUCE, sporting goods manufacturer; b. Ft. Smith, Ark., Jan. 25, 1951; s. Lesfred Lenant Caldwell and Judy Flo (Myatt) Grove; divorced; children: Jaime M., Aaron B. Pres., owner, operator Fiber Sport Inc., Kansas City, Mo., 1976—; cons. to numerous athletes, Kansas City, 1972—. Author: The Elusive Bar, 1972; designer fiber vaulting poles; inventor vaulting pole used by athletes. Avocations: magic, bowling, dancing. Office: Fiber Sport Inc 6740 E Bannister Rd Kansas City MO 64134

CALDWELL, CRAIG HOSKINS, chemist; b. Cleve., May 1, 1951; s. H. VanYorx and Clarice (Hoskins) C.; m. Katherine Elizabeth Wilson, July 26, 1986. BA in Chemistry, Hamilton Coll., 1973; MS in Soil and Water Sci., U. New Hampshire, 1974; MBA in Mgmt., Xavier U., 1983. Environ. scientist PEDCo. Environ. Inc., Cin., 1975-78; group leader PED Co., Cin., 1978-79, group supr., 1979-84; lab coordinator PEI Assocs., Inc., Cin., 1984-86; lab. ops. mgr. PEI/IT, Cin., 1987—. Author, editor: Guidlines for Outings Leaders, 1982. Pres. bd. dirs. Oxford Audubon Soc., 1981. Mem. Am. Chem. Soc., Am. Indsl. Hygiene Assn., Sierra Club (outings leader 1981—, chmn. leader tng. 1986—). Avocations: skiing, backpacking, bicycling, gardening. Home: 12028 Gaylord Dr Cincinnati OH 45240 Office: PEI/IT 11499 Chester Rd Cincinnati OH 45246

CALDWELL, DIANNE DEE, cosmetic company executive; b. Youngstown, Ohio, Jan. 24, 1946; d. Leo William and June Marie (Gakel) Difford; B.S. in Edn., Kent (Ohio) State U., 1968; m. Thomas R. Caldwell, June 22, 1968; children—Ryan Thomas, Reed Jason. High sch. English tchr., Mogadore, Ohio, 1968-69; librarian Ann Arbor (Mich.) Public Schs., 1969-72; cons. Jafra Cosmetics, Inc.-Gillette, Saline, Mich., 1974-79, cons., mgr., 1977-79, regional dir., 1979-82; v.p. The Creative Circle, Saline, 1982—; divisional sales mgr. Jafra Cosmetics, Inc., Saline, 1982—. Pres. Ann Arbor Police Wives Assn., 1971-75; mem. Republican Nat. Com.; mem. Saline Vocat. Edn. Adv. Com., 1979-80; spl. events chmn. Saline March of Dimes, 1973-75. Named Outstanding Mgr., Jafra Cosmetics, Inc.-Gillette, 1978; recipient Jan Day award, 1978, Saline Edn. Adv. award, 1979, 80. Mem. Nat. Assn. Female Execs., Nat. Ruffled Grouse Soc. Methodist. Office: 213 E Michigan Ave Saline MI 48176

CALDWELL, DONALD FROST, psychologist, educator; b. Chgo., Mar. 3, 1933; s. Cal Wayland and Kathryn A. (McAuley) C.; m. Sheryl Bedette Rashleigh, May 20, 1955 (div. 1978); children: Brett Frost, Robin Bedette, Kristen Leigh; m. Cynthia Kay Wood, Jan. 12, 1984. BS, Purdue U., 1955; MA, George Peabody Coll., 1957; PhD, Vanderbilt U., 1960. Licensed consulting psychologist, Mich. Research asst. Vanderbilt U., Nashville, 1957-59; research assoc. Lafayette Clinic, Detroit, 1960-68, mental health research scientist, 1968—; exptl. psychologist Walter Reed Isnt. Research, Washington, 1962-63; prof. psychiatry Wayne State U., Detroit, 1976—, adj. prof. psychology, 1971—; dir. dept. psychobiology Lafayette Clinic, Detroit, 1963—, dir. sleep disorder ctr., 1975—; grad. officer Wayne State U. dept. psychiatry, Detroit, 1985—; vis. prof. Ctr. for Creative Studies, Coll. Art & Design, Detroit, 1982—. Contbr. over 80 sci. publs. in jours. and books. Chmn. recreation adv. bd. City of Huntington Wood, Mich., 1976-77. Served to 1st lt. M.C., U.S. Army, 1962-63. Disting. Speaker, Mercy Coll., Detroit, 1975; NIH predoctoral fellow, 1959-60. Mem. Am. Psychol. Assn., Internat. Soc. Devel. Psychobiology, Soc. Biol. Psychiatry. Congregationalist. Avocations: fine art photography, history. Home: 2043 Golfview Dr #210 Troy MI 48084 Office: Lafayette Clinic 951 E Lafayette St Detroit MI 48207

CALDWELL, JAMES MARSHALL, accountant; b. Chillicothe, Ohio, Aug. 1, 1939; s. Marshall and Emma (Gillette) C.; B.B.A., Ohio U., 1963; m. Pamela Lynne Marsh, June 13, 1963; children—Jennifer Lynne, James Patrick. Dep. auditor Ross County (Ohio), 1960-63, county commr., 1977—; tchr. Jackson (Ohio) City Schs., 1963-64; accountant, Chillicothe, 1961—; pres. James M. Caldwell & Assos. Inc., public accts.; sec. Huston Gifts, Dolls & Flowers Inc.; del. White House Conf. on Small Bus., 1986. City councilman, City of Chillicothe, 1968-75; pres. Ross County Young Republican Club, 1968-69; bd. dirs. Ross County Community Improvement Corp.; trustee Mid-Ohio Health Planning Fedn., 1975-77, Ohio Valley Health Services Found.; pres. Bd. Ross County Commrs., 1979; mem. Ross County Planning Commn.; exec. bd. Ohio Valley Regional Devel. Commn.; mem. citizens policy adv. com. Scioto River Basin, Ohio EPA. Mem. Nat. Soc. Public Accts., Public Acctg. Soc. of Ohio (pres. So. Ohio chpt. 1974-79), Chillicothe-Ross C. of C. (dir. 1970-73, pres. 1973), Chillicothe Jaycees (Citizen of Year 1973), Hon. Ky. Cols. Methodist (mem. adminstrv. bd. 1971-74, chmn. council ministries 1975-76, trustee 1985—). Lodges: Kiwanis, Elks. Home: 306 Fairway Ave Chillicothe OH 45601 Office: 84 W 2d St PO Box 1640 Chillicothe OH 45601

CALDWELL, JAMES WILLIAM, drugstore chain executive; b. Fallis, Ky., Apr. 24, 1935; s. James Hugh and Estelle Bernice (Drugan) C.; m. Delinda Jane Reeves, Mar. 29, 1959. B.S. in Pharmacy, Purdue U., 1957. Registered pharmacist. Asst. mgr. Hook Drugs, Inc., Indpls., 1958-62, mgr., 1962-69, divisional coordinator, 1969-77, asst. v.p. ops. 1977-83, asst. v.p. health care, 1983-84; v.p. health care, 1985—. Bd. dirs. Indpls. Sr. Citizens Ctr., 1984-85, chmn. bldg. com., 1984-85; adv. bd. Warren Performing Arts Ctr., 1986—; fin. chmn. Southport United Methodist Ch., Ind., 1980-83. Served with U.S. Army, 1959-61. Mem. Ind. Pharmacist Assn. Democrat. Lodge: Masons. Avocations: farming; Tennessee walking horses; miniature animals. Home: 8930 Baker Rd Indianapolis IN 46259 Office: Hook Drugs Inc 2800 Enterprise St Indianapolis IN 46226

CALDWELL, MARK DONALD, magazine marketing executive; b. N.Y.C., Nov. 23, 1954; s. Roy Arthur and Beverly Jean (Kline) C. AAS, Morrisville Coll., 1974; BA, SUNY, 1976. Wine mcht. Wine Mchts. Ltd., Syracuse, N.Y., 1977-78; sales rep. Time Inc., Houston and N.Y.C., 1978-81, circulation sales mgr., So. Calif., Laguna Hills, 1981-84, v.p. midwest region, Chgo., 1984-86; exec. v.p. Mag. and Paperback Mktg. Inst., Des Plaines, Ill., 1986—. Mem. Chgo. Art Inst. Mem. Morrisville Coll. Alumni Corp, Mid-Am. Periodical Distbrs., Food Mktg. Inst., Nat. Assn. Convenience Stores. Club: Oak Brook Polo. Home: 555 W Madison #4608 Chicago IL 60606 Office: Mag and Paperback Mktg Inst 701 Lee St Suite 760 Des Plaines IL 60016 Address: 555 W Madison St #4608 Chicago IL 60606

CALDWELL, NANCY LOUISE, air force officer, nurse; b. Monroe, Wis., Dec. 16, 1939; d. Hans and Goldie Marie Johnson; m. Douglas Lorimer Caldwell, July 31, 1965. Diploma, Sparks Sch. Nursing, 1960; BSN, Tex. Christian U., 1976; MA, Okla. U., 1985; grad., Air Command and Staff Coll., 1978, Air War Coll., 1982. R.N. Commd. 1st lt. USAF, 1963, advanced through grades to col., 1983; operating room supr. RAF, Eng., 1976-77, infection control nurse, 1977-79; supr. outpatient clinic USAF Regional Hosp., Minot, N.D., 1979-81; chief nurse USAF Hosp., Misawa Air Base, Japan, 1981-83, USAF Regional Hosp., McDill AFB, Fla., 1983-85, USAF Med. Ctr., Scott AFB, Ill., 1985—; infection control cons. USAF Europe, 1978-79, Pacific Air Forces, 1981-83, TAC, 1983-85, MAC, 1985—; cons. USAF Surgeon Gen., 1987—. Mem. Air Force Assn. (pres. 1982), Assn. Operating Room Nurses, Assn. Practitionaers in Infection Control, Assn. Mil. Surgeons U.S., Am. Nurses Assn., Sigma Theta Tau. Lutheran. Office: USAF Med Ctr Scott Scott AFB IL 62221

CALDWELL, ROBERT BRENTON, dentist; b. Detroit, July 26, 1939; s. Robert Edmond and Marie Theresa (Ardito) C.; m. Carole J. Gross, May 7, 1966; children: Robert D., James P., Patricia T. BS, U. Detroit, 1961; DDS, U. Mich., 1969, postdoctoral sch. pub. health, 1983-84; postdoctoral, L.D. Pankey Dental Inst., Miami, Fla., 1974, 79, 80. Gen. practice dentistry Ann Arbor, Mich., 1969—. Counselor Boy Scouts Am., Ann Arbor, 1978—; chmn. dental sect. Washtenaw United Fund, Ann Arbor, 1977. Served with USN, 1961-65. Recipient Purcell-Hiebert award Ohio Dental Assn., 1972. Fellow Am. Coll. Dentists, Internat. Coll. Dentists (sect. editor 1982-85); mem. Mich. Dental Assn. (trustee 1982-85, chmn. legis. com. 1981), Washtenaw Dist. Dental Soc. (pres. 1977-78, editor newsletter 1972-75), Mich. Soc. Dentistry for Children (pres. 1976-77, editor newsletter 1973-78), Detroit Dental Clinic Club (pres. 1980-81, editor newsletter 1979-81), Univ. Mich. Sch. Dentistry Alumni Soc. (bd. dirs. 1980-86). Roman Catholic. Avocations: photography, nature study, woodworking, sailing, travel. Office: 606 W Stadium Blvd Ann Arbor MI 48103

CALDWELL, WILL M., former automobile company executive; b. Detroit, Dec. 9, 1925; s. Manly Lee and Marjorie Fern (Meadows) C.; m. Jeanne Boren, Sept. 16, 1950; children: Elizabeth (Mrs. Michael Charles Hatz), Sarah (Mrs. Warren Wilson Stickney), Martha (Mrs. David Michael Muñoz). AB, U. Mich., 1948, MBA, 1949. Credit analyst Chase Manhattan Bank, N.Y.C., 1949-50; mgr. budget analysis Ford Motor Co., Dearborn, Mich., 1952-62; controller Lincoln Mercury div. Ford Motor Co., 1962-66, corp. asst. controller, 1967-68; v.p. fin. Ford of Europe, 1968-72, controller internat. automotive ops., 1973-77, v.p. corp. strategy and analysis, 1977-79, exec. v.p., chief fin. officer, bd. dirs., 1979-85; bd. dirs. Air Products and Chems., Inc., 1st Nationwide Fin. Corp., Batts Internat., Ltd. Served to ensign USNR, 1943-46, lt. 1950-52, PTO, MTO. Trustee Harper Grace Hosps., 1980-86; chmn. fin. com., trustee Detroit Med. Ctr., 1986—; mem. vis. com. U. Mich. Grad. Sch. Bus., 1980-86. Mem. Beta Theta Pi. Baptist. Club: Detroit.

CALE, STEVEN JOSEPH, police officer; b. Hartford City, Ind., July 28, 1961; s. Joseph Norman and Beverly Sue (Armstrong) C.; m. Cindy Marie Hook, Apr. 25, 1981; children: Ryan Michael, Matthew Steven. Grad., Ind. Law Enforcement Acad., Plainfield, 1982. Police officer City of Bluffton, Ind., 1982—. Named Patrolman of Yr., Optimists, 1985. Mem. Fraternal Order of Police (sec., treas. 1984—). Democrat. Roman Catholic. Lodge: KC. Avocations: pistol shooting, tennis. Home: 327 W Central Ave Bluffton IN 46714

CALENDINE, RICHARD HARLEY, college administrator; b. Parkersburg, W.Va., Oct. 25, 1939; s. Harley William and Margaret Irene (Armstrong) C.; B.A., W.Va. Wesleyan Coll., 1962; M.A., Ohio State U., 1966; m. Georgeann Allard, Aug. 22, 1964; children—Caren Ferree, Michelle Louise. Terminal clk. Am. Bitumals and Asphalt Co., Marietta, Ohio, 1959-61; asst. dir. student financial aids Ohio State U., Columbus, 1964-67, counseling psychologist Counseling Center, 1967-74; financial aids officer Columbus Tech. Inst., 1974-76, asst. admissions officer, 1976—. Individual practice psychology, Columbus, 1973—. Bd. dirs. Columbus Campaign for Arms Control; mem. Welcome Soc. Pa. Mem. Am., Ohio Psychol. Assns., Nat., Ohio Assns. Student Fin. Aid Adminstrs., First Families of Ohio, Order Crown of Charlemagne in U.S.A., Ohio Geneal. Soc. (v.p. chpt. 1979), Baronial Order of Magna Charta, Nat. Soc. Ams. Royal Descent, Phi Delta Kappa, Omicron Delta Kappa, Psi Chi, Theta Xi, Alpha Phi Omega (chair sect. 58, 1968-70). Presbyterian (chmn. bd. deacons 1973, elder 1980-83). Lodge: Masons (local pres.). Author: College Majors as a Guide to Career Planning, 1972. Home: 111 Webster Park Columbus OH 43214

CALENOFF, LEONID, radiologist; b. Vienna, Austria, Aug. 24, 1923; came to U.S., 1957, naturalized, 1962; s. Albert and Anna (Prover) C.; m. Miriam Arnon, Oct. 30, 1955; children—Jean Zucker, Deborah Lipoff. M.D., U. Paris, 1955. Diplomate: Am. Bd. Radiology. Intern Jewish Hosp., Cin., 1958; resident in radiology U. Ill. Med. Center, Chgo., 1959-61; asst. radiologist Ill. Research and Ednl. Hosp., Chgo., 1961-64; chief radiology Chgo. State Hosp., 1963-68; dir. radiology Sheridan Gen. Hosp., Chgo., 1964-68; attending radiologist West Side VA Hosp., Chgo., 1963-68; attending radiologist Rehab. Inst. Chgo., 1964—, chief diagnostic radiology, 1974-86; attending radiologist Northwestern Meml. Hosp., Chgo., 1968—; chief outpatient diagnostic radiology Northwestern Meml. Hosp., 1979—; chief diagnostic radiology Passavant Pavillion of Northwestern Meml. Hosp., 1972-79; asst. prof. radiology Northwestern U. Med. Sch., 1970-73, asso. prof., 1973-78, prof., 1978—. Author articles in field, chpts. in books.; Editor: Radiology of Spinal Cord Injury, 1981. Fellow Am. Coll. Radiology, Am. Coll. Chest Physicians; mem. Radiol. Soc. N.Am., Am. Roentgen Ray Soc., AMA, Soc. Univ. Radiologists, Soc. Nuclear Medicine, Am. Congress Rehab. Medicine. Home: 1515 Astor St Chicago IL 60610 Office: 250 E Superior St Chicago IL 60611

CALEY, BRUCE B., insurance company executive; b. Menominee, Mich., Sept. 10, 1944; s. William Henes and Florence (Hooker) C.; m. Joan Carley, Nov. 11, 1967; children: Heather, Brea, Catheryn. BA, Mac Murray Coll., 1967; MFA, Temple U., 1972. Instr. Phila. Coll. of Art, 1972-76; pres. Cert. Fin. Planner Assocs., Ltd., Pottstown, Pa., 1976-78, Superior State Life Agy., Inc., Menominee, Mich., 1978—. Pres. united Way, Menominee, 1982; vice chmn. Downtown Devel. Authority, Menominee, 1982—; pres. Hist. Waterfront, Inc., Menominee, 1986—. Served with U.S. Army, 1968-69, Vietnam. Avocations: sailing, skiing, swimming, fishing, camping. Home: 4201 3d St Menominee MI 49858 Office: Superior State Life Agy Inc 1101 11th Ave Menominee MI 49858

CALHOUN, JOHN CHARLES, civil and structural engineer; b. Omaha, May 9, 1941; s. John Harlan and Opal Mae (Leonard) C.; m. Mary Camille Case, Aug. 5, 1962; children—Michael John, Ann Christine. B.S. in C.E., U. Iowa, 1964; M.S., U. Iowa, 1966. Registered profl. engr., Iowa, Mich., Minn., Nebr., Colo. Engr.-in-tng. Powers & Assocs., Iowa City, 1964-66; cons. engr. Powers-Willis & Assocs., Iowa City, 1968-73; county engr. Madison County (Iowa), Winterset, 1973-77; v.p. Terry A. Shuck Structural Engrs., Inc., Des Moines, 1977-82; pres. Calhoun-Burns and Assocs., Inc., West Des Moines, 1982—. Mem. Iowa Hwy. Research Bd., 1974-76; dir. Iowa Good Rds. Assn., 1982—, v.p., 1986—. Active United Way of Greater Des Moines; participant Joint Civilian Orientation Conf. 47, 1982; mem. adv. bd. U. Iowa Coll. Engring. Served to 1st lt., C.E., U.S. Army, 1966-68. Decorated Bronze Star; Nile Kinnick Meml. scholar U. Iowa, 1959. Mem. ASCE (Iowa pres. 1982-83), Am. Cons. Engrs. Council, Cons. Engrs. Council Iowa, Nat. Soc. Profl. Engrs., Iowa Engring. Soc. (pres. 1985-86), Am. Ry. Engring. Assn., Am. Pub. Works Assn., Am. Concrete Inst., Am. Inst. Steel Constrn., Def. Orientation Conf. Assn. (dir.) Republican. Mem. United Ch. of Christ. Lodge: Masons. Office: 1000 73d St Suite 19 Des Moines IA 50311

CALHOUN, JOHN P., manufacturing company executive; b. 1926; married. B.C.E., Clemson U., 1948; advanced mgmt. program, Harvard U., 1980-81. Sales engr. B.L. Montague Co., 1955-56; sales rep. Kieckhefer Container Corp., 1956-57; with Rexnord Co., Milw., 1957—, mgr. sales, 1957-68, div. mgr. mktg., 1968-70, pres. gear div., 1970-74; v.p. sales mktg. ECG-Rexnord Inc., Milw., 1974-79; pres. rotary components group Rexnord Inc., Milw., 1979-81, pres. mech. power div., 1981-82, v.p. sector exec., 1982-85, pres., chief operating officer, 1985—, dir. Served with U.S. Army, 1944-46. Office: Rexnord Inc 350 N Sunny Slope Rd Milwaukee WI 53005

CALHOUN, ROGER L., financial planner; b. Freeport, Ill., June 28, 1945; s. Elwyn E. and Evelyn E. (Glenn) C.; m. Paula R. Willison, June 28, 1969; children: Brian M., Dawn E. AS, Highland Community Coll., Freeport,

1966; BS, U. Ill., 1971, MBA, 1982. Supr. Leichner Industries, Champaign, Ill., 1971-74; v.p., cashier Comml. Bank, Champaign, 1974-82; v.p. agrl. lending 1st Nat. Bank, Robinson, Ill., 1982-84; financial planner IDS Am. Express, Champaign, 1984—. Leader Boy Scouts Am., Robinson, 1983, Champaign, 1985; coach Holy Cross Sch., Champaign, 1985-86. Mem. U. Ill. Alumni Assn., Champaign C. of C. Club: Am. Bus. (Champaign). Avocation: woodworking. Home: 2114 Galen Dr Champaign IL 61821 Office: IDS Am Express 108 Hessel Blvd Champaign IL 61820

CALHOUN, SALLY HANSON, clinical psychologist, educator; b. Wauwatosa, Wis., July 7, 1939; d. Lee Delbert and Olive Elizabeth (Congdon) Hanson; B.A. with distinction in English, U. Mich., 1961, M.A. in English, 1963; M.A. (USPHS fellow), Northwestern U., 1967, Ph.D. in Clin. Psychology, 1970; m. David Redfearn Calhoun, Sept. 5, 1964; children—Douglas David, Julie Katherine. Clin. clk. Hines VA Hosp., 1964; psychologist Ill. State Psychiat. Inst., 1965-69; cons. Nelson Hall Pub. Co., 1972-78, also lectr. Northeastern Ill. U., 1972-77; with Assoc. Psychotherapists of Chgo., 1973-74; pvt. practice clin. psychology, Glenview, Ill., 1978—; assoc. prof., core faculty Forest Inst. Profl. Psychology, 1979-85, assoc. prof. 1985—; editorial review bd. Journal of Training and Practice in Profl. Psychology. Recipient awards for fiction Scholastic Mag., 1954, 56, Avery Hopwood writing award U. Mich., 1958. Mem. Am. Psychol. Assn., Ill. Psychol. Assn., Nat. Council Health Service Providers Psychology, Nat. Soc. Arts and Letters, Mortar Bd., Nat. Soc. DAR, Pi Beta Phi, Psi Chi. Office: 1717 Glenview Rd Suite 200 Glenview IL 60025

CALHOUN, WILLIAM LEE, logistics support analysis manager; b. Chgo., Jan. 3, 1954; s. James Joseph Calhoun and Martha Josephine (Rozowski) Johnson; m. Patricia Lynn Mayall, June 2, 1979; children: Amy Bridget, William John, Kathleen Marie. BS in Electronic Systems, So. Ill. U., 1978; MBA, U. S.D., 1983. Draftsman Commonwealth Edison Co., Maywood, Ill., 1975-76; project. supr. Avon Products, Morton Grove, Ill., 1984-86; mgr. logistics support analysis ITW Linac, Chgo., 1986—. Served to capt. USAF, 1978-84. Mem. Soc. Logistics Engrs., Assn. Old Crows, Air Force Assn., Res. Officer's Assn. Roman Catholic. Avocations: personal computers, sports. Home: 5461 N Mason Chicago IL 60630 Office: ITW Linac 6620 W Dakin Chicago IL 60634

CALLAHAN, MICHAEL THOMAS, construction consultant, lawyer; b. Kansas City, Mo., Oct. 7, 1948; s. Harry Leslie and Venita June (Yohn) C.; B.A., U. Kans., 1970; J.D., U. Mo., 1973, LL.M., 1979; postgrad. Temple U., 1976-77; m. Stella Sue Paffenbach, Mar. 21, 1970; children—Molly Leigh, Michael Kroh. Admitted to Kans. bar, 1973, N.J. bar, 1975, Mo. bar, 1977; v.p. T.J. Constrn., Inc., Lenexa, Kans., 1973-74; sr. cons. Wagner-Hohns-Inglis, Inc., Mt. Holly, N.J., 1974-77, v.p., Kansas City, Mo., 1977-86; exec. v.p. CCL Constrn. Cons., Overland Park, Kans., 1986—; adj. prof. U. Kans.; arbitrator, lectr. in field; mem. Bldg. Industry Adv. Bd. Mem. Am. Bar Assn., N.J. Bar Assn., Mo. Bar Assn., Am. Arbitration Assn., Internat. Wine and Food Soc. Congregationalist. Clubs: Saddle & Sirloin , Indian Hills Country. Lodge: Rotary Internat. Author: Desk Book of Construction Law, 1981; Discovery in Construction Litigation, 1983; Construction Schedules, 1983, Construction Law, 1986, Delay Claims, 1987; contbr. articles to profl. jours. Home: 9011 Delmar St Prairie Village KS 66207 Office: CCL Constrn Cons 4400 College Blvd Suite 150 Overland Park KS 66211

CALLAN, JOHN PATRICK, psychiatrist; b. Dublin, Ireland, Feb. 13, 1939; s. Patrick J. and Bridget M. (Meade) C.; m. Clair M. Mills, Apr. 4, 1964; children: Eoin, Grainne, Colm, Maeve. MD, Nat. U. Ireland, 1963. Med. dir. Blue Hills Hosp., Hartford, Conn., 1979-84, Family Service for McHenry (Ill.) County, 1986—. Author: Your Guide to Mental Health, 1983; editor: The Physician, 1983. Served to col. USAFR, 1982—. Fellow Am. Psychiat. Assn., Am. Med. Writers Assn. Office: Family Service McHenry County 5320 W Elm St McHenry IL 60050

CALLANAN, KATHLEEN JOAN, electrical engineer, airplane company executive; b. Detroit, Feb. 10, 1940; d. John Michael and Grace Marie (Kleehammer) C. B.S.E. in Physics, U. Mich., 1963; postgrad. in physics Northeastern U., 1963-65; M.S.E.E., U. Hawaii, 1971; diploma in Japanese lang. St. Joseph Inst. Japanese Studies, Tokyo, 1973; cert. in mgmt. Boeing Mil. Airplane Co. Employee Devel., 1985. Vis. scholar Sophia U., Tokyo, 1976-79; elec.-electronic components engr. Boeing Mil. Airplane Co., Wichita, Kans., 1979-83, instrumentation design engr., 1983-85, strategic planner for tech., 1985-86, research and engring. tech. supr., 1986-87 ; electromagnetic effects Avionics mgr., 1987—. Contbr. articles to profl. jours. Mem. Rose Hill Planning Commn., Kans., 1982-85; coordinator Boeing Employees Amateur Radio Soc., Wichita, 1982-83. Mem. Soc. Women Engrs. (sr. mem., sect. rep. 1981-83, sec. treas. 1985-86, regional bd. dirs. 1983-85, sect. pres. 1987—), AIAA, Bus. and Profl. Women, Quarter Century Wireless Assn. (communications com. 1985-86). Lodge: Toastmasters (local pres. 1985-86, competent toastmaster 1985). Avocations: amateur radio; singing; bowling. Home: 1201 N West St Rose Hill KS 67133 Office: Boeing Mil Airplane Co 3810 S Oliver Wichita KS 67210

CALLANDER, KAY EILEEN PAISLEY, teacher; b. Coshocton, Ohio, Oct. 15, 1938; d. Dalton Olas and Dorothy Pauline (Davis) Paisley; m. Don Larry Callander, Nov. 18, 1977. BSE, Muskingum Coll., 1960; MA in Speech Edn., Ohio State U., 1964, postgrad., 1964-84. Cert. elem. tchr., Ohio. Tchr. Columbus (Ohio) Pub. Schs., 1960-70, 80-87, drama specialist, 1970-80, classroom, gifted/talented tchr., 1986—. V.p., bd. dirs. Neoteric Dance and Theater Co., Columbus, 1985-87; tchr. advisor Columbus Council PTA's, 1983-86, ch-chmn. reflections com., 1984-87. Named Educator of Yr., Shady Lane PT, 1982; Sch. Excellence grantee Columbus Pub. Schs. Mem. NEA, Ohio Edn. Assn., Ohio PTA, Columbus Edn. Assn., Capital Area Humane Soc., Liturgical Art Guild Ohio. Republican. Lutheran. Avocations: painting, photography, swimming, golfing, playing piano and organ. Home: 570 Conestoga Dr Columbus OH 43213 Office: Columbus Pub Schs Shady Lane Elem Sch 1488 Shady Ln Rd Columbus OH 43227

CALLAWAY, RICHARD EARL, dentist; b. Des Moines, Aug. 9, 1951; s. Grover Earl and Geraldine Anna (Dageforde) C.; m. Nancy Jean Clark, May 2, 1981; children: Scott, Jessica, Lindsey, Rachel. BA, Mo. Western State Coll., 1974; DDS, U. Mo., Kansas City, 1978. Gen. practice dentistry Fremont, Nebr., 1978—. Bd. dirs. Fremont Big Bros./Big Sisters, 1981-87. Named one of Outstanding Young Men of Am., Fremont Jaycees, 1985. Mem. ADA, Nebr. Dental Assn., Omaha Dist. Dental Assn., Tri Valley Dental Soc. (treas. 1980, v.p. 1981), Fremont Jaycees (bd. dirs. 1979-85, v.p. 1985-86, pres. 1986-87), Fremont Tennis Assn. Republican. Lutheran. Lodge: Optimists. Avocations: hunting, boating, skiing, volleyball, tennis. Home: 545 N Platte Fremont NE 68025 Office: 1835 E Military Fremont NE 68025

CALLEN, CRAIG CHARLES, dentist; b. Mansfield, Ohio, June 27, 1956; s. William Charles and Maurine Elizabeth (Beal) C.; m. Linda Marie Mattern, Aug. 14, 1982. BS, Case Western Res. U., 1976, DDS, 1980. Pvt. practice dentistry Mansfield, 1980—; organizer Dental Study Club, Mansfield, 1984—. Div. leader United Way, Mansfield, 1986, YMCA Bldg. Fund, Mansfield, 1986; vol. Save a Child, Mansfield, 1985-86, United Way Clinic, 1980—. Mem. ADA, Ohio Dental Assn. (del. 1985), Cen. Ohio Dental Assn., Mansfield Dental Soc. (chmn. wellness com. 1985), Mansfield C. of C., Jaycees (chmn. parade com. 1980-82, Jaycee of Month 1982). Presbyterian. Club: Liederkrantz (Mansfield), Mansfield Univ. Lodge: Kiwanis (chmn. bd. dirs. 1982—, Kiwanian of Month 1986). Avocations: biking, running, weight lifting, boating, skiing. Home: 76 Sunnyslope Dr Mansfield OH 44907 Office: Family Dental Care 234 Park Ave W Mansfield OH 44907

CALLIF, DAVID MARK, marketing executive; b. Columbus, Ohio, Feb. 9, 1950; s. Neal and Sylvia (Solomon) C.; m. Lynn Scher Bornstein, Sept. 1, 1974; children: Dustin Warren, Robert Charles. BS, Ohio State U., 1972. Sales rep. Procter and Gamble, Cin., 1972-74; unit sales mgr. Procter and Gamble, Cleve., 1974-78; dist. sales mgr. Procter and Gamble, Balt., 1978-81; nat. accounts and sales mgr. Procter and Gamble, Cin., 1981-83; v.p. mktg. and sales Baylis Bros., Cin., 1983-86, Alubec Industries, Inc. (formerly Aluminum Packaging), Cin., 1986—. Exec. com. Jewish Welfare Fund Leadership Council. Cin., 1984-86; mgr. Montgomery/Sycamore Baseball Assn., Cin., 1982-86, commr., 1986; bd. dirs. Jewish Family Service, Cin., 1984—. Democrat. Clubs: North Israel Men's, Adath Israel Men's. Avocations: reading, tennis, basketball, baseball. Home: 13056 Coopermeadow Ln Cincinnati OH 45242 Office: Alubec Industries Inc 635 Main St Cincinnati OH 45202

CALLIGHAN, PHILLIP EDWARD, marketing professional; b. Sterling, Ill., Dec. 10, 1951; s. Charles Edward and Gertine Magdalene (Schlough) C.; m. Janet Kathryn Nelson, Sept. 6, 1975. BA, North Cen. Coll., 1974. Writer, producer Arthur Meriwether Inc., Downers Grove, Ill., 1974-79; v.p. Arthur Meriwether, Inc., Downers Grove, Ill., 1979-84, pres., 1984-85; pres. Ctr. for Communications, Inc., Lombard, Ill., 1985—; Mem. adv. com. on comml. art and advt., Coll. of DuPage, Glen Ellyn, Ill., 1982—. Republican. Methodist. Club: Valley Ad (Aurora, Ill.) (pres. 1983). Avocations: collecting records (78's), audiophile, tennis. Office: Ctr for Communications Inc 954 Springer Dr Lombard IL 60148-6412

CALLIHAN, HARRIET K., medical society executive; b. Chgo., Feb. 8, 1930; d. Harry Louis and Josephine (Olstad) Kohlman; m. Clair Clifton Callihan, Dec. 17, 1955; 1 child, Barbara Claire Callihan. BA, U. Chgo., 1951, MBA, 1953. Personnel dir. Leo Burnett Co., Chgo., 1953-57, John Plain & Co., 1957-62, Follett Pub. Co., 1962-64, Needham, Harper & Steers, N.Y.C., 1966-68, Bell, Boyd, Lloyd, Haddad & Burns, 1964-66; Hume, Clement, Hume & Lee, 1968-70, owner, operator PersD, 1970-75; exec. dir. Inst. Medicine Chgo., 1975—, mng. editor ofcl. med. publ. Proceedings, 1975—. Sec./treas. Interagy. Council on Smoking and Disease. Mem. Chgo. Soc. Assn. Execs., Conf. Med. Soc. Execs. Greater Chgo. (pres.), Am. Med. Writers Assn. (pres.), Nat. Sci. Writer's Assn., Lincoln Park Zool. Soc., Field Mus. Soc. Natural History, Nat. Soc. Fund Raising Exec. Profl. Conv. Mgrs. Assn., Chgo. Council Fgn. Relations, Chgo. Connection, Met. Chgo. Coalition Aging, Midwest Pharm. Advt. Club. Clubs: Westmoreland Country, Michigan Shores; Cliffdwellers. Office: Inst of Medicine of Chicago 332 S Michigan Ave Chicago IL 60604

CALLIHAN, PATRICK J., medical care facilities executive. Chmn., pres. Provincial House Inc., Lansing, Mich. Office: Provincial House Inc 4000 N Grand River Ave Lansing MI 48906 *

CALLIS, BRUCE, insurance company executive; b. Sedalia, Mo., Dec. 4, 1939; s. George Elgin and Jo (Trigg) C.; m. Nancy Williams, Nov. 14, 1959; children: Cheryl, Kevin, Kimberly. B.S., U. Mo., 1961. Plant mgr. Boonslick Mfg. Co., Boonville, Mo., 1961-62; field claim rep. State Farm Mut. Automobile Ins. Co., Rolla, Mo., 1963; asst. personnel mgr. State Farm Mut. Automobile Ins. Co., Columbia, Mo., 1964-66; various personnel, sales positions State Farm Mut. Automobile Ins. Co., Bloomington, Ill., 1966-76, v.p., personnel, 1976-83, v.p. Office of Pres., 1983—; dir. State Farm Life & Annuity, State Farm Internat. Services. Mem. McLean County (Ill.) Bd., 1968-74; chmn. McLean County Republican Com., Bloomington, 1978—; bd. dirs. Brokaw Hosp., Normal, Ill., 1979-82. Recipient appreciation award Am. Compensation Soc., 1969. Mem. Am. Soc. for Personnel Adminstrn. (chmn. adv . com. 1976-83), Ins. Inst. for Hwy. Safety (personnel com. chmn. 1977-83), McLean County Assn. Commerce, Westminster Coll. Alumni Assn. (award 1986). Presbyterian. Home: 4 Tami Ct Bloomington IL 61701 Office: State Farm Mutual Automobile Ins Co 1 State Farm Plaza Bloomington IL 61071

CALLIS, KENNETH RIVERS, clergyman; b. Louisville, Aug. 26, 1925; s. George Washington and Fannie Lou (Hutcherson) G.; student Berea Coll., 1943-44; B.S. in Mech. Engring., U. Mich., 1947, postgrad. (Margaret Kraus Ramsdell fellow), 1947-48; M.Div., Asbury Theol. Sem., 1950; D.D. (hon.), Albion Coll., 1975; m. Annie Ruth Smith, Sept. 1, 1949; children—Kenneth Rivers, Annette, Cheryl Lynn. Ordained to ministry United Methodist Ch., 1949; minister, Mich., 1950—, sr. minister Ypsilanti 1st Meth. Ch., 1965-72, Court St. Meth. Ch., Flint, 1972-77, Utica United Meth. Ch., Sterling Heights, 1977—; trustee Asbury Theol. Sem., 1979—; pres. bd. trustees United Meth. Retirement Homes, Detroit conf., 1979—; dean Mich. Pastors Sch., 1972-75; mem. World Meth. Council, 1971-76; del. Gen. Conf., 1976. Mem. Sterling Heights Housing Commn., 1978-87; exec. bd., council advancement chmn. Clinton Valley council Boy Scouts Am., 1978-80, exec. bd. Tall Pine council, 1974-77; mem. Ypsilanti Housing Commn., 1969-72; bd. dirs. Nat. Ch. REsidences, 1987—. Served to ensign USN, 1943-46. Mem. Utica Ministerial Assn. Contbr. articles to religious mag. Home: 8506 Clinton River Rd Sterling Heights MI 48078 Office: Utica United Meth Ch 8650 Canal Rd Sterling Heights MI 48078

CALLOW, WILLIAM GRANT, state supreme court justice; b. Waukesha, Wis., Apr. 9, 1921; s. Curtis Grant and Mildred G. C.; m. Jean A. Zilavy, Apr. 15, 1950; children: William G., Christine S., Katherine H. Ph.B. in Econs, U. Wis., 1943, J.D., 1948. Bar: Wis. Asst. city atty. Waukesha, 1948-52; city atty. 1952-60; county judge Waukesha, 1961-77; justice Supreme Ct. Wis., Madison, 1978—; mem. faculty Wis. Jud. Coll., 1968-75; asst. prof. U. Minn., 1951-52; Wis. commr. Nat. Conf. Commrs. on Uniform State Laws, 1967—. Served with USMC, 1943-45; Served with USAF, 1948-52. Recipient Outstanding Alumnus award U. Wis., 1973. Fellow Am. Bar Found.; mem. Am. Bar Assn., Dane County Bar Assn. Episcopalian. Office: Supreme Ct of Wis 231 E State Capitol Box 1688 Madison WI 53701 *

CALMESE, LINDA, computer training center executive, consultant; b. East St. Louis, Ill., June 3, 1947; d. Lonnie Daniel and Louise (Anderson) C. BS, So. Ill. U., 1969, MS, 1972, specialist in counselor edn., 1978. Tchr. bus. edn. St. Teresa Acad., East St. Louis, 1969-73, DODDS, Madrid, Spain, 1973-84; computer cons. Scott AFB, Ill., 1984-87, Norton AFB, Calif., 1986; pres. Bits and Bytes Computer Tng. Ctr., Belleville, Ill., 1985—; instr. State Community Coll., East St. Louis, 1986-87; computer cons. Army Aviation Systems Command, St. Louis, 1986-87, Ohio Army N.G., Worthington, Ohio, 1986, Mil. Personnel Records Ctr., St. Louis, 1986. Mem. Nat. Assn. Female Execs., Delta Pi Epsilon, Pi Omega Pi. Democrat. Baptist. Avocations: traveling, computing, reading, aerobics. Office: Bits and Bytes Computer Tng Ctr 56 S 65th St Suite 1 Belleville IL 62223

CALOMENI, DALE ANTHONY, lawyer; b. Detroit, Mar. 31, 1952; s. Anthony David and Annette (Bayliff) C.; B.A. cum laude, Seattle U., 1974; J.D., Thomas M. Cooley Sch. Law 1979. Bar: Mich. 1980, U.S. Dist. Ct. (we. dist.) Mich. 1981. With City Atty.'s Office, Jackson, Mich., 1978-79; asst. pros. atty. Kent County Prosecutor's Office, Grand Rapids, Mich., 1979-81; pvt. practice Grand Rapids, 1981—; legal counsel Grand Rapids Jaycees, 1985-86. Mem. Grand Rapids Bar Assn., Mich. Bar Assn., Assn. Trial Lawyers Am. Republican. Office: 72 Ransom St NE Grand Rapids MI 49503

CALVER, DAVID ROBERT, obstetrician; b. Pontiac, Mich., Oct. 12, 1941; s. Robert Bruce and Mary Jane (Guinan) C.; m. Kathleen Mary Donovan, June 17, 1967; children: Michelle, William. BA, Albion Coll., 1963; MD, U. Mich., 1967. Diplomate Am. Bd. Obstetrics and Gynecology. Dir. obstetrics/gynecology, Ultrasound Pontiac Gen. Hosp., 1977—, chmn. obstetrics/gynecology, 1986—; med. dir. diagnostic Ultrasound Marygrove Coll., Detroit; clin. asst. prof. Wayne State U., Detroit, 1987—. Active Pontiac Gen. Hosp. Generals, 1984. Served as maj. USAF, 1971-73. Fellow Am. Coll. Obstetricians and Gynecologists; mem. AMA, Mich. State Med. Soc., Oakland County Med. Soc. (sec. 1985-86, bd. dirs. 1982-86), Am. Fertility Soc. Episcopalian. Avocations: sailing, horticulture, carpentry. Office: Ob/Gyn Assocs Pontiac 2520 S Telegraph Rd Suite 200 Pontiac MI 48013

CALVERT, ANNIVORY, municipal government administrator; b. St. Louis, July 23, 1954; d. John Warrick Calvert II and Wyvette Kie (Brown Calvert) Porter; 1 child, Joel Loving. BA in Psychology, Pub. Adminstrn., Oakland U., 1977, MA, 1978; postgrad., Wayne State U., 1979—. Mgr. profl. services City of Detroit, 1978-79; sr. govtl. analyst City of Detroit dept. Pub. Works, 1979-81, prin. govtl. analyst, 1981-82, asst. supr., 1982, exec. adminstr., 1982-85, asst. dir., 1985—; instr. Oakland U., Rochester, Mich., 1977, adj. prof., 1978-80. Contbr. articles to profl. jours. Exec. bd. 13th Congl. Dem. Dist., Detroit, 1985-86, vice chair Dem. Endorsement Com., Detroit, 1985-86; co-chairperson Equal Opportunity Task Force for Am. Pub. Works Assn., 1986—. Recipient Matilda R. Wilson award Oakland U., 1977, Freedom award Afro-Am. Mus., 1978, Mayor's award of Merit, City Council's award of Recognition. Mem. Am. Pub. Works Assn. (exec. council mem. 1979—, co-chairperson equal opportunity task force 1986—), Internat. City Mgrs. Assn., Inst. Equipment Services (exec. council mem. 1985—), Nat. Assn. Female Execs., Am. Mgmt. Assn., Assn. Mcpl. Profl. Women (chair 1981—, Appreciation award 1983), Detroit C. of C. (exec. bd. PRIDE 1986-87), NAACP (life). Roman Catholic. Avocations: swimming, painting, calligraphy, automobile collector and refurbisher. Office: City of Detroit Dept Pub Works 8221 W Davison Ave Detroit MI 48238

CALVERT, COLLIN MICHAEL, government agency administrator; b. Geneva, N.Y., Jan. 14, 1952; s. George G. and Diane Carole (Seefeldt) C.; m. Patricia Lynn Miller, Aug. 25, 1975 (div. Dec. 1978); m. Linda Sue Rutherford, Aug. 28, 1982. Student, S.D. Sch. Mines, 1970-71; BS in Econs., S.D. State U., 1974; postgrad., U. S.D., 1974-75. Asst. dir. Greater Sioux Falls (S.D.) Safety Council, 1975-76; budget analyst City of Lincoln, Neb., 1977-81, budget officer, 1981-83; dir. legis. fiscal State Of Neb., Lincoln, 1983—. Democrat. Avocations: golf, fishing. Home: 4218 Garfield Lincoln NE 68506 Office: Legis Fiscal Office State Capitol Room 1007 Lincoln NE 68509

CALVERT, NANCY ANN, public relations executive; b. Michigan City, Ind., Oct. 26, 1939; d. E. Preston and Eloise (Worthington) C. B.A. in Communication Arts, Lindenwood Coll., 1961; postgrad. U. Ariz., summers 1962-64. Dir. pub. relations, tchr. journalism, pub. schs., Michigan City, 1962-65; asst. dir. radio and TV, Batz Hodgson Neuwoehner Advt. and Pub. Relations, St. Louis, 1965-68; dir. pub. relations, pub. sch. dist., St. Charles, 1968-76; staff asst. pub. relations, Electro-Motive div. Gen. Motors Corp., LaGrange, Ill., 1976-79, asst. dir. pub. relations, 1979, dir. pub. relations and advt., 1979—, mem. Gen. Motors Chgo. pub. affairs com., 1979—, mem. steering com. Gen. Motors civic involvement program, 1982—. Trustee Chgo. 4-H Found. Mem. Am. R.R. Found. (chmn. advt. subcom.), Ry. Progress Inst. (pub. relations com.), Assn. Am. R.R.s (pub. relations adv. com.), R.R. Pub. Relations Assn. (v.p. 1982-83, program chmn. 1984, sr. v.p. 1985, pres. 1985-86), Assn. R.R. Advt. Mgrs., Women's Advt. Club Chgo., Pub. Relations Soc. Am., Pub. Relations Clinic, Alpha Epsilon Rho. Episcopalian. Clubs: Chgo. Press; Pottawattomie Country (Michigan City). Office: Gen Motors Electro-Motive Div LaGrange IL 60525

CALVIN, JON DAVID, automotive distribution executive; b. Akron, Ohio, Apr. 3, 1951; s. David Putnam and Charlene (Henderschott) C.; m. Joan Linda White; children: Jennifer, Jason, Jessica. Student, Marshall U., 1970-71; BBA, Kent State U., 1977. Squadron supr. Goodyear Tire and Rubber Co., Akron, 1975-77, tire prodn. planner, 1977-83, asst. mgr., 1983-85, mgr. distbn. automation, 1985—. Founder, pres. Youth Basketball Assn., Tallmadge, Ohio, 1983—; v.p. Tallmadge Little League, 1978—. Mem. Tallmadge Jaycees. Republican. Avocations: boating, golf, hunting, fishing. Home: 348 Tammery Dr Tallmadge OH 44278

CALVIN, ROBERT JOSEPH, management consultant; b. Chgo., Dec. 28, 1936; s. Joseph K. and Pauline (Harris) C.; m. Jane L. Levy, Apr. 27, 1940; children—Susan D., Amy E. B.A., Conn. Wesleyan U., 1956; M.B.A., Columbia U., 1957. Salesman, acct., prodn. mgr. Cryovac div. W.R. Grace Co., Boston, 1958-60; asst. to pres. Lab. for Electronics, Boston, 1960-62; gen. mgr. Mid Continent Leasing, Chgo., 1963-65; pres. Hayward Marum Inc., Lawrence, Mass., 1970-80, Mgmt. Dimensions Inc., Chgo., 1962—, Hartmarx Furnishings Group, 1986—. Lectr. Grad. Sch. Bus., U. Chgo., 1968—. Pres. bd. dirs. Jane Addams Ctr., Chgo.; bd. dirs. Hull House Assocs., Author: Profitable Sales Management and Marketing for Growing Businesses, 1983.

CALVIN, STAFFORD RICHARD, retail mail order house executive; b. St. Paul Apr. 6, 1931; s. Carl and Zelda Ida (Engelson) C.; m. Phyllis Lotwin, Sept. 15, 1958 (div 1970); m. Nancy Pistner, Sept. 21, 1974 (div.); children—Lawrence, Carlton, Loran. B.A.., U. Minn. 1952. Pres. Sibley Co., St. Paul, 1953-58, Dealers Distbrs., St. Paul, 1958-65; v.p. Internat. Systems Assn., N.Y.C., 1965-70, Carlson Cos., Mpls., 1970-74; chmn. bd. Calhoun's Collectors Soc., Inc., Mpls., 1974—. Vice pres. Jewish Family Services, St. Paul, 1982; bd. dirs. Little Bros. of Elderly, Chgo., 1984. Democrat. Office: Calhouns Collectors Soc Inc 7401 Cahill Rd Minneapolis MN 55435

CAMACCI, MICHAEL A., commercial real estate broker, development consultant; b. Youngstown, Ohio, Feb. 6, 1951; s. Martin B. and Viola F. (Conti) C.; m. Susan Hawkins, Oct. 18, 1985; 1 child, Michael Philip. BBA, Youngstown Coll., 1974. Cert. bus. analyst. Acct. U.S. Steel Corp., Youngstown, 1969-80; mgr. sales Soc. Realty, Boardman, Ohio, 1980-81; dir. sales Pop-ins Maid Services, Columbiana, Ohio, 1981-82; bus. broker Eranco Assocs., Girard, Ohio, 1982-86; pres. JMC Realty, Inc., Youngstown, 1986—; broker CAmacci Real Estate, 1986—. Served with U.S. Army, 1971-77. Democrat. Roman Catholic. Club: YMCA. Office: Camacci Real Estate PO Box 3077 Youngstown OH 44511

CAMERON, CRAIG ROBERT, dentist; b. Saginaw, Mich., May 22, 1956; s. Robert John and Maxine (Oligney) C.; m. Laura Jean Reid, May 5, 1984. AS, Delta Coll., 1976; BS in Zoology, Mich. State U., 1978; DDS, U. Detroit, 1983. Gen. practice dentistry Ravenna, Mich., 1983—. Mem. ADA, Mich. Dental Assn., Muskegon Dental Assn., Ravenna C. of C. Republican. Lodge: Lions (bd. dirs. Ravenna 1985—). Avocations: sailing, skiing, reading, fishing, woodworking. Home: 12374 Stafford St Ravenna MI 49451 Office: PO Box 204 Ravenna MI 49451

CAMERON, ROY EUGENE, scientist; b. Denver, July 16, 1929; s. Guy Francis and Ilda Annora (Horn) C.; m. Margot Elizabeth Hoagland, May 5, 1956 (div. July 1977); children: Susan Lynn, Catherine Ann; m 2d Carolyn Mary Light, Sept. 22, 1978. B.S., Wash. State U., 1953, 54; M.S., U. Ariz., 1958, Ph.D., 1961; D.D. (hon.), Ministry of Christ Ch., Delavan, Wis., 1975. Research scientist Hughes Aircraft Corp., Tucson, 1955-56; sr. scientist Jet Propulsion Lab., Pasadena, Calif., 1961-68, mem. tech. staff, 1969-74; dir. research Darwin Research Inst., Dana Point, Calif., 1974-75; dep. dir. Land Reclamation Lab. Argonne Ill. Nat. Lab., 1975-77, dir. energy resources tng. and devel., 1977-85; staff scientist Lockheed Engring. & Mgmt. Services Co., Las Vegas, Nev., 1986—; cons. Lunar Recieving Lab. Baylor U., 1966-68, Ecology Ctr. Utah State U., Desert Biome, 1970-72, U. Alaska Tundra Biome, 1973-74, U. Maine, 1973-76, numerous others; mem. Nat. Agriculture Research and Extension Users Adv. Bd., 1986—. Contrb. articles to sci. books; participated in 7 Antarctic expdns. Served with U.S. Army, 1950-52, Korea, Japan. Recipient 3 NASA awards for tech. briefs; Paul Steere Burgess fellow U. Ariz., 1959; grantee NSF, 1970-74; Dept. Interior, 1978-80. Mem. AAAS, Soil Sci. Soc. Am., Am. Chem. Soc., Am. Soc. Microbiology, Am. Soc. Agronomy, Antarctican Soc., Polar Soc. Am., Am. Scientist Affiliation, World Future Soc., Internat. Soc. Soil Sci., Council Agrl. Sci. and Tech., Am. Inst. Biol. Sci., Sigma Xi. Mem. Christian Ch.

CAMERON, THOMAS JOSEPH, data processing executive; b. Mpls., Jan. 17, 1955; s. Leo Joseph and Rubye Lucile (Rakowski) C. B in Computer Sci., U. Minn., 1976; MBA, Coll. St. Thomas, 1980. Cert. data processor. Programmer/analyst Programs, Inc., St. Paul, 1973-76, mgr. software devel., 1976-77; sr. cons. Ernst & Whinney, Mpls., 1977-82; pres. Synergistic Techs., Mpls., 1982—; publicity chmn. Minn. Joint Computer Conf., Mpls., 1984-85. Mem. Assn. Computing Machinery (chmn. 1981-83). Republican. Avocations: sailing, skiing, amateur radio. Home and Office: 4605 Weston Ln N Plymouth MN 55446-2026

CAMMA, ALBERT JOHN, neurosurgeon; b. Cleve., Dec. 27, 1940; s. August and Amelia (Catalioti) C.; B.S. cum laude, John Carroll U., 1963; M.D., Western Res. U., 1967; m. Sheryl Virginia Doptis, Aug. 27, 1966 (div. Jan. 1986); children—August Leon, Albert David. Intern, surg. resident U. Pitts., 1967-69, resident in neurosurgery, 1971-75; practice medicine specializing in neurosurgery, Zanesville, Ohio, 1975—. Trustee Zanesville YMCA, 1976-82. Served with M.C., USN, 1969-71. Diplomate Am. Bd. Neurol. Surgeons, Nat. Bd. Med. Examiners. Mem. AMA, Ohio State Med. Assn., Muskingum County Acad. Medicine, Congress Neurol. Surgeons, Am. Acad. Thermology, Midwest Pain Soc., Soc. Behavioral Medicine, ACS, Am. Assn. Neurol. Surgeons, Ohio State Neurosurg. Soc. (bd. dirs. 1985—), Mid-Atlantic Neurosurg. Soc., Am. Pain Soc. Office: 855 Bethesda Dr Zanesville OH 43701

CAMMA, PHILIP, accountant; b. Phila., May 22, 1923; s. Anthony and Rose (LaSpada) C.; m. Anna Ruth Karg, July 21, 1956 (dec. Aug. 1960); 1 child, Anthony Philip. BS, U. Pa., 1952. CPA, Ohio, Ky. Acct., Main and Co., CPA's, Phila., 1952-53; in-charge acct. Haskins & Sells, CPA's, Phila., St. Louis, Cin. and Columbus, Ohio, 1953-60; controller Marvin Warner Co., Cin., 1960-61, Leshner Corp., 1961-63; mng. ptnr. Camma & Patrick, CPA's, 1963-66; founder Philip Camma Co., CPA's, Cin., 1966—. Served with USAAF, 1942-45, ETO. Mem. Am. Inst. CPA's, Ohio Soc. CPA's, Ky. Soc. CPA's, Am. Acctg. Assn., Nat. Assn. Accts. Republican. Clubs: Cincinnati; University Pa.; Hamilton City. Home: Phelps Townhouse 506 E 4th St Cincinnati OH 45202 Office: 700 Walnut St Suite 603 Cincinnati OH 45202

CAMMARANO, SAMUEL JOSEPH, JR., project manager, civil engineer; b. Paterson, N.J., Oct. 25, 1950; s. Samuel Joseph Sr. and Mary Ann (Natella) C. m. Lori Beth Rosen, June 14, 1980; children: Christopher Michael, Megan Marie. BSCE, Cleve. State U., 1975; degree in engrng. mgmt., Calif. Inst. Tech., 1987. Registered profl. engr., Ohio, Fla. Structural engr. Davy-McKee, Cleve., 1975-78; project mgr. Ferro Corp., Cleve., 1978—. Mem. ASCE. Republican. Roman Catholic. Home: 3407 Ridgepark Blvd Broadview Heights OH 44147 Office: Ferro Corp 1 Erieview Plaza Cleveland OH 44114

CAMMARATA, WALTER THOMAS, publishing company executive; b. St. Louis, July 2, 1940; s. Walter and Anne (Tucciarello) C.; B.S., St. Louis U., 1964, M.B.A., 1968; m. Gail Ann Leiendecker, Feb. 11, 1961; children—Mark, Dana, Christy. Office mgr. McGraw Hill Book Co., Manchester, Mo., 1967, staff asst., 1968, gen. mgr., 1969, regional v.p., 1980—. Bd. dirs. YMCA. Served with U.S. Army, 1962-68. Mem. Associated Industries of Mo., C. of C., Ballwin Athletic Assn. Republican. Club: Rotary. Home: 651 Tanglewilde Dr Manchester MO 63011 Office: 13955 Manchester Rd Manchester MO 63011

CAMMIN, WILLIAM BENJAMIN, clin. psychologist; b. Saginaw, Mich., Jan. 16, 1941; s. Howard John and Beulah Ione Cammin; B.S., Central Mich. U., 1964; M.A., Western Mich. U., 1966; Ph.D., U. S.C., 1969; m. Joanne Marie Seidel, July 23, 1966; children—Darren William, Kiena Marie, Clane Joseph. Chief psychologist outpatient services Carter Meml. Hosp., Ind. Med. Center, Indpls., 1968-70; cons. clin. psychology Quinco Community Mental Health Center, Columbus, Ind., 1969-70; cons. Community Mental Health Planning, Kokomo, Ind., 1970; exec. dir. Bay-Arenac Community Mental Health Services Bd., Bay City, Mich., 1971—; mem. mental health com. E. Central Mich. Health Systems Agy., 1973—; co-chmn. psychiat. tech. com. Emergency Med. Services Eastern Mich., 1975-78. Mem. Am. Psychol. Assn., Mich. Psychol. Assn., Mich. Assn. Community Mental Health Dirs. (exec. com.). Home: 5578 Mackinaw Rd Saginaw MI 48604 Office: 201 Mulholland St Bay City MI 48706

CAMP, HERBERT LEE, physician; b. Saginaw, Mich., May 27, 1940; s. Harper L. and Ann Agatha (Hardy) C.; m. Jacqueline Anne Nelson, June 17, 1961; children: Jeffrey, Susan, Patricia. BS, Mich. State U., 1962; MD, U. Mich., 1966. Diplomate Am. Bd. Otolaryngology. Otolaryngologist Wilferd Hall Med. Ctr., San Antonio, 1971-73; attending otolaryngologist Ponce de Leon Infirmary, Atlanta, 1973-74; attending physician Midland (Mich.) Hosp. Ctr., 1974—; cons. physician Bay Med. Ctr., Bay City, Mich., 1976—, Clare (Mich.) Community Hosp., 1984—; bd. dirs. Wolverine Savs. & Loan, Midland, 1981—. Served to maj. USAF, 1971-73. Fellow ACS; mem. AMA, Mich. Med. Soc., Midland County Med. Soc., Am. Acad. Otolarngology and Head and Neck Surgery. Republican. Presbyterian. Clubs: Benmark (treas. Roscommon chpt. 1986—, pres. 1987—), Midland Country; Univ. (East Lansing, Mich.); Carlton (Chgo.). Avocation: outdoor sports. Home: 16 Snowfield Ct Midland MI 48640 Office: PO Box 1446 Midland MI 48641

CAMP, WILLIAM LYMAN, psychologist; b. Chgo., May 10, 1938; s. William Lyman and Julia Wiladene (Zellmer) C.; m. Mildred Bell Cavanaugh, Aug. 14, 1965; children: Christine, Jonathan. BS, U. Wis., Platteville, 1960; MS, U. Wis., Madison, 1961, PhD, 1968. Substitute tchr. Webb High Sch., Reedsburg, Wis., fall 1959; dir. guidance and tchr. civics Platteville (Wis.) High Sch., 1959-60; dir. guidance, tchr. Elgin (Ill.) Pub. Schs., 1962-64, dir. research and devel., 1964-67; asst. prof. psychology U. Wis., Platteville, 1968-70, assoc. prof., 1970-81, dir. univ. counseling and testing ctr., 1969-75; clin. psychologist Marinette (Wis.) County Unified Services Bd./Community Mental Health Clinic, 1981—; pvt. practice clin. psychology Platteville, Marinette, 1970—; instr. psychology Elgin Community Coll., 1964-67; extension lectr. child guidance Bradley U. Grad. Sch., 1965-67; cons. Mich. Bur. Social Security Disability Ins., 1982—, Wis. Bur. Social Security Disability Ins., 1982—, Luth. Social Services. Wis. and Mich., 1983—; lectr. No. Mich. U. Extension, Marquette, 1981—, U. Wis., 1980—. Author: (with wife) America's Education Press., 1966; Guide to Periodicals in Education, 1968, Our Children in a Changing World; contbr. articles to profl. jours. Mem. AAUP, Am. Psychol. Assn., Wis. Psychol. Assn. Home: 923 Edwin St Marinette WI 54143 Office: Marinette County Unified Services Bd Counseling Service 400 Wells St Marinette WI 54143

CAMPANELLA, THEODORA, social welfare administrator; b. N.Y.C., Sept. 15, 1943; d. Joseph Louis and Frances Julia (De Monaco) Miklich; m. Joseph Vincent Campanella, Apr. 18, 1964 (div. July 1971); children: Frances Ann, Anthony Joseph. BBA, Queens Coll., N.Y.C., 1971; postgrad., NYCC, 1976-77, Coll. of Ins., 1980. Internal auditor Am. Express Co., N.Y.C., 1961-64; leasing agt. Arlen Mgmt. Corp., Long Island City, N.Y., 1971-74; personnel asst., sr. acct. Foster & Kleiser, Long Island City, 1974-77; assoc. dir. personnel YMCA, N.Y.C., 1977-81; human resources mgr. YMCA of U.S.A., Chgo., 1981-83; dir. personnel Cath. Charities, Chgo., 1985—. Contbr. poetry to arts jours. V.P. Winston Village Assn., Bolingbrook, Ill., 1982-85; chmn. Easter Seals Fund Raiser, Bolingbrook, 1984, United Way, Bolingbrook, 1984; legis. com. mem. DuPage Bd. Realtors, Wheaton, 1984; mem. women's bd. House of Good Shephard, Chgo. Mem. Am. Soc. Personnel Adminstrs., Am. Compensation Assn., Nat. Assn. Female Execs. Roman Catholic. Avocations: swimming, boating, tennis. Office: Cath Charities Archdiocese Chgo 126 N Des Plaines St Chicago IL 60606

CAMPANIZZI-MOOK, JANE, consulting company executive; b. Wheeling, W.Va., Nov. 27, 1947; d. Peter and Jean (Ciesielka) Campanizzi; m. William Harry Mook, Dec. 31, 1978. MA, Ohio State U., 1971, PhD, 1978. Cert. quality analyst. Instr. Barnesville (Ohio) Schs., 1968-70, Columbus (Ohio) Schs., 1971-76; cons. State of Ohio, Columbus, 1978-81; analyst OCLC Inc., Dublin, Ohio, 1981-85; pres. JCM Enterprises, Columbus, 1985—; bd. dirs. Application Innovations Corp., Columbus. Rapi-Serv Cash Systems, Columbus; trustee Artreach Gallery, Columbus, Small Bus. Council, 1987—. Editor Quali-News newsletter, 1986; contbr. articles to profl. jours. Mem. com. Columbus Area Leadership Program, 1985—, sci./math adv. com. Columbus Schs., 1986; convenor Nat. Issues Forum, Dayton, Ohio, 1986—. Mem. Am. Soc. Quality Control, Quality Assurance Inst., AAAS, Columbus C. of C. (exec. club). Roman Catholic. Club: Faculty Ohio State U., Capital. Avocations: astronomy, electronics. Home: 4453 Masters Dr Columbus OH 43220 Office: JCM Enterprises 4627 Executive Dr Columbus OH 43220

CAMPBELL, CAROL NORTON, controller, university administrator; b. Mpls., July 28, 1944; d. Dale Edward and Betty Lorraine (Huntley) Norton; m. George Carl Anderson, May 5, 1963 (div. Aug. 1973); children: Todd Elove, Robb Norton, Mark Edward; m. John Thomas Campbell, June 10, 1976. BSB in Acctg., U. Minn., 1975. CPA, Minn. Mem. audit staff Coopers & Lybrand, Mpls., 1977-79, audit supr., 1979-81, mgr., 1981-84; dir. acctg. U. Minn., Mpls., 1984-86, controller, treas., 1986—. Mem. com. Citizens League, Mpls., 1983-85. Mem. Am. Inst. CPA's, Minn. Soc. CPA's, Cen. Assn. Coll. and Univ. Bus. Officers (exec. com. 1986-87). Office: Univ Minn 302 Morrill Hall 100 Church St SE Minneapolis MN 55455

CAMPBELL, CHALEN J., minister, educator; b. Alton, Ill., Feb. 17, 1937; s. Chalen and Dorothy (Dossett) C.; m. Ellen Stickels, Dec. 13, 1958; children: Annette Ellen, Jayne Renee. Diploma, Moody Bible Inst., 1968; BS, Calvary Bible Coll., 1969; MA, Trinity Theol. Seminary, 1974; DEd, Trinity Bible Coll. Seminary, 1980; DD (hon.), Wesley Coll., 1979. Pastor First Assembly of God, Pocahontas, Ill., 1962-65, Dolton Assembly of God, Dolton, Ill., 1965-68, Bethel Assembly of God, Elmhurst, Ill., 1969-74, First Assembly of God, Merrillville, Ind., 1974—; prof. Christian Life Coll., Mt. Prospect, Ill., 1970—, Berean Coll. of the Bible, Merrillville, 1982—; pres. Living Hope Ministries, Merrillville, Ind., 1983—; founder Good Shepherd Day Care Ctr., 1976, Merrillville Christian Sch., 1978. Bd. dirs. Chgo. Teen Challenge, 1970-74. Served with USN, 1954-57. Mem. Assemblies of God Ministerial Assn., Ross Township Clergy Assn. Avocations: golf, swimming, softball. Office: 7525 Taft St Merrillville IN 46410

CAMPBELL, CHARLES EDWIN, physics educator; b. Columbus, Ohio, Dec. 11, 1942; s. Leslie J. and Florine (Wingate) C.; m. Martha Arlene Hutton, Aug. 15, 1965; children: Derek Brian, Scott Andrew. BS, Ohio State U., 1964; PhD, Washington U., St. Louis, 1969. Research assoc. in physics U. Wash., Seattle, 1969-71, Stanford (Calif.) U., 1971-73; asst. prof. physics U. Minn., Mpls., 1973-76, assoc. prof. physics, 1976-81, prof. physics, 1981—, dir. grad. studies in physics, 1982-83, head sch. physics and astronomy, 1983-86; mem. internat. adv. com. Conf. Series on Recent Progress in Many-Body Theories; chmn. Feenberg Medal Selection Com., 1983-85. Contbr. articles to profl. jours. Alexander von Humboldt fellow, 1981-82; grantee NSF, 1974—, Research Corp. grantee, 1973-75; recipient Alva Smith award Ohio State U., 1964. Mem. Am. Phys. Soc., AAAS, Phi Beta Kappa, Sigma Xi. Office: U Minn Sch Physics and Astronomy 116 Church St SE Minneapolis MN 55455

CAMPBELL, CHARLES GEORGE, banker; b. Andover, Eng., July 16, 1895; s. William T. and Grace (Calder) C.; came to U.S., 1901, naturalized, 1919; grad. Ind. Bus. Coll., 1916; student U. Chgo., 1920-22; hon. degree Wabash Coll., 1980; m. Helen I. Thompson, June 14, 1926; children—Claire E. (Mrs. David Locke, Jr.), Joyce C. (Mrs. Rodney Beals). Sec.-treas. Kamp Motor Co., Mt. Carmel, Ill., 1923-26, pres., 1926-59; v.p. Vigo Motor Co., Terre Haute, Ind., 1944-50; v.p. Security Bank and Trust Co., Mt. Carmel, 1937-59, pres., 1959-64, chmn. bd., 1969—, also dir.; pres. Am. Savs. & Loan Assn., Mt. Carmel, 1939-59, dir., 1937—; dir. Camray, Inc., Mt. Carmel, Mt. Carmel Area Devel. Corp.; dir. Tri-County Indsl. Com., 1965-67. Mem. Mt. Carmel City Commn., 1963—; mayor City of Mt. Carmel, 1965-67. Served with U.S. Army, 1917-19; AEF in France. Named to Mt. Carmel High Sch. Hall of Fame, 1983. Mem. Mt. Carmel C. of C. (dir. 1959-62, 65-68), Am. Legion (comdr. Wabash post 1937), 40 and 8, Wabash Valley Assn. Presbyterian. Lodges: Masons, Shriners, Elks (lodge trustee 1979-80), Moose, Eagles, Kiwanis (pres. Mt. Carmel 1935, dir. 1936). Home: 323 Cherry St Mount Carmel IL 62863 Office: 400 Main St Mount Carmel IL 62863

CAMPBELL, D'ANN MAE, history educator; b. Denver, Dec. 30, 1949; d. Bernard Edward and Eleanor Louise (Mahoney) Campbell; B.A., Colo. Coll., 1972; Ph.D. in History, U. N.C., Chapel Hill, 1979; m. Richard Jensen, July 16, 1976. Asst. dir. Family and Community History Center, Newberry Library, Chgo., 1976-78, assoc. dir., 1978-79; adj. prof. history U. Ill., Chgo. Circle, 1977-79; dean for women's affairs Ind. U., asst. prof. history, 1979-85, assoc. prof., 1985—. Newberry Library fellow, 1975-76, NEH grantee, 1976-79, 81-84; Dept. Edn. grantee, 1979-81, 83-85. Mem. Am. Studies Assn. (nat. council 1979-81), Orgn. Am. Historians (chair com. status women 1977-79, chmn. nominating bd. 1980-82), Am. Hist. Assn., So. Hist. Assn., Social Sci. Hist. Assn. (chmn. nominating bd., co-chmn. program com.), Nat. Hist. Communal Socs. Assn. (pres.), Quantum Internat. Orgn., Coalition for Women in Humanities and Social Scis., Phi Beta Kappa, Pi Gamma Mu. Author: Women at War with America, 1984; contbr. articles to profl. jours.; mem. editorial bd. Newberry Papers, Teaching History. Home: 1109 Longwood Dr Bloomington IN 47401 Office: Dept History Ind U Bloomington IN 47405

CAMPBELL, DENNIS EDWIN, career military officer, educator; b. Hampton, Va., Oct. 26, 1938; s. William Pren and Lula Norine (Stewart) C.; m. Sirkka Anneli Mäkeläinen, Oct. 22, 1960; children: Lisa Ann, Darice Lynn. BS, U. Ala., 1973; MBA, Clark U., 1975; PhD, Ohio State U., 1986. Enlisted U.S. Army, 1958, advanced through grades to maj., 1976, ret., 1978; div. mgr. F.A. Bartlett Co., Stanford, Conn., 1978-81; contract mgr. Falcon Jet Corp., Little Rock, 1981; prof. Air Force Inst. Tech., Wright-Patterson AFB, Ohio, 1982—; pvt. practice cons. Beavercreek, Ohio, 1984—; Southwest regional dir. Ohio Assn. Adult and Continuing Edn. Assn. Decorated Bronze Star, Cross of Gallantry; sustained superior performance award USAF, 1982, 83, 84, 85, 86; Outstanding Tchr. in Ohio Assn. for Adult and Continuing Edn., 1986. Mem. Soc. Logistics Engrs. (sr.), Assn. Psychol. Type, Nat. Univ. Continuing Edn. Assn., DAV (life). Home: 3755 Frostwood Dr Beavercreek OH 45430 Office: Air Force Inst Tech LSM Wright-Patterson AFB OH 45433-6583

CAMPBELL, DONALD WESLEY, accountant; b. Mays, Ind., Aug. 21, 1936; s. James Henry and Laura Agnes (Cross) C.; m. Barbara Lou Feaster, Sept. 9, 1956; children: Steven, Donald Jr., James. BS in Agr. Edn., Purdue U., 1958; MBA, St. Francis Coll., 1971. Sales mgmt. Ralston Purina Co., Lafayette, Ind., 1958-59; corp. fin. planner Cen. Soya, Ft. Wayne, Ind., 1964-72; nat. service mgr. Vindale Corp., Dayton, Ohio, 1972-74; pvt. practice acctg. Dayton, 1974—. Served to capt. U.S. Army, 1959-64, Korea. Mem. Nat. Soc. Income Tax Preparers, Nat. Fedn. Tax Prepareers, Pub. Acct. Soc. of Ohio, VFW. Republican. Methodist. Lodge: Masons. Avocations: boating, walking, motorcycling. Home: 717 Chandler Dr Dayton OH 45426 Office: Campbell Bus Service 2454 Shiloh Springs Rd Dayton OH 45426

CAMPBELL, DOUGLAS BRIAN, dentist; b. Lansing, Mich., Jan. 7, 1956; s. Rolf Corydon and Shirley Elaine (Barr) C.; m. Jill Lynn Pierce, July 30, 1983. BS, Mich. State U., 1978; DDS, U. Ill., 1982. Pvt. practice dentistry Lake Forest, Ill., 1982—. Mem. ADA, Chgo. Dental Soc., Lake County (Ill.) Dental Soc., Acad. Gen. Dentistry. Club: Lake Forest-Lake Bluff Running. Avocations: running, tennis, water skiing, snow skiing, gymnastics. Home: 755 E Highview Terr Lake Forest IL 60045 Office: 1400 N Western Lake Forest IL 60045

CAMPBELL, F(ENTON) GREGORY, university administrator, historian; b. Columbia, Tenn., Dec. 16, 1939; s. Fenton G. and Ruth (Hayes) C.; A.B., Baylor U., 1960; postgrad. (Fulbright grantee), Philipps U., Marburg/Lahn, W. Ger., 1960-61; M.A. (Woodrow Wilson fellow), Emory U., 1962; postgrad. (Exchange fellow) Charles U., Prague, Czechoslovakia, 1965-66; Ph.D., Yale U., 1967; postgrad. Inst. for Ednl. Mgmt., Harvard U., 1981; m. Barbara D. Kuhn, Aug. 29, 1970; children—Fenton H., Matthew W., Charles H. Research staff historian Yale U., New Haven, 1966-68, spl. asst. to acting pres., 1977-78; asst. prof. history U. Wis., Milw., 1968-69; asst. prof. European history U. Chgo., 1969-76, spl. asst. to pres., 1978-87, sec. bd. trustees, 1979-87, sr. lectr., 1985-87; pres. Carthage Coll., 1987—; fellow Woodrow Wilson Internat. Center for Scholars, Smithsonian Instn., Washington, 1976-77; mem. E. European selection com. Internat. Research and Exchanges Bd., 1975-78; rev. panelist NEH, 1983-84, 86. Fulbright grantee, 1973-74; U.S.A.-Czechoslovakia exchange fellow, 1973-74, 85; participant Japan Study Program for Internat. Execs., 1987. Mem. Am. Hist. Assn., Am. Assn. for Advancement Slavic Studies, Czechoslovak History Conf. (pres. 1980-82), Conf. Group on Central European History (sec.-treas. 1980-83), Chgo. Council on Fgn. Relations (com. on fgn. affairs 1979—, exec. com. 1984—), Phi Beta Kappa. Clubs: Mid-Day, Quadrangle (Chgo.). Author: Confrontation in Central Europe, 1975. Contbr. articles, revs. to profl. jours. Joint editor Akten zur deutschen auswartigen Politik, 1918-45, 1966—. Home: 623 17th Pl Kenosha WI 53140 Office: Carthage Coll Kenosha WI 53141

CAMPBELL, HELEN ISABEL, auditor, bank executive; b. Mt. Pleasant, Mich., Sept. 12, 1955; s. Albert Algernon and Vivian Lucille (Graham) C. BSBA in Acctg., Cen. Mich. U., 1977. CPA, Mich., cert. auditor. Staff acct. Page, Cassel & Olson CPA's, Mt. Pleasant, 1975-77; auditor Deloitte Haskins & Sells, Saginaw, Mich., 1977-80; from sr. auditor to audit supr. Mich. Nat. Corp., Lansing, 1980-85; regional audit dir. Mich. Nat. Corp., Farmington Hills, 1985—. Big sister Big Bros. Big Sisters, Lansing, 1981-86. Mem. Am. Inst. CPA's, Mich. Assn. CPA's. Republican. Presbyterian. Avocations: tennis, cross-country skiing. Home: 4254 Somerville Dr West Bloomfield MI 48033 Office: Mich Nat Corp 30445 Northwestern Hwy Farmington Hills MI 48018-9065

CAMPBELL, HELEN WOERNER (MRS. THOMAS B. CAMPBELL), librarian; b. Indpls., Oct. 17, 1918; d. Clarence Julius and Gertrude Elizabeth (Colley) Woerner; student Ind. U., 1935-38; B.S., Butler U., 1967; m. Thomas B. Campbell, Jan. 17, 1942; 1 dau., Martha (Mrs. L. Kurt Adamson). Asst. order librarian Ind. U., Bloomington, 1937-42; librarian Ind. U. Sch. Dentistry, Indpls., 1942-46, cataloger, part-time, 1960-65, asst. librarian, 1965-66, librarian, 1966-80. Mem. Med. Library Assn., Spl. Libraries Assn. (chpt. pres. 1972-73). Home: 1865 Norfolk St Indianapolis IN 46224

CAMPBELL, JACK DEE, insurance agent; b. Lincoln, Nebr., Dec. 21, 1928; s. John D. and Alice H. (Heldt) C.; m. Sally L. Holmes, Mar. 26, 1951; children: John Daniel, Amy Holmes, Peter J. BSBA with distinction, U. Nebr., 1950. CLU, CHFC. Loan officer 1st Nat. Bank, Lincoln, 1950-52; agt. Mass. Mut., Lincoln, 1954-65, gen. agt., 1965—; bd. dirs. Cooper Found., Contact, Inc., Nebr. Interactive Video, Inc., vice chmn. Bd. dirs. Nebr. Pub. TV, Lincoln, 1975-85, U. Nebr. Found., Lincoln, 1983-85. Served to capt. USAF, 1952-54. Recipient Disting. Service award Lincoln Jaycees, 1972; named one of (3) Outstanding Young Men Am., Nebr. Jaycees, 1973. Mem. Am. Soc. CLU's (v.p. 1982-85, pres. Lincoln chpt. 1968-69), Nebr. Gen. Agts. and Mgrs. (pres. 1969-70). Republican. Episcopalian. clubs: Lincoln U. (pres. 1978-79), Country Club of Lincoln (dir. 1980-83). Lodges: Shriner, Elks. Office: Mass Mut Life Ins Co NBC Center Suite 880 Lincoln NE 68508

CAMPBELL, JAMES ARTHUR, professional baseball executive; b. Huron, Ohio, Feb. 5, 1924; s. Arthur A. and Vanessa (Hart) C.; m. Helene G. Mulligan, Jan. 16, 1954 (div. July 1969). B.S., Ohio State U., 1949. Bus. mgr. Thomasville (Ga.) Baseball Club, 1950, Toledo Baseball Club, 1951, Buffalo Baseball Club, 1952; bus. mgr. Detroit Minor League System, 1953; asst. farm dir. Detroit Baseball Club, 1954-56, v.p., farm dir., 1957-61, v.p., gen. mgr., 1962-65; exec. v.p., gen. mgr. Detroit Tigers, 1965-78, pres., gen. mgr., 1978-84, pres., chief exec. officer, 1984—. Served with AC USNR, 1943-46. Named Maj. League Exec. of Year, 1968; named to Mich. Sports Hall of Fame, 1985. Mem. Ohio State U. Varsity O Assn., Assn., Delta Upsilon. Presbyn. Clubs: Detroit Athletic, Detroit Press, Renaissance, Detroit Golf; Lone Palm Golf (Lakeland, Fla.). Office: Tiger Stadium 2121 Trumbull Ave Detroit MI 48216

CAMPBELL, JOHN ROY, animal scientist, educator; b. Goodman, Mo., June 14, 1933; s. Carl J. and Helen (Nicoletti) C.; m. Eunice Vieten, Aug. 7, 1954; children: Karen L., Kathy L., Keith L. B.S., U. Mo., Columbia, 1955, M.S., 1956, Ph.D., 1960. Instr. animal sci. U. Mo., Columbia, 1960-61; asst. prof. U. Mo., 1961-65, assoc. prof., 1965-68, prof., 1968—; asso. dean, dir. resident instrn. Coll. Agr., U. Ill., Urbana, 1978-83; dean Coll. Agr. U. Ill., 1983—. Author: (with J.F. Lasley) The Science of Animals That Serve Humanity 1969, 2d edit., 1975, 3d edit., 1985, In Touch with Students, 1972, (with R.T. Marshall) The Science of Providing Milk for Man, 1975. Recipient Outstanding Tchr. award U. Mo., 1967; Superior Teaching award Gamma Sigma Delta, internat. award for disting. service to agr., 1985. Mem. Am. Dairy Sci. Assn. (dir., pres. 1980-81, Ralston Purina Disting. Teaching award 1973), Nat. Assn. Coll. Tchrs. Agr. (Ensminger Interstate Disting. Tchr. award 1973). Office: U Ill Coll Agr 101 Mumford Hall 1301 W Gregory Urbana IL 61801

CAMPBELL, KEITH EDWIN, computer systems analyst; b. Rockford, Ill., Dec. 5, 1948; s. Alan Howard Campbell and Margery Ann (Franklin) Hampton; m. Maria Therese Piscitelli, June 23, 1979. BS in Engrin. Math., U. Ariz., 1971. Engrng. analyst Tucson Gas & Electric, 1971-77; pvt. practice cons. Tucson, 1977-79; analyst, programmer TRW Controls Inc., Houston, 1979-81, Electronic Ass. Inc., West Long Branch, N.J., 1981-83; systems analyst Teledyne Brown Engrng., Leavenworth, Kans., 1983—. Choir dir. Weston (Mo.) United Meth. Ch., 1984-86. Served to sgt. USNG, 1970-73. Mem. IEEE. Republican. Methodist. Avocations: tennis, racquetball, guitar, reading, antiques, travel. Home: 10536 Bluejacket Overland Park KS 66214 Office: Teledyne Brown Engring 430 Walnut St Leavenworth KS 66048

CAMPBELL, MALCOLM BYRON, educator; b. Flint, Mich., May 25, 1938; s. Malcolm and Marian Marguerite (Smith) C.; m. Lynn Mildred Ufholz, June 29, 1968 (div. 1977); children—Alycia Lynn, Courtney Jessica; m. Rosie Lanette Mapes, May 31. 1986. AB, U. Mich., 1960, AM, 1961, PhD, 1966. Tchr., English elem. schs., Bloomfield Hills (Mich.) Dist. Schs., 1965-66; asst. prof. edn. Bowling Green State U. (Ohio), 1966-70, assoc. prof., 1970-75, prof., 1975—; cons. Tiffin Devel. Ctr. (Ohio). Lyndon Baines Johnson Found. grantee, 1974. Mem. Comparative and Internat. Edn. Soc., Ohio Valley Philosophy of Edn. Soc., Am. Ednl. Studies Assn., Am. Ednl. Research Assn., Spl. Interest Group on Internat. Studies. Democrat. Author: Non-Specialist Study in the New Universities and Colleges of Advanced Technology in England, 1966; co-editor: Jour. of Abstracts in Internat. Edn., 1971—, Ednl. Impressions: Readings, 1977. Home: 729 Ordway Bowling Green OH 43402 Office: Bowling Green State U 556 Ednl Bldg Bowling Green OH 43403

CAMPBELL, MALCOLM (MIKE), sales training consultant; b. Tracy, Minn., Sept. 6, 1925; s. Charles Moore and Stella Leonora Campbell; m. Mary Ellen Duer, June 11, 1947 (div. 1956); children: Daniel, Peggy, Maryann; m. Helen Mary Pivonka, Dec. 7, 1959; children: Jo Ellen, Shelley, Sheila, Michael. BA, St. Olaf Coll., 1950; postgrad., Moorhead (Minn.) State U., 1978—. Safety dir. Honeywell AERO, Mpls., 1950-55; nat. sales dir. Babee-Tenda Corp., Shaker Heights, Ohio, 1955-69; mktg. dir. Fund Aids Co., Audubon, Minn., 1970-78; pres. Successervices, Detroit Lakes, Minn., 1980—; cons. DLAVTI, Detroit Lakes, Minn., 1978—, Personal Dynamics, Mpls., 1980—, Better Than Money, 1982—, Performax, Mpls., 1983—; instr. Wilson Tng., Mpls., 1968—. Author: The Sekim Sales System, 1984, Communicating With People--Not At Them, Self-Esteem: Loving Yourself More, Hospitality/Tourism: The Industry of Tomorrow. Sec., treas. bd. trustees United Methodist Ch., 1984. Served with USN, 1943-46, PTO. Decorated DFC, Purple Heart. Mem. Dist. Edn. Clubs Am. (advisor, recipient Distinguished Advisor award 1984), Sales and Mktg. Club, Detroit Lakes C. of C., Alcoholics Anonymous, VFW, DAV, Am. Legion. Republican. Methodist. Lodge: Optimist (fund raiser Detroit Lakes 1985). Avocation: golf. Home and Office: 1512 Carol Ave Detroit Lakes MN 56501

CAMPBELL, MURDOCH THOMAS, metal distribution company executive; b. Detroit, Mar. 30, 1946; s. John Duncan and Mary (Fahey) C.; div. 1984; children: Mona, Margaret. BA, Mich. State U., 1968; MBA, U. New Orleans, 1970. CPA, Mich. Auditor Peat, Marwick and Mitchell, Detroit, 1970-71; prof. U. New Orleans, La., 1971-72; owner, exec. Brown-Campbell Steel Co., Detroit, 1972—. Mem. Am. Inst. CPA's, La. State Bd. CPA's, Mich. Assn. CPA's, Delta Upsilon. Club: Mercedes-Benz (treas. Colorado Springs, Colo. chpt. 1983—). Avocation: instrument rated private pilot. Office: Brown-Campbell Steel Co 14290 Goddard Detroit MI 48212

CAMPBELL, PAUL BRUCE, construction company executive; b. St. Louis, Mar. 30, 1942; s. Bruce and Evelyn (Pemberton) C.; m. Sarajane McWilliams, Nov. 26, 1966; children: Jill Lynn, Jeffrey Scott. BS in Engring., U. Ill., 1964, MS in Physics, 1965; MBA, U. Santa Clara, 1970; PhD in Applied Econs., U. Calif., Berkeley, 1981. Engr., scientist Douglas Missile and Space, Huntington Beach, Calif., 1965-67; research engr. Lockheed, Sunnyvale, Calif., 1967-69; pres. Greater Mo. Builders, St. Louis, 1970—, also bd. dirs.; asst. prof. So. Ill. U., 1978-83; adj. prof. Washington U., St. Louis, 1983—; bd. dirs. Crunden Martin Mfgs. Pres. Clayton Gardens Assn., Clayton, Mo., 1985—. Mem. Nat. Assn. Real Estate Bds., Home Buildres Assn., U. Ill. Alumni Assn., U. Calif. Alumni Assn. Avocations: jogging, cycling, tennis. Home: 180 N Forsyth Clayton MO 63105 Office: Greater Mo Buildres 3651 N Lindbergh Saint Louis MO 63074

CAMPBELL, RICHARD (MIKE) LEE, county building superintendant; b. Dayton, Ky., Feb. 8, 1928; s. Albert John and Selma Burdette (Carmichael) C.; m. Jeanette Vilma Schnur, Nov. 24, 1949 (div. Aug. 1977); children: Diana Marie, Cynthia Lee, Michael Anthony; m. Roberta May Schaeffer, May 10, 1980. Student, Salmon P. Chase Coll., 1952-53; BS, U. Hawaii, 1947. Supt. Carlton Machine Tool Co., Cin., 1952-75; supt. bldgs. Hamilton County, Ohio, 1975—. Mem. Cheviot (Ohio) City Council, 1960-74, pres. 1975-80; del. to Rep. Conv., 1980, 84. Served to sgt. USMC, 1945-48, PTO, 1950-52, Korea. Mem. Bldg. Owners and Mgrs. Assn. Republican. Roman

Catholic. Lodge: K.C. (Grand Knight Cin. 1958-59, Dist. Dep. Ohio 1960-64). Home: 3806 Dina Terr Cincinatti OH 45211 Office: Courthouse Rm 127 1000 Main St Cincinatti OH 45202

CAMPBELL, ROBERT L., management consultant; b. Haverford, Pa., Jan. 6, 1944; s. Robert L. and I. Lee (Groah) C.; B.S. in Mktg., Loyola U., Chgo., 1964; M.M., Northwestern U., 1978; m. Elizabeth A. Powers, Dec. 20, 1975; 1 dau., Elisabeth. Mgmt. cons. Quirsfeld, Hussey & Manes, Chgo., 1964-70, Peat, Marwick, Mitchell & Co., Chgo., 1970-73, Booz, Allen & Hamilton, Chgo., 1973; founder, owner, mgr. Robert Campbell & Assocs., Chgo., 1973—; lectr. Loyola U., part-time, 1976—; Fin. Inst., part-time, 1972—. Bd. dirs. Youth Guidance Chgo., 1977—; bd. dirs., exec. com. Wyler Children's Hosp. U. Chgo.; bd. dirs. Mental Health Greater Chgo.; chmn. devel. com. Ill. Republican Com., 1970—. Mem. Assn. Bus. Economists, Am. Econometric Assn., Nat. Small Bus. Assn., Am. Prodn. and Inventory Control Soc., Am. Mktg. Assn., Northwestern U. Alumni Assn. (dir. 1978—). Clubs: Chgo. Yacht, University (Chgo.). Contbr. articles on labor econs. to profl. publs. Home: 470 Deming Pl Chicago IL 60614 Office: Robert Campbell & Assocs 18 S Michigan Ave Chicago IL 60603

CAMPBELL, STUART KEATHLEY, accountant; b. St. Louis, Nov. 23, 1961; s. William Murray and Geraldine (Keathley) C. BSBA in Acctg. magna cum laude, U. Mo., St. Louis, 1983. CPA, Mo. Staff acct. Price Waterhouse, St. Louis, 1983-86, sr. acct., 1986—. Mem. fin. com. Ballwin (Mo.) Bapt. Ch., 1985—. Mem. Am. Inst. CPA's, Mo. Soc. CPA's. Avocations: piano, trumpet, racquetball. Office: Price Waterhouse One Centerre Plaza Saint Louis MO 63101

CAMPBELL, WILLIAM EDWARD, state hospital school superintendent; b. Kansas City, Kans., June 30, 1927; s. William Warren and Mary (Bickerman) C.; m. Joan Josselyn Larimer, July 26, 1952; children: William Gregory, Stephen James, Douglas Edward. Student, U. Nebr., 1944-45, M.S., 1975; student, U. Mich., 1945, Drake U., 1948; B.A., U. Iowa, 1949, M.A., 1950; Ph.D. in Psychology, U. Nebr., Lincoln, 1980. Psychologist Dept. Pub. Instrn., State of Iowa, 1951-52; hosp. adminstr. Mental Health Inst., Cherokee, Iowa, 1952-68; dir. planning and research Dept. Social Services, State of Iowa, 1968-69; supt. Glenwood State Hosp. Sch., Iowa, 1969—, Clarinda Mental Health Inst., Iowa, 1979—; adj. prof. Coll. Medicine and Health Adminstrn., Tulane U., 1979—; pres., bd. dirs. River Bluffs Community Mental Health Center; dir. Shared Mental Health Services, Clarinda/Glenwood; founder, chmn. Regional Drug Abuse Adv. Council; adj. prof. Sch. Pub. Health, U. Minn.; also preceptor grad. students in mental health adminstrn.; vis. faculty Avepane U., Caracas, Venezuela. Author works in field. UN spl. cons. to Venezuela for UNESCO.; bd. dirs. Polk County Mental Health; v.p., bd. dirs. Mercy Hosp., Council Bluffs, Iowa; state pres. United Cerebral Palsy; charter mem. bd. dirs. Pub. Broadcasting Sta. KIWR, Council Bluffs, Iowa. Served with AUS, 1944-46; col. Res. Decorated Army Commendation medal; recipient Meritorious Service medal U.S. Army, 1982. Fellow Assn. Mental Health Adminstrs. (nat. com. chmn. 1970); mem. Assn. Med. Adminstrs., Am. Hosp. Assn. (nat. governing bd. psychiat. services sect., charter panelist nat. adv. panel on mental health services, mem. governing body psychiat. services sect.), Iowa Hosp. Assn., Health Planning Council of Midlands, Assn. Univ. Programs in Health Adminstrn. (mem. nat. task force on edn. of mental health adminstrs.), Am. Assn. on Mental Deficiency (chmn. adminstrn. sect. Region 8), Nat. Rehab. Assn., Assn. for Retarded Children, Mental Health Assn., Phi Beta Kappa. Address: Glenwood State Hosp Sch Glenwood IA 51534

CAMPBELL-GLENN, PATRICIA ANN, government official; b. Brandon, Miss., Dec. 15, 1942; d. James Alvin and Eunice Agnes (Finch) Campbell; children—Allison, Jennifer, Lee. B.S. in Edn., Ohio State U., 1971; postgrad. U. Ill., 1980—. Supr., investigator Civil Rights Commn., Columbus, Ohio, 1971-74; tchr. Columbus Bd. Edn., 1974-78; mediator, dep. dir. U.S. Dept. Justice, Chgo., 1979—. Contbr. articles to profl. jours. Tutor Nat. Literacy Campaign, 1985; commr. Boy Scouts Am., 1985-86; speaker Women's Bd., Ill., 1985-86. Recipient Humanitarian award Columbus Met. Action Community Action Orgn., 1980; Human Relations Spl. award Flint Human Relations Bd., Mich., 1985; Cert. of Appreciation, Kiwanis, Chgo., 1985. Mem. Nat. Council Negro Women, Nat. Assn. Female Execs., Ind. Law Enforcement Commn., Soc. for Profls. in Dispute Resolution. A.M.E. Ch. (asst. supt. Bd. Christian Edn.) Club: VFW Ladies Aux. (pres. 1984-85). Home: 6231 Champlain Chicago IL 60637

CAMPBELL-THRANE, LUCILLE WISSOLIK, educational research center administrator; b. Pitts., Jan. 3, 1921; d. Albert and Roselda Blacksmith (Frances) Wissolik; m. Roland George Campbell, June 25, 1943; children—Melanie Campbell Dragan, Kaaren (dec.), George Crawford, Heidi Campbell Fay; m. 2d, William John Thrane, May 5, 1975. B.S. in Home Econs., Carnegie Mellon U., 1942; M.Ed., U. Pitts., 1953; Ed.D., Pa. State U., 1967. Dir., coordinator vocat. edn. State of Pa., 1964; program officer Region 3, Office of Edn., HEW, Phila., 1973-75; assoc. dir. resource devel. Nat. Ctr. for Research in Vocat. Edn., Columbus, Ohio, 1975-79, assoc. dir. devel. research, 1979—; founder, dir. Pitts. Skill Ctr.; cons. Middle State Accreditation. Bd. dirs. Allegheny council Girl Scouts Am., 1955-60, scout leader, 1950-62; supr. jr. vols. St. Margaret Hosp., Pitts., 1958-62; trustee Franklin County Mental Health Assn., Columbus, 1981—. Named Homemaking Tchr. of Yr., Seventeen Mag., 1963; recipient Carnegie Mellon U. merit award, 1971; disting. alumni in edn. award U. Pitts., 1971, 72, 74. Mem. Am. Home Econs. Assn., Am. Vocat. Assn., Pa. Vocat. Adminstrs., Omicron Nu, Pi Lambda Theta, Delta Kappa Gamma, Phi Delta Kappa, Omicron Tau Theta. Episcopalian. Lodge: Order of Eastern Star. Contbr. articles to profl. jours. Home: 1000 Urlin Ave Summit Chase Suite 1006 Columbus OH 43212 Office: Nat Ctr for Research in Vocat Edn 1960 Kenny Rd Columbus OH 43210

CAMPEN, SELDEN WILLIAM, mortgage company executive; b. Cleve., May 1, 1945; s. Richard Newman and Helen Elise (Selden) C.; m. Jacqueline Valorie Patsche, Aug. 30, 1969; children: Peter, Sarah, Andrew. BS, Carnegie Mellon U., 1967; MA, U. Mich., 1968. Systems engr. Westinghouse, Pitts., 1968-71; fin. analyst Mellon Bank, Pitts., 1971-78; controller Mellon Fin. Services, Cleve., 1978-83, chief fin. officer, 1986—; asst. group controller Mellon Nat. Corp., Pitts., 1983-86. Treas. Pitts. Orgn. for Childbirth, 1975-76, Agnon Sch., Cleve., 1981-82. Mem. Phi Kappa Phi. Republican. Club: Moraine Sailing (treas. 1973-75). Avocations: sailing, computers, geneology, philately. Home: 20670 University Blvd Shaker Heights OH 44022 Office: Mellon Fin Services 1255 Euclid Ave Cleveland OH 44115

CANALE, BRIAN A., restaurateur, real estate developer; b. Akron, Ohio, Sept. 19, 1959; s. Jerry Allen Canale and Carolyn (Ball) Canale DeVore; m. Carol Ann Schellenburger, Apr. 11, 1986; stepchildren: Stacy L., Shawna L., Cindy L. BS in Acctg., U. Akron, 1982. Mgr. DeVores Hopocan Gardens, Barberton, Ohio, 1979-82, gen. mgr., 1982-86, v.p., 1986—; owner, operator Quality Properties, Barberton, 1986—. Past pres. Norton (Ohio) F.O.P.A., 1984-85; mem. Barberton Fraternal Order Police Assn., 1984—; charter mem. Barberton Sports Hall of Fame. Mem. First Hungarian Soc. Democrat. Roman Catholic. Avocations: golf, spectator football, reading. Office: DeVorbes Hopocan Gardens 4396 Hopocan Ave Barberton OH 44203

CANDEE, RICHARD ALEXANDER, JR., diversified manufacturing corporation executive; b. Milw., Dec. 13, 1947; s. Richard Alexander and Vi (Egan) C.; m. Mary Linda Brown, May 26, 1979; 1 child, Alexander Darcy. B.A. magna cum laude, Lawrence U., 1970; M.B.A., Harvard U., 1978; student Mich. State U./Barcelona, Spain, 1968. Sales coordinator, asst. plant mgr. Barton Mfg., Inc., Wis. and P.R., 1970-72; v.p., treas. Cormac, S.A., Panama and Wis., 1972-73; export sales mgr. Latin Am., Gehl Co., West Bend, Wis., 1973-76; mktg. analyst Deere & Co., Moline, Ill., summer 1977; mktg. assoc. Eaton Corp., Cleve., 1978-83, planner, sales mgr., mktg. mgr., Brussels and Aurora, Ohio, 1983-86, dir. mktg. durable med. products div., Invacare Corp., Elyria, Ohio, 1986-87; pres. Vintage Motorpress, Inc., Shaker Heights, Ohio, 1982—; dir. Bill's Sporting Goods Inc., Lomira, Wis., Wolf's Auction Galleries, Cleve. Author, pub.: Aston Martin in America (Davis award 1983), 1982; Facel Vega-The Glory That Was France..., 1975. Exec. producer video tape Austin Healeys-On the Road, 1985. Capt. fund raising Cleve. Orch., 1978-85, Cleve. Ballet, 1980-82; trustee Friends of Shaker Square, Cleve., 1980—; jud. candidate rev. com. Citizens League, 1984, 85. Recipient Conn./Pa. driver Aston Martin Owners Club, Lakeville, Conn., 1982, S.C.H. Davis Publs. award, London, 1983, Elisha Walker Trophy, 1985. Mem. Phi Delta Theta. Clubs: Harvard Bus. Sch. (v.p. 1980-85), Skating (Cleve.). Avocation: vintage automobile racing. Home: 13623 Larchmere Blvd Shaker Heights OH 44120 Office: Vintage Motorpress Inc 13623 Larchmere Blvd Shaker Heights OH 44120

CANDRL, RONALD PAUL, financial services executive; b. St. Louis, Mar. 2, 1948; s. Paul Steven and Dolores Bernadine (Sextro) C.; m. Charlotte Marie Ostmann, Aug. 14, 1971; children: Michelle, David. BBA, U. Mo., 1970; MBA, Lindenwood Coll., 1977. Accounts payable supr., sr. acct. Monsanto Co., St. Louis, 1970-77; v.p. Arthur Ostmann Gen. Contractor Inc., St. Charles, Mo., 1977-86; pres. Candrl and Co. Inc., St. Charles, 1984—. Served with U.S. Army, 1970-72. Republican. Roman Catholic. Home: 3320 Town and Country Ln Saint Charles MO 63301

CANE, ROY DOUGLAS, anesthesiology educator, researcher; b. Johannesburg, South Africa, Jan. 29, 1945; s. Francis John and Ruby (Nicholas) C. M.B.B.Ch., U. Witwatersrand, South Africa, 1969. Registered specialist anesthetist. Intern, Coronation Hosp., Johannesburg, 1970; registrar in anesthesia Baragwanath Hosp. and U. Witwatersrand Med. Sch., Johannesburg, 1971-73, sr. med. officer, 1974, anesthetist, dir. intensive care, 1975, prin. anesthetitist, dir. intensive care, 1976-77; resident in anesthesia Northwestern U., Chgo., 1974, asst. prof. clin. anesthesia, 1978-81, assoc. prof., asst. dir. respiratory/critical care, 1981-86 , pres. med. faculty senate, 1983-84; prof. clin. anesthesia, 1986—. mem. assoc. attending staff Northwestern Meml. Hosp., 1979-84, attending staff, 1984—, asst. med. dir. dept. respiratory therapy, 1978-84, assoc. med. dir. dept. respiratory therapy, 1985—; lectr. Cook County Grad. Sch. Medicine, 1980—. Fellow Faculty Anesthetists of Coll. Medicine South Africa, 1973. Fellow Am. Coll. Chest Physicians; mem. Am. Assn. Respiratory Therapy, Ill. Soc. Respiratory Therapy (med. adviser 1980-83), Nat. Assn. Med. Dirs. of Respiratory Care, Soc. Critical Care Medicine, Am. Soc. Anesthesiologists, South African Critical Care Medicine Soc. (founder), South African Soc. Anesthetists (Atherstone prize 1972), South African Med. and Dental Council, Assn. Univ. Anesthetists, Med. Grads. Assn. Johannesburg, Chgo. Thoracic Soc., Ill. Soc. Anesthesiology, Sigma Xi. Co-author: Case Studies in Critical Care Medicine, Clinical Application of Respiratory Care, 3d edit. Reviewer for Jour. AMA, Critical Care Medicine, Chest and Respiratory Care, Am. Inst. Biol. Scis., 1982—, NIH, 1983—; editorial cons. Yr. Book Med. Pubs., Aspen Pubs.; editor Year Book of Anesthesia, 1981; contbr. articles, abstracts to profl. jours., chpts. in books. Office: 250 E Superior St Suite 678 Chicago IL 60611

CANEPA, JOHN CHARLES, financial exec.; b. Newburyport, Mass., Aug. 26, 1930; s. John Jere and Agnes R. (Barbour) C.; m. Marie Olney, Sept. 13, 1953; children—Claudia, John J., Peter C., Milissa L. A.B., Harvard U., 1953; M.B.A., N.Y. U., 1960. With Chase Manhattan Bank, N.Y.C., 1957-63; sr. v.p. Provident Bank, Cin., 1963-70; pres. Old Kent Fin. Corp.; pres., Chief exec. officer also Old Kent Bank & Trust Co., Grand Rapids, Mich., 1970—. Served with USN, 1953-57. Office: Old Kent Bank & Trust Co 1 Vandenberg Center Grand Rapids MI 49503 *

CANFIELD, FRANCIS XAVIER, clergyman, educator; b. Detroit, Dec. 3, 1920; s. Edward and Adelle (Berg) C. B.A., Sacred Heart Sem., Detroit, 1941; M.A., Catholic U., 1945; A.M. in L.S, U. Mich., 1950; Ph.D. U. Ottawa, 1951; spl. courses, Notre Dame U., Wayne U., U. Detroit. Ordained priest Roman Cath. Ch., 1945, named domestic prelate, 1963; with English dept. Sacred Heart Sem., Detroit, 1946-70; librarian Sacred Heart Sem., 1948-63, rector-president, 1963-70; pastor St. Paul's Parish, Grosse Pointe Farms, Mich., 1971—; Instr. library sci. Immaculate Heart Coll., Los Angeles, summers 1955-61; Chaplain Detroit Police Dept., 1965—. Author: Condensed History of the Catholic Church in the Archdiocese of Detroit, 1984; Editor: Philosophy and the Modern Mind, 1961, Literature and the Modern Mind, 1963, Political Science and the Modern Mind, 1963; Author articles, book revs. Bd. dirs. Bon Secours Hosp., Grosse Pointe, Mich., 1982—. Mem. Cath. Library Assn. (chmn. Mich. unit 1950-52, 54-56, exec. council 1957-63, pres. 1961-63), Grosse Pointe Ministerial Assn. (pres. 1972-73), Council Nat. Library Assns. (vice chmn. 1962-63), Am. Friends of Vatican Library (pres. 1981—). Home: 157 Lake Shore Grosse Pointe Farms MI 48236

CANJAR, PATRICIA MCWADE, psychologist, marriage counselor; b. Pitts., Mar. 14, 1932; d. Robert Malachai McWade and Lillian Kathryn (Seidenstricker) Robb; m. Lawrence N. Canjar, Aug. 4, 1951 (dec. Nov. 1972); 1 son, R. Michael; m. James M. McDonald, Sept. 24, 1977. A.A., Carlow Coll., 1951; B.A., U. Detroit, 1973, M.A., 1975. Lic. psychologist, Mich. Psychologist, Robinwood Clinic, Detroit, 1973-77, Psychol. Resources, Birmingham, Mich., 1977-80, Realistic Living Ctr., Warren, Mich., 1983-85, Behavior Ctr., Birmingham, 1980-84. Mem. Nat. YWCA Spl. Commn., Boston, N.Y.C. and Washington, 1967; bd. dirs. YWCA, Pitts., 1961-65, Detroit, 1965-67; asst. coordinator United We Sing, Pitts. Music Festival, 1955-65; pres. Carnegie Mellon Women's Club, Pitts., 1963-65, U. Detroit Faculty Wives' Club, 1968-70. Fellow Am. Psychol. Assn.; mem. Mich. Assn. Profl. Psychologist, Mich. Assn. Alcohol and Drug Abuse Counselors. Democrat. Roman Catholic. Office: Eastwood Community Clinic 888 W Big Beaver Troy MI 48084

CANNADY, EDWARD WYATT, JR., physician; b. East St. Louis, Ill., June 20, 1906; s. Edward Wyatt and Ida Bertha (Rose) C.; A.B., Washington U., St. Louis, 1927, M.D., 1931; m. Helen Freeborn, Oct. 20, 1984; children by previous marriage—Edward Wyatt III, Jane Marie (Mrs. Starr). Intern internal medicine Barnes Hosp., St. Louis, 1931-33, resident physician, 1934-35, asst. physician, 1935-74, emeritus, 1974—; asst. resident Peter Bent Brigham Hosp., Boston, 1933-34; fellow in gastroenterology Washington U. Sch. Medicine, 1935-36, instr. internal medicine 1935-74, emeritus, 1974—; cons. internal medicine Washington U. Clinics, 1942-74; physician St. Mary's Hosp., East St. Louis, 1935-77, pres. staff, 1947-49, chmn. med. dept., 1945-47; physician Christian Welfare Hosp., 1935-77, chmn. med. dept., 1939-53, dir. electrocardiography, 1936-77; dir. electrocardiography Centreville Twp. Hosp., East St. Louis. mem. staff Meml. Hosp., Belleville, Ill., St. Elizabeth Hosp., Belleville; pres. C.I.F. Dir. health service East St. Louis pub. schs., 1936-37; chmn. med. adv. bd. Selective Service, 1941-45; pres. St. Clair County Council Aging, 1961-62; chmn. St. Clair County Home Care Program, 1961-68, St. Clair County Med. Soc. Com. Aging, 1960-70; del. White House Conf. Aging, 1961, 71, 81; mem. Adv. Council Improvement Econ. and Social Status Older People, 1959-66; bd. dirs., exec. com. Nat. Council Homemaker Services, 1966-73, chmn. profl. adv. com. 1971-73; bd. dirs. St. Louis Met. Hosp. Planning Commn., 1966-70; mem. Ill. Council Aging, 1966-74; mem. Gov.'s Council on Aging, 1974-76; mem. Ill. Regional Heart Disease, Cancer and Stroke Com.; mem. exec. com. Bi-State Regional Com. on Heart Disease, Cancer and Stroke; pres. Ill. Joint Council to Improve Health Care Aged, 1959-61; dir. Ill. Council Continuing Med. Edn., 1972-77, v.p., 1974-75. Trustee McKendree Coll., 1971-79; adv. bd. Belleville Jr. Coll. Sch. Nursing, 1970-78; bd. dirs. United Fund Greater East St. Louis, 1953-58. Recipient Disting. Service Award Am. Heart Assn., 1957, Disting. Achievement award, 1957; award Ill. Public Health Assn., 1971; Greater Met. St. Louis award in geriatrics, 1976. Diplomate Am. Bd. Internal Medicine. Fellow Am. Coll. Cardiology, Am. Geriatrics Soc., A.C.P. (gov. 1964-70); mem. AMA (ho. dels. 1961-71, mem. aging com.; editorial adv. bd. Chronic Illness News Letter 1962-70, chmn. Ill. delegation 1964-66, mem. council vol. health agys.), Am. (dir. 1956-62, personnel and personnel tng. com. 1956-60), Ill. (pres. 1950-51) heart assns., St. Clair County (pres. 1952, bd. censors 1953-57), Ill. (sec. cardiovascular sect. 1957, chmn. sect., 1958-59; chmn. com. on aging, 1959-69, speaker Ho. Dels. 1964-68, pres. 1969-70) med. socs., Beta Theta Pi, Nu Sigma Nu, Alpha Omega Alpha. Presbyn. Mason. Clubs: St. Clair Country, Mo. Athletic, Media; Palmbrook Country (Sun City, Ariz.). Contbr. articles to med. jours. Home: 7500 Claymont Ct Apt 2 Belleville IL 62223

CANNADY, ROGER LEON, technical training and services company executive; b. St. Louis, June 5, 1946; s. Wilford Leon and Dorothy Alene (Williams) C.; m. Vicki Storne, Sept. 21, 1966; children—Michael Leon, Marcia Lynn. B.S. in E.E., U. Mo., Rolla, 1968. Service supr. Southwestern Bell Telephone, Kansas City, Mo., 1968-69, service supr., Eldon, Mo., 1975-76, service mgr., Hannibal, Mo., 1976-79; regional service mgr. Gen. Dynamics Communications Co., Chgo., 1979-82; nat. service mgr. Thermotron Industries, Holland, Mich., 1983-86, pres. Cannady and Assocs., 1986—. Served to capt., USAF, 1969-74. Decorated Nat. Def. Service medal USAF, 1969; USAF Outstanding Unit award, 1972; Armed Forces Expeditionary medal Republic of Korea, 1973; Vietnam Service medal with 2 battle stars. Mem. Inst. Environ. Sci., Nat. Assn. Service Mgrs., Nat. Rifle Assn. Club: Michigan United Conservation. Home: 372 Evergreen Dr Holland MI 49423

CANNING, FRED FRANCIS, drug store chain executive; b. Chgo., Apr. 1, 1924; s. Fred and Lillian (Popiolek) C.; m. Margaret Luby, Nov. 23, 1944; children: Jeanette, Laura, Debbie, Terry, Patrick, Marggie, Timothy, Kathleen. Registered Pharmacist, Hynes Sch. Pharmacy, 1950. With Walgreen Co., Deerfield, Ill., 1946—; v.p. Walgreen Co., 1972-76; sr. v.p. Walgreen Co. (Drug Store div.), 1976-78; exec. v.p. Walgreen Co., 1978, pres., chief operating officer, 1978—, also dir. Served with USCG, 1942-45. Mem. Am. Pharm. Assn., Am. Mktg. Assn. Roman Catholic. Office: Walgreen Co 200 Wilmot Rd Deerfield IL 60015 *

CANNING, WILLIAM MATTHEW, psychologist, educator; b. Chgo., Sept. 14, 1921; s. William J. and Edith E. (Williams) C.; B.S. in Edn., Northwestern U., 1947, M.A., 1948, Ph.D., 1955; m. Marian H. Connor, Apr. 23, 1955; children—David, Paul, Peter. Instr. psychology St. Louis U., 1949-51; asst. dean, dir. student counseling Northwestern U., Evanston, Ill., 1951-54; tchr., asst. dean Chgo. Tchrs. Coll., 1954-56; dir. Bur. Child Study, Chgo. Bd. Edn., 1956-81; pvt. practice psychology, Barrington, Ill., 1960—; cons. VA, univs., Am. Psychol. Assn., city public sch. systems, Mayor's Commn. on Human Relations, Gov.'s Commn. on Mental Retardation, State Dept. Mental Health, Office State Supt. Public Instrn., State Psychol. Adv. Com. Served to capt. Chem. Corps, U.S. Army, 1943-46. Diplomate Am. Bd. Profl. Psychology. Fellow Am. Psychol. Assn. (mem. exec. bd. div. sch. psychology); mem. Midwestern Psychol. Assn., Phi Delta Kappa. Contbr. articles in field to profl. jours.

CANNON, BENJAMIN WINTON, lawyer, business executive; b. Muncie, Ind., Sept. 17, 1944; s. Zane William and Gloria Gene (Phillips) C.; B.A., Western Mich. U., 1965; postgrad. Notre Dame Law Sch., 1966-67; J.D., Wayne State U., 1969; M.B.A., Mich. State U., 1979; m. Diane Joan Koenig, June 24, 1967; children—Matthew Zane, Christine Elizabeth, Leslie Joan, Todd Graham. Admitted to Mich. bar, 1970; law clk. labor relations staff Gen. Motors Corp., Detroit, 1966-69; tax atty. Plante & Moran, C.P.A.s, Southfield, Mich., 1969-71; atty. Burroughs Corp., Detroit, 1971-72; assoc. Nine and Maister, Attys., Bloomfield Hills, Mich., 1972-73; atty. Chrysler Fin. Corp., Troy, Mich., 1973-78, sr. atty., 1978-80; corp. counsel CF Industries Inc., Long Grove, Ill., 1980-81; asst. gen. counsel, asst. sec. COMDISCO, Inc., Rosemont, Ill., 1981-82, asst. v.p. and gen. mgr. internat., 1983-86, pres. COMDISCO Internat. Sales Corp., 1983-86; asst. v.p., dir. capital equipment fin., 1987—; instr. law Oakland U., Rochester, Mich., 1980. Mem. ABA, Mich. Bar Assn., Ill. Bar Assn., Gray's Inn Legal Soc., Omicron Delta Kappa, Kappa Delta Pi. Republican. Presbyterian. Home: 21265 N Pheasant Trail Barrington IL 60010-2950 Office: 6400 Shafer Ct Rosemont IL 60018

CANNON, CHARLES EARL, research chemist; b. Sylacauga, Ala., Jan. 30, 1946; s. Eugene and Carrie Lue (Clemons) C.; B.S., Ala. A&M U., 1968; postgrad. Vanderbilt U., 1968-69; Ph.D., U. Wis., Milw., 1974. Chemist, Amoco Chems. Corp., Naperville, Ill., 1974-78, Standard Oil Co. Ind., Amoco Research Center, 1978-85, Elmhurst (Ill.) Coll., 1985—; career day speaker high schs.; sci. fair judge. Recipient John Phillip Sousa music award, 1967; Pres.'s trophy for acad. excellence Ala. A&M U., 1968; Knapp Dissertation award, 1974; Ford Found. fellow, 1973-74. Recipient Alumni award Nat. Assn. Equal Opportunity in Higher Edn., 1983. Mem. Am. Chem. Soc. (vice chmn. Chgo. sect. 1980-81, chmn. 1982-83), Am. Inst. Chemists, Nat. Assn. Negro Musicians (bd. dirs. Central region), So. Christian Leadership Conf., NAACP, Nat. Assn. Advancement Black Chemists and Chem. Engrs., Ala. A&M U. Alumni Assn. (pres. 1984—), Beta Kappa Chi, Alpha Kappa Mu. Democrat. Club: R. Nathaniel Dett Club Music and Allied Arts. Home: 3 S 081 Barkley Ave Warrenville IL 60555 Office: Ill Math and Sci Acad 1500 W Sullivan Rd Aurora IL 60505

CANNON, RAEBURN ANN, manufacturing company executive; b. Ft. Atkinson, Wis., July 20, 1910; s. Anthony Edmund and Mary Ann (Williams) O'Malley; m. William Patrick Cannon, June 28, 1941 (dec. July 1984); children: Mary Ann, Catherine, William Patrick Jr., Michael Francis II. AB, Coll. St. Scholastica, 1933; MA, U. Minn., 1936; PhD, U. Mich., 1940. Licensed elem., secondary and coll. tchr. English tchr. Coll. St. Scholastica, Duluth, Minn., 1937-38, Lake Linden (Mich.) High Sch., 1938-41, Frankton (Ind.) Jr. High Sch., 1957-61; pres. Cannon Products, Inc., Elwood, Ind., 1984—; Spanish tutor Culver (Ind.) Acad., 1937-39. Columnist Our Sunday Visitor, 1954-62. Vol. Mercy Hosp., Elwood, 1984—. Mem. AAUW, Nat. Fedn. Press Women (treas. 1976-80), Women's Press Club (treas. 1982—, Kate Milner Rabb award 1984). Republican. Roman Catholic. Avocations: needlework, rose gardening, travel, gourmet cooking.

CANTER, ARTHUR, psychologist; b. Boston, July 8, 1921; s. Harry and Ida Sarah (Janofsky) C.; m. Miriam Louise Rosenbaum, Jan. 24, 1946; children: Andrea Sherril, Laurence Alan. Student, MIT, 1938-40; BA, U. Iowa, 1946, MA, 1948, PhD, 1950. Instr. Ill. Inst. Tech., Chgo., 1950-52; asst. prof. Vanderbilt U., Nashville, 1952-56, Johns Hopkins U., Balt., 1956-60; prof. U. Iowa, Iowa City, 1960-86, prof. emeritus, 1986—; chief psychologist Vanderbilt Hosp., 1952-56, Henry Phipps Psychiat. Clinic Johns Hopkins U., 1956-60; chief psychology services U. Iowa Psychiat. Hosp., 1960-86. Author neuropsychol. test Background Interference Procedure, 1976; contbr. articles to profl. jours. Pres. Pub. Library Bd. Trustees, Iowa City, 1974-75. Served to sgt. U.S. Army, 1942-45, ETO. Fellow Am. Psychol. Assn., Nat. Acad. Neuropsychology (Bronze Plaque 1981, pres. 1976); mem. Midwest Psychol. Assn., Assn. Advancement of Behavior Therapy, Biofeedback Soc. Am. Avocations: musicology, painting. Home: 30 Brookfield Dr Iowa City IA 52240 Office: U Iowa 500 Newton Rd Iowa City IA 52242

CANTON, IRVING DONALD, management consultant; b. N.Y.C., Feb. 10, 1918; s. Louis and Mollie (Wolf) C.; B.Chem. Engring., Coll. City N.Y., 1940; m. Shelly Terman, Sept. 28, 1958; children—Larry, Diana. Engr., U.S. Navy Dept., 1941-45; research group leader Foster D. Snell Inc., N.Y.C., 1945-49; chem. engring. cons. S.Am., 1949-53; asst. dir. Internat. div. Ill. Inst. Tech., Chgo., 1953-61; founding stockholder, v.p. Indsl. Research Mag., Beverly Shores, Ind., 1961-62; dir. comml. devel. and planning Internat. Minerals and Chem. Co., Skokie, Ill., 1962-67; founder, pres. Strategic Decisions Co. mgmt. cons., Chgo., 1968—. Mem. Am. Mktg. Assn. (dir.; v.p. mktg. mgmt. Chgo.), Midwest Planning Assn. (founding; v.p. 1975), Am. Chem. Soc. Contbr. articles to Harvard Bus. Rev., other bus. and profl. jours. Home: 4141 Grove St Skokie IL 60076 Office: 1 Northfield Plaza Northfield IL 60093

CANTONI, LOUIS JOSEPH, psychologist, poet; b. Detroit, May 22, 1919; s. Pietro and Stella (Puricelli) C.; m. Lucile Eudora Moses, Aug. 7, 1948; children: Christopher Louis, Sylvia Therese. A.B., U. Calif., Berkeley, 1946; M.S.W., U. Mich., 1949, Ph.D., 1953. Personnel mgr. Johns-Manville Corp., Pittsburg, Calif., 1944-46; social caseworker Detroit Dept. Pub. Welfare, 1946-49; counselor Mich. Div. Vocat. Rehab., Detroit, 1949-50; conf. leader, tchr. psychology, coordinator family and community relations program Gen. Motors Inst., Flint, Mich., 1951-56; from assoc. prof. to prof., dir. rehab. counseling Wayne State U., Detroit, 1956—; cons. Social Security Adminstrn., 1986-87. Author books including: Marriage and Community Relations, 1954, (with Mrs. Cantoni) Counseling Your Friends, 1961, Supervised Practice in Rehabilitation Counseling, 1978, Writings of Louis J. Cantoni, 1981; (poetry) With Joy I Called to You, 1969, Gradually The Dreams Change, 1979. Editor: Placement of the Handicapped in Competitive Employment, 1957; co-editor: Preparation of Vocational Rehabilitation Counselors through Field Instruction, 1958; prin. editor: (poetry) Golden Song Anthology, 1985. Editor jours.: Mich. Rehab. Assn. Digest, 1961-63, Grad. Comment, 1963-64; poetry editor Cathedral Digest, 1973-75. Contbr. articles, revs. and poems to jours. Judge Mich. regional and nat. essay and poetry contests, 1965-77; bd. dirs. Mich. Rehab. Assn., 1962-64, 78-79,

Mich. Rehab. Conseling Assn., 1985-87. Served to 2d lt. AUS, 1942-44. Recipient award for leadership and service Mich. Rehab. Assn., 1964, Mich. Rehab. Counseling Assn., 1985, 87; South and West ann. poetry award, 1970; Award for Meritorious Service Wayne State U., 1971, 81, 86, 87; Outstanding Service award Poetry Soc. Mich., 1984. Fellow AAAS; mem. AAUP, Council of Rehab. Counselor Educators (sec. 1957-58, chmn. 1965-66), Am. Psychol. Assn., Am. Assn. Counseling and Devel., Nat. Rehab. Assn., Nat. Assn. Rehab. Profls. in Pvt. Sector, Mich. Rehab. Assn. (pres. 1963-64), Detroit Rehab. Assn. (pres. 1958), World Poetry Soc., Acad. Am. Poets, Detroit Inst. Arts, Poetry Soc. Mich., Phi Kappa Phi, Phi Delta Kappa. Democrat. Episcopalian. Clubs: Faculty, Scarab (Detroit). Home: 2591 Woodstock Dr Detroit MI 48203 Office: Wayne State Univ Detroit MI 48202

CANTOR, BERNARD JACK, patent lawyer; b. N.Y.C., Aug. 18, 1927; s. Alexander J. and Tillie (Henzeloff) C.; m. Judith L. Levin, Mar. 25, 1951; children—Glenn H., Cliff A., James E., Ellen B., Mark E. B. Mech. Engring., Cornell, 1949; J.D., George Washington U., Washington, 1952. Bar: D.C. bar 1952, U.S. Patent Office bar 1952, Mich. bar 1953. Examiner U.S. Patent Office, Washington, 1949-52; practice patent law Detroit, 1952—; partner firm Cullen, Sloman, Cantor, Grauer, Scott & Rutherford, Detroit, 1952—; lectr. in field. Contbr. articles on patent law to profl. jours. Mem. exec. council Detroit Area Boy Scouts Am., 1972—; trustee Fresh Air Soc. of Detroit. Served with U.S. Army, 1944-46. Recipient Ellsworth award patent law George Washington U., 1952, Shofar award Boy Scouts Am., 1975, Silver Beaver award, 1975, Disting. Eagle award, 1985. Mem. Am. Technion Soc. (bd. dirs. Detroit 1970—), ABA, Mich. Bar Assn., Detroit Bar Assn., Mich. Patent Law Assn., Am. Arbitration Assn., Cornell Engring. Soc., Pi Tau Sigma, Phi Delta Phi, Beta Sigma Rho. Home: 5685 Forman Dr Birmingham MI 48010 Office: 2400 City Nat Bldg Detroit MI 48226

CAPALDI, DANTE JAMES, biochemist, researcher; b. Windsor, Ont., Can., Sept. 4, 1957; s. Loreto and Mariangela (Iaconelli) C.; m. Vilma Kathleen Andreolli, July 23, 1983. BS (hon.), U. Windsor, 1980, PhD, 1983. Biochemist U. Mich., Ann Arbor, 1983-84; biochemist, researcher Henry Ford Hosp., Detroit, 1984-85; scientist Nuclear Diagnostics, Troy, Mich., 1985-87, Leeco Diagnostics, Southfield, Mich., 1987—; vis. scholar U. Mich., 1984-85; adj. lectr. in chemistry U. Mich., Dearborn, 1985—. Contbr. articles to profl. jours. Dist. rep. Liberal Party Can., Essex-Windsor, 1979-84. Mem. Am. Chem. Soc., Am. Assn. Clin. Chemistry, Chem. Inst. Can., Canadian Biochem. Soc., Canadian Soc. Clin. Chemists, Soc. Chem. Industry, N.Y. Acad. Sci. Roman Catholic. Avocation: photography. Home: 697 Front Rd N, Amherstburg, ON Canada N9V 2V6 Office: Leeco Diagnostics 21705 Evergreen Southfield MI 48075

CAPALDO, GUY, gynecologist obstetrician; b. Bisaccia, Italy, Jan. 1, 1950; came to U.S., 1958; s. Arturo Nunziante and Maria Carmela (Ciani) C.; m. Kathy Nicita, Apr. 20, 1985. BSEE magna cum laude, U. Dayton, 1972; MS, Ohio State U., Columbus, 1973; MD, Med. Coll. Ohio, 1978. Diplomate Am. Bd. Ob-Gyn. Research asst. Ohio State U., 1973-75; resident in ob-gyn Med. Coll. Ohio, Toledo, 1978-82; practice medicine specializing in ob-gyn Mansfield, Ohio, 1982—; chief ob-gyn dept. Mansfield Gen. Hosp., 1985—. Clinic physician Plan Parenthood, Mansfield, 1982—. Pres. scholar U. Dayton, 1968-72, Univ. fellow Ohio State U., 1972-75. Fellow Am. Coll. Ob-Gyn; mem. AMA, Ohio State Med. Assn., Richland County Med. Soc. Avocation: reading. Office: Mansfield Ob-Gyn Assocs 500 S Trimble Rd Mansfield OH 44906

CAPATI, ANA CAMAYA, physician; b. Guagua, Pampanga, Philippines, July 26, 1937; d. Maximino L. and Leonor (Songo) Camaya; m. Nazario R. Capati, Dec. 10, 1958; children: Anne Marie, Carmel. AA, U. Santo Tomas, Manila, 1954; MD, U. Santo Tomas, 1959. Intern Youngstown (Ohio) Hosp. Assn., 1959-61, resident in gen. practice, 1961-62; resident in anesthesiology St. Joseph's Hosp., Warren, Ohio, 1962-64; practice medicine specializing in anesthesiology Neillsville, Wis., 1967-1976; gen. practice medicine Neillsville, 1976—; med. dir. Fairchild Nursing Homes, Neillsville, 1976—. Named Physician Yr. Wis. Nursing Home Assn., 1986. Mem. AMA, Clark County Med. Soc. (sec. 1968-74, pres. 1975). Roman Catholic. Home: Rt 1 Box 16 Neillsville WI 54456 Office: Neillsville Clinic 216 Sunset Pl Neillsville WI 54456

CAPAUL, RAYMOND WILLIAM, acoustical manufacturing engineer; b. Lambertville, Mich., Nov. 4, 1912; s. William Caspar and Mary (Gess) C.; m. Gertrude May Steakley, June 24, 1939; children: Raymond Jr., Barry Douglas, Marcia Louise Capaul Oliver. BEE, Toledo U., 1936. Cert. electrical engr., Ohio, Ill. Power sales engr. Toledo Edison Co., 1936-48; v.p. mktg. Glass Fibers, Inc., Toledo, 1948-56, cons. engr., 1956-59; pres., chief exec. officer Capaul Corp., Plainfield, Ill., 1959—. Patentee acoustical wall and ceiling panel systems. Mem. Gov. Thompsons Small Bus. Adv. Com. Served to lt. USN, 1943-46. Mem. Acoustical Soc. Am., Am. Soc. Physics, Nat. Fed. Ind. Bus., Ill. Mfg. Assn. Republican. Presbyterian. Lodge: Shriners. Avocations: golf. fishing. Home: Rt 3 Box 643 Wildwood Dr Aurora IL 60504

CAPEK, VLASTIMIL, radiologist, educator; b. Kosice, Czechoslavakia, Jan. 27, 1925; came to U.S., 1968; s. Josef and Marie (Linhart) C.; m. Miloslava Bienerova, 1950; children: Michael, Paul. MD, Charles U., 1950. Head dept. radiology Hosp. Cheb, Czechoslovakia, 1954-57; asst. head dept. radiology Inst. Postgrad. Med. Edn., Prague, Czechoslovakia, 1957-66; head radiology dept. 6th Dist. Health, Prague, 1966-68; staff radiologist U. Ill. Hosp., Chgo., 1968-73, prof., head dept. radiology, 1973—; cons. VA Hosp., Chgo., 1970—, Hinsdale (Ill.) Hosp., 1972—, Portes Cancer Prevention Ctr., Chgo., 1974-78. Contbr. articles to profl. jours. Mem. AMA, Am. Coll. Radiology, Soc. Chmn. Acad. Radiology, Assn. Univ. Radiologists, Roentgen Ray Soc. Office: U Ill Hosp Dept Radiology 1740 W Taylor Chicago IL 60612

CAPLING, ROBERT DAVID, osteopath; b. Kitchener, Ont., Can., Dec. 7, 1922; came to U.S., 1947; s. Ephraim John and Beulah Dell (Eby) C.; m. Betty Marcia Wales, June 19, 1948; children: Mara Lee Searing, Wendy S. Bass, Robin L. Randall, David J. Student, U. Western Ont., 1945-47; DO, Chgo. Coll. Osteo. Medicine, 1951. Intern Chgo. Coll. Osteo. Medicine, 1951-52, resident in ob-gyn, 1952-53; practice medicine specializing in osteopathy Pittsville, Wis., 1954—; health officer City of Pittsville and surrounding twps., 1955—. Clk. Pittsville Pub. Sch. Bd. Edn., 1955-57. Served with Royal Can. Navy, 1943-45. Mem. Wis. Assn. Physicians and Surgeions (pres. 1965-66), Am. Coll. Gen. Practitioners of Osteo. Medicine and Surgery, Assn. Osteo. Physicians and Surgeons, Wis. Soc. Am. Coll. Gen. Practitioners (pres. 1967-68, Gen. Practitioner of Yr. 1977). Republican. Mem. United Ch. of Christ. Lodges: Lions (pres. Pittsville chpt. 1958-59), Masons (master 1961), Order of Eastern Star (worthy patron 1959). Avocations: fishing, camping, golf. Office: 5335 2d Ave PO Box 98 Pittsville WI 54466

CAPONIGRO, JEFFREY RALPH, public relations counselor; b. Kankakee, Ill., Aug. 13, 1957; s. Ralph A. and Barbara Jean (Paul) C.; m. Ellen Colleen Kennedy, Oct. 15, 1982; children: Nicholas J., Michael J. B.A., Cen. Mich. U., 1979. Sports reporter Observer and Eccentric newspapers, Rochester, Mich., 1974-75, Mt. Pleasant (Mich.) Times, 1975-77, Midland (Mich.) Daily News, 1977-79; account exec. Desmond & Assocs., Oak Park, Mich., 1979-80; v.p. Anthony M. Franco, Inc., Detroit, 1980-84; exec. v.p. Casey Communications Mgmt., Inc., Southfield, 1984—. Mem. Pub. Relations Soc. Am. (bd. dirs., officer Detroit chpt.), Adcraft Club of Detroit. Club: Detroit Athletic. Contbr.: Best Sports Stories, 1978. Home: 2873 Mayfair Troy MI 48084 Office: Casey Communications Mgmt Inc 17117 Nine Mile Rd Suite 700 Southfield MI 48075

CAPORALE, D. NICK, state supreme court judge; b. Omaha, Sept. 13, 1928; s. Michele and Lucia (DeLuca) C.; m. Margaret Nilson, Aug. 5, 1950; children: Laura Diane Caporale Stevenson, Leland Alan. B.A., U. Nebr.-Omaha, 1949, M.Sc., 1954; J.D. with distinction, U. Nebr.-Lincoln, 1957. Bar: Nebr. 1957, U.S. Dist. Ct. Nebr. 1957, U.S. Ct. Appeals 8th cir. 1958, U.S. Supreme Ct. 1970. Mem. firm Stoehr, Rickerson, Sodoro & Caporale, Omaha, 1957-66; ptnr. Schmid, Ford, Mooney, Frederick & Caporale, Omaha, 1966-79; judge Nebr. Dist. Ct., Omaha, 1979-81, Nebr. Supreme Ct., Lincoln, 1982—; lectr. U. Nebr., Lincoln, 1982-84. Pres. Omaha Community Playhouse, 1976. Served to 1st lt. U.S. Army, 1952-54, Korea. Decorated Bronze Star; recipient Alumni Achievement U. Nebr.-Omaha, 1972. Fellow Am. Coll. Trial Lawyers, Internat. Soc. Barristers. Office: Room 2222 State House 1445 K St Lincoln NE 68509

CAPPS, NORMAN EDWARD, computer education executive; b. Topeka, June 25, 1933; s. Thomas P. and Mae (McCabe) C.; m. Shirley Lytle, Nov. 24, 1956; children: Linda, Leane. BSA, U. Kans., 1955; BA in Fgn. Trade, Am. Inst. Internatl. Mgmt., 1956. Internatl. sales staff Wilson & Co., Inc., Chgo., London, 1956-65; pres. Electronic Computer Programming Inst., Kansas City, Mo., 1966—; pres. Mo. Assn. Private Career Schs., Kansas City, 1974. Mem. Mo. Job Training Coordinating Council, Jefferson City, 1983—; v.p. Lyric Opera Kansas City, 1984—. Recipient Meritorious Service award Kansas City Police Dept., 1975. Mem. Data Processing Mgmt. Assn. (pres. 1969-70, Performance award), Assn. for Systems Mgmt. (pres. 1977-78, Disting. Service award), Greater Kansas City C. of C. (vice chmn. 1984-86), Omicron Delta Kappa. Clubs: Carriage (Kansas City), Kansas City (pres. 711 Club 1984—). Lodge: Rotary (pres. 1979-80). Home: One Dunford Circle Kansas City MO 64112 Office: Electronic Computer Programming Inst 611 W 39th St Kansas City MO 64111

CAPPY, JOSEPH E., automobile company executive; b. 1934; married. BBA, U. Wis., 1956. With Ford Motor Co., 1956-80, mktg. plans mgr., custom cars and light trucks, 1969-71, gen. field sales mgr. Detroit dist., 1971-72, spl. projects mgr. recreational vehicles, 1972-73, recreational products sales mgr., 1973-74, dir. mktg. staff, sales planning office, 1974-77; dist. sales mgr. Ford Motor Co., Louisville, 1977-78; mktg. plans mgr. Lincoln-Mercury div. Ford Motor Co., 1978-80, gen. mktg. mgr. Lincoln-Mercury div., 1980; v.p. mktg. Am. Motors Corp., Southfield, Mich., 1982-84, group v.p. sales and mktg., 1984-85, exec. v.p., chief operating officer, 1985, chief exec. officer, 1986—; now pres., bd. dirs. Am. Motor Sales Corp. (subs. Am. Motors Corp.), 1985—. Office: Am Motors Corp 27777 Franklin Rd Southfield MI 48034

CAPRA, RICHARD D., electrical equipment company executive; b. St. Louis, Sept. 21, 1932; s. August Francis and Dorothy Ida (Hicks) C.; m. JoAnn Arnold, Oct. 6, 1956; children—Sharilyn, Karen, Michael. B.S. in Commerce, St. Louis U., 1954. Mng. assoc. Arthur Young and Co., N.Y.C., 1960-65; controller Mobil Chem., N.Y.C., 1965-70; group v.p. Gould ITE, Chgo. and Phila., 1970-79; v.p., then pres. Richardson Witco Chem., Des Plaines, Ill., 1979-83; exec. v.p. Advance Transformer, Chgo., 1983, pres., 1983—. Served with U.S. Army, 1954-56. Mem. Am. Inst. C.P.A.s. Office: Advance Transformer Co 2950 N Western Ave Chicago IL 60618

CAPRARO, MICHAEL ANTHONY, chemical engineer; b. Detroit, Nov. 19, 1948; s. Anthony and Lucille (Caporosso) C.; B.S., Wayne State U., 1970, M.S., 1974; m. Myrna Lee Bolton, Aug. 28, 1971; children—Ernest Anthony, Rachel Elaine, Ellen Janelle. With BASF (Mich.) Corp., 1970—, plant technologist, 1979-83, research assoc., 1983-84, research supr., 1984—. Chmn. St. Cyprian Parish Council. Mem. Am. Inst. Chem. Engrs., Tau Beta Pi. Roman Catholic. Home: 13998 Kingswood St Riverview MI 48192 Office: BASF Corp 1609 Biddle St Wyandotte MI 48192

CAPRIOTTI, MARCIA SWANSON, paralegal; b. St. Charles, Ill., Mar. 6, 1951; d. Albert Roy and Estelle Bernice (Drake) Swanson; m. Bruce Warren, May 31, 1980. BA, Clarke Coll., 1973. Cert. paralegal. Staff aide Dem. Congressman Mich., Hon. John Conyers Jr., Washington, 1973-74; tchr. Geneva (Ill.) Sch. Dist., 1974-76; bi-lingual aide Batavia (Ill.) Sch. Dist., 1977; asst. mgr. Lord & Taylor, Aurora, Ill., 1977-80; bailiff Superior Ct., South Bend, Ind., 1984—. Mem. AAUW (bd. dirs. 1984—), Women's Com. on Sexual Offenses (bd. dirs. 1985-87). Roman Catholic. Home: 1410 McKinley South Bend IN 46617

CARAHER, JOHN FRANCIS, manufacturing company executive; b. Chgo., Oct. 2, 1932; s. Edward Patrick and Loretta Celia (Shanahan) C.; m. Catherine Hynes, Dec. 26, 1953; children: John, Catherine, Charles, Patrick, Jeanne. BS in Bus., Chgo. State U., 1979. CPA, Ill. Fire fighter Chgo. Fire Dept., 1959-63, fire engr., 1963-78, fire lt., 1978-84; acct. Pheian, Johnson, McGreal, Oak Lawn, Ill., 1980-84; treas. Advanced Pulver Systems, Chicago Ridge, Ill., 1984—. Served to 1st lt. USAF, 1952-57. Roman Catholic. Avocation: golf. Home: 7617 W Sycamore Dr Orland Park IL 60462 Office: Advanced Pulver Systems 10255 S Ridgeland Chicago Ridge IL 60415

CARANO, JOHN JOSEPH, JR, foundry products sales manager; b. Warren, Ohio, Oct. 19, 1954; s. John Joseph and Theresa Rose (Mattinat) C.; m. Teresa Helen Scott, Oct. 4, 1980. BS in Edn., Youngstown State U., 1979. Sales trainee Nat. Castings div. Midland Ross Corp., Sharon, Pa., 1979-80, coordinator mktg. services , sales rep. RR products, Chgo., 1980-81, sales rep. indsl. castings, Sharon, 1981-82, dist. sales mgr. mining and mill sales, Columbus, Ohio, 1982-86, regional sales mgr. midwest sales, Nat. Castings, Inc., Columbus, 1986—. Mem. Hubbard Vol. Fire Dept., Ohio, 1975-79; active Ohio Hist. Soc., Columbus, 1984—, Cat Welfare Assn., Ind. Coal Mining Inst., Misty Meadows Civic Assn., Northwest Civic Assn. Mem. Am. Mktg. Assn., Am. Foundrymen's Soc., Am. Acad. Polit. and Social Sci., Youngstown State U. Alumni Assn. Democrat. Roman Catholic. Clubs: Columbus Italian, Unity, Toastmasters (Columbus) (v.p. local chpt. 1984, pres. 1987—, Best Pub. Speaker award 1984-85, Pub. Debate speaker award 1984, Best Speaker Evaluator award 1985). Avocations: running, book collecting, home repair and restoration. Home: 2667 Delcane Dr Columbus OH 43220-1712 Office: Nat Castings Inc 1400 S Laramie Ave Cicero IL 60650

CARBONE, ALFONSO ROBERT, construction executive; b. Cleve., Jan. 17, 1921; s. Rosario P. and Carmela (Mandalfino) C.; student Sch. Architecture, Case Western Res. U. and Case Inst. Tech., 1940-42; BArch, 1946; m. Anna Mae Simmons, June 16, 1945; children—Carmela, Florence Roberta, Rosario P. II, Anne Marie. Ptnr., v.p. estimator R.P. Carbone Constrn. Co., Cleve., 1940-77, owner, pres., 1977-82, chmn. bd., 1983—. Alt. builder rep. mem. City of Cleve., Bd. Bldg. Standards and Bldg. Appeals, 1953-64, builder rep. mem., 1964-74, chmn., 1965-74; past chmn. Cleve. Air Pollution Appeals Bd. Mem. Bus. Men's Club, Central YMCA, Cleve.; mem. Nat. UN Day Com., 1971-80; trustee, past chmn. resources and personnel com. Alta House, pres. bd. trustees, 1981-83, chmn. devel. and govt. relations com., 1983—; bd. dirs. Neighborhood Ctrs. Assn., 1981-84; del. Assembly of United Way Services of Cleve., 1981-84; commd. extraordinary minister for adminstrn. of Holy Communion by Cath. Ch., 1974, also councilman, pres. parish council, 1985-87 . Served with U.S. Coast and Geodetic Survey, Washington, 1942-45. Recipient Alpha Rho Chi medal, 1946; decorated cavalier Order Star Solidarity (Italy); papal cavaliere Order St. Gregory. Mem. Cleve. Engring. Soc., Assoc. Gen. Contractors Am., Builders Exchange Cleve., Holy Name Soc., Ohio Bldg. Insps. Assn., Citizen League Cleve., Greater Cleve. Growth Assn., Order Sons Italy Am. (past grand orator, past pres. lodge, grand trustee officer, state parliamentarian), Epsilon Delta Rho. Home: 3324 Aberdeen Rd Shaker Heights OH 44120 Office: 6449 Wilson Mills Rd Cleveland OH 44143

CARDA, DANIEL DAVID, geochemist; b. Tyndall, S.D., Sept. 16, 1943; s. Daniel J. and Mildred (Holy) C. BS, S.D. Sch. Mines and Tech., 1968, MS, 1971, PhD, 1975. Asst. dir. Expt. Sta., S.D. Sch. Mines and Tech., Rapid City, 1975-83; dir. lab. and quality control Lien Metals, Inc., Rapid City, 1983-85; v.p. Chlor-Pure Corp., Rapid City, 1985—. Served with U.S. Army, 1968-70. Mem. Am. Chem. Soc., Nat. Assn. Corrosion Engrs., ASTM, AIME, Sigma Xi, Alpha Chi Sigma. Roman Catholic. Home: PO Box 9283 Rapid City SD 57709 Office: Chlor-Pure Corp 2561 Deadwood Ave Rapid City SD 57702

CARDEN, TERRENCE STEPHEN, JR., physician; b. Scranton, Pa., Mar. 12, 1938; s. Terrence S. and Jean (McGuire) C.; B.S., U. Scranton, 1960; M.S. in Journalism, Columbia U., 1961; M.D., Jefferson Med. Coll., 1971; m. Coralie Hall; children—Terrence Stephen III, Andrea. Copy editor Phila. Inquirer, 1961-63; wire editor Scranton (Pa.) Times 1963-66; public relations dir. Mercy Hosp., Scranton, 1966-67; copy editor Phila. Bull., 1967-69; intern Duke U. Med. Center, Durham, N.C., 1971-72, resident, 1972; practice medicine specializing in emergency medicine and family practice, Highland Park, Ill., 1973—, Lake Forest, Ill., 1974—, Ingleside, Ill., 1978-81, Round Lake, Skokie, Ill., 1980—, Atlanta, 1981-84; Glenview, Ill., 1983—, Chgo., 1983—, Addison, Ill., 1984—, Long Grove, Ill., 1985—; dir. emergency services Highland Park Hosp., since 1974—; med. dir. South Lake County Mobile Intensive Care Program, 1974—; dir. emergency services Lake Forest Hosp., 1974-80; pres. Emergency Physicians Group, Ltd., Prairie View, Ill., 1974—; clin. asso. prof. dept. surgery Chgo. Med. Sch., Downey, Ill., 1977—; mem. adv. bd. Statewide Mobile Intensive Care, Ill. Dept. Health, 1977-78; dir. First Nat. Bank of Lincolnshire, 1978-81. Bd. dirs., chmn. emergency care com. Lake County Heart Assn., 1977-83; state conv. publicity aide Pa. Assn. for Retarded Children, 1966. Diplomate Am. Bd. Family Practice, Am. Bd. Emergency Medicine. Mem. Am. Coll. Emergency Physicians, Am. Acad. Family Physicians, Inst. of Medicine Chgo., Ill. Med. Soc., Am. Trauma Soc., Lake County Med. Soc., U. Assn. Emergency Med. Services, Gibbon Surg. Soc., Physicians Nat. Housestaff Assn. (alt. regional rep. 1972-73), U. Scranton Alumni Soc. (nat. sec. 1967), Jefferson Med. Coll. Alumni Assn., Hobart Amory Hare Honor Med. Soc., Alpha Omega Alpha, Alpha Sigma Nu (v.p. Scranton chpt. 1959-60). Clubs: Chgo. Yacht, Gordon Setter Am., Gordon Highlanders, Fox River Valley Kennel. Author: (with R.H. Daffner and J.A. Gehweiler) Case Studies in Radiology, 1975; contbr. editorials to New Physician publ., 1971-75; contbg. editor Jour. Am. Med. Assn., 1977-80; copy editor Introduction to History of General Surgery, 1968. Home: 23636 N Elm Rd Mundelein IL 60060 Office: 430 Milwaukee Ave Prairie View IL 60069

CARDER, TERRY D., printing company executive. Chmn., pres., chief exec. officer Reynolds & Reynolds Co., Dayton, Ohio. Officer: Reynolds & Reynolds Co 15 S Ludlow St Dayton OH 45402 *

CARDUCCI, BERNARDO JOSEPH, psychology educator, consultant; b. Detroit, May 20, 1952; s. Edward and Mary (Bosco) C.; 1 child, Rozana. AA, Mt. San Antonio Coll., 1972; BA, Calif. State U., Fullerton, 1974, MA, 1976; PhD, Kans. State U., 1981. Asst. prof. psychology Ind. U.-S.E., New Albany, 1979—; textbook mktg. cons.; stress workshop dir.; research supr., tchr. Author: Instructor's Manual to Accompany Mehr's Abnormal Psychology, 1983; mem. editorial bd. Jour. Bus. and Psychology; contbr. numerous articles to profl. jours. Recipient Most Cert. of Merit award Mt. San Antonio Coll. Associated Men Students, 1971; Service award Ingleside Mental Health Ctr., 1976; Outstanding Faculty Contbn. award Ind. U.-S.E., 1981. Mem. Am. Psychol. Assn., Soc. for Personality and Social Psychology, Midwestern Psychol. Assn., Council Undergrad. Psychology Depts. (pres. 1985-87), Southeastern Psychol. Assn., Soc. for Psychol. Study Social Issues, Psi Chi (recipient cert. recognition for outstanding research 1974). Home: 4002 Summer Pl New Albany IN 47150 Office: Dept Psychology Ind U SE New Albany IN 47150

CARELLA, JOSEPH DINO, entrepreneur, export/import company executive; b. Belleville, Ill., Oct. 26, 1955; m. Deborah Kay Moore, July 14, 1984; 1 child, Bryan Anthony. AS in Bus., Waubonsee Community Coll., 1975; BS in Bus. Mktg., No. Ill. U., 1977; cert., DuPage Sch. Real Estate, 1978. Lic. real estate agt., ins. salesman, Ill. Pres., founder JDC Mktg. Internat., Geneva, Ill., 1977—; real estate salesperson Rizzo & Assocs., Chgo., 1978-79; mktg. dir. Acctg. Mgmt. Services, Aurora, Ill., 1984-85; founder, co-owner Orion Specialty Printing, Geneva, Ill., 1986—. Author: 30 Small Business Mistakes, 1981. Coach Tri-Cities Soccer Assn. Mem. Am. Entrepreneurs Assn., Internat. Traders Assn., Waubonsee Community Coll. Alumni Assn. (v.p. 1985-87, pres. 1987—, founding bd. dirs. 1983), Phi Theta Kappa. Roman Catholic. Lodge: Moose. Avocations: camping, fishing, sailing, soccer. Office: JDC Mktg Internat PO Box 361 Geneva IL 60134

CAREY, EDWARD MARSHEL, JR., accounting co. exec.; b. Washington, Pa., June 12, 1942; s. Edward Marshel and Mildred Elizabeth (Bradley) C.; B.S. in Bus. Adminstrn., Greenville (Ill.) Coll., 1964; m. Naomi Ruth Davis, June 1, 1964; children—Martha Ann, Mary Louise. Accountant, Gen. Motors Corp., Anderson, Ind., 1964-68, supr. accounting, 1968-70; staff accountant Carter, Kirlin & Merrill, C.P.A.s, Indpls., 1970-74, partner, 1974—, pres. CKM Mgmt., Inc., Indpls., 1985—. Mem. Am. Inst. C.P.A.s (mgmt. of accounting practice com. 1976-80, chmn. com. 1978-80, mgmt. adv. services com. 1980-83, chmn. com. 1982-83, dir. Indpls. chpt. 1977-83, treas. 1978-79, pres. 1979-80), Nat. Assn. Accountants, Am. Mgmt. Assn., Inst. Internal Auditors (dir.), Greenville Coll. Alumni Assn. (dir., treas. Ind. chpt. 1980-82). Republican. Methodist. Club: Indpls. Athletic. Home: 215 Royal Oak Ct Zionsville IN 46077 Office: 9102 N Meridian St Indianapolis IN 46260

CAREY, GERALD EUGENE, veterinarian; b. St. Joseph, Mo., July 12, 1944; s. Earl Victor and Emma Jean (Ensign) C.; B.S., U. Mo.-Columbia, 1966, D.V.M., 1968; m. Donna Louise Graf, June 3, 1967; children—Jeffrey Jay, Mark Christopher, Allison Beth, Amanda Christine. Unit head dog and cat quarantine unit NIH, Bethesda, Md., 1968-70; individual practice small animal medicine, surgery Kansas City, Mo., 1970-73, Blue Springs, Mo., 1973—. Bd. dirs. Jackson County (Mo.) United Way, 1975-78, Chapel Hill Early Childhood Center; active Boy Scouts Am. Served with commd. corps USPHS, 1968-70. Recipient Pizer award, 1967. Mem. Kansas City (pres. 1977), Mo. (alt. dist. del. 1978-81, chmn. small animal disease control com. 1978-79), Am. vet. med. assns. Mo. Acad. Veterinarians. Presbyterian (elder, pres. bd. trustees 1978), Club: Kiwanis. Home: Route 2 Box 58 Blue Springs MO 64015 Office: Blue Springs Animal Hospital 1201 W 40 Hwy Blue Springs MO 64015

CAREY, GREGORY BRIAN, magazine publisher; b. St. Paul, Jan. 11, 1942; s. George Harris and Kathleen B. (Prew) C.; m. Mary Beth Hearnen, Jan. 24, 1968; children: Stacy, Jason. Student, U. Minn., 1960-62, Metro State U., 1983—. Advt. sales Mpls. Star & Tribune, 1963-69; advt. mgr. Rapid City (S.D.) Jour., 1969-72; v.p. sales Conway Publs., Atlanta, 1972-77; advt. dir. Family Handy Man, St. Paul, 1977-84, publisher, 1984—. Avocations: golf, photography, antiques. Home: 1000 Knob Hill Rd Burnsville MN 55337 Office: The Family Handyman The Webb Co 1999 Shepard Rd Saint Paul MN 55116

CAREY, JOANNA ANTOINETTE, professional society administrator; b. Douglas, Mich., Sept. 1, 1937; d. Edwin Albert and Marion Frances (Koscinski) C. BS in Psychology, Loyola U., 1963, postgrad. in Health Care Law, 1986—. Registrar Loyola U. Med. Sch., Chgo., 1955-59; asst. dir. pub. relations ADA, Chgo., 1959-72; dir. communications Acad. Gen. Dentistry, Chgo., 1972-75; exec. dir. Internat. Assn. Orthodontics, Chgo., 1975—, Am. Acad. Gnathologic Orthopedics, Chgo., 1985—; pub. relations cons. Am. Soc. Oral Surgery, Chgo., 1971-73. Editor Am. Student Dental Assn., 1970-75, Internat. Coll. Dentistry (Gold Pen award 1982). Bd. dirs. Cicero (Ill.) Community Orgn., 1968-75. Mem. ADA (credit union 1960—, pres. 1968-74), Am. Assn. Dental Editors. Chgo. Assn. Health Care Execs. (pres. 1986—), Am. Assn. Women Dentists (hon. 1968), Nat. Dental Assn. (hon. 1972), Pub. Relations Soc. Am. (writer pub. relations campaign, Gold Eagle award 1969). Roman Catholic. Avocations: farming, golf, tennis, horseback riding. Office: Internat Assn for Orthdontics 211 E Chicago Ave #915 Chicago IL 60611

CARGIN, CONNIE LOESCH, nursing home administrator; b. Jefferson City, Mo., Nov. 1, 1955; d. Norman Richard and Donnabell Roseanne (Fischer) Loesch; m. Thomas Clad Cargin, Sept. 13, 1980. BBA, Cen. Mo. State U., 1976; postgrad., U. Mo., Kansas City. CPA, Mo.; licensed nursing home adminstr. Semi-sr. auditor Mo. State Auditor's Office, Jefferson City, 1976-79; sr. auditor Baird, Kurtz & Dobson, Kansas City, 1979-82; dir. fin. Kingswood Manor, Kansas City, 1982—. Mem. Statue of Liberty-Ellis Island Found., N.Y.C., 1983-87. Mem. Am. Inst. CPA's, Am. Bus. Women's Assn. (pres., v.p., treas. 1980-87), Mo. soc. CPA's, Kansas City C. of C. (mem. bus. edn. com.), Alpha Omicron Pi (mem. alumni chpt. corp. bd.). Club: Overland Park Athletic. Avocations: scuba diving, skiing, racquetball. Office: Kingswood Manor 10000 Wornall Rd Kansas City MO 64114

CARICO, WILLIAM L., small business owner; b. Urbana, Ill., Jan. 25, 1936; s. William Herman and Dorothy (Slightom) C.; m. Mary Margaret Franklin (dec. Jan. 1964); m. Pamela Ann Christensen, July 10, 1964; children: Kimry K., Kevin M. Grad. high sch., Champaign, Ill. Installer siding H.E. Moore Co., Champaign, 1964-67; pres. Illini Siding and Insulation,

Champaign, 1977-82, Illini Insulations, Inc., Champaign, 1982—. Served as sgt. U.S. Army, 1953-59, Korea. Named Contractor of Yr. Revere Corp., Chgo., 1980, Contractor of Yr. Vipco Corp., Chgo., 1981. Republican. Baptist. Lodge: Moose. Avocations: fishing, scuba diving, travel. Home and Office: Illini Insulations Inc 2160 NE 39th St Ocala FL 32670-2508

CARL, EARL GEORGE, social worker; b. Wooster, Ohio, Sept. 14, 1924; s. Earl George and Effie (Weible) C.; B.S., Ohio U., 1951; M.S., Simmons Coll., 1955; m. Mary J. Sheehan, Dec. 25, 1950; children—Earl George III, Christopher T., Mary Lisa, Richard S. Boys' supr. Youth Service Bd., State Mass., Boston, 1952-54; psychiat. social worker VA Hosp., Coatesville, Pa., 1955-57, Family Service Chester County, West Chester, Pa., 1957-59; exec. dir. Family Service Pottstown, Pa., 1959-63; asst. dir. social service dept. Newberry (Mich.) State Hosp., 1963-66, dir. field offices, Marquette, Mich., 1966-70; dir. outpatient dept. Coldwater (Mich.) State Home and Tng. Sch., 1970-73; dir. continued care unit Kalamazoo State Hosp., 1973—; guest lectr. in social work No. Mich. U., supr. field lab. in social work, 1967-69; supr. field lab. in social work Western Mich. U., 1974-80. Served with USNR, 1943-46. Mem. Nat. Assn. Social Work, Acad. Cert. Social Workers, Cert. Marriage Counselors Mich. Home: 3815 Oakridge Rd Kalamazoo MI 49008 Office: Kalamazoo Regional Psychiat Hosp Kalamazoo MI 49008

CARL, RICHARD WILLIAM, dentist; b. Evansville, Ind., July 2, 1933; s. Henry Andrew and Aline M.C. (Sander) C.; m. Judith Blake, July 28, 1957; children: Michelle Carl Ver, Patricia Carl Fritz. DDS, Ind. U., 1960. Gen. practice dentistry Ellettsville, Ind., 1960—; bd. dirs. People's State Bank, Ellettsville, Ellettsville Banc Shares Inc. Pres. Monroe County Bd. Health, Bloomington, Ind., 1963-78. Lodges: Elks, Lions (pres. Ellettsville club 1965). Avocations: astronomy, music, woodcutting, backpacking, canoeing. Home: Box 74 Rt 1 Freedom IN 47431 Office: Box 338 Ellettsville IN 47429

CARLEN, ROSALINE ANN, financial analyst, accountant; b. Detroit, July 5, 1938; d. Joseph Aloyious and Hedwig Theresa (Jakubiak) Kowalewski; B.B.A., U. Detroit, 1963; A.Indsl. Engring., Lawrence Inst. Tech., 1973; m. Bernard Albert Carlen, Dec. 31, 1973. Delivery coordinator internat. div. Vickers div. Sperry Rand Corp., 1962-67; supr. prodn. control and inventory control Bryant Computer Products div. Excello Corp., 1968-71; acctg. clk. to sr. fin. analyst, mem. devel. team performance measurement system Vought Corp., 1971-75; sr. fin. analyst EECSG div. Bendix Corp., 1977-78; supr. fin. and cost analysis F. Joseph Lamb Co., Warren, Mich., 1979-83; mgr. cost acctg. Cadillac Products, Inc., 1983-85; pres. Lincoln Tool and Die, Detroit, 1985—; sec.-treas. Evergreen Fin. Services, Sterling Heights, Mich., 1984-85. Mem. St. Clair Shores (Mich.) Budget Com., 1979. Lic. real estate broker, Mich. Mem. Nat. Assn. Female Execs., Am. Mgmt. Assn. Republican. Roman Catholic. Author mil. maintenance manuals. Home: 23221 Doremus Ave Saint Clair Shores MI 48080 Office: Lincoln Tool and Die 5221 Trumbull Ave Detroit MI 48208

CARLETON, GORDON ROBERT, graphic artist; b. St. Clair, Mich., Aug. 2, 1955; s. Monroe Richard and Ruth Evelyn (Bowlby) C.; m. Lori Lee Chapek, Aug. 7, 1976. BFA, Mich. State U., 1980. Artist The State News Mich State U., East Lansing, Mich., 1971-80; editorial cartoonist Lansing Suburban Newspaper Network, 1984, Ingham News Co., East Lansing, 1984; graphic artist Gordon Carleton Studios, East Lansing, 1980-87, Lansing, 1987—. Artist, writer daily comic strip Mich. State U. Shadows, 1976-80; artist mural Silver Dollar Crowd, 1980; contbr. articles to profl. jours. Advisor T'Kuhtian Press Mich. State U., 1980—; co-chmn., art show dir. T'Con, 1978; 2'Con, 1979; Mediawest Con or MediawWest-Con-7, Lansing, 1981-87. Mem. T'Kuhtian Press Mich. State U. (chmn. 1978-80). Avocations: sci. fiction and other media in visual arts, spl. effects, miniatures.

CARLIE, KEVIN STUART, accountant; b. St. Louis, Feb. 26, 1955; s. Carl Jay Antoniette Rose (Gorczyca) C.; m. Robin Stoliar, June 1, 1980. AB in Econs., Dartmouth Coll., 1976; MBA in Taxation, NYU, 1982. CPA, Mo., Ill., N.Y.; cert. fin. planner. Assoc. Stone, Carlie and Co., St. Louis, 1979-84, ptnr., 1984—. Contbr. articles to profl. jours. Mem. Mo. Soc. CPA's (sub-com. chmn. pub. relations, charter mem. personal fin. planning com.), Ill. Soc. CPA's, N.Y. Soc. CPA's, Am. Inst. CPA's, Inst. Cert. Fin. Planners, Internat. Assn. Fin. Planners (internat. bd. standards and practices), Am. Assn. of Individual Investors. Clubs: Dartmouth (St. Louis) (pres. 1987), Sons of Bosses (St. Louis). Avocations: racquetball, antiques. Home: 14061 Deltona Chesterfield MO 63017 Office: Stone Carlie and Co 7710 Carondelet Ave Suite 200 Saint Louis MO 63105

CARLIER, JOHN CARMELO, coal company executive; b. Martins Ferry, Ohio, Aug. 30, 1957; s. John Reynard and Mary Angelina (Monteleone) C.; m. Karen Emma Flowers, July 5, 1986; 1 child, Emily Ann. BSBA, Ohio U., 1979; MBA, Wheeling (W.Va.) Coll., 1984. Asst. controller Follansbee (W.Va.) Steel Corp., 1979-81; controller Aladdin Food Mgmt. Services, Wheeling, 1981-86, Marietta Coal Co., St. Clairsville, Ohio, 1986—; bus. instr. Belmont Tech. Coll., St. Clairsville, 1986—; cons. Carlier Enterprises, Dillonvale, Ohio, 1986—. Adv. council 4-H Club, Harrisville, Ohio, 1977—, pres. 1980-82; mem. council St. Casimir's Parish, 1987; vol. Harrisville Fire Dept. Mem. Jaycees (secs., treas., pres. Adena chpt. 1981—, regional dir. Ohio 1983, Jaycee of Yr. region 6 1983, one of Outstanding Young Men, Tulsa chpt. 1984). Democrat. Roman Catholic. Lodge: KC. Avocations: arts, crafts, camping. Home: 52355 Lakeview Dr Dillonvale OH 43917 Office: Marietta Coal Co 67705 Friends Ch Rd Saint Clairsville OH 43950

CARLILE, ROBERT LESLIE, accountant; b. Boswell, Ind., Oct. 2, 1924; s. Jasper Leslie and Mearl (Smith) C.; m. Olga E. Gize, Aug. 24, 1952; children: Byron, Bradley. Student, Ind. State Tchrs. Coll., 1942-43; BS, Ind. U., 1948. Trainee Goodyear Tire & Rubber Co., Akron, Ohio, 1948-49; office mgr. Goodyear Tire & Rubber Co., Moline, Ill., 1949-51; asst. store mgr. Goodyear Tire & Rubber Co., Waterloo, Iowa, 1951-52; cost acct., chief timekeeper Burgess Battery Co., Freeport, Ill., 1952-55; sr. acct. William T. Bingham, CPA, Freeport, 1956-60; pvt. practice acctg. Freeport, 1960—. Mem. Forestry Commn., Freeport, 1960—; treas. Freeport Community Chest, Freeport Meml. Hosp. Served with USNR, 1943-46. Mem. Am. Inst. CPA's, Ill. Soc. CPA's, No. Ill. Soc. CPA's, Delta Sigma Pi. Methodist. Club: Freeport Country. Lodges: Masons, Rotary. Home: 1713 Manor St Freeport IL 61032 Office: 905 State Bank Ctr Freeport IL 61032

CARLIN, CLAIR MYRON, lawyer; b. Sharon, Pa., Apr. 20, 1947; s. Charles William and Carolyn L. (Vukasich) C.; m. Cecilia Julia Reis, Sept. 21, 1971 (div. Mar. 1982); children—Elizabeth Marie, Alexander Myron; m. Pamela Ann Roshon, Sept. 30, 1982; 1 son, Eric Richard. B.S. in Econs., Ohio State U., 1969, J.D., 1972. Bar: Ohio 1973, Pa. 1973, U.S. Dist. Ct. (so. dist.) Ohio 1973, U.S. Dist. Ct. (no. dist.) Ohio 1975, U.S. Supreme Ct. 1976, U.S. Ct. Claims 1983, U.S. Ct. Appeals (6th cir.) 1983, U.S. Tax Ct. 1985. Staff atty. Ohio Dept. Taxation, Columbus, 1972-73; asst. city atty. City of Warren, Ohio, 1973-75; assoc. McLaughlin, DiBlasio & Harshman, Youngstown, Ohio, 1975-80; ptnr. McLaughlin, McNally & Carlin, Youngstown, 1980—. Mem. Trumbull County Bicentennial Commn., Ohio, 1976; v.p. Services for the Aging, Trumbull County, 1976-77; mem. Pres.' Club Ohio State U. Served to maj. Ohio NG, 1972-84. Mem. ABA, Ohio State Bar Assn., Ohio State Bar Coll., Mahoning County Bar Assn. (chmn. legal edn. com. 1985-86), Am. Acad. Trial Lawyers, Ohio Acad. Trial Lawyers, Ohio State U. Alumni Assn. (pres. Trumbull County chpt. 1985—), Cath. War Vets. (Ohio state commdr.). Democrat. Roman Catholic. Club: Tippecanoe Country (Canfield, Ohio). Lodge: Rotary. Home: 5510 W Boulevard Youngstown OH 44512 Office: McLaughlin McNally & Carlin 500 City Centre One Youngstown OH 44503

CARLIN, JERRY FAY, engineering executive; b. Beloit, Kans., Dec. 12, 1946; s. Thomas Lee and Clara Jane (Grittman) C.; m. Elaine Rose Teasley, Sept. 6, 1967; children: Patricia M., Jeffrey L., Scott T., Jennifer J. BS in Agrl. Engring., Kans. State U., 1970, MME, 1971. Registered profl. engr., Kans. Engr. Westinghouse Electric Co., Pitts., 1973-75; design engr. Cessna Fluid Power, Hutchinson, Kans., 1975-77, project engr., 1977-79, mgr. advanced engring., 1979—. Patentee in field. Served to 1st lt. USAF, 1971-73. NDEA fellow, 1971-72. Mem. NSPE (state dir. 1980-81), Nat. Fluid Power Assn. (mem. tech. bd. 1982-87, chmn. hydraulic systems com. 1986—), ASME, Am. Soc. Agrl. Engrs., Am. Nat. Metric Counsel, Soc. Automotive Engrs. Republican. Methodist. Home: 2403 Colorado Hutchinson KS 67502 Office: Cessna Fluid Power PO Box 1028 Hutchinson KS 67504

CARLIN, JOHN WILLIAM, former governor of Kansas; b. Salina, Kans., Aug. 3, 1940; s. Jack W. and Hazel L. (Johnson) C.; m. Diana Bartelli Prentice, 1987; children: John David, Lisa Marie. BS in Agr., Kans. State U., 1962, PhD (hon.), 1987. Farmer, dairyman Smolan, Kans., 1962—; mem. Kans. Ho. of Reps. (from 93d Dist.), 1971-73; mem. Kans. Ho. of Reps. (from 73d Dist.), 1973-79, speaker of ho., 1977-79; gov. State of Kans., Topeka, 1979-87; vis. prof. pub. adminstrn. and internat. trade Wichita State U.; chmn. Nat. Govs. Assn., 1984-85, Midwestern Govs. Conf., 1982-83. Democrat. Lutheran. Home: Cedar Crest Topeka KS 66606 *

CARLISLE, JOHN RICHARD, electrical engineer; b. Independence, Ky., Nov. 4, 1942; s. John Dwight and Nancy Pearl (Russell) C.; m. Jo Ann Ishmael, Apr. 6, 1963; children: Michelle Ann, Nicole Lynne, Mitchell Clay. BSEE, U. Ky., 1968. Registered profl. engr., Ohio. Field engr. Square D Co., Dayton, 1968-70; engr. Sidney (Ohio) Electric Co., 1970-76, v.p. engring., 1976-84, pres., 1984—. Active various coms. United Way, Sidney, 1974-78, YMCA Bd., Sidney, 1978—; fin. chmn. Boy Scouts Am., Sidney, 1984—. Mem. IEEE, Nat. Electrical Contractors Assn., Profl. Engrs. in Constrn., Nat. Mgmt. Club (various coms.), Sidney C. of C. Lodge: Rotary, Masons, Shriners. Home: 2401 Fair Rd Sidney OH 45365

CARLOCK, MAHLON WALDO, high school administrator; b. Plymouth, Ind., Sept. 17, 1926; s. Thorstine Clifford and Katheryn G. (Gephart) C.; m. Betty L. Dobbs, Aug. 24, 1954; children: Mahlon W. II, Rhena M., Shawn R., Steve. BS, Ind. U., 1951, MS, 1956. Tchr. jr. high Martinsville Sch. Corp., Brooklyn, Ind., 1952-53; tchr. high sch. Indpls. Pub. Schs., 1953-63, asst. to dean of boys, 1963-73, asst. dean of boys, 1973-75, bus. mgr., 1976—. Served as sgt. U.S. Army, 1945-47. Mem. NEA (life), Indpls. Adminstrs., Ind. Bus. Edn. Assn., Indpls. Edn. Assn. (rep. 1958-63). Republican. Baptist. Lodge: Masons. Avocations: investing in real estate, beekeeping, camping. Home: 9705 East Michigan St Indianapolis IN 46229 Office: Arsenal Tech High Sch 1500 E Mich St Indianapolis IN 46201

CARLSON, BARTLEY JAMES, computer software company executive; b. Rockford, Ill., Mar. 4, 1944; s. Alvin B. and Doris E. (Nelson) C.; B.S., No. Ill. U., 1969; children—Jill C., Barbara J., Brenda J. Customer engr. IBM Corp., Glendale, Calif., Janesville, Wis., and Evanston, Ill., 1962-64; field engr. Xerox Corp., Phoenix, 1964-65; systems coordinator Sundstrand Corp., Rockford, 1965-66; programming mgr. No. Ill. Corp., DeKalb, 1966-68; mem. faculty, dir. computer services Waubonsee Coll., Sugar Grove, Ill., 1968-78; dir. computer services Coll. of DuPage, Glen Ellyn, Ill., 1978-80; sr. cons. Deloitte, Haskins & Sells, Chgo., 1980-83; pres. Nat. Systems Labs., Inc., 1983-85, v.p. COMNET/Group 1 Software, 1985-86; pres. Napersoft, Inc., 1986—. mem. Nat. Commn. on Software; chmn. Nat. Task Force on Edn. and Tng. of Software Profls., 1981-82; chmn. Task Force on Adminstrv. Computing, Ill. Higher Bd. Edn., 1971. Cert. data educator. Mem. Internat. Word Processing Assn. (cons. adv. council 1982-83), Assn. Data Processing Service Orgs., Data Processing Mgmt. Assn., Coll. and Univ. System Exchange (dir.), Word Processing Soc.; Ill. Assn. Ednl. Data Systems (dir. 1973-76), Ill. Community Council of Pres.'s, Nat. Ednl. Computer Network, EDUNET Task Force on Electronic Mail, Coll. and Univ. Machine Records Assn., XPLOR Internat. Club: Big Foot Country. Home: 777 Royal St George #116 Naperville IL 60540-2987 Office: Napersoft Inc 1 Energy Ctr Naperville IL 60540-8466

CARLSON, BRIAN JAY, health care executive; b. Mpls., Mar. 21, 1956; s. John Russell and Shirley Mae Joan (Warholm) C.; m. Ann Margaret Grabau, May 26, 1979; children: Daniel Jordan, Katja Mari. BA in Bus. and Hosp. Adminstrn., Concordia Coll., 1978; MSA in Instl. Adminstrn., U. Notre Dame, 1986. Dir. ops. St. Joseph's Med. Ctr., Brainerd, Minn., 1978-80, dir. research and devel., 1980-84, v.p. corp. devel., 1984—; indsl. engring. cons. St. Joseph's Med. Ctr., Brainerd, 1980-84. bd. dirs. Vols. in Partnership, Inc., Brainerd, 1986. Mem. Am. Coll. Healthcare Execs., Am. Mgmt. Assn., Am. Hosp. Assn., Soc. for Hosp. Planning and Mktg., Brainerd C. of C. (mkt. expansion com. 1984—). Democrat. Presbyterian. Avocations: woodworking, tennis, racquetball, golf, softball. Office: St Joseph's Med Ctr 523 N 3d St Brainerd MN 56401

CARLSON, CHARLES A., data processing executive; b. Mpls., Jan. 28, 1933; s. Clifford and Loretta M. (Sengir) C.; m. Marlene G. Carlson, Nov. 1, 1969; children—Susan, Anne, Richard, Patricia, Andrew. B.A. in English, Coll. St. Thomas, St. Paul, 1954; postgrad., U. Iowa. Retail store mgmt. positions Sears Roebuck & Co., Mpls., 1955-66; dept. mgr. positions Sears Roebuck & Co., Chgo., 1966-76; territorial data processing mgr. Sears Roebuck & Co., Atlanta, 1976-80; nat. mgr. computers and communications Sears Roebuck & Co., Chgo., 1980-81, v.p. data processing and communications, 1981—. Bd. dirs. Jr. Achievement of Chgo., 1985—. Woodrow Wilson fellow, 1955. Mem. Nat. Retail Mchts. Assn. (bd. dirs. info. systems. div. 1981—). Republican. Lutheran. Avocations: civil war interests; sports. Home: 908 S Royal Blackheath Ct Naperville IL 60540 Office: Sears Roebuck and Co D-704X Sears Tower Chicago IL 60684

CARLSON, CHARLES LEIGH, electronics executive; b. Chgo., Aug. 16, 1935; s. Vern Julian and Ether Marion (Wilson) C.; m. Catherine Louise Shelley, Aug. 23, 1955; children: Jeffery Leigh, Ronald David, James Vern, Linda Leigh. Student, COll. of Dupage, U. Wis. From expediter to buyer ITT Telecommunications, Chgo., 1957-63; buyer Bell & Howell, Lincolnwood, Ill., 1963-67; purchasing agt. Comtech Corp., Broadview, Ill., 1967-70; salesman Carlson Co. and H. Grubb Co., Ill., 1970-80; asst. mgr. purchasing electronics div. Stewart Warner, Chgo., 1980—. Served with USAF, 1954-57. Republican. Lodge: Moose. Avocations: photography, old cars, coins.

CARLSON, CURTIS L., department store company executive; b. 1915. Student, U. Minn. Adminstr. Procter & Gamble Distbg. Co., Cin., 1937-38; now chmn. bd. dirs. Ardan Inc., Des Moines. Office: Ardan Inc 2320 Euclid Ave Des Moines IA 50310 *

CARLSON, CURTIS LEROY, business executive; b. Mpls., July 9, 1914; s. Charles A. and Leatha (Peterson) C.; m. Arleen Martin, June 30, 1938; children: Marilyn Carlson Nelson, Barbara Carlson Gage. B.A. in Econs., U. Minn., 1937. Salesman, Procter & Gamble Co., Mpls., 1937-39; founder, pres. Gold Bond Stamp Co., Mpls., 1938-84, pres., chmn. bd. dirs., 1938—; chmn. bd. dirs. Carlson Cos., Inc. (formerly Premium Service Corp.), 1972-84, 1984—; pres. MIP Agy., Inc.; chmn. bd. Gold Bond Stamp Co., Radisson Hotel Corp., Radisson Group Inc., Radisson Mo. Corp., Radisson Raleigh Corp., Colony Resorts, Inc., Carlson Properties, Inc., Carlson Mktg. Group, Inc., Carlson Leasing, Inc., Cartan Tours, Inc., Jason Empire, Inc., TGI Friday's Inc., Dallas, CSA, Inc.; dir. Premiums Internat. Ltd., Can., Gold Bond Japan Ltd., Marquette Bank of Mpls., Bank Shares, Inc., Radisson Wilmington Corp., Sr. v.p. U. Minn. Found.; bd. dirs. Fairview Hosp.; chmn. Swedish Council Am.; bd. dirs., founder Boys Club Mpls.; bd. dirs. Minn. Orchestral Assn., Mpls. Downtown Council, Minn. Meetings; mem. adv. bd. U. Minn. Exec. Program; bd. dirs. U.S. Swedish Council; mem. Hennepin Ave. Meth. Ch. Mem. Trading Stamp Inst. Am. (dir., founder, pres. 1959-60), Mpls. C. of C. (exec. com.), Swedish-Am. C. of C. (dir.), U. Minn. Alumni Assn. (honors com.), Sigma Phi Epsilon. (nat. trustee). Methodist (mem. fin. adv. bd.). Clubs: Minneapolis, Minneapolis Athletic; Northland Country (Duluth); Minikahda, Woodhill Country; Ocean Reef Yacht (Key Largo); Palm Bay (Miami). Lodges: Masons, Shriners, Jesters. Office: Carlson Marketing Group Inc 12755 State Hwy 55 Minneapolis MN 55441

CARLSON, DENNIS LEE, dentist; b. Virginia, Minn., Sept. 20, 1946; s. Sanfrid and Lois Eleanor (christensen) C.; m. Carolee Jo Hard, June 7, 1969; children: Brent W., Ross P., Renni J. AA, Virginia Jr. Coll., 1966; BA in Physiology, U. Minn., 1968, BS in Chemistry, 1970, DDS, 1972. Clin. instr. dentistry U. Minn., Mpls., 1972-75; gen. practice dentistry Virginia, 1976—; mem. staff Virginia Regional Med. Ctr., 1976—; chmn. adv. bd. Hibbing (Minn.) Area Vocat. Tech. Inst., 1978-86; mem. adv. bd. Eveleth (Minn.) Area Vocat. Tech. Inst., 1985-86. Mem. ADA, Minn. Dental Assn., Northeast Minn. Dist. Dental Soc., Open Pit Dental Study Club (pres. 1984-87), Virginia Area C. of C. Avocations: flying, fishing, hunting, photography. Home: PO Box 3520 Britt MN 55710 Office: 200 Tini Square Bldg Virginia MN 55792

CARLSON, EDWARD HILL, physicist, educator; b. Lansing, Mich., Apr. 29, 1932; s. Harold Walter and Emily Pauline (Hill) C.; m. Leantha Louise Duke, Aug. 20, 1960; children: Karen, Brian, Melinda. BS, Mich. State U., 1954, MS, 1955; PhD, Johns Hopkin's U., 1959. Asst. prof. U. Alabama, Tuscaloosa, 1960-65; prof. Mich. State U., East Lansing, 1965—. Author (book series) Kids and Computers; contbr. articles to profl. jours. Mem. Am. Physical Soc. Home: 3872 Raleigh Dr Okemas MI 48864 Office: Mich State U Dept Physics East Lansing MI 48824

CARLSON, GUY RAYMOND, minister, religious organization administrator; b. Crosby, N.D., Feb. 17, 1918; s. George and Ragna Louise (Rassum) C.; m. Mae Adeline Steffler, Oct. 7, 1938; children: Gary Allen, Sharon Carlson Bontrager, Paul Raymond. Student, Western Bible Coll., Winnipeg, Man., Can., 1934-35; D. of Div. (hon.), N. Cen. Bible Coll., Mpls., 1968. Ordained to ministry Assemblies of God Ch., 1941. Pastor Assembly of God Tabernacle, Thief River Falls, Minn., 1940-48; Minn. dist. Sunday sch. dir. Assemblies of God Council, Mpls., 1944-48, Minn. dist. supr., 1948-61; asst. gen. supt. Assemblies of God Council, Springfield, Mo., 1970-85, gen. supt., 1986—; pres. N. Cen. Bible Coll., Mpls., 1961-69; chmn. Pentecostal Fellowship of N.Am., 1986. Contbr. articles to profl. jours. Bd. dirs. Cen. Bible Coll., Evangel Coll., Springfield; chmn. bd. dirs. Assemblies of God Theol. Sem. Named to Order of Golden Shield, Evangel Coll., 1977. Mem. Nat. Assn. Evangelicals (exec. com. 1983—). Office: Assemblies of God 1445 Boonville Ave Springfield MO 65802

CARLSON, KENNETH GEORGE, data processing executive; b. Duluth, Minn., Dec. 14, 1949; s. George Bernard and Laura Anna (Larson) C.; m. Stephanie Venn Petersen, Sept. 20, 1969; children: Laura, Anna. BSEE, U. Minn., 1972. Cert. in data processing; cert. systems profl. Systems programmer U. Minn. Computer Ctr., Mpls., 1969-74; dept. mgr. United Computing System, Kansas City, Mo., 1974-80; computer scientist Computer Scis. Corp., Falls Church, Va., 1980-82; pres., chmn. bd. Lake Superior Software, Duluth, Minn., 1982-86; v.p. Minn. Supercomputer Ctr., Mpls., 1986—; data processing advisor Johnson Community Coll., Overland Park, Kans., 1975-78; bd. dirs., chief fin. officer Superior Resources, Duluth, 1985—. Republican. Mem. United Ch. of Christ. Avocations: cross country skiing, downhill skiing, travel. Office: Minnesota Super Computer Ctr 1200 Washington Ave South Minneapolis MN 55415

CARLSON, LARRY PAUL, electric company executive; b. Escanaba, Mich., Apr. 27, 1942; s. Victor Hilding and Eva Lillian (Thibeault) C.; m. Sandra Lee Pierce, Dec. 28, 1964; children: Eric, Scott. BEE, Milw. Sch. Engring., 1965. Sales engr. Allen Bradley Co., Milw., 1965-67, Mpls., 1967-78; mgr. Allen Bradley Co., Grand Rapids, Mich., 1978-80; v.p. sales Fitzpatrick Electric Supply, Muskegon, Mich., 1980-83, pres., 1983—, also bd. dirs. Republican. Roman Catholic. Lodge: Rotary Internat. Avocations: reading, golf, fishing, hunting. Office: Fitzpatrick Electric Supply Co PO Box 657 Muskegon MI 49443

CARLSON, LOREN MERLE, university dean, political science educator, lawyer; b. Mitchell, S.D., Nov. 2, 1923; s. Clarence A. and Edna M. (Rosenquist) C.; m. Verona Gladys Hole, Dec. 21, 1950; children: Catherine Ann, Bradley Reed, Nancy Jewel. B.A., Yankton Coll., 1948; M.A., U. Wis., 1952; J.D., George Washington U., 1961. Bar: S.D. 1961, U.S. Supreme Ct. 1976. Asst. dir. Govt. Research Bur., U. S.D., 1949-51; orgn. and methods examiner Dept. State, Washington, 1951-52; asst. dir. legis. research State of S.D., 1953-55, dir., 1955-59; research asst. to U.S. Senator from S.D., 1959-60, adminstrv. asst., 1960-63; budget officer State of S.D., 1963-68; dir. statewide ednl. services U. S.D., Vermillion, 1968-74; dean continuing edn. U. S.D., 1974-87, assoc. prof. polit. sci., 1968-79, prof., 1979—; mng. editor U.S. D. Press, 1985—; hwy. laws study dir. Law Sch., 1963; sec. Mo. Valley Adult Edn., 1978-79; Chmn. Model Rural Devel. Commn., Dist. II, State of S.D., 1972-74; chmn. Region VII Planning Commn. on Criminal Justice, S.D., 1969-74. Author: (with W.O. Farber and T.C. Geary) Government of South Dakota, 1979; contbr. articles profl. publs. Mem. Vermillion City Council, 1980—, pres., 1982—; bd. dirs. Vermillion Devel. Co., pres., 1987; Rep. cand. State Ho. of Reps., 1986. Served with USNR, 1945-46. Named Outstanding Young Man Pierre Jaycees, 1959. Fellow Nat. U. Continuing Edn. Assn.; mem. S.D. State Bar, Am. Soc. Public Adminstrn., S.D. Adult Edn. Assn. (chmn. 1973-74), Am. Arbitration Assn., U. S.D. Found., Karl Mundt Found., Pi Sigma Alpha, Pi Kappa Delta. Republican. Lutheran. Clubs: Lions, Eagles. Home: 229 Catalina St Vermillion SD 57069 Office: State Wide Educational Services University of South Dakota Vermillion SD 57069

CARLSON, MARK AUGUST, market research contractor, advertising representative; b. Richmond Heights, Mo., Sept. 28, 1948; s. John Victor and Martha Jane (Anderson) C. BA, U. Miami, Coral Gables, Fla., 1971; MS, So. Ill. U., Edwardsville, 1985. Clk., bus. writer Sun-Sentinel, Ft. Lauderdale, Fla., 1972-73; circulation aide Nola Express, New Orleans, 1973-74; editor, pub. Amphibious Prodns., New Orleans, 1974-80; pvt. practice market research New Orleans, 1981-1984, St. Louis, 1984—. Editor, pub. (newspaper) Broken Barriers, 1975-80, monthly poetry mag., 1974-75. Disaster Services vol. ARC, St. Louis, 1986—; mem. task force Confluence St. Louis, 1987. Mem. Mensa. Democrat. Mem. United Ch. of Christ. Avocations: reading, writing, swimming, travel. Home and Office: 3864 Bamberger Ave #2W Saint Louis MO 63116

CARLSON, OSCAR NORMAN, metallurgist, educator; b. Mitchell, S.D., Dec. 21, 1920; s. Oscar and Ruth Belle (Gammill) C.; m. Virginia Jyleen Forsberg, July 30, 1946; children: Gregory Norman, Richard Norman, Karen Virginia. B.A., Yankton Coll., 1943; Ph.D., Iowa State U., 1950. Mem. faculty Iowa State U., Ames, 1943-87, prof., sr. metallurgist Ames Lab.,, 1960-87, prof. emeritus, 1987, chmn. dept. metallurgy, chief metallurgy div., 1962-66; Vis. scientist Max Planck Institut für Metallforschung, Stuttgart, Germany, 1974-75, 83. Bd. regents Waldorf Coll., 1964-74. Mem. Am. Soc. Metals (chmn. Des Moines 1957-58), Am. Chem. Soc., AIME, Iowa Acad. Scis., Sigma Xi, Phi Kappa Phi. Lodge: Lions. Spl. research nuclear metallurgy of vanadium, niobium and yttrium, phase studies binary alloy systems, deformation behavior metals and alloys, mass transport of solutes in metals. Home: 811 Ridgewood Ames IA 50010

CARLSON, RANDY EUGENE, insurance executive; b. Central City, Nebr., Jan. 5, 1948; s. Ned Conrad and Bonnie Lee (Norgard) C.; m. Lorraine Marie Cordsen, Sept. 16, 1967; children: Lance, Brent. BA in Edn., Wayne State Coll., 1970. Tchr., coach Elgin (Nebr.) Pub. Schs., 1970-72, Lewiston (Nebr.) Consol. Schs., 1972-74, North Platte (Nebr.) Pub. Schs., 1974-78; sales assoc. Franklin Life Ins. Co., North Platte, 1977-79; mng. gen. agt. Life Investors Ins. Co., North Platte, 1979—; trustee Fortunaires Found., Davenport, Iowa, 1980—; bd. dirs. Life Investors Ownership Trust, Cedar Rapids, Iowa. Contbr. articles to profl. jours. Mem. North Platte Buffalo Bills, 1980—, North Platte Booster Club, 1983—; adv. bd. Communication for Agr., 1986—. Mem. Nat. Assn. Life Underwriters (local pres. 1985-86, state membership com. 1986—), Nebr. Life Underwriters Assn. (state membership chmn. 1986—), Gen. Agts. and Mgrs. Assn. (1985—), North Platte C. of C. (bd. dirs. 1986). Republican. Lutheran. Club: North Platte Country. Lodge: Elks. Avocations: golf, fishing, spectator sports. Home: 3301 West F St North Platte NE 69101 Office: Carlson and Assocs Inc 717 S Willow North Platte NE 69103

CARLSON, RICHARD GEORGE, chemical company executive; b. Chgo., Sept. 26, 1930; s. Gustav George and Mildred Elisabeth (Englund) C.; m. S. Diane Russell, Oct. 10, 1948; children—Richard G., Pamela, Kurt D.; m. Barbara Jennie, Nov. 1979. B.S., Ill. Inst. Tech., 1956. With Waterway Terminal, Argo, Ill., 1949-56; with Dow Chem. Co., Midland, Mich., 1956—; bus. mgr. organic chems. Dow Chem. Co., 1971-73, dir. process research, 1973—; mem. fossil energy adv. com. Dept. Energy, 1976—; mem. adv. group dept. chem. engring. Ill. Inst. Tech., 1974-77. Adv. Jr. Achievement, 1956-64; Pres. Midland Newcomers Club, 1957-58; scoutmaster Paul Bunyon council Boy Scouts Am., 1956-64; bd. overseers Coll. Engring. Ill. Inst. Tech., 1981—. Inst. Gas Tech. scholar, 1954-56. Mem. Am. Inst. Chem. Engrs., Mich. Energy and Resource Research Assn. (trustee 1974-78), Tau Beta Pi. Methodist. Office: Dow Chem Co 2020 Building Midland MI 48640

CARLSON, ROBERT JOEL, minister, pastoral counselor, administrator; b. Chgo., Feb. 24, 1932; s. Joel Edwin and Faithe Marie (Brehm) C.; m. Leona Phyllis Hershey, Aug. 8, 1953; children: Steven Eric, Chris Carol, Beth Elaine. AB, Upland Coll., 1954; BD, San Francisco Theol. Sem., 1959, DMin, 1977; STM, Wesley Theol. Sem., 1967. Cert. mental health chaplain. Ordained to ministry Gen. Conf. Mennonite Ch., 1960. Acting chaplain Junior Village, Washington, 1959-60; pastor Bethel Coll. Ch., N. Newton, Kans., 1960-64; clinical pastoral supr. Prairie View, Newton, Kans., 1968—, dir. hosp. div., 1975-85, dir. Wichita div., 1985—; vis. lectr. Trinity Theol. Coll., Singapore, 1981. Author: Mental Health Centers and Local Clergy; author column Your Well Being, 1985—; contbr. articles to profl. jours. Mem. Newton Recreation Commn., 1980—, Worship Commn. B.C. Ch., N. Newton, 1985; World Trade Council, Wichita, Kans., 1983—, Pres. Carter's Rural Mental Health Task Panel, 1977-78. Fellow Coll. of Chaplains Am. Protestant Health Assn.; mem. Assn. for Clinical Pastoral Edn. (cert. supv., nat. cert. commn. 1984, regional chmn., Research award 1977), Assn. Mental Health Clergy (cert. mental health chaplain, chmn. com. mental health), Am. Assn. Pastoral Counselors (clinical), Nat. Council Community Mental Health Ctrs., Council of Prevention. Democrat. Mennonite. Avocation: board sailing. Home: 127 S Pine St Newton KS 67114 Office: Prairie View 337 N Waco Wichita KS 67202

CARLSON, ROBERT JOHN, manufacturing company executive; b. Mpls., Sept. 12, 1929; s. C.R. Jr. and Helen (Wahl) C.; m. Joann Ferguson, Jan. 12, 1952; children: Jon, Jodie, Robert, Tom. BBA, U. Minn., 1952. With Deere & Co. and predecessor, Moline, Ill., 1952-54, 58-79, v.p. farm equipment and consumer products div., 1970-72, sr. v.p. and bd. dirs., 1972-79; mgr. Western Implement Co., Wichita, Kans., 1954-58; pres. Pratt & Whitney Aircraft Co., East Hartford, Conn., 1979-80; v.p. power group United Technologies, Hartford, Conn., 1980-82, exec. v.p., 1982-83, pres. and bd. dirs., 1983-84; pres., chmn. and chief exec. officer BMC Industries, Inc., St. Paul, 1985—; bd. dirs. Lee Data Corp., Barris Industries, Inc. Mem. Council Fgn. Relations, N.Y.C., U. Minn. Pres.' Club; exec. com., trustee Com. Econ. Devel., N.Y.C.; bd. dirs. Swedish Council Am., Mpls., Courage Ctr., Golden Valley, Minn., 1986. Served with U.S. Army, 1948-49. Republican. Office: BMC Industries Inc 1100 Am Nat Bank Bldg Saint Paul MN 55101

CARLSON, ROGER ALLAN, manufacturing company executive, accountant; b. Mpls., Dec. 12, 1932; s. Carl Albert and Borghild Amanda (Anderson) C.; m. Lois Roberta Lehman, Aug. 20, 1955; children: Gene, Bradley. BBA, U. Minn., 1954. CPA, Minn. Investment mgr. Mayo Found., Rochester, Minn., 1963-83; controller Luth. Hosp. and Homes Soc., Fargo, N.D., 1983-84; v.p., treas. Crenlo Inc., Rochester, 1984—, also bd. dirs.; instr. seminars, 1971, 82. Pres. Ability Bldg. Ctr., Rochester, 1974-75, United Way, Olmsted County, Minn., 1980; trustee Minn. Charities Rev. Council, Mpls., 1981-83. Served to capt. U.S. Army, 1955-57. Mem. Am. Inst. CPA's, Minn. Soc. CPA's, Nat. Assn. Accts. (pres. So. Minn. chpt. 1969). Methodist. Avocations: photography, fishing, travel. Home: 1208 19th Ave NE Oakcliff Rochester MN 55904 Office: Crenlo Inc 1600 4th Ave NE Rochester MN 55901

CARLSON, ROGER WHITNEY, graphics company executive, manufacturing company executive; b. Rochester, N.Y., Apr. 28, 1943; s. Raymond Laverne and Margaret Reid (Mansfield) C.; m. Millicent Ann Fisher, Jan. 26, 1966 (div. June 1977); m. Barbara Joan Lipcamin, Aug. 1, 1981 (div. July 1985); children: Todd, Scott, Rebecca. BA in English, Franklin (Ind.) Coll., 1965; MS in Journalism, Ohio U., 1967. Dir. pub. relations Plenco, Sheyboygan, Wis., 1972-74; news editor Daily News, Green Bay, Wis., 1974-75; prof. journalism St. Louis Community Coll., 1975-85; pres. NHP Graphics, St. Louis, 1985—. Author: (with others) (textbook) Style, 1977. Served to capt. USAF, 1968-72. Mem. Soc. Profl. Journalists. Presbyterian. Avocations: bridge, music. Home: 530-I Nirk Ave Kirkwood MO 63122 Office: NHP Graphics 483 S Kirkwood Rd Suite 22 Saint Louis MO 63122

CARLSON, ROLLAND SIGFRID, banker; b. Chgo., Apr. 15, 1932; s. Sigfrid and Esther (Peterson) C.; m. Gretchen J. Lindfelt, Mar. 17, 1956 (dec. Oct. 1986); children—Kristine, David, Karin. A.A., North Park Coll., 1952; B.A., Augustana Coll., 1954; M.B.A., U. Chgo., 1960. Cashier Harris Bank, Chgo., 1962-65, asst. v.p., 1965-68, v.p., 1968-76, sr. v.p., 1976-78, exec. v.p., 1978—. Mem. pres.'s adv. council North Park Coll., Chgo.; bd. dirs. Swedish Covenant Hosp., Chgo., Evang. Covenant Ch. Am., United Negro Coll. Fund. Club: Union League. Office: Harris Trust and Savs Bank 311 W Monroe St Chicago IL 60690

CARLSON, VICTOR ROBERT, JR., processing and packaging executive; b. Seattle, May 18, 1937; s. Victor Robert and Hazel Louise (Sivesind) C.; m. Glenda Jo Fuller, June 24, 1964; children: Corey Christine, Christopher Robert. Student, Washington State U., 1955-58; BS, Oreg. State U., 1961. Lic. profl. food technologist. Devel. engr. Cherry-Burrell Corp., Cedar Rapids, Iowa, 1966-71, mgr. research, 1971-74, mgr. application engring., 1974-80; pres., chmn. Astec, Cedar Rapids, Iowa, mgr. devel. div., 1986—; cons. Dean Foods, 1985—, Gen. Foods, 1982—, CCA, 1980-83. Author: CIP, 1968, Aseptic Processing, 1971; contbr. numerous article to profl. jours. Served with USNR, 1955-63. Recipient Cert. of Achievement, Fed. Drug Adminstrn., 1980. Mem. Internat. Assn. Milk, Food, & Environ. Sanitarians, Inst. Food Technologists (profl.), Am. Dairy Sci. Assn., Dairy & Food Industry Supply Assn., Inst., Energy Research & Devel. Adminstrn., Inst. Thermal Processing Specialists, ASME (vice chmn. food, drug & beverage com. 1978—), Alpha Zeta. Methodist. Club: Indian Creek Country (Marion, Iowa). Lodge: Elks. Avocations: boating, golf. Home: 2771 27th Ave Marion IA 52302 Office: Astec Devel Div Astec 4403 1st Ave SE Suite 301 Cedar Rapids IA 52402

CARLTON, DONALD JAMES, communications executive; b. Detroit, May 18, 1947; s. James Albert and Mabel (Johnson) C.; m. Donna Marie Barbrick, Dec. 28, 1985; 1 child, Brendan James. BA in Communication Arts, DePauw U., 1969; MA in Asian Studies, Ind. U., 1979. Assoc. instr., research asst. Ind. U., Bloomington, 1972-77; assoc. publisher Ryder Mag. Prodns., Bloomington, 1977-82; owner Go Enterprises, Bloomington, 1979—; adv. univ. div. Ind. U., 1981—; cons. Querkus Corp., Bloomington, 1985—; bd. dirs. PCB Services, Bloomington. Assoc. publisher restaurant guides, 1980-81; contbr. articles to profl. jours. Trustee Middle Way House Crisis Ctr./Shelter for Women, 1979-86, treas. 1982-85; mem. Monroe County Jail Com., Bloomington, 1984-86, Pledge of Resistance, 1985-86. Democrat. Mem. Soc. of Friends. Avocations: guitar, mathematics, Buddhist arts. Home: 1025 S Manor Rd Bloomington IN 47401 Office: PCB Services/Go Enterprises 104 1/2 Kirkwood #33 Bloomington IN 47401

CARLTON, FRANK ALFRED, II, printing and publishing company executive; b. Chgo., Apr. 6, 1949; s. Howard A. and June (Overlock) C.; m. Caroline F. Szathmary, June 13, 1981; children—Edward A., Robert F. B.A. summa cum laude with exceptional distinction in Classics Yale U. 1970; M.B.A., J.D., Harvard U., 1974. Bar: Ill. 1974. Asst. to sr. v.p., fin. No. Trust Co., Chgo., 1974-75; assoc. atty. Sidley and Austin, Chgo., 1975-78; asst. to pres. Rand McNally & Co., Skokie, Ill., 1978—. Mem. Ill. State Bar Assn., Chgo. Council Fgn. Relations, Phi Beta Kappa. Club: Harvard Bus. Sch. (Chgo.). Home: 3000 N Sheridan Rd Chicago IL 60657 Office: Rand McNally & Co 8255 N Central Park Ave Skokie IL 60076

CARLTON, MARVIN WENDELL, dentist; b. Macedonia, Ill., July 9, 1917; s. Marvin James and Nellie Mae (Mangis) C.; m. Mary Ellen Jones; children: David Wendell, Gwendolyn Ellen, Marvin Jones. BS, So. Ill. U., 1938; DDS, St. Louis U., 1942. Gen. practice dentistry McLeansboro, Ill., 1946—. Mem. Bd. Edn. Unit 10, McLeansboro, 1970-77. Served to maj. (dental corps) U.S. Army, 1942-46, PTO. Mem. ADA, Ill. Dental Soc., So. Ill. Dental Soc. (pres. 1955). Republican. Methodist. Home: 309 E Cherry St PO Box 9 McLeansboro IL 62859 Office: 201 S Jackson St McLeansboro IL 62859

CARLTON, MICHAEL WILL, advertising executive; b. Cleve., Sept. 2, 1936; s. Will Alexander and Emiah Jane (Hopkins) C.; m. Ruth Marie Long, Mar. 3, 1962; children—David (dec.), Andrew, Matthew, James, Sarah, Ann, Daniel, Oscar, Lynetta, Jennifer. B.S. in Bus. Adminstrn., U. Del., 1958. Trainee Carr Liggett, Inc. (now Liggett-Stashower, Inc., Cleve., 1959-61, media buyer, 1961-64, account exec., 1965-67, account supr., 1967-69, v.p., 1969-77, sr. v.p., 1977-84, exec. v.p., 1985-86, gen. mgr., 1987—, dir., 1974—; sr. v.p. Carr Liggett Can., Ltd. (now Ligget-Stashower Can., Inc.), Toronto, Ont., Carr Liggett AG (now Liggett-Stashower A.G.), Zug, Switzerland, Hyde-Liggett Systems, Ltd., London. Trustee Children's Services, Cleve., 1980—; allocation com. United Way, Cleve., 1981-86 ; dir. Chagrin Valley Recreation Council, 1983-86. Mem. Sales and Mktg. Execs. Cleve. (pres. 1987—, dir. 1983—), Bus. Profl. Advt. Assn. Cleve. (pres. 1981-82, dir. 1979-82), Cleve. Council Am. Assn. Advt. Agys. (chmn. 1979-80, 87—), Nat. Assn. Advt. Agys. (chmn. 1987—). Mem. United Ch. of Christ. Clubs: Pine Lake, 13th Street Racquet. Home: 42 E Orange St Chagrin Falls OH 44022 Office: 815 Superior Ave Cleveland OH 44022

CARLTON, YVONNE ANNETTE, contingency planning specialist; b. Mpls., May 23, 1949; s. George Paul and Pearl Rose (Niles) Spano; m. Donald Dean Carlton, Mar. 4, 1972; 1 child, Sarah Ann. BS with honors, St. Cloud State U., 1971; MBA, Coll. St. Thomas, 1987. Claims processor The Travelers, Mpls., 1972-74; asst. mgr. The Spring Co., Mpls., 1974-77; ops. analyst FBS Mortgage, Mpls., 1977-81; project analyst Norwest Bank NA, Mpls., 1981-84; bus. systems planning Red Owl Stores, Inc., Mpls., 1984-86; contingency planning specialist Norwest Info. Services, Mpls., 1986—. Home: 4740 Oakview Ln Plymouth MN 55442 Office: Norwest Info Services 255 2d Ave S Minneapolis MN 55479

CARMICHAEL, CHARLES WESLEY, plant engr.; b. Marshall, Ind., Jan 18, 1919; s. Charles Wesley and Clella Ann (Grubb) C.; B.S., Purdue U., 1941; m. Eleanor Lee Johnson, July 2, 1948 (dec. 1984); 1 dau., Ann Bromley Carmichael Biada; m. Bernadine P. Carlson, Dec. 21, 1985. Owner, operator retail stores, West Lafayette, Ind., 1946-48, Franklin, Ind., 1950-53; mem. staff time study Chevrolet Co., Indpls., 1953-55; indsl. engr. Mallory Capacitor Co., Indpls., 1955-60, Greencastle, Ind., 1960-70, plant engr., 1970-81; contract cons. Northwood Assocs., 1981—; lectr. in field. Chmn. Greencastle br. ARC, 1962-63; bd. dirs. United Way Greencastle, 1976-79, 84-86. Served to capt., F.A., U.S. Army, 1941-46; ETO. Decorated Bronze Star, Purple Heart with oak leaf cluster. Mem. Greencastle C. of C. (dir. 1962-64), Am. Inst. Plant Engrs., Ind. Bd. Realtors (dir. 1983-85), Putnam County Bd. Realtors (pres. 1983-84), Ind. Hist. Soc, Am. Legion. Republican. Methodist. Clubs: John Purdue, Soc. Ind. Pioneers, Windy Hill Country. Lodges: Masons, Shriners, Kiwanis (past pres.). Home: 3628 Woodcliff Dr Kalamazoo MI 49008 Office: 3628 Woodcliff Dr Kalamazoo MI 49008-2513

CARMICHAEL, GREGORY RICHARD, chemical engineering educator; b. Marengo, Ill., June 16, 1952; s. Elsworth Varnes and F. Margaret (Wallace) C.; m. Candace Jerene Pederson, June 14, 1975; 1 child, Emmett. B.S. in Chem. Engring., Iowa State U., 1974; M.S., U. Ky., 1975, Ph.D., 1979. Asst. prof. U. Iowa, Iowa City, 1978-82, assoc. prof., 1982-85, prof., 1985—, chmn. dept., 1982—; vis. scientist Nat. Inst. Environ. Studies, Tsukuba, Japan, 1983, 85, 86. Contbr. numerous articles to profl. jours. Grantee, EPA, NASA, Electric Power Research Inst. Recipient Outstanding Young Alum award Iowa State U., 1986. Mem. AAAS, Am. Inst. Chem. Engrs. (chmn.-elect Iowa sec.), Air Pollution Control Assn., Am. Chem. Soc., Am. Geog. Union, Am. Meteorol. Soc., Am. Soc. Engring. Edn. (Outstanding Young Faculty award, 1986), Sigma Xi, Omega Chi Epsilon Lodge: Rotary. Office: Dept Chem Engring U Iowa 125 A CB Iowa City IA 52242

CARMICHAEL, JOE WILLIAM, architect, health care consultant; b. Henryetta, Okla., Oct. 2, 1928; s. James Guy and Sylvia B. (Baker) C.; m. Jo Saille Grimes, July 5, 1953; children: John Leith, Theron Kent, Dahl Raymond. BArch, Okla. State U., 1953. Registered profl. architect, Kans., Okla., Nebr., Ark., Mich., Mo., Tex. Architect Robert S. Mayberry, Wichita, Kans., 1953-58; prin. Wichita, 1958-59; ptnr. Carmichael, Wheatcroft & Assocs., Wichita, 1959-71, pres., 1971-74; pres. Carmichael Assocs. P.A., Wichita, 1974—; v.p. N. Central Nursing Ctr., Wichita, 1967—, Springfield (Mo.) Nursing Ctr., 1967-68, Halstead (Kans.) Nursing Ctr., 1967-77; treas. Indian Creek Nursing Ctr., Inc., Overland Park, Kans., 1973-74; pres. Salina (Kans.) Nursing Ctr., 1973—, Westview Manor, Inc., Derby, Kans., 1971—, NCH, Inc., Newton, Kans., 1982—, Am. Home Health Care, Wichita, 1985—, Overland Park, 1985—; sec. Triple-Jay Corp., Wichita, 1977—, Lincoln Plaza, Inc., Hesston, Kans., 1974—, 1st Auburn Co., Wichita, 1974—; mng. ptnr. Cherry Creek Village, Wichita, 1976-84, Lancaster, J.V., Wichita, 1981—, Newton Truck Maint. Ctr., 1981—. Bd. dirs. Meadow Creek Assn., Overland Park, 1983-84, Villas of Meadow Creek, Overland Park, 1983-84; deacon Grace Presbyn. Ch., Wichita, 1969-72, trustee, 1972-75, 78-81; mem. Gen. Council Synod of Kans., Presbyn. Ch. USA; corp. mem. Interfaith Forum on Religion, Art and Architecture; scoutmaster Wichita Troop 509 Boy Scouts Am., 1968-76. Served to capt. U.S. Army C.E., 1946-48, ETO. Mem. AIA (corp.), Kans. Soc. Architects div. AIA (mem. various coms.), Constrn. Specifications Inst. (corp.), Kans. Profl. Nursing Home Adminstrs. Assn. (corp., assoc.), Kans. State Bd. Tech. Professions (sec. 1983, 86), Aircraft Owners and Pilots Assn, Am. Legion, Solar Energy Industries Assn. (assoc.), Sigma Alpha Epsilon, other orgns. Democrat. Lodges: Optimists (pres. 1965-66), High-Twelve (pres. 1978—), masons, shriners (mem. flying fezz com.). Avocations: hunting, boating, flying. Home: 4255 Auburn Wichita KS 67220 Office: Carmichael & Assocs PA 2911 E Douglas Wichita KS 67211

CARMICHAEL, RANDY BOB, entertainer; b. Los Angeles, June 27, 1940; s. Howard Hoagland and Ruth Mary (Menardi) C.; m. Suzanne Jensen, Oct. 25, 1963; 1 child, Lisa Marie. Grad. high sch., Palos Verdes, Calif., 1959. Golf prof. Profl. Golf Assn., 1964-77; entertainer Caesars Palace, 1970; participated in golf tourneys including An Evening With Hoagy Carmichael. Council of Sagamore of Wabash, State of Ind., 1987. Served with U.S. Army, 1961-67. Presbyterian. Avocation: sailing. Home: 89 Handy Rd Grosse Pointe MI 48236

CARMICHAEL, VIRGIL WESLY, mining, civil and geological engineer, former coal company executive; b. Pickering, Mo., Apr. 26, 1919; s. Ava Abraham and Rosevelt (Murphy) C.; m. Emma Margaret Freeman, Apr. 1, 1939; m. Colleen Fern Wadsworth, Oct. 29, 1951; children: Bonnie Rae, Peggy Ellen, Jacki Ann. B.S., U. Idaho, 1951, M.S., 1956; Ph.D., Columbia Pacific U., San Rafael, Calif., 1980. Registered geol., mining and civil engr., geologist, land surveyor. Asst. geologist Day Mines, Wallace, Idaho, 1950; mining engr. De Anza Engring. Co., 1950-52; hwy. engring. asst. N.Mex. Hwy. Dept., Santa Fe, 1952-53; asst. engr. U. Idaho, 1953-56; minerals analyst Idaho Bur. Mines, 1953-56; mining engr. No. Pacific Ry. Co., St. Paul, 1956-67; geologist N.Am. Coal Corp., Cleve., 1967-69, asst. v.p. engring., 1969-74, v.p., head exploration dept., 1974-84. Asst. chief distbn. CD Emergency Mgmt. Fuel Resources for N.D., 1968—; bd. dirs., chmn. fund drive Bismarck-Mandan Orch. Assn., 1979-83; 1st v.p., bd. dirs., chmn. fund drive Bismarck Arts and Galleries Assn., 1982-86; mem. and spl. adivsor Nat. Def. Exec. Res., 1983—; mem. Fed. Emergency Mgmt. Agy., 1983—. Served with USNR, 1944-46. Recipient award A for Sci. writing Sigma Gamma Epsilon. Mem. Am. Inst. Profl. Geologists (past pres. local chpt.), Rocky Mountain Coal Mining Inst. (past pres.), N.D. Geol. Soc. (past pres.), AIME (past chmn. local sect.), Am. Mining Congress (bd. govs. western div. 1973-84), N.Y. Acad. Sci., N.D. Acad. Sci., Sigma Xi. Republican. Club: Breezy Shores Resort and Beach (bd. dirs. 1987—). Lodges: Kiwanis (past club pres., dist. lt. gov.), Masons (past master, trustee 1987—), Elks. Home: 1013 N Anderson St Bismarck ND 58501

CARMICHAEL, WILLIAM EDWARDS, marketing director; b. Bedford, Ind., Jan. 25, 1929; s. Ralph and Millie (Marsey) C.; m. Mary Frances McSoley, Oct. 15, 1950 (div.); children—William Wesley, James Edward, Cathi; m. 2d, Betty Jo Withers, Dec. 3, 1982. BSBA, Ind. U., 1955. Sales rep. Black-Hebert Lumber Co., Indpls., 1955-59; sales engr. Acme Refrigeration, Inc., Indpls., 1959-62, sales mgr., 1962-68, v.p. mktg., 1968-74, exec. v.p., 1974-77; pres. Wm. E. Carmichael & Assocs., Indpls., 1977-85; dir. mktg. Black Lumber Co., Inc., Bloomington, Ind., 1985—; dir. Black-Carmichael-Klein Lumber Co., Inc., Bedford, Ind., Black Lumber Co., Martinsville, Inc., Black Lumber Co. Inc., Bloomington, Ind., Black Lumber Co., Inc., Greencastle, Ind., Black Lumber Co., Inc., Sullivan, Ind. Contbr. chpt. to manual. Vice chmn. Wayne Twp. Screening Caucus, Indspl., 1966. Served to lt. U.S. Army, 1950-54. Recipient DeMolay Cross of Honor Internat. Supreme Council of Order of DeMolay, 1972; named Ky. Col., 1980; named Mem. of Honor Bethel 109 Internat. Order Job's Daughters, 1977. Democrat. Methodist. Lodges: Masons, Shriners. Office: Black Lumber Co Inc PO Box 576 Bloomington IN 47402

CARNEAL, THOMAS WILLIAM, historian, educator; b. Plattsmouth, Nebr., Apr. 8, 1934; s. Glen Thomas and Frances Elizabeth (Wetenkamp) C.; B.A., U. Kansas City, 1963; M.A., U. Mo., Kansas City, 1966; postgrad. U. Mo., 1966-70. Mem. faculty Jr. Coll. program Kemper Mil. Sch., Boonville, Mo., 1965-68; asst., then asso. prof. history N.W. Mo. State U., Maryville, 1968—. Pres., Nodaway County Hist. Soc., 1971—; chmn. Nodaway County Bicentennial Com., 1975-77. Served with U.S. Army, 1953-56. Mem. Orgn. Am. Historians, State Hist. Soc. Mo., Econ. History Assn., Delta Chi. Methodist. Author: A Historic Inventory of Nodaway County, 1977; A Historic Inventory of Andrew County, 1978; A Historic Inventory of the Tri-County Area, 1979; A Historic Inventory of Daviess County, Mo., 1979; Saint Joseph Mo.: Landmarks, 1978; A Historic Inventory of DeKalb County, 1979; A Historic Inventory of Holt County, 1980; A Historic Inventory of Worth County, 1980; A Historic Inventory of Harrison County, 1981; A Historic Inventory of Buchanan County, 1981; Historical and Architectural Landmarks of Nodaway County, 1980; contbr. articles to profl. jours. Home: 418 W 2d St Maryville MO 64468 Office: 307 Colden Hall Northwest Missouri State U Maryville MO 64468

CARNER, WILLIAM JOHN, banker; b. Springfield, Mo., Aug. 9, 1948; s. John Wilson and Willie Marie (Moore) C.; m. Dorothy Jean Edwards, June 12, 1976; children: Kimberly Jean, John Edwards Carner. AB, Drury Coll., 1970; MBA, U. Mo., 1972. Mktg. rep. 1st Nat. Bank Memphis, 1972-73; asst. br. mgr. Bank of Am., Los Angeles, 1973-74; dir. mktg. Commerce Bank, Springfield, Mo., 1974-76; affiliate mktg. mgr. 1st Union Bancorp., St. Louis, 1976-78; pres. Carner & Assocs., Springfield, Mo., 1977—; instr. Drury Coll., 1975, 84—, U. Mo., Columbia, 1986—; dir. Ozark Pub. Telecommunications, Inc. 1982—, sec., 1984-85, treas., 1985-86, vice chmn. 1986-87, chmn., 1987—. Bd. dirs. Am. Cancer Soc., Greene County, Mo., 1974-82, crusade chmn., 1982-83, publicity chmn., 1974-78; bd. dirs. Springfield (Mo.) Muscular Dystrophy Assn., 1975-76, Greater Ozarks council Camp Fire Girls, 1980-81. Mem. Bank Mktg. Assn. (service mem. council 1985—), Mo. Banker's Assn. (instr. Gen. Banking sch.), Fin. Instns. Mktg. Assn. (chmn. service mem. com.), Assn. MBA Execs., Drury Coll. Alumni Assn. (v.p. 1985-86, pres. 1986—). Democrat. Mem. Christian Ch. (Disciples of Christ). Club: Hickory Hills Country. Lodges: Masons, Shriners. Home: 1500 S Fairway Ave Springfield MO 65804 Office: PO Box 1005 Springfield MO 65805

CARNEY, BARBARA JOYCE, executive search consultant; b. Chgo.; d. Maurice David and Celia (Baylen) Sachnoff; B.A. cum laude, UCLA, 1964; M.Ed., Nat. Coll. Edn., 1968; children—Michael, Michelle. Tchr., North Suburban Chgo. pub. schs., 1965-68; mfrs. rep. Shardon Mktg. Inc., Chgo., 1976-78; Midwestern regional sales mgr. Superscope, Inc., Chatsworth, Calif., 1977-80; nat. spl. markets sales mgr. Ronco, Inc., Elk Grove Village, Ill., 1980-81; exec. search cons. Womack & Assocs., Inc., Chgo., 1982-85, B. Carney & Assocs., Chgo., 1985—. Bd. dirs. North Shore Mental Health Assn., 1975-76; chpt. v.p., chmn. LWV, 1968-76. Mem. Women in Mgmt., AAUW, Am. Soc. Profl. and Exec. Women, Nat. Assn. Female Execs. Home: 2020 Lincoln Park W Chicago IL 60614

CARNEY, LARRY BRADY, telecommunications manager, accountant; b. Poplar Bluff, Mo., Mar. 15, 1948; s. Brady Elvis and Wanda Pauline (Francis) C.; m. Barbara Sue Foster, June 6, 1968; children—Lisa Anne, Steven Wayne, Karen Brooke. B.S. in Bus. Adminstrn., S.E. Mo. State U., 1970. C.P.A. Auditor, Ernst & Whinney, St. Louis, 1970-73; internal auditor, acctg. mgr., v.p. controller Maritz Inc., St. Louis, 1973-80; staff mgr. Southwestern Bell Telephone, St. Louis, 1980-82, cost analyst, 1984—; staff mgr., industry mgr. AT&T Info. Systems, St. Louis, 1982-84; acctg. instr. Mo. Bapt. Coll., St. Louis, 1981-82, St. Louis Community Coll., 1982—. Served with Army N.G., 1970-76. Mem. Am. Inst. CPA's, Mo. Soc. CPA's. Republican. Baptist.

CARNEY, THOMAS PATRICK, medical instruments company executive, researcher; b. Dubois, Pa., May 27, 1915; s. James Patrick and Margaret Elizabeth (Senard) C.; m. Mary Elizabeth McGuire, Oct. 3, 1942; children—Thomas, Sheila, James, Janet. B.S. in Chem. Engring., Notre Dame U., 1937, LL.D. (hon.), 1969; M.S., Pa. State U., 1939, Ph.D., 1941. Research chemist Reilly Tar and Chem. Corp., Indpls., 1937-39, 41-43; post doctoral fellow U. Wis., Madison, 1943-44; research chemist Eli Lilly & Co., Indpls., 1944-54, v.p., 1954-64; exec. v.p. G.D. Searle & Co., Skokie, Ill., 1964-74; chmn. exec. com. Nat. Patent Devel. Co., N.Y.C., 1974-75; pres. Metatech Corp., Northbrook, Ill., 1976—, also dir., Bioferm, Inc., Northbrook, 1980—, also dir.; dir. ImmunoGenetics, Vineland, N.J.; cons. to Sec. HEW, Washington. Author: Laboratory Fractional Distillation, 1949; Instant Evolution, 1980; False Profits, 1981. Contbr. articles to profl. publs. Patentee in field. Recipient Disting. Service award Assn. Cons. Chemists and Engrs., 1976; Ernest Stewart award Council Advancement and Support of Edn., 1982. Fellow N.Y. Acad. Sci., AAAS, Chem. Soc. London, Am. Inst. Chemists; mem. Am. Chem. Soc. (div. chmn.), Swiss Chem. Soc., London Soc. Chem. Industry, Sigma Xi, Alpha Chi Sigma, Phi Lambda Upsilon. Clubs: Onwentsia; Mid-Am. (Chgo.). Home: 277 Bluff's Edge Dr Lake Forest IL 60045 Office: Metatech Corp 910 Skokie Blvd Northbrook IL 60062

CARONE, GARY THOMAS, psychologist; b. Toledo, Ohio, June 20, 1958; s. Carl Samuel and Bonnie Viola (Stein) C.; m. Jo Anne Jaworski, Aug. 24, 1985. BS, Mich. State U., 1979; MS, Ea. Mich. U., 1985. Cert. limited lic. psychologist, Mich. Therapist Monroe (Mich.) Community Mental Health, 1980-83, psychologist, 1985—; therapist Southeast Mich. Substance Abuse, Allen Park, 1983-85; cons. psychologist Inst. Behavioral Devel., Northville, Mich., 1986—; speaker in field. Mem. Dem. Socialists Am., N.Y.C., 1980. Mem. Assn. for Behavior Analysis. Democrat. Avocations: softball, basketball. Home: 8165 Swan Creek Newport MI 48161

CAROTHERS, CHARLES OMSTED, orthopedic surgeon; b. Medina, N.Y., Aug. 2, 1923; s. Thomas Abbott and Helen Flavia (Olmsted) C.; m. Winifred Ashforth Booker, Dec. 22, 1943 (div. 1970); children—Thomas Abbott, Stephen Cole, Lisa Booker; m. Lucille Klau, June 20, 1971. B.A., Williams Coll., 1944; M.D., Harvard U., 1946; M.S. in Orthopedic Surgery, U. Tenn., 1954. Diplomate Am. Bd. Orthopedic Surgery. Intern Cin. Gen. Hosp., 1946-47; head bone research project Naval Med. Research Inst., Bethesda, Md., 1949; resident in gen. surgery U. Cin., 1949-51; resident in orthopedic surgery U. Tenn., 1951-54; practice medicine specializing in orthopedic surgery Cin., 1954—; chief orthopedic sect. Bethesda Hosps.; pres. Carothers & Carothers Inc., Cin.; mem. staff Drake Hosp., Univ. Med. Sch., Univ. Hosp. Cin. Pres., chief exec. officer Cin. Playhouse in the Park, 1974—. Served with USN, 1949. Recipient Post-Corbett award for Contbn. to the arts, 1986. Mem. Am. Acad. Orthopedic Surgery, Clin. Orthopedic Soc., ACS, Am. Assn. Surgery Trauma, Mid-Am. Orthopedic Assn., AMA, Gen. Soc. Colonial Wars of Ohio (dep. gov. 1979-82, gov. 1975-76). Episcopalian. Clubs: Cin. Country, U. of Cin., Losantiville Country, Wequetonsing Assn. Literary. Home: 1 Walsh Pl Cincinnati OH 45208 Office: 8260 Northcreek Dr Cincinnati OH 45236

CAROW, EDWARD GEROLD, real estate executive; b. Milw., July 20, 1959; s. Edward Raymond and Bernadine Irene (Propp) C.; m. Tammy Lynn Johnson; children: Jennifer Lynn, Nicole Theresa. Grad. high sch., Mukwanago, Wis., 1977. Rental agt. Nat. Realty, Wauwatosa, Wis., 1978-79, site mgr., 1979, field coordinator, 1979-81, sr. field coordinator, 1981-84, dir. ops. western region, 1984-86, nat. dir. ops, 1986—. Adv. bd. Waukesha County Tech. Inst., Pewaukee, Wis., 1986; bd. stewards Christ Lutheran Ch., Big Bend, Wis., 1985; Star Bethlehem Ch., New Berlin, Wis., 1986. Mem. Inst. Real Estate Mgmt. (exec. bd. dirs. 1986-1991). Republican. Avocations: reading, golf, racquetball, softball, hunting. Home: 13085 W Applebiossom Ln New Berlin WI 53151

CARPENTER, ANNA-MARY PASSIER, physician, educator; b. Ambridge, Pa., Jan. 14, 1916; d. Samuel V. and Adele M. (Passier) C. B.A., Geneva Coll., 1936, D.Sc. (hon.), 1968; M.S., U. Pitts., 1937, Ph.D., 1940; M.D., U. Minn., 1958. Research asst. U. Pitts., 1938-40; instr. Moravian Coll. Women, Bethlehem, Pa., 1941-42; chmn. biology curricula Keystone Coll., Scranton, Pa., 1942-44; research assoc. pathology Children's Hosp.; lectr. mycology Sch. Medicine, Pitts., 1944-53; instr. Sch. Medicine U. Minn., Mpls., 1954-57; asst. prof. Sch. Medicine U. Minn., 1957-58, assoc. prof., 1959-65, prof. anatomy, 1965-80; prof. pathology N.W. Center Med.

Edn., Ind. U., 1980-87. Author: Color Atlas of Human Histology, 1968. Mem. AAAS, Am. Diabetes Assn., Histochem. Soc. (sec. 1974-75, treas. 1975-79, pres. 1980-81), Am. Assn. Anatomy, Internat. Soc. Mycology, Internat. Soc. Stereology (sec.-treas. 1971-83, v.p. 1984—). Home: 6424 Hayes St Merrillville IN 46410

CARPENTER, CARMEN OLGA, elementary school counselor; b. Detroit, Dec. 20, 1937; d. Montgomery O'Neal Tarrant and Nellie Louise (Jackson) Tarrant Tribble; B.S., Wayne State U., 1960, M.Ed., 1975; children—Spencer III, Kevin O'Neal, Bert Dorian. Nat. cert. counselor Nat. Bd. for Cert. Counselors. Vocal music tchr. Detroit Bd. Edn., 1960-77; model Hawkins Apparel, Inc., Lynette's Inc., March of Dimes Extravaganza, 1974-79; elem. sch. counselor Keidan Sch., Detroit Bd. Edn., 1977-83; career edn. liaison com. person Region 3, Detroit Bd. Edn. Pres. Courtis Sch. PTA, 1973-74; public relations chairperson Detroit Council PTA, 1976, 79, corr. sec., 1977-79. Democratic Precinct del., 1976, 78—; pres. Oakman Blvd. Homeowners Assn., 1982-85; chmn. MacKenzie Area Prevention Project; pub. relations chmn. Broadstreet Unity Presbyn. Ch.; v.p., pres. elect Oakman Blvd. Community Assn., 1986—. Named Woman of Yr., St. Andrews Presbyterian Ch., 1973; Ms. March of Dimes Model, 1977; recipient Outstanding Mich. Citizen award, 1978, Community Services award Wayne County, 1986, Mayor's Award of Merit, 1986; Cert. of Appreciation, Wayne County Bd. Commrs., 1980; Cert. of Achievement, Detroit Bd. Edn., Guidance and Counseling Dept., 1981; Appreciation Trophy, God's Humanitarian Garden, 1981; citations MacKenzie Area Prevention Project, named Counselor of Month, 1982. Mem. Detroit Fedn. Tchrs. (bldg. rep. 1969, 73), Am. Assn. for Counseling and Devel., Mich. Elem. Sch. Counselor Assn., Mich. Non-White Counselors Assn., Guidance Assn. Met. Detroit, Wayne State U. Alumni Assn., Women of Wayne, State Dem. Educators Caucus, Detroit Assn. to Promote Amateur Boxing (rec.-corr. sec. 1979-82), NAACP (life), Phi Delta Kappa. Presbyterian. Club: Les Cosmopolites Bridge (former pres.). Compiler exhbn., booklet on black scientists and inventors for Afro-Am. Mus., 1974. Office: care Guidance Dept 644 Detroit Schs Center Bldg Detroit MI 48202

CARPENTER, JAMES ALLEN, minister; b. Houston, Sept. 24, 1936; s. Allen Lawrence and Ninnah Leona (Thurmond) C.; m. Dolly Syletta Still, June 7, 1958; children: Lydia, Ninnah. BA, Johnson Bible Coll., 1958; MDiv, Christian Theol. Seminary, 1966; D Ministry, Phillips U., 1982. Ordained to ministry Christian Ch., 1957. Pastor Blvd. Christian Ch., Balt., 1958-62, Christian Ch., Edwardsport, Ind., 1962-66, Bethany Christian Ch., Detroit, 1966-73, Community Christian Ch., Manchester, Mo., 1973-76; sr. pastor Midwest Blvd. Christian Ch., Midwest City, Okla., 1976-86, First Christian Ch., Noblesville, Ind., 1986—. Author: Faith in Action, 1975. Pres. Mid-Del Group Homes, Inc., Midwest City, 1982-84; dir. Hamilton County Emergency Shelter, Noblesville, 1987. Named Outstanding Vol., Okla. Dept Human Services, 1985. Democrat. Lodge: Kiwanis. Home: 7695 Creekside Ct Noblesville IN 46060 Office: First Christian Church PO Box 189 Noblesville IN 46060

CARPENTER, JOHN MARLAND, engineer, physicist; b. Williamsport, Pa., June 20, 1935; s. John Hiram and Ruth Edith (Johnson) C.; children: John Marland, Kathryn Ann, Susan Marie, Janet Elaine. B.S. in Engring. Sci, Pa. State U., 1957; M.S. in Nuclear Engring, U. Mich., 1958, Ph.D., 1963. Fellow Oak Ridge Inst. Nuclear Studies, 1957-60; postdoctoral fellow Inst. Sci. and Tech., U. Mich., 1963-64, mem. faculty univ., 1964-75, prof. nuclear engring., 1973-75; vis. scientist nuclear tech. br. Phillips Petroleum Co., 1965; solid state sci. div. Argonne (Ill.) Nat. Lab., 1971-72, 73; physics div. Los Alamos Sci. Lab., 1973; sr. physicist solid state sci. div., mgr. intense pulsed neutron source project Argonne Nat. Lab., 1975-77, program dir., 1977-78, tech. dir., 1978—; cons. in field; mem. U.S. del. to USSR on fundamental properties of matter, 1977; mem. indsl. and profl. adv. council Coll. Engring., Pa. State U., 1984-87; mem. Nat. Steering Com. for Advanced Neutron Source, 1986—. Author, editor. Recipient Disting. Service award U. Mich. Dept. Nuclear Engring., 1967, L.J. Hamilton Disting. Alumnus award, 1977, Disting. Performance award for work at Argonne Nat. Lab. U. Chgo., 1982. Mem. Am. Phys. Soc., Am. Nuclear Soc. (sect. chmn. 1974-75). Patentee nuclear instrumentation, neutron scattering, time dependent neutron thermalization, pulsed spallation neutron sources, neutron scattering instrumentation, structure and dynamcs of amorphous solids. Office: Intense Pulsed Neutron Source Program Argonne Nat Lab Argonne IL 60439

CARPENTER, PHYLLIS MARIE ROSENAU, physician; b. Hastings, Nebr., Aug. 2, 1926; d. Alvin Benjamin and Sophia Helen (Schmidt) Rosenau; B.S., Hastings Coll., 1948; M.D., U. Nebr., 1951; cert. Gestalt Inst. Cleve., 1970; m. Charles Robert Carpenter, Mar. 24, 1956 (dec. Mar. 1972); children—Charles Robert, Carole Rose, Lucinda Joy. Intern, St. Luke's Hosp., Chgo., 1951-52; resident in pediatrics Children's Meml. Hosp., Chgo., 1952-54; asst. med. dir., also clin. supr. EEG lab., Mcpl. Contagious Disease Hosp., Chgo., 1955-60; tchr. parenting; staff Well Baby Clinics, Infant Welfare, 1960-70; pvt. practice specializing in Gestalt therapy, preventive medicine and biofeedback, Chgo. and Clarendon Hills, Ill., 1970—; mem. staff Grant Hosp., Chgo.; lectr., workshops on stress mgmt. and biofeedback; founding fellow, mem. faculty Gestalt Inst. Chgo., 1970—, faculty chmn., 1981-83; mem. faculty Coll. DuPage, 1975-79, 83—, No. Ill. U., 1979-80, George Williams Coll., Chgo., 1979-85 ; therapist Martha Washington Alcoholic Rehab. Clinic, Chgo., 1969-75. Organizer Community Presbyn. Ch. Nursery Sch., 1965-66. Mem. AAUW, Am. Assn. Biofeedback Clinicians (cert. clinician), Am. Med. Writers Assn., Nat. Writers Club. Author articles in field. Contbg. editor Current Health mag., 1981-85 . Home: 35 Norfolk St Clarendon Hills IL 60514 Office: 35 Norfolk St Clarendon Hills IL 60514 Office: 826 W Armitage Ave Chicago IL 60614

CARPENTER, ROBERT BRUCE, medical technology consultant; b. Miami, Fla., Sept. 20, 1951; s. Homer Frederick and Helen (Grubb) Evenson; m. Kay Radebaugh, Aug. 23, 1972; children: Elias, Catherine, Amanda, Nathan. BA, U. Ill., 1973; med. technologist diploma, Carle Sch. Med. Tech., 1975; MS, Brigham Young U., 1981. Staff technologist Champaign Co. Blood Bank, Urbana, Ill., 1974-75, Little Traverse Hosp., Petoskey, Mich., 1976-79, Utah Valley Hosp., Provo, 1979-81; cons. technologist Lab. of Clin. Medicine, Sioux Falls, S.D., 1981—. scoutmaster Latter Day Saints Ch., Sioux Falls, 1983-85, troop com. chmn., 1985—. Mem. Clin. Lab. Mgmt. Assn. (charter), Am. Soc. for Clin. Pathologists. Republican. Avocations: swimming, running, reading, skiing. Home: 5800 W 40th St Sioux Falls SD 57106 Office: Lab Clin Medicine 1212 S Euclid Sioux Falls SD 57105

CARPENTER, ROBERT WAYNE, manufacturing company executive; b. Evansville, Ind., Sept. 23, 1949; s. Robert Earl and Loyce Jeaneen (DeWeese) C.; m. Theresa Ann Herron, Nov. 19, 1971; 1 child, Sean Adam. BA in Chemistry, U. Evansville, 1971, BS in Chemistry and Bus. Adminstrn., 1980, MBA, 1981. Spl. projects mgr. Windsor Plastics, Inc., Evansville, 1972—. Contbr. articles to profl. jours. Mem. Soc. Plastics Engrs. (sr., speaker 1974-85, pres. tri-state sect. 1979-80), Am. Soc. Electroplated Plastics, Assn. Finishing Processes. Avocations: reading, softball, coaching little league, playing clarinet. Home: 12428 Oak Gate Rd Evansville IN 47711 Office: Windsor Plastics Inc 601 N Congress Ave Evansville IN 47715

CARPENTER, STEVEN RUSSELL, data services executive; b. Neenah, Wis., July 22, 1958; s. Russell Thomas and Marigen Zoe (Braun) C.; m. Abilgail Sallee Forbes, Nov. 7, 1981; 1 child, David Forbes Carpenter. BBA in Computer Sci., U. Wis., Stevens Point, 1980; MBA, U. Wis., Milw., 1986. Supr. corp. data ctr. Wis. Bell, Milw., 1980-81, analyst application support, 1981-82, mgr. info. ctr., 1982-85, mgr. data services provisioning, 1985—. Weekend mgr. Ronald McDonald House, Milw.; leader Boy's Brigade Assn., Neenah, Wis., 1974-80. Mem. Assn. Computing Machinery. Presbyterian. Avocations: photography, nordic skiing, theatre. Home: 1320 N 63d St Wauwatosa WI 53213 Office: Wis Bell Inc N15 W24250 Bell Dr Waukesha WI 53188

CARR, CAREY SCOTT, lawyer, real estate developer; b. Kansas City, Mo., Oct. 26, 1958; s. Lloyd Leroy Carr and Anita June (Scott) Long. BBA, Wash. U., Topeka, Kans., 1980; JD, Wash. U., 1982. Bar: Kans., Nebr., U.S. Supreme Ct. 1986. V.p., gen. counsel The Lockwood Group, Topeka, 1983—. Mem. ABA, Kans. Bar Assn., Nebr. Bar Assn., Phi Delta Theta. Republican. Lodges: Sertoma (v.p. Topeka chpt.), Rotary, Masons, Shriners. Avocations: golf, fishing, hunting. Office: Lockwood Devel 5123 A SW 29th St Topeka KS 66614

CARR, CAROLYN KEHLOR, educational administrator; b. St. Louis, July 23, 1948; d. James Kehlor Jr. and Jean Wheatly (Costen) C. BA in Art History, U. Mo., 1970, MEd in Learning Disabilities, 1971; Cert. in Spl. Edn. Adminstrn. and Supervision, U. Toledo, 1978—; postgrad., Cen. Mo. State U., 1986—. Learning lab. tchr. Jefferson County Pub. Schs., Lakewood, Colo., 1971-72; resource tchr. Littleton (Colo.) Pub. Schs., 1972-75; learning disabilities/behavior disorder spur. Lucas County Sch. Bd., Toledo, 1975-78; spl. edn. cons. Mo. Dept. Elem. and Secondary Edn., Jefferson City, 1978-80, interagy. supr., 1980—; mem. steering com. Mo. Gov.'s. Conf. on Health Edn. for Children, 1986; also presider working session for decision making profls. Mem. Nat. Assn. State Dirs. Spl. Edn. (life), Council Adminstrs. Spl. Edn., Capital Kappans (steering com. chmn. 1980-81), Phi Delta Kappa Club (pres. 1981-82). Episcopalian. Office: Mo Dept Elem and Secondary Edn PO Box 480 Jefferson City MO 65102

CARR, DAWN ELIZABETH, nurse; b. Canton, Ohio, Sept. 7, 1954; d. Harry Russell and Majel Maxine (McConahey) Adams; m. Gregory Allen Carr, Aug. 16, 1975; 1 child, Christa Marie. RN, Aultman Hosp. Sch. Nursing, 1975. Staff RN operating room Aultman Hosp., Canton, 1975-79, asst. patient care coordinator, 1979-86, coordinator patient care, 1986—. Mem. Assn. Operating Room Nurses, Aultman Alumni Assn. Mem. Christian Ch. Avocations: bicycle riding, needlepoint, reading. Home: 7661 Oakdale NW Massillon OH 44646 Office: Aultman Hosp Operating Room 2600 Sixth St SW Canton OH 44710

CARR, GENE EMMETT, school superintendent; b. Madison, S.D., Dec. 6, 1937; s. Emmett A. and Phyllis E. (Heitman) C.; B.S., Dakota State Coll., 1961; M.S., U. Utah, 1964; Edn. Specialist, U. S.D., 1975; m. Carolyn Riley, May 25, 1961; children—Catherine, Robert, Michael, Mark, Patricia, Bradley. Tchr. pub. schs., Garretson, S.D., 1961-63, Dell Rapids, S.D., 1964-70; supt. schs., Oldham, S.D., 1970-76, Hamlin Schs., Hayti, S.D., 1976—. Vice pres. Oldham Fire Dept., 1972-76; mem. agr. com. Sioux Empire Farm Show, 1964-79. Mem. Sch. Adminstrs. S.D., S.D. Sch. Supts. Assn. (dir.), Am. Quarter Horse Assn. Club, Center of Nation Appaloosa Horse Club (pres. 1972-74, 82-83), Pony of Ams. Club. Contbr. articles to equine mags. Home: PO Box 25 Hayti SD 57241 Office: PO Box 298 Hayti SD 57241

CARR, JAMES CHARLES, physician; b. New Hampton, Iowa, Mar. 28, 1939; s. Hubert B. and Anna Mary (McKone) C.; B.A. in English, Loras Coll., 1957-61; M.D., U. Iowa, 1965; m. Mary Kay Peters, June 17, 1961; children—Barbara, Robert, Jane, Susan, David. Intern, Broadlawns Polk County Hosp., Des Moines, 1965-66; resident in family practice, 1966-67; practice medicine specializing in family medicine Med. Assos., New Hampton, Iowa, 1967—; chief staff St. Joseph's Community Hosp., New Hampton, 1972, 1975, 80; instr. family medicine Mayo Med. Sch., U. Minn., Rochester, 1975—; med. advisor Chickasaw Ambulance Service, 1972—. Bd. dirs. N.E. Iowa Council on Substance Abuse, 1976-81. Served to major Iowa N. G., 1966-72. Recipient Distinguished Service Award Jaycees, 1971; recipient Outstanding Young Mem of Am. Award, 1974; diplomate Am. Bd. Family Practice. Fellow Am. Acad. Family Practice; mem. AMA, Chickasaw County, Iowa Med. Socs., N.E. Iowa Emergency Med. Services Assn. (dir. 1979-82, chmn. 1980, 81). Roman Catholic. Home: 414 N Chestnut Ave New Hampton IA 50659 Office: 201 S Linn Ave New Hampton IA 50659

CARR, JOHN MARK, minister, elementary educator; b. Danville, Ill., Mar. 20, 1953; s. John Paul and Betty Lee (Brattain) C.; m. Kathy Jean Iman, Aug. 8, 1981; children: John Michael, James Matthew, Kara Jean, Jared Mark. BA in Christian Ministries, Cin. Bible Coll., 1975; student, Cin. Christian Sem., 1980-81, Ball State U., 1981; BS, Ind. U.-Purdue U., Indpls., 1984. Ordained minister, Churches of Christ, 1975. Assoc. minister Southglen Christian Ch., Anchorage, 1984, Homer (Alaska) Christian Ch., 1984-85; elementary tchr. Indpls. Pub. Schs., 1985—. Ofcl. observer Civil Air Patrol, Homer, 1984-85; mem. South Peninsula Amateur Radio Club, Homer, 1984-85; Insp. Rep. Party, Indpls., 1985-86. Mem. Nat. Edn. Assn., Ind. State Tchrs. Assn., Indpls. Edn. Assn. Avocations: amateur radio, outdoor sports, spectator sports. Office: School #50 75 N Bellevue Pl Indianapolis IN 46222

CARR, LEON CLEMENT, pub. relations exec.; b. Milbank, S.D., Sept. 11, 1924; s. Frank B. and Laura A. (Kohl) C.; B.A. in Journalism, U. Minn., 1951; m. Donnie M. Cronin, May 19, 1956; 1 son, John. Wire editor St. Cloud (Minn.) Daily Times, 1951-52; staff writer Asso. Press, Sioux Falls, Pierre, S.D., 1952-56; copy editor St. Paul Pioneer Press, 1956-57; copy editor St. Paul Dispatch, 1957-60, asst. news editor, 1960-61; with 3M, St. Paul, 1961—, staff publicist, 1965-71, pub. relations coordinator, 1971-73, supr. media relations, 1973-76, mgr. br. pub. relations, 1976-86, program mgr., 1986—. Mem. Pub. Relations Soc. Am. (accredited), U. Minn. Sch. Journalism Mass Communication Alumni Assn. (charter, past pres.), Soc. Profl. Journalists (life). Roman Catholic. Club: Minn. Press (charter). Home: 21 E Logan Ave West Saint Paul MN 55118 Office: 3M Center Box 33600 Saint Paul MN 55133

CARR, M. ROBERT (BOB), congressman; b. Janesville, Wis., Mar. 27, 1943; s. Milton Raymond and Edna (Blood) C. BS, U. Wis., 1965, JD, 1968; postgrad., Mich. State U., 1968-69. Bar: Wis. 1968, Mich. 1969, U.S. Supreme Ct. 1973. Mem. staff of minority leader Mich. State Senate, 1968-69; adminstrv. asst. to atty. gen. State of Mich., Lansing, 1969-70, asst. atty. gen., 1970-72; counsel to spl. joint com. on legal edn. Mich. Legislature, Lansing, 1972; mem. 94th-96th, 98th-100th congresses from 6th Mich. Dist., Washington, 1974-78, 82—; mem. appropriations com. 1982—. Dist Office: 2848 E Grand River Ave Suite 1 East Lansing MI 48823 Office: 2439 Rayburn Bldg Washington DC 20515 *

CARR, ROBERT FRANKLIN, III, fiduciary management company executive; b. Chgo., July 29, 1940; s. Robert Franklin, Jr. and Vesta Culbertson (Morse) C.; B.S. in Bus. Adminstrn., Babson Coll., Wellesley, Mass., 1962; m. Maude Goldsmith; children—Rebecca, Mimi, Robert. Treas., Murine Co., Chgo., 1966-69; mgr. optical dept. Abbott Labs., Lake Bluff, Ill., 1969-72; exec. v.p. mktg. and client services Investment Capital Mgmt. Co., Chgo., 1973-80; chmn. bd. Fiduciary Mgmt. Assocs., Chgo., 1980—; dir. Quincy Coal, Charleston, W.Va., Makalika, Inc., Vero Beach, Fla., Legacy Life Co., Phoenix. Chmn. bd. Grant Hosp., Chgo., 1978; vice chmn. bd. Chgo. Zool. Soc., 1977; bd. dirs., trustee Babson Coll.; assoc. bd. dirs. Northwestern U., 1975; v.p., trustee Graceland Cemetery, Chgo., 1976; trustee Old People's Home, Chgo., 1979, Lake Forest Acad., 1982—. Served with USAR, 1963-69. Mem. Assn. Investment Mgmt. Sales Execs., Better Govt. Assn. (bd. dirs.), Chancellor Soc. U. Denver (bd. dirs.), Econ. Club Chgo. Clubs: Mid-Day (Chgo.); Onwentsia, Winter (Lake Forest); La Cheneaux (Mich.), Old Elm (Ft. Sheridan). Home: 507 Lexington Dr Lake Forest IL 60045 Office: 55 W Monroe St Suite 2550 Chicago IL 60603

CARR, ROY DOUGLAS, steel company executive; b. LaCrosse, Wis., June 15, 1949; s. Franklin G. and June L. (Kircheis) C.; m. V. Susan Rediehs, Dec. 10, 1971; children: Ryan A., Katy C., Romy E. BA in Chemistry, N. Cen. Coll., 1975; MS in Chemistry, Ill. Inst. Tech., 1982, MBA in Ops. Mgmt., 1987. Assoc. chemist Inland Steel, East Chicago, Ind., 1975-76, chemist, 1976-78, analytical chemist, 1978-81, sr. chemist, 1981-83, section mgr., 1983—. Served with U.S Army, 1969-71, VietNam. Mem. ASTM, Am. Soc. for Quality Control. Republican. Lutheran. Avocations: bicycling, golf, swimming, baseball. Home: 8255 Steepleside Dr Burr Ridge IL 60521 Office: Inland Steel Industries 3210 Watling St East Chicago IN 46312

CARR, SALLY ANN, researcher; b. Aurora, Ill., Jan. 1, 1953; d. John Thurman and Grace May (LeCuyer) C. BA, Ea. Ill. U., 1974; MA, Western Mich. U., 1975, MS in Librarianship, 1981. Researcher Library of Internat. Relations, Chgo., 1975-76; fin. analyst No. Trust Co., Chgo., 1976-79; legal researcher Karon, Morrison & Savikas, Chgo., 1979-80; research assoc. Arthur Andersen & Co., Chgo., 1981-85, Fleming Assocs., Miami, Fla., 1985-86, dir. research, 1986—. Mem. Am. Soc. Info. Sci., Spl. Libraries Assn., ALA, Am. Jewish Com., Beta Phi Mu, Pi Sigma Alpha, Alpha Kappa Delta.

CARR, STEVEN ADDISON, communications company executive; b. Madison, Wis., Apr. 22, 1950; s. Hal Noflet and Mary Elizabeth (Smith) C.; m. Diane Kay Schmitz, Nov. 3, 1984; 1 child, Jordon Bentley. BS, Tex. A&M U., 1972; MA, U. Tex., 1980. Sales mgr. Midwest Video Corp., Bryan, Tex., 1972-76; asst. mgr. Capital Cable Corp., Austin, Tex., 1976-80; mktg. mgr. Centel Corp., Chgo., 1980-83; system mgr. Centel Cable of Ill., Des Plaines, 1983-84; dir. mktg. Cox Cable Communications, Moline, Ill., 1984-85; gen. mgr. TCI-Taft Cablevision Assocs., Muskegon, Mich., 1985—; producer, dir. (nat. telecast) Rep. Govs.' Conf., 1979. Mem. Muskegon Civic Theater, New Muskegon Com. Mem. Am. Mktg. Assn., Internat. Indsl. TV Assn., Cable TV Adminstrn. and Mktg. Soc., Phi Kappa Phi. Republican. Episcopalian. Avocations: tennis, sailing, skiing. Home: 575 Franklin St North Muskegon MI 49445 Office: Muskegon Cable TV 700 W Broadway Muskegon MI 49443

CARRAHER, CHARLES JACOB, JR., professional speaker; b. Cin., Sept. 22, 1922; s. Charles Jacob and Marcella Marie (Hager) C.; grad. pub. schs., Norwood, O.; m. Joyce Ann Root, June 13, 1947; children—Cynthia A., Craig J. With Cin. Enquirer, 1937-72, office mgr., circulation mgr., adminstrv. asst. to exec. v.p., 1947-66, dir. employee community relations, 1966-72, corp. sec., 1969-72; exec. v.p., partner Cin. Suburban Newspapers Inc., 1973-77; asst. dir. devel. WCET-TV, 1977-79; v.p. Garrett Computer Inc., 1979-81; participant numerous symposia. Mem. bd., v.p. Cin. Conv. and Visitors Bur., 1966-72; mem. Cin. Manpower Planning Council, 1972. Bd. dirs. Central Psychiatric Clinic, 1970-80, Mental Health Assn., 1970-72, Great Rivers council Girl Scouts U.S.A., 1969-74; v.p. bd. dirs. Neediest Kids of All, 1969-72; bd. dirs. Greater Cin. Urban League, 1971-74, 75-78. Served to lt., USAAF, World War II, ETO. Decorated Air medal with cluster. Mem. Greater Cin. C. of C. (chmn. human resources devel. com. 1972), Beta Gamma Sigma. Republican. Methodist. Home and office: 10848 Lake Thames Dr Cincinnati OH 45242

CARRIER, WILFRED PETER, elec. engr.; b. Faulkton, S.D., July 14, 1923; s. Wilfred P. and Mary (Mundy) C.; E.E., Ill. Inst. Tech., 1952; m. Mary M. Mulcahy, July 17, 1943; children—Patrick, Timothy. Dir. quality Standard Coil Products Co., Chgo., 1951-58; dir. quality, reliability Mallory Capacitor Co., Indpls., 1958-74, dir. engring., 1974—. Served with AUS, 1942-46; CBI. Mem. Electronic Industries Assn., Am. Soc. Quality Control (regional award), IEEE, Am. Def. Preparedness Assn., Nat. Security Indsl. Assn. Roman Catholic. Clubs: Indpls. Athletic, K.C. Home: 9861 Chesterton St N Indianapolis IN 46280 Office: 3029 Washington St E Indianapolis IN 46206

CARRINGER, PAUL TIMOTHY, marketing executive; b. St. Paul, Apr. 8, 1958; s. Donald Fred and Violet Johanna (Wermter) C.; m. Patsy Sue Mullins, Sept. 12, 1986. AA, Columbus Tech. Inst., 1981; BSBA, Franklin U., 1982; MBA, Ohio U., 1986. V.p. Carringer Bus. Service, Columbus, 1981—; mgmt. trainee Farmers Ins. Corp., Columbus, 1985; grad. staff asst. Ohio U., Athens, 1985-86. Served with USAR, 1977-83. Mem. Columbus Area C. of C. (mgr. 1984-85, cons. 1985), Columbus Jaycees. Republican. Pentecostal. Club: Columbus Road Runners. Avocations: running, reading, computer modeling. Office: Carringer Bus Service PO Box 15637 Columbus OH 43215-0637

CARRIVEAU, MICHAEL JON, military officer; b. Lena, Wis., Sept. 29, 1956; s. Roger Walter and Audrey Ann (Frye) C.; m. Judith Ann Steffenhagen, Nov. 14, 1974 (div. Mar. 1979); children: Michelle, Amanda; m. Rhonna Jean Hayden, Feb. 14, 1982; children: Devin, Jonathan. Grad. high sch., Oconto Falls, Wis., 1974. Asst. store mgr. Kinney Shoe Corp., Green Bay, Wis., 1974-75; enlisted USAF, 1975, advanced through grades to staff sgt., 1980; with stock control sect. 601st Tactical Control Wing, Sembach Air Base, Fed. Republic of Germany, 1975-77; base supply customer liaison 3750th Supply Squadron, Sheppard AFB, Tex., 1977-79; with aircraft maintenance material control 52d Tactical Fighter Wing, Spangdahlem Air Base, Fed. Republic of Germany, 1979; enlisted aid to comdr.-in-chief Allied Air Forces Europe, Ramstein Air Base, Fed. Republic of Germany, 1980; with aircraft maintenance material control 388th Tactical Fighter Wing, Hill AFB, Utah, 1984-86; with base contracting 321st Strategic Missle Wing, Grand Forks AFB, N.D., 1986—. Asst. camp ranger Bear Paw Boy Scout Camp, Mountain, Wis., 1972-73. Mem. Air Force Assn., Aircraft Owners and Pilots Assn., Noncommd. Officers Assn. Republican. Roman Catholic. Avocations: playing drums, flying. Home: 4931 Machickanee Ln Lena WI 54139

CARROLL, CARMAL EDWARD, clergyman, educator; b. Grahn, Ky., Oct. 8, 1923; s. Noah Washington and Jessie Laura (Scott) C.; Ph.B., U. Toledo, 1947, M.A., 1950, B.Edn., 1951; M.L.S., UCLA, 1961; Ph.D., U. Calif., Berkeley, 1969; postgrad. in theology Duke U., Episcopal Div. Sch.; m. Greta S. Seastrom, June 11, 1960; 1 adopted child, Mehran Sabouhi. Edn. librarian, U. So. Calif., 1961-62; reference librarian U. Calif. at Berkeley, 1962-65; dir. library So. Oreg. Coll., Ashland, 1965-67; dir. libraries Wichita (Kans.) State U., 1967-70; prof. library sci. U. Mo. at Columbia, 1970—. Named Ky. col. Mem. AAUP, ALA, Assn. Library and Info. Sci. Educators, Mo. Library Assn., N.Y. Acad. Sci., Assn. Info. and Image Mgmt., Internat. Platform Assn., Phi Delta Kappa, Beta Phi Mu. Democrat. Episcopalian. Club: Rotary. Author: Professionalization of Education for Librarianship, 1970. Home: 2001 Country Club Dr Columbia MO 65201

CARROLL, GLADA IROLENE HOUSER, hospital food service director; b. Carson, Iowa, May 24, 1923; d. Jacob Henry and Sarah Viola (Frain) Houser; B.S., Iowa State U., 1944, M.S., 1977; m. Leo Warren Carroll, Apr. 7, 1945 (dec.); children—Philip, Linda, Daniel, Timothy, Beverly, Rita. Dietitian, Stouffer's Food Corp., Cleve., Chgo., N.Y.C., 1944-46; dietitian, asst. dir. food service Mercy Hosp., Des Moines, 1967-78, dir. food service, 1978—. Mem. Am. Dietetic Assn. (registered dietitian), Iowa Dietetic Assn. (treas. 1979-83, pres. 1984-85), Des Moines Dist. Dietetic Assn., Am. Soc. Hosp. Food Service Adminstrs., Omicron Nu. Roman Catholic. Office: Mercy Hosp 6th and University St Des Moines IA 50314

CARROLL, MICHAEL R., radiologist; b. Greensburg, Ind., Oct. 17, 1948; s. William Rea and Henrietta (Moeller) C.; m. Marsha Ann Auter, June 12, 1971; children: Phillip, Brent, Emily. BS, Purdue U., 1971; MD, Ind. U., 1975. Cert. Am. Bd. Radiology. Staff radiologist St. Elizabeth and Good Samaritan Hosps., Dayton, Ohio, 1979—. Mem. AMA, Am. Coll. Radiology, Ohio State Med. Assn. Roman Catholic. Avocations: skeet shooting, antique collecting. Office: 111 W 1st St Suite 918 Dayton OH 45402

CARROLL, NORMAN EDWARD, college dean, educator; b. Chgo., Oct. 17, 1929; s. Ralph Thomas and Edith (Fay) C.; m. Ruth Carlton, July 26, 1960; children—Rebecca, Mark, John. B.S., Loyola U.-Chgo., 1956; M.S.A., Rosary Coll., 1983; M.A., DePaul U., 1965; Ph.D., Ill. Inst. Tech., 1971. Prin. Carroll Assocs., River Forest, Ill., 1956-65; prof. bus. and econs. Rosary Coll., River Forest, 1968-70, dean Grad. Sch. Bus., 1977—, v.p., dean faculty, 1970—. Contbr. articles to profl. publs. Bd. dirs. Oak Park Human Relations Com., Ill., 1965; mem. selection com. Chgo. Archdiocesan Sch. Bd., 1970; mem. adv. com. River Forest Sch. Bd., 1975. Served to cpl. U.S. Army, 1951-53. Mem. Acad. Mgmt., Am. Econ. Assn., Associated Colls. Chgo. Area (pres. 1973-75, treas. 1982—), Indsl. Relations Research Assn., Ill. Tng. and Devel. Assn. (chmn. membership 1983-84). Lodge: Rotary. Office: Rosary Coll 7900 Division River Forest IL 60305

CARROLL, PATRICK TERRENCE, electrical engineer; b. Milw., Nov. 22, 1959; s. Bernard F. and Rita C. (Rudolph) C.; m. Natalie A. Dryfka, May 21, 1983. BSEE, U. Wis., Milw., 1982. Registered profl. engr., Wis. Elec. engr. nuclear power Wis. Electric Power Co., Milw., 1982-84, elec. engr. system protection, 1984—. Mem. Broadcast Music, Inc., Wis. Herpetological Assn. Democrat. Roman Catholic. Avocations: film, photography, poetry, lit. Home: 2928 N Cambridge Ave Milwaukee WI 53211

CARROLL, VALEREE SUE, speech pathologist; b. Kansas City, Mo., Aug. 29, 1946; d. Middleton Scott and Patricia Pauline (Anderson) C.; B.S. in Edn., U. Kans., 1968, M.A. in Speech Pathology, 1970. Speech/lang. pathologist Clay County Health Dept., Liberty, Mo., 1970-71, Kansas City (Mo.) Pub. Schs., 1971—; mem. spl. edn. placement team Kansas City Public Sch. Dist. U.S. Office Edn. fellow, 1968-70. Mem. Am., Greater Kansas City speech hearing assns., Council for Exceptional Children. Republican. Home: 2115 W 78th St Prairie Village KS 66208 Office: 1211 McGee St Kansas City MO 64106

CARROLL, WALLACE EDWARD, instruments and equipment manufacturing company executive; b. Taunton, Mass., Nov. 4, 1907; s. Patrick J. and Katherine (Feely) C.; m. Lelia Holden, Nov. 7, 1936; children: Wallace E., Denis H., Barry J., Lelia K.H. PhB, Boston Coll., 1928, LLD, 1957; post-grad., MIT, 1929; postgrad. in bus., Harvard U., 1930, NYU, 1933; post-grad., Northwestern U., 1936; LLD, DePaul U., 1966. With acctg. dept. N.Y. Telephone Co., 1930-33; indsl. engr. Reed & Barton, 1933-34; with sales dept. Fed. Products, 1934-40; chmn., bd. dirs. Wacker Sales, from 1940, Size Control Co., from 1941, Walsh Press & Die Co., from 1945; chmn., bd. dirs. Am. Gage & Machine Co., Elgin, Ill., 1948—, now also pres.; chmn., bd. dirs. Simpson Electric Co., from 1950, Standard Transformer Co., from 1956; chmn. bd. dirs., chief exec. officer Katy Industries, Inc., Elgin, 1970—; chmn. bd. Hawthorne Bank Wheaton; vice chmn., dir. Ludlow Typograph Co.; vice chmn. bd. dirs. M-K-T R.R., Dallas; treas., dir. G.M. Diehl Machine Co., Champion Pneumatic Machinery Co., 1957—; bd. dirs. numerous cos. including Binks Mfg. Co., Franklin Park, Ill., OEA, Inc., Denver, CRL, Inc., Denver, British LaBour Pump Co., London, Ruttonsha-Simpson Pvt. Ltd., Bombay, Bush Universal, Inc., N.Y.C., Mercantile Nat. Bank Chgo.; dir. metal-working equipment div. BDSA, Dept. Commerce, Washington, 1957; with U.S. Trade Mission to India, 1958-59, UAR, 1960, Ireland and Portugal, 1966, U.S. Council Commerce and Industry, 1973, U.S. Bus. Trade Mission Korea, 1974, Trade and Investment Mission Rep. China, 1975. Chmn. fed. agys. Community Fund drive, 1959; mem. citizen's com. Loyola U.; bd. dirs. Cath. Charities, 1962, Chgo. Boys Club, Chgo. Girls Club, Am. Irish Found., Gregorian U. Found., N.Y.; past bd. regents Boston Coll.; trustee Christine and Alfred Sonntag Found. Cancer Research; past trustee DePaul U. Served with U.S. Army Air Corps, 1929, with N.G., 1930-33. Recipient Civic award Loyola U., 1965, Heinze/Winzeler award, 1982, Dr. Humanities award St. Xavier Coll., 1986; named hon. mem. Chippewa Indian Tribe. Mem. Tool and Die Inst. (pres. 1952-53), U.S. C. of C. (econ. policy com. 1959-62), Nat. Machine Tool Builders Assn. (pres. 1962-63). Roman Catholic. Clubs: Chgo. Athletic, Chgo., Mid-Am., MIT, Harvard, Harvard Bus., Boston Coll., NYU (Chgo.); Burning Tree (Bethesda, Md.); Exmoor Country (Highland Park, Ill.); East Chop Beach, Martha's Vineyard, Edgartown Yacht (Mass.); Everglades, Bath and Tennis (Palm Beach, Fla.); Univ. (N.Y.C.). Office: Katy Industries Inc 2200 E Devon Ave Suite 220 Des Plaines IL 60018 also: Katy Industries Inc 853 Dundee Ave Elgin IL 60120

CARROW, LEON ALBERT, physician; b. Chgo., Jan. 18, 1924; s. Charles and Mollie (Sachs) C.; m. Joan Twaddell, June 21, 1974; children by previous marriage—Elizabeth, James. B.S., U. Chgo., 1945, M.D., 1947. Intern Cook County Hosp. and Chgo. Lying-in Hosp., 1947-48; resident Chgo. Wesley Meml. Hosp., Chgo. Maternity Center, 1949-51; sr. attending physician in obstetrics and gynecology Northwestern Meml. Hosp., 1954—, also past chief of staff; asso. prof. obstetrics and gynecology Northwestern U. Med. Sch., 1967-73, prof. clin. obstetrics and gynecology, 1973—. Contbr. articles to profl. jours. Served with AUS, 1944-46; to capt. USAF, 1952-53. Fellow A.C.S.; mem. Ill., Chgo. med. socs., AMA, Chgo. Gynecology Soc., Am. Soc. Cytology, Central Assn. Obstetrics and Gynecology. Home: 566 Cedar St Winnetka IL 60093 Office: 251 E Chicago Ave Chicago IL 60611

CARRUTHERS, PHILIP CHARLES, lawyer, public official; b. London, Dec. 8, 1953; came to U.S., 1962, naturalized, 1971; s. J. Alex and Marie (Calarco) C. B.A., U. Minn., 1975, J.D., 1979. Bar: Minn. 1979, U.S. Dist. Ct. Minn., 1979, U.S. Ct. Appeals (8th cir.) 1979. Assoc., Nichols & Kruger, and predecessor firm, 1979-81; ptnr. Nichols, Kruger, Starks and Caruthers, Mpls., 1982-84; ptnr. Luther, Ballenthin & Carruthers, Mpls., 1985—; pros. atty. City of Deephaven, Minn., 1979—, City of Woodland, Minn., 1980—; mem. Minn. Ho. Reps., 1987—. Co-author: The Drinking Driver in Minnesota: Criminal and Civil Issues, 1982. Note and comment editor Minn. Law Rev., 1978-79. Mem. Met. Council of Twin Cities Area, St. Paul, 1983-87; Minn. Ho. of Reps., 1987—. Mem. Minn. Trial Lawyers Assn. (bd. govs. 1982-86), Minn. State Bar Assn., Hennepin County Bar Assn., Assn. Trial Lawyers Am. Mem. Democratic Farmer-Labor Party. Roman Catholic. Home: 6931 Willow Ln N Brooklyn Center MN 55430 Office: Luther Ballenthin & Carruthers 4624 IDS Ctr Minneapolis MN 55402

CARRYER, HADDON MCCUTCHEN, physician, educator; b. Unionville, Mo., Aug. 25, 1914; s. Carl Haddon and Margaret Dill (McCutchen) C.; m. Mable Jane Jones, Feb. 15, 1941; children: Haddon Carl, Peter Ward, Diane Elizabeth. BA, Drake U., 1934; MD, MS, Northwestern U., Chgo., 1938; PhD, U. Minn., 1948. Clin. cons. Mayo Clinic, Rochester, Minn., 1943-46; instr. internal medicine Mayo Grad. Sch., Rochester, 1946-51, asst. prof. medicine, 1951-62, assoc., 1962-73; prof. med. Mayo Med. Sch., Rochester, 1973-79; emeritus staff Mayo Clinic, Rochester, 1979—, chmn. various comms., 1958-67. Mem. med. adv. com. Minn. State Dept. Pub. Welfare. Recipient Good Neighbor award Sta. WCCO-Radio, 1975. Fellow ACP, Am. Acad. Allergy and Immunology; mem. AMA, (Minn. del. 1965-72, 1973-78), Minn. Med. Assn. (pres. 1962), Min. Soc. Internal Med., Zumbro Valley Med. Soc. (past pres.). Republican. Episcopalian. Club. University, Golf and Country (Rochester). Home: 1125 Skyline Dr SW Rochester MN 55902

CARSELLO, CARMEN JOSEPH, psychologist, educator; b. Chgo., July 16, 1915; s. Joseph and Mary Domenica (Tomasone) C.; m. Nicoletta Dalesio, June 18, 1939; children: Camille (dec.), Frank, Robert. BPE, DePaul U., 1938, MA, 1953; PhD, U. Sarasota, 1971; degree in gerontology, U. Ill., 1983. Registered psychologist, Ill. Tchr. parochial schs., Chgo., 1939-42; tchr. pub. schs., Cicero, Ill., 1942-43, Chgo., 1950-57; reading specialist Bur. Child Study Pub. Schs., Chgo., 1957-63; counselor, reading specialist U. Ill., Chgo., 1963-85; prof. emeritus Nat. Coll. Edn., Chgo., 1986—; prof. emeritus psychology Triton Coll., River Grove, Ill., 1986—. Contbr. articles to profl. jours. Vol. Loyola U., Chgo., 1960—; northwest rep. Mont-Clare Leyden Srs., Chgo., St. Williams Srs., 1985—; mem. career com. Joint Civic Com. Italian Ams., Chgo., 1985. Served with USN, 1943-45, PTO. Recipient Service award Loyola U., Chgo. Mem. Internat. Reading Assn., Chgo. Psychol. Assn., Asian-Am. Literacy Assn. of Internat. Reading Assn., U. Ill. Retirement Assn., U. Ill. Scholarship Assn., Chgo. Area Reading Assn. Roman Catholic. Club: Gregorians (various offices Chgo. chpt.). Avocations: reading, swimming, dancing, travel, photography. Home and Office: 2154 N Nordica Ave Chicago IL 60635

CARSON, BONNIE L(OU), chemist; b. Kansas City, Kans., Aug. 11, 1940; d. Harold Lee and Lorene Marie (Draper) Bachert; student U. Kansas City, 1958-61; B.A. in Chemistry summa cum laude, U. N.H., 1963; M.S. in Organic Chemistry, Oreg. State U., 1966; m. David M. Carson, June, 1961 (div. 1973); 1 dau., Catherine (Katie) Leslie. Grad. teaching asst. Oreg. State U., 1963-66; organic chem. lab. instr. U. Waterloo, Ont., Can., 1968-69; asst. abstractor in macromolecular chemistry Chem. Abstracts Service, Columbus, Ohio, 1969-71; freelance Russian translator, 1971-73; asst. chemist Midwest Research Inst., Kansas City, Mo., 1973-75, asso. chemist, 1975-80, sr. chemist, 1980—. Mem. Am. Soc. Info. Scientists, Am. Chem. Soc., N.Y. Acad. Sci., Soc. Environ. Geochemistry and Health, Am. Translators Assn. (pres. Mid-Am. chpt. 1984-85), Soc. Tech. Communication. Author and Editor: (with others) Trace Metals in the Environment, 1977-81, Toxicology and Biological Monitoring of Metals, 1986; contbr. in field. Home: 5501 Holmes St Kansas City MO 64110 Office: 425 Volker Blvd Kansas City MO 64110

CARSON, CLAUDE MATTESON (KIT), investment counselor; b. Farley, Mo., Sept. 26, 1907; s. Robert Walter and Mirtle Virginia Carson; student Advanced Mgmt. Program, Harvard U., 1962; m. Helen Long, May 16, 1931. Pres., Hoerner Boxes, Inc., until 1966; sr. v.p. adminstrn., dir. Hoerner Waldorf Corp. (merger Hoerner Boxes, Inc. and Waldorf Paper Products Co.), St. Paul, 1966-73, 76—, also chmn. audit co., mem. exec. com.; chmn. audit com., dir. Puritan-Bennett Corp., Kansas City, Mo. Mem. Bus. Climate Task Force Com., State of Minn., 1971-73; active Boy Scouts Am.; bd. mgrs. Parker B. Francis III Found.; bd. govs. Interlachen, 1976-82. Served with AUS. Fellow Am. Inst. Mgmt. (pres.'s council); mem. Fibre Box Assn. (chmn. bd., past pres.), TAPPI, Fourdrinier Kraft Board Inst., Internat. Corrugated Case Assn. (dir.). Clubs: Union League, Mid-Am. (Chgo.); Interlachen, Question, Minneapolis, St. Paul Pool and Yacht, Harvard Alumni, Rotary. Home: 5209 Schaefer Rd Edina MN 55436 Office: 6500 York Ave Suite 119 Minneapolis MN 55435

CARSON, DIANE EILEEN, communications educator; b. St. Louis, June 10, 1946; d. Edmund Kevin and Marvell Delores (Walchli) C.; m. Willis Lee Loy, June 3, 1978. MA in English, Kans. U., 1970; MA in Media Communications, Webster U., 1979; MA in Film, Ohio U., 1981. Cert. lifetime tchr., Mo. From. instr. to assoc. prof. English St. Louis Community Coll.-Meramec, Kirkwood, Mo., 1970-80, prof. mass communications, 1981—; adj. faculty film Webster U., St. Louis, Mo., 1982—. Contbr. articles to profl. jours. Fulbright fellow; recipient Ford Found. grant, 1986. Mem. Soc. Cinema Studies, U. Film and Video Assn., Popular Culture Assn. Nat. Awards Com., Mo. Assn. Community and Jr. Colls. Democrat. Avocations: sports, jogging, swimming, skiing, horseback riding. Office: St Louis Community Coll at Meramec 11333 Big Bend Blvd Kirkwood MO 63122

CARSON, GORDON BLOOM, reserch institute executive; b. High Bridge, N.J., Aug. 1, 1911; s. Whitfield R. and Emily (Bloom) C.; m. Beth Lacy, June 19, 1937; children—Richard Whitfield, Emily Elizabeth (Mrs. Lee A. Duffus), Alice Lacy (Mrs. William P. Allman), Jean Helen (Mrs. Michael J. Gable). B.S. in Mech. Engring, Case Inst. Tech., 1931, D.Eng., 1957; M.S., Yale U., 1932, M.E., 1938; LL.D., Rio Grande Coll., 1973. With Western Electric Co., 1930; instr. mech. engring. Case Inst. Tech., 1932-37, asst. prof., 1937-40, asso. prof. indsl. engring. charge indsl. div., 1940-44; with Am. Shipbldg. Co., 1936; patent litigation 1937; research engr., dir. research Cleve. Automatic Machine Co., 1939-44; asst. to gen. mgr. Selby Shoe Co., 1944, mgr. engring., 1945-49, sec. of corp., 1949-53; sec., dir. Pyrrole Products Co., 1948-53; dean engring. Ohio State U., Columbus, 1953-58; v.p. bus. and finance, treas. Ohio State U., 1958-71; dir. Engring. Exptl. Sta., 1953-58; exec. v.p. Albion (Mich.) Coll., 1971-76, exec. cons., 1976-77; asst. to chancellor, dir. fin. Northwood Inst., 1977-82; v.p. Mich. Molecular Inst., 1982—. Editor: The Production Handbook, 1958; cons. editor, 1972—; Author of tech. papers engring. subjects. Trustee White Cross Hosp. Assn., 1960-71; bd. dirs. Cardinal Funds, 1966—; bd. dirs. Goodwill Industries, 1959-67, 1st v.p., 1963-64; bd. dirs. Orton Found., 1953-58; v.p. Ohio State U. Research Found., 1958-71; v.p., chmn. adv. council Center for Automation and Soc., U. Ga., 1969-71; Chmn. tool and die com. 5th Regional War Labor Bd., 1943-45; chmn. Ohio State adv. com. for sci., tech. and specialized personnel SSS, 1965-70. Fellow ASME, AAAS, Am. Inst. Indsl. Engrs. (pres. 1957-58); mem. Columbus Soc. Fin. Analysts (pres. 1964-65), Fin. Analysts Fedn. (dir. 1964-65), C. of C. (dir., treas. 1952-53), Am. Soc. Engring. Edn., Asso. U. for Research in Astronomy (dir. 1968-71), Midwestern Univs. Research Assn. (dir. 1958-71), U.S. Naval Inst., Nat. Soc. Profl. Engrs., Romophos, Sphinx, Sigma Xi (fin. com. 1975—, nat. treas. 1979—), Tau Beta Pi, Zeta Psi, Phi Eta Sigma, Alpha Pi Mu, Omicron Delta Epsilon. Lodge: Mason (32 deg.). Home: 5413 Gardenbrook Dr Midland MI 48640 Office: Mich Molecular Inst 1910 W Saint Andrews Rd Midland MI 48640

CARSON, IRWIN KRENGEL, orthopedic surgeon; b. Phila., Dec. 30, 1944; s. George K. and Claire (Althousen) C.; m. Nancy Gilbert Dec. 27, 1969; children—Jonathan, Julie, Joshua. A.B., Harvard U., 1966; M.D., U. Mich., 1970. Diplomate Am. Bd. Orthopedic Surgery. Intern, Kaiser Found. Hosp., San Francisco, 1970-71; resident Michael Reese Med. Ctr., Chgo., 1971-74; fellow U. Toronto, 1974-75; practice medicine, specializing in orthopedic surgery, Arlington Hts., Ill., 1976—; staff Humana Hosp., Hoffman Estates, Ill., Children's Meml. Hosp., Chgo. Mem. Sch. Bd. Caucus, Highland Park, Ill., 1978; recreation Adv. Com., Highland Park, 1983—; bd. dirs. Northbrook Symphone Orchestra, men's council Mus. Contemporary Art, Chgo. Mem. Ill. Orthopedic Soc., Chgo. Orthopedic Soc. Clubs: Harvard of Chgo. (bd. dirs.), U. Mich. of Chgo., Pres.'s. Home: 290 Briar Ln Highland Park IL 60035 Office: 3295 N Arlington Heights Rd Arlington Heights IL 60004

CARSON, MARY SILVANO, educator, counselor; b. Mass., Aug. 11, 1925; d. Joseph and Alice V. (Sherwood) Silvano; B.S., Simmons Coll., Boston, 1947; M.A., U. Chgo., 1961; postgrad. Ctr. Urban Studies, 1970, U. Chgo., 1970, 72, U. Minn., 1977, DePaul U., 1980; m. Paul E. Carson, Feb. 21, 1947 (dec.); children—Jan Ellen, Jeffrey Paul, Amy Jayne. Cert. Nat. Commn. Counselor Cert. Bd., Ill. sch. counselor, Ill. employment counselor III, career testing. Mgr. S.W. Youth Opportunity Center, Dept. Labor, Chgo., 1966-67; careers counselor Gordon Tech. High Sch., Chgo., 1971-74; dir. Career and Assessment Center, YMCA Community Coll., Chgo., 1974-81; project coordinator Career Ctr., Loop Coll., Chgo., 1981-82; adv. bd. City-Wide Coll. Career Center. Bd. dirs. Loop YWCA, Chgo. Mem. Women's Share in Public Service (v.p.), Am. Ednl. Research Assn., Am. Counseling and Devel. Assn., Nat. Vocat. Guidance Assn., Bus. and Profl. Women's Club, Pi Lambda Theta (pres. chpt. 1975). Home: 155 Harbor Dr Chicago IL 60601

CARSTEDT, WILLIAM DOUGLAS, lawyer; b. Chgo., Mar. 9, 1938; s. William E. and Lillian (Smith) C.; m. Mary E. May, July 31, 1981. BS in Law, Northwestern U., 1957, LLB, 1960. Bar: Ill. 1960. Assoc. Shaheen, Lundberg & Callahan, Chgo., 1960-68; ptnr. Springer & Carstedt, Chgo., 1968-85, Defrees & Fiske, Chgo., 1985—. Bd. dirs. Assn. Beverly Shores (Ind.) Residents, 1986—. Mem. ABA, Chgo. Bar Assn., Chgo. Estate Planning Council. Home: PO Box 586 Beverly Shores IN 46301-0586 Office: Defrees & Fiske 72 W Adams Chicago IL 60603

CARSTENS, ROBERT LOWELL, civil engineering consultant, researcher, former educator; b. Sisseton, S.D., July 31, 1922; s. Fred Andrew and Ava Esther (Kulow) C.; m. Marian Helen Kirkendall, Apr. 24, 1948; 1 child, Michael Robert. B.S., Iowa State U., 1943, M.S., 1964, Ph.D., 1966. Registered profl. engr., Iowa. Constrn. engr. Kramme & Jensen Constrn. Co., Des Moines, 1946-48; constrn. engr. Jensen Constrn. Co., Des Moines, 1949-50; maintenance engr., supr. Arabian-Am. Oil Co., Saudi Arabia, 1954-61; hwy. engr. U.S AID, La Paz, Bolivia, 1962-63; prof. civil engring. Iowa State U., Ames, 1964-86; cons. hwy. safety and accident reconstruction; mem. Gov.'s Task Force To Modernize State Transp. System, 1973-74. Contbr. articles to tech. and profl. jours. Served with U.S. Army, 1943-45, 50-54. Decorated Bronze Star; recipient Dir.'s Ann. award Iowa Dept. Transp., 1981. Mem. ASCE, Nat. Soc. Profl. Engrs., Inst. Transp. Engrs., Transp. Research Bd. Republican. Lodges: Masons, Shriners, Kiwanis. Home: 1503 20th St Ames IA 50010

CARSTENSEN, CAROL JEAN, former state agency administrator; b. Cleve., Jan. 31, 1943; d. Herman Samuel and Rose (Offner) Schneider; m. Peter C. Carstensen, July 14, 1968; children: Mary, Jean, Daniel, Steven. BA with honors, U. Wis., 1965, M in Pub. Adminstrn., 1986; M in Teaching, Yale U., 1967. Caseworker Cuyahoga County Welfare, Cleve., 1966; tchr. New Haven (Conn.) Pub. Schs., 1966-68, Washington Pub. Schs., 1968-71; instr. Madison (Wis.) Area Tech. Coll., 1974-83; policy analyst Dept. Industry Labor and Human Relations, Madison, 1986-87. Pres. Elem. Parent Group, Madison, 1981-82, 83-84, Mid. Sch. Parent Group, 1985-87, founder; founder, steering com., Citywide Parent Group, Madison, 1984-87. Recipient Outstanding Performance award State of Wis., 1986. Mem. LWV (unit pres. Dane County 1978-80). Avocations: books, biking, home remodeling. Home: 720 Orton Ct Madison WI 53703

CARSTENSEN, JOHN ROBERT, civil engineer; b. Waverly, Iowa, Feb. 21, 1940; s. Clarence Frederick and Mary Isabel (Bradley) C.; m. MaryBeth Edelman, June 4, 1966; children: Jay, Karen. BCE, Iowa State U., 1962; MCE, Ariz. State U., 1966. Registered profl. engr., Ohio, Iowa, Nebr., Colo. Commd. 2d lt. USAF, 1962, advanced through grades to lt. col., 1978, ret., 1984; constrn. engr. 4600 civil engring. squad USAF, Ent AFB, Colo., 1962-64; constrn. engr. 820 civil engring. squad USAF, Tuy Hoa, Vietnam, 1966-67; civil engr. Civil Engrng. Ctr. USAF, Wright-Patterson AFB, Ohio, 1967-71; base civil engr. HQ The U.S. Logistics Group USAF, Ankara, Turkey, 1971-73; chief requirements and resources br. USAF, Pentagon, Va., 1973-78; chief ops. br. 27th civil engr. squad USAF, Cannon AFB, N.Mex., 1978-79; chief installations br. HQ 6th allied tactical NATO air force, Izmir, Turkey, 1979-81; chief utilities systems HQ SAC USAF, Offutt AFB, Nebr., 1981-83, chief facilities systems HQ SAC, 1983-84; dir. bus. devel. Farris Engring., Omaha, 1985—. Contbr. articles to profl. jours. Mem. Soc. Am. Mil. Engrs., Nat. Soc. Profl. Engrs., Soc. Mktg. Profl. Services, The Retired Officers Assn., Air Force Assn., Engrs.' Club Omaha. Home: 802 Brenton Ave Bellevue NE 68005 Office: Farris Engring 11239 Chicago Circle Omaha NE 68154

CARTEE, THOMAS EDWARD, JR., banker; b. Largo, Fla., Jan. 30, 1960; s. Thomas Edward and JoAnne (Todd) C.; m. Kathryn Armecia Stokes, Aug. 6, 1983; 1 child, Thomas Edward III. AB in Econs., Davidson Coll., 1982; MBA, U. N.C., 1984. Assoc. account rep. First Nat. Bank Chgo., 1984-85; credit analyst, account rep. Swiss Bank Corp., Chgo., 1985, asst. mgr., head credit dept., 1986—; assoc. Robert Morris Assocs., Chgo., 1986—. Treas. Clifton Place Condominium Assn., Chgo., 1985-86. Mem. U. N.C. Alumni Assn. Republican. Office: Swiss Bank Corp 3 1st National Plaza Suite 2100 Chicago IL 60602

CARTER, ARNOLD NICK, cassette learning systems company executive; b. Phila., Mar. 25, 1929; s. Arnold and Margaret (Richter) C.; A.A., Keystone Jr. Coll., 1949; B.S. in Speech and Dramatic Art, Syracuse U., 1951; post-grad. Syracuse U., 1951-52; M.A. in Communications, Am. Univ., 1959; m. Virginia Lucille Polsgrove, Oct. 14, 1955; children—Victoria Lynne, Andrea Joy. Actor Rome (N.Y.) Little Theater, summers, 1951-52; mgr. customer relations Martin Marietta, Orlando, Fla., 1959-70; v.p. communications research Nightingale-Conant Corp., Chgo., 1970—. Served with USNR, 1953-59; Korea. Recipient Continuare Professus Articulatus Excellare award, Nat. Speakers Assn., 1978. Mem. Sales and Mktg. Execs. Chgo. (v.p. 1979-81), Nat. Speakers Assn., Am. Soc. Tng. and Devel., Internat. Platform Assn. Republican. Presbyn. Author: Communicate Effectively, 1978; The Amazing Results-Full World of Cassette Learning, 1980; Sales Boosters, 1981. Home: 1315 Elmwood Ave Deerfield IL 60015 Office: Nightingale-Conant Corp 7300 N Lehigh Chicago IL 60648

CARTER, A(RT) B(RADEN), construction company executive; b. Coraopolis, Pa., Oct. 7, 1939; s. Mortimer J. and Verna (Burch) C.; m. Sandra S. Tidswell, July 2, 1960; children: Andrea B., Stacey L. BS, U. Cin., 1962. Registered profl. civil engr., Ohio. Field engr. Jennings & Churella, New London, Ohio, 1957-62; gen. supt. Butler Constrn. Co., Lima, Ohio, 1962-64; estimator, project mgr., gen. supt. Funk Constrn. Co., New London, 1964-66; supt., project mgr. Mosser Constrn. Co., Fremont, Ohio, 1966-85, v.p., dir. field ops., 1985—; prof. Bowling Green (Ohio) State U., 1980-85. Active Girl Scouts U.S., Fremont, 1966—, area dir. 1980; active Campfire, Fremont, 1966—. Mem. Ohio Contractors Assn. (bd. dirs. 1983-86, chmn. labor exec. com. 1984, Outstanding Chpt. 1983), Assn. Gen. Contractors. Republican. Mehtodist. Home: 1625 Tiffin Fremont OH 43420 Office: Mosser Constrn Co 122 S Wilson Ave Fremont OH 43420

CARTER, CHARLES DOUGLAS, controller; b. Moline, Ill., May 26, 1936; s. Charles Edward and Lila Mae (Reiling) C.; m. Sylvia Kay Stein, July 3, 1960; children: Michael D., James H. BS, Bradley U., 1958; MBA, No. Ill. U., 1973. CPA. Auditor Gauger & Diehl CPA, Rockford, Ill., 1964-68; mgr. acctg. GC Electronics, Rockford, 1968-69, controller, 1969-87; corp. controller Rockford Bolt and Steel Inc. and Jackson Screw div., 1987—. Bd. dirs. small bus. loan com. City of Rockford, 1983—; advisor Jr. Achievement, Rockford, 1969-77; pres. Christian Bus. Men's Com., Rockford, 1981, 83, 84; trustee First. Evang. Free Ch., Rockford, 1985—. Served to capt. USAF, 1958-63. Mem. Am. Inst. CPA's, Ill. Soc. CPA's, Nat. Assn. Accts., Inst. Cert. Mgmt. Accts. Home: 3423 Fawnridge Dr Rockford IL 61111 Office: Rockford and Steel Inc 6483 Falcon Rd Rockford IL 61109

CARTER, CHRISTIE HEISTAND, dentist; b. Springfield, Ohio, June 18, 1923; s. Christie D. and Leona (Moore) C.; m. Vivian Hehl, Aug. 2, 1952; children: Lisa Rae, Christie Neal, Terri Lee. Student, Wittenberg U., Springfield, 1946-48; DDS, Ohio State U., 1952. Gen. practice dentistry Springfield, 1952—; mem. dental staff Mercy Hosp., Springfield; bd. dirs. Home City Fed. Savs. and Loan Assn., Springfield. Fellow Acad. Internat. Dentistry, Acad. Gen. Dentistry, Internat. Coll. Dentists; mem. Ohio Dental Assn., Mad River Valley Dental Soc. (pres. 1960-61), Am. Soc. Dentistry for Children. Republican. Lutheran. Clubs: University (Springfield), Springfield Country. Avocations: skiing, wind surfing, tennis. Home: 1927 Fairway Dr Springfield OH 45504 Office: 1209 Plum St Springfield OH 45504

CARTER, CONSTANCE LAVERNE, office manager; b. Pensacola, Fla., Aug. 6, 1945; d. Robert Henry and Catherine (Lindsay) Grant; m. Robert Carter, Aug. 9, 1968; children: James H., Catherine L., Michelle D. B in Gen. Studies, Roosevelt U., 1984. Mgr. office services Jacobs Suchard/Brach Inc. (formerly E.J. Brach & Sons), Chgo., 1976—; Bd. dirs. Brach Credit Union, Brach Mgmt. Club. Fellow Am. Mgmt. Assn., Nat. Assn. Female Execs. Democrat. Baptist. Avocations: bowling, baseball. Office: Jacobs Suchard/Brach Inc 4656 W Kinzie St Chicago IL 60644

CARTER, DANIEL PAUL, consultant systems management; b. Des Moines, July 7, 1953; s. Delbert Bruce and Doris Jean (Thompson) C.; m. Victoria Lea Kriegler, Sept. 13, 1980; children—Kimberly, Nicholas. BS, Iowa State U., 1975. Cons. staff Arthur Andersen & Co., Chgo., 1975-79, cons. mgr., 1979-82, cons. ptnr., 1982—. Mem. Data Processing Mgmt. Assn., Assn. Systems Mgmt. (v.p. 1982-83, div. dir. 1984—), Am. Correctional Assn. Lodge: Elks. Avocations: fishing, racquetball, chess. Home: 108 Roanoke St Rochester IL 62563 Office: Arthur Andersen & Co 1 N Old State Capitol Plaza Springfield IL 62701

CARTER, DAVID CARLSON, data processing executive; b. Berea, Ky., Nov. 24, 1935; m. Marilyn K. Piech, Jan. 29, 1966; children: Paul, Stephanie. BS, Berea Coll., 1957; MS, U. Ill., 1960. Cert. systems profl. Programmer/systems analyst Procter & Gamble, Cin., 1962-67; dir. info. services Williams Mfg. Co., Portsmouth, Ohio, 1967-76; pres. Pioneer Systems, Inc., Columbus, 1976-81; mgr. tech. support/data processing Nationwise Automotive, Inc., Columbus, 1982—. Served with U.S. Army, 1960-62. Mem. Assn. for Computing Machinery. Avocations: microcomputers, classical music, electronics. Office: Nationwise Automotive Inc 3750 Courtright Ct Columbus OH 43227

CARTER, DENNIS LEE, dentist; b. South Bend, Ind., Nov. 20, 1945; s. Floyd and Leola (Smith) C.; m. Carol Ann Williams, June 13, 1970 (div. 1981); 1 child, Joseph; m. Emma Doris Forrest, Oct. 1, 1981. BS, Alma Coll., 1968; DDS, Ind. U., 1972. Gen. practice dentistry South Bend, 1972-83; in-home dentist, pres. Spl. Patients, South Bend, 1983—; cons., mfr. Spl. Patients, South Bend, 1983—. Inventor patient positioner. Chmn. bd. South Bend Urban League, 1983; bd. dirs. Jr. Achievement, South Bend, 1982; bd. dirs. fin. com. Studebaker's Nat. Mus.; mem. e.a.d. com. United Way of St. Joseph County, South Bend, 1981; mem. profl. adv. bd. Visiting Nurses Assn. Mem. ADA, Nat. Dental Assn., Omicron Delta Kappa, Kappa Alpha Psi. Baptist. Avocation: writing. Office: Spl Patients 726 E Ewing Ave South Bend IN 46613

CARTER, JAMES H., justice state supreme court; b. Waverly, Iowa, Jan. 18, 1935; s. Harvey J. and Althea (Dominick) C.; m. Jeanne E. Carter, Mar. 1959; children: Carol, James. B.A., U. Iowa, 1956, J.D., 1960. Law clk. to judge U.S. Dist. Ct, 1960-62; assoc. Shuttleworth & Ingersoll, Cedar Rapids, Iowa, 1962-73; judge 6th Jud. Dist., 1973-76, Iowa Ct. Appeals, 1976-82; justice Iowa Supreme Ct., Des Moines, 1982—. Office: Supreme Ct State Capitol Des Moines IA 50319

CARTER, JAY DOUGLAS, insurance exective, restaurant industry executive; b. Anderson, Ind., Oct. 12, 1942; s. James V. and Virginia (Williams) C.; m. Ellen Katherine Rigley, Jan. 6, 1972; children: Lynda, Shirley, Jessica. BS in Bus., Ind. U., 1964. Conf. coordinator Ind. U., Bloomington, 1967-68; asst. fed. bank examiner Fed. Deposit Ins. Corp., Chgo., 1968-70; pvt. practice real estate devel. Nashville, Ind., 1970—; prin. Carter Freese & Gredy Ins., Nashville, 1977—; pres. Sunshine Inn of Nashville (Ind.), 1986—; bd. dirs. Midwest Bancorp (formerly Nashville State Bank), ELJA Mgmt., Nashville, sec./treas., 1984—. Mem. Ind. Ins. Agts. of Ind. (bd. dirs. 1984-86). Republican. Avocations: impressionist art collecting, American antiques collecting. Home: PO Box 252 Nashville IN 47448 Office: PO Box 698 Nashville IN 47448

CARTER, JEFFREY ALLYN, academic administrator; b. Dayton, Ohio, Sept. 9, 1955; s. Paul Richard and Sue Ann (Mellage) C.; m. Karen Sue

Amole, June 11, 1983. BSBA magna cum laude, Wright State U., 1977, MBA, 1980. Asst. to dir. alumni assn. Wright State U., Dayton, Ohio, 1979-81; asst. office mgr. Beavercreek (Ohio) Fed. Credit Union, 1981-82; asst. MBA dir. U. Dayton, 1982—. Author MBA Update, 1984—. Mem. Easter Seal Soc., Dayton, 1985—. Wright State U. graduate fellow, 1977; Harry W. and Margaret Moore scholar, 1976, Wright State U. Found. scholar, 1975, Nat. Contract Mgmt. Assn. scholar, 1977; named one of Outstanding Young Men of Am., 1982. Mem. Nat. Assn. Acad. Affairs Adminstrs., Internat. Plastic Modelers Soc., Beavercreek Jaycees (entertainment organizer Fourth of July 1976, 83, 84), Wright State U. Alumni Assn. (Outstanding Service award 1981), Nat. Wildlife Fedn., Beta Gamma Sigma, Phi Eta Tau. Methodist. Clubs: Dayton MBA, U. Dayton Colleagues. Avocations: golf, softball, bowling, model building, guitar. Home: 1322 Meadow Bridge Dr Dayton OH 45432 Office: U Dayton 300 College Park Ave Dayton OH 45469

CARTER, JERRY RALPH, feed ingredient co. exec.; b. Springfield, Mo., Jan. 11, 1930; s. Lloyd Ralph and Atrelle (Ward) C.; B.S., Drury Coll., 1951; m. Blanchelen Campbell, June 15, 1951; children—Cheri Ellen, Thomas Lloyd, Timothy James. Salesman, Nat. Biscuit Co., Springfield, 1954-59; mgr. Southwest Rendering Co., Inc., Springfield, 1959—; mgr. Southwest By-Products, Inc., Springfield, 1959—, pres., 1961—; organizer, dir. Met. Nat. Bank, Springfield, Mo., 1983—. Served with USAF, 1951-54. Mem. Nat. Renderers Assn. (regional pres. 1971-72), Drury Coll. Alumni (pres. 1975). Episcopalian (vestry 1964-65). Lodge: Masons (K.T., Shriner, Jester). Home: 2732 E Seminole St Springfield MO 65804 Office: PO Box 2876 CSS Springfield MO 65803

CARTER, JOHN DALE, organizational development executive; b. Tuskegee, Ala., Apr. 9, 1944; s. Arthur L. and Ann (Bargyh) C.; AB, Ind. U., 1965, MS, 1967; PhD (NDEA fellow), Case Western Res. U., 1974; m. Veronica Louise Hopper, Oct. 12, 1986. Dir. student affairs Dental Sch., Case Western Res. U., Cleve., 1974-75, asst. prof. applied behavioral sci., 1974—, asst. dean orgn. devel. and student affairs, 1975-78; pres. John D. Carter and Assocs., Inc., Cleve., 1985—; ptnr. Portsmouth Cons. Group, 1984—; chmn. bd. Gestalt Inst. Cleve., 1974-80, program dir., fin. dir. 1981-86; mem. exec. bd. Nat. Tng. Labs., 1975-78; faculty Am. U., 1980—; bd. dirs. Behavioral Sci. Found., Cleve., Fielding Inst., 1986—. Mem. Internat. Assn. Applied Social Scientists, (cert. cons. Internat.), Kappa Alpha Psi (pres. alpha chpt. 1964-65), Alpha Phi Omega. Author: Counselling the Helping Relationship, 1975, Managing the Merger Integration Process, 1986. Home: 2995 Scarborough Rd Cleveland Heights OH 44118 Office: PO Box 1822 Cleveland OH 44106

CARTER, JOHN WILLIAM MICHAEL, orthodontist, pedodontist, educator; b. Kansas City, Kans., Nov. 21, 1945; s. William Jay and I'Aleen Gloria (Kramer) C.; m. Colleen Marie O'Rourke, June 25, 1977; children—John Ryan William, Caitlyn Marie. B.F.A., U. Kans., 1967, B.A., 1972; D.D.S. with distinction, U. Mo.-Kansas City, 1978; M.Sc.D. in Oral Biology, grad. cert. in pedodontics, Boston U., 1980; grad. cert. in orthodontics St. Louis U., 1982. Practice dentistry specializing in pedodontics, St. Louis, 1980-82; practice dentistry specializing in pedodontics and orthodontics, Overland Park, Kans., 1982—; asst. prof. orthodontics U. Mo.-Kansas City, 1982—, dir. predoctoral orthodontics, 1984—, asst. prof. grad. orthodontics, 1982—; bd. dirs. St. Louis Edn. and Research Found., 1985—. Author, illustrator: (manual) Practical Biomechanics, 1984; Mixed Dentition Analysis and Treatment, 1984. Contbr. to book Dental Collectables, 1984. Served to maj. USAR, 1978. Mem. ADA, Am. Acad. Pedodontics, Am. Assn. Orthodontists, St. Louis Orthodontic Edn. and Research Found. (v.p. 1987-88), Kans. State Dental Assn., SAR, Omicron Kappa Upsilon, Phi Lambda Upsilon, Psi Omega (pres. 1977, chpt. adviser 1983—nat. committeeman 1984—, province counselor 1987—). Avocations: jogging, cooking, outdoors activities. Office: 8005 W 110th St Suite 214 Overland Park KS 66210

CARTER, LAURIE BETH, accountant executive; b. Cedar Rapids, Iowa, Dec. 16, 1955; d. Jack Keith and Norma Jean (Clayton) Hicks; m. Timothy John Carter, June 5, 1976 (div. July 1981); 1 child, Jacqueline; m. Marty Gene Carter, June 16, 1984. BS, Mt. Mercy Coll., 1979. CPA, Iowa. Staff acct. Davison, Botkin, Koranda & Sieh P.C., Cedar Rapids, 1980-82; asst. v.p. Collins Credit Union, Cedar Rapids, 1982—. Mem. Am. Inst. CPA's, Nat. Assn. Accts., Iowa Soc. CPA's (award for excellence in acctg. at Mt. Mercy Coll. 1980). Democrat. Mem. Christian Ch. Avocations: swimming, cross stitching, crafts. Office: Collins Credit Union 1150 42d NE Cedar Rapids IA 52402

CARTER, MARGUERITE, publishing executive; b. Seattle, Jan. 31, 1899; d. William Whitfield and Minnie (Stafford) Herring; m. Alan C. McConnell, Sept. 29, 1914; 1 child, Alan Richard. Sec., treas. Alan McConnell & Son, Inc., Indpls., 1928—. writer syndicated daily newspaper feature, 1928-39. Office: Alan McConnell & Son Inc 546 S Meridian St #602 Indianapolis IN 46225

CARTER, MICHAEL FRANK, urologist; b. Santa Monica, Calif., Sept. 14, 1939; s. Floyd Arthur and Evelyn Elizabeth (Eager) C.; student U. So. Calif., 1957-62; M.D., Georgetown U., 1966; m. Joan Carol Tedford, Aug. 23, 1959; children—Cristen, Timothy, Richard, Gregory. Intern, resident in surgery Harbor Gen. Hosp., Torrance, Calif., 1966-68; resident in urology Johns Hopkins Hosp., Balt., 1968-72; assoc. prof. clin. urology Northwestern U., Chgo., 1976—; staff physician Northwestern Meml. Hosp., 1972—, exec. com., 1979—; sec., treas. med. staff, 1986-88; chief of urology Lakeside VA Hosp. Troop com. chmn. Boy Scouts Am., 1977-79; mem. Wilmette (Ill.) Sch. Bd. Caucus, 1977-79. Named Outstanding Intern, Harbor Gen. Hosp., 1967; Am. Cancer Soc. fellow, 1970-72. Diplomate Am. Bd. Urology. Fellow A.C.S.; mem. Am. Urol. Soc., AMA, Chgo. Urol. Soc. (exec. com. 1979—, pres. 1986-87), Ill. Med. Assn. Episcopalian. Research on uveal micro circulation in rabbits, androgens in cell cycle of prostate gland, prostatic ultrasound, impotence and penile blood pressure. Home: 720 Ashland Ave Wilmette IL 60091 Office: 251 E Chicago Ave Chicago IL 60611

CARTER, ROBERT LEROY, engineering educator; b. Leavenworth, Kans., Aug. 22, 1918; s. Joseph LeRoy and Viola Elizabeth (Hayner) C.; m. Jewell Mamie Long, June 3, 1941; children—Roberta, Benjamin, Judy Carter Meadows, Frederick, Camille Carter Ronchetto. B.S., U. Okla., 1941; Ph.D., Duke U., 1949. Registered profl. engr., Mo. Testing technician Eastman Kodak Corp., Rochester, N.Y., 1940-42; physicist Tenn. Eastman Corp., Oak Ridge, 1945-46; research scientist-engr. Atomics Internat., Canoga Park, Calif., 1949-63; faculty U. Mo., Columbia, 1962—, now prof. elec. engring., nuclear engring.; chmn. Mo. Low-Level Radiation Waste Task Force, Jefferson City, 1983-84. Contbr. sci. articles to profl. jours. Commr., Gov.'s Task Force on Low Level Waste, 1981-84; mem. ofcl. bd. Mo. United Meth. Ch., Columbia, 1985. Served to 1st lt. AUS, 1942-45, PTO. Mem. Am. Phys. Soc., Am. Nuclear Soc., Nat. Soc. Profl. Engrs., Mo. Soc. Profl. Engrs. (pres. Central chpt. 1978-79, trustee Ednl. Found. 1983—). Republican. Avocations: violinist, violist chamber and symphonic music. Home: 1311 Parkridge Dr Columbia MO 65203 Office: Univ Missouri Dept Elec and Computer Engring Columbia MO 65211

CARTER, SHIRLEY M. BRYANT, counselor; b. Chgo., Nov. 5, 1949; d. Robert L. and Minnie Ferguson (Amerson) Bryant; B.S. with honors, Chgo. State U., 1974; M.S., 1978; m. Naggie L. Carter, Jr., Nov. 18, 1967; children—Kathryn, Nycole, Tiyaka. Unit leader commn. div. Prudential Ins. Co., Chgo., 1969-71; psychotherapist Jackson Park Hosp., Chgo., 1978; tchr. Chgo. Bd. Edn., 1975—, counselor, 1978—. Pres., St. Elthelreda Sch. Bd., 1978-79; youth coordinator 1st Corinthians Ch., Chgo., 1979; mem. So. Bapt. Assn., 1979—, dir. Vacation Bible Sch., 1981, 82; dir. Christian Pre-Sch. Recipient cert. of honor Black Masters Hall of Fame, Chgo. Mem. Assn. Black Psychologists, Am. Personnel and Guidance Assn., Kappa Delta Pi. Baptist. Club: Brainerd Women's. Office: 4214 S St Lawrence Chicago IL 60653

CARTER, THOMAS SMITH, JR., railroad executive; b. Dallas, June 6, 1921; s. Thomas S. and Mattie (Dowell) C.; m. Janet R. Hostetter, July 3, 1946; children: Diane Carter Petersen, Susan Jean, Charles T., Carol Ruth. B.S. in Civil Engring., So. Meth. U., 1944. Registered profl. engr., Mo., Kans., Okla., Tex., La., Ark. Various positions Mo. Kans. Tex. R.R., 1941-44, 46-54, chief engr., 1954-61, v.p. ops., 1961-66; v.p. Kansas City So. Ry. Co., La. and Ark. Ry. Co., 1966—; pres. Kansas City So. Ry. Co., 1973-86, also bd. dirs., chmn. bd., 1981—; pres. La. and Ark. Ry. Co., 1974-86, also bd. dirs., chmn. bd., 1981—, chief exec. officer, 1981—; dir. Kansas City So. Industries. Served with C.E. AUS, 1944-46. Fellow ASCE; mem. Am. Ry. Engring. Assn., Assn. Am. Railroads (dir. 1978—), Nat. Soc. Profl. Engrs. Clubs: Chgo, Kansas City, Shreveport. Home: 9319 W 92d Terr Overland Park KS 66212 Office: Kansas City So Ry 114 W 11th St Kansas City MO 64105

CARTER, WILLIAM LEIGH, JR., nurse, healthcare administrator; b. Henderson, Ky., July 15, 1956; s. William Leigh Sr. and Betty Sharon (Fairchild) C.; m. Sharon Daine Powell, Dec. 27, 1975; children: Jarrod Leigh, Joshua Neal. Assoc. diploma in nursing, U. Ky. U., 1977; BSN, No. Ky. U., 1982; cert. in long-term care administration, Ohio State U., 1984. Dir. personnel and devel. staff Am. Healthcare Ctr., Ohio, 1980-82; nursing instr. Henderson Community Coll., 1982-83; adminstr. nursing and rehabilitation Ohio Valley Manor Convalescent Ctr., Ripley, Ohio, 1983-86; dir. clin. nursing St. Mary's Med. Ctr.-Regina Continuing Care, Evansville, Ind., 1986—; nurse cons. Vocat. Corp of Hillsboro, Ohio, 1985; nurse adminstr., cons. Sunrise Manor Care Ctr., Amelia, Ohio, 1979-82. Dir. Royal Rangers Boys Ministries, Rpley, 1986. Mem. Ohio Health Care Council of Nurses (chmn. seven counties Greater Cin. 1983-86), Ind. Healthcare Nursing Dirs. Council. Avocations: piano, singing, church, travel. Home: Rt 1 Box 183A Robards KY 42452 Office: Regina Continuing Care 3700 Washington Ave Evansville IN 47714

CARTIER, THOMAS NICHOLAS, sales executive; b. St. Paul, May 17, 1950; s. Robert Alvin and Rose Adele (Cardinal) C.; m. Marta Sue Mastel, Sept. 19, 1975; children: Kristin, Kelly. Student, Lakewood Community Coll., White Bear Lake, Minn., 1969-71. Salesman, designer Minn. Toro Inc., Mpls., 1973, mgr. irrigation div., 1974—, v.p. irrigation div., 1977—; pres., founder DesignScapes, Inc., 1987—. Served with USNG Minn., 1968-72. Roman Catholic. Home and Office: 2410 Byrnes Rd Minnetonka MN 55343

CARTLEDGE, CHRISTOPHER BLAIR, retail company executive; b. Wyandotte, Mich., Oct. 22, 1959; s. William Dan and Catherine Marion Louise (Blair) C.; m. Cynthia Ann Marie Scarr, Aug. 12, 1979; children Kathryn Elizabeth, Thomas Francis. BA, Bowling Green U., 1980. Sales rep. A & A Inventory Services, Liberty Ctr., Ohio, 1979-80, sales mgr., 1980-82; retail cons. A & A Enterprises, Liberty Ctr., 1982—, gen. mgr., 1982—; pres. Wedding Decor Ltd., Liberty Ctr., 1983—. Youth coordinator Liberty Ctr. United Meth. Ch., 1980-86; actor, dir. Town Hall Civic Theater, Grand Rapids, Ohio, 1982, dir., asst. Liberty Ctr. United Meth. Ch. Choir, 1986. Mem. Ohio State Pharm. Assn. (assoc.), N.W. Ohio Retail Cons. Assn. Club: Toledo Drug. Avocations: barbershop quartet singing, tennis, cross-country skiing, home gardening. Home: 7 463 Country Rd Box 118 RFD 1 Liberty Center OH 43532 Office: A & A Enterprises 936 East St Liberty Center OH 43532

CARTWRIGHT, HOWARD E(UGENE), association executive; b. Kenosha, Wis., Nov. 19, 1924; s. Raymond W.A. and Theresa (Peterson) C.; m. Evelyn Tieckelmann, June 11, 1949; children—Thomas, Mark, Bradley, Jeffrey. B.A., Carthage Coll., 1946; M.S., Northwestern U., 1950. Reporter LaPorte (Ind.) Herald-Argus, 1949-50; editorial writer Lindsay-Schaub Newspapers, Decatur, Ill., 1950-56; speech writer, dept. head AMA, Chgo., 1956-66; communications dir. A.C.S., Chgo., 1966-67; asst. exec. dir. Coll. Am. Pathologists, Skokie, Ill., 1967-72; exec. dir. Coll. Am. Pathologists, 1972-85, chief exec. officer, 1985—; bd. dirs. Coll. Am. Pathologists Found. Recipient Disting. Alumni award, Cathage Coll. Mem. Am. Soc. Assn. Execs., Am. Assn. Med. Soc. Execs. Presbyterian. Home: 591 Forest Hill Lake Forest IL 60045 Office: 5202 Old Orchard Rd Skokie IL 60077

CARTWRIGHT, INEZ P. GESELL, concrete co. exec.; b. Fosston, Minn., Feb. 25, 1917; d. Elmer Olof and Esther Marie (Peterson) Solberg; student public schs.; m. William John Gesell, Dec. 31, 1938 (dec. 1975); children—William Lester, Gary John, Mary Ann; m. Myron R. Cartwright, Jan. 30, 1982. With Gesell Concrete Products Inc., Bagley, Minn., 1945—, pres., 1975—. Treas. ladies aux. St. Ann Roman Catholic Ch., Bagley. Home: 110 Lakeview Dr Bagley MN 56621 Office: Gesell Concrete Products Inc Route 2 Bagley MN 56621

CARTWRIGHT, MYRON ROGER, accountant, mayor; b. Shevlin, Minn., Apr. 15, 1919; s. Clayton Samuel and Esther Seamuela (Rydeen) C.; m. Winona June Mattson, Oct. 24, 1942 (dec. July 1979); children—Lynn Priscilla, Karen Colette, Tracy April; m. Inez Patricia Solberg, Jan. 30, 1982. Grad. French's Bus. Coll., Bemidji, Minn., 1937; B.A. in Acctg. magna cum laude, Coll. of St. Thomas, St. Paul, 1942. C.P.A., Minn., 1952. Instr. acctg. Coll. of St. Thomas, 1946-53; pvt. practice pub. acctg., St. Paul, 1946-52, as C.P.A., 1952—. Mayor of Bagley, Minn., 1985—; bd. dirs. Bagley Indsl. Devel. Corp. Served to capt. USMCR, 1942-45; maj. Res. Mem. Am. Inst. C.P.A.s, Minn. Soc. C.P.A.s, Am. Legion, Minn. Golf Assn. (dir. 1965-66), Minn. Pub. Golf Assn. (sec. 1965-66). Republican. Lutheran. Club: Twin Pines Golf (Bagley, Minn.). Home: 110 Lakeview Dr Bagley MN 56621 Office: City Hall Bagley MN 56621

CARTY, RAYMOND WESLEY, academic administrator; b. Carlinville, Ill., Jan. 26, 1956. AA, Hannibal-LaGrange (Mo.) Coll., 1977; BS, S.W. Bapt. U., 1979. Registered social worker, Ill. Youth therapist Macoupin County Mental Health Ctr., Ill., 1979-84; minister music and youth Charity Bapt. Ch., Carlinville, 1979-84; assoc. dir. admissions Hannibal-LaGrange Coll., 1984—. Baptist. Lodge: Optimist. Avocations: music, antique automobiles. Home: 15 Fairway Dr Hannibal MO 63401 Office: Hannibal-LaGrange Coll 2300 Palmyra Rd Hannibal MO 63401

CARUTHERS, BARBARA SUE APGAR, physician, educator; b. Guthrie, Okla., Oct. 4, 1943; d. Wallace Duke and Gloria Jayne (Glover) McMillin; m. Charles George Caruthers, Apr. 1, 1976; 1 dau., Larisa Ann. B.A. in Biology, Loretto Heights Coll., 1965; M.S. in Anatomy, U. Mich., 1968; M.D., Tex. Tech. Med. Sch., 1976. Diplomate Am. Bd. Family Practice, Am. Bd. Med. Examiners. Research asst. Parke Davis, Ann Arbor, Mich., 1965-66; research asst. Aerospace Med. Labs Wright-Patterson AFB, Ohio, 1968-70; instr. anatomy dept. Tex. Tech. U. Med. Sch., Lubbock, 1972-74, resident in family practice, 1976-79, clin. asst. prof., 1980-83; physician The Pavilion, Lubbock, 1981-83; sr. physician, dir. gynecology clinic U. Mich. Health Service, 1983-87, instr.dept. family practice U. Mich., 1984—; med. dir. Briarwood Health Ctr., U. Mich., 1986—; steering com. for ambulatory care U. Mich.; mem. staff Meth. Hosp., St. Mary of the Plains Hosp., U. Mich. Hosp. Mem. Soroptimist Internat., 1979-81; adv. bd. Lubbock chpt. March of Dimes, 1972-74. Recipient Upjohn Achievement award, 1976, Psychiatry Achievement award, 1976; Soroptimist Internat. grantee, 1978-79, U. Mich. Dept. Family Practice Tchg. Excellence award, 1985, 87. Mem. Am. Acad. Family Practice, Lubbock County Med. Soc., Tex. Med. Assn., Mich. Acad. Family Practice, Alpha Omega Alpha. Democrat. Mormon. Home: 883 Scio Meadow Ann Arbor MI 48103 Office: U Mich 325 Briarwood Circle Ann Arbor MI 48108

CARVER, GERFORD CHESTER, mechanical engineering consultant; b. Battle Creek, Mich., July 11, 1929; s. Chester Gerford and Gertrude Marguerite (Stock) C.; B.M.E., Mich. Technol. U., 1950; M.S., Chrysler Inst., 1956; m. Eleanor Anne Dunne, June 25, 1955; children—John, James, Marguerite, Elizabeth, William, Sara. Shop liaison engr., detailer Clark Equipment Co., Battle Creek, 1950; test engr. Chrysler Corp., Highland Park, Mich., 1952-55, welding engr., 1955-56; div. project engr. Midland Ross Corp., Cleve., 1956-62; chief engr. R.S.L. Corp., Cleve., 1962; account engr. A.O. Smith Corp., Milw., 1962-87; pvt. practice engring. cons., Milw., 1987—. Served in arty. U.S. Army, 1950-52. Registered profl. engr., Ohio. Mem. Soc. Automotive Engrs., Am. Welding Soc., Am. Soc. Metals, Engring. Soc. Milw. Clubs: Snowstar Ski (asst. head instr.) (Milw.). Home and Office: 880 E Birch St Milwaukee WI 53217

CARVER, MARTIN GREGORY, manufacturing company executive; b. Muscatine, Iowa, May 10, 1948; s. Roy James and Lucille Avis (Young) C. B.A. in Math, U. Iowa, 1970; M.B.A., U. Ind., 1972. Asst. treas. Consol. Foods Corp., 1975-79; Regional v.p. heavy duty parts, then vice chmn. Bandag, Inc. (retreaded tires mfrs.), Muscatine, 1979-81; chmn. bd., chief exec. officer Bandag, Inc. (retreaded tires mfrs.), 1981—. Chmn. bd. dirs. Augustana Coll., 1986—; bd. of visitors U. Iowa Sch. of Bus. Clubs: 33, Chicago. Lodge: Rotary. Office: Bandag Inc Bandag Center Muscatine IA 52761

CARVER, NORMAN FRANCIS, JR., architect, photographer. m. Joan Willson, Aug. 15, 1953; children: Norman F. III, Cristina. Grad., Yale. Practice architecture Kalamazoo; prof. advanced photography Kalamazoo Inst. Arts, 1971—; vis. lectr., critic Carnegie Inst. Tech., Mich. State U., Yale U., MIT; guest lectr. King Faisal U., Saudi Arabia, 1981. Exhibited photography, U.S. and abroad; photographs pub. in Aperture, House Beautiful, Horizon; others.; Author: Form and Space of Japanese Architecture, 1955; Silent Cities of Mexico and the Maya, 1966, rev. edition, 1986, Italian Hilltowns, 1979, Iberian Villages - Spain and Portugal, 1981, Japanese Folkhouses, 1984. Recipient Fulbright awards to Japan, 1953-54, 64; silver medal Archtl. League, 1962; award Archtl. Record, 1960, 61, 62. Home: 3201 Lorraine Kalamazoo MI 49008

CARVER, TODD B., legal administrator; b. Dayton, Ohio, Oct. 25, 1958; s. Ellis B. and Patricia L. (Boggs) C.; m. Deborah K. Tucker, June 21, 1980; children: Edwin, Brittany. BA in Polit. Sci., Wright State U., 1987. Investigator Smith & Schnacke Attys., Dayton, 1978-81, paralegal, 1981-84; litigation paralegal NCR Corp., Dayton, 1984—; civic lectr., hist. researcher. Mem. Community Adv. Council, Bank One of Dayton, 1986—; various positions Boy Scouts Am., Dayton, 1970-86; chmn. local bd. Selective Service Commn., Dayton, 1982—; pres. St. Anne's Hill Hist. Soc., Dayton, 1983-84, Dayton Area Council Hist. Neighborhoods, 1985—. Named one of Outstanding Young Men Am. U.S. Jaycees, 1982; recipient Vigil honor Order of the Arrow, Boy Scouts Am., 1977, Founder's award, 1984, Community Service award City of Dayton, 1987. Mem. Greater Dayton Paralegal Assn. Republican. Methodist. Lodge: Optimists (bd. dirs. 1984-86). Avocations: historic architecture preservation, civic activities. Home: 601 McLain St Dayton OH 45403 Office: NCR Corp 1700 S Patterson Blvd Dayton OH 45479

CARVIN, CHARLES RUSSELL, accountant; b. Columbus, Ind., Aug. 18, 1952; s. Don R. and Nedra Ruth (Ziegler) C.; m. Alice Mae Carvin, July 1975 (div. Dec. 1978); 1 child, Ami; m. Sally Lee Cramer, June 16, 1984. Assoc. in Applied Sci., Ind. U., Indpls., 1975, BS in Acctg., 1978. CPA, Ind. Acctg. mgr. Marvin Johnson & Assocs., Columbus, 1977-78; asst. controller Ind. Cities Water Corp., Greenwood, Ind., 1978-81; staff acct. Pub. Service Commn., Indpls., 1981-83, prin. acct., 1984-86, asst. chief acct., 1986—. Mem. Am. Inst. CPA's, Ind. Soc. CPA's. Republican. Methodist. Club: Decatur Township Community Civic. Avocations: golf, hiking, outdoor sports, computers. Home: 6925 Chauncey Dr Indianapolis IN 46241 Office: Ind Utility Regulatory Commn 901 State Office Bldg Indianapolis IN 46204

CARY, ARLENE D., hotel company sales executive; b. Chgo., Dec. 19, 1930; d. Seymour S. and Shirley L. (Land) C.; student U. Wis., 1949-52; B.A., U. Miami, 1953; m. Elliot D. Hagle, Dec. 30, 1972 (div.). Public relations account exec. Robert Howe & Co., 1953-55; sales mgr. Martin B. Iger & Co., 1955-57; sales mgr., gen. mgr. Sorrento Hotel, Miami Beach, Fla., 1957-59; gen. mgr. Mayflower Hotel, Manomet, Mass., 1959-60; various positions Aristocrat Inns of Am., 1960-72; v.p. sales, McCormick Center Hotel, Chgo., 1972—. Active Nat. Women's Polit. Caucus, Internat. Orgn. Women Execs., membership promotion chmn., 1979-80, bd. dirs., 1980-81. Recipient disting. salesman award Sales and Mktg. Execs. Internat., 1977. Mem. Profl. Conv. Mgmt. Assn., Nat. Assn. Exposition Mgrs., Hotel Sales Mgmt. Assn., Meeting Planners Internat., Am. Soc. Assn. Execs., N.Y. Soc. Assn. Execs., Chgo. Soc. Assn. Execs., Ind. Hotel Alliance (sec. 1986—). Jewish. Home: 1130 S Michigan Ave Apt 3203 Chicago IL 60605 Office: McCormick Center Hotel 23d and Lakeshore Dr Chicago IL 60616

CARY, JOHN MILTON, physician; b. Ewing, Mo., July 11, 1932; s. Milton Madison and Alice (Sells) C.; A.B., Central Coll. Mo., 1954; M.D., St. Louis U., 1958; m. Barbara Ann Dorsey, June 4, 1955; children—Kimberly Anne Cary Kelce, John Madison. Diplomate Am. Bd. Internal Medicine. Intern, Barnes Hosp., St. Louis, 1958-59, resident in internal medicine, 1959-60, subsequently mem. staff; resident in internal medicine St. Lukes Hosp., St. Louis, 1961-62, subsequently mem. staff; fellow in hematology Washington U., St. Louis, 1960-61; practice medicine specializing in internal medicine, St. Louis, 1962—; mem. staff St. Johns Mercy Med. Center; clin. instr. Washington U., 1966—. Mem. ACP, N.Y. Acad. Scis., AAAS, St. Louis Soc. Internal Medicine, Mo. Med. Assn., St. Louis Med. Soc., Alpha Omega Alpha. Congregational. Home: 37 Chesterfield Rd Chesterfield MO 63017 Office: 224 S Woods Mill Rd Saint Louis MO 63017

CASAS, SALVADOR G., marketing professional; b. Havana, Cuba, Mar. 3, 1950; came to U.S., 1962; s. Jose A. and Consuelo (Salvat) C.; m. Alice J. Alexander, Feb. 14, 1981; 1 child, Julia Christine. BBA, Roosevelt U., 1973; MBA, DePaul U., 1976. Buyer Montgomery Ward, Chgo., 1973-80; regional sales mgr. Plaskolite, Inc., Columbus, Ohio, 1980-83, v.p. sales, 1983, v.p. consumer products div., 1983-86; mgr. mktg. Kinkead div. USG Industries Inc., Chgo., 1987—. Recipient four Golden Drummer awards Bldg. Supply and Home Ctr. Mag., 1985. Mem. Assn. Home Improvement Mfrs. (co-chmn. 1985), Nat. Alliance of Bus. (campaigner Chgo. 1975). Republican. Roman Catholic. Avocations: golfing, traveling, scuba diving. Home: 2449 Rio Grande Ct Naperville IL 60565

CASBERGUE, JOHN P., medical educator; b. Angleton, Tex., Jan. 14, 1932; s. Selim F. and Nona (Chase) C.; m. Eugenia Szpieg, Feb. 24, 1962 (div. 1979); children: Paul A., Maria A., Lisa A.; m. Helen E. Hagens, Dec. 21, 1985; children: Jennifer E., Frances A. Burigana. BA, Fla. State U., 1955; MA, Mich. State U., 1961, PhD, 1974. Assoc. prof. Ohio State U., Columbus, 1962-72; assoc. prof. Mich. State U., East Lansing, 1973-78, prof., 1978-81, prof. emeritus, 1981—; v.p. ednl. affairs Applied Med. Data Inc., Ann Arbor, Mich., 1981-86; pres. Casbergue and Assocs. Inc., East Lansing, 1985—; cons. WHO, Colombia, Guatemala, 1971, numerous med. schs. in Eng., Can., U.S., 1972-82, Nat. Library of Medicine, USPHS, Mich. Judicial Inst., Am. Dietetic Assn., Am. Hosp. Assn., Can. Coll. Family Physicians, 1965—. Contbr. articles to profl. jours. Served to 1st lt. USAF, 1955-60. Fellow Soc. Advancement of Food Service Research (pres. 1972-73). Universalist-Unitarian. Home: 1243 Lilac Ave East Lansing MI 48823-5122 Office: Applied Med Data Inc 555 E William St Suite 13D Ann Arbor MI 48104

CASCINO, MARY DORY, business executive; b. Chgo., Dec. 21, 1949; d. V. Paul and Vada L. (Tuttle) Dory; A.B., Loyola U., Chgo., 1971; M.A., U. Chgo., 1972; m. Anthony E. Cascino, Jr., July 28, 1973; children: Anthony E. III, Christine Ann, Caroline Stephanie. Asso. planner, local service specialist Northeastern Ill. Planning Commn., 1972-76; self-employed park and recreation planner, Highland Park, Ill., 1976-80; owner Mary Anne Products, Glencoe, Ill., 1981-87, Exec. Services Unltd., 1987—. Candidate for alderman City of Chgo., 1971; past sec. Glencoe PTA, now v.p.; chairperson Glencoe Village Caucus. Mem. Am. Planning Assn. Author: Bicycle Safety Planning Guide. Home and Office: 385 Lincoln Ave Glencoe IL 60022

CASE, HANK, art educator, wine consultant; b. Danville, Ky., Jan. 12, 1938; s. Will Franklin and Margaret (Whitaker) C.; divorced; 1 child, J. Erin. BS, Ball State U., 1964, MA, 1966. Cert. master tchr., Ind. State Tchrs. Assn. Supr. of fine arts Anderson (Ind.) Community Schs., 1964—; instr. photography Anderson (Ind.) Coll., 1969—; free-lance photographer Anderson, 1956—, cons. wine, 1981—; cons. wine Indpls., 1982-84. Mem. Art Educators Assn. Ind. (life), Confrerie du Chevaliers des Tastevin (chevalier, redacteur 1984—), Commanderie du Bontemps de Medoc et des Graves (commandeur 1982—), Indpls. Wine Soc. (pres. 1981-83). Home: 823 W 7th St Anderson IN 46016 Office: Anderson Community Schools 1301 Lincoln St Anderson IN 46016

CASE, KAREN ANN, lawyer; b. Milw., Apr. 7, 1944; d. Alfred F. and Hilda M. (Tomich) Case. B.S., Marquette U., 1963, J.D. 1966; LL.M.,

N.Y.U., 1973. Bar: Wis. 1966, U.S. Ct. Claims, 1973, U.S. Tax Ct. 1973. Ptnr. Meldman, Case & Weine, Milw., 1973-85; ptnr. Meldman, Case & Weine div. Mulcahy & Wherry, S.C., 1985-87; Sec. of Revenue State of Wis., 1987—; lectr. U. Wis., Milw., 1974-78; guest lectr. Marquette U. Law Sch., 1975-78. Fellow Wis. Bar Found. (dir. 1977—, treas. 1980—); mem. Milw. Assn. Women Lawyers (bd. dirs. 1975-78, 81-82), Milw. Bar Assn. (bd. dirs. 1985-87), State Bar Wis. (bd. govs. 1981-85, 87—, dir. taxation sect. 1981-87, vice chmn. 1986-87), Am. Acad. Matrimonial Lawyers, Nat. Assn. Women Lawyers (Wis. del. 1982-83), Milw. Rose Soc. (pres. 1981, dir. 1981-83), Friends of Boerner Bat. Gardens (pres. 1984—), Clubs: Professional Dimensions (dir. 1985-87), Tempo (sec. 1984-85). Contbr. articles to legal jours. Home: 9803 W Meadow Park Dr Hales Corners WI 53130 Office: 125 S Webster Madison WI 53708

CASE, WELDON WOOD, telephone company executive; b. Hudson, Ohio, Feb. 22, 1921; s. Harry Nelson and Alice (Wood) C.; m. Beatrice Kuhn, Jan. 3, 1942; children: Thomas W., William R. Student, Case Western Res. U., 1939-40, Ohio Wesleyan U., 1940-41. With Western Res. Telephone, Hudson, 1934-56; with Elyria Telephone Co., Ohio, 1956-60; pres. Mid-Continent Telephone Co., Hudson, 1960-83; chmn. bd., chief exec. officer Alltel Corp. formerly Mid-Continent Telephone Corp., Hudson, 1983—. Served to 2d lt. U.S. Army, 1942-46; ETO. Mem. U.S. Ind. Telephone Assn. (bd. dirs., past pres., Disting. Service medallion 1973), Ohio Ind. Telephone Assn. (past pres.). Republican. Congregationalist. Clubs: Royal Palm (Boca Raton, Fla.); Country (Pepper Pike, Ohio). Home: 1200 S Ocean Blvd Apt 17H Boca Raton FL 33432 Office: Alltel Corp 100 Executive Pkwy Hudson OH 44236 *

CASE, WILLIAM ROBERT, county official; b. Mpls., July 15, 1921; s. Delbert V. and Nellie (Castonguay) C.; m. Dorothy A. Sheets, July 15, 1953; children—William, Christopher, Catherine. Student, Grinnell Coll., 1944; B.A. in Polit. Sci., U. Kans., 1949, M.A. in Pub. Adminstrn. (Carnegie fellow), 1950. Assoc., Adache Assocs., Inc., Cleve., 1952-58; sr. assoc., cons. Lawrence-Leiter & Co., mgmt. cons., Kansas City, Mo., 1958-60; asst. to gen. mgr. Pitman Mfg. Co., Grandview, Mo., 1960-62, dir. personnel and indsl. relations, br. mgr., 1964-66; gen. mgr. Case Engring. Assocs., Inc., cons. engrs., 1966-71; dir. dept. pub. works, coordinator EEO Office, County of Midland (Mich.), 1972-74, coordinator CETA office, 1974-79, county treas., 1979—; past chmn. City Commn. on Community Relations. County chmn. Midland County United Way; lector, eucharistic minister Blessed Sacrament Roman Catholic. Ch.; chmn. Adult Continuing Edn. Adv. Council. past chmn.; mem. Midland County Republican Exec. Com., precinct del. 1980, 82, 84; del. Rep. State Conv., 1984, 85. Served with U.S. Army, 1943-46. Decorated European Theatre medal with two bronze stars, Victory medal, Pacific Theatre medal. Mem. Mich. Assn. County Treas. (v.p., trustee), United County Officers Assn. (bd. reps.), Midland County Econ. Devel. Corp. (bd. dirs.), Midland County C. of C., Am. Soc. Pub. Adminstrs., Mcpl. Fin. Officers Assn., Internat. City Mgrs. Assn., Mich. Assn. Govtl. Computer Users. Clubs: Kiwanis (pres. 1984-85), Rep. Breakfast, KC. Home: 4416 Concord St Midland MI 48640 Office: County Courthouse 301 W Main St Midland MI 48640

CASEY, EDWARD PAUL, manufacturing company executive; b. Boston, Feb. 23, 1930; s. Edward J. and Virginia (Paul) C.; m. Patricia Pinkham, June 23, 1950; children: Patricia Estes Casey Shepherd, Lucile Tyler, Jennifer Paul Casey Schwab, Sheila Pinkham Casey McManus, Virginia Louise. A.B., Yale U., 1952; M.B.A., Harvard U., 1955. With Davidson Rubber Co., Dover, N.H., 1950-65; chief operating officer McCord Corp., 1965-78, dir., 1965-78; pres. McCord Corp., Detroit, 1965-78; chief operating officer Ex-Cell-O Corp., Troy, Mich., 1978-81; chief exec. officer, pres., dir. Ex-Cell-O Corp., 1981—, chmn., 1983—; dir. Mfrs. Nat. Corp.,. Trustee Henry Ford Health Care Corp., Detroit; bd. dirs. Detroit Symphony Orch.; adv. council Jr. Achievement of Southeastern Mich.; bd. dirs. United Found., Detroit Renaissance, Machinery and Applied Products Inst., Econ. Club Detroit, Automotive Hall of Fame, Inc.; mem. Detroit Area council Boy Scouts Am. Mem. Engring. Soc. Detroit, Soc. Automotive Engrs., Harvard Bus. Sch. Club Detroit. Clubs: Detroit (Detroit), N.Y. Yacht (N.Y.C.), Yondotega (Detroit), Grosse Pointe; Country Club of Detroit (Grosse Pointe Farms, Mich.), Bloomfield Hills Country, Eastern Yacht (Marblehead, Mass.), Bath and Tennis (Palm Beach, Fla.), Wig and Pen (London, Eng.). Home: 4 Rathbone Pl Grosse Pointe MI 48230 Office: Ex-Cell-O Corp 2855 Coolidge Troy MI 48084 *

CASEY, JOHN MICHAEL, construction company executive; b. Detroit, Dec. 11, 1930; s. Michael John and Agnes Mary (Brodrick) C.; m. Dolores Jean Mancuso, Apr.7, 1954; children—Barbara, Kathleen, Joanne, Sue, Mary, Tim, Martin. B.S., U. Wis.-Madison, 1950; M.B.A., U. Detroit, 1953; postgrad. Harvard U., 1961, Georgetown U., 1966. Vice pres. Perron Constrn. Co., Detroit, 1954-58; pres. Pyramid Constrn. Co., Detroit, 1958-60; mgr. Chrysler Corp., Troy, Mich., 1960-70; pres. Derry Corp., Southfield, Mich., 1970-75, Wellesley Constrn. Co., West Bloomfield, Mich., 1975-82; v.p., dir. mktg. Pioneer Co., Madison Heights, Mich., 1982-86, Sietman, Birmingham, Mich., 1986—; dir. Robotic Peripherals, Troy, Novi Bank and Trust, Mich., Liberty Mfg. Co., Wall Lake, Mich. Author: Building for Profit, 1974; What It Takes To Do Business in China, 1983. Pres. Big Bros., Detroit, 1966-70; bd. dirs. United Way, Detroit, 1971-76, ARC, Detroit, 1974- 78. Named Man of Yr., Jr. C. of C., Detroit, 1966. Mem. Irish-Am. Cultural Inst. (v.p. 1981—), Am. Def. Preparedness Assn., Soc. Automotive Engrs., Am. Home Builders Assn. (v.p. 1974-76), Nat. Home Builders Assn. Republican. Roman Catholic. Clubs: 100, President (Detroit). Lodges: Elks, K.C. Home: 7495 Cabernet Rd West Bloomfield MI 48322

CASEY, JOHN P., educator; b. Pitts., May 26, 1920; s. Patrick F. C.; m. Eileen; children: Charles, Carol. B.A., Bethany (W.Va.) Coll., 1949; M.Ed., U. Pitts., 1950; Ed.D. in Secondary Edn., Ind. U., 1963. Cert. tchr., Ill., Ohio. Tchr. Columbus (Ohio) Public Schs., 1950-59; asst. prof. Ill. State U., Normal, 1959-63; div. chmn. dept. social studies Northwestern Coll., Orange City, Iowa, 1963-64; asst. prof. So. Ill. U., Carbondale, 1964-69; assoc. prof. dept. spl. edn. and profl. ednl. experiences So. Ill. U., 1969-73, prof. curriculum and spl. edn., 1973—, dir. Talent Retrieval and Devel. Edn. Project (TRADE), 1965-85. Co-author: Roles in Off-Campus Student Teaching, 1967; contbr. articles to profl. jours. Served with U.S. Army. Mem. Ill. Assn. Curriculum Devel., Ill. Assn. Tchr. Educators, Phi Delta Kappa. Research in supervision, research and teaching of gifted children. Home: 623 Glenview Dr Carbondale IL 62901 Office: Coll Edn So Ill U Carbondale IL 62901

CASEY, MARY THERESE, nursing educator, nurse; b. Chappell, Nebr., Mar. 28, 1954; d. Lawrence James and Mary Phyllis (Dymond) C. B.S.N., Fort Hays State U., 1975; M.S. in Nursing, U. Tex.-Austin, 1982. Advanced registered nurse practitioner, clin. Nurse Specialist, Aide, grad. nurse, charge nurse obstetrics and surg. St. Anthony's Hosp., Hays, Kans., 1975-78; charge nurse high risk surgery Bay Area Hosp., Coos Bay, Oreg., 1978-79; charge nurse obstetrics St. Anthony's Hosp., Hays, Kans., 1979-80; nursing instr. Fort Hays State U., Hays, 1980-81, asst. prof. nursing, 1982—; staff labor and delivery St. Francis Hosp., Topeka, Kans., 1984-85, clin. nurse specialist in obstetrics, 1985—, mgr. patient care, 1987—; cons. Am. Nursing Resources, Kansas City, Kans., 1983—. St. Anthony's Hosp. scholar, 1975; Wagner fellow Fort Hays State U. Sch. Nursing, 1981-82. Mem. Am. Nurses' Found., Am. Nurses Assn. (council high-risk perinatal nurses 1982—), Nat. League Nursing, Nat. Assn. Pro-Life Nurses, Kans. State Nurses' Assn. (dist. sec., bd. dirs., vice chmn. parent, child conf. 1986-88). exec. bd. 1983-86, rep. to children's Coalition 1983-86, rep. to Kans. Council on Children and Youth 1983-86), Kans. League Nursing, Ft. Hays State U. Faculty Assn., Ft. Hays State U. Faculty Women's Assn., LWV, Nat. Wildlife Fedn., Audubon Soc., Sierra Club, Sigma Theta Tau, Phi Kappa Phi, Alpha Lambda Delta. Roman Catholic. Home: 2233 Westport Pl Topeka KS 66614 Office: St Francis Hosp 1700 W 7th St Topeka KS 66612

CASEY, MURRAY JOSEPH, physician, educator; b. Armour, S.D., May 1, 1936; s. Meryl Joseph and Gladice (Murray) C.; m. Virginia Anne Fletcher; children: Murray Joseph, Theresa Marie, Anne Franklin, Francix X., Peter Colum, Matthew Padraic. Student Chanute Jr. Coll., 1954-55, Rockhurst Coll., 1955-56; A.B., U. Kans., 1958; M.D., Georgetown U., 1962; postgrad. Suffolk U. Law Sch., 1963-64, Howard U., 1965, U. Conn., 1977; MS in Mgmt., Cardinal Stritch Coll., 1984; postgrad. Marquette U., 1983—. Intern, USPHS Hosp.-Univ. Hosp., Balt., 1962-63; staff physician USPHS Hosp., Boston, 1963-64; staff asso. Lab Infectious Diseases, Nat. Inst. Allergy and Infectious Diseases, NIH, Bethesda, Md., 1964-66; virologist, resident physician Columbia-Presbyn. Med. Ctr., also Francis Delafield Hosp., N.Y.C., 1966-69; USPHS sr. clin. trainee, 1969-70; fellow gynecol. oncology, resident dept. surgery Meml. Hosp. Cancer and Allied Diseases, Meml. Sloan-Kettering Cancer Ctr., N.Y.C., 1969-71, Am. Cancer Soc. fellow, 1969-71; ofcl. observer in radiotherapy U. Tex. M.D. Anderson Hosp. and Tumor Inst., Houston, 1971; vis. scientist Radiumhemmet Karolinska Sjukhuset and Inst., Stockholm, 1971; asst. prof. ob-gyn U. Conn. Sch. Medicine, 1971-75, asso. prof., 1975-80, dir. gynecologic oncology, 1971-80, also mem. med. bd.; prof., asso. chmn. dept. ob-gyn U. Wis. Med. Sch., 1980—; chief ob-gyn Mt. Sinai Med. Ctr., Milw., 1980-82, dir. gynecologic oncology, 1980—, also mem. med. exec. com.; chmn. research adv. com., mem. council Conn. Cancer Epidemiology Unit; bd. dirs., mem. exec. com., chmn. profl. edn. com. Hartford unit. Am. Cancer Soc., dir. Milw. div., exec. com. 1985—, v.p., 1985-86, pres.-elect, 1986—; mem. med. services 1980 Winter Olympic Games, Lake Placid, N.Y.; mem. med. supervisory team U.S. Nordic Ski Team. Diplomate Am. Bd. Med. Examiners, Am. Bd. Ob-Gyn. Fellow Am. Coll. Obstetricians and Gynecologists, ACS; mem. AAAS, N.Y. Acad. Scis., Am. Soc. Colposcopy, Am. Fertility Soc., Soc. Gynecologic Oncologists, New Eng. Assn. Gynecologic Oncologists (pres. 1980-81), Am. Radium Soc., Am. Soc. Clin. Oncology, Internat. Menopause Soc., Soc. Meml. Gynecologic Oncologists (exec. bd. 1979-84; pres. 1982-83), Lake Placid Sports Medicine Soc. (v.p. 1981-84, pres. 1984-86), Cedarburg C. of C. (Ambassadors com. 1983—, dir. 1983-85), St. George Soc. Contbr. articles to profl. jours., chpts. to books. Research in oncogenesis and tumor immunology. Home: Cedarburg WI 53012 Office: PO Box 342 Dept Ob-Gyn U Wis Med Sch Milw Clin Campus Milwaukee WI 53201

CASEY, RAYMOND RICHARD, agricultural business executive; b. Wauseon, Ohio, Sept. 18, 1935; s. Raymond John and Esther Elizabeth (Read) C.; m. Clara Jane Patrick, Apr. 26, 1958; children: Patrick, Natalie, Michelle, Brian, Kevin, Eric. BS in Agrl. Econs., Ohio State U., 1956, MBA, 1969. Dir. corp. planning Landmark, Inc., Columbus, 1978, v.p. corp. plannning, treas., 1978-80, v.p. grain div., 1980-85; asst. dir. market research and devel. Ohio Farm Bur. Fedn., Inc., Columbus, 1962-64, assoc. dir. commodity dept., 1964-65, dir. research and devel., 1965-68, dir. market research, 1968-70, asst. to exec. v.p. research and devel., 1970-75, adminstrv. asst., dir. research and devel., 1975-78, v.p. corp. affairs, 1986—; vice chmn. People's Travel Service, Columbus, 1979—. Author: Food as a Tool of Foreign Policy, 1977. Bd. dirs. Columbus Met. YMCA, 1975-85, Columbus Artist in Sch. Program, 1975-76, Internat. Council Mid-Ohio, 1976-84; pres. Camp Willson YMCA, Columbus, 1970-74; trustee, vice chmn., treas. Cen. Ohio Ctr. for Econ. Edn., Columbus, 1979—. Served to capt. USAF, 1957-62. Mem. Am. Mktg. Assn., Scabbard and Blade, Ohio U. Alumni Assn. (life), Gamma Sigma Delta, Alpha Zetz Alumni Assn. (chmn bd. trustees). Home: 3920 Reed Rd Columbus OH 43220 Office: Ohio Farm Bureau Fedn Inc 35 E Chestnut St Columbus OH 43215

CASEY, ROBERT DILLON, JR., advertising publications company executive; b. Evanston, Ill., Apr. 27, 1955; s. Robert Dillon and Rosemary Ann (O'Riley) C.; m. Joan Elizabeth McCarthy, Sept. 28, 1984; 1 child, Elizabeth Rose. B.A. in Fin., U. Ill., 1977. Spl. agt. Northwestern Mut. Life Ins. Co., Chgo., 1978-79; dist. sales rep. Gordon Publs., Chgo., 1979-85, regional office mgr., 1980-85; ind. sales rep. Walker Davis Publs.-Midwest, Chgo., 1985—; group leader sales course Dale Carnegie, Chgo., 1985. Mem. Bus. and Profl. Advt. Assn. Republican. Club: Adult Outdoors (sec. 1984). Avocations: skiing; camping; horseback riding; jogging; reading. Home and Office: Casey & Assocs 507 Opaterny Dr Fox River Grove IL 60021

CASEY, TERRY FRANKLIN, retail executive, pharmacist; b. Chamberlain, S.D., May 13, 1938; d. Delos W. and Lois V. (Shanahan) C.; m. Sharon L. Bargmann, June 13, 1959; children: Michael, Jeanne, Collin, Christian. BS, S.D. State U. Registered pharmacist, S.D., Colo. Pharmacist Casey Drug and Jewelry Store, Chamberlain, 1960-70, pharmacist, owner, operator, 1970; pres. Casey Corp., Chamberlain, 1975—; pres. S.D. Bd. Pharmacy, Pierre, 1973-79. Pres. Chamberlain Sch. Bd., 1976; bd. dirs. St. James Ch., Chamberlain,, 1983—. Mem. S.D. Pharm. Assn., Nat. Assn. Retail Druggists, S.D. Soc. Hosp. Pharmacists, Dist. RX Assn. (pres. 1972-73), S.D. Retailers Assn. (bd. dirs. 1982—), Key Club (advisor 1982—), Chamberlain Jaycees (pres. 1964, recipient Boss of Yr. award 1981), Chamberlain C. of C. (pres. 1981, named Man of Yr. 1981). Democrat. Roman Catholic. Lodge: Kiwanis (pres. 1978), K.C. Avocations: golf, skiing. Home: 1404 S Alcott Chamberlain SD 57325 Office: Casey Corp Box 549 Chamberlain SD 57325

CASH, ALAN SHERWIN, industrial engineer; b. Chgo., Oct. 28, 1938; s. Edward A. and Mildred M. (Miller) C.; m. Carole M. Hoffman, July 31, 1966; children: Susan, Jody. BS in Indsl. Engring., U. Ill., 1961; MBA, Northwestern U., 1969. Registered profl. indsl. engr., Calif. Sr. process engr. Cook Electric Co., Morton Gorve, Ill., 1973-75; sr. indsl. engr. Motorola, Carol Stream, Ill., 1975-77; supr. indsl. engring. def. systems div. Northrop Corp., Rolling Meadows, Ill., 1977-80, mgr. tech. services def. systems div., 1980-84, mgr. advance mfg. tech. def. systems div., 1984-86, mgr. tng. ctr. def. systems div., 1986—. Mem. Am. Inst. Indsl. Engring. (pres. N. Suburban Ill. chpt. 1982-83, program chmn. dist. 8 1984—), Indsl. Engring. Process Soc., Assn. Old Crows, U. Ill. Alumni Assn., Northwestern U. Alumni Assn. Home: 725 Lavergne Wilmette IL 60091 Office: Northrop Def Systems Div 600 Hicks Rd Rolling Meadows IL 60008

CASH, JOSEPH HARPER, university dean, historian; b. Mitchell, S.D., Jan. 3, 1927; s. Joseph R. and Claudia B. (Harper) C.; m. Margaret Ann Halla, Dec. 18, 1952; children—Sheridan Lisa, Joseph Mark, Meredith Ann. B.A., U. S.D., 1949; M.A., 1959; Ph.D., U. Iowa, 1966. Tchr. public schs. S.D., 1951-62; instr. Black Hills State Coll., summer 1961; grad. asst. U. Iowa, 1962-65; assoc. prof. history Eastern Mont. Coll., 1965-68; research asso. Inst. Indian Studies U. S.D., summer 1967, 68, dir. inst. div. Indian research, 1970-77, acting dir. inst., 1976-77, 86-87, asso. prof., 1970-74, Duke research prof. history, 1972—, prof., 1974—, dean Coll. Arts and Scis., 1977-87; dir. Am. Indian Research Project, State of S.D., 1969-74, S.D. Oral History Project, 1970-74, Oral History Center (merger both projects), 1974-77; chmn. S.D. Bd. Hist. Preservation, 1970-73; chmn. council dirs., cultural pres. div. State S.D., 1975-76; mem. S.D. Council on Humanities, 1975-77, S.D. Hist. Records Adv. Bd., 1976-86, S.D. Bd. Cultural Preservation, 1977—, Kampgrounds of Am.-U. Adv. Bd., 1978—. Author: 6 Indian Tribal Series books, 1971-76; author: (with Herbert T. Hoover) To Be An Indian, 1971, Working the Homestake, 1973, The Practice of Oral History, 1974; gen. editor: (with Herbert T. Hoover) American Indian Oral History Collection, 1977; bd. editors: (with Herbert T. Hoover) Rocky Mountain Rev, 1966-68, Midwest Rev, S.D. History. Mem. S.D. Centennial Commn., 1986—. Served with USMCR, 1945-46. Recipient award of merit Am. Assn. State and Local History, 1975. Mem. Am. Hist. Assn., Oral History Assn., Orgn. Am. Historians, S.D. Hist. Soc. (pres. 1977—), Western History Assn., Phi Beta Kappa, Phi Delta Theta. Republican. Home: 609 Catalina St Vermillion SD 57069 Office: Coll Arts and Scis U SD Vermillion SD 57069

CASILIO-LONARDO, EMILIA ELIZABETH, medical research technologist; b. Buffalo, May 10, 1954; d. Mario C. and Rose (Stefanacci) Casilio; m. Anthony Joseph Lonardo, May 19, 1984; 1 child, David Anthony Lonardo. B.S., SUNY-Geneseo, 1975; student in Med. Tech., Buffalo Gen. Hosp., 1977; M.S., Western State Coll., 1981. Cert. med. technologist. Med. technologist, Buffalo Gen. Hosp., 1976-79; med. research tech. leader Cleve. Clinic Found., 1979—. Active St. Gregory Family Ctr., S. Euclid Ohio, 1983-86, St. Joan of Arc, Chagrin Falls, 1986—; mem. S. Euclid Library Assn., 1984-85. Western State Found. research grantee, 1978. Mem. Am. Soc. Clin. Pathologists, Am. Human Genetics Soc., Am. Soc. Histocompatibility and Immunogenetics, N.E. Ohio Transplantation Soc. Roman Catholic. Clubs: Lake Bellwood (Chagrin Falls); Severance Athletic. Avocations: gourmet cooking, cross country skiing, gardening. Office: Cleveland Clinic Found 9500 Euclid Ave Cleveland OH 44106

CASKEY, HAROLD LEROY, state senator; b. Bates County, Mo., Jan. 3, 1938; s. James Alfred and Edith Irene (Anderson) C.; A.B., Central Mo. State U., 1960; J.D., U. Mo., Columbia, 1963; m. Kay Head, 1974; children—Kyle James. Pros. atty., Bates County, 1967-72; city atty., Butler, Mo., 1973-76; individual practice law, Butler, Mo.; asst. prof. NE Mo. State U., 1975-76; mem. Mo. Senate, 1977—. Mem. Mo. Bar Assn., Am. Judicature Soc., Fellowship Christian Politicians, Am. Criminal Justice Educators, Order Coif, Acacia, Phi Alpha Delta, Kappa Mu Epsilon, Alpha Phi Sigma. Baptist. Lodge: Rotary. Office: State Capitol Jefferson City MO 65101

CASON, MARILYNN JEAN, cosmetics company executive; b. Denver, May 18, 1943; s. Eugene Martin and Evelyn Lucille (Clark) C. BA in Polit. Sci., Stanford U., 1965; JD, U. Mich., 1969; MBA, Roosevelt U., 1977. Assoc. Dawson, Nagel, Sherman & Howard, Denver, 1969-73; atty. Kraft, Inc., Glenview, Ill., 1973-75; corp. counsel Johnson Products Co., Inc., Chgo., 1975-86, v.p., 1977-86; mng. dir. Johnson Products Co., Inc., Lagos, Nigeria, 1980-83; v.p. internat. Johnson Products Co., Inc., Chgo., 1986—. Bd. dirs. Ill. chpt. Arthritis Found., Chgo., 1979—, sec. 1985—; bd. dirs. Internat. House, Chgo., 1986. Mem. ABA, Nat. Bar Assn., Chgo. Bar Assn., Cook County Bar Assn. (pres. community law project 1986—). Club: Stanford (Chgo.)(pres. 1985—). Home: 322 Darrow Ave Evanston IL 60202 Office: Johnson Products Co Inc 8522 S Lafayette Ave Chicago IL 60620

CASPER, ELLEN FRANCES, clinical psychologist; b. Camden, N.J., Feb. 16, 1951; d. Seymour Arthur and Rita (Carlin) C. BA, U. Rochester (N.Y.), 1973; MA, Columbia U., 1974; PhD, U. Va., 1981. Lic. psychologist, sch. psychologist, Ohio. Psychologist State of Ohio, Cleve., 1978-82, Cleveland Heights (Ohio) Bd. Edn., 1978-82; clin. psychologist Ctr. Effective Living, Beachwood, Ohio, 1981-85, Behavior Mgmt. Assocs., Beachwood, 1985—; adj. faculty Ursuline Coll., Pepper Pike, Ohio, 1982—. Exec. bd. dirs. Adam Walsh Child Resource Ctr., Cleve., 1984—, Goodwill Found., Cleve., 1986—; bd. dirs. Hebrew Free Loan Assn., Cleve., 1985—. Mem. Am. Psychol. Assn., Ohio Psychol. Assn., Cleve. Psychol. Assn. Democrat. Avocations: tennis, jogging, skiing, sky-diving, scuba diving. Home: 18123 Scottsdale Blvd Shaker Heights OH 44122 Office: Behavior Mgmt Assocs 23200 Chagrin Blvd #225 Beachwood OH 44122

CASPER, REGINA CLAIRE, physician, researcher; b. Berlin, Fed. Rep. Germany, Aug. 13, 1938; came to U.S., 1964; m. Gerhard Casper; 1 child, Hanna. BS, Free U., Berlin, 1959; MD, Albert Ludwig U., Freiburg, Fed. Rep. Germany, 1962. Internship U. Hamburg, Fed. Rep. Germany, 1962-64; postdoctoral fellowship U. Calif., Berkeley, 1965-67; residency Michael Reese Hosp., Chgo., 1967-70; assoc. dir. research Ill. State Psychiat. Inst., Chgo., 1972-83; assoc. prof. psychiatry U. Chgo., 1984—; dir. eating disorders research and treatment program Michael Reese Hosp., Chgo., 1983—. Contbr. articles on depression and eating disorders to profl. jours. Mem. Am. Psychiat. Assn., Am. Coll. Psychoneuropharmacology, Internat. Soc. Psychosomatic Medicine, Physicians Social Responsibility. Office: Michael Reese Hosp 31st St and Lake Shore Dr Chicago IL 60616

CASPERSON, CARL CHRISTIAN, orthodontist; b. Mpls., Nov. 7, 1937; s. Carl Ludwig and Kathryn Harriet (Flaa) C.; m. Kathleen Mae Aaker, July 1, 1960; children: Steven Christian, David M. BA cum laude, Augsburg Coll., 1959; DDS, U. Minn., 1964, MSD, 1968. Diplomate Am. Bd. Orthodontics. Practice dentistry specializing in orthodontics Bloomington, Ind., 1964—. Bd. dirs, chmn. St. Olaf Residence, 1968—, bd. dirs., treas. Bd. Edn. Dist. 271, 1983—. Mem. ADA, Am. Assn. Orthodontics, Am. Coll. Diplomates, Midwest Assn. Orthodontics, Minn. Assn. Orthodontics, Minn. Dental Assn., Mpls. Dist. Dental Soc., Omicron Kappa Upsilon. Avocations: tennis, skiing, hunting, fishing. Office: 4200 W Old Shakopee Rd Suite 220 Minneapolis MN 55437

CASS, OLIVER WILFRED, gastroenterologist; b. Niagara Falls, N.Y., Aug. 2, 1949; s. Oliver Wilfred and Marie (McDonnell) C.; m. Janet Katz, Aug. 28, 1983; 1 child, Alexander Conrad. BA in Chemistry, Oberlin (Ohio) Coll., 1972; D of Medicine, U. Minn., 1978. Diplomate Am. Bd. Internal Medicine, Am. Bd. Gastroenterology. Resident in internal medicine U. Minn. Hosp., Mpls., 1978-81, fellow in gastroenterology, 1981-84; assoc. physician, asst. prof. medicine U. Minn., Mpls., 1984—, Hennepin County Med. Ctr., Mpls., 1984—. Contbr. articles and abstracts to profl. jours. Recipient Mosby Book award and Merck Manual award U. Minn., 1978; research grantee March of Dimes, 1976. Mem. AMA, ACP, Minn. State Med. Assn., Am. Gastroent. Assn. (research grantee 1978), Am. Soc. for Gastrointestinal Endoscopy (ad hoc computer com. 1986, cons. computer com. 1984-85), Hennepin County Med. Soc., Mpls. Soc. Internal Medicine. Office: Hennepin County Med Ctr Dept Medicine 701 Park Ave S Minneapolis MN 55415

CASSADY, CHERYL GALE, small business owner; b. Magee, Miss., Apr. 8, 1949; d. Herbert Finley and Ellen (Plunkett) Gale; m. Francis Neil Cassady, June 17, 1971; children: Kim, Gwen, Ginger, Amanda, Kelly. BS in English, Clemson U., 1971. Owner, sec., treas. Village Clock Shop, Zionsville, Ind., 1973—. Mem. Zionsville C. of C. Republican. Club: Main St. Investors. Avocations: tennis, aerobics, biking, piano. Office: Village Clock Shop 5 N Main Zionsville IN 46077

CASSADY, JOSEPH RUDOLPH, III, radio broadcaster, educator; b. Chicago Heights, Ill., Feb. 15, 1959. BA, Columbia Coll., 1981. Air personality Stas. WCGO and WTAS-FM, Chicago Heights, 1979-82; producer, reporter Lee Communications, Inc., Chgo., 1980-85; producer, announcer Sta. WYEN-FM, Chgo., 1982-83; music dir. Sta. WLAK-FM, Chgo., 1983-84; air personality Sta. WCLR-FM, Chgo., 1984—; voice-over talent Rocklin-Irving, Chgo., 1982—, Prescription Learning, Mt. Prospect, Ill., 1985—; cons. Jim Smith Cons., Chgo., 1984-85; instr. broadcasting Columbia Coll., 1985—. Recipient Cert. Appreciation, CARE, 1984. Mem. AFTRA. Avocations: golf, bowling, writing. Office: Sta WCLR-FM 8833 Gross Point Rd Skokie IL 60077

CASSEL, CHRISTINE KAREN, physician; b. Mpls., Sept. 14, 1945; d. Charles Moore and Virginia Julia (Anderson) C.; A.B., U. Chgo., 1967; M.D., U. Mass., 1976. Intern, resident in internal medicine Children's Hosp., San Francisco, 1976-78; fellow in bioethics, Inst. Health Policy Studies, U. Calif., San Francisco, 1978-79; fellow geriatrics Portland (Oreg.) VA Hosp., 1979-81; asst. prof. medicine and public health U. Oreg. Health Scis. U., 1981-83; asst. prof. geriatrics and medicine Mt. Sinai Med. Ctr., N.Y.C., 1983-85; assoc. prof. medicine U. Chgo., 1985—. Woodrow Wilson fellow, 1967; Henry J. Kaiser Family Found. faculty scholar, 1982-85; diplomate Am. Bd. Internal Medicine. Fellow Am. Geriatrics Soc., ACP; mem. Physicians Social Responsibility (dir. 1983—), Soc. Health and Human Values (pres. 1986). Author: Ethical Dimensions in the Health Professions, 1981; Geriatric Medicine: Principles and Practice, 1984; Nuclear Weapons and Nuclear War: A Sourcebook for Health Professionals, 1984. Office: Sect Gen Internal Medicine Box 12 U Chgo Pritzker Sch Medicine Chicago IL 60637 *

CASSIDY, DWANE ROY, insulation contracting co. exec.; b. Bedford, Ind., Oct. 20, 1915; s. Leo Clayton and Lilly Fay (Robbins) C.; student Roscoe Turner's Sch. Aviation, 1944; m. Mary Catherine Shrout, Aug. 28, 1937; children—Gail (Mrs. Gordon Everling), Cheryl, Duane, Nina (Mrs. Robert McAnulty). With L. C. Cassidy & Son, Inc., Indpls., 1934—, now v.p.; v.p. L.C. Cassidy & Sons, Inc. of Fla., 1963—. Served with USN, 1944-45; PTO. Mem. Gideons Internat. Methodist. (dir.). Club: Optimists (Indpls.). Home: 644 Lawndale St Plainfield IN 46168 Office: 1918 S High School Rd Indianapolis IN 46241

CASSIDY, EUGENE PATRICK, pathologist; b. N.Y.C., July 21, 1940; s. Eugene Zachary and Anita Hilda (Corsi) C.; m. Hollis Elizabeth Ward, Sept. 25, 1965; 1 child, Meredith. BA, Williams Coll., 1962; MD, Yale U., 1966. Diplomate Am. Bd. Pathology. Intern Yale-New Haven Hosp., Conn., 1966-67; resident then fellow in pathology and lab. medicine Yale U. Med. Ctr., 1967-70; dir. pathology Appalachian Lab. for Occupational Respitory Disease, Morgantown, Wis., 1970-72; pathologist Clarkson Hosp., Omaha, 1972-78, Scripps Hosp., Encinitas, Calif., 1978-84; dir. pathology Marshalltown (Iowa) Med. and Surgical Ctr., 1984—; asst. prof. W.Va. U. Sch. Medicine, Morgantown, 1970-72, U. Nebr. Sch. Medicine, Omaha, 1974-78. Contbr. articles to profl. jours. Served with USPHS, 1970-72. Fellow Internat. Acad. Pathology, Coll. Am. Pathologists, Am. Soc. Clin. Pathologists; mem. AMA, Am. Assn. Blood Banks. Republican. Avocations:

music, architecture. Home: Woodfield Rd Marshalltown IA 50158 Office: Marshalltown Med & Surgical Ctr 3 S 4th Ave Marshalltown IA 50158

CASSIDY, GERALD JOSEPH, restaurant chain executive; b. Chgo., Aug. 16, 1941; s. Joseph Patrick and Mary Rita (Gleason) C.; B.S. in Indsl. Econs., Purdue U., 1964; M.B.A., Old Dominion U., 1970; m. Jennie Jones; children—Lisa Kathleen, Mary Elizabeth, Darrin Christopher, Angela Rhonda, Gerald Joseph II. Fin. analyst Gen. Foods Corp., Lafayette, 1970-72; owner, pres. 10 McDonald's Restaurants, Inc., Tipton, Ind., 1973—, charter mem. McDonald's Corp. Operators' Adv. Bd., 1973-74; pres. Central Ind. McDonald's Operators Assn., 1975-76, advt. chmn., 1977-80, 83-86; treas. Ind. bd. dirs. Ronald McDonald House, 1980-83, pres., 1984-86; adv. com. Ronald McDonald Children's Charities Found., 1984—; lectr. Purdue U., 1969. Fin. chmn. Tipton County Republican Party, 1976-80, county chmn., 1980-81; founder Eagle Inst., Ctr. Human Growth and Achievement, 1984—. Served to lt. USN, 1966-70. Recipient McDonald's Ronald award for excellence in mktg., 1979; Sagamore of the Wabash award, Gov. of Ind., 1980 Mem. Tipton C. of C., Ind. Restaurant Assn., Purdue Pres.' Council, Sigma Pi. Republican. Roman Catholic. Clubs: Elks, Jaycees. Home: PO Box 6 Atlanta IN 46031 Office: Cassidy Restaurants PO Box 378 Tipton IN 46072

CASSIDY, JAMES MARK, construction company executive; b. Evanston, Ill., June 22, 1942; s. James Michael and Mary Ellen (Munroe) C.; B.A., St. Mary's Coll., 1963; m. Bonnie Marie Bercker, Aug. 1, 1964 (dl. Dec. 1981); children—Micaela Marie, Elizabeth Ann, Daniel James; m. Patricia Margaret Mary Murphy, Sept. 15, 1984. Estimator, Cassidy Bros., Inc., Rosemont, Ill., 1963-65, project mgr., 1965-67, v.p., 1967-71, exec. v.p., 1971-77, pres., 1978—; trustee Plasterer's Health & Welfare Trust, 1971—. Area fund leader constrn. industry salute to Boy Scouts Am., 1975; mem. pres.'s council St. Mary's Coll.; chmn. labor liaison com. Laborers Internat. Union N.Am. and Assn. Wall and Ceiling Industries, 1982-85, chmn. labor-mgmt. group, 1985—; chmn. Chicagoland Assn. Wall and Ceiling Contractors' Carpenters Union Negotiating Team, 1983—. Served with U.S. Army, 1963-64, N.G., 1964-69. Mem. Chgo. Plastering Inst., Builder Uppers Club (pres. 1973-74), Chicagoland Assn. Wall and Ceiling Contractors (pres. 1976-79), Great Lakes Council, Internat. Assn. Wall and Ceiling Contractors (chmn. 1977), Constrn. Employers Assn. Chgo. (dir. 1976—, chmn. com. labor-mgmt. relations 1983—), Assn. Wall and Ceiling Industries (dir. 1978-81). Roman Catholic. Clubs: Abbey Springs Country (Fontana, Wis.); Park Ridge (Ill.) Country. Office: Cassidy Bros Inc PO Box 570 Rosemont IL 60018

CASSIDY, LAWRENCE R. (LARRY), marketing, advertising consultant; b. Chgo., Jan. 6, 1946; s. Ralph and Anamae (Foster) C. BA in Mktg., Roosevelt U., 1978, M in Mktg. Communications, 1980. With sales communications dept. Libby's, Chgo., 1970-75, mgr. sales planning, 1975-80; mktg., advt. cons. Tactical Mktg. Co., Chgo., 1980—; mem. Internat. Acad. Merchandising and Design, Chgo., faculty Roosevelt U. Served with U.S. Army, 1966-70. Mem. Am. Legion, Nat. Rifle Assn., Beta Gamma Sigma. Avocations: fishing, hunting, musical theater, opera.

CASSIDY, SAMUEL M., banker; b. Lexington, Ky., Aug. 8, 1932; s. Samuel M. Cassidy and Frances Carroll Stevenson; m. Rebecca Jane Hoult, June 9, 1956; children: Francis Cassidy Sabad, James W., Michael, Mary. A.B. in Econs., Duke U., 1958; M.B.A., U. Cin., 1962. Mgmt. trainee 1st Nat. Bank Cin., 1958-62, asst. cashier, 1962-64, asst. v.p., 1964-68, v.p. dept. banks, 1968-74, sr. v.p., 1974-80, exec. v.p., dir., 1980-84, pres., 1984—; dir. Leyman Corp., Cin. Group vice chmn. United Appeal, Cin., 1979—; chmn. devel. com. Santa Maria Community Service, Cin., 1981-83; trustee Greater Cin. Better Bus. Bur., 1983—; corp. chmn. Fine Arts Fund, Cin., 1984. Served as sgt. USMC, 1953-56. Mem. Ohio Bankers Assn. (chmn. BancPac group 1985-86), Cin. C. of C. (leadership com. 1980, vice chmn. steering com. 1982-83, ballot issues com. 1984—). Clubs: Commonwealth, Cin. Country, Bankers, Queen City. Avocation: gardening. Home: 7790 Ivygate Ln Cincinnati OH 45242 Office: 1st Nat Bank Cin 1st National Bank Ctr 5th and Walnut Sts Cincinnati OH 45201 *

CASSIN, JAMES RICHARD, broadcast educator; b. Port Huron, Mich., Oct. 7, 1933; s. Lloyd George Cassin and Gladys Carolyn (Smith) McCarron; m. Winnie Christine Carr, May 2, 1952; children: James R. II, Carolyn Marie Cassin Krecklow. BS in Journalism, Ball State U., 1982; MS in Radio-TV, Butler U., 1984. Enlisted USAF, 1951; served as pub. info. specialist USAF, Japan, Korea, Nev., Tex., Colo., Wis., 1951-71; ret. USAF, 1971; editor internal publs. Am. Fletcher Corp., Indpls., 1972-74; publicity dir. Amateur Athletic Union of U.S., Indpls., 1974-76; prof. broadcasting Def. Info. Sch., Ft. Benjamin Harrison, Ind., 1976—. Editor industry newspaper Dimensions (Best newspaper award Ind. Bus. Communicators, 1972); editor newletter Kaleidoscope (Award of Merit, Ind. Bus. Communicators, June 1972, Mar. 1973); editor Am. Fletcherline (Best newspaper award Ind. Bus. Communicators, 1974); editor AAU News Mag. (award of month Ind. Bus. Communicators, Feb., Apr., Dec. 1975, Mar. 1976). Mem. Radio-TV News Dirs. Assn., Am. Legion, USAF Thunderbird Alumni Assn., Kappa Tau Alpha, Phi Delta Kappa. Republican. Lutheran. Avocations: creative writing, jogging, live theatre and music, amateur sports.

CASSOU, JAMES LEON, airline pilot; b. Santa Barbara, Calif., Apr. 2, 1951; s. Leon Joseph and Dorisedna (Forslund) C.; A.A., Santa Barbara City Coll., 1973; postgrad. Calif. State Coll., 1973-74; m. Norita Ellen Besel, Mar. 13, 1976. Ambulance attendant, dispatcher and orderly Santa Ynez Valley Hosp., Solvang, Calif., 1968-73; chief ground instr., asst. chief pilot Gt. Atlantic and Pacific Aeroplane Co., Van Nuys, Calif., 1973-74; personal pilot, adminstrv. asst. to A. Brent Carruth, Counselor at Law, Encino, Calif., 1974-75; v.p. transp. and shipping, head grower Santa Maria Greenhouses, Inc., Nipomo, Calif., 1975-76; chief ground instr. Bud Walen Aviation, Van Nuys, Calif., 1976; flight instr. ATE of Santa Monica (Calif.), 1976; capt. Air Wis., Inc., Appleton, 1976—; ind. distbr. Shaklee Products; owner Sky Portraits by Jim; also freelance photographer. Mem. Air Line Pilots Assn., Assoc. Photographers Internat. Club: Pace Setters Running. Office: Outagamie County Airport Appleton WI 54911

CASTELE, THEODORE JOHN, radiologist; b. New Castle, Pa., Feb. 1, 1928; s. Theodore Robert and Anne Mercedes (McNavish) C.; m. Jean Marie Willse, Oct. 20, 1951; children: Robert, Ann Marie, Richard, Mary Kathryn, Thomas, Daniel, John. BS, Case Western Res. U., 1951, MD, 1957. Diplomate Am. Bd. Radiology, 1962. Intern then resident U. Hosps. Cleve., 1958-61, fellow, 1958-62; dir. of radiology Luth. Med. Ctr., Cleve., 1968-75, 77—; chief of staff Luth. Med. Ctr., 1975-80; pres. Med. Ctr. Radiologists, Inc., Cleve., 1978—; med. editor sta. WEWS-TV, Cleve., 1975—; chmn. bd. Med. Cons. Imaging Co., Cleve., 1981—; asst. clin. prof. radiology Case Western Res. U. Chmn. Southwestern dist. Greater Cleve. Council Boy Scouts Am., 1969, 73; mem. bd. med. cons. Cleve. Police Dept.; trustee Community Dialysis Ctr., Cleve. Health Edn. Mus., Luth. Med. Ctr. Found., chmn. bd. trustees 1969-75, Case Western Res. U., Blue Cross/Blue Shield Ohio. Served with USN, 1946-47. Recipient Order of Merit award Boy Scouts Am. 1971, Silver Beaver award 1972, Nat. Disting. Eagle Scout award, 1984. Fellow Am. Coll. Radiology; mem. AMA (Physician Speaker Gold award 1978, 80, Silver 1979, Bronze 1978), Ohio State Med. Assn. (5th dist. councilor, 1977-79, Spl. award 1979), Cleve. Radiol. Soc. (pres. 1969-70), Case Western Res. U. Med. Alumni Assn. (pres. 1971-72), Cleve. Acad. Medicine (pres. 1974-75). Home: 18869 Canyon Rd Fairview Park OH 44126 Office: Luth Med Ctr 2609 Franklin Ave Cleveland OH 44113

CASTER, RICHARD JOHN, educational administrator; b. Canton, Ohio, May 12, 1946; s. Peter and Mary (Angelantoni) C.; B.A. in Edn., Walsh Coll., Canton, 1968; M.S. in Tech. Edn., U. Akron (Ohio), 1973, Ed.D., 1979; m. Kathleen Annette; children—Matthew Adam, Scott Michael. Tchr. Columbus (Ohio) City schs., 1968-69; tchr. Canton City schs., 1969-73, coordinator, 1973-74, supr. career edn., 1974-79; asst. prin. Canton McKinley Sr. High Sch., 1979-84; prin. Newark Sr. High Sch., Ohio, 1984-87, asst. supt. Newark City Schs., 1987—; instr. pt. time Xavier Univ. Grad. Sch; keynote speaker Principals Acad. Ohio Dept. Edn., Nat. Honor Soc. State-Wide Conf. Ohio Dept. Edn.; tchr. edn. adv. com. Denison U. Mem. Ohio Assn. Secondary Sch. Adminstrs., Nat. Assn. Secondary Sch. Prins., Newark Adminstrs. Assn., Buckeye Assn. Sch. Adminstrs. Home: 693 Tall Oaks Ct Newark OH 43055 Office: Newark High Sch Wright St Newark OH 43055

CASTIGLIONE, DENNIS JOSEPH, printing company marketing executive; b. Cleve., Oct. 8, 1954; s. Joseph Martin and Antoinette Marie (Piunno) C.; m. Mary Elizabeth Gardner, Aug. 7, 1976; children—Michael A., Lisa E. B.S., Bowling Green State U., 1976. Account exec. Baron Advt., Inc., Cleve., 1976-78; communications mgr. Diamond Shamrock Corp., Cleve., 1978-83; v.p. sales and mktg. Carpenter Res. Printing Co., Cleve., 1983—; dir. dept. mktg. info. and research Printing Industries of Am., Washington, 1983—, mktg. adv. com., 1983—, chmn. sales & mktg. adv. bd. 1987—. Chmn. Cleve. Printing Week, 1982. Mem. Cleve. Advt. Club, Bus. Profl. Advt. Assn. (pres. 1986-87), Sales Mktg. Exec. Internat., Graphic Arts Council Cleve. (pres. 1982-83). Avocations: jogging, racquetball, golf, bowling. Home: 5730 Janet Blvd Solon OH 44139 Office: Carpenter Res Printing Co 7100 Euclid Ave Cleveland OH 44103

CASTILLO, GLORIA JEAN, marketing executive; b. Chgo., Sept. 3, 1954; d. Anastacio and Ramona (Flores) C. Student, Mundelein Coll., 1972-73, Northwestern U., 1974-75; BA, U. Calif., Santa Barbara, 1980. Sr. sales rep. B. Dalton Bookseller, Orlando, Fla., 1975-76; mgr. Louis Barbara D.O., Inc., Port Hueneme, Calif., 1977-80; classified mgr. Crain's Chgo. Bus., 1980-81; account mgr. Redbook Mag., Chgo., 1981-85; v.p., dir. mktg. Monarch Graphics of Ill., Chgo., 1985—. Resource networker Women Employed, Chgo., 1986—. Scholar State of Ill., 1972. Mem. Am. Mktg. Assn., Chgo. Advt. Club, Women's Advt. of Chgo. Club (co-dir. adwoman of yr. com. 1986-87, bd. dirs. 1983, 84), Chgo. Conv. and Visitors Bur., NOW (bd. dirs. Chgo. chpt. 1975-75). Avocations: music, lyricist, golf. Office: Monarch Graphics of Ill Inc 151 N Michigan Ave Chicago IL 60601

CASTINGS, JOHN HENRY, transportation executive; b. Hinsdale, Ill., Jan. 24, 1950; s. Gaylord Hancock and Frieda Helene (Stunkel) C. Student, Rollins Coll., 1968-72, N.Y. Inst. Fin., 1972. Broker Bacon, Whipple & Co., Chgo., 1972-75; v.p. corp. sales Allied Van Lines, Chgo., Beverly Hills, Calif. and Seattle, 1975-78; pres. Castings & Co., Willow Brook, Ill., 1978—, Apollo Transfer Co., Hinsdale, 1985—, Hinsdale Transfer Co., 1985—. Lobbyist Ga. State Legis., Atlanta, 1976-78; mem. Civil Air Patrol, Orlando, Fla., 1968-80. Mem. Nat. Inst. Cert. Moving Cons., Aircraft Owners and Pilots Assn., Delta Nu Alpha. Republican. Presbyterian. Lodge: Rotary. Avocations: flying airplanes, water skiing, swimming, travel, jazz music. Home: 6148 Willowhill Rd Willowbrook IL 60514 Office: Hinsdale Transfer Co 200 Burlington Clarendon Hills IL 60514

CASTLE, ROBERT D., design engineer; b. Marshall, Mo., Oct. 10, 1954; s. Robert Edward and Wilma Jean (Dennis) C. BS, Cen. Mo. State U., 1982. Engring. technician Stahl Specialty Co., Kingsville, Mo., 1982-84; design engr. Eaton Corp., Kearney, Nebr., 1984—; builder, mechanic Team Wanker Motorcycle Endurance Roadracing, Kansas City, Mo., 1979-81. Recipient Nat. Endurance Roadracing Championship award Western-Eastern Roadracing Assn., 1980. Mem. Soc. Mfg. Engrs., Aircraft Owners and Pilots Assn. Avocations: flying (pvt. pilot), volleyball. Home: 114 E 31st St Kearney NE 68847 Office: Eaton Corp E Lincoln Hwy Kearney NE 68847

CASTLE, THOMAS WAYNE, jewelry store owner, gemologist; b. Niles, Mich., Sept. 4, 1952; s. Wayne Calvert and Lena Ruth (Koenigshof) C.; m. Karen Renee Virgil, June 13, 1981. Student, Cen. Mich. U., 1970, Lake Mich. Coll., 1971-72, Andrews U., 1973. Cert. gemologist; cert. quartz watch technician. Teller, with credit dept. Inter City Bank, Buchanan, Mich., 1973-75; owner, operator Castle Jewelry & Gift Shop, Buchanan, 1976—; pres. Buchanan Retail Div., 1985-86. Bd. dirs. Buchanan Area Reps., 1976-79, Niles (Mich.) Buchanan Big Bros. Big Sisters, 1985-87, Buchanan Downtown Devel. Authority, 1983—; bd. dirs. Buchanan C. of C., 1976-79. Club: Orchard Hills Country. Lodges: Lions (bd. dirs. Buchanan club 1985—, v.p. 1987—), Masons. Avocations: golfing, snorkeling, gardening. Home: 16608 Rynearson Buchanan MI 49107 Office: Castle Jewelry & Gift Shop 122 E Front St Buchanan MI 49107

CASTLES, WILLIAM ALBERT, physician; b. Dallas, S.D., Feb. 1, 1911; s. Thomas Ralph and Edna B. (Pabst) C.; student Albia Jr. Coll., 1928-30; M.D., State U. Iowa, 1935; m. Mildred Alyce Owen, Apr. 16, 1932; children—Thomas Ralph, William Albert II. Intern St. Mary's Hosp., Kansas City, Mo., 1935-30; resident Mo. Pacific R.R. Hosp., St. Louis, 1936-37; practice family medicine, Rippey, Iowa, 1939-46, Dallas Center, Iowa, 1946—; mem. staff Iowa Luth. Hosp., Iowa Meth. Hosp., Des Moines; staff physician Midwestern area A.R.C., 1937-39. Dir. Recreational Vehicles Inc., Des Moines, 1972-73. Mem. City Council, Dallas Center, 1948-52. Served from lt. to lt. col. M.C., AUS. 1941-46. Mem. Iowa Med. Soc. (ho. dels. 1952-66), Iowa Acad. Family Practice (dir. 1956-60, pres. 1963-64), Dallas Guthrie County Med. Soc. (pres. 1958), Am. Acad. Family Practice (ho. of dels. 1964-76, commn. membership and credentials). Rotarian (pres. 1959-60). Home: 105 Rhinehart Ave Dallas Center IA 50063 Office: 515 Sycamore St Dallas Center IA 50063

CASWELL, BRUCE EUGENE, mathematics educator; b. Hillsdale, Mich., Oct. 20, 1949; s. Donald Eugene and Eleanor May (Blenz) C.; m. Beth Ann Caulkins, Mar. 23, 1974; children: Mark Owen, Kevin Donald. BA in Math., Mich. State U., 1971, MA in History, 1976. Cert. secondary educator. Math. tchr. N. Adams (Mich.) High Sch., 1971-76; math. tchr., athletic dir. Onsted (Mich.) High Sch., 1976-79; math. instr. Pittsford (Mich.) High Sch., 1979—; football, basketball coach N. Adams High Sch., 1971-76, Onsted High Sch., 1976-79; track coach Pittsford High Sch., 1979—. Supr. Adams Twp., N. Adams, 1980-87; tax appraiser Cambria, Fayette, Adams Twps., 1982—. Mem. Internat. Assn. Assessing Officers, Mich. Twp. Assn. (pres. Hillsdale 1985-86), Am. Legion. Republican. Methodist. Avocations: weightlifting, reading, stock investing. Home: 4540 Knowles Rd North Adams MI 49262 Office: Pittsford High Sch Hamilton St Pittsford MI 49271

CASWELL, JEFFREY PAUL, tariffs administrator; b. Queens, N.Y., Sept. 5, 1962; s. James Paul and Patricia Ann (Sullivan) C. BBA, Iowa U., 1984; MBA, Drake U., 1985. Utilities analyst II Iowa Commerce Commn., Des Moines, 1984-86; access tariffs adminstr. Telephone and Data Systems, Madison, Wis., 1986—; negotiator Ohio Contracts Com., Columbus, 1986—; cons. Bus. Aid Soc., Des Moines, 1984-85. Mem. Assn. MBA Execs., MBA Assn. (pres. 1984-85), Delta Chi (homecoming chmn. 1980-83, Ednl. Merit award 1982-84). Roman Catholic. Home: 6714 Schroeder Rd Apt 20 Madison WI 53711 Office: Telephone and Data Systems PO Box 5158 Madison WI 53705

CATALANO, GERALD, accountant, oil company executive; b. Chgo., Jan. 17, 1949; s. Frank and Virginia (Kreiman) C.; B.S. in Bus. Adminstrn., Roosevelt U., 1971; m. Mary L. Billings, July 4, 1970; children—James, Maria, Gina. Jr. acct. Drebin, Lindquist and Gervasio, Chgo., 1971; jr. acct. Leaf, Dahl and Co., Ltd., 1971-77, prin., 1978—, ptnr. 1980—; prin. Gerald Catalano, C.P.A., Chgo., 1982-83; ptnr. Barbakoff, Catalano & Assocs., 1983—; v.p. Tri-City Oil, Inc., Addison, Ill., 1983—; corp. officer P.I.N.S., Inc., Chgo., Bionic Auto Parts, Inc. Pres. Young Democrats, Roosevelt U., 1967-71; dir. Elmhurst Jaycees, 1976. C.P.A., Ill. Mem. Am. Inst. C.P.A.s, Ill. C.P.A. Soc., Theosophical Soc. Roman Catholic. Office: 6650 N Northwest Hwy Chicago Il 60631

CATALANOTTI, V(INCENT MARIO), health services company executive; b. Detroit, Sept. 26, 1948; s. Gaspare and Rosaria Theresa (Polisano) C.; m. Marian Ruth Main, Aug. 5, 1972; children: Andrea Michelle, Michael Gaspare. AS in Orthopedic Physicians Asst., Marygrove Coll., 1974; BS in Occupational Health and Safety Adminstrn., Madonna Coll., 1983. Cert. orthopedic physician's asst., audiometrist. Clinic supr. Metroclinic, Romulus, Mich., 1972-75; clinic mgr. Detroit Indsl. Clinic, 1975-84; adminstr. Doctors Med-1, Grand Haven, Mich., 1984-85, Grand Rapids, Mich., 1985-86; cons. Systemworx, Grand Rapids, 1986—; instr. CPR, first aid. Fellow Am. Acad. Physician's Assts.; mem. Am. Heart Assn. Club: Ambucs (Grand Haven). Avocations: photography, auto sports.

CATE, S. L., steel manufacturing company executive. Chmn., pres. Gate City Steel Corp., Omaha. Office: Gate city Steel Corp PO Box 14022 Omaha NE 68114 *

CATER, ALLEN WOODBURY, food company executive; b. St. Cloud, Minn., June 24, 1933; s. Harry Woodbury and Marion Allen (Neide) C.; m. Betty Ann Simonson, June 18, 1955; children: Mark Woodbury, Jeffrey Allen, Stephanie Ann. BBA, U. Minn., 1955. Product coordinator Honeywell Inc., Mpls., 1959-61; sales mgr. Energy Internat., Mpls., 1961-66; regional mgr. Stauffer Chem. Co., Chgo., 1966-75; pres. CRS Co., Mpls., 1975—. Served with USN, 1955-59, comdr. Res. Mem. Inst. Food Tech., Am. Assn. Cereal Chemists, Chi Psi. Clubs: Olympic Hills Golf (Mpls.), St. Croix Yacht (Stillwater, Minn.). Avocations: skiing, boating, model railroading. Home: 6316 Post Ln Edina MN 55435 Office: CRS Co 4940 Viking Dr Minneapolis MN 55435

CATES, JOSEPH RICHARD, accountant; b. Mattoon, Ill., Oct. 3, 1931; s. Joseph Raymond and Myrtle W. (O'Connell) C.; m. Nancy Givan Deetz, Nov. 24, 1955; children: Joseph, Elizabeth, Cathy, Mary, John, Thomas. BS, Eastern Ill. State Coll., 1955. CPA, Ill. Auditor Caterpillar Tractor Co., Decatur, Ill., 1955-57; with loan dept. Northtown Bank, Decatur, 1957-61; revenue agent IRS, Decatur, 1961-65; revenue agent IRS, Springfield, 1965-66, conferee appellate div., 1967-69; tax supr. Ernst & Ernst, CPA's, Springfield, 1969-71; mgr. Klein, Brown & Carter CPA's, Springfield, 1972-75; pvt. practice acctg. Springfield, 1971-72, 75-84; appeal officer, appeals div. IRS, 1984—. Mem. exec. com. Sangamon Valley Estate Planning Council, 1974-76. Served with U.S. Army, 1951-52. Mem. Am. Inst. CPA's, Ill. Soc. CPA's (mem. fed. taxation com. 1970-74). Roman Catholic. Lodge: KC. Home: 460 Raintree Ct apt 3R Glen Ellyn IL 60137

CATHER, CHARLES WAYNE, pharmacist; b. Toledo, Sept. 17, 1955; S. Charles Donald and Marilyn (Kapp) C.; m. Kathleen Anne Schmader, July 22, 1978; children: Colleen Marie, Charles Paul, Carrie Lynn. BS in Pharmacy, Ohio No. U., 1978; MBA, Kent State U., 1984. Staff pharmacist Timken Mercy Med. Ctr., Canton, Ohio, 1978-83, mgr. profl. pharmacy, 1985-87; mgr. Brewster Family Pharmacy, Massillon (Ohio) Community Hosp., 1987—; cons. nursing homes, Canton, 1983-87. Mem. Am. Soc. Cons. Pharmacists, Brewster Bus. Assn. Home: 3330 Banyan St NW Massillon OH 44646 Office: Brewster Family Pharmacy 360 N Wabash Brewster OH 44613

CATLIN, WILLIAM ARTHUR, police chief; b. Youngstown, Ohio, Dec. 28, 1941; s. Clyde Macky and Margaret (Loftus) C.; m. Mary Rose Corso, Nov. 9, 1963; children: Janet Marie, Judy Marie, Linda Marie. AAS, Kent (Ohio) State U., 1977, BS, 1979; MS, Youngstown (Ohio) State U., 1983. Capt. Niles (Ohio) Police Dept., 1970-86; chief of police Lordstown (Ohio) Police Dept., 1986—. Contbg. author: The Police Personnel System, 1983. Served with U.S. Army, 1959-62, Korea. Mem. Internat. Assn. Chiefs of Police, Ohio Assn. Chiefs of Police, Mahoning Valley Chiefs of Police. Democrat. Byzantine Catholic. Avocations: bodybuilding, weightlifting, fishing, reading, writing. Home: 3726 Austintown Warren Rd Mineral Ridge OH 44440 Office: Lordstown Police Dept 1583 Salt Springs SW Lordstown OH 44481

CATTANACH, JAMES PHILIP, advertising executive; b. Mt. Clemens, Mich., Oct. 1, 1949; s. Willard A. and Theresa G. (Weiner) C.; m. Roberta J. Long; children: John R., Amy L. BA in Advt., Mich. State U., 1971, MA in Advt., 1972. Writer Herman Miller Co., Zeeland, Mich., 1970; v.p. Wallace-Blakeslee, Grand Rapids, Mich., 1972-77; account supr. Juhl Advt., Elkhart, Ind., 1977-84; v.p., mgmt. supr. Hoffman York & Compton, Milw., 1984—. Home: 4501 N Sheffield Ave Shorewood WI 53211 Office: Hoffman York & Compton 330 E Kilbourn Ave Milwaukee WI 53202

CATTRELL, BETTY JANE, librarian; b. Wichita, Kans., Feb. 27, 1927; d. Vern Hamlin and Orpha Jane (Kerr) Welch; m. Melvin Lee Cattrell, June 26, 1945; children—Kary Lee, Keith Lane(dec.), Kelly Jane, Karla Joyce. Student Kans. Newman Coll. Periodical librarian Boeing Airplane Co., Wichita, Kans., 1952-60; librarian Unified Sch. Dist. #261, Haysville, Kans., 1961-77, Haysville Community Library, 1977—. Mem. Internat. Reading Assn. (pres. 1983—), ALA, Mountain Plains Library Assn., Kans. Library Assn.(library assoc.), DAR, VFW Aux., Assn. Am. Bus. Women. Democrat. Baptist. Home: 132 Wire St Haysville KS 67060 Office: Haysville Community Library 239 E Grand St Haysville KS 67060

CAUCUTT, AMY MEAD CARR, business administration educator; b. Christiansburg, Va., May 12, 1946; d. Francis Lewis and Miriam Mead (Arnold) Carr; m. Greg Caucutt; children—Mary A., Elizabeth M., George N. Student Wellesley Coll., 1964-65, Mich. State U., 1966, U. Wis.-Madison, 1967, U. Md., 1968-69, Rochester Community Coll., 1980-81; B.A. with honors, U. Wis.-Eau Claire, 1969; M.B.A., Winona State U., 1982. Instr. bus. adminstrn. Winona State U., Minn., 1982-84; asst. prof. Winona State U.-Rochester, Minn., 1984—; dir. Small Bus. Devel. Ctr., SBA, Winona, 1985—; cons. Olmsted Co., Rochester, 1982. Pub. mem. admissions com. Mayo Med. Sch., Rochester, 1979-82, Am. Assn. Med. Colls., Washington, 1982-83; bd. dirs., found. mem. Ability Bldg. Ctr., Inc., Rochester, 1984—; chmn., vice-chmn. Rochester Planning and Zoning Commn., 1983—; mem. Rochester Zoning Bd. Appeals, 1984, Recycling Task Force, Olmsted County, Minn., 1980-81; mem. housing com. Rochester- Olmsted Council of Govts., 1978-79; candidate for Olmsted County auditor, 1982; co-chmn. for state legis. campaign, precinct chmn., affirmative action officer Democratic Farmer Labor Party, Rochester, 1972—; active various coms., vol. Rochester Sch. Dist. 535, 1981—; mem. vestry, lay reader, Bible sch. dir., mem. various coms. St. Luke's Episcopal Ch., Rochester, 1970—. Mem. LWV (pres. 1976—, sec. treas. 1980-82, mem. coms., League of Yr. 1982), Minn. Women's Network, Rochester C. of C., Minn. Edn. Assn. Home: 716 28th St NW Rochester MN 55901 Office: Winona State U-Rochester 2220 3d Ave SE Rochester MN 55904

CAULFIELD, JOAN, educational administrator; b. St. Joseph, Mo., July 17, 1943; d. Joseph A. and Jane (Lisenby) Caulfield; B.S. in Edn. cum laude, U. Mo., 1963, M.A. in Spanish, 1965, Ph.D., 1978; postgrad. (Mexican Govt. scholar) Nat. U. Mexico, 1962-63. TV tchr. Spanish, Kansas City (Mo.) pub. schs., 1963-68; tchr. Spanish, French Bingham Jr. High Schs., Kansas City, 1968-78; asst. prin. S.E. High Sch., Kansas City, 1984; prin. Nowlin Jr. High Sch., Independence, Mo., 1984-86, Lincoln Coll. Preparatory Acad., Kansas City, Mo., 1986—; part-time instr. U. Mo.-Kansas City; dir. English Inst., Rockhurst Coll., summers, 1972-75. Mem. Sister City Commn., Kansas City, 1980—; ofcl. translator to mayor on trip to Seville, Spain, 1969; cons. Possum Trot (hist. soc.), 1979-80. Named Outstanding Secondary Educator, 1973; Delta Kappa Gamma state scholar, 1977-78. Mem. Romance Lang. Assn., Assn. for Supervision and Curriculum Devel., Nat. Assn. Secondary Sch. Prins., Modern Lang. Assn. (contbr. jour.), Am. Assn. Tchrs. Spanish and Portuguese, Friends of Seville, Friends of Art, Friends of the Zoo. Phi Sigma Iota, Phi Delta Kappa, Delta Kappa Gamma, Phi Kappa Phi, Sigma Delta Pi. Presbyterian. Home: 431 W 70th St Kansas City MO 64113 Office: 2111 Woodland Kansas City MO 64108

CAUSEY, RODNEY WAYNE, investment broker; b. Peoria, Ill., July 28, 1951; s. Thomas Nolan and Janet Lorraine (Connour) C.; m. Sharon Herman, Sept. 30, 1973; children: Michael Thomas, Mark Allan. AA, Ill. Cen. Coll., 1972. Sales mgr. Noah Herman Sons, Peoria, 1972-77; v.p. Controlled Builders, Peoria, 1977-80; sales mgr. Penn Mut. Life Ins., Peoria, 1980-84; owner R.W. Causey Investments, Peoria, 1984—. Mem. Inst. Real Estate Mgmt., Nat. Assn. Security Dealers, Nat. Assn. Life Underwriters (bd. dirs. Peoria chpt. 1983-86). Republican. Home: 1711 W Tiffany Ct Peoria IL 61614 Office: 4516 N Sterling Ave Peoria IL 61615

CAVALIER, DONALD RICHARD, university administrator; b. Walhalla, N.D., Sept. 28, 1943; s. Amos O. and Francis (McCambridge) C.; B.S., Mayville State Coll., 1965; M.S., Bemidji State U., 1970; m. Mary A. Salisbury, July 23, 1966; children—David Cavalier, Todd. Tchr., coach Warren (Minn.) public schs., 1965-67; tchr., counselor Crookston (Minn.) public schs., 1967-75; edn. dir. N.W. Regional Corrections Center, Crookston, 1975-76; dir. counseling, career planning and placement U. Minn., Crookston, 1976—; group leader, facilitator, The Social Seminar, Adventures in Attitude Tng., 1975-76; humanistic cons. Moorehead State U., 1973-78. Bd. dirs. S.O.S. Club for Teens, 1976-77; chmn. Family Living Center, Crookston, 1972-73; team leader Crookston Community Drug edn. program, 1975-76. PTO scholar, 1961-62. Mem. Am. Sch. Counselor Assn., Am. Assn. Counseling and Devel., Minn. Assn. Counseling and Devel. Northwestern

Minn. Guidance Assn., Minn. Vocat. Guidance Assn., NEA, Nat. Assn. Vocat. Edn. Spl. Needs Personnel, Minn. Coll. Personnel Assn., Minn. Govt. Coll. Council Assn. of Minn. Recruiters and Placement Dirs., Jaycees (pres. 1978-79, named Outstanding Pres. 1979). Democrat. Roman Catholic. Clubs: Lions, K.C., Elks Country, Dance, Town and Country, Eagles, Elks, Toastmaster 600 (pres.). Home: 614 N Ash Ct Crookston MN 56716 Office: U of Minn Bede Hall Room 107 Crookston MN 56716

CAVANAGH, MICHAEL F., judge; b. Detroit, Oct. 21, 1940; s. Sylvester J. and Mary Irene (Timmins) C.; m. Patricia E. Ferriss, Apr. 30, 1966; children: Jane Elizabeth, Michael F., Megan Kathleen. B.A., U. Detroit, 1962, J.D., 1966. Law clk. Ct. Appeals, Detroit, 1966-67; atty. City of Lansing, Mich., 1967-69; ptnr. Farhat, Story, et al., Lansing, Mich., 1969-73; judge 54-A Dist. Ct., Lansing, Mich., 1973-75, Mich. Ct. Appeals, Lansing, 1975-82; justice Mich. Supreme Ct., Lansing, 1983—; supervising justice Sentencing Guidelines Com., Lansing, 1983—, Mich. Jud. Inst., Lansing, 1986—. Chmn. bd. Am. Heart Assn. Mich., Lathrup Village, 1985; bd. dirs. YMCA, Lansing, 1978. Mem. ABA, Ingham County Bar Assn., Inst. Jud. Adminstrn. (hon.), Thomas M. Cooley Law Sch. (bd. dirs.). Democrat. Roman Catholic. Avocations: jogging; racquetball; fishing. Home: 234 Kensington St East Lansing MI 48823 Office: Mich Supreme Ct Law Bldg PO Box 30052 Lansing MI 48909 *

CAVANAH, GARY LYNN, technical services company executive, engineer; b. Kansas City, Mo., Feb. 1, 1941; s. Zillman Gail and Betty Brooke (Burchett) C.; m. Patricia Jane Armbrecht, May 1, 1976. BSEE, Finlay Engrng. Coll., 1966. Registered profl. engr., Calif., Kans., Ill., Ohio. Elec. engr. Bailey Controls Co., Wickliffe, Ohio, 1966-73; cons. Fisher Controls Co., Marshalltown, Iowa, 1973-78; pres. SEGA, Inc., Stanley, Kans., 1973—. Mem. Instrument Soc. Am., Nat. Soc. Profl. Engrs. Office: Sega Inc 15238 Cherry St Stanley KS 66223

CAVANAUGH, DANIEL BERNARD, financial executive; b. Michigan City, Ind., Feb. 7, 1943; s. Bernard Patrick and Margaret (Carbury) C.; m. Donna Jean Tichelaar, Aug. 21, 1965; children—Julie, Brian. B.S. in Acctg., Ind. U., 1971. Div. acct. Joy Mfg., Michigan City, Ind., 1968-70; cost mgr. NIBCO Inc., Elkhart, Ind., 1971-74, acctg. mgr., 1974-79, tax mgr., 1979-83, treas., 1983-84; v.p., controller Holiday Rambler Corp., Wakarusa, Ind., 1984—. Mem. Nat. Assn. Accts. (v.p. 1983). Roman Catholic. Home: 114 S Greenlawn Ave South Bend IN 46617 Office: Holiday Rambler Corp State Rd 19 PO Box 465 Wakarusa IN 46573

CAVANAUGH, DENNIS MILES, railroad company executive; b. Los Angeles, Sept. 19, 1937; s. Edward and Louella (Olson) C.; m. Marilyn J. Scovil, Sept. 11, 1965; children—Ann Louise, Amy Denise. B.S., U. Minn., 1965. Yard clk. Soo Line R.R. Co., Mpls., 1955-57, 61-65, asst. trainmaster, 1965-67, indsl. engr., 1969-72, dir. transp. planning, 1972-73, asst. supt. central div., 1974, gen. supt., 1974-77, asst. to exec. v.p., 1977-78, gen. mgr. transp. and maintenance, 1978, v.p. ops., 1978-81, exec. v.p., 1981-83, pres., chief operating officer, 1983-84, pres., chief exec. officer, 1984—; chmn., pres., chief exec. officer Soo Line Corp., 1986—; dir. Consol. Papers, Inc., Wis. Rapids, Wis., Minn. Bus. Partnership, Inc., Mpls., Remmele Engring., Mpls., Mpls., Soo Line R.R. Co., Mpls., Soo Line Corp., Mpls. Served with USN, 1957-61. Mem. Am. Mgmt. Assn. Clubs: Midland Hills Country, Minneapolis, Minn. Alumni, Transp. Internat. Avocations: sailing; cross-country skiing; skating; golf. Address: Soo Line Corp Soo Line Bldg Box 530 Minneapolis MN 55440

CAVANAUGH, JOHN WILLIAM, II, dentist; b. Oklahoma City, Aug. 20, 1940; s. John William and Catherine Coe (Jacobs) C.; m. Louise Elizabeth Bridges; Sept. 23, 1964; children: Beth A., John M., William P., Jennifer B., Susan K. BS, Rockhurst Coll., 1962; DDS, U. Mo., Kansas City, 1966. Pvt. practice gen. dentistry Topeka, 1968—; bd. dirs. Blue Cross-Blue Shield, Topeka, 1981-86, exec. com. bd. dirs., 1982-85, cons. 1985—. Patentee in field. Served to lt. USN, 1966-68; comdr. Res. discharged 1984. Mem. ADA, Kans. Dental Assn., Topeka Dist. Dental Assn., council Dental Health Care Plans. Republican. Roman Catholic. Avocations: automobile restoration and racing. Home: 5016 Cedar Crest Rd Topeka KS 66606 Office: 5225 N 7th St Topeka KS 66606

CAVANNA, ROBERT CHARLES, educational service executive; b. N.Y.C., Nov. 5, 1943; s. Charles Carmine and Margaret Eleanor (Corsiglia) C.; m. Regina Mary Claire Clipper, Aug. 4, 1973; children: Alison Joy, Megan Leigh. AB, Pace U., 1966; MA, U. N.Mex., 1968; EdD, U. Wyo., 1975. Lic. sch. supt., prin., tchr. Tchr. social studies Fishers Island (N.Y.) High Sch., 1968-73; secondary prin. Ellsworth (Minn.) Schs., 1975-77; supt. Hendrum-Perley (Minn.) Schs., 1977-79, Lake Benton (Minn.) Schs., 1979-82, Norwood-Young Am., Norwood, Minn., 1982-85; exec. dir. Cen. Minn. Ednl. Cooperative Service Unit, St. Cloud, Minn., 1985—; adminstr. intern Albany County Schs., Laramie, Wyo., 1973-75. Contbr. articles to profl. jours. Mem. Assn. for Supn. and Curriculum Devel., Nat. Sch. Pub. Relations Assn. (bd. dirs. Minn. chpt. 1984-85), Minn. Assn. Sch. Adminstrs., Am. Assn. Ednl. Service Agys., Minn. Alliance for Sci. (bd. dirs.), Phi Delta Kappa. Episcopalian. Avocations: skiing, swimming, reading. Home: 3015 20th St S Saint Cloud MN 56301 Office: Cen Minn Ednl Cooperative Service Unit St Cloud State U Coll Edn A-127 Saint Cloud MN 56301

CAVE, PATRICK WILLIAM, engineering sales executive; b. Columbus, Nebr., Sept. 13, 1955; s. William Paul and Maxine (Borowiak) C. BS in Mech. Engring., U. Nebr., 1979. Applications engr. Fisher Controls, Marshalltown, Iowa, 1979-86; sales engr. Rosemount Analytical Div., Mpls., 1986-87, Materials Research Corp., Bridgeton, Mo., 1987—. Asst. scoutmaster Boy Scouts Am., Marshalltown, 1984-85, leader Explorer div., 1985. Mem. Tech. Assn. Pulp and Paper Industry, Instrument Soc. Am. (tech. chmn. 1986), Pacific Coast Gas Assn. (guest tech. speaker 1985-86), Am. Soc. Mech. Engrs. Republican. Roman Catholic. Avocations: fly fishing, waterfowl hunting, skiing, sailing, golf. Home: 8856 Knollwood Dr Eden Prairie MN 55344 Office: Materials Research Corp 3450 Bridgeland Dr Bridgeton MO 63044

CAWNEEN, KEVIN MARTIN, oil company executive, accountant; b. Cleve., Mar. 31, 1960; s. James Francis and Helen Cecilia (Snyder) C.; m. Deborah Van, Aug. 9, 1986. BBA, U. Notre Dame, 1982; postgrad. in Bus. Adminstrn., John Carroll U., 1982—. CPA, Ohio. Staff auditor Arthur Andersen and Co., Cleve., 1982-84; acct. crude oil dept. Standard Oil Co., Cleve., 1984-86, sr. systems acct., 1986—. Mem. Am. Inst. CPA's, Ohio Soc. CPA's. Club: Irish Am. (Euclid, Ohio) (audit com. 1985). Avocation: sports. Office: Standard Oil 200 Public Square 23-4204-A Cleveland OH 44114

CAWTHORNE, KENNETH CLIFFORD, fragrance manufacturing company executive; b. Manistee, Mich., Feb. 13, 1936; s. Clifford Haney and Marie Dorothy (Schimke) C.; m. Martha S. Zielinski, Aug. 23, 1958; children—Steven, Daniel, Cynthia, Thomas. B.S. cum laude, Central Mich. U., 1958. Lic. real estate broker, Ill.; C.P.A., Mich.; registered rep. Nat. Assn. Security Dealers. Sr. acct. Ernst & Ernst, C.P.A.s, Grand Rapids, Mich., 1958-62; controller Grand Rapids Sash and Door Co., 1962-67, Melling Forging Co., Lansing, Mich., 1968-72; controller, treas., v.p. fin. Jovan, Inc. (now Beecham Cosmetics, Inc.), Chgo., 1973-84; corp. v.p. mfg. ops. Jovan, Inc. (now Beecham Cosmetics, Inc.), 1984—. Mem. Am. Inst. C.P.A.s, Nat. Assn. Accts. Home: 503 W Haven Dr Arlington Heights IL 60005 Office: 600 Eagle Dr Bensenville IL 60106

CAYLOR, TRUMAN E., physician; b. Pennville, Ind., Jan. 10, 1900; s. Charles E. and Bessie (Ferree) C.; student Ind. U., 1917-1919; B.S., Wis. U., 1921; M.D., Rush Med. Coll., 1924; m. Julia Gettle, June 28, 1923 (dec. June 6, 1960); children: Carolyn Caylor Wadlington, Charles H., Constance Caylor Carney; m. Eva Abbott, May 29, 1961 (dec. 1979); m. Suzanne Black, 1980. Intern, Evanston (Ill.) Gen. Hosp.; practice medicine specializing in urology, Bluffton, Ind., 1924-81; co-founder, mem. staff Caylor Nickel Clinic, Bluffton, mem. staff Caylor Nickel Hosp., Bluffton, 1939-81, exec. com., 1939-75, also dir.; dir. emeritus Mut. Security Life Ins. Co., Ft. Wayne, Ind. Mem. adv. com. Ind. Commn. on Aging, 1972-80; mem. adv. com. Grace Coll., Winona Lake, Ind., 1970—. Dir. emeritus Yorkfellow Inst., Richmond, Ind., Caylor Nickel Research Found.; pres. emeritus, co-founder Caylor Nickel Research Inst., 1961. Served with AUS, 1918. Fellow A.C.S.; mem. Ind. Council Sagamores, Ind. State Med. Soc. (50th Year Certificate of Distinction 1974), Am. Urol. Assn., Delta Upsilon, Phi Rho Sigma. Clubs: Masons, Shriners, Scottish Rite, Rotary (dist. gov. 1965-66), Elks. Home: 920 River Rd PO Box 292 Bluffton IN 46714 Office: One Caylor-Nickel Square Bluffton IN 46714

CECH, JOSEPH HAROLD, chemical engineer; b. Flint, Mich., Oct. 8, 1951; s. Joseph, Jr. and Margaret Luella (Taphouse) C. B.S. in Chem. Engrng., Mich. Tech. U., 1978. Trainee, Menasha Corp., North Bend, Oreg., 1978-79, project engr. molded products div., Watertown, Wis., 1979-84, plastic devel. engr., 1984-86, composite engr., coordinator, 1986—. Served with USN, 1971-75. Mem. Soc. Plastic Engrs., Am. Inst. Chem. Engrs., Nat. Geog. Soc., Watertown Conservation Club: Methodist. Office: 426 Montgomery St Watertown WI 53094

CECI, LOUIS J., justice state supreme court; b. N.Y.C., Sept. 10, 1927; s. Louis and Filomena C.; m. Shirley; children—Joseph, Geraldine, David; children by previous marriage: Kristin, Remy, Louis. Ph.B., Marquette U., 1951, J.D., 1954. Bar: Wis. 1954, U.S. Dist. Ct. (ea. dist.) Wis. 1954. Sole practice Milw., 1954-58, 63-68; asst. city atty. City of Milw., 1958-63; mem. Wis. Assembly, Madison, 1965-66; judge Milw. County Ct., 1968-73, Milw. Circuit Ct., 1973-82; justice Wis. Supreme Ct., Madison, 1982—; lectr. Wis. Jud. Confs., 1970-79. Lectr. Badger Boys State, Ripon, Wis., 1961, 1982-84; asst. dist. commr. Boy Scouts Am., 1962. Recipient Wis. Civic Recognition PLAV, Milw., 1970; recipient Community Improvement Pompeii Men's Club, Milw., 1971, Good Govt. Milw Jaycees, 1973, Community-Judiciary Pompeii Men's Club, 1982. Mem. ABA, Wis. Bar Assn., Dane County Bar Assn., Am. Legion (comdr. 1962-63). Office: Wisconsin Supreme Court PO Box 1688 Madison WI 53701

CECIL, DORCAS ANN, property manager; b. Greensboro, N.C., Mar. 31, 1945; d. George Joseph and Marianne Elizabeth (Zimmerman) Ernst; m. Richard Lee Cecil, June 8, 1968; children: Sarah, Matthew. BA, U. Ark., 1967. Pres. B & C Enterprises Property Mgmt., Ltd., O'Fallon, Ill., 1977—. Bd. dirs. O'Fallon Pub. Library, 1983—, v.p., 1986-87, pres., 1987—. Mem. Inst. Real Estate Mgmt. (cert.)(v.p.), Accredited Resident Mgr. Com. (sec. 1986), Ill. Apt. Assn., St. Louis Multi-Housing Council, Profl. Housing Mgmt. Assn., Nat. Assn. Realtors, Belleville Bd. Realtors, O'Fallon C. of C. (bd. dirs. 1987-90). Democrat. Roman Catholic. Office: B & C Enterprises One Eagle Ctr PO Box 403 O'Fallon IL 62269

CECIL, STEPHEN DON, minister; b. Sikeston, Mo., Nov. 26, 1958; s. Leeman Donald and Naomi Ruth (Ball) C.; m. Peggy Lee Denny, Aug. 15, 1981; children: Leigh-Ann, Stephanie Michelle. BA, Mid-Am. Nazarene Coll., 1981. Assoc. pastor Community Ch. of Nazarene, San Antonio, Tex., 1981-83; pastor Ch. of Nazarene, Kempton, Ill., 1983-86, Grace Ch. of Nazarene, Inver Grove Heights, Mnn., 1986—; zone youth coordinator San Antonio, 1982, Kankakee, Ill., 1985, Minn. Nazarene Youth Internat., Inver Grove Heights, 1986—. Named One of Outstanding Young Men Am., 1982, 85. Avocation: various sport. Home: 7268 Clay Ave E Inver Grove Heights MN 55075 Office: Grace Ch of Nazarene 7950 Blaine Ave E Inver Grove Heights MN 55075

CEDERBERG, JOHN EDWIN, accountant; b. Osceola, Nebr., Feb. 18, 1943; s. Carl Edwin and Bernita Irene (Burns) C.; m. Bonnie Louise Butler, June 20, 1970; children: Erika Kristine, Kevin Bradley. BA summa cum laude, Dana Coll., 1965; MA, U. S.D., 1967; postgrad., Georgetown U., 1967-68. CPA, Md. Mem. audit staff Arthur Andersen & Co., Washington, 1968-71, mem. tax staff, 1971-73, mgr. taxes, 1973-75; mgr. taxes Touche Ross & Co., Lincoln, Nebr., 1976-78, tax ptnr., 1978—; mem. adv. bd. Nebr. Tax Research Council, 1986—. Mem. editorial com. Bank Tax Bulletin, 1986—. Mem. Am. Inst. CPA's (mem. tax com., sub-com. specialized entities 1985—), Nebr. Soc. CPA's, Nebr. Assn. Commerce and Industry (tax comm. 1985—), Bank Tax Inst. (adv. bd. mem. 1979—), Lincoln C. of C. (mem. state legis. com. 1976—, mem. fed. legis. com. chmn. 1981-82), Sons of Am. Legion. Home: 1916 Devonshire Dr Lincoln NE 68506 Office: Touche Ross & Co 1040 NBC Ctr Lincoln NE 68508

CEDERBURG, MARK STEVEN, clinical social worker; b. Kansas City, Kans., Jan. 25, 1951; s. Ben Harrison and Mary Elizabeth (Davis) C.; m. Jana Lee Kasper, Nov. 18, 1984 (div. Dec. 1985). AA, Longview Community Coll., Kansas City, 1973; BA, U. Mo., Kansas City, 1975; MSW, U. Kan., 1984. Lic. social worker, Kans. Social service worker Mo. Div. Family Services, Kansas City, 1976-84; staff clinician Community Mental Health Ctr., Kansas City, 1984-85; clin. social worker Family and Children Services of Kansas City, 1985-87; dir. therapy services The Spofford Home, Kansas City, Mo., 1987—. Mem. Mo. Assn Social Welfare, Nat. Assn. Social Workers. Democrat. Avocations: long distance running, piano, reading. Home: 4304 Campbell Kansas City MO 64110 Office: The Spofford Home 9700 Grandview Rd Kansas City MO 64134

CELEBREZZE, ANTHONY J., JR., attorney general Ohio; b. Cleve., Sept. 8, 1941; s. Anthony J. and Anne M. C.; m. Louisa Godwin, June 19, 1965; children: Anthony J. III, Catherine, Charles, David, Maria. BS, U.S. Naval Acad., 1963; MS, George Washington U., 1966; JD, Cleve. State U., 1973. Bar: Ohio 1973. Ptnr. Celebrezze and Marco, Cleve., 1975-79; mem. Ohio State Senate, 1975-79; sec. of state State of Ohio, Columbus, 1979-83, atty. gen., 1983—. Pres. Joint Vets. Commn. of Cuyahoga County, Ohio, from 1977; v.p. Lake Erie Regional Transp. Authority, 1972-74; mem. Gt. Lakes Commn., 1975-78, vice chmn., 1977-78. Served with USN, 1963-68. Decorated Navy Commendation medal; recipient Jeffersonian Lodge award, 1977, Man of Yr. award Delta Theta Phi, Freedoms Found. Honor medal, 1980, 86; named 1 of 5 Outstanding Legislators by 2 Ohio mags., 1978. Democrat. Roman Catholic. Office: State Office Tower 30 E Broad St Columbus OH 43215 *

CELEBREZZE, STEVEN JAMES, lawyer; b. Cleve., Feb. 19, 1959; s. Frank Daniel and Mary Ann (Armstrong) C. BA, Ohio Dominican Coll., 1981; JD, Capital U., 1984. Bar: Ohio 1984, U.S. Dist. Ct. (so. dist.) Ohio 1984. Assoc. Teaford, Rich & Dorsey, Columbus, Ohio, 1984-85, Teaford, Rich, Belskis, Coffman & Wheeler, Columbus, Ohio, 1985—; legal cons. Beneficial Ohio Inc., Beneficial Mortgage Co. of Ohio, Capital Savs. & Loan Co., Columbus, 1984—. Recipient Am. Jurisprudence Book award Lawyer's Cooperative Pub. Co., 1983. Mem. ABA, Acad. Trial Lawyers Am., Ohio Acad. Trial Lawyers, Columbus Bar Assn., Ohio State Bar Assn. Democrat. Roman Catholic. Office: Teaford Rich Belskis et al 20 E Broad St Columbus OH 43215

CELESTE, RICHARD F., governor of Ohio; b. Cleve., Nov. 11, 1937; s. Frank C.; m. Dagmar Braun, 1962; children: Eric, Christopher, Gabriella, Noelle, Natalie, Stephen. B.A. in History magna cum laude, Yale U., 1959; Ph.B. in Politics, Oxford U., 1962. Staff liaison officer Peace Corps, 1963; dir. Peace Corps, Washington, 1979-81; spl. asst. to U.S. ambassador to India, 1963-67; mem. Ohio Ho. of Reps., Columbus, 1970-74, majority whip, 1972-74; lt. gov. State of Ohio, Columbus, 1974-79, gov., 1983—. Mem. Ohio Democratic Exec. Com. Rhodes scholar Oxford U., Eng. Mem. Am. Soc. Pub. Adminstrn., Italian Sons and Daus. Am. Methodist. Office: Office of Gov State Capitol Columbus OH 43215 *

CELUSTA, JEFFREY ROBERT, restaurant owner; b. Duluth, Minn., Nov. 10, 1952; s. George Robert and Betty May (Gustafson) C.; m. Holly Jo Hoover; children: Jeffrey George, Jeremy Robert. BBA, U. Wyo., 1975. Gen. mgr. Chart House Inc., Jacksonville, Fla., 1975-78, Atlanta, 1978-79; gen. mgr. Naegele Restaurants, St. Cloud, Minn., 1979-84; owner, operator D.B. Searle's Restaurant, St. Cloud, 1984—. Mem. Nat. Restaurant Assn., Minn. Restaurant Assn., St. Cloud C. of C. Office: DB Searles 18 S 5th Ave Saint Cloud MN 56301

CENA, LAWRENCE, transp. co. exec.; b. San Jose, Calif., Mar. 19, 1922; s. Carl and Teresa (Massetti) C.; m. Patricia H. Hayes, June 19, 1942; children: Lawrie Kathleen, Patrick C., Timothy M., Terry M., Robin Kay. Student, North Central Coll., Naperville, Ill., 1946, Northwestern U., 1947; various mgmt. programs, Northwestern U. With A.T.S.F. Ry., 1948—; asst. gen. mgr. A.T.S.F. Ry., Topeka, 1966-68; asst. v.p. ops. A.T.S.F. Ry., Chgo., 1968; v.p. ops. A.T.S.F. Ry., 1968-78, pres., 1978—. Served with U.S. Navy, 1942-45. Office: The Atchison Topeka & Santa Fe Railway Co 80 E Jackson Blvd Chicago IL 60604 *

CENGEL, JOHN ANTHONY, chemist; b. East Chicago, Ind., July 21, 1936; s. John Felix and Margaret Ruth (Gelon) C.; m. Christine Ellen Lakatos, Aug. 25, 1962; children: John David, Laura Ann, Keith Albert. BSChemE, Purdue U., 1958; MSChemE, Oreg. State U., 1959; PhD in Phys. Chemistry, Purdue U., 1965. Research chemist Amoco Chem. Co., Whiting, Ind., 1965-69; staff research chemist Amoco Chem. Co., Naperville, Ill., 1970-73, sr. research chemist, 1985—; sr. research chemist Amoco Petroleum Additives Co. subs. Amoco Chem. Co., Naperville, 1978-84. Contbr. tech. papers to profl. jours.; patentee in field. Fellow NSF, 1959, AEC, 1961-65. Mem. Am. Chem. Soc., Tau Beta Pi, Sigma Xi, Omega Chi Epsilon. Roman Catholic. Avocations: teaching, gardening, fishing. Home: 1879 Cheshire Ln Wheaton IL 60187 Office: Amoco Chem Co PO Box 400 Naperville IL 60566

CENTA, WILLIAM JAMES, financial executive; b. Cleve., July 17, 1952; s. Andrew Edward and Phyllis Elizabeth (Cleary) C.; m. Renee Maria Halik, Aug. 9, 1975; children: Lauren M., Jennifer M. BBA, Bowling Green (Ohio) State U., 1974; MBA, Cleve. State U., 1977; postgrad., Cleve.-Marshal Law Sch., 1983-84. CPA, Ohio. Dep. dir. acctg. United Way Services, Cleve., 1974-76; sr. mgr. Arthur Andersen & Co., Cleve., 1977-84; v.p. fin. Invacare Internat., London, 1984-86; controller Invacare Corp., Elyria, Ohio, 1986—; cons. Hallmark Fin. Group, Inc., Cleve., 1986—. Mem. Am. Inst. CPA's, Ohio Soc. CPA's, Beta Gamma Sigma, Alpha Tau Omega. Republican. Roman Catholic. Avocations: racquetball, literature, investment research. Home: 12466 Bentbrook Dr Chesterland OH 44026 Office: Invacare Corp 1200 Taylor St Elyria OH 44036

CENTER, JOHN WILLIAM, management educator, consultant; b. Berkeley, Calif., Aug. 4, 1946; s. William Cranford and Thelma May (Ammons) C.; m. Lois Ann Koopmeiners, Nov. 8, 1975; childen: James William, Olivia Ann. BS in Physics, U. Calif., Riverside, 1968; MS in Systems Engring., Calif. State U., Fullerton, 1973; MBA, Coll. St. Thomas, St. Paul, 1982. Registered profl. engr. Physicist USN, 1968-70, 72-73; engr. Control Data Corp., St. Paul, 1973-75; mgr. Medtronic Inc., Mpls., 1975-84; cons. Center Assocs., St. Paul, 1984—; adj. prof. Coll. St. Thomas, St. Paul., 1983—; bd. dirs. Xinotech. Research, Inc., Mpls. Served as sgt. U.S. Army, 1970-72. Mem. NSPE, IEEE, Assn. Computing Machinery, Ints. Mgmt. Sci. Office: Center Assocs 1450 Energy Park Dr Saint Paul MN 55108

CENTERS, LOUISE CLAUDENA, clinical psychologist, lawyer; b. Huntington Park, Calif.. BA, U. So. Calif., 1953, PhD in Psychology, 1958; JD, Detroit Coll. Law, 1979. Bar: Mich. 1979, Fla. 1980; diplomate Am. Bd. Profl. Psychology. Pvt. practice psychology specializing in forensic assessment Southfield, Mich., 1959—; chief, clin. psychology sect. Sinai Hosp., Detroit, 1970—. Contbr. 9 articles to profl. jours. Fellow Am. Orthopsychiat. Assn., Mich. Psychol. Assn. (pres. 1981, Disting. Psychologist award 1984); mem. Am. Psychol. Assn., Mich. Soc. Clin. Psychologists (pres. 1975), Mich. Interprofl. Assn. (pres. 1985). Clubs: Fairlane (Dearborn, Mich.), Women's Econ. (Detroit), Econ. of Detroit. Home: 25052 Sherwood Circle Southfield MI 48075 Office: Sinai Hosp Dept Psychiatry 14800 W McNichols Detroit MI 48235

CENTNER, CHARLES WILLIAM, lawyer; b. Battle Creek, Mich., July 4, 1915; s. Charles William and Lucy Irene (Patterson); m. Evi Rohr, Dec. 22, 1956; children—Charles Patterson, David William, Geoffrey Christopher. A.B., U. Chgo., 1936, A.M., 1936, A.M., 1939, Ph.D., 1941; J.D., Detroit Coll. Law, 1970; LL.B., LaSalle Extension U., 1965. Bar: Mich. 1970. Asst. prof. U. N.D., 1940-41, Tulane U., New Orleans, 1941-42; liaison officer for Latin Am., Lend-Lease Adminstrn., 1942; assoc. dir. Western Hemisphere div. Nat. Fgn Trade Council, 1946-52; exec. Ford Motor Co., Detroit, 1952-57, Chrysler Corp. and Chrysler Internat. S.A., Detroit and Geneva, Switzerland, 1957-70; adj. prof. Wayne State U., U. Detroit, Wayne County Community Coll., 1970—. Served to lt. comdr. USNR, 1942-45. Mem. State Bar of Mich., ABA, Detroit Bar Assn., Oakland County Bar Assn. Republican. Episcopalian. Club: Masons. Author: Great Britain and Chile, 1810-1914, 1941. Home: 936 Harcourt Rd Grosse Pointe Park MI 48230 Office: 100 Renaissance Ctr Suite 1575 Detroit MI 48243-1075

CENTNER, ROBERT WAYNE, computer engineer; b. Dunkirk, N.Y., Dec. 17, 1942; s. Fred L. and Mildred A. (Subjack) C.; m. Beryl Anne Ball, May 19, 1967; children: Douglas, William, Jonathan, Sara. BS, St. Bonaventure U., Olean, N.Y., 1964; MS, U. Detroit, 1967, Iowa State U., Ames, 1969, 71. Research physicist Gen. Motors Corp., Warren, Mich., 1966-67; research and teaching assoc. Iowa State U., 1967-69; research and devel. engr. Uniroyal, Inc., Detroit, 1971-86; research engr. Uniroyal-Goodrich, Troy, Mich., 1986—. Pres. Grosse Pointe (Mich.) War Meml. Chess Club, 1974-76; chess instr. St. Angela Sch., Roseville, Mich., 1975—, soccer dir., 1976, soccer coach, 1976-84; chess instr. Bishop Gallagher High Sch., 1986—. Teaching fellow U. Detroit, 1964-66. Mem. Am. Soc. for Quality Control. Roman Catholic. Home: 26201 Koontz Roseville MI 48066 Office: Uniroyal-Goodrich Tire Co 1305 Stephenson Hwy Troy MI 48084

CENTNER, ROSEMARY LOUISE, chemist; b. Newport, Ky., Sept 23, 1926; d. Alexis F. and Mary Anne (Cloud) Centner; B.A., Our Lady of Cin. Coll., 1947; M.S., U. Cin., 1949. Library asst., tech. library Procter & Gamble Co., 1949-52, br. librarian Miami Valley labs., Cin., 1952-56, tech. librarian, 1956-66, mgr. tech. info. service, 1966-72, mgr. div. info. cons., 1972-73, mgr. NDA coordination, 1973-75, mgr. biomed. communications, 1975-81, mgr. tech. communications, 1981—. Trustee, Edgecliff Coll., 1975-82. Mem. Am. Chem. Soc., Am. Med. Writers Assn. Iota Sigma Pi. Roman Catholic. Home: 2678 Byrneside Dr Cincinnati OH 45239 Office: Winton Hill Tech Center Cincinnati OH 45224

CENTURY, BERNARD AMOS, manufacturing company executive; b. Chgo., May 12, 1926; s. Louis and Julia (Stolar) C.; m. Evelyn Coodin, Nov. 23, 1949; children: Janet, Larry. BS, U. Notre Dame, 1946, MS, 1947. Registered profl. engr., N.J. Instr. U. Ill., Champaign, 1947-50; mgr. research and devel. Hewitt Robins Inc., Passaic, N.J., 1953-63; project engr. Cleve. Trencher, 1963-67; mgr. product devel. Allied Steel & Tractor, Solon, Ohio, 1967-80; pres. Rexrock, Inc., Cleve., 1980—. Patentee in field. Served with USNR. Mem. ASME. Home and Office: 2305 S Overlook Rd Cleveland OH 44106

CERKAS, MICHAEL WILLIAM, computer systems executive; b. Manitowoc, Wis., Apr. 25, 1956; s. Leonard Florian and Agnes Rose (Smith) C.; m. Kathleen Jean Schmidt, Aug. 6, 1977; 1 child, Brandon Michael. BA, U. Wis., Green Bay, 1978; MS in Mgmt., Cardinal Stritch U., Milw., 1986. Customer service mgr. Burroughs Corp., Green Bay, 1978-81; info. cons. Wis. Pub. Service Corp., Green Bay, 1981-84, systems supr., 1984—. Democrat. Roman Catholic. Avocations: water skiing, fishing, bowling, volleyball, basketball. Home: 436 Stonehedge Rd Green Bay WI 54302-5225 Office: Wis Pub Service Corp PO Box 19001 Green Bay WI 54307-9001

CERLING, CHARLES EDWARD, minister; b. Elmhurst, Ill., Oct. 7, 1943; s. Charles Edward and Agnes MacIntosh (Muir) C.; m. Geraldine Lee Bock, June 11, 1966; children: David Bruce, Jonathan Mark, Peter James. AB, Taylor U., 1965; MA, Trinity Sem., 1968; MDiv, Trinity Coll., 1969; D in Ministry, Talbot Theol. Sem., 1984. Lic. social worker, Mich.; ordained to Bapt. ministry, 1978. Minister Hopevale Bapt. Ch., Saginaw, Mich., 1976-78, First Bapt. Ch., Tawas City, Mich., 1978—; profl. advisor Parents without Ptnrs., Tawas City, 1981—. Author: Holy Boldness, 1982, Assertiveness, 1983, The Divorced Christian, 1984, Freedom from Bad Habits, 1985, Cleaning Out Your Mental Closet, 1987. Avocations: golf, hunting, fishing. Home and Office: PO Box 457 405 Second St Tawas City MI 48764

CERNY, JOSEPH CHARLES, urologist, educator; b. Oak Park, Ill., Apr. 20, 1930; s. Joseph James and Mary (Turek) C.; m. Patti Bobette Pickens, Nov. 10, 1962; children—Joseph Charles, Rebecca Anne. B.A., Knox Coll., 1952; M.D., Yale U., 1956. Diplomate Am. Bd. Urology. Intern U. Mich. Hosp., Ann Arbor, 1956-57, resident, 1957-62; practice medicine specializing in urology, Ann Arbor, and Detroit since 1962—; inst. surgery (urology) U.

Mich., Ann Arbor, 1962-64, asst. prof., 1964-66, assoc. prof., 1966-71, clin. prof., 1971—; chmn. dept. urology Henry Ford Hosp., Detroit, 1971—; pres. Resistors, Inc., Chgo., 1960—; cons. St. Joseph Hosp., Ann Arbor, 1973—. Contbr. articles to profl. jours., chpts. in books. Bd. dirs., trustee Nat. Kidney Found. Mich., Ann Arbor, 1980—, chmn. urology council 1987-89, exec. com. 1987-89; bd. dirs. Ann Arbor Amateur Hockey Assn., 1980-83; pres. PTO, Ann Arbor Pub. Schs., 1980. Served to lt. USNR, 1956-76. Recipient Disting. Service award Transplantation Soc. Mich., 1982. Fellow ACS (pres.-elect Mich. br. 1984-85, pres. 1985—); mem. Internat. Soc. Urology, Am. Urol. Assn. (pres. North Cen. sec. 1985-86, Manpower com. 1987-88, Jud. Rev. com. 1987-91, tech. exhibits 1987-88, Best Sci. Exhibit award 1978, Best Sci. Films award 1980, 82), Transplantation Soc. Mich. (pres. 1983-84), ACS (pres. Mich. chpt. 1985-86), Am. Assn. Transplant Surgeons, Endocrine Surgeons, Soc. Univ. Urologists, Am. Assn. Urologic Oncology, Am. Fertility Soc. Republican. Methodist. Clubs: Barton Hills Country; Ann Arbor Raquet (Ann Arbor). Avocations: tennis; fishing; Civil War. Home: 2800 Fairlane Dr Ann Arbor MI 48104 Office: Dept Urology Henry Ford Hosp 2799 W Grand Blvd Detroit MI 48202

CESARE, ANTHONY GIORGI, writer, inventor, puppeteer; b. Chgo., July 31, 1943; s. Anthony Giorgi and Genevieve Stephanie (Lucas) C.; BA in English, Parsons Coll., 1965; m. Margaret Ann Hooks, Sept. 27, 1981. Tech. writer T.M. Pubs., Chgo., 1965-67; copywriter Hilltop Advt., Battle Creek, Mich., 1967-68; mktg. and pub. relations coordinator Ad Art and Design, Kalamazoo, 1968-69; owner Cesare & Assos., Boulder, Colo., 1969-71; free-lance writer, 1973-77; tech. editor Chemetron Fire Systems, Monee, Ill., 1977-79; sr. tech. writer Allis-Chalmers Corp., 1979-80; pres. Snaffle, Inc., Lake Village, Ind., 1982—; with Cole Marionettes, Lake Village, Ind., 1982-85. Mem. Internat. Platform Assn., Am. Advt. Fedn., Writers Guild. Roman Catholic. Author: A White Feather Means Death, 1965, The Feathers Technique, 1980, Capt. Monsewer Weird, 1985, The Kitchen Survival Manual, 1986; editor: Chemetron Fire Systems Halon 1301 Design Manual, 1978; designer The Snaffler Paper Airplane, 1986; inventor card game Snaffle, copyright 1982. Home: Lake Village IN 46349

CESARIO, ROBERT CHARLES, franchise executive, consultant; b. Chgo., Apr. 6, 1941; s. Valentino A. and Mary Ethel (Kenny) C.; m. Emily Carbone (div.); 1 son, Jeffrey; m. Susan Kay DePoutee. B.S. in Gen. Edn., Northwestern U., 1975; postgrad. in bus. adminstrn. DePaul U., 1975. Mgr. fin. ops. Midas Internat. Corp., Chgo., 1968-73; dir. staff ops. Am. Hosp. Supply Corp., McGaw Park, Ill., 1973-76; v.p. Car X Service Systems Inc., Chgo., 1976-78, v.p. oil services, 1983-84; pres. Growth Strategies, Inc., 1984-87; pres. CEO Lube Pro's Internat., Inc., 1987—; v.p. Chicken Unlimited Enterprises Inc., Chgo., 1978-83. Served with USMC, 1960-62. Office: Lube Pros Internat Inc 20 N Wacker Dr Suite 1530 Chicago IL 60606

CHADBOURNE, JOSEPH HUMPHREY, educational association administrator; b. Boston, May 15, 1931; s. Joseph Humphrey and Barbara (Bullard) C.; m. Ann Hopkins Nolan, Sept. 15, 1956 (div. Feb. 1979); children: Gay Kellogg, Scott Holt; m. Mary McConnville, Apr. 19, 1982; 1 child, Caitlin. BS, Yale U., 1952; MS, U. Conn., 1965. Prodn. plant mgr. Danielson (Conn.) Mfg. CO., 1955-58; sales and mktg. Spencer Chem. Co., Kansas City, Mo., 1958-61; prodn. mgr. Moldings & Extrusions, Danielson, 1961-62; tchr. Univ. Sch., Cleve., 1964-68; headmaster Tilton (N.H.) Sch., 1969-71; dir. govt. grants Inst. for Environ. Edn., various cities, 1971-76; pres. Inst. for Environ. Edn., Cleve., 1971—. Publisher (audio visual series) Environ. Edn., 1969-76; editor Tuning Green Machine, 1976. Ford Found. workshop, 1968; recipient Gov.'s award for Community Action, Ohio, 1973. Mem. Ohio Environ. Protection Agy. Task Force, Cleve. Collaboration for Math. (bd. dirs. 1984—). Unitarian. Avocations: competing in Nat. Masters Track and Field Meets. Home: 18554 Haskins Rd Chagrin Falls OH 44022 Office: Inst for Environ Edn 32000 Chagrin Blvd Cleveland OH 44124

CHADDOCK, CHARLES RICHARD, pharmaceutical company executive; b. Canton, Ohio, April 9, 1914; s. Richard Greer and Dora M. (Elser) C.: m. Bessie Jane Kilgore, Sept. 1, 1948; children: Georgia Kay Bailey, Carole Rae Niederkofler. BS in Pharmacy, Ohio State U., 1936; postgrad., Syracuse U., 1959. Registered pharmacist, Ohio. Pharmacist Bowman Bros. Drug Co., Canton, 1936-57; pres. Bowman Braun Pharm. Co., Canton, 1957-61; pres. Bowman Pharm. Inc., 1961-84; pres. CRC Unit Formulas Inc., Canton, 1985—. Developer of new pharm. products, over the counter and prescription items. Mem. Tri-County Health Career Assn. (pres. 1973), Sigma Phi Epsilon (Clifford B. Scott Hon. award), Phi Rho Alpha. Republican. Mem. Ch. of Christ. Lodges: Rotary (edn. com. 1945—), Masons (32 degree). Avocations: swimming, bridge. Home: 2110 Red Coach Dr NW North Canton OH 44720 Office: CRC Unit Formulas Inc 914-18th St NW Canton OH 44703

CHADHA, SANJIV, architect; b. Calcutta, India, Sept. 3, 1956; s. Ashwani and Daman (Puri) C. BS in Architecture, Indian Inst. Tech., Kharagpur, India, 1979; MS in Architecture, Ill. Inst. Tech., Chgo., 1983. Registered architect, India. Architect Satnam Namita Assoc., Chandigarh, India, 1980-81, Gouvis & Assocs., Chgo., 1983-84; graphics and computer-aided design instr. Ill. Inst. Tech., Chgo., 1983-85; real estate agt. Century 21, Chgo., 1986—; computer-aided design and drafting mgr. Neil Wennlund & Slomka, Chgo., 1984—; bd. dirs. Chadha & Co., Calcutta, India; cons. dept. phys. resources Ill. Inst. Tech., Chgo., 1986—. Contbg. editor Tech. News Jour., 1981-82. Mem. North Side Realtors Bd., Indian Inst. Architects, Council Indian Architects, India Assn. Indians in Am., Am. Assn. Indians in Am. Hindu. Avocations: racquetball, cricket, debating. Home: 3101 S Wabash #902 Chicago IL 60616 Office: Neil Wennlund & Slomka 8 S Michigan #3400 Chicago IL 60603

CHADHA, SUJAN SINGH, small business owner; b. Warwal, Panjab, India, Oct. 15, 1923; came to U.S., 1974; s. Grad., U. Panjab Lahore, Pakistan, 1943; BA, U. Panjab Lahore, Pakistan, 1946. Clerical cadre controller mil. accts. N.W. Army, Rawalpindi, Pakistan, 1942-66; acct. SAS Def. Accounts, India, 1967-73; owner Chadha Imports-Exports, Wis., 1974—; ptnr. R. A. Bazar, Meerut, India, 1948-55, R.A. Bazar, Lucknow, India, 1957-60; part owner fleet of taxis, India, 1970-73. Mem. Metro Milw. Assn. of Commerce, Credit Bur. Milw. Inc., Better Bus. Bur. Greater Milw., Internat. Inst. Wis., All India Def. Accts. Employees Assn. Republican. Lodge: Rotary. Avocations: hockey, volleyball. Home: 9308 S 35th St Franklin WI 53132 Office: Chadha Imports-Exports 9661 S 20th St Oak Creek WI 53154

CHAI, WINBERG, political science educator, foundation official; b. Shanghai, China, Oct. 16, 1932; came to U.S., 1951, naturalized, 1973; s. Ch'u and Mei-en (Tsao) C.; m. Carolyn Everett, Mar. 17, 1966; children: Maria May-lee, Jeffrey Tien-yu. Student, Hartwick Coll., 1951-53; B.A., Wittenberg U., 1955; M.A., New Sch. Social Research, 1958; Ph.D., N.Y. U., 1968. Lectr. New Sch. Social Research, 1957-61; vis. asst. prof. Drew U., 1961-62; asst. prof. Fairleigh Dickinson U., 1962-65; asst. prof. U. Redlands, 1965-68, asso. prof., 1969-73, chmn. dept., 1970-73; prof., chmn. Asian studies CCNY, 1973-79; disting. prof. polit. sci., v.p. acad. affairs, spl. asst. to pres. U. S.D., Vermillion, 1979-82; chmn. Third World Conf. Found., Inc., Chgo.; vice chmn. U.S.-Asia Research Inst., N.Y.C. Author: (with Ch'u Chai) The Story of Chinese Philosophy, 1961, The Changing Society of China, 1962, rev. edit., 1969, The New Politics of Communist China, 1972, The Search for a New China, 1975; editor: Essential Works of Chinese Communism, 1969, (with James C. Hsiung) Asia in the U.S. Foreign Policy, 1981; co-editor: (with James C. Hsiung) U.S. Asian Relations: The National Security Paradox, 1983, (with Cal Clark) Political Stability and Economic Growth, 1987; co-editor (with Cal Clark) Political Stability and Economic Growth, 1988; co-translator: (with Ch'u Chai) A Treasury of Chinese Literature, 1965. Ford Found. humanities grantee, 1968, 69; Haynes Found. fellow, 1967, 68; Pacific Cultural Found. grantee, 1978, 86; NSF grantee, 1970; Hubert Eaton Meml. Fund grantee, 1972-73; Field Found. grantee, 1973, 75; Henry Luce Found. grantee, 1978, 80; S.D. Humanities Com. grantee, 1980; Asian Pacific Fund grantee, 1987. Mem. Am. Assn. Chinese Studies (pres. 1978-80), AAAS, AAUP, Am. Polit. Sci. Assn., N.Y. Acad. Scis., Internat. Studies Assn. Democrat. Home: Rural Route 1 Box 22 Vermillion SD 57069 Office: PO Box 53110 Chicago IL 60653

CHAKRABARTI, SUBRATA KUMAR, research engineer; b. Calcutta, India, Feb. 3, 1941; came to U.S., 1969, naturalized, 1981; s. Asutosh and Shefali Chakrabarti; m. Prakriti Bhaduri, July 23, 1967; children—Sumita, Prabal. BSME, Jadavpur U., Calcutta, India, 1963; MSME, U. Colo., 1965, PhD in Mech. Engring., 1968. Registered profl. engr., Ill. Asst. engr. Kulijian Corp., Calcutta, 1963-64; asst. engr. Simon Carves Ltd., Calcutta, 1964; instr. engring. U. Colo., Boulder, 1965-66; hydrodynamacist Chgo. Bridge & Iron Co., Plainfield, Ill., 1968-70, head analytical group, 1970-79, dir. marine research, 1979—; vis. prof. U.S. Naval Acad., Annapolis, Md., 1986; presenter seminars in field. Author: Hydrodynamics of Offshore Structures, 1987; mem. editorial bd. Applied Ocean Research; assoc. editor Energy Resources Tech.; contbr. numerous articles to profl. publs., chpts. to books; patentee in field. Recipient Jadavpur U. Gold medal, 1963; U. Colo. fellow, 1968; named Outstanding New Citizen, 1981-82. Fellow ASCE (publ. com. waterway div., James R. Cross Gold medal 1974, Freeman scholar 1979), AAAS, ASTM, ASME (exec. com., editor jour. offshore mechanics and arctic engring. div. 1986—, chmn. div., 1987-88; mem. awards com. 1983—, tech. session developer, chmn. 1983—, Ralph James award 1984, co-editor proceedings 4th internat. symposium 1985), Sigma Xi. Home: 191 E Weller Dr N Plainfield IL 60544 Office: Chgo Bridge and Iron Co 1501 N Division St Plainfield IL 60544

CHAKRABORTY, ANUP KUMAR, physician; b. Brahmanbaria, Bangladesh, May 23, 1946; came to U.S., 1975; s. Kusum Kumar and Jyotsna (Mayee) C.; m. Sarbani Chakraborty, Feb. 19, 1976; children—Apurba, Amit. M.B.B.S., Bankura Sammilani Med. Coll. Calcutta U., 1969; M.D., Postgrad Inst., Chandigarh, India, 1973. Diplomate Am. Bd. Internal Medicine (pulmonary disease). Resident in medicine VA Med. Ctr., Bklyn., 1975-77; fellow in pulmonary medicine Nat. Jewish Hosp. and U. Colo., Denver, 1977-79; staff physician VA Med. Ctr., Denver, 1979-80, also faculty U. Colo. Med. Ctr. chief med. service VA Med. Ctr., Tomah, Wis., 1980-81; dir. respiratory care VA Med. Ctr., Lincoln, Nebr., 1981-82; practice medicine specializing in pulmonary disease, Lincoln, 1982—; mem. staff Bryan Meml., Lincoln Gen., St. Elizabeth Community Health Ctr. (all Lincoln), cons. physician V.A. Med. Ctr., Lincoln; clin. asst. prof. medicine U. Nebr. Med. Ctr., Omaha. Fellow ACP, Am. Coll. Chest Physicians. Contbr. articles to profl. jours. Home: 6510 Skylark Ln Lincoln NE 68516 Office: 120 Wedgewood Dr Suite A Lincoln NE 68510

CHALBERG-PLUNKETT, SHERRI LINELL, corporation executive; b. Leavenworth, Kans., Mar. 10, 1960; d. Larry Allen and Esther Louise (Martin) C.; m. James Davidson Plunkett, Oct. 25, 1986. BSBA, William Jewell Coll., 1984; postgrad., Rockhurst Coll., 1985—. Personnel dir. Belger Cartage Service, Kansas City, Mo., 1984-86; v.p. Jim Plunkett, Inc., Kansas City, Kans., 1986—; chief exec. officer Wall Systems Corp., Kansas City, Kans., 1986—. Republican. Mem. Unity Ch. Avocations: parachuting, hang gliding, flying, reading. Home: 15313 W 90th St Lenexa KS 66219 Office: Jim Plunkett Inc 1304 Argentine Kansas City KS 66105

CHALKLEY, THOMAS HENRY FERGUSON, ophthalmic surgeon, educator; b. N.Y.C., Nov. 3, 1933; s. Lyman and Katherine (Ferguson) C.; B.A., U. Wis., 1955, M.D., 1958; div. Jan. 1987; children—Ellen Elizabeth, Deborah Katherine. Intern, E. J. Meyer Hosp., Buffalo, 1958-59; resident physician Northwestern U. Med. Sch., 1960-62; practice medicine specializing in ophthalmic surgery, Chgo., 1962—; attending physician Northwestern Meml. Hosp., Chgo., 1962—; courtesy staff Lakeland Hosp., Elkhorn, Wis., 1983—; assoc. prof. clin. ophthalmology Northwestern U. Med. Sch., 1962—; assoc. examiner Am. Bd. Ophthalmology, 1965—.; cons in field. Bd. dirs. Ill. Soc. Prevention Blindness, 1978-79. Served to comdr. USNR, 1966-68. Recipient Disting. Merit award Hadley Sch. for Blind, 1979. Mem. Am. Acad. Ophthalmology Pan Am. Ophthal. Soc., Chgo. Ophthal. Soc. (pres. 1977-78), AAUP, Walworth County Med. Soc., Wis. Med. Soc. Author: Your Eyes, 1973, 2d edit., 1981; also articles; mem. editorial bd. Am. Jour. Ophthalmology, 1965-82, cons. editor, 1982—. Office: 233 E Erie Chicago IL 60611

CHALKLEY, YVONNE, dentist; b. Leicester, Eng.; children: Sheleigh, Benjamin, Sebastian. BS, U. Iowa, 1973, DDS, 1977, MS, 1979. Asst. prof. U. Iowa Coll. Dentistry, Iowa City, 1979-84, assoc. prof., 1984—, coordinator student affairs, 1986—; continuing edn. lectr. on aesthetic dentistry, 1979—. Author: (with others) Operative Dentistry, 1980, 2 edit., 1985; contbr. articles to profl. jours. Mem. ADA, Am. Assn. Women Dentists, Internat. Assn. Dental Research, Univ. Dist. Dental Soc., Johnson County Dental Soc., Omicron Kappa Upsilon. Avocations: piano, guitar, reading, bird watching, theatre arts. Office: U Iowa Coll Dentistry Adminstrn Bldg Iowa City IA 52242 Home: 406 Rockyshore Dr Iowa City IA 52240

CHAMBERLAIN, DAVID HAROLD, research and development company executive; b. East Stroudsburg, Pa., Mar. 2, 1944; s. John Harold and Elizabeth Gertrude (Altemose) C.; m. Jeanne Marie Fleming, Aug. 22, 1966; children: Elizabeth, Mary, Dianne. BA, Cen. Coll., Pella, Iowa, 1976. Project engr. Stresau Lab., Spooner, Wis., 1967-74, gen. mgr., 1974-80, pres., 1980—. Contbr. numerous articles to profl. jours. Mem. Am. Def. Preparedness Assn. Methodist. Office: Stresau Lab Inc Star Rt Box 189 Spooner WI 54801

CHAMBERLAIN, DONALD SHERWOOD, radiologist; b. Cin., May 21, 1935; s. Sherwood Archibald and Christine Carter (Matthews) C.; B.A., Northwestern U., 1956, M.D., 1960; m. Lillian Joyce Knudsen, June 2, 1956; children—Cheryl Ann, Daniel. Intern, U. Cin. Gen. Hosp., 1960-61, resident in radiology, 1961-64; practice medicine, specializing in radiology, Radiology, Inc., South Bend, Ind., 1966—; med. staff Meml. Hosp., South Bend, 1966—, Elkhart (Ind.) Gen. Hosp., 1966—, Parkview Hosp., Plymouth, Ind., 1966-81, South Bend Clinic, 1966—; dir., sec. Ind. Physicians Ins. Co., 1981-83; dir. X-Ray Equipment Inc., South Bend, Radiology, Inc.; chmn. Am. Physicians Life Ins. Co., 1985-87, bd. dirs.; chmn. First Interstate Bank of No. Ind. Bd. dirs. No. Ind. Health Systems Agy., 1978-83, exec. com., 1979-83; bd. dirs. Ind. Med. Edn. and Devel. Info. Center, 1978-81, Ind. State Wide Profl. Standards Rev. Council, 1978; bd. dirs. Ind. Area 2 PSRO Inc., 1974-81, chmn., 1974-79; bd. dirs., chmn. No. Ind. Found. for Health, 1981-87; bd. dirs. Meml. Med. Found., 1982—. Served to capt. M.C., U.S. Army, 1964-66. Diplomate Am. Bd. Radiology. Fellow Am. Coll. Radiology (councilor Ind. 1983—); mem. Ind. Med. Soc. (trustee 1978-83), St. Joseph County Med. Soc. (pres. 1976-77), AMA, Ind. Roentgen Soc. (pres. 1985-86), Radiol. Soc. N.Am., Am. Roentgen Ray Soc., N. Central Ind. Med. Edn. Found., South Bend Med. Found., Am. Radio Relay League, Lambda Chi Alpha, Phi Rho Sigma, Pi Kappa Epsilon. Methodist. Clubs: Profl. Investors, South Bend Country, Masons, Shriners, Signal Point (pres. 1986—). Contbr. articles to med. jours. Home: 54712 Merrifield Dr Mishawaka IN 46545 Office: 707 N Michigan St South Bend IN 46601 also: 52088 Heather Cave South Bend IN 46635

CHAMBERLAIN, JOSEPH MILES, astronomer, educator; b. Peoria, Ill., July 26, 1923; s. Maurice Silloway and Roberta (Miles) C.; m. Paula Bruninga, Dec. 12, 1945; children—Janet Ann, Susan Louise, Barbara Jean. B.S., U.S. Mcht. Marine Acad., 1944; B.A., Bradley U., 1947; A.M., Tchrs. Coll. Columbia, 1950, Ed.D., 1962. Instr. Columbia Jr. High Sch., Peoria, 1943; instr. nav. War Shipping Adminstrn., 1944-45; boys sec. YMCA, Peoria, 1946-47; instr. U.S. Mcht. Marine Acad., Kings Point, N.Y., 1947-50; asst. prof. U.S. Mcht. Marine Acad., 1950-52; asst. curator Am. Museum-Hayden Planetarium, N.Y.C., 1952-53; gen. mgr., chief astronomer Am. Museum-Hayden Planetarium, 1953-56, chmn., 1956-64; asst. dir. Am. Mus. Natural History, 1964-68; dir. Adler Planetarium, Chgo., 1968—; pres. Adler Planetarium, 1977—; prof. astronomy Northwestern U., 1968-78; professorial lectr. U. Chgo., 1968-71; led eclipse expdns. to, Can., 1954, 79, Ceylon, 1955, Pacific Ocean, 1977, astro-geodetic expdns. to, Can., 1956, 57, Greenland, 1958; dean council of sci. staff Am. Mus. Nat. History, 1960-62. Coauthor: Planets, Stars and Space, 1957; author: Time and the Stars, 1964; also articles on popular astronomy. Active Boy Scouts Am., Met. Chgo. YMCA. Served to lt. USNR, 1945-46; staff Naval Res. Officers Sch. 1953-54, N.Y.C. Mem. Am. Astron. Soc., Internat. Astron. Union, Internat. Planetarium Dirs. Conf. (vice chmn. 1968-77, chmn. 1977—), Gt. Lakes Planetarium Assn., Internat. Planetarium Soc., Midwest Museums Conf., Am. Polar Soc., Am. Assn. Museums (mem. council 1965-77, v.p. 1971-74, pres. 1974-75), Phi Delta Kappa, Phi Kappa Phi, Kappa Delta Pi. Republican. Presbyn. (elder). Clubs: University (Chgo.), Tavern (Chgo.), Econ. (Chgo.), Metropolitan (Chgo.); Dutch Treat. Home: 1500 Oak Ave Evanston IL 60201 Office: Adler Planetarium 1300 S Lake Shore Dr Chicago IL 60605

CHAMBERLAIN, MARK WILLIAM, data processing executive; b. Sterling, Ill., Nov. 7, 1947; s. Lourde Harland and Ruth Wilhelmina (Meyer) C.; m. Patricia Ann Dinges, June 28, 1969; children: Michael, Anne, Philip, Ryan. BS, Loras Coll., 1969; MS, St. Louis U., 1971. CLU, CPCU, Chartered Fin. Cons. From data processing specialist to sr. analyst data processing State Farm Mut. Auto Ins. Co., Bloomington, Ill., 1971-79, supt. data processing, 1979-82, mgr. data processing, 1982-86, asst. dir. data processing, 1986—. Mem. bd. edn. Holy Trinity Parish, Bloomington, 1976-82, pres. 1981; coach Prairie Cities Soccer League, Bloomington, 1980—. Mem. Cen. Ill. Chpt. CPCU's, Cen. Ill. Chpt. CLU's. Republican. Roman Catholic. Home: 1922 E Jackson St Bloomington IL 61701 Office: State Farm Mut Auto Ins Co 1 State Farm Plaza Bloomington IL 61701

CHAMBERS, DAVID ALLEN, accounting executive, controller; b. Pontiac, Mich., Sept. 1, 1950; s. Donald Wallace and Donna Maderal (Edison) C.; m. Kathy Suzanne Kinsey, Dec. 30, 1975; children: Christopher D., Stacey B. AA, Washtenaw Community Coll., 1975; BBA, Eastern Mich. U., 1976. CPA, Mich. Staff acct. Gross & Ludwig, CPA's, Adrian, Mich., 1977-78; tax mgr. Wright, Griffin, Davis & Co., Ann Arbor, Mich., 1978-86; v.p., controller Lutz Assocs., Inc., Farmington Hills, Mich., 1986—; pres. Washtenaw Planning Council, Ann Arbor, 1985-86. Mem. Am. Inst. CPA's, Mich. Assn. CPA's, Nat. Assn. Accts. (v.p. 1981-83). Club: Zal Gaz Grotto (Ann Arbor). Lodge: Golden Rule. Avocations: golf, reading, computers. Office: Lutz Assocs Inc 31000 Northwestern Farmington Hills MI 48333-9079

CHAMBERS, EARL RICHARD, personnel administrator; b. Wyoming, Ill., Nov. 4, 1916; s. John Thomas and Margaret Jane (Lawless) C.; B.Ed., Ill. State Normal U., 1938; M.A., U. Ill., 1947, postgrad., 1948-53; m. Jane Margaret Petersen, May 8, 1954 (dec. May 1982); 1 son, Robert. Profl. personnel work Ill. Civil Service Commn., 1947-53, chief of exams. adminstring., employee selection, 1951-53; personnel dir. St. Louis County, Mo., 1953—. Mem. Gov. Mo. Citizens Adv. Council Higher Edn. Act, 1972-73. Served from pvt. to tech. sgt. AUS, 1942-46; Philippines, New Guinea. Mem. Pub. Personnel Assn. (exec. bd. local chapter, 1952-53, regional sec.-treas., 1956-57, regional 1st v.p. 1963-64, regional chmn. 1964-65), Am. Soc. Personnel Adminstrn. (accredited); Am. Soc. Pub. Adminstrn. (exec. bd. local chpt. 1951-52, 59-63, 64-65, 70-71, pres. Met. St. Louis 1963-64), Internat. Personnel Mgmt. Assn. (v.p. St. Louis chpt. 1973-74, pres. 1974-75), Kappa Delta Pi, Pi Gamma Mu. Contbr. articles, abstracts and revs. to profl. jours. Home: 12 Armstrong Dr Glendale MO 63122 Office: 7900 Forsyth Blvd Clayton MO 63105

CHAMBERS, GLENN DARRELL, wildlife photographer, artist; b. Butler, Mo., June 14, 1936; s. E. Glenn and Fern M. (Woods) C.; m. Marilyn Janell Henry, Aug. 29, 1959 (div. Jan. 1980); children—James D., Russell G., Lindell C.; m. Jeannie Bay Erwin, Feb. 27, 1980; stepchildren—Robert Roemer, Matthew Roemer. B.S., Central Mo. State U., 1958; M.A., U. Mo.-Columbia, 1961. Area mgr. Mo. Dept. Conservation, Jefferson City, 1961-62, research biologist, 1962-69, biologist, photographer, 1969-79; regional dir. Ducks Unltd., Columbia, Mo., 1979-83, wildlife photographer, 1984—; pres. Niska Art, Inc., Columbia, 1984—. Films include: (with Charles and Elizabeth Schwartz) Return of the Wild Turkey (2d place award Outdoor Writers Assn. Am.), 1971, The Show-Me Hunter (2d place award Outdoor Writers Assn. Am.), 1972, Wild Chorus: The Story of the Canada Goose (1st place award Outdoor Writers Assn. Am.), 1974, (Best Motion Picture award Wildlife Soc.), 1974; More Than Trees: Ecology of the Forest (2d place award Forestry Film Festival, 1st place award Outdoor Writers Assn. Am.), 1977. Photographs in Audubon mag., others. Contbr. tech. articles to Jour. Wildlife Mgmt., 1961-77. Winner 1984-85 Mo. Waterfowl Stamp Design Contest. Democrat. Baptist. Home: 501 Onofrio Ct Columbia MO 65203 Office: Ducks Unltd 1 Waterfowl Way at Gilmer Long Grove IL 60047

CHAMBERS, JOHN ALBERT, systems analyst; b. Pittsburg, Kans., May 1, 1944; s. John A. and Christine C. (Toliver) C.; m. Wilma K. Graham, Aug. 6, 1966; children: Candee C., John Jason. BS, Pittsburg State U., 1967. CLU, Chartered Fin. Cons., Cert. Data Processor. Underwriter State Farm Ins. Co., Columbia, Mo., 1969-71; programmer State Farm Ins. Co., Bloomington, Ill., 1971-74, system analyst, 1971-80, project mgr., 1980-85, staff asst., 1985—; cons. gifted math, computer Jr. High Sch., Danvers, Ill., 1982—. Section chmn. United Way, Mclean County, 1981; treas. Jr. High Booster Club, Danvers, 1984-86; speech and drama chmn. High Sch. Booster Club, Normal, Ill, 1986—. Served to 1st lt. U.S. Army, 1967-69. Fellow Life Mgmt. Inst.; mem. Nat. Soc. CPCU (Continuing Profl. Devel. award 1984, 87, mgmt. info. services com. 1983—), CPCU's (bd. dirs. local chpt. 1982—, pres. cen. Ill. chpt. 1987—), Data Processing Mgmt. Assn. Avocations: tennis, skiing, reading. Office: State Farm Ins SB4 One State Farm Plaza Bloomington IL 61710

CHAMBERS, LAROYCE FRANCIS, obstetrician, gynecologist; b. Detroit, Dec. 5, 1944; s. Hobart Madra and Alma Bernice (Green) C.; m. Minnie Pearl Smith, July 3, 1971; children: Anthony LaRoyce, Reginald Alan. BS, Wayne State U., 1966; MD, U. Mich., 1970. Diplomate Am. Bd. Ob-Gyn. Intern Chgo. Wesley Meml. Hosp., 1970-71; resident Northwestern U., 1973-76; practice medicine specializing in ob-gyn Ob-Gyn Med. Services, Milw., 1976—; chmn. dept. ob-gyn Good Samaritan Med. Ctr., Milw., 1986—; asst. clin. prof. Med. Coll. Wis., Milw., 1981—. Mem. ethics bd. City of Mequon, Wis., 1986; bd. govs. Wis. affiliate Am. Heart Assn., Milw., 1986; bd. dirs. Univ. Sch. Milw., River Hills, Wis., 1986, Family Services, Milw., 1986. Served to capt., U.S. Army, 1971-73. Baptist. Avocations: bowling, biking. Home: 2720 W Rangeline Ct Mequon WI 53092 Office: Ob-Gyn Med Services 940 N 23d St Milwaukee WI 53233

CHAMBERS, VIRGINIA ANNE, music educator; b. Middlesboro, Ky., Jan. 28, 1931; d. Jason C. and Virginia Claire (Dobyns) C. Mus.B., U. Louisville, 1952; Mus.M., Eastman Sch. Music, 1964; Ph.D., U. Mich., 1970. Gen. elem. music tchr. Oak Ridge Pub. Schs., 1952-63, Rochester (N.Y.) Sch. Dist., 1963-64; prof. music SUNY-Geneso, 1964-66, Eastern Mich. U., Ypsilanti, 1966-68, U. Wis.-Madison, 1968-75, U. Toledo, 1975—; v.p. Tometic Assocs., Ltd., Buffalo. Mem. Music Educators Nat. Conf., Ohio Music Educators Assn., Sonneck Soc. Club: University (Toledo). Author: Words and Music: An Introduction to Music Literacy, 1976; Tometics: Reading Rhythm Patterns, 1979; Piano Accompaniments for A Nichols Worth, Vols. 3 and 4, 1982; editor: A Nichols Worth, Vols. 3 and 4, Reading Tonal Patterns, 1984, Basic Keyboard Accompaniments, 1986. Home: 2129 Brookdale Rd Toledo OH 43606 Office: U Toledo Ctr for Performing Arts Toledo OH 43601

CHAMBERS, WALTER R., investment banker; b. Lancaster, Ohio, May 2, 1931; s. Walter R. and Martha Blanche (Notestone) C.; m. Sue Hartley, Aug. 8, 1953; children—James R., Mark R. B.S., Ohio State U., 1952. With Ohio Co., Columbus, 1961—, adminstr. pub. fin., fixed income and equity trading depts., 1968—, dir., exec. v.p., 1972—; dir. Ohio Equities Inc., Ins. Ohio Co. Agy.; pres., dir. Midwest Parking Inc. Treas., bd. dirs. Health Services Found.; trustee Coll. of Wooster; treas. Upper Arlington Civic Assn., 1966-67; cabinet mem. Franklin County United Way, 1982-83. Served with U.S. Army, 1956-58. Mem. Pub. Securities Assn. (chmn., dir.), Securities Industry Assn. (dir., exec. com.), Mcpl. Fin. Forum Washington, Mcpl. Fin. Forum N.Y. Republican. Episcopalian. Clubs: Muirfield Village Golf, Scioto Country, University (Columbus). Lodge: Masons. Contbr. articles to profl. jours. Office: 155 E Broad St Columbus OH 43215

CHAMBERS, WILLIAM DOUGLAS, dentist; b. Madison, W.Va., Sept. 23, 1945; s. Arlie and Emma Jean (Chandler) C.; m. Sheryl Lynn Leatherman, May 25, 1966; children: Jeffery Douglas, Terin Raphe, Tory Lynn, Lindsey Paige, Cody Lane. BA, Emporia (Kans.) State U., 1973; DDS, U. Mo., Kansas City, 1978. Midwest customer service mgr. Standard Brands Foods, Kansas City, 1973-74; gen. practice dentistry Andover, Kans., 1978—; comml. developer Cloud City Devel., Andover, 1982—; cons. Midwest Dental Consultation, Andover, 1986—. Contbr. articles to Andover Jour. and Kans. Dental Assn. Jour. Coach Andover Little League Baseball Program, 1979—; deacon Cen. Ch. of Christ, Wichita, 1980—; mem. adv. bd. Christ Villa Nursing Home, Wichita, 1980—; fund raiser

Citizens for Alcohol-Drug Abuse Awareness, Andover, 1985-86. Served with USAF, 1963-67. Mem. 7th Dist. Dental Soc. (sec., treas. 1981-83, pres. 1984-85, del. 1986—), Kans. Dental Assn. (co-chmn. com. on dental practice, 1985-86, chmn. 1986—), Andover C. of C., Tri Bete. Avocations: family activities, vocal music, coaching baseball, sports, Indian artifacts. Home: 314 Pineview Andover KS 67002 Office: 310 W Central Suite B Box 246 Andover KS 67002

CHAMBLESS, RICK, sales executive; b. Turlock, Calif., June 15, 1949; s. George Junior Chambless and Ann (Stapp) Van Gorder; m. Susan Elizabeth Rouse, June 9, 1974; children: Kristen S., Lauren E. Student, U. Hawaii, 1971-75; BS in Bus., Calif. State U., Sacramento, 1977. Sales rep. Tamarack Corp., Sacramento, 1978-79, Armour Pharm., Phoenix, 1979, Berlex Labs., Wayne, N.J., 1979-81; regional sales mgr. Surgidev Corp., Mpls., 1981—; dir. rep. devel. program Surgiden Corp., Mpls. Served with U.S. Army, 1969-71, Vietnam. Republican.

CHAMBLISS, JAMES FRANCIS, JR., physician; b. Chgo., Feb. 24, 1937; s. James Francis and Mary Catherine (Curran) C.; m. Elizabeth LaVoo; children: Catherine, Rebecca, Michelle, Michael. BS in Biology, Boston Coll., 1959; MD, Georgetown U., 1964. Diplomate Am. Bd. Radiology, Am. Bd. Nuclear Medicine, Nat. Bd. Med. Examiners. Surgical intern Presbyn.-St. Luke's Hosp., Chgo., 1964-65, resident in radiology, 1967-70; staff radiologist Columbus-Cabrini-Cuneo Med. Ctr., Chgo., 1970-77, dir. dept. radiology, 1977-82, exec. med. dir., 1982—; lectr. in field. Served to lt. USNR, 1965-67. Mem. AMA, Ill. State Med. Soc., Chgo. Med. Soc., Ill. Radiol. Soc., Chgo. Radiol. Soc., Am. Coll. Radiology, Radiol. Soc. N.Am., Soc. Nuclear Medicine. Republican. Clubs: Carlton (Chgo.); Evanston Golf (Skokie, Ill.). Office: Columbus-Cabrini-Cuneo Med Ctr Chicago IL 60600

CHAMNESS, LAWRENCE E., farmer; b. Carbondale, Ill., Jan. 19, 1942; s. Clay M. and Hazel V. Chamness; m. Margaret Anna Sweeney, Oct. 1, 1966; 1 child, Jason Brooke. BS, So. Ill. U., 1964, MS, 1966. Asst. extension advisor U. Ill., Vandalia, 1965-67; tchr. vocat.-agr. Tamaroa (Ill.) High Sch., 1968; farm mgr. Blue Bell Packing Co., DuQuoin, Ill., 1969-75; gen. mgr. Almo Farm, Wayne City, Ill., 1976—. Mem. Ill. Corn Growers Assn. (bd. dirs. 1983). Baptist. Lodge: Ruritan (pres. 1981). Avocations: golf, gardening, woodwork, fishing, hunting. Home and Office: Rural Rt 1 Box 112 Wayne City IL 62895

CHAMPAGNE, BRENDA (JEAN) LAMB, occupational therapist; b. Northampton, Mass., Aug. 14, 1951; d. Frank Gilbert and Gertrude Maria (MacArthur) Lamb; student Winthrop Coll., 1969-70, Boston U., 1970; B.S. in Occupational Therapy, Quinnipiac Coll., 1974; m. Clement Henri Champagne, Nov. 9, 1974; children—Melissa Yolande, Timothée Daniel. Occupational therapist Alexandra Pavilion, Montreal (Que., Can.) Children's Hosp., 1974-75; therapist Area Coop. Ednl. Services, North Haven, Conn., 1975, Trinity Luth. Hosp., Kansas City, Mo., 1976; part time therapist Bethany Med. Center, Kansas City, Kans., 1976-77, dir. occupational therapy, 1977-81; home health therapist, nursing home cons. Crosslands Rehab. Agy., 1984; cons. Med. Splty. Assocs., 1984—; part time asst. prof. dept. occupational therapy, U. Kans., 1977; chmn. Greater Kansas City Occupational Therapy Adminstrv. Council, 1978-79; cons. profl. adv. com. Outreach Rehab. Services, Inc., 1979-80; cons. profl. adv. bd. Crossland Rehab. Agy., Inc., 1980—; council pres. U. Kans. Council on Occupational Therapy Edn., 1980-83, chmn. coms., 1978-81. Mem. Am. Occupational Therapy Assn. (registered occupational therapist, elected commn. on edn. 1980—), Kans. Occupational Therapy Assn. (newsletter editor 1977-79, state long range plan chmn. 1979-81, state v.p. 1979-81). Contbg. author, editor: MidTerm Evaluation of Fieldwork Experience, 1979. Home: 8215 Webster St Kansas City KS 66109 Office: 51 N 12th St Kansas City KS 66102

CHAMPAGNE, JOSEPH ERNEST, university president, industrial psychology consultant; b. Norwich, Conn., May 19, 1938; s. Fred Joseph and Loretta Eva (Lucier) C.; m. Emilie Lind, Dec. 27, 1969; children: Jennifer, Juliana, Johanna. A.B., St. Mary's U., 1960; M.A., Fordham U., 1962; Ph.D., Purdue U., 1966. Lic. cert. psychologist, Tex. Psychology instr., research asst., cons. various orgns. 1962-71; pres. Houston Community Coll. System, 1971-73, pres. emeritus; assoc. dir. Ctr. Human Resources U. Houston, 1969-71, 73-76; coordinator extended acad. and pub. service programs U. Houston System Office, 1977-78, assoc. v.p. office of exec. v.p., 1977-78; prof. dept. organizational behavior and mgmt. U. Houston, 1967-81, v.p. acad. affairs, 1978-81; pres. Oakland U., Rochester, Mich., 1981—; pres. Houston Area Rehab. Assn., 1971; bd. dirs. Tex. Rehab. Assn., 1971-72; mem. adv. com. Community Colls., Houston, 1970-71; mem. task force U. Houston, 1974-75, State of Tex., 1973-75. Contbr. articles to numerous publs. Bd. dirs. Ctr. Multiple Handicapped Children, 1973-81; chmn. bd. dirs. Houston Lighthouse for Blind, 1976-81; trustee Crittenton Hosp., Oakland U.; bd. dirs. Detroit Symphony Orch., Detroit Econ. Club; mem. nat. adv. council Ctr. for Study of Presidency; v.p., bd. dirs. Nat. Accreditation Council for the Blind. Named Citizen of Yr. Houston Area Rehab. Assn. Mem. Am. Psychol. Assn., Am. Assn. Higher Edn. Roman Catholic. Office: Oakland Univ Office of the Pres Rochester MI 48309

CHAMPLIN, GEORGE CHARLES, marketing executive; b. Omaha, Jan. 30, 1938; s. George L. and Eunice (Walker) C.; m. Barbara Hamilton Lewis, Apr. 4, 1964; children: Kelly Hamilton, Lesley Walker, Lindsey Parkes, Matthew C. BA in History, U. Minn., 1960. Sales rep. Internat. Silver Co., Meriden, Conn., 1962-67; regional sales mgr. Hamilton Watch Co., Lancaster, Pa., 1967-71; mgr. incentive sales Faribault (Minn.) Woolen Mill Co., 1971-81, v.p. spl. markets, 1981—. Served to 1st lt. U.S. Army, 1960-62. Recipient Deans Cross award Cathedral of Our Merciful Savior. Mem. Incentive Mfrs. Rep. Assn. (treas. 1976-77), Nat. Premium Sales Execs. (pres. 1984), Nat. Premium Sales Execs. (Cert. Incentive Profl. 1981). Republican. Episcopalian. Club: Minn. Incentive (pres. 1977-78). Lodge: Sertoma (pres. 1977-78, Sertoman of Yr. 1979). Avocations: fishing, golf, hunting. Home: 8 St James Bay Faribault MN 55021 Office: Faribault Woolen Mill Co 1500 2d Ave NW Faribault MN 55021

CHAMPNEY, DON, construction company executive; b. Detroit, Sept. 8, 1927; s. Donald Ole and Marjorie Elaine (Porter) C.; m. Ann Christine Mainland, June 23, 1951; children—Christine Champney Forte, Sarah Ann Champney Sieber. B.Arch., U. Mich., 1951. Design engr. Detroit Steel Products, 1951-52; regional mgr. Lumber Fabricators, Inc., Cin., 1952-53; designer Arcose Homes, Cin., 1953-55; v.p. engring. Style Rite Homes Corp., Columbus, Ohio, 1955-57; regional mgr. Scholz Homes, Cin., 1957-58; br. mgr. Fred M. Cole Corp., Columbus, 1958-66; v.p. engring. Gardner Co., Columbus, 1966—. Pres. pro tem, chmn. fin. com. village council Village of Minerva Park, 1976—; mem. Joint Twp. Hosp. Dist., 1982—. Served with USN, 1945-46; to ensign USNR. Recipient mem. of the Yr. Construction Specifications Inst. (Columbus chpt.), 1975. Mem. Builders Exchange Central Ohio (pres. 1981), U. Mich. Club of Columbus (pres. 1960), Sigma Alpha Epsilon. Republican. Episcopalian. Club: Brookside Country (Worthington, Ohio); Continental Athletic (Columbus). Home: 5386 Park Lane Ct Columbus OH 43229 Office: 4588 Kenny Rd Columbus OH 43220

CHAN, CARLYLE HUNG-LUN, psychiatrist, educator; b. Clarksdale, Miss., July 4, 1949; s. Henry Howe and Jennie (Wong) C.; m. Patricia Meyer, June 18, 1977; children: Christopher, Diana. BS, U. Wis., 1971; MD, Med. Coll. Wis., 1975. Diplomate Am. Bd. Psychiatry and Neurology. Resident in psychiatry U. Chgo., 1975-78; asst. prof. Med. Coll. Wis., Milw., 1980-86, assoc. prof., 1986—; catchment area dir. Milw. County Mental Health Complex, 1981-82; chief psychiatrist psychotherapy ctr. Columbia Hosp., Milw., 1982—, course dir. annual psychiat. conference, 1982—. asst. editor Asian-Am. Psychiatry Newsletter, Washington, 1983-84; contbr. articles to profl. jours. Bd. dirs. Planning Council for Mental Health and Social Service, 1983—. Robert Wood Johnson clin. scholar Yale U., 1978-80; jr. Faculty Devel. award NIMH, 1983-85; Community Devel. award Apple Computer Co., Milw., 1984. Mem. Am. Psychiat. Assn., Assn. Acad. Psychiatry, Wis. State Med. Soc., Milw. County Med. Soc., Wis. Psychiat. Assn. Avocations: tennis, golf, running. Office: Columbia Hosp Psychotherapy Ctr 3521 N Prospect Ave Milwaukee WI 53211

CHAN, CHUN-WAH, social worker; b. Chao-Young, Kwangtung, China, July 22, 1945; s. Hak-Tang and So-Fong (Yeung) C.; came to U.S., 1969, naturalized, 1978; B.S.Sc. cum laude (scholar) Chinese U. Hong Kong, 1967; M.A. (scholar) U. Chgo., 1971; m. Heidi Kwok-Shun Cheng, June 15, 1968. Social work supr. Family Planning Assn. of Hong Kong, 1967-69; with Cook County Hosp., Chgo., 1971—, divisional dir. psychiat. social service div., 1973—, coordinator staff devel. and quality assurance dept. social service, 1978—; pvt. practice individual and family therapy, Chgo., 1977—. Leader Hong Kong Boy Scout Assn., 1964-69; divisional officer St. John Ambulance Brigade, Hong Kong, 1968-69; bd. dirs. Chinese Am. Service League, Chgo., 1977-78, chmn. nominating com., 1978, pres. bd. dirs. 1978—. Cert. social worker, Ill. Mem. Nat. Assn. Social Workers, Acad. Cert. Social Workers, Asian Am. Mental Health Research Center. Home: 405 Jamestown Ave Darien IL 60559

CHAN, DANIEL CHI NGAI, dentist, researcher; b. Hong Kong, Nov. 27, 1953; came to U.S., 1982; s. Chuen Kong and Yuk Mok; m. Eva Hui Chan, Aug. 2, 1986. DDS, U. Philippines, 1979; MS, U. Iowa, 1984. Cert. operative dentistry, 1984. Gen. practice dentistry Hong Kong, 1980-82; postdoctoral assoc. Dows Inst. for Dental Research, Iowa City, 1984—; research assoc. Prince Philip Dental Hosp., Hong Kong, 1986-87. Contbr. articles to profl. jours. Mem. Internat. Assn. of Dental Research, Am. Assn. Dental Research (session co-chmn. 1986), Hong Kong Dental Assn., Electron Microscopy Soc. Am., N.Y. Acad. Sci., Acad. Operative Dentistry, St. Louis Old Boy's Assn. (pres. 1981-82). Roman Catholic. Avocations: fishing, volleyball, swimming. Home: 929 Harlocke St #6 Iowa City IA 52240 Office: U Iowa Coll Dentistry Ctr for Clin Studies Iowa City IA 52242

CHAN, ROY KIN-FAI, accountant, management consultant; b. Hong Kong, Dec. 5, 1951; s. Chow and Fan (Ho) C.; m. Connie M. Jenkins, June 26, 1975; children: Susanne, Roy, Victoria, Michael, Simon. BSBA, Berea Coll., 1976; MS in Acctg., U. Ky., 1978. CPA, Ohio, Ky., Ill. Acct. Head Corp., Berea, Ky., 1978-79; cost acct. Partridge Meats, Inc., Cin., 1979-80; sr. acct. Foxx & Co., Cin., 1980-82; pres. Roy K. Chan, Inc., Cin., 1982—; mgmt. cons. Chan & Co., Cin., 1982—. Treas. PTA Frost Elem Sch., Cin., 1985—. Mem. Am. Inst. CPA's, Inst. Cert. Mgmt. Accountants. Avocation: studies in math. logics. Home: 1882 Mistyhill Dr Cincinnati OH 45240 Office: 8234 Winton Rd Suite 100 Cincinnati OH 45231

CHAN, SHIH HUNG, mechanical engineering educator, consultant; b. Chang Hwa, Taiwan, Nov. 8, 1943; came to U.S., 1964; s. Ping and Fu Zon (Liao) C.; m. Shirley Shih-Lin Wang, June 14, 1969; children: Bryan, Erick. Diploma Taipei Inst. Tech., Taiwan, 1963; MS, U. N.H., 1966; PhD, U. Calif.-Berkeley, 1969. Registered profl. engr., Wis. Asst. to assoc. prof. NYU, N.Y.C., 1969-73; assoc. prof. Poly. Inst. N.Y., N.Y.C., 1973-74; research staff mem. Argonne Nat. Lab., Ill., 1974-75; assoc. prof. U. Wis., Milw., 1975-78, prof. mech. engring., 1978—, chmn. dept., 1979—; cons. Argonne Nat. Lab., Ill., 1975—, Allen-Bradley Co., Milw., 1984, Gen. Electric Co., Schenectady, 1980. Contbr. articles to profl. jours. Bd. dirs. Orgn. Chinese Americans, State of Wis., 1983—; v.p. Civic Club, Milw., 1984—, pres., 1985—. Served to 2d lt. Taiwan M.C., 1963-64. Recipient Outstanding Research award U. Wis.-Milw. Research Found., 1983, Research citation Assembly State of Wis., Madison, 1984, 1st Coll. Research award, 1987; grantee NSF, Dept. Energy, Argonne Nat. Lab., Office of Naval Research, 1969—. Mem. Am. Nuclear Soc. (pres. Wis. 1982-83), Profl. Ergrs. State of Wis., ASME. Avocations: fishing, Tae-Kwon-do. Home: 3416 W Meadowview Ct Mequon WI 53092 Office: U Wis-Milw Dept of Mech Engring Milwaukee WI 53201

CHANCE, RICHARD FRANKLIN, electrical engineer; b. Indpls., May 24, 1931; s. Ernest Thomas and Della May (Kochel) C.; m. Mary Jane Manion, Feb. 7, 1959; children: Marilyn L., Thomas E., Barbara A. BSEE, Purdue U., 1954. Engr. Naval Ordinance, Indpls., 1954-59, R.B. Marshall & Assn., Monticello, Ind., 1959-61; owner Ind. Standards Lab., Indpls., 1961—. Patentee in field. Mem. Instrument Soc. Am. Avocations: hiking, photography. Home: 2244 Woodcrest Rd Indianapolis IN 46227 Office: Ind Standards Lab 3734 Carrollton Ave Indianapolis IN 46205

CHANDAR, KRISHAN, neurologist, educator; b. Shahzada, Pakistan, Jan. 14, 1934; came to U.S., 1972; s. Ishar Dass and Acchran Devi; m. Sneh Lata, Nov. 17, 1968; children: Rupali, Gaurav. Student, Khalsa Coll., Amritsar, India, 1952-54; MBBS, Christian Med. Coll., Ludhiana, India, 1960. Diplomate Am. Bd. Psychiatry and Neurology. Lectr. neurology Postgrad. Med. Inst., Chandigarh, India, 1968-70, asst. prof. neurology, 1970-72; asst. prof. neurology Case Western Res. U., Cleve., 1976—; dir. EEG Lab., Case Western Res. U. Hosp., 1976-79, dir. neurology, 1978-79; asst. neurologist Mt. Sinai Med. Ctr., Cleve., 1979—, dir. EEG Lab., 1985—. Mem. Royal Coll. Physicians, Am. Acad. Neurology, Am. EEG Soc., AAAS, Ohio State Med. Assn., Acad. Medicine Cleve. Home: 5950 Buckboard Ln Solon OH 44139 Office: Mt Sinai Med Ctr One Mt Sinai Dr Cleveland OH 44106

CHANDEL, MAHENDRA KUMAR, surgeon; b. Dhar, India, Jan. 9, 1944; s. C.K. and Yashodhara (Rathore) C.; came to U.S., 1970, naturalized, 1974; BS, U. Indore (India), 1961; MD, M.G.M. Med. Coll., Indore, 1966; m. Carol Ann Lennox, Apr. 29, 1977; children—Leena, Madhur, Michael, Michelle. Intern, St. Luke's Hosp., Fargo, N.D., 1970-71; resident St. Elizabeth Hosp., Youngstown, Ohio, 1971-72, Highland Park (Mich.) Gen. Hosp., 1972-74; chief of surgery McNamara Community Hosp., Warren, Mich., 1975, Clare (Mich.) Osteo. Hosp., 1977, 79; practice medicine, specializing in gen. surgery, family practice, angiology, proctology, Clare, 1976—. Diplomate Am. Bd. Surgery, Am. Bd. Family Practice, Internat. Bd. Proctology; recert. in family practice, 1985. Fellow Internat. Coll. Surgeons, Am. Soc. Abdominal Surgery, Am. Acad. Family Practitioners, Am. Coll. Emergency Physicians, Am. Coll. Internat. Physicians; asso. fellow Am. Coll. Angiology; mem. AMA, Am. Soc. Contemporary Medicine and Surgery, Wayne County Med. Soc., Mich. Med. Soc., Clare/Isabella County Med. Soc. Office: 11128 Mission PO Box 120 Clare MI 48617

CHANDLER, JESSE SAMUEL, gynecologist/obstetrician; b. Oklahoma City, July 5, 1944; s. Jesse Samuel and Thelma Theresa (O'Connor) C.; m. Joyce Carolyn Graves, Sept. 1966; divorced; 1 child, Michelle Renee; m. Alma Elizabeth Buckner, May 11, 1975; 1 child, Christine Elizabeth. BS, U. Md., 1969; MD, Howard U., 1975, postgrad. in microbiology, 1969-71. Intern Cook County Hosp., Chgo., 1975-76; resident Mt. Sinai Hosp., Chgo., 1976-79, attending physician, 1979—, med. dir. family planning service, 1979-82; practice medicine specializing in ob-gyn Chgo., 1979—, Grant Hosp., Chgo., 1979—, Columbus Hosp., Chgo., 1982—, Provident Hosp., Chgo., 1982—, Chgo. Ctr. Hosp., 1982—; cons. sex edn. tng. program Mt. Sinai Hosp., 1979; assoc. prof. ob-gyn Rush Med. Coll. Mt. Sinai Hosp., 1979-82. Mem. sch. health adv. com. Bur. Med. and Sch. Health Service Chgo. Bd. Edn., 1976—. Fellow Am. Coll. Ob-gyn (jr.), Gynecol. Laser Soc.; mem. AMA, Nat. Med. Assn., Cook County Hosp's. Interns' and Residents' Alumni Assn., Internat. Coll. Surgeons (jr.), Nat. Assn. Interns and Residents, Am. Assn. Gynecol. Laparoscopists, Am. Fertility Soc., Chgo. Med. Soc., Ill Med. Soc., Cook County Physicians Assn., Am. Soc. Colposcopy and Cervical Pathology. Democrat. Methodist. Avocations: scuba diving, golf. Office: 30 N Michigan Ave #1329 Chicago IL 60602

CHANDLER, JOHN ROHAN, real estate developer; b. Lakewood, Ohio, Sept. 10, 1952; s. Neville Albert and Dorathy Ann (Rohan) C.; m. Deborah Ann Friel, July 1, 1977; children: John Rohan Jr., Charles Thomas. BS, U. Colo., 1974. V.p. Chandler's Inc., Westlake, Ohio, 1972-78, pres., 1978—; pres. Chandler Realty Co., Rocky River, Ohio, 1978—; v.p. Pinewood Mgmt., Rocky River, 1984—; pres. J.R.C. Investments, Inc., Rocky River, 1985—. Editor: The Syndicator, 1984. Mem. Cleve. Area Bd. Realtors (pres. elect 1987, pres. 1988, bd. dirs. 1985—, treas. 1986, pres. Westside Roundtable, 1984), Real Estate Securities and Syndication Inst. (treas. chpt. 3 1984, v.p. 1985, pres. 1986), Ohio Assn. Realtors (trustee 1984-86). Roman Catholic. Club: Westwood Country (Rocky River). Lodge: Rotary.

CHANDLER, THEODORE ARTHUR, educational psychology educator; b. Indpls., May 21, 1932; s. Myron Benjamin and Elizabeth (Kaplan) C.; m. Yolande Viviane Dahan, Nov. 21, 1962; children: Sonia, Eric, Colette. BS, Northwestern U., 1954; MA, U. Chgo., 1957; PhD, U. Mich., 1971. Cert. psychologist, Ohio. Social worker Contra Costa Social Services Dept., Pleasant Hills, Calif., 1959-61; psychologist U.S. Dependents Schs., Frankfurt, Fed. Republic of Germany, 1963-65; asst. prof. psychology Lindenwood Coll., St. Charles, Mo., 1965-67; asst. prof. edn. InterAm. U., P.R., 1967-71; dir. guidance, spl. edn. Ramey AFB Schs., P.R., 1967-71; prof. ednl. psychology Kent (Ohio) State U., 1971—; cons. numerous sch. systems, Ohio, 1972-80, Caterpillar, Ohio, 1980-81. Contbr. over 50 articles to profl. jours. Mem. sch. bd. Stow-Munroe Falls Pub. Schs., Ohio, 1984—. Mem. Am. Psychol. Assn., Am. Ednl. Research Assn., Midwest Ednl. Research Assn., Phi Delta Kappa, Stow C. of C. Democrat. Lodge: Rotary. Avocations: tennis, skiing, jogging, exercise. Home: 2483 Valleydale Rd Stow OH 44224 Office: Kent State U Coll Edn 407 White Hall Kent OH 44242

CHANDRA, GIRISH, steel company executive; b. Ballia, Uttar Pradesh, India, July 1, 1941; came to U.S., 1970; s. Vindhyachal Prasad; B.Sc., Banaras Hindu U., India, 1959; M.B.A., Case Western Res. U., Cleve., 1972; m. Chander Kiran Sood, July 8, 1973; children—Ankur, Pravir, Nupur. Prodn. supr. New Central Jute Mills Co., Calcutta, 1964-68; office supr., 1968-69; purchase officer Jaipur Metals and Electricals, Ltd. (India), 1969-70; inventory control analyst Alcan Aluminum Corp., Warren, Ohio, 1972-77; inventory mgr. Wheatland Tube Co. (Pa.), 1978-80, mgr. materials mgmt., 1981, dir. materials and systems, 1982-84, dir. materials mgmt., 1985—. Mem. Am. Prodn. and Inventory Control Soc. (v.p. communications Youngstown chpt.). Hindu. Home: 9061 Altura Dr Warren OH 44484

CHANDRA, MICHAEL SUSHIL, cardiologist; b. Ba, Fiji, Apr. 26, 1940; came to U.S., 1969; s. Edward Pratap and Elizabeth Devigi (Nair) C.; m. Lynette Chandra, Feb. 15, 1969; children: Susan Anita, Michael Ajay. DSM, Fiji Sch. Medicine, 1963; BS, MB, Assam Med. Coll., India, 1968. Diplomate Am. Bd. Internal Medicine, Subspecialty Bd. in Cardiovascular Disease. Resident in internal medicine Creighton U., Omaha, 1970-73; fellow in cardiovascular medicine U. Iowa, 1973-75, staff cardiologist, 1975-76; cons., cardiologist Marian Health Ctr., Sioux City, Iowa, 1976—, St Lukes Regional Med. Ctr., Sioux City, 1976—. Fellow Am. Coll. Physicians, Am. Coll. Cardiology, Am. Coll. Chest Physcians, Am. Heart Assn. (council clin. cardiology), Am. Coll. Angiology, Internat. Coll. Angiology, Am. Coll. Internat. Physicians. Avocations: travel, photography. Home: 4406 Manor Circle Sioux City IA 51104 Office: Cardiovascular Assocs 4500 Hamilton Blvd Sioux City IA 51104

CHANDRAMOHAN, NANJAPPA, physician; b. Coimbatore, Madras, India, Aug. 9, 1942; came to U.S., 1966; s. A. Nanjaffa Chettiar and Chinnammal Chandramohan; m. Ananthalakshmi Vellingiri, Mar. 1, 1972; children: Kaladevi, Devamurugan. Student, Sir Theagaraya Coll., Madras, 1959-60; grad., Madras Med. Coll., 1966. Intern Govt. Gen. Hosp., Madras, 1965-66; rotating intern, then resident Queens Gen. Hosp., Jamaica, N.Y., 1966-70; practice medicine specializing in internal medicine, endocronology and metabolism Carthage, Mo., 19670—. chief med. resident Queens Hosp. Ctr., Jamaica, N.Y., 1969. Home: Rt 5 Box 315 Carthage MO 64836 Office: 616 W Centennial Carthage MO 64836

CHANDRAN, SATISH RAMAN, anatomy educator; b. Quilon, Kerala, India, Oct. 6, 1938; came to U.S., 1961.; s. Govind Raman and Ponnamma Pillai; m. Judith Gail Urban, Oct. 1, 1966; children: Pamela Devi, Anjali Devi. BS, Sree Narayana Coll., Kerala, India, 1955; MS, U. Coll. U. Kerala, India, 1958; PhD, U. Ill., 1965. Research assoc. dept. entomology U. Ill., Urbana, 1965-66; asst. prof. biology U. Ill., Chgo., 1966-72; prof. anatomy Kennedy-King Coll., Chgo., 1972—. Contbr. articles to profl. jours. Research assoc. U.S. Pub. Health Services, 1965-66, Nat. Sci. Found., 1968; Nat. Inst. Health, 1962-65, research assistant Nat. Sci. Found., 1968. Mem. Am. Inst. Biological Sci., Entomological Soc. Am., Nat. Assn. Biology Tchrs., Sigma Xi, Omega Beta Pi, Phi Sigma. Democrat. Hindu. Avocations: horticulture, photography, environmental conservation. Home: 1648 Western Ave Flossmoor IL 60422 Office: Kennedy King Coll 6800 Wentworth Chicago IL 60621

CHANDRASEKHAR, SUBRAHMANYAN, theoretical astrophysicist, educator; b. Lahore, India, Oct. 19, 1910; came to U.S., 1936, naturalized, 1953; m. Lalitha, Madras, India, Sept. 1936. M.A., Presidency Coll., Madras, 1930; Ph.D., Trinity Coll., Cambridge, 1933, Sc.D., 1942; Sc.D., U. Mysore, India, 1961, Northwestern U., 1962, U. Newcastle Upon Tyne, Eng., 1965, Ind. Inst. Tech., 1966, U. Mich., 1967, U. Liege, Belgium, 1967, Oxford (Eng.) U., 1972, U. Delhi, 1973, Carleton U., Can., 1978, Harvard U., 1979. Govt. India scholar in theoretical physics Cambridge, 1930-34; fellow Trinity Coll., Cambridge, 1933-37; research asso. Yerkes Obs., Williams Bay and U. Chgo., 1937, asst. prof., 1938-41, assoc. prof., 1942-43, prof., 1944-47, Disting. Service prof., 1947-52, Morton D. Hull Disting. Service prof., 1952-86, prof. emeritus, 1986—; Nehru Meml. lectr., Padma Vibhushan, India, 1968. Author: An Introduction to the Study of Stellar Structure, 1939, Principles of Stellar Dynamics, 1942, Radiative Transfer, 1950, Hydrodynamic and Hydromagnetic Stability, 1961, Ellipsoidal Figures of Equilibrium, 1969, The Mathematical Theory of Black Holes, 1983, Eddington: The Most Distinguished Astrophysicist of His Time, 1983. Mng. editor: The Astrophysical Jour, 1952-71. Contbr. various sci. periodicals. Recipient Bruce medal Astron. Soc. Pacific, 1952, gold medal Royal Astron. Soc., London, 1953; Rumford medal Am. Acad. Arts and Scis., 1957; Nat. Medal of Sci., 1966; Nobel prize in physics, 1983; Dr. Tomalla prize Eidgenössiche Technische Hochschule, Zurich, 1984);. Fellow Royal Soc. (London) (Royal medal 1962, Copley medal 1984); mem. Nat. Acad. Scis. (Henry Draper medal 1971), Am. Phys. Soc. (Dannie Heineman prize 1974), Am. Philos. Soc., Cambridge Philos. Soc., Am. Astron. Soc., Royal Astron. Soc. Club: Quadrangle (U. Chgo.). Address: Lab for Astrophys & Space Research 933 E 56th St Chicago IL 60637

CHANEY, REECE, psychology educator; b. Rowdy, Ky., July 27, 1938; s. Roy and Lola (Hays) C.; B.S., Ohio U., 1962, M.Ed., 1965, Ph.D., 1968; children—Tammy Kaye, Ronald Dean; m. 2d, Mary L. Ross, July 20, 1979; stepchildren—Reid Robert, Erin Leigh. Tchr., Scioto Valley Schs., Piketon, Ohio, 1959-64; NDEA Title IV fellow Ohio U., 1964-68; elem. counselor South Western City Schs., Grove City, Ohio, 1965-66; prof. counseling psychology, chmn. dept. counseling Ind. State U., Terre Haute, 1968—; cons. marriage and family therapy, career edn. and pupil personnel services Ind. Dept. Pub. Instrn. Cert. psychologist, Ind. Mem. Am. Psychol. Assn., Am., Ind. (pres. 1977-78) personnel and guidance assns., Assn. Counselor Edn. and Supervision, Nat. Vocat. Guidance Assn., Am. Assn. Marriage and Family Therapy (approved supervisor) , Assn. Measurement and Evaluation in Guidance, Am. Sch. Counselor Assn., Phi Delta Kappa. Home: 243 Hudson Ave Terre Haute IN 47803 Office: Ind State U Sch Edn Terre Haute IN 47809

CHANG, CHEN-KANG, pathologist; b. Miao-Li, Taiwan, Republic China, Sept. 8, 1945; s. Kai-In and Niemei (Wu) C.; came to U.S., 1972, naturalized, 1979; M.D., Nat. Taiwan U., 1971; m. Julie Huang, July 1, 1973; children—Warren, Peter. Intern, Nat. Taiwan U. Hosp., Taipei, 1970-71; resident in pathology U. Wis. Med. Center, Madison, 1972-76, mem. faculty, 1976—, clin. asst. prof. pathology, 1977—; pathologist St. Mary's Hosp. Med. Center, Madison, Methodist Hosp., Madison, Ft. Atkinson (Wis.) Meml. Hosp., St. Clare's Hosp., Baraboo, Wis., Stoughton (Wis.) Hosp., Richland Hosp., Richland Center, Wis. Served as officer M.C., Chinese Army, 1971-72. Dr. Huang scholar, 1966-69. Mem. Coll. Am. Pathologists, Am. Soc. Clin. Pathologists, Internat. Acad. Pathology, Wis. State Soc. Pathologists. Contbr. articles to med. jours. Home: 21 N Harwood Circle Madison WI 53717 Office: 707 S Mills St Madison WI 53715

CHANG, JAE CHAN, physician, educator; b. Chong An, Korea, Aug. 29, 1941; s. Tae Whan and Kap Hee (Lee) C.; came to U.S., 1965, naturalized, 1976; M.D., Seoul (Korea) Nat. U., 1965; m. Sue Young Chung, Dec. 4, 1965; children—Sung-Jin, Sung-Ju, Sung-Hoon. Intern, Ellis Hosp., Schenectady, 1965-66; resident in medicine Harrisburg (Pa.) Hosp., 1966-69, fellow in nuclear medicine, 1969-70; instr. in medicine U. Rochester, N.Y., 1970-72; chief hematology sect. VA Hosp., Dayton, Ohio, 1972-75; hematopathologist Good Samaritan Hosp., Dayton, 1975—, dir. oncology unit, 1976—, coordinator of med. edn., 1976-77, chief oncology-hematology sect., 1976—; asst. clin. prof. medicine Ohio State U., Columbus, 1972-75; assoc. clin. prof. medicine Wright State U., Dayton, 1975-80, clin. prof., 1980—; staff St. Elizabeth Med. Center, Dayton, Miami Valley Hosp., Dayton; cons. in hematology VA Hosp. Mem. med. adv. com. Greater Dayton Area chpt. Leukemia Soc. Am., 1977—; trustee Montgomery County Soc. for Cancer Control, Dayton, 1976—, Community Blood Ctr., 1982—.

Nat. Cancer Inst. fellow in hematology and oncology, 1970-72; diplomate Am. Bd. Internal Medicine, Am. Bd. Pathology. Fellow A.C.P.; mem. Am. Soc. Hematology, Am. Fedn. Clin. Research, Am. Soc. Clin. Oncologists, Am. Assn. Cancer Research, AAAS, Dayton Oncology Club, Dayton Soc. Internal Medicine. Contbr. articles to profl. med. jours., essays to newspaper columns. Home: 1122 Wycliffe Pl Dayton OH 45459 Office: Good Samaritan Hosp and Health Center 2222 Philadelphia Dr Dayton OH 45406 Office: 2200 Philadelphia Dr Dayton OH 45406

CHANG, JUNG-CHING, research chemist; b. Taipei, Taiwan, Jan. 13, 1939; came to U.S., 1967; s. Tien-Gen and Mien (Huang) C.; B.S., Tamkang Coll., 1963; M.S., U. P.R., 1969; Ph.D., U. Mo., Kansas City, 1975; m. Mei-Chu, Nov. 12, 1965; 1 dau., Edith. Chem. engr. Taiwan Sugar Corp., 1964-67; research asst. U. P.R., Rio Piedras, 1967-69; research asst., teaching asst., research fellow U. Mo., Kansas City, 1971-75; postdoctoral research asso. U. Oreg., Eugene, 1976-77; postdoctoral fellow U. Cin., 1977-79; chemist ICN Pharmaceuticals, Inc., Cin., 1979-81; research chemist Ashland Chem. Co., Dublin, Ohio, 1981—. Served with Nat. Chinese Air Force, 1963-64. Fisher scholar, 1961-63; NSF research fellow, 1967-69; postdoctoral fellow, 1976-77; U. Kansas City trustees' fellow, 1973-75; U.Mo., Kansas City summer research fellow, 1971-75; Office Naval Research postdoctoral fellow, 1977-79. Mem. Am. Chem. Soc., N.Y. Acad. Scis., Sigma Xi. Contbr. research articles to sci. jours. Home: 2555 Sawmill Forest Ave Dublin OH 43017 Office: PO Box 2219 Columbus OH 43216

CHANNER, STEPHEN DYER STANTON, trade association executive; b. Chgo., Nov. 1, 1933; s. George Stanton and Maxine (Dyer) C.; m. Antoinette Persons, June 29, 1957; children: Stephen Persons, Wyndham Harvey. BABA, Colo. Coll., 1956; grad. U.S. Army Officers Sch., 1957. Dir. sales Am. Seating Co., Grand Rapids, Mich., 1958-77; with Bus. and Instn. Furniture Mfrs. Assn., Grand Rapids, Mich., 1977—, exec. dir., 1978—. Contbr. articles to various mags. Served to 1st lt., U.S. Army, 1956-58. Mem. Am. Soc. Assn. Execs. Mem. Christian Ch. (Disciples of Christ). Club: Grand Rapids Racquet, Forest Hills Golf; Mchts. and Mfrs. (Chgo.), Forest Hills Golf (Grand Rapids, Mich.). Home: 7440 Leyton Dr Ada MI 49301 Office: 2335 Burton St SE Grand Rapids MI 49506

CHANNICK, HERBERT S., broadcasting corporation executive; b. Phila., Aug. 27, 1929; s. Maurice and Rose (Rosenberg) C.; m. Nancy Abarbanel Wolfe, Dec. 1, 1950; children: Joan D., Robert L. AB, U. Ill., 1951; JD, Yale Law Sch., 1954. Assoc. Antonow & Weissbourd, Chgo., 1957-59; ptnr. Met. Investment Co., Chgo., 1960—; chmn. Channick Broadcasting Corp., Joliet, Ill., 1979—; bd. dirs. Canisteo Valley Broadcasting Co., Hornell, N.Y., 1980—, Crest Hill Broadcasting, Inc., Joliet, 1983—; comml. arbitrator Am. Arbitration Assn., 1978—. Bd. dirs. Ctr. for Psychosocial Studies, Chgo., 1977—, Monmouth (Ill.) Coll., 1973-75; mem. Highland Park (Ill.) Planning Commn., 1972-74, Ill. Racing Bd., Chgo., 1974-76. Served to capt. USAF, 1955-57. Office: Channick Broadcasting Corp 1520 N Rock Run Dr Joliet IL 60435

CHAO, MARSHALL S., chemist; b. Changsha, Hunan, China, Nov. 20, 1924; came to U.S., 1955; s. Heng-ti and Hwei-yng C.; m. Patricia Hu, July 20, 1968; 1 dau., Anita J. B.S., Nat. Central U., Nanking, China, 1947; M.S., U. Ill., 1958, Ph.D., 1961. Tech. asst. Taiwan Fertilizer Co., Taipei, 1949-55; research chemist Dow Chem. Co., Midland, Mich., 1960-72, research specialist, 1973-80; research leader Dow chem. Co., Midland, Mich., 1980-86; sr. assoc. Omni Tech Internat., Ltd., Midland, 1986—. Author: Taiwan Fertilizers, 1951; articles; patentee in field. Mem. Ch. Council Grace Bapt. Ch., Taipei, 1951-55; deacon 1st Baptist Ch., Midland, 1974-76. Univ. fellow U. Ill., 1957-60. Fellow Am. Inst. Chemists; mem. Am. Chem. Soc., Electrochem. Soc. (sect. chmn. 1973-74, 83-84, councilor 1974-76, 85—, vice chmn. 1964-65), Soc. Electronanalytical chemistry (charter), N.Y. Acad. Scis., Mensa, Sigma Xi, Phi Lambda Upsilon. Clubs: Midland Chinese (chmn. 1975-76), Tittabawassee Toastmasters (sec.-treas. 1976-77). Home: 1206 Evamar Midland MI 48640 Office: Omni Tech Internat Ltd 2715 Ashman St Midland MI 48640

CHAPIN, JOHN THOMAS, food products executive; b. Chgo., June 30, 1947; s. John Ralph and Margie Lois (O'Neill) C.; m. Carol Ann Coccia, June 28, 1969; children: Laura Ann, Lisa Mary. AA, Prairie State Coll., Chicago Heights, Ill., 1971. Mgr. transp. Scot Lad Foods, Lansing, Ill., 1973-80; dir. transp. S.C. Shannon Co., Appleton, Wis., 1980-81; dir. transp., distbn. Ind. Sugars, Inc., Gary, 1982-87; operation mgr. Neill Cartage Co Inc, Berkeley, Ill., 1987—. V.p. Calumet Maintenance and Safety Council, 1984-85, pres. 1985-86; mem. Nat. Rep. Com., Washington, 1987, Ind. Rep. Com., Indpls., 1987. Mem. Property Owners Assn., Teamsters (local 142 grievance bd.), Delta Nu Alpha. Roman Catholic. Club: South Suburban Traffic. Avocations: golf, water sports. Home: 1403 Brandywine Rd Crown Point IN 46307 Office: Neill Cartage Co Inc 5400 Proviso Dr Berkeley IL 46307

CHAPLIK, BARBARA DARE NORTH, psychologist; b. Kingston, R.I., June 28, 1935; d. H.F.A. and Virginia Dare (Long) North; m. John P. Chaplik Jr., Dec. 19, 1969; children: Elizabeth Eckard, Suzanne Rohde. AA, Colo. Woman's Coll., Denver, 1953-55; BA, George Washington U., 1955-58; MS, Iowa State U., 1971, PhD, 1981. Lic. psychologist, Iowa. Biophysics research asst. Carnegie Inst. Washington, 1957-60, U. Wis., 1960-61; tchr. Lineville (Iowa) Pub. Schs., 1968-69; teaching asst. Dept. Psychology, Ames, Iowa, 1969-71; psychologist Des Moines Schs., 1971—; gen. practice psychology Ames, 1978—; cons. psychology Iowa Dept. Vocat. Rehab., Des Moines, 1978—; Disability Determination Services, Des Moines, 1981—. Mem. Des Moines Edn. Assn. (chmn. human relations, 1983—, Iowa Sch. Psychologists Assn. (ethics chmn. 1978—), Iowa Psychologist Assn., Nat. Assn. Sch. Psychologists, Internat. Sch. Psychologist Assn., NOW, Peace Educator's Project (sec. 1986-87), Delta Gamma, Phi Delta Kappa, Psi Chi. Democrat. Methodist. Avocations: reading, fishing. Office: 2825 Arbor Ames IA 50309

CHAPMAN, ALBERT LEE, anatomy educator, university dean; b. Anderson, Mo., Nov. 5, 1933; s. Coleman V. and Lorena (Farley) C.; m. Patsy Joan Pickett, Aug. 31, 1958; children: Gregory Paul, Robin Annette, Janette Lee, Jeffrey Coleman. AA, Joplin Jr. Coll., 1954; BA, U. Mo., 1956, U. Mo., 1959; PhD, U. Nebr., Omaha, 1962. Instr. U. Kans., Kansas City, 1962-64, asst. prof. med. ctr., 1964-69, assoc. prof. dept. anatomy, 1969-74, dir. electron microscopy research ctr., 1973—, prof., 1974—, acting dean grad. studies med. ctr., 1983-85, dean. grad. studies and research med. ctr., 1985—. Mem. Am. Assn. Anatomists, Am. Soc. Cell Biology, Cen. States Electron Microscopy Soc. (pres. 1979-80, 85-86), Electron Microscopy Soc. Am., Sigma Xi (pres. 1978-79). Office: U Kans Med Ctr Office Grad Studies and Research 39th and Rainbow Blvd Kansas City KS 66103

CHAPMAN, ALGER BALDWIN, finance executive, lawyer; b. Portland, Maine, Sept. 28, 1931; s. Alger Baldwin Sr. and Elizabeth (Ives) C.; m. Beatrice Bishop, Oct. 30, 1983; children: Alger III, Samuel P., Andrew I., Henry H. BA, Williams Coll., 1953; JD, Columbia U., 1956. Bar: N.Y. 1957. Pres. Shearson & Co., 1970-74, co-chmn., 1974-81; vice chmn. Am. Express Bank, 1982-85; chmn., chief exec. officer Chgo. Bd. Options Exchange, 1986—. Mem. N.Y. State Bar Assn. Clubs: Metropolitan (N.Y.C.); Attic, Chicago, Glenview. Avocations: golf, skiing, reading. Home: 1500 N Lake Shore Dr Chicago IL 60610 Office: Chgo Bd Options Exchange 400 S LaSalle St Chicago IL 60605

CHAPMAN, ANNE BROWN, adult education coordinator; b. Cleve., Nov. 16, 1939; d. Charles William and Elsie Blanche (Rambo) Brown; m. Robert Anthony Chapman, Aug. 19, 1961; children: Kathleen Anne, Robert Alan. BS, Ohio State U., 1961; MS, Kent State U., 1987. Cert. tchr., Ohio. Tchr. home econs. Eastlake Jr. High Sch., Willoughby, Ohio, 1968-75; dept. mgr. White Sewing Machine Co., Cleve., 1978-79; custom product rep. interior design Kay Trimmer Inc., Mentor, Ohio, 1979-80; coordinator displaced homemaker program Lake County Joint Vocat. Sch., Painesville, Ohio, 1980—. Pres. Ridge PTA, 1976-77; mem. Western Res. Consortium, 1980—; mem. Human Services Forum Geauga County, 1980—. Ohio Vocat. Edn. Dept. grantee, 1981-83. Mem. Am. Bus. Women's Assn., Am. Vocat. Assn., Ohio Vocat. Assn., Ohio State U. Home Econs. Alumni Assn., Ohio State U. Alumni Assn., Zeta Tau Alpha. Club: Parents (liaison 1982—). Home: 7281 Taft St Mentor OH 44060 Office: 8140 Auburn Rd Painesville OH 44077

CHAPMAN, BARBARA DELLA, orthopedic surgeon; b. Lansing, Mich., Jan. 19, 1952; d. Robert James and Ruth R. Chapman; m. Frank Lewis Andrews, Aug. 30, 1980; children: William, S. Ross. BS in Zoology, Mich. State U., 1973, BS in Psychology, 1974, DO, 1977. Intern Pontiac (Mich.) Osteo. Hosp., 1978, resident in orthopedic surgery, 1979-81, chief resident orthopedic surgery, 1983; resident hand surgery Harper Grace Hosp., Detroit, 1982; surgeon Lapeer (Mich.) Orthopedic Assocs., 1984; pres. Barbara D. Chapman, DO, Lapeer, 1985—, also bd. dirs. Mem. Am. Osteo. Assn., Am. Osteo. Acad. Orthopedics. Avocation: gardening. Office: 415 W Nepessing Lapeer MI 48446

CHAPMAN, (GEORGE) BRAINERD (III), lawyer; b. Louisville, Oct. 18, 1911; s. George B. and Kathryn (Schneiderhan) C.; B.A., Amherst Coll., 1933; J.D., Harvard, 1936; m. Martha McCaig, June 11, 1948; 1 son, George Brainerd, IV. Bar: Ill. 1936. Assoc. then ptnr. Lord, Bissell & Brook, and predecessors, 1936-58; pvt. practice, 1959-62; ptnr. Chapman, Pennington, Montgomery, Holmes & Sloan, Chgo., 1962-70, Vedder, Price, Kaufman & Kammholz, Chgo., 1971-83, of counsel, 1984—; former dir. various corps., eleemosynary instns. and founds. Former chmn. bd. Presbyn. Home; past bd. dirs., nat. treas. Mil. Tng. Camps Assn. U.S. Served from capt. to col. JAG'S Dept., AUS, 1942-46. Decorated Bronze Star (U.S.); knight officer of Crown (Italy); recipient medal for eminent service Amherst Coll., 1969, Foster and Mary McGaw award, 1977. Mem. Beta Theta Pi. Presbyn. (elder, trustee). Author: Dream Cruise, 1980. Clubs: Chgo., University, Law, Glen View (Golf, Ill.). Office: 115 S LaSalle St Chicago IL 60603

CHAPMAN, CARL HALEY, anthropology educator; b. Steelville, Mo., May 29, 1915; s. William M. and Estelle Madolin (Haley) C.; m. Eleanor Eliza Finley, Mar. 14, 1942; children: Richard Carl, Stephen Finley. A.B., U. Mo., 1939; M.A., U. N.Mex., 1946; Ph.D. (Horace H. Rackham fellow), U. Mich., 1959. Instr. sociology U. Mo., Columbia, 1946-48; dir. Am. archeology U. Mo., 1946-65, instr. sociology and anthropology, 1948-50, asst. prof. anthropology, 1951-57, assoc. prof. anthropology, 1957-60, prof., 1960-85, prof. emeritus, 1985—, dir. archeology research activities, 1965-75, research prof. Am. archaeology, 1975—; dir. Mus. Anthropology, 1949-50, 51-56; mem. steering com. Miss. Alluvial Valley Archaeol. Program, 1968-72; chmn. adv. council on archaeology to Mo. State Park Bd., 1959-70; ex-officio mem. Adv. Council on Archaeology and History, 1970-72, Adv. Council on Hist. Preservation, 1977-81. Author: (with Eleanor Chapman) Indians and Archaeology of Missouri, 1964, rev. edit., 1983, The Origin of the Osage Indian Tribe, 1974, Archaeology of Missouri, I, 1975, II, 1980, (with David Evans and John Cottier) Investigation and Comparison of Two Fortified Mississippi Tradition Sites in Southeastern Missouri, 1977; contbg. author: The Indomitable Osage in Spanish Illinois, 1973, Cultural Change and Continuity, 1976; contbr. articles on Am. Archaeology to scholarly jours. Gov.'s rep. to Lewis and Clark Trail Commn. meetings State of Mo., 1966-68; sec. Mo. Lewis and Clark Trail Commn., 1966-67; Democratic committeeman 3d Ward, Columbia, 1970-72; bd. dirs. Mo. Heritage Trust, 1977-85. Served with USAAF, 1942-45. Decorated Air medal; recipient Thomas Jefferson award. U. Mo., 1984; grantee Nat. Park Service, 1952-63, NSF, 1961-63, NEH, 1971-75, 82-85. Fellow Am. Anthrop. Assn., AAAS; mem. Soc. Am. Archaeology (Disting. Service award 1975, 50th anniversary award for outstanding contbns), Am. Soc. Conservation Archaeology (Conservation award 1980), Soc. Profl. Archaeologists (pres. 1978-79), Mo. Archaeol. Soc. (Soc. Honor award), Soc. Hist. Archaeology, Central States Anthrop. Assn., Am. Ethnol. Soc., AAUP, Phi Beta Kappa, Sigma Xi, Phi Kappa Phi. Democrat. Unitarian. Home: 211 Edgewood Columbia MO 65203 Office: 205 Swallow Hall University of Missouri Columbia MO 65211

CHAPMAN, CONRAD DANIEL, lawyer; b. Detroit, July 31, 1933; s. Conrad F. and Alexandrine C. (Baranski) C.; m. Carol Lynn DeBash, Sept. 1, 1956; children: Stephen Daniel, Richard Thomas, Suzanne Marie. BA, U. Detroit, 1954, JD summa cum laude, 1957; LLM in Taxation, Wayne State U., 1964. Bar: Mich. 1957, U.S. Dist. Ct. (so. dist.) Mich. 1957. Ptnr. Powers, Chapman, DeAgostino, Meyers, McTigue & Milia and predecessor firms, Troy, Mich., 1964—. Mem. ABA, Detroit Bar Assn., Oakland Bar Assn., Am. Arbitration Assn., Detroit Estate Planning Council, Oakland Estate Planning Council. Clubs: Detroit Athletic, Detroit Golf. Lodge: Elks. Office: Powers Chapman DeAgostino Meyers McTigue & Milia 3001 W Big Beaver Rd Suite 704 Troy MI 48084

CHAPMAN, EMILY ELIZABETH, systems analyst; b. Paris, Ont., Can., Jan. 19, 1921; d. Robert Alexander George and Emily Adabelle (Turnbull) Cale; Asso. in Home Econs., Macdonald Inst., Guelph, Ont., 1941; B.S., U. Wis., Madison, 1957, postgrad. Grad. Sch. Computer Scis., 1966-67; m. R. Keith Chapman, Aug. 22, 1942; children—Robert Wayne, Linda Jean, Susan Gay. Research programmer analyst U. Wis., Madison, 1966-70; exec. sec. Sponsors of Sci. Inc., Madison, 1970-74; programmer analyst Higher Ednl. Aids Bd., State of Wis., 1975-78; systems analyst Bur. Info. Devel., Dept. Adminstrn., State of Wis., Madison, 1978-80, project leader, 1980-84, Computer Support mgr., 1984-87; cons. programmer analyst, 1970-73. Chmn. Cancer Soc.-Heart Fund Health Drives, Verona, Wis., 1956-57; bd. dirs. Central YWCA, Madison, 1965-66. Recipient Exceptional Performance award Dept. Adminstrn., State of Wis., 1981, 83. Mem. Assn. for Systems Mgmt. (treas. Madison chpt. 1979-81), Council for Agrl. Sci. and Tech., Univ. League Madison, Daus. of Demeter. Home: 1119 Waban Hill Madison WI 53711 Office: State of Wis Dept Adminstrn Gen Exec Facility II Madison WI 53702

CHAPMAN, FRANCES ELIZABETH CLAUSEN (MRS. WILLIAM JAMES CHAPMAN), civic worker, writer; b. Atchison, Kans., Feb. 27, 1920; d. Erwin W. and Helen (Hackney) Clausen; B.A., Wellesley Coll., 1941; m. W. MacLean Johnson, Aug. 31, 1940 (dec. Nov. 1965); children—Stuart MacLean, Duncan Scott, Douglas Hamilton; m. 2d, William James Chapman, Dec. 5, 1970. Author: Grandmother's House, 1987. Project dir. Women in Community Service, Inc., St. Louis, 1965-66; pres. Nursery Found., St. Louis, 1956-58, dir., 1953-59, 65-68; adv. com. Mo. State Children's Day Care, 1963—; chmn. day care com. Mo. Council Children and Youth, 1961, chmn. foster care sect., 1961-63; spl. asst. to the pres. Webster Coll., 1966-68. Bd. dirs. New City Sch., 1967-69, Mid-County YMCA, 1967-70, St. Louis Conservatory and Sch. Arts, 1978—; mem. Mo. State Coordinating Bd. Higher Edn., 1982-86 ; mem. steering com. Mo. Council on Children and Youth, 1967-69; trustee Jr. Coll. Dist., St. Louis-St. Louis County, 1968-80, pres. bd. trustees, 1971-73, 76-77; trustee John Burroughs Sch., 1973-79, Wellesley Coll., 1976-82; bd. dirs. Assn. Governing Bds. Univs. and Colls., 1970-80, v.p., 1977-78, chmn. bd., 1978-79, hon. dir., 1982-85; bd. commrs. Nat. Commn. on Accrediting, 1971-72; bd. overseers Center for Research on Women in Higher Edn. and Professions, Wellesley, Mass., 1977-82. Recipient Dem. Woman of Achievement award, St. Louis Globe, 1965. Mem. Nat. Soc. Arts and Letters, Wellesley Coll. Alumnae Assn. (sec., dir. 1958-61). Club: Wellesley Coll. (pres. 1965-67). Home: 10 Overbrook Dr Saint Louis MO 63124

CHAPMAN, JAMES CLAUDE, marine equipment manufacturing executive; b. Detroit, Mar. 16, 1931; s. Claude Byrand and Madolin C. (Werstine) C.; m. Elizabeth Jane Quinley, May 1, 1954; children—Diane, Donna. B.M.E. cum laude, U. Detroit, 1956, M.B.A., 1966. Registered profl. engr., Mich. Plant mgr. Rockwell Internat. Corp., Marysville, Ohio, 1971-74; dir. facilities Rockwell Internat. Corp., Troy, Mich., 1974-78; dir. mfg. Outboard Marine Corp., Waukegan, Ill., 1978, v.p. mfg., 1978-85, pres., chief operating officer, 1985—. Pres. Northeast Ill. council Boy Scouts Am.; bd. dirs. Lake Forest Sch. of Mgmt., Ill., 1984. Served with USNR, 1950-58. Mem. Soc. Mfg. Engrs., Soc. Automotive Engrs., Waukegan-Lake County C. of C. (vice chmn. 1985). Republican. Roman Catholic. Club: Glen Flora Country (Waukegan). Avocations: boating; fishing; golfing; rock hounding; skiing. Home: 937 Sandstone Dr Libertyville IL 60048 Office: Outboard Marine Corp 100 Sea Horse Dr Waukegan IL 60085

CHAPMAN, JANE B., federal office administrator; b. Columbus, ohio, Apr. 11, 1938; d. Henry John and Helen Gertrude (Robbins) Bitterman; m. Ralph Frederic Nelson, Sept. 6, 1958 (div. May 1971); children: Graham, Ralph Jr., Pamela; m. George Courtney Chapman, May 22, 1971. BA, U. Ill., 1958. Staff aide U.S. Ho. Rep., Columbus, 1984—. Pres. PTA, Worthington, Ohio, 1975-78, Service Bd. Buckeye Boys Ranch, Columbus, 1981-86; chmn. Worthington Songsters, Worthington, 1986—. Republican. Avocations: reading, sewing, gardening, knitting, boating. Home: 488 Greenglade Ave Worthington OH 43085 Office: Congressman Chalmers P Wylie 200 N High St Columbus OH 43215

CHAPMAN, JANET MARIE, auditor; b. Wichita, Kans., Jan. 26, 1949; d. Hubert and Goldie Marie (Counterman) Vant Leven; m. Kenneth L. Chapman, July 5, 1974 (div. May 1986); 1 child, Denise Marie. BBA, Washburn U., 1979. Sec. VA, Wichita, Kans. and Washington, 1971-76; grants specialist U.S. Environ. Protection Agy., Kansas City, Mo., 1980-81; auditor U.S. Gen. Acctg. Office, Kansas City, Mo., 1981—; Chairperson, mgr. Fed. Women's Program, Kansas City, 1982-84. Served to cpl. USMC, 1967-69. Avocations: snow skiing, golf. Home: 701 Ida Lansing KS 66043 Office: US Gen Acctg Office 4th and State Kansas City KS 66101

CHAPMAN, JOSEPH DUDLEY, gynecologist, sexologist, author; b. Moline, Ill., Apr. 29, 1928; s. Joseph Dudley and Lillian Caroline (Pruder) C.; m. Mary Kay Sartini, June, 1949 (div.); children—Mary Jo Tucker, Nancy Jo Robinson; m. 2d, Virginia Helene Milius, June, 1958 (div.). B.S., U. Ill. and Roosevelt Coll., Chgo., 1950; D.O., Coll. Osteo. Medicine and Surgery, 1953; D.Sc., 1963; M.D., Calif. Coll. Medicine, 1962, PhD Inst. Advanced Study Human Sexualtiy, 1986. Cert. Am. Osteo. Bd. Ob-Gyn. Intern, resident in ob-gyn Still Coll. Hosp., Des Moines; practice medicine specializing in ob-gyn, North Madison, Ohio, 1973—; clin. prof. ob-gyn Ohio U., 1979—; mem. faculty, acad. bd. Inst. Advanced Study Human Sexuality, San Francisco, 1979—; TV appearances on Phil Donahue Show, Good Morning Am., The Last Word, and others; med. examiner FAA, comml. pilot. Active Boy Scouts Am. Mem. Am. Fertility Soc., Am. Assn. Gynocol. Laparoscopists, Am. Coll. Osteo. Ob-Gyn (Purdue Frederick awards, editor), Acad. Psychosomatic Medicine (bd. govs.), Am. Med. Writers Assn. Lutheran. Author: The Feminine Mind and Body, 1966; The Sexual Equation, 1977; editor-in-chief O.P., 1968-77; editorial cons. Penthouse Forum, J.A.O.A.: Psychosomatic Medicine; contbr. chpts. to books, articles to profl. jours. Home: Box 340 North Madison OH 44057

CHAPMAN, VERNON GLENN, purchasing executive; b. Chgo., July 21, 1950; s. Vernon G. and Anna B. (Dorner) C.; m. Judith Ann Treletsky, Mar. 10, 1974; children: Alyson, Adam. BS in Bus. Mgmt., U. Ill., 1974. Asst. product mgr. W.W. Grainger, Niles, Ill., 1974-76; buyer Am. Hosp. Supply, Des Plaines, Ill., 1976-78; purchasing mgr. Internat. Products, Des Plaines, 1978-83, Interand Corp., Chgo., 1983—. Mem. Nat. Assn. Purchasing Mgrs. (cert.), Purchasing Mgmt. Assn. Chgo. Home: 1321 Joan Dr Palatine IL 60067 Office: Interand Corp 3200 W Peterson Chicago IL 60659

CHAPMAN, WILLIAM A., business executive; b. County of Essex, Eng., 1924. With Ranco Inc., 1960—, mng. dir. U.K. ops., 1969; mng. dir. Ranco Inc., Europe, 1975; exec. v.p. European ops. Ranco Inc., 1976, vice chmn. bd., 1978, pres., chief operating officer, dir., 1979—. Address: Ranco Inc 555 Metro Pl N Suite 550 Dublin OH 43017 *

CHAPMAN, WILLIAM FRANCIS, newspaper editor, consultant; b. Powersville, Mo., Mar. 28, 1925; s. William Bryant and Esther (Coddington) C.; student jr. coll., St. Joseph, Mo., 1942-43, Central Mo. State Coll., 1946, Wayne State U., 1955; m. Lillian Louise Fyler, Aug. 10, 1945 (dec. Sept. 1984); children—Robert Earl, Karen Louise, Sharon Frances; m. Karen Ann Moore, July 13, 1985. News editor Warrensburg (Mo.) Daily Star-Jour., 1946-47; mgr. U.P.I., Jefferson City, Mo., 1949, war corr., Korea, 1950-51, mgr. Seattle, 1952-53; asst. city editor Detroit Free Press, 1954-61; exec. editor Daily Times, Chester, Pa., 1961-63; mng. editor The Times, Hammond, Ind., 1964-75, exec. editor, 1975-85; editorial dir. Howard Publs., Oceanside, Calif., 1971-85; pres. Chapman Report, Merrillville, Ind., 1985—. Founding dir. Mid-Am. Press Inst., So. Ill. U. Carbondale (chmn. 1971); bd. dirs. Youngkwang Ednl. Found., Taegu U., Republic Korea; mem. Internat. Press Inst. Served with USMCR, 1943-46; PTO. Mem. Am. Soc. Newspaper Editors, A.P. Mng. Editors. Home: 7818 Marshall Pl Merrillville IN 46410 Office: 7818 Marshall Pl Merrillville IN 46410

CHAREK, ROBERT STANLEY, business executive, financial consultant; b. Cleve., Aug. 8, 1924; s. Stanley Joseph and Lillian Helen (Prosser) C.; m. Hilda Marie Hoffman, Aug. 9, 1944; children: Barbara C. Charek Reesing, Bonita L. Charek McCormick, Ralph K. Prince, Christopher R. Student, Centre Coll. Ky., 1943, Western Res. U., 1946. Pub. acct., Gold Bros. Co., Cleve., 1946-47, office mgr. 1947-49; with Master Builders div. Martin Marietta, Cleve., 1949-84, acctg. dept. mgr., 1954-58, dir. acctg., 1959-73, internat. controller, 1974-82, internat. acctg. mgr., 1982-84; fin. cons., tax acct., 1984—. Served with USAAF, 1943-45. Mem. Data Processing Mgmt. Assn. (past dir. chpt.). Republican. Roman Catholic. Lodge: KC. Home: 21941 Briarwood Dr Fairview Park OH 44126

CHAREWICZ, DAVID MICHAEL, photographer; b. Chgo., Feb. 17, 1932; s. Michael and Stella (Pietrzak) C.; student DePaul U., 1957, Northwestern U., 1952; MA in Photography, Profl. Photographers Am. Inc., 1986; m. Catherine Uccello, Nov. 8, 1952; children—Michael, Karen, Daniel. Trainee, Merill Chase, Chgo., 1950-51; dark room technician Maurice Seymour, Chgo., 1951-52; photographer Oscar & Assos., Chgo., 1955-63; owner Dave Chare Photography, Park Ridge, Ill., 1963—; pres., owner C&C Duplicating, Inc., 1978—. Pres. Oakton Parent Tchr. Club, 1968-69, del. dist. 64 caucus, 1970, 73; mem. centennial photo com., Park Ridge, Ill., 1973; mem. sponsoring com. Park Ridge Men's Prayer Breakfast 1982—. Served with AUS, 1952-54. Mem. Am. Soc. Photographers, Profl. Photographers Assn., Midstate Indsl. Photographers Assn. (treas. 1981, pres. 1984-85). Home: 739 N Northwest Hwy Park Ridge IL 60068 Office: 1045 N Northwest Hwy Park Ridge IL 60068

CHARLA, LEONARD FRANCIS, auto manufacturing company executive, lawyer; b. New Rochelle, N.Y., May 4, 1940; s. Leonard A. and Mary L. Charla; m. Kathleen Gerace, Feb. 3, 1968; children—Larisa, Christopher. B.A., Iona Coll., 1962; J.D., Cath. U., 1965; LL.M., George Washington U., 1971. Bar: D.C. 1967, N.Y. 1970, Mich. 1971. Tech. writer IRS, Washington, 1966-67; atty. adv. ICC, Washington, 1967, atty., 1968-69; mgmt. intern HEW, Washington, 1967-68; atty. Bowes & Millner, Transp. Cons., Roseland, N.J., 1969-71; atty. legal staff Gen. Motors Corp., Detroit, 1971-85, sr. counsel, 1985-87, asst. gen. counsel, 1987—; faculty Center for Creative Studies, Coll. Art and Design, Detroit, 1978—, adj. asst. prof., 1982—; faculty art U. Mich., 1980, 84, 85, 86, 87. Bd. dirs. Gt. Lakes Performing Artists Assocs., 1983—, Mich. Assn. Community Arts Agys., 1983—; bd. govs. Cath. U. Am. Alumni, 1982—. N.Y. State Regents teaching fellow, 1962; Cath. U. Law Sch. scholar, 1962-65. Mem. ABA, Mich. State Bar Assn. (chmn. arts sect. 1980-81), Assn. ICC Practitioners (pres. Gt. Lakes chpt. 1974-75, v.p. region VIII 1976-77). Office: Gen Motors Legal Staff New Center One Bldg 3031 W Grand Blvd Suite 7104 Detroit MI 48232

CHARLES, JOSE RODOLFO (PEPE), marketing executive; b. Mexico City, Mar. 28, 1953; came to U.S., 1983; s. Alberto and Josefa (Saldivar) C.; m. Pamela Jo Kiland, Aug. 2, 1985. Degree in indsl. engring., Anahuac Coll., Mexico City, 1975; MBA in Internat. Mktg., London U., 1980. Engr. Procter & Gamble, Mexico City, 1975-78; mktg. asst. S.C. Johnson, Toronto, Can., 1980-81, mktg. assoc., 1981-83; mktg. mgr. S.C. Johnson, Racine, Wis., 1983—; Author: Agro Industry in Mexico, 1979. Mem. Assn. MBA's. Clubs: First Thursday, Johnson Internat. (pres.). Office: S.C. Johnson 1525 Howe St Racine WI 53403

CHARLES, SARA CONNOR, psychiatrist; b. Mt. Kisco, N.Y., Nov. 27, 1934; d. James Patrick and Isabel (Roney) C.; m. Eugene Kennedy. BA, St. Mary's of the Springs Coll., 1956; MD, St. Louis U., 1964. Asst. prof. psychiatry U. Notre Dame, South Bend, Ind., 1968-72; assoc. prof. U. Ill., Chgo., 1972—; pvt. practice psychiatry Chgo., 1972-77. Author: (with others) Defendant, 1985; contbr. articles on malpractice litigation and physician stress to profl. jours. Fellow Am. Psychiat. Assn.; mem. AMA. Roman Catholic. Home: 1300 N Lake Shore Dr Chicago IL 60610 Office: U Ill at Chgo 912 S Wood St M/C 917 Chicago IL 60612

CHARLTON, DAVID SAMUEL, geologist; b. Milw., Oct. 10, 1942; s. James Robert and Lucille R. (Kerschner) C.; m. Candace Sue Pierson, July

27, 1985. Student, U. Wis., Whitewater, 1962-63; BS, U. Wis., 1966, MS, 1969, PhD, 1981. Geologist Atlantic Richfield Co., Lafayette, La., 1973-75; environ. coordinator Anchorage, 1976-78; sr. geologist London, 1982-85; project geologist ARCO Alaska Inc., Anchorage, 1979-81; sr. geologist ARCO Norway Inc., Stavanger, 1984-85; cons. geologist Lincoln, Nebr., 1986—; speaker ARCO Speaker's Bur., Anchorage, 1980. Contbr. articles to prof. jours.; inventor in field. vol. photograper Prince's Trust, London, 1986. Grantee NSF, 1968, Geol. Soc. Am., 1970, 71. Fellow Royal Geog. Soc.; mem. Am. Assn. Petroleum Geologists, Soc. Econ. Paleontologists and Mineralogists, Nebr. Geol. Soc., Alaska World Affairs Council (bd. dirs. 1980-82), Lincoln Investors Assn., Sigma Xi, Alpha Gamma Rho (counselor 1970-72). Clubs: Globetrotters (London), Forum 49 (mem. bd. 1980-82) (Anchorage). Avocations: sailing, photography, travel, reading, languages. Home and Office: 3840 Washington St Lincoln NE 68506

CHARPENTIER, DONALD ARMAND, psychologist; b. Bklyn., Mar. 8, 1935; s. Joseph Roche and Grace Viola (Adrience) C.; B.A., Hope Coll., 1956; M.A., Ohio U., 1958; Ed.S., George Peabody Coll., 1964; Ph.D., U. Minn., 1972; m. Janice Lee Getting, May 21, 1961; children—Jennifer Diane, Ian Lee Burke. Asso. dir. Westminster Found. Ohio, 1956-57, acting dir., 1957-58; psychologist, probation officer Cook County Family Court, Chgo., 1961-62; asst. prof. psychology State U. N.Y., Fredonia, 1964-65; asst. prof. U. Wis., River Falls, 1965-72, asso. prof., 1974-80, prof., 1980—. Vis. research fellow, Harvard U., 1973-74. Lic. psychologist, Wis. Mem. Am. Assn. Advancement Social Psychology, Am. Psychol. Assn., Am. Sociol. Assn., Internat. Soc. History of Behavioral and Social Scis., Soc. Psychol. Study Social Issues, Soc. for Advancement Am. Philosophy, N.Y. Acad. Scis. Home: Rt 4 River Falls WI 54022 Office: Dept Psychology Univ Wis River Falls WI 54022

CHARTIER, JANELLEN OLSEN, airline inflight service coordinator; b. Chgo., Sept. 12, 1951; d. Roger Carl and Genevieve Ann (McCormick) Olsen; m. Lionel Pierre-Paul Chartier, Nov. 6, 1982; 1 child, Régine Anne. B.A. in French and Home Econs., U. Ill., 1973, M.A. in Teaching French, 1974; student U. Rouen (France), 1971-72. Cert. tchr., Ill. Flight attendant Delta Airlines, Atlanta, 1974—, French qualified, 1974—, Spanish qualified, 1977-82, German qualified, 1980—, in flight service coordinator, 1980—, European in flight service coordinator, 1983—; French examiner In-Flight Service, 1984—; interpreter Formax, Inc., Mokena, Ill., 1976-82. Bd. dirs. One Plus One Dance Co., Champaign, Ill., 1977-78. Mem. Alliance Maison Francaise de Chgo., Phi Delta Kappa, Alpha Lambda Delta. Roman Catholic. Home: 155 N Harbor Dr Apt 3506 Chicago IL 60601

CHASE, CHARLES AYER, investment advisor; b. Mpls., Oct. 12, 1931; s. Kenneth A. and Irma M. (Brodin) C.; A.B., Ripon Coll., 1954; postgrad. U. Minn., Boston U., Mexico City Coll.; m. Janet Gray, Sept. 17, 1960; children—Anne, Charles Ayer. Contracting officer Boston Ordance Dist., 1955-57; ptnr. Chase Investment Co., 1962-74; owner, propr. Chase Investment Co., Mpls., 1974—; cons. Served with ordnance, AUS, 1955-57. Registered investment advisor. Mem. Nat. Rifle Assn., Exptl. Aircraft Assn. Republican. Congregationalist. Club: Mpls. Athletic. Office: 1115 2d Ave S Minneapolis MN 55403

CHASE, DEBORAH SUE, computer software consultant, trainer; b. Springfield, Ill., Apr. 11, 1962; d. Kenneth Laverne and Grace Elizabeth (Jones) Cain; m. Clifford Steven Chase, Aug. 9, 1980; 1 child, Jacob Aaron. Grad. high sch., Glen Ellyn, Ill. Office mgr. Presdl. Services, Wheaton, Ill., 1979-83, corp. asst. sec., 1982-83; office mgr. and con. DataMgmt., Glen Ellyn, 1983-86; application developer Glenbard Graphics, Carol Stream, Ill., 1986; office mgr. Huron Leasing, Carol Stream, 1986—; corp. sec. Fin. Services Group, Wheaton, 1982-83; corp. asst. sec. Centre Capital, Wheaton, 1982-83, Equity Realty, 1982-83. Baptist. Avocations: cooking, swimming, exercising, ch.-related activities. Home: 660 Iroquois Trail Carol Stream IL 60188 Office: Huron Leasing Inc. 205 E Kehoe Suite 7 Carol Stream IL 60188

CHASE, ERNEST ARTHUR, accountant; b. Galien, Mich., Apr. 10, 1931; s. Samuel M. and Mildred Irene (Morley) C.; student LaSalle Extension U., 1953-57, Lake Michigan Coll., 1974-75; m. Joyce Elaine Winney, July 21, 1951; children—Ernest L., Arthur M., Robert J., William R., James R. Assembly insp. David Products Co., Niles, Mich., 1951; gen. acct. Warren Featherbone Co., Three Oaks, Mich., 1953-55; cost acct. Bendix Products Co., South Bend, Ind., 1955-56; officer mgr. Babbitt Lumber Co., Niles, 1956-57; cost acct. Curtiss Wright Corp., South Bend, 1957-58; mgr. credit office Am. Home and Gray Aretz Co., South Bend, 1958; chief acct. Millburg Growers Exchange (Mich.), 1958-59; sales mgr. S.W. Mich. dist. Nat. Fedn. Ind. Bus., 1959-60; owner Chase Pub. Acctg. Service, Galien, 1958—, Chase Ins. Service Center, Galien, 1960-85, Family Everyday Clothing and Shoe Store, Three Oaks, 1963-65; salesman Kiefer Real Estate, Berrien Springs, Mich., 1962-76. Leader, Boy Scouts Am., 1957-72; sec., treas., coach Galien Little League, 1964-76; clk. Village of Galien, 1963-64; mem. adv. com. Galien Twp. Schs., 1963-70, chmn., 1966-70; mem. tax allocation bd. Berrien County, 1971-72, mem. key man com., 1971-72, chmn. finance com., 1971-72, chmn. budget com., 1969-70, county commr., 1969-72, 77-79, 83-84; mem. Berrien County Pension Bd., 1977-79; mem. regional key man com. Mich. Assn. Counties, 1971-72. Mem. Berrien County Republican Exec. Com., 1969-72, 77-79, 83-84; mem. Berrien County Road Commn., 1985—, chmn. 1986—; mem. Berrien County Parks Commn., 1986—. Served with USN, 1949-50, 52-53. Mem. Ind. Accts. Mich., Mich. Assn. Mut. Ins. Agts., Nat. Soc. Pub. Accts., Am. Legion. Methodist. Lion. Home: Hwy US 12 E Galien MI 49113 Office: 112 N Main St Galien MI 49113

CHASE, JOYCE ELAINE, accountant, nurse; b. Benton Harbor, Mich., Dec. 4, 1931; d. Richard I. and Evelyn Pauline (Hahn) Winney; student Lake Mich. Coll., 1974-75, Mich. State Ins. Sch., 1974, A.A. in Nursing, Lake Mich. Coll., 1986; m. Ernest Arthur Chase, July 21, 1951; children—Ernest L., Arthur M., Robert J., William R., James R. Clk. Gillespie's Drug Store, Benton Harbor, 1945, WoolWorth's Store, Benton Harbor, 1946-47; bookkeeper Reeder's Bookkeeping Service, Benton Harbor, 1949; assembler VM Corp., Benton Harbor, 1950; telephone operator Mich. Bell Co., Benton Harbor, 1951; bookkeeper I & M Electric Co., Buchanan, Mich., 1952, Auto Specialties Co., St. Joseph, Mich., 1953; clk. Galien Drug Store, Galien, Mich., 1955; assembler Electro-Voice Corp., Buchanan, Mich., 1958-62; bookkeeper Chase Bookkeeping & Tax Service, Galien, Mich., 1963-78, sr. tax accountant, 1968—; ins. agt. Chase Ins. Service Center, Galien, Mich., 1974-85, registered nurse, Pawating Hosp., Niles, Mich., 1986—; emergency med. technician and ambulance driver Galien Vol. Ambulance Service, 1974—. Cub. Scout den mother S.W. Mich. council Cub. Scouts Am., 1963-69; mem. Galien Twp. election bd., 1971-78; mem. Galien Sch. Election Bd., 1971—; pres. Galien Athletic Boosters, 1969; mem. Galien High Sch., PTA, 1966—, adv. com., 1965-68. Mem. Nat. Soc. Pub. Accountants, Mich. Emergency Services Health Council, Am. Legion Aux. Republican. Methodist. Home: US Route 12 East Garwood Lake Galien MI 49113 Office: 112 N Main St Galien MI 49113

CHASE, JUDY DARLENE, social worker; b. Salina, Kans., Jan. 1, 1943; s. Walter L. and E. Juanita (Curtiss) C.; 1 child, Mark A. Sabes. BA in Elem. Edn. and Music, Calif. State U., Humboldt, 1965; MSW, U. Kans., 1981. Cert. specialist clin. social worker, Kans., elem. tchr., Calif. Tchr. Humboldt County Schs., Calif., 1965-71; social worker Kans. Dept. Social and Rehab. Services, Topeka, 1973-85, community program cons., 1985-87, social work supr., 1987—; cons., therapy, Topeka, 1986. Vol. Topeka State Hosp., 1983—. Mem. Kans. Conf. Social Welfare, Kans. Assn. Blind and Visually Impaired, Mental Health Assn. Shawnee County. Avocations: gardening, reading, collecting crystal. Office: Kans Dept Social Rehab Services 2700 W 6th St Topeka KS 66606

CHASE, ROBERT HENRY, dentist; b. Evansville, Ind., Oct. 30, 1923; s. John Randall and Hilda Frances (Moutoux) C.; m. Geraldine Campbell, May 28, 1945 (dec. 1970); m. Betty Krause, Feb. 19, 1972; 5 children, 9 stepchildren. DDS, U. Detroit, 1947. Gen. practice dentistry Traverse City, Mich., 1947—; mem. Mich. State Bd. Dental Examiners, 1971-78. Contbr. articles to profl. jours.; also author articles on civic affairs and social justice. Mayor Traverse City, 1963-64; trustee Northwestern Mich. Coll., Traverse City, 1980. Served with USN, 1951-53. Fellow Internat. Coll. Dentists, Acad. Gen. Dentistry, Am. Coll. Dentists; mem. ADA, Mich. Dental Assn. (ho. of dels.), Pierre Fouchard Acad. (hon.). Republican. Roman Catholic. Lodges: Kiwanis, KC. Avocations: writing, skiing, golfing, scuba diving. Home: 757 Wilson Rd Traverse City MI 49684 Office: 876 E Front St Traverse City MI 49684

CHASE, ROCHELLE ANN, advertising agency executive; b. Detroit, Sept. 3, 1961; d. Roger Henry and Patricia Ann (Badaczewski) Robichaud; m. Timothy Mark Chase, Aug. 27, 1983. BBA, Cen. Mich. U., 1983; postgrad., Mich. State U., 1985—. Adminstrv. asst. Denham & Co., Troy, Mich., 1983-84, traffic coordinator, 1984-85, mgr. prodn. and media services, 1985-86, account exec., 1986-87; project mgr. Maritz Communications, Detroit, 1987—; cons. Wolpac, Roseville, Mich., 1986—, Wolverine Products, Roseville, 1986—. Mem. Nat. Assn. Female Execs. Republican. Lutheran. Clubs: Adcraft Club of Detroit, Advt. Prodn. Club of Detroit, Women's Advt. Club of Detroit. Office: Maritz Communications 3031 E Grand Blvd #515 Detroit MI 48202

CHASTAIN, CLAUD BLANKENHORN, educator; b. Stamford, Tex., Oct. 12, 1945; s. Claud Harrison and Jean Ida (Blankenhorn) C.; B.S., U. Mo., 1967, D.V.M., 1969; M.S., Iowa State U., 1972; m. Joyce Busche, June 25, 1977; children—Andrea Lee, Danielle Renee. Instr. public health Taiwan Nat. U., 1971-72; instr. Coll. Vet. Medicine, Iowa State U., 1972-75; asst. prof. La. State U., 1975-76; asst. prof. vet. clin. scis. Iowa State U., 1976-77, assoc. prof., 1977-81, prof., 1981-82; assoc. prof., 1982-86, instructional leader of medicine block Coll. Vet. Medicine, U. Mo., Columbia, 1982-86; prof., 1986—; dir. Small Animal Teaching Hosp. U. Mo., 1986—. Served to capt. USAF, 1969-71. Author: Clinical Endocrinology of Companion Animals, 1986. Mem. Am. Vet. Med. Assn., Am. Acad. Vet. Dermatologists, Am. Assn. Vet. Clinicians, Am. Animal Hosp. Assn., Am. Coll. Vet. Internal Medicine, Nat. Woodcarvers Assn., Nat. Wildlife Fedn., Phi Zeta. Methodist. Office: U Mo Columbia MO 65211

CHATO, JOHN CLARK, mechanical engineering educator; b. Budapest, Hungary, Dec. 28, 1929; s. Joseph Alexander and Elsie (Wasserman) C.; m. Elizabeth Janet Owens, Aug. 1954; children: Christine B., David J., Susan E. ME, U. Cin., 1954; MS, U. Ill., 1955; PhD, MIT, 1960. Co-op sutdent trainee Frigidaire div. GMC, Dayton, Ohio, 1950-54; grad. fellow U. Ill., Urbana, 1954-55; grad. fellow, inst. MIT, Cambridge, 1955-58, asst. prof., 1958-64; assoc. prof. U. Ill., Urbana, 1964-69, prof., 1969—; cons. Industry and Govt., 1958—; dir., founder Biomed. Engrng. Systems Team, Urbana, Ill, 1974-78; assoc. editor Jour. Biomech. Engrng., 1976-82. Patentee in field; contbr. articles to profl. jours., chpts. to books. Elder, trustee 1st Presbyn Ch., Urbana, 1976-78, 82-85; exec. bd. mem. Univ. YMCA, Champaign, Ill., 1976-78, 87—; com. mem. Boy Scout Troop 6, Urbana, 1984—, Urbana Planning Commn., 1973-78; Urbana Park Dist. Adv. com., 1981-84; 2d. v.p. Champaign County Izaak Walton League, 1986, 1st v.p., 1987. Named Disting. Engrng. Alumnus, U. Cin., 1972. Fellow ASME (Charles Russ Richards Meml. award 1978); mem. ASHRAE, IEEE, Am. Soc. Engrng. Education, Internat. Inst. Refrigeration (assoc.). Club: Exchange. Avocations: tennis, photography, bird watching, hiking. Office: U Ill Dept Mech Indsl Engring 1206 W Green St Urbana IL 61801

CHATROOP, LOUIS CARL, data processing scientist; b. Chgo., July 15, 1951; s. Louis Carl and Nellie (Sakota) C.; m. Carol Ann Grant, Nov. 3, 1973; children: Louis, Erik. BEE, Devry Inst. Tech., 1972; M in Computer Sci., DePaul U., 1982. Computer scientist GTE Communication Systems, Northlake, Ill., 1972-86, Siemens Transmission Systems, Northlake, 1986—; instr. computer edn. DePaul U., Chgo., 1981-82; cons. in field. Created computer software (Software Innovation award, 1984). Mem. IEEE, Assn. Computing Machinery. Club: Sundowner's Ski. Avocations: dancing, roller skating, skiing, racquetball. Home: 947 Prairie Des Plaines IL 60016 Office: Siemens Transmission Systems 400 N Wolf Rd Northlake IL 60164

CHATTERTON, ROBERT TREAT, JR., reproductive endocrinology educator; b. Catskill, N.Y., Aug. 9, 1935; s. Robert Treat and Irene (Spoor) C.; m. Patricia A. Holland, June 4, 1956 (div. 1965); children—Ruth Ellen, William Matthew, James Daniel; m. Astrida J. Vanags, June 25, 1966 (div. 1977); 1 son, Derek Scott; m. Carol J. Lewis, May 24, 1985. B.S., Cornell U., 1958, Ph.D., 1963; M.S., U. Conn., 1959. Postdoctoral fellow Harvard U. Med. Sch., 1963-65; research assoc. div. oncology Inst. Steroid Research, Montefiore Hosp. and Med. Ctr., N.Y.C., 1965-70; asst. prof. U. Ill. Coll. Medicine, 1970-72, assoc. prof., 1972-79; prof. Northwestern U. Med. Sch., Chgo., 1979—; mem. sci. adv. com. AID. Contbr. numerous articles to sci. jours.; patentee ovulation detection method, oral contraceptive, method for hormone removal from body fluids. NIH grantee, 1972—. Mem. AAAS, N.Y. Acad. Scis., Am. Chem. Soc., Endocrine Soc., Soc. Gynecologic Investigation, Soc. Study Reprodn. Presbyterian (deacon). Home: 5018 W Agatite Ave Chicago IL 60630 Office: Suite 1121 333 E Superior St Chicago IL 60611

CHAUDHRY, DEWAT RAM, psychiatrist; b. Rajasthan, India, Jan. 5, 1942; s. Mallu Ram and Gomti (Siyag) C.; came to U.S., 1970, naturalized, 1978; m. Lalita Beniwal, May 12, 1967; children: Neena, Suneel. MBBS, Sardar Patel Med. Coll., Bikaner, India, 1966. Diplomate Am. Bd. Psychiatry and Neurology. Intern J.L.N. Hosp., Ajmer, India, 1966-67; resident in psychiatry VA and Provincial hosps., St. John, N.B., Can., 1968-70; intern Aultman Hosp., Canton, Ohio, 1970-71; resident in psychiatry Med. Coll. Toledo Hosp., 1971-73; fellow child psychiatry Hawthorn Center, Northville, Mich., 1973-74; child psychiatrist, coordinator children's services Comprehensive Community Mental Health Center Rock Island (Ill.) and Mercer County, 1974-80; practice medicine specializing in psychiatry, Moline, Ill., 1980—. Fellow Am. Acad. Child Psychiatry; mem. AMA, Ill. State Med. Soc., Am. Psychiat. Assn., Ill. Psychiat. Soc. Hindu. Office: 550 30th Ave Moline IL 61265

CHAWLA, JAG MOHAN, orthodontist; b. Delhi, India, Dec. 5, 1943; came to Can., 1975; s. Ramji Dass and Raj Rani (Malik) C.; m. Rita Chowdhary, Feb. 20, 1973; children: Shalini, Sumit. BS in Dental Surgery, U. Lucknow, Upper Pradesh, India, 1968, MS in Dental Surgery, 1971; diploma in Dental Pub. Health, U. Toronto, Ont., Can., 1977; cert. of speciality, Loyola U., Chgo., 1982. Lic. dentist, Ill. House surgeon Lucknow U., 1968-69, demonstrator in orthodontics, 1971-72; staff dental surgeon Indian Rys., Bombay, 1972-75; instr. orthodontics U. Okla., Oklahoma City, 1979-80; asst. prof. Loyola U. Sch. Dentistry, Maywood, Ill., 1982—, coordinator grad. orthodontic clinic, 1982—; cons. orthodontist Fed. Govt. India, Bombay, 1972-75. Mem. Am. Assn. Orthodontists, Ill. Soc. Orthodontists, Midwestern Orthodontic Soc. Hindu. Avocations: reading, golfing, cricket, community development. Home: 1 South 212 Radford Ln Villa Park IL 60181 Office: Loyola U Sch Dentistry 2160 S First Ave Maywood IL 60153

CHEEK, MALCOLM, electrical engineering consulting company executive; b. Boston, Apr. 12, 1950; s. Bruce M. and Alison M. (Western) C.; m. Stephanie A. Howard, Sept. 9, 1967; children: Malcolm A., Benjamin A. Student, U. Va., 1968-75; BSBA, SUNY, Albany, 1979; postgrad., U. Alaska, 1979-81, Webster Coll., 1982. Pub. utilities specialist USDA Rural Elec. Adminstrn., Washington, 1972-78; gen. mgr. Matanuska Electric Assn., Palmer, Alaska, 1978-81; sr. v.p., chief fin. officer The L.E. Myers Co. Group, Chgo., 1981-84; v.p. corp. devel. Burnup and Sims, Inc., Ft. Lauderdale, Fla., 1984-85; pres., chief exec. officer D. Ralph Young and Assocs., St. Louis, 1985—, also bd. dirs.; chmn. credit com. Rural Elec. Adminstrn., Washington, 1974-76, safety com. Alaska Rural Elec. Assn., Anchorage, 1979-81. Mem. Nat. Investor Relations Inst., Am. Mgmt. Assn., Nat. Assn. Over the Counter Cos. Episcopalian. Club: The Chgo. Avocations: sports, travel. Office: D Ralph Young and Assocs Inc 16301 Fontaine Rd #230 Chesterfield MO 63017

CHEFFER, ROBERT GENE, counselor; b. Kankakee, Ill., Aug. 9, 1936; s. Herman Joseph and Cecilia Marie (Dion) C.; B.S., Eastern Ill. U., 1958; M.Ed., Chgo. State U., 1962; m. Patricia Paris, June 25, 1960; children—Christian, Scott. Tchr., Oak Lawn (Ill.) Community High Sch., 1958-70; counselor Maine Twp. High Sch., Park Ridge, Ill., 1970—, Monacep Alt. High Sch. Program, 1976—. Named Outstanding Secondary Educator, 1973. Mem. Am. Personnel and Guidance Assn., Nat. Vocat. Guidance Assn., Am. Sch. Counselors Assn., Ill. Guidance and Personnel Assn. (pres. 1978-79, pres. N.W. Suburban chpt. 1974-75), Ill. Vocat. Guidance Assn. (pres. 1974-75), Ill. Guidance and Personnel Assn., NEA, Ill. Edn. Assn., Ill. Assn. Adult and Continuing Edn. Counselors, Eastern Ill. U. Alumni Assn., Chgo. State U. Alumni Assn., Pupil Personnel Service Consortium. Home: 153 Chandler St Elmhurst IL 60126 Office: 1111 Dee Rd Park Ridge IL 60068

CHEHVAL, MICHAEL JOHN, surgeon; b. Racine, Wis., June 30, 1941; s. Michael K. and Iva Alma (Makovsky) C.; m. Marijane S. Jakaitis, Sept. 2, 1967; children—Kelley, Michael, Benjamin, Vincent. B.S., Northeast Mo. State U., 1963; M.D., St. Louis U., 1967. Diplomate Am. Bd. Urology. Intern St. Louis U. Hosp., 1967-68; resident U. Iowa Hosps., Iowa City, 1970-75; fellow Am. Cancer Soc., 1973-74; assoc. clin. prof. urology St. Louis U. Sch. Medicine, 1985—; chmn. Div. Urology, St. John's Mercy Med. Ctr., St. Louis, 1983—; sec. med. staff Cardinal Glennon Hosp. for Children, St. Louis, 1985-86; pres. Central Eastern Mo. Peer Rev. Orgn., St. Louis, 1984-86; chmn. med. adv. com. Vis. Nurses St. Louis, 1984-86; staff St. John's Hosp., St. Louis U. Hosp., St. Mary's Health Ctr. Contbr. articles to med. publs. Served with USN, 1968-70. Mem. ACS, Am. Urologic Assn., Soc. Pediatric Urology, AMA, Mo. State Med. Assn., Am. Fertility Soc., St. Louis Med. Soc., St. Louis Urol. Soc. (pres. 1986—), St. Louis Surg. Soc. Lutheran. Home: 1260 Glenvista Pl Saint Louis MO 63122 Office: Michael J Chehval Inc 621 S New Ballas Rd Saint Louis MO 63141

CHELBERG, BRUCE STANLEY, holding company executive; b. Chgo., Aug. 14, 1934; s. Stanley Andrew and Josephine Marie (Mohn) C.; children—Stephen E., David M., Kimberly Anne. B.S. in Commerce, U. Ill., 1956, LL.B., 1958. Bar: Ill. 1958. Atty. Trans Union Corp., Chgo., 1958-64, asst. gen. counsel, 1964-68; pres. Getz Corp., San Francisco, 1968-71; v.p. Trans Union Corp., Chgo., 1971-78, pres., chief operating officer, 1978-81; sr. v.p. IC Industries, Inc., Chgo., 1982-85, exec. v.p., 1985—; Bd. dirs. Exec. Council on Fgn. Diplomats, N.Y.C., 1982—, Chgo. Crime Commn., 1983—, Arlington Heights Pub. Sch Dist 25, Ill., 1974-83; mem. Internat. Exec. Service Corps, Stamford, Conn., 1980—. Mem. ABA, Ill. State Bar Assn. Clubs: Chicago, Metropolitan (Chgo.); World Trade (San Francisco).

CHELNOV, MICHAEL, architect; b. Berlin, Germany, Sept. 13, 1947; s. Anatole and Jean Clark (Potter) C. BA, Yale U., 1970; MArch, U. Calif., Berkeley, 1974. Lic. architect, Iowa. Designer Harry Weese & Assocs., Washington, 1975-77, World Plan Exec. Council, Kansas City, Mo., 1977-81, Interactive Design Corp., Palm Springs, Calif., 1982; pvt. practice architecture Fairfield, Iowa, 1982—. Mem. AIA. Home: 200 W Lowe St Fairfield IA 52556 Office: 200 W Lowe Fairfield IA 52556

CHEN, JOHN TSAN-HSIANG, engineering technology educator; b. Fuchou, Fukien, China, Feb. 11, 1937; came to U.S., 1964; s. Tze-Hong and Pao-Kaun (Liu) C.; m. Yu-Eng Huang, Jan. 6, 1957 (dec. Feb. 1986); children—James P.C., Susan J.L.; m. Ju-Jung Lu, June 1986. BEd, Nat. Taiwan Normal U., 1961; postgrad. U. Ill., 1968; MS in Indsl. Edn., U. Wis.-Stout, 1965; MS in Mech. Engrng., Marquette U., 1970; PhD, U. Mo., 1973. Cert. mfg. engr. Instr., Nat. Taiwan Normal U., Taipei, 1961-62, 63-64, Gateway Tech. Inst., Racine, Wis., 1977-78, 65-76; chmn. mech. engrng. tech. Nat. Taiwan Inst. Tech., Taipei, 1976-77; assoc. prof. Rochester Inst. Tech., N.Y., 1978-81; chmn. tech. dept. Pittsburg State U., Kans., 1981-84, asst. to pres., coordinator grad. studies, 1984—; Regional VII chmn. Mech. Tech. in Engrng. Dept. Heads Com. cons. Westinghouse Corp., 1983, others. Contbr. articles to sci. publs. Chinese Student Assn., Pittsburg, 1981—. Scholar, Chinese Buddhist Assn., 1959; fellow Fukiense Assn., 1960. Mem. ASME, Am. Soc. Engrng. Edn., Soc. Mfg. Engrs., Am. Soc. Metals, Phi Delta Kappa. Avocations: fishing; table tennis. Office: Pittsburg State U Pittsburg KS 66762

CHEN, MIN SHUNG, radiologist; b. Tsinchu, Taiwan, Rep. of China, Oct. 2, 1942; came to U.S., 1973; s. Ming Liang and Dai (Naimei) C.; m. Mary Bihchu Lin, Jan. 5, 1972; children: Betty, Thomas. MD, Taipei Med. Sch., 1970. Diplomate Am. Bd. Diagnostic Radiology. Intern St. Louis City Hosp., 1973-74; resident in diagnostic radiology Meth. Hosp., Indpls., 1974-77; dir. radiology Fairbury (Ill.) Hosp., 1977—, Gibson City (Ill.) Hosp., 1981—. Mem. AMA. Home: 28 Timber Ridge Dr Fairbury IL 61739 Office: Fairbury Hosp 519 S 5th St Fairbury IL 61739

CHEN, MING-KONG, physician; b. Sha-Lu, Taiwan, Apr. 20, 1942; came to U.S., 1971; s. Wu-Chang and Chin-Hua (Lee) C.; m. Mei-Li Lin, May 19, 1973; children: Judy Lynn, Emily Ruth, Carolyn Beth. Student premed., Nat. Taiwan U., Taipei, 1963, MD, 1968. Diplomate Am. Bd. Ob-Gyn. Resident in ob-gyn Nat. Taiwan U. Hosp., Taipei, 1969-71; intern Bklyn.-Cumberland Med. Ctr., 1971-72, resident in ob-gyn, 1972-75; attending physician Man (W.Va.) Appalachian Regional Hosp., 1975-76; attending physician Med. Ctr. Hosp., Chillicothe, Ohio, 1976—, chief dept. ob-gyn, 1983, 87; practice medicine specializing in ob-gyn Chillicoth, Ohio, 1976—. Served to lt. Taiwanese Army, 1968-69. Beta Kapa scholar Nat. Taiwan U., 1963. Fellow Am. Coll. Ob-Gyn; mem. Ohio State Med. Assn., Ross County Med. Soc. (censor 1982-84). Office: Ctr Ob-Gyn Assocs Inc PO Box 969 Station A Chillicothe OH 45601

CHEN, PETER FU MING, surgeon; b. Medan, Indonesia, Dec. 3, 1941; s. Ah Sok and Oei Tan; came to U.S., 1968, naturalized, 1977; M.D., Nat. Def. Med. Center, Taiwan, 1968; m. Shueh-Yen Tien, Apr. 9, 1968; children—Vivian, Calvin. Intern, Barberton (Ohio) Citizens Hosp., 1968; resident in surgery Fairview (Ohio) Gen. Hosp., 1969-73; practice medicine specializing in surgery, Mantua, Ohio; staff Robinson Meml. Hosp., Ravenna, Ohio; clin. asst. prof. surgery Neucom (Ohio) U. Recipient Scholar award Chinese Govt., 1968. Diplomate Am. Bd. Surgery. Fellow A.C.S.; mem. Ohio Med. Assn., Cleve. Surg. Soc., Portage County Med. Soc. Baptist. Home: 4692 Streeter Rd Mantua OH 44255 Office: Portage Surgical Assocs 3973 Loomis Pkwy Ravenna OH 44266

CHEN, SHAU-TSYH, architect; b. Canton, Republic of China, May 16, 1936; came to U.S., 1968; s. Shie-Ling and Cheng-May (Ho) C.; m. Yeong-Fu Chu, Apr. 1, 1967; 1 child, Peng Chen. BSE, Nat. Cheng-Kung U., Republic of China, 1960; MA in Arch and Urban Design, U. Ill., 1969. Asst. prof. Cheng-Kung U., Tainan, Republic of China, 1961-62; from designer to project mgr. various offices, Taipei, Republic of China, 1963-66; supr. project section Air Asia, Tainan, 1966-68; from designer to sr. staff BGA, Chgo., 1969-75; pvt. practice architecture Chgo., 1976-86; prin. architect SCS Assoc., Chgo., 1984-86; ptnr. C.C.H.P. Internat., Chgo., 1985-86; pres. G.C. Internat., Chgo., 1985-86. Precinct capt. New Trier Rep. Organization, Kenilworth, Ill., 1976-86. Recipient Outstanding Service award chmn.'s adv. bd. Am. Security Council, 1982. Fellow Ill. Soc. Architects (sec. 1980-84, v.p. 1985-86, Outstanding Service award 1986); mem. AIA, Ill.-Chinese-Am. C. of C. (exec. v.p. 1985-86), U. Ill. Alumni Assn. (life), Nat. Cheng-Kung U. Alumni Assn. (exec. v.p. 1986). Avocations: painting, photography, electronics, economics, carpentry. Home: 809 Le Claire Ave Wilmette IL 60091 Office: S T Chen Assoc 162 N State St Suite 815 Chicago IL 60601

CHEN, SHOEI-SHENG, engineer; b. Taiwan, Jan. 26, 1940; s. Yung-cheng and A-shu (Fang) C.; m. Ruth C. Lee, June 28, 1969; children: Lyrice, Lisa, Steve. B.S., Nat. Taiwan U., 1963; M.S., Princeton U., 1966, M.A., 1967, Ph.D., 1968. Research asst. Princeton U., 1965-68; asst. mech. engr. Argonne (Ill.) Nat. Lab., 1968-71, mech. engr., 1971-80, sr. mech. engr., 1980—; cons. to Internat. Atomic Energy Agy. to assist developing countries in research and devel. of nuclear reactor systems components, 1977, 79, 80; cons. NASA, NRC, Rockwell Internat., others. Author: Flow-Induced Vibration of Circular Cylindrical Structures; contbr. articles to profl. jours. Recipient Disting. Performance award U. Chgo., 1986. Fellow ASME (chmn. tech. subcom. on fluid/structure interactions, pressure vessel and pipings div.); mem. Am. Acad. Mechanics, Accoustical Soc. Am., Sigma Xi. Home: 6420 Waterford Ct Willowbrook IL 60521 Office: 9700 S Cass Ave Argonne IL 60439

CHEN, WEN FU, otolaryngologist; b. Taiwan, China, Apr. 25, 1942; s. Wainan and Wangchien C.; came to U.S., 1969, naturalized, 1977; M.D., Kaohsiung Med. Coll., Taiwan, 1968; m. Huiying Wu, Sept. 13, 1973; children—David W., Jeffrey W., Justin W. Intern, Augustana Hosp., Chgo., 1969-70; resident in surgery VA Hosp., Dayton, Ohio, 1970-72; resident in otolaryngology Homer Phillip Hosp., St. Louis, 1972-75; asst. chief otolaryngology VA Hosp., Kansas City, Mo., 1975-77; mem. staff Kansas Med. Center, Kansas City, 1975-77; practice medicine specializing in otolaryngology, Chillicothe, Ohio, 1977—. Diplomate Am. Bd. Otolaryngology. Fellow Am. Acad. Otolaryngology, Am. Cosmetic Surgery; mem. Am. Soc. Liposuction Surgery, Ohio State Med. Assn. Home: 22 Oakwood Dr Chillicothe OH 45601 Office: 3 Medical Center Dr Chillicothe OH 45601

CHEN, WILLIAM HOK-NIN, dentist; b. Shanghai, People's Republic of China, July 17, 1950; s. Ling Pao and Shu Yung (Ning) C.; m. Alison Po-Wai Cheng, 1976; children: Audrey Y., Bianca Y. BA in Biology, Washington U., St. Louis, 1973; DMD, Washington U., 1976. Pres. Chen's Assocs., Ltd., Granite City, Ill., 1979—; provisional staff St. Elizabeth's Hosp., Granite City, 1980-81, active staff, 1982—. Fund raiser, dir. dental section Granite City United Way, 1986. Fellow Acad. Gen. Dentistry; mem. ADA, Acad. Gen. Dentistry, Am. Equilibration Soc., Striaghtwire Found. Technique Soc. Lodge: Rotary. Avocations: tennis, soccer, chinese calligraphy. Office: 4168 Nameoki Rd Granite City IL 62040

CHENEVERT, DENISE LENORE, sales executive; b. Syracuse, N.Y., Aug. 21, 1955; d. Wilson Paul and Dorothy Evelyn (Brown) C.; m. Paul A. Gryzwa, Feb. 14, 1981. BS in Edn. with honors, U. Wis., 1976, MBA, 1986. Tchr. Brown Deer (Wis.) Schs., 1977-81; mng. dir. Posner Gallery, Milw., 1981-84; gen. mgr. CAD Systems of Wis., Milw., 1984—; mem. Autodesk Dealer Adv. Council, 1984—. Mem. editorial bd. CADalyst, 1984—. Vol. Pub. TV, Milw., 1977—, Milw. Repertory Theater, 1980. Mem. Autocad User's Group, Phi Kappa Phi. Home: 2756 N 73d St Wauwatosa WI 53210 Office: CAD Systems Wis Inc 150 N Sunnyslope Brookfield WI 53005

CHENG, CHEN CHANG, book salesman; b. Yanshan, Jiangxi, China, Oct. 1, 1926; came to U.S., 1957; s. Yi Wu and Tsu Shou (Hou) C.; m. Jane Kan, Oct. 5, 1958. Student Chung Cheng U., Nanchang, China, 1946-49; B.A., Taiwan U., Taipei, 1954-56; Postgrad. U. Mo., 1957; M.A., DePaul U., 1964. Reporter Chung Hwa Daily News, Tainan, Taiwan, 1950-55; writer China Times, Taipei, Taiwan, 1955-57; editor San Min Daily, Chgo., 1958-65; chmn. bus. dept. Internat. Sch., Bangkok, Thailand, 1965-71; pres., owner Peking Book House, Evanston, Ill., 1971—; acctg. instr. YMCA Coll., Chgo., 1960-61; tchr. social studies Immaculate Heart of Mary High Sch. for Girls, Westchester, Ill., 1964-65; Chinese instr. U. Maryland, Bangkok br., 1969-71. Author: Ten Years Overseas, 1967; A Chinese View of America, 1984; My Hometown and I, 1985. Mem. charter U.S.-China Friendship Assn., Chgo., 1972, Chinese-Am. Assn., Chgo., 1975. Served to capt. Army of China, 1944-46. Mem. Small Businessmen Assn., Evanston C. of C. Avocations: singing; writing; lecturing. Home: 2001 Sherman Ave Evanston IL 60201 Office: Peking Book House 1520 Sherman Ave Evanston IL 60201

CHENG, CHU YUAN, educator; b. Kwangtung Province, China, Apr. 8, 1927; came to U.S., 1959, naturalized, 1964; s. Hung Shan and Shu Chen (Yang) C.; B.A. in Econs., Nat. Chengchi U., Nanking, China, 1947; M.A., Georgetown U., Washington, 1962, Ph.D., 1964; m. Alice Hua Liang, Aug. 15, 1964; children—Anita Tung I, Andrew Y.S. Research prof. Seton Hall U., 1960-64; vis. prof. George Washington U., Washington, 1963; sr. research economist U. Mich., Ann Arbor, 1964-69; assoc. prof. Lawrence U., Appleton, Wis., 1970-71; assoc. prof. econs., chmn. Asian studies com. Ball State U., Muncie, Ind., 1971-73, prof. econs., 1974—; cons. NSF, Washington, 1964—. Bd. dirs., pres. Dr. Sun Yat-sen Inst., Chgo., 1978—. Grantee, NSF, 1960-64, Social Sci. Research Council, 1965-67, 74; recipient Outstanding Research award Ball State U., 1976; Outstanding Educator in Econs., Ball State U., 1981-82. Mem. Am. Econ. Assn., Assn. Asian Studies, Assn. Comparative Econ. Studies, Am. Acad. Polit. and Social Sci., Assn. Chinese Social Scientists in N.Am. (bd. dirs. 1986—), Am. Assn. Chinese Studies, Chinese Acad. and Profl. Assn. Mid-Am. (pres. 1983-84), Ind. Acad. Social Sci., Omicron Delta Epsilon. Author: Scientific and Engineering Manpower in Communist China, 1966; The Machine-Building Industry in Communist China, 1971; China's Petroleum Industry: Output Growth and Export Potential, 1976; China's Economic Development: Growth and Structural Change, 1981; The Demand and Supply of Primary Energy in Mainland China, 1984; Taiwan as a Model for China's Modernization, 1986; Sun Yat-sen's Doctrine in Modern World, 1987; mem. adv. com. Chinese Econ. Studies Quar., 1966—. Home: 1211 Greenbriar Rd Muncie IN 47304 Office: Room 123 Coll Bus Ball State U Muncie IN 47306

CHENG, ELISE, otolaryngolgist; b. Chgo., May 11, 1956; d. Herbert S.Y. and Lily (Hsuing) Cheng. BA, Northwestern U., 1977; MD, Rush Med. Coll., 1981. Intern dept. surgery U. Ill. Hosps., Chgo., 1981-82; from resident to chief resident dept. otolaryngology head and neck surgery U. Ill. Eye and Ear Infirmary, Chgo., 1982-87; practice medicine specializing in otolaryngoloy Knoxville, Tenn., 1987—; coordinator, instr. soft tissue course workshop dept. otolaryngology head and neck surgery U. Ill., Chgo., 1985; lectr. in field. Contbr. articles to profl. jours. Grantee Am. Hearing Research Found., 1985, Hoechst-Roussel Pharmaceuticals, 1985-86. Mem. AMA, Ill. State Med. Soc., Chgo. Med. Soc., Am. Acad. Otolaryngology Head and Neck Surgery, Am. Acad. Facial Plastic and Reconstructive Surgery, Rush Med. Coll. Alumni Assn. (class agt. 1977—), Alpha Chi Omega, Alpha Omega Alpha (pres. 1980-81). Avocation: classical pianist.

CHENG, FRANCIS SHYUE-TSO, physician; b. Kun-Ming, Yunan, China, July 7, 1943; came to U.S., 1971, naturalized, 1978; s. Wen Lo and Jane (Young) C.; m. Sylvia Y. Lam, May 10, 1973; 1 child, Michael. M.D., Kaohsiung Med. Coll., Taiwan, 1971. Diplomate Am. Bd. Internal Medicine, Am. Bd. Cardiovascular Diseases. Rotating intern Vets. Gen. Hosp., Taipei, Taiwan, 1970-71; straight med. intern U. Ill. Hosp., Chgo., 1971-72, resident, 1972-74; asst. in medicine U. Ill. Sch. Medicine, Chgo., 1972-74; fellow in cardiology Michael Reese Hosp. and Med. Ctr., 1974-75, Rush Presbyn.-St. Luke's Hosp., Chgo., 1975-76; instr. Rush Med. Sch., Chgo., 1975-76; med. dir. Cardiac Rehab. Unit, Alexian Bros. Med. Ctr., Elk Grove Village, Ill., 1978—, audit com. chmn. dept. internal medicine, 1981—. Fellow Am. Coll. Cardiology; mem. ACP, Am. Heart Assn., AMA, Cinese-Am. Health Profls. Assn. (pres. 1984). Republican. Club: Meadow. Avocation: computing. Office: 1000 Grand Canyon Pkwy Hoffman Estates IL 60194

CHENG, KUANG LU, chemist; b. Yangchow, China, Sept. 14, 1919; came to U.S., 1947, naturalized, 1955; s. Fong Wu and Yi Ming (Chiang) C.; children: Meiling, Chiling, Hans Christian. Ph.D., U. Ill., 1951. Microchemist Comml. Solvents Corp., Terre Haute, Ind., 1952-53; instr. U. Conn., Storrs, 1953-55; engr. Westinghouse Electric Corp., Pitts., 1955-57; assoc. dir. research metals div. Kelsey Hayes Co., New Hartford, N.Y., 1957-59; mem. tech. staff RCA Labs., Princeton, N.J., 1959-66; prof. chemistry U. Mo., Kansas City, 1966—. Recipient Achievement award RCA, 1963; N.T. Veatch award for disting. research and creative activity U. Mo., Kansas City, 1979; cert. of recognition U.S. office of Naval Research, 1979; cert. of recognition Coll. Engring., Tex. A&M U., 1981; Bd. Trustees fellow U. Kansas City, 1984. Fellow AAAS, Chem. Soc. London; mem. Am. Chem. Soc., Electrochem. Soc., Soc. Applied Spectroscopy, Am. Inst. Physics. Home: 34 E 56th Terr Kansas City MO 64113 Office: Dept Chemistry U Mo Kansas City MO 64110

CHENG, PAUL HUNG-CHIAO, civil engineer; b. China, Dec. 1, 1930; s. Yen-Teh and Shu-Yin (Tsou) C.; came to U.S., 1958, naturalized, 1973; B.S. in Civil Engring., Nat. Taiwan U., 1951; M.S. in Civil Engring., U. Va., 1961; m. Lucial Jen Chen, Aug. 1, 1964; children—Maria, Elizabeth, Deborah, Samuel. Structural engr. Swift & Co., Chgo., 1963-67; sr. structural designer P & W Engring., Inc., Chgo., 1967; sr. structural engr. A. Epstein & Son, Inc., Chgo., 1967-68; staff engr. Interlake, Inc., Chgo., 1968-71, supervising engr., 1971-73, chief structural engr., 1973-80, product engring. mgr., 1980-82, CAD/CAM devel. mgr., 1982-84; CAD/CAM System mgr. Continental Can Co., 1984—. Registered structural engr., Ill.; registered profl. civil engr., Calif. Mem. ASCE, Soc. Mfg. Engrs. (Computer and Automated Systems Assn.), Am. Mgmt. Assn. Home: 1869 Allen Ln Saint Charles IL 60174 Office: Continental Can Co 1700 Harvester Rd West Chicago IL 60185

CHENG, SYLVIA LAM, physician; b. Chung King, China, Aug. 15, 1946; d. Lam Horng-Yip and Yung Wai-Cheng; m. Francis Cheng, Oct. 5, 1973; 1 son, Michael. MD, Kaohsiung Med. Coll., Taiwan, 1972. Cert. Am. Bd. Quality Assurance and Utilization Rev. Physicians. Resident in pediatrics Mercy Hosp. and Med. Ctr., Chgo., 1972-75; practice medicine specializing in pediatrics, Hoffman Estates, Ill., 1975—. Fellow Am. Coll. Utilization Rev. Physicians; mem. AMA, Chgo. Med. Assn., Am. Med. Women's Assn., Orgn. Chinese Am. (hon.). Office: 1000 Grand Canyon Pkwy Hoffman Estates IL 60194

CHENG, YUK-BUN DEREK, electrical engineer; b. Swatow, Kwangtung, China, Aug. 7, 1950; s. Leung-Wing and Wai-Shan (Ma) C.; m. Susanna Wai-Hing Yuen, Aug. 6, 1983. Student E. Tex. State U., 1970-71; B.S.E.E., W.Va. Inst. Tech., 1974; M.S.E.E., W.Va. U., 1976. Grad. research asst. dept. elec. engring. W.Va. U., Morgantown, 1974-77; antenna research engr. Andrew Corp., Orland Park, Ill., 1977-82, sr. antenna research engr., 1982-84, sect. leader antenna analysis, 1984—. Recipient William E. Jackson award Radio Tech. Commn. for Aeronautics, 1976. Mem. IEEE, IEEE Antennas and Propagation Soc., IEEE Microwave Theory Tech. Soc. (sec., treas.), IEEE Chgo. joint chpt. Antennas and Propagation Soc. and Microwave Theory and Techniques Soc. (sec.-treas. 1984-85, chmn. 1985-86), Sigma Xi, Eta Kappa Nu, Tau Beta Pi, Phi Kappa Phi. Mem. Chinese Christian Union Ch. Contbr. articles to profl. jours.; patentee in field. Home: 13905 Cherokee Trail Lockport IL 60441 Office: 10500 W 153d St Orland Park IL 60462

CHENOWETH, ARLENE JOYCE, construction company executive; b. Cass City, Mich., Apr. 1, 1941; d. Robert Melvin and Geraldine Thelma (Bell) Milner; grad. Olivet Nazarene U., Kankakee, Ill., 1963; postgrad. U. Mich., 1963-65; m. Robert R. Chenoweth, Sept. 1, 1962; children—Timothy, Eric, Gregg. Tchr. bus. edn. Swartz Creek (Mich.) Sr. High Sch., 1963-67, Flushing (Mich.) Sr. High Sch., 1969-74; v.p. A & B Enterprises, Fenton, Mich., 1974—; co-owner, exec. v.p. Chenoweth Constrn. Co., Inc., Fenton, 1974—; mem. alumni bd. Olivet Nazarene U., 1983—; lectr. and freelance writer in field. Recipient O Alumni award Olivet Nazarene U., 1986. Founder Fenton Businesswomen's Breakfast Fellowship; dir. Eastern Mich. Dist., Women's Ministries, 1983-86. Mem. Am. Mgmt. Assn., Nat. Assn. Female Execs., Fenton Area Bus. and Profl. Women's Club (charter mem., treas. 1979). Nazarene. Clubs: University (Flint, Mich.); Spring Meadows Country. Home: 12050 White Lake Rd Fenton MI 48430 Office: Chenoweth Constrn Co Inc 265 N Alloy Dr Fenton MI 48430

CHENOWETH, ROBERT DUANE, machinery company executive; b. Bedford, Ind., Oct. 10, 1923; s. Henry Carl and Elizabeth Jane (Barrett) C.; engring. student Internat. Corr. Schs., 1946-48; grad. Approved Supply Pastor's Sch., Garrett Theol. Sch., 1959; B.A., Miami U., 1962, postgrad., 1962-64; m. Shirley Ellen Woods, Sept. 17, 1949; children—Steven Carl, Mark Duane, Paula Jane. Cons. engr. J.E. Novotny Co., Dayton, Ohio, 1955-63; ordained elder United Methodist Ch., 1960, ordained to ministry, 1958; pastor Brookville and Miamitown (Ohio) Meth. Chs., 1958-67; chief tool engr. OPW div. Dover Corp., Cin., 1963-64; chief mfg. engr., mgr. mfg. Campbell-Hausfeld Co., Harrison, Ohio, 1964-68; plant mgr. Sheffer Corp., Blue Ash, Ohio, 1968—. Cons. prodn. engring. Helipebs, Ltd., County of Gloucester (Eng.), 1972. Sec., Brookville Planning Com., 1960-63; mem. adv. com. Great Oaks Joint Vocat. Sch., Warren County (Ohio) Joint Vocat. Sch.; mem. adv. council Miami U. Sch. Applied Sci.; mem. Industry Council, Greater Cin. C. of C.; sec. bd. trustees Thomas Meml. Med. Center, Brookville. Recipient Service award City of Brookville, 1963. Mem. Soc. Mfg. Engrs. (past chmn. Dayton chpt., cert. mfg. engr.), Internat. Platform Assn. Lodge: Optimists. Home: 1759 Maplewood Dr Lebanon OH 45036 Office: 6990 Cornell Rd Blue Ash OH 45242

CHEON, SUNG AI, psychiatrist; b. Seoul, Republic of Korea, Jan. 21, 1950; came to U.S., Apr. 27, 1976; d. Sung B. and Sook (Myung) Kang; m. Byung O. Cheon, Apr. 10, 1976; children: Eric, James. MD, Ewha Woman's U., Seoul, Republic of Korea, 1975. Resident in psychiatry Mount Sinai Hosp., Chgo., 1977-80, Boston U. Hosp., 1980-81; assoc. staff psychiatrist Arbour Hosp., Jamaica Plains, Mass., 1981-82; staff psychiatrist VA Med. Ctr., North Chicago, Ill., 1983—. Recipient Abbie Norman Prince merit award Mt. Sinai Hosp., 1980. Mem. Am. Psychiat. Assn., Ill. Psychiat. Soc. Office: VA Med Ctr North Chicago IL 60064

CHERENZIA, BRADLEY JAMES, radiologist; b. Niagara Falls, N.Y., Aug. 22, 1931; s. Peter and Myrna (Bradley) C.; m. Paula Joyce, Mar. 9, 1978; children: Kevin, Lori, David, Robert, Lisa. BS in Pharmacy cum laude, U. Buffalo, 1953; MD, SUNY Upstate Med. Ctr., Syracuse, 1957. Cert. Am. Bd. Radiology, Am. Bd. Nuclear Medicine. Intern SUNY Upstate Med. Ctr. Hosps., Syracuse, 1957-58; resident in radiology Wayne State U. Sch. Medicine Hosps., Detroit, 1960-63; practice medicine specializing in radiology Drs. Otto, Kurtzman & Assocs., Warren, Mich., 1965—; sr. attending radiologist Detroit-Macomb Hosp. Corp. Served to capt. M.C., U.S. Army, 1958-60. Mem. AMA, Wayne County Med. Soc. (mem. del. bd.), Mich. State Med. Soc., Radiol. Soc. N.Am., Mich. Radiol. Soc., Am. Coll. Radiology, Soc. Nuclear Medicine. Republican. Roman Catholic. Avocations: photography, art, music, golfing, tennis.

CHERF, FRANK MICHAEL, accounting company executive; b. Battle Creek, Mich., Nov. 15, 1925; s. Martin and Nellie Josephine (Horowitz) C.; married, 1950; children: Randon Sue Pintens, Jody Anne Comstock, John Michael. Student, St. Louis U., 1943-44, 46-47; diploma in acctg., Argubright Coll., Battle Creek, Mich., 1949. CPA, Mich. Controller Coll. Drug Stores, Inc., East Lansing, Mich., 1950-51; acct. Miller, Bailey, Smith & Dale, Lansing, Mich., 1951-56, ptnr., 1956-69; mng. ptnr. KMG Main Hurdman, Lansing, Mich., 1969-87, Peat Marwick Main & Co., Lansing, Mich., 1987—. Bd. dirs. Lansing Community Coll. Found., 1984—. Served as sgt. AUS, 1944-46, ETO. Mem. Am. Inst. CPA's, Nat. Assn. Accts., Mich. Assn. CPA's (chpt. chmn. 1959-60, bd. dirs. 1967-70). Republican. Roman Catholic. Clubs: Walnut Hills Country, City, Automobile of Lansing. Lodge: Rotary. Home: 2911 Colony Dr East Lansing MI 48823 Office: Peat Marwick Main & Co Mich Nat Tower Suite 1700 Lansing MI 48933

CHERNIACK, SAUL MARK, barrister, solicitor; b. Winnipeg, Man., Can., Jan. 10, 1917; s. Joseph Arthur and Fannie Golden; m. Sybil Claire Zeal, July 10, 1938; children: Howard David, Lawrence Allan. MA, U. Chgo., 1967, LLB, U. Man., 1977; PhD, U. N.C., 1980. Formerly M.L.A., Minister Fin., Man., Minister Urban Affairs, Man., Minister for Man. Telephone System; chmn. Man. Hydro-Electric, Winnipeg; also bd. dirs.; now mem. Security Intelligence Rev. Com. Bd. dirs. Community Chest, Welfare Planning Council, Winnipeg Auditorium Commn., Winnipeg Pub. Library, Winnipeg Enterprises, Winnipeg General Hosp.; past pres. Jewish Welfare Fund Winnipeg, Peretz-Folk Sch. Parents Assn.; past nat. v.p. Can. Jewish Congress, past nat. chmn. integration and settlement com.; past sch. bd. trustee, alderman, councillor; Queen's Privy Council for Can., 1984. Served to capt. Can. Armed Forces, 1943-46. Recipient Queen's Council award Lt.-Gov.-in-Council, 1963. Mem. New Democratic Party. Jewish. Home: 333 St John's Ave, Winnipeg, MB Canada R2W 1H2 Office: Manitoba Hydro, PO Box 815, Winnipeg, MB Canada

CHERNICOFF, DAVID PAUL, osteopathic physician, educator; b. N.Y.C., Aug. 3, 1947; s. Harry and Lillian (Dobkin) C. A.B., U. Rochester, 1969; D.O., Phila. Coll. Osteo. Medicine, 1973. Rotating intern Rocky Mountain Hosp., Denver, 1973-74; resident in internal medicine Community Gen. Osteo. Hosp., Harrisburg, Pa., 1974-76; fell in hematology and med. oncology Cleve. Clinic, 1976-78; asst. prof. medicine sect. hematology-oncology Chgo. Coll. Osteo. Medicine, 1978-82, assoc. prof., 1982—; co-chmn. tumor task force Chgo. Osteo. Med. Center, 1978—, dir. clin. cancer edn., 1978—; chmn. tumor task force Olympia Fields (Ill.) Osteo. Med. Center. Trustee, mem. clin. exec. com. Ill. Cancer Council; bd. dir. Chgo. unit Am. Cancer Soc., 1981-86. Diplomate Nat. Bd. Osteo. Examiners, Am. Osteo. Bd. Internal Medicine, also in Hematology-Oncology. Mem. Am. Osteo. Assn., Am. Coll. Osteo. Internists, Am. Assn. for Cancer Edn., Ill. Assn. Osteo. Physicians and Surgeons, Eastern Coop. Oncology Group (sr. investigator), Am. Soc. Clin. Oncology. Contbr. articles to med. jours. Office: Chgo Coll Osteo Medicine 5200 S Ellis Ave Chicago IL 60615

CHERNISH, STANLEY MICHAEL, physician; b. N.Y.C., Jan. 27, 1924; s. Michael B. and Veronica (Hodon) C.; m. Lelia M. Higgins, June 19, 1949; 1 child, Dwight. B.A., U. N.C., 1945; M.D., Georgetown U., 1949. Diplomate Nat. Bd. Med. Examiners, Am. Bd. Internal Medicine. Intern Washington Gen. Hosp., 1949-51; resident Marion County Gen. Hosp., Indpls., 1953-55; clin. research div. Eli Lilly & Co., Indpls., 1954—, staff physician, 1955-63, sr. physician, 1963-74, clin. pharmacologist, 1974-85; research cons. Meth. Hosp., Indpls., 1985—; vis. staff Marion County Gen. Hosp., 1965-87; mem. staff Lilly Research Labs.; clin. assoc. prof. medicine Ind. U. Sch. Medicine, 1976-80, assoc., 1980—. Contbr. articles to profl. jours., chpts. to books. Served with USNR, 1943-45, 50-53, comdr. Res. Fellow ACP, Am. Coll. Gastroenterology, Am. Coll. Clin. Pharmacology and Therapeutics; mem. AMA (Physicians Recognition award in continuing med. edn.), Ind. Med. Soc. (mem. com. conv. arrangements, mem. subcommn. on accreditation), Marion County Med. Soc. (mem. commn. on ops. and stock ops.), Am. Pancreatic Study Group, Assn. Am. Physicians and Surgeons, Am. Fedn. Clin. Research, Am. Gastroent. Assn., Am. Soc. for Gastrointestinal Endoscopy, Sigma Xi. Office: Dept Med Research Meth Hosp 1604 N Capitol Ave Indianapolis IN 46204

CHERNISS, MICHAEL DAVID, English educator; b. Los Angeles, Apr. 7, 1940; s. Edward H. and Blanche B. (Cohen) C.; m. Christi Weidling, Jan. 10, 1986. AB, U. Calif., Berkeley, 1962, MA, 1963, PhD, 1966. Asst. prof. English U. Kans., Lawrence, 1966-70, assoc. prof., 1970-76, prof., 1976—. Author: Ingeld and Christ, 1972, Boethian Apocalypse, 1987; also articles. Mem. MLA, Medieval Acad. Am., New Chaucer Soc., Internat. Soc. Anglo-Saxonists. Office: U Kans Dept English Lawrence KS 66045

CHERRY, PETER BALLARD, electrical products corporation executive; b. Evanston, Ill., May 25, 1947; s. Walter Lorain and Virginia Ames (Ballard) C.; m. Crissy Hazard, Sept. 6, 1969; children: Serena Ames, Spencer Ballard. B.A., Yale U., 1969; M.B.A., Stanford U., 1972. Analyst Cherry Elec. Products Corp., Waukegan, Ill., 1972-74, data processing and systems mgr., 1974, treas., 1974-77; v.p. fin. and bus. devel. Cherry Elec. Products Corps., Waukegan, Ill., 1977-80; exec. v.p. Cherry Elec. Products Corp., Waukegan, Ill., 1980-82, pres., chief operating officer, 1982-86; pres., chief exec. officer Cherry Elec. Products Corp., 1986—. Trustee Lake Forest Coll., Ill., 1982—, Lake Forest Hosp., 1982—. Mem. IEEE, Computer Soc. Clubs: Economic (Chgo.); Onwentsia, Old Elm (Lake Forest). Office: Cherry Elec Products Corp 3600 Sunset Ave Waukegan IL 60087

CHERRY, ROBERT DOUGLAS, mathematics educator, consultant; b. Berwyn, Ill., Dec. 8, 1950; s. William John and Ruth (Brown) C.; m. Pamela Lee Ratkovich, Apr. 6, 1974; children: Allison, Brent. BS in Edn., No. Ill. U., 1973, student, 1974-75; student, Lewis U., 1975-76; MA, Wheaton Coll., 1977. Cert. instr., Ill. Math. instr. Sch. Dist. #70, Morton Grove, Ill., 1973-74, Sch. Dist. #54, Schaumburg, Ill., 1974-78, Sch. Dist. #200Wheaton (Ill.) Cen. High Sch., 1978—; vis. prof. Wheaton Coll., 1982—; tutor, advisor Math. Edn., 1973—. Author math. books The Riverside Publ. Co., 1986—; contbr. math. article The Mathematics Teacher, 1979. Committeeman Dupage County Rep. Party, Milton Township, Ill., 1985—; pres. SE Wheaton Homeowners Assn., 1978-81; deacon First United Presbyn. Ch., Wheaton, 1979-82, First United Meth. Ch., Glen Ellyn, Ill., 1987—. Mem. NEA, Ill. Edn. Assn., The Christian Legal Soc., No. Ill. Alumni Assn., Wheaton Coll. Alumni Assn., Ill. Jaycees, Delta Upsilon (pres. 1984—, Alumni of Yr. 1984). Republican. Club: Glen Ellyn Racquet. Avocations: profl. tennis instr., basketball, travel. Home: 27 Venetian Way Circle Wheaton IL 60187

CHERRY, WALTER LORAIN, electrical products corporation executive; b. Cedar Rapids, Iowa, Jan. 31, 1917; s. Walter Lorain and Laura Fox (White) C.; m. Virginia Ames Ballard, May 31, 1941; children: Walter Lorain, Peter B. Catherine Cherry Moore. B. Chem. Engring., Yale U., 1939. Research engr. Cherry-Burrell Corp., Chgo., 1939-42, Zenith Radio Corp., Chgo., 1946-69; co-founder Cherry-Channer Corp., Highland Park, Ill., 1949-53; founder, chmn. The Cherry Corp., Waukegan, Ill., 1953—; dir., past pres. Midwest Indsl. Mgmt. Assn., Westchester, Ill., 1969-79. Zoning bd. Village of Winnetka, (Ill.), 1959-71, village caucus, 1958-59, park bd., 1962-68, chmn., 1967-68, planning commn., 1967-68, trustee, 1970-75; assoc. Rehab. Inst., 1978—; trustee Presbyterian Home, 1980—; pres. Allendale Sch. for Boys, 1975-79, trustee, 1973—; trustee Ill. Inst. Tech., 1977—, chmn. bus. and industry devel. council, 1979-82, vice chmn. devel., 1983-87; trustee Mus. Sci and Industry. Served with U.S. Army, 1943-46. Mem. IEEE, Physics Club. Republican. Congregationalist. Clubs: Economic, Commercial, University (Chgo.). Home: 848 Tower Rd Winnetka IL 60093 Office: Cherry Elec Products Corp 3600 Sunset Ave Waukegan IL 60087

CHERTACK, MELVIN M., internist; b. Chgo., June 19, 1923; s. Nathan and Anna (Wadoplan) C.; m. Orabelle Lorraine Melberg, May 26, 1948; children—Pamela, Craig, Rhonda. B.S., U. Ill., 1944, M.D., 1946, M.S., 1948. Diplomate Am. Bd. Internal Medicine. Intern U. Ill. Hosp., Chgo., 1946-47, fellow and resident in internal medicine, 1947-50; practice medicine specializing in internal medicine Skokie, Ill., 1950—; mem. attending staff Luth. Gen. Hosp., Park Ridge, Ill.; mem. courtesty staff Rush North Shore Hosp.; clin. assoc. prof. U. Ill. Abraham Lincoln Coll. Medicine; chmn. Skokie Bd. Health. Editor: Help Yourself Series; contbr. articles to profl. jours. Served with U.S. Army, 1943-45. Recipient Research award Aaron Fox Found. for Diabetes Screening Program, 1976, recognition award for service to Skokie Health Dept., Ill. Assn. Pub. Health Adminstrn., 1981, Luth. Gen. Hosp.; cert. of merit Village of Skokie, 1982. Fellow ACP; mem. Am. Diabetes Assn. (dir. Chgo. and No. Ill. affiliate, chpt., past pres. Chgo. and No. Ill. affiliate, citation for pub. service 1982, Clinician of Yr. award No. Ill. affiliate 1983, 84, 85), Chgo. Med. Soc., Ill. Med. Soc., AMA, Chgo. Soc. Internal Medicine, Chgo. Heart Assn., Am. Heart Assn. Club: Anvil (Dundee). Home: 440 Whittier Ln Northfield IL 60093 Office: 64 Old Orchard Skokie IL 60077

CHERTOCK, SANFORD LEE, clinical psychologist; b. St. Louis, Aug. 10, 1949; s. Milton and Ann Ruth (Spiegelman) C. BA, Ohio State U., Columbus, 1971; MA, U. Mont., 1974, PhD, 1976. Registered and lic. psychologist, Ohio. Intern clinical psychology VA Hosp., Albany, N.Y., 1975-76; psychology service chief N. Ala. Regional Hosp., Decatur, 1977-78; clinical dir. N. Cen. Ala. Mental Health Ctr., Decatur, 1978-80; pediatric psychology fellow Childrens Hosp. Med. Ctr., Cin., 1980-81; asst. prof. Wilmington (Ohio) Coll., 1983-85; clinical dir. Clinton County Mental Health Ctr., Wilmington, 1982—. Named Outstanding Profl. in Human Services, Am. Acad. Human Services, 1974; recipient hon. faculty citation and stipend, U. Mo., St. Louis, 1967. Mem. Am. Psychol. Assn. Democrat. Jewish. Avocations: dog shows, piano performance (classical). Home: 6811 Fallen Oaks Dr Mason OH 45040 Office: Clinton County Mental Health Ctr 49 W Truesdell St Wilmington OH 45177

CHESEN, CATHERINE SUE, investigative consumer reporting executive; b. Lancaster, Pa., Aug. 26, 1953; d. Irwin Somberg and Doris Marion (Schimmel) C.; m. Allen Mark Morris, June 18, 1972 (div. Mar. 1977). BS, U. Nebr., 1975; BA in Speech Pathology, MA, U. Kans., Kansas City, 1978. Speech pathologist Joan Davis Sch. Spl. Edn., Kansas City, Mo., 1975-78, Rainbow Mental Health Ctr., Kansas City, 1978-79, Clinicare Home Health Care, Kansas City, 1978-79; prin. Inter-Link of Am., Leawood, Kans., 1980-86; pres. Chesen Communications Ctr., Overland Park, Kans., 1986—. Mem. Am. Bus. Women's Assn., Kansas City Multi-Family Apt. Assn., NOW. Democrat. Jewish. Avocations: reading, sports, needlework. Office: Chesen Communications Ctr Inc 9290 Bond #114 Overland Park KS 66212

CHESKI, RICHARD MICHAEL, library director; b. Canton, Ohio, Sept. 29, 1935; s. Sigmund and Henrietta (Makowski) Hiczewski; m. Mary Ella Sica, Aug. 23, 1958; children: Karen, Valerie. B.A., Kent State U., B.S. in Edn, M.A. in L.S. Asst. state librarian State Library of Ohio, Columbus, 1970-74; asst. commr. libraries Colo. State Library, Denver, 1974-76; dir. Oceanside (N.Y.) Free Library, 1976-78, State Library of Ohio, Columbus, 1978—; vis. prof. Kent State U., Denver U.; chmn. legis. com. Chief Officers State Library Agys. Chmn. Ohio Humanities Council; mem. Columbus Cable TV Adv. Commn. Recipient Disting. Alumni award Kent State U. Mem. ALA, Ohio Library Assn., Beta Phi Mu, Tau Kappa Epsilon. Office: Library Bd 65 S Front St Columbus OH 43266-0334 *

CHESLER, CAROL ANN, reading specialist; b. Newark, Feb. 9, 1938; d. Hyman J. and Rose (Klayman) Sward; m. S. Alan Chesler, Aug. 27, 1961; children: Stephen, Ian, Craig. BS, Douglass Coll., 1959; MS, No. Ill. U., 1973. Elem. tchr. Livingston (N.J.) Pub. Schs., 1959-61, Warren Twp. (N.J.) Pub. Schs., 1961-62; instr. Kishwaukee Coll., Malta, Ill., 1973—. Commr.

DeKalb (Ill.) Park Dist., 1985—. Mem. Internat. Reading Assn., LWV (bd. dirs. DeKalb chpt. 1986—). Avocations: tennis, gardening.

CHESLIN, WILLIAM DANA, maxillofacial surgeon, dentist; b. Detroit, Jan. 9, 1948; s. Sigmund John and Olgamarie (Gyzinski) C.; m. Lynne Rosenthal, Mar. 13, 1976. B.S., U. Detroit, 1970; D.D.S., 1970; M.D., Northwestern U., 1980. Diplomate Am. Bd. Oral and Maxillofacial Surgery. Intern, Northwestern Meml. Hosp., Chgo., 1975-78; resident Med. Ctr. Vt., Burlington, 1974-75; Sinai Hosp. of Detroit, 1980-81; practice medicine specializing in oral and reconstructive surgery; chmn. dept. oral and maxillofacial surgery William Beaumont Hosp., Royal Oak, Mich., 1982—. Mem. AMA, ADA, Omicron Kappa Upsilon. Avocations: scuba diving, boating. Home: 954 Canterbury Birmingham MI 48009 Office: Torgerson & Small PC 50 W Big Beaver Birmingham MI 48008

CHESNEY, GARY KENT, railroad company executive; b. Topeka, Jan. 6, 1936; s. Kent King and Regina Catherine (Seitz) C.; m. Norma Eleanor Klukos, Feb. 4, 1967; children: G. Kent II, Laura Ellen. BS in Math. and Psychology, Eastern N.Mex. U., 1961, MA in Psychology and Personnel Adminstrn., 1965; MBA, U. Chgo., 1984. Traveling car agent Santa Fe Railway, Temple, Tex., 1964-66; cost analyst Santa Fe Railway, Chgo., 1966-67, dir. personnel adminstrn., 1967-81, asst. to v.p. personnel, 1981—. mem. planning commn. Village of Homewood, Ill., 1986. Served with USN, 1954-58. Mem. Railroad Personnel Aminstrn. (exec. com. 1983—, pres. 1984-85), Am. Soc. of Personnel Adminstrs., Soc. Human Resource Profls. (v.p. membership com., bd. dirs.), Am. Compensation Assn., Am. Soc. Trng. and Devel. Roman Catholic. Lodge: K.C. Avocations: golf, jazz and classical music, microcomputers. Home: 1331 Jill Terr Homewood IL 60430 Office: Santa Fe Railway 80 E Jackson Blvd Chicago IL 60604

CHESNUT, THOMAS EDWARD, industrial engineer; b. Chgo., Apr. 12, 1928; s. John Sanford and Jean (Pepiot) C.; m. Lola Mae McElroy, May 19, 1954 (div. Jan. 1974); children: David, Marilyn, Carolyn, John, Teresa, Brian; m. Ruth Anne Utley, June 22, 1974. Indsl. engring. technician Navord Syscom, Crane, Ind., 1962-76; indsl. engr. Jenn Air Corp., Indpls., 1976-77; sr. indsl. engr. Franklin Electric Co., Jacksonville, Ark., 1981-83, Borg Warner Corp., Muncie, Ind., 1977-81, 83—. Served with USN, 1946-51, PTO. Recipient Silver Beaver award Boy Scouts Am., 1972. Mem. MTM Assn. (instr. 1979—), Inst. Indsl. Engrs. (sr. mem.). Democrat. Presbyterian. Lodge: Masons. Avocations: woodworking, fishing, computer programming, stamp collecting. Home: 410 Ellenhurst Dr Anderson IN 46012 Office: Borg Warner Corp PO Box 2688 Muncie IN 47302

CHESTER, MARK VINCENT, lawyer; b. Chgo., Apr. 22, 1952; s. Alvin L. and Barbara (Segal) C.; m. Shelly L. Beeber, May 20, 1979; children: Jonathan Harry, Michael Steven. BA, Emory U., 1974, MA, 1974; postgrad. Victoria U. of Manchester, 1972-73; JD, Northwestern U., 1977. Bar: Ill. 1977, U.S. Dist. Ct. (no. dist.) Ill. 1977, Ga. 1979, U.S. Ct. Appeals (7th, 11th and 5th cirs.) 1981, U.S. Supreme Ct. 1981. Asst. state's atty. Cook County (Ill.), 1977-81, spl. asst. state's atty., 1981—; spl. asst. atty. gen. Ill., 1981-83; assoc. Butler, Rubin, Newcomer & Saltarelli, Chgo., 1981-83; ptnr. Johnson and Colmar, Chgo., 1983—. Bd. dirs. Project LEAP, 1976—. Mem. Ill. Bar Assn., Ga. Bar Assn., Chgo. Bar Assn. Home: 1017 Prairie Ave Deerfield IL 60015 Office: Johnson and Colmar 75 E Wacker Dr Suite 1000 Chicago IL 60601

CHESTER, STEPHANIE ANN, lawyer, banker; b. Mpls., Oct. 8, 1951; d. Alden Runge and Nina Lavina (Hanson) C.; divorced. B.A. magna cum laude, Augustana Coll., 1973; J.D., U. S.D., 1977; postgrad. C.F.S.C., ABA Nat. Grad. Trust Sch., Evanston, Ill., 1984. Bar: S.D. 1977, Minn. 1979. Asst. counselor Minnehaha County Juvenile Ct. Ctr., Sioux Falls, S.D., 1972-73; child care worker Project Threshold, Sioux Falls, 1973-74; legal intern Davenport, Evans, Hurwitz & Smith, Sioux Falls, 1976; law clk. S.D. Supreme Ct., Pierre, 1977-78; originations dept. buyer Dain Bosworth, Inc., Mpls., 1978-79; v.p., trust officer 1st Bank of S.D., N.A., Sioux Falls, 1979-86; v.p., First Trust Co., Inc., St. Paul, 1986—; bd. dirs., mem. program com. Sioux Falls Estate Planning Council, 1983-85; Projects and research editor S.D. Law Rev., 1977; author law rev. comment. Mem. fund raising coms. S.D. Symphony, Sioux Falls Community Playhouse, Augustana Coll., 1982-83; mem. S.D. div. Nat. Women's Polit. Caucus; mem. events com. Augustana Coll. Fellows, Sioux Falls, 1984; bd. dirs. YWCA, Sioux Falls, 1984, Sioux Falls Arena/Coliseum, 1985; mem. Sioux Falls Jr. Service League, 1984. Augustana Coll. scholar, 1969-73; Augustana Coll. Bd. Regents scholar, 1973. Mem. S.D. Bar Assn., Minn. Bar Assn., ABA, 2d S.D. Jud. Circuit Bar Assn., Nat. Assn. Bank Women (state conv. com. 1983-85), Phi Delta Phi, Chi Epsilon. Republican. Lutheran. Clubs: Network, Portia (Sioux Falls). Office: First Trust Co Inc 180 E 5th St Saint Paul MN 55102

CHESTERTON, S. KEITH, automation engineer; b. Phila., Apr. 10, 1939; s. Stanley and Mathilde (Silber) C.; m. Doris Vianne Gordon, June 15, 1963; children: Brian Keith, Wendi Kim. BS, Drexel U., 1971; MS, U. Nebr., 1984. Registered profl. engr., Pa., Nebr. Design engr. U.S. Gauge Co., Sellersville, Pa., 1963-70; plant engr. Daley Tube Co., Horsham, Pa., 1970-73; design engr. Wildman-Jacquard, Norristown, Pa., 1973-78; mgr. engring. Dale Electronics Co., Norfolk, Nebr., 1978—. Patentee in field. Warden Trinity Episcopal Ch., Norfolk, 1980-86. Mem. ASME (affiliate), Elkhorn Valley Striders (treas. 1983-85, Runner of Yr. 1985). Republican. Avocations: wine making, camping. Home: 1104 S 3d St Norfolk NE 68701 Office: Dale Electronics 2300 Riverside Blvd Norfolk NE 68701

CHETON, CHARLES WILLIAM, furniture company executive; b. Canton, Ohio, Nov. 23, 1924; s. Simeon and Theodora (Morar) C.; m. Carolyn Popa, July 1, 1945 (div. Apr. 1972); children: Anna, Barbara and Charles (twins), Debra, Michelle, Charles II; m. Catherine Condos Gaston, July 14, 1973. Student, U. Tenn., 1944; exec. mgmt. degree, Northwestern U., 1954. Office mgr. Worshill Auto Parts, Canton, Ohio, 1946-47; gen. mgr. Home Furniture Co., Canton, 1947-52; pres. Cheton Furniture Co., Canton, 1952—; pres. Beachcomber Corp., Fla., 1968-81. Pres. Internat. Festival, Canton, 1980-82; pres. bd. St. George Cath. Ch., Canton, 1968-82; exec. v.p. Save Palace Theater Com., 1981-82. Served to cpl. USAF, 1943-46. Recipient Mayor's Award, Canton, 1981. Republican. Lodge: Cath. Order Foresters (pres. local chpt. 1958-70, 1981—), Traian and Iliu Maniu Soc. Home: 3533 Old Colony Dr NW Canton OH 44718 Office: 2655 S Arlington Rd Akron OH 44319

CHEVALIER, PAUL ANDREW, restaurateur; b. Manchester, Iowa, Mar. 14, 1953; s. Marvin Freeman and Faye Lucille (MacTaggart) C.; m. Debarah Leigh Long, Feb. 26, 1982; children: Heather Samantha, Joshua Jason, Lucas Josiah Christain. BBA in Indsl. Relations, U. Iowa, 1976. Asst. cashier Citizens State Bank, Postville, Iowa, 1976-79, Exchange State Bank, Collins, Iowa, 1979-84; owner Stone Hearth Inn, Decorah, Iowa, 1984—. Mem. Iowa Restaurant and Beverage Assn., State Assn. Beverage Retail Establishments. Lodge: Masons. Avocation: photography. Office: Stone Hearth Inn PO Box 474 Decorah IA 52101

CHEW, WENG CHO, engineering executive; b. Kuantan, Pahang, Malaysia, June 9, 1953; came to U.S., 1973; s. Fatt Sim Chew and Toh Lan Goh; m. Chew-Chin Phua, Dec. 21, 1977; children: Hulbin Amelia, Shinen Ethan. BSEE, MIT, 1976, MSEE, 1978, PhD in Elec. Engring, 1980. Postdoctoral assoc., inst. MIT, Cambridge, 1980-81; mem. profl. staff Schlumberger-Doll Research, Ridgefield, Conn., 1981-83, program leader, 1983-84, dept. mgr., 1984-85; assoc prof. U. Ill., 1985—; presdl. young investigator, 1986; cons. Schlumberger, Ridgefield, 1985—. Contbr. over 50 articles to sci. jourl. Mem. IEEE (sr., assoc. editor, 1984—), Union Raido Sci. Internat. (guest editor 1985). Avocation: badminton.

CHEYNE, VALORIE ELLENOR, counselor, psychotherapist; b. Bloomfield Hills, Mich., Apr. 28, 1944; d. Cyril Gordon Browne and Dorothy Ellenor (Neel) Van Kempen; m. Kenneth McLean, July 22, 1967; 1 child, Casey. BA, Mich. State U., 1966; MEd, Wayne State U., 1978; Psy. S., Ctr. for Humanistic Studies, 1983. Cert. tchr., Mich.; cert. social worker, Mich. Tchr. multiply physically hadicapped and learning disabled Farmington (Mich.) Pub. Schs., 1966-72; counselor, psychotherapist, coordinator attention deficit ctr. Ten-Southfield Clinic P.C., Southfield, Mich., 1968—. Pres. bd. Women's Survival Ctr., Pontiac, Mich., 1985—; bd. dirs. Jr. League, Birmingham, Mich., Jr. Women's Assn. for Detroit Symphony Orch. Mem. Am. Psychol. Assn., Mich. Psychol. Assn., Am. Orthopsychiatr. Assn., Assn. Humanistic Psychology, Mich. Inter-Profl. Assn. Congregationalist. Club: Hill and Dale Garden (Farmington) (Pres. 1977-78). Office: Ten-Southfield Clinic PC 29830 Telegraph Rd Southfield MI 48034

CHIAPPA, FRANCIS WILLIAM, psychologist; b. Bklyn., Dec. 24, 1949; s. John Francis Chiappa and Florence May (Cockeram) Sievwright; m. Dorene Marie Davis, June 3, 1978; children: Tai Jessica, Emma Elaine. BA, SUNY, Buffalo, 1971; PhD, Case Western Res. U., 1977. Psychology asst. Cambridge (Ohio) Mental Health and Mental Retardation Ctr., 1977-78; psychologist Western Res. Psychiat. Rehab. Ctr., Northfield, Ohio, 1978-80; psychologist, pres. Horizons Counseling Services Inc., Parma Heights, Ohio, 1982—; cons. Aftercare Residential Ctr., Cleve., 1982—, Parmadale Children's Village, Parma, 1983-84. Chairperson Cleve. Heights Weapons Freeze Campaign, 1983-86; v.p. Greater Cleve. Nuclear Weapons Freeze, 1985-86, pres., 1987. Mem. Am. Psychol. Assn., Ohio Psychol. Assn., Cleve. Psychol. Assn., Assn. Humanistic Psychology. Democrat. Avocations: musician, skiing, hiker. Home: 2997 Hampshire Rd Cleveland Heights OH 44118 Office: Horizons Counseling Services 5851 Pearl Rd 305 Parma Heights OH 44130

CHIARO, A. WILLIAM, management consultant; b. Chgo., July 12, 1928; s. Anthony Joseph and Marie Anne (Bonario) C.; m. Lyne LaVerne Franke, Aug. 27, 1961; children: David Huntington, Caroline Elizabeth. BS, U. Ill., 1954. Cert. profl. bus. cons. Acct., IBM, Chgo., 1954-55; with Black & Skaggs Assocs., Chgo., 1955—, pres., 1978—; dir. P.M. Chgo., Inc. Contbr. articles to med. and profl. jours. Served with U.S. Army, 1946-47, USAF, 1950-52. Mem. Soc. Advancement Mgmt., Soc. Profl. Bus. Cons., Nat. Soc. Public Accts. Presbyterian. Home: 2721 Iroquois Rd Wilmette IL 60091 Office: PM Chgo Inc 666 Lake Shore Dr Suite 1314 S Chicago IL 60611

CHILA, ANTHONY GEORGE, osteopathic educator; b. Youngstown, Ohio, Dec. 14, 1937; s. Paul and Anne (Jurenko) C.; m. Helen Paulick, Oct. 9, 1965; 1 child, Anne Elizabeth. BA, Youngstown State U., 1960; DO, Kansas City Coll. Osteopathy and Surgery, 1965. Assoc. prof. family medicine Mich. State U. Coll. Medicine, East Lansing, 1977-78; assoc. prof. family medicine Ohio U. Coll. Medicine, Athens, 1978-83, prof. family medicine, 1983, chief clin. research, 1982; chmn. instl. rev. bd. Ohio U., Athens, 1986-88; George C. Kozma Meml. lectr. Cleve. Acad. Osteo. Medicine, 1979. Contbr. numerous articles to profl. jours. Trustee Saint Vladimir's Orthodox Theol. Sem., Tuckahoe, N.Y., 1975—; active Kootaga Area council Boy Scouts Am. Mem. AAAS, Am. Osteo. Assn. (Louisa M. Burns lectr. Clearwater, Fla. 1987), Am. Coll. Gen. Practitioners, Am. Acad. Osteopathy (pres. 1983-84, 85-87, Scott Meml. lectr. Kirksville, Mo. 1984, Thomas L. Northup lectr. Las Vegas, Nev. 1986), Cranial Acad., N.Y. Acad. Scis., N.Am. Acad. Manipulative Medicine, Gen. Charles Grosvenor Civil War Round Table. Republican. Avocations: stamp and coin collecting, chess, Am. Civil War history. Office: Ohio U Coll Osteo Medicine Grosvenor Hall Athens OH 45701

CHILCOTE, JACK WALLACE, saving and loan executive; b. Sidney, N.S., Can., Sept. 18, 1924; s. Chester Mark and Gladys Maude (Shane) C.; m. Iris K. Kolp, June 16, 1951; children: Ted William (dec.), Betsy Jane. Student, Auburn (Ala.) U., 1945-46; BS, Ohio State U., 1948. Fed. examiner Home Loan Bank Bd., Cin., 1949-52; with Park Fed. Savs. and Loan Assn., Columbus, Ohio, 1952-80, pres., chief exec. officer, 1969-80; chmn., chief exec. officer Freedom Fed. Savs. and Loan Assn., Columbus, 1980—. Treas., trustee United Meth. Children's Home, Worthington, Ohio, 1958-75; vice chmn. Bd. of Zoning Appeals, Worthington, 1971-74. Mem. Mid-Ohio Savs. and Loan League (pres., trustee 1970-76), Ohio Savs. and Loan League (trustee 1983—). Republican. Clubs: Scioto Country (Upper Arlington, Ohio), Country at Muirfield (Dublin, Ohio). Lodges: Shriners, Masons, Kiwanis. Avocation: golf. Home: 567 Hallmark Pl Worthington OH 43085 Office: Freedom Fed Savs and Loan Assn 2939 Kenny Rd Columbus OH 43221

CHILDERS, JOHN HENRY, talent company executive, personality representative; b. Hoopston, Ill., July 26, 1930; s. Leroy Kendal and Marie Ann (Sova) C.; m. JoAnn Uhlar, July 27, 1956; children—Michael John, Mark Joseph. Sales rep. Universal Match Corp., Chgo., 1956-59; v.p. sales to pres. Sales Merchandising, Inc., Chgo., 1959-63; chmn. bd., chief exec. officer Talent Services, Inc. and Talent Network, Inc., Skokie, Ill., 1963—. Served as pilot USAF, 1950-56. Mem. Assn. Reps. of Profl. Athletes (v.p.); Internat. Wine and Food Soc., Chaine des Rotisseurs, Les Amis du Vin, Wine finders, Classic Car Club Am., Auburn-Cord-Dusenberg Club. Republican. Roman Catholic. Clubs: Knollwood Country; Big Foot Country; Lake Geneva Country, PGA Country. also: Apt 4G North-of-Nell Aspen CO 81611 also: 219 Club Cottages Palm Beach Gardens FL 33410 Office: 5200 W Main St Skokie IL 60077

CHILDRES, MARY ROSE, marketing professional; b. Livingston, Ala., Apr. 13, 1936; d. Simon and Mary Magdalene (Sanders) Childress; m. Robert Walker Greene. AS in Secretarial Sci., U. Cin., 1973, BS in Adminstrv. Mgmt., 1976; MBA, Columbia Pacific U., 1986. Secretarial positions Hamilton County (Ohio) Welfare Dept., 1954-59, VA Hosp., Cin., 1959-63, Mut. Benefit Life Ins. Co., Cin., 1965-66, Ky. State U., Frankfort, 1966-68; nutrition program asst. W.Va. U., Charleston, 1969-70; with U. Cin., 1970—, bus. adminstr., office of vice provost for continuing edn. and met. services, from 1978, now sr. bus. adminstr. continuing edn. and met. services, chmn. Cornelius Van Jordan Scholarship Fund. Author: Handbook of Office Procedures, 1973, 75, Managing Funded Accounts Electronically for Non-Traditional Programs, 1986. Mem. Nat. Secs. Assn. (charter; cofounder Frankfort chpt.), AAUW, Bus. and Profl. Women, United Black Assn. of Faculty, Adminstrs. and Staff U. Cin. (treas.), Mid-Level Mgrs. Assn. U. Cin., Nat. U. Continuing Edn. Assn. (chmn., treas. 1982 conv.), Adminstrv. Women's Assn. U. Cin., Nat. Assn. Female Execs., Delta Tau Kappa. Mem. Ch. of God. Home: 838 Crowden Dr Cincinnati OH 45224 Office: 223 N Wayne Ave Cincinnati OH 45215

CHILDRESS, BARRY LEE, child psychoanalyst; b. Chgo., Apr. 19, 1941; s. Affie Sylvester and Dorothy Mildred (Rein) C.; m. Gene Ziupsnys, June 29, 1963; children—Brett Lee, Brian Lee. B.S. with honors, U. Ill., 1961, M.D., 1965; grad. Inst. for Psychoanalysis, Chgo., 1983. Diplomate Am. Bd. Psychiatry and Nuerology. Intern Ill. Masonic Hosp., Chgo., 1965-66; resident in adult psychiatry Presbyn.-St. Lukes Hosp., Chgo., 1966-69, fellow in child psychiatry, 1971-72; dir. child psychiatry sect. Rush-Presbyn.-St Lukes Hosp., Chgo., 1975-76; mem. faculty child and adolescent tng. program Inst. Psychoanalysis, Chgo., 1980—, dir., 1985—, core faculty, 1985—, chmn. child and adolescent psychoanalysis program, 1987—; cons. Hephzibah Children's Home Assn., Oak Park, Ill., 1984—. Served to capt. USAF, 1969-71. Mem. Am. Psychoanalytic Assn., Ill. Council Child Psychiatry, Ill. Soc. Adolescent Psychiatry, Chgo. Psychoanalytic Soc. Avocations: camping; hiking; running; computer applications to psychoanalytic practice. Home: 1221 N East Ave Oak Park IL 60302 Office: 520 N Michigan Ave Suite 1420 Chicago IL 60611

CHILDS, GAYLE BERNARD, educator; b. Redfield, S.D., Oct. 17, 1907; s. Alva Eugene and Dora Amelia (Larsen) C.; A.B., Nebr. State Tchrs. Coll., Wayne, 1931; M.A., U. Nebr., 1936, Ph.D., 1949; M.Ed., Harvard, 1938; m. Doris Wilma Hoskinson, Dec. 22, 1930; children—Richard Arlen, George William, Patricia Ann (Mrs. Ronald Bauers). Tchr. sci. Wynot (Nebr.) High Sch., 1928-30; tchr. sci. Wayne (Nebr.) High Sch., 1931-38, prin., 1938-41; supt. Wakefield (Nebr.) pub. schs., 1941-44, West Point (Nebr.) pub. schs., 1944-46; curriculum specialist U. Nebr. extension div., Lincoln, 1946-49, instr. secondary edn. Tchrs. Coll., also curriculum specialist extension div., 1949-51, asst. prof., 1951-53, asso. prof., 1953-56, prof., head class and corr. instrn., 1956-63, prof., asso. dir. extension div., 1963-66, prof., dir. extension div., 1966-74. Nebr. del. White House Conf. on Aging, 1981; Congl. sr. intern First dist. Congl. Office, Washington, 1981; mem. state curriculum com. Nebr. State Dept. Edn., 1951-55. Sr. Fulbright-Hays scholar Haile Sellassie I U., Addis Ababa, Ethiopia, 1974. Mem. Capitol City Edn. Assn. (pres. 1949-50), Nebr. Edn. Assn. (dist. III sec. 1941-42), Nat. U. Extension Assn. (mem. adminstrv. com., div. corr. study 1952-68, chmn. 1963-65, Assn. dir. 1963-65, mem. joint com. minimum data and definitions 1965-70, chmn. 1970-73; Walton S. Bittner award 1971; establishment Gayle B. Childs award div. ind. study 1969; Gayle B. Childs award 1973), Internat. Council on Corr. Edn. (chmn. com. on research 1961-69, program com. 9th internat. conf. 1971-72), Assn. Univ. Evening Colls. (program com. 1971-72, membership com. 1971-73), Nebr. Schoolmasters Club, Phi Delta Kappa (dist. rep. 1957-63, dir., 1963-69, mem. commn. on edn. and human rights and responsibilities 1963-74, mem. adv. panel on commns. 1970-72; Disting. Service award 1970), North Central Assn. Colls. and Secondary Schs. (cons. def. com. 1953-55, mem. panel vis. scholars 1971-73), Fulbright Alumni Assn., U. Nebr. Emeriti Assn. (pres. 1979-80). Club: Kiwanis (bd. dirs. 1978-81). Contbr. articles to profl. jours. Home: 4530 Van Dorn St Lincoln NE 68506 Office: Nebr Ctr for Continuing Edn 33d and Holdrege Sts Lincoln NE 68503

CHILDS, K(ENNETH) ROSS, government manager, management consultant; b. London, Ont., Can., June 17, 1937; came to U.S., 1955; s. William Ross and Catharine Evelyn (Donaldson) C.; m. Helen Ann Randle, June 28, 1958; children: Mary, Susan. BSIndslE, U. Mich., Ann Arbor, 1960. Tax engr. County of Washtenaw, Ann Arbor, 1960-68, asst. county adminstr., 1968-69, county adminstr., 1970-73; asst. gen. mgr. Southeastern Mich. Transp. Authority, Detroit, 1973-74; acting gen. mgr. S.E.M.T.A., Detroit, 1974-75; county coordinator County of Grand Traverse, Traverse City, Mich., 1976—; pvt. practice mgmt. cons., Traverse City, 1980—. Elected to U. Mich. "Dekers" Hall of Fame, 1971; recipient Excellence in County Govt. award Mich. Assn. Counties; named Mich. Pub. Servant of Yr., Govt. Adminstrs. Assn. Mem. Mich. Assn. County Adminstv. Officers (pres. 1984), Nat. Assn. County Adminstrs. Home: 640 Bay E Traverse City MI 49684

CHILDS, LYNN BUCKLEY, accountant; b. Pitts., Feb. 28, 1959; d. G. Donald and Jane Ann (Jennewine) Buckley; m. Clinton Walter Childs, May 3, 1986. BSBA, John Carroll U., 1982. CPA, Ohio. Trainee IRS, Cleve., 1979-82; sr. acct. Deloitte, Haskins & Sells, Cleve., 1982-85, Coopers and Lybrand, Cleve., 1986; spl. projects coordinator Ivy Med. Group, Solon, Ohio, 1986-87; mgr. fin. and internat. acctg. Austin Powder Co., Beachwood, Ohio, 1987—. Mem. Am. Inst. CPAs, Ohio Soc. CPA's. Roman Catholic. Avocations: photography, cross country skiing, swimming. Home: 34440 Ridge Rd C-19 Willoughby OH 44094 Office: Austin Powder Co 3690 Orange Pl Beachwood OH 44122

CHILSTROM, HERBERT WALFRED, bishop; b. Litchfield, Minn., Oct. 18, 1931; s. Walfred Emanuel and Ruth (Lindell) C.; m. Ella Corinne Hansen, June 12, 1954; children: Mary, Christopher. B.A., Augsburg Coll., Mpls., 1954; B.D., Augustana Theol. Sem., Rock Island, Ill., 1958; Th.M., Princeton Theol. Sem., 1966; Ed.D., NYU, 1976; D.D. (hon.), Northwestern Luth. Theol. Sem., Mpls., 1979. Pastor Faith Luth. Ch., Pelican Rapids, Minn., 1958-62; prof., acad. dean Luther Coll., Teaneck, N.J., 1962-70; sr. pastor First Luth. Ch., St. Peter, Minn, 1970-76; pres., bishop Minn. Synod, Luth. Ch. Am., Mpls., 1976—, mem. exec. council, 1978-82; mem. Faith and Order Commn. Nat. Council Chs., N.Y.C., 1982; mem. Commn. for a New Lutheran Ch., 1982—. Author: Hebrews, A New and Better Way, 1984. Recipient Pub. Service award Suomi Coll., Hancock, Mich, 1979; Disting. Alumnus citation Augsburg Coll., Mpls., 1979. Avocations: photography; golf; travel; picture framing; fishing. Office: Luth Ch in America Minn Synod 122 W Franklin St Room 600 Minneapolis MN 55404 *

CHILTON, PHILIP NEAL, accountant, lawyer; b. St. Louis, Apr. 13, 1943; s. Thomas Laverne and Sadie Imogene (Smith) C.; m. Mary Eileen Sarver, June 24, 1967; children: Meghan Neal, Amy Beth. BSBA, U. Mo., 1965, JD, 1968; M in Taxation, Washington U., St. Louis, 1975. Bar: Mo. 1968; CPA, Mo. With Arthur Anderson & Co. CPA's, St. Louis, 1968-71, Medserco, Inc., St. Louis, 1971-78, Gallant Seigel & Mitchell Co. CPA's, St. Louis, 1978-82, Laventhol & Horwath CPA's, St. Louis, 1982-86, Hochschild Bloom & Co., St. Louis, 1986—. Served with U.S. Army, 1968-70, Korea. Mem. Mo. Bar Assn., Bar Assn. Met. St. Louis, Mo. Soc. CPA's (estate planning com. 1987-88), Am. Inst. CPA's, Phi Delta Phi. Clubs: Westglen Swim (St. Louis) (treas. 1979-82), Rockwood Swim (St. Louis) (treas.). Avocations: running, tennis, gardening, basketball, reading. Home: 321 Fox Hollow Woods Dr Ballwin MO 63021 Office: Hochschild Bloom & Co 16100 Chesterfield Village Pkwy Chesterfield MO 63017

CHINN, PHILIP CHARLES, real estate executive; b. Hazel Park, Mich., Apr. 1, 1934; s. Charles Philip Chinn and Louise (Berger) Rapp; m. Linda Hill, Nov. 27, 1982; children from previous marriage: Sue, Karen, Philip, Thomas, Lisa. BA, U. Notre Dame, 1955. Nat. mgr. corp. property ops. Sears, Roebuck & Co., Chgo., 1982—. Founder, pres. H.O.P.E. Inc., 1968-73; pres. DuPage County Comprehensive Health Planning Agy., 1974-76, Suburban Cook-DuPage Counties Health Systems Agy., 1976-80; chmn. new applicants com. United Way of Met. Chgo. Mem. Bldg. Owners and Mgrs. Assn. Chgo. (pres. 1984—, chmn. urban affairs sect. 1985—), Am. Health Planning Assn. (bd. dirs. 1982-84), Ill. Assn. Health Planning Consumers (pres. 1979-82). Avocation: running. Home: 410 N Scoville Ave Oak Park IL 60302 Office: Sears Roebuck and Co Sears Tower D/931 BSC 37-10 Chicago IL 60684

CHIOU, JIUNN PERNG, mechanical engineering educator, laboratory administrator; b. Nanking, China, July 29, 1933; m. Rita Chiou; children—Derek, Jeff. B.S. in Mech. Engring., Nat. Taiwan U., 1954; M.S. in Mech. Engring., Oreg. State U., 1960; Ph.D., U. Wis., 1964. Mech. engr. Keelung Harbor Bur., Taiwan, 1955-58; research asst. U. Wis., Madison, 1960-62, instr. mech. engring., 1963-64; engring. specialist AiResearch Mfg. Co., Los Angeles, 1964-69; prof. mech. engring. U. Detroit, 1969—, dir. Heat Transfer Lab., 1969—. Editor: Military Vehicle Power Plant Cooling, 1975, Solar Energy in Cold Climates, 1977, Heat Transfer and Fluid Flow in Solar Energy System, 1985, Automobile Heating and Cooling, 1986, Heat Transfer in Waste Heat Recovery and Heat Rejection Systems, 1986. Named Engring. Tchr. of Yr., U. Detroit, 1983. Mem. Am. Soc. Mech. Engr. (chmn. 1979-86, exec. com. solar energy div. 1986—), Soc. Automotive Engrs. (chmn. climate control com., passenger car activity, 1980—, Forest R. McFarland award 1987), Internat. Solar Energy Soc., Phi Tau Sigma, Sigma Xi, Tau Beta Pi. Office: Univ Detroit Dept Mech Engring 4001 W McNicholas Rd Detroit MI 48221

CHIPMAN, DEBORAH GONDEK, communications executive; b. Phoenix, Apr. 6, 1953; d. Joseph H. and Dorothy E. (Bradac) G.; B.A. cum laude in Journalism, Duquesne U., 1975; m. John A. Chipman, Oct. 6, 1979; children: Lauren Emily, Kyle Joseph. Dir., performer The Young Tamburitzans ensemble, Phoenix, 1968-71; reporter Phoenix Gazette, 1970-71; newswriter, broadcaster Sta. WDUQ, Pitts., 1973-74; ensemble performer Duquesne U. Tamburitzans, nat. folk arts ensemble, Pitts., 1971-75, European tours, 1971-72; communications/planning Chipman Design, Chgo., 1979—; owner Custom Sources, Park Ridge, Ill., 1980—; writer-editor Fairburn Assos., Inc., Phoenix, 1977-79. Recipient Piano Solo Excellence award Nat. Fedn. Musicians, 1971; Quill and Scroll nat. editorial writing award, 1971. Mem. Women in Communications (treas. Phoenix chpt. 1976-77), Internat. Assn. Bus. Communicators Phoenix award of merit 1979, Gold Four award 1981, Gold Quill award), 1982, Sigma Delta Chi (sec. Duquesne chpt. 1974), Kappa Tau Alpha, Duquesne U. Tamburitzans Alumni Assn. Editor Horizons, 1976-77. Home: 400 S Home Ave Park Ridge IL 60068 Office: 648 Busse Hwy Park Ridge IL 60068

CHIPMAN, JAMES THOMAS, university official; b. Wichita, Kans., Mar. 28, 1952; s. Edwin E. and Mary A. (Johnson) C. BS in Polit. Sci., Kans. State U., 1974, BBA, 1974, MS in Counseling and Student Personnel, 1976; postgrad. Ind. U., 1982—. Asst. dean students, dir. student activities McPherson Coll., Kans., 1976-78; residence hall dir. U. Kans., Lawrence, 1979-81; coordinator for residence life Ind. U., Bloomington, 1981-85, adminstrv. asst. commn. on racial understanding, 1985—, anti-racism trainer, 1985—. Recipient Disting. Service award McPherson Coll., 1978, Outstanding Advisor award U. Kans. Assn. Univ. Residence Halls, 1981; named one of Outstanding Men in Am., 1983. Mem. Am. Coll. Personnel Assn. (state membership chmn. 1984-86), Am. Assn. Counseling and Devel., Assn. for Multicultural Counseling and Devel., Ind. Coll. Personnel Assn. (exec. com. 1982-85), Nat. Orientation Dirs. Assn. (editorial bd. 1972-78, nat. cons.'s com. 1976-78), Phi Delta Kappa. Democrat. Presbyterian. Office: Dean of Students Dept Residence Life 801 N Jordan Bloomington IN 47405

CHIPOCO, ADOLFO MALMBORG, physician; c. Callao, Peru, Dec. 1, 1929; came to U.S., 1955; s. Adolfo and Elisa (Malmborg) Chipoco Meza; m. June Shreiner Badorf, June 1, 1957 (div. Mar. 1973); m. Gladys Mirta Delgado, Oct. 5, 1973. M.D., San Marcos U., Lima, Peru, 1954. Diplomate Am. Bd. Family Practice. Intern, Grasslands Hosp., Valhalla, N.Y., 1955; resident St. Joseph's Hosp., Lancaster, Pa., 1956-59, Henry Ford Hosp., Detroit, 1959-60, Leila Hosp., Battle Creek, Mich., 1960-61; practice family medicine, Detroit, 1968—; mem. staff Grace-Harper Hosp., Detroit, 1968—. Author: Oro Y Sombras, 1976; Los Heroes Y Grau, 1977; El Arbol, 1978; Meditaciones Fernandinas, 1979; Castilla, 1980; La Esfera Azul, The Blue Sphere, 1984; editor: El Amauta, 1979-83; Pams, 1983; Friends of the Arts of Iberoamerica, 1983. Med. chmn. Oakland County unit Am. Cancer Soc., 1968-71; v.p. Friends of Arts Ibero-Am., Bloomfield Hills, Mich., 1983. Recipient Cruz Castilla, Inst. Libertador Castilla, 1982; Valor Humanitario, Peruvian-Am. Council Good Will, 1983. Fellow Am. Acad. Family Practice; mem. AMA, Mich. State Med. Soc., Wayne County Med. Soc., Peruvian Am. Med. Soc. (pres. 1984-85). Roman Catholic. Club: Peruvian of Mich. (pres. 1979-83). Home: 3015 Spring West Bloomfield MI 48033 Office: 17000 S Eight Mile Rd Southfield MI 48075

CHIPPS, MICHAEL ROBERT, college official; b. Grand Island, Nebr., Mar. 28, 1950; s. Robert C. and Kathryn A. (Seifert) C.; m. Susan G. Wescott, Dec. 5, 1970; children—Sean, Angela. Student, U. Nebr., 1968-69, postgrad., 1983—; student Sioux Falls Coll., 1969-70; B.S., Kearney State Coll., 1972; M.S., 1980. Intern, U. Nebr. Med. Center, Nebr. Psychiat. Inst., Omaha, 1978; counselor-examiner div. rehab. services Dept. Edn., Hastings, Nebr., 1975-79; instr. social scis. and coordinator career devel. center Central Community Coll., Hastings, 1979-82, adminstrv. asst., 1982-84, chmn. health div., 1984-86, registrar, 1986, dir. fin. aid and student records, 1986, asst. dean of students, 1986—. Served to comdr. USAR, 1974—. Recipient award Assn. U.S. Army, 1977, Outstanding Leader award Officer Candidate Acad., 1977, 84-85; named one of Outstanding Young Men Am., 1986. Mem. Res. Officers Assn., Assn. U.S. Army, Phi Delta Kappa. Lodge: Masons. Office: PO Box 1024 Hastings NE 68901

CHIRICOSTA, RICK ALAN, financial executive, accountant, educator; b. Springfield, Ohio, Feb. 23, 1956; s. Raymond Carl and Janice Marie (Trenner) C.; m. Sheila Ann Hart, Apr. 30, 1982; 1 child, Matthew Alan. BBA in Acctg., U. Toledo, 1978. CPA, Ohio. Audit supr. Ernst & Whinney, Toledo, 1978-84; corp. internal auditor Blade Communications, Inc., Toledo, 1984-86; asst. v.p., controller Blue Cross & Blue Shield of Ohio Western Div., Toledo, 1986—; instr. acctg. Owens Tech. Coll., Toledo, 1982—, mem. acctg. adv. bd., 1984—. Mem. Am. Inst. CPA's, Ohio Soc. CPA's. Roman Catholic. Club: Can. Friends of Mine (Detroit). Avocations: music, sports. Home: 3902 Grantley Toledo OH 43613 Office: Blue Cross & Blue Shield of Ohio Western Div 3737 W Sylvania Toledo OH 43623

CHISHOLM, GEORGE NICKOLAUS, dentist; b. Pullman, Wash., Sept. 21, 1936; s. Leslie L. and Lila Rene (Cates) C.; D.D.S., U. Nebr., 1960; 1 son, Andrew M. Practice dentistry, Lincoln, Nebr., 1963-83; clin. instr. Coll. Dentistry, U. Nebr., 1976-83. Mem. S.E. Nebr. Health Planning Agy., 1976-82. Served to capt. Dental Corps, USAF, 1960-63. Mem. ADA (del. 1980), Nebr. Dental Assn. (del. 1974-80, trustee 1980-83), Lincoln Dist. Dental Assn. (pres. 1979-80), Sigma Alpha Epsilon, Xi Psi Phi. Mason (32 deg., Shriner). Asst. editor Nebr. State Dental Jour., 1967-69. Home: 1230 Manchester Dr Lincoln NE 68528

CHISHOLM, TAGUE CLEMENT, pediatric surgeon, educator; b. East Millinocket, Maine, Nov. 6, 1915; s. George James and Victoria Mary (Tague) C.; m. Verity Burnett, 1940 (div. 1975); children—Christopher Tague, Penelope Ann, Robin Francis; m. Johanna Lyon Myers, Aug. 9, 1975. A.B. cum laude, Harvard U., 1936, M.D., 1940. Diplomate Am. Bd. Surgery. Intern Peter Bent Brigham Hosp. and Boston Children's Hosp., 1940-41, resident in gen. and pediatric surgery, 1941-46; Arthur Tracy Cabot fellow in surgery Harvard Med. Sch., 1946; practice medicine specializing in pediatric surgery Mpls., 1947—; mem. faculty U. Minn. Sch. Medicine, Mpls., 1947—, clin. prof. surgery, 1965-84; trustee Mpls. Children's Health Ctr. Hosp. Mem. editorial bd. Jour. Pediatric Surgery, 1965-76, Pediatric Digest, 1962-82, Jour. Minn. Med. Assn., 1957-86; contbr. articles in pediatric surgery to profl. jours. and books. Former trustee Bishop Whipple Schs., Faribault, Minn.; former bd. dirs. Wells Found., Mpls.; trustee Minn. Internat. Health Vols., Mpls., Surg. Aid to Children of the World, N.Y.C. Recipient Presdl. award Minn. Med. Assn., 1978; Merit medal U. Rio Grande Norte, Brazil, 1976; Charles Bowles Rogers award Hennepin County Med. Soc., Minn., 1976. Home: 17745 Maple Hill Rd Wayzata MN 55391 Office: 2545 Chicago Ave S Minneapolis MN 55404

CHISM, JAMES ARTHUR, data processor; b. Oak Park, Ill., Mar. 6, 1933; s. William Thompson and Arema Eloise (Chadwick) C.; A.B., DePauw U., 1957; M.B.A., Ind. U., 1959; postgrad. exec. program Wharton Sch. Bus., U. Pa., 1984. Mgmt. engr. consumer and indsl. products div. Uniroyal, Inc., Mishawaka, Ind., 1959-61, sr. mgmt. engr., 1961-63; systems analyst Miles Labs., Inc., Elkhart, Ind., 1963-64, sr. systems analyst, 1965-69, project supr., distbn. systems, 1969-71, mgr. systems and programming for corporate finance and adminstrv. depts., 1971-73, mgr. adminstrv. systems and corp. staff services, 1973-75, group mgr. consumer products group systems and programming, 1975-79; dir. adminstrn. and staff services Cutter/Miles, 1979-81, dir. advanced office systems and corp. adminstrn. 1982-84; dir. advanced office systems Internat. MIS and Adminstrn., 1984-85, dir. advanced office systems, tng. and adminstrn., 1985—. Bd. dirs. United Way Elkhart County, 1974-75. Served with AUS, 1954-56. Mem. Assn. Systems Mgmt. (chpt. pres. 1969-70, div. dir. 1972-77, recipient Merit award 1975, Achievement award 1977, cert. systems profl. 1984, disting. service award 1986), Dean's Assocs. of Ind. U. Sch. Bus.-Bloomington, Assn. Internal Mgmt. Cons., Fin. Execs. Inst., Office Automation Soc. Internat., Nat. Assn. Bus. Economists, DePauw U. Alumni Assn., Ind. U. Alumni Assn., Delta Kappa Epsilon, Sigma Delta Chi, Sigma Iota Epsilon, Beta Gamma Sigma. Republican. Episcopalian. Clubs: Morris Park Country. (South Bend, Ind.); Delta Kappa Epsilon Club (N.Y.C.), Yale of N.Y.C., Vero Beach Country (Fla.); Coast (Melbourne, Fla.); Ind. Soc. of Chgo. Home: 504 Cedar Crest Ln Mishawaka IN 46545 Office: Miles Labs Inc PO Box 40 1127 Myrtle St Elkhart IN 46515

CHISM, NEAL ASA, economist; b. Humboldt, Nebr., Nov. 5, 1924; s. Ralph Asa and Jessie Ann (Graham) C.; student Weber Coll., Ogden, Utah, 1942, Wabash Coll., Crawfordsville, Ind., 1944-46, U. Ill., 1946; B.S., U. Calif., Berkeley, 1947; certificate d'Etude, U. Grenoble (France), 1949; M.A., U. Nebr., 1951, secondary teaching cert., 1963, Ph.D., 1967; cert. Sch. Banking, U. Wis., 1978; m. Joan Johnson, Feb. 27, 1965; 1 son, John Neal Asa. Export-import salesman Getz Bros. & Co., San Francisco, 1947-48; research officer U.S. Govt., Washington, 1951-53, fgn. service res. officer, 1953-59; asst. to v.p. Am. Express Co., N.Y.C., 1959-62; asst. prof. to assoc. prof. econs. Nebr. Wesleyan U., Lincoln, 1965—, also head dept. bus. adminstrn./econs., 1977—. Chmn. ednl. com. Nemeco Credit Union, 1967-75; univ. rep. Lincoln Community Concerts, Lincoln Community Chest, 1972, 73; univ. rep. to liaison com. Mayor's Edn. Com., 1971. Served with USN, 1942-46. Recipient Trustee award Nebr. Wesleyan U., 1972; named Gt. Teaching Prof. 1st Nat. Bank, Lincoln, 1982. Mem. AAUP (pres. Wesleyan chpt. 1965-69), SAR (pres. Lincoln chpt. 1975-76, pres. Nebr. state soc. 1977), Chism Family Assn. (exec. sec. 1962—), Am. Econs. Assn., Midwest Econs. Assn., Nebr. Bus. and Econs. Assn. (sec.-treas. 1978—), Clan Chisholm Soc. in Am., Scottish Am. Soc., Lincoln Lancaster Geneal. Soc., Delta Phi Epsilon, Delta Tau Delta, Tau Kappa Epsilon (faculty adv. Beta Gamma 1969-77, Nat. Advisers award 1974), Omicron Delta Epsilon, Pi Gamma Mu (pres. chpt. 1977, gov. Nebr. province 1978, vice chancellor middle western region 1980, chancellor 1984). Republican. Presbyterian (deacon, elder). Clubs: Filson (Louisville); Masons, Shriners. Home: 5243 Huntington St Lincoln NE 68504 Office: Nebr Wesleyan U 50th St Paul Lincoln NE 68504

CHITWOOD, JULIUS RICHARD, librarian; b. Magazine, Ark., June 1, 1921; s. Hoyt Mozart and Florence (Umfrid) C.; m. Aileen Newsom, Aug. 6, 1944. A.B. cum laude, Ouachita Bapt. Coll., Ark., 1942; M.Mus., Ind. U., 1948; M.A., U. Chgo., 1954. Music supr. Edinburgh (Ind.) Pub. Schs., 1946-47; music and audiovisual librarian Roosevelt Coll., Chgo., 1948-51; humanities librarian Drake U., 1951-53; spl. cataloger Chgo. Tchrs. Coll., 1953; asst. circulation librarian Indpls. Pub. Library, 1954-57, coordinator adult services, 1957-61; dir. Rockford (Ill.) Pub. Library, 1961-79, No. Ill. Library System, Rockford, 1966-76; chmn. subcom. library system devel. Ill. Library Adv. Com., 1965—; adv. com. U. Ill. Grad. Sch. Library Sci., 1964-68; cons. in field, participant workshops. Pres. Rockford Regional Academic Center, 1974-76; Mem. history com. Ill. Sesquicentennial Commn.; mem. Mayor Rockford Com. for UN, 1962-70; sect. chmn. Rockford United Fund, 1966-70; exec. Rockford Civic Orch. Assn., 1962-70. Served to maj., inf. AUS, 1942-45, ETO. Recipient Ill. Librarian of Year award, 1974. Mem. ALA (chmn. subcom. revision standards of materials, pub. library div. 1965-66, pres. bldg. and equipment sect. library adminstrn. div. 1967-68, chmn. staff devel. com. personnel adminstrn. sect., library adminstrv. div. 1964-68, pres. library adminstrn. div. 1969-70), Ill. Library Assn. (v.p. 1964-65, pres. 1965-66), Rockford Area C. of C. Unitarian (pres. 1965-67). Clubs: Rotarian (exec. bd. Rockford 1965-66), Rockford University. Home: 916 Paris Ave Rockford IL 61107 Office: 115 7th St Suite 209 Rockford IL 61104

CHMIELEWSKI, MARGARET ANN, psychology educator; b. Detroit, Dec. 13, 1946; d. Joseph and Mary (Anderanin) Kakaley; m. James Andrew Chmielewski, May 19, 1973; children: Mark James, Elizabeth Ann. BBA, Wayne State U., 1969, MA, 1972. English tchr. Our Lady Star of the Sea High Sch., Grosse Pointe, Mich., 1969-70, Bishop Borgess High Sch., Detroit, 1972-73; instr. in speech Wayne County Community Coll., Detroit, 1972-74; asst. prof. in psychology, counselor Madonna Coll., Livonia, Mich., 1977—; cons. Ford Motor Co., Dearborn, 1979-81; speaker in field. area coordinator Miss Wheelchair Mich. Pageant, 1978-80; trustee Wheelchair Awareness Found., Inc., Columbus, 1979-84, pres. 1982-84; mem. Planning Council for Devel. Disabilities, Lansing, Mich., 1980-84; mem. various coms. Statewide Health Coordinating Council, Lansing, 1980—; chair Consumers Caucus, Malpractice Issue com., exec. com., state health devel. com., various coms. Gov.'s Task Force on Physician Reimbursement, Lansing, 1980-82; chair Task Force on Nursing Personnel, Lansing, 1985; mem. parish council St. John Newman Cath. Ch., Canton, 1983—, pres., 1986-87. Named Miss Wheelchair Michigan, 1976, Miss Wheelchair America, 1978-79; recipient Arkansas Travelors award Gov. Bill Clinton 1979, Gov.'s award State of Mich., 1979, Gov.'s award State of La., 1979, Gov.'s award State of Miss., 1979; recipient Key to the City, Montgomery, Ala., 1979, Key to the City, Mobile, Ala., 1979, Key to the City, New Orleans, 1979. Mem. Nat. Assn. of the Physically Handicapped (life), Wayne State Alumni Assn. (Outstanding Woman of Wayne award 1980), Delta Zeta (adv., dir. Wayne State chpt. 1969-72), U.S. Trotting Assn., Mich. Harness Horseman Assn. Avocations: harness horse racing, bridge. Home: 46730 Strathmore Plymouth MI 48170 Office: Madonna Coll 36600 Schoolcraft Livonia MI 48150

CHMURNY, WILLIAM W., university official. Chancellor U. Wis., Platteville. Office: Univ of Wis-Platteville Office of the Chancellor Platteville WI 53818-3099 *

CHODORKOFF, JOAN, clinical psychologist; b. N.Y.C., Feb. 17, 1929; d. Jacob Ludwig and Cora (Berger) Rosmarin; m. Bernard Chodorkoff, June 11, 1951; children: Catherin, David Jacob. BA, Marietta Coll., 1950; MS, U. Wis., 1954; PhD, Wayne State U., 1960. Lic. psychologist, Mich. Chief psychologist pediatrics PRESCAD Detroit Gen. Hosp., 1967-69; assoc. prof., acting dir. Children's Psychodiagnostic Ctr. U. Detroit, 1970-71; chief psychologist Downriver Guidance Clinic, Lincoln Park, Mich., 1975-84; outpatient supr. Genesee County Community Mental Health Child and Adolescent Services, Flint, Mich., 1984—; adj. asst. prof. psychology Wayne State U., 1967—; adj. assoc. prof. Coll. Medicine Wayne State U., 1967-69; cons. psychologist PRESCAD North Cen. Health Ctr., 1971-73; lectr. Northville State Hosp. first yr. residents in psychiatry, 1972-74; adj. prof. Child Growth and Devel. Macomb Community Coll., 1973. Contbr. articles to profl. jours. Mem. Oak Park (Mich.) Youth Guidance Bd., 1963-64. Fellow Am. Orthopsychiat. Assn.; mem. Am. Psychol. Assn., Council for Nat. Register Health Service Providers in Psychology, Mich. Psychol. Assn., Detroit Psychol. Assn. (sec.-treas. 1958-59), Mich. Assn. Cons. Psychologists (membership chmn. 1975-76).

CHODOS, DALE DAVID JEROME, physician, pharmaceutical company executive; b. Mpls., June 5, 1928; s. John H. and Elvera Isabella (Lundberg) C.; m. Joyce Annette Smith, Sept. 8, 1951; children—John, Julie, David, Jennifer. A.B., Carroll Coll., Helena, Mont., 1950; M.D., St. Louis U., 1954. Diplomate Am. Bd. Pediatrics. Intern U. Utah, Salt Lake City, 1954-55, resident in pediatrics, 1955-57, NIH fellow in endocrinology and metabolism, 1957-58; practice medicine specializing in pediatrics Idaho Falls, Idaho, 1958-62; staff physician Upjohn Co., Kalamazoo, Mich., 1962-64, head clin. pharmacology, 1964-65, research mgr. clin. pharmacology, 1965-68, research mgr. clin. services, 1968-73, group research mgr. med. therapeutics, 1973-81, med. dir. domestic med. affairs, 1981-85, exec. dir. domestic med. affairs, 1985—; chief pediatrics Latter-day Saints Hosp., Sacred Heart Hosp., Idaho Falls, 1962; chnn. med. relations operating com. Nat. Pharm. Council, 1977-80, med. sect. steering com. 1977-80, chmn., 1984-86. Contbr. articles to med. and pharm. jours. Bd. dirs. Family Service Ctr., Kalamazoo, 1965-71. Served with AUS, 1945-46. Recipient W.E. Upjohn award for excellence, 1969, Physician's Recognition award AMA, 1969, 73, 76, 79, 82, 85. Fellow Am. Acad. Pediatrics; mem. Am. Soc. Clin. Pharmacology and Therapeutics, Am. Coll. Clin. Toxicology, AMA, Pharm. Mfrs. Assn. (med. sect. steering com. 1977—). Home: 619 Aqua View Dr Kalamazoo MI 49009 Office: Upjohn Co 7000 Portage Rd Kalamazoo MI 49001

CHOE, KENNETH HONG, physician; b. Taegue, Korea, Jan. 28, 1933; came to U.S., 1965; m. Caroline Yu, Nov. 30, 1974; 1 child, William K. MD, Kyungpook Nat. U., Taegu, 1958. Diplomate Am. Bd. Neurology and Psychiatry. Intern Mt. Sinai Hosp., Chgo., 1966-70; resident dept. psychiatry Northwestern U., Chgo., 1970; gen. practice medicine Oakbrook Terrace, Ill., 1970—. Mem. AMA, Ill. Med. Soc., Chgo. Med. Soc., Am. Acad. Clin. Psychiatrists. Home: 2819 Meyers Rd Oak Brook IL 60521

CHOICE, MICHAEL JOHN, securities exec.; b. Chgo., Sept. 12, 1942; s. Herbert John and Josephine (DeVoto) C.; B.A., Beloit Coll., 1965; M.B.A., Roosevelt U., 1969; m. Nancy Lamson, July 10, 1965; 1 dau., Cynthia. Group div. underwriting supr. Continental Casualty Co., Chgo., 1965-70; asst. v.p. Merrill Lynch, Pierce, Fenner & Smith, Inc., Chgo., 1970-87, v.p., 1987—. Mem. United Ch. Christ. Home: 136 Linden Ave Elmhurst IL 60126 Office: 33 W Monroe Chicago IL 60603

CHOICH, RUDOLPH, JR., pharmacist, educator; b. Ambridge, Pa., Mar. 14, 1945; s. Rudolph and Mary Magdalene (Zgainer) C.; m. Joann Vulich, Apr. 11, 1970; 1 child, Jennifer Ashley. B.S. in Pharmacy, Duquesne U., 1968; M.S., U. Iowa, 1973; M.B.A., Butler U., 1985. Registered pharmacist. Asst. dir. pharmacy Ind. U. Hosps., Indpls. 1973-76, dir. pharmacy, 1976-86; affiliate asst. prof. Purdue U. Sch. Pharmacy, West Lafayette, Ind., 1973-76; dir. pharmacy Univ. Hosps., Cleve., 1986—; symposium faculty Pfi Pharmecs Corp., Dallas, 1984. Contbr. articles to profl. jours. Lectr. Drug Abuse Awareness Program, Indpls. Pub. Schs., 1982-83. Served with U.S. Army, 1969-71. Mem. Am. Soc. Hosp. Pharmacists, Am. Pharm. Assn., Ind. Soc. Hosp. Pharmacists (pres. 1979, Past Pres. award 1980, Hosp. Pharmacist of Yr. 1984), Rho Chi. Roman Catholic. Lodge: Lions. Avocations: racquetball, music, gardening. Home: 13550 Fox Den E Novelty OH 44072

CHONG, WOOK-CHIN, radiologist; b. Sangju, Korea, Sept. 16, 1944; s. Jae-Sun and Myongnam (Song) C.; m. Chongsook (Cecilia) Suh, May 18, 1971; children: Joon, Grace. MD, Cath. Med. Sch., Seoul, Republic of Korea, 1970. Cert. Am. Bd. Radiology. Resident in diagnostic radiology Mt. Sinai Hosp., N.Y.C., 1975-78; radiologist St. Mary's Hosp., Livonia, Mich., 1978-79, Beloit (Wis.) Meml. Hosp., 1979—. Served to capt. M.C. Korea AF, 1970-73. Mem. AMA, Am. Coll. Radiology, Radiol. Soc. N.Am. Roman Catholic. Office: Beloit Meml Hosp 1969 W Hart Rd Beloit WI 55511

CHOO, YEOW MING, lawyer; b. Johore Bahru, Malaysia, Aug. 1, 1953; s. Far Tong and Kim Fong (Wong) C.; LL.B. with honors (first in class), U. Malaya, 1977; LL.M., Harvard U., 1979; J.D., Chgo.-Kent Coll., 1980. Admitted to Malaysia bar, 1977, Ill. bar, 1980; lectr. law U. Malaya Law Sch., Kuala Lumpur, Malaysia, 1977-78, Monash U. Law Sch., Melbourne, Australia, 1978; internat. atty. Standard Oil Co. (Ind.), Chgo., 1979-82; partner firm Anderson, Liu and Choo, Chgo., 1982-84; ptnr. Baer Marks and Upham, N.Y.C., 1984-85; ptnr. Winston and Strawn, Chgo., 1985—; dir. Harvard Bros. Internat. Corp.; Boston; chmn. tax subcom. Nat. Council for US-China Trade, 1980—. Mem. Am. Mining Congress (alt. mem. com. on law of sea 1980-82), ABA, Ill. Bar Assn., Chgo. Bar Assn., Malayan Bar Council, U.S. Chess Fedn., Harvard Law Sch. Alumni Assn. Club: Harvard. Office: Winston & Strawn One First National Plaza Chicago IL 60603

CHORMANN, RICHARD F., bank executive; b. 1937. BS, Western Mich. U., 1959. With First Am. Bank Mich., Kalamazoo, 1959-80, sr. v.p., 1972-76, exec. v.p., 1976-80; pres. First Am. Bank Wayne Oakland, Detroit, 1980-84; exec. v.p. First Am. Bank Corp., Kalamazoo, 1984-85, pres., chief operating officer, 1985—. Office: First of Am Bank Corp 108 E Michigan Ave Kalamazoo MI 49007 *

CHOU, CHEN-LIN, geochemist; b. Kiangsu, China, Oct. 8, 1943; came to U.S., 1966; s. Yun-Chang and Yu-Ying (Liu) C.; m. Susan S. Wen, June 14, 1970; children—Cynthia, Peter. B.S., Nat. Taiwan U., 1965; Ph.D., U. Pitts., 1971. Postdoctoral scholar UCLA, 1971-72, asst. research geochemist, 1972-75; sr. research assoc. U. Toronto (Ont., Can.), 1975, asst. research prof., 1976-79; postdoctoral fellow McMaster U., Hamilton, Ont., Can., 1979-80; lectr. Calif. State U., Fullerton, 1973-74; asst. geologist Ill. State Geol. Survey, Champaign, 1980-84, assoc. geologist, 1984—. Andrew Mellon fellow, 1967-68; recipient Nininger award Ariz. State U., 1971. Mem. Internat. Assn. Geochemistry and Cosmochemistry, Geol. Soc. Am., Geol. Soc. China, Geochem. Soc., Mineral. Soc. Am., Am. Geophys. Union, Meteoritical Soc. Home: 3007 Valley Brook Dr Champaign IL 61821 Office: Ill State Geol Survey 615 E Peabody Champaign IL 61820

CHOU, SHELLEY NIEN-CHUN, neurosurgeon, medical educator; b. Chekiang, China, Feb. 6, 1924; s. Shelley P. and Tse-tsun (Chao) C.; m. Jolene Johnson, Nov. 24, 1956 (div. 1977); children: Shelley T., Dana, Kerry; m. remarried, 1979. B.S., St. John's U., Shanghai, China, 1946; M.D., U. Utah, 1949; M.S., U. Minn., 1954, Ph.D., 1964. Diplomate: Am. Bd. Neurol. Surgery (mem. bd.). Resident U. Minn. Hosps., 1950-55; practice medicine, specializing in neurosurgery Salt Lake City, 1955-58, Bethesda, Md., 1959, Mpls., 1960—; clin. asst. Coll. Medicine U. Utah, 1956-58; vis. scientist Nat. Insts. Neurol. Diseases and Blindness NIH, 1959; mem. faculty U. Minn., 1960—, asso. prof. neurosurgery, 1965-68, prof. neurosurgery, 1968—, head dept. neurosurgery, 1974—; mem. Am. Bd. Neurol Surg., 1974-79; mem. residency rev. com. ACGME, 1984—, chmn., 1987—. Contbr. numerous articles to profl. jours.; Publs. on studies of intracranial lesions using radioactive angiography techniques; malformations of cerebral vasculature; neurol. dysfunctions of urinary bladder. Mem. AMA, A.C.S. (mem. adv. council neurosurgery 1981—, mem. grad. Med. edn. com. 1984—), Congress Neurol. Surgery, Soc. Neurol. Surgeons (pres. 1978-79), Am. Acad. Neurol. Surgery (pres. elect 1985-86, pres. 1986-87), Soc. Nuclear Medicine, Am. Assn. Neurol. Surgeons (bd. dirs. 1980-83, v.p. 1984-85), Neurosurg. Soc. N.Am. (pres. 1977-78), N.Y. Acad. Medicine, Forum Univ. Neurosurgeons (pres. 1968-69), AAAS, Phi Rho Sigma. Home: 12 S Long Lake Trail North Oaks MN 55127 Office: B-590 Mayo Meml 420 SE Delaware St Minneapolis MN 55455

CHOUKAS, CHRIS NICHOLAS, oral and maxillofacial surgeon; b. Chgo., July 17, 1955; s. Nicholas Chris and Lavern Ann (Tumosa) C. DDS, Loyola U., Maywood, Ill., 1980, splty. degree in oral and maxillofacial surgery, 1984. Diplomate Internat. Assn. Oral and Maxillofacial Surgery, Am. Bd. Oral and Maxillofacial Surgery. Examiner Lake County Coroner's Office, Ill., 1984—; pvt. practice oral and maxillofacial surgery Elmwood Park, Antioch and Melrose Park, Ill., 1984—. Fellow Am. Coll. Stomatologic Surgeons (Outstanding Achievements award 1980), Ill. Soc. Oral and Maxillofacial Surgeons; mem. Am. Assn. Oral and Maxillofacial Surgeons (Outstanding Achievement award 1980), Lake County Dental Soc., Chgo. Soc. Oral and Maxillofacial Surgeons, Omicron Kappa Epsilon. Republican. Roman Catholic. Avocations: scuba diving, boating. Home: 42675 Antioch IL 60002

CHOUKAS, NICHOLAS CHRIS, dental educator; b. Chgo., Sept. 5, 1923; s. Chris and Ethel (George) C.; student Wright Jr. Coll., 1941-43, U. Chgo., 1943-44; D.D.S., Loyola U., Chgo., 1950, M.S. in Oral Anatomy, 1958; m. LaVerne Tumosa, Apr. 19, 1951; children—Janet Lynn, Chris Nicholas, Michael John, Nicholas Chris. Fellow in oral surgery Loyola U., 1953; resident in oral surgery Cook County Hosp., Chgo., 1954, 55; practice specializing in oral and maxillofacial surgery, Elmwood Park, Ill., 1956—; asst. prof. Loyola U. Dental Sch., 1957-64, asso. prof., 1964—, chmn. dept. oral and maxillofacial surgery, 1962-83, asso. prof. oral biology Grad. Sch., 1968-69, prof. dept. oral biology, 1969 , prof. dept. oral and maxillofacial surgery, 1969—; attending oral surgeon Hines (Ill.) VA Hosp., 1958-60; asso. attending surgeon Cook county Hosp., 1959-62; cons. VA Hosp., Hines, Ill., 1960—. Served to lt. (j.g.), USNR, 1951-53. Research grantee NIH, 1961, 62, 63. Diplomate Am. Bd. Oral and Maxillofacial Surgery. Fellow Internat. Assn. Oral Surgeons, Am. Coll. Dentists, Inst. Medicine Chgo., Pan Am. Med. Assn., Internat. Coll. Dentists, Internat. Assn. Maxillofacial Surgeons, Am. Coll. Stomatologic Surgeons; mem. Chgo. Soc. Oral Surgeons, Am. Soc. Oral Surgeons, Odontographic Soc., Logan Brophy Meml. Soc., Sigma Xi, Omicron Kappa Upsilon, Delta Sigma Delta. Contbr. articles to profl. jours. Home: 230 Oakdene Rd Barrington Hills IL 60010 Office: 7310 North Ave Elmwood Park IL 60635

CHOW, CHI-MING, mathematics educator; b. Tai-Yuan, Shansi, Republic of China, Nov. 15, 1931; came to U.S., 1959; s. Wei-Han Chow and Lu-Tsen Hsu. Cert. tech. officer, Chinese Air Force Tech. Inst., Republic of China, 1954; BS in Math., Ch. Coll. Hawaii, 1962; MS in Math., Oreg. State U., 1965. Tech. officer Chinese Air Force, Republic of China, 1954-59; prof. math. Oakland Community Coll., Farmington Hills, Mich., 1965—; student advisor Oakland Community Coll., Union Lake, Mich., 1968; mem. scholar com. Oakland Community Coll., Farmington Hills, 1985—. Contbr. articles to prof. jours. Donor United Fund, Mich., and others. Served to 1st lt. Air Force of Republic of China, 1954-59. Mem. NEA, Mich. Edn. Assn., Oakland Community Coll. Faculty Assn., Pi Mu Epsilon. Avocation: piloting aircraft. Home: PO Box 903 Novi MI 48050 Office: Oakland Community Coll Math Dept 27055 Orchard Lake Rd Farmington Hills MI 48018

CHOW, HAU CHEUNG, physics educator; b. Shanghai, Peoples Republic China; Came to U.S., 1964; m. Christa R. Schmidt. BS with high honors, U. Tex., 1968; MS, UCLA, 1970; PhD, British Columbia U., 1977. Cons. Xonics, Inc., Van Nuys, Calif., 1972-74; vis. asst. prof. Okla. State U., Stillwater, 1978-80, vis. assoc. prof., 1984; vis. asst. prof. U. Wis., Madison, 1981; assoc. prof. So. Ill. U., Edwardsville, 1980—; cons. physics Naval Research Lab, 1985. Contbr. over 20 articles to profl. jour. Mem. Am. Phys. Soc., Phi Beta Kappa. Office: So Ill Univ Edwardsville IL 62025

CHOW, JAMES MILTON, otolaryngologist; b. Buffalo, Nov. 5, 1954; s. Wen-Lung and Rhoda (Dai) C.; m. Minda Cabinian, Oct. 3, 1981; children: Christina Rhoda, Rebecca Ann. BS, U. Ill., 1976, MD, 1980. Diplomate Am. Bd. Otolaryngology. Intern, then resident U. Ill. Med. Ctr., Chgo., 1980-84, chief resident, 1983-84, asst. prof., 1984—; dir. head and neck spl. care unit U. Ill., Chgo., 1985—; mem. coms. on electives and quality assurance U. Ill., Chgo., 1980—. Contbr. articles to profl. jours. Bd. dirs. Cardinal Stritch Found. for the Deaf. Recipient hon. award pediatrics Ill. Masonic Hosp., 1979, Walter P. Work Soc. Research award, Ann Arbor, Mich., 1983. Fellow Am. Acad. Otolaryngology; mem. AMA, Am. Acad. Facial Plastic and Reconstructive Surgery, Chgo. Med. Soc., Chgo. Laryngol. and Otol. Soc. (Lederer Pierce Research award 1983, 84), Soc. Univ. Otolaryngologists, Alpha Omega Alpha. Roman Catholic. Avocations: stamp and coin collecting, tennis, golf, fishing, violin. Home: 9 S 557 Dixon Ct Downers Grove IL 60516 Office: U Ill 1855 W Taylor Chicago IL 60612

CHOWDARY, GORANTLA KOTI SWAMY, anesthesiologist; b. Gorantlavaripalem, India, July 1, 1944; came to U.S., 1973; s. Venkata Subbaiah and Pushpavathi (Ambati) C.; m. Kondreddy Krishnaveni, May 22, 1975; children: Kavita, Kalyan. P.U.C., Andhra Loyola Coll., Vijayawada, India, 1962; MBBS, Guntur (India) Med. Coll., 1969, postgrad., 1970-73. Diplomate Am. Bd. Anesthesiology. Resident dept. anesthesiology Cook County

Hosp., Chgo., 1973-77, attending physician, 1977-80, acting chmn. dept. anesthesiology, 1980-83; ptnr. Assoc. Anesthesiologists, Hammond, Ind., 1983—. Fellow Am. Coll. Anesthesiologists; mem. Internat. Anesthesiare Search Soc., Am. Acad. Clin. Anesthesiologists, Ind. Soc. Anesthesiologists, Am. Soc. Anasthesiologists, Soc. for Ambulatory Anesthesia, Anesthesia Patient Safety Found., Soc. Cardiovascular Anesthesiologists, Soc. Critical Care Anesthesiologists. Home: St Margaret Hosp Dept Anesthesia 5454 Hohman Ave Hammond IN 46320

CHOWDHURY, ASHOK KUMAR, economics educator, researcher; b. West Bengal, India, Aug. 15, 1951; came to U.S., 1980; s. Haradhan and Jyotsna C.; m. Shipra Sikdar, Aug. 12, 1978; 1 son, Soumen. B.Sc. in Agr. and Animal Husbandry with honors, G.B. Pant U. of Agr. and Tech., Pantnagar, India, 1973; M.Sc., Indian Agrl. Research Inst., New Delhi, 1975; Ph.D., Iowa State U., 1980. Research assoc. Ctr. Agrl. and Rural Devel., Iowa State U., Ames, 1978-80, vis. asst. prof., summer 1981; asst. prof. econs. Mankato (Minn.) State U., 1980-83, assoc. prof., 1983—. G.B. Pant U. Agr. and Tech. scholar, 1972-73; Indian Agrl. Research Inst. jr. fellow, 1973-75. Mem. Am. Econs. Assn., Am. Agrl. Econs. Assn., Midwest Econs. Assn., Sigma Xi, Gamma Sigma Delta. Author books, the most recent being: An Analysis of the Government Operated Reserve Program For U.S. Crop Commodities Under Various Export Situations for 1980-1990, 1985. 1981; An Analysis of the Government-Operated Reserve Program for U.S. Crop Commodities Under Various Export Situations for 1980-1990, 1985. Home: 151 Bermuda Dr Mankato MN 56001 Office: Box 14 Econs Dept Mankato State U Mankato MN 56001

CHOYKE, ARTHUR DAVIS, JR., manufacturing company executive; b. N.Y.C., Mar. 13, 1919; s. Arthur Davis and Lillian (Bauer) C.; A.B., Columbia, 1939, B.S., 1940; m. Phyllis May Ford, Aug. 18, 1945; children—Christopher Ford, Tyler Van. With indsl. engring. dept. Procter & Gamble Co., S.I., N.Y., 1940-43; instr. Pratt Inst., Bklyn., 1942-45; chief indsl. engr. M & M, Ltd., Newark, 1943-47; ptnr. Ford Distbg. Co., Chgo., 1947-57; incorporator, pres., treas., dir. Artcrest Products Co., Inc., Chgo., 1951—; dir. Gallery Series, Harper Sq. Press. Mem. pres.' com. Landamrk Preservation Council Ill., Hist. Alliance Chgo. Hist. Soc. Clubs: Chgo. Farmers, Arts (Chgo.); John Evans Northwestern U. Lodge: Rotary. Home: 29 E Division St Chicago IL 60610 Office: 500 W Cermak Rd Chicago IL 60616

CHOYKE, PHYLLIS MAY FORD (MRS. ARTHUR DAVIS CHOYKE, JR.), ceiling systems company executive, editor, poet; b. Buffalo, Oct. 25, 1921; d. Thomas Cecil and Vera (Buchanan) Ford; m. Arthur Davis Choyke Jr., Aug. 18, 1945; children: Christopher Ford, Tyler Van. BS summa cum laude, Northwestern U., 1942. Reporter City News Bur., Chgo., 1942-43, Met. sect. Chgo. Tribune, 1943-44; feature writer OWI, N.Y.C., 1944-45; sec. corp. Artcrest Products Co., Inc., Chgo., 1958—, v.p., 1964—, founder, dir. Harper Sq. Press div., 1966—. Bonbright scholar, 1942. Mem. Soc. Midland Authors, Mystery Writers Am. (assoc.), Chgo. Press Vets. Assn., Hist. Alliance of Chgo. Hist. Soc., Phi Beta Kappa. Clubs: Arts (Chgo.); John Evans (Northwestern U.). Author: (under name Phyllis Ford) (with others) (poetry) Apertures to Anywhere, 1979; editor: Gallery Series One, Poets, 1967, Gallery Series Two, Poets—Poems of the Inner World, 1968, Gallery Series Three—Poets: Levitations and Observations, 1970, Gallery Series Four, Poets—I am Talking About Revolution, 1973, Gallery Series Five/Poets—To An Aging Nation (with occult overtones), 1977; (manuscripts and papers in Brown U. Library). Home: 29 E Division St Chicago IL 60610 Office: 500 W Cermak Rd Chicago IL 60616

CHRAPKOWSKI, ROSEMARIE, chemical dependence therapist, art therapist; b. Chgo., Dec. 8, 1935; d. Andrew H. and Charlotte D. (Poterackie) C. BFA, U. Chgo. and Sch. Art Inst. Chgo., 1959, postgrad., 1962-63, 78; student Inst. Psychiatry, Chgo., Inst. Psychoanalysis, Chgo., Cen. States Inst. Addiction, C.G. Jung Inst., Chgo.; grad. alcoholism counselor tng. program Grant Hosp., Chgo., 1981. Cert. alcoholism counselor, Ill.; cert sr. addictions counselor, Ill. Artist various studios and agys., from 1963; staff artist Soc. for Visual Edn., Chgo., 1965-66; supr. picture acquisitions Ency. Brit., Inc., Chgo., 1969-71; alcoholism counselor U. Ill. Alcohol Program, Chgo., 1978; sr. chem. dependence counselor Northwestern Meml. Hosp. Inst. Psychiatry, Chgo., 1979-86, expressive arts therapist, 1986—; pvt. practice therapy, Chgo., 1981-87; therapist Assocs. in Jungian Psychology and Creative Therapies, Chgo., 1987—; cons., workshop presenter, art therapist Northwestern Hosp., 1982—; instr., lectr. Cen. State Inst. Addictions, 1986—. Exhibited paintings various galleries, from 1958. Mem. Nat. Assn. Alcoholism and Drug Abuse Counselors, Ill. Addictions Counselors Assn., Ill. Art Therapy Assn., Chgo. Assn. Psychoanalytic Psychology (assoc.), Assn. Transpersonal Psychology, C.G. Jung Inst., Alumni Assn. Sch. Art Inst. Chgo. (life), Sierra Club, Lincoln Park Zool. Soc., Nat. Anti-Vivisection Soc. (life), Humane Soc. U.S., Wilderness Soc.

CHRISMAN, GEORGE ALBERT, art educator; b. Kansas City, Mo., Aug. 15, 1934; s. Howard Chanslor and Mollie Belle (Ziegler) C.; m. Rachel Caroline Lowman, Aug. 18, 1956; children: Marty Rachelle, Scott Gibson, George Chanslor, Aaron Robert. Student, U. Kans., 1954, Kansas City Art Inst., 1955-56; BA, U. Mo., Kansas City, 1963, MA, 1967. Cert. art tchr., Mo. (life). Dance instr. Arthur Murray, Kansas City, 1955-56; art instr. Grandview (Mo.) Pub. Schs., 1957—; instr. William Nelson Creative Art Ctr., Kansas City, 1958-70, Johnson County Community Coll. Kids Coll. Art Ctr., Unexa, Kans., 1986; instr. Kansas City Art Inst., 1984-85; cons. design S. Aldin Inc., 1986. Mem. NEA (life), Mo. NEA, Grandview NEA (local pres. 1969-70, 74-75, chmn. negotiations 1974-78, 83, Service award 1983). Mem. Disciples of Christ Ch. Home: 310 Raintree Dr Lees Summit MO 64063

CHRISOPULOS, JOHN, food service specialist; b. Oak Park, Ill., Jan. 5, 1946; s. Harry and Nicolette (Kappos) C.; student DePaul U., 1964-65; cert., Washburne Trade Sch., 1968; m. Pamela Sue Towsley, Sept. 17, 1978; 1 dau., Amanda Lynn. Sous-chef Racquet Club of Chgo., 1968-69; food service dir. Szabo Food Service, Chgo., 1970-71; owner Markon's Restaurant and Delicatesson, Chgo., 1971-74; mgr. food service Northwestern Meml. Hosp., Chgo., 1974; dir. food service Holy Family Hosp., Des Plaines, Ill., 1975-78; pres. Connoisseurs Caterers, Inc., Barrington, Ill., 1978-82; dir. food services Westlake Community Hosp., Melrose Park, Ill., 1979-80; assoc. dir. food and nutrition service U. Chgo. Med. Center, 1980-82; food service specialist John Sexton & Co., Elk Grove Village, Ill., 1982—. Recipient Pres.'s Club award, 1984. Mem. Am. Soc. Hosp. Food Service Adminstrs. (bd. dirs. 1975-76, chmn. 10th annual ednl. conf. 1977, pres.-elect 1977, pres. 1978, mem. nat. nominating com. 1978), Internat. Food Service Execs. Assn., Catering Execs. Club. Am. Greek Orthodox. Home and Office: 1106 N Plum Grove Rd Schaumburg IL 60173

CHRISTEN, ARDEN GALE, dental educator, researcher, consultant; b. Lemmon, S.D., Jan. 25, 1932; s. Harold John Christen and Dorothy Elizabeth (Taylor) Deering; m. Joan Ardell Akre, Sept. 10, 1955; children—Barbara, Penny, Rebecca, Sarah. B.S., U. Minn., 1954, D.D.S., 1956; M.S.D., Ind. U., 1965; M.A., Ball State U., 1973. Lic. dentist S.D., Minn., Ind. Commd. 1st lt. U.S. Air Force, 1956, advanced through grades to col., 1972; base dental surgeon Zaragoza Air Base, Spain, 1970-73; dental surgeon, cons. preventive dentistry RAF Bentwaters, Eng., 1973-75; air force preventive dentistry officer Sch. Aerospace Medicine, Brooks AFB, Tex., 1978-80; prof., chmn. dept. preventive dentistry Ind. U., Indpls., 1981—; sr. med. service cons. Surgeon Gen., U.S. Air Force, U.S. and Eng., 1974-80; spl. cons. to asst. surgeon gen. for dental services, Washington, 1975-80. Co-author: Primary Preventive Dentistry, 1987. Contbr. numerous articles to profl. jours. Bd. dirs. Bexar County chpt. Am. Cancer Soc., San Antonio, 1976-80, Marion County chpt., Indpls., 1980—; mem. Ind. div. Pub. Edn. Standing Com., Indpls., 1980. Decorated Service medal with 2 oak leaf clusters; Legion of Merit. Fellow Am. Coll. Dentists; mem. ADA, Am. Acad. Oral Pathology, Internat. Assn. Dental Research, Am. Acad. History of Dentistry (v.p. 1984-85, pres. 1986-87). Democrat. Lutheran. Avocations: photography, classical music, travel, jogging. Home: 7112 Sylvan Ridge Rd Indianapolis IN 46240 Office: Ind U Oral Health Research Inst Sch Dentistry 415 Lansing St Indianapolis IN 46202

CHRISTENSEN, CHERRYL JUNE, physician; b. Muscatine, Iowa, June 7, 1948; d. Wildon Wayne and Lillian June (Hurlburt) H.; m. Doran Michael Christensen, Feb. 14, 1975; children—Julia Anna, Vasthi. B.S. in Pharmacy, U. Iowa, 1971; D.O., Coll. Osteo. Medicine and Surgery, 1975. Head health evaluation occupational medicine service Navy Environ. Health Ctr., Norfolk, Va., 1979-82; occupational and environ. medicine physician U. Cin., 1982—, assoc. dir. Med. Ctr. Health Services, U. Cin., dir. clin. outreach Occupational and Environ. Medicine Dept., asst. clin. prof. occupational medicine, environ. health, Coll. Medicine; pres. Occupational and Environ. Medicine Cons., Cin. Contbr. articles to profl. jours. Mem. AMA, Am. Occupational Med. Assn., Am. Pub. Health Assn., Am. Osteo. Assn. Lutheran. Home: 2736 Grandin Rd Cincinnati OH 45208 Office: Univ Cin Med Ctr ML 705 Cincinnati OH 45267

CHRISTENSEN, DAVID A., clothes manufacturing company executive; b. 1935. BS, S.D. State U., 1957. With John Morrell & Co., 1960-62; with Raven Industries Inc., Sioux Falls, S.D., 1962—, product mgr., 1964-71, pres., chief exec. officer, 1971—. Served with AUS, 1957-60. Office: Raven Industries Inc PO Box 1007 Sioux Falls SD 57101 *

CHRISTENSEN, DAVID ALAN, military officer; b. Yankton, S.D., Dec. 24, 1946; s. Peter Holger and Aves Lorraine (Aune) C.; m. Julaine Faye Elshere, June 23, 1968; children: Nicole Lynne, Jennifer Anne, Chadwick David. BS in Agriculture, S.D. State U., 1968; MBA, Midwestern U., 1972; JD, Creighton U., 1985. Commd.2d lt. USAF, 1969, advanced through grades to maj., 1980; chief of maintenance 2054th Command Squadron, Sheppard AFB, Tex., 1969-72; detachment comdr. Detachment 2, 1962d Command Group, IeShima, Okinawa, Japan, 1972-73; JACC/CP comdr. Joint Communications Support Element, MacDill AFB, Fla., 1975-79; chief of secure integration div. Hdqrs. Def. Communications Agy., Washington, 1982-85; chief of tech. assessment Hdqrs. Strategic Communication Div./XPT, Offutt AFB, Nebr., 1985—. Mem. Rep. Nat. Com.; deacon Bellevue (Nebr.) Assembly of God, 1980-82, 1985—, bd. dirs., 1985—. Mem. Federalist Law Soc., Student Bar Assn., Alpha Gamma Rho. Avocation: golf. Home: 836 Hidden Hills Dr Bellevue NE 68005 Office: HQ SCD/XPT Offutt AFB NE 68113

CHRISTENSEN, DONN DOUGLAS, lawyer; b. St. Paul, June 30, 1929; s. Jonas Jergen and Hildur Minerva (Lundeen) C.; m. Renee E. Pinet, Aug. 31, 1970; children—Keith, Catherine, Eric. B.S., U. Minn., 1950, J.D., 1952. Bar: Minn. 1952, U.S. Fed. Ct. 1955, U.S. Supreme Ct. 1981. Practiced in St. Paul, 1954-68, 70—; dep. atty. gen. State of Minn., 1968-70; justice of peace, City of Mendota Heights, Minn., 1961-66; instr. bus. law Macalester Coll., St. Paul, 1960-67; mediator Minn. Farm Mediation Program, 1986—. Served with U.S. Army, 1952-54. Mem. ABA, Minn. Bar Assn. (chmn. environ. law sect. 1972-73), Ramsey County Bar Assn., Execs. Assn. St. Paul (pres. 1966), Mendota Heights C. of C. (sec. 1965), Delta Theta Phi. Clubs: Athletic, Torch (pres. 1982-83) (St. Paul). Home: 676 Schifsky Rd Saint Paul MN 55126 Office: 3585 N Lexington Ave Suite 155 Saint Paul MN 55126 also: North Branch MN 55056

CHRISTENSEN, DONNA ELIZABETH, health care administrator, small business owner; b. Winnepeg, Man., Can., Jan. 6, 1930; came to U.S., 1933; d. Robert John and Lilah Grace (Smith) Henderson; m. Donald E. Christensen, Dec. 16, 1955 (div. 1983); children: Terry, LuAnn, Thomas, Lori, Todd. Student, U. Minn., 1949-54. Cert. in aquatic adaptations, ARC. Dir. nursing Glenwood Hills Hosp., Mpls., 1955-58; hospice care adminstr. Fairview Hosp., Edina, Minn., 1967—; owner, dir. Grandma's We Sit Better, Spring Park, Minn., 1982—; vol. coordinator West Hennepin County, 1987—; vol. instr. in aquatic adaptation ARC, Golden Valley Courage Ctr., 1986—. Vol. Respite Care for Parents of Handicapped Children, 1975-87; leader Girl Scouts Am., Spring Park, 1978; mem. Heart Fund, Hennepin County, Minn., 1973, Cancer Fund and Edn. Program, Mpls., 1976-86. Mem. Am. Legion, VFW. Republican. Lutheran. Avocations: sewing, knitting, paining, flower gardening, reading. Home: 2052 Commerce Blvd Mound MN 55364

CHRISTENSEN, DONOVAN LEE, jeweler; b. Exira, Iowa, Nov. 6, 1928; s. Edwin Benjamin and Vivian Emalin (Bowen) C.; m. Phyllis Jean Lewis, Sept. 6, 1949; children: Daniel Lee, Ginger Rae, Shager. Grad. high sch., Exira; student, Gemological Inst. Am. Jeweler Christensen Jewelers, Exira, 1946-62, owner, operator, 1962-67; owner, operator Christensen Jewelers, Estherville, Iowa, 1967-81, Baker Jewelers, Eau Claire, Wis., 1981—. Lodge: Elks. Home: Rt 6 Box 272 Chippewa Falls WI 54729 Office: Baker Jewelers 1504 S Hastings Way Eau Claire WI 54701

CHRISTENSEN, GEORGE CURTIS, university official; b. N.Y.C., Feb. 21, 1924; s. Carl Lee and Marie (Larsen) C.; m. Janeth M. Reid, July 19, 1947; children: Curtis Lee, Joyce Janeth, William George, Cheryl Reid. D.V.M., Cornell U., 1949, M.S., 1950, Ph.D., 1953; D.Sc. (hon.), Purdue U., 1978. Instr. vet. anatomy Cornell U., 1949-53; asso. prof. vet. anatomy Iowa State U., 1953-58; prof. vet. anatomy, head dept. Purdue U., 1958-63; dean Iowa State U. Coll. Vet. Medicine, Ames, 1963-65; v.p. acad. affairs Iowa State U., Ames, 1965—; chmn. council on internat. programs, exec. commr. North Central Assn. Colls. and Secondary Schs.; chmn. Iowa Instnl. Com. Ednl. Coordination; mem. com. on costs of educating med. profls. Nat. Acad. Sci.-NRC; mem. Nat. Adv. Research Resources Council, NIH. Co-author: Anatomy of the Dog, 1964. Vice pres. Iowa Bd. Health.; Bd. dirs. Quad Cities Grad. Center, State Hygienic Lab., Iowa, Center for Research Libraries. Served with AUS, 1942-43. Mem. Am. Assn. Anatomists, Am. Assn. Vet. Anatomists, AVMA (past chmn. council on edn.), AAAS, Mid-Am. State Univs. Assn. (v.p., governing council), Nat. Adv. Council on Research Resources, Conf. Research Workers Animal Diseases, Am. Assn. for Accreditation of Lab. Animal Care (chmn.), Nat. Assn. State Univs. and Land Grant Colls. (chmn. council acad. affairs, chmn. com. on open learning, mem. exec. com., com. on ednl. telecommunications, exec. com. council on internat. programs), Assn. Internat. Edn. Adminstrs. (pres.-elect 1986—), N.Y. Acad. Scis., Sigma Xi, Phi Kappa Phi, Phi Zeta, Lambda Chi Alpha, Alpha Psi, Gamma Sigma Delta, Cardinal Key. Lutheran. Club: Rotarian. Research numerous publs. cardiovascular system, genito-urinary system, history vet. med. edn., higher edn. Home: 1025 Gaskill Dr Ames IA 50010

CHRISTENSEN, JAMES MILTON, manufacturing company executive; b. Deadwood, S.D., June 2, 1934; s. Milton Joseph and Florence Ann (Perkovich) C.; m. Nancy Lucille Lervaag, July 25, 1955; children: Marcia Kay, James, Victoria Lynn. BS in Engring., S.D. Tech. U., 1957. Registered profl. engr., S.D. Asst. engr. VA, Fargo, N.D., 1957-62, chief engr., 1962-67; tech. rep. Lennox Industry, Portland, Oreg., 1968-69; v.p. Dunham Assn., Rapid City, S.D., 1970-85, also bd. dirs.; pres. Symcom Inc., Rapid City, 1986—, also bd. dirs.; cons. Am. Arbitrators Assn., Mpls., 1975—. Mem. NSPE (ethics chmn. 1978), ASHRAE (past pres.), S.D. Tech. Alumni Assn. (bd. dirs. 1982—), S.D. Tech. Found. (bd. dirs. 1985—). Republican. Roman Catholic. Club: Arrowhead Country (Rapid City) (bd. idrs. 1979-82). Lodge: Elks. Avocations: golf, squash, music, gardening. Home: 4241 Foothill Dr Rapid City SD 57702 Office: Symcon Inc 522 Kansas City St Rapid City SD 57701

CHRISTENSEN, JERRY MELVIN, agricultural engineer; b. Volga, S.D., May 5, 1949; s. Melvin Nicholi and Louise (Werner) C.; m. Linda Christensen, Apr. 26, 1985. BS, S.D. State U., 1972. Engr. Morton Bldgs., Spencer, Iowa, 1972-73, Morton, Ill., 1973—, livestock housing products mgr., 1981-84, design estimator, 1984-86; asst. bldg. code coordinator with Morton Bldgs. 1986—. Registered profl. engr., Ill., S.D., Wis., Mich., Ind., N.J., N.H., Vt., Ct., Va., Pa., N.Y. Mem. vocat. adv. council Morton High Sch. Mem. Am. Soc. Agrl. Engrs. Democrat. Lutheran. Home: Prairie Village Unit 10 Morton IL 61550 Office: Morton Bldgs Inc 252 W Adams St Morton IL 61550

CHRISTENSEN, ORLA JUNE, educator, psychologist; b. Clarkfield, Minn., June 5, 1934; d. Clifford Arnold and Clara Theoline (Stokke) C.; B.A. in Health and Phys. Edn., Augsburg Coll., Mpls., 1956; M.S. in Counseling (NDEA fellow), Purdue U., 1966; Ed.D. in Counseling and Personnel Services in Higher Edn. (Delta Kappa Gamma scholar), Mont. State U., 1972. Tchr. health and phys. edn. Appleton (Minn.) Pub. Schs., 1956-58, Alexandria (Minn.) Pub. Schs., 1958-65; counselor Irvington (N.Y.) High Sch., 1966-67, Tacoma (Wash.) Pub. Schs., 1967-73; prof. ednl. psychology and counseling U. S.D., Vermillion, 1973—; coordinator, internship program in ednl. psychology and counseling, participant workshops in communications, human relations, cultural awareness, career devel. Mem. Am. Psychol. Assn., Am. Counseling and Devel., S.D. Assn. Counseling and Devel. (pres. elect, pres. 1983-85), Nat. Career Devel. Assn., Assn. Counselor Edn., N.Am. Soc. Adlerian Psychology, Delta Kappa Gamma Internat., Phi Delta Kappa. Contbr. articles in field to profl. jours. Office: Dezell Edn Center U SD Vermillion SD 57069

CHRISTENSEN, ROGER WILLIAM, manufacturing company executive; b. St. Paul, Oct. 26, 1936; s. James Einer and Helen Caroline (Giefer) C.; m. Kristine Elizabeth Skaret, Feb. 23, 1974; 1 child, Eric Joseph. BA, U. Mankato, 1960. Mgr. 3M Co., St. Paul, 1962-68, corp. customer relations mgr., 1968-86. Served with U.S. Army, 1960-66. Mem. Nat. Accounts Mktg. Assn., Am. Mgmt. Assn., Better Bus. Bur., Bus. Econ. Edn. Found., Am. Nat. Standards Inst., Soc. Consumer Affairs Profls. in Bus. (officer 1985—), Delta Sigma Pi. Home: 944 Transit Ave Roseville MN 55113 Office: Minn Mining & Mfg Co Saint Paul MN 55144

CHRISTENSEN, TIMOTHY LEE, electric cooperative executive; b. Des Moines, July 28, 1944; s. Leo Donald and Mildred (Daggy) C.; 1 child, Kristie Rae. Student, U.S. Dept. Agr. Grad. Sch., 1970-71, Superior Tech. Sch., 1970, U. Wis. Extension-Madison, 1975. Acct., Head of the Lakes Coop., Superior, Wis., 1968-71; office mgr. Eau Claire Elec. Coop., Fall Creek, Wis., 1971-73; asst. mgr. Price Electric Coop., Phillips, Wis., 1973-76; exec. v.p., gen. mgr. Cedar Valley Elec. Coop., St. Ansgar, Iowa, 1976-83; exec. v.p., gen. mgr. Ill. Valley Elec. Coop., Princeton, 1983—; dir. Soyland Power Coop., Decatur, Ill., 1983—. Organizer, Phillips Youth Activities, 1975; bd. dirs. St. Ansgar C. of C., 1977-83. Served with USAF, 1962-65. Mem. Am. Legion, Phillips C. of C. (sec. 1976), Wis. REC Office Mgrs. Assn. (pres. 1971-76). Lodges: Lions, Elks. Office: Ill Valley Electric Coop Inc PO Box 70 Princeton IL 61356

CHRISTENSON, ANTHONY STEPHEN, video company executive; b. Wichita, Kans., July 18, 1960; s. Donald Dee and Marilyn Jean (Rend) C.; m. Katherine Marie Taylor, Aug. 30, 1980; children: Karl Alan, Katrina Jean. Grad. high sch., Wichita, 1978. Sales desk clk. S.A. Long Co., Wichita, 1979-84; regional mgr. Capitol Investors COrp., Sioux Falls, S.D., 1985-86; mgr. Popingo Video, Inc., Wichita, 1984-85, mgr., v.p., 1986—. Home: 1755 S Topeka Wichita KS 67207 Office: PARI Corp 7816 E Harry Wichita KS 67207

CHRISTENSON, FABIENNE FADELEY, business executive; b. Washington, June 20, 1951; d. James McNelledge and Catherine Shirley (Sweeney) Fadeley; B.S. cum laude, U. Md., 1976; M.B.A. with honors, Boston U., 1979; m. Gordon A. Christenson, Sept. 16, 1979. With Gen. Electric Aircraft Engine Group, Evendale, Ohio, 1979—, contract adminstr., 1981, 83-84, foreman, 1981, prodn. control specialist, 1980-82, contract adminstr., 1985—, now negotiator for aircraft engine component purchases; pres. Mfg. Tng. Program, 1980. Home: 3465 Principio Ave Cincinnati OH 45226 Office: Gen Electric Aircraft Engine Group Mail Drop A-182C 1 Neumann Way Cincinnati OH 45215

CHRISTENSON, WALLACE LYNNE, dentist; b. Bertha, Minn., Dec. 22, 1936; s. Edward Andrew and Gladys (Lynne) C.; m. Carolyn Joyce Kliewer, Dec. 19 , 1959; children: Lori Ann, Jennifer Lee, Jodi Lynn, Matthew Reed. BS, U. Minn., 1957, DDS, 1961. Dentist Drs. Christenson, Hattstrom, Lindley, Pihlstrom and Wilcox, Mpls., 1963—. Sec., bd. dirs. Mpls. YMCA, 1978—. Served to capt. U.S. Army, 1961-63. Mem. ADA, Minn. State Dental Assn., Mpls. Dist. Dental Soc. Republican. Lutheran. Club: Golden Valley (Minn.) Country (sec., bd. dirs. 1979-82). Lodges: Masons, Shriners. Avocations: music, reading, golf, skiing, tennis. Home: 2455 Brunswick Ave N Golden Valley MN 55422 Office: 6120 Brooklyn Blvd Minneapolis MN 55429

CHRISTIAN, NELSON FREDERICK, chemical engineer; b. Chgo., Sept. 4, 1949; s. Norman Frederick and Blanche (Zach) C.; m. Terryl Lynn Smith, Jan. 11, 1975. BSChemE, Ariz. State U., 1972. Process engr. Farmland Industries, Coffeyville, Kans., 1978-82, sr. ops. advisor, 1982-84, process mgr., 1984—. Served to capt. USAF, 1972-78. Mem. Nat. Petroleum Refiners Assn. (nat. question and answer session). Republican. Lutheran. Avocations: golf, restoring antiques, fishing, gardening. Office: Farmland Industries PO Box 570 Coffeyville KS 67337

CHRISTIAN, RICHARD CARLTON, educator, former advertising agency executive; b. Dayton, Ohio, Nov. 29, 1924; s. Raymond A. and Louise (Gamber) C.; m. Audrey Bongartz, Sept. 10, 1949; children: Ann Christian Carra, Richard Carlton. B.S. in Bus. Adminstrn, Miami U., Oxford, Ohio, 1948; MBA, Northwestern U., 1949; LLD (hon.), Nat. Coll. Edn., 1986; postgrad., Denison U., The Citadel, Biarritz Am. U. Mktg. analyst Rockwell Mfg. Co., Pitts., 1949-50; exec. v.p. Marsteller Inc., Chgo., 1951-60; pres. Marsteller Inc., 1960-75, chmn. bd., 1975-84, chmn. emeritus, 1984—; assoc. dean Kellogg Grad. Sch. Mgmt. Northwestern U., 1984—; dir., chmn. Bus. Publs. Audit Circulation, Inc., 1969-75; Speaker, author marketing, sales mgmt., marketing research and advt. Trustee Northwestern U., 1970-74, Nat. Coll. Edn., Evanston, Ill., 1970—, James Webb Young Fund for Edn., U. Ill., 1962—; pres. Nat. Advt. Rev. Council, 1976-77; bd. adv. council mem. Miami U.; mem. adv. council J. L. Kellogg Grad. Sch. Mgmt., Northwestern U.; v.p., dir. Mus. Broadcast Communications. Served with inf. AUS, 1942-46, ETO. Decorated Bronze Star, Purple Heart; recipient Ohio Gov.'s award, 1977, Alumni medal, Alumni Merit and Service awards Northwestern U. Mem. Am. Mktg. Assn., Indsl. Marketing Assn. (founder, chmn. 1951), Bus./Profl. Advt. Assn. (life mem. Chgo., pres. Chgo. 1954-55, nat. v.p. 1955-58, G.D. Crain award 1977), U. Ill. Found., Northwestern U. Bus. Sch. Alumni Assn. (founder, pres.), Am. Assn. Advt. Agys. (dir., chmn. 1976-77), Am. Acad. Advt. (1st disting. service award 1978), Northwestern U. Alumni Assn. (nat. pres. 1968-70), Council Better Bus. Burs. Chgo. (dir.), Council Fgn. Relations, Bus. Press Ednl. Fedn. (bd. dirs.), Alpha Delta Sigma, Beta Gamma Sigma, Delta Sigma Pi, Phi Gamma Delta. Baptist (trustee). Clubs: Sky (N.Y.C.); Mid-America, Commercial, Chicago, Executives, Economic (Chgo.); Kenilworth; Westmoreland Country (Wilmette, Ill.); Pine Valley Golf (Clementon, N.J.). Office: J L Kellogg Grad Sch Mgmt Northwestern U Leverone Hall Evanston IL 60201

CHRISTIAN, SAMARA MARIE, jewelry designer; b. Sturgeon Bay, Wis., June 8, 1956; d. Earl Otto and L. Rochelle (Fairchild) Philipp; m. Greg Paul Christian, Oct. 24, 1981. BS, U. Wis.-Stout, 1978. Owner gallery Cupola Collection, Egg Harbor, Wis., 1978; art tchr. Eisenhower High Sch., Hopkins, Minn., 1978-79; publs. designer Sch. Home Econs., U. Wis.-Stout, Menomonie, 1979-80; owner, jewelry designer Gold and Silver Creations, Sturgeon Bay, 1981—. Avocations: gardening, crafts, historic home restoration. Home: 742 Jefferson St Sturgeon Bay WI 54235 Office: Gold and Silver Creations 742 Jefferson St Sturgeon Bay WI 54235

CHRISTIAN, TERRY VINCENT, aerospace engineer; b. Delaware, Ohio, Feb. 10, 1954; s. LaVerne Vincent and Doris (Smith) C.; m. Carol Ann Stegner, Oct. 8, 1977; 1 child, Erin. BS in Aero. and Astronautical Engring., Ohio State U., 1977. Simulation engr. flight control div. Air Force Wright Aero. Labs., Wright-Patterson AFB, Ohio, 1977-86; flight control engr. X-29 Air Force Wright Aero. Labs., Wright-Patterson AFB, Ohio, 1986—. Named one of Outstanding Young Men of Am., 1985. Mem. AIAA, Soc. Computer Simulation. Lutheran. Avocations: camping, fishing, archery, golf. Office: Air Force Wright Aero Labs FIGD B-45 Area B Wright-Patterson AFB OH 45433

CHRISTIAN-MICHAELS, STEPHEN, social worker; b. San Francisco, Mar. 3, 1954; s. Richard Houghton Michaels and Madeline Larrabee; m. Andrea Marie Christian, May 24, 1980; 1 child, Matthew. BA, Carnegie-Mellon U., 1977; MA, U. Chgo., 1979; postgrad. cert. family systems program, Inst. for Juvenile Research, 1982. Cert. social worker, Ill. Psychotherapist Leyden Family Services, Franklin Park, Ill., 1979-80; clinician, cons. DuPage County Health Dept., Wheaton, Ill., 1980-83, sr. clinician, cons., 1983-85, supr., 1985—; ptnr., therapist Ctr. for Family Change, Oakbrook Terrace, Ill., 1985—; chmn. high risk child task force Dupage Consortium, Inc., Wheaton, 1982-86, chmn. hosp. subcom., 1986—; cons. Bloomingdale Twp. (Ill.) Com. on Youth, 1983—. Mem. Nat. Assn.

Social Workers, Acad. Cert. Social Workers, Am. Assn. Marriage and Family Therapy. Avocations: camping, hiking. Home: 3919 Custer Lyons IL 60534 Office: DuPage County Health Dept 111 N County Farm Rd Wheaton IL 60187

CHRISTIANSEN, ALAN KEITH, architect; b. Des Moines, Aug. 15, 1946; s. Wallace Wilson and Gertrude Anne (Sandberg) C.; m. Patricia Jo Storey, Oct. 28, 1972; children: Sara Storey, David Matthew, Michael John. Student, Grand View Jr. Coll., 1964-66; B. of Architecture, Iowa State U., 1972. Registered profl. architect, Iowa. Architect in tng. Robert L. VanDeVenter, West Des Moines, Iowa, 1972-75; architect Des Moines, 1975-79, H. Ronald Walker Architects, Des Moines, 1979-82, Bloodgood Group, Des Moines, 1982-87; pvt. practice architecture Des Moines, 1987—. Mem. AIA, Nat. Council Archtl. Registration Bds. (cert.), Des Moines Architects Council. Democrat. Presbyterian. Avocations: hunting, fishing, golf.

CHRISTIANSEN, JANELL JUNE, dentist; b. Alexandria, S.D., June 6, 1940; d. Herbert and Mabel Viola (Sievers) Jucht; m. Richard Christiansen, Aug. 5, 1967; children: Lance, Trent. BS in Nursing, S.D. State U., 1962; M in Nursing Edn., U. Minn., 1966, DDS, 1977. Asst. prof. nursing Meth. Hosp., Mitchell, S.D., 1962, Coll. St. Catherine, St. Paul, 1967-74; practice dentistry Lennox, S.D., 1978—; dentist Added Satellite Clinic, Beresford, S.D., 1984—; cons. in field. Bd. dirs. and health educator West Lincoln unit Am. Cancer Soc., Lennox, 1979—; pres. Lennox PTA, 1982-83; sec. bldg. com. First Bapt. Ch., Chancellor, S.D., 1982-83; trustee N.Am. Bapt. Sem., Sioux Falls, S.D., 1985—; chmn. Career State of Minn. Mobility Task Force, 1971-72. Mem. Am. Dental Soc., Beresford C. of C., Sigma Theta Tau, Omicron Kappa Upsilon. Republican. Club: Lennox Comml. (bd. dirs. 1980-82). Avocations: gardening, farming, reading. Home: Rural Rt 2 Box 28 Lennox SD 57039 Office: Christiansen Dental Clinic 101 S Main Lennox SD 57039

CHRISTIANSEN, LISA, nurse; b. Valparaiso, Ind., May 5, 1961; d. John and Julia (Svensli) C. AS, Anderson Coll., 1983. RN, Ind., Ohio. Nurse ICU St. Anthony Hosp., Michigan City, Ind., 1983-84, Mt. Sinai Hosp., Cleve., 1984-85; nurse ICU, dialysis Ohio State U. Hosps., columbus, 1985—. Vol. Easter Seals, Columbus, 1986-87, Am. Heart Assn., Columbus, 1986; photographer Columbus Zoo, 1987; fundraiser Ohio State U. Mem. Am. Nephrology Nurse Assn. (sec.-treas. 1987), Ohio Nurses Assn., Sons of Norway. Lutheran. Avocations: stamp collecting, photography. Home: 430 E Dunedin Rd Columbus OH 43214 Office: Ohio State U Hosps 410 W Tenth #4623 Columbus OH 43210

CHRISTIANSEN, NORMAN JUHL, newspaper publisher; b. Isle, Minn., Apr. 30, 1923; s. Arthur Theodore and Ingeborg Hansena (Clemensen) C.; m. Margaret Eleanor Whorton, June 13, 1948; children—Gregory Lowell, Susan Joy. B.A. in Journalism, Drake U., Des Moines, 1947. Reporter Bloomington (Ill.) Pantagraph, 1947; spl. agt. FBI, 1948-54; mem. labor relations staff Am. Newspaper Pubs. Assn., 1954-59; with Gannett Newspapers, 1959-67; asst. gen. mgr. Westchester-Rockland Newspaper Group, 1965-67; with Knight-Ridder Newspapers, Inc., 1967-80; group v.p. ops. Knight-Ridder Newspapers, Inc., Miami, Fla., 1975-80; pres., pub. Wichita (Kans.) Eagle and Beacon, 1980—. Bd. dirs. William Allen White Found., United Way, Wichita and Sedgwick, Wichita State U., Endowment Assn. Served with AUS, 1943-45. Mem. Am. Newspaper Pubs. Assn., Inland Daily Press Assn. (dir.). Clubs: Wichita, Wichita Country. Home: 626 N Doreen St Wichita KS 67206 Office: The Wichita Eagle-Beacon Wichita Eagle & Beacon Pub Co Inc 825 E Douglas Ave Box 820 Wichita KS 67201

CHRISTIANSEN, PAUL ALGER, business exec.; b. Detroit, July 3, 1928; s. Alger Cornelius and Gladys Marie (Volz) C.; B.S., Wayne State U., 1948, M.A., 1949; postgrad. U. Minn., 1950-60, Harvard U., 1978-79; m. Irene A. Adams, July 16, 1954; children—Paul Alger II, John Adams. Instr., Va. Poly. Inst. and State U., Blacksburg, 1949-51; accountant Arthur Andersen & Co., Kansas City, Mo., 1952-55; sr. tax accountant Arthur Young & Co., Kansas City, 1956-58; prof. acctg. U. Mo., Kansas City, 1958-80; owner Paul A. Christiansen, C.P.A., Kansas City, 1958—; pres. Metal Engineered Structures, Inc., Kansas City, 1963—, Paul A. Christiansen & Co., Blue Springs, Mo., 1966—, Lake Village Corp., Blue Springs, 1975—. Mem. Jackson County Bond Adv. Commn., 1967-73; chmn. 4th Congl. Dist. Republican Com., 1968; mem. Jackson County Rep. Com., 1968-72; pres. Independence Rep. Club, 1968-72. Decorated King Fredrik II Medal (Norway); C.P.A., Mo. Mem. Am. Inst. C.P.A.'s, Mo. Soc. C.P.A.'s, AAUP (chpt. pres. 1964-65), Nat. Assn. Home Builders, Eastern Jackson County Builders and Developers Assn., Beta Alpha Psi. Contbr. articles to profl. jours. Home: 3333 Lake Shore Dr Blue Springs MO 64015 Office: 333 Lake Village Blvd Blue Springs MO 64015

CHRISTIANSEN, RAYMOND STEPHAN, librarian, educator; b. Oak Park, Ill., Feb. 15, 1950; s. Raymond Julius and Anne Mary (Fusek) C.; m. Phyllis Anne Dombkowski, Nov. 25, 1972; 1 child, Mark David. BA, Elmhurst Coll., 1971; MEd, No. Ill. U., 1974. Dept. dir. Elmhurst Coll., Ill., 1971-73; asst. law librarian media services Lewis U., Glen Ellyn, Ill., 1974-77; asst. prof. edn. Aurora U., Ill., 1977—, media librarian, 1977-82, instructional developer, 1982—; media cons., 1977—. Author video series: Rothblatt on Criminal Advocacy, 1975; book: Index to SCOPE the UN Magazine, 1977. Mem. Assn. Ednl. Communications and Tech., Assn. Tchr. Educators, Assn. Supervision and Curriculum Devel. Home: 424 S Gladstone Ave Aurora IL 60506 Office: Aurora U Library 347 S Gladstone Aurora IL 60506

CHRISTIANSEN, RICHARD DEAN, journalist; b. Berwyn, Ill., Aug. 1, 1931; s. William Edward and Louise Christine (Dethlefs) C. B.A., Carleton Coll., Northfield, Minn., 1953; postgrad., Harvard U., 1954. Reporter, critic, editor Chgo. Daily News, 1957-73, 74-78; editor Chicagoan mag., 1973-74; critic-at-large Chgo. Tribune, 1978-83, entertainment editor, 1983—. Served with U.S. Army, 1954-56. Recipient award Chgo. Newspaper Guild, 1969, 74. Mem. Am. Theatre Critics Assn., Chgo. Acad. TV Arts and Scis. Republican. Lutheran. Clubs: Headline (Chgo.), Arts (Chgo.) (dir.). Home: 666 Lake Shore Dr Apt 1109 Chicago IL 60611 Office: Chgo Tribune 435 N Michigan Ave Chicago IL 60611 *

CHRISTIANSEN, RICHARD LOUIS, orthodontics educator, dean; b. Denison, Iowa, Apr. 1, 1935; s. John Cornelius and Rosa Katherine C.; m. Nancy Marie Norman, June 24, 1956; children—Mark Richard, David Norman, Laura Marie. D.D.S., U. Iowa, 1959; M.S.D., Ind. U., Indpls., 1964; Ph.D., U. Minn., 1970. Prin. investigator Nat. Inst. Dental Research NIH, Bethesda, Md., 1970-73, chief craniofacial anomalies, 1973-81, assoc. dir. extramural Nat. Inst. Dental Research, 1981-82; prof. dept. orthodontics U. Mich., Ann Arbor, 1982—, dean, Sch. Dentistry and dir. W.K. Kellogg Found. Inst., 1982—; organizer state-of-the-art workshops in field of craniofacial anomalies and other aspects of oral health. Contbr. chpts. to books and articles to profl. jours. Chmn. Region III United Way, U. Mich., Ann Arbor, 1984; chmn., v.p. Trinity Lutheran Ch., Rockville, Md., 1975, planning task force Trinity Luth. Ch., Ann Arbor. Served with USPHS, 1959-82. Recipient Commendation medal USPHS, 1980; Cert. of Recognition NIH, 1982. Fellow Internat. Coll. Dentists, Am. Coll. Dentists, Pierre Fauchard Acad.; mem. Am. Assn. Dental Sch., ADA, Mich. Dental Assn., Am. Assn. Dental Research (dir. craniofacial biology group 1975-79, v.p. 1979-80, pres. 1981-82), Omicron Kappa Upsilon. Republican. Avocations: reading, jogging, tennis, sailing, econs. Home: 5612 N Dixboro Rd Ann Arbor MI 48105

CHRISTIANSEN, RUSSELL, utility company executive; b. Jefferson, S.D., May 19, 1935; s. Milton and Grace Marie (Rosenburger) C.; m. Marilyn Grace Connors, Oct. 6, 1956; children: Lori, Lynn Christiansen Lanning, Lisa, Russell P. B.S. in Engring., S.D. State U., 1959. Various engring. positions Iowa Pub. Service Co., Sioux City, 1959-76, prodn. mgr., 1976-79, v.p. prodn., 1979-81, v.p. trans. and dist., 1981-83, sr. v.p. consumer services, 1983-84, exec. v.p., chief operating officer, 1984, pres., chief operating officer, 1984—; exec. v.p. Midwest Energy Co., Sioux City, 1984, pres., 1985, chmn., pres., chief exec. officer, 1986—; bd. dirs. Security Nat. Bank, Sioux City, Alexander Energy Corp. Chmn. United Way of Siouxland Campaign, Sioux City, 1984; bd. dirs. Sioux City Aid Ctr., 1983-86, Sioux City Symphony, 1984—, Gordon Chem. Dependency Ctr., Sioux City, 1984—. Served with U.S. Army, 1954-56. Mem. Am. Gas Assn. (bd. dirs. 1986—), Midwest Gas Assn., Edison Electric Inst., Siouxland Assn. Bus. & Industry (bd. dirs. 1984—, chmn. 1986-87). Republican. Roman Catholic. Club: Country (Sioux City). Lodges: Lions, Rotary. Avocations: backpacking; fly fishing; tennis; skiing. Office: Midwest Energy Co 401 Douglas St PO 1348 PO Box 1348 Sioux City IA 51106

CHRISTIANSON, BONITA RAE, systems engineer; b. Austin, Minn., Nov. 14, 1953; s. Marion Selmer and Bertha Arlee (Ballantyne) C.; m. Paul Edward Pederson, May 24, 1986. BA, St. Olaf Coll., 1977. Systems engr. IBM, Minn., 1977—. Mem. Phi Beta Kappa. Democrat. Lutheran. Avocation: reading, piano. Home: 2305 Irving Ave S Minneapolis MN 55405-2529 Office: IBM Corp 100 Washington Sq Suite 900 Minneapolis MN 55401

CHRISTIANSON, ELIN BALLANTYNE, librarian, civic worker; b. Gary, Ind., Nov. 11, 1936; d. Donald B. and Dorothy May (Dunning) Ballantyne; B.A., U. Chgo., 1958, M.A., 1961, certificate advanced studies, 1974; m. Stanley David Christianson, July 25, 1959; children—Erica, David. Asst. librarian, then librarian J. Walter Thompson Co., Chgo., 1959-68; library cons., 1968—; part-time lectr. Grad. Library Sch., U. Chgo., 1981—, Sch. Library and Info. Sci., Ind. U., 1982—. Chmn. Hobart Am. Revolution Bicentennial Commn., 1974-76; bd. dirs. Hobart Hist. Soc., 1973—, pres., 1980-85; pres. LWV, Hobart, 1977-79. Recipient Laura Bracken award Hobart Jaycees, 1976; cert. achievement Ind. Am. Revolution Bicentennial Commn., 1975; Woman of Yr. award Hobart Bus. and Profl. Women, 1985. Mem. Am. Assn. Info. Sci., ALA, Ind. Library Assn., Spl. Libraries Assn. (chmn. advt. and mktg. div. 1967-68), English Spl. Libraries Assn., Assn. Library and Info. Sci. Edn., AAUW (pres. Hobart br. 1975-77), U. Chgo. Grad. Library Sch. Alumni Assn. (v.p. 1971-74, 76-77, pres. 1977-79). Unitarian. Author: Non-Professional and Paraprofessional Staff in Special Libraries, 1973; Directory of Library Resources in Northwest Indiana, 1976; Old Settlers Cemetery, 1976; New Special Libraries: A Summary of Research, 1980; Daniel Nash Handy and the Special Library Movement, 1980; co-author: Subject Headings in Advertising, Marketing and Communications Media, 1964; Special Libraries: A Guide for Management, 1981, rev. 2d edit., 1986; mem. editorial adv. bd. New Standard Encyclopedia, 1986—. Address: 141 Beverly Blvd Hobart IN 46342

CHRISTIANSON, JAMES DUANE, real estate developer; b. Bismarck, N.D., Aug. 18, 1952; s. Adolph M. and Elizabeth M. (Barnes) C. Student, Bismarck Jr. Coll., 1970, 1971-72, U. N.D., 1971. Lic. pvt. pilot. Gen. mgr. and supr. Nutrition Search, Bismarck, 1974-76; gen. mgr. Home Still, Inc., Bismarck, 1976-78; v.p. Good Heart Assocs., Bismarck, 1978-82; pres. N. W. Devel. Group, Bismarck, 1982—; chmn. bd. Basin State Bank, Stanford, Mont., 1986—. Supr. editor: Nutrition Almanac, 1975. Mem. Bismarck Centennial Com., 1986-89. Recipient Outstanding Citizen award Mayor and City Commn., Bismarck, 1982. Avocations: traveling, reading, computers, golf. Office: N W Devel Group Inc 412 1/2 E Main Box 1097 Bismarck ND 58502

CHRISTIE, ADRIAN JOSEPH, pathologist; b. Cardiff, Wales, Dec. 1, 1940; s. Maxwell and Sonia (Samuel) C.; came to U.S., 1973; M.D., Welsh Nat. Sch. Medicine, 1964; m. Mynetta Ann Michaelson, Dec. 12, 1965; children—Helen, Leona, Gavin. Resident in pathology Mt. Sinai Hosp., N.Y.C., 1967-68; asst. lectr. pathology Middlesex Hosp. Med. Sch., London, 1968-69; sr. registrar Southmead Hosp., Bristol, Eng., 1970-73; pathologist Grace and I.O.D.E. hosps., Windsor, Ont., Can., 1973-75, Detroit-Macomb Hosps. Assn., Detroit, 1976, Cottage Hosp., Grosse Pointe, Mich., 1976—; clin. asst. prof. Wayne State U. Med. Sch., Detroit. Diplomate Am. Bd. Pathology. Fellow Royal Coll. Physicians and Surgeons (Can.), Am. Soc. Clin. Pathologists, Coll. Am. Pathologists, Internat. Acad. Pathology, Royal Coll. Pathologists; mem. AMA, Wayne County Med. Soc., Mich. Soc. Pathologists, N.Y. Acad. Scis. Jewish. Club: H.M.C.S. Hunter (Windsor). Author papers complications silicone joint implants. Home: 1010 W Lincoln St Birmingham MI 48009 Office: 11800 E 12 Mile Rd Warren MI 48093

CHRISTIE, GARY ALBERT, marketing executive; b. Hazleton, Pa., July 30, 1952; s. Ector Joseph and Jean Christie; widowed; 1 child, Allison. BS in Civil Engring., U. Pitts., 1974; MBA, Baldwin Wallace Coll., 1977. Jr. project engr., bus. devel. specialist, corp. planner Davy McKee Corp., Independence, Ohio, 1974-81; bus. devel. specialist Babcock & Wilcox Internat., Barberton, Ohio, 1981-82; mktg. mgr. Union Metal Mfg. Co., Canton, Ohio, 1982-84; dir. mktg. Shanafelt Mfg. Co., Canton, 1984—. Roman Catholic. Avocations: photography, golf, reading, music. Home: 13530 Inverness Ave NW Uniontown OH 44685 Office: Shanafelt Mfg Co 2600 Winfield Way NE Canton OH 44705

CHRISTIE, MICHAEL JAE, advertising executive; b. Des Moines, July 19, 1956; s. James Edward and Barbara Kay (Spence) C.; m. Silvia Consuegra, May 26, 1974 (div. Feb. 1981); m. Kimberly Ann Saiger, June 15, 1985; children: Elizabeth Anne, Brandon Michael. Gen. mgr. Advanced Lighting, Inc., Altamonte Springs, Fla., 1976-80; mgr. Custom Shop, Chgo. and Dearborn, Mich., 1980-82; sr. account exec., regiional sales mgr. Pocket Savers Plus, Inc., Madison Heights, Mich., 1984-85; pvt. practice mktg. cons. 1984—; dir. franchising Hungry Howies Pizza, Inc., Plymouth, Mich., 1984. Co-developer Anonymous Self Help Group for Recovering Addicts, Detroit, 1982. Mem. Am. Mensa Ltd. Avocations: reading, computers. Home: 5458 Neckel Dearborn MI 48126 Office: Pocket Savers Plus Inc PO Box 71625 Madison Heights MI 48071

CHRISTIE, WALTER SCOTT, state official; b. Indpls., 1922; s. Walter Scott and Nina Lilian (Warfel) C. B.S. in Bus. Adminstrn., Butler U., 1948. With Roy J. Pile & Co., C.P.A.s, Indpls., 1948-56, Howard E. Nyhart Co., Inc., actuarial consultants, Indpls., 1956-62; with Ind. Dept. Ins., Indpls., 1962—, dep. commr., 1966-74, adminstrv. officer, 1974-79, sr. examiner 1979-81, adminstrv. asst., 1981-82, chief auditor, 1982—; bd. dirs. Sr. Enterprises. Bd. dirs. Delt House Corp., Butler U. Served with AUS, 1942-45. Named Ky. Col.; C.P.A., Ind.; cert. fin. examiner. Mem. Ind. Assn. C.P.A.s, Soc. Fin. Examiners (state chmn.), Indpls. Actuarial Club, Nat. Assn. Ins. Commrs. (chmn. Zone IV life and health com. 1970-75), Internat. Platform Assn. Episcopalian (assoc. vestryman 1948-60). Club: Optimist (dir.). Home: 620 E 53d St Indianapolis IN 46220 Office: Indiana Dept Ins 113 E Washington St Suite 300 Indianapolis IN 46204

CHRISTISON, WILLIAM HENRY, III, lawyer; b. Moline, Ill., Aug. 30, 1936; s. William Henry and Gladys Evelyn (Matherly) C.; m. Mary Proctor Stone, Sept. 16, 1958; children—William Henry IV, Elizabeth S., Caroline S. B.A., Northwestern U., 1958; LL.B., U. Iowa, 1961. Bar: Ill. 1961, Iowa. Ptnr. Baymiller, Christison & Radley, Peoria, Ill., 1961—; permanent trustee in bankruptcy U.S. Dist. Ct., Cen. Dist. Ill., Peoria, 1967—; v.p., dir. W.H.C., Inc., Moline, 1958-86, pres., 1987—; dir., mem. exec. com., trust investment com. 1st Nat. Bank, Peoria, 1967—; dir. 1st Peoria Corp. Mem. Peoria Sesquicentennial Commn., 1968; bd. dirs., vice chmn. John C. Proctor Endowment, 1964—, pres., 1972—; bd. dirs. Meth. Med. Ctr. Found. (chmn. bd. 1987—), Ill. Masonic Youth Found., 1976-82; trustee Meth. Med. Ctr. Ill. Mem. ABA, Ill. Bar Assn. (dist. sec. 1966), Iowa Bar Assn., Peoria Bar Assn. (dir. 1968-69), Greater Peoria Legal Aid Soc. (dir. 1971-74), Peoria Hist. Soc., Phi Gamma Delta, Phi Delta Phi. Club: Country (Peoria). Lodges: Masons (master 1970—), Shriners (potentate 1984), Jesters, Rotary (pres. 1979). Home: 3217 W Prince George Ct Peoria IL 61615 Office: 700 1st Nat Bank Bldg Peoria IL 61602

CHRISTMAN, KENNETH DANIEL, plastic and reconstructive surgeon; b. Honolulu, Jan. 8, 1949; s. Donald R. and Dorothy (Daniel) C. BA, Southwestern Union Coll., 1970; MD, Loma Linda U., 1973. Intern in gen. surgery Baylor U. Coll. Medicine, Houston, 1974-77, resident in plastic surgery, 1978-79; resident in plastic surgery Kettering (Ohio) Med. Ctr., 1980-81; pvt. practice specializing in plastic and reconstructive surgery Dayton, Ohio, 1981—. Mem. Am. Soc. Plastic Surgery, Ohio Valley Soc. Plastic Surgery, Ohio State Med. Assn., Montgomery County Med. Soc. Republican. Seventh Day Adventist. Avocation: playing and collecting violins. Office: 5441 Far Hills Ave Dayton OH 45429

CHRISTMAN, WILLIAM I., data processing executive; b. Omaha, Nebr., Feb. 15, 1937; s. Daniel Irving and Dorothy Edna (Brady) C.; m. Laurie Ann Jackson, Sept. 17, 1966; children: Desiree, Danial, Melodee, Sheri, Patricia, Sean, Barbara. BGS, Roosevelt U., 1976, MBA, 1982. Clk. Belt Railway, Chgo., 1955-56; asst. supr. Standard Oil Ind., Chgo., 1956-67; mgr. data processing St. Mary of Nazareth Hosp., Chgo., 1967-77, asst. adminstr., 1977-80; mgr. data processing Am. Hosp. Supply, Evanston, Ill., 1980-84; dir. data processing Edgewater Hosp., Chgo., 1984—. Roman Catholic. Avocations: swimming, tennis, racquetball, aerobics, jogging. Office: Edgewater Hosp 5700 N Ashland Chicago IL 60660

CHRISTNER, DAVID LEE, utilities executive; b. Millersburg, Ohio, Apr. 9, 1949; s. George and Nettie (Swartzentruber) C.; m. Carol Kay Gerber, May 2, 1970. Student, United Electronics Inst., 1970. Cert. elec. safety inspector, Ohio. Electrician Kauffman Supply Co., Millersburg, 1971-73, Charm (Ohio) Plumbing, 1973-75, Dave's Elec. and Plumbing, Berlin, Ohio, 1975-80; quality control officer Skyline Corp., Holmesville, Ohio, 1980-81; elec. safety inspector State of Ohio, Columbus, 1981—; class instr. Berlin, Ohio, 1984—. V.p. Full Gospel Businessmen's Fellowship Hdqrs., Costa Mesa, Calif., 1984—; treas. Ohio Mennonite Relief Sale, Kidron, Ohio, 1985—. Mem. Internat. Traders. Republican. Avocations: coin collecting, bird watching, sports. Home: PO Box 116 US 62 Berlin OH 44610 Office: State of Ohio Dept Indsl Relations 2323 W 5th Ave Columbus OH 43216

CHRISTOFFERSEN, ARTHUR LYNN, insurance holding company executive; b. Maquoketa, Iowa, Nov. 20, 1946; s. Frank Sorne and Frances Leona (Fayram) C.; m. Theresa Ann Seng, June 6, 1970; children—Dawn, Eric. A.A. magna cum laude, Eastern Iowa U., 1970; B.B.A., U. Iowa, 1972. C.P.A., Iowa. Tax acct. Touche Ross & Co., Mpls., 1972-75; tax dir. Life Investors, Cedar Rapids, Iowa, 1975-81, v.p., sec., 1981-83, exec. v.p., 1983—; dir. Leaseamerica Corp., Cedar Rapids, Electronic Tech. Corp., Life Investors Ins. Co. Am. Served with AUS, 1966-68; Ger. Mem. Iowa C.P.A. Soc., Am. Soc. C.P.A.s, Iowa C.P.A. Fed. Tax Com., Iowa Life Ins. Assn. (steering com. 1983), Cedar Rapids C. of C. (bd. dirs. 1983-86, treas. 1984-85), Nat. Assn. O-T-C Cos. (bd. dirs., sec.). Republican. Roman Catholic. Club: Jaycees. Home: 810 E Main St Marion IA 52302 Office: Life Investors Inc 4333 Edgewood Rd NE Cedar Rapids IA 52499

CHRISTOPHER, GLENN A., publishing company executive. Vice chmn. Pulitzer Pub. Co., St. Louis. Office: Pulitzer Pub Co 900 N Tucker Blvd Saint Louis MO 63101 *

CHRISTOPHER, NORMAN FRANKLIN, engineer; b. Irvine, Ky., Sept. 23, 1930; s. Thomas Ashcraft and Anna Maude (Turner) C.; m. Jane Anne Dean, June 16, 1952; children—Paula, Phyllis. B.A., Ky. Wesleyan Coll., 1952; M.S., Ohio U., 1969. Shift chemist Liberty Powder Def. Corp., Baraboo, Wis., 1952-54; shift supr. Goodyear Atomic Corp., Piketon, Ohio, 1954-57, sect. head mass spectrometry dept., 1957-79, asst. gen. mgrs.' staff, 1979-81, supr. mass spectrometry dept., 1982-84, supt. nuclear materials engring., 1984-85, supt. analytical services, 1985-86, Martin Marietta Energy Services, Inc., Piketon, 1986—. Mem. Inst. Nuclear Material Mgmt., Am. Assn. Indsl. Hygiene. Home: 406 S Market St Waverly OH 45690 Office: PO Box 628 Piketon OH 45661

CHRISTOPHER, WILLIAM GARTH, lawyer; b. Beaumont, Tex., Oct. 14, 1940; s. Garth Daugherty and Ollye Mittie (Harkness) C.; m. Elizabeth O'Hara, June 9, 1962; children—John William, David Noah, Michael O'Hara. B.S. in Engring., U.S. Mil. Acad., 1962; J.D., U. Va., 1970. Bar: Va. 1970, D.C. 1970, U.S. Supreme Ct. 1975, Mich. 1977. Assoc. Steptoe & Johnson, Washington, 1970-77; ptnr. Honigman Miller Schwartz & Cohn, Detroit, 1977—. Pres. Birmingham (Mich.) Hockey Assn., 1982-84; mem. Episcopal Diocese of Mich. Commn. on Ministry, 1983—, co-chmn. 1987—. Served to capt. C.E. U.S. Army, 1962-67. Elected to Raven Soc., U. Va., 1970. Mem. ABA, Fed. Bar Assn., Va. Bar Assn., D.C. Bar Assn., Mich. Bar Assn., Detroit Bar Assn. (trustee 1984—, sec. 1986-87), Order of Coif, Phi Delta Phi. Episcopalian. Contbr. article to legal publ. Home: 7290 Parkhurst Dr Birmingham MI 48010 Office: Suite 2290 First Nat Bldg Detroit MI 48226

CHRISTY, JOHN PAUL, surgeon; b. Gary, Ind., Oct. 10, 1937; s. Paul Andrew and Ruth (Hagemeyer) C.; m. Pauline Walz, June 20, 1959 (div. June 1967); children: Paul Sutherland, Jennifer Lynne; m. Mary Jane Mackley, Oct. 15, 1967; children: Mary Ruth, Lara Anne. AB, Washington U., 1959, MD, 1963. Diplomate Am. Bd. Surgery. Intern in surgery Barnes Hosp., St. Louis, 1963-64, resident surgery, 1964-68; surgeon Kneibert Clinic, Poplar Bluff, Mo., 1971—; mem. exec. com. Kneibert Clinic, 1985—, Doctors Med. Ctr., Poplar Bluff, 1985—, 686 Partnership, Poplar Bluff, 1985—. Trustee United Meth. Ch., Poplar Bluff, 1985-87. Served to maj. M.C., U.S. Army, 1968-71. Fellow ACS; mem. Am. Med. Soc., Mo. Surgical Assn., St. Louis Surgical Soc. Republican. Methodist. Avocaitons: astronomy, fishing, gardening. Home: Rural Rt #2 Box 295 C Poplar Bluff MO 63901

CHRISTY, PERRY THOMAS, lawyer, air transport company executive; b. Cin., Nov. 7, 1941; s. Thomas Perry and Mary (Vatsures) C.; m. Patricia K. Lolas, Jan 7, 1968; children: Thomas Perry, Stephanie Ann. BBA, U. Cin., 1961; MBA, U. Pa., 1962; JD, U. Mich., 1966. Bar: Mich. 1967, U.S. Supreme Ct. 1970. Fin. analyst Ford Motor Co., Dearborn, Mich., 1967-69; ptnr. Christy & Robbins, Dearborn, 1969—; pres. Air Am., Inc., Dearborn, 1979—; adj. prof. mgmt. U. Mich. Mem. Rep. State Com., 1977—; chmn. 16th Rep. Congl. Dist. Com., 1984— . Served to lt. col. USAR, 1982—. Mem. Mich. Bar Assn., Comml. Law League, Econ. Club of Detroit. Greek Orthodox. Club: Dearborn Country. Home: 21711 Wildwood Dearborn MI 48128 Office: Village Plaza Towers 5th Floor Dearborn MI 48124

CHRISTY-CHAMPAGNE, DEBRA LYNN, nurse; b. Sandusky, Mich., Aug. 7, 1956; d. Elmer Francis and Arlene Marie (Rickett) Champagne; m. Coke James Geilhart, Jan. 28, 1975 (div. 1977); m. Brad Thomas Christy; 1 child, Brandon Thomas. Student, Mich. State U., 1977-79; grad., Oakland Community Coll., 1984. RN Med. Offices of Robert R. Roman, Farmington, Mich., 1979—; asst. head nurse State of Mich. Fairlawn Ctr., Pontiac, 1984-85. Served with U.S. Army, 1974-77. Mem. Am. Nursing Assn. Roman Catholic. Avocations: skiing, needlepoint. Office: Robert R Roman MD 30335 13 Mile Farmington Hills MI 48018

CHRON, GUSTAV NICHOLAS, principal; b. Chgo., June 6, 1926; s. Nicholas Constantine and Jennie (Athans) C.; B.A., DePaul U., 1952; M.A., Northwestern U., 1954; B.A. in Aeros., Stanton U., 1965, Ph.D., 1976; M.Ed., Loyola U., Chgo., 1969; J.D. (hon.), Clinton U., 1971; D.Phil., Met. Coll. Inst., London, 1974; m. Helen Hoegerl, Sept. 18, 1948; children—Edward, Karen, Timothy. Mem. staff Chgo. Better Bus. Bur., 1954-58; tchr. Northbrook (Ill.) elem. schs., 1958-60, Northbrook Jr. High Sch., 1960-63, Glenbrook South High Sch., Glenview, Ill., 1963-64; adminstrv. asst. Comsat div. trust dept. Continental Ill. Nat. Bank, Chgo., 1964-65; prin. Westmoor Sch., Northbrook, 1966—; dir. Northbrook Dist. 28 Summer Sch., 1971, 77; asst. prof. aeros. Grad. Research Inst., East Coast U., 1975-79. Mem. adv. bd. Am. Security Council. Served with USNR, 1943-46, 52, 63-64. Decorated Air medal, Purple Heart, Navy Commendation medal, Legion of Merit, Bronze Star; named to Aviation Hall of Fame. Mem. Nat., Ill. sch. prins. assns., Am. Security Council, Navy League, Navy Inst., Am. Legion, Assn. Naval Aviation, Am. Mil. Inst., Nat. Rifle Assn., Vets. OSS, Assn. Former Intelligence Officers, Nat. Intelligence Study Center, Internat. Naval Research Orgn., Am. Hist. Found., U.S. Naval Acad. Found., 82d Airborne Div. Assn., Aerospace Edn. Assn., Nat. Eagle Scout Assn., Air Force Assn., Spl. Forces Assn., Mil. Order of Purple Heart, Am. Philatelic Soc., Phi Delta Kappa, Delta Theta Phi, Pi Gamma Mu. Club: Moose. Home: 7110 N McAlpin Ave Chicago IL 60646 Office: 2500 Cherry Ln Northbrook IL 60062

CHRONISTER, STEPHEN HALL, dentist; b. Kansas City, Mo., July 13, 1958; s. Irvin Graves and Betty Jean (Park) C.; m. Kimberly Ann Septer, Dec. 27, 1981 (div. Sept. 1984). BA magna cum laude, Westminster Coll., Fulton, Mo., 1980; DDS with honors, U. Mo., Kansas City, 1984. Licensed dentist, Kans., Mo. Assoc. dentist Kansas City, Mo., 1984-86; gen. practice dentistry Topeka, 1985—; clin. researcher, 1984—. Vol. dentist inner city area John Knox Kirk Presbyn. Ch., Kansas City, 1984—, elder, 1986-88, mem. Habitat for Humanity program. Mem. ADA, Am. Prosthodontic Soc., Kans. Dental Assn., Omega Kappa Upsilon, Alpha Chi. Republican. Avocation: house renovation. Home: 845 Illinois Lawrence KS 66044 Office: 1005 S Topeka Topeka KS 66612

CHRYSTAL, JOHN, banker. Pres., chief exec. officer Bankers Trust Co., Des Moines. Office: Bankers Trust Co Des Moines IA 50309 *

CHRYSTLER, JOSEPH ANTHONY, accountant, federal court officer; b. Kalamazoo, Oct. 5, 1935; s. Leo Louis and Frances Christina (Miller) C.; m. Constance Kreling, Aug. 28, 1965; children: Rebecca, Mark. BBA, Western Mich. U., 1965; postgrad., Wayne (Mich.) State U., 1965. CPA, Mich. Acct. Ernst & Whinney, Kalamazoo, 1965-71; controller Boylan Leasing, Inc., Kalamazoo, 1972, Titus Constrn., Inc., Galesburg, Mich., 1973-75; pvt. practice acctg. Kalamazoo, 1975—; chpt. 12 and 13 trustee U.S. Bankruptcy Ct. western dist. Mich., Grand Rapids, Mich., 1975—; panelist and speaker numerous bankruptcy practice seminars. Mem. budget and allocations com. Greater Kalamazoo United Way; bd. dirs., coach, mgr. Milwood Little League, Kalamazoo.Served with U.S. Army, 1958-60. Mem. Am. Inst. CPA's, Mich. Assn. CPA's, Nat. Assn. Chpt. 13 Trustees. Avocations: golf, bridge, collecting matchbooks, coins. Home: 1110 Homecrest Ave Kalamazoo MI 49001 Office: Chpt 13 Trustee US Bankruptcy Ct 906 E Cork St Kalamazoo MI 49001

CHU, JOSEPH Q., mechanical engineer; b. Phanrang, Ninhthuan, Vietnam, May 27, 1955; came to U.S., 1973, naturalized, 1981; s. Thuc Nang and Cuoi Thi (Pham) C. BA, William Jennings Bryan Coll., 1977; MS, U. Tenn., 1979, PhD, 1982. Lab. asst. William Jennings Bryan Coll., Dayton, Tenn., 1975-77; sr. project engr. Allison Gas Turbine Gen. Motors Corp., Indpls., 1982—. Contbr. articles to profl. jours. Mem. AIAA, ASME (assoc.), Phi Kappa Phi. Republican. Roman Catholic. Avocations: canoeing, soccer, photography, hiking, sailing. Home: 8175 Pascal Ct Indianapolis IN 46268 Office: PO Box 420 Speed Code T23 Indianapolis IN 46206-0420

CHUA, CHENG LOK, educator; b. Singapore, Jan. 5, 1938; s. Yew Cheng and Kuo Hui (Tan) C.; came to U.S., 1956; B.A., DePauw U., 1960; M.A., U. Conn., 1962, Ph.D., 1968; m. Gretchen Taeko Sasaki, July 26, 1965; children—Iu-Hui Jarrell, Poh-Pheng Jaime. Part-time instr. English, U. Conn., Storrs, 1960-65; asst. prof. English, U. Mich., Ann Arbor, 1965-72; lectr., sr. lectr. English, U. Singapore, 1972-74; lectr. English, Calif. State U. at Fresno, 1974-76; Nat. Endowment Humanities postdoctoral fellow Yale U., 1976-77, vis. fellow comparative lit., 1976-77; assoc. prof. Moorhead (Minn.) State U., 1977-81, prof., chmn. dept. English, 1982-85; vis. prof. Asian Am. Studies, U. Calif., Santa Barbara, 1985-86. Australasian Univs. Lang. and Lit. Assn. grantee, 1975; Am. Council Learned Socs. grantee, 1978; Nat. Endowment Humanities summer fellow, 1980; fellow East Asia Inst., Hamline U., 1981. Mem. MLA (exec. com. Ethnic Studies Div.), Nat. Council Tchrs. English, Multi-Ethnic Lit. of U.S., AAUP, Nat. Assn. Interdisciplinary Ethnic Studies. Office: Moorehead State U English Dept. Moorehead MN 56560

CHUANG, RICHARD YO, political scientist, educator; b. Shanghai, China, Mar. 9, 1939; came to U.S., 1962; s. Han K. and Rose C.; LL.B., Nat. Taiwan U., 1961; M.A. (fgn. student scholar), U. Minn., 1964, Ph.D. (fgn. student scholar), 1970; cert. (scholar) Parker Sch. Fgn. and Comparative law, Columbia U., 1973; m. Elsie Yao Chuang, Sept. 4, 1965; children—Erik, Cliff, Fleur. Vis. asso. prof. law Nat. Taiwan U., 1971-72; vis. asso. prof. polit. sci. Nat. Chung Hsin U., Taipei, Taiwan, 1973-74; asst. prof. No. State Coll., Aberdeen, S.D., 1968-71, assoc. prof., 1971-76, prof. polit. sci., 1976—, acting chmn. dept. social sci., 1979-81, chmn. dept. social sci., 1981-83, interim chmn. faculty social and natural scis., 1983-84, dean Faculty Arts and Scis., 1984—; NSF vis. prof. Republic of China, 1973-74; participant, scholar Diplomat Seminars, U.S. Dept. State, 1981; participant program for tchrs. of Am. govt. Am. Judicature Soc., 1985; cons. Bush Summer fellow, 1987. Mem. Am. Polit. Sci. Assn., Am. Soc. Internat. Law. Democrat. Buddhist. Club: Mason. Author: The International Air Transport Association, 1972; editor No. Social Sci. Rev., 1975—; contbr. numerous articles to profl. jours. Home: 216 21st Ave NE Aberdeen SD 57401 Office: No State Coll Aberdeen SD 57401

CHUBB, GERALD PATRICK, engineering executive; b. Columbus, Ohio, Mar. 30, 1941; s. Richard Kanaga and Mary Elizabeth (Corbett) C.; m. Suzanne Lee Parks, Dec. 12, 1961; children: Mark D., Christopher B., Laura L., Lynette M. BS, Ohio State U., 1962, MA, 1963, PhD, 1981. Cert. quality engr., Calif.; registered psychologist, Ohio. Engring. research pyschologist human engr. div. Aerospace Med. Research Lab., Wright-Patterson AFB, 1963-67, 68-80, gen. engr., 1980-82; sr. analyst Serendipity Assocs., Chatsworth, Calif., 1967-68; gen. mgr. ALPHATECH, Inc., Dayton, Ohio, 1982-85; prin. cons. SofTech, Inc., Fairborn, Ohio, 1985—. Author govt. tech. reports and symposia papers. Chmn. Bible Inst. Christian Missions, Shelbyville, Ind., 1983—; mem. Greene County Transit Bd., Xenia, Ohio; vice chmn. Greene County Mental Health Ctr Bd., Xenia; scoutmaster Boy Scouts Am., Spring Valley, Ohio; pres. Grand Oak Estate Owners' Assn., Xenia, 1986—. Mem. Am. Assn. for Artificial Intelligence, Human Factors Soc., Computer Simulation Soc., Am. Helicopter Soc., Mil. Ops. Research Soc. Avocations: piano, canoeing. Office: SofTech Inc 3100 Presidential Dr Fairborn OH 45324-2039

CHUBICK, LESLEY IRWIN, advertising executive; b. Clinton, Iowa, Nov. 17, 1943; s. Delvin Dow and Anna Belle (Nichols) C.; B.S., Central Mo. State U., 1967; seminar cert. Fiway Modular Brace System, 1983; m. Markey Lou Ewing, July 11, 1980; children by previous marriage—Lesley Irwin, Jeannette Louise; 1 stepchild, Carol Ann. Lay-out artist/copywriter Sears, Roebuck & Co., Kansas City, Mo., 1973-75; advt. artist/copy writer Medco Jewelry Corp., Overland Park, Kans., 1975-78; free-lance work in advt., Merriam, Kan., 1978-79; advt. mgr. Knit-Rite Inc., Kansas City, Mo., 1979—, trade show and seminar dir., 1982—. Bd. dirs. Quail Valley Coop., 1980-82, sec., 1980-82, editor bi-weekly Quail Valley Newsletter, 1980-82; mem. ann. exhibit com. Nat. Scupture Exhibition, Lenexa, Kans., 1986—, com. on promotion AOPA Ann. Conv.; mem. com. Dimensions 3 Dimensional Outdoor Art Exhibit, Lenexa, 1986-87. Recipient Award of Excellence, Advt. Artists Guild of Kansas City, Mo., 1970; cert. of completion Avila Coll. Seminar in Coop. Mgmt., 1980, course in fitting camp orthotic supports, 1980. Mem. Plains Assn., Print Prodn. Club of Kansas City. Clubs: Ad of Kansas City, Art Dirs., Sportscar. Home: 14620 W 93d St Lenexa KS 66215 Office: PO Box 208 2020 2020 Grand Ave Kansas City MO 64141

CHUN, SHUNEUI, obstetrician, gynecologist; b. Seoul, Dem. Rep. Korea, June 23, 1950; d. Chong Hwee and Eun Sook (Hahn) C.; m. David E. Pautz, June 13, 1976; children: Christina M. Chun Pautz, Andrew J. Chun Pautz. BA, Macalester Coll., 1973; MD, U. Minn., 1977. Resident U. Minn., Mpls., 1977-81; obtetrician, gynecologist Paul Larson Ob-Gyn Clinic, Mpls., 1981—; clin. instr. U. Minn. Hosps., 1982—. Fellow Am. Coll. Ob-gyn; mem. Minn. Council Ob-gyn, Minn. Med. Assn., Hennepin County Med. Soc., Minn. Women Physicians. Home: 5701 Long Brake Trail Edina MN 55435 Office: Paul Larson Ob-Gyn Clinic 6517 Drew Ave S Edina MN 55435

CHUNG, JACK CHUN-HSIEN, petroleum company scientist; b. Taiwan, Apr. 29, 1953; s. Ti Chung and Chou-Yang Lee; m. Chiung-Lan Huang, Nov. 14, 1980; 1 child, Ingrid. H. College diploma, Ming-Chi Inst. Tech., Taiwan, 1974; MS, U. Tex., Arlington, 1982; PhD, Purdue U., 1984. Sr. engr. Nan-Ta Plastics Corp., Taiwan, 1976-80; research asst. U. Tex., 1981-82, Purdue U., West Lafayette, Ind., 1982-84; project leader The Standard Oil Co., Cleve., 1984—. Mem. ASME (assoc.), Inst. Electronics and Elec. Engrs. (assoc.). Home: 7258 Selworthy Solon OH 44139 Office: The Standard Oil Co 4440 Warrensville Rd Cleveland OH 44128

CHUNG, RONALD ALOYSIUS, home economics educator; b. Brownstown, Clarendon, Jamaica, Sept. 30, 1936; came to U.S., 1956; s. Henry and Norah (Young) C.; m. Cecile Sheila Lee Sue, May 19, 1963; children: Paula A., Denise A., Sandra A. BS in Chemistry, Coll. of Holy Cross, 1959; MS in Food Sci., Purdue U., 1961, PhD in Food Sci., 1963. Asst. prof., head dept. food sci. Tuskegee (Ala.) U., 1963-65, assoc. prof., head dept. food sci., 1965-68, prof., 1968-86, div. head, 1969-84, prof., head dept. home econs., 1984-86; prof., head dept. home econs. U. No. Iowa, Cedar Falls, 1986—; cons. Biochem Analyst, Huntsville, Ala., 1975—; alt. rep. grad. dean council Ala. Higher Edn. Council, Birmingham, 1973-75. Recipient Research/Teaching award Tuskegee Inst., 1968, Morrison-Evans Outstanding Scientists award 1890 Tuskegee Inst. Research Dirs., 1984. Fellow AAAS; mem. Am. Chem. Soc., Inst. Food Technologists, Poultry Sci. Assn. (Research award 1968), Sigma Xi (pres. 1970-73). Lodge: Rotary. Avocations: tennis, cross-country skiing. Home: 7263 Hudson Dr Hudson IA 50643 Office: Univ No Iowa Home Econs Cedar Falls IA 50614

CHUNPRAPAPH, BOONMEE, physician, educator; b. Songkhla, Thailand, Nov. 23, 1938; came to U.S., 1966; s. Yen Hua Tseng and Chou Sou Chen; m. Kaysorn Suttajit, July 29, 1944; children: Benj, Kabin. MD, U. Med. Sci., Bangkok, 1964. Diplomate Am. Bd. Orthopedic Surgery. Rotating intern Samaritan Hosp., Troy, N.Y., 1966-67; pvt. practice gen. surgery Youngstown (Ohio) Hosp. Assn., 1967-68; pvt. practice specializing in orthopedic surgery Univ. Hosp., Mobile, Ala., 1968-71; assoc. prof. U. Ill., Chgo., 1980—. Contbr. articles to profl. jours. Fellow ACS, Internat. Coll. Surgeons; mem. AMA, Acad Orthopedic Surgeons, Am. Soc. Surgery of the Hand. Avocations: photography, gardening, tennis. Office: U Ill Hosp 901 S Wolott Ave Chicago IL 60612

CHURCH, ANNAMARIA THERESA, pediatrician; b. Detroit, Feb. 1, 1955; d. Gerhard Alois and Barbara Lenore (Siegert) Blass; m. Richard Joseph Church, May 17, 1975; children—Christopher, Sarah. B.S., U. Detroit, 1975; M.D., Wayne State U., Detroit, 1979. Diplomate Nat. Bd. Med. Examiners, Am. Bd. Pediatrics. Pediatric resident William Beaumont Hosp., Royal Oak, Mich., 1979-82; practice medicine specializing in pediatrics Brighton-Ann Arbor Med Assn., Brighton, Mich., 1982-83; dir. ambulatory pediatrics William Beaumont Hosp., Royal Oak, 1983-84, attendant staff pediatrician, 1984—; resident staff physician Providence Hosp., Southfield, Mich., 1984—; practice medicine specializing in pediatrics Child Health Assocs., Southfield, 1984—; clin. instr. Wayne State U. Sch. Medicine, Detroit, 1985—. Mem. Suspected Child Abuse and Neglect Team, Royal Oak, 1983—; mem. Adv. Com. on Parent Edn., Royal Oak, 1983—; mem. Pediatric Utilization Rev. Com., Royal Oak, 1983-86; mem. Oakland County Council Children at Risk, Oakland County, Mich., 1983. Fellow Am. Acad. Pediatrics; mem. Ambulatory Pediatric Assn., Christian Med. Soc. Roman Catholic. Office: Child Health Assocs 16800 W Twelve Mile Rd Southfield MI 48072

CHURCH, GLENN J., lawyer; b. Grand Island, Nebr., Aug. 20, 1932; s. Glenn Jennings and Rachel Frances (Cochran) C.; m. Norma Ann Ray; children: Susan Jo, Zackary William. AB, U. Ill., 1954, JD, 1959. Bar: Ill. 1959, U.S. Dist. Ct. (cen. dist.) Ill. 1960, U.S. Ct Appeals (7th cir.) 1967, U.S. Supreme Ct. 1971, Ohio 1983. Assoc. Kavanaugh, Bond, Scully, Sudow & White, Peoria, Ill., 1959-62; ptnr. Smith, Whitney & Church, Peoria, 1962-66; sole practice Peoria, 1966-70; prin. Glenn J. Church Ltd., Peoria, 1970-86; spl. asst. atty. gen. water pollution div. State of Ill. , 1960-61; hearing officer Am. Arbitration Assn., Chgo., 1966—; mem. Ill. Fair Employment Practice Commn., 1974-79. Liasion officer Air Force Acad., Colorado Springs, Colo., 1968-82; bd. dirs. W.D. Boyce council Boy Scouts Am., 1970-86, Heart of Ill. Fair and Exposition Gardens, Peoria, 1978-84; exec. bd. chmn. eagle rev. com. Boy Scouts Am. , Peoria, 1977-86. Served to lt. col. USAF, 1954-82. Mem. Ill. Bar Assn., Ohio Bar Assn., Peoria Bar Assn., Assn. Trial Lawyers Am., Phi Alpha Delta. Republican. Methodist. Lodge: Sertoma. Home: 4709 N War Meml Dr Peoria IL 61615 Office: 1000 Savings Ctr Tower Peoria IL 61602

CHURCH, IRENE ZABOLY, personnel services company executive; b. Cleve., Feb. 18, 1947; d. Bela Paul and Irene Elizabeth (Chandas) Zaboly; children: Irene Elizabeth, Elizabeth Anne, Lauren Alexandria Gadd, John Dale Gadd II. Student pub. schs. Personnel cons., recruiter, Cleve., 1965-70; chief exec. officer, pres. Oxford Personnel, Pepper Pike, Ohio, 1973—, Oxford Temporaries, Pepper Pike, 1979—; guest lectr. in field, 1974—; expert witness for ct. testimony, 1982—. Troop leader Lake Erie council Girl Scouts Am., 1980-81; mem. Christian action com. Federated Ch., United Ch. Christ, 1981-85, sub-com. to study violence in relation to women, 1983, creator, presenter programs How Work Affects Family Life and Re-entering the Job Market, 1981, mem. Women's Fellowship Martha-Mary Circle, 1980—, program dir., 1982-84; chpt. leader Nat. Coalition on TV Violence, 1983—. Mem. Nat. Assn. Personnel Consultants (cert., mem. ethics com. 1976-77, co-chairperson ethics com. 1977-78, mem. bus. practices and ethics com. 1980-82, mem. cert. personnel cons. soc. 1980-82), Ohio Assn. Personnel Consultants (trustee 1975-80, 85—, sec. 1976-77, 85—, chairperson bus. practices and ethics com. 1976-77, 81-82, 1st v.p., chairperson resolutions com. 1981-82, chairperson membership com. 1985—), Greater Cleve. Assn. Personnel Consultants (2d then 1st v.p., 1974-76, state trustee 1975-80, pres. 1976-77, bd. advisor 1977-78, chairperson bus. practices and ethics com. 1974-76, nominating com. ,1983, membership com. 1984-85, arbitration com., 1980, fundraising, 1980——, bd. dirs. 1980—, , trustee 1985—), Vi Pender Outstanding Service award 1977), Euclid C. of C. (small bus. com. 1981, chairperson task force com. evaluating funding in social security and vet.'s benefits 1981), Internat. Platform Assn., Am. Bus. Women's Assn., Nat. Assn. Temp. Services, Chagrin Valley C. of C., Greater Cleve. Growth Assn. Council Small Enterprises. Lodge: Rotary. Home: 8 Ridgecrest Dr Chagrin Falls OH 44022 Office: Oxford Personnel Exec Commons 2945 Chagrin Blvd Pike OH 44122

CHURCH, JAY KAY, psychologist, educator; b. Wichita, Kans., Jan. 18, 1927; s. Kay Iverson and Gertrude (Parrish) C.; B.A., David Lipscomb Coll., 1948; M.A., Ball State U., 1961; Ph.D., Purdue U., 1963; m. Dorothy Agnes Fellerhoff, May 21, 1976; children—Karen Patrice Church Edwards, Caryn Annice Church Casey, Rex Warren, Max Roger. Chemist, Auburn Rubber Corp., 1948-49; salesman Midwestern United Life Ins. Co., 1949-52; owner, operator Tour-Rest Motel, Waterloo, Ind., 1952-66; tchr., guidance dir., public schs., Hamilton, Ind., 1955-61; counselor Washington Twp. (Ind.) Schs., Indpls., 1961-62; asst. prof. psychology Ball State U., 1963-67, assoc. prof., 1967-71, prof., 1971—, chmn. dept. ednl. psychology, 1970-74, dir. advanced grad. programs in ednl. psychology, 1978-81; pvt. practice psychology, 1963—. Mem. Am. Psychol. Assn., Midwest Psychol. Assn., Ind. Psychol. Assn., Nat. Assn. Sch. Psychologists. Home: 8501 N Ravenwood Dr Muncie IN 47303 Office: Ball State U Muncie IN 47306

CHURCH, THOMAS WAYNE, hospital executive; b. Las Vegas, Feb. 24, 1949; s. Robert Wayne and Florence (Loranne) C.; divorced; children: Thomas W., Christopher T., Nicholas M., Shawn M. AA, U. Nev., Las Vegas, 1976. Registered nurse. Med. dir. Mercy Ambulance, Las Vegas, 1976-79; emergency nurse Suburban Med. Ctr., Overland Park, Kans., 1979-80; flight nurse USAFR, Scott AFB, 1980—; program dir. med. air res. corps. St. Louis U. Hosp., 1982-85, aeromed. cons., 1986-87; program dir. Harris Meth. Hosp., Ft. Worth, 1987—; bd. dirs. St. Louis Emergency Med. council, 1986; pres. Progressive Systems, Inc., 1985—. Served to sgt. USAF, 1968-72, Korea. Fellow Aerospace Med. Assn. (mem. flight nurse sect. 1984—), mem. Soc. Aerospace Physiologists, Nat. Flight Assn. (edn. com. 1982—), Ashbeams (standards and clin. practice com.), Reserve Officers Assn. State Ill. (pres. 1983-86, bd. dirs. 1986—). Republican. Lodge: Elks. Avocations: mountain climbing, water skiing. Home: 2538 Mariner Dr #1314 Saint Louis MO 63129

CHURCHILL, ANDREW CALDWELL, architect; b. Madison, Wis., Apr. 20, 1957; s. Don Warren and Lee Baldwin (Caldwell) C.; m. Lynne Ainsley Murray, Apr. 19, 1986. BArch, U. Cin., 1984. Reg. architect, Ind. Pres. Churchill Masonry, Indpls., 1976-80; archtl. designer Everett L. Brown, Indpls., 1981-82, Archonics, Indpls., 1982-83, Leech Architects, Indpls., 1984-85; project. arch. United Cons. Engrs., Indpls., 1985—. Mem. Nature Conservancy Consumers Union, 1985—, Beech Grove (Ind.) Main St. Revitalization Com., 1985-86. Mem. AIA, Constrn. Specifications Inst., Apt. Assn. Ind., Bldg. Owners and Mgrs., Cert. Comml. Investment Mgrs., Nat. Trust for Hist. Preservation. Episcopalian. Avocations: music, exercise, computers. Office: United Cons Engrs 5332 N Temple Indianapolis IN 46220

CHURCHILL, JAMES PAUL, judge; b. Imlay City, Mich., Apr. 10, 1924; s. Howard and Faye (Shurte) C.; m. Ann Muir, Aug. 30, 1950; children: Nancy Ann Churchill Nyquist, David James, Sally Jo. B.A., U. Mich., 1947, J.D., 1950. Bar: Mich. Sole practice Vassar, Mich., 1950-65; circuit judge 40th Jud. Circuit Mich., 1965-74; U.S. dist. judge Eastern Dist. Mich., Detroit, 1974—; ct. commr. Tuscola County Cir., 1963-65; adj. prof. Detroit Coll. Law, 1980-81. Served with U.S. Army, 1943-46. Mem. Fed. Judges Assn., Fed. Bar Assn., 40th Jud. Cir. Bar Assn. Office: US Dist Ct 214 Fed Bldg Bay City MI 48707 *

CHURCHILL, RUEL VANCE, mathematician; b. Akron, Ind., Dec. 12, 1899; s. Abner C. and Meldora (Friend) C.; m. Ruby F. Sicks, 1922 (dec. 1969); children: Betty Churchill McMurray, Eugene S.; m. Alice B. Warren, 1972. B.S., U. Chgo., 1922; M.S., U. Mich., 1925, Ph.D., 1929. Faculty U. Mich., Ann Arbor, 1922—; prof. math. U. Mich., 1942-65, emeritus, 1965—; vis. lectr. U. Wis., 1941; research U. Freiburg, Germany, 1936, Calif. Inst. Tech., 1949; research specialist USAAF, 1944; mem. NRC, 1947-50. Author: books including Complex Variables and Applications, 1948, 4th edit. (with J.W. Brown),1984, Japanese edit., 1975, Spanish edit., 1978; Operational Mathematics, 1944, Japanese edit. 1950, Fourier Series, 1941, 4th edit. (with J.W. Brown) 1987, Japanese edit., 1960, Spanish edit., 1966, Portuguese edit., 1978. Home: 1200 Earhart Rd #255 Ann Arbor MI 48105 Office: U Mich Dept Maths Ann Arbor MI 48109

CHURRAY, EDWARD JOHN, systems and programming manager; b. Canonsburg, Pa., Apr. 22, 1944; s. John Bernard and Elizabeth Joan (Simko) C.; m. Catherine E. Warner, July 16, 1966; children: Jennifer Lyn, Keith Edward. AA, Macomb County (Mich.) Community Coll., 1981. EAM operator Mellon Bank, Pitts., 1963-65; computer operator, programmer Associated Food Stores, Jamaica, N.Y., 1965-68; programmer, analyst Mfrs. Nat. Bank, Detroit, 1968-76, systems and programming mgr., 1976—. Served with USAF, 1962. Mem. Assn. Systems Mgmt. Avocation: stamp collecting. Office: Mfrs Nat Bank 411 W Lafayette Detroit MI 48231

CHUTE, ROBERT DONALD, electrical engineering educator; b. Detroit, Nov. 29, 1928; s. George Maynard and Josephine Chute; B.S. in Elec. Engring., U. Mich., 1950; M.S., Wayne State U., 1966; m. Marion Louise Price, June 17, 1950; children—Janet Louise, Lawrence Robert. Control engr. indsl heating div. Gen. Electric Co., Shelbyville, Ind., 1950-57; group leader Chrysler Corp., Warren, Mich., 1957-59; chief product engr. internat. div. Burroughs Corp., Detroit, 1959-73; asso. prof. elec. engring. Lawrence Inst. Tech., Southfield, Mich., 1973—; cons. in indsl. controls, 1969—. Instl. rep. Detroit Met. Area council Boy Scouts Am., 1964-68. Registered profl. engr., Mich., Ind. Mem. IEEE, Am. Soc. Engring. Edn., Nat. Soc. Profl. Engrs., Engring. Soc. Detroit. Presbyterian. Clubs: Just Right, Economic of Detroit. Author: (with George M. Chute) Electronics in Industry, 1971, 5th edit., 1979; patentee in field. Office: 21000 W Ten Mile Rd Southfield MI 48075

CHUTIS, LAURIEANN LUCY, social worker; b. Detroit, Nov. 30, 1942; d. Paul J. and Helen Marie (Shilakes) C.; A.B., U. Mich., 1964, M.S.W., 1966. Community worker Tuskegee (Ala.) Inst., 1966; social worker Catholic Sch. Bd. Head Start, Chgo., 1966; community worker Cath. Charities, Chgo., 1966-70; asst. to dir. Ravenswood Hosp. Community Mental Health Center, Chgo., 1970-72, coordinator consultation and edn. dept., 1972, dir. consultation and edn. dept., 1972—, also cons., trainer therapist; instr. Chgo. Bd. Edn., Northeastern Ill. U., 1974—; guest lectr. various profl. assn. groups, corps., 1975—; pvt. practice individual group and family therapy; 1976—; cons. NIMH, mental health centers, bus. and industry, 1977—. Coordinator Nat. Consultation and Edn. Net working; mem. Salvation Army Community Services Bd., 1978-80; mem. com. Chgo. Health Systems Agy., 1980—; mem. Ill. Alcohol Prevention Task Force, 1980-82. Mem. Nat. Assn. Social Work, Acad. Certified Social Work, World Fedn. Mental Health, Registry Clin. Social Workers, Nat. Council Community Mental Health Centers (council on Prevention 1977-79), Assn. Consultation-Edn. Service Providers (pres. 1978-79). Contbg. author: To Your Good Health. Contbr. articles to profl. jours. Office: 4550 N Winchester Chicago IL 60640

CHYLASZEK, ROBERT JOSEPH, manufacturing executive; b. Dunkirk, N.Y., Nov. 19, 1935; s. John and Lillian (Latos) Czarnecki; m. Rosalie Anne Batten, Nov. 25, 1964; children: Melissa, Aimee, Alexander. BSME, Tri-State U., 1963; MSE, MBA, U. Cin., 1972. Design engr. N. Am. Aviation, El Segundo, Calif., 1963-64, Pratt & Whitney, West Palm Beach, Fla., 1964-66, Gen. Electric Co., Cin., 1966-78; v.p., gen. mgr. Morris Machine Co., Indpls., 1978-83, pres., chief exec. officer, 1983—. mem. Nixon for Pres. com. Cin. Rep. Party, 1968. Served with USAF, 1954-58, Korea. Roman Catholic. Club: Columbia (Indpls.). Avocations: tennis, jogging. Home: 4068 Serenity Way Greenwood IN 46142 Office: Morris Machine Co Inc 6480 S Belmont Ave Indianapolis IN 46227

CIANCIOLA, CHARLES SAL, paper manufacturing company executive; b. Milw., Apr. 15, 1933; s. Salvatore S. and Mary R. (Torcivia) C.; m. June A. Reynolds, Jan. 21, 1956; children: Mary, Ann, Charles Jr., Chris. BS, Lawrence U., Appleton, Wis., 1955. Sales promotion mgr. Wis. Tissue Mills Inc., Menasha, 1965-67, western region sales mgr., 1967-77, v.p. mktg. devel., 1977-79, v.p. sales and mktg., 1979-83, exec. v.p., 1983—; bd. dirs. Associated First Bank, Neenah, Wis., Webex Co., Neenah. Co-founder Yards for Youth football program, Menasha; bd. dirs. YMCA, Neenah, 1977-79; gen. chmn. United Way, Neenah, 1977-79; trustee Lawrence U., 1984-88. Recipient Disting. Service award U.S. Jaycees, 1969. Mem. Fox Cities C. of C. (bd. dirs.). Clubs: Lawrence U. Viking Bench, N. Shore Golf. Lodge: Elks. Avocation: golf. Home: 1616 S Park Dr Neenah WI 54952 Office: Wis Tissue Mills Inc PO Box 489 Menasha WI 54952

CIARALDI, STEPHEN WILLIAM, metallurgical engineer; b. Ft. Monmouth, N.J., Sept. 30, 1954; s. Guy Alexander Ciaraldi and Letty Jean (Miller) Putnam. BS in Metall. Engring. with high hons., U. Ill., 1976, PhD in Metall. Engring., 1980. Research asst. U. Ill., Urbana, 1976-80; research engr. Amoco Corp. Research, Naperville, Ill., 1980-83, staff research engr., 1983-87, sr. research engr., 1987—. Contbr. articles in field. Mem. Nat. Assn. Corrosion Engrs. (chmn. 1987—), Am. Iron and Steel Inst., Alpha Sigma Mu. Roman Catholic. Avocations: skiing, weight-lifting, cooking, golfing. Office: Amoco Corp Research PO Box 400 Naperville IL 60566

CIATTEO, CARMEN THOMAS, psychiatrist; b. Clifton Heights, Pa., May 25, 1921; s. Ralph and Grace (Manette) C.; A.B. in Chemistry, U. Pa., 1947; M.D., Loyola U., Chgo., 1951; m. Lucille Dolores Ranum, Nov. 1, 1957; children—William, Jane, Thomas. Intern, Mercy Hosp., Chgo.; resident Fitzsimons Army Hosp., Denver, 1952-53, Hines (Ill.) VA Hosp., 1957-59; practice medicine specializing in psychiatry, Joliet, Ill., 1959-72; correctional and forensic psychiatrist, 1966, 77—; psychiatrist VA hosps., 1959; cons. Dept. Vocat. Rehab., 1959-72, Matrimonial Tribunal Diocese Joliet, 1959-76, Cath. Archdiocese Ft. Wayne and South Bend, Ind., Assn. Retarded Citizens, Wells and Adams Counties, Ind.; cons. Fed. Prison System, U.S. Dept. Justice, Chgo., 1975-76, 77-82; tchr. nursing tng. Hines VA Hosp., 1957-59; med. dir. Community Counseling Service, Inc., Ft. Wayne, Adams County Meml. Hosp. Psychiatric unit, Decatur, Ind. Served with USAF, 1942-46, 51-56. Diplomate Am. Bd. Psychiatry and Neurology. Mem. Ill. Psychiat. Soc., Am. Psychiat. Assn., Am. Acad. Psychiatry and Law, Am. Correctional Assn. Democrat. Roman Catholic. Home: Route 2 135 Little Creek Lockport IL 60441 Office: 815 High St Ste D Decatur IN 46733

CIAVARELLA, BRADLEY ALAN, architect; b. Bismarck, N.D., May 13, 1960; s. Joseph Clemens and Elizabeth Della (Belohlavek) C.; m. Karol Jo Gohner, July 26, 1981; 1 child, Grant Austin. BArch, N.D. State U., 1983. Assoc. engr. PanAm World Services, Houston, 1983-84; intern architect Mutchler & Lynch Assocs., Fargo, N.D., 1984-85, Hanson & Foster Architects, Bismarck, 1985—. Mem. AIA (N.D. chpt. Draftsman award 1982), Bismarck C. of C. (coll. relations com., chmn. ednl. exposition 1987). Club: Eagles (Mandan., N.D.). Avocations: photography, fishing, skiing, basketball. Office: Hanson & Foster Architects PC 322 E Main Bismarck ND 58501

CICCONE, WILLIAM, data processing executive; b. St. Louis, Apr. 11, 1937; s. Gerardo and Frances (Caputo) C.; student parochial schs., St. Louis;

m. Marcia L. Ciccone; children—Anna Maria, Anthony William, Mary Frances, Mark Olan. Data processing mgr. Comml. Union-N. Brit. Group, Kansas City, Mo., Chgo., 1958-61; data processing mgr. Electronic Pub. Co., Inc., Chgo., 1961; data processing cons. Mgmt. Assistance, Inc., Chgo., 1961-62; data processing mgr. Cruttenden Podesta & Miller, Chgo., 1962-63; v.p. Data Systems Tng. Corp., Hammond, Ind., 1963; pres., chmn. Illiana Data Processing Services, Inc., Tinley Park, Ill., 1963—; sec. Personal Touch Computer Sales, Inc., Tinley Park, Ill., 1984—. Trustee Twp. of Orland (Ill.), 1977-83, collector, 1976-77, chmn. youth commn., 1976-81, youth service bur. adv. bd., 1978-81; trustee Village of Orland Park, 1983—; Ill. State rep. legis. aide, 1977-81; bd. dirs. Cath. Grad. Sch. Conf., 1975-78; chmn./pres. Cath. Central Parochial Basketball League, 1966-78; chmn. Sch. Dist. 135 Sch. Bd. Caucus, 1978; sec. Village of Orland Park Planning Commn., 1965-69. Served with USAF, 1955-58. Cert. data processor. Mem. Twp. Ofcls. of Ill. (2d v.p. collector div. 1976-77, dir. 1979-83), Twp. Ofcls. of Cook County (hon. mem., dir. 1979-83, sec. 1981-83). Democrat. Roman Catholic. Home: 14535 Greenland Ave Orland Park IL 60462 Office: 16860 Oak Park Ave Tinley Park IL 60477

CICERO, FRANK, JR., lawyer; b. Chgo., Nov. 30, 1935; s. Frank and Mary (Balma) C.; m. Janice Pickett, July 11, 1959; children—Erica, Caroline. Student Amherst Coll., 1953-54; A.B. with honors, Wheaton Coll., 1957; M in Pub. Affairs, Woodrow Wilson Sch. of Pub. and Internat. Affairs, 1962; J.D., U. Chgo. Law Sch., 1965. Bar: Ill., Colo.U.S. Dist. Ct. (no. dist.) Ill., 1965, U.S. Ct. Appeals (7th cir.), U.S. Ct. Appeals (5th cir.), U.S. Supreme Ct. Polit. sci. instr. Wheaton Coll., Ill., 1957-58; spl. asst. Gov. Richard J. Hughes of N.J., 1962; assoc. Kirkland & Ellis, Chgo., 1965-70, ptnr., 1970—; mem. vis. com. U. Chgo. Law Sch., 1971-74; del. to 6th Ill. Constl. Conv., 1969-70. Bd. editors U. Chgo. Law Rev., also author articles. Recipient Joseph Henry Beale prize U. Chgo., 1963, Outstanding Young Man award Evanston Jaycees, 1970. Fellow Am. Coll. Trial Lawyers, Internat. Acad. Trial Lawyers; mem. ABA, Ill. State Bar Assn., Bar Assn. 7th Fed. Circuit, Am. Polit. Sci. Assn., Am. Acad. Polit. and Social Sci. Clubs: Chicago, Mid-Am. (gov. 1981-84), Saddle and Cycle (gov. 1984). Office: Kirkland & Ellis 200 E Randolph Dr Chicago IL 60601

CIESLAK, JAMES LAWRENCE, educator, lawyer, accountant; b. Cleve., Dec. 13, 1944; s. Frank Stanley and Bernice (Kuczek) C.; m. Sue Ellen Foster, Dec. 26, 1980. BBA, Kent State U., 1965; MBA, Xavier U., 1968; JD, Cleve. State U., 1977. Bar: Ohio; CPA, Ohio. Tax examiner Ohio Bur. of Employment Services, Cleve., 1970-78; assoc. Carson, Bockanil & Carson, Bedford, Ohio, 1978-79; sole practice law Parma, Ohio, 1979-86; asst. prof. acctg. Cuyahoga Community Coll., Warrensville Twp., Ohio, 1983—. Served to capt. U.S. Army, 1966-70. Mem. ABA, Ohio Bar Assn., Am. Inst. CPA's, Ohio Soc. CPA's, Am. Acctg. Assn., Am. Bus. Law Assn. Roman Catholic. Avocations: photography, travel. Home: 1415 North Ave Parma OH 44134 Office: Cuyahoga Community Coll 4250 Richmond Rd Warrensville Township OH 44122

CILLIE, JOHN JAMES, car rental agy. ofcl.; b. Martins Ferry, Ohio, Jan. 4, 1940; s. John Peter and Margaret C.; student Cleve. State U.; m. Janice Kudley, Sept. 30, 1961; children—Sheila, John James. With City Loan and Savs., Cleve., 1961-65, Avco Delta Corp., Cleve., 1965-70, Bobbie Brooks Inc., Cleve., 1970-74, Allstate Ins., Cleve., 1974-76; used vehicle sales mgr. Rent-a-Car Agy., Bedford, Ohio, 1976—. Ky. Colonel. Office: Agency Rent A Car 30000 Aurora Rd Solon OH 44139

CILLO, LARRY JOSEPH, brokerage house executive; b. Chgo., June 19, 1955; s. Joseph Jr. and Tillie Cillo. BS, U. Ill., Chgo. Trading mgr. Fidelity Investments, Chgo., 1982-85; chief operating officer Continental Brokerage Services Inc., Chgo., 1985—. Office: Continental Brokerage Services Inc 231 S LaSalle St Chicago IL 60697

CILLUFFO, JOHN MARIANO, neurosurgeon; b. Detroit, Sept. 8, 1950; s. Antony and Rose Veronica (Parisi) C.; m. Jennifer Jean Rafeld, Oct. 3, 1975; children: Penny Kathryn, Rebecca Rose. BS in Zoology, U. Mich., 1972; MS in Biology, Wayne State U., 1973, MD, 1977; MS in Neurosurgery, U. Minn., Rochester, 1982. Diplomate Am. Bd. Neurol. Surgery. Intern St. Mary's Hosp. Mayo Clinic, Rochester, Minn., 1977-78; resident Mayo Clinic, Rochester, Minn., 1977-82; neurosurgeon Burns Clinic, Petoskey, Mich., 1982-86; mem. staff Munson Hosp., Traverse City, Mich.; practice medicine specializing in neurosurgery Petoskey, Mich., 1987—. Contbr. articles to profl. jours. Mem. Mich. State Med. Soc., Am. Assn. Neurol. Surgeons, Congress Neurol. Surgeons, Mich. State Neurol. Assn. Democrat. Roman Catholic. Avocations: piano, golf, computers. Office: 2202 Mitchell Park Dr Petoskey MI 49770

CIOTOLA, NICHOLAS ANTHONY, financial executive; b. Hazleton, Pa., Oct. 29, 1946; s. Anthony John and Marie Theresa (Fescina) C.; m. Rita Frances Von Ville, Apr. 21, 1979; children: Nicholas Anthony Jr., Phillip John. BS in Math., Lafayette Coll., 1968; MBA, Northwestern U., 1970; JD, DePaul U., 1980. Bar: Ill. 1980; CPA, Ill. Auditor Arthur Young & Co., Chgo., 1970-75; comptroller Chgo. Urban Transp. Dist., 1975-81; treas. GDC, Inc., Chgo., 1981—; panel atty. Chgo. Vol. Legal Services Found., 1986—; treas. HYCRUDE Corp., Chgo., 1984—. Treas. 1169 South Plymouth Ct. Condominium Assn., Chgo., 1982-85. Mem. ABA, Chgo. Bar Assn., Am. Inst. CPA's, Ill. CPA Soc. Roman Catholic. Avocations: tennis, bridge. Home: 18 W 125 Rodgers Ct Darien IL 60559 Office: GDC Inc Chicago IL 60616

CIPKUS, LORETTA ANN, biochemist; b. Cleve., Apr. 27, 1957; d. Stanley John and Dona (Gelgotas) C. BS, John Carroll U., 1979, MS, 1987. Cert. tchr., Ohio; lic. real estate broker, Ohio. Jr. research asst. Case Western Res. U., Cleve., 1982-83, from research asst. I to research asst. II, 1983-85; research assoc., biochemist Upjohn CO., Kalamazoo, 1985—, also corp. catalyst rep. Editor Newsletter Grow Catalyst. Asst. coordinator religious edn. St. Mary Magdalene Ch., Willowick, Ohio. Mem. AAAS, Am. Assn. Univ. Women, Assn. Women in Sci., Mich. Soc. Med. Research (chairperson sci. edn. com. 1985—), Kalamazoo Network (program com. 1985—). Roman Catholic. Club: Willowick Clown (pres. 1984-85). Avocations: photography, naturalist, wild life supporter, stamp collecting. Home: 118 E Candlewyck Apt 1001 Kalamazoo MI 49001 Office: Upjohn Co 301 Henrietta St 7243 209 3 Kalamazoo MI 49001

CIPOLLA, LAWRENCE JOHN, human resources development services company executive; b. Hartford, Conn., Nov. 30, 1943; s. Anthony Francis and Rose Marie (Alesi) C.; A.A. with honors, Manchester Community Coll., 1968; B.A. with high honors, U. Conn., 1970; M.A. with honors (Regent's Fund scholar), U. Minn., 1972; m. Judith L. Peterka, June 24, 1972. Spencer Found. research fellow U. Minn., Mpls., 1971-72; cons., sr. instructional analyst 3M Co., St Paul, 1972-74, supr., 1974-76; v.p. learning systems div. Golle & Holmes, 1976-79, pres. Cipolla Cos., Inc., Mpls., 1979—; mem. grad. sch. faculty U. Minn., Coll. St. Thomas, St. Paul; cons. in sales and mgmt. performance systems, productivity systems, negotiation strategies, team bldg., communication skills, orgnl. transformation and devel., leadership assessment surveys; lectr., author in field. Served with USAF, 1961-65. Mem. Am. Soc. Tng. and Devel., Am. Soc. Performance Improvement, Sales and Mktg. Execs. Internat., Phi Beta Kappa. Home: 7021 Comanche Ct Edina MN 55435

CIPOLLA, ROBERT PRIMO, physician; b. Milano, Italy, July 31, 1951; came to U.S., 1982; s. Renato and Alba (Bertelli) C.; m. Luisella Raffo, July 1, 1974; children: Laura, Henry John. BA, Liceo Carducci, Milano, Italy, 1970; MD, U. Milano, 1981. Resident physician Beth Israel Med. Ctr., N.Y.C., 1982-84; practice medicine specializing in family practice Paxton, Ill., 1984—. Mem. AMA, Ill. State Med. Soc., Am. Acad. Family Physicians, Am. Coll. Medicine. Avocations: opera and classical music. Office: 114 S Market St Paxton IL 60957

CIRCLE, SYBIL JEAN, psychiatrist; b. Peoria, Ill., July 2, 1945; d. Sidney Joseph and Sydell C.; B.A., Northwestern U., 1967, M.D., 1971. Diplomate Am. Bd. Psychiatry and Neurology. Intern, Passavant Meml. Hosp., Chgo., 1971-72; resident in psychiatry Northwestern U. Med. Sch., Chgo., 1972-74; practice medicine specializing in psychiatry, Maywood, Ill., 1975-82, Chgo., 1982—; mem. faculty Loyola U. Med. Sch., Chgo., 1975—, asst. prof., 1977-81, clin. asst. prof., 1981-82, lectr., 1982—; dir. undergrad. edn., dept. psychiatry, 1977-82; staff psychiatrist West Side VA Hosp., 1982—; asst. prof. dept. psychiatry U.-Ill. Med. Sch., 1982—; staff Ill. Masonic Med. Ctr., St. Joseph Hosp., Chgo. Mem. AMA, Am. Psychiat. Assn., Am. Med. Soc. on Alcoholism and Other Drug Dependencies (cert.), Ill. Psychiat. Soc., Chgo. Med. Soc. Office: 600 N McClurg Ct #506A Chicago IL 60611

CIRICILLO, SAMUEL FRANCIS, manufacturing company executive; b. Newark, Nov. 14, 1920; s. Michael Edward and Madeline Vicenza (Rosa) C.; m. Rose Ann Casale, June 15, 1948 (div. Mar. 1958); children: Linda, Michael; m. Eileen Theresa Butfiloski, Apr. 16, 1958; children: Denise, Glennis, Samuel Jr., Nadine, Brett. BSME cum laude, Newark Coll. Engring., 1942; Cert. Indsl. Design, Newark Sch. Fine and Indsl. Arts, 1948; cert. mgmt., Ohio State U., 1967. Registered profl. engr., N.J., Ohio. Section engr. Gen. Electric Co., Bloomfield, N.J., 1942-44, dept. supr., 1946-52; project engr. Kellex Corp., Jersey City, 1944-46; chief engr. Emerson Radio & Phonograph Co., Jersey City, 1952-58; dir. research Ranco, Inc., Pompano Beach, Fla., 1958-61; v.p., dir. engring. Ranco Controls div. Ranco, Inc., Columbus, Ohio, 1961—; Adv. com. Underwriters Labs., Northbrook, Ill., 1961—; standards com. Am. Nat. Standards Inst., N.Y.C., 1967—. Contbr. articles to profl. jours. Awards chmn. Boy Scouts Am., Columbus, 1970—; advisor Columbus Jaycees, 1971. Recipient Presdl. Citation Manhattan Project, Jersey City, 1944. Fellow ASHRAE (life, disting. service award 1979); mem. ASME (life), Alpha Phi Delta, Delta Sigma Zeta, Tau Beta Pi. Democrat. Roman Catholic. Club: Teorese Social. Avocations: golf, art, sculpting. Home: 3277 Somerford Rd Columbus OH 43221 Office: Ranco Controls 8115 US Rt 42 Plain City OH 43064

CIRINO, JOHN MICHAEL, management information services executive; b. Detroit, Dec. 31, 1940; s. Louis and Marie Antoinette (Sancolla) C. BS, U. Detroit, 1965, postgrad., 1965-66, Wayne State U., 1966-68. Cert. systems profl. Systems analyst, programmer Automobile Club of Mich., Detroit, 1965-68; sr. systems analyst Chrysler Corp., Detroit, 1968-69; mgr. data processing Stroh Brewery Co., Detroit, 1969-74; dir. data processing, 1974-82; dir. mgmt. info. services B & E Sales Co., Bloomfield Hills, Mich., 1982-85, v.p. mgmt. info. services, 1986—. Mem. Assn. Systems Mgmt. Republican. Roman Catholic. Avocations: model bldg.; art; tennis; skiing; handball. Home: 24900 N Cromwell Franklin MI 48025 Office: B & E Sales Co 200 E Long Lake Bloomfield Hills MI 48013

CISCO, RONALD RAY, computer information scientist; b. Alpena, Ark., July 24, 1940; s. R.C. Cisco and Helen Jean (Buell) Smith; m. Gail Elaine Butler, Feb. 14, 1969; children: Marc Ronald, Scott Jefferson, Elaine JoAnne. BA, U. Nebr., Omaha, 1971; MA, Ball State U., 1978. Commd. U.S. Army, 1961, commd. 2d lt., 1967, advanced through grades to maj., 1980, ret., 1981, served as scientist aeromed. research lab., 1978-81, retired, 1981; zone mgr. Motorola C&E, Overland Park, Kans., 1982-86; system analyst Answer Jefferson City, Mo., 1984—. Mem. Human Factors Soc., Nat. Rifle Assn. (life). Republican. Club: United Sportsman. Avocations: hunting, fishing, camping, photography. Office: Answer Jefferson City Jefferson City MO 65101

CISKEY, DEBRA JUNE, association administrator; b. Sandusky, Ohio, Feb. 2, 1957; d. Robert Leroy and Jeanette Irene (Beers) Betz; m. Mark Louis Ciskey, July 28, 1979; 2 children. BA, Iowa State U., 1979. Asst. dir. pub. affairs Am. Collectors Assn., Inc., Mpls., 1980-85, dir. edn., 1985—. Contbr. articles to Collector Mag. Vice chmn. Dem. precinct, Apple Valley, Minn., 1986. Mem. Am. Soc. Assn. Execs., Minn. Fedn. Bus. and Profl. Women (legs. chmn. 1986-87), Minn. Bus. and Profl. Women (1st v.p. 1986-87). Democratic Farm Labor Party. Roman Catholic. Avocations: camping, aviation. Office: Am Collectors Assn Inc 4040 W 70th St Minneapolis MN 55435

CISLAK, GREGORY NOBLE, finance executive; b. Chgo., Jan. 31, 1956; s. Peter John and Margaret F. (Noble) C.; m. Catherine Ann Boyd, June 25, 1977; children: Clifton Boyd, Mary Margaret. BS, Purdue U., 1977; MBA, U. Chgo., 1979. CPA, Ind. With internat. fin. Eli Lilly and Co., Indpls., 1979-80; v.p. fin., ops. Bacompt Systems, Inc., Indpls., 1980—. Pres.'s council Purdue U., West Lafayette, Ind., 1979—. Mem. Am. Inst. CPA's, Nat. Assn. Accts., Nat. Assn. Purchasing Mgrs., Data Processing Mgrs. Assn., Ind. CPA Soc. (adv. bd. 1986—), U. Chgo. Alumni Assn. (bd. dirs. 1987—). Republican. Clubs: Meridian Hills Country, Columbia (Indpls.). Avocation: flying. Office: Bacompt Systems Inc 8561 Zionsville Rd Indianapolis IN 46268

CISZCZON, WILLIAM JOSEPH, lawyer, accountant; b. Cleve., May 26, 1950; s. Stanley and Helen (Throm) C.; m. Toshiko Kanenaga, June 12, 1982; children: Andrew, Erika. BBA, Cleve. State U., 1973, JD, 1983; MBA, Case Western Res. U., 1978. CPA, Ohio 1983; cert. mgmt. acct., internal auditor. Internal auditor Kennecott Copper, Cleve., 1973-79; mgr., dir. internal audit Scott Fetzer, Lakewood, Ohio, 1979-84; counsel, corp. atty. Scott Fetzer/United Consumer Fin. Services, Westlake, Ohio, 1984—; bd. dirs. Merchants Research Council, Chgo., 1987. Mem. ABA, Ohio Bar Assn., Am. Soc. CPA's, Ohio Soc. CPA's. Republican. Home: 3189 Bay Landing Westlake OH 44145 Office: United Consumer Fin Services 865 Bassett Rd Westlake OH 44145

CITRIN, PHILLIP MARSHALL, lawyer; b. Chgo., Nov. 1, 1931; s. Mandel Hirsch and Birdie (Gulman) C.; m. Judith Goldfeder, Dec. 23, 1967 (div. 1984); 1 child, Jeffrey Scott Levin. B.S., Northwestern U., 1953, J.D., 1956. Bar: Ill. 1957. Ptnr. Davis, Jones & Baer, Chgo., 1961-80; sole practice law specializing in domestic relations Chgo., 1980—. Republican candidate for judge circuit ct., Cook County, Ill., 1976, 78. Served with USNR, 1956-58. Fellow Am. Acad. Matrimonial Lawyers (founding); mem. Chgo. Bar Assn. (bd. mgrs. 1974-76, chmn. entertainment com. 1971, co-author ann. satire program 1963—, matrimonial law com. 1963—), Ill. Bar Assn. (mem. assembly of dels. 1972-73, family law com. 1964—), ABA (gavel awards com.), Internat. Soc. Family Law (exec. com. of domestic relations mgmt., adv. com. Cir. Ct. Cook County, chmn. ct. facilities security subcom. 1986—), Phi Delta Phi. Office: 30 N LaSalle St Chicago IL 60602

CIULEI, LIVIU, theatrical dir. Artistic dir. The Guthrie Theater, Mpls. Office: The Guthrie Theater 725 Vineland Place Minneapolis MN 55403 other: Teatrul Lucia Sturdza Bulandra,, Bd Schitu Magureanu Nr 1,, Bucharest Romania *

CIZEK, DAVID JOHN, sales engineer; b. Chgo., Sept. 29, 1959; s. John Jacob and Cecelia Ursula (Shway) C.; m. Kimberly Ann Kral, May 12, 1984. BSEE, U. Ill., 1981. Asst. sales engr. control div. Westinghouse Electric Co., Chgo., 1981-83; product line engr. control div. Westinghouse Electric Co., Fayetteville, N.C., 1983-85; sales engr. field sales div. Westinghouse Electric Co., Chgo., 1985-86, aerospace and def. automation specialist, 1987—. Mem. Am. Inst. Plant Engrs., Soc. Mfg. Engrs./Robotics, U. Ill. Alumni Assn., Kappa Sigma Alumni Assn. Republican. Presbyterian. Avocations: real estate investing, fishing, hunting, tennis. Home: 8409 Willow West Dr Willow Springs IL 60480 Office: Westinghouse Electric Corp 10 S Riverside Plaza Chicago IL 60606

CLAASSEN, MELVIN L., management accountant; b. Beatrice, Nebr., Oct. 12, 1954; s. Louis and Elsie (Linsenmeyer) C.; m. Lorna Louise Snyder, June 4, 1977; children: Jeffrey, Heidi. AA, Hesston (Kans.) Coll., 1975; BBA, Eastern Mennonite Coll., Harrisonburg, Va., 1977; MBA, U. Nebr., Lincoln, 1982. Asst. adminstr. Menno Housing, Elmira, N.Y., 1977-80; controller L. Goossen Surge Dairy, Beatrice, 1980-83; asst. v.p. bus. Martin Luther Home, Beatrice, 1983—; vice chmn. Homestead Village, Beatrice, 1984—. Mem. ch. bd. dirs. First Mennonite Ch., Beatrice, 1983-85. Mem. Nat. Assn. Accts. Avocations: sports, computers, reading, learning. Home: 123 Reed Beatrice NE 68310 Office: Martin Luther Home 804 S 12th St Beatrice NE 68310

CLAGETT, GARY ALLAN, sales and advertising executive; b. Zanesville, Ohio, Aug. 25, 1939; s. Kenneth Ray and Elizabeth M. (Dickson) C.; m. Lois Marie Patterson; children: Deborah, Jo, Iseli. BME, Ohio Mechanics Inst., 1959. Sales mgr. Arvin Diamond, Lancaster, Ohio, 1970-72, internat. sales mgr., 1972-74, asst. gen mgr., 1975; sales mgr. Ohio Semitronics, Inc., Columbus, Ohio, 1975—. Contbr. to profl. jours. Speaker Lancaster Speakers Bur., Lancaster, 1965; candidate City Council, Lancaster, 1967. Mem. Instrument Soc. Am., Cen. Ohio Indls. Marketers, Jaycees. Republican. Methodist. Club: Internat. Edsel (Ohio). Home: 261 Amity Rd Galloway OH 43119 Office: Ohio Semitronics Inc 1205 Chesapeake Ave Columbus OH 43212

CLANCY, DANIEL FRANCIS, retired journalist; b. Logansport, Ind., May 8, 1918; s. Joseph Francis and Daisy C. (Strecker) C.; student pub. schs.; m. Okodell Glads Salyer, Apr. 12, 1947; children—Cassandra Sue, Holly Eve. Reporter Logansport Press, 1942-46, Springfield (Ohio) Daily News, 1946-47, Springfield Sun, 1947-56; reporter, Columbus (Ohio) Dispatch, 1956-80, ret. 1980. Dir. Nat. Com. Against Limiting the Presidency, 1949-54. Served to lt. col. Ohio Def. Corps. Decorated French Nat. Merit, Gold medal, La Renaissance Francaise, medal Honor and Merit, knight Order of Lion of Ardennes, Cross of Lorraine and Companis of Resistance, Soc. Encouragement Arts, Scis., Letters Silver medal (France); knight Order of Crown of Stuart (Eng.); Assn. Am. Friendship Bronze medal, Trieste; count Ho. of Deols (Italy); knight Delcassian Order (Ireland); medal Institute of Libertador Ramon Castilla (Peru); medal Internat. Eloy Alfaro Found. (Panama); silver medal spl. membership Japanese Red Cross Soc.; Ohio Faithful Service ribbon; recipient Nat. Headliner award, 1948, 49; 1st place award for editorial columns Nat. Found. for Hwy. Safety, 1970; cert. of appreciation Ohio Vets. World War I, 1971; Appreciation plaque Ohio N.G., 1976; Meritorious service medal SSS; spl. recognition award Ohio VFW, 1981; Ohio Disting. Service medal; named hon. Ky. col., hon. adm. Nebr. Navy, hon. col., hon. adm. Tex. Navy, hon. N.Mex. col., hon. Miss. col., hon. lt. col. Ala., Ga., lt. gov. Ohio, Ind. Sagamore; commodore Okla., Ohio. Mem. Am. Mil. Inst., Orders and Medals Soc. Am., Ohio Mil. Res. Officers Assn., State Defl. Force Assn. U.S., Nat. Flag Found., Am. Internat. Acad., Brazilian Acad. Polit. and Social Sci., Nat. Citizens for State 51; (P.R.), Inst. Heraldry (Spain), Internat. Inst. Study and Devel. Human Relations, Brazilian Acad. Econs. and Adminstrv. Scis., Sons Union Vets. Civil War (past state comdr.), Continental Confedn. Adopted Indians (co-founder, past continental chief), Civil War Press Corps (founder, past comdr.), Assn. U.S. Army, Am. Indian Lore Assn. (hon.), U.S. Horse Cavalry Assn., 7th U.S. Cavalry Assn. (assoc. life), Cass County (Ind.) Hist. Soc., My Country Soc., Ohio Soc. Military History, Smokers' Freedom Soc. Clubs: National Headliners; Honolulu Press. Author: Two Term Tradition, 1940; Collected Poems, 1937-47, 1948. Columnist; contbr. articles to mags. Home: 2420 Zollinger Rd Columbus OH 43221

CLANTON, STEPHEN LANCE, accountant; b. Alexandria, La., Aug. 1, 1951; s. Arthur Lee and Grace Dexter (Lance) C.; m. Debra Jeanne Hudson, Oct. 3, 1981; children: Eric, Clayton, Trisha. BSBA, U. Mo., St. Louis, 1975. CPA, Mo. Adminstrv. asst. Mercantile Trust Co., St. Louis, 1975-76; staff auditor Arthur Andersen & Co., St. Louis, 1976-80, audit mgr., 1980-82; mgr. fin. acctg. Emerson Electric Co., St. Louis, 1982-85, dir. fin. electronic speed control div., 1985—. Active Big Bros. St. Louis, 1976-79, fin. cons., 1977-79; foster parent St. Louis Family Services, 1978-79; career guide various high schs., univs., St. Louis, 1981-83; treas. Danbury Assn., St. Louis, 1982-84. Mem. Am. Inst. CPA's, Mo. Soc. CPA's, Nat. Assn. Accts. (bd. dirs. 1979-84). Avocations: boating, tennis. Home: 214 Monroe Mill Ballwin MO 63011 Office: Emerson ESC Div 12301 Missouri Bottom Rd Saint Louis MO 63042

CLARE, STEWART, research biologist, educator; b. nr. Montgomery City, Mo., Jan. 31, 1913; s. William Gilmore and Wardie (Stewart) C.; m. Lena Glenn Kaster, Aug. 4, 1936. B.A. (William Volker scholar), U. Kans., 1935; M.S. (Rockefeller Research fellow, teaching fellow), Iowa State U., 1937; Ph.D. (Univ. fellow), U. Chgo., 1949. Dist. survey supr. entomology bur. entomology and plant quarantine CSC, 1937-40, tech. cons., 1941-42; instr. meteorology USAAF Weather Sch., 1942-43; research biologist Midwest Research Inst., Kansas City, Mo., 1945-46; spl. study, research Kansas City Art Inst., U. Mo., 1946-49; instr. zoology U. Alta., 1949-50, asst. prof. zoology, lectr.-instr. sci. color, dept. fine arts, 1950-53; interim asst. prof. physiology Kansas City Coll. Osteopathy and Surgery, 1953; lectr. zoology U. Adelaide, S. Australia, 1954-55; sr. research officer and cons. entomology Sudan Govt. Ministry Agr., Khartoum, Sudan and Gezira Research Sta., Wad Medani, Sudan, N.Africa, 1955-56; sr. entomologist and cons. Klipfontein Organic Products Corp., Johannesburg, Union S.Africa, 1957; prof., head dept. biology Union Coll., 1958-59, chmn. sci. div., prof., head biology, 1959-61, spl. study grantee, 1960; prof., head dept. biology Mo. Valley Coll., Marshall, 1961-62; research grantee Mo. Valley Coll., 1961-62; lectr., instr. biology, meteorology, sci. of color Adirondack Sci. Camp and Field Research Sta. at Twin Valleys, SUNY, Plattsburgh, 1962-66; dir. acad. program SUNY, 1963-66, research facilities grantee, 1963-66; Buckbee Found. prof. biology Rockford (Ill.) Coll., lectr. biology evening coll., 1962-63, spl. research grantee, 1962-63; prof., chmn. dept. biochemistry, mem. research div. Kansas City (Mo.) Coll. Osteopathy and Surgery, U. Health Scis., 1963-67; also NIH basic research grantee, 1963-67; prof. biology Coll. of Emporia, Kans., 1967-74; dir. biol. research Coll. of Emporia, 1972-74, prof. emeritus, 1974—; research biologist, cons. 1974—; research study grantee, 1967-74, spl. research grantee study in, Arctic, 1970, 72, C. Am. and Mexico, 1973; cons. VITA, 1962—, Adirondack Research Sta., 1962-66, Nat. Referral Center for Sci. and Tech., other orgns. Contbr. over 100 papers and monographs on capillary movement in porous materials, physiology and biochemistry of arthropoda; numerous local, nat., internat. exhbns. on color, also articles to profl. jours. Mem. adv. bd. Fine Art Registry Soc. N.Am. Artists. Served with USNR, 1943-45. Recipient Certificate of Service Vols. Internat. Tech. Assistance, 1970; Creativity Recognition award Internat. Personnel Research, 1972; Distinguished Achievement and Service awards for edn. and research in biology; Certificate of Merit in Art Internat. Biog. Centre, Cambridge, 1968, 72, 73, 76; Outstanding Service to Community award Am. Biog. Inst., 1975, 76, 77, 79-80; Notable Ams. of Bicentennial Era award, 1976; Book of Honor award, 1978; named Outstanding Educator Coll. of Emporia, 1973; research grantee Alta. Research Council, 1951-53; research facilities grantee U. Alaska, 1970; research facilities grantee No. Research Survey Arctic Inst. N.Am., 1970, 72. Fellow Internat. Biog. Assn. (life), Am. Biog. Inst., Explorers Club, Anglo-Am. Acad. (hon.); mem. N.Y. Acad. Scis. (life), Brit. Assn. Adv. Sci. (life), Am. Entomol. Soc. (life), Nat. Assn. Biology Tchrs., AAUP, Arctic Inst. N.Am., Am. Polar Soc., Inter-Soc. Color Council, Sigma Xi, Phi Sigma, Psi Chi, numerous others. Spl. research sci. of color and design of color. Home: 405 NW Woodland Rd Indian Hills in Riverside Kansas City MO 64150

CLARIZIO, MICHAEL JOSEPH, lawyer; b. Chicago Heights, Dec. 11, 1957; s. Joseph Michael and Carmella Ann (DeScorpio) C. BS in Criminal Justice and Polit. Sci., Ill. State U., 1980; JD, Drake U., 1984. Bar: Ill. 1984, U.S. Dist. Ct. (no. dist.) Ill. 1984. Law clk. to chief judge U.S. Dist. Ct., Iowa, 1983; asst. state's atty. Cook County, Chgo., 1984—. Mem. ACLU. Named one of Outstanding Young Men Am., U.S. Jaycees, 1983. Mem. ABA, Ill. Bar Assn., Chgo. Bar Assn., Assn. Trial Lawyers Am. Avocations: tennis, auto racing. Home: 30 E Division Suite 14E Chicago IL 60610

CLARK, CAROL MORROW, investment executive; b. Mpls., Feb. 12, 1962; d. Glen Marvin and Elaine Ruth (Strehlow) Morrow; m. Gregory Loren, Dec. 20, 1986. BBAS, William Woods Coll., 1983. Chartered fin. analyst. Market strategist Piper, Jaffray & Hopwood, Mpls., 1983-87; investment research officer First Trust, Inc., St. Paul, 1987—. Editor The Informed Investor newsletter, 1983-87. Instr. swimming local sch. dists. ARC, Mound and Minnetonka, Minn., 1983—; coordinator ARC Swim-a-Cross Campaign, Mpls., 1985-86; mem. Minnetonka Choral Soc., 1983—. Fellow Fin. Analysts Fedn.; mem. Twin Cities Soc. Securities Analysis. Lutheran. Avocations: boating, skiing, biking, camping, art. Office: First Trust Inc First Nat Bank Bldg S-5E540 Saint Paul MN 55101

CLARK, CHARLES EDWARD, arbitrator; b. Cleve., Feb. 27, 1921; s. Douglas John and Mae (Egermayer) C.; student Berea Coll., 1939-41, King Coll., 1945; LLB, U. Tex., 1948; m. Nancy Jane Hilt, Mar. 11, 1942; children: Annette S. (Mrs. Paul Gernhardt), Charles Edward, John A., Nancy P., Paul R., Stephen C., David G. Bar: Tex. 1948, Mass. 1956, U.S. Supreme Ct. 1959. sole practice, San Antonio, 1948-55; writer legal articles, editor NACCA Law Jour., Boston, 1955-58; legal asst. to vice chmn., chief voting sect. U.S. Commn. on Civil Rights, Washington, 1958-61; spl. counsel Pres.'s Com. on Equal Employment Opportunity, 1961-65; sr. compliance officer Office Fed. Contract Compliance, 1965-66; regional dir. Equal Employment

Opportunity Commn., Kansas City, Mo., 1966-79; arbitrator, 1979—; prof. law, asst. dean St. Mary's U. Sch. Law, 1948-55; lectr. Rockhurst Coll., 1980—. Active Boy Scouts Am. Served with AUS, 1943-44. Mem. Soc. Profls. in Dispute Resolution, State Bar Tex., Nat. Acad. Concillators, Am. GI Forum (D.C. vice chmn. 1962-63), Indsl. Relations Research Assn. (exec. bd. Kansas City 1976—, pres. chpt. 1986), Phi Delta Phi (province pres. 1951-55). Contbr. articles to legal jours. Home and Office: 6418 Washington St Kansas City MO 64113

CLARK, DANIEL MARTIN, military officer; b. Jersey City, N.J., Apr. 10, 1958; s. Chester Howard and Ann Elizabeth (Loehwing) C.; m. Lynne Ellen Nuber, Oct. 23, 1982; 1 child, Daniel Martin Jr. BA in Geology, Rutgers U., 1980; MA in Govt. and Nat. Security, Georgetown U., 1985. Commd. 2d lt. USAF, 1980, advanced through grades to capt., 1984; imagery analyst Defense Intelligence Agy. div. USAF, Washington, 1981-85; intelligence instr. air tng. command USAF, Offutt AFB, Nebr., 1985—; Pres., co-founder Jr. Officer Council, Defense Intelligence Agy., 1985. Mem. Nat. Mil. Intelligence Assn., Mensa. Republican. Methodist. Lodges: Order of Demolay (dep. state master councilor N.J. 1978), F&AM. Avocations: reading, cycling, golf, hiking, philately. Home: 1108 Tanglewood Ct #74 Bellevue NE 68005 Office: 3428 th TTS Offutt Air Force Base NE 68113

CLARK, DELORIS ANN (DEE), interior decorator; b. St. Louis, Sept. 3, 1937; d. George William Sr. and Wanetta Ann (Locke) Huntington; m. Wayne Charles Clark, Aug. 30, 1958; children: Bret Wayne, Berry Huntington. A in Applied Sci., Western Wis. Tech. Inst., 1974; postgrad., Viterbo Coll. Interior designer AC Johnson Co., LaCrosse, Wis., 1974-80, VA Med. Ctr., Tomah, Wis., 1980—; night sch. tchr. Western Wis. Tech. Inst., LaCrosse, 1974-79; cons. interior design VA Med. Ctr., St. Cloud, 1979, Mpls., 1979, Tomah, 1974-80. Avocations: golf, cooking, gardening, weaving, travel. Home: Rt 1 Stoddard WI 54658 Office: VA Med Ctr Tomah WI 54660

CLARK, DONALD CAMERON, diversified company executive; b. Bklyn., Aug. 9, 1931; s. Alexander and Sarah (Cameron) C.; m. Jean Ann Williams, Feb. 6, 1954; children: Donald, Barbara, Thomas. B.B.A., Clarkson U., 1953; M.B.A., Northwestern U., 1961. With Household Fin. Corp., Chgo., 1955—, sec., asst. treas., 1965-72, treas., 1972-74, sr. v.p., office of chief exec. officer, 1974-76, exec. v.p., chief fin. officer, 1976-77, pres., 1977—; pres., dir. holding co. Household Internat., Inc., Prospect Heights, Ill., 1981—, chief operating officer, chief exec. officer, 1982—, chmn., 1984—; dir. Sq. D. Co., Warner-Lambert Co. Bd. dirs. Lyric Opera of Chgo.; trustee Clarkson U., Evanston Hosp., Com. Econ. Devel., Northwestern Univ. Served to lt. U.S. Army, 1953-55. Mem. Econ. Club Chgo. (dir., pres. 1985-87), Chgo. Council Fgn. Relations (dir.), Conf. Bd. Clubs: Chgo., Westmoreland Country, Mid-Am., Commercial (Chgo.). Home: 2828 Blackhawk Rd Wilmette IL 60091 Office: Household Fin Corp 2700 Sanders Rd Prospect Heights IL 60070

CLARK, DOUGLAS O., gynecologist/obstetrician; b. Toledo, Oct. 31, 1936; s. Walter J. and Fern (Spitler) C.; m. Mary Judith Adams; children: Christi Lynn, Lori Jo. BA, Ohio State U., 1957, MD, 1961, M in Med. Edn., 1966. Diplomate Am. Bd. Ob/Gyn. Rotating intern Milw. County Gen. Hosp., 1961-62; resident in ob-gyn Ohio State U. Hosp., Columbus, 1962-66; instr. The Med. Coll. Wis., Milwaukee, 1968, asst. prof., 1968-72, asst. clin. prof., 1972—; physician Med. Assocs. Health Ctr., Menomonee Falls, Wis., 1972—; cons., lectr. Planned Parenthood, Milwaukee, 1969—; adv. ob/gyn Nurse Practitioner Program, Milwaukee, 1980—; researcher Inst. Biol. Research and Devel., 1983—; med. cons. Nat. Testing Lab., 1983—; mem. speakers bur. Med. Soc., Milwaukee Community Meml. Hosp., 1982—. Presented numerous papers to profl. orgns. Mem. AMA, Soc. Sterility and Fertility, Wis. State Ob/Gyn Soc., Cen. Assn. Ob/Gyn, Milwaukee Gynecol. Soc., Am. Coll. Ob/Gyn. Home: 3660 Mary Cliff Brookfield WI 53005 Office: Med Assocs Health Ctr 7950 Town Hall Rd Menomonee Falls WI 53051

CLARK, EDWARD JAMES, marketing executive; b. N.Y.C., Jan. 11, 1932; s. John Alfred and Ellen Agnes (Gorman) C.; m. Bertha M. Clark, Feb. 16, 1956; children: Edward, Karen, David. BBA, Seton Hall U., 1960. Sales rep. to br. sales mgr. Honeywell, Inc., N.Y.C., 1960-67; dir. sales Comten Inc., Washington, 1967-69; v.p. sales NCR Comten Inc., Washington, 1969-78, nat. v.p. sales, 1979-82, nat. v.p. mktg., 1983—. Fund raiser Gutheric Theatre, Mpls., 1982—; bd. dirs., 1983—. Served to cpl. U.S. Army, 1950-51. Republican. Roman Catholic. Club: Excelsior Bay Yacht, North Oaks Golf (Mpls.). Avocations: jogging, sailing. Home: 23 E Oak Rd Saint Paul MN 55110 Office: NCR Comten Inc 2700 N Snelling Ave Roseville MN 55113

CLARK, ELIZABETH ANN, nurse; b. Alton, Ill., Dec. 10, 1950; d. Angelo Thomas and Josephine Ann (Lombardo) Alben; grad. St. Joseph's Sch. Nursing, Alton, 1971; B.S. in Nursing, McKendree Coll., 1985; m. Gary Daniel Clark, Aug. 20, 1970; children—Nicole Leigh, Jason Andrew. Staff nurse obstetrics-gynecology S.W. Tex. Meth. Hosp., San Antonio, 1971; staff nurse operating room Kansas City (Mo.) Gen. Hosp., 1971-73; staff nurse obstetrics, recovery room, med.-surg. Spelman Meml. Hosp., Smithville, Mo., 1974-76; staff nurse operating room Alton Meml. Hosp., 1976-85, head nurse operating room, 1985-86, dir. surgery services, 1986—; sec. Anestat, Inc., 1975-76. Treas. Alton Area Swim Team, 1985—. Mem. Assn. Operating Room Nurses (nominating com. 1985-86, bd. dirs. 1986-87, v.p./pres.-elect 1987—), Phi Theta Kappa. Roman Catholic. Home: 2915 Gilbert Ln Alton IL 62002

CLARK, FRANK RAY, manufacturing and construction company executive; b. Des Moines, Sept. 5, 1944; s. Thomas M. and Vivian (Lewis) C.; m. Carole F. Williams, Aug. 5, 1972; 1 child, Brian A. B.S., Drake U., 1966. C.P.A., Iowa, Wis. Auditor, Ernst & Whinney, Des Moines and Mpls., 1966-69; mgr. corp. acctg., mgr. planning, div. controller Applied Power Inc., Milw., 1970-78; group controller McQuay Inc., Milw., 1978-79; v.p., chief fin. officer, treas. Realex Corp. Kansas City, Mo., 1979-85; v.p. fin. sec. Layne Western Co., Inc., Mission, Kans., 1985—. Solicitor, United Way, Kansas City, Mo., 1983. Mem. Am. Inst. C.P.A., Fin. Execs. Inst. (pres. Kansas City chpt. 1984-85). Republican. Methodist. Office: Layne Western Co Inc 5800 Foxridge Dr Mission KS 66201-4411

CLARK, HENRY OGDEN, architect; b. Berwyn, Ill., Dec. 29, 1944; s. Charles Dhority and Agnes Theresa (Ogden) C.; m. Susan Jean Longini, Aug. 1967 (div. Aug. 1970). Student, Reed Coll., 1962-64; BArch, U. Mich., 1969; MS in Creative Intelligence, Maharishi European Research U., Weggis, Switzerland, 1980. Registered architect, Ga., Iowa, Washington (D.C.). Intern Anderson, Notter, Boston, 1970-71, Enteleki, Salt Lake City, 1971-73; ctr. chmn. Internat. Meditation Soc., Traverse City, Mich., 1973-75; architect Sizemore Assocs., Atlanta, 1975-79; campus architect., asst. prof. art Maharishi Internat. U., Fairfield, Iowa, 1979—; v.p., bd. dirs. Merlin's Enterprises Internat., Fairfield, 1985—; pres. Traverse Bay Group, Fairfield, 1982—. Co-author: Energy Planning for Buildings, 1978. Recipient State Energy award State of Iowa, 1986. Mem. AIA. Avocations: skiing, swimming, running, sailing, transcendental meditation. Home and Office: Maharishi Internat U Faculty Fairfield IA 52556

CLARK, JACK ANTHONY, professional baseball player; b. Nov. 10, 1955; m. Tamara C., Nov. 3, 1979; children—Danika, Rebekah, Anthony. Profl. baseball player San Francisco Giants, Nat. League, 1976-84; profl. baseball player St. Louis Cardinals, Nat. League, 1985—. Player, Major League All-Star Game, 1978, 79. Office: care St Louis Cardinals Busch Stadium 250 Stadium Plaza Saint Louis MO 63102 •

CLARK, JAMES ROBERT, JR., osteopathic physician, radiologist; b. Harrisburg, Pa., May 19, 1946; s. James Robert and Mary Jane (Rudy) C.; m. Marcia Allerdice, Aug. 17, 1968; children—Benjamin, Emily, Elizabeth. B.S. in Pharmacy, U. N.C., 1969; D.O., Phila. Coll. Osteo. Medicine, 1977. Cert. in radiology Am. Osteo. Bd. Radiology. Rotating intern Grandview Hosp., Dayton, Ohio, 1977-78, resident in radiology, 1978-81; practice osteo. medicine specializing in radiology, Dayton, 1981—; chmn. radiology sect. Grandview Hosp. and Med. Ctr., Dayton; mem. Dayton Assocs. in Radiology, Inc.; mem. vol. faculty Ohio U. Coll. Osteo. Medicine. Served to capt. USAF, 1970-73. Mem. Am. Osteo. Assn., Ohio Osteo. Assn., Dayton Dist. Acad. Osteopathy, Am. Osteo. Coll. Radiology, Radiological Soc. of N.Am. Republican. Episcopalian. Office: 405 Grand Ave Dayton OH 45405

CLARK, JANE COLBY, English educator; b. Smith County, Kans., July 22, 1928; d. Noel Barclay and Velma Matilda (Helfinstine) Colby; B.S., Kans. State U., 1951; postgrad. Colo. State U., 1955-56, U. Colo., summers 1957-59; m. William Kline Clark, May 27, 1951; children—Courtney, Hilary. Tchr. rural sch., Smith County, 1946-47; sec., home service worker ARC, Boulder, Colo., 1952-55; tchr. public schs., Manhattan, Kans., 1956-59; temporary instr. in English, Kans. State U., 1968-74, instr., 1974—, asst. dir. writing lab. dept. English, 1974-85, dir. writing lab., 1985—. Mem. Nat. Council Tchrs. English, Nat. Writing Ctrs. Assn. (exec. bd.), Midwest Writing Ctrs. Assn. (exec. bd.), Riley County Humane Soc., Mortar Bd. Alumnae, Phi Kappa Phi. Methodist. Contbr. book revs. to newspaper, Manhattan Mercury; editorial bd. The Writing Ctr. Jour. Home: 2105 McDowell Ave Manhattan KS 66502 Office: 102 Denison Hall Kans State U Manhattan KS 66506

CLARK, JOHN EARL, banker, consultant; b. Columbus, Ohio, June 19, 1951; s. Earl W. and Juanita (Wolford) C.; m. Donna M. Weimann, June 12, 1971; children—Carol, Andrea. A.A., Columbus Tech., 1971; cert. Am. Inst. Banking, 1977, Ohio Sch. Consumer Credit, Kent State U., 1978, Ohio Sch. Banking, Ohio U., 1984. Br. asst. City Loan Co., Newark, Ohio, 1969-74; asst. mgr. Creditthrift of Am., Lancaster, Ohio, 1974-75; asst. v.p. Central Trust Co., Lancaster, 1975—; freelance photographer, Lancaster, 1977-84; pres. J.E. Clark & Assocs., Inc., Lancaster, 1984—; ptnr. C & E Devel., Gameboard Gallery, Lancaster, 1984—; pres. Lancaster Deli, Inc. Cons. Jr. Achievement, Lancaster, 1979-83, bd. dirs. 1983—86, pres. 1985-86; mem. sales com. Fairfield County Jr. Fair Bd. Recipient Gold award United Way, Lancaster, 1977, Citation of Service, Am. Diabetes Assn., 1983. Mem. Lancaster Downtown Merchants Assn., Fairfield County C. of C., Buckeye Lake C. of C. Baptist. Lodge: Lions (pres. 1984-85). Avocations: photography; fishing; antique collecting. Home: 333 W Fair Ave Lancaster OH 43130 Office: Central Trust Co PO Box 188 Millersport OH 43046

CLARK, JOHN HAMILTON, chemist; b. San Gabriel, Calif., Nov. 22, 1949; s. Charles Warren and Nellie May (Hamilton) C.; m. Piyanud Ruth Hyssey, June 12, 1971; 1 child, Cynthia Alison. A.B. with highest honors, U. Calif.-Santa Barbara, 1971; Ph.D. Physics and Chemistry, U. Calif.-Berkeley, 1976. J. Robert Oppenheimer research fellow Los Alamos Sci. Lab, 1976-79; asst. group leader laster photochemistry Los Alamos Sci. Lab., 1979; asst. prof. phys. chemistry U. Calif.-Berkeley, 1979-85, sr. scientist chem. biodyanamics div. Lawrence Berkeley Lab., 1979-85; research supr. photon processes group Amoco Corp., Naperville, Ill., 1985-87; dir. research and devel. Amoco Laser Co., Naperville, 1987—. Co-author: Laser Chemistry, 1977, Chemical and Biochemical Applications of the Laser, 1980; contbr. numerous articles to profl. jours.; patentee laser chemistry. Nat. Merit Scholar, 1967-71; Regents scholar, 1967-71; Pres.'s fellow, 1970-71; Chancellor's Sci. fellow 1971-72; Kofoid Eugenics fellow 1973-74; grantee Research Corp., 1980-81, Dept. Energy, 1980-83, Am. Heart Assn., 1980-82, Dow Chem. Co., 1981-84, Gen. Atomic Co, 1981, Office Naval Research, 1982-85, Gas Research Inst., 1982-85, U.S. Dept. Energy, 1980-83; Alfred P. Sloan research fellow, 1982-84; Camille and Henry Dreyfus tchr.-scholar, 1981-86. Mem. Am. Chem. Soc., Am. Phys. Soc., AAAS, Optical Soc. Am., Phi Beta Kappa, Sigma Xi. Office: Amoco Corp Amoco Research Ctr Naperville IL 60187

CLARK, JOHN ROBERT, management psychologist; b. Pitts., Oct. 23, 1943; B.A., U. Notre Dame, 1965; M.B.A., Loyola U., 1974; Ph.D., Ill. Inst. Tech., 1979; m. Mary Diorio, Nov. 24, 1966. Supr. manpower procurement Hyster Co., Portland, Oreg., 1967-70, sales rep., Chgo., 1970-79; v.p. Mark Silber Assos. Ltd., 1979-81; sr. assoc., Witt Assos., Inc., Oak Brook, Ill., 1981-86, mgr. health care exec. search, Coopers & Lybrand, Inc., Chgo., 1986—. Mem. Am. Psychol. Assn., Am. Theatre Organ Soc. Roman Catholic. Club: Notre Dame (Chgo.). Home: 125 Saddlebrook Dr Oak Brook IL 60521 Office: 203 N LaSalle St Chicago IL 60601

CLARK, LARRY DALTON, civil engineer; b. Sask., Can., May 12, 1942; s. Albert Ray and Christina Emily (Marum) C.; B.S. in Civil Engring., S.D. Sch. Mines, Rapid City, 1971; m. Janice Martina Kettleson, Aug. 16, 1969; children—Tamara Dayrie, Laura Janelle, Jennifer Lynette, Daniel Jerod. Engr. in tng. Iowa Hwy. Commn., Ames, 1971-75; asst. resident engr. Iowa Dept. Transp., New Hampton, 1975-79, acting resident engr., 1977-78; county engr. Black Hawk County, 1979—. Active local United Way campaign, 1976-77. Recipient award Nat. Assn. Counties Bridge Rehab., 4 awards Asphalt Paving Assn. Iowa. Registered profl. engr., Iowa; registered land surveyor. Mem. ASCE, Nat., Iowa socs. profl. engrs., Sigma Tau. Lutheran. Home: 338 Longview Dr Waterloo IA 50701 Office: Black Hawk County Courthouse Waterloo IA 50703

CLARK, LARRY GORDON, food service executive; b. Bay Village, Ohio, Mar. 15, 1958; s. Gordon David and Carol Johanna (Wriedt) C. Student, Muskingham Coll., 1979-80. Exec. chef Matter of Taste, Columbus, Ohio, 1977-79, Specialty Restaurants Corp., Columbus, 1980-81, Marriot Corp., Columbus, 1981-82; pres. Custom Auto, Dublin, Ohio, 1984-86; chmn. bd. Made From Scratch, Inc., Dublin, 1982-86; food service cons., Columbus, 1985-86. Pres. bd. Learning Juncture, Worthington, Ohio, 1980-86; mem. Columbus Conv. and Visitors Bur., 1983. Mem. Am. Culinary Fedn., Nat. Restaurant Assn., Ohio Restaurant Assn., Internat. Food Service Execs. Assn., Columbus C. of C., Worthington C. of C., Dublin C. of C. Lodge: Rotary. Avocation: sculpting. Office: Made From Scratch Inc 6175 Shamrock Ct Dublin OH 43017

CLARK, LEWIS SIDNEY, manufacturing company executive; b. Columbus, Ohio, Sept. 23, 1942; s. Robert Wayne and Viola M. (Klass) C.; m. Carol Marie Hartwig, Feb. 24, 1968; children: Matthew Scott, Kimberly Ann. BS in Indsl. Engring., U. Dayton, 1965, MBA, 1971. Registered profl engr., Ohio. Plant facilities engr. NCR, Dayton, Ohio, 1968-73; mgr. plant engring. Outdoor Power div. FMC, Port Washington, Wis., 1973-75; foreman power house Allis-Chalmers ESD Inc., Milw., 1975-80, cons. mech. engring., 1980-83, mgr. fin. and adminstrn., 1983—. Republican. Roman Catholic. Club: Toastmasters (pres. 1980). Avocations: micro-computers, reading. Home: N95 W6550 Fieldcrest St Cedarburg WI 53012 Office: Allis-Chalmers ESD Inc 1126 S 70th St 1805 JC West Allis WI 53214

CLARK, LINDA MARIE, cons.; b. Chgo., June 9, 1940; d. Harold Dean and Edith M. (Nystrom) C.; B.S., U. Mich., 1962; M.B.A., U. Chgo., 1969. Analyst, Biol. Scis. Computation Ctr., Billings Hosp., U. Chgo., 1962-65; dir. math. and statis. services Armour & Co., Chgo., 1965-68; pvt. practice cons., Chgo., 1968-69; pres. LMC Cons. Co., Flossmoor, Ill., 1969—; dir. Internat. Computer Edn. Corp., Ill., 1971-75; mem. Ill. Small Bus. Delegation to China, 1986. Bd. govs. Internat. House, U. Chgo., 1976—; sec.-treas. U. Chgo. Alumnae Council Exec. Com., 1976-77; del. White House Conf. Small Bus., 1980; mem. Pvt. Industry Council Suburban Cook County, 1980-81; mem. delegation to China Ill. Small Bus., 1986. Mem. Am. Statis. Assn. (pres. Chgo. chpt. 1972-73, dir. 1971-74), Optical Soc. Am. (mem. nat. com. computers 1976-77), AAAS, Ill. Del. Small Bus., Ind. Bus. Assn. Ill. (dir., v.p. state issues 1982-84), Chgo. Assn. Commerce and Industry (dir. 1974-79), U. Chgo. Women's Bus. Group, Alpha Chi Omega. Club: P.E.O. (pres. chpt. HH 1981-83). Contbr. articles to profl. jours. Pub. Met. Chgo. Maj. Employer's Directory, 1977. Home: 1127 Dartmouth Rd Flossmoor IL 60422

CLARK, MARTIN BELL, printing company executive, consultant; b. Duluth, Minn., Mar. 18, 1955; s. Thomas Ferguson and Barbara Jean (Barclay) C.; m. Leigh Ann Schlich, Sept. 24, 1977; children—Andrew Charles, Megan Leigh, Casey Thomas, Colin Patrick. B.S. in Bus. Administrn., Miami U.-Oxford, Ohio, 1977. Pres., owner Profl. Flagpole Painting, Dayton, Ohio, 1975-76; mgr., coach Trailsend Club, Kettering, Ohio, 1973-77; sr. sales engr. Kettering Material Handling, Dayton, 1977-81; v.p. mktg. Fabspec, Dayton, 1982-85; pres. Alan-Laf, Inc., Dayton, 1985—; cons. Sperotech, Spring Valley, Ohio, 1982-84; dir., sec. Fabrication Specialties, Dayton, 1982—. Recipient Salesman of Yr. award Kettering Material Handling, 1979. Mem. Robotics Internat. of Soc. Mech. Engr. Republican. Roman Catholic. Club: Quail Run Leisure Ctr. (v.p., bd. dirs. 1982—). Avocations: swimming; skiing; tennis. Home: 1248 Timber Hawk Trail Spring Valley OH 45370 Office: Alan-Laf Inc 3127 Encrete Ln Dayton OH 45439

CLARK, MARY ROMAYNE SCHROEDER, communication consultant, civic worker; b. Fergus Falls, Minn.; d. Christian Frederick and Dorothy Genevieve (Miller) Schroeder; B.A., Coll. St. Teresa, 1944; diploma fine arts Conservatory St. Cecelia, 1944; M.A., Marquette U., 1978; postgrad. U. Salzburg (Austria); m. Donald Arthur Clark, Aug. 24, 1946 (dec. Jan. 1975); children—Donald Arthur, Anne Elizabeth, Christopher John. Instr., Ottumwa (Iowa) Heights Coll., 1944-46; instr. U. N.D., Grand Forks, 1946-48, Marquette U., Milw., 1948-52, Milw. Area Tech. Coll., 1962-66, Mt. Mary Coll., Milw., 1976-81; dir. tng. and devel. First Bank, Milw., 1981-84; instr., seminar leader Div. Continuing Edn., Marquette U., 1984—, U. Wis. Ext., 1984—; communications cons. 1978-80, coordinator community relations, 1980—. Mem. com. on edn. U.S. Cath. Conf., Washington, 1971-75; state vol. adviser Nat. Found., 1971—; mem. adv. bd. Sickle Cell Disease Center, Deaconess Hosp., Milw., 1970-73; mem. nat. alumnae bd. Coll. St. Teresa, Winona, Minn., 1970—; mem. bd. edn. Archdiocese Milw., 1965-71, pres., 1967-71; bd. dirs. Woman to Woman Inc.; adv. bd. Mgmt. Inst., U.Wis.-Milw., 1983—. Named Wis. Woman of Year, Wis. Cath. War Vets., 1963, Alumna of Year, Coll. St. Teresa, 1969, Outstanding Vol. Nat. Found., 1974, Vol. Activist Germaine Monteil, 1974; Presdl. award Nat. Cath. Edn. Assn., 1981; Excellence in Tng. award Am. Soc. Tng. and Devel., 1983, 84. Mem. Archdiocesan Confraternity Christian Mothers (pres. 1961-63), Archdiocesan League Cath. Home and Sch. Assns. (pres. 1963-65), Archdiocesan Council Cath. Women (dist. pres. 1965-67), Nat. Forum Cath. Parents Orgns. (v.p. 1979), Internat. Fedn. Cath. Alumnae, Am. Soc. Tng. and Devel. AAUW, Marquette U. Women's Club (pres. 1959). Home: 317 N Story Pkwy Milwaukee WI 53208

CLARK, MAURICE COATES, hospital chaplain, educator; b. Stamford, Conn., Feb. 4, 1921; s. Loyal Brown and Ada Agnes (Coates) C.; m. Cynthia Ann Reed, Aug. 25, 1945 (div. 1965); children: Steven, Judith, Daniel, Peter; m. Harriett Anne Stovall, Oct. 17, 1965. BA, Wesleyan U., 1942; M Div., Yale U., 1945. Ordained to ministry United Ch. of Christ, 1945. Chaplain Columbus (Ohio) State Hosp., 1950-68; pastoral counselor Bay County Guidance Clinic, Panama City, Fla., 1968-70; dir. pastoral services Brevard County Mental Health Ctr., Rockledge, Fla., 1970-77; teaching chaplain Toronto (Can.) Inst. Pastoral Tng., 1977-79; chaplain supr. Hosp. Chaplaincy Council, Troy, Ohio, 1979-80, Cen. Ohio Psychiat. Hosp., Columbus, 1980—; mental health cons. Roman Cath. Diocese of Columbus, 1981—, Trinity Luth. Sem., Columbus, 1984—; mem. dept. ministry United Ch. Christ; exec. dir. Council Clin. Tng., N.Y.C., 1962-67. Contbr. articles to profl. jours. Mem. Am. Acad. Psychotherapists, Am. Assn. Pastoral Counselors (diplomate), Am. Group Therapy Assn., Am. Protestant Hosp. Assn. (coll. of chaplains), Assn. Clin. Pastoral Edn. (chaplain supr. 1948—), Assn. Mental Health Chaplains (profl. mem.). Office: Cen Ohio Psychiat Hosp Pastoral Services 1960 W Broad St Columbus OH 43223

CLARK, MAXINE, retail executive; b. Miami, Fla., Mar. 6, 1949; d. Kenneth and Anne (Lerch) Kasselman; m. Robert Fox, Sept. 1984. B.A. in Journalism, U. Ga., 1971. Exec. trainee Hecht Co., Washington, 1971, hosiery buyer, 1971-72, misses sportswear buyer, 1972-76; mgr. mdse. planning and research May Dept. Stores Co., St. Louis, 1976-78, dir. mdse. devel., 1978-80, v.p. mktg. and sales promotion Venture Stores div., 1980-81, sr. v.p. mktg. and sales promotion Venture Stores div., 1981-83, exec. v.p. mktg. and softlines, 1983-85; exec. v.p. apparel Famous-Barr, St. Louis, 1985-86; v.p. mcdsg. Lerner Shops div. Limited Inc., N.Y.C., 1986—. Sec., Lafayette Sq. Restoration Com., 1978-79. Mem. Nat. Assn. Female Execs., St. Louis Women's Commerce Assn., Advt. Club Greater St. Louis, St. Louis Forum.

CLARK, MICHAEL HAROLD, academic administrator; b. Columbus, Ohio, Oct. 25, 1940; s. Harold Hine and Marian Evelyn (Winzeler) C.; m. Saundra Jean Jones, Sept. 4, 1960; children: Shari Diane, Julie Lynn. AB, Ind. U., Bloomington, 1963; MA, U. Wis., 1973. Commd. 2d lt. U.S. Army, 1964; served as pub. affairs officer U.S. Army, Vietnam, Washington, Rep. of Germany, 1968-72, 74-77, 82-85; advanced through grades to lt. col. U.S. Army, 1980, retired, 1985; dir. communications No. Mich. U., Marquette, 1985—; chief press inquiry br. Dept. of the Army, Washington, 1982-84. Decorated Bronze Star, Legion of Merit. Mem. Pub. Relations Soc. Am. (accredited), Council for the Advancement and Support of Edn. Methodist. Lodge: Kiwanis. Avocations: physical fitness, genealogy. Home: 1604 Bayview Dr Marquette MI 49855 Office: No Mich U Cohodas Bldg Room 607 Marquette MI 49855

CLARK, MONTAGUE GRAHAM, JR., former college president; b. Charlotte, N.C., Feb. 25, 1909; s. Montague G. and Alice C. (Graham) C.; m. Elizabeth Hoyt, May 2, 1933; children: Elizabeth (Mrs. Joe Embser), Alice (Mrs. Harold Davis), Margaret (Mrs. William Miller), Julia (Mrs. Cecil Hampton). Student, Ga. Tech. Sch. Engring.; LL.D., Drury Coll., 1957; Ed.D., S.W. Bapt. Coll., 1972; Litt.D., Sch. of the Ozarks, 1975, D.Sc., 1986; D.D., Mo. Valley Coll., 1977; DSc, Sch. Ozarks, 1986. Ordained to ministry Presbyn. Ch., 1950. V.p. W.R. Hoyt & Co., Atlanta, 1934-46; v.p. Sch. of Ozarks, Point Lookout, Mo., 1946-52, pres., 1952-81, sec. bd. trustees, 1957-71, pres. emeritus, chmn. bd. emeritus, 1981—; past dir. Bank of Taney County.; Past mem. Commn. on Colls. and Univs., North Central Assn. Colls. and Secondary Schs.; former moderator Lafayette Presbetery and Synod of Mo., Presbyn. Ch. of U.S.; Past mem. nat. adv. council on health professions edn. NIH; dir. Empire Gas Corp. Mem. Nat. council Boy Scouts Am.; also mem. adv. bd. Ozarks Empire Area council; mem. Wilson's Creek Battlefield Nat. Commn., 1961—; mem. bd., exec. com., sec. Blue Cross; hon. mem. Mo. Am. Revolution Bicentennial Commn.; former v.p., dir. Am. Heart Assn., mem. exec. com., chmn. fund raising adv. and policy com., Gt. Plains regional chmn.; chmn. Mo. Heart Fund; past chmn. bd. Mo. Heart Assn.; mem. adv. council Council on Am. Affairs.; mem. South Central/Lakes County Med. Services System; mem. security panel Aircraft War Prodn. Council, N.Y.; v.p., vice chmn. Thomas Hart Benton Homestead Meml. Commn.; bd. dirs. St. Louis Scottish Towers Residence Found.; chmn. burns prevention com. Shrine of N.Am.; hon. chmn. So. Mo. div. Am. Cancer Soc.; pres. Youth Council Atlanta; mem. exec. com. Atlanta Christian Council; mem. Park and Recreation Commn. Fulton County; chmn. planned giving and legacies Mo. div. Am. Cancer Soc., hon. edn. chmn. So. Mo. div., chmn. planned giving and legacy Mo. div. Served to maj. Internal Security, World War II. Named Ark. traveler, 1962; recipient Silver Beaver award Boy Scouts Am., Gold Heart award Am. Heart Assn., George Washington certificate Freedoms Found., 1974, 78, In God We Trust award Family Found., Red Cross of Constantine York Rite, Disting . Service award Am. Legion Dept. of Mo., numerous other awards; named to Ozark Hall of Fame. Mem. Royal Order Scotland; Mem. S.A.R. (past pres. gen. nat. soc., hon. v.p. Mo. Soc., patriotic com., Nat. Soc. Good Citizenship medal, Patriot medal, Minute Man award, Va. Soc. medal), Acad. Mo. Squires, Navy League U.S., Mo. C. of C., Branson C. of C. (econ. devel. com.), Assn. Grand Jurors of Fulton County, Atlanta Sunday Sch. Supts. Assn. (pres., treas.), Mo. Pilots Assn. (1st chmn. bd.), Civil Air Patrol (dir. adv. bd.), White River Valley Hist. Soc. (past pres.), Soc. Colonial Wars, Order Founders and Patriots Am., Air Force Assn., Assn. U.S. Army, Mo. Assn. State Troopers Emergency Relief Soc., Internat. Assn. Chiefs of Police, Nat. Gavel Soc., Red Cross Constantine. Clubs: Masons (33 deg., awards, grand chaplain 1980-81, chmn. Americanism Com., others), Shriners (past imperial chaplain, others), K.T, Rotary (past local pres., dist. gov. 1966-67), DeMolay. Address: Sch of the Ozarks Point Lookout MO 65726

CLARK, NATHAN BRUCE, military officer; b. Tampa, Fla., Sept. 16, 1947; s. Elmo Earl and Ina Erma (Myers) C.; m. Joan Louise Howard, Dec. 28, 1971 (div. Sept. 1981); m. Diana Lynn (Strobel) Desautels, Jan. 20, 1986; step children: Jacqueline Gail, Jo-Anne Cheryl. BS in Computer Sci., USAF Acad., 1969; MS in Aerospace Systems Mgmt., St. Mary's U., San Antonio, 1975; MS in Computer Systems, Air Force Inst. Tech., 1977. Commd. 2d lt. USAF, 1965, advanced through grades to maj.; T-38 instr. pilot 64th Flying Tng. Wing, Reese AFB, Tex., 1970-73; acad. course designer 3305th Sch. Sq. HQ ATC, Randolph AFB, Tex., 1973-75; lab. contract mgr. Rome Air Devel. Ctr., Griffiss AFB, N.Y., 1977-81; aircrew & flight commdr. 906th Air Refueling SQ, Minot AFB, N.D., 1981-85; chief tanker mission devel. 5th Bomb Wing, Minot AFB, 1985—; pvt. practice cons. Architectronics, 1979-85. Systems adminstr. ARC, Minot, 1986. Mem. Air Force Assn.,

NRA. Republican. Lodge: Elks. Avocations: computer hacking. Home: 1433 16th St Northwest Minot ND 58701 Office: 5th BMW/DOTTK Minot AFB ND 58705

CLARK, PAUL ALAN, accountant; b. Ft. Wayne, Ind., Nov. 15, 1943; s. Harold L. and C. Ruth (Kantzer) C.; m. Patricia L. Martin, Sept. 13, 1980. BS, Ind. U., 1967, postgrad., 1967-68. CPA, Ohio, Ind. Staff acct. Arthur Young & Co., Toledo, 1969-74; ptnr. Chastain, Due & Thomas, CPA's, Anderson, Ind., 1974-81; prin. Paul A. Clark, CPA, Anderson, 1981—. Bd. dirs. March of Dimes, 1975-76; treas. House of Hope, 1986-87. Mem. Am. Inst. CPA's, Ind. CPA Soc., Ohio Soc. CPA's, Ind. U. Alumni Assn. (life), Evans Scholars Alumni, Nat. Rifle Assn. (life, cert. instr.), Alpha Kappa Psi. Lodges: Lions (local pres. 1985-86), Elks. Avocations: golf, hunting, community service. Office: 2527 E 10th St Anderson IN 46012

CLARK, PAUL EDWARD, publisher; b. Metropolis, Ill., Mar. 7, 1941; s. Paul E. and Lillie Jean (Melcher) C.; B.A., So. Ill. U., 1963, M.A., 1965; M.Div., Northwestern U., 1970; D.Mus., Inst. Musical Research (London), 1973; Ph.D., U. Ill., 1978. Staff accompanist The Story (TV series) and White Sisters (Word Records), 1959-62; staff accompanist voice faculty So. Ill. U., Carbondale, 1961-65; ordained to ministry, Meth. Ch., 1966; pastor Stockland (Ill.) United Meth. Ch., 1966-70; minister of music First United Meth. Ch., Watseka, Ill., 1972-76; dir. choral activities Unit 3, Donovan (Ill.) schs., 1970-79; studio musician Chgo., Nashville, Los Angeles, 1966—; pres. Clark Music Pub. and Prodn., Watseka, 1973—; bus. mgr., transp. dir. Community Unit 3 Schs., 1980—; cons. for workshops, univs. Named Piano Tchr. of the Year, So. Ill. U., 1970; Gospel Music Instrumentalist award, 1971; Ill. Chess Coach award, 1973, 74; U. Calif. at Los Angeles fellow, 1971. Mem. Am. Choral Dirs. Assn. (dist. chmn. 1977-80), Am. Fedn. Musicians, Music Educators Nat. Conf., Ill. Music Educators Assn., U.S. Chess Fedn., So. Ill. U. Alumni Assn., Broadcast Music Inc., Phi Mu Alpha, Mu Alpha Theta. Republican. Methodist. Contbr. articles in field to profl. jours. music reviewer, critic, columnist The Illiana Spirit (newspaper), 1976-83 ; composer; The Voice That Calls His Name, 1961; Jesus Dear Jesus, 1971; Spring Was But A Child, 1977; Country Living, 1976; Losing is the Hurting Side of Love, 1977; Use Me Lord, 1978; Come On In, 1978; All I Ask of You, 1979. Office: PO Box 299 Watseka IL 60970

CLARK, ROBERT BADEN, manufacturing company executive; b. Detroit, Jan. 30, 1933; s. Arthur Baden and Midred Grace (Sanford) C.; m. Kathleen Patricia Waite, June 1, 1956; children: Gregory, Shawn, Todd. BS in Indsl. Engring., U. Mich., 1955. Engr. Gen. Motors Corp., Janesville, Wis., 1958-65; sales engr. Mid West Conveyor, Kansas City, Kans., 1965-72, v.p., 1972—. Inventor, patentee in field. Served with U.S. Army, 1956-57. Mem. Pi Tau Sigma, Tan Beta Phi. Avocation: sailing. Home: 11001 W 100th St Overland Park KS 66214 Office: Mid West Conveyor Co 2601 Mid West Dr Kansas City KS 66112

CLARK, ROBERT EUGENE, religion educator; b. Cheyenne, Wyo., Aug. 19, 1931; s. Glen E. and Anna W. (Shaw) C.; m. Marian A. Anderson, June 13, 1954; children: Kathleen, Kevin, Kristine, Karen, Ken, Kraig. BA, Wheaton Coll., 1961; MS, U. Nebr., Omaha, 1965; EdD, U. Denver, 1968. Dir. Christian edn. Bethel Bible Ch., Hammond, Ind., 1954-58; instr. Faith Bapt. Bible Coll., Ankeny, Iowa, 1958-59, chmn. Christian edn. dept., 1961-69; prof. Christian edn. faculty Moody Bible Inst., Chgo., 1969—. Author: (with others) Understanding People, 2d edit., 1981; editor Childhood Education in the Church, 1975, rev. edit., 1986, Teaching Preschoolers, 1983; contbr. to publs. in field. Recipient Faculty Citation award Moody Bible Inst., 1983. Baptist. Home: 1044 Garner Ave Wheaton IL 60187 Office: Moody Bible Inst 820 N LaSalle Dr Chicago IL 60610

CLARK, ROBERT LOY, human services executive; b. Kansas City, Mo., July 2, 1937; s. Robert William and Donna Lavonna (Loy) C.; A.B., No. Colo. U., 1959; postgrad. Syracuse U., 1959; M.S. in Psychology, Ft. Hays (Kans.) State U., 1963; postgrad. U. Nebr., 1963; m. Connie Lou Davis, Sept. 3, 1960; children—Vicki Marie, Robert Scott, Angie Linn. Vocational rehab. counselor Hays (Kans.) Div. Rehab. Services, 1960-62, Lincoln (Nebr.) Div. Rehab. Services, 1964-65, Glenwood (Iowa) Hosp.-Sch. for Mentally Retarded, 1965-66; exec. dir. Greater Omaha Assn. Retarded Citizens, 1966-71; dir. Douglas County (Nebr.) Dept. Mental Health Resources, Omaha, 1971-74; asst. dir. human services Eastern Nebr. Human Services Agy., Omaha, 1974-75; adminstr. human services Lincoln-Lancaster County (Nebr.), 1975-85; v.p. planning and allocations United Way Cen. Iowa, Des Moines, 1986—; co-founder Nebr. Coalition for Community Human Services, 1982, pres., 1982, 1st v.p., 1983; community services cons. U. Nebr. Coll. Medicine, 1971-74, instr. med. psychology, dept. psychiatry, 1975-79; adv. mem. governing bd. Eastern Nebr. Community Office of Retardation, 1970-74; mem. Nebr. Gov.'s Citizens' Study Com. Mental Retardation, 1967-69; mem. Lincoln-Lancaster County Emergency Med. Services Council, 1975-78; mem. adminstrv. team human services coordinating bd. United Way Cen. Iowa and State Dept. Human Services, Polk County, Des Moines; bd. dirs. Mental Health Assn. Nebr., 1972-86, treas., 1974-76, 84-85; bd. dirs. Lincoln Action Program, 1976-80, Combined Health Agencies Drive of Nebr., 1985-86. Mem. Rehab. Assn. Nebr. (past dir., treas. 1964-72). Democrat. Home: 1100 50th St #1205 West Des Moines IA 50265 Office: 700 6th Ave Des Moines IA 50309

CLARK, ROBERT WESLEY, neurologist; b. Jamestown, N.Y., Apr. 16, 1946; s. Robert Wesley and Dorothy (Depue) C.; m. Linda Gray, June 15, 1968 (div. Jan. 1982); 1 child, Jennifer Marie; m. Marcia Ramm, June 10, 1983; 1 child, Robert Scott. BS in Biology, John Carroll U., 1968; MD, Ohio State U., 1972. Diplomate Am. Bd. Psychiatry and Neurology, Am. Bd. Med. Examiners. Intern Barnes Hosp., St. Louis, 1972-73, resident, 1973-74; resident in neurology Ohio State U. Coll. Medicine, Columbus, 1974-77, clin. instr. neurology and psychiatry, 1977-78, asst. prof., 1978-81; med. dir. clin. sleep lab. St. Anthony Med. Ctr., Columbus, 1981-85, dir. clin. sleep and electroencephalography labs., 1985—; cons. neurology Columbus Children's Hosp., Columbus, 1982—, Doctor's Hosp., Columbus, 1984—; med. advisor Ohio Narcolepsy Assn., Akron, Ohio, 1983—; cons. Nat. Insts. Health Gen. Clin. Research Com., Bethesda, Md., 1979. Contbr. articles on neurology, other topics; also reviewer. Recipient Nu Sigma Nu award Ohio State U. Coll. Medicine, 1969, John Edwin Brown award Ohio State U. Coll. Medicine, 1972. Mem. Am. Acad. Neurology (Weir Mitchell award 1977), Am. Narcolepsy Assn. (bd. dirs. 1986—), Ohio Narcolepsy Assn., Assn. Profl. Sleep Socs. (accredited clin. polysomnographer), Epilepsy Found. Ohio, Epilepsy Found. Franklin County. Roman Catholic. Club: Jaleistas (San Diego). Avocations: flamenco guitar, photography. Office: St Anthony Med Ctr 1492 E Broad St Columbus OH 43205

CLARK, ROBERT WILSON, manufacturing executive; b. Greeley, Colo., Jan. 7, 1925; s. Edgar Wilson and Florence Mary (Huntington) C.; m. Margaret Ella Swope, Aug. 20, 1950; children: Matthew Wilson, John Huntington. B.S. in Mech. Engring, U. So. Calif., 1945; postgrad., Stanford U. With Goodyear Aerospace Corp., 1946—, v.p. ops., 1977-80; exec. v.p., chief operating officer Goodyear Aerospace Corp., Akron, Ohio, 1980-81; pres., chief exec. officer Goodyear Aerospace Corp., 1981—. Sr. warden Episcopal Ch., Dayton, Ohio, 1966. Mem. Nat. Security Indsl. Assn. (trustee 1979-80), Aviation Distbg. and Mfg. Assn. (trustee 1976-77), Aerospace Industries Assn. Office: Goodyear Aerospace Corp 1210 Massillon Rd Akron OH 44315 *

CLARK, ROGER GORDON, educational administrator; b. St. Louis, Nov. 1, 1937; s. Frank E. and Bernice A. (Ervin) C.; m. Jane F. Carfagno, Sept. 6, 1968 (div. 1976). BA, U. Mo., 1959, MA, 1961; PhD, U. Colo., 1969. Project mgr. Nat. Council Tchrs. English Ednl. Resources Info. Clearinghouse, Champaign, Ill., 1967-69; asst. prof. English U. Ill., Urbana, 1969-80, asst., then assoc. dean Grad. Coll., 1969-75, 76-80, acting dir. Sch. Library Sci., 1978-79; assoc. dir. U. Ill. Press, Champaign, 1980-85; dir. Com. Instl. Cooperation between Big Ten Univs. and U. Chgo., Champaign, 1985—. Home: 801 S Coler St Urbana IL 61801 Office: Com Instl Coop 302 E John St Suite 1705 Champaign IL 61820

CLARK, ROGER LLOYD, university program administrator; b. Washington, Ind., Dec. 1, 1952; s. Lloyd Lewis and Violet Elizabeth (Wuertz) C.; m. Wanda L. Harder, June 30, 1974; 1 child, Beth E. B of Music Edn., U. Evansville, Ind., 1974; M of Music, So. Ill. U., Edwardsville, 1977, EdS, 1984. Prof. music St. Louis Christian Coll., Florissant, Mo., 1975-82, dean of students, 1982-84, v.p. for student affairs, 1985—; dean of students Milligan (Tenn.) Coll., 1984-85; minister Christian Ch., 1975—; past pres., v.p. Christian Student Fellowship Greater St. Louis Area, 1984, 86. Mem. Nat. Assn. Student Personnel Adminstrs., Assn. Supervision and Curriculum Devel., Assn. Christians in Student Devel. Office: St Louis Christian Coll 1360 Grandview Florissant MO 63033

CLARK, RUSSELL GENTRY, U.S. dist. judge; b. Myrtle, Mo., July 27, 1925; s. William B. and Grace Frances (Jenkins) C.; m. Jerry Elaine Burrows, Apr. 30, 1959; children: Vincent A., Viki F. LL.B., U. Mo., 1952. Bar: Mo. 1952. Mem. firm Woolsey, Fisher, Clark, Whiteaker & Stenger, Springfield, Mo., 1952-77; U.S. dist. judge Western Dist. of Mo., Kansas City, 1977—. Served to 2d lt. U.S. Army, 1944-46. Mem. ABA, Mo. Bar Assn. (continuing legal edn. com. 1969), Greene County bar assn. (dir. 1968-71). Democrat. Methodist. Club: Kiwanis (past pres. Springfield chpt.). Office: US Dist Ct 654 US Courthouse 811 Grand Ave Kansas City MO 64106 also: 320 US Courthouse 870 Booneville St Springfield MO 65801 *

CLARK, RUSSELL LEWIS, landscape architect; b. Sheridan, Mich., Nov. 28, 1950; s. Erwin Dale and Jo Lena (Ross) C.; m. Karen Sue Yeasley, Mar. 17, 1972; children—R. Jason, Jeremy H., Karyann L. Student Ferris State Coll., 1969-71; B. Landscape Architecture with honors, Mich. State U., 1974. Registered landscape architect, Mich. Landscape architect Grabeck, Bell & Kline, Traverse City, Mich., 1974-75; planner Leelanau County Planning Commn., Leland, Mich., 1975-78; sr. planner Metcalf & Eddy Internat., Al-Khobar, Saudi Arabia, 1983; prin., owner R. Clark Assocs., Inc., Traverse City, 1979-84; v.p. spl. projects Traverse Devel. Co., Acme, Mich., 1984—. Bd. dirs. Traverse City Osteopathic Hosp., 1983-85. Mem. Am. Soc. Landscape Architects, Mich. Soc. Planning Ofcls., Mich. Bd. Landscape Architects (past chmn.). Home: 2706 Hartman Rd Traverse City MI 49684 Office: Grand Traverse Condominium Developers Inc PO Box 366 Acme MI 49610

CLARK, SAMUEL SMITH, urologist; b. Phila., Sept. 2, 1932; s. Horace E. and Jane (Mullin) C.; m. Heather Jean Ogilvy, June 21, 1957; children: Ross Angus, Erin, Brian Mullin. B.S., McGill U., 1954, M.D., 1958, C.M., 1958. Diplomate: Am. Bd. Urology. Intern Bethesda (Md.) Naval Hosp., 1958-59; resident Royal Victoria Hosp., Montreal, Can., 1962-67; practice medicine specializing in urology Munster, Ind., 1967-68, Chgo., 1969—; attending urologist Central DuPage Hosp., Winfield, Ill., 1976—; asst. prof. urology Abraham Lincoln Sch. Medicine, U. Ill., 1968-71, asso. prof., 1971-73, prof., 1973-81, head div. urology, 1971-77; chief urology West Side VA Hosp., Chgo., 1969-77, U. Ill. Hosp., Chgo., 1971-77; clin. prof. urology Loyola U., Chgo., 1981—; med. dir. Crescent Counties Found. Med. Care, 1979-83; dir. urol. services, dir. neurogenic bladder clinic Marianjoy Rehab. Hosp., Wheaton, Ill., 1983-87, bd. dirs., 1979-84. Contbr. articles to profl. jours. Served to lt. MC USN, 1958-62. Fellow ACS; mem. Am. Urol. Assn. (exec. com. North Central sect. 1974-77), Ind. Med. Soc., DuPage Med. Soc., AMA, Chgo. Urol. Soc. (pres.). Episcopalian. Club: Glen Oak Country. Home: 592 Turner St Glen Ellyn IL 60137 Office: 399 Schmale Rd Carol Stream IL 60187

CLARK, SANDRA LEE, health facility administrator; b. Adrian, Mich., Dec. 17, 1949; d. Thomas W. III and Alice J. (Culver) Warren; m. Frank L. Clark, Sept. 1, 1974; children: Casey, Anna, Sarah. BA, Wayne State U., 1978. Social worker Zieger Hosp., Detroit, 1977-78; owner, adminstr. C.F.S. Internat., Benton Harbor, Mich., 1981—; co-owner, adminstr. MEC-1, Benton Harbor, 1983—; pres. Data Solutions, Benton Harbor, 1987—; v.p. Americare Med. Assn., Valparaiso, Ind., 1987—. Fundraiser Twin Cities Symphony, St. Joseph, Mich., 1986, United Way, St. Joseph, 1986. Mem. Nat. Assn. Ambulatory Care (bd. dirs. Mich. chpt. 1985-86), Century Club Wayne State U., In Home Health Care Assn., Phi Beta Kappa. Republican. Avocations: raising and showing Great Danes, travel, art, singing, literature. Home: 544 Onondaga Benton Harbor MI 49022 Office: Midwest Emergency Ctr MEC-1 872 E Napier Ave Benton Harbor MI 49022

CLARK, TERRY NICHOLAS, sociology educator; b. Chgo., Nov. 26, 1940. Student, U. Paris, 1960-61, U. Frankfort, U. Berlin and U. Munich, 1962; BA in Psychology, Bowdoin Coll., 1962; MA in Sociology, Columbia U., 1965, PhD in Sociology, 1967. Asst. prof. sociology U. Chgo., 1966-71, assoc. prof., 1971—; sr. study dir. Nat. Opinion Research Ctr., 1974—; vis. assoc. prof. dept. govt. Harvard U., summer 1972, UER de Scis. Sociales U. Paris Sorbonne, spring 1973; vis. assoc. prof. depts. polit. sci. and sociology and instn. for social and policy studies Yale U., fall 1972; vis. scholar Centre Universitaire Internat., Paris, spring 1965, summer 1965, 69, Brookings Instn., summer, 1975; coordinator fiscal austerity and urban innovation project US and world; dir. comparative study community decision-making U. Chgo., 1967—; chmn. com. on community research and devel. Soc. for Study Social Problems, 1970-71; vis. researcher Urban Inst. Pub. Fin. Group, Washington, summer 1970; cons. to Office Policy Devel. and Research HUD, Washington, summer 1975, Pub. Adminstrn. Service, Real Estate Research Corp., U.S. Conf. Mayors; lectr., cons. to various orgns., 1975—. Author: Prophets and Patrons: The French University and the Emergence of the Social Sciences, 1973, Community Power and Policy Outputs, 1973, Leadership in American Cities: Resources, Interchanges and the Press, 1973; co-author: (with Irving P. Leif) Community Power and Decision-Making: Trend Report and Bibliography, 1974, A Mayor's Financial Management Handbook, 1982, (with Lorna Crowley Ferguson) City Money: Political Processes, Fiscal Strain and Retrenchment, 1983, (with Paul David Schumaker and Russell W. Getter) Policy Responsiveness and Fiscal Strain in 51 American Communities: A Manual for Studying City Politics Using the MORC Permanent Community Sample, 1983; co-author, editor: Community Structure and Decision-Making: Comparative Analyses, 1968, Comparative Community Politics, 1974, Urban Policy Analysis: Directions for Future Research, 1981, Coping with Urban Austerity, Research in Urban Policy, 1984; co-author, co-editor: (with Charles M. Bonjean and Robert L. Lineberry) Community Politics: A Behavioral Approach, 1971, (with Joseph Ben-David) Culture and Its Creators: Essays in Honor of Edward Shils, 1977; editor: Gabriel Tarde on Communication and Social Influence, 1969; editor Research in Urban Policy ann., 1983—; mem. editorial bd. Am. Jour. Sociology, 1966—, Adminstrv. Sci. Quarterly, 1968-72, Social Sci. Quarterly, 1967-70, Comparative Urban Research, 1972—, Policy and Politics, 1973-77, Jour. Urban Affairs, 1982—, Urban Affairs Quarterly, 1980—, Urban Interest, 1979-82; series editor Wiley Series in Urban Research, 1973-79; contbr. articles to profl. jours. Mem. Am. Sociol. Assn. (chmn. sect. on community 1974-76, com. on internat. cooperation 1969-72, 78—, council sect. sociol. theory 1970-73), Internat. Sociol. Assn. (chmn. com. for community research 1964—, research com. 1968—), The Toqueville Soc. (council 1983-85). Office: Univ Chgo 332 Social Sci Bldg 1126 E 59th St Chicago IL 60637

CLARK, THOMAS ROLFE, clinical psychologist; b. Detroit, Oct. 30, 1947; s. Edward Rolfe and Ruth Ann (Spurr) C.; m. Mary Franzen, July 15, 1972. A.B. magna cum laude, Greenville Coll., 1963; Ph.D. (Robards Doctoral fellow), U. Windsor (Can.), 1972. Diplomate Am. Bd. Psychology. Intern Wayne County Psychiat. Hosp., Detroit, mem. staff, 1972-77; chief psychologist Heritage Hosp., 1978-81; dir. mental health, program dir. Marian Manor Med. Center, exec. and clin. dir. Alpha Psychol. Services, Livonia, Mich.; pvt. pvt. practice clin., forensic and police psychology and psychotherapy, Detroit, 1972—; dir. Alpha Psychol. Services, 1982—; faculty Henry Ford Community Coll., Dearborn, Mich., 1972-76; dir. clin. services Met. Guidance Center, Livonia, Mich., 1978-82; mental health cons. People's Community Hosp. Authority, various police depts. Organist 1st United Meth. Ch., Dearborn, 1965-83; concert organist, 1975—; bd. dirs. Meth. Children's Home Soc., Livonia, Mich., 1974-84. Fellow Am. Orthopsychiat. Assn., Am. Coll. Psychology, Masters and Johnson Inst., Christian Assn. Psychol. Studies; mem. Am., Southeastern, Southwestern, Western, Mich. psychol. assns., Internat. Therapy Behavior Assn., Am. Assn. Sex Edn. Counselors, Acad. of Psychologists in Marital, Sex, and Family Therapy, Mich. Soc. Lic. Psychologists, Mich. Alcoholism and Addiction Assn., Am. Guild Organists, Internat. Council Psychologists, Mich. Profl. Police Assn., Mich. Sheriffs Assn., Internat. Law Enforcement Stress Assn. Contbr. articles to profl. jours.; rec. artist. Recipient awards in music, psychology. Office: Suite 150 29555 W Six Mile Rd Livonia MI 48152

CLARK, TIMOTHY JOE, financial executive; b. Seymour, Ind., Apr. 13, 1952; s. Joe Richard and Beulah May (Snyder) C.; m. Kathryn Lynn McKinney, Aug. 11, 1973; children: Jeremy Benjamin, Courtney Elisha. BS in Acctg., Ind. U., 1974. CPA, Ind. Mem. audit staff Arthur Young & Co., Indpls., 1974-79, audit mgr., 1979-83, audit prin., 1983-85; dir. fin. planning RCA Consumer Electronics div. RCA Corp., Indpls., 1985-86, acting div. v.p. fin., 1986; mgr. fin. planning and analysis Gen. Electric Co., Indpls., 1986—. Treas. Career Edn. Ctrs. Builders, Inc., Indpls., 1983-85; instr. Project Bus. Jr. Achievement Ind., Indpls., 1984. Mem. Am. Inst. CPA's, Ind. CPA Soc., Indpls. C. of C., Justack Aviation Flying Club (pres. 1986—). Republican. Lutheran. Club: Royal Oak Country. Avocations: flying, golf, reading. Home: 966 Santa Maria Dr Greenwood IN 46143 Office: Gen Electric CEB 600 N Sherman Dr Indianapolis IN 46201

CLARK, TONY GERALD, radio executive; b. Washington, Ind., Sept. 13, 1955; s. George Robert and Vonda Laverne (McBride) C.; m. Mary Ann Gauer, Dec. 10, 1977; children: Sarah, Nicholas. Student, Ind. State U., 1973-79. Sales cons. Sta. WTHI-AM-FM, Terre Haute, Ind., 1981-82; sales cons. Broadcasting Corp. of Ind. (WPFR), Terre Haute, 1982-83, local sales mgr., 1983-84, gen. sales mgr., 1984-85; gen. mgr. Oak Ridge Boys, Terre Haute, 1985—; v.p., gen. mgr. Power Rock Broadcasting Corp. Ind., 1987—. Bd. dirs. Terre Haute Boys Club, 1984-87, March of Dimes, Terre Haute, 1985-87, Jr. Achievement, Terre Haute, 1986. Named one of Outstanding Young Men of Am., 1986, Can. Club Man of Yr. Hiram Walker Inc., Windsor, Ontario, 1980. Fellow Advt. Fedn. Terre Haute (bd. dirs. 1985—); mem. Radio Advt. Bur. (WPFR rep. mng. sales conf. 1985, 86), Nat. Assn. Broadcasters (WPFR rep. 1985). Avocations: basketball, golf, sales research, reading. Office: WPFR-AM-FM 643 Ohio St Terre Haute IN 47807

CLARK, WAYNE HERBERT, school system administrator; b. Towanda, Kans., May 15, 1928; s. Russle H. and Eliza M. Clark; m. Shirley A. Morley, Nov. 22, 1951; children: Craig, Debra, Kevin. BA, Southwestern Coll., Winfield, Kans., 1950; MEd, Wichita State U., 1959, postgrad. in spl. edn., 1971; EdD, U. Kans., 1975. High sch. tchr. Peirceville and Benton, Kans., 1950-51, 1955-63; asst. prin. Cirle High Sch., Towanda, 1963-65; supt. Unified Sch. Dist. 375, Towanda, 1965-73, Unified Sch. Dist. 254, Medicine Lodge, Kans., 1974-81, Unified Sch. Dist. 262, Valley Ctr., Kans., 1981—. Served with U.S. Army, 1951-53, Korea. Mem. Am. Assn. Sch. Adminstrs., Kans. Assn. Sch. Adminstrs. (bd. dirs. 1983—), United Sch. Adnminstrs. of Kans. Republican. Methodist. Lodge: Lions. Avocations: golf, photography, gardening. Home: 9 Ora Ct Valley Center KS 67147 Office: Unified Sch Dist 262 132 S Park Valley Center KS 67147

CLARK, WILLIAM GEORGE, judge; b. Chgo., July 16, 1924; s. John S. and Ita (Kennedy) C.; m. Rosalie Locatis, Nov. 28, 1946; children: Merrilee, William George, Donald, John Steven, Robert. Student, Loyola U., Chgo., 1942-43, 44; J.D., DePaul U., 1946; J.D. (hon.), John Marshall Law Sch., Chgo., 1962. Bar: Ill. 1947. Mem. firm Crane, Kearney, Korzen, Phelan & Clark (and predecessor), Chgo., 1947-56; atty. for Pub. Adminstr. Ill., 1949-53; mem. Ill. Ho. of Reps. from Austin Dist. of Chgo., 1952-54, 56-60; mem. Senate, 1954-56, majority leader, 1959; atty. gen. Ill., 1960-69; partner firm Arvey, Hodes & Mantynband, Chgo., 1968-76; justice Supreme Ct. Ill., 1976—, chief justice, 1984—. Served with AUS, 1942-44. Mem. Ill., Chgo., bar assns., AMVETS, Celtic Legal Soc., Am. Legion, Irish Fellowship Club (pres. 1961-62), Catholic Lawyers Guild Chgo., Delta Theta Phi. Office: Supreme Court Office Ill Supreme Ct Richard J Daley Center Chicago IL 60602

CLARK, WILLIAM MERLE, baseball scout; b. Clinton, Mo., Aug. 18, 1932; s. Merle William and Beulah (Wilson) C.; student George Barr Umpire Sch., 1950, Central Mo. State U., 1950-51; B.J., U. Mo., 1958; postgrad. Somers Umpire Sch., 1962; m. Dolores Pearl Denny, Aug. 11, 1955; children—Patrick Sean, Michael Seumas, Kelly Kathleen, Kerry Maureen, Casey Connor. Umpire, Central Mexican League, Neb. State League, 1956; sportswriter, Lexington (Ky.) Leader, 1958, Columbia (Mo.) Missourian, 1958-60, Columbia (Mo.) Tribune, 1963-73; recreation dir. City of Columbia, Mo., 1962-68. Umpire, Pioneer League, 1962; partner J.C. Stables, Columbia, Mo., 1965—; scouting supr. Pitts. Pirates, 1968, Seattle, 1969, Milw., 1970, Cin., 1971—. Served with AUS, 1951-54. Mem. Amateur Athletic Union (life), Mo. Sportswriter's Assn. (pres. 1958), Mo. Archeol. Soc., Mo. Hist. Soc., Columbia Audubon Soc., Mo. Aubundon Soc. (bd. dirs. 1983—). Unitarian-Universalist. Address: 3906 Grace Ellen Dr Columbia MO 65202

CLARKE, CHARLES FENTON, lawyer; b. Hillsboro, Ohio, July 25, 1916; s. Charles F. and Margaret (Patton) C.; m. Virginia Schoppenhorst, Apr. 3, 1945; children: Elizabeth, Margaret, Jane, Charles Fenton, IV. A.B. summa cum laude, Washington and Lee U., Lexington, Va., 1938; LL.B., U. Mich., 1940; LL.D. (hon.), Cleve. State U., 1971. Bar: Mich. 1940, Ohio 1946. Pvt. practice Detroit, 1942, Cleve., 1946—; ptnr. firm Squire, Sanders & Dempsey, 1957—, adminstr. litigation dept., 1979-85; trustee Cleve. Legal Aid Soc., 1959-67; pres. Nat. Assn. R.R. Trial Counsel, 1966-68; life mem. 6th Circuit Jud. Conf.; chmn. legis. com. Cleve. Welfare Fedn., 1961-68; bd. dirs. W.M. Brode Co., Park Mfg. Co. Pres. alumni bd. dirs. Washington and Lee U., 1970-72; pres. bd. dirs. Free Med. Clinic Greater Cleve., 1970-86; trustee Cleve. Citizens League, 1956-62; bd. dirs. citizens adv. bd. Cuyahoga County (Ohio) Juvenile Ct., 1970-73; bd. dirs. George Jr. Republic, Greenville, Pa., 1970-73, Bowman Tech. Sch., Cleve., 1970—; vice chmn. Cleve. Crime Commn., 1973-75; exec. com. Cuyahoga County Republican Orgn., 1950—; councilman Bay Village, Ohio, 1948-53; pres., trustee Cleve. Hearing and Speech Center, 1957-62; Laurel Sch., 1962-72, Fedn. Community Progress, 1984—; trustee Cleve. chpt. ACLU, 1986—. Served to 1st lt. AUS, World War II. Fellow Am. Coll. Trial Lawyers; mem. Greater Cleve. Bar Assn. (trustee 1983-86), Cleve. Civil War Round Table (pres. 1968), Cleve. Zool. Soc. (dir. 1970), Phi Beta Kappa. Presbyterian. Clubs: Skating, Union (Cleve.); Tavern. Home: 2262 Tudor Dr Cleveland Heights OH 44106 Office: Huntington Bldg Cleveland OH 44115

CLARKE, CHARLES PATRICK, electronics co. exec.; b. Chgo., Oct. 3, 1929; s. James Patrick and Elizabeth (McLaughlin) C.; student U. Ill., 1948-50; BS, DePaul U., 1953. Auditor, Baumann Finney Co., CPA's, Chgo., 1953-55; with Cuneo Press, Inc., Chgo., 1955-66, successively asst. gen. accounting supr., asst. chief corp. accountant, gen. auditor, 1955-61, systems, procedures and audit mgr., 1961-64, asst. to treas., 1964-66; comptroller Internat. Couriers Corp. (formerly Bankers Utilities Corp.), Chgo., 1966-69, treas., 1969-72, financial v.p., 1972-75; pres. C.P. Charles & Assos., 1975-76; treas., corp. controller DC Electronics, Inc., Aurora, Ill., 1976-86; corp. controller, chief fin. officer Aurora Cord and Cable Co., Yorkville, Ill., 1986—. CPA, Ill. Mem. Am. Inst. CPA's, Ill. Soc. CPA's, Nat. Assn. Accountants, Financial Execs. Inst. Democrat. Roman Catholic. Home: 36 Parliament Dr W Palos Heights IL 60463 Office: 205 Beaver St Yorkville IL 60560

CLARKE, DAVID JOHN, obstetrician-gynecologist; b. Ann Arbor, Mich., Sept. 2, 1952; s. A. Bruce and Florence (Myres) C.; m. Diane Helen Lipka, June 4, 1974; children: Chandra Lynn, Colin Michael. AB with honors, Brown U., 1974; MD, Wayne State U., 1978. Diplomate Am. Bd. Ob-Gyn. Resident ob-gyn. Wayne State U. Hosp., Detroit, 1978-82; pvt. practice Livonia, Mich., 1982—; resident instr. Providence Hosp., Southfield, Mich., 1985—; med. staff St. Mary Hosp., Livonia, 1982—, Hutzel Hosp., Detroit, 1982—, Providence Hosp., Southfield, 1985—. Fellow Am. Coll. Ob-Gyn. Office: 10533 Farmington Rd Livonia MI 48150

CLARKE, DAVID SCOTT, management educator; b. Kenosha, Wis., Jan. 2, 1942; s. Donald Edwin and Martha Jean (Chatterton) C.; m. Ingrid Gadway Rebholz, Dec. 24, 1984. BS in Philosophy, U. Wis., 1966; BArch, U. Oreg., 1969; M in Urban Design, Cath. U. Am., Washington, 1980, M in Mgmt. Sci., 1981. Exec. dir., spl. projects dir. Assn. Collegiate Schs. Architecture, Washington, 1970-80; chmn. dept. comprehensive planning, design So. Ill. U., Carbondale, 1980-81, prof. tech. careers, 1981—; vis. scholar Yale U., 1977-78. Author: L'Education Architecturale en France, 1979, Arguments in Favor of Sharpshooting, 1985; editor: Life Experiences in Environ. Design, 1975, (with others) Architectural Schools in North America, 1973, Architecture in Community and Junior Colleges, 1975; contbr. articles, book reviews to profl. jours. Active White House Com. on Barrier-Free Environments, Washington, 1973. Research fellow Nat. Endowment for the Arts, Washington, 1978-79; recipient George Washington

Honor Medal for Excellence in Econ. Edn. Freedom Found., Valley Forge, Pa., 1986. Mem. AIA (Henry Adams medal 1969, research fellow 1978-79), Assn. Collegiate Schs. Architecture, Nat. Council Archtl. Registration Bds., European Policy Studies Assn. Avocations: tennis, skiing. Office: So Ill U Sch Tech Careers Carbondale IL 62901

CLARKE, GEORGE PATRICK, controller; b. Kansas City, Mo., July 15, 1949; s. Raymond F. and Katherine J. (Hayes) C.; m. Vonnie Lea Morris, Dec. 27, 1973; children: Megan Elizabeth, George Patrick III, Rebecca Ann. BA in Econs., U. Mo., Kansas City, 1972, MBA in Acctg., 1976. CPA, Mo., Kans. Clk. B.C. Christopher & Co., Kansas City, 1965-78; staff acct. Alexander Grant & Co., Kansas City, 1978-80, Mize, Houser, Topeka, Kans., 1980-83; controller Action Products Co., Inc., Odessa, Mo., 1983—. Served with USCGR, 1969-75. Mem. Am. Inst. CPA's, Mo. Soc. CPA's, Am. Prodn. and Inventory Control Soc. Roman Catholic. Home: 1804 Chief Circle Blue Springs MO 64015 Office: Action Products Co PO Box 100 Odessa MO 64076

CLARKE, LLOYD E., real estate developer; b. Medicine Lodge, Kans., Sept. 11, 1929; s. Lloyd L. and Geraldine E. (Wilson) C.; m. Carol L. Colby, Aug. 30, 1952; 1 child, John J. Chmn. Clarke Cos., Des Moines, 1954—; bd. dirs. FNMA, Washington, 1st Interstate Bank, Des Moines, 1982—; chmn., bd. dirs. H.O.W. Corp., Washington, 1975-78, Iowa Fin. Authority, Des Moines, 1985—. Mem. NAHB (pres. 1968, Nat. Housing Hall of Fame, 1975). Republican. Episcopalian. Club: Des Moines Country. Home: 5000 Grand Ave West Des Moines IA 50265 Office: 950 Office Park Rd #333 West Des Moines IA 50265

CLARKE, MICHAEL STEWART, orthopaedic surgeon; b. Chgo., Sept. 3, 1943; s. Michael James and Kathryn (Stewart) C.; m. Katherine Elizabeth Hawkins, Dec. 16, 1967; children: Elizabeth Stewart, Katherine Lewis. BA, Northwestern U., 1965; MD, U. Mo., 1969. Diplomate Nat. Bd. Med. Examiners, Am. Bd. Orthopaedic Surgery. Intern in gen. surgery Vanderbilt U. Med. Ctr., 1969-70; resident in gen. surgery Vanderbilt U., Nashville, 1970-71; resident in orthopaedic surgery Willis C. Campbell Clinic, U. Tenn., Memphis, 1971-74; pres. Ozark Area Orthopaedic Assocs., Springfield, Mo., 1974—; clin. assoc. prof. U. Mo. Med. Sch., Columbia, 1977—; mem. staff, surgeon Mo. Crippled Children's Service, Springfield, 1975—,St. John's Regional Health Ctr., chief surgery, 1979-81, chief osteo. surgery, 1980-81; mem. staff Springfield Community Hosp., chief of staff, 1987—; cons. team. physician Springfield Pub. High Schs. Contbr. articles to profl. jour. Bd. dirs. Ozarks council Boy Scouts Am., 1977—, pres. 1983-85; cons. orthopedic surgeon Easter Seal Soc., Regional Cerebral Palsy Ctr.; chmn. United Way of Ozarks; founder Springfield Regional Opera; pres. Ozarks Medicine Bus. Coalition; bd. dirs. Springfield-Greene County Library System, Springfield Area C. of C., 1982-85. Served to maj. USAR. Recipient Silver Wreath award Nat. Council Boy Scouts Am., 1983, Silver Beaver award Nat. Council Boy Scouts Am., 1984-85. Fellow ACS, Am. Acad. Orthopedic Surgeons, Am. Acad. Pediatrics, Am. Assn. Surgery of the Hand, Clin. Orthopedic Soc., Soc. Mil. Orthopedic Surgeons ; mem. AMA, Mid. Cen. States Orthopedic Soc., Mo. State Orthopedic Assn., So. Orhopedic. Assn., Mid-Am. Orthopedic Assn., Nat. Arthritis Found., So. Med. Assn., Greene County Med. Soc., Am. Philatelic Soc. Clubs: Ozark Mountain Ridge Running. Lodges: Rotary Internat. (Paul Harris fellow), Masons, Shriner. Home: 1227 S Delaware Springfield MO 65804 Office: Ozarks Area Orthopaedic Assocs, Inc 1900 S National Springfield MO 65804

CLARKE, OSCAR WITHERS, physician; b. Petersburg, Va., Jan. 29, 1919; s. Oscar Withers and Mary (Reese) C.; m. Susan Frances King, June 18, 1949; children—Susan Frances, Mary Elizabeth, Jennifer Ann. B.S., Randolph Macon Coll., 1941; M.D., Med. Coll. Va., 1944. Intern Boston City Hosp., 1944-45; resident internal medicine Med. Coll. Va., 1945-46, 48-49, fellow in cardiology, 1949-50; practice medicine specializing in internal medicine and cardiology Gallipolis Holzer Med. Ctr., Ohio, 1950—; dir. Ohio Valley Devel. Co., Gallipolis, Community Improvement Corp.; pres. Ohio State Med. Bd.; chmn. Ohio Med. Edn. and Research Found.; pres. Gallipolis City Bd. Health, 1955—, Gallia County Heart Council, 1955—. Contbr. articles to med. jours. Vice pres. Tri-State Regional council Boy Scouts Am., 1957; pres. Tri-State Community Concert Assn., 1957-59; trustee Med. Meml. Found., Holzer Hosp. Found. Served as capt. M.C., AUS, 1946-48, ETO. Recipient John Stewart Bryant pathology award Med. Coll. Va., 1943. Fellow ACP, Royal Soc. Medicine; mem. Gallia County Med. Soc. (pres. 1953), AMA, Am. Heart Assn., Central Ohio Heart Assn. (Merit medal 1960, trustee), Ohio Med. Assn. (pres. 1973-74), Am. Soc. Internal Medicine, Ohio Soc. Internal Medicine, Alpha Omega Alpha, Sigma Zeta, Chi Beta Phi. Presbyterian. Club: Rotary (pres. 1953-54). Home: Spruce Knoll Gallipolis OH 45631 Office: Box 344 Holzer Med Clinic Gallipolis OH 45631

CLARKE, ROBERT THORBURN, medical center president; b. Edmonton, Alta., Can., May 9, 1945; came to U.S., 1946; s. Edwin Cameron and Agnes Currie (Thornburn) C.; m. Carolyn Elizabeth Copeland, May 11, 1966 (div. 1973); 1 child, Shawn Margaret; m. Phoebe Jane Moseman, Aug. 11, 1973; children—Margo Suzanne, Lindsay Moseman. B.S. in Biology, Geneva Coll., 1967; M.H.A., U. Mich., 1969. Asst. dir. Community Hosp. Ind., Indpls., 1969-72, assoc. dir., 1972-75, v.p. profl. services, 1975-76, sr. v.p., 1977-80, exec. v.p., chief operating officer, 1980-83; pres., chief exec. officer Meml. Med. Ctr., Springfield, Ill., 1983—; bd. dirs. Vol. Hosps. Am., 1985—. Contbr. articles to profl. jours. Bd. dirs. United Way Sangamon County, Springfield, 1984—, Kids at Heart, Springfield, 1984-86, Springfield Cen. Area Devel. Assn., 1984-86, Springfield Zool. Assn., 1984-86. Fellow Am. Coll. Healthcare Execs. Republican. Presbyterian. Home: 34 Meander Pike Chatham IL 62629 Office: Meml Med Ctr 800 N Rutledge Springfield IL 62781

CLARY, ROSALIE BRANDON STANTON, timber farm executive, civic worker; b. Evanston, Ill., Aug. 3, 1928; d. Frederick Charles Hite-Smith and Rose Cecile (Liebich) Stanton; B.S., Northwestern U., 1950, M.A., 1954; m. Virgil Vincent Clary, Oct. 17, 1959; children—Rosalie Marian, Frederick Stanton, Virgil Vincent, Kathleen Elizabeth. Tchr., Chgo. Public Schs., 1951-55, adjustment tchr., 1956-61; faculty Loyola U., Chgo., 1963; v.p. Stanton Enterprises, Inc., Adams County, Miss., 1971—; author Family History Record, genealogy record book, Kenilworth, Ill., 1977—; also lectr. Leader, Girl Scouts, Winnetka, Ill., 1969-71, 78-86, Cub Scouts, 1972-77; badge counselor Boy Scouts Am., 1978—; election judge Republican party, 1977—. Mem. Nat. Soc. DAR (Ill. rec. sec. 1979-81, nat. vice chmn. program com. 1980-83, state vice regent 1986—), Am. Forestry Assn., Forest Farmers Assn., North Suburban Geneal. Soc. (governing bd. 1979—), Winnetka Hist. Soc. (governing bd. 1978—), Internat. Platform Assn., Delta Gamma (mem. nat. cabinet 1985—). Roman Catholic. Home: 509 Elder Ln Winnetka IL 60093 Office: PO Box 401 Kenilworth IL 60043

CLARY, THOMAS SIDWELL, diversified company executive; b. Brazil, Ind., May 1, 1951; s. William M. and D. JoAnn (Jacks) C.; m. Elizabeth J. Shurter, May 26, 1978; children: Thomas II, Allison, Lauren, Kristen. BS in Acctg., Ind. State U., 1973. CPA, Ind. Staff acct. Ernst & Ernst, Indpls., 1973-74; dir. auditing Sackrider and Co., Terre Haute, Ind., 1974-85; treas., chief fin. officer Green Constrn. Ind., Inc., Oaktown, Ind., 1986—; pres., bd. dirs. Ernest Johnson Fuel and Supply Corp., Terre Haute; sec. and bd. dirs. The Boston Connection, Inc., Terre Haute. bd. dirs., chmn. fin. com. Terre Haute Boys Club, 1985—. Mem. Am. Inst. CPA's, Ind. CPA Soc. (bd. dirs. edn. found. 1983-84, chmn. agribus. com. 1983, pres. Terre Haute chpt. 1984). Democrat. Presbyterian. Club: Terre Haute Country. Lodge: Elks. Avocations: horse racing, tennis. Home: 106 Southridge Rd Terre Haute IN 47802

CLATWORTHY, F. JAMES, human resources development educator; b. Detroit, Dec. 14, 1935; s. Frank and Lucy Luisa Elizabeth (House) C.; m. Juliana Marie Shepardson, Aug. 25, 1962; 1 child, Jennifer Anne. BA, U. Mich., 1960, MA, 1961, PhD, 1970. Instr. to asst. prof. Oakland U., Rochester, Mich., 1966-, assoc. prof.; co-chairperson new charter coll. Oakland U., 1970-75; coordinator edn. specialties in sch. admintrn. Oakland U., 1985—. Author: Formulation of British Colonial Policy 1923-48, 1971. Alternate mem. Point Creek Trailway Commn., Rochester, 1985—; mem. legis. adv. com. State Bd. Edn., Lansing, Mich., 1986—. Fellow U.S. Office Edn. Mem. Am. Soc. for Tng. and Devel., Mich. Assn. Sch. Adminstrs., Chi Psi. Office: Oakland U Dept Human Resources Devel Rochester MI 48063

CLAUER, CALVIN ROBERT, consulting engineer; b. South Bend, Ind., Sept. 8, 1910; s. Calvin Kingsley and Etta (Fiddick) C.; B.S. in Civil Engring., Purdue U., 1932; postgrad. Columbia U., 1944-45; m. Rosemary Y. Stultz, June 23, 1934; 1 son, Calvin Robert. Project engr. Ind. State Hwy. Commn., 1932-35; engr. Erie R.R. Co., 1935-36; dist. chief engr. Truscon Steel Co., Indpls., 1936-42; chief engr. United Steel Fabricators, Inc., 1945-55, div. sales mgr., 1955-57; pres. Clauer Assos., Engrs. for Industry, Wooster, Ohio, 1957-60, chief product engr. Mfg. group Republic Steel Corp., Youngstown, Ohio, 1960-75; prin. Clauer Assos., Youngstown, 1975-79; prin. Midgley-Clauer & Assos., Youngstown, 1979—. Chmn. civil engring. tech. indsl. adv. com. Youngstown State U., 1971-76. Served to col. USAR, 1932-60. Fellow ASCE; mem. Internat. Assn. for Bridge and Structural Engring., ASTM, Am. Iron and Steel Inst., Am. Concrete Inst., Internat. Materials Mgmt. Soc., Soc. Profl. Journalists-Sigma Delta Chi, Chi Epsilon. Republican. Christian Scientist. Club: Northcliffe. Lodges: Masons, Shriners. Holder patent on sheet metal box beam. Office: 860 Boardman Canfield Rd Youngstown OH 44512

CLAUS, ALVIN HERBERT, dentist; b. Chgo., July 19, 1921; s. Max and Mary (Cable) C.; m. Natalie Becker, Dec. 11, 1949; children: Jeffrey, Marcie Ruth, Joan Maxine Claus Selz. AA, Sprinfield Coll., 1940; BA, U. Ill., 1944, DDS, 1945. Practice dentistry Morton Grove, Ill., 1947-66, Skokie, Ill., 1966—; lctr. Am. Acad. Euporean Dentists, 1983; pres., chmn. bd. Skokie Dental, North Chgo., 1974—; dir. L.I.C.D., North Suburban Chgo., 1981-84. Served to lt. USN, 1945-47. Fellow Acad. Gen. Denstry, Ill. Dental Soc., Am. Legion, Alpha Omega. Jewish. Home: 8546 Laramie Ave Skokie IL 60077 Office: 64 Old Orchard Bldg Skokie IL 60077

CLAUSEN, ROBERT WILLIAM, allergist, immunologist, internist; b. Englewood, N.J., June 18, 1947; s. Richard William and Elsie Bertha (Kramer) C.; m. Barbara Ann Kraemer, Aug. 3, 1975; 1 child, Amalia Kaye. BS, Valparaiso (Ind.) U., 1969; MedB, B in Surgery, Kasturba Med. Coll., Manipal, South India, 1974; fifth pathway cert., Rutgers U., 1975. Diplomate Am. Bd. Internal Medicine, Am. Bd. Allergy and Immunology. Intern, then resident in internal medicine Henry Ford Hosp., Detroit, 1975-78, fellow in allergy and clin. immunology, 1978-80, sr. staff physician, instr., 1978-82; ptnr., physician The South Bend (Ind.) Clinic, 1982—; teaching attending physician family practice residency program Meml. Hosp., South Bend, 1983—, St. Joseph's Med. Ctr., South Bend, 1983—; clin. instr. dept. medicine U. Mich., Ann Arbor, 1980-83; guest asst. prof. dept. biol. scis. U. Notre Dame, Ind., 1984—; clin. asst. prof. dept. medicine Ind. U., Notre Dame, 1986—. Contbr. articles to profl. jours. Bd. dirs. Am. Lung Assn. North Cen. Ind., South Bend, 1984—, Fischoff Chamber Music Assn., South Bend, 1986—; mem. pres.' adv. council Valparaiso U., 1984—, chmn. med. alumni assn., 1982—; mem. AIDS Task Force St. Joseph County, South Bend, 1985—; active Internat. Student Host Family Program U. Notre Dame. NSF grantee. Fellow Am. Coll. Physicians (gov.'s adv. council Ind. chpt. 1985-87, program com. 1985-86), Am. Acad. Allergy and Immunology (insect allergy com, Hymenoptera Sting Fatality com.), Am. Coll. Allergists (stinging insect com.); mem. AMA, Ind. Med. Soc., Mich. Allergy Soc. (program com. 1985—), Nat. Hospice Orgns., Lutheran Acad. Scholarship, Phi Delta Epsilon. Avocations: music, racquetball, fishing, photography, internat. travel and affairs. Home: 52790 Brooktrails Dr South Bend IN 46637 Office: The South Bend Clinic 211 N Eddy at LaSalle Ave South Bend IN 46634-1755

CLAUS-GRAY, ROSEMARY BARR, social worker; b. Chgo., Mar. 18, 1942; d. Irving Stanley and Phoebe Virginia (Coppage) Barr; m. Gary C. Claus, Apr. 11, 1962 (div. Oct. 1974); children: Robert C., David G., Suzanne V.; m. Donald I. Gray, May 14, 1977. BS, No. Ill. U., 1973; MSW, George Williams Coll., 1977. Cert. social worker, Ill. Therapist Ctr. for Psychotherapy, Geneva, Ill., 1976-79; pvt. practice family therapist Doniphan, 1982-87; therapist Permanency Planning div. of Family Services, Doniphan, 1982; cons. local hosps. 1982—; chair profl. seminars, 1977—, lectr. community orgns., 1980—; cons. dir. family services, 1980-82. Author: Barns, 1986. Mem. Nat. Assn. Social Workers (diplomate), Acad. Cert. Social Workers, Bus. and Profl. Women. Methodist. Avocations: animal lover, writing, photography, hiking, canoeing.

CLAUSSEN, HOWARD BOYD, recruiting company executive; b. Kansas City, Mo., May 12, 1946; s. Harry Ben and Mary Loraine (Shipley) C.; m. Virginia Ione Nehf, July 21, 1973; children: Paul, Rebecca, Debora, Arienne, John, Jennifer. BA in Econs., Yale U., 1968. Salesman Sperry Corp., Kansas City, 1970-72; sr. salesman Honeywell Inc., Kansas City, 1972-73; dist. mgr. Singer Bus. Machines, Kansas City, 1973-75; pres. 'C' Cons., Inc., Kansas City and Terre Haute, Ind., 1975-80, 82—; nat. sales mgr. Delta Systems, Seattle, 1980-82; cons. CBS, Inc., N.Y.C., 1976-80, Southwestern Bell Telephone Co. subs. AT&T, St. Louis, 1978-80, Convergent Tech., San Jose, Calif., 1983—, Multiflow Computer, Branford, Conn., 1986—. Republican. Methodist. Avocation: gardening. Home and Office: 4519 Park Ln Ct Terre Haute IN 47803

CLAUSSEN, VERNE EVERETT, JR., optometrist; b. Wilson, Kans., Aug. 10, 1944; s. Verne E. and Dorothy Louise (Soukup) C.; student (Santa Fe scholar, Union Pacific scholar), 1962-65; B.S., U. Houston Coll. Optometry, 1966, certificate in optometry, 1968; certificate (Gesell fellow) in pediatrics, 1969; D.Optometry, U. Houston, 1970; m. Patricia Mary Williams, Aug. 26, 1966; children—Verne Everett III, Mary Chris. Practice optometry U. Houston Coll. Optometry, mem. clin. staff, 1970; optometrist, Wamego and St. Mary's, Kans., 1970—. Lectr. optometry Eastern Seaboard Conf., Washington, U. Houston, 1969; vision cons. Briarwood Sch. for learning problems, Houston, 1967-69. Councilman, Alma City (Kans.), 1971-73. Bd. dirs. Optometric Extension Program Found.; mem. USD 329 Sup. Council, 1986. Recipient Contest award Kans. Optometric Jour., 1971. Mem. Am., Kans. optometric assns., Heart of Am. Contact Soc., Alma, Wamego (dir.), St. Mary's (pres.) chambers commerce, Farm House Assn. (v.p. 1976-77), Phi Theta Upsilon, Farm House Frat. (dir.; found. pres. 1986). Republican. Methodist. Club: Dutch Mill Swingers Square Dance. Home: Route 2 Alma KS 66401 Office: 5th and Elm Wamego KS 66547

CLAWSON, ROBERT WAYNE, political science educator; b. Glendale, Calif., Dec. 21, 1939; s. Charles Vernor and Ada Fern (Hower) C.; m. Judith Louise Lisy, June 25, 1961; children—Deborah Marie, Gregory Scott. Student, Tex. A&M U., 1957-58; A.B., UCLA, 1961, M.A., 1961-64, Ph.D., 1969; Exchange Scholar, U.S. Def. Lang. Inst., 1963-64, State U. Moscow, 1966. Research asst. Russian and East European Studies Ctr., UCLA, 1961-65; from asst. prof. to assoc. prof. polit. sci. Kent State U., Ohio, 1966-83, prof., 1983—, assoc. dir. Lemnitzer Ctr. NATO Studies, dir. Ctr. Internat. and Comparative Programs, coordinator Soviet and East European studies program; v.p. research, internat. trade INTERTAG INC., 1973-75; cons. editor Houghton Mifflin. Editor scholarly books; contbr. articles to profl. publs. Charles Fletcher Scott fellow, 1961-64, Acad. yr. research fellow Kent State U., spring 1971. Mem. Am. Assn. for Advancement Slavic Studies, Internat. Studies Assn., AAUP (pres. Kent State chpt. 1975). Democrat. Presbyterian. Home: 7336 Westview St Kent OH 44240 Office: Ctr for Internat Programs Kent State U Kent OH 44242

CLAXON, MICHAEL WILLIAM, electronics engineer; b. Litchfield, Ill., Aug. 15, 1951; s. William Russell Claxon and Suzanne Rae (Swank) Duzan. BS, Ill. Inst. Tech., 1981, MS, 1983. Quality engring. mgr. Bally Mfg., Chgo., 1976-78; test engr. Cummins-Allison Corp., Elk Grove, Ill., 1978-79; proj. engr. Northrop DSD, Rolling Meadows, Ill., 1979—. Mem. Chi Psi (chmn. Rush, 1973). Republican. Club: Duck Unltd. Avocations: camping, fishing, hunting. Home: 218 Walnut Lane Elk Grove Village IL 60007 Office: Northrop Def Systems Div 600 Hicks Rd Rolling Meadows IL 60008

CLAXTON, BARBARA JANE, mental health educator; b. Peoria, Ill., Apr. 25, 1951; s. Charles Beverly and JoAnn (White) Vanatta; m. Timothy Arthur Claxton, Jan. 20, 1979; 1 child, Seth Michael. BS in Edn., Northwestern U., 1973; MA, Bradley U., 1976. Tchr. lang. arts Creve Coeur (Ill.) Sch. Dist., 1973-77; guidance counselor Farmington (Ill.) High Sch., 1977-80; ednl. cons. Community Mental Health Ctr., Canton, Ill., 1980—. Deaconess First Christian Ch., Canton, 1979-85; mem. bd. edn. Canton Christian Sch., 1983—. Named one of Outstanding Young Women of Am. Mem. Am. Assn. for Counseling and Devel., Ill. Assn. for Counseling and Devel. (exec. bd. 1983—, co-chmn. conv. program 1985), Am. Sch. Counselors Assn., Ill. Sch. Counselors Assn. (senator 1980-82, pres. 1981-82, newsletter editor 1978-80), Alpha Lambda Delta, Kappa Delta Pi. Avocations: writing, sewing, sports. Office: Community Mental Health Ctr 229 Martin Ave Canton IL 61520

CLAY, HENRY ALLEN, lawyer, systems analyst, consultant; b. Tarentum, Pa., Sept. 10, 1930; s. Henry Clevenger and Mary Eleanor (Shingledecker) C.; m. Christine Ann Brooks, Jan. 3, 1953; children—Stephen Henry, Carol Ann, Andrew Robert. Student Carnegie-Mellon U., 1948-49; B.A., U. Pa., 1952, J.D., 1957. Bar: Washington 1959, Pa. 1961; C.L.U. Trainee, Employee Relations Devel. Program, Gen. Electric Co., Lynn, Mass. and Phila., 1957-59; asst. counsel Provident Mut. Life Ins. Co. Phila., 1959-65, dir. adminstrv. systems, 1965-68; dir. law student div. ABA, Chgo., 1968-69; dir. office mgmt. systems Penn Mut. Life Ins. Co., Phila., 1969-73, dir. variable annuities, pres. Penn Mut. Equity Services, 1973-76; bus. mgr., bd. dirs. Lower Merion Sch. Dist., Ardmore, Pa., 1976-78; ptnr. in charge adminstrn. firm Dykema, Gossett, Spencer, Goodnow & Trigg, Detroit, 1978—; lectr. in work measurement Am. Mgmt. Assn.; circuit exec. qualifier U.S. Circuit Cts. Appeals, 1972-73. Mem. Marple Newtown Sch. Bd., Newtown Square, Pa., 1971-77, pres., 1973-77; judge elections Marple Twp., Broomall, Pa.; pres. Grosse Pointe (Mich.) Newcomers Club, 1982-83; pres. Citizens Against Recall Effort, Grosse Pointe Farms, Mich., 1983-84. Served to maj. JAGC, USAR, 1952-68; Korea. Decorated Army Commendation medal. Fellow Life Mgmt. Inst.; mem. ABA, Phila. Bar Assn., Assn. Internal Mgmt. Cons., Am. Arbitration Assn., Assn. Life Ins. Counsel. Republican. Episcopalian. Clubs: Masons, Shriners (Phila.); Players (Detroit). Office: Dykema Gossett Spencer Goodnow & Trigg 35th Flr 400 Renaissance Ctr Detroit MI 48243

CLAY, STEVEN THOMAS, dentist; b. Columbus, Ohio, Oct. 27, 1953; s. John Robert and Margaret Ellen (Kirkland) C.; m. Dianne Marie Conway, Sept. 17, 1977; children: Jennifer Marie, Elizabeth Ann. BS in Chemistry, Denison U., 1975; DDS, Ohio State U., 1978. Gen. practice dentistry Nelsonville, Ohio, 1978-80, Hilliard, Ohio, 1980—; clin. instr. Ohio State U., Columbus, 1982—. Republican. Baptist. Avocations: swimming, chess, French horn. Home: 5961 Hayden Run Rd Hilliard OH 43026 Office: 3736 Main St Hilliard OH 43026

CLAY, WILLIAM LACY, congressman; b. St. Louis, Apr. 30, 1931; s. Irving C. and Luella (Hyatt) C.; m. Carol A. Johnson, Oct. 10, 1953; children: Vicki, Lacy, Michelle. B.S. in Polit. Sci, St. Louis U., 1953. Real estate broker from 1964; mgr. life ins. co., 1959-61; alderman 26th Ward St. Louis, 1959-64; bus. rep. state, county and municipal employees union 1961-64; edn. coordinator Steamfitters local 562, 1966-67; mem. 91st-100th congresses from 1st Mo. Dist., 1969—. Served with AUS, 1953-55. Mem. NAACP (past exec. bd. mem. St. Louis), CORE, St. Louis Jr. C. of C. Democrat. Office: US Ho Reps 2470 Rayburn House Office Bldg Washington DC 20515 *

CLAY, WILLIAM LACY, JR., state legislator; b. St. Louis, July 27, 1956; s. William L. and Carol Ann (Johnson) C.; m. Leslie Renee Lubiano, Dec. 17, 1983. BS in Polit. Sci., U. Md., Coll. Park, 1983. Cert. paralegal; lic. real estate salesman, Mo. State rep. Mo. Gen. Assembly, Jefferson City, 1983—; real estate marketer W.A. Thomas Realty, St. Louis, 1986—. Vice chmn., bd. dirs. Metro Community Health Ctr., St. Louis, 1985—; treas. 26th Dem. Ward, 1984—. Mem. Ams. Dem. Action (Outstanding Legis. Mo. chpt. 1985, 86). Roman Catholic. Avocations: dominoes, basketball, golf, swimming, card playing. Office: Mo Ho of Reps State Capitol Bldg Jefferson City MO 65101

CLAYBURGH, BEN JAMES, orthopaedic surgeon; b. Scobey, Mont., Jan. 31, 1924; s. Marcus and Anna (Horvick) C.; m. Mina Tennison, June 7, 1948 (dec. Feb. 1968); children: James, Robert, John, Richard; m. Beverly Manternach, Jan. 3, 1970. BA, U. N.D., 1946, BS, 1947; MD, Temple U., 1949; MS in Orthopaedic Surgery, U. Minn., 1956. Diplomate Am. Bd. Orthopaedic Surgery, Nat. Bd. Med. Examiners; lic. physician Minn., N.D. Intern Anchor Gen. Hosp., St. Paul, Minn., 1949-50; resident gen. surgery St. Luke's Hosp., St. Paul, 1950-51; fellow orthopaedic surgery U. Minn., Rochester, 1953-56; orthopaedic surgeon Grand Forks Clinic, Grand Forks, N.D., 1956-66, The Orthopaedic Clinic, Grand Forks, 1966—; mem. staff United Hosp.; mem. staff Rehab. Hosp., vice chief staff, mem. exec. com.; clin. prof. U. N.D. Sch. Med.; cons. USAF, USPHS, Minn. Crippled Children's Services; mem. adv. com. Gillette State Hosp. for Crippled Children, St. Paul; mem. rehab. service nat. adv. com. HEW, 1976-77. Mem. Rep. Nat. Com., N.D., 1968-76, 80-84, mem. exec. com., 1971-72, 75-76, 81-84; del. Rep. Nat. Conv., 1964, 72, 76, 84, alternate del., 1968, 80, mem. numerous coms.; chmn. Grand Forks Area Rep. Coordinating Com., 1977-80; regional chmn. Physicians for Reagan-Bush, 1980, 84; 1st chmn. N.D. Com. on Med. Polit. Action. Served to capt. M.C., USAF, 1951-53. Recipient special award Govs. Com. for Employment of Handicapped, Recognition award Med. Ctr. Rehab. Hosp., 1979. Mem. AMA, Am. Acad. Orthopaedic Surgeons (N.D. councilor), 3d. Dist. Med. Soc. (past pres.), N.D. Med. Assn., Minn.-Dakota-Manitoba Orthopaedic Soc. (past pres.), Clin. Orthopaedic Soc., Mid-Am. Orthopaedic Assn. (founder, 2d. v.p.), Bone and Joint Soc. (past pres.). Lutheran. Avocation: hunting. Home: 1626 Belmont Rd Grand Forks ND 58201 Office: Orthopaedic Clinic 960 Columbia Rd S Grand Forks ND 58201

CLAYBURGH, JOHN EDWARD, dentist; b. Rochester, Minn., Aug. 11, 1956; s. Ben and Mina (Tennison) C. BA, Concordia Coll., 1978; DDS, Loyola U., Maywood, Ill., 1982. Gen. practice dentistry Grand Forks, N.D., 1982—; dental cons. Devel. Homes, 1985—, Valley Meml. Homes, 1985—. Chmn. Citizens Nutrition Adv. Com., 1985-86. Mem. ADA, Acad. Gen. Dentistry, N.D. Dental Assn., N.E. Dist. Dental Soc. (sec., treas. 1985—). Republican. Lodge: Lions. Avocations: skiing, photography, hunting, sailing. Office: 667 Demers Ave Grand Forks ND 58201

CLAYBURN, MARGINELL POWELL, librarian; b. Nashville, Jan. 20, 1937; d. James Murphy and Marie (Huff) Powell; m. Kenneth J. Clayburn, Mar. 14, 1962. BA in Liberal Arts & Sci., Southern U., 1959; MA in Library Sci., U. Iowa, 1981; MGS, Drake U., 1983. Cert. librarian, language resource specialist. Asst. librarian Pub. Library of Des Moines, 1962-76, children's librarian, 1976-83, young adult librarian, 1983-84, librarian I, 1984-86, sr. librarian, 1986—, supervising librarian, 1987—. Mem. ALA, Iowa Library Assn., Am. Bus. Women of Am., Beta Phi Mu, Delta Sigma Theta. Democrat. Roman Catholic. Club: Toastmasters. Home: 985 28th St Des Moines IA 50312 Office: East Side Branch Library 2559 Hubbell Ave Des Moines IA 50317

CLAYMORE, BETTY JANE, psychologist, social worker; b. Ashland, Wis., Apr. 24, 1935; d. Phil S. and Gertrude M. (Acker) Halls; m. James L. Claymore, Dec. 31, 1965; children: David, Vickie. BA in Sociology, William and Mary Coll., 1957; MSW, U. Wis., 1960; PhD in Psychology, Union U., 1978. Cert. social worker. Casework supr. Rock County Welfare, Janesville, Wis., 1960-63; agy. social worker Bur. Indian Affairs, Rosebud, S.D., 1963-66; social worker Bur. Indian Affairs, Anchorage, Alaska, 1966-70; mental dir. Indian Health Services, Eagle Butte, S.D., 1971-79; area mental health officer Indian Health Services, Aberdeen, S.D., 1979—. Mem. Nat. Assn. Social Workers, Assn. Cert. Social Workers. Democrat. Episcopalian. Lodges: Elks, Eastern Star. Avocation: bridge. Home: 124 Elizabeth Dr Aberdeen SD 57401 Office: Indian Health Service Fed Bldg Aberdeen SD 57401

CLAYTON, BRUCE DAVID, educator; b. Grand Island, Nebr., Mar. 9, 1947; s. John David and Eloise Regnier (Camp) C.; student Hastings Coll., 1965-67; B.S., U. Nebr., 1970; D.Pharmacy, U. Mich., 1973; m. Francine Evelyn Purdy, June 19, 1971; children—Sarah Elizabeth, Beth Anne. Resident U. Mich., 1972-74; asst. prof. clin. pharmacy Creighton U., Omaha, 1974-77; assoc. prof. Coll. Pharmacy, U. Nebr. Med. Center, Omaha, 1978—, viee chmn. dept. pharmacy practice, 1978-84, interim chmn., 1984-85, prof., chmn. dept. pharmacy practice, U. Ark. Med. Scis., Little Rock, 1985-87; unit coordinator perinatal pharmacy services Univ. Hosps., Omaha, 1978-80; Ciba-Geigy vis. prof., Australia and N.Z., 1979; S.E. Wright traveling fellow Pharm. Soc. Australia, 1983; lectr. in field. Recipient Bristol award for professionalism, 1970; named Nebr. Hosp. Pharmacist of Yr., 1978. Mem. Nebr. Soc. Hosp. Pharmacists (pres. 1978-79, dir. 1979-80), Ark. Pharmacists Assn., Am. Soc. Hosp. Pharmacists (council on organizational affairs 1979-82, com. on nominations 1980-85, chmn. 1985, ho. of dels. 1980—, council on ednl. affairs 1987—), Am. Pharm. Assn., Nebr. Pharm. Assn., Am. Assn. Colls. of Pharmacy, Rho Chi. Author: (with S.A. Ryan): Handbook of Practical Pharmacology, 1977, 2d edit., 1980; (with J.E. Squire) Basic Pharmacology for Nurses, 7th edit., 1981; Handbook of Pharmacology in Nursing, 1984, Handbook of Pharmacology, 1987; Basic Pharmacology for Nurses, 1985. Contbr. articles to profl. jours.

CLAYTON-RANDOLPH, HARVEY JAMES, health and safety educator, consultant; b. Detroit, Dec. 1, 1933; s. Lawrence and Alice (Harvey) R.; m. Susan Elizabeth Clayton, June 9, 1978; children: Genie, Shawn, Brenda. BS in Health/Safety Mgmt., U.N.Y., Albany, 1977; MS in Health/Safety Mgmt., Ind. U., 1983. Cert. hazard control mgr. Enlisted ensign USN, 1952, advanced through grades to chief petty officer 2d class, 1980, retired, 1980; indsl. hygienist Navy Weapons Support Ctr., Crane, Ind., 1985; hazard control specialist Ind. U., Bloomington, 1981-85, 85—; cons. Clayton-Ran & Asscos., Bloomington, 1983—. Mem. Am. Soc. Safety Engrs., Cert. Hazard Control Mgrs. Assn., Pollution Engring. Assn. Republican. Methodist. Avocation: industrial and public photography. Home: Rural Rt 4 Box 797 Bloomfield IN 47424 Office: Ind U 400 E 7th St Room 617 Bloomington IN 47405

CLAY-TURLEY, PAMELA ANN, telephone co. exec.; b. Ames, Iowa, Apr. 22, 1944; d. Roger Leon and Barbara Ruth (Hunt) Clay; B.A., Grinnell Coll., 1966; m. Jack Turley, Sept. 13, 1980; 1 dau., Krista. With Gen. Telephone Co. Ill., Bloomington, 1966—, dir. tng., 1980-82, state mgr. tng., 1982—. Pres. bd. dirs. McLean County YWCA, 1986-87. Mem. Am. Soc. for Tng. and Devel., Bus. and Profl. Women's Club. Home: 1305 Schroeder Normal IL 61761 Office: Gen Telephone Co Ill 404 Brock Dr Bloomington IL 61701

CLEARY, PATRICK JAMES, newspaper editor; b. Momence, Ill., Jan. 20, 1929; s. James Augustine and Nellie DeWitt (Liston) C.; student U. Chgo., 1946-48; m. Alice Marie Duval, Oct. 1, 1955; children—Mary Elizabeth, James Augustine, Michael John. Reporter, wire editor, city editor Kankakee (Ill.) Daily Jour., 1945-52; reporter Gary (Ind.) Post-Tribune, 1952-53; staff asst. Ill. Senate, 1953-57; dir. pub. relations Plumbing Contractors Assn. Chgo. Cook County (Ill.), 1957-59; city clk. City of Kankakee, 1955-57, clk., county and probate cts. County of Kankakee, 1959-63; editor Farmers Weekly Rev., Joliet, Ill., 1963—; editor Compass Newspapers Inc., Kankakee, 1977, Herscher (Ill.) Rev., 1963-69; editor Crete (Ill.) Record, Steger (Ill.) News, 1963-64; chmn. bd. rev. Ill. Dept. Labor, 1969-73. Office: 100 Manhattan Rd Joliet IL 60433

CLEARY, ROBERT EMMET, gynecologist, infertility specialist; b. Evanston, Ill., July 17, 1937; s. John J. and Brigid (O'Grady) C.; M.D., U. Ill., 1962; m. June 10, 1961; children—William Joseph, Theresa Marie, John Thomas. Intern, St. Francis Hosp., Evanston, 1962-63, resident, 1963-66; practice medicine specializing in gynecology and infertility, Indpls., 1970—; head Sect. of Reproductive Endocrinology and Infertility, Chgo. Lying-In Hosp., U. Chgo., 1968-70; head Sect. of Reproductive Endocrinology and Infertility, Ind. U. Med. Center, Indpls., 1970-80; prof. ob-gyn Ind. U., Indpls., 1976-80, clin. prof. ob-gyn, 1980—. Recipient Meml. award Pacific Coast Obstetrical and Gynecol. Soc., 1968; diplomate Am. Bd. Ob-Gyn, Am. Bd. Reproductive Endocrinology and Infertility. Fellow Am. Coll. Ob-Gyn, Am. Fertility Soc.; mem. Endocrine Soc.,Soc. Gynecol. Investigation, Pacific Coast Fertility Soc., Soc. Reproductive Endocrinologists, Soc. Reproductive Surgeons, N.Y. Acad. Scis., Sigma Xi. Roman Catholic. Contbr. articles in field to med. jours. Home: 7036 Dubonnet Ct Indianapolis IN 46278 Office: 8091 Township Line Rd Indianapolis IN 46260

CLEARY, WILLIAM RICHARD, superintendent of schools; b. Wagoner, Okla., Sept. 24, 1933; s. William R. and Tressie (Bird) C.; m. Barbara J. Berry, June 2, 1956; 1 child, Richard Bryant. BA, Cen. State U., Edmond, Okla., 1959, ThM, 1963; PhD, Nat. Christian U., 1974. Tchr. Unified Sch. Dist. 259, Wichita, Kans., 1966-68; supt. Unified Sch. Dist. 462, Burden, Kans., 1968-75, Unified Sch. Dist. 402, Augusta, Kans., 1975-79, Unified Sch. Dist. 368, Paola, Kans., 1979—; Chmn. East Cen. Kans. Spl. Coop., Paola, 1979—; joint commn. Law Related Edn., Topeka, Kans., 1985—; mem. Council of Supts., Topeka, 1985—. Served to sgt. U.S. Army, 1952-55. Mem. Am. Assn. Sch. Adminstrs., Kans. Assn. Sch. Adminstrs. (bd. dirs. 1973-75), Kans. Assn. Supervision and Curriculum Devel. Republican. Methodist. Lodge: Lions (pres. 1985-86). Home: 602 E Miami Paola KS 66071 Office: Unified Sch Dist 368 202 E Wea Paola KS 66071

CLEELAND, RAYMOND THEODORE, china company executive; b. Providence, Dec. 4, 1925; s. Raymond and Mary (McVicker) C.; m. Margaret Mary Walsh, May 5, 1951 (dec. Jan. 1978); children: Cathleen, Nancy, Kevin, Theresa, Patricia, Carol; m. Betty Louise Goodwin, Jan. 2, 1982. BSBA, U. R.I., 1950. Mgr. sales Wallace Silversmith's, Wallingford, Conn., 1952-63; pres. Ekco Products Internat. Corp., N.Y.C., 1963-72; chmn. bd. dirs. Johann Haviland China Corp., Des Plaines, Ill., 1972—; chmn. bd. dirs. Renaissance Glass Co., Des Plaines, Super Mktg., Inc., Des Plaines. Served to cpl. U.S. Army, 1944-46, ETO. Mem. Am. Mgmt. Assn., Soc. Profl. Mktg. Specialists, Sigma Chi (cons. 1948-50). Republican. Roman Catholic. Clubs: Itasca Country (Ill.); Chgo. Health (Rosemont, Ill.). Avocations: scuba diving, racquetball, golf, running. Home: 610 N Euclid Ave Oak Park IL 60302 Office: Johann Haviland China Corp 2200 S Mount Prospect Rd Des Plaines IL 60018

CLEGG, WILLIAM HOOVER, business educator; b. Toledo, Dec. 30, 1925; s. Raymond V. and Margaret K. (Hoover) C.; m. Pauline R. Uhorczuk, Aug. 2, 1952; children: William K., Kathleen A. BS in Gen. Engring., U.S. Naval Acad., 1947; MBA, U. Toledo, 1973, EdD, 1978. Commd. ensign USN, 1947, advanced through grades capt., 1968, with Res., 1974; indsl. engr. Owens-Ill. Inc., Toledo, 1950-58, mgr. quality control, 1958-59, mgr. prodn. control, 1959-60, corp. indsl. engr., 1960-61, mgr. indsl. engring., 1961-65, mgr. ops., 1965-70, mgr. indsl. engring./cost control, 1970-74, mgr. adminstrv. services, 1974-77, mgr. indsl. engring./prodn. planning/facilities planning, 1977-82; assoc. prof. bus. adminstrn. U. Toledo, 1982—; cons. in field. Contbr. articles to profl. jours. Mem. Am. Soc. Quality Control (sr.), Mensa, Phi Kappa Phi, Beta Gamma Sigma, Kappa Delta Pi. Home: 2647 Barrington Dr Toledo OH 43606

CLEGHORN, GEORGE EDWARD, apartment management executive; b. Terre Haute, Ind., Sept. 15, 1950; s. Edward Melle and Dorothy Pearl (Jones) C.; m. Laura Maureen Boyke, Dec. 18, 1971; children—Kathleen Mary, Corey Bruce. A.A.S. in Electronics Engring., SAMS Tech. Inst., 1970; A.A.S. in Mid Mgmt., Coll. Lake County, 1981, A.A.S. in Indsl. Supervision, 1983; Supr. Imperial Towers, Waukegan, Ill., 1976-84, gen. mgr., 1984—. Served with USN, 1970-76. Mem. Waukegan/Lake County C. of C. (investing mem. 1985), Phi Theta Kappa. Republican. Home: 560 Forest View Dr Lindenhurst IL 60046 Office: Gen Mgr Imperial Towers 805 Baldwin Ave Waukegan IL 60085

CLEM, NANCY GAYLE, educator; b. Princeton, Ind., Feb. 27, 1941; d. Gaylord Elliott Kirk and Elsie Isabel (Dunning) McDowell; m. Larry Jay Clem, Aug. 10, 1963; children: Jay Michael, Jana Michelle. BS in Vocat. Home Econs., Purdue U., 1963; MS in Vocat. Home Econs., Ind. State U., 1966. Vocat. home econs. tchr. Petersburg (Ind.) High Sch., 1963-74; vocat. home econs. tchr., dept. head Pike Central High Sch., Petersburg, 1974—; dist. coordinator Ind. Home Econs. and Future Homemakers Am.; cons. Harcourt, Brace, Jananovich, Inc. Mem. Am. Home Econs. Assn., Ind. Home Econs. Assn. (Home Econs. Tchr. Yr. 1976), Am. Vocat. Assn., Ind. Vocat. Assn., Nat. Assn. Vocat. Home Econs., NEA, Ind. Vocat. Home Econs. Assn. (v.p., pres.-elect, pres.), Ind. Tchrs. Assn., Ind. Assn. Future Homemakers Am., Delta Kappa Gamma. Republican. Presbyterian. Lodge: Daus. Nile. Home: Rural Route 2 Princeton IN 47670 Office: Pike Central High Sch Rural Rt 3 Petersburg IN 47567

CLEMENS, NORMAN ANDREW, psychiatrist, educator; b. Kingston, Pa., July 3, 1933; s. Norman Weaver and Gertrude Mellita (Beagle) C.; m. Julia Strong Taylor, June 23, 1956; children: David Taylor, George Andrew. Ba, Wesleyan U., 1955; MD, Harvard U., 1959. Diplomate Am. Bd. Psychiatry and Neurology. Practice medicine specializing in psychiatry Cleve., 1963—; instr. to assoc. clin. prof. Case Western Res. U., Cleve., 1964—; bd. dirs. Mental Health Rev., Inc., Columbus, Ohio, Cleve. Acad. Medicine. Contbr. articles to mental health publs. Pres. Choral Arts Performing Soc., Cleveland Heights, 1982-85, trustee, 1985—; chmn. Mental Illness and Substance Abuse Task Force, Cleve., 1983—. Fellow Am. Psychiat. Assn.; mem. AMA, Ohio Psychiat. Assn. (pres. 1986-87, Meritorious Service award 1981, Disting. Service award 1983), Cleve. Psychiat. Soc. (pres. 1978-79). Avocations: sailing, tennis, computer programming, writing, skiing, photography. Home: 2258 Lamberton Rd Cleveland Heights OH 44118 Office: Univ Suburban Health Ctr 1611 S Green Rd South Euclid OH 44121

CLEMENS, ROBERT CHARLES, accounting executive; b. Xenia, Ohio, June 13, 1950; s. John Ewart and Ruth Drake (Barry) C.; m. Leslie Rebecca Loan, May 26, 1974; 1 child, David. BS in Acctg., Wright State U., 1972. CPA, Ohio. Acct. Grismer Tire Co., Dayton, Ohio, 1974-76; v.p., comptroller Able Pest Control, Dayton, 1976—. State of Ky. grantee, 1986. Mem. Am. Inst. CPA's, Ohio Soc. CPA's. Republican. Methodist. Lodge: Masons (worthy patron new Burlington chpt. 1981-82, trustee 1982-85). Avocations: hiking, spelunking. Home: 2066 Malibu Trail Xenia OH 45385

CLEMENS, T(OM) PAT, manufacturing company executive; b. Hibbing, Minn., July 26, 1944; s. Jack LeRoy and Mildred (Coss) C.; m. Marianne Paznar, Oct. 1, 1966; children—Patrick Michael, Heather Kristen. B.S. in Econs. and Mgmt., St. Cloud State U., 1968, student, Coll. St. Thomas, 1985-87. Sales adminstr. Transistor Electronics Co., Eden Prarie, Minn., 1969; head instnl. sales Chiquita Brands, Edina, Minn., 1970; dist. sales mgr. Menley & James Labs., Phila., 1971-75; owner, pres. T. P. Clemens Labs., Eagan, Minn., 1975—; instr community edn. Rosemount, Minn., 1979—; lectr. econs. to corps., high schs. and colls. in U.S., Scotland, Ireland, and Jamaica, 1979—. Author, editor: How Prejudice and Narcissism Control Economics of the United States and the World, 1979. Mem. Rosemont Community Edn. Bd., 1985, chmn. 1986-87; chmn. speakers bur. Citizens Steering Com., 1984-85; little League coach, 1970-82; high sch. weight lifting coach, 1982—; vol. worker with comatose children. Mem. Internat. Platform Assn. Home and Office: 1276 Vildmark Dr Eagan MN 55123

CLEMENT, DAVID JOSEPH, dentist; b. Hettinger, N.D., May 19, 1955; s. Joseph Leon and Alleyne Anna (Anderson) C.; m. Annette Mary Lapinski, Apr. 2, 1977. BA, Jamestown Coll., 1977; DDS, U. Minn., 1981. Pvt. practice dentistry Beach, N.D., 1981—; cons. Golden Valley County Hosp., Beach, 1985—. Mem. mus. singing group Silhoutte's In Sound. Mem. N.D. Dental Assn., Omicron Kappa Upsilon. Lutheran. Lodge: Lions. Avocations: aviation, camping, fishing. Home: 459 2d Ave SE Beach ND 58621 Office: Family Dentistry 22 S Central Ave Beach ND 58621

CLEMENT, DONALD LEE, personnel administrator; b. Salem, Oreg., Dec. 11, 1943; s. Henry H. and Mildred L. (Cross) C.; m. Diane C. Cliffe, July 26, 1969; 1 child, Matthew D. BA, Seattle Pacific U., 1966; MEd, Cleveland State U., 1979. Cert. elem. tchr., prin., supr., Ohio. Dir. outdoor edn. Cleve. Bd. Edn., 1968-70, tchr., 1970-78, dir. desegregation monitoring, 1981-85, supr. elem. orgn., 1985—; adminstrv. asst. Office on Sch. Monitoring, Cleve., 1978-81. Vol. U.S. Peace Corps, India, 1966-68. Educational Policy fellow, 1980. Mem. Am. Assn. Sch. Personnel Adminstrs., Ohio Assn. Sch. Personnel Adminstrs., Northeast Ohio Assn. Sch. Personnel Adminstrs., Ohio Assn. Elem. Sch. Adminstrs., Cleve. Council Adminstrs. and Suprs. Democrat. Home: 1189 Teakwood Ln Brunswick OH 44212 Office: Cleve Bd Edn 1380 E 6th St Cleveland OH 44114

CLEMENTI, PETE JOHN, data processing specialist; b. Detroit, Oct. 3, 1952; s. Charles and Lila Mae (Denney) C.; m. Denise Ann Schuetze, June 8, 1980; children: Lynn, Kimberly. BS, Northeastern Ill. U., 1979. Assoc. systems cons. Allstate Ins. Co., Northbrook, Ill., 1980—. V.p. Courtland Square Condominiums, Des Plaines, Ill., 1980-83. Office: Allstate Ins Co G2B Allstate Plaza Northbrook IL 60056

CLEMENTS, ROBERT EUGENE, JR., physician; b. Hartford City, Ind., Oct. 5, 1948; s. Robert Eugene and Geraldine Ellen (Needler) C.; m. Heidi Jane Webb, July 12, 1975; children: Ryan Scott, Allison Brooke. BA, Hanover Coll., 1970; MD, Ind. U., 1974. Intern Marion County Gen. Hosp., Indpls., 1974-75; emergency physician Hancock Meml. Hosp., Greenfield, Ind., 1975-79, gen. practice medicine, 1978—; gen. practice medicine Community Hosp., Indpls., 1985—; pharmacy-therapeutics com. Hancock Meml. Hosp., Greenfield, Ind., 1984—; mem. emergency dept. dir. Hancock Meml. Hosp., 1977-79, lab. com., 1980-84, exec. com., 1986—, pharmacy-therapeutics com., 1984—. Recipient Physicians Recognition award AMA, 1982-84, 85—. Mem. Am. Acad. Family Physicians, Ind. State Med. Assn., Hancock County Med. Soc. (pres. 1982), Ind. U. Alumni Assn. Republican. Methodist. Avocations: computing, golf, snow skiing, autocross. Home: 10935 Ridge Ct Indianapolis IN 46256 Office: 120 W McKenzie Greenfield IN 46140

CLEMINSHAW, HELEN K. MARIE, psychologist, educator; b. Elizabeth, N.J., May 16, 1938; d. Fred A. and Helen W. (Bittner) Kronseder; m. John G. Cleminshaw, June 24, 1960; children: John David, Suzanne Christine. BS, Rutgers U., 1960; MA, Kent (Ohio) State U., 1972, PhD, 1977. Lic. psychologist, Ohio. Sch. psychologist Maple Heights (Ohio) Schs., 1972-75; assoc. prof. U. Akron, Ohio, 1976—; psychologist Hudson (Ohio) Psychol. Assocs., 1980—; bd. dirs. Child Life Specialist Tng. Program, Akron, 1979—, Ctr. Family Studies, Akron, 1981—. Co-editor: Alcoholism: New Perspectives, 1983; contbr. articles to profl. jours. U. Akron faculty research grantee, 1978-79, NIMH grantee, 1979-84, AAUW Ednl. Found. grantee, 1986—. Mem. Am. Psychol. Assn., Nat. Council Family Relations, Assn. for Care of Children's Health. Office: U Akron Schrank Hall S 215 Akron OH 44325

CLESEN, GERARD FOSTER, naval officer; b. Chgo., May 19, 1941; s. Joseph William and Dorothy Katherine (Donohoe) C.; m. Mary Jo Lacey, July 16, 1966; children: Sean, Timothy, Erin Anne. BA, St. Ambrose Coll., 1965; MA, U. Cen. Mich., 1979. Commd. ens. USN, 1965, advanced through grades to capt., 1986, aviator, 1965—; comdg. officer Tng. Squadron Nine, Meridian, Miss., 1982-85; comdg. officer Navy Recruiting Dist., Kansas City, Mo., 1985-86, Chgo., 1986—. Decorated 2 Meritous Service medals, 4 Air medals, Navy Achievement medal, Humanitarian Service medal. Mem. Order of Daedalians, Naval Inst., Tailhook Soc. Democrat. Roman Catholic. Home: 1346 Shermer Rd Glenview IL 60025 Office: Navy Recruiting Dist Chgo Bldg 41 Naval Air Sta Glenview IL 60026-5200

CLEVELAND, CARL S., III, academic administrator; b. Kansas City, Mo., Oct. 7, 1946; s. Carl S. Jr. and Mildred G. (Allison) C.; m. Elizabeth Louise Fields, Apr. 3, 1971; children: Carl IV, Cynthia, Ashley, Alexandra, Christian. AS, Met. Jr. Coll., 1967; BS in Biology, U. Mo., 1970; D of Chiropractic, Cleveland Chiropractic Coll., 1975; postgrad., U. Mo., U. Colo., U. Kans., 1972-74. Instr. U. Mo., Kansas City, 1974; instr. in labs. Cleveland Chiropractic Coll., Kansas City, 1974-75, dean of academic affairs, 1975-78, exec. v.p., 1978-82, pres., 1982—. Mem. Assn. Chiropractic Colls. (pres. 1984-87), Nat. Bd. Chiropractic Examiners (chmn. principles and practices com.), Am. Chiropractic Assn., Internat. Chiropractors Assn., Acad. Mo. Chiropractors, Mo. Chiropractors Assn., Council on Chiropractors Edn. (chmn. postgrad. panel 1984-85). Avocations: classical piano, foreign languages, jogging.

CLEVELAND, DONALD LESLIE, insurance broker, reinsurance intermediary and consultant; b. Omaha, Nebr., July 16, 1938; s. Albert Leslie and Lucille Arlene (Fancher) C.; B.S. in Polit. Sci. and Journalism, Creighton U., 1961; M.A. in Polit. Sci., U. Nebr., 1968; m. Christa Anita Wahl, Oct. 9, 1965; children—Christopher Leslie, Stephan Donald. Adminstrv. asst. Clarkson Hosp., Omaha, 1965-67; adminstrv. asst. Assn. Minn. Counties, St. Paul, 1967-68; asst. dir. house research dept. Minn. Ho. of Reps., St. Paul, 1968-71; exec. dir. Iowa State Assn. Counties, Des Moines, 1971-80; chmn. Cleveland Research and Devel. Corp., 1975-84; v.p. domestic ops. GIF Ins. Co. Ltd., 1980-84; chief exec. officer Multi-County Services Agy., Joint County Unemployment Compensation Fund, County Liability Indemnification Fund, Local Govt. Research Found., 1975-80; pres. Cleveland Group, West Des Moines, Iowa, 1980—. Pres., St. Paul Beautiful Coordinating Com., 1970-71; county rep. Mid Continent Fed. Regional Council, Kansas City, 1977-80. Served to capt. U.S. Army, 1961-66. Mem. Am. Soc. Assn. Execs., Am. Soc. Public Adminstrn., Acad. Polit. Sci., Council Fgn. Relations, Internat. Personnel Mgmt. Assn., Nat. Assn. Counties, Nat. Assn. County Assn. Execs. (sec.-treas. 1978—, 2d v.p. 1979-80, 1st v.p. and pres. 1980), Captive Ins. Cos. Assn. (bd. dirs. 1984). Democrat. Roman Catholic. Editor The County, 1971-80. Office: Cleveland Group 1200 35th St Suite 602 West Des Moines IA 50265

CLEVELAND, JERRY LESTER, hospital official; b. Ft. Dodge, Iowa, Nov. 1, 1949; s. Lester Jessie and Maxine Evelyn (Burch) C.; A.A., Area XI Community Coll., Ankeny, Iowa, 1977; m. Adella Lynn Lara, Dec. 19, 1970; children—Michael, Timothy, Frank. Asst. chief, then chief supply, processing and distbn. VA Hosp., Des Moines, 1973-77; dir. central service St. Luke's Methodist Hosp., Cedar Rapids, 1977-86, chmn. safety com., 1979, chmn. products improvement com., 1980-84, chmn. assocs. activities com., 1980, treas., 1981-86, gen. mgr. home health care services/St. Luke's Home Care 1986—. Served with USN, 1969-73. Mem. Am. Soc. Hosp. Central Service Personnel (membership com. 1980-81, dir. region II 1982-83, pres-elect 1984, pres. 1985), Central Service Assn. Iowa (chmn. membership 1978, pres. 1979-81, membership dir. 1985-86), Am. Legion. Roman Catholic. Club: Los Amigos (v.p. 1978-79 pres. 1980-81) (Cedar Rapids). Office: 105 Tenth St NE Cedar Rapids IA 52402

CLEVEN, DONALD LE ROY, pension fund executive; b. Kendall, Wis., Mar. 11, 1931; s. Morris Edward and Anne Marie (Preuss) C.; Master of Accounts, Madison (Wis.) Bus. Coll., 1950; postgrad. Madison Area Tech. Coll., 1968-73, U. Wis., Madison, 1973-77; m. Maxine Eileen Schuchmann, May 18, 1958; children—Gina, Paul, Ruth. Acct. trainee, distbr. sales acct. Borden Co., Madison, Wis., 1950-57, internal auditor, Chgo., 1958; acct. Vogel Bros. Bldg. Co., Madison, 1958-69, treas., 1969-83; controller Munz Corp., Madison, 1983-84; portfolio/property mgr. real estate and mortgages div. State of Wis. Investment Bd., 1984—. Bd. dirs. Leigh Roberts Transitional House, Madison, 1983—. C.P.A. Mem. Am. Inst. C.P.A.'s, Wis. Inst. C.P.A.'s. Lutheran. Home: 1706 Wendy Ln Madison WI 53716 Office: 340 W Washington Ave Madison WI 53703

CLEVENGER, THOMAS RAMSEY, banker; b. Wichita, Kans., Jan. 24, 1935; s. Raymond Charles and Mary Margaret (Ramsey) C.; m. Linda Lee, Feb. 6, 1965; children: John C., Christopher. B.S., Kans. U., 1957. Asst. cashier, asst. v.p. Republic Nat. Bank, Dallas, 1961-65; v.p. First Nat. Bank, Topeka, Kans., 1965-68, exec. v.p., 1969-71, pres., 1971—; dir. KPL Gas Services, Topeka, Security Benefit Life Ins. Co., Topeka, Gas Service Co., Kansas City, Mo. Trustee, Menninger Found., Topeka, 1974—, MRI, Kansas City, Mo., 1978—. Served as 1st lt. USMC, 1957-60, Okinawa. Republican. Roman Catholic. Home: 3101 W 17th St Topeka KS 66604 Office: Bank IV Topeka 1 Townsite Plaza Topeka KS 66603 *

CLIFFORD, THOMAS JOHN, university president; b. Langdon, N.D., Mar. 16, 1921; s. Thomas Joseph and Elizabeth (Howitz) C.; m. Florence Marie Schmidt, Jan. 25, 1943 (dec. 1984); children: Thomas John, Stephen Michael. B.C.S., U. N.D., 1942, J.D., 1948; M.B.S., Stanford U., 1957, Stanford exec. fellow, 1958; LLD (hon.), Jamestown (N.D.) Coll., 1973. CPA, N.D. Instr. accounting U. N.D., 1946-47, counselor men, 1947-49, head accounting dept., 1948-49, dean sch. commerce, 1950-71, pres. univ., 1971—; dir. Red River Nat. Bank, Grand Forks, N.D., Ottertail Power Co., Fergus Falls., Western States Life Ins. Co.; pres., bd. dirs. Nodak Trust. Bd. dirs. Greater N.D. Assn., Fargo, Bush Found., St. Paul, Minn.; pres., No. Lights council, Boy Scouts Am., 1981—. Served from 2d lt. to maj. USMC, 1942-45. Decorated Purple Heart, Bronze Star medal, Silver Star. Mem. N.D. C.P.A. Soc. (pres. 1953-54), A.I.M., Am. Inst. Accountants, Am. Bar Assn., Beta Gamma Sigma, Beta Alpha Psi, Phi Eta Sigma, Kappa Sigma, Blue Key, Order Coif. Club: K.C. Office: Univ North Dakota Box 8193 Univ Sta Grand Forks ND 58201

CLIFTON, JO ELLEN, social worker; b. Storm Lake, Iowa, Feb. 22, 1940; d. Clyde Calvin and Mary Patience (Fierk) Leeds; m. Kenwood Glenn Foster, Aug. 19, 1961 (div. Oct. 1970); children: John Derek, Dulce Jo; m. Robert Dale Clifton, Dec. 1, 1975. BA, Culver-Stockton Coll., 1962; postgrad., Fla. State U., 1962-63; MSW, U. Ala., Tuscaloosa, 1975. Social worker Dept. Pensions and Security, Birmingham, Ala., 1964-65, Children's Aid Soc., Birmingham, 1965-66, 70-76; dir. social work Lloyd Noland Hosp., Fairfield, Ala., 1976-78; sch. social worker Area Edn. Agy. 9, Davenport, Iowa, 1980-81; med. social worker Dept. Health and Environ. Control, Orangeburg, S.C., 1981-84; social worker VA Med. Ctr., Grand Island, Nebr., 1985—; mem. adv. com. Protective Services, Orangeburg, 1982-84, S.W. accountability com. Dept. Health and Environ. Control, Orangeburg, 1982-84, family stability com. Clemson Extension, Orangeburg, 1983-84. Nat. treas. rep. Baha'is of the U.S., S.C. and Nebr., 1982—; local spiritual assembly mem. Baha'is of Grand Island, 1985-86; local spiritual assembly sec. Baha's of Greater Orangeburg, 1983-84; active Orangeburg Part Time Players, 1982-84. Mem. Nat. Assn. Social Workers (cert.). Avocations: piano, clarinet, knitting, community theater, community band.

CLINARD, JOHN WILSON, III, marketing, public relations professional; b. High Point, N.C., Oct. 4, 1947; s. John Wilson Jr. and Lelia Shore (Thomas) C.; m. Linda McCorkel, Aug. 19, 1972; children: Anne, Jeffrey, Trevor. BS in Econs., Guilford Coll., 1969; MBA, Ind. U., 1971; M of Internat. Affairs, Columbia U., 1972. Mgr. zone sales Lincoln-Mercury div. Ford Motor Co., Dearborn, Mich., 1972-77; mgr. market devel. Ford Mid-East & Africa, Inc., Dearborn, 1977-79; sr. market anaylst Ford Motor Co., Dearborn, 1979-81; mktg. mgr. spl. vehicles ops. Ford Motor Co., Allen Park, Mich., 1981-87; product info. mgr., pub. affairs staff Ford Motor Co., Dearborn, Mich. Republican. Founder Italian Happening Car Show, Greenfield Village, Dearborn, 1979—. Office: Ford Motor Co 20000 Rotunda Dr Dearborn MI 48121

CLINE, BYRON WALDO, physician; b. Houston, Mar. 25, 1951. AA, Alvin Jr. Coll., 1971; BS magna cum laude, Houston Bapt. U., 1973; MD with honors, U. Tex., Galveston, 1977. Diplomate Am. Bd. Ob-Gyn. Resident in ob-gyn U. Kans. Sch. Medicine, Wichita, 1977-81; gen. practice medicine specializing in ob-gyn Wichita, 1981—; dir. colposcopy and laser clinic, dept. ob-gyn Wesley Med. Ctr., Wichita, 1982—. Fellow Am. Coll. Obstetricians and Gynecologists (vice chmn Kans. sect. 1977-78,sec., treas. 1978-79, various coms.); mem. Kans. Med. Soc., Med. Soc. Sedgwick County, Wichita Ob-Gyn Soc., Phi Theta Kappa, Theta Kappa Psi, Mu Delta, Alpha Omega Alpha. Office: 550 N Lorraine St Wichita KS 67214

CLINE, CHARLES WILLIAM, poet; b. Waleska, Ga., Mar. 1, 1937; s. Paul Ardell and Mary Montarie (Pittman) C.; m. Sandra Lee Williamson, June 11, 1966; 1 son, Jeffrey Charles. Student, U. Cin. Conservatory of Music, 1957-58; A.A., Reinhardt Coll., 1957; B.A., George Peabody Coll. for Tchrs., 1960; M.A., Vanderbilt U., 1963; Litt.D., World U., 1981. Asst. prof. English Shorter Coll., Rome, Ga., 1963-64; instr. English West Ga. Coll., Carrollton, 1964-68; manuscript procurement editor Fideler Co., Grand Rapids, Mich, 1968; assoc. prof. English Kellogg Community Coll., Battle Creek, Mich., 1969-75, prof. English and resident poet, 1975—; chmn. creative writing sect. Midwest Conf. on English, 1976; condr. poetry readings and workshops. Author: Crossing the Ohio, 1976, Questions for the Snow, 1979, Ultima Thule, 1984; editor: Forty Salutes to Mich. Poets, 1975; contbr. poems to jours. and anthologies. Recipient Poetry awards Modus Operandi, 1975, Internat. Belles-Lettres Soc., 1975, Poetry Soc. Mich., 1975, N.Am. Mentor, 1977, 78, Literary Prize World Inst. Achievement, 1986; resolutions recognition Kalamazoo City Commn., Mich. Ho. of Reps. and Senate, 1981, others. Fellow World Literary Acad. (founding, prize 1983), Internat. Soc. Lit. (life); mem. Tagore Inst. Creative Writing Internat. (life), Midwest Conf. on English, NEA, Mich. Edn. Assn., Mich. Assn. Higher Edn., World Poetry Soc. Intercontinental, Centro Studi e Scambi Internazionali (poet Laureate award, Diploma di Benemerenza, Diploma d'Onore), Accademia Leonardo da Vinci, Poetry Soc. Am., Poets and Writers Inc., Acad. Am. Poets, Associated Writing Programs, Am. Biog. Inst. Research Assn. (dep.

gov.), Internat. Biog. Assn. (life patron), Am. Biographical Inst. (life). Presbyterian. Office: Kellogg Community Coll 450 North Ave Battle Creek MI 49016

CLINE, DOROTHY MAY STAMMERJOHN (MRS. EDWARD WILBURN CLINE), educator; b. Boonville, Mo., Oct. 19, 1915; d. Benjamin Franklin and Lottie (Walther) Stammerjohn; grad. nurse U. Mo., 1937; B.S. in Edn., 1939, postgrad., 1966-67; M.S., Ark. State U., 1964; m. Edward Wilburn Cline, Aug. 16, 1938 (dec. May 1962); children—Margaret Ann (Mrs. Rodger Orville Bell), Susan Elizabeth (Mrs. Gary Lee Burns), Dorothy Jean. Dir. Christian Coll. Infirmary, Columbia, Mo., 1936-37; asst. chief nursing service VA Hosp., Poplar Bluff, Mo., 1950-58; tchr.-in-charge Tng. Center No. 4, Poplar Bluff, 1959-66, Dorothy S. Cline State Sch., Boonville, 1967-85; instr. U. Mo., Columbia, 1973-74; cons. for workshops for new tchrs., curriculum revision Mo. Dept. Edn. Mem. Butler County Council Retarded Children, 1959-66; v.p. Boonslick Assn. Retarded Children, 1969-72; sec.-treas. Mo. chpt. Am. Assn. on Mental Deficiency, 1973-75. Mem. NEA, Mo. Tchrs. Assn., Am. Assn. on Mental Deficiency, Council for Exceptional Children, AAUW (v.p. Boonville br. 1968-70, 75-77), Mo. Writers Guild, Creative Writer's Group (pres. 1974—), Columbia Creative Writers Group, Eastern Center Poetry Soc., Laura Speed Elliott High Sch. Alumni Assn., Bus. and Profl. Women's Club, Smithsonian Assn., U. Mo. Alumni Assn., Ark. State U. Alumni Assn., Internat. Platform Assn., Mo. Hist. Soc., Boonslick Hist. Soc., Friends Historic Boonville, Delta Kappa Gamma. Mem. Christian Ch. Home: 603 E High St Boonville MO 65233

CLINE, JAYSON HOWARD, coin dealer; b. Richlands, Va., Sept. 21, 1934; s. George Henry and Rachael Elizabeth (Ray) J.; student public schs., Richlands; m. Vicki Ann Coleman Hyer, Jan. 30, 1981; children by previous marriage—Carlotta Bernard, Quinton Bennett, Carmellia Loyd; stepchildren—Brian Hyer, Keith Hyer. Apprentice, Sunshine Biscuit Co., Dayton, Ohio, 1954-55; with Nat. Cash Register Co., Dayton, 1955-65; owner, operator Cline's Rare Coins, Dayton, 1955—; lectr. numismatics Wilberforce Coll. Cedarville Coll. Mem. Am. Numismatic Assn. (life), Blue Ridge Numismatic Assn. (life), Penn-Ohio Gt. Eastern Numismatic Assn. (life), So. Calif. Numismatists, Tex. State Numismatists, Mich. State Numismatists, Central States Numismatists, Fla. United Numismatists. Republican. Mem. Brethren Ch. Club: Green County Coin, Penn-Ohio Coin, Inc. (v.p.). Author: Standing Liberty Quarters, 1976; contbr. articles to profl. publs. Office: 4421 Salem Ave Dayton OH 45416

CLINE, LINDA BLAIR, accountant; b. Nashville, Nov. 1, 1950; d. Frank Williamson and Mary Elizabeth (Hayes) Blair; m. William Chambers Cline, July 3, 1971; children: Polly, Sarah, William, Blair. AB, Duke U., 1971; MA, George Peabody Coll., 1972; M of Mgmt., Northwestern U., 1978. CPA, Ill. Sr. acct. Touche Ross & Co., Chgo., 1978-80; prin. Linda B. Cline, CPA, Glencoe, Ill., 1980—. Treas., bd. dirs. Nat. Lekotek Ctr., Evanston, Ill., 1981—; active Duke U. Alumni Adv. Com., Durham, N.C., 1979—, Jr. League of Chgo., 1972—. Mem. Am. Inst. CPA's, Ill. CPA Soc., Northwestern U. Profl. Women's Assn. Episcopalian. Home and Office: 536 Dundee Rd Glencoe IL 60022

CLINE, RICHARD GORDON, business executive; b. Chgo., Feb. 17, 1935; s. William R. and Katherine A. (Bothwell) C.; m. Carole J. Costello, Dec. 28, 1957; children: Patricia, Linda, Richard, Jeffrey. BS, U. Ill., 1957. With Jewel Cos., Inc., Chgo., 1963-85; pres. Osco Drug, Inc. subs., 1970-79, sr. exec. v.p., 1979, vice chmn., 1979, pres., 1980-84, chmn., pres., chief. exec. officer, 1984-85; pres. NICOR Inc., Naperville, Ill., 1985-86, chmn., pres., chief exec. officer, 1986—, also bd. dirs.; chmn., bd. dirs. No. Ill. Gas and subs.; bd. dirs. IC Industries Inc., Pet Inc. and Hussmann Corp. Trustee Rush-Presbyn.-St. Luke's Med. Ctr.; gov. and former chmn. bd. Cen. DuPage Hosp.; bd. dirs. U. Ill. Found.; gov. Ill. Council on Econ. Edn.; mem. Northwestern Univ. Assocs., Chiagoland United Way/Crusade of Mercy. Mem. Am. Gas Assn. Clubs: Econ., Chgo., Chgo. Golf, Comml., Commonwealth (Chgo.). Office: NICOR Inc 1700 W Ferry Rd Naperville IL 60566

CLINE, WALTER QUAINE, geologist, oil producer, real estate developer and appraiser; b. Mount Vernon, Ill., May 19, 1926; s. Orval Kellous and Vandora (Wheeler) C.; m. Frances Shaw (dec. 1974); children—Cynthia, John, Robert. B.A., Evansville Coll., 1952; postgrad. U. Ga., 1972, U. Colo., 1972, U. Ind., 1974. Scout-geologist Stanford Oil Co., Evansville, Ind., 1952-53; area geologist Cities Service Oil, Midland, Tex., 1953-58, exploration geologist, supr. oil drilling and exploration, Evansville, Ind., 1958—; pres. Kellous Corp., Evansville, 1980—. Contbr. articles to profl. publs. Served as cpl. U.S. Army, 1944-46, Res., 1946-60. Mem. Am. Inst. Profl. Geologists, Am. Assn. Petroleum Geologists, Ill. Geol. Soc., Ind.-Ky. Geol. Soc., Ind. Bd. Realtors, VFW, Am. Legion. Lodge: Eagles. Avocations: swimming, camping, reading. nature study. Office: Kellous Corp Box 363 Evansville IN 47703

CLINGAN, GREGORY LEE, insurance agent, real estate broker; b. Danville, Ill., Oct. 8, 1959; s. James Leroy and Thelma (Tucker) C.; m. Pamela Dawn Perry, Nov. 5, 1983; 1 child, Amanda. Ins. agent Clingan Ins., Covington, Ind., 1979—; auctioneer Clingan Auction and Real Estate, Covington, 1981—, real estate broker, 1984—. Named one of Outstanding Young Men in Am. Mem. Ind. Auctioneers Assn. Democrat. Lodge: Lions (pres. Covington 1984). Home: 421 Johnson Covington IN 47932 Office: Clingan Agy 121 Elm Dr Covington IN 47932

CLINGAN, MELVIN HALL, lumber exec., publisher; b. Atchison, Kans., July 12, 1929; s. Frank E. and Hazel Ellen (Hall) C.; B.S. in Bus. (Summerfield scholar), U. Kans., 1951; m. Athelia Roberta Sweet, Apr. 7, 1956; children—Sandra, Scott, Kimberly, Marcia. Pres., Holiday Homes, Inc. and Clingan Land Co., Shawnee Mission, Kans., 1956—; former pub. Johnson County Herald, Gardner News, De Soto News, Spring Hill New Era; dir. R.L. Sweet Lumber Co. and subs., Kansas City, Kans., 1959—, exec. v.p., 1973-80, pres., 1981—. Vice pres. Westwood View Sch. Bd., 1965-68; Republican congl. dist. chmn., mem. state exec. com., 1966-72; bd. dirs. Johnson County Community Coll. Found., 1973-82. Served with USAF, 1951-55. Mem. Home Builders Assn. Greater Kansas City (past pres.), Home Builders Assn. Kans. (past pres.), Nat. Assn. Home Builders (nat. life dir.), Mission C. of C. (pres. 1971), Sigma Nu (grand officer 1961-68, ednl. found. 1980-85 , trustee 1982-85), Omicron Delta Kappa, Beta Gamma Sigma, Republican. Mem. Disciples of Christ Ch. Club: Mission Hills Country. Home: 5345 Mission Woods Rd Shawnee Mission KS 66205 Office: 4500 Roe Blvd Kansas City KS 66103

CLINGERMAN, THOMAS BURDETTE, avionics manufacturing company executive; b. Beech Grove, Ind., Feb. 26, 1948; s. Cleo Burdette and Ruth Veronica (Beach) C.; m. Karen Marie Slanika, May 22, 1976; 1 child, Michael Thomas. BA, Va. Mil. Inst., 1970; MPA, Boise State U., 1980; postgrad. in mgmt. USAF Air Command and Staff Coll., 1975-79. Commd. 2d lt. U.S. Air Force, 1970; advanced through grades to maj., 1984; assigned Del Rio, Tex., 1970-74, Nellis AFB, Las Vegas, 1974-76, Mt. Home, Idaho, 1977-80; resign, 1980; with USAFR, 1980—; indsl. engr. Rockwell Internat. Collins div., Cedar Rapids, Iowa, 1980, mgr. process engring., 1980-82, mgr. flight control, 1983, program mgr. Peoples Republic of China, 1984, program mgr. railroad system, 1984—; advisor CAP, 1982—. Mem. Robotics Internat. (sr.), Exptl. Aircraft Assn., Iowa Sled Dog Drivers (pres. 1982—). Republican. Roman Catholic. Avocations: flying, scuba diving, sailing, skiing, dog sled racing. Home: RR 1 Box 269C Solon IA 52333 Office: Rockwell Internat Collins Div 400 Collins Rd 108-157 Cedar Rapids IA 52498

CLINKSCALES, J(AMES) RANDALL, lawyer; b. Hillsboro, Tex., Mar. 12, 1954; s. Ronald Orr Clinkscales and Vallee (Wafer) Hefner; m. Barbara Jean Stucky, Sept. 28, 1980; 1 child, Joshua Lane. BS in Polit. Sci., Howard Payne U., 1976; JD, Washburn U., 1980. Bar: Kans. 1980, U.S. Dist. Ct. Kans. 1980. Assoc. Hiatt & Carpenter, Topeka, 1980-83, Ken Havner, Hays, Kans., 1983-85; sole practice Hays, 1985—. Mem. ABA, Kans. Bar Assn., Ellis County Bar Assn. Lodge: Kiwanis (pres. elect 1986). Home: 323 W 32d Hays KS 67601 Office: 2604 General Hays Rd Hays KS 67601

CLINTON, FRANK LEE, mayor; b. Chgo., July 29, 1937; s. Francis Ring and Eva (Strohl) C.; BS, U. Ill., 1960. Credit analyst Marshall Field & Co., Chgo., 1961-62; with trust dept. Edgar County Nat. Bank, Paris, Ill., 1962-64; purchasing mgr., accountant Bastian-Blessing Co., Chgo., 1965-71; production mgr. McCann Engring. & Mfg. Co., Glendale, Calif., 1971-74; exec. v.p. Paris (Ill.) C. of C., 1975-80; pres. Charleston (Ill.) Area C. of C., 1980-81; mayor City of Paris, 1983—; sports announcer Paris Broadcasting Corp., 1953—. Bd. dirs. Edgar County Fair Assn., 1966-78, v.p., 1970-73; bd. dirs. Covered Bridge council Girl Scouts U.S., 1977-86; pres. Young Republican Orgn., Edgar County, 1964. Served to sgt. Army N.G., 1960-66. Execs. Presbyterian. Lodges: Masons, Rotary (bd. dirs. 1976-80). Home: 1002 S Main St Paris IL 61944

CLINTON, WILLIAM CHRISTOPHER, physicist; b. Dubuque, Iowa, Aug. 19, 1937; s. William Milford and Mary Avo (Thorpe) C.; B.A., William Jewell Coll., 1966; student Ill. Inst. Tech., 1967, M.I.T., 1968; m. Lisa DeWandel, July 8, 1978. Med. lab. technician U.S. Air Force, Aeromed. Research Lab., Holloman AFB, N.Mex., 1961-65; physicist U.S. Bur. Mines, Rolla (Mo.) Metallurgy Research Center, 1966—. Chmn., Rolla Combined Fed. Campaign, 1976-78, 83-84 ; bd. dirs. Rolla Civic Theatre, 1976-78, Alamogordo (N.Mex.) Players Workshop, 1963-65, Bus. Opportunities for Mo. Blind, 1982-86 ; bd. govs. Eye Research Found. Mo., 1979—. Mem. Microbeam Analysis Soc., Internat. Metallographic Soc., AAAS, Sigma Xi. Club: Rolla Lions (treas. 1971-77, sec. 1977-83, dist. gov. 1979-80). Contbr. articles to tech. jours. Home: PO Box 1125 Rolla MO 65401 Office: Bur Mines PO Box 280 Rolla MO 65401

CLOKE, THOMAS HENRY, mech. engr.; b. Chgo., Oct. 17, 1921; s. Thomas Henry and Lillian Clara (Krez) C.; B.S., U. Ill., 1943; m. Frances Irene Fox, Dec. 19, 1942; children—Deborah Cloke Kalbow, Thomas Myron. With Shaw, Naess & Murphy and Naess & Murphy, architects, Chgo., 1946-62, chief mech. engr., 1954-62; chief engr. Jensen & Halstead, architects, Chgo., 1962-64; prin. Neiler, Rich & Bladen, Inc., cons. engrs., Chgo., 1964-68, Gritschke & Cloke, Inc., cons. engrs., Chgo., 1968-79, Loebl Schlossman & Hackl, architects, Chgo., 1979—. Cons. engr. U.S. Air Force in Japan, 1963. Mem. Glen Ellyn (Ill.) Park Bd., 1957-60, pres., 1961; mem. Recreation Commn., Village of Glen Ellyn, 1965-74, chmn., 1974-75, mem. Bldg. Bd. of Appeal, 1973-77. Served to capt. AUS, 1943-46. Decorated Bronze Star. Registered profl. engr., Ill. Fellow ASHRAE (life mem., research promotion com. 1969-75, research and tech. com. 1976-77, chmn. 1977-78, tech. council 1980-83, long range planning com., Disting. Service award); mem. Air Pollution Control Assn., Nat. Fire Protection Assn., Am. Mgmt. Assn., Soc. Am. Mil. Engrs., Am. Gas Assn., U.S. Power Squadron, U.S. Naval Inst., U. Ill. Alumni Assn., Theta Chi. Home: 950 Roslyn Rd Glen Ellyn IL 60137 Office: 130 E Randolph Chicago IL 60601

CLONINGER, FRANKLIN DALE, plant breeder, research director; b. Hartshorn, Mo., Sept. 25, 1938; s. George Franklin and Patsy Jane (Derryberry) C.; B.S., U. Mo., Columbia, 1960, M.S., 1968, Ph.D., 1973; m. Marion Ruth Haas, May 19, 1962; children—Carla Sue, Mary Jane. Materials insp. Mo. Hwy. Dept., Kirkwood, 1964-65; research asst. P.A.G. Seeds Co., Carrollton, Mo., 1965-66; grad. asst. in agronomy U. Mo., Columbia, 1966-68, research specialist, 1968-74; plant breeder Golden Harvest, J.C. Robinson Seed Co., Waterloo, Nebr., 1974-84, dir. research and devel., 1985—. Elder Faith Christian Ch., Omaha, 1983—. Served with AUS, 1960-63. Mem. Am. Soc. Agronomy, Crop Sci. Soc. Am., Genetics Assn. Am., Can. Seed Growers Assn. Plant Breeder, Sigma Xi, Gamma Sigma Delta. Mem. Disciples of Christ Ch. Home: 602 Westridge St Elkhorn NE 68022 Office: JC Robinson Seed Co Waterloo NE 68069

CLOONAN, JAMES BRIAN, investment executive; b. Chgo., Jan. 28, 1931; s. Bernard V. and Lauretta D. (Maloney) C.; student Northwestern U., 1949-52, B.A., 1957, Ph.D., 1972; M.B.A., U. Chgo., 1964; m. Edythe Adrianne Ratner, Mar. 26, 1970; children—Michele, Christine, Mia; stepchildren—Carrie Madorin, Harry Madorin. Prof., Sch. Bus., Loyola U., Chgo., 1966-71; pres. Quantitative Decision Systems, Inc., Chgo., 1972-73; chmn. bd. Heinold Securities, Inc., Chgo., 1974-77; prof. Grad. Sch. Bus., DePaul U., Chgo., 1978-82; chmn. Investment Info. Services, 1981-86; pres., founder Am. Assn. Individual Investors, 1979—; pres. Mktg. Systems Internat., Inc., 1985—, Analytics Systems, Inc., 1987—. Served with U.S. Army, 1951-54. Mem. Ops. Research Soc., Inst. for Mgmt. Sci., Am. Fin. Assn., Am. Mktg. Assn. Author: Estimates of the Impact of Sign and Billboard Removal Under the Highway Beautification Act of 1965, 1966; Stock Options - The Application of Decision Theory to Basic and Advanced Strategies, 1973; An Introduction to Decision-Making for the Individual Investor, 1980; Expanding Your Investment Horizons, 1983. Home: 950 N Michigan Ave Chicago IL 60611 Office: 612 N Michigan Ave Chicago IL 60611

CLOSE, ELIZABETH SCHEU, architect; b. Vienna, Austria, June 4, 1912; came to U.S., 1932, naturalized, 1938; d. Gustav and Helene (Riesz) C.; m. Winston A. Close, 1938; children—Anne Miriam (Mrs. Milton Ulmer), Roy Michel, Robert Arthur. Student, Technische Hochschule, Vienna, 1931-32; B.Arch., Mass. Inst. Tech., 1934, M.Arch., 1935. Draftsman Oscar Stonorov, Architect, Phila., 1935-36; designer Magney & Tusler, Mpls., 1936-38; partner, architect Elizabeth and Winston Close (changed to Close Assos., Inc., 1969), Mpls., 1938—; instr. Mpls. Sch. Art, 1936-37; instr. design U. Minn. Sch. Architecture, 1938-39. Prin. works include Garden City Devel, Brooklyn Center, Minn., 1957, Duff House, variety structures Met. Med. Center Complex, 1960-75, Golden Age Homes, 1960, Peavey Tech. Center, Chaska, Minn., 1970, Gray Freshwater Biol. Inst., Orono, Minn., 1974, U. Minn. Music Bldg., Mpls., 1985. Bd. dirs. Civic Orch. Mpls., 1951-68; bd. dirs. Minn. Opera Co.; past pres. New Friends Chamber Music; mem. Commn. on Minn.'s Future. Recipient Honor award Pub. Housing Adminstrn., 1964; hon. mention F.D. Roosevelt Meml. competion, 1960; named Outstanding Woman of Yr., YWCA, 1983. Fellow AIA (dir. Mpls. chpt. 1964-69, jury of Fellows 1986-87); mem. Minn. Soc. Architects (pres., Honor award 1975), Minn. Hist. Soc. (jury bldg. competition 1986). Home: 1588 Fulham St Saint Paul MN 55108 Office: Close Assocs Inc 3101 E Franklin Ave Minneapolis MN 55406

CLOSE, KEVIN JOHN, quality assurance engineer; b. Chgo., Feb. 8, 1937; s. John Joseph and Mildred Jean (Thurn) C.; m. Christine Janeteas, May 5, 1962; 1 child, Carla. BEE, Am. Inst. Engring., 1960. Registered profl. engr., Ill.; cert. quality and reliability engr. With Knight Electronics, Maywood, Ill., 1960-66, successively quality mgr., prodn. mgr. and asst. v.p. and gen. mgr.; with Advance Transformer, Chgo., 1966—, successively mgr. quality control and mgr. engring., now dir. quality assurance; instr. North Park Coll., Chgo. Author: Vendor Quality Handbook, 1985; also author several manuals and papers in field. Mem. adv. bd. Chgo. Commons Tech. Inst., 1984—; mem. sch. bd. St. Louise de Marrilac, La Grange Park, Ill., 1982-85; pres. United Way Brookfield, 1980-85; trustee Village of Brookfield, Ill.; bd. dirs. Brookfield Library, 1981-83. Served with USMC, 1954-57. Named Outstanding Jaycee Wis. State Jaycees, 1967. Fellow Am. Soc. Quality Control (chmn. by laws com. 1980—, sr., instr.); mem. Internat. Assn. Quality Circles (pres. 1984—, regional dir.), Monroe Jaycees. Roman Catholic. Lodge: Kiwanis (pres. Brookfield 1980-81). Home: 3628 Prairie Brookfield IL 60513 Office: Advance Transformer Co 2950 N Western Ave Chicago IL 60618

CLOSEN, MICHAEL LEE, law educator, lawyer; b. Peoria, Ill., Jan. 25, 1949; s. Stanley Paul and Dorothy Mae (Kendall) C.; B.S., Bradley U., 1971, M.A., 1971; J.D., U. Ill., 1974. Bar: Ill. 1974. Instr. U. Ill., Champaign, 1974; jud. clk. Ill. Appellate Ct., Springfield, 1974-76, 77-78; asst. states atty. Cook County, Chgo., 1978; prof. law John Marshall Law Sch., Chgo., 1976—vis. prof. No. Ill. U., 1985-86; reporter Ill. Jud. Conf., Chgo., 1981—; arbitrator Am. Arbitration Assn., Chgo., 1981—; lectr. Ill. Inst. Continuing Legal Edn., Chgo., 1981—. Author casebook Agency, Employment and Partnership Law, 1984, (with others) Contracts, 1984; co-author: The Shopping Bag: Portable Art, 1986; contbr. articles to profl. jours. Recipient Service award Am. Arbitration Assn. 1984; named one of Outstanding Young Men in Am., 1981. Mem. ABA, Ill. Bar Assn., Appellate Lawyers Assn. Home: 1247 N State #204 Chicago IL 60610 Office: John Marshall Law Sch 315 S Plymouth Ct Chicago IL 60604

CLOUD, JACK LESLIE, realtor, publisher; b. Fremont, Ohio, Mar. 15, 1925; s. Wesley James and Mildred Elizabeth (Miller) C.; grad. Walsh Coll. Acctg., 1948; m. Janet Sorg, Apr. 1, 1944; children—Jack Leslie, Charles Robert. V.p. Nat. Lithograph Co., Detroit, 1946-57; sales mgr. Shelby Lithograph Co., Detroit, 1957-62; v.p. Calvert Lithograph Co., Detroit, 1962-70; with Litho-Graphics, Detroit, 1970-75; with Odyssey Internat. Gallery, Livonia, Mich., 1975-79, pres., chmn. bd. dirs., 1975-80; with Candlelite Inc., Birmingham, Mich., 1977-79, pres., chmn. bd. dirs., 1977-80; real estate broker, mgr. Weir, Manuel, Snyder & Ranke, Troy, Mich., 1980—. Served with AUS, 1943-46. Mem. Rockport Art Assn., Internat. Platform Assn., Am. Printing History Assn., U. Mich. Artist Guild. Espicopalian (sr. warden 1977-78, trustee endowment trust 1979—). Clubs: Elks (chmn. bd. trustees 1966-67), Detroit Athletic. Home: 4253 Brandywyne Dr Troy MI 48098 Office: 4700 Rochester Rd Troy MI 48098

CLOUD, STEPHEN REED, bearing and transmission company executive, state legislator; b. Kansas City, Kans., Mar. 11, 1949; s. Forrest L. and Bonnie L. (Simpson) C.; m. Barbara Anne Verron, Aug. 26, 1972; children—Matthew Brian, Kevin Michael, Jeffrey David. B.S., U. Kans., 1971. Vol., VISTA, 1971-72; with Indsl. Bearing and Transmission Co., Inc., Merriam, Kans., 1972—, corp. v.p., 1977-86, pres., chief exec. officer, 1986—; mem. Kans. Ho. of Reps., 1980-86. Bd. dirs. Turner House, Inc., 1972—; chmn. Johnson County Planning Commn., 1978-81. Named Lambda Chi Alpha of Yr., 1971; recipient Johnson County Service award Johnson County Bd. Commrs., 1980. Mem. Delta Sigma Pi. Republican. Episcopalian. Office: IBT Inc 9400 W 55th St Merriam KS 66203

CLOUGH, DAVID WILLIAM, molecular biologist; b. Schenectady, N.Y., Dec. 27, 1952; s. David William and Constance Marie (Patnaude) C.; m. Jane M. Holmblad, June 15, 1974 (div. June 1983); Diane M. Powell, Jan. 28, 1985; children: Rebecca Ruth. BS, U. Ariz., 1974; PhD, Med. Coll. Wis., 1979. Fellow Harvard Med. Sch., Boston, 1979-81; instr. U. Ill. Coll. Medicine, Chgo., 1981-83, research asst. prof., 1983-87; asst. prof. cell biology and anatomy Northwestern U. Med. Sch., Chgo., 1987—. Reviewer and contbr. profl. jours. Named Basil O'Connor scholar Nat. Found. March of Dimes, 1986-88. Mem. Am. Soc. Microbiology, AAAS. Avocation: sports. Office: Northwestern U Med Sch 303 E Superior St Chicago IL 60611

CLOUSE, JOHN DANIEL, lawyer; b. Evansville, Ind., Sept. 4, 1925; s. Frank Paul and Anna Lucille (Frank) C.; m. Georgia L. Ross, Dec. 7, 1978; 1 child, George Chauncey. AB, U. Evansville, 1950; JD, Ind. U., 1952. Bar: Ind. 1952, U.S. Supreme Ct. 1962, U.S. Ct. Appeals (7th cir.) 1965. Assoc. firm James D. Lopp, Evansville, 1952-56; pvt. practice law, Evansville, 1956—; guest editorialist Viewpoint, Evansville Courier, 1978-86, Evansville Press, 1986—, Focus, Radio Sta. WGBF, 1978-84; 2d asst. city atty. Evansville, 1954-55; mem. appellate rules sub-com. Ind. Supreme Ct. Com. on Rules of Practice and Procedure, 1980. Pres. Civil Service Commn. of Evansville Police Dept., 1961-62, Ind. War Memls. Com., 1963-69; mem. jud. nominating com. Vanderburgh County, Ind., 1976-80. Served with inf. U.S. Army, 1943-46. Decorated Bronze Star. Fellow Ind. Bar Found.; mem. Evansville Bar Assn. (v.p. 1972), Ind. Bar Assn., Selden Soc., Pi Gamma Mu. Republican. Methodist. Club: Travelers Century (Los Angeles). Home: 819 S Hebron Ave Evansville IN 47715 Office: 1010 Hulman Bldg Evansville IN 47708

CLOUTEN, NEVILLE HENRY, architecture educator; b. Toronto, New South Wales, Australia, Feb. 10, 1940; came to U.S., 1980; s. Herbert and Pearl (Hawkins) C. BArch, U. Sydney, Australia, 1962; MArch, Ohio State U., 1966; PhD, Edinburgh U., Scotland, 1968. Registered architect, Australia. Architect Gösta Åbergh Sar, Stockholm, 1963-64; researcher Edinburgh U., 1966-68; lectr. architecture U. Newcastle, Australia, 1969-70, sr. lectr., 1971-80; pvt. practice architecture Newcastle, 1969-80; prof., chmn. dept. architecture, cons. Andrews U., Berrien Springs, Mich., 1980—; researcher Sydney Opera House, 1962-63. Contbr. articles on architecture to profl. jours., 1967—. Recipient Research award Australian Inst. Aboriginal Studies, 1973, 74, 75. Fellow Royal Australian Inst. Architects; mem. Architect Accreditation Council Australia, Royal Inst. Brit. Architects. Avocations: travel, photography. Home: 8695 Maplewood Dr Berrien Springs MI 49103 Office: Andrews U Dept Architecure Berrien Springs MI 49104

CLOW, DONALD SPENCER, SR., advertising agency executive; b. Milw., Nov. 29, 1933; s. John Cecil and Rose (Preisinger) C.; m. Peggy Ann Littleton, July 1, 1955; children: Diana, Dale, Donald Jr., Dean, Douglas. Grad. high sch., Milw. Media clk. Cramer-Krasselt Co., Milw., 1956-58, media buyer, 1958-64, mgr. media dept., 1964-71, dir. media, 1971-79, v.p., media dir., 1979—. Served as sgt. USAF, 1952-56. Mem. Nat. Retail Hardware Assn. (advt. council 1986-87), Bus. Profl. Advt. Assn. (Milw. chpt.), Milw. Advt. Club (sales mgr. monthly mag. 1971-72). Republican. Roman Catholic. Avocation: golfing. Home: 8543 Avalon Ln Cedarburg WI 53012 Office: The Cramer-Krasselt Co 733 N Van Buren St Milwaukee WI 53202

CLOYD, GEORGE THOMAS, dentist; b. Hattiesburg, Miss., Dec. 14, 1944; s. Carl Franklin and Mary Louise (Craig) C.; m. Victoria Casady, June 16, 1973; children: Benjamin, Ross, Adam. BS, Ind. State U., 1968; DDS, Ind. U., Indpls., 1972. Gen. practice dentistry Clinton, Ind., 1972—; staff dentist Vermillion County Hosp., Clinton, 1972-87; chief dental staff Vermillion Convalescent Ctr., Clinton, 1975-87. V.p. S. Vermillion Sch. Bd., 1980-83; bd. dirs. Clinton Little League, 1985, 86, 87, Kathryn Hamilton Mental Health Ctr., 1986, 87; mem. Vermillion County Hosp. Found., Vermillion County Hosp. planning com., 1985, 86, 87; coach S. Vermillion Youth Baseball, 1982-87. Mem. ADA, Internat. Orthodontic Assn., Am. Orthodontic Soc., Am. Endodontic Soc., Acad. Gen. Dentistry, Mid-E. Soc. Orthodontics for Gen. Practice, Ind. Dental Assn., Chgo. Dental Soc., Western Ind. Dental Assn., Mid East Soc. Orthodontics for Gen. Practitioner, Clinton C. of C., Ducks Unltd. (local pres. 1985—). Democrat. Club: Cen. Ind. Functional Jaw Orthopoedic Study. Home: Rural Rt 2 Grady Ln Clinton IN 47842 Office: State Hwy 163 Clinton IN 47842

CLUKEY, CATHERINE ANN, nurse; b. Cin., Mar. 27, 1954. BS in Biology and Chemistry, Mary Washington Coll., 1976; AD in Nursing cum laude, Raymond Walters Gen. Tech. Coll., 1981; BS in Mgmt., Coll. Mt. St. Joseph, Cin., 1987. Registered nurse. Hemodialysis staff St. Barnabas Dialysis, Pinebrook, N.J., 1975-77, Limited Care Dialysis, Cin., 1977-81; hemodialysis nurse intensive care unit Bethesda Hosp., Inc., Cin., 1981—, continuing edn. instr., 1984-87, basic life support instr., 1985-86. Active Cin. Zoo, 1983-87, Cin Nature Ctr., 1984-87, Sta. WCET-TV, Cin., 1985-87, Milford Children's House, Cin., 1986-87. Mem. Am. Assn. Critical Care Nurses (programs com. Greater Cin. chpt. 1983). Republican. Avocations: gourmet cooking, nature enthusiast. Home: 707 Floral Ave Terrace Park OH 45174 Office: Bethesda Hosp 619 Oak St Cincinnati OH 45206

CLUNE, JERE, sales and marketing executive; b. Drexill Hill, Pa., July 9, 1952; d. Alexander Joseph and Mary Lou (Hammann) C. AA in Gen. Edn., Ricks Coll., Rexburg, Ind., 1975; BA in Broadcasting cum laude, Brigham Young U., 1977, MBA, 1980. Asst. buyer Target Stores Dayton Mo., Mpls., 1980-81; nat. sales mgr., v.p. sales Harvest Maid APS Corp., Mpls., 1981-83; nat. sales mgr. Waterloo (Iowa) Beatrice Corp., 1983-84, 86—, also bd. dirs.; dir. sales Chgo. Beatrice Corp., 1985. Dist. del. Utah Republican Orgn., Provo, 1974; water safety instr. Internat. Red Cross, Provo, 1975-77. Served with USMC, 1971-73. Recipient Presdl. Unit Citation USMC, 1972; recipient Acad. Leadership scholarship Brigham Young U., 1975-77. Mormon. Avocations: youth counseling, water safety. Office: Waterloo Industries Beatrice Corp 300 Ansborough Waterloo IA 50704

CLYBURN, LUTHER LINN, real estate broker; b. Evansville, Ind., May 17, 1942; s. Luther and Robbie (Cobb) C.; children: Lisa Michelle Clyburn Swain, Luther Brent. Grad., Am. Savs. and Loan Inst., 1970; ABA, Pontiac (Mich.) Bus. Inst., 1972; BS, Detroit Coll. Bus., 1972; M of Bus. Mgmt., Cen. Mich. U., 1983. Chief loan officer First Fed. Savs. and Loan Assn. Oakland, Pontiac, 1964-74; assoc. broker Bateman Real Estate Corp., Pontiac, 1975-77; regional rep. United Guaranty Residential Ins., Troy, Mich., 1977-83; sr. account mgr. Investors Mortgage Ins. Co., Boston, 1983-87; real estate broker, appraiser Pontiac, 1977—. Project dir., capt.: (documentary film) Angels of the Sea, 1982 (N.Y. Film Festival award 1983). Capt., comdr. "Noble Odyssey" Tng. Ship, Mt. Clemens, Mich., 1977—; dir., comdr. U.S. Naval Sea Cadet Corps Great Lakes div., Southfield, Mich., 1973—; project dir. Interseas Inc., Pontiac, 1982. Recipient Cert. Appreciation award Southfield Bicentennial Commn., 1976, Letter of Commendation award Sec. of Navy, 1983. Mem. Mich. League Savs. Insts., Mich. Mortgage Bankers Assn., Internat. Ship Masters Assn., Navy League of U.S. Club: Detroit Econs. Home and Office: 9000 Gale Rd Pontiac MI 48054

CLYDE, PAYSON JAMES, civil engineer; b. Columbus, Ohio, Sept. 6, 1930; s. Paul Hibbert and Mildred Rebecca (Smith) C.; B.S. in Civil Engring., Pa. State U., 1952; m. Marilyn Jean Ashley, Nov. 19, 1965; 1 dau. by previous marriage, Alberta Ann Sanders. Sales engr. Armco Drainage & Metal Products, Inc., Detroit, Tucson, 1957-63; exec. sec., dir. engring. Wis. Concrete Pipe Assn., Madison, 1963-66; project engr., customer service engr., safety engr., mgr. marine and indsl. spare parts sales spl. program coordinator Gen. Electric Co., Cin., 1966—, now tech. documentation specialist; expert witness; vocat. sch. counselor. Served with USN, 1952-55. Registered profl. engr., Wis., Ind., Calif., Ohio. Fellow ASCE; mem. Naval Res. Assn., Res. Officers Assn., Navy League. Republican. Roman Catholic. Club: Elks. Author: OSHA and the Safety Engineer, 1977; OSHA and Its Impact, 1978. Home: 11269 Marlette Dr Cincinnati OH 45249 Office: Gen Electric Co Mail Drop-In N-155 Cincinnati OH 45215

CLYMER, JOHN M., finance company executive; b. Indpls., July 8, 1960; s. Richard Marion and Jean (Archibald) C. AB in Religion and Econs., Wabash Coll., 1982. Registered fin. planner. Mktg. rep. Springs Industries, Youngstown, Ohio, 1982-83, Grand Rapids, Mich., 1983-84; sr. mktg. rep. Springs Industries, Columbus, Ohio, 1984-85, Mpls., 1985; fin. cons. Indpls. Fin. Group, 1986—. Author: Escape!, 1981. Youth dir. Hudnut Mayoral Campaign, Indpls., 1975; mem. staff Ford Presdl. Campaign, 1976, Reagan Presdl. Campaign, 1980; Rep. precinct capt., Indpls. Named Eagle Scout, 1973. Mem. Nat. Assn. Life Underwriters, Ind. Assn. Life Underwriters, Econ. Club Indpls., Nat. Assn. Wabash Men (bd. dirs.). Republican. Methodist. Club: Indpls. Athletic. Avocations: politics, writing, charitable fundraising, sports. Office: Indpls Fin Group 400 Marott Ctr 342 Massachusetts Ave Indianapolis IN 46204-2161

CLYNE, JOHN CLAYTON, real estate/financial corporation officer; b. Chgo., Dec. 16, 1946; s. John Clayton and Marilyn Paula (Matt) Clyne-Lee; m. Nancy Ann McCrory, Nov. 27, 1970; children: Jennifer Diane, Heidi Jo. BS, U. Nebr., 1970. Salesman, decorator Matt Furniture Co., Marshalltown, Iowa, 1970-73; tng. specialist Mil. Dept. of Nebr., Lincoln, 1973-80; asst. dir. facilities planning and mgmt. U. Nebr., Lincoln, 1980-82; v.p., property mgr. Am. Charter, Lincoln, 1982—; v.p., gen. mgr. State Realty, Inc., Lincoln, 1982—. Sr. Counselor Cornhusker Boys State, Lincoln, 1975; sr. advisor Explorer Post #1, Lincoln, 1985; loaned exec. United Way of Lincoln, 1983-86; bd. dirs. Downtown Lincoln Assn., 1984—. Mem. Internat. Facilities Mgmt. Assn., Soc. of Coll. and Univ. Planners, Am. Amateur Racquetball Assn. (state bd. dirs. 1986—), Nebr. State Racquetball Assn. (Player of Yr. 1984, Sportsman of Yr. 1984, pres. 1986—). Democrat. Roman Catholic. Lodge: Sertoma (pres. Lincoln Ctr. 1987—). Avocations: racquetball, handball. Home: 6020 Dogwood Dr Lincoln NE 68516 Office: Am Charter Fed 206 S 13th St Lincoln NE 68508

COALE, ROBERT PEERLING, librarian; b. Chgo.; s. Robert Peerling Coale and Rita (Goeppner) Milbourne. BA, U. Chgo., MA, 1964. Dep. chief cataloger Newberry Library, Chgo., 1962-66; librarian Olive-Harvey Coll., Chgo., 1966—; adj. bibliographer for Latin-Am. history Newberry Library, Chgo., 1980—. Sec. Old Masters Soc. Art Inst. Chgo., 1981—. Research grantee Hispanic Found. Library of Congress, 1962. Clubs: Alliance Française (Chgo.), The English-Speaking Union; Victorian Soc. (Phila.). Home: 1150 N LaSalle Chicago IL 60610 Office: Olive-Harvey Coll Library 10001 S Woodlawn Chicago IL 60610

COASH, RONALD JAMES, electrical engineer; b. Clifton, Kans., May 15, 1939; s. Russell Francis and Hazel Marie (Scouten) C.; B.S., Kans. State U., 1972, A.M.; m. Linda Ann Dieker, June 26, 1965; children—Russell E., Jennifer M., Christopher J. Engring. technician environ. research Kans. State U., 1968-70; chief engr. Raincat Engring. Co., Greeley, Colo., 1974, Reinke Mfg. Co., Deshler, Nebr., 1974-82; with Notifrer Corp., Lincoln, Nebr., 1982—; applications, service and mfg. engr. IC/MIDWEC, 1978. Served with USAR, 1961-63. Mem. Am. Soc. Agrl. Engrs., Internat. Brotherhood Elec. Workers, Am. Legion. Roman Catholic. Club: K.C. Author handbook, articles in field. Patentee in field. Home: 4311 Antelope Creek Rd Lincoln NE 68506 Office: 6050 N 56th St Lincoln NE 68507

COATES, GLENN RICHARD, lawyer; b. Thorp, Wis., June 8, 1923; s. Richard and Alma (Borck) C.; m. Dolores Milburn, June 24, 1944; children—Richard Ward, Cristie Joan. Student, Milw. State Tchrs. Coll., 1940-42, N.M.A. and M.A., 1943-44; LL.B., U. Wis., 1948, S.J.D., 1953. Bar: Wis. 1949. Atty. Mil. Sea Transp. Service, Dept. Navy, 1951-52; pvt. practice law Racine, Wis., 1952—; dir. Pioneer Savs. & Loan Assn., Racine Federated, Inc.; lectr. U. Wis. Law Sch., 1955-56. Author: Chattel Secured Farm Credit, 1953; contbr. articles to profl. publs. Chmn. bd. St. Luke's Meml. Hosp., 1973-76; pres. Racine Area United Way, 1979-81; mem. bd. dirs. Racine County Area Found., 1983—; bd. curators State Hist. Soc. Wisc., 1986—. Served with AUS, 1943-46. Mem. State Bar Wis. (bd. govs. 1969-74, chmn. bd. 1973-74), Wis. Jud. Council (chmn. 1969-72), ABA, Am. Law Inst., Order of Coif. Methodist (chmn. fin. com. 1961-67). Club: Racine Country. Lodge: Masons. Home: 2830 Michigan Blvd Racine WI 53402 Office: 840 Lake Ave Racine WI 53403

COATES, ROGER SPENCER, psychologist; b. Ann Arbor, Mich., June 26, 1955; s. Randall Fitzgerald and Pauline Rosanna (Rogers) C.; B.A., Western Mich. U., 1976, M.A., 1978, Ed.S., 1982. Psychologist, Van Buren Intermediate Sch. Dist., Lawrence, Mich., 1978—; resource person Schoocraft Schs., Western Mich. U., 1976-78. Mem. Nat. Assn. Sch. Psychologists, Mich. Assn. Sch. Psychologists, Assn. Behavior Analysis. Office: 701 S Paw Paw St Lawrence MI 49064

COATS, DANIEL R., congressman; b. Jackson, Mich., May 16, 1943; s. Edward R. and Vera E. C.; m. Marcia Crawford, Sept. 4, 1965; children: Laura, Lisa, Andrew. B.A., Wheaton (Ill.) Coll., 1965; J.D. cum laude, Ind. U., 1971. Bar: Ind. 1972. Mem. 97th-100th Congresses from 4th Dist. Ind., Washington, 1981—; Dist. rep. U.S. Congressman Dan Quayle, 1976-80. Pres., Big Bros./Big Sisters, Ft. Wayne, Ind. Served with U.S. Army, 1966-68. Office: House of Reps 1417 Longworth House Office Bldg Washington DC 20515

COATS, STEPHEN E., gynecologist/obstetrician; b. Winchester, Ind., Mar. 24, 1948; s. Charles Edward and Martha Voss (Grove) C.; m. Margaret Louise Chmielowiec, Jan. 31, 1971; children: Alison, David, Aaron, Glenn. AB, Ind. U., Bloomington, 1970; MD, Ind. U., Indpls., 1974. Intern Meml. Hosp. of South Bend, 1974-75; residency Meth. Hosp., Indpls., 1975-78; practice medicine specializing in ob-gyn Ft. Wayne, Ind., 1978—; bd. dirs. Three Rivers Neighborhood Health Services, Ft. Wayne, 1982—. Fellow Am. Coll. Obstetricians and Gynecologists. Home: 12202 Sylvan Meadows Dr Fort Wayne IN 46804 Office: 2828 Fairfield Ave Fort Wayne IN 46807

COBB, CAROLYN ANN, communications consultant; b. St. Louis, Feb. 21, 1950; d. Vincent Atlee and Margaret Elizabeth (Ottinger) Knopp; m. Richard Joseph Cobb, Aug. 7, 1976; children: Richard Joseph, Cassandra Ann. BA, Harris Tchrs. Coll., 1973; MA, Webster Coll., 1975. Tchr. St. Louis Pub. Schs. 1973-74; programmer Gen. Am. Life, 1974-75, Mercantile Trust Co., N.A. 1975-78; programmer/analyst Mo. Pacific R.R. 1979-81; data base adminstr. staff specialist Southwestern Bell, St. Louis 1981-84; sr. cons. CAP Gemini Am., 1984-87; sr. cons. Codd & Date Cons. Group, 1987—. Editor: Fundamentals of Data Communications and Networking. Fin. chmn., mem. various coms. United Ch. of Christ, Oakville, Mo., also softball and volleyball coach, mem. choir and adult fellowship; youth group leader Grace United Ch. of Christ; adviser Drop-In Ctr.; data processing adviser Explorer Post, Boy Scouts Am. Mem. Assn. Systems Mgmt., Data Processing Mgmt. Assn., Assn. Women in Computing (charter), Heart of Am. DB2 Users Group (founder), St. Louis DB2 Users Group (participant DB2 forum Dallas), Kappa Delta Pi. Republican. Home: 6520 Galewood Ct Saint Louis MO 63129 Office: 1034 S Brentwood Blvd Suite1750 Saint Louis MO 63117

COBB, GREGORY JOSEPH, convenience store executive; b. Indpls., Dec. 27, 1956; s. Glenn Edward and Mary Ann (Bernhauer) C.; m. Sheila Hyde, May 19, 1979; 1 child, Jennifer. BS in Mktg., U. Evansville, 1979. Supr. Crystal Flash, Indpls., 1979-83, retail ops. mgr., gen. mgr., 1983-86, v.p. ops., 1986—. Mem. Ind. Assn. Convenience Stores (1st v.p. 1984-85, pres. 1985-86, treas. 1986—). Roman Catholic. Home: 970 Tillson Zionsville IN 46077 Office: Crystal Flash Petroleum PO Box 684 Indianapolis IN 46206

COBLE, PAUL ISHLER, advertising agency executive; b. Indpls., Mar. 17, 1926; s. Earl and Agnes Elizabeth (Roberts) C.; A.B., Wittenberg U., 1950; postgrad. Case-Western Res. U., 1950-53; m. Marjorie M. Trentanelli, Jan. 27, 1951; children—Jeff, Sarah Anne, Doug. Reporter, Springfield (Ohio) Daily News, 1944; reporter, feature writer Rockford (Ill.) Register-Republic, 1947-48; account exec. Fuller & Smith & Ross, Inc., Cleve., 1949-57; dir. sales promotion McCann Erickson, 1957-63; dir. sales devel. Marschalk Co., 1963-65, v.p., 1965-70, sr. v.p., 1970-73; pres. Coble Group, 1973—; chmn. bd., sec.-treas. Hahn & Coble. Inc., advt., mktg. and pub. relations, 1977—; pub. Islander mag., Hilton Head Island, S.C., 1973-83; asst. prof. advt. W.Va. U., 1982-83. Chief instr. Cleve. Advt. Club Sch., 1961-73. Active fund raising drives for various charitable and youth orgns. Served with AUS, 1944-46. Mem. Sales and Marketing Internat., Assn. Indsl. Advertisers, Cleve. Advt. Club, Newcomen Soc. Clubs: River Oaks Racquet; Sea Pines (Hilton Head Island, S.C.); Cleve. Rotary. Contbr. articles to profl. pubs. Home: 22683 Meadowhill Ln Rocky River OH 44116 Office: Hanna Bldg Cleveland OH 44115

COCCIA, MICHAEL ANTHONY, controller; b. Columbus, Ohio, Nov. 5, 1954; s. Alfred P. and Elia (Blateri) C.; m. Betsy Sheppard, May 27, 1978; children: Jeffrey Michael, Leslie Jane. BSBA, Ohio State U., 1976. CPA, Ohio. Staff acct. Haskins & Sells, Columbus, 1976-78; acct., asst. controller Geupel Constrn. Co., Columbus, 1978-83, controller, 1983—. Mem. Am. Inst. CPA's. Roman Catholic. Avocations: running, golf, landscaping, gardening. Home: 5463 Redwood Rd Columbus OH 43229

COCCO, RONALD ALLEN, architect; b. Lorain, Ohio, May 13, 1951; s. Anthony Daniel and Mary Marie (DeLeonardis) C.; m. Linda Sue Minnich, Jan. 21, 1978; children: Mindi Marie, Christopher Clark. BArch, Kent State U., 1974. Registered architect, Ohio. Draftsman Smith & Clark, Elyria, Ohio, 1973-78; v.p., architect Clark & Post Architects Inc., Lorain, 1978—, also bd. dirs.; cons. Preservation Code City of Lorain, 1985, design rev. bd. chmn., 1987. Columnist newspaper series Church Architecture and Religion in Lorain County, 1986. Active Leadership Lorain County, 1985; trustee Leadership Lorain County Alumni Assn., 1985, Lorain County Hist. Soc., 1986; vol. Lorain County United Way, 1985; mem. Lorain Chamber of Council. Mem. AIA, Nat. Council Archtl. Bds. Democrat. Roman Catholic. Avocations: jogging, swimming. Home: 3317 Tressa Ave Lorain OH 44052 Office: Clark & Post Architects Inc 6125 S Broadway Lorain OH 44053

COCHLAN, STEVEN JAMES, accounting company executive; b. Barberton, Ohio, Mar. 25, 1955; s. James Burkham and Marjorie (Whipple) C. BS in Bus. Administrn., Bowling Green State U., 1977. CPA, Mich. Acct. Price-Waterhouse, Detroit, 1977-82; sr. v.p., chief fin. officer Clark/Bardes Orgn., Inc., Chgo., 1986—. Chmn. Berkley (Mich.)/Huntington Woods Youth Assn. Com., 1979-82; co-founder Big Bros./Sisters program People Listening Understanding and Sharing, Berkley, 1980-82; bd. dirs., treas. Meth. Childrens Home Soc., Detroit, 1982—. Recipient Pres. Club award Bowling Green State U. Alumni. Mem. Nat. Assn. Life Underwriters (Million Dollar Round Table award 1984—, Top of Table award 1986—, Internation Forum award 1986—), Chgo. Assn. Life Underwriters, Am. Inst. CPAs. Republican. Avocations: skiing, deep sea fishing, athletics, football. Home: 1030 N State St Unit 30E Chicago IL 60610 Office: Clark/Bardes Orgn Inc 205 N Michigan Ave Suite 4207 Chicago IL 60601

COCHRAN, DONALD EARL, lawyer; b. Chgo., Sept. 17, 1939; s. John Roy and Ruth (Miller) C.; m. Nancy Helburn Stein, Dec. 29, 1984. B.S. in C.E., Ind. Inst. Tech., 1961; M.S., Mich. State U., 1963; J.D., DePaul U., Chgo., 1972. Registered profl. engr., Ind., Ohio, Mich.; profl. land surveyor, Ind. Engring., surveying cons., 1964—; dir. engring. and legal depts. Suburban Homes Corp., Valparaiso, Ind.; dir. South Haven Waterworks; engr. Drainage Bd. Adams County (Ind.), 1966-68; asst. prof. Ind. Inst. Tech., 1962-68; asst. prof. constrn. tech. Calumet campus Purdue U., Hammond, Ind., 1968-73; owner Cochran Enterprises Co., Gary; pvt. practice law, Gary and Westville, Ind., 1972—; pres., dir. M.V.M.H.P., Inc., Valparaiso. Mem. ASCE, Nat. Soc. Profl. Engrs., Am. Congress on Surveying and Mapping, Ind. Soc. Profl. Land Surveyors (chmn. com. on edn. and registration exams 1966-70, v.p. 1968, pres. 1970 Ill., Ind. bar assns. Home: 576 Fargo Rd Jackson Farm Westville IN 46391 Office: 375 W US #6 South Haven Valparaiso IN 46383

COCHRAN, DWIGHT EDWIN, II, veterinarian; b. East Chicago, Ind., May 18, 1948; s. Dwight Edwin and Laura Eileen (Meyer) C.; student Baylor U., 1966-68; D.V.M., Purdue U., 1973; m. Glenda Kay Boyd, May 19, 1973. Gen. practice veterinary medicine, herd health cons., Boswell, Ind., 1973—; cons. Ind. Dairy Goat Assn. Recipient Leadership award 4-H Clubs, 1978. Mem. Ind. Acad. Veterinary Medicine, Acad. Vet. Cons., Am. Assn. Swine Practitioners, Am. Assn. Sheep, Goat Practitioners, Am. Assn. Bovine Practitioners, Am., Ind., West Central Ind. veterinary med. assns., Am. Registry Cert. Animal Scientists, Am. Soc. Agrl. Cons. Presbyterian. Club: Rotary Internat. (dir. Boswell chpt.). Author: Common Diseases of Dairy Goats, A Guide to Their Prevention, Treatment, and Control For the Herdsman, 1977. Home: 402 E North St Boswell IN 47921 Office: 104 E Main St Boswell IN 47921

COCHRAN, JOHN R., bank executive. Chmn. bd. dirs. NW Bank, Omaha. Office: Norwest Bank Omaha NA 1919 Douglas St Omaha NE 68102 *

COCHRAN, MALCOLM LOWELL, psychologist; b. Crawfordsville, Iowa, Oct. 17, 1941; s. Vaun Wesley and Pearl Ida (Robertson) C.; B.A., Iowa Wesleyan Coll., 1963; M.S., Municipal U. of Omaha, 1965; m. Barbara Sue Stotts, Apr. 17, 1966; children—Teresa Marie, Gary Lowell, Debra Sue, Patricia Diane. Intern sch. psychometrist, Child Study Service Municipal U. of Omaha, 1963-64; research psychometrist, sch. psychologist Glenwood State Hosp.-Sch., Glenwood, Iowa, 1964-68, cons. psychologist, diagnostic and evaluation clinic, 1968-74, dir. employee testing program, 1968-72, dir. psychol. testing center, 1974—, lectr.,-in-service training, child devel., 1968-72. Cubmaster Boy Scouts Am., Glenwood, 1976-77. Served with Army N.G., 1961. Recipient Explorer Scouts Silver Award Boy Scouts Am., 1958; certified sch. psychologist, Iowa; licensed psychologist, Iowa. Fellow Am. Assn. Mental Deficiency. Republican. Methodist. Contbr. articles to profl. jours. Home: 225 W Florence Ave Glenwood IA 51534 Office: 711 S Vine St Glenwood IA 51534

COCHRANE, LADD LOREN, educator; b. Hastings, Nebr., Feb. 19, 1932; s. Alex Joy and Irma Henrietta (Harris) C.; m. Delores Ann DeJarnett, Aug. 14, 1955; children—Carrie Eileen Cochrane Ciecior, Patrick Gaylen. Registered physical therapist Mayo Clin. Sch. Physical Therapy, 1957; B.A., Hastings Coll., 1958; M.A., Western Mich. U., 1963; Ph.D., Ariz. State U., 1972. Chief physical therapist, pub. schs., Kalamazoo, Mich., 1958-63; sci. tchr. East Jr. High Sch., Casper, Wyo., 1963-66, sr. vice prin., 1966-70; coordinator edn. field experiences U. Northern Colo., 1972-77, dir. external degrees, conferances and insts., 1977-80, coordinator edn. field experiences, 1980-82; chmn. edn. dept. Hastings Coll., Nebr., 1982—, tchr. cert. officer, 1982—; staff assoc. Colo. Assn. Sch. Execs., Aurora, 1978-79; cons. in field. Contbr. articles to profl. jours. Served to cpl. USAF, 1950-54. Mem. Nat. Edn. Assn., Schoolmasters Nebr., Assn. Supervision and Curriculum Devel., Assn. Tchr. Educators, Nebr. Council Tchr. Edn. (statutory com. 1982—), Nebr. Post-Secondary Edn. (ad hoc com. 1982—), Nebr. Assn. Colls. of Tchr. Edn. (chief instl. rep. 1982—), Am. Assn. Colls. of Tchr. Edn. (chief instl. rep. 1982—), Phi Delta Kappa. Republican. Presbyterian. Avocations: furniture refinishing; antique collecting; music; athletics. Home: 310 North Shore Dr Hastings NE 68901 Office: Hastings Coll 7th and Turner Hastings NE 68901

COCKLIN, WILLIAM CLINTON, international finance executive, accountant; b. Creston, Iowa, Apr. 21, 1948; s. Raymond Leon and Edyth Patricia (Denison) C.; m. Constance Marie Hart, Oct. 3, 1981; 1 child, Douglas Paul. BS in Fin., Iowa State U., 1970. CPA, Iowa, Minn. Acct. Schmidt & Co., Atlantic, Iowa, 1970-71, 73-75; audit cons. Control Data Corp., Bloomington, Minn., 1975-79, mgr. internal acctg., 1979-82, mgr. internat. fin., 1982—; ptnr. LaCoy & Cocklin Devel., Hayward, Wis., 1983—. Served to capt. U.S. Army, 1971-73. Mem. Am. Inst. CPA's, Minn. Soc. CPA's, Lambda Chi Alpha, Am. Legion. Republican. Methodist. Avocations: outdoor activities. Home: 4108 Poplar Bridge Rd Bloomington MN 55437 Office: Control Data Corp 8100 34th Ave S Bloomington MN 55420

COCKRELL, RONALD SPENCER, scientist, educator; b. Kansas City, Mo., June 26, 1938; s. Robert Spencer and Jean (Hammond) C.; B.S., U. Mo., 1960, B.Med.Sci., 1964; Ph.D., U. Pa., 1968; m. Florence Barbara Hanline, June 7, 1960; children—Richard, Synthia. Asst. prof. biochemistry St. Louis U. Sch. Medicine, 1969-74, assoc. prof., 1974—. Nat. Cancer Inst. grantee, 1970-81 . Mem. Am. Soc. Biol. Chemists. Home: 8560 Webshire Ln Saint Louis MO 63123 Office: St Louis U Sch Medicine Dept Biochemistry 1402 S Grand Blvd Saint Louis MO 63104

COCKRUM, ROBERT BARRETT, lawyer, accountant, educator; b. Chgo., Dec. 14, 1947; s. Barrett William and Mabel Marie (Wheeler) C.; m. Jamie Brereton Burgoon, Aug. 15, 1970; children: Robert B. Jr., Alice Wheeler. BS in Bus., Ind. U., 1970, JD and MBA, 1974. Bar: Ind. 1978; CPA, Ind. 1978. Tax staff Arthur Young & Co., Milw., 1974-77; prof. taxation Ind.-Purdue U., Ft. Wayne, 1977—; pres. R.B. Cockrum, Inc., CPA, Ft. Wayne, 1980—; chair acctg. dept. Ind.-Purdue U., Ft. Wayne, 1980-84. Contbr. articles to profl. jours. Pres. Alpha Sigma Phi Alumni Corp., Bloomington, Ind., 1984—; bd. dirs. Encore, Ft. Wayne, 1981, Make A Wish Found., Ft. Wayne, 1986. Mem. ABA, Ind. Bar Assn., Am. Inst. CPA's, Ind. CPA Soc. Club: The Board. Avocation: coin collecting. Home: 3119 Marias Dr Fort Wayne IN 46815 Office: 3522 Stellhorn Fort Wayne IN 46815

CODDING, PEGGY ANN, music educator, therapist; b. Denver, Mar. 11, 1953; d. James Leland Codding and Betty June (Currence) Danyew. B in Music Edn., Phillips U., 1975; MM, Fla. State U., 1982, PhD, 1985. Cert. music therapist. Lectr. music therapy U. Wis., Eau Claire, 1979-82; research assoc. ctr. music research Fla. State U., Tallahassee, 1985-86; dir. music therapy Ohio U., Athens, 1986—; cons. music therapy, Athens, 1982—. Contbr. articles to profl. jours. Active various orgns. for handicapped. Mem. Nat. Assn. Music Therapy (assembly of delegates 1982, 87), Music Educator's Nat. Conf. Avocations: travel, photography, calligraphy. Office: Ohio U Sch of Music Athens OH 45701

CODDINGTON, THOMAS TUCKER, automotive co. exec.; b. Columbus, Ohio, Jan. 1, 1938; s. Gilbert Harold and Louise (Hazen) C.; B.M.E., Ohio State U., 1961; M.Automotive Engring., Chrysler Inst., Highland Park, Mich., 1964; m. Cecelia Ann McLaughlin, Aug. 31, 1968; children—Maureen Louise, Kevin Ward. With Chrysler Corp., Detroit, 1961—, engring. coordinator, spl. vehicle devel., 1969-74, supr. fuel metering systems, engring. office, 1974-78, product planner, truck produce planning, 1978-80; partner, v.p. engring. Specialize Vehicles, Inc., Troy, Mich., 1980—. Served in USAF, 1961-62. Mem. Soc. Automotive Engrs., Ohio State U. Alumni Assn., SAR. Patentee fuel filter, rollover valve, emergency fuel line closure. Home: 6179 Herbmoor St Troy MI 48098 Office: 2468 Industrial Row Troy MI 48084

CODE, ARTHUR DODD, astrophysics educator; b. Bklyn., Aug. 13, 1933; 4 children. MS, U. Chgo., 1947, PhD, 1950. Asst. Yerkes Obs. U. Chgo., 1946-49; instr. U. Va., Charlottesville, 1950; instr. then asst. prof. astronomy U. Wis., Madison, 1951-56, prof., 1969—; mem. staff Mt. Wilson and Palomar Obs. Calif. Inst. Tech., Pasadena, 1956-58, prof., 1958-69. Recipient Pub. Service award NASA. Office: Univ of Wis Washburn Obs 475 N Charter St Madison WI 53706 *

CODER, CAMERON HAYES, food service executive; b. Indpls., July 2, 1956; s. Terry R. and Geraldine D. (Williams) C. Student in hotel and restaurant mgt., Northwood Inst., 1977. Service technician Food Equipment Parts, Honolulu, 1979; chef Racoon Lake Restaurant, Rockville, Ind., 1979-80; mgr. Greenbriar, Crawfordsville, Ind., 1980-81; chef, mgr. Kendalls Musicale, Indpls., 1981-83; dir. food service Kappa Sigma Frat., Crawfordsville, 1983-86; instr. Atterbury Job Corp, Edinburgh, Ind., 1986—. Club: Gatling Gun (Indpls.) (mgr.). Lodges: Masons, Shriners. Avocations: reading, flying. Home: 1850 N 600 E Danville IN 46122

CODISPOTI, ANTHONY, dentist; b. St. Andrews, Calabria, Italy, Nov. 19, 1946; s. Vincent S. and Maria T. (Magisano) C.; divorced; children: Vincent, Anthony, Jospeh, Maria, Richard, Julie. DDS, Ohio State U. Coll. Dentistry, 1972. Gen. practice dentistry Canton, Ohio, 1974—; v.p. Baron Fin. Corp., North Canton, 1985—; pres. Olympic Leasing Corp., Canton, 1986—; bd. dirs. M.S. Harmon Co., Columbus, 1984—, Martrey Inc., Canton, 1985—. Served to capt. U.S. Army, 1972-74. Fellow Acad. Gen. Dentistry; mem. Am. Dental Soc., Ohio Dental Assn., Stark County Dental Soc. Roman Catholic. Club: Unique, Arrowhead Country (Canton). Home: 2347 Chestnut Hill North Canton OH 44720

CODO, EDWARD ANTHONY, JR., dentist; b. Joliet, Ill., June 16, 1954; s. Edward Anthony Sr. and Jeanne Marie (Donoghue) C. BS, Loyola U., Chgo., 1976; DDS, Marquette U., 1982. Gen. practice dentistry Naperville, Ill., 1985—. MEm. ADA, Ill. Dental Soc., Chgo. Dental Soc. Naperville C. of C. Republican. Roman Catholic. Office: 10 W Martin Suite 212 Naperville IL 60540

CODY, GORDON PATRICK, controller; b. N.Y.C., Dec. 12, 1943; s. Joseph Gordon and Alice Frances (Granahan) C.; m. Maureen Grace Rowell, June 24, 1967 (div.); children: Colleen A., Allison M.; m. Susan E. Kane. BBA, Bernard M. Baruch Coll., 1970. CPA, N.Y. Loan clerk Morgan Guaranty, N.Y.C., 1967-68; sr. auditor Fox & Co., N.Y.C., 1968-72; controller Transgraphics Inc., Carlstadt, N.J., 1972-73; mgr. corp. accounts Dun & Bradstreet Co., N.Y.C., 1973-75; dir. budgets and analysis Tech. Pub., N.Y.C., 1975-85; controller Community Telephone Directory, Kenilworth, Ill., 1985—. Served as sgt. USMCR, 1963-68. Mem. Am. Inst. CPA's, N.Y. State Soc. CPA's (printing and pub. com. 1984-85), Am. Bus. Press (fin. com. 1976-83). Home: 9921 Amanda Ln Algonquin IL 60102 Office: Community Telephone Directories 512 Green Bay Rd Kenilworth IL 60043

COE, CHRISTOPHER LANE, psychiatry researcher; b. N.Y.C., Jan. 4, 1951; s. Samuel Peter and Katherine (Diamond) C.; m. Lyn Bromley, Aug. 25, 1980; children: Ian Andrew, Kieran Michael. B.A., CCNY, 1971; Ph.D., SUNY-Bklyn., 1976. Postdoctoral fellow Stanford U. Med. Sch., Calif., 1977, asst. dir. Stanford Primate Facility, 1977-79, research assoc. dept. psychiatry, 1979-81, asst. prof. dept. psychiatry, 1981-85; assoc. prof. U. Wis., Madison, 1985—, chmn. Harlow Primate Lab., 1985—; outside reviewer NSF, Washington, 1982—. Author: Handbook of Squirrel Monkey Research, 1984; contbr. chpts. to books, 50 articles to profl. jours. Biomed. research grantee NIH, 1983; NIMH grantee, 1983-86. Mem. Internat. Soc. Developmental Psycholgy, Am. Soc. Primatology, Am. Psychology Assn. Home: 5525 Varsity Hill Madison WI 53705 Office: U Wis Dept Psychology Madison WI 53706

COE, JAMES GALE, business educator; b. Ft. Wayne, Jan. 29, 1948; s. Russell Gale and Gladys Cleora (Flickinger) C.; m. Linda Jeanne Chapman, May 29, 1971; children: Sarah Lynn, Matthew James Gale. BS, Ind. U., Bloomington, 1972; MS, Nat. Coll. Edn., Evanston, Ill., 1981. Cert. profl. in Huamn Resources Personnel Accreditation Inst., 1986. Budget analyst International. Harvester, Melrose Park, Ill., 1974-83; asst. prof. bus. Taylor U., Upland, Ind., 1983—; adj. prof. McHenry County Coll., Crystal Lake, Ill., 1983; cons. Nat. Coll. Edn., Evanston, 1982, Lakeview Wesleyan Ch., Marion, Ind., 1985. Editor, adv. bd. Macroeconomics Annual, 1987-88. Coach Eastbrook Soccer Team, Upland, 1986. Faculty Res. grantee Taylor U., 1986-87. Mem. Acad. Mgmt., Ind. Acad. Social Scis., Ind. U. Alumni Assn. (life), Christian Ministries Mgmt. Assn. Mem. Evangelical Free Ch. Lodge: Kiwanis. Avocation: breeding sheep and organic farming. Home: 10390 E 500 S Upland IN 46989 Office: Taylor U 1 Reade St Upland IN 46989

COE, JOHN WILLIAM, management consultant; b. Highland Park, Mich., Oct. 2, 1924; s. C. Leroy and Grace Lamont C.; B.S. in Indsl.-Mech. Engring., U. Mich., 1949; m. Sally Childs, Oct. 24, 1953; children—John Childs, Daniel William. Acct., Charles L. Coe and Assos., 1949; buyer J.L. Hudson Co., Detroit, 1950-58, div. mdse. mgr., 1959-81, v.p., gen. mgr. stores, 1981-83; v.p. retail mktg. Champion Home Builders; dir. Champion Home Builders, I.T.C.O. Inc; pres. Coe and Assocs., 1984—; chmn. Urban Devel. Corp.; bd. dirs. Champion Enterprises, Inc. Dist. chmn. United Found., 1971-72; bd. dirs. Planned Parenthood League, Inc. Served to lt. (j.g.) USNR, 1943-46. Mem Northland-Eastland Mchts. Assn. (dir., past pres.), Mensa, Phi Alumni Assn. Psi Upsilon (dir.). Republican. Anglican. Clubs: Country of Detroit, Econ. Detroit; Pere Marquette Rod and Gun; Rotary (past pres.)(Harper Woods, Mich.). Home: 281 Stephens Rd Grosse Pointe Farms MI 48236 Office: Coe & Assocs -Urban Devel Corp PO Box 36252 Gross Pointe Farms MI 48236

COE, ROBERT WILLIAM, state official.; b. Johnston City, Ill., Feb. 19, 1927; s. Myron John and Lola Oneida (Cothern) C.; B.S., No. Ill. U., 1965, M.S., 1966; m. Dorothy L. Thorson, June 8, 1947; children—Sandra Coe Freedman, Ronald, Cheryl Coe Gray, Dena Coe Carter. Sanitarian, Ill. Dept. Public Health, Carbondale, 1950-54, Rock Island, 1954-64, Aurora, 1964-71, Springfield, 1971-72, exec. adminstr., Chgo., 1972—; prof. mgmt. No. Ill. U. at DeKalb, 1966-67. Asst. scoutmaster Cub Scouts Am., 1957-59; asst. scoutmaster Boy Scouts Am., 1959-61, scoutmaster, 1961-64, dist. commr., 1964-66. Served with AUS, 1945-47. Mem. Ill. Pub. Health Assn., Assn. Ill. Milk, Food and Environmental Sanitarians (sec., treas. 1968-80), AAUP. Author: A Study to Determine the Effect of Appropriations Upon Program Administration, 1966. Editor: Office Management (Clarence Sims), 1965. Home: 206 Boulder Hill Pass Montgomery IL 60538 Office: Ill Dept Public Health 2121 W Taylor Chicago IL 60612

COELHO, RICHARD JOHN, psychologist, research; b. Providence, Jan. 10, 1952; s. Jean Mae (Raybon) C.; m. Denise Patrica Kee, Aug. 2, 1980; children: Richetta Marie, Clifford John. BA, Seton Hall U., 1974, MA, 1976; PhD, Mich. State U., East Lansing, 1983. Rehab. counselor Cath. Community Services, Newark, 1975-76, Clinic Mental Health, Paterson, N.J., 1976-78; sr. research asst. Mich. State U., East Lansing, 1979-84; therapist Professional Psychol. Assocs., East Lansing, 1979-81; evaluation specialist CEI Community Mental Health, Lansing, 1984—; research cons. State Mich., 1980-84; adj. prof. Mich. State U., East Lansing, 1986—, Lansing Community Coll., 1987—; editorial cons. Jour. Applied Rehab. Counseling, 1986—; clin. cons. Mich. Correctional Mental Health Project, 1986—. Author: Quitting Smoking, 1985; contbr. articles to profl. jour.; mem. editorial bd. Jour. Rehab., 1986—. Bd. dirs. Cen. Handicapped Affairs, Lansing, 1984—, Mich. Rehab. Counseling Assn., 1986—. NIMH fellow, 1978-82. Mem. Am. Psychol. Assn., Assn. Black Psychologist, Nat. Rehab. Assn., Am. Assn. Mental Deficiency, Am. Pub. Health Assn. Home: 714 Pkwy Dr Lansing MI 48910 Office: CEI Community Mental Health Bd 838 Louisa St Lansing MI 48910

COELSCH, GERARD CHRISTOPHER, retail executive; b. Plymouth, Mass., Sept. 3, 1943; s. Eugene Gerard and Dolores Eileen (Longhi) C.; m. Joanne Kathryn Epstein, Mar. 21, 1970. B.A. in History and Math., Calif. State U.-Northridge, 1969; postgrad. Pepperdine U., 1979. Store dir. Food Giant Markets, Los Angeles, 1961-70; mktg. mgr. fast foods Southland Corp., Dallas, 1970-80; dir. gen. Visa Group, Monterrey, Mex., 1980-82; sr. v.p. ops., mktg. Lawson Co. div. Dairy Mart, Cuyahoga Falls, Ohio, 1982—; cons. Cadena Comml., Monterrey, 1980-82; dir. Internat. Soap Box Derby, Akron, Ohio, 1982—. Cons. Jr. Achievement Project Bus., Ohio, 1982—, div. chmn., 1983; trustee Amateur Athletic Union Found., 1986—. Republican. Roman Catholic. Home: 7407 McShu Ln Hudson OH 44236 Office: Lawson Co 210 210 Broadway Cuyahoga Falls OH 44222

COFFEE, CHARLENE DAUGHERTY, accountant; b. Athens, Tenn., Feb. 3, 1943; d. Charles McGee and Alma (Millsaps) Daugherty; B.S., U. Tenn., Knoxville, 1964; m. Joe Donald Coffee, Apr. 9, 1966 (div. Mar. 1986). Buyer trainee Castner-Knott Co., Nashville, 1964-66; asst. buyer, buyer Harvey's, Nashville, 1966-67; mdse. control clk., supr. Sears Roebuck, Nashville, 1967-73, acctg. mgmt. trainee, 1973-74, mem. point of sale implementation team So. ter., 1974-77, controller acctg. and processing center, Atlanta, 1977-80, staff asst., field report consolidation, Chgo., 1980-81, staff asst. acctg. policy and procedure, 1981-83, sr. staff asst. acctg. services, 1983-86; hdqtrs. dept. controller, 1986—. Vice-pres. council Ch. of the Living Christ-Lutheran, 1985-86; dist. bd. dirs. Family Care Services Met. Chgo. Mem. DAR (rec. sec. Sarah's Grove chpt. 1985-86), AAUW, Delta Zeta. Home: 405 S Home Ave #102 Oak Park IL 60302 Office: Sears Tower BSC 12-21 Chicago IL 60684

COFFEE, JAMES FREDERICK, retired lawyer; b. Decatur, Ind., Mar. 6, 1918; s. Claude M. and Frances N. (Butler) C.; m. Jeanmarie Hackman, Dec. 29, 1945 (dec. 1978); children: James, Carolyn, Susan, Sheila, Kevin, Richard, Elizabeth, Thomas, Claudia; m. Marjorie E. Masterson, Oct. 4, 1980. B.C.E., Purdue U., 1939; J.D., Ind. U., 1947. Bar: Wis. 1947, Ill. 1952. Patent atty. Allis Chalmers Mfg. Co., Milw., 1947-51; mem. firm Anderson, Luedeka, Fitch, Even & Tabin (and predecessors), Chgo., 1951-64; partner Anderson, Luedeka, Fitch, Even & Tabin (and predecessors), 1956-64; individual practice law Chgo., 1964-71; partner law firm Coffee & Sweeney, Chgo., 1971-76; partner, gen. counsel design firm Marvin Glass & Assos., Chgo., from 1973, now ret. Served to capt. AUS, 1941-46, Japanese prisoner of war, 1942-45. Mem. ABA, Ill. Bar Assn., Chgo. Bar Assn. (chmn. com. patents, trademark and unfair trade practices 1967), Am. Patent Law Assn., Patent Law Assn. Chgo. (chmn. com. copyrights 1969), Am. Judicature Soc. Club: Tower of Chgo. (bd. govs. 1978—, sec. 1982-83, treas. 1983-85). Home: 320 Earls Ct Deerfield IL 60015

COFFEE, VIRGINIA CLAIRE, civic worker, former mayor; b. Alliance, Nebr., Dec. 8, 1920; d. James Maddigan and Adelaide Mary (Forde) Kennedy; B.S., Chadron State Coll., 1942; m. Bill Brown Coffee, June 21, 1942; children—Claire, Sara, Virginia Anne, Sue. High sch. prin., Whitman, Nebr., 1942; sec., bookkeeper Coffee & Son, Inc., Harrison, Nebr., 1965—, officer, 1967—; mayor City of Harrison, 1978-80. Leader, Girl Scouts U.S.A., 1953-63; mem. Harrison Elem. Sch. bd., 1958-64; mem. liaison com. Chadron State Coll., 1975—; pub. relations chmn. Nebr. Cowbelles, 1968; sec. Northwest Stock Growers, 1971-73; corp. officer Ft. Robinson Centennial, 1973—; officer Gov.'s Fort Robinson Centennial Commn., 1973-75; hon. gov. Nebr. Centennial, 1967; chmn. Sioux County Bicentennial, 1973-77; trustee Nebr. State Hist. Soc. Found., 1975—, Village of Harrison, 1973-80; bd. dirs. Harrison Community Club, Inc., 1983-86, officer, 1984-86. Mem. Nebr. State Hist. Soc. (life, dir. 1979-85, 2d v.p. 1982-84, 1st v.p. 1984-85, com. for marker to honor Harrison centennial 1985-86), Sioux County Hist. Soc. (dir. 1975-81, 83-84, past pres., Sioux county history book com. 1985-86, contbr. articles, dir., v.p. 1987—), Wyo. Hist. Soc. Cardinal Key Honor Frat. Roman Catholic. Clubs: Sioux County Cowbelles, Nebr. Cowbells, Ladies Community, Harrison Community (dir. 1983—, officer 1984—), Contbr. articles to area newspapers; chmn. compilation com. book Sioux County Memoirs of Its Pioneers, 1967. Address: PO Box 336 Harrison NE 69346

COFFEY, DANIEL PATRICK, architect; b. Chgo., Jan. 11, 1954; s. Robert and JoAnn (Drazoga) C.; m. Robin Lynn Stokes, July 3, 1982. BArch, U. Ill., 1976; postgrad., Ecole Des Beaux Arts, Versailles, France, 1976, Aachen Technische Hochshule, Fed. Rep. Germany, 1977-78; MArch, Harvard U., 1980. Project architect Metz Train Youngren, Chgo., 1981-82, Jack Train Assocs., Chgo., 1982-83; sr. assoc. Sisco Lubotsky Assocs., Chgo., 1983-84; prin., chief exec. officer Daniel P. Coffey & Assocs., Chgo., 1984—. V.p. Friends of Downtown Chgo., 1981—; mem. southside task force Chgo. Cen. Area Com., 1985. Fulbright Hays fellow Fed. Govt. and Deutscher Akademischer Austausch Dienst, Aachen, Fed. Rep. Germany, 1977-78; Kate Neal Kinley fellow in Fine Arts U. Ill., 1979-80; recipient Young Chgo. Architect Designer Chgo. Bar Assn., 1982, 85, 87. Mem. AIA, Internat. Facilities Mgmt. Assn., Nat. Council Archtl. Accrediting Bd., Chgo. Assn. Commerce and Industry, St. Petersburg C. of C., Fulbright Alumni Assn., Urban Land Inst. Club: Harvard (Chgo.). Avocations: language, art. Office: 205 W Wacker Suite 1500 Chicago IL 60606

COFFEY, JOHN LOUIS, judge; b. Milw., Apr. 15, 1922; s. William Leo and Elizabeth Ann (Walsh) C.; m. Marion Kunzelmann, Feb. 3, 1951; children: Peter Lee, Elizabeth Mary Coffey Robbins. B.A., Marquette U., 1943, JD, 1948; M.B.A. (hon.), Spencerian Coll., 1964. Bar: Wis. 1948, U.S. Dist. Ct. 1948, U.S. Supreme Ct. 1980. Asst. city atty. Milw., 1949-54; judge Civil Ct., Milw. County, 1954-60, Milw. Mcpl. Ct., 1960-62; judge Circuit Ct. (criminal div.), Milw. County, 1962-72, sr. judge, 1972-75, chief presiding judge, 1976; circuit ct. judge Circuit Ct. (civil div.), Milw. County, 1976-78; justice Wis. Supreme Ct., Madison, 1978-82; circuit judge U.S. Ct. Appeals (7th cir.), Chgo., 1982—; mem. Wis. Bd. Criminal Ct. Judges, 1960-78, Wis. Bd. Circuit Ct. Judges, 1962-78. Chmn. adv. bd. St. Joseph's Home for Children, 1958-65; mem. adv. bd. St. Mary's Hosp., 1964-70; mem. Milwaukee County council Boy Scouts Am.; chmn. St. Eugene's Sch. Bd., 1967-70, St. Eugene's Parish Council, 1974; mem. vol. services adv. com. Milwaukee County Dept. Public Welfare; bd. govs. Marquette U. High Sch. Served with USNR, 1943-46. Recipient Disting. Service award Cudworth Post Am. Legion, 1973, Alumni Merit award Marquette U., 1985; named Outstanding Law Alumnus of Yr., Marquette U., 1980. Fellow Am. Bar Found.; mem. Alpha Sigma Nu. Roman Catholic.

COFFIN, ROBERT PARKER, architect; b. Chgo., Aug. 6, 1917; s. Charles Howells and Irene (Parker) C.; m. Emily Elizabeth Magie, Jan. 2, 1944; children: Betsy, Robert Jr., Barbara John. BEngring., Yale U., 1939. Registered architect, Ill., Wis., Minn., Mo., Ind., Mich.; registered engr., Ill. Field engr. Commonwealth Edison, Chgo., 1939-50; architect Shaw Metz and Dolio, Chgo., 1950-56; ptnr. Coffin and Scherschel, Barrington, Ill., 1956—. Pres., sec. Long Grove (Ill.) Sch. Bd., 1950-56; trustee Long Grove Village, 1956-59, pres., 1959-81, chmn. plan commn., 1981—. Served to lt. (j.g.) USN Air Corps, 1942-46. Recipient 3 Gold Key awards Nat. Home Builders Assn. Mem. AIA, ASCE (life), Am. Soc. Archtl. Historians, Interfaith Forum on Ch. Architecture. Avocations: sailing, gardening, archeology, anthropology. Office: Coffin and Scherschel 119 North Ave Barrington IL 60010

COFFING, JAMES LEE, retail executive; b. Peru, Ind., Dec. 9, 1946; s. J. Richard and Gladys Marie (Strong) C.; m. Ann Christine Aiken, Aug. 19, 1967 (div. Aug. 1980); children: Tara Lynn, Andrew John; m. Sharon Karl, Mar. 23, 1984; 1 child, Lauren Ashley. BS in Indsl. Mgmt., Purdue U., 1969. System rep. Burroughs Corp., Louisville, 1969-74; sr. acctg. mgr. UCCEL Corp., Dallas, 1974-85; v.p. Sterling Software, Dallas, 1985-87; mgr. Peat Marwick Main & Co., Chgo., 1987—. Served with U.S. Army, 1969-75. Avocations: boating, golf, stamp collecting, coin collecting. Home: 39056 Cedarcrest Lake Villa IL 60046 Office: Peat Marwick Main & co 303 E Wacker Dr Chicago IL 60601

COFFMAN, CURT WRAY, health care consulting company executive; b. Charles City, Iowa, June 4, 1959; s. Jack W. and Karen L. (Pedersen) C.; m. Tammy Sue Gannon, Aug. 8, 1981; 1 child, Kathryn Elizabeth. BS, Kearney (Nebr.) State Coll., 1983. Counselor adolescents Lincoln (Nebr.) Gen. Hosp., 1981-85; cons. Selection Research, Inc. Gallup, Lincoln, 1985—; mem. bd. profl. interviewers Selection Research, Inc., 1986—. Bd. dirs. Lincoln Council on Alcoholism and Drugs, 1986, Community Builders, 1986. Named one of Outstanding Young Men of Am., 1984, 86. Mem. Am. Mktg. Assn. Democrat. Methodist. Home: 2241 N 78th Lincoln NE 68505 Office: SRI Gallup 301 S 68th Lincoln NE 68510

COFFMAN, KENNETH MORROW, mechanical contractor; b. Ann Arbor, Mich., Aug 3, 1921; s. Harold Coe and Aletha (Morrow) C.; B.S., Lawrence U., 1943; m. Barbara Ann Porth, Dec. 30, 1943 (dec. 1983); children—Gregory, Deborah Coffman Greene, Jenifer Coffman Dillon. Exec. v.p. Stanley Carter Co. Ohio, Toledo, 1957-59; v.p. sales Wenzel & Henoch Co., Milw., 1959-64; exec. v.p. Milw. W & H Inc., 1964-70; exec. v.p. Downey Inc., Milw., 1970-76, pres., 1977-85, chmn. bd. dirs., 1986—. Bd. dirs. YMCA, Milw., 1965-87, Tri County, 1973-78; chmn. bd. mgrs. Camp Minikani, 1965-82; chmn. Am. Cancer Soc. Council, 1987—. Served with USMC 1943-46. Named Layman of year, Tri County YMCA, 1973, Disting. Service award Tri County YMCA, 1979. Mem. Nat. Cert. Pipe Welders Bur. Wis. (bd. dirs. 1973-86), Mech. Contractors Assn. South East Wis. (dir. 1970-80, pres. 1974-75), Mech. Contractors Devel. Fund. (bd. dirs. 1972-87, pres. 1972-73), Wis. Constrn. Employers Council (bd. dirs. 1973-87), Mech. Contractors Assn. of Wis. (bd. dirs. 1977-86, pres. 1983-84), Nat. Fire Protection Assn., Nat. Assn. Plumbing, Heating, Cooling Contractors, Mech. Contractors Assn. Am. (bd. dirs. 1982-86, pres. elect 1987—), Nat. Mech. Equipment Service and Maintenance Bur. (bd. dirs. 1982-87), Sheet Metal and Air Conditioning Contractors Nat. Assn. Congregationalist. Home: 925 E Wells St Milwaukee WI 53202 Office: Box 1155 Milwaukee WI 53201

COFFMAN, PHILLIP HUDSON, professor music; b. Lincoln, Nebr., Nov. 27, 1936; s. Rowland Francis and Elberta (Hudson) C.; m. Carolyn J. Nimmo, July 23, 1983; children by previous marriage: Phillip C., Catherine L. B.Mus. Edn., U. Nebr., 1958; M.Mus., U. Idaho, 1962; Ph.D., U. Toledo, 1971. Tchr. public schs. Rushville, Nebr., 1958-59; instr. Doane Coll., Crete, Nebr., 1959-60; teaching asst. U. Idaho, Moscow, 1960-62; instr. U. Idaho, 1962-65; asso. prof., chmn. dept. music Jamestown (N.D.) Coll., 1965-68; adminstv. intern U. Toledo, 1968-71; asso. prof., head dept. music U. Minn., Duluth, 1971-76; prof., dean Sch. Fine Arts, 1976-86, asst. to chancellor, 1987—; mem. Lincoln Symphony, 1954-60, Toledo Symphony, 1969-71; guest artist Ednl. TV; instr. Internat. Music Camp, 1967-68. Contbr. articles to profl. jours. Pres. Civic Music Assn., 1967, Minn. Coll. and Univ. Council for Music, 1976; music adjudicator, interviewer Bush Leadership Fellows Program, 1977—; chmn. bd. Duluth Festival of Arts, 1979-81; mem. Gov.'s Commn. on Econ. Vitality in the Arts, 1984-86 ; mem. adv. panel Minn. State Arts Bd., 1985—. F.E. Olds scholar, 1963; Bush Found. fellow, 1973. Mem. Internat. Council Fine Arts Deans, Theta Xi, Phi Mu Alpha, Pi Kappa Lambda, Kappa Kappa Psi. Home: 4601 Woodland Duluth MN 55803 Office: School Fine Arts U Minn Duluth MN 55812

COFFMAN, WARD DENVER, III, lawyer; b. Zanesville, Ohio, Jan. 12, 1953; s. Ward Denver Jr. and Patricia Delphine (Sayer) C.; m. Lesa Kaye Luke Castagnetto, Nov. 15, 1986. Student, U. Ariz., 1971-72, Ohio State U., 1972-73; BA, Bowling Green (Ohio) State U., 1975; JD, Ohio No. U., 1978. Bar: Ohio 1978, U.S. Dist. Ct. (so. dist.) Ohio 1979. Assoc. Kincaid, Cultice & Assocs., Zanesville, 1978-82; sole practice Zanesville, 1982-86; ptnr. Coffman, Lewis, Graham, Watson, Vinsel & Erhard Co., Zanesville, 1986—. Bd. dirs. Zanesville High Sch. Quarterback Club, 1986. Mem. ABA, Ohio State Bar Assn. (mem. eastern mineral law conf.), Ohio Oil and Gas Assn., Muskingum County Bar Assn. (sec. 1984, v.p. 1985, pres. 1986). Republican. Episcopalian. Avocations: golf, skiing. Office: Coffman Lewis Graham Watson et al BancOhio Nat Bank Bldg PO Box 1110 Zanesville OH 43702-1110

COHEN, ALBERT DIAMOND, merchandising executive; b. Winnipeg, Man., Can., Jan. 20, 1914; s. Alexander and Rose (Diamond) C.; m. Irena Kankova, Nov. 6, 1953; children: Anthony Jan, James Edward, Anna Lisa. LLD (hon.), U. Man., Can., 1987, 1987. Pres. Gendis Inc., Winnipeg, 1953—; chmn., chief exec. officer Gendis, Inc., Winnipeg, 1987—; chmn. exec. com. Met. Stores of Can., Ltd., Winnipeg, 1961—, Greenberg Stores Ltd.; sec., treas., dir. Saan Stores Ltd.; chmn., chief exec. officer Sony of Can. Ltd., 1975—. Pres. Winnipeg Clin. Research Inst., 1975-80, Paul H.T. Thorlakson Research Found., 1978-80.; hon. chmn. St. John's Ravenscourt Sch., 1984. Served with Royal Can. Navy, 1942-45. Recipient Order of Can., 1984. Office: Gendis Inc, 1370 Sony Pl, Winnipeg, MB Canada R3C 3C3

COHEN, ALBERTO, cardiologist; b. Rio de Janeiro, Aug. 12, 1932; came to U.S., 1959; s. Nessim and Anneta (Rabischoffsky) C.; m. Bertha Kalichztein, Dec. 27, 1958; children: Deborah Cohen Stein, Annabel, Miriam Cohen Disner. BS, Edn. Rui Barboza, Rio de Janero, 1952; MD, Brazil U., Rio de Janero, 1958. Diplomate Am. Bd. Internal Medicine, Am. Bd. Cardiovascular Disease; cert. bd. med. examiners, Ariz., Fla., Tex., Calif. Intern Middlesex Gen. Hosp., New Brunswick, N.J., 1959-60; resident Detroit Meml. Hosp., 1960-61; fellow cardiology medicine Harper Hosp., Detroit, 1961, Detroit Receiving Hosp., Wayne State U., 1963-65; practice medicine specializing in cardiology and internal medicine Mt. Clements, Mich., 1966—; attending staff St. Joseph Hosp., Mt. Clements, 1966—, Hutzel Hosp., Detroit, 1966—; courtesy staff Detroit-Macomb Hosp. Assn., Warren, Mich., 1966—; staff Detroit Gen. Hosp., 1966—; instr. medicine Wayne State U., Detroit, 1964-65, asst. prof. medicine, 1965-67, clin. asst. prof. medicine, 1967—. Contbr. numerous articles to profl. jours. Pres. Macomb County Heart Unit, 1974-77. Fellow Am. Coll. Chest Physicians, Am. Coll. Angiology, Am. Coll. Internat. Physicians, Am. Coll. Cardiology, Am. Coll. Internal Angiology Internat. Coll. Angiology; mem. AMA, Brazilian Soc. Medicine, Brazilian Soc. Cardiology, Am. Soc. Internal Medicine, Mich. Soc. Internal Medicine (trustee 1974-77), Mich. State Med. Soc., Wayne County Med. Soc., Macomb County Med. Soc., Am. Heart Assn. (assoc. fellow scientific council clin. cardiology). Jewish. Club: Detroit Heart. Avocations: music, art, reading. Home: 1477 Lochridge Dr Bloomfield Heights MI 48013

COHEN, ALDEN M., advertising executive; b. Chgo., Apr. 30, 1934; s. Laurence I. and Myra P. (Littmann) C.; m. Susanne Zoloto, July 29, 1961; children: Jordin S., Laura E., Adam A. AB, Carleton Coll., 1956; MBA, U. Chgo., 1959. Stock div. prioritizer Bagcraft, Chgo., 1959-62, mgr. coffee div., 1962-67, mgr. advt., 1967—; dir. NKI Industries, St. Louis, 1980-85. Bd. dirs. Mid-Am. chpt. ARC, Chgo., 1978-80, co-chmn. tng. com., 1972—, instr./trainer first aid, 1955—, tng. mgr. multi-media tng., 1965—; bd. dirs. N. Cook Dist. ARC, Mt. Prospect, Ill., 1980-82; dist. com. Boy Scouts Am., Evanston, 1974—. Served with U.S. Army, 1957-59. Recipient 1,000 Hours of Service award ARC, 1980, Chmn.'s award Boy Scouts Am., 1978, Max Pheyline Tng. award 1987; named Silver Arrowhead Trainer Boy Scouts Am., 1972. Mem. Paper/Plastic Adv. Com., Am. Trauma Soc. (founder 1974), Sixteen Ten Soc. (v.p. 1980-85). Club: Brighton Luncheon Soc. (Chgo.) (v.p., treas., mgr. 1976—). Avocations: photography, high vector tuners, camping, scouting. Home: 1610 Seward Ave Evanston IL 60202 Office: Bagcraft Corp Am 3900 W 43d St Chgo IL 60632

COHEN, ALLAN RICHARD, lawyer; b. Chgo., Feb. 25, 1923; s. Louis and Ruth (Cohen) C.; m. Audrey Doris Levy, Oct. 14, 1960; children: Joseph, David, Gale. B.A., U. Wis., 1947, J.D., 1949; postgrad., Northwestern U., 1953-54. Bar: Ill. 1950. Assoc. Blum, Jacobsen & Shkoler, Chgo., 1950-53; ptnr. Cohen & Cohen, Chgo., 1953—. Served with AUS, 1943-45. Decorated Presdl. citation with oak leaf cluster. Mem. Fed. Bar Assn., Ill. Bar Assn. (vice chmn. comml. banking and bankruptcy sect. 1977—), Chgo. Bar Assn. (vice chmn. com. bankruptcy 1972-73, chmn. 1973-74, panelist bankruptcy seminars 1968, 72, 74, 82, 83), Zeta Beta Tau, Tau Epsilon Rho. Club: Elms Swim Tennis (Highland Park, Ill.). Office: Cohen & Cohen 55 W Monroe Chicago IL 60603

COHEN, ASHLEY VAUGHAN, computer executive, consultant; b. Norwich, Norfolk, Eng., Dec. 9, 1954; came to U.S., 1977; s. Maurice and Joan Mary (Pitt) C.; m. Victoria Cohen, Dec. 23, 1984 (div.). Test engr. Computing Techniques, Billingshurst, Eng., 1972-75, Transdata Ltd., Havant, Hants, Eng., 1975-77; customer engr. Sweda Internat., Detroit, 1977-78; systems engr. Unitote/Regitel, Detroit, 1978; area supr. Datatrol, Inc., Detroit, 1978-79; supr. Detroit Free Press, 1979—; pres. computer cable andnetworking service Ashley Services, Fairhaven, Mich., 1983—. Mem. IBEW. Office: Detroit Free Press 321 W Lafayette St Detroit MI 48231

COHEN, BARBARA GLORIA, management consultant, marketing executive; b. Bklyn., Dec. 17, 1952; d. Herbert and Ruth (Schwartz) C. BA in Speech/Communications, Pa. State U., 1974, MBA, 1977. Product mgr. Procter and Gamble, Cin., 1977-82; mgmt. cons. Booz, Allen & Hamilton, N.Y.C., 1982-85, Chgo., 1985—; bd. dirs. Morgan Reed, N.Y.C. Mem. N.Y.C. Wharton Alumni Club, League Women Voters (co-chair N.Y.C. health study group 1984-95), Phi Beta Kappa. Avocations: hiking, travel.

COHEN, BERNARD CECIL, political scientist, educator; b. Northampton, Mass., Feb. 22, 1926; s. Louis Mark and Lena (Slotnick) C.; m. Laura Mae Propper, Sept. 1, 1947; children: Barbara Ellen, Janie Louise. B.A., Yale, 1948, M.A., 1950, Ph.D., 1952. Research asst. Yale, 1950-51; research asst., then research asso. Princeton, 1951-59, asst. prof., 1957-59; mem. faculty U. Wis., 1959—, prof. polit. sci., 1963-73, Quincy Wright prof. polit. sci., 1973—, chmn. dept., 1966-69, assoc. dean Grad. Sch., 1971-75, vice chancellor acad. affairs, 1984-86, interim chancellor, 1987—; vis. research scholar Carnegie Endowment Internat. Peace, 1965-66; mng. editor World Politics, 1956-59, mem. bd. editors, 1959-60, 72-78; mem. bd. editors Internat. Studies Quar., 1966-78. Author: The Political Process and Foreign Policy, 1957, The Press and Foreign Policy, 1963, The Public's Impact on Foreign Policy, 1973; Editor: Foreign Policy in American Government, 1965. Served with AUS, 1944-46. Ford Found. Faculty Research fellow, 1369-70; fellow Center Advanced Study Behavioral Scis., 1961-62, 69-70; Fulbright-Hays research scholar Netherlands, 1975-76; Guggenheim fellow, 1981-82. Mem. Am., Midwest polit. sci. assns., Internat. Studies Assn. Home: 1034 Seminole Hwy Madison WI 53711 *

COHEN, BURTON DAVID, franchising executive, lawyer; b. Chgo., Feb. 12, 1940; s. Allan and Gussy (Katz) C.; B.S. in Bus. and Econs., Ill. Inst. Tech., 1960; J.D., Northwestern U., 1963; m. Linda Rochelle Kaine, Jan. 19, 1969; children—David, Jordana. Admitted to Ill. bar, 1963; staff atty. McDonald's Corp., Oak Brook, Ill., 1964-69, asst. sec., 1969-70, asst. gen. counsel, 1970-76, asst. v.p., 1976-78, dir. legal dept., 1978-80, v.p. licensing, asst. gen. counsel, asst. sec., 1980—; lectr. Practising Law Inst. Served with AUS, 1963-64. Mem. Am. Bar Assn., Ill. Bar Assn., Chgo. Bar Assn., Internat. Franchise Assn. (lectr.), Assn. Nat. Advertisers, Chgo. Council Fgn. Relations, Tau Epsilon Phi, Phi Delta Phi. Club: Executives (Chgo.). Author: Franchising: Second Generation Problems, 1969. Office: McDonalds Plaza Oak Brook IL 60521

COHEN, EDWIN ROBERT, financial executive; b. St. Louis, Apr. 13, 1939; s. Harry W. and Sally (Robinson) C.; m. Sheilah Renee Aron, Aug. 20, 1961; children—David Brian, Scott Alan, Craig Aron. B.S., Washington U., St. Louis, 1966; C.L.U., 1973. Chartered fin. cons., 1985. Pres. Edwin R. Cohen & Assocs., St. Louis, 1966—; gen. agt. Central Life Assurance Co., Des Moines, 1969—, B.C. Christopher Securities, 1985—, The Whitestone Corp., 1985—; registered rep. Nat. Assn. Securities Dealers. Author: The New Agents Survival Manual, 1987. Arbitrator, Better Bus. Bur. St. Louis, 1976—; chmn. local SSS, 1982—. Mem. Million Dollar Round Table, 1972-74; recipient certs. of appreciation Better Bus. Bur. St. Louis, 1979-87. Mem. Am. Soc. C.L.U.s, Nat. Assn. Life Underwriters (Nat. Quality award 1987, Nat. Sales Achievement award 1983), Gen. Agts. and Mgrs. Assn., St. Louis Life Underwriters Assn. (dir. 1978-81), Am. Legion. Jewish. Lodge: Jaycees (v.p. 1963-64) (St. Louis). Home: 10256 Lylewood Dr Ladue MO 63124 Office: 7710 Carondelet Ave Clayton MO 63105

COHEN, GERALD JAY, social services administrator; b. Milw., May 15, 1952; s. Hyman Harold and Lena (Zeitz) C.; m. Ruth Christman, May 29, 1977; 1 child, Sarah Beth. BA, U. Wis., 1974; JD, Washington U., St. Louis, 1977; MPA, U. Mo., Kansas City, 1985. Bar: Mo. 1977. Legal counsel Mo. Div. Aging, Jefferson City, 1978-82; mng. atty. Legal Aid, Kansas City, 1982-84; cons. Med. Systems, Inc., Kansas City, 1983-86; asst. dir. U. Mo. Inst. for Human Devel., Kansas City, 1984—. Advisor People First, 1984—; bd. dirs. Family Friends, Voluntary Action Ctr., Career Guild, Nat. Council Silver Haired Legislature. Mem. Mo. Bar Assn., Assn. Pub. Adminstrn., Mid-Am. Congress Aging, Older Woman's League, Gray Panthers. Jewish. Home: 14 W 61 Terr Kansas City MO 64113 Office: U Mo Inst Human Devel 2220 Holmes Kansas City MO 64108

COHEN, GERALD N., allergist; b. Chgo., June 25, 1929; m. Muriel Cohen; children: Marci, Marc, Elliott, Lorin. AB, U. Ill., Urbana, 1950, MS, 1954; MD, U. Ill., Chgo., 1958. Diplomate Am. Bd. Allergy and Immunology. Intern Michael Reese Hosp., Chgo., 1958-59, resident in internal medicine, 1959-61, resident in chest and pulmonary medicine, 1961-62, resident in allergy and immunology, 1962-63; practice medicine specializing in allergy Chgo., 1963—. Contbr. over 25 articles to med. jour. Served with U.S. Army, 1951-53. assoc. prof. U. Ill. Med. Sch., Chgo., 1964-72; cons. clinical allergy. Office: 1029 Howard St Evanston IL 60202

COHEN, HARRY, gynecologist obstetrician, anesthesiologist; b. Balt., Jan. 15, 1918; s. Myer and Anna Cohen; m. Mitzie Polakoff, Feb. 5, 1950; children: Judith, Howard, Deborah. BS, U. Md., 1939, MD, 1943. Diplomate Am. Bd. Ob-Gyn, Am. Bd. Anesthesiology. Intern and resident U. Md. Hosp., 1943, 66-68; resident in ob-gyn South Balt. Gen. Hosp., 1945-46, Balt. City Hosp., 1946-48, Luth. Hosp. Md., 1948-50; fellowship Columbia Presbyn. Hosp., N.Y.C., 1968-70; med. faculty U. Miami, Fla., 1970-81, Northwestern U., Chgo., 1981—. Contbr. articles to profl. jours. Served to capt. U.S. Army, 1944-46, ETO. Mem. Am. Coll. Ob-Gyn, Am. Soc. Anesthesiology. Home: 990 N Lake Shore Dr 8A Chicago IL 60611 Office: Northwestern Meml Hosp Prentice Pavilion 333 E Superior St Chicago IL 60611

COHEN, JEFFREY, hospital chaplain; b. Sydney, Austrialia, Jan. 4, 1950; s. Leonard and Gwen (Abbott) C.; m. Edith Feldman, June 27, 1982; children: Len, Miriam. B in Commerce, U. New South Wales, Australia, 1973; Dr. Ministries, Eden Theol. Sem., 1986. Ordained rabbi, 1979. Exec. dir. Assn. Internat. des Etudiants Sciences Economiques et Commerciales, South Pacific, 1972-74, Europe World Council Synagogues, London, 1979-80; assoc. rabbi Congregation B'Nai Amoona, St. Louis, 1980-82; chaplain Jewish Fedn., St. Louis, 1983-84; coordinator pastoral services St. Louis State Hosp., 1984—. Active Holocaust Commn., St. Louis; bd. dirs. Solomon Schechter Day Sch. St. Louis, Sr. Service Bd., University City, Mo.; Jewish Community Relations Council, St. Louis. Jewish Fedn. fellow, 1981, 86. Fellow Assn. Jewish Chaplains in Spl. Settings (pres. 1986), Coll. Chaplains (clinical mem.); mem. Assn. Mental Health Clergy, Assn. for Clin. Pastoral Edn., Rabbinical Assembly St. Louis (pres. 1985-86), U. New South Wales Alumni Assn. (award 1974), Leo Baeck Coll. Alumni Assn. (bd. dirs.). Home: 7822 Stanford Saint Louis MO 63130 Office: St Louis State Hosp 5400 Arsenal Saint Louis MO 63139

COHEN, JEROME, electronic business equipment company executive; b. Kansas City, Mo., Oct. 9, 1913; s. Rueben and Helen (Silverstein) C.; grad. Kansas City (Mo.) Jr. Coll., 1931; student Huffs Bus. Coll., 1932, Central Bus. Coll., 1933; m. Jeannette Baier, Nov. 25, 1934; children—Rosalyn Jean, Elaine Marie. Asst. mgr. Burts Shoe Store, Kansas City, Mo., 1932-34; sec. to State Senator of Mo., 1934-35; chief clk. Mo. Old Age Assistance Div., 1935-37, Jackson County (Mo.) Welfare Office, Kansas City, 1937-38; founder Tempo Co., Kansas City, Mo., 1938, pres., 1938—, chief exec. officer, 1938—; pres., chief exec. officer Electronic Bus. Equipment, Inc., Kansas City, Mo., 1957—, Jefferson City, Mo., 1960-86, Saint Joseph, Mo., 1961—; commr. Kansas City (Mo.) Park Bd., 1955-72. Vice pres. Am. Humanics Found., Kansas City, Mo., 1956-80; chmn. Kansas City (Mo.) Jewish Chautauqua Drive, 1962-64; mem. Nat. Com. for Support of Public Schs., 1967-78; mem. exec. com. Kansas City Safety Council, 1958-86; chmn. Mayor's Christmas Tree Assn., Kansas City, 1955-86; mem. adv. bd. Met. Jr. Coll., 1972-78; Kansas City chmn. Richards Gebaur AFB Community Council, 1960-61; mem. Kansas City Bus. and Indsl. Commn., 1955-62; pres. Temple B'nai Jehudah, 1980-81; mem. exec. bd. Sr. Citizens Corp. of Kansas City, 1954-65, Kansas City Recreation Commn., 1955-70, Citizens Assn., 1940-86, Child's World, 1969-81, Camp Fire Girls, 1956-66, Starlight Theatre, 1950-86, v.p., 1978-86; chmn. Kansas City Soap Box Derby, 1947-64; bd. dirs. U. Kans. Sch. of Religion, 1971-86, Scottish Rite Found. of Mo., 1969-86; hon. trustee Heart of Am. council Boy Scouts Am., 1960-86. B'nai Jehudah Brotherhood Hall of Fame Honoree, 1976; named Kansas City (Mo.) Mktg. Exec. of Year, 1981. Hon. fellow Harry S. Truman Library Inst.; mem. Mo. C. of C., Kansas City (Mo.) C. of C., Kansas City (Kans.) C. of C., Native Sons of Kansas City (Mo.), Conservation Fedn. of Mo., Mo. U. Assos., Bus. Dist. League (pres. 1963-65), Jackson County Execs. (exec. council), Jackson County Hist. Soc., Audubon Soc., Am. Assn. of Zoos and Aquariums, Bus. Products Council Assn. (pres. 1970-72), Mid-Town Assn. (v.p. 1964-65), Friends of the Zoo (pres. 1973-74), Navy League, Kansas City (Mo.) Lyric Theatre Guild, Japan Am. Soc., Jewish Chautauqua Soc., Hebrew Acad. of Kansas City, Hyman Brand Hebrew Acad., Piscator's Soc. (pres. 1970-71), Sci. Pioneers, Friends of Art, NCCJ, Air Force Assn., U.S. China Friendship Assn., Am. Royal Assn. (bd. govs. 1955-86). Clubs: Masons (33 degrees), Shriners, Kansas City Athletic, Meadowbrook Country, Elmers Fishing (pres. 1968-69). Home: 6616 Ward Parkway Kansas City MO 64113 Office: 1500 Grand Ave Kansas City MO 64108

COHEN, JEROME LEONARD, management consultant; b. Jacksonville, Ill., Nov. 25, 1923; s. Herman H. and Ida Marie (Horen) C.; m. Pauline Kessler, Sept. 1, 1946 (dec. July, 1965); children: Bernard H., James M., Frank R., David H. BA, Ill. Coll., Jacksonville, 1948. Prin. Jacob Cohen's Sons, Jacksonville, 1946-63; v.p. Stephen Crane Assocs., Beverly Hills, Calif., 1963-65, Mauna Loa Restaurants Inc., Detroit, 1965-72, Roth Young Personnel Service, Chgo, 1972-74; pres. Blecha, Cohen, Tokarz & Assocs., Chgo., 1974-76, Consultant Services Inc., Lincolnwood, Ill., 1976—. Served to cpl. U.S. Army, 1942-45, PTO. Republican. Jewish.

COHEN, MELVIN FRANK, psychiatrist; b. Detroit, July 18, 1925; s. Morris and Hilda (Kazdan) C.; m. Lillian Taylor, Sept. 14, 1952; Jan Ellen, David, Brian. Student, Tufts U., 1943-44; MD, U. Mich., 1948. Intern Michael Reese Hosp., Chgo., 1948-49; resident Wayne County Gen. Hosp., Eloise, Mich., 1949-50; attending physician Sinai Hosp., Detroit, 1957—, William Beaumont Hosp., Royal Oak, Mich., 1969—; bd. dirs. Adult Psychiat. Clinic, Detroit, 1953-57, Beacon Hill Clinic, Southfield, Mich., 1975-80. Served to capt. USAF, 1950-52. Mem. AMA, Mich. Med. Soc., Am. Psychiat. Assn., Mich. Psychiat. Soc., Oakland County Med. Soc. (com. 1979-82), Phi Delta Epsilon. Avocations: tennis, golf, swimming, sailing. Home: 28590 Rivercrest Dr Southfield MI 48034 Office: 31555 W 14 Mile Rd Farmington Hills MI 48018

COHEN, MILLARD STUART, diversified manufacturing company executive; b. Chgo., Jan. 17, 1939; s. Lawrence Irmas and Myra Paula (Littmann) C.; B.S. in Elec. Engring., Purdue U., 1960; m. Judith E. Michel, Aug. 2, 1970; children—Amy Rose, Michele Lauren. Design engr. GTE Automatic Electric Labs., Northlake, Ill., 1960-66; chief elec. engr. Nixdorff Krein Industries, St. St. Louis, 1966-68, dir. data processing, 1968-72, treas., 1970—, v.p., 1980-85, pres., 1985—, exec. v.p. Nixdorff Chain, 1972-76, pres. Grape Expectations, 1976—, also dir. Dist. commr. Boy Scouts Am., 1968-72; judge Mo. State Fair; mem. Mo. State Wine Adv. Bd., 1980—, vice-chmn., 1983; mem. St. Louis County Restaurant Commn., 1979—, Augusta (Mo.) Wine Bd., 1981—. Recipient award of merit French Wine Commn., 1972. Mem. ACM, IEEE, Mensa, Les Amis du Vin, Chaine des Rotisseurs, Commanderie de Bordeaux. Jewish (trustee temple). Club: St. Louis. Home: 11233 Ladue Rd Creve Coeur MO 63141 Office: PO Box 27479 Saint Louis MO 63141

COHEN, MORLEY MITCHELL, chain store executive; b. Winnipeg, Man., Can., Jan. 2, 1917; s. Alexander and Rose (Diamond) C.; m. Rita Lillian Stober, Nov. 4, 1957; children: Joanne (Mrs. Barry Goldmeir), Donna Susan (Mrs. Graeme Low). Ed., St. John's Tech. Sch.; Ph.D., Haifa U., 1985. Pres. Saan Stores, Ltd., Winnipeg, 1954-57; exec. v.p. Gen. Distbrs., Ltd., Montreal, 1958-63, Met. Stores of Can., Ltd., Montreal, 1964-68; pres. Met. Stores of Can., Ltd., 1969—, chmn., 1979—; chmn. Hineni of Can., 1984—; dir. Gen. Distbrs., Ltd., Montreal Bd. Trade, 1973-75. Chmn. Combined Jewish Appeal, Montreal, 1970, mem. campaign cabinet, 1980; treas. YMHA and YWHA, Montreal, 1971; chmn. capital fund drive, 1980; treas. United Israel Appeal, 1970-71; chmn. Arthritis Soc., Que., 1981; bd. dirs., v.p. Jewish Community Fund Found., 1980; bd. dirs. Jewish Gen. Hosp., Montreal, Que. Safety League; chmn. Univ. Grad. Employment Agy.-Jewish Vocat. Service, 1984. Served with RCAF, 1940-45. Mem. Internat. Golf Soc. (founder). Clubs: B'nai B'rith (Montreal), Elmridge Golf and Country (Montreal) (past pres.), Montefiore (Montreal). Office: Met Stores of Can Ltd, 1370 Sony Place, Winnipeg, MB Canada R3C 3C3

COHEN, MYRON AARON, musician; b. Denver, Mar. 28, 1918; s. Goodman and Rose (Cohen) C.; student De Paul U. Sch. Music, 1936-38, Am. Conservatory of Music, Chgo., 1939-42, Juilliard Sch. Music, 1947; B.A., U. Omaha, 1947; Mus.M., U. Nebr., Lincoln, 1960; violin student Richard Czerwonky, Scott Willits, Louis Persinger, others. Concertmaster following orchs.: Omaha Symphony Orch., 1947-77, Omaha Opera Co. Orch., 1959-79, Lincoln (Nebr.) Symphony Orch., 1951-60; organized String Quartet, 1978; asst. condr. Omaha Youth Orch., 1958-66; part-time faculty U. Omaha, 1951-52, U. Nebr., Lincoln, 1958-59, Coll. St. Mary, 1980-84; soloist radio, TV; pvt. violin tchr., Omaha, 1946-82. Served with AUS, 1943-45. Winner commencement contest for violinists Am. Conservatory Music, 1940. Mem. Omaha Musicians Assn. (past mem. exec. bd.), Nebr. Music Tchrs. Assn. (past pres.), Am. String Tchrs. Assn. (past pres. Nebr. chpt.), Pi Kappa Lambda. Democrat. Jewish. Author: The Beginning Violinist's Left Hand Technique, 1956; Finger Relationships through Patterns and Keys for Violin, 1964; also revs. and articles. Home: 3925 S 24th St Omaha NE 68107

COHEN, PAUL G(ERSON), management consultant; b. N.Y.C., July 23, 1938; s. Henry A. and Esther (Reiner) C.; B.A., Union Coll., Schenectady, 1960; children—David Mark, Deborah Esther. With Northwestern Bell Tel. Co., Omaha, 1966-74, revenue supr. long distance and WATS, 1971-74; asst. v.p., sec. S. Riekes & Sons, Inc., Omaha, 1974-75, gen. ops. mgr., 1975-76; v.p. ops., Riekes Crisa Corp., Omaha, 1976-81; pres. Mid-Am. Bus. Enterprises, Inc., Omaha, 1981—. Treas., youth sports program Omaha Suburban Athletic Assn., 1976-77; bd. dirs. Cystic Fibrosis Assn. Nebr., 1977-79; bd. dirs. Jewish Fedn. Omaha, 1973-76, v.p., 1977-81, pres., 1982-84; trustee Nat. Jewish Hosp./Nat. Asthma Center, Denver; bd. dirs. Council Jewish Fedns. Served with USAF, 1960-66; col. Nebr. Air N.G., 1967—, now dep. chief staff Hdqrs. Nebr. Air N.G. Mem. Air Force Assn., Nebr. N.G. Assn. (dir. 1973-76, pres. 1979). Clubs: B'nai B'rith (pres.); regional pres. 1974-75, dist. bd. govs., 1976-78), Rotary. Home: 12406 Burt Plaza #12 Omaha NE 68154

COHEN, PHILIP EDWARD, social worker; b. Chgo., May 26, 1948; s. Morris and Miriam Ann (Wolfson) C.; student Parsons Coll., 1966-67; B.S., Murray State U., 1970; m. Elaine E. Biegacz, Oct. 8, 1972; 1 dau., Miriam Esther. Clk., Bur. of Census, U.S. Dept. Commerce, Jeffersonville, Ind., 1970-71; social work asso. VA Med. Center, Chillicothe, Ohio, 1971—; mem. supervisory com. Chivaho Fed. Credit Union, 1976-80, chmn., 1978, sec. credit com., 1983-85, mem. 1985—. VA Med. Center rep. Internat. Yr. of Child, 1979; mem. ad hoc com. Internat. Yr. of Disabled Persons, VA Med. Center; trustee Beth Jacob Congregation, 1981—; pres. Beth Jacob Brotherhood, 1984-86. Recipient Superior Performance award VA Med. Center, 1978, 83, 85, 86, VA Adminstrs.'s Hands and Heart award, 1984. Mem. Nat. Assn. Social Workers, VA Employees Assn. (pres. 1977-79, dir. 1979-80), Central Ohio Diabetes Assn., Murray State U. Alumni Assn. (life), Fraternal Order Police Assos., Ky. Col. Democrat. Jewish. Club: B'nai B'rith (Pres.'s award 1973, Community Service award 1975, historian 1973-74, community service v.p. 1975-76, v.p. membership 1978-79), Beth Jacob Young Couples. Home: 5114 Teddy Dr Columbus OH 43227 Office: VA Medical Center 17273 State Rt 104 Chillicothe OH 45601

COHEN, ROBERT SELDON, chemical executive, consultant; b. Rochester, N.Y., Sept. 23, 1923; s. Samuel J. and Jean Eleanor (Goldstein) C.; m. Roberta Joan Klar, May 4, 1958; children: Matthew Stuart, Mardah Beatrice. BS in Chem. Engring., U. Mich., 1944, MS in Physics, 1947. Registered profl. engr., Pa., Ohio. Founder, pres. Dover (Ohio) Chem. Corp., 1949-74; founder Power Grip Co., 1960; v.p. ICC Industries (merger The Ansul Co. and Dover Chem. Corp.), 1975-77; founder Enterprise Chem. Corp., Ltd., 1977-84; pvt. cons. to chem. industry Dover, 1984—; chmn. bd. dirs. Cripple Creek Trout Farm, Inc., Rural Retreat, Va., 1985—; mem. nat. adv. council Consumer Products Safety Commn., 1975-77. Patentee in chlor hydrocarbons field. Pres. bd. dirs. Jr. Achievement, Inc., Tuscarawas County, Ohio; trustee Wilderness Ctr., Wilmot, Ohio. Fellow Am. Inst. Chem. Engrs.; mem. Fire Retardant Chems. Assn. (founding mem), Ohio Soc. Profl. Engrs. Avocations: tennis, fishing, boating. Home: 4 Parkview Dr Dover OH 44622

COHEN, RONALD S., accountant; b. Lafayette, Ind., July 13, 1937; s. William and Stella (Fleischman) C.; m. Nancy Ann Plotkin, May 29, 1960; children: Philip, Douglas. BS in Acctg., Ind. U., 1958. CPA, Ind. Staff acct. Crowe, Chizek & Co., South Bend, Ind., 1958-65, ptnr., 1965-82, mng. ptnr., 1982—. Commr. Housing Authority of South Bend, 1976-85, also vice-chmn.; pres. Jewish Fedn., 1979-82; bd. dirs. United Way of South Bend, 1987—. Served to lt. USAR, 1958-66. Mem. Am. Inst. CPA's, Ind. Soc. CPA's, South Bend Estate Planning Council. Democrat. Jewish. Office: Crowe Chizek & Co PO Box 7 South Bend IN 46624

COHEN, SIDNEY SIMON, accountant; b. St. Louis, Nov. 12, 1901; s. Isaac and Jennie (Radlove) C.; m. Sadie Lillian Margulis, June 9, 1925; children: Helen M., Ilene Janice. BS in Bus., Washington U., 1922. CPA, Mo. Reporter Globe-Dem., St. Louis, 1918-19, St. Louis (Mo.) Star, 1919-22; agt. IRS, Springfield, Ill., 1922-24; sr. ptnr. Sidney S. Cohen and Co., St. Louis, 1924-81; acct. Grant-Thornton, St. Louis, 1981—. Mem. Police Bd. Retirement Fund, St. Louis, 1951-55, Beautification Bd., St. Louis, 1967; mem., treas. Land Clearance Authority, St. Louis, 1956-60; commr. Art Mus., St. Louis, 1978-86. Named Disting. Alumnus Bus. Sch. Washington U., 1973; recipient Award of Yr. John Burroughs Sch., 1986, Award of Yr. St. Louis Art Mus., 1986. Mem. Am. Inst. CPA's, Mo. Soc. CPA's. Jewish. Lodges: B'nai B'rith (pres. 1925-29), Mo. Avocations: football, golf, squash, basketball. Office: Grant-Thornton 500 Washington Ave Suite 1200 Saint Louis MO 63101

COHEN, STEVEN RICHARD, government official; b. Haverhill, Mass., Dec. 14, 1940; s. Kaufman and Celia (Richer) C.; B.A. cum laude, U. Mass., 1962, postgrad., 1962-63; m. Carole Simons, Mar. 21, 1970; children—Scott Michael, Lisa Michelle. With U.S. Office Personnel Mgmt. (formerly U.S. Civil Service Commn.), 1962—, investigator, varied personnel mgmt. and staffing positions, Boston region, 1962-65, adminstrv. officer, bur. recruiting and examining, Washington, 1965-70, mgr. Norfolk (Va.) Area Office, 1970-73, asst. to dep. exec. dir., Washington, 1973-75, dep. regional dir. Great Lakes Region, Chgo., 1975-81, regional dir., 1981—. Mem. Chgo. Fed. Exec. Bd., 1981—, chmn., 1983-84; chmn. Chgo. Combined Fund Campaign, 1983; fed. coordinator Ill. Savs. Bonds Campaign, 1984—. Mem. Internat. Personnel Mgmt. Assn., Am. Soc. Public Adminstrs., Chgo. Fed. Exec. Bd., Chgo. Fed. Personnel Council, Tau Epsilon Phi. Home: 1542 Orth Ct Wheaton IL 60187 Office: 230 S Dearborn St Chgo IL 60604

COHEN, SUSAN ELAINE, social service administrator; b. Los Angeles, July 20, 1953; d. Leo and Norma (Levin) C.; m. Daniel L. Stillings, June 13, 1981; children: Nicholas Loren, Joshua Adam. BS, U. Ill., 1975, MSW, 1978. Marriage and family therapist Family Service Assn. Brown County, Green Bay, Wis., 1978-85, supr. crisis ctr., 1984-85, program dir. crisis and sexual assault ctr, runaway project, 1985—. Mem. Acad. Cert. Soc. Workers (clin.), Am. Assn. Marriage and Family Therapy (clin.). Home: 2546 Laredo Ln Green Bay WI 54304 Office: Family Service Assn Brown County 131 S Madison Green Bay WI 54301

COHEN, TOBE MICHAEL, financial analyst; b. Chgo., Nov. 4, 1960; s. Bernard R. and Bess Rose (Nidetz) C. BS in Acct., U. Ill., 1982; MBA in Fin., DePaul U., 1983. CPA, Ill. Fin. rate analyst Nicor Inc. div. NI Gas, Naperville, Ill., 1984-86; sr. fin. analyst Kitchens of Sara Lee, Deerfield, Ill., 1986—. Jewish. Avocations: music, golf, baseball, photography. Home: 1310 Valley Lake Dr Suite 426 Schaumburg IL 60195 Office: Kitchens of Sara Lee 500 Waukegan Rd Deerfield IL 60015

COHILL, DONALD FRANK, surgeon; b. Darby, Pa., Dec. 1, 1934; s. Raymond Harris and Agnes Mae (Smith) C.; A.B. in Chemistry, Haverford (Pa.) Coll., 1956; M.D., U. Pa., 1960; m. Lorna Westcott, Feb. 15, 1957; children—Karen Lea, Linda Lea, Julie Lea, Andrew Scott. Intern, U. Pa.-Presbyn. Hosp., Phila., 1960-61; surg. resident Abington (Pa.) Meml. Hosp., 1966-70, assoc. surgeon, 1969-70; practice medicine specializing in gen. surgery, Racine, Wis., 1970—; surgeon St. Mary's, St. Luke's hosps.; chief of surgery St. Mary's Med. Ctr., Racine, 1986—; dir. med. edn. St. Mary's Hosp.; exec. com. Kurten Med. Group; adv. bd. Life Line, Racine. Bd. dirs. S.Am. Mission, Lake Worth, Fla. Served with M.C., USAF, 1962-64. Decorated Commendation medal; named Flight Surgeon of Yr., SAC, USAF, 1963-64. Fellow A.C.S., Milw. Acad. Surgery; mem. AMA, Wis., Racine County med. socs., Racine Acad. Medicine, Wis. Surg. Soc. Mem. Evang. Ch. Home: 1902 Crestwood Dr Caledonia WI 53108 Office: 2405 Northwestern Ave Racine WI 53404

COHN, ALAN, radiologist; b. Phila., June 9, 1940; s. Arthur Cohn and Hilda (Levy) Cramer; m. Nancy Lynn Bleecker, June 16, 1963 (dec. 1983); children: Matthew Paul, Justin Alexander; m. Diane Marjorie Stifter, Feb. 10, 1985. AB in Chemistry, U. Pa., 1961; DO, U. Osteo. Medicine and Surgery, 1965. Cert. Am. Osteopathic Coll. Radiology. Intern Pontiac (Mich.) Osteo. Hosp., 1965-66, resident in radiology, 1966-69, assoc. radiologist, 1969-73; chmn. dept. radiology and nuclear medicine Lansing (Mich.) Gen. Hosp., 1973-81, vice chmn. dept. medicine, chmn. tumor bd., 1975-77, mem. med. edn. com., 1979-81; asst. chief radiologist Park Med. Group, Detroit, 1981-87, Outpatient Imaging, Mich. Health Care Corp., 1987—; pres. Mich. Radiology, PC, 1973—; asst. clin. prof. radiology Coll. Osteo. Medicine Mich. State U., 1973-80; cons. radiologist Oakland County Health Depts., 1969-83; cons. Mich. Hosp. Assn. Mut. Ins. Co. Contbr. articles to profl. jours. Mem. Am. Osteo. Assn. (editorial cons.), Am. Osteo. Coll. Radiology (lectr.), Radiol. Soc. N.Am., Mich. Radiol. Soc., Mich. Osteo. Soc. Radiology, Mich. Assn. Physicians and Surgeons, Ingham County Assn. Osteo. Physicians and Surgeons, Am. Arbitration Assn., Am. Contract Bridge League (life master). Jewish. Club: Wabeek Country (Bloomfield Hills). Home: 1923 Pine Ridge Ln Bloomfield Hills MI 48013 Office: Mich Radiology PC 9221 E Jefferson Detroit MI 48214

COHN, ALVIN W., food company executive; b. 1921; married. Attended, DePaul U. With CFS Continental, Inc., Chgo., 1936—, v.p., 1948-58, pres., 1958—, chmn., 1968-81, chief operating officer, 1981, also dir. Served to 1st lt. U.S. Army, 1943-46. Office: CFS Continental Inc 100 S Wacker Dr Chicago IL 60606

COHN, ANN ROCHELLE, psychologist; b. N.Y.C., Apr. 16, 1941; d. Harry and Eleanor Rochelle; m. Ronald Ira Cohn, Dec. 20, 1970; 1 child, Henry Ian. BS, Temple U., 1962; PhD in Psychology, Ill. Inst. Tech., 1975. Editorial asst. Babcock & Wilcox, N.Y.C., 1962-64; creative dir. Comdine Corp., N.Y.C., 1964-68; v.p. Rowland Co., N.Y.C., 1968-70; intern psychology Ill. Masonic Med. Ctr., Chgo., 1974-75; psychologist Rehab. Inst. Chgo., 1975-77; pvt. practice clin. and cons. psychology Chgo., 1977—; media psychologist NBC Radio, Chgo., 1982—. Mem. Am. Psychol. Assn., AFTRA, Nat. Register Health Service Providers, Ill. Psychol. Assn. Office: 1030 N State St Chicago IL 60610

COHN, ANNE HARRIS, health planner, health science association administrator; b. Evanston, Ill., Jan. 16, 1945; d. Nathan and Marjorie (Kurtzon) C.; m. Michael Teitz, Mar. 25, 1973 (div. Dec. 1978). BA in Sociology, U. Mich., 1967; MA in Med. Sociology, Tufts U., 1970; MPH in Health Adminstrn., U. Calif., Berkeley, 1972, DrPH in Health Adminstrn., 1975. Lectr. sch. pub. health U. Calif., Berkeley, 1975-78; legis. aide Senator Albert Gore, Jr., Washington, 1978-79; spl. asst. to sec. HHH, Washington, 1979-80; exec. dir. Nat. Com. Prevention Child Abuse, Chgo., 1980—; adv. bd. Nat. Resource Ctr. Child Abuse, Denver, 1986—, Nat. Assn. Children of Alcoholics, South Laguna, Calif., 1987—. Contbr. articles to profl. jours., newspapers, encys. Assoc., bd. dirs. Berkeley Planning Assocs., 1973-78; bd. dirs. Nat. Congress Parents and Tchrs., Chgo., 1985—. White House fellow, 1979-80. Fellow AAAS (Congl. sci. fellow 1978-79); mem. Internat. Soc. Prevention Child Abuse and Neglect (sec. 1986—), Am. Pub. Health Assn., Soc. Research in Child Devel. Avocations: photography, triathlons. Office: Nat Com Prevention Child Abuse 332 S Michigan Ave Suite 950 Chicago IL 60604

COHN, BERT MARTIN, consulting engineering company executive; b. Stralsund, Germany, May 3, 1930; came to U.S., 1941, naturalized 1951; s. Fritz A. and Ilse (Joseph) C.; m. Holly Renald, Feb. 8, 1964; children—Helise, Judith. B.S. in Engring., Ill. Inst. Tech., 1952. Registered profl. engr. Ill., N.Y., N.J., Va.; cert. fallout shelter analyst Fed. Emergency Mgmt. Agy. Engr., Mo. Inspection Bur., St. Louis, 1950-53; chief fire protection br. U.S. Army No. Command, 8th Army, 1955-57; sr. v.p., treas., dir. Gage-Babcock & Assocs. Inc., Elmhurst, Ill., 1963-85, pres., 1985—; v.p., treas., dir. Gage-Babcock Internat. Ltd., Elmhurst, 1982—; mem. rev. panel on Nat. Bur. Standards Fire Research Ctr., NRC; lectr., expert witness, research investigator, fire and safety issues; engring. cons. fire protection and security. Mem. Bd. Fire and Police Commrs., Elmhurst, 1970-80, 84-86, chmn., 1977-80. Served with U.S. Army, 1953-54. Fellow ASTM (chmn. combustibility standards), Soc. Fire Protection Engrs.; mem. Am. Soc. Safety Engrs., Am. Soc. Indsl. Security (cert. protection profl.), Nat. Fire Protection Assn. Home: 346 Prospect Ave Elmhurst IL 60126 Office: Gage-Babcock & Assocs 135 Addison Ave Elmhurst IL 60126

COHN, BRIAN ROBERT, investment banker; b. Youngstown, Ohio, June 27, 1957; s. Stanley and Carolyn (Fried) C.; m. Nancy Listorti, Dec. 1, 1985. BA, Ohio U., 1974. Investment exec. Butler Wick & Co., Youngstown, Ohio, 1979-80, Paine, Weber, Youngstown, 1980-81, Paine, Westchester, N.Y., 1981-82, L.F. Rothschild, N.Y.C., 1982-84; pres., prin. Brian Cohn Inc., Ohio, Md., Washington, N.Y., Fla., Calif., 1984—; cons. Depositer Fin. Services, Cleve., Kasko Inc., Venture Capital, Ohio and Fla., Adult Congregate Living Group, Youngstown. Active United Jewish Appeal. Mem. Nat. Assn. Security Dealers, Security Investor Protection Corp., Fin. Planning Investment Banking and Brokerage Assn. Lodge: B'nai B'rith. Avocations: art, tennis, sailing, equestrian. Office: City Centre One Youngstown OH 44504 also: 112 Cove Creek Kent Island MD 21871

COHN, ROBERT H., food company executive; b. 1926; married. Entire career with CFS Continental, Inc., Chgo., pres., 1968-81, chmn. bd., chief exec. officer, 1981—, also dir. Office: CFS Continental Inc 100 S Wacker Dr Chicago IL 60606 *

COHN, WILLIAM ELLIOTT, engineering executive; b. Chgo., Apr. 10, 1951; s. Henry R. Cohn and Celia (Kalman) Rich; m. Patricia Alice Walsh, June 15, 1973 (div. Feb. 1981); 1 child, Alexander Walsh; m. Linda Sue Carl, Dec. 3, 1983; children: Glenn Jospeh, Hayden Ross. BEE, U. Ill., 1973; MBA, Roosevelt U., 1982. Broadcast engr. U. Ill., Urbana, 1971-73; design engr. Zenith Radio Corp., Chgo., 1973-81; engr. field ops. Zenith Electronics Corp., Glenview, Ill., 1981-83, mgr. field engring., 1983—. Patentee in field. Mem. IEEE, Soc. Cable TV Engrs., Heath Users Group. Avocations: micro computers, home repair, collecting antique radio. Home: 185 Grovenor Dr Schaumburg IL 60193 Office: Zenith Electronics Corp 699 Wheeling Rd Mount Prospect IL 60056

COHOAT, JOHN STEPHEN, health services executive; b. Indpls., Jan. 8, 1954; s. John Joseph and Mary Arlene (Stieff) C.; m. Adrienne Allyce Berg, June 19, 1976; children: Adair Lynn, John Thomas, Mary Kathryne. BBA, U. Notre Dame, 1976; MBA, U. Pitts., 1987. CPA, Pa., Ind. Auditor Coopers & Lybrand, South Bend, Ind., 1976-82; auditor, cons. Coopers & Lybrand, Pitts., 1982-84; v.p. fin. Med-Chek Lab., Inc., Pitts., 1984-86; pres., treas. Cardiac Fitness, Inc., Pitts., 1985-86; pres., chief exec. officer OMNI Healthcare Systems, Inc., South Bend, 1986—. Mem. mgmt. assistance program United Way St. Joseph County, South Bend, 1987. Mem. Am. Inst. CPA's, Am. Osteo. Hosp. Assn. (mem. affairs council 1987), Healthcare Fin. Mgmt. Assn., Vis. Nurse Assn. (bd. dirs. 1986—), Beta Alpha Psi, Beta Gamma Sigma. Republican. Roman Catholic. Clubs: Knollwood Country (Granger, Ind.), Summit (South Bend). Avocations: golf, racquetball, running. Home: 51411 Pebble Beach Ct Granger IN 46530 Office: OMNI Healthcare Systems Inc 202 S Michigan #850 South Bend IN 46601

COIL, CURTIS EDWIN, JR., pattern company executive; b. Paulding, Ohio, Feb. 19, 1936; s. Curtis Edwin Coil and Opal Berniece (McCullough) Hill; m. Martha Jean Sigmon, Nov. 7, 1958; 1 child, Gary Eugene. Grad. high sch., Ft. Wayne, Ind. Cert. journeymen patternmaker. Patternmaker Process Pattern, Ft. Wayne, 1955-65, Erler's Industries, Anderson, Ind., 1965-67; owner, patternmaker Modern Pattern Works, Inc., Richmond, Ind., 1967—; Lodge: Elks (exalted ruler Webb lodge 1979-80, numerous others), Shriners, Masons. Avocations: reading, boating, hunting. Home: 2309 Parkdale Dr Richmond IN 47374 Office: Modern Pattern Works Inc 1400 NW 5th St PO Box 1341 Richmond IN 47375

COIL, LOWELL MICHAEL, pharmacist; b. Iowa, June 11, 1929; s. Michael Moses and Ethel Mae (Lindsey) C.; m. Janelle Kay Seidel, June 16, 1962; children: Lowell Michael II, Melissa Kay. BS in Pharmacy, BS in Edn., Drake U., 1961. Prin., owner Mike's Pharmacy, Omaha, 1962-74, Des

Moines, 1977—; owner Janelle's Maternity, Omaha, 1965—, Des Moines, 1980—. Leader Boy Scouts Am. Omaha council, 1971-75; coach football, softball, track, basketball YMCA, Omaha, 1974-77, football, Little All-Am. League, Des Moines, 1977-80; founder/coach West Des Moines Track Club, 1978—; founder, charter mem. Iowa Athletic Congress, 1979; pres. Iowa Youth Athletics Jr. Olympics, 1979-85, exec. dir., 1979—; official Athletic Congree Nat. level Track and Field. Named Hon. Football Coach of Yr. Omaha YMCA, 1976. Mem. Nat. Assn. Retail Druggists, Polk County Pharmacy Assn., Pi Kappa Alpha. Republican. Methodist. Home: 1716 Plaza Circle Des Moines IA 50322 Office: Mikes Pharmacy 3510 University Ave Des Moines IA 50311

COIN, SHEILA REGAN, management consultant; b. Columbus, Ohio, Feb. 17, 1942; d. James Daniel and Jean (Hodgson) Cook; m. Tasso H. Coin, Sept. 17, 1967 (div.); children—Tasso, Alison Regan; m. Robert James Hall, Feb. 28, 1987. B.S., U. Iowa, 1964. R.N. Staff nurse VA Hosp., Boston, 1964-66; field rep. ARC, Chgo., 1966-67, adminstr., 1967; asst. div. dir. Am. Hosp. Assn., sec. Am. Soc. Hosp. Dirs. Nursing, Chgo., 1967-69; owner Coin & Assocs., Chgo., 1975-77; ptnr. Coin, Newell & Assocs., Chgo., 1977—; instr. dept. continuing edn. Loyola U., Chgo., 1975-77, Rock Valley Coll. Mgmt. Inst., Rockford, Ill., 1978-80, Ill. Central Coll. Inst. Personal and Profl. Devel., Peoria, 1979—, Triton Coll. Continuing Edn., River Grove, Ill., 1983-86, No. Ill. U. Continuing Edn., DeKalb, 1983—. Vol. Art Inst., Chgo., 1968-69; mem. Chgo. Beautiful Com., 1968-73; chmn. Mayor Daley's Chgo. Beautiful Awards Project, 1972; mem. jr. bd. Girl Scouts Assn., Chgo., 1975-76; mem. jr. governing bd. Chgo. Symphony Orch., 1971—, pres., 1977-78; governing mem. Orchestral Assn., Chgo., 1977-81; bd. dirs. Mid-Am. chpt. ARC, Chgo., 1979-81, vice chmn. 1986—; bd. dirs. Chgo. dist., 1981—, chmn. fin. devel. com., 1982-85, vice chmn. dist. bd., 1986—; dir. Com. for Thalossemia Chgo. Bd., 1981-82; mem. Women's bd. Nat. Com. Prevention Child Abuse, Chgo., 1981-82. Mem. Am. Mgmt. Assn., Am. Soc. Tng. and Devel., Ill. Tng. and Devel. Assn. Democrat. Roman Catholic. Avocations: piano; tennis; national and international travel; spectator sports; family activities. Home: 1037 W North Shore Ave Chicago IL 60626 Office: Coin Newell & Assocs 919 N Michigan Ave Chicago IL 60611

COL, JEANNE-MARIE, public administration educator; b. San Jose, Calif., Apr. 18, 1946; d. Raymond Thompson and Elizabeth Jean (Peter) C. BA cum laude, U. Calif., Davis, 1968, MA, 1969; PhD, U. S.C., 1977. With dept. political sci. and pub. adminstrn. Makerere U., Kampala, Uganda, 1972-76; with dept. political sci. Calif. State U., San Jose, 1977; asst. prof. SUNY, Albany, 1977-81; assoc. prof. pub. adminstrn. program Sangamon State U., Springfield, Ill., 1981—; cons. United Nations, N.Y.C., 1980-81, 86-87. Co-author: (videotape) Dealing with Differences in the Heterogenous Workplace, 1984; contbr. articles to profl. jours. Recipient Outstanding Demonstration award Nat. Conf. on Teaching Pub. Adminstrn., 1985. Mem. Internat. Assn. Schs. and Insts. of Adminstrn. (project dir., 1987—), Am. Soc. Pub. Adminstrn. (nat. council 1985—, chmn. women in pub. adminstrn. sect. 1984-85, tng. com. 1986-87, vice-chmn. pubs. com., 1987—, commn. on orgn. and structure 1987—), Midwest Polit. Sci. Assn. (exec. com. 1987—), Internat. Political Sci. Assn. (project leader 1982—), Pi Alpha Alpha, Pi Sigma Alpha. Democrat. Episcopalian. Avocations: swimming, cooking, travel. Home: 28 Trailridge Ln Springfield IL 62704 Office: Sangamon State U Pub Adminstrn Program Shepherd Rd Springfield IL 62708

COLARCO, RICHARD FRANK, military officer, engineer; b. N.Y.C., June 9, 1949; s. Frank Salvatore and Angelina (Mammano) C.; m. Linda Irene Gensinger, Sept. 5, 1970; children: Peter, Susan. BS in Physics, Manhattan Coll., 1970; MS in Ops. Research, Air Force Inst. Tech., 1980; EdS, Troy State U., 1986. Commd. 2d lt. USAF, 1972, advanced through grades to maj., 1984; instr. electronic warfare USAF, Grand Forks, N.D., 1974-78; chief attrition analysis modeling br. SAC USAF, Omaha, 1980-83, chief sci. and tech. electronic intelligence ops., 1983-85, chief electronic combat systems engring. div. SAC, 1986—; adj. faculty Buena Vista Coll., Council Bluffs, Iowa, 1980-85, Embry Riddle U., Offutt AFB, Nebr., 1981-84. Vol. probation officer Juvenile Ct., Grand Forks, 1975-78; com. mem. Boy Scouts Am., Offutt AFB, 1983-85. Decorated Air medal. Mem. Air Force Assn. (life), Assn. of Old Crows. Republican. Roman Catholic. Avocations: competitive shooting, computers, photography. Home: 2303 Whitted Dr Omaha NE 68123 Office: USAF HQ SAC/DOJS Offutt AFB NE 68113

COLAW, EMERSON S., clergyman. Bishop N. Central jurisdiction United Methodist Ch., Mpls. Office: 122 W Franklin Ave Rm 400 Minneapolis MN 55404 *

COLBER, RUSSELL HOWARD, writer, advertising executive; b. Milw., June 21, 1938; s. Ralph Howard and Margaret Marie (Hoppens) C.; B.A. (WLOL Broadcasting scholar), U. Minn., 1965; M.S. (Nat. Acad. of TV Arts and Scis. fellow), Newhouse Sch. Pub. Communications, Syracuse U., 1966; m. Bonita Elizabeth Cheesebrough, Sept. 1, 1963 (div. July 1986); children—Newell, Geoffrey, Charles, Nelson. Asst. to v.p. corp. communications Dayton Hudson Corp., Mpls., 1966-70; v.p., Advertisers Diversified Services, Mpls., 1970-73; chmn. communications div. The Mpls. Inst. of Arts, 1973-75; pres., Russ Colber & Assos., Mpls., 1975-78; dir. pub. relations Sielaff/Johnson Advt., 1978-79; dir. advt. Salkin & Linoff, 1979-80, EO Inc., 1981-82, PSG Medtronic Inc., Mpls., 1982-87; programs mgr. Worldwide Communications, Inc., 1987—; convenor Twin Cities Journalism Conf., Nat. Model Cities Conf.; panelist Minn. Advt. Fedn. Trade Press Day, 1983. Recipient Fisher-Stevens Nat. Mail Works Achievement award, 1983; Excellence award Soc. Tech. Communications, 1986. Mem. Pub. Relations Soc. Am. (health sect., accredited in pub. relations), Am. Med. Writers Assn., Advt. Fedn., Bus. and Profl. Advt. Assn. (Oliver award 1984). Home: 4828 Xerxes Ave S Minneapolis MN 55410 Office: 6951 Central Ave NE Minneapolis MN 55432

COLBERT, CAROL SUGAR, psychologist; b. Cleve., Nov. 1, 1933; d. Alfred and Esther (Reiter) Sugar; m. Charles E. Colbert, Oct. 14, 1956 (div. Apr. 1967); children: Paul Andrew, Jeremy Stephen, Daniel Todd, Thomas Michael; m. James M. Shulman, Apr. 20, 1985; stepchildren: Andrew James, Jonathan Ira, Ruth Eileen. BA, Cornell U., 1955; MA, Case Western Res. U., 1968, PhD, 1973. Lic. psychologist, Ohio. Sec., editor Univ. Hosps., Cleve., 1955-57; sr. psychologist Beech Brook Treatment Ctr., Cleve., 1969-77; pvt. practice psychology Cleve., 1974—; lectr. Cleve. State U., 1973-75; cons. Cath. Service Bur., Painesville, Ohio, 1977-81, Guardian ad Litum Project Cuyhoga County Juvenile and Domestic Relations Cts., 1982—; assoc. adj. prof. Case Western Res. U., Cleve., 1977-81, Marriage Clinic Univ. Hosps. Psychiat. Out Patient Dept., 1981—; co-dir. Family Divorce Ctr., Cleve., 1979—. Mem. Am. Psychol. Assn., Ohio Psychol. Assn., Cleve. Psychol. Assn. (bd. dirs.), Cleve. Acad. Cons. Psychologists, Council for Nat. Register of Health Service Providers in Psychology, Cleve. Soc. Psychoanalytic Psychology. Office: Hillcrest Med Bldg Suite 550 6801 Mayfield Rd Mayfield Heights OH 44124

COLBERT, THOMAS ALBERT, mental health facility administrator; b. Shelbyville, Ind., Sept. 22, 1935; s. Leo Harter and Antoinette Marie (Pitman) C.; m. Patricia Lucille Breeze, Dec. 27, 1958; children: Teresa, Mary Agnes, Daniel Patrick. AB, Millikin U., 1958; MSW, U. Ill., 1964. Supr. Ill. Dept. Children and Family Service, Champaign, 1964-66; exec. dir. North Country Mental Health, Berlin, N.H., 1966-68, Stephenson-Jo Davies Mental Health, Freeport, Ill., 1968-74, Branch County Mental Health, Coldwater, Mich., 1974-80, Monroe (Mich.) County Mental Health, 1980-82; pvt. practice social work Monroe, 1982-85; dir. Cath. Family Service of the Thumb, Caro, Mich., 1985—. Mem. Nat. Assn. Mental Health Adminstrs., Nat. Assn. Social Workers (cert.), Sigma Zeta. Avocations: writing, traditional jazz. Home: 15 Custer Ct Monroe MI 48161

COLBURN, DAVID WAYNE, vocational educator; b. Detroit, Aug. 26, 1950; s. Harry Wayne and Leona Irene (Hunter) C.; m. Rosemary Marie Mayer, Jan. 10, 1951. A.S., Macomb County Community Coll., 1970; B.S., Wayne State U., 1972, M.Ed., 1976, Specialist cert. in Edn., 1980, Ed.D., 1982. Detailer, Cross Co., Fraser, Mich., 1973, Proficient Products, Inc., Warren, Mich., 1978-80; drafting tchr. Detroit Bd. Edn., 1972—, tchr. adult edn., 1973—; mem. task force vocat. edn. service Mich. Dept. Edn., 1981-82, mem. task force tchr. facilitator for Vocat. Tech. Edn. Service, 1983. Mem. Am. Vocat. Assn., Mich. Occupational Edn. Assn., Mich. Curriculum Leaders, Mich. Trade and Tech. Edn., Mich. Indsl. Edn. Soc. (regional adminstrv. officer 1984—; Region Tchr. of Yr. 1983-84). Roman Catholic. Lodge: KC. Home: 32814 Beacon Ln Fraser MI 48026

COLBURN, MICHAEL JOHN, management consultant; b. Columbus, Ohio, June 13, 1941; s. John Lawrence and Edna Marie (Eviston); m. Sharon Ann Murray, Apr. 22, 1967; children: Dennis, Kathryn, Danial, Nora. B in Indsl. and Systems Engring., Ohio State U., 1964, MS, 1986. Registered profl. engr., Ohio. Indsl. engr. Timken Co., Columbus, 1964-67; indsl. engring. mgr. Anchor Hocking, Jacksonville, Fla., 1967-70, Ross Labs., Columbus, 1970-73; grad teaching assoc. Ohio State U., Columbus, 1984-86; grad. research assoc. The Nat. Ctr. for Research in Vocat. Edn., Columbus, 1986—; pres. Colburn and Assocs., Columbus, 1973—. Author and co-author mgmt. tng. manuals. Chmn. Franklin County Rural Zoning Commn., Ohio, 1981-86; vice chmn. Franklin County Dem. Party, Columbus, 1977-81, exec. com., 1976-85; ch-chair Ohio CoalitionAdult Learning, 1987. Named Cath. Young Man of Yr., Columbus Dioceson Council Cath. Youth, 1966, Committeeperson of Yr., Franklin County Dem. Party, 1981; recipient Pres.'s Leadership award Jacksonville Jaycees, 1969. Mem. Am. Soc. Tng. and Devel. (pres. cen. Ohio chpt. 1985), Ohio Assn. Adult and Continuing Edn. (bd. dirs. 1985—). Democrat. Roman Catholic. Avocation: academics. Home: 2992 Upton Rd W Columbus OH 43232

COLBY, GAGE, dentist; b. St. Paul, June 28, 1923; s. Woodard L. and Ruth (Gage) C.; m. Sylvia Chaney, Nov. 25, 1950 (dec. Sept. 1978); children: Christopher, Gregory, Katherine, Rebecca; m. Virginia Manke, Oct. 5, 1979. BA, U. Minn., 1944, DDS, 1946. Commd. lt. (j.g.) USN, 1946, advanced through grades to capt., 1963, ret., 1970; general practice dentistry St. Paul, 1970—. Pres.' council Children's Hosp. Assn. Found., St. Paul, 1986. Fellow Internat. Coll. Craniomandibular Orthopedics; mem. Acad. Gen. Dentistry (master), Minn. Acad. Gen. Dentistry (pres. 1975-76, chmn. continuing dental edn. 1977-86), Retired Officers Assn. (life), U. Minn. Alumni Assn. (life), U. Minn. Sch. Dentistry Century Club (life), Am. Legion, VFW. Episcopalian. Lodge: Rotary (Paul Harris fellow St. Paul chpt.). Office: 408 Saint Peter St 412 Hamm Bldg Saint Paul MN 55102

COLBY, ROBERT LESTER, psychologist; b. N.Y.C., Jan. 21, 1941; came to Can., 1966; s. Allen Michael and Beatrice Dorethea (Kalkut) C. BA, NYU, 1963; MS, L.I. U., 1965. Research fellow Ctr. for Ednl. Disabilities, Guelph, Ont., Can., 1967-69; lectr. U. Guelph, 1967-69; dir., chief psychologist Psychol. Services of County Sch. Bd., Brantford, Ont., Can., 1969-83; pvt. practice psychology Vancouver, B.C., Can., 1980—; clin. field placement supr. Simon Fraser U., Vancouver, 1984—, lectr. Justice Inst. B.C., 1984—; clin. dir. Personnel Inst. Can., Vancouver, 1984—; pres. Grad. Tests Tng., Inc., Vancouver, 1984—, Colby Gallagler & Assocs., Vancouver, 1984—; cons. to govt. agys. and depts., Can., 1984—. Chmn. Interagy. Coordinating Com., Brantford, 1975-77; bd. dirs. Ont. Antipoverty Coordinating Com., Brantford, 1975-77. Mem. Am. Psychol. Assn., Can. Psychol. Assn., B.C. Psychol. Assn. (bd. dirs. 1985—, chmn. ethics com. 1985—), N.S. Psychol. Assn., Can. Mental Health Assn., Soc. for Psychol. Study of Social Issues.

COLE, ANNA MARIE, English language educator; b. Berryville, Ark., Feb. 21, 1944; d. William Riley and Lucy Marie (Cain) Walters; m. Harold David Cole, Aug. 2, 1965; 1 child, Eleanor. BA, U. Tulsa, 1966; MA, Case Western Res. U., 1981. Lectr. English Case Western Res. U., Cleve., 1977-81; tchr. ESL Am. Lang. Acad., Berea, Ohio, 1981—, dir. acad. counseling and placement, 1983—; lectr. Baldwin-Wallace Coll., Berea, Ohio, 1983—. Mem. MLA, Nat. Council Tchrs. English. Unitarian. Avocations: reading, traveling. Office: Baldwin-Wallace Coll Berea OH 44017

COLE, DONALD WHEELER, management psychologist; b. Cleve., Dec. 30, 1929; s. Lawrence Chester and Mabel Louise (Wheeler) C.; A.B., U. R.I., 1950; M.S., Boston U., 1952; 3d year cert. Smith Coll., 1955; D.S.W., Washington U., St. Louis, 1964; m. Norma Gale Skoog, July 11, 1953; 5 children. Mgr. mgmt. devel. TRW, Inc., Cleve., 1963-71; mgmt. psychologist, cons., pres. Don Cole & Assocs., Cleve., 1968—; dir. personnel and orgn. devel. Bobbie Brooks, Cleve., 1974-76; mem. sci. and tech. council Am. Industries Corp., Cleve., 1969-71; mem. faculty Cleve. State U., 1966-73; dir. Orgn. Devel. Inst., 1968—; pres. Internat. Registry Orgn. Devel. Profls., Cleve., 1968—, pub., 1974—. Lic. psychologist, Ohio. Fellow Am. Orthopsychiat. Assn. (life); mem. Société Internationale pour le Développement des Organisations (N.Am. dir. 1977—), Am. Psychol. Assn., Cleve. Psychol. Assn., Orgn. Devel. Network (trustee 1978-81). Author: Professional Suicide, 1981; Improving Profits Through Organization Development, 1982; Conflict Resolution Technology, 1983; pub. Orgn. Devel. Jour., 1983—; editor Orgns. and Change, 1974—; assoc. editor Leadership and Orgn. Devel. Jour., 1979—. Home: 11234 Walnut Ridge Rd Chesterland OH 44026 Office: 6501 Wilson Mills Rd Suite K Cleveland OH 44143

COLE, EUGENE ROGER, clergyman, author; b. Cleve., Nov. 14, 1930; s. Bernard James and Mary Louise (Rogers) C.; B.A., St. Edwards Sem., 1954; student John Carroll U., 1957; M.Div., Sulpician Sem. N.W., 1958; A.B., Central Wash. U., Ellensburg, 1960; M.A., Seattle U., 1970; Litt.D. (hon.), 1983. Ordained priest Roman Catholic Ch., 1958; Newman moderator and cons. Central Wash. U., Ellensburg, 1958-59; bus. mgr. Experiment Press, Seattle, 1959-60; chaplain St. Elizabeth Hosp., Yakima, Wash., 1959-61; chmn. English dept. Yakima Central Cath. High Sch., 1959-66, Marquette High Sch., Yakima, 1966-68; poetry critic Nat. Writers Club, Denver, 1969-72; poet in service Poets & Writers Inc., N.Y.C., 1974—; founder Godspeople, Inc., 1985, dir. 1985—, originator, anapoem, 1985; instr. contract bridge, Ind., 1975-79; freelance writer, editor, researcher, 1958—; researcher Harvard, 1970; religious counselor. Recipient Poetry Broadcast award, 1968, Musical Expertise award, 1970, Lorraine Harr Haiku award, 1974, Ann. Mentor Poetry award, 1974, Pro Mundi Beneficio award, 1975, Readers Union award, 1976, Diploma di Merito, 1982, Marathon award Cleve. Orchestra, 1983. Authors Guild, Poetry Soc. Am. (judge 1970), Western World Haiku Soc., Acad. Am. Poets, World Acad. Poets, World-Wide Acad. Scholars, Internat. Poetry Soc., Soc. for Scholarly Pub., Internat. Platform Assn., Eighteen Nineties Soc. (London), Friends of the Lilly Library, Expt. Group, Soc. for Study of Midwestern Lit., Nat. Fedn. State Poetry Socs., Poetry Soc. (London), Sir Thomas Beechom Soc., Chgo. Symphony Orch. Assn., Cleve. Mus. Art, Ohioana Library Assn., No. Ohio Bibliophilic Soc., Century Club of Cleve. State Univ., Poets' League Greater Cleve., Am. Contract Bridge League, Kappa Delta Pi. Composer: Werther: Tone Poem for Piano, 1948; Chronicle for Tape, 1960. Author: Which End, the Empyrean?, 1959; April Is the Cruelest Month, 1970; Falling Up: Haiku & Senryu, 1979; Act & Potency (poems), 1980; Ding an sich: anapoems, 1985; Uneasy Camber: Early Poems & Diversions 1943-50, 1986; Godspeople: Not a Church but a People, 1987; lyrics for male prodn. Finian's Rainbow, 1958; 3 hymns on Bach melodies, 1958; editor: Grand Slam: 13 Great Short Stories about Bridge, 1975; In the Beginning, 1978; assoc. editor: The Harvester, 1955; guest editor Experiment: An Internat. Rev., 1961; editorial staff This Is My Best, 1970; contbr. Your Literary I.Q. Saturday Rev., 1970-72; author religious monograph, also contbr. articles, poetry and drama to numerous lit. jours. and anthologies. Home: 9810 Cove Dr North Royalton OH 44133 Office: PO Box 91277 Cleveland OH 44101

COLE, FRANK CRUNDEN, mfg. co. exec.; b. St. Paul, May 14, 1922; s. Wallace H. and Mary (Crunden) C.; B.A., Williams Coll., 1943; m. Ardath Starkloff, May 23, 1959; children—Maria C., Catherine L., Wendy F., Mary C., Caroline B. Vice pres. Crunden Martin Mfg. Co., St. Louis, 1954-64, pres., 1964—, chmn. bd., 1971—; mng. partner Riverfront Realty Co. Bd. dirs. Jefferson Expansion Meml., 1965—. Served to lt. (j.g.), USNR, 1943-46. Clubs: St. Louis Country, Noonday, Deer Creek, Stadium. Office: Crunden Martin Mfg Co PO Box 508 Saint Louis MO 63166

COLE, HAROLD DAVID, art history educator; b. Tulsa, Feb. 28, 1940; s. William Harold and Ida Mae (Cronin) C.; m. Anna Marie Walters, Aug. 2, 1965; 1 child, Eleanor Melissa. BA in Art Criticism, U. Tulsa, 1963, MA in Art Criticism, 1966; MA in Art History, Ohio State U., 1972, PhD in Art History, 1982. Instr. Art History Philbrook Art Ctr., Tulsa, 1964-66; asst. dir. art gallery U. Tulsa, 1963-66; instr. to assoc prof. of art history Baldwin-Wallace Coll., Berea, Ohio, 1966-84, prof. art history, 1985—. Ohio State U. Regents fellow, 1977, Lazarus fellow 1972. Mem. Coll. Art Assn., Internat. Ctr. Medieval Art, Mid-West Art Assn., Ohio Arts Council, Alpha Sigma Lambda (Faculty Excellance award 1986). Office: Baldwin Wallace Coll 95 Eastland Rd Berea OH 44017

COLE, JEFFREY A., retail stores executive; b. 1914. BA, Harvard U., 1963, MBA, 1965. With Cole Nat. Corp., 1969—, chmn. exec. com., treas., 1977-78, chmn. exec. com., treas., chief fin. officer, 1978-83, pres., 1983—, vice-chmn. bd., chief exec. officer, 1984—, also bd. dirs. Office: Cole Nat Corp 29001 Cedar Rd Cleveland OH 44124 *

COLE, JOSEPH EDMUND, specialty retail company executive; b. Cleve., Jan. 4, 1915; s. Solomon and Sarah (Miller) C.; m. Marcia Newman, Oct. 31, 1937; children: Jeffrey, Stephan. Student, Ohio State U., 1932, Fenn Coll., Cleve., 1933. Salesman Waldorf Brewing Co., 1933-35; office mgr., then gen. mgr. Nat. Key Shops, Inc., 1935-44; partner, sales dir. Curtis Industries, 1944-50; pres., now chmn. Cole Nat. Corp., Cleve., 1950—; past chmn. Shelter Resources Corp.; past dir. BancOhio Nat. Bank, Cleve. Past pub. The Cleveland Press. Active Jewish Welfare Fund, Cleve., 1963-64; Chmn. Ohio Citizens for Kennedy, 1960; chmn. Hubert Humphrey for Pres., 1972; mem. Cuyahoga County Democratic Exec. Com., 1960—; chmn. finance com. Dem. Nat. Com., 1973-74; Bd. dirs. Jewish Community Fedn., Cleve., Notre Dame Coll., Playhouse Sq. Found., Cleve., Palm Beach Ctr. for the Performing Arts, Fla.; past trustee Cleve. State U.; past chmn. scholarship fund Ohio State Coll.; life mem. Brandeis U. Mem. Cleve. C. of C. Jewish (trustee temple). Clubs: Masons, (32 deg.), Shriners, Oakwood Country City (Cleve.); Standard (Chgo.); Palm Beach (Fla.) Country. Office: Cole Nat Corp 29001 Cedar Rd Cleveland OH 44124

COLE, KATHLEEN ANN, social worker, advt. agy. exec.; b. Cin., Nov. 22, 1946; d. James Scott and Kathryn Gertrude (Borisch) Cole; B.A., Miami U., 1968; M.S.W., U. Mich., 1972; M.M., Northwestern U., 1978; m. Brian Brandt, Mar. 21, 1970. Social worker Hamilton County Welfare Dept., Cin., 1969-70, Lucas County Children Services Bd., Toledo, 1970-74, East Maine Sch. Dist., Niles, Ill., 1974-77; account supr. Leo Burnett Advt. Agy., Chgo., 1978—; field instr. Loyola U., Chgo., 1976-77. Mem. Acad. Cert. Social Workers, Nat. Assn. Social Workers, Miami U. Alumni Assn. (dir. 1976—), Northwestern U. Mgmt. Club. Home: 414 Kelling Ln Glencoe IL 60022 Office: Leo Burnett Advt Agy Prudential Plaza Chicago IL 60601

COLE, NEWTON V., military officer, chaplain; b. Marks, Miss., Sept. 7, 1928; m. Sue Vernon; children: David, Charles, Susan. BS, Tex. A&M U., 1947; BD and M of Religious Edn., Southwestern Bapt. Sem., 1951; M of Pub. Adminstrn., George Washington U.; postgrad., Army-Air Force Chaplain Sch., Ft. Slocum, N.Y., 1951, Air Command and Staff Coll., 1964. Commd. USAF, 1951, advanced through grades to col., 1974; chaplain USAF, Chanute AFB, Ill., 1951; chaplain 1805 AACS Group USAF, McAndrew AFB, Nfld., Can., 1951-55; chaplain USAF, McCoy AFB, Fla., 1959-61; installation staff chaplain USAF, Bruntingthrope, Eng., 1961-65, Gunter AFB, Ala., 1965-67, Nakhon AFB, Thailand, 1967-68; sr. Protestant chaplain USAF, Randolph AFB, Tex., 1968-72; from chief spl. activities and tng. to chief profl. div. hdqurs air fef. command USAF, Colorado Springs, Colo., 1972-77; installation staff chaplain USAF, Homestead AFB, Fla., 1977-79; staff chaplain U.S. Forces and 5th Air Force USAF, Japan, 1979-82; command chaplain mil. airlift command USAF, Scott AFB, Ill., 1982—; pastor First Bapt. Ch., Whitewright, Tex., 1955-58; — Bellevue Bapt. Ch., Colorado Springs, 1958-59. Decorated Legion of Merit with oak leaf cluster. Office: USAF Mil Airlift Command Office of Command Chaplain Scott AFB IL 62225

COLE, PATRICIA ANN SHANNON, educational administrator; b. Trenton, Mich., Sept. 5, 1948; d. James Norman and Virginia Ruth (Davis) Shannon; B.S., U. Mich., 1970, Ph.D., 1981; M.A., Eastern Mich. U., 1974. Jr. high sch. bus. edn. tchr. Wyandotte (Mich.) Schs., 1970-72, adult edn. tchr. bus. edn., 1970-72, bus. edn. tchr. Roosevelt High Sch., 1972-78, dir. vocat./career edn., 1978-85, summer adminstr. summer youth employment program four-city consortium, co-op coordinator, 1982-84; dir. state and fed. programs, pub. relations, curriculum, profl. devel., summer gifted coordinator Wyandotte Pub. Schs., 1985—; instr. Detroit Coll. Bus., Dearborn, Mich., 1974-82; adj. instr. grad. research Ea. Mich. U., 1974-82. Cert. profl. sec., 1975; recipient certificates of appreciation for service in field; named outstanding bus. edn. student U. Mich., 1970. Mem. Mich. Council Vocat. Adminstrs. (rep. to Vocat. Edn. Study Task Force, 1980-81), Vocat. Edn. Planning Com. (chmn. Wayne County, Mich. chpt.), S.E. Regional Vocat. Educators (sec./treas.), Mich./Nat. Assn. State/Fed. Program Suprs., Wayne County State/Fed. Progam Suprs. (chmn.). Guest speaker profl. confs.; contbr. articles to profl. publs. in field. Home: 424 Riverside Dr Wyandotte MI 48192 Office: 639 Oak St Wyandotte MI 48192

COLE, PAUL LEON, office equipment company executive, marketing engineer, consultant; b. Lansing, Mich., June 25, 1946; s. Leslie Arthur and Alice Margaret (LeBoeuf) C.; m. Candace Ann Denhof, June 15, 1968; children. B.S.E., U. Mich., 1970, M.B.A., U. Mont., 1975. Registered profl. engr., Mich. Engr., Brunswick Corp., Muskegon, Mich., 1967-70; product planner, crane and hoist ops. Dresser Industries Inc., Muskegon, 1976-78, mgr. product planning, 1978-82; product mgr. Shaw Walker Co., 1983-87, mgr. mktg., planning and devel., 1987—; cons. Cole & Assocs. Served to capt. USAF, 1970-76. Mem. Nat. Soc. Profl. Engrs., Mich. Soc. Profl. Engrs., Soc. Mfg. Engrs. (sr.). Home: 4283 Carolyn Dr Muskegon MI 49444

COLE, RONALD ALLEN, mechanical engineer, consultant; b. Chgo., Feb. 26, 1941; s. Sol and Faye (Weintraub) C.; m. Hinda Halpern, May 11, 1963; children: Brian, Jason. BSME, U. Ill., 1964. Registered profl. engr., Ill. Dist. sales mgr. Vilter Mfg. Corp., Milw., 1964-67; product mgr. Crepaco, Inc., Chgo., 1967-71; pvt. practice mech. engring. Evanston, Ill., 1971-73; chief engr. Imeco, Inc., Polo, Ill., 1973-76; sales mgr. Bohn Heat Trans. Div., Danville, Ill., 1976-82; pres. R. A. Cole & Assoc., Inc., Champaign, Ill., 1982—. Mem. ASME, ASHRAE (chmn. com. 1981-83, Disting. Service award 1987), Internat. Inst. Ammonia Refrigeration (dir. 1984-87, assoc. dir. indsl. refrigeration conf. 1982-87, dir. Refrigerating Engrs. & Technicians Assn. Indsl. Refrigeration Sch. for Users 1985-87), NSPE. Avocations: reading, interior decorating, gourmet cooking, motorcycle riding. Home and Office: 1111 W Church St Champaign IL 61821

COLE, WILLIAM PORTER, librarian; b. St. Louis, Sept. 11, 1929; s. Saxon and Mary Porter (Moore) C.; m. Alexandra Melpomene Vasos, June 9, 1973; children—Julia Ellen, William Kendall, Heather, Jason Antares. B.A., Washington U., St. Louis, 1952; M.A.L.S., U. Mich., 1962. Pres. Cole Bros. Constrn. Co., Inc., St. Louis County, Mo., 1950-61; adminstrv. asst. Washington U., 1962-63, asso. dir. libraries, 1968-70, dir. libraries, 1970—; mng. editor Library Tech. Reports, ALA, Chgo., 1964-68. Served with USAF, 1948-49. Home: 701 Cherry Tree Ln Olivette MO 63132 Office: St Louis Univ Pius XII Meml Library 3650 Lindell Blvd Saint Louis MO 63108

COLEMAN, B. R., provincial judge. Judge Ct. of Queen's Bench, Winnipeg, Manitoba, Can. Office: Court of Queen's Bench, Law Courts Bldg, Winnipeg, MB Canada R3C 0V8 *

COLEMAN, BRUCE FREDERICK, economist, municipal bond trader; b. Pontiac, Mich., Aug. 13, 1944; s. Frederick George and Edith Maud (Eley) C.; B.S., U. Mich., 1967; m. Diane Marie Base, May 18, 1968; children—Christine, Carrie, Christopher, Craig, Amanda. With Mfrs. Nat. Bank of Detroit, 1975-76; asst. v.p. Ann Arbor Bank and Trust (Mich.), 1976-78; exec. v.p. Mich. Mcpl. Bond Corp., Ann Arbor, 1978-80; gen. partner Roney & Co., Detroit, 1980-87, 1st v.p. Mich. Nat. Bank, Farmington Hills, Mich., 1987— . Mem. Fin. Analysts Soc. Detroit, Bond Club Detroit, Nat. Security Traders Assn., Basis Club Detroit. Office: c/o Mich Nat Bank PO Box 9065 Farmington Hills MI 48018

COLEMAN, CHARLES MICHAEL, contracts manager, military official; b. Youngstown, Ohio, Dec. 30, 1950; s. Charles Philip and Helen (Kohut) C.; m. Holly Jean Dutton, Aug. 25, 1973; 1 child, Sarah. BS, U.S. Mil. Acad., 1972. Commd. 2d lt. U.S. Army, 1972, advanced through grades to maj., 1983; spl. agt. Def. Investigative Service, New London, Conn., 1974-75; asst. personnel officer U.S. Army, Fort Bragg, N.C., 1975-77; contract mgr. Babcock & Wilcox Co., Barberton, Ohio, 1978—. Mem. Nat. Guard Assn.

U.S., Ohio Army Nat. Guard Assn., Nexus, Assn. Grads. U.S. Mil. Acad. Democrat. Roman Catholic. Home: 5483 S Raccoon Rd Canfield OH 44406-9227 Office: Youngstown State U Dept Military Sci Youngstown OH 44555-0001

COLEMAN, CLARENCE WILLIAM, banker; b. Wichita, Kans., Mar. 24, 1909; s. William Coffin and Fanny Lucinda (Sheldon) C.; m. Emry Regester Inghram, Oct. 2, 1935; children—Rochelle, Pamela, Kathryn Sheldon. Student, U. Kans., 1928-32; LL.D., Ottawa U., 1973; D.H.L., Friends U.; D. Laws, Ottawa U. bd. dirs. Union Blvd. Nat. Bank, 1987—. With Coleman Co., Inc., Wichita, 1932—; v.p. charge mfg. Coleman Co., Inc., 1944, dir., 1935—, asst. gen. mgr., 1951-54; pres. Union Nat. Bank, Wichita, 1957-72; vice chmn. bd. Union Nat. Bank, 1972—; chmn. bd. dir. Cherry Creek Inn, Inc., Denver, 1961-69, Kans. Devel. Credit Corp.; bd. dirs. Union Blvd. Nat. Bank, 1987—. Bd. dirs. Inst. Logopedics, 1940-74, chmn. bd., 1947-48; bd. dirs. Wichita Symphony Soc.; trustee Wichita Symphony Soc. Found.; bd. dirs. Found. for Study of Cycles, Pitts., Wichita Mental Health Assn., 1956-74, United Fund Wichita and Sedgewick County, 1957-74, Friends U., 1956-74; bd. dirs. Wichita Crime Commn., 1953-74, pres., 1958; mem. Nat. Budget Com., 1952; chmn. State Mental Health Fund Kans., 1953; Trustee Peddie Sch., Hightstown, N.J., chmn. bd. trustees, 1972-76, chmn. emeritus, 1981. Mem. Mid-Ark. Valley Devel. Assn. (treas.), Wichita C. of C. (pres. 1956, dir. 1947-74), Phi Kappa Psi. Club: Rotarian. Office: 1005 Union Ctr Wichita KS 67202

COLEMAN, DAVE ALLEN, video specialist, artist; b. Roseau, Minn., Apr. 24, 1959; s. John Harry and Marion Faye (Gulander) C.; m. Martha Kurtz, Oct. 5, 1985. BA, Moorehead State U., 1982. Producer Prairie Pub. TV, Fargo, N.D., 1980-82; asst. supr. Moorehead (Minn.) U. TV Ctr., 1980-82; producer, dir. Computer Video Prodns., Mpls., 1982—; ptnr. M.O.S. Prodns., Mpls., 1986, DMC Prodns; founder Chubby Diver Prodsn., 1987. Director, editor Escape From Ubadistan, 1985, Closer To Me, 1986; producer, writer documentary Colleen Moore: The Perfect Flapper, 1980. Recipient Monitor award U.S. Indsl. Film Fest. Mem. Soc. for Cinefiles, Univ. Film Soc., Ind. Video and Film Makers, Walkers Art Ctr., Mus. Modern Art. Avocation: watching films. Home: 5028 37th St S Minneapolis MN 55417 Office: Computer Video Prodns 1317 Clover Dr Bloomington MN 55420

COLEMAN, DAVID MANLEY, chemistry educator; b. Duluth, Minn., Mar. 24, 1948; s. Richard Bonar and Virginia Ann (Hocking) C.; m. Linda Marie Mason, Dec. 27, 1969; children: Shannon, Maren, John. BS, So. Ill. U., 1970; MS, U. Wis., 1972, PhD, 1976. Postdoctoral fellow U. Wis., Madison, 1976-77; asst. prof. chemistry Wayne State U., Detroit, 1977-87, assoc. prof., 1987—; cons. Jarrell-Ash, Waltham, Mass., 1977-79, Detroit Edison, 1980-87. Contbr. 38 articles to profl. jours. Sr. warden Christ Ch., Detroit, 1985, mem. standing com. Episc. Diocese of Mich., Detroit, 1987—; bd. dirs. Detroit Indian Village Assn., 1982-85. Recipient J. Lee Barrett award City of Detroit and the Met. Detroit Conv. and Vis.'s Bur., 1986. Mem. Fedn. Analytical Chemistry and Spectroscopy Socs. (chmn. 1986-87), Assn. Analytical Chemists. Democrat. Clubs: Wayne State U. Faculty (pres. 1985, 1987—), Detroit Yacht. Home: 2910 Iroquois Detroit MI 48214 Office: Wayne State U Dept Chemistry-175 Detroit MI 48202

COLEMAN, E. THOMAS, congressman; b. Kansas City, Mo., May 29, 1943; s. Earl T. and Marie (Carlson) C.; m. Marilyn Anderson, June 8, 1968; children: Julie Anne, Emily Catherine, Megan Marie. A.B. in Econs., William Jewell Coll., 1965; M.P.A., NYU, 1969; J.D., Washington U., 1969. Bar: Mo. 1969. Practiced in Gladstone 1973-76; asst. atty. gen. Mo., 1969-73; mem. Mo. Ho. of Reps., 1973-76; mem. 95th-100th Congresses from 6th Mo. Dist., 1977—, mem. agr., edn. and labor coms., 1977—; chmn. Republican Task Force on Fgn. Policy. Office: US Ho Reps 2344 Rayburn House Office Bldg Washington DC 20515 *

COLEMAN, GEORGE HUNT, chemist; b. San Gabriel, Calif., Oct. 15, 1928; s. Thomas and Grace Muriel (Love) C.; A.B., U. Calif., Berkeley, 1950; Ph.D., UCLA, 1958; m. Lois Mae Tarleton, Feb. 14, 1953; children—David Howe, Thomas George, Margaret Rose. Microanalyst, U. Calif., Berkeley, 1950-51; nuclear chemist Calif. Research and Devel. Corp., 1951-53; sr. nuclear chemist Lawrence Livermore Lab., 1957-69; assoc. prof. chemistry Nebr. Wesleyan U., Lincoln, 1969-78, prof., 1979—, acting head dept., 1976-78, head dept. chemistry, 1978-80. Mem. Am. Chem. Soc., AAAS. Democrat. Presbyterian. Home: 5920 Margo Dr Lincoln NE 68510 Office: Nebr Wesleyan U 50th and St Paul St Lincoln NE 68504

COLEMAN, GEORGE MICHAEL, oil company executive; b. Cleve., Mar. 5, 1953; s. George M. and Patricia A. (Harrold) C.; m. Deborah M. Zalar, Feb. 19, 1977; children: Sean, Kate. BS in Biology, John Carroll U., 1975. Prodn. supr. Republic Steel Copr., Cleve., 1975-79; acct. rep. Calgon Corp. div. Merck and Co., Cleve., 1979-81; mktg. mgr. Calgon Corp. div. Merck and Co., Pitts., 1981-82, regional sales mgr., 1982-83, mgr. mktg., comml. devel., 1983-84; mgr. new bus. devel. biotechnology Standard Oil Chem Co Specialties div, Cleve., 1984-87, gen. mgr. Adhesive Products div., 1987—. Patentee in field. Republican. Roman Catholic. Clubs: Cleve. Yachting, Holden Arboretum. Avocations: sailing, racing, skiing , scuba, travel. Home: 21565 Avalon Dr Rocky River OH 44116 Office: Standard Oil Chem Co Specialties Div 200 Public Square Cleveland OH 44114

COLEMAN, JAMES REGIS, sales executive; b. Bethlehem, Pa., Dec. 8, 1946; s. James Regis and Viva Vola (Kehley) C.; m. Kathleen O'Brien, Nov. 30, 1968; children: James, Michael. BS in Phys. Edn., Appalachian State U., 1969; postgrad., Western Carolina U., 1969, U. Va., Charlottesville, 1971. Tchr, coach Craig County Schs., New Castle, Va., 1969-71, Buena Vista (Va.) Sch., 1971-74; salesman Lees Carpets, Beckley, W.Va., 1974-78; dist. sales mgr. Phila. Carpets, Cin., 1978—. Republican. Mem. United Ch. Christ. Avocations: coin colleting, racquetball, coach of youth sports. Home and Office: 1276 Eagle Ridge Rd Milford OH 45150

COLEMAN, JOYCE JONES, tax examiner, consultant, nurse, civic worker; b. Selma, Ala., Apr. 3, 1941; d. John Wesley and Vera (Thomas) Jones; m. Milton C. Coleman, Jr., Aug. 6, 1966; children: Geoffrey S., Allyson A. Student Villa Madonna Coll., 1958-59, Mercy Sch. Nursing, 1959-61, U. Cin., 1961-63; grad. practical nurse No. Ky. State Vocat. Sch., 1965. Lic. practical nurse. Staff nurse St. Mary's Hosp., Cin., 1961-65; surg. nurse Good Samaritan Hosp., Cin., 1965; med. office nurse, Cin., 1966-67; tax examiner adjustment br., spl. processing refund inquiry group IRS, Cin.; cons. NIH, Washington. Pres., chmn. bd. dirs., coordinator, co-founder Sickle Cell Awareness Group of Greater Cin., 1972—; mem. adv. bd. Comprehensive Sickle Cell Ctr. Cin.; 3d v.p. Nat. Assn. Sickle Cell Disease Inc., 1985, 2d vice chmn., 1986-87; mem. steering com. Midwest Regional Genetic Systems Network, 1986, Women's Inst. Religion and Social Issues, 1986; pres. PTA; treas. chpt. 73 Nat. Treasury Employees Union; past sec. hosp. bond issue com. Ohio chpt. Nat. Health Agys.; mem. parish council, bd. dirs. St. Agnes Fed. Credit Union, chmn. supervisory com.; v.p. St. Agnes Bd. Edn., 1977-79; mem. admissions com. for minority students Kent State U. Med. Sch.; co-founder Bond Hill Child Devel. Ctr., 1973; cons. M.E.T. Cons. and Assocs., Indpls., 1974, Ebon Research Assos., 1976; mem. policy and rev. bd. lay pastoral ministry program Mt. St. Mary's Sem., 1976-82; neighborhood writer Paddock Hills Press, 1980-83. Named Fed. Employee of Yr., 1981, Omega Psi Phi Citizen of Yr., 1981, Citizen of Day, Sta. WLW and WCPO; recipient Bicentennial award for community involvement, 1976, Outstanding Achievement in Community Affairs award, 1976, McDonald award, 1978, Excellence in Leadership award Sickle Cell Awareness Group Greater Cin., 1983. Mem. Nat. Treasury Employees Union, Nat. Assn. Sickle Cell Disease, Nat. Assn. Fund Raising Execs. Roman Catholic. Clubs: Parents, Homemakers, Paddock Hills Assembly. Home: 1323 Westminster Dr Cincinnati OH 45229

COLEMAN, MARILYN (ADAMS), poultry science consultant; b. Lancaster, S.C., Mar. 27, 1946; d. Coyte and Jill J.D. (Lyon) Adams; B.S. in Biology, U. S.C., 1968; Ph.D. in Physiology, Auburn U., 1976; postgrad. U. Va., summer, 1971, 72, Va. Poly. Inst., 1972; m. George Edward Coleman III, Jan. 27, 1968; children—Jill Ann Marie, George Edward IV. Teaching asst. U. S.C., 1967-68; research technician Va. Poly. Inst. and State U., Blacksburg, 1968, teaching asst. biology, 1970-72; tchr. biology and basketball coach Brunswick County (Va.) Pub. Schs., 1968-69; research asst. poultry sci. Auburn (Ala.) U., 1973-76; asst. prof. poultry sci. Ohio State U., Columbus, 1977-81, adj. asso. prof., 1982—; propr. MAC Assos., Columbus, Ohio, 1974—; cons. to poultry industry throughout U.S. and 60 fgn. countries, 1974—. Pianist, New Cut Presbyn. Ch., Lancaster, 1960-64; tchr.'s aide Mountview Baptist Ch., Upper Arlington, Ohio, 1964. Nat. winner 4-H, 1964; NSF grantee, 1967, 71-72. Named Top 10 Young Execs., Esquire Mag., 1985. Mem. Poultry Sci. Assn., Am. Physiol. Assn., World Poultry Sci. Assn., Assn. of Southeastern Biologists, Auburn U. Alumni Assn., U. S.C. Alumni Assn., Sigma Xi, Phi Sigma. Republican. Contbr. numerous articles poultry sci. to profl. publs. Home and office: 2532 Zollinger Rd Columbus OH 43221

COLEMAN, MELVIN DOUGLAS, psychologist; b. Cleve., Oct. 9, 1948; s. James P. and Neda (Tidmore) C. BS, U. Wis.-Stout, 1969, MS, 1971; cert., U. Minn., 1979. Social worker Cuyahoga County Welfare, Cleve., 1969; parole officer State of Ohio, Cleve., 1970; vocat. rehab. counselor State of Minn., Mpls., 1972-78; psychologist Harley Clinic of Minn., Mpls./St. Paul, 1978—; cons. Bryn Mawr and Queen Nursing Home, Mpls., 1985—, Pilgrim and Zion Bapt. Ch., Mpls., 1984—. Named one of Outstanding Young Men of Am., 1983; named to Basketball Hall of Fame, U. Wis.-Stout, 1978. Mem. Minn. Behavioral Analysis Assn. Avocation: music. Home: 3828 Clinton Ave S Minneapolis MN 55409

COLEMAN, PAMELA, investment advisor; b. Wichita, Kans., July 17, 1938; d. Clarence William and Emry Regester (Inghram) Coleman; student U. Okla., 1956-57, U. Mo., 1962-65, Wichita State U., 1972-73; children—Cristy Jeanne Coleman, Cathryn Coleman. Teller, Union Nat. Bank, Wichita, 1959, 1st Nat. Bank, Charleston, S.C., 1959-61, 1st Nat. Bank of New London (Conn.), 1961-62; acct., bookkeeper Greenbaum & Assos., Sydney, Australia, 1966-68; pres., chief exec. officer Sweet Peach Prodns. Pty., Ltd., Sydney, 1968-72; fin. mgr. Clarence Coleman Investments, Wichita, 1972-75, registered investment adv., office mgr., 1976—; bd. dirs. Coleman Co., Inc. Formerly active Project Bus. of Jr. Achievement; bd. dirs. Goodwill Industries of Wichita, 1978-80, sec., 1978-79, treas., 1979-80; 1st v.p. Angel Fire Guild, Santa Fe Opera, 1983-84, treas., 1984-85; pres. Guilds of the Santa Fe Opera, 1984-85; 1st v.p. N.Mex. Opera Guilds, Inc., 1984-85. Mem. Midwest Geneal. Soc., DAR, Soc. Mayflower Descs., Daus. Am. Colonists, Nat. Soc. Colonial Dames of Am. (Kans., bd. mgrs. N.Mex. chpt. 1986—). Clubs: Wichita, Wichita Country. Home: PO Box 41 Eagle Nest NM 87718 Office: 1005 Union Center Wichita KS 67202

COLEMAN, RAYMOND JAMES, international trade institute administrator, educator; b. Bethel, Kans., Jan. 8, 1923; s. Leonard George and Jo Hannah (Poulsen) C.; m. Katherine Elizabeth Dietrich, Apr. 8, 1945; children—Katherine Anne Coleman Morehead, Jayne Elaine Coleman Lewis, Christopher Lynn. B.B.A., U. Kans., 1948; M.B.A., Central Mo. State U., 1963; Ph.D. in Bus. Adminstrn., U. Ark., 1967. Mem. mktg. staff Gen. Mills Feed Div., Kansas City, Mo., 1949-56; supr. Investors Diversified Service, Mpls., 1956-63; prof. mktg. Kans. State U., Manhattan, 1963—, dir. Internatl. Trade Inst., 1980—; exec. v.p. Internat. Trade Council of Mid-America, Inc., Manhattan, 1980—. Author: M.I.S.: Management Dimensions, 1973. Vice pres. Kans/Paraguayan Ptnrs., 1984—. Served to lt. (j.g.), USN, 1943-46, PTO. Decorated Air medals (5). Fellow Fin. Analysts Fedn.; mem. Acad. Internat. Bus., Beta Gamma Sigma, Delta Mu Delta. Republican. Presbyterian. Lodge: Masons. Office: Internat Trade Council Mid-Am Inc 1627 Anderson Ave Manhattan KS 66502

COLEMAN, RICHARD WALTER, educator; b. San Francisco, Sept 10, 1922; s. John Crisp and Reta (Walter) C.; B.A., U. Calif., Berkeley, 1945, Ph.D., 1951; m. Mildred Bradley, Aug. 10, 1949 (dec.); 1 dau., Persis C. Research asst. div. entomology and parasitology U. Calif., Berkeley, 1946-47, 49-50; ind. research, 1951-61; prof. biology, chmn. dept. Curry Coll., Milton, Mass., 1961-63, chmn. div. scis. and math. Monticello Coll., Godfrey, Ill., 1963-64; vis. prof. biology Wilberforce U., Ohio; 1964-65; prof. sci. Upper Iowa U., Fayette, 1965—; collaborator natural history div. Nat. Park Service, 1952; spl. cons. Arctic Health Research Center, USPHS, Alaska, 1954-62; apptd. explorer Commr. N.W. Ty., Yellowknife N.W. Ty., Can., 1966. Mem. Nat. Health Fedn., Iowa Acad. Sci., Geol. Soc. Iowa (affiliate), AAAS, AAUP, Am. Inst. Biol. Scis., Nat. Sci. Tchrs. Assn., Ecol. Soc. Am., Am. Soc. Limnology and Oceanography, Am. Bryological and Lichenological Soc., Arctic Inst. N.Am., N.Am. Benthological Soc., Am. Malacological Union, Assn. Midwestern Coll. Biology Tchrs., The Nature Conservancy, Société de Biologie de Montréal, Nat. Assn. Biology Tchrs., Sigma Xi. Methodist. Contbr. articles to profl. reports. Home: PO Box 156 Fayette IA 52142

COLEMAN, ROBERT LEE, lawyer; b. Kansas City, Mo., June 14, 1929; s. William and Edna (Smith) C. B.Mus. Edn., Drake U., 1951, LL.B., U. Mo., 1959. Bar: Mo. 1959, Fla. 1973. Law clk. to judge U.S. dist. ct. (we. dist.) Mo., 1959-60; assoc. Watson, Ess, Marshall & Enggas, Kansas City, Mo., 1960-66; asst. gen. csl. Gas Service Co., Kansas City, Mo., 1966-74; corp. csl. H & R Block, Inc., Kansas City, Mo., 1974—. Served with U.S. Army, 1955-57. Mem. ABA, Kansas City Bar Assn., Lawyers Assn. Kansas City.

COLES, RICHARD W(ARREN), biology educator, research administrator; b. Phila., Sept. 16, 1939; s. Henry Braid and Katherine Warren (Baker) C.; m. Mary Sargent, June 16, 1962; children—Christopher Sargent, Deborah Walton. B.A. with highest honors, Swarthmore Coll., 1961; M.A., Harvard U., 1967, Ph.D., 1967. Teaching fellow Harvard U., 1961-65; asst. prof. biology Claremont Coll., Calif., 1966-70; dir. Tyson Research Ctr., prof. biology Washington U., St. Louis, 1970—; vis. instr. Nature Place, Florissant, Colo., 1981—; participant ornithropical field trips, Venezuela, 1986-87; cons., sec.-treas. Orgn. Biol. Field Stas.; cons. NSF, Nat. Geographic Soc., book pubs., park planners. Contbr. articles to profl. jours. Grantee in field. Mem. AAAS, Am. Inst. Biol. Scis., Am. Soc. Mammalogists, Am. Ornithol. Assn., Ecol. Soc. Am., Wilderness Soc., Animal Behavior Soc., Phi Beta Kappa, Sigma Xi. Quaker. Clubs: Explorers (N.Y.C.); Naturalists (St. Louis). Home: 11 Hickory Ln Eureka MO 63025 Office: Washington U Tyson Research Ctr PO Box 258 Eureka MO 63025

COLEY, RONALD FRANK, waste management consultant; b. Chgo., Dec. 27, 1941; s. Leslie William Coley and Florence Ruth (Sontag) Jennings; m. Carol Marie Purtell, Sept. 1, 1962; children: Terry, Sherry, Peter, Eric. BS in Chemistry, Ill. Benedictine Coll., 1963; PhD in Physical and Inorganic Chemistry, Iowa State U., 1969. Research asst. Ames (Iowa) Lab., 1965-69; research assoc. Argonne (Ill.) Nat. Lab, 1969-70; various positions Commonwealth Edison, Chgo., 1970-85; pres. RLD Cons. Inc., Bolingbrook, Ill., 1984—; cons. in field, 1984—. Contbr. articles to profl. jours. Mem. Am. Chem. Soc., Am. Nuclear Soc., AAAS. Avocation: golf. Office: RLD Cons Inc 620 Keystone Dr Bolingbrook IL 60439-1256

COLLER, GARY HAYES, osteopathic physician; b. Detroit, June 5, 1952; s. Eldon Hayes and Shirley Elaine (Makima) C.; m. Mary Elaine Irrer, Oct. 15, 1977; children—Christopher, Michael, Kimberly, Jonathon. B.S. with honors, Mich. State U., 1974, D.O., 1978. Diplomate Nat. Bd. Examiners for Osteopathic Medicine. Gen. practice osteopathic medicine, Montague, Mich., 1979—; mem. staff Muskegon (Mich.) Gen. Hosp.; trainee in preventive medicine Farmington (Mich.) Med. Center. Mem. Nat. Republican Com., 1975-83. Mem. Am. Osteo. Assn., W. Mich. Osteo. Assn., Mich. Osteo. Assn., Am. Acad. Med. Preventics, Internat. Acad. Preventive Medicine, Northwest Acad. Preventive Medicine, Am. Soc. Gen. Laser Surgeons, N.Y. Acad. Scis., Christian Med. Soc., Nat. Health Service Corp., U.S. C. of C. Contbr. articles on osteopathy to profl. jours. Home: 1424 Waukazoo Holland MI 49424 Office: 9883 US 31 N Montague MI 49437

COLLETTE, RENÉE ANN, nurse; b. Ashtabula, Ohio, Mar. 18, 1951; d. Tony Goiello and Helen Sadie (Simon) C.; m. G. John Balogh, Apr. 25, 1980. BA in Sociology Correction Parole and Probation, Kent (Ohio) State U., 1973; BS in Nursing, U. Akron, 1986. RN, Ohio. Paraprofl. trainer Portage County Drug Edn. and Crisis Intervention Ctr., Kent, 1972-77, treas., bd. trustees; paraprofl. trainer counseling and group resources Kent State U., 1973-77; casework coordinator Residential Intervention Ctr., Akron, Ohio, 1975-76; exec. dir. Akron Rape Crisis Ctr., 1976-79; RN Cleve. Clinic Found., 1986—, Akron City Hosp., 1986—; instr. Honor and Exptl. Coll., Kent State U., 1977-78. Registrar bd. elections Summit County, Ohio, 1986; mem. Coalition Revision Nurse Practice Act., Ohio, 1986. Recipient Mary Giadwin award U. Akron, 1986. Fellow Emergency Nursing Assn., Am. Assn. Critical Care Nurses, U. Akron Collegiate Nursing Club (pres. 1985-86), Sigma Theta Tau. Democrat. Roman Catholic. Home: 17266 Egbert Rd Walton Hills OH 44146 Office: Akron City Hosp Emergency Dept 525 E Market St Akron OH 44304

COLLETTI, MICHAEL THADDEUS, dentist; b. Ft. Knox, Ky., Dec. 23, 1957; s. Joseph John and RoseMarie (Paoletti) C.; m. Jean Diane Pattermann, Sept. 1, 1984; children: Kristen Rose, Vincent Chester. Student, U. Wis., Whitewater, 1979; DDS, Loyola U., Maywood, Ill., 1984. Assoc. practitioner Richard N. PiPia, Chgo., 1984; mem. dental staff Union Dental Clinic, LaGrange, Ill., 1985—; clin. instr. Am. Inst. of Dental Edn., Chgo., 1985—; gen. practice dentistry Lombard, Ill., 1985—. Rep. Parent and Child Ednl. Soc., Western Springs, Ill., 1986. Fellow Am Cancer Soc. (oral cancer div.); mem. ADA, Acad. Gen. Dentistry, Ill. Dental Soc., Chgo. Dental Soc. (rep. speaker's bur. 1984—), Gamma Mu (pres. 1977—). Roman Catholic. Lodges: Kiwanis (sec. Whitewater chpt. 1979), KC (3d degree). Avocations: fishing, scuba diving, golf, tennis. Home: 22 W 441 Arbor Ln Glen Ellyn IL 60137 Office: 901 S Main St Lombard IL 60148

COLLEY, LYNN ALLAN, insurance agent; b. Sanford, Maine, Oct. 31, 1945; s. Leonard V. and Phyllis A. (Treadwell) C.; student S.E. Mo. U., 1963-67; m. Saundra L. Cumpton Brunke, Dec. 14, 1974; 1 dau., Brooke Anne Nix. Owner, Sikeston (Mo.) Coin & Stamp Co., 1965-68; owner Principal Mut. Fin. Services, Sikeston, 1986—; agt. Met. Life Ins. Co., Sikeston, 1968-86; owner C & C Stationery Supply, Sikeston, 1968—, Statewide Pest Control, Sikeston, 1979-81. Chmn., Scott County Rep. Com., 1968-74, vice chmn., 1966-68; treas. bd. dirs. Sikeston Activity Center, 1975-79; mem. Channey-Harris Meml. Com., Sikeston, 1978-80; chmn. adv. bd. Chaney-Harris Cultural Ctr., 1980-86; chmn., trustee Sikeston Pub. Library, 1984-87. Recipient Am. Legion History award, 1962; Dr. Tom L. Chidester award Sikeston Little Theatre, 1965; Nat. Assn. Life Underwriters Nat. Quality award, 1974, 78, 79, 80, 81, 82, 83, 84, Nat. Health Quality award, 1976, Nat. Sales Achievement award, 1976. Mem. Sikeston Assn. Life Underwriters (sec.-treas. 1975—), Mo. Assn. Life Underwriters, Nat. Assn. Life Underwriters, Sikeston Little Theatre (pres. 1967—), Mo. Arts Council (adv. com. 1981-85), Sikeston Arts and Edn. Council (treas. 1975-86), St. Louis Symphony in Sikeston Com. (treas. 1975-86). Jehovah's Witness. Home: 916 Alexander St Sikeston MO 63801 Office: Principal Mut Fin Services PO Box 74 Sikeston MO 63801

COLLIE, JOHN, JR., insurance agent; b. Gary, Ind., Apr. 23, 1934; s. John and Christina Dempster (Wardrop) C.; student Purdue U., 1953; A.B. in Econs., Ind. U., 1957; m. Jessie Fearn Shaw, Aug. 1, 1964; children—Cynthia Elizabeth, Douglas Allan Hamilton, Jennifer Fearn. Operator, Collie Optical Lab., Gary, 1957-62; owner, operator Collie Ins. Agy., Merrillville, Ind., 1962—; pres. Collie Realty and Investment;v.p. Med Scan Northwest Ind., 1986—; lectr. High Frontier. Lt. col. U.S. Army Res., 1957-85; instr. Command and Gen. Staff Coll., 1973-77. Mem. Profl. Ins. Agts. Assn. Ind. (dir.), Mil. Order World Wars, Res. Officers Assn. (sec., v.p. Ind. chpt., pres. N.W. Ind.), Leadership Council Am., bd. dirs.; Nat. Fedn. Ind. Bus., Guardian, Merrillville C. of C., Phi Kappa Psi. Republican. Presbyterian. Clubs: Masons (32 deg.), Shriners, Elks. Home: 717 W 66th Pl Merrillville IN 46410 Office: 5600 Broadway PO Box 10148 Merrillville IN 46410

COLLIER, NATHAN MORRIS, musician, music educator; b. Clinton, Okla., July 23, 1924; s. Lotan Morris and Annie Carlletta (Willsey) C.; m. Frances Aleta Snell, June 24, 1955; children—Susan Aleta Kowalski, Ray Morris. Mus.B., U. Okla., 1949; Mus.M., Eastman Sch. Music, U. Rochester, 1951. String music cons. Lincoln (Nebr.) Pub. Schs., 1951-68; asst. concertmaster Lincoln Symphony Orch., 1953—; assoc. concertmaster Omaha (Nebr.) Symphony, 1977-78, first violin, 1956-79; first violinist Lincoln String Quartet, 1951—; concertmaster Lincoln Symphony, Lincoln Little Symphony, 1977-78; asst. prof. violin and theory Nebr. Weslyan U., Lincoln, 1968-84; now string tchr. St. John Luth. Sch., Seward, Nebr., vis. instr. music Concordia Tchrs. Coll., Seward, 1985; asst. concertmaster Nebr. Chamber Orch., 1973—, acting concertmaster on occasion; guest prin. violinist DesMoines Symphony, 1979, guest violinist and violinist with Myron Cohen string quartet, Omaha, 1985—; asst. prof. music Kans. State U., Manhattan, 1980-81, condr. symphony orch., 1980-81; pvt. tchr. and ensemble coach, Lincoln, 1951—; cons., lectr. in field. Tchr. co-organizer Brownville (Nebr.) Summer Music Festival, 1972-77. Served with USN, 1943-46. U.S. Govt. grantee 1966-67. Mem. Am. String Tchrs. Assn., Music Tchrs. Nat. Assn., Music Educators Nat. Conf., Violin Soc. Am., Lincoln Music Tchrs. Assn., Nat. Sch. Orch. Assn., NEA, Nebr. State Edn. Assn., Lincoln Musicians Assn., Omaha Musicians Assn., Internat. Soc. of Bassists. Democrat. Methodist. Composer various musical pieces. Home: 4544 Mohawk Lincoln NE 68510

COLLIER, ROBERT GEORGE, educator; b. Stockton, Calif., Aug. 23, 1944; s. Laurence Donald and Dorothy Mary (Braghetta) C.; A.A., San Joaquin Delta Coll., 1965; B.A. in Psychology, U. Calif., Riverside, 1967; M.A. in Elem. Edn., Calif. State U., Los Angeles, 1973; Ph.D. in Edn., Claremont Grad. Sch., 1978; m. Sandra LaVaughn Haller, July 22, 1972; children—Steven Edward, Brian James. Asst. football coach U. Calif., Riverside, 1967-68, instr. univ. extension, 1979; elem. tchr. Riverside Unified Sch. Dist., 1968-74, 75-79; research asst. Claremont Grad. Sch., 1974-75; tchr. Lovett's Presch., Riverside, summer 1979; assoc. prof. early childhood edn. Western Ill. U., 1979—; mem. rev. com. Erikson Inst., Chgo.; mem. McDonough County Council Child Devel.; mem. governing bd. Wee Care Center, Macomb, Ill. Served with USAR, 1968-74. Recipient Peter L. Spencer award Phi Delta Kappa at Claremont Grad. Sch., 1978; Western Ill. U. Faculty Devel. Office mini grantee, 1980; Western Ill. U. Research Council grantee, 1981; cert. elem. tchr., Calif. Mem. Assn. Childhood Edn. Internat., Assn. Supervision and Curriculum Devel., Assn. Anthropol. Study Play, Council Exceptional Children, Nat. Assn. Edn. Young Children, Phi Delta Kappa (v.p.-elect. Western Ill. U. chpt. 1981-82). Home: 30 Briarwood Pl Macomb IL 61455 Office: Elem Edn Dept Western Ill U Macomb IL 61455

COLLIER, WILLIAM JEWELL, physician; b. Albany, Mo., Apr. 25, 1925; s. Ora and Mabel (Adkisson) C.; B.S., Tulane U., 1947; M.D., Bowman Gray Sch. Medicine, Wake Forest U., 1949; m. Mary Evelyn Fisher, Mar. 29, 1952; children—William Jewell II, Sherry Lynn, Terri Lee, Linda Lorraine. Intern, U.S. Naval Hosp., Great Lakes, Ill., 1949-50; resident internal medicine VA Hosp., Wadsworth, Kans., 1950-51, resident gen. surgery, 1951-52, 54-57; asst. chief surgery VA Hosp., Wichita, Kans., 1957-58; pvt. practice gen. and thoracic surgery, McPherson, Kans., 1958—. Dir. Home State Bank & Trust. Former mem. aviation adv. bd. McPherson City-County Airport. Served from lt. (j.g.) to lt. M.C., USNR, 1952-54. Diplomate Am. Bd. Surgery. Fellow Southwestern Surg. Congress, ACS, Internat. Coll. Surgeons; mem. C. of C. Mem. Christian Ch. Rotarian. Home: 302 S Walnut St McPherson KS 67460 Office: 400 W 4th St McPherson KS 67460

COLLINS, CARDISS, congresswoman; b. St. Louis, Sept. 24, 1931; ed. Northwestern U.; m. George W. Collins (dec.); 1 son, Kevin. Stenographer, Ill. Dept. Labor; sec. Ill. Dept. Revenue, then accountant, revenue auditor; mem. 93d-100th Congresses from 7th Ill. Dist., 1973—, mem. Govt. Ops. com., Energy and Commerce com.; chmn. Manpower and Housing com., former majority whip-at-large; past chmn. Congressional Black Caucus; former chmn. Mems. of Congress for Peace through Law. Bd. dirs. Greater Lawndale Conservation Commn., Chgo. Mem. NAACP, Nat. Council Negro Women, Chgo. Urban League, Alpha Kappa Alpha. Baptist. Democrat. Office: US Ho Reps 2264 Rayburn Washington DC 20515 *

COLLINS, CYNTHIA LYNNE, health care company executive; b. Alton, Ill., Apr. 13, 1958; d. Peter and Delores June (Neibel) Perica; m. Robert Marshall Collins, June 14, 1980. BS in Microbiology, U. Ill., 1980; postgrad., U. Chgo., 1985—. Materials planner Abbott Labs, North Chicago, Ill., 1982, specialist rare reagent planning, 1983-85, planning coordinator new products, 1985, mgr. inventory planning, 1985-86; dir. materials mgmt. Pandex div. Travenol Labs, Mundelein, Ill., 1986—. Recipient Gen. Assembly scholarship Ill. Ho. Reps., 1976-78. Mem. Am. Soc. Microbiology. Avocations: golf, racquetball, swimming, horseback riding. Home: 2838 N

Mildred Chicago IL 60657 Office: Travenol Labs Pandex Div 909 Orchard St Mundelein IL 60060

COLLINS, DANA JON, controller; b. Grand Rapids, Mich., July 15, 1956; s. Daniel Hiltz and JoAnne M. (Smee) Collins. BBA with honors, U. Mich., 1978. CPA, Mich. Staff acct. Ernst & Whinney, Jackson, Mich., 1978-82, mgr., 1982-86; controller, sec.-treas. Fetzer Broadcasting Service, Inc., Kalamazoo, 1986—, also bd. dirs. Mem. Am. Inst. CPA's, Nat. Assn. Accts. (treas. Lansing and Jackson, Mich. chpt. 1984-86, bd. dirs. 1987—), Mich. Assn. CPA's. Republican. Avocations: golf, tennis, sports, square dancing. Home: 3739 Greenleaf Circle #304 Kalamazoo MI 49008 Office: Fetzer Broadcasting Service Inc 590 W Maple St Kalamazoo MI 49008

COLLINS, DANIEL W., accountant, educator; b. Marshalltown, Iowa, Sept. 1, 1946; s. Donald E. and Lorine R. (Metge) C.; m. Mary L. Packer, June 27, 1970; children—Melissa, Theresa. B.B.A. with highest distinction, U. Iowa, 1968, Ph.D., 1973. Asst. prof. acctg. Mich. State U., East Lansing, 1973-76, assoc. prof., 1976-77; vis. assoc. prof. U. Iowa, Iowa City, 1977-78, assoc. prof., 1978-81, prof., 1981-83, Murray chaired prof. acctg., 1983—. Assoc. editor Acctg. Rev., 1980-86; mem. editorial bd. Jour. Acctg. and Econs., 1978—, Jour. Acctg., Auditing and Fin., 1986—; contbr. articles to profl. jours. Served to 2d lt. U.S. Army, 1972. Recipient All Univ. Tchr. scholar award Mich. State U., 1976; Gilbert Maynard Excellence in Teaching award U. Iowa, 1985; Univ. Faculty scholar U. Iowa, 1980-82. Mem. Am. Acctg. Assn. (disting. vis. faculty mem. Doctoral Consortium 1980). Avocations: jogging; gardening. Home: 11 Wildberry Ct Iowa City IA 52240 Office: U Iowa Coll Bus 305 Phillips Hall Iowa City IA 52242

COLLINS, DAVID RAYMOND, educator, author, lecturer; b. Marshalltown, Iowa, Feb. 29, 1940; s. Raymond Amby and Mary Elizabeth (Brecht) C.; B.S., Western Ill. U., 1962, M.S., 1966. Instr. English, Woodrow Wilson Jr. High Sch., 1962-83, Moline (Ill.) Sr. High Sch., 1983—; founder, dir. Miss. Valley Writers Conf., 1973—, Children's Lit. Festival, 1979—; sec., Quad Cities Arts Council, 1971-75; pres. Friends of Moline Pub. Library, 1965-66. Recipient writing award Writer's Digest, 1967, writer of the year award Writers' Studio, 1971, award Bobbs-Merrill Pub. Co., 1971, writer of the year award Quad-Cities Writers Club, 1972, writing awards Judson Coll., 1971, Jr. Literary Guild awards, 1980, 82. Mem. Nat., Ill., Moline (dir. 1964-67) Edn. Assns., Ill. PTA (life; Outstanding Ill. Educator award 1975), Ill. Hist. Soc., Black Hawk Div. Tchrs. English (pres. 1967-68), Writers Studio (pres. 1967-71), Children's Reading Roundtable, Authors Guild, Soc. Children's Book Writers, Juvenile Forum, Quad-Cities Writers Club (pres. 1973-75, 77-78), Am. Amateur Press Assn., Book Lures, Inc., Schoolmasters, Nat. Council Tchrs. English, Kings' Men, Blackhawk Reading Council, Western Ill. U. Alumni (dir. 1968-74, Outstanding Achievement award 1973), Kappa Delta Pi, Sigma Tau Delta, Alpha Delta, Delta Sigma Phi. Democrat. Roman Catholic. Author: Kim Soo and His Tortoise, 1970; Great American Nurses, 1971; Walt Disney's Surprise Christmas Present, 1972; Linda Richards, America's First Trained Nurse, 1973; Harry S. Truman, People's President, 1975; Football Running Backs, 1975; Abraham Lincoln, 1976; Illinois Women: Born to Serve, 1976; Joshua Poole Hated School, 1977; Charles Lindbergh, Hero Pilot, 1978; A Spirit of Giving, 1978; If I Could, I Would, 1979; Joshua Poole and Sunrise, 1979; The Wonderful Story of Jesus, 1980; A Special Guest, 1980; The Only Thing Wrong with Birthdays, 1980; George Washington Carver, 1981; George Meany, Mr. Labor, 1981; Dorothy Day, Catholic Worker, 1982; Thomas Merton, Monk with a Mission, 1982; Super Champ! The Story of Babe Didrickson Zaharias, 1982; Notable Illinois Women, 1982; Francis Scott Key, 1982; Joshua Poole and the Special Flowers, 1982; The Golden Circle, 1983, Florence Nightingale, 1984, Johnny Applessed, 1984, Jane Addams, 1987, Clara Barton, 1985, Not Only Dreamers, 1986, Lyndon Baines Johnson-No Ordinary Man, 1987, Ride a Wild Dinosaur, 1987, The Wisest Answer, 1987. Home: 3403 45th St Moline IL 61265 Office: 3600 23d Ave Moline IL 61265

COLLINS, DEAN TRACY, psychiatrist; b. Junction City, Kans., Mar. 19, 1928; s. Laurence Edwin and Alverda Patience (Tracy) C.; m. Elisabeth Bartholdi, May 16, 1959. B.A. U. Kans., Lawrence, 1950; MD, U. Kans., Kansas City, 1955. Staff psychiatrist Winfield (Kans.) State Hosp. and Tng. Ctr., 1960-62, acting chief dept., supt., 1962-63; cons. psychiatrist Kans. Neurol. Inst., Topeka, 1963-70; staff psychiatrist Menninger Meml. Hosp., Topeka, 1963-70; sect. chief Menninger Meml. Hosp., Topeka, 1970—. Assoc. dir. edn. Menninger Found., 1982—, dir. psychiatry, 1986—. Served with U.S. Army, 1946-47. Fulbright scholar, 1950-51; A.V. Humboldt scholar, 1957-58. Fellow Am. Psychiat. Assn.; mem. AMA, Kans. Psychiat. Assn. (pres. 1980-82), Shawnee County Med. Soc. (pres. 1975-76). Office: The Menninger Found 5800 SW 6th PO Box 829 Topeka KS 66601

COLLINS, DON CARY, lawyer; b. Christopher, Ill., Sept. 10, 1951; s. Everett Hugh, Jr. and Evelyn Loriene (Wootton) C. Student Western Ky. U., 1969-70; BA, Ill. State U., Normal, 1972; JD, So. Ill. U., 1976. Bar: Ill. 1976, Mo. 1977, U.S. Supreme Ct., U.S. Ct. Appeals (7th cir.), U.S. Dist. Ct. (so. dist.) Ill. Pub. relations/media chmn. S.W. Ill. Regional Spl. Olympics, 1979. Mem. ABA, Ill. Bar Assn., Mo. Bar Assn., St. Clair County Bar Assn., East St. Louis Bar Assn., Met. St. Louis Bar Assn., Trial Lawyers Assn. Am., Ill. Trial Lawyers Assn., Am. Judicature Soc., So. Ill. U. Sch. Law Alumni Assn. (bd. dirs. 1984—, v.p. 1986-87, pres. 1987—). Home: B3 Hidden Valley Dr #4 Belleville IL 62223 Office: 126 W Main St Belleville IL 62220

COLLINS, DOROTHY JANE, economic development association executive; b. Shreveport, La., Oct. 23, 1937; d. Albert Hews and Cecile (Nelken) McCann; m. Robert Herrick, 1959 (dec. Aug. 19, 1963); m. Edward J. Collins Jr., Sept. 19, 1964; children: Dorothy Loraine, Edward J. III. Student, Centenary Coll., 1957-58; cert. dental assistant, Laney Coll., 1964-65; cert in econ. devel., U. Okla., 1982-84. Dir. Vol. Pool Deerfield (Ill.), 1977-81; exec. sec. Nat. Assn. Installation Devel., Schiller Park, Ill., 1981-85; v.p. Am. Econ. Devel. Council, Schiller Park, Ill., 1981—; exec. dir. Mid-Am. Econ. Devel. Council, Schiller Park, Ill., 1981—; mem. Deerfield Village Ctr. Devel. Commn., Deerfield, 1977-81; dir. Kensington (Calif.) Commn. Service Dist., 1975-77; instr. Econ. Devel. Inst., Norman, Okla., and Cleve., Ohio. Mem. Am. Soc. Assn. Execs., Chgo. Soc. Assn. Execs., Metafile Users Group (pres. 1983-86), Deerfield LWV (bd. dirs. 1977-79). Republican. Episcopalian. Avocations: computers, crossword puzzles. Home: 617 Indian Hill Rd Deerfield IL 60015

COLLINS, EDWARD JAMES, JR., association executive; b. Lawrence, Mass., Mar. 17, 1933; s. Edward James and Mary Elizabeth (Rogers) C.; m. Dorothy Jane McCann, Sept. 19, 1964; 1 son, Edward James; 1 stepdau., Dorothy Lorraine. A.B. in Journalism, U. Calif.-Berkeley, 1959. Mng. editor Brawley Daily News, (Calif.), 1959-62; assoc. exec. dir. Calif. Veterinary Med. Assn., Moraga, Calif., 1962-65; exec. dir. Marin Med. Soc., San Rafael, Calif., 1965-66; asst. dir., prof., pub. relations Calif. Med. Assn., San Francisco, 1966-68; v.p. Assn. Western Hosps., San Francisco, 1968-76; exec. dir. Am. Assn. Med. Soc. Execs., Chgo., 1977-81; pres., chief adminstrv. officer Am. Econ. Devel. Council, Chgo., 1981—. Recipient Agrl. Writers award, 1961; recipient Key Man award Oakland Jaycees, (Calif.), 1964. Mem. Am. Soc. Assn. Execs., No. Calif. Soc. Assn. Execs. (pres. 1973), Chgo. Soc. Assn. Execs. Avocations: amateur radio (KC 9RL). Home: 617 Indian Hill Rd Deerfield IL 60015 Office: 4849 N Scott St Suite 22 Schiller Park IL 60176

COLLINS, FRANCIS BERNARD, sales executive; b. Lohrville, Iowa, Dec. 23, 1924; s. Maurice Joe and Rose Collins; m. Juanita Faye, Apr. 18, 1946; children: Bernice, Delores, Sandra, Donna, Rosemary, Beverly. Grad. high sch., Lohrville, Iowa, 1944. Farmer Cleve., 1946-65; salesman Kent Industries, Cleve., 1965-82; regional sales mgr. H&H Supply, New Hudson, Mich., 1982—. Democrat. Roman Catholic. Lodge: Eagles, K.C., Moose. Home and Office: Rt 5 Box 212A Chariton IA 50049

COLLINS, JAMES DUANE, electrical engineer; b. Saginaw, Mich., Feb. 27, 1952; s. Bernard Duane and Dolores Laura (Tucker) C.; m. Janet Marie King, Apr. 28, 1973; children: Amy, James II. BSEE with honors, Lawrence Inst. Tech., 1975. Project engr. Lear/Siegler Home Div., Holland, Mich., 1975-77; staff engr. Rowe Internat. Inc., Grand Rapids, Mich., 1977—; cons. in field, Holland, 1977—. Inventor universal document validator, improved universal document validator. Mem. Tau Beta Pi. Avocations: reading, golfing, travelling. Office: Rowe Internat Inc 1500 Union Ave SE Grand Rapids MI 49507

COLLINS, JAMES DUFFIELD, engineer, editor; b. Logansport, Ind., Dec. 20, 1919; s. Louis Duffield and Gaynelle May (Mobley) C.; m. Barbara Cook, Mar. 12, 1949; children: Barbara Collins Allemenos, James Duffield II. BS in Marine Engring., U.S. Mcht. Marine Acad., 1946. Process engr. Gen. Motors Corp., Indpls., 1940-44; marine engr. Moore McCormack Lines, N.Y.C., 1946; sr. project engr. research and devel. Gen. Motors Corp., Indpls., 1946-82; editor-at-large Marcel Dekker, Inc., N.Y.C., 1986—. Contbr. author: Materials and Processes, 1985; author: Bowline Knot, 1972; contbr. articles to profl. jours; patentee in field. Served to lt. (j.g.) USNR, 1946-57. Mem. Soc. Naval Architects and Marine Engrs. Lodge: Masons. Avocations: music, concert master, orchestra and symphony member. Home and Office: 5228 Belvedere Dr Indianapolis IN 46208

COLLINS, JERRY HOLMAN, research pharmacist; b. Indpls., Nov. 8, 1939; s. Leon Leonard and Dollie (Holman) C.; m. Carol Ann Lynn, Apr. 25, 1959; children: Cathy, Lori Ann, Jennifer, Steven. BS in Pharmacy, Butler U., 1961, MS in Pharm. Chemistry, 1963; PhD in Med. Chemistry, U. Kans., 1968. Registered pharmacist, Ill., Wis. Research chemist Esso Research, Linden, N.J., 1968-70, Ansul Co., Madison, Wis., 1970-72, Abbott Labs., North Chgo., Ill., 1973—. Inventor in field. Mem. Am Chem. Soc., Am. Assn. Pharm. Soc., Rho Chi, Sigma Xi. Avocation: hiking. Home: 2035 Poplar St Waukegan IL 60087 Office: Abbott Labs PPD 1400 Sheridan Rd D497 North Chicago IL 60064

COLLINS, JOHN DAVID, court director, probation officer, consultant; b. Cin., May 8, 1937; s. W. Jack and Mary Louise (Langland) C.; m. Bonnie Rita Anderson, Sept. 30, 1961; children: Kelly Collins McCullough, Wendy, Kristin, Kathleen. BS in Criminal Justice, U. Cin., 1973, MEd, 1974, EdD, 1983. Asst. service dir. City of Wyoming, Ohio, 1958-59; patrol officer Cin. Police, 1959-63, patrol tng. officer, 1967-78, criminal investigator, 1968-76; dep. sheriff Hamilton County, Cin., 1963-66, chief probation officer, dir. ct. services, 1980—; engr. safety Employers Ins. Co., Cin., 1966-67; dir. pub. safety Greenhills, Ohio, 1977-81; asst. prof. U. Cin., 1978-80; adj. asst. prof. criminal justice Wilmington Coll., 1984—; cons. Cin. Tech. Coll., 1978—, coordinator pvt. police tng., Covington Police Dept., Ky., 1979. Author: Police Internal Affairs, 1983. Coach baseball St. James Sch., 1958-60; commr. Ohio Valley Bantam Football League, 1964; chmn. youth service Avondale Community Council, 1968; mem. Gov.'s Com. of Deaf, 1980-82; dir. transp. St. Rita's Sch. for Deaf, Cin., 1975-85. Served with USN, 1955-58. Recipient Commendation Cin. C. of C., 1970, 74. Mem. Am. Probation and Parole Assn. (bd. dirs. 1982—), Am. Correction Assn., Hamilton County Police Assn. (tng. com. 1978), Acad. Criminal Justice Scis., Ohio Chief Probation Officer Assn. (charter), Ohio Valley Officers Assn. (exec. sec. 1982-86), Ohio High Sch. Athletic Assn., Ohio Football Assn., Ohio Valley Officials Assn. (exec. sec., past pres.), Queen City Assn. Baseball Umpires (tng. com.), Ky. Col. Assn. Republican. Roman Catholic. Lodge: Kiwanis (adv. bd. Greenhills/Forest Park club). Avocations: sports officiating, teaching criminal justice. Home: 2 Hamlin Dr Cincinnati OH 45218 Office: Hamilton County Probation Dept 222 E Central Pkwy 4th Cincinnati OH 45218

COLLINS, MARIANNE NELSON, psychologist; b. Batavia, N.Y., Oct. 24, 1942; d. Leonard and Violet Marie (Pedersen) N.; divorced; children: Cathy Lee, Robert Jeffrey. BA, La. State U., New Orleans, 1973; MA, Ohio State U., 1975, PhD, 1977; postgrad., Wright State U., 1982. Lic. psychologist, Ohio. Asst. prof. Ohio State U., Columbus, 1978-81; pvt. practice psychology Columbus, 1982—; cons. to various bus., edn. and govt. orgns. Ohio State U. fellow, 1973-77. Mem. Am. Psychol. Assn., Ohio Psychol. Assn., Cen. Ohio Cons. Psychologists. Office: 2000 W Henderson Rd Suite 470 Columbus OH 43220

COLLINS, MARY ALICE, psychiatric social worker; b. Everett, Wash., Apr. 20, 1937; d. Harry Edward and Mary (Yates) Caton; B.A. in Sociology, Seattle Pacific Coll., 1959; M.S.W., U. Mich., 1966; Ph.D., Mich. State U., 1974; m. Gerald C. Brocker, Mar. 24, 1980. Dir. teenage, adult and counseling depts. YWCA, Flint, Mich., 1959-64, 66-68; social worker Catholic Social Services, Flint, 1969-71, Ingham Med. Mental Health Center, Lansing, Mich., 1971-73; clin. social worker Genesee Psychiat. Center, Flint, 1974-82, Psychol. Evaluation and Treatment Ctr., East Lansing, Mich., 1982-84; pvt. practice, East Lansing, 1984—; instr. social work Lansing Community Coll. and Mich. State U., 1974; vis. prof. Hurley Med. Center, 1979-84; cons. Ingham County Dept. Social Services, 1971-73; instr. Mich. State U., 1987. Advisor human relations Youth League, Flint Council Chs., 1964-65; sec. Genesee County Young Democrats, 1960-61, pres. Round Lake Improvement Assn., 1984-87. Mem. Nat. Assn. Social Workers, Acad. Cert. Social Workers, Registry Clin. Social Workers, Registry Health Care Workers, Phi Kappa Phi, Alpha Kappa Sigma. Contbr. articles to profl. jours. Home: 5945 Round Lake Rd Laingsburg MI 48848

COLLINS, MARY ELLEN KENNEDY, librarian, educator; b. Pitts., Feb. 28, 1939; d. Joseph Michael and Stella Marie (Kane) Kennedy; m. Orpha Collins. BA, Villa Maria Coll., 1961; MLS, U. Pitts., 1970, PhD, 1980. Tchr., Pitts. Catholic Schs., 1962-65; tchr., Anne Arundel County Schs., Annapolis, 1965-67; legal sec., firm Joseph M. Kennedy, Pitts., 1967-70; cataloger Newport News (Va.) Library System, 1970-71; reference librarian Glenville (W.Va.) State Coll., 1971-80; asst. prof. library sci. Ball State U., Muncie, Ind., 1980-83; reference librarian, asst. prof. Purdue U., West Lafayette, Ind., 1983—. Contbr. articles to profl. jours. Sec. Presbyn. Ch., 1973-74, pres., 1974-76, bd. deacons, 1979-80; chmn. library com., Muncie, 1981-83; mem. belle com. W.Va. Folk Festival, 1973-80. Recipient Title III advanced study grant, 1977-78. Mem. ALA (reference books rev. com. 1979-82, profl. devel. com. 1983-87, mem. Ednl. Behavioral Scis. Sect.-Problems of Access and Control of Ednl. Materials 1984-88), Ind. Library Assn., Spl. Libraries Assn., Assn. Coll. and Research Libraries, Am. Assn. U. Profs., Assn. Ind. Media Educators, Assn. Am. Library Schs., AAUW (corr. sec. 1981-82), Delta Kappa Gamma, Sigma Sigma Sigma. Republican. Office: HSSE Library Purdue Univ West Lafayette IN 47907

COLLINS, MOIRA ANN, graphics and communications company executive, calligrapher; b. Washington, Dec. 16, 1942; d. Peter William and Louise (Carroll) Collins; m. Andrew Joseph Griffin, Aug. 21, 1965; children—Andrew Fitzgerald, Timothy. B.A., U. Toronto (Ont., Can.), 1964; M.A. in Teaching, Northwestern U., 1965; M.Ed. in Urban Studies, Northeastern U., Chgo., 1968. Tchr., Chgo. Bd. Edn., 1965-68; apprentice to profl. calligraphers, scribes and illuminators, U.S. and Eng., 1971-75; freelance calligrapher, 1974-78; mem. publicity and promotional staff Swallow Press, Chgo., 1978-79; owner Letters, Chgo., 1979—; pres. Astrogram, Chgo. 1986. HEW fellow Northeastern U., 1967-68. Author, contbr.; Celebration: Anais Nin, 1975; contbr. to Goodfellow Rev. of Crafts, 1979. Calligrapher: Erotica, 1976, Chgo. Rev., 1978. Chmn. fund-raising Van Gorder Walden Sch., Chgo., 1979-80. Mem. Chgo. Calligraphy Collective (co-founder, chmn. 1976-77, pres. 1978-79, hon. mem.), Soc. Scribes N.Y., Soc. Calligraphers, Soc. Scribes and Illuminators (Eng.), Friends Calligraphy Calif. Democrat. Roman Catholic. Home: 834 W Chalmers Pl Chicago IL 60614 Office: 429 W Ohio St Suite 555 Chicago IL 60610

COLLINS, PAUL DOUGLAS (DOUG COLLINS), professional basketball coach; b. Christopher, Ill., July 28, 1951. Student, Ill. State U. Profl. basketball player Phila. 76ers, NBA, 1973-81; asst. basketball coach U. Pa., University, 1981-82, Ariz. State U., Tempe, 1982-84; basketball commentator CBS-TV, 1982-85; profl. basketball announcer Sta. WPHL, Phila.; head coach Chgo. Bulls, NBA, 1986—. Mem., capt. U.S. Olympic Basketball Team, 1972; Coll. All-Am., 1972-73; mem. NBA All-Star Team, 1976-79. Office: care Chgo Bulls 333 N Michigan Suite 1325 Chicago IL 60601 *

COLLINS, ROBERT CLARKSON, II, packaging engineer; b. Buffalo, May 27, 1949; s. Richard Thurlow and June (Shearer) C.; m. Michelle Reed, Dec. 20, 1974; 1 child, Robert Clarkson III. BS in Indsl. Tech., U. Wis., Menomonie, 1971. Designer Packing Corp. Am., Grandville, Mich., 1972-76; sr. packaging engr. Baxter Travenol Labs., Round Lake, Ill., 1976-78; engr., group leader Amway Corp., Ada, Mich., 1978-85; sr. packaging engr. The Drackett Co., Cin., 1985—. Patentee in field. Den. leader Loveland (Ohio) Cub Scouts, 1985-86; asst. coach S.A.Y. Soccer, Loveland, 1985-86. Mem. Soc. Packaging and Handling Engrs. (cert. bd. dirs. 1982-84, cert. chmn. 1983-85, design competition award 1982). Republican. Presbyterian. Avocations: cabinet making, golf, camping. Office: The Drackett Co 5020 Spring Grove Ave Cincinnati OH 45232

COLLINS, THOMAS M., insurance holding company executive. Chmn. Life Investors, Inc., Cedar Rapids, Iowa. Office: Life Investors Inc 4333 Edgewood Rd NE Cedar Rapids IA 52499 *

COLLINS, THOMAS WILLIAM, caterer, consultant; b. Lewiston, Idaho, Nov. 4, 1926; s. William James and Mary (Egan) C.; m. Mary Charlene Tracy, Aug. 1, 1947 (dec. Apr. 1984); children: Kathleen, William, Charles. Grad. high sch., Staples, Minn., 1944. Owner Collins Cafe, Park Rapids, Minn., 1947-63, Tom Collins Restaurant, Walker, Minn., 1963-83, Tom Collins Catering, Walker, 1983—. Author: Collins Cooking Secrets, 1981. Fundraiser DFL, 1976-83; dir. Lake Country Food Bank, Mpls., 1981-86. Served with USN, 1945-46, 51-52. Tom Collins Day proclaimed Minn. Gov. Rudy Perpich, 1977; recipient Recognition award Mont. Gov. Ted Schwinden, 1978. Mem. Assn. Great Lakes Outdoor Writers, Am. Legion. Lodge: Masons (sr. warden 1958), Shriners. Avocations: hunting, fishing, photography. Home and Office: PO Box 33 Walker MN 56484

COLLIVER, GARY WINSTON, agronomist; b. Tina, Mo., Apr. 29, 1942; s. C. Leroy and Mary Ruth (Dempsey) C.; m. Judy Ann Breeding, Aug. 26, 1962; children: Deeann E. Gay Lynn, George Winston. BAgr, U. Mo., 1964, MS in Soil Fertility, 1966; PhD, U. Ill., 1969. Cert. profl. agronomist. Research specialist Ciba-Geigy Corp, Ardsley, N.Y., 1969-72; regional agronomic dir. Potash-Phosphate Inst., Atlanta, 1973-74; assoc. prof. agronomy U. Mo., Columbia, 1974-79; chief agronomist Farmland Industries, Kansas City, Mo., 1979—. Contbr. numerous papers and articles to profl. jours. Mem. Am. Soc. Agronomy (numerous com. and memberships), Soil Sci. Soc. Am., Mo. Forage and Grassland Council (pres. 1986-87), Gamma Sigma Delta, Sigma Xi. Lodge: Masons, Shriners. Home: 807 Adams Dr Liberty MO 64068 Office: Farmland Industries Inc PO Box 7305 Kansas City MO 64116

COLMENERO, CHARLES, business consultant; b. N.Y.C., Dec. 30, 1931; s. Aurelio and Consuelo María (Fernández) C.; B.S., N.Y.U., 1957; student U. Miami, 1957-58, Fairleigh Dickinson U., 1962-63; m. Sabra Ann Pryor, Feb. 20, 1954; children—Laura, Elena, Charles, Elisa, Mercedes, Anita, Aurelio. Indsl. engr. Pan-American, Miami, Fla., 1957-58; mgr. systems and procedures Radiation, Inc., Palm Bay, Fla., 1958-62; gen. analyst Continental Can Co., N.Y.C., 1962-64; mgr. logistics and ops. Xerox Corp. (Latin-Am.), Rochester, N.Y., 1964-68; dir. ops. Xerox De Mexico, S.A., Mexico City, 1968-71; exec. v.p., chief exec. officer Koehn Mfg. Inc., Watertown, S.D., 1971-77; chmn. bd., pres. Mattson's Inc., Grafton, N.D., 1977-82, Repsel Assos. Inc., Watertown, 1982—; bd. dirs. Baltic Overseas, Watertown. Chmn. Dist. Export Council S.D. Served with USAF, 1951-55. Mem. S.D. Mfrs. Assn. (charter dir., chmn. articles and by-laws com., chmn. membership com.), Watertown Mgmt. Council, Farm Equipment Mfrs. Assn., Nat. Assn. Mfrs., Am. Legion, Alpha Kappa Psi. Republican. Presbyterian. Club: Elks. Author: Technology-Its Impact on Enterprise, 1959. Home: 406 2d Ave SE Watertown SD 57201 Office: PO Box 274 Watertown SD 57201

COLOMBERO, DONALD FRANK, health care products company executive; b. Rochester, N.Y., July 5, 1953; s. Frank S. and Rosemarie D. (Ferrara) C.; m. Patricia I. Thornton, July 5, 1975; children—Corrie B., Brandon A., Carly M. B.A. in Advt., Western Ky. U., 1975. Expeditor, Harris Corp., Rochester, N.Y., 1975-76, sales adminstr., 1976-77, sales promotion mgr., 1977-79; conv. mgr. Zimmer Inc. div. Bristol Myers, Warsaw, Ind., 1979-81, mktg. services mgr., 1981-83, dir. meeting services, 1983—. Recipient exhibit awards Bus. Mktg. Mag., 1st pl., 1980, 2d pl., 1981, 82. Mem. Nat. Trade Show Exhibitors Assn., Health Care Exhibitors Assn. (cert. exhibit specialist), Alpha Kappa Psi (Indpls.). Roman Catholic. Devised transp. modules for cross country shipments. Office: Zimmer Inc 2801 Fortune Circle E Suite F Indianapolis IN 46241

COLONNA, WILLIAM MARK, accountant; b. Joliet, Ill., Jan. 18, 1956; s. William and Lorraine (Govednik) C. BA in Acctg., Lewis U., 1974-78. Cost acct., asst. acctg. mgr. Insta-Foam Products, Joliet, Ill., 1978-86; cost acct. Durkee Foods, Joliet, 1986—; sec. Joliet St. Anne Credit Union, Crest Hill, Ill., 1980—. Lodge: Elks. Home: 1718 Dearborn Crest Hill IL 60435

COLOSIMO, ANTONIO, architect; b. Dayton, Ohio, Apr. 3, 1949; s. Joseph Antonio and Maria Antonietta (Guerri) C.; divorced; 1 child, Marcus Antonio. BS in Architecture, Ohio State U., 1974. Registered architect, Ohio, Ill. Founder, pres. 3D/Group, Inc., Columbus, 1978—. Mem. AIA, Nat. Cert. Archtl. Registration Bds. (cert.1980), Architects Soc. of Ohio, Urban Land Inst. Roman Catholic. Home: 3440 Olentangy Blvd Columbus OH 43202 Office: 3D/Group Inc 17 S High St #200 Columbus OH 43215-3413

COLSON, PATRICIA MARY (BECK), insurance administrator; b. Chgo., Mar. 22, 1938; d. Charles Joseph Beck and Katherine Harwood (Norton) Beck Ennis; m. Allan Hilding Hanson, 1962 (div. 1974); children—Terrance Allan, Tracy Michele, Eric Stephen; m. Donald Lee Colson, June 27, 1975. Student Marquette U., 1956-58; R.N., St. Francis Hosp. Sch. Nursing, 1974. Tchr., Holy Cross Sch., Deerfield, Ill., 1960-62; charge nurse Martha Washington Hosp., Chgo., 1974-76; asst. dir. nursing Riverwoods Ctr., Mundelein, Ill., 1976-78; asst. dir., mgr. Concerned Care, Inc., Evanston, Ill., 1979-81; dir. nursing Am. Home Health Service, Arlington Heights, Ill., 1982-83; program innovator, developer Home Care Evaluation, Inc. Subs. Republic Service Bur., Naperville, Ill., 1983-84; disability claim rev. cons. Jewel Food Stores, Melrose Park, Ill., 1984—; cons. New Eng. Mut. Life Ins. Co., Rolling Meadows, Ill., 1983. Fellow Nat. League for Nursing. Roman Catholic. Home: 129 S Harvard Ave Arlington Heights IL 60005 Office: Jewel Food Stores 1955 W North Ave Melrose Park IL 60160

COLTON, DOUGLAS GRANT, pharmacologist, consultant; b. Council Bluffs, Iowa, Apr. 10, 1944; s. Everett Lewis and Lois Evelyn (Meadows) C.; m. Felita Salcedo, Oct. 21, 1967; children: Christine, Alexander, Carolyn. BS in Chemistry, Physics, Mich. State U., 1965; MS in Biophysics, U. Chgo., 1967; PhD in Biochemistry, U. Neb., 1973. Research assoc. Okla. State U., Stillwater, 1973-76; research investigator G.D. Searle, Skokie, Ill., 1976-80; sr. research scientist Bristol-Myers, Syracuse, N.Y., 1980-85; assoc. research prof. Med. Coll. Wis., Milw., 1985—; cons. independently. Mem. AAAS, Am. Chem. Soc. (treas. 1982-83, chmn. Syracuse chpt. 1985), Am. Soc. Pharmacology Exptl. Therapeutics, Soc. Exptl. Biology and Medicine, N.Y. Acad. Scis. Home: 17700 Royal Crest Dr Brookfield WI 53005 Office: Childrens Hosp Wis 1700 W Wisconsin Ave Milwaukee WI 53233

COLTON, FRANK BENJAMIN, retired chemist; b. Bialystok, Poland, Mar. 3, 1923; came to U.S., 1934, naturalized, 1934; s. Rubin and Fanny (Rosenblat) C.; m. Adele Heller, Mar. 24, 1950; children—Francine, Sharon, Laura, Sandra. B.S., Northwestern U., 1945, M.A., 1946; Ph.D., U. Chgo., 1949. Research fellow Mayo Clinic, Rochester, Minn., 1949-51; with G.D. Searle & Co., Chgo., 1951-86, asst. dir. chem. research, 1961-70, research advisor, 1970-86. Contbr. articles to profl. jours. Pioneer in organic and steroid chemistries. Patentee first oral contraceptive. Recipient Discovery medal for first oral contraceptive Nat. Assn. Mfrs., 1965, Profl. Achievement award U. Chgo., 1978, Achievement award Indsl. Research Inst., 1978. Mem. Am. Chem. Soc., Chgo. Chemists Club. Home: 3901 Lyons St Evanston IL 60203

COLTON, JEFFREY JAMES, facial cosmetic surgeon; b. Saginaw, Mich., Mar. 20, 1948; s. Howard John and Nan (Doughty) C.; m. Cynthia Gale Martin, May 31, 1975; children: Sarah Nanette, Jeffrey James. BS with distinction, U. Mich., 1970, MD, 1974. Diplomate Am. Bd. Otolaryngology. Physician & surgeon Henry Ford Hosp., Detroit, 1980-83; clin. instr. U. Mich., Ann Arbor, 1980—; instr. Henry Ford Hosp., Detroit, 1980—. Contbr. articles to various jours. and books. Fellow Am. Coll. Surgeons, Am. Acad. Facial Plastic and Reconstructive Surgery, Am. Acad. Otolaryngology-Head and Neck Surgery, Am. Acad. Cosmetic Surgery; mem.

Am. Soc. for Liposuction Surgery. Republican. Presbyterian. Clubs: Centurion, Barton Hills Country (Ahh Arbor). Avocations: music, art, piano, gardening. Home: 2541 Londonderry Rd Ann Arbor MI 48104 Office: 30700 Telegraph #4566 Birmingham MI 48010

COLWELL, WILLIAM S., JR., data processing executive; b. Indpls., Jan. 4, 1935. Data processing operator Allison div. Gen. Motors Corp., Indpls., 1955-60, programmer, 1960-65; programmer, analyst Gen. Motors Corp., N.Y.C., 1965-70, supr. data processing programming and ops., 1970-81; supr. info. ctr. GMAC, Detroit, 1981-85; mgr. EDS/GMAC Info. Ctr., Detroit, 1985—; mgr. Devel. End User Computing Facility GMAC, Detroit, 1982. Asst. scout master Boy Scouts Am., Hempstead, N.Y., 1967-79, scout master, New Agausta, Ind., 1959-61. Avocations: private piloting, travel. Home: 43235 Candlewood Ct Canton MI 48187

COMAN, EDWARD JOHN, real estate and accounting company executive; b. Chgo., Dec. 7, 1939; s. Edward John and Agnes Marie (Martin) C.; m. Maxine Margaret Mikols, Dec. 29, 1962; children: Martin Edward, Daniel Gerard, Timothy Joseph, Amy Marie. BS in Acctg., Walton Sch. Commerce, 1961; postgrad., MIT, 1967; MBA, U. Chgo., 1969. CPA, Ill. Mgr. Glen Ingram & Co., Chgo., 1961-64; fin. exec. Jewel Cos., Melrose Park, Ill., 1964-69; pres. Edward J. Coman & Assocs., Lombard, Ill., 1969—, also chmn. bd. dirs.; pres. Real Estate Mgmt. Co., Lombard, 1981—, also chmn. bd. dirs. Author: How To Make Money Doing Tax-Free Exchanges of Real Estate, 1987, How To Make Money Giving Real Estate To Charity, 1987. Served with USNG, 1961. Mem. Lombard C. of C. (bd. dirs. 1978-80). Roman Catholic. Lodge: Rotary (bd. dirs. 1979-81, pres. 1980). Avocations: reading, travel. Home: 555 Prince Edward Rd Glen Ellyn IL 60137 Office: 1100 S Main St Lombard IL 60148

COMBER, FRANK JOHN, real estate development executive; b. Paris, Tenn., July 22, 1940; s. Frank John and Sophia (Deresiewicz) C.; m. Virginia Kathryn Hackl, Aug. 24, 1968; children: Marsha, Darchelle. BArch, U. Ill., 1968; MBA, Loyola U., Chgo., 1974. Registered architect, Ill. Draftsman E. Zisook & Assocs., Chgo., 1964-67; architect A.M. Kinney & Assocs., Chgo., 1967-73; architect Homart Devel. Co., Chgo., 1973-75, dir., 1975-82, officer, 1982—; cons. Sears Roebuck, Mexico City, 1980. Mem. planning bd. City of Deer Park, Ill., 1984-86; campaign assoc. United Way, Chgo., 1986. Served with Air N.G., 1963-68. Recipient Cert. of Appreciation, Chgo. Builders Assn., 1986. Mem. Internat. Council of Shopping Ctrs. (cons. 1982-84), Am. Constrn. Owners Assn. Roman Catholic. Club: Terrace Hill Golf (Elgin, Ill.). Avocations: golf, boating. Home: 42 Lea Rd Barrington IL 60010 Office: Homart Devel Co 55 W Monroe Chicago IL 60603

COMBS, DON EDGAR, banker; b. Reinersville, Ohio, Nov. 2, 1929; s. Everett Alva Combs and Bessie (Gorrell) Young; m. Marilyn Elizabeth Price, Nov. 22, 1962; children—Susan Michelle, Michael Don, James Paul, John Price. Asst. cashier 1st Nat. Bank, McConnelsville, Ohio, 1953-61; chief exec. officer Citizens Bank Co., Beverly, Ohio, 1961-72, pres., 1972-82, Malta Nat. Bank, Ohio, 1983—. Corp. mem. Marietta Meml. Hosp., Ohio, 1969—; pres. Friend of Library, Beverly, 1967—. Served to sgt. U.S. Army, 1951-53, Korea. Recipient Boss of Yr. award, Beverly-Waterford Jaycees, 1966. Mem. M&M Jaycees (pres. 1959), Ohio Bankers Assn., Ohio Community Bankers (treas. 1975-81). Republican. Presbyterian. Lodges: Lions, Rotary, Masons. Home: 530 Mitchell Ave Rt 1 Box 9 Beverly OH 45715

COMBS, JOE DENTON, psychiatrist; b. Greenfield, Mo., June 14, 1905; s. Thaddeus Denton and Carolyn Marie (Robertson) C.; m. Fay Madgel Meshew, Mar. 1, 1945; 1 child, Julia Carolyn. AB, Drury Coll., 1929; MA, U. Ill., 1931, PhD, 1934; MD, U. Ga., 1941. Asst. prof. microanatomy U. Ga. Sch. Med., Augusta, 1934-41; gen. practice medicine Lockwood, Mo., 1941-45; resident Ball Meml. Hosp., Muncie, Ind., 1945; sr. physician, clin. dir. Milledgeville (Ga.) State Hosp., 1945-59; resident Yale U., New Haven, 1948, The Menninger Inst. Psychiatry, Topeka, 1950, The Inst. Pa. Hosp., Phila., 1951-52; clin. dir., asst. supt. Nevada (Mo.) State Hosp., 1959-81; dir. psychiatry Nevada (Mo.) Mental Health Services, 1981—; cons. Nevada (Mo.) State Hosp., 1981—, Nevada (Mo.) City Hosp., 1984—. Fellow Am. Psychiat. Assn. (life), mem. Alpha Omega Alpha, Sigma Xi. Avocation: painting. Home: Rt Bronaugh MO 64728 Office: Nevada Mental Health Services 815 S Ash St Nevada MO 64772

COMBS, THOMAS NEAL, lawyer; b. Dallas, Nov. 30, 1942; s. Thomas James and Edith (Gibson) C.; m. Dorothy Elaine Bell, Mar. 12, 1965; children—Thomas Neal, James, John. J.D. with honors, So. Meth. U., 1968. Bar: D.C. 1968, U.S. Supreme Ct. 1975, Mich. 1976. Assoc. Alston, Miller & Gaines, Washington, 1968-70, Marmet & Webster, Washington, 1970-73; from assoc. to ptnr. Webster, Kilcullen & Chamberlain, Washington, 1973-75; v.p., gen. counsel, sec. Fruehauf Corp., Detroit, 1975-85, exec. v.p. fin. and legal, chief fin. officer, sec., 1985-86, pres., chief adminstrv. and fin. officer, 1986—, also bd. dirs.; bd. dirs. Fruehauf Corp., Fruehauf Internat. Ltd., Fruehauf Can., Kelsey Hayes Can.; lectr. various tax insts., 1968—. Contbr. articles to profl. publs. Bd. visitors So. Meth. U. Sch. Law. Mem. ABA, Mich. Bar Assn., Bar Assn. D.C., Am. Judicature Soc., Am. Soc. Corp. Secs., Fin. Exec. Inst., Order of Coif. Clubs: Metropolitan (Washington); Detroit, Detroit Athletic, Country of Detroit. Home: 169 Stephens Rd Grosse Pointe Farms MI 48236 Office: PO Box 33238 Detroit MI 48232-5238

COMER, FREDERICK RAY, education association executive; b. Lapeer, Mich., Aug. 3, 1942; s. Arthur Raymond and Lorraine Helen (Kesler) C.; m. Sally Lou Ost, Dec. 18, 1965; children—Allison Lee, Justin Arthur. B.S., Central Mich. U., 1964; M.A., Western Mich. U., 1968. Tchr. Wayland Union Schs., Mich., 1967-70; UniServ dir. Mich. Edn. Assn., Holland, 1970-73, asst. exec. dir., Traverse City, 1973-78, assoc. exec. dir., East Lansing, 1978-81; exec. dir. Iowa State Edn. Assn., Des Moines, 1981—; evaluator Nat. Council Accrediation Tchr. Edn., Washington, 1982; cons. on instrn. Nat. Edn. Assn., Washington, 1983—. Contbr. to booklets. Com. mem. Legis. Com. Collective Bargaining, 1984, Govs. Com. Local Govt., 1983, Planning com. Iowa Edn. Forum, 1983. Mem. Nat. Council State Edn. Assns., Central Mich. U. Alumni Assn. Democrat. Mem. United Ch. Christ. Avocations: Travel; reading; college athletics. Home: 1111 11th St West Des Moines IA 50265 Office: Iowa State Edn Assn 4025 Tonawanda Dr Des Moines IA 50312

COMER, ROBERT MARLIN, publishing company purchasing executive; b. Dayton, Sept. 27, 1932; m. Jean L. Miller, Apr. 16, 1955; children: Pamela Horsley, Amy, Brian. A in Applied Scis., Sinclair Community Coll., 1977. Chief machinist Dayton (Ohio) Newspapers, Inc., 1970-75, purchasing agt., 1975-78, dir. purchasing, 1978—. Contbr. articles to newsletters. Mem. Dem. Cen. Com., Dayton, 1962-64. Mem. Newspaper Purchasing Mgmt. Assn., Inc. (bd. dirs. 1981-83, treas. 1983-84, 2d v.p. 1984-85, 1st v.p. 1985-86, pres. 1986-87, Pres.' award 1987), Nat. Assn. Purchasing Mgmt. (local chpt. bd. dirs. 1978-81, treas. 1981-82, elected pres. 1982-83, pres. 1983-84, dir. nat. affairs 1984-85, Presidents award 1984), Minority Purchasing Council. Republican. Roman Catholic. Lodge: Kiwanis (bd. dirs. local chpt. 1983-84). Avocations: golf, weight lifting, walking, running. Office: Dayton Newspapers Inc 45 S Ludlow St Dayton OH 45401

COMIENSKI, JAMES SIGMON, educator; b. Cleve., Nov. 6, 1948; s. Sigmon James and Martha Helen (Chernus) C.; m. Barbara Ann Lutz, July 1, 1978. B.A. in Geology, Case Western Res. U., 1970; postgrad. Ohio State U., Cleve. State U., U. Akron, 1974—. Traffic checker schedule dept. Regional Transit Authority, Cleve., 1966-68, 69-70, 72; sci. tchr., planetarium dir. Lakewood (Ohio) Schs., 1973—; cons. earth sci. curriculum North Ridgeville, 1977; lectr. bird migration; asst. instr. Ohio Sea Grant Edn., summer, 1981. Ruling elder Lakewood Presbyterian Ch., 1981—. Served with U.S. Army, 1970-72. Mem. Nat. Sci. Tchrs. Assn., Great Lakes Planetarium Assn. (edn. com.), Cleve. Astron. Assn. (exec. council), Assn. Astronomy Educators, Internat. Soc. Planetarium Educators, Cleve. Mus. Natural History, Cleve. Regional Council Sci. Tchrs., Cleve. Regional Assn. Planetarians, Lakwood Tchrs. Assn., Ohio Educators Assn., Nat. Earth Sci. Tchrs. Assn., Aerospace Educators Assn., Western Res. Hist. Soc., Nat. Geog. Soc., Planetary Soc., Ctr. Environ. Edn., NEA, Bay Village Hist. Soc., Smithsonian Assoc. Democrat. Co-writer sci. project activities. Home: 420 Bassett Rd Bay Village OH 44140 Office: Lakewood Schs 14100 Franklin Blvd Lakewood OH 44107

COMPAAN, PEARL JOAN, oncologist; b. Hull, N.D., Mar. 27, 1939; divorced; children: Maria, Michele. BA, Hope Coll., 1960; MD, U. Mich., 1964. Diplomate Am. Bd. Radiology. Intern Christ Hosp., Cin., 1964-65; resident U. Minn., Mpls., 1966-67; resident U. Cin., 1967-69, instr. radiology, 1969-70; asst. radiotherapist Good Samaritan Hosp., Cin., 1970-73; pres., practice medicine specializing in radiology Oncology Assocs. Inc., Cin., 1973—; physician coordinator Clin. Chemotherapy in Cancer Control, Cin., 1973-76; mem. com. Children's Cancer Study Group, Nat. Wilms Tumor Study, Providence, 1985—; mem. Ohio State Radiol. Exec. Council, 1986—. Mem. Am. Soc. Therapeutic Radiologists and Oncologists, Am. Coll. Radiology, Am. Soc. Clin. Oncology, Ohio State Med. Assn., Ohio State Radiol. Soc., Cin. Acad. Medicine. Office: Oncology Assocs Inc PSC 3120 Burnet Ave Suite 103 Cincinnati OH 45229

COMPTON, CHERYL LYNN, social worker; b. Shelbyville, Ill., Aug. 16, 1950; d. Junior Harold and Ruth Esther (Norman) Cushman; m Richard Lyle Compton, May 5, 1973; children: Nicholas, Nathan. BSW, So. Ill. U., 1972; MSW, U. Ill., 1977. Cert. social worker, Ill. Social worker Pleasant Acres Nursing Home, Altamont, Ill., 1972-73; social services dir. CEFS Econ. Opportuntiy Corp., Effingham, Ill., 1973-78; social worker, head dept. social services Sarah Bush Lincoln Mental Health Ctr., Mattoon, Ill., 1978-79; sch. social worker Ea. Ill. Spl. Edn. Coop., Mattoon, 1980; exec. dir. Effingham County (Ill.) Guidance and Counseling Ctr., 1980—; cons. Luth. Care Ctr., Altamont, Ill., 1975-77, Effingham Care Ctr., 1977; pres. Heartland Hospice, Effingham, 1982-85. U. Ill. fellow 1975. Mem. Nat. Assn. Social Workers, U. Ill. Alumni Assn. Democrat. Methodist. Club: Jr. Women (Altamont) (Woman of the Yr. nominee 1981). Avocations: reading, cooking. Home: Rural Rt #5 Box 67FF Effingham IL 62401 Office: Effingham County Guidance and Counseling Ctr 1108 S Willow Effingham IL 62401

COMPTON, WALTER A., manufacturing company executive. BS, Princeton U., 1933; MD, Harvard U., 1937. With Miles Labs. Inc., Elkhart, Ind., 1938—, v.p. research med. div., 1946-61, exec. v.p., 1961-64, chief exec. officer, 1964-81, pres., 1964-73, chmn. bd. dirs., 1973-81, hon. chmn. bd. dirs., 1981—. Served to lt. col. AUS, 1942-46. Office: Miles Labs Inc 1127 Myrth St Elkhart IN 46515 *

COMSTOCK, JACQUOLINE MARGARET, podiatrist; b. St. Louis, Apr. 10, 1923; d. William Thomas Comstock and Julia Beatrice (Schuetz) Van Hole; m. Oscar August Meinhardt, July 28, 1956 (dec. Oct. 1975); children: Chris Meinhardt, Greg Thomas Meinhardt, Julie Ann Sell. Student, Washburn U., 1941-43, Kans. State U., 1943-45; D in Podiatric Medicine, Ill. Coll. Podiatry and Foot Surgery, 1951. Practice medicine specializing in podiatry Topeka, 1951—; cons. VA Hosp., Topeka, 1958-61, Menninger Clinic, Topeka, 1965-85. Served with USN, 1944-48. Mem. Am. Podiatric Med. Assn., Kans. Podiatry Med. Assn. (sec. 1953). Democrat. Roman Catholic. Lodge: Soroptomists. Avocations: golf, bowling, cooking, antique collecting, travel. Home and Office: 908 Washburn Topeka KS 66606

CONANT, HOWARD ROSSET, steel company executive; b. Chgo., Sept. 30, 1924; s. Louis J. and Fredericka (Rosset) Cohn; m. Doris S. Kaplan, Dec. 14, 1947; children: Alison Sue, Howard R., Meredith Ann. B.S., U. Pa., 1947. Pres., dir. Interstate Steel Co., Des Plaines, Ill., 1947-71; chmn. bd. Interstate Steel Co., 1971—; pres., dir. Elliott Paint & Varnish Co., Chgo., 1961-76; dir. Valspar Co., Mpls., Interstate Steel Supply Co., Facets Multimedia, Inc.; chmn. bd. dirs. White Products Corp., 1965-67. Discussion leader Center Study of Continuing Edn., 1955-62; dir. Com. for Sane Nuclear Policy, 1964-69; mem. Bus. Execs. Move for Vietnam Peace, 1965-73. Served with AUS, 1943-46, PTO. Mem. World Bus. Council, Chgo. Pres.'s Orgn., Chgo. Assn. Commerce and Industry (dir.). Clubs: Ridge and Valley Tennis (Glenview); Carlton (Chgo.); East Bank. Home: 736 Greenacres Ln Glenview IL 60025 Office: 401 E Touhy Ave Des Plaines IL 60017

CONANT, STEVEN GEORGE, psychiatrist; b. Elkhart, Ind., July 8, 1949; s. Hubert Eugene and Ruth (Weaver) C. BA in Zoology with distinction, DePauw U., 1971; MD, Ind. U., 1975. Diplomate Am. Bd. Psychiatry and Neurology. Intern Ind. U. Med. Ctr., Indpls., 1975-76, resident in psychiatry, 1976-78; asst. prof. psychiatry Ind. U., Indpls., 1978-80; cons. psychiatry Gallahue Mental Health Ctr., Indpls., 1979-85; staff psychiatrist Metro Health, Indpls., 1983—; staff privileges at Community Hosp., Indpls., 1979—; cons. psychiatrist Ind. Prison Systems, 1986, social security div. Ft. Benjamin Harrison Army Hosp. Mem. Conductor's Circle of the Indpls. Symphony, 1984—, Indpls. Symphonic Choir Orch., 1876-83, Ensemble Music Soc., 1983—. Mem. Am. Psychiat. Assn., Ind. Psychiat. Soc., Am. Acad. Clin. Psychiatrists, Mensa, The Hoosier Group. Republican. Presbyterian. Avocations: European and Am. lit., classical piano, Am. Impressionist and Post-impressionist Art, Chinese Export Porcelain. Home: 3651 Totem Ln Indianapolis IN 46208 Office: Metro Health 3266 N Meridian 9th Floor Indianapolis IN 46208

CONARD, ARLYN MARK, minister, historian; b. Ashland, Kans., June 22, 1948; s. Arlyn Elmer and Mary Lockie (Mast) C.; m. Joyce Marie Fieser, Aug. 21, 1971; children: Jonathan, Andrew, Kristin. BA, Southwestern Coll., Winfield, Kans., 1970; MDiv, St. Paul Sch. Theology, Kansas City, Mo., 1974; ThM, Union Theol. Sem. in Va., 1975, ThD, 1979. Ordained to ministry United Methodist Ch., Deacon, 1971, elder, 1979. Pastor United Meth. Ch., Geneseo, Kans., 1978-81, Maize, Kans., 1981-87; pastor Pleasant Valley Ch., Wichita, 1987—; chmn. conf. commn. on archives and history, United Meth. Ch., 1980—, vice chmn. jurisdictional com. on archives and history, 1984—, mem. gen. commn. on archives and history, 1984—. Contbr. articles and book revs. to profl. jours. Grad. fellow Union Theol. Sem. in Va. 1975-78. Mem. Am. Soc. Ch. History, Am. Assn. for State and Local History, Conf. on Faith and History, Assn. Records Mgrs. and Assocs., Kans. State Hist. Soc. Avocation: philately. Home: 3160 Carlock Wichita KS 67204 Office: Pleasant Valley Ch 2801 Coolidge Wichita KS 67204

CONARD, BRENDA RUTH, education consultant; b. Sedalia, Ohio, Aug. 1, 1940; d. Herman Kenneth and Ruth Aurdry (Gossard) Dorn; m. Dennis Eric Conrad, Aug. 14, 1971; children: Hilary Paige, Timothy Alexander. BS in Elem. Edn., Ohio State U., 1961, MA in Phil. Edn., 1974, postgrad., 1968—. Cert. tchr., Ohio. Tchr. elem. Columbus City Schs., 1962-63, 1968-69, TV tchr., resource cons., 1969-78, tchr. elem., 1970-78, cons. multicultural edn., 1978—; tchr. elem. Orange County Schs., Orlando, Fla., 1962-68. Author parenting booklet for Columbus council PTA, 1986. Youth leader Franklin County 4-H Club, 1983—; council del. Ridgeview Sch. PTA, 1985—; guest appearances on local radio and TV stations, 1978—. Mem. Assn. Supervision and Curriculum Devel., Cen. Ohio Council Social Studies, Colo. Edn. Assn., Ohio Edn. Assn., Nat. Edn. Assn., Phi Delta Kappa. Congregationalist. Club: Hunt (Upper Arlington, Ohio) (pres., sec. 1974-86). Lodge: Order Eastern Star. Avocations: tennis, oil painter, writer, aerobic dancer. Office: Columbus City Schs Alum Crest Ctr 2200 Winslow Dr Columbus OH 43207

CONDON, THOMAS SAMUEL, accountant, corporate professional; b. Parkersburg, W.Va., Jan. 10, 1957; s. Harry F. and Barbara A. (Clark) C. BS with honors, Ferris State Coll., 1980. Staff acct. Howell Osbourne & Co., Hillsdale, Mich., 1980-83, sr. acct., 1983-85, mgr., 1985—; treas. Hillsdale Terminal Products, Jonesville, 1980—; bd. dirs. Penbridge Assocs., Hillsdale. Mem. Am. Inst. CPA's, Mich. Assn. CPA's. Club: Hillsdale Golf and Country. Lodge: Elks. Office: Howell Osbourne & Co 184 Carleton Hillsdale MI 49242

CONDREN, PATRICK JOSEPH, banker; b. Cin., June 22, 1951; s. Joseph Patrick and Charlotte Katherine (LeMonn) C.; m. Linda Ann Wohlfrom, Dec. 14, 1973; children: Jennifer Lynn, Joseph Patrick, Jeffrey Michael. BBA, U. Cin., 1973. CPA, Ohio. Credit mgr. Early & Daniel Co., Cin., 1975-79; acct. Clark, Schaefer & Hackett, Cin., 1979-85; v.p., controller Union Savs. Bank, Loveland, Ohio, 1985-86; treas. Oak Hills Savs. and Loan Co., Cin., 1986—; pvt. practice tax cons., Cin., 1980—. Mem. Am. Inst. CPA's, Ohio Soc. CPA's. Roman Catholic. Club: Westwood Athletic (Cin.) (pres. 1985-86). Avocations: golf, tennis. Home: 5082 Nighthawk Dr Cincinnati OH 45247 Office: Oak Hills Savings and Loan Co 6581 Harrison Ave Suite 310 Cincinnati OH 45247

CONE, MARK DOUGLAS, data processing executive; b. Oklahoma City, July 26, 1959; s. Ralph Dale and Barbara Ann (Reser) C. BS, BA in Data Processing, Cen. Mo. State U., Warrensburg, 1981. Mini-computer specialist Computer Scis. Corp., Kansas City, Mo., 1981-84; programmer analyst Iowa Beef Products, Inc., Shawnee Mission, Kans., 1984-85, analyst, 1985-86, project mgr., br. mgr., 1986—; cons. in field, Kansas City, 1982-85. Youth leader St. Mark's Ch., Independence, Mo., 1985-86, also lector, lay minister. Mem. Data Processing Mgmt. Assn., Data Processing Mgmt. Assn. (student orgns. com. 1982-84, pub. relations com. 1985). Democrat. Roman Catholic. Avocations: reading, softball, racquetball, choir, church activities. Home: 3603 S Spring Independence MO 64055 Office: Iowa Beef Processing Inc 6400 Glenwood Shawnee Mission KS 66202

CONERLY, RICHARD PUGH, corporation executive; b. Jackson, Ala., May 6, 1924; s. William L. and Eunice (Pugh) C.; m. Iva Jean Brightwell, Aug. 12, 1956; children: William Edward, Robert Andrew, Christopher Brightwell, Elizabeth Anne. Student, Howard Coll., Birmingham, Ala., 1942; B.J., U. Mo., 1949; LL.B., Harvard U., 1952. Bar: Mo. 1952. Practice in St. Louis, 1952-65; assoc., partner Thompson & Mitchel, 1952-65; v.p., gen. counsel, exec. v.p. Peabody Coal Co., St. Louis, 1965-69; pres. Pott Industries Inc., St. Louis, 1969—; vice-chmn. Houston Natural Gas Corp., 1979-85. Served with USAAF, 1942- 46. Home: 339 Hawthorne St Webster Groves MO 63119 Office: 3010 Mercantile Tower Saint Louis MO 63101

CONFER, OGDEN PALMER, feed and flour mill executive; b. Mpls., Nov. 14, 1921; s. Ogden Armour and Ruth (Palmer) C.; m. Elizabeth McElhenny, Dec. 20, 1941; children: Ogden William, Kay Confer Lamb, Richard Palmer, Carol Confer Greenwald. Student, Westminster Coll., Mo., 1939-40; B.B.A., U. Minn., 1943. Mgr. feed div., v.p. Hubbard Milling Co., Mankato, Minn., 1946-58, pres., 1958-70, chmn. bd., chief exec. officer, 1970—; dir. Norwest Bank, Mankato. Trustee Gustavus Adolphus Coll. Mem. N.W. Feed Mfrs. Assn. (past pres.), Am. Feed Industry Assn. (dir., chmn. bd. 1970), Millers Nat. Fedn. (past dir.), Mankato C. of C. (past dir.). Presbyterian (trustee, elder). Club: Mankato Golf (past dir.). Lodges: Kiwanis; Elks. Home: 20 Trail Dr Mankato MN 56001 Office: Hubbard Milling Co 424 N Front St Mankato MN 56001

CONGER, WILLIAM FRAME, artist, educator; b. Dixon, Ill., May 29, 1937; s. Robert Allen and Catherine Florence (Kelly) C.; m. Kathleen Marie Onderak, May 23, 1964; children: Sarah Elizabeth, Clarisa Lynn. Student, Art Inst. Chgo., 1954, 56-57, 60, 62; B.F.A., U. N.Mex., 1960; M.F.A., U. Chgo., 1966. asst. prof. Rock Valley Coll., Rockford, 1966-71; vis. lectr. Beloit Coll., 1969; prof., chmn. dept. art DePaul U., Chgo., 1971-85; vis. artist U. Chgo., 1976, 83, Cornell U., 1980; Sch. Art Inst. Chgo., 1985; adj. prof. So. Ill. U., 1984; prof., chmn. dept. art theory and practice Northwestern U., Evanston, Ill., 1985—; numerous lectures. One man shows Burpee Mus., Rockford, Ill., 1971, Douglas Kenyon Gallery, Chgo., 1974, 75, Krannert Center for Arts, Urbana, Ill., 1976, Zaks Gallery, Chgo., 1978, 80, 83, Roy Boyd Gallery, Chgo., 1985, group shows include Art Inst. Chgo., 1963, 71, 73, 78, 80, 84, 85 Mus. Contemporary Art, Chgo., 1976, Krannert Mus., Urbana, 1976, Ill. State Mus., 1978, E.B. Crocker Gallery, Sacramento, 1977, Phoenix Mus., 1977, Mitchell Mus., 1980, Notre Dame U., 1981, Sonoma State U., 1983, Cowles Mus., 1983, Arts Club Chgo., 1983, 84, 85, Sheldon Meml. Gallery, U. Nebr., 1984, Anchorage Fine Arts Mus., 1985, Ark Art Ctr., 1985, Block Gallery, Northwestern U., 1986; represented in permanent collections, Art Inst. Chgo., Ill. State Mus., Chgo., No. Ill. U., DePaul U., Jonson Mus., U. N.Mex., Block Gallery, others, also pvt. collections U.S. and worldwide.; numerous catalogs, revs. and commentary in Arts mag., Art Forum, Art in Am., Ciamese, Art News, Art Criticism; others; author essays in Whitewalls, Chicago/Art/Write, Psychoanalytic Perspectives on Art, other jours. Bd. dirs. Ox Bow Art Sch., 1982-86. Recipient Bartels award Art Inst. Chgo., 1971; Clusmann award, 1973; Friedman awards U. Chgo., 1965, 66. Mem. Coll. Art Assn. Am., Phi Sigma Tau. Office: Northwestern U Dept Art Theory and Practice Room 216 and 251 Kresge Hall Evanston IL 60201

CONKLIN, JOSEPH JUSTINE, JR., journalist; b. Jackson, Mich., Oct. 8, 1950; s. Joseph Justin and Lucille Virginia (Surque) C.; m. Deborah Sue Goldsberry, June 2, 1972; children: Heather Marie, Matthew Ryan. BA in Journalism, Cen. Mich. U., 1972. Sports editor Traverse City (Mich.) Record-Eagle, 1972-83; sports copy editor, feature writer Grand Rapids (Mich.) Press, 1983—. Named Mich. Sports Columnist of Yr., AP, 1983. Roman Catholic. Avocations: family activities.

CONKLIN, ROBERT EUGENE, electronics engineer; b. Loveland, Ohio, Apr. 21, 1925; s. Charles and Alberta (Reynolds) C.; m. Virginia E. McCann, June 14, 1952; children—Carl Lynn, Jill Elaine Conklin Bradford. B.S. in Edn., Wilmington Coll., 1949, B.S. in Sci., 1949. Electronic scientist Electronic Technol. Lab., Wright-Patterson AFB, Ohio, 1951-55; electronic engr. AF Avionics Lab., Wright-Patterson AFB, 1956-60 supervisory elec. engr., 1960-72, cons. electronic engr., 1972-78, supervisory electronic engr., 1978-82, electronic engr. (VHSIC), 1982-84; cons. engr. REC Electronics, Fairborn, Ohio, 1984—; mem. Inst. Nav., 1968-72. Mgr. Babe Ruth Boys' Baseball, 1969-74; mgr. and pres. Little League, Fairborn, 1965-68. Served with USAAC, 1943-46. Mem. IEEE. Republican. Quaker. Lodge: Lions (Fairborn) Home: 114 Wayne Dr Fairborn OH 45324 Office: 47 N Broad St Fairborn OH 45324

CONKLIN, WILLIAM EARL, JR., hospital administrator; b. Charleston, W.Va., Sept. 12, 1937; s. William Earl and Myrtle Lee (Hanson) C.; m. Leila Darlene Ash, Dec. 15, 1957; children—William Earl, Amy Denise. B.S.B.A., W.Va. U., 1960; M.Pub. Adminstrn., Ind. State U., 1981. Adminstrv. extern, acting personnel dir. Meml. Hosp., Charleston, 1960-61; personnel dir., adminstrv. asst. Luth. Hosp., Cleve., 1961-68; dir. personnel Presbyn. Hosp., Charlotte, N.C., 1968-70, Deaconess Hosp., Evansville, Ind., 1970—; cons. in field. Com. chmn., asst. scoutmaster Buffalo Trace council Boy Scouts Am., Evansville, 1973-78; bd. dirs. Lutheran Found., 1974-77, Evansville Assn. Retarded Citizens, 1986—. Mem. Evansville C. of C. (legis. com. 1980—), Am. Soc. Hosp. Personnel Adminstrn. (lit. award 1978; charter; dir. 1983-85, pres.-elect 1985-86), Ind. Soc. Hosp. Personnel Adminstrn. (pres. 1978-79), Evansville Personnel Assn. (pres. 1978-79), Am. Soc. Personnel Adminstrn., Am. Soc. Healthcare Adminstrn. (pres. 1986-87), Ind. Personnel Assn., Profl. Secs. Internat. (dir.). Republican. Co-author: A Basic Guide to Health Care Personnel Policies & Procedures, 1983; contbr. articles to profl. jours. Home: 4155 Pine Dr Newburgh IN 47630 Office: 600 Mary St Deaconess Evansville IN 47747

CONKRIGHT, GARY WILLIAM, manufacturing executive; b. Lafayette, Ind., July 20, 1954; s. Charles William and Shirley Lynn (Feaster) C.; m. Marilyn Ruth Johnson, Oct. 23, 1982; 1 child, Chad William. BS, Purdue U., 1976; MBA, U. Chgo., 1982. Engr. Sargent & Lundy, Chgo., 1976-78; dir. engring. Midwesco, Niles, Ill., 1978-86; v.p. engring. Rovanco, Joliet, Ill., 1986, exec. v.p., 1986—. Mem. Am. Soc. Heating and Refrigeration Engrs., Am. Soc. Testing and Materials, N.Am. Dist. Heating and Cooling Assn. Republican. Methodist. Home: 1009 Augustana Naperville IL 60565 Office: Rovanco I-55 and Frontage Rd Joliet IL 60436

CONLEY, CAROLYN PATTON, accountant; b. Detroit, Mar. 5, 1944; d. Carl D and Roberta Jean (Kennedy) Patton; B.B.A., Wichita State U., 1966, M.S., 1967; m. Norman Eddy Conley, Nov. 19, 1967; 1 son, Sean Peter. Mem. audit staff Fox & Co., C.P.A.s, Wichita, 1967-69; controller Central Computing Inc., Wichita, 1969-70, Campus Activity Center, 1970-72, Inst. Logopedics, 1972-74; mgr. mgmt. services George U. Landis C.P.A., Wichita, 1974-76; tax analyst Dynatax div. Tymeshare, Wichita, 1976-78; pvt. practice acctg., Wichita, 1978—; mem. gov's. task force Kans. White House Conf. Small Bus., 1986, taxation moderator, 1986; del. Nat. White House Conf. Small Bus., 1986, mem. project beauty, 1984—. Mem. Commn. Status of Women, 1975-81, pres., 1976; bd. dirs. Historic Wichita, 1981—, sec.-treas., 1982-83, v.p., 1983-84, pres., 1984-87; bd. dirs. YWCA, 1978—, treas., 1978-85, 1st v.p. 1987—; mem. Friends Botanica; campaign treas., local polit. campaigns; treas. Wichita Free U., 1981-84; participant Leadership 2000, 1983, Leadership Kans., 1987. Mem. Nat. Assn. Women Bus. Owners (pres. 1982-83, dir. pub. affairs 1986-88), Adminstrv. Mgmt. Soc. (membership chmn. 1981-82, v.p. fin. 1982-83), Nat. Assn. Accts., Am. Inst. C.P.A.s, Kans. Soc. C.P.A.s, League Women Voters(dir. fin. 1987-88), NOW, Wichita Area C. of C. (seminar chmn. 1984, chair White House Conf.

Small Bus. 1986). Clubs: Sports Car Am. (treas. dir.; Midwest div. Class A Rallye champion, 1974, 75, 76).Lodge: Soroptimists. Home: 2916 W 21st St Wichita KS 67203 Office: 2916 w 21st Wichita KS 67203

CONLEY, ELIZABETH JOAN, physician; b. Monett, Mo., Sept. 2, 1947; s. Martin William and Mary Ann (Belt) C. BS in Biology, Pitts State U., 1974; DO, Kirksville Coll. Osteopathic Med., 1979; diploma registered nursing, Mount Carmel Sch. Nursing, Pitts., 1968. Nurse intensive care unit Baxter Meml. Hosp., Baxter Springs, Kans., 1968-74; gen. practice osteo. medicine Baxter Springs, Kans., 1980-83; osteopath Baxter Meml. Hosp., Baxter Springs, Kans., 1983-84; gen. practice osteo. medicine Jefferson City, Mo., 1983-85, Saint Elizabeth, Mo., 1984—, St. Elizabeth, Mo., 1985—; med. dir. Staint Elizabeth Care Ctr., 1984—; med. advisor Meta (Mo.) Ambulance, 1986. Active Jefferson City United Way, 1984. Served to maj. USNG. Mem. Am. Osteopahtic Assn., Mo. Osteopathic Assn., Nat. Guard Assn., Sigma Sigma Phi, Phi Kappa Phi. Democrat. Roman Catholic. Avocations: camping, swimming, target shooting, cross country skiing. Home and Office: Saint Elizabeth Clinic PO Box 57 Saint Elizabeth MO 65075

CONLEY, JAMES P., accountant; b. Boston, Oct. 26, 1938; s. James and Eleanor Dorothy (Lewis) C.; m. Christine Zanone, July 14, 1973; 1 child, Peter J. BSBA, Northeastern U., 1961. CPA, Mass. Sr. mgr. Ernst & Whinney, Boston, 1968-72, ptnr., 1972-86; ptnr. Ernst & Whinney, Cleve., 1986—. Bd. dirs. Morgan Meml. Goodwill Industries, Boston, 1979-85. Mem. Nat. Assn. Accts. (bd. dirs. 1980-82, pres. Boston chpt. 1979-80), Am. Inst. CPA's, Mass. Soc. CPA's. Home: 15900 S Woodland Rd Shaker Heights OH 44120 Office: Ernst & Whinney 2000 National City Center Cleveland OH 44114

CONLEY, PATRICIA L., software support company executive; b. Dayton, Ohio, Oct. 6, 1954; s. Jerry C. and Joyce E. (Powell) Brock; m. Frank Conley, June 23, 1973 (div. July 1985); 1 child, Eric Douglas. Student, Sinclair Community Coll., Dayton, 1972-82. CPA, Ohio. Bookkeeper various firms, Lexington, Ky., 1975-79; acct. Battelle and Battelle, Dayton, 1979-84; support technician DayProm Computer, Dayton, 1984-86; pres. Data Tech. Support Group, Inc., Dayton, 1986—. Mem. Am. Inst. CPA's, Nat. Assn. Accts., Ohio Soc. CPA's. Republican. Avocations: writing children's stories, home remodeling, showing dogs, sewing, woodworking. Office: Data Tech Support Group Inc 3490 S Dixie Hwy Dayton OH 45439

CONLIN, ROXANNE BARTON, lawyer; b. Huron, S.D., June 30, 1944; d. Marion William and Alyce Muraine (Madden) Barton; m. James Clyde Conlin, Mar. 21, 1964; children: Jacalyn Rae, James Barton, Deborah Ann, Douglas Benton. B.A., Drake U., 1964, J.D., 1966, M.P.A., 1979; LL.D. (hon.), U. Dubuque, 1975. Bar: Iowa 1966. Assoc. firm Davis, Huebner, Johnson & Burt, Des Moines, 1966-67; dep. indsl. commr. State of Iowa, 1967-68, asst. atty. gen., 1969-76; U.S. atty. So. Dist. Iowa, 1977-81; assoc. firm James, Galligan & Conlin, P.C., 1983—; gen. counsel Legal Def. and Edn. Fund, NOW, 1985-86, pres., 1986—; adj. prof. law U. Iowa, 1977-79; guest lectr. numerous univs. Chmn. Iowa Women's Polit. Caucus, 1973-75, del. nat. steering com., 1973-77; cons. U.S. Commn. on Internat. Women's Year, 1976-77. Contbr. articles to profl. publs. Nat. committeewoman Iowa Young Democrats; also pres. Polk County Young Dems., 1965-66; del. Iowa Presdl. Conv., 1972; Dem. candidate for gov. of Iowa, 1982; nat. policy chmn. John Glenn for Pres. Com., 1983-84; bd. dirs. Riverhills Day Care Center, YWCA; chmn. Drake U. Law Sch. Endowment Trust, 1985-86 ; bd. counselors Drake U., 1982-86; pres. Civil Justice Found., 1986—. Recipient award Iowa Civil Liberties Union, 1974; named to Iowa Women's Hall of Fame, 1981; other awards.; Fischer Found. scholar, 1965-66; Readers Digest scholar, 1963-64. Mem. ABA, Iowa Bar Assn., ACLU, NAACP, Common Cause, Assn. Children Learning Disabilities, Assn. Trial Lawyers Iowa (bd. dirs.), Assn. Trial Lawyers Am. (chmn. consumer and victims coalition com. 1985—), Women's Equity Action League, NOW (dir. 1969), NOW Legal Def. and Edn. Fund (gen. counsel 1985-86, pres. 1986—), Phi Beta Kappa, Alpha Lambda Delta, Chi Omega (Social Service award). Office: 610 Equitable Bldg Des Moines IA 50309-3790

CONMY, PATRICK A., federal judge; b. 1934. BA, Harvard U., 1955; JD, Georgetown U., 1959. Ptnr. Lundberg, Conmy et al, Bismarck, N.D., 1959-86; mem. Bismarck City Commn., 1968-76; state rep. N.D. House Reps., Bismarck, 1976-86; judge U.S. Dist. Ct. of N.D., Bismarck, 1986—. Office: US Dist Ct 411 U S Courthouse 3rd St & Rosser Ave PO Box 1578 Bismarck ND 58502 *

CONNAR, JEFFREY WALTER, data processing educator; b. Milw., Dec. 19, 1956; m. Margaret R. Connar; 1 child, Christopher. Student, Marquette U., 1975-77; cert. instructional design, U. Wis., Eau Claire, 1986. Staff supr. Wis. Bell Telephone Co., Milw., 1977-83; ednl. dir. Marshall & Isley Data Services, Inc., Milw., 1983—; cons. MGIC, Milw., 1983, Old Kent Bank, Grand Rapids, 1985-86, 1st Nationwide Bank, San Francisco, 1986—, S.C. Johnson & Sons, Racine, Wis., 1986—; advisor U. Wis. Sch. Bus., Madison. Mem. Milw. Area Tng. Orgn., Am. Soc. Tng. and Devel. Lodge: KC. Avocations: golf, tennis, bowling. Home: 1127 S 95th St West Allis WI 53214

CONNELL, DAVID F., steel company executive; b. Hamilton, Ohio, June 23, 1942; s. Bob Lee and Eileen M. Connell; m. Nancy L. Williams, Apr. 6, 1962; children: John, Chris, Jennifer. BS, U. Cin., 1964; MBA, Xavier U., Cin., 1976. Indsl. engr. Gen. Motors Corp., Fairfield, Ohio, 1965-71; supt. Beckett Paper Corp., Hamilton, 1971-78; dir. ops. Southwestern Ohio Steel Industries, Hamilton, 1978—. Office: Southwestern Ohio Steel Industries PO Box 148 Hamilton OH 45012

CONNELL, FRED JOPLING, statistician; b. Dallas, Aug. 18, 1944; s. Louis Fred and Geraldine (Jopling) C.; m. Tschera Harkness, Jan. 3, 1974; children: Ruth, Beth. BA, Rice U., 1966; MS, U. Chgo., 1967, PhD, 1971. Registered profl. engr. Spl. asst. prof. U. Colo., Boulder, 1971-73; asst. prof. math. Millikin U., Decatur, Ill., 1973-78; forecast specialist Ill. Power Co., Decatur, 1978—. Contbr. articles to profl. jours. Elder Presbyn. Ch., 1977—; treas. PTO, Decatur, 1985—. NSF fellow, 1966-70; Sigma Xi research grantee, 1972. Mem. Am. Statisticial Assn. (cen. Ill. chpt.). Avocations: reading, cooking, camping. Home: 1644 W Forest Decatur IL 62522 Office: Ill Power Co 500 S 27th St Decatur IL 62525

CONNELL, JAMES PAUL, advertising executive; b. Boston, July 1, 1943; s. James Jeremiah and Elizabeth Jane (Fitzgerald) C.; m. Diane Marqua Guenther, Aug. 12, 1967; 1 child, James Paul II. BS, U.S. Mil. Acad., West Point, N.Y., 1966; M in Pub. Affairs, U. Cin., 1973. Commd. 2d lt. U.S. Army, 1966, advanced through grades to maj., 1976, resigned, 1977; media asst. Procter & Gamble Co., Cin., 1977-78, media supr., 1978-82, asst. media mgr., 1982-86, media mgr., 1986—. pres. Green Township (Ohio) Hist. Assn., 1979—, chmn. S.W. Ohio and N.Ky. chpt.Multiple Sclerosis Soc., Cin., 1976-79, Green Township Cable TV Commn., 1979-83. Decorated Purple Heart, Air medal. Mem. Nat. Assn. TV Program Execs., Cin. Jaycees (v.p. 1973-78), Delta Tau Kappa. Republican. Roman Catholic. Avocations: golf, scuba diving, banjo playing. Home: 5909 Gaines Rd Cincinnati OH 45247 Office: Media Section Procter & Gamble Co 1 Procter & Gamble Plaza Cincinnati OH 45202

CONNELLY, JAMES THOMAS, archivist, priest; b. Louisville, Ky., Dec. 15, 1937; s. James Bernard and Hazel (Horan) C. BA, U. Notre Dame, 1960, MA, 1968; STB, Pont. U. Gregoriana, Rome, 1963; PhD, U. Chgo., 1977. Ordained priest Roman Cath. Ch., 1964. Instr. U. Notre Dame, Ind., 1965-66; asst. prof. King's Coll., Wilkes-Barre, Pa., 1972-76; lectr. Alokolum Nat. Sem., Gulu, Uganda, 1977-79; archivist Province Archives Ctr., Notre Dame, 1980—. Mem. Soc. Am. Archivists, Midwest Archives Conference, Holy Cross History Assn. (pres. 1984-85). Democrat. Home: Holy Cross Mission House Notre Dame IN 46556 Office: Ind Province Archives Ctr PO Box 568 Notre Dame IN 46556

CONNELLY, JOHN DOOLEY, social service organization executive; b. Chgo., Sept. 8, 1946; s. John Joseph and Mary (Dooley) C. B.S., Xavier U., 1968; M.A., Northeastern Ill. U., 1973; Ph.D., Cornell U., 1976. Spl. edn. tchr. Spl. Edn. Dist., Lake County, Gurnee, Ill., 1969-73; asst. prof. spl. edn. Eastern Ky. U., Richmond, Ky., 1973-76; div. dir., acting exec. dir. City of Chgo. Health System, 1977-80; exec. dir. Jobs for Youth Chgo., 1980—; mgr. Emergency Loan Fund, Chgo., 1983—. Editor jour. Health and Medicine, 1984. Chmn. Pegasus Players Theatre, Chgo., 1982-87; bd. dirs. Health and Medicine Policy Research Group, Chgo., 1983-84; Clarence Darrow Community Ctr., Chgo., 1983—. Roman Catholic. Office: Jobs for Youth Chicago 67 E Madison St Chicago IL 60603

CONNER, GENE PATRICK, consultant; b. Morgantown, W.Va., Apr. 20, 1940; s. Gilbert Lionel and Esther Ruth (Mayfield) C.; m. Amy Elizabeth Evans, June 6, 1970. BS in Bus., Mountain State Coll., 1967. Pres. Conner Farm's, Columbus, Ohio, 1968—, BARCode Data Systems, Columbus, Ohio, 1984—, Data Acquisition Technology, Columbus, Ohio, 1986—; cons. Automation Identification Systems Inc., Indpls., 1986—, dir. health and med. div., 1987—; cons. Conat, Inc., Stuart, Fla., 1984—. Designer: (software) BDS-BARCode Systems, 1984; 10 mil. amp Date Decoder, 1984, Executive Decoder, 1985. Club: Central Ohio 4WD (Columbus) (pres. 1974-76), East Coast 4WD (regional chmn. 1975-76). Avocations: reading, music. Office: Data Acquisition Technology Assocs PO Box 144 Columbus OH 43216-0144

CONNER, H. CLINTON, mental health facility administrator; b. Mansfield, Ohio, June 11, 1937; s. Holly E. and Mildred Emma (Nichols) C.; m. Patricia Sue McClenathan, June 11, 1961 (div. June 1968); children: David, Jonathan; m. Bonnie Marie Lowles, July 5, 1969; 1 child, Corrie Bethany. BS, Bowling Green State U., 1957-60; MA, U. Chgo., 1960-62. Lic. independent counselor. Caseworker I Salvation Army Family Service, Chgo., 1962-64; caseworker II Evang. Ch. Welfare Agy., Chgo., 1964-67; caseworker III Marion (Ohio) Counseling Ctr., 1968-75; pvt. practice counselor Marion, 1975-83; dir. Christian Mental Health Clinic of Ohio, Lancaster, 1983—; adj. prof. Ohio State U., Columbus, 1964-79. Author: Not Without Cure, 1978; contbr. articles to profl. jours. Mem. Lic. Counselors Ohio, Ohio Counselors Conf. (founder 1984), Epsilon Pi Tau. Republican. Home: 570 Morningside Dr Lancaster OH 43130 Office: Christian Mental Health Clinic Ohio 114 Mt Ida Box 784 Lancaster OH 43130

CONNER, JANET CHESTELYNN, financial broker; b. Albany, Ky., Nov. 24, 1953; d. Kathleen (Stearns) C. Student, Purdue U. V.p. mktg. Brandon Polo Club, Fla., 1981-82; asst. Puller Mortgage, Indpls., 1982-83; pres., owner Excalibur Fin., New Castle, Ind., 1983—. Appointed mem. Ind. Venture Capital Conf., Indpls., 1983. Named Hon. Lt. Gov., Lt. Gov. Mutz of Ind., 1983. Mem. Nat. Assn. Women Bus. Owners, Network Women in Bus., Nat. Assn. Sec. Services, Internat. Enterpreneurs Assn., Delta Sigma Pi. Republican. Methodist. Clubs: Brandon (Fla.) Polo; Ind. Sanyo Users (Indpls.) (chmn.). Avocations: polo, business, fox-hunting, computers, airplanes. Home: PO Box 48 New Castle IN 47362

CONNER, MICHAEL EDWARDS, human resources professional, educator, consultant; b. Xenia, Ohio, Mar. 26, 1952; s. Thomas Robert and Beulah May (Bowles) C.; m. Cynthia Louise Bistline, May 24, 1980; children: Michael Edwards Jr., Matthew Loren. BSBA, Wright State U., Dayton, Ohio, 1980; MA in Indsl. Relations, U. Cin., 1984. Tech. recruiter Cin. Electronics, 1980-81; human resources mgr. Kenner Products, Cin., 1981—; instr. human resource mgmt. and personnel mgmt. So. Ohio Coll., Cin., 1985. Mem. YMCA, Lebanon, Ohio. Mem. Greater Cin. Human Resources Council, Employment Recruitment Council, Coll. Placement Council. Avocations: softball, golf, basketball, boating, water sports. Home: 5117 Carter Ct Mason OH 45040 Office: Kenner Products 1014 Vine St Cincinnati OH 45202

CONNOR, CATHERINE, automotive executive; b. Champaign, Ill.; d. Ernst Garland and Jeanne Juliette (Hazard) Mathews; m. Dean Wayne Nelson, Dec. 7, 1985. BS, U. Ill., 1969, MEd, 1973, MBA, 1985. Vis. scientist U. Ill., Urbana, 1970-79, instr., 1983-84; tng. mgr. Rogers Chevrolet Pontiac Buick, Rantoul, Ill., 1985—; pvt. practice cons. Urbana, 1985—; instr. U. Ill., Urbana, 1983-84; mem automotive adv. bd. Parkland Coll., Champaign, 1986—. Editor U. Ill. Commerce Alumni Newletter, Urbana, 1984-85. Mem. citizen's adv. com. Urbana Sch. Bd., 1981—; trustee First Presbyn. Ch., Urbana, 1983-86. NSF fellow, 1969-70. Home: 2207 S Anderson Urbana IL 61801 Office: Rogers Chevrolet Pontiac Buick 101 Congress Rantoul IL 61866

CONNOR, JAMES ALLEN, utilities executive; b. Mpls., Oct. 27, 1941; s. William Albert Sr. and Anne Marie (Asmundson) C.; m. Maureen Dianne Froelke, May 15, 1965; children: Mark Allen, Christopher Wade. BS in Bus. Econs., N.D. State U., 1969; BA in Hosp. Adminstrn., Concordia Coll., 1977. Project supt. Westchester Corp., Houston, 1971-74; asst. constrn. mgr. S.I.P., Houston, 1974-76; project mgr. Levering & Reid, Houston, 1977-80; project control supr. No. States Power, Mpls., 1980—. Bd. dirs. Hudson (Wis.) Booster Assn., 1984. Mem. Hudson Hockey Assn. (constrn. bd. 1987). Roman Catholic. Avocations: skiing, hunting, fishing. Home: Rt 1 Box 97 Hudson WI 54016 Office: Northern States Power 920 Second Ave S Minneapolis MN 55402

CONNOR, JAMES RICHARD, university administrator; b. Indpls., Oct. 31, 1928; s. Frank Elliott and Edna (Felt) C.; m. Zoe Ezopov, July 7, 1954; children: Janet K., Paul A. B.A., U. Iowa, 1951; M.S., U. Wis., 1954, Ph.D., 1961. Asst. prof. history Washington and Lee U., 1956-57, Va. Mil. Inst., 1958-61; asst. dir. Salzburg Seminar in Am. Studies, 1961-62; joint staff mem. Wis. Coordinating Com. Higher Edn., 1962-63; dir. Inst. Analysis; asst. prof. history U. Va., 1963-66; asso. prof. history, asso. provost No. Ill. U., 1966-69; provost, acad. v.p., prof. history Western Ill. U., 1969-74; chancellor, prof. history U. Wis.-Whitewater, 1974—; asso. dir. Va. Higher Edn. Study Com., 1964-65; Am. Council Edn. intern acad. adminstrn. Stanford U., 1965-66; staff dir. Study of Governance of Acad. Med. Center, Josiah Macy, Jr., Found., 1968-70; mem. commn. on higher edn. North Central Assn., 1970-75, 79-84, cons.-examiner, 1972—. Author: Studies in Higher Education, 1965; contbr., Ency. Brit. Served with AUS, 1946-47, 51-53. Woodrow Wilson fellow, 1953-54; So. fellow, 1957-58. Mem. Am. Hist. Assn., Orgn. Am. Historians, AAUP, Phi Beta Kappa, Phi Eta Sigma, Phi Kappa Phi, Phi Delta Kappa, Beta Gamma Sigma, Phi Alpha Theta, Delta Sigma Pi. Home: Route 2 Linden Dr Whitewater WI 53190 Office: U Wis Whitewater WI 53190

CONNOR, JUDITH HOLT, researcher; b. New Orleans, July 11, 1943; d. Harold Bert and Rhea Marie (Weilbaecher) Holt; m. David Thomas Connor, June 17, 1967; children: Kevin David, Jane Elizabeth. BA in Maths., Duchesne Coll., 1965; MA, U. Chgo., 1967; MBA, U. Mich., 1983. Ref. librarian Chgo. Pub. Library, 1967-68; research asst. Survey Research Ctr., U. Mich., Ann Arbor, 1978-81, research assoc., 1981—. Roman Catholic. Avocations: theatre, reading. Home: 2453 Antietam Dr Ann Arbor MI 48105 Office: U Mich Inst Social Research Sampling Sect PO Box 1248 Ann Arbor MI 48106

CONNOR, LAWRENCE STANTON, journalist, editor; b. Indpls., Aug. 31, 1925; s. Nicholas John and Agnes (Peelle) C.; m. Patricia Jean Alandt, Nov. 3, 1956; children—Carolyn, Julia, Lawrence Stanton, Maureen, Janet, Michael Connor. Student, Butler U., summers, 1943, 47, U. Ky., 1943, Miss. State U., 1944; A.B., U. Notre Dame, 1949; postgrad., Fordham U., 1949. With Indpls. Star, 1949—, chief copy desk, news editor, city editor, 1963-79, editor, 1979, mng. editor, 1979—. Served with USAAF, 1943-46. Mem. Am. Soc. Newspaper Editors, AP Mng. Editors Assn. Roman Catholic. Clubs: Indpls. Press, Indpls. Athletic. Office: The Indpls Star Indpls Newspapers Inc 307 N Pennsylvania St Indianapolis IN 46206

CONNOR, MARSHA J., advertising professional; b. Bklyn., Mar. 25, 1954; d. Lorenzo and Marie Louise (Edwards) Jamerson; m. Walter J. Connor III, July 1976. BA in English, Journalism, Dillard U., 1976; MA in Mass Communication, U. Minn., 1983. Reporter Times-Picayune Pub., New Orleans, 1973-75; account exec. advt. Bozell & Jacobs, Inc., Minn. and Wis., 1976-80; supr. advt. Northwestern Bell, Mpls., 1984—. Fellow U. Minn., 1981, WCCO, 1981-82. Mem. Am. Mgmt. Assn., Nat. Assn. for Female Execs., Minn. Black Mgrs. Assn. (vice chmn. 1986—), U. Minn. Alumni Assn., Mpls. Jaycees. Office: Northwestern Bell 100 S 5th St Room 680 Minneapolis MN 55402

CONNOR, MAUREEN FROELKE, nurse, hospital administrator; b. Rush City, Minn., Feb. 4, 1942; d. Leonard Robert and Mary Louise (Delmore) Froelke; m. James Allen Connor; children—Mark Allen, Christopher Wade. Diploma Northwestern Hosp. Sch. Nursing, 1963; B.A., Metro U., 1983. Cert. nursing adminstr. Am. Nurses Assn. Nursing supr. Dakota Hosp., Fargo, N.D., 1966-69; dir. nurses St. Mary's Hosp. and Home, Winsted, Minn., 1970-72; asst. adminstr. Houston N.W. Med. Ctr., 1972-80; assoc. adminstr. St. Croix Valley Meml. Hosp., St. Croix Falls, Wis., 1980—; bd. dirs. Western Wis. Health Services Agy. Mem. Am. Soc. Hosp. Nursing Services Adminstrs., Wis. Nurses Assn. (bd. dirs.), Wis. Orgn. for Nursing Execs. Roman Catholic. Home: Rural Rt #1 Box 97 Hudson WI 54016 Office: St Croix Valley Memorial Hospital Saint Croix Falls WI 54024

CONNOR, WILLIAM SHAUN, construction company executive; b. Indpls., Sept. 22, 1953; s. Robert Ambrose and Antoinette Loretta (Scheller) C.; m. Telene A. Edington, June 16, 1979; children: Colin Edington, Moira Elizabeth. BA, Ind. U., 1975. Tchr. St. Gabriel Grade Sch., Indpls., 1976-79; free-lance painter, carpenter Indpls., 1979-80; owner Connor & Crew, Indpls., 1980—; pvt. practice gen. contractor Indpls., 1982—. Pres. St. Joseph Neighborhood Park Assn., 1984-85, Meridian Park Neighborhood Assn., 1986-87; bd. dirs. Cathedral Arts, Inc., Indpls., 1984, Riley Area Revitilzation Area, Indpls., 1986. Club: Athletic (Indpls.). Home: 3173 N Delaware St Indianapolis IN 46205 Office: Wm S Connor & Co Inc 218 E 10th St Indianapolis IN 46202

CONNOR, WILLIAM STEPHEN, food industry executive; b. Chgo., Oct. 11, 1945; s. William Stephen Jr. and Mary Jane (Sheridan) C.; m. Margaret Cordula Carney, Nov. 25, 1973. B.S., So. Ill. U., 1972. Dist. sales mgr. Pepperidge Farm Inc., Chgo., 1979-83; sales mgr. Evans Food Products, Chgo., 1983—. Served with USMC, 1966-69. Mem. Potato Chip Snack Food Assn. Roman Catholic. Avocations: golf; racquetball. Home: 14450 Country Club Ln Orland Park IL 60462 Office: Evans Food Products 4118 S Halsted St Chicago IL 60609

CONNORS, DORSEY (MRS. JOHN E. FORBES), TV and radio commentator, newspaper columnist; b. Chgo.; d. William J. and Sarah (MacLean) C.; m. John E. Forbes; 1 dau., Stephanie. B.A. cum laude, U. Ill. Floor reporter WGN-TV Republican Nat. Conv., Chgo., Democratic Nat. Conv., Los Angeles, 1960. Appeared on: Personality Profiles, WGN-TV, Chgo., 1948, Dorsey Connors Show, WMAQ-TV, Chgo., 1949-58, 61-63, Armchair Travels, WMAQ-TV, 1952-55, Homeshow, NBC, 1954-57, Haute Couture Fashion Openings, NBC, Paris, France, 1954, 58, Dorsey Connors program, WGN, 1958-61, Tempo Nine, WGN-TV, 1961, Society in Chgo, WMAQ-TV, 1964; writer: column Hi! I'm Dorsey Connors, Chgo. Sun Times, 1965—; Author: Gadgets Galore, 1953, Save Time, Save Money, Save Yourself, 1972. Founder Ill. Epilepsy League; mem. woman's bd. Children's Home and Aid Soc., mem. women's bd. USO. Mem. AFTRA, Screen Actor's Guild, Nat. Acad. TV Arts and Scis., Soc. Midland Authors, Chgo. Hist. Soc. (guild com., costume com.), Chi Omega. Roman Catholic. Office: Chgo Sun Times 401 N Wabash Chicago IL 60611

CONNORS, JAMES DANIEL, JR., manufacturing company executive; b. Bklyn., May 1, 1938; s. James Daniel and Ann Frances (Mullins) C.; m. Mary Frances Landor, Jan. 8, 1966 (div. June 1986); children: Colleen Mary, Michael Patrick, Kevin Daniel, Shannon Mary. BS, U.S. Merchant Marine Acad., 1960; postgrad., St. John's U., 1962-63, L.I. U., 1964-65. Lic. USCG marine Engr. Sales engr. Babcock & Wilcox, N.Y.C., 1964-72; div. mgr. Chas. Lowe Co., Cleve., 1972-75; v.p. Reliable Products Co., Cleve., 1975-76; pres. Helfrich Die Casting Co., North Canton, Ohio, 1976-83; v.p. Investors Growth Corp., Hudson, Ohio, 1976—; also bd. dirs. Investors Growth Corp., Hudson; v.p. Gen. Die Casters, Inc., Peninsula, Ohio, 1983—. Cofounder Port Jefferson (N.Y.) Montessori Sch., 1970. Served to lt. commdr. USNR, 1960-70. Mem. Soc. Die Casting Engrs., Soc. Naval Architects and Marine Engrs. Republican. Roman Catholic. Club: Hudson Country. Avocations: sailing, golf. Home: 358 Atterbury Blvd Hudson OH 44236 Office: Gen Die Casters Inc PO Box 155 Peninsula OH 44264

CONOMY, JOHN PAUL, neurologist; b. Cleve., July 31, 1938; s. John and Marie Conomy; m. Jeannette Melchior, Oct. 19, 1963; children: John, Lisa, Christopher. BS cum laude, John Carroll U., 1960; MD, St. Louis U., 1964. Diplomate Am. Bd. Psychiatry and Neurology (examiner 1975—). Student research fellow in neurology St. Louis U., 1963-64; intern in straight medicine St. Louis U. Hosps., 1964; resident in neurology U. Hosps. of Cleve., 1965-68; fellow in neuropathology Cleve. Met. Gen. Hosp. and Case Western Res. U., Cleve., 1968; career teaching fellow dept. medicine Case Western Res. U. at U. Pa., University Park, Pa., 1970; asst. prof. neurology Case Western Res. U. Med. Sch., Cleve., 1972-77, assoc. clin. prof., 1979; chmn. dept. neurology Cleve. Clinic Found., 1975—, chmn. clin. research projects and instl. rev. com., 1978-82, chmn. neurosensory ctrs. task force, 1982—, mem. research program com., neurosci. study sect., 1982, dir. Mellen Ctr. Multiple Sclerosis Treatment and Research, 1984—, exec. dir., 1987—, also dir. consortium of multiple sclerosis ctrs., mem. task force on fund raising, 1985—; attending physician U. Hosps. Cleve., 1968, attending neurologist, 1972—, mem. bd. govs. dept. medicine, 1974-75; attending physician Highland View Hosp., Cleve., 1968; assoc. neurologist Hosp. U. Pa., 1970; sr. staff neurologist Scott and White Clinic and Hosp., Temple, Tex., 1971; cons. in neurology VA Ctr., Temple, 1971; clins. attending neurologist Parkland Hosp., Dallas, 1971-72; clin. instr. neurology U. Tex. Southwestern Med. Sch., Dallas, 1971-72; vis. lectr. neuroscis. U. Tex. Med. Sch., San Antonio, 1971-72; cons. physician evaluation bd. Whittaker Internat. Services for Saudi Arabia and United Arab Emirates, 1980; mem. physician evaluation bd. Whittaker Corp., 1980-85, sci. adv. bd. Communicative Disorders Found., 1980—; conf. participant health services utilization study Rand Corp., Santa Monica, Calif., 1984; med. advisor Huntington's Disease Found., Cleve., 1984—; mem. biotech. adv. bd. State of Ohio, 1983-85; participant Manpower in Neurology Conf., San Diego, 1985; mem. adv. bd. Internat. Health Resources Crop., 1985—; vis. prof. neurology Meml. Med. Ctr., Savannah, Ga., 1973, 77, 79, 80, 81, 83, 85, Bethesda (Md.) Naval Hosp., 1973, 78, U. Okla Dept. Medicine, 1976, U. Aris. Dept. Neurology, 1977, U. Ill. Rockford Med. Sch., 1978, Med. Coll. Va., 1978, Uniformed Sch. Med. Scis. and Bethesda Naval Med. Ctr., 1979, U. Rochester (N.Y.), 1979, Med. Coll. Ga., 1980, U. Western Ont. (London, Can.), 1981, Brooke Army Med. Ctr., San Antonio, Tex., 1981, George Washington U., Washington, 1981, Bowman-Gray Med. Sch. Wake Forest U., Winston-Salem, N.C., 1981, U. Eastern Va., 1982, VA Hosp., Montgomery, Ala., 1982, London Hosp. Med. Sch., 1982-83, U. Louvain, Belgium, 1983, Oxford (Eng.) U., 1983, Nat. Ctr. Nervous, Mental and Muscular Disorders, Tokyo, 1984, Kyoto (Japan) U., 1984, Kyushu U., Fukuoka, Japan, 1984, numerous others; guest lectr. numerous orgns, hosps., colls. and univs.; vis. neurologist numerous univs. and colls.; mem. organizing com. First Internat. Brain-Heart Symposium, Jerusalem, 1980, 2d Internat. Brain-Heart Symposium, Jerusalem, 1983, 3d Internat. Heart-Brain Symposium, Trier, Fed. Republic Germany, 1985; hon. cons. The London Hosp. and Tower Hamlets Health Dist., 1982-83; co-investigator neurogenic factors in the pathogenesis of arterial hypertension NIH, 1978, efficacy of guanabenz in the prophylaxis of migraine headaches, Wyeth Corp., 1977, randomized controlled clin. trial of prostacyclin in acute thromboembolic strokes and embolic strokes of cardic origin The Upjohn Co., 1983-84; sr. investigator quantitation of Cutaneous Sensation VA Hosp., Cleve., 1974, neuroscis. research program Cleve. Clinic Found., 1975—, guanabenz in migraine headaches: parallel, double-blind, multi-instl. trial in the prophylaxis of migraine headaches Wyeth Corp., 1979-82, others. Contbr. numerous articles to profl. jours.; rers.) Postgrad. Medicine, 1975—, Neurology, 1977—, Cleve. Clinic Quar., 1977—, Neurosurgery, 1979—, Am. Jour. Physiology, 1980-81, Archives of Neurology, 1982—, Residency Rev. Com. in Psychiatry and Neurology, 1983—. Served as capt. USAF, 1968-70. Recipient Francis M. Grogan prize St. Louis U. Med. Sch., 1964, Clin. Tchr. of Yr. award U. Hosps. Cleve., 1973; grantee Mary B. Lee Fund, 1973, Reinberger Found., 1976-82, Mellen Fund, 1976, 84. Fellow ACP (invited speaker 1979, 85, reviewer health care delivery programs 1984), Royal Soc. Medicine (London, hon., sect. neurology 1983), Am. Acad. Neurology, Am. Heart Assn. (stroke council); mem. AAAS, AMA (sect. council on neurology 1977-81, vice chmn.-sec. 1979-81; del. Health Policy agenda for the Am. People, 1983), Soc. Neurosci. (pres. Cleve. chpt. 1975-79), Am. Assn. History Medicine, Ohio State Med. Assn., Cleve. Acad. Medicine, No. Ohio Neurologic Soc., Assn. Research in Nervous and Mental Disease, Internat. Soc. Tech. Assessment in Health Care (founder), Royal Coll. Medicine (London, vis. mem.), Am. Neurol.

Assn. (chmn. pub. relations com. 1981—, attended joint meeting with Assn. Brit. Neurologists 1985), Can. Neurol. Soc. (hon.), Soc. Clin. Neurologists (councillor 1976-79, program chmn. 1982), Assn. U. Profs. Neurology, Am. Electroencephalographic Soc., Internat. Assn. Study Pain, Am. Acad. Neurology (ethics com. 1973—, chmn. ethics com. 1973-77, membership com. 1973—, chmn. membership com. 1977—, chmn. assoc. membership 1973—, asst. sec. treas. 1977-81, editor newletter 1979-85, practice com. 1977—, non-physician health care profl. com. 1981—, 1st v.p. 1983-85, chmn. legis. council 1985—), Cleve. Med. Library Assn. (trustee 1980—, chmn. pubs. com. 1984, joint exec. council Cleve. Health Scis. Library, exec. com. 1984-86), Behavioral Neurology Soc. (founder), Nat. Multiple Sclerosis Soc. (nat. med. adv. bd. 1985—, invited speaker 1985, chmn. profl. adv. council 1987—), Worshipful Soc. Apothecaries London, Council Med. Specialty Socs. (chmn. health care delivery com. 1979-81, chmn. by-laws com. 1981-82, mem. com. grad. med. edn., health manpower, 1984—, chmn. ad hoc com. tech. assessment 1985—), Am. Assn. Neurol. Surgeons (assoc., assoc. membership bd. 1982—), Inst. Clin. Neuroscis. London, Alpha Omega Alpha. Avocations: travelling, biking, racquetball, photography, music.

CONRAD, JEROME CHARLES, operations resources management executive; b. Chgo., Mar. 20, 1947; s. William G. Conrad and Patricia Teresa (Geiser) Nicol; m. Judith Blanche Brudek, Dec. 11, 1971; Children: Matthew Jerome, Daneen Judith. AA, Chgo. City Coll., 1973; BFA in Environ. Design, No. Ill. U., 1976. Asst. to chief exec. officer Equipment Mfg. Co., Chgo., 1976-77; assoc. Fulton and Partners, Inc., Toledo, 1977-80, v.p. facility planning and mgmt. group, gen. mgr. br. ops., 1980-83; chief exec. officer Conrad & Wood Techs. Inc., Toledo, 1983—. Bd. dirs. Environ. Design Inst. Purdue U., 1979-83; bd. dirs. Ops. Mgmt. Edn. and Research Found., Richardson, Tex., 1984—. Mem. Inst. Bus. Designers, Assn. Systems Mgmt. Republican. Avocations: reading, woodworking. Home: 2055 South Ave Toledo OH 43609 Office: Conrad and Wood Techs Inc 7 South Superior St Toledo OH 43602 also: 723 Phillips Ave Bldg E Toledo OH 43612

CONRAD, JON WILLIAM, dentist; b. Smithville, Mo., May 9, 1953; s. Marshall Dean and Evelyn Myrtle (Steneck) C.; m. Deborah Lynne Leeds, June 8, 1974; children: Michael William, Kimberly Lynne. Student, William Jewell Coll., 1974; DDS summa cum laude, U. Mo., Kansas City, 1978. Gen. practice dentistry Coffeyville, Kans., 1978—. Pres. Neosho Valley Study Club, Chanute, Kans, 1983. Mem. ADA, Kans. Dental Assn., Am. Orthodontic Soc., Coffeyville C. of C. (membership com. 1986—). Republican. Avocations: photography, snowskiing, marathon running, golf, boating. Home: 303 Michele Ln Coffeyville KS 67337 Office: 808 Willow St Coffeyville KS 67337

CONRAD, KELLEY ALLEN, industrial and organizational psychologist; b. N.Y.C., June 29, 1941; s. Allen and Dorothy Etta (McAtee) C.; m. Barbara Rae Bedessem, July 8, 1976. BS in Behavioral Science, Mont. State U., 1963; MA in Psychology, SUNY, Geneseso, 1970; PhD in Psychology, Iowa State U., 1973. Lic. psychologist, Wis. Cons. indsl. psychologist Humber, Mundie & McClary, Milw., 1973—. Contbg. author Learning by Experience-What, Why, How, 1978; contbr. articles to profl. jours. Served to lt. USN, 1964-68, Vietnam. Recipient Eli Tash award Wis. Assn. for Children with Learning Disabilities, 1979; Outstanding Contbn. recognition Alverno Coll., 1983. Mem. Am. Psychol. Assn., Am. Soc. Tng. and Devel. (bd. dirs. 1980), Nat. Psychol. Cons. to Mgmt., Midwest Psychol. Assn., Midwest Human Resources Planning Assn., Wis. Psychol. Assn. (sec. 1984—, pres. indsl. organizational div. 1984-85), Milw. Area Psychol. Assn. (pres. 1985-86), Acad. Mgmt., Sigma Xi, Psi Chi. Republican. Congregationalist. Lodge: Kiwanis (bd. dirs Milw. 1978-80, com. chair 1980, 81). Avocations: computer programming, jogging, skiing, photography, reading. Home: N22 W22 347 Rosewood Ct Waukesha WI 53186 Office: Humber Mundie & McClary 111 E Wisconsin Ave Suite 1950 Milwaukee WI 53202-4889

CONRAD, KENNETH DEAN, real estate executive; b. Dayton, Iowa, June 12, 1938; s. Don Orville and Viola Marie (Swanson) C.; m. Claudia Kea Spirek, Aug. 11, 1962; 1 child, Gregory John. BS, Iowa State U., 1960. Agrl. economist U.S. Dept. Agriculture and U.S. Tariff Commn., Washington, 1962-69; prof. farm mgr., v.p., co-owner Iowa Farms Assocs., Ft. Dodge, 1970—. Mem. Am. Soc. Farm Mgrs. and Rural Appraisers (accredited farm mgr., chairperson farm income com. Iowa chpt. 1983-85). Lutheran. Home: 1023 25th Ave N Fort Dodge IA 50501 Office: Iowa Farms Assocs Inc Warden Plaza Fort Dodge IA 50501

CONRAD, KENT, U.S. senator; b. Bismarck, N.D., Mar. 12, 1948; m. Lucy Calantti, Feb. 1987; 1 child, Jessamyn Abigail. Student, U. Mo., 1967; BA, Stanford U., 1971; MBA, George Washington U., 1975. Asst. to tax commr. State of N.D. Tax Dept., Bismarck, 1974-80, tax commr., 1981-86; U.S. senator from N.D. Washington, 1987—. Office: US Senator Office of Senate Members Washington DC 20510 *

CONRAD, KEVIN JOHN, publishing company financial executive; b. Evanston, Ill., July 25, 1960; s. Ralph William and Marilyn Carol (Meyer) C. BS in Commerce, DePaul U., Chgo., 1982; MBA, DePaul U., 1987. CPA, Ill. Supr. acctg. Torco Oil Co., Chgo., 1982-87; asst. controller Hitchcock Pub. Co., Wheaton, Ill., 1987—. Mem. Am. Ins. CPA's, Ill. CPA Soc., Assn. MBA Execs. Roman Catholic. Avocations: golf, skiing. Office: Hitchcock Pub Co 25 W 550 Geneva Rd Wheaton IL 60188

CONRAD, LORETTA JANE, educational administrator; b. Wooster, Ohio, Aug. 9, 1934; d. Donald William and Celia Irene (Smith) C.; B.Mus.Edn. cum laude, Coll. of Wooster, 1956; M.Mus.Edn., U. Colo., 1969; postgrad. cert. supervision/adminstrn. (Univ. scholar), John Carroll U., 1978. Tchr., Avon Lake (Ohio) public schs., 1956-61, Dept. Def., Europe and Far East, 1961-64, Bay Village (Ohio) Bd. Edn., 1964-73, Elyria (Ohio) public schs., 1973-78; asst. prin. Bay Village Bd. Edn., Bay High Sch., 1978-84, Bay Middle Sch., 1984—; music clinician, adjudictor; pvt. tchr. piano; accompanist, dir. Ch. Choir, Luth. Ch., 1966-80. Area rep. for recruitment, mem. music com. Coll. of Wooster. Presser scholar, 1955-56; Annie Webb Blanton scholar, Delta Kappa Gamma, 1968. Mem. Ohio Assn. Secondary Sch. Prins., Nat. Assn. Secondary Sch. Prins., Assn. Secondary Curriculum Devel., Ohio Middle Schs. Assn., Phi Delta Kappa, Delta Kappa Gamma, Alpha Delta (state music rep.). Democrat. Lutheran. Club: Quota (pres. 1985-87). Home: 1650 Cedarwood Dr Westlake OH 44145 Office: 27725 Wolf Rd Bay Village OH 44140

CONRAN, JOSEPH PALMER, lawyer; b. St. Louis, Oct. 4, 1945; s. Palmer and Theresa (Bussmann) C.; m. Daria D. Conran, June 8, 1968; children: Andrew, Lisabeth, Theresa. BA, St. Louis U., 1967, JD with honors, 1970. Bar: Mo. 1970, U.S. Ct. Mil. Appeals 1971, U.S. Ct. Appeals (8th cir.) 1974. Assoc. Husch, Eppenberger, Donohue, Elson & Cornfeld, St. Louis, 1974-78, ptnr., 1978—; mem. faculty Trial Practice Inst. Served to capt., JAGC, USAF, 1970-74. Mem. Bar Assn. Met. St. Louis recipient Merit award 1976,77). Roman Catholic. Club: Mo. Athletic (pres. 1986-87). Home: 2306 E Royal Ct Saint Louis MO 63131 Office: 100 N Broadway #1800 Saint Louis MO 63102

CONROE, HENRY GERALD, psychiatrist; b. Newark, N.J., Nov. 22, 1946; s. William Randolph and Sylvia (Wolt) C.; m. Harriet Gonzer, Aug. 17, 1969; children: Andrew, Gabriel, Daniel. BS, Rutgers U., 1968; MD, Hahnemann U., 1972. Diplomate Am. Bd. Psychiatry and Neurology. Intern Phila. Gen. Hosp., 1972-73; resident in psychiatry Michael Reese Hosp., Chgo., 1973-76, attending psychiatrist, 1976—; practice medicine specializing in psychiatry Chgo., 1976—; cons. Social Security Adminstrn., Chgo., 1980—, Jewish Vocat. Service, Chgo., 1986; clin. asst. prof. U. Chgo., 1982—. Mem. Am. Psychiatry Assn., Am. Psychoanalytic Assn. Democrat. Jewish. Avocations: reading, jazz, fitness. Office: 55 E Washington #3105 Chicago IL 60602

CONROY, ROBERT WARREN, psychiatrist; b. Syracuse, N.Y., Sept. 27, 1938; s. John William and Mary Elizabeth (Warren) C.; m. Beverly Joan Huney, Sept. 5, 1959; children: Robert William, Stephen John, Andrew Joseph. BS cum laude, Coll. St. Thomas, St. Paul, 1960; MD, U. Minn., 1964. Diplomate Am. Bd. Psychiatry and Neurology. Intern William Beaumont Gen. Hosp., El Paso, 1964-65, chief mental hygiene, 1968-70, chief dept. psychiatry, 1970-71; resident in psychiatry Walter Reed Gen. Hosp., Washington, 1965-68; staff psychiatrist C. F. Menninger Meml. Hosp., Topeka, 1971-74, sect. chief long term unit, 1974-87, section chief eating disorders unit and chem., 1982-87, assoc. dir., 1982-87; dir. Will Menninger Ctr for Applied Behavioral Scis., 1987—. Contbr. articles to profl. jours. Served to maj. U.S. Army, 1964-71. Mem. Am. Psychiatric Assn., Shawnee County Med. Soc. Roman Catholic. Avocations: reading, exercise, religious studies. Home: 6800 SW 40th St Topeka KS 66610 Office: The Menninger Found Box 829 Topeka KS 66601

CONROY, THOMAS HYDE, lawyer; b. Beloit, Kans., Feb. 6, 1922; s. Thomas Emmett and Ida Ruth (Hyde) C.; m. Helen Regina Supple, Nov. 27, 1952; children: Thomas William, Sheila Anne, Regina Marie, Joseph Patrick. AB, U. Kans., 1945, LLB, 1949. Bar: Kans. 1949. Assoc. Ralph H. Noah, Beloit, 1949-52; city atty. City of Beloit, 1953-55, 67-81; county atty. County of Mitchell, Kans., 1957-65; ptnr. Hamilton & Conroy, 1965; sole practice Beloit, 1965—; owner, developer Conroy Place, 1965—; bd. dirs. First Nat. Bank, Beloit. Bd. dirs. Mitchell County Hist. Soc., Inc. 1972—, 1st v.p., 1972-75, pres., 1975-77; trustee Mitchell County Hosp., 1965-87, pres. 1965-73, Marymount Coll. of Kans., 1983—. Mem. Am. Legion, Phi Kappa, Phi Delta Phi. Lodges: Elks, Lions, KC (state adv. 1958-59). Home: 721 E 3d St Beloit KS 67420 Office: 209 E Main St Beloit KS 67420

CONRY, THOMAS FRANCIS, mechanical engineering educator, consultant; b. West Hempstead, N.Y., Mar. 7, 1942; s. Thomas and Bridget Anne (Walsh) C.; m. Sharon Ann Silverwood, June 10, 1967; children—Christine Elizabeth, Carolyn Danielle, Anne Marie. B.S., Pa. State U., 1963; M.S., U. Wis.-Madison, 1967, Ph.D., 1970. Registered profl. engr., Wis., Ill. Engr., Gen. Motors Corp., Milw., 1963-66; sr. research engr., Indpls., 1969-71; asst. prof. gen. engrng. U. Ill., Urbana, 1971-75; assoc. prof. gen. and mech. engrng., 1975-81, prof. gen. and mech. engrng., 1981—, co-dir. mftg. engrng. program, Coll. Engrng., 1986—, head dept. gen. engrng., 1987—; sr. visitor U. Cambridge (Eng.), 1978; cons. Zurn Industries, 1974-83; staff cons. Sargent & Lundy, Engrs., 1977, 79; cons./evaluator commn. on instns. of higher edn. North Ctl. Assn., 1983—; cons. indsl. firm on machine dynamics, optimization and tribology. Contbr. articles to profl. jours. Mem. Bd. Edn. St. Matthews Parish Roman Catholic Ch., Champaign, 1981-84. NSF trainee, 1968-69; NASA/ASEE summer faculty fellow, 1974-75. Mem. ASME (chmn. design engrng. div. 1979-80, tech. editor Jour. Vibration, Acoustics, Stress and Reliability in Design), Am. Soc. Engrng. Edn., Sigma Xi, Lambda Chi Alpha. Home: 3301 Lakeshore Dr Champaign IL 61821 Office: 104 S Mathews Ave Urbana IL 61801

CONSIDINE, FRANK WILLIAM, container corporation executive; b. Chgo., Aug. 15, 1921; s. Frank Joseph and Minnie (Regan) C.; m. Nancy Scott, Apr. 3, 1948. Ph.B., Loyola U., Chgo., 1943. Owner F. J. Hogan Agy., Chgo., 1945-47; asst. to pres. Graham Glass Co., Chgo., 1947-51; owner F.W. Considine Co., Chgo., 1951-55; v.p. Metro Glass div. Kraftco, Chgo., 1955-60; v.p., dir. Nat. Can Corp., Chgo., 1961-67; exec. v.p. Nat. Can Corp., 1967-69, pres., 1969—, chief exec. officer, 1973—, chmn., 1983—, also mem. fin. com., chmn. exec. com., mem. corp. devel. com.; vice chmn. Triangle Industries, Inc. (parent corp.), New Brunswick, N.J., 1985—; dir. Allis Chalmers Corp., Ency. Brittanica, 1st Chgo. Corp., 1st Nat. Bank Chgo., Internat. Minerals & Chem. Corp., Maytag Co., Tribune Co. Past chmn. U.S. sect. Egypt Bus. Council; trustee, mem. exec. com. Mus. Sci. and Industry Chgo.; bd. dirs. Can Mfrs. Inst., Evanston Hosp., Lyric Opera of Chgo., Field Mus. Natural History, Jr. Achievement Chgo., Econ. Devel. Com. Chgo. Served to lt. USNR, 1943-46. Mem. Econ. Club Chgo., Chgo. Assn. Commerce and Industry (past pres.). Clubs: Economic, Chicago, Commercial, Mid-Am.; Glen View (Golf, Ill.). Office: Nat Can Corp 8101 Higgins Rd Chicago IL 60631 *

CONSIDINE, TIMOTHY PATRICK, lawyer; b. Champaign, Ill., Oct. 8, 1957; s. James Lloyd and Lois Catherine (Morrissey) C. BS, Lewis U., 1975-79; JD, So. Ill. U., 1983. Bar: Ill. 1983, U.S. Dist. Ct. (cen. dist.) Ill. 1984, U.S. Dist. Ct. (no. dist.) Ill. 1986. Asst. states atty. Peoria County, Peoria, Ill., 1983-85; assoc. J.A. Morrissey & Assocs., Rockford, Ill., 1985—. Asst. village mgr. Village of Romeoville, Ill., 1978-80; sec. planning commn., Romeoville, 1978-80, zoning bd. appeals, Romeoville, 1978-80, econ. devel. commn., Romeoville, 1978-80. Mem. ABA, Ill. State Bar Assn., Ill. Trial Lawyers Assn., Assn. Trial Lawyers Am., Nat. Dist. Attys. Assn. Democrat. Roman Catholic. Avocations: swimming, running, team sports. Office: Joseph A Morrissey & Assocs 321 W State Suite 1208 Rockford IL 61101

CONSIDINE, WILLIAM HOWARD, health care adminstrator; b. Akron, Ohio, July 7, 1947; s. G. Howard and Gene Marie (Nelson) C.; m. Rebecca Diane Krenrick, Oct. 14, 1972; children—Michael, Cathryn, Matthew. B.A., Akron U., 1969; M.S., Ohio State U., 1971. Program cons. USPHS, Bethesda, Md., 1971-73; with patient care mgmt. N.C. Meml. Hosp., Chapel Hill, 1973-75, with gen. services, 1975-76, dir. ambulatory care, 1977-79; pres. Children's Hospital, Akron, Ohio, 1979—; cons. search com. Children's Hosp., Nat. Med. Ctr., Washington, 1982, Robert Wood Johnson Found. on Ambulatory Care Dental Program, 1978-79. Chmn. Akron Health Coordinating Council, 1978-79, EEO com. NIH, 1972-73. Served to lt. USPHS, 1971-73. Recipient Appreciation award Ohio State U. Alumni in Health Services Adminstrn., 1975, Outstanding Hoban Alumni award, 1984; research asst. grantee Kellogg Found., 1971. Mem. Am. Coll. of Hosp. Adminstrs., Am. Hosp. Assn., Assn. of Am. Med. Colls., Nat. Assn. of Children's Hosps. and Related Insts., Children's Hosp. Executive Council, Assn. of Univ. Programs in Health Adminstrn., Ohio Hosp. Assn., Ohio State U. Alumni Assn., North Hosp. Assn., Chapel Hill C. of C. Roman Catholic. Clubs: Casad, University, Portage Country (Akron). Office: Children's Hosp Med Ctr of Akron 281 Locust St Akron OH 44308

CONSTAN, LOUIS LEONARD, physician; b. Chgo., Jan. 11, 1947; s. Peter Louis Constan and Kyra Aris (Brown) Kaptur; m. Karen Leigh West, June 21, 1969; children: Zachary, Megan. BS, U. Chgo., 1968, MD, 1972. Diplomate Am. Bd. Family Practice. Intern, then resident Saginaw (Mich.) Coop. Hosps., 1972-75; assoc. dir. Family Practice Ctr., Saginaw, Mich., 1977-80; asst. prof. dept. family practice Mich. State U., East Lansing, 1977-80; chief dept. family practice St. Lukes Hosp., Saginaw, 1981—; med. officer Saginaw County Juvenile Ctr., 1976—. Editor Bulletin Saginaw County Med. Soc. Recipient Outstanding Voluntary Physician Educator award Saginaw Coop. Hosps. Inc., 1984. Fellow Am. Acad. Family Physicians; mem. AMA, Saginaw Acad. Family Physicians, Saginaw County Med. Soc. (bd. dirs. 1986—).

CONTE, EUGENE THOMAS, osteopath, dermatologist; b. N.Y.C., May 11, 1953; m. Michele A. O'Brien; children: Nachie, Chad, Jadea. BS, St. Johns U., Jamaica and N.Y.C., 1975; DO, Mich. State U., East Lansing, 1978. Intern Pontiac (Mich.) Osteopathic Hosp., 1979-80, resident in dermatology, 1980-83; chmn. dept. of dermatology Grandview and Southview Hosps., Dayton, Ohio, 1983—; vol. clinical faculty Ohio U. Coll. of Osteo. Medicine, Dayton, 1983—, Wright State U. Coll. Medicine, Dayton, 1983—. Contbr. articles to profl. jours. Served as lt. USN, 1977-78. Grantee N.Y. Inst. Scis., 1967. Mem. Am. Osto. Assn., Am. Acad. Osteopathy, Am. Coll. Osteo. Medicine, The Skin Cancer Found., Ohio Osteo. Assn., Soc. for Pediatric Dermatology. Republican. Roman Catholic. Home: 3369 Penenil Rd Spring Valley OH 45370 Office: Dermatology Cons Inc Southview Hosp Suite 133 1997 Miamisburg-Centerville Rd Dayton OH 45459

CONTE, LOU, artistic director, choreographer; b. DuQuoin, Ill., Apr. 17, 1942; s. John and Floy Mae (Saunders) C. Student Ellis DuBoulay Sch. Ballet, Chgo., 1961-68, So. Ill. U., 1960-62, Am. Ballet Theatre Sch., N.Y.C., 1964-66. Choreographer musicals Mame, 1972, Boss, 1973; choreographer Milw. Melody Top, 1966; dir. Lou Conte Dance Studio, Chgo., 1974—; artistic dir. Hubbard St. Dance Co., Chgo., 1977—; lectr. Mem. Actors Equity Assn., AFTRA. Office: Hubbard Street Dance Co 218 S Wabash Ave Chicago IL 60604

CONTIE, LEROY JOHN, JR., judge; b. Canton, Ohio, Apr. 2, 1920; s. Leroy John and Mary M. (DeSantis) C.; m. Janice M. Zollars, Nov. 28, 1953; children: Ann L., Leroy John III. B.A., U. Mich., 1941, J.D., 1948. Bar: Ohio 1948. Law dir. City of Canton, 1952-60; chmn. Canton City Charter Commn., 1963; mem. Stark County Bd. Elections, Canton, 1964-69; judge Common Pleas Ct., Stark County, 1969-71, U.S. Dist. Ct., No. Dist. Ohio, Cleve., 1971-82, U.S. Ct. Appeals (6th cir.), Cin., 1982—. Trustee Stark County Legal Aid Soc., Canton chpt. ARC; adv. bd. Walsh Coll., Canton, Ohio, U. Akron Law Coll. Served with AUS, 1942-46. Mem. Am., Ohio, Stark County, Summit County, Cuyahoga County, Akron bar assns., Am. Judicature Soc., U.S. Jr. C. of C. (internat. senator), Canton Jr. C. of C. (trustee), Stark County Hist. Soc., Stark County Wilderness Soc., Am. Legion, Sigma Phi Epsilon (Nat. citation award), Phi Alpha Delta., Omicron Delta Kappa. Roman Catholic. Clubs: K.C. (4 deg.), Elks. Office: US Courthouse Akron OH 44308

CONTINO, VINCENT NICHOLAS, controller; b. Chgo., Jan. 5, 1952; s. Louis Joseph and Margaret Florence (Guiffre) C.; m. Linda Jean Schmidt, Jan. 31, 1981; 1 child, Jennifer Lyn. AA, S.W. City Coll., 1974; BSBA, Loyola U., Chgo., 1975; MBA, Keller Grad. Sch., 1982. CPA, Ill. Staff acct. Exchange Nat. Bank, Chgo., 1976-77; mgr. internat. acctg. Maremont Corp., Chgo., 1977-81; controller Extel Corp., Northbrook, Ill., 1981-86, Handi-Foil Corp., Wheeling, Ill., 1986—. Mem. Am. Inst. CPA's, Ill. CPA Soc., Ill. State C. of C. Avocations: gardening, reading, computers. Home: 1060 Weeping Willow Dr Wheeling IL 60090 Office: Handi-Foil Corp 135 E Hintz Wheeling IL 60090

CONTRATTO, SUSAN, psychologist; b. Boston, June 20, 1943; d. Andrew William and Doris (Masters) C.; m. Thomas E. Weisskopf, Jan 17, 1970; children: Nicholas, Jonah. BA magna cum laude, Harvard U., 1965, EdD, 1972. Lic. psychologist, Mich. Dir. women's studies program U. Mich., Ann Arbor, 1977-79, fellow Nat. Inst. Mental Health, 1980-81, adj. assoc. prof. women's studies, 1980-81, 84-86; fellow Nat. Inst. Mental Health U. Calif., Berkeley, 1979-80; practice clin. psychology Ann Arbor, 1980—; lectr. on feminist psychology various locations. Contbr. articles to profl. jours. Chmn. bd. Pound House Children's Ctr. U. Mich, 1976-79; v.p. bd. dirs. Domestic Violence Project, Washtenaw County, 1981-86; vice chairperson for issues Ann Arbor Dems., 1986—. Mem. Am. Psychol. Assn., Nat. Women's Studies Assn., Assn. for Women in Psychology (midwest regional coordinator, 1981—), Phi Beta Kappa. Avocations: skiing, sailing, swimming. Home and Office: 1320 Brooklyn Ann Arbor MI 48104

CONVERSE, THOMAS ISALY, architect; b. Tulsa, May 8, 1949; s. Edward E.a nd Anna Marie (Isaly) C.; m. Nancy Emily Fields, June 13, 1970. BArch, Miami U., Oxford, Ohio, 1972. Registered architect, Ohio. Project mgr. Trautwein Assocs., Worthington, Ohio, 1976-78; v.p. ops. Nitschke Assocs. Inc., Columbus, Ohio, 1978-85; pres. Renouveau Design, Inc., Columbus, 1985—. Served to lt. USN, 1972-76. Mem. AIA, Architects Soc. Ohio, Alpha Chi Omega (fine Arts award 1972). Clubs: Swim and Racquet (Columbus); Leatherlips Yacht (Dublin, Ohio). Avocations: sailing, tennis. Office: Renouveau Design Inc 261 E Livingston Ave Columbus OH 43215

CONVERY, PATRICK GEORGE, orthopedic surgeon; b. Paterson, N.J., July 4, 1953; s. Patrick Hugh and Constance (Donato) C.; m. Marilyn Jean Glaser, Aug. 3, 1975; children: Kristen, Ellen, Matthew, Steven. BA in Chemistry, Montclair State Coll., 1975; MD, Bowman Gray Sch. Medicine, 1979. Diplomate Am. Bd. Orthopedic Surgery. Resident Pa. State U., Hershey, 1979-84; practice medicine specializing in orthopedic surgery Budd Lake, N.J., 1984-85; orthopedic surgeon Mednet/Euclid (Ohio) Clinic, 1985—; cons. staff Ridgecliff Hosp., Willoughby, Ohio, 1986—; assoc. staff Euclid Gen. Hosp., 1986—; active staff Lake County Hosp., Willoughby, 1986—; med. adv. bd. Kerr Brumbaugh Rehab. Ctr., Mentor, Ohio, 1987—. Mem. Ohio State Med. Assn., Lake County Med. Soc. Democrat. Roman Catholic. Avocation: sports. Home: 9941 Cypress Circle Mentor OH 44060 Office: Mednet/Euclid Clinic 18599 Lake Shore Blvd Euclid OH 44119

CONWAY, GERALD ALLEN, state legislator, finance educator; b. Sioux City, Iowa, July 20, 1947; s. C. Patrick and Helen (Manning) C.; m. Kathleen Lynch, Aug. 26, 1967; 1 child, Jennifer. BS, U. S.D., 1973; MS, Chadron (Nebr.) State Coll., 1974; postgrad., U. Nebr., 1977-80. Program dir. Chadron State Coll., 1973-75; asst. prof. fin. Wayne (Nebr.) State Coll., 1975—; mem. Nebr. Legislature, Lincoln, 1984—; vol. Action Corps of Execs., 1977—; cons. Nebr. Bus. Devel. Ctr., Wayne, 1978—; bd. dirs. Old West Underwriters. Served with U.S. Army, 1968-69, Vietnam. Mem. Midwest Fin. Assn., Midwest Bus. Adminstrn. Assn., Am. Legion, VFW. Democrat. Roman Catholic. Lodges: KC, Kiwanis. Avocations: flying, scuba diving, woodworking. Home: 1115 Lawndale Dr Wayne NE 68787 Office: Nebr Legislature State Capitol Bldg Lincoln NE 68509

CONWAY, JAMES JOSEPH, physician; b. Chgo., July 1, 1933; s. Frank and Mary (Tuohy) C.; m. Dolores Mazer, June 30, 1956; children: Laurie, John, Cheryl. BS, DePaul U., 1959; MD, Northwestern U., 1963. Asst. instr. U. Pa., 1964-68; assoc. in radiology McGaw Med. Ctr. Northwestern U., Chgo., 1968-71, asst. prof. to assoc. prof. radiology, 1974-80; attendant radiology, chief nuclear medicine div. Children's Meml. Hosp., Chgo., 1968—, prof. radiology, 1980—; cons. radiologist Hines (Ill.) VA Hosp., 1972—. Contbr. 94 articles to profl. jours.; pub. Internat. Wine Rev. Served with U.S. Army, 1953-55. Fellow Am. Coll. Nuclear Physicians, Am. Coll. Radiology; mem. Puerto Rico Soc. Nuclear Medicine (hon.), Radiol. Soc. N.Am. (Scroll of Appreciation award 1983), Soc. Nuclear Medicine, AMA. Avocation: collector of Chgo. memorabilia. Office: Children's Meml Hosp 2300 Children's Plaza Chicago IL 60614

CONWAY, JAMES WALTER, accountant; b. Berwyn, Ill., May 1, 1955; s. Raymond J. and Hettie (McMillan) C.; m. Pamela A.M. Feige, Oct. 25, 1980; children: Kathleen Ann, Brendan Paul. BS in Acctg., U. Ill., 1979; MS in Taxation, DePaul U., 1984. CPA, Ill.; registered fin. planner. Acct. Pritzker & Pritzker Co., Chgo., 1978-79; sr. acct. Ronald J. Borden & Co., Chgo., 1980-83; controller Callaghan Paving, Inc., Orland Park, Ill., 1983-85; ptnr. Moticka & Ralph, Inc., Brookfield, Ill., 1985—. Mem. Am. Inst. CPA's (tax div.), Ill. Soc. CPA's, Am. Assn. Personal Fin. Planners, Internat. Assn. Fin. Planners. Office: Moticka & Ralph Inc 9040 W Ogden Ave Brookfield IL 60513

CONWAY, NEIL JAMES, III, title company executive, lawyer, writer; b. Cleve., Feb. 15, 1950; s. Neil J. and Jeanne Lewis (Gensert) C. BSBA, John Carroll U., 1972; MBA, Suffolk U., 1974; JD, Antioch Sch. Law, 1982. Bar: Ohio, 1983, U.S. Dist. Ct. (no. dist.) Ohio, 1983, U.S. Supreme Ct., 1987. Auditor U.S. Dept. Interior, Arlington, 1974-77; systems acct. Mil. Dist. Washington, 1978-79; legal intern Govt. Accountability Project, Washington, 1981; judicial intern presiding judge U.S. Dist. (no. dist.) Ct. Ohio, 1982; v.p. Conway Land Title Co., Painesville, Ohio, 1984-85, pres., 1985—; staff writer Schanachie mag., Euclid, Ohio, 1986—. Editor-in-chief: Antioch Law Jour., 1982-83; also articles. Served to capt. U.S. Army Reserve, 1981. Mem. ABA, Am. Soc. Internat. Law (Dean Rusk award 1980), Ohio Bar Assn., Lake County Bar Assn., Ohio Land Title Assn. (real property sect.), Lake County Bd. Realtors (program com., Affiliate of Yr. 1986), Painesville Title Assn. (pres. 1985-86), Women's Council Realtors (treas. 1984-86), Lake-Geauga Legal Aid Soc. (adv. bd. 1984—), Amnesty Internat., Nat. Trust for Hist. Preservation, Smithsonian Inst., Irish Am. Cultural Inst. St. Paul, Irish Nat. Caucus (past del.), Ancient Order Hibernians (dep. polit. edn. chmn. Cleve. chpt. 1986—), North Coast Pipe Band (drummer, mgr.). Democrat. Roman Catholic. Club: Irish American, Irish Heritage. Avocations: playing drums, racquetball, rugby. Home: 762 Mentor Ave #2 Painesville OH 44077

CONWAY, WILLIAM EDWARD, mineral company executive; b. Oct. 16, 1927; s. Timothy J. and Margaret Mary (Nelson) C.; m. Mary French, Dec. 28, 1950; children: Peter F., William T., Jane C. Barber, Anne N. BS, Yale U., 1949. Exec. v.p. Pickands Mather, Cleve., 1950-70; exec. v.p., adminstr. Diamond Shamrock, Cleve., 1970-74; group v.p., capital goods Midland Ross, Cleve., 1974-78; chmn. bd. dirs., chief exec. officer Fairmount Minerals Ltd., Chardon, Ohio, 1978—; bd. dirs. First Union Real Estate, Cleve. Electric Illuminating, Huntington Nat. Bank, Cleve. Clinic. Trustee Univ. Sch., Pepper Pike, Ohio, 1975—. Office: Fairmount Minerals Ltd 11833 Ravenna Rd Chardon OH 44124

CONYERS, JOHN, JR., congressman; b. Detroit, May 16, 1929; s. John and Lucille (Simpson) C. B.A., Wayne State U., 1957, J.D., 1958; LL.D., Wilberforce U., 1969. Bar: Mich. 1959. Legis. asst. to Congressman John Dingell, 1959-61; sr. partner firm Conyers, Bell & Townsend, 1959-61; referee Mich. Workmen's Compensation Dept., 1961-64; mem. 89th-99th congresses from 1st Dist. Mich.; sr. mem. Judiciary Com., chmn. subcom. on criminal justice, mem. subcom. on civil and constl. rights; mem. Govt. Ops. Com., mem. subcom. on commerce, consumer and monetary affairs, mem. subcom. on intergovtl. relations; Past dir. edn. Local 900, U.A.W.; mem. adv. council Mich. Liberties Union; gen. counsel Detroit Trade Union Leadership Council; vice chmn. nat. bd. Ams. for Democratic Action; vice chmn. adv. council ACLU; an organizer Mems. Congress for Peace through Law; bd. dirs. numerous other orgns. including African-Am. Inst., Commn. Racial Justice, Detroit Inst. Arts, Nat. Alliance Against Racist and Polit. Repression, Nat. League Cities. Sponsor, contbg. author: Am. Militarism, 1970, War Crimes and the American Conscience, 1970, Anatomy of an Undeclared War, 1972; contbr. articles to profl. jours. Trustee Martin Luther King Jr. Center for Non-Violent Social Change. Served to 2d lt. AUS, 1950-54, Korea. Recipient Rosa Parks award SCLC. Mem. NAACP (exec. bd. Detroit), Kappa Alpha Psi. Democrat. Baptist. Office: 2313 Rayburn House Office Bldg Washington DC 20515

CONYNE, ROBERT KARLTON, psychologist, university administrator; b. Amsterdam, N.Y., May 21, 1944; s. Robert Karlton and Elizabeth Maida (Brownell) C.; m. Lynn Suzanne Rapin, July 26, 1980; children: Suzanne Lynn Conyne-Rapin, Zachary Robert Conyne-Rapin. AB, Syracuse U., 1966; MS, Purdue U., 1968, PhD, 1970. Lic. psychologist, Ohio, Ill. Psychologist, prof., counselor Ill. State U., Normal, 1971-79; assoc. vice provost, prof. counseling U. Cin., 1980-87, head dept. Sch. Psychology and Counseling, 1987—. Author: Environmental Assessment, 1981; editor: Jour. Specialists in Group Work, 1979-85, Group Workers Handbook, 1985; contbr. articles to profl. jours. Mem. Am. Psychol. Assn., Am. Assn. Counseling and Devel. Avocations: running, sailing. Home: 1134 Cryer Ave Cincinnati OH 45208 Office: U Cin Mail Loc 02 Cincinnati OH 45221

CONZELMAN, DOROTHY ROSTRON, pediatrician; b. Waukegan, Ill., Sept. 13, 1930; d. John Wilson and Dorothy Evelyn (Rostron) C.; m. Abdullah Walid Burhani, Dec. 26, 1958 (div. 1976); children: Mary Jamila, John Zeki Burhani. BA, Lake Forest Coll., 1952; MD, Med. Coll. Pa., 1956. Intern St. Luke's Hosp., Chgo., 1956-57, resident pediatrics, 1957-58; resident pediatrics Children's Meml. Hosp., Chgo., 1958-59, fellow pediatrics, 1959-60; sole practice pediatrics Kenosha, 1961—; active staff Kenosha Meml. Hosp., 1961—, St. Catherines Hosp., 1961—. Mem. AMA, Am. Women's Med. Assn., Women in Medicine Wis., Wis. Med. Soc., Kenosha County Med. Soc. Republican. Episcopalian. Avocation: organ playing. Home: 200 68th St Kenosha WI 53140 Office: 3618 8th Ave Kenosha WI 53140

COOK, ALEXANDER BURNS, educator, museum curator; b. Grand Rapids, Mich., Apr. 16, 1924; s. Gorell Alexander and Harriette Florence (Hinze) C.; B.A., Ohio Wesleyan U., 1949; M.S., Case Western Res. U., 1967. Editorial cartoonist, artist Cleve. Plain Dealer, 1949-55; account exec. Edward Howard & Co., Cleve., 1955-61; spl. art tchr. Cleve. Pub. Schs., 1964—; curator exhibits Gt. Lakes Mus., Vermilion, Ohio, 1970-78, curator, 1978—, chmn. mus. operating com., 1977—. Trustee, Berkshire Condominium Owners Assn., 1981-83, pres., 1982-83. Served with AUS, 1943-45. Recipient award of honor Ohio Wesleyan U., 1955; Distinguished Achievement award Gt. Lakes Hist. Soc., 1973; 1st pl. award for editorial cartoons Union Tchr. Press Assn., 1980, 81, 82. Mem. Gt. Lakes Hist. Soc. (exec. v.p. 1959-64, v.p. 1964—, trustee, mem. exec. com. 1959—), Ohioana Library Assn., Akron Art Mus., Cleve. Mus. Art, Am. Soc. Marine Artists, Delta Tau Delta, Pi Delta Epsilon, Pi Sigma Alpha. Republican. Episcopalian. Contbr. editorial cartoons to Reid Cartoon Collection, U. Kans. Jour. Hist. Center, The Critique, 1975—; editorial adviser, numerous articles to Inland Seas, 1957—, The Chadburn, 1976—; cover illustrations for Ohioana Quar., 1979—; book cover illustrations Dodd, Mead & Co., 1984. Paintings represented in pvt. collections, 1960—; executed mural depicting Gt. Lakes shipping Gt. Lakes Mus., 1969. Mem. The English Speaking Union. Home: 11820 Edgewater Dr Lakewood OH 44107

COOK, BEVERLY BLAIR, political science educator; b. Chgo., Dec. 10, 1926; d. Ross J. and Nita L. (Hanson) Ulman; m. Cornelius P. Cotter, July 31, 1966; children: C. Randall, Linda G., David S., Gary A., Cornelia Calvert, Lawrence P., Charles, Steven A. BA, Wellesley Coll., 1948; MA, U. Wis., Madison, 1949; PhD, Claremont Grad. Sch., 1962. Instr. Iowa State U., Ames, 1949-50; asst. prof. polit. sci. Calif. State U., Fullerton, 1962-66; assoc. prof. U. Wis., Milw., 1967-74, prof., 1974—; vis. prof. UCLA, 1984; bd. advisers NOW Legal Aid and Def. Fund Project on Jud. Edn. Bd. overseers NSF Supreme Ct. Project; bd. dirs. Bicentennial Constn. Project '87. Pendleton scholar, 1944-48, Wellesley scholar, 1948; Ford Found. fellow, 1960-62, 72-73; Fromkin grantee, 1973, Florence E. Eagleton grantee, 1976-77, grantee Am. Philos. Soc., 1967, 71, Social Sci. Research Council, 1969-70. Mem. Am. Polit. Sci. Assn., Internat. Polit. Sci. Assn. (v.p. 1986-87), Midwest Polit. Sci. Assn., Western Polit. Sci. Assn., Law and Soc. Assn., U.S. Supreme Ct. Hist. Soc., NOW, Am. Judicature Soc., Pi Sigma Alpha (bd. dirs.). Author: The Judicial Process in California, 1967; contbr. chpts., articles to profl. publs. Home: 3965 N Harcourt Pl Milwaukee WI 53211 Office: Dept Polit Sci U Wis Milwaukee WI 53201

COOK, CHRISTOPHER WYATT, computer education specialist, bilingual education consultant; b. Midland, Mich., Nov. 14, 1959; s. James Wyatt and Barbara Marie (Collier) C.; m. Mary Sharon Twohey. BS in Edn. with honors, U. Mich., 1982; MS in Edn., Nat. Coll. Edn., 1986. Cert. elem. tchr., Ill., bilingual tchr., Ill., Mex. Tchr. ESL Colegio Arjí, Villahermosa and Tabasco, Mex., 1980-81; tchr. bilingual edn., computer coordinator Waukegan (Ill.) Pub. Schs., 1982-85; cons. bilingual edn. Weidner Communications Corp., Northbrook, Ill., 1985—; specialist computer edn. PLATO/WICAT Systems Co., Downers Grove, Ill., 1986-87, WICAT Edn. Systems Co., Chgo., 1986—. Mem. Ill. Computing Educators. Avocations: music, guitar. Home: 2129 N Racine #2R Chicago IL 60614 Office: WICAT Edn Systems Co 4750 N Milwaukee St 7 Chicago IL 60630

COOK, DANIEL CURTIS, foundation administrator; b. Moorhead, Minn., May 26, 1960; s. Curtis Leroy and Dorothy June (Mulcahy) C.; m. Sheryce Lynn Gustafson, Mar. 10, 1984; 1 child, Spencer. BS in Acctg., Moorhead (Minn.) State U., 1982. Regional dir. Miss Teen of Am. Pageant, Mpls., 1981-85; salesman Computerland, Aberdeen, S.D., 1985; exec. dir. Brown County United Way, Aberdeen, 1985—. Trustee Zion Luth. Ch., Aberdeen, 1987—. Mem. Nat. Soc. Fundraising Execs., Aberdeen C. of C. (com. chmn. 1985-87), Aberdeen Jaycees. Republican. Avocations: volleyball, basketball, softball, singing, camping. Home: 725 NE 18th St Aberdeen SD 57401 Office: Brown County United Way 12 4th Ave SE Aberdeen SD 57402-1065

COOK, DAVID CHARLES, III, publisher and editor; b. Elgin, Ill., June 11, 1912; s. David Charles, Jr. and Frances Lois (Kerr) C.; m. Nancy L. Nagel, Nov. 11, 1983; children: Margaret Anne, Martha L., Bruce L., Gregory D., Rebecca; 1 stepson: Todd Erin Cahill. Student, Occidental Coll., 1930-32; Ph.B., U. Chgo., 1934; Lit.D., Judson Coll., 1965. Chmn. bd. David C. Cook Pub. Co. (founded by grandfather 1875), Elgin, Ill., 1934; editor-in-chief of its 35 curriculum publs. David C. Cook Pub. Co. (founded by grandfather 1875). Author: Walk the High Places, 1964, Invisible Halos, 1975. Dir. youth study tour Cultural Travel Found., 1955; v.p. Elgin Council Chs., 1954, pres., 1956-57; governing bd. Elgin Community Chest; pres. David C. Cook Found.; trustee Conf. Point Camp, Judson Coll., Elgin, Laubach Literacy, 1st Methodist Ch. Mem. Phi Kappa Psi. Office: David C Cook Pub Co 850 N Grove Ave Elgin IL 60120

COOK, DAVID MICHAEL, dentist; b. Evansville, Ind., Mar. 3, 1950; s. Melfred Leroy and Frances Jean (Leathers) C.; m. Diana May McFall, July 2, 1978; children: Melissa May, Philip Michael. DDS, U. Ill., Chgo., 1974, BS in Dentistry, 1983. Gen. practice dentistry Harrisburg, Ill., 1978—; allied health care staff Harrisburg Med. Ctr., 1979—. Active with choir First Bapt. Ch., Harrisburg, 1979—. Served to capt. USAF, 1974-77. Fellow Acad. Gen. Dentistry (fellowship 1982); mem. ADA, Ill. State Dental Soc., So. Ill. Dental Soc., Chgo. Dental Soc. (assoc.), Greater Harrisburg C. of C. Lodge: Kiwanis (bd. dirs. local chpt. 1983—, v.p. 1984-85, pres. 1986—). Avocations: arranging music, singing, bridge. Home: 102 Mohawk Dr Harrisburg IL 62946 Office: 410 W Poplar PO Box 188 Harrisburg IL 62946

COOK, GREGORY ALAN, dentist; b. Cleve., Mar. 6, 1947; s. Clyde Udall Cook and Thelma Aileen (DeGroodt) Keister; m. Marianne Ziska, June 14, 1969; children: Amy, Amanda. BA, Albion Coll., 1969; DDS, Case Western Res. U., 1979. City planning cons. Community Devel. Assn., Inc., Cin., 1969-72; planner, systems analyst City of Dayton, Ohio, 1972-75; city planner Northeastern Ohio Areawide Coordination Agy., Cleve., 1975-76; mem. med. staff Benjamin Rose Inst., Cleveland Heights, Ohio, 1979—; gen. practice dentistry Mayfield Heights, Ohio, 1980—. Inventor adult logic game. Vol. educator various city schs., 1976—. Mem. ADA, Ohio Dental Soc., Cleve. Dental Soc., Am. Assn. Clin. Hypnosis. Unitarian Universalist. Club: Heights Sailfish Swim (Cleveland Heights) (pres. 1985—). Avocations: running, swimming, guitar, piano, photography. Home: 3068 Euclid Heights Blvd Cleveland Heights OH 44118

COOK, HENRY FRANKLIN, communications executive; b. Terre Haute, Ind., Sept. 27, 1922; s. Harold Guy and Pansy Audrey (Estes) C. m. Nelle M. Bailey, Aug. 4, 1944; children: Candice Lynn, Cynthia Rae, Gregory Franklin. BS in Art Edn., Ind. State U., 1946. Tchr. art city schs. Terre Haute, 1946-47, Indpls., 1950-52; instr. art Ind. State U., Terre Haute, 1948; mgr. prodn. Spencer-Curtis Advt., Indpls., 1952-53; v.p. Pictorial Pubs., Indpls., 1953-71; chmn. bd. dirs. Four Winds Distbg., Inc., Indpls., 1964—; pres. Nat. Aero Service, 1948-52; v.p. Art Directors Ind., 1953-54; chmn. Pro-Net, Inc.; bd. dirs. United Mobile Power, Wash, Inc., Grand Rapids, Mich., 1987—; chmn. bd. dirs. Hoosier United Mobile Power Wash, Inc. Editor: Pilot's Cross Country Guide, 1948-52. V.p. Plainfield (Ind.) Sch. Bd., 1969-66. Served to 1st lt. USAAF, 1943-46, CBI. Decorated D.F.C., Air medal with two oak leaf clusters. Mem. Circle Systems Internat. (founding chmn. 1981-87), Direct Distbrs. Assn. (voting), Flying Tigers of the 14th Air Force Assn. (squadron officer). Republican. Methodist. Club: Columbia (Indpls.). Lodge: Elks. Avocations: flying, art, skiing, Indian relic collecting. Home: 5721 Lakeland Blvd Indianapolis IN 46234 Office: Four Winds Distbg 5721 Lakeland Blvd Indianapolis IN 46234

COOK, JOHN RONALD, consulting civil engineer; b. Evanston, Ill., Sept. 21, 1957; s. Ronald Edward and Shirley Ann (Pregl) C.; m. Linda Marie Olsiewicz, Oct. 11, 1981. B.S. in Civil Engring., U. Ill., 1980; M.B.A., Roosevelt U., 1984. Registered profl. engr., Ill., Calif. Civil engr., Doyen & Assocs., Inc., Chgo., 1980-81, project engr., 1981-83, sr. mgr. computer ops., 1982-83, project mgr., 1983-84; sr. mgmt. engr. Surety Support Services, Inc., Oak Brook, Ill., 1984—; pres. Diversified Mgmt. Cons., Naperville, 1979—. United Airlines scholar, 1975. Mem. U. Ill. Alumni Assn., Am. Concrete Inst., Ill. Soc. Profl. Engrs., Nat. Soc. Profl. Engrs., ASCE, Beta Gamma Sigma. Republican. Lutheran. Office: Surety Support Services Inc 1333 Butterfield Rd Suite 130 Downers Grove IL 60515

COOK, JULIAN ABELE, JR., federal judge; b. Washington, June 22, 1930; s. Julian Abele and Ruth Elizabeth (McNeill) C.; m. Carol Annette Dibble, Dec. 22, 1957; children: Julian Abele III, Peter Dibble, Susan Annette. B.A., Pa. State U., 1952; J.D., Georgetown U., 1957. Bar: Mich. 1957. Law clk. to judge Pontiac, Mich., 1957-58; sole practice Detroit, 1958-78; judge U.S. Dist. Ct. (ea. dist.) Mich., Detroit, 1978—; spl. asst. atty. gen. State of Mich., 1968-78; adj. prof. law U. Detroit Sch. Law, 1971-74; gen. counsel Sta. WTVS (Public TV), 1973-78; labor arbitrator Am. Arbitration Assn. and Mich. Employment Relations Commn., 1975-78; mem. Mich. State Bd. Ethics, 1977-78. Contbr. articles to legal jours. Mem. exec. bd. dirs., past pres. Child and Family Services Mich.; bd. dirs. Mich. Heart Assn., Brighton Health Services Corp., Brighton Hosp., Hutzel Hosp., Georgetown U. Law Ctr.; chmn. Mich. Civil Rights Commn., 1968-71; mem. adv. council Ashland Theol. Sem. Served with Signal Corps U.S. Army, 1952-54. Recipient merit citation Pontiac Area Urban League, 1971, Pathfinders award Oakland U., 1977, Service award Todd-Phillips Home, Inc., 1978, Disting. Alumnus award Pa. State U., 1985, Focus and Impact award Oakland U., 1985; resolution Mich. Ho. of Reps., 1971; named Boss of Yr. Oakland County Legal Secs. Assn., 1973-74. Fellow Am. Bar Found.; mem. NAACP (Disting. Citizen of Yr. 1970, mem. state constl. revision and legal redress com. 1963), Mich. Bar Assn. (chmn. constl. law com. 1969, vice-chmn. civil liberties com. 1970, co-chmn. profl. devel. task force 1984—), Oakland County Bar Assn. (chmn. continuing legal edn. com. 1968-69, jud. liaison Dist. Ct. com. 1977, continuing legal edn. com. 1977, unauthorized practice law com. 1977), ABA, Nat. Bar Assn., Fed. Bar Assn., Wolverine Bar Assn., Mich. Assn. Black Judges, Am. Inn of Ct. (pres., master of bench, chmn. 6th cir. com. on standard jury instructions), Georgetown U. Alumni Assn. (bd. dirs.), Pa. State. U. Alumni Assn. (bd. dirs.).

COOK, KENNETH JOHN, communications executive; b. Milw., Sept. 4, 1941; s. Kenneth Alfred and Ruth Louise (Tetzlaff) C.; m. Jean H. Evers, Apr. 10, 1982. BSEE, Purdue U., 1964; MBE, Claremont Grad. Sch., 1967. V.p. indsl. mktg. Ken Cook Co., Milw., 1967-71; v.p. U.S. ops. Planaprint Internat., Deerfield, Ill., 1971-74; exec. v.p. Ken Cook Co., Milw., 1975—. Tchr. Jr. Achievement Project Bus., Milw., 1985. Fellow Soc. Tech. Communication (Robert G. Frank award Chgo. Chpt. 1975, named Outstanding Communicator Wis. Chpt. 1983, pres. 1982-83); mem. Am. Soc. Tng. Devel. Avocations: music, golf, swimming, tennis, sailing, sports cars. Home: 2306 W Dickinson Ct Mequon WI 53092 Office: Ken Cook Co 9929 W Silver Spring Dr Milwaukee WI 53225

COOK, M(ORREECE) ELAINE, medical social worker; b. Owosso, Mich., June 17, 1946; d. Charles M. and Freda Belle Saunders. BA in Psychology, Mercy Coll., Detroit, 1971; MSW, Wayne State U., Detroit, 1972. Cert. social worker, Mich. Social worker Sinai Hosp., Detroit, 1972—. Mem. Nat. Hospice Orgn., Nat. Assn. Social Workers (sec. med. council 1979), Mich. Pub. Health Assn., Mich. Soc. Clin. Social Workers. Club: Social Worker's (Detroit) (v.p. 1979, pres. 1978). Avocations: music, art, travel.

COOK, NOEL ROBERT, manufacturing company executive; b. Houston, Mar. 19, 1937; s. Horace Berwick and Leda Estelle (Houghton) C.; student Iowa State U., 1955-57; B.S. in Indsl. Engring., U. Mich., 1960; children—Laurel Jane, David Robert. Engr. in tng. Eaton Mfg., Saginaw, Mich., 1960-61; mgr. mfg. and contracting J. N. Fauver Co., Madison Heights, Mich., 1961-65; pres. Newton Mfg., Royal Oak, Mich., 1965—; soc. Indsl. Piping Contractors, Birmingham, Mich., 1969-75; pres. RNR Metal Fabricators, Inc., Royal Oak, Mich., 1974-78; chmn. bd. Kim Internat. Sales Co., 1978—; pres. Newton Sales Co., Royal Oak, 1978—, Power Package Windsor Ltd., Windsor, Ont., Can., 1981—. Served with U.S. Army, 1960-61. Registered profl. engr., Mich. Mem. Fluid Power Soc., Nat. Fluid Power Assn., Birmingham Jr. C. of C. (past bd. dirs.). Patentee in field. Home: 4481 W Cherry Hill Dr Orchard Lake MI 48033 Office: 4249 Delemere Blvd Royal Oak MI 48073

COOK, PAUL M., chemical manufacturing company executive; b. Ridgewood, N.J.. B.S. in Chem. Engring, M.I.T., 1947. With Stanford Research Inst., Palo Alto, Calif., 1949-53, Sequoia Process Corp., 1953-56; with Raychem Corp., Menlo Park, Calif., 1957—, former pres., now chmn., chief exec. officer, bd. dirs. Office: Raychem Corp 300 Constitution Dr Menlo Park CA 94025 *

COOK, ROBERT E., diversified manufacturing executive. Pres., chief exec. officer, chief. operating officer, dir. Roper Corp., Kankakee, Ill. Office: Roper Corp 1905 W Court St Kankakee IL 60901 *

COOK, THOMAS J., computer specialist; b. Shelbyville, Ky., Nov. 9, 1944; s. Charles G. and Martha M. (Martin) C.; m. Sydney J. Bruce, Aug. 15, 1966. BA, Vanderbilt U., 1966; PhD in Phys. Chemistry, U. Chgo., 1972. Postdoctoral researcher AT&T Bell Labs., Murray Hill, N.J., 1972-74; software devel. mgr. AT&T Bell Labs., Columbus, Ohio, 1974—. Contbr. articles to profl. jours. Dir. Bible teaching Metro Columbus Bapt. Assn., 1984-87; commr. City of Gahanna, Ohio, 1986. Fellow Woodrow Wilson Found., 1966-67, NSF, 1966-72. Mem. IEEE, Sigma Xi, Phi Beta Kappa. Home: 477 Uxbridge Ave Gahanna OH 43230 Office: AT&T Bell Labs 6200 E Broad St Columbus OH 43213

COOKE, DAVID WILLIAM, medical group practice consultant b. Detroit, May 31, 1935; s. Edward Goddard and Helen (Vredeveld) C.; m. Mary Kathryn Cooke; children—David W., Judith A., Thomas J. B.S., Franklin U., 1974; M.B.A., U. Dayton, 1975. With sales mgmt. dept. Ciba Pharm. Co., Pitts., Detroit and Columbus, Ohio, 1961-68; adj. prof. Franklin U., 1976—; pres. University Med. Mgmt., Inc., Columbus, Ohio, 1981-85 ; exec. dir. Dept. Medicine Found. Inc., Ohio State U., Columbus, 1981-86; pres. David W. Cooke Assocs., 1986— ; dir. Alternative Health Care Systems, Inc., Columbus, 1986—. Mem. Med. Group Mgmt. Assn., Ohio Med. Group Mgmt. Assn., Central Ohio Med. Group Mgmt. Assn., Am. Mgmt. Assn. Mem. Reformed Ch. Home: 158 Corbin's Mill Dr Dublin OH 43017 Office: 1631 Northwest Profl Plaza Columbus OH 43220

COOKE, EVELYN KATHLEEN CHATMAN, educator; b. Jackson, Tenn.; d. Charles Elijah and Josie (Bond) Chatman; B.A. cum laude, Lane Coll., 1955; M.Ed., Xavier U.; m. James T. Cooke, Apr. 21, 1954 (div. Aug. 1970); 1 dau., Madelyn LaRene. Tchr. public schs., Chattanooga, 1957-67, Cin., 1967—; cons. career edn. Public Schs., Cin. Pres., Harriet Tubman's Black Women's Democratic Club; mem. upper grade sch study council. Recipient Spirit of Detroit award, 1981, Outstanding Educator award Phi Delta Kappa. Mem. Fellowship United Meth. Musicians, NAACP, Council for Co-op Action, Am., Ohio Fedn. Tchrs. Cin. Fedn. Tchrs., Cin. Council Educators, Nat. Council Negro Women, Top Ladies of Distinction (outstanding service award 1981, nat. 2d v.p. chmn. info. com., pres. Cin. chpt.), Sigma Gamma Rho (nat. constn. and by-laws com., anti-basileus Epsilon Lambda Sigma chpt.), Gamma Theta, Sigma Rho Sigma. Methodist (dir. music ch.). Home: 6748 Elwynne Dr Cincinnati OH 45236

COOLIDGE, JOSEPH LEXINGTON, mathematics educator; b. Cleve., May 24, 1932; s. Joseph Lexington and Elizabeth (Hoffman) C.; m. Virginia Bartou Low, Sept. 2, 1961; children: Elizabeth, Amy. AB, Williams Coll., Williamstown, Mass., 1954; MA, La. State U., 1965. Math. tchr. and coach Gov. Dummer Acad., Byfield, Mass., 1954-66, Maumee Valley Country Day Sch., Toledo, 1966-73, Cin. Country Day Sch., 1973—. Mem. Nat. Council Tchrs. Math., Math. Assn. Am., Nat. Soccer Coaches Assn., Southwestern Ohio Soccer Coaches Assn. (treas. 1973—). Democrat. Episcopalian. Avocations: hiking, camping, fly fishing. Home: 6255 Orchard Ln Cincinnati OH 45213 Office: Cin Country Day Sch 6905 Given Rd Cincinnati OH 45243

COONEY, GEORGE AUGUSTIN, lawyer; b. Detroit, July 12, 1909; s. Augustin W. and Mary (McBride) C.; m. Julia Grace Starrs, Oct. 26, 1940; children: George Augustin Jr., Michael Edward, Timothy John. A.B., U. Detroit, 1932, J.D., 1935. Bar: Mich. 1935, Fed. 1935. Practice Detroit, 1935—; mem. firm Cooney & Cooney (P.C.), Detroit, 1969—; lectr. in field. Former editor news and comment sect.: Probate and Trust Law Jour. Served with USAAF, World War II. Recipient Tower award U. Detroit, 1973. Fellow Am. Coll. Probate Counsel; mem. Am., Detroit, Fed. bar assns., State Bar Mich., Cath. Lawyers Soc. Detroit, Soc. Irish-Am. Lawyers, Am. Judicature Soc., Selden Soc., Mich. Assn. Professions, Am. Philatelic Soc., Royal Can. Philatelic Soc., Detroit Zool. Soc. Clubs: K.C. (4 deg.), Stoney Point (Ont.) Sportsmans, Detroit Golf; Nat. Lawyers (Washington). Home: 8832 St Clair Rd, Stoney Point, ON Canada N0R 1N0 Office: 2329 One Kennedy Sq Detroit MI 48226

COONEY, THOMAS MICHAEL, greeting card company executive; b. N.Y.C., Feb. 7, 1926; s. Michael Joseph and Ellen Florence (McIntyre) C.; m. Mary Lynn Sullivan, Dec. 26, 1953; children—Michael, Thomas, William, John. B.S., U. Va., 1945; LL.B., Columbia U., 1949; M.B.A., NYU, 1959. Group v.p. Pfizer, Inc., N.Y.C., 1955-71; group v.p. Am. Home Products, N.Y.C., 1971-74; exec. v.p., chief exec. officer Fairmont Foods Co., Des Plaines, Ill., 1974-78; pres., chief exec. officer Gibson Greeting Cards, Inc., Cin., 1978-86, chmn., chief exec. officer, 1986—, chmn. bd., 1987—; dir. Harris Pub., N.Y.C., Aircap Industries, Inc. Office: Gibson Greeting Cards Inc 2100 Section Rd Cincinnati OH 45237

COONS, ELDO JESS, JR., recreational vehicle manufacturing company executive; b. Corsicana, Tex., July 5, 1924; s. Eldo Jess and Ruby (Allison) C.; student engring. U. Calif., 1949-50; m. Beverly K. Robbins, Feb. 6, 1985; children by previous marriage—Roberta Ann, Valerie, Cheryl. Owner C & C Constrn. Co., Pomona, Calif., 1946-48; sgt. traffic div. Pomona Police Dept., 1948-54; nat. field dir. Nat. Hot Rod Assn., Los Angeles, 1954-57; pres. Coons Custom Mfg., Inc., Oswego, Kans., 1957-68; chmn. bd. Borg-Warner Corp., 1968-71; pres. Coons Mfg., Inc., Oswego, 1971-84; pres. E.B.C Mgmt. Cons., Grove, Okla., 1984—. Mem. Kans. Gov.'s Adv. Com. for State Architects Assn. Served with C.E., AUS, 1943-46. Named to Exec. and Profl. Hall Fame, Recreational Vehicle/Mobile Homes Hall of Fame; recipient Paul Abel award Recreation Vehicle Industry Assn., 1978, 1st Ann. New Product award Kans. Gov.'s Office and Kans. Engring. Soc. 1982-83. Mem. Oswego C. of C. (dir.), Nat. Juvenile Officers Assn., Municipal Motor Officers Assn., Am. Legion, AIM (fellow pres.'s council), Young Pres.'s Orgn. Mason (K.T., Shriner), Rotarian (pres. Oswego 1962-63). Originator 1st city sponsored police supervised dragstrip. Home: Rt 4 Box 246 Grove OK 74344 Office: 2300 W 4th St Oswego KS 67356

COONTZ, ERIC JOHN, periodontist; b. Worcester, Mass., Mar. 22, 1949; s. Gustaf and Clare Elliot (McSheehy) C.. BA in Biology cum laude, Assumption Coll., Worcester, 1971; DDS, Loyola U., Maywood, Ill., 1976, MS in Oral Biology, 1981, Cert. in Periodontics, 1981. Practice dentistry specializing in periodontics Bourbonnais, Ill., 1982—; mem. staff Foster G. McGaw Hosp., Maywood, Riverside Med. Ctr., Kankakee, Ill., St. Mary's Hosp., Kankakee; from asst. prof. periodontics to clin. assoc. prof. periodontics Loyola U. Med. Ctr., Maywood, 1981—. Served to capt. U.S. Army, 1976-79. St. Louis U. anatomy fellow, 1971. Mem. ADA, Chgo. Dental Soc., Kankakee Dist. Dental Soc., Acad. Gen. Dentistry, Am. Acad. Periodontology, Midwest Soc. Periodontists, Ill. Soc. Periodontology, Am. Acad. Implant Dentistry, Delta Sigma Delta (Chgo. grad. chpt. officer). Republican. Roman Catholic. Avocations: travel, photography, golf. Home: 375 Yale Ct Bourbonnais IL 60914 Office: 555 W Court St Kankakee IL 60901

COOPER, CLARINDA RYNN, retail company executive; b. Bloomington, Ind., Mar. 6, 1955; d. Dale Dallas and Catherine (Starbuck) C. B.A., Ind. U., 1978. Sales rep. Sears Roebuck & Co., Bloomington, Ind., 1974-80; asst. mgr. K-Mart, Speedway, Ind., 1980-81; salesperson FAS Auto Works, Bloomington, 1982; retail mgr. Deb Shops, Inc., Bloomington, 1982-86, dist. mgr., 1986—; cons. Ind. U. Sch. Arts and Scis., Bloomington, 1985—. Mem. Nat. Assn. Female Execs., Career Track. Republican. Mem. Ch. of Christ. Avocations: music; reading; calligraphy; photography; fashion. Home: 904 Arcadia Dr #2 Bloomington IL 61701

COOPER, DAVID BOOTH, newspaper editor; b. N.Y.C., May 15, 1933; s. Charles Gray and Dorothy (Booth) C.; m. Frances Whinery, June 15, 1954; children: David B. Jr., Charles G. III. BA, U. N.C., 1954. Reporter The Raleigh (N.C.) News & Observer, 1955-56, 59-64; capital correspondent Winston-Salem Jour. & Sentinel, Raleigh, 1964-68; city hall bur. chief The Detroit Free Press, 1968-70, asst. city editor, 1970-71; state capital bur. chief The Detroit Free Press, Lansing, Mich., 1971-73; assoc. editor The Detroit Free Press, 1973-77; assoc. editor, edit. page editor Akron (Ohio) Beacon Jour., 1977—; dep. conv. mgr. Knight-Ridder Newspapers, 1976, 80, 84. Author (mus. catalog) Robert Frank and Am. Politics, 1985 (1st place Ohio Mus. Catalogs). Trustee The Akron Roundtable, 1977—; treas., trustee John S. Knight Meml. Jour. Fund, Akron, 1981—. Served to 1st lt., USAF, 1956-58. Recipient 1st Place Edit. Writing award Cleve. Press Club-SDX, 1980, Akron Press Club, 1981, Ohio AP, 1982. Mem. Am. Soc. Newspaper Editors, Nat. Conf. Edit. Writers. Episcopalian. Clubs: Cascade (Akron); Deep Springs Trout (Chardon, Ohio). Avocations: fishing, music, art, reading, sailing. Home: 2942 Silver Lake Blvd Cuyahoga Falls OH 44224 Office: Akron Beacon Journal 44 E Exchange Akron OH 44328

COOPER, ELAINE JANICE, physical therapist; b. Detroit, Apr. 26, 1937; s. Morris and Sally (Mack) Braverman; m. Morley Allen Cooper, Sept. 5, 1959; children: Jeffrey, Michael, Jonathan. BS, U. Mich., 1959. Supr. Rehab. Inst., Detroit, 1959-61; cons. Redford (Mich.) Community Hosp., 1963-73; cons. in field Detroit, 1970-78; asst. dir. William Beaumont Hosp., Royal Oak, Mich., 1979-81; pres., cons. Cooper & Assoc. Physical Therapy

P.C., Farmington Hills, Mich., 1981—; cons. Drs. Sobel & Castle, Detroit, 1965-66. Mem. Am. Physical Therapy Assn. (edn. com. 1969), Mich. Physical Therapy Assn., Biofeedback Soc. Mich., Mich. Dance Assn. Club: Brookfield Highlands (chmn. land devel., restrictions coms. 1979-85). Avocations: dance, running, aerobics, skiing, golf. Office: Cooper & Assocs Physical Therapy PC 31800 Northwestern Hwy Suite 110 Farmington Hills MI 48018

COOPER, GARRETT WAYNE, real estate executive; b. Yuma, Ariz., Nov. 27, 1952; s. Charles Edwin and Martha Lou (Smith) C.; m. Jennifer Ann Johnson, June 26, 1976; children: Michelle Marie, Benjamin Garrett. BS, Rose Hulman Inst. Tech., Terre Haute, 1975; MBA, Ariz. State U., 1980. Cert. fin. planner. Tchr. bus. math. Ariz. State U., 1978-80; asst. prof. maths. and computer sci. Ind. Inst. Tech., Ft. Wayne, 1980-81; v.p. property mgmt. Sturges, Griffin, Trent & Co., Inc., Ft. Wayne, 1981-83, v.p. ops. comml. indsl. real estate, 1983-86, mgr. mortgage loan portfolio, 1986—. Lay pastor First Missionary Ch., Ft. Wayne, 1985—; chmn. Christian Businessmen's Com., Ft. Wayne, 1986. Mem. Inst. Real Esate Mgmt., Bd. Realtors, Tau Beta Pi. Office: Mut Security Life Ins Co 3000 Coliseum Blvd E Fort Wayne IN 46808

COOPER, GEORGE KILE, educator; b. Bushnell, Ill., Apr. 5, 1920; s. George Kile and Lula Belle (Robinson) C.; m. June Anna Cardell, June 12, 1948; children: Kyle, Ernest, Ruth Anne, William, Jeanne, Andrew. BEd, Western Ill. State U., 1942; MBA, Ind. U., 1951; PhD, U. Mich., 1962. Cert. secondary sch. tchr., Ill. Bus. tchr. Reynolds (Ill.) Community High Sch., 1946-47; student teaching coordinator Western Mich. U., Kalamazoo, 1948-55, head bus. edn. dept., 1955-62; head bus. edn. and adminstrv. office mgmt. dept. Eastern Ill. U., Charleston, 1962-73, prof. bus. edn. and adminstrv. office mgmt., 1962-82, prof. emeritus, 1982—; vis. research and devel. specialist Ctr. for Vocat. and Tech. Edn., Ohio State U., Columbus, 1973-74. Treas. Wesley United Meth. Ch., Charleston, 1983—. Served with AUS, 1942-46. Mem. Ill. Bus. Edn. Assn. (pres. 1971-72, disting. service award 1975), Ill. Vocat. Assn. (treas. 1965-69), Ill. State U. Annuitants Assn. (pres.-elect 1986—), Eastern Ill. U. Annuitants Assn. (pres. 1984-86), Pi Omega Pi (nat. pres. 1966-68), Delta Pi Epsilon (pres. Kappa chpt. 1960-61), Phi Delta Kappa (pres. EIU chpt. 1980-81, alt. del. 1986). Home: 708 Taft Ave Charleston IL 61920

COOPER, IVAN LEVESON, publisher, retired architect; b. Stoke-on-Trent, Staffordshire, Eng., July 25, 1925; s. John and Annie Eliza (Walker) C.; m. Peggy Reneta Murray Hinett, July 25, 1949; children: Susan Louise, Ella Rosamund, Margaret Olivia. Student, Christ Ch., Oxford, Eng., 1943, Liverpool U., Eng., 1947-52. Registered architect, N.J., Pa. Architect Keele (Eng.) U., 1962-67; sr. assoc. Kramer, Hirsch & Carchidi, AIA, Trenton, N.J., 1967-76; prin. Ivan L. Cooper, AIA, Morrisville, Pa., 1976-86; pres., chief exec. officer PC Research Services, Traverse City, Mich., 1986—; mem. archtl. adv. commn. Mercer County Coll., Trenton, 1973-86. Served as navigator RAF, 1944-47. Mem. Ch. of England.

COOPER, JAMES DAVID, accountant; b. Hastings, Nebr., Jan. 20, 1948; s. Clarence V. and Lola L. (Louis) C.; m. Kathleen L. Sparks, July 31, 1970; children: Justin, Brock. BBA, Wichita (Kans.) State U., 1970. CPA, Kans. Staff acct. Kirkpatrick, Sprecker & Co., Wichita, 1970-76, ptnr., 1977—. Adv. bd. Wichita Children's Home, 1986-87. Mem. Am. Inst. CPA's, Nat. Assn. Accts., Kans. Soc. CPA's (pres. Wichita chpt. 1980-81). Republican. Club: Air Capital Cosmopolitan Internat. Wichita (pres. 1985-86).

COOPER, JOE L., paper products company executive; b. 1934. BS, Tex. A&M U., 1956. With Mobil Oil Corp., N.Y.C., 1956-79; v.p. U.S. Supply and Transp. Corp., 1979-83; with Container Corp. Am., 1983—, pres., chief exec. officer, 1985—, bd. dirs. Office: Container Corp of America One 1st National Plaza Chicago IL 60603 *

COOPER, JOHN GARY, television director; b. Cin., Oct. 16, 1948; s. John G. and Blanche C. (Combs) C.; m. Patricia Lynn Weddle, Apr. 7, 1972; children: Audrey K., Kathryn M., Ashley L. BA, U. Colo., 1979. Dir. Wright State U., Dayton, Ohio, 1971-72, Sta. WLWD-TV, Dayton, 1973-75, Sta. KOA-TV, Denver, 1976-80, Sta. WXYZ-TV, Detroit, 1980—. Bd. dirs. Franklin Community Assn., Franklin Village, Mich., 1986. Recipient Emmy for Outstanding Late News, Nat. Assn. TV Arts and Scis., 1983, 85. Mem. Dirs. Guild Am. (chmn. and steward Detroit 1983—, bd. dirs. and coordinating com. Detroit 1984—), Am. Film Inst. Avocations: film, theater, books, travel, photography. Home: 32500 Haverford Dr Franklin Village MI 48025 Office: WXYZ-TV 20777 W 10 Mile Rd Southfield MI 48237

COOPER, JOHN IRELAND, pharmaceutical company executive; b. Pikeville, Ky., Oct. 30, 1955; s. John Allan and Frances Lyvonne (Elkins) C.; m. Cathy Jean Hammon, Apr. 18, 1981; children: Joshua Ireland, Joseph Richard, Nicholas Mitchell. BS in Chem. Engring., U. Ky., 1979; MBA, Ind. U., 1983; diploma energy mgmt., Va. Polytechnic Inst., 1984. Project engr. Miles Labs., Elkhart, Ind., 1979-82, sr. environ./energy engr., 1982-83, mgr. wastewater treatment plant, 1983-84, mgr. corp. energy, 1984-85, mgr. utility ops., 1985—. Contbr. articles to profl. jours. Chmn. Elkhart Energy Conservation Commn., 1985. Mem. Am. Inst. Chem. Engrs., Assn. Energy Engrs., Internat. Assn. Energy Economists, Ind. Indsl. Energy Consumers (past vice chmn., chmn., founder 1983—). Avocation: basketball. Home: 15 St Joseph Manor Elkhart IN 46516 Office: Miles Labs Inc 1127 Myrtle St Bldg 120 Elkhart IN 46515

COOPER, JOHN SENTER, JR., insurance company executive; b. Detroit, Sept. 20, 1940; s. John S. and Susan W. (White) C.; m. Gail K. Landis, May 3, 1950; children: Christine, Gage, Bradley. BSBA, Cen. Mich. U., 1962. CPCU. Underwriter Fremont (Mich.) Mut. Ins. Co., 1963-78, v.p., 1978-81, pres., 1981—, also bd. dirs.; bd. dirs. Old Kent Bank of Fremont, Lincoln Mut. Casualty Co., Troy, Mich. Bd. dirs. Newaygo County Assn. Retarded Citizens, Fremont, 1985, Newaygo County Community Services; mem. adv. com. Ferris State Coll., Big Rapids, Mich., 1983. Served to lt. Mich. N.G., 1962-68. Mem. Soc. CPCU, West Mich. Chpt. CPCU, Fremont Jaycees (senator 1980). Lodge: Rotary (bd. dirs. 1982-85). Avocation: hunting. Home: 2221 S Warner Fremont MI 49412 Office: Fremont Mut Ins Co 933 E Main St Fremont MI 49412

COOPER, KENNETH CARLTON, training consultant; b. St. Louis, May 2, 1948; s. George Carlton and Mary Frances (Kavanaugh) C.; B.S., U. Mo. Columbia, 1970, M.S. in Indsl. Engring., 1971; Ph.D. in Adminstrn. and Mgmt., Columbia Pacific U., 1985; m. Susan Ann Bujnak, Sept. 6, 1969; children—Jeffrey Carlton, Daniel Stephen, Mara Elizabeth. Mktg. rep. IBM, St. Louis, 1971-76; account exec. Downtowner Newspaper, St. Louis, 1976; pres. Ken Cooper Communications, Chesterfield, Mo., 1976—; adj. faculty St. Louis U., 1972-73, Columbia Coll., 1976-79, Webster Coll., 1977-79; speaker in field. Roy P. Hart Scholar-Athlete grantee, 1970-71; registered profl. engr., Mo.; cert. adminstrv. mgr.; cert. speaking profl. Mem. ASTD, Nat. Writers Club, Nat. Speakers Assn., Mensa. Republican. Methodist. Author: Nonverbal Communication For Business Success, 1979, Spanish edit., 1982; (with Lance Humble) The World's Greatest Blackjack Book, 1980; Body Business, 1981; Kroppsspråket, 1981; Always Bear Left, 1982; Stop It Now, 1985. Home: 16408 Brandsford Point Chesterfield MO 63017

COOPER, PERL RICHARD, psychiatric social worker; b. St. Louis, Jan. 25, 1933; s. Leroy Elijah and Corinne (Morris) C.; m. Juanita Billingsley, Jan. 6, 1958 (div. Apr. 1978); m. Geraldine Jackson, Nov. 4, 1979; 1 child, Vanessa Annette Jackson. BA in Social Welfare, Calif. State U., Los Angeles, 1981; MSW, Washington U., St. Louis, 1983. Psychiat. social worker VA Med. Ctr., St. Louis, 1982; med. social worker St. Louis State Hosp., St. Louis, 1983; social service worker Mo. div. Family Services, St. Louis, 1984; asst. employee cons. PRC Employee Assistance Cons., St. Louis, 1984—. Served with USN, 1950-53, USAF, 1954-60. Grantee Nat. Inst. Alcohol Abuse and Alcoholism. Mem. Nat. Assn. Social Workers. Baptist. Avocations: reading, attending profl. conventions, symphony concerts. Home and Office: PO Box 8171 Saint Louis MO 63156

COOPER, RALPH DAYTON, osteopathic surgeon; b. Haigler, Nebr., July 18, 1927; s. Charles Wilbur and Etta Mae (Sampson) C.; m. Anna R. Weber, June 26, 1953 (div. Apr. 1972); children: Wesley Harold, Annette Marie. BS, N.E. Mo. State U., 1952; DO, Kirksville Coll. Osteo. Medicine, 1953. Diplomate Am. Bd. Osteo. Surgery. Mem. surg. staff Mineral Area Osteo. Hosp., Farmington, Mo., 1960-64, Eastmoreland Gen. Hosp., Portland, Oreg., 1964-69; mem. staff Oak Hill Osteo. Hosp., Joplin, Mo., 1969—. Fellow Am. Coll. Osteo. Surgeons; mem. Am. Osteo. Assn., Mo. Assn. Osteo. Physicians. Republican. Lodge: Elks. Office: 118B Frisco Bldg Joplin MO 64801

COOPER, RICHARD ALAN, lawyer; b. Hattisburg, Miss., July 19, 1953; s. H. Douglas and Elaine (Reece) C.; m. Margaret Jeanne Luth, May 9, 1981. B.A., B.S., U. Ark.-Little Rock, 1976; J.D., Washington U., St. Louis, 1979. Bar: Mo. 1979, Ill. 1980, U.S. Dist. Ct. (ea. dist.) Mo. 1980. Law clk. U.S. Dist. Ct., St. Louis, 1979-80; assoc. William R. Gartenberg, St. Louis, 1980-81, Danis, Reid, Murphy, Tobben, Schreiber, Mohan & Cooper, St. Louis, 1983-87, ptnr. 1987—; liaison to Washington U. Sch. Law, Mo. Assn. Trial Attys., St. Louis, 1983-85 . Bus. mgr. Urban Law Jour., 1978-79; editor Bankruptcy Law Reporter, 1983—, co-mgr., editor, 1984—. Recipient Milton F. Napier trial award Lawyers Assn. of St. Louis, 1979. Mem. ABA, Mo. Bar Assn., Am. Assn. Trial Attys., Nat. Orgn. Social Security Claimants Reps., Ill. State Bar Assn. Clubs: Clayton, Media (St. Louis). Avocation: basketball. Home: 330 Stark Ct Webster Groves MO 63119 Office: Danis Reid Murphy et al 8850 Ladue Rd Ladue MO 63124

COOPER, RICHARD WAYNE, SR., utility executive; b. Hammond, Ind., Feb. 19, 1940; s. Harry E. and Myrtle Irene (Stiles) C.; m. Ema Sue Bradley, June 28, 1958; children: Richard W. Jr., Sheryl Ann, Virginia Anne, Gregory Lee, Sara Christine. Profl. foremanship cert., Purdue U., 1975, A in Applied Sci., 1977, A in Applied Sci. Indsl. Engring., 1978, BS in Supervision, 1978. Mechanic, groundman, groundman operator No. Ind. Pub. Service Co., Hammond, 1958-62; asst. instr. tng. and utilization No. Ind. Pub. Service Co., LaPorte, Ind., 1969-73, instr. then tng. supr., 1973-81; mgr. mgmt. system control No. Ind. Pub. Service Co., Hammond, 1981-82, dir. mgmt. system control, 1982—. Chmn. steering com. Heritage Christian Acad., New Buffalo, Mich., 1978-80; Sun. sch. supr. Bible Bapt. Ch., New Buffalo, 1978-80, choir dir., 1980-83; choir dir. Lake Hills Bapt. Ch., Schererville, Ind., 1986—. Mem. IEEE, Am. Inst. Indsl. Engrs., Am. Productivity Mgmt. Assn., Soc. Am. Value Engrs. Home: 2615 Roma Ct Schererville IN 46375 Office: No Ind Pub Service Co 5265 Hohman Ave Hammond IN 46320

COOPER, ROBERT DEAN, architect; b. Riverside, N.J., July 25, 1944; s. William Jr. and Kathryn Bertha (Broderson) C.; m. Roberta Ann Roeske, Nov. 9, 1974; children: Peter William, Jennifer Ann. BArch, Carnegie-Mellon U., 1967; MArch, U. Pa., 1968. Registered architect, Wis., Fla. Draftsman Vincent G. Kling & Assocs., Phila., 1969; designer Miller Waltz Diedrich, Architects, Milw., 1972-77, architect, 1977-80; exec. v.p. Miller Meier & Assocs., Milw., 1980-85, Miller Meier Kenyon Cooper Architects & Engrs., Milw., 1985—. Prin. works include Broward County Main Library (Wis. Soc. Architects honor award 1985, ALA award 1987), archtl. addition Manpower Hdqrs. (Wis. Soc. Architects merit award 1973), Mitchell Field Airport (Wis. Soc. Architects 1986). Mem. Milw. bldg. code com., 1976; pres. bd. Greenfield (Wis.) Pub. Library, 1985, 86. Served to lt. USN, 1969-72, Vietnam. Mem. Wis. Soc. Architects (pres. elect 1986, chpt. pres. 1983), Sigma Alpha Epsilon. Home: 3666 S 56 St Greenfield WI 53220 Office: 756 N Milwaukee St Milwaukee WI 53202

COOPER, TERRY DALE, food products executive; b. Kankakee, Ill., Oct. 18, 1955; s. Chester D. and Alice M. (Holtgreve) C.; m. Kimberly A. Koester, June 10, 1978; children: Jeffrey, Christopher. BBA magna cum laude, U. Mo., St. Louis, 1978. CPA, Mo. Mem. audit staff Peat, Marwick, Mitchell & Co., St. Louis, 1978-82; dir. auditing Wetterau Inc., St. Louis, 1982-84; v.p. fin. Hazelwood div. Wetterau Inc., St. Louis, 1984-87; v.p. Higdon Gocery Co. subs. Wetterau, Inc., 1987—. Fellow mem. Mo. Soc. CPA's; mem. Am. Inst. CPA's, Nat. Assn. Accts. Home: 1432 Westbrooke Terr Dr Manchester MO 63021 Office: Hazelwood div Wetterau Inc 7100 Hazelwood Ave Hazelwood MO 63042

COOPERRIDER, TOM SMITH, botanist; b. Newark, Ohio, Apr. 15, 1927; s. Oscar Harold and Ruth Evelyn (Smith) C.; m. Miwako Kunimura, June 13, 1953; children: Julie Ann, John Andrew. B.A., Denison U., 1950; M.S., U. Iowa, 1955, Ph.D. (NSF fellow), 1958. Instr. biol. scis. Kent State U., Ohio, 1958-61; asst. prof. Kent State U., 1961-65, asso. prof., 1965-69, prof., 1969—, dir. exptl. programs, 1972-73, curator herbarium, 1968—; dir. Bot. Gardens and Arboretum, 1972—; mem. editorial bd. Univ. Press, 1976-79; on leave as asst. prof. dept. botany U. Hawaii, 1962-63; NSF researcher Mountain Lake Biol. Sta., U. Va., summer 1958; faculty mem. Iowa Lakeside Lab., U. Iowa, summer 1965; cons. endangered and threatened species U.S. Fish and Wildlife Service, Dept. Interior, 1976—; cons. Davey Tree Expert Co., 1979-85, Ohio Natural Areas Council, 1983. Author: Ferns and Other Pteridophytes of Iowa, 1959, Vascular Plants of Clinton, Jackson and Jones Counties, Iowa, 1962; editor: Endangered and Threatened Plants of Ohio, 1983. Active YMCA-YWCA Students in Govt., Washington, 1950, personnel placement U.S. Census Bur., Washington, 1950-51; Quaker Internat. Vol., Fed. Republic Germany, 1951; YMCA-YWCA Students in Govt., Washington, summer 1950; personnel placement U.S. Census Bur., Washington, 1950-51, Am. Friends Service Com., Germany, summer, 1951. Served with U.S. Army, 1945-46. NSF predoctoral fellow, 1957-58; NSF research grantee, 1965-72. Fellow AAAS, Ohio Acad. Scis. (v.p. 1967), Explorers Club; mem. Am. Soc. Plant Taxonomists, Internat. Assn. Plant Taxonomists, Bot. Soc. Am., Nature Conservancy, Wilderness Soc., Blue Key, Sigma Xi. Home: 548 Bowman Dr Kent OH 44240

COOPERSMITH, BERNARD IRA, gynecologist/obstetrician; b. Chgo., Oct. 19, 1914; s. Morris and Anna (Shulder) C.; m. Beatrice Klass, May 26, 1940; children: Carol, Cathie. BS cum laude, U. Ill., 1936, MD cum laude, 1938. Diplomate Am. Bd. Ob-Gyn. Intern Michael Reese Hosp., Chgo., 1938-39, resident in ob-gyn, 1939-42; practice medicine specializing in ob-gyn Chgo., 1942—; mem. staff Prentice Women's Hosp. of Northwestern Meml. Hosp., Michael Reese Hosp., Mt. Sinai Hosp., Chgo. Maternity Ctr.; asst. prof. ob-gyn Northwestern U. Med. Sch., Chgo., 1948—. Contbr. articles to profl jours. Pres. Barren Found. Chgo., 1971-73. Fellow ACS; mem. AMA, Ill. Med. Soc., Chgo. Med. Soc., Chgo. Gynecol. Soc., Cen. Assn. Ob-Gyn, Am. Coll. Ob-Gyn, Alpha Omega Alpha. Jewish. Clubs: Bryn Mawr Country, Carleton. Home: 1110 N Lake Shore Dr Chicago IL 60611 Office: 333 E Superior St Suite 444 Chicago IL 60611

COOPERSMITH, JEFFREY ALAN, distribution corporation executive; b. N.Y.C., Mar. 23, 1946; s. Jack J. and Anita S. (Selikoff) C.; m. Marjorie Myers, July 5, 1987; children: Jarred, Aubrey. B in Mgmt. Engring., Rensselaer Poly. Inst., 1967; MBA, Ohio State U., 1979. Security arbitrage Arnhold and S. Bleichroeder, Inc., N.Y.C., 1967-70; with Pfizer, Inc., N.Y.C., 1970-72, asst. controller Minerals, Pigments and Metals div.; with Distbn. Ctrs., Inc. subs. Distek, Inc., Westerville, Ohio, 1972—, v.p., controller, 1975-77, v.p., treas., 1977-78, v.p. fin., 1978-80, exec. v.p. Distek, Inc., 1980-83, pres., chief operating officer, 1983—, also bd. dirs. pres. Directel, Inc.; bd. dirs. Yassenduf Jewish Ctr., Columbus, Ohio, Quick, CPS Freight. Mem.Young Pres. Orgn., Council Logistics Mgmt., Warehousing Edn. and Research Council, Fin. Execs. Inst. (past dir.), Direct Mktg. Assn., Young Pres.'s Orgn. Office: 229 Huber Village Blvd Westerville OH 43081

COOVER, DANIEL ALAN, civil engineer; b. Chambersburg, Pa., Jan. 9, 1954; s. William Daniel and Helen Louise C.; m. Sonya Kay Fowler, Sept. 5, 1981; children: Aleischa Louise, Aaron Daniel. BSCE, Bucknell U., 1975; MSCE, Carnegie Mellon U., 1977. Registered profl. engr., Ohio. Structural engr. Korda, Nemeth, Kadakia & Jezerinac, Ltd., Columbus, Ohio, 1976-79; structural engr. United McGill Corp., 1979-82, asst. project mgr., 1982-83, mgr. mech. engring., 1983-86, mgr. engring., 1986—. Mem. ASME, ASCE. Republican. Presbyterian. Office: United McGill Corp 2400 Fairwood Ave Columbus OH 43216

COPE, ANTHONY LEON, credit union executive; b. Cleve., June 17, 1911; s. Leone and Rosalia (Lupica) Coppolino; m. Frances Louise Scott, June 13, 1936; children: Virginia Lee Cope Smith, Ronald Anthony. BA cum laude, Adelbert Coll., 1934; MA, Case Western Res. U., 1941; postgrad., Kent State U., 1966, 68; postgrad., John Carroll U., 1971. Cert. secondary tchr., Ohio. Tchr. bus. edn. John Hay High Sch., Cleve., 1934-61; guidance counselor West Tech. High Sch., Cleve., 1961-76, chmn. guidance dept., 1965-76, counselor, adminstr. adult div., 1961-76; pres. bd. dirs. Cleve. N.E. Ohio Ednl. Credit Union. Pres. bd. trustees MidAm. Automated Payments Systems, Cleve., 1986—; mem. Ohio Credit Union League, chmn. legis. com. 1985, pres. Cleve. chpt. 1983-85, bd. dirs. 1985, treas. 1986. Named Oustanding Credit Union Vol. of Yr., Cleve. chpt. Ohio Credit Union, 1982. Mem. Am. Personnel and Guidance Assn., Soc. Motion Picture and TV Engrs. (life) Ohio Bus. Tchrs. Assn. (pres. 1963-64), Nat. Bus. Tchrs. Assn. (2d v.p. 1959-60), Cleve. Area Bus. Tchrs. Assn. (pres. 1959), Sigma Delta Chi (life), Alpha Phi Delta. Avocations: photography, tech. writing, writing motion pictures scripts. Home: 1143 S Belvoir Blvd South Euclid OH 44121 Office: Cleve NE Ohio Ednl Credit Union 3010 Project Ave Cleveland OH 44115

COPE, LLOYD JOHNSON, dentist; b. Provo, Utah, July 6, 1933; s. James Austin and Irma (Shumway) C.; m. Kathleen Wallentine, June 7, 1955; children: Jeff, Jim, Kevin, Stephen, Lisa, Janet, Michelle, Wendy, Jennifer. BS, Utah State U., 1955, postgrad., 1959-60; DDS, Case Western Res. U., 1965. Gen. practice dentistry Paradise, Calif., 1965-85; mission pres. Latter-day Saints Ch., Independence, Mo., 1985-87. Stake pres. Latter-day Saints Ch., Paradise, 1972-81, regional rep., 1981-85; pres. No. Calif. council Boy Scouts Am., 1980-81. Served with USAF, 1955-60. Recipient Silver Beaver award Boy Scouts Am., 1980. Republican. Lodge: Rotary. Avocations: jogging, reading, writing, lecturing. Home: 5787 Bower Ave Kansas City MO 64133 Office: Latter-day Saints Mission 517 W Walnut Independence MO 64050

COPE, RAY, radiologist; b. Liverpool, Eng., Aug. 9, 1930; came to U.S., 1977; s. Joseph and Helen Christine (Halpin) C.; m. Frances Bell, May 27, 1972. MBChB, U. Liverpool, Eng., 1954, DTM&H, 1959; DMRD, U. Edinburgh, Scotland, 1969. Diplomate Am. Bd. Radiology. Med. resident Walton Hosp., Liverpool, 1961-65, Aberdeen (Scotland) Royal Infirmary, 1965-67; resident in radiology Edinburgh (Scotland) Royal Infirmary, 1967-69; sr. resident in radiology United Bristol (Eng.) Hosps., 1969-72; cons. radiologist Southmead Hosp., Bristol, Eng., 1972-74; sr. radiologist Southport and Ormskirk Hosps., Lancs, Eng., 1974-77; staff radiologist Met. Gen. Hosp., Cleve., 1977-78; assoc. prof. radiology Oreg. Health Scis. U., Portland, 1978-84; assoc. prof. U. Mo., Columbia, 1984—. Contbr. articles to profl. jours. Served to surg. lt. comdr. Royal Navy, 1955-58. Fellow Royal Coll. Physicians Edinburgh; mem. Am. Coll. Radiology, Radiolog. Soc. N.Am., Assn. Univ. Radiologists, S.E. Soc. Skeletal Radiology. Roman Catholic. Home: 908 Martin Dr Columbia MO 65203 Office: Univ Mo Sch Medicine Dept Radiology Columbia MO 65221

COPE, W(ILLIAM) ROBERT, lawyer; b. St. Louis, Apr. 14, 1942; s. Carma N. and Virginia M. (Moore) C.; m. Jan Beth Levy, Mar. 2, 1968; children: Kristin Lynn, Robin Ann. BSEE, U. Mo., Rolla, 1965; JD, U. Mo., Columbia, 1968. Bar: Mo. 1968. Ptnr. Oliver, Oliver and Jones, Cape Girardeau, Mo., 1970-75, Summer, Cope and Walsh, Poplar Bluff, Mo., 1975—; Asst. prosecuting atty, Cape Girardeau County, 1970-73. Served to capt. U.S. Army, 1968-70. Mem. ABA, Mo. Bar Assn., Cape Girardeau County Bar Assn., Butler County Bar Assn., Poplar Bluff C. of C. (pres. 1983, Outstanding Service award 1983), U. Mo. Alumni Assn. (mem. nat. bd. 1981—), Ducks Unltd. (chmn. Poplar Bluff 1977—). Democrat. Methodist. Lodge: Rotary (local pres. 1986-87, dist. gov. 1979-80). Avocations: hunting, fishing. Home: 29 Tomaro Trail Poplar Bluff MO 63901 Office: Summers Cope & Walsh PC 106 S Second PO Box 1 Poplar Bluff MO 63901

COPELAND, BRIAN CHARLES, accountant; b. Kalamazoo, Aug. 14, 1956; s. Milburn Charles and Gloria Ann (Redmond) C.; m. Carol Ann Glocheski, July 5, 1980; children: Elizabeth Marie, Sara Ann. BBA cum laude, Western Mich. U., 1978, postgrad. in Bus., 1986—. CPA, Mich. Audit supr. Touche Ross & Co., Grand Rapids, Mich., 1979-84; v.p. Arnie's Inc., Grand Rapids, 1984—. Mem. Am. Inst. CPA's, Mich. Assn. CPA's. Republican. Roman Catholic. Avocations: tennis, basketball, softball, travel, reading. Home: 5811 Appleview SE Kentwood MI 49508 Office: Arnie's Inc 722 Leonard NW Grand Rapids MI 49504

COPELAND, JAMES CLINTON, development executive; b. Chgo., Nov. 15, 1937; s. Wallace J. and Ann T. (Tuka) C.; m. Ella G. Greene, Apr. 30, 1961; children: Catherine, Carolmarie, Christina, James Jr., Jeffrey. BS, U. Ill., 1959; MS, U. Tenn., 1961; PhD, Rutgers U., 1965; MBA, U. Chgo., 1981. Assoc. geneticist Argonne (Ill.) Nat. Labs., 1967-72; assoc. prof. microbiology Ohio State U., Columbus, 1972-77; dir. research, devel. Corn Products Internat. Corp., Argo, Ill., 1977-81; pres. Enzyme Tech. Corp., Ashland, Ohio, 1981-86, Tech. Investments Inc., Ashland, 1986—. Author, co-editor: (text) Regulatory Biology, 1976; contbg. author reference articles Ency. Britannica Book of Yr., 1968-71; editor Microbial Genetics Bulletin, 1973-77; contbr. articles to profl. jours. Trustee Samaritan Hosp., Ashland, 1986—; chmn. indsl. div. United Appeal, Ashland, 1985, mem. adv. com., 1986. Oak Ridge Inst. fellow, 1961, Am. Cancer Soc. fellow, N.Y.C., 1962-65, NIH Predoctoral fellow, Bethesda, Md., 1965-67; recipient NIH Career Devel. award, 1973-78. Mem. AAAS, Ohio Acad. Sci., Sigma Xi. Clubs: Mohican Sailing (Mifflin, Ohio); Country of Ashland. Lodge: Rotary. Avocations: sailing, jogging, racquetball. Home: 298 N Countryside Dr Ashland OH 44805 Office: Tech Investments PO Box 899 Ashland OH 44805

COPELAND, JOSEPH CONRAD, obstetrician-gynecologist; b. Algood, Tenn., July 9, 1944; s. D. Osborne and Annie Myrtle (Gilliam) C.; m. Kathleen Marie Hoffman, Apr. 25, 1977; children: Laura, Kirsten, Courtenay, Kathryn, Jamie, Jason. BA, U. South Fla., 1966; MS, Ind. U., 1969; MD, UCLA, 1971. Pvt. practice medicine specializing in ob-gyn. Anderson, Ind., 1976—; chief ob-gyn. dept. Community Hosp., Anderson, 1983-84. Fellow Am. Coll. Ob-Gyn.; mem. Pacific Coast Fertility Soc., Madison County Med. Soc. (pres. 1982-84), Ind. State Med. Assn. (mem. impaired physicians council 1985—). Republican. Methodist. Home: 1401 Van Buskirk Anderson IN 46011 Office: 1210 Med Arts Blvd Anderson IN 46012

COPELAND, PHILIP RUSSELL, social worker; b. Philipsburg, Pa., Aug. 29, 1937; s. Goodrich Russell and Ivern (Donlon) C.; m. Anna Lois Zimmerly, June 21, 1969. BA, U. Miami, 1960; MSW, U. Tenn., 1967. Lic. ind. social worker, Ohio. Staff social worker N.C. State Commn. Blind, Raleigh, 1962-65, 67-70; counselor, therapist W.G. Nord Mental Health Ctr., Lorain, Ohio, 1970-85; pvt. practiice clin. social worker Elyria, Ohio, 1985—. Contbr. articles on disability to local newspaper, 1984-85. V.p. Ctr. for Visually Impaired, Elyria, 1984—; mem. Handitalk Com., Avon Lake, Ohio, 1983—. Mem. Nat. Assn. Social Workers (Lorain County chpt. Social Worker of Yr. 1984), Nat. Fedn. Blind (Lorain County chpt. pres. 1982—), Acad. Cert. Social Workers. Democrat. Roman Catholic. Lodge: Lions (bd. dirs. 1975). Avocations: travel, reading, music. Home: 110 Indiana Ave Elyria OH 44035 Office: 40667 Griswold Rd Elyria OH 44035

COPELAND, WILLIAM MACK, hospital administrator, lawyer; b. Harriman, Tenn., Jan. 21, 1937; s. John Hyder and Margaret Elizabeth (Gardner) C.; m. Barbara Ann Leurck, 1980; children: Elizabeth, William, Brian, George, Carolyn. B.A., So. Colo. State U., 1965; M.S., U. Colo., 1969; J.D., No. Ky. State U., 1977. Bar: Ohio 1978, U.S. Dist. Ct. (so. dist.) Ohio 1978. Commd. 2d lt. U.S. Air Force, 1954, advanced through grades to capt., 1968, ret., 1975; assoc. adminstr. St. George Hosp., Cin., 1976-77, adminstr., 1977-78; pres. St Francis-St. George Hosp., Inc., Cin., 1978—, St. Francis-St. George Health Services, Inc., 1983—; chmn. Ohio Cath. Health Services Inc., 1986—, Greater Cin. Hosp. Council, 1984-85, Health Industry Bar Code Council, 1987—; charter pres. Dayton Area Adminstrs., 1972-74. Group; adj. faculty Xavier U., InterAm. U.; lectr. patients' rights. Contbr. articles to profl. jours. Vice chmn. dept. health affairs Ohio Catholic Conf., 1981-84, 86—; chmn. strategic plan com. and mem. legis. com. Decorated Meritorious Service medal; decorated Air Force Commendation medal with oak leaf cluster; recipient Monsignor Griffin award Ohio Hosp. Assn., 1979. Fellow Am. Coll. Healthcare Execs., ; mem. Nat. Health Lawyers Assn., Am. Acad. Hosp. Attys., Soc. Ohio Hosp. Attys. (mem. govt. liaison com.), Ohio Hosp. Assn. (trustee, mem. planning com.), Am. Hosp. Assn. (council mgmt. 1986), Cath. Health Assn. U.S. (govt. relations com. 1980-82, health planning com., nominating com. 1985-87), Health Industry Bar Code

Council (bd. govs. 1984-87, exec. com. 1985-87, chmn.-elect 1987), Am. Soc. Law and Medicine, Am. Coll. Cath. Healthcare Leadership (chmn. nominating com. 1985-86), ABA, Ohio Bar Assn., Cin. Bar Assn. Lodge: Kiwanis. Office: 3131 Queen City Ave Cincinnati OH 45238

COPENHAVER, IDA LOUISE, chemical information company executive; b. Johnson City, Tenn., Oct. 19, 1945; d. Lawrence L. and Ida L. (Wolff) C.; m. James L. Ginter. BA in Chemistry, Agnes Scott Coll., 1967; MS in Chemistry, Emory U., 1969. Asst. editor Chem. Abstracts Services, Columbus, Ohio, 1969-72, assoc. editor, 1973-76, sr. assoc. editor, 1976-78, mgr. product specifications and services, mgr. processing coordination, 1978, mgr. product specifications and services, 1978-86, mgr. physical-inorganic-analytical chemistry, 1986—. Com. chair, bd. dirs. Jr. League, Columbus, 1969—, CALL, Columbus, 1980-83; pres., com. chair, bd. dirs. CALLVAC Services, Columbus, 1984—; sec., bd. dirs Columbus Area Leadership Program, 1977-83; steering com. chair Skills Bank, Columbus, 1982-86. Recipient Pres. award Jr. League Columbus, 1985, CALP Columbus Area Leadership award, 1985; named one of 10 Outstanding Young Citizens, 1977. Mem. Am. Chem. Soc., Am. Soc. Info. Sci. Clubs: Met. Women's Ctr., Columbus Met., Conestoga. Avocations: gardening, collecting antique dolls. Home: 2448 Edington Rd Columbus OH 43221 Office: Chem Abstracts Service PO Box 3012 Columbus OH 43210

COPPLE, MICHAEL ANDREW, marketing executive; b. St. Louis, Aug. 30, 1951; s. Samuel John and Dorothy (Segermann) C. BA in Asian Studies and BS in Internat. Bus., U. Pa., 1973; MA in Asian Studies and MBA, Washington U., St. Louis, 1981. Rep. internat. banking Mercantile Bank, St. Louis, 1973-75; mgr. export mktg. Acco, Salem, Ill., 1975-79; mgr. adminstrn. Coaliquid, Inc., Louisville, 1981-82; project dir. George S. May Internat. Co., Chgo., 1982-86; ops. analyst Maritz Motivation Co., St. Louis, 1986—; pres. Michael A. Copple Internat., St. Louis, 1976—. Vol. cons. Mgmt. Assistance Ctr. United Way, St. Louis, 1986. Mem. Sierra Club. Democrat. Roman Catholic. Club: World Trade (St. Louis). Home: 2927 Greentop Ct Saint Louis MO 63119 Office: Maritz Motivation Co 1375 N Highway Dr Saint Louis MO 63026

COPUS, LINDA M., accountant; b. Gary, Ind., Oct. 25, 1958; d. Elmer W. and Phyllis M. (Smith) Gee; m. Donald E. Copus, Sept. 25, 1982. BS in Acctg., Ball State U., 1980. CPA, Mich., Ind. Sr. auditor Ernst & Whinney, Indpls., 1980-83; asst. controller Detroit-Macomb Hosp. Corp., Detroit, 1983-85, dir. reimbursement and budget, 1985—. Mem. Am. Inst. CPA's, Healthcare Fin. Mgmt. Assn. Office: Detroit-Macomb Hospital Corp 7815 E Jefferson Detroit MI 48214

CORBET, DONALD LEE, technical systems educator; b. Dayton, Ohio, Dec. 1, 1959; s. John R. and Barbara L. (Timmerman) C.; m. Julie Kay Miller, June 5, 1982. Computer cons. Radio Shack, Dayton, 1981-82; computer service tech. Reynolds and Reynolds, Peoria, Ill., 1982-84; tech. systems instr. Reynolds and Reynolds, Dayton, 1984—; owner D. L. Corbet Audio, Dayton, 1980—; career developer Success Motivation Inst., Waco, Tex., 1986—; bd. dirs. Mgmt. Documentation Assn., Dayton; cons. SIGI Wittenburg U., Springfield, Ohio, 1982. Co-author: Everybody's Guide to P.C.'s, 1986; composer (recordings) Thunder Road Theme, 1985, Twister film soundtrack, 1986. Recipient Dayton Music Link award Hands Across Am., 1986. Mem. Am. Mgmt. Assn., Soc. Tech. Communication. Home: 4220 Cleveland Ave Dayton OH 45410

CORBETT, BARBARA LOUISE, advertising agency executive; b. Sioux City, Iowa, May 6, 1947; d. Bayliss and Shirley Louise (Wiese) Corbett; m. Henry F. Terbrueggen, Nov. 22, 1976. B.A. in Polit. Sci., Antioch Coll., 1969. Cert. bus. communicator. Copywriter, J.L. Hudson Co., Detroit, 1969-72, Patten Co., Southfield, Mich., 1972-73; copywriter/producer Campbell Ewald, Detroit, 1973-75; free lance writer, 1975-76; pres. Corbett Advt., Inc., Rochester, Mich., 1977—; tchr. Barbizon Sch., Southfield, 1979; prof. advt. Oakland Community Coll., 1980-82; judge Detroit News Scholastic Writing Awards competition, Detroit, 1979-80, 11th ann. BPAA Pro-Comm. awards, 1985; lectr. in field. Recipient award for Ad of the Year, J.L. Hudson Co., 1971; Merit award Seklemian, 1971; Gold Award Creative Advt. Club of Detroit, 1974; others. Mem. Greater Rochester C. of C. (dir.), Indsl. Marketers of Detroit (past pres.), Mich. Advt. Agy. Council (past pres.), Midstates Agy. Network (past pres.), Adcraft. Republican. Unitarian. Home: 6175 Sheldon Rd Rochester MI 48063 Office: Corbett Advt Inc 800 W University Dr Suite F Rochester MI 48063

CORBETT, DENNIS DALE, advertising executive; b. Evansville, Ind., Apr. 11, 1944; s. Cecil W. and Gertrude M. (Jackson) C.; m. Dwana Sue Yates, Jan. 27, 1973; 1 child, Koelle Kristen. BS in Bus., U. Evansville, 1966; BS in Econs., Henry George Sch., 1969; theol. cert., Ambassador Coll., 1970. Spl. investigator Research Assocs., 1963-65; detective Internat. Films, 1968-71; owner Corbett Enterprises, Evansville, Ind., 1963—. Probation counselor Vanderburgh County Vol. Counselors Program, 1972—; campaign dir. March of Dimes, 1968; mem. nat. adv. com. Am. Security Council; mem. citizens adv. com. for Right to Keep and Bear Arms; bd. dirs. Community Action Program Evansville; chmn. Smile Transp. founder Archtl. Barriers Research; bd. dirs. Evansville Area Council Chs., mem. mass media com.; asst. lay leader Seventh Day Adventist Ch.; bd. dirs. Concern for Haiti (orphanage); mem. Rep. Citizens Fin. Com. Ind.; chmn. Title I parnets adv. council Harwood Sch., 1980-81; spl. advisor troop 505 Boy Scouts Am., 1980—. Recipient Key Man award Jr. C. of C., 1966. Mem. Am. Mgmt. Assn. (pres.'s assn.), Direct Selling Legion, Internat. Speakers Network, Nat. Wildlife Fedn., ACLU, Nat. Rifle Assn., Ams. Against Union Control of Govt., Council on Religion and Internat. Affairs, Conservative Caucus, Security and Intelligence Fund, Council Inter-Am. Security, Interam. Soc. OAS, Nat. Right to Work Com., Internat. Platform Assn., Am. Film Inst., Assn. Supervision and Curriculum Devel., Inst. Soc., Ethics and Life Scis., Inst. Am. Relations, Target '76, Evansville Mus., Evansville Zool. Soc. Home: 2605 Box D Old Bridge Ct Evansville IN 47710 Office: 1639 N California St Chicago IL 60647

CORBETT, GERARD FRANCIS, electronics company executive; b. Phila., Apr. 6, 1950; s. Eugene Charles and Dolores Marie (Hoffmann) C.; m. Marcia Jean Serafin, July 9, 1983. A.A., Community Coll. of Phila., 1974; B.A. in Pub. Relations, San Jose State U., 1977. Sci. programmer Sverdrup Inc., NASA Ames Research Ctr., Moffett Field, Calif., 1970-77; sr. writer Four-Phase Systems, Inc., Cupertino, Calif., 1977-78; with Nat. Semicondr. Corp., Santa Clara, Calif., 1978-79; sr. account exec. Creamer Dickson Basford, Providence, 1979-81; mgr. tech. and exec. communications Internat. Harvester Co., Chgo., 1981-82; mgr. corp. tech. communications Gould Inc., Rolling Meadows, Ill., 1982-83, dir. corporate pub. relations, 1983-86, dir. corp. communications 1986—; pub. relations and communications cons. on high tech. Recipient Vice Presdl. award of honor Calif. Jaycees, 1977. Mem. Pub. Relations Soc. Am. (accredited; Pres.'s citation 1981), AIAA, Nat. Assn. Sci. Writers, AAAS, Kappa Tau Alpha. Republican. Roman Catholic. Clubs: Capital Hill, Commonwealth of Calif. Home: 4610 Tall Oaks Ln Rolling Meadows IL 60008 Office: Gould Inc 10 Gould Ctr Rolling Meadows IL 60008

CORBETT, JAMES JOHN, neurologist, neuroophthalmologist; b. Chgo., July 2, 1940; s. Maxwell Melville and Rose Marie (Evanchak) C.; m. Joyce Roberta Zymali, Dec. 29, 1962; children: John Christopher, Jill Stephanie, Jennifer Sarah. BA, Brown U., 1962; MD, Chgo. Med. Sch., 1966. Diplomate Am. Bd. Neurology and Psychiatry. Instr., clin. asst. prof. Jefferson Med. Coll., Phila., 1973-77; asst. prof. neurology U. Iowa, Iowa City, 1977-80, assoc. prof. neurology, 1980-85, prof. neurology and ophthalmology, 1985—. Served to lt. comdr. USNR, 1971-73. Fellow Am. Neurol. Assn., Am. Acad. Neurology. Democrat. Episcopalian. Home: 316 Lee St Iowa City IA 52240 Office: U Iowa Dept Neurology Iowa City IA 52242

CORBETT, JULES JOHN, microbiology educator; b. Natrona, Pa., Apr. 12, 1919; s. Anthony and Theodosia (Kuczynski) C.; m. Gabrielle Ann Wengel, June 24, 1950; children: Brian Lee, Alan Jeffrey, Christine Marie. AA, North Park Coll., 1941; cert. med. tech. Franklin Sch. Sci. and Arts, 1946; SB, U. Chgo., 1950; MS, Ill. Inst. Tech., 1957. Med. technologist St. Bernard Hosp., Chgo., 1947-49; microbiologist Englewood Hosp., Chgo., 1949-52; dir. labs. Beverley Arts Bldg., Chgo., 1954; microbiologist Borden Co., Hammond, Ind., 1955-64; instr. Roosevelt U., Chgo., 1956-59, asst. prof., 1959-64, assoc. prof., 1964-72, prof. biology, 1972-87, prof. emeritus, 1987—, chmn. biology dept., 1974-79; cons. Metro Labs., Chgo. Served with U.S. Army, 1937-39, with USNR, 1941-45. HEW grantee, 1969-72, Ill. Bd. Higher Edn. grantee, 1971-72. Mem. Am. Soc. Microbiology, Ill. Soc. for Microbiology, AAAS, N.Y. Acad. Scis., Ill. State Acad. Sci., Am. Legion (4th dist. comdr. 1975, dep. vice comdr. 1980), La Societe des 40 Hommes et 8 Chevaux Cheminot, VFW, Sigma Xi. Republican. Roman Catholic. Clubs: Immaculate Conception Men's, Clown Unit, Voiture 220 (Chgo.). Home: 8318 S Komensky Ave Chicago IL 60652 Office: Roosevelt U 430 S Michigan Ave Chicago IL 60605

CORBETT, KEITH EDWARD, lawyer; b. Bklyn., Sept. 4, 1949; s. Thomas Anthony and Marie Therese (Westgarth) C.; m. Adrienne D. Schmuhl, Sept. 2, 1972; 1 child, Erik. BA in Polit. Sci., Canisius Coll., 1971; JD, U. Notre Dame, 1974. Bar: Mich. 1974, U.S. Dist. Ct. (ea. dist.) Mich. 1975. Asst. prosecutor Oakland County Pros. Office, Pontiac, Mich., 1974-77; asst. U.S. atty. U.S. Atty.'s Office, Detroit, 1977-78, sr. litigation counsel, 1987—; spl. atty. organized crime sect. U.S. Dept. Justice, Detroit, 1978-87; guest lectr. law Wayne State U., Detroit, 1985, U. Mich., Ann Arbor, 1986; guest instr. U.S. Atty. Gen.'s Advocacy Inst., Washington, 1986—. Recipient Spl. Achievement award U.S. Dept. Justice, 1981, 85. Mem. Fed. Bar Assn. (lectr. 1985-86), Mich. Bar Assn. Roman Catholic. Club: Huntington Woods Men's (Mich.). Avocations: sports, golf, racquetball. Home: 10025 Borgman Huntington Woods MI 48070

CORBETT, RANDI REBECCA, communications manager; b. Chgo., Nov. 28, 1957; d. Leslie and Sandra Jean (Feiges) Perlman; m. Timothy Corbett, Oct. 3, 1982. Student, U. Mo., 1978; BS in Journalism and Advt., So. Ill. U., 1980; postgrad., Roosevelt U., 1985—. Promotion and publicity coordinator Am. Dental Hygeinists Assn., Chgo., 1980-81; mktg. communications coordinator Kay-Ray Inc., Arlington Heights, Ill., 1981-83, mktg. communications adminstr., 1983, mktg. communications mgr., 1984—. Mem. Bus. Profl. Advt. Assn. (asst. treas. 1986—), Nat. Assn. Female Execs., Sigma Kappa. Home: 123 Windwood Ct Buffalo Grove IL 60089 Office: Kay-Ray Inc 8399 Holbrook Dr Wheeling IL 60090

CORBETT, ROBERT EARL, appliance manufacturing executive, engineer; b. Anderson, Ind., Aug. 1, 1926; s. Will Lee and Lavinia Mary (Bevan) C.; m. Frances K. Corbett, July 14, 1956; children: Carol, Brian. BS in Aero. Engring., Purdue U., 1951. Cert. mfg. engr. Design and mfg. engr. Westinghouse Electric Co., Sharon, Pa., 1951-55; gen. foreman Westinghouse Electric Co., Athens, Ga., 1956-62; supt. Westinghouse Electric Co., Metuchen, N.J., 1962-63; gen. foreman Westinghouse Electric Co., Mansfield, Ohio, 1963-78; mgr. mfg. engring. Mansfield Products Co. div. White Consol. Industries, 1979-85, mgr. indsl. engring., 1986—. Pres. SW Little League, Mansfield, 1979-80; announcer Mansfield High Sch. Marching Band, 1984—; pres. Mansfield Schs. Vocat. Adv. Council, 1987. Served to 2d lt. inf. U.S. Army, 1944-46, PTO. Named to Hon. Order Ky. Cols. (v.p. Mansfield chpt. 1975-86); recipient Appreciation award, Mansfield City Schs., 1986. Mem. Soc. Mfg. Engrs. (life), Nat. Rifle Assn. (endowment), Japanese Sword Soc. U.S., Infantry Mus. Soc. (life), DAV (life). Republican. Lutheran. Club: Univ. (Mansfield). Lodge: Masons (32 degree). Avocation: mil. history. Home: 1179 Burkwood Rd Mansfield OH 44907 Office: WCI Laundry div Mansfield Plant 246 E 4th St Mansfield OH 44902

CORBIN, GARY GEORGE, state legislator; b. Bedford, Ind., Dec. 13, 1941; s. George and Mamie (Saltz) C.; m. Sheila Buck, 1962; children: Susan, Sally. BA, Anderson (Ind.) Coll., 1963, MDiv., 1967. Ordained to Ch. of God, 1968. Pastor Community Ch. of God, Clio, Mich., 1967-74; commr. Genesee County, Mich., 1970-74; mem. Mich. State Senate, Lansing, 1975-86, Exec. Office Mich. Dept. Labor, 1987—; asst. majority leader, Mich. State Senate, 1976-82, majority leader, 1983—. Mem. Mich. Job Tng. Coordinating Council, 1983—; trustee Olivet (Mich.) Coll., 1979—. Recipient Patty Bleecker award Social Services for Hearing Impaired, 1983, Meritorious Service award Mich. Alcohol Fuels Assn., 1983. Mem. Nat. Conf. State Legislatures (ethics and elections com. 1977-82, conf. liaison 1983—), Council State Govts., Legis. Council. Home: 11500 Colonial Woods Dr Clio MI 48420

CORBOY, PHILIP HARNETT, lawyer; b. Chgo., Aug. 12, 1924; s. Harold Francis and Marie (Harnett) C.; m. Doris Marie Conway, Nov. 26, 1949 (div. 1985); children—Philip Harnett, Joan Marie, John, Thomas. Student, St. Ambrose Coll., 1942-43, U. Notre Dame, 1945; J.D., Loyola U., 1948. Bar: Ill. bar 1949. Asst. corp. counsel City Chgo., 1949-50; individual practice 1950-82; ptnr. Corboy & Demetrio, Chgo., 1982—. Contbr. articles to profl. jours. Trustee Roscoe Pound Found. Served with AUS, 1943-45. Fellow Am. Coll. Trial Lawyers; mem. ABA. (chmn. litigation sect. 1979-80), Ill. Bar Assn., Chgo. Bar Assn. (pres. 1972-73), Law Sci. Acad., Am. Judicature Soc., Am. Trial Lawyers Assn., Ill. Trial Lawyer Assn. (pres. 1963-64), Nat. Inst. Trial Advocacy (vice chmn. 1971-72), Internat. Acad. Trial Lawyers, Internat. Soc. Barristers, Inner Circle Advs. Clubs: Evanston Golf, Chgo. Athletic Assn. Office: Corboy & Demetrio Suite 630 33 N Dearborn St Chicago IL 60602

CORBY, MICHAEL CHARLES, architect; b. Grand Rapids, Mich., June 3, 1960; s. Justin Thomas and Norma Jean (Zigmont) C.; Debra Ann Bennett, June 29, 1985; 1 child, Michael Charles II. BS, U. Mich., 1982, MArch, 1984. Registered architect, Mich. Planning designer Meijer, Inc., Grand Rapids, Mich., 1982-84; project architect Hobbs and Black Assocs., Ann Arbor, Mich., 1984—. Vol. Washtenaw United Way, Ann Arbor, 1985-86. Mem. AIA, Mich. Soc. Architects. Republican. Lutheran. Avocations: golf, squash, racquetball, downhill skiing, reading. Home: 112 E Davis Ann Arbor MI 48104 Office: Hobbs and Black Assocs Inc 100 N State St Ann Arbor MI 48104

CORCORAN, BARBARA CONNOR, social work director; b. Hammond, Ind., July 29, 1951; d. John Neeson and Barbara (Singleton) Connor; m. Russell M. Corcoran, June 11, 1977; 1 child, Meghann Catherine. Student, Ind. U., 1970; BA, Clarke Coll., 1973; MA, Gov.'s State U., 1987. Tchr. Carmel High Sch., Mundeline, Ill., 1976-78; coordinator sr. citizens Calumet City (Ill.) Youth and Family Services Dept., 1980-86, dir., 1986—; mem. Nat. Council on Aging. Mem. adv. bd. Suburban Cook County Area On Aging, 1984—; mem. State's Atty. Community Adv. Council, 1985—; mem. adv. council Sr. Citizen's Legal Services, 1985—; exec. dir. United Way Calumet City, 1981—. Recipient Treasure award South Suburban Focus Com., 1986, Cert. Appreciation, Cook County State's Atty.'s Office, 1984, Youth in Action award Cook County Sherrif's Dept., 1986. Mem. Gerontol. Soc. Am., Am. Assn. for Counseling and Devel., Kappa Kappa Kappa. Roman Catholic. Club: Lansing (Ill.) Women's. Home: 200 Park Ave 228 Calumet City IL 60409 Office: Calumet City Youth & Family Services Dept 687 Wentworth Calumet City IL 60409

CORCORAN, DENNIS MICHAEL, urologist; b. Ottawa, Ill., Oct. 16, 1945; s. Leo Michael and Beverly June (Thumm) C.; m. Marylou Stapleton; children: Erin, Michaela, Moira, Craig. BS, No. Ill. U., 1967; MD, U. Ill., Chgo., 1971. Diplomate Am. Bd. Urology. Intern in urologic surgery Providence Hosp., Portland, Oreg., 1972-73; resident in surgery Med. Coll. Wis., 1973-77; practice medicine specializing in urology Rockford Urol. Assocs., Ltd., Rockford, Ill., 1977—; clin. researcher in erectile dysfunction and neurogenic bladder dysfunction; clin. asst. prof. surgery U. Ill. Coll. Medicine, Rockford. Mem. AMA, Winnebago County Med. Assn., Am. Urol. Assn., Ill. State Med. Assn., North Cen. Am. Urol. Assn., Chgo. Urologic Soc., Am. Fertility Soc. Avocations: music, the trumpet, woodworking, photography. Office: Mulford Village Office Park 6090 Strathmoor Dr Rockford IL 61107

CORCORAN, MARY ELIZABETH, educational psychology professor; b. Providence, Aug. 15, 1921; d. Charles M. and Katherine (Weeden) C. BA cum laude, Hunter Coll., 1947; MA, Stanford U., 1948; PhD, U. Minn., 1957. Lic. cons. psychologist, Minn. Instr. psychology U. Vermont, Burlington, 1948-50; assoc., editor Edn. Testing Service, Princeton, N.J., 1950-53; asst., then assoc. prof. U. Minn., Mpls., 1957-67; prof. edn. psychology and higher edn. U. Minn., 1967—; research dir. internat. study univ. admissions Internat. Assn. Univs., Paris, 1961-63; vis. prof. Ont. Inst. Studies in Edn., Toronto, 1968-69, Ind. U., Bloomington, 1975-76; cons. various colls., higher edn. systems and research projects. Contbr. articles to profl. jours. Mem. Assn. Instl. Research (bd. dirs., Disting. Mem. 1981), Assn. Studies in Higher Edn. (bd. dirs., chmn., Merit award 1980), Am. Ednl. Research Assn., Am. Psychol. Assn. Episcopalian. Avocation: nature study. Home: 400 Groveland Ave #209 Minneapolis MN 55403 Office: U. Minn. 178 Pillsbury Dr SE Minneapolis MN 55455

CORCORAN, PATRICK ARNOLD, company executive; b. Mpls., Mar. 15, 1937; s. Alvin Byron and Evelyn Victoria (Jensen) C.; B.A., St. Olaf Coll., 1959; m. Carol Ruth Willard, Jan. 9, 1963; children—Pamela Sue, Patrick Sean. Sales corr. 3M Co., St. Paul, 1961, salesman, Wis., 1961-64, account exec., 1964-66; v.p. Color Arts Inc., Racine, Wis., from 1966, now pres., chief exec. officer; organizer, dir. Village Bank of Elm Grove (Wis.), 1979—. Chmn. Recreation Com., Village of Elm Grove, 1974-82; life mem. Republican Party; chmn. bd. trustees Screen Printing Tech. Found., 1986—. Mem. Screen Printing Assn. Internat. (dir., sec., v.p., Certificates of Merit 1973-78, Magnus award 1983 chmn. bd. dirs. 1983-84), Am. Soc. Agrl. Engrs., Alumni Assn. St. Olaf Coll. (bd. mem. 1974-78). Republican. Lutheran. Home: 1005 Verdant Dr Elm Grove WI 53122 Office: 1840 Oakdale Ave Racine WI 53406

CORDELL, STEVEN MARK, sales engineer; b. Kansas City, Mo., Aug. 18, 1955; s. Arthur Orville and Eva (Miller) C.; m. Sandra Sue Price, Oct. 24, 1981; 1 child, Elizabeth Ann. AA, Penn Valley Coll., 1975; BA, U. Mo., 1977. Store mgr. Radio Shack, Kansas City, 1977-78; sales rep. Harris-Hansen Co., Grandview, Mo., 1978-80; jr. ptnr. Palatine Engring., Mission, Kans., 1980-82; sales engr. T. L. Dowell and Assoc., Overland Park, Kans., 1983-85; sales mgr. Independent Electric, Kansas City, 1985—. Mem. Disciples of Christ Ch. Club: Kansas City Blues Soc. Avocations: hunting, travel, history of music. Home: 1929 Osage Circle Olathe KS 66062 Office: Independent Electric Co PO Box 412047 Kansas City MO 64141

CORDES, BROCK VALENTINE, publisher; b. Milw., Sept. 1, 1942; s. Henry Carl and Mary Elizabeth (Munk) C.; m. Georgia Felice Church, Feb. 19, 1966; children—Erika Hillary, Trevor Eaton. B.A., U. Alaska, 1965; M.B.A., U. Oreg., 1968. Engring. technician, surveyor Alaska Dept. Hwys., Fairbanks, 1963-67; lectr. U. Man., Winnipeg, 1968-72; life underwriter Monarch Life Assurance Co., Winnipeg, 1972-74, br. mgr., Winnipeg, 1974-78; pres., chief exec. officer Seabrook Industries Ltd., Winnipeg, 1978—; pres., pub. Reliance Press Ltd., 1978—; pres. Web Graphics West Ltd., 1978—, Edan Restaurants Ltd., 1978—. Served with USN, 1960-61, USMCR, 1962-65. Mem. Can. Community Newspaper Assn., Printing Industries Am. Progressive Conservative. Presbyterian. Home: 62 Paradise Dr, Winnipeg, MB Canada R3R 1L1 Office: 386 Broadway, Suite 602, Winnipeg, MB Canada R3C 3R6

CORDES, JAMES F., gas transmission company executive; b. 1940. BS, St. Louis U., 1963; MBA, Creighton U., 1968; MS, U. Maine, 1976. Indsl. engr. A.E. Staley Mfg. Co., Decatur, Ill., 1963-65; research analyst No. Natural Gas Co., 1965-77; with ANR Pipeline Co., Detroit, 1977—; now pres., chief exec. officer. Office: ANR Pipeline Co 1 Woodward Ave Detroit MI 48226 *

CORDES, LOVERNE CHRISTIAN, interior designer; b. Cleve., Feb. 13, 1927; d. Frank Andrew and Loverne Louise (Brown) Christian; m. William Peter Cordes, Nov. 14, 1959; children: Christian Peter, Carey Pomeroy. B.S., Purdue U., 1949. Owner, mgr. Loverne Christian Cordes, Chagrin Falls, Ohio, 1967—; tchr. John Carroll U., Cleve., 1976-77. Interior designer, Fred Epple Co., Cleve., 1949-67. Fellow Am. Soc. Interior Designers, AIA, Nat. Home Fashion League (past pres. Ohio chpt.), Am. Inst. Interior Designers (past pres. Ohio chpt., nat. bd. dirs. 1969-75, nat. v.p. East Central region 1972-75, nat. exec. bd. 1972-75, recipient 1st Presdl. citation 1973, 74, 75); mem. Soc. Collectors Dunham Tavern Mus. (bd. dirs. 1961-62), Dunham Dames (past pres.), Western Reserve Hist. Soc., Cleve. Mus. Art, Cleve. Garden Center, Chagrin Falls Hist. Soc., Nat. Trust for Historic Preservation, Internat. Platform Assn., Arcadian, Kappa Kappa Gamma. Republican. Congregationalist. Clubs: Chagrin Valley Country, Dogwood Garden. Avocations: golf, cross country skiing, wine maker, caligraphy. Address: 60 S Franklin St Chagrin Falls OH 44022

CORE, HARRY MICHAEL, psychiatric social worker, mental health administrator; b. Core, W.Va., Oct. 7, 1933; s. Earl Lemley and Freda Bess (Garrsion) C.; m. Jane Ann Boggs, Oct., 1976; children: Kevin M., Brian D. BS, W.Va. U., 1955; MSW, U. N.C., 1957. Psychiat. social worker Lake County Mental Health Ctr., Mentor, Ohio, 1960-67, asst. dir., 1967-72, exec. dir., 1972—; psychiat. social worker Simon & Bertschinger MDs, Inc., Eastlake, Ohio, 1966—; trustee Tri-Care, Inc., Westlake, Ohio, 1986—. Served to 1st lt., U.S. Army, 1957-60. Fellow Am. Orthopsychiat. Assn.; mem. Acad. Cert. Social Workers, Nat. Assn. Social Workers Ohio Council of Community Mental Health Agencies (trustee 1981-84, v.p. 1984). Democrat. Mem. Disciples of Christ Ch. Home: 6707 Stratford Rd Painesville OH 44077 Office: Lake County Mental Health Ctr 8445 Munson Rd Mentor OH 44060

COREN, ARTHUR, electrical manufacturing company executive; b. Chgo., Oct. 16, 1933; s. Lewis and Celia (Wolfson) C.; m. Judith Strauss, Mar. 8, 1955; children: Linda, David. BS in Bus. and Engring. Adminstrn., MIT, 1954; MBA, Northwestern U., 1965. Various positions Zenith Controls Inc., Chgo., 1954-70, pres., 1970—. Mem. Elec. Generating Systems Assn. (pres. 1978-79), Beta Gamma Sigma. Avocations: travel, tennis, reading. Office: Zenith Controls Inc 830 W 40th St Chicago IL 60609

COREY, JOHN CHARLES, finance executive; b. Ft. Leavenworth, Kans., Sept. 28, 1947; s. Robert R. and Ann (Glen) C. BA in Acctg., Sacred Heart U., 1973; MBA in Fin., George Washington U., 1977. Acct. Price Waterhouse, Stamford, Conn., 1973-76; analyst new car prodn. Ford Motor Co., Dearborn, Mich., 1977-79; fin. mgr. Gen. Foods Corp., White Plains, N.Y., 1979-82; v.p. IFINT U.S.A., Inc., N.Y.C., 1982—; sr. v.p. fin. and adminstrn. Moog Automotive, Inc., St. Louis, 1982—. Mem. Am. Inst. CPA's, Conn. Soc. CPA's, Assn. for Corp. Growth, Fin. Execs. Inst. Office: Moog Automotive Inc 6565 Wells Ave Saint Louis MO 63133

CORLEY, DIANA KAY, speech communication educator; b. Russellville, Ark., Dec. 4, 1946; d. Robert Eston and Claudie (Cates) C. BS, Ill. State U., Normal, 1968, MS, 1970; PhD., U. Md., 1986. Tchr. Davenport (Iowa) Schs., 1968-69; prof. speech communication Black Hawk Coll., Moline, Ill., 1970—; cons. U.S. Army Corps Engrs., Hosp. Groups, Cooperative Extension Service, Moline, Rock Island, East Moline, 1973—. Contbr. articles to profl. jours. Vol. Sta. WQPT-TV, Luth. Hosp., Moline, 1983-85; tchr., coordinator Moline Ch. Christ, 1980-86; bd. dirs. Towncrest Homeowners Assn., Moline, 1983-86. Mem. Speech Communication Assn., Internat. Listening Assn., Smithsonian Inst. Democrat. Avocations: reading, collecting art objects, walking. Home: 1315 C 9th St Moline IL 61265 Office: Black Hawk Coll 6600 34th Ave Moline IL 61265

CORLEY, WILLIAM EDWARD, hospital administrator; b. Pittsburgh, Sept. 2, 1942; s. Robert Ray and Helen (Wise) C.; m. Angela Irvine Blose, Mar. 22, 1969; children—Laura, Matt. B.A. in Bus. and Econs., Coll. of William and Mary, 1964; M.H.A. in Hosp. Adminstrn., Duke U., Durham, 1966. Adminstrv. asst. Duke U., Durham, N.C., 1965-66; mgmt. cons. Booz, Allen & Hamilton, Chicago, 1968-71; assoc. hosp. dir. U. Ky., Lexington, 1971-75; hosp. dir. Milton S. Hersey Med. Ctr. of Pa. State U., Hershey, 1975-78; pres. Akron Gen. Med. Ctr., Ohio, 1978-84, Community Hosps. of Ind., Inc., 1984—; Bd. dirs. Vol. Hosps. Am., Irving, Tex., 1982—; chmn. United Hosp. Services, Indpls., 1984—; lectr. Ind. U.-Purdue U. at Indpls., 1984—. Contbr. articles to profl. jours. Served to 1st lt. U.S. Army, 1966-68. Mem. Am. Coll. Hosp. Adminstrs. Presbyterian. Lodge: Rotary (Indpls.). Avocations: photography, basketball, coaching, running. Home: 13570 N Gray Rd Carmel IN 46032 Office: Community Hosps Ind Inc 1500 N Ritter Ave Indianapolis IN 46219

CORLEY, WILLIAM GENE, research engineer; b. Shelbyville, Ill., Dec. 19, 1935; s. Clarence William and Mary Winifred (Douthit) C.; m. Jenny Lynd Wertheim, Aug. 9, 1959; children: Anne Lynd, Robert William, Scott Elson. BS, U. Ill., 1958, MS, 1960, PhD, 1961. Registered profl. engr., Ill., Va., Wash., Calif., Miss., Fla. Devel. engr. Portland Cement Assn., Skokie,

Ill., 1964-66, mgr. structural devel. sect., 1966-74, dir. engring. devel. div., 1974-86; v.p. Constrn. Tech. Labs., Inc. (formerly Portland Cement Assn.), Skokie, 1986—, also bd. dirs.; mem. adv. panels NSF. Contbr. aritcles to tech. and profl. jours. Pres. caucus Glenview (Ill.) Sch. Bd., 1971-72; elder United Presbyn. Ch., 1975-79; sec. bd. dirs. Assn. House, Chgo., 1976, treas., 1977, pres., 1978-79; chmn. bd. dirs. North Cook dist. ARC; bd. dirs. Mid-Am. chpt. ARC. Served to 1st lt. U.S. Army, 1961-64. Recipient Wason medal for Research, 1970; Martin Korn award Prestressed Concrete Inst., 1978; Reinforced Concrete Research Council Arthur J. Boase award, 1986. Fellow ASCE (T.Y. Lin award 1979), Am. Concrete Inst. (Bloem award 1978, Reese Structural Research award 1986); mem. Réunion Internationale des Laboratoires d'Essais et Recherchas sur Matériaux Construction, NSPE, Earthquake Engring. Research Inst. (chpt. sec., treas. 1980-82, chmn. 1984—), Internat. Assn. Bridge and Structural Engring., Structural Engrs. Assn. Ill. (pres. 1986-87), Post-Tensioning Inst., Chgo. Com. High-Rise Bldgs. (vice-chmn. 1978-82, chmn. 1982-84, Bldg. Seismic Safety Council (vice-chmn. 1983-85, sec. 1985—). Presbyterian. Home: 744 Glenayre Dr Glenview IL 60025 Office: Constrn Tech Labs Inc 5420 Old Orchard Rd Skokie IL 60077

CORMAN, WARREN WILLIAM, facilities director; b. Kansas City, Kans., July 31, 1926; s. Emmett J. and Miriam E. (Twineham) C.; divorced; children: Becky, Cathy, David, Nancy; m. Mary Ella Chrisman, June 13, 1979; children: Traci, Bill. BArch, U. Kans., 1950. Registered architect, Kans.; registered profl. engr., Kans. Project architect State of Kans., Topeka, 1950-57, E.I. DuPont De Nemours, Wilmington, Del., 1957-59; ptnr., architect Williamson-Corman, Topeka, 1959-63, Howells-Hale-Corman, Topeka, 1963-66; dir. facilities State of Kans. Bd. of Regents, Topeka, 1966—; chmn. bldgs. and grounds Brewster Place Retirement Complex, Topeka, 1982—. Author: Energy-1977, Energy-1980. pres. PTA of Topeka, 1964; chmn. United Fund Drive, Topeka, 1967; chmn. fin. com. 1st Presbyn. Ch., Lawrence, Kans., 1985—. Served with USN, 1944-46, PTO. Mem. AIA (Topeka sect. sec.-treas. 1967-68), Nat. Assn. Univ. Architects (pres. 1986). Lodge: Rotary (bd. dirs. Topeka chpt. 1969-72, pres. 1973) (Paul Harris fellow, 1986). Avocations: tennis, jogging. Home: 844 Highland Dr Lawrence KS 66044 Office: Kans Bd of Regents 400 SW 8th Topeka KS 66603

CORNA, MARK STEVEN, construction company executive; b. Columbus, Ohio, July 21, 1949; s. Albert and Ann Elizabeth (Amicon) C.; m. Margaret Ann Igoe, July 18, 1970 (div. Apr. 1986); children: Joshua Daniel, Sophia Ann. With Corna and DiCesare Builders, Inc., Columbus, 1970-76; pres. The M.S. Corna Co., Columbus, 1976-85, Corna and DiCesare Construction Co., Columbus, 1985—; mem. Gov.'s Blue Ribbon Com. to Investigate Delays in Bldg. Plan Approval, State of Ohio, 1980. Coach soccer Immaculate Conception Sch., Columbus, 1982-83, basketball, 1983-85, com. chmn. Mem. Associated Gen. Contractors (bd. dirs. 1980—, pres. 1986), Builders Exchange Cen. Ohio (bd. dirs. 1981—, v.p.). Democrat. Roman Catholic. Clubs: Athletic, Columbus Italian. Avocations: triathlons, reading, music, traveling, golf. Office: Corna and DiCesare Construction Co 1621 W 1st Ave Columbus OH 43212

CORNELIUS, ALLEN FINLEY, industrial engineer; b. Dayton, Ohio, Oct. 14, 1960; s. Dale Finley and Leona Fay (Rogers) C. B in Tech. Indsl. Engring. Tech., U. Dayton, 1983. Indsl. engr. Forma Sci., Marietta, Ohio, 1983-87; mfg. engr. Spectra-Physics, Dayton, Ohio, 1987—. Mem. Am. Inst. Indsl. Engrs., Tau Alpha Pi. Republican. Pentecostal. Avocations: phys. fitness, motorcycling.

CORNELIUS, WILLIAM EDWARD, utilities company executive; b. Salt Lake City, Sept. 6, 1931; s. Edward Vernon and Gladys (Bray) C.; m. Mary Virginia Bunker, June 13, 1953; children: Mary Jean, Linda Anne. B.S., U. Mo., 1953; M. Liberal Arts, Washington U., St. Louis, 1983. C.P.A., Mo. Mgr. Price Waterhouse & Co., St. Louis, 1955-62; asst. comptroller Union Electric Co., St. Louis, 1962-64, dir. corporate planning, 1964-67, exec. v.p., 1968-80, pres., 1980—, chief exec. officer, 1984—, also dir.; dir. Centerre Bank N.A., Centerre Bancorp., Gen. Am. Life Ins. Co., McDonnell Douglas Corp. Bd. dirs. St. Louis Children's Hosp.; trustee Washington U. Served to 1st lt. AUS, 1953-55. Mem. Beta Theta Pi. Clubs: Bellerive Country, St. Louis, Log Cabin. Home: 2 Dunlora Ln Saint Louis MO 63131 Office: Union Electric Co PO Box 149 Saint Louis MO 63166

CORNELL, HARRY M., JR., mattress company executive; b. 1928; married. Grad., U. Mo., 1950. With Leggett & Platt, Inc., 1950—, salesman, 1950-53, gen. mgr., 1953-55, v.p., 1955-60, pres., gen. mgr., from 1960; now chmn., chief exec. officer Leggett & Platt, Inc., Carthage, Mo. Office: Leggett & Platt Inc 1 Leggett Rd PO Box 757 Carthage MO 64836 *

CORNELL, WILLIAM DANIEL, mechanical engineer; b. Valley Falls, Kans., Apr. 17, 1919; s. Noah P. and Mabel (Hennessy) C.; m. Barbara L. Ferguson, Aug. 30, 1942; children—Alice Margaret, Randolph William. B.S. in Mech. Engring., U. Ill., 1942. Registered profl. engr., N.Y. Research engr. Linde Air Products Co., Buffalo, 1942-48, cons. to Manhattan Dist. project, 1944-46; project engr. devel. of automatic bowling machine Am. Machine and Foundry, Buffalo, 1948-55; cons. Gen. Electric Co., Hanford, Wash., 1949-50; project engr. devel. of automatic bowling machine Brunswick Corp., Muskegon, Mich., 1955-59, mgr. advanced engring., 1959-72; mgr. advanced concepts and tech. Sherwood Med. Industries div. Am. Home Products Corp., St. Louis, 1972-85; mem. faculty Coll. Engring., U. Buffalo, 1946-47; cons. Cornell Engring., St. Louis, 1985—. Patentee numerous inventions, including automatic golf and bowling game apparatus, med. instruments; developer new method of measuring hemoglobin. Recipient Navy E award, 1945, Manhattan Project Recognition award, 1945, Merit award Maritime Commn., 1945. Republican. Presbyterian. Home: 907 Camargo Dr Ballwin MO 63011 Office: 11802 Westline Ind Dr Saint Louis MO 63141

CORNELSEN, PAUL FREDERICK, manufacturing and engineering company executive; b. Wellington, Kans., Dec. 23, 1923; s. John S. and Theresa Albertine (von Klatt) C.; m. Floy Lila Brown, Dec. 11, 1943; 1 son, John Floyd. Student, U. Wichita, 1939-41, 45-46; B.S. in Mech. Engring, U. Denver, 1949. With Boeing Airplane Co., 1940-41, Ralston Purina Co., St. Louis, 1946—; v.p. internat. div. Ralston Purina Co., 1961-63, adminstrv. v.p., gen. mgr. internat. div., 1963-64, v.p., 1964-68, dir., 1966—, exec. v.p., 1968-78, vice chmn. bd., chief operating officer, 1978-81, pres. internat. group, 1964-77; pres., chief exec. officer Moehlenpah Industries Inc., St. Louis, 1981-82, M.Tek Industries (formerly Moehlenpah), St. Louis, 1982—; bd. dirs. DeKalb (Ill.) Corp., Sunmark Cos., St. Louis, Petrolite Corp., St. Louis, Carlin Foods, Inc., Chgo.; founding mem. Latin Am. Agribus. Investment Corp., 1970—; founding mem. industry coop. program UN Agys., Rome, Italy. Mem. Nat. 4-H Council Adv. Com.; trustee Ill. Coll., Jacksonville. Served to 1st lt. AUS, World War II; Served to 1st lt. AUS, also Korean War. Decorated Silver Star. Home: 506 Fox Ridge Rd Saint Louis MO 63131 Office: 11710 Old Ballas Rd Creve Coeur MO 63141

CORNER, BRUCE EDWARD, financial executive; b. Wisconsin Rapids, Wis., Oct. 31, 1949; s. Harold John and Dorothy (Herman) C.; m. Marlene Marie Bushmaker, June 19, 1971; children: Mackenzie Ann, Kaitlin Elise. BBA, U. Wis., Stevens Point, 1971; MS in Acctg., U. Wis., Madison, 1973. CPA, Wis. With Price Waterhouse, Milw., 1973-84, staff acct., 1973-76, sr. staff acct., 1976-78, mgr., 1978-81, sr. audit mgr., 1981-84; from asst. corp. controller to corp. controller Western Pub. Co., Inc., Racine, Wis., 1984-86; v.p. fin. and adminstrn., sec.-treas. Lake Shore Inc., Kingsford, Mich., 1986—; instr. Milw. Area Tech. Coll., 1974-75. Mem. Friends of Channel 10/36, Milw., 1980—. Served with USAR, 1971-77. Mem. Am. Inst. CPAs, Wis. Inst. CPAs (competence rev. com.), Ind. Bus. Assn. Wis. (chmn. adminstrv. rules com. 1982-84), Univ. Wis. Bus. Alumni Assn. Roman Catholic. Avocations: tennis, fishing, cycling, gardening. Home: 1000 Woodward Ave Iron Mountain MI 49801 Office: Lake Shore Inc 900 W Breitung Ave Kingsford MI 49801

CORNET, HANK, marketing professional; b. Peoria, Ill., Nov. 16, 1940; s. Marion George and Marian Margaret (Morrison) C.; m. Kathleen Ann Taylor, Sept. 5, 1964; children: Douglas, Erik, Jac, Patrick. BS in Mktg., Calif. State U., Long Beach, 1966. Designer Little Giant Products, Peoria, Ill., 1958-63, Lockheed, Redlands, Calif., 1963-64, F.M.C. Corp., Riverside, Calif., 1964; research and devel. mgr. Scholle Corp., Northlake, Ill., 1964-70; dir. mktg. services Scholle COrp., Northlake, Ill., 1970—. Asst. scoutmaster Boy Scouts Am., Honover Park, Ill., 1983; dep. Rep. committeman, Schaumburg, Ill., 1975; campaign coordinator, 1975. Republican. Roman Catholic. Lodge: KC (fin. sec. 1985). Avocations: canoeing, fishing, camping. Home: 33 Woodworth Pl Roselle IL 60172 Office: Scholle Corp 200 W North Ave Northlake IL 60164

CORNS, ALAN EDWARD, dentist; b. Pitts., Oct. 6, 1939; s. Rex. C. and Ann G. (Dickinson) C.; m. Sharon Arlene Carl, July 19, 1969; children: Christine, Robert. DDS, Ind. U., 1963. v.p. Denpac Systems Inc., Valparaiso, Ind., 1980. Co-author: Computer Software Denpac 80, 1980. Bd. dirs. Christian Community Action, Valparaiso, 1972-76. Recipient Pierre Faucado Acad., 1979. Fellow: Internat. Coll. Dentists; mem. ADA (del. 1976), Ind. Dental Assn. (del. 1972), Northwest Ind. Dental Assn. (pres. 1975), Omicron Kappa Upsilon. Republican. Roman Catholic. Lodge: Kiwanis Internat. Avocations: gardening, music. Home and Office: 809 Wall St Valparaiso IN 46383

CORNYN, JOHN EUGENE, accounting company executive; b. San Francisco, Apr. 30, 1906; s. John Eugene and Sara Agnes (Larkin) C.; B.S., St. Mary's Coll., 1934; M.B.A., U. Chgo., 1936; m. Virginia R. Shannahan, Sept. 10, 1938 (dec. May 1964); children—Virginia R., Kathleen R. Cornyn Arnold, John Eugene, Madeleine A. Cornyn Shanley, Carolyn G. Cornyn Clemons; m. 2d, Marian C. Fairfield, Aug. 21, 1965. Partner, John E. Cornyn & Co., C.P.A.s, Winnetka, Ill., 1951-73; pres. John E. Cornyn & Co. Ltd., 1973—. Exec. sec. North Shore Property Owners Assn., 1953—. C.P.A., Ill. Mem. Am. Inst. C.P.A.s, Ill. Soc. C.P.A.s, Am. Acctg. Assn., Am. Tax Assn., Fellowship Cath. Scholars. Catholic (Byzantine Rite). Home: 126 Bertling Ln Winnetka IL 60093-4299

CORRALES, PATRICK, professional baseball manager; b. Los Angeles, Mar. 20, 1941; s. David and Josephine (Rivera) C.; m. Sharon Ann Grimes, Sept. 23, 1960 (dec. July 22, 1969); children: Rena M., Michele D., Patricia A., Jason P.; m. Donna Ardene Myers, Mar. 7, 1983; 1 son, Patrick David Parker. Grad., Fresno High Sch., Calif., 1959. Signed with Phila. Phillies, 1959, profl. baseball player, 1959-78; mgr. Tex. Rangers, Arlington, 1978-80, Phila. Phillies, 1982-83, Cleve. Indians, 1983-87; coach Am. League All-Stars, Seattle, 1979, Nat. League All-Stars, Chgo., 1983; coach Am. League All-Stars, Houston, 1986, Oakland, Calif., 1987. Holder Am. Karate Acad. Brown Belt. Democrat. Roman Catholic. Office: Cleveland Indians Boudreau Blvd Cleveland OH 44114

CORRELL, BRUCE, accounting firm executive; b. Highland, Mich., Aug. 9, 1943; s. George William and Dorothy Emma (Bunting) C.; m. Janis Elaine Furlonge, Feb. 8, 1964 (div. Apr. 1972). BS, Wayne State U., 1967. CPA, Mich. Ptnr. Plante & Moran, Southfield, Mich., 1963-76; mng. ptnr. Correll, Krywko, Harrell, Morgante & Button, Southfield, 1976—. Mem. Am. Inst. CPA's, Mich. Assn. CPA's (Gold medal 1967). Club: Detroit Athletic. Office: Correll Krywko Harrell Morgante & Button 26261 Evergreen Suite 200 Southfield MI 48076

CORRELL, DAVID WILLIAM, architect; b. Noblesville, Ind., Oct. 29, 1942; s. James Leander and Velma Belle (Day) C.; m. Jeri Kay Couden, Aug. 16, 1964; children: Scott David, Curtis Ryan, Matthew J. BArch, U. Cin., 1968. Registered architect, Ind., Ohio, Ky. Corp. sec. David B. Hill & Assocs. Inc., Seymour, Ind., 1971-81, pres., 1981-86; pres. Correll/Bradley Architects, Seymour, 1986—; bd. dirs. Seymour Ind. Corp.; com. chmn. Target 2000, Seymour. Coach Seymour Youth Baseball, 1975—, Emerson Elem. Sch. Football, Seymour, 1985—. Republican. Club: Seymour Country. Lodge: Elks (house com. 1982-84). Avocations: golf, fishing, coaching. Office: Correll/Bradley Architects 202 1/2 W 2d PO Box 178 Seymour IN 47274

CORSER, GEORGE ALBERT, engineering educator, consultant; b. Hibbing, Minn., June 13, 1934; s. Albert and Mary Ann (Argir) C.; m. Maureen Kay Slagg, Apr. 8, 1962; children—George Patrick, John Kevin, Carin Glendyne. B.S. in Civil Engring., U. Colo., 1958; M.S. in Civil Engring., Wash. State U., 1963. Registered profl. engr., Mich. Asst. prof. Wash. State U., Pullman, 1958-64; assoc. prof. Gen. Motors Inst., Flint, Mich., 1964-81; chmn. mech. engring. Saginaw Valley State Coll., Mich., 1981—. Mem. Mayor's Task Force for Efficiency in City Govt., 1971; mem. Community Edn. Day com., 1980; citizen observer, Interfaith Action Council, 1970-71. Recipient Faculty Innovative Teaching award, Gen. Motors Inst., 1975. Mem. ASCE, AAUP, Am. Soc. Engring. Edn. (chmn. edn. research and methods div. 1973-75, dir. N. Central sect. Effective Tching. Insts., 1972), Mich. Soc. Profl. Engrs. (chmn. profl. engrs. in edn. 1974-76, Engr. of Yr. Flint chpt. 1984), Nat. Soc. Profl. Engrs., Sigma Xi, Phi Delta Kappa. Democrat. Unitarian. Lodge: DeMolay. Author: (with others) Mechanical Engineering Laboratory II, 1974. Office: Saginaw Valley State Coll Pioneer Hall 2250 Pierce Rd University Center MI 48710

CORSON, THOMAS HAROLD, recreational vehicle manufacturing company executive; b. Elkhart, Ind., Oct. 15, 1927; s. Carl W. and Charlotte (Keyser) C.; m. Dorthy Claire Scheide, July 11, 1948; children: Benjamin Thomas, Claire Elaine. Student, Purdue U., 1945-46, Rennsselaer Poly. Inst., 1946-47, So. Meth. U., 1948-49. Chmn. bd. Coachmen Industries, Inc., Elkhart, Ind., 1965—; also chmn. bd. Coachmen Industries, Inc. (numerous subs. cons.); bd. dirs. First State Bank Middlebury, Canton Drop Forge Co. (Ohio), Elkhart, Olofsson Corp., Lansing, Mich., R.C.R. Scientific Inc., Goshen, Ind.; chmn., sec. Greenfield Corp., Middlebury. Adv. council U. Notre Dame; Ttrustee Ball State U., Interlochen (Mich.) Arts Acad. and Nat. Music Camp. Served with USNR, 1945-47. Mem. Ind. Mfrs. Assn. (dir.), Elkhart C. of C. (past dir.). Methodist. Clubs: Masons, Shriners, Elcona (past dir.); Capitol Hill (Washington); Imperial Golf (Naples, Fla.). Home: PO Box 504 Middlebury IN 46540 Office: Coachman Industries Inc 601 E Beardsley Ave Box 3300 Elkhart IN 46514

CORTE, JAMES CHARLES, electrical construction company executive; b. Blue Island, Ill., July 17, 1948; s. S. Charles and Amelia (Costalunga) C.; B.A., St. Mary's Coll., Winona, Minn., 1970; m. Darcy L. DeYoung, Oct. 3, 1971; children—Mark Charles, Jaime Leigh. With Super Electric Constrn. Co., Chgo., 1971—, asst. controller, 1975-79, controller, 1979—. Mem. Ill. High Sch. Assn., South Suburban Ofcls. Assn., Oak Forest Baseball Assn. (v.p.). Roman Catholic. Home: 17010 S Cicero Ave Tinley Park IL 60477 Office: 4300 W Chicago Ave Chicago IL 60651

CORTELLESSA, GARY R., insurance executive; b. Mt. Vernon, N.Y., June 26, 1947; s. Vincent James and Elizabeth J. (Siegfried) C. BA, U. Bridgeport, 1969; JD, N.Y. Law Sch., 1974; M in Mgmt., Northwestern U., 1986. Bar: N.J. 1975, N.Y. 1976, Va. 1977, D.C. 1980. Divisional counsel Chgo. Title Ins. Co., Arlington, Va., 1979-80, v.p., regional counsel, 1980-83; v.p., dir. corp. mktg. Chgo. Title Ins. Co., Chgo., 1984—. Bd. dirs. Newberry Plaza Condo. Assn., 1984—, sec. 1985, pres. 1986—. Mem. Nat. Assn. Indsl. and Office Parks, Nat. Assn. Corp. Real Estate Execs., Va. Land Title Assn. (v.p. 1981-82, pres. 1982-83), Va. Bar Assn., N.J. Bar Assn., D.C. Bar. Assn., Urban Land Inst. Avocations: skiing, tennis, running. Home: 1030 N State St #25B Chicago IL 60610 Office: Chgo Title Ins Co 111 W Washington St Chicago IL 60602

CORTESE, JOSEPH SAMUEL, II, lawyer; b. Des Moines, Aug. 17, 1955; s. Joseph Anthony and Kathryn Mary (Marasco) C.; m. Diane Caniglia, Aug. 5, 1978; children: Joseph III, James David, Kathryn Elizabeth. BA, Ind. U., 1977; JD with honors, Drake U., 1980. Bar: Iowa 1981, U.S. Dist. Ct. (no. and so. dists.) Iowa 1981, U.S. Ct. Appeals (8th cir.) 1984. Assoc. Jones, Hoffman & Davison, Des Moines, 1981-85, ptnr., 1985—. Pol. activist, vol. Iowa Dem. party, 1971—; asst. coordinator Birch Bayh presdl. campaign, Iowa and Ind., 1975-76. Mem. ABA, Iowa State Bar Assn., Polk County Bar Assn., Def. Research Inst. Roman Catholic. Home: 6526 Allison Ave Des Moines IA 50322 Office: Jones Hoffman & Davison 1000 Des Moines Bldg Des Moines IA 50322

CORTESE, THOMAS ANTHONY, surgeon; b. Mesoraca, Italy, Feb. 20, 1908 (parents Am. citizens); s. Joseph and Mary (Schipani) C.; A.B., Ind. U., 1930, B.S., 1931, M.D., 1933. Intern, resident in surgery Columbus Hosp., Chgo., 1933-34; intern St. Francis Hosp., Indpls., 1932-33; practice medicine specializing in surgery, Indpls., 1934—; mem. staff St. Francis, Community, Univ. Heights hosps.; mem. Pres. Johnson's Commn. on Cardiovascular Disease, 1966-67. Mem. Pres. Johnson's Council on Youth Opportunity, 1966-67. Served with M.C., U.S. Army, World War II. Recipient Cavaliere di Merito, Republic of Italy, also commendatore. Diplomate Am. Bd. Surgery, Am. Bd. Abdominal Surgery, Internat. Coll. Surgeons. Fellow Internat. Fertility Assn.; mem. Indpls., Marion County med. socs., Am. Soc. Contemporary Medicine and Surgery, Am. Soc. Study of Sterility, Am. Fedn. Scientists, N.Y. Acad. Scis., Am. Assn. Clinics, AAAS, World Med. Assn. (founder), Ind. State Med. Assn., AMA, Fedn. of Italian Am. Socs. Ind. (pres., founder), Am. Legion, St. Francis Pathol. Soc., Am. Atomic Scientists. Club: Indpls. Athletic. Author: Hiatus Hernia, 1947; contbr. articles to profl. jours. Home: 3525 Payne Dr Indianapolis IN 46227 Office: 1550 E County Line Rd Suite 240 Indianapolis IN 46227

CORVO, NICOLANGELO, chemist, consultant; b. Italy, Dec. 5, 1950; s. Giuseppe and Mariatonia (Malatesta) C.; m. Felecia M. Hollifield, Sept. 5, 1970; children: Antoinette, Gina. BS in Chemistry, Cleve. State U., 1978. Lab. asst. Cleve. State U., 1976-78; chem. sales Dearborn Chem. Co. div. W.R. Grace & Co., Cleve., 1978-80; tech. dir. Dearborn Chem. Co. div. W.R. Grace & Co., Lake Zurich, Ill., 1980-86, sr. tech. dir., 1986—. Served as staff sgt. USAF, 1970-73. Mem. Am. Chem. Soc., Nat. Assn. Corrosion Engrs., Paper Chemists. Democrat. Roman Catholic. Avocations: skiing, swimming, softball, jogging, bicycling. Office: Dearborn Chem Co 300 Genesee St Lake Zurich IL 60047

CORWIN, BERT CLARK, optometrist; b. Rapid City, S.D., Oct. 4, 1930; s. Meade and Adeline (Clark) C.; m. Lydia M. Forehand; children: Bert C. II, Kelly Linette. AS, S.D. State U., 1952; BS, Ill. Coll. Optometry, Chgo., 1956, OD, 1957. Pvt. practice optometry Rapid City, 1957—; projects chmn. S.D. Lions Sight and Service Found., 1964; chmn. med. adv. com. to S.D. Dept. Pub. Welfare, 1968-76; mem. S.D. Adv. Council for Regional Med. and Health Planning, 1971. Contbr. articles to profl. jours. Pres. Cleghorn PTA, Rapid City, 1968-69, Knife & Fork, Rapid City, 1969-70. Fellow Am. Acad. Optometry (diplomate contact lens sect., local chpt. sec./treas. 1986—, pres. elect); mem. Am. Optometric Assn. (exec. com. 1974-76), S.D. Optometric Soc. (pres. 1970-71), N. Cen. State Optometric Conf. (bd. dirs. 1970-71), Black Hills Optometric Soc. (sec./treas. 1958-69), S.D. State Bd. Examiners (pres. 1982-86). Republican. Methodist. Club: Black Hills (pres. 1963). Lodges: Masons, Elks, Lions (pres. Rushmore chpt. 1961-62). Avocations: skiing, water skiing, hunting, piloting, public speaking. Home: 5436 Timberline Rapid City SD 57702 Office: 810 Mountain View Rd Rapid City SD 57702

CORWIN, EVERETT FRANKLIN, JR., architect; b. Kansas City, Mo., Sept. 23, 1928; s. Everett Franklin and Helen Pearl Marie (Gruver) C.; m. Samira Van der Klok, Jan. 26, 1957; children: Dvak, Shawn. Student, William Jewell Coll., 1947, 49; BArch, U. Kans., 1953, MA in Anthropology, 1986; M in Pub. Adminstrn., U. Mo., Kansas City, 1975. Registered architect, Mo., Kans. Draftsman, designer Howard Needles et al, Kansas City, 1955-56; draftsman L.B. Taylor, Miami, 1957-60; chief draftsman Browne and Buford, Kansas City, 1960-63; project architect Marshall and Brown, Kansas City, 1963-67; architect dept. parks and recreation City of Kansas City, 1967—. Contbr. articles to profl. jours. Served with U.S. Army, 1947-48. Guy I. Bromley Residuary Trust grantee, 1975. Mem. AIA, Soc. Archtl. Historians (founder, pres. Mo. Valley Chpt. 1967), Internat. Assn. Childs Right to Play, Phi Kappa Phi, Phi Gamma Delta. Home: 513 NE 55th St Kansas City MO 64118 Office: City of Kansas City Parks and Recreation Dept 5606 E 63d St Kansas City MO 64130

CORWIN, ROBERT GILBERT, dermatologist; b. Dayton, Ohio, July 27, 1942; s. Charles Frederick Snyder and Josephine Harshaman (Kiefaber) C.; m. Marilyn Louise Nagare, June 21, 1969 (div.); children: Robert P., Michael T. AB, Princeton U., 1964; MD, Case Western Res. U., 1968. Intern then resident internal medicine U. Hosp., Cleve., 1968-70; resident dermatology Cleve. Metro Gen. Hosp., 1972-75, mem. staff; practice medicine specializing in dermatology Cleve., 1975—; mem. staff Southwest Gen. Hosp.; asst. clin. prof. Case Western Res. U., 1975—. Served to maj. USAF, 1970-72. Mem. AMA, Am. Acad. Dermatology, Ohio Med. Assn., Cleve. Dermatology Assn., Cleve. Acad. Medicine, Alpha Omega Alpha. Avocation: horseback riding. Office: 7155 Pearl Rd Middleburg Heights OH 44130

CORY, DELBERT JASON, labor investigator, manufacturing executive; b. New Castle, Ind., Jan. 7, 1934; s. Harold Eugene Cory and Ruth Florence (Thornburg) Kidder; m. Miriam Elaine Bradfield, June 23, 1956; children: Stephen, Nadine, Catherine, Karen. BSME, U.S. Naval Acad., 1956; M Theology, Oberlin (Ohio) Grad. Sch. Theology, 1964; cert. programmer, Brown Inst., Mpls., 1977. Ordained to ministry Christian Ch.; ordained elder Reorganized Ch. of Jesus Christ of Latter-day Saints, 1959. Commd. ensign USN, 1956, advanced through ranks to lt., 1964, line officer, 1956-60, chaplain, 1961-70, served in Korea and Vietnam, 1956-70, resigned, 1970; dir. settlement house Matthews Ctr., Mpls., 1971-73; engring. crib mgr. Control Data Corp., Roseville, Minn., 1974-76; sr. labor investigator Minn. Dept. Labor and Industry, St. Paul, 1976—; pres. Future Trend Industries, Cottage Grove, Minn., 1985—; pastor Reorganized Ch. of Jesus Christ of Latter-day Saints, Elyria, Ohio, 1961-63, com. on ministry to armed forces personnel, 1964-70, com. on war and peace, 1962-64, dir. Christian edn. Minn. dist., 1979-85; chaplain Scientology, Mpls., 1980-86, chmn. camp fire com., St. Paul, 1975-85. Contbr. articles in field to profl. jours. Avocations: canoeing, camping, hiking, fishing. Home: 8346 Isleton Ct Cottage Grove MN 55016 Office: Minn Dept Labor and Industry div Labor Standards 444 Lafayette Rd Saint Paul MN 55101

CORYELL, ORLANDO T., data processing executive; b. Richmond, Ind., June 11, 1931; s. Orlando F. and Lillian (Wesson) C.; m. Caroline Francis Smith, Sept. 19, 1964; children—Jane Ellen, Catherine Rebecca. Ph.B., Northwestern U., 1964; M.B.A., U. Chgo., 1967. Cert. data processing, system profl. Mgr. data processing Chgo. Rawhide, 1968-70; project mgr. Land & Assoc., Chgo., 1970-73; sr. cons. William Kordsiemon Assoc., Chgo., 1973-74; pres. The Colour Shop, Inc., La Grange, Ill., 1974-78, treas., 1978—; v.p. Comp-U-Mart, La Grange, 1982—; pres. Exbridge Group, La Grange; v.p. C.B.I. Assoc., La Grange, 1977-82. Candidate village pres., La Grange, 1973; treas. La Grange Caucus, 1976-78; dir., treas. bd. dirs. Chamber Ballet Ensemble, Evanston, Ill., 1984—. Mem. Assn. Systems Mgmt. (pres. Chgo. chpt. 1971-72, achievement award 1971), Chgo. Lyric Opera. Republican. Lutheran. Avocations: duplicate bridge; boating; travel. Home: 115 S Spring La Grange IL 60525

CORZIN, HAROLD ALLEN, lawyer, educator; b. N.Y.C., Oct. 29, 1946; s. Michael and Sally (Levine) C.; m. Lee Ann Vogel, Sept. 10, 1978. B.A., U. Akron, 1968; J.D., U. Toledo, 1975. Bar: Ohio 1975. Assoc. Nadler, Sokolsky, Bahas, Balantzow & Holub, Akron, Ohio, 1976-78; ptnr. Meador, Corzin & Lowrey and predecessor firm Meador & Corzin, Fairlawn, Ohio, 1978—; instr. Kent State U., Ohio, 1984—; U.S. bankruptcy trustee U.S. Bankruptcy Ct., No. Dist. Ohio, 1976—; asst. atty. gen. State of Ohio, 1980-85. Bd. dirs. United Cerebral Palsy, Akron, 1979. Served with USN, 1968-72. Recipient Am. Jurisprudence award, 1974. Mem. Akron Bar Assn., Ohio State Bar Assn. Democrat. Jewish. Avocation: flying. Home: 2514 Smith Rd Akron OH 44313 Office: Meador Corzin & Lowrey 2770 W Market St Fairlawn Akron OH 44313

COSCO, JOHN ANTHONY, hospital administrator; b. Cin., July 13, 1947; s. Adolph John and Pasqualina Marie (Saluppo) C.; m. Anne Patricia Ward, Aug. 5, 1978; children—Jon Francis, Stephen Ward, Justin Thomas. B.S., Xavier U., Cin., 1969, M.Ed., 1972, M.B.A., 1975; postgrad. U. Cin., 1972, PhD in Health Services, Columbia-Pacific U., 1986. Notary public. Asst. dir. edn. and staff devel. Jewish Hosp., Cin., 1972-77; exec. dir. Region IX Peer Rev. Systems, Inc., Portsmouth, Ohio, 1977-78; exec. dir. Region II Med. Rev. Corp., Dayton, Ohio, 1978-81; asst. adminstr. Mercy Hosp., Tiffin, Ohio, 1981-87, sr. v.p., 1987—; adj. faculty mem. in bus. mgmt. Xavier U., Sinclair Community Coll., Tiffin U.; Bd. dirs. Tiffin Area Physicians Placement Fund.; mem. Seneca County Health Coordinating Council. Served to lt. AUS, 1969-71. Decorated Bronze Star. Mem. Am. Coll. Hosp. Adminstrs., Am. Hosp. Assn., Tiffin C. of C., Ohio Hosp. Assn., 1st Cav. Div.

Assn. Lodges: Elks. Home: 289 Ella St Tiffin OH 44883 Office: 485 W Market St Tiffin OH 44883

COSENTINO, ANTHONY V., controller; b. Columbus, Ohio, Aug. 16, 1961; s. Paul Milton and Barbara Ruth (Van Fleet) C.; m. Lisa Renee Alsip, May 22, 1982. BS in Acctg., Miami U., 1983. CPA, Ill., Ohio. Sr. auditor Continental Ill. Nat. Bank, Chgo., 1983-86; br. controller Bank One, Columbus (Ohio) NA, 1986—. Mem. Am. Inst. CPA's, Ill. Soc. CPA's, Delta Chi. Republican. Roman Catholic. Club: Agonis. Home: 1705 Hickory Creek Ln Columbus OH 43229 Office: Bank One Columbus NA 100 E Broad St Columbus OH 43271-1048

COSENTINO, JERRY, state treasurer; b. Chgo., June 13, 1931; m. Charlotte Cosentino; children: Carla, Carey, Claudia, Carolyn, Collette. Chmn. bd. dirs. Fast Motor Service, Brookfield, Ill.; commr. Met. Sanitary Dist., Chgo., 1975-79; treas. State of Ill., Springfield, 1979-83; dem. committeeman Palos Twp., Palos Heights, Ill., 1979—; treas. State of Ill., Springfield, 1987—. Co-chmn. Com. to Re-elect Pres. Carter, 1980; mem. Field Mus. Bd. Mem. Ill. Citizens Animal Welfare League. Office: Treasurer's Office 219 State House Springfield IL 62706 *

COSENTINO, LOUIS CIRO, biomedical engineer; b. Bklyn., Mar. 23, 1944; s. Louis and Lucy Cosentino; m. Judi Reiss, Sept. 5, 1965; children: Daniel, Lisa, Jack, Allen. BSEE, Poly. Inst. Bklyn., 1965, MSEE, 1967, PhD in Bioengring., 1972. Biomed. engr. Hoffmann La Roche, Nutley, N.J., 1967-69; mgr. profn. devel. Datascope Corp., Saddle Brook, N.J., 1969-70; biomed. engr. Roche Med. Electronics, Cranbury, N.J., 1970-72; dir. advanced research and devel. Medtronic, Inc., Mpls., 1972-74; pres. Minntech., Inc. formerly Renal Systems, Inc., Mpls., 1974—. Patentee in field; contbr. articles on med. instrumentation and biomed. engring. to profl. jours. Named Outstanding Citizen City of Plymouth (Minn.), 1979, One of 10 Outstanding Minnesotans, 1979, One of 10 Outstanding Young Men Am., U.S. Jaycees, 1980. Mem. IEEE, Assn. Advancement Med. Instrumentation, Nat. Assn. Pub. Health Technicians, U.S. Power Squadron (exec. com. Minnetonka chpt. 1980-81). Office: Renal Systems Inc 14905 28th Ave N Minneapolis MN 55441

COSENTINO, PATRICIA LEE, lawyer, accountant; b. Chgo., June 17, 1957; d. James Frank and Dorothy Gladys (Sypniewski) C. BS in Acctg., U. Ill., Chgo., 1979; JD, John Marshall Law Sch., 1985. Bar: Ill.; CPA, Ill. Controller Waste Mgmt., Oakbrook, Ill., 1979-83; gen. counsel, controller Travelers and Immigrants Aid of Chgo., 1983—. Mem. ABA, Ill. Bar Assn., Chgo. Bar Assn., Am. Inst. CPA's, Ill. CPA Soc. Democrat. Roman Catholic. Home: 5241 S Kostner Chicago IL 60632 Office: Travelers & Immigrants Aid Chgo 327 S LaSalle St Suite 1500 Chicago IL 60604

COSGRIFF, ROBERT P., fund raising consultant; b. Iowa City, Feb. 16, 1926; s. Harold F. and Elizabeth (Phelan) C.; student Washington U., St. Louis, 1946-48; B.S.C., U. Iowa, 1950; postgrad. St. Louis U., 1950-51; children—Kevin, Ann, Jean. Mem. Beaver Assos., Chgo., 1954-60; founder, pres. Cosgriff Co., Omaha, 1960—. Served with USMC, 1944-46. Mem. Nat. Soc. Fund Raising Execs., Am. Public Relations Assn., Iowa C. of C. Execs. Assn., Omaha C. of C., Am. Fund Raising Council (dir.), Am. Legion. Clubs: Omaha, Happy Hollow Country, Lake Shore Country. Office: Cosgriff Co 1480 1st Nat Center Omaha NE 68102

COSGROVE, JOSEPH WILLIAM, JR., state agency administrator; b. St. Paul, Sept. 29, 1947; s. Joseph William and Grace Catherine (Streng) C.; m. Lois Jean Johnson, June 5, 1970; children: Bridget, Andrew. BS, St. Cloud State U., 1970, MS, 1971. Adult probation agt. Blue Earth County Cts., Mankato, 1975-77; spl. parole agt. Minn. Dept. of Corrections, Mankato, 1975; correctional counselor Minn. Dept. of Corrections, St. Cloud, 1977-79; sr. correctional counselor Minn. Dept. of Corrections, Stillwater, 1979-86, corrections supr., 1986—. Co-author: Behavioral Analysis of Vocational Dysfunction, 1971. Mem. Minn. Valley Mental Health Ctr. Chem. Dependency Task Force, Mankato, 1975-77. Served to lt. comdr. USCGR, 1977—. Mem. Minn. Assn. Profl. Employees (v.p. 1986—, Disting. Service award 1983, 85), Am. Corrections Assn., Minn. Corrections Assn. (sec. 1985-86), Indsl. Relations Research Assn. Lutheran. Club: Boy Lake Sportsmen's. Avocations: fishing, hunting, camping. Home: 702 N 4th St Stillwater MN 55082 Office: Minn Correctional Facility Box 55 Stillwater MN 55082

COSKY, JUDITH ANN, clinical nurse specialist; b. Farmington, Mich., Jan. 20, 1953; d. Thaddeus Anthony and Elizabeth Joann (Delinski) C. BS in Nursing, Oakland U., 1978; MS in Nursing, Wayne State U., 1982. Registered nurse. Clin. faculty Mercy Coll., Detroit, 1981-82; psychotherapist, researcher U. Mich. Hosps., Ann Arbor, 1982-83; psychotherapist, coordinator infant program Fairlawn Ctr., Pontiac, Mich., 1983-85; referral coordinator Havenwyk Hosp., Auburn Hills, Mich., 1985—; lectr. in field, various locations. Democrat. Roman Catholic. Avocations: tennis, photography, needlepoint. Home: 600 E 14 Mile Clawson MI 48017 Office: Havenwyk Hosp 1525 E University Dr Auburn Hills MI 48057

COSS, JOHN EDWARD, archivist; b. Spring Valley, Ill., Apr. 2, 1947; s. Edward Francis and Doris (Leonard) C.; m. Sherry Lee Ushman, June 4, 1973 (div. May 1979); 1 child, Stephen John; m. Brenda Lynn Gibson, May 30, 1981; 1 stepchild, Anthony Robert. AA, Ill. Valley Community Coll., 1967; BA, Northwest Mo. State U., 1970. Archivist Ill. State Archives, Springfield, 1971-81, records analyst, 1982—. Mem. ASsn. Records Mgrs. and Adminstrs. (cen. Ill. chpt.). Methodist. Avocations: music, reading, golf. Home: 3401 Ridge Ave Lot #29 Springfield IL 62702 Office: Ill Sec State Dept Archives and Records Archives Bldg Springfield IL 62756

COSTANZO, W. KENNETH, chemical company executive; b. Scranton, Pa., Dec. 28, 1952; s. Michael and Josephine Marie (Mecca) C.; m. Linda Abernethy, Feb. 26, 1983. BA in Psychology, Mansfield U., 1973; MS in Corp. Law, Newport U., 1987. Asst. personnel mgr. Schott Technologies, Duryea, Pa., 1974-75; mgr. personnel benefits Zenith Radio Corp., Watsontown, Pa., 1975-78; dir. human resources Dearborn Chem. Co., Lake Zurich, Ill., 1978-81, v.p. human resources, 1981-83; v.p. adminstrn. Dearborn div. W.R. Grace & Co., Lake Zurich, 1983—; cons. Walter V. Clarke Assoc., Providence, 1978—. Mem. Am. Soc. Personnel Adminstrn., Midwest Indsl. Mgmt. Assn., Northwest Indsl. Council, Am. Mgmt. Assn., Internat. Found. Employee Benefit Plans. Republican. Avocations: writing, bowling, golf, sports. Home: 45 Meadow Ln Barrington IL 60010 Office: WR Grace & Co Dearborn Div 300 Genesee St Lake Zurich IL 60047

COSTARELLA, ADAM EARLE, emergency physician; b. Youngstown, Ohio, Apr. 8, 1949; s. Adam Earle and Lucy (Woodley) C. BS in Engring. summa cum laude, Youngstown State U., 1972; MD, Ohio State U., 1975. Diplomat Am. Bd. Internal Medicine, Am. Bd. Emergency Medicine. Resident in internal medicine Cleve. Clinic, 1975-78, peripheral vascular Ds., 1978-79; emergency physician St. Vincent's Charity Hosp., Cleve., 1976-80, Youngstown Hosp. Assn., 1980—. Fellow Am. Coll. Emergency Physicians; mem. AMA, Ohio Med. Assn., Mahoning Valley Med. Assn. Democrat. Avocations: fishing, skiing. Home: 821 Krehl Ave Girard OH 44420

COSTELLO, JOHN MICHAEL JR., insurance executive; b. Cin., May 13, 1961; s. John Michael and Mary Frances (Gessing) C.; m. Rebecca Joan Hiles, Aug. 18, 1984. BBA magna cum laude, U. Cin., 1983. Actuarial analyst Ohio Casualty Ins. Group, Hamilton, 1983—; stringer The Cin. Post, 1979—. Mem. Moeller High Sch. Alumni Assn. (editor, bd. dirs. 1982—, Gold Shield award 1979), Gamma Iota Sigma (alumni assn., treas. 1980-83, Warren L. Weeks scholar 1982). Democrat. Roman Catholic. Avocations: coin collecting, landscaping. Home: 4318 Glenway Ave Cincinnati OH 45236 Office: Ohio Casualty Ins Group 136 N Third St Hamilton OH 45025

COSTELLO, JUDITH ELAINE, corporate professional; b. East St. Louis, Dec. 28, 1946; d. Joseph A. O'Guinn and Lawanda I. (Brooks) Beckman; m. Michael Thomas Costello, Oct. 9, 1965. Grad. high sch., East St. Louis. Office clk. Liberstein Jewelers, East St. Louis, 1965-69; asst. mgr., office buyer Becherer's Jewelers, Belleville, Ill., 1969-76, ptnr., 1976-83; pres. Mike Costello Inc., Belleville, 1981-85; sales assoc. MacGregor Century 21 Realty, Ltd., Fairview Heights, Ill., 1985—. Mem. Ill. Retail Jewelers Assn., Belleville C. of C. Democrat. Roman Catholic. Home and Office: 1908 E C St Belleville IL 62221

COSTIKYAN, ANDREW MIHRAN, film director; b. N.Y.C., Oct. 10, 1922; s. Mihran Nazar and Berthe (Muller) C.; m. Kathryn Reed, Sept. 11, 1948; children: Robert McNeil, Nancy Kathryn. BA, Columbia U., 1943. Dir. photography Encyclopedia Britannica Films, Wilmette, Ill., 1946-55; dir., v.p. VPI of Ill., Chgo., 1964-67; free-lance dir. photography Chgo., 1955-64, 67—; dir., dir. photography, pres. V.I. Prodns. Inc., Northfield, Ill., 1967—. Served to capt. U.S. Army Air Corps, 1943-46, ETO. Mem. Dirs. Guild Am. (nat. bd. dirs. 1979—, v.p. 1971-73, trustee ednl. and benevolent Found. 1981—). Democrat. Avocations: photography, scuba diving.

COSTOFF, THEODORE, hardware company executive; b. 1925. Student, Bryant & Stratton Bus. Coll. Ptnr. Certified Grocers, 1949-55; with Ace Hardware Corp., Hinsdale, Ill., 1957—, chmn. bd., 1983—. Office: Ace Hardware Corp 2200 Kensington Ct Oak Brook IL 60521 *

COTE, BRUCE STEVEN, human resources development manager; b. Burlington, Vt., May 24, 1955; s. Maxim Cote and Nancy Annette (Laramee) Lague. BS, U. Vt., 1978; MEd, Bowling Green State U., 1980; PhD, U. Minn., 1984. Cert. tchr, Vt. Tchr. South Burlington High Sch., South Paul, Vt., 1977-78; equipment designer Durgin & Brown Industries, Burlington, 1979; instr. Bowling Green State U., Ohio, 1980-81; mgr. human resources Hutchinson Technol., Inc., Minn., 1984—; cons. Onan Corp., Fridley, Mn., 1981-84, U. Minn., Mpls., 1981-84; dir. CETA Youth Employment Program, Bowling Green, 1980. Auhtor: Introduction to Technology, 1980; contbr. articles to profl. jours. Tutor Neighborhood Improvement Program, Mpls., 1983-84. Mem. Am. Soc. for Tng. and Devel., Nat. Soc. for Performance and Instrn., Am. Mgmt. Assn. Republican. Roman Catholic. Avocations: woodworking, skiing, tennis, basketball, architecture design. Home: 4808 Sparrow Rd Minnetonka MN 55345 Office: Hutchinson Tech Inc 40 W Highland Park Hutchinson MN 55350

COTE, JOHN CHARLES, hospital administrator; b. Flint, Mich., June 17, 1957; s. Edward John and Doris E. (Bugbee) C.; m. Leslie Anne Richards, Nov. 12, 1983. BS, No. Mich. U., 1979; MS in Bus., Cen. Mich. U., 1985. Adminstrv. asst. Hurley Med. Ctr., Flint, 1980-85, mgmt. engr., 1985, mgmt. analyst, 1986—; adj. prof. bus. adminstrn. Baker Coll., Flint, Mich., 1986—. Named one of Outstanding Young Men of Am., 1985. Mem. Am. Hosp. Assn., Am. Coll. Healthcare Execs., Am. Mgmt. Assn., Hosp. Mgmt. Soc. Am. Hosp. Assn., Mich. Hosp. Mgmt. Soc., Sigma Iota Epsilon. Republican. Roman Catholic. Office: Hurley Med Cr 1 Hurley Plaza Flint MI 48502

COTMAN, ROBERT JOHN, food service company executive; b. Cleve., Oct. 31, 1945; s. John Earnest and Esther Marie (Fleischer) C.; m. Janet Christie Muhleman, Mar. 12, 1982 (div.); 1 son, John Phillip Muhleman. Student U. Mich., 1963-67; B.S., Ohio State U., 1973, M.F.A., 1978. Research assoc. Ctr. for Vocat. Edn., Columbus, Ohio, 1973-75; founder, pres. Group 243 Design, Inc., Ann Arbor, Mich., 1974-81; sr. v.p. Domino's Pizza, Inc., Ann Arbor, 1981-85, also dir.; pres. The Sponsers Report, Inc., 1985—; chmn. bd. Joyce Julius & Assocs. Inc., 1985—, Ashlar Devel., Inc., 1986—; dir. Visual Communications Processes, Inc., Cubecraft Furniture Makers, Inc.; Served with U.S. Army, 1968-70. Decorated Commendation medal. Mem. Am. Inst. Graphic Artists, Ann Arbor C. of C., Sigma Nu. Office: Joyce Julius & Assoc Inc 2010 Hogback Rd Suite 3 Ann Arbor MI 48105

COTNER, DAN BARRETT, dentist; b. Cape Girardeau, Mo., Apr. 11, 1923; s. Barrett and Bertha Alma (Kassel) C.; m. Thelma Paulette Sturgeon, Dec. 25, 1948; children: Danna P., Danice C. Dean, Danel C. Burch, Paul B. DDS, St. Louis U., 1949; BSS, Southeast Mo. State U., 1979. Gen. practice dentistry Cape Girardeau, 1949—; forensic dentist Southeast Mo. Regional Crime Lab., Cape Girardeau, 1972—. Organist Westminster Prebyn. Ch., Cape Girardeau, 1964—; dental rep. Mo. Emergency Preparedness Com., Jefferson City, Mo., 1985, sub-com. med. mortuary, earthquake disaster. Served to 1st lt. USAF, 1951-54. Recipient Dingeldein award Southeast Mo. Arts Council, Cape Girardeau, 1982. Mem. ADA, Mo. Dental Assn., Midwestern Assn. Forensic Scientists (dental coordinator 1983), Mo. Dental Assn., Southeast Mo. Dental Soc. (pres. 1961-62), Am. Guild Organists. Lodge: Rotary (pres. Cape Girardeau 1961-62). Avocations: music, jewelry, fishing, hunting. Home: 1222 Hillcrest Dr Cape Girardeau MO 63701 Office: 310 Broadway 6th Floor Cape Girardeau MO 63701

COTT, BURL GENE, transportation company executive; b. Wichita, Kans., Dec. 2, 1940; s. T. Otho and Leona F. (Binford) C.; m. Marsha J. Thomason, Dec. 27, 1975; 1 son, John. B.A., Wichita State U., 1963. Mgr. Arthur Andersen and Co., Kansas City, Mo., 1963-75; controller Terminal Transport Co., Atlanta, 1975-77; v.p., treas. Am. Freight System Inc., Overland Park, Kans., 1977-80; pres. Sioux Falls Service Ctr. Inc., S.D., 1982—; sr. v.p. Am. Carriers Inc., Overland Park, Kans., 1980—; dir. Am. Freight System Inc., Overland Park, Sioux Falls Service Ctr. Inc. Mem. Am. Trucking Assn. (nat. acctng. finance council), Am. Inst. C.P.A.s. Office: Am Carriers Inc 9393 W 110th St Overland Park KS 66210

COTTELEER, MICHAEL ALEXANDER, lawyer; b. Chgo., Feb. 4, 1944; s. Alexander Charles and Helen Lucille (Schmitt) C.; B.A., No. Ill. U., 1968; J.D. (Alumni scholar), Loyola U., Chgo., 1971; children—Jennifer, Amy, Kevin. Bar: Ill. 1971. Atty. Chgo. Title & Trust Co., 1971-72; atty. firm Herrick, McNeill, McElroy & Peregrine, Chgo., 1972-74, Daniels, Hancock & Faris, Elmhurst, Ill., 1974-75; asst. dean, assoc. prof. law No. Ill. U. Coll. Law, Glen Ellyn, 1975-78; sole practice, Wheaton, Ill., 1978-81, 82—; ptnr. Borenstein, Cotteleer, Greenberg & Young, Chgo. and Wheaton, 1981-82. Bd. dirs. No. Ill. U. Found., 1979—, mem. pres.'s legis. action com., 1978—; bd. dirs. Festival Theater, Oak Park, Ill., 1981-82. Served with U.S. Army, 1962-65. Recipient award for service Ill. Bd. Regents, 1979. Mem. ABA, Ill. Bar Assn. (vice chmn. sect. council on corps. and securities law 1981-82), Chgo. Bar Assn., DuPage County Bar Assn., No. Ill. U. Alumni Assn. (v.p., bd. dirs. 1977-82, pres. 1985—), Sigma Alpha Epsilon. Roman Catholic. Office: 209 N Washington St Wheaton IL 60187

COTTER, BARBARA JOANN, accountant; b. DeKalb, Mo., May 1, 1934; d. Ivyal Paul and Eva Evelyn (Hale) C.; m. Ralph Edward Peasley, Feb. 11, 1952 (div. 1968); children—Rhonda Eileen, Arthur Paul. Student Johnson County Community Coll., 1969-70; B.A., Rockhurst Coll., 1972. Asst. controller Rickel Inc., Kansas City, Mo., 1972-81; acct., mdse. dir. Seaboard Allied Milling, Shawnee Mission, Kans., 1981-82; data processing mgr. Physicians Assoc., Overland Park, Kans., 1982-83; owner, operator B.J. Cotter Services, Shawnee, Kans., 1983—; trust acct. Merrigan & Assocs., Kansas City, 1983-86; sec., treas. Chesen Communications Ctr., Inc., Overland Park, 1986—. Pres. Bonner Springs Jaycee Jaynes, Kans., 1965-66; music dir. children's choir First Christian Ch., 1960. Mem. Am. Bus. Women's Assn. (treas. 1986-87), Nat. Assn. Accts. Republican. Mem. Christian Ch. Clubs: Barcelona Townhomes Assn. (treas. 1976). Lodges: Order Eastern Star, DeMolay Mothers. Avocations: golf; bowling; bridge; reading; acting. Home: 6621 Bluejacket Shawnee KS 66203 Office: BJ Cotter Services 8301 W 95th Shawnee Mission KS 66212

COTTER, DANIEL A., diversified company executive; b. Duluth, Minn., Dec. 26, 1934. B.A., Marquette U., 1957; M.B.A., Northwestern U., 1960. With Cotter & Co., Chgo., 1959—, pres., chief executive officer. Office: Cotter & Co 2740-52 N Clybourn Ave Chicago IL 60614 *

COTTER, JOHN M., diversified company executive; b. 1904. With Dayton's Bluff Hardware Co., 1916-23; salesman Raymer Hardware Co., 1923-28; gen. ptnr. Kohloop Hardware, 1928-31; gen. mdse. mgr. Kelly-How-Thompson Co., 1933-42; v.p., gen. mgr. Oakes & Co., 1942-48; with Cotter & Co., Chgo., 1948 -, chmn. bd. dir., 1978 -. Office: Cotter & Co 2740 N Clybourn Ave Chicago IL 60614*

COTTINGHAM, RICHARD ALLAN, radiologist; b. Hastings, Nebr., Dec. 5, 1934; s. Quentin Clifford and Inez Mae (Schultz) C.; m. Jean Ellen Ashton, Sept. 7, 1956 (div. Sept. 1982); children: Shawna Marie, Kevin Craig. BA, Hastings Coll., 1955; MD, U. Nebr., 1959. Diplomate Am. Bd. Radiology. Intern Nebr. Meth. Hosp., Omaha, 1960; resident in radiology Orange County Med. Ctr., Orange, Calif., 1964-67; staff radiologist Long Beach (Calif.) Vets. Hosp., 1967-68; cons. radiologist Community hosp., McCook, Nebr., 1968—; Cons. radiologist to hosps., S.W. and N.W. Nebr., 1968-83; bd. dirs. Gemini Oil Co., McCook and Denver. Mem. McCook County Airport Adv. Bd., 1981. Served to lt. comdr. USN, 1960-64, S.E. Asia. Mem. AMA, Am. Coll. Radiology (accredited surveyor 1980), Nebr. Med. Assn. (councilor 1980-84), S.W. Nebr. County Med. Soc. (pres. 1970-71), Rocky Mountain Radiol. Soc., Exptl. Aircraft Soc. (life). Lodge: Elks. Avocations: sailing, photography, scuba diving, skiing, poetry writing. Home: Rural Rt 1 McCook NE 69001 Office: Community Hosp Radiology Div 1301 E H St McCook NE 69001

COTTON, HUGH ARTHUR, emeritus educator; b. Allen County, Ind., June 1, 1918; s. Elmer Knox and Mamie (Arnold) C.; m. Helen Mildred Rogers, July 1, 1945; children: Judit Ann Cotton Dorsey, Barry A., Jeffrey A. BS in Pharmacy, Purdue U., 1941; MBA in Bus., U. Colo., 1962. Lic. pharmacist, Ariz., Kans. Pharmacist, asst. dept. head Abbott Labs., North Chicago, Ill., 1941-44; pharmacist Tooele (Utah) Drug Store, 1944-45; pharmacist, ptnr. Elko (Nev.) Drug Store, 1945-46; pharmacist, mgr. Stockman's Hotel Drug Store, Elko, 1946-49; pharmacist Eagle Drug Store, Prescott, Ariz., 1949-50; med. service rep. E.R. Squibb and Sons, N.Y.C., 1950-58; chief pharmacist, instr. sch. pharmacy, Wardenburg Student Health Ctr. U. Colo., Boulder, 1958-68; asst. dean, lectr. sch. pharmacy U. Kans., Lawrence, 1968-70, assoc. dean, assoc. prof., 1968-86, prof. emeritus, 1986—, chairperson various coms., 1974-76, mem. univ. council, 1975-78, mem. scholarly publs. com., 1978, mem. jud. bd., 1982-85; cons. drug studies div. Social Security Adminstrn., HEW, 1972, cons. in field; advisor State Dept. Social Welfare, 1970-72; field dir. Market Measures, Inc., West Orange, N.J. Co-author: Pharmacy Management, A Case Study, 1968; author: Pharmacy Law Review, 1983, Financial Management for Pharmacy, A Course Outline, 1984; editor: Effective Pharmacy Mgmt., 1983; contbr. articles to profl. jours.; developer pharmacy computer programs, 1983; researcher in field. Mem. Am. Pharm. Assn. (policy com. for profl. affairs, 1983-85), Kans. Pharmacist Assn. (govtl. affairs com., third party pay com.), Am. Assn. Colls. Pharmacy, Rho Chi, Kappa Psi. Avocations: computer, photography, traveling, swimming. Home: 926 Wellington Rd Lawrence KS 66044 Office: Univ Kans Sch Pharmacy Lawrence KS 66045

COTTON, STEVEN FORST, engineering executive; b. Bluffton, Ind., Oct. 1, 1950; s. Lyle Jerome and Gladys Rennette (McAfee) C.; m. Judy Ann Croy, Aug. 16, 1969; children Matthew Shane, Joshua Frost, Daniel Croy. B in Indsl. Engring. Tech., Purdue U., 1968-79. Indsl. engr. Bucyrus Erie Co., Polatello, Idaho, 1974-78; mgr. quality control Gen. Electric Co., Ft. Wayne, 1978-79; mgr. tech. services Sheller Globe Corp., Portland, Ind., 1979-82; mgr. design div. Sheller Globe Corp., Detroit, 1982—; mgr. engineering Sheller Globe Corp., Grabill, Ind., 1984—; adv. com. Ind. Vocat. Tech. Coll., Ft. Wayne, 1985—. Patentee in field. Trustee 1st United Meth. Ch., Bluffton, 1984—. Mem. Nat. Rifle Assn. Republican. Club: Parlor City Country (Bluffton). Lodge: Elks. Avocation: golf. Home: 7256 E State Rd 316 Bluffton IN 46714 Office: Sheller Globe Corp PO Box 500 Grabill IN 46741

COTTON, W(ILLIAM) PHILIP, JR., architect; b. Columbia, Mo., July 11, 1932; s. William Philip and Frances Barbara (Harrington) C. AB, Princeton U., 1954; MArch, Harvard U., 1960. Registered architect, Mo. Pvt. practice architecture St. Louis, 1964—. Author (book) 100 Historic Buildings in St. Louis County, 1970. Treas. New Music Circle, St. Louis, 1968—, Pub. Revenue Edn. Council, St. Louis, 1977—. Mem. AIA (Cen. states spl. honor award 1981). Roman Catholic. Club: Valley Sailing (commodore 1985). Home: 5145 Lindell Blvd Saint Louis MO 63108 Office: 217 N 10th St Saint Louis MO 63101

COTTRELL, PHILIP EDGAR, chemical company executive; b. Greenville, Ohio, Jan. 3, 1933; s. William Claude and Lucy Francis (Toman) C.; m. Thelma Louise Turk, July 12, 1951 (div. Apr. 1978); m. Naomi Ruth Campton, Jan. 3, 1980; children: Susan, Tomas, Debra, Joseph. Student, Eastern Mich. U., 1957, Western Mich. U., 1957, John Wesley Coll., 1977. Prison guard State of Mich., Jackson, 1956-64; salesman Hoag Bookbindery, Springport, Mich., 1964-69; ins. agent Cottrell Agy., Jackson, 1969-79; pres., chief operating officer, salesman Hydroplex Chem. Corp., Massillon, Ohio, 1979—. Formulator chem. compounds. Named Top Producer, Sentry Ins. Co., 1972-73. Mem. Gideons Internat. (sec. 1984-85). Baptist. Lodges: Masons (master 1964-65), Lions (sec. 1976-77). Home: 10701 Corundite St NW Massillon OH 44646

COUCH, FRANCES GENE, obstetrician, gynecologist; b. Bremerton, Wash., Dec. 13, 1942; d. Richard Bailey and Harriet Frances (Gilmore) C.; children: Jon Couch, Richard James Zamberlan. BS, Coll. Pharmacy U. Mich., 1967; MD, U. Mich., 1977. Pharmacist VA Hosp., Ann Arbor, Mich., 1967-69; resident in ob-gyn St. Joseph Mercy Hosp., Ann Arbor, 1977-81; practice medicine specializing in ob-gyn Ann Arbor, 1981-87, Boardman, Ohio, 1987—; dir. Womens Health Ctr., Chelsea, Mich. 1986—; Womens Care Ctr., Western Res. Care System, Youngstown, Ohio, 1986—, Menopause Clinic, Saline, Mich. 1986—. Fellow Am. Coll. Ob-Gyn (jr.); mem. Am. Fertility Soc., Am. Med. Assn., Am. Laparoscopy Soc., Am. Laser Soc. Office: 6505 Market St Boardman OH 44512

COUCH, JAMES RUSSELL, JR., neurology educator; b. Bryan, Tex., Oct. 25, 1939; married; 2 children. BS, Texas A&M U., 1961; MD, Baylor U., 1965, PhD in Physiology, 1966; postgrad., Nat. Inst. Neurol. Diseases and Stroke, 1969-72. Diplomate Am. Bd. Psychiatry and Neurology; lic. physician, Tex., Md., Kans., Mo., Ill. Intern Barnes Hosp., St. Louis, 1966-67; resident in neurology Washington U. Sch. Medicine, St. Louis, 1969-72; mem. staff Kans. U. Med. Ctr., Kansas City, asst. prof. div. neurology, 1972-76, assoc. prof., 1976-79; prof., chief div. neurology So. Ill. U. Sch. Medicine, Springfield, 1979—; mem. staff VA Hosp., Kansas City, Mo., Marion, Ill., St. Joseph (Mo.) Hosp., Atchison (Kans.) Hosp., Kansas City Gen. Hosp.; mem. staff Meml. Med. Ctr., Springfield, dir. EEG lab., muscular dystrophy clinic, cons. speech and hearing lab., 1979—; mem. staff St. John's Hosp., Springfield; investigator Mental Retardation Research Ctr. Kans. U. Med. Ctr., Kansas City, 1972-79; dir. postgrad. neurology course Continuing Med. Edn.; examiner Am. Bd. Psychiatry and Neurology, 1975-77, 79, 84-85, Am. Bd. Neurosurgery, 1977; cons. Richland Meml. Hosp., Olney, Ill., 1981-85, Abraham Lincoln Meml. Hosp., Lincoln, Ill., 1981—; staff cons. Lincoln Devel. Ctr., Outpatient Clinics, Lincoln, 1981—; vis. prof. Northwestern U., Chgo., 1982; presenter at profl. confs.; mem. various coms. Kans. U. Med. Sch., 1972-79, So. Ill. U. Sch. Medicine, 1980—. Mem. editorial bd. Headache, 1979—; contbr. numerous articles to profl. jours. Mem. med. adv. bd. Lincoln Land Epilepsy Assn., 1980—. Served to surgeon, USPHS, 1967-69. Recipient award Am. Neurologic Assn.; fellow Nat. Heart Inst., 1965-66, NIH and NIMH, 1967-69; recipient numerous grants for neurology research, 1969—. Fellow Am. Acad. Neurology (asst. sec.-treas. 1985-87, sec.-treas. 1987—), Stroke Council of Am. Heart Assn.; mem. AMA, Am. Assn. for Study of Headache (exec. com. ad hoc 1982, dir. winter headache course, membership com. 1983-85, faculty Continuing Med. Edn. courses 1983-84, edn. com. 1983-85, 86—, achievement recognition com., publs. com. 1986—, bd. dirs. 1983-85, 86—), Am. Geriatric Soc., Am. Assn. Univ. Profs. Neurology, Neurosci. Soc. (sec. Kansas City chpt. 1976-77, pres. 1977-78), Ill. Med. Soc., Sangamon County Med. Soc., Baylor U. Med. Alumni Assn., Washington U. Med. Alumni Assn., Sigma Xi, Alpha Omega Alpha, Phi Eta Sigma, Phi Kappi Phi. Home: 2109 Illini Rd Springfield IL 62704 Office: So Ill Univ Sch of Medicine Dept of Neurology 801 N Rutledge PO Box 3926 Springfield IL 62708

COUCH, TOM, food products company executive. Pres. Early & Daniels Industries, Inc., Indpls. Office: Early & Daniel Co 525 Carr St Cincinnati OH 45203 *

COUEY, DUANE EMERSON, church administrator; b. Milw., Sept. 13, 1924; s. Ralph Emerson and Hazel Viola (Lindsey) C.; m. Edith Rosalyn Griswold, Sept. 6, 1947 (dec. Sept. 1982); children: Patricia Louise, Ralph Floyd. Student, U. Wis., 1946-47; B.A. in Religious Studies, Park Coll., 1978. Lithographer, Moebious Printing Co., Milw., 1942; fabricator Product Miniature Co., Inc., Milw., 1946-54, supt. mfg., 1947-54; ch. adminstr.

Memphis dist. Reorganized Ch. Jesus Christ of Latter Day Saints, 1954-57; asst. to first presidency Reorganized Ch. Jesus Christ of Latter-day Saints, 1958, pres. Los Angeles Stake, 1959-60, mem. council Twelve Apostles, 1960, mem. first presidency, 1966-82, presiding patriarch, 1982—. Contbr. articles to religious jours. Mem. Citizens' Adv. Com. Selection Chief of Police, Independence, Mo., 1968; bd. corporators Independence Regional Health Ctr., trustee, 1966-72. Served with USNR, 1943-51. Mem. U.S. Naval Inst. Office: The Auditorium PO Box 1059 Independence MO 64051

COUGHLAN, KENNETH LEWIS, lawyer; b. Chgo., July 8, 1940; s. Edward James and Mary Virginia (Lewis) C.; m. Therese Koziol, Oct. 11, 1981; 1 son, Kevin Edward. BA, U. Notre Dame, 1962; JD, Northwestern U., Chgo., 1966. Bar: Ill. 1967. Trust officer Am. Nat. Bank & Trust Co., Chgo., 1969-72; sec. bd., sr. v.p., gen. counsel, cashier Cen. Nat. Bank, Chgo., 1972-82; sec., gen. counsel Cen. Nat. Chgo. Corp., 1976-82; sr. v.p., gen. counsel Exchange Nat. Bank, Chgo., 1982-83; gen. counsel Exchange Internat. Corp., Chgo., 1982-83; chmn. bd., pres. Union Realty Mortgage Co., Inc., Chgo., 1981-83; ptnr. DeHaan & Richter P.C., 1983—. Mem. aux. bd. North Ave. Day Nursery, 1980-85. Served to capt. U.S. Army, 1966-68. Fellow Ill. Bar Found.; mem. ABA, Ill. Bar Assn. (chmn. sect. on comml., banking and bankruptcy law 1981-82), Chgo. Bar Assn. (chmn. fin. instns. com. 1980-81, comml. law com. 1979-80). Clubs: Law of Chgo., Chgo. Athletic Assn. Office: DeHaan & Richter 55 W Monroe St Chicago IL 60603

COUGHLIN, JOSEPH JAMES, obstetrician-gynecologist; b. Evergreen Park, Ill., Aug. 15, 1954; s. James F. and Dorothy M. (Motschman) C.; m. Anne Marie McEvoy, May 21, 1976; children: Christopher, Therese. BS summa cum laude, Bradley U., 1976; MD, So. Ill. U., 1979. Diplomate Am. Bd. Ob-Gyns. Resident in ob-gyn. Loyola U. Med. Ctr., Maywood, Ill., 1979-83; pvt. practice specializing in ob-gyn. Resurrection Hosp., Chgo., 1983—, Luth. Gen. Hosp., Park Ridge, Ill., 1984—; clin. instr. ob-gyn. Loyola U., Maywood, 1984—. Fellow Am. Coll. Ob-Gyns. (jr.); mem. AMA, Ill. Med. Soc., Chgo. Med. Soc., Phi Kappa Phi. Office: Resurrection Profl Bldg 7447 W Talcott Suite 405 Chicago IL 60631

COUKOULIS, MARILYN A., social worker; b. Wichita, Kans., July 26, 1941; d. Lynn A. and Marguerite A. (Tally) Johnson; m. Gary Coukoulis, Nov. 24, 1958 (div. Apr. 1967) (dec.); children: Lori Pamela, Gary, Marcus, Monique, Christopher. BA in Psychology, Wichita State (Kans.) U., 1974; MSW, U. Kans., 1979. Lic. specialist clin. social worker, Kans. Income maintenance worker social and rehab. services State of Kans., 1974-76; protective services Dept. Family Services, State of Mo., Kansas City, 1977; acting coordinator transitional living unit Western Mo. Mental Health Ctr., Kansas City, 1979-84; clin. social worker The VA Med. Ctr., Leavenworth, Kans., 1984-85; clin. social worker, family therapist, cons. The Kans. Inst., Olathe, 1985-87; pvt. practice social work Mission, Kans., 1987—; mem. task force Soc. Traumatic Stress Studies, Dayton, Ohio, 1985—. Sr. mem. Univ. Yr. for Action, Wichita State U., 1974; vol. Wichita Area Community Action Program, 1969, Wesley Med. Ctr., Wichita, 1968. NIMH scholar U. Kans., 1978. Mem. AAUW, Nat. Orgn. Women, Nat. Assn. Social Workers (diplomate), Kans. Assn. Social Workers, Registered Clin. Social Workers, Woman's Awareness Orgn., Psi Chi. Democrat.

COULSON, JOHN C(ARL), real estate developer, investor; b. Sullivan, Ind., July 10, 1939; s. M. Allan and Mary Ellen (Thompson) C.; m. Sue Ellen Frew, Nov. 4, 1961; children—Dan T., Jeff A., John A. B.S. in Indsl. Econs., Purdue U., 1961; grad. Realtors Inst., 1979. Cert. residential specialist; lic. real estate broker. Territorial mgr. Hess & Clark div. Vick Chems., Ashland, Ohio, 1961-66; dist. mgr. Allis Chalmers Mfg. Co., Columbus, Ohio, 1966-68, dist. mgr., Lansing, Mich., 1969-70; store mgr. Plantation Supply, Ft. Wayne, Ind., 1968-69; lot mgr. Thomas Mobile Homes, Kokomo and Lafayette, Ind., 1970-71; real estate broker Coldwell Banker/Sycamore-Realty, West Lafayette, Ind., 1971—; pres. New Vintage Homes, West Lafayette, 1977—; owner Vintage Investments, West Lafayette, 1979—; sec. SAE House Corp., West Lafayette, 1979—. Chmn. West Lafayette Parks and Recreation Adv., West Lafayette, 1977. Served with U.S. Army, 1961-62. Mem. Lafayette Bd. Realtors (pres. 1980-81, bd. dirs. 1975-84, Realtor of Yr. 1985) Ind. Assn. Realtors (bd. dirs. 1981-83), Greater Lafayette C. of C. (com. chmn.), Jaycees (v.p. 1971-73, keyman 1972, dir. 1971-73). Republican. Presbyterian (deacon, trustee, elder). Lodges: Kiwanis (bd. dirs. 1974-77), Elks. Home: 619 Wilshire Ave West Lafayette IN 47906 Office: Coldwell Banker/Sycamore-Mason 120 Sagamore Pkwy W West Lafayette IN 47906

COULTER, PAUL DAVID TODD, chemical company executive; b. Dayton, Ohio, Apr. 4, 1938; s. Todd W. and Catherine Jeannett (Starry) C.; m. Geraldine Nelson Miles, June 6, 1959; children: Jerri-Lynn, Catherine Marie Coulter Lambert, Paula Dianne. BS in Chemistry, U. Dayton, 1960; PhD in Analytical Chemistry, U. Kans., 1965. Program mgr. CLF Union Carbide Corp., Parma, Ohio, 1973-76; plant mgr. Union Carbide Corp., Greenville, S.C., 1976-78, Clarksburg, W. Va., 1978-80; pres. UC Grafito Union Carbide Corp., Yabucoa, Puerto Rico, 1980-83; dir. technology Union Carbide Corp., Parma, 1983-86, v.p. technology, 1986—. Patentee Sorption Analysis Apparatus and Method. Mem. Am Chemical Soc., Am. Acad. for Advancement of Sci. Avocations: photography, flying. Home: 23891 Stonehenge Dr Westlake OH 44145 Office: Union Carbide Corp 12900 Snow Rd Parma OH 44130

COULTER, RONALD MILTON, transportation executive; b. Chattanooga, June 30, 1943; s. Bruce Brewer and Opal Lucille (Haynes) C.; m. Syvella Laverne Helms, June 18, 1966; children: Reneé, Cory Helms, Kevin Haynes, John Abel, Julie. BS in Edn., U. Tenn., 1966; M of Forest Resources, U. Wash., 1971. Coordinator of interpretation The Morton Arboretum, Lisle, Ill., 1967-69, 71-78; materials supr. The Major Corp., Northbrook, Ill., 1978-80; materials mgr. Chgo. Fluid Power Corp., Streamwood, Ill., 1980-84; dir. purchases and material Chgo. South Shore & South Bend R.R., Michigan City, Ind., 1984—, Chgo., Mo. and Western R.R., Chgo., 1986—; cons./advisor Endless Summer Tour Corp., Michigan City, 1985—. Author: Spring-flowering Herbaceous Plants of the Morton Arboretum, 1975, Planning a Wilderness Canoe Trip, 1976. Precinct chmn., sec. Lisle Twp. Reps., 1976-78; precinct capt. Palatine (Ill.) Twp. Reps., 1978-80. Mem. Am. Prodn. and Inventory Control Soc., Nat. Assn. Purchasing Mgrs. Mormon. Avocations: photography, bicycling, canoeing, backpacking, fishing. Home: 3876 N 625 West LaPorte IN 46350 Office: Chgo South Shore & South Bend RR N Carroll Ave Michigan City IN 46360

COULTER, THOMAS H(ENRY), former association executive, management consultant; b. Winnipeg, Man., Can., Apr. 21, 1911; s. David and Sarah Anne (Allen) C.; B.S., Carnegie Inst. Tech., 1933; M.A., U. Chgo., 1935; m. Mary Alice Leach, Nov. 24, 1937; children—Sara, Anne, Jane, Thomas II. Investment analyst Shaw & Co., Chgo., 1935-36; sales engr. Universal Zonolite Insulation Co., Chgo., 1936-39, sales promotion mgr., 1939-40, gen. sales mgr., 1940-41, v.p., 1941-45; mgr. devel. div. Booz, Allen & Hamilton, Chgo., 1945-48, partner, 1948-50; pres. Am. Bildrok Co., 1950-54; chief exec. officer Chgo. Assn. Commerce and Industry, 1954-81; exec. v.p. Lester B. Knight & Assos., Chgo., 1981-84; pub. Commerce mag.; lectr. mktg., exec. program U. Chgo.; chair bd. Mytmar & Co., Inc., Chgo.; dir. Chgo.-Tokyo Bank. Mem. State Dept.'s Top Mgmt. Seminar Team, Israel, 1956, Japan, 1958; mem. Dist. Export Council. Mem. Mayor's Commn. Rehab. Persons; mem. Chgo.-Cook County Criminal Justice Commn., Cook County Real Estate Tax Study Commn., Ill. Gov.'s Council on Health and Fitness, Chgo. Dept. Human Services Bd. dirs. Chgo. Crime Commn.; bd. dirs. Chgo. chpt. ARC, 1953-59, USO of Chgo.; mem. citizens bd., council Sch. Bus. Assn.; bd. govs. Internat. House, U. Chgo.; mem. citizens com. U. Ill.; exec. council Chgo. Civil Def. Corps; exec. com. Ill. Council Econ. Edn.; hon. trustee Skokie Valley Community Hosp., pres., 1955-57, 66-70; bd. dirs. Better Bus. Bur. Met. Chgo., Hosp. Planning Council Met. Chgo., Chgo. Council Fgn. Relations; mem. Northwestern U. Assos.; trustee Village of Golf (Ill.), 1951-55; mem. nat. adv. bd. Am. Security Council Edn. Found.; mem. adv. bd. Chgo. Area council Boy Scouts Am.; mem. Cook County Home Rule Commn.; mem. Rehab. Inst. Chgo. Assos.; mem. adv. com. U. Chgo. Met. Inst.; mem. nat. adv. council Nat. Legal Center for Pub. Interest; mem. Cook County Econ. Devel. Adv. Com., Ill. Devel. Bd. Decorated comdr.'s cross Order of Merit (Germany); knight Order of Merit (Italy); knight Order of Lion (Finland); knight 1st class Royal Order of Vasa, comdr. Royal Order Vasa (Sweden); chevalier Nat. Order of Merit (France); 3d class Order of Sacred Treasure (Japan); recipient Silver Ann. All-American award Sports Illustrated, 1957; Outstanding Civilian Service medal U.S. Army, 1961; Gold Badge of Honor for Merits (Austria), 1962, (Province of Vienna), 1971; citation pub. service U. Chgo.; Alumni merit award for outstanding profl. achievement Carnegie Inst. Tech.; Indsl. Statesman award U.S.-Japan Trade Council, 1976; Citizen Fellowship award Inst. Medicine, 1976. Mem. Nat. Sales Execs., Newcomen Soc. N.Am., U.S. C. of C. (banking, monetary and fiscal affairs com.), Nat. Planning Assn., U.S. Olympians (dir. Midwest chpt.), Geog. Soc. Soc. Chgo. (dir.), Internat. Bus. Council, Midwest-Japan Assn., Japan-Am. Soc. Chgo. (dir., pres.), French-Am. C. of C. in U.S. (dir. Midwest chpt.), Am. Austrian Soc. of Midwest, Finnish Am. C. of C. of Midwest, Ill. Assn. C. of C. Execs., Am. Mgmt. Assn., Royal Hort. Soc., Chgo. Hist. Soc., Chgo. Architecture Found, Field Mus. Natural History, Art Inst. Chgo., Mus. Sci. and Industry, Chgo. Council on Fgn. Relations (Chgo. com.), Mid-Am. Swedish Trade Assn., Lambda Alpha. Clubs: Mid-Am., Comml., Execs. (pres. 1950-51), Sales and Mktg. Execs. (pres. 1953-54, award 1979), Internat. Trade, Canadian Univ., Economic, Univ. (Chgo.); Glenview (Golf, Ill.), Circumnavigators.

COULTON, MARTHA JEAN GLASSCOE (MRS. MARTIN J. COULTON), librarian; b. Dayton, Ohio, Dec. 11, 1927; d. Lafayette Pierre and Gertrude Blanche (Miller) Glasscoe; student Dayton Art Inst., 1946-47; m. Martin J. Coulton, Sept. 6, 1947; children—Perry Jean, Martin John. Dir., Milton (Ohio) Union Public Library, 1968—. Active, West Milton (Ohio) Cable TV Com. Named Outstanding Woman Jaycees, 1978-1979. Mem. ALA, Ohio Library Assn., Miami Valley Library Orgn. (sec. 1981, v.p. 1982, pres. 1983), Internat. Platform Assn., West Milton C. of C., DAR. Home: 1910 N Mowry Rd Pleasant Hill OH 45359 Office: 560 S Main St West Milton OH 45383

COUNTS, SAMUEL HAROLD, dentist; b. Lockesburg, Ark., Oct. 12, 1939; s. Willie Henry and Georgie Ada (Thompson) C.; m. Velma Alexander, Nov. 26, 1970 (div. May 1980). BS, U. Detroit, 1975, DDS, 1979. Programmer, analyst Pontiac (Mich.) Schs., 1968-74; dentist, assoc. Harold F. Farrow DDS, Ferndale, Mich., 1979-83; pvt. practice Oak Park, Mich., 1983—. Mem. Oak Park Health Council, 1984—; pres. Oakland County Ednl. Data Processor, Pontiac, 1973. Served with USAF, 1960-64. Recipient Cert. of Appreciation Mich. Consol. Gas, Detroit, 1982, Oak Park Health Council, 1985. Mem. ADA, Mich. Dental Assn., Oakland County Dental Soc., Acad. of Gen. Dentistry. Methodist. Avocations: flying, bowling, hunting, fishing. Office: 25101 Coolidge Oak Park MI 48237

COURECH, ARLETTA BERNICE, advertising salesperson; b. Isle, Minn., Nov. 11, 1924; d. John Bernard and Eda Marie (Ziesmer) Carlson; m. Arnold John Courech (div.); children—Raymond, Greggory, Wendy, Renee. Student Cambridge Bus. Coll., 1965, Macomb County Community Coll., 1966-67, U. Mich.-Dearborn, 1976. Real estate sales staff Durbin Co., Birmingham, Mich., 1973-75; payroll supr. ITT, Oak Park, Mich., 1975-76; new home sales rep. Harry Carlson Assocs., Troy, Mich., 1975-77; furniture sales rep. Montgomery Ward Co., Pontiac, Mich., 1977-83; advertising dir. Women's Clubs Pub. Co., Inc., Chgo., 1983—. Home: 114 Waterly Ave Pontiac MI 48053 Office: Women's Clubs Pub Co Inc 323 S Franklin St Chicago IL 60606

COUREY, FRED SAMUEL, management consultant, former mayor; b. Lennox, S.D.; s. Samuel Thomas and Mabel (Salem) G.; student Lennox pub. schs. With Courey's Food Mart, Inc., Lennox, 1934-83, co-owner, 1946-83; city auditor, Lennox, 1948-50, mayor, 1960-80; with Fred Courey & Assocs., gen. cons., 1983—; past mem. Urbanized Devel. Commn., S.Eastern Criminal Justice Commn., S.Eastern Health Planning Council (all of S.E. Council Govts. S.D.); past mem. S.D. State Local Govt. Study Commn.; past mem. S.D. adv. council SBA, 1969-82, ACE mgmt. assistance counselor, 1969-84. Gen. chmn. Lennox Diamond Jubilee, 1954; past mem. parish council St. Magdalen Roman Cath. Ch., Lennox; project coordinator, program dir. Lennox Area Med. Center, 1975—; past mem. bd. dirs. Lennox Area Devel. Corp. Served with AUS, 1941-45; PTO. Decorated Army Commendation medal. Mem. Am. Water Works Assn., S.D. Water and Wastewater Conf. (past dir.), Am. Fedn. Police, Am. Legion. Small Towns Inst., Smithsonian Instn., Nat. Rifle Assn., Nat. Wildlife Fedn., Early Am. Soc., Lennox L.E.E. Com., Inc. (bd. dirs. 1983—), VFW. Republican. Club: Lennox Comml. (past pres.), Nat. Travel, S.D. Auto. Address: Box 56 Lennox SD 57039

COURNOYER, BARRY ROGER, social work educator, clinical social worker; b. Woonsocket, R.I., Mar. 29, 1947; s. Armand A. and Marjory Martha (Murphy) C.; m. Catherine Hughes; 1 child, John Paul. BS, Middle Tenn. State U., 1973; MSW, U. Tenn., 1974; DSW, U. Utah, 1979. Cert. clin. social worker; diplomate clin. social work; cert. stress mgmt. cons. Clin. social worker Jackson (Tenn.) Mental Health Ctr., 1974-77; assoc. prof. social work Ind. U., Indpls., 1979—; pvt. practice clin. social work Indpls., 1980—. Contbr. articles to profl. jours. Treas. Ind. polit. action com. for human services, 1982-85. Served as sgt. USAF, 1968-72. Mem. Assn. for Advancement of Behavior Therapy, Nat. Assn. Social Workers (treas., bd. dirs., exec. com. Ind. chpt. 1986—), Phobia Soc. Am., Mental Health Assn. of Marion County, Phi Kappa Phi. Home: 8417 Spring Mill Rd Indianapolis IN 46260 Office: Ind U Sch Social Work 902 W New York St Indianapolis IN 46223

COURT, WILMA CONSTANCE GRIFFITHS, social service administrator; b. Dayton, Nov. 1, 1928; d. Edwin Kingsley and Olive Virginia (Flory) Griffiths; m. Robert Frank Court, Mar. 18, 1951; children: Gary Robert, Gayle Lynn, Susan René. BS in Elem. Edn., Eastern Mich. U., 1950, MA in Edn., 1968. Cert. tchr., social worker. Tchr. Plymouth (Mich.) Pub. Schs., 1950-53; tchr. High-Scope Edn. Found., Ypsilanti, 1968-70, researcher, 1977-79; educator Ea. Mich. U., Ypsilanti, 1970-71; dir. homemakers service Child and Family Services, Washtenaw County, Mich., 1971-76; program coordinator Salvation Army, Washtenaw County, 1980-85; program dir. Cornerstone Ctr., Washtenaw County, 1984—, Christian Horizons, Inc. of Mich., Washtenaw County, 1984—; cons. student-parent services, Ann Arbor, Mich., 1982-84; counseling Family Life Services, Ann Arbor, 1986—. Exec. bd. County Council on Aging, Ann Arbor, 1974-76; pres. bd. dirs. Mich. Assn. Community Councils, Ann Arbor, 1980-82; pres. Huron Valley Nursery Sch. Council, Washtenaw County, Mich., 1967. Republican. Avocations: folk art, oil painting. Home: 547 Brookside Ypsilanti MI 48197

COURTNEY, KATHIE SUE, athletic trainer/consultant; b. Aberdeen, S.D., Aug. 4, 1952; d. Robert Charles and Margaret Malvena (Day) Demery; m. Robert James Courtney, Jr., Mar. 22, 1975; children—Amanda Kathleen, Patrick Michael, Alicia Marie. B.S., S.D. State U., 1974; M.S., Ind. State U., 1975. Grad. asst. trainer Ind. State U., Terre Haute, 1974-75; tchr., coach, trainer West Vigo High Sch., West Terre Haute, Ind., 1975-76; athletic trainer/instr. Dakota State Coll., Madison, S.D., 1976—; athletic trainer cons. Madison High Sch., 1981—, S.D. State U., 1976—, Parent Tchr. Orgn. Mem. Am. Legion Aux., Am. Heart Assn., S.D. Athletic Trainers Assn. (pres. 1985—), Nat. Athletic Trainers Assn., S.D. Emergency Med. Tech. Assn., AAUW (membership v.p.). Democrat. Roman Catholic. Clubs: Dakota State Coll. Women's (pres. 1978-79). Home: 209 NW 7th St Madison SD 57042 Office: Room 8 Fieldhouse Dakota State Coll Madison SD 57042

COURTNEY, NELSON WARN, physician, radiologist; b. Kalamazoo, June 19, 1936; s. Nelson J. and Gladys M. (Warn) C.; m. Jean Louise Hilton, June 24, 1961; children: Catherine, Susan, Karen. BA, Kalamazoo Coll., 1958; MD, U. Mich., 1963. Cert. Am. Coll. Radiology. Intern Blodgett Meml. Hosp., Grand Rapids, Mich., 1963-64; resident U. Mich. Hosp., 1964-67; radiologist Kalamazoo Radiology P.C., 1969—; chief of radiology Bronson Meth. Hosp., Kalamazoo, 1974-76, 80-82; vice chief of staff Bronson Meth. Hosp., 1984-86, chief of staff, 1986—, trustee, 1984—; bd. dirs. Bronson Clin. Investigation Unit, Kalamazoo, Southwestern Mich. Area Health Edn. Ctr., Kalamazoo. Served to capt. USAF, 1967-69. Mem. AMA, Mich. State Med. Soc. (del. 1976-86, jud. commn.). Republican. Roman Catholic. Club: Kal-Country. Avocations: tennis, bird watching, chess, travel. Home: 1410 Holiday Ln Kalamazoo MI 49008 Office: Kalamazoo Radiology PC 524 S Park St Kalamazoo MI 49007

COURTOIS, STEPHEN VINCENT, psychologist; b. Cape Girardeau, Mo., Nov. 27, 1941; s. Gilbert Vincent and Chloe Henrietta (Chappuis) C.; m. Joyce Ann Baker, Feb. 26, 1977; children: Michael, Matthew. BS, S.E. Mo. State U., 1964; MA, N.E. Mo. State U., 1967; PhD, U. Mo., Kansas City, 1973. Registered psychologist, Ill. Psychologist St. Joseph (Mo.) Schs., 1973-74, Thresholds, Chgo., 1974-75, Moultrie County Counseling, Sullivan, Ill., 1975-78; coordinator, psychologist Decatur (Ill.) Mental Health, 1978—; Mem. Regional Tng. Com., Champaign, Ill., 1976—; cons. psychologist Human Service Orgn., Decatur, 1980-85, R.B. King Found., Decatur, 1985—; adj. prof. Millikin U., Decatur, 1986—; cons. psychologist Pratt County Mental Health Ctr., Monticello, Ill., 18-986—. Pres. Cath. Charities, Decatur, 1986—; chmn. St. Patrick's Ch. bldg. com., Decatur, 1986—. Mem. Am Psychol. Assn. (Am. Law Soc. div., family psychology div.), Am. Soc. Clin. Hypnosis, Cen. Ill. Psychol. Soc. Club: Camera (Decatur) (pres. 1979-80). Avocation: photography. Home: 256 S Austin Decatur IL 62522 Office: Decatur Mental Health Ctr 2300 N Edward Decatur IL 62526

COURTRIGHT-WHYTE, PAUL, retired optometrist; b. Kimberly, Idaho, Jan. 4, 1914; s. John Joseph and Mary Della (Courtright) W.; m. Betty Jane Ripley, July 31, 1947; children: Daniel Paul, Deborah Jane Bowers, Dallas Courtright, Darcy Dell McGraw, Diana Dee. Student, N.D. State U., 1931-34; OD, No. Ill. Coll. Optometry, 1940; grad. advanced AUS mil. govt. career course, Ft. Gordon, Ga., 1956; BS, U. Wis., 1972. Salesman Lever Bros. Co., Cambridge, Mass., 1937-38; pvt. practice optometry Oshkosh, Wis., 1940-85; pres. Oshkosh Swimpool, Inc., 1958-59; exec. dir. Trautmann-Lee Natural Food Fund, Inc., Oshkosh, 1963—. Author: A 21st Century Philosophical Handbook for Living, 1973; lectr. philosophy and use of health practices including natural foods; contbr. articles to jours. and mags. Active City-County Taxpayers Union, Oshkosh, 1972—; chmn. Winnebago County Democratic Orgn., 1964. Served with AUS, WWII; retired lt. col. res. Mem. Natural Food Assn. (pres. Wis. chpt. 1987—). Lodge: Toastmasters (founding pres. 1955), Optimists (founding pres. 1948). Address: 317 Waugoo Ave Oshkosh WI 54901

COUSINS, ALBERT NEWTON, sociology educator; b. Cleve., May 7, 1919; s. Harry and Anna (Roth) C.; m. Rose Demetra Manitsas, May 18, 1944; children—Julia, Daniel. A.B., Ohio State U., 1942; M.A., Harvard U., 1949, Ph.D., 1951. Asst. prof. sociology Fla. State U.-Tallahassee, 1949-51; asst. prof. to prof. sociology Fenn Coll., Cleve., 1951-65; prof. sociology Cleve. State U., 1965—; co-dir. NDEA tng. project, 1966-69; dir. Anti-Poverty Inst., Cleve., 1967. Pres. bd. trustees United Area Citizens Agy., Cleve., 1978-82; bd. dirs. Citizen's League for Nursing, 1979-83. Recipient Disting. Faculty award Cleve. State U., 1985-86. Mem. Am. Sociol. Assn., N. Central Sociol. Assn., Phi Beta Kappa. Author: Urban Life, 1979; editor; Urban Man and Society, 1970. Contbr. articles to profl. jours. Home: 2595 Charney Rd University Heights OH 44118 Office: Cleve State Univ Cleveland OH 44115

COUTO, C. DOUGLASS, military officer; b. Feb. 28, 1950; s. Edward D. and Darlene D. (Douglass) C.; m. Katharine E. Couto, Aug. 18, 1973. BBA in Indsl. Relations, U. Iowa, 1972; MSA in Govtl. Adminstrn., George Washington U., 1976, MBA, 1983. Commd. USAF, 1972; chief of base adminstrn. communications USAF, Langley AFB, 1972-75, commdr. squadron sect., 1975-77; exec. support officer USAF, Washington, 1977-81, asst. prof. aerospace studies Howard U., 1981-84; hdqrs. squadron commdr., chief of staff USAF, Thule Air Base, Greenland, 1984-85; dir. adminstrn. hdqrs. strategic communications USAF, Offutt AFB, Nebr., 1985—; instr. bus. adminstrn. Park Coll., Hampton, Va., 1977-79; instr. mgmt. No. Va. Community Coll., Alexandria, 1978-81; instr. exec. writing program, Pentagon, Washington, 1979-81. Founder, editor The Air Force Adminstr., 1977-81; speaker, lectr. on mgmt. and leadership. Advisor Andrew D. Turner Squadron Arnold Air Soc., Washington, 1983-84; mem. speakers' bur. Presdl. Inaugural Com., Washington, 1981. Recipient Dist. award of Merit Boy Scouts Am., 1976. Mem. Air Force Assn., Eagle Scout Alumni Assn., Am. Legion (Americanism award 1977), Alpha Phi Omega. Lodge: Toastmasters Internat.(area gov., div. lt. gov., ed. lt. gov., adminstrv. lt. gov., Disting. Toastmaster award 1981). Avocations: racquetball, stamp collecting, speechwriting. Home: 5102 Underwood Ave Omaha NE 68132 Office: HQ SCD/KSD Offutt AFB NE 68113

COUZIN, SHARON, filmmaker; b. Detroit, Apr. 19, 1943; d. Joseph and Ruth Barnes; m. Dennis Couzin, July 17, 1965; children: Nimbus, Odilon, Gradiva. BFA, Sch. of Art Inst. Chgo., 1976, MFA, 1977. Prof. film U. Calif., Santa Barbara, 1975-77; assoc. prof. film Sch. of Art Inst. Chgo., 1978—; freelance filmmaker, Santa Barbara and Chgo., 1975-86; vis. artist San Francisco Art Inst., 1980-81; vis. prof. film U. Wis., Milw., 1984. Films include Roseblood, 1975, Deutschland Spiegel, 1980, Salve, 1981, A Trojan House, 1981, Odilon Odilon, 1985, Pauline, 1985, Shells and Rushes, 1987. Judge various nat. film festivals; panelist regional NEA Dayton-Hudson Found. and Ill. Arts Council; pres. Exptl. Film Coalition, Chgo., 1983—. Fellow Ill. Arts Council, 1981, 83, 84, 85; grantee NEA, 1984. Avocations: photography, organic gardening. Office: Sch of Art Inst Chgo Jackson and Columbus Chicago IL 60603

COVERT, CALVIN C., manufacturing company executive; b. 1924. With Woodward Governor Co., Rockford, Ill., 1942—; supr. green house and ground, asst. sec., 1970-75, chmn. bd., chief exec. officer, 1976—, pres., 1982—. Office: Woodward Governor Co 5001 N 2nd St Rockford IL 61125 *

COVERT, RICHARD PERRY, hospital association executive; b. Rapid City, S.D., May 26, 1928; s. Simon Perry and Eda Luella (Edzards) C.; m. Mary Jean Mertz, Aug. 6, 1961; children: Ralph Scott, Cheryl Ann, Nancy Elizabeth. Student, Norfolk Jr. Coll., 1946-47; BSEE, Iowa State Coll., 1950; MS, U. Iowa, 1959, PhD, 1964. Jr. engr. Iowa-Ill. Gas & Electric Co., Davenport, 1950-51; asst. engr. Moline, Ill., 1952-54, Iowa City, 1955; design engr. Convair, Ft. Worth, 1956; instr. mech. engring. U. Iowa, Iowa City, 1957-61; assoc. prof. indsl. engring. U. Mo., Columbia, 1961-67; prof. mech engring. S.D. State U., Brookings, 1967-73; vis. assoc. prof. U. Iowa, 1973-74; with Am. Hosp. Assn., Chgo., 1974—, from assoc. dir. to dir. Ctr. for Hosp. Mgmt. Engring., 1976-83, dir. Hosp. Mgmt. Systems Soc., 1978—. Contbr. articles on engring. to profl. jours. Served with USN, 1945-46, 51-52. Mem. Inst. Indsl. Engrs. Republican. Mem. United Ch. of Christ. Office: Am Hosp Assn 840 N Lake Shore Dr Chicago IL 60611

COVEY, FRANK MICHAEL, JR., lawyer; b. Chgo., Oct. 24, 1932; s. Frank M. and Marie B. (Lorenz) C.; m. Patricia Ann McGill, Oct. 7, 1961; children: Geralyn, Frank Michael III, Regis Patrick. BS with honors, Loyola U., Chgo., 1954, JD cum laude, 1957; SJD, U. Wis., Madison, 1960. Bar: Ill. 1957, U.S. Supreme Ct. 1965. Research assoc. Wis. Gov.'s Com. on Revision Law of Eminent Domain, 1958; law clk. Ill. Appellate Ct., 1959; assoc. Belnap, Spencer, Hardy & Freeman, Chgo., 1959-60; assoc. McDermott, Will & Emery, Chgo., 1960-64, ptnr., 1965—, mem. exec. com., 1979-81, mgmt. com., 1979-82; instr. Northwestern U. Sch. Law, 1958-59, Loyola U. Coll., 1958-69, 79-80; assoc. gen. counsel Union League Civic and Arts Found., 1967-69, v.p., 1969-72, 73-75, pres., 1972-73, mng. dir., 1975-80; co-dir. Grant Park study team Nat. Commn. on Causes and Prevention of Violence, 1968. Author: Roadside Protection Through Access Control, 1960, (with others) Federal Civil Practice in Illinois, 1974, 6th edit., 1987, Business Litigation I: Competition and Its Limits, 1978, Class Actions, 1979, 2d edit., 1986, Architect and Engineer Liability; Claims Against the Design Professional, 1987; contbr. articles to profl. jours. Mem. bd. athletics Loyola U., 1970-72, mem. estate planning com., 1969-81, mem. com. on the future of the law sch., 1975-76, trustee, 1979—, mem. citizens bd., 1979—; bd. dirs. Chgo. Bldg. Congress, 1978-82, sec., 1982-84; mem. revenue adv. com. Chgo City Council, 1983-84; mem. Spl. Commn. on Adminstrn. Justice in Cook County, 1984—. Recipient Conf. on Personal Fin. Law award, 1955, Founders Day award Loyola U., 1976, Disting. Service award Loyola U. Dept. Polit. Sci., 1979, Disting. Service award Loyola U. Dept. Socio-legal Studies, 1980, Excellence medal Loyola U. Law Sch., 1979. Charter fellow Ill. Bar Found.; mem. ABA, Ill. State Bar Assn. (Lincoln award 1963, Bd. Govs. award 1986), Chgo. Bar Assn., Fed. 7th Circuit Bar Assn., Catholic Lawyers Guild, Chgo. Council Lawyers, Am. Judicature Soc., North Shore Bd. Realtors (affiliate), Internat. Assn. Defense Counsel, Def. Research Inst., Ill. Hist. Soc., Air Force Assn., U.S. Navy League, Loyola U. Alumni Assn. (pres. 1965-66), Loyola U. Law Sch. Alumni Assn. (chmn. alumni fund campaign 1967-68, v.p. alumni 1968-69, pres. 1969-70, chmn. Thomas More Club 1973-75; award 1957), Western Soc. Engrs. (assoc.), Chgo. Architecture Found., The Forum for Architecture, Blue Key, Phi Alpha Delta, Alpha Sigma Nu, Pi Gamma Mu, Delta Sigma Rho. Clubs: Union League (Chgo.) (bd. dirs. 1977-80, chmn. house com. 1977-80), Legal (Chgo.), Law (Chgo.). Home: 1104 W Lonnquist Blvd Mount Prospect IL 60056 Office: McDermott Will & Emery 111 W Monroe St Chicago IL 60603

COVEY, GERALD GRANT, construction company executive; b. Euclid, Ohio, May 1, 1931; s. Gerald Grand and Edith Althea (Tiffany) C.; m. Gail Ramsdell, Dec. 28, 1963; children: Christopher R., Carrie A., Cathy L., Kellie A. Student, Miami U., Oxford, Ohio, 1950-53, Case Inst. Tech., 1953-54, Fenn Coll., 1958-64. Pres. Gerald G. Covey Co., Rocky River, Ohio, 1957—; mng. ptnr. Covey 57, Rocky River, Ohio, 1970—; v.p. Rossborough Mfg. Co., Cleve., 1973-75, Wescon Inc., Lakewood, Ohio, 1976080; gen. mgr. Esch Constrn. Co., Cleve., 1975-80; owner, mgr. James Hardware Co., Rocky River, Ohio, 1979—. Served with U.S. Army, 1954-57. Mem. Builders Exchange, Cleve. Growth Assn., C. of C. Republican. Methodist. Clubs: Avon Oaks Country, River Oaks Racquet, Founders and Patriots. Lodges: Masons, Kiwanis. Home: 21040 Lake Rd Rocky River OH 44116 Office: The Gerald G Covey Co 20119 Lake Rd Rocky River OH 44116

COVINGTON, CALVIN BLACKWELL, agricultural association administrator; b. Winston-Salem, N.C., Sept. 24, 1955; s. Calvin Roger and Ruth (Walker) C.; m. Lorraine Simms, Mar. 29, 1980. BS, N.C. State U., 1977. Area rep. Am. Jersey Cattle Club, Columbus, Ohio, 1977-78, equity specialist, 1978-82, exec. asst., 1982-84, asst. sec., 1984—, treas., 1985—. Deacon Ch. of Christ, Columbus, 1984-86, com. chmn., 1985—. Mem. World Jersey Bur., Dairy Shrine, N.C. State Wolfpack Club, N.C. State Alumni Assn., Jaycees (Columbus chpt. bd. dirs. 1984), Wis. Jersey Breeder Assn. (Disting. Service award 1987). Republican. Avocation: farming. Home: 470 Beaver Ave Columbus OH 43213 Office: Am Jeney Cattle Club 2105 S Hamilton Columbus OH 43227

COVINGTON, GEORGE MORSE, lawyer; b. Lake Forest, Ill., Oct. 4, 1942; s. William Slaughter and Elizabeth (Morse) C.; m. Shelagh Tait Hickey, Dec. 28, 1966; children: Karen Morse, Jean Tait, Sarah Ingersoll Covington. AB, Yale U., 1964; JD, U. Chgo., 1967. Assoc. Gardner, Carton & Douglas, Chgo., 1970-75, ptnr., 1976—; Pres. Chgo. Acad. Scis., 1982-84; bd. dirs., sec. Grant Hosp., Chgo., 1976—. Trustee Ill. Chpt. Nature Conservancy, Chgo., 1974—; bd. dirs. Open Lands Project, Chgo., 1972-86. Served with U.S. Army, 1967-69. Mem. ABA, Ill. Bar Assn., Chgo. Bar Assn., Lambda Alpha. Club: University (bd. dirs. 1985—), Cliff Dwellers (Chgo.); Shoreacres (Lake Bluff, Ill.), Les Cheneaux (Cedarville, Mich.). Office: Gardner Carton & Douglas 321 N Clark St Chicago IL 60610

COVINGTON, JEFFREY LEROY, school systems administrator; b. Washington, Aug. 8, 1958; s. Ethel (Covington) Mason. BEd, Youngstown State U., 1979; postgrad., Kent State U., 1984. Phys. edn. instr. Leonard Kirtz Sch., Youngstown, Ohio, 1980-83; minority recruiter Trumbull Campus, Kent State U., Warren, Ohio, 1984-85; phys. edn. instr. Ashtabula (Ohio) Sch., 1983-85, asst principal, 1985—. Active Big Bros. Am., Youngstown, 1981. Named one of Outstanding Young men Am., Montgomery, 1985. Mem. Assn. Secondary Sch. Adminstrs., Nat. Alliance Black Educators Inc., Phi Delta Kappa. Democrat. Baptist. Office: 1231 W 47th St Ashtabula OH 44004

COVINGTON, PATRICIA ANN, educator, program director, artist; b. Mount Vernon, Ill., June 21, 1946; d. Charles J. and Lois Ellen (Combs) C.; m. Burl Vance Beene, Aug. 10, 1968 (div. 1981). BA, U. N.Mex., 1968; MS in Ed., So. Ill. U., 1974, PhD, 1981. Lab dir. Anasazi Origins Project, Albuquerque, 1969; tchr. pub. schs., Albuquerque, 1969-70; teaching asst. So. Ill. U., Carbondale, 1971-74, prof. art, 1974—; dir. Artist of the Month for U.S. rep. Paul Simon, Washington, 1974-81; vis. curator Mitchell Mus., Mount Vernon, Ill., 1977-83; panel mem. Ill. Arts Council, Chgo., 1982; faculty advisor European Bus. Seminar, London, 1983; edn. cons. Ill. Dept. Aging, Springfield, 1978-81, Apple Computer, Cupertino, Calif., 1982-83. Exhibited papercastings in nat. and internat. shows in Chgo., Fla., Calif. Tenn. N.Y. and others, 1974—; author: Diary of a Workshop, 1979, History of the School of Art at Southern Ill. Univ. at Carbondale, 1981. Bd. dirs. Humanities Council John A. Logan Coll., Carterville, Ill., 1982—. Grantee Kresge Found., 1978, Nat. Endowment for the Arts, 1977, 81; named Outstanding Young Woman of Yr. for Ill., 1981. Fellow Ill. Ozarks Craft Guild (bd. dirs. 1976-83); mem. Ill. Higher Edn. Art Assn. (chmn. bd. dirs. 1978-85), Ill. Art Edn. Assn., Am. Craft Council, Nat. Art Edn. Assn., Coll. Art Assn., Phi Kappa Phi. Presbyterian. Home: 352 Lake Dr Rt 6 Murphysboro IL 62966 Office: So Ill Univ Sch of Art Carbondale IL 62966

COVY, KAREN ANN, lawyer; b. Detroit, June 4, 1959; d. Stanley F. and Helene (Lach) C. BA, Western Mich. U., 1981; certificat d'etudes, L'institute de Tourraine, Tours, France, 1980; JD, Notre Dame U., 1984. Bar: Ill. 1984. Assoc. Querrey, Harrow, Gulank & Kennedy (name now Querrey & Harrow, Ltd.), Chgo., 1984—. Mem. ABA, Ill. Bar. Assn., Chgo. Bar Assn., Ill. Def. Council, Am. Trial Lawyers Assn. Office: Querrey Harrow Gulanik & Kennedy 135 S LaSalle Chicago IL 60603

COWHERD, LONNIE PHILIP, youth services coordinator; b. Columbia, Ky., July 13, 1947; s. Robert Louis and Edna Woodrun (Bault) C.; m. Gwendolyn Gwen Schock, Feb. 10, 1968; children: Alexander, Melanie, Manda, Shanda. BA, S.D. Wesleyan U., 1969; MEd, S.D. State U., 1971. Cert. tchr., counselor. Tchr. Tri-Valley Schs., Lyons, S.D., 1969-70; secondary counselor, tchr. Bristol (S.D.) Sch., 1970-71; sr. employment counselor Work Incentive Program, Duluth, Minn., 1971-79; counselor statewide vocat. sch. program Minn. Dept. Econ. Security, St. Paul, 1979-80; program analyst Minn. Work Equity Program, St. Paul, 1980-81; youth program coordinator Minn. Job Service, St. Paul, 1981—; employment tchr. St. Thomas Coll., St. Paul, 1982—; youth cons. Minn. Dept Jobs and Tng., 1983-86. Author tng. manual Job Seeking Skills, 1979. Mem. Minn. Assn. Counseling and Devel. (govt. relations com. 1985—). Democrat. Lutheran. Avocations: collecting stamps and coins, outdoors work. Office: Minn Job Service 390 N Robert 1st Floor Saint Paul MN 55101

COWLE, ARCH E., surgeon; b. Madison, Wis., Aug. 29, 1920; s. Arch Evan and Blanche E. (Stotts) C.; m. Janice Sherritt, Dec. 18, 1943; children: Patricia Sue, Jennifer Lee, Bonnie Ann. BA, U. Louisville, 1942, MD, 1944. Diplomate Am. Bd. Orthopedic Surgery. Intern Oak Knoll Naval Hosp., Oakland, Calif., 1944-45; resident in gen. surgery Louisville Gen. Hosp., 1946-48, resident in orthopedic surgery, 1948-50; resident in orthopedic surgery Kosair Childrens' Hosp., Louisville, 1950-51; clin. asst. dept. orthopedic surgery U. Wis., Madison, 1973-80; practice orthopedic surgery Madison, 1951—. Served to lt. USN, 1944-46, PTO, 1953-54. Mem. Am. Acad. Orthopedic Surgeons, Clin. Orthopedic Soc., Am. Med. Assocs., Wis. Orthopedic Soc. Avocations: water colors, drawing, gardening. Home: 2358 Fitchburg Rd Verona WI 53593 Office: Quisling Clinic 2 W Gorham St Madison WI 53703

COX, BERT G., apparel company executive. Pres. Joseph & Feiss Co., Cleve. Office: Phillips-Van Husen Corp 1290 Ave of Americas New York NY 10104 *

COX, CHARLES EDWARD, data processing executive, consultant; b. Indpls., Feb. 1, 1960; s. H. Keith and Loraine (Loomis) C.; m. Lisa Sue York, July 17, 1982. BS, Ball State U., 1982, MBA, 1984. Computer systems analyst Ameritech Services, Arlington Heights, Ill., 1984-85; cons. info. ctr. Elgin, Ill., 1985-87; asst. mgr. Decision Support Systems, Schaumburg, Ill., 1987—. Author: PC, WP and You, 1983. Avocations: running, weight tng., personal computers. Home: 845 St John Elgin IL 60120 Office: 1900 E Golf Rd Schaumburg IL 60195

COX, CONSTANCE MARIE, accountant; b. Danville, Ill., July 12, 1962; d. W. Dean and M. Christine (Campbell) C. BS, U. Ill., 1984. CPA, Ill.; cert. mgmt. acct. Cost acct. Carle Hosp., Urbana, Ill., 1984-87; sr. acct. Fearn Internat., Franklin Park, Ill., 1987—. Mem. Am. Inst. CPA's, Am. Women's Soc. CPA's, Ill. State Soc. CPA's. Avocations: flag football, reading, cooking. Home: 1098 Tamarack Apt #509 Mount Prospect IL 60056 Office: Fearn Internat 9353 Belmont Franklin Park IL 60131

COX, DAVID CARSON, communications executive; b. Orange City, N.J., July 31, 1937; s. Earl Byron and Ruth Elinor (Carson) C.; m. Vicki Bever, Aug. 29, 1959; children: Brian Bever, Carson Burns. A.B., Stanford U., 1959; M.B.A., Harvard U., 1961. Internat. v.p. Lawry's Foods, Inc., Los Angeles, 1962-72; mktg. mgr., dir. planning, corp. sec. Lawry's Foods, Inc., Paris, 1972-75; v.p., gen. mgr. internat. div. Litton Microwave Cooking Products, Mpls., 1975-78; v.p., gen. mgr. consumer products div. The Toro Co., Mpls., 1979-81; exec. v.p., chief operating officer Cowles Media Co., Mpls., 1981-84, pres., chief operating officer, treas., 1984-85; pres., chief exec. officer Cowles Media Co., 1985—, corp. sec., 1983-84, dir., 1982—; dir. Nat. Computer Systems. Bd. dirs. Spring Hill Ctr., 1981—; bd. dirs. Guthrie Theater, 1977—, v.p., 1982, pres., 1983-85, chmn., 1985—; bd. dirs. Minn. Bus. Partnership, Inc., 1985—. Served to lt. U.S. Army, 1962-64. Mem. Greater Mpls. C. of C. (dir. 1981—, exec. com. 1985, 1st vice chmn. 1986, vice chmn. transp. div.), Council Fgn. Relations Mpls., Harvard Bus. Sch. Club, Stanford Alumni Club. Club: Minneapolis. Office: Cowles Media Co 329 Portland Ave Minneapolis MN 55415 *

COX, DAVID EUGENE, federal agency administrator; b. Eldon, Mo., Aug. 2, 1949; s. C. Wayne and Berlie M. (Greenway) C.; m. Anita Marie Cox, Jan. 24, 1970; 1 child, Timothy E. BS in Agronomy, U. Mo., 1972. Asst. county dir. Agrl. Stblzn. Conservation Service USDA, Columbia, Mo., 1976-77; asst. county supr. Farmers Home Administrn. USDA, Columbia, Mo., 1977-79; county supr. Farmers Home Administrn. USDA, Fayette, Mo., 1979-87; farmer program specialist Farmers Home Administrn. USDA, Columbia, 1987—. Served with USNG, 1970-76. Mem. Mo. Soc. Rural Appraisers and Farm Mgrs., Columbia Jaycees. Avocations: woodworking, horse riding, water skiing. Home: Rt 1 Box 170 Harrisburg MO 65256 Office: USDA Farmers Home Administrn 555 Vandiver Dr Columbia MO 65202

COX, DAVID FRANK, chiropractor, radio executive; b. Kenosha, Wis., Mar. 3, 1946; s. Charles Russell and Ellen E. (Fortimo) C.; m. Sandra Louise Ingram, Aug. 7, 1971 (div.); children—Aimee, Angela, Amanda. A.A., Kemper Mil. Sch., 1966; B.S. in Human Biology, D. Chiropractic, Nat. Coll. Chiropractic, 1973. Diplomate Nat. Bd. Chiropractic Examiners, Am. Bd. Chiropractic Cons.; lic. chiropractor Ill., Ind. Pvt. practice chiropractic physician, Winchester, Ind., 1974-76, Lansing, Ill., 1976—; sec., treas. DBC Broadcasting, 1982, also dir.; owner, operator sta. WDND-FM, Wilmington, Ill., 1982—; ins. cons.; team physician Thornton (Ill.) Fractional South and St. Francis de Sales High Sch. Trustee, Village of Lansing, chmn. pub. works, 1981-83, chmn. fin. com., 1983—; fund devel. chmn. Girl Scouts U.S.; mem. Ill. Peer Rev. Com. Recipient Rebel Helmet award, Dedicated Service to Athletes award Thornton Fractional South Booster Club, award Thornton Fractional South Hockey Club; bd. dirs. Calumet Council Girl Scouts U.S.A., 1986-87; hon. emergency med. technician Ill. Dept. Pub. Health. Mem. Nat. Assn. Disability Evaluating Physicians (charter), Am. Chiropractic Assn., Ill. Chiropractic Soc., (bd. dirs. 1982-84), Chgo. Chiropractic Soc. (treas. 1977-80, pres. 1982-84), Am. Coll. Sports Medicine, Lansing C. of C. (dir.), Am. Coll. Chiropractic Cons. (sec.), Jaycees (Jaycee of Yr. 1978-79, Presdl. award of honor, 1981, past pres., state dir.), Ill. Peer Review Com. Lodge: Lions (pres. Lansing 1984-85). Office: 18037 Torrence Ave Lansing IL 60438

COX, DAVID WALTER, lawyer; b. Columbus, Ohio, July 30, 1951; s. James F. and Mary J. (Brown) C.; m. Florence E. Poland, June 10, 1972; children: Christine L., Adam David. BA, Ohio Wesleyan U., 1972; JD, Ohio State U., 1975. Bar: Ohio 1976. Ptnr. Cox & Chappars, Xenia, Ohio, 1975—. Pres. Xenia Bd. Edn., 1977-81, Greene Vocat. Bd. Edn., Xenia, 1977-81, Greene County Bd. Elections, Xenia, 1980-84, Golden Age Sr. Citizens, Inc., Xenia, 1977—; chmn., sec. Greene County Dem. Party, 1978—. Named Hon. Ky. Col., Xenia, 1986. Mem. Ohio Bar Assn., Greene County Bar Assn., Phi Beta Kappa, Omicron Delta Epsilon. Methodist. Lodge: Elks. Avocation: golf. Home: 1383 Regency Dr N Xenia OH 45385 Office: Cox & Chappars Allen Bldg Xenia OH 45385

COX, GALEN R, import sales company executive; b. Kyoto, Japan, May 11, 1957; s. Ralph Emerson and Stella Mae (Sluder) C.; m. Elizabeth Bailey Paton, Aug. 9, 1981 (div. July 7, 1986); 1 child, Michael Whitney; m. Sharon Ann Meldrum, Oct. 4, 1986. AA, John Brown U., Sildam Springs, Ark., 1977. Interpreter Asano Labs., Nagoya, Japan, 1978-81; pres. United Steel and Metals, Nagoya, Japan, 1981-84, Enkei Internat., Madison Heights, Mich., 1984—; bd. dirs. Koyo Corp. Republican. Avocations: bird watching, darts. Office: Enkei Internat 31800 Research Park Dr Madison Heights MI 48071

COX, JOHN MICHAEL, cardiologist; b. Toledo, June 21, 1952; s. William E. and Laura M. (Carroll) C.; m. Sandra Helen Kemner, Aug. 19, 1972 (div. Mar. 1978); 1 child, Justin Michael; m. Vickie Diane Humphreys, May 27, 1978; children: Sarah Elizabeth, Aaron Alexander. BA magna cum laude, Westminster Coll., 1974; DO, Kirksville Coll. Osteo. Medicine, 1978. Cert. Am. Bd. Osteo. Cardiology, Internal Medicine. Intern in internal medicine Riverside Hosp., Trenton, Mich., 1978-79, resident, 1979-81, fellow in cardiology, 1981-83; practice medicine specializing in cardiology Sedalia, Mo., 1983—; chmn. dept. internal medicine Bothwell Regional Health Ctr., 1985—. Grantee Detroit Osteo. Hosp. Corp., Burroughs Wellcome Fellowship, Meade Johnson Fellowship. Mem. Am. Coll. Osteo. Internists, Am. Heart Assn., Am. Osteo. Assn., Mo. Assn. Osteo. Physicians and Surgeons (v.p. west cen. dist. 1985-87, pres. 1987), Am. Soc. Echocardiography, Am. Thoracic Soc., Psi Sigma Alpha, Sigma Sigma Phi. Methodist. Office: West Cen Internal Medicine Clinic 1701 S Lafayette Sedalia MO 65301-7228

COX, KENNETH R., state agency administrator; b. Ohio, Oct. 8, 1928; s. Dexter L. and Ila B. Cox; m. Marjorie L. Cox; children: Timothy, Patricia. Student, U. Akron, Ohio. Mgr. advt. prodn. B.F. Goodrich Co.; mem. city council City of Barberton, Ohio, 1960-66; mayor City of Barberton, 1966-72; mem. Ohio Ho. of Reps., 1973-76, Ohio Senate, 1977-82; dir. Ohio Dept. Hwy. Safety, 1983-85, Ohio Dept. Commerce, 1985—. Mem. exec. com. Summit County (Ohio) Dems.; mem. adv. bd. Coll. of Nursing U. Akron; mem. Summit County Mental health Assn.; trustee Portage Path Community Mental Health Ctr. Mem. Nat. Conf. State Legislators, Akron Area Bd. Realtors, Barberton (Ohio) Jaycees, Barberton C. of C. Lodges: Elks, Kiwanis. Office: Commerce Dept 2 Nationwide Plaza Columbus OH 43266-0544

COX, LANA SUE, accountant; b. Lindsborg, Kans., Nov. 1, 1950; d. Landvis Earl and Lois (Wiebe) Ferm; m. James Martin Cox., Mar. 11, 1983; 1 child, Patrick Earl. BS in Bus. Edn., Wichita State U., 1972; MS, Emporia State Coll., 1973. Tchr. bus. edn. Coffeyville (Kans.) Jr. Coll., 1973-74; acctg. clk. Indian Wells Oil Co., Wichita, Kans., 1974-76; revenue acctg. supr. Indian Wells Oil Co., Liberty, Mo., 1976-86; teaching asst. Emporia (Kans.) State Coll., 1972-73. Mem. Lindsborg 4-H (held various positions from song leader to pres.). Republican. Lutheran. Avocations: sewing, knitting, water and snow skiing, swimming. Home: 838 Marilyn Liberty MO 64068 Office: One Liberty Plaza Liberty MO 64068

COX, LANDON GREAUD, JR., defense contractor; b. Portsmouth, Ohio, Jan. 2, 1940; s. Landon Greaud and Virginia (Boyd) C.; m. Marjorie Carole Evans, Dec. 15, 1962 (div. Oct. 29, 1980); children: Kimberly Sue, Robert James; m. Patricia Ann Malone, Nov. 15, 1980; 1 child, Emily Catherine. BS, U.S. Naval Acad., 1963; MS, Naval Postgrad. Sch., 1974. Commd. naval aviator USN, 1964; maintenance officer Attack Squadron 66, Lemoore, Calif., 1971-72; advanced through grades to comdr. USN, 1978; ops. officer Attack Squadron 94, Lemoore, Calif., 1976-77; budget coordinator Office of Chief Naval Ops., Washington, 1977-80; weapons officer USS Independence, Norfolk, Va., 1980-82; dep. dir. aviation programs Asst. Sec. Navy Dept. Navy, Washington, 1982-85; ret. USN, 1985; exec. program mgr. Emerson Electric Co., St. Louis, 1985—. Decorated Legion of Merit, Air medal (6). Mem. Assn. Naval Aviation, Ret. Officers Assn., U.S. Naval Acad. Alumni Assn. Episcopalian. Home: 1515 Hudson Landing Saint Charles MO 63303 Office: Emerson Electric Co ATE Program Mgmt Sta 1944 8100 W Florissant Saint Louis MO 63136

COX, LAWRENCE KOSSUTH, II, dentist; b. Mar. 12, 1936. BA in Chemistry and Biology, Albion Coll., 1959; DDS, U. Detroit, 1963. Pvt. practice dentistry Adrian, Mich., 1965—; health occupations adv. Lenawee County Vocat. Tech. Inst., 1968—, chmn., instr. dental div. 1968-75; sec./treas. Bixby Hosp. Dental Staff, 1969-72, chief, 1973-74; instr. U.S. Dental Inst., 1977—. Dentist rep. planning com. Mid-Mich. South Health System Agy., 1982-83; chmn. Adrian Election com., 1978—. Served to capt. USAF, 1963-65. Mem. ADA, Mich. Dental Assn. (ho. dels. 1985—), Jackson County Dental Soc., Detroit Dist. Dental Soc., Am. Soc. of Dentistry for Children, Pierre Fauchard Acad., Internat. Assn. Orthodontists, Am. Assn. Dental Research, 1986—, Vietnam Vets. Am., Fedn. Orthodontic Assn.,Am. Acad. Head Facial and Neck Pain and TMJ Orthopedics (bd. dirs. 1987—), Mich. Assn. Professions, Acad. Stress and Chronic Disease, Sutherland Cranial Found., 1986—, U. Detroit Alumni Assn. (treas. 1969-71, pres. 1973-74), Psi Omega, Alpha Tau Omega. Club: Lenawee Country (bd. dirs. 1981-84). Lodge: Kiwanis (pres. Adrian 1970-71), Circle K (chmn. Mich. dist. 1972-75). Office: 225 S Main St Adrian MI 49221

COX, LESTER LEE, broadcasting executive; b. Springfield, Mo., Nov. 6, 1922; s. Lester Edmund and Mildred Belle (Lee) C.; m. Claudine Viola Barrett, Jan. 19, 1946; 1 son, Lester Barrett. A.B. in Econs., Westminster Coll., 1944, LL.D., 1974; postgrad., U.S. Mil. Acad., 1944-46; M.B.A., Drury Coll., 1965. Pres. Springfield TV, Inc. (KYTV), 1952-79, K.C. Air Conditioning, North Kansas City, 1968-85; Pres., Mid-Continent Telecasting, Inc. (KOAM-TV), Pittsburg, Kans., 1958-85, Pittsburg Broadcasting Co. (KOAM); Pres., Ozark Motor & Supply Co., Springfield, Modern Tractor & Supply Co.; bd. dirs. Commerceshares, Inc., Kansas City, Mo., TWA. Mem. Mo. Bd. Health, 1968-73, past chmn.; mem. Commn. on Higher Edn. for Mo., 1977-83; pres. Ozark Empire council Boy Scouts Am., 1960; chmn. bd. Lester E. Cox Med. Center; bd. dirs. Westminster Coll., 1949-79, Drury Coll., 1965-79, Midwest Research Inst., Kansas City. Served with AUS, 1943-46, to capt. 1951-53. Recipient Silver Beaver award Boy Scouts Am., 1961; named Hon. col. Gov. of Mo., 1960-64, 68-72. Mem. Central States Shrine Assn. (pres. 1970). Club: Hickory Hills Country. Lodges: Masons, Shriners. Office: 440 E Tampa St Springfield MO 65806

COX, MARILYN LESLIE MCELHANEY, financial planner; b. Eldorado, Ill., Apr. 23, 1945; d. Ernest D. and Emily (Robison) McElhaney; m. Robert G. Cox, Feb. 6, 1965; children: Leslie Jo, Traci Jane. BS in Home Econs. Edn., So. Ill. U., 1980. Owner, operator Depot Inn, Eldorado, 1968-76; instr. nutrition Southeastern Ill. Jr. Coll., Harrisburg, 1981; extension advisor, home economist Cooperative Extension Service, Gallatin County, Ill., 1981-86; personal fin. planner IDS Fin. Services Inc., Eldorado, 1986—. Author numerous home econs. programs. Treas. So. Ill. 4-H Camp Assn., 1983-86, leader, 4-H Program, Gallatin and Saline Counties; ruling elder Presbyn. Ch., Eldorado. Mem. Ill. Assn. Extension Home Economists (Peer Award 1984), Nightingales Homemakers Extension Unit (treas., sec.), Beta Sigma Phi (v.p., pres. Beta Omega chpt.). Avocations: cooking, sewing, collecting and refinishing antiques. Home: 2121 Illinois Ave Eldorado IL 62930

COX, MYRON KEITH, educator; b. Akron, May 6, 1926; s. Carney F. and Nina Castilla (Kenny) C.; B.S., Va. Poly. Inst., 1949; B.S., Pa. State Coll., 1952; M.S., M.I.T., 1957; D.Sc., London Coll., Eng., 1964; m. Emma A. Edwards, July 2, 1950; children—Carney K., Myron D., Eric L., Brett W. Commd. staff sgt. U.S. Air Force, 1950, advanced through grades maj., 1964; radar meteorology staff Hanscom AFB, Mass., 1964-66; electronic countermeasures Wright Patterson AFB, Ohio, 1966-69; ret., 1969; faculty Wright State U., Dayton, Ohio, 1969—, prof. mgmt. sci., quantitative bus. analysis, 1981—. Bd. govs. Fairborn (Ohio) YMCA, 1972-73. Served with USN, 1944-46. Registered profl. engr., Mass. Fellow Acad. Mktg. Sci.; mem. Inst. Mgmt. Sci., Am. Statis. Assn., Assn. Inst. Decision Sci., So. Mktg. Assn., Phi Kappa Phi, Tau Beta Pi, Sigma Xi, Eta Kappa Nu, Beta Gamma Sigma, Alpha Iota Delta. Club: Lions, Masons, Shriners. Patentee surface friction tester; contbr. mktg., mgmt., forecast modeling and simulation. Home: 2527 Grange Hall Rd Beavercreek OH 45431 Office: Wright State Univ Dayton OH 45435

COX, THOMAS J., accountant; b. Advance, Mo., Feb. 23, 1930; s. Thomas Isom and Clarissa Elizabeth (Zimmerman) C.; m. Mary June Whittle, Sept. 22, 1956; children: Leslie Ann, Thomas J. Jr., Donna Gail, Lori Leigh. BS, Ark. State U., 1956. CPA, Mo. Owner, mgr. T.J. Cox, CPA, Poplar Bluff, Mo., 1961-68, 78-85; sr. ptnr. Cox, Stewart et al, CPA's, Poplar Bluff, 1968-78, Cox & Eads, CPA's, Poplar Bluff, 1985—; mem. adv. council SBA, 1969. Chmn. Butler County (Mo.) Rep. Party, 1978-83; treas. Mo. 10th Dist., Cape Girardeau, 1978-83; del. Rep. Nat. Conv., 1980. Mem. Am. Inst. CPA's, Mo. Soc. CPA's (chmn. ethics com. 1961-62, mem. exec. bd. 1963-64), S.E. Mo. Chpt. CPA's (pres. 1963), Tenn. Soc. CPA's. Republican. Methodist. Lodge: Masons. Avocations: golf, fishing. Home: 1810 Big Bend Poplar Bluff MO 63901 Office: Cox & Eads CPAs 1902 Northwood Poplar Bluff MO 63901

COX, THOMAS JOSEPH, oil executive; b. Youngstown, Ohio, Mar. 5, 1946; s. John Charles and Margaret Pearl (Reese) C.; m. Della Jean Sympson, Feb. 17, 1968; children: Amy Leigh, Thomas Joseph Jr. Student, Youngstown State U., 1968-69. V.p. Apartment Home Protection Co.Inc., Youngstown, 1969-71; ptnr. Pershing-Cox Ins. Co., Boardman, Ohio, 1971-75; asst. to pres. Park Ohio Industries, Cleve., 1975-78; pres. Landmark Petroleum Mgmt. Co. Inc., Canfield, Ohio, 1978—; ptnr. B&C Pipeline, Marietta, Ohio, 1981—. Served to cpl. USMC, 1965-68. Mem. Ohio Oil and Gas Assn., Builders Assn. Democrat. Roman Catholic. Lodge: Ancient Order Hibernians in Am. (pres. Youngstown 1968). Home: 7973 Spartan Dr Youngstown OH 44512 Office: Landmark Petroleum Mgmt Co Inc 3770 Starrs Centre Dr Canfield OH 44406

COX, WILLIAM CLARENCE, dentist; b. Alton, Ill., Oct. 28, 1952; s. Clarence Albert and Bernice Leona (Fisher) C.; m. Mary Thomas Mullin, Dec. 28, 1974; children: Sarah E., Ellen M., Jody A. BA, MacMurray Coll., 1974; DDS, So. Ill. U., Alton, 1976. Lic. dentist, Ill. Gen. practice dentistry Wood River, Ill., 1976—; clin. instr. So. Ill. U., Alton, 1979-82, clin. asst. prof., 1982-87, clin. assoc. prof., 1987—; courtesy staff Alton Meml. Hosp., 1980—. Chmn. Nat. Children's Dental Health Week, 1982; v.p. Wood River Devel. Corp., 1983-85, treas., 1985—. Mem. ADA, Ill State Dental Soc., Madison Dist. Dental Soc., So. Ill. U. Alumni Assn. (bd. govs. 1985), MacMurray Coll. Alumni Assn. (bd. dirs. 1983-85). Home: 2309 Fairview Dr Alton IL 62002 Office: 22 S 2d Wood River IL 62095

COYLE, EDWARD JOHN, electrical engineer; b. Bryn Mawr, Pa., Apr. 22, 1956; m. Patricia J. Sommer, July 20, 1985. BEE, U. Del., 1977; MS in Elec. Engring., Computer Sci., Princeton U., 1980, PhD in Elec. Engring., Computer Sci., 1982. Asst. prof. Purdue U., W. Lafayette, Ind., 1982-86, assoc. prof., 1986—; pres. Info. Sci. and Systems, Inc., Lafayette, Ind., 1985—. Contbr. articles to profl. jours.; patentee digital filtering by threshold decomposition. Recipient Scott Paper Co. Leadership award Scott Paper Co. and U. Del., 1975-77; Wallace fellow in Engring., Princeton U., 1980-82; Research Initiation grantee NSF, 1983-85. Mem. IEEE (Scholastic Achievement award 1977), Assn. Computing Machinery. Avocations: bicycling, art history. Home: 505 S 7th St Lafayette IN 47901 Office: Purdue U Sch Elec Engring West Lafayette IN 47907

COYLE, MARTIN ADOLPHUS, JR., lawyer, electronic and engring. co. exec.; b. Hamilton, Ohio, June 3, 1941; s. Martin Adolphus and Lucille Baird C.; m. Sharon Sullivan, Mar. 29, 1969; children—Cynthia Ann, David Martin, Jennifer Ann. B.A., Ohio Wesleyan U., 1963; J.D. summa cum laude, Ohio State U., 1966. Bar: N.Y. bar 1967. Asso. firm Cravath, Swaine & Moore, N.Y.C., 1966-72; chief counsel securities and fin. TRW Inc., Cleve., 1972-73; sr. counsel, asst. sec. TRW Inc., 1973-75, asst. gen. counsel, asst. sec., 1976, asst. gen. counsel, sec., 1976-80, v.p., gen. counsel, sec., 1980—; sec. TRW Found., 1975-80, trustee, 1980—. Pres., trustee Judson Retirement Community; nat. chmn. Ohio Wesleyan U. Assocs., 1987—; chmn., sec. Martin A. Coyle Found. Mem. ABA, Am. Soc. Corporate Secs. (pres. Ohio regional group 1978-80, nat. dir. 1981—, nat. chmn. 1985-86), Assn. Gen. Counsel, Ohio Bar Assn., Bar Assn. Greater Cleve., Ohio Wesleyan Assocs. (nat. chmn. 1987). Clubs: Mayfield Country, Union. Coinventor voting machine. Home: 23175 Laureldale Rd Shaker Heights OH 44122 Office: TRW Inc 1900 Richmond Rd Cleveland OH 44124

COYLE, RHONDA MAY, computer programmer/analyst; b. Monmouth, Ill., Apr. 29, 1957; d. Merlyn Hoyt Anderson and Jennie Ann (Torrance) McKee; m. Richard David Coyle, July 22, 1978. BS in Math., Ill. State U., 1978, BS in Applied Computer Sci., 1984. Tchr. math. Lourdes High Sch., Chgo., 1978-80, Richwoods High Sch., Peoria, Ill., 1980-81; tchr. math. and sci. Toluca (Ill.) High Sch., 1981-83; programmer/analyst State Farm Ins. Co., Bloomington, Ill., 1983—. Stewardship com. First Meth. Ch., Normal, Ill., 1986. Avocations: travel, sewing, reading. Office: State Farm Ins LDMK 1 State Farm Plaza Bloomington IL 61701

COYNE, ANN, social work educator; b. Medford, Mass., June 26, 1936; d. Edward James Jr. and Catherine Mary (Stokes) Gaffey; m. Dermot Patrick Coyne, June 15, 1957; children: Patrick J., Brian D., Thomas M., James E., Catherine A., Gerard W. BA, Cornell U., 1958; MSW, U. Nebr., 1975, PhD, 1980. Dir. community services Lancaster Office Mental Retardation, Lincoln, Nebr., 1971-75; assoc. prof. social work U. Nebr., Omaha, 1975—; dep. dir. State Dept. Social Services, Lincoln, 1981-82; pres. Coyne & Assocs., Lincoln, 1978—; project dir. Child Welfare Tng. Inst., Lincoln, 1982-87; bd. dirs. Hispanic Community Ctr., Lincoln, 1982—. Contbr. articles to profl. jours. Bd. dirs. Child Guidance Ctr., Lincoln, 1975-81, Crime and Community, Lincoln, 1983-85, Nebraskans for Peace, Lincoln, 1985, Nebraskans for Nicaraguan Children, 1987—, Voices for Children in Nebr., 1987—; chmn. Gov.'s Planning Council on Devel. Disabilities, 1986—. Mem. Nat. Assn. Social Workers, Am. Orthopsychiat. Assn., Child Welfare League of Am. (cert.), Sigma Xi. Democrat. Catholic. Avocation: photography. Home: 1130 N 79 St Lincoln NE 68505 Office: Univ Nebr Sch Social Work Annex 40 Omaha NE 68182-0293

COYNE, DERMOT PATRICK, horticulture educator; b. Ireland, July 4, 1929; m. Ann Coyne, June 15, 1957; children: P.J., Brian, Thomas James, Catherine, Gerard. BS, Univ. Coll., Dublin, Ireland, 1953, MS, 1954; PhD, Cornell U., 1958; DSc, Nat. U. Ireland, 1981. Asst. mgr. agrl. research Campbell Soup Co., England, 1958-60; asst. prof. horticulture U. Nebr., Lincoln, 1961-65, assoc. prof., 1965-68, prof., 1968—, acting chmn. dept. horticulture, 1974-75. Assoc. editor HortSci., 1974-78; editorial bd. Horticulture Revs., 1980-81, Plant Breeding Revs., 1981-82; contbr. numerous articles to profl. jours. Recipient numerous awards and research grants, 1975—. Fellow AAAS, Am. Soc. Hort. Sci.; mem. Crop Sci. Soc., Am. Soc. Agronomy, Am. Assn. Univ. Profs., Am. Genetic Assn., Internat. Soc. Hort. Sci., Bean Improvement Coop., Nebr. Statewide Arboretum, Cucurbit Genetics Coop., Sigma Xi, Gamma Sigma Delta, Eucarpia. Office: U Nebr Dept Horticulture 366 PS Lincoln NE 68583-0724

COYNE, M. JEANNE, state supreme court justice; b. Mpls., Dec. 7, 1926; d. Vincent Mathias and Mae Lucille (Steinmetz) C. B.S. in Law, U. Minn., 1955, J.D., 1957. Bar: Minn. 1957, U.S. Dist. Ct. Minn. 1957, U.S. Ct. Appeals (8th cir.) 1958, U.S. Supreme Ct. 1964. Law clk. Minn. Supreme Ct., St. Paul, 1956-57; assoc. Meagher, Geer & Markham, Mpls., 1957-70, ptnr., 1970-82; assoc. justice Minn. Supreme Ct., St. Paul, 1982—; mem. Am. Arbitration Assn., 1967-82; mem. bd. conciliation Archdiocese St. Paul and Mpls., 1981-82; instr. U. Minn. Law Sch., Mpls., 1964-68; mem. Lawyers Profl. Responsibility Bd., St. Paul, 1982; chmn. com. rules of civil appellate procedure Minn. Supreme Ct., St. Paul, 1982—. Editor: Women Lawyers Jour., 1971-72. Mem. ABA, Minn. State Bar Assn., Nat. Assn. Women Lawyers, Nat. Assn. Women Judges, Minn. Women Lawyers Assn. (dir.), U. Minn. Law Alumni Assn. Office: Minn Supreme Ct 230 State Capitol Saint Paul MN 55155

COYNE, TERRANCE CHARLES, pharmaceutical research and development executive; b. Racine, Wis., Mar. 22, 1946; s. Edward Charles and Joyce Lilah (DuBois) C.; m. Gayle Maurine Ryder, June 19, 1971; children—Angelique, Genaviece, Alexander. B.S., U. Wis., 1968, M.D., 1972. Intern, U.S. Pub. Health Service Hosp., New Orleans, 1972-73; practice family medicine Grantsburg Clinic, Wis., 1973-74; assoc. dir. clin. research Abbott Labs., North Chgo., Ill., 1974-76, dir. clin. research, 1976-78; dir. med. affairs Riker Labs., 3M, St. Paul. 1978-82, tech. dir., 1982—; v.p. and Treas. Coyne's Creative Collections, Inc. Bd. dirs. Mississippi Valley Chamber Orch., St. Paul, 1984-85; mem. Citizens League, Mpls., 1985; bd. dirs. 3M Polit. Action Com., 1984—. Recipient Physicians Recognition award, AMA, 1984. Fellow Am. Soc. Clin. Pharmacology and Therapeutics; mem. AAAS, AMA, Am. Mgmt. Assn., Internat. Soc. for Antiviral Research, Am. Heart Assn., Drug. Info. Assn., N.Y. Acad. Scis., Wis. Med. Alumni Assn., Pharm. Mfrs. Assn. (research and devel. sect. steering com. 1984—, commn. on drugs for rare diseases 1986—), Found. for Health Care Evaluation, Harold Bruun Soc. for Med. Research, U. Wis. Alumni Assn. Republican. Methodist. Avocations: piano, music, gardening, water sports, tennis. Home: 1355 Medora Rd Mendota Heights MN 55118 Office: Riker Labs Inc 3M Center Saint Paul MN 55144

COYNE, THOMAS EDWARD, oil company executive; b. Cleve., Sept. 16, 1936; s. Thomas Edward and Eileen M. (O'Connell) C.; m. Ursula Mary Jeffers, Nov. 9, 1957; children: Kathleen, Michael, Thomas, Michele, John, Timothy, Patrick. BSEE, Cleve. State U., 1976. Engr. Standard Oil Co., Cleve., 1976-78, dist. engr., 1978-82, project engr., 1982—. Officer St. Thomas More PTA, 1975-79, Athletic Assn., 1979—; mem. Brooklyn (Ohio) City Council, 1977—; mem. exec. com. Cuyahoga (Cleve.) Dem. Party, 1977—. Served with U.S. Army, 1955-57. Mem. Cleve. Engring. Soc. Roman Catholic. Lodge: KC. Avocations: weight lifting, fishing, computer finance. Home: 4829 Autumn Lane Brooklyn OH 44144 Office: Standard Oil Co Cleveland OH 44144

CRABB, BARBARA BRANDRIFF, U.S. dist. judge; b. Green Bay, Wis., Mar. 17, 1939; d. Charles Edward and Mary (Forrest) Brandriff; m. Theodore E. Crabb, Jr., Aug. 29, 1959; children: Julia Forrest, Philip Elliott. A.B., U. Wis., 1960, J.D., 1962. Bar: Wis. bar 1963. Assoc. firm Roberts, Boardman, Suhr and Curry, Madison, 1968-70; research asst. Law Sch. U. Wis., 1968-70; research asst. Am. Bar Assn., Madison, 1970-71; U.S. magistrate Madison, 1971-79; U.S. dist. judge Western Dist. Wis., 1979—, chief judge, 1980—; mem. Gov. Wis. Task Force Prison Reform, 1971-73. Membership chmn., v.p. Milw. LWV, 1966-68; mem. Milw. Jr. League, 1967-68. Mem. Am. Bar Assn., Nat. Council Fed. Magistrates, Nat. Assn. Women Judges, State Bar Wis., Dane County Bar Assn., U. Wis. Law Alumni Assn. Home: 741 Seneca Pl Madison WI 53711 Office: US District Court Box 591 Madison WI 53701

CRABB, KENNETH WAYNE, obstetrician-gynecologist; b. Glendive, Mont., June 17, 1950; s. Kenneth Willard and Marjorie Jane (Martin) C.; m. Gwen Aldean Wendelschafer, June 8, 1974; children: Kenneth Wendel, Richard David. BS with honors in Biochemistry, U. Iowa, 1971, MD, 1975. Diplomate Am. Bd. Ob-Gyn. Intern, then resident in ob-gyn St. Paul Ramsey Med. Ctr., 1975-79; practice medicine specializing in ob-gyn St. Paul, 1979—; clin. asst. prof. Dept. Ob-gyn, U. Minn., Mpls., 1981—; vice chmn. Dept. Ob-gyn United Hosp., St. Paul, 1984-86, chmn. edn. and research com., 1986, ob-gyn liason to family practice dept., 1981-82, pharm. and therapeutics com., 1980-84; preceptor family practice res'., St. John's Hosp., St. Paul, 1979—, maternal health com., 1979—, cancer com., 1984-85; quality assurance com. St. Joseph's Hosp., St. Paul, 1981-83. Trustee Actors Theatre of St. Paul, 1980—, bd. dirs, 2d v.p., 1984-85; mem. council Grace Luth. Ch., 1984—; bd. dirs. Indianhead Council Boy Scouts Am., 1986—. Recipient Eagle Scout award, Boy Scouts Am., 1966, Appreciation award Am. Acad. Family Physicians, 1979, 85. Fellow Am. Coll. Ob-Gyn (jr. fellow dist. chmn. 1978-79, jr. fellow adv. council 1978-80, chmn. 1989 Dist. VI meeting, appreciation award 1978-79), Am. Fertility Soc.; mem. AMA (physicians recognition award 1985), Cen. Assn. Obstetricians & Gynocologists, Am. Soc. Coloscopy & Cervical Pathology, Am. Assn. Gynecologic Laparoscopists, Am. Acad. Family Physicians (appreciation award), Minn. Med. Soc., Minn. Obstetric & Gynecologic Soc.(program com. 1984), Ramsey County Med. Soc. (med. practice com. 1982—, del. 1983, fin. com. 1984—, med. service com. 1986—), Assn. Profs. Ob-gyn, Found. Health Care Evaluation, Phi Beta Sigma, Omicron Delta Kappa, Phi Beta Phi (sec., U. Iowa chpt. 1972-73, 2d vice archon 1982-83, supreme sec. treas. 1984—). Club: St. Paul Athletic. Lodge: Rotary (various coms. chmn. 1983-85, bd. dirs. 1984-86, sgt. at arms 1986—). Avocations: volleyball, skiing, theatre, sci. fiction. Home: 6411 Glen Rd Woodbury MN 55125 Office: 355 Sherman St Suite 300 Saint Paul MN 55102

CRABB, LARRY WAYNE, school system administrator; b. Plymouth, Ind., Feb. 28, 1937; s. Ernest L. and Hazel (Renas) C.; m. Barbara Sue Burkett, Aug. 23, 1958; children: Jeffrey, Jill. BA, Grace Coll., Winona Lake, Ind., 1960; MS, Ind. U., 1967, EdD, 1973. Cert. sch. supt. Asst. prin. Culver (Ind.) Community Schs., 1962-66; prin. Penn, Harris, Madison, Osceola, Ind., 1966-72; grad. asst. Ind. U., Bloomington, 1972-73; asst. supt. Monroe Community Schs., Bloomington, 1973-75; supt. Hanover Community Schs., Cedar Lake, Ind., 1975-80, Warsaw (Ind.) Community Schs., 1980—. Contbr. articles to profl. jours. Sec. Boys Club, Warsaw; bd. dirs. Ind. U. Sch. Edn., Bloomington, 1984-86, Ivy Tech, Warsaw, 1980-86, Pvt. Industry Council, Goshen, 1984-86, Pres.'s Council Grace Coll., Winona Lake, Ind., 1980-86; chmn. bd. Kosciusko County United Way, Warsaw, 1985-86, pres., 1984, campaign chmn., 1983. Named Alumnus of Yr. Grace Coll., 1982; recipient Service award Kosciusko County United Way, 1984, 85, 86, Cedar lake Jaycees, 1979. Mem. Ind. Sch. Supts. (mem. exec. com. 1978-80), Lake County Supts. (pres. 1977-78), Ind. Sch. Supts. (sec. 1976-77), Ind. Pub. Relations. Lodge: Kiwanis (v.p. 1985-86). Avocations: antiques and collectibles. Home: 205 Kelly Dr Warsaw IN 46580 Office: Warsaw Community Schs PO Box 288 One Administration Dr Warsaw IN 46580

CRABB, WINSTON DOUGLAS, physician; b. Waukegan, Ill., May 15, 1943; s. Wilfred Dayton and Leona Irene (Keckler) C.; m. Millicent B., Sept. 23, 1965; chidlren—Wesley David, Laura Elizabeth, William Charles. B.S. in Medicine, Northwestern U., 1965, M.D., 1967. Diplomate Am. Bd. Ob-Gyn. Rotating intern Evanston Med. Sch. Hosp., Ill., 1967-68; resident in ob-gyn Kans. U. Med. Ctr., Kansas City, 1970-73; attending physician ob-gyn Lincoln Clinic, Nebr., 1973—; attending physician Bryan Hosp., Lincoln, 1973—, chmn. ob-gyn Dept., 1978-80; mem. courtesy staff Lincoln Gen. Hosp., St. Elizabeth's Hosp., 1973—. Mem. med. adv. bd. Planned Parenthood of Lincoln, 1975—. Served with USNR, 1968-70. Fellow Am. Coll. Ob-Gyn; mem. Lancaster County Med. Soc., Nebr. Med. Soc. Democrat. Presbyterian. Avocations: Duplicate bridge; stamp collecting.

CRACIUM, JOHN ODIE, accountant, health care facility executive; b. Royal Oak, Mich., Sept. 12, 1944; s. John Eli and Carlene Mae (Grace) C.; m. Roberta Kristine Width, Feb. 19, 1966; children: John R., Eric A., Kelly L. Cert. acctg. and fin., Walsh Coll., 1968. CPA, Mich. Staff acct. Thurley Allen CPA, Rochester, Mich., 1962-64; sr. acct. Allen & Roberts CPA's, Rochester, 1964-67; asst. controller Jim Robins Co., Troy, Mich., 1967-71; pvt. practice acctg. Rochester, 1971-80; pres., chief exec. officer Profl. Breathing Assocs., Inc., Rochester, 1978—; also bd. dirs. Profl. Breathing Assocs., Inc.; bd. dirs. Madison Gen. Service, Rochester, Fleet Battery Inc., Rochester; v.p., bd. dirs. Amico & Assocs., Rochester. Coach Rochester Youth Soccer League, 1979-83; chmn. GRRU Chpt. Mich. Lupus Found., Rochester, 1981; treas. Com. to Elect Cliff Lilly, Rochester, 1982; Served with USAR, 1967-72. Recipient Cert. of Appreciation, Mich. Dept. Edn., 1973, 77. Mem. Am. Inst. CPA's (lectr. continuing edn.), Mich. Assn. CPA's (lectr. continuing edn.), Nat. Assn. Med. Equipment Supplies, Health Industry Distbrs. Assn., Mich. Assn. Durable Med. Equipment Cos., Walsh Coll. Alumni Assn., Nat. Rifle Assn., Past Exalted Rulers Assn. (treas. 1975-76). Club: Hix-N-Chix (Rochester) (treas. 1963-64). Lodge: Elks (life, Exalted Ruler 1971-72, various offices 1967-71). Avocations: hunting, fishing, reading, golf. Home: PO Box 8066 Rochester MI 48308-8066 Office: Profl Breathing Assocs 1703 Star Batt Dr Rochester MI 48063

CRADDOCK, JAMES RICHARD, minister; b. Chatham, Va., Oct. 7, 1921; s. Richard Irvin and Elna May (Cox) C.; m. Frances Smith, Aug. 20, 1943; 1 child, Lynn Josephine. BSME, Va. Poly. Inst., 1942; BD in Theology, Lexington (Ky.) Theol. Sem., 1951; D of Ministry, Eden Theol. Sem., Webster Groves, Mo., 1973. Ordained to ministry Christian Ch., 1951. Aero. engr. G.L. Martin Co., Balt., 1945-48; mech. engr. Aberdeen (Md.) Proving Grounds, 1948; minister Christian Ch., Willisburg, Ky., 1948-51, First Christian Ch., Richmond, Mo., 1951-57, Cen. Christian Ch., Granite City, Ill., 1957-70, First Christian Ch., Centralia, Ill., 1970-74, Augusta Christian Ch., Indpls., 1975-86; pres. Greater Indpls. Disciples Housing, Inc., 1985-86; bd. dirs. Christian Ch., Indpls., 1980-84. Bd. dirs. Lenoir Home, Columbia, Mo., 1969-73, Greater Indpls. Disc. Housing Bd., 1980-84, Nat. Benefit Assn., St. Louis, 1986. Served to capt. USAF, 1942-45. Mem. Am. Assn. Pastoral Counselors, Assn. Clin. Pastoral Edn. Democrat. Lodges: Kiwanis, Optimists, Masons, Shriners. Home: 6439 Chapelwood Ct Indianapolis IN 46268-4002 Office: Robin Run Village 5354 W 62d St Indianapolis IN 46268

CRAFT, LEWIS JOHN, lawyer; b. Clayton, Ill., Feb. 24, 1927; s. Lewis John and Mamie Elizabeth (Anderson) C.; m. Clara Ellen Adrian, Sept. 4, 1949; children: Phyllis, Ruth, Beth, Carl, Donna, Don. BSEE, BSME, U. Ill., 1949, MEE, 1950; JD, Ill. Inst. Tech., 1964. Bar: Ill.; registered profl. engr. With mgmt. dept. Sunbeam Corp., Chgo., 1950-78; sole practice Villa Park, Ill., 1964—. Chmn. Christian Ch. Villa Park, 1979; bd. dirs. Sch. Dist. 48, Villa Park, 1973-85; com. mem. DuPage County Sch., Wheaton, Ill., 1985-86. Mem. IEEE, Ill. Bar Assn., DuPage County Bar Assn., Pi Tausigma, ETA Kappa Nu. Lodges: Kiwanis, Masons. Avocations: Mechanical and electrical projects, camping, boating. Home: OS481 Ardmore Villa Park IL 60181 Office: Lewis John Craft & Assocs 205 E St Charles Rd Villa Park IL 60181

CRAFT, RICHARD EARL, utility company manager; b. East Cleveland, Ohio, Feb. 1, 1947; s. Earl L. and Lenora D. (Brown) C.; m. Linda J. Barth, Nov. 28, 1970; children: Teresa, Marc. BA, The Coll. of Wooster, 1969; MBA, U. Akron, 1982. Asst. analyst Ohio Bell Telephone Co., Cleve., 1969-70; asst. analyst Ohio Bell Telephone Co., Brecksville, 1973-79, mgr., 1979-85, 85—; mgr. Ohio Bell Telephone Co., Akron, 1985. Former treas., pres., bd. dirs. Concern for Children, Inc., northeastern Ohio, 1980—; corp. solicitor United Way of Summit County, Akron, 1985; alumni admissions rep. The Coll. of Wooster, 1985—. Served to lt. (j.g.) USNR, 1970-72. Mem. Sigma Iota Epsilon. Avocations: music, reading, physical fitness. Home: 6626 Meadow Farm Dr Hudson OH 44236 Office: Ohio Bell Telephone Co 6889 Snowville Rd Brecksville OH 44141

CRAFT, ROBERT MERRILL, lawyer; b. Jackson, Mich., Sept. 12, 1958; s. Robert David and Sandra Sue (Fransted) C. BA, Albion (Mich.) Coll., 1980; JD, Detroit Coll. of Law, 1983. Bar: Mich. 1983. Atty. Curtis, Curtis, Falahee & Craft, P.C., Jackson, Mich., 1983—; bd. dirs. Bridgeway Ctr., Inc., Jackson; pub. speaker Mich. Bar, 1983—. Bd. dirs., pres. Mich. Child Search, Jackson, 1985—; big brother Big Brothers/Big Sisters of Am., Jackson, 1985—; county dir. Bill Lucas for Gov., Detroit, 1986. Mem. ABA, Mich. Bar Assn., Am. Judicature Soc., Jackson Bar Assn., Jackson Jaycees (bd. dirs. 1984-85, Mich. Speaker's award 1984). Republican. Roman Catholic. Avocations: politics, sports, photography. Home: 1002 S Brown St Jackson MI 49203 Office: Curtis Curtis Falahee & Craft PC 1500 Jackson County Tower Bldg Jackson MI 49201

CRAGG, NELSON RANDOLPH, JR., architect; b. Cin., May 1, 1944; s. Nelson Randolph Sr. and Ruth Gertrude (Tewell) C.; m. Rosa Song, June 22, 1974; children: Nelson, Michael. BArch, Ohio State U., 1968. Architect Roth Partnership, Inc., Cin., 1972—. Vice chmn. State of Ohio Modernization/Renovation Cert. Need Task Force, 1984. Served to lt. USN, 1968-72. Mem. AIA (pres. Cin. chpt. 1986—), Am. Assn. Hosp. Planning. Republican. Avocations: family activities, coaching soccer. Home: 3810 Miami Rd Cincinnati OH 45227 Office: Roth Partnership Inc 128 E 6th St Cincinnati OH 45202

CRAGUN, IRMA MARY K., resort executive; b. Powell River, B.C., Can., Sept. 1, 1934; d. Angelo and Elena Culos; m. Merrill K. Cragun, Dec. 29, 1965. RN, St. Paul's, Vancouver, B.C., Can., 1956; postgrad., U. Hawaii, San Francisco State U. RN Powell River Gen. Hosp., 1956-59, 62-63, French Hosp., San Francisco, 1959-65, Hahnemann Hosp., San Francisco, 1959-65, Poly Clinic, San Francisco, 1959-65; asst. gen. mgr. Cragun's Lodge Conf. Ctr., Brainerd, Minn., 1965—; mem. adv. bd. 1st Am. Bank Baxter. Mem. Heartland Symphony Orgn., Brainerd Arts Alliance; vol. various campaigns for State Reps. and U.S. Senators from Brainerd area. Recipient honors for services Minn. Vocat. Rehab. Mem. Minn. Resort Assn. (bd. dirs.), Brainerd C. of C. Avocations: bareboat cruise sailing, supporting the arts. Home and Office: 2001 Pine Beach Rd Brainerd MN 56401

CRAIG, DALE K., transportation company executive; b. Pennville, Ind., Apr. 16, 1927; s. Norwood S. and Emma M. (Chipman) C.; m. Gail M. Seely, Nov. 30, 1952; children: Michael L., Brian D., Lance C. BS, Ind. U., 1950. Exec. v.p. Craig Trucking, Inc., Albany, Ind., 1960-62; pres. Hofer Motor Transp., Perrysburg, Ohio, 1962-73, Craig Transp. Co., Perrysburg, 1973—; pres. MBL Corp., Perrysburg, 1963—, chmn., 1964—, Airport Travel Agy., Perrysburg, 1972—, chmn., 1972—, Nat. Perishable Transp. Assn., Chgo., 1984-85; chmn. 1973—. Mem. bus. adv. council U. Toledo, 1983-85. Mem. Am. Trucking Assns., Inc. (various coms. and task forces 1984—, chmn. bd. dirs. 1984-85), Ohio Trucking Assn. (trustee 1972-80), Common Carrier Conf. (chmn. exec. com. 1971-72, trustee edn. fund 1972-80), Canned Goods Shippers Conf. (chmn. motor carrier 1983-85), Toledo Area C. of C. (chmn. various coms., trustee 1983-85, Aviation award 1983), Perrysburg C. of C. (bd. dirs. 1975-76, exec. com. 1976), Mo. Trucking Assn., Aricraft Owners and Pilots Assn. Republican. Methodist. Club: Toledo Transp. Lodge: Lions. Office: Craig Transp Co 26699 Eckel Rd PO Box 709 Perrysburg OH 43551

CRAIG, JUDITH, clergywoman; b. Lexington, Mo., June 5, 1937; d. Raymond Luther and Edna Amelia (Forsha) C. BA, William Jewell Coll., 1959; MA in Christian Edn., Eden Theol. Sem., 1961; MDiv, Union Theol. Sem., 1968; DD, Baldwin Wallace Coll., 1981; DHL, Adrian Coll., 1985. Youth dir. Bellefontaine United Meth. Ch., St. Louis, 1959-61; intern children's work Nat. Council of Chs. of Christ, N.Y.C., 1961-62; dir. christian edn. 1st United Meth. Ch., Stamford, Ct., 1962-66; inst. adult basic edn. N.Y. Schs., N.Y.C., 1967; dir. christian edn. Epworth Euclid United Meth. Ch., Cleve., 1969-72, assoc. pastor, 1972-76; pastor Pleasant Hills United Meth. Ch., Middleburg Heights, Ohio, 1976-80; conf. council dir. East Ohio Conf. United Meth. Ch., Canton, 1980-84; bishop United Meth. Ch., Detroit, 1984—. Contbr. articles to ministry mags. Bd. dirs. YWCA, Middleburg Heights, 1976-80. Recipient Citation of Achievement William Jewell Coll., 1985. Mem. Internat. Women Minister's Assn. Office: United Meth Ch 155 W Congress Suite 200 Detroit MI 48226 *

CRAIG, TIMOTHY JAMES, advertising consultant; b. Grinnell, Iowa, Sept. 12, 1956; s. John Hill and Vivian Gail (Judy) C.; m. Cynthia Lorene Kriegel, Aug. 13, 1977; children: Kelly Gail, Mallory Rochelle, Timothy Ryan. Student, U. No. Iowa, 1974-76; BS in Journalism, S.D. State U., 1977-80. Advt. sales Eagle Printing Co., Marinette, Wis., 1980-84, advt. dir., 1984-86; advt. cons. Thomson Newspapers, Inc., Des Plaines, Ill., 1986—. Vol. George McGovern for Senate, Brookings, S.D., 1980. Mem. Soc. Profl. Journalists, Mich. Press Assn. Methodist. Avocations: golf, outdoors, family activities. Home: 196 Mulford Dr Elgin IL 60120

CRAIGHEAD, WENDEL LEE, educational and business film producer and director; b. Burr Oak, Kans., May 30, 1936; s. Alfred and Eva May (Burton) C. Student, Kans. State U., 1954-55; BA, Bethany (Okla.) Nazarene Coll., 1959; postgrad., U. Mo., Kansas City, 1962-63. Film editor Calvin Prodns., Kansas City, 1959-63, film dir., 1963-68; v.p., mgr. producer services Calvin Communications, Kansas City, 1968-75, producer, 1975-80, producer, v.p. sales, 1980-82; owner Craighead Films, Prairie Village, Kans., 1982—. Dir. A Place in History, 1969 (Cine award 1970); producer, dir. 60 motion pictures. Mem. Smoky Hill. Ry. Hist. Soc., Greater Kansas City. Mem. Assn. N.Am. Radio Clubs (nat. exec. sec. 1970-72), Greater Kansas City C. of C. Republican. Nazarene. Avocations: shortwave radio, classical music, trains. Home and Office: 2110 W 74th Terr Prairie Village KS 66208

CRAIN, JAMES WALTER, industrial engineer; b. Waukegan, Ill., June 8, 1949; s. Walter James and Gladys Mary (Snyder) C.; m. Victoria Ann Teale, May 3, 1969; children: Stephanie Lee, David James. Cert., Racine/Kenosha Teachers Coll., Union Grove, Wis., 1970; BA, Carthage Coll., Kenosha, 1974; postgrad., Milw. Sch. Engring., 1981-82. Edn. coordinator Urban League of Racine, 1976-79; indsl. engrs. Am. Motors Corp., Kenosha, 1979-82, Schweiger Industries, Jefferson, Wis., 1982, Exide Corp., Racine, 1983-84; sr. indsl. engr. Internat. Register Intermatic Inc., Spring Grove, Ill., 1984—; instr. maths. Gateway Tech. Inst., Kenosha, 1976-82, Milw. Area Tech. Coll., 1982—; cons. maths. Ironworkers #43, 1976—, Milw. Graphic Arts Inst., 1982—. Author: Concepts of The Metric Systems, 1978, Math For Ironworkers, Ironworkers, 1976, Math For The Graphic Arts, 1985. V.p. Human Rights Commn., Racine, 1977, pres. 1978. Mem. Inst. Indsl. Engrs. (sec. 1985-86). Republican. Roman Catholic. Avocations: woodworking, camping, hunting, canoeing. Home: 2712 Dwight St Racine WI 53403 Office: Internat Register Intermatic 7777 Winn Rd Spring Grove IL 60081

CRAIN, LARRY WAYNE, telecommunications company executive; b. Poplar Bluff, Mo., June 2, 1949; s. Harry C. and Lola E.C.; B.S. magna cum laude, SE Mo. State U., 1975; M.B.A., U. Mo., 1976. New product planner Hallmark Cards, Kansas City, Mo., 1977-78, bus. planning project mgr., 1978-80; mgr. planning United Telecommunications, Inc., Kansas City, Mo., 1980-83; dir. corp. planning, mktg. and regulatory affairs Republic Telcom, Bloomington, Minn., 1983-84, v.p. corporate planning and mktg., 1984-86, sr. v.p. corp. planning and human resources, Teleconnect Co., 1986, group and exec. v.p. mktg. and sales, 1987—; pres. Carrier Services Group, 1987—; bd. dirs. Prime Health, health maintenance orgn., 1980-83; instr. mktg. Served with USN, 1968-72; lectr. in field. Gregory fellow. Mem. Am. Mktg. Assn., CompTel Industry Assn. (bd. dirs. 1984—, vice chmn. 1986—, treas. 1986—), Planning Execs. Inst., Am. Numismatic Assn., Mensa. Club: Kansas City Ski. Author fiction. Home: 2407 Buckingham Dr NW Apt 323 Cedar Rapids IA 52405 Office: Teleconnect Co 500 2d Ave SE Cedar Rapids IA 52406

CRAIN, M. ELISE, construction company administrator; b. Aurora, Mo., Aug. 19, 1942; d. Joseph C. and Helen F. (Gough) C.; m. James E. Estes, Aug. 30, 1963 (div. 1965). BS in Polit. Sci., Drury Coll., 1975. Office mgr. W&A Inc., Springfield, Mo., 1967-77, Razorback Constrn., Harrison, Ark., 1977-80; pres. CLA Inc., North Little Rock, Ark., 1980; office mgr. PNH Joint Ventures, Greensboro, N.C., 1980-83, Bramer Constrn. Co., Springfield, 1983—; v.p., corp. sec. Bramer Constrn. Co. and Unistructures, Inc., 1986—. Zoning and planning commr. City of Ozark, Mo., 1984-86; sec.-treas. Sun Ridge South Homeowners Assn., Ozark, 1986; elected to serve as Alderman City of Ozark. Mem. Nat. Assn. Women in Constrn. (bd. dirs. Springfield chpt. 1985-86, treas. Springfield chpt. 1984-85, chmn. regional com. 1985-86), Greater Ozarks Bldg. Systems Assn., FORUM Women's Network (sec.-treas. 1984-86). Republican. Mem. Christian Ch. Home: 1007 Amy Ln PO Box 455 Ozark MO 65721 Office: Bramer Constrn Co 2531 W Bennett PO Box 671 Springfield MO 65801

CRAIN, THOMAS SPENCER, investment counselor; b. Cin., June 4, 1940; s. Lairy Leslie and Thelma (Bailey) C.; m. Sally Pathe, Apr. 27, 1968; children: Andrew Paul, Elizabeth Hillery. BS, U.S. Mil. Acad., 1964; MBA in Fin., U. Cin., 1970. Chartered fin. analyst; chartered investment counselor. Commd. 2d lt. USAF, 1964, advanced through grades to capt., resigned, 1969; portfolio mgr. Scudder, Stevens and Clark, Cin., 1969-78, v.p. investments, 1978-83, gen. ptnr., 1983-84, mng. dir. Midwest div., 1984—. Served to capt. USAF, 1964-69. MEm. Cin. Soc. Fin. Analysts. Republican. Clubs: Cin. Athletic, Coldstream Country, Queen City (Ohio). Office: Scudder Stevens & Clark 540 Carew Tower Cincinnati OH 45202

CRAINER, HERCHEL AMERICUS, III, insurance company agent; b. Pasadena, Tex., Aug. 9, 1955; m. Herchel Americus Crainer Jr. and Naomi Gaynell Pearce; m. Kristine Ann Oldehoeft, Nov. 25, 1978; children: Caleb J., Holly R. AA, Butler County Community Coll., Eldorado, Kans., 1975; BA, Wichita State U., 1977; MSW, U. Kans., 1981. Social work adminstr. State of Kans., Hutchinson, 1981-84; ins. agt. State Farm Ins., Hutchinson, 1984—. Bd. dirs. Kans. Conf. on Social Welfare, 1983-84, Mental Health Assn. Reno County, Hutchinson, 1983-86, Community Improvement Commn., Hutchinson, 1986. Mem. Hutchinson Assn. Life Underwriters (bd. dirs.), Hutchinson Jaycees. Democrat. Lutheran. Home: 604 E 15th Hutchinson KS 67501 Office: 216 E 30th Hutchinson KS 67502

CRAM, MARC ERIC, personnel manager; b. LaCrosse, Wis., Mar. 4, 1951; s. Harold Raymond and Elena (Chavez) C.; m. Karin Kay Nelson, May 20, 1972; children: Stacy, Cristyn. BA in Philosophy, U. Wis., LaCrosse, 1973; postgrad., U. Wis., 1975; cert. indsl. relations, U. Minn., 1984. Store mgr. Holiday Village Inc., Medford, Wis., 1976-81; personnel mgr. Erickson Petroleum Corp., Mpls., 1981—; advisor Mpls. Area Tech. Ctr., Mpls., 1981—. Pre-unit chairperson Minn. Ind. Rep. Party, Eden Prairie, 1984—; chmn.

United Way, Medford, 1979-80. Mem. Twin City Personnel Assn. Avocations: gardening, woodworking, video and audio recording, amateur theater. Home: 8681 Meadowvale Dr Eden Prairie MN 55344

CRAMER, ELVIN W., distributing company executive; b. Glasco, Kans., July 26, 1919; s. Ralph Whistler and Margaret May (Cundiff) C.; m. Ruth Alene Woodhull, June 12, 1949; children: Douglas Elvin, Jane Leslie Cramer Williams. BS, Kansas State U., 1942. Salesman Siebert & Willis, Wichita, 1947-58; pres. The Cramer Co., Wichita, 1958. Served to lt. USNR, 1942-46, PTO. Republican. Lodge: Kiwanis (pres. Downtown Wichita chpt. 1982-83), Masons. Home: 8610 Huntington Wichita KS 67206 Office: The Cramer Co 811 E Waterman Wichita KS 67202

CRANDALL, JOHN LYNN, insurance company executive; b. Chgo., Apr. 17, 1927; s. Paul Bertram and Olga (Bliech) C.; m. Irene Anze Ruenne, Dec. 26, 1973; children by previous marriage: Deborah Crandall Schmude, Jeffrey, Lynne Crandall Blais; stepchildren: George Ruenne, Helgi Ruenne Becker. BS in Fire Protection Engring., Ill. Inst. Tech., 1951. CPCU; cert. in gen. ins. Highly protected risk inspector FIA, Chgo., 1951-53, asst. engring. supr., 1953-56, engring. supr., 1956-59, underwriting supr., special agt., 1959-65; HPR engr., underwriter Kemper Group, Chgo., 1965-67, HPR sales specialist, 1967-71; asst. to dir. underwriting Protection Mutual Ins. Co., Park Ridge, Ill., 1971-73, v.p. underwriting, 1973-78, v.p., dir. underwriting, 1978—. Served with USN, 1945-46. Mem. Soc. Fire Protection Engrs. (charter), Soc. CPCU's (chpt. pres. 1980-81, nat. dir. 1987—). Republican. Lutheran. Home: 24 Lambert Dr Schaumburg IL 60193 Office: 300 S Northwest Hwy Park Ridge IL 60068

CRANDALL, TIMOTHY F., accountant; b. Chicago Heights, Ill., Oct. 8, 1962; s. Joseph Christopher and Geraldine Marie (Becker) C.; m. Patricia Sue Utz, May 4, 1985. BS in Acctg., No. Ill. U., 1984. CPA, Ill. Ptnr. Crandall & Crandall, Geneva, Ill., 1980—. Treas. Sch. Dist. 304, Geneva, 1986-87, United Meth. Ch., Geneva, 1986—. Mem. Am. Inst. CPA's, Ill. Soc. CPA's. Republican. Methodist. Avocations: computers, outdoor activities. Home: 808 Manchester Course Geneva IL 60134 Office: 312 W State PO Box 490 Geneva IL 60134

CRANDALL, YVETTE BIRS, physical education educator; b. Key West, Fla., May 20, 1939; s. Louis Benjamin and Rosalina (Sawyer) Birs; m. Warren Linneer Crandall, Nov. 4, 1966; children: Deborah, Rebecca, Matthew, Julia, Andrea, Lucas. BS, U. Wis., 1962, MS, 1967; Edn. Specialist, Cen. Mich. U., 1987. Instr. Cen. Mich. U., Mt. Pleasant, 1964-65, dir. dance programs, 1970—, asst. prof. phys. edn. and sport-dance, 1972—; tchr. Bd. Edn., Madison, Wis., 1965-66; artistic dir. Orchesis Dance Theatre, Cen. Mich. U., 1967—; dance resp. Mich. Youth Arts Festival, 1972-83. Critic dance Midland Daily News, Mich., 1985—; choreographer The Object, 1981 (regional award 1981), For My Children, 1983 (regional award 1983), Mensurum, 1985 (regional award 1985), Forms I, 1986 (nat. award 1986). Mem. Am. Coll. Dance Festival Assn., Sag Valley Dance Council. Episcopalian. Office: Cen Mich U 127 Rose Ctr Mount Pleasant MI 48859

CRANE, ALISON ROGERS, gemologist, jeweler, goldsmith, enamelist; b. Louisville, Ky., Nov. 7, 1940; d. Vincent Muir and Frances (Cheatham) R.; m. Thomas Michael Crane, Sept. 22, 1962; children—Kevin Muir, Brook Jennifer. Student Northwestern U., 1956-59, Pine Manor, 1956; grad. Gemological Inst. Am., 1985. Apprentice goldsmith, salesstaff Michael Banner Inc., Glencoe, Ill., 1972-73; owner, operator Jewels By Alison, Glenview, Ill., 1973—. Recipient Golden Horseshoe award Equestrian Assn., 1961, citation Mayor Daley of Chgo., 1959. Mem. Ill. Jewelers Assn. (vigilante com. 1975—), Nat. Assn. Jewelery Appraisers (sr. mem.), Gemological Inst. Am. Alumni Assn. (sec. Ill.-Wis. chpt. 1987-88), Jewelers Assn. Republican. Avocations: scuba diving; tennis; horseback riding. Home and Office: 1410 Pleasant Ln Glenview IL 60025

CRANE, EDWARD J., airline executive; b. 1928; m. Margaret Struif; children: Steven, Edward J., Mary Ann, John. Grad., St. Louis U. Sch. Commerce and Fin., 1951. Accounting dept. comptroller Ozark Air Lines, Inc., St. Louis, 1951-60, v.p., comptroller, 1960-65, v.p., treas., 1965-68, exec. v.p., treas., 1968-71, pres., chief exec. officer, 1971—; also dir. Ozark Air Lines, Inc.; dir. Bank of St. Louis, Valley Industries, Gen. Bancshares Corp. Mem. pres.'s council, trustee St. Louis U.; bd. dirs. United Way, 1977-83, Regional Commerce and Growth Assn. St. Louis, St. Louis Council Boy Scouts Am.; trustee Incarnate Word Hosp. Served with USMC, World War II. Mem. Assn. Local Transport Airlines (past chmn., bd. dirs.), Air Transport Assn. (bd. dirs.), Air Conf. (bd. dirs.). Office: Ozark Airlines PO Box 10007 Lambert Field Saint Louis MO 63145 *

CRANE, FAYE, small business owner; b. Amery, Wis., Dec. 2, 1947; d. Vaemond Hall and Irene C. (L'Allier) C.; 1 child, Camille Mills Seifert. Grad. high sch., Milltown, Wis. Premiums statistical clk. State Farm Ins., St. Paul, 1968-73; pension adminstrn. asst. Mutual Service Ins., St. Paul, 1973-78; dist. dir. Avon Products, Inc., Morton Grove, Ill., 1978-79; sales rep. Midwest Bus. Systems, Duluth, Minn., 1979-84, REM's Inc., Grand Rapids, Minn., 1984; pres. production Presto Print, Grand Rapids, 1984—. Mem. Northern Minn. Citizen's League, Grand Rapids, 1984-86. Mem. Minn. Fedn. Bus. and Profl. Women (promotion com., 1982—, emblem chmn. 1982-83, found. chmn. 1983-84, exec. dir. chmn., 1984-85, editor 1987—), Grand Rapids Bus. and Profl. Women (pres. 1985-86). Home: PO Box 404 Grand Rapids MN 55744 Office: Presto Print 3 Golf Course Rd Grand Rapids MN 55744

CRANE, JAMES KENNETH, physician; b. Evanston, Ill., Dec. 30, 1950; s. Robert Lamar and Helena (Slater) C.; m. Phyllis Ann Davis, Jan. 29, 1972; children: Matthew James, Suzanne Michelle. BS, U. Ill., 1972; MD, U. Ill., Chgo., 1977. Diplomate Am. Bs. Ob-Gyn. Resident Ohio State U., Columbus, 1977-81; clinical instr. U. Ill., Peoria, 1981—. Author: (chpts.) Drug Therapy in Obstetrics and Gynecology, 1986. Fellow Am. Coll. Ob-Gyn, Am. Fertility Soc.; mem. AMA. Home: 4502 W Broyhill Ct Peoria IL 61615 Office: Murphy Saad Crane SC 4809 N Sheridan Rd Peoria IL 61614

CRANE, PHILIP MILLER, congressman; b. Chgo., Nov. 3, 1930; s. George Washington III and Cora (Miller) C.; m. Arlene Catherine Johnson, Feb. 14, 1959; children: Catherine Anne, Susanna Marie, Jennifer Elizabeth, Rebekah Caroline, George Washington V, Rachel Ellen, Sarah Emma, Carrie Esther. Student, DePauw U., 1948-50; B.A., Hillsdale Coll., 1952; postgrad., U. Mich., 1952-54, U. Vienna, Austria, 1953, 56; M.A., Ind. U., 1961, Ph.D., 1963; LL.D., Grove City Coll., 1973; Doctor en Ciencias Politicas, Francisco Marroquin U., 1979. Advt. mgr. Hopkins Syndicate, Inc., Chgo., 1956-58; teaching asst. Ind. U., Bloomington, 1959-62; asst. prof. history Bradley U., Peoria, Ill., 1963-67; dir. schs. Westminster Acad., Northbrook, Ill., 1967-68; mem. 91st-100th congresses, 12th Ill. Dist.; mem. ways and means com. Author: Democrat's Dilemma, 1964, The Sum of Good Government, 1976, Surrender In Panama: The Case Against the Treaty, 1977; contbr.: Continuity in Crisis, 1974, Crisis in Confidence, 1974, Case Against the Reckless Congress, 1976, Can You Afford This House?, 1978, View from the Capitol Dome (Looking Right), 1980, Liberal Cliches and Conservative Solutions, 1984. Dir. research Ill. Goldwater Orgn., 1964; mem. nat. adv. bd. Young Ams. for Freedom, 1965—; bd. dirs., chmn. Am. Conservative Union, 1965-81, Intercollegiate Studies Inst.; bd. dirs. Ashbrook Ctr., Ashland Coll., 1983—; founder, chmn. Rep. Study Com., 1984—; commr. Commn. on Bicentennial U.S. Constn., 1986; trustee Hillsdale Coll. Served with AUS, 1954-56. Recipient Distinguished Alumnus award Hillsdale Coll., 1968, Independence award, 1974, William McGovern award Chgo. Soc., 1969, Freedoms Found. award, 1973; named Ill. Statesman's Father Yr., 1979. Mem. Am. Hist. Assn., Orgn. Am. Historians, Acad. Polit. Sci., Am. Acad. Polit. and Social Scis., Phila. Soc., ASCAP, VFW (award 1978), Phi Alpha Theta, Pi Gamma Mu. Lodge: B'nai B'rith (award 1978). Office: 1035 Longworth House Office Bldg Washington DC 20515

CRANE, ROBERT SELLERS, JR., plastic company executive, civic worker; b. Dayton, Ohio, June 9, 1922; s. Robert Sellers and Helen (Jameson) C.; m. Lois Ann Woods, Aug. 14, 1948; children—Robert Sellers III, Thomas W., Ann B., Mary Jameson. B.S. in Bus. Adminstrn., Ohio State U., 1948. Pres. Crane Plastics, Inc., Columbus, Ohio, 1963-67, chmn., 1967—; chmn. Taytec Corp., Columbus, 1976—; bd. dirs. State Savs., Columbus, Buckhorn Industries, Inc., Columbus, Care Ctr., Inc., Dayton. Trustee Franklin U., Columbus; pres. United Franklin County, Columbus, 1977, campaign chmn., 1974; chmn. governing bd. First Community Ch., Columbus, 1976, mem. governing com. Columbus Found., 1980—, vice chmn., 1982-83, chmn., 1984—; campaign chmn. United Way, Columbus, 1974 . Served to 2d lt. U.S. Army, 1945-46. Mem. Soc. Plastic Industry, Presidents Club Ohio State, Presidents Assn. Am. Mgmt. Assn., Columbus Area C. of C. (vice chmn. 1979-83, Columbus award 1977), Phi Gamma Delta. Republican. Home: 2740 Edington Rd Columbus OH 43221 Office: Crane Platics Corp 2141 Fairwood Ave Columbus OH 43207

CRATCHA, DANIEL STANLEY, counseling center clinical supervisor; b. Cleve., Mar. 7, 1956; s. Stanley George and Alice (Kalafatis) C.; m. Shelby Jean Heleen, Feb. 14, 1986. BA in Psychology, Ohio U., 1981; MEd in Counseling, Cleve. State U., 1983; cert., Gestalt Inst., 1986. Counseling supr. Teamsters Assistance Program, Cleve., 1984-85; designate dir. Deaconess Hosp. Weekend Intervention Program, Cleve., 1986; clin. supr. Neighborhood Counseling, Cleve., 1985—. Served with USNG, 1978-85. Greek Orthodox. Avocations: running, reading, crossword puzzles, motorcycles. Home: 37 Middleton Dr Painesville OH 44077 Office: Neighborhood Counseling 1885 Fulton Rd Cleveland OH 44113

CRATIN, THOMAS LEE, dentist; b. Detroit, Aug. 2, 1952; s. William S. Cratin and Barbara (Estes) Watters; m. Christy Ann Smith, June 23, 1978; children: Peter, Catherine. BA in Biology, Drake U., 1974; DDS, Loyola U., Maywood, Ill., 1978. Staff Hinsdale (Ill.) Hosp., 1979—; gen. practice dentistry Hinsdale, 1979—. Fellow Acad. Gen. Dentistry; mem. ADA, Am. Soc. Dentistry Children, Am. Equilibration Soc., Ill. State Dental Soc., Chgo. Dental Soc. Office: 522 Chestnut St Hinsdale IL 60521

CRAVEN, PAUL DAVID, dentist; b. Atlantic, Iowa, Sept. 24, 1954; s. Norman Porter and Kathryn (Maus) C. B in Elected Studies, U. Minn., 1976, DDS, 1980. Gen. practice dentistry Circle Pines, Minn., 1981—. Mem. ADA, Minn. Dental Assn., Mpls. Dist. Dental Assn. Club: North Star Study. Office: 9085 S Highway Dr Circle Pines MN 55014

CRAVENS, JAMES HEWITT, pediatrician, educator; b. St. Louis, July 11, 1919; s. Harvey Mudd and Marie Elise (Zingre) C.; m. Ann Schnake, Feb. 12, 1944; children—Patricia Ann Cravens Kiser, Carol Lynn Cravens Johnson, James Charles. B.S., U. Ill., 1941; M.D., Washington U., St. Louis, 1943. Diplomate Am. Bd. Pediatrics. Intern U. Chgo. Clinics, 1944; resident in pediatrics St. Louis Children's Hosp., 1947-48; pediatrician Physicians and Surgeons Clinic, Quincy, Ill., 1948—, chmn. bd., 1957-62; instr. pediatrics Washington U., 1948; clin. assoc.in pediatrics So. Ill. U. Sch. Medicine, 1977—. Pres. Swanberg Med. Found., 1971—. Served to capt. AUS, 1944-46. Fellow Am. Acad. Pediatrics (sec. Ill. chpt. 1980-83, pres. 1986—), mem. AMA, Ill. Med. Soc., Adams County Med. Soc. (pres. 1965), Downstate Ill. Pediatric Soc. (pres. 1973-75), Soc. for Acad. Achievement, Phi Eta Sigma, Phi Lambda Upsilon, Omega Beta Pi, Delta Chi, Phi Rho Sigma. Presbyterian. Club: Quincy Country. Lodge: Rotary (pres. Quincy 1953-54). Home: 62 Lincoln Hill NE Quincy IL 62301 Office: 1101 Maine St Quincy IL 62301

CRAVENS, JOE BOB, environmental engineer; b. Guthrie, Okla., May 13, 1952; s. George Vernon and Audrey Blanch (Mustain) C.; m. Lynette Naomi Sinclair, Jan. 22, 1984. BS in Aquatic Biology and Chemistry, Okla. State U., 1974, MS in Environ. Engring., 1977. Engr. environ. research Rexnord Corp. Research and Devel., Environ. Research Ctr., Milw., 1977-82; project engr. Envirex Systems div. Rexnord S.A. (Pty.) Ltd., Johannesburg, South Africa, 1982-84; project officer EPA, Dallas, 1984-85; sr. environ. engr. Dames & Doore, Cin., 1985—. Mem. Am. Water Pollution Control Fedn., Cen. States Water Pollution Control Fedn., Am. Water Works Assn., Wis. Wastewater Treatment Plant Operators Assn., Nat. Soc. Profl. Engrs., Wis. Soc. Profl. Engrs., U.S. Ski Assn., Am. Soc. Johannesburg, Johannesburg Jaycees (v.p. programs, exec. v.p.), Milw. Jaycees (external v.p., bd. dirs. 1981-82, Spoke of Yr. award 1980-81, Dir. of Yr. Award 1981-82, Project Co-Chmn. of Yr. award 1981-82), Milw. Met. Civic Alliance (bd. dirs. 1981-82). Democrat. Baptist. Home: 7218 Adena Hills Dr Westchester OH 45069 Office: Dames & Moore 644 Linn St Suite 501 Cincinnati OH 45203

CRAVER, JAMES STEPHEN, lawyer; b. Centerville, Iowa, Mar. 28, 1943; s. Harlan B. and Jean (Shanks) C.; m. Jennifer Cogis, June 22, 1968; children: Michael, Marc, Matthew. BBA, U. Iowa, 1965; JD, Drake U., 1968. Bar: Iowa 1968. Ptnr. Milani & Craver, Centerville, 1968—; atty. City of Centerville, 1973—, City of Moravia, Iowa, 1978—. Mem. ABA, Iowa Bar Assn., Iowa Mcpl. Attys. Assn., Centerville C. of C. Methodist. Clubs: Appanoose County Baseball Assn. (treas. 1986—); Appanoose County Country (Centerville) (pres. 1980). Lodge: Elks. Avocations: golf, swimming, baseball, tennis. Home: Rural Rt #3 Rock Valley Rd Centerville IA 52544

CRAWFORD, DOUGLAS NATHAN, community college administrator; b. Ann Arbor, Mich., Oct. 7, 1942; s. Ferris Nathan and Eileen Bessie (Icheldinger) C.; m. Lois Ann Hart, June 19, 1970; children—Nathan Robert, Andrea Marie, Kimberly Diane. BA, Central Mich. U., 1964; M in Pub. Adminstrn., U. Mich., 1969; PhD, Mich. State U., 1979. Tchr. govt. and history Petoskey High Schl., Mich., 1968-70; instr. polit. sci. Jackson Community Coll., Mich., 1970-72; assoc. prof. polit. sci. Lansing Community Coll., Mich., 1971-78; chmn. div. gen. and pub. service studies Edison State Community Coll., Piqua, Ohio, 1979-85, dean acad. services, 1985—, mem. chancellor's adv. commn. on two-yr. acad. programs, 1985—, mem. bd. regents task force on social studies, 1981-82; mem. North Central Assn. visitation team, Greenville Ohio, 1983 and Arcanum, Ohio, 1985. Pres. Human Services Council, Miami County (Ohio), 1984-85; instl. rep. and convener Domestic Policy Assn., Piqua, 1984-85; capt. membership campaign Miami County YMCA, 1984-85; del. Mich. Rep. Conv., 1974. Served as 1st lt. U.S. Army, 1965-67, Vietnam. Mem. Am. Soc. Pub. Adminstrn. (chpt. sec. 1974-76), Nat. Council Instrnl. Adminstrs. (Ohio council chief instrntl. officers), Am. Tech. Edn. Assn., Phi Delta Kappa. Episcopalian. Lodge: Rotary (bull. editor 1983-85, trustee 1986—, dir. 1986-87). Avocations: camping, boating, racquetball, collecting old textbooks. Home: 28 S 7th St Miamisburg OH 45342 Office: Edison State Community Coll 1973 Edison Dr Piqua OH 45356

CRAWFORD, FERRIS NATHAN, educator; b. Frankfort, Mich., Nov. 1, 1912; s. Nathan Jennings and Mary Elizabeth (Lentz) C.; m. Eileen Bessie Icheldinger, June 25, 1941; children: Douglas Nathan, Barbara Ann (Mrs. David E. Ellies), Susan Marie (Mrs. William E. Tharr Jr.), Thomas Alfred. AB, Cen. Mich. U., 1935; MA, U. Mich., 1940; DEd, Mich. State U., 1959. Tchr. Rose City (Mich.) High Schs., 1935-36; tchr. Fairgrove (Mich.) High Schs., 1936-37, prin., 1937-39; tchr. Dearborn (Mich.) High Schs., 1939-42; adminstr. Ford Airplane Sch., Willow Run, Mich., 1942-45; dir. selective psychol. testing Ford Motor Co., Dearborn, 1945-46; dir. community sch. service programs Mich. Dept. Edn., Lansing, 1946-54, chief higher edn., 1954-58, asst. supt. gen. edn., 1958-65, assoc. supt. ednl. services, 1966-76; dir. Mid-Am. Cons. Assocs., Lansing, 1977—; lectr. U. Mich. and Mich. State U., 1960-65, U. Tex., 1963; exec. sec. Mich. Commn. on Coll. Accreditation, 1961-66. Author: (with Maurice Seay) The Community School and Community Self-Improvement, 1954; contbr. numerous articles to profl. jours. Named to Mich. Edn. Hall Fame, 1976; recipient Disting. Pub. Service award Mich. Congress Parents and Tchrs., 1959, Mich. Council Community Coll. Pres., 1963, Gov.'s award Commn. Disting. Pub. Employees, 1974, Mich. Council Exceptional Children, 1975, Disting. Service award Mich. Legis., 1976. Mem. Mich. Assn. Sch. Bds. (Disting. Service award 1976), Mich. Sch. Adminstrs (Disting. Service award 1976), Mich. Community Coll. Assn. (Disting. Service award 1976), Phi Delta Kappa. Home and Office: 2958 Mayfair Dr Lansing MI 48912

CRAWFORD, HELEN MARIETTA, teacher, artist, writer, retired; b. Lincoln, Mo., Jan. 22, 1907; d. Robert Finley and Margaret Eliza (Moore) Wilson; m. Hugh Byron Hudelson, Nov. 30, 1933 (dec. Apr. 1959); children: Robert Lee, Donna May, David Martin, Ralph Allen, James Arthur; m. John Hindman Crawford, Aug. 26, 1962 (dec. Sept. 1974); stepchildren: John William, George Wesley. BS, Sterling Coll., 1927, BA, 1930; postgrad., Wyo. U., 1932, 59, Portland State U., 1964-65. Tchr. Torrington (Wyo.) Pub. Sch., 1930-33, 1959-64, West Hills Christian Sch., Portland, Oreg., 1964-67; pres. Woman's Christian Temperance Union, Portland, 1973-80; editor, lectr. Oreg. Woman's Christian Temperance Union, Portland, 1973-80; art tchr. pvt. classes, Wyo., Oreg., Kans., 1930-83. Author: Discovering Young Life, 1986; also illustrator. County coordinator I Love Kans., Topeka, 1986—. Republican. Presbyterian. Club: Garden (Sterling, Kans.). Avocations: gardening, culturing flowers, quilting, painting, creative ceramics. Home: 117 N 8th St Sterling KS 67579

CRAWFORD, JAMES WELDON, psychiatrist, educator, administrator; b. Napoleon, Ohio, Oct. 27, 1927; s. Homer and Olga (Alderman) C.; m. Susan Young, July 5, 1955; 1 child, Robert James. A.B., Oberlin Coll., 1950; M.D., U. Chgo., 1954, Ph.D., 1961. Intern Wayne County Hosp. and Infirmary, Eloise, Mich., 1954-55; resident Northwestern U., Chgo., 1958-59, Mt. Sinai Hosp./Chgo. Med. Sch., 1959-60; practice medicine specializing in psychiatry Chgo., 1961—; mem. staff Mt. Sinai Hosp., Chgo., Ravenswood Hosp., Chgo., Louis A. Weiss Meml. Hosp., Chgo., St. Lukes-Presbyterian Med. Ctr.; clin. assoc. prof. dept. psychiatry Abraham Lincoln Sch. Medicine, U. Ill., 1970—; assoc. prof. dept. psychiatry, dept. psychology and social scis. Rush Med. Coll., Chgo., 1984—; chmn. dept. psychiatry Ravenswood Hosp. Med. Ctr., 1973-79; chmn. J.W. Crawford Assocs. Inc., 1979-82. Contbr. articles to profl. jours. Bd. dirs. Pegasus Player, Chgo., 1978—, chmn. bd. dirs., 1979-84; bd. dirs. Bach Soc., 1985—. Served with MC, AUS, 1945-46. NIH Inst. Neurol. Diseases postdoctoral fellow, 1955-59. Fellow Am. Psychiat. Assn., Am. Orthopsychiat. Assn. (nat. council on family relations); mem. AAAS, Assn. Am. Med. Colls., Ill. Psychiat. Soc., AAUP, Sigma Xi. Lodge: Rotary. Home and Office: 2418 Lincoln St Evanston IL 60201 Office: 440 N Michigan Ave Chicago IL 60611

CRAWFORD, JEAN ANDRE, counselor; b. Chgo., Apr. 12, 1941; d. William Moses and Geneva Mae (Lacy) Jones; student Shimer Coll., 1959-60; BA, Carthage Coll., 1966; MEd, Loyola U., Chgo., 1971; postgrad. Nat. Coll. Edn., Evanston, Ill., 1971-77, Northwestern U., 1976-83; m. John N. Crawford, Jr., June 28, 1969; cert. counselor Nat. Bd. Cert. Counselors. Med. technologist, Chgo., 1960-62; primary and spl. edn. tchr. Chgo. Pub. Schs., 1966-71, counselor maladjusted children and their families, 1971—; counselor juvenile first-offenders, 1968—. Vol., Sta. WTTW-TV; vol. counselor deaf children and their families. Cert. elem. edn., spl. edn. and pupil personnel services, Ill. Mem. Ill. Assn. Counseling and Devel., Am., Ill. sch. counselors assns., Council Exceptional Children, Am. Assn. Counseling Devel., Coordinating Council Handicapped Children, Shimer Coll. Alumni Assn. (sec. 1982-84), Phi Delta Kappa. Home: 601 E 32d St Chicago IL 60616 Office: 2131 W Monroe St Chicago IL 60612

CRAWFORD, JOHN GEORGE, III, pediatric dentist, orthodontist; b. Evergreen Pk., Ill., Oct. 29, 1945; s. John G. and Helen A. (Skoog) C.; m. Susan Marie Machamer, Aug. 27, 1963; 1 child, Andrea Jean. B.S., U. Ill. Med. Ctr.-Chgo., 1968, D.D.S., 1970, M.S., 1974. Cert. pedodontics, Ill., Orthodontics, Ill. Asst. prof. pedodontics, orthodontics U. Ill. Coll. of Dentistry, Chgo., 1974-79, dir. div. of growth and devel., 1975-79; practice dentistry specializing in pediatric dentistry and orthodontics, Oak Park, Ill., 1979—; pedodontic cons. State of Ill. Dept. of Registration and Edn., Springfield, 1982-85. Fellow Am. Acad. Pediatric Dentistry; mem. Ill. Soc. Pediatric Dentists (pres. 1985-86), Chgo. Dental Soc. (pres. west side br. 1983-84), Am. Assn. Orthodontists. Home: 155 N Taylor Ave Oak Park IL 60302 Office: 505 N Ridgeland Ave Oak Park IL 60302

CRAWFORD, MARTHA JEANNE, architectural interior designer; b. Rockford, Ill., June 25, 1925; d. Woodruff Lynden and LaVerna (Means) C. Student Vassar Coll., 1943-45, Rockford Coll., 1945, Parsons Sch. Design, 1945-48, Columbia U. Sch. Architecture, 1951-53. Asst. interior designer Eleanor LeMaire Assocs., N.Y.C., 1948-49; head color dept. Amos Parrish & Co., N.Y.C., 1950-52; contract interior designer Beeston and Patterson, N.Y.C., 1952-53, Welton Becket & Assocs., N.Y.C., 1952-53; cons. interior designer, N.Y.C., 1953-58; owner Martha Crawford and Assocs., comml. design co., N.Y.C., 1958-66; cons. interior designer Joseph Maxwell Assocs., Ft. Lauderdale, Fla., 1969-70, VVKR Ptnrship., Alexandria, Va., 1972-74, Design for Bus. Interiors, Washington, 1973-74; archtl. interior designer, Waukesha, Wis., 1975—;cons. color coordinator Timbertone Corp., N.Y.C., 1958-61, R.C.A. Rubber Co., Akron, Ohio, 1954-59; brochure cons. Rockcote Paints, Rockford, 1960-61. Contbr. to profl. publs. Vol. Inst. for Crippled and Disabled, N.Y.C., 1950-53; sec. Child Care Found., Fort Lauderdale, Fla., 1968-69; co-founder, coordinator Job Hunter's Network, Waukesha, Wis., 1982-86. Recipient hon. mention award for outstanding interior of yr. S.M. Hexter Co., Cleve., 1959; 2d place award Dow Chem. Co., N.Y.C., 1960. Mem. Constrn. Specifications Inst. (D.C. bd. dirs. 1975, President's plaque 1975), N.Y.C. AIA (assoc.), Archtl. League N.Y. (co-chmn. current work 1959-60). Club: Altrusa (pres. 1969-70) (Fort Lauderdale). Avocations: paint jazz pastels; listening to jazz; book discussion groups. Home and Office: W305 S4522 Brookhill Rd Waukesha WI 53188

CRAWFORD, MICHAEL E., university official. Chancellor Adminstrn. Ctr. St. Louis Community Coll. Office: St Louis Community Coll Adminstrn Ctr 5801 Wilson Ave Saint Louis MO 63110 *

CRAWFORD, PAUL ANCIL, computer consultant; b. Oklahoma City, Okla., Jan. 25, 1952; s. Othel and Lola Mary (Harris) C.; m. Wanda Delores Pearson, Aug. 22, 1971 (div. May 1979); children: Jon Paul, Jeffery Lee; m. Jeri Lynn Jones, July 21, 1979. BS in Engring., Northeastern State U., Tahlequah, Okla., 1975; postgrad., Okla. State U., 1975-76. Staff engr. Seismograph Services Corp., Tulsa, 1975-76; engr. Tex. Instruments, Richardson, 1976-78; cons. Dallas, 1979-80, CAMSCO, Inc., Dallas, 1979-80; group engr. Martin Marietta Aerospace, Orlando, Fla., 1980-85; cons. Collins div. Rockwell Internat., Cedar Rapids, Iowa, 1985—. Served as sgt. U.S. Army, 1969-71. Decorated Bronze Star. Mem. Acad. Model Aeronautics, Radio-Operated Auto Racing, Sigma Pi Sigma, Kappa Mu Epsilon. Republican. Presbyterian. Avocations: radio controlled cars and airplanes, computers, motorcycling. Home and Office: 348 Norman Dr NE Cedar Rapids IA 52402

CRAWFORD, RALPH CHRISTOPHER, advertising executive; b. Marion, Ohio, Sept. 9, 1959; s. Melton and Roberta Marie (Cramer) C.; m. Laurie Lynn Boxwell, Oct. 20, 1984. BA in Mktg., Ohio State U., 1982. Sales inspector Rollins Inc., Columbus, Ohio, 1982-83; acct. exec. Scantland Communications, Marion, 1983—; bd. govs. Marion Cadets. Chmn. Marion Popcorn Festival, 1986-87; asst. commr. Marion U.S. Open, 1986-87; com. mem. Cancer Sterethon, Marion, 1985—; bd. mem. Marion Cadets Drum and Bugle Corps. Recipient Highest Achievement award Dale Carnegie, 1985; named one of Outstanding Young Men Am. award, 1985. Mem. Sales Advt. Club, Ohio State Alumni Assn., Cadet Alumni Assn. Republican. Avocations: fishing, camping, golf, boating. Office: Scantland Communications 355 E Center St Marion OH 43302

CRAWFORD, RAYMOND JOHN, gas measurement company executive; b. West Frankfort, Ill., May 11, 1927; 6. Raymond John and Emma (Grazulis) C.; m. Joyce Marguerite Tyler, July 31, 1954; children: Janet Crawford Podrasky, Catherine, David, Robert. Various positions No. Ill. Gas Co., Bellwood, Ill., 1950-67; dir. measuremet No. Ill. Gas Co., LaGrange, Ill., 1967-84; v.p. ops. Measurement Services Inc., Neponset, Ill., 1984—. Served with USN, 1945-46. Recipient Joe Harper award Rockwell Internat., 1977. Mem. Am. Gas Assn. (chmn. measurement com. 1976-77, Merit Award 1978), Midwest Gas Assn. (chmn. measurement and control 1972-73), Internat. Sch. Hydrocarbon Measurement (chmn. 1982). Avocations: woodworking, golf. Home: 811 S Euclid Ave Princeton IL 61356 Office: Measurement Services Inc PO Box 298 208 W Bureau St Neponset IL 61345

CRAWFORD, RAYMOND MAXWELL, JR., nuclear engineer; b. Charleston, S.C., July 28, 1933; s. Raymond Maxwell and Mary Elizabeth (Bates) C.; m. J. Denise LeDuc, Mar. 10, 1951; children: Denis, Michael, Deborah, Peter, Elizabeth. B.S., Wayne State U., 1958, M.S., 1960; Ph.D., UCLA, 1969. Instr. Wayne State U., 1960-63; asst. prof. Calif. State U., Northridge, 1963-66; mem. tech. staff Atomics Internat., 1969-71; nuclear engr. Argonne Nat. Lab., Ill., 1971-74; assoc. and asst. head nuclear safeguards and licensing div. Sargent & Lundy, Chgo., 1974-80; v.p. Sci. Applications, Inc., Oak Brook, Ill., 1980-83; engring. dir. Nutech, Chgo., 1983-86; pres. Engring. Research Group, Naperville, Ill., 1986—; tech. cons.

Atomic Power Devel. Assn., 1962-63; summer fellow NASA Lewis Research Ctr., 1965-66. Contbr. articles to profl. jours. Scoutmaster, counsellor Boy Scouts Am., 1963-66; active YMCA, 1966-69, Recs. for Blind, 1964-65. Recipient numerous awards. Mem. Western Soc. Engrs., Am. Nuclear Soc., Am. Inst. Chem. Engrs., Am. Chem. Soc., Nat. Soc. Profl. Engrs., Am. Sci. Affiliation, N.Y. Acad. Sci., AAAS, Sigma Xi, Tau Beta Pi, Phi Lambda Upsilon. Home: 1005 E Kennebec Ln Naperville IL 60540

CRAWFORD, RODERICK JAMES, engineer; b. Wellington, Kans., Oct. 17, 1952; s. James S. and Dorothy (James) C.; m. Waunita Ann Jackson, Dec. 28, 1974; children: Aaron, Sally, Wendy. Student, Washburn U., 1970-72; BSEE, Kans. State U., 1974. Registered profl. engr., Kans., Mo. Engr. Burns & McDonnell, Kansas City, Mo., 1975-76; project engr. Solid State Sonics & Electronics, Inc., Topeka, 1976—. Chmn. bd. deacons 1st Presbyn. Ch., Topeka, 1985. Mem. IEEE, Am. Soc. Non-Destructive Testing. Republican. Club: Kans. Valley Amateur Radio. Office: Solid State Sonics & Electronics Inc 4137 Lower Silver Lake Rd Topeka KS 66618

CRAWFORD, RONALD LYLE, microbiology educator, consultant; b. Santa Anna, Tex., Sept. 28, 1947; s. Lester Crawford and Doris Delores (Smith) Crawford Norman; m. Onie Ann Thompson, Dec. 30, 1967; 1 child, Lisa Brooks. B.A. in Biology cum laude, Oklahoma City U., 1970; M.S. in Bacteriology, U. Wis.-Madison, 1972, Ph.D. in Bacteriology, 1973. Research assoc. U. Minn. St. Paul, 1973-74; research scientist N.Y. State Dept. Health, Albany, 1974-75; asst. prof. microbiology U. Minn.-Twin Cities, 1975-79, assoc. prof., 1979-83, prof., 1983-86; head dept. bacteriology and biochemistry, U. Idaho, Moscow, 1987—; research dir. Chem Waste Control, Wayzata, Minn., 1984-85; cons. to industry, 1975—; adviser on environ. pollution to U.S. Senator David Durenberger, Mpls., 1983. Author: Lignin Biodegradation and Transformation, 1981; also book chpts., numerous articles. Editor: (with R.S. Hanson) Microbial Growth on C1 Compounds, 1984; Applied and Environ. Microbiology, 1982—. Weyerhaeuser fellow U. Wis.-Madison, 1970-73. Mem. Am. Soc. Microbiology, Blue Key, Sigma Xi, Beta Beta Beta. Democrat. Avocations: playing guitar and banjo, long distance running.

CRAWFORD, THOMAS PAUL, draftsman; b. Youngstown, Ohio, Sept. 13, 1955; s. Paul Floyd and Donna Jean (Doyle) C.; m. Judith Jayne Bales, Nov. 4, 1975; children: April Elizabeth, Paul Joseph. Student, U. Nebr., Lincoln, 1973-75, U. Nebr., Omaha, 1975-77. Shipper Valmont Industries, Valley, Nebr., 1977, draftsman, 1984—; assembler Stormor, Inc., Fremont, Nebr., 1977-79, drafter, 1979-84. Designer bio-mass drying system for grain dryers, 1981. Vol. youth activities YMCA, Fremont, 1984—; mem. PTA, Fremont. Presbyterian. Lodge: Eagles. Avocations: softball, volleyball, golf, fishing, soccer coach. Office: Valmont Industries Hwy 275 Valley NE 68064

CRAY, CLOUD LANOR, JR., grain products company executive; b. Detroit, Nov. 7, 1922; s. Cloud Lanor and Edna (Reinoehl) C.; m. Sara Jane Hunter, Feb. 12, 1944; children: Karen Lee Cray Seaberg, Susan Hunter Cray Robbins, Cathy Lynn Cray Freund, Jr. BS in Chem. Engring. cum laude, Case Western Res. U., 1943. With Dow Chem. Co., Midland, Mich., 1943-44, Midwest Grain Products, Inc., Atchison, Kans., 1947—; pres. Midwest Grain Processing Equipment Co., 1972—; pres., chmn. bd. Atchison Leather Products Co., 1976-86, Midwest Solvents Co. Ill., Inc., Pekin, 1980—; pres. Midwest Grain Asset Co., Inc., 1980—; bd. dirs. Distilled Spirits Inst., Security Benefit Life Ins. Co., KPL Gas Service, Commerce Bancshares. Mem. Human Relations Commn. Atchison, 1965-69, chmn. 1965-67; v.p. Unified Dist. #409 Sch. Bd., 1970-75, bd. dirs. 1967-75; bd. dirs. YMCA, Atchison, 1963-72; orgn. chmn. United Way, Atchison, 1977; co-chmn. Benedictine Coll.-Atchison Community Support Program, 1984-85; mem. Kans. Diabetes Adv. Council, 1985—; trustee Coll. Emporia, Kans., 1962-73, fin. chmn. 1970-73; trustee Atchison Hosp. Assn., 1966—; chmn. Rep. Fin. Com., Atchison County, 1966; pres. Cray Med. Research Found., 1981—. Served with AUS, 1944-46. Recipient Kans. Exporter of the Yr. award 1981—. Mem. Atchison C of C. (bd. dirs. 1962-64, v.p. civic affairs 1964), Young Pres. Orgn. (vice chmn. 1968-69, western area conference edn. chmn. 1971-72), Distillers Feed Research Council (bd. dirs. 1949-72, pres.), Tau Beta Pi, Alpha Chi Sigma, Sigma Xi, Tau Kappa Alpha. Republican. Presbyterian. Clubs: Bellevue Country, Fellowship (pres.), Saddle & Sirloin, Kansas City. Lodge: Kiwanis (past pres.), Elks, Masons. Designed first vodka plant in Mexico. Avocations: golf, swimming, sailing, racquetball, traveling. Home: Rural Rt 1 Potatoe Hill Atchison KS 66002 Office: Midwest Grain Products Inc 1300 Main St Atchison KS 66002

CRAYTON, BILLY GENE, physician; b. Holden, Mo., May 15, 1931; s. John Reuben and Carrie Zona (Head) C.; student Central Mo. State Coll., 1948-49; B.S., Stetson U., 1958; postgrad. U. Kansas City, summer 1955; M.D., U. Mo., 1962. Intern, Mound Park Hosp., St. Petersburg, Fla., 1962-63; practice gen. medicine Latham Hosp., California, Mo., 1963-64, Kelling Clinic and Hosp., Waverly, 1964-86, vice chief of staff, 1980-86; preceptor in community health and med. practice U. Mo. Sch. Medicine, Waverly, 1968—; sec., dir. Kelling Hosp., Inc., 1969-80; pres. Kelling Clinic, 1971—; med. dir. Waverly Ambulance Co., 1985-86; pres. Riverview Heights, 1972—. Adviser, Mo. chpt. Am. Assn. Med. Assts., 1973-79. Adviser, Explorer Post Boy Scouts Am., 1968-70. Served with AUS, 1952-54. Fellow Am. Acad. Family Physicians. Baptist. Home: PO Box 41 Waverly MO 64096 Office: Kelling Clinic Inc Waverly MO 64096

CREAHAN, DAVID JOSEPH, lawyer; b. Cleve., July 4, 1916; s. John Thomas and Eva (Grothaus) C.; m. Ruth Janice Winterman, Jan. 15, 1944; children—David, Thomas, Mary, Kathleen, Julie, Kevin, Ann, John. B.B.A., U. Cin., 1939; J.D., No. Ky. U., 1975. Bar: Ohio 1975, U.S. Dist. Ct. 1975, U.S. Supreme Ct. 1984; C.P.A., Ohio. Pres. Techne Corp., Plainview, Tex., 1963-69, Cherokee Nitrogen Co., Pryor, Okla., 1969-75; v.p., treas., assoc. gen. counsel N.Ren Corp., Cin., 1975-78; gen. mgr. Sudan-Ren Chem. and Fertilizer Ltd., Khartoum, 1978-81; assoc. Simon, Namanworth and Bohlen, Cin., 1981—. Served to capt. USN, 1941-45, 52-53. Mem. Cin. Bar Assn. Democrat. Roman Catholic. Avocations: politics, civil rights, history. Home: 6600 Corbly Rd Cincinnati OH 45230 Office: Simon Namanworth & Bohlen 602 Main St Cincinnati OH 45202

CREAMER, ANDREW G., bank executive. Pres. Pontiac (Mich.) State Bank. Office: Pontiac State Bank 28 N Saginaw St Pontiac MI 48058 *

CREAMER, JACK MAJOR, sales executive; b. Detroit, Feb. 15, 1954; s. Cary Rowland and Virginia (Major) C.; m. Zane Griffin, Aug. 1, 1981; children: Cary, Troy, Mont. BS in Indsl. Engring., Syracuse U., 1975; MBA, Rensselaer Poly. Inst., 1976. Sales trainee Gen. Electric Co., Milw. and Cleve., 1976-79; sales engr. Gen. Electric Co., Pitts. and Louisville, 1979-81; area sales mgr. Gen. Electric Co., Bloomington, Ill., 1981-84, mgr. market devel., 1984-86, regional sales mgr., 1986—. Contbr. articles to tech. jours. Bd. dirs. Blooming Grove Acad., Normal, Ill., 1986; men. new bldg. com. College Park Christian Ch. Republican. Avocations: golf, volleyball, basketball. Home: 5 Somerset Ct Bloomington IL 61701 Office: Gen Electric Co 1601 GE Rd Bloomington IL 61701

CREASON, TIMOTHY T., college track coach; b. Kokomo, Ind., Apr. 7, 1959; s. Paul L. and Marilyn J. (Todd) C. BS in Pub. and Corp. Communications, Butler U., 1981. Sports editor Tri-Weekly News, Berne, Ind., 1981-82; gen. assignment reporter Evening News-Banner, Bluffton, Ind., 1982-86, sports editor, 1986; coach women's track Butler U., Indpls., 1986—; asst. track coach South Wells High Sch., Poneto, Ind., 1984, 86, Norwell High Sch., Ossian, Ind., 1985; correspondent Indiana Runner mag., Indpls., 1983—. Pres. Wells County Teenage Reps., 1974-77; mem. Environ. Action, 1978—. Named one of Outstanding Young Men Am. 1983, 84, 85. Mem. Nat. Rifle Assn., Sierra Club. Roman Catholic. Avocations: photography, running. Office: Butler U Dept Athletics 4600 Sunset Ave Indianapolis IN 46208

CREEL, DAVID RUSSEL, advertising and public relations company executive; b. Detroit, June 26, 1949; s. Russell Keith and Catherine (Robertson) C.; m. Shelley Anne Gersick, Aug. 3, 1975 (div. Sept. 1984); 1 child, Lauren Elizabeth. BS, U. Ill., 1971; MBA, DePaul U., 1977. Account exec. Martin E. Janis & Co., Chgo., 1972-73; dir. pub. relations First Ogden Corp., Naperville, Ill., 1973-76; exec. v.p. Creel Assocs., Inc., Oakbrook, Ill., 1976-84, pres., 1984—. Bd. dirs. Naperville YMCA, 1976-82. Served to lt. U.S. Army, 1971-72. Republican. Presbyterian. Clubs: Suburban Press (Chgo.) (gov. 1975—, Service award 1982), Lodge: Kiwanis (Oakbrook Pres.'s award 1982). Avocations: softball, racquetball, skiing. Office: Creel Assocs Inc 900 Jorie Blvd Oakbrook IL 60521

CREEL, ROGER E., data processing executive; b. Ocheyedan, Iowa, Aug. 9, 1933; s. Wyman Ulmer and Hilda Sophie (Wassman) C.; m. LaDonna Mae Pederson, June 16, 1956; children: Suzanne Kay Creel Thompson, Stuart Roger. AA, Worthington Jr. Coll., 1956-58; BS in Math. and Sci., S.D. State U., 1960. Various systems and programming positions Wausau (Wis.) Ins. Cos., 1960—, asst. v.p. systems and data processing, 1975-79, v.p., systems and data processing, 1979—; Mem. IBM's Ins. Adv. Council, 1980, Raytheons Ins. Adv. Council, 1981. Contbr. articles to profl. jours. Sr. vice comdr. Marine Corps League, Wis., 1970-71. Served as sgt. USMC, 1953-56. Mem. Data Processing Mgmt. Assn. (bd. dirs. 1969-72, 74-76, treas. 1970-71, pres. 1975-76, nat. council subcom. data processing 1971-82, chrmn. 1981-82, individual performance award 1977), Life Office Mgmt. Assn. (property & casualty com. 1975—, chmn. 1983-84), Ins. Acctg. and Systems Assn. (ins. com. chmn. 1984-85), Am. Legion. Republican. Lutheran. Clubs: Wausau Country, Wausau. Lodges: Kiwanis (bd. dirs. 1979-82, pres. 1980-81), Elks. Avocations: hunting, fishing. Office: Wausau Ins Cos 2000 Westwood Dr Wausau WI 54401

CREELMAN, MARJORIE BROER, psycologist; b. Toledo, Dec. 5, 1908; d. William F. and Ethel (Griffin) Broer; m. George Douglas Creelman, June 29, 1932 (div. Dec. 1958); children: Carleton Douglas, Stewart Elliott, Katherine George Skrobela. AB, Vassar Coll., 1931; MA, Columbia U., 1932; PhD, Western Res. U., 1954. Asst. psychologist N.Y. Psychiat. Inst., N.Y.C., 1932-33, Sunny Acres Sanitorium, Cleve., 1947-48; clin. asst. dept. psychology Case Western Res. U., Cleve., 1947-49, supr. field work, dir. practicum tng. program, 1949-54; asst. to dir. parent edn. program Children's Aid Soc., Cleve., 1952-53; ptnr., sr. assoc. Creelman Assocs., Cleve., 1954-58; pvt. practice psychology Cleve., 1954-64, Washington, 1964-69; research psychologist behavioral studies St. Elizabeth's Hosp., Washington, 1963-65, dir. psycho-physiology, clin. and behavioral studies, 1965-67; dir. psychol. services Alexandria Community Mental Health Ctr., 1967-69; mem. policy and planning com. Midwest Tng. Ctr. in Human Relations, 1954-60; prof. psychology Cleve. State U., 1969-76, prof. emeritus, 1976—; pvt. practice psychology 1969—; mem. profl. staff Gestalt Inst. Cleve., 1969-81; hon. fellow, 1981—. Author: The Experimental Investigation of Meaning, 1965; editor: Ohio Psychologist, 1956-59; contbr. articles to profl. jours. Mem. Citizen's Adv. Bd. Case Western Res. U. Psychiat. Habilitation Ctr., 1979-81. Fellow Internat. Council Psychologists (sec. 1964-65), Am. Soc. Group Psychotherapy and Psychodrama, Ohio Psychol. Assn.; mem. Internat. Soc. Gen. Semantics (v.p. Cleve. chpt. 1950-61), Am. Acad. Psychotherapists (life, publs. com. directory editor 1963-67), Cleve. Acad. Cons. Psychologists (pres. 1957-58), Sigma Delta Epsilon, Psi Chi, Alpha Chi Omega. Club: Cleve. Skating.

CREMERS, ALBERT LOUIS, manufacturing company executive; b. Columbus, Mich., July 16, 1940; s. Albert and Virginia Mary (Fraley) C.; m. Veronica Jean Galvin, May 1, 1965; children: John Albert, Kimberly Ann. Grad. cum. laude, Port Huron Jr. Coll., 1959; BS, U.S. Merchant Marine Acad., 1963; MBA, U. Akron, 1971. Engr. Am. Export, N.Y.C., 1963-64, Burns & Roe, N.Y.C., 1964-65, Western Electric, N.Y.C., 1965-67; program mgr. Babcock & Wilcox, Barberton, Ohio, 1967—. Mem. Jaycees. Republican. Roman Catholic. Lodges: K.C., Elks. Avocation: reading, gardening. Home: 4105 Meadowview Dr NW Canton OH 44718 Office: Babcock & Wilcox Co 91 Stirling Ave Barberton OH 44203

CREPEAU, JOYCE ANN, nurse; b. Charles City, Iowa, Nov. 24, 1945; d. Dale Irvin and Christine (Menken) Crosby; m. Henry J. Crepeau III, July 16, 1977 (div. Apr. 1984); children: Joel William, Jeffrey Dana, Amy Christine. BA with honors, U. Ill., Chgo., 1977; RN, Ravenswood Sch. Nursing, 1979. Nurse Luth. Gen. Hosp., Park Ridge, Ill., 1979-83, utilization rev. coordinator, 1983-86, coordinator diagnosis related group, 1986—. Mem. Ill. Assn. Quality Assurance Profls. Democrat. Lutheran. Avocations: needlework, woodwork, sewing. Home: 1239 Oak St Evanston IL 60202 Office: Luth Gen Hosp 1775 Dempster St Park Ridge IL 60068

CREPEAU, LAURENCE RENE, accountant; b. Mpls., June 2, 1942; s. Rene A. and Genevieve R. (Benias) C.; m. Sharry Marie Gozola, Sept. 7, 1963; children: Laurence Jr., Susannah. BA, Coll. of St. Thomas, 1964. Mgr. Peat, Marwick, Mitchell & Co., Mpls., 1964-75; ptnr. McGladrey, Hendrickson & Co., St. Paul, 1975-86. Treas. Boy Scouts of Am., Golden Valley, 1982-83. Mem. Minn. Soc. CPA's (bd. dirs. 1985—, chmn. fed. and state tax com. 1982), Am. Inst. CPA's (minority bus. devel. com.), Minn. Acctng. Aid Soc. (pres. 1984). Office: Laurence R Crepeau Ltd 4000 Meml Hwy Suite 511 Golden Valley MN 55422

CRESSEY, BRYAN CHARLES, lawyer; b. Seattle, Sept. 28, 1949; s. Charles Ovington and Alice Lorraine (Serry) C.; m. Christina Irene Petersen, Aug. 19, 1972; children—Monique Joy, Charlotte Lorraine, Alicia Lin. B.A., U. Wash., 1972; M.B.A., Harvard U., 1976, J.D., 1976. Bar: Ill. 1977, Wash. 1976. Sr. investment mgr. First Chgo. Investment Corp., Chgo., 1976-80; ptnr. Golder, Thoma and Cressey, Chgo., 1980—; dir. Nu-Med, Inc., Encino, Calif., Superior Electromechanical, Long Island, N.Y., Continental Med. Systems, Inc., Mechanicsburg, Pa., Intercole, Inc., Laguna Hills, Calif., Phenix Venture Acquisitions, Columbus, Ohio, Interspec, Inc., Conshohocken, Pa., Crystal Diagnostic Systems, Inc., Anthony's Mfg., San Fernando, Calif., REB Industries, Inc., Glastonbury, Conn., Proxy Message Ctr., Brisbane, Calif. V.p. Planning Infant Welfare Soc., Chgo., 1984—. Home: Rural Rte 2 Bateman Circle Barrington Hills IL 60010 Office: Golder Thoma & Cressey 120 S La Salle St Suite 630 Chicago IL 60603

CREWS, JOHN ERIC, rehabilitation administrator; b. Marion, Ind., Aug. 4, 1946; s. Odis Earl and Beatrice True (Wright) C.; m. Nancy J. Murphy, Aug. 9, 1975; 1 dau., Katherine. B.A. in English, Franklin Coll., 1969; M.A. in English, Ind. U., 1971; M.A. in Blind Rehab. with honors, Western Mich. U., 1977, postgrad in pub. administrn., 1983—. Mem. English faculty Ball State U., Muncie, Ind., 1971-73, S.W. Mo. State U., Springfield, 1973-76, Western Mich. U., Kalamazoo, 1976-77; rehab. tchr. Mich. Commn. for the Blind, Saginaw, 1977-80, program mgr. Sr. Blind Program, Saginaw, Southeastern Mich. Ctr. for Ind. Living, Detroit, 1980—; v.p. bd. Midland County Council on Aging, 1982-84; bd. dirs. Saginaw Valley Spl. Needs Vision Clinic, 1981—; mem. adv. bd. rehab. continuing edn. program So. Ill. U., Carbondale, 1985—. Mem. editorial bd. Jour. Visual Impairment and Blindness, 1984—. Contbr. to book and profl. publs. Recipient Grant award Ind. Living Services for Older Blind Rehab. Services Administrn., 1986; grantee Ctr. Ind. Living U.S. Dept. Edn., 1980, 82, Ind. Living for Elderly Blind, 1986. Mem. Nat. Council Aging, Assn. Retarded Citizens (pres. Midland 1981—; Ann. Appreciation award 1981). Methodist. Home: 5502 Whitehall Midland MI 48640 Office: Mich Commn for the Blind 411-G E Genesee Saginaw MI 48607

CRIBBS, DAVID DALE, insulation company executive; b. Halfway, Mo., Feb. 13, 1939; s. Clifford C. and Sadie Irene (Seiner) C.; m. Betty Kay Johnson, Dec. 9, 1961; children: Sandy, Michael, Susan, Betsy. Student, Draughon Bus. Sch., 1958-59, Drury Coll., 1959-60; PhD in Bus. (hon.), S.W. Bapt. U., 1986. Rate clk. Yellow Transit Co., Springfield, Mo., 1958-59; salesman Bolivar Insulation Co. Inc., Springfield, 1959-61, supt., owner, 1961-64, pres., owner, 1964—; bd. dirs. Commerce Bank, Springfield; advisor Owens/Corning Co., Toledo. Bd. dirs. Citizens Meml. Hosp., Bolivar, Mo.; pres. Bolivar Nursing Home; fund raiser John Ashcroft Election, Bolivar, 1972; fund raiser, pres. bldg. program Assembly of God Ch., Bolivar, 1980. Served with U.S. Army, 1957-58. Named Entrepreneur of Yr., Nat. Free Enterprise, 1986. Mem. Insulation Contractors Am. Republican. Lodge: Kiwanis (pres. Bolivar club 1968). Avocations: golfing, snow skiing, cattle ranching. Home: Rt 3 Box 568 Bolivar MO 65613 Office: Bolivar Insulation Co Inc 2050 E Trafficway MPO Box 887 Springfield MO 65801

CRIDER, LESLIE RAY, hospital executive; b. Stella, Mo., Dec. 11, 1949; s. Charles McKinley and Zelpha Rae (Hyden) C.; m. Katherine Louise Schaughency, Apr. 29, 1974; children: Charles Sean, Katherine Rayann, Leslie Colleen. BBA, U. Mo., 1972; MA, Cen. Mich. U., 1983. Sr. medicare auditor Blue Cross of Kansas City, 1972-74; chief acct. Dept. Mental Health, Nevada, Mo., 1974-83; asst. supt. administrn. Dept. Mental Health, St. Louis, 1983-85; asst. hosp. dir. Mo. Rehab. Ctr., Mt. Vernon, Mo., 1985—. Mem. Healthcare Fin. Mgrs. Assn. (bd. dirs. Show-Me, Shawnee chpt. 1986—). Republican. Methodist. Lodge: Rotary, Optimist (pres. Nevada 1980). Avocations: snow skiing, gardening. Home: 624 N Main Mount Vernon MO 65712 Office: Mo Rehab Ctr 600 N Main Mount Vernon MO 65712

CRIDER, ROBERT AGUSTINE, international financier, colonel law enforcement; b. Washington, Jan. 3, 1935; s. Rana Albert and Terasa Helen (Dampf) C.; student law enforcement U. Md., 1959-63; m. Debbie Ann Lee, Feb. 1960. Police officer Met. Police Dept., Washington, 1957-67; substitute tchr., bldg. trades instr. Maries R-1 Sch., Vienna, Mo., 1968-70; vets. constrn. tng. officer VA Dept. Edn., Mo., 1968-70; constrn. mgr. Tectonics Ltd., Vienna, 1970-79; owner, dir. R-A Crider & Assocs., St. Louis, 1979—; bd. dirs. TI-CO Investment Corp., Langcaster Corp., Barclay Coll., St. Ann., Mo. Served with USAF, 1952-56. Mem. Assn. Ret. Policemen, Internat. Conf. Police, Internat. Assn. Chiefs of Police, Nat. Police Assn., World Future Soc., Internat. Platform Assn., Mo. Police Chiefs Assn., Mo. Sheriff's Assn., Am. Correctional Assn., Law Enforcement Intelligence Assn., Internat. Drug Enforcement Assn., Nat. Assn. Fin. Cons., Internat. Soc. Financiers, Am. Legion, St. Louis Honor Guard. Roman Catholic. Clubs: Lions, K.C. (4th deg.). Home: PO Box 109 Vienna MO 65582 Office: R-A Crider & Assocs PO Box 3459 2644 Roseland Terr Saint Louis MO 63143 Office: Barclay Coll 10403 International Plaza Dr Saint Ann MO 63074

CRIGER, NANCY S., banker; b. Ypsilanti, Mich., Apr. 16, 1951; d. Douglas D. and Edith (Nicoll) Smith; m. Dane Criger, July 9, 1982; children: Amanda L. Denomme, William G. Denomme, Jr. Student, Mich. State U., 1969-71; BS in Elem. Edn., Wayne State U., 1973. Asst. v.p. Nat. Bank of Detroit, 1978-87, Comerica Bank, Detroit, 1987—. Asst. treas. Jr. League of Detroit, 1985-86, treas., 1986-87; treas. women's assn. Detroit Symphony Orch., 1987—; mem. Assistance League N.E. Guidance Ctr. Detroit Symphony League, past bd. dirs.; mem. Friends of Greenfield Village, Detroit Inst. Arts, Detroit Artist Market, Detroit Zool. Soc., Detroit Sci. Ctr., Smithsonian Instn. Archives of Am. Art. Mem. Detroit Hist. Soc., Chi Omega. Office: Comerica Bank 211 W Fort St Detroit MI 48275-1034

CRIM, LINDA KAY, accountant; b. Albia, Iowa, Apr. 23, 1947; d. Francis Emanual and Gladys Amelia (Mahin) Lane; m. Lyle William Crim, Jan. 31, 1969 (div. Oct. 1985); 1 child, Terry Francis. BBA, U. Iowa, 1969. CPA, Iowa. Computer programmer U. Iowa, Iowa City, 1969-72; staff acct. L.A. Greenwood, P.C., Iowa City, 1974-78; owner, CPA Greenwood & Crim, P.C., Iowa City, 1978—. Treas., bd. dirs. Big Bros./Big Sisters Johnson County, Iowa City, 1984—; mem. bd.-at-large, pres.-elect Friends of the Library, Iowa City, 1987—. Mem. Am. Inst. CPA's (small bus. taxation subcom.), Iowa Soc. CPA's (Hawkeye chpt.), Nat. Assn. Women Bus. Owners (treas. Iowa City 1987—). Democrat. Methodist. Club: Pilot (com. chairperson 1983—, treas. 1987-88) (Iowa City). Avocations: reading, fitness, golf. Home: 1305 Brookwood Dr Iowa City IA 52240 Office: Greenwood & Crim PC 518 S Clinton Iowa City IA 52240

CRINKLAW, DON HENRY, writer, reporter; b. Kansas City, Mo., July 15, 1939; s. Archie DeLos and Vera Margarite (Donegan) C.; m. Elaine Viets, Aug. 6, 1971. BA, Marquette U., 1961, MA, 1963. Tech. and promotional writer Clayton Commodity Services, St. Louis, 1964-65; advt. and pub. relations writer Weintraub & Assocs., St. Louis, 1965-68; instr. English U. Mo., St. Louis, 1969-75; writer-reporter St. Louis Mag., 1975-79, St. Louis Weekly, 1980—. Contbr. freelance articles to Nat. Rev., Marriage and Family Living, others. Served with U.S. Army, 1964-66, with res. 1964. Democrat. Roman Catholic. Home: 3867A Utah Pl Saint Louis MO 63116 Office: St Louis Weekly 222 S Meramec Saint Louis MO 63105

CRIPE, DAVID LYLE, optometrist; b. Goshen, Ind., Mar. 23, 1952; s. Edwin C. Cripe and Helen Naomi (Armstrong) Rice; m. Erika Kitchik Alibek, July 30, 1977; children: Geoffrey David, Brittany Leigh. AB in Psychology, Ind. U., 1974, OD, 1979. Spl. agt. Exec. Ins. Services, Indpls., 1974-76; contact lens specialist Fredricksburg (Va.) Eye Assocs., 1984; assoc. optometrist Dr. Nancy Graves, Woodbridge, Va., 1983-84; pvt. practice optometry Goshen, 1984—; mem. adj. faculty Ind. U. Optometry Sch., Bloomington, 1982-83, Pa. Coll. Optometry, Phila., 1981-83. Served to lt. comdr. USNR, 1979-83. Mem. North Cen. Ind. Optometric Soc. (v.p. 1986-87), Ind. Optometric Assn., Am. Optometric Assn. Republican. Roman Catholic. Lodges: Kiwanis (v.p. Goshen club. 1986-87), Lions (sight chmn. Stafford club 1983-84). Avocations: guitar, basketball, racquetball. Home: 2213 Cambridge Dr Goshen IN 46526 Office: 1524 Bashor Rd Goshen IN 46526

CRIPE, JANICE LEE, nurse; b. South Bend, Ind., June 19, 1942; d. Wayne A. and Virginia V. (Miller) Shoemaker; m. Rodger L. Cripe, June 15, 1963; children: Carrie Sue, Scott Douglas. BS in Nursing, DePauw U., 1964. Cert. sch. nurse, Ill. Instr. nursing St. Joseph's Hosp., South Bend, 1970-71, Ind. Vocat. Tech. Coll., South Bend, 1971-75, Ind. Cen. Coll., Indpls., 1978-79; nurse spl. edn. Raymond Sch., Bloomington, Ill., 1979-85; nurse community health McLean County Health Dept., Normal, Ill., 1985—. Deacon Second Presbyn. Ch., Bloomington, 1984—. Mem. Ill. Pub. Health Assn., Kappa Kappa Kappa (past sec., past pres.). Lodge: Order Eastern Star. Avocations: piano, boating, swimming, water-skiing, drama. Home: Rural Rt 1 Box 101A 37 Edgewater Dr Carlock IL 61725

CRIST, CYNTHIA LOUISE, academic administrator; b. Waukesha, Wis., Sept. 30, 1950; d. George Philip and Evelyn Pauline (Schultz) C.; m. Andy Driscoll, June 27, 1987. BS in Edn., Ill. State U., 1972, MS in Edn., 1977. Tchr. Peoria (Ill.) Pub. Schs., 1972-78; spl. edn. tchr. North St. Paul-Maplewood Pub. Schs., Minn., 1978-82; asst. dir. Govs. Office of Sci. and Tech., St. Paul, 1983-86, acting dir., 1986-87; asst. to chancellor for policy research Minn. State U. System, St. Paul, 1987—; Mem. Equity and Edn. Task Force Commn. on the Econ. Status of Women, Minn., 1984, Govs. Adv. Com. on tech. in edn., 1985—, Govs. issue team for people with disabilities, 1985—. Author: (directory) High Technology in Minnesota: A Directory of Programs, Policies, and Services, 1984, Disabilities and Technology: Report of the Governor's Issues Team on Technology for People with Disabilities, 1986; editor: Interdisciplinary Methods of Teaching, 1981; contbr. articles to profl. jours. Dir. 4th Congl. Dist. Dem. Farmer Labor Party, St. Paul, 1981-85; del. Minn. State Dem. Farmer Labor Cen. Com., 1983-85; chair Ramsey County Human Services Adv. Com., Minn., 1985-87. Mem. Minn. Alliance for Sci. (bd. dirs. 1986—), Minn. Acad. Sci., Minn. Orchestral Assn. (guarantor 1985—), Minn. Wellspring (edn. and tech. com. 1981-82). Avocations: reading, guitar, piano, gardening. Office: Minn State U System 555 Park St Suite 230 Saint Paul MN 55103

CRIST, JOHN MICHAEL, physical education educator; b. Hammond, Ind., Feb. 25, 1955; s. Jackie Lee and Patricia Ann (Zimmerman) C.; m. Julie Lynn Zacharias, June 16, 1984; 1 child, John Zacharias. BS, Ind. U., 1977, MS, 1978. Asst. swim coach Counsilman Swim Camp, Bloomington, Ind., 1977-78; tchr. and swim coach Zionsville (Ind.) High Sch., 1978—, physical edn. dept. head, 1985—; head swim coach Zionsville Swim Club, 1978—. Mem. NEA, Nat. Interscholastic Swim Coaches Assn., Ind. Swim Coaches Assn. (v.p. 1982). Presbyterian. Home and Office: 6635 Foxfire Ct Indianapolis IN 46214

CRISWELL, DENISE ELAINE, athletic trainer, physical education educator; b. Marion, Ohio, Aug. 29, 1956; d. Jerald Wayne and Betty Jean (Williams) C. B.S. in Phys. Edn./Health, Miami U., Oxford, Ohio, 1978; M.S. in Phys. Edn./Ednl. Adminstrn., Ft. Hays State U., Hays, Kans., 1979. Cert. First Aid/CPR, Water Safety Instr., ARC. Asst. athletic trainer Valparaiso U. (Ind.), 1979—, instr. phys. edn., 1979—, athletic trainer Sports Camps, 1980—; athletic trainer-cons. Porter County Schs. (Ind.), 1979—; trainer White River Park State Games, 1986; coordinator Valparaiso U./Cramer Athletic Injury Clinic, 1986; cons. Nautilus Fitness Club, Merrillville, Ind., 1980-81. Med. coordinator INdpls. Peace Games, 1986. Mem. Nat. Athletic Trainers Assn., Inc., Ind. Athletic Trainers Assn., Kappa Psi Omega. Democrat. Lutheran. Office: Valparaiso Univ Athletics-Recreation Ctr Valparaiso IN 46383

CRITELLI, PAUL JOSEPH, psychologist; b. Rochester, N.Y., Mar. 11, 1949; s. Joseph and Mary (Campanozzi) C. BA, Iona Coll., 1970; MA, Fordham U., 1972, PhD, 1978. Lic. clin. psychologist, Mich. Chief psychologist Care Unit, Grand Rapids, Mich., 1978-81; pvt. practice psychology Grand Rapids, 1979-87, Greenville, Mich., 1987—; asst. dir. Terrap of Mich., Grand Rapids, 1986—; adj. lectr. Holy Family Coll., Phila., 1976-78. Producer: (TV series) Psychology in Focus, 1986, (1st place Philo T. Farnsworth Competition, 1986), Magic with Paul, 1986 (1st place Philo T. Farnsworth Competition, 1986). Mem. Am. Psychol. Assn., Mich. Psychol. Assn., Soc. Am. Magicians, Psychic Entertainers Assn. Avocation: magic. Home: 858 Iroquois SE Grand Rapids MI 49506 Office: 103 College St Grand Rapids MI 49503

CRITTENDEN, LEE JOHN, finance company executive; b. Kalamazoo, Mich., June 20, 1945; s. Jack L. and Evelyn B. (Wohlfert) C.; m. Mary Ann Frescura, Jan. 31, 1970 (div. Aug. 26, 1982); 1 child, Alexandra N. B.S., No. Ill. U., 1968; cert. modern bus. Alexander Hamilton Inst., N.Y.C., 1973. Publs. editor Uniroyal Inc., Joliet Army Ammunition Plant (Ill.), 1968-70; staff editor Employee Communications, Uniroyal, Inc., N.Y.C., 1970-71, assoc. editor employee publs., Middlebury, Conn., 1971-73, pub. relations mgr., tire and automotive products, Allen Park, Mich., 1973-76; v.p. APC Cons., Inc., Joliet, Ill., 1976-81; pres., gen. mgr. Bee Newspapers, Inc., Joliet, Ill., 1978-80; v.p. corp. communications Assocs. Comml. Corp., Chgo., 1981—. Mem. citizens adv. council Selective Investigation and Prosecution Unit, Will County, Ill., 1979-83; bd. dirs. exec. com. Profl. Truck Driver Inst. Am., Inc., chmn., fin. com.; bd. dirs. Regional Distbn. and Carriers Conf. Inc.; mem. exec. com. Alliance for Simple, Equitable and Rational Truck Taxation. Mem. Am. Trucking Assn. (communications adv. com.), Trucking Industry Alliance (coordinating com., chmn., communications com.), Am. Truckers Benevolent Assn. (bd. dirs. exec. com.), Chgo. Conv. and Vis. Bur., Inc., Truck Renting and Leasing Assn. (supplier adv. council, bd. dirs. regional and distbn. ctrs. conf.), Pub. Relations Soc. Am. Clubs: Publicity (Chgo.), Chgo. Press Club. Office: Assocs Ctr 150 N Michigan Ave Suite 3500 Chicago IL 60601

CRITZ, NANCY WIER, social service consultant; b. Cin., Feb. 13, 1954; d. Robert Charles and Judy (Phillips) Wier; 1 dau., Kelly Suzanne. A.S. in Social Work, U. Cin., 1974, B.S. in Social Work, 1976. Children's protective social worker Hamilton County (Ohio) Welfare Dept., 1977-79; dir. social services Our Lady of Mercy Hosp., Cin., 1982-86; cons. social work students U. Cin. Mem. Am. Hosp. Assn., Soc. Social Work Dirs., Ohio Hosp. Assn. Hosp. Social Work Dirs., Sigma Delta Tau (alumni pres.). Methodist. Home and Office: 3966 Piccadilly Circle Cincinnati OH 45230

CRIVELLONE, SALVATORE CARMEN, newspaper publisher; b. Chgo., July 11, 1927; s. Vincent and Angeline (Sangiacomo) C.; m. Geraldine Rose, Sept. 8, 1951; children: Margaret, James, John. Student, Ray Vogue Design Sch., Chgo., 1946-48, Chgo. Acad. Art, 1948-50. Salesman Commonwealth Edison, Chgo., 1950-53, Englewood Electric, Chgo., 1953-71; pub. Suburban Graphics Inc., Oak Lawn, Ill., 1972-86; gen. mgr. Pulitzer Community Newspapers Inc., Oak Lawn, 1986—. Served as cpl. U.S. Army, 1945-47. Mem. Oak Lawn C. of C. (pres. 1981, bd. dirs. 1982-87). Democrat. Roman Catholic. Lodge: Rotary. Avocations: photography, hunting. Office: Pulitzer Community Newspapers 4740 W 95th St Oak Lawn IL 60454

CRIVITS, JAMES H., restaurant executive; b. 1942. BA, U. Minn. Pres. Consul Restaurant Corp., Mpls., 1979-84, pres., chief exec. officer, 1984—, also bd. dirs. Office: Consul Restaurant Corp 4815 W 77th St Minneapolis MN 55435 *

CROAT, THOMAS BERNARD, botanical curator; b. St. Marys, Iowa, May 23, 1938; s. Oliver Theodore and Irene Mary (Wilgenbush) C.; m. Patricia Swope, Sept. 16, 1965; children—Anne Irene, Thomas Kevin. B.A., Simpson Coll., 1962; M.A., U. Kans., 1966, Ph.D., 1967. Tchr. sci. pub. schs., Virgin Islands and Iowa, 1962-64; research botanist Mo. Botanical Garden, St. Louis, 1967—, P.A. Schulze curator of botany, 1977—; vis. fellow Smithsonian Tropical Research Inst., Ancon, Canal Zone, 1968-71; adv. com. NSF Resources in Systematic Botany, 1972-74; faculty assoc. biology Washington U., St. Louis, 1970-84; adj. faculty U. Mo., St. Louis, 1974-84; adj. assoc. prof. St. Louis U., 1982-84. Author: Flora of Barro Colorado Island, 1978. Contbr. articles to profl. jours. Served as pfc U.S. Army, 1956-58, Fed. Republic Germany. Recipient Research award Soc. Sigma Xi, 1975. Grantee NSF, 1972-83, Nat. Geog. Soc., 1973, 84, Nat. Endowment Arts, 1975, 79. Mem. Am. Soc. Plant Taxonomists, Assn. Tropical Biology, Internat. Soc. Plant Taxonomists, Internat. Aroid Soc. (hon. bd. 1978-84), Botanical Soc. Am. Republican. Roman Catholic. Club: Republican (St. Louis) (pres. 1982-84). Avocations: Welding; electronics; auto repair; construction. Home: 4043 Parker Saint Louis MO 63116 Office: Mo Botanical Garden Box 299 Saint Louis MO 63166

CROCKER, DIANE WINSTON, pathologist, educator; b. Cambridge, Mass.; d. Richard M. and Rose (Fisher) Winston; children: Deborah, Kimberly, Anne. BA, Wellesley (Mass.) Coll., 1947; MS, Brown U., 1948; MD, Boston U., 1952. Diplomate Am. Bd. Pathology. Intern Boston City Hosp., Mallory Inst. Pathology, 1952-53; resident in pathology New Eng. Deaconess Hosp., Boston, 1953-54, Los Angeles Children's Hosp., 1954-56, Columbia U.-Presbyn. Med. Ctr., N.Y.C., 1956-58; from instr. to asst. prof. pathology Harvard U. Med. Sch., Cambridge, 1958-70; surg. pathologist, chief cytology lab. Peter Bent Brigham Hosp., 1958-70; co.-dir. Boston Sch. Cytotech., 1969-70; chief pathology Temple U. Hosp., 1970-73; chief anatomic pathology, data process and surg. pathologist Los Angeles County/U. So. Calif. Med. Ctr., 1973-77; prof. pathology U. So. Calif., Los Angeles, 1973-77; prof., chmn. dept. pathology U. Tenn., Memphis, 1977-80, prof., 1980-85; chmn. pathology, assoc. chmn. lab. medicine Cook County Hosp., Chgo., 1985—; bd. dirs. Am. Cancer Soc., Memphis, 1977-85; vis. prof. Rush Med. Sch. Editor UP Report, 1967-73, Crocker Reports, 1973-74; mem. editorial bd. Am. Jour. Surg. Pathology, 1979—; contbr. articles to profl. jours. Recipient Disting. Alumnus award Boston U. Sch. Medicine, 1982. Fellow Royal Soc. Medicine, Internat. Coll. Surgeons; mem. AMA, Internat. Acad. Pathology, Am. Assn. Pathologists, Am. Soc. Clin. Pathologists, Am. Soc. Cytology, Am. Heart Assn., Arthur Purdy Stout Soc. Surg. Pathologists (chmn. fin. com. 1981—), Memphis and Shelby County Med. Soc. (program com. 1981—), Harvard Med. Alumni Assn., AAAS, Phi Beta Kappa, Sigma Xi. Office: Cook County Hosp 627 S Woods St Chicago IL 60612

CROCKETT, ADRIENNE JONES, sch. prin.; b. Hamtramck, Mich., Dec. 7, 1946; d. Sidney Minrose and Rosa Eileen (McKinney) J.; m. John William Crockett, June 27, 1981; 1 child, April Eileen. BA, U. Mich., 1969, MA, 1973. Tchr. Bloomfield Hills (Mich.) Schs., 1969-77, adminstrv. intern, 1977-78, prin., 1978—. V.p. Bloomfield Hills Adminstrv. Council, 1980-81, treas., 1986-87. Organist, St. Peters African Meth. Episc. Zion Ch., 1974-79; fin. sec., treas. Brazeal Dennard Chorale, 1973—; dir. music Resurrection United Meth. Ch., 1986—, coordinator of children, 1986; U.S. adult rep. to Leeds, Eng., for Children's Internat. Summer Village, 1974. Recipient Opportunity grant U. Mich., 1965-69. Mem. Internat. Reading Assn., Nat. Assn. Elem. Sch. Prins., Mich. Elem. and Middle Sch. Prins Assn., U. Mich. Alumni Club, One Hundred Club U. Mich. Home: 22950 Mapleridge St Southfield MI 48075 Office: 1101 Westview St Eastover Sch Bloomfield Hills MI 48013

CROCKETT, GEORGE WILLIAM, JR., congressman; b. Jacksonville, Fla., Aug. 10, 1909; s. George William and Minnie A. (Jenkins) C.; m. Ethelene Jones (dec.); children: Elizabeth Ann Crockett Hicks, George William III, Ethelene C.; m. Harriette Clark, Aug. 1980. A.B., Morehouse Coll., 1931, LL.D., 1972; J.D., U. Mich., 1934; LL.D., Shaw Coll., 1973. Bar: Fla. 1934, W.Va. 1935, Mich. 1944, U.S. Supreme Ct. 1940. Practiced law Jacksonville, 1934-35, Fairmont, W.Va., 1935-39; sr. atty. Dept. Labor, 1939-43; hearings officer Fed. Fair Employment Practices Commn., Washington, 1943; founder, dir. Internat. UAW Fair Employment Practices Dept.; adminstrv. asst. to internat. sec-treas. UAW; assoc. gen. counsel Internat. UAW, 1944-46; sr. mem. firm Goodman, Crockett, Eden and Robb, Detroit, 1946-66; judge Recorder's Ct., Detroit, 1966-78; presiding judge Recorder's Ct., 1974-79; vis. judge Mich. Ct. Appeals, 1979; acting corp. counsel City Detroit, 1980; mem. 97th-99th Congresses from Mich.; mem. com. fgn. affairs, com. judiciary, select com. on aging. Mem. exec. bd. Democratic Study Group, U.S. Congress; mem. Congl. Black Caucus, Congl. Auto Caucus, Congl. Arts Caucus; hon. mem. Congl. Hispanic Caucus. Trustee Morehouse Coll. Mem. Nat. Bar Assn. (founder and 1st chmn. Jud. Council), Nat. Lawyers Guild, N.E.-Midwest Econ. Coalition, Congress For Peace Through Law, Phi Beta Kappa, Kappa Alpha Psi. Democrat. Baptist. Office: US Ho Reps 1531 Longworth House Office Bldg Washington DC 20515 *

CROCKETT, JAMES EDWIN, physician, educator; b. Kansas City, Kans., Oct. 20, 1924; s. John Edward and Orva Rose (Ramsey) C.; m. Martha Adam, June 8, 1949; children—Kevin, Brian, Cara. B.A., Park Coll., 1945; M.D., U. Kans., 1949. Diplomate Am. Bd. Internal Medicine and Cardiovascular Diseases. Intern U.S. Naval Hosp., Long Beach, Calif., 1949-50; resident U. Kans. Med. Ctr., Kansas City 1950-56; asst. prof. medicine U. Kans. Sch. Medicine, Kansas City, 1956-58, assoc. prof., 1958-63, dir. cardiology, 1960-63; clin. prof. medicine U. Mo.-Kansas City Sch. Medicine, 1972—; mem. adv. bd. Chinese Inst. Cardiology, Beijing, 1984—; cofounder, cons. cardiologist Mid-Am. Heart Inst., Kansas City; sr. cons. cardiology Scripps Clinic, LaJolla, Calif. Author: Your Heart, 1983; contbr. articles to profl. jours. Bd. dirs. St. Lukes Hosp. Research Found., 1973-75. Served to lt. USN, 1949-57. Fellow ACP, Am. Coll. Cardiology (bd. trustees 1965-67, 71-73, assoc. editor Accel. 1969-81, Cummings Internat. Teaching award, 1967). Republican. Episcopalian. Clubs: River, Carriage. Avocations: music; reading; tennis. Home: 1233 W 63 Terr Kansas City MO 64113 Office: Cardiovascular Cons Office Pres 4320 Wornall Kansas City MO 64111

CROFFOOT, KIRK ALLEN, heating and air conditioning executive; b. Belleville, Ill., Apr. 5, 1959; s. Francis Keith Sr. and Dorothy Faye (Stephens) C.; m. Susan Elaine Thompson, Aug. 9, 1980; 1 child, Kristel. Degree in heating, ventilation and air conditioning, Ranken Tech., St. Louis, 1979. Serviceman Koerner & Sons Heating, DuQuion, Ill., 1979-81, Ham Heating & Cooling, Granite City, Ill., 1981; pres. Croffoot Heating & Air Conditioning, Troy, Ill., 1981—. Mem. Ch. Christ. Avocations: bowling, flying, golf. Office: Croffoot Heating & Air Conditioning 302-A W Hwy 40 Troy IL 62294

CROFTS, INEZ ALTMAN, composer, contralto; b. Portsmouth, Ohio; d. John Louis and Hazel Opal (Walters) Altman; B.Mus., Chgo. Conservatory, 1958, Mus.M., 1960; m. Philip Hague Crofts; 1 son, Philip Hague. Tchr. piano, Portsmouth; organist, choir dir. Temple Bapt. Ch., Portsmouth; TV program Twilight Time, Sta. WNHC, New Haven, 1951-53; dir. Woman's Dept. Club Chorus, Terre Haute, Ind., 1953-55; toured with N.Y.C. Opera Co. in role of Bertha in Barber of Seville, 1957; contralto soloist North Shore Bapt. Ch., 1959-81; composer opera Mission in Burma, premiered Judson Coll., Elgin, Ill., 1970; Quartette of Chgo. Lyric Opera premiered Musicians Club Women, 1986; faculty mem. music dept. Judson Coll., 1968-74, Chgo. Conservatory Coll., 1967-74; dir. choral activities Sigma Alpha Iota (Sword of Honor 1959, Rose award 1971); composer music centennial pageant, Riverside, Ill., 1975. Active Heart Assn. solicitations; bd. dirs. North Shore Bapt. Ch., 1985—. Mem. Internat. Soc. Contemporary Music (dir. Chgo. chpt. 1961—), Lake View Mus. Soc. (pres. 1977-78, dir.), Chgo. Artists Assn. (pres. 1960-62), Musicians Club of Women (pres. 1982-84, program chmn.), Am. Opera Soc., 19th Century Woman's Club. Home: 277 Gatesby Rd Riverside IL 60546

CROIS, JOHN HENRY, village government official; b. Chgo., Jan. 13, 1946; s. Henry F. and Dorothy M. (Priebe) C.; B.A., Elmhurst (Ill.) Coll., 1969; M.A., U. Notre Dame, 1972. Asst. village mgr. Village of Oak Lawn (Ill.), 1975-85, village of Westchester (Ill.), 1985-87, village mgr. Village of Westchester, 1987—; coordinator Oak Lawn Swine Flu Immunization Program, 1976. Mem. Internat. City Mgmt. Assn., Am. Soc. Public Adminstrn., Am. Econ. Assn., Ill. City Mgmt. Assn., Ill. Assn. Mcpl. Mgmt. Assts., Metro-Mgrs. Assn. Roman Catholic. Clubs: St. Germaine's Men's, Cath. Alumni. Home: 10233 S Karlov Ave Oak Lawn IL 60453 Office: 10240 W Roosevelt Rd Westchester IL 60153

CROLAND, ROGER CLARK, optometrist; b. Paterson, N.J., Mar. 21, 1944; s. Herman Harry and Rose Jean (Koningswood) C.; m. Nancy Russo, Feb. 1, 1969 (div. 1979); children: Joshua Adam, Melissa Rose; m. Patricia Louise Harmon, Apr. 21, 1985. BS in Biology, Albright Coll., 1965; OD, Pa. Coll. Optometry, 1969. Gen. practice optometry Drs. Boni & Croland, Mountain Lakes, N.Y., 1969-77; dir. of optometrists Weisser Eyecare, Peoria, Ill., 1977—. Club: Wharf Harbor Yacht (Peoria) (commodore). Lodge: Masons. Avocations: tennis, boating. Home: Foot of Alexander St PO Box 215 Peoria IL 61601 Office: Weisser Eyecare 5001 N University Peoria IL 61614

CROLL, ROBERT FREDERICK, educator, economist; b. Evanston, Ill., Feb. 3, 1934; s. Frederick Warville and Florence (Campbell) C.; B.S. in Bus. Adminstrn., Northwestern U., 1954; M.B.A. (Burton A. French scholar) with high distinction, U. Mich., 1956; D.B.A., Ind. U., 1969; D.Litt., John F. Kennedy Coll., 1970; m. Sandra Elizabeth Bell, June 15, 1968; 1 son, Robert Frederick. Instr. Ind. U. Sch. Bus., Bloomington, 1956, researcher in bus. econs., 1960-62; mng. dir. Motor Vehicle Industry Research Assocs., Evanston, 1962-63; personal asst. to speaker Ill. Ho. of Reps., 1963-65; asst. prof. bus. adminstrn. Kans. State U., 1965-66; asst. prof. Inst. Indsl. Relations, Loyola U. Chgo., 1966-70; assoc. prof. Sch. Bus. Adminstrn., Central Mich. U., 1970-76, prof., 1976—. Mem. platform committee Ind. Republican Com., 1958; Ind. del. Young Rep. Nat. Conv., 1959; nat. chmn. Youth for Goldwater Orgn., 1960-61; chmn. coll. clubs Young Rep. Orgn. Ill., 1960-62; asst. chief page Rep. Nat. Conv., 1964; mem. Mt. Pleasant City Charter Commn., 1973-76. Trustee estate of F.W. Croll, Chgo., 1959—; bd. govs. Clarke Hist. Library, 1986—. Recipient Grand prize Gov. of Ind., 1958. Accredited personnel diplomate Am. Soc. Personnel Adminstrn. Accreditation Inst. Mem. Soc. Automotive Engrs., Am. Inst. Mgmt., Soc. Advancement Mgmt., Am. Econ. Assn., Mt. Pleasant C. of C., Young Ams. for Freedom (founder 1960, vice chmn. 1962-63), Phila. Soc. (founder 1964), Beta Gamma Sigma, Delta Sigma Pi Key, Phi Delta Kappa, Phi Kappa Phi, Pi Sigma Alpha, Delta Mu Delta, Sigma Pi, Alpha Kappa Psi, Sigma Iota Epsilon, Phi Chi Theta. Episcopalian. Clubs: Little Harbor (Harbor Springs, Mich.); Mount Pleasant Country. Author: Fall of an Automotive Empire: A Business History of the Packard Motor Car Company, 1945-1958, others. Contbr. articles to profl. jours. Address: 1224 Glenwood Dr Mount Pleasant MI 48858

CROMIE, WILLIAM JOSEPH, freelance writer; b. N.Y.C., Mar. 12, 1930; s. Harry Joseph and Margaret Cecil (Terrifoy) C.; m. Alicia Marie Connors, Dec. 28, 1958; 1 child, Steven William. BS, Columbia U., 1957. Geophysicist Arctic Inst. N.Am., Little Am., Antarctica, 1957-58, Lamont-Doherty Geol. Observatory Columbia U., Sta. Charlie, Arctic Ocean, 1958-60; freelance writer N.Y.C., 1960-62; pub. info. dir. Project Mohole Brown and Root, Houston, 1962-64; various positions World Book Encyclopedia Sci. Service, Houston, 1964-70; pres. Universal Sci. News, Houston, 1970-74; pub. Tribune Newspapers, Houston, 1970-74; v.p. Universal Publ. Co., Houston, 1970-74; dir. research and devel. Field Enterprises Ednl. Corp., Chgo., 1974-75; exec. dir. Council for the Advancement of Sci. Writing, Oak Park, Ill., 1975—; cons Exec. for Edn. Chgo. United, 1976-77; freelance writer 1977—; participate- in U.S-French geophys. exploration of Lake Tanganyika, East Africa, 1981; served as navigator of oceanic research vessel Tatarrax, 1978; mem. U.S. del. to the Soviet Union to discuss cooperative research in materials and metallurgy under the US/USSR Sci. and Tech. Agreement, 1977; cons., editor Washington Post-Los Angeles News Service, 1976; worker Operation Green Turtle, Costa Rica, 1966-67; participant expedition to Mt. Ararat, Turkey, 1964. Author: (TV script) America's Achievements in Space, 1986, (books) Earthquakes, 1962, Volcanos, 1962, Exploring the Secrets of the Sea, 1964, Why The Mohole, 1964, Living World of the Sea, 1966, Steven and the Green Turtle, 1970, Secrets of the Sea, 1972, Skylab, 1976, About the Solar System, 1985; editor La Grange Centennial History, 1979; contbr. articles on the astronauts, U.S. Space Program, sci., medicine, technology, bldg. and constrn. to World Book Encyclopedia, World Book Year Book, World Book Sci. Year; contbr. articles to mags. including Readers Digest, Newsweek, Sci. Digest, Paris Match (France), Twen (Germany), Sci. 80, Discover; author news and feature articles for newspapers including N.Y. Times, N.Y. Herald Tribune, Houston Chronicle; columnist Chgo. Daily News, 1974-76; syndicated columnist Newspaper Enterprise Assn., 1974-78. Mt. Cromie Trans-Antarctic Mountains named in his honor.

CROMLEY, JON LOWELL, lawyer; b. Riverton, Ill., May 23, 1934; s. John Donald and Naomi M. (Mathews) C.; B.S., U. Ill., 1958; J.D., John Marshall Law Sch., 1966. Real estate title examiner Chgo. Title & Trust Co., 1966-70; admitted to Ill. bar, 1966; practiced in Genoa, Ill., 1970—; mem. firm O'Grady & Cromley, Genoa, 1970—; dir. Genoa State Bank, Kingston Mut. County Fire Ins. Co. Bd. dirs. Genoa Day Care Center, Inc. Mem. Am. Judicature Soc., Am., Ill., Chgo., DeKalb County bar assns. Home: 130 Homewood Dr Genoa IL 60135 Office: 213 W Main St Genoa IL 60135

CROMWELL, NORMAN HENRY, chemist, educator; b. Terre Haute, Ind., Nov. 22, 1913; s. Henry and Ethel Lee (Harkelroad) C.; m. Grace N. Newell, Jan. 29, 1955; children: Christopher Newell, Richard Earl. B.S. with honors (Rea scholar 1932-35), Rose-Hulman Inst., 1935; Ph.D., U. Minn., 1939; DSc (hon.), U. Nebr., 1987. Teaching asst. U. Minn., 1935-39; instr. organic chemistry U. Nebr., Lincoln, 1939-42; asst. prof. U. Nebr., 1942-45, assoc. prof., 1945-48, prof., 1948—, Howard S. Wilson regents prof., 1960-70, chmn. dept. chemistry, 1964-70, exec. dean for grad. studies and research, 1970-72, v.p., dean Grad. Coll., 1972-73, Regents prof. chemistry Grad. Coll., 1973-83, Regents prof. emeritus, 1983—; interim dir. Eppley Inst. for Cancer Research, Med. Center, Omaha, 1979-80, dir., 1981-83; guest dept. chemistry MIT, 1967; hon. research assoc. Univ. Coll., London, 1950-51, 58-59; hon. research assoc. Calif. Inst. Tech., 1958; Am. Chem. Soc. tour lectr., 1952-70; frontiers of chemistry lectr. Wayne State U., 1958; research lectr. U. Coll., Dublin, Ireland, 1958; vis. prof. U. Calif. Med. Center, 1961; Gordon Research Conf. lectr., 1961, conf. discussion leader, 1970, 77; Hungarian Chem. Soc. lectr., 1962, Sigma Xi nat. lectr., 1964; Keynote speaker Nat. Com. Adminstrn. Research Conf., 1970; cons. Parke Davis & Co., 1943-46, Smith, Kline & French Labs., 1946-51, Am. Cancer Soc., 1956-58, Philip Morris, Inc., 1964-79, USPHS, 1952-64, chmn. medicinal chem. study sect., 1960-64; Nat. Cancer Inst., 1964-70; pres. 2d Internat. Congress Heterocyclic Chemistry, Montpellier, France, 1969; plenary lectr. 5th Internat. Congress, Ljubljana, Yugoslavia, 1975; U.S.-India exchange scientist, 1977; dir. coop. coll. tchr. devel. program for Nebr. NSF, 1960-63. Asst. editor: Jour. Heterocyclic Chemistry, 1967—; Contbr. articles to research publs. Mem. bd. Lincoln Bryan Hosp. Fulbright advanced research scholar, 1950-51; Guggenheim Meml. fellow, 1950, 58; recipient Outstanding Alumnus Achievement award U. Minn., 1975; Outstanding Research and Creativity award U. Nebr., 1978. Mem. Am. Chem. Soc. (plenary lectr. nat. meeting 1983, 40th Midwest award 1984), Chem. Soc. London, Nebr. Art Assn. (trustee 1958—, v.p. 1971), Sigma Xi, Phi Lambda Upsilon, Sigma Tau, Gamma Alpha, Tau Nu Tau, Alpha Chi Sigma, Alpha Tau Omega. Home: 6600 Shamrock Rd Lincoln NE 68506 Office: 2417 S 70th St Lincoln NE 68506

CRONE, WILLIAM FREDRICK, manufacturing engineer; b. Adrain, Mich., May 3, 1929; s. William H. and Clara (Knoblouch) C.; m. Jacqueline Sue Cather, Dec. 9, 1950; children: Rebecca L. Crone Rupert, James M., Susan A. Rupert, Amy L. Reed, William Bradley. BSEE, Toledo U., 1957; BS, Bowling Green State U., 1953, MBA, 1971. Electrical engring. supt. Libbey-Owens-Ford-Glass, East Toledo, Ohio, 1952-72; plant engr. Libbey-Owens-Ford-Glass, East Toledo, 1972-74; mfg. supt. Libbey-Owens-Ford, East Toledo, 1974-82; glass mfg. mgr. Libbey-Owen-Ford Co., Rossford, Ohio, 1982-84; mfg. engring. mgr. Libbey-Owen-Ford Co., Toledo, 1984—. Patentee in field. Chmn. bd. dirs. pub. utilities City of Bowling Green, Ohio, 1967-79; bd. dirs., v.p. bd. edn. Bowling Green Pub Schs., 1970-78. Mem. IEEE, Instrument Soc. Am., Inst. Plant Engrs. Republican. Presbyterian. Club: Bowling Green Ski (pres.). Lodge: Masons. Avocations: skiing, fishing, woodworking. Home: 1066 Melrose Dr Bowling Green OH 43402 Office: Libbey Owens Ford Co 140 Dixie Hwy Rossford OH 43460

CRONENWORTH, CHARLES DOUGLAS, manufacturing company executive; b. Mohawk, Mich., Aug. 7, 1921; s. Jacob and Margaret (Therien) C.; m. Lorraine Evelyn DeBruyne, May 18, 1946; children: Carol, Linda, Mary, Charles. B.S. in Mech. Engring., Mich. Tech. U., 1944. Registered profl. engr., Mich. Design engr. Chrysler Corp., Detroit, 1946-47; project engr. Gen. Foods, St. Clair, Mich., 1947-50; plant mgr. Diamond Crystal Salt Co., St. Clair, Mich., 1950-68, gen. mgr. prodn., 1968-75, pres., chief exec. officer, 1975-85, vice chmn., 1985-86; founder, pres. Mohawk Plastics, 1987—; dir. Comml. & Savs. Bank, St. Clair, Maritek Corp., Corpus Christy, Tex., Worldwide Protein Bahamas, Nassau, Diamond Crystal Salt, St. Clair. Mem. chmn. Mich. Mineral Well Adv., Lansing, Mich., 1970-78; mayor City of St. Clair, 1962-63, councilman, 1955-58. Recipient Silver medal Mich. Tech. U., 1976. Mem. Mich. Soc. Profl. Engrs. (alt. dir. 1958-62), Nat. Soc. Profl. Engrs., Nat. Assn. Mfrs. (dir. 1980—). Republican. Roman Catholic. Lodge: Rotary Internat. (St. Clair pres. 1979-80, St. Clair dir. 1976-82). Home: 129 E Meldrum Circle Saint Clair MI 48079 Office: Diamond Crystal Salt Co 916 S Riverside Saint Clair MI 48079

CRONIGER, JAMES DEWEY, electrical engineer; b. Cleve., Apr. 20, 1930; s. Wilbur and Elloree A. (Dewey) C.; m. Patricia A. O'Donnell, Sept. 3, 1960; children—Mary Eileen, Colleen, James. B.Sc., Case Inst. Tech., 1952. Registered profl. engr., Ohio. Control engr. Clark Controller, Cleve., 1952-60; systems engr. Reliance Electric, Cleve., 1961-68, supr. fed. marine dept., 1968-74, product mgr., 1974-80, project mgr., 1980—. Precinct committeeman Republican Party, Euclid, Ohio, 1960-65. Served with U.S. Army, 1953-55. Mem. IEEE, Assn. of Iron and Steel Engrs. Republican. Roman Catholic. Club: Euclid Hockey Assn. (pres. 1979-80). Avocations: photography; skeet; ice skating; baseball; watercolor painting. Home: 75 E 217 St Euclid OH 44123 Office: Reliance Electric 24703 Euclid Ave Euclid OH 44117

CRONIN, JAMES WATSON, educator, physicist; b. Chgo., Sept. 29, 1931; s. James Farley and Dorothy (Watson) C.; m. Annette Martin, Sept. 11, 1954; children: Cathryn, Emily, Daniel Watson. A.B., So. Methodist U. (1951); Ph.D., U. Chgo. Asso. Brookhaven Nat. Lab., 1955-58; mem. faculty Princeton, 1958-71, prof. physics, 1965-71; prof. physics U. Chgo., 1971—; Loeb lectr. physics Harvard U., 1967. Recipient Research Corp. Am. award, 1967; John Price Wetherill medal Franklin Inst., 1976; E.O. Lawrence award ERDA, 1977; Nobel prize for physics, 1980; Sloan fellow, 1964-66; Guggenheim fellow, 1970-71, 82-83. Mem. Am. Acad. Arts and Scis., Nat. Acad. Sci. Participant early devel. spark chambers; co-discover CP-violation, 1964. Home: 5825 S Dorchester St Chicago IL 60637 Office: Univ of Chgo Enrico Fermi Inst 5630 S Ellis Ave Chicago IL 60637 *

CRONON, E(DMUND) DAVID, JR., educator, historian; b. Mpls., Mar. 11, 1924; s. Edmund David and Florence Ann (Meyer) C.; m. Mary Jean Hotmar, May 13, 1950; children: William John, Robert David. Student, Macalester Coll., 1942-43; A.B., Oberlin Coll., 1948; A.M., U. Wis., 1949, Ph.D., 1953; postgrad., Manchester (Eng.) U., 1950-51. Instr., then asst. prof. history Yale U., 1953-59; asso. prof., then prof. history U. Nebr., 1959-62; prof. history U. Wis., Madison, 1962—; dean Coll. Letters and Sci. U. Wis., 1974—, chmn. dept., 1966-69, dir. Inst. Research in Humanities, 1969-74; lectr. for State Dept., Europe and Near East, 1966; Fulbright-Hays lectr. Moscow State U., 1974. Author: Black Moses: The Story of Marcus Garvey and the Universal Negro Improvement Association, 1955, Josephus Daniels in Mexico, 1960, Government and the Economy: Some Nineteenth Century Views, 1960, Contemporary Labor-Management Relations, 1960, The Cabinet Diaries of Josephus Daniels, 1913-1921, 1963, Labor and the New Deal, 1963, Twentieth Century America; Selected Readings, 2 vols, 1965-66, The Political Thought of Woodrow Wilson, 1965, Marcus Garvey, 1973. Mem. exec. com. Wis. Am. Revolution Bicentennial Commn.; adv. bd. Franklin D. Roosevelt Library, 1971-76, Wis. Humanities Com., 1973-77, Council for Internat. Exchange Scholars, 1977-80; mem. Commn. Instns. Higher Edn. N. Central Assn. Colls. and Schs., 1978-82, cons., examiner, 1970—; bd. dirs. Council of Colls. of Arts and Scis., 1978-80, pres., 1981-82; mem. Commn. Arts and Scis., Nat. Assn. State Univs. and Land Grant Colls., 1984—; trustee Ripon Coll. Served to 1st lt., inf. AUS, 1943-46. Fulbright fellow, 1950-51; Stimson fellow, 1958-59. Fellow Soc. Am. Historians; mem. Am. Hist. Assn., Orgn. Am. Historians (exec. bd.), Wis. Hist. Soc. (bd. curators, pres.), So. Hist. Assn. (exec. council, bd. editors), Phi Beta Kappa. Unitarian. Home: 5601 Varsity Hill Madison WI 53705 *

CROOKS, KERRY ANDERSON, air force officer; b. Castle AFB, Calif., May 23, 1955; s. Kenneth Elmer and Kathleen Violet (Aagaard) C.; m. Viviene Wilkinson, Dec. 23, 1985. BS in Edn., Ohio State U., 1979; postgrad., U. Alaska, 1982, U. Okla., 1984-85; grad., Squadron Officer's Sch., 1985. Cert. tchr., Ohio. Enlisted USN, 1973; commd. capt. USAF, 1979; petty officer nav. nuclear fleet ballistic missle submarine USS James K. Polk USN, Charleston Naval Base, S.C., 1973-75; instr. electronic warfare, flight evaluator 6th strategic wing USAF, Eielson AFB, Alaska, 1980-83, dep. comdr. ops., exec. officer, 1981-82; instr., crew comdr. electronic warfare 343d strategic reconnaissance squadron USAF, Offutt AFB, 1983—. Author: (audio-visual multi screen) History of the 55th Strategic Wing, 1985; contbr. articles to profl. jours. Active Joselyn Art Mus., Omaha. Decorated Airman's medal, Air medal with 6 oak leaf clusters; recipient Comdrs. Cup award Ariz. State U., 1979, Am. Legion award, Columbus, 1979; named 15th USAF Jr. Officer Yr., 1982. Mem. Assn. Old Crows (Gold Cert. of Merit award 1986), Air Force Assn. (Rickenbacker chpt. award 1979, Maj. Norman C. Miller award 1981, Lt. Gen. Glen R. Birchard award 1982), Am. Polit. Sci. Assn. Avocations: travel, photography. Home: PO Box 46931 Papillion NE 68046 Office: 343d Strategic Reconnaissance Squadron Offutt AFB NE 68113

CROPPER, REBECCA LYNN, radiological engineer, radioactive waste engineer; b. LaGrange, Ky., Nov. 8, 1958; d. Clyde Carter and Dorothy Jean (Neblett) C. B.A. in Physics, Hanover Coll., Ind., 1979; M.S. in Health Physics, Ga. Inst. Tech., 1982. Radiol. control and safety technician U.S. Ecology, Inc., Louisville, 1979-81; research asst. Ga. Inst. Tech., Atlanta, 1981-82; radiol. engr. Bechtel Nat., Inc., Oak Ridge, 1982-85; lead sr. engr. Impell Corp., Lincolnshire, Ill., 1985—. Mem. Health Physics Soc., Am. Nuclear Soc., Nat. Assn. Female Execs. Home: 711 Wakefield Gurnee IL 60031 Office: Impell Corp 300 TriState Internat Suite 400 Lincolnshire IL 60015

CROSBY, BENJAMIN GRATZ, electronics executive; b. Lexington, Ky., May 9, 1936; s. Ben Gratz Crosby and Myra (Smith) Brooking; m. Susan Lee Nichols, Nov. 21, 1962 (div. June 1978); children: Alex Russell, Ben R., Elise M., Joanna D., Dawn N.; m. Jane White Firestone, Feb. 2, 1984. BS in Engring., U.S. Mil. Acad., 1958; cert., Armed Forces Staff Coll., 1972. Cert. fin. planner. Commd. 2d lt. U.S. Army, 1958, advanced through grades to lt. col., 1973, retired, 1978; v.p. F.L. Putnam & Co., Boston, 1978-81; pres. Blue Cactus Mining Corp., Las Vegas, 1981-84; exec. Oneac Corp., Libertyville, Ill., 1984—. Mem. Rep. Inner Circle, Washington, 1985—; bd. dirs. Citizen Scholarship Found., St. Paul, 1980—. Decorated two Silver Stars, four Bronze Stars, two Legions of Merit. Mem. Am. Fedn. Hosps., Am. Hosp. Assn., Hosp. Engring. Soc., Inst. Cert. Fin. Planners, Am. Inst. Ultrasound in Medicne, Assn. Advancement of Med. Instrumentation. Republican. Episcopalian. Avocations: skiing, tennis, racquetball. Office: Oneac Corp 27944 N Bradley Rd Libertyville IL 60048

CROSBY, FRED MCCLELLAN, retail home and office furnishings executive; b. Cleve., May 17, 1928; s. Fred Douglas and Marion Grace (Naylor) C.; m. Phendalyne D. Tazewell, Dec. 23, 1958; children: Fred, James, Lionicia. Grad. high sch. Vice pres. Seaway Flooring & Paving Co., Cleve., 1959-63; pres., chief exec. officer Crosby Furniture Co., Inc., Cleve., 1963—; dir. First Bank Nat., First Intercity Banc Corp., Cleve. Auto Systems. Dir. adv. council Ohio Bd. Workmen's Compensation, 1974-82; chmn. Minority Econ. Devel. Corp., 1972-83; bd. dirs. Council Smaller Enterprise, 1973-80, Goodwill Industries, 1973-80, Woodruff Hosp., 1975-82, Cleve. Devel. Found., Greater Cleve. Growth Assn., Pub. TV, Surveyors Telecom., Inc., Sta. WVIZ-TV, Cleve.-Cuyahoga Port Authority, 1986—; chmn. bd. dirs. Glenville YMCA, 1973-76; trustee Cleve. Play House, Eiza Bryant Ctr., Cleve. Small Bus. Incubator; bd. dirs., treas. Urban League Cleve., 1971-78; mem. adv. council Small Bus. Assn., adv. bd. Salvation Army, 1980; bd. dirs. Forest City Hosp. Found., Cleve. State U. Found.; Commr. Ohio State Boxing Commn., 1985, Pvt. Industry Council, 1985, Nat. Small Bus. Adv. Council, 1980; bd. advocates Antioch Coll.; county commrs. appointee to Community Adv. Bd., 1987—; mem. Cleve. Opera Council, 1987—. Served with AUS, 1950-52. Recipient award bus. excellence Dept. Commerce, 1972; Presdl. award YMCA, 1974; Gov. Ohio award community action, 1973; First Class Leadership Cleve., 1977. named Family of Yr. Cleve. Urban League, 1971. Mem. Greater Cleve. Growth Assn. (dir.), Cleve. C. of C., NAACP (v.p. Cleve. 1969-78), Ohio Council Retail Mchts. (dir.), Ohio Home Furnishing and Appliance Assn. (pres.), Exec. Order Ohio Commodore. Clubs: Mid-Day, Cleve. Play House, Harvard Bus. Sch., Clevelander, Bratenahl, Univ. (Cleve.). Lodge: Rotary. Home: 2530 Richmond Rd Beachwood OH 44122 Office: 12435 St Clair Ave Cleveland OH 44108

CROSBY, MICHAEL HUGH, priest; b. Fond du Lac, Wis., Feb. 16, 1940; s. Hugh John and Blanche Hannah (Bouser) C. BA, St. Mary's Capuchin Coll., 1963; ThM, St. Anthony Coll., 1967; M in Econs., New Sch. Social Research, 1985; postgrad. in theology, Theol. Union, 1986—. Ordained priest Roman Cath. Ch., 1966. Assoc. pastor St. Elizabeth Ch., Milw., 1968-73; staff Justice & Peace Ctr., Milw., 1973-83, coordinator beatitudes program, corp. responsibilities, 1983—; mem. governing bd., exec. com. Interfaith Ctr. on Corp. Responsibility, N.Y., 1973—; mem. peace and justice coms. Province of St. Joseph, Detroit, 1982—; mem. Justice and Peace Com. Conf. of major supervising men, Washington, 1982—. Author six books on spirituality and theology; contbr. articles on spirituality, theology and corp. responsibility to profl. jours. Avocations: racquetball, swimming. Home and Office: 1016 N 9th Milwaukee WI 53233

CROSIER, DALE FINLEY, manufacturing executive; b. Sioux City, Iowa, Feb. 18, 1931; s. Dale Theron and A. Marie (Finley) C.; m. Alice Florence Smith, June 24, 1956; children: Susan, Andrew, Scott, Steven. Student, U. Iowa, 1949-51; BS in Engring., U.S. Naval Acad., 1955; postgrad., U. Minn., 1960-62; MBA, Drury Coll., 1971. Commd. ensign USN, 1955, advanced through grades to lt., 1959, retired, 1959; process engr. 3M Co., St. Paul, 1959-65; quality control supr. 3M Co., Springfield, Mo., 1966-74; prodn. supr. 3M CO., Springfield, Mo., 1974; quality, process engr. supr. 3M CO., Aberdeen, S.D., 1974-79, prodn. control supr., 1980-85; adminstr. quality control div. 3M CO., St. Paul, 1985—; adj. faculty SW Mo. State U., Springfield, 1971-74, Presentation Coll., Aberdeen, 1976-78; mem. tech. adv. bd. No. State Coll., Aberdeen, 1979-85; tech. recruiting liason 3M Co., Aberdeen, 1979-85. Author Supplier Improvement Guide, 1985. Chmn., pres. ARC, Aberdeen, 1975-85, Boy Scouts, Aberdeen, 1975-85, Substance Abuse Council, Aberdeen, 1975-85, Foster Grandparents, Aberdeen, 1975-85; campaign chmn. United Way, Aberdeen, 1977. Mem. Am. Soc. for Quality Control, Cottage Grove Jaycees (pres. 1964-65). Democrat. Presbyterian. Lodges: Kiwanis (pres. Aberdeen club 1984-85), Masons, Shriners. Avocations: travel, hiking, swimming, reading, playing the drum. Home: Rt 5 Box 114B Audubon Ct Hudson WI 54016 Office: 3m Co 3M Ctr OH&SP 553 Saint Paul MN 55144

CROSS, ALVIN F., supermarket chain executive; b. 1927. With Nat. Tea Co., Des Plaines, Ill., 1946—; now pres. Office: Nat Tea Co 9701 W Higgins Rd Rosemont IL 60018 *

CROSS, JANET LAVERN, nurse; b. East St. Louis, Ill., Aug. 8, 1944; d. Henry Edward and Gustava Lucille (Titus) Pritchett; m. Robert Lee Cross, Dec. 10, 1967 (div. Dec. 1976); 1 dau., Ja'Net Annette. B.N., So. Ill. U., 1972. Staff nurse Vets. John Cochran Hosp., St. Louis, 1972-73, St. Mary's Hosp., East St. Louis, 1974; staff nurse-pub. health East Side Health, East St. Louis, 1974-76; staff nurse Incarnate Word Hosp., St. Louis, 1976—. Mem. parent group, project follow-through Dunbar Sch., East St. Louis, 1981-83. Mem. Ill. Nurses Assn., Am. Nurses Assn., Am. Nurses Found. Baptist.

CROSS, SHELLEY ANN, neurologist, neuro-ophthalmologist; b. Beacon, N.Y., Dec. 2, 1948; s. A.J. and Anna L. (Geering) C. AB, Wellesley (Mass.) Coll., 1970; MD, Med. Coll. Pa., 1975. Intern Montreal (Can.) Gen. Hosp., 1975-76; resident in medicine Royal Victoria Hosp., Montreal, Can., 1976-78; resident in neurology Mass. Gen. Hosp., Boston, 1978-81; fellow in neuro-ophthalmology Bascom Palmer Eye Inst., Miami, Fla., 1981-82; cons. in neurology Mayo Clinic, Rochester, Minn., 1982—. Contbr. articles to profl. jours. Fellow Royal Coll. Physicians; mem. Am. Coll. Physicians, N.A. Neuro-ophthalmological Soc., Am. Acad. Neurology and Psychiatry. Avocations: classical music, travel, literature, languages. Office: Mayo Clinic Dept Neurology Rochester MN 55905

CROSSET, JAMES M., accountant, real estate investor; b. Cin., June 13, 1958; s. Robert J. and Mary P. (Wagner) C. BS, Ind. U., 1980; MBA, U. Cin., 1982. CPA, Ill. Acct. Wilson Foods Co., Cedar Rapids, Iowa, 1980-81; internal auditor SFN Cos., Inc., Glenview, Ill., 1982-84; sr. acct. South-Western Pub. Co., Cin., 1984—. Coach high sch. basketball, Knox Ch., Cin., 1984—, advisor high sch. youth, 1985—; asst. scoutmaster Troop 5 Boy Scouts Am., Cin., 1986—. Mem. Am. Inst. CPAs. Democrat. Presbyterian. Avocation: running. Home: 3601 Edwards Rd Cincinnati OH 45208 Office: South-Western Pub Co 5101 Madison Rd Cincinnati OH 45227

CROSSMAN, DOUGLAS MICHAEL, dentist; b. Detroit, Aug. 9, 1941. DDS, U. Detroit, 1967. Gen. practice dentistry Livonia, Mich., 1970—. Fellow Acad. Gen. Dentistry; mem. ADA, Internat. Assn. Orthodontists (nat. sec. 1976), Detroit Clinic Club (periodontal sect. (co-dir. 1985-87). Office: 36180 Five Wile Rd Livonia MI 48154

CROUCHER, DAVID WAYNE, religion educator; b. St. Paul, Dec. 19, 1961; s. Dennis Wayne and Evelyn Marie (Trapp) C.; m. Carrie Ann Peters, June 2, 1980 (dec. Nov. 1983); m. Shawna Kay Fisher, Oct. 20, 1984. BTh., Ind. Bible Coll., 1984. Mgr. Rose Acre Farms, Seymour, Ind., 1980-83; tchr. Ind. Bible Coll., Seymour, 1983—. Republican. Pentecostal. Home: 526 Ends Rd Seymour IN 47274 Office: Ind Bible Coll 501 N Walnut St Seymour IN 47274

CROUSE, FREDERICK LYNN, claims examiner; b. Red Oak, Iowa, July 2, 1960; s. Richard Glen and Lucille Marie (Ritnour) C.; m. Deirdre Lynne Martin, Oct. 12, 1985. BA in Polit. Sci., Iowa State U., 1982. Dist. mgr. Des Moines Register, 1984; claims examiner Am. Republic Ins. Co., Des Moines, 1984—. Mem. Des Moines Jaycees. Home: 4216 Ingersoll Ave Des Moines IA 50312 Office: Am Republic Ins Co 6th and Keoway Des Moines IA 50334

CROUTER, ELAINE FAYE, hospital supervisor; b. Hancock, Mich., July 27, 1943; d. Toivo Edward and Esther Ada (Maki) Siponen; m. William Harold Crouter, Sept. 2, 1967. BS in Med. Tech., Mich. Tech. U., 1965. Registered med. technologist Am. Soc. Clin. Pathologists. Med. technologist Botsford Hosp., Farmington, Mich., 1965-66, U. Mich. Hosp., Ann Arbor, 1966-67, William Beaumont Hosp., Royal Oak, Mich., 1967-76; supr. blood bank St. Joseph Mercy Hosp., Pontiac, Mich., 1976—, supr. serology, 1986—. Mem. Am. Assn. Blood Banks (inspector blood banks 1976—, mem. Midwest adv. bd.), Mich. Assn. Blood Banks (co-coordinator ann. meeting 1978—, program com. 1978—, Founders award 1986). Lutheran. Home: 3027 St Jude Dr Drayton Plains MI 48020 Office: St Joseph Mercy Hosp 900 Woodward Ave Pontiac MI 48053

CROW, RICHARD RONALD, management consultant; b. Point Marion, Pa., Aug. 19, 1915; s. Benjamin K. and Alice (Richards) C.; B.S., California (Pa.) U., 1936; M.A., Ohio State U., 1938; m. Mary Grace Jessup, Aug. 16, 1951; children—Megan Leslie, Philip Edward. Tng. dir. Curtiss-Wright Corp., Columbus, Ohio, 1941-45; corporate tng. dir. U.S. Rubber Co., N.Y.C., 1945-53; mgmt. devel. dir., asst. mgr. indsl. relations, regional mgr. indsl. relations Continental Oil Co., Houston and Ft. Worth, 1953-59; v.p. personnel Stouffer Foods Corp., Cleve., 1959-68; corporate v.p.-human resources Sherwin-Williams Co., Cleve., 1968-78; pres. R.R. Crow Co., Inc., Rocky River, Ohio, 1978—. Mem. council on devel., edn. and tng. Nat. Conf. Bd. Accredited personnel exec. Recipient Laureate citation award Epsilon Pi Tau, 1946. Mem. Am. Mgmt. Assn. (manpower planning and devel. commn.). Home: 3858 W Surrey Ct Rocky River OH 44116 Office: RR Crow Co Inc 3858 W Surrey Suite 22 Rocky River OH 44116

CROW, SAM ALFRED, federal judge; b. Topeka, May 5, 1926; s. Samuel Wheadon and Phyllis K. (Brown) C.; m. Ruth M. Rush, Jan. 30, 1948; children—Sam A., Dan W. B.A., U. Kans., 1949; J.D., Washburn U., 1952. Bar: Kans. 1952, U.S. Dist. Ct. Kans. 1952, U.S. Supreme Ct. 1962, U.S. Ct. Appeals (10th cir.) 1963, U.S. Mil. Ct. Appeals 1953. Ptnr. Rooney, Dickinson, Prager & Crow, Topeka, 1953-63; ptnr. Dickinson, Crow, Skoog & Honeyman, Topeka, 1963-70; sr. ptnr. Crow & Skoog, Topeka, 1971-75; part-time U.S. magistrate 1973-75, U.S. magistrate, 1975-81; judge U.S. Dist. Ct. Kans., Wichita, 1981—; lectr. Washburn U. Sch. Law, also assns., convs. Bd. rev. Boy Scouts Am., 1960-70, cubmaster, 1957-60; mem. vestry Grace Episcopal Ch., Topeka, 1960-65; chmn. Kans. March of Dimes, 1959, bd. dirs. 1960-65; bd. dirs. Topeka Council Chs., 1960-70; mem. Mulvane Art Soc., 1965—, Kans. Hist. Soc., 1960—; pres., v.p. PTA. Served to col. JAGC, USAR, ret. Fellow Acad. Internat. Law and Sci.; mem. ABA (del. Nat. Conf. Spl. Ct. Judges 1978, 79), Kans. Bar Assn. (trustee 1970-76, chmn. mil. law sect. 1965, 67, 70, 72, 74, 75), Assn. Trial Lawyers Am., Kans. Trial Lawyers Assn. (sec. 1959-60, pres. 1960-61), Nat. Assn. U.S. Magistrates (com. discovery abuse), Topeka Bar Assn. (chmn. jud. reform com., chmn. bench and bar com., chmn. criminal law com.), Wichita Bar Assn., Wichita Lawyers Club, Topeka Lawyers Club (sec. 1964-65, pres. 1965-66), Res. Officers Assn., Am. Legion, Delta Theta Phi, Sigma Alpha Epsilon. Club: Shawnee Country, Wichita Lawyers. Office: 401 Market St Suite 322 Wichita KS 67202

CROWDER, BARBARA LYNN, lawyer; b. Mattoon, Ill., Feb. 3, 1956; d. Robert Dale and Martha Elizabeth (Harrison) C.; m. Lawrence Owen Taliana, Apr. 17, 1982; children: Paul Joseph, Robert Lawrence. BA, U. Ill., 1978, JD, 1981. Bar: Ill. 1981. Assoc., Louis E. Olivero, Peru, Ill., 1981-82; asst. state's atty. Madison County, Edwardsville, Ill., 1982-84; ptnr. Robbins & Crowder, Edwardsville, 1985-87; ptnr. Robbins, Crowder & Bader, Edwardsville, 1987—. Chmn. City of Edwardsville Zoning Bd. Appeals, 1986-87; mem. City of Edwardsville Planning Commn., 1985—. Named Best Oral Advocate, Moot Ct. Bd., 1979, Outstanding Sr., Phi Alpha Delta, 1981, Young Career Women, Ill. Bus. and Profl. Women, 1986; recipient Parliamentary Debate award U. Ill., 1978, Alice Paul award Alton-Edwardsville NOW, 1987. Mem. ABA, Ill. Bar Assn., Assn. Trial Lawyers Am., Phi Alpha Delta, Women Lawyers Assn. Met. East (v.p. 1985, pres. 1986), LWV, Edwardsville Bus. and Profl. Women (Woman of Achievement 1985, Jr. Service award 1987). Democrat. Home: 982 Surrey Dr Edwardsville IL 62025 Office: PO Box 451 Edwardsville IL 62025

CROWE, RAYMOND RIGGAN, psychiatrist, educator; b. Nashville, May 31, 1942; s. Raymond R. and Lola O. Crowe; m. Sally R. Crowe, June 9, 1966; children: Nancy, Kimberly, Amy. BA, Vanderbilt U., 1963, MD, 1966. Diplomate Am. Bd. Psychiatry. Resident in psychiatry U. Iowa, Iowa City, 1967-68, 70-72; postdoctoral in human genetics U. Mich., Ann Arbor, 1973-75; prof. psychiatry U. Iowa, 1975—. Contbr. articles to profl. jours. Served to capt. USAF, 1968-70, Vietnam. Human Genetics fellow Found. Fund Research in Psychiatry, 1973-75. Mem. AMA, AAAS, Am. Psychiat. Assn., Psychiat. Research Soc., Am. Psychopathological Assn., Soc. Biol. Psychiatry. Office: U Iowa Dept Psychiatry 500 Newton Rd Iowa City IA 52242

CROWLEY, CORNELIUS JOSEPH, emeritus linguistics educator, publishing company executive; b. N.Y.C., Mar. 21, 1911; s. Florence Francis and Helen (Sheehan) C.; m. Frances Felicia Geyer, Sept. 28, 1948; children—Veronica, Robert. B.A., CUNY, 1938; M.A., NYU, 1941, Ph.D., 1951. Cert. secondary tchr., N.Y. Tchr. English, Spanish and Latin, Kohut Sch., Harrison, N.Y., 1942-43; sr. translator Naval Censorship, N.Y.C., 1943-45; instr. Bergen Coll., Teaneck, N.J., 1946-48; asst. prof. U. Wyo., Laramie, 1948-50; asst. prof. to prof. linguistics St. Louis U., 1950-75, prof. emeritus, 1975—; pres. and editor in-chief Heartland Books, Cape Girardeau, Mo., 1972—. Author: Legend of the Wanderings of the Spear of Longinus, 1972. Translator: A Choice of Propertius, 1976, rev. 1981. Contbr. articles to profl. jours. Recipient Cert. of Merit, U.S. Govt., 1945. Mem. Linguistic Soc. of Am., Renaissance Soc. of Am., Am. Oriental Soc., Medieval Acad. of Am., Internat. Linguistic Assn., Phi Sigma (moderator 1952-60) Romance Language Soc. Democrat. Roman Catholic. Avocations: toy trains; studying unusual languages; attempting to decipher Minoan Linear A. Home: 515 North Sprigg Cape Girardeau MO 63701

CROWLEY, DAVID HARMAN, social worker; b. Pitts., May 17, 1954; s. Henry Francis and Helen Laurine (Harman) C. B in Social Work, So. Ill. U., Carbondale, 1976; MSW, U. Ill., 1984. Cert. social worker. Supr. emergency program Janet Wattes Mental Health Ctr., Rockford, Ill., 1977-84; after hours clinician, crisis line coordinator Champaign (Ill.) County Mental Health Ctr., 1984—; pvt. practice therapy Counseling Inst., Champaign, 1985—; staff mem. mental health div. U. Ill., Urbana, 1984—. Mem. Nat. Assn. Social Workers, Acad. Cert. Social Workers, Alpha Delta Mu. Avocations: softball, golf, ski, jogging, guitar. Office: Champaign County Mental Health Ctr 600 E Park Champaign IL 61820

CROWLEY, JOSEPH MICHAEL, electrical engineer, educator; b. Phila., Sept. 9, 1940; s. Joseph Edward and Mary Veronica (McCall) C.; m. Barbara Ann Sauerwald, June 22, 1963; children: Joseph W., Kevin, James, Michael, Daniel. B.S., MIT, 1962, M.S., 1963, Ph.D., 1965. Vis. scientist Max Planck Inst., Goettingen, W.Ger, 1965-66; asst. prof. elec. engring. U. Ill., Urbana, 1966-69, assoc. prof., 1969-78, prof., dir. Applied Electrostats. Research Lab., 1978—; pres. JMC Inc., 1981—, Electrostatic Applications, 1986—; cons. to several corps. Contbr. articles to profl. jours.; patentee ink jet printers. Pres. Champaign-Urbana Bd. Cath. Edn., 1978-80. Recipient Gen. Motors scholarship, 1958-62; AEC fellow, 1962-65; NATO fellow, 1965-66. Mem. IEEE (sr.), Electrostats. Soc. Am., Am. Phys. Soc., Soc. Inf. Display, Mensa. Roman Catholic. *

CROWN, SUSAN M., social services administrator; b. Chgo., May 14, 1958; d. Lester and Renee (Schine) C.; m. William Kunkler, May 2, 1981. Student, U. de Salamanca, Spain, 1979; BA, Yale U., 1980; MA, NYU, 1982. Mental health worker N.Y. Hosp., Cornell Med. Ctr., White Plains, 1980; psychology intern Psychiat. Services Ctr., White Plains, 1980-81; researcher Albert Einstein Hosp., Bronx, 1981-82; staff assocs. Chgo. Community Trust, 1983-84; exec. dir. charitibal grants, v.p. Henry Crown and Co., Chgo., 1985—. Bd. dirs. Family Focus, Evanston, Rush Presbyn. St. Luke's Med. Ctr., Chgo.; bd. govs. Northwestern U. Library Council, Evanston. Mem. Chgo. Found. for Women (chmn. investment com.), Council on Founds., Juvenile Protection Assn. (bd. dirs.), Jerusalem Found. (chmns. com.). Clubs: Yale, Met., Lincoln Park Boat (Chgo.). Office: 300 W Washington St Chicago IL 60606

CROWNER, DAVID WELLS, dentist; b. Toledo, Oct. 28, 1935; s. Harold Penniman and Jeanette Helen (Bremer) C.; student Purdue U., 1953-55, U. Toledo, 1955-56; D.D.S., Ohio State U., 1960; m. Barbara Ann Prickman, Dec. 27, 1958; children—Susan Lynne, John David. Pvt. practice dentistry, Toledo, 1962-72, Sylvania, Ohio, 1972—. Pres., Renworc, Inc., Sylvania, 1969—. Finance chmn. Sylvania Sch. Bd. Levy, 1973; pres. St. Paul's Lutheran Ch., Toledo; pres. Sylvania Downtown Bus. Assn.; gen. chmn. Holiday Parade, Sylvania, 1983 Served with Dental Corps, USNR, 1960-62, comdr. Res. Decorated Navy Commendation medal. Mem. Am., Ohio, Toledo (program chmn. 1971-72, clinic day chmn. 1968-69, chmn. continuing edn. 1976-77) dental assns., Beta Beta Beta, Alpha Epsilon Delta, Phi Gamma Delta (bd. dirs.). Club: International Torch (membership chmn. 1975—, dir. 1981—, pres.) (Toledo). Home: 6739 Fifth Ave Sylvania OH 43560

CROWSON, WALTER COLLON, dentist; b. Detroit, Oct. 12, 1932; s. Walter Stanley and Leone (Collon) C.; B.A., Mich. State U., 1957; D.D.S., U. Mich., 1958; m. Bonnie Lou Kremer, Nov. 30, 1974; 1 dau. by previous marriage—Jony Collon. Practice dentistry, Ferndale, Mich., 1958—. Dental dir. Detroit Orthopaedic Clinic, 1959—; chmn. Dental Adv. Bd. to Ferndale, 1968-74; chmn. Oakland County Dental Vocational Adv. Com.; cons. Dept. Edn. State of Mich.; cons. dental hygiene program Oakland Community Coll., 1975-76; cons. Hartland Center for Handicapped, 1978—; dental surgery staff Detroit Children's Hosp., 1979—; cons. Spl. project U. Mich., 1981. Pres. Graefield Condominium Assn., Birmingham, Mich., 1972-78; bd. dirs. Tri-County Dental Health Council, 1975—, Spirit of Detroit Assn., 1983—. Recipient Citizen of Year award Clawson Troy Elks Club, 1974. Sigma Gamma Found. grantee, 1972. Mem. Am., Mich. dental assns., Mich. Assn. Professions, Oakland County Dental Soc. (chmn. aux. personnel 1974-76), Acad. of Dentistry for Handicapped, Birmingham Power Squadron, Lambda Chi Alpha, Delta Sigma Delta. Elk. Clubs: Detroit Boat (rear commodore 1982, vice commodore 1984, commodore 1985, bd. dirs. 1982—, v.p. 1987), Huron Pointe Yacht (Mt. Clemens, Mich.), Detroit River Yachting Assn. Home: 1970 Graefield St Birmingham MI 48008 Office: Detroit Orthopaedic Clinic 26789 Woodward Ave Huntington Woods MI 48070

CRUICKSHANK, JOHN THOMAS, sales executive; b. N.Y.C., Mar. 22, 1930; s. John Thomas and Marie (Odegaard) C.; m. Marilyn O. Head, June 13, 1953 (div. May 1967); children: Kathy R. Bennett, Karen M. Bottoms, Pamela L.; m. Laura Kathryn Lang, Dec. 31, 1968. BSBA, U. Denver, 1953. Sales rep. NuTone, Inc., Denver, El Paso (Tex.) and Phoenix, 1956-61; dist. mgr. NuTone, Inc., San Francisco, 1961-66; regional mgr. NuTone, Inc., Los Angeles, 1966-71, western sales mgr., 1971-77; v.p., mgr. gen. sales and mktg. Scovill div. NuTone, Inc., Cin., 1977—. Served to cpl. U.S. Army, 1947-50, ETO. Mem. Am. Mgmt. Assn., Am. Home Lighting Inst. Republican. Lutheran. Avocations: golf, swimming, gardening, travel. Home: 9100 Indian Ridge Rd Cincinnati OH 45243 Office: NuTone Inc Madison & Red Bank Rds Cincinnati OH 45227

CRUMMER, MURRAY THOMAS, JR., insurance company executive; b. Eldorado, Kans., Aug. 27, 1922; s. Murray Thomas and Bertha Ellen (Sandifer) C.; m. Elliott Downs, Aug. 16, 1952; children—Elizabeth, Ellen, Barbara, Carolyn, Murray Philip. Student, U. Nebr., 1940-43. Underwriter, salesman Central Investment Co. Tex., Dallas, 1946-49; salesman Central Investment Co. Tex., Omaha, 1949-53; various positions United Benefit Life Ins. Co., Omaha, 1953-82; chief investment officer Mut. of Omaha Ins. Cos., 1982—. Served as sgt. inf. U.S. Army, 1943-46. Republican. Episcopalian. Home: 5115 Lafayette Ave Omaha NE 68132 Office: Mut of Omaha Ins Co Mutual of Omaha Plaza Omaha NE 68175

CRUMP, JOHN GEORGE, JR., engineering company executive; b. St. Louis, Nov. 10, 1948; s. John George and Marilyn (Phelan) C.; m. Maureen Ann Shaugnessy, July 23, 1971. BSEE, U. Ill., 1971; MBA, Northwestern U., 1974. Systems engr. Kay-Ray, Inc., Arlington Heights, Ill., 1971-73, mgr. engring., 1973-77, v.p. engring., 1977-80, v.p. sales and mktg., 1980-84, pres., 1984—, also bd. dirs.; bd. dirs Kay Elemetrics, Pine Brook, N.J. Patentee in field, 1977. Mem. Am. Mgmt. Soc., Instrument Soc. Am., Assn. Elec. Engrs., Profit Sharing Council of Am. Republican. Roman Catholic. Avocatins: running, skiing, reading, stamp collecting, sailing. Home: 73D Braeburn Ln Barrington Hills IL 60010 Office: Kay-Ray Inc 590 Holbrook Dr Wheeling IL 60010

CRUMPTON, SANDRA ANN, financial services company executive; b. Greenville, S.C., Oct. 12, 1945; d. James Albert and Elizabeth Mae (Surett) C. B.A., Mich. State U., 1968; postgrad. U. Calif.-Berkeley, 1976-77, Am. U., 1972-74. Cert. tchr., Mich., Calif.; cert. adminstr., Calif. Tchr., Okemos (Mich.) Pub. Schs., 1968-70, Crete (Ill.) Pub. Schs., 1970-72; master tchr. Am. Community Sch., Athens, Greece, 1972-74; bus. dir. Crested Butte, Colo., 1974-76; mktg. rep. data processing div. IBM, San Francisco, 1977-80; dir. customer support Walker Interactive Products, San Francisco, 1980-85; v.p. prodn. ops. SEI Corp., Chgo., 1985—; Mem. Am. Mgmt. Assn., Nat. Assn. Female Execs., Women in Bus., AAUW, Women's Exec. Network, Chgo. Council on Fgn. Relations, Alliance Francaise. Republican. Clubs: Corp. Connections Exec., Execs. of Chgo. Office: 2 N Riverside Plaza Suite 500 Chicago IL 60606

CRUTE, CHRISTY LYNN, systems analyst, educator; b. Martins Ferry, Ohio, July 5, 1957; d. Frank Jr. and Nancy Lee (LaRue) Faldowski; m. Michael Everett Crute Sr., Jan. 5, 1985; 1 child, Michael Everett Jr. BA in Edn., U. Akron, 1980; MBA, Kent State U., 1986. Postgrad., 1986—. Programmer Ohio Edison, Akron, 1980-83, programmer analyst, 1983, systems analyst, 1986—; instr. Kent State U., 1986—. Mem. ORSA, TIMS. Office: Kent State U Kent OH 44240

CRUTHIRD, ROBERT LEE, sociology educator; b. LeFlore County, Miss., Dec. 10, 1944; s. Harvie and Mary Florence (Black) C.; m. Julie Mae Boyd,

Dec. 17, 1965; 1 son, Robert Lee. M.A., U. Ill.-Chgo., 1976. Correctional counselor Ill. Dept. Corrections, Joliet, 1977-78; instr. in sociology Kennedy-King Coll., Chgo., 1978-80, 81-84, asst. prof., 1984-87, assoc. prof., 1987—, dir. instl. research, 1980-81; cons. Ednl. Mgmt. Assocs., 1981-82. Served with U.S. Army, 1965-67. Crime and delinquency research tng. fellow U. Ill.-Chgo., 1976-77; NEH fellow, summer 1983. Mem. Am. Sociol. Assn., Assn. Instl. Research, Nat. Assn. Devel. Edn., Assn. Study of Afro-Am. Life and History, U. Ill. Chgo. Alumni Assn. (life), Alpha Phi Alpha, Phi Theta Kappa (named to Ill. Hall of Honor 1984, 86). Democrat. Baptist. Home: 5050 S Lake Shore Dr #3203S Chicago IL 60615 Office: 6800 S Wentworth Suite 326E Chicago IL 60621

CRUTSINGER, ROBERT KEANE, diversified food wholesale company executive; b. St. Louis, Sept. 2, 1930; s. Robert Matthews and Gertrude (Keane) C.; m. Mary Lou Hopkins, Feb. 2, 1957; children—Cary Anne, Robert H., Kathryn P. B.S. in Bus. Adminstrn., Quincy Coll., 1955. With Nat. Cash Register Corp., 1956-70, div. mgr. corp. accounts, 1970; owner, operator IGA food store, 1965-69; with Wetterau Inc., Hazelwood, Mo., 1970—, exec. v.p., 1974-78, pres. food services div., 1978-79, pres., chief operating officer, 1979—, also dir.; dir. Centerre Bank of Florissant, Mo. Trustee Quincy Coll., 1985—. Served with U.S. Army, 1952-54. Mem. Am. Mgmt. Assn., Nat. Am. Wholesale Grocers Assn., Knights of Cauliflower Ear. Club: Bellerive Country. Office: Wetterau Inc 8920 Pershall Rd Hazelwood MO 63042 *

CUBBERLY, FRED DONALD, JR., restaurant equipment company official; b. Dayton, Ohio, Aug. 10, 1948; s. Fred D. and Lucile R. (Fitzgerald) C.; m. Deborah K. Redrick, Mar. 4, 1972; children—Dana N., Diane M. A.A., Sinclair Community Coll., 1970, Assoc. Sci. in Bus. Adminstrn., 1972, Assoc. Applied Sci. in Mgmt., 1974, Assoc. Applied Sci. in Procurement and Materials Mgmt., 1980; B.S. in Mgmt., Wright State U., 1978. Prodn. scheduler Dayton-Walther Corp., Dayton, Ohio, 1967-69, prodn. control supr., 1969-72, prodn. control specialist, 1978-79, corp. sr. buyer, 1979-81; purchasing mgr. Monarch Marking Co., Dayton, 1981-84, bus. unit mgr., 1984-85, mgr. purchased materials Henny Penny Corp., Eaton, Ohio, 1985—; adj. assoc. prof. mgmt. Wright State U.; lectr. Sinclair Community Coll. Chmn., Miamisburg (Ohio) Community Devel. Adv. Council, 1979-82; mem. Miamisburg Library Renovation Com., 1982; coach Little League baseball, Miamisburg; chmn. Monarch Marking Co. United Way campaign, 1983, 84. Named Outstanding Mgmt. Grad., Wright State U., 1978. Fellow Am. Prodn. and Inventory Control Soc. (cert.); mem. Purchasing Mgmt. Assn. Dayton, Nat. Assn. Purchasing Mgmt. (cert.), Miami Valley Mgmt. Assn., Phi Theta Kappa, Beta Gamma Sigma. Democrat. Mem. Ch. of Christ. Home: 704 Evans Ave Miamisburg OH 45342 Office: 1219 W Sr35 Eaton OH 45320 Office: PO Box 608 Dayton OH 45401

CUCCO, ULISSE P., obstetrician and gynecologist; b. Bklyn., Aug. 19, 1929; s. Charles and Elvira (Garafalo) C.; m. Antoinette DeMarco, Aug. 31, 1952; children—Carl, Richard, Antoinette Marie, Michael, Frank, James. B.S. cum laude, L.I. U., 1950; M.D., Loyola U., Chgo., 1954. Diplomate Am. Bd. Ob-Gyn. Intern Nassau County Hosp., Hempstead, N.Y., 1954-55; resident in ob-gyn Lewis Meml. Mercy Hosp., Chgo., 1955-58; practice medicine specializing in ob-gyn Mt. Prospect, Ill., 1960—; mem. staff Resurrection Hosp., Chgo., N.W. Community Hosp., Arlington Heights, Ill.; past pres. med. staff, now chmn. dept. ob-gyn Holy Family Hosp., Des Plaines, Ill.; clin. asst. prof. Stritch Sch. Medicine, Loyola U. Contbr. articles to med. jours. Mem. ACS, Am. Fertility Soc., AAAS, Central Assn. Ob-Gyn, N.Y. Acad. Scis., Ill. Med. Soc., Chgo. Med. Soc., Chgo. Gynecol. Soc., Chgo. Inst. Medicine. Roman Catholic. Club: Sunset Ridge Country. Office: 221 W Prospect Ave Mount Prospect IL 60056

CUDAHY, RICHARD D., judge; b. Milw., Feb. 2, 1926; s. Michael F. and Alice (Dickson) C.; m. Ann Featherson, July 14, 1956 (dec. 1974); m. Janet Stuart, July 17, 1976; children: Richard Dickson, Norma Kathleen, Theresa Ellen, Daniel Michael, Michaela Alice, Marguerite Lois, Patrick George. B.S., U.S. Mil. Acad., 1948; J.D., Yale U., 1955; LL.D. (hon.), Ripon Coll., 1981. Commd. 2d. lt. U.S. Army, 1948, advanced through grades to 1st lt., 1950; law clk. to presiding judge U.S. Ct. Appeals (2d cir.), 1955-56; asst. to legal adv. Dept. State, 1956-57; assoc. firm Isham, Lincoln & Beale, Chgo., 1957-60, ptnr., 1976-79; pres. Patrick Cudahy, Inc., Wis., 1961-71; ptnr. firm Godfrey & Kahn, Milw., 1972; commr., chmn. Wis. Pub. Service Commn., 1972-75; judge U.S. Ct Appeals (7th cir.), Chgo., 1979—; lectr. law Marquette U. Law Sch., 1961-66; vis. prof. law U. Wis., 1966-67; prof. lectr. law George Washington U., Washington, D.C., 1978-79;. Commr. Milw. Harbor, 1964-66; pres. Milw. Urban League, 1965-66; trustee Environ. Def. Fund, 1976-79 chmn. Wis. Democratic party, 1967-68; Dem. candidate for Wis. atty. gen., 1968. Mem. ABA (spl. com. on Energy Law 1978-84, council adminstrv. law sect. 1986—), Am. Law Inst., Wis. Bar Assn., Milw. Bar Assn., Chgo. Bar Assn. Roman Catholic. Office: US Courthouse and Fed Office Bldg 219 S Dearborn St Chicago IL 60604

CUDDEBACK, GEORGIA LUCK, psychologist, educator; b. Hillsboro, Ill., Jan. 16, 1936; d. Lester Earl and Cordelia Catherine (Bailey) Luck; m. Charles Eugene Butts, Apr. 10, 1954 (div. Feb. 1965); 1 child, Terri Lynn Butts Landry; m. Byron Edgar Cuddeback, June 28, 1966, 1 child, Beth Ann. Student, Ill. State U., 1953-54, Kans. State U., 1966-68; BA, Colo. State U., Fort Collins, 1969; EdM, PhD, U. Ill., 1973-78. Lic. psychologist. Tchr. Pub. Schs., Fort Collins, 1969-70, Dept. of Def., Friedberg, Republic of GErmany, 1970-73; therapist Decatur (Ill.) Mental Health, 1978-81; asst. prof. Sch. Medicine, So. Ill. U., Decatur, 1980—; bd. dirs. Progress Resources Ctr., Decatur, 1982—, pres. 1986—. Mem. affiliate Planned Parenthood, Decatur, 1985—. Mem. Nat. Orgn. for Women, Profl. Women's Network, Am. Psychol. Assn., Ill. Psychol. Assn., Macon County Mental Health Assn., Soc. Tchrs. Family Medicine. Democrat. Avocations: travel, reading. Home: 4810 Hayden Dr Decatur IL 62521 Office: Decatur Family Practice Ctr 1314 N Main Suite 201 Decatur IL 62526

CUDLIPP, ALICE VERNER, health care executive; b. Richmond, Va., Nov. 1, 1941; d. Joseph Henry and Mary Irene (Mills) C. BA, Bridgewater (Va.) Coll., 1962; MA, U. Richmond, 1968. Tchr., dept. head Chesterfield (Va.) County Pub. Schs., 1967-71, Nansemond County Pub. Schs., Va., 1962-66; v.p. acad. div. Smithdeal-Massey Coll., Richmond, 1974-78; instr. J. Sargeant Reynolds Coll., Richmond, 1982-84; asst. to v.p. patient services Columbia Hosp., Milw., 1982-84; pres., chief exec. officer Med. Placement Services Inc., Milw., 1984—; pres. Cons. Resources, Inc., Richmond, 1974-81; gen. ptnr. Courtland Ltd., Richmond, 1981—; cons. and lectr. in field. Mem. Clovernook Homeowners Assn. Named one of Outstanding Young Women of Am., U.S. Jaycees, 1974; DuPont fellow U. Va., 1972. Mem. Columbia Coll. Nursing Alumni Assn. (chmn. 1984-85), Nat. League Nursing, Am. Mgmt. Assn., Nat. Assn. for Home Care, Wis. Home Care Orgn., Nat. Assn. Female Execs., Assn. Professional Saleswomen, Phi Delta Epsilon, Alpha Psi Omega, Delta Kappa Gamma. Presbyterian. Club: YMCA (Brown Deer, Wis.). Office: Med Placement Services Inc 710 N Plankinton Ave Milwaukee WI 53203

CUELLAR, LUIS LORETTO, JR., dentist; b. Gary, Ind., June 17, 1956; s. Luis L. Sr. and Marian Norma (Spradling) C.; m. Elizabeth L. Arnold, Mar. 2, 1985; children: Luis L. III, Jillian. BS, Valparaiso (Ind.) U., 1978; student, Marquette U. Sch. Dentistry, 1979-81; DDS, Ind. U., 1983. Gen. practice dentistry Merrillville, Ind., 1983—, Chesterton, Ind., 1985—; instr. anatomy and physiology Ind. U. NW, Gary. Named one of Outstanding Young Men Am., 1985. Mem. ADA, Ind. Dental Assn., Porter County Dental Assn., Northwest Ind. Dental Soc., Acad. Gen. Dentistry. Office: 7891 Broadway Suite C Merrillville IN 46410

CULBERTSON, FRANCES MITCHELL, psychology educator; b. Boston, Jan. 31, 1921; d. David and Goldie (Fishman) Mitchell; m. John Mathew Culbertson, Aug. 27, 1947; children: John David, Joanne, Lyndall, Amy. BS, U. Mich., 1947, MS, 1949, PhD, 1955. Lic. clin. psychologist, Wis. Clin. child psychologist Wis. Diagnostic Ctr., Madison, 1961-65; chief clin. psychologist dept. child psychiatry U. Wis., Madison, 1965-66; resident psychologist NIMH, Berkeley, Calif., 1966-67; psychologist Madison Pub. Schs., 1967-68; prof. psychology U. Wis., Whitewater, 1968—; clin. psychologist Mental Health Assn., Madison, 1987—; clin. psychologist Counseling and Psychotherapy Assn., Madison, 1982—; clin. hypnotherapy cons. Family Achievement Ctr., Oconomowoc, Wis., 1984—. Author: Voices in International School Psychology, 1985. Mem. Dane County Mental Health Bd., Madison, 1980-82. Fellow Am. Psychol. Assn.; mem. Madison Hypnotherapy Soc. (pres. 1986—), Internat. Council Psychologists, Nat. Assn. Sch. Psychologists, Sigma Xi, Pi Lambda Theta. Avocations: skiing, walking, hiking, reading, gardening. Home: 5305 Burnett Dr Madison WI 53705 Office: U Wis Dept Psychology N Prairie Whitewater WI 53190

CULBERTSON, RANDALL LEE, family physician; b. Kansas City, Mo., July 27, 1952; s. Calvin Lee and Loretto (Vann) C.; m. Barbara Ann Turner, June 7, 1975; children: Scott David, Christopher Lee. BS in Chemistry, Southwest Mo. State, 1974; Do, U. Health Scis., 1982. Diplomate Nat. Bd. Examiners Osteo. Physicians. Chemist Jensen-Salsberry Labs., Kansas City, 1974-75; pharm. rep. Ives Labs., N.Y.C, 1975-78; intern Lakeside Hosp., Kansas City, 1982-83; gen. practice osteo. medicine Blue Springs, Mo., 1983—; med. dir. Emergency Preparedness, Blue Springs, 1984; med. cons. City of Blue Springs, 1986. Team physician Blue Springs High Sch., 1983—; vol. Spl. Olympics Basketball, Blue Springs, 1985; panel mem. Community Anti-Drug Campaign, Blue Springs, 1984. Mem. Am. Osteo. Assn., Mo. Assn. Osteo. Physicians, Southwest Clin. Soc., Jackson County Osteo. Assn. Methodist. Club: Mens Breakfast. Lodge: Rotary. Office: Blue Springs Family Clinic 1218 N 7 Hwy Blue Springs MO 64015

CULL, DAVID GAIL, structural engineer; b. Louisville, July 15, 1947; s. Franklin David and Margaret Lucille (Moreland) C.; m. Linda Jane Turner, Mar. 23, 1968; children—Daniel, Elizabeth, Kathleen. B.C.E., U. Louisville, 1971, M.Engring., 1975. Registered profl. engr., numerous states. Engr., then asst. chief engr. Caldwell Tanks, Inc., Louisville, 1971-76; structural engr. Universal Tank & Iron Works, Inc., Indpls., 1976-80, chief structural engr., 1980-83; v.p. engring. Tank Industry Cons., Inc., Speedway, Ind., 1984—; guest lectr. Brownsburg Community Sch. Corp. Cons. Jr. Achievement Project Bus., 1977-78; mem. bd. zoning appeals Town of Brownsburg (Ind.), 1983-86, v.p., 1985, pres., 1986; mem. planning commn. Town of Brownsburg, 1986. Mem. Am. Water Works Assn., (3 revision task forces, D100 steel tanks standard com.), Steel Plate Fabricators Assn., Am. Arbitration Assn. (constrn. arbitrator), Steel Structures Painting Council. Republican. Mem. Christian Ch. Home: 6 Woodstock Dr Brownsburg IN 46112 Office: 6 Woodstock Dr Brownsburg IN 46112

CULLEN, CHARLES THOMAS, historian, librarian; b. Gainesville, Fla., Oct. 11, 1940; s. Spencer L. and Blance J. Cullen; m. Shirley Harrington, June 13, 1964; children: Leslie Lanier, Charles Spencer Harrington. BA, U. of South, 1962; MA, Fla. State U., 1963; PhD, U. Va., 1971. Asst. prof. history Averett Coll., 1963-66; assoc. editor Papers of John Marshall Inst. Early Am. History and Culture, Williamsburg, Va., 1971-74, co-editor, 1974-77, editor, 1977-79; lectr. history Coll. William and Mary, 1971-79; editor Papers of Thomas Jefferson Inst. Early Am. History and Culture, Williamsburg, Va., 1979-86; sr. research historian Princeton U., 1979-86; pres., librarian Newberry Library, Chgo., 1986—; vice chmn. bd. trustees Founding Fathers Papers, Inc.; mem. N.J. Hist. Commn., 1985-86. Nat. Hist. Publs. and Records Commn. fellow, 1970-71. Mem. Assn. Documentary Editing (pres.), Orgn. Am. Historians, Am. Soc. Legal History, Am. Hist. Assn., So. Hist. Assn. Office: The Newberry Library 60 W Walton St Chicago IL 60610

CULLEN, DONNA MARIE, accountant, governmental auditor; b. Thief River Falls, Minn., Feb. 28, 1953; d. Peter Claude and Helen Bertha (Bruneau) C. BA, Moorhead (Minn.) State Coll., 1975. CPA, Minn. Auditor Office of Minn. State Auditor, St. Paul, 1975-77, sr. auditor, 1977-79, prin. auditor, 1979-84, mgr., 1984—. Del. Dem. Farmer Labor Polit. Conv., Duluth, Minn., 1986. Mem. Am. Inst. CPA's, Minn. Soc. CPA's, Minn. Govt. Fin. Officers Assn. Roman Catholic. Avocations: biking, hiking, reading. Home: 177 Wheelock Pkwy W Saint Paul MN 55117 Office: Office of the State Auditor 555 Park St Saint Paul MN 55103

CULP, BETHANY KELLY, lawyer; b. Niles, Mich., May 24, 1951; d. William T. and Mary (Ketcham) Kelly; m. John P. Culp, Oct. 31, 1969; children: Paul M., Mary K. Student, U. Mich., 1969-72; B of Fine Arts summa cum laude, So. Meth. U., 1974; JD magna cum laude, William Mitchell Coll. Law, 1983. Bar: Minn. 1984, U.S. Dist. Ct. Minn. 1984. Assoc. Oppenheimer Wolff Foster Shepard and Donnelly, St. Paul, 1983—. Editor newspaper The View, 1977-79. Precinct chmn. Dem. Farm Labor Party, St. Paul. Mem. Am. Trial Lawyers Assn., ABA (vice-chmn. dirs. and officers liability sect. on torts and ins. 1986—), Minn. Bar Assn., Fed. Bar Assn., Kappa Tau Alpha. Office: 1700 West First Nat Bank Bldg Saint Paul MN 55101

CULVER, JAMES EDWARD, orthopedist; b. Milford, Del., Sept. 29, 1938; s. James Edward and Catherine (Jones) C.; m. Anne Clayton Brower, May 30, 1962 (div. Aug. 1974); children: Leigh, James Linwood; m. Sheryl Rodrigue, Sept. 7, 1974; children: Emily, Brinn. Diplomate Am. Bd. Orthopaedic Surgery. Instr. orthopaedic surgery U. Va. Hosp., Charlottesville, 1972-73, asst. prof. orthopaedic surgery, 1973-74; head hand surgery sect. dept. orthopaedic surgery Cleve. Clinic Found., 1974—. Contbr. articles profl. jours. Served to maj. U.S. Army, 1967-69. Fellow ACS, Am. Acad. Orthopaedic Surgeons; mem. Am. Soc. for Surgery of the Hand. Office: Cleve Clinic Found 9500 Euclid Ave Cleveland OH 44106

CULVER, MAC ALLEN, retail drug store executive. Pres., gen. mgr. Gray Drug Fair, Inc., Cleve. Office: Gray Drug Fair Inc 666 Euclid Ave Cleveland OH 44114 *

CULVER, ROBERT ELROY, osteopathic physician; b. Toledo, Oct. 1, 1926; s. Elroy and Helen Mary C.; m. Sallie Jane Corder, June 10, 1972; children: Diana L., Galen R., Ronald A., Richard A., Patricia A., Robert B. B.S., U. Toledo, 1951; D.O., Chgo. Osteo. Medicine, 1959. Intern Sandusky Meml. Hosp., Ohio, 1960; practice medicine specializing in family practice and sports medicine Oregon, Ohio, 1960—; mem. staff Parkview Hosp., Riverside Hosp., Toledo Hosp.; physician Oreg. Sch. System; Oregon police surgeon; chief dep. coroner, 1978-80; chmn. wrestling div. physicians Nat. AAU; U.S. med. rep. Federation Internationale Lute Amateur; physician U.S. World Wrestling Team; med. dir. World Cup of Wrestling; pres. Northwestern Ohio AAU; 3d v.p. Ohio AAU. Mem. Air Force Mus., Toledo Mus. Art; dir. Toledo Zoo; mem. Smithsonian Instn. Served with C.E., U.S. Army, 1944-46; col. Ohio Def. Service. Recipient commendation Ohio Ho. of Reps., 1983, honor award Oregon Sch. System, 1983. Mem. Am. Osteo. Assn., Ohio Osteo. Assn., 1st Dist. Acad. Osteo. Medicine (state trustee, past pres.), Am. Coll. Gen. Practitioners in Osteo. Medicine and Surgery, Ohio Osteo. Assn. Physicians and Surgeons, Chgo. Coll. Osteo. Med. Alumni Assn., Nat. Rifle Assn. (life), U. Toledo Alumni Assn. (life), Air Force Assn., Aircraft Owners and Pilots Assn., Nat. Hist. Soc., Ohio Hist. Soc., Am. Legion. Methodist. Club: Atlas. Lodges: Masons, Elks, Shriners. Office: 5517 Corduroy Rd Oregon OH 43616

CUMBER, CAROL JANE, business and economics educator; b. Jamestown, N.D., Nov. 24, 1956; d. Robert James and Alice Anna (Lira) C.; m. Craig Lee Fairbanks, May 29, 1982; 1 child, Benjamin Cumber Fairbanks. BA, N.D. State U., 1979, MBA, 1984. Office mgr. job site Allison Constrn., West Memphis, Ark., 1980-84; instr. bus. and econs. U. Minn., Morris, 1984—; cons., researcher in field; adj. prof. S.W. State U., Marshall, Minn. Mem. exec. bd. dirs. Countryside Council, Marshall, Minn., 1985—. Mem. Indsl. Relations Research Assn., Bus. and Profl. Women. Roman Catholic. Avocations: music, motorcycle touring, traveling. Home: 630 County Rd 9 Watson MN 56295 Office: U Minn Div Social Scis Morris MN 56267

CUMMIN, ALFRED S(AMUEL), chemist; b. London, Sept. 5, 1924; came to U.S., 1940, naturalized, 1948; s. Jack and Lottie (Hainesdorff) C.; m. Sylvia E. Smolok, Mar. 24, 1945; 1 dau., Cynthia Katherine. B.S., Poly. Inst. Bklyn., 1943, Ph.D. in Chemistry, 1946; M.B.A., U. Buffalo, 1959. Research chemist S.A.M. labs, Manhattan Project, Columbia U., 1943-44; plant supr. Metal & Plastic Processing Co., Bklyn., 1946-51; research chemist Gen. Chem. div. Allied Chem. & Dye Corp., N.Y.C., 1951-53; sr. chemist Congoleum Nairn, Kearny, N.J., 1953-54; supr. dielecs-advance devel. Gen. Elec. Co., Hudson Falls, N.Y., 1954-56; mgr. indsl. products research dept. Spencer Kellogg & Sons, Inc. (Textron), Buffalo, 1956-59; mgr. plastics div. Trancoa Chem. Corp., Reading, Mass., 1959-62; asso. dir. product devel. service labs. chem. div. Merck & Co., Inc., Rahway, N.J., 1962-69; dir. product devel. Borden Chem. div. Borden Inc., N.Y.C., 1969-72; tech. dir. Borden Chem. div. Borden Inc., 1972-73; tech. dir. Borden Inc., 1973-78, v.p. product safety and quality, 1978-81, v.p. sci. and tech., 1981—; mem. exec. com. Food Safety Council, 1976-81, trustee, chmn. membership com., 1976—; bd. dirs. Formaldehyde Inst., 1977—, vice chmn., 1982—, mem. exec. com., 1981—, mem. med. com., 1977—, steering com., 1977—; bd. dirs. Internat. Life Scis. Inst., 1986—, Nutrition Found., 1986—; instr. Poly. Inst. Bklyn., 1946-47; asst. prof. Adelphi Coll., 1952-54; prof. math. sci. U.S. Merchant Marine Acad., 1954; seminar leader Am. Mgmt. Assn.; prof. mgmt. N.Y. U. Sch. Mgmt., 1968—. Contbr. articles to profl. jours. Recipient cert. award Fedn. Socs. Paint Tech., 1965. Mem. Am. Chem. Soc. Fedn. Coatings Tech., Inst. Food Tech., ASTM, Synthetic Organic Chems. Mfg. Assn. (dir. 1977-84), Paint Research Inst., Delta Sigma Pi, Gamma Sigma Epsilon, Beta Gamma Sigma, Phi Lamda Upsilon. Research in polymers, electrochemistry, food packaging Research in polymers, electrochemistry, food packaging. Office: 960 Kings Mill Pkwy Columbus OH 43229

CUMMINGS, ERWIN KARL, data processing executive; b. Toledo, Ohio, June 19, 1954; s. Idell and Mae Sue (Jones) C. AS in Electronic Engring., U. Toledo, 1976, BS in Bus. Services, 1981. Telecommunications analyst Owens-Ill. Inc., Toledo, 1975-78, ops. and planning analyst, 1978-81, software systems analyst, 1981-83, sr. data communications analyst, 1983-86, lead data communicatons analyst, 1986—. Mem. Christian Youth Fellowship, Phillips Temple, 1968-72, pres., 1971-72, young adult tchr., 1971-79, supt. Sunday sch., 1979-81, asst. supt., 1983—, asst. Ch.treas., 1985—, head coach basketball, 1986—. Named one of Outstanding Young Men of Am., 1985, 86. Mem. DAV (Commdrs. Club 1985, 86). Democrat. Methodist. Home: 1323 Oak Hill Ct #153 Toledo OH 43614 Office: Owens-Ill Inc 1 Seagate Sq Toledo OH 43666

CUMMINGS, PATRICK, telecommunications company executive; b. Chgo., Aug. 8, 1944; s. Douglas William and Anne (Claire) C.; m. Carol Louise Estes, Oct. 14, 1978; children from previous marriage: Laura Anne, Erin Kathryn. BS in Biology and Chemistry, North Park Coll., Chgo., 1969. Field sales rep. Armour Pharm. Co., Phoenix, 1969-72, dist. sales mgr., 1972-78; dist. sales mgr. McGraw-Hill, N.Y.C., 1978-83; exec. v.p. CTS, Inc., Elmhurst, Ill., 1983—; sales and tng. dir. Armour Pharm., Phoenix, 1973. Served with U.S. Army, 1967-71. Mem. Mensa. Avocations: motorcycle touring, sports, reading sci. fiction. Office: CTS Inc 597 W York Rd Elmhurst IL 60126

CUMMINGS, RICHARD J., otologist; b. Topeka, Nov. 18, 1932; s. John Edward and Mary J. (Harrington) C.; m. Laura Roberta Herring, Dec. 21, 1956; children: Thomas, Anne, William, John. BA, U. Kans., 1954, MD, 1957. Intern St. Benedict Hosp., Ogden, Utah, 1957-58; resident U. Okla. Med. Ctr., Oklahoma City, 1959-62; practice medicine specializing in ear, nose, throat Colorado Springs Med. Clinic, Colo., 1961-62; practice medicine specializing in otology Wichita (Kans.) Ear Clinic, 1962—; clin. asst. prof. U. Kans. Sch. Medicine; pres. med. staff St. Francis Hosp., Wichita, 1974-75; host M.D. Radio program, Wichita, 1978-79. Contbr. articles to med. jours. Chmn. St. Joseph Charity Classic Tournament, 1981; physician's group chmn. United Way Campaign, 1968, 69, 77, 84; bd. dirs. Wichita Rotary Club, 1978-79; mem. U. Kans. Nat. Alumni Bd., 1979-84. Served with USPHS, 1958-59. Fellow ACP, ACS, Am. Acad. Otolaryngology; mem. AMA, Am. Audiological Soc., Kans. Med. Soc., Kans. Ear Nose Throat Soc. (pres. 1975), Wichita Surg. Soc., Hearing Conservation Assn., Pan Am. Soc. Otolaryngology. Home: 1258 Burning Tree Wichita KS 67214 Office: 427 N Hillside Wichita KS 67214

CUMMINGS, TERRY (ROBERT TERRELL), professional basketball player; b. Chgo., Mar. 15, 1961; m. Vonnie Cummings; children: Robert Tyrell, Sean. Student, DePaul U., 1979-82. Profl. basketball player San Diego Clippers, Nat. Basketball Assn., 1982-84, Milw. Bucks, Nat. Basketball Assn., 1984—. Player Nat. Basketball Assn. All-Star Game, 1985. Office: Milw Bucks 901 N 4th St Milwaukee WI 53203 *

CUMMINGS, WALTER J., U.S. circuit judge; b. Chgo., Sept. 29, 1916; s. Walter J. and Lillian (Garvy) C.; m. Therese Farrell Murray, May 18, 1946 (dec. Nov. 1968); children: Walter J. III, Keith M., Mark F.; m. Marie Campbell Krane, Sept. 6, 1975. A.B., Yale U., 1937; LL.B., Harvard U., 1940. Bar: Ill. 1940. Mem. staff U.S. solicitor gen., Washington, 1940-46; spl. asst. to U.S. atty. gen. 1944-46; ptnr. Sidley, Austin, Burgess & Smith, Chgo., 1946-66; solicitor gen. U.S., 1952-53; judge 7th circuit U.S. Ct. Appeals, Chgo., 1966—; chief judge 7th circuit U.S. Ct. Appeals, 1981-86; former mem. Joint Coms. Jud. Articles and Uniform Comml. Code; former grievance commr. Ill. Supreme Ct.; former mem. U.S. Jud. Conf.; chmn. Conf. Chief U.S. Cir. Ct. Judges, 1985-86, also subcom. judicial improvements, chmn. ad hoc com. on disposition of ct. records. Former mem. vis. com. Harvard Law Sch.; former mem. bd. visitors Stanford Law Sch.; past mem. vis. com. Northwestern U. Law Sch., U. Chgo. Law Sch. Past nat. bd. dirs., vice chmn. Ill. div. Am. Cancer Soc.; past bd. govs. Citizens Greater Chgo.; governing life mem. Art Inst. Chgo. Named knight of Malta, knight of Holy Sepulchre. Mem. ABA (past chmn. spl. com. fed. rules procedure, past chmn. com. jud. center, mem. com. consumer credit, nat. ct. assistance com., Ross essay contest, mem. ad hoc com. on award of litigation costs), Fed. Bar Assn. (bd. dirs. Chgo. chpt.), Ill. Bar Assn. (past chmn. internat. law sect., past chmn. antitrust sect., comml. and bankruptcy law com., com. jud. ethics), Chgo. Bar Assn. (com. on judiciary, past chmn. com. constl. revision, grievance com. div. III A, bd. mgrs., past chmn. com. founds.), Bar Assn. 7th Fed. Cir. (past pres.), Chgo. Bar Found., Am. Bar Found., Harvard Soc. Ill. (past dir.), Thomas More Assn. (dir.), Am. Law Inst., Am. Judicature Soc., Appellate Lawyers Assn., Fed. Judges Assn. (bd. dirs.). Roman Catholic. Clubs: Law, Legal, Racquet, Tavern, Standard, Union League, Saddle and Cycle (Chgo.); Metropolitan (Washington); Yale (N.Y.C.). Office: U S Ct of Appeals Dirksen Fed Bldg 219 S Dearborn St Chicago IL 60604

CUNIN, JOHN RAYMOND, industrial distributing company executive; b. Akron, Ohio, Sept. 11, 1924; s. Earl Augusta and Mary Elizabeth (McAlonan) C.; m. Marilyn Ann McGuigan, Aug. 30, 1952; children: John M., Mary Catherine, Thomas K., Jane D., William E. Student, John Carroll U., Cleve., 1946-47, Akron U., 1947-48, Gen. Motors Inst., 1967. With Bearings, Inc., Cleve., 1948—; dist. mgr., then gen. sales mgr. Bearings, Inc., 1972-80, pres., chief operating officer, after 1980, chmn., chief exec. officer, 1980—, also dir. Mem. adv. bd. Our Lady of the Wayside Homes for the Handicapped, Avon, Ohio, 1968; bd. dirs. Cleve. State U. Devel. Found.; trustee St. Vincent Charity Hosp. and Health Ctr., Cleve. Tomorrow; chmn. adv. bd. sch. bus. John Carroll U.; v.p., dir. Midtown Corridor; pres. Cleanland Cleve. Served with USAAF, 1942-45, ETO. Decorated D.F.C., Air medal. Mem. Power Transmission Distbrs. Assn., Associated Industries Cleve. (bd. dirs.), Bearing Specialist Assn. (bd. dirs.), Greater Cleve. Growth Assn. (bd. dirs.). Democrat. Clubs: Rotary, Univ, Caterpillar. Office: Bearings Inc PO Box 6925 Cleveland OH 44101 *

CUNNINGHAM, ALEXANDER ALAN, retired automotive company executive; b. Sofia, Bulgaria, Jan. 7, 1926; came to U.S., 1930; s. Leslie Charles and Vera (Malinov) C.; m. Dorothy I. Keehn (div.); children: Lesli D. Cunningham Weber, Mary L., Richard A., Julie J.; m. Mary Helen Durkee. BS in Indsl. Engring., Gen. Motors Inst., 1952. Mng. dir. Adam Opel, A.G., Ruesselsheim, Fed. Republic Germany, 1970-74; gen. dir. European ops. Gen. Motors Corp., N.Y.C., 1974-76, v.p., gen. mgr. overseas group, 1976-78, group exec. overseas group, 1978-80; v.p., group exec. body and assembly group Gen. Motors Corp., Detroit, 1980-84, exec. v.p. N.Am. automotive ops., 1984—, also bd. dirs. Trustee Detroit Symphony Orch., 1983—, Gen. Motors Engring. and Mgmt. Inst., Flint, Mich. Mem. Soc. Automotive Engrs., Soc. Mfg. Engrs., Engring. Soc. Detroit. Office: Gen Motors Corp 3044 W Grand Blvd Detroit MI 48202

CUNNINGHAM, CHARLES FREDERICK, dentist; b. Indpls., Dec. 16, 1950; s. Albert Frederick and Ann (Farrell) C.; m. Toni Williams, Aug. 20, 1972; children: Chad, Andy, Antonia Jacqueline. BA, Ill. Wesleyan U., Bloomington, 1972; DDS, Loyola U., Maywood, Ill., 1976. Gen. practice dentistry Bloomington, Ill., 1976—. Dental missionary to Haiti, St. John's Luth. Ch., Bloomington, 1984, 85; coach Youth Soccer, Normal, Ill., 1984—, Youth Baseball, Hudson, Ill., 1985—; cubmaster Normal (Ill.) council Boy Scouts Am., 1985—. Named One of Outstanding Young Men of Am., 1986. Mem. ADA, McLean County Dental Soc., Chgo. Dental Soc. Avocation: marathon running. Home: Rural Rt 1 Box 249 Hudson IL 61748 Office: 202 Eldorado Rd Bloomington IL 61701

CUNNINGHAM, EDWARD PRESTON, JR., food manufacturing company personnel executive; b. Hammond, Ind., Sept. 24, 1945; s. Edward Preston and Louise Catherine (Kohler) C.; B.B.A., U. Wis., Madison, 1968, M.B.A., 1969; m. Julie Cunningham; children—Scott, Jennifer. Personnel supr. Quaker Oats Co., Rockford, Ill., 1972-75, employee relations mgr., 1975-79, employee and community relations mgr., Lawrence, Kans., 1979—. Met. bd. dirs. Nat. Alliance Bus., 1976-78; bd. dirs. U. Kans. Concert Series, 1980—, Lawrence chpt. ARC, 1983—, Douglas County Vis. Nurses, 1983—; chmn. commerce and industry unit Lawrence Multiple Sclerosis, 1981—; bd. dirs. Cotttonwood Inc. Served to capt. U.S. Army, 1969-72; Vietnam. Decorated Bronze Star; named Outstanding Young Man Am., U.S. Jaycees, 1981. Mem. Ill. Employment Service, Midwest Indsl. Mgmt. Assn. (instr. 1978-79), Am. Soc. for Tng. and Devel., Lawrence C. of C. (chmn. edn. com. 1980), Lawrence Personnel Club. Republican. Congregationalist. Club: Cosmopolitan. Home: 2904 W 27th Terr Lawrence KS 66044 Office: 727 Iowa St Lawrence KS 66044

CUNNINGHAM, ERSKINE, credit manager; b. Talladaga, Ala., Oct. 3, 1955; s. Frank and Dorothy (Ragland) C. BBA, Northwood Inst., 1977; MBA, Rosary Coll., 1981. Asst. mgr. Detroit Bank and Trust, 1979; accounts rep. Ford Motor Credit, Park Ridge, Ill., 1979-84; mgr. family bus. Detroit, 1984-85; credit mgr. Rowntree Demet's, Chgo., 1985—. Named one of Outstanding Young Men in Am., 1984. Mem. Chgo. Midwest Credit Assn., Nat. Black MBA Assn., Rosary Coll. Grad. Assn. (election com. 1985—). Avocations: horseback riding, tennis, basketball, chess, reading.

CUNNINGHAM, JAMES FRANCIS, JR., accounting company executive; b. Chgo., June 26, 1953; s. James F. and Laura (DiPasquale) C.; m. Karen L. Carleton, Sept. 13, 1975; children: Kelly, James III. AA, Coll. DuPage, 1976; BS, U. Ill., Chgo., 1978; M in Taxation, De Paul U., 1982. CPA, Ill. Staff acct. Servicemaster Industries Inc., Downers Grove, Ill., 1974-77; supr. Peat, Marwick & Mitchell, Chgo., 1977-81; pres. and owner James F. Cunningham & Co., Glen Ellyn, Ill., 1981—. Mem. Am. Inst. CPA's, Ill. Soc. CPA's (chmn. edn. com. Fox Valley chpt. 1986-87, pres. 1987—). Home: 1551 Concord Ct Saint Charles IL 60174 Office: 800 Roosevelt Rd E-114 Glen Ellyn IL 60137

CUNNINGHAM, LOUIS MORRIS, psychologist; b. Charleston, W.Va., Jan. 3, 1931; s. Louis M. and Maude Virginia (Seay) C.; m. Mary Catherine Bernlohr, Aug. 13, 1955; children: Mary, Catherine, William, David. MA, Ohio State U., 1960, PhD, 1969; Cert., Universite de Geneve, Switzerland, 1973, Mason des Petits, Geneva, 1973; postgrad. cert., U. Akron, Ohio, 1984. Lic. psychologist, Ohio. Counselor Columbus (Ohio) Pub. Schs., 1957-65; instr. Ohio State U., Columbus, 1962-65; prof., dean Muskingum Coll., New Concord, Ohio, 1965-84; pvt. practice psychology New Concord, 1984—; cons. N.Am. Rockwell, Columbus, 1963-67, Bur. Vocat. Rehab., Zanesville, Ohio, 1980—, Bur. Disability, Columbus, 1982—, Zanesville Schs., 1984—. Author: Readings in Human Growth, 1968, Counseling Theories, 1973; contbr. articles to profl. jours. Served with USN, 1955-57. NDEA fellow, 1960. Mem. Am. Assn. Univ. Profs., Nat. Sch. Psychologists Assn., Ohio Sch. Psychologists Assn., Assn. Measurement and Evaluation, Am. Personnel and Guidance Assn. Lutheran. Avocations: tennis, golf, skiing, photography. Home and Office: 107 Eastview Dr New Concord OH 43762

CUNNINGHAM, PATRICK JOSEPH, JR., addictions counselor; b. Chgo., Nov. 29, 1950; s. Patrick Joseph and Sally Mary (Kmiotek) C. BS, Western Ill. U., 1975; MA, Governors State U., 1979. Cert. tchr., Ill.; cert. addictions counselor. Acad. advisor Triton Coll., 1975-80, biofeedback trainer, 1976-80, acting records evaluator, 1978-79, mem. faculty, 1980; alcoholism counselor The Abbey, Winfield, Ill., 1981, St. Joseph Hosp., Joliet, Ill., 1981-84; addictions counselor Pape and Assocs., Wheaton, Ill., 1984-87; instr. addiction counselor tng. Coll. of DuPage, Glen Ellyn, Ill., 1985-87; dir. addictions counselor tng. program Coll. of DuPage, Glen Ellyn, 1986-87; pvt. practice addictions counselor Lisle, Ill., 1987—. Mem. Nat. Assn. Alcoholism and Drug Abuse Counselors, Nat. Assn. for Children of Alcoholics, Assn. Labor-Mgmt. Adminstrs. and Cons. on Alcoholism. Office: 3060 Ogden Ave Suite 307 Lisle IL 60532

CUNNINGHAM, RICHARD THOMAS, lawyer; b. Akron, Ohio, Mar. 19, 1930; s. Ernest L. and Hazel A. (Coates) C.; m. Mary Lou Mackin, June 13, 1953; children—Susan, Elizabeth, Amy, David, Diane, Christine. Student Western Res. U., 1948, Columbia U., 1950; L.L.B., U. Ill., 1953. Bar: Ohio 1953, Ill. 1953. Legal officer USN, Norfolk, 1953-56; asst. atty. gen. State of Ohio, Columbus, 1956-57; mng. ptnr. Amer Cunningham Brennan Co., L.P.A., Akron, 1957—; del. Fed. 6th Jud. Conf., 1983—. Trustee Kent State U., chmn. 1984-86; mem. Family Services of Cuyahoga Falls, Ohio, 1964-70, pres. 1968, Bd. Edn., Cuyahoga Falls, 1972-76. Fellow Am. Coll. Trial Lawyers; mem. Akron Bar Assn. (pres. 1976-77), Ohio State Bar Assn. (del. 1977-79), ABA, Assn. Trial Lawyers Am., Ohio Trial Lawyers Assn. Republican.

CUNNINGHAM, ROBERT EDWIN, graphic design educator; b. Oil City, Pa., Sept. 5, 1948; s. Carl Newman and Myrna Effie (Vandevort) C.; m. Pamela Charlene Deaton, May 23, 1970 (div. Dec. 1984); 1 child, Ethan Lucas. Student, Broward Jr. Coll., 1966-67; BS, Towson State U., 1970. Tchr. art Balt. City Schs., 1970; layout artist Acme Mkts., Inc., Balt., 1973; design dir. Cunningham & Sullivan, Balt., 1973; creative dir. nat. Thompson Recruitment Advt., Inc., Balt., 1973-86; v.p., sr. art dir. Williams Co., Terre Haute, Ind., 1986; graphic design instr. Coll. of Fine Arts Ball State U., Muncie, Ind., 1986—; employment/career advisor Md. Inst. Coll. Art, Balt., 1983-85. Served with U.S. Army, 1970-71. Recipient awards Art Direction Mag., 1977, 78, 79, 80, So. Creativity Show, Barney awards, 1979, 80, 81, The Best in Balt. Merit awards, 1980, Desi awards Graphics Design U.S.A. Mag., 1977, 80, 81, 82, 84, 85. Avocations: design, fine art, reading, traveling, tennis, the beach. Home: 1417 W 16th St Muncie IN 47302 Office: Ball State U Coll of Fine Arts Muncie IN 47306

CUNNINGHAM, STANLEY VERNON, mathematics educator; b. Karlsruhe, W.Ger., Aug. 29, 1953; s. Stanley Vernon and Anna Josephine (Hoffmann) C.; m. Susan J. Wisdom, Mar. 22, 1985; 1 child, Sara Ann; stepchildren: David Loren, Benjamin Robert, Erica Rachell. BS, Kearney State Coll., 1977, MS, 1979. Cert. tchr. in math., physics, Nebr. Grad. asst. Kearney State Coll. (Nebr.), 1977-78; mem. programming staff AT&T, Kansas City, Mo., 1979; instr. math. Three Rivers Community Coll., Poplar Bluff, Mo., 1980—. Mem. Am. Math. Assn Two Year Colls., Nat. Council Tchrs. Math., Mo. Assn. Community and Jr. Colls., Three Rivers Amateur Radio Assn., Kappa Mu Epsilon, Sigma Pi Sigma. Democrat. Lutheran. Home: 1102 White Oak Dr Poplar Bluff MO 63901 Office: Three Rivers Community Coll Dept Math Poplar Bluff MO 63901

CUPURO, JEFFREY GREGORY, accountant; b. Chgo., Jan. 15, 1955; s. Angelo Joseph and Rita Amelia (Guidarelli) C.; m. Linda Jean Karp, Oct. 7, 1978; children: Kelly, Kristen, Katie. AA, Wright Jr. Coll., Chgo., 1976; BA, Northeastern Ill. U., 1979. CPA, Ill. Staff acct. Hoyt Greenberg and Friedman, Ltd., Chgo., 1980, James V. Hoey, Ltd., Schiller Park, Ill., 1980-81; sr. auditor Schneider, Kleinberg, Horwitz & Assocs., Chgo., 1981—. Contbr. articles to profl. jours. Mem. Am. Inst. CPA's, Ill. CPA Soc. (membership com. 1983-84, govtl. acctg. federally assisted programs com. 1984-85, govtl. acctg. local govtl. units com. 1985-86). Office: Schneider Kleinberg Horwitz & Assoc 55 E Monroe Chicago IL 60603

CURATO, RANDY JOSEPH, lawyer; b. Rumford, Maine, Nov. 5, 1958; s. Lawrence J. and Adelia M. (Meisner) C. BA, Manhattanville Coll., 1981; JD, U. Notre Dame, 1984. Assoc. Wildman, Harrold, Allen & Dixon, Chgo., 1984—. Mem. ABA, Ill. Bar Assn. Roman Catholic. Club: Manhattanville Coll. Alumni (pres. Chgo. chpt. 1986—). Home: 1255 W Eddy Chicago IL 60657 Office: Wildman Harrold Allen & Dixon 1 IBM Plaza Suite 3000 Chicago IL 60611

CURCI, WILLIAM, architect; b. Canton, Ohio, Mar. 21, 1931; s. Angelo Rocco and Mary Katherine (Schuffenecker) C.; m. Zita Jane Riggs, July 2, 1966; 1 child, Erica Jane. B in Archtl. Engring., Catholic U. Am., 1953, M in Archtl. Engring., 1955. Engring. asst. U.S. Army, Washington, 1955-57; archtl. assoc. Keith Haag & Assoc., Cuyahoga Falls, Ohio, 1958-62; prin. Wm. Curci AIA-Architect, Canton, Ohio, 1962—; owner Wilcur Systems, Canton, 1985—; instr. Kent (Ohio) State U., 1962. Patentee "Hatch" Fly File. Bd. advisors Preservation Soc., Canton, 1979—; mem. planning commn. Meyers Lake (Ohio) Village, 1980—. Mem. AIA (pres. Eastern Ohio chpt. 1971-72). Roman Catholic. Avocations: fly fishing, hunting. Home: 3820 20th St NW Canton OH 44708

CURCIO, BARBARA A., physical education educator; b. Sharon, Pa., Mar. 14, 1945; d. Frank Orlando and Irene (Alongi) Curcio. B.S. cum laude, Slippery Rock State Coll., 1967, M.Ed., 1968; D.Edn., Ball State U., 1980. Tchr. Moniteau High Sch., West Sunbury, Pa., 1967-68; tchr., coach Pa. State U.-Behrend, Erie, Pa., 1968-70; assoc. prof., coach Ball State U., Muncie, Ind., 1970—, women's volleyball head coach, 1972-83, bd. dirs. Credit Union, 1983—; volleyball master clinician Northeastern Jr. Coll., Sterling, Colo., 1979, various high sch. camps, Wyoming, Mich., Ind., 1973-78; fencing cons. Nat. Thespian Meeting, Muncie, 1982, Muncie Civic Theatre, 1986; fitness cons. elem. sch., 1986; mem. speaker's bur. Pan-Am. Games, 1986. Mem. Ind. Assn. Intercollegiate Athletics for Women (treas. 1981-83, coach state championship volleyball team, 1973, 77), Am. AHPERD, Collegiate Volleyball Coaches Assn., Delta Zeta, Delta Psi Kappa, Kappa Delta Pi. Roman Catholic. Editor chpt. in Phys. Edn. Handbook, 1980; contbr. articles to profl. jour. Office: Ball State U 200F Ball Gym Muncie IN 47306

CURD, PHILIP LOGAN, lawyer; b. St. Louis, Sept. 19, 1937; s. Logan Woodson Curd and Gladys V. Ballard. BBA, Washington U., St. Louis, 1959, JD, 1962. Bar: Mo. 1962, Ohio 1966. Field atty. NLRB, St. Louis, 1965-66; field atty. Burke, Haber & Berick Co., LPA, Cleve., 1966—, pres., chief exec. officer, 1986—. Mem. Citizen's League, Cleve., 1966. Served to capt. USAF, 1962-65. Mem. ABA, Ohio Bar Assn., Mo. Bar Assn., Cleve. Bar Assn.; Greater Cleve. Growth Assn. Republican. Clubs: City, Commerce (treas. 1984—), Mid-Day (Cleve.). Avocation: computers. Office: Burke Haber & Berick 300 National City Bank Bldg 629 Euclid Ave Cleveland OH 44114

CURL, DANIEL ARTHUR, pharmacist; b. Dec. 2, 1953; s. Earl Stanley and Patricia Anne (Schindler) C.; m. Mariann Woodruff, Sept. 17, 1982; 1 child, Carter James. B.S. in Pharmacy, Ohio No. U., 1977. Staff pharmacist Hatton & Enright Pharmacy, Urbana, Ohio, 1973-78; chief pharmacist, mgr. St. Paris Pharmacy, Ohio, 1978; staff pharmacist Howards Pharmacy, Huber Heights, Ohio, 1979-80, Community Hosp., Springfield, Ohio, 1980-84, Western Pharmacy, Springfield, 1984; chief pharmacist, mgr. Wendt-Bristol Pharmacy, Springfield, 1984-85; staff pharmacist Ohio Masonic Home, Springfield, 1985—; cons. pharmacist Hatton & Enright Pharmacy, Urbana, 1974—. Mem. Urbana Downtown Bus. Assn., 1984, U Urbana Boosters Club, 1984. Mem. Clark County Pharm. Assn. Republican. Methodist. Clubs: Optimist, Shrine. Lodge: Demolay (order of chevalier). Avocations: collecting auto racing memoribilia, off-road driving. Home: 145 Taft Ave Urbana OH 43078 Office: Ohio Masonic Home Springfield OH 45506

CURLER, HOWARD J., business executive; b. 1925; (married). B.S. in Chem. Engring, U. Wis., 1948. With research dept. Marathon Corp., 1948-58; pres. Curwood Inc., 1958-68; corp. v.p. Bemis Co. Inc., 1965-76, exec. v.p., chief operating officer, 1976, pres., chief operating officer, 1977, pres., chief exec. officer, 1978-87, chmn., chief exec. officer, 1987—. Office: PO Box 1154 Appleton WI 54912

CURLIN, L(EMUEL) CALVERT, III, chemical executive; b. Chgo., Oct. 8, 1941; s. Lemuel Calvert Jr. and Carol (Baldwin) C.; m. Billie Jeanne Mahoney, Aug. 30, 1967; children: John Calvert, David Moore. Student, U. Mich., 1961; BA in Chemistry, Hope Coll., 1964; MBA in Bus. Chemistry, Western Mich. U., 1966. Area supr. Diamond Shamrock Corp., Painesville, Ohio, 1966-73; ops. mgr. Electrode Corp., Chardon, Ohio, 1973-79; bus. mgr. chlorine systems Eltech Systems, Chardon, 1979-84, sales and mktg. mgr., 1984-86; bus. mgr. Oxy Tech Systems Inc., Chardon, 1986—. Author Chlorine/Ullmanns Ency., 1986. Served with U.S. Army, 1967-69, Vietnam. Mem. Chlorine Inst., Tech. Assn. Pulp and Paper Industry, Am. Mktg. Assn., Am. Assn. Individual Investors, Chi Phi. Republican. Club: Madison (Ohio) Country. Lodge: Elks. Avocations: golf, coin collecting. Home: 1186 Foxfire Dr Painesville OH 44077 Office: Oxy Tech Systems Inc 470 Center St Chardon OH 44024

CURRAN, THOMAS FREDERICK, psychotherapist; b. LaCrosse, Wis., Feb. 6, 1948; s. Lawrence Griggs and Eleanor (Gibson) C.; B.S., U. Wis., 1970; M.S.W., Mich. State U., 1972, Ph.D., 1974. Cons., Ingham Med. Center-Community Mental Health Center, Lansing, Mich., 1973-74; asst. prof. Fla. State U., Tallahassee, 1974-77; psychotherapist Genesee Psychiat. Center, Flint, Mich., 1977-81; pres. Northbank Counseling Services, Flint, 1981—; cons. Nat. Council on Alcoholism, 1978—, St. Joseph Hosp., Hurley Hosp., 1984—. Mich. State U. Dean's Office fellow, 1972, 73. Mem. Nat. Assn. Social Workers, Am. Psychol. Assn., Council on Social Work Edn. Editorial adv. bd. Jour. of Humanics, 1977—; contbr. articles to profl. jours. Office: Suite 300 Northbank Center 400 N Saginaw Flint MI 48502

CURRAN, THOMAS J., federal judge. B of Natural Scis., Marquette U., 1945, LLB, 1948. Lawyer, Curran, Curran and Hollenback, Mauston, Wis., 1948-83; judge, U.S. Dist. Ct. (ea. dist.) Wis., Milw., 1983—. Office: U S Dist Ct 250 US Courthouse 517 E Wisconsin Ave Milwaukee WI 53202 *

CURRIS, CONSTANTINE WILLIAM, university president; b. Lexington, Ky., Nov. 13, 1940; s. William C. and Mary (Kalpakis) C.; m. Roberta Jo Hern, Aug. 9, 1974. B.A., U. Ky., 1962, Ed.D., 1967; M.A., U. Ill., 1965. Vice pres., dean of faculty Midway (Ky.) Coll., 1965-68; dir. ednl. programs W.Va. Bd. Edn., Charleston, 1968-69; dean student personnel programs Marshall U., Huntington, W.Va., 1969-71; v.p., dean of faculty W.Va. Inst. Tech., Montgomery, 1971-73; pres. Murray (Ky.) State U., 1973-83, U. No. Iowa, 1983—. trustee Midway Coll.; charter mem. adv. council Nat. Small Bus. Devel. Center. Recipient Algernon S. Sullivan medallion U. Ky., 1962; named outstanding young man in Ky., Jaycees, 1974. Mem. Phi Beta Kappa, Omicron Delta Kappa, Sigma Chi. Democrat. Greek Orthodox. Club: Rotary. Office: Univ of No Iowa 1222 W 27th St Cedar Falls IA 50614 *

CURRIVAN, JOHN DANIEL, lawyer; b. Paris, Jan. 15, 1947. B.S. with distinction, Cornell U., 1968; M.S., U. Calif.-Berkeley, 1969, U. West Fla., 1971; J.D. summa cum laude, Cornell Law Sch., 1978. Bar: Ohio 1978. Mng. ptnr. Southwest Devel. Co., Kingsville, Tex., 1971-76; note editor Cornell Law Review, Ithaca, N.Y., 1977-78; prosecutor, Naval Legal Office, Norfolk, Va., 1978-79, chief prosecutor, 1979-81; sr. atty. USS Nimitz, 1981-83; trial judge Naval Base, Norfolk, 1983-84; tax atty. Jones, Day, Reavis & Pogue, Cleve., 1984—. Recipient Younger Fed. Lawyer award Fed. Bar Assn., 1981. Mem. ABA, Ohio State Bar Assn., Nat. Assn. Bond Lawyers, Order of Coif, Tau Beta Pi, Eta Kappa Nu. Home: 2842 Sedgewick Rd Shaker Heights OH 44120 Office: Jones Day Reavis & Pogue 901 Lakeside Ave Cleveland OH 44114

CURRY, DAN PAUL, film editor; b. Chgo., Mar. 6, 1953; s. Patrick John and LaVern Marie (Wolf) C.; m. Kimberley Ann Loughlin, Dec. 20, 1975. AA, Moraine Valley Coll., 1973; BS, Northwestern U., 1976, MFA in Film, 1979. Asst. prof. Va. Tech. U., Blacksburg, 1978-82; vis. artist Ohio U., Athens, 1982-83; asst. prof. U. Miami, Fla., 1983-84, Grand Valley State, Allendale, Mich., 1984-86; film editor Sinnott & Assoc., Chgo., 1987—. Films include Saturday Morning, 1978, Waiting, 1978, Zones, 1983, Southwestern Ballet, 1986. Prodn. grantee Ala. Film Co-op, 1982, Fla. Endowment for the Humanities, 1984, Appalshop/NEA, 1984, Am. Film Inst., 1985. Mem. Ctr. for New TV (prodn. grantee 1985), Assn. Independent Video and Filmmakers, Soc. Motion Picture and TV Engrs. Avocations: motorcycling, swimming, writing letters, traveling in the Western U.S. Home: 5756 N Washington Chicago IL 60659 Office: Sinnott & Assocs 676 N LaSalle St Chicago IL 60610

CURRY, JOHN PATRICK, insurance company executive, management consultant; b. Logan, W.Va., May 3, 1934; s. Albert Bruce and Mary Naomi (Shugert) C.; m. Patricia Jean Blessington, Oct. 26, 1956; children—Joseph Patrick, Mary Patricia. Kathleen Anne, Carmen Frances, John Gregory. Student St. Charles Coll., Catonsville, Md., 1949-52; B.A., U. Notre Dame, 1956; M.S. in Ops. Research, Western Mich. U., 1976. Lic. profl. cons., Mich. Agt., Conn. Mut. Life Ins. Co., 1959-65; gen. agt. Occidental Life Ins. Co., Los Angeles, 1965-66; pres. Investment Assocs. Inc., 1966-69; gen. agt. Fed. Life Ins. Co., Peoples Home Life Ins. Co. and Home Assurance Cos., 1969-71; actuarial cons. Am.-Brit. Ins. & Annuity Co., Ltd. (Bermuda), Battle Creek, Mich., 1979—; mgmt. cons., 1971—; owner, mgr. Nat. Search Cons., exec. search firm, Kalamazoo and Chgo.; owner, operator Curry Supply Co., Portage, Mich., 1978-83; pres. The Consulting Group, Inc. (Del.), Kalamazoo, 1985—; pres. The Pilot Co., Bermuda, 1985—; dir. Anglo-Am. Ins. Co., Ltd. (Bermuda). Served with U.S. Army, 1957-59. U. Notre Dame scholar, 1952-55; Pat O'Brien scholar, 1956. Republican. Roman Catholic. Clubs: Sertoma (charter dir. 1961-64) (Kalamazoo). Home: 7226 Rockford St Kalamazoo MI 49002

CURTIS, GEORGE C., psychiatry educator; b. St. Petersburg, Fla., Dec. 10, 1926; s. George Clifton and Anne Mildred (Perry) C.; m. Marion Margaret Johnson, Sept. 24, 1955; children: Paul Jefferson, Andrew Warren, Brian Ross. BA, Lambuth Coll., 1950; MD, Vanderbilt U., 1953; MS, McGill U., Montreal, Que., Can., 1959. Diplomate Am. Bd. Psychiatry and Neurology. From assoc. in psychiatry to assoc. prof. psychiatry U. Pa., Phila., 1959-72; prof. psychiatry U. Mich., Ann Arbor, 1972—; External reviewer NIMH, Bethesda, Md., 1985, 86. Editor: Psychiatric Clinics of North America, 1985; manuscript reviewer for many sci. jours., 1965-86; contbr. articles to profl. jours. Served with USN, 1945-46. Fellow Am. Psychiat. Assn. (mem. revision com. Diagnostic and Statistical Manual of Mental Disorders III); mem. AAAS, Am. Psychosomatic Soc. (council 1969-72, mem. program com. 1969), Soc. Biol. Psychiatry, Phobia Soc. Am. (bd. dirs. 1981—, chmn. sci. adv. com. 1985—). Club: Barton Hills Country (Ann Arbor). Avocations: golf, fishing, skiing, history. Home: 8711 Scully Rd Whitmore Lake MI 48189 Office: Univ Mich Dept Psychiatry Ann Arbor MI 48189

CURTIS, JAMES RICHARD, flight engineer; b. Champaign, Ill., Feb. 2, 1930; s. John Wesley and Jessie May (Quackenbush) C.; m. Constance Ann Sticher, Jan. 10, 1954; children: Christie Lynn, James Richard Jr., Stephen Lawrence. Student, U. Ill., 1947-48. Profl. flight engr.; cert. airframe and power plant mechanic, commercial pilot. Plant mgr. Dean's Dairy, Champaign, 1947-50; draftsman C.S. Johnson Co., Champaign, 1955; aircraft mechanic Am. Airlines, Ft. Worth, 1955; flight engr. Chgo., 1956—; check airman, flight engring. instr. Am. Airlines, Chgo., 1964—; examiner designee, FAA, Chgo., 1966-67. Served as sgt. USAF, 1950-54. Mem. Flight Engrs. Internat. Assn.

CURTIS, RICHARD D., mechanical engineer; b. Lafayette, Ind., Sept. 11, 1942; s. William D. and Lucille M. (MaCurdy) C.; m. Maureen D. Shriebak, Jan. 27, 1973; children: Diane, Brian, Suzanne. BSME, Purdue U., 1964, MSME, 1978; MBA, Ind. U., 1975. Registered profl. engr., Ind. Various engring. positions Pullman Standard Corp., Chgo., engring. mgr., 1964-80; dir. new car projects N.Am. Car Corp., Chgo., 1980-81; mgr. mech. engring., gen. supt. research and engring. Ill. Cen. Gulf, Chgo., 1981-84; v.p. engring. Thrall Car Mfg. Co., Chicago Heights, Ill., 1984—. Served with Ordinance Corps. U.S. Army, 1965-67. Mem. ASME, Nat. Soc. Profl. Engrs., Beta Gamma Sigma. Home: 8731 Crestwood Ave Munster IN 46321 Office: Thrall Car Mfg Co PO Box 218 Chicago Heights IL 60411

CURTIS, ROBERT JAMES, architect; b. Chgo., Mar. 28, 1927; s. Charles Mathew and Caroline Agnes (McVey) C.; m. Eileen Patricia Farrington, May 24, 1952; children: Charles, Mark, Patrick, Christopher, Colleen, Maureen, KellyAnn, Sean. BS in Archtl. Engring., U. Ill., 1950. Registered architect, Ill. Draftsman Hewitt & Bastian, Peoria, Ill., 1950-53; field supr. Nicol & Nicol, Chgo., 1953-58; chief draftsman Connor & Assocs., Harvey, Ill., 1958-61, Thomas Cooke, Chgo., 1961-64; pres. Curtis Architects & Planners, Burr Ridge, Ill., 1964—; mem. archtl. curriculum com. Prairie State Jr. Coll., Chicago Heights, Ill., 1975-79; cert. examination evaluator Nat. Council Architecture Registration Bd., St. Charles, Ill., 1977. Commr. Bldg. and Zoning Bd., Tinley Park, Ill., 1961-64, 67-69. Mem. AIA (sec. 1976-77, v.p. 1978-79, pres. 1980). Republican. Roman Catholic. Lodges: Rotary (local pres. 1979), KC (sec. 1954). Avocation: sailing. Home: 6924 W 176 Pl Tinley Park IL 70477 Office: 401 Frontage Rd Burr Ridge IL 60521

CURTISS, CHARLES WALLACE, jeweler; b. Urichsville, Ohio, Mar. 29, 1924; s. LeRoy Osborn and Irma L. (Guthrie) C.; m. Evelyn Mae Keller, May 19, 1946. Student, Kent State U., 1942-43, NYU, 1950—. Pres. Curtiss Jewelers, Newcomerstown, Ohio, 1946—. Mem. area council Boy Scouts Am., 1950-57. Served with USN, 1943-46, ATO, PTO. Mem. Am. Nat. Retail Jewelers, Ohio Retail Jewelers, Ind. Retail Jewelers, Retail Mchts., Ohio Watchmakers Assn. (bd. dirs. 1982—), Am. Watchmakers Assn., Newcomerstown C. of C. Republican. Methodist. Lodges: Masons, Elks, Rotary. Avocations: golf; hunting; fishing; gardening. Office: Curtiss Jewelers 120 Main St Newcomerstown OH 43832

CURTISS, JEFFREY EUGENE, pharmaceutical company executive; b. Plainview, Nebr., Aug. 23, 1948; s. Eugene Herbert and Jan Beverly (Jeffrey) C.; m. Margaret Mary Karpowicz, Apr. 10, 1976; children: Anthony, Gene. BSBA, U. Nebr., 1970, JD, 1971; LLM in Taxation, Washington U., St. Louis, 1975. Bar: Nebr. 1972, Colo. 1973, Mo. 1973, Ill. 1981; CPA, Colo., Ill.; lic. real estate broker, Ill. Acct. Peat, Marwick & Mitchell, Denver, 1970-71; assoc. Nelson & Harding, Lincoln, Nebr., 1971-73; mgr. tax, treasury Monsanto Co., St. Louis, 1973-79; v.p. fin. G.D. Searle & Co., Skokie, Ill., 1979-86, 1986—. Pres. bd. advisors Countryside Montessori Schs., Northbrook, Ill., 1985—; sec. Boy Scout Am. pack 163. Mem. Fin. Execs. Inst. Home: 2195 Landwehr Rd Northbrook IL 60062 Office: G D Searle & Co 5200 Old Orchard Rd Skokie IL 60076

CUSACK, GREGORY DANIEL, state agency administrator; b. Davenport, Iowa, May 6, 1943; s. Daniel Ignatius and Jeanette (Heeney) C. BA, St. Ambrose Coll., 1965; MA, U. Iowa, 1967. History tchr. Briar Cliff Coll., Sioux City, Iowa, 1967-68, Marycrest Coll., Davenport, 1969-70; mem. (81st dist.) Iowa Ho. of Reps., 1973-81; history tchr. St. Ambrose Coll., Davenport, 1976-81; exec. dir. Nat. Cath. Rurul Life Conf., Des Moines, 1981-87; dir. adminstrv. div. Iowa Dept. Agrl. and Land Stewardship, 1987—; v.p. Prairie Fire Rural Action, Des Moines, 1985—; vice chmn. Land Stewardship Project, St. Paul, 1985—. Mem. Davenport City Council, 1969-72. Mem. Am. Hist. Soc., U.S. Cath. Conf. (social devel., world peace coms.). Democrat. Avocations: reading, writing, hiking. Office: Nat Cath Rural Life Conf 4625 NW Beaver Dr Des Moines IA 50310

CUSHING, RALPH HARVEY, chemical company executive; b. Buffalo, Nov. 3, 1922; s. Benjamin Ralph and Ella Mabel (Lukens) C.; m. Edith Elizabeth Smith, Nov. 27, 1947; children: Sharonrose, Paul Ralph. BS ChemE, Drexel U., 1952. Chem. engr. Bristol Labs., Syracuse, N.Y., 1952-60; project engr. Mobay Chem. Co., Pitts., 1960-63; sr. project engr. Gulf Research Co., Harmarville, Pa., 1963-65; sr. researcher, mgr. engring., dir. coordinated computer services, sr. cons. Enron Corp. (formerly No. Nat. Gas Co.), Omaha, 1965-86; pres. CISSCO, Inc., Omaha, 1968—. Patentee corrosion protection of pipelines; contbr. articles to profl. jours. Lay minister Meth. Ch., Pitts., 1960-63. Served to cpl. U.S. Army, 1944-46, CBI. Mem. Am. Inst. Chem. Engrs., Am. Assn. Cost Engrs., Nat. Assn. Corrosion Engrs. (corrosion specialist 1978—). Republican. Avocations: photography, computer art.

CUSHMAN, JEFFREY DEAN, radiologist; b. Johnstown, Pa., Nov. 17, 1957; s. Raymond Michael and Theresa Marie (Iacaruso) C.; m. Melinda Wracar, June 26, 1983; 1 child, Lauren Nicole. BA in Chemistry, Washington and Jefferson Coll., 1979; DO, Phila. Coll. Osteo. Medicine, 1983.

Now radiologist Grandview Hosp., Dayton, Ohio. Mem. Am. Osteo. Assn., Am. Osteo. Coll. Radiology, Radiologic Soc. N.Am. Republican. Roman Catholic. Avocations: golf, music. Home: 908 Shroyer Rd Dayton OH 45419 Office: Grandview Hosp 405 Grand Ave Dayton OH 45405

CUSHMAN, ORIS MILDRED, nurse, hospital education administrator; b. Springfield, Mass., Nov. 22, 1931; d. Wesley Austin and Alice Mildred (Vaile) Stockwell; m. Laurence Arnold Cushman, Apr. 16, 1955; children—Lynn Ann Cushman Crandall, Laurence Arnold III. Diploma in nursing Hartford Hosp. Sch. Nursing (Conn.), 1953; B.S., Western Mich. U., 1978, M.A., 1980. Staff nurse Wesson Maternal Hosp., Springfield, 1953-54, acting supr., 1954-55; staff nurse Hartford Hosp., 1955-56, head nurse, 1956, staff nurse, 1957-59; staff nurse, charge nurse Reed City Hosp. (Mich.), 1961-67; supr. Meml. Hosp., St. Joseph, Mich., 1967-75, clin. supr. maternal/child health, 1975-77, dir. maternal/child health 1977-80; dir. edn. Pawating Hosp., Niles, Mich., 1980—. Sec. Women's aux. Reed City Hosp., 1964-65, v.p., 1965-66, pres., 1966-67; mem. adv. bd. on family life edn. St. Joseph Sch. Bd. (Mich.), 1979-80. Mem. Nurses Assn. Am. Coll. Obstetricians and Gynecologists, Perinatal Assn. Mich., S.W. Mich. Perinatal Assn. (founding; v.p. 1979-80, pres. 1980), S.W. Mich. Healthcare Edn. Council (sec. 1983-85), Tri-County Continuing Edn. Council Southwestern Mich. (founding, chairperson 1983-84), Mich. Soc. Healthcare Edn. and Tng. (sec. 1985-86), Am. Soc. Healthcare Edn. and Tng., Mich. Health Council. Republican. Office: Pawating Hosp 31 N St Joseph Ave Niles MI 49120

CUSTIN, RICHARD RANDALL, television reporter and producer; b. Milw., Sept. 22, 1960; s. James Randall and Lorraine Genevieve (Miller) C. Student, Albert Ludwigs Universität, Freiburg, Fed. Republic Germany, 1980-81; BA in Journalism with distinction, U. Wis., 1982; postgrad., Johannes Gutenberg Universität, Mainz, Fed. Repiblic Germany, 1982-83. Freelance producer NBC News, Frankfurt, Fed. Republic Germany, 1983; news anchor, reporter Sta. WGNW, Milw., 1983-84, Sta. WPBN-TV, Traverse City, Mich., 1984-86; reporter, producer Sta. WUHQ-TV, Battle Creek, Mich., 1986-87; reporter Sta. WZZM-TV, Grand Rapids, Mich., 1987—; vol. Sta. WHA Pub. Radio, Madison, Wis., 1979, 81-82. Harry J. Grant scholar, 1982; German Acad. Exchange Service grantee, 1982. Mem. Phi Beta Kappa, Phi Kappa Phi. Avocations: traveling, reading, cooking, skiing. Home: 437 Chasseral NW Apt #2A Comstock Park MI 49321 Office: Sta WZZM-TV PO Box Z Grand Rapids MI 49501

CUTHBERT, WILLIAM R., consumer goods manufacturing company executive. Chmn. bd. dirs. Newell Co., Freeport, Ill. Office: Newell Co Newell Ctr Freeport IL 61032 *

CUTILLETTA, THOMAS PAUL, paper company executive; b. Chgo., July 5, 1943; s. Santo and Benedetta (Falzone) C.; m. Bernadine Paluch, Apr. 16, 1966; children—Sheryl, Laura, Jennifer. B.S. in Acctg., U. Ill., 1965; M.B.A., Northwestern U., 1966. C.P.A., Ill. Fin. analyst Standard Oil of Ind., Chgo., 1966-70, supr. div. level, 1970-72, supr. corp. level, 1973-74; dir. profl. planning Norlin Industries-Gibson Div., Lincolnwood, Ill., 1974-75, v.p. and controller, 1975-80; corp. controller Stone Container Corp., Chgo., 1980-83, v.p., corp. controller, 1984—. Tuition scholar Northwestern U., 1966. Mem. Am. Inst. C.P.A.s., Fin. Execs. Inst. Office: Stone Container Corp 150 N Michigan Chicago IL 60601

CUTLER, NORMAN BARRY, funeral service executive; b. Chgo., Mar. 5, 1942; s. Jerome and Hannah (Feinberg) C.; B.S.B.A., Northwestern U., 1964, M.B.A., 1965; m. Gail Weinstein, June 30, 1965; children—Brett, Rebecca. Mgmt. trainee First Nat. Bank of Chgo., 1965-66; with Weinstein Bros., Inc., Wilmette, Ill., 1966—, v.p., 1972—; v.p. Levitt-Weinstein, Inc., North Miami Beach, Fla., 1979—; exec. v.p. Beth David Meml. Gardens, Hollywood, Fla., 1985—; gen. ptnr. Wilmette Computer Assocs., Dixie Ptnrs., N.M.B. Assocs.; faculty Worsham Coll., Skokie, Ill., 1981-82. Bd. dirs. North Suburban Jewish Community Center, 1975—, also past pres.; gen. co-chmn. Channel 11 Public TV Auction, 1974-75; bd. govs., v.p., pres., 1986— Congregation Am Shalom, Glencoe, Ill., Mem. Jewish Funeral Dirs. Am. (pres.1986—, bd. govs.). Lodge: B'nai B'rith (v.p.). Office: 111 Skokie Blvd Wilmette IL 60091

CUTLER, ROBERT RICHARD, III, health products company executive; b. Columbus, Ohio, Dec. 9, 1935; s. Robert Richard Jr. and Julia (Bourne) C.; m. Maria Constance Monachino, June 24, 1961; children: Jennifer Ann, Robert R. IV. BS in Biophysics, Yale U., 1958; cert., Oak Ridge (Tenn.) Inst. Nuclear Studies, 1959; cert. track II mgmt., Case Western Res. U., 1980. Mgr. cen. region Atomium Corp., Boston, 1962-64; with Picker X-Ray Corp., White Plains, N.Y., 1964-79, mgr. internat. sales, 1979-80; dir. sales and mktg. ATC Med. Group, Cleve., 1980-81; nat. sales mgr. Computer Industries Corp. subs. Control Data Corp., Cleve., 1981-84; pres., chief exec. officer Sonostics Corp., Broadview Heights, Ohio, 1984—; bd. dirs. Merritt Med., Cleve. Mem. Greater Cleve. Growth Assn.; trustee The Cleve. Ballet, 1973-84; bd. dirs. No. Ohio Opera League, 1980-83; past chmn., vice chmn. Yale Schs. Com.; chmn. tech. sales continuing edn. Cleve. State U. and U. Akron, 1973-74; mem. adv. bd. continuing engring. mgmt. edn. Mem. Sales and Mktg. Execs. Cleve., Ohio Venture Assn., Am. Assn. Ultrasound in Medicine, Am. Assn. Physicists in Medicine, Soc. Nuclear Medicine, Nat. Mgmt. Assn., Cleve. World Trade Assn., Council Smaller Enterprises. Clubs: Shaker Heights (Ohio) Country, Mid Day; Cotillion Soc. Home: 21522 S Woodland Rd Shaker Heights OH 44122 Office: Sonostics Corp 3201 E Royalton Rd Broadview Heights OH 44147

CUTTER, JOHN MICHAEL, dentist; b. Columbus, Ohio, May 28, 1952; s. John Raymond and Betty Mae (Paripovich) C.; m. Alice May Mcquitty, Aug. 6, 1977 (div. May 1984); 1 child, John David Benjamin. BA, Ohio State U., 1974, DDS, 1976. Practice gen. dentristy Fairfield, OH, 1976—; assoc. staff dental outpatient dept. Jewish Hosp. Cin., 1977-80, courtesy staff mem. 1980-84; also dental outpatient rep. to med. records and ambulatory care com.; instr. radiology div. dental hygiene U. Cin., 1977, supervising dentist clin. affairs; cons. Loveland Health Care Ctr., Tri-County Extended Care Ctr., Sunnybreeze Nursing Home and others; also provided yearly in-services to nursing staff for devel. of dental care for homebound and institutionalized. Contbr. articles to profl. jour. Sr. clin. dentist Cin. Bd. Edn.; mem. programming com. Southwestern Ohio chpt. Am. Heart Assn., 1983; co-chmn. fin. com., ch. bd. Lindenwald United Meth. Ch., 1982;. Mem. ADA, Ohio Dental Assn., Acad. Gen. Dentistry (nat. spokesdentist in hypertension and geriatric dental care), Am. Endodontic Soc., Internat. Endodontic Soc., Cin. Dental Soc. (assoc.), Keely Dental Soc. (co-chmn. programming com. 1980, chmn. continuing edn. 1979-82, editor Keely Bulletin 1982-85, mem.-at-large KDS council 1982), Psi Omega. Republican. Avocations: cross-country bicycling, collecting antique banks and toys, racquetball. Office: 1251 Niles Rd Fairfield OH 45014

CUTTER, THOMAS FRANKLIN, controller; b. Lafayette, Ind., Sept. 22, 1955; s. Willard and Leona (Hoefer) C.; m. Janet S. Collins, Aug. 22, 1981. BBA, Western Mich. U., 1977. CPA, Ind. Acct. Wolf & Co., Lafayette, 1978-79, Girardot, Strauch & Cox, Lafayette, 1979-86; controller Adminstrs. and Benefit Cons., Lafayette, 1986—. Bd. dirs. YMCA, Lafayette, 1984-86. Named one of the Outstanding Young Men in Am., U.S. Jaycees, 1984. Mem. Am. Inst. CPA's, Ind. CPA Soc., Estate Planning Council of Tippecanoe County. Club: Lafayette Country. Avocations: basketball, raquetball, golfing. Home: 920 N Wagon Wheel Trail Lafayette IN 47905 Office: Adminstrs and Benefit Cons 731 Main St Lafayette IN 47901

CYGAN, STEVE JOHN, physical therapist; b. Toledo, Sept. 16, 1947; s. Steve John and Marjorie Marie (Diehl) C.; m. Charla Faye Malcomb, Sept. 15, 1973; children: Kristen Elizabeth, Matthew Steven. BS, BA, U. Toledo, 1970, MEd, 1983; cert. phys. therapy, Ohio State U., 1973. Lic. phys. therapist Ohio, Fla. Staff phys. therapist St. Vincent Hosp., Toledo, 1973-74; chief phys. therapy Humana Hosp., Jacksonville, Fla., 1974-75; adminstrv. dir. dept. phys. medicine and rehab. The Toledo Hosp., 1975—; asst. prof. phys. therapy profl. curriculum Med. Coll. Ohio; mem. clin. faculty phys. therapy prog. Med. Coll. Ohio, 1981—, Ohio State U., 1976—. Dist. rep. fed. and local Peer Standards Rev. Orgn. Coms., 1976-77; mem. admissions com. phys. therapy program Med. Coll. Ohio, 1982-85, chmn. admissions com. 1982-83. Mem. Toledo Soc. Handicapped (bd. dirs. 1986—, mem. program com. 1984—), Toledo Area Wheelchair Athletic Assn., Inc. (mem. adv. com.), Am. Phys. Therapy Assn. (judicial com. Ohio state chpt. 1981-83), Ohio Phys. Therapy Assn. (exhibit chmn. chpt. conv. 1978). Democrat. Lutheran. Lodges: Rotary (chmn. handicap service com. Toledo club 1983-85, vice chmn. running and fitness com. 1983-84), Masons, Shriners. Avocations: running, biking, swimming, racquetball, home remodeling. Home: 5006 Fairway Ln Sylvania OH 43560 Office: The Toledo Hosp Dept Phys Medicine and Rehab 2142 N Cove Blvd Toledo OH 43606

CYPLIK, CLIFFORD ANDREW, teacher; b. Detroit, June 11, 1952; s. Eugene Andrew and Sylvia J. (Spisz) C.; m. Jennifer Mae Sorensen, June 21, 1985; 1 child, Rebecca Jane. BA cum laude, U. Mich., 1975; MA, Oakland U., 1979. Cert. tchr., Mich. Cons. Avondale Schs., Auburn Hills, Mich., 1976-79; program coordinator Oakland U., Rochester, Mich., 1979-80; cons. Oxford (Mich.) Community Schs., 1980-82; supr. instr. U. Detroit, 1984; chmn. English dept. St. Mary's Prep. Sch., Orchard Lake, Mich., 1984-86; tchr. Troy (Mich.) Sch. Dist., 1986—; reading support services Avondale Schs., 1976-78, g.e.d. instr., 1978, 79, 83, 84; grad. asst. Oakland U., 1979; intern Oakland Intermediate, Pontiac, Mich., 1978, Learnings Cons., Inc., Detroit, 1977; supr. St. Mary's Prep. Sch., 1984; conferee Mich. Ednl. Assessment Program, Grand Blanc, 1977. Editor: This Winter of Grace, 1975; author: (book) By Its Solemn Shine, 1981. Named one of Outstanding Young Men Am., 1985. Mem. Mich. Council of Tchrs. of English, Nat. Council of Tchrs. of English, Internat. Reading Assn., The New Alchemy Inst., World Future Soc., The Planetary Soc., Nat. Writers' Club. Democratic. Roman Catholic. Avocations: writing, piano. Home: 1404 Leupp Rochester MI 48063 Office: Troy Sch Dist 4400 Livernois Troy MI 48098

CZAJA, RITA JANE, accountant; b. Chgo., May 24, 1952; d. John Frank and Loretta Catherine (Koterski) C. BS, Bowling Green (Ohio) State U., 1974. CPA, Ill. Audit supr. Touche, Ross & Co., Chgo., 1974-82; acctg. mgr. Montgomery Ward, Chgo., 1983—. Trustee Margaret Keldie Scholarship Fund. Named one of Outstanding Young Women of Am., 1976. Mem. Am. Inst. CPA's, Am. Soc. Women Accts. (chmn. 1976-82, chpt. pres. 1982-84), Am. Woman's Soc. CPA's, Chgo Soc. Women CPA's. Avocations: photography, travel, sailing. Home: 7515 Nantucket #410 Darien IL 60559 Office: Montgomery Ward One Montgomery Ward Plaza Chicago IL 60671

CZAJA, SALLY JOAN, accounting systems consultant professional, infosystems specialist; b. Chgo., May 24, 1952; d. John Frank and Loretta Catherine (Koterski) C. BS summa cum laude, Bowling Green State U., 1974. CPA, Ill. From staff acct. to sr. cons. Arthur Andersen & Co., Chgo., 1974-77, sr. cons., 1977-81, mgr., 1981—. Mem. Am. Inst. CPA's, Am. Woman's Soc. CPA's (co-editor nat. newsletter 1983-84, historian 1982-86, Edn. Found. 1984-85, sec. 1984-85, treas. 1985-86, v.p. 1987—), Am. Soc. Women Accts. (chmn. data processing steering com. nat. chpt. 1982-84, dir. Chgo. chpt. 1977-79, officer 1980-85), Chgo. Soc. Women CPA's. Avocations: crafts, travel, photography, hiking. Office: Arthur Andersen & Co 69 W Washington St Chicago IL 60602

CZARNECKI, JOHN TEDDY, engineer; b. Akron, Ohio, May 31, 1942; s. Teddy Joseph and Genevieve (Pawlak) C.; m. Patricia Ann Dalaski, APr. 20, 1965 (div. Oct. 1974); m. Rita Marie Reymann, Oct. 22, 1982; 1 child, Annemarie. BS in Chem., U. Akron, 1968. Compounder Goodyear Tire and Rubber Co., Akron, 1967-70, chief compounder, 1978-87, chief engr., 1987—; compounder Goodyear Tire and Rubber Co., Jackson, Mich., 1970-78. Mem. Am. Chem. Soc. (rubber div.), Akron Rubber Group, Soc. for Preservation and Encouragement of Barbershop Quartet Singing in Am. Democrat. Roman Catholic. Club: SPEBSQSA. Lodge: Alliance of Poles. Avocations: singing, barbershop harmony, gardening, wood work. Home: 154 Hollywood Ave Akron OH 44313 Office: Goodyear Tire & Rubber Co 1144 E Market St Akron OH 44316

CZARNEZKI, JOSEPH JOHN, state legislator; b. Milw., Sept. 27, 1954; s. Gerald J. and Eleanor Helen (Lietz) C.; m. Mary Ann Schroeder, Dec. 20, 1975; children: Jason, Jamie Marie. BA, U. Wis., Milw., 1975, MA, 1977. Project asst. U. Wis., Milw., 1976-78, specialist, 1978-79; grant coordinator Milwaukee County, Wis., 1979-80; mem. Wis. Assembly, Madison, 1981-83, Wis. Senate, Madison, 1983—. Mem. Citizens Utility Bd. Named Friend of Edn., Wis. Dept. Pub. Instrn., 1986, Environ. Legislator of 1986, Wis.' Environ. Decade. Mem. Am. Soc. Pub. Adminstrn., U. Wis. at Milw. Alumni Assn. Democrat. Roman Catholic. Home: 7004 W Van Beck Ave Milwaukee WI 53220 Office: Wis State Senate State Capitol Room 12 S Madison WI 53707-7882

DAAB-KRZYKOWSKI, ANDRE, pharmaceutical and nutritional company engineering administrator; b. Warsaw, Poland, May 16, 1949; came to U.S., 1973, naturalized, 1981; s. Aleksy Czeslaw crest Polkozic and Zofia (Dyszkiewicz crest Kudrys) Krzykowski; m. Susan Elizabeth Reed, June 26, 1987. MSChemE, Tech. U. Warsaw, 1973; MBA, Memphis State U., 1979. Research chemist Schering-Plough, Memphis, 1974-77; process control mgr. Ralston Purina Co., Memphis, 1977-80; dir. Pharm. projects indsl. div. Bristol Myers, Bristol-Myers Co., Evansville, Ind., 1980—. Served to 2d lt. Polish Army Res. Mem. Am. Mgmt. Assn., Am. Chem. Soc. Republican. Lutheran. Club: Toastmasters (pres. local chpt. 1986). Avocations: sailing, scuba diving, karate, macrobiotics. Office: Bristol Myers Indsl Div 2404 Pennsylvania Ave Evansville IN 47721

D'ABATE, JOANN THERESE, information systems specialist; b. Cleve., Aug. 1, 1946; d. John Patrick and Jean Veronica (Stevens) Thiel; m. Douglas F. D'Abate, June, 1, 1974. BA in Math., Miami U., Oxford, Ohio, 1969. Programmer Chase Brass & Copper, Cleve., 1969-72; systems analyst, designer Standard Oil Co., Cleve., 1972-78, mgr. retail dispersed systems, 1984-85, mgr. retail systems, 1985—; systems project leader Republic Steel Corp., Cleve., 1978-84. Bd. dirs. Fairmount Ctr. for Creative and Performing Arts, Novelty, Ohio, 1985—. Mem. Data Processing Mgmt. Assn., Phi Beta Kappa (local trustee 1980—, treas. 1981-83, v.p. 1983-84, 86-87, pres. 1984-85). Republican. Roman Catholic. Avocations: aerobics, reading, guitar, wines, gourmet food. Home: 10283 Johnnycake Ridge Rd Concord OH 44077 Office: Standard Oil Co 200 Public Square Cleveland OH 44114-2375

DABERKO, DAVID A., bank executive. Student, Denison U., Case Western Res. U. Chmn. bd. dirs. BancOhio Nat. Bank, Columbus. Office: BancOhio Nat Bank 155 E Broad St Columbus OH 43265 *

DABILL, PHILLIP ALVIN, wholesale foods executive; b. Pequot Lakes, Minn., Sept. 14, 1942; s. Gaylord D. and Faith A. (Brant) D.; m. Judith Salfisberg (dec.); children: Julie, Barbara, Tom, Paul. A.B.A., Dakota Bus. Coll., 1962. Devel. mgr., store engr. Super Valu Stores, Inc., Fargo, N.D., 1962-72; dir. retail devel. Food Mktg. Corp., Ft. Wayne, Ind., 1972-74; retail ops. mgr. Super Valu Stores, Inc., Bismarck, N.D., 1974-77; gen. mgr. Plainfield Super Valu div., Ill., 1977-79; pres. Food Mktg. Corp., Ft. Wayne, 1979-85; corp. v.p., pres. wholesale foods Super Valu Stores, Inc., Eden Prairie, Minn., 1985—; dir. Brotherhood Mutual Ins. Co., Ft. Wayne. Mem. planning com. ARC, 1980—; capt. United Way, 1981—. Mem. Plainfield C. of C. (dir. 1978). Republican. Lodge: Rotary. Home: 3067 Farview Ln Long Lake MN 55356 Office: Super Valu Stores Inc PO Box 990 Minneapolis MN 55440

DABKOWSKI, JOHN, electrical engineer, consultant, researcher; b. Chgo., Feb. 15, 1933; s. John and Harriet (Sierakowski) D.; m. Cecilia Klonowski, June 26, 1976. B.S.E.E., Ill. Inst. Tech., 1955, M.S.E.E., 1960, Ph.D. in Elec. Engring., 1969. Sr. research engr. Ill. Inst. Tech. Research Inst., Chgo., 1957-79; ops. mgr. Sci. Applications Internat. Corp., Hoffman Estates, Ill., 1979-85, dir. EM effects research, 1985-87, div. mgr., 1987—; instr. Grad. Sch., Ill. Inst. Tech., Chgo., 1962-79. Research, publs. in field. Served with U.S. Army, 1955-57. Mem. IEEE (sr. mem.), Nat. Assn. Corrosion Engrs., Am. Geophys. Union, Sigma Xi. Roman Catholic. Home: 7021 Foxfire Dr Crystal Lake IL 60012

DABNEY, JACK LEE, psychologist; b. Dubuque, Iowa, Jan. 27, 1929; s. Claude Oruin and Naomi Helen (Stoker) D.; m. Lucille Marie Clarence, June 7, 1952. BS in Bus. and Engring. Adminstrn., U. Nebr., Omaha, 1951, MA in Psychology, 1957. Lic. psychologist, Nebr. Mental health coordinator Douglas County Hosp., 1961-71, clin. psychologist, 1955—; supr. alcoholism treament program Douglas County, Omaha, 1956-57. Served with U.S. Army, 1953-55. Mem. Am. Psychol. Assn. (assoc.), Nebr. Psychol. Assn. (affiliate). Avocations: fishing, camping, gardening. Home: 1879 S 133 St Omaha NE 68144 Office: Douglas County Hosp 4102 Woolworth Ave Omaha NE 68144

DABY, RALPH EDWARD, finance company executive; b. Clarkfield, Minn., Aug. 13, 1956; s. Donald Francais and Doris Audrey (Hedla) D. BS in Acctg. and Fin., Mankato (Minn.) State U., 1979; JD cum laude, William Mitchell Coll. Law, 1986. Bar: Minn, 1986; CPA, Minn. Staff acct. Field's Hokanson and Co., Edina, Minn., 1980-81; auditor House and Nezurka, CPA's, Edina, 1981-82; pvt. practice fin. cons. Bloomington, Minn., 1985-86; equity broker Dataserv, Inc., Mpls., 1986—. Mem. Am. Inst. CPA's, Minn. Soc. CPA's. Democrat. Avocations: reading, fishing, running, hunting, computers.

DA COSTA, MARGARET ANNE, packaging executive; b. Elmhurst, Ill., Sept. 13, 1941; d. Malvern J. and Margaret E. (Barrett) Hiler; m. Flavio O. da Costa, Oct. 31, 1964 (div.); children—Kathryn (dec.), Flavio J.; m. 2d, Walter A. Gamble, Jr., Dec. 27, 1982. B.A., Miami U., Oxford, Ohio, 1962. Flight attendant Pan Am., N.Y.C., 1962-65; clk. typist City of East Lansing (Mich.), 1974-75; ct. coordinator East Lansing Police Dept., 1975-77; adminstrv. asst. Mich. Co., Lansing, 1977-78; sec.-treas. ASI Packaging Co., Pontiac, Mich., 1978-82, pres.-treas., Grand Blanc, Mich., 1982—; ptnr. Holly-75, 1982—. Mem. Clarkston Zoning Bd. Appeals, 1985. Mem. Clarkston Community Hist. Soc. (treas., bd. dirs. 1980-82), Delta Zeta. Republican. Office: ASI Packaging Co 9311 Holly Rd Grand Blanc MI 48439

DADA, YASMINE, controller; b. Karachi, Pakistan, May 31, 1952; came to U.S., 1972; s. Abdur Razzak and Rabia (Diwan) D.; m. M. Mohsin Dada, Mar. 5, 1976. BA in Polit. Sci., Sangamon State U., 1973, BA in Acctg., 1979; MA, Eastern Ill. U., 1975. CPA, Ill. Acct. Roosevelt Nat. Co., Springfield, Ill., 1975-77; supr. acctg. So. Ill. U., Springfield, 1977-79; fin. mgr. State of Ill., Chgo., 1979-85; sr. acct. Gray Hunter Stenn, Chgo., 1982-85; controller Dry Ice Inc., Hinsdale, Ill., 1985-86, Zwiren and Ptnrs., Chgo., 1986—. Vol. Rep. party, Chgo., 1984. Mem. Am. Inst. CPA's, Ill. CPA Soc. Home: 3256 Venard Rd Downers Grove IL 60515 Office: Zwiren and Ptnrs 211 E Ontario Chicago IL 60611

DADO, CLAUDIA MARIA, dentist; b. Evergreen Park, Ill., Mar. 12, 1957; d. Ralph Natale Sr. and Violet Mary (Mlejnek) D. BS in Biology, St. Xavier Coll., 1979; DDS, Loyola U., Maywood, Ill., 1983. Gen. practice dentistry Chgo., 1983—; instr. histology Loyola U., Maywood, 1983-84. Mem. ADA, Ill. Dental Soc., Chgo. Dental Soc.

DADO, DIANE VALENTINA, pediatric plastic and reconstructive surgeon; b. Chgo., Feb. 14, 1952; d. Ralph N. and Violet M. (Mlejnek) D.; m. Joseph L. Giacchino Jr., May 22, 1976; 1 child, Joseph. BA, St. Xavier Coll., Chgo., 1973; MD, Loyola U., Maywood, Ill., 1976. Cert. Am. Bd. Plastic and Reconstructive Surgeery. Intern in surgery Loyola U. Med. Ctr., Maywood, 1976-77, resident in surgery, 1977-79; resident plastic surgery Loyola U. Med. Ctr., 1979-82; fellow plastic surgery Children's Meml. Hosp., Chgo., 1982-83; instr. surgery Stritch Sch. Medicine Loyola U., Maywood, 1983, asst. prof. surgery, 1983—; bd. dirs. Loyola U. Cleft Palate/Craniofacial Team, 1983—; attending physician Loyola U. Med. Ctr. div. plastic surgery, 1983—, Children's Meml. Hosp. div. plastic surgery, 1983—. Contbr. articles to profl. jours. Mem. AMA, Am. Med. Women's Assn., Ill. Med. Soc., Chgo. Med. Soc., Am. Soc. Plastic and Reconstructive Surgeons, Am. Acad. Pediatrics, Am. Burn Assn., ACS, Am. Cleft. Palate Assn., Ill. Assn. Craniofacial Teams, Chgo. Soc. Plastic Surgery, Desmond A. Kernahan Soc. (founding). Avocations: sailing, skiing. Office: Loyola U Med Ctr 2160 S 1st Ave Maywood IL 60153

DAGAMA, STEVEN ALEXANDRE DE SALDANHA, artist, poet; b. Akron, Ohio, Sept. 11, 1943; s. Francis August and Louise Betty (Butler) Osterlund. Student, Ashland (Ohio) Coll., 1961, 62-65, Akron U., 1962, Akron Art Inst., 1962, Kent (Ohio) State U., 1966-67. Reference librarian Akron Pub. Library, 1960-65, U. Western Ont., London, Can., 1967; copywriter Sta. CKJD, Sarnia, Ont., 1969; reporter The Sarnia Observer, 1970-71; instr. creative writing Fanshawe Coll. London, Sarnia, 1976-77; instr. communications arts Lambton Coll., Sarnia, 1969. Author: Sign on a Door, 1971, Twenty Love Poems, 1976, Pendulum/New Poems, 1977, Black Ice, 1978, A Scroll for the Flood Season, 1983, A Window Facing the Sea (English-Portugese), 1987; contbr. poems to numerous jours.; one-man shows include exhibit of paintings and poems Thielsen Art Gallery, Inc., London, Ont., 1977. Grantee Abraham Woursell Found., 1972-76, Ont. Arts Council, 1976, 77; recipient Poet of Yr. award The U.S.A. Mainline, 1985-86. Home and Office: 1767 23d St Cuyahoga Falls OH 44223

DAGAR, RONALD MICHAEL, manufacturing company executive; b. Canonsburg, Pa., Nov. 24, 1940; s. Michael Albert and Symaria Sonja (Namy) D.; m. Patricia Beverly Cherok, Oct. 6, 1962; children: R. Scott, Danielle. BA in Econs., Washington (Pa.) & Jefferson Coll., 1962. Product specialist Tex. Instruments, Detroit, 1969-72, area sales mgr., 1972-75; dir. mktg. and sales Met div. P.R. Mallory, Indpls., 1975-80; v.p. mktg. and sales Micro Poise div. Ransburg Corp., Indpls., 1980-85; pres. and gen. mgr. Roto Finish Co. div. Ransburg Corp., Kalamazoo, Mich., 1985—. Served to 1st lt. U.S. Army, 1962-64. Republican. Presbyterian. Club: Country of Indpls. Avocations: golf, sports, family activities. Home: 1517 Brewster Rd Indianapolis IN 46260 Office: Ransburg Corp Roto-Finish Div 3700 E Milnam Rd Kalamazoo MI 49003

DAGENBACK, THOMAS JACK, accountant; b. Cin., Jan. 7, 1958; s. G. Jack and Clara Ruth (Holtkamp) D.; m. Linda Jean Tolle, June 6, 1980; children: Lauren Emily, Steven Thomas. BBA in Acctg., U. Cin., 1981. CPA, Ohio. With Grant Thornton (formerly Alexander Grant & Co.), Cin., 1978—, intern, 1978, mgr., personnel dir., 1981—. Treas. Comprehensive Community Child Care, Cin., 1983—. Mem. Am. Inst. CPA's, Inst. Internal Auditors, Ohio Soc. CPA's. Avocations: softball, basketball, volleyball. Home: 5861 Cedaridge Dr Cincinnati OH 45247 Office: Grant Thornton 1600 Atrium One Cincinnati OH 45202

DAGER, MICHAEL BESHARA, small business owner; b. Bucyrus, Ohio, Jan. 28, 1943; s. Charles Joseph and Josephine Mary (Farage) D. Student, Ohio State U., 1960-62, Columbus Bus. U., 1963-64, Coll. Art and Design, Columbus, Ohio, 1964-65. Owner Velvet Ice Cream Co., Utica, Ohio, 1963—. Active Licking County Hist. Soc., Newark, Ohio; bd. dirs. Licking County Convention Bur., Newark, 1985-87, Old Town West Soc., Newark; v.p. Town Franklin Assn., Columbus, 1983-85. Mem. Ohio Dairy Products Assn, Internat. Assn. Iec Cream Mfrs. Republican. Roman Catholic. Home: 329 E College St Granville OH 43023 Office: Velvet Ice Cream Co State Rt 13 Utica OH 43080

DAGGETT, RICHARD PARKER, television station executive; b. Madison, Wis., Oct. 11, 1944; s. Parker R. and Frances (Usher) D.; m. Pamela Rene Hall, Aug. 27, 1977; children: Kristin, Lindsay. BBA, U. Wis., 1967. Buyer, planner Leo Burnett Advt. Co., Chgo., 1967-70; account exec. Petry TV, Chgo., 1970-72, Sta. WLS-TV, Chgo., 1972-74; gen. sales mgr. Sta. KVOA-TV, Tucson, Ariz., 1974-75; eastern sales mgr. Sta. NBC-TV, N.Y.C., 1975-76; local sales mgr. Sta. WMAQ-TV, Chgo., 1976-79, dir. sales, 1979—, also editorial bd., 1985—. Served to lt. USN, 1969-75. Club: Broadcast Advt. (Chgo.) (bd. dirs., membership chmn. 1982-86). Avocation: golf. Office: Sta WMAQ-TV Merchandise Mart Chicago IL 60654

DAGHESTANI, AMIN NASRALLAH, psychiatrist; b. Aleppo, Syria, Feb. 29, 1944; came to U.S., 1970; Hikmat N. and Madiha (Dahan) D.; m. Ann M. Smessaert, May 31, 1973; children: Omar, Khaled, Aliya. MD, Damascus (Syria) U., 1969. Dir. outpatient psychiatry Med. Sch. Loyola U., Chgo., 1985-86, dir. grad. edn., 1986—; coordinator Quality Assurance Psychiatry, Hines, Va., 1986—; cons. Affective Disorder Program, Loyola U., 1986—. Mem. AMA, Am. Psychiatric Assn., Am. Assn. of Dirs. of Psychiatric Residency Program. Contbr. numeours papers to profl. jours. Avocations: reading, travel. Office: Loyola U Med Ctr 2160 S First Ave Maywood IL 60153

D'AGOSTINO, ANTHONY MICHAEL, psychiatrist; b. Chgo., Feb. 10, 1941; s. Anthony J. and Neva (Gennaro) D'A.; m. Beverly J. Schumacher, Oct. 26, 1968; children: Michael, Christopher, Jonathan. Student, Loyola U., Chgo., 1958-61; MD, U. Ill., Chgo., 1965. Practice medicine specializing in psychiatry Elk Grove Village, Ill., 1977—; chmn. dept. psychiatry Alexian Bros. Med. Ctr., Elk Grove Village, 1979—. Served to lt. comdr. USN, 1969-71. Fellow Am. Psychiat. Assn.; mem. Ill. Psychiat. Soc. (pres. 1986-87). Office: Alexian Bros Med Ctr 800 Biesterfield Rd Elk Grove Village IL 60007

DAGUE, LINDA JO CLARK, lawyer; b. Muncie, Ind., Apr. 12, 1947; d. Gene Phillip and Dorothy Catherine (Griffin) Clark; A.B., Ind. U., 1968, J.D., 1982; m. Jerry Halsey Dague, June 15, 1968 (div. May 1979); children—Mary Louise, Robert Clark; m. Michael D. Smith, Aug. 15, 1987. Reporter, Tri City Jour., Delaware County, Ind., 1968; teaching asst. Ind. U. Sch. Journalism, 1968-69; editor RCA, Bloomington, Ind., 1969-70, Tri City Jour., 1970-71; asst. editor Pi Lambda Theta, Bloomington, 1974-75, nat. editor, 1975-80; research asst. Ind. U., 1981-82; assoc. Warner, Wallace, McLaren & Dague, Muncie, 1982-85, ptnr. 1986—. V.p. Friends of Library, Martinsville, 1975-76; bd. dirs. Tulip Trace council Girl Scouts U.S., 1981-82, Ret. Srs. Vol. Program, 1983—, Wepehani Girl Scouts council, 1984-87; bd. dirs. Delaware County Council for Arts, 1984-86, sec., 1985-86, YWCA, Muncie, 1987; parliamentarian Del. County Rep. Women's club, 1986—. Mem. ABA, Ind. State Bar Assn., Muncie Bar Assn., Women in Communications (pres. chpt. 1978-79), Soc. Profl. Journalists, Ednl. Press Assn. Am. (regional rep. 1979-80), Am. Soc. Assn. Execs. (communicators sect.), Ind. U. Sch. Journalism Alumni Assn. (dir., treas., class agt. 1975-77, pres. 1982-83), Pi Lambda Theta, Zeta Tau Alpha. Republican. Club: Altrusa. Editor Ednl. Horizons, 1975-80; assoc. Ind. U. Law Jour., 1981-82. Home: 301 Pasture Ln Muncie IN 47304 Office: 400 E Jackson St Muncie IN 47305

DAHL, CHRISTINE LOUISE, dentist; b. Washington, Jan. 22, 1951; d. Roy Arthur and Molly Christine (Woie) D. BA magne cum laude, Northeast La. U., 1972; DDS, U. Iowa, 1980. Gen. practice dentistry Bettendorf, Iowa, 1980—. Mem. 7th Jud. Dist. Nominating Com., Davenport, Iowa, 1984—. Mem. ADA, Iowa Dental Assn. (Clinician award 1984), Am. Assn. Women Dentists, Acad. Gen. Dentistry (membership chmn. 1984), Acad. Geriatric Dentistry, Am. Acad. Clin. Hypnosis. Democrat. Unitarian. Club: Flying Country (Moline, Ill.). Avocations: guitar, literature, art, camping, biking. Home: 5085 Crestview Heights Ct Bettendorf IA 52722 Office: 2415 18th St Suite 206 Bettendorf IA 52722

DAHL, EUGENE, manufacturing company executive; b. 1924. BS, U. N.D., 1948. Gen. ptnr. Melroe Mfg.; with Stelger Tractor Inc., Fargo, N.D., 1970—, chief exec. officer, 1970-77, chmn. bd. dirs., 1977—. Served with AUS, 1943-45. Office: Steiger Tractor Inc 406 Main Fargo ND 58126 *

DAHL, GERALD LUVERN, consultant; b. Osage, Iowa, Nov. 10, 1938; s. Lloyd F. and Leola J. (Painter) D.; B.A., Wheaton Coll., 1960; M.S.W., U. Nebr., 1962; PhD in psychotherapy (Hon.), Internat. U. Found., 1987; m. Judith Lee Brown, June 24, 1960; children—Peter, Stephen, Leah. Juvenile probation officer Hennepin County Ct. Services, 1962-65; cons. Citizens Council on Delinquency and Crime, Mpls., 1965-67; dir. patient services Mt. Sinai Hosp., Mpls., 1967-69; clin. social worker Mpls. Clinic of Psychiatry, 1969-82, G.L. Dahl & Assocs., Inc., Mpls., 1983—; asso. prof. social work Bethel Coll., St. Paul, 1964-83; spl. instr. sociology Golden Valley Luth. Coll., 1974-83; pres. Strategic Team-Makers, Inc., 1985—. Founder, Family Counseling Service, Minn. Baptist Conf.; bd. dirs. Edgewater Baptist Ch., 1972-75, chmn., 1974-75. Mem. Nat. Assn. Social Workers, AAUP, Pi Gamma Mu. Author: Why Christian Marriages Are Breaking Up, 1979; Everybody Needs Somebody Sometime, 1980. Office: 4825 Hwy 55 Suite 140 Golden Valley MN 55422

DAHL, GREGORY L., lawyer, state legislator; b. Mpls., Mar. 25, 1952; s. Frederick Andrew and Lee May (Stratmoen) D. BA summa cum laude, St. Olaf Coll., Northfield, Minn.; JD, Stanford (Calif.) U. Atty. Leonard, Street & Deinard, Mpls.; sole practice Coon Rapids, Minn.; venture capital cons. Control Data Corp., Bloomington, Minn.; mem. Minn. State Senate, St. Paul, 1980—. Mem. ABA, Minn. Bar Assn., Anoka County Bar Assn., Phi Beta Kappa. Democrat-Farm-Laborer. Lutheran. Lodge: Lions. Avocations: carpentry, woodworking, photography, cross-country skiing,. Office: 942 120th Ln NW Coon Rapids MN 55433

DAHL, HARRY WALDEMAR, lawyer; b. Des Moines, Aug. 7, 1927; s. Harry Waldemar and Helen Gerda (Anderson) D.; m. Bonnie Sorensen, June 14, 1952; children: Harry Waldemar, Lisabeth (dec.), Christina. BA, U. Iowa, 1950; JD, Drake U., 1955. Bar: Iowa 1955, U.S. Dist. Ct. (no. and so. dists.) Iowa 1955, U.S. Supreme Ct 1965, Fla. 1970, Nebr. 1983, Minn. 1984. Sole practice Des Moines, 1955-59, 70—, Miami, Fla., 1972—; ptnr. Steward & Crouch, Des Moines, 1955-59; Iowa dep. indsl. commr. Des Moines, 1959-62; commr. 1962-71; ptnr. Underwood, Gillis and Karcher, Miami, 1972-77; adj. prof. law Drake U., Des Moines, 1972—; exec. dir. Internat. Assn. Indsl. Accident Bds. and Commns., 1972-77; pres. Workers Compensation Studies, Inc., 1974—, Workers' Compensation Services, Inc., 1978—, Hewitt, Coleman & Assocs. Iowa, Inc., 1975-79; mem. adv. com. Second Injury Fund, Fla. Indsl. Relations Commn. Author: Iowa Law on Workmen's Compensation, 1975; editor: ABC Newsletter, 1964-77. Served with USNR, 1945-46. Recipient Adminstrs. award, 1967. Mem. Am. Trial Lawyers Assn., ABA, Iowa Bar Assn., Fla. Bar Assn., Nebr. Bar Assn., Minn. Bar Assn., Internat. Bar Assn., Am. Soc. Law and Medicine (council 1975-82), Iowa Assn. Workers' Compensation Lawyers (co-founder, past pres.), Def. Research Inst., Coll. of Workers Compensation Inc. (co-founder, regent), Swedish Pioneer Hist. Soc., Am. Swedish Inst., Des Moines Pioneer Club, East High Alumni Assn. (pres. 1975-76), Order of Coif. Lutheran. Lodges: Masons, Shriners, Sertoma (chmn. bd. dirs. 1974-75). Home: 3005 Sylvania Dr West Des Moines IA 50265 Office: 974 73 St #16 Des Moines IA 50312

DAHL, JOHNNY MALCOLM, military officer; b. Lake Forest, Ill., Nov. 7, 1958; s. Malcolm Gibbs and Barbara Jean (Kopveiler) D.; m. Suzan Aysegül Apaydin, Sept. 28, 1985. BS, USAF Acad., 1981. Commissioned to 2d lt. USAF, 1981, advanced through grades to capt., 1985; fighter pilot Mt. Home AFB, Idaho, 1986—; mobility officer 21st Tactical Air Support Squadron, Shaw AFB, S.C., 1983-85, air liason officer, 1983-86, summary court officer, 1984-85, weapons officer, 1985-86. Republican. Avocations: golf, sports.

DAHLBERG, ALBERT ARCHER, dentist, dental anthropologist; b. Chgo., Nov. 20, 1908; s. Albert Edward Dahlberg and Edith Ann Carlson; m. Thelma Elizabeth Ham, Jan. 2, 1934; children: Cordelia Thelma, Albert Edward, James Eric. BS, DDS, Loyola U., Chgo., 1931. Intern then, resident U. Chgo. Clinic, Chgo., 1932-36; attending dental surgeon Chgo. Meml. Hosp., 1937-53; research assoc., prof. Mus. Natural History, Chgo., 1942—; research assoc., assoc. prof. Dept. Anthropology, Zoller Meml. Clinic, U. Chgo., 1949—, prof. emeritus, 1972—. Contbr. articles to profl. jour. Fellow Chgo. Inst. Medicine; mem. ADA (emeritus), Am. Assn. Phys. Anthropology, Internat. Symposium Dental Morphology, Am. Acad. Forensic Scis., Delta Sigma Delta. Home: 885 W Stone Barn Rd Franklin Grove IL 61031 Office: U Chgo Zoller Meml Clinic 1126 E 59th St Chicago IL 60637

DAHLBERG, BARRY ANDREW, SR., electrical engineering executive; b. Chgo., Sept. 27, 1932; s. Everett Axel and Evelyn M. (Forster) D.; m. Evelyn Vera Trojanek, July 5, 1953; children: Robert, Barry Jr., Andrew, Mi-a. BSEE, Tri-State Coll., 1959. Engr. Warner Electric, South Beloit, Ill., 1966-70, Gibbs Mfg., Janesville, Wis., 1970-76; cons. elec. engring. Rockton, Ill., 1976-84; pres., founder Aware Services, Inc., Chgo., 1984—. Inventor textile drive mechanism, 1969. Served with USN, 1953-57. Mem. IEEE. Office: Aware Services Inc 1500 S Western Chicago IL 60608

DAHLBERG, GILBERT EDWARD, priest; b. Chgo., Oct. 11, 1933; s. Gilbert Edward and Helen Miriam (Watkiss) D.; m. Pat Aitken, July 11, 1965 (div. Mar. 1984); children: Martha Aitken, Anne Aitken; m. Mary Garrett Price, Feb. 2, 1985. AB, U. Chgo., 1954; MDiv., Seabury Western Theol. Sem., Evanston, Ill., 1962. Ordained priest Episcopal Ch., 1962. Chgo. area dir. U. Chgo. Alumni Found., 1956-57; curate St. Gregory's Episcopal Ch., Deerfield, Ill., 1962-65; rector St. Barnabas Episcopal Ch., Denver, 1965-83; v.p. Extensive Care Inc., Dayton, Ohio, 1984—; founding dir., treas. Capitol Hill Community Ctr., Denver, 1977-82; bd. dirs., treas. ch. community service Colo. Council Chs., Denver, 1979-81. Bd. dirs. Rocky Mountain Kidney Found., Denver, 1968-72; mem. Huffman Hist. Area Soc., Dayton. Served with U.S. Army, 1957-58. Named one of Outstanding Young Men of Am., U.S. Jaycees, 1965. Fellow Coll. of Preachers of Washington Nat. Cathedral; mem. Phi Delta Theta (treas. 1952-54). Republican. Home: 1721 E 4th St Dayton OH 45403 Office: Extensive Care Inc PO Box 3018 Dayton OH 45401

DAHLE, JOHANNES UPTON, university director; b. Ada, Minn., Nov. 28, 1933; s. Upton Emmanuel and Marte (Golee) D.; m. Arlene Isabel Powell, Dec. 27, 1956; children—Randall Douglas, Lisa Johanna. B.S., U. Minn., 1956, M.A., 1966. Choral dir. U. Minn., Mpls., 1960-62, 63-66; dir. choirs Macalester Coll., St. Paul, 1962-63; dir. student activities and univ. programs U. Wis.-Eau Claire, 1966-71, dir. univ. ctrs., 1971-84, dir. devel., 1984—. Pres., dir. Eau Claire Conv. Tourism Bur., 1979-84; v.p., dir. Eau Claire Regional Arts Council, 1982-84; bd. dirs. United Way of Eau Claire. Served to capt. USAF, 1956-60. Mem. Internat. Assn. Coll. Unions, Council for Advancement and Support Edn., Phi Kappa Phi (sec. 1982-84), Omicron Delta Kappa (sec. 1981-84), Phi Mu Alpha Sinfonia. Mem. United Ch. of Christ. Lodge: Kiwanis (pres. Eau Claire chpt. 1975-76). Home: 1725 Coolidge Ct Eau Claire WI 54701 Office: U Wis Eau Claire 214 Schofield Hall Eau Claire WI 54701

DAHLEM, VALENTINE, aerospace engineer; b. Louisville, Sept. 5, 1935; s. Valentine and Ethel Margarette (Elder) D.; m. Shirley Marie Cissell, Oct. 20, 1956; children: Gregory A., Andrew M. Valerie M., Jennifer A. BS in Aero. Engring., St. Louis U., 1956; MS, Ohio State U., 1973. Assoc. engr. Marquardt Corp., Van Nuys, Calif., 1956, aero. engr., 1959-61; aerospace engr. Flight Dynamics Lab., Wright-Patterson AFB, Ohio, 1961-65, supervisory aerospace engr., 1965—; mem. U.S.-U.K. Tech. Coordinating Panel. Contbr. articles to profl. jours. Served with USAF, 1956-59. Reciepient Engring. Achievement award Research Soc. Am., 1967. Mem. AIAA, Sigma Xi. Roman Catholic. Home: 7594 Chambersburg Rd Dayton OH 45424 Office: Flight Dynamics Lab Wright-Patterson AFB OH 45433

DAHLEN, ELIZABETH MARGARET, speech and language pathologist; b. Moline, Ill., July 23, 1953; d. William Eric and Dorothy Ellen (Reed) D. B.A. cum laude, Augustana Coll., Rock Island, Ill., 1975; M.S., Eastern Ill. U., 1976. Cert. spl. edn. tchr., Ill., Iowa. Speech and lang. pathologist Wyanet Pub. Schs. (Ill.), 1976-87Wyanet, Tiskilwa Western and Manilus Dist. Coop., 1981-87, Hall Twp. High Sch., Spring Valley, Ill., 1987—. Cons. in field; speech therapy inservice resource person Bureau-Marshall-Putnam Counties Spl. Edn. Coop.; staff Summer Speech and Hearing Clinic, Augustana Coll., 1975, 78, 79, 81. Active Bureau County Chorus, 1977—, bd. dirs., 1982—; active Perry Meml. Hosp. Aux., 1980-85. Mem. Ill. Speech-Lang.-Hearing Assn. (sec. 1983-84), Am. Speech-Lang.-Hearing Assn. (cert.), Delta Kappa Gamma (chpt. pres. 1984-86, state nominating com. 1987—). Republican. Lutheran. Home: 20 E Peru St Apt 3 Princeton IL 61356 Office: Hall High Sch Spring Valley IL 61362

DAHLGREN, JOHN ROBERT, military officer; b. Washington, Feb. 26, 1959; s. John Onsgard and Lois Faye (Reed) D.; m. Judy Neuman Prescott, Apr. 26, 1986. AA, N.Mex. Mil. Inst., 1980; BA, W.Va. U., 1983. Commd. 2d lt. U.S. Army, 1980, advanced through grades to capt., 1985; forward observer F.A., Fairmont, W.Va., 1981-82; with ordinance officer basic course Ordinance Corp., Aberdeen, Md., 1984; mgr. weapons systems matrix Ordinance Corp., Rock Island, Ill., 1984—. Mem. Nat. Hist. Preservation Trust, Ducks Unlimited, Phi Theta Kappa (hon.). Republican. Lutheran. Clubs: Officer's, Arrowhead Hunt, BMW. Avocation: hunting, traveling. Home: 3430 Winston Dr #4 Bettendorf IA 52722 Office: Hdqrs Armanent Munitions and Chem Command Rock Island Arsenal 390 Redman Ave Rock Island IL 61299

DAHLINGER, RANDOLPH, bank examiner; b. Milw., Aug. 11, 1953; s. Fred and Barbara (Perkl) D.; m. Alice Frances Betzhold, June 30, 1984; 1 child, Carolanne. BBA, U. Wis., Milw., 1976; postgrad. in banking, U. Wis., Madison, 1986. Commd. bank examiner. Acct. rep. Midland Nat. Bank, Milw., 1975-76; sr. bank examiner FDIC, Chgo., 1976—; tchr. FDIC Tng. Ctr., Washington, 1985—; tng. coordinator FDIC, Madison, 1986—. Mem. Madison Jaycees (treas.).

DAHLKE, DANIEL FRANK, auditor; b. Orlando, Fla., May 21, 1954; s. Howard Carl and Doris (Joanne) D. BS in Acctg., Bradley U., 1975. Sr. acct. Peat Marwick Mitchell, Peoria, Ill., 1975-78; audit supr. County Nat. Bancorp., Clayton, Mo., 1978-80; dir. audit dept. County Tower Corp., Clayton, 1980-84; audit mgr. ITT Fin. Corp., St. Louis, Mo., 1984—. Active Child Ctr. of Our Lady, St. Louis, 1983—. Mem. Inst. Internal Auditors, Sigma Alpha Epsilon. Republican. Lutheran. Avocations: softball, boating, coin collecting. Home: 1609 Thrush Terr Brentwood MO 63144 Office: ITT Fin Corp 12555 Manchester Saint Louis MO 63131

DAHLKE, JANE BRUSH, child psychiatrist; b. Omaha, Feb. 17, 1945; d. John Hobart and Louise (Mackey) Brush; m. Helmuth W. Dahlke, Dec. 18, 1971; children—Ann, Rachel. B.A., Wheaton Coll., Norton, Mass., 1967; M.D., U. Nebr., 1972. Intern, U. Nebr., Omaha, 1972-73, resident in psychiatry, 1973-75, fellow in child psychiatry, 1974-76; staff child psychiatrist Nebr. Psychiat. Inst., 1976-78, part-time, 1978-82; pvt. practice medicine specializing in psychiatry, Omaha, 1978—; asst. prof. psychiatry U. Nebr. Coll. Medicine; cons. psychiatrist Episcopal Diocese Nebr.; cons. child psychiatrist Boys Town, Immanuel Mental Health Ctr. Mem. AMA, Am. Psychiat. Assn., Nebr. Psychiat. Soc., Am. Acad. Child Psychiatry (com. pvt. practice). Clubs: North Hills Hunt, Odd Couples Dance. Office: 6801 N 72d St Suite 15 Omaha NE 68122

DAHLMAN, DENNIS ARNOLD, educator, personnel administrator; b. St. Paul, Jan. 28, 1947; s. Louis Henry and Margaret (Ostrom) D. BS in Vocal Music, St. Cloud State U., 1969. Tchr. vocal music Dassel Cokato (Minn.) Schs., 1969-73, St. Francis (Minn.) Middle Sch., 1973-84, East Bethel Sch., Cedar, Minn., 1984—; mem. office personnel Norwest Agencies, Inc., Edina, Minn., 1983—. Dir. music Bethany Luth. Ch., Mpls., 1984—. Recipient Third Place award Nat. Assn. Tchrs. of Singing, 1968. Mem. Twin Cities Choir Dirs. Assn., Minn. Music Edn. Assn., Automatic Musical Instruments Collectors Assn. (sec. 1986—), Minn. Music Educators Assn., Phy Mu Alpha. Avocations: tennis, computers, antiques, travel. Home: 3906 52d Ave N Brooklyn Center MN 55429 Office: East Bethel Community Sch 21210 Polk St NE Cedar MN 55429

DAHLMAN, STEVEN RAY, advertising executive, consultant; b. Newton, Iowa, Oct. 8, 1961; s. Ray Albert and Bonnie Sue (East) D. Prodn. dir. KCDR/KQCR Radio, Cedar Rapids, Iowa, 1980-81; reporter news KCJJ Radio, Iowa City, 1981-82; gen. mgr. Dahlman Creative Media, Iowa City, 1983—; reporter news KIOA/KDWZ Radio, Des Moines, 1983—; bus. mgr. LaughLine, Des Moines, 1987—; freelance journalist, Des Moines, 1978—; writer TV, performer KDSM-TV, Des Moines, 1985-86. Producer assorted radio comedy dramas, 1984—; contbr. numerous stories to ABC Rock Radio Network, 1984—. Mster of Ceremonies, Riff's, Des Moines, 1985. Named Stringer of Month, UPI, 1984. Republican. Avocations: student pilot, computer programming, electronics design. Home and Office: 1000 School St #53 Des Moines IA 50309

DAHLQUIST, HORTON ALBERT, fire chief; b. Omaha, Mar. 12, 1928; s. Horton and Mercedes D.; m. Catherine Dahlquist, June 15, 1957; children—Robert, Catherine, Mercedes, Patricia, William. B.S., U. Nebr.-Omaha, 1964. Firefighter, Omaha Fire Div., 1955-66, capt. 1966-73, bn. chief, 1973-76, asst. chief, 1976-82, fire chief, 1982—; chmn. fire protection tech. dept. U. Nebr.-Omaha. Served with USNR, 1945-47. Mem. Missouri Valley Fire Chiefs Assn., Tri Mut. Aid Assn., Nebr. Emergency Med. Services Council, Internat. Assn. Fire Chiefs. Democrat. Roman Catholic. Club: Omaha Business Men's. Office: Office of the Fire Chief 1516 Jackson St Omaha NE 68102

DAHLSTEIN, DAVID KEITH, minister; b. Indepedance, Mo., Dec. 24, 1959; s. Richard Oscar and Hilda Darlene (Richardson) D.; m. Vanessa Faye Lowe, June 5, 1982; children: Mary Elizabeth, Sarah Dianne. B in Biblical Literature, Ozark Bible Coll., Joplin, Mo., 1982; M of Ministry, Cin. Christian Sem., 1986. Ordained to ministry Grain Valley Christian Ch., 1981. Asst. basketball coach Cin. Bible Coll., 1982-83; minister Ch. of Christ, St. Mary's, Ohio, 1983—; instr. Christian Tng. Ctr., St. Mary's, 1985—. Mgr. St. Mary's Little League, 1986. Named one of Outstanding Young Men Am., 1985. Mem. St. Mary's Ministerial Assn. Republican. Avocations: golf, baseball card collecting. Home: 620 W Spring Saint Mary's OH 45885 Office: Ch of Christ Rt 2 Box 21 Saint Mary's OH 45885

DAHLSTROM, NATALIE RUTH BAKER, school psychologist; b. LaPorte, Ind., Feb. 2, 1931; d. Oscar Roland and Ruth Winifred (Peterson) Baker; m. Kenneth Dahlstrom, Sept. 30, 1950 (div. June 1976); children: Victoria, Virginia, Kimberly, Alison. BS in Elem. Edn., U. Wis., River Falls, 1971, MEd in Sch. Psychology, 1973; MEd in Adminstrn., U. Wis., Superior, 1981. Teaching asst. U. Wis., River Falls, 1971-73; sch. psychologist Superior Sch. Dist., 1974—; adj. instr. U. Wis., Superior, 1984—. Mem. Wis. Sch. Psychologist Assn. (regional rep. 1983-86), Indianhead Sch. Psychologist Assn. (treas. 1981-84), Douglas County Mental Health Assn. (pres. 1980-86), LWV, Phi Delta Kappa (treas. 1983-84). Methodist. Avocations: sewing, travel, reading, writing poetry. Home: 2634 John Ave Superior WI 54880 Office: Superior Sch Dist 3025 Tower Ave Superior WI 54880

DAHMS, LESTER LOYD, consultant; b. Gladbrook, Iowa, Mar. 9, 1920; s. Henry August and Alvena Pauline (Bern) D.; m. Ardis Alvina Mueller, Oct. 12, 1947; children—Beverly J. Dahms Thompson, Kathleen Ann Dahms Carpenter. Student Marshalltown Community Coll., 1964-65. Clk. and rural mail carrier U.S. Postal Service, Marshalltown, Iowa, 1947-75; exec. dir. Am. Inst. Parliamentarians, Inc., Des Moines, 1972-83; pres. Dahms and Bierbaum Assocs., Inc., Norwalk, Iowa, also Dryden, N.Y., 1983—; cons., profl. parliamentarian to various orgns.; tchr. parliamentary procedure; lectr. in field. Served with USMC, 1941-45. Mem. Am. Inst. Parliamentarians (dir. 1964-84, pres. 1970-72). Lutheran. Author parliamentary law charts. Home: 1137 Pinehurst Circle Norwalk IA 50211

DAHN, CARL JAMES, aero. engr.; b. Chgo., June 22, 1936; s. Carl E. and Genevieve (Bardon) D.; B.S. in Aero. Engring., U. Minn., 1959; m. Rose E. Kucenski, May 25, 1974. Cert. chem. engr., registered profl. engr. Rocket propulsion devel. engr. Aerojet Gen. Corp., Azusa, Calif., 1959-61, propulsion and explosives devel. engr., 1962-63; chief engr. Omega Ordanace Co., Azusa, 1961-62; propulsion and explosives specialist Honeywell, Inc., Mpls., 1963-68; system safety research engr. IIT Research Inst. Systems Hazard Analysis, Chgo., 1968-74; hazards engring. specialist Polytechnic, Inc., Chgo., 1974-77; pres. Safety Cons. Engrs., Inc., Rosemont, Ill., 1977—; instr. explosives, guns and ballistics; cons. in same field; researcher dust explosions. Asst. scout master Mpls. St. Paul council Boy Scouts Am., 1962; area dir. Parents Without Partners, 1973; ward chmn. Republican party, 1964; ward chmn. Democratic party, 1973. Mem. Am. Soc. Safety Engrs., ASTM (com. sec.), System Safety Soc., Soc. Explosives Engrs., Nat. Soc. Profl. Engrs. Democrat. Methodist and Roman Catholic. Club: N.W. Divorced Catholic Group. Researcher, patentee in explosives field. Home: 6118 W Melrose St Chicago IL 60634 Office: 5240 Pearl St Rosemont IL 60018

DAILEY, MILLARD, utilities company executive. Pres. Minnkota Power Coop. Inc., Grand Forks, N.D. Office: Minnkota Power Coop Inc Grand Forks ND 58201 *

DAILEY, ROBERT FRANCIS, educator, systems engineer; b. Cleve., May 26, 1951; s. Robert Francis and Patricia Jean (Kennedy) D.; B.S. with high honors, U. Notre Dame, 1974; M.S. in Indsl. and Systems Engring., Ohio State U., 1979, Ph.D., 1985. Tchr., head math. dept. Hoban High Sch., Akron, Ohio, 1974-77; asst. to dean Coll. Engring. Ohio State U., Columbus, 1977-79; mem. tech. staff Bell Telephone Labs., Naperville, Ill., 1979-81; counselor Ill. Benedictine Coll., Lisle, Ill., 1979-81; grad. teaching assoc. dept. indsl. and systems engring. Ohio State U., 1981-84; asst. prof. math. scis. Loyola U., Chgo., 1985—. Provincial council Midwest Province Brothers of Holy Cross, 1985—; bd. dirs. Voice of the People in Uptown, Chgo., 1985—. Recipient Grad. Assoc. Teaching award Ohio State U., 1983. Mem. Ops. Research Soc. Am., Sigma Xi, Phi Kappa Phi, Alpha Pi Mu. Roman Catholic. Home: Brothers of Holy Cross PO Box 460 Notre Dame IN 46556 Office: Dept Math Scis Loyola U Chicago IL 60626

DAILY, ADELE FAUTH, dentist; b. Worms, Fed. Rep. of Germany, June 28, 1940; came to U.S., 1967; d. Jakob and Margaret (Michel) Fauth; m. Hugh Carlon Daily; children: Nora, Thomas. BA, Hochschule für Bildende Künste, Hamburg, Fed. Rep. Germany, 1964; BS, Bowling Green State U., 1979; DDS, Ohio State U., 1983. Dentist City of Detroit, 1983—. Avocations: photography, bicycling. Office: 1151 Taylor Detroit MI 48202

DAILY, FAY KENOYER, botany educator; b. Indpls., Feb. 17, 1911; d. Fredrick and Camellia Thea (Neal) Kenoyer; A.B., Butler U., 1935, M.S., 1952; m. William Allen Daily, June 24, 1937. Lab. technician Eli Lilly & Co., Indpls., 1935-37, Abbott Labs., North Chicago, Ill., 1939, William S. Merrell & Co., Ohio, 1940-41; lubrication chemist Indpls. Propellor div. Curtiss-Wright Corp., 1945; lectr. botany Butler U., Indpls., 1947-49, instr. immunology and microbiology, 1957-58, lectr. microbiology, 1962-63, mem. herbarium staff, 1949-87, curator cryptogamic herbarium, 1987—. Ind. Acad. Sci. research grantee, 1961-62. Mem. Am. Inst. Biol. Sci., Bot. Soc. Am., Phycol. Soc. Am., Internat. Phycol. Soc., Ind. Acad. Sci., Torrey Bot. Club, Sigma Xi, Phi Kappa Phi, Sigma Delta Epsilon. Republican. Methodist. Coauthor book on sci. history. Contbr. articles on fossil and extant charophytes (algae) to profl. jours. Home: 5884 Compton St Indianapolis IN 46220

DAITCH, PEGGY, magazine executive; b. Detroit, Aug. 20, 1946; d. Stanley B. and Miriam L. Friedman; m. Marvin C. Daitch; children—Joshua, Karen. Degree, Universite de Grenoble (France), 1966; B.A., U. Mich., 1967. Producer Sta.-WTAK, Detroit, 1968-70; pub. relations mgr. Sta. WTVS-TV, Pub. Broadcasting System, Detroit, 1970-72; broadcast producer/writer Loren/Snyder Advt., Detroit, 1976-78; broadcast producer/writer D'Arcy MacManus & Masius, Bloomfield Hills, Mich., 1978-79, account exec., 1979-84, account supr., 1984-86, v.p. 1985-86; mgr. Vogue Mag., Detroit, 1986—. Adv. Bd. dirs. Founders Jr. Council, Detroit Inst. Arts, 1976—, sec., 1978, v.p., 1980. Mem. Adcrat Club Detroit, Women's Advt. Club Detroit, The Fashion Group, Detroit Zool. Soc., Detroit Artists Market. Jewish. Home: 8621 Hendrie Huntington Woods MI 48070 Office: 3310 E Big Beaver Rd Troy MI 48084

DAKE, ANN BARBRA, insurance and risk manager; b. Edgewood, Iowa, June 18, 1952; d. Raymond George and Gretchen Winona (Taylor) Hochhaus, Robert Neil Dake, Sept. 2, 1972; children—Jennifer Ann, Kimberly Michelle. Clerical records dept. Iowa Nat. Mutual Ins. Co., Cedar Rapids, Iowa, 1970-72; customer service rep. Trissel, Graham & Toole, Inc., Davenport, Iowa, 1972-74; rep. comml. lines Friedman Ins. Inc., Dubuque, Iowa, 1974-78; agent The Dave Harper Agy. Inc., Manchester, Iowa, 1978-84, mgr., owner br. office, Strawberry Point, Iowa, 1980-84; ins. and risk mgr. Seedorff Masonry, Strawberry Point, Iowa, 1985—; cons. in field. Mem. Ind. Ins. Agents Iowa (instr. comml. lines rating 1979—), Ins. Women of Dubuque, Ins. Inst. Am. (cert. gen. ins. 1981), Nat. Assn. Ins. Women (cert. profl. ins. woman 1981), Ind. Ins. Agents Am., Strawberry Point C. of C. (sec./treas. 1982—). Republican. Methodist. Office: Seedorff Masonry Inc 408 W Mission St Strawberry Point IA 52076

DALE, JAN AUSTIN, psychologist; b. Grinnell, Iowa, Oct. 22, 1941; s. William Tracey and Evalena Mae (McIlrath) D.; m. Donna Kay Dolmage, July 21, 1963; Children: Kristin Joanne, Jeffrey William, Jon Matthew. BA, Simpson Coll., 1963; BST, Boston U., 1966, PhD, 1972. Lic. psychologist. Asst. pastor Congregational Ch., Walpole, Mass., 1965-66; pastor Cen. United Meth. Ch., Saugus, Mass., 1969-71; chief psychologist Cen. Iowa Mentla Health Ctr., Ames, Iowa, 1971—; dir. consultation and edn. Cen. Iowa Mental Health Ctr., Ames, Iowa, 1980—; psychol. cons. Beloit of Iowa Children's Home, Ames. 1971-80, Youth and Shelter Services, Ames, 1971-81, Boone County (Iowa) Head Start, 1971-80. V.p. Iowa State 4-H Clubs,

Ames, 1960-61; pres. S. Iowa Meth. Ch. Fellowship, Des Moines, 1958-59; family life coordinator Collegiate United Meth. Ch., Ames. 1972-73. Mem. Community Mental Health Ctrs. Assn. Iowa (continuing edn. chmn. 1979-81, Staff award 1981), Iowa Psychol. Assn. (adv. com. 1978-80), Iowa Mental Health Authority (standards adv. task force 1980-81), Cen. Iowa Guidance Counsellors Assn. (Outstanding Lay Person award 1976-77). Democrat. Club: Mr. and Mrs. Ch. (Ames)(chmn. 1976-77, 80-81). Mem. New Christy's Minstrels and Sons of the Pioneers singing groups. Home: Rt 3 Ames IA 50010 Office: Cen Iowa Mental Health Ctr 713 S Duff Ames IA 50010

DALEIDEN, JAMES PATRICK, obstetrician; b. Mason City, Iowa, Oct. 12, 1943; s. Herbert Mathias and Mary Alice (Nerby) D.; m. Jeanne Mary Hammes, Apr. 23, 1966; children: Patrick, Eric, Sara, David. BS, Marquette U., 1965; MD, U. Minn., 1969. Diplomate Am. Bd. Ob-Gyn. Intern St. Joseph's Hosp., Milw., 1969-70, resident, 1969-73; obstetrician Moreland Ob-Gyn Assocs., Waukesha, Wis., 1973—. Fellow ACS, Am. Coll. Ob-Gyn; mem. AMA, Am. Fertility Soc. Roman Catholic. Avocations: computers, skiing. Home: 212 Westminster Waukesha WI 53186 Office: Moreland Ob-Gyn Assocs 1111 Delafield Waukesha WI 53188

DALEY, JAMES KENT, consultant; b. Chgo., Jan. 25, 1952; s. James LeRoy and Sydney Dorcus (Carlton) D.; B.S. in Math., Ill. State U., 1974; M.S. in Biostats., U. Pitts., 1976; M. in Finance, Northwestern U., 1984. Research asst. Nat. Safety Council, Chgo., 1976-78; research analyst Central States Health, Welfare and Pension Fund, Chgo., 1978-84; pension systems cons. Hewitt Assocs., Lincolnshire, Ill., 1984—. USPHS scholar, 1974-76. Mem. Am. Statis. Assn., Ill. State Alumni Assn., U. Pitts. Alumni Assn., Northwestern U. Alumni Assn., Beta Gamma Sigma, Alpha Kappa Lambda. Republican. Evangelical. Lodge: Lions. Avocations: Bicycling; skiing; tennis; golf. Office: Hewitt Assocs 100 Half Day Rd Lincolnshire IL 60015

DALEY, VINCENT RAYMOND, JR., real estate executive, consultant; b. Evanston, Ill., June 21, 1940; s. Vincent R. and Carole V. (Johnson) D.; m. Violo Elizabeth Bursiek, May 6, 1967; children: Kathleen Marie, Colleen Patricia. AA, Lincoln Coll., 1961; BS, Loyola U., Chgo., 1963; student in real estate, Roosevelt U., 1964. From salesman to store mgr. Sears Roebuck & Co., Chgo., 1962-73; v.p., cons. Kencoe Corp., Des Plaines, Ill., 1973-74; pres. Daley & Assocs., Chgo., 1974—. Trustee Lincoln Park Coop. Sch., Chgo., 1979—; mem. edn. council Chgo. Pub. Sch. System, 1981—; mem. Econ. Devel. Com., State of Ill., Springfield, 1985—; legis. asst. 8th Legis. Dist., Chgo., 1985—. Served with USNG, 1961-67. Mem. Chgo. Bd. Realtors (life) (bd. dirs.), Nat. Assn. Realtors (bd. regents), Ill. Assn. Realtors, Realtors Land Inst. (bd. govs.), Realtors Nat. Mktg. Inst. (sr. cert.). Democrat. Roman Catholic. Avocation: traveling. Home: 2130 Lincoln Park West Chicago IL 60614 Office: Daley & Assocs 77 W Washington Chicago IL 60602

DALIA, VERA, clinical psychologist; b. Brno, Czechoslovakia, Nov. 19, 1935; d. Aharon and Helen (Grun) Wollner; came to U.S., 1963, naturalized, 1970; m. Zol F. Muskovitch, Dec. 23, 1958 (dec. 1969); children—David, Debby. Student Hebrew U., Jerusalem, 1956-58; B.A., U. Toronto, 1961; M.A., U. Evansville, 1971; Ph.D., U. Mich., 1974. Clin. community psychologist Sudbury (Ont., Can.) Algoma Sanatorium, 1974-76; clin. coordinator Bangor (Maine) Mental Health Inst., 1976-78; dir. behavioral sci. family practice residency St. Joseph Hosp., Flint, Mich., 1978-79; clin. and cons. psychologist Flint, Birmingham, Southfield, Mich., 1979-84; clin. faculty U. Maine, 1978. Horace B. Rackham grantee, 1973-74. Mem. Am. Psychol. Assn., Mich. Psychol. Assn., Mich. Soc. Cons. Psychology, Soc. Tchrs. Family Medicine. Office: 1621 E Court St Flint MI 48503

DALICANDRO, JOHN JOSEPH, state agency official; b. Chgo., June 26, 1957; s. John Robert Dalicandro and Josephine (Sabatino) Pusateri. Student, Oakton Community Coll., 1975-77; BA, Loyola U., 1981. Police officer Triton Coll., River Grove, Ill., 1980-81; revenue collector Ill. Dept. Revenue, Chgo., 1981-83; promotions dir. Ill. State Lottery, Chgo., 1983-84; asst. dir. personnel Gov.'s Office, Chgo., 1984-87; bur. chief mktg. and devel. Project Chance Ill. Dept. Pub. Aid, Chgo., 1987—. Legis. liason Young Voter Orgn. Leyden Township, Elmwood Park, 1985—. Named Outstanding Young Man of Am., 1985. Mem. Italian-Am. Nat. Union Chgo. Avocations: golf, hockey. Home: 8633 Orchard Dr Hickory Hills IL 60457 Office: Ill Dept Pub Aid 624 S Michigan Chicago IL 60605

DALLAS, DANIEL GEORGE, social worker; b. Chgo., June 8, 1932; s. George C. and Azimena P. (Marines) D.; B.A., Anderson (Ind.) Coll., 1955; B.D., No. Bapt. Theol. Sem., 1958; M.S.W., Mich. State U., 1963; M.Div., No. Bapt. Theol. Sem., 1972, D.Min., 1981; m. G. Aleta Leppien, May 26, 1956; children—Paul, Rhonda. Mem. faculty Mich. Dept. Corrections, Mich. State U., 1963-66; med. social adminstr. Med. Services div. Mich. Dept. Social Services, 1966-68; cons. Outreach Center of DuPage County, 1976—, also dir. social service Meml. Hosp. of DuPage County, Elmhurst, Ill., 1968—; therapist, lectr. Traffic Sch., Elmhurst Coll.; pvt. practice; indsl. cons. Mem. Elmhurst Sr. Citizen Commn., 1976—. Recipient Outstanding Service award Mental Health Assn. Ill., 1978. Mem. Nat. Assn. Social Workers, Soc. Hosp. Social Work Dirs., Am. Hosp. Assn., Nat. Registry of Health Care Providers, Mental Health Assn. Chgo. Club: Rotary. Contbr. articles to profl. jours. Office: 242 N York St Room 203 Elmhurst IL 60126

DALLAS, JULIE FAY, accountant; b. Crosby, Minn., Aug. 3, 1952; d. Robert George and Mabel Helmi (Hill) Erickson; m. Edward Dwain Dallas, Dec. 25, 1973; children: Karen, Jay. BS in Bus. and Acctg., U. Minn., 1974. CPA. Sr. acct. Touche Ross & Co., Anchorage, 1974-76, Mpls., 1977-78; mgr. Donald Engen CPA., Pequot Lakes, Minn., 1979—. Bd. dirs. Cuyuna Range Dist. Hosp. and Home, Crosby, Minn., 1980—. Mem. Am. Inst. CPA's, Minn. Soc. CPA's. Democrat. Methodist. Avocations: skating, gardening. Home: PO Box 155 Deerwood MN 56444 Office: Donald H Engen CPA's Box 171 Pequot Lakes MN 56472

DALLMEYER, A(LVIN) RUDOLPH, JR., management consultant; b. St. Louis, Nov. 15, 1919; s. Alvin Rudolph and Sarah Lucille (Ford) D.; B.S. in B.A., Washington U., St. Louis, 1941; M.B.A. with distinction, Harvard U., 1947; children—Richard L., R. Ford, J. Scott, P. Suzanne. Exec. asst. Automatic Electric Co., Chgo., 1947-52; cons., assoc. Booz, Allen & Hamilton, Chgo., 1952-59; v.p. Spencer Stuart & Assos., Chgo., 1959-63; v.p., pres. Donald R. Booz & Assocs., Chgo., 1963-77; pres. Dallmeyer & Co., Inc., Chgo., 1977—; pres. Euro-Am. Mktg. Group Inc., Chgo., 1985—; dir. Maritz, Inc., Federated Foods, Inc., Microseal, Inc. Served to maj. U.S. Army, 1941-45. Cert. mgmt. cons. Mem. Inst. Mgmt. Cons. (chpt. pres.), Chgo. Assn. Commerce and Industry, Internat. Bus. Council MidAm., Chgo. Council on Fgn. Relations, French-Am. C. of C., German Am. C. of C., Belgian-Am. C. of C., Phi Delta Theta. Republican. Presbyterian. Clubs: University, Metropolitan, Harvard Bus. Sch. Chgo. (dir.). Home: 861 Bryant Ave Winnetka IL 60093 Office: 20 N Wacker Dr Chicago IL 60606

DALRYMPLE, HAROLD RAY, speech educator; b. Akron, Ohio, Dec. 28, 1944; s. Harold Ray and Betty J. (Carter) D.; m. Rhea Irene Gaunt, Mar. 16, 1970; children: Siobhan Rhea, Sean Ernest. BA, Heidelberg Coll., 1966; MA, Bowling Green State U., 1970; PhD, Kent State U., 1980. Tchr. Firelands High Sch., Oberlin, Ohio, 1967-68; instr. Heidelberg Coll., Tiffin, Ohio, 1969-70; prof. speech Kent State U., Ashtabula, Ohio, 1970—. Chmn. preventive edn. com. Northeast Ohio Council on Alcoholism, Youngstown, 1986—, bd. dirs. 1981—, sec. 1987—. Mem. Speech Communication Assn., Internat. Listening Assn. (treas. 1987), Ohio Assn. Gifted Children (Service award 1984-86), Am. Assn. Gifted/Social and Emotional Needs of Gifted. Avocations: aerobics, racquetball, walking, swimming. Office: Kent State U 3325 W 13th St Ashtabula OH 44004

DALTON, HARRY, baseball exec.; b. Springfield, Mass., Aug. 23, 1928. Grad., Amherst Coll., 1950. With Balt. Orioles, 1953-71, v.p. and player personnel dir., 1965-71; exec. v.p., gen. mgr. Calif. Angels, 1971-77, Milw. Brewers, 1977—. Served as 1st lt. USAF. Decorated Bronze Star. Office: care Milw Brewers Milw County Stadium Milwaukee WI 53214 *

DALY, CHARLES JOSEPH, professional basketball coach; b. St. Mary's, Pa., July 20, 1933. Student, St. Bonaventure U., 1948-49, Bloomsburg State Coll., 1949-52, Pa. State U. Asst. coach Duke U., Durham, N.C., 1963-69; coach Boston Coll., 1969-71, U. Pa., Phila., 1971-77; asst. coach Phila. 76ers, NBA, 1977-81; coach Cleve. Cavaliers, NBA, 1981-82, Detroit Pistons, NBA, 1983—. Office: Detroit Pistons Pontiac Silverdome 1200 Featherstone St Pontiac MI 48057 *

DALY, DENNIS STANFORD, health care administrator; b. Detroit, Oct. 6, 1944; s. Stanford F. and Doris I. (Seitz) D.; m. Gail Ellen Murphy, Aug. 9, 1969. BS in Engring., U. Mich., 1967. Mgmt. trainee Chrysler Corp., Ann Arbor, Mich., 1965-66; assoc. CSF, Ltd., Ann Arbor, 1966-79; sr. cons. JRB Assocs., McLean, Va., 1979-80; sr. systems analyst Fairview Hosps. and Healthcare Services, Mpls., 1980-81; assoc. dir. mgmt. info. systems div. Fairview Community Hosps., Mpls., 1981-85, corp. dir. mgmt. services, 1985—. Author: Comprehensive Program for Capital and Property Management, 1979; contbr. articles to profl. jours. Mem. Am. Hosp. Assn., Hosp. Fin. Mgmt. Assn., Am. Inst. Indsl. Engrs., Hosp. Mgmt. Systems Soc. (info. systems com., conservation of energy in hosps. com.). Avocations: golf, bowling, painting, reading. Home: 6712 Sioux Trail Edina MN 55435 Office: Fairview Hosps and Healthcare Services 2312 S 6th St Minneapolis MN 55454

DALY, JAMES MICHAEL, III, computer programmer analyst; b. Evanston, Ill., Dec. 5, 1958; s. James Michael II and Mary Helen (FitzGerald) D. BSBA, Marquette U., 1981; postgrad., DePaul U., 1985—. Programmer analyst, Info. Services Am. Hosp. Supply Corp., McGaw Pk., Ill., 1981-82, sr. programmer analyst, 1983-84, systems analyst, 1985-86; sr. programmer/analyst Travenol Labs. Info. Resources, McGaw Pk., 1986-87; tech. cons. Baxter Info. Resources, McGaw Pk., 1987—. Chmn. Marquette U. Alumni Admissions Recruiting Chpt., Chgo., 1982—; pres. Prince of Peace Sch. Bd., Lake Villa, Ill., 1985-87. Mem. Data Processing Mgmt. Assn. (dir. communications 1981-82, v.p. communications, North Shore sect. 1982-83). Republican. Roman Catholic. Club: Marquette U. of Chgo. (bd. dirs. 1983—). Home: 36376 N Traer Terr Gurnee IL 60031-1343 Office: Baxter Info Resources 1400 Waukegan Rd McGaw Park IL 60085-6784

DALY, JOHN FRANCIS, industrial manufacturing company executive; b. N.Y.C., Dec. 13, 1922; s. John F. and Caroline (Pohl) D.; m. Casilda Boyd, July 16, 1953; children—Jo-Ann, Avis, Carol, Peter, Alexia. B.S., Rensselaer Poly. Inst., 1943. Vice pres. Internat. Steel Co., Evansville, Ind., 1956-59; exec. v.p. Universal Wire Spring Co., Bedford, Ohio, 1959-60; v.p. Hoover Ball & Bearing Co. (name Hoover Universal Inc. 1978), Ann Arbor, Mich., 1960-66; exec. v.p. Hoover Ball & Bearing Co. (name Hoover Universal Inc. 1978), 1966-68, pres., 1968—, chmn., chief exec. officer, 1972—, also dir.; vice chmn. Johnson Controls, 1985—; dir. Comerica Bank, Detroit, Comerica Inc., Comerica Ann Arbor, Mich. Mut. Ins. Co., Amerisure Cos., Cross & Trecker Corp., Bloomfield Hills, Mich., Handleman Co., Troy, Mich., Plasti-Line, Knoxville; vice-chmn., dir. Johnson Controls. Trustee Indsl. Tech. Inst., Ann Arbor, Citizens Research Council of Mich., Siena Heights Coll., Adrian, Mich. Served to capt. USAAF, 1943-46. Mem. Theta Xi. Home: 18 Southwick Ct Ann Arbor MI 48105 Office: PO Box 1003 Ann Arbor MI 48106

DALY, JOSEPH MICHAEL, biochemist, biologist, educator; b. Hoboken, N.J., Apr. 9, 1922; m. Cecelia Reiger, 1951; eight children. BS, U. R.I., 1944; MS, U. Minn., 1947, PhD, 1952. Instr. plant pathology U. Minn., Mpls., 1947-52; asst. prof. biology U. Notre Dame, South Bend, Ind., 1952-55; asst. prof. plant pathology U. Nebr., Lincoln, 1955-56, prof. plant pathology, 1958-64, prof. botany, 1960-65, chmn. dept. plant pathology, 1962-64, prof. agrl. biochemistry, 1964-66, C. Petrus Peterson prof. biochemistry, 1966—, interim dir. Sch. Life Scis., 1973-74; cons. FMC corp., 1962-79; lectr. and participant in numerous symposiums and workshops throughout the world. Co-editor: (with others) Biochemical and Cytology of Plant-Parasite Interaction, 1976, Recognition and Specificity in Plant Host-Parasite Interactions, 1979, Toxins and Plant Pathogenesis, 1983; assoc. editor Plant Physiology, 1981-86; editorial bd. Physiological Plant Pathology and Phytopathology; reviewer Phytopathology, Can. Jour. Botany, Physiological Plant Pathology; contbr. numerous articles to textbooks, sci. books and profl. jours. Recipient Elvin Charles Stakman award, 1986. Fellow Am. Phytopathology Soc.; mem. AAAS, Am. Soc. Plant Physiologists, Soc. Am. Microbiologists, Nat. Acad. Scis., Am. Acad. Arts and Scis. Office: Univ of Nebr Dept Biochem & Nutrition 211 ABH Lincoln NE 68583-0718

DAMASKUS, CHARLES WILLIAM, biochemist; b. Blue Island, Ill., Oct. 28, 1924; s. Frederich and Johanna Damaskus; children—Linda, Craig, Diane. B.A., Valparaiso U., 1949. Research chemist Baxter Labs., Morton Grove, Ill., 1949-51; sr. scientist Armour Pharm. Co., Chgo., 1951-63; clin. research scientist Am. Hosp. Supply Co., Mt. Prospect, Ill., 1963-66; pres. Alper Labs., Inc., LaGrange, Ill., 1966—. Contbr. articles to sci. jours. Patentee in field. Elder St. John's Lutheran Ch., LaGrange, 1950-58, chmn. elders, 1959-61, pres. congregation, 1962-64. Served with USCG, 1942-44, as aviator USNR, 1944-47. Mem. Am. Chem. Soc., AAAS. Home: 132 S Kensington Ave LaGrange IL 60325 also: 4745 S Atlantic Ponce Inlet FL 32018 Office: PO Box 232 LaGrange IL 60525

D'AMATO, A. S., chemical company executive. Pres. Borden Chem. Div., Columbus, Ohio. Office: Borden Chem Div 180 E Broad St Columbus OH 43215 *

DAMBACH, VIRGINIA LEE, public broadcasting executive; b. Beckley, W.Va., Aug. 19, 1949; d. William Jack and Mary Virginia (Bennett) Carman; m. Patrick G. Mulloy, Nov. 27, 1969 (div. 1976); m. Robert O. Dambach, June 12, 1982; 1 child, Mary RIta. BS in English/Speech, U. Nevada, 1974. Program coordinator Clark County Library, Las Vegas, 1976-79; br. adminstr. City of Las Vegas, 1979; devel. dir. radio sta. KNPR, Las Vegas, 1979-84, Prairie Pub. Broadcasting, Fargo, N.D., 1985—; mktg. cons. Lincoln Trails Library System, Ill., 1983; mem. NPR Pub. Info. Adv. Com., Washington, 1980-82, Downtown Bus. Assn., Fargo, 1984—. V.p. Allied Arts Council, Las Vegas, 1982-84; fundraiser ETCOM pub. radio, El Paso, 1983, various non-profit agencies, Las Vegas, 1980-84; bd. dirs. Devel. Exchange Inc., Washington, 1983—, Lake Agassiz Arts Council, Fargo, 1984—. Mem. Devel. Exchange Inc. Democrat. Club: Quilter's Guild N.D. (Fargo) (chmn. edn. 1986—). Avocations: quilting, reading, gardening. Home: 806 S 9th St Fargo ND 58103 Office: Prairie Pub Broadcasting 207 N 5th St Fargo ND 58108-3240

DAMBERG, JOHN PAUL, architect; b. Mpls., May 1, 1930; s. Paul S. and Vanda (Nelson) D.; m. Virginia McElfish; children: William, Kathryn, Paul. BArch, U. Minn., 1953. Registered architect, Minn. Architect Thorshov & Cerny, Mpls., 1953-57, Damberg & Damberg, Virginia, Minn., 1957-68, Damberg & Peck, Virginia, 1968-83, Damberg, Scott, Peck & Booker, Virginia, 1983—. Bd. dirs. Virginia C. of C., 1981-84, Camp Warren, Eveleth, Minn., 1973—. Mem. Minn. Soc. Architects (bd. dirs. 1973-76). Lodges: Rotary (pres. Virginia club 1976-77, sec. 1981-86, dist. gov. 1987—), Shriners. Avocation: photography. Home: 3268 Cedar Island Dr Eveleth MN 55734 Office: Damberg Scott Peck & Booker 3200 Lincoln Bldg Virginia MN 55792

DAMER, LINDA K., educator; b. Springfield, Ill., Dec. 5, 1938; d. J. Fred and Mary Jane (Thurmond) Welsh; B.A., William Jewell Coll., 1959; M.A., Boston U., 1967; Ed.D., U. N.C., Greensboro, 1979; children—Diana, Cynthia and John Damer. Tchr., Kearney (Mo.) Public Schs., 1959-60, Consolidated Sch. Dist. 1, Kansas City, Mo., 1960-63, Wellesley (Mass.) Pub. Schs., 1963-64, Newton (Mass.) Pub. Schs., 1966-67, Smyth County (Va.) Pub. Schs., 1969-72, Washington County (Va.) Pub. Schs., 1973-76, Burlington (N.C.) Pub. Schs., 1978-79; grad. teaching asst. U. N.C., Greensboro, 1977-78; assoc. prof. music Ind. State U., Terre Haute, Ind., 1979—. U. N.C., Greensboro fellow, 1976-77. Mem. Music Educators Nat. Conf., Ind. Music Educators Assn. (exec. bd., pres.), Am. Orff Schulwerk Assn., Pi Kappa Lambda (pres.), Phi Delta Kappa, Sigma Alpha Iota. Clubs: University , Faculty Women's. Home: 9048 Arrowood Ct Terre Haute IN 47802 Office: Ind State U Dept Music Terre Haute IN 47809

DAMIANOV, VLADIMIR BLAGOI, mechanical engineer; b. Sofia, Bulgaria, Sept. 19, 1938; came to U.S., 1971; s. Blagoi Petrov and Bona Krasteva (Stereva) D.; m. Millie N. Melanov, Sept. 16, 1972; 1 child, William. BSME, U. Sofia, 1961, MSME, 1967. Dept. mgr. R&D Ctr. Lift Trucks, Sofia, 1961-70; project engr. MTD Products, Inc., Cleve., 1972-74; chief engr. Canton (Ohio) Stocker Corp., 1974-77; sr. project engr. McNeil Akron (Ohio), Inc., 1977-81; sr. devel. engr. Goodyear Aerospace, Akron, 1981—. Patentee in field. Pres. St. Thomas Ch., 1980-82. Mem. ASME, Soc. Mech. Engrs., ASTM. Eastern Orthodox Catholic. Clubs: Businessmen (Akron) (v.p. 1980-82), Fort Island (Fairlawn, Ohio) (bd. dirs. 1980-83). Avocations: bridge, biking, traveling, tennis, swimming. Home: 3021 Morewood Rd Fairlawn OH 44313 Office: Goodyear Aerospace Corp D/461-C2E 1210 Massillon Rd Akron OH 44315

D'AMICO, LARRY JOHN, chef; b. Cleve., July 29, 1950; s. Arthur and Helen Marie (Kaczmarek) D'A.; m. Jenifer Lynn Diedrich, Aug. 18, 1985; children: Amanda Lynn. BA in History, Ohio State U., 1975. Chef D'Amico's Restaurant, Medina, Ohio, 1975-79, 1980-83; exec. chef Westwood Country Club, Rocky River, Ohio, 1979-80; corp. chef D'Amico & Ptnrs., Mpls., 1984—; exec. chef Primavera Restaurant, Mpls., 1984—; cons. Mrs. Appleton's Restaurants, Ft. Meyers and Sarasota, Fla., 1985—, The Driscoll, St. Paul, 1986—, Minnetonka Boat Workers, Wayzata, Minn., 1986—, Edinburgh Club, Brooklyn Park, Minn., 1986—. Author: American Bistro Cookbook, 1986; contbr. articles to profl. jours. Recipient Best New Generation Restaurant award Esquire magazine, 1985; named one of 40 Best Am. Restaurants, Food and Wine mag., 1985. Mem. Soc. Am. Cuisine (assoc.), Geneva Soc., Nat. Restaurant Assn. Roman Catholic. Club: Sport (pres. 1986—).

DAMON, SARA ELLEN, chemical executive; b. Rapid City, S.D., Sept. 22, 1926; d. Samuel and Sara Anna (Johnston) Crabb; m. Jack Almon Damon, Feb. 2, 1952; children: Alan Jay, Janice Ann, Kenneth Lew, Keith Jeffrey. BA in Journalism and Spanish, Cornell Coll., Mt. Vernon, Iowa, 1948. Teen-age program dir. YWCA, Alliance, Ohio, 1950-52; sec., treas. Damon Chem. Co., Alliance, Ohio, 1953—. Contbr. poems and articles to Sharing Mag., 1980—. Mem. Ch. Women United, chmn. com. 1982-83; council rep. Alliance of Chs., 1980—; gov. region IV council Order of St. Luke the Physician, 1982—, convenor, 1982, sec. Alliance chpt., 1983—, workshop leader, 1984—; counselor Inner Healing and Healing of Memories, 1980—; deaconess First Bapt. Ch., 1985—, spiritual healing minister, 1982—. Republican. Club: Am. Univ. Women (charter mem., first v.p.). Avocations: reading, needle-point, singing, travel, skiing. Home: 1100 Fernwood Blvd Alliance OH 44601 Office: Damon Chem Co Inc 12435 Rockhill NE Alliance OH 44601

DAMRON, GLENN E., data processing executive; b. Pikeville, Ky., Feb. 4, 1933; s. Harvey E. and Louanna (Prater) D.; m. Patty J. Maggard, Apr. 19, 1952; children: Keith, Trese. Student, U. Md., 1955; BA in Bus., Ohio State U., 1957; BA, Franklin U., 1983. Data processing trainee Rockwell Internat., Columbus, Ohio, 1957-58; computer ops. supr. Ohio Hwy. Dept., Columbus, 1958-65; ops. mgr. Chemical Abstracts Service, Columbus, 1965-68; salesman Honeywell & Mohawk Data, Columbus, 1968-70; pres., chief exec. officer Data Entry Processing Service, Inc., Columbus, 1970-85, Data Input Leasing, Inc., Grove City, Ohio, 1985—. Republican. Baptist. Home and Office: 2777 White Rd Grove City OH 43123

DAMROW, RICHARD G., advertising executive; s. Donald C. and V. June (Miller) D.; m. Kimberly Anne Millhollin, Oct. 13, 1982; children—Andrew, Anthony, Adam. B.A. cum laude, Hastings Coll., 1970; postgrad. Creighton U., 1970-72. Cert. bus. communicator. Pub. relations assoc. Western Electric Co., Omaha, 1970-71; mgr. employee and pub. relations Gate City Steel Corp., Omaha, 1971-72; advt. mgr. Ag-tronic, Inc., Hastings, Nebr., 1972-74; v.p. Fletcher/Mayo Assocs., St. Joseph, Mo., 1974-80; pres. Mark, Morris & Co., Mpls., 1980-82; sr. v.p., mng. dir. Carmichael Lynch Advt., Mpls., 1982-86; sr. v.p., gen. mgr. Miller Meester Mktg. Support Group, St. Paul, 1986—. Mem. Midwest Direct Mktg. Assn., Bus. and Profl. Advt. Assn., Nat. Agrimktg. Assn., Direct Mktg. Assn., Pub. Relations Soc. Am. Republican. Presbyterian. Club: Flagship Athletic. Home: 2420 Winter Circle Wayzata MN 55391 Office: 531 S Snelling Ave Saint Paul MN 55116

DAMSCHROEDER, ALLEN DALE, orthopaedic surgeon; b. Gibsonburg, Ohio, Feb. 19, 1937; s. Floyd Howard and Pauline (Kinker) D.; m. Jane Mae Terrill, June 14, 1959; children: Spencer, Kurt, Susan. BS, Ohio State U., 1959, MD, 1963. Diplomate Am. Bd. Orthopaedic Surgery. Orthopaedic surgeon Burns Clinic, Petoskey, Mich., 1970—; bd. dirs. Old Kent Bank, Petoskey. Served to lt. USNR, 1965-66. Fellow Clin. Orthopaedic Soc., Am. Acad. Orthopaedic Surgeons; mem. Sierra-Cascade Trauma Soc. (v.p. 1986—), Woodcock Boscage Benevolent Soc., Petoskey C. of C. (chmn. 1980). Republican. Presbyterian. Avocations: hunting, farming. Home: 7737 Indian Garden Rd Petoskey MI 69770 Office: Burns Clinic 560 W Mitchell Petoskey MI 49770

DAMSTEEGT, DON CALVIN, psychologist, educator; b. Waupun, Wis., July 31, 1946; s. Cornelius and Della (Navis) D. BA, Hope Coll., 1968; MDiv, Western Theol. Sem., Holland, Mich., 1972; MA, U. Nebr., 1976, PhD, 1981. Lic. psychologist, Iowa. Minister Pilgrim Congl. Ch., Lincoln, Nebr., 1974-81; pvt. practice psychotherapy Cedar Rapids, Iowa, 1982—; prof. psychology Mt. Mercy Coll., Cedar Rapids, 1981—; cons. The Help Ctr., Marion, Iowa, 1986—. Contbr. articles to profl. jours. Bd. dirs., pres. Found. II Crisis Counseling and Youth Shelter, 1985-87. Mem. Am. Psychol. Assn., Am. Assn. for Marriage and Family Therapy, Iowa Psychol. Assn. Democratic. Presbyterian. Avocations: tennis, racquetball, aerobics. Home: 701 27th St NE Cedar Rapids IA 52402 Office: Mt Mercy Coll 1330 Elmhurst Dr NE Cedar Rapids IA 52402

DANA, DEBRA LYNN, commodity executive; b. Evanston, Ill., Oct. 1, 1954; d. Warren C. and Ramona O. (Anderson) D.; m. Neal E. Hoffman; children: Bret, Mason. BA magna cum laude, No. Ill. U., 1977, MA, 1979. Exec. recruiter W.P. Assocs., Chgo., 1979; mgr. employment and tng. Chgo. Bd. of Trade, 1981—. Mem. Save the Park Community Group, Evanston, 1986. Mem. Nat. Soc. Performance Instruction. Avocations: soccer, broomball.

DANCA, JOHN ARTHUR, psychotherapist, educator; b. Chgo., Apr. 19, 1950; s. John Joseph and Josephine Rose (Bartolotta) D.; 1 son, Matthew John. B.A., DePaul U., 1972; M.A., Governors State U., 1975; C.A.S., No. Ill. U., 1978, Ed.D., 1982. Mem. counseling faculty Fenwick High Sch., Oak Park, Ill., 1973-75; instr. psychology, counselor Triton Coll., River Grove, Ill., 1975-78; assoc. dir. Ball Found., Glen Ellyn, Ill., 1978-79; assoc. prof. student devel. Oakton Coll., Des Plaines, Ill., 1979—; cons. Moley Internat., 1986; lectr. in field. Bd. dirs. Chgo. Bd. of Mental Health, Northwest, 1974-75; mem. Oakton Coll. Crusade of Mercy Appeal, 1982. Sears grantee, 1986—. Mem. NEA, Ill. Edn. Assn., Am. Psychol. Assn., Midwest Psychol. Assn., N.Am. Assn. Adlerian Psychology, Ill. Guidance and Personnel Assn., Ill. Coll. Personnel Assn., Ill. Assn. Tests and Measurements, Phi Delta Kappa. Contbr. articles to profl. jours. Home: 520 Butterfield Rd Elmhurst IL 60126 Office: 1600 East Golf Rd Des Plaines IL 60016

DANCIE, WAYNE LEE, financial executive; b. Cleve., June 22, 1959; s. Kay F. (Pearson) Spates; m. Paula K. Garden, Aug. 11, 1984. BBA, Miami U., Oxford, Ohio, 1981. Acctg. systems coordinator Standard Oil Corp., Cleve., 1981-82, refinery analyst, 1983, sr. fin. analyst, 1983-85, fin. analyst, 1985-87; account officer leaveraged capital group Citicorp Indsl. Credit, Inc., Cleve., 1987—; treas. Blamenco Investment Group, Cleve., 1983-86; instr. Dale Carnegie & Assoc., Cleve., 1987. Bus. advisor Inroads of Northeast Ohio, Cleve., 1982—, Jr. Achievement, Cleve., 1982-83. Mem. Planning Forum (bd. dirs. 1986—), Nat. Assn. Accts., Ohio CPA Soc., Nat. Assn. Black Accts. (chmn. 1984-85). Futurist Soc. Republican. Home: 3304 Archwood Ave Cleveland OH 44109 Office: Citicorp Indsl Credit Inc 1300 E 9th Cleveland OH 44114

DANDREA, CARMINE, English educator, poet, antique dealer; b. Elmira, N.Y., July 30, 1929; s. Carmine S. and Mary E. (DiPetto) D.; m. Nancy R. McMann, Jan. 1, 1976; children—Michael, Karen, Anne, Jane. B.A. in English summa cum laude, Hobart Coll., 1956; postgrad. in Am. Civilization, Brown U., 1956-57; M.S. in Edn., Elmira Coll., 1961; M.F.A. in Creative Writing, Cornell U., 1969. English tchr. Elmira (N.Y.) Free Acad., 1959-65; spl. lectr. in English and social sci. Elmira Coll., 1961-65, asst. prof. English,

1965-72, mem. faculty evening and summer sessions, 1965-75; lectr. in English and audio-visual lab. coordinator Corning (N.Y.) Community Coll., 1972-73; mem. faculty Independent Study Program, SUNY, 1972-73; mem. faculty Lake Michigan Coll., Benton Harbor, Mich., 1973—, instr. English, 1973-75, English staff coordinator, 1973-75, assoc. prof. English, 1975, prof. English, 1976—, chmn. dept. humanities, 1980-85. Served with USMC, 1948-52. Decorated Purple Heart. Spl. univ. scholar, Brown U., 1956-57; N.Y. State Regents War Vet. Scholar, 1959-62; HEW/Fulbright faculty grantee, India, 1970; nat. winner N.Y. Poetry Ctr. Discovery 69 Program, 1969; Mayves Zantell Lyric award N.Y. Poetry Forum, 1972; Nat. Fedn. of State Poetry Socs. awards, Bicentennial Patriotism award, 1976; Tradition Poetry award, 1976; Ariz. State Poetry Soc. award, 1972; Rose Magnoni Marinoni Meml. award, 1972; Tenn. Poetry Contest award, 1974; Ill. State Poetry Soc. award, 1976, 77, Walter Lovel Meml. award, 1976; N.Y. State Poetry Forum award, 1976; Shel McDonald Dramatic Poetry award, 1977; Macomb Fantasy Factory ann. awards, 1976, 77, 79, 81, 84, 86, 87. Mem. N.J. Poetry Soc., Phi Beta Kappa, Pi Gamma Mu, Phi Theta Kappa (hon.). Author: (poetry) Heart's Crow, 1972; contbr. poetry to various anthologies. Home: 153 Windsor Rd Benton Harbor MI 49022 Office: 2755 E Napier Ave Benton Harbor MI 49022

DANDY, ALEX, food products executive; b. Mt. Hope, W.Va., July 18, 1928; s. Samuel K. and Godley (El-Kadri) D.; m. Lilah Aekle Hazemy, Sept. 11, 1948; children: Samuel A., Cathy A., D. Michael, Richard, Barbara A., Susan. Grad. pub. schs., W. Va. Chmn. of the bd. Hamady Bros. Food Markets Inc., Flint, Mich., 1974—, Durant Enterprises Inc., Flint, 1974—. Bd. dirs. Faith and Hope Children's Rehab. Hosp., Cairo; mem. Rep. Leadership Council, Washington, Rep. Eagles., Washington, Inner Circle Pres. Club, Washington. Recipient Mayoral award City of Flint, 1982, Man of Yr. award St. Jude's Children's Research Hosp., Los Angeles, 1983. Mem. Islamic Assn. of N.Am. (Man of Yr. 1978). Lodge: Masons (bd. mgrs. Md.). Office: Hamady Bros Food Markets Inc 3301 S Dort Hwy Flint MI 48507

DANEY, WILLIAM CHESTER, physician; b. Pueblo, Colo., Nov. 18, 1934; s. William Lawrence and Isabel (Stevenson) D.; m. Barbara Julia Packan, July 27, 1956; children—Colette Marie, Tamra Kay, William C. Jr., Randall Todd. B.A. magna cum laude in Zoology, U. Colo.-Boulder, 1956; M.D., U. Colo.-Denver, 1960. Diplomate Am. Bd. Emergency Medicine Am. Bd. Family Practice. Intern St. Anthony Hosp., Denver, 1960-61; resident in internal medicine St. Mary-Corwin Hosp., Pueblo, 1961; pvt. practice, Pueblo, Colo., 1962-76; Staff St. Mary-Corwin Hosp., Pueblo, 1972-82, dir. emergency dept., 1976-82; chmn. dept. emergency medicine St. Mary's Hosp., Grand Rapids, Mich., 1982—, dir. Emergency Care Ctr., 1983—; project med. dir. Kent County Emergency Med. Services, 1985—; chmn. Kent County Med. Soc. Emergency Med. Services com.; pres. Grand River Emergency Med. Group, Grand Rapids, 1982—; del. to Colo. State Med. Soc., Pueblo, 1968; asst. prof. medicine Mich. State U., Lansing, 1983—; examiner Am. Bd. Emergency Medicine, Lansing, 1981—. Mem. Pueblo Arts Council, Colo., 1969-71; Pueblo Civic Symphony, Colo., 1968-72; patron Grand Rapids Opera, Mich., 1984—; mem. advanced cardiac life support com. Mich. Heart Assn. Recipient Physicians Recognition award AMA, 1984; Spl. Recognition award Scenic Trails Council Boy Scouts Am., Mich., 1984. Fellow Am. Coll. Emergency Physicians (bd. dirs. Mich chpt., Spl. Service award Colo. chpt. 1981); mem. Kent County Med. Soc., Kent County Emergency Med. Services Council, Am. Acad. Med. Dirs. Club: Cascade Country (Grand Rapids). Avocations: Fly fishing, photography, astronomy, camping, travel. Home: 1631 Mont Rue SE Grand Rapids MI 49506 Office: Dir Emergency Care Ctr 200 Jefferson SE Grand Rapids MI 49503

DANFORTH, JOHN CLAGGETT, U.S. senator, lawyer, clergyman; b. St. Louis, Sept. 5, 1936; s. Donald and Dorothy (Claggett) D.; m. Sally B. Dobson, Sept. 7, 1957; children: Eleanor, Mary, Dorothy, Johanna, Thomas. B.A. with honors, Princeton U., 1958; B.D., Yale U., 1963, LL.B., 1963, M.A. (hon.); M.A. hon. degrees; L.H.D., Lindenwood Coll., 1970; L.H.D., Ind. Central U.; LL.D., Drury Coll., 1970, Maryville Coll., Rockhurst Coll., Westminster Coll., Culver-Stockton Coll., St. Louis U.; D.D., Lewis and Clark Coll.; H.H.D., William Jewell Coll.; S.T.D., Southwest Bapt. Coll. Bar: N.Y. 1964, Mo. 1966. With firm Davis Polk Wardwell Sunderland & Kiendl, N.Y.C., 1964-66, Bryan, Cave, McPheeters and McRoberts, St. Louis, 1966-68; atty. gen. State of Mo., 1969-76; U.S. senator from Mo. 1976—; chmn. Senate com. commerce, sci. and transp.; ordained deacon Episcopal Ch., 1963, priest, 1964; asst. rector N.Y.C., 1963-66; assoc. rector Clayton, Mo., 1966-68, Grace Ch., Jefferson City, 1969; hon. assoc. St. Albans Ch., Washington, 1977—; chmn. Mo. Law Enforcement Assistance Council, 1973-74. Republican nominee U.S. Senate, 1970. Recipient Distinguished Service award St. Louis Jr. C. of C., 1969, Disting. Missourian and Brotherhood awards NCCJ, Presdl. World Without Hunger award, 1985; Disting. Lectr. award Avila Coll.; named Outstanding Young Man Mo. Jr. C. of C., 1968; Alumni fellow Yale U., 1973-79. Mem. Mo. Acad. Squires, Alpha Sigma Nu (hon.). Republican. Office: 497 Russell Senate Bldg Washington DC 20510

DANG, MINH NGOC, minister; b. Quang-Nam, DaNang, Socialist Republic of Vietnam, May 3, 1958; came to U.S., 1975; s. Cang Ngoc Dang and Duyen Thi Nguyen. BS, U. Akron, 1980; M Divinity, Grace Theol. Sem., 1983; D Ministry, Ashland Theol. Sem., 1987. Ordained minister. Dir. Vietnamese Evangelistic Outreach, Akron, 1984—; bd. leadership Vietnamese Christian Youth Assn. Am., Des Moines, 1986—. Author: The Evacuation Route 1975, 1978. Mem. Vietnamese Pastor Assn. Am. Mem. Ind. Ch. Avocations: writing, reading, ping pong. Home: 105 Mayfield Ave Akron OH 44313

DANGELO, CHARLES MICHAEL, neurosurgeon; b. M rlboro, Mass., Apr. 8, 1942; m. E. Betsy Curtis, Aug. 29, 1964. BA, Johns Hopkins U., 1964; MD, U. Vt., 1968. Cert. Am. Bd. Neurol. Surgery. Intern Yale U. Med. Ctr., 1968-69, resident in surgery, 1969-70, resident in neurosurgery, 1970-75; sr. attending surgeon, assoc. prof. neurosurgery Rush Med. Sch., Chgo., 1975—. Served to capt. U.S. Army. Mem. AMA, ACS, Neurol. Soc. Am., Assn. Neurol. Surgeons, Congress Neurol. Surgery. Office: 1725 W Harrison Chicago IL 60612

DANGELO, THOMAS ANTHONY, data processing executive; b. Salem, Ohio, Apr. 3, 1962. BS, Youngstown (Ohio) State U., 1984. Systems analyst Trinova Corp., Toledo, 1984-86, Libbey-Owens Ford Co., Toledo, 1986—. Mem. Assn. Sysytems Mgmt., Alpha Phi Delta. Lodge: KC. Avocations: softball, basketball, golf. Home: 3652 Harley Rd Toledo OH 43613 Office: Libbey-Owens Ford Co 811 Madison Ave Toledo OH 43695

DANI L, DAVID LOGAN, retired state welfare agency administrator; b. Columbia, Tenn., Jan. 2, 1906; s. David and Mahalah (Lloyd) D.; B.A., Fisk U., 1928; M.A., U. Chgo., 1954, postgrad., 1955-56; m. Mary Beatrice Evins, Aug. 4, 1935. Caseworker, casework supr., dist. office asst. adminstr. Chgo. Relief Adminstrn., Cook County Bur. Welfare and Dept. Pub. Aid, 1933-48; asst. div. dir., pub. assistance div. Cook County Dept. Pub. Aid, Chgo., 1948-66, dir., services programs, 1966-67, dep. dept. dir., 1967-69, dir., 1969-74; asst. dir. Ill. Dept. Pub. Aid, 1974-83. Mem. bd. mgrs. Youth Guidance, 1948—; bd. dirs. Chgo. Commons Assn., Big Bros./Big Sisters of Met. Chgo., 1970-83; Joint Negro Appeal; mem. adv. council Dept. Aging and Disability City of Chgo., 1983—; mem. citizens' adv. com. Ill. Dept. Pub. Aid; mem. info. and referral com. United Way of Chgo.; chmn. state employees campaign United Way/Crusade of Mercy, 1976-83; bd. dirs. Met. Chgo. Coalition on Aging, 1979—; mem. Exec. Service Corps, 1983; mem. citizens adv. com. Ill. Dept. Pub. Aid. Served with AUS, 1943-46; capt. Res. ret. Recipient Service award Vets. Assistance Commn. Cook County, 1973, Chgo. Area Manpower Planning Council, 1974; Past Pres.'s award City Club Chgo., 1974; Holy Angels award Holy Angels Catholic Ch., 1976; Stamps Service award Joint Negro Appeal, 1976; Golden Alumnus Meritorious award Fisk U., 1982; honors award United Way/Crusade of Mercy, 1984, others. Mem. Nat. Assn. County Welfare Dirs. (pres. 1973-74), Nat. Assn. Social Workers, Acad. Certified Social Workers, Chgo. Urban League, Am. Pub. Welfare Assn., NAACP (life), Ill. Welfare Assn. (pres.), Amvets (former comdr. greater Chgo. post #1), Alpha Phi Alpha (life; past chpt. pres.). Methodist. Clubs: City of Chgo. (dir., past pres.), Chgo. Umbrian Glee (pres. 1946—). Home: 5839 S Michigan Ave Chicago IL 60637

DANIEL, FREDERICK RICHARD, JR., lawyer; b. Tiffin, Ohio, May 15, 1953; s. Frederick Richard Sr. and Florence Alberta (Albright) D.; m. Cheryl Ellen Hamrick, July 27, 1974; children: Nathan Andrew, Gideon Richard. BA, U. Notre Dame, 1975, JD, 1978. Bar: Ohio, U.S. Dist. Ct. (no. dist.) Ohio, U.S. Ct. Appeals (6th cir.). Sole practice Tiffin, 1978—. Mem. ABA, Ohio Bar Assn., Seneca County Bar Assn. (treas. 1985—). Roman Catholic. Lodge: KC (council adv. 1980-84). Avocations: backpacking, photography, reading, fishing, boating, tennis. Home: 27 Ella St Tiffin OH 44883 Office: 36 Madison St Tiffin OH 44883

DANIEL, SHARON REBECCA ROSE, educational administrator; b. Detroit, Aug. 28, 1955; d. James Edward and Wilma Jo (Thacker) D. A.B. in Edn., Marion Coll., Ind., 1976; M.A. in Edn., Ball State U., 1983. Cert. tchr., Ind. Tchr., dept. head Westside Christian Sch. and Noah's Ark Day Care Ctr., Marion, Ind., 1980-82, asst. dir., 1982-84, adminstrv. dir., 1984—; pvt. music tchr. Band dir. Am. Legion Hoosier Girl's State, Marion, 1982. Mem. Christian Instrumental Dirs. Assn., Assn. Supervision and Curriculum Devel. Republican. Mem. Assemblies of God. Avocations: music, travel. Home: 906 S Norton St Marion IN 46953 Office: Westside Christian Sch 2011 W 10th St Marion IN 46953

DANIELL, SANDRAL, physical scientist, educator; b. St. Louis, July 29, 1940; d. Willie Davis and Catherine (Robnett) Allen; m. Maurice Digby Daniell, Jan. 29, 1982. B.S., Lincoln U., 1962; M.A., Webster U., 1975; M.S., Washington U., St. Louis, 1980. Cartographer, Def. Mapping Agy., St. Louis, 1962-74, geodesist, 1974-82, phys. scientist, 1982—; affiliate prof. Civil engring. (geometric geodesy) Washington U., St. Louis, 1982—. Mem. Am. Soc. Photogrammetry (exec. bd. 1978-80), Am. Geophys. Union, Beta Kappa Chi. Methodist. Avocations: playing flute; music; poetry. Home: 85 Depot Dr Edwardsville IL 62025

DANIELS, ARTHUR PRESTON, data processing executive; b. Bklyn., Mar. 7, 1946; s. Arthur Preston and Jeannette (Farina) D.; m. Geraldine Ann Mascari, May 2, 1964; children—Joseph Gerard, Christopher Preston. Transp. technician Tri-State Commn., N.Y.C., 1963-67; systems specialist Ins. Data Processing Ctr., N.Y.C., 1967-69; systems planner Borden Inc., N.Y.C., 1969-71, systems project mgr., Columbus, Ohio, 1971-75, mgr. systems support, 1975-80, mgr. info. ctr., 1980-85, mgr. decision support, 1985—; project mgr., speaker Guide 41, Denver, 1976; cons. Borden Can., Toronto, Ont., 1983-84. Coach Pickerington Athletic Assn., Ohio, 1972, Reynoldsburg Little League, Ohio, 1974; vol., booster Bishop Hartley High Sch., Columbus, Ohio, 1984. Mem. Data Processing Mgmt. Assn., Am. Mgmt. Assn., Columbus Info. Ctr. Assn. Roman Catholic. Lodge: K.C. Avocations: sports; Am. history; music. Office: Borden Inc 180 E Broad St Columbus OH 43215

DANIELS, DAVID WILDER, music educator; b. Penn Yan, N.Y., Dec. 20, 1933; s. Carroll Cronk and Ursula (Wilder) D.; m. Jimmie Sue Evans, Aug. 11, 1956; children—Michael, Abigail, Andrew. A.B., Oberlin Coll., 1955; M.A., Boston U., 1956; M.F.A., U. Iowa, 1963, Ph.D., 1963. Instr. music Culver-Stockton Coll., Canton, Mo., 1956-58; music librarian Berkshire Athenaeum, Pittsfield, Mass., 1958-61; asst. prof. U. Redlands, Calif., 1963-64, Knox Coll., Galesburg, Ill., 1964-69; asst. prof. Oakland U., Rochester, Mich., 1969-71, assoc. prof., 1971-85, prof., 1985—, chmn. dept., 1982—; music dir. Warren Symphony, Mich., 1974—, Pontiac-Oakland Symphony, Pontiac, Mich., 1977—; pres. Mich. Orchestra Assn., 1981-83. Author: Orchestral Music, 1972, rev. edit., 1982; editor: Avanti newsletter, 1982-86. Mem. Am. Symphony Orchestra League, AAUP, Coll. Music Soc., Conductors Guild (bd. dirs. 1986—). Home: 1215 Gettysburg Rochester MI 48064 Office: Oakland U Dept Music Theater and Dance Rochester MI 48063 also: Warren Symphony Orch 4504 E Nine Mile Rd Warren MI 48091

DANIELS, KENNETH RICHARD, communications executive; b. Ludden, N.D., Mar. 18, 1943; s. Joe and Emma Sofia (Hoikkala) D.; m. Jane Elaine Neufeld, Mar. 5, 1965; children: Christopher, Sonja, Jennifer, Erikki. Student, N.D. State U., Fargo, 1961-63, 70-71; grad. in elec. engring., Brown Inst., Mpls., 1965. Staff engr. Sta. KXJB-TV, Fargo, N.D., 1970-72; engring. supr. Sta. WHA-TV, U. Wis., Madison, Wis., 1972-81, Hubbard Broadcasting, St. Paul, 1981-82; chief engr. Computer Video Prodns., Mpls., 1982-85, v.p. engring., 1985—. Active Energy Commn., Blaine, Minn., 1984-85; adv. bd. Mpls. Pub. Schs. Indsl. Tech. Council, 1983—, Internat. Lang. Village Concordia Coll., Moorhead, Minn., 1985—. Served as staff sgt. USAF, 1965-70. Mem. Soc. Broadcast Engrs. Democrat. Lutheran. Avocations: softball, reading. Home: 770 96th Ln NE Blaine MN 55434 Office: Computer Video Prodns 1317 Clover Dr S Minneapolis MN 55420

DANIELS, STEPHEN DOUGLAS, banker, accountant; b. Decatur, Ill., Dec. 8, 1955; s. Charles Edward Daniels and Joe Ann (Pope) Stephens; m. Carol Lynn Stogsdill, Dec. 18, 1976; 1 child, Jillian Michael. BA, Milliken U., 1979. CPA, Ill. Sr. acct. Arthur Andersen & Co., Chgo., 1979-82; controller Mt. Prospect (Ill.) State Bank, 1982-85, v.p., 1983-84, sr. v.p., 1984-86; asst. treas., sr. v.p., chief fin. officer First United Fin. Services, Inc., Arlington Heights, Ill., 1985—. Mem. Am. Inst. CPA's, Ill. CPA Soc., Nat. Assn. for Bank Cost Analysts. Avocations: skiing, photography, flying. Office: First United Fin Services Inc 2355 S Arlington Heights Rd Arlington Heights IL 60005

DANIELSON, CHARLES IRVIN, controller; b. Decorah, Iowa, June 22, 1931; s. Carl Ole and Ida Marie (Strand) D.; m. Virginia Ruth Perau, Feb. 27, 1956; children: Michael, Allison, Lori. BA, Luther Coll., 1953. CPA, Iowa. Treas. Am. Litho Co., Des Moines, 1961-64; asst. controller Sheller-Globe Corp., Keokuk, Iowa, 1964-69; treas. Midwest Carbide Corp., Keokuk, 1969-86; corp. controller Reif Oil Co., Burlington, Iowa, 1986-87; plant controller Foote Mineral Co., Keokuk, 1987—; tax cons., Keokuk, 1975—. Pres. Jr. Achievement, Keokuk, 1976. Served as cpl. U.S. Army, 1953-55. Am. Inst. CPA's, Iowa Soc. CPA's. Republican. Lutheran. Lodge: Elks. Avocations: golf, coin and stamp collecting. Home: 311 Hawthorne Pl Keokuk IA 52632 Office: Foote Mineral Co Commercial St Keokuk IA 52632

DANIELSON, DAVID GORDON, health science facility administrator; b. Minot, N.D., Dec. 18, 1954; s. Gordon Everett and Myla Eunice (Torgerson) D.; m. Lisbeth Annette Roehrich, June 9, 1979; children: Michael, Katherine. BSBA, U. N.D., 1977, JD, 1980; postdoctoral, U. Minn., 1980-82. Bar: N.D. 1980, U.S. Dist. Ct. N.D. 1983; CPA, Minn., N.D. Tax specialist Deloitte, Haskins & Sells, Mpls., 1980-82, Eide Helmeke and Co., Fargo, N.D., 1982-84; adminstr. Med. Arts Clinic, Minot, 1984—; bd. dirs. Teamcare HMO, Inc., Minot. Mem. ABA, N.D. Bar Assn., Am. Inst. CPA's (area IV planning com.), N.D. Soc. CPA's (chmn. legis. com. 1986—). Lodge: Rotary, Elks. Avocations: golf, tennis, reading. Home: 2513 Bel Air Pl Minot ND 58701 Office: Med Arts Clinic PC Box 1489 Minot ND 58702-1489

DANIELSON, ELIZABETH KAY, psychology educator; b. Van Nuys, Calif., Oct. 5, 1949; d. Joe Henry and Margaret Louise (Owens) Bull; m. Scott G. Danielson, Dec. 27, 1984. BA, Baylor U., 1970; MA, U. Colo., 1977, PhD, 1982. Lic. cons. psychologist, Minn., psychologist, N.D., sch. psychologist, Minn., La. VISTA vol. Sp. Peaks Mental Health Ctr., Peublo, Colo., 1971-72; vol. Peace Corps, Khemisset, Morocco, 1974-75; sch. psychologist Northeast Colo. BOCES, Haxtun, Colo., 1978-80, Boulder (Colo.) Valley Schs., 1980-82; asst. prof. Moorhead (Minn.) State U., 1982—; cons. Rape/Abuse Crisis Ctr., Fargo, N.D., 1986—. Mem. Nat. Assn. Sch. Psychologists (mem. exec. bd. 1986—), Am. Psychol. Assn., Am. Ednl. Research Assn., North Cen. Assn. Sch. Psychologists (pres. 1985), Colo. Soc. Sch. Psychologists (sec. 1981). Democrat. Episcopalian. Home: 915 2d Ave S #5 Fargo ND 58103 Office: Moorhead State U Dept Psychology Moorhead MN 56560

DANIHER, FRANCES ANDERSON, hospital administrator, educator; b. Madrid, Spain, Jan. 7, 1953; (parents Am. citizens); s. Claude Ellery and Ruby Stewart Anderson; m. William Joseph Daniher Jr., Oct. 29, 1983. Student, Am. U., 1971-72; BA, U. Wis., 1975; MBA, Cornell U., 1980. Adminstrv. fellow Met. Hosp. and Health Ctrs., Detroit, 1980-81; asst. adminstrv. dir. Sheridan Rd. Hosp., Chgo., 1981-83; asst. adminstr. Rush-Presbyn.-St. Lukes Med. Ctr., Chgo., 1983-85; v.p. ops. St. Francis Hosp., Evanston, Ill., 1985—; assoc. prof. dept. health systems mgmt. Rush U., Chgo., 1982—. Mem. Am. Coll. Health Care Execs., Am. Hosp. Assn., Chgo. Health Execs. Forum (program chmn. 1984, sec. 1985, pres. 1986). Roman Catholic. Home: 7446 N Washtenaw Chicago IL 60645 Office: St Frances Hosp 355 Ridge Ave Evanston IL 60202

DANNEMILLER, JOHN C., transportation company executive; b. Cleve., May 17, 1938; s. John Charles and Jean I. (Bage) D.; m. Jean Marie Sheridan, Sept. 22, 1962; children—David, Peter. B.S., Case Western Res. U., 1960, M.B.A., 1964; postgrad., Stanford U., 1975, Columbia U., 1974, Tuck Exec. program Dartmouth Coll., 1976. Vice pres. foods div. Diamond Shamrock, 1978-81, dir. planning, 1981-83; v.p. SDS Biotech Corp., Cleve., 1984-85; group v.p. leasing group Leaseway Transp., Cleve., 1984-85, pres., chief operating officer, 1985—, also dir.; dir. Bearings, Inc., Cleve. Bd. dirs., advisor Jr. Achievement, Cleve., 1962-64; fund raiser United Way, Cleve. and St. Louis. Mem. Am. Trucking Assns., Beta Gamma Sigma. Republican. Presbyterian. Clubs: Cleve. Athletic, Lakewood Country, Firestone Country. Avocations: tennis; water skiing; boating; snow skiing; golf. Office: Leaseway Transp Co 3700 Park East Dr Beachwood OH 44122

DANNER, DAVID C., retail executive; b. Indpls., Mar. 1, 1951; s. Ray Junior and Garnet Elizabeth (Smith) D.; m. Teresa A. Ward, Aug. 10, 1985. BSBA, Butler U., 1976. Asst. mgr. Danners, Inc., Valparaiso, Ind., 1976-77; asst. dir. store planning Danners, Inc., Indpls., 1977-82, asst. v.p. store planning, 1982-83, v.p. store planning, 1983-85, v.p. adminstrn., 1985-86, v.p. adminstrn., sec., 1986—, also bd. dirs., 1986—. Bd. dirs. Boys Club Indpls., 1984; adv. bd. dirs. Atkins Boys' Club, Indpls., 1980—. Served with U.S. Army, 1971-73. Methodist. Lodge: Rotary. Avocations: racquetball, skiing, swimming. Office: Danners Inc 6060 N Guion Rd Indianapolis IN 46254

DANNER, DEAN WILSON, electrical engineer, manufacturing executive; b. Milw., June 9, 1950; s. George Wilson and Hazel B. (Damisch) D.; m. Bonita Mae Albert, June 19, 1971; children: Elizabeth, Matthew, Jonathan. BSEE, Marquette U., 1976. Registered profl. engr., Wis. Field engr. GTE Automatic Electric, Waukesha, Wis., 1972-74, purchasing agt. and tech. liason, 1974-76, mgr. product shop, 1976-78, mgr. engring., 1978-80; v.p. and dir. engring. Electronic Tele-Communications, Inc., Waukesha, 1980-86, exec. v.p., 1986—, also bd. dirs. Patentee in field. Bd. dirs. Waukesha United Way, 1986—. Mem. IEEE, Nat. Soc. Profl. Engrs., Wis. Soc. Profl. Engrs., Independent Telephone Pioneer Assn., Roadrunners Internat. Republican. Roman Catholic. Lodge: Rotary (pres. 1983-84). Office: Electronic Tele-Communications Inc 1915 MacArthur Rd Waukesha WI 53188

DANNER, DONALD PHILLIP, controller; b. St. Louis, July 2, 1948; s. Clifford Phillip and Virginia (Deters) D.; m. Susan Jean Hoehn, July 3, 1970; children: Laurie, Amy, John. BS in Commerce, St. Louis U., 1970; MBA, U. Mo., St. Louis, 1979. CPA, Mo. Staff acct. Haskins & Sells, CPA's, St. Louis, 1970-71; sr. acct. Massie, Fudemburg, Goldberg, St. Louis, 1971-75; controller Telecommunication Services Inc., St. Louis, 1975-78; v.p. fin. Rolm-Mid., Rolm-Ill., Chgo., 1979-84; region controller Rolm Corp., Dallas, 1984-85, Schaumburg, Ill., 1986-87; mgr. acctg. IBM Corp., Schaumburg, 1987—; adj. asst. prof. St. Louis U., 1973-78. Mem. Am. Inst. CPA's, Mo. Soc. CPA's. Roman Catholic. Avocations: baseball, reading. Home: 101 Thompson Wheaton IL 60187 Office: IBM Corp 1253 E Golf Rd Schaumburg IL 60194

DANSBY, EUNICE LILLITH, music educator, consultant; b. Springfield, Mass., Jan. 11, 1927; d. Benjamin and Theo Maud (Amsbury) Heideman; m. Ellsworth Harry Dansby, Jr., Sept. 24, 1949; children—Deborah Dale, Ellsworth Harry. B.Applied Music magna cum laude, Millikin U., 1948; M.Mus. Edn., 1953; postgrad. U. Ill., Roosevelt U., U. Wis., Nat. Coll. Edn. Mem. faculty Millikin U., Decatur, Ill., 1945-49, adj. prof. music, 1987—, Maroa (Ill.) High Sch., 1947-48, Cerro Gordo (Ill.) Pub. Schs., 1948-49, Chgo. Pub. Schs., 1952-53, Mattoon (Ill.) Pub. Schs., 1953-55, Decatur Pub. Schs., 1957-59, Bethany (Ill.) Pub. Schs., 1959-69, Wheaton-Warrenville (Ill.) Pub. Schs., 1969-83, ret., 1983; guest condr. orchs. and choruses; judge music contests, Ill., Ind., Wis. Mem. Decatur Mcpl. Band; bd. dirs. Millikin-Decatur Symphony Guild. Gen. mgr. Millikin-Decatur Civic Orch., 1987—. Recipient Tchr.'s Writing Contest prizes Reader's Digest and NEA, 1970, 71, 72. Mem. NEA (life), Ill. Edn. Assn., Music Educators Nat. Conf., Ill. Music Educators Assn. (rec. sec. 1978-80, Disting. Service award 1985), Am. String Tchrs. Assn., Ill. String Tchrs. Assn. (editor Scroll 1976-82), In-and-About Chgo. Music Educators Assn., Ill. Project for Sch. Reform, Citizens Utility Bd., NOW, LWV (v.p. Decatur chpt.), Phi Kappa Phi, Sigma Alpha Iota (chpt. pres.). Presbyterian. Contbr. articles to Music Educators Jour., Ill. Music Educators Jour., Scroll, Sch. Musician mag.; editor Southeastern Sounds; composer, arranger woodwind ensembles. Home and Office: 1044 W Tuttle St Decatur IL 62522

DANTO, HAROLD NEWTON, environmental engineer; b. Cleve., Jan. 1, 1927; s. Joseph Bernard and Anna (Stotsky) D.; m. Muriel Elaine Sobol, Sept. 6, 1947 (dec. Sept. 1986); children—Charlotte Elizabeth, Allan Howard. B.S. in Chem. Engring., Case Western Res. U., 1950. Prin., H.N. Danto Cons., Cleve., 1954-70; air pollution engr. Ohio EPA, Cleve., 1970-76; sr. environ. engr. Sherwin Williams Co., Cleve., 1976-78; v.p. Danto Environ. Corp., Cleve., 1978-84, pres., 1985-86; sec.-treas. Insulation Removal Co., 1986—. lectr. in field. Bd. dirs. Eagle Scout Assn., Cleve., 1973-84; active Boy Scouts Am. Served with U.S. Army, 1944-46. Mem. Am. Pollution Control Assn., Water Pollution Control Fedn. Advocations: swimming; hiking; computer programming. Address: 4022 Stonehaven Rd Cleveland OH 44121

DANZIG, JEFFREY A., lawyer; b. Lebanon, Penn., Mar. 23, 1959; s. Howard S. and Tr dy (Frankel) D.; m. Wendy Hope Ketai, May 4, 1986. BA with honors, Mich. State U., 1981; JD, U. Detroit, 1984. Bar: Mich. 1984, U.S. Dist. Ct. (ea. dist.) Mich. 1984. Assoc. Lopatin, Miller, et al, Detroit, 1984-85; in house counsel The Mains Group, Detroit, 1985—, v.p. adminstrv. affairs, 1985—. Bd. dirs. Greenbrooke Condo Assn., Southfield, Mich., 1986—. Mem. ABA, Assn. Trial Lawyers Am., Mich. Trial Lawyers Assn., Nat Law Jour. Soc. Avocations: reading, sports, plants, gardening. Home: 25276 Maplebrooke Southfield MI 48034 Office: Lopatin Miller et al 511 E Larned Detroit MI 48226

DANZIGER, GERTRUDE, metal fabricating mfg. co. exec.; b. Chgo., Oct. 24, 1919; d. Isidor and Clara (Fuchs) Seelig; student Northwestern U., 1937-40, U. Wis., 1945; m. Sigmund H. Danziger (dec.); children—Robert, Steven, James, Charles. Sec., treas. Homak Mfg. Co., Chgo. 1955-78, pres., 1979—, also dir. Patentee mech. and design process. Office: 4433 S Springfield St Chicago IL 60032

DAOUD, GEORGE JAMIL, hotel and motel consultant; b. Beirut, Oct. 20, 1948; came to U.S., 1958, naturalized, 1970; s. Jamil G. and Shafika E. Daoud; B.S., N.Y.U., 1967; M.P.S., Cornell U., 1969; m. Barbara A. Fisco, Apr. 30, 1972; 5 children. Gen. mgr. Holiday Inn, New London and Groton, Conn., 1974-75, Gentle Winds Beach Resort, St. Croix, V.I., 1975-78; pres., cons. Motor Inn Mgmt., Inc., Dayton, Ohio, 1973—; pres. Central Services Group, Inc., First Group, Inc., Host Mgmt., Inc., The Inn Group, Inc., , 1981—, Metro Markets, Inc., Triad Ventures, Inc. (all Dayton), 1980-86; v.p. V.I. Hotel and Motel Assn., 1976. Mem. Am. Hotel and Motel Assn. (mem. Ednl. Inst., cert. hotel adminstr.), Ohio Hotel and Motel Assn., Nat. Assn. Rev. Appraisers, Cert. Real Estate Rev. Appraisers. Republican. Roman Catholic. Club: Masons. Office: Host Mgmt Inc 18 W 1st St Suite 100 Dayton OH 45402

DARCHUN, LINO AUKSUTIS, nightclub owner; b. Chgo., Mar. 4, 1942; s. Joseph and Ursula (Shimkus) D.; m. Patricia Marcy Sobel, Sept. 1, 1978 (div. Sept. 1979); m. Mary Lynn Burchette, Nov. 11, 1983; 1 child, Matthew. Student, So. Ill. U., 1960-62, 65, U. Ill., Chgo., 1966. Agt. Eastern Airlines, Chgo., 1967-68; sta. mgr. World Airways, Oakland, Calif., 1968-71; mgr. The Bulls Restaurant-Nightclub, Chgo., 1971-73; pres. The Bulls Restaurant, Chgo., 1977—; v.p. Leber-Darchun, Inc., Chgo., 1973-74; adminstr. dept. aviation City of Chgo., 1974-77. Chmn. com. Old Wicker Park, Chgo., 1972-73; vol. Grant Hosp., Chgo.; bd. dirs. St. Joseph's Hosp. Early Guidance Program, Chgo., Lincoln Park Inter-Agy. Council. Served to sgt. U.S. Army, 1962-65. Mem. Nat. Restaurant Assn., Ill. Restaurant Assn., Chgo. Conv. and Visitors Bur., Lincoln Park C. of C. (chmn. human services com. 1987—, bd. dirs.), Lincoln Park Zool. Soc., Lincoln Park Conservation Assn. (bd. dirs.). Democrat. Unitarian. Avocations: travel, music, epicure, arts. Home: 3100 N Sheridan Rd Chicago IL 60657 Office: Candide Inc/Bulls Jazz Nightclub 1916 N Lincoln Park W Chicago IL 60614

D'ARCY, JOHN MICHAEL, bishop; b. Brighton, Mass., Aug. 18, 1932. Student, St. John's Sem., Brighton, 1949-57; ThD, Angelicum U., Rome, 1968. Ordained priest Roman Cath. Ch., 1957. Spiritual dir., prof. theology St. John's Sem., 1968-85; ordained titular bishop of Mediana and aux. bishop of Boston Archdiocese of Boston, 1975-85; bishop Archdiocese of Ft. Wayne-South Bend, Ind., 1985—. Office: Diocese of Ft Wayne-South Bend PO Box 390 Fort Wayne IN 46801

DARICHUK, W. M., provincial judge. Judge Ct. of Queen's Bench, Dauphin, Man., Can. Office: Court of Queen's Bench, Court House Box 604, Dauphin, MB Canada R7N 2V4 *

DARK, T. R., brokerage house executive; b. Grand Rapids, Mich., Jan. 24, 1934; s. C. Maurice and E. Ruth (Hogan) D.; m. Sharon A. Kelly, Oct. 15, 1971; 1 child, Nancy A. BBA, Aquinas Coll., 1956; MBA in Fin., U. Mich., 1958. Trust investor Old Kent Bank, Grand Rapids, Mich., 1958-61; security analyst R.F. Newman, Milw., 1962-64; research dir. William C. Roney & Co., Detroit, 1965-70, broker, 1971-78; security analyst Security Supervisors, Chgo., 1970; v.p. research First Heritage Corp., Southfield, Mich., 1978—; Pres. Corporate Appraisals, Inc., Troy, Mich., 1978—. Contbr. fin. column Detroit Free Press. Commr. Grand Rapids Pub. Lib., 1964. Served to sgt. Mich. N.G., 1952-70. Mem. Nat. Assn. Security Dealers (prin.), Detroit Soc. Security Analysts, Inst. Bus. Appraisers. Home: 2556 Charnwood Dr Troy MI 48098-2109 Office: First Heritage Corps 26877 Northwestern Hwy PO Box 5077 Southfield MI 48086

DARLEY, JOHN GORDON, psychologist, educational administrator; b. Pitts., Feb. 20, 1910; s. William Watson and Edith (Gordon) D.; m. Kathleen Berry McConnon, Aug. 15, 1936 (div. May 1975); children: John McConnon Darley, Janet Berry Darley Griffith; m. Janet M. Hively, Nov. 26, 1976. BA, Wesleyan U., 1931; MA, U. Minn., 1932, PhD, 1937. Diplomate Am. Bd. Profl. Psychology; lic. consulting psychologist, Minn. Dir. student counseling bur. U. Minn., Mpls., 1935-43, 46-47, assoc. dean grad. sch., 1947-59, chmn. psychology dept., 1963-75, prof. psychology, 1975-78, prof. emeritus, 1978—; exec. officer Am. Psychol. Assn., Washington, 1959-62. Author numerous monographs, books, tech. reports, articles to profl. and scholarly jours.; editor Jour. Applied Psychology, 1955-60, Am. Psychologist, 1959-62, Psychol. Documents, 1982-85. Served to lt. USNR, 1944-46. Decorated Strong Meml. medal for research in interest measurement, 1966. Fellow Am. Psychol. Assn., Minn. Psychol. Assn. (award for disting. contbns. 1982), Phi Beta Kappa, Sigma Xi. Club: Cosmos (elected mem.). Avocations: detective stories, golf, bridge. Home: 1200 Nicollet Mall #201 Minneapolis MN 55403

DARLEY, WILLIAM JOSEPH, fire apparatus and municipal supplies manufacturing company executive, mechanical engineer; b. Chgo., July 17, 1928; s. William Stuart and Mary Josephine (Bartik) D.; m. Francis B. Darley; children—Stephen, Peter, Thomas, Paul, Krina, James, Anne. M.E., Purdue U., 1950. Engr., W. S. Darley & Co., Chippewa Falls, Wis., 1950-51, Chgo., 1951-55, sales mgr., Melrose Park, Ill., 1955-70, v.p., 1970-79, pres., 1979—; tech. com. Nat. Fire Protection Assn., Quincy, Mass., 1980—. Pres., River Forest Service Club, River Forest, Ill., 1978-80; bd. mem. Soc. Samaritans, Chgo., 1980-84; bd. mem. World Without Wars, Chgo., 1980-84. Recipient Outstanding Service award Cuerpo de Bomberos, Valparaiso, Chile, 1973, Small Bus. Man of Yr. award region V GSA, 1986. Mem. Fire Apparatus Mfrs. Assn. (v.p. 1983-86, pres. 1986-87), Internat. Assn. Fire Instrs., Soc. Automotive Engrs., Truck Body and Equipment Assn., Chgo. C. of C. and Industry, Central Am. Fireman's Assn. (hon.). Roman Catholic. Office: WS Darley & Co 2000 Anson Dr Melrose Park IL 60160

DARLING, ALBERTA STATKUS, art museum executive; b. Hammond, Ind., Apr. 28, 1944; d. Albert William and Helen Anne (Vaicunas) Statkus; m. William Anthony Darling, Aug. 12, 1967; children—Elizabeth Suzanne, William Anthony. B.S., U. Wis., 1967. English tchr. Nathan Hale High Sch., West Allis, Wis., 1967-69, Castle Rock High Sch., Colo., 1969-71; community vol. work, Milw., 1971—; cons. orgn. devel., Milw., 1982—; dir. mktg. and communications Milw. Art Mus., 1983—. A founder Goals for Greater Milw. 2000, 1980-84; co-chair Action 2000, 1984-86; bd. dirs., exec. com. United Way, Milw., 1982—, chair project 1985, 1984-85; founder Today's Girls/Tomorrow's Women, Milw., 1982—; pres. Jr. League Milw., 1980-82, Planned Parenthood Milw., 1982-84, Future Milw., 1983-85. Recipient Vol. Action award Milw. Civic Alliance, 1984, Community Service award United Way, 1984, Leader of Future award Milw. Mag., 1985, Nat. Assn. Community Leadership Orgn. award, 1986.Mem. Greater Milw. Com., TEMPO Profl. Women, Am. Mktg. Assn. (Marketer of Yr. 1984), Pub. Relations Soc. Am., Internat. Assn. Bus. Communicators. Republican. Avocations: travel, art history, contemporary American literature, golf, tennis. Home: 1325 W Dean Rd Milwaukee WI 53217 Office: Milw Art Mus 750 N Lincoln Memorial Pkwy Milwaukee WI 53217

DARLING, CHARLES DAVID, III, facilities and services planner; b. Elkhart, Ind., Nov. 2, 1949; s. Charles David Jr. and Marilyn May (Busenburg) D.; m. Melissa Ann Meece, Sept. 12, 1970; children: Megan Jennifer, Charles David IV. BArch, U. Cin., 1974. Registered architect, Ohio. Head bldg. dept. City of Loveland, Ohio, 1975-76; plans examiner Hamilton County, Cin., 1976-80; dir. design and constrn. Univ. Hosp., Cin., 1980-85; asst. dir. design and constrn. U. Cin., 1985-86, dir. facilities and services planning, 1986—; cons. mem. facilities adv. com. Bd. Edn., Cin., 1985—. Mem. AIA. Republican. Episcopalian. Clubs: Faculty (U. Cin.), North Hills Swim (Cin.). Avocations: sailing, writing fiction. Home: 1611 Peaslee Ave Cincinnati OH 45224 Office: U Cin 3333 Vine St ML 186 Cincinnati OH 45221

DARLING, LAWRENCE DEAN, engineer, computer aided design manager; b. Springfield, Ill., Dec. 20, 1936; s. John Darling and Virginia (Siltman) Vice; divorced; 1 child, Tena Louise. BSME, Northwestern U., 1960. Registered profl. engr., Ill. With Allis-Chalmers, Springfield, 1956-74; product engr. Fiat-Allis, Springfield, 1974-83; computer aided design mgr. controls div. Singer (name now Eaton), Schiller Park, Ill., 1984—. Named Outstanding Dir., Springfield Jaycees, 1964. Mem. Am. Soc. Mech. Engrs. Baptist. Avocations: bowling, reading, motorcycle and auto racing. Office: Eaton Controls Div 191 E North Ave Carol Stream IL 60188

DARLING, ROBERT HOWARD, lawyer; b. Detroit, Oct. 29, 1947; s. George Beatson and Jeanne May (Mainville) D.; m. Cathy Lee Trygstad, Apr. 30, 1970; children—Bradley Howard, Brian Lee, Kara Kristine, Blake Robert. B.S. in Mech. Engring., U. Mich., 1969, M.S. in Mech. Engring., 1971; J.D., Wayne State U., 1975. Bar: Mich. 1975, U.S. Dist. Ct. (ea. dist.) Mich. 1975, U.S. Ct. Appeals (6th cir.) 1975. Engr., Bendix Corp., Ann Arbor, Mich., 1970, Ford Motor Co., Dearborn, Mich., 1972-73; ptnr. Philo, Atkinson, Darling, Steinberg, Harper and Edwards, Detroit, 1975-81; sr. ptnr. Sommers, Schwartz, Silver & Schwartz, Southfield, Mich., 1981—. Author: Michigan Products Liability, 1982; Michigan Premises Liability, 1984. Mem. ABA, Assn. Trial Lawyers Am., Mich. Trial Lawyers Assn. (exec. bd. 1981—, publs. chmn. 1981-85, products liability chmn. 1986—), Met. Detroit Trial Lawyers Assn. (mem. exec. bd. 1981—), Oakland County Trial Lawyers Assn., State Bar Mich., Detroit Bar Assn., Plymouth Hist. Soc., Pi Tau Sigma. Episcopalian. Avocations: numismatics; history; golf. Home: 12940 Portsmouth Crossing Plymouth MI 48170 Office: Sommers Schwartz Silver Schwartz 1800 Travelers Tower Southfield MI 48076 Office: 747 S Main St Plymouth MI 48170

DARMODY, ROBERT GEORGE, science educator; b. Washington, Nov. 29, 1949; s. Philip A. and Ruth E. (Schorr) D.; m. Susan M. Thomas, June 24, 1978. BS, U. Md., 1972, MS, 1975, PhD, 1980. Asst. prof. U. Ill., Urbana, 1981—. Contbr. articles to sci. jour. Mem. Am. Soc. Agronomy, Soil Sci. Soc. Am., Ill. Soil Classifises Assn. (newsletter editor). Avocations: photography, camping. Home: 809 W Clark Champaign IL 61820 Office: U Ill Dept Agronomy 1102 S Goodwin Ave Urbana IL 61801

DARNALL, ROBERT J., steel company executive. married. BA in Math., DePauw U., 1960; BCE, Columbia U., 1962; MBA, U. Chgo., 1973. With Inland Steel Co., Chgo., 1963—; gen. mill foreman Inland Steel Co., East Chicago, Ind., 1967-68, asst. supt., 1969-1970, supt., 1971-75, then asst. to v.p. steel mfg., asst. gen. mgr. flat product mills, gen. mgr., 1979, v.p. engring and corp. planning, 1981; exec. v.p. Inland Steel Co., Chgo., 1982, pres., 1984-86, chief operating officer integrated steel segment, 1984-86; pres., chief operating officer Inland Steel Industries, Inc., Chgo., 1986—, also bd. dirs. Active Flossmoor (Ill.) Community Ch., Jr. Achievement, Calumet Coll., Whiting, Ind.; assoc. Northwestern U., Chgo. Theol. Sem.; bd. dirs., United Way, Crusade of Mercy, United Way Suburban Chgo.; trustee DePauw U., Glenwood Sch. for Boys. Mem. Am. Iron and Steel Inst., Assn. Iron and Steel Engrs., Ill. Mfrs. Assn. (bd. dirs.). Office: Inland Steel Industries Inc 30 W Monroe St Chicago IL 60603 *

DARNALL, THOMAS STEELE, JR., financial executive; b. Birmingham, Ala., Aug. 9, 1936; s. Thomas Steele and Janice (Dollins) D.; m. Carol Jane Baker, Sept. 30, 1967. B.A. in Econs., U. of South, 1957. Chartered fin. analyst. Ptnr. W. E. Hutton & Co., N.Y.C., 1963-70; pres. Standard & Poors Counseling Corp., N.Y.C., 1971-73; sr. v.p. Centerre Trust Co., St. Louis, 1973—. Trustee U. of South, Sewanee, Tenn., 1976-84, bd. regents, 1983—. Served with U.S. Army, 1957-58. Republican. Episcopalian. Clubs: Old Warson Country (St. Louis); University (N.Y.C.). Home: 201 Graybridge Saint Louis MO 63124 Office: Centerre Trust Co 510 Locust Saint Louis MO 63101

DARNELL, GERALD THOMAS, automotive company executive, consultant; b. Detroit, Apr. 21, 1942; s. William C. and Nadine L. (Evans) D.; m. Janet M. Harns, Feb. 14, 1981; 1 child, Rebecca F. AB, Wayne State U., 1971; BA, Faith Coll., Morgantown, Ky., 1973; MA, Pacific Western U., 1986. Various supr. and adminstrv. positions Chevrolet Motor Div., Detroit, 1968-84; mgr. Quality Inst., Gen. Motors, Troy, Mich., 1984—; instr. Wayne State U., Detroit, 1976-84; cons. Darnell Assocs., Clarkston, Mich., 1979-84. Bd. dirs. Northcrest Condominium Assn., Clarkston, 1981-86; chmn. Clarkston Downtown Devel. Authority, 1986-87. Mem. Am. Soc. Tng. and Devel., Inst. Cert. Profl. Mgrs. (cert.), Am. Soc. for Quality Control, Orgn. Devel. Inst. (cert.), Nat. Mgmt. Assn. Avocation: travel. Home: 8753 Sharon Dr Union Lake MI 48085 Office: Gen Motors Quality Inst 5700 Crooks Rd Troy MI 48098

DARNELL, PATRICIA ANN, laboratory director; b. South Bend, Ind., Apr. 18, 1944; d. Michael Joseph and Irene Veronica (Dombkowski) Pecsi; m. James Lee Lezak, July 23, 1966 (div. Aug. 1973); children: Keli Ann, Juli Ann; m. Thomas Michael Darnell, Feb. 28, 1976. BS in Med. Tech., Marquette U., 1966; MA, Western Mich. U., 1985. Registered med. technologist. Lab technologist aide Milw. County Gen. Hosp., 1965-66; med. technologist Meml. Hosp., South Bend, Ind., 1966-67; med. technologist, asst. to chief Meml. Hosp., St. Joseph, Mich., 1967-72; chief technologist Meml. Hosp., St. Jospeh, Mich., 1972-83; lab. dir. Mercy Meml. Hosp., St. Joseph, 1983—; advisor Lake Mich. Coll., Benton Harbor, Mich., 1976—; tchr. Andrews U., Berrien Springs, Mich., 1983—. pub. relations Berrien Horseback Riding for Handicapped, St. Joseph, 1985-86, v.p. 1986—; sec. Berrien County Sheriff Posse Auxillary, St. Joseph, 1987—. Mem. Am. Soc. Med. Technologists, Am. Soc. Clin. Pathologists, Clin. Lab. Mgmt. Assn. Republican. Roman Catholic. Lodge: Civitan. Avocations: needlework, sewing, reading, horse shows, camping. Office: Mercy Meml Med Ctr 1234 Napier Ave Saint Joseph MI 49085

DARRAGH, JOHN K., printing company executive; b. 1929. BS, Ariz. State U., 1959. Account auditor Arthur Anderson and Co., 1959-64; v.p. fin. Sorg Paper Co., Middletown, Ohio, 1964-74; with Standard Register Co., Dayton, Ohio, 1974—, treas., 1974-80, v.p. fin., 1976-80, exec. v.p., 1980-83, chief fin. officer, 1980-81, chief operating officer, 1981-83, pres., chief exec. officer, 1983—. Served to lt. USAF, 1950-56. Office: The Standard Register Co 600 Albany St Dayton OH 45408 *

DARROW, GREGORY LEIGH, physician; b. Terre Haute, Ind., June 13, 1950; s. Norman Luther and Harriet Marcella (Driskell) D.; m. Beverly Louise Hilt, Jan. 30, 1971; children: Amy Louise, Amanda Leigh, Rachel Elaina. BA, Ind. U., Bloomington, 1971; MD, Ind. U., Indpls., 1974. Diplomate Am. Bd. Family Practice. Family physician AP&S Clinic, Terre Haute, 1975-77; practice medicine specializing in family practice Terre Haute, 1977-78, Janesville, Wis., 1978—. Contbr. articles to profl. jours. Bd. dirs. Am. Cancer Soc., North Rock, Wis., 1985. Recipient Outstanding Med. Paper award Bayfront Med. Ctr., 1974, Socioeconomic Med. award Med. Econs. Mag., 1981-83; named on of Outstanding Young Men Am., Jaycees, 1979. Fellow Am. Acad. Family Physicians (chmn. Mead-Johnson com. 1984-85, pub. relations and mktg. com. 1985—); mem. Wis. Med. Soc., Wis. Acad. Family Physicians (bd. dirs. 1983—, chmn. sci. com. 1983-84, chmn. pub. relations com. 1984-85), Am. Geriatrics Soc. Home: 305 Seminole Rd Janesville WI 53545 Office: 2000 E Racine St Janesville WI 53545

DAS, MAN SINGH, sociology educator; b. Mainpuri, India, May 6, 1932; m. Promilla Das; children: Anjali, Sanjay. BS, U. Allahabad, India, 1955; G.Th., Leonard Theol. Coll., 1958; BD, Serampore U., India, 1958; Th.M., Princeton Theol. Seminary, 1960; MA in Edn., Morehead (Ky.) State U., 1961; MA in Sociology, U. Ill., 1963; PhD in Sociology, Okla. State U., 1969. Instr. sociology Okla. State U., Stillwater, 1968-69; asst. prof. sociology No. Ill. U., DeKalb, 1969-72, assoc. prof. sociology, 1972-80, prof. sociology, 1980—; lectr. in field. Author: Brain Drain in International Students, 1972; editor: Research Studies in Marriage and the Family, 1979, Contemporary Sociology in the United States, 1983, (with others) The Family in Asia, 1978, Sociocultural Change Since 1950, 1978, Communes: Historical and Contemporary, 1979, The Family in Latin America, 1980, A Legacy of Knowledge: Sociological Contributions of T. Lynn Smith, 1980, Homosexuality in International Perspective, 1980, Sociology in Eastern Europe, 1984; editor (jours.) Internat. Rev. Modern Sociology, 1971—, Internat. Jour. Sociology of Family, 1971—, assoc. editor Jour. Polit. Military Sociology, 1972—, Internat. Jour. Contemporary Sociology, 1972—, cons. editor Indian Jour. Social Research, 1971—, Free Inquiry in Creative Sociology, 1979—, editorial advisor Internat. Jour. Comparative and Applied Criminal Justice, 1977—, The Third World Rev., 1975—; contbr. articles to profl. jours. Pres. Internat. Jours., Inc., 1972—; chmn. Bishop Pryor Scholarship for Indian Christian Students, 1971; cons. Marriage and Family Counseling Service, 1975—; ordained minister No. Ill. Conf. United Meth. Ch.; minister of edn. Fourth St. United Meth. Ch., 1974-76, chmn. Commn. Religion and Race, 1978—, cons. Curriculum Resource Materials, Bd. Discipleship, Fourth St. Meth. Ch., 1981; mem. Aurora Dist. Council Ministries, United Meth. Ch., 1975-76, No. Ill. Conf. Bd. Ministries., 1975-76. Named Outstanding New Citizen of Yr., Citizenship Council Met. Chgo., 1975; Dean's Grant, No. Ill. U., 1970. Mem. Internat. Union for Sci. Study Population, Internat. Inst. Sociology, Internat. Sociol. Assn. (com. Family Research, com. Ethnic, Race and Minority Relations, com. Sociology of Migration), Internat. Assn. Family Sociolgy (gen. sec. 1972—), Internat. Sci. Commn. on Family, Internat. Conf. for Sociology of Religion, World Future Reserch Conf., Internat. Assn. Prejudice and Peace Research, Am. Sociol. Assn., Population Assn. Am., Nat. Council Family Relations, Soc. Study Social Problems, Groves Conf. Marriage and Family, Indian Sociol. Soc., Indian Anthrop. Soc., South Asian Sociologists (midwest rep. 1976—), Midwest Sociol. Soc. (chmn. Comparative Family Sociology session 1974), N. Cen. Sociol. Assn., Ill. Sociol. Assn. (chmn. spring colloquim 1971), Ill. Council Family Relations, No. Ill. Conf. of United Meth. Ch., Delta Tau Kappa, Alpha Kappa Delta. Home: 11 Fernilee Ct Aurora IL 60506 Office: No Ill U Dept Sociology DeKalb IL 60115

DAS, RATHIN C., molecular and cellular biologist, research scientist; b. Jorhat, India, Jan. 1, 1948; came to U.S., 1978, naturalized, 1984; s. Ramesh C. and Kadambini Das; m. Sushila Kanodia, Nov. 24, 1979; 1 child, Rishiraj K. B.S., Gauhati U., India, 1967, M.S., 1969, Ph.D., 1975. Lectr. U. Gauhati Coll. System, Shillong, India, 1969-75; research assoc. India Inst. Sci., Bangalore, 1975-78, U. Iowa, Iowa City, 1978-81, MIT, Cambridge, 1981-84; research scientist, Miles Labs., Elkhart, Ind., 1984-85, sr. research scientist, 1985— . V.p. Am. Soc. Microbiology, INd. Branch, 1985-86, pres. 1986-97, organizer symposium, 1986. Mem. Am. Soc. Microbiology (v.p. Ind. br. 1985-86, pres. Ind. br. 1986-87, co-organizer conf. on molecular aspects of protein secretion and membrane assembly 1985), AAAS, Soc. for Complex Carbohydrates, Soc. Indsl. Microbiology (nat. coms.), Nat. Geog. Soc. Club: Toastmasters. Avocations: philately; chess. Home: 2321 Kenilworth Dr Elkhart IN 46514 Office: Miles Labs Inc PO Box 932 Elkhart IN 46515

DASCHLE, THOMAS ANDREW, senator; b. Aberdeen, S.D., Dec. 9, 1947; m. Linda Hall Daschle; children: Kelley, Nathan, Lindsay. B.A., S.D. State U., 1969. Fin. investment rep.; chief legis. aide, field coordinator Sen. James Abourzek, 1973-77; mem. 96th-97th Congresses from 1st S.D. Dist., 98th-99th Congresses at large, 1983-87; U.S. senator from S.D. 1987—. Served to 1st lt. USAF, 1969-72. Democrat. Office: US Senate 317 Hart Bldg Washington DC 20510

DASH, RAYMOND, computer scientist; b. Phila., Oct. 5, 1932; s. Joseph and Ida (Weinberg) D.; m. Mary A. Karon; children: marlene, Suzanne, Richard. BS in Math., Temple U., 1954; postgrad., U. Pa., 1959-61. Cert. data processor. Mathematician Gen. Electric, Phila., 1958-59; systems mgr. RCA Corp., Chery Hill, N.J., 1959-67; assoc. dir. computer ctr. Northwestern U., 1967-68, adj. prof., 1975—; sr. v.p. info. systems Benefit Trust Life, Chgo., 1968—. Served to 1st lt. U.S. Army, 1954-58. Mem. IEEE, Assn. Computing Machines (chmn. bd. Chgo. and Phila. chpts., chmn. com. on chpts.). Home: 2120 Wilmette Ave Wilmette IL 60091 Office: Benefit Trust Life 1771 Howard St Chicago IL 60626

DASH, SITA KANTHA, nutritionist; b. Tunpur, Orissa, India, Nov. 15, 1942; came to U.S., 1969, naturalized, 1977; s. Nila K. and Duti (Sarangi) D.; m. Kalpana M. Mohapatra, June 18, 1967; children—Rajesh, Dave S. D.V.M., Orissa Vet. Coll., Bhubaneswar, India, 1964; M.S., S.D. State U., 1970, Ph.D., 1973. Cert. animal scientist. Vet. surgeon Kakatpur Vet. Clinic, India, 1964-68; asst. project officer Orissa Vet. Service, Bhubaneswar, India, 1968-69; research asst. S.D. State U., Brookings, 1969-73; dir. regulatory services S.D. Dept. Agr., Pierre, 1973-81; pres. UAS Labs. and United Agri-Services, Inc., Mpls., 1981—. Mem. AVMA, Am. Dairy Sci. Assn., Am. Soc. Animal Sci., Assn. Am. Feed Control Ofcls., S.D. Acad. Sci., Minn. Veterinary Med. Assn., S.D. Veterinary Med. Assn., Council Agrl. Sci. and Tech., North Central Assn. Dairy, Food, Feed and Drug Control Ofcls., Am. Feed Mfrs. Assn., Nat. Feed Ingredient Assn., N. Cen. Food Mfrs. Assn., Sigma Xi. Democrat. Hindu. Club: Lions. Contbr. articles to profl. jours. Developed DDS-acidophilus tablets and capsules for human use: Keto-Nutri-Aid, Calf Lacto Bolus, others. Home: 210 E 107th St Circle Bloomington MN 55420 Office: UAS Labs 9201 Penn Ave S Suite 10 Bloomington MN 55431

DASHNER, RICHARD FRANCIS, architecture and design company executive; b. Oak Park, Ill., Sept. 26, 1931; s. Francis J. and Margaret (Tompkins) D.; m. Alice Turner, July 11, 1954; children: Margaret Ruth, John Robert. BS, U. Ill., 1953. Sales engr. U.S. Gypsum Co., Chgo., 1956-59; with sales dept. Nat. Gypsum Co., Buffalo, 1959-67; constrn. sales G.E. Silicones, Waterford, N.Y., 1967-75, mgr. archtl. sales, 1975-77; pres. Archtl. Design Coating Sales, Wheaton, Ill., 1977—. Patentee in field; contbr. articles to profl. jours. Scoutmaster Boy Scouts Am., Wheaton, 1976; mem. camping, fundraising coms., 1977-80. Served to 1st lt. U.S. Army, 1954-56. Mem. Constrn. Specification Inst. (bd. dirs., v.p. Chgo. chpt. 1975-80, bd. dirs. No. Ill. chpt. 1980-83, pres. 1985-86, past pres. 1986-87). Republican. Presbyterian. Home: 919 N Washington Wheaton IL 60187 Office: A&D Coating Sales 215 N Washington Unit F Wheaton IL 60187

DASKAL, JAY LEONARD, obstetrician-gynecologist; b. Chgo., Apr. 14, 1938; s. Nathan and Gertrude (Brooks) D.; m. Lee Francis Mason, Sept. 3, 1961; children: Meryl, Ellyn, Sharyn. BS, U. Ill., Urbana, 1959; MD, U. Ill., Chgo., 1963. Cert. Am. Bd. Ob-Gyn. Clin. asst. prof. ob-gyn U. Ill., Chgo., 1969—; asst. chief ob-gyn dept. Ill. Masonic Med. Ctr., Chgo., 1975—. bd. dirs. United Way, Northfield, Ill., 1986. Served to capt. U.S. Army, 1965-66, Vietnam. Decorated Bronze Star. Mem. AMA, Am. Coll. Ob-Gyn (treas. Ill. sect. 1985—), Am. Fertility Soc., Inst. of Medicine of Chgo. Jewish. Home: 93 Coventry Rd Northfield IL 60093 Office: 166 E Superior Chicago IL 60611

DATTILO, JEROME JOSEPH, insurance executive; b. Cin., Mar. 25, 1942; s. Jerome Salvadore and Ruth Catherine (Holderbach) D.; m. Phyllis May Ladnow, Sept. 9, 1961; children: Dawn Marie, Kristine Lynn, Lori Ann, Karen Lee. Grad. high sch., Newport, Ky., 1960. 2d v.p. Western-Southern Life Ins. Co., Cin., 1960—. Republican. Roman Catholic. Avocations: bass fishing, photography, health and physical fitness. Office: Western Southern Life Ins Co 400 Broadway Cincinnati OH 45202

DAUB, HAL, congressman; b. Fayetteville, N.C., Apr. 23, 1941; s. Harold John and Eleanor M. (Hickman) D.; m. Cindy S. Shin, Apr. 7, 1968; children: Natalie Ann, John Clifford, Tammy Renee. B.S. in Bus. Adminstrn, Washington U., St. Louis, 1963; J.D., U. Nebr., Lincoln, 1966. Bar: Nebr. Asso. firm Fitzgerald, Brown, Leahy, McGill & Strom, 1968-71; v.p., gen. counsel Standard Chem. Mfg. Co., 1971-80; mem. 97th-99th congresses from 2d Nebr. Dist.; mem. ways and means com., subcoms. on health and social security, select com. 97th Congress from 2d Nebr. Dist.; Staff intern to U.S. Senator Roman Hruska from Nebr., 1966. Jr. pres. Nebr. Founders' Day, 1971; mem. exec. com., dir. Combined Health Agys. Drive, 1976; pres. Douglas-Sarpy unit Nebr. Heart Assn.; treas. Douglas County (Nebr.) Republican Party, 1970-73, chmn., 1974-77; mem. Nebr. Rep. Central Com., 1974-77, Congl. Rep. Agrl. Task Force, 1981—, Liability Ins. and Tort Reform Task Force, 1986 ; mem. exec. com. Rep. Nat. Congl. Com., 1981—. Served to capt. U.S. Army, 1963-68. Decorated Army Commendation medal with oak leaf cluster; named Outstanding Nebraskan, 1966; recipient Service award SAC, 1976; Outstanding Vol. of Yr. award Douglas-Sarpy unit Nebr. Heart Assn., 1976; Recipient Leadership award Coalition for Peace Through Strength, Guardian of Small Bus. award Omaha C. of C., four Watchdog of Treasury awards, 1981-86. Mem. Nat. Assn. Credit Mgmt. (1st v.p. 1977), Omaha Bar Assn., Am. Legion, 40 and 8, VFW, NAACP, Urban League Nebr. Presbyterian. Clubs: Optimists, Masons. Office: 1019 Longworth Bldg Washington DC 20515 *

DAUGHERTY, SUSAN LORRAINE, sales consultant; b. Chgo., Sept. 25, 1955; d. Forest Allan and Betty Grace (Dillman) D. Student Bradley U., 1972-76; B.A., Avila Coll., 1980, B.S., 1981; postgrad. Keller Grad. Bus. Coll., 1987—. Hemodialysis technician St. Francis Hosp., Peoria, Ill., 1975-77; saleswoman Environ. Internat., Kansas City, Mo., 1977-78; cons. APC Cons., West Palm Beach, Fla., 1978-79; saleswoman Honeywell Corp., Kansas City, Mo., 1979-83, Computerland, St. Charles, Ill., 1983-84; pvt. practice sales cons., West Chicago, Ill., 1984—. Vol. in edn. Kansas City Sch. Dist., Mo., 1978. Mem. Nat. Assn. Female Execs. Democrat. Avocations: photography; collecting music; collecting artwork. Home: PO Box 1244 Lombard IL 60148

DAUM, ROBERT MATHEW, park ranger; b. Evergreen Park, Ill., Sept. 25, 1955; s. Donald Greogory and Joan Marie (Roethel) D.; m. Mary Ann Kryscio, Oct. 11, 1980; children: Kevin, Rose. BA in Environtl. Sci., Gov.'s State U., 1977, MA in Media Communications and Photography, 1978. Park ranger Nat. Park Service, various locations, 1979—; photographer Daum Photography, Chesterton, Ind., 1979—; supervisory park ranger Nat. Park Service, Ind. Dunes, 1986—; Instr. photography workshops, various locations, 1980—. Contbr. photographs to books, calendars. Mem. Save the Dunes Council (bd. dirs. 1981-82). Avocations: running, biking, windsurfing, hiking. Office: Ind Dunes Nat Lakeshore 1100 N Mineral Springs Rd Porter IN 46304

DAUNTER, MARIA TERESA, clinical psychologist; b. Zabbar, Malta, Oct. 26, 1946; d. Azaria and Evan (Sherry) G.; m. James A. Daunter, Mar. 1, 1969; children: Dominic J., Kelly D. AS, N. Cen. Mich. Coll., 1978; BS, Lake Superior State Coll., Mich., 1980; MA, Cen. Mich. State U., 1982; PhD in Clin. Psychology, Union Grad. Sch., Cin., 1985. Clin. dir. Family Med. and Mental Health Clinic, Traverse City, Mich., 1982-84; prin., dir. Family Psychol. Services, Traverse City, 1984—; adj. faculty Northwestern Mich. Coll., 1984—; cons. Traverse City Ct. Systems, 1984—. Mem. Am. Psychol. Assn., Am. Assn. Marriage and Family Therapists, Mich. Assn. Marriage and Family Therapists, Mich. Psychol. Assn., Mich. Assn. Profl. Psychologists, World Fedn. Mental Health Workers. Avocations: skiing, reading, swimming, meditation, walking, sunset watching. Office: Family Psychol Services 3491 Hartman Rd Traverse City MI 49684

D'AURORA, JAMES JOSEPH, psychologist, consultant; b. Canton, Ohio, Feb. 10, 1949; s. James Joseph Sr. and Arsilia (Lombardi) D'A.; m. Denise Marie Linkenhoker, Dec. 28, 1974; children: Andrew David, Elizabeth Clare. BA, U. Notre Dame, 1971; MEd, Kent State U., 1974; PhD, U. Minn., 1984. Licensed cons. psychologist. Pre-major adv. Coll. of Liberal Arts U. Minn., Mpls., 1974-75; intern Bach Inst., Mpls., 1975-77, staff psychologist, 1977-79; psychologist Loring Family Clinic, Mpls., 1979-81; pvt. practice psychology Mpls., 1981-86; cons. psychologist Solstice: A Ctr. for Psychotherapy and Learning, St. Paul, 1986—; Cons. in field, 1975—; researcher Family Renewal Ctr., Mpls., 1982-85. Lectr. eucharistic minister Newman Ctr., Mpls.; co-chair Baptismal Preparation, eucharistic minister, Christ the King Ch. Mem. Am. Psychol. Assn., Minn. Psychol. Assn. Mem. Democratic Farm Labor Party. Roman Catholic. Club: Notre Dame of Minn. (bd. dirs. 1986—, sec. 1987—). Avocations: running, rock climbing, windsurfing, snorkeling, cross country skiing. Home: 1007 W 53d St Minneapolis MN 55419 Office: Solstice - A Ctr for Psychotherapy and Learning 821 Raymond Ave Suite 200 Saint Paul MN 55114

DAUT, STEVEN WILLIAM, geophysicist, geologist; b. Davenport, Iowa, May 1, 1951; s. Glenn Paul and Anna May (Herwig) D.; m. Rebecca Angeline Lannom, June 25, 1983; 1 child, William. BS in Geology, U. Iowa, 1978, MS in Geology, 1980. Geologist Mobil Oil Corp., Dallas, 1978; research geologist Iowa Geol. Survey, Iowa City, 1978-80; geologist, geophysicist Marathon Oil Co., Casper, Wyo., 1980-81; geophysicist NOMECO, Jackson, Mich., 1981-86; prin., geophys. cons. Steve Daut Consl, Inc., Jerome, Mich., 1986—. Chmn. edn. com. Sommerset Ctr. (Mich.), 1985-86; mem. allocations com. Jackson County United Way, 1985-86, adv. bd. Jackson Salvation Army, 1986. Mem. Am. Assn. Petroleum Geologists (edn. com. 1986—), Soc. Exploration Geophysicists, Internat. Brotherhood Magicians, U.S. Golf Assn. Avocations, writing, computers, magic, golf. Home and Office: 11769 Greenbriar Dr Jerome MI 49249

DAUTERMAN, STEVEN LYNN, banker; b. Bowling Green, Ohio, Jan. 28, 1954; s. James Franklin and Fannie (Smaltz) D.; m. Donna K. Gillette, Mar. 10, 1984. BA summa cum laude, Muskingum Coll., 1975; JD, Ohio State U., 1978. Bar: Ohio, 1978. Trust officer The Fifth Third Bank, Cin., 1979—. Producer Annie, Cin. Music Theatre, 1985, Barnum, 1986. Vice chmn. bd. trustees Cin. Music Theatre, 1983-87; chmn. music com. Hyde Park Community United Meth. Ch., Cin., 1987—; mem. Cin. May Festival Chorus, 1981—. Mem. Cin. Bar Assn. Republican. Avocations: choral singing, photography. Home: 7807 Heatherglen Dr Cincinnati OH 45255 Office: Fifth Third Bank Dept #00850 Cincinnati OH 45263

DAVENPORT, DONALD LYLE, engring. and real estate co. exec.; b. Eau Claire, Wis., Oct. 9, 1930; s. Douglas Benjamin and Leona Margaret (Fairbanks) D.; B.A. in Social Studies, Coll. St. Thomas, St. Paul, 1955; children—Ann, Martin, John, Donna, Jennifer. Adminstrv. asst. to regional mgr. Butler Mfg. Co., Mpls., 1955-58; corp. sec., gen. mgr. Spencer Corp., Eau Claire, 1958-60; sales mgr. Russell Structures Co., Madison, Wis., 1960; former pres. Bldg. Systems, Inc., Middleton, Wis., from 1960; pres. D Davenport Ltd., Madison, 1980—; Former chmn. bd., pres. Jr. Achievement. Served with USAF, 1950-54. Registered profl. engr., Wis.; lic. real estate broker, Wis. Mem. Metal Bldg. Dealer Assn. (pres. 1971), Profl. Engrs. in Constrn., Wis. Soc. Profl. Engrs. (former pres. practice sect.), Johns Manville Dealer Council (chmn.), ARMCO Steel Corp. Dealer Council. Republican. Roman Catholic. Club: Exchange. Home: 6646 W Chestnut Circle Windsor WI 53598 Office: 2320 Darwin Rd Madison WI 53704

DAVENPORT, GORDON, III, lawyer; b. Madison, Wis., Nov. 16, 1956; s. Gordon Jr. and Marjorie Ann (Dawley) D.; m. Jeanne Marie Lund, May 31, 1980. BBA, U. Wis., 1980, JD, 1983. Bar: Wis. 1983, U.S. Dist. Ct. (we. and ea. dists.) Wis. 1983, U.S. Ct. Appeals (7th cir.) 1983. Assoc. Foley & Lardner, Madison, 1983—. Author: Johnson vs. Misericordia Community Hospital: Corporate Liability of Hospitals Arrives in Wisconsin. Hearing examiner community devel. authority City of Madison, 1985—. Mem. ABA, Order of Coif. Club: Madison. Home: 3834 Cherokee Dr Madison WI 53711 Office: Foley & Lardner 1 S Pinchney St Madison WI 53701

DAVERMAN, ROBERT WARREN, architect; b. East Grand Rapids, Mich., Aug. 19, 1952; s. Robert James and Kathleen Morley (Hartmann) D.; m. Kathleen Anne Bolenbaugh, May 1, 1977. BS, U. Mich., 1975, MArch., 1977. Registered architect, Mich. Draftsman Osler-Milling, Inc., Ann Arbor, 1978-81; architect Bechtel Power Corp., Ann Arbor, Mich., 1981-83; group supr. Bechtel Power Corp., Ann Arbor, 1983-84; v.p. Fry Assocs., Inc., Ann Arbor, 1984—. Active Planning Commn. Manchester, Mich., 1986—; Hist. Dist. Commn. Manchester, 1985—. Mem. AIA (cert.). Republican. Methodist. Avocations: carpentry, winter sports, travel, Am. arts and crafts. Home: 421 Riverside Manchester MI 48158

DAVEY, ALICE LYNNETTE, accountant; b. Dallas, Dec. 14, 1956; d. Kenneth Roger and Susan Adele (Putman) D.;. BBA, U. Tex., 1978, MBA, 1980. CPA, Tex. Mgr. Ernst & Whinney, Houston, 1980-86; sr. mgr. Ernst & Whinney, Cleve., 1986—. Vol. Tex. Accts. and Lawyers for the Arts, Houston, 1984—; Mem. Art Symposium of Houston, 1982-86; chmn. Trees for Houston charity benefit, 1985, Jr. Com. Cleve. Orch, 1987. Named one of Outstanding Young Women in Am., 1985. Fellow Life Mgmt. Inst., mem. Houston Jr. C. of C. (membership dir. 1985-86, Best Project chmn. 1986), Am. Inst. CPA's, Tex. Soc. CPA's. Episcopalian. Clubs: Women's City (Cleve.), Cotillion of Houston (pres. 1986, dir. membership 1985). Avocations: scuba diving, aerobics, reading, politics. Home: 1801 E 12th St #919 Cleveland OH 44117 Office: Ernst & Whinney 2000 National City Ctr Cleveland OH 44114

DAVEY, WILLIAM PATRICK, physician; b. Ponca, Nebr., June 5, 1912; s. Joe and Abbie Mabel (Twohig) D.; m. Mary Joe Meyers; children: Barbara, Abbie, Patrick, Peter. BS, Creighton U., 1936, MD, 1938. Intern Creighton Meml. Hosp., Omaha, 1938-39; resident Douglas County, Omaha, 1939-40; eye, ear, nose and throat fellow N.Y. Hosp., N.Y.C., 1944-46; practice medicine specializing in ear, eye, nose and throat Sioux City, Iowa, 1938—. Served to lt. comdr. M.C., USN, 1942-47. Fellow ACS (pres. Iowa chpt.), Internat. Coll. Surgeons; mem. Iowa Med. Soc., Woodbury County Med. Soc., Iowa Acad. Ophthalmology and Otolaryngology (pres.), Sioux Valley Acad. Ophthalmology and Otolaryngology (pres.), Woodbury County Med. Soc. Home: 4714 Country Club Blvd Sioux City IA 51104 Office: 420 Davidson Bldg Sioux City IA 51101

DAVI, ANNA MARY, educator; b. Poplar Bluff, Mo., July 13, 1926; d. George Francis and Bertha Louise (Franck) AuBuchon; A.A., Three Rivers Community Coll., 1984, B.S. in Edn., U. Mo., Columbia, 1986; m. Roy Emerson Baygents, May 11, 1968 (dec. 1978); 1 son, Ralph George (dec.); step-children—Steven Warren, Edris Marie, Roy Emerson, William Michael, Jeffrey Thomas, Timothy Gregory, Patricia Joy; m. Peter Joseph Davi, Mar. 14, 1987; step-children: Carla Frances, Dennis Michael. Lab. technician, chairside asst., secretarial asst. to dentist, 1944-68; bookkeeper Baygents Holiday Inn Texaco, Poplar Bluff, 1968-78; instr. dental assisting Three Rivers Community Coll., Poplar Bluff, part-time 1972-76, full time 1976—; owner, bus. mgr., bookkeeper Baygents Mobil Service Co., Poplar Bluff, 1978-83. Sec., Butler County United Fund Bd., 1960-61, chmn. budget com., 1959-61; chmn. reunion com. Poplar Bluff High Sch. Class of 1944, 1969, 74, 79, 84; active Butler County Assn. for Retarded Children, 1974—, pres., 1981, 82, 85, 86, v.p., 1983, 84; troop com. chmn. Boy Scouts Am., Girl Scouts U.S.A., 1979-82; mem. parish council Sacred Heart Ch., 1984-86; organizing bd., sec., treas. Willhaven Residential Complex, Inc., 1982—. Mem. Am. Dental Assts. Assn. (life, treas. 1963-68, Achievement award 1967), Mo. Dental Assts. Assn. (life, pres. 1956-57, Cooperation award 1974, Achievement award 1976), S.E. Mo. Dental Assts. Soc. (life), Am. Vocat. Assn., Mo. Vocat. Assn., Mo. Dental Assisting Educators (pres. 1985-86), Mo. State Tchrs. Assn., Mo. Assn. Community and Jr. Colls., Butler County Geneal. Soc. (1st v.p. 1980-83, sec. 1985—), DAR (treas. Poplar Bluff chpt. 1980-81, chaplain 1983-86, vice regent 1987—), Butler County (Mo.) Hist. Soc. Democrat. Roman Catholic. Contbr. articles to profl. jours. Home: 725 Kinzer St PO Box 506 Poplar Bluff MO 63901 Office: Three Rivers Community Coll Three Rivers Blvd Poplar Bluff MO 63901

DAVIAS, ENRICO ESTRONDOS, small business owner; b. South Bend, Ind., July 14, 1949; s. Clifford D. and Eleanor (Williams) DaV.; m. Nery Gonzalez, June 6, 1978; children: Erico Jr., Joshua, Natasha. Cert. in Computer Concepts, Millard Fillmore Coll., 1969; BA in Sociology, Empire State Coll., 1972, BA in Elem. and Secondary Edn., 1976; Cert., U. Wis., Milw., 1982. Owner DaVias Enterprises, Buffalo, 1977—. Dir. children's plays Langston Hughes Inst., Buffalo, 1979; pres. Playwright Fireside Theatre Group, U. Wis., Milw., 1984-85; mem. Rep. Nat. Com., Zool. Soc. Milw. County. Phillip Morris grantee, 1982. Mem. N.Y. State Tchr. Placement Assn., Tchr.'s Assn. Nat. Cath. Edn. Assn. Club: Fortune Soc. Home: 2120 E Menlo Blvd Shorewood WI 53211

DAVIAS, NERY GONZALEZ, business executive; b. Buffalo, Oct. 18, 1952; d. Concepcion Gonzalez and Rosita (Leon) Glosek; m. Erico Estrondos DaVias, June 6, 1978; children—Jason, Layla, Erico Jr., Joshua, Natasha. B.A. in Sociology, Empire State Coll., 1979. Rep., DaVias Enterprises, Buffalo, 1977-81; organizer, dir. pub. relations Fireside Theatre Group/United Theatre Artist Group, Milw., 1986—. Active Rich for Poor Fundraisers, Milw., 1985; mem. Republican Nat. Com. Recipient Pub. Relations award Fireside Theatre Group, 1986. Avocation: performing arts. Office: Fireside Theatre Group/United Theatre Artist Group PO Box 92563 Milwaukee WI 53202

DAVID, BRUCE EDWARD, publishing company executive; b. El Paso, Tex., Jan. 18, 1952; s. Raymond F. and Joyce (Albright) D. Student, Kent State U., 1971, Ariz. State U., 1974. Prin. Worthprinting Pubs. Ltd., Twinsburg, Ohio, 1981—; instr. mktg. U. Akron, Ohio, 1986. Author: Profitable Advertising, 1982; editor/pub. (newsletter) Shoestring Marketer, 1984; pub. (newspaper) Akron Bus. Reporter, 1982 (Small Bus. Media Adv. award 1986). Mem. N.E. Ohio Women's Bus. Owners Assn. (bd. trustees 1986), N.E. Ohio Entrepreneurs Assn., Akron Regional Devel. Bd., Cleve. Advt. Club, Akrom Advt. Club. Home: 1791D Rolling Hills Dr Twinsburg OH 44087 Office: 82 Lincold St Akron OH 44308

DAVID, CATHY KOMISAR, financial services account manager; b. Milw., Oct. 31, 1956; d. Norman Joseph and Suzanne (Meissner) Komisar; m. Edward N. David, Aug. 11, 1985. BS in Acctg., Miami U., Oxford, Ohio, 1979. CPA, Wis.; cert. bank auditor. Audit officer Marshall & Ilsley Bank, Milw., 1979-87; acct. mgr., fin. services officer Marshall & Ilsley Data Services, Milw., 1987—. mem. planning com. Jewish Nat. Fund, 1986—; advisor Sigma Delta Tau Nat. Sorority, 1986—. Mem. Am. Inst. CPA's, Wis. Inst. CPA's, Inst. Internal Auditors (chmn. hospitality com. 1984-85). Avocations: biking, cooking. Home: 2929A N Shepard Ave Milwaukee WI 53211 Office: Marshall & Ilsley Data Services 770 N Water St Milwaukee WI 53202

DAVID, CLAYTON CUNNINGHAM, corporation executive, community college administrator; b. Topeka, July 19, 1919; s. James Cunningham and Gladys Faye (Zinn) D. B.S. in Agr., Kans. State U., 1941; student Mo. So. Coll., 1970; postgrad. W.Va. U., 1979, 81, 82. Fieldman, Pet Milk Co., Fremont, Ohio, 1945-46, head fieldman, Bryan, Ohio, 1946-48, area fieldman, Greeneville, Tenn., 1948-61, dist. field supt., Salt Lake City, 1961-65, dist. field supt., Nosho, Mo., 1965-71; owner, pres. The Youcan Co., Neosho, Mo., Columbus, Ohio, and St. Clairsville, Ohio, 1971—; assoc. prof. W.Va. No. Community Coll., Wheeling, 1976-85, dir. community edn. and coll. exploration, 1979-81; condr. mgmt. and personal devel. seminars bus. and industry. Author, pub. My Life, 1975. Pres. Greeneville United Way, 1959, Greeneville Exchange Club, 1960; mem. Utah state com. Am. Dairy Assn., 1963-65; mem. dairy adv. com. U. Mo., 1969-70; ruling elder Presbyterian Ch. Served to lt. col. USAAF, 1941-45. Decorated Purple Heart. Mem. Am. Soc. Tng. and Devel., 303d Bomb Group assn., 8th Air Force Hist. Soc., Res. Officers Assn. U.S., Air Forces Escape and Evasion Soc. (bd. dirs.), Am. Legion. Republican. Home: 19 Oak Ridge Pond Hannibal MO 63401

DAVID, NEAL, amusement company executive, architect; b. Lansing, Mich., July 19, 1950; s. Hugo John and Fyrmith Winona (Blaseck) D. BS, U. Mich., 1972, MArch, 1974. Registered architect, Mich., Colo. Project mgr. Wickes Corp., Wheeling, Ill., 1974-75; project planner Daverman Associs., Grand Rapids, Mich., 1975-78; gen. mgr. Haertl Devel., Portland, Oreg., 1978-80; marketing mgr. Auto-Trol Tech. Corp., Denver, 1980-84; v.p. marketing Skok Systems, Boston, 1984-86; dir. new product devel. Six Flags Corp., Chgo., 1986—. Mem. Am. Inst. Architects, Chgo. Found. Architecture. Republican. Club: Exec. Health (Chgo.). Avocations: piano, cooking, water skiing. Home: 900 N Lake Shore Dr #2409 Chicago IL 60611 Office: Six Flags Corp 8700 N Bryn Mawr Ave Chicago IL 60631

DAVID, RICHARD GEORGE, accountant; b. Detroit, July 29, 1956; s. George Asa and Marie (Kirdahy) D.; m. Denise Ann Anton, Aug. 14, 1983. B.B.A., U. Mich., 1978. C.P.A., Mich. Sr. mgr. Peat, Marwick, Mitchell & Co., Detroit, 1978—; pres. Ascot Assocs., Inc. Editor: Preparing for the National Model United Nations, 1980-81. Pres., Nat. Collegiate Conf., N.Y.C., 1979-82; bd. dirs. UN Assn. U.S.A. Recipient Medal of Merit, U.S. Congress, 1974. Mem. Internat. Assn. Hospitality Accts., Am. Inst. C.P.A.s, Nat. Assn. Accts. (bd. dirs. 1979-80), Retail Fin. Execs. Detroit (bd. dirs.), Mich. Assn. C.P.A.s (com. chmn. 1984-87), Southeastern Mich. Venture Group (v.p.), Mich. Tech. Council, Inventors Council of Mich. Home: 13557 Ascot Dr Sterling Heights MI 48077 Office: Peat Marwick Mitchell & Co 200 Renaissance Ctr Suite 3400 Detroit MI 48243

DAVIDSON, BARBARA TAYLOR, real estate sales agent; b. Ames, Iowa, Jan. 30, 1920; d. Harvey Nelson and Ruby (Britten) Taylor; m. Donald Thomas Davidson Sr., May 22, 1942 (dec. Oct. 1962); children: Donald Thomas Jr., John Taylor, Ann Elizabeth Davidson Costanzo. BS in Home Econs., Iowa State U., 1943. Assoc. tchr. Ames (Iowa) Pub. Schs., 1970-73; retail mgr. Gen. Nutrition Ctr., Ames, 1974-77; sales assoc. Century 21 Real Estate, Ames, 1978-82, Friedrich Realty, Ames, 1982—. Pres. Ames City PTA Council, 1950; leader, advisor Boy Scouts Am., Ames, 1952-58; chmn. Campfire Leaders' Assn., Ames, 1959-61; sec. bd. dirs. Campfire Girls, Ames, 1964-66; cons. Delta Zeta Corp. Bd., Ames, 1954-60, property com. United Meth. Ch., Ames, 1964-67; mem. Octagon for the Arts, Brunier Gallery, Med. Ctr. Auxiliary. Mem. Nat. Assn. Realtors, Iowa Assn. Realtors, Ames Multiple Listing Service, Nat. Home Econs. in Homemaking (chmn. fgn. student relations com.), Internat. Orchestra Assn. Republican. Avocations: floriculture, wildlife and forest conservation, Indian culture, fitness and nutrition, gerentology. Home: 1416 Harding Ave Ames IA 50010 Office: Friedrich Realty Sixth at Duff Ave Ames IA 50010

DAVIDSON, BRENT NORMAN, obstetrician-gynecologist; b. Louisville, May 1, 1956; s. Myles Harold and Elaine Rosemond (Goldberg) D.; m. Karen Beth Salem, Aug. 1, 1982; children: Amanda Rachel, Stephanie Elaine. BS, U. Wis., 1977; MD magna cum laude, U. Louisville, 1981. Intern then resident Women's Hosp., U. Mich., 1981-85; sr. staff physician Henry Ford Hosp., Detroit, 1985—; adminstrv. chief resident U. Mich., Ann Arbor, 1984-85. Jr. Fellow Am. Coll. Ob-Gyn (chmn. Mich. sect. 1985-86); mem. AMA, Mich. State Med. Soc., Am. Fertility Soc. (assoc.), Phi Beta Kappa, Phi Kappa Phi, Alpha Omega ALpha. Republican. Jewish. Avocations: racquetball, photography. Home: 3187 Winchester West Bloomfield MI 48033 Office: Henry Ford Hosp 6777 W Maple West Bloomfield MI 48033

DAVIDSON, ELOISE GROGG, foundry executive; b. Pontiac, Mich., Dec. 26, 1925; d. Roger Vernon amd Wanda (Leiter) Grogg; m. Carroll Frick Davidson, Oct. 3, 1951 (dec. Oct. 1979); children: Gregg Randall, Bradd Jeffrey. AS in Acctg., Ivy Tech. Coll., 1976; student, Ind. U., 1977—. Sec., treas. Foley Pattern Co., Auburn, Ind., 1967—. Trustee, bd. dirs. Auburn Presbyn. Ch., 1984—. Mem. Auburn C. of C., Entre Nous Literary Club. Republican. Avocations: reading, sewing, home decorating, sports. Home: 1304 Kiblinger Pl Auburn IN 46706 Office: Foley Pattern Co Inc 500 W 11th St Auburn IN 46706

DAVIDSON, GORDON ALAN, real estate manager; b. Storm Lake, Iowa, Dec. 2, 1946; s. Everett Claire and Eleanor Lucille (Kaufmann) D.; m. Debra Herby Daman, Dec. 1, 1973; 1 child, Pilar Meggan. B.A., U. No. Iowa, 1974; postgrad. Inst. Real Estate Mgmt., 1980. Accredited resident mgr. Asst. mgr. Kinney Shoes, Omaha, Des Moines, 1974-75; resident mgr. Iowa Realty, Des Moines, 1975-80; property mgr. Elkhorn Property Service, Waterloo, Iowa, 1980-86, pres., 1986—.Decorated Vietnam Cross of Gallantry, Nat. Def. medal, Navy Expeditionary medal, Vietnam Service medal, Vietnam Campaign medal, Meritorious Unit Commendation. Ruling elder Westminster Presbyterian Ch., Waterloo, 1985-87. Home: 1521 E Mitchell Ave Waterloo IA 50702 Office: Elkhorn Property Services Corp 1521 E Mitchell Ave Waterloo IA 50702

DAVIDSON, HAROLD FRENCH, JR., firearm company executive; b. Chgo., July 26, 1920; s. Harold French and Hazel Louise (Ward) D.; m. Clara I. Wendling, July 18, 1948 (dec. Apr. 1981); children: Harold French III, Doulgas, Roger, Kenneth, William II. Student, U. Minn., 1946, U. Ill., 1947-48. With Brink's Inc., Chgo., 1946-80; owner Harold Firearm Service/ Supply CO., Chgo., 1980—; police firearm instr., 1948-81. Served with U.S. Army, 1941-45. Mem. Nat. Sporting Goods Assn., Nat. Shooting Sports Found., Nat. Def. Preparedness Assn., Am. Legion (comdr. 1954-55). Lutheran. Lodge: Moose. Home and Office: 7295 Catherine St Merrillville IN 46410

DAVIDSON, JAMES DOUGLAS, sales professional; b. Syracuse, N.Y., Aug. 8, 1952; s. James Albert and Elizabeth Ann (Meehan) D.; m. Pamela Jean Mitchell, Aug. 31, 1974; children—Emily Ann, Alison Jean. B.S., Clarkson Coll., 1974. With Eaton Corp, 1974-80; sales rep. Midwest Tech. Sales, Lenexa, Kans., 1985—. Mem. Assn. of Old Crows, Internat. Platform Assn. Republican. Lutheran. Avocations: golf; gardening, woodworking. Home: 10422 W 52d Circle Shawnee KS 66203 Office: Midwest Tech Sales Inc 15301 W 87th St Pkwy Suite 200 Lenexa KS 66219

DAVIDSON, JOHN A., state senator, chiropractor; b. Westpoint, Miss., Aug. 31, 1924; s. Homer F. and Anna (Grosboll) D.; D.C., Nat. Coll. Chiropractic, 1951; m. Shirley Beard, 1953; children—Ann, Jane, John. Chiropractor, Springfield, Ill.; trustee, Found. Chiropractic Edn. and Research, 1967—. Mem. and asst. supr. for Capital Twp., Sangamon County (Ill.) Bd. Suprs., 1959-72, chmn., 1970-72; mem. Ill. State Senate, 1973—; asst. minority leader. Served in AC, USN, 1943-46; PTO. Decorated Air medal, others. Fellow Internat. Coll. Chiropractic; mem. Ill. Chiropractic Soc. (Chiropractor of Yr. 1962), Am. Chiropractic Assn. (Chiropractor of Yr. 1973), Am. Legion. Methodist. Lodges: Masons, Elks. Office: 721 Myers Bldg Springfield IL 62701

DAVIDSON, JOHN HUNTER, agriculturist; b. Wilmette, Ill., May 16, 1914; s. Joseph and Ruth Louise (Moody) D.; m. Elizabeth Marie Boynton, June 16, 1943; children—Joanne Davidson Hildebrand, Kathryn Davidson Bouwens, Patricia. B.S. in Horticulture, Mich. State U., 1937, M.S. in Plant Biochemistry, 1940. Field researcher agrl. chems. Dow Chem. Co., Midland, Mich., 1936-42, with research and devel. dept. agrl. products, 1946-72, tech. adviser research and devel. agrl. products, 1972-80, tech. adviser govt. relations, 1980-84, cons., 1984—. Active Republican Party, Mich. Served to lt. USNR, 1945. Mem. Am. Chem. Soc., Am. Soc. Hort. Sci., Weed Sci. Soc., Am. Pathol. Soc., N.Y. Acad. Sci., Phi Kappa Phi, Alpha Zeta. Presbyterian. Club: Exchange of Midland. Contbr. articles on plant pathology and weed control to profl. jours. Home: 4319 Andre Midland MI 48640 Office: Dow Chem Co PO Box 1706 Midland MI 48640

DAVIDSON, JOHN KENNETH, SR., sociologist, educator; b. Augusta, Ga., Oct. 25, 1939; s. Larcie Charles and Betty (Corley) D.; m. Josephine Frazier, Apr. 11, 1964; children: John Kenneth, Stephen Wood. Student, Augusta Coll., 1956-58; B.S. in Edn, U. Ga., 1961, M.A., 1963; Ph.D., U. Fla., 1974. Asst. prof. dept. psychology and sociology Armstrong State Coll., Savannah, Ga., 1963-67; asst. prof. sociology Augusta Coll., 1967-74; acting chmn., asst. prof. dept. sociology Ind. U., South Bend, 1974-76; asso. prof. sociology U. Wis., Eau Claire, 1976-78; prof. U. Wis., 1978—, spl. projects asst. to dean grad. studies and univ. research, 1987—, chmn. dept. sociology, 1976-80; cons. family life edn.; research cons. dept. ob-gyn Med. Coll. Ga., Augusta, 1969-74, pediatrics, 1972-73, also asso. dir. health care project, 1971-73, research instr., summer 1971, research asso., summer 1972-73, research cons. dept. community dentistry, 1974-79; program coordinator Community Devel. in Process Phase II and III, Title I Higher Edn. Act of, 1965, 1970; mem. sociology and anthropology com. Univ. System Ga., 1970-74, chmn. curriculum sub-com., 1970-72; dir. Sex Edn., The Public Schs. and You project Ind. Com. on Humanities, 1975. Assoc. editor: Jour. Marriage and the Family, 1975-85, Jour. Deviant Behavior, 1979—, Sociological Inquiry, 1986—; contbr. articles to profl. jours. Past state chmn. public affairs Ind. Assn. Planned Parenthood Affiliates, 1975-76; past mem. Eau Claire Coordinating Council.; Former bd. dirs. Planned Parenthood North Central Ind., also past chmn. public affairs com., 1975-76; former bd. dirs., former 1st v.p., mem. resources allocation com. Wis. Family Planning Coordinating Council; bd. dirs., former mem. exec., info., internat. and edn. coms., chmn. social sci. research com. Assn. for Vol. Sterilization; bd. dirs. Planned Parenthood of Wis., Inc.; former mem. Eau Claire County Adv. Health Forum, Eau Claire County Task Force on Family Planning. Mem. Am. Sociol. Assn., Am. Home Econs. Assn., Wis. Econs. Assn., Wis. Sociol. Assn., So. Sociol. Soc., Mid-South Sociol. Assn., Midwest Sociol. Soc., Nat. Council Family Relations (past chmn. com. standards and criteria for cert., former mem. devel. com. and cert. com.), Wis. Council Family Relations (bd. dirs., exec. com., past pres.), Soc. Sci. Study Sex, Soc. Study Social Problems, Augusta Coll. Alumni Soc., U. Fla. Alumni Soc., U. Ga. Alumni Soc., Groves Conf., Pres.'s Club U. Wis.-Eau Claire, Kappa Delta Pi, Phi Kappa Phi, Phi Theta Kappa, Alpha Kappa Delta (editor nat. newsletter 1979-83, past mem. exec. council). Episcopalian. Home: 1305 Nixon Ave Eau Claire WI 54701 Office: Dept Sociology U Wis Eau Claire WI 54701

DAVIDSON, JOHN ROBERT, dentist; b. Peru, Ind., Apr. 28, 1947; s. John Howard and Kathryn (Loughran) D.; m. Jean-Marie Dobler, Jan. 23, 1965 (div. Oct. 1972); children: James Michael, Jennifer Renee; m. Linda Mary Seasock, Oct. 22, 1977; children: Kathryn Cherise, John Richard. BS, Purdue U., 1969; DDS, UCLA, 1972. Gen. practice dentistry Granada Hills, Calif., 1972-74; prof. clin. and community dentistry, dir. of clinics Ferris State Coll., Big Rapids, Mich., 1974-75; pvt. practice dentistry specializing in oral implantology Peru, Ind., 1975—; dental staff mem. Dukes Meml. Hosp., Peru, 1975—. Drive chmn. United Way of Miami County, Peru, 1977, 78, bd. dirs., 1977-84; mem. Utility Service Bd., Peru, 1984—, chmn., 1986; trustee 1st Bapt. Ch., Peru, 1979-82, 84—, chmn. bd. trustees, 1986. Recipient Citizen of Yr. award, Peru, 1978, Pride award, Grissom AFB Community Council, Peru, 1980. Fellow Internat. Congress of Oral Implantologists, Am. Coll. Oral Implantologists (assoc.); mem. Am. Dental Assn., Ind. Dental Assn., Wabash Valley Dental Soc., Peru Area C. of C. (bd. dirs. 1976-83, Outstanding Service award 1979), Mensa. Republican. Lodges: Masons, Elks, Rotary (chmn. scholarship com., Peru, 1975—), Scottish Rite. Home and Office: 27 N Park Ave Peru IN 46970

DAVIDSON, JUDITH ANNE, physical education educator; b. N.Y.C., Nov. 7, 1944; d. James Harold and Miriam Ruth (Karansky) D. B.S., U. N.H., 1966; cert. Chelsea Coll., Eastbourne, Eng., 1967; M.Ed., Boston U., 1974; Ph.D., U. Mass., 1983. Tchr. high sch. N. Rockland Bd. Edn., Haverstraw, N.Y., 1967-68, Newton (Mass.) Bd. Edn., 1968-76; teaching assoc., head field hockey coach U. Mass., Amherst, 1976-78; asst. prof., head field hockey coach U. Iowa, Iowa City, 1978—; owner, mgr. Atalanta Sports Ltd., Iowa City, 1979—. Contbr. articles to profl. jours. Mem. AAU Jr. Olympics Com., Iowa City, 1985, U.S. Olympic Com. Named Coach of Yr., Field Hockey, Big 10 Conf., Chgo., 1983, Coach of Yr. Big 10 Conf., 1984; nat. runner-up NCAA Final Four Field Hockey, 1984; nat. champion NCAA Div. 1 Field Hockey, 1986; nat. indoor hockey champion, 1984. Mem. N.Am. Soc. Sport History, U.S. Field Hockey Assn. (adminstrv. v.p. 1981-83, pres. 1985—, nat. runner-up in indoor hockey 1985), AAHPER, N.Am. Soc. Sport History, Popular Culture Assn. Jewish. Democrat. Home: 1106 Yewell St Iowa City IA 52240 Office: Carver Hawkeye Arena University of Iowa Iowa City IA 52242

DAVIDSON, MORRIS, surgeon; b. Milw., May 25, 1914; s. Mandel and Sophie (Dunn) D.; m. Louise B. Boettcher, June 5, 1943; children: Richard,

Susan, Elizabeth, Sallie. BS, Ind. U., 1936; MD, Ind. U., Indpls., 1938. Diplomate Am. Bd. Otolaryngology. Practice medicine specializing in surgery St. Louis, 1947—. Served to lt. col. USAF, 1939-46. Fellow ACS, Am. Acad. Otolaryngology, Am. Laryngological, Rhinological, Otological Soc. Home: 128 Frontenac Forest Saint Louis MO 63131 Office: 35 N Central Ave Saint Louis MO 63105

DAVIDSON, PAUL PATRICK, manufacturing company executive, consulting engineer; b. Goshen, Ind., May 28, 1956; s. Walter Loyal and Marian Ellen (Knecht) D. BS in Indsl. Engring. and Mgmt., Ill. Inst. Tech., 1979. V.p. Diversified Industries of Am., Syracuse, Ind., 1979-81; pres. Acutech Corp. div. Texam Corp., Houston, 1981-85; mfg. supt., cons. Labelette Co., Chgo., 1986—; Cen. Am. cons. San-Per Trading, Texam Corp., Miami, Fla., 1977—; prodn. cons. Texam Petroleum, 1982—; cons. mfg. engring. Mem. Alph Pi Mu. Roman Catholic. Club: Carlton (Chgo.). Avocations: sports, travel, flying.

DAVIDSON, VERNON A., apparel holding company executive. Pres. Apparel Mktg. Industries, Mission, Kans. Office: Apparel Mktg Industries 5700 Broadmoor Mission KS 66202 *

DAVIDSON, WILLIAM M., diversified company executive; b. 1921; divorced. LL.B., Wayne State U.; B.B.A., U. Mich. Pres. chief exec. officer Guardian Glass Co., Northville, Mich., 1957-68; pres., chief exec. officer, dir. Guardian Industries Corp., Northville, Mich., 1968—. Served with USN. Office: Guardian Industries Corp 43043W Nine Mile Rd Northville MI 48167 *

DAVIES, ROGER, geoscience educator; b. London, Aug. 29, 1948; came to U.S., 1972, naturalized, 1985; s. Trevor Rhys and Gracie Rhys (Beaton) D.; m. Corinne Marie Scofield, Oct. 29, 1977; children: Colin, Gavin. BS with honors, Victoria U., Wellington, N.Z., 1970; PhD, U. Wis., 1976. Meteorologist, New Zealand Meteorol. Service, Wellington, 1971-77; scientist U. Wis., Madison, 1977-80; asst. prof. atmospheric sci. Purdue U., West Lafayette, Ind., 1980-86, assoc. prof. 1986—; mem. Earth Radiation Budget Expt. Sci. Team, 1980—, First Internat. Satellite Cloud Climatology Project, Regional Exptl. Sci. Team, 1984—. Assoc. editor Jour. Geophys. Research, 1987—; contbr. articles and book revs. to profl. publs. Research grantee NASA. Mem. Am. Meteorol. Soc., Am. Geophys. Union, Optical Soc. Am. Avocation: sailing. Office: Purdue U Dept Earth and Atmospheric Scis West Lafayette IN 47907

DAVIES, TERENCE CARMAN, medical educator; b. Llanelly, Wales, Aug. 5, 1935; came to U.S., 1966; s. William David and Effie Amelia (Carman) D.; m. Sylvia Margaret Francis, Oct. 17, 1960; children: Nicola Jane, Lisa Anne, Rhiannon Patricia. MB, ChB, Victoria U., Manchester, Eng., 1959. Diplomate Am. Bd. Family Practice. Instr. U. W.I., Kingston, Jamaica, 1963-66; asst. prof. Med. Coll. S.C., Charleston, 1966-70, assoc. prof., 1970-76; prof. U. South Ala., Mobile, 1976-78; prof., chmn. dept. family practice U. Mich., Ann Arbor, 1978—. Contbr. over 30 articles to profl. jours. Fellow Am. Acad. Family Practice; mem. Soc. Tchrs. Family Medicine, Mich. Health Found. (sec. 1986). Republican. Episcopalian. Avocations: med. history and philosophy, classical music, fishing, sailing. Home: 2562 Blueberry Ln Ann Arbor MI 48103 Office: Dept Family Practice 1018 Fuller St Ann Arbor MI 48109

DAVIN, JOHN WILLIAM, marketing professional; b. Lockport, N.Y., Apr. 19, 1938; s. John William and Helen Margaret (McGaugh) D.; m. Mary Sharon Ryan, Nov. 24, 1963 (div. Apr. 1981); m. Ava S. Berstein, Oct. 12, 1984; children: Kristin M., Timothy J., Amy R., Patrick J., Robert P., Wendy J. BS, Canisius Coll., Buffalo, 1960, Gen. Motors Inst., Flint, Mich., 1961; MBA, SUNY, Buffalo, 1966. Product planning mgr. Philco div. Ford Motor Co., Blue Bell, N.J., 1970-73; dir. mktg. Rollei of Am., N.J.; v.p. and ptnr. Jaeger Home Ctrs., Madison, N.J., 1975-77; v.p. bus. devel. Pace div. W.R. Grace, Cleve., 1977-79; pres. Bochin-Davin & Assoc., Chagrin Falls, Ohio, 1979-82; v.p. mktg. and sales Crown div. Allen Group, Wooster, Ohio, 1982—; cons., 1970—. Mem. Soc. Automotive Engrs., Robotics Internat., Am. Mgmt. Assn., Mensa. Clubs: Fairlane, Chagrin Valley Athletic. Lodge: Elks. Avocation: antique car restoration. Home: 8890 Tanglewood Trail Chagrin Falls OH 44022 Office: Crown div Allen Group 315 Gasche St Wooster OH 44691

DAVIS, ALAN RICHARD, controller; b. Boston, Feb. 18, 1949; s. Clarence Hoyt and Estella May (Pearson) D.; m. Marcia Ann Epperson, Oct. 7, 1971; children: James Norbin, John Michael, Rebecca Ann. BA, U. Kans., 1971; MSA, U. Houston, 1976. CPA, Mo., Tex. Controller Hosp. Affiliates Internat., Houston, 1976-81; v.p. fin. HEI Corp., Houston, 1981-86; dir. fiscal services Cardinal Glennon Children's Hosp., St. Louis, 1986—. Leader Cub Scouts, Houston, 1984-86, St. Louis, 1987—. Mem. Am. Inst. CPA's, Tex. Soc. CPA's, Hosp. Fin. Mgmt. Assn. Republican. Presbyterian. Avocations: woodworking, computers. Home: 15472 Long Castle Forest Ct Chesterfield MO 63017 Office: Cardinal Glennon Children's Hosp 1465 S Grand Ave Saint Louis MO 63017

DAVIS, ALVIA B., JR., hospital system executive; b. Hutchinson, Kans., Feb. 15, 1929; s. Alvia B. and Marie (Maresch) D.; m. Jacquelyn Aurell, June 17, 1950; children: Elizabeth, Stephanie, Grant. B.A., U. Kans., 1950. Wage and salary supr. Beech Aircraft Co., Wichita, Kans., 1951-55; with Wesley Med. Ctr., Wichita, 1955—, adminstr., 1970-76, exec. v.p., 1976-81, chief exec. officer, pres., 1982-85; chmn., chief exec. officer Wesley Med. Ctr., 1985—; pres., chief exec. officer Health Frontiers, Inc., Wichita, 1982-85; govt. appt. Statewide Health Coordinating Council, Topeka, 1976-87; dir. Central Bank & Trust Co., Wichita, 1971—, Vol. Hosp. Am., Irving, Tex., 1982-85. Fellow Am. Coll. Hosp. Adminstrs. (regent 1975-81); mem. Am. Hosp. Assn., Kans. Hosp. Assn. (chmn. 1977). Lodge: Rotary. Office: HCA Wesley Med Ctr 550 N Hillside Ave Wichita KS 67214

DAVIS, ALVIN GEORGE, international trade consultant; b. Chgo., May 10, 1918; s. Isadore and Mary (Wasserman) D.; m. Rose Lorber, Dec. 14, 1940 (dec. 1980); children—Fred Barry, Glenn Martin; m. 2d, June Elizabeth, May 24, 1982. With Sears Roebuck & Co., 1936-40; gen. partner, sales mgr. Ritz Mfg. Co., 1940-41; buyer hobby dept. The Fair, 1941-43; mgr. hobby div. Central Camera Co., wholesalers, 1944; pres., gen. mgr. Nat. Model Distbrs., Inc., 1945-63; pres. Hobbycraft Exports, 1946-62; pub., editor Cyclopedia Pub., Inc., 1949-62; dir. internat. operations Aurora Plastics Corp., 1951-62, v.p. internat. div., 1962-70; v.p. Aurora Plastics Can., Ltd., 1963-70; mng. dir. Aurora Plastics Nederland N.V., 1964-70, Aurora Plastics Co. U.K. Ltd., Croydon, Eng.; expert cons. U.S. and Fgn. Comml. Service, Hong Kong; EDP internat. trade and distbn. cons.; internat. trade cons. until 1984; sr. internat. trade specialist U.S. Comml. Service, U.S. Dept. Commerce, 1971-84; lectr. Stuart Sch. of Bus. Adminstrn., Ill. Inst. Tech.; dir. Rowe Industries (HK) Ltd., Rowe Industries (Taiwan) (Singapore), Rowe Industries Ltd. Mem., chmn. People to People Com.; scoutmaster, past mem. fin. com. Chgo. council Boy Scouts Am.; info. officer, dep. comdr. CAP. Recipient Berkeley award, 1957, Hobbies award of merit Hobby Industry Assn., 1960, Meritorious award of honor, 1975. Fellow Inst. Dirs. (London), Hobby Industry Am. (hon. life); mem. Nat. Rifle Assn. (life), Soaring Soc. Am., Airplane Owners and Pilots Assn., Acad. Model Aeros. (contest dir. 1936-70), Nat. Model R.R. Assn. (life), Model Industry Assn. (dir. 1952-60, sec. 1954-57, pres. 1957-59), Hobby Industry Assn. (hon. life; pres. 1957-59), Chgo. Aeronuts (hon.). Lodges: Masons (32 deg.), Shriners. Contbr. articles on internat. merchandising to trade mags. Pub., Cyclopedia of Hobbies, 1946-62; editor Dartnell-Internat. Trade Handbook; contbg. editor Brittanica Jr., 1949. Office: 3601 W Devon 300N Chicago IL 60659

DAVIS, BARBARA SNELL, school system administrator, educator; b. Painesville, Ohio, Feb. 21, 1929; d. Roy Addison and Maybelle Irene (Denning) Snell; div.; children—Beth Ann, James L., Polly Denning. B.S., Kent State U., 1951; M.A., Lake Erie Coll., 1981; postgrad. Cleve. State U., 1982-83. Cert. reading specialist, elem. prin., Ohio. Dir. publicity Lake Erie Coll., Painesville, 1954-59; tchr. Mentor (Ohio) Exempted Village Sch. Dist., 1972-86, prin., 1986—. Trustee Old Mentor Found. Mem. Delta Kappa Gamma (pres. 1982-84), Theta Sigma Phi (charter). Methodist. Contbr. articles to profl. jours. Home: 7293 Beechwood Dr Mentor OH 44060 Office: Center St Village Sch 7482 Center St Mentor OH 44060

DAVIS, BOB J., transportation educator; b. Grand Saline, Tex., June 27, 1927; s. Frank H. and Minnie Kathryn (Crocker) D.; B.B.A., U. Houston, 1957, M.B.A., 1961, J.D., 1966; m. Alice Joyce Reagan, Oct. 22, 1948; 1 dau., Paula Lynn. Admitted to Tex. bar, 1966; traffic rep. Texaco, Inc., Houston, 1951-61; traffic mgr. Republic Steel Corp., Cleve., 1961-67; mem. faculty Western Ill. U., Macomb, 1967—, prof. transp., 1970-83, dir. exec. devel., 1970-83; mem. Macomb Planning Commn., 1971-75, Macomb Mcpl. Airport Authority, 1980-84. Served with USNR, 1944-47. Recipient Sam Harper award Purchasing Agts. Assn. Houston, 1957; named Traffic Man of Yr., Transp. Club Houston, 1966; Regional Educator of Yr., Delta Nu Alpha, 1980, 81, Regional Man of Yr., 1982, Mayleben award, 1982; Coll. Bus. Tchr. of Yr., Western Ill. U., 1981. Mem. Assn. ICC Practitioners (Clyde B. Aitchison award 1966), Am. Soc. Traffic and Transp., Internat. Material Mgmt. Soc., Ill. Pub. Airports Assn. (bd. dirs. 1982-84), Phi Kappa Phi (disting. mem. 1982). Methodist. Club: Masons. Author books, bibliographies, reports, articles in field. Home: 1111 E Grant St Macomb IL 61455 Office: Western Ill U 900 W Adams St Macomb IL 61455

DAVIS, BRUCE ALLEN, psychologist; b. Monett, Mo., Aug. 13, 1948; s. William Lester and Mable Caroline (Frederickson) D. AB in Psychology, Drury Coll., 1970, MBA, 1980; MS in Guidance and Counseling, So. Mo. State U., 1974. Lic. psychologist, sch. psychol. Examiner; cert. marriage & family therapist. Prison psychologist U.S. Bur. Prisons, Springfield, Mo., 1976; staff psychologist Greene County Guidance Clinic, Springfield, 1975-80; clin. psychologist Davis Psychol. Testing Service, Springfield, 1975—; child clin. psychologist Springfield Park Cen. Hosp., 1985-87; divorce psychologist Springfield Divorce Ctr., 1987—; psychol. cons. Social Security Adminstn., Springfield, 1981-86, Mo. Div. Family Servics, Springfield, 1985, Syntex Corp., Springfield, 1984m, Springfield Pub. Sch., 1984-86. Contbr. articles to profl. jour. Cons. Greene County Mental Health Soc., Springfield, 1985-86. Mem. Am. Psychol. Assn., Mo. Psychol. Assn., Ozark Area Psychol. Assn., Am. Assn. Marriage and Family Therapists, Mo. Assn. Marriage and Family Therapists, Ozark Area Marriage and Family Therapists, Mensa (test adminstr. 1984—), Kappa Alpha. Republican. Mem. Christian Ch. Avocation: tech. analysis of stocks and bonds for investments. Home: 1240 S Saratoga Springfield MO 65804

DAVIS, CHARLES JOSEPH, security specialist; b. Portland, Oreg., July 8, 1948; s. Melvin E. and Eloise (Pashak) D.; m. Scottie Lynn Nix, July 31, 1970 (div. 1978); children—Jeffrey S., Amy L.; m. Sheryl Marie Dwyer, Sept. 2, 1980. B.A., Western Wash. U., postgrad. U. So. Calif., 1983, Northwestern U., 1985, S.D. State U., 1986—. Enlisted in U.S. Air Force, 1971; security specialist, Korea, 1971-73, Spokane, Wash., 1973-74, Thailand, 1975, W.Ger., 1977-80, Marysville, Calif., 1981-85, Ellsworth AFB, S.D., 1985—. Tchr., asst. preacher Ch. of Christ, Rapid City, S.D., 1984. Decorated Meritorious Service medals, others. Mem. Air Force Assn., Wilderness Soc., Bibl. Archaeology Soc., Nat. Wildlife Assn. Home: 9708 A Madison Ellsworth AFB SD 57706

DAVIS, CORNELIA HAVEN CASEY, civic leader; b. Greenville, Ill., Sept. 17, 1909; d. George Farnum and Cornelia (Ravold) Casey; m. Frank V. Davis, May 9, 1936; children: James Casey, Thomas Wait (dec.), Andrew Waggoner. AB, Millikin U., 1931. Statistician Bond County (Ill.) Emergency Relief Commn., 1934-36; sec.-treas. E.H. Paul Co., Hookdale, Ill., 1957-67, Davis & Royer, Inc., Greenville, 1967-73. Pres. Greenville PTA, 1944-45; mem. Utlaut Meml. Hosp. Found., 1957, Aux. historian, 1958-59, pres. 1966-67, rec. sec., 1969-70; chmn. Bond County ARC, 1962-64, vice chmn. Ill. fund, 1966, chmn. territorial fund, 1967-68, 69, mem. resolutions com.; bd. dirs. Bond County Tb Assn., 2d v.p., 1965-67, pres. 1969-70; 1st v.p., chmn. Christmas Seals fund drive Heritage Trail Tb and Respiratory Disease Assn., 1970-71; chmn. Greenville and Bond County Bicentennial Commn.; bd.dirs. Greenville Sesquicentennial, 1965. Recipient Good Citizenship medal SAR, 1962, Disting. Service award Greenville Jaycees, 1981. Mem. Ill Hist. Soc. (life), Bond County Hist. Soc. (charter, pres., bd. dirs.), Bond County Fair Assn. (life), DAR (various coms. and offices 1935—, including dir. 6th div. 1955-56, state corr. sec. 1956-58, state chmn. 50-Yr. Club nat. chpt. 1963—), Children Am. Revolution (various offices 1955—, hon. sr. state pres.), U.S Daus. War of 1812 (various offices 1963—, hon. state pres.), Ill. Ct. Women Descs. Ancient and Hon. Arty. Co. (various coms. and offices), Daus. Am. Colonists (chmn. Ill. colonial com.), Col. Daus. 17th Century (various com. and offices 1961—, hon. pres. gen.), Colonial Dames of Am. (rec. sec. local chpt. 1969-71, 77-81, pres. 1981-83), Nat. Soc. Magna Charta Dames, Soc. Descs. Colonial Clergy, Ill. Geneal. Soc., bond County Art and Cultural Assn. (bd. dirs., sec.), Sons and Daus. Pilgrims (chmn. constn. and bylaws com. 1977), Nat. Gavel Soc., Nat. Soc. Daus. Colonial Wars, Order of Crown in Am., South Cen. Ill. Women's Golf Assn. (chmn. 1953, 66, 71) Nat. Trust Hist. Preservation, Cousteau Soc., Delta Delta Delta. Republican. Episcopalian. Club: Greenville Garden (pres. 1954-56). Home and Office: Rural Rt 2 Box 44 Greenville IL 62246

DAVIS, CRAIG STEVEN, lawyer; b. Mpls., Jan. 7, 1957; s. Gordon Louis and Eunice R. (Anderson) D. BS in Indsl. and Labor Relations, Cornell U., 1979; JD, Washington and Lee U., 1982. Bar: Pa. 1982, U.S. Dist. Ct. (ea. dist.) Pa. 1982, Minn. 1983, U.S. Dist. Ct. Minn. 1983. Jud. clk. 3d Jud. Dist. Ct., State of Minn., Austin, 1983-84; sole practice Mpls., 1985—. Vol. atty. Judicare Sr. Citizen Project, Phila., 1982. Balfour Nat. scholar, 1981. Mem. ABA, Pa. Bar Assn., Minn. Bar Assn. Office: 701 Fourth Ave S 5th Floor Minneapolis MN 55415

DAVIS, D. BARRY, manufacturing company executive; b. 1928. MBBS, Sydney U., Australia. With Squibb Corp., Princeton, N.J., 1969-79, v.p. comml. devel., 1969-71; pres., chief exec. officer E.R. Squibb and Son, Princeton, 1971-74; pres., chief operating officer Squibb Corp., 1974-79; cons. in field 1979-84; with Sun Electric Corp., Crystal Lake, Ill., 1984—. Office: Sun Electric Corp One Sun Pkwy Crystal Lake IL 60014 *

DAVIS, DAVID BRET, industrial engineer, manufacturing company executive; b. Pueblo, Colo., May 31, 1952; s. Francis Leon and Amelia (Millson) D.; m. Denise Ceceille Nelson, July 24, 1976; 1 child, Brandon Lee. BS in Indsl. Engring., Iowa State U., 1979. Systems engr. John Deere Co., Des Moines, 1980-86; project mgr. Gen. Electric Co., Ft. Wayne, Ind., 1986—; speaker Central Coll., Pella, 1985. Avocations: jogging, golf, tennis. Home: 7515 Hope Farm Rd Fort Wayne IN 46815 Office: Gen Electric Co Box 1701 Fort Wayne IN 46801

DAVIS, DAVID COLEMAN, minister, chaplain supervisor; b. Portsmouth, Ohio, Sept. 9, 1932; s. Edward Thomas and Julia Alveretta (Fox) D.; m. Barbara Kathryn Redinger, Dec. 19, 1952; children: Kathryn Sue, Kimberle Anne, Karyn Dawn. BA, Otterbein Coll., 1955; MDiv, United Theol. Sem., 1958; M of Sacred Theology, Trinity Sem., 1973. Pastor of chs. Evangel. United Brethern Ch., Ohio and Pa., 1952-68; staff chaplain St. Elizabeths Hosp., Washington, 1968-75; dir. human relations Bronson Meth. Hosp., Kalamazoo, 1975-83; staff chaplain Meth. Hosp., Jacksonville, Ill., 1983-84; dir. pastoral care Carle Found. Hosp., Urbana, Ill., 1984—. Bd. dirs. Mich. Hospice Orgn., 1978-83; bd. dirs., founder Hospice Greater Kalamazoo, 1978-83; me. clergy com. Am. Cancer Soc., Mich., 1980-82. Named Chaplain of Yr., United Meth. Health and Welfare, 1981. Fellow Coll. Chaplains (com. mem. 1981-83); mem. Assn. Clin. Pastoral Edn. (cert. supr.), Assn. Mental Health Clergy (mag. editor 1977-82). Club: Toastmasters (local officer 1979-86). Avocations: golf, photography, horseshoe nail art, camping, speaking. Home: 2508 Valkar Ln Champaign IL 61821 Office: Carle Found Hosp 611 W Park St Urbana IL 61801

DAVIS, DONALD ROBERT, accounting educator; b. St. Louis, Apr. 8, 1935; s. Howard Allen and Maude (Crow) D.; m. Mary Susannah Fleenor, July 21, 1962; children—Brian Robert, Valerie Ann. B.A.E.E., Washington U., St. Louis, 1957, M.B.A., 1960. Corp. sec. Cox-Ware Corp., Kirkwood, Mo., 1960; v.p. Mid-States Bus. Capital Corp., St. Louis, 1960-65; pres. Davco Auto Parts, Inc., Farmington, Mo., 1965-67; faculty St. Louis Community Coll., 1967—, prof. acctg., 1981—; writer software Dryden Press, Chgo., 1984—. Creater acctg. software programs. Served to 1st lt. AUS, 1958-59. Washington U. honor scholar, 1954-57; Boatman's Bank fellow, 1958, Weinheimer fellow, 1959. Mem. NEA, Nat. Assn. Accts., Mo. Bus. Edn. Assn., Mo. Assn. Acctg. Educators, Mo. Assn. Community and Jr. Colls., Tau Beta Pi, Sigma Alpha Epsilon. Office: Dept Acctg St Louis Community Coll at Meramec 11333 Big Bend Blvd Kirkwood MO 63122

DAVIS, DONALD WOODROW, healthcare consultant; b. Lamar County, Miss., July 15, 1937; s. Ewal Woodrow and Verlee (Aultman) D.; m. Vera Craig Phelps, Nov. 23, 1961; children: Deanna Lyn, Craig Woodrow. BS, U. So. Miss., 1959. Sales rep. McKesson & Robbins, Jackson, Miss., 1959-65; sales mgr. USV Pharm., Houston, 1965-74; asst. pres. Danal Lab., St. Louis, 1974-77; gen. mgr. Advanced Health, St. Louis, 1977-82; owner DWD Enterprises, St. Louis, 1982—; Owner Aunt Vera's Attic of Chesterfield (Mo.), Medi-Crush Co. of Hattiesburg, Miss., Horn Vitamin Co., Chesterfield. Patentee in field. Mem. Baxter Village Trustees, St. Louis County, 1981-84. Mem. Inst. Health Mgmt. (bd. dirs.), Univ. So. Miss. Alumni Assn. (pres. St. Louis chpt.), Delta Sigma Pi. Republican. Methodist. Avocations: running, tennis, reading. Home: 15692 Summer Lake Dr Chesterfield MO 63017 Office: DWD Enterprises 7750 Clayton Rd Suite 305 Saint Louis MO 63117

DAVIS, E. M., manufacturing company executive. Pres., chief operating officer Hobart Corp., Troy, Ohio. Office: Hobart Corp World Hdqrs Ave Troy OH 45374 *

DAVIS, EARON SCOTT, editor, publisher, environmental health law consultant; b. Chgo., Sept 7, 1950; s. Milton and Grayce Davis; m. Gilla Prizant, May 29, 1977; children—Jeremy Adam, Jonathan Michael, Daniel Benjamin. B.A., U. Ill., 1972; J.D., Washington U., St. Louis, 1975; M.P.H., UCLA, 1978. Bar: Ill., Mo., D.C. Asst. to chmn. Ill. Pollution Control Bd., Chgo., 1975-77; environ. cons. Fred C. Hart Assos., Washington, 1979-80; atty. coordinator Migrant Legal Action Program, Washington, 1980-81; environ. cons., Evanston, Ill., 1981—; editor, pub. Ecol. Illness Law Report, Evanston, 1982—. Exec. dir. Human Ecology Action League, Evanston, Ill., 1983-84; mem. nat. adv. bd. Environ. Task Force, Washington, 1984—. Author: Toxic Chemicals: Law and Science, 1982. Contbr. articles to various publs. Mem. adv. com. D.C. Lung Assn., Washington, 1980-82; Clean Air Coalition, Phila., 1983-85, spl. commendation D.C. Lung Assn., 1981. Recipient Presdl. award Am. Acad. Environ. Medicine, 1983. Mem. Environ. Law Inst. (assoc.), Air Pollution Control Assn., Assn. Trial Lawyers Am., Mo. Bar Am. Pub. Health Assn., ABA (co-chmn. com. on pub. and employee health 1981-83). Office: Ecol Illness Law Report Box 1796 Evanston IL 60204

DAVIS, EVAN CROOKS, packaging company executive; b. Elizabeth, N.J., May 12, 1938; s. Donald Graham and Eleanor Mitchel (Crooks) m. Juanita Pickett, Sept. 10, 1960; children: Brian Michael, Bradley Edward, Donald Graham, Kristin Lee. BME, Stevens Tech., 1960; JD, Detroit Coll., 1968. Prodn. supr. Gt. Lakes Steel, Detroit, 1960-62; plant mgr. Mobil Oil Corp., Detroit, 1962-69; mgr. employee relations Mobil Oil Corp., Chgo. and Phila., 1969-74; area mgr. indsl. relations Packaging Corp., Evanston, Ill., 1974-75, corp. dir. labor relations, 1975-81, v.p. employee relations, 1981—. Bd. dirs. Mt. Prospect (Ill.) Football Assn., 1980-84; commr. Mt. Prospect Police and Fire Commn., 1983-85;chmn. bd. Emmaus Bible Coll., Dubuque, Iowa, 1981—; bd. dirs. Christian Witness Support Team, Sterling, Va., 1983—. Mem. Ill. State Bar Assn., Mich. State Bar Assn., Pa. State Bar Assn., Am. Paper Inst. (employee relations com. 1981—). Republican. Mem. Plymouth Brethren. Avocations: football, baseball coaching, hist. reading. Home: 1307 Santee Ln Mount Prospect IL 60056 Office: Packaging Corp Am 1603 Orrington Ave Evanston IL 60204

DAVIS, EVELYN MARGUERITE B., artist, organist, pianist; b. Springfield, Mo.; d. Philip Edward and Della Jane (Morris) Bailey; student pub. schs., Springfield; student art Drury Coll.; piano student of Charles Cordeal; m. James Harvey Davis, Sept. 22, 1946. Sec., Shea and Morris Monument Co., before 1946; past mem. sextet, soloist Sta. KGBX; past pianist, Sunday sch. tchr., mem. choir East Avenue Bapt. Ch.; tchr. Bible, organist, pianist, vocal soloist and dir. youth choir Bible Bapt. Ch., Maplewood, Mo., 1956-69, also executed 12 by 6 foot mural of Jordan River; pvt. instr. piano and organ, voice, Croma Harp, Affton, Mo., 1960-71, St. Charles, Mo., 1971-83; Bible instr. 3d Bapt. Ch., St. Louis, 1948-54; pianist, soloist, tchr. Bible, Temple Bapt. Ch., Kirkwood, Mo., 1969-71; asst. organist-pianist, vocal soloist, tchr. Bible, Bible Ch., Arnold, Mo., 1969; faculty St. Charles Bible Bapt. Christian Sch., 1976-77; ch. organist, pianist, soloist, Bible tchr., dir. youth orch., music arranger Bible Bapt. Ch., St. Charles, 1971-78; organist, vocal soloist, floral arranger, Bible tchr. Faith Missionary Bapt. Ch., St. Charles, 1978-82; organist, floral arranger Bellview Bapt. Ch., Springfield, Mo., 1984—; tchr. piano, organ, voice, organist, Springfield, Mo., 1983-84; interior decorator and floral arranger. Fellow Internat. Biog. Assn. (life), Am. Biog. Inst. Research Assn. (life). Mem. Nat. Guild Organists, Nat. Guild Piano Tchr. Auditions, Internat. Platform Assn. Composer: I Will Sing Hallelujah, (anthems cala) I Am Alpha and Omega, Prelude to Prayer, My Shepherd, O Sing unto The Lord A New Song, O Come Let Us Sing unto The Lord, The King of Glory; The Lord Is My Light and My Salvation; O Worship the Lord in the Beauty of Holiness; The Greatest of These is Love; also numerous hymn arrangements for organ and piano. Home: RFD 2 Box 405 Rogersville MO 65742

DAVIS, FLOREA JEAN, social worker; b. Crossett, Ark., Jan. 10, 1953; d. Richard Davis and Geneva (Bedford) Williams. BA in psychology and social work cum laude, Park Coll., Parksville, Mo., 1975; MSW, Kans. U., 1982. Cert. tchr. social studies secondary level; lic. social worker, Kans. Asst dir. Northeast Counseling and Devel. Ctr., Kansas City, Kans., 1975; asst. dir., clin. supr. DRAG Alcohol Ctr., Kansas City, 1975-83; substance abuse counselor Johnson County Substance Abuse Ctr., Shawnee, Kans., 1983-85; clin. social worker Family & Children Services, Inc., Kansas City, 1975—; agy.'s field practicum instr. U. Kans., Lawrence, 1976; substance abuse specialist, cons., Kansas City area, 1985—; part time instr. Avila Coll., Kansas City, Mo., 1987—. Vol. mem. United Way Speakers Bur., 1986—. Mem. Acad. Cert. Social Workers, Nat. Assn. Female Execs. Avocations: reading, singing, tennis, travel. Home: 3196 Coronado Rd Kansas City KS 66104 Office: Family & Children Services Inc 3217 Broadway Kansas City MO 64111

DAVIS, F(RANCIS) GORDON, public relations executive; b. Bloomfield, Ind., May 21, 1908; s. Francis Gordon and Grace (Bryan) D.; m. Margaret Aletha Smith, July 13, 1931; children: Margaret Jayne Davis Johnson, Marilyn Grace Davis Johnson. Student Wayne State U., 1925-27, postgrad., 1929-30; BA, U. Mich., 1929, postgrad., 1930, 42; postgrad. Cleve. Inst. Art, 1936-37, Western Res. U., 1938-39. Reporter, aviation editor, editorial writer Buffalo Times, 1930-33; feature, editorial, sci. writer Cleve. Press, 1934-42; pub. relations dir. Mich. Blue Cross-Blue Shield, Detroit, 1942-46; exec. dir. Mich. Health Council, Detroit, 1943-46; owner F. Gordon Davis & Assocs., Roscommon, Mich., 1946—. Mem. Pub. Relations Soc. Am., Am. Hosp. Assn. (life; chmn. pub. relations adv. com. 1965, mem. 1968-71, chmn. Conf. Affiliated Soc. Pres. 1969), Ohio Hosp. Assn. (hon.), Am. Soc. Hosp. Pub. Relations (pres. 1968-69), Mich. (pres. 1975-76), Southeastern Mich. (pres. 1973-74) hosp. pub. relations assns. Club: Higgins Lake Boat (dir. 1962-65). Contbr. articles to profl. jours. Home and Office: 127 Forest Trail Roscommon MI 48653

DAVIS, F(RANCIS) KEITH, civil engineer; b. Bloomington, Wis., Oct. 23, 1928; s. Martin Morris and Anna (Weber) D.; BSCE, S.D. State U., 1950; m. Roberta Dean Anderson, May 25, 1957; 1 child, Mark Francis. With firm Howard, Needles, Tammen & Bergendoff, Kansas City, Mo., 1950—, asst. chief structural designer, 1960-65, project mgr., sect. chief, 1965-76, dep. chief structural engr., 1976-79, chief engr., 1979—. Bd. advisers N.W. Kans. Area Vocat. Tech. Sch., 1977-80, chmn., 1979-80. Served with AUS, 1951-53. Registered profl. engr., Mo., Iowa, Ind., Nebr., Mich., Colo., Ariz., Oreg. Fellow ASCE; mem. NSPE, Mo. Soc. Profl. Engrs., Am. Ry. Engring. Assn. (tech. com. 1981—). Club: Homestead Country. Home: 5024 Howe Dr Shawnee Mission KS 66205 Office: 9200 Ward Pkwy PO Box 299 Kansas City MO 64141

DAVIS, GARY WAYNE, college administrator; b. Bismarck, N.D., June 15, 1944; s. Gale Wayland and Mary Lorraine (McGillic) D.; m. Amy C. Johnson, Aug. 7, 1965 (div. Dec. 1983); 1 child, Alexandra Ellen; m. Karen J. Sams, July 9, 1987. BA magna cum laude, Morningside Coll., 1965;

postgrad., Duke U., 1965-67; PhD, U. Iowa, 1972; postgrad., N.W. Mo. State U., 1977-79, U. Mich., 1980. Teaching asst. U. Iowa, Iowa City, 1968-70; from asst. to assoc. prof. humanities N.W. Mo. State U., Maryville, 1970-78, chmn. dept. humanities and philosophy, 1972-76, chmn. faculty hearing com., 1977-80, dir. univ. honors program, 1978-81; assoc. prof. philosophy, asst. provost, asst. v.p. acad. affairs, dir. summer sessions Ill. State U., Normal, 1981-83; asst. to pres., sec. to bd. control Saginaw Valley State Coll., University Center, Mich., 1984-86; exec. dir. Ill. Community Colls. Trustees Assn., Springfield, 1986—; cons. State Com. for the Humanities, Northwest Mo. State U., mem. gen. edn. com., faculty salary com., affirmative action com., student placement com., vice presdl. search com., retention task force, rep. Coll. Arts and Scis. Council, coordinator community coll. recruitment; dir. advanced coll. experience program, Saginaw Valley State Coll., Mich., chmn. commencement com., campus ministry com. Chmn. Health Systems Agy., Northwest Mo. State U., Mayor's Task Force on Youth, Saginaw, Mich., 1985; bd. dirs. United Way, Saginaw, drive chmn., 1984-86; co-chmn. Nat. Issues Forum, 1985-86; cons. Explorer Scouts, 1985. Mem. AAUP (pres. Mo. Conf.), Am. Assn. Higher Edn., Am. Acad. Religion, Assn. Governing Bds., Am. Assn. State Colls. and Univs., Pi Kappa Delta (life). Home: 410 Mayfair Dr Lincoln IL 62656 Office: Community Coll Trustees Assn 509 S Sixth St Suite 426 Springfield IL 62704

DAVIS, GEORGE BENJAMIN, business educator; b. Cleve., Jan. 29, 1919; s. Benjamin Franklin and Julia Rebecca (Guilfoyle) D.; m. Margaret Owen Easton, Sept. 10, 1946 (dec. Feb. 1954); 1 son, Benjamin; m. Nancy Bayliss Easton, Sept. 10, 1954; children—William, David, Rachel. B.B.A., Cleve. State U., 1941, M.B.A., 1981. C.P.A., Ohio. Controller Ford Motor Co., Cleve., 1947-59; dir. budgets Lubrizol, Wickliffe, Ohio, 1960-62; v.p., treas. Donn, Inc., Westlake, Ohio, 1962-82; dir. Exec. M.B.A. program Cleve. State U., 1981-82, vis. instr., 1983—; dir. Donn, Inc., Westlake, Ohio. Pres. So. Hills YMCA, Brecksville, Ohio, 1974; bd. dirs. Cleve. State U. Devel. Found. Served to 1st lt. USAF, 1942-46, ETO. Decorated DFC. Mem. Fin. Execs. Inst., Cleve. State U. Alumni Assn. (pres. 1986). Lodges: Kiwanis (treas. 1978-82), Masons, Shriners.

DAVIS, GLENN GALLERY, library/museum facility consultant; b. Mexico City, Aug. 29, 1955; s. Glenn Tappenden and Marion Isabel (Gallery) D.; m. Megan J. MacQuilkin, Sept. 13, 1986. B.A., Lake Forest Coll., Ill., 1979; M.A., U. Chgo., 1981; postgrad. Harvard U., 1982, Northwestern U., 1984. Planning asst. Newberry Library, Chgo., 1979-81, planning librarian, 1981-82, dir. planning, 1982-85; sr. facility cons. Facility Systems Inc., Schaumburg, Ill., 1985-87, v.p. Kilian Corp., Glendale Heights, Ill., 1987—; planning cons. Harvard U./Radcliffe U., Cambridge, Mass., 1983—. Patentee in field. Fellow English Speaking Union; mem. ALA, Am. Mgmt. Club, Chgo. Library Club, Republican. Roman Catholic. Club: Caxton. Home: 1120 N Lake Shore Dr Chicago IL 60611

DAVIS, HARRY LEONARD, investment company executive; b. Hammond, Ind., Dec. 15, 1941; s. Harry L. Davis and Helen (Chizmadia) Davis Christian; m. Lissa Knudsen, Dec. 22, 1976; 1 son, Anthony Michael; m. Loretta Nelson, June 15, 1961 (div. 1967); children—Gregory A., Minette. Student pub. schs., Downey, Calif. Account exec. Internat. Precious Metals Corp., Fort Lauderdale, Fla., 1975-77; prin., exec. v.p. First Nat. Monetary Group, Southfield, Mich., 1977—, and subs. First Nat. Securities Corp., First Nat. Trading Corp., First Nat. Prodns., Inc., First Nat. Real Estate Corp., Internat. Registry Systems, Fin. Instns. Div., First Ctr. Office Plaza (all Southfield), First Nat. Home Theatres, Inc., Livonia, Mich., Franklin (Mich.) Savs. Bank. Office: 1st Ctr Office Plaza 26913 Northwestern Hwy 6th Floor Southfield MI 48075

DAVIS, HOWARD WELLS, child psychiatrist; b. Indpls., Feb. 7, 1945; s. Howard W. and Elizabeth L. (Kehn) D.; m. Susan M. Huelsbeck; children: Adam, Erik. AB, Wabash Coll., 1967; MD, Ind. U., 1971. Diplomate Am. Bd. Psychiatry and Neurology. Intern and resident Ind. U. Med. Ctr. Hosps., Indpls., 1971-75; asst. prof. Ind. U. Sch. Medicine, Indpls., 1975-82; clin. dir. Brown County Mental Health Ctr., Green Bay, Wis., 1982—. Mem. Am. Psychiat. Assn., Brown County Med. Soc. Avocations: radio control model airplanes, computer programming. Office: Psychiat Services of Green Bay Bellin Bldg Suite 501 Green Bay WI 54301

DAVIS, IRVIN, public relations, advertising executive; b. St. Louis, Dec. 18, 1926; s. Julius and Anna (Rosen) D.; m. Adrienne Bronstein, Apr. 25, 1968; 1 child, Jennifer Alison. BSBA, Washington U., 1950; postgrad., St. Louis U., 1952; D Humanities (hon.), Nat. Coll., 1981. Pres. Clayton-Davis & Assoc., Inc., St. Louis, 1953—, Admiral Broadcasting Corp., St. Louis, 1983—; v.p., bd. dirs. Nat. Acad. TV Arts and Scis., 1982—. Author: (books) Room for Three, Comprehensive Tng. in Advt. and Pub. Relations; producer (film) Family Album, 1974, Use It in Good Health, Charlie, 1975. V.p. Boys Town Mo., St. James, 1976-86, Make Today Count, 1985-86; bd. dirs. Crusade Against Crime, St. Louis, 1984-86. Served to capt. USAF, 1945-47, PTO. Recipient Freedom Found. award, 1975, Internat. Film and TV Festival award, 1973-75, Internat. Broadcasting award Hollywood Advt. Club., 1965, 77, 82, 83, Cinegolden Eagle award Council on Internat. Non-Theatrical Events, 1975. Mem. Pub. Relations Soc. Am. (accredited), Advt. Club, Press Club, Am. Med. Writers Assn. Office: Clayton-Davis & Assoc Inc 8229 Maryland Ave Saint Louis MO 63105

DAVIS, JACK, congressman; b. Sept. 6, 1935; m. Virginia Ann Griffin, 1960; children: Jill, Heather, Jack II. BA, So. Ill. U., 1956; PhD, London Acad. Scis. Mem. Ill. House Reps., Springfield, 1977-87, 100th Congress from Ill., 1987—. Served with USN. Office: US House of Reps Office of House Mems Washington DC 20515 *

DAVIS, JAMES ALLEN, concert producer and director, musician; b. Fremont, Nebr., June 1, 1955; s. Jack Gilbert and Janice Elizabeth (Myers) D.; m. Debra Ann Reding, Nov. 24, 1979. Student, U. Nebr., N.D. State U. Band leader NOAH, Omaha, 1973-76; composer, pianist Johnny Holm Band, Mpls., 1979-83; agt., owner Davis Entertainment, Omaha, 1976-79, McCarthy, Davis, Fargo, N.D., 1983-85; entertainment dir. Don Romeo Agy., Omaha, 1985—. Rec. artist The Red Ryder Band, 1979, The Johnny Holm Band, 1981, When Love Made a Fool, 1982. Named to dean' list U. Nebr.; recipient Hubert Humphrey medal Hubert Humphrey Meml. Found., Mpls., 1983. Mem. Nat. Assn. Coll. Artists (assoc.), Am. Fedn. Musicians, Rho Epsilon. Avocations: Furniture building; boating; biking. Office: 8504 Cass St Omaha NE 68114

DAVIS, JAMES CASEY, lawyer; b. Bloomington, Ind., Feb. 23, 1937; s. Frank Vivian and Cornelia Haven (Casey) D.; m. Delores Mae Evans, 1961 (div. 1975); 1 child, Sarah Haven; m. Frances Joyce Budreck, Aug. 21, 1977; 1 child, Felicia Louisa Budreck. B.A., U. Iowa, 1959, J.D., 1962. Bar: Iowa 1962, U.S. Supreme Ct. 1976. Ptnr. law firm France, Nady & Davis, Tipton, Iowa, 1963-65; exec. sec., gen. counsel Iowa Jr. C. of C., Newton, Iowa, 1965-66; assoc. firm Swanson & Davis, Newton, Iowa, 1966-69, ptnr., 1969-70; Justice of Peace, Newton, Iowa, 1967-70; asst. atty. gen. Iowa Dept. Justice, Des Moines, 1970-79; pvt. practice law, Des Moines, 1979-84; ptnr. Woodward, Davis & Rossi, 1984—; assoc. Environmental Law Inst., 1980-86 ; mediator Iowa Pub. Employment Relations Bd., 1980—, arbitrator, 1983—. Bd. dirs. Iowa chpt. Arthritis Found., 1971—, mem. exec. com., 1976-81, mem. govtl. affairs com., 1976—, chmn. 1977-83, mem. adv. com. 1981-84, , mem. nat. bd. 1976-77; Nat. Vol. Service citation 1984; mem. Iowa State Central Com. Young Republicans, 1970-75; mem. Polk County Rep. Central Com., 1984—, exec. com. 1985—, asst, county co-chmn., 1987—; Rep. candidate Iowa Atty. Gen., 1986; bd. dirs. Newton Community Theatre, 1970-73; leader Explorer Scouts Am., 1963-65. Mem. ABA (chmn. interface com. computer div. econs. sect. 1984-85, editor nat. newsletter, 1985—), Fed. Bar Assn. (pres. Iowa chpt. 1982-83, nat. v.p. 1983—, chmn. nat. computer com. 1984-86, chmn. communication & intellectual property sec. 1986—), Iowa Bar Assn. (computer subcom. 1985—), Polk County Bar Assn., Assn. Trial Lawyers Am., Assn. Trial Lawyers Iowa, Iowa Assn. Arbitrators (treas. 1983—), SAR, Sons and Daus. of Pilgrims, Descs. Colonial Clergy, Order of Crown in Am., Trout Unltd. (pres. Iowa chpt. 1974—), Delta Theta Phi. Home: 931 32d St West Des Moines IA 50265 Office: Skywalk Suite 203 700 Walnut St Des Moines IA 50309

DAVIS, JAMES J., osteopathic physician, educator; b. Niagara Falls, N.Y., Apr. 13, 1923; s. Frank and Antonina (Anteczka) Rogozinski; m. Betty A. Dombrowski, Aug. 10, 1946; children—Kingman P., Bruce J., Bradley J., Douglas P. Student Niagara U., 1941-43, U. Rochester, 1943-44, Cornell U., 1944; B.S., Canisius Coll., 1948; postgrad. U. Buffalo, 1948-50; D.O., Phila. Coll. Osteo. Medicine, 1965. Hosp. rep. Parke, Davis Co., 1951-61; gen. practice osteo. medicine, Grand Rapids, Mich., 1965-75; prof. dept. family medicine Coll. Osteo. Medicine, Mich. State U., East Lansing, 1975—; dir. three ambulatory clinics; developer, coordinator courses. Served to lt. (j.g.) USN, 1943-46. Recipient Rose Bowl prize Parke, Davis Co., 1956, 58; Deans award Phila. Coll. Osteo. Medicine, 1965. Fellow Am. Osteo. Assn., Am. Coll. Gen. Practitioners; mem. Mich. Assn. Osteo. Physicians and Surgeons, Ingham County Assn. Osteo. Physicians and Surgeons, Am. Coll. Gen. Practitioners. Roman Catholic. Club: University (East Lansing, Mich.). Contbr. articles to profl. jours. Home: 4726 Arapaho Trail Okemos MI 48864 Office: Mich State U Coll Osteopathic Medicine Fee Hall East Lansing MI 48824

DAVIS, JAMES KEITH, beef cattle breeder; b. Logan, Ohio, Sept. 29, 1939; s. Delbert Pearl and Frieda Belle (Moore) D.; m. Jan Elaine Henderson, Dec. 28, 1963; children: Kimberly Lynne, Keith Eric, Kristen Leigh. BS in Agr., Ohio State U., 1961, PhD in Animal Nutrition and Physiology, Ohio State U., 1970; MS in Animal Breeding, U. Ga., 1963. 4-H county extension agt. Ohio Coop. Extension Service, Wilmington, 1965-66; asst. prof., coordinator animal sci. Wilmington Coll. (Ohio), 1966-69; dir. research and mktg. Schearbrook Land & Livestock Inc., Clayton, Ohio, 1969-76, v.p., 1976-83, pres., 1983-84; gen. ptnr., Schearbrook Land & Livestock, Co., 1984—; pres., chief exec. officer Ankina Breeders, Inc., Clayton, 1975—; pres. Buckeye Beef Improvement Fedn., Columbus, 1978-82, Agridex, Inc., Clayton, 1981-84; v.p., sec. Deramo Properties, Inc., Clayton, 1981—; v.p. Anglais Breeding Herds, Ltd., 1976-83, pres., 1983-84; mem. exec. com., chmn. program com. Buckeye Beef Congress, 1976-78; mem. animal sci. adv. com. Agrl. Tech. Inst., Ohio State U., 1977—. Developer Ankina breed of cattle; research and publs. in field of beef cattle sci. Advisor 4-H Club, Montgomery County, Ohio; pres. Montgomery County Extension Adv. Com., Dayton; mem. prin.'s adv. com., academic policy com. Brookville High Sch.; lay leader Concord United Meth. Ch., 1980-82, chmn. council on ministries, 1983, chmn. pastor-parish relations com., 1984-85, gen. co-chmn., 1987, chmn. fin., 1987; mem. North Cen. accreditation com. Brookville High Sch., adv. com. animal sci. dept. Ohio State U. Mem. Am. Soc. Animal Sci., Am. Angus Assn., Am. Chianina Assn. (rec. sec., mem. nat. bd.), Miami Valley Angus Assn. (bd. dirs.), Ohio Angus Assn. (bd. dirs.), Green Key, Sigma Xi, Alpha Gamma Sigma, Gamma Sigma Delta. Avocations: woodworking; gardening. Home: 5229 Diamond Mill Rd Brookville OH 45309 Office: Schearbrook Land & Livestock Co 5803 Oakes Rd Clayton OH 45315

DAVIS, JEFFREY COLLEEN, businessman; b. Morris, Ill., Dec. 2, 1952; s. Clarence Colleen and Eva Mae (Yahnke) D.; m. Karen Anne Hemberger, July 5, 1975; 1 son, Jonathan Allen. B.A. in Bus. Adminstrn., Greenville Coll. (Ill.), 1975. Asst. mgr. S.S. Kresge Corp., Troy, Mich., 1975-76; inside sales rep. David C. Cook Pub. Co., Elgin, Ill., 1976-77; sr. cons. Accu Exec. Search, Inc., Oak Brook, Ill., 1977-79; personnel rep. Travenol Labs., Inc., Deerfield, Ill., 1979-81, asst. to v.p. personnel, 1981-82, sr. compensation analyst, 1982-84; owner Davis Custom Decorators, 1984—. Bd. dirs. Butterfield Manor Homeowners Assn., 1984-87. Republican. Lodge: Lions (bd. dirs. Glen Ellyn 1986-87, treas. 1987—). Home and Office: 423D Ramblewood Dr Glen Ellyn IL 60137

DAVIS, JODINE MARIE, physical therapist; b. Janesville, Wis., Nov. 9, 1959; d. Alvin Walter and Joann Ruby (Rabiola) Haeberlin; m. Kerry LeRoy Davis, Oct. 27, 1984. BS, U. Wis., 1982. Lic. physical therapist, Wis. Physical therapist Beloit (Wis.) Meml. Hosp., 1982-84, Southwest Health Ctr., Cuba City, Wis., 1984—. Roman Catholic. Avocations: reading, singing, art. Home: 282 N 4th St Platteville WI 53818 Office: Southwest Health Ctr 808 S Washington Cuba City WI 53807

DAVIS, JOHN JAMES, religion educator; b. Phila., Oct. 13, 1936; s. John James and Cathryn Ann (Nichols) D.; m. Carolyn Ann. BA, Trinity Coll., Dunedin, Fla., 1959, DD (hon.), 1968; MDiv, Grace Coll. & Grace Theol. Sem., Winona Lake, Ind., 1962, ThM, 1964, ThD, 1967. Instr. Grace Coll. & Grace Theol. Sem., 1963-65, prof. of Old Testament, 1965—, exec. v.p., 1976-82; exec. dean Near East Sch. Archaeology, Jerusalem, 1970-71; area supr. Tekoa Archeol. Expdn., Jordan, 1968, 70, Raddana Expdn., Jordan, 1974, Meshbon Expdn., Jordan, 1976, Abilo Archeol. Expdn., Jordan, 1982, 84. Author: Paradise to Prison, 1975 (Book of Yr.), The Perfect Shepherd, 1979 (Book of Yr.), 8 other books. Recipient Gold award United Way, 1980, Conservation award Barbee Property Owners Assn., 1983; named Outdoor Writer of Yr., Ind. Dept. Natural Resources, 1986. Mem. Am. Schs. of Oriental Research, Near East Archeol. Soc., Outdoor Writers Assn., Hoosier Outdoor Writers Assn. (pres. 1984-86). Avocations: fishing, hunting, stamp collecting, photography. Home: PO Box 635 Winona Lake IN 46590 Office: Grace Theol Sem 200 Seminary Dr Winona Lake IN 46590

DAVIS, JULIA, psychologist; b. Passaic, N.J., Sept. 12, 1952; d. Horace Raymond Jr. and Joyce Darlene (Beckman) D.; m. Jon Gottesman, July 17, 1976; 1 child: Adria Claire. AB, Oberlin Coll., 1974; PhD, U. Minn, 1984. Lic. cons. psychologist, Minn. Sr. counselor vocat. assessment clinic U. Minn., Mpls., 1978-83; psychologist Minn. Psychotherapy and Consultation Services, St. Paul, 1984—; Chmn. parent adv. bd. U. Minn. Child Care Ctr., Mpls., 1985-86; Cons. Genesis II for Women, Mpls., 1986—. Mem. Dem. Farm Labor Feminist Caucus. U. Minn. fellow, 1983. Mem. Am. Psychologists Assn., Minn. Psychologists in Pvt. Practice (prog. chmn. 1985-86), Minn. Women Psychologist, ACLU, Planned Parenthood, Sigma Xi. Avocations: bibliophile, amateur musician, writing, poetry. Home: 2810 Xenwood Ave Saint Louis Park MN 55416 Office: Minn Psychotherapy and Consultation Services 2550 University Ave W Saint Paul MN 55114

DAVIS, JUNE LEAH, psychologist; b. Craigsville, W.Va, Nov. 10, 1922; d. Ernest Layton and Bessie May (Bostic) Taylor; m. Charles William Heasley, Jan. 16, 1943 (div. 1961); children: Denasse Ann Heasley Dugan, Wanda Lori Heasley Schwartz; m. Theodore R. Davis, Nov. 20, 1971. BA, Glenville (W.Va.) State Coll., 1962; MA, Ohio State U., 1967. Cert. psychologist, Ohio. Tchr. Nicholas County Bd. Edn., Summersville, W.Va., 1943-46, 1958-60; tchr. Columbus (Ohio) Bd. Edn., 1962-70, sch. psychologist, 1970—. Active First Baptist Ch., Columbus, 1975—. Mem. Sch. Psychologists Cen. Ohio (pres.), Ohio Sch. Psychologists Assn. (mem. various coms.), Cen. Ohio Psychologists Assn. Democrat. Club: Heart of Ohio Smocking (Columbus). Avocations: smocking, camping, walking. Home: 432 S Weyant Ave Columbus OH 43213 Office: Columbus Pub Schs Psychol Services 2571 Neil Ave Columbus OH 43202

DAVIS, JUSTINA, manufacturing executive; b. Highland Park, Mich., Dec. 8, 1955; d. John Edward and Catherine (Golden) D. AA, Highland Park Community Coll., 1982; A of Commerce and Cert. in Transp. and Traffic Mgmt., Henry Ford Community Coll., 1983; BS in Mktg., Madonna Coll., Livonia, Mich., 1984; Cert. Statistical Process Control and Interaction Mgmt., Chrysler Mgmt. Program, Warren, Mich., 1985; postgrad., Cen. Mich. U., 1985—. Recruiter Highland Park Adult Edn., 1980-84; production supr. truck plant Chrysler Corp., Warren, 1985—. Democrat. Baptist. Avocations: tennis, bicycling, boating. Home: 92 California St Highland Park MI 48203

DAVIS, KENNETH ROY, industrial engineer; b. Gary, Ind., Sept. 12, 1950; s. Budd Roy and Anna (Kadelak) D.; m. Connie S. Smith, Oct. 14, 1972 (div. Apr. 1980). AAS in Indsl. Engring. Tech., Purdue U., 1983, AAS in Supervision, 1985, BS in Indsl. Engring. Tech., 1985. Cert. profl. supr. Basic laborer Bethlehem Steel, Burns Harbor, Ind., 1969-70; dept. mgr. Hannah's Bldg. Ctr., Merrillville, Ind., 1970-78; purchasing agt. Gary Steel Products Corp., 1978-79; sr. indsl. engr. Combustion Engring., East Chicago, Ind., 1979-86, Johnson Controls, Inc., Milw., 1986—; indsl. engr. Bo-ke Cons., Hobart, Ind., 1983-86. Mem. Am. Soc. Profl. Supervision, Soc. Mfg. Engrs., Inst. Indsl. Engrs. Presbyterian. Lodge: Order of DeMolay (master council 1966-67). Home: 8519 W Grantosa Dr Apt 2 Milwaukee WI 53225 Office: Johnson Controls Inc 5757 N Green Bay Ave Milwaukee WI 53209

DAVIS, LAURENCE LAIRD, coal company executive; b. Cin., June 6, 1915; s. Thomas Jefferson and Jane (Brown) D.; m. Charlotte Rowe Nichols, Oct. 12, 1940 (dec. Sept. 1973); children: Sally Laird (Mrs. Arthur D. Pratt), Laurence Laird, Thomas Jefferson II; m. Onlee Partin, Nov. 7, 1973; 1 dau., Nancy Matilda Kathleen; stepchildren: Rickey Lee Foland, Stella Logan Turner, Samuel J. Logan, Gregory C. Logan. Grad., St. Mark's Sch., 1934; A.B., Harvard, 1938; postgrad., London (Eng.) Sch. Econs., 1939. With First Nat. Bank Cin., 1939-42, 46-70, v.p., 1949-64, vice chmn. bd., dir., 1964-70; also dir.; vice consul, econ. analyst State Dept., 1943-45; financial cons. 1970—; pres., dir. Roberta Coal Co., Elkhorn Collieries Co., Millers Creek Mineral Devel. Co., Burning Springs Land Co.; Chmn. English Speaking Union, 1965-72. Pres. Symphony Orch., 1965-68; Bd. dirs. Christ Hosp. Mem. Greater Cin. C. of C. (pres. 1965-68). Clubs: Commonwealth (Cin.), Camargo (Cin.), Queen City (Cin.). Home and Office: 7844 Remington Rd Cincinnati OH 45242 also: Treasure Cay, Abaco Bahamas

DAVIS, LAWRENCE (LARRY), educator; b. Blossburg, Pa., Aug. 17, 1932; s. Harold Irving and Carrie Mae (Rude) D.; B.S., Black Hills State Coll., 1957; M.A., U. S.D., 1958; m. Shirley Leone Blodgett, May 24, 1957; children—Shirleen Deanna (dec.), Darrell Eugene. Speech clinician Sioux City (Iowa) Pub. Schs., 1958-68; asst. prof. speech and hearing sci. Briar Cliff Coll., Sioux City, 1968-74; instr. gen. edn. Western Iowa Tech. Community Coll., Sioux City, 1974—. Past pres. Sioux City Noon Lions, 1971, zone chmn., 1977, dep. dist. gov., 1978, dist. gov., 1979-80, 86-87, mem. Dist. 9 Council Govs. Lions of Iowa Dist. 9; pres. Lions Gavel Club, 1983-84; mem. Sioux City Human Rights Commn., 1979-82. Served with USAF, 1950-54. Mem. Am., Iowa vocat. assns., Council for Exceptional Children (past pres. N.W. Iowa chpt.), Sioux City Schoolmasters Club (past pres.), AF Assn., Am. Legion, Phi Delta Kappa (pres. 1984-85). Methodist (chmn. fin. 1980, trustee 1981-84, adminstrv. bd. 1985—). Home: 3416 Pierce St Sioux City IA 51102 Office: Box 265 Sioux City IA 51106

DAVIS, LINDA LONSDORF, computer systems sales executive, executive to sales; b. Wausau, Wis., Apr. 25, 1953; d. Geroge John and Dolores Marguerite (Litzer) Lonsdorf; m. Robert Edwin Davis, Feb. 15, 1986. BA, U. Wis., 1976. Tech. writer Systems by Graber, Madison, 1974-77; sales support word processing Benchmark Computers, Mpls., 1977-78; mgr. office automation Digital Info. Systems, Mpls., 1978—. Contbr. mag. articles. Bd. dirs. Big Sisters of Greater Mpls., 1986. Mem. Mpls. Office Systems Assn. Club: Decathlon Athletic (Bloomington, Minn.). Avocations: skiing, horseback riding, vol. work. Office: Digital Info Systems 7555 Market Pl Dr Eden Prairie WI 55344

D'AVIS, LUIS M., physician, surgeon, immediate care consultant; b. Cochabamba, Bolivia, June 10, 1944; came to U.S., 1971, naturalized, 1976; s. Luis and Adela (Medeiros) d'A.; m. Amalia Lourdes Reyes, May 16, 1969; children—Monique Marie, John-Andrew, Edward-Joseph. B.S., San Agustin Indsl. Coll., 1961; M.D., San Simon U. Med. Sch., Bolivia, 1969. Postgrad. tng., Evanston, Ill., 1971-80; med. staff Ravenswood, hosps., Chgo.; owner, med. dir. Med. Ctr., Chgo. Pres. Bolivian Friendship Club, 1981-83; hon. mem. Internat. Red Cross. Mem. AMA, Ill. Med. Soc., Chgo. Med. Soc., Fellow Am. Acad. Family Practice, Ill. Acad. Family Practice (pres. Lincoln Park br.), Interam. Coll. Physicians and Surgeons, Bolivian Med. Soc. (dir. 1982-83). Republican. Roman Catholic. Home: 8241 N Kildare Ave Skokie IL 60076 Office: 4315 N Lincoln Ave Chicago IL 60618

DAVIS, MARY HELEN, psychiatrist, educator; b. Kingsville, Tex., Dec. 2, 1949; d. Garnett Stant and Emogene (Campbell) D. BA, U. Tex., 1970; MD, U. Tex., Galveston, 1975. Cert. Nat. Bd. Med. Examiners, Am. Bd. Psychiatry and Neurology, Child and Adolescent Psychiatry. Asst. prof. Med. Coll. Wis., Milw., 1980—; med. dir. adolescent treatment unit Milw. Psychiat. Hosp., 1981-86; med. dir. Schroeder Child Ctr., 1986—. Named one of Outstanding Young Women of Am., 1985. Mem. Am. Psychiat. Assn., Am. Soc. Adolescent Psychiatry, Am. Acad. Child and Adolescent Psychiatry, Am. Med. Women's Assn. Baptist. Club: Univ. (Milw.). Avocations: music, computers, crochet. Office: Milw Psychiat Hosp 1220 Dewey Ave Wauwatosa WI 53213

DAVIS, MAYNARD PARKER, educator; b. Bethlehem, Pa., Apr. 15, 1930; s. William Henry and Gertrude Marion (Brunner) D.; m. Elsie Mai Carpenter, Dec. 31, 1952; children—Jeanette, Deborah. B.S. in Secondary Edn., Austin Peay State U., 1957; M.B.A. in Mktg., Bradley U., 1960; postgrad. U. Tenn., 1961, U. Ill., 1972-75. Tchr., Sch. Dist. 150, Peoria, Ill., 1957—; sales promotion mgr. Modern Home TV & Appliances, Inc., 1963-72; pres., treas., chief exec. officer A.R.M.S. of Ill., Inc., Peoria, 1967—; sec. La Cantina Italiana, Inc., 1975-77; dir. Peoria County Sch. Employees Credit Union, 1985—. Served with USMC, 1948-49, 50-52. Mem. Nat. Rifle Assn. (life), Nat. Assn. Federally Lic. Firearms Dealers, NEA (life), Ill. Edn. Assn., Peoria Edn. Assn. (dir., exec. com. 1968-75, negotiator 1970-75), Am. Legion, Midwest Gun Collectors Assn., Kappa Delta Pi. Republican. Club: River Valley Sportsman's (East Peoria). Office: 624 W Lake St Peoria IL 61614

DAVIS, MICHAEL HAROLD, biochemist, researcher; b. Denison, Tex., June 18, 1953; s. Kenneth Richard and Margaret Alice (MacMahon) D.; m. Carol Marie Solie, June 23, 1979; 1 child, Helen Ruth. BS, Wash. State U., 1975; PhD in Biochemistry, Iowa State U., 1979. Postdoctoral asst. U. Cin., 1979-81, postdoctoral fellow, 1982; asst. prof. Phila. Coll. Osteopathic Medicine, 1982-86; research assoc. Ohio State U., Columbus, 1986—. Contbr. articles to profl. jours. Cons. med. adv. bd. Lupus Found. Delaware County, Ardmore, Pa., 1985-86, treas., 1984-85, bd. dirs. 1983-86; mem. Common Cause, Washington, 1983-87. Muscular Dystrophy Assn. fellow, 1982; grantee Phila. Coll. Osteopathic Medicine, 1983. Mem. AAAS, Am. Chem. Soc., Union Concerned Scientists, Phi Kappa Phi. Democrat. Episcopalian. Home: 1505 Lealand Dr Marion OH 43302 Office: Ohio State U Dept Physiol Chemistry 333 W 10th Ave 5170 Graves Hall Columbus OH 43210

DAVIS, MULLER, lawyer; b. Chgo., Apr. 23, 1935; s. Benjamin B. and Janice (Muller) D.; m. Jane Lynn Strauss, Dec. 28, 1963; children: Melissa Jane, Muller, Joseph Jeffrey. Grad. with honors, Phillips Exeter (N.H.) Acad., 1953; B.A. magna cum laude, Yale U., 1957; J.D., Harvard U., 1960. Bar: Ill. 1960, U.S. Dist. Ct. (no. dist.) Ill. 1961. Practice law Chgo., 1960—; assoc. Jenner & Block, 1960-67; ptnr. Davis, Friedman, Zavett, Kane & MacRae, 1967—; lectr. continuing legal edn., matrimonial law and litigation Legal adviser Michael Reese Med. Research Inst. Council, 1967-82. Contbr. articles to law jours.; author (with Sherman C. Feinstein) The Parental Couple in a Successful Divorce; mem. editorial bd. Equitable Distbn. Jour., 1984—. Bd. dirs. Infant Welfare Soc., 1975—, pres., 1978-82. Served to capt. U.S. Army, Ill. N.G., 1960-67. Fellow Am. Acad. Matrimonial Lawyers; mem. Fed. Bar Assn., ABA, Ill. Bar Assn., Chgo. Bar Assn. (matrimonial com., sec. civil practice com. 1979-80, vice chmn. 1980-81, chmn. 1981-82), Chgo. Estate Planning Council, Law Club Chgo. Republican. Jewish. Clubs: Tavern, Lake Shore Country. Home: 1020 E Westleigh Rd Lake Forest IL 60045 Office: 140 S Dearborn St Chicago IL 60603

DAVIS, ORVAL CLIFTON, diversified energy company executive; b. Rosiclare, Ill., May 7, 1920; s. Luther and Elizabeth (St. John) Rumfelt D.; m. Thelma Sherry, Nov. 24, 1942 (div. 1983); children: Henry T., Jon F.; m. Loretta Jean Molter, July 31, 1984. B.S. in Mech. Engring., Tex. A&M U., 1947. Area mgr. Thompson, Starrett & Co., N.Y.C., 1942-43; constrn. engr. Natural Gas Pipeline Co. of Am., Geneseo, Ill., 1947-49; plant engr., chief insp. Natural Gas Pipeline Co. of Am., Great Bend, Kans., 1949-50, Wharton, Tex., 1950-51; sta. supt. Natural Gas Pipeline Co. of Am., Conroe, Tex., 1951-52; resident engr. Natural Gas Pipeline Co. of Am., Centralia, Ill., 1952-53, Herscher, Ill., 1953-55; supt. storage Natural Gas Pipeline Co. of Am., Chgo., 1955-61, asst. v.p., 1962-63, v.p., 1963-66, exec. v.p., 1966-69, pres., 1969-73; pres. Peoples Gas Co., Chgo., 1973-77, chmn. bd. dirs., 1977-80; chmn., pres., chief exec. officer Peoples Energy Corp., Chgo., 1980-81; chmn., pres., chief exec. officer MidCon Corp., Chgo., 1981-85, chmn., chief exec. officer, 1985—; exec. v.p. Occidental Petroleum Corp. (parent), Los Angeles, 1986—; dir. Amsted Industries Inc., Chgo., 1975—, Continental Ill. Corp., Chgo., 1985—, Continental Ill. Nat. Bank & Trust Co., Chgo., 1985—. Served to capt. USAF, 1942-46, ETO. Mem. Am. Inst. Mining & Metall. Engrs. Republican. Clubs: Chicago, Commercial, Economic (Chgo.). Avocations: golf; hunting; fishing. Home: 501 Burr Ridge Club Dr Burr Ridge IL 60521 Office: MidCon Corp 701 E 22d St Lombard IL 60148 *

DAVIS, PATTIE ANN, shopping center manager; b. Owensboro, Ky., Feb. 18, 1939; d. Leo John and Annie Sue (Jennings) Weaver; m. John Edward Davis, Aug. 24, 1957 (div. May 1976); children: Deborah, Daniel, Mark. Student, Mich. State U., 1984, Indiana Vocat. Coll., 1986. Account exec. WJPG Radio, Evansville, Ind., 1966-67, Evansville Printing Corp., 1967-71; mktg. dir. Washington Sq. Mall, Evansville, 1971-84; gen. mgr. Washington Sq. Complex, Evansville, 1984—. Created promotional materials for shopping ctr., 1972. Mem. exec. bd., sec. Evansville Freedom Festival, 1975-86; mem. adv. bd. Welfare Dept., Evansville, 1984-86. Recipient Service to Mankind award Sertoma Club, 1982, Ed Addy award Evansville Advt. Club, 1978, 80, 81, Silver medal, 1985, Meritorial Achievementaward Ind. Fun. Dirs., 1983. Republican. Roman Catholic. Club: Triad Advt. (Evansville), Ski (social dir.). Lodge: Rotary (Evansville) (pres. women's club 1985-86). Avocations: boating, snow skiing, tennis, volleyball. Home: 1105 S Frederick Evansville IN 47715 Office: Washington Sq Mall 1138 Washington Sq Mall Evansville IN 47715

DAVIS, RALPH, research chemist; b. Huntington, Ind., Aug. 14, 1917; s. Floyd Anderson and Rozella (Burton) D.; m. Muriel Evelyn Wait, Aug. 11, 1940 (dec. 1975); children—Robert S., Norman W. B.A., Huntington Coll., 1939; M.A., Ind. U., 1942. Tchr. Leo High Sch., Ind., 1939-41; research asst. in chemistry Ind. U., Bloomington, 1941-42; analytical chemist Dow Chem. Co., Midland, Mich., 1942-49, chem. researcher, 1949-82, ret. 1982. Patentee in field of fluorine and halogen chemistry. Contbr. articles to sci. jours. Active Boy Scouts Am., 1950-63. Mem. Am. Chem. Soc., AAAS, Sigma Xi. Republican. Methodist. Avocations: gardening; photography. Address: 1160 Poseyville Rd R7 Midland MI 48640

DAVIS, RANDALL JAMES, data processing professional; b. Delphos, Ohio, Dec. 21, 1952; s. John Sherman and Virginia May (Colmbs) D.; m. Kathy Lou Kirkpatrick, Oct. 3, 1975; children: Chad Allen, Jeremy Stuart. Grad. high sch., Gahanna, Ohio, 1970; student, Miami U., Oxford, Ohio, 1973. Missile tech. U.S. Army, 1970-72; instr. Elec. Computer Programming Inst., Columbus, Ohio, 1975-76; analyst, project leader Landmark Inc., Columbus, 1976-83, Ross Labs. div. Abbott Labs, Columbus, 1983—; cons., developer Balaton Mktg., Washington, 1984—, various cos. Columbus area, 1984—, Needle in a Haystack, Washington/Columbus, 1985—; v.p. research and devel. Info. Profile Sysytems, Columbus, 1985—. Sci. fair judge Rosemore Jr. High Sch., Whitehall, Ohio, 1979—; data processing services cons. Johnstown (Ohio) Youth League, 1986—. Roman Catholic. Avocations: stamp collecting, electronics, audio. Home: 266 Upham Dr Johnstown OH 43031 Office: Ross Labs 625 Cleveland Ave Columbus OH 43216

DAVIS, RICHARD LEE, insurance executive; b. Neola, Iowa, July 20, 1933; s. Harold Harrie and Clara (Jacobsen) D.; m. Marianne Dorothy Lobeck, June 22, 1958; children: Joseph, Kristine, Patrick. BS, U. Omaha, 1958, MS, 1962. Cert. ins. counselor. Tchr., coach Council Bluffs (Iowa) Schs., 1958-68; owner, salesman Smith-Davis Ins. Agy., Council Bluffs, 1964—. V.p. Vocat. Devel. Bd., Council Bluffs, 1985-86. Served with U.S. Army, 1955-57. Named to Iowa Coaches Hall of Fame, 1968. Mem. Ind. Ins. Agts. Assn. Council Bluffs (pres. 1976-77). Republican. Lutheran. Avocation: golf. Home: 526 Cogleywood Ln Council Bluffs IA 51501 Office: 532 1st Ave Council Bluffs IA 51502

DAVIS, ROBERT LOUIS, lawyer; b. Wichita, Kans., June 16, 1927; s. Carl H. and Maria (Francisco) D.; m. Marian Frances Larson, June 26, 1955; children—Martha F., Alison L., Carl B., Janet E. A.B., U. Kans., 1950, J.D., 1952. Bar: Kans. 1952, Utah 1953. Atty. Gulf Oil Corp., 1952-53; ptnr. firm Davis & Davis, Wichita, 1954-61, Davis, Bruce & Davis, Wichita, 1962-70, Davis, Bruce, Davis & Cather, 1971-72, Davis, Bruce, Davis & Winkler, Wichita, 1973-77, Bruce, Davis & Gilhousen, Wichita, 1977-85, Bruce & Davis, Wichita, 1985—; mcpl. judge City of Goddard, Kans., 1979—; lectr. bus. law Friends U., Wichita, 1967; leader Kans. Lawyers China Mission, 1981. Editor The Logos jour., Alpha Kappa Lambda, 1950-60. Pres. Goodwill Industries Greater Wichita, 1965-66, 71-73; mem. Wichita Bd. Edn., 1963-71, also pres., 1969-70; bd. dirs. Wichita Guidance Ctr., 1964-70, Friends Com. on Nat. Legis., Washington, 1970-82, Community Planning Council Wichita, 1972-76; trustee Friends U., 1959-77, chmn. bd., 1965-74; trustee Kans. Found. Pvt. Colls., Mid-Am. Yearly Meeting of Friends, Wichita Scottish Rite Bodies. Served with USNR, 1945-46. Mem. Wichita Bar Assn., Kans. Bar Assn., Utah Bar Assn., ABA, Assn. Governing Bds. Univs. and Colls., Nat. Assn. Coll. Attys., Phi Beta Kappa, Omicron Delta Kappa. Clubs: Knife and Fork, University (pres. 1984-85), Petroleum, Keystone High-Twelve (pres. 1981) (Wichita). Lodges: Lions, Shriners, Masons (33 degree), Knights York Cross of Honor. Home: Route 1 Box 66A Colwich KS 67030 Office: Bruce & Davis 2121 W Maple St Wichita KS 67213

DAVIS, ROBERT PHELPS, surgeon; b. Evanston, Ill., Nov. 9, 1942; s. Carl Braden and Marianne Williams (Hoover) D.; B.A., U. of the South, 1964; M.D., Northwestern U., 1969; Intern, Chgo. Wesley Meml. Hosp., 1969-70; resident in surgery Northwestern U., Chgo., 1970-75; staff surgeon VA Lakeside Hosp., Chgo., 1975—; sr. attending surgeon Columbus Cuneo Med. Center, Chgo., 1975—; asst. med. dir. research and edn., dir. med. edn. Columbus Hosp.; assoc. prof. clin. surgery Northwestern U. Med. Sch., 1975—. Diplomate Am. Bd. Surgery. Fellow A.C.S.; mem. Soc. Acad. Surgery, Assn. Vets. Surgeons, Soc. Surgery of Alimentary Tract, Cen. Surg. Assn., Western Surg. Assn., AMA. Republican. Episcopalian. Clubs: Racquet of Chgo., Saddle and Cycle. Home: 1442 N Dearborn St Chicago IL 60610 Office: 467 W Deming Pl Suite 919 Chicago IL 60614

DAVIS, ROBERT W., congressman; b. Marquette, Mich., July 31, 1932; student No. Mich. U., 1950, 52, Hillsdale Coll., 1951-52; B.S., Coll. Mortuary Sci., Wayne State U., 1954; m. Martha Cole, 1976; children—Robert W., Jr., Lisa, George, Alexandra. Funeral dir. Davis Funeral Home, St. Ignace, Mich., 1954-66; mem. St. Ignace City Council, 1964-66; mem. Mich. Ho. of Reps., 1966-70; mem. Mich. Senate, 1970-78, majority whip, 1970-74 minority leader, 1974-78; mem. 96-100th Congresses from 11th Dist. Mich.; mem. N.E.-Midwest Econ. Advancement Coalition, Congressional Tourism Caucus, Republican Study Club, Conf. Gt. Lakes Congressmen, Environ. Study Conf., Coalition for Peace Through Strength, Congressional Shipyard Coalition, Congressional Steel Caucus. Bd. dirs. Mich. Cystic Fibrosis Assn.; adv. bd. Young Ams. for Freedom. Mem. Mich. Funeral Dirs. Assn., Nat. Rifle Assn. Republican. Clubs: Lions, Eagles, Elks, Masons, Ducks Unlimited. Office: 2417 Rayburn Washington DC 20515

DAVIS, RONALD FARLANDI, JR., health science facility administrator; b. Arlington, Va., Dec. 10, 1946; s. Ronald Farlandi and Mary Anne (Reynolds) D.; m. Annabella C. Ozbun, Dec. 30, 1965 (div. Nov. 1984); children: Wendy Ann, Kimberly Ann; m. Constance Jeanne Phelps, Feb. 14, 1986. B Health Services, U. Mo., 1982. Fingerprint technician FBI, Washington, 1964-66; enlisted U.S. Army, 1966, advanced through grades to chief warrant officer, 1971; spl. agt. U.S. Army, U.S. and Vietnam, 1966-75; adminstr. Sunset Nursing Home, Union, Mo., 1975—. Alderman City of Union, 1977-85; active Franklin County Youth Fair Bd., Union, 1986—. Named Nursing Home Adminstr. of Yr. ADAPT Inst. Am., 1985. Mem. Am. Health Care Assn., Mo. Health Care Assn. (bd. dirs. 1977-81), Mo. League Nursing Home Adminstrs., Mo. Police Chiefs Assn., Union C. of C., Am. Legion (sgt. at arms 1985—). Republican. Roman Catholic. Lodge: Rotary (pres. 1979-80, sec. 1985—). Avocations: instrumental music, flying. Home: 402 Gruber Ave Union MO 63084 Office: Sunset Nursing Home 400 W Park Ave Union MO 63084

DAVIS, SAM V., food products company executive. Pres. Hyplains Dressed Beef Inc., Dodge City, Kans. Office: Hyplains Dressed Beef Inc PO Box 539 Dodge City KS 67801 *

DAVIS, SARA JANE, utility company official; b. Jackson, Mich., Feb. 24, 1948; d. Leonard William and Margery Barbara (Smith) Lashley. AA in Bus. Mgmt. and Data Processing, Lansing Community Coll., 1978; BA, Spring Arbor Coll., 1984. Computer programmer Consumers Power Co., Jackson, 1968-79, computer analyst, 1979-82, supr. software services, 1982-83, supr. energy supply systems support, 1984-85, project mgr. customer info., 1986—. Mem. mktg. com. United Way; mem. exec. com. Employees for Better Govt. PAC; bd. dirs. Jackson Community Leadership Acad. Mem. Assn. for Systems Mgmt. (chpt. sec.), Nat. Fedn. Bus. and Profl. Women (chpt. pres.). Office: Consumers Power Co 1945 Parnall Rd Jackson MI 49201

DAVIS, SHARON ANN, social services program coordinator; b. Chgo., July 10, 1959; d. Amos and Charlotte Lorraine (Davis) Boseman; m. Glenn Bernard Davis, Feb. 14, 1986. BA, Western Ill. U., 1982. Camp dir., head tchr. Children's World, Bolingbrook, Ill., 1983-84; tng. supr. Oak/Leyden Devel. Services, Franklin Park, Ill., 1984-85; program coordinator Northwestern U. Settlement House, Chgo., 1985—; teen counselor Shalom Ministries, Chgo., 1983-85. Author: Plays and Poems, Lessons for Us All, 1986. Democrat. Avocation: writing children's plays. Home: 423 S Taylor Ave Apt 1-E Oak Park IL 60302 Office: Northwestern U Settlement House 1400 Augusta Blvd Chicago IL 60622

DAVIS, STANLEY STANTON, real estate developer; b. Janesville, Wis., Sept. 9, 1925; s. Ferrell Thornton and Hazel Gladys (Stevens) D.; m. Eloise Jeanette Larson, Nov. 6, 1949; children—William Allen, Jeffrey Stanton. Student U. Pitts., 1944, U. Wis., 1946-47, Madison Coll., 1948-49. Auditor, Kroger Co., Madison, Wis., 1949-54; realtor Badger and Lucey Realty, Madison, 1954-58; pres., owner Empire Realty Co., Madison, 1958-65, Stanton-Fritz Corp., Madison, 1964-74, Highlander Bldg. Devel. Co., Madison, 1975—; owner, mgr. Interior Design and Supply Studio, Madison, 1969—. Served with USAF, 1944-45. Mem. Greater Madison Bd. Realtors, Nat. Assn. Realtors, Wis. Exchange Club, Fla. Real Estate Exchangors. Republican. Lutheran. Lodge: Rotary. Avocations: aviation; hunting; camera; bowling; golf. Home: 3365 Crystal Ct W Palm Harbor FL 33563 also: 3018 Irvington Way Madison WI 53713 Office: Highlander Bldg Devel Co 4343 W Beltline Hwy Madison WI 53711

DAVIS, STARKEY DEE, pediatrics educator; b. Atlanta, Tex., Jan. 29, 1931; s. Sidney Rush and Veda Louise (Nichols) D.; m. Kathryn Maegli, Apr. 3, 1982. BA, Baylor U., 1953, MD, 1957. Diplomate Am. Bd. Pediatrics. Fellow in pediatric medicine U. Wash., 1962-65, mem. faculty, 1965-75; prof. pediatrics Medical Coll. Wis., 1975—, chmn. pediatrics, 1983—. Contbr. numerous sci. papers. to profl. jours. Mem. Am. Pediatrics Soc. Avocations: sailboat racing, downhill skiing. Office: Children's Hosp Wis PO Box 1997 Milwaukee WI 53201

DAVIS, ULILLAH ELMORE, pharmacist; b. Ashland, Miss., Mar. 15, 1932; d. Hayse and Graftee (McKenzie) Elmore; m. Edward Davis, Jr., Dec. 5, 1959; children—Karen Lynn, Keith Edward. B.S. in Pharmacy, Xavier U., New Orleans, 1955. Registered pharmacist, La., Ohio. Instr. chemistry, biology, dean of women, Miss. Indsl. Coll., Holly Spring, 1956-57; asst. mgr. Shauter Drug Co., Cleve., 1958-59; staff pharmacist Highland View Hosp., Warrensville, Ohio, 1960-70, asst. dir. pharmacy, 1971-78; sr. staff pharmacist Cleve. Met. Gen. Hosp., 1979; dir. pharmacy Kenneth W. Clement Ctr., Cleve., 1980—; SunnyAcres Skilled Nursing Facility, 1985—; treas. Phillis Wheatley Assoc., 1985. Trustee Lee Seville Ch., 1985. Recipient Super Achievement award Highland View Hosp, 1975. Mem. Cleve. Soc. Hosp. Pharmacists, Ohio Soc. Hosp. Pharmacists, Am. Soc. Hosp. Pharmacists, Nat. Pharm. Assn., Cleve. Pharm. Assn. (sec. 1984—, pres. 1985), Xavier Alumni Assn., Cleve. Tots and Teens (v.p. 1973-75, Super Performance award 1979), East End Settle Coop. (pres. 1975-78), NAACP, Nat. Council Negro Women, Phillis Wheatley Aux., Alpha Kappa Alpha Achievement award 1982). Democrat. Baptist. Avocations: gourmet cooking; jogging. Home: 20150 S Woodland Rd Shaker Heights OH 44122 Office: Sunnyacres Skilled Nursing Facility 4310 Richmond Rd Warrensville Township OH 44122

DAVIS, WILLIAM DOYLE, JR., real estate appraiser; b. Kansas City, Mo., Sept. 24, 1934; s. William D. Sr. and Lindalou (Turner) D.; m. Mary Camille Bronaugh. BS, U. Mo., 1956, MS, 1957. Ptnr. Appraisal Assocs., Kansas City, 1957—; pres. Farm Mgmt. Assocs., Kansas City, 1981—. Served with 1st lt. U.S. Army, 1956-57. Mem. Mo. Soc. Farm Mgrs., Agrl. Hall of Fame (pres., chmn. bd. 1976-81). Mem. Christian Ch. Avocation: music. Home: 1400 NE 76th Terr Kansas City MO 64118 Office: Appraisal Assocs 1009 Baltimore Suite 316 Kansas City MO 64105

DAVIS, WILLIAM HARRY, watch repairman, jeweler; b. Clarks Hill, Ind., Dec. 12, 1921; s. Ora Lee and Lola Bethel (Street) D.; m. Ella Kathryn Whitteberry, Sept. 12, 1946; children: Nancy Marie Davis Cottrell. Grad. high sch., Rossville, Ind. Mgr., watchmaker Nicewander Jewelry, Mulberry, Ind., 1948-61; owner Davis Jewelry, Mulberry, Ind., 1961—. Served with U.S. Navy, 1942-44. Methodist. Lodge: Masons. Avocations: fishing, traveling. Home: 305 S Clinton St Mulberry IN 46058 Office: Davis Jewelers 124 E Jackson St Mulberry IN 46058

DAVISON, DANIEL THOMAS, physician; b. Grand Rapids, Mich., Sept. 27, 1951. AS, Grand Rapids Jr. Coll., 1971; BS with honors, Mich. State U., 1973, DO, 1978. Cert. Am. Osteo. Bd. Gen. Practitioners. Intern Flint (Mich.) Osteo. Hosp., 1978-79; fellow in adolescent medicine Rush-Presbyn. Saint Luke's Med. Ctr., Chgo., 1982-84; resident in family medicine Chgo. Osteo. Med. Ctr., 1979-80, attending physician emergency room, 1980-82, dir. sports medicine and family fitness ctr., 1984—; team physician U. Ill., Chgo., 1984—. Mem. AMA, Am. Osteo. Acad. Sports Medicine (bd. dirs. 1985—), Am. Coll. Sports Medicine, Am. Osteo. Assn. Office: Chgo Osteo Med Ctr 5200 S Ellis Chicago IL 60615

DAVISON, M(ARY) JO, environmental research laboratory executive, educator, writer; b. Middletown, Ohio, Nov. 8, 1935; d. Harry Edmund and Marie Angeline (Caswell) D. BS, Miami U., Oxford, Ohio, 1957; MA in Sci. Edn., Environ. Studies, Counseling & Guidance, W.Va. U., 1974. Cert. high sch. sci. tchr., W.Va., Ohio. Sci. tchr. Los Angeles Schs., 1958-61; with sales, advt. and pub. relations staff Bell and Gen. Telephone, Columbus, Ohio and Long Beach, Calif., 1962-69; sci. tchr. Summers County (W.Va.) Schs., 1970-76; sci. and environ. edn. specialist Fayette County (W.Va.) Schs., 1976-84; pres., research dir. Lambda Group, Inc., Columbus, Ohio, 1984—, Lambda of Am., Inc., Columbus, 1984—; pres., owner Lambda Environ. Tech., Morgantown, W.Va., 1987—; pres. Lambda Prodn. Corp., Dayton, Columbus, Ohio, 1987—, Lambda of Can., Vancouver, B.C., Calgary, Alta., 1987—; environ. edn. cons. Columbus City Schs., 1984—. Author: The Colony Trilogy, 1974, Against The Odds, 1978; contbr. articles to sci. jours.; inventor coal and water cleaning processes, microbial delivery system. Advisor Women's Outreach, Columbus, 1983—; adv. com. W.Va. Dems. in State Sen. and Ho.of Reps., Oak Hill and Charleston, 1979-84; dist. rep. W.Va. Conservation Edn. Council, Oakhill, 1979-84. Recipient several Sci. and Environ. Educator of Yr. awards, 1973-84; Dept. of Energy grantee, 1985-86. Mme. Nat. Assn. Biologist, Am. Assn. Scientists, Ohio Acad. Sci. (sci. fair judge, 1983—), W.Va. Acad. Sci., Sierra Club, Nature Conservancy, NOW, Nat. Orgn. Female Execs. Home: 5683 Jousting Ln Columbus OH 43229 Office: Lambda Group Inc 1445 Summit St Columbus OH 43201

DAVISON, THOMAS CORNELL BARRINGER, software systems design manager; b. Durham, N.C., Aug. 9, 1948; s. Alexander Thayer and Mary Laura (Cline) D.; m. Marilyn Bauer, Nov. 24, 1972. BA, Duke U., 1970; MA, Bradley U., 1973; PhD, Ohio State U., 1977. Mem. tech. staff AT&T Bell Labs., Columbus, Ohio, 1977-82, supr., 1982—. Contbr. articles to profl. jours. Pres. Friends of Grandview Heights Library, Columbus, 1981. Mem. Human Factors Soc., Phi Kappa Phi. Club: Leatherlips Yacht (Delaware, Ohio) (fleet capt. 1985—). Avocations: sailing, tennis. Home: 1064 Baumock Burn Dr Worthington OH 43085 Office: AT&T Bell Labs 6200 E Broad St Columbus OH 43213

DAVISSON, SHARON RYAN, county official, accountant; b. St. Louis, Aug. 13, 1940; d. Tom E. and Eleanor (Rudolph) Ryan; m. Walter F. Davisson, 1963; children: Patricia, Valerie, Ann. BS, St. Louis U., 1962. CPA, Mo. Computer programmer McDonnell Douglas, St. Louis, 1962-64; computer programmer biomed lab. Washington U., St. Louis, 1964-66; pvt. practice acctg. Jefferson City, Mo., 1983—; auditor Cole County, Jefferson City, 1984-86, presiding commr., 1987—. Treas. Heart of Mo. council Girl Scouts U.S., Jefferson City, 1984-87; bd. regentys St. Mary's Health Ctr., Jefferson City, 1987—. Mem. Am. Inst. CPA's, Mo. Soc. CPA's, Govtl. Accting. Assn. Republican. Roman Catholic. Club: Pachyderms (treas. 1987—). Avocation: landscaping. Home: Star Rt 2 Schott Rd Jefferson City MO 65101 Office: Cole County Commission 301 E High St Jefferson City MO 65101

DAW, JOHN LAWRENCE, architect; b. Des Moines, Feb. 12, 1927; s. John Francis and Ruth (Lawrence) D.; m. Alberta J. James, June 4, 1954; children: Kathleen, Deirdre, Brigid, Sean, Megan. BArch, U. Notre Dame, 1952. Registered architect, Mo., Kans., La., Fla., Tex., Ill., Ohio, Ariz. Prin. John Lawrence Daw & Assocs., Inc., Kansas City, Mo., 1956—. Commr. Kansas City Mcpl. Art Commn., 1972-78. Served to capt. USNR. Constrn. Industry Producers Council award, 1961, James F. Lincoln Arc Welding award, 1961. Mem. AIA (pres. Kansas City chpt. 1976-77, internat. relations com., Bldg. Medal awards 1961, 68, 72). Roman Catholic. Clubs: Univ. (pres. Kansas City chpt. 1979-80), Mission Hills Country, Notre Dame (pres. 1974-75), Montabaur (pres. 1970). Avocations: squash, auto racing. Home: 812 W 60th Terr Kansas City MO 64113 Office: John Lawrence Daw & Assocs Inc 912 Baltimore Ave Kansas City MO 64105

DAWE, ROBERT BRUCE, dentist; b. Pontiac, Mich., Aug. 3, 1953; s. Arthur James and Lottie Mildred (Key) D.; m. Patricia Joyce Mirtich, July 15, 1978; children: Amber, Bobby. DDS, U. Ill., Chgo., 1977. Gen. practice dentistry Granville, Ill., 1983—. Pres. bd. dirs. Granville Pre-Sch., 1986; bd. dirs. Putnam County Bd. Health, Hennepin, Ill., 1986. Mem. ADA, Ill. State Dental Soc., Ill. Valley Dental Soc. (program chmn. 1986), Granville Jaycees. Roman Catholic. Avocations: gardening, racquetball, waterskiing. Home: 303 W Hopkins Granville IL 61326 Office: 315 S McCoy Granville IL 61326

DAWES, DARYL ANN, personnel executive; b. Detroit, Aug. 7, 1952; d. Raymond J. and Elizabeth Ann (Marnik) Jeanguenat; m. Ronald Charles Dawes, July 22, 1978. BS, Western Mich. U., 1973; postgrad., Oakland U., Rochester, Mich., 1974-75. Tchr. math and Spanish Rochester, Oak Park and Centerline (Mich.) Pub Schs., 1974-76; pub. relations coordinator Gen Motors Tech. Ctr., Warren, Mich., 1976-84, pub. relations staff asst., 1984-85; adminstr. tng. and communications Gen. Motors Facilities, Detroit, 1985—. Mem. Internat. Assn. Bus. Communicators, Warren C. of C. (membership com. 1976-84). Club: Women's Econs. (Detroit). Avocations: cross country skiing, boating, aerobics, tennis, knitting. Office: GM Facilities Argonaut A Bldg 9th Floor 485 W Milwaukee Detroit MI 48202

DAWLEY, DONALD LEE, business educator, information systems specialist; b. Amanda, Ohio, Feb. 21, 1936; s. Stanley Bernel and Alice Opel (Santee) D.; m. T. Jane Bokay, Nov. 24, 1957; children: Donald Wayne, Douglas Lee, Denise Jane. BS in Edn., Kent State U., 1959; AA in Bus., U. Calif., Victor Valley, 1966; MBA in Bus., U. Hawaii, Far East div., 1968; MS in Logistics Engring., Air Force Inst. Tech., Dayton, Ohio, 1970; D in Bus. Adminstrn., George Washington U., 1980-81. Cert. systems profl., data processor. Enlisted USAF, 1959, advanced through grades to lt. col.; with data processing and logistics inspection Hdqrs. USAF, Washington, 1973-75; with data processing plans Def. Logistics Agy., Washington, 1973-75, Air Force Logistics, Dayton, 1978; resigned USAF, 1979; from instr. to assoc. prof. decision scis. Miami U., Oxford, Ohio, 1979—, asst. chair Mgmt. Info. Systems, 1985—; cons. J.M. Smucker Co., Orville, Ohio, 1982, McCullough-Hyde Hosp., Oxford, 1986—. Author: Auditor Data Processing Knowledge Requirements, 1984; also articles. Decorated Medal of Honor (foreign), Bronze Star. Mem. Data Processing Mgmt. Assn. (internat. com., sec./treas. 1987), Assn. for Systems Mgmt., Assn. for Ednl. Data Systems, Soc. Data Educators, Assn. Computing Machinery, Ohio Mgmt. Info. Systems Dirs. Assn. (founder, past pres.). Baptist. Avocations: computers, reading, gardening, fishing, traveling. Home: 323 Sandra Dr Oxford OH 45056 Office: Miami Univ Decision Scis Dept 221 Culler Oxford OH 45056

DAWSON, JAMES RICHARD, fire and safety engineer; b. Fond du Lac, Wis., July 1, 1936; s. Cecil V.and Helen (Greider) D.; m. Martha Bromley, June 10, 1959; children: Heather Joy, Jamie Ruth. Cert. safety profl., master fire fighter. With Mut. Fire Inspection Bur. New Eng., Salem, Mass., 1959-61, Home Ins. Co., Milw., 1961-65; safety dir. Amron Corp. div. Gulf and Western Co., Waukesha, Wis., 1965-69; fire and safety engr. Ind. U., Bloomington, 1969—. Pres. Waukesha Safety Council, 1969. Mem. Am. Soc. Safety Engrs., Nat. Fire Protection Assn., Vets. of Safety, Ind. Twp. Trustees Assn. (Twp. Trustee of Yr. 1985), Ind. Vol. Fireman's Assn., Fraternal Order Police. Republican. Presbyterian. Home: 3899 E Bethel Ln Bloomington IN 47401 Office: Ind U 840 State Rd 46 Bypass Bloomington IN 47405

DAWSON, NANCY B., health science association administrator; b. Cin.. Student, Purdue U., 1970-72; BS in Nursing, Coll. Mt. St. Joseph, 1974; MEd in Bus., Xavier U., 1985. RN. Clin. supr. Planned Parenthood, Cin., 1974-76; team leader Cin. Health Dept., 1974-76; asst. dir. ARC, Cin., 1976-78, dir. health services, 1978-85, dir. workplace services, 1985-87; dir. women's care ctr. for health and medicine Deaconess Hosp., Cin., 1987—. Mem. adv. bd. Dartmouth Coll., 1985—; mem. Montana Hills Community Orgn., Cin., 1976-86, Westwood Community Assn., Cin., 1985-86; bd. dirs. Big Bros/Big Sisters, Cin., 1973-76, Cin. Assn. Edn. Young Children, 1981-84; trustee Lower River Community Agy., Cin., 1984-86. Mem. Am. Mktg. Assn., Assn. of Fitness in Bus., Am. Pub. Health Assn., Nat. League for Nursing, Am. Soc. for Health Edn. and Tng. Home: 3428 Ferncroft Dr Cincinnati OH 45211 Office: ARC 720 Sycamore St Cincinnati OH 45202

DAWSON, PETER JOHN, pathologist, educator; b. Wolverhampton, Eng., Feb. 17, 1928; came to U.S., 1960; s. Sydney and Bertha (Richards) D.; m. Elizabeth Ann Coombs, Mar. 1, 1982; m. Nancy Sexton Taylor, Apr. 10, 1953 (div. 1969). B.A., Cambridge U., 1949, M.A., 1953, M.B.,B.Ch., 1952, M.D., 1960. Diplomate Am. Bd. Pathology. Intern, Royal Berkshire Hosp., Reading, Eng., 1952-53, Victoria Hosp. for Children, London, 1953; resident St. George's Hosp., London, 1953-54, Royal Postgrad. Med. Sch., 1954-55, 58-59; vis. asst. prof. U. Calif., San Francisco, 1960-62; lectr. U. Newcastle, Eng., 1962-64; assoc. prof. U. Oreg., Portland, 1964-67, prof. pathology, 1967-76; prof. pathology, dir. lab. surg. pathology U. Chgo., 1977—. Contbr. articles to profl. jours. Fellow Royal Coll. Pathologists; mem. Chgo. Pathology Soc (v.p. 1984-86, pres. 1986—), Internat. Acad. Pathology, Am. Assn. Cancer Research, Am. Assn. Pathologists. Episcopalian. Clubs: Burnham Park Yacht, Quadrangle. Avocation: sailing. Office: Lab Surg Pathology Univ Chicago 5841 Maryland Ave Chicago IL 60638

DAWSON, WAYNE LOWELL, minister; b. Independence, Mo., Mar. 29, 1961; s. Lowell Allison Dawson and Marian (Rosbrugh) Walker; m. Robin Kay Jensen, June 5, 1982; children: Roxanne L., Michelle L. Student, Mid-Am. Nazarene Coll. Music minister Ch. of the Nazarene, Omaha, 1977-79; with pub. relations Mid-Am. Nazarene Coll., Olathe, Kans., 1979-81; music minister Ch. of the Nazarene, Overland Park, Kans., 1982; assoc. pastor music and youth First Ch. of the Nazarene, Independence, Kans., 1982—. Sr. Youth Dir. Nazarene Ch. Joplin dist., 1984—. Fellow Independence Ministerial Alliance. Republican. Avocations: automobiles, photgraphy, outdoor activities, woodworking. Home: 316 S 12th Independence KS 67301 Office: 3200 S 10th St Box 595 Independence KS 67301

DAWSON, WILLIAM JAMES, hand and orthopaedic surgeon; b. Oak Park, Ill., May 29, 1937; s. E. James and Esther (Rakow) D.; m. Beverly E. Roberts, Sept. 10, 1961; 1 child, Susan Leigh-Elizabeth. BS cum laude, Elmhurst Coll., 1958; MD, U. Ill. Coll. Medicine, 1962. Cert. Am. Bd. Orthopaedic Surgery (examiner); cert. Nat. Bd. Med. Examiners. Practice medicine specializing in hand surgery Evanbrook Orthopaedics, Evanston, Ill., 1969—; asst. prof. orthopaedic surgery Northwestern U. Med. Sch., Chgo., 1976—; sr. attending staff Evanston Hosp. Corp., 1969—; hand surgery cons. Northwestern U. varsity teams, Evanston, 1984—; lectr. hand and orthopaedic subjects, various nat. and regional groups. Contbr. articles on hand and orthopaedic surgery. Prin. bassoonist Chgo. Symphonic Wind Ensemble, 1986—. Served to capt. U.S. Army, 1963-65. Mem. AMA, Ill. State Med. Soc., Chgo. Med. Soc., Internat. Arts Medicine Assn., Am. Burn Assn., Internat. Platform Soc., Chgo. Orthopaedic Soc., Ill. Orthopaedic Soc. (pres. 1982-83), Am. Acad. Orthopaedic Surgeons, Mid-Am. Orthopaedic Assn., Am. Trauma Soc. (founding), Chgo. Soc. for Surgery of the Hand (pres. 1983-84). Lodge: Masons. Avocations: music, genealogy, electric railroading. Office: Evanbrook Orthopaedic Assocs 2500 Ridge Ave Suite 109 Evanston IL 60201

DAY, REGINA MARGARET, elementary school teacher; b. Creston, Iowa, Oct. 5, 1936; d. Joseph Gabriel and Margaret Regina (Treanor) Hawks; m. Robert Aaron Day, Oct. 19, 1957; children: Edward Robert, Charles Anthony, Michael Joseph, Thomas Aaron, Kevin William. AA, S.W. Community Coll., Creston, 1971; BS magna cum laude, N.W. Mo. State U., 1973. Cert. elem. tchr., Iowa. Elem. tchr. Creston Community Schs., 1973—. Active Creston Hosp. Aux., Creston Hospice. Mem. NEA, Iowa State Edn. Assn., Creston Edn. Assn. Democrat. Roman Catholic. Avocations: reading, needlecraft, crocheting, camping, volunteer work. Home: Rural Rt #1 Box 116 Creston IA 50801 Office: Irving Elem Sch 801 N Elm St Creston IA 50801

DAY, ROBERT JENNINGS, mineral company executive; b. 1925. B.A., Pa. State U., 1947. With U.S. Gypsum Co., 1950—, dist. sales mgr., 1956, mktg. mgr. steel products, 1958, staff mktg. mgr. plastering materials, 1960, mdse. mgr., 1961, dir. product mgmt., 1966; div. gen. mgr. western div. U.S. Gypsum Co., Los Angeles, 1969; corporate v.p. mktg. U.S. Gypsum Co., 1974-77, sr. v.p., 1977-79, exec. v.p., 1979-81, pres., chief operating officer, 1981-85, also dir.; chmn., chief exec. officer USG Corp, 1985—; bd. dirs. Fed. Res. Bank Chgo., 1983—, chmn. bd. dirs., 1986—; dir. BPB Industries, Plc, London, CBI Industries, GATX Corp., Can. Gypsum Co. Bd. dirs. Chgo. Lyric Opera, Great Books Found.; trustee George Williams Coll., Robert Crown Ctr., Hinsdale, Ill. Served to capt. USAFR, 1943-45, 51-53. Address: USG Corp 101 S Wacker Dr Chicago IL 60606

DAY, ROLAND BERNARD, justice Wis. Supreme Ct.; b. Oshkosh, Wis., June 11, 1919; s. Peter Oliver and Joanna King (Wescott) D.; m. Mary Jane Purcell, Dec. 18, 1948; 1 dau., Sarah Jane. B.A., U. Wis., 1942, J.D., 1947. Bar: Wis. 1947. Trainee Office Wis. Atty. Gen., 1947; asso. mem. firm Maloney & Wheeler, Madison, Wis., 1947-49; 1st asst. dist. atty. Dane County, Wis., 1949-52; partner firm Day, Goodman, Madison, 1953-57; firm Wheeler, Van Sickle, Day & Anderson, Madison, 1959-74; legal counsel mem. staff Sen. William Proxmire, Washington, 1957-58; justice Wis. Supreme Ct., 1974—; Mem. Madison Housing Authority, 1960-64, chmn., 1961-63; regent U. Wis. System, 1972-74. Served with AUS, 1943-46. Mem. Am. Bar Assn., State Bar Wis., Am. Trial Lawyers Assn., Am. Judicature Soc., Ygdrasil Lit. Soc. (pres. 1968). Mem. United Ch. of Christ. Clubs: Madison, Madison Lit. Office: Supreme Ct Chambers 231 E State Capitol Madison WI 53702 and: PO Box 1688 Madison WI 53701 *

DAY, STANLEY R., construction company executive; b. 1925. BA, Kenyon Coll., 1948. With Aluminum Alloys Corp., 1948-66; with Champion Home Builders Co., Dryden, Mich., 1971—, chmn. bd. dirs., 1977—. Office: Champion Home Builders Co 5573 North St Dryden MI 48428 *

DAY, WILLIAM ELMER, lawyer; b. Sioux City, Iowa, Mar. 22, 1931; s. Winfred Elmer and Franciska (Croot) D.; m. Shirley J. Lindley, June 2, 1952 (div. 1976); m. H. Joanne Rickord, Aug. 17, 1979; children: Debra, Sue Ellen, David. BS, U. S.D., 1953, JD, 1956. Bar: Iowa 1983. Adjuster State Farm Ins. Co., Sioux City, 1956-82; sole practice Sioux City, 1982—. Served to 1st lt. U.S. Army, 1953-55. Republican. Methodist. Lodge: Kiwanis (pres. Sioux City club 1986—). Home: 3730 Pawnee Pl Sioux City IA 51106 Office: 2004 S Saint Aubin Sioux City IA 51106

DAYAL, SARAT, advertising executive; b. Patna, Bihar, India, Aug. 12, 1952; came to U.S., 1973; s. Lakhsmeswar and Usha (Prasad) D.; m. Mohini Seereeram, July 30, 1972. MA, U. Fla., 1974, MBA, 1975. Advt. mgr. AAR Corp., Elk Grove, Ill., 1976-77; mktg. mgr. Dyrotech, Inc., Joliet, Ill., 1977-82; pres., owner Dayal & Assocs., Lemont, Ill., 1982—. Avocations: travel, gourmet cooking. Office: Dayal & Assocs Inc 111 Stephen St Lemont IL 60439

DAYANI, ELIZABETH LOUISE CROW, nurse, executive, educator; b. Birmingham, Ala., Apr. 28, 1950; d. Jon Killough and Flora Louise (Worthington) Crow; m. John H. Dayani, June 13, 1970; 1 son, John H. B.S.N., Vanderbilt U., 1971, M.S.N. cum laude, 1972. Instr., Vanderbilt U. Sch. Nursing, Nashville, 1972-74; dir., practitioner Moore County Primary Care Center, Lynchberg, Tenn., 1974-75; family nurse practitioner Metro Health Dept., Nashville, 1975-76; asst. prof. Wayne State U. Sch. Nursing, Detroit, 1976-77; asst. prof. U. Kans. Sch. Nursing, Kansas City, 1977-81, assoc. prof., 1981-82; co-owner, exec. dir. Am. Nursing Resources, Kansas City, Mo., 1982—. Bd. dirs. Midwest Bioethics Ctr., Kans. Nurses Found.; mem. adv. bd. Cradles and Crayon. Recipient Service award Moore County Health Council, 1975, Exceptional Performance award Am. Nursing Resources, 1986; named one of Outstanding Young Women Am. Good Housekeeping mag., 1985. Mem. Am. Nurses Assn., Am. Pub. Health Assn., Nat. Assn. Home Care, Nat. League Nursing, Nat. Assn. Women Bus. Owners, Sigma Theta Tau (Leadership award 1986). Republican. Presbyterian. Clubs: Central Exchange. Author: (with Betty R. Riccardi) The Nurse Entrepreneur, 1982; contbg. editor: The Nurse Practitioner, 1979-83, mem. editorial bd., 1983—; mem. editorial bd. Nursing Economics, 1983, assoc. editor, 1985—; mem. editorial bd. The Kansas Nurse, 1983—.

DAYRINGER, RICHARD LEE, medical educator, Baptist minister; b. Carthage, Mo., Feb. 3, 1934; s. Joseph Allen and Sarah Marlin (Ruppert) D.; m. Evelyn Janet Hymer, Jan. 26, 1952; children: Stephen Lee, David Carter, Deborah Evelyn, Daniel Hymer, James Ray. AA, Southwest Bapt. Coll., Bolivar, Mo., 1953; AB, William Jewell Coll., 1955; MDiv, Midwestern Bapt. Theol. Sem., 1961; ThD, New Orleans Bapt. Theol. Sem., 1968. Ordained to ministry Bapt. Ch., 1952. Pastor various Bapt. Chs. Mo., Kans., La., 1951-65; interim pastor Santa Fe Hills Bapt. Ch., Kansas City, Mo., 1968-69; intern So. Bapt. Hosp., New Orleans, 1961-63; resident in psychiatry East La. State Hosp., Jackson, 1963-64; instr. pastoral care Immaculate Conception (Mo.) Sem., 1967-72; clin. instr. in pastoral care, then adj. prof. Midwestern Bapt. Theol. Sem., Kansas City, 1968-74, guest prof., 1967, 69; instr. religion and pastoral counseling sch. medicine U. Mo., Kansas City, 1971-74; dir. dept. pastoral care and counseling Bapt. Meml. Hosp., Kansas City, 1965-74; adj. prof. human devel. counseling Sangamon State U., Springfield, Ill., 1979—; dir. clin. edn. in psychosocial care sch. medicine So. Ill. U., Springfield, 1974—, assoc. prof., 1974-82, prof., depts. of family practice and med. humanities, 1982—; assoc. dir. Alcohol Edn. Project, Nat. Inst. Alcoholics Anonymous Assn., 1977-79; mem. adv. com. on tenure grievance, 1976; mem. promotion and tunure com. 1977-79, 84—; mem. student progress com., 1979-84; chmn. med. edn. dept. rev. com., 1982; mem. med. student faculty advisory program, 1983—; mem. med. service and research plan, 1984—; med. staff affiliate and clin. counselor St. John's Hosp., Springfield, 1975—; founder and supr. Interfaith Counseling, Inc., Springfield, 1979—; tchr. Boyce Bible Sch., Springfield, 1980-82. Author: God Cares for You, 1983; editor: Pastor and Patient, 1982; contbr. numerous chpts. to books, articles to profl. jours. Served as asst. scoutmaster, then scoutmaster, Troop 11 Boy Scouts Am., Springfield, 1978-84; also v.p. Abraham Lincoln council, 1985, council chaplain, 1986—. Recipient Cen. Research award So. Ill. U. Sch. Medicine, 1979-81, Research award Joint Council for Research in Pastoral Care and Counseling, 1981, Humanitarian Service award for 1985, Greater Springfield Interfaith Assn.; grantee Midwestern Bapt. Theol. Sem., 1959-61, New Orleans Bapt. Theol. Sem., 1961-62, East La. State Hosp., 1963-64, Eastern Star Lodge, 1961-62, NEH, 1977. Fellow Coll. Chaplains Am. Protestant Hosp. Assn. (chair nat. research com. 1968, nat. editorial com. 1973-74); mem. Am. Assn. Marriage and Family Therapy (supr. 1983—, chair Ill. div. devel. com. 1983-84, 87), Am. Assn. Pastoral Counselors (diplomate 1969—, chair membership com. cen. region 1970-82), Am. Assn. Sex Educators, Counselors and Therapists (cert. sex therapist 1979—), Am. Soc. Clin. Hypnosis, Assn. Clin. Pastoral Edn., Inc. (chaplain supr. 1964—, various coms., 1968—, Researcher of Yr. award 1984), Assn. Bapt. Chaplains (pres. 1970), Assn. Mo. Chaplains (pres. 1967-68), Jackson County Med. Soc. (mem. mediation com. 1974), Kaw Valley Bapt. Assn. (moderator 1960), Ministers in Med. Edn. (newsletter editor 1978-81), Nat. Found. Sudden Infant Death (bd. dirs. Kansas City chpt. 1973-74), Soc. Health and Human Values (publs. com. 1979-80), Soc. Tchrs. Family Medicine (mem. task force on humanities, 1981—), So. Bapt. Conv. Democrat. Lodge: Optimist (program chmn. Kansas City chpt. 1970-73). Home: 3221 Dorchester Springfield IL 62704 Office: So Ill U Sch Medicine Box 3926 Springfield IL 62708

DAYTON, ROBERT JACKSON, retail executive; b. Mpls., Feb. 4, 1942; s. Donald C. and Lucy (Jackson) D.; m. Joan Layng, May 19, 1964; children: James, Tobin, Scott. BA, Yale U., 1964. V.p. and gen. mgr. Dayton-Hudson Store, Mpls., 1964-77; chmn. and chief exec. officer Harold Corp., Mpls., 1977-85; ptnr. Conservatory Devel. Project, Mpls., 1985—; bd. dirs. Williams-Sonoma. Chmn. Downtown Council of Mpls., 1984—; bd. dirs. United Way of Mpls., 1985—, Mpls. Found.; trustee Carleton Coll., Northfield, Minn., 1984—. Office: Harold Corp 808 Nicollet Mall Minneapolis MN 55402

DAYTON, TIMOTHY JOHN, merchant marine officer; b. Port Clinton, Ohio, Aug. 8, 1954; s. Lloyd John and Audrey (Hallier) D.; m. Regina Laudi, July 28, 1978. BS, U.S. Merchant Marine Acad., 1976; postgrad., Cleve. State U., 1983—. Lic. U.S. Coast Guard Great Lakes Master; 3d mate Oceans. 1st mate, relief master Ford Motor Co./Rouge Steel, Dearborn, Mich., 1976—. Recruiting rep. U.S. Merchant Marine and Naval Acads. Served to lt. comdr. USNR. Mem. Great Lakes Hist. Soc., U.S. Naval Inst., U.S. Naval Res. Assn., Internat. Shipmasters Assn., Kings Point Alumni Assn., Beta Gamma Sigma. Avocation: travel. Home: PO Box 36742 Strongsville OH 44136 Office: Ford Motor/Rouge Steel Marine Office Dearborn MI 48121-1699

DAYVAULT, DAVID MARCUS, JR., oil company executive; b. Wichita, Kans., June 15, 1954; s. David Marcus and Rachel Lou (Wright) D.; m. Amy Lou Gladden, July 26, 1986. BBA, U. Okla., 1975. CPA, Mo., Kans. Acct. Fox & Co., St. Louis, 1975-77; tax mgr. Fox & Co., Wichita, 1978-82; fin. mgr. Am. Energies, Wichita, 1982—. Mem. Peteroleum Accts. Soc. Kans. (v.p. 1985-86, bd. dirs. 1983-86), Kans. Soc. CPA's, Petroleum Accts. Soc. Kans. Avocations: camping, sailing, music. Home: 904 Shadyway Wichita KS 67203 Office: Am Energies Corp 155 N Market Suite 710 Wichita KS 67202

DCAMP, CHARLES BARTON, educator, musician; b. Fairfield, Iowa, Feb. 16, 1932; s. Glenn Franklin and Nina Clarice (Larson) DC.; student Bradley U., 1950-51; B.S., U. Ill., 1956, M.S., 1957; Ph.D., U. Iowa, 1980; m. Ruth Joyce MacDonald, June 27, 1953; children—James Charles, Douglas Kevin, David Michael, Richard Manley, Paul Frederick, Jon Barton. Tchr., Watervliet (Mich.) Pub. Sch., 1958-61; tchr. music United Twp. High Sch., East Moline, Ill., 1961-63; band dir. Pleasant Valley (Iowa) Schs., 1963-74; prof. music St. Ambrose Coll., Davenport, Iowa, 1974—, also dir. bands, chmn. div. fine arts and chmn. dept. music; guest dir., adjudicator festivals, music contests Iowa, Ill., Minn.; producer Quad-City Music Guild, 1973-77, music dir., 1967-81; chmn. Iowa All-State Band, 1971-74; tchr. woodwinds Bemidji State Coll. Band Camp, 1969—. Mem. Riverdale Vol. Fire Co., 1966-75, pres., 1971-73; founder, first conductor Quad-City Wind Ensemble, 1987—. Served with AUS, 1952-55. Recipient Karl King Disting. Service award Iowa Bandmasters, 1987. Mem. Iowa (past pres.), Nat. Cath. bandmasters assns., Coll. Band Dirs. Nat. Assn., Music Educators Nat. Conf., Iowa Music Educators (pres.), Am. Fedn. Musicians, Am. Sch. Band Dirs. Assn., Nat. Band Assn., N.E.A. (life), Phi Mu Alpha Sinfonia, Phi Delta Kappa, Tau Kappa Epsilon. Republican. Methodist. Editor, Iowa Music Educator mag., 1978-80 ; contbr. articles to profl. jours. Home: 301 Circle Dr Riverdale Bettendorf IA 52722 Office: St Ambrose Coll Davenport IA 52803

DEAL, MARY HOLMAN, urban planner, writer, historian; b. Evanston, Ill., Feb. 5, 1944; d. George Varnum and Emily L. (Sedlacek) D.; A.B., U. Chgo., 1965, M.A., 1966. Adminstrv. asst. Am. Soc. Planning Ofcls., Chgo., 1966-67; asst. planner Genesee County Met. Planning Commn., Flint, Mich., 1967-70; individual practice as planner and designer, Akron, Ohio, 1970-73; housing planner N.E. Ohio Areawide Coordinating Agy., Cleve., 1973-74; regional planner Miami Valley Regional Planning Commn., Dayton, Ohio, 1974-79; project mgr. nat. competition identifying and promoting urban planning activities and designs for women in urban environments HUD, 1980-81; project mgr. Women and Urban Planning: A Bibliography, HUD and Council Planning Librarians, 1980-81. Mem. Am. Planning Assn. (nat. task force mag.; contbr. to Ency. of Cleveland History. planning for women 1979, dir. planning and women div. 1979-81), NOW (treas. Ohio 1975-77), Ohio Women, Inc. (bd. dirs. 1977-78. treas. 1978-79). Contbr. articles to profl. jours. and nat. mags.; contbr. to Ency. of Cleveland History. Home: 2062 Ayers Ave Akron OH 44313

DEAL, MAX EDWARD, auditor; b. Terre Haute, Ind., Oct. 4, 1947; s. George Curtis and Inez Ellen (Jones) D.; m. Cynthia Leuse Weathers, Sept. 22, 1972; children: Eric Curtis, Jeffrey Ryan. BS in Acctg., Ind. State U., 1970; MBA, Butler U., 1983. CPA, Ind.; cert. internal auditor, Ind. Sr. asst. Deloitte Haskins and Sells, Indpls., 1969-72; mgr. provider audit Blue Cross Blue Shield of Ind., Indpls., 1972-77, dir. gen. acctg., 1977-82, dir. Civilian Health and Med. Program for the Uniformed Services, 1982-83, corp. internal auditor, 1983—. Served with U.S. Army, 1970-71. Mem. Am. Inst. CPA's, Inst. Internal Auditors (2d v.p. Indpls. chpt. 1985-86, pres. 1986—). Avocations: small game hunting, fishing, golf, chess. Home: 6710 E 52d Place Indianapolis IN 46226 Office: Blue Cross Blue Shield Ind 120 W Market St Indianapolis IN 46204

DEAL, WILLIAM THOMAS, school psychologist; b. Canton, Ohio, Dec. 18, 1949; s. Richard Lee and Rheta Lucille (Gerber) D.; m. Paula Nespeca, Aug. 5, 1972. B.S., Bowling Green State U., 1972; M.A., John Carroll U., 1977; postgrad. Kent State U., 1979—. Sci. tchr. Westlake Schs., 1972-76, head bldg. sci. dept., 1974-76; intern sch. psychologist Garfield Heights Schs., 1976-77, sch. psychologist, 1977—; pvt. practice psychology, Parma Heights, Ohio, 1982-84. Alternate mem. adv. council Cuyahoga County Spl. Edn. Service Ctr., 1977—. Recipient Cert. of Recognition, Garfield Heights Bd. Edn., 1980; Outstanding Achievement award Cleve. Assn. for Children with Learning Disabilities, Inc., 1980. Mem. Nat. Assn. Sch. Psychologists, Am. Orthopsychiat. Assn., United Teaching Profession, Ohio Sch. Psychology Assn., Cleve. Assn. Sch. Psychologists, Phi Delta Kappa. Republican. Mem. Reformed Ch. Home: 5290 Kings Hwy Fairview Park OH 44126 Office: 5640 Briarcliff Dr Garfield Heights OH 44125

DEAN, ALBERTA LAVAUN, nurse; b. Lafayette, Ind., Apr. 12, 1925; d. Edward Louis and Leona May (Delong) Anderson; m. Guy Dean, Oct. 16, 1948; children—Gregory A., Rebecca A., Eulonda S., Melissa K., Marcia L., Valerie A. R.N., Hurley Med. Ctr., 1948. Staff nurse Hurley Med. Ctr., Flint, Mich., 1948-53, McLaren Gen. Hosp., 1953-54, Lafayette (Ind.) Home Hosp., 1954—; resolve through sharing counselor for perinatal loss, 1985—. Mem. Southside Wesleyan Ch. Mem. Nurses Assn. of Am. Coll. Obstetricians and Gynecologists. Republican. Home: 276 Dayton Rd Dayton IN 47941 Office: Lafayette Home Hosp 2400 South St Lafeyette IN 47941

DEAN, DAVID J., data processing and systems analysis educator; b. Madison, Wis., Feb. 8, 1948; s. Donald Walter and Melody (Kuehl) D.; div., 1979; children: Diane, Dory; m. Stephanie A. Brown, Aug. 4, 1984; 1 child, Charles C. BBA, U. Wis., Whitewater, 1971. Systems analyst The Milw. Rd., Chgo., 1972-74, Verex, Madison, 1974-77, Oscar Mayer and Co., Madison, 1977-78; instr. Madison Area Tech. Coll., 1978—. Mem. Data Processing Mgmt Assn., Madison Area Tech. Coll. Tchrs. Union (pres. 1982—), Wis. Fedn. Tchrs. (v.p. Madison 1984-85, pres. 1986—). Democrat. Avocation: coin collecting. Home: 1406 Dover Dr Waunakee WI 53597 Office: Madison Area Tech Coll 3550 Anderson St Madison WI 53704

DEAN, ERIC, philosophy and religion educator; b. London, Oct. 30, 1924; came to U.S., 1947, naturalized 1971; s. Francis Ernest and Mabel Johanna (Ritchie) D.; m. Betty Jane Garrett, July 30, 1948; children—Daphne, Eric Jr., Jonathan. Student North Park Coll., Chgo., 1947-58; A.B., U. Chgo., 1950, B.D., 1953, Ph.D., 1959; D.D. (hon.) Hanover Coll., 1978, Christian Theol. Sem., 1979. Ordained to ministry Presbyterian Ch., 1955. Instr. philosophy, asst. prof. No. Central Coll., Naperville, Ill., 1956-57; prof. philosophy, religion Wabash Coll., Crawfordsville, Ind., 1957—; overseer St. Meinrad Archabbey, Ind., 1968—; dir. Wabash Exec. Program, 1983—. Author: The Good News about Sin, 1982. Contbr. articles to profl. jours. Served with RAF, 1942-47. Mem. Am. Theol. Soc. (pres. 1968-69), Ind. Acad. Religion (pres. 1966-67), Am. Soc. Ch. History, N. Am. Acad. Ecumenists. Democrat. Presbyterian. Avocations: monasteries, bicycle touring, backpacking. Office: Wabash Coll Crawfordsville IN 47933

DEAN, JAMES LEA, retired obstetrician-gynecologist; b. Madison, Wis., Nov. 3, 1916; s. James Phillip and Maud Luella (Lea) D.; m. Margaret Joan Woodhead (div. 1952); children: Barbara, James Jr., Peter, Michael, Mary; m. Ruth Eleanor Ubbelohde, Jan. 28, 1954. Student, U.S. Naval Acad., 1935-37; BS in pre-medicine, U. Wis., 1939, MD, 1943. Practice medicine specializing in ob-gyn Dean Med. Ctr., Madison, 1947-78; clin. instr. ob-gyn U. Wis., Madison, 1956-78; practice medicine specializing in ob-gyn Sturgeon Bay, Wis., 1978-83; bd. dirs. 1st Fed. Savs. and Loan, Madison. Served to lt. MC, USN Med. Corps., 1943-47, PTO. Fellow Am. Coll. Ob-Gyn (life, founding fellow); mem. Wis. Soc. Obstetricians and Gynecologists. Republican. Roman Catholic. Club: Sturgeon Bay Yacht (sec. 1982—). Lodge: Rotary. Avocations: piano, hiking, reading, golfing, sailing. Home: 3866 Glidden Dr Sturgeon Bay WI 54235

DEAN, ROBERT WALTER, JR., licensing company executive; b. Milw., July 8, 1950; s. Robert W. and Kathleen M. (Manion) D.; m. Karen Lois Turner, Apr. 7, 1973; children: Matthew S., Elizabeth E. BA, U. Wis., Madison, 1972; MBA, U. Wis., Milw., 1979. Sales rep. Best Block Co., Milw., 1972-79, sales mgr., 1979-80, v.p. mktg., 1980-83; pres., owner Designer Blocks, Inc., Milw., 1983—; v.p. Concrete Masonry Industries, Milw., 1982-83. Patentee building structure blocks. Mem. Wis. Concrete and Products Assn. (treas., bd. dirs. 1980-83), U. Wis. Milw. Alumni Assn. (bd. dirs. 1981—), U. Wis. Milw. Bus. Alumni Assn. (pres., bd. dirs. 1985—). Lodge: Kiwanis (bd. dirs. Milw. club 1986—). Avocations: basketball, softball, tennis. Office: 3934 N Ridgefield Circle Milwaukee WI 53211

DEANE, LARRY ALLEN, accountant; b. Grand Rapids, Mich., Sept. 5, 1944; s. Donald A. and Mary B. (Humbarger) D.; m. Susan Marie Tibbets, Aug. 16, 1968; children: Brenda Sue, Tracie Lynn. Assoc., Grand Rapids Jr. Coll., 1965; BBA, Western Mich. U., 1967. CPA, Mich. Staff mem. Beene, Garter & Hrouda, Grand Rapids, Mich., 1967-72; controller Cascade Data, Inc., Grand Rapids, 1972-73; tax mgr. Beene, Garter & Co., Grand Rapids, 1973-76, ptnr., 1976—; adv. com. Grand Valley State Coll. Grad. Sch. of Taxation, Allendale, Mich. Named one of Outstanding Local Pres., Mich. Jaycees, 1979. Mem. Am. Inst. CPA's, Mich. Assn. CPA's, Internat. Assn. Fin. Planners, West Mich. Estate Planning Council (bd. dir. 1981-83), West Mich. Pension Conference, Grand Rapids Area C. of C. (chmn. 1984), Grand Rapids Jaycees (pres. 1978-79). Roman Catholic. Club: Peninsular, Blythefield Country, Belmont, Mich. Lodge: KC. Avocations: reading, basketball, racquetball. Home: 549 Russwood NE Grand Rapids MI 49505 Office: Beene Garter & Co 50 Monroe NW Suite 600 Grand Rapids MI 49503

DE ANGELIS, ANTHONY ALEXANDER, brokerage executive; b. Kenosha, Wis., Apr. 10, 1938; s. Domineck and Angeline Victoria (Ciotti) De A.; m. Judith Jean Krause, June 9, 1962; children: Mark, Lisa, Jennifer. BS, U. Wis., 1962; postgrad, U. Wis., Whitewater. Pub. relations supr. Wis. Bell, Milw., 1967-72; v.p. advt., pub. relations First Fin. Savs., Milw., 1972-75; manpower asst. U.S. Dept. Labor, Waukesha, Wis., 1975-77; asst. corp. relations dir. MGIC Investment Corp., Milw., 1977-81; v.p. Blunt, Ellis and Loewi, Milw., 1981-86; bd. govs. Am. Fedn. Musicians, Waukesha and Washington, 1970-80. V.p. polit. contact Assn. Retarded Citizens, Oconomowoc, Wis, 1970-72; co-chmn. Southeastern Wis. United Cerebral Palsy, 1971. Served with USN, 1963-64. Recipient Humanitarian Service award United Cerebral Palsy, Milw., 1972, Disting. Service award Boy Scouts Am., Waukesha, 1981, Youth Work award, Western Lakes Boy Scouts Am., Waukesha, 1982. Roman Catholic. Club: Milw. Press (trustee). Home: 1221 Saratoga Pkwy Oconomowoc WI 53066

DEANS, THOMAS SEYMOUR, lawyer; b. St. Louis, Mar. 21, 1946; s. Thomas Ellison and Eva May (Seymour) D.; m. Barbara Jean Wilson, Aug. 10, 1974; children: Katherine, Tyler. BA, Northwestern U., 1968; JD cum laude, U. Minn., 1973. Bar: Minn. 1973, U.S. Dist. Ct. Minn. 1978. Senate counsel Minn. State Senate, St. Paul, 1973-78; ptnr. Knutson, Flynn, Hetland & Deans, St. Paul, 1978—. Mem. ABA, Minn. Bar Assn., Ramsey County Bar Assn. (chmn. legis. com. 1984-85), Nat. Assn. Bond Lawyers, Nat. Sch. Bds. Assn. Council Sch. Attys. Lutheran. Home: 1401 June Ave S Minneapolis MN 55416 Office: Knutson Flynn Hetland & Deans 345 Cedar Suite 800 Saint Paul MN 55101

DEARDORFF, CLARE ANN, pediatric physical therapist; b. Johnstown, Pa., Aug. 24, 1942; d. William Joseph and Marian (Moore) Larrimer; m. Howard Lee Deardorff, Aug. 21, 1965; children: David Scott, Amy Elizabeth. BS in Phys. Therapy, U. Pitts., 1964; MA in Child Devel. and Family Life, Eastern Mich. U., 1983. Lic. physical therapist. Phys. therapist Pa. Vocat. Rehab. Ctr., Johnstown, 1964-65, St. Joseph's Mercy Hosp., Ann Arbor, Mich., 1965-66; pediatric phys. therapist Northville (Mich.) Schs., 1976-77; dir. phys. therapy dept. Woodford Mem.. Hosp., Versalles, Ky., 1977-78; pvt. practice specializing in phys. therapy Lexington, Ky., 1977-80; pediatric phys. therapist Ypsilanti (Mich.) Pub. Schs., 1980—. Family life educator, pre-marital counselor Ypsilanti Free Meth. Ch., 1983—. Mem. NEA, Mich. Assn. Sch. Therapists, Am. Phys. Therapy Assn., Assn. Couples for Marriage Enrichment. Avocations: quilting, sailing, cross country skiing. Home: 2547 Meade Ct Ann Arbor MI 48105 Office: New Horizon Ednl Ctr 1555 W Cross St Ypsilanti MI 48197

DEARDORFF, DARRYL K., business consultant, accountant; b. Canton, Ohio, June 3, 1945; s. Harry H. and Gladys M. (Kinsley) D.; m. Juanita S. Huber, Dec. 9, 1966; children: Duane L., Dana L. BS, Manchester Coll., 1967. CPA, Ohio. Sr. acct. Ernst & Ernst, Dayton, Ohio, 1967-71; tax mgr., then controller, then v.p. fin. Dayton Press Inc., 1971-84, v.p. adminstrn. and fin., 1984—; bd. dirs. Cardinal Tool, Dayton, Dodds Monument, Dayton. Bd. dirs., chmn. Dist. of So. Ohio Ch. of the Brethren, Dayton, 1980—; moderator Emmanuel Ch. of the Brethren, Dayton, 1986; organizer, chmn. 400 Club, Dayton, 1983-84. Mem. Am. Inst. CPA's, Ohio Soc. CPA's. Home: 6888 Jonetta St Dayton OH 45424 Office: Dayton Press Inc 6750 Brandt Pk Dayton OH 45424

DEASEY, STEPHEN MICHAEL, food products executive; b. Pitts., Dec. 26, 1954; s. John Plummer and Shirley Jeanne (Allen) D.; m. Mary Elizabeth Nelson, Sept. 19, 1981; children: Stephen Michael Jr., Brendon Patrick. BA in Econs., Yale U., 1976; MBA, Harvard U., 1978. Mgmt. trainee CFS Continental Inc., Seattle, 1978-79; regional v.p. Sugar Food Corp. div. CFS Continental Inc., Columbus, Ohio, 1979-83, sr. v.p. adminstrn., 1984-86, sr. v.p., 1986—. Mem. Council Logistics Mgmt. Roman Catholic. Club: Yale, Harvard. Avocations: flying, golf. Home: 5517 Preswick Dr Dublin OH 43017 Office: Sugar Food Corp 2000 Westbelt Dr Columbus OH 43228

DEASY, THERESA, law firm financial executive; b. N.Y.C., May 19, 1958; d. Thomas Edward Deasy and Dorothy Beatrice (Federico) Deasy Cox; m. Dennis James Stanton, May 29, 1983. BS in Commerce, DePaul U., 1981; postgrad. Keller Grad. Sch. Acctg. clk. Kirkland & Ellis, Chgo., 1977-80; fin. div. clk. Talman Home Fed. Savs. & Loan, Chgo., 1980-81; staff acctg. Sachnoff Weaver & Rubenstien, Chgo., 1981-83, asst. controller, 1984—. Vol. dir., treas. The Commons of Evanston, 1985-87; leader Ravenswood Hosp. Mental Health Ctr., Chgo., 1984 . Mem. Am. Soc. Women Accts., Nat. Assn. Female Execs., Chgo. Council Fgn. Relations, Ill. Notaries Assn., Assn. Legal Adminstrn., Law Office Mgrs. Assn. Avocations: travel, photography, skiing, racquetball. Home: 1408 W Norwood Chicago IL 60660 Office: Sachnoff Weaver & Rubenstein Ltd 30 S Wacker Dr 29th Floor Chicago IL 60606

DEATON, ROBERT LEE, II, obstetrician, gynecologist; b. Indpls., Aug. 5, 1949; s. Robert Lee and Grace Vonna (Davis) D. AB in Zoology, Ind. U., 1970, MD, 1974. Asst. prof. ob-gyn Ind U. Med. Ctr., Indpls., 1978-79; physician Henry County Hosp., New Castle, Ind., 1979-81; practice medicine specializing in ob-gyn Indpls., 1981—. Author: Post-Operative Gynecological Care, 1981. Fellow Am. Coll. Ob-Gyn. Republican. Methodist. Avocations: sailing, skiing. Home: 1711 Wood Valley Dr Carmel IN 46032 Office: Ob-Gyn Assocs 3850 Shore Dr #203 Indianapolis IN 46254

DEBARTOLO, EDWARD J., SR., real estate developer; b. Youngstown, Ohio, May 17, 1919; s Michael and Rose (Villani) DeB.; m. Maria Patricia Montani, Dec. 18, 1944; children: Edward J., Marie D. Grad., U. Notre

Dame; D.Sc. hon., Fla. Inst. Tech., 1981. Registered profl. engr. registered surveyor. Ptnr. Michael DeBartolo Constrn. Co., Youngstown, 1936-41; pres. Michael DeBartolo Constrn. Co., 1946-48, Edward J. DeBartolo Corp., Youngstown, 1958-79; chmn. bd., chief exec. officer Edward J. DeBartolo Corp., 1979—; owner (3 race tracks), U.S. Football League franchise, (soccer team), (hockey team). 2d lt. C.E. U.S. Army, 1941-46, Okinawa. Named Man of Yr. Mahoning Valley Econ. Devel. Corp., 1983; named Man of Yr. City of Pitts., 1983. Mem. Urban Land Inst., Nat. Realty Com., Internat. Council Shopping Ctrs. Roman Catholic. Office: The Edward J. DeBartolo Corp 7620 Market St Youngstown OH 44512 *

DEBARTOLO, HANSEL MARION, JR., otorhinolaryngology surgeon; b. Aurora, Ill., May 13, 1947; s. Hansel Marion and Rosemary (Boetto) D.; m.Susan Elizabeth Debartolo, June 26, 1977; children: Doré, Hansel III, Merrit, Janae, Raquel. BA cum laude, U. Minn., 1969; MD, Loyola U., Chgo., 1972. Fellow in surgery Mayo Clinic., Rochester, Minn.; fellow in otorhinolaryngology Geisinger Clinic, Danville, Pa.; chief of staff AmSurg, Joliet, Ill.; ptnr. Chgo. White Sox, H.M.D. Racing Stables; attending surgeon Delnor Community Hosp., Geneva, Ill. Contbr. articles to profl. jours. Fellow Deafness Research Assn. (life.), Am. Acad. Otorhinolaryngology, Chgo. Larynigol. and Otological Soc., Am. Rhinologic Soc., Priestly Surgical Soc., Drs. Mayo Soc.; mem. Ill. Soc. Opthalmology and Otolaryngology (exec. council, sec.-treas.), Pa. Acad. Ophthalmology and Otolaryngology. Roman Catholic. Club: Aurora Country. Avocations: tennis, skiing, golf. Home: 20 Dorchester Ct Aurora IL 60504 Office: 45 S Lincoln Aurora IL 60505

DEBEAR, RICHARD STEPHEN, library planning consultant; b. N.Y.C., Jan. 18, 1933; s. Arthur A. and Sarah (Morrison) deB.; m. Estelle Carmel Grandon, Apr. 27, 1951; children—Richard, Jr., Diana deBear Fortson, Patricia deBear Talkington, Robert, Christopher, Nancy. B.S., Queens Coll. CUNY, 1953. Sales rep. Sperry Rand Corp., Blue Bell, Pa., 1954-76; pres. Library Design Assocs., Plymouth, Mich., 1976—, Am. Library Ctr., Plymouth, 1981—; bldg. cons. to numerous libraries, 1965—. Mem. ALA, Mich. Library Assn. Office: Library Design Assocs Inc 859 S Main St Plymouth MI 48170

DEBENEDICTIS, DEBRA CERGOL, teacher; b. Cleve., Nov. 28, 1951; d. Carl Clarence and Mary Mildred (Ondracek) Cergol; m. Leonard Michael DeBenedictis, May 31, 1980; children: Jeremy, Michael. BS in Edn., Ohio U., 1972; MA in Polit. Sci., U. Akron, 1982. Cert. elem. tchr., Ohio. Tchr. Nordonia Hills Schs., Northfield, Ohio, 1972—; Mem. Reading Textbook/ Competency Testing Com., 1984—. Mem. Community Intervention, Northfield, 1984—. Mem. NEA, Ohio Edn. Assn., Nordonia Hills Edn. Assn. (former grievance chairperson). Democrat. Roman Catholic. Avocations: piano, swimming, bicycling, reading, tennis. Home: 4205 Ellsworth Rd Stow OH 44224 Office: Rushwood Elementary 8200 Rushwood Ln Northfield OH 44067

DEBLANDER, DAVID JOHN, bakery owner; b. Pitts., June 3, 1951; s. Alex A. and Madeline M. (Ducsay) DeB.; m. Kathryn Kahn, Feb. 8, 1953; 1 child, Kahlia. Student, Wittenberg U., 1969-72, Schiller Coll., 1971-72. Owner, pres. Livin Bread Bakery, Madison, Wis., 1976—. Home: 18 Merrill Crest Madison WI 53705

DEBOLD, VICKI SUE, insurance broker; b. Macomb, Ill., Sept. 14, 1947; d. Robert Melvin and Laura Mae (Magnuson) Pollock; student public schs.; m. Neil C. Goforth, July 18, 1969 (dec. Mar. 1971); m. 2d, David Loran DeBold, Nov. 18, 1978. Lic. ins. producer, Ill. Broker-owner Goforth Ins. Agy., Bushnell, Ill., from 1971; sales exec. WJEQ-FM Radio, McDonough Broadcasting, Inc., 1983; profl. singer with group Life, 1972-74. Judge Miss Quincy Pageant, 1974. Named Young Career Woman of Yr., Bus. and Profl. Women Macomb (Ill.), 1972; Miss Macomb of 1966-67. Mem. Ill. Assn. Nat. Campers and Hikers Assn. (hon., Wild Life Refuge award 1975), Nat. Fedn. Small Businesses, Nat. Assn. Female Execs., Ind. Ins. Agts. Ill., Profl. Ins. Agts. Ill., Bushnell Ind. Ins. Agts. Assn., Macomb Ind. Ins. Agts. Assn., McDonough County Geneal. Soc.. Republican. Presbyterian. Home: 1227 W Adams St Macomb IL 61455

DEBOTH, CAROL JEAN, investment executive; b. Milw., Dec. 29, 1950; d. Raymond F. and Loretta (Petrie) DeB.; m. Roger L. Dominowski, Sept. 19, 1984. BA, U. Ill., Chgo., 1972, MBA, 1985.; MA, Northeastern U., 1977. Asst. to editor Jour. of Abnormal Psychology, Chgo., 1974-76; tchr. remedial reading Mendel High Sch., Chgo., 1976-77; tchr. spl. edn. Roosevelt Jr. High Sch., Bellwood, Ill., 1977-79; program adminstr. U. Ill., Chgo., 1979-86; account exec. Dean Witter Reynolds, Schaumburg, Ill., 1986—. Pres. Oak Park (Ill.) Tennis Assn., 1985-86. Mem. Nat. Network Women in Sales. Home: 1142 Wenonah Oak Park IL 60304 Office: Dean Witter Reynolds Inc 1900 E Golf Rd Schaumburg IL 60173

DEBREY, ANDREW DALE, die casting company executive; b. Baraboo, Wis., Sept. 20, 1922; s. Michael and Lucille (Graff) D.; m. Francis Adele Whitfill, May 15, 1942; children: Drew, Elizabeth, Julie. AA, U. Ill., 1942. Engr. Ametek, E. Moline, Ill., 1947-48; pres. Quad City Die Casting Co., Moline, Ill., 1948—, also bd. dirs.; bd. dirs., pres. Red Oak (Iowa) Die Casting, 1986—; pres. Thermizer, Davenport, Iowa, 1982—. Patentee in field. Served to pvt. U.S. Army, 1943-45. Republican. Roman Catholic. Club: Davenport. Avocation: sailing. Home: 2531 37th Ave Rock Island IL 61201

DEBREY, DREW STEPHEN, die casting company executive; b. Moline, Ill., Oct. 29, 1953; s. Andrew Dale and Francis Adele (Whitfill) D.; m. Cynthia Anne Dudley, Apr. 19, 1986. BA, Knox Coll., 1975; MBA, Tulane U., 1977. Asst. gen. mgr. Quad City Die Casting Co., Moline, 1977-84, treas., 1977—, asst. sec., 1981—, gen. mgr., 1984—. Named Outstanding Am., Outstanding Young Men U.S., 1986. Mem. Am. Die Casting Inst. (Cert. Appreciation 1983, dir. 1986—), Am. Prodn. and Inventory Control Soc. (chmn. 1983-84), Beta Gamma Sigma, Beta Alpha Psi. Republican. Presbyterian. Club: Davenport (Iowa). Avocations: piano, community theater. Home: 3225 14th St Rock Island IL 61201 Office: Quad City Die Casting Co 3800 River Dr Moline IL 61265

DE BRULER, ROGER O., justice Ind. Supreme Ct.; b. 1934. A.B., LL.B., Ind. U. Bar: Ind. 1960. Dep. city prosecutor City of Indpls., 1960-63; judge Ind. Circuit Ct., Steuben County, 1963-68; Now justice Supreme Ct. of Ind., has also served as chief justice, 1968—. Office: Supreme Court of Indiana 321 State House Indianapolis IN 46204 *

DE BYLE, THOMAS DEWAYNE, accountant; b. Rhinelander, Wis., Jan. 24, 1960; s. DeWayne Murley and Janet Elizabeth (Cleary) De B. BBA, St. Norbert Coll., 1982; postgrad., Marquette U. CPA, Wis.; lic. real estate broker, Wis. Acct. Eugene B. Frank, Milw., 1982-83, Ritz, Holman, Butala & Fine, Milw., 1983-86, Sattell, Johnson, Appel & Co., S.C., Milw., 1986—. Mem. Am. Inst. CPA's, Wis. Inst. CPA's, MBA Execs. Inc. Republican. Roman Catholic. Avocations: tennis, skiing. Home: 2518 N Farwell Apt #1 Milwaukee WI 53211 Office: Sattell Johnson Appel & Co SC 777 E Wisconsin Ave Suite 3200 Milwaukee WI 53202

DECARLO, DOROTHY ANN, restaurant executive; b. Chgo., June 26, 1947; d. Rocco and Frances (Lagori) DeC.; m. Frank E. Peters Jr., Aug. 28, 1971 (div. Dec. 1980); m. David Eckhardt Houle, Apr. 27, 1985; children: Christopher DeCarlo Houle. BBA, Loyola U., Chgo., 1969. Account executive Chgo. Sun Times, 1971-74, Sta. NBC-TV, Chgo., 1974-77; account exec., asst. mgr. John Blair TV, Chgo., 1977-83; pres., co-owner Mama Mia! Pasta Restaurant Co., Chgo., 1981—. Active Bus. Mobilized for Loyola U. Mem. Ill. Restaurant Assn. (bd. dirs.), Roundtable for Women in Foodservice, Juvenile Protection Assn. (bd. dirs.). Club: The Fortnightly Chgo. Avocations: skiing, aerobic, reading, cooking. Home: 1721 N Cleveland Chicago IL 60614 Office: Mama Mia! Pasta Restaurant Co 116 S Michigan Ave Chicago IL 60603

DECELLIS, SUZANNE KAY, travel agency executive; b. LaPorte, Ind., Apr. 15, 1945; s. Walter Raymond Carl and Margaret M. (Bundy) Blanda; m. Anthony DeCellis, Aug. 6, 1965; 1 child, Nicole Renee. Student, Ind. U., 1972-82. Cert. travel cons., tour profl. Airline sales agt. Trans World Airlines, N.Y.C., 1965-70; travel agt. Diners/Fugazy, Indpls., 1970-75; travel mgr. Ind. Nat. Bank, Indpls., 1975-79; gen. mgr. AAA Travel Agy., Indpls., 1974-79, v.p., 1979—; Conf. speaker Ind. Dept. Tourism, 1984-86, mem. Pan-Am. Games com., 1986; speaker AAA Nat. Hdqrs., Falls Church, Va., 1980—. Mem. Nat. Tour Assn. (speaker 1980—), Am. Soc. Travel Agts., Am. Bus. Women's Assn. Republican. Clubs: Indpls. Skal (mem. coms.). Avocations: travel, reading, writing, swimming. Office: AAA Travel Agy 3750 Guion Rd Indianapolis IN 46222

DECIO, ARTHUR JULIUS, manufacturing executive; b. Elkhart, Ind., Oct. 19, 1930; s. Julius A. and Lena (Alesia) D.; m. Patricia George, Jan. 6, 1951; children: Terrence, Jamee, Linda, Jay, Leigh Allison. Student, DePaul U., 1949-50; D.B.A. (hon.), Salem Coll., W.Va.; LL.D., U. Notre Dame, Ind. State U., Terre Haute. Pres. Skyline Corp., Elkhart, 1956-72; chmn. bd., chief exec. officer Skyline Corp., 1959—; bd. dirs. Schwarz Paper Co., Morton Grove, Ill., Banc One Ind. Corp., Indpls., Rodman & Renshaw Capital Group, Inc., Chgo., Greencroft Found., Elkhart, Ind.; past dir. Michiana Public Broadcasting Corp., South Bend, Ind., Foremost Corp. Am., Grand Rapids, Mich., Midwest Commerce Banking Co., Elkhart, Fed. Res. Bank Chgo.; adv. council Coll. Commerce DePaul U.; bd. govs. NFL Alumni. Dir. Spl. Olympics Internat., Washington; trustee U. Notre Dame; adv. bd. Goshen (Ind.) Coll., Ind. U., South Bend; past chmn. Elkhart Urban League Membership Drive, Elkhart Gen. Hosp. Major Expansion Drive, Bicentennial Commn. Elkhart County, Salvation Army New Hdqrs. Bldg. Drive; past hon. chmn. Salvation Army Christmas Fund Drive; past mem. Commn. on Presdl. Scholars; pres. Elkhart Gen. Hosp. Found.; past dir. Nat. Italian-Am. Found., Washington; chmn. adv. council United Way, Elkhart, past dir., campaign chmn., 1966; past dir. Cath. Diocese of Fort Wayne-South Bend, Ind.; trustee Aux Chandelles Village Found., Elkhart; life mem. adv. bd. Nat. Salvation Army, Verona, N.J.; life mem. NAACP, exec. bd. Elkhart County chpt., 1980-82; life mem. bd. trustees Marmion Mil. Acad., Aurora, Ill.; past dir. Elkhart Urban League; past dir. Jr. Achievement Elkhart, pres. 1965-66; past dir. Elkhart Gen. Hosp., N. Central Ind. Med. Edn. Found., South Bend, Nat. Jr. Achievement; past trustee Stanley Clark Sch., South Bend, LaLumiere Sch., Laporte, Ind.; mem. Council on Devel. Choices for the 80's, Urban Land Inst., Presdl. Task Force on Low Income Housing, 1970; Presdl. appointment Christopher Columbus Quincentenary Jubilee Commn., Washington; mem. Internat. Summer Spl. Olympics Com., Inc., 1987; co-chmn. capital campaign Assn. for Disabled of Elkhart County, 1985; exec. bd. dirs. Elkhart County NAACP, 1980-82; hon. chmn. Capital Campaign for Elkhart Community Day Care Ctr. Recipient U. Portland (Oreg.) medal, 1972, Golden Plate award Acad. Achievement Dallas, 1967, Others award Salvation Army, 1972, William Booth award, 1987Alexis de Tocqueville Soc. award United Way Am., 1987, Sagamores of the Wabash award State of Ind., 1977, Community Service award Elkhart County br. NAACP, 1980, Marmion Centurion award Marmion Mil. Acad., 1979 Achievement award Jr. Achievement, 1974, Humanitarian award Elkhart Urban League, 1981, Community Service award Elkhart Urban League, 1977 Disting. Am. award NFL Found. and Hall of Fame, 1984, Book of Golden Deeds award Elkhart Noon Exchange Club, 1984, E. M. Morris award Div. Bus. and Econs., Ind. U.-South Bend, 1985, Alumni Leadership award Marmion Mil. Acad., 1964, Wall of Fame award Assn. for the Disabled, 1985; Salvation Army Hon. Adv. Bd. Mem. award, 1971, Columbus Day award for outstanding Italian-Am., 1973, Elkhart Bar Assn. Liberty Bell award, 1976, Aux Chandelles Village Found. OK award, 1976, Life Hon. Membership award Elkhart Urban League, 1980, Outstanding Contbn. award Elkhart Urban League, 1982, Nat. Italian-Am. Found. Career Achievement award, Washington, 1984, Ind. Individual Philanthropist of Yr. award, 1984, Mobile Home Hall of Fame, 1975, Industry Man of Yr. award Iowa Manufactured, William Booth award The Salvation Army, 1987. Housing Assn., 1976, Calif. Manufactured Housing Assn., 1977, N.J. Manufactured Housing Assn., 1977. Mem. Manufactured Housing Inst., Mobile Home Mfrs. Assn. (past dir., past pres., past chmn. Washington affairs com.), Ind. Acad., Chgo. Presidents Orgn., Chief Execs. Orgn. Inc., World Bus. Council, Assn. for Disabled (Wall of Fame award 1987). Roman Catholic. Clubs: Knights of Malta; Chicago, Tavern (Chgo.); Country of Fla. (Village of Golf); Delray Beach Yacht (Fla.); Ocean of Fla. (Ocean Ridge); Signal Point Country (Niles, Mich.); Indpls. Athletic. Home: 3215 Greenleaf Blvd Elkhart IN 46514 Office: Skyline Corp 2520 ByPass Rd Elkhart IN 46514

DECK, JENNIFER LOU, artist, carver; b. West Branch, Mich., Mar. 22, 1949; d. Alden Louis and Eleanore Breese (Jones) Matthews; m. Edward George Deck Jr., Aug. 15, 1975; children: Edward Alden, Mitchell Eric. BA, Adrian Coll., 1971. Cert. social worker, Mich. Social worker Mich. Dept. Social Services, Monroe, 1973-76; artist JMD Studio, Flat Rock, Mich., 1979—. Exhibited in group shows at Mich. Artist Collection, Battle Creek, 1980, Grand Rapids Pub. Mus., 1983, Mich. State U., 1986. Mem. Nat. Carousel Assn., Am. Carousel Soc., Mich. Woodworkers Guild. Methodist. Office: JMD Studio 26240 Gibraltar Rd Flat Rock MI 48134

DECKER, BERNARD MARTIN, U.S. dist. judge; b. Highland Park, Ill., Apr. 2, 1904; s. Martin C. and Florence (Bryant) D.; m. Louise Armstrong, Aug. 15, 1928; children—Janine L. (Mrs. Jack G. Collins), Martin C. II. Student, Northwestern U., 1922-23; A.B., U. Ill., 1926; LL.B., Harvard, 1929. Bar: Ill. bar 1929. Law clk. Ralph J. Dady, 3d and 4th dists. Appellate Ct. Ill., 1938-43; gen. practice law firm Decker & Decker, Waukegan, Ill., 1929-51; judge Circuit Ct., 17th Circuit Ill., 1951-57; presiding judge (19th Circuit), 1957-62; U.S. judge No. Dist. Ill., Chgo., 1962—; Chmn. organizing com. Ill. Jud. Conf., 1957, mem. exec. com., 1958-62, chmn. conf., 1959; exec. com. Nat. Conf. State Trial Judges, 1961-63, del., 1961, 62; mem. com. ct. adminstrn. U.S. Cts., 1968-75, mem. rev. com., 1974-78, mem. jud. ethics com., 1978—. Pres. bd. edn. Waukegan Twp. High Sch., 1946-49. Mem. Harvard Law Soc. Chgo. (pres. 1964-65), ABA, Ill. Bar Assn., Lake County Bar Assn. (pres. 1955), Phi Beta Kappa, Delta Tau Delta. Office: U S Dist Ct 219 S Dearborn St Chicago IL 60604

DECKER, JOHN WILLIAM, steel company executive; b. Cleve., July 15, 1948; s. James William and Betty Erdmann (Smith) D.; m. Elaine Marie Metz, Aug. 30, 1971; children: Amanda Elaine, Gregory John. BS, Lincoln Meml. U., 1966-70; MEd, Kent (Ohio) State U., 1970-72. Cert. tchr., adminstr., Ohio. Elem. tchr. Parma (Ohio) City Schs., 1970-78; corp. sec., treas. Decker Steel & Supply, Inc. (formerly Decker Reichert Steel & Supply, Inc.), Cleve., 1978-83, v.p., 1983-85, chmn., chief exec. officer, 1985—. Ruling elder Parma South Presbyn. Ch., Parma Heights, Ohio, 1979-81, clk. of session, 1983—; mem. Am. Theater Orgn. Soc., Playhouse Square Vol. Group. Mem. Greater Cleve. Growth Assn. Republican. Lodge: Masons. Avocations: choral group singing, pipe organ playing, repair and building. Home: 9634 Greenbriar Dr Cleveland OH 44130 Office: Decker Steel & Supply Inc 4500 Train Ave Cleveland OH 44102

DECKER, PETER W., Bible college official, former chemical company executive; b. Grand Rapids, Mich., Mar. 20, 1919; s. Charles B. and Ruth E. (Thorndill) D.; B.S., Wheaton Coll., 1941; postgrad. Northwestern U., 1942-43, U. Mich., 1958-60; D.Sc. (hon.), London Inst. Applied Research, 1973, LL.D., 1975; m. Margaret I. Stainthorpe, June 10, 1944; children—Peter, Marilyn, Christine, Charles. Advt. dept. Hotels Windermere, Chgo., 1942, Princess Pat Cosmetics, Chgo., 1943; market research investigator A.C. Nielson Co., Chgo., 1944-48; pres. Peter Decker Constrn. Co., Detroit, 1948-60; sales mgr. Century Chem. Products Co., Detroit, 1961-62, v.p., 1962-63, pres., 1963-75; sr. partner G & D Advt. Assos., 1967-78; v.p., treas., exec. dir. Christian Edn. Advancement, Inc., 1975-77, exec. dir., 1978—; registrar, instr. N.T. Greek and Theology Birmingham (Mich.) Bible Inst., 1973—; prof. Midwestern Baptist Coll., 1984—, dir. student fin. aid, 1984—, trustee, 1985—; mem. exec. com., 1986—. Neighborhood commr. Boy Scouts Am., 1961-66, merit badge counselor; emeritus, 1979—; mem. Bd. Rev., Beverly Hills, Mich., 1957-63; chmn. bd. review Southfield Twp., Mich., 1964-67; bd. dirs., past pres. Beverly Hills Civic Assn.; bd. dirs. Mich. Epilepsy Center and Assn., 1957-71, exec. com., 1962-67. Mem. Detroit Soc. Model Engrs. (pres. 1958, 62, dir. 1955-71), Chem. Splty. Mfg. Assn., AAAS, Nat. Geog. Soc., Internat. Platform Assn., ASTM, Smithsonian Instn. Assos., Archaeol. Inst. Am., Bibl. Archaeol. Soc., Bible-Sci. Assn., Creation Research Soc., Mich. Student Fin. Aid Assn., Midwest Assn. Student Fin. Aid Adminstrs. Republican (sustaining mem. Oakland County, Mich.). Baptist (trustee, instr. Bible Inst.). Author: Getting To Know New Testament Greek. Home: 32210 Rosevear Dr Beverly Hills Birmingham MI 48009 Office: 280 E Lincoln Birmingham MI 48009

DECKER, WILLIAM ADRIAN, psychiatrist; b. Sully, Iowa, May 3, 1921; s. Dick William and Mary (Verkow) D.; m. Florence Nancy Bukowski, Sept. 8, 1943 (dec. 1980); 1 child, Sheila Ann; m. Greta Louise Johnson, Feb. 12, 1982. BS cum laude, Western Mich. U., 1948; MD, Wayne State U., 1952. Diplomate Am. Bd. Psychiatry and Neurology. Intern City of Detroit Gen. Hosp., 1952-53; resident in psychiatry Kalamazoo Regional Psychiat. Hosp., 1953-55, Lafayette Clinic, Detroit, 1955-57; staff psychiatrist Kalamazoo Regional Psychiat. Hosp., 1957-60; asst. med. supt. Pontiac (Mich.) State Hosp., 1960-61; clin. dir., dir. children's services Kalamazoo Regional Psychiat. Hosp., 1960-74, asst. med. supt., 1974, med. supt., 1974-87; clin. instr. Dept. Occupational Therapy Western Mich. U., Kalamazoo, 1957-58, assoc. adj. prof., 1968—; spl. instr. Dept. Spl. Edn. Western Mich. U., 1967-70; lectr. Nat. Inst. Mental Health, 1966-70; cons. cts. of southwestern Mich., 1960—, Juvenile Ct. Services for Kalamazoo, Barry, Allegan, Branch and St. Joseph Counties, 1970-74. Producer weekly TV series "Your Mental Health," (Media award, 1985). Chmn. Gov.'s Subcom. on Adminstrv. Reorganization of Dept. Mental Health. Served as pvt. U.S Army, 1942-43. Fellow Am. Psychiat. Assn.; mem. AMA, Mich. Med. Soc., Southwest Mich. Psychiat. Assn., Mich. Psychiat. Assn., Am. Acad. Forensic Scis., Am. Soc. Psychiatry and Law. Republican. Roman Catholic. Home: PO Box 97 Kalamazoo MI 49005

DECKER-SPANGENBERG, BARBARA JEAN, artist, forms analyst; b. Ft. Snelling, Minn., Sept. 27, 1941; d. Lawrence Joseph and Margaret Christene (Menger) Decker; m. Robert J. Spangenberg, Aug. 31, 1968; children: Lisa, Gary. BA in Sociology, Coll. St. Catherine, St. Paul, 1963; BFA in Sculpture, U. Minn., 1978, postgrad. in library sci., 1978-82. Caseworker mil. services ARC, St. Paul, 1963-65; adoption caseworker Cath. Welfare Services, Mpls., 1965-67; home finder Wilder-Children Services, St. Paul, 1967-68; assoc. forms analyst St. Paul Cos., 1979-85, analyst, 1985-87; trainer spl. projects-graphics, 1981-83; founding mem., gallery coordinator WAVE Art Gallery, St. Paul, 1983-84; exhibited in one-woman show: St. Paul YWCA, 1981; group shows: U. Minn., 1975, 77, 78, Coll. St. Thomas, 1978, St. Paul YWCA, 1980; represented in permanent collections: St. Paul Cos., Winter & Assocs., Mpls.; gallery cons., juror YWCA, St. Paul, 1975, 83-85; cons. graphics Coll. St. Catherine, 1981. Community organizer Highland Neighbors, St. Paul, 1972-78, cons., 1978-82; cons. Highland Area Resident Bus. Ptnrs., St. Paul, 1982-83. Mem. Minn. Artists Exhbn. Program, Art Librarians, Mpls. Inst. Arts, Walker Art Ctr., Women's Art Registry Movement (assoc., WAVE coordinator 1983). Home: 2130 Pinehurst Ave Saint Paul MN 55116

DE COSTA, EDWIN J., physician, surgeon; b. Chgo., Mar. 25, 1906; s. Lewis M. and Grace (Myers) DeC; m. Mari H. Bachrach, Jan. 5, 1935 (dec. 1970); children: Mari Jane De Costa Terman, Catherine De Costa Burstein, Louise De Costa Wides, John Lewis; m. Alyce H. Heller, Feb. 1, 1971. B.S., U. Chgo., 1926; M.D., Rush Med. Coll., 1929. Diplomate: Am. Bd. Obstetricians and Gynecologists (examiner 1955—). Intern Cook County Hosp., Chgo., 1929-30; resident obstetrics and pathology Cook County Hosp., 1930-32; resident gynecology Michael Reese Hosp., Chgo., 1932-33; attending Northwestern Meml. Hosp., Prentice Women's Hosp., Cook County Hosp.; prof. ob-gyn Northwestern U. Med. Sch., 1946—. Author: (with J.I. Brewer) Gynecology, 4th edit., 1967. Served as officer USNR, 1933-66; capt. ret. Mem. Chgo. Gynecol. Soc., Central Assn. Obstetricians and Gynecologists, Am. Coll. Obstetricians and Gynecologists, Am. Gynecol. and Obstetrical Soc., ACS, AMA, Ill., Chgo. med. socs., Central Travel Club, Chgo. Inst. Medicine, Pan-Pacific Surg. Assn., Pan-Am. Med. Assn., Phi Beta Kappa, Sigma Xi, Alpha Omega Alpha; hon. mem. Ark., Nebr. obstetrical and gynecol. socs., Am.-Brit. Cowdray Med. Soc., Tex. Assn. Obstetricians and Gynecologists. Home: 1540 N Lake Shore Dr Chicago IL 60610 Office: 166 E Superior Chicago IL 60611

DE COSTER, MILES MCCALL, artist, publisher; b. California, Mo., Mar. 13, 1950; s. Richard Joseph and Jane Delores (Herst) DeC. BFA, Washington U., St. Louis, 1972; MFA, Sch. Art Inst. Chgo., 1979. Editor, printer Sch. Art Inst. Publs. Office, Chgo., 1977-79; editor Argot mag., Chgo., 1979—; artist-in-residence Chgo. Council Fine Arts, 1979-80; asst. dir. Word City, 1980-82; pres. Art Equity Inc., 1980—; vis. faculty U. Ill., Chgo., 1980-81, Art Inst. Chgo., 1981; co-founder Permanent Press, Chgo., 1978—; dir. Bookspace, 1981-83; art dir. In These Times, 1983—. Bd. dirs. N.A.M.E. Gallery, 1982-83, WhiteWalls, 1983—. Recipient Post-Newsweek Media fellowship. Author: Scotoma, 1978, Photoaccuracy, 1978, Coloraccuracy, 1979, The Cereal Wars, 1979, Sleight of Hand, 1980, Iconomics: Money, 1984, Television, 1985. Home: 2723 N Kenmore Chicago IL 60614

DECRAENE, ROBERT G., accountant; b. Detroit, Jan. 19, 1935; s. George Paul and Evelyn Rose (DeVos) D.; m. Geraldine Ann Flanigan, Sept. 8, 1956; children: Daniel, James, Susan, Robert, Diane, Michael. BS in Acctg., U. Detroit, 1956. CPA Mich. Acct. Coopers & Lybrand, Detroit, 1956-68, ptnr., 1968-75; mng. ptnr. Coopers & Lybrand, Indpls., 1975-83; regional mng. ptnr. Midwest Coopers & Lybrand, Detroit, 1983—. Trustee Mich. Accountancy Found., Detroit, 1984—, U. Detroit, 1986—, Marian Coll., Indpls., 1981-83; bd. dirs. Commn. for Downtown, Indpls., 1981-83. Mem. Am. Inst. CPA's, Mich. Assn. CPA's (chmn. Detroit chpt. 1973). Roman Catholic. Clubs: Plum Hollow Golf (Southfield, Mich.) (bd. dirs. 1973-75); Meridian Hills Country (Indpls.) (pres. 1982). Avocation: golfing. Home: 104 Manorwood Bloomfield Hills MI 48013 Office: Coopers & Lybrand 400 Renaissance Ctr Detroit MI 48243

DECRANE, VINCENT FRANCIS, construction co. executive; b. Cleve., Aug. 27, 1927; s. Alfred Charles and Verona Ida (Marquard) DeC.; m. Flora Elizabeth Friday; children—Barbara Bumbacco, Peter, Donna Panzica, Michael, Melinda Capone, Melissa, Joan, Mary Jean. B.S. in Archtl. Engring., U. Notre Dame, 1950. Field engr., Gt. Lakes Dredge & Dock Co., Cleve., 1950; engr., estimator Dunlop & Johnston, Inc., Cleve., 1952-59, sec.-treas., 1959-75, exec. v.p., sec., 1975-86, pres., treas., 1986—; gen. ptnr. Sawmill Creek Lodge Co., Cleve., 1971—. Chmn. com. United Way Cleve., 1971—; chmn. bd., pres. Brentwood Hosp., 1981-85; pres. Catholic Charities Corp., 1980-82; trustee Community Dialysis Ctr., Inc., Gilmour Acad.; mem. Lyndhurst (Ohio) Planning Commn.; trusteeship com. Greater Cleve. Hosp. Assn.; bd. dirs. parents council St. Mary's Coll., Notre Dame, Ind.; bd. overseers St. Mary's Seminary, Cleve. Served with AUS, 1946-47, 50-52. Named Notre Dame Man of Yr. Notre Dame Club Cleve. Mem. Builders Exchange (pres. 1981-83), Cleve. Engring. Soc. (Hall of Fame award 1986), Constrn. Employers Assn., Am. Inst. Constructors, Constrn. Industry Affairs Com., Greater Cleve. Growth Assn., Warrensville Heights C. of C. (hon. dir.). Roman Catholic. Club: Mayfield Country. Office: 17900 Miles Ave Warrensville Heights OH 44128

DE DECKERE, DORIS C., public relations executive; b. Grosse Pointe, Mich., Aug. 21; d. George Joseph and Lillian Anna (Pipper) Clutterbuck; ed. Wayne State U.; student U. Mich. Extension, Detroit Inst. Musical Arts; m. Robert O. DeDeckere, Sept. 9, 1950; children—Robert, David, James, Adrienne. Exec. sec. Recorder's Court, Detroit, from 1968; vice chmn. Mayor's Narcotics Com., Detroit; chmn. Pub. Health Commn., Detroit, 1970-73; asso. dir. Mayor's Com. Human Resources Devel., 1973-74; dir. pub. relations Metro Detroit March of Dimes, 1974-77, 78-81 Detroit Inst. Tech., 1977-78, Island of Boblo, 1981-84; pres. Jade/Assocs., Inc., 1984—; coordinator ethnic classroom project at Wayne State U.; pub. relations cons. to community theatre groups, colls. and businesses; free lance writer, 1965—. Chmn. Housing Poor Peoples March for Eastside of Detroit, 1967; chmn. Christian Services St. Matthews Ch., 1969-72; pres. bd. trustees Detroit Community Music Sch., 1979-81; bd. dirs. Eastwood Clinic, Greater Mich. Found. Recipient Spirit of Detroit medal, 1973, Gov.'s Minute Man award, 1981; certs. of appreciation Mem. Women in Communication, Women in Advt. Pub. Relations Soc. Am., Mich. Women's Hall of Fame (ad hoc adv. com.), Univ. Cultural Center Assn., Detroit Press Club, Econ. Club of Detroit, Friends of Detroit Library, Friends of Natural History Mus. Roman Catholic. Club: Breakfast of Detroit. Contbr. poetry to various mags. and articles to community publs.

DEDERICH, GERARD JOHN, data processing executive; b. Plain, Wis., Sept. 24, 1935; s. Lawrence Anthony and Grace Olive (Thering) D.; m. Patricia Viola Deppeisse, Aug. 23, 1963; children: Jill Judith, Jodi Kay, Jason Thomas. Study in Korean linguistics, Army Lang. Sch., Monterey, Calif., 1955; degree in Geology, Marquette U., 1961; BS, U. Wis., 1961.

Dist. mgr. Harnischfeger Corp., Milw., 1961-64; group br. mgr. SBC div. IBM Corp., Chgo., 1964-74; v.p. decimus div. Bank of Am., Elk Grove, Ill., 1974-76; pres. GJD Inc., Northbrook, Ill., 1976-81, Niakwa Mgmt. Services, Mundelein, Ill., 1981—; mng. dir. software com. Basic 2, Chgo., 1984—. Author: (book kits) Sales Ideas, 1968, Chicago Data Center, 1975. Pres. Riverside Found., Lincolnshire, Ill., 1983. Served with U.S. Army, 1955-58, Korea. Mem. CFA Homeowners Assn. (pres. 1978), Aircraft Owners and Pilots Assn., Midwest Flight Instrs. Assn., Nat. Corvette Owners Assn., Am. Motorcycle Assn., CAmbridge Forest Assn. Republican. Roman Catholic. Club: Midwest Antigue & Classic Motorcycle (DeKalb, Ill.) (pres. 1984-85). Avocations: racquetball, golf, investments. Home: 39 Canterbury Rd Lincolnshire IL 60015 Office: Niakwa 23600 N Milwaukee Ave Mundelein IL 60060

DEDERT, STEVEN RAY, small business owner, management consultant; b. Franklin, Ind., Feb. 17, 1953; s. Ralph Edward and Martha Elizabeth (Weisman) D.; m. Brenda Kay Deutsch, June 2, 1974; children: Eric Allen, Tammi Michelle. AA, St. John's Coll., Winfield, Kans., 1973; BSBA, U. Denver, 1975. CPA, Ind. Audit sr. Coopers & Lybrand, Indpls., 1975-78; controller Am. Med. Mgmt., Inc., Indpls., 1978-82, Moorfeed Corp., Indpls., 1982-84; chief fin. officer, controller Midwest Energy Mgmt., Indpls., 1984-86; pres. Cleaning Solution, Inc., Indpls., 1986—; cons. acct., 1980—. Treas. bd. dirs. Greater Indpls. Assn. for Luth. Secondary Edn., 1978-82; mgr. Franklin Twp. Little League, 1985-86. Mem. Ind. CPA Soc., Am. Inst. CPA's. Avocation: family activities. Home: 4254 S Eaton Ave Indianapolis IN 46239 Office: Cleaning Solution Inc PO Box 90031 Indianapolis IN 46290

DEDEURWAERDER, JOSE JOSEPH, automotive executive; b. Brussels, Belgium, Dec. 31, 1932; s. Louis and Philippine (Pater Not) D.; m. Nelly Antoinette Clemens, May 15, 1954; 1 child, Joelle Cabassol. Grad. in tech. engring, Ecole Technique Moyenne Superieure, Belgium, 1953. Mfg. dir. Renault, Belgium, 1958-67; indsl. dir. Renault, Argentina, 1967-73; chief exec. officer Renault Mexicana, Mexico, 1973-76; plant dir. Renault, Douai, France, 1976-81; exec. v.p. Am. Motors Corp., Detroit, 1981-82, pres., chief operating officer, 1982-84; pres., chief exec. officer Am. Motors Corp., Southfield, Mich., 1984-86, vice chmn., chmn. exec. com., 1986—. Served as officer Belgium Navy, 1952-53. Mem. Automotive Hall of Fame (bd dirs.). Office: American Motors Corp 27777 Franklin Rd Southfield MI 48034

DEDLOFF, JAMES THOMAS, public administrator; b. Buffalo, Aug. 28, 1938; s. Ellsworth Frederick and Marie Ann (McHugh) D.; m. Edeltraud Amalie Wuttkowski, Apr. 3, 1965; children: Wayne, Melissa. BS in Journalism/Mass Communication, U. Nebr., 1979; MSW, U. Kans., 1980-82. Commd. 2d lt. U.S. Army, 1967, advanced through grades to maj., 1977, ret., 1981; dir. child services Kans. Social Services, Leavenworth, Kans., 1982-84; prevention cons. Employee Assistance Programs, Leavenworth, 1984-85; prevention, alcohol/drug program cons. N.E. Kans. Mental Health Ctr., Leavenworth, 1984-85; dir. Community Corrections, Leavenworth, 1985—; mem. faculty criminal justice adminstrn. Park Coll., Parkville, Mo., 1987; mem. exec. com. Leavenworth County Alcohol and Drug Abuse Adv. Council, 1981-85; cons. Leavenworth County Substance Abuse Program, 1981-86; bd. dirs. Kans. Alcohol and Drug Coalition, Topeka, 1985-86; chmn. legis. platform task force Kans. Community Corrections, 1987—; pres. adv. bd. adolescent treatment St. John's Hosp., Leavenworth. Contbr. articles to mags. and newspapers. Decorated Bronze Star medal, army commendation for heroism; recipient Liberty Bell award; Harry S. Truman Library Inst. hon. fellow. Mem. Kans. Correctional Assn., Kans. Prevention Profls., Am. Parole and Probation, Kans. Assn. Community Corrections, Retired Officers Assn., U. Kans. Alumni Assn. Republican. Protestant. Avocations: golf, boating, raquetball, water skiing. Office: Leavenworth County Community Corrections 624 Olive Leavenworth KS 66048

DEDMON, ROBERT ERNEST, diversified company executive; b. Fairbury, Nebr., Jan. 6, 1931; m. Helen Boudry, June 23, 1957; children: Sharon, Mary Dee, Susan. AB, Ind. U., 1953, MD, 1956. instr. medicine U. Ill., 1961-64, instr. medicine and microbiology, 1963-64; clin. asst. prof. U. Wis., 1964-72. Intern Presby. Hosp., Chgo., 1956-57; resident in internal medicine Presby. St. Luke's Hosp., Chgo., 1957-59, 61-62; research fellow USPHS, Chgo., 1959-60; fellow in endocrinology and metabolism Presby. St. Luke's Hosp., Chgo., 1960-61, fellow in arthritis and immunology, 1962-64; physician Nicolet Clinic, Neenah, Wis., 1964-76; staff v.p. med. affairs Kimberly-Clark Corp., Neenah, 1976—; instr. medicine U. Ill., Chgo., 1961-64, instr. medicine and microbiology, 1963-64; clin. asst. prof. U. Wis., 1964-72; gen. practice specializing in intenal medicine and rheumatology; mng. ptnr., pres. Twin City Clinic, Neenah, 1965-74; pres. med. staff Theda Clark Regional Med. Ctr., Neenah, 1973-75. Assoc. editor Presby. St. Luke's Hosp. Bulletin; contbr. numerous articles to profl. jour. Instr. advanced cardiac life support Am. Heart Assn., 1978; bd. dirs. Nicolet Clinic, 1974-76; elder, assoc. organist Presby. Ch., Neenah, 1970-80. Fellow ACP; mem. AMA, AAAS, Am. Occupational Med. Assn., Wis. State Med. Soc., Winnebago County Med. Soc., Am. Soc. Internal Medicine, Wis. Soc. Internal Medicine, Vox Valley Acad. Medicine, Ill. State Med. Soc., Chgo. Med. Soc., Chgo. Gas Chromatography Discussion Group (co-founder, sec., treas. governing bd.), N.Y. Acad. Scis., Am. Fedn. Clin. Research, Chgo. Rheumatism Soc., Am. Hosp. Assn. (adv. com. cen. office on internat. classification deseases 1964-80, chmn. 1977-80),Winnebago County Med. Soc. (pres. 1974-75, chmn. ins. adv. com. 1970-73), Sigma Xi. Office: Kimberly-Clark Corp 2100 Winchester Rd Neenah WI 54956

DEDONATO, DONALD MICHAEL, obstetrician-gynecologist; b. Bridgeport, Conn., Apr. 25, 1952; s. Michael Anthony and Mary Jane (Zawadski) DeD.; m. Susan Mary Naulty, June 15, 1974; 1 child, Mark Dominic. BA in Chemistry cum laude, Coll. Holy Cross, 1974; MD, Loyola U., Maywood, Ill., 1977. Intern Loyola Foster McGaw Hosp., Maywood, Ill., 1977-78; resident Ohio State U. Hosp., Columbus, Ohio, 1978-81; ob-gyn. Ob-Gyn. Assocs., Arlington Heights, Ill., 1981-87, DeDonato MD and Goodnough MD, Ob-Gyn, Arlington Heights, 1987—; Clin. instr. Northwestern U. Med. Ctr., Chgo., 1981—. Recipient CIBA award. Mem. AMA, Am. Assn. Med. Colls. (Loyola rep.), Chgo. Med. Soc., Ill. State Med. Soc., Am. Bd. Ob-Gyn., Phi Beta Kappa, Alpha Sigma Nu. Club: Garden Camera (pres. 1985-86). Avocation: photography. Office: DeDonato MD and Goodnough MD Ob-Gyn 1614 W Central Rd Arlington Heights IL 60005

DEDONDER, LEON GERARD, training program developer; b. Emporia, Kans., July 13, 1951; s. Leo Francis and Helen Josephine (Trear) DeD.; m. Kathleen Jean Bock, May 12, 1979. BS in Agr. Econs., Kans. State U., 1973. Mgmt. trainee Ralston Purina Co., Beatrice, Nebr., 1973-74; terr. mgr. Ralston Purina Co., Denison, Iowa, 1974-76; mgr. field tng. Ralston Purina Co., St. Louis, 1976-84; mgr. tng. program devel. Purina Mills, Inc., St. Louis, 1984—. Mem. Am. Soc. Tng. and Devel. Democrat. Roman Catholic. Avocation: baseball. Home: 322 Village Creek Dr Ballwin MO 63021 Office: Purina Mills Inc 1401 South Hanley Saint Louis MO 63166

DEDRICK, DONALD EARL, physical plant administrator; b. Madison, Wis., Feb. 26, 1930; s. Calvert Lampert and Ruth Marion (Larson) D.; m. Barbara Joane Hobelmann, Dec. 29, 1952; children: Dale Katherine, Margaret Lynn, Susan Marlene. BS, Am. U., 1952. With machine systems Litton Industries, Washington, 1956-59; bus. mgr., phys. plant dir. Am. U., 1959-78; phys. plant dir. U. Notre Dame (Ind.), 1978—. Served to lt. USN, 1953-56. Mem. Assn. Phys. Plant Adminstrs., Nat. Assn. Coll. and Univ. Bus. Officers. Home: 15595 Hearthstone Dr Mishawaka IN 46545 Office: Univ Notre Dame Notre Dame IN 46556

DEEMS, DELMAR L., municipal official; b. Sciota, Ill., Aug. 15, 1919; s. Gilbert Aaro and Ethel Viola (Burg) D.; m. Josephine Hodges, Feb. 2, 1947; children: Douglas, Gregory. County clk., recorder McDonough County, Macomb, Ill. Served to 1st lt. USAF, 1942-45. Republican. Lodge: Masons. Avocations: golf, fishing. Home: Rural Rt #1 Blandinsville IL 61420 Office: McDonough County Ct House Office Clk/Recorder Macomb IL 61455

DEEN, JAMES ROBERT, nuclear engineer; b. Dallas, Mar. 1, 1944; s. James Young and Dorothy Faye Deen; m. Katy James Pavlidou, Aug. 14, 1971; children: Dorothy, Christina, David, Joshua, Priscilla, Joy. B in Engring. Sci., U. Tex., 1966, BSME, 1970, PhD, 1973. Registered profl. engr., Calif. Sr. engr. Gen. Electric, San Jose, Calif., 1972-76; asst. nuclear engr. Argonne (Ill.) Nat. Lab, 1976-81, nuclear engr., 1981—. Mem. Am. Nuclear Soc. Republican. Mem. Evang. Free Ch. Avocation: classical music instrn. Home: 593 Cambridge Bolingbrook IL 60439 Office: Argonne Nat Lab 9700 S Cass Ave Argonne IL 60439

DEENY, MICHAEL CHARLES, data processing executive; b. Waterloo, Iowa, May 8, 1957; s. Donald Francis and Corrine (Bodensteiner) D. BS in Computer Sci. and Math., Mankato State U., 1979. Assoc. programmer Sperry Univac, Roseville, Minn., 1980-82; programmer analyst Northwest Airlines, Mpls., 1982-84, ops. coordinators, 1984-86, supr. prodn., 1986, mgr. ops. tech., 1986—. Home: 14580 Elysium Pl Apple Valley MN 55124 Office: Northwest Airlines MS C3650 Mpls St Paul Internat Airport Communications/Computer Services Saint Paul MN 55111

DEEULIS, DANIEL RAYMOND, accountant; b. Lakewood, Ohio, Jan. 23, 1945; s. Jay and Hazel Rose (Moley) DeE.; m. Anne Karin Pedersen, June 17, 1972; 1 child, Jason. BBA, Tulane U., 1967. Plant acct. Inmont Corp., Morganton, N.C., 1972-73; mgr. gen. acctg. and fin. analysis Inmont Corp., Detroit, 1973-76, mgr. aftermarket distn. and planning, 1976-78; area mgr. UTC Inmont, San Juan, P.R., 1978-81; plant controller SAR products UTC Automotive, St. Louis, 1982-86; mgr. capital and fin. planning BASF-Inmont Div., OEM Products, Troy, Mich., 1986—. Served with USN, 1969-70. Mem. Inst. Cert. Mgmt. Accts., Nat. Assn. of Accts., San Juan Jaycees (Civic Achievement award, 1981), Trout Unlimited. Club: Carchdelet Fly and Bait Casting (St. Louis). Office: BASF-Inmont Div OEM Products 3221 W Big Beaver Troy MI 48099

DEFABIIS, SUSANNE MARIE, nurse; b. N.Y.C., Mar. 22, 1943; d. Emidio DeFabiis and Maria Verdiglione. B.S. in Nursing, D'Youville Coll., 1967; M.S. in Psychiat. Nursing, St. Xavier Coll., 1974. Registered profl. nurse, Ind., Ill., N.J., N.Y. Asst. dir. nursing service Nazareth Nursing Home, Buffalo, 1967-69; staff nurse Ill. State Psychiat. Inst., Chgo., 1971; psychiat. supr. Jackson Park Hosp., Chgo., 1971-72; asst. head nurse Little Co. of Mary Hosp., Evergreen Park, Ill., part-time 1972-73; instr. psychiat. nursing DePaul U., Chgo., 1973-75; clin. specialist psychiatry Christ Hosp., Oak Lawn, Ill., 1975-79; clin. coordinator mental health Mercy Hosp. and Med. Ctr., Chgo., 1977-78; cons. psychiat. mental health Bethany-Garfield Park Community Hosp., Chgo., part-time, 1978-79; dir. psychiat. nursing Our Lady of Mercy Hosp., Dyer, Ind., 1979-80; practitioner, tchr. psychiat. nursing Rush-Presbyterian-St. Luke's Med. Ctr., Chgo., 1980-81, practitioner, tchr. med. nursing, 1981-82, coordinator nursing systems mgmt., 1982; med./psychiat. liaison nurse, clin. specialist Loyola U. Med. Ctr., Maywood, Ill., 1982-84, nurse, psychotherapist, Mercy Hosp. and Med. Ctr., 1984—; instr. nursing Rush U., Chgo., 1980—; lectr. in field to profl. assns. Recipient continuing edn. recognition units Ill. Nursing Assn., 1977-79. Mem. Am. Nurses Assn. (cert. clin. specialist in adult psychiat. nursing), Sigma Theta Tau. Club: Riviera Country (Orland Park, Ill.).

DEFFEYES, ROBERT JOSEPH, manufacturing company executive; b. Oklahoma City, Aug. 16, 1935; s. Joseph Alfred and Hazel (Stover) D.; m. Ethel Black, Aug. 2, 1958; children—Joan Elizabeth, Suzanne Carol. B.S., Calif. Inst. Tech., 1957. Devel. engr. Dow Chem. Co., Pittsburg, Calif., 1957-63; mgr. tech. services Memorex Co., Santa Clara, Calif., 1963-69; sr. v.p. tech. Graham Magnetics, Graham, Tex., 1969-77; pres. Graham Magnetics, Fort Worth, 1978-84, Carlisle Cos., Inc., Cin., 1985—. Patentee in field. Served with U.S. Army, 1958. Avocations: swimming; photography; underwater photography; music. Home: 701 Tusculum Ave Cincinnati OH 45226 Office: Carlisle Corp 1600 Columbia Plaza 250 E 5th St Cincinnati OH 45202

DEFINO, NICHOLAS, accountant; b. N.Y.C., Nov. 4, 1953; s. Anthony and Norma (Quattrochii) DeF.; m. Mary Lou Miller, July 19, 1975; 1 child, Mia Christine. BS in Acctg. and Fin., Marquette U., 1975. CPA, Wis. Acct. Touche, Ross & Co., Milw., 1975-79; asst. v.p. First Bank, Milw., 1979-81; controller Miller & Meier & Assocs., Milw., 1981—; sr. real estate acct. Northwestern Mutual Life. Ins. Co., Milw., 1984—. Mem. Am. Inst. CPA's, Wis. Inst. CPA's, Marquette Bus. Admnstrn. Alumni Bd. (bd. dirs. 1985—). Avocations: racquetball, tennis, sailing. Home: 2937 N Hackett Ave Milwaukee WI 53211 Office: Northwestern Mutual Life 720 E Wisconsin Ave Milwaukee WI 53201

DEFLEUR, LOIS B., university provost, sociology educator; b. Aurora, Ill., June 6, 1936; d. Ralph Edward and Isabel Anna (Cornils) Begitske; m. Melvin L. DeFleur (div.). AB, Blackburn Coll., 1958; MA, Ind. U., 1961; PhD in Sociology, U. Ill., 1965. Asst. prof. sociology Transylvania Coll., Lexington, Ky., 1963-67; assoc. prof. Wash. State U., Pullman, 1967-74, prof., 1975-86, dean Coll. Arts and Scis., 1981-86; provost U. Mo., Columbia, 1986—; disting. vis. prof. U.S. Air Force Acad., 1976-77; vis. prof. U. Chgo., 1980-81; mem. sociology grad. record com. Ednl. Testing Service, 1980-86. Author: Delinquency in Argentina, 1965; (with others) Sociology: Human Society, 3d edit. 1981, 4th edit., 1984, The Integration of Women into All Male Air Force Units, 1982, The Edward R. Murrow Heritage: A Challenge for the Future, 1986; contbr. articles to profl. jours. Mem. Wash. State Bd. on Correctional Standards and Edn., 1974-77. Recipient Alumni Achievement award Blackburn Coll., 1985; grantee NIMH, 1969-79, NSF, 1972-75, Air Force Office, 1978-81. Mem. Am. Sociol. Assn. (pubs. com. 1979-82, nominations com. 1984-86), Pacific Sociol. Assn. (pres. 1980-82), Sociologists for Women in Society, Law and SocietyAssn., Soc. Study Social Problems, Inter-Univ. Seminar on Armed Forces and Soc., Council Colls. of Arts and Scis. (dir. 1982-84, pres. 1985-87), Am. Soc. Criminology, Internat. Orgn. Women Pilots, Aircraft Owners and Pilots Assn., Internat. Comanche Soc. Office: U Mo 114 Jesse Hall Columbia MO 65211

DEFLON, RICHARD LANE, architect; b. Monett, Mo., May 17, 1953; s. Jon R. and Marylyn L. (Weston) deF.; m. Linda Marie Schmidt, July 28, 1973; children: Alicia Christine, Sara Nicole, Jennifer Ann. B in Environ. Design, U. Kans., 1975, BArch, 1976. Architect various firms, Kansas City, Mo., 1973-81; architect, project mgr. HNTB Architects, Kansas City, 1981-83; prin., v.p. Hellmuth, Obata & Kassabaum Architects, Inc., Kansas City, 1983—. Mem. AIA, Mo. Council of Architects. Avocations: woodworking, sports cars. Home: 610 Camelot Liberty MO 64068 Office: Hellmuth Obata Kassabaum Architects Inc 323 W 8th St Suite 700 Kansas City MO 64105

DEFONSO, LENORE EMILIA, psychology educator; b. Pitts., Mar. 31, 1941; d. Leonard and Amanda Marie (Cercone) DeF. BA in Psychology, Pa. State U., 1963; PhD in Clin. Psychology, Ind. U., 1973. Lic. psychologist, Wis., Ind. Staff psychologist, outpatient supr. Rock County Guidance Clinic, Janesville, Wis., 1972-75; instr. psychology St. Francis Coll., Ft. Wayne, Ind., 1976-78; dir. tng. Ft. Wayne Mental Health Ctr., 1978-80; instr. psychology Ind.-Purdue U., Ft. Wayne, 1981—; pvt. practice psychology, Ft. Wayne, 1981—; mem. Ind. State Bd. Examiners Psychology, Indpls., 1979-85. Mem. Ft. Wayne Philharmonic Chorus, 1976—. Recipient Profl. Devel. grant Ind.-Purdue U., Ft. Wayne, summer 1983; honored as Sagamore of the Wabash Gov. Ind., 1986. Mem. Am. Psychol. Assn., Midwestern Psychol. Assn., Ind. Psychol. Assn. Democrat. Avocations: singing, piano. Home: 930 W Oakdale Dr Fort Wayne IN 46807

DEFORD, DAVID WAYNE, data processing executive; b. Ellettsville, Ind., Nov. 23, 1952; s. Frederick Wayne and Phyllis LaVerne (Justis) DeF.; m. Katherine Lynn Ferrara, June 10, 1972; children: Sarah Katherine, Matthew David, William Jay, Adam Michael. AA in Bus. Data Processing, Lexington Tech. Inst., 1982. Computer operator Bluegrass Data Service, Lexington, Ky., 1973-79, data processing mgr., 1979-82; data processing mgr. Indpls. Airport Authority, 1982-85; data processing mgr. ARA Living Ctrs., Carmel, Ind., 1985-86, remote ops. mgr., 1986—. Bishop Ch. of Jesus Christ of Latter-Day Saints, Lexington, 1975-78, high councilor, Lexington, 1978-82, Indpls., 1982-87. Named Outstanding Young Man of Am., U.S. Jaycees, 1976. Mem. Data Processing Mgmt. Assn. (bd. dirs. 1983-86, pres. 1985, Recognition award 1984, Individual Performance award 1985, 87), Profl. Secs. Internat. (exec. adv. bd.). Avocations: hiking, children's athletics, reading. Home: 617 Nelson Dr Mooresville IN 46158 Office: ARA Living Ctrs 11350 N Meridian St Carmel IN 46032

DEFOREST, PATRICIA ANN, library director; b. Danville, Ill., June 6, 1927; d. Clarence Eugene and Lily White (Hampton) Schien; m. John Searle DeForest (div. 1981); children: Carol, Dan, John, Diane, Andrew. BA, Macalester Coll., St. Paul, 1949; MLS, Wayne State U., 1975. Cert. librarian, Mich. Librarian asst. VA Hosp. Library, Allen Park, Mich., 1972-73, Burroughs Corp., Detroit, 1973-74; librarian Wayne-Oakland (Mich.) Library Fedn., 1975-79; dep. dir. Sterling Heights (Mich.) City Library, 1979-85, dir., 1985—. Pres. Sterling Heights Cultural Arts Council, 1984-86. Recipient Cert. of Recognition, U.S. Dept. Edn., 1984; State of Mich. grantee, 1985, 86. Mem. ALA, Mich. Library Assn. (subcom. chmn. 1986-87), Spl. Libraries Assn., Sterling Heights C. of C. Club: Toastmasters. Avocations: classical music, promotion of arts activities. Office: Sterling Heights Pub Library 40255 Dodge Park Rd Sterling Heights MI 48078-4496

DEFOSSET, DANIEL, mechanical engineer; b. St. Louis, Jan. 28, 1952; s. Donald and Marilyn (Herzog) DeF.; m. Susan Marting, Aug. 6, 1977; children: Daniel Robert, Timothy Marting. BSBA, U. Mo., 1974; BSME, U. Mo., Rolla, 1977. Registered profl. engr. Systems engr. Black & Veatch Cons. Engrs., Kansas City, Mo., 1978-81; project engr. Sverdrup & Parcel Cons. Engrs., St. Louis, 1981-84; lead project engr. Monsanto, St. Louis, 1985-86; mgr. facilities and plant engring. Emerson Electric Co., St. Louis, 1986—. Solicitor United Way, St. Louis, 1984-85. Grantee NSF, 1977. Mem. ASME, ASHRAE, Engrs. Club St. Louis, Tau Beta Pi, Phi Kappa Phi. Lutheran. Avocations: sports, house restorations. Home: #2 Wedgewood Ln Creve Coeur MO 63141 Office: Emerson Electric Sta 2475 8100 W Florissant Saint Louis MO 63136

DEFOUW, EUGENE ALLEN, manufacturing company executive; b. Berrien Springs, Mich., Dec. 9, 1941; s. Arthur John and Myrtle Edna (Bolks) De F.; m. Lucille Mae Van Ess, July 12, 1968; children: Sandra Lynn, Karen Sue, Laura Jean. AA, Ferris State Coll., 1962, BS, 1964; BSME, U. Mich., 1969; MSME, Wayne State U., 1972. Cert. mfg. engrs. Sr. engr. Ford Motor Co., Dearborn, Mich., 1964-75; chief engr. Borroughs div. LSI, Kalamazoo, 1975-79; dir. mfg. engr. Haworth, Inc., Holland, Mich., 1979-81; div. gen. mgr. Keeler Brass Co., Grand Rapids, Mich., 1981-82; v.p., gen. mgr. Benteler/Slagboom, Grand Rapids, 1982-85; pres., chief exec. officer, owner Alofs Mfg. Co., Grand Rapids, 1985—. Mem. Am. Soc. Mech. Engrs., Soc. Mfg. Engrs. (sr.), Trout Unlimited (state treas. 1985-86), Fed. Fly Fishermen, Grand Rapids C. of C. Republican. Clubs: Grand Rapids Economic, Lotus. Lodge: Rotary. Office: Alofs Mfg Co 345 32d St SW Grand Rapids MI 49508-1083

DE GEORGE, RICHARD THOMAS, philosophy educator; b. N.Y.C., Jan. 29, 1933; s. Nicholas and Carmelina (D'Ippolito) De G.; m. Fernande I. Melanson, June 15, 1957; children: Rebecca, Anne Marie, Catherine. B.A., Fordham U., 1954; Ph.B., U. Louvain, Belgium, 1955; M.A., Yale U., 1958, Ph.D., 1959. Mem. faculty U. Kans., 1959—, prof. philosophy, 1964-72, Univ. prof., 1972—, chmn. dept., 1966-72; co-dir. Ctr. for Humanistic Studies, 1977-82, dir., 1982-83; Dirksen vis. prof., U. Santa Clara, 1986; lectr., sr. research fellow Columbia U., 1965-66; asso. Inst. E. European Studies, Fribourg, Switzerland, 1962-63; dir. summer research inst. NEH, 1976, 77, 80, 81. Author: Patterns of Soviet Thought, 1966, The New Marxism, 1968, Soviet Ethics and Morality, 1969, A Guide to Philosophical Bibliography and Research, 1971, The Philosopher's Guide, 1980, Business Ethics, 1981, Japanese edit., 1985, 2d edit., 1986; The Nature and Limits of Authority, 1986; also articles.; editor: Ethics and Society, 1966, Classical and Contemporary Metaphysics, 1962, Semiotic Themes, 1981; editor, contbr.: Reflections on Man, 1966; co-editor: The Structuralists, 1972, Marxism and Religion in Eastern Europe, 1976, Ethics, Free Enterprise and Public Policy, 1978. Served to 1st lt. AUS, 1955-57. Fulbright fellow, 1954-55, Ford fellow, 1962-63, NEH fellow, 1969-70, Rockefeller Found. fellow, 1976-77, research fellow Yale U., 1969-70, project grantee, 1972-73; recipient Hope Teaching award U. Kans., 1965, Balfour Jeffrey Research Achievement award U. Kans, 1986. Mem. Am. Philos. Assn. (exec. com. 1976-79, nat. bd. officers 1982-85), Internat. Fedn. Philos. Socs. (governing bd. 1978—, v.p. 1983—), Internat. Assn. Philosophy Law and Social Philosophy (pres. Am. sect. 1977-79), Metaphys. Soc. Am. (v.p. 1981-82, pres. 1982-83). Home: 945 Highland Dr Lawrence KS 66044

DEGERSTROM, JAMES MARVIN, health service orgn. exec.; b. Owosso, Mich., Aug. 9, 1933; s. John Marcellus and Emma Judith (Folkadahl) D.; B.S. in M.E., Mich. State U., 1955; M.B.A., DePaul U., 1966; m. Ann Blandford, July 3, 1964. Adminstrv. asst. Sunbeam Corp., Chgo., 1955-61; mfg. supt. Internat. Register Co., Inc., Chgo., 1961-65; sr. engr. Kitchens of Sara Lee, Inc., Deerfield, Ill., 1965-71; pres. Edmanson Bock Caterers, Chgo., 1972; mgr. bldg. ops. Jewel Cos., Inc., Barrington, Ill., 1972-81; dir. plant ops. Copley Meml. Hosp., Aurora, Ill., 1981-86; dir. plant ops. Little Co. Mary Hosp., Evergreen Park, Ill., 1986—; bd. dirs., treas. Credit Union, Kitchens of Sara Lee, 1966-70. Served with USAF, 1957-65. Recipient cert. of recognition, Am. Inst. Plant Engrs. Nat. Conf., 1977. Mem. Am. Inst. Indsl. Engrs., Am. Inst. Plant Engrs. (sec. 1977-79). Club: Toastmasters (dist. officer 1982—, pres. 1981, area gov. 1982, lt. gov. 1983-84, dist. gov. 1984-85). Home: 102 Knollwood Ct Oak Brook IL 60521 Office: 2800 W 95th St Evergreen Park IL 60642

DEGRIJS, LEO CHARLES, banker; b. Batavia, Java, 1926; married. Grad. Vrijzinning Christelijk Lyceum, The Hague, Netherlands, 1943. With Netherlands Post Tel & Tel Co., 1943-45, Netherlands-Indies Civil Adminstrn., 1945-49, Nederlandsche Handel-Maatschappij, bankers, Amsterdam, 1951-63, Continental Ill. Nat. Bank and Trust Co., Chgo., 1963—; internat. banking dept., 2d v.p. and head Continental Ill. Nat. Bank and Trust Co., Tokyo and Osaka, 1964; v.p. Continental Ill. Nat. Bank and Trust Co., Chgo., 1967; head Far East group Continental Ill. Nat. Bank and Trust Co., 1968; with Continental Devel. Bank SAL, Beirut, Lebanon, 1970; head Asia Pacific and Africa-Middle East groups, 1973, sr. v.p., 1974, head internat. banking dept., 1976, head internat. banking services dept., 1980, exec. v.p., 1981—, chmn. country exposure com., head sovereign risk mgmt., 1983—; dir. Continental Bank SA, Brussels, Continental Ill. Securities Ltd., Hong Kong, Continental Internat. Fin. Corp. Address: Continental Illinois Corp 231 S LaSalle St Chicago IL 60697

DE HAAN, DEBORAH LEE, orthodontist; b. Pontiac, Mich., June 28, 1956; d. Robert Frances and Dorothy Aleda (Skeels) De H.; m. Bradford Harry Strohm, July 31, 1982; 1 child, Deanna Dorothy. BS, Oakland U., Rochester, Mich., 1979; DDS, U. Mich., 1984, MS, 1986. Licensed dentist, Mich.; licensed orthodontist, Mich. Research asst. anatomy U. Mich., Ann Arbor, 1979-84, research assoc. oral biology, 1984-85, clin. instr. orthodontics, 1985-86; practice dentistry specializing in orthodontics Dearborn, Mich., 1986—. Mem. ADA, Am. Assn. Orthodontists, Omicron Kappa Upsilon. Home: 1322 McIntyre Dr Ann Arbor MI 48105

DEHAAN, JON HOLDEN, vacation exchange executive; b. Ann Arbor, Mich., July 7, 1940; s. William and Kathleen Helen (Holden) DeH.; m. Christel Stark, July 16, 1973; children—Keith, Tim, Kirsten. B.A. with honors, Claremont Men's Coll., 1963; M.B.A. with distinction Ind. U., 1966; postgrad. U. Pa. Wharton Sch. Fin., 1966-69. Cons. Econ. Research Assocs., Los Angeles, 1969-70; dir. camping div. Brynmawr Parks Corp. affiliate Ramada Inns, 1970-71; dir. fin. community devel. div. Intertherm Corp., 1972-73; chmn. bd. Resort Condominiums Internat., Indpls., 1974—; founding dir. Nat. TimeSharing Found.; founding dir., v.p. pub. relations Internat. Found. for TimeSharing, 1984-85; speaker in field. Honored with mayoral proclamations City of Miami (Fla.), 1982, City of Indpls., 1983, 84. Mem. Am. Soc. Travel Agts., Am. Resort and Residential Assn. (dir., co-chmn. Camp Coast-to-Coast program), Nat. TimeSharing Council (dir. 1976—), Am. Hotel/Motel Assn., Indpls. C. of C., Fla. C. of C. Republican. Episcopalian. Office: One RCI Plaza 3502 Woodview Trace Indianapolis IN 46268

DEHART, DAVID GLENN, accountant; b. Springfield, Ohio, Dec. 17, 1958; s. Glenn Wood and Florence Joan (Rosell) DeH. BSBA in Acctg. summa cum laude, Wright State U., 1981. CPA, Ohio. Jr. staff acct. Flagel, Huber, Flagel & Co., Dayton, Ohio, 1981-85; sr. staff acct. Flagel, Huber, Flagel & Co., Dayton, 1985-86; audit mgr. Duvall & Assocs., Inc., Dayton, Ohio, 1986—; treas. Full Gospel Bus. Men's Fellowship Internat., Springfield, Ohio, 1987—, Full Gospel Community Ch., 1977—. Mem. Am. Inst. CPA's, Nat. Assn. Accts., Ohio Soc. CPA's, Beta Gamma Sigma.

Republican. Avocations: swimming, playing piano, bicycling, singing. Home: 6925 Joseph Dr Enon OH 45323 Office: Duvall & Assocs 5335 Far Hills Ave Dayton OH 45429

DEHAVEN, CLARK EDWIN, business educator; b. Hartford, Mich., Feb. 12, 1922; s. Edwin and Kathryn (Call) DeH.; m. Virginia Marie Mills, June 1940 (div. 1963); m. Daisy Corinne Schoolcraft, Oct. 17, 1964; children: Clark, Craig, Susan. BS in Pharmacy, Ferris State Coll., 1950; MA in Mgmt., Mich. State U., 1953. Asst. prof. pharmacy, dir. alumni affairs Ferris State Coll., Big Rapids, Mich., 1950-57; instr. bus. Mich. State U., East Lansing, 1957-66, dir. exec. programs, 1966—; cons. Pub. Sector Cons., 1982—; bd. dirs. Mich. State U. Employees Credit Union, 1975-82; mem. nursing licensing bd. Mich. Dept. Licensing and Registration, Lansing, 1981-84. Elder First Presbyn. Ch., Lansing, 1975—; mem. acad. council Inst. Cert. Travel Agts., Wellesley, Mich., 1975—. Recipient Outstanding Faculty award Ferris State Coll., 1956; named Mem. of Yr. Mich. State U. Employees Credit Union, 1976. Mem. Nat. Assn. Colls. and Univs. Food Services (exec. dir. 1984—, adminstrv. sec. 1971-84, Theodore S. Minah award 1976), Am. Mgmt. Assn. (pres. 1966), Sales and Mktg. Assn. (pres. 1984-85). Republican. Avocations: travel, golf, cultivating roses. Home: 1625 N Fairview Lansing MI 48912 Office: Exec Programs Mich State U 7 Olds Hall East Lansing MI 48824-1047

DEHAVEN, EARL RUSSELL, data processing executive; b. Wichita, Kans., Apr. 3, 1926; s. Charles Wesley and Verna Lucile (Monasmith) DeH.; m. Barbara Lou Smith, Sept. 3, 1948; children: William R., Leslye E., Gary R., Kathleen F., Nancy K., Thomas C., Paul B., Joel D. Student, Wichita U., 1957-58. Cert. data processing. IBM equipment operator Fed. Land Bank, Wichita, 1947-48; service bur. mgr. IBM Corp., Wichita, 1948-53, St. Louis, 1953-55; computer program mgr. Cessna Aircraft Co., Wichita, 1955-1970; v.p. mgmt. systems St. Joseph Med. Ctr., Wichita, 1970-87. Mem. Prairie Garden Bd. Edn., Sumner County, Kans., 1963-64; mem. computer adv. com. Wichita Bd. Edn., 1969—. Democrat. Mem. Ch. Christ. Avocations: forestry, carpentry, geneaology, hunting, fishing. Home: Rural Rt 2 Box 673 Mulvane KS 67110 Office: St Joseph Med Ctr 3600 E Harry St Wichita KS 67218

DEHAVEN, ERNEST THOMAS, association executive; b. Hiram Twp., Ohio, Aug. 7, 1928; s. Ernest Roy and Bertha Catherine (Thomas) DeH.; m. Barbara Ann Hoskin, Aug. 21, 1955; children—Matthew, Stephen, Catherine. A.B., Hiram Coll., 1949; M.H.A., Va. Commonwealth U., 1957. Lic. nursing home adminstr., Iowa. Adminstr. Albert Schweitzer Meml. Hosp., St. Mark, Haiti, 1958-59, Jackman Meml. Hosp., Bilaspur, India, 1959-64; asst. adminstr. Lake County Meml. Hosp., Painesville, Ohio, 1965-67; adminstr. Carroll County Meml. Hosp., Carrollton, Ky., 1967-77; exec. dir. Wesley Manor, Frankfort, Ind., 1977-82; adminstr. Ramsey Meml. Home, Des Moines, 1982—; regional ops. dir. Nat. Benevolent Assn., 1985—. Served with AUS, 1953-54. Mem. Am. Coll. Health Care Adminstrs., Am. Coll. Hosp. Adminstrs. (cert.), Am. Mgmt. Assn., Des Moines Choral Soc. Mem. Christian Ch. (Disciples of Christ). Avocation: Choral singing. Home: 7008 Townsend St Des Moines IA 50322 Office: Ramsey Home 1611 27th St Des Moines IA 50310

DEHNKE, RONALD EARL, educator; b. Detroit, Jan. 29, 1934; s. Earl Clifford and Rose Jean (Ambuehl) D.; m. Eileen Elizabeth Purder, June 16, 1956; children: Lori Elizabeth, Bradley Earl, Gregory David. BA, Eastern Mich. U., 1956; MEd, Wayne State U., 1963, EdD, 1966. Cert. secondary tchr., Mich. Tchr. English Lake Shore High Sch., St. Clair Shores, Mich., 1956-63; instr. Wayne State U., Detroit, 1963-66; asst. prof. English U. Colo., Colorado Springs, 1966-70; assoc. prof. Ind./Purdue U., Indpls., 1970—, dir. student teaching, lab field experiences, 1982—. Contbr. articles to profl. jours. Mem. Ind. Assn. Tchr. Educators (pres. 1987—), Nat. Council Tchrs. of English, Assn. Tchr. Educators, Phi Delta Kappa,. Avocations: reading, sports, camping. Home: 7335C Lions Head Dr Indianapolis IN 46260 Office: Ind U/Purdue U Sch of Edn 902 W New York Indianapolis IN 46223

DEIBERT, ALVIN NELSON, psychologist; b. Highland, Ill., Sept. 24, 1938; s. Alvin Fredon and Viola (Mueller) D.; m. Margaret Dean, Dec. 29, 1975. BA, Elmhurst Coll., 1960; MA, Hollins Coll., 1962, So. Ill. U., 1980; PhD, Washington U., St. Louis, 1968. Cert. psychologist, Ill. Clin. dir. Hancock County Mental Health Ctr., Carthage, Ill., 1976-79; faculty Ark. State U., Jonesboro, 1980-84; clin. coordinator Alton (Ill.) Mental Health Ctr., 1985—. Auhtor: New Tools for Changing Behavior, 1972, B.J. and Language of Woodland, 1984. NIMH fellow, 1962-65. Mem. Am. Psychol. Assn. Lodge: Kiwanis (bd. dirs. 1983-85). Home: 848 Danforth Alton IL 62002

DEININGER, JOHN, manufacturing company executive; b. 1932; married. BS, Bradley U., 1954. V.p. sales Signode Canada Ltd., 1969-70, pres., 1970; with Signode Industries, Inc., 1956—, field mgr., 1956-58, sr. field engr., 1958-63, mgr. brick industry sales, 1963-67, asst. gen. mgr. industry sales services, 1967, gen. mgr., 1967-70, pres., 1970-73; v.p. & gen. mgr. Paslode div. Signode Industries, Inc., from 1973; corp. v.p. Signode Industries, Inc., 1974-81, chief operating officer, 1979—, now also pres., dir. Served with U.S. Army, 1954-56. Office: Signode Industries Inc 3600 W Lake Ave Glenview IL 60025 *

DEINZER, GEORGE WILLIAM, public welfare organization administrator; b. Tiffin, Ohio, Nov. 1, 1934; s. Harvey Charles and Edna Louise (Harpley) D.; A.B., Heidelberg Coll., 1956; postgrad. Washington U., 1956-57. Asst. to dir. phys. plant Heidelberg Coll., 1957-58, admissions counselor, 1958-60, dir. admissions, 1960-71, dir. fin. aids, asso. dir. admissions, 1971-80; exec. dir. Tiffin-Seneca United Way, 1980-85; adminstr. Seneca County (Ohio) Dept. Human Services and Children's Services, 1986—. Voting rep. Coll. Entrance Examination Bd., 1963-80; fin. aid cons. Nat. Collegiate Athletic Assn.; cons. Ohio Scholarship Funds, 1960-61. Pres., chmn. allocations com., bd. dirs. United Way; pres. lay bd. Mercy Hosp.; treas., bd. dirs. N.W. Ohio Health Planning Assn., co-chmn. steering com., 1984; mem. legis. com. Ohio Citizens Council, 1981—, human services task force, 1984—; pres. Seneca County Mus.; treas. Tiffin Theatre, Inc.; mem. Seneca Indsl. and Econ. Devel. Corp. Bd., 1983—; chmn. Tiffin Area Devel. and Pub. Relations Dirs., 1984—. Mem. Nat., Ohio (regional coordinator, treas., state trainer, chmn. needs analysis com.) assns. student fin. aid adminstrs., Ohio Athletic Conf. Fin. Dirs. (past chmn.), Internat. Platform Assn., Am. Personnel and Guidance Assn., Am. Coll. Personnel Assn., Council Ohio United Way Execs., Farm Bur., Ohio Hist. Soc., N. Cen. Ohio Regional Council on Alcoholism, U.S. Naval Inst., Buckeye Sheriffs Assn., N.W. Ohio and Ohio Human Service Dirs., Beta Beta Beta. Republican. Lodges: Rotary (dir., pres. 1982-83), Elks. Contbr. articles to profl. jours. Home: 197 Jefferson St PO Box 904 Tiffin OH 44883

DEITZ, ROBERT DAVID, protective coatings manufacturing company executive; b. Cleve., Dec. 26, 1926; s. Joseph H. and Irene (Mates) D.; m. Sallie Eisen, Jan. 26, 1950; children—Jo-Anne Deitz Daniels, Diana Deitz Russel. B.B.A., Case Western Res. U., 1948. Export mgr. Consol. Paint and Varnish Corp., Cleve., 1948-57; v.p. Consol. Protective Coatings Corp. and subs. Consol. Inter-Continental Corp., Consol. Protective Coatings Ltd., Cleve., Montreal, Que., Can., 1957, pres., 1958—; dir. Hastings Pavement corp., L.I., N.Y. Chmn. budget com. United Way Services, Cleve., 1972-75; trustee Mt. Sinai Med. Ctr., Cleve., 1971-78; pres. Jewish Vocat. Service, 1970-73; vice chmn. Dist. Export Council, Dept. Commerce, 1975-83; pres. Menorah Park Jewish Home for Aged, Beachwood, Ohio, 1976-78. Served with USMC, 1945-46. Recipient Kane award Jewish Community Fedn., 1965; Man of Yr. award Orgn. Rehab. Tng., 1981. Office: Consol Protective Coatings Corp 202 Ohio Savs Plaza Cleveland OH 44114

DEJESUS-BURGOS, SYLVIA TERESA, information systems specialist; b. Rio Piedras, Puerto Rico, Jan. 13, 1941; came to U.S., 1961; d. Luis deJesus Correa and Maria Teresa (Burgos) deJesus. BA, Cen. U., Madrid, 1961. Sr. systems analyst H.D. Hudson Mfg. Co., Chgo., 1974-76; mgr. software engring. Morton Thiokol, Chgo., 1976-87; sr. mgr. systems devel. Kraft, Inc., Glenview, Ill., 1987—. Editor U. Minn. Mgmt. Info. Systems Jour., 1984—. Pres. Chgo. chpt. Nat. Conf. Puerto Rican Women, 1980-83, nat. v.p. 1981-82; bd. dirs. Midwest Women's Ctr., 1980-82, YWCA, Chgo., 1982-84, Gateway Found. Substance Abuse Prevention and Rehab., 1986-87; v.p. communications Hispanic Alliance for Career Enhancements, 1986-87, bd. dirs. 1982-84; 1st v.p. Campfire Met. Chgo., 1982, bd. dirs. 1980-82; appointed to Selective Service Bd. by Ill. Gov. James Thompson, 1982; alt. del. Dem. Nat. Conv., N.Y.C., 1980. Served with USN, 1961-64. Recipient Youth Motivation award Chgo. Assn. Commerce and Industry, 1978-82, 86, YWCA Leadership award 1980, 84. Mem. Women in Computing, Info. Systems Planners Assn., Navy League, Am. Legion. Republican. Roman Catholic. Home: 35 Wildwood Dr S Prospect Heights IL 60070 Office: Kraft Inc Kraft Ct Glenview IL 60025

DEJMEK, LINDA MARIE, optometrist; b. Memphis, June 2, 1953. BS in Optometry, Ind. U., 1975, OD, 1977. Owner, operator Appleton (Wis.) Eye Clinic, 1977—. Med. illustrator System for Ophthalmic Dispensing, 1979; illustrator Diver Mag., 1985, Skin Diver mag., 1985; exhibited in group shows at Appleton Gallery Arts, 1979—. Recipient Harold Bailey Award Am. Optometric Found., 1977; named Hon. Citizen, City of Clarksville, Tenn., 1976. Mem. Am. Optometric Assn., Wis. Optometric Assn., Fox Cities Optometric Soc. (pres. 1984-86), Wis. Fedn. Bus. Profl. Women (chmn. state membership com. 1985-86, state 1st v.p. 1986-87, pres. elect 1987—), Mid-Day Bus. and Profl. Women (treas. 1980-81, found. chmn. 1981-84, pres. 1984-86), Fox Cities C. of C. (mem. govtl. relations com. 1986-87), Appleton Jr. Women's Club (illustrator 1981-82). Avocations: scuba diving, art, photography, travel, camping. Office: Appleton Eye Clinic 509 Chain Dr Appleton WI 54915

DEJONG, BRUCE ALLEN, architect; b. Sully, Iowa, June 17, 1946; s. Floris Donald and Margaret (Van Roeckel) DeJ. BArch, Iowa State U., 1969. Registered architect, Minn. Architect Charles Herbert & Assocs., Des Moines, 1968-70, Parker Klein Assocs., Mpls., 1970-71; v.p., project architect Perrenoud Architects Inc., Mpls., 1971-81; assoc., project architect Frederick Bentz, Milo Thompson, Robert Rietow, Inc., Mpls., 1981—. Mem. arts adv. com. Met. Council, St. Paul, 1986—. Mem. AIA (dir. Minn. chpt. 1977-79, chmn. annual conv. 1985-87), Am. Arbitration Assn., Constrn. Specifications Inst. Home: 3853 Aldrich Ave S Minneapolis MN 55409 Office: Frederick Bentz Milo Thompson Robert Rietow Inc 1234 Dain Tower Minneapolis MN 55402

DE JONG, RUSSELL NELSON, neurologist; b. Orange City, Iowa, Mar. 12, 1907; s. Conrad De Jong and Cynthia J. Bursma; m. Madge Anna Brook, Apr. 23, 1938; children: Mary C. Obuchowski, Constance J. Armitage, Russell N. Jr. AB, U. Mich., 1929, MD, 1932, MS in Neurology, 1936. Diplomate Am. Bd. Psychiatry and Neurology. Intern in neurology U. Mich., Ann Arbor, 1932-33, resident, 1933-36, instr. neurology, 1936-37, asst. prof., 1937-41, assoc. prof., 1941-50, prof., chmn. dept., 1950-76, prof. emeritus, 1977—; mem. World Fedn. of Neurology research group on Headache, research group on Huntington's Chorea; cons. neurology and psychiatry Surgeon Gen. U.S. Army Far East Command, 1949; Stephen W. Ranson lectr. Northwestern U. Med. Sch., 1964; vis. prof. neurology U. Calif. Sch. Medicine, San Francisco, 1961, UCLA, 1966. Author: The Neurologic Examination, 1950, A History of American Neurology, 1982; editor-in-chief Neurology, 1951-76; neurology editor Yearbook of Neurology and Neurosurgery, 1969—; contbr. articles to profl. jours. Mem. U.S. Pharmacopeia Adv. Panel on Neuropsychiatry, mem. med. adv. bd. Nat. Multiple Sclerosis Soc., 1955—, chmn. 1967-69. Mem. Deutsche Gesellschaft für Neurologie (hon.), Instituto Neurologico de Guatemala (hon.), AMA, Nat. Acad. Sci. (drug efficacy com., nat. research council), Am. Assn. for History of Medicine, Am. Acad. Neurology (hon., v.p. 1961-63), Am. Epilepsy Soc. (pres. 1955-56), Am. Med. Writers Assn. (bd. dirs. 1962-64), Am. Neurol. Assn. (hon., v.p. 1957-58, pres. 1964-65), Am. Psychiat. Assn. (chmn. sect. convulsive disorders 1950-52), Cen. Neuropsychiat. Assn., Mich. Neurol. Assn., Alpha Omega Alpha, Phi Kappa Psi, Sigma Xi. Home: 1526 Harding Rd Ann Arbor MI 48104 Office: Univ Hosp Univ Mich Ann Arbor MI 48109

DE JONG, STUART DONALD, small business owner; b. Grand Rapids, Mich., Mar. 27, 1932; s. Dewey S. and Winnie (Bouma) De J.; m. Jean Marie Tilma, June 5, 1952; children: Daniel, David, Joel, Mark, Janna. Student, Calvin Coll., 1949-50. Owner Millbrook TV Service, Grand Rapids, 1954-61; pres. Electro Med. Services, Inc., Grand Rapids, 1961—. Pres. Grand Rapids Bapt. Acad. Found., 1986-87. Served with U.S. Army, 1952-54. Mem. Assn. for Advancement of Med. Instrumentation. Republican. Avocations: flying, boating, tennis. Office: Electro Med Services Inc 1260 Burton St SW Grand Rapids MI 49509

DEKKER, RANDALL M., bank executive. Chmn. bd. dirs. 1st Mich. Bank Corp., Zeeland. Office: First Mich Bank Corp 101 E Main St Box 300 Zeeland MI 49464 *

DELABRE, KEVIN MICHAEL, financial institution executive; b. Kankakee, Ill., May 25, 1952; s. Richard Victor Sr. and Theresa Ann (Marlaire) D.; m. Carol Marie Surprenant, Sept. 20, 1974; children: Heather, Aaron. AA, Kankakee Community Coll., 1972; BBA, Govs. State U., 1974, M in Pub. Service, 1980. Lic. life ins. broker. With Kankakee Fed. Savs. and Loan Assn., 1973—, mgr. investment services, 1983—, ins. risk mgr., 1985—. Chmn. sustaining membership program Kankakee Trials Dist. Boy Scouts Am., 1981-83, dist. chmn., 1984-85, exec. mem. Rainbow Council, 1984—; chmn. fin. com. St. George's Ch., 1985—, choir mem.; mem. Kankakee County Farm Bur.; mem. Dist. 258 Sch. Bd., 1985—. Mem. Inst. Fin. Edn. (pres. Kankakee chpt. 1981-82), Nat. Assn. Securities Dealers (registered). Roman Catholic. Lodges: Moose, Rotary (bd. dirs. 1986—). Avocations: golf, guitar, furniture refinishing, wood working. Office: Kankakee Fed Savs & Loan Assn PO Box 552 Kankakee IL 60901

DE LANCEY, JOHN OLIVER LANG, gynecologist/obstetrician; b. Ann Arbor, Mich., Sept. 7, 1951; s. Oliver Samuel and Mary (Wacker) DeL.; m. Barbara Lang, May 30, 1980; 1 child, John Oliver Lang. BA, Oberlin Coll., 1973; MD, U. Mich., 1977. Diplomate Am. Bd. Ob-Gyn. Resident in ob-gyn. U. Mich., Ann Arbor, 1977-81; faculty physician dept. ob-gyn. U. Mich., Ann Arbor, 1981—. Mem. Am. Coll. Ob-Gyn, Soc. Gyn. Surgeons, Normal F. Miller Gyn. Soc. (sec. 1985), Washtenaw Ob-Gyn Soc. (program chmn. 1982-84), Internat. Continence Soc., Phi Beta Kappa, Sigma Xi. Avocations: woodworking, drawing.

DELANEY, DANIEL LYNN, management consultant; b. Owosso, Mich., Mar. 25, 1950; s. Carl F. and Ann (Svarc) D.; m. Catherine R. Chabica, Aug. 28, 1971; children: Erik, Ryan, Tara. AA, Ferris State Coll., 1970; BS, Mich. State U., 1972; JD, Thomas Cooley Law Sch., 1979. Mng. dir. Urban Health Services, Flint, Mich., 1976-78; bus. cons. Profl. Cons., Lansing, Mich., 1978-81; bus. cons., owner Med.-Dental Cons., Okemos, Mich., 1981—. Soccer coach YMCA, Owosso, 1983—; basketball coach St. Joseph Sch., Owosso, 1984—; pres. St. Joseph Athletic Assn., 1985—. Roman Catholic. Avocations: softball, fishing. Home: 700 Riverbend Owosso MI 48867 Office: Med-Dental Cons 4295 Okemos Rd #8 Okemos MI 48864

DELANEY, MARY MURRAY (LANE, MARY D.), author, travel agency executive; b. New Richmond, Wis., Jan. 1, 1913; d. Christopher James Murray and Rachel (Newell) Turner Murray; m. Thomas James Delaney, Jr., June 1, 1932; children—Thomas James III, Joni Mary Delaney O'Connell. Grad. Twin City Bus. Coll., 1931; student Macalester Coll., St. Paul, 1955-56, 1958. Sec. Montgomery Ward & Co., St. Paul, 1930-32; auditor E. I. duPont de Nemours, Rosemount, Minn., 1942; v.p., tour escort Delaney J Joyce & O'Dell Travel, 1963—; author: Of Irish Ways, 1986; contbr. short stories mags., U.S., England, Australia, Norway, Sweden, Denmark, Italy. Contbr. articles to profl. jours. Mem. Nat. League Am. Pen Women. Home: 1606 Highland Pkwy St Paul MN 55116 Office: 249 S Snelling Ave Saint Paul MN 55105

DELANEY, MICHAEL JOSEPH, bank executive; b. Evergreen Park, Ill., Feb. 7, 1952; s. Patrick Michael and Mildred Catherine Delaney; m. Patricia Elizabeth Bradac; children: Michael, John, Joseph. BS, DePaul U., 1975, MBA, 1977, MST, 1981. Systems, research analyst Commonwealth Edison, Chgo., 1970-80; project leader CNA, Chgo., 1978-80; applications mgr. United Ins., Chgo., 1980-84, Am. Nat. Bank, Chgo., 1984—. Roman Catholic. Home: PO Box 741 Tinley Park IL 60477 Office: Am Nat Bank 33 N LaSalle Chicago IL 60690

DELANEY, PHILIP ALFRED, banker; b. Chgo., Nov. 18, 1928; s. Walter J. and Kathryn M. (McWilliams) D.; m. Patricia O'Brien, June 21, 1952; children—Sharon Ann, Philip A., Nancy, Mary Beth. B.S. magna cum laude, U. Notre Dame, 1950; M.B.A., U. Chgo., 1956; postgrad., U. Wis. Grad. Sch. Banking, 1960. Trainee A.G. Becker & Co., Chgo., 1950; broker/dealer A.G. Becker & Co., 1951-52; with Harris Trust & Savs. Bank, Chgo., 1952—; exec. v.p., chief credit officer Harris Trust & Savs. Bank, 1980-84, pres., 1984—; pres. holding co. Harris Bankcorp, Inc., Chgo., 1984—, dir.; dir. DeSoto, Inc., Des Plaines, Ill.; prin. Chgo. United. Bd. dirs. Catholic Charities Chgo., Chgo. Conv. and Visitors Bur., Ill. Council Econ. Edn., Evanston Hosp.; mem. Chgo. Com., Chgo. Council Fgn. Relations; assoc. Northwestern U.; Chief Crusader United Way/Crusade of Mercy; mem. adv. council Chgo. Urban League; mem. citizens bd. Loyola U., Chgo. Served to 2d lt. USMC, 1951. Mem. Am. Bankers Assn., Am. Inst. Banking, Am. Mgmt. Assn., Assn. Res. City Bankers, Bankers Club Chgo., Chgo. Assn. Commerce and Industry, Robert Morris Assocs., U. Chgo. Alumni Assn., Mid Am. Com., Chgo. United, Chgo. Urban League Bus. Adv. Council., Econ. Club of Chgo. Roman Catholic. Clubs: Commercial, Commonwealth, Economic, Notre Dame (Chgo.), North Shore Country, Chgo. Office: Harris Bankcorp Inc 111 W Monroe St PO Box 755 Chicago IL 60690

DELANO, WILLIAM RICHARD, manufacturing company engineer; b. Chgo., Feb. 1, 1951; s. William Stevens and Louise Catherine (Uccello) D. BSEE, Ill. Inst. Tech., 1973. Sr. automatic test engr. Northrop Def. Systems Div., Rolling Meadows, Ill., 1974-79; sr. project leader Genrad Co., Schaumburg, Ill., 1979-81; systems engr. Tex. Instruments Corp., Arlington Heights, Ill., 1981-82; tech. support mgr. Sun Electric Co., Chgo., 1982-83; sr. automatic test engr. Oak Switch Systems, Inc., Crystal Lake, Ill., 1984-86; sr. cons. Computing Architects Inc., Bloomingdale, Ill., 1986; cons. Sundstrand Aviation, Rockford, Ill., 1986; incoming inspection sr. automatic test engr. Digital Appliance Controls Inc., Elgin, Ill., 1986—; software designer Delano Cons. Inc., Hoffman Estates, Ill., 1983—. Designer Tri-Ped robot, 1978, water fall and fountain, 1980. Mem. Rep. Task Force, Washington, 1983-84. Roman Catholic. Avocations: music, gardening, movies, sports, robotics. Home: 3730 Whispering Trails Hoffman Estates IL 60195 Office: Digital Appliance Controls Inc 2401 Hassell Rd Hoffman Estates IL 60195

DE LANOY, CHARLES JAMES, accountant; b. Detroit, May 26, 1956; s. Robert Le Roy and Helen Marie (Maciag) D.L. BA, Mich. State U., 1979. CPA, Mich. Fin. analyst Control Data Corp., Rochester, Mich., 1979-81; tax mgr. Seidman & Seidman, Grand Rapids, Mich., 1981—; v.p. Checker Drugs, Westland, Mich., 1981—. Com. mem. Kent Skills Ctr., Grand Rapids, 1986—. Mem. Am. Inst. CPA's, Mich. Assn. CPA's.

DELAPORTE, EDWARD CHARLES, IV, telecommunications systems programmer; b. Rockford, Ill., Aug. 20, 1958; s. Edward Charles III and Doris Ann (Dolan) D.; m. Karen Ruth Hatch, Oct. 27, 1978; children: Sarah Elizabeth, Edward Charles V. Student, Rock Valley Coll., 1978. Shop floor coordinator Sundstrand Aviation, Rockford, 1977-78, contracts adminstr., 1978, service analyst, 1979, bus. application programmer, 1980-83, systems programmer, 1983-86; telecommunications systems programmer Sundstrand Corp., Rockford, 1986—; instr. data processing, Rock Valley Coll., 1981-86; instr. safety, No. Ill. U., DeKalb, 1981-86. Mem. Data Processing Mgmt. Assn. (bd. dirs. 1983-84). Republican. Mem. Assembly of God Ch. Clubs: Sundstrand Micro Computer (pres. 1983-86). Avocations: microcomputers, motorcycling. Office: Sundstrand Corp 4751 Harrison Ave Rockford IL 61125

DELATTRE, DWIGHT DAVID, architect; b. Ebensburg, Pa., Apr. 1, 1943; s. Clement George and Mary Marie (Rambeau) DeL.; m. Sheila Mary O'Donnell, Sept. 18, 1965; children—Steven Dwight, Brian David. B.S.A.E., Chgo. Tech. Coll., 1965. Cert. architect, Ill. Draftsman, Jensen & Halstead, Chgo., 1965-66, Kennedy Co., Deerfield, Ill., 1966-69, DelBianco, Schwartz & Donatoni, Chgo., 1969-72; with Kennedy Co., Kennedy Bros., Northbrook, Ill., 1972-75, mgr. drafting dept., 1975-78; owner, architect New Horizons Inc., Arlington Heights, Ill., 1978—. Coach, Little League, Elk Grove Village, Ill., 1975-78; leader Northwest Suburban council Boy Scouts Am., 1975-78. Recipient Archtl. award Des Plaines C. of C., 1982, Mem. AIA, AIA (Chgo. chpt.), Nat. Assn. Home Builders, Home Builders Assn. Greater Chgo. (Bronze Key Design award 1984, 2 Silver Key Design awards 1984). Roman Catholic. Avocations: sailing; scuba diving; skiing; woodworking. Office: New Horizons Inc 1600 N Arlington Hts Rd Arlington Heights IL 60004

DELAY, JOHN LYNN, electrical engineer; b. Pekin, Ill., June 9, 1954; s. Oakley Freemont and Carmen Violet (Stone) DeL.; m. Tamara Sue Paden, Dec. 2, 1978; 1 child, Aimeé Jo. AS in Broadcast Electronics Tech., John Wood Community Coll., 1984; BS in Electronics Engring. Tech., Culver Stockton Col., 1986. Engr. asst. Dickey John Corp., Auburn, Ill., 1973-76; engr. Harris Corp., Quincy, Ill., 1976—; keynote speaker Soc. Women Engrs., 1987. Mem. Am. Soc. Quality Control (program chmn. 1984—, vice chmn. 1985-86, chmn. 1987—). Republican. Avocaitons: softball, basketball.

DELAY, WILLIAM RAYMOND, communications executive; b. Texarkana, Tex., June 16, 1929; s. Raymond Wallace and Flora Thomas (Greenwood) DeL.; m. Mary Elinor Dolson, Oct. 2, 1954; children—Martha, Nancy. B.S. in Journalism, U. Kans., William Allen White Sch. Journalism, 1951; postgrad. Mead Johnson Inst., 1958-59, Counter Intelligence Corps. Sch., 1951. Reporter Kansas City Kansan, 1951; reporter, copy editor Kansas City Times, 1953-56; pub. relations mgr. Mead Johnson & Co., 1956-60; dir. pub. relations Am. Acad. Family Physicians, 1960-71, dir. communications div., 1971—, founder Am. Acad. Family Physicians Reporter, 1974; advt. promotion mgr. Am. Family Physician mag., 1962-69; instr. pub. relations U. Mo.-Kansas City, 1979; lectr. pub. relations NYU, U. Kans. U. Nev. Chmn. pub. info. com. and exec. com. Am. Cancer Soc., West Met. Area Mo. div. Served with U.S. Army, 1951-53. Recipient U.S. C. of C. Disting. Achievement award, 1962; Gold medal N.Y. Film Festival, 1967. Mem. Pub. Relations Soc. Am. (Silver Anvil award 1980; Prism award Kansas City chpt. 1980, 85; Profl. of Year award 1982, President's award 1985), Soc. Profl. Journalists, Kansas City Press Club, Nat. Assn. Sci. Writers, Am. Assn. Med. Soc. Execs., Soc. Tchrs. Family Medicine, Acad. Health Services Mktg., Sigma Delta Chi. Roman Catholic. Contbr. to book: Kansas City Out Loud. Office: 1740 W 92d St Kansas City MO 64114

DEL CASTILLO, JULIO CESAR, neurosurgeon; b. Havana, Cuba, Jan. 21, 1930; s. Julio Cesar and Violeta (Diaz de Villegas) Del C.; came to U.S., 1961, naturalized, 1968; B.S., Columbus Sch., Havana, 1948; M.D., U. Havana, 1955; m. Rosario Freire, Sept. 18, 1955; children—Julio Cesar, Juan Claudio, Rosemarie. Intern, Michael Reese Hosp., Chgo., 1955-56; resident Cook County Hosp., Chgo., 1957, Lahey Clinic, Boston, 1957-58, U. Pa. Grad. Hosp., 1958-60; research asst. dept. gen. surgery Jackson Meml. Hosp., Miami, Fla., 1962-64; practice medicine, specializing in neurosurgery, Havana, 1960-61, Quincy, Ill., 1965—; mem. staff Blessing Hosp., Quincy, pres. staff, 1972-74; mem. staff St. Mary's Hosp., Quincy, trustee, 1987; owner Top Hat Hobbies, Inc., Quincy. Bd. dirs. Western Ill. Found. for Med. Care, 1970-73; trustee Blessing Hosp., 1972-74. Mem. Am. Acad. Model Aeros., Congress Neurol. Surgeons, AMA, A.C.S., Adams County Med. Soc. (sec., treas. 1966-75, pres.), Ill. Med. Soc., Exptl. Aircraft Assn. Rotarian (dir. 1970-72, pres. 1976-77). Home: 14 Curved Creek Quincy IL 62301 Office: 1235 Broadway Quincy IL 62301

DELCOURT, BENOIT RENÉ, business executive; b. Lille, France, Apr. 11, 1947; m. Sarah Lindsay Cooper, Oct. 19, 1975; children: Alice, Emilie, David. Diploma, Ecole Superieure de Commerce de Paris, 1969; MBA, NYU, 1971. Mktg. specialist Leroy-Somer Ltd., Skelmersdale, Lancashire, Eng., 1974, Leroy-Somer S.A., Angouleme, France, 1974; regional mgr. Leroy-Somer S.A., Bangkok, Thailand, 1975-76; v.p. sales Leroy-Somer Inc., Arlington Heights, Ill., 1977-81; pres. Crouzet Controls Inc., Schaumburg, Ill., 1982—. Case coordinator Amnesty Internat., Palatine Ill., 1984—. Mem. French-Am. C. of C., Ill. C. of C., Small Motor Mfrs. Assn. Avocations: photography, tennis, sailing. Home: 27 Wychwood Ln South Barrington IL 60010 Office: Crouzet Controls Inc 1083 State Pkwy Schaumburg IL 60173

DE LERNO, MANUEL JOSEPH, elec. engr.; b. New Orleans, Jan. 8, 1922; s. Joseph Salvador and Elizabeth Mabry (Jordan) De L.; B.E. in Elec. Engring., Tulane U., 1941; M.E.E., Rensselaer Poly. Inst., 1943; m. Margery Ellen Eaton, Nov. 30, 1946 (div. Oct. 1978); children—Diane, Douglas. Devel. engr. indsl. control dept. Gen. Electric Co., Schenectady, 1941-44; design engr. Lexington Electric Products Co., Newark, 1946-47; asst. prof. elec. engring. Newark Coll. Engring., 1948-49; test engr. Maschinenfabrik Oerlikon, Zurich, Switzerland, 1947-48; application engr. Henry J. Kaufman Co., Chgo., 1949-55; pres. Del Equipment Co., Chgo., 1955-60; v.p. Del-Ray Co., Chgo., 1960-67; pres. S-P-D Services Inc., Forest Park, Ill., 1967-81, S-P-D Industries, Inc., Berwyn, Ill., 1981—; mem. standards making coms. Nat. Fire Protection Assn. Internat. Served as lt. (j.g.) USNR, 1944-45, to lt. comdr., 1950-52. Registered profl. engr., Ill. Mem. IEEE (sr.), Ill. Soc. Profl. Engrs., Soc. Fire Protection Engrs., Am. Water Works Assn. Home: 36 W 760 Stonebridge Ln Saint Charles IL 60174 Office: 3105 S Ridgeland Ave Berwyn IL 60402

DELESPINASSE, DORIS BARNES, accounting educator; b. Torrington, Conn., July 3, 1941; d. Raymond Barnes and Doris (Orr) Stringham; m. Paul F. deLespinasse, Aug. 5, 1967; children: Cobie Ann, Alan Fredrick. BA, Stanford U., 1963; MA, U. Oreg., 1965, postgrad., 1965-67. CPA, Mich. Staff acct. Lonzella Seaburge, CPA, Adrian, Mich., 1977-79, Gross & Ludwig, CPA's, Adrian, 1980-81; prof. acctg. Adrian (Mich.) Coll., 1979—. Bd. dirs. Adrian Symphony, 1986-87. Mem. Am. Inst. CPA's, Alpha Kappa Psi. Home: 1142 College Adrian MI 49221 Office: Adrian Coll 110 S Madison Adrian MI 49221

DELGADO, JOSEPH RAMON, business executive; b. Chgo., Mar. 4, 1932; s. Joseph Ramon and Florence (Nelson) D. BA in English, U. Ill., 1958. With Campbell-Mithun Advt., Chgo., 1960-68, purchasing agt., dir. office services, 1964-68; purchasing agt., asst. to pres., asst. to treas. Maxant Button & Supply Co., Chgo., 1968-70; asst. purchasing agt., administrv. asst. Soiltest, Inc., Evanston, Ill., 1970-82; v.p., asst. to pres. S.W. Chgo. Corp., 1982—. Mem. Lyric Opera Subscription Com., 1957; observer Joint Civic Com. on Elections, 1965; election judge primary and gen. elections, 1968, 70. Served with AUS, 1952-54. Mem. Purchasing Agts. Assn. Chgo. (co-chmn. publicity and pub. relations com. 1963-64), U. Ill. Alumni, Illiniweks, Chgo. Symphony Soc. (charter). Lutheran. Republican. Clubs: Whitehall, Barclay, Ltd., International (Chgo.). Dance choreographer for various groups and individuals. Home and Office: 900 Lake Shore Dr Chicago IL 60611 Address: 3605 NE 32d Ave Fort Lauderdale FL 33308

DELGIORNO, MICHAEL, hotel executive; b. Bklyn., Aug. 18, 1949; s. Robert and Ann (Santori) D.; m. Barbara Musiol, May 21, 1973; children: David, Diane. Student, Southampton (N.Y.) Coll., 1967-69. Gen. mgr. Wilmington (Del.) Hilton, 1975-78, Facilities Leasing Corp., Princeton, N.J., 1978-81, Sheraton Univ. Inn, Ann Arbor, Mich., 1981-82, Cleve. Hilton, 1982-83; dir. ops. The Springe Group, Cleve., 1983-85, v.p. ops., 1985—. Mem. Am. Hotel and Motel Assn. (cert.). Club: Columbia Hills Country. Avocations: golf, football, music. Home: 15214 High Point Strongsville OH 44136

DELLACQUA, RICHARD LEE, sales executive; b. Chgo., Apr. 14, 1945; s. Joseph C. and Evelyn R. (Templin) D.; m. Eileen Roberta Farmilant, Mar. 22, 1970; children: Bradley, Gina Marie, Anthony. Student, Wright Jr. Coll., 1963-65, Montgomery Coll., 1974. Br. mgr. Gaybar Electric Inc., Washington, 1969-75; dist. sales mgr. Panasonic Co., Elk Grove, Ill., 1975-77; asst. sales mgr. Atlanta Stone Works, 1977-80; regional sales mgr. Borg Erikson Co., Chgo., 1980-81; nat. sales mgr. Alpha Metals Inc., Jersey City, 1981-84; v.p. Dickson Weatherproof Nail Co., Evanston, Ill., 1984—. Served to sgt. USAF, 1965. Roman Catholic. Avocations: music, trumpet player. Home: 3985 Huntington Blvd Hoffman Estates IL 60195 Office: Dickson Weatherproof Nail Co 1900 Greenwood Ave Evanston IL 60204

DELLA MARIA, JOSEPH PETER, JR., lawyer; b. Chgo., Oct. 11, 1940; s. Joseph Peter and Mary Margaret (Kelley) Della M.; m. Martha Elizabeth Woodall, Jan. 2, 1971; children: Laura Rawn, Katherine Kelley. AB, U. Notre Dame, 1962, JD, 1966. Bar: Ill. 1966, U.S. Dist. Ct. (no. dist.) Ill. 1971, U.S. Ct. Mil. Appeals 1968, U.S. Ct. Appeals (7th cir.) 1967, U.S. Supreme Ct. 1974, U.S. Ct. Appeals (9th cir.) 1979. Law clk. to Judge Roger Kiley U.S. Ct. Appeals (7th cir.), 1966-67; instr. U.S. Naval Justice Sch., 1967-71; assoc. Rothschild, Barry & Myers, Chgo., 1971-78, ptnr., 1978—. Served to lt. comdr. JAGC, USNR, 1967-71. Mem. ABA, Ill. Bar Assn., Chgo. Bar Assn., U.S. Naval Inst. Roman Catholic. Club: Dunham Woods (Wayne, Ill.).

DELLANDE, WILLIAM DREW, optometrist; b. Dyersburg, Tenn., Jan. 20, 1926; s. Armand Joseph and Georgianna (Collins) D.; m. Alice Hassebrock, Oct. 1, 1947; children—Brian William, Elaine Alison. O.D. Ill. Coll. Optometry, 1949; M.A. U. Mo., 1966. Diplomate Am. Acad. Optometry. Pvt. practice St. Louis, 1950-54, Columbia, Mo., 1955—; instr. reading improvement progam U. Mo., Columbia, 1963-68; mem. adv. com. Sch. Optometry U. Mo.-St. Louis, 1982-84. Contbr. articles profl. jours. Fellow Am. Acad. Optometry; mem. Am. Optometric Assn. (mem. contact lens com. 1972-73, assoc. editor Contact Lens sect. 1983-84), St. Louis Optometric Soc. (pres. 1952), Heart of Am. Contact Lens Soc. (pres. 1970-71, man of the year 1975), Mo. Chapt. Am. Acad. Optometry (pres. 1983-84), Cen. Mo. Optometric Soc. (pres. 1986). Club: Webster Groves Toastmaster (Toastmaster of Yr. 1953). Home: 811 Cornell Columbia MO 65203 Office: 205 Executive Bldg 601 E Broadway Columbia MO 65203

DELL'ANTONIA, JON C., information services executive; b. Pittsburg, Kans., June 3, 1941; s. Stenie and Katherine Marie (Seibert) Dell'A.; m. Mary Jo Rienbolt, June 18, 1960; 1 child, Karin. BBA, Pitts. State U., 1963. V.p. Ennis Brandon Computer Services, Dallas, 1969-71; dir. mgmt. info. services Gen. Portland, Dallas, 1971-77, Harte-Hanks, San Antonio, 1977-80, Seaboard Allied Mill, Shawnee Mission, Kans., 1980-82; v.p. mgmt. info. systems The Coleman Co., Wichita, Kans., 1982—. Co-chmn. State of Kans. Computer Adv. Com., Topeka, 1985—; mem. bd. advisors Kelce Sch. Bus., Pitts. State U., 1985—; mem. City Air Service Strategy Task Force, Wichita, 1985. Served to 1st lt. U.S. Army, 1964-66. Mem. Alpha Kappa Psi (life). Republican. Methodist. Avocations: tennis, collecting model trains. Office: The Coleman Co Inc PO Box 1762 Wichita KS 67201

DELLA PIA, MAX HAROLD, lawyer; b. Manistee, Mich., July 11, 1953; s. John Lawrence and Mary Sue (Flarity) D.; m. Nancy Jean Knepel, June 23, 1984; 1 child, Michael Alexander. BS in Econs., USAF Acad., 1975; JD cum laude, Marquette U., 1984. Bar: Wis. 1984, U.S. Dist. Cts. (ea. and we. dists.) Wis. 1984, U.S. Ct. Appeals (7th cir.) 1984. Commd. 2d lt. USAF, 1975, advanced through grades to capt., 1979, resigned, 1981; capt. USAF Reserves, 1984—; sole practice Milw., 1984-86; assoc. Ruder, Ware, Michler, & Forester, S.C., Wausau, Wis., 1986—; legal research asst. Def. Research Inst., Milw., 1982-84. Ins. Trial Counsel of Wis. scholar 1982-83, Thomas J. Weithers Meml. scholar Def. Research Inst., 1983-84. Mem. ABA, Wis. Acad. Trial Lawyers, Wis. Bar Assn., Assn. Trial Lawyers of Am., Def. Research Inst., Civil Trial Counsel Wis. Lutheran. Avocation: piloting. Home: 4222 N 68th Milwaukee WI 53216 Office: Ruder Ware Michler & Forester SC PO Box 8050 First Am Ctr Wausau WI 54401-8050

DELO, ROBERT PAUL, accountant, consultant; b. Fremont, Mich., July 8, 1952; s. Haldon Leslie and Elizabeth Carolyn (Beckett) D.; m. Rose Marie Culley, Sept. 1, 1985. BA in English, DePaul U., 1974; MBA, Keller Grad. Sch. Mgmt., Chgo., 1983. CPA, Ill. Sr. bus. cons. Deloitte Haskins & Sells, Chgo., 1983-86; internal auditor Chgo. Tribune Co., 1986-87, sr. acct., gen. acctg. dept., 1987—. Served to capt. U.S. Army, 1974-78. Mem. Am. Inst. CPA's, Ill. CPA Soc., Inst. Internal Auditors, News Media Internal Auditors Assn. Roman Catholic. Office: Chgo Tribune Co 435 N Michigan Ave Chicago IL 60611

DE LONG, DALE RAY, chemical executive; b. Oelwein, Iowa, Dec. 11, 1959; s. Jack Rollis De Long and Shirley Jean (Follitt) Miller; m. Joyce Lynn Bazan, Aug. 15, 1981; children: Nicolas, Kymberly, Sabrina. Office mgr. 3D Inc., St. Joseph, Mich., 1978-82; v.p. 3D Inc., Benton Harbor, Mich., 1982—. Republican. Clubs: Exchange. Avocations: weight lifting, aerobics. Office: 3D Inc 1007 Nickerson Ave Benton Harbor MI 49022

DELONG, ERIKA VENTA, psychiatrist; b. Riga, Latvia, Oct. 14, 1925; came to U.S., 1949; d. Janis and Ida Cielens; m. Mark Eldridge DeLong, Apr. 12, 1952; 1 child, Ruth Ellen. Cand. Med., Gustav Adolf U., Göhingen, Federal Rep. Germany, 1948; MD, U. Vienna, Austria, 1957. Diplomate Am. Bd. Psychiatry and Neurology. Intern Trumbell Meml. Hosp., Warren, Ohio, 1958-59; resident in psychiatry Cleve. Psychiat. Inst., 1963; practice medicine specializing in psychiatry Fairview Park and Parma, Ohio, 1963—; chief psychiat. dept. Fairview Gen. Hosp., Cleve., 1981—. Cardiovascular research fellow Mt. Zion Hosp., San Francisco, 1957-58. Mem. AMA, Ohio State Med. Assn., Cleve. Psychiat. Assn., Cleve. Acad. Medicine. Republican. Lutheran. Clubs: Playhouse, Ski Docs. Avocations: skiing, horseracing. Home: 4495 Valley Forge Dr Fairview Park OH 44126 Office: 20800 Westgate Plaza Fairview Park OH 44126

DELONG, MICHAEL BEN, clergyman, college president; b. Bellefonte, Pa., Sept. 24, 1956; s. Bernard Lincoln and Priscilla (Hobson) DeL.; m. Terry Arlene Stone, Dec. 3, 1978; children—Benjamin, Jonathan, Matthew, Samuel. Student Centerville Bible Coll., 1975-78; B.A., Temple Baptist Coll., 1981, M.A., 1985. Ordained to ministry Baptist Ch. 1979. Minister of music First Bapt. Ch. Centerville, 1978—; instr., registrar Centerville Bible Coll., 1978—, pres., 1985—; asst. pastor First Bapt. Ch. Centerville, 1983—. Editor The Light, 1981-83. Republican. Avocations: tennis, flying, racquetball. Home: 148 Washington Mill Rd Bellbrook OH 45305 Office: First Baptist Ch Centerville 38 N Main St Centerville OH 45459

DE LONG, PAUL TERRY, mechanical engineer, manufacturing company executive; b. Waterloo, Iowa, Apr. 2, 1946; s. Arthur Paul and Alice May (White) De L.; m. Judith Ann Baer, Aug. 5, 1963; children: Donald Jay, Richard Paul. BSME, Iowa State U., 1972. Designer John Deer, Waterloo, 1965-68, mgr. quality engring., 1975-83, project mgr., 1983-86, mgr. product assurance, 1986—; sr. project engr. Gen. Motors Corp., Milford, Mich., 1972-75. Mem. Soc. Automotive Engrs. (pres. Ames, Iowa chpt. 1970-72), Am. Soc. Quality Control (scholarship chmn. 1987). Avocations: hunting, fishing, cycling, running, skiing. Office: John Deere Engine Works PO Box 5100 Waterloo IA 50704

DELOUGHERY, GRACE LEONA, nursing educator; b. Allison, Iowa, Jan. 17, 1933; d. Ed F. and Alma K. (Kampman) Meinen; B.S., U. Minn., 1955, M.P.H., 1960; Ph.D., Claremont Grad. Sch., 1966; m. Henry O. Deloughery, Nov. 30, 1962; children—Paul Edward, Michael, Kathleen. Staff nurse Mpls. Dept. Pub. Health, 1955-59; research fellow U. Minn. Sch. Pub. Health, 1960-63; sch. nurse Val Verde Sch. Dist., Perris, Calif., part-time 1963-66; community coordinator, nurse in Title I pilot project in San Jacinto, Riverside (Calif.) County Schs., 1966, cons. Title I, 1966-67; assoc. prof. U. N.C. Coll. Nursing, 1967-68; asst. prof. U. Calif. Sch. Nursing, Los Angeles, 1968-72; dean Center Nursing Edn., Spokane, 1972-74; prof., head dept. nursing Winona (Minn.) State U., 1975-77; adminstr. Deloughery Home Sr. Adults, 1977-84; assoc. prof. Ind. U., New Albany, 1984—, Bellarmine Coll., Louisville, Ky.; participant seminars, condr. workshops, cons. in field. Recipient award for research Calif. Edn. Research and Guidance Assn., 1967. Fellow Am. Pub. Health Assn., Am. Assn. Social Psychiatry (treas. 1974-78); mem. Am. Nurses Assn., Nat. League Nursing, Am. Sch. Health Assn., Internat. Mental Health Fedn., Wash. Pub. Health Assn., Acad. Polit. and Social Sci., Acad. Polit. Sci., Pi Lambda Theta, Sigma Theta Tau. Lutheran. Club: Winona Country. Contbr. to profl. jours. Home: Route 2 Box 402 Georgetown IN 47122

DELOYE, JAMES MICHAEL, association administrator; b. Milw., Sept. 18, 1960; s. James Frederick and Jule Cathryn (Kennedy) D. BS in Communication Arts, U. Wis., 1983. Freelance prodn. asst. Chgo., 1983-86; prin., designer Go Outfitting, Chgo., 1984—; 1st asst. dir. Dir.'s Guild of Am., Hollywood, Calif., 1986—; Mem. Chi Psi.s. Outside Mag., Chgo., 1985—, Early Winters Inc., Buffalo Grove, Ill., 1986—. Avocations: boardsailing, photography, guitar, art, travelling. Home and Office: 4317 N Paulina Chicago IL 60613

DELP, ARLEN RUSH, osteopath; b. Norristown, Pa., Feb. 17, 1933; s. Enos Price and Catherine (Rush) D.; m. Shirley Ann Jamison, Oct. 15, 1960; children: Dorothea Jane, Janelle Leanne, Sharon Louise. BS, Eastern Mennonite Coll., 1960; DO, Phila. Coll. Osteopathic Medicine, 1967. Diplomate Am. Bd. Family Practice. Gen. practice osteopathic medicine Lexington, Ky., 1979-86; practice osteopathic medicine Miskego (Wis.) Med. Clinic, 1968—. Mem. State Bd. Med. Examiners, Madison, Wis., 1986. Mem. Am. Osteopathic Assn., Wis. Assn. of Osteopathic Physicians and Surgeons (pres. 1980-81, Gen. Practitioner of Yr. 1979). Mennonite. Home: 3767 Shady Ln New Berlin WI 53151 Office: Muskego Med Clinic SC W186 S8055 Racine Ave Muskego WI 53150

DELUCA, AUGUST FRANK, financial executive; b. Balt., Oct. 10, 1943; s. August F. and Harriet (Logue) DeL.; m. Carolyn Ann Coffman, May 22, 1965; children: August F. III, Anthony P. BS in Engring. and Math., U. Mich., 1966; MBA, U. Wash., 1972; MS in Engring., U. So. Calif., 1968. V.p., treas. Kent-Moore Corp., Warren, Mich., 1972-83; v.p. fin. and adminstrn. Medstat System, Ann Arbor, Mich., 1983=85; v.p. fin. MSL Industries Inc., Oak Brook, Ill., 1985—. Mem. Fin Execs. Inst. Home: 333 E 59th Hinsdale IL 60521 Office: MSL Industries Inc 2122 York Rd Oak Brook IL 60521

DE LUCA, HECTOR F., biochemistry educator. Prof. dept. biochemistry U. Wis., Madison. Office: Univ of Wisconsin Dept of Biochem Madison WI 53706 *

DE LUCA, RICHARD ANTHONY, securities broker; b. Columbus, Ohio, Sept. 10, 1961; s. Joseph and Carolyn J. (Sloan) De L. BS in Aviation Adminstrn., Embry Riddle Aeronautical U., 1984; grad., Longman Fin. Sch., 1985. With aircraft sales div. Pgae Uajet, Orlando, Fla., 1984-85; fin. cons. The New York Life, Columbus, Ohio, 1985—; fin. cons. New York Life, Columbus 1985—. Mem. annual campaign Children's Hosp., Glen Civic Assn. Republican. Roman Catholic. Home: 3330 Noreen Dr Columbus OH 43220 Office: The New York Life 140 E Town Suite 1500 Columbus OH 43215

DELUCCA, LEOPOLDO ELOY, otolaryngologist, surgeon; b. Santurce, P.R., Nov. 1, 1952; s. Leopoldo Claudio and Laura Iris (Juncos) DeL.; m. Judith Lynn McClellan, June 11, 1977; children: Lauren Denise, Gina Fay. Pre-med. degree, U. P.R., 1973; MD, Jefferson Med. Coll., Phila., 1977. Diplomate Am. Bd. Otolaryngology. Otolaryngologist Ft. Dodge (Iowa) Med. Ctr., 1981-86; practice medicine specializing in otolaryngology Ft. Dodge, 1986—; active med. staff Trinity Regional Hosp., Ft. Dodge, 1981—, chief of surgery, 1985—; vol. faculty Coll. Osteo. Medicine and Surgery, Des Moines, 1981-82. Fellow ACS, Am. Acad. Otolaryngology-Head and Neck Surgery, Am. Acad. Facial Plastic and Reconstructive Surgery. Democrat. Roman Catholic. Avocation: guitar. Home: 2626 Woodland Dr Fort Dodge IA 50501 Office: Physicians Office Bldg Suite K S Kenyon Rd Fort Dodge IA 50501

DE LUCE, JUDITH, classicist, educator; b. Boston, June 9, 1946; d. Hollinshead and Martha Thacher (Hudson) de L. A.B., Colby Coll., Waterville, Maine, 1968; student Dartmouth Coll., 1967-68; M.A., U. Wis., 1971, Ph.D., 1974. Research editor Grolier Info. Service, N.Y.C., 1968-69; asst. prof. classics Miami U., Oxford, Ohio, 1974-81, assoc. prof., 1981—, coordinator women's studies, 1979-85, acting chmn. dept., 1983-84, chmn. dept., 1984—. Mem. Oxford Choral Ensemble, also trustee; trustee United Campus Ministry, 1980-83; bd. dirs. Planned Parenthood Assn. Butler County. Recipient John B. Foster prize Colby Coll., 1967; Hugh E. Pillinger prize U. Wis., 1972; named Outstanding Univ. Woman, Miami U., 1981; Knapp fellow, 1969-70; Ford fellow, 1971, 72; U. Wis. fellow, 1973-74; Bixler scholar, 1967-78; Miami U. grantee. Mem. Am. Philol. Assn., Archaeol. Inst. Am., Ohio Classical Conf., Vergilian Soc., Classical Assn. Middle West and South, Nat. Women's Studies Assn., Am. Legal Studies Assn., Cin. Assn. Tchrs. Classics, Phi Beta Kappa, Omicron Delta Kappa. Editor: (with Hugh T. Wilder) Language in Primates, 1983; contbr. articles, transls. to classical lit., also articles in feminist studies. Home: 4869 Somerville Rd Oxford OH 45056 Office: Miami U Classics Dept Oxford OH 45056

DE LUCIA, JOSEPH JAMES, psychology educator; consultant; b. Jersey City, Apr. 30, 1921; s. Vincent and Catherine (Hughes) De L.; m. Kathleen O'Neil (div.); 1 dau., Kathy Ann De Lucia Hug; m. Elizabeth Loebs Maisack, May 5, 1961. B.S., St. Peter's Coll., 1943; M.S., U. Ill., 1949, Ph.D., 1951. Instr. psychology U. Ill.-Urbana, 1950-52; asst. prof. psychology Marquette U., Milw., 1952-56; pvt. practice psychology, Milw., 1956-63; dir. Area Mental Health Ctr., Garden City, Kans., 1963-66; exec. dir. Douglas County Guidance Ctr., Superior, Wis., 1966-67; prof. psychology U. Wis.-Superior, 1967—, chmn. dept. psychology, 1967-74; tchr., cons. in field. Chmn. adv. bd. Sta. WDSE-TV (pub. TV), Duluth, Minn., 1982—; pres. bd. dirs. Djorkje Kostic Inst. Audiolinguistic Studies, Inc., Superior, 1980—. Served with USMC, 1942-45. Mem. Am. Psychol. Assn. Republican. Roman Catholic. Home: 823 4th Ave E Superior WI 54880 Office: U Wis Superior WI 54880

DEMAIO, CHARLES PAUL, sales professional; b. Freeport, N.Y., Sept. 23, 1950; s. Paul and Charlotte (Cordy) DeM.; m. Carol Davies, Nov. 22, 1975. BS, Ind. State U., 1973. Tchr. Union Free Schs. #17, Franklin Sq., N.Y., 1973-74; sales person Mass. Mutual Life Ins. Co., Terre Haute, Ind., 1974-76; product mgr. Marcraft Corp., Indpls., 1976—; guest lectr. Ind. State U., Terre Haute, 1983—; guest speaker Pack-Expo, Chgo., 1982, 84, N.Y.C., 1986. Sustaining mem. Rep. Nat. Com., Washington, 1980-86. Mem. Packaging Machine Mfrs. Inst., Soc. Packaging and Handling Engrs. (cons.), Lambda Chi Alpha. Republican. Lodges: Masons, Shriners. Avocations: jogging, racquetball, reading, music, travel. Home: 3379 Eden Village Dr Carmel IN 46032 Office: Marcraft Corp 2915 Tobey Dr Indianapolis IN 46219

DEMAREE, JACK LEE, bank executive; b. Indpls., Aug. 14, 1948; s. Jack H. and Virginia M. (Buis) D.; m. Patricia A. Harrold, June 15, 1967; children—Jeannine, Jay. Student Ball State U., 1967-71; grad. Am. Inst. Banking, 1975; grad. U. Wis. Grad. Sch. Banking, 1981; grad. Jr. Bank Officers Seminar, 1970. With Mchts. Nat. Bank, Muncie, Ind., 1967—, asst. cashier, 1972-75, asst. v.p., 1975-81, v.p., 1981—, mgr. consumer services, 1978-80, v.p. and div. head Comml. Lending dept., 1980—; chmn. underwriting com. WIPB Telesale. Bd. dirs. Delaware County Tb Assn. (Ind.), 1980—, pres., 1982—; chmn. Ball State U. Pres.'s Club, Muncie; chmn. United Way Div. VIII, Muncie; bd. dirs. Muncie-Delaware County ARC, Muncie Children's Mus. Named one of 10 Outstanding Young Hoosiers, Ind. Jaycees, 1981; recipient Benny award Ball State U., 1984. Mem. Ind. Bank Mktg. Assn., YMCA, Muncie-Delaware County C. of C. (chmn. welcome to the community com.), Muncie Jaycees (Disting. Service award 1981), Consumer Bankers Assn. Am. Methodist. Clubs: Cardinal Varsity, Catalina, Muncie Advt. Lodges: Kiwanis, Elks. Home: 3412 Riverside Ave Muncie IN 47304 Office: Merchants Nat Bank PO Box 792 Muncie IN 47305

DEMARIA, ALFRED ANTHONY, JR., neurologist; b. Sewickley, Pa., Mar. 27, 1952; s. Alfred Anthony Sr. and Helen J. (Goray) DeM.; m. Katherine Grace Bridge, June 25, 1977; children: Genevieve, Gabrielle. BA in Biology, John Hopkins U., 1973; MD, Ohio State U., 1976. Diplomate Am. Bd. Med. Examiners, Am. Bd. Psychiatry and Neurology. Intern in internal medicine N.C. Bapt. Hosp., Winston-Salem, 1976-77; resident in neurology N.C. Meml. Hosp., Chapel Hill, 1977-80; fellow in electroencephalography Mayo Clinic, Rochester, Minn., 1980-81; attending neurologist, med. dir. electroencephalography lab. Riverside Meth. Hosp., Columbus, Ohio, 1981, clin. competency com., 1983—. Contbr. articles to profl. jours. Fellow Am. Electroencephalography Soc.; mem. Cen. Assn. Electroencephalographers (future sites com. 1983-85), Am. Acad. Neurology, Am. Epilepsy Soc., Epilepsy Assn. Cen. Ohio (chmn. profl. adv. bd. 1985—, v.p. exec. com.), Am. Soc. Neuroimaging. Roman Catholic. Avocations: music, handball. Home: 7755 Southwick Dr Dublin OH 43017-9562 Office: Neurol Assocs 931 Chatham Ln Columbus OH 43221-2486

DEMASCIO, ROBERT EDWARD, judge; b. Coraopolis, Pa., Jan. 11, 1923; s. Peter and Rosa (Baretta) DeM.; m. Margaret Loftus, Aug. 6, 1955; children: Thomas, Robert, Mary. Student, Wayne State U., 1942-43, 47-51, LL.B., 1951; student, U. Ill., 1944. Bar: Mich. bar 1951. Practice law Detroit, 1951-53, 61-66, asst. U.S. atty., chief criminal div., 1954-61; judge Recorders Ct., Detroit, 1967-71; U.S. dist. judge Eastern Dist. Mich., 1971—. Served with USNR, 1943-46. Mem. Am., Fed., Detroit bar assns., State Bar Mich. Office: U S Dist Ct U S Courthouse 231 W Lafayette Blvd Room 707 Detroit MI 48226

DEMBER, CYNTHIA FOX, clinical psychologist; b. N.Y.C., Feb. 15, 1934; d. Joseph and Florence (Davidson) Fox; m. William Norton Dember, Dec. 21, 1958; children: Joanna, Laura, Greg. AB, Vassar Coll., 1954; MS, Yale U., 1955, PhD, 1959. Dir. psychology Children's Psychiat. Ctr., Cin., 1961-80; pvt. practice Cin., 1962—; adj. prof. U. Cin., 1961—. Contbr. articles to profl jour. Mem. Am. Psychol. Assn., Midwestern Psychol. Assn., Ohio Psychol. Assn., Cin. Acad. Profl. Psychology (pres. 1984), Cin. Soc. Child Clin. Psychologists (pres. 1982-84). Home: 920 Oregon Trail Cincinnati OH 45215 Office: 36 E Hollister St Cincinnati OH 45219

DEMBER, WILLIAM NORTON, educator, psychologist; b. Waterbury, Conn., Aug. 8, 1928; s. David and Henrietta (Siegel) D.; m. Cynthia Fox, Dec. 21, 1958; children: Joanna, Laura, Gregory. A.B., Yale U., 1950; M.A., U. Mich., 1951, Ph.D., 1955. Instr. dept. psychology U. Mich., 1954-56; asst. prof. Yale U., 1956-59; mem. faculty U. Cin., 1959—, prof. psychology, 1965—, asst. dean, grad. sch., 1965-67, head dept. psychology, 1968-76, 79-81, dean Coll. Arts and Scis., 1981-86. Author: Psychology of Perception, 1960, 2d edit., 1979, Visual Perception, 1964, General Psychology, 1970, 2d edit., 1984, Exploring Behavior and Experience, 1971; also articles. Fellow AAAS, Am. Psychol. Assn.; mem. Midwest Psychol. Assn. (pres. 1976), Eastern Psychol. Assn., Psychonomic Soc., N.Y. Acad. Scis. Developed and tested theory of motivation applying to behavior human beings and animals. Home: 920 Oregon Trail Cincinnati OH 45215 Office: U Cin Dept Psychology Cincinnati OH 45221-0376

DEMEESTER, TOM RYAN, thoracic surgeon, medical educator; b. Grand Rapids, Mar. 7, 1938; s. Ryan J. and Ruth (Van't Hof) DeM.; m. Carol Walburg, Aug. 29, 1958; children—Steven Ryan, Sara Lyn, Scott Ryan, Susan Lyn. A.B., Calvin Coll., 1959, M.D., U. Mich., 1963. Diplomate Am. Bd. Surgery, Am. Bd. Thoracic Surgery. Intern, Johns Hopkins Hosp., Balt., 1963-64, resident, 1968-71; asst. prof. thoracic surgery U. Chgo. Pritzker Sch. Medicine, 1974-76, assoc. prof., 1976-78, prof., 1978-83, chief thoracic surgery, 1974-83; prof. thoracic and cardiovascular surgery, chmn. dept. surgery Creighton U. Sch. Medicine, Omaha, 1983—; chief of surgery St. Joseph Hosp., 1983—. Served to lt. col. U.S. Army, 1971-74. Fellow ACS, Am. Coll. Chest Physicians; mem. Assn. Acad. Surgery, AMA, Am. Heart Assn., Johns Hopkins Med. Surg. Soc., Lukes Soc., Chgo. Surg. Soc., Soc. Univ. Surgeons, Soc. Surg. Chmn., Assn. Surg. Edn., Soc. Thoracic Surgeons, Am. Assn. Thoracic Surgery, Am. Assn. Cancer Research, Soc. Surgery Alimentary Tract, Internat. Assn. Study Lung Cancer, Pan-Pacific Surg. Assn., Central Surg. Assn., Western Surg. Soc., Am. Thoracic Soc., Met. Omaha Med. Soc., Nebr. Thoracic Soc., Southwestern Surg. Congress, Nebr. Med. Assn., Collegium Internationale Chirurgiae Digestivae, Internat. Cardiovascular Soc., Am. Soc. Clin. Oncology, Omaha Mid-West Clin. Soc. Soc. Clin. Surgery, Surg. Biology Club II, Internat. Bronchoesophagological Soc., Societe Internationale de Chirurgie, Am. Surg. Assn., Inst. Medicine Chgo., Soc. Surg. Oncology. Research in lung cancer. Home: 11127 Woolworth Plaza Omaha NE 68144 Office: Dept Surgery Creighton U 601 N 30th St Omaha NE 68131

DE MENESES, MARY ROADES, nursing educator; b. Alton, Ill., Apr. 16, 1939; d. Charles Franklin and Eunice Lorea (Nolan) Roades; m. William C. Meneses, May 31, 1973; children: Luis Alberto, Daniel William. Diploma, St. Luke's Sch. Nursing, St. Louis, 1960; BS in Nursing, DePaul U., 1970, MA, 1973, MS in Nursing, 1975; EdD in Leadership and Ednl. Policy Studies, No. Ill. U., 1982. Supr., head nurse St. Joseph's Hosp., Alton, Ill., 1964-66; head nurse St. Joseph's Hosp., Chgo., 1966-69; head instr. nursing Michael Reese Med. Ctr., Chgo., 1969-73; assoc. prof. DePaul U., Chgo., 1973-82; assoc. prof. So. Ill. U., Edwardsville, 1982—, coordinator grad. nursing program, 1985—; med. cons. VA, St. Louis, 1986—. Author: (book) Nursing Process, 1986; contbr. articles to profl. jours. Mem. Am. Nurses Found., Am. Heart Assn. (bd. dirs. Edwardsville unit 1982—), Am. Assn. Critical Care Nurses (treas. So. Ill. chpt. 1983-85), Ill. Nurses Assn. (med.

cons. 1982—, v.p. local dist. 1985-87), DePaul U. Nursing Alumni (pres. 1980-81), Kappa Delta Pi, Sigma Theta Tau, Phi Kappa Phi, Phi Delta Kappa. Republican. Roman Catholic. Home: 4710 Fantasy Ln Alton IL 62002 Office: So Ill U Sch Nursing Box 1066 Edwardsville IL 62026

DEMERANVILLE, MARK IRVING, systems analyst; b. Biloxi, Miss., Oct. 17, 1952; s. Marshall Irving and Mildred Lucille (Weiss) D.; m. Jana Ponsell McDonald, Nov. 24, 1974; children: Marshall Irving III, Heather Nicole, Scott Langford. BS in Computer Sci., Miss. State U., 1975, MS in Computer Sci., 1976. Assoc. programmer, Roseville Software Devel. Ctr. UNISYS (formerly Sperry), St. Paul, 1976-78, sci. programmer def. systems div., 1978-79, sr. sci. programmer def. products group, 1980—; sr. systems programmer McDonald Douglas Automation Co., St. Louis, 1979-80. Chmn., trustee Crystal Lake Rd. Bapt. Ch., Burnsville, Minn., 1983—; pres. Winds Crossing Home Owners Assn.; mem. Initial Graphics Exchange Specifications Com. Recipient Outstanding Achievement award U.S. Geol. Survey, 1975. Mem. Nat. Computer Graphics Assn., Nat. Model R.R. Assn., Upsilon Pi Epsilon, Triangle Frat. (chpt. pres. 1973-74, regional advisor 1978-79). So. Bapt. Home: 15611 Cornell Trail Rosemount MN 55068 Office: UNISYS-Def Systems Div Box 64525 MS U2N27 Saint Paul MN 55164-0525

DEMERS, JACQUES, hockey league coach; b. Montreal, Que., Can., Aug. 25, 1944; s. John Demers and Marie Bergeron; m. Linda Stone, June 24, 1973; children—Brandy, Stefanie, Jason. Student Cote St. Luc High Sch., Montreal. Data processor IBM, Montreal, 1977; coach Quebec Nordiques, Quebec, Can., 1978-83, St. Louis Blues, NHL, 1983-86, Detroit Red Wings, 1986—. Recipient Spirit of St. Louis Bus. Community award, 1984. Home: 5700 Oakland Ave Saint Louis MO 63110 Office: Detroit Red Wings 600 Civic Center Dr Detroit MI 48226 *

DEMETRIUS, ANABEL STAFFORD, association executive, trainer, consultant; b. Chgo., July 2, 1941; d. Philip Truesdale and Joanna Bartlett (Rogers) Stafford; m. Kris Demetrius, Feb. 2, 1970 (div. 1978); 1 child, Rebecca Bartlett. B.A. in Edn., U. N.Mex., 1967; M.P.A., Ind. U., 1983. Personnel officer City of Los Angeles Community Redevel. Agy., 1970-73; cons. supr. Houston-Harris County Community action Assn., 1966-69; U.S. Peace Corps vol., Philippines, 1962-64; exec. dir. Santa Barbara Community Action Assn., Calif., 1974-78; dir. community devel. tng. Santa Barbara County Schs., 1978-81; asst. exec. dir. Ind. Health Care Assn., Indpls., 1983-84; exec. dir. Pi Lambda Theta, Bloomington, Ind., 1984—; instr. Santa Barbara City Coll., 1978-81; participation trainer Ind. U., Bloomington, 1982—. Author: Job Hunter's Guide, 1973. Chmn. Adult Day Health Care Planning Com., Santa Barbara, 1976; pres. sub-area council Health Systems Agy., Santa Barbara, 1979; precinct committeeman Monroe County Democratic Party, Ind., 1982; chmn. social concerns com. Unitarian Ch., Santa Barbara, 1978; bd. dirs. Santa Barbara Dem. League, 1977-79. Named to Outstanding Young Women Am., U.S. Jaycees, 1965. Mem. Am. Soc. Assn. Execs., Sch. Pub. and Environ. Affairs (v.p.), Alumni Assn. of Ind. U. (bd. dirs.), Central Ind. Assn. Tng. and Devel., Nat. Assn. Female Execs., Spurs (chpt. pres. 1960-61), Pi Lambda Theta, Phi Kappa Phi. Club: Alpine Ski (Bloomington). Avocations: skiing, ski racing, real estate, art, politics. Home: 6636 E State Rd 46 Bloomington IN 47401 Office: Pi Lambda Theta 4101 E Third Bloomington IN 47401

DE MEUSE, DONALD H., paper products manufacturing executive; b. 1936. With Ft. Howard Paper Co., Green Bay, Wis., 1959—; v.p. ops. 1977-79, exec. v.p., from 1979, now pres., dir. Office: Ft Howard Paper Co 1919 S Broadway Box 19130 Green Bay WI 54307 *

DEMKE, THOMAS ALAN, scientist; b. Hillsboro, Wis., Sept. 15, 1956; s. Robert L. and Frances L. (Moutoux) D. Student, U. Wis., Stevens Point, 1973-76; DDS, Marquette U., Milw., 1980. Gen. practice dentistry Stevens Point, 1980-82; dentist Midwest Dental Care, Stevens Point, 1982-83; research scientist U. Wis., Madison, 1984-86, LUNAR Radiation Corp., Madison, 1986—; cons. Wis. Pvt. Sector Initiative Program, Stevens Point, 1981. Author: (record) From The Heart, 1981. Mem. ADA, Broadcast Mus. Inc., Planetary Soc., Omicron Kappa Upsilon (hon.). Lutheran. Avocations: writing music, sports. Home: 4913 Chalet Gardens Rd #101 Madison WI 53711 Office: LUNAR Radiation Corp 313 W Beltline Hwy Madison WI 53713

DEMKOVICH, PAUL BRYAN, management analyst; b. East Chicago, Ind., Aug. 1, 1959; s. Paul Andrew and Margaret Ann (Litecky) D.; m. Sheila Ellen Nevers, May 7, 1977; 1 child, Amanda. A in Archtl. Tech., Purdue U., 1976, A in Supervision, 1977, BS in Constrn., 1978. Asst. mgr. Van Til's Supermarket, Hammond, Ind., 1973-78; operator Amoco Oil Co., Whiting, Ind., 1976; scheduler Brown & Root, Inc., Oak Brook, Ill., 1978-82; analyst Envirodyne Engring., Chgo., 1983—; guest lectr. Purdue U., Hammond, 1981-82; cons. Ill. State Toll Hwy. Authority, Oak Brook, 1983-85; cons., analyst O'Hare Assocs., Chgo., 1983—. Mem. Assn. Profl. Planners and Schedulers, Am. Assn. Cost Engrs. (nat. coms. chmn. 1985-86, planning and scheduling com., Cert Appreciation, 1986). Roman Catholic. Avocations: home remodeling, home computers, birds, photography. Home: 240 Willow Rd Elmhurst IL 60126

DEMLOW, CHARLES EDWARD, police detective; b. Inpls., Dec. 22, 1942; s. Edwin Merritt and Nellie Ester (DeLong) D.; m. Jean Ellen McKinstray, Jan. 22, 1962 (div. Jan. 1970); children—Kevin E., Kenneth J.; m. Jacqueline Kaye Foertsch, Aug. 23, 1972; children: Shay L., Robert M. Student in criminal justice Ind. U. S.E., New Albany, 1971-74. Trooper, Ind. State Police, Charlestown, 1964-70, detective, Indpls., 1970-74, trooper, 1974-83, detective, Sellersburg, 1982—. Recipient Prosecutors award for Excellence Washington County Inc. Pros. Atty., 1982. Republican. Methodist. Lodge: Masons. Avocations: reading; sports; farming; photography. Home: Rural Route 1 Box 197 Scottsburg IN 47170 Office: Ind State Police 8014 Hwy 311 Sellersburg IN 47172

DEMOS, TERRENCE CONSTANT, radiologist; b. Chgo., Dec. 9, 1936; s. Constant and Berenis (Cartner) D.; m. Carol J. Jellies, Nov. 20, 1959 (div. Feb. 1972); m. Virginia Budinger, Nov. 26, 1978; children: Terrence C.P., Christine C. Student, Knox Coll., 1955-58; BS, Roosevelt U., 1959; MD, U. Ill., Chgo., 1963. Cert. diagnostic radiology, Am. Bd. Radiology, 1972. Rotating intern Cook County Hosp., Chgo., 1963-64; resident in radiology U. Wis., Madison, 1966-69, VA Hosp., Hines, Ill., 1969-70; staff radiologist VA Hines (Ill.) Hosp., 1970-75; attending radiologist Loyola U. Med. Ctr., Maywood, Ill., 1975—; prof. radiology Loyola Stritch Sch. Medicine, Maywood, 1979—; asst. prof. Chgo. Med. Sch., 1974-78; cons. VA Hines Hosp., 1978—; relief examiner Am. Bd. Radiology, 1981, guest examiner, 1982, 84, 85; dir. edn. dept. radiology Foster G. McGaw Hosp., Maywood, 1986. Author: Bone Radiology Case Studies, 1982; assoc. editor (jour.) Orthopedics, Thorofare, N.J., 1979—; contbg. editor Ill. Med. Jour., Chgo., 1980—; contbr. chpts. to books and articles to profl. jours. Served to comdr. USCG, 1964-66. Fellow Am. Coll. Chest Physicians; mem. AMA, Am. Coll. Radiology, Radiolgic Soc. N.Am., Internat. Skeletal Soc., Soc. Thoracic Radiology (founding mem.), Assn. Univ. Radiologists, Am. Roentgen Ray Soc. Office: Loyola U Med Ctr 2160 S First Ave Maywood IL 60153

DEMOSS, JON W., lawyer; b. Kewanee, Ill., Aug. 9, 1947; s. Wendell and Virginia Beth D.; m. Eleanor T. Thornley, Aug. 9, 1969; 1 son, Marc Alain. B.S., U. Ill., 1969, J.D., 1972. Bar: Ill. 1972, U.S. Dist. Ct. (cen. dist.) Ill. 1977, U.S. Supreme Ct. 1978, U.S. Dist. Ct. (no. dist.) Ill. 1983. In house counsel Assn. Ill. Electric Coop., Springfield, 1972-74; registered lobbyist Ill. Gen. Assembly, 1972-74; asst. dir. Ill. Inst. for Continuing Legal Edn., Springfield, 1974-85; exec. dir. Ill. State Bar Assn., 1986—. Bd. dirs. Springfield Symphony Orch., 1982—. Served to capt. U.S. Army, 1972. Fellow Ill. Bar Found. (bd. dirs. 1983-85); mem. ABA (mem. ho. of dels. 1979-85, fellow Am. Bar Found. 1979—, co-chmn. projects to prepare Appellate Handbook, 1978, 80), Ill. State Bar Assn. (pres. 1984-85, bd. govs. 1975-85 , chmn. com. on scope and correlation of work 1982-83, chmn. budget com. 1983-84, chmn. legis. com. 1983-84, chmn. com. on merit selection of judges, 1977, del. long-range planning conf. 1972, 78, liason to numerous coms. and sects.), Chgo. Bar Assn., Sangamon County Bar Assn., Hancock County Bar Assn., U. Ill. Dean's Club. Presbyterian. Clubs: Monroe (Chgo.); Sangamo, Illini Country, La Chaine des Rotisseurs (Springfield), Ordre Mondial des Gourmet Degustateurs (St. Louis). Home: 1633 Bates Ave Springfield IL 62704

DEMPSEY, DERREL L., aviation consultant, air traffic controller, pilot; b. Gilson, Ill., Apr. 19, 1932; s. Loren Albert and Mary Ardella (Sniff) D.; children: Darrell Dan, Guy Wayne, Tamera Sue Dempsey Luth, Minda Kay Dempsey Lawson, Lisa Grace. BS, Bradley U., 1950-54. Lic. pilot, air traffic controller. Commd. 2d lt. USAF, 1954, advanced through grades to col.; pilot trainee USAF, Greenville, Miss., 1955-56; pilot, air traffic controller USAF, various locations worldwide, 1956-84; mem. air command and staff Air Univ. USAF, Montgomery, Ala., 1966-67; student Air War Coll. USAF, Montgomery, 1971-72; ret. USAF, 1984; aviation cons. Unisys Corp., Great Neck, N.Y., 1984—; owner Dempsey Assocs., O'Fallon, Ill. Author terps automation instrumentation flight procedures, Senior Executive, 1983 (Duckworth award 1983). Chmn. bd. trustees First United Meth. Ch., O'Fallon, Ill., 1985-87. Decorated D.F.C., Legion of Merit, Air medal, Meritorious Service medal. Mem. Air Traffic Control Assn., Air Force Assn., Armed Forces Communications and Electronics Assn., Ret. Officers Assn., Am. Assn. Ret. Persons, Sheriff's Assn., Daedalians. Republican. Club: Officers (Scott AFB, Ill.).

DEMPSEY, JOHN CORNELIUS, manufacturing company executive; b. Cleve., July 14, 1914; s. John Henry and Anna Gertrude (Donavon) D.; children: Virginia Agnes (Mrs. Richard J. Ragan) Patricia Marie, Mary Theresa (Mrs. William J. McAlpin), Maureen Anne (Mrs. Daniel Phillip Kendall), Judith Marie (Mrs. Cecil J. Petitti), Michael Henry. Student, John Carroll U., 1932-35. With U.S. Steel Corp., Cleve., 1932-40; auditor Ernst & Ernst, Cleve., 1940-45; asst. comptroller Werner G. Smith, Cleve., 1945; sec. Greif Bros. Corp., Delaware, Ohio, 1946; chmn. bd., chief exec. officer Greif Bros. Corp., 1947—. Trustee Central Ohio council Boy Scouts Am.; trustee St. Ann Maternity Hosp.; trustee Cleve. City Hosp., chmn. bd. trustees, 1949. Office: Greif Bros Corp 621 Pennsylvania Ave Delaware OH 43015 *

DEMPSEY, JOHN NICHOLAS, packaging company executive; b. St. Paul, June 16, 1923; s. Mark V. and Mabel M. (Stehly) D.; m. Marian V. Lind, June 5, 1948; children—Barbara Dempsey McCarrier, Mary Dempsey Santiago, Patricia Lee. B.S., St. Thomas Coll., 1948; Ph.D., U. Iowa, 1951. Teaching asst. AEC fellow U. Iowa, Iowa City, 1948-51; research chemist Ethyl Corp., Detroit, 1951-52; research physicist Honeywell, Inc., Mpls., 1952-56, research sect. head, 1956-60, asst. dir. research, 1960-61, dir. research, 1961-65, v.p. research, 1965-67, v.p. sci. and engring., 1967-72; v.p. tech. services Bemis Co., Inc., Mpls., 1972-75, v.p. sci. and tech., 1975—, also dir.; trustee Midwest Research Inst., Kansas City, Mo. Served to lt. (j.g.) USN, 1943-46, PTO. Mem. North Star Research Found. (pres., bd. dirs.). Indsl. Research Inst. (rep.), Dirs. Indsl. Research, Am. Mgmt. Assn. (trustee), Am. Chem. Soc., Inst. Environ. Scis., Sigma Xi, Phi Lambda Upsilon, Gamma Alpha. Clubs: Mpls., Interlachen. Avocations: hunting, skeet shooting. Home: 4926 Westgate Rd Minnetonka MN 55345 Office: Bemis Co Inc 800 Northstar Ctr Minneapolis MN 55402

DEMPSEY, MARGARET A., broadcasting executive; b. La Junta, Colo., Apr. 9, 1950; d. Oliver James and Elisabeth Ann (Clevenger) Cuddy. BA in Communications, Loyola U., New Orleans, 1971; MBA in Mktg. and Econs., U. Wash., 1977. Continuity dir. Sta. KALB, Sta. KSLI-FM, Alexandria, La., 1972-73; merchandise and promotion dir. Sta. KTAC, Sta. KBRD-FM, Seattle, Tacoma, Wash., 1977-78; account exec. Sta. KTAC, Seattle, Tacoma, 1978-80, gen. sales mgr., 1980-83; gen. sales mgr. Sta. KTAC, Sta. KBRD-FM, Seattle, Tacoma, 1983-84; v.p., gen. mgr. Sta. KMFY, Sta. WAYL-FM, Mpls., 1984—. Mem. Mpls. Advt. Fedn. Office: WAYL-FM/KMFY-AM 2110 Cliff Rd Eason MN 55122

DEMPSTER, KEITH WILLIARD, restauranteur; b. Grinnell, Iowa, Oct. 16, 1932; s. Keith Greer and Fran (Seager) D.; m. Jean Varles, Apr. 1, 1961 (div. Apr. 1969); 1 child, Greer Elizabeth. Student, Grinnell Coll., 1950-52, 55-56, Drake U., 1952, U. Iowa, 1956-57. Owner The Mill Restaurant, Iowa City, 1962—. Served with U.S. Army, 1953-55. Mem. BMW Motorcycle Owners Am. (bd. dirs. 1973-75, v.p. 1976-79, pres. 1979—). Home: Rural Rt 1 Iowa City IA 52240 Office: The Mill Restaurant 120 E Burlington Iowa City IA 52240

DENAMUR, THOMAS JOSEPH, dentist; b. Green Bay, Wis., Aug. 20, 1950; s. Lloyd Francis and Muriel Janet (Delfosse) DeN.; m. Lynn Marie Vetter, Aug. 26, 1972; children: Christopher Thomas, Nicole Lynn. BS in Chemistry, St. Norbet Coll., 1972; DDS, Marquette U., 1976. Lic. dentist, Wis. Gen. practice dentistry Algoma, Wis., 1976—; cons. dentist Algoma Meml. Hosp., 1985-86. Contbr. articles to profl. jours. Mem. Concerned Citizens Com. St. Mary's Ch., 1982, Algoma Citizens Together, 1984. Fellow Acad. Gen. Dentistry; mem. Am. Equilibration Soc., Soc. Occlusal Studies, Wis. Dental Assn. (alternate del. 1986), Bay Lakes Dental Soc., Chgo., Brown Door Kewanee Dental Soc. (bd. dirs. 1983-86, peer rev. com. 1984-86), Chgo Dental Soc. (assoc.), Am. Assn. Functional Orthodontists (Hon. Mention Case Solvers 1986), Omicron Kappa Soc. Lodges: Algoma Optimists (v.p. 1979-80, pres. 1980-81, Honor Club mem. 1981). Avocations: building wooden model sailing ships. Home: 520 Ohio St Algoma WI 54201 Office: 800 Jefferson St Algoma WI 54201

DENBROCK, LINDA SUZANNE, advertising executive; b. Lansing, Mich., Sept. 11, 1961; d. Dennis John and Georgianna (Thompson) Holcomb; m. Stephen Allen Denbrock, June 4, 1983. BA, Adrian (Mich.) Coll., 1983. Account exec. Sta. WABJ-AM Radio, Adrian, 1983-84; media mgr. Brewer Assoc. Adv., Dearborn, Mich., 1984, account exec., 1984—. Mem. Adcraft Club Detroit. Republican. Home: 48825 W Twelve Mile Southfield MI 48034 Office: Brewer Assoc Adv 806 Oakwood Dearborn MI 48124

DENDINGER, DONALD CHARLES, educational administrator, social work educator; b. Coleridge, Nebr., Nov. 4, 1937; s. David Camillus and Regina Marcella (McCluskey D.; m. Mary Jo Fitzgerald, Aug. 6, 1975; children: Suzanne Marie, Regina Marie. BA, Creighton U., 1959; MA in Religious Edn., St. Thomas Seminary, 1962; MSW, U. Md., 1971; PhD in Social Work, U. Denver, 1977. Priest Archdiocese of Omaha, 1963-75; case worker Cath. Social Services, Omaha, 1971-73, exec. dir., 1973-75; prof. U. Nebr., Omaha, 1977-83, dir. Goodrich Scholar Program, 1983—. Contbr. articles to profl. jours. Mem. Nat. Assn. Social Workers (pres. Nebr. chpt. 1979-81), Acad. Cert.Social Workers, Nebr. Welfare Assn. (pres. 1985). Democrat. Roman Catholic. Home: 1025 S 117th Ave Omaha NE 68154 Office: Univ Nebr 60th and Dodge Omaha NE 68182

DENES, ALEX EUGENE, oncologist; b. Miskolc, Hungary, Apr. 18, 1947; came to U.S., 1956; s. Lajos Bela and Katherine (Clyne) D.; m. Mary Grace Tully, Aug. 29, 1970; children: Christen, Alex, Magda, Lawrence. BA, Washington U., St. Louis, 1969; MD, U. Mo., 1973. Diplomate Am. Bd. Internal Medicine. Intern Johns Hopkins Sch. Medicine, Balt., 1973-74, resident, 1974-75; epidemiologist Ctr. for Disease Control, Atlanta, 1975-77; fellow in hematology-oncology Washington U., St. Louis, 1977-79, asst. prof. clin. medicine div. hematology-oncology, 1979-85; attending physician St. John's Mercy Med. Ctr., St. Louis, 1985—. Contbr. articles to profl. jours. Served to lt. commdr. USPHS, 1975-77. Fellow Am. Coll. Physicians; mem. Am. Soc. Clin. Oncology, Am. Oncology Assn., Am. Soc. Hematology, St. Louis Soc. Med. Oncology (pres. 1984-85), Am. Assn. Cancer Edn., Southwest Oncology Group, Nat. Surgical Adjuvant Breast Project, SIgma Xi, Alpha Omega Alpha. Home: 1215 Hampton Park Dr Saint Louis MO 63117 Office: 621 S New Ballas Saint Louis MO 63141

DENGER, ELSIE SUE, nursing administrator; b. Iowa Falls, Iowa, July 12, 1936; d. Ray Lester and Elsie Mae (Brighton) Denger. R.N., Broadlawns Polk County Sch. Nursing, 1956; B.S. in Nursing, U. Iowa, 1966, M.A., 1968. Dir. nursing services Emma L. Bixby Hosp., Adrian, Mich., 1969-76; asst. hosp. adminstr., dir. nursing services Milton S. Hershey Med. Ctr., Hershey, Pa., 1976-79; asst. exec. dir. nursing services U. Louisville Hosp., 1979-83; v.p. St. Francis Regional Med. Ctr., Wichita, Kans., 1983—. Mem. Nat. League for Nursing, Am. Nurses Assn., Am. Orgn. Nurse Execs. Home: 7700 E 13th St #83 Wichita KS 67206

DENINNO, JOHN LOUIS, manufacturing company executive; b. Pitts., July 6, 1933; s. Louis Peter and Suzanne P. (Maurice) DeN.; m. Patricia Ann Guaghan, June 6, 1959; children: Karen L., Lynn S., Lisa A., Gregory J. Sr. BS, U. Pitts., 1956; MS, Case Western Res. U., 1973. Sr. indsl. engr. Jones & Laughlin Steel Corp., Pitts., 1956-61; mgr. indsl. engring. Cyclops Corp., Pitts., 1961-65; plant mgr. The Stanley Works, Conn., 1965-70; dir. mfg. engring. Warner & Swasey Co., Cleve., 1970-72; pres. Reliable Products Co., Cleve., 1972-76, Crystaloid Electronics Co., Stow, Ohio, 1976, Investors Growth Corp. and subs., Hudson, Ohio, 1976-84; prin. Enterprise Achievement Assocs., Hudson, 1984—; lectr. Sch. Bus., Cuyahoga Community Coll., Cleve., State U., Stark Tech. Coll., U. Akron, Hiram Coll.; adj. prof. Kent (Ohio) State U. Chmn. library bd., Scott Twp., 1963. Served to capt. USAF, 1957-60. Mem. Am. Inst. Indsl. Engrs. Roman Catholic. Clubs: Country (Hudson), Univ. (Pitts.). Home: 2259 Danbury Ln Hudson OH 44236 Office: PO Box 244 Hudson OH 44236

DENMARK-FRIEDMAN, BONNIE, social worker; b. Steubenville, Ohio, May 26, 1945; d. Samuel and Renee (Felder) Denmark; m. Gary Howard Friedman, July 23, 1967; children: Jennifer Lyn, Ellen Beth. BA, Goucher Coll., 1967; MSW, U. Wis., 1979. Perinatal social worker Madison (Wis.) Gen. Hosp., 1980-81, med. social worker, 1983—; cons. Childbirth Parent Edn. Assn., Madison, 1978—; social worker Bereaved Parents, Madison, 1981-85. Treas. Temple Beth El Sisterhood, Madison, 1974-78, chairperson fundraiser, 1976. Mem. Nat. Orgn. Social Workers, Acad. Cert. Social Workers. Avocations: needlework, travel, piano, biking. Home: 3401 Nottingham Way Madison WI 53713 Office: Madison Gen Hosp 202 S Park St Madison WI 53715

DENNARD, JAMES RICHARD, photography lab manager; b. Macon, Ga., Oct. 2, 1949; s. Charles Richard and Margie (Hargrove) D.; m. Anne Hays, Sept. 5, 1971; children: Charles Richard II, Ashley Anne. ABJ, U. Ga., 1974. Owner J. Richard Dennard Photo, Bainbridge, Ga., 1975-85; nat. sales dir. Garrett and Lane Color Labs, Columbus, Ga., 1985; mgr. Midwest ops. Garrett and Lane Color Labs, St. Peters, Mo., 1985—. Served as sgt. USMC, 1967-71, Vietnam. Named Master of Photography Profl. Photographers Am., 1986; recipient numerous photographic competition awards. Mem. Southeastern Profl. Photographers Assn. (bd. govs. 1982-83), Ga. Profl. Photographers Assn. (pres. 1981-82), Comml. Photographers Assn. of St. Louis (2d v.p. 1987). Lodge: Lions (treas. Bainbridge, Ga. 1983). Avocations: photography, computers. Office: Garrett and Lane Color Labs 230 Turner Blvd Saint Peters MO 63376

DENNER, MELVIN WALTER, science educator; b. North Washington, Iowa, Aug. 27, 1933; s. Norbert William and Petronella Nettie (Eischeid) D.; m. N. Anne Greer, June 19, 1965; children: Mark Andrew, Michael Alan (twins). B.S., Upper Iowa U., 1961; M.S. (NSF fellow), U. Ky., 1963; Ph.D., Iowa State U., 1968. Asst. prof. life scis. U. So. Ind., Evansville, 1968-71; chmn. dept. U. So. Ind., 1969—, assoc. chmn. div. scis. and math., 1975—, assoc. prof., 1971-76, prof., 1976—, acting chmn. div. scis. and math., 1976-77, chmn., 1979—; Eucharistic minister Corpus Christi Ch., 1981—. Contbr. articles to profl. jours. Vice chmn. Iowa Young Dems., 1958-60; bd. dirs. Deaconess Hosp. Allied Health Programs, chmn. radiation tech. adv. com., 1987—; bd. dirs. Evansville Mus. Arts and Scis.; mem. alumni adv. bd. U. So. Ind., 1982—; spl. minister Corpus Christi Ch., 1981—. Served with USN, 1953-57. NSF fellow 1962, 64, NIH fellow, 1966-67; Alumni Achievement fellow, 1967-68. Mem. Internat. Soc. Invertebrate Pathology (founding), Am. Soc. Parasitologists, Am. Micros. Soc. (nat. treas.), North Cen. Assn. Colls. and Secondary Schs. (visitation team 1976—), AAAS (film critic), Am. Inst. Biol. Sci., Sigma Xi (pres. So. Ind. chpt.), Sigma Zeta. Home: 100 S Peerless Rd Evansville IN 47712 Office: Univ So Indiana Div Sci and Math Evansville IN 47712

DENNEY, CHARLES EUGENE, state agency supervisor; b. Ava, Mo., Oct. 31, 1951; s. Owen Elwin and Norma Lou (Flynn) D.; m. Sharon Dawn Sampson, Oct. 9, 1975; children: Amy Lyn, Andrew Lee. BS in Social Studies, S.W. Mo. State U., 1973. Probation and parole officer Mo. Bd. Probation and Parole, Rolla, 1973-79, dist. supr., 1979—; Chmn. regional adv. council Div. Alcohol and Drug Abuse, Jefferson City, Mo., 1985—. Vice chmn. New Horizons Residential Treatment Ctr., Vichy, Mo., 1984—; pres. Mo. Ozarks Community Action Agy., Richland, Mo. 1986—; bd. dirs. Cen. Ozark Mental Health Services, Inc., Rolla, 1980-83. Mem. Am. Corrections Assn., Mo. Corrections Assn. (sec. 1984-85). Democrat. Home: PO Box 532 Rolla MO 65401 Office: Mo Bd Probation and Parole PO Box 366 Rolla MO 65401

DENNEY, LUCINDA A., corporate professional; b. Akron, Aug. 7, 1938; d. Charles Andrew and Madora Heinretta (Frederick) Shetter; m. Jon E. Denney; children: Mary, Jon, Andrew. BA cum laude, Ohio Wesleyan U., 1960. Exec. v.p. Exec. Arrangements, Inc., Cleve., 1978—. Mem. adv. council to pub. relations com. Mus. Arts Assn.; exec. com. Cleve. Orch.; mem. adv. com. Rock'n Roll Hall of Fame, Cleve., 1986—, Shaker Heights (Ohio) Citizens League, Cleve. Opera Council; trustee Boy Scouts Am., Inc., 1984—, Shaker Heights Youth Ctr., 1982—, also v.p.; trustee Jr. League of Cleve., 1968-84, Big. Bros./Big Sisters of Greater Cleve., 1968-84, St. Luke's Hosp. Jr. Bd., 1968-84. mem. jr. com. Cleve. Orch., 1968-84. Named one of 77 Most Interesting Persons Cleve. Mag., 1977; recipient Outstanding Pace Setter award Directory of Greater Cleve.'s Enterprising Women, 1985. Mem. Cleve. Convention and Vis. Bur., Mortar Bd., Alpha Theta Pi, Kappa Alpha Theta. Republican. Methodist. Clubs: 20th Century, Midday. Avocations: tennis, golf, pub. speaking. Home: 2705 Dryden Rd Shaker Heights OH 44122 Office: Exec Arrangements Inc 13221 Shaker Sq Cleveland OH 44120

DENNING, GARY R., transportation company executive; b. 1939. Terminal mgr. Crouch Bros., St. Joseph, Mich., 1960-64; div. v.p. Yellow Freight System Inc., Overland Pk., Kans., 1964-79; with Associated Truck Lines Inc., Grand Rapids, Mich., 1979—; exec. v.p. 1979-81, pres., chief exec. officer, 1981—, also bd. dirs. Office: Associated Truck Lines Inc 200 Monroe NW Grand Rapids MI 49503 *

DENNIS, GENE WINFIELD, engineering and construction company executive; b. Akron, Ohio, Oct. 28, 1943; s. Wilfred and Helen Mary (Smith) D.; m. Janice K. Severin, Dec. 18, 1965; children: Scott, Todd, Sean, Chad. BSEE, U. Mich., 1965. Registered profl. engr., Mich. Engr. Universal Elect. Constrn. Co., Flint, Mich., 1966-69, v.p., 1970-79, pres., 1980—, also bd. dirs., 1969—; bd. dirs. Mich. Nat. Bank Mid-Mich., Flint, 1985—. Campaign chmn. United Way of Genesee and Lapeer Counties, Mich., 1985; pres. Flint YMCA, 1983-84. Recipient Disting. Service award Flint YMCA, 1980. Mem. Mich. Soc. Profl. Engrs. (Flint chpt. Young Engr. of Yr. award, 1974, pres. 1972-73), Flint Jaycees (pres. 1969-70). Lodge: Rotary (v.p., 1987—, Paul Harris fellow 1986). Avocations: pilot hot air balloons, tennis. Office: Universal Systems Corp 1401 E Stewart Ave Flint MI 48505

DENNIS, RALPH EMERSON, JR., lawyer; b. Marion, Ind., Dec. 19, 1925; s. Ralph Emerson Sr. and Martha Elnora (Bahr) D.; m. Virginia Lea Harter, June 19, 1949 (dec. Oct. 1981); children: Nancy J. Barefoot, Kathleen Ann Polk, Amel Joseph, Mary Elizabeth Saler, Ralph E. III; m. Barbara Grose, May 31, 1985. BS, Dartmouth Coll., 1946; JD, Ind. U., 1950. Bar: Ind. 1950, U.S. Supreme Ct. 1971. Sr. ptnr. Dennis, Cross, Raisor, Jordan & Marshall, P.C., Muncie, Ind., 1956-80, Dennis, Raisor, Wenger & Haynes, P.C., Muncie, 1980-85, Dennis & Wenger, P.C., Muncie, 1985-86, Dennis, Wenger & Orlosky, P.C., Muncie, 1986—; bd. dirs. Bahr Bros. Mfg. Inc., Marion; pres. Eastern Electric Supply Inc., Muncie; pres., chmn. bd. dirs., chief exec. officer Lift-A-Loft Corp., Muncie. City judge, Muncie, 1951-59, city atty., 1964-67; trustee Muncie Community Schs., 1960-63. Served with USN, 1944-46. Recipient Disting. Service award, Muncie Jaycees, 1959, Good Govt. award, Muncie Jaycees, 1959. Mem. ABA, Ind. Bar Assn. Republican. Lutheran. Club: Del. Country (Muncie). Lodges: Elks, Masons. Home: 411 Wildwood Ln Muncie IN 47304 Office: Dennis Wenger & Orlosky PC 201 E Jackson Suite 300 Muncie IN 47305

DENNY, JAMES MCCAHILL, retail executive; b. Mpls., Oct. 25, 1932; s. Charles and Mary (McCahill) D.; m. Catherine Mary Florance, Aug. 19, 1961; children: James, Philip, Sarah, Matthew, Catherine, William. Student, Princeton U., 1950-54; AB, U. Minn., 1957; LLB, Georgetown U., 1960. Assoc. Dewey Ballantine, N.Y.C., 1960-68; treas. Firestone Tire and Rubber Co., Akron, Ohio, 1968-78; exec. v.p., chief fin. and planning officer G.D.

Searle & Co., Skokie, Ill., 1978-85; v.p. fin. Sears, Roebuck & Co., Chgo., 1986—; bd. dirs. Gen. Binding Corp., Northbrook, Ill. Trustee Ravinia Festival Assn., Highland Park, Ill., 1985—. Served to cpl. U.S. Army, 1954-56, Korea. Mem. ABA, Am. Soc. Internat. Law, Assn. Bar City N.Y., Fin. Execs. Inst. Republican. Roman Catholic.

DENOYER, ARSÉNE J., former community relations executive; b. Limestone Twp., Kankakee County, Ill., Dec. 21, 1904; s. Arsene and Julia (Clark) D.; student parochial schs. of Kankakee and Bourbonnais, Ill. Field dir. Am. Nat. Red Cross, 1943-48; sales United Educators, Inc., 1932-42, community relations, 1948-63, asst. treas., community relations director, 1963—; asst. treas. Book House for Children, 1963—. Life bd. dirs. NCCJ; past pres. Chgo. Civitan Club; chmn. Lake County chpt. ARC, Lake County Adv. Bd. for Spl. Edn.; mem. Ill. Gov.'s Adv. Bd. for Devel. Disabilities, Commn. for Interstate Edn. Served as 1st sgt. USAAF, 1942-43. Mem. Am. C. of C. Execs., Chairs of Pvt. Enterprise, D.A.V. (life), Ill. Assn. C. of C. Execs., Chgo. Assn. Commerce and Industry (govtl. affairs com., mass transp. com.), Kankakee County Hist. Soc. (life, hon. mem. found. bd.), North La. Hist. Soc. (life), Iroquois County Hist. Soc. (life), Waukegan-Lake County C. of C. Home: 805 Baldwin Ave Waukegan IL 60085

DENSMORE-WULFF, LINDA KIMMONS, educational administrator; b. Clovis, N.Mex., Dec. 10, 1946; d. Lee Hugh and Alta Lou (McDaniel) Kimmons; m. Jerry Paul Densmore, Aug. 21, 1965; 1 child, Stefan Christian; m. Stephen Wayne Wulff, May 23, 1981; 1 child, Whitney Abigail Kimmons. BS, Olivet Nazarene Coll., Kankakee, Ill., 1968; MEd, U. Cin., 1978, PhD, 1985. Cert. tchr., supr., elem. prin., personnel dir., ednl. researcher, Ohio. Tchr. Jessamine County, Ky., 1968-69; tchr. Mt. Orab Elem. Sch., Western Brown County, Ohio, 1971-74; tchr. Greenhills-Forest Park Sch. Dist., Cin., 1974-80, instructional specialist, 1980-81, project dir. ednl. adminstrn., 1981-85, adminstrv. asst. instructional services, 1985—; hostess PBS-TV series Dragons, Wagons and Wax, 1977—. Mem. adminstrv. bd. United Meth. Ch.; rep. Children's Internat. Summer Village, Stockholm, 1978. Named Outstanding Adminstr., Greenhills-Forest Park City Sch. Dist., 1987. Mem. Assn. Supervision and Curriculum Devel., Ohio Sch. Bds. Assn., Nat. Coalition Sex Equity in Edn., Am. Ednl. Research Assn., Phi Delta Kappa. Home: 1090 Hickory Ridge Ln Cincinnati OH 45140 Office: 1501 Kingsbury Dr Cincinnati OH 45240

DENT, WARREN THOMAS, data processing executive; b. Sydney, Australia, Jan. 12, 1944; came to U.S., 1966; s. Ronald Thomas and Elizabeth Margaret (Lawrence) D.; m. Vicki Carol Anderson, Sept. 2, 1967; children: Arlene, Karin, Rani, Minissa. BS in Econs. with honors, Australian Nat. U., Canberra, 1964; MS in Econs., U. Adelaide, Australia, 1966; PhD, U. Minn., 1971. Asst. prof. mgmt. U. Rochester, N.Y., 1970-71; prof. econs. and statictics U. Iowa, Iowa City, 1971-78; assoc. prof. econs. U. Wis., Madison, 1975-76; mgr. bus. planning Asia Eli Lilly & Co., Indpls., 1979-80, mgr. info. systems, 1984—; dir. ops. Eli Lilly & Co., London, 1981-83; v.p. HANSA Assoc.s, Iowa City, 1973-78; cons. Australian Wool Bd., Melbourne, 1974-78. Editor Jour. Econometrics; contbr. articles to profl. jours. Bd. dirs. Park Tudor Sch., Indpls., 1979—, Ind. Vocat. Tech. Coll., Indpls., 1986—. Amelia Earhardt fellow, 1966-70; NSF grantee, 1974-75. Avocations: aviculture, pottery, tennis, computing. Home: 1318 Tishman Ln Indianapolis IN 46260 Office: Eli Lilly & Co Lilly Corp Ctr Indianapolis IN 46285

DENTON, RAY DOUGLAS, insurance company executive; b. Lake City, Ark., May 16, 1937; s. Ray Dudney and Edna Lorraine (Roe) D.; B.A., U. Mich., 1964, postgrad., 1969-70; J.D., Wayne State U., 1969, postgrad., 1964-65; m. Cheryl Emma Borchardt, Mar. 9, 1964; children—Ray D., Derek St. Clair, Carter Lee. Claims rep. Hartford Ins. Co., Crum & Forster, Detroit, and Am. Claims, Chgo., 1962-73; partner Chgo. Metro Claims, Oak Park, Ill., 1974-75; founder, pres. Ray D. Denton & Assocs., Inc., Hinsdale, Ill., 1975—. Mem. Pi Kappa Alpha, Phi Alpha Delta. Home: 4532 Howard Western Springs IL 60558 Office: 930 N York Suite 1 Hinsdale IL 60521

DENZEL, KEN JOHN, lawyer, corporate executive; b. Chgo., Jan. 21, 1940; s. John E. and Estelle K. D.; m. Mary Sue Plummer, Feb. 1, 1964; children—Michael B., Kyle J., Kristyn M., Karyn L., Mark R. B.S. in Econs. and Bus. Adminstrn., St. Ambrose Coll., 1962; J.D., Loyola U. of Chgo., 1967. Bar: Ill. 1968, U.S. Dist. Ct. (no. dist.) Ill. 1978, U.S. Ct. Appeals (7th cir.) 1978. Assoc. Yates, Haider, Hunt & Burke, Chgo., 1968-69, Philip H. Corboy & Assocs., Chgo., 1969; poverty lawyer Neighborhood Legal Services Program of Legal Aid Bur. (OEO), 1969-71; of counsel Burditt & Calkins, Chgo., 1971-78; ptnr. Ken J. Denzel & Assocs., Chgo., Des Plaines and Park Ridge, Ill., 1971—; rep. to U.S. Mil. Acad., West Point, N.Y., 1976-80; consul adviser, lectr. in sports, sports law; arbitrator Am. Arbitration Assn.; lectr. sports law Ill. Inst. Continuing Legal Edn., De Paul U. Sch. Law. Mem. adv. bd. Passionists Religious Community, 1981—; mem. U.S. Olympic Com., arbitrator 1984 Olympics; founder Internat. Center for Athletic and Ednl. Opportunities, 1967—; bd. mgrs. King Chgo. Boys Clubs, 1967-80; mem. parish sch. bd., 1973-74, mem. parish council, chmn. athletic bd., 1977-78; v.p. Orgn. of NW Communities, 1966-68; pres. Pulaski Civic Club, 1965-66; mem. O.L.S. Youth Council, 1968-75; coach Crane High Sch. Basketball Team, Chgo., 1969-72, Chgo. City Champs, 1972; coach Chgo. team in Nat. Neighborhood Invitational Basketball Tournament, 1972, Prairie State Games (Ill. Olympics), 1984—; founding mem., dir., atty. Cen. for Students Rights and Responsibilities U. Ill., Chgo., 1972; active numerous civic and community orgns. Recipient Loyola Law Sch. award for Outstanding Leadership and Scholastics Achievement, 1967; award for assistance to Chgo. Police Dept. Youth Program, 1970. Mem. Chgo. Bar Assn. (founding chmn. sports law com. 1981-84, mem. nominating com. 1983, judiciary com.), Ill. Bar Assn., ABA, Am. Judicature Soc., Ill. Trial Lawyers Assn., Am. Trial Lawyers Assn., Assn. of Evening Law Students (pres. 1965-67), Phi Alpha Delta (outstanding mem. and Nat. Justice award 1967). Roman Catholic. Contbr. articles to legal jours. Home: PO Box 141 Park Ridge IL 60068-0141 Office: 3 South Prospect Park Ridge IL 60068-4101

DEPOISTER, RANDY MURRA, investment advisor; b. Mt. Vernon, Ill., Sept. 6, 1951; s. Donald Leo Depoister and Marjorie Lucille (Shelton) Schuchardt; m. Sara Ann Hertenstein, June 3, 1978. AA, Rend Lake Coll., 1971; BS, Ill. State U., 1973; cert. fin. planner, Coll. for Fin. Planning, 1986. Registered Investment advisor, Ill.; registered securities prin., Ill. Pres. Depoister & Assocs., Dixon, Ill., 1982—, Fin. Resources Adv., Inc., 1984—, Integrated Fin. Services, Oakbrook Terrace, Ill., 1985—; registered rep. Dreher & Assocs., Oakbrook Terrace, 1985—; pres. Holloway Found., Dixon, 1985—. Pres. St. Patrick Day Fin. Com., Dixon, 1984. Named one of Outstanding Young Men In Am. Outstanding Young Men in Am. Adv. Bd., 1985. Mem. Internat. Assn. for Fin. Planners, Registry of Fin. Planners, Nat. Assn. Securities Dealers, Inst. Cert. Fin. Planners, Rock River Life Underwriters, Dixon C.of C. Republican. Roman Catholic. Lodge: Rotary (classification chmn.). Avocations: golf, boating, woodworking. Home: 855 Riverside Dr Dixon IL 61021 Office: Fin Resources Adv Inc 215 E First St Suite 100 Dixon IL 61021

DEPOUW, DONALD CHARLES, boat manufacturing executive; b. Oconto, Wis., Sept. 10, 1942; s. William Phillip and Marie Louise (Detaege) D.; m. Lois Mae Mueller, June 8, 1968; children: Sarah, Kristin. Salesman Cruisers, Inc., Oconto, 1961-67, sales coordinator, 1967-72, asst. sales mgr., 1972-75, sales mgr., 1975-80, v.p. mktg., 1980—. Served with USNG, 1964-68. Mem. Nat. Marine Mfrs. Assn. (shows com. 1984—). Roman Catholic. Home: 5584 County N Oconto WI 54153 Office: Cruisers Inc 804 Pecor St Oconto WI 54153

DEPP, ROBERT EUGENE, manufacturing engineering executive; b. Selma, Ohio, June 15, 1932; s. William Henry and Fonetta (Upthegrove) D.; m. JoAnne C. Sutton, Oct. 10, 1960 (div. Mar. 1973); 1 child, Lloyd Garrett. BS in Physics, Cen. State U., Wilberforce, Ohio, 1969; MS in Logistics Mgmt., Air Force Inst. Tech., 1973. With Def. Electronics Supply Ctr., Dayton, Ohio, 1969—, br. chief assignee activity, 1978-82, chief qualification div., 1982-86, dir. quality assurance, 1986—; com. mem. Internat. Wire and Cable Symposium, Eatontown, N.J., 1982—; mem. group electronics parts NATO, Brussels, 1984—, fiber optics, 1980-82. Contbr. articles to profl. jours.; author invited paper on standardization of fiber optics, Dept. of Def., 1981. Tutor under privileged persons Fair Lane Pk. Dist., Dayton, 1974—; organizer West Dayton Self-Help Ctr., 1968. Served with U.S. Army, 1952-54. Def. Logistics Agy. fellow, 1971; recipient Outstanding Fed. Supervision award, Am. Mgmt. Assn., Dayton, 1979, 8 Outstanding Performance awards, Def. Electronics Supply Ctr., 1964—. Mem. IEEE (standard rev. com. N.Y. 1984—), Soc. Logistics Engrs. Avocations: collecting coins and firearms, hunting, fishing. Home: 635 Majestic Dr Dayton OH 45427 Office: Def Electronics Supply Ctr 1507 Wilmington Pike Dayton OH 45441

DEPPISCH, LUDWIG MICHAEL, pathologist; b. N.Y.C., May 18, 1938; s. Ludwig Adam and Rose (Moyka) D.; m. Rosemarie Granelli, Sept. 24, 1965; children—Carl, Barbara Ann. A.B. Fordham U., 1960; M.D. Johns Hopkins, 1964. Diplomate Am. Bd. Pathology. Intern, Henry Ford Hosp., Detroit, 1964-65; resident in pathology Mt. Sinai Hosp., N.Y.C., 1967-69, assoc. pathologist, 1971-75, asst. prof., 1971-75; assoc. pathologist William Beaumont Hosp., El Paso, Tex., 1969-71; assoc. pathologist Youngstown Hosp., Ohio, 1975-80, vice chmn. pathology dept., 1980-83, chmn. dept. pathology and lab. medicine, 1983—; assoc. prof. pathology Northeast Ohio U. Coll. Medicine, Rootstown, Ohio, 1977-82, prof., 1982—. Author: (with others) Malignant Alteration in Benign Cystic Teratoma, 1983. Contbr. articles to profl. jours. Bd. dirs. Ballet Western R Reserve, Youngstown, 1979-82; charter class Leadership Youngstown, 1984. Served to maj. U.S. Army, 1969-71. Coll. Am. Pathologists fellow; mem. Am. Soc. Clin. Pathologists, Internat. Soc. Gynecol. Pathologists, Group for Research Pathology Ed., Gastrointestinal Pathology Club. Roman Catholic. Club: Sierra (exec. com. chpt. 1976-80) Avocation: ornithology. Home: 685 Blueberry Hill Dr Canfield OH 44406 Office: Youngstown Hosp Association Youngstown OH 44501

DE PREE, MAX O., furniture manufacturing company executive; b. 1924. BA, Hope Coll., 1947. With Herman Miller Inc., Zeeland, Mich., 1947—, exec. v.p., sec., 1962-71, chmn. bd. dirs., 1971-80, 82—, chief exec. officer, 1980—, pres., 1982—. Office: Herman Miller Inc 8500 Byron Rd Zealand MI 49464 *

DEPUKAT, THADDEUS STANLEY, optometrist; b. Chgo., Feb. 3, 1936; s. Stanley Frank and Genevieve Josephine (Skorupinski) D.; m. Melanie Ann Gadomski, Sept. 7, 1963 (dec. Jan. 1987); children—Brian Ted, Todd Steven. Student Loyola U., 1954-56; B.S., Ill. Coll. Optometry, 1960, O.D., 1960. Clin. instr. Ill. Coll. Optometry, Chgo., 1960-61, assoc. prof., 1961-66; optometrist, Downers Grove, Ill., 1966—; trustee Ill. Coll. Optometry, 1982—. Contbr. articles to profl. jours. Active mem. United Fund Bd., Downers Grove, 1966-69, Suburban Cook County-Dupage County Health Systems Agy., 1976-77; del. White House Conf. on Children, Washington, 1970. Recipient Tribute of Appreciation Ill. Coll. Optometry Alumni Assn., 1982. Fellow Am. Acad. Optometry, AAAS, Coll. Optometrists in Vision Devel.; mem. Ill. Optometric Assn. (Disting. Service award, 1982; pre. 1978-80, v.p. pub. health 1974-76), Ill. Coll. Optometry Alumni Assn., Am. Optometric Assn., West Suburban Optometric Assn. (pres. 1974), Optometric Extension Program. Lodge: Lions (v.p. 1982-85, pres. 1985-86, named Lion of Yr. 1986, award of appreciation 1986). Avocations: camping; computers; reading. Office: 1043 Curtiss Downers Grove IL 60515

DERAAD, DALE LEE, accountant; b. Albert Lea, Minn., May 17, 1951; s. Eldert and Avis Marie (Larson) DeR.; m. Cindy Susan Mickelson, June 21, 1975; children: Michelle Christine, Shanda Marie. Sr. acctg. degree, Area Vocat.-Tech. Inst., Mankato, Minn., 1971. Office mgr. Farmers Union, Augusta, Wis., 1971-72; acctg. clk. Lyle Sign Co., Mpls., 1972-73; acct. Hoffman Electric, Eden Prairie, Minn., 1973; corp. acct. Erickson Petro Corp., Bloomington, Minn., 1973-76; mgr. Clapper Kitchenmaster, Waseca, Minn., 1976-80; sr. ptnr. DeRaad, Goetz, Haefner & Co., Waseca, 1980—; customer rep. PBS Computing, Arden Hills, Minn., 1980-86; expert tax witness Waseca County Ct., 1980-86; mem. State Senate Adv. Com., Mpls., 1980-86. Bd. dirs. Waseca County Fair, 1980-85, United Way, Waseca, 1986, Miss Minn. Scholarship Pageant, Austin, 1986; chmn. County Sheriff Re-Election, Waseca, 1982, 86. Recipient Disting. Service award City of Waseca, 1985. Mem. Nat. Soc. Pub. Accts., Nat. Soc. Income Tax Preparers, Minn. Assn. Pub. Accts., Waseca C. of C. (pres., dir. 1979-82, Ambassador of Yr. 1983-84), Minn. Jaycees (Ten Outstanding Young Minnesotans 1985, Outstanding Young Man of Am., 1985). Lutheran. Clubs: Lake Preservation (Ellendale, Minn.); Waseca Ambassadors (pres. 1980-86). Lodges: Rotary, Masons. Avocations: golf, fishing, wrestling. Home: 3 Summit Ln Waseca MN 56093 Office: DeRaad Goetz Haefner & Co 212 15th Ave NE Suite 1040 Waseca MN 56093

DERAMUS, WILLIAM NEAL, III, railroad executive; b. Pittsburg, Kans., Dec. 10, 1915; s. William Neal and Lucile Ione (Nicholas) D.; m. Patricia Howell Watson, Jan. 22, 1943; children: William Neal IV, Patricia Nicholas Fogel, Jean Deramus Wagner, Jill Watson Dean. A.A., Kansas City Jr. Coll., 1934; A.B., U. Mich., 1936; LL.B., Harvard U., 1939. Transp. apprentice Wabash R.R. Co., St. Louis, 1939-41; asst. trainmaster Wabash R.R. Co., 1941-43; asst. to gen. mgr. K.C.S. Ry. Co., Kansas City, Mo., 1946-48; asst. to pres. C.G.W. Ry. Co., Chgo., 1948; pres., dir. C.G.W. Ry. Co., 1949-57, chmn. exec. com., 1954-57; pres., dir. M.-K.-T. R.R., 1957-61; chmn. bd. MAPCO, Inc., Tulsa, 1960-73, chmn. exec. com., 1973-81, now dir.; pres., dir. Kansas City So. Lines, Mo., 1961-73; chmn. bd. Kansas City So. Lines, 1966-80; pres. Kansas City So. Industries, Inc., Mo., 1962-71, chmn. bd., 1966—; dir. Bus. Men's Assurance Co., Kansas City, Kansas City Royals. Served from capt. to maj. Transp. Corps, Mil. Ry. Service AUS, 1943-46, overseas, India. Mem. Beta Theta Pi. Clubs: Chicago; Kansas City (Kansas City), River (Kansas City), Mission Hills Country (Kansas City), Mercury (Kansas City), Rotary (Kansas City). Home: 37 LeMans Ct Prairie Village KS 66208 Office: 114 W 11th St Kansas City MO 64105

D'ERCOLI, GENO CARLO, lighting company executive; b. Chicago Heights, Ill., Sept. 7, 1933; s. Raniero and Ersilia (Moscardella) D'E.; m. Nan Jean Linzenmeyer, Oct. 3, 1964; children: Rachele Ann, Nicole Renee, Gina Carla. BA, U. Ill., 1956. Designer LTJ, Chgo., 1960-62; exec. v.p. Reinecke Assocs., Chgo., 1962-73; dir. design Halo Lighting div. Cooper Industries, Elk Grove, Ill., 1973-80, mktg. mgr., 1980-82, dir. advt., pub. relations, 1982—. Patentee in field. Avocations: hunting, golf. Home: 2055 Vermont Rolling Meadows IL 60008 Office: Halo Lighting div Cooper Industries 400 Busse Rd Elk Grove IL 60007

DERDEYN, EUGENE DUNCAN, map company executive, cartographer; b. Natchez, Miss., Feb. 10, 1929; s. Roman Quinn and Agnes (Eidt) D.; m. Kay Ann Turner, Mar. 9, 1957; children: David, Denise. Student, Am. Acad. Art, Chgo., 1950-53, Art Inst. Chgo., 1953-54. Owner Universal Art Distbrs., Natchez, 1948-50; sign painter Waggoner Sign Co., Natchez, 1956-57; comml. artist Pontiac Graphics, Chgo., 1957-58; artist, writer, producer Ency. Brittanica Films, Chgo., 1958-67; pres., chief exec. officer Perspecto Map Co., Inc., Richmond, Ill., 1967—. Copyright numerous city, county, college campus and varied facilities maps. Served with U.S. Army, 1954-56. Avocations: pub. speaking, oil and watercolor painting. Home and Office: Perspecto Map Co Inc 5702 George St Richmond IL 60071

DERHAM, ROBERT EMMETT, financial executive, financial and tax consultant; b. Evanston, Ill., Dec. 10, 1944; s. Francis Emmett and Helen (Dreelan) D. B.B.A. in Acctg., Loyola U., Chgo., 1971. C.P.A., Ill. Auditor Arthur Young & Co., Chgo., 1971-74; field controller McDonald's Corp., Oak Brook, Ill., 1975-81; chief fin. officer Mediatech, Inc., Chgo., 1981—; dir. Midcoast Producers Services, Inc., Chgo., 1981-84, Travel Tech. Group, Chgo., 1984—. Served with USMC, 1962-66. Mem. Am. Inst. C.P.A.s, Ill. Soc. C.P.A.s, Beta Alpha Psi, Beta Gamma Sigma, Phi Theta Kappa. Avocations: travel; skiing. Home: 915 W Webster St Chicago IL 60614 Office: Mediatech Inc 110 Hubbard St Chicago IL 60610

DERLACKI, EUGENE L(UBIN), physician; b. Chgo., Mar. 16, 1913; s. Walter and Jadwiga (Pamulowna) D. B.S., Northwestern U., 1936, M.D., 1939. Diplomate: Am. Bd. Otolaryngology. Intern Cook County Hosp., Chgo., 1939-40; jr. resident Cook County Hosp., 1941, sr. resident, 1942-43; postgrad. otolaryngology Rush Med. Coll., 1940, U. Ill., 1941-42; sr. attending staff Northwestern Meml. Hosp., 1946—; prof. otolaryngology Northwestern U. Med. Sch., 1957—. Served with M.C. AUS, 1943-46. Mem. AMA, Am. Acad. Otolaryngology, Coll. Allergists. Home: 1 The Mews Franklin St Geneva IL 60134 Office: 55 E Washington St Chicago IL 60602

DERPINGHAUS, PATRICK JAMES, auditor; b. Green Bay, Wis., Oct. 20, 1955; s. Merle Francis and Mary Rose (Achten) D. B, St. Norbert Coll., 1979. CPA; chartered bank auditor. Auditor Valley Bancorp., Appleton, Wis., 1979-81, audit officer, 1983-84; controller Valley Bank, Appleton, Wis., 1981-83; gen. auditor Davenport (Iowa) Bank & Trust Co., 1984; audit mgr. Mercantile Bancorp. Inc., St. Louis, 1985—. Served as sgt. USMCR, 1977-83. Mem. Am. Inst. CPA's, Wis. Inst. CPA's, Inst. Internal Auditors. Republican. Roman Catholic. Lodge: Lions (treas. Wrightstown, Wis. chpt. 1983). Home: 902 Carr St Saint Louis MO 63101 Office: Mercantile Bancorp Inc PO Box 524 Saint Louis MO 63166

DERR, KENNETH LEROY, architect; b. Akron, Ohio, Dec. 24, 1923; s. Dwight L. and Hazel (Boise) D.; married; children: Linda J. Derr Hummer, Lora K. BArch, U. Mich., 1950. Ptnr. Derr, Stueber, Cornachione & Brown and predecessor firms, Akron, 1954—; owner K.L. Derr & Assocs., Akron, 1980—; plan examiner Five County Bldg. Ofcls., Akron, Ohio Bd. Architects, Columbus, Wayne County Bldg. Dept., Wooster, Ohio. Prin. works include Steiner Youth Ctr., 1975, Portage County Mental Workshop, 1975, Wadsworth High Sch. Phys. Edn. Bldg., 1979. Served with U.S. Army, 1943-45. Mem. AIA (profl.), Am. Arbitration Assn. (arbitrator 1970—), Nat. Woodcarvers Assn. Republican. Lutheran. Lodge: Rotary (bd. dirs. Wadsworth club). Avocations: wood carving, fishing. Home: 10099 Dale Dr Wadsworth OH 44281 Office: 251 Main St Wadsworth OH 44281

DERRICK, WILLIAM STUART, JR., maintenance consultant, project mangaer, computer consultant; b. Calgary, Alta., Can., Oct. 24, 1950; s. William Stuart Sr. and Helen Louise (Hartney) D.; m. Mary Esther Arizpe, Aug. 1, 1981; 1 child, Alison Ray. B.A., Westminster Coll., 1972; student U. Houston, 1973, U. Colo., 1982-83. With Brown & Root, internat. constrn., 1971-76, in project mgmt. Houston, 1978-79; materials mgr. Occidental Engring. Co., Scotland, 1976-77; estimator Payne & Keller, Houston, 1979-80; sr. systems analyst Stearns-Catalytic, Denver, 1980-86, Heery Program Mgmt., Columbus, Ohio, 1986-87, area mgr. Super Mgmt. Services; pres. Tekbuild Inc, 1987—; bankruptcy mgr. Pin Oaks Condos, Houston, 1979-80 Vice pres. Trenton Pl. Town Homes, Bellaire, Tex., 1980. Mem. Westminster Coll. Alumni Assn. (pres. 1983-87). Republican. Presbyterian.

DERRY, MICHAEL LOUIS, management consultant; b. Detroit, July 6, 1949; s. Charles Louis and Samuella Dale D.; BA, No. Mich. U. 1972; m. Margaret Leigh Sowers, Apr. 26, 1980. Founder, M.L. Derry & Assocs., Inc., Detroit 1972—; pres. Info. Mgmt. Corp., Farmington Hills, Mich. 1978—; chmn. bd. Sales Devel. Corp., Farmington Hills, 1982, Mgmt. Devel. Corp.; guest instr. Wayne State U. Mem. Pres.'s Assn., Am. Mgmt. Assn. Clubs: Univ. of Detroit (founder); No. Mich. U. Dean's. Contbr. in field. Office: 31500 W 13 Mile Rd #135 Farmington Hills MI 48018

DERTIEN, JAMES LEROY, librarian; b. Kearney, Nebr., Dec. 14, 1942; s. John Ludwig and Muriel May (Cooley) D.; m. Elaine Paulette Mohror, Dec. 26, 1966; children—David Dalton, Channing Lee. A.B., U. S.D., 1965; M.L.S., U. Pitts., 1966. Head librarian Mitchell Pub. Library, S.D., 1966-67; head librarian Sioux Falls Coll., S.D., 1967-69; acting dir. libraries U. S.D., Vermillion, 1969-70; head librarian Vets. Meml. Pub. Library, Bismarck, N.D., 1970-75, Bellevue Pub. Library, Nebr., 1975-81; city librarian Sioux Falls Pub. Library, S.D., 1981—. Roundtable commr. Sioux council Boy Scouts Am., 1981—. Mem. ALA, Mountain Plains Library Assn. (pres. 1978-79, editor newsletter 1982—), S.D. Library Assn. (pres. 1986-87). Unitarian. Lodge: Rotary. Avocations: backpacking; reading; gardening. Home: 1602 Carter Pl Sioux Falls SD 57105 Office: Sioux Falls Pub Library 201 N Main Ave Sioux Falls SD 57102

DERWINSKI, DENNIS ANTHONY, dentist; b. Chgo., Oct. 18, 1941; s. Anthony Joseph and Julie Donata (Pochron) D.; m. Mary Pamela Butler, Feb. 11, 1964 (div. Dec. 1975); children: Julie, Nancy, John, Amy, Mollie, Camy; m. Gayle Marie Sondelski, Oct. 8, 1977; 1 child, Anthony. DDS, Marquette U., 1965. Resident Cook County Hosp., Chgo., 1967-68; dentist Riverview Dental Assocs., Wausau, Wis., 1968-81; also pres. Riverview Dental Assocs., Wausau, 1971-81; dentist Hosp. Dental Assocs., Wausau, 1981—, also pres., 1981—; vice chmn. Wausau Hosps. Dental Staff, Wausau, 1983-87, chmn. 1987—. Contbr. articles to profl. jours. Dental chmn. United Way, Wausau, 1983; pres. Montessori Sch. Wausau, 1984; bd. dirs. St. Francis Cabrini Sch., 1978-85. Served to capt. USAF, 1965-67. Fellow Acad. Gen. Dentistry (cert.); mem. Soc. Occlusal Studies, ADA, Wis. Dental Assn. (Continuing Edn. award), Am. Equilibration Soc. Republican. Roman Catholic. Club: Wausau. Avocations: sailing, skiing, hunting, fishing. Home: 1209 E Crocker St Wausau WI 54401 Office: Hosp Dental Assocs 425 Pine Ridge Blvd Wausau WI 54401

DESAI, PRAKASH NAVINKANT, psychiatrist, educator; b. Baroda, India, Feb. 18, 1940; s. Navinkant and Snehlata (Mehr) D.; m. Alice Meara, Nov. 12, 1971; children: Reshma, Natasha. MS, U. Baroda, 1957, MB, BS, 1963. Jr. lectr. in psychiatry B.J. Med. Sch., Ahmedabad, India, 1962-63; intern W. Suburban Hosp., Oak Park, Ill., 1964; resident in psychiatry Northwestern U. Hosp., Chgo., 1965-67; resident grad. in psychiatry Mental Health Ctr., Chgo., 1968; asst. dir. outpatient dept. Ill. State Psychiat. Inst., Chgo., 1969; sr. psychiatrist B.M. Inst., Ahmedabad, 1969-70; assoc. dir. Community Psychiat. Program, Chgo., 1970-72, dir., 1972-73; regional dir. Chgo. Met. Area Ill. Dept. Mental Health, 1973-78; chief psychiat. services VA W. Side Med. Ctr., Chgo., 1978—; assoc. mem. Com. on S. Asia, U. Chgo., 1981-84; assoc. prof. Psychiatry U. Chgo. Sch. Medicine. Author: Cross Cultural Psychiatry, 1980; co-author: Cross Cultural Psychiatry, 1982, 84, 86. Pres. Am. Assn. S. Asia, 1977-79; mem. India Forum Found. Fellow Am. Psychiat. Assn. Avocations: cricket, bridge, travel. Home: 1043 N Lathrop River Forest IL 60305

DE SANTOS, ROBIN KING, manufacturing executive; b. Columbus, Ohio, Nov. 3, 1958; s. Robert Lawrence de Santos and Martha Jean (King) Veitch; m. Cynthia Marie Walters, Sept. 20, 1986. Student, Ohio State U., 1974-76, 79-80, MIT, 1976-77. Patient services coordinator Ohio State U. Hosp., Columbus, 1977-81; project engring., N.Am. aircraft ops. Rockwell Internat., Columbus, 1981-85, supr. planning, 1985—. Mem. Rep. Nat. Com., Washington, 1980—. Mem. Astron. League (sec. 1984, 1985), AAAS, Reynoldsburg (Ohio) Jaycees. Republican. Lutheran. Home: 127 S James Rd Columbus OH 43213-1622 Office: Rockwell Internat N Am Aircraft Ops PO Box 1259 Columbus OH 43216-1259

DESAULNIERS, MARC JOSEPH, industrial engineer, microcomputer consultant; b. Woonsocket, R.I., May 8, 1951; s. Norman Omer Desaulniers and Muriel Margarette (Drainville) Marien; m. Deborah Ann Cross; 1 child, Jennifer Green; m. Jennifer Kay Schwank; 1 child, Adam Norman. BS in Indsl. Engring., Northeastern U., 1974; MBA, U. New Haven, 1979. Jr. indsl. engr. Chesebrough-Pond's, Inc., Clinton, Conn., 1974-75, supr. stores, 1975-76, sr. divisional engr., 1976-78; indsl. engring. mgr. Chesebrough-Pond's, Inc., Jefferson City, Mo., 1978-87; quality assurance mgr. Volume Shoe Corp., Topeka, Kans., 1987—; mem. Industry Rev. Group, U. Mo., 1983—. Author: (microcomputer system) The Home Address Book, 1982. Bd. dirs. Sheltered Workshop, Jefferson City, 1982—; head EDP com. United Way, Jefferson City, 1984—. Fellow Am. Inst. Indsl. Engrs. (pres. 1981, bd. dirs. 1982-83); mem. Alpha Pi Mu. Roman Catholic. Avocations: tennis, skiing, microcomputers, woodworking, golf. Home: 1311 Stone Meadows Dr Lawrence KS 66046 Office: Volume Shoe Corp 3231 E 6th St Topeka KS 66608

DESENBERG, LOUIS ARTHUR, lawyer; b. Niles, Mich., Sept. 2, 1943; s. B.R. and Marjorie Minnie (Hetler) D.; m. Catherine Ann Franklin, July 9, 1966; children: Louis F., B. Robert. BA, U. Notre Dame, 1966; JD, U. Valparaiso, 1970. Ptnr. Desenberg & Desenberg, Buchanan, Mich., 1970-76, Desenberg, Marrs & Colip, Buchanan, 1976-84, Desenberg & Colip, Buchanan, 1984—; bd. dirs, counsel Inter-City Bank, Benton Harbor, Mich.; atty. Village of Galian, Mich., 1974—, City of Buchanan, 1979-87, City of Bridgman, Mich., 1986—. Trustee Berrien County Intermediate Sch. Dist., Berrien Springs, Mich., 1976-82, 87—; bd. dirs. Buchanan Area Found.,

1976—. Mem. ABA, Mich. Bar Assn., Berrien County Bar Assn. Republican. Roman Catholic. Lodge: Lions (pres. Buchanan 1973, treas. 1974-76). Avocations: golf, softball. Office: Desenberg & Colip PO Box 72 Buchanan MI 49107

DES HARNAIS, GABRIEL ALFRED, clinical social worker; b. River Rouge, Mich., Sept. 1, 1933; s. Armand François and Therese Ubaldine (Fournier) D.; m. Mary Bernadette LaJeunesse, Mar. 22, 1968; children: Denis Martin, Armand Gabriel. BA, Sacred Heart Sem. Coll., Detroit, 1955; MSW, Wayne State U., 1969, PhD, 1979; M of Div., St. John Provincial Sem., Plymouth, Mich., 1980. Assoc. pastor St. Mary Magdalen Ch., Melvindale, Mich., 1959-64, St. John the Evangelist Ch., Detroit, 1964-67; caseworker Family Service of Oakland, Berkley, Mich., 1967-69; pvt. practice clin. social work Southfield, Mich., 1969—; cons. Neighborhood Legal Services, Detroit, 1981. Mem. Nat. Assn. Social Workers,, Am. Assn. Marriage and Family Therapy (state treas. 1982, state pres. 1983). Democrat. Episcopalian.

DE SIMONE, LIVIO DIEGO, diversified mfg. co. exec.; b. Montreal, Que., Can., July 16, 1936; s. Joseph D. and Maria E. (Bergamin) De S.; B.Chem. Engring., McGill U., Montreal, 1957; m. Lise Marguerite Wong, 1957; children—Daniel J., Livia D., Mark A., Cynthia A. With Minn. Minning & Mfg. Co. St. Paul, now exec. v.p. Office: Indsl & Consumer Sector 3M Center St Saint Paul MN 55144

DESMOND, KATHLEEN KADON, art educator, artist; b. Marshfield, Wis., Sept. 2, 1950; d. John Charles and Ann (Preller) Kadon; m. William Dean Desmond, Aug. 8, 1970 (dec.). B.A. in Art Edn., Photography, U. Wis.-Madison, 1973; M.A. in Art Edn., Ariz. State U., 1976, Ed.D. in Art Edn., 1981. One woman art exhbns. include: Ind. U., 1985, Scottsdale Community Coll., 1980, U. Wis., 1978; numerous group and juried exhbns., France, Ariz., Colo., Ohio., Ky., Ill.; art instr. Scottsdale (Ariz.) Community Coll., 1974-81; instr. photography dept. art U. Wis., summer 1978; teaching assoc. art edn. Ariz. State U., Tempe, 1978-81; assoc. prof. art edn. Ohio State U.-Newark, 1981—; researcher in teaching art and photography for exhbns. Recipient nat. and regional grants and awards. Mem. Nat. Art Edn. Assn., Ariz. Art Edn. Assn., Soc. Photog. Edn., Columbus Art League, Coll. Art. Assn., Phi Delta Kappa. Contbr. articles profl. jours. Office: Ohio State U Newark OH 43055

DESOMBRE, EUGENE ROBERT, organic chemistry educator; b. Sheboygan, Wis., May 6, 1938; s. George August and Viola Ann (Schmidt) DeS.; m. Nancy Cox, Sept. 10, 1960; children: Elizabeth, Michael. BS, U. Chgo., 1960, MS in Chemistry, 1961, PhD in Organic Chemistry, 1963. Instr. Ben May Inst., U. Chgo., 1964-67, asst. prof., 1967-73, assoc. prof., 1974-79, prof., 1980—, dir. Biomed. Computation Facility, 1980—; chmn. breast cancer task force Nat. Cancer Inst., 1978-80, mem. breast cancer diagnosis com., 1974-78;. Patentee estrogen receptor antibodies for diagnosis; contbr. articles to profl. jours. Cancer Research grantee Nat. Cancer Inst., 1979—, Reproductive Research grantee NIH, 1981—. Mem. Endocrine Soc., Am. Assn. for Cancer Research (mem. editorial bd. 1975-79), Internat. Assn. Breast Cancer Research (mem. bd. govs. 1980-86), Internat. Soc. for Endocrinology (mem. cen. com. 1982—), Am. Cancer Soc. (mem. biochemistry and carcinogenesis adv. com. 1978-82, mem. personnel adv. com. 1985—). Home: 1021 N Elmwood Ave Oak Park IL 60302 Office: Univ Chgo 5841 S Maryland Ave Chicago IL 60637

DESOMOGYI, AILEEN ADA, retired librarian; b. London, Nov. 26, 1911; d. Harry Alfred and Ada Amelia (Ponten) Taylor; immigrated to Can., 1966; B.A., Royal Holloway Coll., U. London, 1936, M.A., 1939; M.L.S., U. Western Ont., 1971; m. Leslie Kuti, Nov. 22, 1958; m. 2d, Joseph DeSomogyi, July 8, 1966. Librarian in spl. and public libraries, Eng., 1943-66; sr. instr. Nat. Coal Bd., 1957; charge regional collection S.W. Ont., Lawson Library, U. Western Ont., 1967-71; cataloger Coop. Book Centre Can., 1971; mem. staff E. York (Ont.) Public Library, 1971-74; librarian Ont. Ministry Govt. Services Mgmt. and Info. Services Library, 1975-78, Sperry-Univac Computer Systems, Toronto (Ont.) Central Library, 1980-81. Mem. Internat. Platform Assn., English Speaking Union, Can. Orgn. for Devel. Through Edn., Royal Can. Geog. Soc., Consumers Assn. Can., Can. Wildlife Fedn., Ont. Humane Soc., Internat. Fund Animal Welfare, Endangered Animal Sanctuary, U. Western Ont. Alumni Assn., Royal Holloway and Bedford New Coll. Assn., Am. Biog. Inst. Research Assn. (dep. gov., nat. bd. advisors), Can. Mental Health Assn., John Howard Soc., Met. Toronto Zool. Soc., Toronto Humane Soc. Roman Catholic. Contbr. articles to profl. jours. Home: 9 Bonnie Brae Blvd, Toronto, ON Canada M4J 4N3

DESSIMOZ, RICHARD EDMUND, transportation executive; b. Chgo., May 22, 1947; s. Rene Edmund and Mary Catherine (Finnegan) D.; m. Eileen Mermelstein, Aug. 2, 1970 (div. Feb. 1975); m. Carolyn Joyce Fitzpatrick, Dec. 17, 1977. BA in Econs., U. Ill., Chgo., 1969; LLB, Northwestern U., 1972; MBA, U. Chgo., 1980. Bar: Ill. 1972. Pvt. placement analyst Combined Ins. Co., Chgo., 1972-76; atty. N.Am. Car Corp., Chgo., 1974-76; group atty. Evans Products, Rolling Meadows, Ill., 1976-80; v.p., gen. mgr. trailer leasing Evans Transp., Rolling Meadows, 1980-85, pres. railcar div., 1985—. Mem. Nat. Freight Transp. Assn. Roman Catholic. Club: Meadows (Rolling Meadows). Home: 1218 Barclay Circle Inverness IL 60010 Office: Evans Transp Co 2550 Golf Rd Rolling Meadows IL 60007

DESSOUKY, IBTESAM A. R., librarian; b. Cairo, July 29, 1941; came to U.S. 1963; d. Abdul Rahman Kolali and Tafida El Kahal; m. Mohamed I. Dessouky, Oct. 9, 1958; children: Sherif, Maged, Yasser, Dahlia. BA in French and History, U. Ill., 1973, MLS, 1977. Librarian Nat. Acad. Arts, Champaign, Ill., 1978, Arab Planning Inst., Kuwait City, Kuwait, 1978-80; head librarian Indsl. Bank Kuwait, Kuwait City, 1980-83, Ill. State Water Survey, Champaign, 1984—; library cons. Kuwaiti Internat. Investment Co., Kuwait, 1983. leader Cub Scouts Am., Urbana, 1972; asst. leader Girl Scouts U.S., Urbana, 1976. Mem. ALA, Ill. Library Assn., Spl. Library Assn. Avocations: jogging, swimming, aerobics, reading. Home: 1106 Michem Dr Urbana IL 61801 Office: Ill State Water Survey 2204 Griffith Dr Champaign IL 61820

DE STEFANO, MICHAEL JOSEPH, obstetrician, gynecologist; b. Chgo., Sept. 28, 1945; s. Michael and Helen (Clarke) De S.; children: Michael J. Jr., Nicole, Thaddeus. BA, St. Mary's Coll., Winona, Minn., 1967; MD, U. Ill., Chgo., 1971; MSA, U. Notre Dame, 1986. Diplomate Am. Bd. Ob-Gyn. Staff Ob-Gyn Assocs. Inc., South Bend, Ind., 1977—; dir. perinatal services Meml. Hosp., South Bend, 1984-86. Served to maj. U.S. Army, 1975-77. Fellow Am. Coll. Ob-Gyn; mem. Am. Acad. Med. Dirs. Roman Catholic. Avocations: literature, history, golf, skiing. Office: Ob-Gyn Assocs Inc 912 E LaSalle South Bend IN 46617

DE TAR, DAVID LAWRENCE, dentist; b. Jplin, Mo., Apr. 9, 1946; s. Burleigh Eli De Tar and Alma LaMora (Coulter) Terry; m. Katherine Jean Wilson, Mar. 18, 1972; children: Amanda Wyatt, Joshua Gipson, Katherine Lawrence. BA, U. Kans., 1968; DDS, U. Detroit, 1972. Practice gen. dentistry Joplin, 1974—; chmn. dental dept. Saint Johns Med. Ctr. Joplin, 1984-85; clin. lectr. Cub scouts den leader Boy Scouts Am.; chmn. Joplin Bd. Health, 1982-84; pres. Columbia Sch. PTA, Joplin, 1985, Southwest Mo. Swim Team, Joplin, 1985-86. Served to lt. USN, 1972-74. Fellow Acad. Gen. Dentistry, Internat. Coll. Dentists; mem. ADA, Southwest Mo. Dental Soc. (pres. elect 1986), Mo. Dental Assn. (mem. lab. com. 1980—, clinician state meeting 1984, del. 1982), Mo. Acad. Gen. Dentistry (trustee 1986—). Republican. Presbyterian. Club: Twin Hills Country (Joplin). Lodge: Kiwanis. Avocations: backpacking, skiing, fishing. Home: 1250 Crest Dr Joplin MO 64801 Office: 2700 McClelland Blvd Joplin MO 64804

DETHLOFF, KAREN LOUISE, hospital engineer; b. Cleve., June 3, 1952; s. Louis John and Eleanor Alice (Ducosky) Vesel; m. Thomas Charles Dethloff, June 24, 1978. BS in Agriculture, Ohio State U., 1974; MSEE, Cleve. State U., 1978. Clin. engr. intern Cleve. Metro Gen. Hosp., 1978; clin. engr. Huron Run Hosp., Cleve., 1978-80; dir. engring. and maintenance Huron Rd. Hosp., Cleve., 1980-87, adminstrv. dir. ops., 1987—. Career Day speaker Cleve. Pub. Schs., 1985. Mem. Am. Soc. Hosp. Engring. (regional bd. rep. 1987—), Ohio Soc. Hosp. Engring. (pres.-elect 1986—), N.E. Ohio Soc. Hosp. Engring. (treas. 1985-86), Nat. Fire Protection Assn. (health care sect.). Avocations: equitation, boating, swimming, skiing. Home: 7279 Maple St Mentor OH 44060 Office: Huron Road Hosp 13951 Terrace Rd Cleveland OH 44112

DETTLAFF, BARBARA JEAN, banker; b. Davenport, Iowa, July 22, 1955; s. Robert Franklin and Mary Ann (Winchell) Murphy; m. Michael Paul Dettlaff, May 23, 1981; children: Kathryn Anne, Kimberly Kristeen. BA, Marycrest Coll., 1977. Tchr. U. So. Calif., Los Angeles, 1977-80; fin. service rep. Northwest Bank & Trust, Davenport, 1980-81, fin. service rep. trainer, 1981-82, ednl. trainer, 1982-83, tng. officer, 1983—; tchr. Scott Community Coll., Bettendorf, Iowa, 1984—; tchr. Blackhawk Coll., Moline, Ill., 1982-84; lectr., 1983—. Dir. (community play) House of Blue Leaves, 1978; actress (community play) California Suite, 1978. Named Best Dir. Davenport Maycrest Community Theatre, 1978, Best Actress, 1978. Mem. Am. Inst. Banking (v.p. edn. 1986-87). Roman Catholic. Avocations: directing and performing in community theater. Home: 4125 31st St Bettendorf IA 52722 Office: Northwest Bank & Trust 100 E Kimberly Rd Davenport IA 52806

DETTMAN, ROBERT MARKS, II, financial executive, corporate treasurer; b. Los Angeles, May 3, 1944; s. Robert Marks and LaVerne Marie (Froula) D.; m. Linda Carol Webster, Apr. 1, 1967 (div. Feb. 1974); m. Mary Renea Getz, Nov. 14, 1975; children: Robert III, Robin. Student, U. Phillipines, Luzon, 1965, U. Md., 1966; BBA, North Tex. State U., 1972. CPA, Tex., Wis. Mgr. acctg. Docutel, Irving, Tex., 1972-77; controller Laminated Plastics, Dallas, 1977-78, Med. Computer Systems, Dallas, 1978-83; dir. fin. Mgmt. Systems Wausau, Wis., 1983-85; pres. 1st Leasing and Investment , McFarland, Wis., 1986—, also bd. dirs.; treas. Amtel Communications, McFarland, 1986—; cons. Health Data Systems, Wausau, 1986-87. Mem. Young Reps., Denton, Tex., 1970; patrolman Dallas Police Res., 1972-76. Served with USAF, 1964-68. Mem. Am. Inst. CPA's, Nat. Assn. Accts. (dir. pub. relations 1973-74), Beta Alpha Psi. Roman Catholic. Home: 3601 Hart Circle McFarland WI 53558 Office: Amtel Communications 4800 Curtin Dr McFarland WI 53558

DETTMANN, FREDERICK GUSTAV, obstetrician, gynecologist; b. Milw., Dec. 24, 1934; s. Norbert Frederick and Hertha (Strandt) D.; m. Brenda Boughton, Dec. 30, 1961; children: Curtis Warren, Dianne Ruth, Jami Lynn. AB, Ripon Coll., 1956; MD, Marquette U., 1960; M of Med. Sci., Ohio State U., 1965. Diplomate Am. Bd. Ob-Gyn. Intern Ohio State U. Hosps.; resident U. Washington Hosp.; practice medicine specializing in ob-gyn Milw., 1969—; med. dir. Found. Med. Care, Milw., 1969-84, Wis. Peer Rev. Orgn., Madison, Wis., 1984—; dir. Fertility Clinic Southwest Wis., Milw., 1973—; cons. Govt. Acct. Office, Washington, 1985—, Health Care Fin. Adminstrn., Washington, 1985—; project leader Tech. Assistance Task Force, HMO Rev. Task Force, Washington, 1985—. Chmn. N. Shore Paramedics, Inc., Glendale, Wis., 1976-79; pres., bd. dirs. Big Bros. and Big Sisters Greater Milw. Area., 1970-72. Served to capt. USAF, 1965-67. Mem. Am. Med. Peer Rev. Assn. (bd. dirs., chmn. med. dirs. sect.), Am. Med. Rev. Research Ctr. (bd. dirs.), Am. Coll. Ob-Gyn, Am. Fertility Soc., Am. Coll. Quality Assurance and Utilization Rev. Physicians (dir. Samaritan Health plan), Samaritan Physicians Assn. (adminstr), Ohio State Med. Soc., Wis. State Med. Soc. Home and Office: 105 W Silver Springs Dr Milwaukee WI 53217

DETWILER, PAUL NORMAN, real estate investor; b. St. Louis, Jan. 1, 1952; s. Laurin Edwin and Lena Elizabeth (Saviors) D.; m. Sally Lu Spahr, Mar. 23, 1974; 1 child, Christopher Paul. Student, Ball State U., 1970-72. Freelance painting contractor Elberfeld, Ind., 1968-72; salesman Jim Walter Homes, Henderson, Ky., 1972-73; purchasing agt. Spahr Distbg., Portland, Ind., 1973-80; owner, operator Applegate Properties, Portland, Ind., 1978—; restored and leased empty dept. store bldg. as hist. landmark, Portland, 1984-86. Supt. Sunday Sch. Blaine (Ind.) United Meth. Ch., 1976-81, chmn. adminstrv. council, 1981—. Republican. Home: Rural Rt 2 PO Box 30A Portland IN 47371 Office: Applegate Properties One Weiler Sq Suite 150 Portland IN 47371

DETWILER, RONALD LEE, optometrist; b. Salem, Ohio, Jan. 17, 1948; s. Donald Lee and Virginia May (Prouty) D.; m. Marilou Douglass, Nov. 26, 1977; children—Kristin, Jeffrey, Daniel. B.S., Kent State U., 1970; B. in Visual Sci., Ill. Coll. Optometry, 1975, O.D., 1975. Gen. practice optometry, East Liverpool, Ohio, 1975—; pres. Vision League of Ohio, Columbus, 1978. Bd. dirs. Columbiana County Mental Health Assn., Lisbon, Ohio, 1982—; exec. bd. dirs. Columbiana County council, Boy Scouts Am. 1984—; county chmn. Columbiana County Cystic Fibrosis Assn., East Liverpool, 1979, 80, 85; bd. dirs. Northeast Ohio Regional Council on Alcoholism, Warren, 1980-82. Mem. Northeast Ohio Optometric Assn. (pres. 1979-80, Zone Activity award 1980), Ohio Optometric Found., Better Vision Inst., Ohio Optometric Assn. (chmn. pub. info. 1979, trustee 1980-84, sec.-treas. 1984, pres. 1985—), Salem Jaycees (pres. 1977-78, Outstanding Local Pres. award 1978, Disting. Service award 1978), Council on Sport Vision. Republican. Methodist. Lodges: Kiwanis (East Liverpool) (trustee 1979-80); Elks. Avocation: breeding Arabian horses. Home: 3437 W Garfield Rd Columbiana OH 44408 Office: 122 W 5th St East Liverpool OH 43920

DEUBELL, G. ROBERT, university administrator, puchasing consultant; b. Cin., Nov. 4, 1930; s. George Leonard and Eleanor (Keating) D.; m. Linnea Breeze, Mar. 2, 1957; children: Robert Marcus, Laurette Renee. BS, Xavier U., 1962, MBA, 1965; EdD, U. Cin., 1984. Commodity trader Emery Industries, Cin., 1960-64, commodity forecaster, 1964-67; dir. purchases U. Cin., 1967-71, dir. material mgmt., 1971-80, asst. v.p., 1980—. Mem. Nat. Assn. Purchasing Mgmt., Am. Opera Assn. (bd. dirs.), Ohio Inter Univ. Council, Am. Mgmt. Assn. Republican. Roman Catholic. Home: 10501 Adventure Ln Cincinnati OH 45242 Office: U Cin M L 89 Cincinnati OH 45221

DEUBERRY, LAURA ANNE, college administrator; b. St. Paul, Aug. 23, 1948; d. William N. and Neenann A. (Burns) D. Student, St. Mary's Coll., Mpls.; AA, Metro State Coll. Materiel mgr. Divine Redeemer Hosp., South St. Paul, Minn., 1972-76; buyer The Webb Co., St. Paul, 1976-83; dir. purchasing Coll. of St. Thomas, St. Paul, 1983—; dir. purchasing receiving stores Coll. St. Thomas. Singer St. Paul Opera Workshop, 1974-75, Coppertones, Mpls., 1979-82; advisor St. Paul Jr. Achievement, 1977-82; vol. Little Bros. of the Poor, Mpls., 1985; mem. St. Paul Jr. League, 1986—. Recipient Community Leader award St. Paul YWCA, 1983. Mem. Nat. Assn. Purchasing Mgmt., Nat. Assn. Ednl. Buyers (regional pres. 1986, editorial bd. 1986—, Leader award 1986), Twin City Purchasing Mgmt. Assn. (seminar chairperson 1984-86, Recognition award 1986), Associated Colls. of Twin Cities (chairperson joint purchasing com. 1986). Office: Coll of St Thomas 2115 Summit Ave Box 5045 Saint Paul MN 55105

DEUEL, DAVID JOHN, tool manufacturing company executive; b. Bay City, Mich., Sept. 24, 1945; s. Raymond David and Marie June (Gibas) D.; m. Debra Kay Hugo, May 27, 1972; children—Ashley Lynn, Erik Michael. Sales clk. Walgreen Drugs, Bay City, Mich., 1963-64; insp. Chevrolet Mfg., Bay City, Mich., 1964-67; with Wieland Furniture, Bay City, Mich., 1969-70; tool maker Gil Ray Tools, Bay City, Mich., 1970-80, owner, pres., 1981—. Contbr. articles to tech. jours. Mem. edn. com. Bay City Right to Life, 1981; lay pastor Calvary Fellowship Christian Ch., 1976-82, treas., 1972-81. Served with USNR, 1967-68. Mem. Soc. Mfg. Engrs., Associated Locksmiths Am. (assoc.), Bay Area C. of C. Republican. Lodge: Elks. Home: 204 Sharpe St Essexville MI 48732 Office: Gil Ray Tools Inc 1306 McGraw St PO Box 801 Bay City MI 48707

DEUPREE, MICHAEL HAROLD, newspaper columnist; b. Council Bluffs, Iowa, Mar. 23, 1946; s. Harold Hubert and Margaret Jane (Royer) D.; m. Anne Kathryn Perry, Aug. 16, 1969. Student, Iowa State U., 1964-67; BA in Journalism, U. Iowa, 1969. Sports editor The Blackfoot (Idaho) News, 1969-73; reporter The Cedar Rapids (Iowa) Gazette, 1973-78, state editor, 1978-82, editorial writer, 1982-87, columnist, 1987—. Mem. Nat. Soc. Newspaper Columnists, Iowa NEwspaper Assn. (master columnist 1984). Mem. Ch. of Christ. Avocations: amateur radio, scuba diving, travel, bowling. Home: 1716 Morris Ave SW Cedar Rapids IA 52405 Office: The Cedar Rapids Gazette 500 3d Ave SE Cedar Rapids IA 52406

DEUSCHLE, THOMAS ARTHUR, state government official; b. Sedalia, Mo., Dec. 15, 1957; s. Arthur Junior Deuschle and Violet Lee (Shaver) Livingston; m. Denise Jean Holzem, Oct. 22, 1983. AS in Bus. Mid-Mgmt., State Fair Community Coll., Sedalia, 1978; BSBA in Personnel Adminstrn., Cen. Mo. State U., 1980. Support enforcement adminstr. Pettis County Pros. Atty., Sedalia, 1979-81; adminstrv. asst. Mo. Atty Gen., Jefferson City, 1981-84; dep. campaign mgr. Ashcroft for Gov., Jefferson City, 1984; dir. personnel Mo. Transition Govt., Jefferson City, 1984-85; asst. for appointments and personnel Office of Gov., Jefferson City, 1985—; atty. gen.'s rep. Mo. Housing Devel. Commn., Kansas City, 1982-84; gov.'s rep. Mo. Housing Devel. Commn., Kansas City, 1985—. Chmn. Environ. Quality Commn., Sedalia, 1977-80, City Rep. Com., Sedalia, 1978-80, Sedalia Housing Authority, Sedalia, 1980-81; pres. Capital Area Young Reps., Jefferson City, 1982-83. Named One of Outstanding Young Men of Am., 1985. Republican. Roman Catholic. Avocation: jogging. Home: 402 Norris Jefferson City MO 65101 Office: Office of Gov State Capitol Bldg Jefferson City MO 65102

DEUSHANE, JOHN CHARLES, sales executive; b. Canton, Ill., Jan. 24, 1957; s. Ralph Franklin and Wilma Marie (St. Clair) D. BS in Broadcast Mgmt. and Journalism magna cum laude, Bradley U., 1979. Producer, dir. WEEK-TV, East Peoria, Ill., 1980-82, prodn. mgr., 1982-84, account exec., 1984-85, local sales mgr., 1985-86, gen. sales mgr., 1986-87; v.p., gen. mgr. KRCG-TV, Jefferson City, Mo., 1987—; prof. advt., journalism Bradley U., 1985—. Dir., producer railroad documentary, 1984 (Adam award 1984). Mem. Peoria Advt. and Selling Club, Bloomington Normal Ad Club, Phi Beta Phi. Republican. Roman Catholic. Avocations: reading, bicycling, skiing. Home: 13022 Duggins Rd Dunlap IL 61525 Office: KRCG-TV Hwy 54N Box 659 Jefferson City MO 65102

DEUSINGER, ROBERT HENRY, physical therapy educator, researcher, clinician; b. Newark, June 3, 1944; s. Donald Jay and Elizabeth Violet (Lidlow) D.; children from a previous marriage: Christopher James, Marcus Jay, Leigh Elizabeth; m. Susan Schaefer, Mar. 15, 1980. BS, Slippery Rock (Pa.) State Coll., 1967; MS, U. Mass., 1968; PhD, U. Iowa, 1981. Lic. phys. therapist. Cons. phys. therapist Dept. Orthopedics U. Iowa Hosps. and Clinics, Iowa City, 1972-77; coordinator kinesiology/pathokinesiology lab, mem. faculty SUNY, Buffalo, 1977-79; dir. advanced kinesiology lab. Washington U. Med. Sch., St. Louis, 1979-82, mem. faculty, 1979—; facility dir. Medic Ctr. Rehab., St. Louis, 1984-85; pres. RSD Enterprises, Allenton, Mo., 1985—; cons. phys. therapist USN Regional Med. Ctr., Oakland, Calif., 1974; cons. task force on restructure therapeutic horsemanship, St. Louis, 1982-83. Contbr. articles to profl. jours. Pres. Audobon Residents Council, Amherst, N.Y., 1978-79. Served to lt. commdr. USNR, 1969-72. NIH grantee. Mem. Am. Phys. Therapy Assn. (N.Y. chpt. del. 1979, sec. orthopaedic sect. 1982-84, del. 1984, pres. 1985-87, Outstanding Service award 1984), Mo. Phys. Therapy Assn. (del. 1980). Avocations: electronics, reading, jogging, basketball, volleyball. Home: 18162 Meramec Vista Ln Pacific MO 63069 Office: RSD Enterprises 308 Main St Box 98 Allenton MO 63001

DEUTCH, RICHARD STEPHAN, optometrist; b. Teaneck, N.J., Jan. 27, 1953; s. Frederick Joseph Jr. and Margaret Mary (Imerito) D.; m. Maureen Ann McGinty, June 30, 1979; children: Carolan Margaret, Richard Stephan Jr. BS, U. Dayton, 1974, MS, 1977; OD, Ohio State U., 1983. Cert. optometrist, Ohio, Va. Clin. instr. Ohio State U. Coll. Optometry, Columbus, 1983-84; staff optometrist Group Health Assocs., Cin., 1984-85, chief eyecare, 1985—. Named one of Outstanding Young Men Am., 1981. Mem. Am. Optometric Soc., Ohio Optometric Assn., Cin. Optometric Assn. (pres. 1987). Avocations: reading, golf, camping. Office: Group Health Assocs 375 Glensprings Dr Cincinnati OH 45246

DEUTSCH, THOMAS ALAN, ophthalmologist; b. Nagoya, Japan, Aug. 11, 1954; (parents U.S. citizens); . William E. and Natasha S. (Sobotka) D.; m. Judith Silverman, Dec. 6, 1986. AB, Washington U., 1975; MD, Rush Med. Coll., Chgo., 1979. Diplomate Am. Bd. Ophthalmology. Asst. prof. ophthalmology U. Ill., Chgo., 1983-84; asst. prof. ophthalmology Rush Med. Coll., Chgo., 1984-87, assoc. prof., 1987—; lectr. in ophthalmology, U. Ill., Chgo., 1984—; adj. asst. prof. biomed. engring., Northwestern U., Evanston, Ill., 1986-87, adj. assoc. prof., 1987—. Assoc. editor Key Ophthalmology, 1986—, Year Book Ophthalmology, 1986; author 4 books, 35, articles, 15 sci. abstracts. Recipient Chancellor's award Washington U., 1975, Henry Lyman award Rush Med. Coll, 1978. Mem. Am. Acad. Ophthalmology, Assn. Research Vision Ophthalmology, Chgo. Ophthalmol. Soc. (chmn. clin. conf. 1986), Rush Alumni Assn. (pres. elect 1987—). Office: Rush Presbyn St Luke's Med Ctr 1725 Harrison St Suite 950 Chicago IL 60612

DEV, AKANT, ceramics engineer; b. Jullundur, India, Sept. 22, 1945; s. Kundan Lal and Bimla Devi (Gupta) D.; m. Anju Basil, Aug. 3, 1973; children: Artee, Amol. Profl. engr. Plant ceramic engr. Ohio Brass Co., Niagara Falls, Can., 1972-76, McGraw Edison Power Systems, Macomb, Ill., 1977-79; mgr. process engring. Cooper Industries, Macomb, 1979-83, mgr. product and process engring., 1984—; project coordinator Porelca, Ojeda, Venezuela, 1979-83; cons. Productos Industrialos, Montrey, Mexico, 1979-84. Recipient Govt. India research award, 1969. Mem. Assn. Profl. Engrs. Ontario-Can., Nat. Inst. Ceramic Engrs., Am. Ceramic Soc. Club: India of Macomb (pres. 1984). Avocations: photography, sports. Home: 145 Holden Dr Macomb IL 61455 Office: McGraw Edison Power Systems 510 N Pearl St Macomb IL 61455

DEVARAJAN, ANANTHANARAYAN DAVE, record company executive; b. Nemmara, India, May 18, 1938; s. Anantha and Meenakshy Vadyar; m. Prema Kumari Chandran, Jan. 19, 1969; children: Sharmila, Anand. BS MechE, Kerala U., 1960; diploma ops. research, ASTEF, Paris, 1967; MS in Mgmt., Purdue U., 1972. Registered profl. engr., Ind.; CPA, Ind. Cons. Nat. Productivity Council, New Delhi, India, 1963-69; tool and planning engr. The Boeing Co., Seattle, 1969-71; chief indsl. engr. Johnson Products, Chgo., 1972-73; ops. dir., chief engr. RCA Records, Indpls., 1973—. Contbr. articles to profl. mags. Recipient scholarship Govt. of India, 1950-60, French Govt., Paris, 1966-67. Mem. Am. Inst. CPA's, Am. Inst. Indsl. Engrs. (sr.), Audio Engring. Soc. Home: 211 S Sunblest Blvd Noblesville IN 46060 Office: RCA 6550 E 30th St Indianapolis IN 46219

DE VAULT, DENNIS ROBERT, heavy equipment company management; b. Abilene, Tex., July 11, 1941; s. Robert Martin and Muriel Dorothy (Sutherland) DeV.; m. Mary Ann Douglas, Aug. 30, 1963 (div. July 1979); children—Kimberly Jo, Brian Douglas; m. Robyn Renee Suchy, Aug. 25, 1982. B.S. in Agr., U. Ariz., 1968. Factory worker Southwestern Paint Co., Tucson, summers 1956-62; assembler Hughes Aircraft Co., Tucson, 1963; dispatcher El Paso Natural Gas Co., Tucson, 1963-66; research asst. U. Ariz., Tucson, 1966-68; design engr. Internat. Harvester Co., Memphis, 1968-73; design engr. Melroe Co. div. Clark Equipment Co., Bismarck, N.D., 1973-75, engring. services supr., 1975-83, designer, 1983-85, group technology coordinator, 1985—. Advisor, Jr. Achievement, Memphis, 1970. Served with USN, 1959-62. Mem. Nat. Mgmt. Assn. (charter, bd. dirs.), Bismarck Mandan Hist. and Geneal. Soc. (pres. 1975, 84, bd. dirs.), Soc. Mayflower Descs. Republican. Methodist. Lodge: Elks. Avocations: genealogy; computers; sports; horseback riding. Home: 1420 E Divide Bismarck ND 58501 Office: Melroe Co PO Box 1215 Bismarck ND 58502

DEVELLANO, JAMES CHARLES, professional hockey manager; b. Toronto, Ont., Can., Jan. 18, 1943; came to U.S., 1979; s. James Joseph and Jean (Piter) D. Ont. scout St. Louis Blues NHL, Toronto, 1967-72; eastern Can. scout N.Y. Islanders, Toronto, 1972-74, dir. scouting, 1974-82; asst. gen. mgr. Islanders, L.I., N.Y., 1981-82; gen. mgr. Detroit Red Wings, 1982—; v.p., gen. mgr. Indpls. Checkers, 1979-81. Home: 1300 E Lafayette St Apt 1203 Detroit MI 48207 Office: Detroit Red Wings Hockey Club Joe Louis Arena 600 Civic Center Dr Detroit MI 48226

DEVENOW, CHESTER, manufacturing executive; b. Detroit, Mar. 3, 1919; s. Samuel and Bessie (Aronoff) D.; m. Marilyn Fruchtman, Apr. 20, 1947 (div. Feb. 1977); children: Mark F., Jeffrey A., Sara Devenow Abrams, Susan P.; m. Maudette Shapiro, Dec. 18, 1978. B.A., NYU, 1941; postgrad., Harvard Law Sch., 1941-42; D.B.A. (hon.), Siena Heights Coll., Adrian, Mich., 1977. Pres. Globe Wernicke Industries, Toledo, 1954-67; pres. Sheller-Globe Corp., Toledo, 1967-72; chmn., chief exec. officer Sheller-

Globe Corp., 1972—, also bd. dirs.; bd. dirs. Toledo Edison, Toledo Trust Co., Toledo Trustcorp., Centerior Energy Corp. Bd. dirs. Tech. and Productivity Ctr. Ohio, Columbus, 1982—; trustee, chmn. bd. trustees Ohio State U., Columbus, 1972-82; mem. Labor-Mgmt. Citizens Com., Toledo, 1972; chmn. bd. Blue Cross NW Ohio, 1975-82. Served to 1st lt. U.S. Army, 1942-45. Recipient Heritage award Yeshiva U., 1971, Gov.'s award State of Ohio, 1981; named Hon. Prof., Ohio State U., 1982. Mem. Toledo Area C. of C. (pres. 1976, sr. council), Soc. Automotive Engrs., Nat. Energy Found. (bd. dirs.). Clubs: Renaissance (bd. govs. 1974—), Economic (Detroit); Toledo; Jockey (Miami, Fla.). Office: Sheller-Globe Corp 1505 Jefferson Ave Toledo OH 43697 *

DEVEREUX, GEORGE DEBARR, financial executive; b. Omaha, Jan. 13, 1922; s. Ellsworth Wilson and Metta Christine (Jorgensen) D.; m. Phyllis Esther Griess, Sept. 6, 1943; children—Susan, Barbara, Catherine. B.Sc. in Commerce, Creighton U., 1947. C.P.A., Nebr. Bus. mgr. Bi-State Distbg. Corp., Omaha, 1951-56, KETV-TV, Omaha, 1957-64; sec.-treas. Kirkham, Michael & Assocs., Omaha, 1964—. Bd. dirs. Camp Fire Girls, Omaha, 1957-67. Served to 1st lt. U.S. Army, 1943-46, ETO. Mem. Am. Soc. C.P.A.s, Nebr. Soc. C.P.A.s. Republican. Episcopalian. Lodges: Masons, Shriners. Home: 12117 Y Plaza Omaha NE 68137 Office: Kirkham Michael & Assocs 9110 W Dodge Rd Omaha NE 68114

DEVERY, KIERAN MATTHEW, paper manufacturing company executive; b. Yonkers, N.Y., Dec. 18, 1937; m. Carol Ann Stefan, Nov. 23, 1963; children: Lora, Michael, Steven. BS in Econs., Villanova U., 1959; postgrad. exec. edn., Stanford U., 1986. Various sales positions St. Regis Paper Co., 1960-66; sales mgr. Continental Can Co., Phila., 1966-71; product mgr. Mead Papers, Dayton, Ohio, 1971-72, mktg. and sales mgr., 1973-76; mktg. mgr. Mead Paperboard Products, Dayton, 1976-80; pres. Kieffer Paper Mills, Brownstown, Ind., 1980—, also bd. dirs. Served with USAR, 1959-65. Mem. Am. Paper Inst. (exec. com. 1982—, recycled paperboard div., paper recycling com.). Republican. Roman Catholic. Avocations: golf, hunting. Office: Kieffer Paper Mills 1220 N Spring St Brownstown IN 47220

DE VINE, JOHN BERNARD, lawyer; b. Ann Arbor, Mich., Feb. 5, 1920; s. Frank Bernard and Elizabeth Catherine (Doherty) DeV.; A.B., U. Mich., 1941; J.D., Harvard U., 1948; m. Margaret Louise Burke, Apr. 23, 1949; children—Margaret Louise DeVine Mumby, Ann Elizabeth, Kathleen Kennedy, Susan Joan, John Kennedy. Bar: Mich. 1948. Ptnr. DeVine, DeVine, Kantor and Serr, Ann Arbor, 1948-84; ptnr. Miller, Canfield, Paddock and Stone, 1984—; asst. pros. atty. County of Washtenaw, Mich., 1948-52; dir. NBD, Ann Arbor, N.A.; mem. Detroit adv. bd. Mich. Consol. Gas Co. Founder NCCJ, Ann Arbor; chmn. Catholic Social Services, Washtenaw County, 1960-64; bd. dirs. Ann Arbor Devel. Council, Nat. Inst. for Burn Medicine. Served to lt. U.S. Navy, 1942-46. Mem. ABA, Mich. Bar Assn., Washtenaw County Bar Assn., Am. Acad. Hosp. Attys. (pres. 1981), Mich. Soc. Hosp. Attys. (past pres.), Mich. Hosp. Assn. Roman Catholic. Club: Barton Hills Country, Crystal Downs. Home: 2121 Wallingford Rd Ann Arbor MI 48104 Office: 300 National Bank & Trust Bldg Ann Arbor MI 48104

DEVINE, MICHAEL BUXTON, lawyer; b. Des Moines, Oct. 25, 1953; s. Cleatie Hiram, Jr., and Katherine Ann (Buxton) D. Student St. Peter's Coll., Oxford U., Eng., 1975; B.A. cum laude, St. Olaf Coll., 1976; M.P.A., Drake U., 1980, J.D., 1980; diploma in Advanced Internat. Legal Studies, U. Pacific extension Salzburg, Austria, 1986. Bar: Iowa 1980, U.S. Dist. Ct. (no. and so. dists.) Iowa 1980, U.S. Ct. Appeals (8th cir.) 1980, Nebr. 1985, Supreme Ct. 1985, Minn. 1986, D.C. 1986. N.Y. 1987; Assoc. Bump & Haesemeyer, P.C., Des Moines, 1980-85; sole practice, Des Moines, 1985—; legal intern Herbert Oppenheimer, Nathan & Vandyk, London, England, 1986. Scholar St. Olaf Coll., 1972-76; nat. alt. U.S. Presdl. Mgmt. Intern Program, 1980. Mem. ABA, Fed. Bar Assn. (chmn. state of Iowa SBA export assistance program 1983-85, treas. Iowa chpt. 1984-85, exec. com. 1985—), Iowa Bar Assn., Nebr. Bar Assn., Minn. Bar Assn., D.C. Bar Assn., Internat. Bar Assn., Polk County Bar Assn., Phi Alpha Theta, Pi Alpha Alpha, Phi Alpha Delta. Presbyterian.. Home and Office: 2611 40th St Des Moines IA 50310

DEVINE, MICHAEL J., state historic preservation agency director; b. Aurora, Ill., Jan. 5, 1945; s. Richard J. and Elayne Marie (Esser) D.; m. Maija Rhee, Nov. 7, 1970; children: Bret, Christopher, Mia, Lisa, T. Brian. BA, Loras Coll., Dubuque, Iowa, 1967; MA, Ohio State U., 1968, PhD, 1974. Vol. Peace Corps, 1969-70; from instr. to asst. prof. history Ohio U., Athens, 1972-74; program adminstr. Ohio Hist. Soc., Columbus, 1974-77, asst. dir., 1977-79; exec. dir. Cin. Consortium Colls., 1979-82; dep. dir. Hist. St. Mary's (Md.) City, 1982-85; dir. State of Ill. Hist. Preservation Agy., Springfield, 1985—; adj. lectr. history Xavier U., Cin., 1979-82; sr. lectr. Fulbright Commn., Argentina, 1983. Author: John W. Foster, 1981; editor: (with others) Ohio: The Next 25 Years, 1978. Mem. St. Mary's County Library Planning Commn., 1984-85; sec. Abraham Lincoln Assn., Springfield, 1985—; trustee Cin Fire Mus., 1980-82. Am. Philos. Soc. grantee, 1978, NEH fellow, 1980. Mem. Am. Hist. Assn., Am. Assn. State and Local History, Ill. State Hist. Soc. (exec. bd. dirs. 1985—). Avocation: painting. Home: 252 Maple Grove Springfield IL 62707 Office: Ill Hist Preservation Agy Old State Capitol Springfield IL 62701-1507

DEVINEY, MARVIN LEE, JR., chemical company research scientist, administrator; b. Kingsville, Tex., Dec. 5, 1929; s. Marvin Lee and Esther Lee (Gambrell) D.; B.S. in Chemistry and Math., S.W. Tex. State U., San Marcos, 1949; M.A. in Phys. Chemistry, U. Tex. at Austin, 1952, Ph.D. in Phys. Chemistry, 1956; cert. profl. chemist; m. Marie Carole Massey, June 7, 1975; children—Marvin Lee III, John H., Ann-Marie K. Devel. chemist Celanese Chem. Co., Bishop, Tex., 1956-58; research chemist Shell Chem. Co., Deer Park, Tex., 1958-66; sr. scientist, head group phys. and radiochemistry Ashland Chem. Co., Houston, 1966-68, mgr. sect. phys. and analytical chemistry, 1968-71, mgr. sect. phys. chemistry div. research and devel., Columbus, Ohio, 1971-78, research assoc., supr. applied surface chemistry, Ashland Ventures Research and Devel., 1978-84, supr. electron microscopy, advanced aerospace composites, govt. contracts, 1984—; adj. prof. U. Tex., San Antonio, 1973-75. Mem. sci. adv. bd. Am. Petroleum Inst. Research Project 60, 1968-74. Mem. edn. adv. com. Columbus Tech. Inst., 1974-84, Central Ohio Tech. Coll., 1975-82. Served to lt. col., USAR. Humble Oil Research fellow, 1954. Fellow Am. Inst. Chemists (pres. Ohio Inst. 1978-82, nat. com. mem. 1985—); mem. Ohio, Tex. acads. scis., Am. Def. Preparedness Assn., Electron Microscopy Soc. Am., Materials Research Soc., SAMPE Composite Soc., N.Am. Catalysis Soc., Am. Soc. Composites, Am. Chem. Soc. (chmn. chpt. exec. bd. 1969, bus. mgr. nat. div. Petroleum Chemistry, 1986—, Best Paper award rubber div. 1967, 70, Hon. Mention awards 1968, 69, 73; symposia co-chmn., co-editor books on catalysis-surface chemistry 1985, carbon-graphite chemistry 1975), Engr.'s Council Houston (sr. councilor 1970-71), Sigma Xi, Phi Lambda Upsilon, Alpha Chi, Sigma Pi Sigma. Co-author govt. research contract reports; contbr. numerous articles to profl. jours.; patentee in field. Home: 6810 Hayhurst Worthington OH 43085 Office: Box 2219 Columbus OH 43216

DEVISÉ, PIERRE ROMAIN, city planner, educator; b. Brussels, Belgium, July 27, 1924; came to U.S., 1935, naturalized, 1958; s. Victor Pierre and Madeleine (Cupers) deV.; m. Margaret Ahern, Nov. 17, 1978; children: Peter Charles, Daniel Romain. B.A., U. Chgo., 1945, M.A., 1958; Ph.D., U. Ill., 1985. Chancellor Belgian Consul, Chgo., 1945-47; comml. attache Belgian Consul, 1947-56, Belgian Consulate Gen., Chgo.; planning dir. Hyde Park-Kenwood Conf., 1956-57; research planner Northeastern Ill. Planning Commn., 1958-60; sr. planner Chgo. City Planning Dept., 1961-63; asst. dir. Hosp. Planning Council for Met. Chgo., 1964-70, Ill. Regional Med. Program, 1971-73; prof. urban scis. U. Ill., 1973-81; prof. pub. adminstrn. Roosevelt U., Chgo., 1982—; Lectr. De Paul U., 1962—; vis. lectr. U. Mich., 1966, U. Hawaii, 1968, U. Ill., 1969, 70, U. Iowa, 1971, U. Chgo., 1972; prin. investigator Chgo. Regional Hosp. Study, 1966—; exec. dir. Chgo. Commn. to Study Conv. Week Disorders, 1968-70; cons. Chgo. Commn. on Human Relations, 1966—, Chgo. Model Cities Program, 1968—, Cook County Council Govts., 1968—, Comprehensive Health Planning, Inc., 1971—; Census Bur., 1973—, U.S. Senate Health Subcom., 1974, HEW, 1975—, Ho. Ways and Means Com., 1975—, Senate Banking Com., 1976—. Author: monographs including Suburban Factbook, 1960, Social Geography of Metropolitan Chicago, 1960, Chicago's People, Jobs and Homes, 1963, Chicago's Widening Color Gap, 1967, Chicago's Apartheid Hospital System, 1968, Chicago, 1971, Ready for Another Fire, 1971, Misused and Misplaced Hospitals and Doctors, 1973, Chicago's Future, 1976, Chicago: Transformations of an Urban System, 1976, Chicago in the Year 2000, 1978; Descent From the Summit, 1985. Mem. Am. Statist. Assn., Chgo. Assn. Commerce and Industry, Am. Soc. Pub. Adminstrn., Am. Pub. Health Assn., Assn. Am. Geographers, Nat. Council Geog. Edn., Planned Parenthood Assn. Chgo., Old Town Boys Club. Club: City (Chgo.). Home: 1712 W Henderson Chicago IL 60657 Office: Roosevelt U 430 S Michigan Ave Chicago IL 60605

DEVITT, JOHN MARTIN, financial institution executive; b. L.I., N.Y., May 27, 1937; s. Patrick Simeon and Nora Mary (O'Sullivan) D.; m. Mary Helen Lynch, Aug. 6, 1960; children: Mary E., John M, Maureen A., Timothy P., Erin P., Margaret M., Jane E. BS in Mktg. Mgmt., U. Scranton, 1960; MA in Mgmt., Webster U., 1979, MA in Computer Data Mgmt., 1984. Commd. 2d. lt. U.S. Army, 1960, advanced through grades to lt. col., 1975; project analyst U.S. Army, Ft. Benning, Ga., 1974-78; chief exec. officer U.S. Army, Ft. Sheridan, Ill., 1978-80, chief tng. and devel., 1980-82, chief tng. officer, 1982-85, ret., 1985; chief adminstrv. officer Olympic Fed., Berwyn, Ill., 1986—; cons. Corson Research, Ft. Wayne, Ind., 1985-86. Decorated Legion of Merit, Bronze Star with four oak leaf clusters, Air medal with two oak leaf clusters, Combat Inf. badge. Mem. Assoc. Employers of Ill., Nat. Fedn. Inter Scholastic Officials, Highland Park/Deerfield Sch. Bd. Avocations: reading, high sch. football ofcl. Home: 912 Talbot Rd Lake Bluff IL 60044 Office: Olympic Federal 6201 W Cermak Rd Berwyn IL 60402

DEVOL, THOMAS IRVING, psychologist; b. Wooster, Ohio, Sept. 18, 1944; s. William Thomas and Gertrude E. (Greene) DeV.; m. Letty Vosotros, July 23, 1983; children: DeAnn, Marc, Tommy. BS, Drury Coll., 1969; MA, U. Mo., 1971, PhD, 1979. Lic. psychologist, Mo. Trainee Cleve. Psychiat. Inst., 1980-83; vis. prof. U. S.E. Philippines, Davao, 1983-84; pvt. practice psychology Counseling and Missionary Consultation Assoc., Inc., Springfield, Mo., 1984—; assoc. pastor Mintel/Foursquare Gospel Ch., Davao, 1984. Mem. Am. Psychol. Assn. Home: Rt 1 Box 148 Brighton MO 65617

DEVORE, MICHAEL A., real estate publishing company executive; b. Marion, Ind., Sept. 3, 1951; s. Earl Frederick DeVore and Martha Joan (Jordan) Stead. BA in Econs., U. Wis., Milw., 1979. Cert. real estate broker. Rental counselor Rent Search, Milw., 1978-80; pres. Rent Pro Corp., Milw., 1980—. Avocations: golf, reading, chess, swimming, econ. polit. analysis. Office: Rent Pro Corp 3306 S 27th St Milwaukee WI 53215

DE VRIES, DEAN ELDEN, pastor; b. Chgo., May 9, 1958; s. Robert Edwin and June Elaine De Vries; m. Elaine Patrice Paton, Apr. 20, 1985—. BA in Theology, Moody Bible Inst., 1981; BS in Psychology, Ill. State U., 1983. Assoc. pastor Evang. Free Ch., Bloomington, Ill., 1979—; area Christian edn. coordinator Evang. Free Ch. of Am., 1984-86. Republican. Avocations: tennis, history. Office: Evang Free Ch 1910 E Lincoln Bloomington IL 61701

DEVRIES, GERRIT HENRY, optometrist; b. Chgo., Sept. 16, 1952; s. Gerrit and Leona (Ebbens) DeV.; m. Dianne Sue Kiekover, Aug. 10, 1974; children—Jennifer Sue, Ryan Gerrit. Student Calvin Coll., 1970-73. BS, Calvin Coll., 1973; OD, Ill. Coll. Optometry, Chgo., 1977. Assoc. Dr. Henry R. DeBoer, Lansing, Ill., 1977-79; ptnr. Drs. Sayre & DeVries, DeMotte, Ind., 1979-83; pres. Dr. Gerrit H. DeVries, Optometrist, DeMotte, Ind., 1984—. Pres., DeMotte Park Bd., 1980-81; mem. DeMotte Bd. Zoning Appeals, 1983—; pres. DeMotte Christian Sch. PTA, 1984-85, mem. sch. bd., 1984—, sec. sch. bd., 1985-86, pres. sch. bd. 1986-87. Mem. Am. Optometric Assn., Ind. Optometric Assn., Northwest Ind. Optometric Soc. (pres. 1986-87), Demotte C. of C.(treas. 1986—, pres. 1987) Beta Sigma Kappa. Republican. Christian Reformed. Avocations: Camping, carpentry. Home: 617 Cedar St NW DeMotte IN 46310 Office: 329 N Halleck St PO Box 154 DeMotte IN 46310

DEVRIES, GLENN FREDRICK, podiatrist; b. Waupun, Wis., Feb. 27, 1952; s. George and Julia Marie (Minnema) DeV.; m. Patricia Joan Van der Kamp, Aug. 11, 1973; children: Jason, Erin, Michael. BA, Trinity Christian Coll., 1974; D of Podiatric Medicine, Ill. Coll. Podiatric Medicine, Chgo., 1980. Diplomat Am. Bd. Podiatric Surgens. Practice podiatric medicine Waupun, 1981—. Fellow Am. Coll. Foot Surgeons. Mem. Christian Reformed Ch. Avocation: tropical fish. Home: 717 Beekman St Waupun WI 53963 Office: 608 Fern St Waupun WI 53963-1018

DEVRIES, MARK HENRY, hospital executive; b. Grand Rapids, Mich., Mar. 22, 1939; s. Henry M. and Anne (Boersema) D.; m. Joyce Ann Huizingh, Oct. 28, 1965; children: Martha A., Joel M., Jonathan E. Student, Calvin Coll., 1957-59; AS in Bus., Davenport Coll., 1961. Mgr. zone acctg. White Consol., Grand Rapids, 1965-67; data processing coordinator Blodgett Meml. Med. Ctr., Grand Rapids, 1967-78; mgr. patient acctg. Blodgett Hosp., Grand Rapids, 1978-80, dir. data processing, 1980—. Treas. Cascade Christian Reformed Ch., Grand Rapids, 1982; bd. dirs. Christian Learning Ctr., Grand Rapids, 1983-86; mem. Calvin Coll. Alumni Players, Grand Rapids. Served with U.S. Army, 1962-64. Fellow Data Processing Mgmt. Assn., Lake Mich. Users Group. Republican. Home: 6950 Cimarron Dr SE Grand Rapids MI 49506 Office: Blodgett Hosp 1840 Wealthy St SE Grand Rapids MI 49506

DEVRIES, NICHOLAS, neuroradiologist; b. Orange City, Iowa, June 15, 1953; s. George Jr. and Kathleen June (Wielenya) deV. BA summa cum laude, Northwestern Coll., Orange City, Iowa, 1975; MD, U. Iowa, 1979. Diplomate Am. Bd. Internal Medicine, Am. Bd. Radiology. Intern U. Utah Med. Ctr. and Affiliated Hosps., 1979-80; resident in internal medicine U. Utah Hosp. and Affiliated Clinics, Salt Lake City, 1979-82; resident in radiology U. Utah Med. Ctr., Salt Lake City, 1982-85; fellow in neuroradiology N.Y. State U.—Upstate Med. Ctr., Syracuse, 1985-86; neuroradiologist Mercy Hosp. Med. Ctr. Dept. Radiology, Des Moines, 1986—. Contbr. articles to profl. jours. Mem. health legis. com. Iowa Dem. Com., Des Moines, 1987. NIH Research Assistantship grantee, 1974. Mem. ACP, Radiol. Soc. N.Am., Am. Soc. Head and Neck Radiologists, Sigma Tau. Mem. Reformed Ch. Am. Club: Bohemian (Des Moines). Avocations: hist. fiction, skiing, running, piano, jazz music. Office: Mercy Hospital Medical Ctr Dept Radiology Sixth & University Des Moines IA 50314

DEW, RANDALL KEITH, ruminant nutritionist; b. Aledo, Ill., Nov. 27, 1954; s. Keith Erskine and Dorothy Virgene (Anderson) D.; m. Nancy Creviston, Sept. 3, 1977. B.S. in Animal Sci., Western Ill. U., 1976; M.S. in Animal Sci., Mont. State U., 1981; postgrad. in ruminant nutrition U. Ky., 1985. Nutrition counselor Moorman Mfg. Co., Quincy, Ill., 1976-79; research asst. Mont. State U., 1979-81; beef projects mgr. Internat. Multifoods, Inc., Mpls., 1981. Mem. Am. Soc. Animal Sci. (cert.), Dairy Sci. Assn., Sigma Xi, Alpha Gamma Sigma, Gamma Sigma Delta. Republican.

DE WAART, EDO, conductor; b. Amsterdam, Netherlands, June 1, 1941. Grad. with honors for oboe, Amsterdam Conservatoire, 1962. Oboist, Concertgebouw Orch., Amsterdam, 1963-64, asst. condr., 1966-67; asst. to Leonard Bernstein, N.Y. Philharm., 1965-66; condr. Rotterdam (Netherlands) Philharm., 1967-79, also prin. condr., music dir.; founding condr. Netherlands Wind Ensemble, 1967-71; condr., music dir., San Francisco Symphony Orch., 1977-85; music dir. Minn. Orch., 1986—; guest condr., Amsterdam Concertgebouw, Berlin Philharm., Boston Symphony, Chgo. Symphony, London Symphony, Cleve. Orch., N.Y. Philharm., Phila. Orch.; condr.: new prodn. Lohengrin, Beyreuth Festival, summer 1979; new prodn. Wagner's Ring, San Francisco Opera, 1985; rec. artist, Philips Records, rec. with major European orchs. including, New Philharmonia, English Chamber Orch., Royal Philharmonic Orch., Dresden State Orch. Recipient 1st prize Metropoulos Competition, N.Y.C., 1964. Office: Minnesota Orch 1111 Nicollet Mall Minneapolis MN 55403 Address: Essenlaan 68,, 3016 Rotterdam Netherlands

DEWALD, HOWARD DEAN, chemistry educator and researcher; b. Casper, Wyo., Aug. 11, 1958; s. Derold Dean and Maryann (Schrantz) D.; m. Elaine Frances Saulinskas, June 7, 1986. BS, U. Wyo., 1980; PhD, N.Mex. State U., 1984. Postdoctoral asst. U. Cin., 1984-86; asst. prof. chemistry Ohio U., Athens, 1986—. Author: History of Circle K International, 1980; contbr. numerous articles to profl. jours. Mem. Am. Chem. Soc., Soc. For Electroanalytical Chemistry, Sigma Xi. Democrat. Ecumenical. Club: Circle K Internat. (Wyo. and N.Mex.) (internat. v.p. 1979-80, pres.'s award 1980). Lodge: Kiwanis (pres. Las Cruces, N.Mex. 1983-84, Disting. Club Pres. award 1985). Avocations: reading, U.S. history, swimming, philately, numismatics.

DEWALD, RONALD L., physician, educator; b. Aurora, Ill., Oct. 4, 1934; s. Lee H. and Elsie (Kellen) DeW.; B.S., U. Ill., 1955, M.D., 1959; m. Mary Lee Johnstone, July 21, 1956; children—Ann Elise, Lee Fraser, Christopher James, Ronald Lee. Intern, Presbyn. St. Lukes Hosp., Chgo., 1959-60; resident U. Ill. Hosp., Chgo., 1960-62, 64-65; asst. prof. orthopaedic surgery, 1965-67, asso. prof., 1967-71; prof., chmn. dept., Stritch Sch. Medicine Loyola at Chgo., 1972-73; prof. Rush Med. Coll., Chgo., 1973—. Cons. surgeon Ill. Div. Services for Crippled Children, 1967—, Ill. Childrens Hosp. Sch., Chgo., 1968-84, Holy Family Hosp., Des Plaines, 1972-78, Hines (Ill.) VA Hosp., 1972—; asso. surgeon Shriners Hosp. for Crippled Children, Chgo., 1972—. Served to capt. M.C., AUS, 1962-64. Diplomate Am. Bd. Orthopaedic Surgery (bd. examiners 1973—). Fellow A.C.S.; mem. A.M.A. (Hektoen Silver medal 1971), Chgo., Ill. med. socs., Chgo., Clin. orthopaedic socs., Scoliosis Research Soc. (founding, dir.), Am. Acad. Orthopadic Surgeons (regional admissions chmn. 1975—), Ill. Orthopaedic Assn., Am. Orthopaedic Assn. Contbr. articles to profl. jours. Office: 1725 Harrison St Chicago IL 60612

DEWALT, MARK DOUGLAS, architect; b. Pitts., Aug. 18, 1951; s. Warren Richard and Jean Louise (Crissman) D.; m. Gail Sue Stack, May 13, 1978; children: Jessica Ellen, Kara Anne. Student, Milliken U., 1969-72, U. Ill., Champaign, 1972-73; BArch, U. Ill., Chgo., 1977. Registered architect, Ill. Intern Hinds, Schroeder & Whitaker, Chgo., 1976-77; architect Metz, Train & Youngren, Chgo., 1977-82; architect, prin. Jack Train Assocs., Chgo., 1982—; vis. design critic U. Ill., Chgo., 1977-86; mem. restoration com. Frank Lloyd Wright Home Found., Oak Park, Ill., 1978-80. Mem. AIA. Democrat. Methodist. Club: University (Chgo.). Home: 217 Randolph Oak Park IL 60302 Office: Jack Train Assocs 111 W Washington Suite 2030 Chicago IL 60601

DEWANE, JOHN RICHARD, manufacturing company executive; b. Cooperstown, Wis., Mar. 4, 1934; s. Clarence John and Arvilla Anne (Gannon) D.; B.S.M.E., U. Wis., 1957; M.B.A., U. Minn., 1973; m. Judith Anne Arnold, Mar. 17, 1974; 1 dau., Kelly Susanne. Dir. mktg. planning Honeywell, Inc., Washington, 1974-76, dir. mktg., Mpls., 1976-78, v.p. service engring., 1979-81, v.p. bus. devel., 1981-82, v.p., gen. mgr., 1982—; mem. NASA Aeronautics Adv. Com. Vice chmn. Community Long-Range Improvement Com., Maple Grove, Minn., 1980-81, chmn. Econ. Devel. Commn., 1982—; mem. Polit. Action com., Honeywell, 1979-83; mem. U. Wis. Alumni Adv. Council; mem. tech. adv. com. on transp. equipment U.S. Dept. Commerce. Served with USN, 1957-60. Navy scholar, 1952-57. Lic. pvt. pilot. Mem. Assn. Unmanned Vehicles, U.S. Navy League, Air Force Assn., Assn. U.S. Army, Am. Def. Preparedness Assn., Aircraft Owners and Pilots Assn., Gen. Aviation Mfrs. Assn. (dir. 1983—, chmn. forecasting com., chmn. airport ops. com.). Mpls. C. of C. (aviation com. 1980—). Office: 5775 Wayzata Blvd Minneapolis MN 55440

DEWAR, NORMAN ELLISON, chemical company executive; b. Rochester, N.Y., Nov. 14, 1930; s. Donald C. and Agnes M. (McLean) D.; m. Joan E. Lehman, Jan. 2, 1955; children: Harold, Joyce, Carol. BS in Chemistry, Syracuse U., 1952; MS in Microbiology, Purdue U., 1955, PhD in Microbiology, 1959. Group leader microbiology Vestal Labs div. Chemed Corp., St. Louis, 1959-60, sect. leader microbiology and product devel. solutions, 1960-62, dir. research, 1962-69, v.p., dir. research, 1969-76, v.p., tech. dir., 1976-87; v.p. ops. DuBois Chems. div. Chemed Corp., Cin., 1987—; mem. antimicrobial program adv. com. EPA. Fellow NIH, AEC, Royal Soc. Health (Eng.); mem. Chem. Spltys. Mfrs. Assn. (chmn. disinfectant sanitizers div. 1971-72), Am. Chem. Soc., Soc. Indsl. Microbiology (nat. counselor Mo. br. 1970-74), Am. Soc. Microbiology, ASTM, Sigma Xi, Phi Lambda Upsilon. Office: DuBois Chems div Chemed Corp 1100 DuBois Tower Cincinnati OH 45202

DEWEES, JAMES H., retail company executive; b. 1933. Student, U. Iowa. Store mgr., sales mgr. Super Value Stores, Eden Prairie, Minn., 1960-72; asst. gen. mgr., then pres., chief exec. officer United Foods Inc., Bells, Tenn., 1972-82; exec. v.p., pres. Roundy's Inc. (div. United Foods Inc.), Wauwatosa, Wis., 1982-84; pres., chief operating officer Godfrey Co., Waukesha, Wis., 1984—. Office: Godfrey Co 1200 W Sunset Dr Waukesha WI 53186 *

DEWEES, LAURA DECOU, art therapist, consultant; b. Phila., July 15, 1959; d. Samuel Coleman III and Ann (Denworth) DeCou; m. Lawrence Allen Dewees, Aug. 10, 1985. BA in Psychology, Earlham Coll., 1981; MA in Expressive Therapies, Lesley Grad. Sch., 1983. Registered art therapist. Intern in expressive therapy Cen. Hosp., Somerville, Mass., 1981-82, intern, tchr. presch. unit, 1982-83; asst. Lesley Grad. Sch., Cambridge, Mass., 1981-83; art therapist Emerson A. North Hosp., Cin., 1984—; cons. Eating Disorder Recovery Ctr., Cin., 1987—; lectr. Music Therapy Assn., Adoptive Parent Support Group, Shriners Burn Inst.; speaker in field. Mem. Am. Art Therapy Assn. (credentialed), Buckeye Art Therapy Assn. Quaker. Avocations: hockey, lacrosse, drawing, photography, tennis. Office: Emerson A North Hosp 5642 Hamilton Ave Cincinnati OH 45224

DEWEY, PATRICK RONALD, librarian; b. Pontiac, Mich., Mar. 4, 1949; s. Wilbur Joseph and Hazel (Stuart) D. A.A., Oakland Community Coll., 1971; B.S. in Psychology, Oakland U., 1971; postgrad. Wayne State U., 1973. Paraprofl. II, Oakland Community Coll., Bloomfield Hills, Mich., 1971-74; editorial librarian Playboy Enterprises, Inc., Chgo., 1974-75; reference librarian Eckhart Park Library, Chgo., 1975-76, Toman Library, Chgo., 1976-78; head librarian North Austin Library, Chgo., 1978-81, North-Pulaski Library, Chgo., 1981-84; adminstrv. librarian Maywood Pub. Library, 1984—; lectr. in field. Author: Public Access Microcomputers: A Handbook for Librarians, 1984, Essential Guide to Bulletin Board Systems, 1987, 101 Software Packages to Use in Your Library; Essential Guide to the Library Apple Applications, 1987; editor Public Computing; columnist Wilson Library Bull., 1984-86, Library Software Rev., Small Computers in Libraries; contbr. articles to profl. jours. Recipient Career Service award, Chgo. Pub. Library, 1983; Chgo. Pub. Library grantee, 1981. Mem. Pub. Library Assn. (mem. com. task force on microcomputers 1982-85). Office: Maywood Pub Library 121 S 5th Ave Maywood IL 60153

DEWEY, RONALD DUANE, sculptor, foundry owner; b. Ludington, Mich., Nov. 7, 1934; s. Daniel Volney and Georgia Alice (Grey) D.; m. Jeannene Beebe, Sept. 28, 1955 (div. Dec. 1968); children: Laura, Pamela, Gregory. BS, Western Mich. U., 1956; BFA, U. Wash., 1972. Product devel. engr. Carrom Industries, Ludington, 1957-60; dir. research and devel. Joerns Furniture Co., Stevens Point, Wis., 1960-67; dir. graphics and sales promotion Educators dev. E.H. Hallserman, Tacoma, 1967-70; designer, engr. Am. Seating Co., Grand Rapids, Mich., 1970-72; owner, operator The Studio Foundry, Cleve., 1973—; products design cons. Affiliated Hosp. Products, St. Louis, 1972-75; instr. sculpture Cleve. Inst. Art, 1978-80; lectr. and workshop giver in field. One man shows include Wentworths Gallery, Rocky River, Ohio, 1971; group shows include Lake Erie Coll., 1978, Bonfoys on the Sq., 1978, Sandusky Cultural Ctr., 1980, Massillon Mus., 1981, Cleve. Inst. Art, 1978-80, Mt. Sinai Invitational Show, 1982; outdoor sculptures include Ashtabula (Ohio) Art Ctr., Sisters of Notre Dame, Toledo; inventor hospital bed safety side, hospital bed, electric hospital bed, manual hospital bed. Mem. jury Ohio Arts Council, Columbus, 1978; pres. New Orgn. Visual Arts, Cleve., 1976-77. Recipient Readership award Archtl. Record, 1969, 3M Print Job of Yr., 1969. Mem. Internat. Sculpture Soc. Office: The Studio Foundry 1001 Old River Rd Cleveland OH 44113

DEWINE, RICHARD MICHAEL, congressman, lawyer; b. Springfield, Ohio, Jan. 5, 1947; s. Richard and Jean DeWine; m. Frances Struewing, June 3, 1967; children—Patrick, Jill, Rebecca, John, Brian, Alice, Mark. B.S. in Edn., Miami U., Oxford, Ohio, 1969; J.D., Ohio No. U., 1972. Bar: Ohio 1972, U.S. Supreme Ct. 1977. Asst. pros. atty. Greene County, Xenia, Ohio,

1973-75, pros. atty., 1977-80; mem. Ohio Senate, 1981-82, 99th Congress from 7th Ohio dist., Washington, 1983—; ptnr. DeWine, Rose, Haller & Sidell, Xenia. Republican. Roman Catholic. Home: 2587 Conley Rd Cedarville OH 45314 Office: 1705 Longworth Office Bldg Washington DC 20515

DEWINE, SUE, communications educator; b. Xenia, Ohio, June 27, 1944; s. Gilbert and Eva (Kepley) Ogilvie; m. Mike DeWine, Aug. 20, 1966; children: Leigh Anne, James Gilbert. BA, Miami U., Oxford, Ohio, 1966, MA, 1967; PhD, Ind. U., 1975. Teaching asst. Miami U., 1966-67; instr. Miami U., Middletown, Ohio, 1967-72, sr. instr., 1972-75; teaching assoc. Ind. U., Bloomington, 1975-77; asst. prof. communications Ohio U., Athens, 1977-80, assoc. prof., 1980-85, prof., 1985—; pres. Communications Cons., Athens, 1972—; mem. and office holder numerous coms. with Ohio U.; cons. in field. Author: (with Jackie Rumbly) Ten Designs for Integration in Experience Based Learning Environments, 1976, (with Lynn Phelps) Interpersonal Communication Journal, 1976, (with Tom Tortoriollo and Steve Blatt) Instructor's Manual: Communication in the Organization: An Applied Approach, 1978, (with others) Women in Organizations, 1983; editor Ohio Speech Jour., 1980-82; contbr. numerous articles to profl. jours. Co-chmn. Athens Taxpayers for a Service Orientated Budget; mem. exec. bd. PTO: asst. leader Girl Scouts U.S., Athens; mem. Civitan. Named Outstanding Tchr., Ind. U., 1977, Outstanding Grad. Faculty Mem., 1986; Ohio U. grantee, 1984. Mem. Internat. Communication Assn. (exec. bd. 1980-84, chmn. orgnl. communication div. 1984—), Speech Communication Assn. (exec. bd. 1980-84), Am. Soc. Tng. and Devel. (chpt. advisor), Cen. States Speech Assn., Ohio Speech Communication Assn., Am. Psychology Assn., Acad. Mgmt., LWV. Avocation: playing piano. Home: 8 York Dr Athens OH 45701 Office: Ohio U Sch Interpersonal Communication Kantner Hall Athens OH 45701

DEWITT, ARNIE MATTHEW, manager information systems; b. Stevens Point, Wis., Apr. 27, 1954; s. Marvin Arnold and Gertrude (Collum) DeW.; m. Chris Margaret Rusch, Sept. 16, 1978; children: Theresa, Katrina. BS in Computer Sci. and Math., U. Wis., Eau Claire, 1981. Programmer aide Cray research, Chippewa Falls, Wis., 1980-81, programmer, analyst, 1981-83, systems analyst, 1983-85, mgr. info. systems, 1985—. Served with USAF, 1973-77. Mem. Am. Prodn. and Inventory Control Soc., Kappa Mu Epsilon, Sigma Gamma Zeta I. Home: Route 7 Box 461-C6 Chippewa Falls WI 54729 Office: Cray Research Inc 913 First Ave Chippewa Falls WI 54729

DE WITT, JESSE R., clergyman; b. Detroit, Dec. 5, 1918; s. Jesse A. and Bessie G. (Mainzinger) DeW.; m. Annamary Horner, Apr. 19, 1941; children: Donna Lee (Mrs. William Wegryn), Darla Jean (Mrs. William Inman). B.A., Wayne State U., 1948; B.D., Garrett Theol. Sem., 1948; D.D., Adrian Coll., 1965, Northland Coll., 1976, Wiley Coll., 1981; H.H.D. (hon.), North Central Coll., 1977. Ordained deacon, received in full membership Methodist Ch. (Detroit conf.), 1945, ordained elder, 1948; student pastor 1944-46; minister Aldersgate Ch., Detroit, 1946, Faith Ch., Oak Park, Mich., 1952-58; exec. sec. Detroit Conf. Bd. Missions, 1958-67; dist. supt. Detroit Conf. Bd. Missions (West dist.), 1967-70; asst. gen. sec. sect. ch. extension Nat. Bd. Missions, 1970-72; bishop United Meth. Ch.; resident bishop United Meth. Ch. (Wis. area), 1972-80; bishop United Meth. Ch. (Chgo. area), 1980—; del. gen. conf. Meth. Ch., 1964, 66, 68, 70, 72, 76; past epis. rep. Commn. on Status and Role Women; epis. rep. Consultation on Ch. Union, Bd. Ch. and Society (other coms. and task forces); pres. nat. div. Bd. Global Ministries, 1976-80, pres., 1980—; past pres. North Central jurisdiction Coll. Bishops; chmn. pastoral concerns com. Council Bishops, United Meth. Ch. Trustee North Central Coll., Naperville, Ill., Garrett Evang. Sem.; bd. dirs. No. Ill. Conf., Meth. Youth Services, Marcy-Newberry Assn., United Meth. Homes and Services, Lake Bluff-Chgo. Homes for Children. Address: No Ill Conf United Meth Ch 77 W Washington St Suite 1806 Chicago IL 60602 *

DEWITT, ROBERT DUANE, electrical engineer; b. Hamden, Conn., Sept. 22, 1930; s. Russell Alan and Margaret (Griffiths) DeW.; m. Janet Lee McConaghey, Feb. 7, 1959; children: Brian Thomas, David Alan, Timothy Robert. BSEE, U. Pa., 1953; postgrad., U. Pitts., 1956-59. Application engr. Elliot Co., Pitts., 1953-61, Reliance Electric Co., Cleve., 1961-73; computer systems engr. Reliance Electric Co., Ann Arbor, Mich., 1973-76; control engr., group mgr. Reliance Electric Co., Cleve., 1976-81; div. mgr. elec. engring. Foil div. Gould Inc., Eastlake, Ohio, 1981—. Contbr. articles to profl. jours. Served to sgt. U.S. Army, 1954-56. Mem. IEEE. Republican. Presbyterian. Home: 1167 Roland Rd Lyndhurst OH 44124 Office: Foil div Gould Inc 35129 Curtis Blvd Eastlake OH 44094

DEWITT, RONALD LEE, military officer; b. Des Moines, Nov. 20, 1947; s. James Alfred and Virginia Marie (Argo) DeW.; m. Patricia Taylor, Aug. 2, 1969; children: Courtney Elyse, Suzanne Nicole, Nathan Wesley. BBA, U. Iowa, 1970; MBA, U. Mo., 1974. CPA, Iowa. Commd. 2d lt. USAF, 1970, advanced through grades to lt. col., 1987; missile launch control officer Minuteman Missiles, Whiteman AFB, N.M., 1970-74; auditor A.F. Audit Agy., Incirlik, Turkey, 1976-78, Robins AFB, Ga., 1975-76; mgmt. analyst Holloman AFB, Alamogordo, N.Mex., 1978-79, budget officer, 1979-81; budget officer Hdqrs. Tactical Air Command, Langley AFB, Va., 1981-84; fin. plans and programs officer Hdqrs. JUSMMAT, Ankara, Turkey, 1984-86; base comptroller McConnell AFB, Wichita, Kans., 1986—. Coordinator Boy Scouts, Holloman AFB, 1980-81, coordinator Tiger cub, Ankara, 1984, dist. commr., Ankara, 1985-86. Named Budget Officer of Yr., 1981. Mem. Am. Inst. CPA's, Iowa Soc. CPA's, Am. Soc. Mil. Comptrollers (disting. performance for budgeting award). Republican. Methodist. Avocations: reading, chess, stamp collecting, music, racquetball. Home: 2808 Foulois Dr Wichita KS 67210-1740 Office: 384 BMW/AC McConnell AFB KS 67221-5000

DEWOLFE, ALAN S(TEYAART), psychology educator, researcher, consultant; b. Madanapelle, India, Aug. 12, 1930; came to U.S., 1933; s. Martin Arend and Ruth (Scudder) D.; m. Ruthanne Katherine Sobota, Aug. 24, 1952 (div.); children: Kyle Arend, Hillary Stuart, Elena Maria. BA, Oberlin Coll., 1952; MS, Northwestern U., 1958, PhD, 1960. Lic. psychologist, Ill., Pa. Staff psychologist VA Hosp., Hines, Ill., 1960-63; sr. psychologist Inst. Pa. Hosp., Phila., 1963-65; research psychologist VA Hosp., Downey, Ill., 1965-74; prof. psychology Loyola U., Chgo., 1974—; mem. exec. com. VA Coop. Research Project, 1960-64; cons. Loeb Ctr., Montefiore Hosp., N.Y.C., 1968-73, Ednl. Devel. Program Lake Forest Coll., 1975-78, Legal Assistance Found., 1975-79, clin. psychology tng. program Ill. State Psychiat. Inst., 1979-86, VA Med. Ctr., North Chicago, 1980—; research cons. U.S. Commn. Civil Rights, Midwestern Regional Office, 1979-81; spl. cons. on creativity L.I. Poetry Jour., 1973-76. Editorial cons. Jour. Abnormal Psychology, 1973—, Jour. Cons. and Clin. Psychology, 1975-81; contbr. numerous sci. articles profl. jours. Trustee Evanston Meeting of Friends, 1975-85, mem. coordinating com. Midwest region Am. Friends Service Com., 1986—. Served to cpl. M.C., U.S. Army, 1953-55. Hall-Mercer Found. grantee, 1963-64, NIMH grantee, 1964-68; VA Cen. Office grantee, 1966-74. Mem. Am. Psychol. Assn., Sigma Xi. Mem. Soc. of Friends. Home: 720A Hinman 3-N Evanston IL 60202 Office: Loyola U Psychology Dept Chicago IL 60626

DEWOLFE, GEORGE FULTON, lawyer; b. Oak Park, Ill., Jan. 22, 1949; s. John Chauncey and Dorothy Sinclair (Fulton) DeW. A.B., Yale U., 1971; LL.B., U. Toronto, Ont., Can., 1974. Bar: Ill. 1975, U.S. Dist. Ct. (no. dist.) Ill. 1975, U.S. Dist. Ct. (ea dist.) Wis. 1976, U.S. Ct. Appeals (7th cir.) 1980, N.Y. 1983, U.S. Supreme Ct. 1985. Assoc. DeWolfe, Poynton & Stevens, Chgo., 1975-80, ptnr., 1980—; legal adviser Brit. Consulate Gen., Chgo., 1984—; gen. counsel Suburban Hosp., Hinsdale, Ill., 1984—; adj. prof. law DePaul U., 1985—; mem. adv. bd. Health Law Inst., DePaul U., 1986—. Assoc. editor U. Toronto Faculty of Law Rev., 1973-74, Hospital Law, 1986—. Bd. dirs., sec. St. Leonard's House of Episc. Diocese of Chgo., 1975-83; mem. Chgo. Area AIDS Task Force, 1987—. Mem. ABA, Ill. Bar Assn., Chgo. Bar Assn. (cert. appreciation 1983-84), Ill. Assn. Hosp. Attys., Nat. Health Lawyers Assn., Am. Soc. Law and Medicine, Am. Acad. Hosp. Attys. Club: University (Chgo.). Home: 880 N Lake Shore Dr Chicago IL 60611 Office: DeWolfe Poynton & Stevens 135 S LaSalle St Chicago IL 60603

DEWOLFE, RUTHANNE K. S., lawyer, psychologist; b. Milw., Aug. 14, 1933; d. Erich Max and Mary Elizabeth (Stork) Sobota; m. Alan S. Dewolfe Aug. 24, 1952 (div. July 1986); children: Kyle A., Hillary S., Elena M. BA, Heidelberg Coll., Tiffin, Ohio, 1954; PhD, Northwestern U., 1960; JD, DePaul U., Chgo., 1976; LLM, DePaul U., 1985. Bar: Ill. 1976, U.S. Dist. Ct. (no. dist.) Ill. 1976, U.S. Ct. Appeals (7th cir.) Ill. 1980, U.S. Supreme Ct. 1982, D.C. 1983; registered psychologist, Pa., Ill. Staff psychologist Hines VA Hosp., 1960-62; pvt. parctice psychology Chgo., 1962—; staff atty. Legal Asst. Found., Chgo., 1975-77, supr. atty., 1980—; regional atty. U.S. Civil Rights Commn., Chgo., 1977-80; adj. faculty criminal justice dept. U. Ill., Chgo., 1980—; lectr. in field. Contbr. numerous articles and papers to various publs. treas. North Shore Chamber Orchestra, Evanston, Ill., 1981—; pres. Northeast Evanston Neighborhood Assn., 1982—. Mem. ABA, Ill. State Bar Assn. (chairperson com. on corrections 1985-86, chairperson com. on mentally disabled 1982-83), Chgo. Bar Assn. (chairperson com. on civil rights 1981-82), Chgo. council of Lawyers, Women's Bar Assn. (com. on corps. and taation), Internat. Fedn. Women Lawyers, Lawyers Alliance for Nuclear Arms Control, John Howard Assn. (v.p. 1985—), Am. Psychol. Assn., Internat. Psychol. Assn., Nat. Assn. Ins. Commrs., Sigma Xi. Home: 811 Colfax Evanston IL 60201

DEXTRAS, MARY LOU, religious organization coordinator; b. Youngstown, Ohio, Sept. 20, 1922; d. Guido and Catherine (Spagnola) Bernard; m. Albert Raymond Dextras, Feb. 9, 1946; children—Suzanne, Paul A., Cathie, Mary Alice, Dee Anne. Student Youngstown Bus. Sch., Wichita State U., 1984—. Exec. sec. U.S. Air Force, Kadena, Okinawa, 1957-62; youth dir. McConnell AFB, Wichita, Kans., 1963-64; real estate agt. Egan Realtors, Derby, Kans., 1965-80; coordinator Congregation Sisters of St. Joseph Coordinated Services, Wichita, 1980—. Served to sgt. USMCWR, 1942-45. Mem. Derby Arts Council, Kans. Named Mother of Yr., Bergstrom AFB, Austin, 1956; recipient Koza Shi Fujenkai award Women's Fedn., Okinawa, 1960; People-to-People award Pres. Eisenhower, 1961. Mem. Derby Bd. Edn., pres., 1978-79, 84-85. Democrat. Roman Catholic. Lodges: Soroptimists, K.C. Aux. (Derby, Kans.). Avocations: Tap dancing; piano. Office: Congregation of Sisters of St Joseph Coordinated Services 3720 E Bayley Wichita KS 67218

DE YAGER, PETER WILLIAM, candy company executive; b. Hawarden, Iowa, Apr. 16, 1950; s. Albert and Minnie (DeRoon) DeY.; m. Betty Jean Kerr, May 31, 1974; children: Bridget Nicole, Gabriel Shannon, Noah Seth. AB, Dordt Coll., 1971. Tchr. Phila. Montgomery Christian Acad., Dresher, Pa., 1971-73, Western Christian High Sch., Hull, Iowa, 1973-80; pres., chief exec. officer The Fgn. Candy Co., Inc., Hull, 1978—. Recipient 500 award Inc. Mag., Boston, 1985-86; named Small Bus. Person of Yr., State of Iowa, 1987. Mem. Nat. Candy Wholesalers Assn., Nat. Food Distbrs. Assn., Direct Mtkg. Assn., Nat. Assn. Specialty Food Trade, Nat. Assn. Tobacco Distbrs., Nat. Automatic Merchandising Assn., Nat. Assn. Concessionaries, Gen. Msde. Distbrs. Council, Retail Confectioners Internat. Republican. Mem. Christian Reformed Ch. Club: Hull Bus. and PRofl. (Employer of Yr. award 1982). Office: The Foreign Candy Co Inc 451 Highway 18 W Hull IA 51239

DEYER, KIRK DONALD, manufacturing execuitve; b. Berwyn, Ill., July 23, 1947; s. Donald Everett and Arlene Helen (Kirk) D.; m. Laurie-Ann Delores Strach, Oct. 19, 1985; children from previous marriage: Michael, Steve, Shannon. BS, De Paul U., 1969; M in Mgmt., Northwestern U., 1979. CPA, Ill., Mo. Auditor Arthur Andersen & Co., Chgo., 1968-72; div. controller Sealed Power Corp., Muskegon, Mich., 1972-81, dir. fin. control, 1981-83, dir. info. services, 1983-85, sr. mgr. fin. and planning, 1985-87; v.p. fin. Alloy Tek Inc., Grandville, Mich., 1987—. Bd. dirs. Muskegon County Easter Seals Soc., 1986—. Mem. Am. Inst. CPA's, Mich. Assn. CPA's, Nat. Assn. Accts., Fin. Execs. Inst. Home: 1943 Hendricks Rd Muskegon MI 49441 Office: Alloy Tek Inc 2900 Wilson Ave SW Grandville MI 49418

DEYOUNG, MARY KAY, therapist, educator; b. Chgo., Aug. 11, 1949; d. Kenneth Jay and Doris Mae (Leyen) DeY. BS, Grand Valley State Coll., Allendale, Mich., 1971; MA, U. Chgo., 1972; ArtsD, Western Colo. U., 1975. Therapist Youth Contact Ctr., Grand Rapids, Mich., 1975-77; instr. Grand Rapids Jr. Coll., 1977-85; assoc. prof. social thought and pub. affairs Grand Valley State Coll., 1985—; cons. in field, 1977—. Author: The Sexual Victimization of Children, 1982, Incest: An Annotated Bibliography, 1985; contbr. articles to profl. jours. Mem. Am. Soc. Criminology, Am. Assn. Sex Educators, Counselors and Therapists, Soc. Scientific Study of Sex, Internat. Conf. Prevention of Child Abuse and Neglect. Avocations: writing fiction, theatre, classical music. Home: 2226 Saginaw Rd SE Grand Rapids MI 49506 Office: Grand Valley State Coll 222 Mackinac Hall Allendale MI 49401

DEYOUNG, ROBERT JAMES, electric company executive; b. Hamilton, Mich., Feb. 22, 1934; s. John Weaver and Delia Margaret (Lampen) DeY.; m. Naomi Ruth Stewart, June 28, 1958; children: Marilyn, Linda, Mark. AB in Math., Hope Coll., 1956; MS in Math., U. Cin., 1973. Sr. programmer Aeronca Mfg., Middletown, Ohio, 1961-64; programmer Gen. Electric Co., Cin., 1960-61, sr. programmer, 1964-67, engring. systems analyst, 1967-68, sr. computations analyst, 1968-84, sr. mfg. geometric specialist, 1984—. Republican. Mem. Ch. Nazarene. Avocations: organ playing, gardening, collecting coins. Home: 7330 Elkwood Dr West Chester OH 45069 Office: Gen Electric Co 1 Neumann Way Cincinnati OH 45215

DEYOUNG, YVONNE MARIE, computer programmer/analyst; b. Milw., Dec. 9, 1951; d. Eugene Owen and Julia Ann (Mann) DeY.; m. Randy Dean Schwartz, Aug. 9, 1980. BBA in Acctg. and Data Processing, U. Wis., 1975. Acct. Lab. Computing Inc., Madison, Wis., 1975-78, Telephone & Data Systems, Madison, 1978-79; programmer Wis. Dairy Herd Improvement Coop., Madison, 1979-80; programmer/analyst Profl. Ins. Mgmt. Co., Jacksonville, Fla., 1980-81; sr. programmer/analyst Rayovac Corp., Madison, 1981—; sec. bd. dirs. Rayovac Office Employees Credit Union, 1985-87, chmn. 1987—; sales rep. Avon Products, Inc., Morton Grove, Ill., 1986—. Active Madison Civic Music Assn., 1975—; mem. St. Bernard's Sr. Choir, Madison, 1975—. Mem. Data Processing Mgmt. Assn. Roman Catholic. Club: Tuesday Night Live (treas. 1986—) (Madison). Avocations: performing arts, bowling, aerobics. Home: 5216 Piccadilly Dr Madison WI 53714-2018 Office: Rayovac Corp PO Box 4960 Madison WI 53711-0960

DEZORT, JACQUELYN LOUISE LINK, Bank executive; b. Woodriver, Ill., Sept. 12, 1950; d. Albert Frances and Margaret Josephine (Schafer) Link; m. Tom Edward Dezort, Nov. 24, 1973; children: Catherine Leigh, Josef Mattew, Amanda Blair. BS in acctg., U. Ill., 1972. CPA, Ill. Staff acct. Peat, Marwick, Mitchell, Chgo., 1972-73; sr. supr. Peat, Marwick, Mitchell, St. Louis, 1973-76; asst. auditor Centerre Bank, St. Louis, 1976, auditor, 1980-84, v.p. productivity, 1984-86; v.p. strategic planner Centerre Bancorp, St. Louis, 1986—. Avocations: tennis, jogging, needlework, cooking. Office: Centerre Bank 1 Centerre Plaza Saint Louis MO 63101

DHARSI, KAZIM HASSANALI, architect; b. Zanzibar, Tanzania, Aug. 17, 1953; came to U.S., 1981; s. Hassan and Lila (Bhalloo) D.; m. Razina Hemraj, July, 27, 1985. BArch, U. Bombay, India, 1979; MArch, SUNY, Buffalo, 1984. Architect Sumar Varma Assocs., Dar-es-Salaam, 1979-81; archtl. asst. John Weting AIA, Marquette, Mich., 1981-82, Moyer Assocs., Glencoe, Ill., 1984, Heard & Assocs., Chgo., 1984-85; asst. prof. Ferris State Coll., Big Rapids, Mich., 1986—. SUNY Research fellow, Buffalo, 1982-83. Moslem. Avocations: cross-country skiing, traveling. Home: 901 Colburn Ave Big Rapids MI 49307 Office: Ferris State Coll Big Rapids MI 49307

DHILLON, PAM S., biochemist; b. Toungoo, Burma, Mar. 14, 1938; m. Sharon Ann Stellner, Feb. 15, 1942; children: Christina Jennifer, Timothy Hayes. PhD, Purdue U., 1965. Research dir. Devel. Cons. Internat., Washington, 1965-69; mgr. devel. FMC Corp., Middleport, N.Y., 1969-74; area mgr. Cen. Soya Co., Inc., Ft. Wayne, Ind., 1973-79; biochemist, pres. Am. Techs. Inc., Ft. Wayne, 1979—. Fellow Am. Inst. Chemists; mem. The Council for Agrl. Sci. and Tech., N.Y.Acad. Scis., Am. Chem. Soc., Am. Assn. Cereal Chemists, Am. Oil Chemists Soc., Assn. Official Analytical Chemists, Am. Soc. Animal Sci., Am. Dairy Sci. Assn., Poultry Sci. Assn., Am. Soc. Fisheries, Am. Assn. Feed Microscopists, World Aquaculture Soc., Am. Soc. Limnology and Oceanography, Xi Sigma Pi, Sigma Xi. Home: 11226 Trails North Dr Fort Wayne IN 46825 Office: Am Techs Inc 6029 Stoney Creek Dr Fort Wayne IN 46825

DIAL, ELEANORE MAXWELL, foreign language educator; b. Norwich, Conn., Feb. 21, 1929; d. Joseph Walter and Irene (Beetham) Maxwell; B.A., U. Bridgeport (Conn.), 1951; M.A. in Spanish, Mexico City Coll., 1955; Ph.D., U. Mo., 1968; m. John E. Dial, Aug. 27, 1959. Mem. faculty U. Wisc.-Milw., 1968-75, Ind. State U., Terre Haute, 1975-78, Bowling Green (Ohio) State U., 1978-79; asst. prof. dept. fgn. langs. and lits. Iowa State U., Ames, 1979-85, assoc. prof. 1985—; cons. pub. co.; participant workshops; del. 1st World Congress Women Journalists and Writers, Mex., 1975, also mem. edn. commn. NDEA grantee, 1967; Center Latin Am. grantee, 1972; Nat. Endowment Humanities summer seminar UCLA, 1982, U. Calif.-Santa Barbara, 1984. Mem. Am. Assn. Tchrs. Spanish and Portuguese, Midwest MLA, MLA, N. Central Council Latin Americanists, Midwest Assn. Latin Am. Studies, Clemont County Geneal. Soc., Ohio Geneal. Soc., Caribbean Studies Assn., Phi Sigma Iota, Sigma Delta Pi. Contbr. articles and revs. to scholarly jours. Home: 921 Burnett Ave Ames IA 50010 Office: Iowa State U Ames IA 50010

DIAMOND, DARROUGH BLAIN, marketing executive; b. Kankakee, Ill., July 27, 1941; s. Noel A. and Sarah Lois (Wertz) Johnson; m. Linda Mann, Aug. 1, 1964; children: Laura Lynn, Julia True. BS in Communications, U. Ill., 1963, MS in Advt., 1967; postgrad. Northwestern U., 1963-64. Account exec. Leo Burnett Co., Chgo., 1967-73; nat. advt. mgr. McDonald's Corp., Oak Brook, Ill., 1974-76; dir. food service mktg. Walgreen Co., Deerfield, Ill., 1976-77; pres., chief exec. officer Arby's Franchise Assn., Pitts., 1977-80; sr. v.p. mktg. Wendy's Internat., Dublin, Ohio, 1980-81; pres. Darrough Diamond Enterprises, Inc., Columbus, 1981—; bd. dirs. Tidbit Alley, Inc.; cons. in field. Mem. James Webb Young Fund, Chgo./Urbana, 1967-74; deacon First Community Ch., Marble Cliff, Ohio, 1987—. Served to 1st lt. U.S. Army, 1964-66. Named Marketer of Yr., Adweek Mag., 1981. Mem. Am. Mgmt. Assn., Columbus Maenaerchor, Alpha Delta Sigma, Kappa Tau Alpha, Sigma Nu. Republican. Home and Office: 4066 Fenwick Rd Upper Arlington OH 43220

DIAMOND, EUGENE CHRISTOPHER, hospital lawyer and administrator; b. Oceanside, Calif., Oct. 19, 1952; s. Eugene Francis and Rosemary (Wright) D.; m. Mary Theresa O'Donnell, Jan. 20, 1984; children: Eugene John, Kevin Seamus. B.A., U. Notre Dame, 1974; M.H.A., St. Louis U., 1978, J.D., 1979. Bar: Ill. 1979. Staff atty. AUL Legal Def. Fund, Chgo., 1979-80; adminstrv. asst. Holy Cross Hosp., Chgo., 1980-81, asst. adminstr., 1981-82, v.p., 1982-83, counsel to adminstr., 1980—, exec. v.p., 1983—; cons. Birthright of Chgo., 1979—; mem. exec. bd. Hosp. Risk Mgmt. Soc. of Met. Chgo., 1982—, pres., 1984—. Mem. benefit com. Birthright of Chgo., 1981—. Mem. ABA, Am. Acad. Hosp. Attys., Nat. Health Lawyer's Assn., Ill. State Bar Assn., Chgo. Bar Assn. Roman Catholic. Office: Holy Cross Hosp 2701 W 68th St Chicago IL 60629

DIAMOND, R. N., pharmacist, pharmacy owner, real estate investor; b. Toledo, July 12, 1944; s. Robert Elliot Diamond and Dorothy Bernice (Hamilton) O'Grady; m. Maria Merced Gonzalez, Aug. 13, 1966; 1 child, Robert Douglas. BS in Pharmacy, Ferris State U., 1975. Registered pharmacist. Ptnr. Westown Pharmacy, Mt. Pleasant, Mich., 1975-76; owner, operator South Shore Pharmacy, Holland, Mich., 1977—; lectr. on drug abuse, drugs and hyperkinetic children, Holland, 1979—; treas. EVS COmmunications, Saugatuck, Mich., 1985—; pres. Equity Investment Co., Holland, 1986—. Contbr. articles to profl. jours. Pres. North Side Youth Orgn., Muskegon, 1970-72, Bus. and Merchants Assn., Southside Holland, 1979-81. Served with U.S. Army, 1966-68. Mem. Mich. Pharmacists Assn., Western Mich. Pharmacists Assn. (chmn. 1978—), Pharmacists and Legislators Conf. (organizer 1985-86). Avocations: golf, tennis, fishing, writing, downhill skiing. Home: 391 W Mae Rose Holland MI 49424 Office: South Shore Pharmacy 505 W 17th St Holland MI 49423

DIAMOND, SEYMOUR, physician; b. Chgo., Apr. 15, 1925; s. Nathan Avruum and Rose (Roth) D.; m. Elaine June Flamm, June 20, 1948; children: Judi, Merle, Amy. Student, Loyola U., 1943-45; M.B., Chgo. Med. Sch., 1948, M.D., 1949. Intern White Cross Hosp., Columbus, Ohio, 1949-50; gen. practice medicine Chgo., 1950—; dir. Diamond Headache Clinic, Ltd., Chgo., 1970—; mem. staff St. Joseph Hosp., Chgo.; dir. inpatient headache unit Weiss Meml. Hosp., Chgo.; prof. neurology Chgo. Med. Sch., 1970-82, adj. prof. pharmacology, 1985—; lectr. dept. community and family medicine Loyola U. Stritch Sch. Medicine, 1972-78; cons. mem. FDA Orphan Products Devel. Initial Rev. Group. Co-author: The Practicing Physician's Approach to Headache, 4th edit. 1986, More Than Two Aspirin: Help for Your Headache Problem, 1976, Advice from the Diamond Headache Clinic, 1982, Coping with Your Headache, 1982, Headache in Contemporary Patient Mgmt. series, 1983; editor: Keeping Current in the Treatment of Headache; mem. editorial bd. Headache, Clin. Jour. Pain, editorial cons. BIOSIS, 1986; contbr. numerous articles on headache and related fields to books and profl. jours. Pres. Skokie (Ill.) Bd. Health, 1965-68. Recipient Disting. Alumni award Chgo. Med. Sch., 1977; Nat. Migraine Found. lectureship award, 1982. Mem. AMA (Physicians Recognition awards 1970-73, 74, 77, 79, 82, del. sect. clin. pharmacology and therapeutics, mem. health policy agenda for Am. People, mem. Cost Effectiveness Conf.), Am. Assn. Study of Headache (exec. dir. 1971-85, pres. 1972-74, regent 1984), Nat. Migraine Found. (pres. 1971-77, exec. dir. 1977—), World Fedn. Neurology (exec. officer 1980—, research group on migraine and headache), Ill. Acad. Gen. Practice (chmn. mental health com. 1966-70), Ill., Chgo. med. socs., Biofeedback Soc. Am., Internat. Assn. Study of Pain, Am. Soc. Clin. Pharmacology and Therapeutics (chmn. headache sect. 1982—, mem. com. coordination sci. sects. 1983—), Postgrad. Med. Assn. (pres. 1981). Office: Diamond Headache Clinic 5252 N Western Ave Chicago IL 60625

DIAMOND, SUSAN Z., management consultant; b. Okla., Aug. 20, 1949; d. Louis Edward and Henrietta (Wood) D.; A.B. (Nat. Merit scholar, GRTS scholar), U. Chgo., 1970; M.B.A., DePaul U., 1979; m. Allan T. Devitt, July 27, 1974. Dir. study guide prodn. Am. Sch. Co., Chgo., 1972-75; pubis. supr. Allied Van Lines, Broadview, Ill., 1975-78, sr. account services rep., 1978-79; pres. Diamond Assocs. Ltd., Melrose Park, Ill., 1978—; condr. seminars Am. Mgmt. Assn. Mem. Nat. Assn. Accts., Adminstrv. Mgmt. Soc., Assn. Records Mgrs. and Adminstrs., Internat. Records Mgmt. Council, Records Mgmt. Soc. Gt. Britain, Bus. Forms Mgmt. Assn., Assn. Info. and Image Mgmt., Delta Mu Delta. Author: How to Talk More Effectively, 1972; Preparing Administrative Manuals, 1981; How to Manage Administrative Operations, 1981; How to be an Effective Secretary in the Modern Office, 1982; Records Management: A Practical Guide, 1983; co-author: Finance Without Fear, 1983; editor Mobility Trends, 1975-78; contbr. numerous articles to profl. jours. Office: 2851 N Pearl Ave Melrose Park IL 60160

DIAMOND, WILLIAM JAMES, financial executive; b. Chgo., Aug. 10, 1955; s. John Wesley and Margaret Mary (O'Grady) D.; m. Judy Ellen Jacob, Sept. 5, 1982; children: Emily Joy, Joseph William. BS in Indsl. Supervision, No. Ill. U., 1979; MS in Accountancy, De Paul U., 1984. CPA, Ill. Prodn. supr. Motorola Corp., Franklin Park, Ill., 1978-81, Packaging Corp. Am., Burlington, Wis., 1981-82; acct. Jerrold Zisook, Ltd., Chgo., 1983-84; staff acct. Thomas Havey & Co., Chgo., 1984-87; asst. controller Waste Mgmt. N.Am., Oak Brook, Ill., 1987—. Mem. Am. Inst. CPA's, Ill. Soc. CPA's. Avocations: golf, travel, camping. Home: 433 S Gables Wheaton IL 60187 Office: Waste Mgmt N Am 3003 Butterfield Rd Oak Brook IL 60521

DIB, ALBERT JAMES, lawyer; b. Detroit, Oct. 14, 1955; s. James Benjamin and Salma (Nacoud) D. B.A., U. Mich., 1977; J.D., Wayne State U., 1980; cert. U. Exeter, Eng., 1980. Bars: Mich. 1981, U.S. Dist. Ct. (ea. dist.) Mich. 1981, U.S. Ct. Appeals (6th cir.), U.S.Supreme Ct., 1986. Law clk. Lopatin, Miller, Freedman, Bluestone, Erich, Rosen & Bartnick, Detroit, 1978-80, assoc., 1981—; moot ct. judge Detroit Coll. Law, 1984. Vestryman Christ Episcopal Ch., Detroit, 1974-77; charter mem. Republican Presdl. Task Force, 1985—. Recipient Cert. Achievement Mich. High Sch. Mock Trial Tournament, 1984. Mem. Assn. Trial Lawyers Am. (cert. trial advocacy 1984), ABA, Mich. Trials Lawyers Assn., Detroit Bar Assn. (speakers bur. com. 1986, Negligence law com. 1986), Oakland Bar Assn., Macomb

Bar Assn. (speaker 1984); Office: Lopatin Miller Freedman Bluestone Erich Rosen & Bartnick 511 E Larned Detroit MI 48226

DIBAL, ERNEST L., engineer; b. Kansas City, Mo., Nov. 16, 1951; s. Ernest L. Sr. and Rose B. (Hallouer) D.; m. Di edre Allen, June 14, 1984; children: Jessica L., Priscilla H. BSES, Rockhurst Coll., 1973. Registered profl. engr., Kans. Engr. Massaglia, Neustrom, Bredson, Kansas City, 1973-75; staff engr. George Butler Assocs., Kansas City, 1976—. Mem. Am. Soc. Heating Refrigeration and Air Conditioning Engrs. Roman Catholic. Avocations: reading, automobiles, golf, photography. Home: 5420 Vista Kansas City KS 66106 Office: George Butler Assocs City Ctr Square Suite 1100 Kansas City MO 64105

DIBENEDETTO, STEPHEN LOUIS, university financial executive; b. Chgo., July 31, 1951; s. Stephen and Rochina (Curcio) DiB.; m. Karen Patricia Lauders, Oct. 7, 1978; children: Nicole Susan, Lauren Elizabeth, Stephen Jack. B.A., Western Ill. U., 1973. Collection supr. Cole-Parmer Inst. Co., Chgo., 1974-76; regional credit mgr. Sony Corp. Am., Niles, Ill., 1976-78; sales rep. Gen. Binding Corp., Lombard, Ill., 1978-80; nat. credit mgr. Globe Amerada Glass Co., Elk Grove Village, Ill., 1980-83; asst. dir. student loans Northwestern U., Evanston, Ill., 1983—. Mem. Ill. Student Loan Administrators' Assn. (founding), Chgo. Midwest Credit Mgmt. Assn. Roman Catholic. Office: Northwestern U 1801 Hinman Evanston IL 60201

DIBIAGGIO, JOHN A., university administrator; b. San Antonio, Sept. 11, 1932; s. Ciro and Acidalia DiBiaggio; m. Carolyn Mary Enright, June 29, 1957; children: David John, Dana Elizabeth, Deirdre Joan. AB, Eastern Mich. U., 1954, D of Edn. (hon.), 1985; DDS, U. Detroit, 1958, LHD (hon.), 1985; MA, U. Mich., 1967; DSci. (hon.), Fairleigh Dickinson U., 1981; LLD (hon.), Sacred Heart U., Bridgeport, Conn., 1984, U. Md., 1985; DHL (hon.), U. New Eng., 1987. Gen. practice dentistry New Baltimore, Mich., 1958-65; asst. prof., asst. to dean, dept. chmn. sch. dentistry U. Detroit, 1965-67; asst. dean student affairs U. Ky., Lexington, 1967-70; prof., dean sch. dentistry Va. Commonwealth U., Richmond, 1970-76; v.p. for health affairs, exec. dir. health ctr. U. Conn., Farmington, 1976-79; pres. U. Conn., Storrs, 1979-85, Mich. State U., East Lansing, 1985—; mem. Mich. Council of State Coll. Pres., 1985—; mem. project for pub. and community services Edn. Commn. of States, 1985—; mem. Nat. Bd. Examiners, 1987; bd. dirs. Mich. Biotech. Inst., 1985—, Mich. Materials and Processing Inst., 1985—, Am. Council on Edn, 1987—; mem. Mich. China Council, 1985—; mem. MUCIA Council of Pres., 1987-88. Author: (with others) Applied Practice Management: A Strategy for Stress Control, 1979; edit. bd. Michigan Woman, 1987—; contbr. articles to profl. jours. Chmn. adv. com. dental scholars R.W. Johnson Found; mem. Pres. Com. for Argonne Nat. Lab. 6, 1986—; trustee U. Detroit, 1979-86; bd. overseers Sch. Dentistry, U. Pa., 1979-86. Decorated Order of Merit, Italy; recipient Leadership award Sacred Heart U., Disting. Profl. of Yr. award Mich. Assn. Profls., 1985, Disting. Alumni award Eastern Mich. U., 1986; named Man of Yr., City of Detroit, 1985. Fellow Am. Coll. Dentists, Internat. Coll. Dentists; mem. ADA (cons. jour.), Mich. Dental Assn., Am. Assn. Dental Schs., Internat. Assn. Dental Research, Am. Pub. Health Assn., Am. Assn. Higher Edn., Assn. Acad. Health Ctrs., Nat. Assn. State Univs. and Land Grant Colls. (chmn. 1986-87), Nat. Assn. State Univs. and Land-Grant Colls., Phi Kappa Phi, Omicron Kappa Upsilon, Beta Gamma Sigma, Alpha Omega, Alpha Sigma Chi, Alpha Lambda Delta. Avocation: tennis. Home: 1 Abbot Rd East Lansing MI 48824 Office: Mich State U Office of Pres 450 Administration Bldg East Lansing MI 48824

DIBLEY, PAUL DALE, dentist; b. Milw., Aug. 16, 1950; s. Chester Dale and Elizabeth Jane (Purdy) D.; m. Geraldine Mary Gmoser, Aug. 18, 1973; children: Laura Ann, Kristen Marie, Brian Paul. DDS, Marquette U., 1974. Pvt. practice dentistry Shawano, Wis., 1974—; pres. Health Systems Agy., Shawano, 1979-80; dental cons. Maple Ln. Health Care Facility, Shawano, 1981—, Woodland Village Nursing Home, Suring, 1983—, emergency room staff Shawano Community Hosp., 1984—. med. advisor County Cancer Soc., Shawano, 1986—;. Wis. scholar, 1968; recipient award Acad. Gold Foil Operators, 1974. Mem. ADA, Wis. Dental Assn., Shawano County Dental Soc. (sec. 1977-78, pres. 1978-79, peer rev. com.), Shawano County C. of C. (bd. dirs. 1985—). Republican. Roman Catholic. Lodge: Rotary (dir. fgn. exchange student program 1986—, bd. dirs. 1986—). Avocations: swimming, skiing, coaching basketball, reading, boating. Home: N1931 Old Keshena Rd Shawano WI 54166 Office: 920 E Fifth St Shawano WI 54116

DICK, BRADLEY LANCE, communications executive; b. Wichita, Kans., Mar. 13, 1948; s. Roderick Earl and Nellie Mae (McLaughlin) D.; m. Linda Marlene Haberly, Aug. 9, 1969; children: Kathy, David, Jeremy. AS, DeVry Inst. Tech., Chgo., 1970; BA, Wichita (Kans.) State U., 1971; MA, U. Kans., 1983. Chief engr. KMUW-FM Wichita State U., 1968-72; dir. engring. ops. KANU-FM and KFKU-AM U. Kans., Lawrence, 1972-85; radio tech. editor Broadcast Engring., Overland Park, Kans., 1985—; broadcast cons. KHCC-FM, Hutchinson, Kans., 1979—, KBRG-AM, Borger, Tex., 1970-71, K30AM-TV, Lawrence, 1984—; lectr. U. Kans., 1983-85. Contbr. over 100 articles to profl. jours.; design engr. stereo broadcast transmitter, 1984. Recipient Minority Tng. grant Corp. Pub Broadcasting, Facilities grants Nat. Telecommunications and Info. Agy. Mem. Soc. Broadcast Engrs., Audio Engring. Soc., Nat. Assn. Radio and TV Engrs. (sr.). Baptist. Lodge: Elks. Avocations: computer programming, lecturing, writing, running marathons. Home: 1745 W 20th Lawrence KS 66046 Office: Broadcast Engring Mag 9221 Quivira Rd Overland Park KS 66215

DICK, CURTIS WAYNE, restaurant owner; b. Clinton, Okla., Oct. 3, 1952; s. Paul Ervin and Vera Lee (Reinschmeidt) D.; m. Sparla Jo Lacey, June 8, 1973; children: Shanna, Aaron. BS in Acctg., Southwestern Okla. State U., 1974. Internal auditor Conoco, Inc., Ponca City, Okla., 1974-81; owner Ken's Pizza, Winfield, Kans., 1981-83, Western Sizzlin Steak House, Winfield, 1985—. Chmn. Sunflower Bowl, Winfield, 1982; mem. fin. com. First United Meth. Ch.; mem. Unified Sch. Dist. 465 ad hoc com. on athletics, 1984, no. cen. accreditation com., 1986; mem. adv. bd. Spl. Olympics, Winfield, 1983-86; mem. citizens' adv. bd. Winfield State Hosp. and Tng. Ctr., 1986; bd. dirs. Winfield United Way, 1986. Recipient Disting. Service award Outstanding Young Men Am., 1986. Mem. Winfield C. of C. (retail com. 1985-86). Republican. Club: Winfield Country (bd. dirs. 1983—). Lodge: Optimists. Avocation: golf. Home: 1605 E 19th Winfield KS 67156

DICK, DAN SHERIDAN, service executive; b. Parsons, Kans., Nov. 16, 1940; s. Max Sheridan and Edith Blanche (Johnson) D.; m. Mary Marlene Heck, Apr. 1, 1967; children: Kathryne Ann, Christopher David, Susan Marlene. BSBA, Kans. State Coll., Pittsburg, 1967. CPA, Kans. Staff acct. Mize, Houser, Reed, CPA's, Topeka, 1967-71; pvt. practice CPA St. Paul, Kans., 1971-73; sr. v.p., controller Topeka Inn Mgmt., Inc., 1973-79; sr. v.p., dir. ops. Calif. Inn Mgmt., Inc., Lawrence, Kans., 1979-85; v.p., dir. ops. Sunway Hotel Mgmt., Inc., Kansas City, Mo., 1985—. State campaign treas. Carlin for Gov., Topeka, 1974. Served with USAF, 1958-63, Vietnam. Mem. Am. Inst. CPA's, Kans. Soc. CPA's. Democrat. Roman Catholic. Avocations: fishing, hunting. Office: Sunway Hotel Mgmt Inc 800 W 47th Suite 717 Kansas City MO 64112

DICK, DAVID WILLARD, computer specialist, project leader; b. Blue Earth, Minn., Dec. 2, 1947; s. David and Julia (Willard) D.; m. Anita L. Hissam, July 31, 1975; children: Michael, Elizabeth. BS, Mankato (Minn.) State Coll., 1970. Analyst Ops. Research, Inc., Mpls., 1973-76; analyst Murphy Motor Freight Lines, Inc., St. Paul, 1976-78, systems programmer, 1979-84, project leader, 1985—, mgr. data processing, 1987—; cons. in field, 1980—. Creator computer software. Office: Murphy Motor Freight Lines Inc PO Box 64640 Saint Paul MN 55164-0640

DICK, DENNIS RAY, accountant; b. Muncie, Ind., June 19, 1956; s. Marvin Rischel Dick and Carole Jean (Bauer) Wade. B.B.A., Western Ill. U., 1978; M.B.A., DePaul U., 1981. Mgmt. trainee Continental Bank, Chgo., 1978-79, budget analyst, 1979-80; acctg. supr. Continental Ill. Leasing, Chgo., 1980-82, acctg. mgr., 1982-84; acctg. mgr. Sanwa Bus. Credit Corp., 1984—. Avocation: Golf. Home: 2182 Stonehaven Way Lisle IL 60532 Office: Sanwa Bus Credit Corp 1 South Wacker Dr Chicago IL 60606

DICK, JAMES CLIFFORD, printing company executive; b. Lansing, Mich., Aug. 24, 1933; s. Clifford William and Mary Ellen (Richards) D.; children: Cheri Le Nill, Teresa Lynn, Lori Kay Ridenour, Steven James; m. Joyce Marie Banish-Borowy, June 26, 1987. Student, Mich. State U., 1951-52. Compositor Myers Printing Service, Lansing, 1952, owner, 1973; pres. Myers Printing Inc., Lansing, 1978. Served to corp. U.S. Army, 1953-54. Mem. Internat. Assn. Printing House Craftsmen (dep. gov. 1980-82, dist. sewc., treas. 1982-85, gov. Internat. fifth dist. 1985-87, Internat. Gov. of Yr. 1986), Lansing Club Printing House Craftsmen (pres. 1979-80, Craftsman of Yr. 1978, 83, Premier Craftsman 1984). Lodge: Kiwanis. Home: 5360 Blue Haven Dr East Lansing MI 48823 Office: Myers Printing Inc 914 E Gier St Lansing MI 48906

DICK, NEIL ALAN, architectural and engineering services company executive; b. Cleve., June 15, 1941; s. Harvey L. and Rose (Flom) D.; B.Arch., Ohio State U., 1965; M.B., Cleve. State U., 1966: m. Bonnie M. Natarus, Sept. 3, 1967; 1 dau., Rory D. Exec. v.p. J.R. Hyde & Assos., Pitts., 1967-70; dir. tech. and market devel. Stirling Homex Corp., Avon, N.Y., 1970-72; sr. housing coordinator Nat. Housing Corp., Cleve., 1972-74; fin. and estate analyst Conn. Gen. Corp., Cleve., 1974-76; sr. v.p., dir. mktg. Cannon Design Inc., Grand Island, N.Y., 1976-82, also dir.; pres. Daverman Assocs., Inc., Grand Rapids, Mich., 1983—; regional dir. Greiner Engring. Inc., Dallas, 1983—. Bd. dirs. West Mich. Telecommunications Found.; mem. bd. trustees Kendall Sch. Design; Grand Rapids C. of C. Found. (bd. dirs.), treas., Amherst (N.Y.) Democratic Com.; zone chmn., county fin. chmn., mem. exec. com. Erie County Dem. Com.; mem. Mich. Dem. State Com.; treas. Mich. 5th Congl. Dist. Dem. Com. Recipient Service award Erie County Dem. Com., 1979, Mem. Soc. Mktg. Profl. Services (regional coordinator), Buffalo Area C. of C., Am. Hosp. Assn., Nat. Trust Hist. Preservation, Ohio State U. Alumni Assn., Mich. C. of C., Grand Rapids Art Mus., Buffalo Mus. Sci., Albright Knox Art Gallery, Alpha Rho Chi. Jewish. Clubs: Economic, Rotary (Grand Rapids). Home: 1642 Pontiac Rd SE East Grand Rapids MI 49506 Office: 82 Iona Ave NW Grand Rapids MI 49503

DICK, RAYMOND DALE, psychology educator; b. Toledo, Ohio, July 16, 1930; s. Floyd Edward and Clara Belle (Spilker) D.; m. Beverly Ann Sparks, June 18, 1955; children: Gregory Dale, Jeffrey Clayton. B.S., Northwestern U., 1952; M.A., U. Mo., 1955, Ph.D., 1958. Asst. prof. psychology Fort Hayes (Kans.) State Coll., 1958-62, assoc. prof., 1962-64, prof., 1964-66, acad. chmn. psychology dept., 1959-66; prof. psychology U. Wis., Eau Claire, 1966-81, dean Sch. Grad Studies, 1966—; assoc. Danforth Found., 1962-84, also chmn. Upper Midwest selection com., 1969-72; mem. com. liberal arts edn. North Central Assn. Colls. and Secondary Schs., 1963-66, coordinator liberal arts com., 1965-68, cons-examiner, 1971—. Contbr. profl. jours. Mem. Am., Midwestern, Wis. psychol. assns., AAUP, AAAS. Home: 2823 Irene Dr Eau Claire WI 54701

DICKASON, ROBERT HART, osteopathic physician, surgeon; b. Louisville, Aug. 4, 1948; s. Jack Hart and Carol Matilda (Drake) D.; m. Frieda Ann Koubal, July 17, 1971; 1 son, Karl Hart. B.S. in Biology, Baldwin-Wallace Coll., 1970; med. research asst. Case Western Res. U., 1971; D.O., Chgo. Coll. Osteo. Medicine, 1975. Intern, Detroit Osteo. Hosp., 1975-76; resident in gen. surgery Riverside Osteo. Hosp., Trenton, Mich., 1976-80; fellow in colon and rectal surgery William Beaumont Hosp., Royal Oak, Mich., 1980-81; practice osteo. medicine specializing in gen. surgery, colon and rectal surgery, Trenton, Mich., 1981—; mem. teaching staff Riverside Osteo. Hosp., instr. emergency med. technician, 1977—; asst. clin. prof. surgery Mich. State U.; physician examiner colon and rectal cancer screening program Gen. Motors Corp., 1981—; free-lance photographer, 1969-76; lectr. in field; vol. CPR instr., 1977—; vol. physician Downriver Community Health Service Referral Network, 1982-83; med. examiner Am. Cancer Soc., 1982—, vol. pub. speaker, 1981—; physician advisor Mich. Peer Rev. Orgn., 1985—; vol. med. advisor, pub. speaker United Ostomy Assn., Nat. Found. for Ileitis and Colitis; instr. emergency med. technician Grosse Ile Fire Dept., 1979; unit chmn. Nat. Cancer Prevention Study II, Am. Cancer Soc., 1982. Mem. St. Thomas Lutheran Ch. Council, 1983, tchr. Sunday sch., 1985. Named one of Outstanding Young Men Am., 1983. Mem. Am. Osteo. Assn., Mich. Assn. Osteo. Physicians and Surgeons, Am. Acad. Osteopathy, Am. Coll. Osteo. Surgeons, Am. Assn. Osteopathic Specialists, Mich. Soc. of Colon and Rectal Surgeons, Wayne County Osteo. Assn., Jaycees (Grosse Ile pres. 1981-82, numerous awards), Sigma Sigma Phi (pres. 1974), Atlas Club, Sigma Sigma Phi, Alpha Phi Omega. Co-author manual for physicians on hyperalimentation and nutritional support; contbr. articles to local newspapers. Home: 9672 Waterway St Grosse Ile MI 48138 Office: 2171 W Jefferson Suite 203 Trenton MI 48183

DICKERSON, ALLEN BRUCE, interior designer, consultant; b. St. Joseph, Mich., June 8, 1938; s. Harold Clyde and Lucille Anne (Thornton) D.; m. Arlene Virginia Bator, Mar. 26, 1965; children—Scott Denek, Maribeth Anne. B.S. in Indsl. Engring., U. Mich., 1961, M.B.A., 1962; cert. N.Y. Sch. Interior Design, 1967. Sr. indsl. engr. Bohn Aluminum & Brass Co., Detroit, 1962-65, engring. ctr. adminstr., 1965-68, prodn. mgr., 1968-70, asst. plant mgr., 1970-72; plant mgr. DuWel Products Co., Bangor, Mich., 1972-74, corp. chief indsl. engr., 1974-75; contract and residential interior designer Klingman's, Grand Rapids, Mich., 1975—; tchr. South Haven Community Edn. Program, 1977, Western Mich. U., 1975, Am. Soc. Interior Designers, 1980-81. Author: Rental Condominiums-Interior Design for Fun and Profit, 1978. Trustee First United Meth. Ch., South Haven, Mich.; bd. dirs. Van Buren County (Mich.) ARC, 1965-68. Mem. Am. Inst. Indsl. Engrs., Am. Soc. Interior Designers, Nat. Council Interior Design Qualification, South Haven C. of C. (com. chmn.), Internat. Lightning Class Assn. Republican. Methodist. Clubs: South Haven Yacht; Shrine (Grand Rapids); Rotary. Home: Route 5 999 North Shore Dr South Haven MI 49090 Office: PO Box 888 Eastbrook Mall 28th St Grand Rapids MI 49508

DICKERSON, KITTY GARDNER, textile and apparel educator; b. Willis, Va., Mar. 30, 1940; d. Lonnie Kavilla and Virgie Lee (Keith) Gardner; m. Harman Carless Dickerson, Mar. 18, 1962; children: Derek Len, Donya Lyn. BS, Va. Poly. Inst. & State U., 1962, MS, 1963; PhD, St. Louis U., 1973. Adminstrv. asst. to v.p. Stix, Baer & Fuller, St. Louis, 1963-64; extension home economist U. Mo. Extension div., St. Louis, 1964-69; off-campus instr. U. Mo., St. Louis, 1969; asst. prof. home econs. Va. Poly. Inst. & State U., Blacksburg, 1976-81; assoc. prof., chmn. dept. U. Mo., Columbia, 1981-86, prof., chmn. dept., 1986—; cons. various industry groups, 1982—; vis. lectr. numerous univs., 1982—. Contbr. more than 40 articles to profl. jours. Co-chairperson New Haven PTA, Columbia, 1983-84; leader Harg Hustlers 4-H Club, Columbia, 1984-85; active Bapt. chs., St. Louis, Blacksburg, 1972-81; mem. Students Opposed to Drugs and Alcohol. Recipient Textile award of merit Va. Textile Industry, 1985, Nat. Research award Man-Made Fiber Producers, 1985, Disting. Service in Adminstrn. award Gamma Sigma Delta, 1986; Congl. Research Fund grantee, 1987; St. Louis U. teaching fellow, 1970, NDEA research fellow, 1971-73. Mem. Assn. Coll. Profs. Textiles and Clothing (sec. cen. region 1984-85, pres. cen. region 1986-87, nat. restructuring com. 1986-87). Avocations: spending time with family, gardening, travel. Home: Rt 2 Box 56 Columbia MO 65201 Office: Univ Mo 137 Stanley Hall Columbia MO 65211

DICKEY, JULIA EDWARDS, management and promotional consultant; b. Sioux Falls, S.D., Mar. 6, 1940; d. John Keith and Henrietta Barbara (Zerell) Edwards; student DePauw U., 1958-59; A.B., Ind. U., 1962, M.L.S., 1967, postgrad., 1967—; m. Joseph E. Dickey, June 18, 1959; children—Joseph E., John Edwards. Asst. acquisitions librarian Ind. U. Regional Campus Libraries, 1965-67; head tech. services Bartholomew County Library, Columbus, Ind., 1967-74; dir. reference services Southeastern Ind. Area Library Service Authority, Columbus, 1974-78, exec. dir., 1978-80; pres. Jedco Enterprises, 1981—; legis. strategy chmn. Ind. Library Coop. Devel., 1975; dir. Ind. Library Trustees Assn. Governance Project, 1982. Mem. Columbus exec. bd. Mayor's Task Force on Status of Women, 1973—; del. Ind. Sch. Nominating Assembly, 1973-75, 75-77; sec. bd. dirs. Human Services Inc. (Bartholomew, Brown and Jackson Counties community action program), 1975, pres., 1976, 77, 78; mem. adv. council Ind./Nat. Network Study, 1977-78; bd. dirs. Columbus Women's Center; precinct coordinator Vols. For Bayh, 1974; sheriff Columbus 1st precinct, 1975, clk., 1976-77, insp., 1978, judge, 1980-83; treas. Hayes for State Rep. Com., 1978, 82, 84, 86. Named Outstanding Young Woman Am., 1973. Mem. ALA, Ind. Library Assn. (dist. chmn. 1972-73, chmn. library edn. div. 1980-81, ad hoc com. on legis. effectiveness, 1982, various coms.), Library Assts. and Technicians Round Table (chmn. 1968-69), Tech. Services Round Table (chmn. 1971-72, sec. library planning com. 1969-72), AAUW (pres. 1973-75), Bartholomew County Library Staff Assn. (pres. 1975-76), Exptl. Aircraft Assn. (charter pres. chpt. 729 1981, pres. Ind. council 1984—, major achievement award Oshkosh), 1983), Ind. EAA Council (pres. 1982—), Antique Airplane Assn., First Tuesday, Psi Iota Xi. Club: Zonta. Home and office: 511 Terrace Lake Rd Columbus IN 47201

DICKHANS, MAUREEN JEANNE, nurse, educator; b. St. Louis, Dec. 16, 1954; d. Marvin Lawrence and Shirley Jean (Dacus) D. AB in Biology, St. Louis U., 1976, MS in Anatomy, 1978, BSN, 1981. RN, Mo. Staff nurse pediatrics dept. Cardinal Glennon Hosp., St. Louis, 1981-82; clin. nurse transplant dept. St. Louis U. Hosp., 1982-85; clin. nurse research dept. Washington U., St. Louis, 1985—; instr. anatomy Palmer Coll., Davenport, Iowa, 1978-79, Deaconess Nursing Sch., St. Louis, 1981-82, Logan Coll., Chesterfield, Mo., 1981-84, asst. prof. anatomy 1979-80. Contbr. articles to profl. jours. Named one of Outstanding Young Women In Am., 1985. Mem. N.Am. Transplant Coordinators Orgn., Midwest Assn. Anatomists, Beta Beta Beta, Eta Sigma Phi, Sigma Phi Chi, Sigma Alumni Club. Avocations: volleyball, piano.

DICKHONER, WILLIAM HAROLD, utility company executive; b. Cin., Sept. 2, 1921; s. Harry Frank and Matilda (Klicke) D.; m. Helen Emma Ludwig, Feb. 20, 1944; children: William H., Thomas Lee. B.S. in Mech. Engring., U. Cin., 1950. With Cin. Gas & Electric Co., 1941-86, supt. power plant, 1961-64, dept. electric prodn., 1964-68, mgr. electric ops., 1968-70, v.p. electric engring. and prodn., 1970-72, sr. v.p. electric engring. and ops., 1972-74, exec. v.p., 1974-75, pres., chief exec. officer, 1975-86, chmn. bd., 1986—; bd. dirs. Cen. Bancorp., Inc., Ohio Nat. Life Ins. Co., Ohio Valley Electric Corp.; chmn. bd. Union Light, Heat & Power Co., Covington, Ky. Mem. adv. bd. Greater Cin. Salvation Army, Boys/Girls Clubs of Greater Cin., Inc.; bd. dirs. Millcreek Valley Conservancy Dist.; mem. bd. advisors U. Cin. Coll. Bus. Adminstrn.; trustee Clovernook Home and Sch. for Blind, Greater Cin. Ctr. for Econ. Edn., Zool. Soc. Cin., U. Cin. Found., DINAMO/OVIA, Pitts. Served to capt., inf. AUS, World War II, Korea. Mem. ASME, Engring. Soc. Cin. Clubs: Queen City (Cin.), Cincinnati (Cin.), Western Hills Country (Cin.). Office: Cin Gas & Electric Co 139 E 4th St Cincinnati OH 45202

DICKIE, JOHN PETER, chemist, corporation executive; b. Waseca, Minn., Apr. 4, 1934; s. John Lewis and Martha (Mortensen) D.; m. Peggy Ann Buhrman, Sept. 6, 1956 (div. 1967); children—Joan E., Anne C.; m. Barbara Lee Brueckman, June 8, 1968 (div. 1978); children—Allison, Kimberly. B.A. cum laude, U. Minn., 1956; M.S., U. Wis.-Madison, 1958, Ph.D., 1960. Postdoctoral fellow U. Wis., Madison, 1960-61; fellow Mellon Inst., 1961-68; group mgr. exploratory research Koppers Co., Monroeville, Pa., 1968-74; dir. basic research Carnation Co., Los Angeles, 1974-78; pres. John Dickie Assocs., St. Paul, 1978-84; v.p., chief operating officer, dir., sec. ATR Electronics Co., St. Paul., 1984-86; research specialist, U. Minn., St. Paul, 1986—. Contbr. articles to profl. jours. Patentee in field. Advisor, Koppers sci. Explorer Scout Post, Monroeville, Pa. Mem. Am. Chem. Soc. (bd. dirs. 1967-68), Pitts. Chemists Club (pres. (1967), Minn. Alumni Assn. (pres. 1970-71). Presbyterian. Avocation: music. Home: 1261 Ingerson Rd Arden Hills MN 55112 Office: Univ Minnesota Dept Biochemistry 356 Gorter Labs Saint Paul MN 55108

DICKIESON, WILLIAM HAROLD, podiatrist; b. Ypsilanti, Mich., Apr. 24, 1956; s. Thomas W. and Joyce A. (Peterson) D.; m. Marcy E. Weingarden, Aug. 15, 1981. AA, Henry Ford Coll., 1976; student, U. Mich., 1976-77; BS, DPM, Ill. Coll. Podiatric Medicine, 1981. Pvt. practice podiatry Dearborn, Mich., 1981—. Fellow Assn. Ambulatory Foot Surgeons, Am. Coll. Foot Surgeons; mem. Am. Podiatric Med. Assn., Southeastern Mich. Podiatric Med. Assn. Presbyterian. Avocations: softball, football, basketball, swimming, reading. Home: 6137 University Dr Dearborn Heights MI 48127 Office: 1213 Mason Dearborn MI 48124

DICKINSON, DAVID FREEMAN, lawyer; b. Jackson, Mich., Jan. 23, 1939; s. Dale Freeman and Zelma Mae (Moore) D.; m. Margaret Lee Hicks, Sept. 12, 1964 (div. 1976); children: Jennifer Lynn, Douglas Freeman; m. Helen Dimanin, Nov. 1, 1980; 1 child, Alexandra Mae. BA, Mich. State U., 1962; JD, Wayne State U., 1967. Bar: Mich. 1967. Trial atty. Giltner & Dickinson, Detroit, 1967-73, Charfoos & Charfoos, Detroit, 1973-79, Lopatin Miller, Detroit, 1979—. Mem. ABA, Detroit Bar Assn., Oakland Bar Assn., Mich. Trial Lawyers, Assn. Trial Lawyers Am. Democrat. Episcopalian. Office: Lopatin Miller et al 547 E Jefferson St Detroit MI 48226

DICKINSON, DAVID WALTER, engineering educator; b. Troy, N.Y., Mar. 29, 1946; s. Edward Irwin and Charlotte Crescentia (Raschke) D.; m. Christine Ann Donnelly, Nov. 18, 1972; children—Kara Ann, Rebecca Jane, Johanna Lee. B.S. in Materials Engring., Rensselaer Poly. Inst., 1967, Ph.D., 1972. Engring. specialist Olin Corp. Research, New Haven, 1972-74; sr. welding research engr. Republic Steel Research, Independence, Ohio, 1974, group leader welding, 1974-79, supr. cold rolled, 1979-83, sect. chief flat rolled, 1983-84; prof. Ohio State U., Columbus, 1984—; dir. research Edison Welding Inst., 1985-87; chmn. dept. welding engring. Ohio State U., 1987—. Author: Welding in the Automotive Industry, 1981. Patentee in field. Mem. adv. bd. Lakeland Community Coll., Mentor, Ohio, 1979-82, Cuyahoga Vocat. Sch., Brecksville, Ohio, 1975-83; mem. acad. bd. Highland Sch. Dist., Hinckley, 1983-84; swim team coach YMCA, Wallingford, Conn., 1972-74; youth advisor Lutheran Ch., Hinckley, 1978-83; synod del. Lutheran Ch. Am., Ohio, 1983; del. Ch. council Lutheran Ch., Hinckley, 1979-84. Recipient Excellence in Oral Presentation award Soc. Automotive Engrs., 1981, Lasting Significance award, 1982; Painter Meml. fellow ASTM, 1970. Mem. Am. Welding Soc. (chmn. Cleve. sect. 1979-80, dir. 1982—; Dist. Meritorious award 1981, McKay-Helm award, 1982), Welding Research Council, Internat. Inst. Welding, Am. Soc. for Metals, Welding Acad. Am. Welding Soc. (chmn. 1980—), Joining Div. Council Am. Soc. Metals, Alpha Sigma Mu (pres. 1970-71). Home: 195 Stonefence Ln Dublin OH 43017 Office: Edison Welding Inst 1100 Kinnear Rd Columbus OH 43212

DICKINSON, JOHN RICHARD, optometrist; b. Danville, Ill., May 10, 1947; s. Robert Dean and Virginia Ruth (Stanton) D.; m. Pamela Jean Smith, June 12, 1971; children—Corey Samuel and Colin Charles. B.S., Ind. U., 1970, D. of Optometry, 1972. Practice assoc. M.D. Bair & Assoc., Findlay, Ohio, 1972-73; resident Martin Luther King Clinic, Cin., 1973-75, gen. practice pediatric optometry, Dayton, Ohio, 1972-84. Contbr. column to Belmont Times, 1985—. Mem. Am. Optometric Assn., Ohio Optometric Assn., Optometric Extension Program (clinic assoc.). Republican. Methodist. Clubs: Toastmasters Internat. (Dayton) (adminstrv. v.p. 1984, pres. 1985), Indian Guides (Xenia) (chief 1983-84). Lodges: Sertoma (corresponding sec. Dayton 1972, sec. Dayton 1973), Lions. Avocations: Golf; bowling; traveling to historically significant destinations. Home: 2493 Coldsprings Dr Beaver Creek OH 45385 Office: Dr John R Dickinson Optometrist 1109 Watervliet Ave Dayton OH 45420 Office: 49 N Howard St Sabina OH 45169

DICKINSON, LANCE DE FORREST, management consultant, educator; b. Johnson City, N.Y., Oct. 31, 1945; s. Clarence B. and Jacqueline A. (Quinn) Sweeney; m. Dorothy L. Burruss, Oct. 5, 1968; children—Nathan K., Lauren W., Sarah A. B.S., U. R.I., 1972; M.A., Central Mich. U., 1981. Personnel mgmt. specialist Naval Underwriter System Ctr., Newport, R.I., 1972-74, Def. Property Disposal Service, Battle Creek, Mich., 1974-76, Def. Contracts Region, Chgo., 1976-78; sr. level personnel mgmt. specialist Def. Logistics Agency, Columbus, Ohio, 1978-82; mng. dir. Lance Dickinson & Co., Columbus, 1982—; adj. prof. Franklin U., Columbus. Bd. dirs. Columbus Opera, 1984 ; mem. vestry St. Albans Episcopal Ch., Bexley, Ohio, 1984—. Served with U.S. Army, 1966-69, Vietnam. Decorated Bronze Star, Purple Heart, Air medal. Mem. Am. Soc. Personnel Adminstrn. (accredited), Nat. Speakers Assn., Am. Soc. Tng. Devel., Am. Mgmt. Assn., Assn. Mgmt. Consultants. Republican. Clubs: University (Columbus); Binghamton. Avocations: pilot; polo; building airplanes. Office: Lance Dickinson & Co 214 E State St Columbus OH 43215

DICKMAN, MARY ANN, nurse, educator; b. Wheeling, W.Va., Feb. 21, 1940; d. George Carl and Elmina G. (Mozena) Bruhn; m. Norman William Dickman, Aug. 11, 1962; children: Amy, Matt. BS in Nursing, Capital U., 1962. Registered Nurse. Pub. health nurse Columbus (Ohio) Pub. Health Nurse Service, 1962-63; charge nurse Community Med. Ctr., Marion, Ohio, 1963-64; instr. Sch. of Practical Nursing, Marion, 1964-65; obstet. nurse Marion Gen. Hosp., 1966-67; office nurse Smith Clinic, Marion, 1967-69; coordinator, instr. Marion Tech. Coll., 1972—. mem. Cen. Ohio Psychiat. Hosp. Adv. Bd., 1985-86, Marion Gen. Hosp. Jr. Woman's Bd. 1979—, Bd. Commrs., 1983; pres. Marion County Mental Health Bd., 1981—. Democrat. Lutheran. Avocations: reading, boating, music. Home: 445 Forest St Marion OH 43302 Office: Marion Tech Coll 1465 Mount Vernon Ave Marion OH 43302

DICKMEYER, KERRY DAVID, land surveyor; b. Ft. Wayne, Ind., June 29, 1948; s. David Paul and Alice Joan (Minser) D.; m. Linda Lou Vonder Haar, Aug. 31, 1968; children: Douglas David, Stacy Theresa. Assoc. Applied Sci. Civil Engring., Purdue U., 1970, BS, 1972. Registered profl. land surveyor, Ind. Instrument man, draftsman Coil Engrs., Inc., Ft. Wayne, 1970-72, survey crew chief, office mgr., 1972-76, chief surveyor (now Coil & Dickmeyer, Inc.), 1976-86, pres., 1986—; mem. assoc. faculty Purdue U., 1980-86. Pres. Hillsboro Community Assn., Ft. Wayne, 1983, 84. Mem. Ind. Soc. Profl. Land Surveyors (v.p. N.E. chpt. 1983, pres., 1984), Am. Congress Surveying and Mapping, Nat. Soc. Profl. Surveyors, Ft. Wayne Ballet, Friends of Allen County Library. Republican. Roman Catholic. Club: Omni (Ft. Wayne). Avocations: philately, computer programming, racquetball, sports. Home: 6734 Hillsboro Ln Fort Wayne IN 46815 Office: Coil & Dickmeyer Inc 6044 East State Fort Wayne IN 46815

DICKSON, BRENT E., state judge. Judge Ind. Supreme Ct., Indpls., 1986—. Office: Ind Supreme Ct State House Indianapolis IN 46204 *

DICKSON, DORIS ROSE, psychologist; b. Cleve., Dec. 7, 1922; adopted d. Herman and Lydia Kathryn (Smith) Lustig; divorced; children: Suzanne Joyce Germond, Terry Marc. BS, U. Toledo, 1958, MEd, 1963; PhD, Walden U., 1978. Lic. psychologist, Ohio. Psychologist Columbus (Ohio) Pub. Schs., 1957—; pvt. practice psychology Columbus, 1980—. Mem. Internat. Transactional Anaylsis Assn., Ohio Psychol. Assn., Nat. Sch. Psychol. Assn., Cen. Ohio Cons. Psychologists, Cen. Ohio Psychol. Assn., AAUW. Avocations: gardening, sewing, cooking, pets. Home: 5623 Chowning Way Columbus OH 43213 Office: 3942 E Main St Columbus OH 43213

DICKSON, NANCY STARR, teacher; b. Frankfort, Ind., Apr. 3, 1936; d. Harley Ledger and Geneve (Daugherty) Fickle; m. Sam W. Dickson, Aug. 23, 1959; 1 child, Hal S. BS, Ball State U., 1958, MA, 1964, cert. reading specialist, 1972. Cert. elem. tchr., Ind. Tchr. Edgelea Elem. Sch., Lafayette, Ind., 1958-59, McKinley Elem. Sch., Muncie, Ind., 1959-65; tchr. spl. reading Garfield Elem. Sch., Muncie, 1967-78; tchr. remedial reading and math. various schs., Muncie, 1978—. Author: (textbook) Our Language Today- Grade 3, 1966, Our Language Today- Grade 4, 1966. Mem. Internat. Reading Assn. (recipient literacy award 1986), Ind. Reading Assn. (coordinator 6 councils 1975—, recipient outstanding service award 1986), Muncie Area Reading Council (membership dir. 1974—, past pres.), Ind. Tchrs. Assn., Nat. Edn. Assn. (life), Muncie Tchrs. Assn., Pi Lambda Theta (v.p. 1985-87), Delta Kappa Gamma, Alpha Sigma Alpha (pres. alumnae 1986-87, advisor 1986—), Ball State U. Wives. Democrat. Methodist. Avocations: reading, sewing, swimming. Home: 3315 W Petty Rd Muncie IN 47304 Office: Garfield Elem Sch 1600 S Madison St Muncie IN 47302

DICKSON, ROBERT FRANK, nursing home executive; b. Carbondale, Ill., Oct. 23, 1933; s. Jason Milburn and Elizabeth (Krysher) D.; m. Roberta Joan Mellican, May 16, 1964; children: Kevin, Craig, Angela, Rebecca. BS, So. Ill. U., 1960. With Farm Credit System, Ill., 1960-67; credit. rep. Fed. Intermediate Credit Bank, St. Louis, 1967-70; adminstr. Union County Hosp., Anna, Ill., 1970-72; v.p. Heritage Enterprises, Inc., Bloomington, Ill., 1972-85, exec. v.p., 1985—. Contbr. articles to mag. Served with USN, 1952-56. Mem. Ill. Health Care Assn. (bd. dirs. 1975-82, 85-86, pres. 1979, 85), Am. Health Care Assn. (bd. dirs. 1979-82, 86). Republican. Presbyterian. Lodge: Kiwanis. Avocations: boating, camping, gardening, reading. Home: 705 Bradley Bloomington IL 61701 Office: Heritage Enterprises Inc 525 N East St Bloomington IL 61701

DIDIER, DONALD EUGENE, social services administrator; b. Grand Forks, N.D., Oct. 10, 1931; s. Eugene Ralph and Frances Flora (Peck) D.; m. Joyce Eddington, Jan. 12, 1952; children: Denise Didier Winsett, Dawn. BA, Belleville (Nebr.) Coll., 1968; MEd, U. Hawaii, 1971. Enlisted USAF, 1954, advanced through ranks to master sgt., retired, 1975; exec. dir. Children's Ctr. for Behavioral Devel., East St. Louis, Ill., 1978-80; dir. consultation and edn. Yeatman/Union-Sarah Mental Health Ctr., St. Louis, 1980-85; exec. dir. St. Clair County Mental Health Bd., Belleville, Ill., 1985—; adj. instr. psychology Park Coll., Kansas City, Mo., 1979-85. Lodges: Lions, Optimists. Office: St Clair County Mental Health Ctr 307 E Washington St Belleville IL 62220

DIDIER, JAMES WILLIAM, college administrator, consultant; b. Detroit, Dec. 25, 1932; s. Charles Louis and Frances (Towne) D.; m. Joan Marie Meylan, Aug. 7, 1954; children: J. Marcus (dec.), Grant Cameron, Fredric Charles. AA, Bay City (Mich.) Jr. Coll., 1952; BA, Alma (Mich.) Coll., 1955; M in Div., No. Bapt. Sem., 1958, ThM, 1959; PhD, Mich. State U., 1965. Dir. higher edn. Mich. Bapt. Conv., Lansing, Mich., 1963-67; dean of student affairs Judson Coll., Elgin, Ill., 1967—, exec. v.p., 1980—; univ. chaplain Am. Bapt. Student Found., East Lansing, Mich., 1960-67; cons. Council Ind. Colls., Washington, 1976—. Bd. dirs. Ecker Ctr. for Mental Health, Elgin, 1984—. Mem. Am. Psychol. Assn., Am. Higher Edn. Assn., Am. Ednl. Research Assn., Am. Personnel and Guidance Assn., Am. Assn. Counseling and Devel., Am. Arbitration Assn. (arbitrator), Mid-West Council on the Ministry, Phi Delta Kappa, Phi Theta Kappa. Lodge: Rotary. Avocations: travel, gardening. Home: 420 Hazel Dr Elgin IL 60123 Office: Judson Coll 1151 N State St Elgin IL 60123

DIDIER, NICHOLAS LEO, real estate developer, consultant; b. White River, S.D., Aug. 24, 1928; s. Nicholas John and Nellie M. (Spear) D.; m. Evelyn E. Beach, Sept. 10, 1949; children—James, Thomas, Barbara. B.B.A., Nat. Coll., Rapid City, S.D., 1948. Dist. mgr. Black Hills Power and Light, Sturgis, S.D., 1952-60, dist. mgr., Hot Springs, S.D., 1960-65, mktg. dir., Rapid City, S.D., 1965-73; owner, gen. mgr. Tip Top Motor Hotel, Rapid City, 1973-83; pres. Interwest Devel. Co., Rapid City, 1983—, Didier and Assoc., Rapid City, 1983—; pres., dir. So. Hills Mining Co., Rapid City, 1981—. Chmn. Fall River County Republican Orgn., Hot Springs, 1962-65. Recipient Disting. Service award Sturgis Jr. C. of C., 1958. Mem. Rapid City C. of C. (bd. dirs., treas. 1979-83). Roman Catholic. Club: Arrowhead. Lodge: Elks. Avocations: golf, swimming. Home: 4618 Ridgewood Dr Rapid City SD 57702 Office: Interwest Devel Co 621 6th St Rapid City SD 57701

DIDZEREKIS, PAUL PATRICK, lawyer; b. Chgo., Mar. 17, 1939; s. Louis Joseph and Estelle (Traczyk) D.; m. Heather Joy Izod, Aug. 8, 1969; children—Alexandria, Alexis. B.B.A., Loyola U., Chgo., 1963, J.D., 1964. Bar: Ill. 1964, U.S. Sup. Ct. 1971. Atty. govt. affairs law and tax depts. Sears, Roebuck & Co., 1960-65; mem. Ashcraft & Ashcraft, Chgo., 1965-72; sole practice, Chgo., 1972-74; pres., ptnr. Didzerekis & Douglas Ltd., Chgo., 1974-78, sole practice, Chgo. and Wheaton, Ill., 1978—; mem. paraprofl. adv. bd. Lewis U. Coll. Law, Glen Ellyn, Ill., 1975, adj. prof. legal ethics in action program 1976-77. Bd. dirs., gen. counsel The Eleanor Assn., 1970—, pres., 1983-84. Recipient David C. Hilliard award Chgo. Bar Assn. 1973-74. Fellow Am. Acad. Matrimonial Lawyers; mem. DuPage County Bar Assn. Contbr. articles to profl. jours. Home: 2 S 209 Stuarton Dr Wheaton IL 60187 Office: 610 W Roosevelt Rd Suite B-2 Wheaton IL 60187

DIECK, DANIEL WILLIAM, search company executive; b. Clintonville, Wis., July 19, 1951; s. Harold Gustav and Jean Lucille (Rohan) D.; m. Kathleen Virginia Goelden, Nov. 3, 1973; children: Ryan Patrick, Benjamin James, Angela Marie, Timothy Daniel. BA cum laude in Mktg. Communications and Drama, U. Wis., Stevens Point, 1973. Dist. sales rep. Mass. Mutual, Springfield, 1973-76, Paul Bunyon Co., Mpls., 1976-83; nat. sales mgr. Browning, Morgan, Utah, 1982-83; v.p. sales and mktg. HCA, Green Bay, Wis., 1983-85; chief exec. officer Corp. Recruiters Inc., Elm Grove, Wis., 1985—; bd. dirs. Summer Breeze Ltd., Brookfield, Wis., 1986—. Mem. Tech. Assocs. Pulp and Paper Industry, Paper Industry Mgmt. Assn., Nat. Assn. Personnel Cons., Wis. Personnel Cons., Nat. Personnel Assocs. Republican. Unitarian. Avocations: hunting, fishing, golf, tennis, travel. Home: 15370 W Linfield Ln New Berlin WI 53151-5857 Office: 890 Elm Grove Rd Suite 212 Elm Grove WI 53122-5100

DIEDERICHS, JANET WOOD, public relations executive; b. Libertyville, Ill.; d. J. Howard and Ruth (Hendrickson) Wood; B.A., Wellesley Coll., 1950; m. John Kuensting Diederichs, 1953. Sales agt. Pan Am. Airways, Chgo., 1951-52; regional mgr. pub. relations Braniff Internat., Chgo., 1953-69; pres. Janet Diederichs & Assocs., Inc., pub. relations cons., Chgo., 1970—; lectr. Harvard U.; mem. exec. com. World Trade Conf., 1983, 84. Com. mem. Nat. Trust for Historic Preservation, 1975-79, Marshall Scholars (Brit. Govt.), 1975-79; trustee Northwestern Meml. Hosp., 1985—; bd. dirs., mem. exec. com. Chgo. Conv. and Visitors Bur. 1978—; bd. dirs. Internat. House, U. Chgo., 1978-84, Com. of 200, 1982-84, Latino Inst., 1986—, Chgo. Network, 1987—; com. mem. Art Inst. Chgo., 1980-83; mem. exec. com. Vatican Art Council Chgo., 1981-83; pres. Jr. League Chgo., 1968-69. Mem. Nat. Acad. TV Arts and Scis., Soc. Am. Travel Writers, Chgo. Assn. Commerce and Industry (bd. dirs. 1982—, exec. com. 1985—), Pub. Relations Soc. Am., Pub. Relations Exchange, Publicity Club Chgo., Chgo. Network. Clubs: Economic, Mid-Am. (dir. 1977-79), Woman's Athletic (Chgo.). Home: 229 E Lake Shore Dr Chicago IL 60611 Office: 333 N Michigan Ave Chicago IL 60601

DIEDRICK, MARCELLA ALICE, educator, reading specialist; b. Vesper, Wis., Dec. 22, 1929; d. William A. and Catherine I. (Wirtz) Brockman; m. Robert W. Diedrick, Dec. 4, 1976. B.S., Edgecliff Coll., Cin., 1968; M.A. in Reading, Cardinal Stritch Coll., Milw., 1975; postgrad. St. Thomas Coll., St. Paul, 1976, U. Wis.-Superior, U. Wis.-Stevens Point, 1977-81. Cert. tchr., prin., reading specialist, Wis. Tchr. St. John the Evangelist Elem. Sch., Deer Park, Ohio, 1959-68, Rhinelander (Wis.) Catholic Central, 1968-74, St. Robert Bellarmine, Merrill, Wis., 1974-75, St. Johns, Edgar, Wis., 1975-76; prin., tchr. St. Peter the Fisherman, Eagle River, Wis., 1976-79; reading specialist, Elcho (Wis.) Pub. Schs., 1979—. Mem. Internat. Reading Assn., Wis. State Reading Assn., Headwater Reading Council (pres. 1970-71, 82-83), Delta Kappa Gamma. Roman Catholic.

DIEHL, GERALD GEORGE, architect; b. Highland Park, Mich., July 24, 1916; s. George Frederick and Alice Veronica (Nolan) D.; m. Marie Josephine Irving (dec. Feb. 1987); children: Rosemary, Martha, Patricia, Elizabeth, Paul, James, Daniel, Frederick. Student, Lawrence Inst. Tech.; LHD (hon.), Siena Heights Coll., 1976. Registered architect, Mich. Draftsman Giffels & Vallet, Detroit, 1941-44, Harley Ellington, Detroit, 1944-45, Sarben & Sarben, Bloomfield Hills, Mich., 1954-47; v.p. Diehl & Diehl, Arch., Detroit, 1947-76, pres., 1976—; chmn. planning com. Siena Heights Coll., Adrian, Mich., 1974—. Chmn. properties com. Boys' & Girls' Clubs, Southeastern Mich., 1982—, torch drive div. United Found., Detroit, 1955-86; chmn., mem. City Plan Commn., Detroit. Fellow AIA (pres. Detroit chpt., Gold Medal Detroit chpt. 1965); mem. Mich. Soc. Architects (sec.), Engring. Soc. Detroit. Roman Catholic. Clubs: Detroit Athletic, Renaissance (Detroit). Avocations: travel, photography, history. Office: Diehl & Diehl Architects Inc 28 W Adams Suite 903 Detroit MI 48226

DIEHL, JAY CORMAN, electrical engineer; b. Detroit, June 26, 1952; s. Corman James and Lucille (DiBacco) D.; m. Barbara Anne Barnes, Sept. 20, 1980. B.E.E., Gen. Motors Inst., 1975; M.B.A., Eastern Mich. U., 1983. Registered profl. engr., Mich. Sr. engr. HydraMatic div. Gen. Motors Corp., Ypsilanti, Mich., 1970-84; mgr. plant and process engring. MAC Valve, Inc., Wixom, Mich., 1984-86, mgr. engring., 1986—. Republican. Roman Catholic. Avocation: competitive water skiing. Home: 8305 Ledgewood Ct Fenton MI 48430 Office: MAC Valve 30569 Beck Rd Wixom MI 48096

DIEHL, PAUL EUGENE, optometrist; b. Belleville, Ill., Sept. 23, 1936; s. Carl and Lucille (Bell) D.; m. Sharon Lee Busekrus, Apr. 8, 1961; children: Deborah Paulette, David Paul, Jonathan Brian. AA, Belleville Area Coll., 1956; BS, Ill. Coll. Optometry, 1958, DO, 1959. Pvt. practive optometry Belleville, 1962—, Cahokia, Ill., 1963—; v.p. Dale Everett Ministries, Belleville, 1982—, also bd. dirs. Speaker Full Gospel Mens Fellowship Internat., 1980—; bd. dirs. Mens Fellowship of Grace World Outreach Ctr., St. Louis, 1984—. Served to capt. USAF, 1959-62. Mem. Am. Optometric Assn., Ill. Optometric Assn., Southwestern Ill. Optometric Assn., Ill. Coll. Optometry (Tomb and Key Honor Frat.), Phi Kappa Theta. Republican. Mem. Ind. Charismatic Ch. Lodge: Rotary (bd. dirs. Belleville chpt. 1977-80). Avocations: golf, tennis, photography, music, radio controlled aviation. Home: 8 Conway Village Ct Creve Coeur MO 63141 Office: 2801 W Main St Belleville IL 62223 Office: 1153 Camp Jackson Rd Cahokia IL 62206

DIEHL, WILLIAM GEORGE, financial executive, consultant; b. Grosse Pointe, Mich., Dec. 10, 1951; s. Wilbert R. and Alice E. (Wells) D.; m. Judith Heedt, Sept. 8, 1983; children: Theresa Lynn, Catherine Marie. BS in Acctg., Wayne State U., 1977; MA in Bus., Cen. Mich. U., 1984. CPA, Mich. Acct. Plante & Moran, Southfield, Mich., 1978-81; controller Dollar Electric Co., Madison Heights, Mich., 1981-83; v.p. fin., treas. Dollar Corp., Troy, Mich., 1984—; cons. small bus., 1981—. Served with USAF, 1971-75. Mem. Nat. Assn. Accts. (pres. Macomb County chpt. 1984-85), Am. Inst. CPAs, Mich. Assn. CPAs. Roman Catholic. Office: Dollar Corp 1835 Technology Dr Troy MI 48083

DIEKEMPER, GREGORY ROBERT, corporate professional; b. Belleville, Ill., May 26, 1958; s. Robert Frank and Arlene Mildred (Rickert) D.; m. Rita Kay Garbs, Feb. 14, 1987. BSBA in Acctg. magna cum laude, U. Mo., 1980. CPA, Mo. Audit supr. Touche Ross and Co., St. Louis, 1980-86; treas., asst. sec. Guarantee Elec., St. Louis, 1986—. Chmn. internat. ops. V.P. Fair, St. Louis. Mem. Am. Subcontractors, Constrn. Fin. Mgmt. Assn., Assn. Corp. Growth, Am. Inst. CPA's, Mo. Soc. CPA's. Avocation: sports. Office: Guarantee Elec PO Box 14351 Saint Louis MO 63178

DIEL, DELORES KAY, elementary teacher; b. May 29, 1953; d. Donald Duane and Mildred Bryant (Willig) B.; m. Rex J. Diel, Aug. 14, 1979. BSEd, Ft. Hay Kans. State U., 1977; postgrad, Northwestern Okla. State U. Owner, operator Dairy Bar, Kiowa, Kans., 1978-84; tchr. South Barber Schs., Kiowa, 1985-86; tchr. mentally handicapped Puls Elem. Sch., Attica, Kans., 1986—; para-profl. South Barber High Sch., 1985. Brownie leader Girl Scouts of U.S., Kiowa, 1984-87; mother advisor Rainbow Girls, 1978-82; bd. Christian edn. Congl. Ch., Kiowa, 1987. Recipient Danforth award, Kiowa, 1971. Mem. Phi Delta Kappa. Republican. Congregationalist. Lodge: Eastern Star. Avocations: reading, crafts, sewing, snow and water skiing. Home: 816 Dickenson Kiowa KS 67070 Office: Puls Elem Sch Attica KS 67009

DIEL, VERNON M., dentist; b. Alamotta, Kans., Jan. 8, 1932; s. Jacob and Pauline (Schegel) D.; m. Lois F. Brosemer, Aug. 31, 1957; children—Thomas McKay, Scott Evan. B.A., U. Kans., 1958; D.D.S., Kansas City U., 1962. Diplomate Am. Bd. Denistry. Oral surgery tng. Gen. Hosp., Kansas City, Mo., gen. practice denistry, Lawrence, Kans., 1962-84. Pres. Cosmopolitan Internat., Lawrence, 1973; precinct committeeman Republican Central Com., Lawrence, 1968-70. Served with U.S. Army, 1954-56. Recipient Disting. Service award Cosmopolitan Internat., 1974. Mem. ADA, Kans. State Dental Assn., Douglas County Dental Assn. (pres. 1964-65), Delta Sigma Delta, Theta Chi (charter). Club: Lawrence Country. Lodge: Elks. Avocations: antique and classic atuos; model airplanes. Office: Vernon M Diel DDS 2711 W 6th St Lawrence KS 66044

DIELEMAN, WILLIAM WILBUR, state legislator; b. Oskaloosa, Iowa, Jan. 19, 1931; s. Garret Jan and Jozena (DeGeus) D.; B.A., Calvin Coll., Grand Rapids, Mich., 1959; M.A., State U. Iowa, Iowa City, 1966; m. Emily June Langstraat, Aug. 30, 1951; children—Wendell E., Cynthia E. Dieleman DeYoung, Kristen E. Dieleman Gandrow. Tchr. social studies Pella (Iowa) Christian High Sch., 1959-74; agt. Guarantee Mut. Life Ins. Co. Nebr., 1974—; mem. Pella City Council, 1970-75; mem. Iowa Ho. of Reps. from 70th Dist., 1974-81, state senator from 35th Dist., 1982—; owner, pub. Diamond Trail News, Sully, Iowa. Del. local and state Democratic Convs., 1963—; mem. Iowa Capitol Planning Commn., 1979-82, 84—. Served with U.S. Army, 1953-55. Asian Affairs Inst. grantee, 1972. Mem. Central Iowa Regional Assn. Local Govt. (vice chmn. 1974), Am. Legion, Iowa Assn. Life Underwriters, Nat. Assn. Life Underwriters, Nat. Conf. State Legislators, Council State Govts., Farm Bur. Democrat. Mem. Christian Reformed Ch. (elder 1978-80, 84-86). Office: PO Box 220 1201 High Ave W Oskaloosa IA 52577

DIERCKS, EILEEN KAY, educational media coordinator; b. Lima, Ohio, Oct. 31, 1944; d. Robert Wehner and Florence (Huckemeyer) McCarty; m. Dwight Richard Diercks, Dec. 27, 1969; children: Roger, David, Laura. BSEd, Bluffton Coll., 1962-66; MS, U. Ill., 1968. Tchr. elem. grades Kettering City Schs. (Ohio), 1966-67; children's librarian St. Charles County, St. Charles, Mo., 1968-69; librarian Rantoul High Sch. (Ill.), 1970-71; elem. tchr. Elmhurst Sch. Dist. (Ill.), 1971-72; media coordinator Plainfield Sch. Dist. (Ill.), 1980—. Founder, treas. FISH orgn., Plainfield, 1975-78; pres. Ch. Women United, 1974; treas. Plainfield Congl. Ch., 1983—; bd. dirs. Cub Scouts, 1983-86; leader Girl Scouts U.S., Plainfield, 1985—; mem. Bolingbrook (Ill.) Community Chorus, 1986—. Mo. State Library scholar, 1967. Mem. Ill. Library Assn., ALA, NEA, Ill. Edn. Assn., Plainfield Assn. Tchrs., Pi Delta, Beta Phi Mu. Clubs: LeWood Homemakers (pres. 1973-74), Plainfield Athletic (sec. 1984-86). Home: 13440 S Rivercrest Dr Plainfield IL 60544 Office: Plainfield Sch Dist #202 612 Commercial St Plainfield IL 60544

DIERINGER, ROBERT LEE, bank executive; b. Celina, Ohio, Feb. 2, 1935; s. Glenn and Elizabeth (Davis) D.; m. Patricia Louise Bidwell, Aug. 9, 1057; children: Tracy, Craig, Marc, Scott,. Student, U. Dayton, 1954-55; BS in Banking, Wis. U., 1984. Br. mgr. Dayton Newspapers, Dayton, Ohio, 1955-57; asst. mgr. Third Nat. Bank, Dayton, 1957-66; exec. v.p. Peoples Nat. Bank, Versailles, Ohio, 1966-83, Arcanum (Ohio) Nat. Bank, 1983-85; sr. v.p. Greenville (Ohio) Nat. Bank, 1985—; bd. dirs. Darke County Mental Health Clinic; instr. Wright State U., Celina, 1979-84. Pres. Versailles Devel. Assn., 1970-72. Mem. Community Bankers Assn. of Ohio (bd. dirs., v.p. 1985-86, pres.-elect 1987—), Darke County Bankers Assn. (pres. 1974-76). Republican. Lutheran. Lodges: Lions (bd. dirs. Versailles chpt. 1979-85), Masons (master 1972-73), Shriners, Elks. Avocation: golf. Home: 11 Elmwood Dr Versailles OH 45380 Office: Greenville Nat Bank Fourth and Broadway Greenville OH 45331

DIERMEIER, JEFFREY JAMES, investment manager; b. Appleton, Wis., Oct. 1, 1952; s. Clair Hubert and Mary Helen (Quella) D.; m. Julie Margaret Evans, Jan. 16, 1982; children: Erica Rae, Jeremy Daniel. BBA with distinction, U.Wis.-Madison, 1974, MBA, 1975. Chartered fin. analyst. Staff strategy and methods First Nat. Bank Chgo., 1975-79, div. head, v.p., 1979-84; mng. dir. First Chgo. Investment Advisors, 1984—. Mem. Candidate Curriculum Com.; bd. dirs. U. Wis. Bus. Alumni, 1987—. Recipient Roger F. Murray award Inst. Quantitative Research, 1986, Graham and Dood award Fin. Analysis Fedn., 1984; T. Doig fellow U. Wis.-Madison, 1974; W. Kies scholar U.Wis., 1973. Mem. Inst. Chartered Fin. Analysts (chmn. econs. subcom. 1986—), Fin. Analysts Fedn., Chgo. Analysts Soc., Investment Tech. Symposium Chgo., Chgo. Options/Futures Soc. Roman Catholic. Club: Young Execs. (Chgo.) (pres. 1982-83). Home: 2650 N Lakeview #902 Chicago IL 60614 Office: First Chicago Investment Advisors 3 First Nat Plaza Suite 0146 Chicago IL 60670

DIERSEN, DAVID JOHN, internal auditor; b. Chicago Heights, Ill., Sept. 29, 1948; s. John Robert and Esther Dorothy (Balgemann) D.; m. Karen Annette Gassner, Apr. 1, 1978. Student, U. Ill., Chgo., 1966-1968; BS in Mgmt., No. Ill. U., 1970; MBA, Loyola U., Chgo., 1976; MS in Acctg., De Paul U., 1980. CPA, Ill.; cert. internal auditor. Mgr. retail sales Firestone Stores, Chgo. Heights, Ill., 1970-71; revenue officer IRS, Chgo., 1971-76, collection div. advisor, 1976-80; evaluator U.S. GAO, Chgo., 1980—. Mem. Assn. Govt. Acct. (bd. dir. 1983—, Recognition Plaque award 1986), Inst. Internal Auditors, Ill. CPA Soc., Am. Inst. CPA's (tax div.), Am. Soc. Pub. Adminstrn., Nat. Assn. Accts., Am. Acctg. Assn. Lutheran. Avocations: reading, walking, travel, Corvettes. Home: 915 Cove Ct Wheaton IL 60187 Office: GAO 10 W Jackson 5th Floor Chicago IL 60604

DIESTERHEFT, RICHARD ROBERT, restaurant company executive; b. Chgo., Feb. 22, 1949; s. Richard William and Evelyn Ruth (Harrer) D.; m. Linda Joy Koenig, Apr. 8, 1975; children: Lindsy, Amy, Richard John. Student, U. London Sch. Econs., Eng., 1969; BA in Edn. and Social Scis., Nat. Coll. Edn., Evanston, Ill., 1972, MS in Edn. Adminstrn., 1973. Cert. secondary tchr., Ill. Pres. Poor Richard's Pub, Gurnee, Ill., 1975—, UBAA Tap and Liquors, Skokie, Ill., 1985—. Pres. Gurnee (Ill.) Days Orgn. Mem. Lake County Tavern Assn. (bd. dirs. 1981-82), Gurnee Liquor Lic. Assn. (pres. 1976—), Gurnee Jaycees (v.p. 1983). Republican. Lodges: Rotary (editor 1974), Exchange (pres. 1982-83). Avocations: nautilus, running, writing, philosophy, physical fitness. Office: Poor Richard's Pub and Restaurant 4610 Grand Ave Gurnee IL 60031

DIETER, RAYMOND ANDREW, JR., physician, surgeon; b. Chebanse, Ill., June 19, 1934; s. Raymond Augustus Sr. and Emma Rose (Witt) D.; m. Bette Renée Myers, Sept. 29, 1961; children: Raymond, David, Lisa, Lynn, Deanna, Robert. Student, U. Ill., 1952-56, MA, 1966; MD, Loyola U., 1960. Diplomate Am. Bd. Thoracic Surgery, Am. Bd. Surgery. Intern Cook County Hosp., Chgo., 1960-61; resident in gen. surgery VA Hosp., Hines, Ill., 1963-67, sr. resident in cardiopulmonary surgery, 1967-69; practice medicine specializing in thoracic, cardiovascular medicine Glen Ellyn (Ill.) Clinic, 1969—, pres., 1982-85, also bd. dirs.; mem. staff Hines (Ill.) VA Hosp., 1963-74, Cen. DuPage Hosp., Winfield, Ill., 1969—, Loyola U. Med. Ctr., Maywood, Ill., 1969-80, Meml. Hosp. DuPage County, Elmhurst, Ill., 1969—, Delnor Hosp., St. Charles, Ill., 1970-79, Community Hosp., Geneva, Ill., 1970—, Alexian Bros. Med. Ctr., Elk Grove Village, Ill., 1975-79, Good Samaritan Hosp., Downers Grove, Ill., 1976—, Glendale Heights (Ill.) Community Hosp., 1980—; clin. instr. Stritch Sch. Medicine Loyola U., 1966-71, clin. asst. prof., 1971-80; trustee Ctr. Bank, Glen Ellyn, Glen Ellyn Found., Glen Ellyn Facilities. Author: (with B.R. Dieter and A.C. Mickelson) Mickelson and Peterson Family Sketch, 1970, (with M.C. Sorensen and E.R. Dieter) A Sorensen and Jensen Family Tree, 1975, (with B.R. Dieter, C. Myers, U. Myers, and D. Dieter) A Myers and Remley Family Tree, 1978; contbr. numerous articles to profl. jours. Mgr. Glen Ellyn baseball team, 1970, 71, 78-82; asst. leader 4-H Club, 1975-83; mem. Glenbard South High Sch. Boosters, World Fedn. Drs. Who Respect Human Life, 1980—. Served with USPHS, 1961-63, with Res. 1982—. Fellow ACS, Internat. Coll. Angiology 1969, Internat. Coll. Surgeons; mem. AMA (Physician's Recognition award 1969, 73, 76, 80, 83), Internat. Soc. Circumpolar Health, Internat. Soc. Outdoor Health, Am. Coll. Angiology, Am. Coll. Chest Physicians, Assn. Academic Surgeons, Am. Soc. Circumpolar Health (charter), Assn. Mil. Surgeons, Assn. Res. Officers, Am. Heart Assn. (counsil 1974—), Nat. Assn. Interns and Residents, Soc. Med. Hist. Chgo., Soc. Critical Care Medicine, Soc. Thoracic Surgeons, Ill. State Med. Soc. (trustee 1983—), Ill. Thoracic Surgical Soc. (sec. 1981-83, pres. 1984-85), DuPage County Med. Soc. (pres. 1977, mem. numerous coms.), Chgo. Med. Soc., Charles B. Puestow Surgical Soc. (sec., treas. 1966-67, v.p. 1968), Good Samaritan Soc., Ala. Geographic Soc., Kankakee Valley Geneal. Soc., Ill. Geneal. Soc., U. Ill. Alumni Assn., Am. Rabbit Breeders Assn. Republican. Roman Catholic. Club: Century (Elmhurst). Lodge: Lions. Home: 22 W 240 Stanton Circle

Glen Ellyn IL 60137 Office: Glen Ellyn Clinic 454 Pennsylvania Ave Glen Ellyn IL 60137

DIETRICH, GEORGE CHARLES, chemical company executive; b. Detroit, Feb. 5, 1927; s. George Sylvester and Catherine Elizabeth (Cable) D.; B.S., U. Detroit; m. Dorothy Ann Flanigan, Aug. 21, 1954; children—Linda Marie, Elizabeth Ann, George Charles. Field sales mgr. Allied Chem. Co., Chgo., 1960-64; dir. sales Aerosol Research Co., North Riverside, Ill., 1964—; pres. Aeropres Corp., Chgo., 1964-65, Diversified Chems. & Propellants Co., Westmont, Ill., 1965—, also dir.; chmn. bd. ChemSpec Ins. Ltd.; dir. Am. Nat. Bank, De Kalb, Ill., Diversified CPC Internat., Anaheim, Calif., Klockner CPC Internat.; bd. dirs., chmn. Consumers Specialties Ins. Co., Wilmington, Del., Expert Mgmt. Systems, Phoenix; pres., chief exec. officer Gen. Energy Internat. Served with USNR, 1945-46. Mem. Chem. Splty. Mfrs. Assn. (gov., chmn. bd.), Chgo. Drug and Chem. Assn., Chgo. Perfumery Soap and Extract Assn., Nat. Paint and Coatings Assn., World Univ. Roundtable, Internat. Platform Assn., Econs. Club Chgo., Execs. Club Chgo. Roman Catholic. Clubs: Butler Nat. Golf; Boca Raton (Fla.) Hotel and Club; Butterfield Country. Home: 1 Charleston Rd Hinsdale IL 60521 Office: 350 E Ogden Ave PO Box 447 Westmont IL 60559

DIETRICH, SUZANNE CLAIRE, instructional designer; b. Granite City, Ill., Apr. 9, 1937; d. Charles Daniel and Evelyn Blanche (Waters) D.; B.S. in Speech, Northwestern U., 1958; M.S. in Pub. Communication, Boston U., 1967; postgrad. So. Ill. U., 1973—. Intern, prodn. staff Sta. WGBH-TV, Boston, 1958-59, asst. dir., 1962-64, asst. dir. program Invitation to Art, 1958; cons. producer dir. dept. instructional TV radio Ill. Office Supt. Pub. Instruction, Springfield, 1969-70; dir. program prodn. and distbn., 1970-72; instr. faculty call staff, speech dept. Sch. Fine Arts So. Ill. U., Edwardsville, 1972—, grad. asst. for doctoral program office of dean Sch. Edn., 1975-78; research asst. Ill. public telecommunications study for Ill. Public Broadcasting Council, 1979-80; cons. and research in communications, 1980—; exec. producer, dir. TV programs Con-Con Countdown, 1970, The Flag Speaks, 1971. Roman Catholic. Home: 1011 Minnesota Ave Edwardsville IL 62025

DIETSCHE, DELMAR ALLEN, business executive; b. Bloomer, Wis., Feb. 11, 1931; s. Harold Charles and Minnie (Boese) D.; m. Irene Alma Tiller, Jun 8, 1952; children—Catherine, David, James. B.S. in Chemistry, U. Wis.-River Falls, 1952; B.S. in Physics, U. Wash., Seattle, 1953. Project engr. elec. div. Gen. Mills, Mpls., 1956-63; tech. service engr. visual products div. 3M Co., St. Paul, 1963-70, product devel. mgr., 1970-76, lab. mgr. nat. advt. div., 1977-82, sign materials project, 1982-85, lab. mgr. comml. graphics div., 1986—. Team leader overhead projector invention, 1977 (Golden Step award), flexible sign face prodn. system, 1977 (Trade Secret); patentee in field. Active mem. Parks and Recreation Com., Shoreview, Minn., 1969-70. Served to capt. USAF, 1953-56. Mem. Jaycees. Republican. Lutheran. Club: Hudson Golf (Wis.). Avocations: golf; Canadian fishing. Home: 3976 MacKubin St Saint Paul MN 55126 Office: 3M Co Comml Graphics Div Bldg 207-BN-03 Saint Paul MN 55144

DIFATE, HELEN KESSLER, architect; b. Mt. Vernon, N.Y., Jan. 23, 1942; d. Lawrence Victor and Helen de Forestal (McKernan) Kessler; B.A., Coll. of New Rochelle, 1963; B.Arch., Cooper Union, 1968; m. Victor George DiFate, Jr., June 5, 1966; children—Eric Victor, Kristen Helen. Designer, Bro. Cajetan J.B. Baumann O.F.M. Architect, FAIA, N.Y.C., 1962-70; project dir. Philip J. Wilker Architect & Assos., Bronxville, N.Y., 1970-71; designer Robert A. Green & Philip G. McIntosh AIA, Architects, N. Tarrytown, N.Y., 1971-72; architect Fleagle and Kaeyer, Architects, Yonkers, N.Y., 1972-74, Anselevicius/Rupe/Assos., St. Louis, 1974-75; architect Helen Kessler DiFate AIA Architect, St. Louis, 1971—; part time faculty engr. div., archtl. option, St. Louis Community Coll. Meramec, 1975-76, also mem. drafting and design tech. adv. com.; mem. Women's Assn. of St. Louis Symphony Soc., Friends of St. Louis Art Mus., Friends of St. Louis Sci. Mus. Registered architect, N.Y., Mo., Ill.; certified Nat. Council Archtl. Registration Bds. Mem. AIA (corporate mem.; dir. Westchester, N.Y., chpt., 1974, officer St. Louis chpt. 1984, 85), Mo. Council Architects, Alliance of Women in Architecture, Clayton (Mo.) C. of C. Roman Catholic. Archtl. project published in books: Buildings Reborn: New Uses, Old Places (Barbaralee Diamonstein), 1978, The Building Art in St. Louis: Two Centuries (George McCue), 1981. Office: 131 N Bemiston Ave Saint Louis MO 63105

DIFINO, RICHARD EDWARD, journalist, food consultant; b. Chgo., Dec. 26, 1933; s. Giacomo John and Mary Rosa D. Student, Marquette U., 1952-54, Northwestern U., 1964-65. Radio personality Migala Communications, Chgo., 1980-83; journalist Pioneer Press, Inc., Wilmette, Ill., 1983—; food cons. Speco Products, Inc., Chgo., 1983—, Spring/Switzerland, Chgo., 1985—; prodn. coordinator Group W Cable TV, Chgo., 1984—; host TV cooking program Cooking with Class, 1980-81. Author: Brick Oven Cookbook, 1983; editor: Italian Heritage Cookbook, 1983, Straight From The Heart Cookbook, 1984. Democrat. Roman Catholic. Avocations: music, opera, TV. Home and Office: 601 Rose Dr Melrose Park IL 60160

DIGGS, MATTHEW O'BRIEN, JR., air conditioning and refrigeration manufacturing executive; b. Louisville, Jan. 11, 1933; s. Matthew O'Brien and Dorothy (Leary) D.; m. Nancy Carolyn Brown, Nov. 5, 1955; children: Elizabeth, Joan, Judith, Matthew III. Student, Hanover Coll., 1950-52; BSME, Purdue U., 1955; MBA, Harvard U., 1961. With Lincoln Electric, Cleve., 1957-59, Toledo Scale Corp., 1961-63; cons., assoc., v.p., then v.p. and mng. officer East Cen. Region Booz, Allen & Hamilton, Inc., Cleve., 1963-72; v.p. mktg. Copeland Corp., Sidney, Ohio, 1972-74, exec. v.p., 1974, pres., chief exec. officer, 1975—. Served to 1st lt. U.S. Army, 1955-57. Home: 1160 Lytle Ln Kettering OH 45409 Office: Copeland Corp 1675 W Campbell Rd Sidney OH 45365

DIGIACOMO, JAMES JOSEPH, accountant; b. Chgo., June 18, 1960; s. Nicholas and Frances Madeline (Liquori) DiG. BS in Acctg., U. Ill., Chgo., 1982; postgrad., Sch. of Mortgage Banking, 1987. CPA, Ill. Acct. residential mortgage div. Draper & Kramer, Inc., Chgo., 1983—. Mem. Am. Inst. CPA's, Ill. CPA Soc. Roman Catholic. Avocations: Italian-Am. history, sports, reading. Office: Draper & Kramer Inc 33 W Monroe Chicago IL 60603

DIGIOVANNI, ANTHONY MICHAEL, physician, gastroenterologist; b. Detroit, Sept. 26, 1942; s. Michael Anthony and Agatha (Ciaramitaro) DiG.; m. Sharon Anne Sakuta, Aug. 22, 1964; children: Michael, Anthony, Joseph, James. BS in Chemistry, U. Detroit, 1964; DO, Chgo. Coll. Osteopathy, 1968. Mem. staff Bi-County Hosp., Warren, Mich., 1973—, vice chmn. internal medicine dept., 1975-78; sect. chief gastroenterology dept. William Beaumont Hosp., Troy, Mich., 1983—, chmn. endoscopy dept., 1983—; mem. staff Mt. Clemens (Mich.) Gen. Hosp.; asst. clin. prof. Mich. State U., 1973—. Contbr. articles to profl. jours. U. Mich. fellow Mich. State Coll., 1972-73. Mem. Am. Coll. Osteo. Internists, Am. Osteo. Physicians, Mich. Assn. Osteo. Physicians and Surgeons, Am. Soc. Gastrointestinal Endoscopy, Mich. Soc. Gastroent. (pres. 1978-79). Roman Catholic. Club: Pine Lake Country (West Bloomfield, Mich.), Amelia Plantation Country (Amelia Island, Fla.). Lodge: Elks. Avocations: golf, photography, water and snow skiing, study of Italian. Office: Tri-County Gastroent PC 13552 Martin Suite A Warren MI 48093

DIGMAN, LESTER ALOYSIUS, management educator; b. Kieler, Wis., Nov. 22, 1938; s. Arthur Louis and Hilda Dorothy (Jansen) D.; m. Ellen Rhomberg Pfohl, Jan. 15, 1966; children: Stephanie, Sarah, Mark. BSME, U. Iowa, 1961, MSIE, 1962, PhD, 1970. Registered profl. engr., Mass. Mgt. cons. U.S. Ameta, Rock Island, Ill., 1962-67; mgmt. instr. U. Iowa, Iowa City, 1967-69; head applied math. dept. U.S. Ameta, Rock Island, Ill., 1969-74, head managerial tng. dept., 1974-77; assoc. prof. mgt. U. Neb., Lincoln, 1977-84; dir. grad. studies in mgmt. U. Neb., 1982—; prof. mgt. U. Neb., Lincoln, 1984—; cons. various orgns., 1963-72; sec. treas. Mgmt. Services Associates Ltd., Davenport, Iowa, 1972-77; owner L.A. Digman and Assocs., Lincoln, 1977—; gen. ptnr. Letna Properties, Madison, Wis., 1978—. Author: Strategic Management, 1986; Network Analysis for Management Decisions, 1982; also articles. Recipient Dist. award SBA, 1980, certs. of appreciation Dept. of Def., 1972. Mem. Decision Scis. Inst. (charter) (assoc. program chmn. 1985-86, program chmn. 1986, pres. 1987-88), Strategic Mgmt. Soc. (founding), Acad. of Mgmt. The Planning Forum, Pan Pacific Bus. Assn. Roman Catholic. Clubs: Hillcrest Country (Lincoln). Avocations: gardening, photography, wine tasting. Home: 7520 Lincolnshire Rd Lincoln NE 68506 Office: U Nebr 219 CBA Lincoln NE 68588

DILAURA, KENNETH ANTHONY, controller; b. Detroit, Dec. 16, 1945; s. Tony Tulleo and Violet Marie (Qualtieri) DiL.; m. Veronica Elizabeth Moses, Apr. 7, 1972; children: Brian, Christina. BBA, U. Notre Dame, 1968; MBA, Wayne State U., 1970. CPA, Mich. Tchr. elem. sch. St. Margaret's, St. Clair Shores, Mich., 1968-70, St. David's, Detroit, 1970-71; audit staff Ernst & Whinney, Detroit, 1971-72, auditor-in-charge, 1972-73, audit sr., 1973-75, audit supr., 1975-76; v.p. and control rev. officer Mich. Nat. Bank of Detroit, Bloomfield Hills, 1976-78; asst. controller Mich. Nat. Corp., Bloomfield Hills, 1978-80; controller Mich. Nat. Corp., Bloomfield Hills., 1980-85; v.p. and controller Mich. Nat. Corp., Bloomfield Hills, 1985—; 1st v.p., controller Mich. Nat. Corp., Farmington Hills, 1987—. Mem. Am. Inst. CPA's, Mich. Assn. CPA's, Fin. Execs. Inst., Bank Adminstrn. Inst., Nat. Assn. Accts. Clubs: Economic, Notre Dame (Detroit). Office: Mich Nat Corp 30665 Northwestern Hwy PO Box 9065 Farmington Hills MI 48018-9065

DILCHER, DAVID L., paleobotany educator; b. Cedar Falls, Iowa, July 10, 1936; m. Katherine Swanson, 1961; children—Peter, Ann. B.S. in Natural History, U. Minn., 1958, M.S. in Botany, Geology and Zoology, 1960; postgrad., U. Ill., 1960-62; Ph.D. in Biology, Geology, Yale U., 1964; participant field course in field dendrology, Costa Rica, 1968. Teaching asst. U. Minn., Mpls., 1958-60; teaching asst. U. Ill., Urbana, 1960-62, Yale U., New Haven, Conn., 1962-63; Cullman-Univ. fellow Yale U., 1963-64, instr. biology, 1965-66; NSF postdoctoral fellow Senckenberg Mus., Frankfurt am Main, Federal Republic Germany, 1964-65; asst. prof. botany Ind. U., Bloomington, 1966-70; assoc. prof. Ind. U., 1970-76, assoc. prof. geology, 1975, prof. paleobotany, 1977—; Guggenheim fellow Giessen, Federal Republic Germany, 1972-73, Imperial Coll., London, 1972-73, Ind. U., 1972-73, 87—; disting. vis. research scholar U. Adelaide, Australia, 1981; Guggenheim fellow Brit. Mus. Natural History, London, 1987—; panel mem. for systematic biology program, NSF, 1977, 78, 79, panel mem. for selecting NATO postdoctoral fellow, 1982; vis. lectr. to People's Republic of China Nat. Acad. Sci. com. on scholarly communications with China, 1986. Author: (with D. Redmon, M. Tansey and D. Whitehead) Plant Biology Laboratory Manual, 1973, 2d edit., 1975; editor: (with Tom Taylor and Theodore Delevoryas) Plant Reproduction in the Fossil Record, symposium vol., 1979, (with T. Taylor) Biostratigraphy of Fossil Plants: Successional and Paleoecological Analysis, 1980, (with William L. Crepet) Origin and Evolution of Flowering Plants, Symposium Volume, 1984, (with Michael S. Zavada) Phylogeny of the Hamamedidae, symposium vol., 1986; contbr. numerous articles and abstracts to profl. jours. and books. Mem. utilities bd. City of Bloomington, 1974-76; ruling elder First Presbyn. Ch. Bloomington, 1975-77; bd. dirs. United Campus Ministries, 1971-72; mem. council Monroe County United Ministries, 1975-77. Grantee Sigma Xi, 1961, 62, 66, Ind. U., 1967-68, Orgn. Tropical Studies, 1971; travel grantee Ind. U., 1968, 71, 77, 80; research grantee NSF, 1966-69, 69-71, 71-74, 75-77, 77-79, 79, 79-80, 79-84, 82-83, 83-84, 85—, Amax Coal Found., 1980-81; Eaton-Hooker fellow, 1963; Cullman-Univ. fellow, 1963-64, Guggenheim fellow, 1972-73, 87—. Fellow Ind. Acad. Sci., Linnean Soc.; mem. Bot. Soc. Am. (chmn. paleobot. sect. 1974, sec.-treas. 1975-77, rep. to jour. editorial bd. 1978-79, mem. jour. editorial bd. 1981-82, mem. conservation com. 1978-81, chmn. conservation com. 1981, 82, program dir. 1982-84, mem. exec. bd. 1982—, sec. 1985-88), Paleontol. Soc., Paleontol. Assn., AAAS, Internat. Orgn. Paleobotanists (N. Am. rep. 1975-81), Assn. Tropical Biology, Am. Inst. Biol. Scis., Am. Assn. Stratigraphic Palynologists, Internat. Assn. Angiosperm Paleobotany (pres. 1977-80), Soc. Vertebrate Paleontology, Geol. Soc. Am. (com. on collection and collecting 1978—), Ky. Acad. Scis., Sigma Xi (pres.-elect Ind. chpt. 1985-86, pres. 1986-87). Office: Ind Univ Dept Biology Bloomington IN 47405

DILIDDO, BART A., chemical engineer, business executive, consultant; b. Cleve., Mar. 5, 1931; s. Donato and Lucia (Simone) DiL.; m. Roseann L. Canalaz, Aug. 13, 1955; children: Kara Marie, David Anthony. B.S. in Chem. Engring., Cleve. State U., 1954; M.S., Ill. Inst. Tech., 1956; Ph.D., Case-Western Res. U., 1960. With Brecksville Research and Devel. Ctr. B.F. Goodrich Co., 1956-67, With Avon Lake Tech. Ctr., 1967-70; process mgr. B.F. Goodrich Co., Orange, Tex., 1970-72; dir. latex chems. B.F. Goodrich Co. (Cleve. office), 1972-73; dir. R&D B.F. Goodrich Co., Cleve., 1973-75; div. v.p. tire tech. B.F. Goodrich Co., Akron, 1975-78; div. v.p. spl. projects B.F. Goodrich Co., Cleve., 1978, div. v.p. plastics, 1978-79, sr. v.p. and gen. mgr. plastics, 1979-80; exec. v.p. B.F. Goodrich Co., 1980-86; pres. Chem. Group, 1980-85; cons. Philip Crosby Assocs., Inc., Winter Park, Fla., 1986 . Mem. Am. Inst. Chem. Engrs., Bluecoats Inc. Republican Roman Catholic. Patentee in field. Office: 3604 N Fork Akron OH 44313

DI LIELLO, SALVATORE, data processing executive, educator; b. Naples, Campania, Italy, Dec. 29, 1958; came to U.S., 1974; s. Antonio and Concetta (Strazzullo) Di L. BS, Youngstown State U., 1984. Cert. systems profl. Microfilm supr. City of Warren, Ohio, 1980-81, data processing operator, 1981-82, data processing coordinator, 1982-83, data processing supr., 1983-85, data processing mgr., 1985—; instr. Bd. Edn., Warren, 1983—. Writer computer software Final Billing Utility System, 1981. Mem. Data Processing Mgmt. Assn. (pres. 1985-86, Plague 1986), U.S. Jaycee's Warren Chpt. (fellow). Roman Catholic. Avocations: reading, computer programming, golf. Home: 926 Terra Alta NE Warren OH 44483 Office: City of Warren 391 Mahoning Ave NW Warren OH 44483

DILL, MARY ALYSON, infomation analyst; b. Aug. 30, 1951. BLS, Edinboro (Pa.) State U., 1973; MS in Instl. Communications, Shippensburg (Pa.) State U., 1979; MLS, Case Western Res U., 1982. Librarian elem. schs. Bd. Cooperative Ednl. Services, Stamford, N.Y., 1973-76; librarian West Point Elem. Sch. U.S. Mil Acad., N.Y.C., 1976-81; info. specialist, records analyst Sohio Info. Ctr., Cleve., 1981-83; info. analyst Standard Oil Corp. (formerly Sohio Info. Ctr.), Cleve., 1983—. Mem. ALA, Library Adminstrn. Mgmt. Assn., Library Info. Tech. Assn. Home: 1823 Lee Rd Cleveland Heights OH 44118 Office: Standard Oil Corp 200 Public Sq Cleveland OH 44114-2375

DILL, WILLIAM JOSEPH, newspaper editor; b. Carmi, Ill., May 8, 1935; s. Hurshell Lloyd and Alma Lucille (Newby) D.; m. Marie Emilie Hubert, Aug. 14, 1965; children: Kevin Joseph, Kathleen Marie, Lisa Marie, Christopher Hubert. BS in Journalsim, So. Ill. U., 1961. Reporter, editor AP, Chgo., 1961-65, asst. bur. chief, 1965-69; bur. chief AP, Balt., 1969-71, Nashville, 1971-73, Charlotte, N.C., 1973-76, Mpls., 1976-81; editor The Forum, Fargo, N.D., 1981—; juror Pulitzer prize, 1985-86, 86-87. Served with USN, 1953-57. Named Journalism Alumnus of Yr., So. Ill. U., 1970. Fellow Am. Soc. Newspaper Editors; mem. Sigma Delta Chi. Roman Catholic. Avocations: reading, gardening. Home: 105 19th Ave N Fargo ND 58102 Office: The Forum PO Box 2020 Fargo ND 58107

DILLARD, JERRY WAYNE, corporate health and safety executive; b. Chattanooga, Oct. 17, 1944; s. John and Sarah Wilma (Witt) D.; m. Susan Michelle Andree, Aug. 31, 1974; children—John M., Stephen C., Jeffrey W. B.A. in Chemistry, U. Chattanooga, 1966; postgrad. in metall. engring. U. Tenn. Space Inst., 1966-67; M.A. in Personnel Mgmt., Central Mich. U., 1982. Cert. safety profl., Ill. Operating engr. City of Chattanooga, 1962-66; research asst. U. Tenn. Space Inst., Tullahoma, 1966-67; safety engr. ARO, Inc., Arnold Air Force Sta., Tenn., 1967-72; sr. safety engr. Ford Motor Co. Nashville (Tenn.) Glass Plant, 1972-75, employee program rep. Dearborn (Mich.) Glass Plant, 1975-76; div. safety engr. Ford Motor Co., Dearborn, 1976-78, corp. safety engr. N.Am. Automotive Ops., 1978-86; corp. health and safety mgr. Budd Co., Troy, Mich., 1986—; guest lectr. safety engring. studies Mercy and Madonna Colls.; chmn. suprs. sect. Safety Council Southeast Mich., 1980—. Aide de Camp gov.'s staff Gov. Winfield Dunn, State of Tenn., 1974, Gov. Lamar Alexander, 1979. Mem. Am. Soc. Safety Engrs. (mgmt. div.). Methodist. Lodges: Masons, Shriners. Home: 21248 Summerside Ln Northville MI 48167 Office: The Budd Co 3155 W Big Beaver Rd Troy MI 48084

DILLE, EARL KAYE, elec. utility exec.; b. Chillicothe, Mo., Apr. 25, 1927; s. George Earl and Josephine Christina (Kaye) D.; m. Martha Virginia Merrill, Sept. 8, 1951; children—Thomas Merrill, James Warren. B.S., U.S. Naval Acad., 1950; M.S., St. Louis U., 1961. With Union Elec. Co., St. Louis, 1957—; exec. v.p. Union Elec. Co., 1971—, also dir.; dir. Elec. Energy, Inc., Union Colliery Co., Merc. Bank, Merc. Bancorp. Inc.; pres. Asso. Industries Mo., 1974-76. Mem. adv. council Coll. Engring., U. Mo.; mem. exec. bd. St. Louis Area council Boy Scouts Am.; bd. dirs. St. Louis Symphony Soc., Bethesda Hosps. and Homes, Webster U., Regional Commerce and Growth Assn. Served with USN, 1950-57; comdr. Res. Recipient Disting. Service in Engring award U. Mo., 1973, Alumni Merit award St. Louis U., 1974, Outstanding Engr. in Industry award Mo. Soc. Profl. Engrs., 1976, Silver Beaver award Boy Scouts Am., 1987. Mem. IEEE, Engrs. Club St. Louis (pres. 1977-78), Mo. Hist. Soc. (bd. dirs.), Sigma Xi. Episcopalian. Clubs: Mason. (Grand master Mo. 1982-83), Bellerive Country, Noonday, St. Louis.

DILLE, ROLAND PAUL, coll. pres.; b. Dassel, Minn., Sept. 16, 1924; s. Oliver Valentine and Eleanor (Johnson) D.; m. Beth Hopeman, Sept. 4, 1948; children—Deborah, Martha, Sarah, Benjamin. B.A. summa cum laude, U. Minn., 1949, Ph.D., 1962. Instr. English U. Minn., 1953-56; asst. prof. St. Olaf Coll., Northfield, Minn., 1956-61; asst. prof. English Calif. Lutheran Coll., Thousand Oaks, Calif., 1961-63; mem. faculty Moorhead (Minn.) State U., 1963—, pres., 1968—. Author: Four Romantic Poets, 1969. Treas. Am. Assn. State Colls. and Univs., 1977-78, bd. dirs., 1978-80, chmn., 1980-81; mem. Nat. Council for Humanities, 1980-86. Served with inf. AUS, 1944-46. Disting. Service to Humanities award given by Minn. Humanities Commn. named in his honor. Mem. Phi Beta Kappa. Home: 516 9th St S Moorhead MN 56560 Office: Moorhead State Univ Moorhead MN 56560-9980

DILLENBURG, MARK ANTHONY, architect; b. Casco, Wis., Sept. 27, 1951; s. Edward John and Marie Helen (Guenzel) D.; m. Susan Alice Shields, Nov. 11, 1972; children: Paul Edward, Rebecca Sue. AA, Milw. Sch. Engring., 1971. Registered architect, Wis. Archtl. technician Superior-Kuetemeyer, Milw., 1971-72; technician, architect Kuskowski & Assoc., Green Bay, Wis., 1972-80; pvt. practice architect De Pere, Wis., 1980-81; architect, sect. mgr. Foth & Van Dyke, Green Bay, 1981—; lectr. Am. Inst. Civil Engring., Oshkosh, Wis., 1984; architects adv. bd. Northeast Wis. Tech. Inst., Green Bay, 1983—. Mem. AIA, Wis. Soc. Architects, Constrn. Specifications Inst. (bd. dirs. 1982—, v.p. 1983-84, pres. 1985-86. Roman Catholic. Club: Interfaith Seaman's Ministry (v.p. 1973-74). Avocations: fishing, boating. Office: Foth & Van Dyke Engrs Architects PO Box 19012 Green Bay WI 54307

DILLER, EROLD RAY, cardiovascular pharmacologist; b. May 4, 1922; s. Waldo and Mary Ann (Zimmerman) D.; m. Geneva W. Wuensch, Mar. 18, 1944; children—Cynthia Ann, David Mark. B.A., Bowling Green U., 1949; M.S., Ind. U., 1951. Biochemist Lilly Research Labs., Indpls., 1955-62, sr. biochemist, 1962-66, research scientist, 1966-71, research assoc., 1971—; mem. adv. bd. Devel. Conf. on Lipids, San Francisco, 1980-85, chmn., 1985—. Contbr. articles to profl. jours. Mem. Council on Arteriosclerosis Am. Heart Assn., N.Y. Acad. Sci., Sigma Xi, Phi Lambda Upsilon, Sigma Nu. Mem. Christian Ch. Avocation: photography. Office: Lilly Research Labs Lilly Corp Ctr Indianapolis IN 46285

DILLEY, TIMOTHY EUGENE, minister; b. Auburn, Ind., Nov. 25, 1958; s. David Eugene and Judy Ann (Duncan) D.; m. Deborah Ann Feher, July 11, 1981. BA summa cum laude, United Wesleyan Coll., Allentown, Pa., 1981; postgrad., Ashland (Ohio) Theol. Sem., 1983-86, Meth. Theol. Sch., Del., Ohio, 1986. Minister visitation Zion Wesleyan Ch., Bath, Pa., 1979-81; sr. minister Deland Wesleyan Ch., Temperance, Mich., 1981-85, Epworth United Meth. Ch., Bluffton, Ind., 1986—. Named one of Outstanding Young Men of Am., 1985. Mem. Wesleyan Theol. Soc., Wells County Ministerial Assn. Republican. Methodist. Lodge: Masons. Avocations: piano, boating, fishing, reading. Home: 1211 W Cherry St Bluffton IN 46714 Office: Epworth United Meth Ch 1204 W Cherry St Bluffton IN 46714

DILLIN, SAMUEL HUGH, U.S. judge; b. Petersburg, Ind., June 9, 1914; s. Samuel E. and Maude (Harrell) D.; m. Mary Eloise Humphreys, Nov. 24, 1940; 1 dau., Patricia Jane. A.B. in Govt, Ind. U., 1936, LL.B., 1938. Bar: Ind. bar 1938. Partner firm Dillin & Dillin, Petersburg, 1938-61; U.S. dist. judge So. Dist. Ind., 1961—; Sec. Pub. Service Commn. Ind., 1942; mem. Interstate Oil Compact Commn., 1949-52, 61. Mem. Ind. Ho. of Reps. from Pike and Knox County, 1937, 39, 41, 51, floor leader, 1951; mem. Ind. Senate from Pike and Gibson County, 1951, 61, floor leader, pres. pro tem, 1961, candidate for gov. Ind., 1956. Served to capt. AUS, 1943-46. Mem. Am. Bar Assn., Am. Judicature Soc., Delta Tau Delta, Phi Delta Phi. Democrat. Presbyn. Club: Indianapolis Athletic. Office: U S Dist Ct U S Courthouse 46 E Ohio St Room 255 Indianapolis IN 46204 *

DILLING, KIRKPATRICK WALLWICK, lawyer; b. Evanston, Ill., Apr. 11, 1920; s. Albert W. and Elizabeth (Kirkpatrick) D.; m. Betty Ellen Bronson, June 18, 1942 (div. July 1944); m. Elizabeth Ely Tilden, Dec. 11, 1948; children—Diana Jean, Eloise Tilden, Victoria Walgreen, Albert Kirkpatrick. Student, Cornell U., 1939-40; B.S. in Law, Northwestern U., 1942; postgrad., DePaul U., 1946-47, L'Ecole Vaubier, Montreux, Switzerland; Degre Normal, Sorbonne U., Paris. Bar: Ill. 1947, Wis., Ind., Mich., Md., La., Tex., Okla., U.S. Dist. Ct. (ea. dist.) Wis., U.S. Ct. Appeals (2d, 3d, 5th, 7th, 8th, 9th, 10th, 11th, D.C. cirs.), U.S. Supreme Ct. Mem. firm Dilling, Gronek and Armstrong, Chgo., 1948—; gen. counsel Nat. Health Fedn., Am. Massage and Therapy Assn., Cancer Control. Soc.; dir. Adelle Davis Found., Dillman Labs.; v.p. Midwest Medic-Aide, Inc.; spl. counsel Herbalife (U.K.) Ltd., Herbalife Australasia Pty., Ltd.; lectr. on pub. health law. Contbr. articles to profl. publs. Bd. dirs. Nat. Health Fedn., Adele Davis Found. Served to 1st lt. AUS, 1943-46. Mem. ABA, Ill. Bar Assn., Chgo. Bar Assn., Assn. Trial Lawyers Am., Cornell Soc. Engrs., Am. Legion, Air Force Assn., Pharm. Advt. Club, Navy League, Delta Upsilon. Republican. Episcopalian. Clubs: Lake Michigan Yachting Assn., Tower, Cornell U., Club Chgo. Home: 1120 Lee Rd Northbrook IL 60062 Winter Home: Casa Dorado Indian Wells CA 92260 Office: 150 N Wacker Dr Chicago IL 60601

DILLINGOFSKI, MARY SUE, film company executive, strategic marketing consultant; b. Madison, Wis., Dec. 27, 1944; d. Albert F. and Camille M. (Blott) D. B.A., Lawrence U., 1967; M.S., U. Wis., 1970, Ph.D., 1980. Tchr. English, Madison Pub. Schs. (Wis.), 1967-70; tchr. reading Niles Pub. Schs. (Ill.), 1971-72, Kamehameha Schs., Honolulu, 1972-77; lectr. U. Wis., Madison, 1977-80; cons. Scott, Foresman & Co., Glenview, Ill., 1980-81, mktg. mgr., 1981-86; dir. mktg. Films Inc., Chgo., 1986-87; pres. Dillingofski and Assocs., 1987—; cons. diagnostician Univ. Hosp. Learning Disability Clinic, Madison, Wis., 1977-80; ednl. cons. Kalihi Palama Adult Edn. Ctr., Honolulu, 1973-75; Author: Nonprint Media and Reading, 1979; Sociolinguistics and Reading (W.S. Gray Research award 1980), 1978; also articles in profl. jours. Active Apollo Chorus, Chgo., 1983—, Friends of Sta. WHA, Madison, 1978-80, Mem. Art Deco Soc. Chgo., Internat. Reading Assn. (com. chmn. 1979-81), Wis. Reading Assn. (membership com. 1978-80), North Shore Reading Assn., Bus. Vols. for Arts, Women in Mgmt., Am. Mktg. Assn. Club: City (Chgo.).

DILLON, DAVID JOSEPH, theatrical producer; b. Chgo., Mar. 8, 1957; s. John Charles Dillon and Mary Louise (Pauwels) Pope. Student, Coe Coll., 1975-77, Loyola U., Chgo., 1977-78. Adminstrv. asst. Victory Gardens Theater, Chgo., 1977-78; co-founder, mng. dir. City Lite Theater Co., Chgo., 1979-83; co-founder, v.p. Dillon/Carroll Prodns., Chgo., 1983—; cons. Piven Theater Workshop, Evanston, Ill., 1981, Pary Prodn. Co., Chgo., 1981-83, Silent Song Assocs., Chgo., 1982; lectr. U. Chgo., 1982; artist in residence Del. Arts Council, 1982; vice chmn. bd. David Puzsh Dance Co., 1986—. Producer (play) The Domestic Contentions of Frank O'Connor, 1980, Why I Live at the P.O., 1980, The Outstation, 1981, Big Blonde, The Constant Reader, 1982, An Evening with Quentin Crisp, 1983, Normal Heart, 1987; actor (play) The Unseen Hand, 1979, Steambath, 1979, Johns, 1981 (Artisan of Yr. Chgo. Acad. Theater Artists and Friends, 1982), Roomies, 1984. Mem. Dramatists Guild. Home and Office: 655 W Irving Park Rd #4312 Chicago IL 60613

DILLON, GARY G., manufacturing company executive; b. Eaton, Ohio, May 21, 1934; s. M.H. and E.L. (Clensy) D.; m. Beverly Mulholland, Jan. 2,

1954; children: Kristen, Deborah, Kirk. BSBA, Miami U., Oxford, Ohio, 1955. With Philip Carey Corp., Cin., 1955-57, Pillsbury Co., Mpls., 1957-78; exec. v.p., chief operating officer King-Seeley Thermos Co. subs. Household Internat., Chgo., 1978-81; pres., chief exec. officer King-Seeley Thermos Co. subs. Household Internat., Prospect Heights, Ill., 1981-82, Household Mfg. Inc. subs. Household Internat., Prospect Heights, 1982—; bd. dirs. Household Internat. Office: Household Mfg Co 2700 Sanders Rd Prospect Heights IL 60070

DILLON, HOWARD BURTON, civil engineer; b. Hardyville, Ky., Aug. 12, 1935; s. Charlie Edison and Mary Opal (Bell) D.; m. Bonny Jean Garard, May 19, 1962; 1 child, Robert Edward. BCE, U. Louisville, 1958, MCE, 1960; postgrad., Okla. State U., 1962, Mich. State U., 1962-65. Registered profl. engr., Ind. Instr. U. Louisville, Ky., 1958-60; from assoc. prof. to prof. Ind. Inst. Tech., Ft. Wayne, 1960-62; NSF fellow Okla. State U., Stillwater, 1962; NSF grantee, instr. Mich. State U., East Lansing, 1962-67; head civil engring. dept. MW Inc. Cons. Engrs., Indpls., 1967-83; project mgr. civil div. SEG Engrs. & Cons., Indpls., 1983—; asst. dir. to local pub. road needs study for Ind., 1970; mem. design com. for dams in Ind., 1974—; spl. cons. to Ind. Dept. Nat. Resources on dams, 1980—; mem. infrastructure com. for State of Ind., 1984—. Committeeman Wayne 52 precinct, Indpls., 1972-86; vice-ward chmn. Wayne South Twp., Indpls., 1986-87. Hazelett and Erdal scholar, 1957-58. Mem. ASCE, NSPE, Am. Soc. Engring. Edn., Am. Soc. for Testing and Materials, Internat. Soc. Found. Engrs., Chi Epsilon. Democrat. Baptist. Lodge: Optimists (pres. Suburban West chpt. 1972-74, bd. dirs. Suburban West 1974-78, lt. gov. Ind. dist. 1973-74). Avocations: fishing, traveling, photography, lecturing, coin collecting. Home: 6548 Westdrum Rd Indianapolis IN 46241 Office: SEG Engrs and Cons Inc Century Bldg 36 S Pennsylvania St Suite 360 Indianapolis IN 46204

DILLON, JAMES RICHARD, health science facility administrator, obstetrician, gynecologist; b. Chgo., Dec. 7, 1921; s. Walter J. and Mary Agatha (McLoone) D.; m. Helen L. McSharry, Apr. 18, 1949; children: Mary, James, Catherine, Charles, Margaret, Thomas, Michael, Elizabeth, Robert. MD, Stritch Sch. Medicine, 1951. Diplomate Am. Bd. Ob-Gyn. Intern 1951-52, resident, 1952-55; pres. med. and dental staff St. Francis Hosp., Evanston, Ill., 1976, dir. obstetrics, 1980—; clin. asst. prof. Loyola U., Chgo., 1974—. Served to 1st lt. U.S. Army, 1941-46. Fellow Am Coll. Ob-Gyn; mem. AMA, Chgo. Med. Soc. (pres. North Suburban br. 1974), Ill. State Med. Soc., Chgo. Gynecol. Soc., Am. Soc. Pro-Life Ob-Gyns. Roman Catholic. Home: 9449 Avers Evanston IL 60203 Office: 800 Austin Evanston IL 60202

DILLON, JOHN RALPH, marketing executive, consultant; b. Indpls., June 26, 1955; s. John Loren and Maria Concepcion (Rico) D.; m. Araceli Jordan Dillon, Aug. 16, 1986. BBA, U. Monterey, 1978. Market researcher Cuauhtemoc Brewery, Monterey, Mexico, 1978-79; adminstrv. asst. Gen. Steel Co., Indpls., 1979-80; internat. trading rep. Hylsa Internat. Corp., Houston, 1980-82; corp. procurement supt. Mexican Cements, Monterey, 1982-84; regional sales mgr. Panam. Foods Co., Houston, 1984—; pvt. practice cons., Chgo., 1984—. Mem. U.S.-Hispanic C. of C., Mexican-Am. C. of C. Roman Catholic. Avocations: fishing, traveling, automobiles. Office: PO Box 709 Evanston IL 60204-0709

DILLON, JOSEPH GERALD, realtor, real estate developer; b. Chgo., Sept. 1, 1934; s. Joseph Gerald and Anne (Dwyer) D.; m. Beverly Tanty, Jan. 2, 1960; children: Joseph, Kathleen, David, Daniel. Student, John Carroll U., 1952-54; BA, Loyola U., Chgo., 1956. Mem. real estate staff Material Service div. Gen. Dynamics Corp., Chgo., 1959-60; v.p. Monticello Realty div. Henry Crown & Co., Chgo., 1960-67; ptnr. Harrington, Tideman & O'Leary, Chgo., 1967-75; v.p. dir. Arthur Rubloff & Co., Chgo., 1975-79; pres. Joseph Dillon & Co., Bensenville, Ill., 1979-82; ptnr. Bennett & Kahnweiler, Inc., Rosemont, Ill., 1982—. Served to capt. AUS, 1956-57. Mem. Nat. Assn. Indsl. and Office Parks (pres. Chgo. chpt. 1978), Soc. Indsl. and Office Realtors (bd. dirs. 1975-77, pres. 1987—), Assn. Indsl. Real Estate Brokers Chgo. (pres. 1974), Urban Land Inst., Indsl. Devel. and Research Council, Realty Club of Chgo., Realtors 40, Lambda Alpha. Clubs: Chgo. Athletic Assn.; Skokie Country (Glencoe, Ill.),.

DILLON, PHILLIP MICHAEL, construction company executive; b. Ypsilanti, Mich., July 15, 1944; s. Robert Timothy and Maxine Helen (Elliott) D.; student Mich. State U., 1962-66; m. Phyllis Louise Brooks, Jan. 21, 1978; children—Richard, Debora, Michael, Robert, Karen. Store mgr. Morse Shoe, Inc., Detroit, 1964-68, asst. dir. store planning and constrn., Canton, Mass., 1968-72; dir. store planning and constrn. Stride Rite Corp., Boston, 1972-74; sr. v.p. Capitol Cos., Inc., Arlington Heights, Ill., 1974-81; chmn. bd., chief exec. officer Standard Cos., Inc., Palatine, Ill., 1982-83; co-owner, sr. v.p. Eagle Constrn. Corp., 1983—. Mem. Inst. Store Planners. Roman Catholic. Club: Green Acres Sportsman. Office: 110 Main St Lemont IL 60439

DILLON, RICHARD NEIL, mechanical engineer; b. Alliance, Ohio, May 7, 1954; s. James Richard and Marjorie May (Watson) D.; m. Diane Elise Tate, June 21, 1975; children—Katie Ann, Joshua Richard. Student U. Mo. Rolla, 1972-74; B.S.M.E., U. Akron, 1977; E.M.T., Aultman Hosp., 1984. Registered profl. engr., Ohio. Design engr. Alliance Electric, Ohio, 1977-81, chief engr., 1981-85; chief engr. Davis Engring., Alliance, 1985—; treas. Alliance Electric, 1972-84, Davis Engring., 1984-85; mgr. Speco Investment Services, 1977-85. Co-worker Cystic Fibrosis Found., Alliance, 1981-85; com. mem. First Immanuel United Ch. Christ, 1977—. Mem. ASME, Nat. Soc. Profl. Engrs., Ohio Soc. Profl. Engrs. Mem. Christian Ch. Lodge: Order of DeMolay. Home: 15350 Salem Church St Homeworth OH 44634 Office: Davis Engring Inc 22623 Lake Park Blvd Alliance OH 44601

DILLON, ROBERT JOHN, consumer products manufacturing executive; b. Mpls., Aug. 26, 1919; s. James John and Mary Stella (Hogan) D.; m. Florence Marie Kelley, Jan. 10, 1942; children: Anne, James, Patrick, Thomas, Joan, Mike, Tim. BS in Mining and Metall. Engring., Case Inst. Tech., 1941. Purchasing, sales mgr. The West Bend Aluminum Co., West Bend and Hartford, Wis., 1946-65; v.p., plant mgr. Chrysler Outboard Corp., Hartford, Wis., 1965-68; gen. mfg. mgr. Marine Group Chrysler Corp., Detroit, 1968-79; v.p. Chrysler Outboard Corp., Chrysler Can. Outboard Ltd., 1968-79, Chrysler Boat Corp., 1968-79; v.p. ops. The Eska Co., Dubuque, Iowa, 1979-81, pres., chief exec. officer, vice-chmn. bd., 1981—, also bd. dirs. Bd. dirs. Southeastern Mich. chpt. ARC, Detroit, 1969-73, Pvt. Industry Council Dubuque and Delaware Counties, Iowa, 1983-85. Served to lt. comdr. USNR, 1941-46, PTO. Mem. Am. Cancer Soc. (pres. Washington County 1956-57), Milw. Archdiocesan Council of Cath. Men (pres. 1963), Hartford C. of C. (pres. 1959). Home: 998 Spires Dr Dubuque IA 52001 Office: The Eska Co 2400 Kerper Blvd Dubuque IA 52001

DILLON, THOMAS RAY, financial planner; b. Alton, Ill., Dec. 16, 1948; s. Elmer Charles Dillon and Doris Jean (Autery) Drewes; m. Eileen Frances Fudala, June 1, 1974; 1 child, Brett. BS in Indsl. Mgmt., Purdue U., 1971. Cert. fin. planner. Account exec. Merrill Lynch, St. Louis, 1975-77, Dean Witter, St. Louis, 1977-82; dir. fin. services div. Bruno, Stolze & Co., St. Louis, 1982—. Contbr. articles to fin. jours.; author, editor radio show Tip of the Week, 1980-82. Speaker various civic orgns., St. Louis, 1980-86; bd. dirs. Optimists Club of West Port, St. Louis, 1978-82. Mem. Internat. Assn. Fin. Planners (v.p. St. Louis chpt. 1982-84, pres. 1984-86, bd. dirs. Atlanta hdqrs. 1986-87), Inst. Cert. Fin. Planners (bd. dirs. St. Louis chpt. 1984-86), Registry Fin. Planning Practitioners. Republican. Avocations: athletics, adventure travel. Office: Bruno Stolze & Co Inc 425 N New Ballas Rd #230 Saint Louis MO 63141

DILWORTH, JAMES LEE, ski resort executive, consultant, engineer; b. Charlevoix, Mich.; s. Forest Wesley and Kathryn Lee (Kennedy) D.; m. Mary Dell Saunders, Oct. 18, 1952; children—Wesley James, David Saunders. B.C.E., U. Mich., 1951. Registered profl. engr., Mich., Mont., Ind., Colo., N.Mex., Wis., Nev., Utah. Engr. Charlevoix County Rd. Commn., Boyne City, Mich., 1952-57; forest engr. U.S. Forest Service, Cadillac, Mich., 1957-60; constrn. supt. Kendall Constrn., Cadillac, 1960-61; cons. engr. Norton & Kobbins, Cadillac, 1961-63; area mgr. Boyne Highlands, Harbor Springs, Mich., 1963-77; gen. mgr. Nubs Nob Ski Area, Harbor Springs, 1977—; prin. James L. Dilworth Ltd., Ski Area Cons., Harbor Springs, 1977—. Patentee snow machine equipment, 1976, 81, 83, 84. Mem. Ski Area Safety Bd., Mich., 1981—, vice chmn. 1984—; bd. dirs. Midwest Ski Area Assn., 1984—; mem. Emmet County Planning Commn., 1981-84; bd. dirs. Little Traverse Conservancy, Mich., 1985—, Lake Charlevoix Assn., 1986—. Mem. Mich. Soc. Profl. Engrs., Mich. Assn. Professions. Presbyterian. Home: 901 Sunset Ct Petoskey MI 49770 Office: Nubs Nob Ski Area 4021 Nubs Nob Rd Harbor Springs MI 49740

DIMARTINI, JOSEPH JOHN, urologist; b. Phila., Nov. 12, 1941; s. Joseph Samual and Margaret (Engle) D.; m. Barbara Jean Sullivan, June 21, 1966; children: Joseph, Danielle, Michael. BS in Biology, St. Joseph's U., 1964; MD, L'universitá di Bologna, Italy, 1972. Diplomate Am. Bd. Urology. Intern Brookdale Hosp. Med. Ctr., Bklyn., 1973; resident in gen. surgery Jewish Hosp. and Med. Ctr., Bklyn., 1973-74, resident in urology, 1974-77; assoc. physician Monroe (Wis.) Clinic, 1977-79; practice medicine specializing in urology Dimartini & Nagale, Waterloo, Iowa, 1980—; mem. active staff Sartori Meml. Hosp., Cedar Falls, Iowa, Allen Meml. Hosp., Waterloo, mem. exec. com.; mem. courtesy staff Schoitz Med. Ctr., Waterloo, St. Francis Hosp., Waterloo, Palmer Meml. Hosp., West Union, Iowa, Winneshiek County Meml. Hosp., Decorah, Iowa. Mem. AMA, Iowa State Med. Soc., Black Hawk County Med. Soc., Green County Med. Soc. (sec.-treas. 1978-79). Club: Black Hawk County Stoma (bd. dirs.). Avocations: swimming, cycling, reading history. Office: Allen Profl Bldg 212 W Dale Waterloo IA 50703

DIMICK, JAMES RICHARD, accountant, basketball coach; b. Madison, Wis., Nov. 29, 1952; s. James Richard and Nancy Weston (Hopkins) D. BA in Math., St. Olaf Coll., Northfield, Minn., 1975; postgrad. in Acctg., Macalester Coll., 1984. CPA, Minn. Head basketball coach and math tchr. LeSueur High Sch., Minn., 1976-81; asst. basketball coach Macalester Coll., St. Paul, 1983-84; acct. Blanski, Peter, Kronlage & Zoch, CPA's, 1985-86; asst. basketball coach Coll. St. Thomas, St. Paul, 1987—; pvt. practice acctg., artist, house painter St. Paul, 1987—. Mem. Am. Inst. CPA's, Minn. Soc. CPA's. Avocations: weightlifting, gardening, reading, bicycling, traveling.

DIMMERLING, HAROLD J., bishop; b. Braddock, Pa., Sept. 23, 1914. Ed., St. Fidelis Prep. Sem., Herman, Pa., St. Charles Sem., Columbus, Ohio, St. Francis Sem., Loretto, Pa. Ordained priest Roman Catholic Ch., 1940; consecrated bishop 1969; bishop Diocese of Rapid City, S.D., 1969—. Office: Chancery Office 606 Cathedral Dr PO Box 678 Rapid City SD 57709 *

DIMON, DIANE ELIZABETH, publishing company executive; b. Memphis, Feb. 8, 1957; s. Charles GRayson and Elizabeth (Fitzgibbon) D. BS, Portland State U., 1980. V.p. Am. City Bus. Jours, Kansas City, Mo., 1980—. Democrat. Roman Catholic. Avocation: equestrian. Home: 4340 Holly Kansas City MO 64111 Office: Am City Bus Jours 3535 Broadway Kansas City MO 64111

DIMOND, MARGARET ANN, social worker; b. Dearborn, Mich., Oct. 14, 1958; s. George Edward and Irene Wlihelmina (Bayor) D. BA, St. Mary's Coll., 1980; MSW, Boston Coll., 1982. Cert. social worker, Mich. Med. social worker Holy Cross Hosp., Detroit, 1982-83, St. Joseph Hosp., Chgo., 1983-84; social work supr. Henry Ford Hosp., Detroit, 1984—; social worker Rogers Park Home Health Care, Chgo., 1984; cons. Cath. Social Services, Warren, Mich., 1984—. com. mem. Am. Heart Assn., Southfield, Mich., 1985. Mem. Nat. Assn. Social Workers. Avocations: running, golf, tennis.

DINAN, THOMAS EDWARD, importing company executive; b. Buffalo, May 9, 1940; s. Edward Thomas and Agnes Mary (McMahon) D.; m. Judy Cleary, Jan. 18, 1964; children: Susan, Timothy. BS in Sociology, Canisius Coll., 1967; MS in Social Scis., SUNY, 1972. Sales supr. Regal Beverage Co., Buffalo, 1968-70, sales mgr., 1970-74, gen. mgr., 1974-76; sales mgr. Lake Erie Distbrs., Inc., Lackawanna, N.Y., 1976-77; regional sales mgr. Dribeck Importers, Inc., Greenwich, Conn., 1977—. Mem. Nat. Assn. Beer Wholesalers, Canisius Coll. Alumni Assn. Democrat. Roman Catholic. Office: 701 Roanoke Ct Naperville IL 60565

DINDO, KATHRYN WARTHER, accountant; b. Dover, Ohio, May 1, 1949; d. Donald Carl and Ruth (Krantz) Warther; m. Thomas William Dindo, Sept. 27, 1969; children: Carl, Paul, Joyce. Student, Bowling Green (Ohio) State U., 1967-69; BS in Acctg., Akron (Ohio) U., 1971. CPA, Ohio. Assoc. Ernst & Whinney, Akron, 1971-85, ptnr., 1985—. Treas., bd. dirs. Terry House, Akron, 1983-85; bd. dirs. small bus. council Akron Regional Devel. Bd., Jr. Achievement Akron Area, Inc. Mem. Am. Inst. CPA's, Ohio Soc. CPA's,. Republican. Roman Catholic. Club: Cascade (Akron). Avocation: travel. Home: 218 Brook Bend Akron OH 44313 Office: Ernst & Whinney 1 Cascade Plaza Akron OH 44308

DINGEE, SARAH ELIZABETH, accountant; b. Rock Hill, S.C., Jan. 8, 1925; d. William Parnell and Charlotte Emilie (Laurey) Branigan; m. William A. Dingee, Oct. 18, 1945; children—William A. Jr., Barbara M., Charles E. Student Winthrop Coll., 1941-42, Ind. Vocat. Tech. Coll., 1980-81. Student acct. So. Bell Telephone Co., 1942-43; clk., acct. White Printing Co., 1943-44; sec., acct. Dingee Co., Hobart, Ind., 1953—; sec., counselor, dir. The Answer, Inc., Hobart, 1980—. Mem. Citizens Action Coalition, United Way Vol. Action Bur. Mem. DAR, VFW Aux, Daus. Confederacy, Daus. Isabella, St. Anns Archconfraternity. Roman Catholic. Office: PO Box 157 Hobart IN 46342

DINGELL, JOHN DAVID, JR., congressman; b. Colorado Springs, Colo., July 8, 1926; s. John D. and Grace (Bigler) D. B.S. in Chemistry, Georgetown U., 1949, J.D., 1952. Bar: D.C. bar 1952, Mich. bar 1953. Park ranger U.S. Dept. Interior, 1948-52; asst. pros. atty. Wayne County, Mich., 1953-55; mem. 84th-88th congresses from 15th Dist. Mich., 1955-65, 89th-100th congresses from 16th Dist. Mich., 1965—; mem. migratory bird conservation commn., chmn. Com. on energy and commerce, sub. com. chmn. oversight and investigation; mem. Office Tech. Assessment. Served as 2d lt. inf. AUS, 1945-46. Home: Trenton MI 48121 Office: US Ho Reps Room 2221 Rayburn House Office Bldg Washington DC 20515 *

DINGLE, KEVIN STUART, manufacturing company executive; b. Detroit, May 29, 1952; s. Stuart Frank and Rae Helen (Hansen) G.; m. Joan Nancy Parrott, May 19, 1973 (div. 1979); m. Barbara Annette Chavey, Apr. 18, 1981; children—Meghan Elisabeth, Patrick Kevin. B.S., U. Detroit, 1974, M.B.A., 1981. Exec. asst. J.W. Crusoe Investments, Birmingham, Mich., 1974-77; acctg. mgr. Handleman Co., Clawson, Mich., 1977-79, ops. planning analyst, 1979-82; gen. mgr. Premier Malt Products, Grosse Pointe, Mich., 1982-83; controller, chief fin. officer Foamade Industries, Auburn Hills, Mich., 1983-86; pres., owner Small Bus. Assistance, Southfield, Mich., 1986-87; v.p., chief fin. officer DST Industries Inc., Romulus, Mich., 1987—. Mem. Assn. MBA Execs., Nat. Assn. Accts., Assn. Computer Users, Assn. Planning Execs., Automotive Industry Action Group, Mich. C. of C. Congregationalist. Home: 17386 Avilla Lathrup Village MI 48076 Office: DST Industries Inc 34364 Goodard Rd Romulus MI 48174

DINGMAN, MAURICE J., bishop; b. St. Paul, Iowa, Jan. 20, 1914; s. Theodore and Angela (Witte) D. Ed., St. Ambrose Coll., Davenport, Iowa, 1936, N.Am. Coll. and Gregorian U., Rome, Catholic U. Am. Ordained priest Roman Cath. Ch., 1939; instr. St. Ambrose Acad., 1940-43; vice chancellor Diocese of Davenport, Iowa, 1942-45; prin. Hayes High Sch., Muscatine, Iowa, 1950-53; domestic prelate 1956; appointed bishop Diocese of Des Moines, 1968-87. *

DIONNE, LEO VINCENT, accountant; b. Sarnia, Ont., Can., Dec. 1, 1928; came to U.S., 1948; s. Michael Vincent and Helena Rita (Langan) D.; m. Lois Elainge Boshaw, June 22, 1948; children: Kyran S., Daniel L., Richard M., Janine M., Jeffery A., Anita L., Michelle R., Shon B. Student, Sarnia Bus. Coll., 1947-48, Lasalle Extension U., 1950-53. Pres., acct. Dionne Acctg. Service Inc., Port Huron, Mich., 1959—; v.p. Marysville (Mich.) Plating Co., 1959—; sec. Serve All Appliance Service, Port Huron, 1985—, Mich. Indsl. Controls, Port Huron, 1986—; acct. Stevenson Electric, Inc., Port Huron, 1983—; distbr. Amway Corp., Ada, Mich., 1978—. Mem., acct. Marydale Ctr. for Aged, 1963—; coach Port Huron Little League, 1961-66, Port Huron Minor Hockey Assn., 1971-81. Mem. Nat. Assn. Enrolled Agts., Jacques Cousteau Soc. (sustaining), Nat. Rifle Assn. (sustaining). Republican. Roman Catholic. Clubs: Old Grand Dad (N.Y.C.); Lehigh (Fla.) Country. Lodge: Elks. Avocation: bowling. Home: 2330 Elk St Port Huron MI 48060 Office: Dionne Acctg Service Inc 2338 Elk St Beside Blue Water Bridge Port Huron MI 48060

DI PRIMA, STEPHANIE MARIE, educational administrator; b. Chgo., Aug. 29, 1952; d. Joseph and Ann Marie (Albate) DiP. BA in English, Rosary Coll., 1974; MEd in Adminstrn. and Supervision, Loyola U., Chgo., 1979. Tchr., St. Vincent Ferrer Sch., River Forest, Ill., 1974-78; Our Lady of Hope Sch., Rosemont, Ill., 1978-81, Sacred Heart Sch., Winnetka, Ill., 1981-84, prin., St. Monica Sch., Chgo., 1984—. Mem. Nat. Cath. Educators Assn., Nat. Assn. Elem. Sch. Prins., Assn. Supervision and Curriculum Devel., Women in Mgmt., Prins. Support Group, Adminstrs. Growth Group, Archdiocesan Prins. Assn., Smithsonian Inst., Art Inst. Chgo., Chgo. Zool. Soc. Avocations: piano, reading, theatre and fine arts, needlecrafts, travelling. Office: 5115 N Mont Clare Ave Chicago IL 60656

DIRLAM, GORDON AUBREY, real estate facility planner; b. Mpls., Aug. 28, 1950; s. Aubrey William and Hazelle Marie (Menz) D.; m. Mary Kathryn Johnson, Apr. 20, 1974; children—Alexandra, Adam. B.S., U. Minn., 1973. Mus. photographer Minn. Hist. Soc., St. Paul, 1973-74; with real estate leasing, Northwestern Bell, Mpls., 1974-75, real estate bldg. constrn., 1978-81, real estate facility planning, St. Paul, 1981—. Vol. Ind. Republicans, Redwood Falls, Minn., 1964-72. Mem. Internat. Facility Mgmt. Assn. (profl.), Delta Phi Delta. Avocations: golf; carpentry; reading on investing; swimming. Office: Northwestern Bell 70 W 4th St Room 1-C Saint Paul MN 55102

DISABATO, JOHN MICHAEL, marketing education coordinator; b. Cleve., June 21, 1950; s. John Devito and Teresa Marie (Vittantonio) DiS. BBA, BSEd, Bowling Green State U., 1973, MEd, 1975. Cert. secondary bus., mktg. edn. tchr. Advt. mgr. Montgomery Ward, Toledo, 1972-73; distributive edn. coordinator pub. schs., Dayton, Ohio, 1973-74, Athens, Ohio, 1976-81; sales cons. Marino Bros. Furniture, Willoughby, Ohio, 1981-82; distributive edn. coordinator city schs., Elyria, Ohio, 1982-83, Lakewood, Ohio, 1983—; mktg. instr. Hocking Tech. Coll., Nelsonville, Ohio. Bloodmobile chmn. Athens County chpt. ARC, 1980-81; participant Ohio Retail Mchts. Anti-Shoplifting campaign, 1976-81, 85. Mem. Distributive Edn. Clubs Am. (dist. chmn.), Am. Vocat. Assn., Ohio Vocat. Assn., NEA, Delta Pi Epsilon, Pi Kappa Alpha. Roman Catholic. Club: Lake Erie Dart Assn. Lodges: Moose, K.C. Contbr. articles to profl. jours. Office: Lakewood High Sch 14100 Franklin Blvd Lakewood OH 44107

DISBROW, JANET ALICE, controller, accountant, data processing manager; b. Battle Creek, Mich., July 30, 1946; d. Casper H. and Marian Frances (Chilson) Uldriks; m. Gerald Dan Kline, Nov. 29, 1963 (div. Dec. 1970) 1 child, Gerald James; m. Richard Alan Disbrow, Jan. 30, 1971. Cert. in acctg., Kellogg Community Coll., 1978, cert. EDP., 1985. Clk., sec. Kalamazoo (Mich.) Pub. Schs., 1964-67; sec. Battle Creek Pub. Sch., 1970-72; controller Converter Systems div. Masco Corp., Battle Creek, 1972-78; v.p. fin. Associated Constrn., Inc., Battle Creek, 1978-84; controller X-Rite, Inc., Grand Rapids, Mich., 1984-86, Comp-Aire Systems, Grand Rapids, 1986—. Mem. Nat. Assn. Women in Constrn. (chartered), Am. Bus. Women's Assn. Presbyterian. Avocations: arts and crafts, seashell collecting, water sports. Home: 7135 Cascade Rd SE Grand Rapids MI 49506 Office: Comp-Aire Systems Inc 4185 44th St SE Grand Rapids MI 49508

DISBROW, RICHARD EDWIN, utility executive; b. Newark, Sept. 20, 1930; s. Milton A. and Madeline Catherine (Segal) D.; m. Patricia Fair Warner, June 27, 1953 (div. Sept. 1972); children: John Scott, Lisa Karen; m. Teresa Marie Moser, May 12, 1973. B.S., Lehigh U., 1952; M.S. in Elec. Engring., Newark Coll. Engring., 1959; M.S. in indsl. mgmt., MIT, 1965. With Am. Electric Power Service Corp., N.Y.C., 1954-80, Columbus, Ohio, 1980—; transmission and distbn. mgr. Am. Electric Power Service Corp., 1967-70, controller, 1970-71, v.p., controller, 1971-74, exec. v.p., 1974-75, vice chmn. bd., 1975-79, pres., chief adminstrv. officer, 1979-84, pres., chief operating officer, 1985—, dir.; pres., dir. Am. Electric Power Co.; dir. Banc Ohio Nat. Bank, 1986; instr. Newark Coll. Engring., 1959-64; mem. N.J. Engrs. Com. For Student Guidance, 1960-64; indsl. commr., Piscataway, N.J., 1960-64; mem. vis. com. dept. mech. engring. and mechanics Lehigh U., 1960-64; trustee Franklin U.; bd. visitors N.J. Inst. Tech. Served to 1st lt. USAF, 1952-54. Sloan fellow MIT. Mem. Edison Electric Inst. (dir.), Psi Upsilon, Eta Kappa Nu. Clubs: Columbus Athletic, Worthington Hills Country. Office: Am Electric Power Service Corp 1 Riverside Plaza Columbus OH 43216 *

DISHOP, RICHARD THOMAS, automotive dealer; b. Wauseon, Ohio, Aug. 24, 1942; s. Albert Henry and Amelia A. D.; m. Janice Elain Longstreet, July 5, 1973; children: Teresa, Anthony, Jodi. Student U. Automotive Mgmt., New Orleans, 1980. Barber, 1961-64; gen. mgr. Turnpike Travelers, Bowling Green, Ohio, 1967-71; owner, operator Dishop Ford Yugo Nissan, Bowling Green, 1972—; owner, operator RTD & Assos., collection agy., 1972-75; mem. Mid Am. Bank Adv. Bd., 1971-80, pres., 1972. Mem. Rep. Nat. Task Force. Named to Outstanding Young Men Am., U.S. Jaycees, 1973; recipient Quality Dealer award Datsun, 1975, 80, 82-83, 86, Quality Dealer award Ford Motor Co., 1985, Disting. Dealer award Ford Motor Co., 1985. Mem. Am. Imported Automobile Dealers Assn., Nat. Auto Dealers Assn., Bowling Green Auto Dealers (sec.-treas. 1978-87), Ohio Auto Dealers Assn. Lutheran. Clubs: Falcon, Bowling Green State U. Pres.'s. Lodge: Elks. Home: 14251 Gorrill Rd Bowling Green OH 43402 Office: Dishop Ford-Yugo-Nissan Rt 25 Bowling Green OH 43402

DISKIN, ROBERT JOSEPH, electronics company executive; b. Parsons, Kans., June 5, 1957; s. Patrick Thomas and Berniece Claire (O'Brien) D.; m. Karen Gayle Harnish, Apr. 28, 1981; 1 child, Eric Michael. BS in Music Edn., Pitts. State U. Cert. tchr. Kans., Iowa. Asst. instr. Am. Inst. Profl. Edn., 1980-81; mgr. J.S. Latta Co., Cedar Falls, Iowa, 1981-83; dist. sales mgr. Panasonic Indsl. Co., Arlington Heights, Ill., 1983—. Mem. Internat. TV Assn., Soc. Broadcast Engrs., Wis. Video Assn., Instrument Soc. Am. Roman Catholic. Avocations: music, karate. Home: 6255 Springfield Lodi Rd Waunakee WI 53597 Office: Panasonic Indsl Co 425 E Algonquin Rd Arlington Heights IL 61312

DI SPIGNO, GUY JOSEPH, psychologist, consultant; b. Bklyn., Mar. 6, 1948; s. Joseph Vincent and Jeanne Nina (Renna) DiS.; BS, Carroll Coll., 1969; MA (fellow), No. Ill. U., 1972; MEd, Loyola U., 1974; PhD, Northwestern U., 1977; m. Gisela Riba, May 23, 1979; children: Michael Paul, Abie Francis. Instr., No. Ill. U., DeKalb, 1969-70; chmn. humanities dept. Quincy (Ill.) Boys' High Sch., 1970-71; dir. religious edn. St. Mary's Ch., DeKalb, 1971-72; dir. edn. Immaculate Conception Parish, Higland Park, Ill., 1972-77; dir. human resources Am. Valuation Cons., Des Plaines, Ill., 1977-79; psychologist Hay Assocs., Chgo., 1979-80; v.p. psychol. services Exec. Assets Corp., Chgo., 1980-82; dir. mgmt. devel. and personnel services Borg-Warner Corp., Chgo., 1982-84; cons. psychologist Medina & Thompson, Chgo., 1984—. Mem. Highland Park Human Relations Commn., 1975-77, Home Owners and Businessmen's Assn., Highland Park, 1976-77; mem. legis. com. Vernon Hills (Ill.) Sch. Bd.; soccer coach, Am. Youth Soccer Orgn., Glenview, Ill. Clifford B. Scott scholar, 1967. Mem. Community Religious Edn. Dirs. (nat. vice chmn. 1971-73), Am. Psychol. Assn., Ill. Psychol. Assn., Nat. Registry Health Service Providers in Psychology, Am. Personnel and Guidance Assn., Carroll Coll. Alumni Counsel, Phi Alpha Theta, Sigma Phi Epsilon. Contbr. articles to profl. jours. Home: 3710 Maple Leaf Dr Glenview IL 60025 Office: 100 S Wacker Dr Suite 1710 Chicago IL 60606

DISS, MICHELLE A., dental hygienist; b. Detroit, Mar. 25, 1949; d. Basil F. and Rosemary M. (Gardner) Cahill; m. William F. Diss, June 28, 1968; 1 child: Brigitte Michelle. Assoc. Liberal Arts, Macomb Community Coll., 1982; Assoc. Applied Scis., Oakland Community Coll., 1984. Dental hygienist Dr. Kolin, Sterling Heights, Mich., 1984, Dr. Regiony, Ortonville, Mich., 1984, Dr. Lahey, Detroit, 1984-85, Dr. Weiss, Warren, Mich., 1985—; lectr. children with behavioral problems, U. Detroit, 1985, Perio Seminar I, 1985, Perio Seminar II, III, 1986; lectr. fearful patients U. Mich., Ann Arbor, 1986. Republican. Roman Catholic. Clubs: Lifestyles, Acapulco Sun. Avocations: weight lifting, corvettes, suntanning, shopping. Home:

58107 Dulwich Washington MI 48094 Office: Warren Family Dental 27600 Hoover Warren MI 48093

DISSER, PAUL J., trust company executive; b. Tulsa, June 12, 1951; s. Robert Kelly and Marjorie C. (Obergfell) D.; m. Michele Sue Glindmeyer, Oct. 19, 1974; children: Evan Joseph, Hollace Marie. BBA, Xaiver U., Cin., 1973. Account exec. T.L.A., Inc., Cin., 1975-78; gen. mgr. sales div. T.L.A., Inc., Kansas City, Mo., 1978-79, v.p., 1979-81, pres., 1981-82; pres., chmn. bd. Trust Benefits Mgmt. Corp., Kansas City, Mo., 1982—; bd. dirs. FAHC, Inc., Phoenix. Contbr. articles to indsl. publ. Mem. adv. council St. Joseph Hosp., Kansas City, Mo., 1982—. Republican. Roman Catholic. Club: Leawood (Kans.) South Country. Avocations: skiing, tennis, cycling, family activities. Home: 12115 Madison Ct Kansas City MO 64145 Office: Trust Benefits Mgmt Corp 1200 E 104th St Kansas City MO 64131

DITKA, MICHAEL KELLER, professional football coach; b. Carnegie, Pa., Oct. 18, 1939; s. Mike and Charlotte (Keller) D.; m. Margery Ditka, Jan. 21, 1961 (div. 1973); children: Michael, Mark, Megan, Matthew; m. Diana Ditka, July 8, 1977. Student, U. Pitts. Profl. football player Chgo. Bears, 1961-66, Phila. Eagles, 1967-68; profl. football player Dallas Cowboys, 1969-72, asst. coach, 1973-81; head coach Chgo. Bears, 1982—; coach Chgo. Bears Superbowl Championship Team, 1985; owner Ditka's Restaurant, Chgo., 1986—. Named Rookie of Yr., NFL, 1961; named to Pro Bowl, 1962-66. Roman Catholic. Office: Chgo Bears Football Club 55 E Jackson St Suite 1200 Chicago IL 60604

DITMEYER, STEVEN ROLAND, railroad executive; b. St. Louis, Nov. 4, 1941; s. Roland John and Mabel Elizabeth (Hermeling) D.; m. Martha Stark Draper, May 26, 1979; children—Anne, David. B.S., MIT, 1963; cert. in transp. Yale U., 1965, M.A., 1965. Ops. research analyst Fed. R.R. Adminstrn., Washington, 1968-74, assoc. adminstr. policy, 1977-79, assoc. adminstr. research and devel., 1980-81; transp. economist The World Bank, Washington, 1974-77; acting gen. mgr. The Alaska R.R., Anchorage, 1979-80; dir. research and devel. Burlington No. R.R., St. Paul, 1981-86, chief engr. research, communication and control systems, 1986—. Co-author pub. reports on R.R. industry. Served to capt. USAR, 1966-68. Recipient Spl. Commendation, Fed. R.R. Adminstrn., 1980. Fellow The Permanent Way Inst.; mem. Am. R.R. Engring. Assn., Tau Beta Pi. Episcopalian. Club: Metropolitan (Washington). Office: Burlington Northern RR 9401 Indian Creek Pkwy Overland Park KS 66201-9136

DITMORE, QUINTON MICHAEL, neurological surgeon; b. Neosho, Mo., May 29, 1944; s. Quint B. and Mary Lorene (Curry) D.; divorced; children: Quinton Michael II, Joshua Curry. Student, U. Okla., 1962-65, MD, 1969. Diplomate Am. Bd. Neurol. Surgery. Intern U. Tex. Health Scis. Ctr., Dallas, 1969-70, resident in neurol. surgery, 1975-79; neurosurgical fellow Univ. Western Ont. (Can.), London, 1977; practice medicine specializing in neurol. surgery Columbia, Mo., 1982—. Contbr. articles to profl. jours. Served to lt. USN, 1970-73. Fellow Am. Coll. Surgeons, Am. Heart Assn. (stroke council). Republican. Unitarian. Avocations: tennis, hunting, fishing. Office: 1701 E Broadway Columbia MO 65201

D'ITRI, FRANK MICHAEL, environmental research chemist; b. Flint, Mich., Apr. 25, 1933; s. Dominic and Angelina (Cosanza) D.; m. Patricia Ann Ward, Sept. 10, 1955; children: Michael Payne, Angela Kathryn, Patricia Ann, Julie Lynn. BS in Zoology, Mich. State U., 1955, MS in Analytical Chemistry, 1966, PhD, 1968. Lab. technician Dow Indsl. Service Labs., Midland, Mich., 1960-62; research asst. dept. chemistry Mich. State U., East Lansing, 1963-68, asst. prof. dept. fisheries and wildlife, 1968-72, assoc. prof. dept. fisheries and wildlife, 1973-76, prof. dept. fisheries and wildlife, 1977—; cons. U.S. Dept Energy, Washington, 1983-85, EEC, United Nations, Geneva, 1982—; vis. prof. Tokyo U. Agr., 1980, 84-85, mem. adv. bd. Lewis Pubs., Inc. Author: (with P.A. D'Itri) Mercury Contamination: A Human Tragedy, 1977, (with A.W. Andren, R.A. Doherty, J.M. Wood) Assessment of Mercury in the Environment, 1978, Acid Precipitation, 1982, Artificial Reefs, 1985; editor (with J. Aguirre M., M. Athie L.) Municipal Wastewater in Agriculture, 1981, Land Treatment of Municipal Wastewater: Vegetation Selection and Management, 1982, Acid Precipitation: Effects on Ecological Systems, 1982, (with M.A. Kamrin) PCBs: Human and Environmental Hazards, 1983, Artificial Reefs: Marine and Freshwater Applications, 1985, A System Approach to Conservation Tillage, 1985, (with H.H. Prince) Coastal Wetlands, 1985; contbr. numerous articles to profl. jours. Mem. critical materials adv. subcom. Mich. Water Resources Commns. Mich. Dept. Natural Resources, 1971-79, mem. subcom. Mich. State U. Waste Control Authority Chem. Waste, 1971—, mem. solid waste com. Mich. Dept. Nat. Resources, Lansing, 1971-79. NIH summer fellow, 1964-67, Socony-Mobil fellow Mich. State U., 1967-68, Japan Soc. Promotion Sci. fellow, 1980; Rockefeller Found. Bellagio Resident scholar, 1972, 75. Mem. Am. Chem. Soc., Am. Soc. Limnology and Oceanography, Assn. Analytical Chemists, Water Pollution Research Soc., Midwest Univs. Analytical Chemists Conf., Mich. Acad. Sci., Arts and Letters, Sigma Xi. Home: 4395 Elmwood Dr Okemos MI 48864 Office: Mich State U Inst Water Research 334 Natural Resources Bldg East Lansing MI 48824

DITTMAN, MARK ALLEN, clinical engineer, hospital safety officer; b. Green Bay, Wis., Aug. 18, 1950; s. Paul William and Norma Jean Dittman; m. Theresa Petri, Aug. 19, 1978. BS in Biology, U. Wis., Stevens Point, 1972; BS in Biomed. Engring., Milw. Sch. Engring., 1978. Clin. engr. Lakeland Hosp., Elkhorn, Wis., 1978-80; clin. engr. Henry Ford Hosp., Detroit, 1980-86, safety officer, 1986—; cons. engr. TerMar & Assocs., Detroit, 1986—. Inventor anesthia gas machine monitor. Mem. Am. Soc. Hosp. Engrs., Assn. Advancement Medicine Inst., Engring. Soc. Detroit (scientific com.). Republican. Roman Catholic. Avocation: gardening. Office: Henry Ford Hosp 2799 W Grand Blvd Detroit MI 48202

DITTMANN, PHILIP ALBERT, oil company executive; b. Chgo., June 1, 1954; s. William Andrew and Marcella Mae (Evans) D.; m. Joan Cecelia Racevice, Aug. 12, 1980. BSME, Ill. Inst. Tech., 1977. Registered profl. engr., Ill., Ind. With engring. dept. Amoco Oil Co., Whiting, Ind., 1977-80, project engr., 1980-84, maintenance engr. constrn. dept., 1984-85, maintenance planner, 1985, project repress engr., 1985-86, supr. contract adminstrn. div., 1986—. Mem. Christ The King Parish Folk Choir, Chgo., 1983—; mem. Art. Inst. Chgo., 1980—. Mem. Gary Regional Purchasing Council. Roman Catholic. Avocations: sailing, traveling. Home: 9015 S Hoyne Ave Chicago IL 60620 Office: Amoco Oil Co 2815 Indpls Blvd Whiting IN 46394

DITTMER, ROBERT LEE, accountant; b. Peoria, Ill., July 14, 1950; s. Warren Donald and Phyllis (Bouton) D.; m. Joan Irene Kearney, Apr. 23, 1978; children: Timothy, Christine, Katherine, Michael (dec.). BS in Indsl. Mgmt., Purdue U., 1972; MS in Accountancy, DePaul U., 1980. CPA. Instr. Purdue U., Lafayette, Ind., 1972-74; cons. Touche Ross & Co., Chgo., 1974-78; systems mgr. CNA Ins., Chgo., 1978-80; prin. Dittmer Profl. Corp., Morton, Ill., 1980—. Named one of Outstanding Young Men of Am., 1985. Mem. Am. Inst. CPAs, Ill. Soc. CPAs, Morton C. of C. (treas. 1984, bd. dirs. 1984—, v.p. 1985, 86), Beta Gamma Sigma, Phi Kappa Phi. Lodge: Rotary (local bd. dirs. 1984-85). Home: 1200 Parkside Ave Morton IL 61550 Office: 617 W David St Morton IL 61550

DITTON, DELORES ELAINE, insurance agent; b. Bedford, Ind., Apr. 6, 1934; d. Haase John and Beulah Glen (Guthrie) Benzel; m. Louis George Ditton, Nov. 8, 1958; children—Cynthia, Ryan. R.N., Lutheran Hosp., Ft. Wayne, 1957; B.S. in Health Arts, Coll. of St. Francis, Joliet, 1980; grad. Bill Miller Sch. Real Estate, 1981, Midwest Ins. Sch., 1983, Ft. Wayne Ground Sch., 1978. Lic. nurse, real estate, ins., Ind.; lic. pvt. pilot. Nurse, surg., coronary, critical care areas, Ft. Wayne, Ind., 1957-83; head nurse geriatric facility, Ft. Wayne, 1983; Sci. Fair judge Aerospace Edn. Council, 1983, 84, 85; vol. Ft. Wayne Children's Zoo; charter men. Greater Ft. Wayne Aviation Mus., Ninety Nines (co-founder Three Rivers chpt., sec. 1983-85, membership, chpt. chmn.), Aircraft Owners and Pilots Assn., Cherokee Pilots Assn., Fort Wayne Aviation Assn. Home: 5417 Inland Trail Fort Wayne IN 46825

DITZER, PAUL DAVID, data processing executive; b. Chattanooga, Dec. 21, 1950; s. Earl D. and Marie Nell (Garrett) D.; m. Pamela A. Kline, Nov. 18, 1972; 1 child, Heather Nicole. Grad. high sch., Russellville, Ky., 1968. Enlisted USMC, 1970, adv. through grades to staff sgt.; systems programmer USMC, various cities, 1970-78; resigned USMC, 1978; systems programmer Hallmark Cards, Kansas City, Mo., 1978-80, United Data Services, Kansas City, 1980-83, Payless Cashways, Kansas City, 1983-85; mgr. systems programming Johnson County Data Services, Olathe, Kans., 1985-87; ops. systems programming supr. House of Lloyd, Grandview, Mo., 1987—. Southern Baptist. Avocation: Clydesdales. Home: Rt #3 Box 4050 Holden MO 64040 Office: House of Lloyd 11901 Grandview Rd Grandview MO 64034

DIUGUID, LEWIS WALTER, editor, reporter, photographer; b. St. Louis, July 17, 1955; s. Lincoln Isaiah and Nancy Ruth (Greenlee) D.; m. Valerie Gale Words, Oct. 25, 1977; children:Adrianne, Leslie Ellen. B.J., U. Mo., 1977. Reporter, photographer Campus Digest, Columbia, Mo., 1974-75, St. Louis Sentinel, 1976; reporter, photographer, copy and automotive editor Kansas City Times, Mo., 1977—; asst. minority recruiting coordinator Kansas City Times and Star, 1985, asst. bur. chief Johnson County office The Kansas City Star, 1985—. Inst. for Journalism Edn. fellow U. Ariz.-Tucson, 1984. Mem. Nat. Assn. Black Journalists, Kansas City Assn. Black Journalists (pres. 1986). Roman Catholic. Avocations: jogging; weight lifting; bike riding; woodworking. Home: 3944 Charlotte St Kansas City MO 64110 Office: Kansas City Times 1729 Grand Ave Kansas City MO 64108

DIUGUID, LINCOLN ISAIAH, chemist; b. Lynchburg, Va., Feb. 6, 1917; m. Nancy Ruth Diuguid, July 8, 1955; children: David, Lewis, Renee, Vincent. BS magna cum laude, W. Va. State U., 1938; MS, Cornell U., 1939, PhD, 1945, post doctorate, 1945-47. Head chemistry dept. Ark. State Coll., Pine Bluff, 1939-43; analytical chemist Pine Bluff Arsenal, 1942-43; pres., founder Du-Good Chem. Lab. and Mfrs., St. Louis, 1947—; chmn. phys. sci. dept. Harris Stowe State Coll., St. Louis, 1949-82, prof. emeritus, 1982—; vis. prof. chemistry Washington U., St. Louis, 1966-68; cons. chemist VA Hosp., Jefferson Barricks (Mo.) Hosp., 1968-78, Intertherm Co., St. Louis, 1964—. Contbr. numerous articles to profl. jours.; chpts. to books; patentee in field. V.p. Leukemia Guild Mo. and Ill., St. Louis, 1963; trustee Leukemia Guild Am., St. Louis, 1968-82. Recipient Disting. Educators award Harris Stowe Alumnae, 1985, Carver award Sigma Gamma, 1979. Fellow Am. Inst. Chemists; mem. AAUP, Am. Chem. Soc., Assn. Cons. Chemists and Chem. Engrs., Ethical Soc., Sigma Xi, Phi Kappa Phi, Omega Psi Phi (v.p. 1950-51, Man of Yr. award 1960). Avocations: golfing, tennis, swimming. Home: 3645 Lafayette Saint Louis MO 63110 Office: Du-Good Chem Lab and Mfrs 1215 S Jefferson Saint Louis MO 63104

DI VENERE, CATHERINE LENA, administrative manager, planner; b. Chgo., Oct. 6, 1941; d. Joseph and Josephine (Zucchero) Di V. Participant Am. Mgmt. Inst., Dible Mgmt. and Drake U. Exec. programs, 1981, 82. Sales asst. to asst. sales mgr. Blair TV, Chgo., 1961-69, sales asst. to v.p. Midwest Sales Mgr., 1969-74, adminstrv. asst. to pres. market div., 1974-76, adminstrv. mgr. Chgo. office, 1976-80; v.p., mgr. office adminstrn. John Blair and Co., Chgo., 1980—. Bd. cons. Park Ridge Ct. Condominium Assn. Mem. Joint Civic Com. Italian-Ams., Am. Women in Radio and TV, Nat. Assn. Female Execs., Apostolate of Women. Office: John Blair & Co 645 N Michigan Ave Suite 700 Chicago IL 60611

DIVERDE, JOSEPH JOHN, advertising executive; b. Bellwood, Ill., Dec. 30, 1938; s. Andrew and Frances (Lobulgio) D.; m. Cynthia Ann Jacobson, Aug. 26, 1967; children: Carissa, Dina, Andrew. Student, Am. Acad. Art, 1958. Artist Whitaker Guernsey Studios, Chgo., 1958-62; staff artist, designer Do All Co., Des Plaines, Ill., 1964-68; art dir. Indsl. Research, Inc., Beverly Shores, Ind., 1968-70, Clapper Pub. Co., Park Ridge, Ill., 1970-79; owner Joe Diverde Advt. Art, Blommingdale, Ill., 1979—. Served with U.S. Army, 1962-64. Home and Office: 153 Longridge Dr Bloomingdale IL 60108

DIVITO, AUGUST, financial planning executive; b. Cleve., Aug. 30, 1929; s. Joseph and Mary (Coreno) DeV.; m. Jane Edith Kelley, June 9, 1951; children: Catherine Sudnik, Donna Jereb, Christopher J. BS, Kent State U., 1951, MA, 1954; MSFS, Am. Coll., Bryn Mawr, Pa., 1979. CLU, chartered fin. cons. Tchr., coach Collinwood High Sch., Cleve., 1952-64; gen. agt. Columbus Mut. Life Ins. Co., Cleve., 1964—; fin. planner Advance Planning Concepts, Inc., Cleve., 1982—; registered prin. Nat. Assn. Security Dealers, Cleve., 1983—, Lowry Fin. Services Corp., Cleve., 1985—; mem. gen. agts. Columbus Mut. Life Ins. Co., 1987—; adv. com. Ins. Co. Elec. Industry, 1985—, also bd. dirs.; spkr. various organizations, 1987—. Contbr. articles to profl. jours. Mem. legacy com. Cuyahoga County Unit Am. Cancer Soc., Cleve., 1983—, devel. com. YMCA, Cleve., 1970. Served as sgt. U.S. Army, 1954-56. Recipient Nat. Sales Achievement award Nat. Assn. Life Underwriters, 1987, Nat. Quality award Nat. Assn. Life Underwriters, 1987. Mem. Estate Planning Council, Soc. Pension Actuaries, Internat. Assn. Fin. Planners, Soc. of CLU's, Soc. of Underwriters, Million Dollar Round Table (life). Republican. Roman Catholic. Avocations: golf, tennis. Home: 12500 Edgewater Dr Apt 707 Lakewood OH 44107 Office: Advance Planning Concepts Inc 601 Rockefeller Bldg 614 Superior Ave NW Cleveland OH 44113

DIVNEY, HERBERT PHILLIPS, clinical psychologist; b. Columbus, Ohio, Apr. 3, 1923; s. James Joseph and Narelle (Phillips) D.; m. Dorothy Smith; children: James, Marc, Ann, Malcolm. BA, Kent State U., 1948; MA, Catholic U., 1952. Lic. psychologist, Ohio. Chief psychologist Apple Creek State Hosp., Wooster, Ohio, 1952-66; unit psychologist Falls View Mental Health Ctr., Cuyahoga Falls, Ohio, 1966-68; adminstrv. psychologist S.E. Colorado Guidance Ctr., La Junta, Colo., 1968-73; chief psychologist Apple Creek State Sch., Wooster, 1973-77, Tiffin Devel. Ctr., Tiffin, Ohio, 1977—. Served with AUS, 1942-46. Mem. Am. Assn. Mental Deficiency, Am. Legion. Lodge: Elks. Home and Office: Tiffin Devel Ctr 600 North River Rd Tiffin OH 44883

DIX, ALAN RICHARD, data processing executive, accountant; b. Quincy, Ill., July 10, 1955; s. Richard E. and martha Kay (Kendall) D.; m. Linda Lou Stutsman, Sept. 20, 1980; children: Aimee Jo, Bradley Alan. BS, Ill. State U., 1977. CPA, Ill. Accountant Price Waterhouse, Peoria, Ill., 1977-83; chief fin. officer Customer Devel. Corp., Peoria, Ill., 1983—. Bd. dirs. Miracles on the March. Mem. Am. Inst. CPA's, Ill. Soc. CPA's. Republican. Methodist. Lodge: Masons. Avocations: hunting, fishing, golf. Office: Customer Devel Corp 240 W Altorfer Dr Peoria IL 61615

DIX, RALPH EUGENE, office supply company executive; b. Leavenworth, Kans., July 16, 1926; s. Grover Webster and Mary Alice Dix; student public schs., Leavenworth; m. Mary Margaret DeCoursey, Dec. 2, 1944; children—Ralph Eugene, Carey Ann. Grocery store clk., 1947-48; owner Ralph's Grocery, 1948-60; in material control Gen. Motors Corp., 1949-59; salesman Sears Roebuck & Co., Leavenworth, 1959-68; owner Dix & Son Office Supply, Leavenworth, 1968—; sr. partner Platte Office Supply, Parkville, Mo., 1978—; partner Discount Carpet Warehouse, Leavenworth, 1978—; consul for Guatemala, 1981—. Mem. Leavenworth Urban Renewal Bd., 1969—; bd. dirs. Leavenworth Downtown Assn., 1974-75; Guatemalan consul Midwest region. Served with U.S. Army, 1944-46. Mem. Leavenworth C. of C. (dir. 1970-72), V.F.W., Am. Legion. Republican. Lodge: Eagles. Home: 2608 S 14th St Leavenworth KS 66048 Office: 413-415 Delaware St Leavenworth KS 66048

DIX, ROLLIN C(UMMING), mechanical engineering educator, consultant; b. N.Y.C., Feb. 8, 1936; s. Omer Houston and Ona Mae (Cumming) D.; m. Elaine B. VanNest, June 18, 1960; children: Gregory, Elisabeth, Karen. B.S.M.E., Purdue U., 1957, M.S.M.E., 1958, Ph.D., 1963. Registered profl. engr., Ind., Ill. Asst. prof. mech. engring. Ill. Inst. Tech., Chgo., 1964-69, assoc. prof., 1969-80, prof., 1980—, assoc. dean for computing, 1980—; cons. mech. design Bronson & Bratton, Inc., Chgo., 1965—; dir. Bimet Corp., Morris, Ill. Patentee road repair vehicle, method for vestibular test. Served to 1st lt. U.S. Army, 1960-61. Fellow ASME; mem. Am. Soc. Engring. Edn., Soc. Mfg. Engrs. Home: 10154 S Seeley Ave Chicago IL 60643 Office: Ill Inst Tech 10 W 31st St Chicago IL 60616

DIXON, ALAN JOHN, U.S. Senator; b. Belleville, Ill., July 7, 1927; s. William G. and Elsa (Tebbenhoff) D.; m. Joan Louise Fox, Jan. 17, 1954; children: Stephanie Jo, Jeffrey Alan, Elizabeth Jane. B.S., U. Ill., 1949; LL.B., Washington U., St. Louis, 1949. Bar: Ill. 1950. Practiced in Belleville, 1950-76; police magistrate City of Belleville, 1949; asst. atty. St. Clair County, Ill., 1950; mem. Ill. Ho. of Reps., 1951-63, Ill. Senate, 1963-71; minority whip; treas. State of Ill., 1971-77, sec. of state, 1977-81; U.S. Senator from Ill., 1981—. Mem. Am. Legion, Belleville C. of C. Democrat. Office: US Senate 316 Hart Senate Bldg Washington DC 20510

DIXON, BILLY GENE, educator; b. Benton, Ill., Oct. 25, 1935; s. John and Stella (Prowell) D.; m. Judith R. McCommons, June 7, 1957; children: Valerie J., Clark A. BS, So. Ill. U., 1957, PhD, 1967; MS, Ill. Wesleyan U., 1961. Tchr. math., chmn. dept. Cahokia (Ill.) High Sch., 1960-61; tchr. Univ. Sch., So. Ill. U., Carbondale, 1961-67, chmn. dept. math., 1963-67; dir. research and evaluation ESEA Title II Project Uplift, Mt. Vernon, Ill., 1967-69; coordinator profl. edn. experiences Coll. Edn. So. Ill. U., Carbondale, 1968-75, mem. faculty, coordinator grad. program in secondary edn., 1975-78, departmental exec. officer curriculum and instrn., 1978—. Pres. Benton Community Park Dist., 1974—. Named Citizen of Yr. Benton C. of C., 1982. Mem. Ill. Assn. Tchr. Eductors (exec. council 1976-79, pres. 1973, Disting. mem. 1984), Assn. Tchr. Educators (exec. bd. 1983-86, chmn. nat. rev. panel Disting. Program in Tchr. Edn. 1976-86, Pres.'s award 1983, 84), Pi Mu Epsilon, Phi Kappa Phi, Phi Delta Kappa, Kappa Delta Pi. Democrat. Methodist. Home: Rural Rt 2 Benton IL 62812 Office: So Ill U Dept Curriculum and Instrn Carbondale IL 62901

DIXON, CARL FRANKLIN, lawyer; b. Mansfield, Ohio, Feb. 17, 1948; s. Carl Hughes and Elizabeth (Kauffman) D.; m. Barbara Wagner, Dec. 27, 1969; children—Clare Elizabeth, Jane Allison. B.A., Ill. Wesleyan U., 1970, B.S., 1970; M.A. Fletcher Sch. Law and Diplomacy div. Tufts U., 1974; JD, U. Chgo., 1974. Bar: Ill. 1975, U.S. Dist. Ct. (no. dist.) Ill. 1975, Ohio 1983. Assoc., Keck, Mahin & Cate, Chgo., 1974-78; ptnr. Dixon & Kois, Chgo., 1978-82; assoc. Porter, Wright, Morris & Arthur, Cleve., 1982-85, ptnr., 1986-87; v.p., sec., gen. counsel Weston Ltd., Inc., Cleve., 1987—. Recipient Adlai E. Stevenson award UN Assn., 1970; Edward R. Murror fellow, 1971. Mem. ABA, Greater Cleve. Bar Assn., Phi Kappa Phi. Republican. Episcopalian. Club: Union League (Chgo.); Clifton (Lakewood, Ohio). Home: 31011 Manchester Ln Bay Village OH 44140 Office: Weston Ltd Inc 3615 Superior Ave Cleveland OH 44114

DIXON, FRED LEROY, communications designer, consultant; b. Grand Ledge, Mich., Jan. 15, 1937; s. Fred A. and Nellie M. (Sanders) D.; m. Pauline A. Doxsie, May 10, 1958; children: Tony, Alan, Lisa. Owner Projection Repair, Lansing, Mich.; chief engr. Mich. State U., E. Lansing, Newman Communications, Grand Rapids, Mich.; pres. Dixon Media System Design, Eagle, Mich. Named Outstanding Citizen Mich. Legislature, 1982. Mem. Internat. Communication Industry Assn. (coarse chmn. annual inst. 1982-86, profl. devel. com. 1980-86), Interior Bus. Designers, 4-H (Outstanding Leader 1976-78). Office: Dixon Media Systems & Design Inc 13701 Hinman Eagle MI 48822

DIXON, GEORGE DAVID, radiologist; b. Valley City, N.D., Mar. 27, 1936; s. George Sherman and Isabel Ruth (Eaton) D.; m. Carol Marie Vennerstrom, Feb. 28, 1958; children: Barbara Sarah, George David Jr. Student, Willamette U., 1954-55; BA, U. N.D., 1959; MD, Tulane U., 1961. Diplomate Am. Bd. Radiology. Intern St. Luke's Hosp., Duluth, Minn., 1961-62; gen. practice Lenont-Peterson Clinic, Cook, Minn., 1962-64; resident in radiology Mayo Clinic, Rochester, Minn., 1964-66, 68-70; radiologist St. Luke's Hosp. Radiol. Group, Inc., Kansas City, Mo., 1970—, sec., 1971—; clin. prof. radiology U. Mo. Sch. of Medicine, Kansas City, 1985—. Mem. edit. adv. bd. Miller-Freeman Pubs., Inc., 1979—; contbr. articles to med. jours. Pres. Interdenominational Christian Youth Council, Fargo, N.D., 1953-54; lay leader Indian Heights United Meth. Ch., Overland Park, Kans., 1977-79. Served to capt. U.S. Army, 1966-68, Vietnam. Mem. AMA, Mo. State Med. Soc., Mo. Radiol. Soc., Soc. Cardiovascular and Interventional Radiology, Am. Coll. Radiology, Jackson County Med. Soc., Greater Kansas City Radiol. Soc. (pres., sec. 1978-79, treas. 1977-78), Radiol. Soc. N.A., Am. Roentgen Ray Soc., Phi Beta Kappa, Phi Beta Pi, Beta Theta Pi, New Eng. Historic Genealogical Soc. Republican. Club: Wally Byan Caravan (Kansas City). Lodge: Masons. Avocations: traveling by trailer, genealogy. Home: 10416 Mohawk Ln Leawood KS 66206 Office: St Lukes Radiol Group Inc 4320 Wornall Rd Suite 710 Kansas City MO 64111

DIXON, GEORGE FRANCIS, JR., manufacturing company executive; b. Jersey City, Feb. 24, 1918; s. George F. and Frances (Martin) D.; m. Lottie Ivy Carter, Dec. 1, 1950; children: George Francis III, Richard Elliott, Marshall Lawrence, Charlotte Ivy. B.S., U.S. Mil. Acad., 1940; M.S., Cornell U., 1947; D.Eng., Grenoble U., France, 1949. Dist. engr. Vicksburg Dist. Corps Engrs., 1949-53; pres. Dart Truck Co., Kansas City, Mo., 1955-57; also dir.; with Carlisle Corp., Pa., 1954—; pres., chief exec. officer Carlisle Corp., 1957-70, chmn. bd., 1970—, also dir.; dir. Dauphin Deposit Trust Co., Harrisburg, Pa., CDI Corp., Phila.; Chmn. Pa. Div. Trauma. Trustee Dickinson Sch. Law; trustee Gettysburg Coll. Served at lt. col. AUS, World War II; div. engr., comdg. officer 65th Engrs., 25th Inf. Div. Mem. ASCE, Assn. Grads. U.S. Mil. Acad. (trustee, pres.), Soc. Automotive Engrs., Soc. Am. Mil. Engrs. Home: Box 6 Boiling Springs PA 17007 Office: Carlisle Corp 250 E Fifth St Cincinnati OH 45202

DIXON, JAMES JASON, physician; b. Kansas City, Mo., July 6, 1920; s. Otto Jason and Olive (Robertson) D.; A.B., U. Kans., 1943, M.D., 1947; m. Kathryn May Hanna, May 2, 1948; children—David Jason, William Nelson, Robert Grant, Mary Christine. Intern, Toledo Hosp., 1947-48, resident, 1948-50; resident Henry Ford Hosp., Detroit, 1950-52; pathologist, dir. labs. Ashtabula (Ohio) Gen. Hosp., 1952-84, Lake County Meml. Hosp., Painesville, Ohio, 1952-58; pathologist Brown Meml. Hosp., Conneaut, Ohio, 1961-70; cons. pathologist Geneva (Ohio) Meml. Hosp., 1961-68; mem. regional adv. com. Cleve. Red Cross Blood Program; dep. sheriff Ashtabula County. Past v.p. Ashtabula Fine Arts Center; active ARC. Diplomate Am. Bd. Pathology. Mem. Ohio, Ashtabula County (sec., treas. 1956, pres. 1960) med. socs., Am. Soc. Clin. Pathologists, Coll. Am. Pathologists, Ohio, Cleve. socs. pathologists, Am. Cancer Soc. (med. dir. Ashtabula County), Am. Assn. Blood Banks, AAAS, Ashtabula Power Squadron (comdr. 1966), Nat. Rifle Assn. (life), Nat. Assn. Federally Licensed Firearms Dealers, Ohio Gun Collectors Assn., Smith and Wesson Collectors Assn., Ohio Rifle and Pistol Assn. (life), Tau Kappa Epsilon, Nu Sigma Nu. Republican. Episcopalian (sr. warden 1960-63). Elk, Rotarian. Clubs: Ashtabula Country, Ashtabula Yacht; Redbrook Boat, Ashtabula Rod and Gun. Home: 1724 Highland Ln Ashtabula OH 44004

DIXON, JOHN FULTON, village manager; b. Bellingham, Wash., Dec. 17, 1946; s. Fulton Albert and Patricia (Broderick) D.; m. Karen Elizabeth Creagh, May 19, 1973; children: Neil, Craig. BS, Bradley U., 1971; M in Mgmt., Vanderbilt U., 1973. Asst. village mgr. Village of Hoffman Estates, Ill., 1974-76, village mgr., 1980-86; dir. village services Village of Roselle, Ill., 1976-79; asst. village mgr. Village of Schaumburg, Ill., 1979-80; village adminstr. Village of Lake Zurich, Ill., 1986-87; village mgr. Village of Mt. Prospect, Ill., 1987—; mgr. exec. bd. dirs. N.W. Suburban Mcpl. Joint Action Water Agy., Hoffman Estates, 1980—; mem. exec. bd. dirs. N.W. Cen. Dispatch, Arlington Heights, Ill., 1987—. Recipient Chief Scout's award Gov. Gen. Jamaica, Kingston, 1970; Adminstrv. fellow Woodrow Wilson Found., 1973-74, Houston fellow Vanderbilt U., 1972-73; Baker scholar Vanderbilt U., 1971-73. Mem. Met. Chgo. City Mgrs. Assn. (bd. dirs., pres. 1986-87), Ill. City Mgmt. Assn. (bd. dirs.). Roman Catholic. Avocations: golf, travel. Home: 1935 Fairway Ct Hoffman Estates IL 60195 Office: Village of Mount Prospect 100 S Emerson St Mount Prospect IL 60056

DIXON, MARY ELLEN, consultant; b. Olney, Ill., Nov. 8, 1940; d. Charles D. and Harriet (Dotson) Combs; m. Larry L. O'Dell, July 1, 1958 (div. 1968); children: Debra, Gary; m. William J. Dixon, May 1, 1976. AS in Bus., Olney Cen. Coll., 1968; BS, Eastern Ill. U., 1971; MS in Indsl. Relations, Loyola U., Chgo., 1985. Personnel adminstr. Booz, Allen & Hamilton, Chgo., 1974-77; personnel mgr. ITW, Chgo., 1977-80, Sara Lee, Chgo., 1980-83; dir. personnel TSR, Inc., Lake Geneva, Wis., 1983-85; cons. William M. Mercer-Meidinger Hansen Inc., Chgo., 1985—. Mem. Am. Soc. Personnel Adminstrn., Am. Compensation Assn. Republican. Avocations: sailing, reading, gardening, home decorating. Home: 3908 W Lakeshore Dr Wonder

Lake IL 60097 Office: Mercer-Meidinger Hansen 222 S Riverside Plaza Chicago IL 60606

DIXON, TERRY PHILLIP, higher education consultant; b. Cin., May 8, 1946; s. Henry Phillip and Annabel (Kincaid) D.; m. Evelyn Bowman, Dec. 23, 1969. BS in Chemistry, Biology, Cumberland Coll., 1968; MS in Elem. Edn., Ill. State U., 1978; postgrad., U. Nebr. Cert. elem. tchr., Mo., Ill.; cert. secondary sci. tchr. Tchr. biology, coach Cissna Park (Ill.) High Sch., 1968-69; tchr. Gilman (Ill.)Elem. Sch., 1969-78; chmn. div. Tarkio (Mo.) Coll., 1978—; cons. higher edn. Williams Dixon Assocs., Tarkio, 1979—; chief exec. officer XL Software, Tarkio, 1983—. Mem. Community Revitilization Com., Tarkio, 1985—; vice chmn. bd. dirs. N.W. Mo. Learning Ctr., Tarkio, 1986—. Mem. Assn. Tchr. Educators, Nebr. Educators Assn., Mo. Unit Assn. Tchr. Edn., Phi Delta Kappa. Baptist. Avocations: software design, writing, research. Home: Box 361 Tarkio MO 64491 Office: Tarkio Coll McNary St Tarkio MO 64491

DIXON, WENDELL L., financial company executive; b. Harrisburg, Ill., Aug. 2, 1923; m. Martha Anne Dixon; 4 children. Grad., U. Evansville. Mgmt. trainee Credithrift Fin., Inc., Houston and Evansville, Ind., 1946, br. mgr., 1947-53, dist. mgr., 1953-54; personnel dir. Credithrift Fin., Inc., Houston and Evansville, 1954-55; dir. ops. Credithrift Fin., Inc., Houston and Evansville, Ind., 1955-68; v.p., chief ops. Credithrift Fin. Corp., Houston and Evansville, Ind., 1968-71, exec. v.p., chief ops., 1971, pres., chief ops., 1971-73, chmn., chief exec. officer, 1973—; pres., dir. Credithrift Fin. Mgmt. Corp., Houston and Evansville, Ind., 1968—; dir. Citizens Nat. Bank; mem. Ind. Dept. Fin. Instns. Trustee U. Evansville; bd. dirs. Evansville's Future, Welborn Bapt. Hosp.; past pres. Welborn Bapt. Hosp. Found. Mem. Am. Fin. Services Assn. (chmn. 1984-85), Evansville C. of C. (dir.). Baptist. Lodge: Shriners. Office: Credithrift Fin Inc 601 NW 2nd St Evansville IN 47701

DIZENHUZ, ISRAEL MICHAEL, child psychiatrist, educator; b. Toronto, Ont., Can., May 20, 1931; came to U.S., 1957; Student, U. Toronto, 1949-51, MD, 1955. Diplomate Am. Bd. Psychiatry and Neurology. Intern E.J. Meyer Meml. Hosp., Buffalo, 1955-56; resident in psychiatry Hamilton (Ont.) Hosp., 1956-57; resident in psychiatry U. Cin., 1957-58, fellow in child psychiatry, 1959-60, from instr. to assoc. prof. child psychiatry, 1961—; practice medicine specializing in child psychiatry Cin., 1961—; asst. dir. child psychiatry Cen. Psychiat. Clinic, Cin., 1963-66, assoc. dir., 1966-78; psychiatrist cons. staff Children's Hosp., Cin., 1966—; sr. assoc. staff psychiatrist, dir. dept. psychiatry The Jewish Hosp., Cin., 1978; dir., chief clinician child and adolescent service Cin. Gen. Hosp., 1973-78, attending child psychiatrist, clinician, 1978—; mem. Precocious Pregnancy research team U. Cin., 1959-60, Adolescents in Families of Alcoholics research team Family Service, Cin., 1967-71; co-prin. investigator research project, Cancer Family Care, Cin., 1974-75; lectr. Vol. Training for Community Mental Health Services, Cin., 1963-68; asst. examiner Am. Bd. Psychiatry and Neurology, 1967—; cons. Hamilton County Ct. Domestic Relations Conciliation Service, 1974-78, Health Maintenance Plan of Cin., 1976-77; seminar leader Family Service, Cin., 1963-67, Jewish Family Service, Cin., 1963-68; seminar leader, cons. rehab. ctr. program U. Cin., 1973-78; mem. numerous rev. coms. Contbr. articles to profl. jours. Trustee Cin. Ctr. for Devel. Disabilities, 1963-83; trustee Bur. Jewish Edn., 1971-85, v.p. 1974-77. Fellow Am. Psychiat. Assn., Am. Acad. Child Psychiatry (mem. com. on tng. in Child Psychiatry 1972-78); mem. Royal Coll. of Physicians and Surgeons of Ont., Med. Council of Can., Am. Assn. Psychiat. Services for Children (pres. 1971-73), Am. Orthopsychiat. Assn., Ohio Psychiat. Assn., Ohio State Med. Assn., Cin. Soc. Neurology and Psychiatry, Cin. Council Child Psychiatry (pres. 1965-66). Office: The Jewish Hosp 3220 Burnet Ave Cincinnati OH 45229

DLOUHY, ROBERT PAUL, administration director; b. Cleve., Feb. 2, 1951; s. Robert P. and Laverne D.; children: Amanda, Nicholas. BBA, Ohio State U., 1973. Gen. acct. Eagle Stamp Co., Cleve., 1973-74; adminstrv. mgr. Chase Metals Services, Cleve., 1974-76; fin. analyst Morse Contorls, Hudson, Ohio, 1976-77; adminstrv. mgr. Chase Metals Service, Cleve., 1977-79; fin. mgr. Premier Indsl., Cleve., 1979-80; mgr. adminstr. Mgmt. Recruiters, Cleve., 1980—. Republican. Roman Catholic. Avocations: skiing, sailing. Office: Mgmt Recruiters Internat 1127 Euclid Ave Suite 1400 Cleveland OH 44115-1122

DMYTERKO, BOHDAN IHOR, lawyer, environmental engineer; b. Salzburg, Austria, Apr. 25, 1948; s. Roman Jaroslav and Romana (Karavan) D.; m. Kate Ann Jnwood, Jan. 21, 1972. BSCE, Ill. Inst. Tech., 1970; JD, Loyola U., Chgo., 1974. Fuel buyer Commonwealth Edison, Chgo., 1975-77, engr. air quality, 1977-83, engr. solid waste and toxics, 1983-85, sr. environ. engr., 1985—; chmn. tech. com. Potentially Responsible Parties for Refinery Products Hazardous Waste Site, Chgo., 1986; mem. com. for Lenz Oil Hazardous Waste Site, Chgo., 1987. Mem. ABA, Ill. Bar Assn. Office: Commonwealth Edison Corp PO Box 767 Chicago IL 60690

DOAN, GARY MICHAEL, marketing professional; b. Mpls., Apr. 20, 1952; s. Glen Norman and Helen Rose (Mosher) D. Student, Mankato (Minn.) State U., 1971-72. Sales rep. MMS Inc., Los Angeles, 1976; br. mgr. MMS Inc., Santa Clara, Calif., 1977-79; sales rep. electronics Anixter Bros., Mpls., 1980-82; sr. sales engr. Computer System Products, Mpls., 1983-84, sales mgr., 1984-85, mktg. dir., 1986—. Del. Dem. Farm Labor Party, Blue Earth, Minn., 1972. Mem. Data Processing Mgmt. Assn., Electronic Connector Study Group. Avocations: golf, flying. Home: 4201 Lakeside Ave N Brooklyn Center MN 55429 Office: Computer System Products 740 Washington Ave N Minneapolis MN 55401

DOANE, CHARLES ARTHUR, mental health facility administrator; b. St. Paul, Apr. 1, 1956; s. Charles William and Sharon Lee (Callan) D. BA in Psychology, St. Louis U., 1978. Program dir. Dungadin Inc., St. Paul, 1981-84; program coordinator P.A.L. Inc., St. Paul, 1984-86; psychiat. technician Fairview Hosp., Mpls., 1986—; mental health worker Wellspring Therapeutic Communities. Writer, dir. (film) Frank, 1986. Democrat. Avocations: sports, scriptwriting, film making. Home: 940 Grand Ave Saint Paul MN 55106

DOBBERT, DANIEL JOSEPH, data analyst, researcher, educator; b. Chgo., Feb. 2, 1946; s. Daniel Benjamin and Mary Jane (Miller) D.; m. Marion Lynne Lundy, Dec. 21, 1969; 1 child, Joan Ellen. BA, Aurora (Ill.) U., 1967; MEd, No. Ill. U., 1970, EdD, 1975. Cert. elem. tchr., secondary tchr., spl. edn. tchr., Ill. From research asst. to asst. prof. U. Minn., Mpls., 1973-85; gen. mng. ptnr. Old Highland Restoration and Old Highland Ltd., Mpls., 1981—; data/research analyst Met. Mosquito Control Dist., St. Paul, 1986—; cons. in field. Contbr. chpts. to books, articles to profl. jours. Mem. Will County First Aid and Safety Com., Joliet, Ill., 1967-69; bd. dirs. Northside Residents Redevel. Council, Mpls., 1974-77, Pilot City Regional Ctr., Mpls., 1976. Mem. NEA (life), Am. Evalution Assn. (charter), Phi Delta Kappa (life). Mem. Democratic-Farmer-Labor Party. Mem. Soc. Friends. Lodge: Masons. Avocations: camping, canoeing, traveling, photography.

DOBBIN, JAMES EDWARD ALMOND, management consultant; b. Chgo., Mar. 16, 1953; s. Robert Archibald Dobbin and Jo (Morril) Clemons; m. Lynn Adele Wittchen, apr. 17, 1982; 1 child, Ashley Layne; stepchildren: Holly Christine, Carrie Anne. BA in Speech, Bradley U., 1975. Sr. counsel Am. City Bur., Inc., Rosemont, Ill., 1981—. Mem. Nat. Soc. Fund Raising Execs. Republican. Avocations: racquetball. Office: Am City Bur Inc 9501 W Devon Ave Rosemont IL 60018

DOBBINS, DAVID JOSEPH, dentist; b. Highland Park, Mich., Dec. 22, 1953; s. Edgar Leroy and Anne Marie (Discenna) D.; m. Judith Carole Stine, Aug. 12, 1978; children: Alisha, Krista, Darin, Brandon. DDS, U. Mich., 1978. Gen. practice dentistry Saint Clair Shores, Mich., 1978—; bus. mgr. Macomb Dental Jour., 1985—; owner advt. splty. bus. Contbr. articles to profl. jours. Mem. ADA, Mich. Dental Assn., Macomb Dental Soc., U.S. Jaycees (pres. 1982-83). Avocations: sports, reading, motivational series. Office: 23915 Jefferson Saint Clair Shores MI 48080

DOBBINS, JAMES EDWARD, psychologist, educator; b. Cin., Apr. 4, 1946; s. Levi Edward and Eula (Anderson) D.; m. Linda Lee Dobbins, Jan. 2, 1971; children: Garvey, Amon-Ra, Afi. BS, Ohio State U., 1969; MS, U. Pitts., 1975, PhD, 1978. Lic. psychologist, Ohio. Research assoc. U. Pitts., 1978-79; assoc. prof. Wright State U., Dayton, Ohio, 1979—; dir. parenting labs. Inst. for the Black Family, Pitts., 1978-79, Parent-Adolescent Child Program, Dayton, 1983—, Univ. Psychol. Services Community Clinic, Dayton, 1985—. Contbr. articles to profl. jours. Bd. dirs. Ohio Youth Advocate Program, Wapakoneta, 1980-81. Mem. Am. Psychol. Assn., Dayton Psychol. Assn., Assn. Black Psychologists (Dayton chpt. pres. 1981-82, regional rep. 1984-85, bd. dirs. 1986, Leadership award 1985, Cert. Appreciation 1984-85), Nat. Coalition Black meeting Planners. Avocations: choir director, pub. speaking. Office: Wright State U Sch Profl Psychology Dayton OH 45435

DOBBINS, WILLIAM THOMAS, JR., architect; b. Chgo., Aug. 21, 1956; s. William Thomas and Anne (Youngren) D.; m. Suzanne Phyllis Surkamer, Dec. 19, 1981. BS in Archtl. Studies, U. Ill., Champaign, 1978; MArch, U. Ill., Chgo., 1981; postgrad., Northwestern U. Registered profl. architect, Ill., Tex. Draftsman H.G. Schnohrich Jr., Lake Bluff, Ill., summers 1979, 80, 81; job capt. Sikes, Jennings, Kelly, Houston, 1982-83; project architect Ambrose and McEnany, Houston, 1983-86; sr. architect The Austin Co., Chgo., 1986—; coordinator Houston Skyline Exhibit, 1983; co-chmn. Licensing seminar, Houston, Dallas, 1984. Dir. high sch. design competition, Houston, 1984-86. Mem. AIA (Young Architect 1985, Pres.'s Citation 1985), Ill. Council Architects, Nat. Council Archtl. Registration Bds., Nat. Trust Hist. Preservation, Jaycees, U. Ill. Alumni Assn. Avocations: photography, running, golf. Home: 2541 N Burling Chicago IL 60614 Office: The Austin Co 401 S LaSalle #1500 Chicago IL 60605

DOBBS, DAVID LOYLE, infosystems specialist; b. Mpls., June 28, 1923; s. Loyle Duncan and Florence May (Quinn) D.; m. Ann Cornwallis Leslie, Nov. 15, 1953; children: Debra Leslie, Michael David, John Robert. BS in Chemistry, U. Minn., 1948. Research info. asst. Merrell-Nat. Labs., Cin., 1957-77, coordinator info. retrieval, 1977-79, mgr. info. storage and retrieval, 1979-81; mgr. info. storage and retrieval Merrell Dow Research Inst., Cin., 1981-84, sr. info. scientist, 1984—. Patentee in field. Served with U.S. Army, 1943-46, ETO. Mem. Am. Soc. Info. Sci. (chpt. chmn. 1981), Am. Chem. Soc., Assn. Image and Info. Mgmt. Avocations: amateur radio, gardening. Home: 6612 Pleasant St Cincinnati OH 45227 Office: Merrell Dow Research Inst 2110 E Galbraith Rd Cincinnati OH 45215

DOBBS, DONALD EDWIN ALBERT, public relations executive; b. Ft. Wayne, Ind., Oct. 8, 1931; s. Edmund F. and Agnes (Stempnick) D.; B.S., Marquette U., 1953; m. Beatrice A. Spieker, July 27, 1957; children—Margaret L. Howard, Christopher E.J., Laura C. Pribe. Reporter, Cath. Chronicle, Toledo, 1953; with pub. relations dept. Nat. Supply Co., Toledo 1955-59; employee communications exec. Prestolite Co., an Eltra Co., Toledo, 1959-61, public relations dir., 1961-80, dir. communications, 1980-83; mgr. external affairs Allied Electronic Components Co., an Allied Corp. Co.; pres. Dobbs & Assocs., 1984—. Past chmn. Maumee Valley Hosp. Sch. Nursing Com.; pres. Internat. Inst., Toledo, 1970-73; past chmn. Child Nutrition Center, Toledo; past mem. Ohio Adv. Council Vocat. Edn.; vice chmn. Mayor's Citizen Devel. Forum; chmn., past pres. Mercy Hosp.; past pres. bd. dirs. Crosby Gardens; past pres. Ohio Friends of Library; past chmn. Salvation Army; past pres. Toledo Council of World Affairs, Toledo Hearing and Speech Center, Friends of Toledo/Lucas County Library; past pres. bd. dirs. Internat. Park; v.p. Toledo Opera Assn. Served with AUS, 1953-55. Mem. Marquette U. Alumni Assn. N.W. Ohio (past pres., area dir.), Soc. Profl. Journalists, Public Relations Soc. Am. (past pres. N.W. Ohio), Automotive Public Relations Council (past pres.), Cath. Interracial Council (past pres.). Democrat (past nat. com. Wis. Young Dems.). Roman Catholic. Kiwanian (past pres. Toledo, Mid-City Athletic League, Kiwanis Youth Found.; lt. gov. 1974-75). Home: 2433 Meadowwood Dr Toledo OH 43606 Office: PO Box 2964 Toledo OH 43606

DOBIE, EDWARD RAYMOND, advertising agency executive, office equipment company executive, business engineering firm executive; b. Lakewood, Ohio, Dec. 8, 1918; s. George Norman and Yerda (Lonn) D.; m. Gertrude A. Getz, Nov. 25, 1938 (dec.); children—Patricia L., Edward R.; m. 2d, Beth Ann Winters, May 25, 1979. Chief engr. ARO Equipment Corp., Bryan, Ohio, 1940-47; owner, operator Supervision Toledo, 1947—; ptnr. Associated Office Supply, Monroe, Mich., 1948—; pres. Dobie Co. of Mich., Monroe, 1949—; sec.-treas. Eazy-Way Corp., Cleve., 1955—, also dir.; v.p. Sales Builders Corp., Detroit, 1956—, also dir.; dir. Erie Shores Corp., Monroe. Patentee in field. Vice chmn. ARC, Monroe, 1973-74, chpt. chmn., 1975-76; trustee St. Paul's Methodist Ch., Monroe, 1976-77; del. Monroe Republican County Conv., 1975-76, Mich. State Repub. Conv., 1976-77. Served with U.S. Army, 1944-45, ETO. Mem. Monroe C. of C., Nat. Office Dealers Assn., Internat. Traders, VFW. Lodge: Masons. Avocations: philatelist; numismatist. Home: 3617 Lake Shore Dr Monroe MI 48161 Office: The Dobie Co 421 S Monroe St Monroe MI 48161

DOBNER, DONALD JOSEPH, electrical engineer; b. Milw., May 24, 1940; s. Joseph M. and Anne M. (Lescanec) D.; m. Karen Marie Lange, July 1, 1961; children: David D., Shelly Ann Dobner Harper. BEE, Gen. Motors Inst., 1964; MS, Auburn U., 1964, PhD, 1967. Research engr. Delco Electronics div. Gen. Motors Co., Milw., 1967-72; devel. engr. Diesel Allsion div. Gen. Motors Corp., Warren, Mich., 1972-76; staff engr. research labs. Gen. Motors Corp., Warren, 1976-84; mgr. systems engr. mil. vehicles ops. Gen. Motors Corp., Troy, Mich., 1984—. Patentee in field. Mem. Soc. Automotive Engrs., Soc. Computing Simulation, Internat. Soc. Terrain Vehicle Systems, Am. Def. Preparedness Assn., Assn. of the U.S. Army, Gen. Motors Inst. ALumni Assn. Avocations: running, stock car racing.

DOBRIN, SHELDON L., architect; b. Chgo., June 2, 1945; s. Max and Sophie (Schuman) D.; m. Marlene K. Smith, Jan. 26, 1969; children: Stefanie, Jonathan. BArch, Ill. Inst. Tech., 1969, BS, 1970. Registered architect, Ill. Architect Form Assocs., Chgo., 1969; tchr. Chgo. Bd. Edn., 1969-72; architect Robert L. Friedman, Chgo., 1972-78, v.p., 1978-84; prin. Friedman, Dobrin & Assoc., Northbrook, Ill., 1984—. Contbr. articles to profl. jours. Docent Chgo. Archtl. Found., 1972-78; mem. Highland Park Sch. Dist. #107 Caucas Bd. Recipient Spl. Recognition for Archtl. Design award, 1985. Mem. AIA, Nat. Council Archtl. Registration Bds. (cert.), Alpha Epsilon Pi. Avocations: bicycling, travel. Office: Friedman Dobrin & Assocs Ltd 105 Revere Dr Suite A Northbrook IL 60062

DOBSON, DANIEL LOUIS, lawyer; b. Louisville, Feb. 19, 1951; s. David and Pauline (Levin) D. BA in Econs., Ohio Wesleyan U., 1973; JD, St. Louis U., 1976; MS in Journalism, Columbia U., 1978. Bar: Ky. 1976, Washington 1978, Minn. 1980. Mng. atty. Minn. Met. Legal Ctr., Mpls., 1980-83; atty. Firemen's Fund Ins. Co., Golden Valley, Minn., 1983-84; prin., ptnr. Daniel L. Dobson & Assocs., Mpls., 1985—; sec., treas. Land Fingerprint Systems, Inc., Mpls., 1986—; sec. The Clean Co. Inc., Mpls., 1986—; hearing officer Mpls. Dept. Civil Rights, 1987. Patentee fingerprint system. Mem. Washington Bar Assn., Minn. Bar Assn., Minn. Trial Lawyers Assn. Democrat. Jewish. Home: 479 Iglehart Saint Paul MN 55103 Office: Daniel L Dobson & Assocs 312 Central Ave SW Suite 592 Minneapolis MN 55414

DOBSON, WARREN THEODORE, II, manufacturing executive; b. Flint, Mich., June 29, 1958; s. Warren Theodore and Phyllis (Phoenix) D. BA, U. Mich., 1980; MBA, Atlanta U., 1983. Mktg. mgmt. trainee Whirlpool Corp., Benton Harbor, Mich., 1983, consumer affairs mgmt. trainee, 1984, customer relations rep., 1984-85; plastics buyer Whirlpool Corp., St. Joseph, Mich., 1986—. Advisor Jr. Achievement, St. Joseph, Mich., 1986—. All Am.-Track award Nat. Collegiate Athletic Assn. award, 1980. Baptist. Avocations: running, golf, bowling, woodworking. Home: 2484 Roncy Rd Benton Harbor MI 49022 Office: Whirlpool Corp Upton Dr Saint Joseph MI 49085

DOBZYNSKI, JOSEPH MARTIN, coporate food and beverage executive; b. Chgo., Jan. 30, 1954; s. Walter and Alice (Brace) D.; m. Debra Ruth Crawford, Apr. 16, 1977; children: Joseph Jr., Mindy. AA in hotel-motel mgmt., Career Acad., 1973; wine diploma, Italian Trade Commn., French Trade Commn., Calif. Wine Inst. Sous chef Playboy Club Internat., Chgo., 1973-75; exec. chef The Bradly House, Palm Beach, Fla., 1975-77; chef dir. East Indian Co., Winter Park, Fla., 1977-80, Ellwood Greens Club, Genoa, Ill., 1980-84; food dir. Bally Corp., Chgo., 1984-85; corp. food and beverage cir. Riverwalk Corp., Geneva, Ill., 1985—; instr. Kishwaukee Jr. Coll., Malta, Ill., 1981-82; vocat. food judge Ill. Dept. Edn., Springfield, 1983; speaker Bremen (Ill.) High Sch. Career Day, 1982. Contbr. articles to profl. jours.; inventor hibernate freezing. vice chmn. Genoa Kingston Vocat. Council, 1981; wine chmn. Festival of the Vine Geneva C. of C., 1986. Recipient Silver medal Am. Culinary Fedn., 1982, Medals (4), Chgo. Culinary Arts Salon, 1981-83, Second place Crab Cooking Olympics, San Francisco, 1982, Entree award Boyle's Co., 1986. Mem. Les Amis du Vin (chpt. dir. 1981—, Cavalier award 1982), The Am. Inst. Food (assoc.) Chgo. Chef Apprentice Program (chmn. 1981-82, Plaque, 1982), Soc. Wine Educators, Am. Wine Soc. Avocations: collecting old cookbooks, creating special menus for civic groups. Home: 306 S Genoa St Genoa IL 60135 Office: Riverwalk Corp 207 S Third Geneva IL 60134

DOCKHORN, ROBERT JOHN, physician; b. Goodland, Kans., Oct. 9, 1934; s. Charles George and Dorotha Mae (Horton) D.; m. Beverly Ann Wilke, June 15, 1957; children: David, Douglas, Deborah. A.B., U. Kans., 1956, M.D., 1960. Diplomate: Am. Bd. Pediatrics. Intern Naval Hosp., San Diego, 1960-61; resident in pediatrics Naval Hosp., Oakland, Calif., 1963-65; resident in pediatric allergy and immunology U. Kans. Med. Center, 1967-69, asst. adj. prof. pediatrics, 1969—; resident in pediatric allergy and immunology Children's Mercy Hosp., Kansas City, Mo., 1967-69; chief div. Children's Mercy Hosp., 1969—; practice medicine specializing in allergy and immunology Prairie, Kans., 1969—; clin. prof. pediatrics and medicine U. Mo. Med. Sch., Kansas City, 1972—. Contbr. articles to med. jours.; co-editor: Allergy and Immunology in Children, 1973. Fellow Am. Acad. Pediatrics, Am. Coll. Allergists (bd. regents 1976—, v.p. 1978-79, pres.-elect 1980-81, pres. 1981-82), Am. Acad. Allergy; mem. AMA, Kans. Med. Soc., Johnson County Med. Soc., Kans. Allergy Soc. (pres. 1976-77), Mo. Allergy Soc. (sec. 1975-76), Joint Council Socio-Econs. of Allergy (dir. 1976—, pres. 1978-79). Home: 8510 Delmar Ln Prairie Village KS 66208 Office: 5300 W 94th Terr Prairie Village KS 66207

DOCKING, THOMAS ROBERT, lawyer, former state lieutenant governor; b. Lawrence, Kans., Aug. 10, 1954; s. Robert Blackwell and Meredith (Gear) D.; m. Jill Sadowsky, June 18, 1977; children: Brian Thomas, Margery Meredith. B.S., U. Kans., 1976, M.B.A., J.D., 1980. Bar: Kans. Assoc. Regan & McGannon, Wichita, Kans., 1980-82; ptnr. Regan & McGannon, 1982—; lt. gov. State of Kans., Topeka, 1983-87; Dem. nominee for Gov. of Kans., 1986; mem. Gov.'s Task Force on High Tech. Devel.; mem. adv. commn. Kans. Dept. Econ. Devel.; chmn. Kans. Tax Rev. Commn.; mem. Adv. Commn. to Kans. Security Commr. Mem. Big Bro.-Big Sister Program. Mem. Kans. Bar Assn., ABA, Kans. Cav. (bd. dirs., v.p. adminstrn.), U. Kans. Alumni Assn., Pi Sigma Alpha, Beta Gamma Sigma, Beta Theta Pi. Presbyterian. Home: 8525 Limerick Ln Wichita KS 67206 Office: Regan & McGannon Suite 1400 KSB Bldg 125 N Market Wichita KS 67202 Also Office: 222 State Capitol Topeka KS 66612

DOCTON, MAURICE HAMILTON, veterinarian; b. Monroe, La., Aug. 20, 1945; s. Frank Leslie and Alice Elizabeth (Willett) D.; m. Candi Jones, May 19, 1974; children: Jennifer Irene, Rachel Elizabeth. AA, Valley Forge Mil. Acad., 1965; BS, U.S. Naval Acad., 1969; DVM, Ohio State U., 1978. Commd. ensign USN, 1969, resigned, 1974; resident in surgery Tennessee Ave. Animal Hosp., Cin., 1978-86; staff veterinarian, cons. surgeon Docton Animal Clinic, Xenia, Ohio, 1978—; cons. surgeon Port William (Ohio) Animal Hosp., 1981—, Waynesville (Ohio) Animal Hosp., 1983—, Yellow Springs (Ohio) Vet. Services, 1984—, Hopewell Animal Hosp., 1986—. Mem. adminstrv. bd. Faith Community Meth. Ch., Xenia, 1984-86, Sunday sch. tchr., 1985-86. Decorated Bronze Star, Purple Heart; Cross of Gallantry (Vietnam). Mem. AVMA, Dayton Vet. Medicine Assn. (sec. 1983-84), Ohio State U. Vet. Alumni Assn. (bd. dirs. 1981). Republican. Avocations: motorcycles, weightlifting. Home: 238 Corwin Ave Xenia OH 45385 Office: Docton Animal Hosp 10 Kinsey Rd Xenia OH 45385

DODDS, CLAUDETTE LA VONN, broadcast executive; b. Lenapah, Okla., Sept. 2, 1947; d. Willie Lee and Dora (Harrell) Davis; m. Donald Howard Dodds, Jan. 14, 1965 (div. June 1982); children: Clarence Adam, Donyielle Alana, Erin Michelle. AAS with honors, Kennedy-King Coll., Chgo., 1984. Newscaster, newswriter Sta. WKKC-FM, Chgo., 1983-84, news dir., 1984-85, program and music dir., 1985, sta. mgr., 1985—; mem. adv. com. Coll. Broadcasting, 1985—. Mem. Dem. Student Task Force, Chgo., 1984, Student Disciplinary Bd. Chgo., 1986; coordinator Concerned Students for Broadcasting Equipment, 1984. Mem. Ill. Broadcasters Assn., Broadcasters Edn. Assn., Communications Arts Guild (corr. sec. 1982-83), Phi Theta Kappa. Club: WKKC Social (treas., founder 1983-84). Lodge: Order of Eastern Star, Heroines of Jericho. Avocations: reading, horseback riding, swimming, chess. Office: Sta WKKC-FM 6800 S Wentworth Ave Chicago IL 60621

DODDS, DOROTHYMAE, educator; b. Mankato, Minn., Nov. 4, 1927; d. William McKinley and Frances Mathilda (Leslie) Grimes; B.S., Moorhead (Minn.) State U., 1948, M.S., 1979; m. Robert Warren Dodds, Aug. 21, 1948; children—Laura Leslie, Michael Robert. Elem. instr. Mpls. Public Schs., 1948-53; sec.-treas. Dodds Drug, Inc., Red Lake Falls, Minn., 1954—; instr. sales, mktg. and mgmt., program head Thief River Falls (Minn.) Area Vocat. Tech. Inst., 1979-84, dir. adult edn., 1984-85; asst. dir. Dakota County Tech. Inst., Rosemount, Minn., 1985—. Com. chmn. Grand Forks (N.D.) council Girl Scouts U.S.A., 1963-70, neighborhood chmn., 1960, v.p., 1970-75, Thanks badge, 1972; com. chmn. Civic and Commerce Assn. of Red Lake Falls, 1971-74; mem. Region I Minn. Arts Adv. com., 1976-80; bd. trustees Citizens for the Arts, St. Paul, 1978—. Recipient awards for painting. Mem. Am. Vocat. Assn., Distributive Edn. Clubs Am. (cert. of appreciation Minn., nat. plaque of appreciation), Burnsville C. of C. (ambassador). Republican. Lutheran. Home: 14601 Portland Ave S Burnsville MN 55337 Office: 1300 145th St E Rosemount MN 55068

DODGE, STEPHEN CHARLES, historian, educator; b. Bronx, N.Y., Dec. 27, 1940; s. Stephen Dearborn and Grace Helen (Havranek) D.; m. Marjorie Ann Ruch, Sept. 7, 1963; children: Jonathan, Jeffrey. BA, U. Dubuque, 1963; MA, U. Minn., 1964, PhD, 1968. Asst. prof. history Millikin U., Decatur, Ill., 1968-76, assoc. prof., 1976-84, prof., 1984—, Griswold Disting. prof. History, 1986—; dir. Carleton Point Bicentennial Project, Abaco, Bahamas, 1983. Co-pres. New Sch., 1973-74. Mem. Assn. Caribbean Historians, Caribbean Studies Assn., Wyannie Malone Hist. Mus. Clubs: Decatur Yacht, Hope Town Sailing. Author: Abaco: The History of an Out Island and Its Cays, 1983, (with V. Malone) Hope Town: A Walking Tour and Brief History, 1985; editor: The Bahamas Index: 1986, 1987, (with Dean Collinwood) Modern Bahamian Society, 1987. Office: Millikin Univ Decatur IL 62522

DODSON, MICHAEL GENE, psychologist; b. Terre Haute, Ind., Nov. 18, 1948; s. Jack Louis and Helen Louise (Bailey) D.; m. Amy Lou Ratcliff, Aug. 17, 1968 (div. 1978); 1 child, Michael T.; m. Lynn Marie Corrigan, May 17, 1980. BA, Case Western Res. U., 1970; MEd, Bowling Green State U., 1972; PhD, U. Toledo, 1983. Lic. psychologist, Ohio; limited lic. psychologist, Mich. Asst. and clin. dir. New Rescue Crisis Services, Toledo, 1982-85; pvt. practice psychotherapy Adrian, Mich., 1985—; asst. prof. grad. dept. Siena Heights Coll., Adrian, 1984—, cons., therapist, 1986—; dir. Talbot Outpatient Ctrs. of Mercy and St. Charles Hosps., Toledo, 1986—; cons., therapist Siena. Mem. adv. bd. Mental Health Technology dept. U. Toledo Community and Tech. Coll. Served to staff sgt. U.S. Army, 1970-76. Mem. Am. Assn. for Counseling and Devel., Am. Psychol. Assn. Republican. Lutheran. Avocations: triathlons, golf, travel. Home: 6955 Dorr St Suite 8 Toledo OH 43615 Office: 127 S Winter St Adrian MI 49221

DODSON, OSCAR HENRY, numismatist, museum consultant; b. Houston, Jan. 3, 1905; s. Dennis S. and Maggie (Sisk) D.; m. Pauline Wellbrock, Dec. 17, 1932; 1 child, John Dennis. B.S., U.S. Naval Acad., 1927; grad., U.S. Naval Postgrad. Sch., 1936; M.A. in History, U. Ill., 1953. Commd. ensign USN, 1927, advanced through grades to rear adm., 1957; moblzn. planning officer Bur. Naval Personnel, 1945-48; comdg. officer U.S.S. Thomas Jefferson, 1949-50; prof. naval sci. U. Ill., 1950-53; comdr. Landing Ship Flotilla, Atlantic Fleet, 1954-55; chief staff U.S. Naval mission to Greece, 1955-

56, 1st Naval Dist., Boston, 1956-57; ret. 1957; asst. prof. history U. Ill., 1957-59; dir. Money Mus., Nat. Bank Detroit, 1959-65; dir. World Heritage Mus., U. Ill., Urbana, 1966-73, now dir. emeritus; acting dir. Champaign County Hist. Mus., 1980; mem. numis. adv. com. Smithsonian Instn., 1946; mem. Ann. Assay Commn., 1948, U. Ill. Found. Pres.'s Council, U.S. Naval Acad. Found.; visited numis. socs. under auspices State Dept., USSR, Finland, Poland, Austria, Denmark, 1959. Author: Money Tells the Story, 1962; contbg. editor: Coinage Mag., 1973—; asst. editor Bridge Mag., 1985—; bd. advs. New Eng. Jour. Numismatics; contbr. articles to profl. and numis. jours. Decorated Silver Star. Fellow Am., Royal (London) numis. socs., Explorers Club; mem. Am. Numis. Assn. (life, Farran Zerbe award 1968, bd. govs. 1950-55, pres. 1957-61), Am. Mil. Inst., Archeaol. Inst. Am., U. Ill. Alumni Assn. (Loyalty award 1966), U.S. Naval Acad. Alumni Assn. Clubs: Rotary (pres. Champaign 1972-73), Yacht (N.Y.C.); Army-Navy (Washington); Champaign Country, Circumnavigators, Torch. Office: 486 Lincoln Hall U Ill 702 S Wright St Urbana IL 61801

DODSON, W(ILLIAM) EDWIN, child neurology educator; b. Durham, N.C., Dec. 23, 1941; s. Howard William and Mildred (Sorrell) D.; m. Doreen Carol Davis, June 4, 1964 (div. May 1976); children: Anna Elizabeth, William Edwin Jr., Jason David; m. Sandra Schorr; children: Steven Gage, Matthew Sorrell. AB, Duke U., 1963, MD, 1967. Intern Children's Hosp., Boston, 1967-68, resident in pediatrics, 1970-71; resident, fellow in child neurology Barnes Hosp. and St. Louis Children's Hosp., 1971-75; asst. prof. child neurology Washington U., St. Louis, 1975-80, residentin pediatrics, 1970-71, assoc. prof., 1980-86, prof. child neurology, 1986—; bd. dirs. Family Resource Ctr., St. Louis, Physicians Corp., Washington U. Alliance Corp., First Tier Health Corp., Nat. Com. to Prevent Child Abuse (Mo. chpt.); pres. bd. dirs. St. Louis Child Abuse Network. Mem. editorial bd. Annals of Neurology and Clinical Neuropharmacology; contbr. numerous articles to profl. jours. Bd. dirs. City St. Louis Bd. Children's Welfare, 1984—, Children's Trust Fund Mo., Jefferson City, 1985—, Child Neurology Soc., 1985—; mem. profl. adv. bd. Epilepsy Found. of Am., 1987—. Served to lt. USPHS, 1968-70. Recipient Spl. Recognition award State of Md., 1971, Career Academic Devel. award NIH, 1975. Fellow Am. Acad. Neurology, Am. Acad. Pediatrics; mem. Child Neurology Soc., Am. Neurol. Assn., Soc. Pediatric Research, Cen. Soc. Neurol. Research (sec., treas. 1985), Alpha Omega Alpha. Avocations: fly fishing, water sports, photography. Office: St Louis Childrens Hosp 400 S Kings Hwy Saint Louis MO 63110

DOE, EILEEN MARIE, educator; b. St. Louis, Mar. 9, 1953; d. John Andrew and Kathleen Appalona (Layton) Hoffman; m. Larry Junior Doe, Aug. 14, 1976. B.S., U. Mo., 1976, postgrad., 1982—. Tchr. mentally handicapped children Northview Sch., Spl. Sch. Dist. St. Louis County, 1976-84; tchr. Highland Sch., 1984—. Mem. Community Tchrs. Assn., Delta Zeta. Roman Catholic. Home: 2 Locust Dr Florissant MO 63031

DOEBLER, WILLIAM DANIEL, plastic surgeon; b. Highland Park, Mich., Mar. 30, 1943; s. Maurice Carl and Marion Anna (Jelneck) D.; m. Carolyn Jean Fredricks, June 5, 1971; children: Jeffrey, Daniel, Megan. BS, Wayne State U., 1966; MD, U. Mich., 1970. Diplomate Am. Soc. Plastic Surgery. Intern Butterworth Hosp., Grand Rapids, Mich., 1970-71, resident in surgery, 1971-74; resident in plastic surgery Providence Hosp., Southfield, Mich., 1974-76; practice medicine specializing in plastic surgery Holland, Mich., 1977—. Mem. Mich. Acad. Plastic Surgeons. Republican. Mem. Reformed Ch. Am. Avocation: photography. Home: 356 Waukazoo Dr Holland MI 49424 Office: 533 Michigan Ave Holland MI 49423

D'OENCH, RALPH FREDRICK, real estate consultant; b. St. Louis, Oct. 22, 1901; s. Harry Fredrick and Clara (Schmitz) D'O.; m. Mabel Estelle Nichols, Dec. 30, 1926; children—Gloria Nichols D'Oench James, Jean Linda D'Oench Field. B.A., Washington U., St. Louis, 1922. Cert. property mgr., real estate broker, Mo. Property mgr. R.E. Mgmt. Co., St. Louis, 1927-34; pres. Ralph D'Oench Co., St. Louis, 1934-77, cons., 1978—; instr., lectr. real estate U. Ill.-Belleville, 1958-59; instr. Washington U., 1955-67. Assoc. Miss. River Pkwy. Planning Commn., 1954-69; bd. dirs., trustee Washington U., St. Louis, 1955-57. Mem. Real Estate Bd. Met. St. Louis (recipient plaque; emeritus), Inst. Real Estate Mgmt. (plaque; emeritus). Republican. Club: University (St. Louis). Avocations: color slide shows; historical themes; travelogs. Home: 1 Normton Dr Saint Louis MO 63124

DOEPKER, J(OHN) FREDERICK, JR., plastic surgeon; b. Lima, Ohio, Mar. 22, 1949; s. John Frederick and Elizabeth (Merritt) D.; m. Cheryl Lynn Bing, Dec. 31, 1982; children: John, Justin, Ashley, Derek. BA in Math., Ind. U., 1971; MD, Ind. U., Indpls., 1976. Diplomate Am. Bd. Plastic Surgery. Resident in gen. and plastic surgery Butterworth Hosp., Grand Rapids, Mich., 1976-81; fellow in plastic surgery Vanderbilt U., Nashville, 1981-82; practice medicine specializing in plastic surgery Evansville, Ind., 1982—. V.p. Vanderburgh County, Am. Cancer Soc., Evansville, 1984—. Fellow ACS; mem. Am. Soc. Plastic and Reconstructive Surgeons, Vanderburgh County Med. Soc., Am. Med. Assn., John B. Lynch Soc., Lipolysis Soc. N.Am., Ferris Smith Soc., Phi Rho Sigma Med. Soc. Home: One Johnson Pl Evansville IN 47714 Office: Evansville Plastic Surg Assocs Inc 3700 Bellemeade Ave Evansville IN 47715

DOERFLER, DOUGLAS MARK, bank executive; b. Ft. Scott, Kans., Aug. 9, 1958; s. Donald Joseph and Shirley Clydene (Snyder) D.; m. Cheryl Ann Jensen, June 12, 1982; children: Dustan Mark, Derek Matthew. BBA, Pittsburg (Kans.) State U., 1980. CPA, Kans. Audit mgr. Diehl, Banwart, Bolton, Jarred & Bledsoe, Ft. Scott, 1980-86, R.L. Quint, CPA, Mission, Kans., 1986-87; chief ops. officer Midland Bank, Lee's Summit, Mo., 1987. Author: (manual) Statistical Sampling, 1982, Internal Auditing, 1987. Mem. Am. Inst. CPA's, Kans. Soc. CPA's, Am. Bankers Assn., Delta Mu Delta, Omicron Delta Epsilon. Republican. Roman Catholic. Avocations: softball, volleyball, weight lifting, drawing. Home: 212 NW Monroe Lee's Summit MO 64063 Office: Midland Bank 740 NW Blue Pkwy Lees Summit MO 64063

DOERING, GEORGE W., agricultural products company executive. Pres., chief operating officer ConAgra Agri-Products Cos., Omaha. Office: Conagra Inc One Central Park Plaza Omaha NE 68102 *

DOERING, LEROY WILLIAM, window manufacturing executive; b. Merrill, Wis., Oct. 27, 1931; s. Harry G. and Catherine (Bloechl) D.; m. Nancy L. Haan, July 11, 1959; children: Susan M., Thomas M. BA, St. Thomas Coll., St. Paul, 1953. Sales rep. Curtis Co., Inc., Clinton, Iowa, 1953-61; mgr. sales and mktg. Carad Co., Inc., Rantoul, Ill., 1961-77; v.p. sales and mktg. Hurd Milwork Co., Medford, Wis., 1977—. Mem. Nat. Home Mgrs. Assn. (bd. dirs. 1980-84), Nat. Wood Window and Door Assn. Clubs: Tee Hi Golf (Medford, Wis.); Dubuque Golf and Country (bd. dirs. 1973-75). Avocations: golf, tennis. Home: 385 Leila Cir Medford WI 54451

DOERNBERGER, WILLIAM LECLAIRE, financial executive; b. Pitts., May 16, 1951; s. George LeClaire and Betty Jane (Miller) D.; m. Mary Jacqueline Fries, Oct. 20, 1979; 1 child, William LeClaire Jr. BA in Econs., Allegheny Coll., 1973; MBA, U. Chgo., 1975. CPA, Ill. Auditor Arthur Andersen & Co., Chgo., 1975-77; gen. acctg. mgr. Am. Hosp. Supply Co., Evanston, Ill., 1977-83; controller Execunet, Chgo., 1983-84; v.p. fin. Am. Louver Co., Chgo., 1984-87; controller Delice De France, Buffalo Grove, Ill., 1987—; bd. dirs., treas. Leader Mfg. Co. Precinct capt. Evanston Reps., 1984-85; treas. Northminster Presby. Ch., Evanston, 1984, tchr., 1986—. Mem. Am. Inst. CPA's, Ill. Soc. CPA's. Avocations: baseball cards, coin and stamp collecting, golf. Home: 3320 Harrison Evanston IL 60201 Office: Delice De France 1111 Busch Pkwy Buffalo Grove IL 60015

DOERSHUK, CARL FREDERICK, physician, professor of pediatrics; b. Warren, Ohio, Dec. 24, 1930; s. Carl Frederick and Eula Blanche (Mahan) D.; m. Emma Lou Plummer, Aug. 21, 1954; children: Rebecca Lee, John Frederick, David Plummer. BA, Oberlin Coll., 1952; MD, Case Western Res. U., 1956. Postdoctoral fellow USPHS, Washington, 1961-63; sr. instr. to prof. pediatrics Case Western Res. U., Cleve., 1963—; pvt. practice specializing in pediatrics Cleve., 1963—. Co-editor Pediatric Respiratory Therapy, 1974, 3d edit., 1986; contbr. numerous articles to profl. jours. Chmn. med. adv. council Cystic Fibrosis Found., Washington, 1966-72, bd. trustees, 1969—, exec. com., 1969-74, v.p. med. affairs Cleve. chpt., 1965—. Served to lt. M.C., USN, 1956-59. Named Young Man Yr. Cystic Fibrosis Found., 1970. Mem. Am. Pediatric Soc., Soc. Pediatric Research, Am. Acad. Pediatrics (exec. com. chest sect.), Am. Thoracic Soc. (chmn. pediatric pulmonary sect. 1971), No. Ohio Pediatric Soc., Acad. Medicine. Avocations: sailing, raising dahlias. Office: Rainbow Babies Hosp 2101 Adelbert Rd Cleveland OH 44106

DOETTLING, ROBERT LESTER, financial executive; b. East St. Louis, Ill., Feb. 6, 1937; s. Clarence and Edna (Nowotny) D.; m. Vera Stanishoff, June 2, 1962. BS in Acctg., Syracuse U., 1959. CPA, N.Y. Acct. Ernst & Whinney, Syracuse, 1959-66; v.p., treas. True Temper Co., Cleve., 1966-80; v.p. fin. Midland Enterprises, Inc., Cin., 1980—. Served with USAR, 1960-66. Mem. Am. Inst. CPA's, N.Y. State Soc. CPA's, Fin. Execs. Inst., Nat. Assn. Accts., Water Transport Assn. (treas. Cin. br. 1983—). Club: Kenwood (Ohio) Country. Avocations: golf, reading, personal investing. Office: Midland Enterprises Inc 580 Bldg Suite 1400 Cincinnati OH 45202

DOGGETT, JOHN NELSON, JR., clergyman; b. Phila., Apr. 3, 1918; s. John Nelson and Winola (Ballard) D.; B.A., Lincoln U., 1942; M.Div., Union Theol. Sem., N.Y.C., 1945; M.Ed., St. Louis U., 1969, Ph.D., 1971; m. Juanita Toley, Aug. 2, 1973; children by previous marriage—Lorraine, John, William, Kenneth Riddick. Ordained to ministry United Methodist Ch., 1943; civilian chaplain South Gate Community Ch., San Francisco, 1945-47; organizing pastor Downs Meml. Meth. Ch., Oakland, Calif., 1947-49; pastor Scott Meml. Meth. Ch., Pasadena, Calif., 1950-53, Hamilton Meml. Meth. Ch., Los Angeles, 1953-64, Union Meml. United Meth. Ch., St. Louis, 1964-76; dist. supt. United Meth. Ch., St. Louis, 1976-82; sr. pastor Grace United Meth. Ch., St. Louis, 1982-85; ret. pastor Cabanne United Meth. Ch., 1986—; staff Pastoral Counseling Inst., St. Louis, 1968—; instr. foundations of edn. Harris Tchrs. Coll., St. Louis, 1971-75; assoc. prof. practical theology Met. Coll., St. Louis, 1976-77; commr. Nat. Council Chs. of Christ, 1981-84. Pres. bd. dirs. St. Louis Christian Med. Ctr., Central Med. Ctr. Hosps., St. Louis, 1973-86 ; pres. St. Louis NAACP, 1973-81; bd. dirs. United Way St. Louis, 1974-81; mem. Commn. on Alternatives to Prison, 1981, Citizens Com. Mo. Dept. Corrections, 1974-80, Mayor's Task Force on Hunger, 1981; adv. com. St. Louis U. Sch. Social Work; advisor John N. Doggett Scholarship Found.; mem. Interfaith Clergy Council, World Meth. Council; pres. Council St. Louis U.; mem. mayor's ambassadors Regional Commerce and Growth Assn., 1980—, Family Planning Council, Am. Lung Assn. Eastern Mo., Nat. Family Planning and Reproductive Health Assn., Epilepsy Fedn. Eastern Mo. Named Minister of Year, St. Louis Argus Newspaper, 1971; recipient Outstanding Alumni award St. Louis U., 1981, Martin Luther King Alpha/Anheuser-Busch Spl. Plaque. Mem. Am. Assn. Pastoral Counselors, Mo. Council Chs., Met. Ministerial Alliance, UN Assn. (clergy-pub. edn. com.), Chi Alpha Lit. Forum, Phi Delta Kappa, Alpha Phi Alpha (nat. chaplain, D. Bowles/R. Anderson Service award, regional hall fame 1987), Democrat. Lodges: Mason, Shriner. Home: 4466 W Pine Blvd #2C Saint Louis MO 63108 Office: 5760 Bartmer Ave Saint Louis MO 63112

DOGGETTE, JACKSON MICHAEL, JR., minister; b. Ardmore, Okla., Mar. 24, 1957; s. Jackson Michael Sr. and Edythe Marie (Young) D.; m. Emily Kaye Dunn, Dec. 23, 1984. Student, Calif. State U. Los Angeles, 1982; BTh, Oakwood Coll., 1982; postgrad., Loma Linda (Calif.) U., 1983, Indian U., 1985; MA in Religion, Andrews U., 1986. Ordained to ministry Adventist Ch., 1986. Pastor, evangelist, mem. sch. bd. Seventh-Day Adventist Ch., Los Angeles, 1979-83, pastor, evangelist, 1979-85; pastor, evangelist Seventh-Day Adventist Ch., Ft. Wayne, Ind., 1985-86; pastor, evangelist, mem. sch. bd. Seventh-Day Adventist Ch., Detroit, 1986—; cons. So. Calif. Conf. of Seventh-Day Adventists, Glendale, Calif., 1979. Contbr. articles to profl. jours. Co-founder Children's Ednl. Watch, Ft. Wayne, 1986; bd. dirs. Met. Open Housing Commn., Ft. Wayne, 1985, Gingerbread House, Inc., Ft. Wayne, 1985, Learning Acad., Ft. Wayne, 1986. Named one of Outstanding Young Men of Am., U.S. Jaycees, 1980. Mem. NAACP, Lake Region Ministerial Alliance (Excellence award 1985-87), Inkster Ministerial Alliance. Democrat. Avocations: flying airplanes, musician, athlete, author. Office: PO Box 19677 Detroit MI 48219-0677

DOHACK, RICHARD ARTHUR, restaurant company executive; b. St. Louis, July 11, 1931; s. Ernest William and Josephine (Marlotte) D.; m. Diane Mary Gansmann, Sept. 8, 1951; children: Richard, Mary, Michael, David, Robert, Timothy, Stephen, Carol, Joann, Diane, Chris. BS in Commerce, St. Louis U., 1952. Pres. Dohack Ins. Agy., St. Louis, 1954-55; asst. v.p. Food Service Mgmt. Inc., St. Louis, 1955-65; pres. Dohack's Restaurants, St. Louis, 1965—, Dohack Mgmt. Corp., St. Louis, 1968—; bd. dirs. Lemay Bank, St. Louis; cons. Chars Restaurant, Collinsville, Ill., 1975—; del. to White House conf. on small bus., 1980. Trustee Nazareth Home; chmn. Resource Devel. Council, Sisters of St. Joseph, St. Louis, 1986; bd. dirs. White House Retreat; mem. Marine Corps Scholarship Fund com., citizens advisory council, Mehlville Sch. Dist.; mem. bd. Gregorian U. Found., Mo, Archdiocesan High Sch. Found. Served to 1st lt. USAF, 1952-54. Mem. Mo. Restaurant Assn. (permanent dir., treas. 1974, man of yr. award 1977). Roman Catholic. Club: Norwood Hills Country. Avocations: golf, fishing, charity work. Home: 1112 Sunhaven Dr Saint Louis MO 63129 Office: 4000 Lemay Ferry Rd Saint Louis MO 63129

DOHENY, DONALD ALOYSIUS, lawyer, business exec.; b. Milw., Apr. 20, 1924; s. John Anthony and Adelaide (Koller) D.; m. Catherine Elizabeth Lee, Oct. 25, 1952; children: Donald Aloysius, Celeste Hazel Doheny Kennedy, John Vincent, Ellen Adelaide, Edward Lawrence II, William Francis, Madonna Lee. Student U. Notre Dame, 1942-43; BME, Marquette U., 1947; JD, Harvard, 1949; postgrad., Washington U., St. Louis, 1950-56. Bar: Wis. 1949, Mo. 1949, U.S. Supreme Ct. 1970; registered prof. engr., Mo. Asst. to civil engr. Shipbuilding div. Froemming Bros., Inc., Milw., 1942-43; draftsman, designer The Heil Co., Milw., 1944-46; assoc. Igoe, Carroll & Keefe, St. Louis, 1949-51; asst. to v.p. and gen. mgr., chief prodn. engr., gen. adminstr., dir. adminstrn. Granco Steel Products subsidiary Granite City Steel, Granite City, Ill., 1951-57; asst. to pres. Vestal Labs., Inc., St. Louis, 1957-63; exec. v.p., dir. Moehlenpah Engring., Inc., Hydro-Air Engring., Inc., 1963-67; pres. dir. Foamtex Industries, Inc., St. Louis, 1967-75; exec. v.p., dir. Seasonal Industries, Inc., N.Y.C., 1973-75; sole practice, St. Louis, 1967-81; ptnr., Doheny & Doheny, Attys., St. Louis, 1981—, Doheny & Assocs. Mgmt. Counsel, St. Louis, 1967—; pres., dir. Mktg. & Sales Counsel, Inc., St. Louis, 1975—; pres., dir. Mid-USA Sales Co., St. Louis, 1976—; pres., bd. dirs. Profl. Bus. Exchange, Inc., St Louis, 1986, Prestige Offices and Properties, Inc., St. Louis, 1987; lectr. bus. orgn. and adminstrn. Washington U., 1950-74; lectr. Grad. Sch. Bus., St. Louis U., 1980—. Served with AUS, 1943-44; 1st lt. Res., 1948-52. Mem. ABA, Am. Judicature Soc., Am. Marketing Assn. (nat. membership chmn. 1959), Mo. Bar Assn., Wis. Bar Assn., Fed. Bar Assn., Bar Assn. St. Louis (gen. chmn. pub. relations 1955-56, vice chmn., sec.-treas. jr. sect. 1950, 51), Marquette Engring. Assn. (pres. 1946-47), Engring. Knights, Am. Legion, Tau Beta Pi, Pi Tau Sigma. Clubs: Notre Dame (pres. 1955, 56), Marquette (pres. 1961), Harvard (St. Louis); Stadium, Engineers, Mo. Athletic. Office: Heritage Bldg 12000 Westline Industrial Dr Suite 330 Saint Louis MO 63146 Office: Mchts Laclede Bldg 408 Olive St Suite 400 Saint Louis MO 63102

DOHERTY, DENNIS CARL, county official; b. Mpls., July 24, 1940; s. Lawrence Anthony Anna Marie (Billstein) D.; m. Olivia Ann Herzan, Dec. 26, 1964; children: Stephen, Mark, Timothy. BS, U.S. Naval Acad., 1963; postgrad., Bryant Coll., 1970-71; MBA, Coll. St. Thomas, St. Paul, 1982. Cert. safety profl. Commd. USN, 1963, advanced through grades to comdr., 1979, resigned, 1971; sr. engring. rep. Travelers Ins., Mpls., 1971-76; asst. risk mgr. Dayton Hudson Corp., Mpls., 1976-79; risk mgr. Hennepin County, Mpls., 1980—. Contbg. editor: (textbook) Risk Management and Insurance, 1985. Cub master Boy Scouts Am., Minnetonka, Minn., 1972-77; bd. dirs. IHM Dayschool, , Minnetonka, 1976-77; function chmn. IHM Ch. Festival, Minnetonka. Decorated Bronze Star with V. Mem. Nat. Safety Council, Minne. Safety Council, Risk and Ins. Mgmt. Soc. (bd. dirs. 1978-80, legis. chmn. 1984—), Pub. Risk and Ins. Mgmt. Assn. (legis. chmn. 1982—), Minn. Self Insurers Assn., U.S. Naval Acad. Alumni Assn. (pres. 1979-80). Roman Catholic. Club: Northwest Raquet and Swim (Golden Valley, Minn.). Avocations: auto restoration, reading, swimming.

DOHERTY, J. PATRICK, marketing and publishing executive; b. Altoona, Pa., Feb. 25, 1937; s. James M. and Evelyn P. (McBrien) D.; m. Jeanne M. Houlihan, July 9, 1966; children: Daniel, Brian, Nancy. BS in Mktg., U. Notre Dame, 1958. Salesman Best Foods Co., Buffalo, 1958-59, Chgo. Tribune, 1959-65, So. Living, Chgo., 1965-67, Good Housekeeping, Chgo., 1967-69, U.S. News and World Report, Chgo., 1969-79; pres. Doherty & Co. Pubs. Reps., Chgo., 1979—. Commr. Village of Northfield (Ill.) Plan Commn., 1982—; pres. St. Philip's Sch. Athletic Bd., Northfield, 1985-86, chmn. St. Philip's $300,000 fund drive, 1986; chmn. Northfield Caucus, 1979-81, Northfield Cub Scouts, 1976-77; chmn. materials Loyola Ramble, 1985. Republican. Roman Catholic. Clubs: Agate of Chgo. (past pres., v.p., treas.), Cinciama (bd. dirs.). Home: 197 Avon Ave Northfield IL 60093 Office: Doherty & Co 307 N Michigan Ave Chicago IL 60601

DOHMEN, FREDERICK HOEGER, retired wholesale drug co. exec.; b. Milw., May 12, 1917; s. Fred William and Viola (Gutsch) D.; B.A. in Commerce, U. Wis., 1939; m. Gladys Elizabeth Dite, Dec. 23, 1939 (dec. 1963); children—William Francis, Robert Charles; m. 2d, Mary Alexander Holgate, June 27, 1964. With F. Dohmen Co., Milw., 1939-82, successively warehouse employee, sec., v.p., 1944-52, pres., 1952-82, dir., 1947—, chmn. bd., 1952-82. Bd. dirs. St. Luke's Hosp. Ednl. Found., Milw., 1965-83, pres., 1969-72, chmn. bd., 1972-73; bd. dirs. U. Wis.-Milw. Found., 1976-79, bd. visitors, 1978—; asso. chmn. Nat. Bible Week, Laymen's Nat. Bible Com., N.Y.C., 1968-82, council of adv., 1983—. Mem. Nat. Wholesale Druggists Assn. (chmn. mfr. relations com. 1962, resolutions com. 1963, mem. of bd. control 1963-66), Nat. Assn. Wholesalers (trustee 1966-75), Druggists Service Council (dir. 1967-71), Wis. Pharm. Assn., Miss. Valley Drug Club, Beta Gamma Sigma, Phi Eta Sigma, Delta Kappa Epsilon. Presbyn. Clubs: University, Town (Milw.). Home: 3903 W Mequon Rd 112 N Mequon WI 53092

DOLAN, DANIEL LEE, manufacturing executive; b. Charleston, W.Va., July 9, 1944; s. Kenneth Thorn and Mary Ann (Gilliand) D.; m. Coralea Farthing, July 1965; children: David M., Scott A., Timothy C. BSEE, W.Va. Inst. Tech., 1966; MS, Union U., 1973. Various mfg. positions Gen. Electric, 1966-76; engring. mgr. FMC, South Charleston, W.Va., 1976-79; dir. mfg. Lancaster Colony, Coshocton, Ohio, 1979-85; v.p. mfg. Chgo. Rawhide Mfg. Co., Elgin, Ill., 1985—. Mem. Soc. Mfg. Engrs. (sr., Robotics Inst.), Internat. Assn. Quality Control Circles (facilitator), Automotive Industry Action Group. Avocations: hunting, fishing. Home: 4916 Valerie Dr Crystal Lake IL 60014 Office: Chgo Rawhide Industries 900 N State St Elgin IL 60123

DOLAN, DENNIS JOSEPH, airline pilot, lawyer; b. St. Louis, Mar. 19, 1946; s. Robert Glennon and Lucille Anne (Stanley) D.; m. Aura Maritza Vargas, June 8, 1974; children: Dennis J. Jr., Rebecca and Robert (twins). BCS, Spring Hill Coll., Mobile, Ala., 1967; JD cum laude, St. Louis U., 1985. Bar: Mo., 1985. Commd. 2d lt. USMC, 1967, advanced through grades to capt., 1972, resigned, 1976; served to maj. USMCR; airline pilot Western Airlines, Los Angeles, 1976-87, Delta Airlines, Atlanta, 1987—; sole practice Clayton, Mo., 1985—. Mem. ABA, Assn. Trial Lawyers Am., Airline Pilots Assn. Republican. Roman Catholic. Avocations: skiing, woodworking. Home: 123 Greenbriar E Dr Saint Louis MO 63122 Office: 11 S Meramec Suite 1100 Clayton MO 63105

DOLAN, DONALD EDWARD, chiropractor; b. Breckenridge, Mo., Oct. 11, 1914; s. Edward Dixon and Bonnie Mable (De Vaul) D.; m. Romola Blanche Wantland, July 6, 1936; children—Winnona Marguerite, Karon Pomalee, Sherry Darlene. D. Chiropractic Medicine, Cleve. pvt. trucker, 1936-38; Coll., 1946. Self-employed as cement, constrn. worker, decorator, paper hanger and painter, and fender and body shop worker, Chillicothe, Mo., 1933-34; pvt. trucker, 1936-38; operator Corn Products Co. Refinery, North Kans. City, Mo., 1938-50; gen. practice chiropractic medicine, Kansas City, Mo., 1947-49, Leavenworth, Kans., 1949—. Candidate for Coroner, City of Leavenworth, Kans., 1954. Mem. Kans. Chiropractic Assn. Republican. Mem. Christian Ch. Lodges: Masons (Proficiency Examiner, Dist. 2, Grand Chpt. Kans., 1981-82; Service award 1983), Order Eastern Star.

DOLAN, JAMES PATRICK, investment banker; b. Trinidad, Colo., June 13, 1949; s. Andrew Patrick and Ethel Josephine (Riggs) D.; m. Sylvia Marie Razien, Jan. 4, 1971. BA in Journalism, U. Okla., 1971. Reporter, exec. editor Express News Corp., San Antonio, Tex., 1971-82; dir. New Media Group News Am. Pub., N.Y.C., 1982-84; pres., pub. Keycom Electronic Pub., Schaumburg, Ill., 1984-86; chmn. bd. JPD Holdings, Inverness, Ill., 1986—; ptnr. Kummerfeld Assocs. Investment Bankers, N.Y.C. and Chgo., 1986—; bd. dirs. Hydro-Tone, Inc., Oklahoma City, 1986—. Founding editor Tex. Examiner, 1976; creator two weekly mags. in San Antonio, 1979 (now defunct), 80. Recipient two Charles E. Green Headliner awards, 1973, 74, eighteen San Antonio Press Club awards, 1971-82, two Fund for Investigative Journalism grants, 1975, 76. Mem. Am. Soc. Newspaper Editors, Assoc. Press Mng. Editors (v.p., treas. Tex. chpt.), Info. Industry Assn. (bd. dirs. videotex div. 1985-86). Clubs: Meadow (Chgo.); Headliners (Austin, Tex.). Avocations: computer programming, architecture, anitque maps and books. Home: 353 Ayrshire Ln Inverness IL 60067 Office: Kummerfeld Assocs 980 N Michigan Ave Chicago IL 60611

DOLAN, JOHN JOSEPH, manufacturing company executive; b. Milw., Apr. 23, 1929; s. John Joseph and Julia Betty (Lebowitz) D.; m. Jane Penn, July 14, 1951; children: John, Louise, Ellen, Julia. PhB, U. Chgo., 1948; BA, U. Wis., 1952; postgrad., Yale U., 1952-53. Communications exec., writer various orgns., Milw. and Chgo., 1954-65; adminstr. advt. and sales promotion Gen. Electric, Milw., 1965-68; mgr. advt. and sales promotion Waukesha (Wis.) Engine div. Dresser Industries, Inc., 1968-73, dir. mktg. services, 1973-85, dir. market planning, 1985—. Mem. ASCAP. Republican. Roman Catholic. Avocations: history, reading, swimming, golf. Office: Waukesha Engine Div Dresser Industries Inc 1000 W St Paul Ave Waukesha WI 53188

DOLAN, KENNETH DEWAYNE, radiology educator; b. Cedar Rapids, Iowa; s. Joseph Raymond and Hazel Irene (Peterson) D.; m. Arlene Rose Pisney, June 20, 1954; children: Catherine Rae, Ann Louise, Christopher Kent. BA, U. Iowa, 1952, MD, 1956. Diplomate Am. Bd. Radiology. Radiology chief VA Hosp., Iowa City, 1963-65; radiologist Univ. Hosp., Iowa City, 1965—. Author Radiology of Maxillofacial Injuries, 1984, Craniovertebral Junction, 1986; contbr. 80 articles to profl. jours. Vestryman Trinity Episc. Ch., Iowa City, 1980-83. Served to commdr. USN, 1959-62. Fellow Am. Coll. Radiol., Am. Acad. Otolaryngology (assoc.); mem. Radiol. Soc. N.Am., Am. Roentgen Ray Soc., Iowa Med. Soc. (councilor), Iowa Radiol. Soc. (pres. 1982-83), Iowa City C. of C. Republican. Lodge: Rotary (pres. Iowa City 1976-77). Avocations: reading, sports, fishing. Office: U Iowa Hosps and Clinics 650 Newton Rd Iowa City IA 52242

DOLAN, THOMAS IRONSIDE, manufacturing company executive; b. Hastings, Mich., Mar. 31, 1927; s. Clifford and Katherine (Ironside) D.; m. Barbara Jane Sisson, June 11, 1948; children—Nancy, Sarah. B.S. in Indsl.-Mech. Engring, U. Mich., 1949. Pres. Kelvinator, Inc., Grand Rapids, Mich., 1969-75; sr. group v.p. White Consol. Industries, Inc., Cleve., 1975-80; sr. v.p. A.O. Smith Corp., Milw., 1980-82, pres., dir., 1982-84, chmn., chief exec. officer, 1984—, also chmn. bd., 1984—, also dir. subs.; trustee Northwestern Mut. Life Ins. Co.; bd. dirs. First Wis. Nat. Bank. Mem. Greater Milw. Com.; corp. mem. Milw. Sch. Engring; bd. dirs. Med. Coll. Wis. Mem. Met. Milw. Assn. Commerce (bd. dirs.), Machinery and Allied Products Inst. (exec. com.), Soc. Automotive Engrs., Hwy. Users Fedn. (trustee), Internat. Exec. Service Corps. (council), Bus. Council, Bus. Roundtable. Clubs: Milwaukee, Milw. Country, Milw. University. Lodge: Rotary.

DOLCE, RICHARD LEE, JR., stockbroker, insurance broker; b. Chgo.; s. Richard Lee and Gloria (Marshall) D. Student in bus. and econs., North Cen. Coll., Naperville, Ill., 1975-78. Tax analyst Clow Corp., Oak Brook, Ill., 1980-81; fin. planner JPM Industries, Bridgeview, Ill., 1981-83; v.p., chief fin. officer Westech, Chgo., 1983-85; pres. R.L. Dolce Inc., Alsip, Ill., 1985—; tchr. ABI Inc., Chgo., 1986—; cons. PRI Inc., Chicago Ridge, Ill., 1985-86, Deli Snacks, Burr Ridge, Ill., 1985-86, Manto Inc., Palatine, Ill., 1985-86, Finest Cons., Downers Grove, Ill., 1986—, Payline, Itasca, Ill.,

1985-86. Treas. Young Reps., Worth-Palos Twp., Ill., 1985—; fin. chmn. Citizens to Elect Dixon, 1986; mem. legis. com. for legal reform Halt. of Ill. Office: R L Dolce Inc 4550 W 122d St Alsip IL 60658

DOLDER, MICHAEL FRANCIS, civil engineer; b. Evanston, Ill., Nov. 23, 1953; s. Lawrence Paul and Virginia Rose (Quick) D.; m. Marilyn Wantroba, May 29, 1982; children: Andrew Michael, Brian Christopher. BSCE cum laude, Marquette U., 1976. Engring. technician Sargent & Lundy Engrs., Chgo., 1973-75; assoc. engr. Inland Steel Co., East Chicago, Ind., 1976-77, engr., 1977-81, project engr., 1981-85, sr. engr., 1985—. Advisor St. James Cath. Youth Orgn., Highland, Ind., 1980-81, St. Michael's Cath. Youth Orgn., Schererville, Ind., 1982-84; sec. adv. drainage bd. Town of Schererville, 1984-85, chmn. 1986. Mem. Alpha Sigma Nu, Tau Beta Pi, Chi Epsilon. Roman Catholic. Club: Inland Steel Ski (pres. 1979-80). Avocations: golf, travel, attending classes. Home: 322 E Joliet St Schererville IN 46375 Office: Inland Steel Co 3210 Watling St East Chicago IN 46312

DOLE, ROBERT J., U.S. Senator; b. Russell, Kans., July 22, 1923; s. Doran R. and Bina D.; m. Elizabeth Hanford, Dec. 1975. Student, U. Kans., U. Ariz.; A.B., Washburn Mcpl. U., Topeka, 1952, LL.B., 1952; LL.D. (hon.), Washburn U., Topeka, 1969. Bar: Kans. Mem. Kans. Ho. of Reps., 1951-53; sole practice Russell, Kans., 1953-61; Russell County atty. 1953-61; mem. 87th Congress from 6th Dist., Kans., 88th-90th congresses from 1st Dist., Kans.; mem. U.S. Senate from Kans., 1968—, Senate majority leader, 1984—, Senate Rep. leader, 1987—; chmn. Republican Nat. Com., 1971-73; Rep. vice-presdl. candidate, 1976. Chmn. Dole Found. Served with AUS, World War II. Decorated Purple Heart (2), Bronze Star with cluster. Mem. Am. Legion, VFW, DAV, 4-H Fair Assn., Kappa Sigma. Methodist. Clubs: Masons, Shriners, Elk, Kiwanis. Home: Russell KS 67665 Office: 141 Hart Senate Office Bldg Washington DC 20510

DOLE, ROBERT PAUL, appliance manufacturing company executive; b. Freeport, Ill., Nov. 12, 1923; s. Herman Walter and Louise Marie (Bornemeier) D.; m. Joyce Lindsay, Mar. 14, 1947; 1 child, Luanne Dole Cloyd. BA, Cornell Coll., Mt. Vernon, Iowa, 1948. Personnel mgr. Green Giant Co., Lanark, Ill., 1948-50; controller Green Giant Co., 1951-52; asst. treas. Henney Motor Co., Inc., Freeport, 1952-53, Eureka Williams Corp., Bloomington, Ill., 1954-62; v.p. and asst. gen. mgr. The Eureka Co., Bloomington, 1962-79; sr. v.p. The Eureka Co., 1980, pres., 1980—; exec. v.p., dir. parent co. Nat. Union Electric Corp., 1980-84, pres., dir., 1980-85, chmn. bd., pres., dir., 1985—; group v.p., dir. Dometic Inc., Bloomington, Ill., 1984-86; group pres., dir. White Consol. Industries, Cleve., 1987—; trustee Internat. Assn. Machinists Nat. Pension Fund, 1972-80; dir. Euroclean of Can., Ltd., Cambridge, Ont., 1980—, Swan Services, Inc., Atlanta, Appliance Components S.A. de C.V., Juarez, Mex., Air Machine Corp., Cold Spring Harbor, N.Y., First Fed. Savs. & Loan Assn., Bloomington. Served in U.S. Army, 1943-46. Republican. Lodges: Masons, Elks. Office: Nat Union Electric Corp 1201 E Bell St Bloomington IL 61701

DOLEZAL, DALE FRANCIS, truck manufacturing company executive; b. Ronan, Mont., Apr. 9, 1936; s. Henry Lewis and Regina Marie Dolezal; B.S. in Indsl. Engring., Mont. State U., 1961; student Program for Mgmt. Devel., Bus. Sch., Harvard U., 1974; m. Patricia Louise Johnson, Aug. 27, 1960; children—Craig, Kelly, Kathleen, Kari. Indsl. and methods engr. Westinghouse Electric Corp., Sunnyvale, Calif., 1961-63; chief indsl. engr. Clarke Equipment Corp., Spokane, Wash., 1963-65; mgr. materials Freightliner Corp., Portland, Oreg., 1965-67; with Internat. Harvester Co., 1967—, dir. purchasing and inventory mgmt., Chgo., 1977-80, dir. materials and ops. planning, 1980-81; gen. mgr. parts and retail Indsl. Trucks div. Eaton Corp., Phila., 1981—; dir. Real Am. Corp.; mem. bd. bus. and indsl. advisers U. Wis., Madison; bd. dirs. Ops. Tng. Inst. Mem. parents adv. bd. Naperville (Ill.) Central High Sch., 1977—; mem. adv. bd. Sch. Dist. 203, Naperville, 1978—. Served with USMC, 1954-57. Registered profl. engr., Oreg. Mem. Am. Inst. Indsl. Engrs., Am. Prodn. and Inventory Control. Soc. Republican. Roman Catholic. Clubs: Rotary, K.C., Harvard (Chgo.). Contbr. articles to trade jours.

DOLEZAL, GERALD DEAN, mechanical engineer; b. Chester, Mont., June 19, 1944; s. John D. and Viviann Ann (Rockman) D.; m. Cheri D. Childs, May 24, 1974; children: Jeff, Julie, Danielle, Natasha. BSME, Gonzaga U., 1969, postgrad. Service rep. Hyster Co., Cherry Hill, N.J., 1969-72; service mgr. Hyster Co., Portland, Oreg., 1972-73; with spl. mktg. group Hyster Co., Peoria, Ill., 1977-85; gen. product mgr. Hyster Co., Kewanee, Ill., 1977-85, mgr. engring., 1987; owner, mgr. Cher Dol, Inc., 1987—. Mem. Constrn. Industry Mfrs. Assn., Farm and Indsl. Equipment Bur., Soc. Automotive Engrs. Roman Catholic. Lodges: Rotary Internat., KC. Home: 9 Lawanee Estates Rural Rt #1 Kewanee IL 61443 Office: Hyster Co 2000 Kentville Rd Kewanee IL 61443

DOLEZAL, HUBERT, psychologist, educator; b. Aug. 29, 1941; s. Hubert and Leonora Dolezal; m. Renée Cargerman; children: Christopher Hubert, Robert Sterling. BA, SUNY, Albany, 1966, MA, 1968; PhD, Cornell U., 1976. Lic. psychologist, Ill. Instr. Cornell U., Ithaca, N.Y., 1971; postdoctoral research and teaching fellow MIT, Cambridge, 1973-75; visiting asst. prof. Brandeis U., Waltham, Mass., 1974; prin. investigator, researcher USAF Research Lab., Dayton, Ohio, 1983-84; prin. investigator, research psychologist NASA, Houston, 1985—; prof. Northeastern Ill. U., Chgo., 1976—; cons. psychologist Orchard Village for Retarded, Skokie, Ill., 1982—, Little City Found., Palatine, Ill., 1985—; introduced parenting program. Author: Living in a World Transformed, 1982, Acad. Press, Univ. Presdl. award for Disting. Scholarly Publ., 1982; contbr. articles to profl. jours. Humanities and Social Sci. fellow Cornell U., 1968-72. Mem. Phi Sigma Phi. Avocations: chess, opera, plays. Home and Office: 1960 Lincoln Park W Chicago IL 60614 Office: Northeastern Ill Univ 5500 N Saint Louis Chicago IL 60625

DOLEZAL, WILBUR FRANCIS, dentist; b. Chgo., July 23, 1928; s. John and Mathilda Anna (Benes) D.; m. Geraldine Clara Viskocil, Dec. 26, 1953; 1 child, Stephen John. AS, Morton Jr. Coll., 1948; BS, U. Ill., 1950; DDS, Loyola U., 1954. Gen. practice dentistry Morris, Ill., 1957—; instr. prosthethics crown and bridge operative dentistry Loyola U., Chgo., 1957-59. Bd. dirs. Am. Cancer Soc.-Grundy County, Morris, 1959-85, Home Health Care Task Force, Joliet, 1972-75; dist. mem. Morris Bd. Edn., 1974-80; v.p. Grundy County Bd. Health, 1985—. Served to capt. USAF, 1954-56. Fellow Internat. Coll. Dentists, Am. Coll. Dentist; mem. ADA (spokesperson), Ill. State Dental Soc. (exec. council, relief com., v.p. com. for pub. info. 1981-85, spl. com. ethics 1987—), Ill. Valley Dental Soc. (pres. 1971-72). Republican. Roman Catholic. Club: Morris Country (bd. dirs. 1967-71). Lodges: Rotary (pres. 1961-62), KC. Home: 200 Briar Ln Morris IL 60450 Office: 417 W Jefferson St Morris IL 60450

DOLGINOW, YALE T., retail stores executive; b. 1942. BS, U. Kans., 1964, MBA, 1966. Pres., chief operating officer Modern Merchandising Inc., 1978-80; with Dolginows Inc., 1980-81; asst. to pres. Dayton Hudson Corp., Mpls., 1981-82; pres., chief exec. officer Dolginows of Mo., Inc., 1982-84; pres., chief exec. officer, dir. Ardan Inc., Des Moines, 1984—. Office: Ardan Inc 2320 Euclid Ave Des Moines IA 50310 *

DOLIN, PAUL ROBERT, dentist; b. Chgo., Oct. 9, 1923; s. Morris and Bertha Dolin; m. Marilyn Miller, Apr. 13, 1957; children: Linda, Laura Lisa. DDS, Loyola U., Maywood, Ill., 1948. Commd. USAF, 1949, advanced through grades to col., retired, 1985; gen. practice dentistry Chgo., 1952-85. Mem. Jewish Community Ctr., Skokie. Served with USAF, 1949-53, to col. Res. Mem. Amvets, Mil. Order World Wars, Disabled Am. Veterans, Jewish War Veterans, Alpha Omega. Club: UCC (Skokie, Ill.). Avocations: volleyball, travel, racquetball.

DOMADIA, MANSUKHLAL, surgeon; b. Vadal, India, June 18, 1934; s. Jamnadas Ranabhai and Kashiben (Viradia) D.; m. Pramila A. Patel, June 1, 1963; children: Sanjay, Sonal. Student, N. Wadia Coll., Poona, India, 1951-55; MBBS, B.J. Med. Coll., Poona, 1962. Gen. practice medicine Bilkha, Ind., 1964-70; intern Robinson Meml. Hosp., Ravenna, Ohio, 1970-71; resident in gen. surgery Fairview Gen. Hosp., Cleve., 1971-75; chief surgery Geauga Hosp., Chardon, Ohio, 1983-86, mem. credentials com., 1983-86; staff Lake County Hosp., Painesville, Ohio, 1986—. Bd. dirs. Western Res. Health Plan Ins. Mem. Ohio State Med. Assn., Geauga Med. Soc. (sec.). Hindu. Lodge: Rotary. Home: 12245 Sperry Rd Chesterland OH 44026 Office: 14577 E Park St Burton OH 44021

DOMASK, MARY ELLEN, nurse; b. Fond du Lac, Wis.; d. John Harold and Evelyn Amanda (Schiller) Harbridge; m. Jerome Harold Domask, Oct. 19, 1963; children: Lisa M., James Jerome, Joseph Jeffrey. Diploma in nursing, St. Mary's Hosp., Milw., 1963; AA, Brevard Community Coll., 1973; BS in Nursing, George Mason U., 1980; MS, Ohio State U., 1986. Registered nurse, Mich. Clin. instr. coronary unit Henry Ford Hosp., Detroit, 1980-82; head nurse emergency, dir. critical care nursing Mercy Hosp., Columbus, Ohio, 1982-86; dir. nursing systems, research Good Samaritan Hosp., Dayton, Ohio, 1986—. Mem. Emergency Nurses Assn. (founder and pres. local chpt. 1983), Dayton Area Nurse Adminstrs., Sigma Theta Tau. Roman Catholic. Home: 7158 Hunters Creek Dr Dayton OH 45459 Office: Good Samaritan Hosp 2222 Phildelphia Dr Dayton OH 45406

DOMBROWSKI, DAVID MICHAEL, mechanical engineer, utilities executive; b. Hartford, Conn., Apr. 20, 1959; s. Edward Alexander and Helen C. (Ozirsky) D.; m. Nancy Ellen James, Oct. 13, 1984. BSME, Worcester (Mass.) Poly. Inst., 1981; MSME, MIT, 1983; MBA, Xavier U., 1986. Registered profl. engr., Ohio. Mfg. engr. machining Northwest Conn. Mfg., Inc., Winsted, 1975-81; advanced machinability engr. Gen. Electric Co., Lynn, Mass., 1983-84; mgr. tech. modernization Gen. Electric Co., Cin., 1984—. Contbr. articles to profl. jours; patentee in field. Mem. Am. Soc. Mech. Engrs. (dir. public affairs 1985—), Soc. Mfg. Engrs., Tau Beta Pi. Avocations: scuba diving, teaching. Home: 1070 Marcie Ln Milford OH 45150 Office: Gen Electric Co MDA272 1 Neumann Way Cincinnati OH 45215

DOMBROWSKI, MITCHELL PAUL, physician, inventor; b. Detroit, Apr. 24, 1953; s. Mitchell Stanley and Dorothy Julia (Silarski) D.; m. Jocelyn McKinley, Mar. 7, 1981; children: Michael, Jacqueline. BS, U. Mich., 1975; MD, Wayne State U., 1979. Resident in obstetrics and gynecology Detroit, 1979-84, fellow in perinatology, 1984-86; asst. prof. Wayne State U. Sch. Medicine, Detroit, 1986—. Contbr. articles to med. publs.; inventor fetal blood sampling device, 1984, suction sampling device, 1985, reagent test strip, 1987. Recipient Research award NIH, 1986. Fellow Am. Coll. Obstetrics and Gynecologists, Soc. Perinatal Obstetricians. Home: 103 Mapleton Grosse Pointe Farms MI 48236 Office: Hutzel Hosp 4707 St Antoine Detroit MI 48204

DOMEIER, JOHN L., savings and loan association executive. Chmn., pres., mng. officer Gt. Am. Fed. Savs. and Loan Assn., Oak Park, Ill. Office: Gt Am Fed Savs & Loan Assn 101 Lake St Oak Park IL 60301 *

DOMINGO, CAROLYN KAY VATH, health services association administrator, nursing consultant; b. Cimarron, Kans., Mar. 23, 1940; d. Irwin Glenn and Muriel Lucille (Baker) Vath; m. Francis Julian Domingo, Oct. 6, 1984; 1 child, David Ross (stepson). BSN, U. Kans., 1962; MS, U. Colo., 1974. Staff nurse U. Kans. Med. Ctr., Kansas City, 1962-64, night supr., 1964-65, head nurse, 1965-74, head nurse, clin. nurse specialist, 1975-77; nursing cons. Dept. Health and Environment, Crippled and Chronically Ill Children's Program, Topeka, 1977—. Bd. dirs. Childbirth Edn. Assn., Kansas City, Mo., 1964-65, Topeka Art Guild, 1982-84, Melody Brown Meml., Inc., Topeka, 1982—, pres., 1985. Mem. Am. Nurses Assn., Kans. State Nurses Assn. (pres. 1981-83, by-laws chmn. 1986-88, sec. 1982-83, other offices), Kans. Pub. Health Assn. (Ross award 1983), Sigma Theta Tau. Baptist. Home: 1631 SW 28th St Topeka KS 66611 Office: Dept Health and Envionment Crippled & Chronically Ill Children's Program 700 Jackson Topeka KS 66620-0001

DOMIR, SUBHASH CHANDRA, research plant physiologist; b. India, Mar. 19, 1944; came to U.S., 1962; s. Ram Lal and Sheela Devi (Sikka) D.; m. E. Loraine Burton, Nov. 16, 1974; 1 child, Meera Elizabeth. BS, George Washington U., 1968; MS, Eastern Ky. U., 1971; PhD, Va. Poly. Inst. and State U., 1975. Research fellow Agrl. Research Service div. USDA, Beltsville, Md., 1974-75; plant physiologist Agrl. Research Service div. USDA, Delaware, Ohio, 1975—. Contbr. articles to profl. jours. Grantee Elec. Power Research Inst., Palo Alto, Calif., 1979, Horticulture Research Inst., Washington, 1985. Mem. Internat. Assn. Plant-Tissue Culture, Internat. Soc. Arbor. Home: 29 Mason Ave Delaware OH 43015 Office: USDA Agrl Research Service 359 Main Rd Delaware OH 43015

DOMJAN, LASZLO KAROLY, newspaper executive; b. Kormend, Hungary, Apr. 19, 1947; came to U.S., 1956; s. Frank and Violet (Pinter) D.; m. Louise Replogle, June 6, 1969; children: Andrew P., Eric S. BJ, U. Mo., 1969. Copy editor St. Louis Globe-Democrat, 1969; reporter, bureau chief UPI, St. Louis, 1969-81; reporter, night city editor St. Louis Post-Dispatch, 1981—, exec. city editor, 1987—. Journalistic writings include: author, editor Dioxin: Quandary for the 80's, 1983 (numerous awards), author, reporter series Hungary: Thirty Years After, 1986. Active Leadership St. Louis, 1987—. Recipient Herb Trask award Sigma Delta Chi, St. Louis, 1968. Roman Catholic. Avocations: reading, freelance writing, music. Office: St Louis Post-Dispatch 900 N Tucker Blvd Saint Louis MO 63101

DOMKE, GARY EDWARD, securities company executive; b. St. Louis; s. Charles Fred and Eleanor (Webbers) D.; m. Yvonne Anderson; m. Constance Lowe, Dec. 10, 1978; children: Jill Michelle Domke Nave, Yvette Lynn. Student, U. Mo., St. Louis, 1971-76, St. Louis U., 1977-80. Registered principal. Registered rep. R. G. Mills and Co., St. Louis, 1969-71, R. Rowland & Co., St. Louis, 1971-80; v.p. tax shelters, mut. funds WZW Cornerstone, St. Louis, 1980-82; v.p. regional fin., service coordinator Thomson McKinnon, St. Louis, 1982—; cons. various CPA and lawfirm. Served to capt. U.S. Army, 1965-69. Mem. Internat. Assn. Fin. Planners. Republican. Methodist. Lodge: Lions (treas. St. Louis chpt. 1974-75). Avocations: golf, skiing, computers, motorcycles, woodworking, photography. Office: Thomson McKinnon Securities #11 S Meramec Clayton MO 63105

DOMMEL, JAMES H., assets and risk management executive; b. Dana, Iowa, Sept. 14, 1936; s. Homer K. and Marion F. Podmore D.; m. Darlene O. Dommel, Oct. 15, 1961; children: Diann, Christy, David. BA, U. No. Iowa, 1958, MA, 1964. Tchr. Grinnel (Iowa) Sch. Dist., 1958-60; adminstr. Orono Sch. Dist., Long Lake, Minn., 1962-69, Nat. Car Rental, Mpls., 1969-74; mgr. corp. ins. Internat. Corp. Foods, Mpls., 1974-79; dir. fixed assets and risk mgmt. H.B. Fuller, St. Paul, 1979—. Mem. St. Paul Dist. 12 Council, 1983—, St. Anthony Block Nurse Bd., St. Paul, 1984-86; chmn. ins. com. Greater Mpls. YMCA, 1985—. Served with U.S. Army, 1960-62. Mem. Risk and Ins. Mgmt. Soc. (nat. coms.), Am. Soc. for Indsl. Security, Phi Delta Kappa (life). Lutheran. Home: 510 Westwood Dr N Golden Valley MN 55422 Office: HB Fuller Co 1200 W County Rd E Saint Paul MN 55112

DOMMERMUTH, WILLIAM PETER, marketing consultant, educator; b. Chgo.; s. Peter R. and Gertrude (Schnell) D.; m. H. Joan Hasty, June 6, 1959; children: Karin Jo, Margaret, Jean. B.A., U. Iowa, 1948; Ph.D., Northwestern U., 1964. Advt. copywriter Sears, Roebuck & Co., Chgo., 1949-51; sales promotion mgr. Sears, Roebuck & Co., 1951-58; asst., then asso. prof. mktg. U. Tex., Austin, 1961-67; asso. prof. U. Iowa, Iowa City, 1967-68; prof. So. Ill. U., Carbondale, 1968-86, U. Mo., St. Louis, 1986—; Cons. bus. firms. Author: (with Kernan and Sommers) Promotion: An Introductory Analysis, 1970, (with Andersen) Distribution Systems, 1972, (with Marcus and others) Modern Marketing, 1975, Modern Marketing Management, 1980, Promotion: Analysis, Creativity and Strategy, 1984; contbr. articles to profl. jours. Mem. Am. Mktg. Assn. (v.p. St Louis chpt.), Am. Psychol. Assn., So. Mktg. Assn., Midwest Mktg. Assn., Phi Beta Kappa, Beta Gamma Sigma, Theta Xi, Delta Sigma Pi. Club: Court, Frontenac Racquet. Home: 7242 S Roland Blvd Pasadena Hills MO 63121 Office: U Mo 1304 Tower Blvd 8001 Natural Bridge Rd Saint Louis MO 63121

DOMPKE, NORBERT FRANK, photography studio executive; b. Chgo., Oct. 16, 1920; s. Frank and Mary (Manley) D.; grad. Wright Jr. Coll., 1939-40; student Northwestern U., 1946-49; m. Marjorie Gies, Dec. 12, 1964; children—Scott, Pamela. Cost comptroller, budget dir. Scott Radio Corp., 1947; pres. TV Forecast, Inc., 1948-52, editor Chgo. edit. TV Guide, 1953, mgr. Wis. edit., 1954; pres. Root Photographers, Inc., Chgo., 1955—. Adv. com. photography & audiovisual tech., So. Ill. U., 1980-81; adv. bd. Gordon Tech. High Sch., 1979-86. Served with USAAC, 1943-47. C.P.A., Ill. Mem. United Photographers Orgn. (pres. 1970-71), Profl. Photographers Am., Profl. Sch. Photographers Am. (v.p. 1966-67, 87—, sec.-treas. 1967-69, pres. 1969-70, dir. 1971-78, treas. 1985-86, sec. 1986-87), Ill. Small Bus. Men's Assn. (dir. 1970-73), Chgo. Assn. Commerce and Industry (edn. com. 1966—), NEA, Nat. Sch. Press Assn., Ill. High Sch. Press Assn., Nat. Collegiate Sch. Press Assn., North Cen. Assn. (visitation com. 1986), Chgo. Bible Soc. (bd. advisors), Ill. C. of C. Co-founder T.V. Guide, 1947. Clubs: Carlton, Barclay, Whitehall, International; Tonquish Creek Yacht. Home: 990 N Lake Shore Dr Chicago IL 60611 Office: 1131 W Sheridan Rd Chicago IL 60660

DOMPKE, RICHARD KENNETH, management consultant; b. Chgo., May 13, 1929; s. Bernard Stephen and Margaret Dorothy (Granner) D.; student in Architecture, Ill. Inst. Tech., 1947-49, Wright Jr. Coll., 1949-52; B.S. in Indsl. Engring., Northwestern U., 1955; m. Gayle Mary Kenney, Jan. 18, 1956. Indsl. engr. Reynolds Metals Co., Phoenix, 1956-59, plant indsl. engr., McCook, Ill., 1959-67; partner/dir. Deloitte Haskins & Sells, Chgo., 1967-85, ret. Republican committeeman, 1960-61; mem. Lake Forest (Ill.) Bldg. Rev. Bd., 1981-85. Cert. mgmt. cons.; cert. compensation profl.; registered profl. indsl. engr. Mem. Am. Inst. Indsl. Engrs. (dir. Chgo. chpt. 1962-65), Inst. of Mgmt. Consultants, Am. Production and Inventory Control Soc., Am. Compensation Assn., Tau Beta Pi. Clubs: University Club of Chgo., Northwestern Alumni Club of Chgo., Alpha Delta Phi. Contbr. articles to profl. publs.

DONAHUE, CHARLES BERTRAND, II, lawyer; b. Hampton, Iowa, Apr. 17, 1937; s. Charles Bertrand and Alta Margaret (Sykes) D.; m. Brenda K. Kumpf, July 18, 1961 (div. 1980); children—Kaylie Elizabeth, Megan Elizabeth; m. Kathleen L. Komnenovich, June 27, 1987. A.B., Harvard Coll., 1959; J.D. cum laude, Cleve.-Marshall Coll. Cleve. State U., 1967. Bar: Ohio 1967, Fla. 1973. Subcontract mgr. Westinghouse Corp., Pitts., 1962-63; contract mgr. TRW, Inc., Cleve., 1963-67; ptnr. Calfee, Halter & Griswold, 1967-79; mng. ptnr. Donahue & Scanlon, Cleve., 1979—; adj. faculty Cleve.-Marshall Coll., 1973-79; dir. DeSantis Coatings Inc., Life Systems, Inc., Lortec Power Systems, Inc., Vitec, Inc. Served to capt. USAF, 1959-62. Delta Theta Phi scholar, 1967; recipient Spl. Merit award, Cleve. State U., 1973, Spl. Merit award, Ohio Legal Ctr. Ins., 1972, 74. Mem. Ohio State Bar Assn., Fla. State Bar Assn., Greater Cleve. Bar Assn., Estate Planning Council, Cleve.-Marshall Law Alumni (pres., trustee 1972). Republican. Episcopalian. Clubs: Harvard (Boston and Cleve.). Avocations: traveling; cooking; reading. Home: 827 Brick Mill Run Rd Westlake OH 44145 Office: Donahue & Scanlon 1500 One Erieview Plaza Cleveland OH 44114

DONAHUE, JOHN LAWRENCE, JR., paper company executive; b. Chgo., Nov. 9, 1939; s. John Lawrence Sr. and Margaret (Bollinger) D.; m. Maureen Anne Forbes, June 20, 1964; children: John L. III, Thomas James, Michael Patrick, Margaret Anne. BS in Marine Engring., U.S. Merchant Marine Acad., 1961. Lic. marine engr. Marine engr. Am. Export Lines, N.Y.C., 1961-64; chief engr. Gen. Box Co., Des Plaines, Ill., 1964-74; dir. engring. Mead Container Corp., Cin., 1974-82; pres. Donahue & Assocs. Internat., Inc., Milford, Ohio, 1982—. Trustee, treas. Milford Community Fire Dept. Inc., 1983—. Served to lt. USNR. Mem. Tech. Assn. Pulp and Paper Industry, Assn. Ind. Corrugated Converters. Republican. Roman Catholic. Avocation: yachting. Home and Office: 415 Mill St Milford OH 45150

DONAHUE, LAURA KENT, state senator; b. Quincy, Ill., Apr. 22, 1949; d. Laurence S. and Mary Lou (McFarland) Kent; m. Michael A. Donahue, July 16, 1983. B.S., Stephens Coll., 1971. Mem. Ill. State Senate, Quincy, 1981. Mem. Lincoln Club of Adams County, Ill. Fedn. Republican Women. Mem. P.E.O. Lodge: Altrusa. Office: State Senator Laura Donahue 400 Maine St Quincy IL 62301

DONAHUE, MICHAEL JAMES, marketing executive; b. Ottawa, Ill., Jan. 29, 1954; s. Thomas Mathew Donahue and Frances (Fitzgerald) Cook; m. Carrie Lynn Solberg, Jan. 18, 1986. BS in Mktg., Fla. State U., 1976. System engr. Electronic Data Systems Corp., Columbus, Ohio and Dallas, 1976-77; dist. mgr. Phoenix-Hecht, Chgo., 1977-78; sales engr. Tektronix, Inc., Chgo., 1978-83, tng. mgr., 1983-84; tng. dir. Bruning CAD, Tulsa, 1984-86; dir. sales, mktg. Advanced Computer Graphics, Milw., 1986—. Editor: A Practical Guide to CAD Management, 1984. Mem. Nat. Computer Graphics Assn., Sales and Mktg. Execs. Milw., AM/FM Internat. Office: Advanced Computer Graphics Inc 9816 N 107th St Milwaukee WI 53224

DONAHUE, MICHAEL RICHARD, marketing and management consultant; b. Jamestown, N.D., May 20, 1949; s. Richard Dwight and Alma (Heer) D. BBA in Mktg., U. Ill., 1977, MS in Fin., MS in Econs. Pres., cons. Tamarack Mgmt. Services, Danville, Ill. and Traverse City, Mich., 1977—, Mgmt. and Mktg. Perspectives, Petoskey, Mich. and Danville, 1984—; dir. cons. ops. ROBETTA Corp., Chamapign, Ill., 1985—. Columnist: Personnaly Speaking, 1972-73, Champaign County Bus. Reports, 1985-87; Contbr. articles to profl. jours. and mags. Cons. Nat. Rep. Congl. Com., Washington, 1980; mem. staff Congl. Polit. Campaign, Ill., 1978; bd. dirs. Vermilion County Bd. Rev., Danville, 1980-81. Recipient Cert. Merit Ill. Dept. Conservation, Springfield, Ill., 1982. Mem. Internat. Council Small Bus., Audubon Council Ill. (bd. dirs. 1980-83), Small Bus. Council C. of C. (chmn. 1986, 87—). Avocations: hiking, canoeing, photography, tennis, golf, wine, nature study. Home: 519 Chester Danville IL 61832 Office: ROBETTA Corp The Manor Bldg 311 W University Foyer Suite 2 Champaign IL 61820

DONAHUE, PENNY FREMONT, teacher; b. Westport, Conn., June 15, 1960; d. Henry Albert and June (Lemon) Fremont; m. Albert Allen Donahue II, June 29, 1985. BS, Miami U., 1983. Art tchr., volleyball and tennis coach Washington City Schs., Washington Court House, Ohio, 1983—; tennis instr. Washington Country Club, Washington Court House, 1983—. Tennis organizer Washington City, 1983—; mem. bd. Community Edn., Washington City, 1986—. Mem. Ohio State Volleyball Coaches Assn., Ohio State Tennis Assn., U.S. Tennis Assn., Ohio Art Edn. Assn., Alpha Phi. Avocations: sailing, painting, tennis, volleyball, travel. Home: 735 Fairway Dr Washington Court House OH 43160 Office: Washington High Sch 1200 Willard Sr Washington Court House OH 43160

DONAHUGH, ROBERT HAYDEN, library administrator; b. St. Paul, May 20, 1930; s. Robert Emmett and Elmyra Elanore (Hayden) D. B.A., Coll. St. Thomas, 1952; M.A., U. Minn., 1953. Instr. English and speech Robert Coll., Istanbul, Turkey, 1956-57; head tech. services Canton (Ohio) Public Library, 1957-62; asst. dir. Public Library of Youngstown and Mahoning County, Ohio, 1962-79; dir. Public Library of Youngstown and Mahoning County, 1979—. Author: Evaluation of Reference Resources in 8 Public Libraries in 4 Ohio Counties, 1970; contbr. book revs. to Library Jour., 1958—; contbr. radio program WYSU-FM, 1976—. Served with M.P. U.S. Army, 1954-56. Mem. ALA, Ohio Library Assn. (pres. 1975, Ohio Librarian of Yr. 1983-84), Midwest Fedn. Library Assns. (pres. 1979-83). Lodges: Elks, Rotary. Home: 509 Ferndale Ave Youngstown OH 44511 Office: 305 Wick Ave Youngstown OH 44503

DONAKER, JOHN CHAPMAN, JR., manufacturing executive; b. Berwyn, Ill., June 29, 1943; s. John C. and Doris P. (Perrin) D.; m. Leigh D. Pengelly, Sept. 21, 1968; children: Christine, Jeremy. BA, Princeton U., 1965. Ops. officer Continental Ill. Nat. Bank, Chgo., 1966-71; mgmt. cons. Deloitte Haskins & Sells, Chgo., 1972-75; pres. Johnston & Chapman Co., Chgo., 1976—. Bd. mem. Community Chest Oak Park-River Forest (Ill.), 1973-83; mem. bd. Sch. Dist. 97, Oak Park, 1976-79. Mem. Indsl. Perforators Assn. (bd. dirs.; pres. 1985-87). Office: Johnston & Chapman Co 2925 W Carroll Chicago IL 60612

DONALD, MILTON LOUIS, lawyer; b. Tuskegee, Ala., Sept. 20, 1946; s. Robert Jackson and Mayme (Lee) Donald; m. Robyn DeBorah Williams, July 18, 1964 (div. Nov. 1980); 1 child, Sa Borria Lynne; m. Karen Lee

Oden, Aug. 23, 1981; children: Marcus, Ashley Nicole. BSBA, Ala. State U., 1979; JD, U. Wis., 1983. Bar: Wis. 1983, U.S. Dist. Ct. (we. and ea. dists.) Wis. 1983. Corrections officer N.Y.C. Dept. Corrections, 1969-72; law advocate Equal Opportunity Adv. Program, Madison, Wis., 1980-82; legis. aide Wis. State Assembly, Madison, 1981-83; legal counsel Wis. Dept. Natural Resources, Madison, 1983—. Pres. South Madison Neighborhood Ctr., 1982—; mem. Com. on Human Relations, Madison, 1983—; treas. com. to elect Jerry E. Smith, Madison, 1986—; sec. Blacks for Polit. and Social Action, Madison, 1983—. Named one of Outstanding Young Men of Am., 1982; recipient Disting. Service award Badger Boys State, 1984, 85, 86, 87. Mem. ABA, Wis. Bar Assn., Assn. Trial Lawyers Am. Democrat. Baptist. Home: 1809 Prairie Rd Madison WI 53711 Office: Wis Dept Natural Resources 101 S Webster St Madison WI 53707

DONALD, PAUL AUBREY, insurance company executive; b. Prince Frederick, Md., July 6, 1929; m. Anne Harris, Nov. 5, 1966; children: Cynthia Binz, Jan Donald, Glenn White, Mike Donald, Ken Donald, Steve Donald. B.Com., U. Balt., 1956. C.L.U.; C.P.C.U. Vice pres., regional mgr. Nationwide Ins., Lynchburg, Va., 1975-79; v.p. property casualty mktg. Nationwide Ins., Columbus, Ohio, 1979-80, v.p. western devel., 1980-81, v.p., adminstrv. asst. to pres., 1981, pres., gen. mgr., 1981—, also dir., 1981—; chmn. bd. Neckura Life Ins. Co., Auto Direkt Ins. Co., Employers Ins. of Wausau, Beaver Pacific Corp., Colonial Ins. Co., Scottsdale Ins. Co.; vice chmn. Farmland Ins. Co., Farmland Life Ins. Co.; pres. Nationwide Found., Nationwide Transport, Inc.; trustee Ins. Services Office, 1986—; dir. Farmland Mut. Ins. Co., NECKURA, numerous subs. and affiliates. Pres. United Way of Franklin County, Inc., Columbus, 1984-85, trustee, 1982-86; trustee Columbus Symphony Orch., 1982-86, Meth. Theol. Sch., Delaware, Ohio, 1983-86, Franklin U., 1986, INROADS/Columbus, Inc., 1986; officer Council for Study of Ethics and Econs., Columbus, 1983-86. Mem. Nat. Assn. Health Underwriters, Am. Soc. C.L.U.s, Soc. C.P.C.U.s. Methodist. Home: 737 Old Oak Trace Worthington OH 43085 Office: Nationwide Ins Co 1 Nationwide Plaza Columbus OH 43216

DONALD, WILLIAM CLYDE, II, clergyman; b. Battle Creek, Mich., Nov. 28, 1918; s. William Clyde and Louella (Shattuck) D.; A.B., Albion Col, 1940; B.D., Garrett Bibl. Inst., 1943; D.D., Northwestern U., 1947; m. Carolyn Marie Fosberg, July 28, 1943; 1 dau., Pamela Marie (Mrs. John Gislason). Chaplain Deaconess Hosp., Milw., 1948-56; pastor Bethel Evangelical and Reformed Ch., Milw., 1949-57, Bethel Evangelical and Reformed Ch., Detroit, 1957-70, Peoples Ch. Chgo., 1970-73, 1st Congl. Ch., Benton Harbor, Mich., 1973-77; interim pastor specialist Plymouth Congl. Ch., Mpls., 1977-79; seasonal pastor Little Stone Ch., Mackinac Island, Mich., 1986—; part-time faculty Wayne State U., 1950-70; chmn. bd. Third Securities Corp., Rockford, Ill., 1965-77. Mem. Am. Protestant Hosp. Assn. (fellow coll. chaplains), Nat. Assn. Congl. Christian Chs. (commn. on ministry 1978-82), Tau Kappa Epsilon. Mem. B'nai B'rith (hon.). Home: 1116 Lakeside Dr Mackinaw City MI 49701

DONALDSON, FRANK COOMBS, obstetrician, gynecologist; b. Lebanon, Ind., May 25, 1922; s. Fred Raymond and Esther Anne (Coombs) D.; m. Loraine Kalow, May 21, 1948 (dec. Feb. 1979); children: Fred, Frank Jr., Tom, Susan, David; m. Anne Decker, Aug. 4, 1983; stepchildren: Tom, Jacquie, Marti. BS, De Pauw U., 1943; MD, Ind. U., 1946. Diplomate Am. Bd. Ob-Gyn. Intern St. Elizabeth's Hosp., Lafayette, Ind., 1946, resident in ob-gyn, 1949-50; resident in ob-gyn William Beaumont Hosp., El Paso, 1947-49, Ind. U. Med. Ctr., 1950-51; pres., chief of staff St. John Hosp., Anderson, Ind., 1968-73, Community Hosp., Anderson, 1974-75; practice medicine specializing in ob-gyn Anderson, 1975—; vol. physician Frances Newton Hosp., Ferozore, Punjab, India, 1968. Bd. dirs. Madison County Planned Parenthood, 1968-75, Anderson C. of C., 1972-75; chmn. Madison County United Way, 1970-86. Served to capt. M.C., U.S. Army, 1943-49. Fellow ACS, Am. Coll. Ob-Gyn; mem. AMA, Ind. State Med. Soc., Anderson C. of C. (bd. dirs. 1972-75). Republican. Roman Catholic. Clubs: Anderson Country (bd. dirs. 1969-72), Tippicanoe Lake Country. Avocation: golfing. Home: #2 Windridge Anderson IN 46011 Office: 2009 Brown St Anderson IN 46014

DONALDSON, LESLIE WELLINGTON (LES), JR., research institute executive; b. Washington, Dec. 29, 1953; s. Leslie W. and Conchita (Newman) D.; m. Karen E. Mitchell, June 19, 1976; 1 dau., Adrienne S. Donaldson. B.S. in Chem. Engring., N.J. Inst. Tech., 1974; postgrad. in bus. Seton Hall U., U. Louisville, Loyola U. Chgo. Research engring. asst. E. I. duPont, Inc., Newark, N.J., 1973; process engr. Airco, Inc., Murray Hill, N.J., 1974-77; project engr. Celanese Corp., Louisville, 1977-83; project mgr. indsl. research and devel. Gas Research Inst., Chgo., 1983-86, mgr., 1986—. Mem. Rep. Senatorial Com. Mem. Am. Inst. Chem. Engrs., Am. Ceramic Soc. Republican. Avocations: racquetball, entrepreneurship. Office: Gas Research Inst 8600 W Bryn Mawr Ave Chicago IL 60631

DONALDSON, ROBERT H., management consultant; b. N.Y.C., Dec. 5, 1929; s. Cortlandt Beekman and Virginia (Macdonald) D.; m. Dorothy DeGreef, Dec. 10, 1955 (dec. Mar. 1964); m. Ardeth Daly, Feb. 28, 1967 (div. Aug. 1977); children: Evan, Courtney, Cooper; m. Elayne Marks Egar, Sept. 1, 1983. BSChemE, Clarkson U., 1951; MS, U. Rochester, 1957. Registered profl. engr., N.Y., Ohio, N.J. Devel. engr. Eastman Kodak, Rochester, N.Y., 1953-64; assoc. McKinsey & Co., Washington, 1964-67; asst. gen. mgr. internat. div. Diamond Shamrock, Cleve., 1967-72; v.p. Prescott Ball Turben Co., Cleve., 1972-74, Clarion Capital, Inc., 1974-79; pres. Delta Planning, Inc., Denville, N.J. and Beachwood, Ohio, 1979—; lectr. in field, U.S. and Can.; bd. dirs. TWM Mgmt. Services Ltd. Contbr. articles to profl. jours. Served with U.S. Army, 1951-53, Korea. Mem. N.Am. Soc. Corp. Planning (bd. dirs. 1970-80, pres. 1975, 79), Ohio Venture Assn. (founder, trustee, pres.), Venture Assn. N.J. (founder, trustee, pres.), Washington Soc. Investment Analysis, Planning Forum, Omega Chi Epsilon, Delta Upsilon, Tau Beta Pi. Republican. Presbyterian. Club: Park East Racquet. Avocations: tennis, sailing, skiing. Home: 24023 Letchworth Rd Beachwood OH 44122 Office: Delta Planning Inc PO Box 22618 Beachwood OH 44122

DONALSON, JAMES RYAN, real estate broker; b. Kansas City, Mo., Jan. 7, 1945; s. Joseph Elmer and Betty Lee (Cousins) D.; B.S. (Mo. Real Estate Assn. scholar), U. Mo., 1967; m. Sandra Lynn Yockey, Dec. 26, 1964; children—Kimberly Kay, Debra Lynn, Jennifer Lee. Loan officer City Wide Mortgage Co., Kansas City, 1967; interviewer personnel Panhandle Eastern Pipe Line Co., Kansas City, 1968; partner Donalson Realtors, Kansas City, 1969—; pres. Classic Homes, Kansas City, 1973—, Donalson Devel. Co., 1980—, Diversified Investments (formerly Donalson & Assos. Realtors), 1980—; bd. dirs. Multiple Listing Service Greater Kansas City, 1971-75, treas., 1972-73. Bd. dirs. Platte County unit Am. Cancer Soc., 1973-75. Mem. Nat. Assn. Real Estate Bds., Mo. Assn. Realtors (dir. 1974-75), Real Estate Bd. Kansas City (dir. 1978-80), Platte County Bus. and Profl. Men's Assn., U. Mo. Alumni Assn., Homebuilders Assn. Greater Kansas City. Baptist. Lion (dir. 1974-76).

DONATI, ROBERT MARIO, physician, educational administrator; b. Richmond Heights, Mo., Feb. 28, 1934; s. Leo S. and Rose Marie (Gualdoni) D. B.S. in Biology, St. Louis U., 1955, M.D., 1959. Diplomate: Am. Bd. Nuclear Medicine, bd. dirs., 1980-86, vice chmn. 1984-85, chmn. 1985-86. Intern St. Louis City Hosp., 1959-60; asst. resident John Cochran Hosp., St. Louis, 1960-62; fellow in nuclear medicine St. Louis U., 1962-63; practice medicine specializing in nuclear medicine St. Louis, 1963—; mem. staff John Cochran Hosp., 1963-83, St. Louis U. Hosp., 1963—; mem. faculty St. Louis U. Sch. Medicine, 1963—, asst. prof. internal medicine, 1965-68, assoc. prof., 1968-74, prof., 1974—, prof. radiology, 1979—, dir. div. nuclear medicine, 1968—, sr. assoc. dean, 1983—; exec. assoc. v.p. Med. Ctr., 1985—; acting v.p. Med. Ctr., 1986; chief nuclear medicine services St. Louis VA Med. Center, 1968-79, chief of staff, 1979-83; adj. prof. medicine Washington U. Sch. Medicine, 1979-83; Del. Am. Bd. Med. Spltys., 1982—, fin. com., 1984-87; councilor Federated Council Member Medicine Orgns., 1981-85. Editor: (with W. T. Newton) Radioassay in Clinical Medicine, 1974; Contbr. articles to profl. jours. Mem. Presdl. Adv. Commn. on VA, 1972; Bd. dirs. Inst. for Health Mgmt., Inc., 1976-78, Alliance for Community Health Inc., 1986—, Ind. Colls. and Univs. of Mo., 1985, Affiliated Med. Transport, Inc., 1985—; mem. HEW Task Force on Health Effects of Ionizing Radiation, 1978-79; mem. desegregation monitoring and adv. com. U.S. Dist. Ct., 1980-82; mem. Multi-Hosp. Systems Nat. Adv. Com., 1982-84. Served to capt. AUS, 1966-68. Decorated Army Commendation medal; recipient VA Disting. Service award, 1983. Mem. AMA (residency rev. com. for nuclear medicine 1978-80), St. Louis Med. Soc., Am. Fedn. for Clin. Research (councilor 1967-70), Central Soc. Clin. Research, AAUP, N.Y. Acad. Scis., Soc. Exptl. Biology and Medicine, Soc. Nuclear Medicine (acad. council 1970—, bd. trustee 1977-81, assoc. chmn. sci. program 1978, mem. publs. com. 1979—, chmn. 1982-83), Am. Coll. Nuclear Physicians, Am., Internat. socs. hematology, Soc. Med. Consultants to Armed Forces, Sigma Xi, Alpha Omega Alpha. Roman Catholic. Clubs: Cosmos (Washington); Racquet (St. Louis). Research in clin. investigative nuclear medicine and humoral control of cellular proliferation. Home: 5335 Botanical Ave Saint Louis MO 63110 Office: St Louis U Sch Medicine 1325 S Grand Blvd Saint Louis MO 63104

DONDANVILLE, WILLIAM MARTIN, dentist; b. Detroit, Apr. 26, 1951; s. Joseph Martin and Lorelie (Stien) D.; m. Mary Elizabeth Deem, Apr. 5, 1975; children: Thomas, Jeffrey. BS, Gonzaga U., 1973; cert. in bus., Lewis & Clark Community Coll., Godfrey, Ill., 1974; DMD, So. Ill. U., Alton, 1978. Gen. practice dentistry Brighton, Ill., 1978—. Mem. ADA, Ill. State Dental Soc., Madison Dist. Dental Soc. Avocations: reading, fishing, hunting. Home: 5 Frontenac Godfrey IL 62035 Office: PO Box 667 Brighton IL 62012

DONEAUD, ANDRE ALEXANDRU, meteorologist, educator, researcher; b. Bucharest, Romania, June 3, 1929; came to U.S., 1978; s. Ernest Alexandre and Marcella Elena (Macovei) D.; m. Alexandrina Sirbu, 1954 (div.); m. 2d, Doina Armida Stan, Aug. 17, 1958. Diploma in Atmospheric Physics, U. Bucharest, 1952, Ph.D., 1971. Research scientist Meteorol. Inst., Bucharest, 1952-78, sci. dir., 1962-72; assoc. prof. U. Bucharest., 1972-78; research sci. tchr., then assoc. prof. S.D. Sch. Mines and Tech., Rapid City, 1978; cons. World Meteorol. Orgn. Served to lt. Romania Air Force, 1952, Recipient Sci. Merit/award Romania Acad. Sci., 1969. Mem. Am. Meteorol. Soc., Am. Geophys. Union, Sigma Xi. Roman Catholic. Club: 39 (Rapid City). Co-author: Numerical and Graphical Methods, 1962; Synoptic, Dynamic and Aeronautic Meteorology, 1966; Prevention and Control of Frost in Vegetable and Fruit Growing, 1968; The Microclimate in Greenhouses, 1977; others; contbr. numerous articles profl. publs. Home: 507 E Chicago St Rapid City SD 57701 Office: 500 St Joseph St Rapid City SD 57701

DONEWALD, MARIAN, speech and hearing clinician, educator; b. St. Louis, July 1911; d. Harry William and Daisy Elizabeth (Eissler) Donewald; student U. Colo., 1937-38; A.B., U. Evansville, 1948; M.S., Purdue U., 1950. Tchr. Wheeler Sch., Evansville, Ind., 1935-48; speech and hearing clinician Evansville-Vanderburgh Sch. Corp., 1948—; lectr. speech Purdue U., Lafayette, Ind., 1952-64, dir. summer workshops, 1952-64; lectr. speech Community Coll., U. Evansville, 1955-76, ret., 1976; cons., pvt. therapist, 1976—. Mem. Christian edn. com. 1st Presbyterian Ch., Evansville, 1965-68, altar com., 1969—; Dem. precinct committeeman, mem. adv. bd. Evansville Knight Twp., 1975-79; trustee Campground Cemetery, Evansville, 1966—, sec. bd., 1970—; historian Old Court House, 1976-87; coordinator Docents Reitz House Mus., 1986—. Mem. Am. Speech and Hearing Assn. (state del. 1966-68), Cen. States Speech and Hearing Assn., Ind. Speech and Hearing Assn. (pres. 1958-60), Internat. Council for Exceptional Children, NEA, Ind. State, Evansville tchrs. assns., Speech Communication Assn., Cleft Palate Assn., Internat. Platform Assn., Assn. Tchr. Educators, Embroiderers Guild Am. (chpt. sec. 1982-83), AAUW, Evansville Rose Soc. (sec. 1969—), Kappa Kappa Iota (Ind. pres. 1977-79, 82-83). Clubs: Flower Growers Garden (pres. 1985-88), Oak Meadow Country. Lodge: Rotary. Author: See and Say Book, 1961. Home: 2900 Bellemeade Ave Evansville IN 47714

DONHOWE, PETER ARTHUR, editor; b. Columbus, Nebr., Feb. 5, 1938; s. Joseph Oliver and Nada Vira (Graham) D.; m. Gail Ramsay, Feb. 3, 1962 (div. Sept. 1965); m. Marcia Kay Farrell, Aug. 1, 1979; children: Joseph Farrell, Helen Nada. Student, Princeton U., 1975-76; BA in Am. Civilization, U. Iowa, 1962, postgrad., 1962-63. Editor Iowa Defender, Iowa City, 1961-63; reporter So. Illinoisan, Carbondale, Ill., 1963; reporter St. Louis Post-Dispatch, 1964-71, editorial writer, 1971-85; bus. and econs. editor U. Ill., Urbana, 1985—; exec. bd. Newspaper Guild Local 47, St. Louis, 1970-72; founding editor St. Louis Journalism Rev., 1972—; visitor program European Communities, Belgium, Eng., Fed. Republic Germany, France, 1983. Contbr. numerous articles to mags., newspapers. Discussion leader Great Decisions Series, St. Louis, 1969, 83-84; exec. com. Euclid Montessori Sch., St. Louis, 1983. Served with USN, 1956-58. Recipient Sloan fellowship in Econs. Princeton U., 1975-76, Outstanding Service award Coalition for the Environment, St. Louis, 1985, Appreciation award St. Louis Journalism Rev., 1985. Club: Princeton (St. Louis and Chgo.). Home: 1909 Harding Dr Urbana IL 61801 Office: Univ Ill News Bur 807 S Wright St Champaign IL 61820

DONIS, PETER P., agricultural machinery manufacturing company executive; b. Madison, Wis., May 30, 1924; s. Peter A. and Katherine A. (Gray) D.; m. Mildred Eva Niesen, June 23, 1948; children: David Lee, Diana Louise, Paul Andrew. B.B.A., U. Wis., 1948. With Caterpillar Tractor Co., 1956—; plant mgr. Caterpillar Tractor Co., Joliet, Ill., 1963-74; v.p. Caterpillar Tractor Co., Peoria, Ill., 1975-77, exec. v.p., 1977-85; pres., chief operating officer Caterpillar Tractor Co., 1985—; dir. Home Fed. Savs. and Loan Assn., Peoria. Trustee Joint Council on Econ. Edn.; trustee Western U. Regional Adv. Council, Adv. Council of Ill. 2000 Found. Mem. Ill. State C. of C. (bd. dirs.). Club: Country (Peoria). Office: Caterpillar Tractor Co 100 NE Adams St Peoria IL 61629 *

DONLON, JAMES PETER, management consultant; b. Utica, N.Y., Sept. 25, 1957; s. James Kendrick and Irene (Mahanna) D. BA in Econs., Union Coll., 1979; MBA in Fin. and Mktg., Northwestern U., 1985. Supr. ops. Utica Nat. Ins., Utica and Dallas, 1981-83; diversification analyst Tata Oil Mills, Bombay, India, 1985; sr. cons. Ernst and Whinney, Chgo., 1985—; cons., speaker Internat. Assn. Amusement Parks, New Orleans, 1980; cons. Chem. Bank, N.Y.C., 1984. Contbr. articles on the European amusement park industry to profl. jours. Thomas J. Watson European fellow, 1979-80. Mem. Northwestern Mgmt. Club. Roman Catholic. Avocations: current events, travel, reading, tennis, basketball. Home: 625 W Wrightwood #518 Chicago IL 60614 Office: Ernst and Whinney 150 S Wacker Chicago IL 60606

DONNEL, KENNETH EUGENE, farmer, beekeeper; b. Shelbyville, Ill., Nov. 7, 1945; s. Dale Delbert and A. Imogene (Askins) D.; m. Joan Ellen Littlejohn, Sept. 7, 1965 (div. Oct. 3, 1984); children: Michael E., Suzanne E., Teresa D.; m. Amy Jo Forcum Stephens, June 7, 1985; stepchildren: Brandon E., Misty D. AS in Electronics Tech., So. Ill. U., 1965. Electronic technician Gen. Electric Corp., Decatur, Ill., 1965-66; technician, rep. Nat. Cash Register, Decatur, 1970-73; field service rep. Le Febure Corp., St. Louis, 1973-77; farmer Findlay, Ill., 1977—. Mem. petition drive, Shelby County, Ill., 1983. Served with USN, 1965-72, Vietnam. Mem. Am. Dairy Goat Assn., So. Ill. Dairy Goat Assn. Republican. Avocation: breeding quality French Alpine dairy goats. Home and Office: Rural Rt 1 Box 34A Findlay IL 62534

DONNELL, ROBERT HART, radiologist; b. Hillsboro, Mo., Mar. 18, 1912; s. Robert Hart and Grace Ernestine (Adams) D.; m. Dorothy Evelyn McDonald, June 15, 1947; children: Robert Hart III, James H., Richard J., David W., Brian C. BA, U. Mo., 1933, BS, 1934; MD, Washington U., St. Louis, 1936. Diplomate Am. Coll. Radiology. Gen. practice medicine Crystal City, Mo., 1937-41; practice medicine specializing in radiology Crystal City, 1946—; radiologist Jefferson Meml. Hosp., 1957-79, pres. staff, 1960-62. Served to lt. col. M.C., U.S. Army, 1941-46, ETO. Mem. AMA, Jefferson County Med. Soc. (pres. 1950-53), Mo. Radiol. Soc., Am. Coll. Radiology, Festus (Mo.) C. of C. Methodist. Lodges: Lions, Masons. Home: 1113 Crystal Heights Rd Crystal City MO 63019 Office: 112 Mississippi Crystal City MO 63019

DONNELLEY, BARBARA COLEMAN, civic worker; b. Chgo., May 20, 1941; d. Walter Cobb Coleman and Barbara (Stanley) Behr; m. Christopher Bayne Clark, July 3, 1965 (div. 1973); children—Barbara Stanley Coleman, Christopher Bayne; m. Thomas E. Donnelley II, Aug. 18, 1979. B.A., Wheaton Coll., Norton, Mass., 1963. With sales staff Max Futorian, Chgo., 1978-79, Lee Rosenberg, Highland Park, Ill., 1977-78, Bartley Collection, Lake Forest, Ill., 1976-77; Vice-pres. Open Lands Project, Chgo., 1983-85, Wetlands Research, Inc., Chgo., 1984-85; chmn. Smith Symposium adv. com. Edward L. Ryerson Conservation Area, Deerfield, Ill., 1984—, pres. Gaylord Lockport Co., Chgo., 1985—; hist. preservation adviser Lockport Area Devel. Commn., Ill., 1984—. Bd. of trustees Salisbury (Conn.) Sch., 1987—. Recipient Friend award Nat. Assn. County Park and Recreation Ofcls., 1985. Republican. Episcopalian. Clubs: Onwentsia (Lake Forest); Cliff Dwellers, Casino (Chgo.). Avocations: travel; photography; fishing; skiing; golf; squash.

DONNELLI, GERALD MICHAEL, dentist; b. Rockford, Ill., June 24, 1954; s. Joseph William and Georgette (Deschmaker) D.; m. Kathryn Mary Ingardona, Sept. 1, 1973; children: David, Kristen. AS, Rock Valley Coll., 1974; BS, No. Ill. U., 1976, postgrad., 1976-77; DDS, Northwestern U., 1981. Assoc. dentist Dr. L.J. Ginestra, Rockford, 1981-83; owner Rockford, 1983—; Mem. TMJ Clinic Swedish Am. Hosp., Rockford, 1986. Mem. Am. Acad. Gold Foil Operators (Achievement award 1981), Acad. Gen. Dentistry, Internat. Assn. Orthodontics, Rockford Gnathological Soc. (founding), Rockford Area C. of C., Jaycees (bd. dirs. 1975-76). Office: 1728 E Riverside Blvd Rockford IL 61111

DONNELLY, ROBERT TRUE, state supreme court justice; b. Lebanon, Mo., Aug. 31, 1924; s. Thomas John and Sybil Justine (True) D.; m. Wanda Sue Oates, Nov. 16, 1946; children: Thomas Page, Brian True. Student, Tulsa U., 1942-43, Ohio State U., 1943; J.D., U. Mo., 1949. Bar: Mo. 1949. Mem. firm Donnelly & Donnelly, Lebanon; city atty. Lebanon, 1954-55; asst. atty. gen. Mo., 1957-61; justice Supreme Ct. Mo., Jefferson City, 1965—; chief justice Supreme Ct. Mo., 1973-75, 81-83; bd. govs. Mo. Bar, 1957-63. Mem. Lebanon Bd. Edn., 1959-65; trustee Sch. Religion, Drury Coll., Springfield, Mo., 1958-66, Mo. Sch. Religion, Columbia, 1971-72. Served with inf. AUS, World War II. Decorated Purple Heart. Mem. Am., Mo. bar assns., Phi Delta Phi. Presbyterian. Club: Mason. Home: PO Box 6818 Jefferson City MO 65102 Office: Supreme Ct Bldg Jefferson City MO 65101

DONNELLY, THOMAS HENRY, chemistry educator, consultant; b. Endicott, N.Y., Apr. 20, 1928; s. Paul John and Dorcas Alida (Gardiner) Donnelly (Donley); m. Jean Marilyn Saunders, May 14, 1955; children—Mary Kathleen, Susan Jean, James Paul, Sarah Elizabeth. B.S. in Chemistry, Rensselaer Polytech Inst., 1950; Ph.D., Cornell U., 1955. Mgr. phys. chem., research and devel. ctr. Swift & Co., Chgo./Oakbrook, Ill., 1965-72, mgr. gelatin and stabilizers, 1967-72, gen. mgr., sci. services, Oakbrook, 1972-78, mgr. applied chemistry, 1978-79; vis. prof. chemistry Loyola U., Chgo., 1979-84, lectr. chemistry, 1984-87, assoc. prof., dept. chmn., Mundelein Coll., Chgo., 1987—; mem. food enzymology del. to China People to People, Spokane, Wash., 1985. Contbr. articles, referee Jour. Phys. Chem., 1959—. Patentee in field. Lector, commentator, cantor St. John of the Cross Parish, Western Springs, Ill., 1961—; former pres. area Home-owners Assn., Western Springs. Served to lt. USNR, 1950-70. Recipient Merit award Chgo. Assn. Tech. Socs., 1984. Mem. AAAS, Inst. Food Technologists, Am. Chem. Soc. (past chmn. and other offices Chgo. sect., mem. div. agrl. and food chemistry, food biochemistry subdiv., chmn. 21st Great Lakes Regional Meeting, 1987). Democrat. Roman Catholic. Office: Loyola U Dept Chemistry 6525 N Sheridan Chicago IL 60626

DONNEM, SARAH LUND, consultant; b. St. Louis, Apr. 10, 1936; d. Joel Y. and Erle Hall (Harsh) Lund; B.A., Vassar Coll., 1958; m. Roland W. Donnem, Feb. 18, 1961; children—Elizabeth Prince, Sarah Madison. Tech. aide Bell Labs., Whippany, N.J., 1959-60; chmn. placement vol. opportunities N.Y. Jr. League, 1972-73, asst. treas. 1974-75, chmn. urban problems relating to mental health, 1967-69, mem. project research com., 1967-71, chmn., 1973-74, mem. bd. mgrs. 1973-74; chmn. community research D.C. Jr. League, 1970-71, mem. bd. mgrs., 1970-71; mem. Stratford Hall (N.Y.) Com., 1970—; bd. dirs. East Side Settlement House, Bronx, N.Y., 1972—, v.p., 1975-76, chmn. Antiques Show com., 1972—, chmn. Nat. Horse Show Benefit, 1976; bd. dirs. Stanley M. Isaacs Neighborhood Center, N.Y.C., 1973-76, v.p., 1975-76; bd. dirs. Presbyn. Home for Aged Women, N.Y.C., 1974-76, v.p., 1976; mem. exec. bd. N.Y. Aux. of Blue Ridge Sch., 1971-75, sec., 1965-67, pres., 1973-75; budget and benevolence com. Brick Presbyn. Ch., N.Y.C., 1973-76, mem. social service com., 1973-74, chmn. fgn. students com., 1963-64. Bd. dirs. Search and Care, N.Y.C., 1973-76, Project LEARN, Cleve., 1978-82; Friends of Project LEARN, 1986—; mem. Fedn. Community Planning, Cleve., Council on Older Persons, 1978-82, mem. Future Planning Task Force, 1980-81, Commn. on Social Concerns, 1982-84; trustee Golden Age Centers Greater Cleve., 1979—, women's council, 1978—, 1st v.p., 1980-81, pres., 1981-85, chmn. Western Res. Antiques Show, 1979, 80, chmn. devel. and pub. relations, 1987—; mem. women's com. Cleve. Inst. Arts, 1983—; mem. women's com. Cleve. Orch., 1979—, Vassar Coll., 1986—; bd. dirs. Cleve. Ballet, 1980—, exec. com., 1981, chmn. legis. advocacy com., 1981-83, sch. com., 1981-85, fin. com., 1982—, mem. ballet sch. com., 1985—; co-chmn. Yale Ball, 1983; bd. advisers Ret. Sr. Vol. Program, 1982, trustee, 1983—, mem. strategic planning com., 1986; mem. Family Friends Adv. Council, 1987—; trustee Fairmount Presbyn. Ch., 1985—; mem. long range planning com. United Way, Cleve., 1985—; chmn. Johns Hopkins Parents Fund, 1986-87. Named Vol. of Year, N.Y. Jr. League, 1975. Mem. Nat. Inst. Social Scis. (mem. memberships com. 1972—, trustee 1984—). Nat. Soc. of Colonial Dames, Western Res. Hist. Soc. (mem. women's advisory council 1977; corr. sec. 1978). Republican. Clubs: Colony (N.Y.C.); Chevy Chase (Washington); Intown, Vassar (sec. 1980-82, v.p. 1983, pres. 1984-86, coll. liaison com.), Jr. League Cleve., Kirtland (Cleve.), Tuxedo. Address: 2945 Fontenay Rd Shaker Heights OH 44120

DONNER, FRED MCGRAW, history educator; b. Washington, Sept. 30, 1945; s. George Robert and Myrtilla Herrick (McGraw) D.; m. Elvira Venables, Dec. 14, 1982. Cert. in Arab Studies, Middle East Centre for Arab Studies, Shimlan, Lebanon, 1967; AB, Princeton U., 1968; postgrad., U. Erlangen, Fed. Republic West Germany, 1970-71; PhD, Princeton U., 1975. Asst. prof. history Yale U., New Haven, Conn., 1975-81, assoc. prof. history, 1981-82; assoc. prof. near eastern languages and civilizations U. Chgo., 1982—. Author: The Early Islamic Conquests, 1981; contbr. articles to profl. jours. Served with U.S. Army, 1968-70. Woodrow Wilson scholar, 1968; fellow NEH., 1987—. Mem. Am. Oriental Soc., Middle East Studies Assn., Phi Beta Kappa. Office: U Chgo Oriental Inst 1155 E 58th St Chicago IL 60637

DONOGHUE, JOHN PETER, marketing executive; b. Winthrop, Mass., Oct. 3, 1939; s. John Francis and Althea (Hartley) D.; m. Juanita Isabella Sierra, Mar. 16, 1966; children: Daniel, Diane, Patrick. BSME, Tufts U., 1961. Various positions Fiatallis Construction Machinery, Carol Stream, Ill., 1961-80, gen. mgr. eastern div., 1980-82, dir. product mktg., 1982-85, dir. planning and devel., 1985-86, v.p. product support, 1986—. Bd. dirs. Chgo. Metro Hockey League, Northbrook, Ill., 1984—. Mem. Construction Industry Mfgrs. Assn. (mem. exec. com. Power Crane and Shovel Assn. bur. 1986—, chmn. 1986—), Barrington Hockey Club (pres. 1985-86, bd. dirs. 1984—), Barrington Quarterback Club (bd. dirs. 1983-86). Roman Catholic. Avocations: gardening, skiing. Home: 433 Signal Hill Rd Barrington IL 60010 Office: Fiat Allis N Am 245 E North Ave Carol Stream IL 60188

DONOHO, BURNETT WILLINGHAM, retail executive; b. Paducah, Ky., July 22, 1939; s. Glen B. and Estelle (Willingham) D.; m. Jane P. Kirkpatrick, Aug. 25, 1962; children—Ann, Burnett W., Kirk. B.A., Vanderbilt U., 1961; M.A., U. Ky., 1964. With Maas Bros., Tampa, Fla., 1964-74; sr. v.p. personnel Joske's, Dallas, 1975; pres. Gimbels, Milw., 1975-84; pres. Marshall Field's, Chgo., 1984—; dir. First Bank, Milw. Bd. dirs. Chgo. Conv. and Tourism Bur., 1985—, Chgo. Crime Commn., 1984; adv. bd. dirs. DePaul U., Chgo., 1984. Mem. Vanderbilt U. Alumni Assn. (bd. dirs. 1987—). Republican. Presbyterian. Office: Marshall Field & Co 111 N State St Chicago IL 60690

DONOHOO, DONOVAN L., accountant; b. Buford, Ohio, Dec. 23, 1936; s. Lawrence Earl and Mary Elizabeth (Remley) D.; m. Beverly Ann Thatcher, Mar. 8, 1958; children: Douglas, Donovan Jr., Dennison, Duane, Daren. BBA in Acctg., Cin. U., 1960. CPA, Ohio, Fla. Asst. treas., controller Am. Fin. Corp., Cin., 1962-66; treas. Thriftway Supermarkets,

Cin., 1962-66; ptnr. Storch, Donohoo & Storch, Cin., 1966-73; pres. D.L. Donohoo & Co., Batavia, Ohio, 1973—; v.p. Donohoo Computer Services, Batavia, 1984—. Deacon Ch. of Christ, Owensville, Ohio, 1960—; pres. Clermont Christian Assembly, Amelia, Ohio, 1973; bd. dirs. YMCA, Batavia, 1985. Fellow Ohio Soc. CPA's (v.p. Cin. 1982, sec. Cin. 1983, bd. dirs. 1985—); mem. Am. Inst CPA's., Fla. Inst. C.P.A.'s. Republican. Lodges: Rotary, Masons, Shriners (mem. clown unit 1961—, dir. 1980-84). Home: 4691 S Rt 132 Batavia OH 45103 Office: D L Donohoo & Co 247 Main St Batavia OH 45103-2978

DONOHUE, CARROLL JOHN, lawyer; b. St. Louis, June 24, 1917; s. Thomas M. and Florence (Klefisch) D.; m. Juanita Maire, Jan. 4, 1943 (div. July 1973); children: Patricia Carol Donohue Stevens, Christine Ann Donohue Smith, Deborah Lee Donohue Wilucki; m. Barbara Lounsbury, Dec. 1978. A.B., Washington U., 1939, LL.B. magna cum laude, 1939. Bar: Mo. 1939. Assoc. Hay & Flanagan, St. Louis, 1939-42; asso. Salkey & Jones, 1946-49; partner Husch, Eppenberger, Donohue, Cornfeld & Jenkins, St. Louis, 1949—. Author articles in field. Campaign chmn. ARC, St. Louis County, 1950; mem. adv. com. Child Welfare, St. Louis, 1952-55; exec. com. Slum Clearance, 1949, bond issue com., 1955; bond issue com. St. Louis County Bond Issue, screening and supervisory coms., 1955-61, county citizen's com. for better law enforcement, 1953-56, chmn. com. on immigration policy, 1954-56, Mayor, Olivette, Mo., 1953-56; chmn. Bd. Election Commrs., St. Louis County, 1960-65; chmn. com. Non-Partisan Ct. Plan; vice-chmn. bd. Regional Commerce and Growth Assn.; bd. dirs. Downtown St. Louis, Inc., Civic Entrepreneurs Orgn. Served to lt. USNR, 1942-45. Decorated Bronze Star medal, Navy and M.C. medal. Mem. Mo. Bar Assn. (past mem. bd. govs., chmn. annual meeting, editor jour. 1940-41), ABA, St. Louis Bar Assn. (past pres., v.p., treas.), Order of Coif, Omicron Delta Kappa, Sigma Phi Epsilon, Delta Theta Phi. Club: Mo. Athletic. Address: 100 N Broadway Saint Louis MO 63102

DONOHUE, TERENCE, research chemist; b. Altadena, Calif., Oct. 15, 1946; s. Jerry and Patricia Ann (Schreier) D.; m. Ann E. O'Hara, Aug. 3, 1974; 1 child, Carolyn. BS in Chemistry, UCLA, 1968; PhD, Cornell U., 1973. Teaching research asst. then postdoctoral research assoc. Cornell U., 1968-75; research chemist Naval Research Lab., Washington, 1975-85; from staff research chemist to supr. photon processes group Amoco Research Ctr., Naperville, Ill., 1985—; lectr. U. Md., U. Lausanne (Switzerland), U. Va., U. Pa., Los Alamos Labs.; session chmn. profl. confs. Contbr. articles to profl. jours., chpts. to books; patentee in laser elemental separation, noble gas purification. Fellow NSF, summers, 1966, 67. Mem. Inter-Am. Photochem. Soc., Am. Chem. Soc., Musical Heritage Soc., ACLU, Sigma Xi. Club: BMW Car of Am. Home: 27 W 771 Washington Ave Winfield IL 60190 Office: Amoco Research Ctr Naperville IL 60566

DONOIAN, HARRY AVEDIS, labor union administrator, economist; b. N.Y.C., Feb. 17, 1935; s. Harry and Helen (Pilibosian) D.; m. Patricia DiCio, Sept. 3, 1963 (div. Dec. 1978); children: David, Michael; m. Elizabeth E. Stephens, June 30, 1979. BS, NYU, 1961; MA, Cath. U., 1968. Economist Bur. Labor Statistics, Dept. Labor, N.Y.C., 1961-63, Washington, 1963-68; asst. dir. edn. Am. Fedn. Govt. Employees, Washington, 1968-72; research dir. Allied Indsl. Workers Am., Milw., 1972-76; assoc. dir. dist. council 48 Am. Fedn. State, County, Mcpl. Employees, Milw., 1976-77; exec. dir. Allied Indsl. Workers Reg. H&W Fund, Brookfield, Wis., 1977—. Author: The Government Employees' Council, 1968; also articles. Served as cpl. U.S. Army, 1953-56. Mem. Indsl. Relations Research Assn. (adv. bd. 1972-76). Mem. Armenian Apostolic Ch. Avocation: soccer referee. Home: 1633 N Prospect Ave 14-D Milwaukee WI 53202 Office: AIW Reg H&W Fund 3540 D N 126th St Brookfield WI 53005

DONOVAN, FRANK WILLIAM, lawyer; b. Washington, Sept. 12, 1905; s. Frank Dennis and Catherine (Connor) D.; m. Helen Turner, June 25, 1938 (div. May 1947); children: Frank William, Julia Donovan Darlow, Russell Hodges; m. Elizabeth Chetwoode Hodges, June 19, 1947 (dec. Nov., 1968); m. Ana Maria Fuentes-Munizaga, Dec. 8, 1969. A.B., Notre Dame U., 1926; JD, Harvard U., 1929. Bar: Mich. 1930. Ptnr. Yerkes, Goddard & McClintock, Detroit, 1932-38; sole practice Detroit, 1938-41; ptnr. Fulton & Donovan, Detroit, 1941-50, McClintock, Fulton, Donovan & Waterman, 1950-73, McClintock, Donovan, Carson & Roach, 1973-80, Donovan, Hammond, Carson, Ziegelman, Roach & Sotiroff, 1980-81, Donovan, Hammond, Ziegelman, Roach & Sotiroff, 1981-86; of counsel Pepper, Hamilton & Scheetz, 1986—; bd. dirs. Zenith Labs, Inc., Northvale, N.J., Ryerson & Haynes, Inc., Jackson. Chmn. Italian Flood Relief Com., Detroit, 1966; chmn. Grosse Pointe War Meml. Assn., 1966-69; chmn. bd. Detroit Grand Opera Assn., Detroit Symphony Orch., Etruscan Found., Mich. Opera Theatre, David T. Chase Found.; mem. senate Stratford Shakespearean Fest. Found., Can.; mem. Met. Opera Assn. N.Y.; trustee Shakespearean Drama Festival Found., Inc., N.Y.C.; bd. govs. Am. Mental Health Found. Recipient award merit Am. C. of C. for Italy, 1967, citation appreciation Greater Mich. Found., 1963; Frank W. Donovan Day in recognition cultural contbns. City of Detroit, 1963. Clubs: Detroit (Detroit), Country of Detroit (Detroit), Renaissance (Detroit); Grosse Pointe (Mich.); La Coquille (Palm Beach, Fla.). Home: 8 Donovan Pl Grosse Pointe MI 48230 Office: 100 Renaissance Center Suite 3600 Detroit MI 48243-1157

DONOVAN, JAMES JOSEPH, III, accountant; b. St. Louis, Jan. 16, 1954; s. James Joseph Jr. and Margaret Joyce (Laub) D.; m. Carrie Davis, Sept. 29, 1978; children: James Joseph IV, Katie Eileen. BS, U. Notre Dame, 1976; B in Gen. Studies, U. Mo., St. Louis, 1978. CPA, Mo. Staff acct. Stone, Carlie & Co., Clayton, Mo., 1978-79; tax mgr. Rubin, Brown, Gornstein & Co., Clayton, 1979—. Contbr. articles to profl. jours. Mem. Am. Inst. CPA's, Mo. Soc. CPA's (taxation com.), Beta Alpha Psi. Roman Catholic. Club: Notre Dame (dir. St. Louis chpt. 1985—, treas. St. Louis chpt. 1986). Avocation: woodworking. Home: 15872 Cedarmill Dr Chesterfield MO 63017 Office: Rubin Brown Gornstein & Co 230 S Bemiston Clayton MO 63105

DONOVAN, JAMES ROBERT, business equipment company executive; b. Wichita, Kans., Apr. 11, 1932; s. Karl Genevay and Louise (Silcott) D.; A.B., Harvard U., 1954, M.B.A., 1956; m. Ottilie Schreiber, July 2, 1955; children—Amy Louise, Robert Silcott; m. Margaret Jones Esty, Oct. 31, 1981. Mgr. sales adminstrn., market research Hickok, Inc., Rochester, N.Y., 1956-59, regional sales mgr., 1959-62, asst. nat. sales mgr., 1963-65; group program mgr. Xerox Corp., Stamford, Conn., 1965-68, mktg. mgr. spl. products, 1968-70, mgr. copier products, 1970-72, dir. corp. pricing and competitive activity, 1972-78, dir. corp. mktg. strategy and planning, 1978-83; sr. v.p. corp. mktg. McDonnell Douglas Automation Co., St. Louis, 1983-84; v.p. mktg., planning Info. Systems Group, McDonnell Douglas Corp., St. Louis, 1984—. Vice pres. Family Service, Rochester, 1971-72; dir. Family and Children's Services, Stamford, 1972-79; dir. Rochester Sales Execs. Club, 1966-71; mem. mktg. adv. bd. Columbia U. Bus. Sch., 1978-86; v.p. United Way of New Canaan, 1982-83; bd. dirs. Family Service Am., 1986—. Mem. Harvard Alumni Assn. (dir. 1978-83), Harvard Bus. Sch. Alumni Assn. (exec. council 1982-85). Clubs: Harvard (pres. Rochester 1971-72, pres. Fairfield County 1976-78, pres. St. Louis 1986-87), Harvard Bus. Sch. (pres. Rochester 1972, chmn. Westchester/Fairfield 1973-74, sec. St. Louis 1986-87); Old Warson Country (St. Louis); Woodway Country (Darien, Conn.). Home: 9834 Old Warson Rd Saint Louis MO 63124 Office: McDonnell Douglas Corp Saint Louis MO 63166

DONOVAN, JOHN, lawyer; b. Toledo, Dec. 31, 1957; s. James and Louise (Zbylot) D.; m. Mary Francis Jakary, Feb. 29, 1984; children: Alanna, Damien. AB with high honors and distinction, U. Mich., 1980; JD, Case Western Res. U., 1983. Bar: Ohio 1983, U.S. Dist. Ct. (no. dist.) Ohio 1983. Law clk. Nat. Aeros. and Space Adminstrn., Cleve., 1982; ptnr. Meekison & Donovan, Napoleon, Ohio, 1983—. Editor Case Western Res. Law Rev., 1982-83. Pres. Am. Heart Assn., Henry County, Ohio br., 1984—. Mem. ABA, Henry County Bar Assn., Assn. Trial Lawyers Am., Ohio Trial Lawyers Assn. Democrat. Avocations: guitar, model rocketry. Home: 315 1/2 W Washington Napoleon OH 43545 Office: Meekison & Donovan 609 N Perry Napoleon OH 43545

DONOVAN, PAUL V., bishop; b. Bernard, Iowa, Sept. 1, 1924; s. John J. and Loretta (Carew) D. Student, St. Joseph Sem., Grand Rapids, Mich.; B.A., St. Gregory Sem., Cin., 1946; postgrad., Mt. St. Mary Sem. of West, Cin.; J.C.L., Pontifical Lateran U., Rome, 1957. Ordained priest Roman Catholic Ch., 1950; asst. pastor St. Mary Ch., Jackson, Mich., 1950-51; sec. to bishop of Lansing Mich.; and adminstr. St. Peter Ch., Eaton Rapids, Mich., 1951-55; sec. to bishop 1957-59; pastor Our Lady of Fatima Ch., Michigan Center, Mich.; and St. Rita Mission, Clark Lake, Mich., 1959-68; pastor St. Agnes Ch., Flint, Mich., 1968-71; bishop of Kalamazoo 1971—; mem. liturgical commn. Diocese of Lansing, chmn., 1963; mem. Cath. Bd. Edn., Jackson and Hillsdale counties; mem. bishop's personnel com., priests' senate. Bd. dirs. Family Services and, Mich. Children's Aid. Office: Chancery Office 215 N Westnedge Ave PO Box 949 Kalamazoo MI 49005 *

DONOVAN, THOMAS PATRICK, accountant; b. South Bend, Ind., Oct. 23, 1935; s. Frank J. and Louise S. (Sattler) D.; m. Donna Duffield, Feb. 16, 1965 (div. May 1984); 1 child, George; m. Carolyn Coleman, Jan. 17, 1986. BBA, U. Miami, Fla., 1958. CPA, Mich. Acct. Alexander Grant & Co., Kalamazoo, 1967-70; treas. Grelac Industries, Inc., Kalamazoo, 1970-77; ptnr. Clawson & Donovan, P.C., Kalamazoo, 1977-81; sole practice acctg. Kalamazoo, 1981-86; pres. Donovan & Poindexter, P.C., Kalamazoo, 1986—. Mem. St. Augustine Fin. Com., Kalamazoo, 1965-86, St. Augustine Sch. Bd., Kalamazoo, 1979-81, pres., 1980; mem. Barbour Hall Found., Kalamazoo, 1967-77, pres., 1974; mem. Hackett Athletic Boosters, Kalamazoo, 1976-78, pres., 1977. Mem. Am. Inst. CPA's, Mich. Inst. CPA's. Roman Catholic. Lodges: Rotary, Elks. Home: 2377 Strathmore Kalamazoo MI 49007 Office: Donovan & Poindexter PC 229 E Michigan #340 Kalamazoo MI 49007

DONOVAN, TRACY W., electronics company executive; b. 1941. BS, Stanford U., 1963. With Commonwealth Edison Co., Lincoln, Nebr., 1963—; elec. estimator 1963-65, dir. Cooper Nuclear Sta., 1965-73, mgr. constrn. ops., 1973-77, sr. v.p., 1977-82, pres., chief exec. officer, dir., 1982—. Office: Commonwealth Electric Co 1901 Y St Lincoln NE 68503 *

DOODY, DANIEL JOHN, publishing executive; b. Oak Park, Ill., July 4, 1952; s. Francis Arthur and Mary Lois Jeanne (Squibbs) D.; m. Carol Armbrust, May 30, 1976; children: Adam, Rachel, Sara. BA summa cum laude, U. Notre Dame, 1974; MS in Journalism, Northwestern U., 1977. Aquisitions editor, asst. to chmn. bd. Marcel Dekker, Inc., N.Y.C., 1977-79; med. editor Yr. Book Med. Pub., Inc., Chgo., 1979-82, exec. editor, 1982-83, v.p. editorial, 1983-87, sr. v.p., gen. mgr., 1987—; bd. dirs. Wolfe Pub., Ltd., London, 1987—. Bd. dirs. Cana Conf. Chgo., 1982-86, Family Ministries of Chgo. Archdiocese, 1986—. Mem. Am. Med. Pub. Assn., Assn. Am. Pub. Sci. Tech. Medicine Pub. Roman Catholic. Avocations: racquetball, tennis. Office: Yr Book Med Pub Inc 35 E Wacker Dr Chicago IL 60601

DOOLEY, EDNA MELLICK, hospital pharmacy director; b. Albia, Iowa, Feb. 25, 1927; d. George and Anna (Zezok) Mellick; m. John W. Dooley, Aug. 13, 1949 (div.); children—Patrick, Michael, Terrance, Ellen, Jane, James. B.S. in Pharmacy, U. Iowa, 1949. Registered pharmacist. Pharmacist Mercy Hosp., Iowa City, 1949-51; Cleve. Clinic, 1951-53 Gilmour Danielson Co., Lincoln, Nebr., 1954-61; dir. pharmacy Oakdale Sanatorium, Iowa, 1961-66; asst. dir. Mercy Hosp., Iowa City, 1966-74, Illini Hosp., Silvis, Ill., 1974-79; dir. Mason Dist. Hosp., Havana, Ill., 1979—; dir. Home Health Services, Havana, 1978-85. Recipient Pharmacist of Yr., Hosp. Pharmacy Inst., 1981. Mem. Am. Soc. Hosp. Pharmacists, Ill. Council Hosp. Pharmacists, Am. Soc. Enteral and Parental Nutrition, Bus. Profl. Women Assn. (v.p. 1986-87), Sugar Creek Soc. Ill. Council Hosp. Pharmacists (past pres.), Miss. Valley Ill. Council Hosp. Pharmacists (past pres.), Pilot Club. Democrat. Roman Catholic. Avocations: jogging; needle arts; gardening. Home: Route 1 Havana IL 62644 Office: Mason Dist Hosp 520 E Franklin St Havana IL 62644

DOOLEY, J. GORDON, food scientist; b. Nevada, Mo., Nov. 15, 1935; s. Howard Eugene and Wilma June (Vanderford) D.; B.S. with honors in Biology, Drury Coll., Springfield, Mo., 1958; postgrad. (NSF grantee) U. Mo., Rolla, 1961, (NSF grantee) Kirksville (Mo.) State Coll., 1959; M.S. in Biology (NSF grantee), Brown U., 1966; postgrad. bus. mgmt. Alexander Hamilton Inst., 1973-75, No. Ill. U., 1964. Tchr. sci. Morton West High Sch., Berwyn, Ill., 1963-64; dairy technologist Borden Co., Elgin, Ill., 1964-65; project leader Cheese Products Lab., Kraft Corp., Glenview, Ill., 1965-73; sr. food scientist Wallerstein Co. div. Travenol Labs., Inc., Morton Grove, Ill., 1973-77; mgr. food sci. GB Fermentation Industries, Inc., Des Plaines, Ill., 1977-79, mgr. product devel., 1979-82; group leader Food Ingredients div. Stauffer Chem. Co., Clawson, Mich., 1982-84; sr. research scientist Schreiber Foods, Inc., Green Bay, Wis., 1984-87, Ridgeview, LaCrosse, Wis., 1987—; sci. lectr. seminars, Mexico, 1975; assoc. mem. Ad Hoc Enzyme Tech. Com., 1978—; dairy research adv. bd. Utah State U. Recipient Spoke award Nevada (Mo.) Jr. C. of C., 1960. Mem. Am. Dairy Sci. Assn., Inst. Food Technologists, Am. Chem. Soc., Cousteau Soc., Am. Inst. Biol. Scis., Nat. Sci. Tchrs. Assn., Whey Products Inst., Beta Beta Beta, Phi Eta Sigma. Republican. Presbyterian. Clubs: Toastmasters Internat. (pres. Baxter Labs. club 1976-77); Brown U. (Chgo.). Patentee in food and enzyme tech. field; contbr. sci. articles to profl. jours. Home: 723 Pleasant Ct Onalaska WI 54602 Office: Ridgeview 2340 Enterprise Ave LaCrosse WI 54602

DOOLEY, THOMAS WALTER, management consultant; b. Covington, Ky., June 28, 1932; s. Thomas Christian and Clara Eleanor (Smith) D.; m. Loraine Rita Rehkamp, June 17, 1955; children—Mary Alyce, Michael Patrick, Martin George, Matthew Walter. A.B., Thomas More Coll., 1952; M.A., U. Toronto, 1954; M.B.A., Xavier U., 1962. Exec. v.p. Gallery of Homes Inc., Elmhurst, Ill., 1970-76; pres. The Real Estate Place, Dublin, Calif., Islin, N.J., 1976, TWD & Assocs., Arlington Heights, Ill., 1976—; dir. grad. studies Lewis U., 1982—; dir. ETA Engrg., Westmont, Ill., The Personal Mktg., Inc., Inc., Houston. Author: Survival Among the Giants, 1980. Contbr. chpts. to books, articles to mags. and profl. jours. Chmn. Civil Service Commn., City of Covinoton, Ky., 1960-62, mayor pro tem, 1962-69; library trustee Arlington Heights, 1973-82. Served with U.S. Army, 1954-56. Recipient Dir. of Yr. award SBA, 1982. Mem. Real Estate Educators, ASTD, Am. Soc. Assn. Execs. (cert.), Delta Sigma Phi, Omega Tau Rho. Roman Catholic. Home and Office: 431 S Patton Ave Arlington Heights IL 60005

DOOLING, JAMES TERRENCE, accountant; b. Alton, Ill., Nov. 2, 1944; s. David Henry and Elizabeth (Fitzgerald) D.; m. Marilyn Jean Manns, June 13, 1970 (dec. Mar. 1975); 1 child, David; m. Noncy Ellen Jensen, Dec. 27, 1980; children: Megan, Bryan. BS, St. Benedict's Coll., 1966; MBA, U. Ill., 1972. CPA, Ill., Mo. Staff acct. Haskins & Sells, CPA, St. Louis, 1972-77; ptnr. C.J. Schlosser & Co., CPA, Alton and St. Louis, 1977—. Trustee St. Anthony's Hosp., Alton, 1978—; mem. adv. bd. Marian Heights Retirement Apts., Alton, 1982—; treas. bd. dirs. Madison County Mental Health Ctr., Alton, 1980-84, pres. bd. dirs., 1984-85. Served with USN, 1966-70. Mem. Am. Inst. CPA's, Ill. Soc. CPA's, Mo. Soc. CPA's, Health Care Fin. Mgmt. Assn., Mo. Health Care Assn. Roman Catholic. Club: Lockhaven Country (Godfrey, Ill.) (treas. 1987). Lodge: Rotary (treas., sec., v.p., pres. Alton-Godfrey club 1981-84). Avocations: golf, reading, gardening. Home: 3302 Whiteclif Ln Godfrey IL 62035 Office: C J Schlosser & Co CPA 233 E Center Dr Alton IL 62002

DOONER, EDWARD THOMAS, accountant; b. Garfield Heights, Ohio, Sept. 18, 1950; s. Edward T. and Dorothy E. (Frankhauser) D. BS in Bus. Adminstrn., Ohio State U., 1973. Coordinator div. advanced mgmt. systems Gen. Electric Co., Independence, Ohio, 1973-75; staff acct. J.J. Frankhauser Co., Bedford, Ohio, 1976-79; acct. A. Schulman, Inc., Akron, Ohio, 1980—. Fin. advisor Jr. Achievement, Akron, 1986. Mem. Am. Inst. CPA's, Ohio Soc. CPA's, Sierra Club, Beta Gamma Sigma. Club: Suburban Ski (Cleve.). Avocations: aviation, scuba diving, golf, tennis. Home: 945 Shepard Hills Blvd Macedonia OH 44056 Office: A Schulman Inc 3550 W Market St Akron OH 44313

DORAIS, GERALDINE, postmaster; b. Detroit, Apr. 21, 1937; d. Stephen Frank and Ethel (Jozsa) Smolnik; m. William Edward Dorais, Jan. 20, 1956 (div. Oct. 1964); children: Stephen, William, Charles. Grad. high sch., Dearborn, Mich. Postal clk. U.S. P.O., Dearborn, 1965-71, supr., 1971-79; postmaster U.S. P.O., Dundee, Mich., 1979-84, South Lyon, Mich., 1984—; cert. postmaster trainer U.S. P.O., Detroit, 1982—. Pres. Dundee Women's Civic Assn., 1984-85. Mem. Nat. Assn. Postmasters of U.S. (bd. dirs. Wayne County br. 1980-84, v.p. 1980-81), Nat. League Postmasters, South Lyon C. of C., Dundee Bus. and Profl. People (v.p. 1983-84). Democrat. Roman Catholic. Avocations: gardening, traveling. Home: 22313 Brookfield Dr South Lyon MI 48178 Office: US Postal Service 350 S Lafayette South Lyon MI 48178-9998

DOREN, DENNIS MITCHELL, psychologist; b. Buffalo, Sept. 9, 1953; s. Louis Sanford and Sylvia (Kaminker) D.; m. Susan B. McDonald, June 18, 1983. BA magna cum laude, SUNY, Buffalo, 1975; MA, Bucknell U., 1978; PhD, Fla. State U., 1983. Lic. psychologist, Wis. Psychology intern VA Med. Ctr., Dallas, 1982-83; chief maximum security treatment unit Mendota Mental Health Inst., Madison, Wis., 1983—; psychology intern supr. Mendota Mental Health Inst., 1984—. Author: Understanding and Treating the Psychopath, 1987; contbr. articles to profl. jours. Mem. Am. Psychol. Assn., Internat. Differential Treatment Assn. (hon.), Psi Chi, U.S. Chess Fedn. (bd. dirs. New Windsor, N.Y. 1973, life). Avocations: correspondence chess, photography, racquetball, swimming, tennis. Office: Mendota Mental Health Inst 301 Troy Dr Madison WI 53704

DORFMAN, HENRY S., meat products company executive; b. 1922; married. With Sausage Mfg. Bus., 1944-49, Gen. Machines Co., 1949-50, Hudson Motor Car Co., 1950-51, B.M. Shindler Meats Co., 1951-52; chmn. bd., pres., chief exec. officer Thorn Apple Valley, Inc., Southfield, Mich., 1952—. Office: Thorn Apple Valley Inc 18700 W Ten Mile Rd Southfield MI 48075 *

DORGAN, BYRON LESLIE, congressman; b. Dickinson, N.D., May 14, 1942; s. Emmett P. and Dorothy (Bach) D.; children: Scott, Shelly. BBA, U. N.D., 1965; MBA, U. Denver, 1966. Exec. devel. trainee Martin Marietta Corp., Denver, 1966-67; dep. tax commr., then tax commnr. State of N.D., 1967-80; mem. 97th-100th Congresses from N.D., mem. ways and means com.; instr. econs. Bismarck (N.D.) Jr. Coll., 1969-71; chmn. Multistate Tax Commn., 1972-74, Gov. N.D. Commn. Air Transp., 1973. Contbr. articles to profl. jours. Recipient Nat. Leadership award Office Gov. N.D., 1972. Mem. Nat. Assn. Tax Adminstrs. (exec. com. 1972-75). Office: 238 Cannon House Office Bldg Washington DC 20515

DORIAN, NANCY MARILYN, psychologist; b. Shaker Heights, Ohio, May 27, 1933; d. Alex and Elsa (Guttman) Frank; m. Alex Dorian, Aug. 6, 1960 (div. Sept. 1961); 1 child, Andrea McIlwaine. AB, U. Chgo., 1954; MA, Case Western Res. U., 1966. Lic. psychologist, Ohio. Psychologist Euclid (Ohio) Pub. Schs., 1965-74; office mgr. Realtek Industries, Cleve., 1974-77; psychologist Vocat. Guidance and Rehab. Services, Cleve., 1977-79; coordinator psychol. services Townhall II-Drug Edn. and Crisis Intervention Ctr., Kent, Ohio, 1979-81; chief psychologist Trumbull County (Ohio) Children's Services Bd., Warren, 1982—. Bd. dirs. Ohio Dist. XI Forensic Bd., Youngstown, 1985—. Recipient Commendation Ohio Bd. Edn., 1972. Mem. Am. Psychol. Assn. (assoc.). Democrat. Jewish. Clubs: Sugarbush Kennel (Chardon, Ohio) (sec. 1980-82), German Wirehaired Pointer of Am. Avocation: breeding show dogs. Home: 15481 Riddle Ln Chagrin Falls OH 44022 Office: Trumbull County Children Services 2282 Reeves Rd NE Warren OH 44483

DORL-ADAMS, DONNA MARIE, college adminstrator; b. Chgo., May 27, 1948; d. Edward Nicholas and Lorraine Josephine (Kranich) Dorl; m. Thomas O. Adams, May 10, 1986. BS in Chemistry, U. Wis., Eau Claire, 1970; MS in Ednl. Adminstrn., SUNY, Albany, 1975. Activities asst. U. Wis., Eau Claire, 1970-73; dir. student activities Rensselaer Poly. Inst., Troy, N.Y., 1973-78; asst. dean students Loyola U., Chgo., 1978-83, tng. mgr., 1983-85, info. ctr. analyst, 1985—, instr. guidance and counseling, 1979-81, instr. math, 1986; seminar leader nursing staff devel. Foster McGaw Hosp., Maywood, Ill., 1987. Mem. Art Inst. Chgo. Grantee Loyola Mellon Found., 1981-82. Mem. Assn. for Computing Machinery, Chgo. Area Microcomputer Profls., Midwest DISOSS Users Group (steering com.), NOW. Democratic. Methodist. Avocations: reading, sewing, gardening. Office: Loyola Univ of Chgo 820 N Michigan Ave Chicago IL 60611

DORMAN, DAVID KENT, physician; b. Milw., Dec. 1, 1942; s. Clifford Warren and Lassie (Beese) D.; m. Donna Lynn Graff, Nov. 16, 1974; 1 dau., Natalie Lynn. B.S., Marquette U., 1964; M.D., Med. Coll. Wis., 1968. Diplomate Am. Bd. Plastic Surgery. Intern Kern County Gen. Hosp., Bakersfield, Calif., 1968-69; resident in gen. surgery Med. Coll. Wis., Hosp., Milw., 1969-75; resident in plastic surgery U. Tex., Galveston, 1975-78; practice medicine specializing in plastic and reconstructive surgery, Milw., 1978—; mem. staffs Elm Brook Meml. Hosp., Brookfield, Community Meml. Hosp., Menomonee Falls. Served to maj. M.C., U.S. Army, 1970-72. Fellow ACS; mem. AMA, Am. Soc. Plastic and Reconstructive Surgery, Am. Assn. Hand Surgery. Avocations: HO model railroading; weather forecasting; stamp collecting. Home: 3200 Jerri Ct Milwaukee WI 53005 Office: 2323 N Mayfair Rd Suite 503 Milwaukee WI 53226

DORN, EDWARD HARVEY, design engineer, illustrator; b. Youngstown, Ohio, May 20, 1952; s. James D. and Muriel S. (Hooper) D.; m. Elaine J. Beaulieu, Jan. 21, 1984; children—Timothy Edward Beaulieu-Dorn, Rachel Elaine Beaulieu-Dorn. B.F.A., Roger Williams Coll., 1979, B.A. in Psychology, 1980, A.S. in Engring. Tech., 1980; M.F.A. candidate in design Southeastern Mass. U., 1984. Design engr. Dorn Designs, Fall River, Mass., 1977—, Behavior Research Inst., Providence, R.I., 1981-82; dir. research and devel. Boardman Stress & Research Ctr., 1984-85; design cons. Equiptect Inc., Canfield, Ohio, 1985; art therapist Crystal Springs Sch., Assonet, Mass., 1980-81; cons. UNICEF, Air Nat. Guard, others. Author: The Eighth Decade, 1980. Editor Nemesis Art Mag., 1977-81. Inventor solar desalinator, 1977. Mem. adv. com. for disabled R.I. State Council on Arts, 1982-83; spl. constable Fall River Police, 1983-84. Served with USN, 1971-73. Recipient numerous art-related awards. Mem. August Derleth Soc., Vols. in Tech. Assistance, Roger Wiliams Coll. Honor Soc. (alumni rep. 1979—).

DORN, RAYMOND EDWARD, publications designer; b. St. Charles, Ill., Aug. 17, 1921; s. August and Ann Sophia (Lukesh) D.; m. Vera Ernestine Hogan, Nov. 20, 1948; children—Michael David, Tamara Jane. Worked in all phases of pub., 1946-76; pres. Dorn Workshops (design studio), Lombard, Ill., 1976—; instr. publ. design Printing Industries Inst. Ill. Served with 13th Airborne, U.S. Army, 1942-45. Decorated Am. Campaign, Good Conduct, Victory medals. Mem. Am. Soc. Bus. Press Editors. Lutheran. Author: How to Design and Improve Magazine Layouts, 1974, 3d edit., 1983; 20/20-Problems and Solutions, 1980; Tabloid Design for the Organizational Press, 1983; designer Universal Layout Sheet for mags. and tabloids, 1983; How to be your own Artist, 1985; contbr. articles on publ. design to profl. jours. Home and Office: 1013 S Ahrens Ave Lombard IL 60148

DORNER, DOUGLAS BLOOM, vascular surgeon, educator; b. Iowa City, Iowa, Aug. 4, 1941; s. Ralph A. and Gene (Bloom) D.; married, 1970; children: Gillian Austin, Hillary Howell. BA magna cum laude, Amherst Coll., 1963; MD cum laude, Harvard U., 1967. Diplomate Am. Bd. Surgery, Am. Bd. Gen. Vascular Surgery, Nat. Bd. Med. Examiners. Physician intern in surgery U. Calif., San Francisco, 1967-68, asst. resident in surgery, 1968-70, sr. resident, 1971-72, chief resident, 1972-73; surg. registrar St. James' Hosp., London, 1970-71; practice medicine specializing in vascular surgery Des Moines, 1974—; chief surgery Broadlawns-Polk County Hosp., Des Moines, 1977-78; co-dir. peripheral vascular lab. Iowa Meth. Med. Ctr., Des Moines, 1977—, chief surgery, 1980-81; co-dir. peripheral vascular lab. Iowa Luth. Hosp., Des Moines, 1980—; instr. surgery U. Iowa, Iowa City, 1973, clin. asst. prof., 1981—; vis. prof. Gunderson Clinic, La Crosse, Wis., 1984, St. James' Hosp., London, 1985, Dublin, Ireland, 1987; cons. VA Med. Hosp., Des Moines, 1980—. Contbr. numerous articles to profl. and scholarly jours. Served to capt. USAR, 1967-77. Nat. Merit scholar, 1959. Fellow ACS (Iowa chpt. scholarship award com., credentials com., chmn. Iowa com. on applicants 1976—); mem. AMA, Naffziger Surg. Soc., Polk County Med. Soc. (councillor 1979-81, trustee 1981-83, pres.-elect 1983, pres. 1984), Iowa Med. Soc. (chmn. program com. sci. session 1982), Am. Trauma Soc., Iowa Acad. Surgery (program chmn. 1981, resident paper award com.), Midwest Surg. Assn. (councillor 1983-85, sec. 1985—), Internat. Soc. for Cardiovascular Surgery, Midwestern Vascular Surg. Soc. (membership com.), Soc. Non-Invasive Vascular Tech., Western Surg. Assn., Peripheral Vascular Surg. Soc., Med. Library Club Des Moines, Phi Beta Kappa, Sigma Xi. Republican. Lutheran. Clubs: Des Moines, Wakonda. Avocations: tennis, travel. Home: 5220 Waterbury Rd Des Moines IA 50312 Office: 1215 Pleasant St Suite 616 Des Moines IA 50312

DOROSCHAK, JOHN Z., dentist; b. Solochiw, Ukraine, Feb. 11, 1928; s. William and Anna (Stroczan) D.; came to U.S., 1950, naturalized, 1954; student U. Minn., 1955-57, B.S., 1959, D.D.S., 1961; m. Nadia Zahorodny, June 30, 1962; children—Andrew, Michael, Natalie, Maria. Pvt. practice dentistry, Mpls., 1961—. Cons., St. Joseph's Home for Aged, Mpls., 1974-77, Holy Family Residence, St. Paul, 1977-84. Mem. steering com. St. Anthony West Neighborhood, Mpls., 1971-72; chmn. Mpls. dentists com. Little Sisters of the Poor Devel. Program, 1975; Webelos leader troop 50, Boy Scouts Am., 1975-76; pres. N.E. Regional Sch. Assn. Parents and Tchrs., 1978-79; bd. dirs. East Side Neighborhood Service, 1972; treas. Plast Inc., Ukrainian youth orgn., Mpls., 1979-83; mem. Sr. Citizen Centers Health Adv. Com., Mpls., 1979-83. Served with AUS, 1953-55. Mem. Am. Dental Assn., Minn. Dental Assn. (com. on dental care access 1980-83), Minn. Soc. Preventive Dentistry (dir. 1977-83, treas. 1979-83), Am. Soc. Dentistry for Children, Mpls. Dist. Dental Soc. (nursing home com. 1974—, chmn. 1979-82, 84—, emergency care com. 1983-84), Ukrainian Med. Assn. (sec.-treas. Minn. chpt. 1971-75), Ukrainian Profl. Club, Psi Omega. Mem. Ukrainian Catholic Ch. (campaign chmn. 1966-80, mem. ch. com. 1965—). Club: University Minnesota Alumni (charter mem.). Home: 919 Main St NE Minneapolis MN 55413 Office: Broadway and University Profl Bldg 230 NE Broadway Minneapolis MN 55413

DORR, ROBERT WILLIAM, osteopathic physician; b. Detroit, May 30, 1952; s. William Curtis and Laurel Jean (Thompson) D.; m. Deborah Jean Boyce, May 30, 1980. B.A., Albion Coll., 1974; D.O., Mich. State U., 1977. Cert. aviation med. examiner. Intern, Southeastern Med. Ctr., North Miami Beach, Fla., 1978; gen. practice osteo. medicine Jackson (Mich.) Northwest Clinic, P.C., 1978-86, Jackson Family Med. Care Clinic, P.C., 1986—; med. dir. Medistation Jackson P.C., 1982—; chmn. credentials com. Jackson Osteo. Hosp. Bd. dirs. Jackson YMCA; bd. advs. Jackson County chpt. MADD (Mothers Against Drunk Driving). Mem. Southcentral Osteo. Assn., Mich. Osteo. Assn. Physicians and Surgeons, Am. Osteo. Assn., Flying Physicians Assn., Am. Coll. Sports Medicine, Civil Aviation Med. Assn., So. Med. Assn., Jackson County Med. Soc., Am. Coll. Gen. Practicioners in Osteo. Medicine and Surgery, Osteo. Gen. Practitioners Mich., AMA. Home: 1786 Lochmoor Blvd Jackson MI 49201 Office: Professional Centre E 900 E Michigan Ave Jackson MI 49201

DORRIS, ALBERT FRANCIS, executive; b. Utica, N.Y., Oct. 25, 1936; s. J.A. Francis and Hope Frances (Earl) D.; m. Nancy Ann Dunston, June 9, 1962; children: Jacqueline Kay, Kelly Elizabeth, Alexandra Jane. BS, U. S. Mil. Acad., West Point, N.Y., 1959; MS in Civil Engring., U. Ill., Urbana, 1963, PhD in Civil Engring., 1965; cert. advanced mgmt., Emory U., 1978; MS in Adminstrn., George Washington U., 1980. Registered profl. engr., Minn., N.Y. Commd. 2d lt. U.S. Army, 1959, advanced through grades to col.; mgr. internat. program Dept. of Army, London, 1972-74; gen. mgr. Constrn. Commd., Fed. Republic Germany, 1974-76; mgr. strategic planning research devel. and adminstrn. The Pentagon, Washington, 1977-79; mng. dir. Mobility Equipment Research and Devel. CM U.S. Army, Ft. Belvoir, Va., 1979-81; ret. U.S. Army, Mpls., 1981; exec. v.p., gen. mgr. Proform, Inc., Mpls., 1981-84; pres. Xerkon Inc., Mpls., 1984—, IcnyTex Inc., Mpls., 1987—; shelter analyst Fed. Emergency Mgmt. Agy., 1965-86. Author: Response Horizontally Oriented Buried Cylinders, 1965, Response Prototype Communications Conduct, 1965; co-author: The Elastic Response of Buried Cylinders, 1965; Editor Material Selection Design and Tooling for Structural Plastics, 1984. Fund raiser Ind. Rep. Party, Edina, 1981-86. Decorated Legion of Merit; Disting. Alumni award Utica Free Acad., 1977. Mem. ASCE (lectr. various confs.1983-86, chmn. com. on structural Plastics 1983-86), Soc. Plastic Engrs., Soc. Am. Mil. Engrs. (pres. 1975), Soc. Advancement Material and Process Engring., Soc. Plastics Industry, So. Mfg. Engrs., U.S. Mil. Acad. Alumni Assn., U. Ill. Alumni Assn. Avocations: tennis, racquetball, skiing, hiking. Home: 5721 View Ln Edina MN 55436

DORSEY, CLINTON GEORGE, counselor, minister; b. N.Y.C., Oct. 29, 1931; s. Calvin Dorsey and Gertrude (Gilbert) Brown; m. Elaine Franklin, Nov. 1953 (div. 1962). BS in Edn., Wilberforce U., 1966; MDiv, United Theol. Sem., 1970; postgrad. guidance and counseling, Wright State U., 1971-73. Press operator New Gen. Army Depot, New Cumberland, Pa., 1953-62; sch. counselor Troy (Ohio) High Sch., 1970—; pres. Clinton Dorsey & Assocs., Troy, 1976—. Contbr. articles and columns to local publs. Dem. nominee 4th Congl. Dist., Ohio, 1976. Served with USAF, 1949-53. Mem. Nat. Edn. Assn., NAACP (life), Ohio Edn. Assn., Troy City Edn. Assn., Ohio Counselors Assn. Democrat. Avocations: tennis, reading, writing, swimming, backgammon. Home: 1334 Custer Ct Troy OH 45373 Office: Troy High Sch 151 Staunton Rd Troy OH 45373

DORSEY, WILBUR CHARLES, school system adminstrator; b. Wichita, Kans., Oct. 16, 1926; s. Charles Wilbur and Mabel Woodruff (Andrews) D.; m. Luella Jean Cook, Dec. 26, 1946; children: John Wilbur, Robert Howard, Deaune Marie. BS in Edn., Emporia (Kans.) State U., 1950, EdS, 1960; MA, U. Denver, 1956. Cert. tchr. and adminstr., Kans. Tchr. and coach Beverly (Kans.) Rural High Sch., 1950-51; tchr. Unified Sch. Dist. 259, Wichita, 1951-56, asst. prin., 1956-65, div. dir., 1965—; tchr. Wichita State U., 1956-60; pres. Mid-Am. ACE, 1982-83, treas., 1984—. Served with USN, 1944-46. Mem. NEA (life), Kans. Educators Assn., Kans. Bus. Officals, Phi Delta Kappa. Democrat. Lodge: Kiwanis (pres. Wichita chpt. 1976-77). Avocations: camping, fishing, golf, travel. Office: Unified Sch Dist 259 432 W 3d St Wichita KS 67203

DOSÉ, FREDERICK PHILIP, JR., art historian; b. Chgo., Sept. 9, 1946; s. Frederick P. and Alfa Elaine (Bahr) D.; m. Jean Hardisty, May 17, 1969 (div. Nov. 1979); m. Dee Hampton Keehn, June 8, 1985. BA, Northwestern U., 1968, MA, 1981. Faculty, art historian Northeastern Ill. U., Chgo., 1974-75, Colgate U., Hamilton, N.Y., 1976-80, Ray Coll., Chgo., 1984—; fine arts and antiques appraiser Evanston, Ill., 1980—; curator, dir. Chgo. br. Daniel B. Grossman Gallery, 1983; agent, broker Charles Lipson Antiquities, Jamaica Plain, Mass., 1985—. Author: (catalogue) Wilson Irvine, 1984; contbr. articles to profl. jours. Faculty grantee Colgate U., 1979. Mem. Coll. Art Assn., Internat. Soc. Appraisers (contributing editor bull. 1981—), Newberry Library Assocs., Friends of Brit. Library, Soc. for Ancient Numismatics, Am. Numismatics Assn., Archaeol. Inst. Am., Napoleonic Soc. Am. (designated appraiser).

DOSHI, MANSUKHLAL, tax planning, investment and immigration consultant; b. Mahuva, Gujarat, India, Dec. 27, 1919; came to U.S., 1979; s. Amritlal and Puriben Doshi; m. Indira Leela, June 18, 1943 (dec. Dec. 1982); children: Ashok, Niru, Chetan, Dipak; m. Neela Doshi, Dec. 17, 1985. BA with honors, Samaldas Coll., Bhavnagar, Gujarat, 1941; MA, U. Bombay, 1947; cert., Indian Statis. Inst., Bombay, 1950, State Trading Corp., New Delhi, 1964; postgrad. bus. sch., Roosevelt U., Chgo., 1971. Asst. dir. industries Govt. of Gujarat, Ahmedabad, 1968-76; adminstrv. officer Arat Electro Chems. (P) Ltd., Ahmedabad, 1976-79, advisor, 1979—; tax planning, investment and immigration cons. Chgo., 1979—; hon. lectr. Local Self-Govt. Inst., Baroda, 1956-57; hon lectr. Jain Soc., Chgo., 1983—, chmn. edn. com., 1984-86; exec. com. mem. Engring. Export Promotion Council Bombay, 1964-68. Editor Indsl. Bull., 1962-67; also articles on industries. Exec. com. mem. Jain Social Group, Chgo., 1985. Republican. Mem. Jainism faith. Club: Ellisbridge Gymkhana (Ahmedabad). Avocation: traveling. Home: 3025 Parkside Dr Highland Park IL 60035 Office: 354 Shelburne Carol Stream IL 60688

DOSS, HOWARD JAY, agricultural safety educator, consultant; b. Lansing, Mich., June 8, 1926. M.S., Mich. State U., 1969. Agrl. safety specialist dept. agr. Mich. State U., East Lansing, 1969—, mem. faculty dept. agrl. engring., 1969—; agrl. safety cons. Mem. Am. Soc. Safety Engrs., Am. Soc. Agrl. Engrs., Nat. Inst. Farm Safety. Club: Clear Creek Ranch Hunt. Author: Agricultural Machinery Safety, 1974. Office: Mich State U Agrl Engring Dept East Lansing MI 48824

DOSS, JEROME FAULKNER, obstetrician-gynecologist; b. Memphis, Dec. 17, 1933; s. William Norman and Sarah Lorena (Simmons) D.; m. Dorothy Ann Carlson, Aug. 24, 1955; children: J. Ann Doss Helms, Paul N. BA, U. Iowa, 1955, MD, 1958. Diplomate Am. Bd. Obstetrics and Gynecology. Intern, then resident Ind. U. Med. Ctr., Indpls., 1958-63; practice medicine specializing in ob-gyn Kokomo, Ind., 1965—; med. affairs coordinator Howard Community Hosp., Kokomo, 1986—; mem. mgmt. com. Physicians Health Network, Indpls., 1986—; bd. dirs. 1st Care Health Plan of Ind., Inc., Indpls., M.C. Med. Found., Indpls. Mem. Howard County Bd. Health, 1978—. Served to capt. USAF, 1963-65. Fellow Am. Coll. Ob-Gyn.; mem. AMA, Am. Fertility Soc., Ind. Med. Assn. (pres. ob-gyn sect. 1971-72), Howard County Med. Soc. (pres. 1971). Office: Gynecology of Kokomo PC 3415 S Lafountain St Kokomo IN 46902

DOTHAGER, DANIEL DUANE, electrical engineer; b. Vandalia, Ill., Sept. 3, 1952; s. Wilbert Herman and Jaynece Margaret (Blankenship) D.; m. Aurelia Johanna Sparks, Aug. 16, 1974; children: Theresa Renee, Tracie Ann, Kevin Daniel, Clara Jaynece. BA, Greenville (Ill.) Coll., 1974; MSEE, So. Ill. U., 1978. Asst. programmer Ill. Power Co., Decatur, 1977-78, engr., 1978-81, elec. engr., 1981, systems project leader, 1981—, mem. speakers bur., attended Am. Power Club, 1979, attended Power Industry Computer Applications, 1981. Deacon Prairie View Bapt. Ch., Lake City, Ill., 1984, treas., 1985; treas. United Bapt. Ch., Long Creek, Ill., 1987. Avocations: fishing, reading, mechanics, gardening, woodworking. Home: Rt 1 PO Box 66 Lovington IL 61937 Office: Ill Power Co 500 S 27th St Decatur IL 62525

DOTY, DAVID SINGLETON, lawyer; b. Anoka, Minn., June 30, 1929. B.A., U. Minn., 1961, LL.B., 1961. Bar: Minn. 1961, U.S. Ct. Appeals (8th and 9th cirs.) 1976, U.S. Supreme Ct. 1982. V.p., dir. Popham, Haik, Schnobrich, Kaufman & Doty, Mpls., 1962-86; pres. Popham, Haik, Schnobrich, Kaufman & Doty, 1977-79; instr. William Mitchell Coll. Law, Mpls., 1963-64; mem. com. public edn. and info. Minn. Supreme Ct., 1978-81; judge U.S. District Court for Minnesota, Minneapolis, 1987—. Trustee Mpls. Library Bd., 1969-79, Mpls. Found., 1976-83. Fellow ABA Found.; mem. ABA, Minn. Bar Assn. (gov. 1976-87, sec. 1980-83, pres. elect 1983, pres. 1984-85), Hennepin County Bar Assn. (pres. 1975-76), Am. Judicature Soc. Home: 23 Greenway Gables Minneapolis MN 55403 Office: 4344 IDS Center Minneapolis MN 55402 *

DOTY, RONALD NELS, nightclub executive; b. Mpls., July 3, 1942; s. LaTelle August and Edna May (Michaelson) D.; children: Cindy, Steven, David. Grad. high sch., Sioux Falls, S.D. Bartender Happy Hour Bar, Sioux Falls, 1963-70; prin. Hurdy Gurdy Saloon, Mankato, Minn., 1971-82, R.J. Noodles & Co., Mankato, 1982-84, T.J. Finnegan's, Mankato, 1976—, Caledonia Lounge, Mankato, 1986—; pres. Midwestern States Fedn. Beverage Lics., Mpls., 1977—; bd. dirs. Minn. Lic. Beverage Retailers, Mpls. Lobbyist Midwestern States Fedn. Beverage Lics., Mpls., 1977—. Lutheran. Avocations: golfing, scuba diving, hunting, travelling. Home: 20 Carolyn Ct Mankato MN 56001 Office: TJ Finnegan's Pub 520 S Front Mankato MN 56001

DOUGAN, JULIE JEAN, training coordinator; b. Evansville, Ind., Sept. 21, 1946; d. Russell and Margie (Riecken) Redman; m. Gregory C. Dougan, Sept. 21, 1986; 1 child, Scott Michael Roudebush. BA, U. Evansville, 1968, postgrad., 1969-72. Tchr. Evansville-Vanderburgh County Sch. Corp., 1968-72; teller, tng. coordinator Citizens' Nat. Bank, Evansville, 1978—. Participant, past v.p. Leadership Evansville. Mem. Am. Soc. Tng. and Devel. (asst. regional dir. 1985-86, com. chairperson 1983-85, past pres., v.p., publicity chairperson River Cities chpt., tri-chair region 5 conf.). Mem. United Ch. of Christ. Avocations: bicycling, creative sewing. Office: Citizens Nat Bank 20 NW 3d St Evansville IN 47708

DOUGHERTY, CHARLOTTE ANNE, financial planner, insurance and securities representative; b. Canton, Ohio, Nov. 9, 1947; d. Myron Martin and Wilma Rose Brown; m. John Edwin Dougherty, Jr., Feb. 14, 1976; 1 son, John Edwin. B.A., Miami U., Oxford, Ohio, 1969; postgrad. Kent State U. (Ohio), 1971-73. Cert. fin. planner. Social worker Summit County Welfare, Akron, Ohio, 1971-73; research coordinator Tufts U., Medford, Mass., 1973-74; corp. recruiter Lincoln Nat. Sales Corp., Ft. Wayne, Ind., 1976-79; agt. Lincoln Nat. Life, Cin., 1980—; registered rep. Lincoln Nat. Pension, Cin., 1981—; v.p. Assocs. Benefit Corp., Cin., 1982—; account exec. Integrated Resources Equity Corp., Englewood, Colo., 1983—. Contbr. articles to profl. jours. Mem. Inst. Cert. Fin. Planners, Internat. Assn. Assn. Fin. Planning, Nat. Assn. Life Underwriters, Cin. Assn. Life Underwriters. Republican. Roman Catholic. Office: Oxford Fin Group 8040 Hosbrook Rd Suite 400 Cincinnati OH 45236

DOUGHERTY, MARK ALLEN, minister; b. Wichita, Kans., Sept. 30, 1960; s. Raymond Joseph and Claudeen V. (Martin) D.; m. Melony Joan Williams, May 28, 1983; 1 child, Kyle Allen. Diploma in emergency medicine, Wichita State U., 1979; student, Mo. So. State Coll., 1985; BTh in Preaching Ministry, B in Biblical Lit., Ozark Christian Coll., 1986. Ordained to ministry Christian Ch., 1985. Firefighter Sedgwick County Fire Dept., Wichita, 1979-81; youth minister Salina (Okla.) Christian Ch., 1982-83; minister McCune (Kans.) Christian Ch., 1984-86; Youth worker 1st Christian Ch., Derby, Kans., 1980-81; acctg. clk. Tamko Asphalt Products, Joplin, Mo., 1983-86. Program dir. Joplin Family YMCA, 1986—. Mem. McCune Ministerial Alliance, Joplin C. of C. (leadership Joplin '87, membership Blitz. 1987). Club: Joplin Tips. Avocation: exercise. Home: 1917 Empire Joplin MO 64801 Office: Joplin Family YMCA 510 Wall Joplin MO 64801

DOUGHERTY, RICHARD MARTIN, library administrator; b. East Chicago, Ind., Jan. 17, 1935; s. Floyd C. and Harriet E. (Martin) D.; m. Ann Prescott, Mar. 24, 1974; children—Kathryn E., Emily E.; children by previous marriage—Jill Ann, Jacquelyn A., Douglas M. B.S., Purdue U., 1959; M.L.S., Rutgers U., 1961, Ph.D., 1963. Head acquisitions dept. Univ. Library, U. N.C., Chapel Hill, 1963-66; assoc. dir. libraries U. Colo., Boulder, 1966-70; prof. library sci. Syracuse U., N.Y., 1970-72; univ. librarian U. Calif-Berkeley, 1972-78; dir. univ. library, prof. library sci. U. Mich., Ann Arbor, 1978—, acting dean. Sch. Library Sci., 1984-85; cons. UPM, Dhahran, Saudi Arabia, Nat. U., San Diego, Fla. State U. Systems, Rutgers U. Sch. Library and Info. Sci., New Brunswick, N.J.; bd. of govs. Research Libraries Group, 1979—, chmn. bd. dirs., 1986-87; founder, pres. Mountainside Publ. Corp., 1974—. Author: Scientific Management of Library Organizations, 2d edit., 1983; editor Coll. and Research Libraries jour., 1969-74, Jour. Acad. Librarianship, 1974. Recipient Disting. Alumnus award Rutgers U., 1980; named Acad. Librarian Yr., Assn. Coll. and Research Libraries, 1983. Fellow Council on Library Resources; mem. ALA (exec. bd. 1972-76, endowment trustee 1986—, Esther Piercy award 1969), Assn. Research Libraries (bd. dirs. 1977-80), Found. Library Com., Research Libraries Group (bd. govs. 1979—, chmn. bd. 1986-87), Mountainside Publ. Corp. (founder, pres. 1974). Home: 6 Northwick Ct Ann Arbor MI 48105 Office: U of Mich Univ Library Ann Arbor MI 48109-1205

DOUGLAS, ANDY, state justice; b. Toledo, July 5, 1932; 4 children. J.D., U. Toledo, 1959. Bar: Ohio 1960, U.S. Dist. Ct. (no. dist.) Ohio 1960. Former ptnr. Winchester & Douglas; judge Ohio 6th Dist. Ct. Appeals, 1981-84; justice Ohio Supreme Ct., 1985—; former spl. counsel Atty. Gen. of Ohio. Served with U.S. Army, 1952-54. Recipient award Maumee Valley council Girl Scouts U.S., 1976, Outstanding Service award Toledo Police Command Officers Assn., 1980, Toledo Soc. for Autistic Children and Adults, 1983, Extra-Spl. Person award Central Catholic High Sch., 1981, Disting. Service award Toledo Police Patrolman's Assn., 1982, award Ohio Hispanic Inst. Opportunity, 1985; named to Woodward High Sch. Hall of Fame. Mem. Toledo Bar Assn., Lucas County Bar Assn., Ohio Bar Assn., Lagrange Bus. and Profl. Men's Assn., Toledo U. Alumni Assn., U. Toledo Law Alumni, St. John's High Sch. Dads' Club, Macomber High Sch. Boosters, Internat. Inst., Pi Sigma Alpha, Delta Theta Phi. Lodges: North Toledo Old Timers Assn., Old Newsboys Goodfellow Assn., 4th Ward Old Timers Assn. Office: Ohio Supreme Ct 30 E Broad St Columbus OH 43215 *

DOUGLAS, GEORGE HALSEY, writer, educator; b. East Orange, N.J., Jan. 9, 1934; s. Halsey M. and Harriet Elizabeth (Goldbach) D.; A.B. with honors in Philosophy, Lafayette Coll., 1956; M.A., Columbia U., 1966; Ph.D., U. Ill., 1968; m. Rosalind Braun, June 19, 1961; 1 son, Philip. Tech. editor Bell Telephone Labs., Whippany, N.J., 1958-59; editor Agrl. Expt. Sta., U. Ill., Urbana, 1961-66, instr. Dept. English, 1966-68, asst. prof. English, 1968-77, assoc. prof. English, 1977—. Mem. Am. Studies Assn., MLA, Am. Bus. Communication Assn. Author: H.L. Mencken Critic of American Life, 1978; The Teaching of Business Communication, 1978; Rail City: Chicago and Its Railroads, 1981; Edmund Wilson's America, 1983; Women of the Twenties; editor Jour. Bus. Communication, 1968—, The Early Days of Radio Broadcasting, History of Bus. Writing; contbr. articles to profl. jours. Home: 1514 Grandview Dr Champaign IL 61820 Office: U Ill Dept English English Bldg Urbana IL 61801

DOUGLAS, JOE J., JR., fire chief; b. Topeka, June 9, 1928; s. J.J. Sr. and Imogene (Taylor) D.; m. Nathalia Jean Washington, Jan. 29, 1950; 1 child, Shelly J. Douglas Wilder. Student, Washburn U., 1948-50. Firefighter Topeka Fire Dept., 1950-83, chief, 1983—. Chmn. com. on religion and race United Meth. Ch., Topeka, 1974; bd. dirs. Topeka Boys' Club, 1975, United Sch. Dist. 501, Topeka, 1977-85, pres. 1980-81, 83-84; bd dirs. Boy Scouts Am., Topeka, 1987—. Served as pvt. U.S. Army, 1946-48. Mem. Internat. Assn. Fire Chiefs, Missouri Valley Fire Chiefs Assn., Nat. Fire Protection Assn. Democrat. Avocations: golf, photography. Office: Office of the Fire Chief 324 Jefferson St Topeka KS 66607-1185

DOUGLAS, JOHN BRADBURY, dentist; b. Floydada, Tex., May 31, 1949; s. Dale Wooley and Virginia (Arlene) D. BA, Miami U., Oxford, Ohio, 1971; DDS, U. Mich., 1975. Assoc. dentist Wayne (Mich.) Dental Group, 1975-82; gen. practice dentistry Westland, Mich., 1982—. Fellow ADA, Chgo. Dental Soc.; mem. Mich. Dental Soc., Detroit Dist. Dental Soc., Westland C. of C. Republican. Presbyterian. Avocations: scuba diving, skiing, ballooning. Home: 2740 Lookout Circle Ann Arbor MI 48104 Office: 6622 Wayne Rd Westland MI 48185

DOUGLAS, KENNETH JAY, food company executive; b. Harbor Beach, Mich., Sept. 4, 1922; s. Harry Douglas and Xenia (Williamson) D.; m. Elizabeth Ann Schweizer, Aug. 17, 1946; children: Connie Ann, Andrew Jay. Student, U. Ill., 1940-41, 46-47; J.D., Chgo. Kent Coll. Law, 1950; grad., Advanced Mgmt. Program, Harvard, 1962. Bar: Ill. 1950, Ind. 1952. Spl. agt. FBI, 1950-54; dir. indsl. relations Dean Foods Co., Franklin Park, Ill., 1952-64; v.p. fin. and adminstrn. Dean Foods Co., 1964-70, chmn., 1970—; dir. Centel Corp., Am. Nat. Bank & Trust Co., Am. Nat. Corp., Milk Industry Found. Life trustee West Suburban Hosp., Oak Park, Ill.; bd. overseers Ill. Inst. Tech. Chgo.-Kent Coll. Law. Served with USNR, 1944-46. Republican. Clubs: Chicago, Economic, Executives, Commercial (Chgo.); Oak Park Country, River Forest Tennis (Ill.); Steamboat Springs Country (Colo.); Old Baldy (Wyo.). Office: Dean Foods Co 3600 N River Rd Franklin Park IL 60131

DOUGLAS, MICHAEL WILLIAM, education administrator; b. Ft. Atkinson, Wis., June 5, 1945; s. Stanton C. and Agnes L. (Mulcaney) D.; m. Mary E. Martin, Jan. 3, 1982; children: Michael Patrick, Meghan Kathleen. BA, Loras Coll., 1967; MEd, No. Ill. U., 1979. Sr. probation officer DuPage County Probation Dept., Wheaton, Ill., 1979-84; exec. dir. Hospice of DuPage, Glen Ellyn, Ill., 1984-86; dir. edn. Wheaton Franciscan Services, Inc., 1986—. Mem. Am. Assn. for Counseling and Devel., Am. Mental Health Counselors Assn., Kappa Delta Pi. Roman Catholic. Office: Wheaton Franciscan Services Inc PO Box 667 Wheaton IL 60189

DOUGLAS, WILLIAM RUSSELL, professional association executive; b. Columbus, Ohio, Dec. 31, 1947; s. Russell Edwin and Sara Kathryn (Hill) D.; m. Cheryl Lynn Sands, Dec. 26, 1971; children: Scott, Sean. BS in Communications, Ohio U., 1970. Sales mgr. SCM, Columbus, 1974-77, Allen Refractories, Columbus, 1977-80; dir. meetings Am. Ceramic Soc., Columbus, 1980—. Served to 1st lt. U.S. Army, 1971-74. Mem. Meeting Planners Internat. (chpt. pres. 1986—), Council Engring. and Scientific Soc. Execs. (chmn. program com. 1985-86). Republican. Methodist. Lodge: Masons. Avocations: fishing, coaching, youth baseball. Home: 961 Ruskin Dr Reynoldsburg OH 43068 Office: Am Ceramic Soc 757 Brooksedge Plaza Dr Westerville OH 43081-2821

DOUMA, HARRY HEIN, social service agency administrator; b. Richmond, N.Y., Mar. 12, 1933; s. Hein and Ida D. (Van Der Veer) D.; m. Carole Marie Piening; June 21, 1958; children:Daniel H., Deborah Joy, Crystal A. BA in Philosophy, Shelton Coll., 1960; MDiv, Faith Theol. Sem., 1965. Ordained to ministry, 1965. Pastor Port Monmouth (N.J.) Ch., 1958-60; chaplain Edward R. Johnstone Tng. and Research Ctr., Bordentown, N.J., 1960-65; pastor Times Beach (Mo.) Bible Ch., 1965-67, Ist Bapt. Ch., Pilot Knob, Mo., 1967-76; founder, pres., pastor Penuel, Inc., Ironton, Mo., 1973—. Author The Book of Revelation for the Layman, 1971. Mem. Rep. Presdl. Task Force. Served with USN, 1953-55. Mem. Full Gospel Bus. Men's Fellowship Internat. Avocations: travel, swimming, fishing, music. Home: 326 Michael Ln Rt 1 Box 593 Ironton MO 63650 Office: Penuel Inc Box 367 Lake Killarney-Ironton MO 63650

DOUMANIAN, HERATCH OHANNES, radiology administrator; b. Beirut, Feb. 11, 1934; s. Ohannes Toros Doumanian and Hripsime Kupelian; m. Sonya L. Dermenjian, Mar. 17, 1967; children: Greta, John, Leo. MD, Am. U. Beirut, Lebanon, 1957. Diplomate Am. Bd. Radiology. Resident in radiology U. Chgo. Hosp., Chgo., 1962-65; fellow in cardiovascular radiology U. Minn. Hosp., Mpls., 1965-66; dir. radiology St. Mary Med. Ctr., Gary and Hobart, Ind., 1967—. Served to capt. M.C. U.S. Army, 1960-62, Germany. Mem. AMA, Radiol. Soc. N.Am., Am. Coll. Radiology. Armenian Orthodox. Club: Innsbrook Country. Home: 6451 Arthur St Merrillville IN 46410 Office: St Mary Med Ctr 540 Tyler St Gary IN 46402

DOURAS, CAROLE LYNN, personnel director; b. El Paso, Tex., Dec. 4, 1944; d. William O. Jr. and Martha L. (Hutchinson) Johnson; m. James H. Douras, June 6, 1965 (div. Feb. 1978); children: Jenny Rebecca, Alison Lynn. BS, Wayne State U., 1966, MBA, 1985. Tchr. Detroit Bd. Edn., 1966-67; corp. tng. exec. J.L. Hudson Co., Detroit, 1967-68; exec. sec. Detroit Police Officer's Assn., 1976-77; personnel asst. Mich. HMO, Detroit, 1977-79; personnel dir. John V. Carr and Son, Inc., Detroit, 1979—. Mem. personnel com. Camp Fire Detroit Area Council. Mem. Internat. Assn. Personnel Women (treas. 1984-85, pres. 1986-87), Detroit Grand Prix Assn., Riverfront West Bus. Dist. Assn. (sec. 1985-86). Office: John V Carr & Son Inc 1600 W Lafayette Detroit MI 48216

DOURLET, ERNEST F., rubber and plastic products manufacturing executive; b. Lancaster, Ohio, 1924. B.S. Chem. Engring., W.Va. U.; postgrad., U. Pa. Wharton Sch. Pres. Cadillac Plastic & Chem. Co., 1957-71; exec. v.p. Dayco Corp., Dayton, Ohio, 1972-73, pres., chief operating officer, dir., 1973—; dir. Price Bros. Co., Bank One N.A. Address: Dayco Corp 333 W 1st St Dayton OH 45402 *

DOUTT, GERALDINE MOFFATT, educational administrator; b. Warren, Mich., Apr. 16, 1927; s. Stanford and Wilhelmine (Ewaldt) Moffatt; married, 2 children. B.S. in Occupational Therapy, Eastern Mich. U., Ypsilanti, 1952, M.A. in Edn., 1959; E.D.S. in Spl. Edn., Wayne State U., Detroit, 1968; m. Robert G. Doutt; children—Eric Robert, Gerald George. Tchr., Van Dyke Pub. Schs., Warren, 1963-65, tchr. educable mentally impaired, 1965-67, tchr. cons. for emotionally impaired, 1967-69, dir. spl. edn., 1969—. Chmn. Macomb County Interagy. Council, 1968-69. Mem. Mich. Assn. Dirs. Spl. Edn., Nat. Council Exceptional Children, Delta Kappa Gamma. Home: 22919 Playview St St Clair Shores MI 48082 also: Treasure Island Higgins Lake PO Box 412 Higgins Lake MI 48627 Office: 22100 Federal St Warren MI 48089

DOVORANY, RICHARD J., manufacturing company executive; b. Racine, Wis., Nov. 3, 1946; s. Joseph M. and Tekla J. (Sadowski) D. BBA, U. Notre Dame, 1968; MBA, U. Chgo., 1970. Profit analyst Inland Steel Co., Chgo., 1974-75; pres., chief exec. officer Acme Die Casting Corp., Racine, 1976—, chmn. bd., 1981—; mem. adv. bd. dirs. Motorola, Inc., Schaumburg, Ill., 1985—. Bd. dirs. Lakeshore Counties ARC, Racine, 1981-84; capt. capital funds campaign St. Catherine's High Sch., Racine, 1984. Served to lt. USN, 1970-73. Mem. Soc. Die Casting Engrs. (bd. dirs. internat. show com. 1984—, Service award 1985), Nat. Assn. Nfrs. (taxation com. 1984—), Racine Area Mfrs. (bd. dirs. 1982—), Racine Area C. of C. (bd. dirs. 1980-82). Clubs: Racine Country, Milw. Athletic. Avocations: golf, reading, tennis. Home: 3657 Hennepin Pl Racine WI 53402 Office: Acme Die Casting Corp 5626 21st St Racine WI 53406

DOWD, DAVID D., JR., federal judge; b. Cleve., Jan. 31, 1929; m. Joyce; children—Cindy, David, Doug, Mark. B.A., Coll. Wooster, 1951; J.D., U. Mich., 1954. Ptnr. Dowd & Dowd, Massillon, Ohio, 1954-55, ptnr., 1957-75; asst. pros. atty. Stark County, 1961-67, pros. atty., 1967-75; judge Ohio 5th Dist. Ct. Appeals, 1975-80, Ohio Supreme Ct., 1980-81; ptnr. Black, McCuskey, Souers & Arbaugh, Canton, Ohio, 1981-82; judge U.S. Dist. Ct. (no. dist.) Ohio, 1982—. Office: U S Dist Ct 510 Fed Bldg & U S Courthouse 2 S Main St Akron OH 44308

DOWD, JAMES PATRICK, bookseller; b. Chgo., Apr. 26, 1937; s. James Patrick and Mary Margaret (Healy) D.; m. Frances Marie Allevato, Aug. 4, 1962; children—Mary Frances, Daniel James, Matthew Joseph. Student Wright Jr. Coll., 1956-58, Harper Coll., 1984, Elgin Community Coll., 1986. With Spraying Systems Co., Wheaton, Ill., 1958-78, owner operator Dowd's Book Shoppe, St. Charles, Ill., 1978-80; tech. specialist Fermi Nat. Accelerator Lab., Batavia, Ill., 1980—, task order adminstr., 1986—, fabrication specialist, 1986—; mem. SSC task force, 1984—, Elgin (Ill.) Community Coll., 1986—; hist. cons. Potawatomi Indian Statue Com., St. Charles. Editor: Life of Black Hawk, 1974. Author: Built Like A Bear, 1979; Custer Lives, 1983. Contbr.: Images of the Mystic Truth, 1981. Served with U.S. Army, 1961-63. Mem. Midwest Bookhunters. Roman Catholic. Chgo. Corral of Westerners (hon.). Avocations: collector of scarce and rare western Americana. Home: 38W 281 Toms Trail Dr Saint Charles IL 60174 Office: Fermi Nat Accelerator Lab PO Box 500 MS 316 Batavia IL 60510

DOWDY, JOHN WESLEY, JR., minister; b. Muskogee, Okla., Nov. 15, 1935; s. John Wesley and Floy Weaver (Thurston) D.; m. Joycelyn Adele Pinnell, June 9, 1956; children: Barbara Annette, Gina Marie (dec.). AA, Southwest Baptist Coll., 1954; BA, Southwest Mo. State U., 1956; M in Div., Midwestern Baptsit Theol. Sem., 1962, D in Ministries, 1974. Pastor Cedar City (Mo.) Baptist Ch., 1956-59, First Baptist Ch., Maysville, Mo., 1959-64, Tabernacle Baptist Ch., Kansas City, Mo., 1964-75; dir. Christian social ministries Metro Mission Bd., Kansas City, 1975-78; dir. Christian social ministries Mo. Baptist Convention, Jefferson City, Mo., 1978-80, dir. mission dept., 1980—; field supr., adj. prof. D of Ministries program Midwestern Baptist Theol Sem., Kansas City, Mo., 1976—; cons. SBC Home Mission Bd., Atlanta, 1976—. Pres. Inter Faith CHaplian's Commn. of Mo., Jefferson City, 1983—; bd. dirs. Am. Field Service, Jefferson City, 1985—. Mem. So. Baptist Convention Research Soc., So. Baptist Social Service Soc., Futurist Soc. Am. Avocation: avid reader. Home: 1004 Winston Dr Jefferson City MO 65101 Office: Mo Baptist Convention 400 E High Jefferson City MO 65101

DOWDY, WALTER, college administrator, educator; b. Oceola, Ark., Aug. 21, 1930; s. Walter Sr. and Ora Lee (Moore) D.; m. Roberta Caffray, June 8, 1952; children: Terrence, Debra, Marsha, Kevin, Alberta. AS, Lake Mich. Coll., 1953; BS, Western Mich. U., 1955. Supr. casework Kalamazoo County Juvenile Ct., 1961-69; dir. special programs Kalamazoo Valley Community Coll., 1969-72, dir. internat. students, 1972—, also cons., 1968; cons. Agy. Internat. Devel., Washington, 1976-78, Sienna Heights Coll., Adrian, Mich., 1981-82, Govt. of Jordan, Amman, 1985—. Author: (with others) Placement of Students From Selected Arab Countries, 1975. Bd. dirs. Pretty Lake Vacation Camp, Kalamazoo. Served as cpl. U.S. Army, 1948-51, Korea. Grantee Kalamazoo Valley Community Coll., 1986; recipient Edn. award South Western Mich. Council Boyscouts of Am., Kalamazoo, 1978. Mem. Nat. Assn. Fgn. Student Affairs (grantee 1973), Am. Assn. Collegiate Registrars and Admission Officers (research com. 1979-80, orientation com. 1978-80, grantee 1975). Lodge: Kiwanis. Avocations: camping, fishing, travel, reading. Office: Kalamazoo Valley Community Coll 6767 W O Ave Kalamazoo MI 49009

DOWELL, DAVID RAY, library administrator; b. Trenton, Mo., Nov. 14, 1942; s. Clarence Ray and Ruth Lucille (Adams) D.; m. Arlene Grace Taylor, May 9, 1964 (div. Aug. 1983); children—Deborah Ruth, Jonathan Ray; m. Denise Jaye Christie, Aug. 19, 1983; stepchildren—David Lee, Jason Alan. BA in History, Okla. Bapt. U., 1964; AM in History, U. Ill., 1966, MLS, 1972; PhD, U. N.C., 1986. Tchr. Wilson Jr. High Sch., Tulsa, 1964-65; head library adminstrv. services Iowa State U., Ames, 1972-75; asst. univ. librarian Duke U., Durham, N.C., 1975-81; dir. libraries Ill. Inst. Tech., Chgo., 1981—; cons. County Commr.'s Library Planning Com., Durham, 1976, Gov.'s Conf. on Libraries and Info. Services, Raleigh, N.C., 1978, Biblioteca do Centro Batista, Goiania, Brazil, 1978; chmn.-elect Chgo. Library System Affialiates Council, 1986—. Contbr. articles to profl. jours. Trustee Glenwood-Lynwood Pub. Library Dist., Ill., 1985-87. Served to capt. USAF, 1967-71. Mem. ALA (chmn. profl. ethics com. 1977-78, chmn. election com. 1982-83, chmn. library personnel adv. com. 1979-80), Assn. Coll. and Research Libraries (nominating com. 1979-80), Library Adminstrn. and Mgmt. Assn. (bd. dirs. 1981-83, chmn. personnel adminstrn. sect. 1982-83, exec. com. library orgn. sect. 1979-81), Met. Chgo. Library Assembly (bd. dirs. 1981-82), Chgo. Acad. Library Council (treas. 1981—), Chgo. Library System Affiliates Council (chair-elect 1986-87), Internat. Fedn. Library Assns. (chmn. registration com. 1984-85), Kappa Delta Pi, Phi Alpha Theta, Beta Phi Mu. Democrat. Baptist. Avocation: tennis. Home: 823 Terrace Dr Glenwood IL 60425 Office: Paul V Galvin Library Ill Inst Tech Chicago IL 60616

DOWGIALLO, WILLIAM WALTER, project manager; b. Portchester, N.Y., June 9, 1955; s. William V. and Anne (Koot) D.; m. Mary Kelly, Sept. 27, 1980; children: Thomas William, Brian Patrick, Kerri Anne. BArch., Ill. Inst. Tech., 1978, MBA, 1980. Asst. to dean Ill. Inst. Tech., Chgo., 1978-79; facilities designer IBM, Tarrytown, N.Y., 1980-83, project mgr., Dobbs Ferry, N.Y., 1983-85, Chgo., 1985—. Recipient Ill. Inst. Tech. 1978. Roman Catholic. Home: 12649 S Massasoit St Palos Heights IL 60463 Office: IBM One IBM Plaza Suite 3100 Chicago IL 60611

DOWGIEWICZ, MICHAEL JOHN, bank executive; b. Worcester, Mass., Nov. 23, 1952; s. Henry and Gladys (Komorek) D.; m. Susan Goyette; children: Kathryn, Joseph. BSBA, Nichols Coll., 1974; postgrad., U. Del., 1986, Mich. State U. Corp. staff acct. Guardian Industries, Northville, Mich., 1974-76; asst. v.p. fin., corp. risk mgr. Bank of the Commonwealth, Detroit, 1976-79; v.p. Mfrs. Nat. Bank, Detroit, 1979—; Mem. editorial adv. bd. Bus. Ins., Detroit, risk mgmt. com. Magic Line Inc., Detroit, security com. Detroit Clearing House Assn. Mem. Am. Soc. for Indsl. Security, Am. Bankers Assn., Risk and Ins. Mgmt. Soc., Delta Mu Delta, Omicron Delta Epsilon. Office: Mfrs Nat Bank 100 Renaissance Ctr 39th Floor Detroit MI 48243

DOWHOWER, RODNEY DOUGLAS, professional football coach; b. Santa Barbara, Calif., Apr. 15, 1943; m. Nancy Dowhower; children: Brian, Deron. Student, Santa Barbara City Jr. Coll.; B.A., San Diego State U., 1971; Master's degree, U.S. Internat. U., 1971. Grad. asst. San Diego State U., 1966-67, asst. football coach, 1968-72; asst. coach St. Louis Cardinals, NFL, 1973, 83, 84, UCLA, 1974-75, Boise State U., 1976; asst. coach Stanford U., 1977-78, coach, 1979; asst. coach Denver Broncos, NFL, 1980-82; coach Indpls. Colts, NFL, 1985—. Address: care Indpls Colts PO Box 24100 Indianapolis IN 46224-0100

DOWLEY, JOEL EDWARD, manufacturing executive, lawyer; b. Jackson, Mich., Apr. 27, 1952; s. William J. and Beth E. (Morell) D.; m. Janelle Smith, Nov. 12, 1983; 1 child, Kara Marie. B.A., Spring Arbor Coll., 1974; J.D., U. Notre Dame, 1977. Bar: Mich. 1977. Atty. Fraser, Trebilcock, Davis and Foster, P.C., Lansing, Mich., 1977-83; exec. v.p., gen. counsel Dowley Mfg. Inc., Spring Arbor, Mich., 1983-87; chmn., chief exec. officer, 1987—. Pub. mem. Mich. Bd. Psychology, 1978-82, vice chmn., 1980, chmn., 1981-82; pub. mem. ethics com. Am. Assn. Marriage and Family Therapy, 1980; mem. Ingham County Republican Exec. Com., Mich., 1978-84, 3d Dist. Rep. Exec. Com., 1983-85; Rep. candidate for Ingham County commr., 1978, 82; trustee Highfield's, Inc., youth opportunity camp, Onondaga, Mich., 1983—, sec., 1984-85, pres., 1986-87; trustee BoarsHead Theater, Lansing, 1983—, treas., 1985-87. Mem. ABA, Mich. Bar Assn., Ingham County Bar Assn., Spring Arbor Coll. Alumni Assn. (trustee 1979-82, pres. 1981-82, Young Leader award 1983), Hand Tools Inst. (bd. dirs. 1986—). Methodist. Home: 1864 Cimarron Dr Okemos MI 48864 Office: Dowley Mfg Inc 7750 King Rd Spring Arbor MI 49283

DOWLING, PHILIP LEE, programmer, analyst; b. Madison, Wis., Sept. 10, 1956; s. Philip and Cecile (Schlough) D.; m. Debbie Lorraine Breininger, Oct. 18, 1980; children: Brian Michael, Kimberly Sue. AA, Madison Area Tech. Coll., 1976. Limited time employee programmer/analyst Dane County, Madison, 1976-77; programmer, analyst Datamatic, Madison, 1977-79, Wis. Physicians Service, Madison, 1979-80; sr. programmer, analyst Rayovac Corp., Madison, 1980-87; lead programmer, analyst Foremost Guaranty Corp., Madison, 1987—; ptnr. Software Connection, Madison, 1985—. Mem. Data Processing mgmt. Assn. (bd. dirs. 1985—). Democrat. Roman Catholic. Clubs: Rayovac Office (treas. 1985, pres. 1984). Avocations: sports, broadcasting. Home: 110 Garnet Ln Madison WI 53714 Office: Foremost Guaranty Corp 131 W Wilson St Madison WI 53703

DOWLING, RICHARD CORNELL, service executive; b. Wilmington, Del., Aug. 7, 1950; s. Thomas III and Evelyn (Cornell) D.; m. Alyce Christine Harris, May 27, 1972. BS in Hotel and Restaurant Mgmt., U. Wis., Menomonie, 1972. Asst. hotel mgr. Sheraton Corp., Columbus, Ohio, 1972-73; regional dir. ops. Red Roof Inns, Columbus, 1973-79; hotel resort search specialist Bryant Bur., East Lansing, Mich., 1979-82; owner, hotel resort search specialist Lake Assocs., Lansing, Mich., 1982—. Mem. Mich. Lodging Assn. (assoc.), Lansing Regional C. of C. Republican. Presbyterian. Avocations: tennis, boating. Home: 1021 N Shore Dr Springport MI 49284 Office: Lake Assocs 1 Michigan Ave Suite 740 Lansing MI 48933

DOWLING, TERENCE DENNIS, realtor; b. Aug. 13, 1946; s. Robert E. and Helen M. Dowling; m. Margaret V. O'Gorman, July 10, 1971; children: Heather, Todd, Tyler. BA, U. Denver, 1969; postgrad., John Marshall Sch. Law, 1969-71. Real estate broker Farnsworth, Palmer & Co., Chgo., 1970-75; pres. Dowling & Co. Realtors, River Forest, Ill., 1975—; co-owner Dowling Bus. Co., Bus. Appraisers and Brokers, Chgo., 1975—. Mem. Nat. Assn. Pealtors, Ill. Assn. Realtors, Oak Park Bd. Realtors, Bldg. Owners and Mgrs. Assn. of Oak park, Jr. Real Estate Bd. of Chgo. (bd. dirs., officer), Realtor 40 Club of Chgo., Real Estate Securities Syndicate Inst. (past pres. Ill. chpt.), Internat. Snooker League. Avocations: skiing, fishing, hunting, boating, golfing. Office: Dowling & Co 400 Lathrop River Forest IL 60305

DOWNEY, DOUGLAS WORTH, editor, publishing executive; b. Oakland, Calif., Nov. 28, 1929; s. John Joseph and Margaret Cudworth (Perley) D.; m. Anne Storrs Reynolds, July 14, 1956; children—Storrs Whitworth, Donald Reynolds. A.B. cum laude, Kenyon Coll., 1951; M.S., U. Wis., 1952. Asst. editor Assoc. Equipment Distbrs., Chgo., 1954-55; assoc. editor Standard Ednl. Corp., Chgo., 1955-57, asst. editorial dir., 1957-60, mng. editor, 1960-63, editor-in-chief, 1963—, v.p., 1964—. Mem. Northbrook Library Bd. (Ill.), 1963-71, 75-79, treas., 1964-67, pres., 1967-71; pres. Glenbrook High Sch. Caucus, 1973. Served with AUS, 1952-54; Korea. Decorated Bronze Star. Republican. Episcopalian. Author: Things to Make and Do, 1974. Home: 2236 Maple Ave Northbrook IL 60062 Office: 200 W Monroe St Chicago IL 60606

DOWNEY, JOHN PHILLIP, optometrist; b. Milw., June 8, 1955; s. William Sloan and Phyllis Ernestine (Teske) D.; m. Linda Ann Forrest, Aug. 13, 1977; children: Alanna, Conor. BA in Econs., U. Wis., Milw., 1977; OD, Ind. U., 1981. Ptnr. Drs. Hayes, Godich, Downey, Hales Corners, Wis., 1981—; peer rev. cons. Optometric IPA, Milw., 1985—. Mem. Wind Lake (Wis.) Mgmt. Dist., 1986; chmn. worship com. Norway Luth. Ch., 1984—. Mem. Am. Optometric Assn., Wis. Optometric Assn., Kettle Moraine Optometric Soc., Windlake Jaycees. Lodge: Lions. Avocations: sailing, computer programming, cycling. Home: 25827 W Loomis Rd Wind Lake WI 53185 Office: Drs Hayes Godich & Downey 10555 W Parnell Hales Corners WI 53130

DOWNING, FRANKLIN J., county official; b. Dearborn, Mo., Sept. 24, 1924; s. Franklin Jesse and Jessie Fay (Frakes) D.; children—Ronald P., Melody Lynne. Student Platte Bus. Coll., St. Joseph Jr. Coll. Field rep. U.S. Dept. Agr., Maryville and Chilicothe, Mo., 1966-71; owner, mgr. Dearborn Oil Co., Dearborn and Smithville, Mo., 1971-77; with Platte County Mapping Dept., Platte City, Mo., 1979—, planning and zoning dir., 1980—. Mayor, City of Dearborn (Mo.), 1980—. Democrat. Baptist. Club: Platte-Buchanan Sportsmen. Lodge: Masons. Home: 412 E 3d St Dearborn MO 64439 Office: Platte County Planning Dept 324 Main St Platte City MO 64079

DOWNING, HAROLD SEARS, III, data processing executive; b. Pitts., July 9, 1951; s. Harold Sears Jr. and Jane (McCall) D.; m. Barbara Ann Tallberg, May 2, 1981. BS in Math and Biology, U. Alaska, 1974; cert., Inst. Cert. of Computer Profls. Avocations: skiing, skating, flying small aircraft, bicycling.

DOWNING, REBEKAH ROGENE, business executive; b. Eureka, Kans., Nov. 23, 1961; d. Jack T. and Linda C. (Huston) D.;. BBA, Kans. State U., 1983. Computer operator Downing's, Inc., Eureka, Kans., 1983-84, bus. mgr., 1984-85, v.p., 1985—. Bd. adminstrn. United Meth. Ch., Eureka, 1985—. Mem. Pi Beta Phi. Republican. Home: 408 Berentz Dr Eureka KS 67045 Office: Downings Inc 1225 E River Eureka KS 67045

DOWNS, ROBERT BINGHAM, librarian; b. Lenoir, N.C., May 25, 1903; s. John McLeod and Clara Catherine (Hartley) D.; m. Elizabeth Crooks, Aug. 17, 1929 (dec. Sept. 13, 1982); children: Clara Downs Keller, Mary Roberta Downs Andre.; m. Jane Bliss Wilson, Sept. 16, 1983. A.B., U. N.C., 1926, LL.D., 1949; B.S., Columbia U., 1927, M.S., 1929; Litt.D., Colby Coll., 1944; D.L.S., U. Toledo, 1953; L.H.D., Ohio State U., 1963, So. Ill. U., 1970; Litt.D., U. Ill., 1973. Asst. U. N.C. Library, 1922-26, N.Y. Pub. Library, 1927-29; librarian Colby Coll., Waterville, Maine, 1929-31; asst. librarian U. N.C., 1931-32, librarian and assoc. prof. library sci., 1932-34, librarian, prof., 1934-38; dir. libraries N.Y. U., 1938-43; dir. Library and Library Sch.; prof. library sci. U. Ill., Urbana, 1943-58; dean library adminstrn. U. Ill., 1958-71; assoc. Columbia Sch. Library Service, 1942-43; cons. Kabul U., Afghanistan, 1963; adviser U. Tunis, 1973; chmn. ALA Bd. on Resources Am. Libraries, 1939-42, 45-50; pres. Assn. Coll. and Reference Libraries, 1940-41; spl. cons. civil information and edn. sect. SCAP, Japan, 1948, 1950; vis. chief Union Catalog Div.; cons. in bibliography Library of Congress, 1949; adviser Nat. Library and Nat. U. Mexico, 1952; library adviser to Turkish Govt., 1955, 68, 71. Author: The Story of Books, 1935, Resources of Southern Libraries, 1938, Resources of New York City Libraries, 1942, Am. Library Resources, 1951-81, Books that Changed the World, 1956, 2d edit., 1978, Molders of the Modern Mind, 1961, Famous Books, Ancient and Medieval, 1964, Family Saga, 1958, Resources of North Carolina Libraries, 1965, How To Do Library Research, 1966, 2d edit. (with Clara D. Keller), 1975, Resources of Missouri Libraries, 1966, Resources of Canadian Academic and Research Libraries, 1967, Books That Changed America, 1970, Famous American Books, 1971, British Library Resources, 1973, Horace Mann, Champion of Public Schools, 1974, Books and History, 1974, Guide to Illinois Library Resources, 1974, Heinrich Pestalozzi, Father of Modern Pedagogy, 1975, Famous Books, 1975, Books That Changed the South, 1976, Henry Barnard, 1977, Friedrich Froebel, 1978, In Search of New Horizons, 1978, Australian and New Zealand Library Resources, 1979, British and Irish Library Resources, 1981, Landmarks in Science, 1982, (with others) Memorable Americans, 1983, Perspectives on the Past, an Autobiography, 1984; (with Ralph E. McCoy) The First Freedom Today, 1984; More Memorable Americans, 1985, Images of America, 1987; editor: Library Specialization, 1941, Union Catalogs in the United States, 1942, Status of American College and University Librarians, 1958, The First Freedom, 1960, The Bear Went Over the Mountain, 1964, (with Frances B. Jenkins) Bibliography, Current State and Future Trends, 1967; Contbr. articles to library jours. Recipient Clarence Day award, 1963, Joseph W. Lippincott award, 1964; Centennial medal Syracuse U., 1970; Melvil Dewey award, 1974; decorated Order of Sacred Treasure (Japan); Guggenheim fellow, 1971-72; hon. adm. Tex. Navy, 1971. Mem. ALA (1st v.p. 1951-52, pres. 1952-53), Ill. Library Assn. (pres. 1955-56), Southeastern Library Assn., AAUP, Authors League Am., Phi Beta Kappa, Beta Phi Mu, Phi Kappa Phi. Democrat. Clubs: Dial (Urbana); Caxton (Chgo.). Lodge: Rotary. Home: 708 W Pennsylvania Ave Urbana IL 61801

DOYEL, CHARLES LYNN, nursing home administrator; b. Albany, Ga., Mar. 12, 1948; s. Melvin Charles and Oka R. (Fry) D.; m. A. Lea Smith, Oct. 15, 1971; children—Dawn Lea, Ryan Charles. B.S., S.W. Mo. State U., 1975. Machine operator Kraft Inc., Springfield, Mo., 1979-81; asst. adminstr. Chastain's of Highland (Ill.), 1981, adminstr., 1981-82; asst. adminstr. Clayton House Health Care, Manchester, Mo., 1982-83; adminstr. Charlevoix Nursing Ctr., St. Charles, Mo., 1983-86, Gambrill Gardens, Ellisville, Mo., 1986—. Named Officer of Yr., USAR Med. Service Corps, 1983. Mem. Mo. Assn. for the Aged (nursing home ombudsman's program adv. bd. 1985—, edn. com.) Home: 13484 Forestlac Creve Coeur MO 63141 Office: Gambrill Gardens 1 Strecker Rd Ellisville MO 63011

DOYLE, ALMA LUCILLE, construction contracts administration and claims executive; b. Okfuskee County, Okla., Jan. 11, 1929; d. Robert Richard and Chloe Erle (Williams) Klutts; m. Andy Hugh Doyle, Oct. 1945; children—Doris June Doyle Fiorini, James Lee, Robert Jeffrey. Student Pueblo Jr. Coll., 1958-59, So. Colo. State Coll., Pueblo, 1971-72. Sec. to supt. Sch. Dist. #70, Pueblo, 1959-63; sec. to pres. Savs. & Loan Assn., Pueblo, 1971-72; engring. clk., sec. Stearns Roger Inc., Pueblo, 1972-76; sec. CF&I Steel Corp., Pueblo, 1976-79; contract adminstr. Stearns Roger Inc., Beulah, N.D., 1979-83; gen. mgr. Egan & Sons, Co., Mandan, N.D., 1983-85. Pres., bd. dirs. Columbine Girl Scouts, Pueblo, 1956-71; v.p., bd. dirs. United Way, Pueblo, 1972-76; bd. dirs. YWCA, Pueblo, 1978-79. Republican. Clubs: Bismark Personal Computer Users Group, Beulah Women of Today. Avocations: Skiing, golf, photography.

DOYLE, ARTHUR JAMES, utility company executive; b. Boston, June 19, 1923; s. M. Joseph and Grace M. (McPhee) D.; m. Glenda M. Luehring, Oct. 14, 1950; children: Teresa, Kevin, Kelley, Conaught, Briana, Michael, Brian, Christopher. J.D., Boston Coll., 1949. Bar: Mo. 1949, Mass. 1949. Assoc. Johnson, Lucas, Graces & Fane, Kansas City, Mo., 1949-51, Spencer, Fane, Britt & Browne, Kansas City, 1951-57; ptnr. Spencer, Fane, Britt & Browne, 1957-73; v.p., gen. counsel Kansas City Power & Light Co., 1973-77, dir., 1976—, exec. v.p., 1977-78, pres., 1978-87, chmn. bd., chief exec. officer, 1979—; bd. dirs. Businessmens' Assurance Co. Am. Served to lt. (j.g.) USN, 1942-46. Mem. Mo. Bar Assn. (chmn. adminstrv. law sect. 1973-74, vice chmn. 1969-73), Fed. Power Bar Assn., Mo. C. of C. (dir. 1968-70). Roman Catholic. Clubs: Kansas City, Mission Hills.

DOYLE, CHARLES THOMAS, process/quality engineer; b. Phoenix, Ariz., Aug. 19, 1961; s. CHarles Edward and Lorraine Ann (Janis) D. BS Indsl. Mgmt., Lawrence Inst. Technology, 1984; postgrad., Cen. Mich. U., 1987—. Mgmt. trainee, materials supr., process/quality engr. Chrysler Corp., Warren, Mich., 1984—. Mem., choreographer Grosse Pointe (Mich.) Theatre, 1985. Mem. Am. Prodn. and Inventory Control Soc., Soc. Automotive Engrs., Sigma Phi Epsilon. Avocations: sports, theatre, dance, travel, education. Home: 37363 Charter Oaks Mount Clemens MI 48043 Office: Chrysler Corp 21500 Mound Rd Warren MI 48091

DOYLE, CONSTANCE TALCOTT JOHNSTON, physician; b. Mansfield, Ohio, July 8, 1945; d. Frederick Lyman IV and Nancy Jean Bushnell (Johnston) Talcott; m. Alan Jerome Demsky, June 13, 1976; children—Ian Frederick Demsky, Zachary Adam Demsky. B.S., Ohio U., 1967; M.D., Ohio State U., 1971. Diplomate Am. Bd. Emergency Medicine. Intern, Riverside Hosp., Columbus, Ohio, 1971-72; resident in internal medicine Hurley Hosp. and U. Mich., Flint, 1972-74, emergency physician Oakwood Hosp., Dearborn, Mich., 1974-76, Jackson County (Mich.) Emergency Services, 1975—; survival flight physician U. Mich. helicopter rescue service, 1983—; disaster cons., co-chmn. emergency med. services disaster com. Region II EMS, 1978-79; course dir. advanced cardiac life support and chmn. advanced life support com. W.A. Foote Meml. Hosp., Jackson, 1979—, others; clin. instr. emergency services, dept. surgery U. Mich., 1981—; instr. Jackson County Emergency Med. Technician refresher courses, Jackson Community Coll. Bd. dirs. Jackson County Heart Assn., 1979-83. Mem. ACP, Am. Med. Women's Assn., Am. Coll. Emergency Physicians (Mich. disaster com., dir. Mich. 1979—, chmn. Mich. disaster com. 1979-85; nat. ad hoc disaster com. 1983-85; chmn. nat. ad hoc com. on disaster services, 1986-87; cons. Fed. Emergency Mgmt. Agy. disaster mgmt. course 1982—, treas. 1984-85, emergency med. services com. 1985, pres. 1986-87, councillor 1986—), ACP, Mich. Assn. Emergency Med. Technicians (dir. 1979-80), Mich. State, Jackson County med. socs., Sierra Club. Jewish. Contbg. author: Clinical Approach to Poisoning and Toxicology, 1983; contbr. articles to profl. publs. Home: 1665 Lansdowne Rd Ann Arbor MI 48105 Office: WA Foote Hospital East Emergency Dept Jackson MI 49201

DOYLE, DONALD VINCENT, state senator; b. Sioux City, Iowa, Jan. 13, 1925; s. William E. and Nelsine E. (Sparby) D.; B.S., Morningside Coll., Sioux City, 1951; J.D., U. S.D., 1953; m. Janet E. Holtz, Aug. 9, 1963; 1 dau., Dawn Renee. Admitted to S.D., Iowa bars, 1953; pvt. practice, Sioux City, 1953—; mem. Iowa Ho. of Reps. from Woodbury County, 1956-80, Iowa Senate, 1981—. Served with USAAF, 1943-46. Recipient award Woodbury County Peace Officers, 1974, Restoration Club Sioux City, 1964, Outstanding Elected Ofcl. award Iowa Corrections Assn., 1979. Mem. Iowa, Woodbury County bar assns., CBI Vets. Assn. (past nat. judge adv.), Am. Legion, VFW, DAV, 40 and 8. Democrat. Office: PO Box 941 Sioux City IA 51102

DOYLE, GERTRUDE ILEENE, hospital administrator; b. Monon, Ind., Feb. 14, 1933; d. Samuel Elmer and Goldia Mae (Raines) Johns; m. Leo Francis Doyle, Apr. 16, 1955; children—Leo Edward, Phillip Wayne. R.N., Methodist Hosp., 1954; B.S.N., Ind. U., 1970, M.S., 1975. R.N., Ind. Office nurse, Indpls., 1954-55; asst. head nurse urology Meth. Hosp., Indpls., 1955-56; occupational health nurse Western Electric Co., Indpls., 1959-68; clin. instr. cardiovascular nursing Meth. Hosp., 1970-75, patient instr. and coordinator cardiovascular rehab. program, 1975-82, program developer, ednl. coordinator noninvasive testing and edn. dept., 1982-86; cons. program devel., cardiac rehab. vol., mem. exec. com., chmn. bd. dirs. Marion County chpt. Am. Heart Assn., bd. dirs. Ind. affiliate Am. Heart Assn., also instr. basic and advanced cardiac life support. Mem. U. Alumni Assn., Meth. Hosp. Council Cardiovascular Nursing Assn., Am. Heart Assn. (recipient Vol. Instr. CPR 5-Yr. award, 1981). Democrat. Roman Catholic. Clubs: St. Michael's Ladies Aux. (Greenfield); Our Lady of Fatima Ladies Guild (Indpls.). Author: (with Jack Hall) Manual of Cardiovascular Rehabilitation, 1975. Home: 2143 W 100 N Greenfield IN 46140 Office: Methodist Hosp 1604 N Capitol Ave Indianapolis IN 46202

DOYLE, RICHARD HENRY, IV, lawyer; b. Elgin, Ill., Aug. 8, 1949; s. Richard Henry and Shirley Marian (Ohms) D.; m. Debbie Kay Cahalan, Aug. 2, 1975; children—John Richard, Kerry Jane. B.A., Drake U., 1971, J.D., 1976. Bar: Iowa 1976, U.S. Dist. Ct. (no. and so. dists.) Iowa 1977, U.S. Ct. Appeals (8th cir.) 1977, U.S. Supreme Ct. 1986. Asst. atty. gen. Iowa Dept. Justice, Des Moines, 1976-77; assoc. Lawyer, Lawyer & Jackson, Des Moines, 1977-79; assoc. Law Offices of Verne Lawyer & Assocs., Des Moines, 1979—. Contbr. articles to profl. jours. Served with U.S. Army, 1971-73. Fellow Iowa Acad. Trial Lawyers; mem. Assn. Trial Lawyers Am., Assn. Trial Lawyers Iowa, ABA (jud. adminstrn. and tort and ins. practice sects.), Am. Judicature Soc., Iowa Bar Assn., Polk County Bar Assn. (law library trustee 1986—), SAR (registrar Iowa 1983—), Phi Alpha Delta (chpt. pres. 1975), Republican. Presbyterian. Home: 532 Waterbury Circle Des Moines IA 50312 Office: Law Offices Verne Lawyer & Assocs 427 Fleming Bldg Des Moines IA 50309

DOYLE, RICHARD J., manufacturing company executive. Pres. Borg-Warner Automotive Inc., Troy, Mich. Office: Borg-Warner Automotive Inc 3001 W Big Beaver Rd Troy MI 48084 *

DOYLE, RICHARD LEE, architect, engineer; b. Franklin Park, Ill., May 1, 1919; s. Richard Earl and Mildred Cleone Doyle; m. Donna Alberta Draland; children: Rebecca Ann, Mary Agnes. BA, U. Ill., 1949. Registered architect, Ill. Clk. of the works Lankton Zeigele Architects, Peoria, Ill., 1950-54; architect, engineer Doyle Assocs. Architects/Engrs., Peoria, 1955—; planning cons. Peoria Heights Planning Commn., 1965—. Prin. works include Pleasant Valley Schs., Peoria High Rehab., also designed various high schs., churches, public works, libraries. Served with U.S. Army, 1939-45, PTO. Mem. AIA, Am. Arbitration Soc. (sr., arbiter), Am. Architects Soc. (arbiter), Ill. Sch. Bds. Assn. (service assoc.), Constrn. Coordinating Council (chmn. 1968-69). Lodge: Kiwanis (pres. Peoria 1985).

Home: 501 Prospect Ln Peoria IL 61614 Office: Doyle Assocs Architects/Engrs 4916 Hamilton Rd Peoria IL 61614

DOYLE, THOMAS JOHN, optometrist; b. St. John's, Mich., Dec. 25, 1952; s. Gaylord John and Rita Mary (Stackpole) D.; m. Deborah Witwer, Jan. 18, 1980 (div. Dec. 1983); children: Scott, Shelby; m. Julie Ann Doyle, Nov. 15, 1986. BS in Optometric Sci., Ill. Coll. Optometry, Chgo., 1977; OD, Ill. (Chgo.) Coll. Optometry, Chgo., 1978. Lic. OD, Mich. Optometrist Health Cen. Inc., Lansing, Mich., 1978-79; gen. practice optometry DeWitt, Mich., 1979—. Roman Catholic. Lodge: Lions (past pres. breakfast club). Avocation: golf. Office: 13109 Shavey Rd #2 DeWitt MI 48820

DOYLE, THOMAS JOSEPH, marketing executive; b. St. Louis, Mar. 10, 1952; s. Charles Richard and Elizabeth (McMahon) D.; m. Linda Marie Markus, Aug. 5, 1977; children: Erin, Patrick, Brian. BS in Fin., U. Santa Clara, 1974. Product mktg. Hall-Mark Electronics, St. Louis, 1977-81; acct. rep. TRW Components Group, St. Louis, 1981-84; regional mktg. mgr. Mylee Systems Co., St. Louis, 1984—. mem. bd. edn. St. Peters Sch., Kirkwood, Mo., 1985-86. Roman Catholic. Home: 511 E Jefferson Kirkwood MO 63122 Office: Mylee Systems Co 155 Weldon Pkwy Maryland Heights MO 63043

DOYLE, WENDELL E., teacher; b. Higbee, Mo., July 8, 1940; s. Travis E. and Hattie Erma (Webb) D.; m. Julia Ann Vail, June 23, 1963; children: Dora Michelle, Michael E., Melissa Kae. BS in Edn., Northeast Mo. State U., 1962; MEd in Music, U. Mo., 1967. Cert. lifetime tchr., Mo. Band dir. Braymer (Mo.) C-4, 1962-68, Brookfield (Mo.) R-3, 1968-72, Platte County (Mo.) R-III, 1972—; exchange tchr. Platte County R-III Schs., Warwickshire, Eng., 1984. Pres. Barry Heights Homes Assn., 1986—; minister of music Park Bapt. Ch., Brookfield, 1968-72, Northgate Bapt. Ch., Kansas City, 1972-85. Mem. Mo. State Tchrs. Assn. (pres. Greater Kans. City dist. 1978), Music Educators Nat. Conf., Mo. Music Educators Assn., Phi Delta Kappa. Democrat. Lodge: Rotary (sec., treas. Braymer, Mo., 1966-68). Avocations: fishing, reading, golfing, travel. Home: 2330 NW Powderhorn Dr Kansas City MO 64154

DOYLE, WILLIAM JAY, II, business consultant; b. Cin., Nov. 7, 1928; s. William Jay and Blanche (Gross) D.; B.S., Miami U., Oxford, Ohio, 1949; postgrad. U. Cin., 1950-51, Xavier U., 1953-54, Case Western Res. U., 1959-60; m. Joan Lucas, July 23, 1949; children—David L., William Jay, III, Daniel L. Sales rep. Diebold, Inc., Cin., 1949-52, asst. br. mgr., 1953-57, asst. regional mgr., Cin., 1957-62, regional mgr., Cin., 1962-74; founder, chief exec. officer Central Bus. Group div. Central Bus. Equipment Co., Inc., Cin., 1974—, dir. parent co. and divs.; mem. area contractor's council Spacesaver Corp., 1985-87; speaker on bus systems, security concepts. Mem. Armstrong Chapel, Methodist ch., Indian Hill, Ohio, adminstrv. bd, 1987-88. Mem. Bus. Systems and Security Mktg. Assn. (nat. dir. 1977-79, 81-83, nat. pres. 1981-83, 84-85), Nat. Assn. Accts. Republican. Clubs: Kenwood Country, Masons, Shriners. Contbr. articles to co. and trade publs.; developer new concepts in tng., cash and securities handling, mobile and mechanized storage and filing, and other areas of bus. systems. Home: 6250 S Clippinger Dr Cincinnati OH 45243 Office: 10839 Indeco Dr Cincinnati OH 45241

DRACH, DEANNE ELMIRA, records storage and service company executive; b. Dodge City, Kans., Sept. 12, 1940; d. Elmer A. and Elda E.N. (Weiss) Wetzel; m. Roger Henry Drach, Aug. 20, 1960; 1 child, Douglas D. AA, Dodge City Community Coll., 1960. Mktg. mgr. Underground Vaults and Storage, Hutchinson, Kans., 1972-86; gen. mgr. Records Ctr. Kansas City Div. Underground Vaults and Storage, Kansa City, 1986—; cons. in field. Mem. Assn. Records Mgrs. and Adminstrs. (pres., sec., program chmn. Wichita Kans. chpt. 1976—). Home: 7604 Goddard #01 Shawnee KS 66214

DRAEGER, GARY ALLAN, accountant; b. Racine, Wis., Oct. 19, 1953; s. Robert Frederick Draeger and Ruth Marie (Flanery) Julson; m. Kimberly Jean Miller, Aug. 12, 1978; children: Jennifer, Lindsey. BBA, U. Wis., Eau Claire, 1974. CPA, Wis. Staff acct. Arthur Andersen & Co., Milw., 1974-77; acct. Vrakas, Blum & Co., S.C., Waukesha, Wis., 1978-85, ptnr., 1985—. Chmn. Waukesha Small Bus. Council, 1986—. Mem. Am. Inst. CPA's, Wis. Inst. CPA's (chmn. various coms., 1977—), Waukesha Area C. of C. Lutheran. Avocations: fishing, golf. Office: Vrakas Blum & Co SC Deer Creek Office Ctr 445 S Moorlnd Rd Brookfield WI 53005

DRAEMEL, MICHAEL CHARLES, electric wholesale company executive; b. Fremont, Nebr., Sept. 5, 1946, s. Myron Charles and Donna Joan (Dunbar) D.; m. Pamela Kay Stunkel, Feb. 11, 1978; children—Darren Reese, Grif Lee. B.A., Midland Lutheran Coll., Fremont, 1968; M.A., Pepperdine U., Malibu, Calif., 1969. Tchr. high sch., Santa Ana, Calif., 1968-69; profl. golfer, 1971-74; div. mgr. Kriz-Davis Elec. Wholesale Co., Fremont, 1974—. Served with U.S. Army, 1969-71. Republican. Episcopalian. Home: 21318 Brentwood Rd Elkhorn NE 68022 Office: 810 S Schneider Fremont NE 68025

DRAGO, CARL J., prosthodontist; b. Yonkers, N.Y., Aug. 14, 1952; s. Rosario Phillip and Elizabeth (Brisgal) D.; m. Kathryn Sue Lammers, Mar. 11, 1978; children: Stephanie Ann, Matthew Brisgal. BA cum laude, Ohio State U., 1974, DDS, 1976; MS, U. Tex., San Antonio, 1981. Diplomate Am. Bd. Prosthodontics. Intern Northwestern U., Evanston, Ill., 1976-77; asst. prof. U. Tex. Dental Sch., San Antonio, 1979-81, resident, 1979-81; staff prosthodontist Gundersen Clinic, Ltd., La Crosse, Wis., 1981—; cons. St. Paul Dist. Dental Soc., 1982; guest lectr. VA Hosp., Milw., 1986. Author chpt. Advances in Occlusion, 1981. Grantee Research and Edn. Found. for Prosthodontics, 1980. Fellow Am. Coll. Prosthodontists. Republican. Roman Catholic. Avocations: photography, racquetball, biking, travel. Home: 400 S 28th St La Crosse WI 54601 Office: Gundersen Clinic Ltd 1836 South Ave La Crosse WI 54601

DRAGOO, JOHN WILLIAM, steel forging company executive; b. New Castle, Ind., Oct. 18, 1949; s. Wayne F. Dragoo and Marjorie Maxine (Hutchison) Walker; m. Jane Edith Morrison, June 7, 1969; children: Brittany, John, Robert. BS in English, Ball State U., 1972, MA in Higher Edn., 1976; postgrad., S.E. Mo., 1977-78, Ind. U., 1978-79, 86—. Tchr. English, coach Union City (Ind.) Schs., 1972-74; tchr. English East Noble Schs., Kendallville, Ind., 1974-75; mgr. computer services S.E. Mo. U., Cape Girardeau, 1976-78; systems analyst Farm Bur. Ins., Indpls., 1978-79, Borg-Warner, Muncie, Ind., 1979-81, Gen. Motors Corp., Anderson, Ind., 1981-82; dir. mgmt. info. systems Teledyne Portland (Ind.) Forge, 1982—; cons. data processing, Portland, 1982—, Ind. Vocat. Coll., Muncie, 1979-82; instr. data processing S.E. Mo. U., 1977-78. Bd. dirs. Portland Area C. of C., 1985—, Wapehani council Girl Scouts U.S., Muncie, 1985-86; founder, dir. Portland Area Girls' Sports Assn., 1984—; chmn. econ. devel. Portland Strategic Planning, 1984-85. Recipient Citation, Mayor of Portland, 1984, 85, 87. Mem. Forging Industry Assn. (chmn. com. 1984-86), Data Processing Mgmt. Assn., Status IBM Minicomputer User Group, Common IBM Minicomputer User Group. Lodge: Rotary. Avocations: reading, tennis, softball, golf, youth activities. Home: 415 E Arch Portland IN 47371 Office: Teledyne Portland Forge PO Box 905 Portland IN 47371

DRAGOSH, A. JAMES, chiropractor; b. Milw., Aug. 30, 1951; s. Anthony James and Pearl B. (Tobin) D.; m. Marilyn Rae Breitbach, Oct. 6, 1973; children—Ann, Chris. A.A., U. Wis.-Stevens Point, 1972; D.C., Palmer Coll. Chiropractic, Iowa, 1976; postgrad. Nat. Coll. Chiropractic. Diplomat Nat. Bd. Chiropractic. Practice chiropractic, Kaukauna, Wis., 1976—; head tennis coach Kaukauna High Sch., 1984—. Vice-pres. bd. adminstrn. Methodist Ch., Kaukauna, 1983, 84; bd. dirs. Thousand Island Environ. Ctr., Kaukauna, 1984—. Mem. Am. Chiropractic Assn., Wis. Chiropractic Assn. (peer rev. com., chmn. workers compensation), Northeast Dist. Chiropractic Assn. (pres. 1980). Lodge: Kiwanis (Kaukauna) (pres. 1982-83). Home: 510 Sanitorium Rd Kaukauna WI 54130 Office: 500 Lawe St Kaukauna WI 54130

DRAKE, CHERYL SUSAN, English language educator, free-lance technical writer; b. Salem, Ohio, Dec. 21, 1950; d. Hubert Nelson and Dorothy Jean (Lewton) Brown; m. Richard Lee Drake, Dec. 23, 1972; children: Miles Richard, Jennifer Lyn. BA, Mt. Union Coll., Alliance, Ohio, 1972; MEd, U. Cin., 1984. Secondary tchr. Avon (Ind.) Community Schs., 1972-75; sec. devel. MIT, Cambridge, 1975-77; asst. dir. devel. Univ. Sch. Milw., 1977-79; instr. Milw. Area Tech. Coll., 1979-81; instr. English So. Ohio Coll., Fairfield, 1984—; seminar leader tech. communications Mosler Internat., Fairfield, 1985. Active with Monfort Heights Elem. Sch., Cin., 1984-86, Monfort Heights United Meth. Ch., Cin., 1984-86. Mem. Nat. Council Tchrs. of English, Soc. for Tech. Communication. Avocations: reading, skiing, swimming, travel. Home: 5597 Vogel Rd Cincinnati OH 45239 Office: So Ohio Coll 4641 Bacher Sq Fairfield OH 45014

DRAKE, DOUGLAS JAMES, research scientist; b. Prairie du Chien, Wis., May 31, 1948; s. James Leroy and Bette Lee (Silberhorn) D.; m. Sylvia Ina Zimmermann, May 22, 1976; children: Raymond, Julia, Robert. Research asst. U. Wis., 1978-82; research scientist KMS Fusion, Inc., Ann Arbor, Mich., 1982-85, mgr. target design group, 1985—. Contbr. articles to profl. jour. Served to capt. U.S. Army, 1970-75. Mem. Am. Phys. Soc. Home: 1465 Hiawatha Jackson MI 49201 Office: KMS Fusion Inc 3621 S State Rd Ann Arbor MI 48106

DRAKE, ELAINE CARLSON, dentist; b. Chgo., June 16, 1954; d. Raymond Frank and Maximiliane Katherine (Koehler) Carlson; m. Dale Addison Drake, Dec. 18, 1977; children: Christa, Lindsay, Adam, Andrew. BS with honors, U. Ill., 1976; DDS, Loyola U., Maywood, Ill., 1980. Gen. practice dentistry Belvidere, Ill., 1980—. Elder First Presbyn. Ch., Belvidere, 1982-84. Mem. Belvidere Panhellenic Assn. (pres. 1981-82), Pi Beta Phi, Belvidere C. of C. Lodge: Zonta. Avocations: reading, sewing, singing, swimming. Home: 7646 Bel-Mar Dr Belvidere IL 61008 Office: 515 Pearl St Belvidere IL 61008

DRAKE, ELLET HALLER, cardiologist; b. Omaha, May 26, 1914; s. Ellet Bradley and Ruth Patterson (Haller) D.; m. Frances Margaret Moyer, Aug. 15, 1944; children: Frances Haller, Patricia Moyer. Student, Grinnell Coll., 1931-34; BS in Medicine, U. Nebr., Omaha, 1935, MD, 1939. Diplomate Am. Bd. Internal Medicine, Am. Bd. Cardiology. Intern Henry Ford Hosp., Detroit, 1939-40, resident in cardiology, 1946-49, mem. staff, 1949-71, chief of staff, 1972-78; chief of staff Wausau (Wis.) Hosp. Ctr., 1978—; med. dir. A. Ward Ford Meml. Inst., Wausau, WI, 1976-84, v.p., 1984, also bd. dirs., cons., 1984—; mem. edn. bd. Lasers in Surgery and Medicine, N.Y.C., 1984—, Clinical Laser Monthly, Atlanta, 1984—; adv. bd. Med. Laser Industry Report, Redondo Beach, CAl., 1986—. Contbr. numerous articles to profl. jours. Vol. United Way, 1985. Served to surgeon USPHS, 1942-46. Fellow ACP, Am. Coll. Cardiology, Am. Soc. Laser Medicine and Surgery (sec. 1981, Recognition award 1986); mem. AMA. Republican. Episcopalian. Club: Doberman Pinscher of Am. (pres. 1960-61). Avocation: raising and training purebred dogs. Home: 706 Spring Wausau WI 54401 Office: 813 2d St Suite 200 Wausau WI 54401

DRAKE, GEORGE ALBERT, college president, historian; b. Springfield, Mo., Feb. 25, 1934; s. George Bryant and Alberta (Stimpson) D.; m. Susan Martha Ratcliff, June 25, 1960; children: Christopher George, Cynthia May, Melanie Susan. A.B., Grinnell Coll., 1956; Fulbright scholar, U. Paris, 1956-57; A.B. (Rhodes scholar), Oxford U., 1959, M.A., 1963; B.D., U. Chgo., 1962, M.A., 1963, Ph.D. (Rockefeller fellow), 1965; LL.D. (hon.), Colorado Coll., 1980, Ripon Coll., 1982; L.H.D. (hon.), Ill. Coll., 1985. Instr. history Grinnell Coll., Iowa, 1960-61; pres., prof. history Grinnell Coll., 1979—; asst. prof., assoc. prof., prof. history Colo. Coll., Colorado Springs, 1964-79, acting dean of Coll., 1967-68, dean, 1969-73. Trustee Grinnell Coll., 1970-79, Penrose Hosp., 1876-79, 80-84, Grinnell Gen. Hosp., 1980—. NEH fellow, 1974. Mem. Am. Hist. Assn., Am. Ch. History Soc., Nat. Coll. Athletic Assn. pres. commn., 1984—.

DRAKE, JUDETH A(NN), accountant; b. Glen Ridge, N.J., Mar. 10, 1952; d. Walter Vincent and Virginia Anna (Cumming) Tyminski; m. Neil L. Drake, Jan. 3, 1987. BS cum laude, Kans. State U., 1975; MBA, U. Mich., 1977. CPA, Ill. Sr. fin. analyst Lester B. Knight & Assoc., Chgo., 1977-79; supr. Alexander Grant & Co., Chgo., 1979-84; mgr. Deloitte Haskins & Sells, Chgo., 1984—. Contbr. articles to Bus. Age mag.; contbr. to fin. column in local newspaper, 1985—. Mem. Am. Inst. CPA's, Ill. CPA Soc. Office: Deloitte Haskins & Sells 200 E Randolph Chicago IL 60601

DRAKE, RICHARD LEE, anatomy and cell biology educator, research scientist; b. Columbus, Ohio, Feb. 25, 1950; s. M. Richard and Nina Louise (Drake) D.; m. Cheryl Susan Brown, Dec. 23, 1972; children—Miles Richard, Jennifer Lyn. B.S., Mt. Union Coll., 1972; Ph.D., Ind. U., 1975. Postdoctoral fellow MIT, Cambridge, Mass., 1975-77; asst. prof. anatomy Med. Coll. Wis., Milw., 1977-81; asst. prof. anatomy and cell biology U. Cin. Coll. Medicine, 1981-85, assoc. prof. anatomy and cell biology, 1985—, dir. body donation program, 1982—, co-dir. freshman med. gross anatomy course, 1982-84, dir. freshman med. and grad. gross anatomy course, 1984—, course dissection coordinator, continuing edn. course for orthopaedic surgeons, 1983—. Mem. Mt. Union Coll. Alumni Council, Alliance, Ohio, 1980-81. Mem. AAAS, Am. Soc. Cell Biology, Am. Assn. Anatomists, Am. Diabetes Assn., Sigma Xi. Methodist. Contbr. articles, abstracts to profl. publs.; research in field of insulin regulation of cellular metabolism. Office: U Cin Coll Medicine Dept Anatomy and Cell Biology 231 Bethesda Ave ML 521 Cincinnati OH 45267

DRAKE, WILLIAM DEPUE, foundation administrator, educator; b. Evanston, Ill., Apr. 13, 1936; s. Charles Francis II and Helen (Depue) D.; m. Susan York, July 3, 1964; children: William Depue, Elizabeth Dean, Mark, Michael. BS, U. Mich., 1959, MBA, 1960, PhD, 1964. Dep. exec. sec. Pres. Com on Tech. Automation and Econ. Progress, 1965-66; asst. prof. Sch. Nat. Resources U. Mich., Ann Arbor, 1966-67, assoc. prof., 1968-69, prof., 1970—, assoc. dean. for research, 1972-75; cons. bd. Consumers Union of USA, 1966-71; chmn. Univ. Wide PhD Program in Urban and Regional Planning, 1968-72; organizer Mich. Savs. and Loan Assn., chmn. bd. 1980—; mem. bldg. research adv. bd. NRC. Chmn. Ann Arbor Met. Transport Authority, 1972-76; sec., treas., trustee Community Systems Found., 1973-78, pres. 1978—. Mem. AAAS, Ops. Research Soc. Am., Inst. Mgmt. Scis. Home: 1321 Brooklyn Ave Ann Arbor MI 48104

DRANNEN, KATHLEEN ANN, banker; b. Grand Forks, N.D., Aug. 12, 1958; d. John William and Elinor Margaret (Grimes) D. BBA, U. Minn., 1980. Asst. v.p. First Bank Mpls., 1980—. Advisor Kappa Kappa Gamma, Mpls., 1986. Mem. Nat. Assn. Indsl. Office Parks, Jr. League St. Paul, Inc. Office: First Bank Mpls Real Estate Dept First Bank Pl Minneapolis MN 55480

DRAPER, JOHN COTTREL, food products executive; b. Detroit, Dec. 9, 1950; s. Cottrel and Ethel Marie (Griffin) D.; m. Deborah Herlene Rawlings, Nov. 19, 1970; children: Angela Deshawn, John Cottrel II. BBA, Wayne State U., 1982; dental specifications course, Acad. Health Sci., Houston, 1973. Asst. mgr. All-Pro Food Services, Inc., Detroit, 1971-73, restaurant mgr., 1973-78, dist. mgr., 1978-83, v.p., 1983—; career developer Detroit Pub. Schs., 1981-83. Pres. Council Marygrove Coll., Detroit, 1985; mem. ecec. bd. student motivational program Detroit Pub. Schs., 1987; hon. mem. com. Inner City Sub-Ctr., Inc., Detroit. Served with USAR, 1972-78. Mem. Kappa Alpha Psi. Democrat. Avocations: model car and antique furniture collecting, racquetball. Office: All-Pro Services Inc 23828 W Seven Mile Detroit MI 48219

DRAPER, WALTER DILLAWAY, librarian; b. Chgo., Sept. 9, 1928; s. Walter Dillaway and Jessie Durant (Johnston) D. B.A., Amherst Coll., 1950; M.Ed., Nat. Coll. Edn., 1954; M.A.L.S., U. Wis., 1965. Cert. tchr., Ill., Ind., Fla. Tchr. Burbank Sch., Oak Lawn, Ill., 1954-56; tchr. Dade County, Miami, Fla., 1956-57; tchr. Sch. City, Hammond, Ind., 1957-60; tchr. Bd. Edn., Chgo., 1966; asst. librarian Rio Grande Coll. (Oh.), 1967-68; reference librarian Pub. Library, Gary, Ind., 1969—. Choir mem. Chopin Chorus, Merrillville, Ind., 1973—, Millenium Chrous, Munster, Ind., 1976—. Winner Sawyer prize Amherst Coll. (Mass.), 1948. Mem. ALA, Ind. Library Assn. Office: Wildermuth Library 501 S Lake St Gary IN 46403

DRAYTON, FRANK JAMES III, marketing professional; b. Jacksonville, Fla., July 8, 1958; s. Frank James Jr. and Joyce Elinor (Johnson) D. BA, Mich. State U., 1980; MS, U. Ill., 1981. Research asst. Young & Rubicam Inc., Detroit, 1981-82, acct. exec., 1982-83, acct. supr., 1983-85; mgmt. dir. Group 243 Inc., Ann Arbor, Mich., 1986-87; mktg. dir. The Beznos Cos., Farmington Hills, Mich., 1987—. Mem. Adcraft Club of Detroit, Am. Mktg. Assn., Mich. State U. Alumni Assn., Univ. Ill. Alumni Assn. Methodist. Avocations: golfing, sailing, skiing. Home: 25055 Pimlico Farmington Hills MI 48018 Office: The Beznos Cos 31731 Northwestern Hwy Farmington Hills MI 48018

DRESCH, STEPHEN PAUL, economist; b. East St. Louis, Ill., Dec. 12, 1943; s. Lester Wilson Reuben and Leonore Marie (Steege) D.; m. Linda Carol Ness, May 18, 1963; children: Soren K., Stephanie Elizabeth, Phaedra Augusta, Karl Friedrick Johannes. A.B. Philosophy, Miami U., Oxford, Ohio, 1963; M.Phil. Econ., NSF fellow, Yale U., 1966, Ph.D., 1970. Mem. faculty dept. econs. Miami U., Oxford, Ohio, 1963-64; mem. Yale U., New Haven, Conn., 1966-67, South Conn. State Coll., New Haven, 1968-69, Rutgers U., New Brunswick, N.J., 1970; researcher Nat. Bur. Econ. Research, N.Y.C. and New Haven, 1969-77; cons. in residence Ford Found., N.Y.C., 1970-72; dir. reserch in econs. of higher edn. Yale U., 1972-75, chmn. Inst. for Demographic and Econ. Studies, 1975—; dean, prof. econs. and bus. Sch. Bus. and Engring. Adminstrn., Mich. Technol. U., 1985—; research scholar Internat. Inst. Applied Systems Analysis, Austria, 1983-85. Author: Substituting a Value Added Tax for the Corporate Income Tax, 1977, Occupational Earnings, 1967-81, 1986; Occupational Earnings, 1967-81, 1986; contbr. articles to profl. jours. Mem. Am. Econ. Assn., AAAS, Fedn. of Am. Scientists, Assn. for Pub. Policy Analysis and Mgmt. Libertarian. Mem. United Ch. Christ. Home: 318 Cooper Ave Hancock MI 49930 Office: SBEA/MTU Houghton MI 49931

DRESSEL, IRENE EMMA RINGWALD, alcoholism and family therapist; b. Enderlin, N.D., Oct. 26, 1926; d. Albert William and Emma Anna Magdelena (Trapp) Ringwald; m. Clarence Irvin Dressel, Jr., Mar. 13, 1946 (div. Nov. 1972); 1 son, Keith Alan. Student pub. schs., Casselton, N.D. Cert. Master addiction counselor, N.D.; cert. chem. dependency counselor, Minn. Alcoholism counseling trainee Heartview Found., Mandan, N.D., 1974-75, family therapy intern, 1975-76, family counselor, 1976-77, supr. family mems. program, 1978; designer, supr. family program The Meadows, Wickenburg, Ariz., 1978-79; treatment programs cons., dir. consultation dept. Johnson Inst., Mpls., 1979-81; assoc. dir. chem. dependency unit Presbyn. Hosp., Oklahoma City, 1981-83; supr. adolescent counseling staff United Recovery Ctr., Grand Forks, N.D., 1983-85; dir. Irene Dressel Counseling, 1985—. cons. S.W. Inst. Alcohol Studies, Norman, Okla., Kans. Alcoholism Counselors Assn., Okla. Assn. Alcoholism and Drug Abuse; lectr. U. N.D., Grand Forks, N.D. Sch. Alcohol Studies. Mem. N.D. Alcoholism Counselors Assn., Nat. Alcoholism and Drug Addiction Counselors Assn., Am. Assn. Counseling and Devel., Nat. Mental Health Counselors Assn. Democrat. Lutheran. Office: 407 DeMers Ave PO Box 6145 Grand Forks ND 58206-6145

DRESSEL, MARGARET (PEGGY) SCHOCHOW, editor; b. Virginia, Minn., July 21, 1955; d. Orville Otto and Edia (Varani) Schochow; m. Brian William Dressel, June 29, 1985. BA, U. Minn., 1977. Copy writer Fingerhut Corp., Mpls., 1977-79; editor Potentials in Mktg. mag. Lakewood Publs., Mpls., 1979-86; editor Machalek Pub., Mpls., 1986—. Mem. Minn. Press Club, Minn. Incentive Club (bd. dirs. 1984—, 1st v.p. 1986—), Nat. Premium Sales Execs., Incentive Mfgs. Rep. Assn. Roman Catholic. Home: 4913 Upton Ave S Minneapolis MN 55410 Office: Machalek Publs 15 S 9th St Minneapolis MN 55402

DRESSLER, DONALD GENE, civil engineer; b. Iola, Ks., July 29, 1936; s. Paul Eugene and Velva Lorene (Paugh) D.; m. Alta Lou Krause; children: Darrin, Kristin, David. Pre-engring. student, Kans. State Coll., 1955-58; BS in Civil Engring., Kans. State U., 1960; MA in Engring., Kans. U., 1986. Registered profl. engr., Kans., Mo., Tex., Ark., Okla., Iowa. Safety dir. Havens Steel, Kansas City, Mo., 1963-66; project engr. Atlas Chems., Joplin, Mo., 1966-67; control engr. ICI, Joplin, 1967-72; corp. engr. ICI, Wilmington, Del., 1972-73; chief engr. Bayvet, Shawnee Mission, Kans., 1973-80; owner Dressler Cons. Engrs., Leawood, Kans., 1973—. Patentee in field. Chmn. Appeals Com., Leawood, 1973—; mem. Bldg. Code Com., Leawood, 1973—. Mem. NSPE, ASCE, Kans. Cons. Engrs., Soc. Explosive Engrs., Am. Arbitration Assn. (arbitrator Chgo., Dallas 1986). Republican. Prebyterian. Club: Cosmopolitan. Avocations: boating, fishing, jogging. Home: 10328 Cherokee Ln Leawood KS 66206 Office: Dressler Cons Engrs 4425 Indian Creek Pkwy Overland Park KS 66207

DREVENSTEDT, JEAN, psychology educator; b. Louisville, July 13, 1927; d. Eduard A. and Suretta (Redmon) D. BS in Bus., Ind. U., 1949; PhD, Vanderbilt U., 1965. From. asst. to prodn. mgr. to traffic mgr. Zimmer-McClaskey-Lewis Advt. Agy., Louisville, 1949-58; clin. psychologist Children's Asthma Research Inst., Denver, 1964-65; asst. prof. Ohio U., Athens, 1965-71, assoc. prof., 1971—. Contbr. articles to profl. jours. Mem. Am. Psychol. Assn., Midwestern Psychol. Assn., Gerontol. Soc. Am., Mortar Bd., Sigma Xi, Beta Gamma Sigma, Omicron Delta Kappa, Alpha Omicron Pi. Presbyterian. Home: 20 Ohio Ave Athens OH 45701 Office: Ohio U Dept Psychology Porter Hall Athens OH 45701-2979

DREW, JIM L., accountant, manufacturing executive; b. Lake Forest, Ill., May 22, 1945; s. Herman L. and Amelia (Bulik) D.; m. Corinne Lipa, June 15, 1967; 1 child, James. BS in Fin., So. Ill. U., 1968; MBA in Fin., No. Ill. U., 1970. CPA, Ill. Acct. Bell & Howell Co., Lincolnwood, Ill., 1970-72, fin. analyst, 1972-73; controller micro design div. Bell & Howell Co., Hartford, Wis., 1973-86, mgr. new products and mktg. micro design div., 1986—. Bd. dirs. Hartford Hosp. Found., 1986—. Mem. Am. Inst. CPA's, Ill. CPA Soc. Lodge: Lions (bd. dirs. Hartford chpt. 1977-79). Avocations: golf, skiing. Office: Bell & Howell Micro Design Div 857 W State St Hartford WI 53027

DREW, MARY JANE HURT, health science association administrator; b. Boonville, Mo.; d. Henry Prezell and Florence Cardelia (Nelson) Hurt; m. George Lee Drew, May 31, 1953; children: Toni L., Bruce E., L'Tanya L. Drew Osborn, Trisha. AA in Applied Sci., Penn Valley Community Coll., Kansas City, Mo., 1977. Dir. human resources Carver Ctr., Kansas City, 1967-77, social worker, 1977-78, dir. program, 1978-82, acting exec. dir., 1980, dir. emergency services, 1982—. Recipient Cultural Devel. award Black Archives of Mid-Am., 1985, Outstanding Vol. Service award Vol. Action Ctr., 1986. Mem. Mo. Assn. for Social Welfare (bd. dirs.), Gray Panthers (hon.). Democrat. Baptist. Avocations: reading, bowling, traveling. Home: 3714 Benton Kansas City MO 64128 Office: Carver Neighborhood Ctr 4115 E 43d St Kansas City MO 64130

DREWERY, IDA M., health science facility administrator; b. Munson, Fla., Nov. 15, 1927; d. Isaiah Moore and Gertrude (Flowers) Johnson; divorced; children: Marcalene R. Dickerson, Edward Aubrey McBride. Grad. high sch., Pensacola, Fla. Comml. cook Kings Nursing Home, Detroit, 1958-66; supr., machine operator McCarthy Plastic Co., Detroit, 1966-74; adminstr. adult foster care home Detroit Dept. Social Services, 1974—. Mem. Women of Concerned Citizens, Detroit, 1984—, Mus. of African Am. Hist., fund raiser, 1965—. Named Provider of Yr., State of Mich., 1940; recipient Resolution County of Wayne, Mich., 1947. Home: 731 E Grand Blvd Detroit MI 48207

DREWES, TOM CHARLES, small business owner; b. Oak Park, Ill., June 20, 1941; s. Karl Alfred Drewes and Ella Alma (Jensen) Armstrong; m. Roberta Merrill Steinberg; children: Michelle, Deborah. Student, Elmhurst Coll., 1981; diploma exec. devel. program, Northwestern U., 1983. Founder, pres. Quality Books, Inc., Lake Bluff, Ill., 1964—; bd. dirs. Iroquois Popcorn Co., Elk Grove Village; mem. adv. bd. Semler Industries, Inc., Melrose Park, 1981—, C. Cretors, Inc. Chgo., 1981—. Contbr. numerous articles to profl. jours. Vol. tutor Lake County Literacy program, 1986. Served with USAF, 1959-63. Mem. ALA, Indsl. Peer Council. Jewish. Club: Chief Exec. Officers of Chgo. Avocations: sky diving, soaring, sailing. Home: 744 Carriage Way Deerfield IL 60015 Office: Quality Books Inc 918 Sherwood Dr Lake Bluff IL 60044-2204

DREXEL, WILLIAM ALLEN, iron foundry executive, accountant; b. Cleve., Feb. 8, 1922; s. William Edward and Florence Lynette (Lohr) D.; m. Janet Lee Phillips, Sept. 6, 1947; children: Deanna Lynn Drexel Green, Katherine Lee Drexel Holt. Student, Kent State U., 1941-42; BS, Ohio State U., Columbus, 1947. CPA, Ohio. Enlisted U.S. Army, 1941, advanced through grades to sgt., 1941, resigned, 1946; from jr. to sr. acct. Keller, Kirschner, Martin & Clinger, CPA's, Columbus, 1947-55; treas., dir., v.p. Orr, Brown & Price, Columbus, 1955-64; asst. treas. Keifer, Stewart Co., Indpls., 1964-67; mgr. ins. and tax Shatterproof Glass Corp., Detroit, 1967-69; gen. acctg. mgr. The Budd Co., Detroit, 1969-73; controller Waupaca (Wis.) Foundry, Inc., 1973—. Mem. Iron Casting Soc., Am. Inst. CPA's, Ohio Soc. CPA's. Republican. Club: Waupaca Country (bd. dirs. 1978-80, pres. 1980). Avocations: golf, dry fly trout fishing. Home: N 2273 Sky View Ln Waupaca WI 54981 Office: Waupaca Foundry Inc Tower Rd Waupaca WI 54981

DREXLER, RICHARD ALLAN, manufacturing company executive; b. Chgo., May 14, 1947; s. Lloyd A. and Evelyn Violet (Kovaloff) D.; m. Dale Sue Hoffman, Sept. 4, 1971; children: Dan Lloyd, Jason Ian. B.S., Northwestern U., 1969, M.B.A., 1970. Staff v.p. Allied Products Corp., Chgo., 1973-75, sr. v.p. adminstrn., 1975-79, exec. v.p., chief fin. officer, adminstrv. officer, 1979-82, exec. v.p., chief operating officer, 1982, pres., chief operating officer, 1982-86, pres., chief exec. officer, 1986—. Home: 2051 Clavey Rd Highland Park IL 60035 Office: Allied Products Corp 10 S Riverside Plaza Suite 1600 Chicago IL 60606

DREZDZON, WILLIAM LAWRENCE, mathematics educator; b. Milw., Feb. 19, 1934; s. Edward Kenneth and Mildred Mary (Schneider) D.; B.S. in Math., St. Mary's U., 1957; M.S. in Math. (Esso Oil Co. fellow), Ill. Inst. Tech., 1964; m. Frances Anita Sikes; children—Gregory Francis, Andrea Louise. Tchr. math., chemistry St. Michael's High Sch., Chgo., 1957-59, Lane Tech. High Sch., Chgo., 1959-66; software design engr. A.C. Electronics div. Gen. Motors, Oak Creek, Wis., 1966-67; prof. math., chmn. dept. Kennedy-King Coll., Chgo., 1967-71; prof. math. and learning lab. coordinator Oakton Community Coll., Des Plaines, Ill., 1971—; vis. prof. U. New Orleans, 1982-84; cons. nat. calculus survey, 1975. NSF grantee, 1961-65; Chgo. Bd. Edn. grantee, summer 1964; NSF coop. program, 1971, 72; Chautauqua Course grantee, 1975-80. Mem. Math. Assn. Am. (chmn. jr. coll. com. Ill. sect., 1971-74), No. Ill. Math. Assn. Community Colls. (founding pres., 1971, 72), Am. Math. Assn. Two-Yr. Colls. (chmn., 1975, pres. 1979), Nat., Ill. councils tchrs. math., Ill. Assn. Community Colls. (pres. 1979), Met. Mathematics Club of Gtr. Chgo., Adler Planetarium Soc., Ill. Assn. Personalized Learning Programs, Analytic Psychology Club of Chgo., Delta Epsilon Sigma. Regional editor Math. Assns. of Two-Year Colleges Jour., 1970-82; author: Curriculum Guide of Transfer Courses for the Ill. Community College Board, 1974; Math. Research and Teaching Techniques, 1973, 76; contbr. articles to jours. Home: 1600 Ashland Ave Des Plaines IL 60016 Office: Oakton Community College 1600 E Golf Rd Des Plaines IL 60016

DRISCOLL, DANIEL DELANO, photographer, inventor, manufacturer; b. Williamsburg, Iowa, Mar. 19, 1946; s. Vincent Edmund and Hilda Gertrude (Schmidt) D.; student U. Iowa, 1964-66; B.A., Loras Coll., 1969; student Winona Sch. Profl. Photography, summers 1969-71: m. Constance Elizabeth Kelleher, Feb. 28, 1970 (div. 1983); children—Duree Danielle, Darren Daniel. With Hilda's Photography, Williamsburg, Iowa, 1969-72; owner Driscoll Gallery, Williamsburg, 1973—, Kent Studio, Iowa City, 1975-76; founder, owner, pres. Four Horsemen Ltd., 1985—; exhibited Epcot Ctr., 1984. Named Iowa Photographer of Yr., 1975, 76, 77; Iowa Fellow of Photography, 1975; Iowa Master of Photography of Yr., 1979; named Heart of Am. Photographer, 1976, 77; recipient Frank W. Medlar Meml. trophy for best portrait, 1975, 76, 77; Internat. Tetrahedron award Eastman Kodak Co., 1984. Mem. Minn. (sweepstakes winner 1973, 74), Nebr. (photographer of year 1974), Pa. (top out of state photographer 1974), Va., Am. (Master of Photography degree 1977) profl. photographers assns. Contbr. articles to profl. jours. Inventor in bioelectronics field. Home: 302 W State St Williamsburg IA 52361 Office: 302 W State St Williamsburg IA 52361

DRISCOLL, THOMAS FRANK, editor; b. Chgo., June 16, 1925; s. Edward Joseph and Helen (Brozicek) D.; m. Margaret Mae Wagner, Dec. 28, 1946; children—Carol, Paul, David, Jane, Peter, Mary, Joseph, Elizabeth, Daniel, Ellen. B.S., Northwestern U., 1948, M.S., 1949. Reporter Jour. Star, Peoria, Ill., 1949-54; asst. city editor Jour. Star, 1954-56, city editor, 1956-70, asst. mng. editor, 1970-73, mng. editor, 1973-79, exec. editor, 1979—; Bd. dirs. Peoria Journal Star, 1987. Served as aviation cadet USN, 1943-45. Mem. Am. Soc. Newspaper Editors. Home: 1001 Holland Rd Metamora IL 61548 Office: Journal Star Peoria Journal Star Inc 1 News Plaza Peoria IL 61643

DRISKELL, CLAUDE EVANS, dentist; b. Chgo., Jan. 13, 1926; s. James Ernest and Helen Elizabeth (Perry) D., Sr.; B.S., Roosevelt U., 1950; B.S. in Dentistry, U. Ill., 1952, D.D.S., 1954; m. Naomi Roberts, Sept. 30, 1953; 1 dau., Yvette Michele; stepchildren—Isaiah, Ruth, Reginald, Elaine. Practice dentistry, Chgo., 1954—. Adj. prof. Chgo. State U., 1971—; dean's aide, adviser black students Coll. Dentistry U. Ill., 1972—; dental cons., supervising dentist, dental hygienists supportive health services Bd. Edn., Chgo., 1974. Vice pres. bd. dirs. Jackson Park Highlands Assn., 1971-73. Served with AUS, 1944-46; ETO. Fellow Internat. Biog. Assn., Royal Soc. Health (Gt. Britain), Acad. Gen. Dentistry; mem. Lincoln Dental Soc. (editor), Chgo. Dental Soc., ADA, Nat. Dental Assn., (editor pres.'s newsletter; dir. pub. relations, publicity; recipient pres.'s spl. achievement award 1969) dental assns., Am. Assn. Dental Editors, Acad. Gen. Dentistry, Soc. Med. Writers, Soc. Advancement Anesthesia in Dentistry, Omega Psi Phi. Author: The Influence of the Halogen Elements upon the Hydrocarbon, and their Effect on General Anesthesia, 1962; History of Chicago's Black Dental Professionals, 1850-1983. Asst. editor Nat. Dental Assn. Quar. Jour., 1977—. Contbr. articles to profl. jours. Home: 6727 S Bennett Ave Chicago IL 60649 Office: 11139 S Halsted St Chicago IL 60628

DROMPP, JOSEPH DANIEL, biomedical engineering executive; b. Detroit, Dec. 22, 1948; s. Benjamin Wayne and Ruth (Lewis) D.; m. Judy Lynn Carroll, July 26, 1980. BA, U. Ark., Little Rock, 1972; Assoc. in Tech., St. Clair Community Coll., 1973; BS in Med. Sculptures (hon.), U. Mich., 1980. Sales rep. Zimmer U.S.A., Walsaw, Ind., 1974-76; dir. sales and mktg. Med. Arts, Detroit, 1977-79, dir. advt., 1980-82; material mgr. Wright & Filippis, Detroit, 1979-80, Drayton Plains, Mich., 1979-80; sales mgr. midwest Hosmer-Dorrance, Campbell, Calif., 1982-85; nat. dir. sales and mktg. Becker Orthopedic, Troy, Mich., 1985—; faculty guest Variety Club Myoelectric Symposium, Detroit, 1984. Developed casting technique, 1984 (Ohio Acad. award, Midwest Acad. award 1984), socket liner, 1984; designer total hip brace, 1985; developer, designer post-operative upper extremity, 1985. Active Boy Scouts Am., Little Rock, 1962-67, New Baltimore Hist. Soc., Mich., 1980-85; rep. interfraternity council U. Ark., Little Rock, 1968-72. Recipient Eagle Scout award Boy Scouts Am., Little Rock, 1965, Order of the Arrow award, 1965. Mem. Am. Orthopedic and Prosthetic Assn. (com. mem. 1983-85), Assn. Biomedical Sculptors, Alpha Kappa Psi (alumni), Sigma Alpha Epsilon (alumni, pres.). Methodist. Avocations: gardening, fishing, boating, photography.

DROTNING, PHILLIP THOMAS, retired oil company official, business and government consultant; b. Deerfield, Wis., July 4, 1920; s. Edward Clarence and Martha (Skaar) D.; student U. Wis., 1937-41; m. Loretta Jayne Taylor, Nov. 3, 1964; children—Meredith Anne, Maria Kristina, Misya Kerri. Reporter, Wis. State Jour., Madison, 1943-44; editorial page writer Milw. Jour., 1944-45; freelance author, 1945-47; exec. sec. to gov. Wis., 1948-55; v.p. Northwest Airlines, Inc., 1956-61; spl. asst. to adminstr. NASA, Washington, 1961-65; exec. communications cons. Standard Oil Co. (Ind.), 1965-66; mgr. communications Am. Oil Co., Chgo., 1967-68; dir. urban affairs Amoco Corp., Chgo., 1968-72, dir. pub. affairs ops., 1973, dir. corp. social policy, 1973-85; ret., 1985; vis. fellow Am. Enterprise Inst. for Pub. Policy Research, Washington, 1985—; cons. to bus. and govt., 1985—. Bd. dirs., first v.p. Child Care Assn. Ill., 1973-76, pres., 1976-78; bd. dirs. T.R.U.S.T., Inc., 1976—, pres., 1979-81. Served with USMCR, 1941-43. Mem. Pub. Relations Soc. Am., Nat. Assn. Mfrs. (chmn. urban affairs com. 1969-71), Nat. Minority Purchasing Council (dir. 1972-84, pres. 1972-77). Clubs: National Press, International, Federal City (Washington); Plaza (Chgo.). Author: A Guide to Negro History in America, 1968; Black Heroes in our Nation's History, 1969; A Job with a Future in the Petroleum Industry, 1969; Up from the Ghetto, 1970; New Hope for Problem Drinkers, 1977; Taking Stock: A Woman's Guide to Corporate Success, 1977; Putting the Fun in Fundraising, 1979; How To Get Your Creditors off Your Back without Losing Your Shirt, 1979; You Can Buy a Home Now, 1982; editorial advisory bd. The Chicago Reporter, 1971-85. Contbr. numerous articles to pubs.

DROUBIE, GEORGE B., educational administrator; b. St. Paul, Dec. 1, 1935; s. George and Marie (Bab) D.; m. JoAnne Carol Capeti, July, 1959; children: Karen, Alan, Michael. BS, U. Minn., 1958, MA, 1959, EdD, 1972. Tchr. Nekoosa (Wis.) pub. schs., 1959-61, Wayzata (Minn.) pub. schs., 1961-66; mgr., dir., tchr. licensing and placement Minn. Dept. Edn., St. Paul, 1966—. Pres., v.p. St. George Church Parish Council, West St. Paul, Minn. Mem. Nat. Assn. State Dirs. of Tchr. Edn. and Cert. (v.p. 1977-78). Avocations: reading, fishing. Office: Minn Dept Edn 550 Cedar St Saint Paul MN 55101

DROUILLARD, THOMAS JAMES, federal telecommunications regulations specialist; b. Mich., Aug. 16, 1960; s. John Edwin and Patricia Kathryn (White) D.; m. Theresa Irene D'Angelo, Oct. 27, 1984. BBA in Mktg., U. Notre Dame, 1982, MBA in Fin., 1986. Acct. exec. Ind. Bell Telephone, Indpls., 1982-84, product delivery mgr., 1984-85; mgr. fed. regulatory issues Ameritech Services, Inc., Chgo., 1986—. Roman Catholic. Home: 1415 Potter Park Ridge IL 60068 Office: Ameritech Services Inc 30 S Wacker Suite 3916 Chicago IL 60606

DROZDA, JOSEPH MICHAEL, cemetery-funeral home executive; b. Chgo., Aug. 3, 1943; s. Albert and Bozena J. (Milonski) D.; m. Cynthia Elizabeth Gartin, Aug. 21, 1971; children: Joseph M. Jr., Patricia B. BS, Ind. U., 1969. Sales rep. EBSCO Industries, Columbus, Ohio, 1969-70; pres. The Stewart Howe Alumni Service, West Lafayette, Ind., 1970-79, Drozda Burchell Advt., Lafayette (Ind.) and Indpls., 1974-79; chmn. fin. Dole For Pres. Com., Alexandria, Va., 1979; sales mgr. Gibraltar Mausoleum Corp., Ind., Minn., Pa., 1980-84; asst. v.p. sales Gibraltar Mausoleum Corp., Indpls., 1984—. Author, editor: Chi Omega 50 Years at Indiana, 1972, Hub City History, 1984; contbr. articles to profl. jours. Precinct committeeman Rep. Party, Lafayette, 1979; cons. Haig for Pres. Com., Alexandria, 1979; v.p. Downtown Bus. Ctr. Corp., Lafayette, 1979. Served to maj. U.S. Army, 1966-69, Vietnam. Mem. Pub. Relations Soc. Am. Presbyterian. Lodge: Rotary (pres. Republic, Pa. club 1983-84). Avocations: golf, painting, reading, book collecting, art collecting. Office: Gibraltar Mausoleum Corp 8435 Keystone Crossing Indianapolis IN 46240

DRUCE, HOWARD MARTIN, physician; b. Salford, Eng., Mar. 28, 1953; came to U.S., 1979.; s. Edward and Beatrice Druce; m. Deborah E. Greisman, July 20, 1978; children: David, Benjamin. BA with honors, U. Oxford, Eng., 1974, MA, 1978; MBBS with honors, U. London, 1977. Diplomate Am. Bd. Internal Medicine; Am. Bd. Allergy. Intern Middlesex Hosp., London, 1978; resident United Manchester Teaching Hosps., Eng., 1978-79; intern and resident in internal medicine Booth Meml. Med. Ctr., Flushing, N.Y., 1979-82; attending physician St. Louis U. Med. Ctr., 1985—; asst. prof. internal medicine, dir. nasal and paranasal sinus physiology lab. St. Louis U. Sch. Medicine, 1985—. Contbr. articles on nasal physiology, allergic disease, asthma to profl. jours. Research fellow NIH, Bethesda, Md., 1982-85. Mem. ACP, Am. Acad. Allergy and Immunology (mem. nasal provocation com.), Am. Fedn. Clin. Research, Am. Thoracic Soc., Asthma and Allergy Found. (mem. med. adv. council 1985—). Avocation: photography. Office: St Louis U Sch Medicine 1402 S Grand Saint Louis MO 63104

DRUDE, KENNETH PAUL, psychologist; b. Ponchatoula, La., Dec. 20, 1945; s. Carl Joseph Jr. and Ruby Catherine (Shafer) D.; m. Sharon M. Hilding, June 8, 1968; children: Diane Elizabeth, Kris Andre Michael. BA, La. State U., 1968; MS, PhD, U. Ill., 1972. Lic. psychologist, Ohio. Mental health worker Adler Zone Ctr., Champaign, Ill., 1968-69; staff psychologist Moundbuilders Guidance Ctr., Newark, Ohio, 1972-75, Children's Hosp., Columbus, Ohio, 1975-77; chief research and evaluation Eastway Community Mental Health Ctr., Dayton, Ohio, 1977-79; assoc. prof. Wright State U., Dayton, 1979-87; dir. psychology Dayton Mental Health Ctr., 1979-87; assoc. dir. Mental Health Services N.W., Cin., 1987—; Cons. Newark Drug Forum, 1974-77. Editor Pub. Service Psychology newsletter, 1983-86; contbr. articles on mental health to profl. jours. Trustee Community Support Systems, Inc., Dayton, 1984-85. Mem. Am. Psychol. Assn. (psychologists in pub. service div., Disting. Service award 1986), Ohio Psychol. Assn. (fin. officer 1983-86, pres. elect 1986, pres. 1987), State Assn. Psychologists and Psychology Assts. (Milton McCollough award 1985). Avocations: woodcarving, reading. Home: 723 Britton Ave Dayton OH 45429 Office: Mental Health Services NW 6922 Hamilton Ave Cincinnati OH 45231

DRUETZLER, CRAIG L., computer programmer; b. Niles, Mich., Nov. 26, 1956; s. Warren O. and Patricia (Fearnside) D.; m. Laura Loree Kottkamp, Oct. 27, 1979; children: Charles Joseph, Katharine Michelle. BS in Indsl. Engrng., Purdue U., 1982. Mfg. engr. Owatonna (Minn.) Tool Co., 1982-84, programmer analyst, 1984-86, supv. engring. applications, 1986—. Home: 239 Phelps St Owatonna MN 58060 Office: Owatonna Tool Co div SPC 655 Eisenhower Dr Owatonna MN 55060

DRUGAN, CORNELIUS BERNARD, school administrator, psychologist, musician; b. Youngstown, Ohio, July 23, 1946; s. Francis Edward and Erminia (Costarella) D.; m. Kathleen Anne Cowhard, Aug. 17, 1968; children: Jonelle Kathryn, Noelle Marie. BS, Heidelberg Coll., 1968; AM, John Carroll U., 1970; PhD, Walden U., 1980. Cert. supt.; lic. psychologist. Tchr. Warrensville City Schs., Warrenville Heights, Ohio, 1968-72; intern psychologist Garfield Heights (Ohio) City Schs., 1972-73; psychologist Belmont (Ohio) County Schs., 1973-80; supr. Union Local Schs., Belmont, 1980-83, pupil personnel dir., 1983—; tchr. Warrenville Heights Recreation Dept., 1968-72, Southgate Music, Maple Heights, Ohio, 1970-73; instr. Cleve. State U., 1970-72; advisor Belmont County Career Ctr., St. Clairsville, Ohio, 1980-86. First place piano competition Portage Music Tchr. Assn., Ravenna, Ohio, 1964. Mem. Ohio Assn. Suprs. of Spl. Edn., Ohio Sch. Psychologists Assn., Buckeye Assn. Sch. Adminstrs., Jaycees (Jaycee of month, St. Clairsville, Ohio chpt. 1975), Wheeling Musical Soc., Ohio Assn. Elem. Sch. Adminstrs. Democrat. Avocations: part-time profl. musician, guitar building. Home: 68488 Woodcroft Dr Saint Clairsville OH 43950 Office: Union Local Schs 66859 Belmont Morris Rd Belmont OH 43718

DRUKKER, BRUCE H(IGHSTONE), obstetrics and gynecology educator; b. Passaic, N.J., Sept. 8, 1934; s. Henry L. and Sylvia H. Drukker; m. Esther Verna VanManen, June 19, 1956; children: Stephen, Cynthia, Jeffery. BS, Calvin Coll., 1956; MD, Cornell U., 1959. Diplomate Am. Bd. Ob-Gyn, Nat. Bd. Med. Examiners. Resident physician Henry Ford Hosp., Detroit, 1960-64, sr. staff physician, 1966-73, chmn. dept. ob-gyn, 1973-84; prof., chairperson dept. ob-gyn, coll. human medicine Mich. State U., East Lansing, 1984—; Clin. prof. ob-gyn U. Mich., Ann Arbor, 1976-83. Contbr. articles to profl. jours. Served to capt. U.S. Army M.C., 1964-66. Fellow Am. Coll. Obstetricians and Gynecologists; mem. Cen. Assn. Obstetricians and Gynecologists (trustee 1986—), Assn. Profs. of Gynecology and Obstetrics, Soc. for the Study of Breast Disease. Office: Mich State Univ Dept of Ob/Gyn and Reproductive Biology Clin Ctr East Lansing MI 48824-1315

DRULEY, NICHOLAS HENRY, biology educator; b. Richmond, Ind., Apr. 15, 1940; s. Byron T. and Virginia (Rodefeld) D.; m. Patricia Ann Breit, July 28, 1962; children: Angela, Kristine. BS, Purdue U., 1962; MA, Ball State U., 1967. lic. tchr. with permanent licenses in Ind., Ohio. Tchr. Salamonie Schs., Warren, Ind., 1962-63, Blue River Valley Sch., Mt. Summit, Ind., 1963-64, Richmond (Ind.) Community Schs., 1964-67, C.R. Coblentz Local Sch. Dist., New Paris, Ohio, 1967—. Mem. NEA, Nat. Assn. Biology Tchrs. (Ohio Outstanding Biology Tchr. award 1986), Coblentz Classroom Tchrs. (pres. 1979-82, bldg. rep. 1986-87), Ohio Edn. Assn. Democrat. Lutheran. Avocation: sports. Home: 2707 W Main St Richmond IN 47374 Office: Nat Trail High Sch 6940 Oxford-Gettysburg Rd New Paris OH 45347

DRURY, CHARLES E., manufacutirng company executive; b. 1921. BS, U. Ill., 1949. Mgr. Cen. Foundry div. Gen. Motors Corp, 1949-69; with Hayes-Albionb Corp., Jackson, Mich., 1969—, pres., chief operating officer, 1969-72, pre., chief exec. officer, 1972-76, chmn. bd., chief exec. officer, pres., 1976-82, chmn. bd., chief exec. officer, 1982-83, chmn. bd., dir., 1983—. Served to capt. AUS, 1942-46. Office: Hayes-Albion Corp 2701 N Dettman Rd Jackson MI 49201 *

DRURY, DOLORES ANN, foot care specialist; b. St. Louis, Mo., June 19, 1947; d. Alphonse Joseph and Virginia Christine (Koke) D.; m. Donald Albert Hoguet, Aug. 19, 1967 (div. Aug. 1978); children: Reneé Francine, Daniel Alphonse; m. Richard Hamilton Davis, Oct. 25, 1986. Nursing diploma, DePaul Hosp. Sch. Nursing, 1965-68; BSN, Maryville Coll., 1980-86. Foot nurse specialist Barnes Hosp., St. Louis, 1975-86; foot care specialist Washington U., St. Louis, 1986—; foot care cons. Med. Care Group, St. Louis, 1981-86; cons. Diabetes Research and Tng., St. Louis., 1980—, lectr. Diabetes Educators, 1980—. Mem. Am. Nurses Assn., St. Louis Assn. Diabetes Educators. Avocations: bicycling, photography, dancing. Home: 2220 Riverwood Trails Dr Florissant MO 63031 Office: Washington U Dept Orthopedic Surgery 4949 Barnes Hosp Plaza Saint Louis MO 63110

DRYDEN, PAUL E., medical device company executive; b. Devil's Lake, N.D., Apr. 12, 1953; s. Gale Emerson and Clara Jeannette (Harrell) D.; m. Barbara Jeanne Kuder, Dec. 18, 1976; children: Matthew Reid, Anne Michelle. BS in Microbiology, Purdue U.; MBA, Butler U. With prodn. dept. Dryden Corp., Indpls., 1975-77, v.p. mktg., 1977-80, pres., 1980—; com. chmn. Corp. for Sci. & Tech., Indpls., 1984—; with Corp. Sci. and Tech., Indpls. Mem. Am. Mgmt. Assn. Pres.'s Club, Ind. World Trade. Presbyterian. Avocations: golf, family activities. Home: 10415 Brigs Ct Indianapolis IN 46256 Office: Dryden Corp 10640 E 59th Indianapolis IN 46236

DRYER, JOHN EDWARD, engineer; b. Indpls., Mar. 2, 1931; s. George Lindley and Lucile Lucy (La Follette) D.; m. Beverly Ann Grant, Dec. 20, 1955; children: Charles Grant, David Andrew. BS, U.S. Mil. Acad., 1955. Commd. 2d lt. U.S. Army, 1955, advanced through ranks to capt., resigned, 1965; various positions Euclid/Terex div. Gen. Motors, Milford, Mich. and Hudson, Ohio, 1966-73; supt. assembly Terex div. Gen. Motors, Hudson, 1974-76, mgr. product engring. Terex div., 1977-78; gen. mgr. Saudi-Am. Machinery Maintenence Co., Jeddah, Saudi Arabia, 1979-82; sr. adminstr. Truck & Bus Group div. Gen. Motors, Pontiac, Mich., 1983—. Mem. Soc. Automotive Engrs., Engring. Soc. Detroit, Assn. Graduates USMA. Club: Army Navy Country (Alexandria). Home: 7349 Oak Forest Dr Clarkston MI 48016 Office: Truck and Bus Group Gen Motors 660 South Blvd Pontiac MI 48016

DUANGPLOY, ORAPIN, accounting educator; b. Bangkok, June 18, 1946; married; 1 child. BA in Acctg., Stephens Coll., 1971; MS in Acctg., U. Mo., 1972, PhD in Acctg., 1977. CPA, Kans. Staff acct. Harry Winfrey, CPA, 1973; chief acct. OATS, Inc., Columbia, Mo., 1973-74; lectr. Nat. Inst. Devel. and Administrn., Bangkok, 1976-77; asst. prof. acctg. U. Wis., Oshkosh, 1977-78; asst. v.p. dept. planning, systems, research Bangkok Bank, Ltd., 1978-80; spl. lectr. Thammasat U., Bangkok, 1979-80; asst. prof. Pittsburg (Kans.) State U., 1980-81, assoc. prof., 1984—; cons. Office Extended Edn. Calif. State U., Fullerton, 1981-83, assoc. prof., 1981-84; participant Touche Ross-Trueblood Seminar, 1984. Author: (software and user's manual) Interactive Intermediate Accouting II Templates, 1985, Interactive Advanced Accounting Templates, 1986; (with others) (workbook) TRICALC: Integrated Microcomputer Applications for Principles of Accounting, 1987; contbr. articles to profl. jours. Recipient Hunt-Wesson Manuscript Award Orange County chpt. Nat. Assn. Accts.; Sch. Bus. Administrn. and Econs. Calif. State U. grantee, 1983; Price Waterhouse Faculty fellow. Mem. Am. Acctg. Assn. (moderator Western Regional Ann. Meeting 1982, reviewer 1983, chmn. Calif. membership com. 1982-83, mem. notable contbns. to literature nominations com. 1982-83, presenter Nat. S.W. Regional Ann. Meeting 1985, 87, named one of outstanding membership com. mems. 1982-83), Am. Inst. CPA's, Am. Women's Soc. CPA's (mem. literary award com. 1986-87), Am. Soc. Women Accts., Beta Alpha Psi. Home: 502 Hobson Pl Pittsburg KS 66762 Office: Pittsburg State U Pittsburg KS 66762

DUB, MICHAEL, chemical company executive; b. Opaka, Austria, Mar. 11, 1917; came to U.S., 1949; s. Eustachius and Anna (Kyiv) D.; m. Gertrude M. Tomasi, June 12, 1949; 1 child, Christine V. PharmM, U. Vienna, Austria, 1944; BS, CCNY, 1954. Research chemist N.Y. Quinine, Newark, N.J., 1952-55; lit. chemist Monsanto Co., Dayton, Ohio, 1955-61; sr. lit. chemist Monsanto Co., St. Louis, 1961-82; pres., cons. Chem-Info. Services, St. Louis, 1983—. Editor: Organometallic Compounds, 1966-75. Mem. Am. Chem. Soc., Sigma Xi. Avocation: table tennis. Home and Office: Chem-Info Systems 1060 Orchard Lakes Saint Louis MO 63146

DUBAY, GWEN ANN, sales and marketing professional; b. Lewiston, Maine, Mar. 25, 1951; d. Ronald N. and Alice M. (Fellows) Johnson; widowed Feb. 1985; children: Ty Brandon, Tara Lee. BA in Sociology, U. Maine, Orono, 1972. Social worker State of Maine, Bangor, 1972; office mgr. S.C. Clayton Co., Marlboro, Mass., 1972-74; sec., treas. Dubay Sales & Mktg., Zionsville, Ind., 1983-85, pres., 1985—; sales adminstr. Woods Wire Products, Inc., Carmel, Ind., 1985—; vis. artist intern Ind. Arts Commn., Indpls., 1983-84. treas. PTO, Zionsville, 1982-83; vol. tchr. for gifted Eagle Elem. Sch., Zionsville, 1983-85. Republican. Methodist. Avocations: running, tennis. Home and Office: 200 Governors Ln Zionsville IN 46077 Office: Woods Wire Products Inc 510 Third Ave SW Carmel IN 46032

DUBEC, GEORGE EDWARD, entrepreneur; b. Youngstown, Ohio, Nov. 30, 1946; s. George Joseph and Frances (Gradski) D.; m. Susan Elizabeth McGowan, June 17, 1967 (div. May 1976); children: Suzanne Elizabeth, Mark Edward; m. Cathy Lynn Barauskas, Nov. 3, 1979. BSBA, Youngstown State U., 1974. Elect. engr. Packard Electric div. Gen. Motors, Warren, Ohio, 1967-79, materials mgmt. supr., 1979-83, prodn. control supr., 1983-86; owner GiO Enterprises, Warren, 1986—; chmn. bd. dirs. Starworks, Inc., Aurora, Ohio, 1986—; cons. in field. Author: (audio cassette) Find-A-Mate, 1984; creator: (social interaction games) Personality Probe, 1986, Sexuality Probe, 1986, Personality Probe—Kids' Edition, 1987. Mem. career awareness program Pvt. Industry Council, Trumbull County, 1984—; campaign dir. YMCA, Warren, 1984—. Avocations: skiing, racquetball, reading, weightlifting, running.

DUBERT, MARY JULIA, social worker; b. Dubuque, Iowa, July 14, 1949; d. Leo J. and Margaret M. (Garvey) Dubert. B.A., U. Iowa, 1975, M.S.W., 1976. Juvenile parole social worker Dubuque County Dept. Social Services, 1976-77; families and children social worker Tama County Dept. Social Services, Toledo, Iowa, 1977; family therapist Dist. IV Dept. Social Services,

Bettendorf, Iowa, 1977-78; adult services supr. Scott County Dept. Social Services, Davenport, Iowa, 1978-82, supr. social work treatment and diversion, 1982-84; dir. displaced homemaker program Blak Hawk Coll., 1985-86; field cons. Iowa Dept. Pub. Health, 1986—; practicum instr. Sch. Social Work, U. Iowa, Iowa City; mem. Adult Protective Services Com., Elderly Services Task Force; mem. evaluation com. Vis. Nurses Assn., Homemaker Services of Scott County. Sec., chmn. loan com. Inner City Devel. Corp.; mem. allocations panel United Way. Democrat. Roman Catholic.

DUBINA, SISTER MARY REGINA, head of religious order; b. Chgo., Dec. 5, 1922; s. John Joseph and Anna (Sirovatka) D. BA, DePaul U., 1967, MEd, 1972. Elem. sch. tchr. various schs., Chgo. and Wis., 1946-62; elem. sch. prin. various schs., Wis., Tex., 1962-64; high sch. tchr. Benet Acad., Lisle, Ill., 1965-85; sixth prioress Benedictine Sisters, Lisle, 1984—; Community treas. Benedictine Sisters, Lisle, 1966-85; mem. Benet Acad. Bd., Lisle, 1967—, Benedictine Sisters council, Lisle, 1967—, bd. dirs. St. Benedict's Home, Niles, Ill., 1986—; treas. Conf. Religious Treas. Region 8, 1980-84. Mem. Leadership Conf. of Women Religious. Avocations: swimming, crafts, visiting sick and shut-ins. Home: 1910 Maple Ave Lisle IL 60532

DUBOIS, JOHN ROGER, communications engineer; b. Eau Claire, Wis., Aug. 16, 1934; s. George Frank and Lillian Mary (Craney) DuB.; married; Debaran, Jan Marie, Jodette. BEE, U. Wis., 1957, MEE, 1959, PhD EE, 1963. Registered profl. engr., Wis., Ill., Minn., Mont., N.D., Ohio. Instr. U. Wis., Madison, 1957-65; dir. electronics N. Star R&D Inst., Mpls., 1963-71; communications mgr. Hennepin County Data Processing, Mpls., 1971—; pvt. practice communication cons. Mpls., 1971—. Contbr. numerous articles on communications engring. to profl. jours. Mem. IEEE, Minn. Telecommunications Assn., APCO (mem nat. hwy. com., 1985—). Home: 7005 Heatherton Trail Minneapolis MN 55435 Office: Hennepin County Data Processing A-2309 Govt Ctr 300 S 6th St Minneapolis MN 55487

DUBOIS, LAURENCE ROBERT, corporate financial executive; b. Bellaire, Ohio, July 20, 1927; s. Charles Lorain and Marie (Stratter) DuB.; m. Irene Milash, 1954; children: Laurence Gregory, Karen, Linda, Brian. BSBA, Ohio State U., 1948. CPA, Ill., Ohio. CPA Haskins & Sells, Chgo., 1949-55; comptroller Detroit Brass & Malleable, Wyandotte, Mich., 1955-57; chief gen. acct. Ormet Corp., Hannibal, Ohio, 1957-66, controller, 1966-67, treas., controller, 1967-78, v.p. fin., 1978—. Pres. Monroe County (Ohio) Tuberculosis and Health Assn., 1960-63; sec. Ohio Pub. Expenditure Council, Columbus, 1966—; trustee Monroe County Bd. Mental Retardation, 1975-80. Served with USMCR, 1945-46. Mem. Nat. Assn. Accts.

DUBOIS, MARK BENJAMIN, utility official; b. Peoria, Ill., Sept. 27, 1955; s. Benjamin John and Marjorie Abigail (Black) DuB.; m. Jeri Rene Simmons, May 24, 1975; 1 son, Benjamin Robert. B.S. with high distinction, U. Ariz., 1977; M.A., U. Kans., 1981. Research asst. State Biol. Survey Kans., Lawrence, 1978-81; systems programmer Central Ill. Light Co., Peoria, 1982-84, operating software supr., 1984-85, gen. supr. data processing ops. sect., 1985—; part-time instr. nat. sci. and computer literacy Midstate Coll., 1987—. Bd. dirs. Spl. People Encounter Christ, Peoria, 1982-83; treas. Religious Edn. Activities for Community Handicapped, Peoria, 1978-81; cons. Jr. Achievement, 1987—. Mem. AAAS, Data Processing Mgmt. Assn., Internat. Union for Study Social Insects, Entomol. Soc. Am., Cen. States Entomol. Soc., Kans. Acad. Sci., Soc. Systematic Zoology, Sigma Xi. Contbr. articles on entomology and personal computer software to profl. jours. Home: 208 Oakwood Circle Washington IL 61571 Office: Central Illinois Light Co 300 Liberty St Peoria IL 61602

DUBOIS, THOMAS RAYMOND, manufacturing company executive; b. Worcester, Mass., Mar. 13, 1955; s. Raymond N. and Elaine M. (Patenaude) D; m. Deborah L. Williams, May 17, 1980; children: Aimee, Michelle. AA, Lakeland Community Coll., Mentor, Ohio, 1976; BS, Ashland (Ohio) COll., 1984. Disc jockey Sta. WCLW Radio, Mansfield, Ohio, 1978-79; mgr. internal pubs. Ohio Brass Co., Mansfield, 1979-84, mgr. mining advt., 1984-85, prodn. planner mining, 1985-87; salesman plastics div. Greif Bros. Corp., Hebron, Ohio, 1987—. Mem. Am. Welding Soc. Avocations: music, golf, reading. Home: 173 Malone Rd Mansfield OH 44907

DU BOIS, WILLIAM FREDERICK, II, physician; b. Grand Rapids, Mich, Jan. 26, 1952; s. William Frederick Sr. and Wilma Marie (Venlet) Du Bois; children: Mary Jo, Crystal Jo. BA, Calvin Coll., 1970-74; MD, Wayne State U., 1974-78. Diplomate Am. Bd. Family Practice. Resident in family practice medicine Midland (Mich.) Hosp., 1978-81; family practice physician Big Rapids, Mich., 1981-86; physician, mgr. Eastside Family Med. Inc., Stanwood, Mich., 1986—; also bd. dirs. Eastside Family Med. Inc., Stanwood; mgr. Sattelite Clinic, Mecosta County Gen. Hosp., Stanwood, 1986—; vice chief of staff Mecosta County Hosp. Fellow Am. Bd. Family Practice; mem. AMA, Mich. State Med. Soc. Lodge: Elks. Office: Eastside Family Med Inc 8513 100th Ave Stanwood MI 49346

DUCHOSSOIS, RICHARD LOUIS, manufacturing executive, service executive; b. Chgo., Oct. 7, 1921; s. Alphonse Christopher and Erna (Hessler) D.; widower; children: Craig J., Dayle, R. Bruce, Kimberly. Student, Washington & Lee U. Chmn. bd. dirs. Duchossois Industries, Elmhurst, Ill.; chmn., chief exec. officer Duchossois Enterprises; chmn. Chamberlain Tech. Cos., Arlington Park Racetrack; chmn. Transportation Corp. Am., Chamberlain Tech. Cos., Chamberlain Consumer Products, Duchossois Communications Co., Arlington Park Racetrack; bd. dirs. LaSalle Nat. Bank, Hill 'n Dale Farm. Served with U.S. Army, 1942-46, ETO. Decorated Purple Heart with cluster, Bronze Star with clusters. Mem. Chief Execs. Orgn., Thoroghbred Racing Assns. (bd. dirs.). Republican. Methodist. Clubs: Economic, Executives (Chgo.) (bd. dirs.); Jockey (N.Y.C.). Office: Duchossois Enterprises Inc 845 Larch Ave Elmhurst IL 60126

DUCKWORTH, CLIFTON LEON, accountant, educator; b. Ewing, Ill., Dec. 1, 1942; s. Fred Lomax and Una Delores (Stewart) D.; m. Pauletta Reivley, Dec. 21, 1962; children: Terri Jo, Thomas Wayne, Tamara Kay, Timothy Larry. BS, So. Ill. U., 1964. CPA, Ill. Field auditor Ill. Agrl. Auditing Assn., Champaign, 1964-69; audit mgr. Ill. Agrl. Auditing Assn., Bloomington, 1972—; internal auditor So. Ill. U., Carbondale, 1969-72. Author: Grain Inventory Observation, 1980, Grain Obligation & Accounting, 1981, Grain Inventory Valuation, 1983, Grain Accounting & Bookkeeping, 1987. Mem. Am. Inst. CPA's, Ill. CPA Soc. (bd. dirs. 1984-86), Nat. Soc. Accts. for Coops. (bd. dirs. 1983-85). Office: Ill Agrl Auditing Assn PO Box 1582 Bloomington IL 61702-1582

DUDERSTADT, MACK HENRY, stained glass artist; b. Kansas City, Mo., Aug. 7, 1918; s. Henry and Valera (McCleary) D.; m. Katharine S. Johnson, Apr. 19, 1940; children: James J., Jane Ray, John C. Mack, Jr. AB, U. Mo., 1939. Advt. Daily Dem., Ft. Madison, Iowa, 1939-41; safety engr. Iowa Arsonal, Burlington, Iowa, 1941; pres. Duderstadt Constn. Co., Carrolltons, Mo., 1945-80; owner Duderstadt Stained Glass, Carrollton, 1979—. Served to lt. USNR, 1941-45, ETO, PTO. Mem. Nat. Wildlife Fedn., Mo. Wildlife Artists Soc., Hon. Soc. Ky. Cols., Nat. Audobon Soc., Ducks Unlimited, Sigma Chi. Democrat. Avocations: hunting, photography. Home and Office: 1310 N Jefferson Carrollton MO 64633

DUDGEON, GARY ALLAN, software systems analyst, electronic data processing educator and researcher; b. Newark, Ohio, Apr. 19, 1939; s. Paul Emerson and Mary Nelda (Shaw) D.; m. Marilyn Kay Beeney, July 16, 1966 (div. Feb. 1986); children: Hopeann, Steven Michael; m. Delores Jean Padgett, May 17, 1986. BA in Econs., DePauw U., 1961. Cert. data processor, Ohio, Ind. Cost analyst Western Electric Co., Columbus, Ohio, 1964-68, info. systems staff, 1968-76; programmer, analyst Automated Data Services, Cin., 1976-78; project programmer, analyst Cin. Milacron, 1978-83; sr. software analyst Hill-Rom Co., Inc., Batesville, Ind., 1983—; instr. So. Ohio Coll., Cin., 1979—. Mem. industry adv. bd. So. Ohio Coll., 1986—. Served with U.S. Army, 1961-64. Mem. Data Processing Mgmt. Assn., Assn. Insts. for Certification Computer Profls., Columbus Jaycees (chmn. activity com. 1968-76). Republican. Methodist. Club: Toastmasters (bd. govs. local chpt., 1975-76, dist. gov.). Lodge: Masons. Avocations: scrabble, sports, walking. Home: PO Box 206 Batesville IN 47006-0206 Office: Hill-Rom Co Inc Rt 46 E Batesville IN 47006

DUDLEY, DURAND STOWELL, librarian; b. Cleve., Feb. 28, 1926; s. George Stowell and Corinne Elizabeth (Durand) D.; B.A., Oberlin Coll., 1948; M.L.S., Case Western Res. U., 1950; m. Dorothy Woolworth, July 3, 1954; children—Jane Elizabeth, Deborah Anne. Librarian, Marietta (O.) Coll. Library, 1953-55, Akron (O.) Pub. Library, 1955-60; librarian Marathon Oil Co., Findlay, O., 1960-74, sr. law librarian, 1974-86; supr. tech. services dept. Findlay-Hancock County Pub. Library, Findlay, 1986—. Mem. Spl. Libraries Assn., Am. Assn. Law Libraries. Presbyterian (deacon). Home: 865 Maple Ave Findlay OH 45840 Office: Findlay-Hancock County Library 206 Broadway Findlay OH 45840

DUDLEY, GORDON DUNCAN, insurance agency executive, underwriter; b. Battle Creek, Mich., July 20, 1953; s. John Duncan and Mary Katherine (Willson) D.; m. Maureen Ann Cochrane, Apr. 29, 1978; children: Erin Katherine, Ian Duncan. Student, Kellogg Community Coll., 1971-73, Ferris State Coll., 1973-74, The Coll. Ins., 1976. Cert. ins. counselor; lic. surpus lines agt., ins. counselor. Underwriter personal lines Mich. Mut. Ins., Grand Rapids, 1974; underwriter commercial lines Saginaw, 1974, Transam. Ins. Co., N.Y.C., 1976; owner, exec. v.p. commercial sales Dudley Ins. Agy., Battle Creek, 1976—. Active fundraiser Boy Scouts of Am., Battle Creek, United Arts Council, Battle Creek, YMCA, Battle Creek, United Way, Battle Creek, 1976—. Mem. Mich. Assn. Property and Liability Ins. Counselors (bd. dirs. 1987-89), Mich. Pub. Risk and Ins. Mgmt. Assn. (editor, writer monthly publ. 1985), Battle Creek Jaycees (pres. 1987-88). Roman Catholic. Avocations: snowmobiling, skiing, golf, wood cutting, maple syrup making. Home: 1065 Cloverdale Hastings MI 49058 Office: Dudley Ins Agy Inc 1321 W Mich Ave Battle Creek MI 49017

DUDLEY, PAUL V., bishop; b. Northfield, Minn., Nov. 27, 1926; s. Edward Austin and Margaret Ann (Nolan) D. Student, Nazareth Coll., St. Paul Sem. Ordained priest Roman Cath. Ch., 1951. Titular bishop of Ursona, aux. bishop of St. Paul-Mpls 1977-78; bishop of Sioux Falls S.D., 1978—. Office: Chancery Office 423 N Duluth Ave PO Box 5033 Sioux Falls SD 57117 *

DUDNIK, ELLIOTT ELIASAF, architectural educator; b. Tel Aviv, Israel, July 24, 1943; came to U.S., 1947; s. Isaac and Sabina (Frank) D.; m. Laura Susan Mall, June 4, 1972; children: Nina Simone, Sara Arona. BArch, Ill. Inst. Tech., 1965, MS, 1967; PhD, Northwestern U., 1982. Lic. architect, Ill., Wis. Architect C. F. Murphy, Chgo., 1964-66, Skidmore Owings & Merrill, Chgo., 1966-69; lectr. U. Ill., Chgo., 1967-70, asst. prof., 1970-73, assoc. prof., 1973-80, prof., 1980—, dir. grad. studies, 1982-87, assoc. dir. sch. architecture, 1984-85; prin. Elliott Dudnik & Assoc., Evanston, Ill., 1974—; vis. lectr. Loyola U., Chgo., 1975, vis. assoc. prof. U. Sydney, Australia, 1976, vis. prof. U. Newcastle, Australia, 1976. Author: Symap User's Reference Manual, 1973; contbr. numerous papers and articles to profl. jours.; prin. works include north br. Evanston Pub. Library, 1985, Evanston Police Hdqrs., 1984-87, Adler Planetarium, Chgo., 1985-7—. Recipient Nat. Endowment Arts award, 1979; Fullbright-Hays lectr., lectr. fellow Inst. Internat. Exchange Scholars, 1976; Walter Murphy fellow Northwestern U., 1970-71. Mem. AIA, CSI, Internat. Solar Energy Soc., Am. Inst. Steel Contrn. (Hands on Steel award 1978), Am. Solar Energy Soc., Assn. Computing Machinery. Home: 1325 Main Evanston IL 60202

DUER, LORRAINE LURZ, advertising executive; b. Rochester, N.Y., Sept. 10, 1956; d. Robert A. Lurz and Marilyn (Moss) McCarthy; m. Timothy K. Duer, May 4, 1985. BA, Ohio Wesleyan U., 1978. Remedial tchr. Laurel Park High Sch., Martinsville, Va., 1978-80; tchr. Suffolk Elem. Sch., Central Islip, N.Y., 1980-81; tchr. sci. Immaculate Conception High Sch., Elmhurst, Ill., 1981-83; account exec. Piqua (Ohio) Daily Call, 1983-85; market mgr. Root Outdoor Advt., Piqua, 1985—. Mem. Am. Bus. Women Assn. (rec. sec. 1985—). Presbyterian. Home: 901 Maple Piqua OH 45356 Office: Root Outdoor Advt PO Box 4246 Sidney OH 45365

DUERRE, JOHN ARDEN, biochemist; b. Webster, S.D., Aug. 21, 1930; s. Dewey H. and Stella M. (Barber) D.; m. Benna Bee Harris, June 16, 1957; children: Gail, Dawn, Arden. B.S., S.D. State U., 1952, M.S. (Lederle fellow), 1956; Ph.D., U. Minn., 1960. Research asso., AEC fellow Argonne (Ill.) Nat. Lab., 1960-61; research bacteriologist NIH Rocky Mountain Lab., Hamilton, Mont., 1961-63; asst. prof. microbiology U. N.D. Med. Sch., 1963-65, assoc. prof., 1965-71, prof. microbiology, 1971—; vis. scientist neuropsychiat. research unit Research Council Lab., Carshalton, Surrey, Eng., 1969-70; vis. scientist Walter Reed Army Inst. Research, Washington, 1984-85. Contbr. numerous articles to profl. publs. Chmn. Grand Forks County (N.D.) Wildlife Fedn., 1965-67, 77-78, Grand Forks chpt. Ducks Unltd., 1970, 77-78; dist. dir. N.D. Wildlife Fedn., 1976-77. Served with U.S. Army, 1953-55. Recipient Career Devel. award NIH, 1965-75; NIH grantee, 1966, 71-83; NSF grantee, 1963-71, 86—; U.S. Dept. Agr. grantee, 1983-84. Mem. N.D. Acad. Scis., Am. Soc. Microbiologists, Fedn. Am. Socs. Exptl. Biology, Henrici Soc., Sigma Xi (Outstanding Research award 1977). Clubs: Grand Forks Curling, Grand Forks Gun. Lodge: Elks. Home: 918 N 26th St Grand Forks ND 58201 Office: U ND Med Sch Grand Forks ND 58202

DUFF, BRIAN BARNETT, federal judge; b. Dallas, Sept. 15, 1930; s. Paul Harrington and Frances Ellen (FitzGerald) D.; m. Florence Ann Buckley, Nov. 27, 1953; children: F. Ellen, Brian Barnett Jr., Roderick FitzGerald, Kevin Buckley, Daniel Harrington. AB in English, U. Notre Dame, 1953; JD, DePaul U., Chgo., 1962. Bar: Ill. 1962, Mass. 1962, U.S. Dist. Ct. (no. dist.) Ill. 1962, U.S. Supreme Ct. 1968. Mgmt. trainee Continental Casualty Co., Chgo., 1956-60; mgmt. cons. Booz, Allen and Hamilton, Chgo., 1960-62; asst. to chief exec. officer Bankers Life and Casualty Co., Chgo., 1962-67; exec. v.p., gen. counsel R.H. Gore Co., Chgo., 1968-69; atty. Brian B. Duff & Assocs., Chgo., 1969-76; judge Cir. Ct. Cook County Ill., Chgo., 1971-76, U.S. Dist. Ct. (no. dist.) Ill., Chgo., 1985—; rep. Ill. Gen. Assembly, Springfield, 1971-76; vis. com. Coll. Law U. Chgo., 1977-79; lectr. Law Sch. Loyola U.; adj. prof. John Marshall Law Sch., 1985—. Served to lt (j.g.) USN, 1953-56. Mem. ABA, Chgo. Bar Assn., Fed. Judges Assn., Am. Judicature Soc., Nat. Lawyers Club, Inc., (hon.)., Legal Club Chgo. (hon.). Roman Catholic. Avocations: fishing, reading, travel, teaching children of all ages. Office: U S Dist Ct 219 S Dearborn St Rm 1886 Chicago IL 60604

DUFF, JAMES GEORGE, automobile company executive; b. Pittsburg, Kans., Jan. 27, 1938; s. James George and Camilla (Vinardi) D.; m. Linda Louise Beeman, June 24, 1961 (div.); children: Michele, Mark, Melissa; m. Beverly L. Pool, Nov. 16, 1984. B.S. with distinction (Sunray Mid-Continent Scholar; Bankers Scholar), U. Kans., 1960, M.B.A., 1961. With Ford Motor Co., Dearborn, Mich., 1962—; various positions fin. staff Ford Motor Co., 1962-71; dir. product, profit, price, warranty Ford of Europe, 1972-74; controller Ford Div., 1974-76, controller car ops., 1976, controller car product devel., 1976-80; exec. v.p. Ford Motor Credit Co., 1980—, also dir.; chmn. Ford Equipment Leasing; dir. Ford Credit Can. Ltd., Fairlane Life Ins. Co., Am. Rd. Equity Co., Ford Consumer Discount Co., Philco Fin. Co., Am. Rd. Ins. Co., Ford Life Ins. Co., Vista Life Ins. Co., Vista Ins. Co., Am. Rd. Services Co., Ford Consumer Credit Co. Mem. adv. bd. Sch. Bus., U. Kans., 1980—; chmn. bus. devel. unit United Found., 1980-85, chmn. edn. and local govt. unit, 1986—. Home: 1505 Ashford Ln Birmingham MI 48009 Office: Ford Motor Credit Co American Rd Suite 2013 Dearborn MI 48121

DUFF, JOHN BERNARD, city official, former university president; b. Orange, N.J., July 1, 1931; s. John Bernard and Mary Evelyn (Cunningham) D.; m. Helen Mezzanotti, Oct. 8, 1955; children: Michael, Maureen, Patricia, John, Robert, Emily Anne. B.S., Fordham U., 1953; M.A., Seton Hall U., 1958; Ph.D., Columbia U., 1964. Sales rep. Remington-Rand Corp., 1955-57, dist. mgr., 1957-60; faculty Seton Hall U., 1960-70, prof. history, 1968-70, acad. v.p., 1970-71, exec. v.p., acad. v.p., 1971-72, provost, acad. v.p., 1972-76; pres. U. Lowell, Mass., 1976-81; chancellor of higher edn. State of Mass., 1981-86; commr. Chgo. Pub. Library System, 1986—; mem. Gov.'s Commn. to Study Capital Punishment, 1972-73; chmn. bd. dirs. Mass. Corp. Ednl. Telecommunications, 1983—; dir. Mass. Tech. Park Corp., Bay State Skills Corp. Author: The Irish in the United States, 1971, also articles.; Editor: (with others) The Structure of American History, 1970, (with P.M. Mitchell) The Nat Turner Rebellion: The Historical Event and the Modern Controversy, 1971, (with L. Greene) Slavery: Its Origin and Legacy, 1975. Democratic candidate to U.S. Congress, 1968; mem. State Bd. Edn., 1981-86; chmn. Livingston Town Democratic Com., 1972-76; bd. dirs. Merrimack Regional Theatre, 1981-84, Mass. Higher Edn. Assistance Corp., 1981-86; trustee Essex County Coll., 1966-70, Mass. Community Coll. System., St. John's Prep. Sch., Danvers, Mass.; chmn. Lowell Hist. Preservation Commn., 1979-86; mem. adv. bd. Wang Inst., 1979-81; mem. nat. adv. com. on accreditation and indsl. eligibility U.S. Dept. Edn., 1981-82. Served with U.S. Army, 1953-55. Mem. Am. Hist. Assn., Orgn. Am. Historians, AAUP, Acad. Polit. Sci., Am. Catholic Hist. Assn., Am. Assn. State Colls. and Univs. (chmn. cultural affairs com. 1979-86), Immigration History Research Group. Club: K.C. Home: 2650 N Lakeview Chicago IL 60614 Office: Chicago Pub Library 425 N Michigan Ave Chicago IL 60611

DUFFNER, STEVEN RICHARD, graphic design executive, illustrator; b. Chgo., July 3, 1958; s. Richard Bay and Phyllis Ann (Dore) D. BFA, No. Ill. U., 1981, MFA, 1983. Designer, illustrator Midweek Publs., Dekalb, Ill., 1981-82, Morel Media, Dekalb, 1982-83, Moore Bus. Systems, Northbrook and Glenview, Ill., 1984-86; pres. Cor De Graphics, Elmhurst, Ill., 1986—; cons. RBD and Assocs., Ltd., Summit, Ill, 1986—. Mem. Soc. Typographic Arts., Soc. Real Estate Appraisors (candidate). Democrat. Roman Catholic. Avocations: musical appreciation, rendering, lithography. Home: PO Box 1345 Elmhurst IL 60126 Office: Cor De Graphics 292 Montrose E-2 Elmhurst IL 60126

DUFFNEY, RICHARD EDWARD, architect; b. Detroit Lakes, Minn., Aug. 5, 1937; s. George Anthony and Tillie Bergette (Soreng) D.; m. Joyce Elaine Paulson, July 3, 1959; children—Richard A., Nancy, Paul, Sally. Diploma, N.D. State Sch. Sci., Wahpeton, 1960. Registered architect Minn., N.D., S.D. Assoc. Winston Larson and Assocs., Detroit Lakes, 1960, Kurke Assocs., Fargo, N.D., 1961-64, Kegel Assocs., Detroit Lakes, 1964-83; prin. Duffney Architecture, Detroit Lakes, 1983—. Mem. drafting dept. adv. com. Detroit Lakes Vocat. Tech. Inst., 1968-75, chmn., 1972-75; bd. dirs. Becker County Day Activity Ctr., Detroit Lakes, 1969-73, pres., 1972-73; mem. ch. council Grace Lutheran Ch., Detroit, 1967-69, 75-77, 80-83, 85—, pres., 1969, 77, 82; precinct chmn. Becker County Ind. Reps., 1980-87, county vice chmn., 1983-87, county chmn., 1987—. Mem. AIA, Constrn. Specifications Inst., Minn. Bldg. Ofcls., Nat. Council Archtl. Registration Bds., Detroit Lakes Regional C. of C., Detroit Lakes Jaycees (bd. dirs. 1966-73, pres. 1971-72), Minn. Jaycees (v.p. region 17 1972-73, nat. dir. N.W. region 1973-74, chmn. N.W. Water Carnival 1975, internat. senator 1974), Becker County Hist. Soc., Plains Art Mus., Walker Art Ctr., Gideons Internat. (local v.p. 1975, state zone leader 1976-78, local sec. 1978-81, local pres. 1981—, state meml. Bible coordinator 1987—). Club: Toastmasters (v.p. local club 1975). Lodge: Sons of Norway Internat. (bd. dirs. 1979-82, v.p. 1979-82).

DUFFY, EUGENE CHARLES, mineral company executive; b. Newark, Sept. 29, 1942; s. Eugene Charles Sr. and Cecilia Elizabeth (Curran) D.; m. Rita M. Roma, Feb 11, 1967; children: LuAnn, Diana, Matthew John. BS in Bus. Adminstrn., Seton Hall U., 1964. Credit analyst U.S. Steel, Newark, 1965; jr. acct. Fed. Electric subs. ITT, Paramus, N.J., 1965-66; div. v.p. and controller Interpace Corp., Parsippany, N.J., 1966-79; v.p. fin. Processed Minerals, Hutchinson, Kans., 1979-81, also bd. dirs.; pres. Carey Salt div. Processed Minerals, Inc., Hutchinson, 1981—; bd. dirs. Underground Vaults & Storage, Hutchinson, H&N Railway Co., Hutchinson, Lake Crystal Salt Co., Ogden, Utah. Mem. fin. com. Trinity High Sch., Hutchinson, 1981—; bd. dirs. Hutchinson Hosp., 1986. Served to lt. USNR, 1964-77. Mem. Am. Mgmt. Assn., Salt Inst. (chmn. agr. com. 1983-85). Republican. Roman Catholic. Home: 3404 Arrowhead Dr Hutchinson KS 67502 Office: Carey Salt div Processed Minerals Inc 1800 Carey Blvd Hutchinson KS 67501

DUFFY, JAMES PATRICK, manufacturing executive; b. Columbus, Ohio, Mar. 20, 1942; s. Joseph Charles and Henrietta (Lisska) D.; m. Kay Marie Fleischman, Sept. 8, 1962; children: Karen, Caroline, William. BSBA, Calif. Coast U., 1984. Buyer Speco div. Kelsey-Hayes Co., Springfield, Ohio, 1962-67; pres. Champion Garden Towne, Perry, Ohio, 1974-76; adminstrv. asst. Upson Machine Products, Inc., Painesville, Ohio, 1967-74, quality mgr., 1976-77, exec. v.p., 1977—, also bd. dirs. Bd. dirs. United Way of Lake County, Mentor, Ohio, 1986—; mem. adv. bd. Cath. Service Bur., Painesville, 1969—. Mem. USN League (life), Air Force Assn. (patron). Roman Catholic. Club: Serra (pres. 1986—). Avocations: golf, fishing, photography. Home: 3021 Blue Spruce Ct Perry OH 44081 Office: Upson Machine Products Inc 572 S Saint Clair St Painesville OH 44077

DUFFY, PATRICK CHARLES, automotive executive; b. Grafton, W.Va., Jan. 31, 1937; s. Charles Patrick and Ethel Louise (Dean) D.; m. Nancy Marie Byrne, Aug. 22, 1959; children: John Patrick, Lynne Marie, Michael Francis, Mark Daniel. BS in Bus. Adminstrn., W.Va. U., 1961; MBA, Fla. Inst. Tech., 1968; grad. exec. devel. program, Cornell U., 1978. Planning mgr. Martin Co., Cape Canaveral, Fla., 1963-66; launch integration mgr. space div. Chrysler Corp., Cape Kennedy, Fla., 1966-72; mgr. engring. space div. Chrysler Corp., New Orleans, 1972-76, gen. mgr., 1976-80; pres. Switches, Inc., Logansport, Ind., 1980-82; pres., chief exec. officer, chmn. bd. Switches, Inc., Indpls., 1982—; sec. Tune-up Mfr's Inst., Teaneck, N.J., 1985—. Bd. dirs. United Way, Logansport, 1984-86, Mental Health Assn., Indpls., 1986. Mem. Automotive Parts and Accessories Assn. (bd. dirs. 1984—, govt. affairs com.), Nat. Assn. of Bd. Dirs. Republican. Roman Catholic. Lodges: KC, Elks, The Pointe. Avocations: tennis, fishing, sailing, scuba diving. Home: 1828 Waters Edge Dr Bloomington IN 47401 Office: Switches Inc 6131 W 80th St Indianapolis IN 46278

DUFFY, PAUL GERALD, food services executive; b. Boston, Aug. 28, 1930; s. Charles Gavin and Marie Francis (Sullivan) D.; m. Mary Jo Mack, Nov. 22, 1958; children: Michael Kevin, Pamela, Kathleen. BS, SUNY, Bronx, 1953. Dist. sales mgr. Canteen Corp., Chgo., 1958—. Served to lt. USN, 1953-57, Korea. Mem. Internat. Franchise Assn. (bd. dirs. 1979-83). Club: Knollwood (Lake Forest) (bd. dirs. 1980-83). Home: 750 Waukegan Rd Lake Forest IL 60045 Office: Canteen Corp 222 N LaSalle Chicago IL 60607

DUFFY, RITA MARIE, psychologist; b. Newark, Sept. 1, 1946; d. Michael Joseph and Helen Katherine (Skelly) Fratantuno; m. John George Duffy, Aug. 12, 1967; children: John Michael, Laura Michelle. BS in Edn., Seton Hall U., 1968; MS in Counseling, U. Dayton, 1978. Cert. tchr. and sch. psychologist, Ohio; lic. profl. counselor. Tchr. Belleville (N.J.) Schs., 1968, Incarnation Sch., Centerville, Ohio, 1975-77; counselor Mad River Schs., Dayton, 1978-82; intern psychologist Blanchester (Ohio) Schs., 1982-83, Wilmington (Ohio) Schs., 1982-83; psychologist Valley View Schs., Germantown, Ohio, 1983—. Leader Miami Valley council Girl Scouts U.S., Dayton, 1982-84; exec. bd. Alter High Sch. Music Assn., Kettering, 1984-85; Twigs vol. Children's Med. Ctr., Dayton, 1983-85. Mem. Nat. Assn. Sch. Psychologists, Southwest Ohio Sch. Psychologists (mem. pub. relations com. 1986—), Ohio Sch. Psychologists Assn. (exec. bd. 1986—), Miami Valley Counseling & Devel. Assn. (exec. bd. 1979-82). Roman Catholic. Avocations: embroidery, gardening, piano. Home: 1563 Frontier Ct Spring Valley OH 45370 Office: Valley View Local Sch 64 Comstock St Germantown OH 45327

DUFFY, WILLIAM EDWARD, JR., educator; b. Fostoria, Ohio, Aug. 30, 1931; s. William Edward and Margaret Louise (Drew) D.; B.S., Wayne State U., 1958, M.Ed., 1960; Ph.D., Northwestern U., 1967; m. Sally King Wolfe, Nov. 21, 1958 (div. 1978). Tchr., Detroit pub. schs., 1957-61; instr. social studies Northwestern U., Evanston, Ill., 1961-65; asst. prof. edn. U. Iowa, Iowa City, 1965-70, assoc. prof., 1970—, coordinator Soc. Found. Edn. program, 1978—, chmn. div. founds., postsecondary edn., 1981—; lectr. in field. Served with USAF, 1951-54. Fellow John Dewey Soc., Philosophy of Edn. Soc.; mem. AAAS, Am. Ednl. Research Assn., History of Edn. Soc.,

Am. Ednl. Studies Assn. Editorial bd. Ednl. Philosophy Theory, 1969-71; contbr. book revs. and articles to profl. publs. Home: 376 Samoa Pl Iowa City IA 52240 Office: N 438 U LC Iowa Iowa City IA 52242

DUFOUR, BRUCE ANTHONY, marketing professional; b. Blackfoot, Idaho, June 1, 1946; s. Hugh Anthony and Laurel (Wray) D.; m. Ann McIntosh, Apr. 19, 1969; children: Nicole, Brian. BSBA, La. Poly. U., 1969. Sr. quality engr. Ford Motor Co., Livonia, Mich., 1974-76; quality control mgr. Clark Equipment, Jackson, Mich., 1976-78, mgr. product planning, 1978-80, mgr. sales, 1980-81; gen. sales mgr. Kysor of Cadillac, Cadillac, Mich., 1981-84, v.p. mktg., 1984—. Cubmaster Cadillac den Boy Scouts Am., 1984-85. Mem. Soc. Automotive Engrs. Republican. Roman Catholic. Club: Cadillac Country (bd. dirs. 1986—). Avocations: sports, reading. Home: 6417 Sherwood Cadillac MI 49601 Office: Kysor of Cadillac 1100 Wright St Cadillac MI 49601

DUFRESNE, DEWAYNE JOSEPH, manufacturing executive; b. Kingsford, Mich., Jan. 14, 1930; s. Joseph E. and Isabelle (Raiche) D.; m. Judith Marie Smith, Aug., 24, 1957; children: Mark J., Gerald D., Kim Marie, David J., Marie A. BBA, Spencerian Coll., 1952; MS in Taxation, Walsh Coll., 1978. CPA, Mich. Auditor Ernst & Whinney, Detroit, 1954-59; controller, treas. Whitehead Stamping Co., Detroit, 1959-63, pres., treas., gen. mgr., chmn. bd., 1963-72; pres., treas. Republic Sales and Mfg., Detroit, 1967-69; v.p., chief fin. officer, dir. Whitehead Mfg. Co., Detroit, 1972-87; pres., chief exec. officer Whitehead Mfg. Co., Dtroit, 1987—. Served with AUS, 1952-54. Mem. Am. Inst. CPA's, Mich. Assn. CPA's, Mich. Professions Assn. Home: 26768 Timber Trail Dr Dearborn Heights MI 48127 Office: Whitehead Mfg Co 6100 Ranspach Ave Dearborn Heights MI 48209

DUGAN, DONALD STEWART, videographer and cable TV executive; b. Evanston, Ill., June 9, 1951; s. Donald Stewart Dugan and Helen Ann (Couch) Barry; m. Stephanie Lee Edwards, Aug. 27, 1976 (div. June 1984). BS, Carroll Coll., Waukesha, Wis., 1974. Newspaper columnist Okaukchee, Wis., 1975-77; newspaper reporter Milw., 1977-80; sales cons. cable TV Wauwatosa, Wis., 1980-82; cameraman, writer prodn. co., West Allis, Wis., 1983—; videographer Waukesha County Tech. Inst., Pewaukee, Wis., 1985—; cons. video production, Milw., 1981—; program dir. local cable channel, Hartland, Wis., 1981—; instr. video prodn. Waukesha County Tech. Inst. producer: (video) Halloween in Hartland, 1982; dir.: (video) WCTI Schwcase, 1986; contbr. articles to various publs. Mem. Hartland Cable Commn., 1981—. Mem. Internat. TV Assn., Nat. Fedn. Local Cable Programmers, Wis. Edn. Assn. Council, Midwest Badminton Assn., Nat. Badminton Assn. Club: Greater Milw. Badminton (pres. 1983—). Avocations: reading, physical fitness, writing. Home: 108 Hill St Hartland WI 53029 Office: Waukesha County Tech Inst 800 Main St Pewaukee WI 53072

DUHM, KENNETH DAVID, industrial engineering consultant; b. Sterling, Ill., Jan. 8, 1952; s. Kenneth Frank Duhm and Janet Ella (Marcy) Rempe; m. Marceia Elaine Jarrard, June 15, 1974; children: Janette Marie, Kristen Leigh-Ann. BS in Applied Sci. and Engring., U.S. Mil. Acad., 1974; MA in Mgmt. and Human Relations, Webster U., 1980. Commd. 2d lt. U.S. Army, 1974, advanced through grades to capt., 1979, resigned, 1981, active Res., 1981—; advanced through grades to maj. USAR, 1986; indsl. engr. Barber-Colman Co., Rockford, Ill., 1981-85, US Army Mgmt. Engring. Tng. Activity, Rock Island, Ill., 1985—. Mem. Assn. U.S. Army, Field Artillery Assn., West Point Soc. Chgo., Assn. Grads. West Point. Mem. Evang. Free Ch. Avocations: marathons, triathlons, camping. Home: 3401-11 Ave A Moline IL 61265 Office: US Army Mgmt Engring Tng Activity Attn AMXOM-SE Rock Island IL 61299-7040

DUHRING, JOHN LEWIS, obstetrician; b. Plainfield, N.J., May 7, 1933; s. Edwin Leslie and Florence Emma (Uber) D.; m. Penelope J. Smith, June 21, 1956; children: Christopher, Susan, Karen. BS, McGill U., Montreal, Que., Can., 1955; MD, U. Pa., 1959. Cert. Am. Bd. Ob-Gyn. Asst. prof. U. Ky., Lexington, 1963-67, assoc. prof., 1970-73, prof., dir. ob-gyn, 1973-77; attending staff Tripler Gen. Hosp., Honolulu, 1967-70; prof., dept. chmn. Med. Coll. Ohio, Toledo, 1978—; faculty chmn., adminstrv. dir. The Toldeo Hosp. Ctr. for Women and Children, 1984—. Contbr. articles to profl. jours. Served to lt. col. U.S. Army, 1967-70. Fellow Am. Coll. Ob-Gyn (chmn. dist. V 1981-84); mem. AMA, Ohio Med. Assn. Ohio Perinatal Assn., Cen. Assn. Obstetricians and Gynecologists (v.p. 1984), Am. Bd.Family Practice (bd. dirs. 1984—). Avocation: photography. Office: Med Coll Ohio 3000 Arlington Ave Toledo OH 43614

DUKE, TIMOTHY EARL, management consulting firm executive; b. Marion, Ind., Dec. 5, 1946; s. Earl Eugene and Martha Elizabeth (Gaddis) D.; m. Paula Lane Pedersen, Sept. 29, 1969 (div. 1975); 1 child, Jennifer Lane; m. Danette Louise Willard, Apr. 12, 1986. B.S. in Indsl. Mgmt., Purdue U., 1972. Salesman Dow Chem. Co., Atlanta, 1972-75; sales engr. Wilson-Fiberfil Internat., Rochester, N.Y., 1976-78, mktg. specialist, 1979-80, Evansville, Ind., 1981, mktg. mgr., 1981-84, mgr. licensing and original equipment mfrs., 1984-85, mgr. cen. region sales, 1985-86; pres. and founder D&T Inc., 1986—; dir. bus. devel. Cookson Performance Plastics, Worcester, Mass., 1986—. Recipient Best Speaker award Dale Carnegie Inst., 1982. Sr. mem. Soc. Plastic Engrs. (program com. 1974-75, appreciation award 1981). Republican. Club: Oak Meadow. Avocations: skiing, tennis, chess, scuba diving. Home: 2335 Bayard Park Dr Evansville IN 47714 Office: D&T Inc 2335 Bayard Park Dr Evansville IN 47714

DUKES, JACK RICHARD, history educator; b. Indpls., Jan. 21, 1941; s. Richard Eugene and Kathleen (Cox) D.; B.A., Beloit Coll., 1963; M.A., No. Ill. U., 1965; Ph.D., U. Ill., 1970; m. Joanne Petty, June 15, 1963; children—Gregory Scott, Richard Aaron. Asst. prof. Macalester Coll., St. Paul, 1969-70; asst. prof. Carroll Coll., Waukesha, Wis., 1970-75, assoc. prof., 1975-83, prof. 1983—, chmn. dept. history, 1972—, dir. Russian Area Studies program, 1972-75; vis. asso. prof. U. Calif., Santa Barbara, 1980-81; Scholar-Diplomat Program participant U.S. Dept. State. Nat. Endowment for Humanities fellow, 1974; U. Ill. assoc. in Russian history, 1977; fellow in residence, U. Calif., Santa Barbara, 1977-78. Mem. Am. Hist. Assn., Am. Assn. for Advancement Slavic Studies, Conf. Group Study Central European History, Soc. History Am. Fgn. Relations. Author: (with Joachim Remak) Another Germany: A Reconsideration of the Imperial Era, 1987; Contbr. articles to profl. jours. Home: 114 W Laflin St Waukesha WI 53186 Office: Dept History Carroll Coll Waukesha WI 53186

DULANEY, WALTER FRENCH, information services executive; b. Chgo., Jan. 23, 1953; s. Donald Cameron and Doris Marion (French) D.; m. Luz Emilia Ibarra, Apr. 19, 1980; children: Kenneth Walter, James Walter, Steven Walter. BS with honors, Marquette U., 1975; M in Mgmt., Northwestern U., 1976. CPA, Ill. Sr. cons. Arthur Andersen, Chgo., 1976-80; mgr. fin. reporting Trans Union, Chgo., 1980-81; asst. treas. Marmon Group, Chgo., 1981-84; dir. info. services Bally Mfg., Chgo., 1984—. Little League coach. Mem. Am. Inst. CPA's, Ill. CPA Soc. (subcom. chmn., EDP edn. com. 1986). Republican. Lutheran. Club: Northwestern (Evanston, Ill.). Avocations: golf, woodworking, jogging, weight lifting. Home: 610 Buckthorn Terr Buffalo Grove IL 60089 Office: Bally Mfg Corp 8700 W Bryn Mawr Ave Chicago IL 60631

DULEY, ALVIN JOSEPH, educator; b. St. Joe, Fond du Lac County, Wis., Jan. 12, 1916; s. Marie (Mary) (Steffes) D. Diploma U. Wis.-Oshkosh, 1940; B.S., Brigham Young U., 1951; M.A., Ariz. State U., 1960; B.S., Marian Coll., 1981. Cert. in adminstrn., secondary schs. and counseling, Utah.; sch. psychology, English, social studies, Hawaii; counseling, social studies, N.Y., social scis., counseling, psychology, Calif. Jr. Colls. Tchr., U.S. Indian Service, 1946-60; reading specialist McNary Sch. Dist., Ariz., 1960-64; tchr. and dormitory counselor high schs., Lahainaluna, Maui, Hawaii, and psychol. services, Hilo and Kailua-Kona, Hawaii, 1964-80. Active Cub Scouts, Boy Scouts Am., Utah, Ariz., Mont., Miss., Wis., Hi-Y, Hawaii. Recipient awards from Boy Scouts Am., Hi-Y, Dept. Interior. Fellow Can. Psychol. Assn. (hon. life), A.B.I.; mem. Am. Assn. Ret. Persons, Hawaii Psychol. Assn., Nat. Assn. Gifted Children (life mem.), Assn. Supervision and Curriculum Devel., Am. Rabbit Breeders Assn., Pyramid Soc. (Arabian Horses), Hawaii Edn. Assn. Roman Catholic, Internat. Reading Assn. Author: Adult Education Reading Series (bilingual). Home: 953 Meadow Creek Ln Fond du Lac WI 54935

DULL, WILLIAM MARTIN, engineer; b. Buchanan, Mich., June 24, 1924; s. Curtis Frank and Daisy Julia (Sharp) D.; m. Margaret Ann McMillan, Apr. 10, 1976; children: Richard William, Beverly Ann, William McMillan. BSME, U. Mich., 1945. Registered profl. engr., Mich. Dir. tech. staff Detroit Edison, 1951-66, asst. gen. supt. cen. plants, 1960-66, gen. supt. underground lines, 1966-71, mgr. employee relations, 1971-74, mgr. orgn. planning and devel., 1974—. Bd. dirs. World Med. Relief, Detroit, 1971-87, Jr. Achievement, Southeastern Mich., 1971-87; bd. trustees Detroit Sci. Ctr., Inc., 1979-85. Served to lt. (s.g.) USN, 1942-51, PTO. Recipient Silver Leadership award Jr. Achievement, 1985. Fellow Engring. Soc. Detroit (pres. 1970-71, Disting. Service 1980); mem. ASHRAE (pres. 1964-65, Outstanding Engr. award 1965), Architects, Engrs., Surveyors Registration Council (chmn. 1968-69), Mich. Soc. Profl. Engrs. (bd. dirs. 1973-75, Disting. Engr. 1980), IEEE (chmn. nat. conf. 1971, U. Mich. Alumni Assn. (Disting. Service award 1970). Republican. Methodist. Clubs: Detroit Yacht, Econ. of Detroit. Home: 4399 Chisholm Trail Brimingham MI 48010 Office: Detroit Edison Co 2000 2d Ave Detroit MI 48226

DUMAS, TYRONE PIERRE, architect, construction manager, consultant; b. Milw., July 11, 1952; s. Augustus Elerby and Darlene (Elerby) Ingram; m. Ceciel Harrell Dumas, Aug. 18, 1973; children: Maurice A., Danielle S.; foster children: Latrice Harrell, Stonia Harrell. AArch, Milw. Area Tech. Coll., 1975; BArch, U.Wis., Milw., 1977. Construction bldg. inspection dept. City Milw., 1977-79; corporate engr. Miller Brewing Co., Milw., 1979-86; constrn. mgr. Heike/Design Assn. Inc., Brookfield, Wis., 1986; with Dumas Cons. Specialties, Milw., 1986—. Vol., speaker United Way, Milw., 1984-86; vol. speaker Milw. Pub. Schs., 1984-86; asst. basketball coach Bethlehem Luth. Sch.; trustee Bethlehem Luth. Ch., steward various coms. Recipient Merit award State of Wis., 1973, Role Model of Yr. award Milw. Pub. Sch., 1983-84, Community Service award Miller Brewing Co., 1985. Mem. AIA (assoc.), Wis. Soc. Architects (assoc.), Project Mgmt. Inst., U.S. Brewers Acad., Constrn. Specifications Inst. (assoc.), U.W. Milw. Alumni Assn. Lutheran. Avocations: stand-up comedy, motivational speaking. Home and Office: 5963 N 78th St Milwaukee WI 53218

DUMAY, RONALD LOUIS, real estate executive; b. Sikeston, Mo., Sept. 11, 1934; s. Oliver Louis and Edith Margaret (Frey) D.; m. Ann Gentry, June 15, 1957; children: David, Susan. BBA, U. Mo., 1960. Lic. real estate broker; cert. property mgr. Credit mgr. Comml. Credit Corp., Cape Girardeau, Mo., 1955-57; budget dir. Hallmark Cards Inc., Kansas City, Mo., 1960-73; v.p. ops. Crown Ctr. Redevel. Corp. subs. Hallmark Cards, Inc., Kansas City, 1973—. Adv. bd. Parents Anonymous of Kansas City, 1981—; mem. Downtown Council, 1984—, Mayor's Adv. Com. Capital Improvements, Kansas City. 1986. Served with U.S. Army, 1957-59. Mem. Kansas City Real Estate Bd., Urban Land Inst., Inst. Real Estate Mgmt. (v.p. 1980-83), Kansas City C. of C. (Man of Yr. Sikeston 1984), Am. Royal Assn. (bd. govs. 1983—), N.E. Kansas Quarter Horse Assn. (pres. 1982-84). Roman Catholic. Avocations: fishing, horses, real estate investments. Home: 4117 Brookridge Dr Fairway KS 66205 Office: Crown Ctr Devel Corp 2440 Pershing Rd Suite 500 Kansas City MO 64108

DUMKE, MELVIN PHILIP, dentist; b. Sleepy Eye, Minn., Jan. 23, 1920; s. Herman Gustav and Else Ida (Battig) D.; D.D.S., U. Minn., 1943; m. Phyllis Lorraine Steuck, June 25, 1950; children—Pamela, Bruce, Shari. Practice dentistry, Sleepy Eye, 1946-50, Morgan, Minn., 1950-66, Mankato, Minn., 1966—. Lectr. dental assts. Mankato State Coll., 1967-69. Mem. Town Council, Morgan, 1960-65. Bd. control Martin Luther Acad., New Ulm, Minn., 1965-79; bd. dirs. The Luth. Home, Belle Plaine, Minn., 1981—. Served to capt., Dental Corps, AUS, 1943-46. Fellow Royal Soc. Health, Internat. Coll. Dentists, Am. Coll. Dentists; mem. ADA (ho. of dels. 1977—), Minn. Dental Assn. (chmn. peer rev. com. 1973-79, mem. ho. of dels. 1978—, pres. 1983-84), So. Dist. Dental Soc. (exec. council), South Cen. Dental Study Club (pres. 1970), Fedn. Dentaire Internationale, Pierre Fouchard Acad., Mankato C. of C., U. Minn. Alumni Assn., V.F.W. (recipient Distinguished Service award 1966, comdr. 1965), Am. Legion, Psi Omega. Lutheran (pres. congregation 1970). Lion (pres. 1965, 74, zone chmn. 1975). Clubs: Mankato Golf, U. Minn. Sch. Dentistry Century. Home: 364 Carol Ct Mankato MN 56001 Office: 430 S Broad St Mankato MN 56001

DUMMER, ROBERT WILLIAM, mechanical engineer; b. Redwood Falls, Minn., Apr. 18, 1952; s. E. Robert and Shirley Ann (Routhe) D.; m. Paulette Ceceil Janke, June 27, 1975; children: Brian, Kevin, Michelle. BS in Aeronautics, U. Minn., 1975. Registered profl. engr., Minn. Product engr. Lear-Siegler, Inc., Mammoth, Plymouth, Minn., 1975-76; design engr. ADC Telecom, Bloomington, Minn., 1976-79; mech. engr. Magnetic Peripherals, Inc. subs. Control Data Corp., Bloomington, 1979-81, mgr. product support, 1981-1983, mgr. mech. process devel., 1983-85, research and devel. and sr. mech. engr., 1985—; cons. Methods Automation, New Brighton, Minn., 1983-84. Inventor mini plug, precision polisher. Mem. Minn. Jaycees (dist. dir. 1981, Gopher editor 1983, regional dir. 1986, U.S. Ambassador 1982, Best State Pub. 1983), ASME. Lodge: Masons. Avocations: photography, writing, remodeling, golf, bowling. Home: 3430 Texas Ave Saint Louis Park MN 55426 Office: Magnetic Peripherals Inc 7801 Computer Ave S Minneapolis MN 55435

DUMONTELLE, PAUL BERTRAND, geologist; b. Kankakee, Ill., June 22, 1933; s. Lester Vernon and Helen (McKinstry) DuM.; m. Dollie Louise Bridgewater, June 5, 1955; children—John, Jeffrey, Jo, James, Jay. B.S., DePauw U., 1955; M.S., Lehigh U., 1957. Lic. geologist, Calif. Geologist, Lehigh Portland Cement Co., Allentown, Pa., 1956, 57, Homestake Mining Co., Lead, S.D., 1957-63; asst. geologist, then assoc. geologist Ill. State Geol. Survey, Champaign, 1963-70, coordinator environ. geology, geologist, 1975, head engring. geology sect., 1979—; dir. Ill. Mine Subsidence Research Program, 1985—; vice chmn. Ill. Mapping Adv. Com., Springfield, 1986—; mem. Prime 750 Policy Com., Champaign, 1983-86 . Contbr. brochures, handbooks and articles to profl. jours. Commr. Boneyard Creek, Urbana, Ill., 1984. Fellow Geol. Soc. Am.; mem. Am. Inst. Profl. Geologists (cert.), Assn. Engring. Geologists (nat. awards com. 1974-76, chmn. North Cen. sect. 1987), Internat. Assn. Engring. Geologists (vice chmn. North Cen. sect.), Soc. Mining Engrs., Ill. Mining Inst., Ill. Geol. Soc., AIME, Soc. for Ill. Scientific Surveys, Am. Congress on Surveying and Mapping, Sigma Xi. Methodist. Lodges: Masons, Kiwanis (bd. dirs. 1983-84). Home: 2020 Burlison Dr Urbana IL 61801 Office: Ill State Geol Survey 615 E Peabody St Champaign IL 61820

DUNBAR, DAVID JOE, internist, educator; b. Findlay, Ohio, Jan. 20, 1951; s. Howard Clay Dunbar and Alice Marie (Kear) Molter; m. Dianne Louise Rine, May 27, 1978; children: Richard, Andrew, Alan, Angelia, Theodore. BA, Ohio No. U., 1974; MD, Ohio State U., 1978. Diplomate Am. Bd. Internal Medicine. Resident internal medicine Duke U., Durham, N.C., 1978-81; practice medicine specializing in internal medicine Lancaster, 1981—; staff physician Lancaster Fairfield (Ohio) Hosp., 1981—; asst. clin. prof. medicine Ohio State U., Columbus, 1983—; Bd. dirs. Fairfield County Hosp., Lancaster, 1984—. Mem. Ohio State Med. Soc., Fairfield County Diabetic Assn. (bd. dirs. 1982—). Home: 1531 Kensington Ln Lancaster OH 43130 Office: 1500 E Main St Lancaster OH 43130

DUNCAN, ALAN L., manufacturing executive; b. Dayton, Ohio, Dec. 10, 1949; s. Willard S. and Betty J. (Harvey) D.; m. Donna M. Miller, Aug. 5, 1972; children: Jason, Aaron. BS in Edn., Kent State U., 1972; MBA, U. Akron, 1980. Designer Firestone Tire, Akron, Ohio, 1974-79, systems engr., 1979-80, fin. analyst, 1981-83, mgr. fin. services, 1984-85; bus. systems cons. TRW, Inc., Lyndhurst, Ohio, 1985—. Youth coach Medina (Ohio) Basketball Assn., 1983-84; treas. First Bapt. Ch., Medina, 1978—. Mem. Epsilon Pi Tau. Republican. Avocations: golf, volleyball, architecture. Home: 830 Andrews Medina OH 44256 Office: TRW Inc 1900 Richmond Rd Lyndhurst OH 44124

DUNCAN, DAVID FRANK, community health specialist, educator; b. Kansas City, Mo., June 26, 1947; s. Chester Frank and Maxine (Irwin) D.; B.A., U. Mo., Kansas City, 1970; postgrad. Sam Houston State U., 1971; Dr.P.H., U. Tex., 1976; 1 foster son, Kevin Rheinboldt. Research asst. U. Kans. Bur. Child Research, 1967-68; supr. Johnson County Juvenile Hall, Olathe, Kans., 1968-70; asst. to warden Draper Correctional Center, Elmore, Ala., summer 1970; supr. Harris County Juvenile Hall, Houston, 1970-71; project dir. Who Cares, Inc. Drug Abuse Treatment Center, Houston, 1971-73; exec. dir. Reality Island Halfway House, Houston, 1974-75; research asso. Tex. Gov.'s Office, Austin, summer 1975; research asso. Inst. Clin. Toxicology, clin. toxicologist Ben Taub Gen. Hosp., Houston, 1975-76; asst. prof. health sci. SUNY, Brockport, 1976-78, asso. prof., 1978, acting chmn. dept. health sci., summer 1978; vis. prof. health environ. research U. Cologne, Fed. Republic Germany, 1986; prof. health edn., coordinator community health program So. Ill. U., Carbondale, 1978—; chmn. So. Ill. Health Edn. Task Force, 1979—; bd. dirs. Ill. Pub. Health Continuing Edn. Council; cons. to numerous health, edn. instns. Mem. Am. Public Health Assn. (past chmn. sect. mental health, mem. action bd.), Ill. Public Health Assn. (exec. council), Am. Coll. Epidemiology, Soc. Epidemiologic Research, AAAS, Ill. Acad. Sci., N.Y. Acad. Sci. Democrat. Methodist. Author: Drugs and the Whole Person, 1982, Health Education: A Transatlantic Perspective, 1987; contbr. articles to profl. jours.; editorial bd. Health Values, 1980—, Jour. Drug Edn., 1981—, Internat. Jour. Mental Health, 1982-83. Home: 306A S Oakland Carbondale IL 62901 Office: So Ill U Health Edn Dept Carbondale IL 62901

DUNCAN, DENIS JULIAN, accountant; b. Kennett, Mo., Nov. 10, 1958; s. Arnold Julian and Martha Sue (Sawyer) D.; m. Tamara Lee Dever, Nov. 28, 1981. BS summa cum laude, David Lipscomb Coll., 1981. CPA, Ohio. Mgr. fin. services Ernst and Whinney, Cleve., 1981—. Editor newsletter FSI Update, 1987. Mem. membership council Fairbount Presbyn. Ch., Cleveland Heights, Ohio, 1987. Mem. Am. Inst. CPA's, Nat. Assn. Accts., Tenn. Soc. CPA's (asst. treas. 1982-83), Nashville Area Jr. C. of C. Republican. Clubs: Canterbury Golf (Shaker Heights)(Jr. bd. dirs. 1986-87). Avocations: golf, squash, tennis, platform tennis. Home: 3016 Chadbourne Shaker Heights OH 44120 Office: Ernst & Whinney 2000 Nat City Ctr Cleveland OH 44114

DUNCAN, DONALD LYNN, agricultural products executive; b. Van Wert, Ohio, Feb. 8, 1955; s. Junior Clair and Patricia Joan (Bagley) D.; m. Sue Ellen Whitmore, June 26, 1976; children: Andrea Dawn, Adam Troy. Student, Bowling Green U., 1973-74; student in customer relations, Ohio State Coll. Agr., 1980. Custom operator Convoy (Ohio) Equity Exchange, 1975-80, asst. mgr., 1980-81, mgr. plant food, 1981—. Mem. Van Wert (Ohio) Civic Theater, 1984, 85, 86; v.p. Aid Assn. Luth., Convoy, 1984, 85, 86; mem. ch. council Trinity Luth., convoy, 1981—. Mem. Country Mark Inc., Ohio Fertilizer and Pesticide Assn., Farm Bur., Farm Focus. Democrat. Lodge: Moose. Avocations: fishing, volleyball, music. Home: Rural Rt #1 Box 79 Scott OH 45886 Office: Convoy Equity Exchange Box 98 W Tully St Convoy OH 45832

DUNCAN, FRANK MARTIN, educational administrator; b. Blue Earth, Minn., June 30, 1943; s. Frank Martin Duncan and Helen Marie (Houghaling) Peterson; m. Carolynn Lee Swensrud, Aug. 21, 1966; children—Derek Andrew, Darcy Lee. B.A., Mankato State U., 1967, M.A.T., 1969, Ed.S., 1975. Cert. supt., prin., tchr., Minn. Tchr., Pomona Pub. Schs., Calif., 1969-70, Prescott Pub. Schs., Ariz., 1970-71, Fairmont Pub. Schs., Minn., 1971-74; prin. Sherburn Pub. Schs., Minn., 1975-77; supt. Amboy-Good Thunder Schs., Amboy, Minn., 1977-80, Howard Lake-Waverly Schs., Howard Lake, Minn., 1980-85, Olivia Sch., Minn., 1985—. Bd. dirs. Howard Lake Cable Commn., 1983-85; mem. Community Corrections Task Force, Mankato, Minn., 1979-80. Served with U.S. Navy, 1961-67. Bush Found. fellow, 1984-85. Mem. Minn. Assn. Sch. Adminstrs., Am. Assn. Sch. Adminstrs. Lutheran. Avocations: archeology, writing. Office: Olivia Pub Sch 701 S 9th Olivia MN 56277

DUNCAN, JON ALLAN, lawyer; b. Auburn, Ind., July 27, 1954; s. Frank A. and Sigrid (Nelson) D. BA, DePauw U., 1976; JD, DePaul U., 1980. Bar: Ill. 1980, U.S. Dist. Ct. (no. dist.) Ill. 1980, U.S. Tax Ct. 1984, U.S. Ct. Appeals (7th cir.) 1986. Editor Instl. Investor, Washington, 1981-82; assoc. Rieck & Crotty, P.C., Chgo., 1983-84, Mass, Miller & Josephson, Ltd., Chgo., 1984—. Mem. ABA, Chgo. Bar Assn., Chgo. Council of Lawyers, Soc. Profl. Journalists, Sigma Delta Chi. Democrat. Club: Chgo. Headline. Home: 3639 N Sheffield #2 Chicago IL 60613 Office: Mass Miller & Josephson Ltd 333 W Wacker Dr #810 Chicago IL 60606

DUNCAN, RICHARD FRED, law educator; b. Fall River, Mass., June 6, 1951; s. Richard Fred and Anne Angela (Rogers) Dunkelberger; m. Gail Holly Cummings, June 30, 1970 (div. Feb. 1981); 1 child, Casey Dwight. BA magna cum laude, U. Mass., 1973; JD cum laude, Cornell U., 1976. Assoc. White & Case, N.Y.C., 1976-79; prof. law U. Nebr., Lincoln, 1979—; vis. prof. Notre Dame Law Sch., South Bend, Ind., 1985-86; chmn. Nebr. State adv. com. to U.S. Commn. on Civil Rights, Lincoln, 1985—. Author: (with Lyons) The Law and Practice of Secured Transactions, 1987; contbr.law rev. articles to profl. jours; mem. editorial bd. Jour. of Contemporary Health Law and Policy. Mem. Rep. Nat. Lawyers Assn., The Heritage Found. (resource bank), Washington Legal Found. (nat. acad. adv. bd.), The Federalist Soc. (faculty). Roman Catholic. Avocations: weightlifting, reading polit. theory. Home: 6431 Skylark Ln Lincoln NE 68516 Office: Univ Nebr Coll Law Lincoln NE 68583-0902

DUNCAN, ROBERT GENE, lawyer; b. Helena, Mo., Nov. 22, 1932; s. Chester Frank and Maxine I. (Henry) D.; m. Anita Fay Woerz, Dec. 11, 1960 (div. 1981); 1 son, Stephen; m. Mary Carol Bradford, Nov. 10, 1983; stepchildren—Marc, Michelle and Misti Montgomery. A.A., Jr. Coll. Kansas City, 1951; B.S. in Edn., Central Mo. State U., 1953; J.D., U. Mo.-Kansas City, 1959. Bar: Mo. 1959, U.S. Supreme Ct. Assoc. Quinn, Peebles & Hickman, Kansas City, Mo., 1960-62, Simon and Pierce, Kansas City, Mo., 1962-65; ptnr. Pierce, Duncan, Bietling & Shute, Kansas, City, Mo., 1965-72, Duncan & Russell, Gladstone, Mo., 1972-81; of counsel Coulson & Chick, Kansas City, Mo., 1981-85; ptnr. Duncan, Coulson & Scholss, 1985—; city atty. City of Gladstone, 1961-74, mcpl. judge, 1974-81; v.p. Northland Ct. Referal Service, Kansas City, Mo., 1970-83. Editor: Missouri Criminal Law, 1984 (2 vols.). Chmn. Clay County Sheltered Facilities Bd., Gladstone, 1970—. Served to sgt. U.S. Army, 1953-55. Fellow Am. Bd. Criminal Lawyers; mem. Mo. Assn. Criminal Def. Lawyers (pres. 1983-84), Nat. Assn. Criminal Def. Lawyers, Clay County Bar Assn. (pres. 1978), Order Bench and Robe. Democrat. Lodge: Elks. Avocations: reading; travel. Home: 4248 NE Davidson Rd Kansas City MO 64116

DUNCAN, THEODORE NORMAN, fluid power company executive; b. N.Y.C., Dec. 18, 1921; s. William F. and Sarah L. (Moore) D.; m. Perdema Mauree Miller, June 15, 1946; children—Claudia Mauree Burckard, Sara Diane Klepper, Jennifer Lynn Salter. B.S.M.E., Stevens Inst. Tech., 1943; postgrad. U. Tulsa, 1950-51, Drury Coll., 1956-57. Registered profl. engr., Okla. Gen. mgr. aerospace div. Sperry Vickers, Troy, Mich., 1965-66, v.p., 1966-68, v.p., gen. mgr. Mobile div., 1968-73, v.p. internat., 1973-80; pres. Vickers, Inc., Troy, 1980—; chmn. Vickers S.Y.S. Can.; dir. overseas subs. Bd. dirs. Milw. Sch. Engring., 1984-85, Master Data Ctr., Inc., Southfield, Mich., 1984-85. Served to lt. USN, 1942-47, PTO. Mem. Am. Soc. Metals, ASME, Soc. Mfg. Engrs., Constrn. Industry Mfg. Assn. (tech. bd. 1984—), Nat. Fluid Power Assn. (bd. dirs. 1983-86, chmn. 1986—, chmn. adv. panel for hydraulic competitiveness and compatability 1983-84), Internat. Ops. Council Machinery and Allied Products Inst. (bd. dirs. 1984-86), Internat. Rd. Fedn. (bd. dirs. 1984-86), Am. Nat. Standards Inst. (exec. council 1983-86), Mich. C. of C. (bd. dirs. 1983-87), Greater Detroit C. of C. Club: Bloomfield Open Hunt (Mich.). Avocations: golf; horseback riding; sailing. Office: Vickers Inc 1401 Crooks Rd Troy MI 48084

DUNDAS, HARVEY LESTER, systems analyst; b. Duluth, Minn., Mar. 28, 1942; s. Lester Harvey and Dorothy Evelyn (Kraft) D.; m. Rosalie Marie Bunge, Feb. 14, 1976. Student, U. Wis., Stevens Point, 1960-62; BS, St. Cloud (Minn.) State U., 1966; BA, Met. State U., St. Paul, 1980. Programmer 3M Co., St. Paul, 1970-78, systems analyst, 1979—. Served to lt. USN, 1967-69. Unitarian. Avocations: ornithology, skiing, fishing. Home: 880 Mound St Saint Paul MN 55106 Office: 3M Co IS&DP SD&S 224-4E-02 3M Ctr Saint Paul MN 55144

DUNHAM, JON LYNN, accountant; b. St. Louis, Sept. 5, 1960; s. Charles Chester and Estelle Lucille (Simon) D.; m. Cheryl Lee Little, Sept. 20, 1986. BS in bus. adminstrn., U. Mo., St. Louis, 1983. CPA, Mo. Staff acct. Tiger, Fireside, Stone, Carlie & Co., St. Louis, 1983-84; tax acct. Schowalter & Jabouri, St. Louis, 1984—. Recipient Eagle Scout award Boy Scouts Am., St. Louis, 1974. Mem. Mo. Soc. CPA's, Am. Inst. CPA's. Republican.

Baptist. Avocations: golf, camping. Home: 2387 Wesglen Estates Dr Saint Louis MO 63043 Office: Schowalter & Jabouri 11777 Gravois Rd Saint Louis MO 63127

DUNLAP, DAVID HOUSTON, judge; b. Columbia, Mo., Apr. 24, 1947; s. James Vardeman and CYnthia May (Roby) D.; m. Dana Sue Coburn, Apr. 23, 1982. BA, Southwest Mo. State U., 1969, MA, 1971; JD, U. Mo., 1975. Assoc. Campbell, Morgan & G, Kansas City, Mo., 1975-82; editor Mo. Law Tape, Inc., Kansas City, 1982-86; judge Howell County Cir. Ct. (37th cir.), West Plains, Mo., 1986—; cons. appellate law, Mo., 1982-86. Author, editor: (audio tapes) Legal Ednl., 1974-86. Spkr. Mo. Right-to-Work Comn., Kansas City, 1978; bd. dirs. St. Francis' Farm, West Plains, Mo., 1986—. Am. Forensic Assn. grantee, 1971. Mem. Mo. Bar Assn., Mo. Judicial Conf., Ozark Gastronomic Soc. (bd. dirs. 1983—). Avocations: gastronomy, horticulture. Home: 728 Monks St West Plains MO 65775 Office: Circuit Ct Assoc Div Howell County Courthouse West Plains MO 65775

DUNLAP, PAUL D., bank holding company executive; b. 1930. LLB, U. Nebr., 1956. With First Nat. Bank Clinton (Iowa), 1967—, now chmn.; vice chmn. Hawkeye Bancorp, Des Moines. Office: Hawkeye Bancorporation 6 Floor First Bldg 319 7th St Des Moines IA 50307 *

DUNN, DANA LEONE, food company manager; b. Elmira, N.Y., Mar. 29, 1949; d. Robert Leon and Georgia Mae (Adams) Hazlett; m. Douglas Eugene Briggs, July 13, 1968 (div. 1979); children: Douglas Eugene Jr., Rebecca Lynn; m. Terrence George Dunn, June 29, 1982. AS, Culinary Inst. Am., 1980. Food prodn. mgr. Neiman-Marcus, White Plains, N.Y., 1980-81; sr. nutrition supr. Canteen Co., Grand Rapids, Mich., 1981-82; asst. store mgr. Koeze Co., Kentwood, Mich., 1986—. Bd. dirs. Garfield Park Neighborhoods Assn., 1985-86. Republican. Avocations: music, crafts, cooking, flying, gardening. Home: 5836 Bramalea Dr SE Kentwood MI 49508 Office: Koeze Co 2880 E Paris SE Kentwood MI 49508

DUNN, EDDIE LYNN, probation manager; b. Clarksville, Tenn., Aug. 10, 1937; s. Ivy Ruble and Vera Mae (Harrison) D.; m. Carole Ann Evans, Aug. 12, 1961 (div. Mar. 1982); children: Lynette, Raila, Jenny; m. J. Scottie Martin Henderson, Apr. 21, 1984. BA, Harding U., 1959. Ordained minister, 1959; lic. social worker, Mich. Minister Ch. of Christ, Helsinki, Finland, 1960-69, Detroit, 1969-70; probation officer Mich. Dept. Corrections, Wayne, Oakland, and Kent Counties, 1971-77; probation supr. Mich. Dept. Corrections, Oakland County, 1977-81, probation mgr., 1981—. Vol. counselor Crossroads, Detroit, 1986—. Mem. Am. Correctional Assn., Mich. Corrections Assn. Avocations: running, handball, singing. Home: 1032 Allen Dr Northville MI 48167 Office: Oakland County Probation Dept 111 S Troy St Royal Oak MI 48067

DUNN, FLOYD EMRYL, neurologist/psychiatrist, consultant; b. Wilkes-Barre, Pa., Apr. 25, 1910; s. Adrian Anson and Frances Amanda (Culver) D.; m. Wilda Kathryn Lauer, Aug. 14, 1943; children—Kathryn Alice (dec.), Deborah Lee. Student, Temple U., 1929-32; D.O., Phila. Coll. Osteo. Medicine, 1936. Diplomate Am. Osteo. Bd. Neurology and Psychiatry. Resident in neurology, psychiatry Still-Hildreth Hosp., 1941-45, staff psychiatrist, 1945-49; chmn. div. neurology, psychiatry Kirksville Coll. Osteo. Medicine, 1945-48, Kansas City Coll. Osteo. Medicine, U. Health Scis., Mo., 1949-68; mem. staff VA Hosp., Knoxville, Iowa, 1968-76, chief psychiatry service, 1970-76; clin. prof. neurology, psychiatry Coll. Osteo. Medicine, Des Moines, 1970-74; mem. Nat. Bd. Examiners for Osteo. Physicans and Surgeons, 1965-74, Excellence award, 1974, cons. neurology, psychiatry, Chgo., 1974—; cons., examiner sect. of disability determinations Mo. Dept. Elem. and Secondary Edn., Jefferson City, 1985—. Author: (monograph) History of the American College of Neuropsychiatrists, 1984. Contbr. articles to profl. jours. Mem. Iowa Adv. Council on Mental Health Ctrs., Des Moines, 1972-78, Central Regional Adv. Council for Comprehensive Psychiat. Services, Columbia, Mo., 1978—. Fellow Am. Coll. Neuropsychiatrists (life, sec.-treas. 1948-52, pres. 1954-55, 63-64, Disting. Service award 1967, Disting. Fellow award 1984), Am. Assn. on Mental Deficiency; mem. Am. Osteo. Assn. (life, editorial cons. publs. 1958—, del. 1960-69, pres.'s adv. council 1973), Mo. Assn. Osteo. Physicians and Surgeons (hon. life, del. 1958-69, v.p. 1969-70), Phi Sigma Gamma (pres. grand council 1952-53, council sec.-treas. 1953-59, editor Speculum 1959-65, Meritorious Service award 1965), Phi Sigma Sigma (exec. sec.-treas. grand council 1980—), Alpha Phi Omega. Republican. Methodist. Lodges: Lions (pres. Gravois Mills, Mo. chpt. 1984-85, sec. 1985—, del. to internat. conv. 1985, 86, 87), Masons, Elks. Avocations: photography; travel; journalism. Home: Route 3 Box 504-A Gravois Mills MO 65037

DUNN, HORTON, JR., organic chemist; b. Coleman, Tex., Sept. 3, 1929; s. Horton and Lora Dean (Bryant) D. B.A. summa cum laude, Hardin-Simmons U., 1951; M.S., Case Western Res. U., 1975, Ph.D., 1979. Research chemist Lubrizol Corp., Cleve., 1953-70, dir. tech. info. ctr., 1970-79, supr. research div., 1980—; chmn. bd., bus. mgr. Isotopics, Cleve., 1964-67, editor, 1961-63. Contbr. articles to profl. jours.; patentee (in field). Fellow Am. Inst. Chemists; mem. Am. Chem. Soc. (Cleve. sect. treas. 1968-70, chmn. 1987); mem. Am. Soc. for Info. Sci. (chpt. pres. 1973-74), AAAS, Nat. Council Met. Opera, SAR, Royal Oak Soc. (life), Cleve. Play House, Cleve. Tech. Soc. Council (treas. 1987), Alpha Chi. Clubs: Univ., Cleve., Play House (Cleve.). Home: 530 Sycamore Dr Cleveland OH 44132 Office: 29400 Lakeland Blvd Wickliffe OH 44092

DUNN, JAMES BERNARD, mining company executive, state legislator; b. Lead, S.D, June 27, 1927; s. William Bernard and Lucy Marie (Mullen) D.; m. Elizabeth Ann Lanham, Sept. 5, 1955; children: Susan, Thomas, Mary Elizabeth, Kathleen. BS in Bus. Adminstrn. and Econ., Black Hills State Coll., 1962. Heavy equipment mechanic Homestake Mi ng Co., Lead, 1947-62, asst. dir. pub. relations, 1962-78, dir. pub. affairs, 1978; mem. S.D. Ho. Reps., Pierre, 1971-72, S.D. State Senate, Pierre, 1973—; exec. com. Nat. Conf. State Legislatures, 1979-81, Council State Govt., 1983—; chmn. Midwestern Conf. Council of State Govts., 1984; bd. dirs. S.D. Blue Shield, S.D. Automobile Assn. Editor: Homestake Gold Mine 1876-1976, 1976, Bulldog Mountain Silver Mine, 1978. Bd. dirs. S.D. State Hist. Soc., Pierre, 1971—; chmn. bd. trustees Adams Mus., Deadwood, S.D., 1962—s. Served as pvt. U.S. Army, 1945-47. Republican. Roman Catholic. Avocations: hunting, fishing, hiking, historical research. Home: 619 Ridge Rd Lead SD 57754 Office: PO Box 887 Lead SD 57754

DUNN, ROBERT GEARHART, sales professional; b. Mpls., Jan. 25, 1923; s. George Robert and Marguerite (Gearhart) Morrow D.; m. Mary Louise Caley, June 23, 1951 (dec. 1969); children: Ruth Caley, Susan Lydia, George Robert, Elizabeth Ann, William Campbell; m. Bette Joyce Lee, Nov. 11, 1972; stepchildren: Robert Paul Hedenstrom, Mary Lee Hedenstrom Leirmo. BA, Amherst (Mass.) Coll., 1948. Gen. mgr. Inland Lumber Co., Princeton, Minn., 1953-66, pres., 1967—. State rep. Minn. Ho. of Reps., St. Paul, 1965-72; senator Minn. Senate, 1973-80; chmn. Princeton Planning Commn., 1960, Minn. Waste Mgmt. Bd., Mpls., 1980-85; mem. Gov.'s Commn. on the Outdoors, 1986, Minn. Environ. Quality Bd., 1986—. Served to capt. USMCR. Republican. Episcopalian. Home: 708 4th St S Princeton MN 55371 Office: Inland Lumber Co Hwy 169 S Princeton MN 55371

DUNN, ROBERT SIGLER, engineering executive; b. Cin., Aug. 13, 1926; s. John W. and Mirian S. (Sigler) D.; m. Barbara A. Rigdon, June 26, 1949; children: Anne Dunn Stockman, John R., Mark A. BSME, BSEE, Purdue U., 1949. With Collins Radio Co., Cedar Rapids, Iowa, 1949-72; regional v.p., gen. mgr. Collins Radio Co., Cedar Rapids; v.p. ops. King Radio Corp., Olathe, Kans., 1973—; also bd. dirs. King Radio Corp., Olathe. V.p., bd. dirs. Olathe Community Hosp., 1981—. Served with USN, 1945-46. Mem. IEEE, NSPE, Soc. Mfg. Engrs., Am. Soc. Quality Control, Pi Tau Sigma, Eta Kappa Nu, Tau Beta Pi. Lodge: Rotary. Home: 15320 Melrose Pl Shawnee Mission KS 66221 Office: King Radio Corp 400 N Rogers Rd Olathe KS 66062

DUNN, SIDNEY N., fraternal organization administrator; b. Detroit, Nov. 12, 1946; s. Albert and Janet (Pollak) D.; m. Linda C. Cohen, Aug. 31, 1969; children: Kari M., Stacie N. BS, Wayne State U., 1964. Tchr. Westside Community Schs., Omaha, 1969-74; exec. v.p. Alpha Epsilon Pi, Omaha, 1974—; bd. dirs. Fraternity Execs. Assn., Indpls., 1985—; cons. Western Regional Greek Conf., Reno, 1982—. Editor: The Lion of Alpha Epsilon Pi, 1977—. Jewish. Office: Alpha Epsilon Pi Fraternity Inc 11128 John Galt Blvd #385 Omaha NE 68137

DUNN, STEPHEN MICHAEL, data processing consultant; b. Boston, June 13, 1950; s. Reginald and Catherine Susan (McCabe) D.; m. Rose Marie Schaumburg, July 3, 1983; 1 child, Stephen Michael II. AS, Blue Hills Inst., 1970; BA, Curry Coll., 1978. Sr. operator Bay Bank, Dedham, Mass., 1969-70; sr. programmer ABT, Cambridge, Mass., 1973-76, Saddle Brook, Cambridge, 1977-78; staff cons. Contract Computer Profl., Kansas City, Mo., 1978-80; exec. v.p. Systems Design & Mgmt. Inc., Am. Computer Systems and Software Assocs. Inc., Praire Village, Kans., 1980-85; pres., chief exec. officer Bids, Inc., Kansas City, 1985—, also bd. dirs. Author: Software Options, 1985. Mem. Rep. Presl. Task Force, Rep. Nat. Com. Served as Sgt. USMC, 1970-73. Mem. Am. Security Council, Am. Against Union Controlled Govt., Curry Coll. Alumni Assn. Baptist. Club: Senatorial. Avocations: racquetball, sailing, reading, photography. Home: 301 W 115th Terr Kansas City MO 64114 Office: Bids Inc PO Box 10714 Kansas City MO 64118

DUNN, WILLIAM EDWARD, dentist; b. Elkton, S.D., July 22, 1921; s. John Eligah and Jane (Horine) D.; m. Charlotte Walsh, Sept. 22, 1948; children: James, Thomas, Catherine, Patrick, Maureen, Michael. Student, St. John's U., Collegeville, Minn., 1938-40; DDS, Creighton U., 1943. Gen. practice dentistry Pierre, S.D., 1948—; mem. gov.'s emergency health service commn., Pierre, 1970-73; mem. policy commn. Headstart, Sioux Falls, S.D., 1971-74. Author: Dentistry In South Dakota, 1970, History of South Dakota Dental Assn., 1983; assoc. editor N.W. Dental Jour., 1981-86. Served to lt. USNR, 1944-46. Fellow Am. Coll. Dentists, Internat. Coll. Dentists; mem. S.D. Dental Assn. (pres. 1969-70, sec. 1974-77, newsletter editor 1974-77, Honored Guest award 1983, Presdl. Citation award 1984, Gold Tooth award 1986), Pierre Fauchard Acad. (state chmn. 1985-86), Sioux Falls C. of C. Roman Catholic. Lodge: Optimists, K.C. Home: 1312 S Center Ave Sioux Falls SD 57105 Office: 2200 S Minnesota Sioux Falls SD 57105

DUNNETTE, MARVIN DALE, psychologist, educator; b. Austin, Minn., Sept. 30, 1926; s. Rodney Arthur and Mildred Geneva (Notestine) D.; m. Leaetta Marie Hough, Feb. 2, 1980; children by previous marriage—Nancy Dawn, Peggy Jo, Sheryl Jean. B.Ch.E., U. Minn., 1948, M.A., 1951, Ph.D., 1954. Research fellow dept. metallurgy U. Minn., 1948-49, research fellow, asst. prof. psychology, 1951-55; adviser employee relations research Minn. Mining and Mfg. Co., St. Paul, 1955-59; vis. assoc. prof. U. Calif.-Berkeley, 1962; chmn. bd. Decision Systems, Inc., Mpls., 1963-65; pres. Personnel Decisions, Inc., Mpls., 1966-75, chmn. bd., 1975-83, vice chmn., head research group, 1982—; pres. Personnel Decisions Research Inst., Mpls., 1975-83, chmn. bd., dir. research, 1983—; prof. psychology U. Minn., Mpls., 1961—; mem. research and devel. adv. group Army Research Inst. Social and Behavioral Scis., 1972-76, chmn. sci. adv. panel, ad hoc com. on personnel research and tng., 1975; mem. personnel research adv. group Bur. Naval Research, 1970-75. Author: (with W.K. Kirchner) Psychology Applied to Industry, 1965; Personnel Selection and Placement, 1966; (with J.P. Campbell and E.E. Lawler, D.E. Weick) Managerial Behavior, Performance and Effectiveness, 1970; editor: Work and Non Work in the Year 2001, 1973, Handbook of Industrial and Organizational Psychology, 1976; cons. editor Jour. Applied Psychology, 1950-75; contbr. articles to profl. jours. Served with USMC, 1944-46. Recipient James A. Hamilton Outstanding Book award Am. Coll. Hosp. Adminstrs., 1972; Ford Found. fellow, 1964-65. Mem. Am. Psychol. Assn. (pres. div. 14, 1966-67, div. 14 award for outstanding sci. contbn. 1985; mem. bd. sci. affairs 1975-77, James McKeen Cattell award 1965), AAAS. Home: 370 Summit Ave Saint Paul MN 55102 Office: 43 Main St SE River Pl Suite 405 Minneapolis MN 55414

DUNNINGTON, MICHAEL GERARD, marketing executive; b. St. Louis, Jan. 14, 1946; s. Joseph Anthony and Olive Minette (Spies) D.; m. Jann Jacoby, May 10, 1980; children: Laurel Elizabeth, Deirdre Ann. BA, St. Louis U., 1969, MA in Am. History, 1970; MBA, So. Ill. U., 1975. Asst. dir. mktg. research Lincoln div. McNeil, St. Louis, 1971-73, asst. sales mgr., 1971-76; dist. sales mgr. Lincoln div. McNeil, Lexington, Ky., 1976-84; nat. sales mgr. Aro Corp., Bryan, Ohio, 1984-87, product mgr. fluid handling, 1987—. Mem. Assn. for Finishing Processes of Soc. Mfg. Engrs. Episcopalian. Avocations: civil war history, bicycling. Office: Aro Corp One Aro Ctr Bryan OH 43506

DUPES, PHILIP LOWELL, consulting firm executive; b. Hobart, Ind., Aug. 13, 1937; s. Lowell Edgar and Mary Louise (Cherrington) D., m. Mary Lou Barrie, June 27, 1970. B.S. in Mech. Engring., Purdue U., 1960; M.B.A., U. Mo.-Kansas City, 1983. Registered engr. in tng., Calif. Project engr. Spreckels Sugar div. Am. Sugar Refining Co., San Francisco, 1960-76; sr. project engr. Russell Stover Candy Co., Kansas City, Mo., 1976-81; pres. Philip Lowell Assocs., Inc., Leawood, Kans., 1984—; computer systems, programming services cons. Author: (with others) Beet Sugar Technology, 1971, 3d edit., 1982. Mem. Am. Statis. Assn., Fin. Mgmt. Assn., Beta Gamma Sigma. Office: Philip Lowell Assocs Inc 12742 Overbrook Rd Leawood KS 66209

DUPUIS, FRANCOISE-ARMANDE, minister, languages and culture educator; b. Paris, Mar. 31, 1924; came to U.S., 1948, naturalized, 1962; d. Armand Alexandre and Genevieve Augustine (Blanchet) D.; m. Edward M. Smith, Feb. 19, 1949 (dec. 1971); 1 child, Michele Dupuis Smith Weyant. B.Philosophy-Lettres, Sorbonne, U. Paris, 1944, P.C.B., Faculte des Sciences de Paris, 1946, postgrad. Faculte de Medecine de Paris, 1947; postgrad. in edn. U. No. Iowa, 1962, Upper Iowa U., 1963; cert. in ministry Seabury Western Theol. Sem., 1983. Chmn. dept. langs. and culture Upper Iowa U., Fayette, 1965—, assoc. prof. langs. and culture, 1968—, chmn. humanities div., 1976-80, acting chmn. dept. religion, 1983—. Layreader, chalice bearer Episcopal Ch., Oelwein, Iowa, 1978—; mem. Fayette Betterment Com., 1982. Mem. AAUP, AAUW, Friends of France-Amerique.

DUPUY, ELBERT NEWTON, obstetrician, gynecologist, educator; b. Parral, W.Va., Oct. 19, 1904; s. Elbert Stephenson and Lillian (Dixon) DuP.; m. Ruth Christine Griffenhagen, May 7, 1938; children: James Newton, Karl Frederick Griffenhagen, William Edwin Stuart. BS, U. W.Va., 1930, Duke U., 1932. Diplomate Am. Bd. Ob/gyn. Intern Ch. Home and Infirmary, Balt., 1933; resident in obstetrics U. Hosp., Balt., 1934-36; fellow Rotunda Hosp., Dublin, Ireland, 1931; practice medicine specializing in Ob/gyn Beckley, W.Va., 1936-42, Quincy, Ill., 1946-84; mem. staff Blessing Hosp., 1946-84, chief ob/gyn, 1975-77; assoc. clin. prof. ob/gyn So. Ill. U., Springfield. Mem. Nat. Council Boy Scouts Am., 1968—; trustee Robert Morris Coll., Carthage, Ill., 1964-69, Spastic Paralysis Research Found., 1956—. Served with M.C., U.S. Army, 1942-46. Decorated Silver Star, Bronze Star; recipient Silver Beaver award Boy Scouts Am., 1972. Fellow Am. Coll. Ob/gyn. (founder), ACS, Royal Soc. Medicine (Eng.), Am. Acad. Geriatrics, Am. Acad. Psychosomatic Medicine, Royal Soc. Health (Eng.), Edn. and Sci. Found. if Ill. Med. Sco. (founder); mem. AMA (Physician's Recognition award), World Soc. Med. Assns., Cen. Assn. Obstetricians and Gynecologists, Assn. Mil. Surgeons, Ill. State Med. Soc. (past pres., past chmn. bd. trustees), Adams County Med. Soc. (past pres.). Clubs: University (Chgo.); Quincy Country. Lodges: Masons, Shriners, Jesters. Home: 18 Country Club Dr Quincy IL 62301

DUQUETTE, RODERICK DANIEL, community health educator; b. Schenectady, N.Y., Nov. 17, 1956; s. Roderick Daniel and Nola Jean (Thomas) D.; m. Debra Sue Morris, Jan. 10, 1981; 1 child Laura Michele. AS, Schenectady County Community Coll., 1977; BS, SUNY, Brockport, 1979; MS, U. R.I., 1981; EdD, SUNY, Buffalo, 1984. Teaching asst. U. R.I., Kingston, 1980-81; teaching asst. SUNY, Buffalo, 1981-84, research asst., 1982-84; asst. prof. U. Wis., La Crosse, 1984—. Del. Am. Cancer Soc., La Crosse, 1985-86, chmn. pub. edn. com. 1985—, fresh start facilitator, 1985-86, bd. dirs. 1985—; com. mem. Am. Lung Assn., Buffalo, 1983-84; alcohol and drug com. chairperson U. Wis., 1986-87. Named one of Outstanding Young Men Am., 1985. Mem. AAAS, Am. Pub. Health Assn., Am. Alliance Health Phys. Edn. Recreation and Dance, N.Y. Acad. Scis., The N.Am. Assn. for Environ. Edn. Avocations: running, reading, music, basketball. Office: U Wis La Crosse Room 219 Mitchell Hall La Crosse WI 54601

DURBIN, RICHARD JOSEPH, Congressman; b. East St. Louis, Ill., Nov. 21, 1944; s. William and Ann D.; m. Loretta Schaefer, June 24, 1967; children: Christine, Paul, Jennifer. B.S. in Econs., Georgetown U., 1966, J.D., 1969. Bar: Ill. 1969. Chief legal counsel Lt. Gov. Paul Simon of Ill., 1969; mem. staff minority leader Ill. Senate, 1972-77, parliamentarian, 1969-77; practice law 1969—; mem. 98th-100th Congresses from 20th Dist. Ill., 1983—; assoc. prof. med. humanities So. Ill. U., 1978—. Campaign worker Sen. Paul Douglas of Ill., 1966; staff Office Ill. Dept. Bus. and Econ. Devel., Washington; candidate for Ill. Lt. Gov., 1978; staff alt. Pres.'s State Planning Council, 1980; advisor Am. Council Young Polit. Leaders, 1981; mem. YMCA Ann. Membership Roundup, YMCA Bldg. Drive, Pony World Series; bd. dirs. Cath. Charities, United Way of Springfield, Old Capitol Art Fair, Springfield Youth Soccer; mem. Sch. Dist. 1986 Referendum Com., Springfield NAACP. Democrat. Roman Catholic. Office: US Senate 417 Cannon House Office Bldg Washington DC 20515 *

DURBNEY, CLYDROW JOHN, clergyman; b. St. Louis, Sept. 27, 1916; s. Earl Elmer and Conetta Mae D.; A.B., Gordon Coll. Theology and Missions, 1950; B.D., Eden Theol. Sem., 1953; S.T.M., Concordia Theol. Sem., 1954, postgrad. 1954-59; postgrad Eden Sem., 1973-75; D.D., Am. Bible Inst., 1980; Cultural doctorate in Sacred Philosophy, World U., 1982; m. Mattie Lee Neal, Oct. 27, 1968. Ordained to ministry Nat. Bapt. Ch., 1952. Clk., U.S. Post Office, St. Louis, 1941-54; instr. Western Bapt. Bible Coll., St. Louis, 1954-67; asst. pastor Central Bapt. Ch., St. Louis, 1954, pastor, 1983; ghetto evangelist Ch. on Wheels, 1952-84; pastor, founder Saints Fellowship Ch., 1984—. Served with AUS, 1942-46; ETO. Decorated Bronze Star. Recipient Disting. World Service award Central Bapt. Ch. Prayer Aux., 1974. Mem. Internat. Platform Assn., Inst. Research Assn., Gordon Alumni Assn., Anglo Am. Acad., Nat. Geog. Soc., Smithsonian Instn. Republican. Author: With Him in Glory, 1955; Adventures in Soul Winning, 1966; contbr. to New Voices in Am. Poetry, 1972—. Home: 8244 Addington Dr Berkeley MO 63134

DURCHHOLZ, DALE LEROY, agricultural research economist, consultant; b. Lincoln, Ill., Nov. 16, 1948; s. Elmer Wayne and Marilyn Marie (Buckles) D.; m. Dawn Robin Vogel, June 4, 1983. BS in Agriculture, U. Ill., 1971, MBA, 1975. Grain analyst, cons. Farmers Grain and Livestock, West Des Moines, Iowa, 1976-79; dir. commodity research Maduff & Sons Inc., Chgo., 1979-84; research dir. G.H. Miller & Sons, Chgo., 1984-86; market research analyst AgriVisor Services Inc., Bloomington, Ill., 1986—. Mem. Nat. Futures Assn. (registered commodity trading advisor). Office: AgriVisor Services Inc 1701 Towanda Ave PO Box 2901 Bloomington IL 61701

DURCHHOLZ, PATRICIA, sociologist; b. Cin., Apr. 5, 1933; d. Robert Patrick and Helen (Lippert) White; m. Richard Francis Durchholz, Aug. 9, 1952 (dec. May 1982); children—Kim Benz, Leslie Chamberlain, Mark, Andrea Harpen, Theresa Hill, Anthony, Amy. B.A., U. Cin., 1973; Ph.D., Union Grad. Sch., Yellow Springs, Ohio, 1977. Ford Found. intern, U. Cin., 1973-74, asst. to pres., 1974-76; dir., adj. prof. U. Ky., Lexington, 1977-79; cons. Cin. Family Health Care, Mason, Ohio, 1983-86; v.p. RFD Enterprises, Mason, Ohio, 1984—; cons. Trillium Hills Coop., Clarksville, Ohio, 1985—; lectr. English, Clermont Coll., Batavia, Ohio, 1986—. Danforth fellow, 1975. Mem. Soc. Values in Higher Edn., Am. Sociol. Assn., U. Cin. Library Guild, Phi Beta Kappa. Democrat. Roman Catholic. Avocations: biking; running; gardening. Home: 9307 Greenhedge Ln Loveland OH 45140

DUREAULT, A., provincial judge. Judge Ct. of Queen's Bench, Winnipeg, Man., Can. Office: Court of Queen's Bench, Law Courts Bldg, Winnipeg, MB Canada R3C 0V8 *

DURENBERGER, DAVID FERDINAND, U.S. senator; b. St. Cloud, Minn., Aug. 19, 1934; s. George G. and Isabelle M. (Cebulla) D.; m. Gilda Beth (Penny) Baran, Sept. 4, 1971; children by previous marriage: Charles, David, Michael, Daniel. B.A. cum laude in Polit. Sci, St. Johns U., 1955; J.D., U. Minn., 1959. Bar: Minn. bar 1959. Mem. firm LeVander, Gillen, Miller & Durenberger, South St. Paul, 1959-66; exec. sec. to Gov. Harold LeVander, 1967-71; counsel for legal and community affairs, corporate sec. H.B. Fuller Co., St. Paul, 1971-78; mem. U.S. Senate from Minn., 1978—. Co-chmn. NAIA Football Bowl Playoff, 1963; div. chmn. United Fund of South St. Paul, 1965; chmn. citizens sect. Minn. Recreation and Park Assn., 1971-72; mem. South St. Paul Parks and Recreation Commn., 1971-72; chmn. Metro Council Open Space Adv. Bd., 1972-74; commr. Murphy-Hanrehan Park Bd., 1973-75; chmn. Save Open Space Now, 1974, Close-Up Found. Minn., 1975-76, Social Investment Task Force, Project Responsibility, 1974-76, Spl. Service div. St. Paul Area United Way, 1973-76; chmn. bd. commrs. Hennepin County Park Res. Dist.; vice chmn. Met. Parks and Open Space Bd.; exec. vice chmn. Gov.'s Commn. on Arts; exec. dir. Minn. Constl. Study Commn., Supreme Ct. Adv. Com. on Jud. Responsibility; pres. Burroughs Sch. PTA, Mpls.; chmn. Dakota County Young Republican League, 1963-64; dir., legal counsel Minn. Young Rep. League, 1964-65; co-chmn. State Young Rep. League, 1965; del. State Rep. Conv., 1966, 68, 70, 72; first vice chmn. 1st Dist. Rep. Party, 1970-72; vice chmn. 13th ward Rep. Party Mpls., 1973-74; bd. dirs. Met. Parks Found., Pub. Service Options, Inc., St. Louis Park AAU Swim Club, Minn. Landmarks, 1971-73, Pub. Affairs Leadership and Mgmt. Tng., Inc., 1973-75, U. Minn. YMCA, 1973-75, Community Planning Orgn., Inc., St. Paul, 1973-76, Project Environment Found., 1974-75, Urban Lab., Inc., 1975, Nat. Recreation and Park Assn., Within the System, Inc., 1976-77; trustee Children's Health Center and Hosp., Inc., Mpls.; mem. exec. com. Nat. Center for Vol. Action, Minn. Charities Rev. Council. Served as 2d lt. U.S. Army, 1955-56; as capt. Res., 1957-63. Named Outstanding Young Man in South St. Paul, 1964, One of Ten Outstanding Yc ng Men in Minn., 1965. Mem. Am., Minn., 1st Dist. bar assns., Corp. Counsel Assn., St. Johns U. Alumni Assn. (pres. Twin Cities chpt. 1963-65, nat. pres. 1971-73), Mpls., St. Paul Area chambers commerce, Gamma Eta Gamma (chancellor 1958-59, v.p. Alumni Assn. 1965-75). Roman Catholic. Club: K.C. Office: US Senate 154 Russell Senate Bldg Washington DC 20510 *

DURHAM, LEON, professional baseball player; b. Cin., July 31, 1957; m. Angela Golightly. Profl. baseball player St. Louis Cardinals, Nat. League, 1980, Chgo. Cubs, Nat. League, 1981—. Mem. Nat. League All-Star Team, 1982-83. Office: Chgo Cubs Wrigley Field Chicago IL 60613 *

DURHAM, STEVEN H., investment company executive; b. Omaha, Mar. 14, 1943; s. Charles W. and Margre (Henningson) D.; m. Barbara Smith; children: Charles W. II, Julie Ann, Peter H. BS, U. Nebr., 1965. Investment banker Kirkpatrick Pettis, Omaha, 1968-70; dir. acquisitions Continental Care Ctrs., Inc., Omaha, 1970-73, Henningson, Durham & Richardson, Omaha, 1973-76; pres. Durham Resources, Omaha, 1976—; bd. dirs. Bank of Park Forest, Ill., Bank of Homewood, Ill., GPNG Co., Fergus Falls, Minn.; bd. govs. Nebr. Wesleyan U., Lincoln. Chmn. fund-raising dr. Jr. Achievement, Omaha; gov. Boys Club, Omaha; pres. adv. commn. U. Nebr., Omaha. Named one of Outstanding Young Nebraskans, 1978. Mem. Nebr. Young Pres.'s Orgn. (chmn. orgn. com. 1984-85, chmn. membership com. 1985-86). Republican. Lodge: Shriners. Home: 304 S 92d St Omaha NE 68114 Office: Durham Resources Inc 8401 W Dodge Rd #100 Omaha NE 68114

DURNIL, GORDON KAY, lawyer, political party official; b. Indpls., Feb. 20, 1936; s. J. Ray and E. Merle Durnil; m. Lynda L. Powell, Mar. 1, 1963; children—Guy S., Cynthia L. B.S., Ind. U., 1960, J.D., 1965. Bar: Ind. 1965. Sales rep. Franklin Life Ins. Co., 1956, Moore Bus. Forms, Inc., 1960; sole practice, Indpls., 1965—; active Republican Party, 1960—, publicity com. Marion County com. (Ind.), 1966-67, campaign coordinating com., mem. campaign coordinating com. Ind. State Com., 1968-80, mem. congressional coordinating com., 1973-74, campaign dir., 1978, state chmn., 1981—, campaign mgr. for numerous candidates; mem. Exec. Council Rep. Nat. Com., 1985—; v.p. Ind. Ornamental Iron Works, Inc., 1960-65; dep. prosecutor Marion County (Ind.), 1965-66; legal counsel Ind. Fedn. Young Republicans, 1965-68; spl. asst. Office of Bus. Service U.S. Dept. Commerce, 1971. Pres. Emmerich Manual High Sch. Alumni Assn., 1968; justice of peace Washington Twp. (Ind.), 1967-70; bd. dirs. Our House, Inc. (Ind.

Ronald McDonald House); chmn. Marion County Election Bd., 1978-81. Served with U.S. Army; Korea. Mem. Ind. Bar Assn., Am. Assn. Polit. Cons. Presbyterian. Editor: The Marion County Republican Reporter, 1966-71. Office: One N Capitol St 1260 Indianapolis IN 46204

DURRETT, ANDREW MANNING, consulting designer, inventor; b. Clarksville, Tenn., Jan. 7, 1924; s. Andrew Manning and Betty Ann (Empson) D.; m. Jean E. Lanning, May 14, 1949; children—Cheryl A. Durrett Yurs, Griffith Lynn, Susan Elizabeth Durrett Pantle, Robert Tracy, Vicki Jean Durrett Robinson. Student U. Tenn., 1946-48; B.F.A., Art Inst. Chgo., 1951. Mech. engr. Werthan Bag Corp., Nashville, 1951-52; designer C.F. Block, Chgo., 1952-53, Advt. Metal Display, Chgo., 1953-55; artist, poster designer Gen. Outdoor Advt. Co., Chgo., 1956-58; with sales, tng. films and scripts. Ross Wetzel Studios, Chgo., 1958-60; sales mgr. indsl. design Palma-Knapp Design, River Forest, Ill., 1961-65; founder, pres. Manning Durrett Design Assocs., R&D med. equipment, Spring Grove, Ill., 1965—. Author: (with Don Gilbert) Industrial Insectology, 1980; producer films on insect control; patentee in field; exhibited med. and indsl. products Mus. Sci. and Industry, Chgo., 1970. Bd. dirs., sec. Brookfield Citizens Mgmt. Assn. (Ill.), 1953-54; committeeman Oaks Assn., Libertyville, Ill., 1970-76, chmn. service com.; co-author flood plane ordinance, Libertyville, 1975. Served with USN, 1943-46. Recipient Excellence in Design awards Indsl. Design Rev., 1969, 69. Mem. Sch. Art Inst. Chgo. Alumni Assn., Chgo. Assn. Commerce and Industry, Internat. Platform Assn., Phi Kappa Phi. Republican. Methodist. Clubs: Oak Bus. Men's (Ill.); Cambridge Country (Libertyville). Office: Manning Durrett Design Assocs 38625 Forest Ave Spring Grove IL 60081

DURRETT, WILLIAM WARD, college admissions director; b. Lakewood, Ohio, June 23, 1950; s. William R. and Elizabeth (Ward) D.; m. Chris Scott, July 21, 1979. BS, Millikin U., Decatur, Ill., 1976; postgrad., VanderCook Coll., Chgo., 1983-86. Regional sales mgr. McCormick Enterprises, Arlington Heights, Ill., 1976-80; ednl. dir. Slingerland Drums, Niles, Ill., 1980-83; pvt. practice music educator Glenview, Ill., 1983-86; admissions dir. VanderCook Coll., 1986—; orginator indoor marching percussion festival, 1979; owner W.D.P. Music Ltd., Glenview, 1983—; clinician, cons. Yamaha Internat., Grand Rapids, Mich., 1985—. Composer: Excerpts from Petrowshka, 1985 (Nat. Championship award 1985); contbr. articles to music trade publs. Sr. deacon New Life Luth. Ch., Hoffman Estates, Ill., 1979-81. Served with USN, 1971-74. Named one of Outstanding Young Men of Am., 1984, 85. Mem. Percussive Arts Soc. (pres. Ill. chpt. 1982-83, nat. bd. dirs. 1986—), Cen. State Judges Assn., Bands of Am. Judges Assn. Home: 17 N Howard St Hillside IL 60162 Office: VanderCook Coll 3209 S Michigan Ave Chicago IL 60616

DURST, JAMES R., musician, recording artist, small business owner; b. Pasadena, Calif., Nov. 6, 1945; s. LaVern Harold and Marie Virginia (Farnum) D. BA, Calif. State U., Long Beach, 1969. Mem. Am. Fedn. Musicians, Am. Soc. Composers, Authors and Pubs., Nat. Acad. Recording Arts and Scis. Avocations: music, writing, drawing, travel, photography. Office: PhoeniXongs PO Box 2601 Northbrook IL 60065

DURST, MILO GERALD, physician; b. Rochester, Minn., Jan. 16, 1951. BA summa cum laude, Mankato (Minn.) State U., 1973; MD, U. Minn., 1976. Diplomate Am. Bd. Psychiatry and Neurology, 1983; lic. Wis., N.C., Minn. Resident gen. psychiatry Med. Coll. Wis. Hosps., Milw., 1976-79; adminstrv. resident dept. psychiatry Med. Coll. Wis., Milw., 1977, chief resident, adminstrv. resident dept. psychiatry, 1978-79; staff psychiatrist Milw. County Mental Health Complex, 1979-80; psychiatrist Family, Social and Psychotherapy Services, Milw., 1980-84; practice psychiatry EastTown Therapy Services, Milw., 1984-86; med. dir. Met. Clinic of Counseling, Mpls., 1986—; asst. clin. prof. psychiatry Med. Coll. Wis., Milw.; speaker in field. Mem. AMA, Am. Psychiat. Assn., Minn. Psychiat. Assn., ACLU, Union of Concerned Scientists, Am. Assn. Physicians for Human Rights, Northland Bus. Assn. Home: 110 Bank St SE Minneapolis MN 55414 Office: Met Clinic of Counseling 625 Hwy 10 Minneapolis MN 55434

DURVE, MOHAN JAGANNATH, allergist; b. Bombay, Sept. 7, 1948; s. Jagannath Gajanan and Tara Jagannath (Karnik) D.; m. Jayshree Mohan Gupte, June 6, 1972; children: Anisha, Anuja, Namita. MBBS, GS Med. Sch., Bombay, 1971. Diplomate Am. Bd. Allergy and Immunology, Am. Bd. Pediatrics. Resident Children's Hosp. Med. Ctr., Boston, 1974-75; resident Cleve. Clinic, 1975-77, fellow, 1977-79; practice medicine specializing in allergy Parma, Ohio, 1979—; clin. faculty Case Western Res. U., Cleve., 1979—; clin. instr. Cleve. Met. Gen Hosp., 1979—; allergist St. Luke's Hosp., Cleve., 1979—, Parma Community Hosp., 1980—, Marymount Hosp., Cleve., 1980—, Deaconess Hosp., Cleve., 1980—. Fellow Am. Acad. Allergy Immunology, Am. Coll. Allergists; mem. Acad. of Medicine of Cleve., No. Ohio Pediatric Soc., Assn. of Indian Physicians of No. Ohio (exec. bd., chmn. continuing edn. com.). Avocations: travel, swimming. Home: 20 Stonehill Ln Moreland Hills OH 44022 Office: 6789 Ridge Rd Parma OH 44129

DUSEK, FRANK ARTHUR, accountant, financial consultant; b. Evergreen Park, Ill., Oct. 26, 1946; s. Robert Frank and Dorothy Leah (Marsh) D.; m. Faith Ballman; children: Nathan, Laurel. BA in Acctg., U. Ill., Chgo., 1971; MBA, Roosevelt U., 1983. CPA, Ill. Sr. auditor Wolf & Co., Chgo., 1971-75, Hurdman & Cranstoun, Chgo., 1975-76; sec./treas. Allstate Erectors, Inc., Norhtbrook, Ill., 1977-84; sr. cons. The Brenner Group, Chgo., 1984-86; pres. Terrell, Weiss & Sugar, Ltd. (formerly Frank Dusek, Ltd.), Chgo., 1986—. Served with U.S. Army, 1966-68. Mem. Am. Inst. CPA's, Ill. CPA Soc., Nat. Assn. Pub. Accts., Am. Subcontractors Assn. (bd. dirs. 1984—). Evangelical. Home: 1067 Cedar Ln Northbrook IL 60062 Office: Terrell Weiss & Sugar Ltd 10 S Riverside Plaza Chicago IL 60606

DUSH, DAVID MICHAEL, psychologist, researcher; b. St. Johns, Mich., Dec. 27, 1953; s. George E. and Hellen Marie (Fabus) D.; m. Billie R. Hothem, Jan. 2, 1982; 1 child, Elayna Hothem. BS, Mich. State U., 1976; MA, U. Man., Winnipeg, Can., 1978; PhD, Kent State U., 1981. Asst. prof. Drake U., Des Moines, 1981-84; adj. asst. prof. Cen. Mich. U., Mt. Pleasant, 1984—; program evaluator Midland-Gladwin (Mich.) Ctr. Mental Health, 1984—; pres. Health Scis. Corp., Sanford, Mich., 1985—; editor The Hospice Jour., Midland, 1985—; cons., advisor various hospices, orgns., and corps.; pub. Mature Health mag., Sanford, 1986—. Contbr. articles to profl. jours. Mem. Am. Psychol. Assn., Midwestern Psychol. Assn., Nat. Hospice Orgn., Mich. Hospice Assn. (chmn. research and evaluation com. 1986-87), Soc. Behavioral Medicine. Office: The Hospice Journal 2620 W Sugnet Midland MI 48657

DUSSMAN, JUDITH ANN, publishing executive; b. Chgo., Aug. 23, 1947; d. Thomas Raymond and Dorothy M. (Stalzer) D.; div. 1985; children: John Thomas, Douglas Jude, Luke Price, Katherine Cannon. BA, Northwestern U., 1969; postgrad., Fordham U., 1974; JD, Loyola U., 1975. Advt. sales mgmt. Chgo. Sun Times, Daily News, 1970-77, New York Trib, 1977-78, New York Times, Golf Digest, Tennis, 1979-81; assoc. pub. Ofcl. Airline Guides mag. div. Dun & Bradstreet, Oak Brook, Ill., 1981-83; circulation dir. Ofcl. Airlines Guide mag. div. Dun & Bradstreet, Oak Brook, Ill., 1985—; pub. New Connections mag. Dun & Bradstreet, N.Y.C., 1984. Contbg. editor: (book) Where The Fun Is, 1968; footnote editor: (book) Re-issue Of The Impending Crisis Of The South, 1969. Local officer Parents without Ptnrs.; bd. dirs., chmn. legal com. Kemeys Cove Condominium, Scarborough, N.Y., 1976-80; mem. Friends of Brookfield Zoo. Mem. Chgo. Assn. Direct Mktg., Am. Soc. Travel Agts. Educators Forum, Direct Mktg. Assn., Women in Mgmt., Advt. Women of N.Y., Loyola Law Alumni, Northwestern U. Alumni Assn., Chi Omega. Roman Catholic. Club: Sales and Mktg. Exec. N.Y. Avocations: flying, travel, hiking, running, pets. Home: 46 S Madison St Hinsdale IL 60521 Office: Ofcl Airline Guides 2000 Clearwater Oak Brook IL 60521

DUTKEWYCH, JAROSLAV IHOR, health services executive; b. Ellwanger-Jagst, Fed. Republic Germany, Sept. 6, 1948; s. Myron and Mary (Halich) D.; m. Myroslawa Tanya Kowal, June 1, 1974. BA, Wayne State U., 1970, MPA, 1972. Personnel rep. Henry Ford Hosp., Detroit, 1972-74, coordinator mgmt. devel., 1974-76, dir. staff services, 1976-77, asst. adminstr., 1977-81, assoc. adminstr., 1982-86; v.p. Fairlane Health Services Henry Ford Health Care Corp., Detroit, 1986—; cons. Bernie Hoffmann Assoc., Southfield, Mich., 1977-81; guest lectr. Detroit Coll. Bus., Dearborn, Mich., 1976-80; lectr. U. Minn., 1978-85; adj. prof. Lawrence Inst. Tech., Southfield, Mich., 1976-81. Manuscript reviewer Personnel Adminstr. Jour.; contbr. articles to profl. jour. bd. dirs. City of Troy Personnel Bd., 1978-86, Met. Detroit Youth Found., 1979—. Recipient Cert. Appreciation City of Troy, 1986. Mem. Am. Soc. for Personnel Adminstrn., Am. Arbitration Assn., Hosp. Personnel Adminstrn. (Communications award 1983, 84, 85, 87), Hosp. Personnel Adminstrn. Assn. (Pres. award 1986, 87), Alumni Leadership Detroit. Avocations: travel, cross country skiing, gardening, music. Home: 2160 Chestnut Ct West Bloomfield MI 48033 Office: Fairlane Health Services Corp 31780 Telegraph Rd Birmingham MI 48010

DUTTON, BOBBY RAY, real estate developer; b. Nauvoo, Ala., Feb. 4, 1938; s. James Archie and Esther Mae (Duncan) D.; m. Judith Lynn Kidder, July 7, 1956; children: Randall R., Teri Lynn, Michael J. Student, Ind. U., South Bend, 1961-63. Owner, pres. Dutton Painting Service, Ocala, Fla., 1957-60, Duttons Sandblasting Co., Elkhart, Ind., 1957-60; pres. B and D Paint Co. Inc., Hemet, Calif., Elkhart, 1960-64, Mobilcraft Wood Product Inc., Elkhart, 1963-68, Brentwood Inc., Continental Trailers Inc., Elkhart, 1969-73; vice chmn. Citizens No. Bank, Elkhart, 1973-76, Dutton Industries Inc., Elkhart, 1973-81; pres., bd. chmn., chief exec. officer Bent Oak Corp., Elkhart, 1983—; cons. mfg. various cos.; vice chmn. Citizens No. Bank, Elkhart, 1973-76; sec., bd. dirs. Peddler Pub. Co. Ft. Wayne, Ind.; advisor 2d grade ednl. book, 1986. Mem. Ind. Mfg. Housing Assn. (chmn. recreational vehicle com. 1971-73, presidents award 1972). Democrat. Methodist. Clubs: Maple Crest (long range planning 1981-83), Bent Oak (pres. 1983—). Lodge: Lions (No. Ind. presidents award 1984). Avocations: fishing, golf. Home: 3512 Bent Oak Trail Elkhart IN 46517 Office: Bent Oak Corp 3610 Bent Oak Trail Elkhart IN 46517

DU VAIR, PAUL JOHN, science educator; b. Colmar, France, Dec. 14, 1937; came to U.S., 1951; s. Pierre Louis and Kathryn Henrietta (Bussmann) de la Ney du Vair; m. Marcia Lynne Halverson, June 27, 1964; children: Suzanne Michelle, Elise Catherine. BS in Biology, St. Norbert Coll., DePere, Wis., 1959; Cert. in Edn., U. Wis., 1964. Cert. secondary tchr. Research asst. Am. Found. Biological Research, Madison, Wis., 1960-63; tchr. Madison Pub. Schs., 1964-76, 80—; pres. Wis. Edn. Assn., Madison, 1976-80; adj. instr. U. Wis., Madison, 1964-66; commr. Edn. Commn. of States, Wis., 1978-80; bd. dirs. Wis. CAPE, Madison, 1973-80. Author: Investigations in Field Biology, 1965; contbr. articles to profl. jours. Pres. bd. trustees Madison Library, 1973; bd. dirs. Coalition Am. Pub. Employees, Madison, 1973-80; sec., treas. Citizens Utility Bd., Madison, 1980-82; sec. City-Wide Orgn. Neighborhoods, Madison, 1982. Recipient Legislative Citation, Wis. Assembly and Senate, 1981, Disting. Achievement in Edn. award St. Norbert Coll., 1983, Norman Bassett award Wis. Acad. Scis., 1985. Mem. NEA (nat. bd. dirs. 1973-76, Disting. Service award 1976), Wis. Edn. Assn., Madison Teachers Inc. (pres. 1971-72, Leadership award 1972), Nat. Sci. Tchrs. Assn., Coaltion of Am. Pub. Employees, Holy Name Soc. (pres. 1971-72), Phi Sigma Soc., Beta Scholars. Avocations: scuba diving, collecting art, hunting, fishing, photography. Home: 3130 Grandview Blvd Madison WI 53713 Office: Madison East High Sch 2222 E Washington Ave Madison WI 53704

DUVALL, CHARLES ROBERT, education educator; b. Washington, Pa., Apr. 28, 1929; m. Wilda Carroll, June 18, 1955; children: Suxanne Carroll DuVall Godown, Stephanie Carroll DuVall Mauck. BSE, U. Pitts., 1951, MEd, 1956; PhD in Elem. Edn., Ohio U., 1966. Elem. tchr. Canon-MacMillan Sch. Dist., Canonsburg, Pa., 1953-57; supt. schs. Somerset (Pa.) Twp. Sch. Dist. Eighty-four, 1957-61; elem. supr. Knox County Schs., Mt. Vernon, Ohio, 1961-63; lectr., teaching fellow Ohio U., Athens, Lancaster, 1963-66; from asst. to assoc. prof. edn. Ind. U., South Bend, 1966-79, prof. edn., 1979—; cons. in field. Author: (with Wayne J. Krepel) Education and Education-Related Serials: A Directory, 1977, Free Materials and Education, 1978; contbr. articles to profl. jours. Ruling elder First Prebyn. Ch., South Bend, 1982-84. Served with U.S. Army, 1951-53, with Res. Mem. NEA, Nat. Assn. Industry-Edn. Cooperations (bd. dirs.), Nat. Council Social Studies, Am. Assn. Univ. Profs., Am. Edn. Research Assn., Assn. Supervision and Curriculum Devel., Ind. Assn. Tchr. Educators, Ind. Council Social Studies, Ohio Edn. Assn., Phi Delta Kappa. Avocations: collecting autographs of baseball players, traveling with family. Home: 1520 Berkshire Dr South Bend IN 46614

DUVALL, RUSSEL WILEY, international trade development executive; b. Indpls., Sept. 8, 1940; s. Russel Franklin and Margaret Helen (Hedges) D.; m. Gay Lynn Halbert, Oct. 25, 1969. A.B., Wabash Coll., 1962; M.B.A. with distinction, Keller Grad. Sch. Mgmt., 1979. Merchandise handling mgr. Lane Bryant, Inc., Indpls., 1969-71; founder, pres. PerfaCime, Inc., Indpls., 1971-72; v.p., dist. mgr. A.W.D., Inc., Indpls., 1972-74; asst. to pres. Crooks Terminal Warehouses, Inc., Chgo., 1975-76; plant and logistics mgr. Flavor Tree Foods, Inc., Chgo., 1976-77; plant mgr. Lawry's Foods, Inc., Chgo., 1977-79; v.p. prodn. and distbn. Monogram Models, Inc., Chgo., 1979-82; pres., chief exec. officer Reach Electronics, Inc., Lexington, Nebr., 1982-86, also dir.; pres., chief exec. officer Veetronix, Inc., Lexington, 1982-86, also dir.; pres., chief exec. officer CRV Corp., Lexington, 1984—, also dir.; gen. mgr. DRV Communications Co., Ltd., Beijing, China, 1986—, also dir. Charter mem. Keller Grad. Sch. Alumni Council, Chgo., 1982—. Served to lt. comdr. USN, USNR, 1962-79. Recipient Small Bus. of Yr. Nebr. award Small Bus. Adminstrn., 1984, Boss of Yr. award Jaycees, 1983, "E" award for exporting U.S. Dept. Commerce, 1983. Avocations: reading, music, participating in sports. Office: CRV Corp PO Box 717 Lexington NE 68850

DUWE, FRANK ARTHUR, gynecologist; b. Detroit, Dec. 6, 1920; s. Frank and Helen G. (Plotske) D.; m. Rita C. Miller; Jan. 29, 1943; children: Rita Ann, Helene, Donna, Mary Elizabeth, Deborah. BS, U. Detroit, 1942; MD, U. Mich., 1945. Diplomate Am. Bd. Ob-Gyn. Intern St. Mary's Hosp., Detroit, 1945-46; resident in ob-gyn Providence Hosp., Detroit, 1949-52; practice medicine specializing in ob-gyn Detroit. Served to capt. U.S. Army, 1947-48. Fellow ACS, Am. Coll. Ob-Gyn. Home: 17580 Avilla Lathrup Village MI 48076 Office: 25321 Fenkel Detroit MI 48239

DUY, WALTER FRED, pharmaceutical company executive; b. Bethlehem, Pa., Jan. 2, 1945; s. Charles Gookins and Anita Weaver (Kannberg) D.; m. Phyllis Anne Albrecht, May, 25, 1974. Student, Miami U., Oxford, Ohio, 1963-64; BS, Ohio State U., 1967, MBA, 1968. Fin. analyst Ross Labs., Columbus, Ohio, 1968-70, mgr. new products, 1970-72; mgr. mktg. planning Roxane Labs. Inc., Columbus, 1972-75, mgr. purchasing, 1975-76, adminstrv. asst. pres., 1976-80, v.p., 1980—. Ace. vol. Small Bus. Adminstrn., Columbus, 1971-73. Clubs: Athletic (Columbus), Racquet (Columbus).

DVORAK, ALLEN DALE, radiologist; b. Dodge, Nebr., Mar. 13, 1943; s. Rudolph Charles and Mildred B. (Misek) D.; m. Carol Ann Cockson, July 22, 1967; children: Kristin Ann, Andrea Marie, Ryan Allen. Grad., Creighton Coll. Arts and Scis., Omaha, Nebr., 1961-64; MD, Creighton Sch. Medicine, Omaha, Nebr., 1964. Intern Creighton Meml. St. Joseph Hosp., Omaha, 1969-70; resident Ind. U. Med. Ctr., Indpls., 1970-73; asst. prof. radiology Creighton U. Sch. Medicine, Omaha, 1973-83; diagnostic radiologist Nebr.-Iowa Radiology Cons., Papillion, Nebr., 1983—; staff radiologist Midlands Community Hosp., Papillion, 1983—. AUthor: (chpt.) Ultrasound, 1981; contbr. articles to profl. jours. Chmn. Midlands Area Health Adv. Council, State of Nebr., 1982—. Fellow Am. Coll. Radiology; mem. Nebr. Radiological Soc. (pres. 1980-81), Omaha Midwest Clinical Soc. (pres. 1982), Nebr. Assn. Nuclear Physicians (pres. 1976-78, del. 1984—), Met. Omaha Med. Soc. (mem. exec. com. 1973—), Nebr. Med. Assn. (del. 1986—) AMA. Club: Regency Lake and Tennis (Omaha) (bd. dirs. 1981-85, chmn. bd. 1983-85). Avocations: tennis, boating. Home: 9733 Brentwood Rd Omaha NE 68114 Office: Nebr-Iowa Radiology Cons 401 E Gold Coast Rd Papillion NE 68046

DVORAK, JANE ANN, commercial property manager; b. Cin., Dec. 19, 1955; d. Ralph Harold and Mary Elizabeth (Rodenburg) Teke; m. Alan Eugene Dvorak, Mar. 19., 1977. BBA, Ohio U., 1977. Part-time emergency med. tech. Southeast Ohio Emergency Med. Services, Athens, Ohio, 1977-80; patient coordinator O'Bleness Hosp., Athens, 1977; loan officer Athens Credit Union, 1978-79; mgr. Athens Mall JMB Property Mgmt. Corp., 1980—; bd. dirs. Athens Pvt. Industry Council. Pub. relations coordinator Athens County Disaster Services, 1985—. Mem. Internat. Council Shopping Ctrs., Athens C. of C. (bd. dirs. 1983—), Athens Crime Solvers Anonymous, Phi Mu Sorority (house corp v.p. 1984—). Avocations: camping, boating, water skiing, motorcycling. Home: 14525 Kincade Rd Athens OH 45701 Office: JMB Property Mgmt Corp Athens Mall E State St Athens OH 45701

DVORIN, HAROLD LEWIS, financial executive; b. Chgo., Dec. 17, 1939; s. Joseph L. and Thelma (Davies) D.; m. Sarah Jane King, July 10, 1982. B.S. in Mgmt., U. Ill.-Urbana, 1961, M.Acctg.Sci., 1967. Staff acct. Alexander Grant & Co., Chgo., 1964-65; profit analyst Inland Steel Co., Chgo., 1965-68; mgr. cost. acctg. Gen. Felt Industries, Chgo., 1968-71, Internat. Products, Palatine, Ill., 1972-73; asst. controller switch div. Oak Industries, Crystal Lake, Ill., 1973-81; controller-treas. Redington, Inc., Bellwood, Ill., 1982-84; controller-treas. C.F.O. Dycast Inc., Lake Zurich, Ill., 1985—; instr. William R. Harper Coll., Palatine, 1974-77, Triton Coll., River Grove, Ill., 1973, Elgin Community Coll., Ill., 1984-86. Vol., Chgo. Symphony Orch. Marathon, 1980-83; mem. Jazz Inst. Chgo., Chgo. Symphony Soc. Served in U.S. Army, 1961-64. Home: 663 Cunningham Dr Palatine IL 60067 Office: 320 E Main St Lake Zurich IL 60047

DVORSAK, GREGORY ROBERT, accountant; b. Alexandria, Minn., July 31, 1956; s. Robert Joseph and Jane Ellen (Krienke) D.; m. Suzanne Marie Sieg, Jan. 3, 1981; children: Matthew, Nicole. Student, St. Cloud (Minn.) State U. CPA, Minn. Staff acct. Peat, Marwick, Mitchell, Mpls., 1978-81; mgr. acctg. Amhoist, St. Paul, 1981-84; mgr. fin. Minstar, Inc., Mpls., 1984-85, asst. controller, 1985-86, asst. treas., 1986—. Mem. Am. Inst. CPA's, Nat. Assn. Accts., Min. Soc. CPA's, New Hope Jaycees (v.p. 1983, pres. 1984, Jaycee of Yr. 1985). Roman Catholic. Lodge: KC. Avocations: hunting, fishing, golfing. Home: 15100 42d Ave N Plymouth MN 55446 Office: Minstar Inc 100 S 5th St Minneapolis MN 55402

DWIGHT, GARY HAROLD, oral and maxillofacial surgeon; b. Lansing, Mich., Sept. 30, 1947; s. Wendell Harold and Margaret Louise (Glasser) D.; m. Mary Lynn Reppa, Nov. 17, 1973; 1 child, Courtney. Student, U. Mich, 1965-68; DDS, U. Mich., 1972, MS, 1976. Clin. instr. U. Mich., Ann Arbor, 1973-77; practice dentistry specializing in oral and maxillofacial surgery Lansing, Mich., 1976—; adj. prof. Mich. State U., East Lansing, 1986—. Fellow Am. Assn. Oral and Maxillofacial Surgeons, Am. Soc. Oral Surgeons; mem. Mich. Dental Assn. (del. 1981—, chmn. ethics com. 1987—), Cen. Dist. Dental Soc. (pres. 1985-86), Chalmers Lyons Acad. Club: Vet. Motor Car (local pres. 1980-81). Lodge: Kiwanis. Avocation: antique automobiles. Office: 1400 E Michigan Lansing MI 48912

DWORAK, THOMAS JOSEPH, radiologist; b. Omaha, July 16, 1952; s. Thomas Edward and Margaret Mary (Barta) D.; m. Charlene Ann Camerato, Aug. 10, 1978; children: Alex, Curt, Eric. Student, Creighton U., 1970-73; MB, MD, U. Nebr., 1976. Diplomate Am. Bd. Radiology. Intern U. Mo., Columbia, 1976-77, resident in radiology, 1977-80; assoc. Nebr.-Iowa Radiology Cons., Papillion, Nebr., 1980—; treas. Nebr.-Iowa Radiology Cons., Papillion, 1985—. Sec. St. Columbkille Sch. Bd., Papillion, 1986. Mem. AMA, Am. Coll. Radiology, Radiol. Soc. N.Am., Nebr. Med. Assn. (del. 1980—), Sarpy County Med. Soc. (v.p., program chmn. 1984—). Republican. Roman Catholic. Club: St. Columbkille Mens (v.p. 1983-87, pres. 1987—) (Papillion). Office: Nebr-Iowa Radiology Cons 401 Gold Coast Rd Papillion NE 68046

DWORKIN, JONATHAN, labor arbitrator; b. Cleve., June 13, 1936; s. Harry and Claire Beth (Safier) D.; m. Ernestine Rae Greenberger, Apr. 4, 1960 (div. 1971); children: Jennifer, James David, Deborah; m. Judith Marion Daniels, Feb. 19, 1983. BA, Case Western Res. U., 1960, LLB, 1962. Bar: Ohio, 1962, U.S. Dist. Ct. (no. dist.) Ohio 1963. Sole practice Cleve., 1962-70, pvt. practice mgmt.-labor arbitration, 1976—; regional arbitrator U.S. Postal Service, 1978—; arbitrator State Employment Relations Bd., Ohio, 1984—, fact-finder, 1984—, conciliator, 1984—; permanent umpire-State Employment Relations Bd., Ohio, Ohio State Hwy. Patrol, Ohio State Panels, Ohio Atty. Gen. and others; system bd. chmn. NW Orient Airlines-Air Line Pilots Assn., Internat., Mpls., 1986—, Republic Airlines-Air Line Pilots Assn., Internat., Mpls., 1986—; panel mem. Ill. Ednl. Labor Relations Bd., 1985—, Nat. Mediation Bd., 1986—, Pub. Employees Relation Bd. Iowa, 1987. Candidate for Ohio Legis., Cuyahoga County, 1964; press sec. Stokes for Congress Com., Ohio, 1969. Recipient recognition award Internat. Mgmt. Council, 1977. Mem. Nat. Acad. Arbitrators (chmn.-elect region 9 Ohio 1987), Am. Arbitration Assn., Indsl. Relations Research Assn. (several recognition awards 1978-85), Soc. for Profls. in Dispute Resolution, Cleve. Bar Assn. (labor law sect., recognition award 1982). Lodge: KP. Avocations: short-story writing, cycling. Home: 18705 Van Aken Blvd Shaker Heights OH 44122 Office: 16828 Chagrin Blvd Shaker Heights OH 44120

DWORKIN, SIDNEY, retail executive; b. Detroit, 1921; married. B.A., Wayne State U., 1942. Ptnr. Dworkin Boone & Gross, 1950-66; indsl. acct. 1966; with Revco Drug Stores Inc. (now Revco D.S., Inc.), Twinsburg, Ohio, 1956—, exec. v.p., 1963-66, pres., 1966-85, chief exec. officer, 1966—, chmn., 1983—, also bd. dirs.; chmn. Wright Airlines, Inc.; bd. dirs. Fabri-Ctrs. Am., Eclipse Industries, Inc., Planco, Inc., Neutrogena Corp., Northern Instruments Corp., Nat. City Bank Corp. Served with U.S. Army, 1943-45. Mem. Nat. Assn. Chain Drug Stores (bd. dirs.). Office: Revco DS Inc 1925 Enterprise Pkwy Twinsburg OH 44087 *

DWORSCHACK, JAMES FRANCIS, chemical engineer; b. Peoria, Ill., Dec. 27, 1953; s. Robert George and Elizabeth (Sweet) D. BS in ChemE, Iowa State U., 1975. Sole proprietor Bio-Process Engring. Co., 1982—. Club: Nash Car of Am. (pres. 1970-77, 84-87). Home and Office: Rt 1 Box 253 Clinton IA 52732

DWYER, JOHN WILLIAM, JR., accountant; b. Chgo., Aug. 21, 1952; s. John William and Margaret Josephine (Cain) D.; m. Joan Mary Gillespie, Oct. 28, 1978. BS, DePaul U., 1974. CPA, Ill. Various positions Arthur Young, Chgo., 1974-86, ptnr., 1986—. Adv. bd. Bus. Adminstrn. Program DePaul U., 1986—; mem. fin. com. St. Alexander's Ch., Villa Park, Ill., 1984—. Mem. Am. Inst. CPA's, Ill. CPA Soc. (mem. not-for-profit com. 1986). Roman Catholic. Clubs: DePaul Ledger & Quill, Chgo. Soc. of Clubs. Avocations: golf, racketball, tennis, spectator sports, music. Office: Arthur Young & Co 1 IBM Plaza Chicago IL 60611

DWYER, MARGRETTA, psychologist; b. Omaha, Dec. 9, 1934; d. Thomas Francis and Ann (Holterhaus) D. BS in Edn., Coll. St. Mary, Omaha, 1965; MA in Psychology, U. No. Colo., 1970; postgrad., U. Pa., 1980. Lic. psychologist, sex therapist. Tchr. Cath. schs., various locations, 1955-70; therapist Cath. Charities, Omaha, 1970-73; dir. marriage, family dept. Cath. Charities, New Orleans, 1973-77; personnel dir. Sisters of Mercy, Omaha, 1977-79; dir. sex offenders treatment U. Minn., Mpls., 1982—. Contbr. articles on sex offender treatment and sexuality to profl. jours. Mem. Am. Assn. Sex Educators, Counselors and Therapists (local pres. 1985-87), Am. Assn. Marriage and Family Therapists. (clin.). Office: U Minn 2630 University Ave SE Minneapolis MN 55414

DWYER, ROBERT FRANKLIN, II, arts administrator; b. Lake City, Fla., Dec. 7, 1943; s. Robert Franklin and Maxine Delores (Stenberg) D.; children—Erin Adair, Robert Franklin III. A.B., U. Calif.-Berkeley, 1967; M.T.S., Harvard U. Div. Sch., 1969; cert in arts mgmt., U. Chgo., 1981. Pub. affairs dir. Sta. KYDO-TV 3, Salem, Oreg., 1969-74; dir. mktg. Specialists Internat., Reno, Nev., 1974-77; dir. devel. Sierra Arts Found., Reno, 1977; bd. dirs. Nev. Alliance for Arts, 1979—, v.p., 1980; now exec. dir. Quincy (Ill.) Soc. Fine Arts; cons. in field. Named Arts Adminstr. of Yr., Arts Mgmt. mag., 1982. Mem. Am. Council on Arts, Assn. Coll., Univ. and Community Arts Adminstrs., Nat. Assembly Community Arts Agys. Editor: Snow Peach, 1980; producer, writer TV documentary: Art Works, 1981.

DYBEL, MICHAEL WAYNE, biochemist, biotechnology company executive, consultant; b. Hammond, Ind., July 19, 1946. B.A., Wabash Coll., 1968; M.S., Northwestern U., 1969; postgrad. U. Notre Dame, 1969-71; M.B.A., U. Chgo., 1978. Biochemist, Internat. Minerals and Chem., Mundelein, Ill., 1971-72; biochemist I, Abbott Labs., North Chicago, Ill., 1972-78; assoc. Technonic Cons., Chgo., 1978-81; v.p. Centaur Genetics Corp., Chgo., 1981; pres. Strategic Techs. Internat., Libertyville, Ill., 1982—; pres. Coal Biotech Corp., Libertyville, 1984—. Lubrizol scholar Wabash Coll., 1968. Mem. Am.

Chem. Soc., AAAS. Office: Strategic Techs Internat Inc 800 S Milwaukee Rd Libertyville IL 60048

DYCK, GEORGE, medical educator; b. Hague, Sask., Can., July 25, 1937; came to U.S., 1965; s. John and Mary (Janzen) D.; m. Edna Margaret Krueger, June 27, 1959; children: Brian Edward, Janine Louise, Stanley George, Jonathan Jay. Student, U. Sask., 1955-56; B. Christian Edn., Can. Mennonite Bible Coll., 1959; M.D., U. Man., 1964; postgrad., Menninger Sch. Psychiatry, 1965-68. Diplomate Am. Bd. Psychiatry and Neurology, Royal Coll. Physicians and Surgeons (Can.) in Psychiatry. Fellow community psychiatry Prairie View Mental Health Center, Newton, Kans., 1968-70; clin. dir. tri-county services Prairie View Mental Health Center, 1970-73; prof. U. Kans., Wichita, 1973—; chmn. dept. psychiatry U. Kans., 1973-80; med. dir. Prairie View, Inc., 1980—. Bd. dirs. Mennonite Mut. Aid, Goshen, Ind., 1973-85, Chmn., 1982-85; bd. dirs. Mid-Kans. Community Action Program, 1970-73, Wichita Council Drug Abuse, 1974-76. Fellow Am. Psychiat. Assn. (pres. Kans. dist. br. 1982-84, dep. rep. 1984-86, rep. 1986—, cert. in adminstrv. psychiatry 1984); mem. AMA, Kans. Med. Soc., Kans.-Paraguay Ptnrs. (treas. 1986). Mennonite. Home: 1505 Hillcrest Rd Newton KS 67114 Office: Prarie View Inc 1901 E 1st St Newton KS 67114

DYCK, PETER JAMES, neurologist; b. Georgia, USSR, Oct. 10, 1927; came to U.S., 1959; s. Jacob and Katherine (Jansen) D.; m. J. Isabelle Bonham, Sept. 11, 1954; children: Ernest Carl, Fred Howard, P. James B., M. Katherine E. BA, U. Saskatchewan, 1951; MD, U. Toronto, 1955. Diplomate Am. Bd. Psychiatry and Neurology. Intern, then resident in neurolog; prof. neurology Mayo Med. Sch., Rochester, Minn., 1973; cons. neurology Mayo Clinic, Rochester, 1961—. Editor: Peripheral Neuropathy, 1975, 85, Diabetic Neuropathy, 1987. Mem. Am. Neurol. Assn. (2d v.p. 1976, 1st v.p. 1983-84), Am. Acad. Neurology, Peripheral Neuropathy Assn. Am. (organizer 1975—, pres. 1984—). Baptist. Avocation: music. Home: 1933 11th St SW Rochester MN 55903 Office: Mayo Clinic Neurology 200 1st St SW Rochester MN 55905

DYDEK, PAUL ANTHONY, accountant; b. East Chicago, Ind., July 14, 1956; s. Joseph and Sally (Bogucki) D.; m. Stephanie Marie Gavrilos, May 14, 1983. B.S. in Acctg. magna cum laude, Calumet Coll., Whiting, Ind., 1978; M.B.A. in Fin., DePaul U., Chgo., 1982. C.P.A., Ill. Acctg. trainee Republic Steel Corp., Chgo., 1978-80, cost acct., 1981-82, supr. budgets, 1982-84, fin. analyst, 1984-85, supr. gen. acctg., 1985-86, supr. fin. analysis, 1986; spl. projects mgr. Lever Bros. Co., Inc., Chgo., 1986, mgr. fin. acctg. personal products div., 1986—; v.p. LTV Steel Suprs. Club until 1986. Mem. Zeta Beta Tau, Delta Mu Delta. Roman Catholic. Lodge: K.C. Home: 1630 Roberts Ave Whiting IN 46394

DYE, CARL MELVYN, educational association executive; b. Cedar Rapids, Iowa, Oct. 7, 1940; s. Floyd Carmen and Inger Marie (Johansen) D.; BA, Parsons Coll., 1962; MEd, No. Ill. U., 1967. Dir. admissions counselors Parsons Coll., Fairfield, Iowa, 1962-68; acad. dean Bryant and Stratton Coll., Milw., 1968-69; pres. Coll. of the South, Pascagoula, Miss., 1969-70; acad. dean Massey Jr. Coll., Atlanta, 1970-71; pres. Am. Schs. Assn., Chgo., 1971—; dir., founder The Job Group, 1982. Served with U.S. Army, 1963-64. Mem. Am. Cons. League, Phi Kappa Phi. Home: 2252 N Fremont St Chicago IL 60614

DYE, CAROL J., psychologist; b. St. Louis, Dec. 18, 1934; d. Guenther Frederick and Jeanette (Grossman) Bemberg; m. David Wayne Dye, Dec. 17, 1960; children: David Bradford, Molly Susan. BS in Edn., Washington U., St. Louis, 1958, MA in Psychology, 1961, PhD in Psychology, 1963. Lic. psychologist, Mo. Postdoctoral intern VA Med. Ctr., St. Louis, 1963-64, staff psychologist, 1976-83, asst. chief of psychology, 1983—; pvt. practice cons. psychology St. Louis, 1967-76; assoc. adj. prof. psychology St. Louis U., 1974—; adj. prof. Inst. Applied Gerontology, Grad. Sch. Social Work, St. Louis U., 1974—; adj. research prof. Washington U., 1977—; mem. adv. research rev. com., 1979—; assoc. clin. prof. U. Mo., St. Louis, 1985—. Cons. editor: (mags.) Experimental Aging Research, 1981—, Profl. Psychology, 1981—; mem. editorial bd. Jour. Gerontology; editor newsletter Adult Devel. and Aging News, 1983—; contbr. articles to profl. jours. Fellow: Am. Psychol. Assn. (newletter editor Aging and Human Devel. div. 1983—, chmn. continuing edn. com. 1982-83), Mo. Psychol. Assn., Gerontological Assn., Midwest Psychol. Assn., Soc. St. Louis Psychologists (pres. 1976), Mo. Assn. for the Prevention of Adult Abuse (bd. dirs. 1982-84), Sierra Club. Avocations: interior decorating, gardening, gourmet cooking. Home: 8 Prado Dr Ladue MO 63124 Office: VA Med Ctr Saint Louis MO 63125

DYE, DAVID ALAN, lawyer, educator; b. Lexington, Mo., Sept. 11, 1950; s. Donald Alfred and Dorothy Sue D.; m. Julia Yolanda Zapata, June 21, 1979; 1 child, Soyal Chaski. B.A., U. Mo., 1972, J.D., 1976. Sole practice, Kansas City, Mo., 1976—; prof., coordinator Legal Asst. Program, Mo. Western State Coll., St. Joseph, 1977—; lawfirm cons. Co-founder, pres. Mid-Coast Radio Project, Inc., 1978-79, bd. dirs., 1978-80, chmn. adv. council, 1980—; legal cons. Greater Kansas City Epilepsy League, pres., 1982-84, mem. exec. com., 1984—, bd. dirs. 1978—; mem. ho. of dels. Epilepsy Found. Am., 1982-83; trustee Legal Aid Western Mo., 1987. State of Mo. grantee, 1980, 82. Mem. ABA, Mo. Bar Assn. (vice chmn. legal asst. com.), Kansas City Met. Bar Assn., Am. Assn. for Paralegal Edn. (organizer, pres. 1987—, bd. dirs. 1983—, chair membership com. 1986), Nat. Assn. of Legal Assts. (assoc.). Editor: (with John Calvert) Systems for Legal Assistant: A Resource Manual of Selected Articles and Materials., 1980; author articles on paralegal edn. and profession; organizer, condr. nat. and regional seminars, confs., workshops on legal assts. programs. Home: 6220 Harrison Kansas City MO 64110 Office: Mo Western State Coll St 4525 Downs Dr Saint Joseph MO 64507

DYE, PEGGIE LOU, elementary educator; b. Kennett, Mo., Oct. 20, 1934; d. Henry Curtis Green and Hazel Delia (Sallee) Green Fullerton; m. James David Dye, Jan. 30, 1954; children—Debra Rene Dye McKone, Susan Kay Dye Storms. B.A., Mich. State U., 1974, M.A. in Classroom Teaching, 1977; postgrad. Mich. Montessori Tng. Ctr., 1977-78. Tchr.-aide follow-through program Flint (Mich.) Community Schs., 1968-73, tchr. grades K-2, 1974-77, Montessori tchr. grades K-2 1977-87, learning strategies tchr. grades K-6, 1987—. Mem. state adv. council Women's Missionary Union of So. Baptists in Mich.; Women's Missionary Union dir. Genesee Baptist Assn. Mem. Nat. Assn. Ret. People (assoc.), United Tchrs. Flint (mem. task force for excellence in edn.), NEA, Nat. Audubon Soc., Mich. Edn. Assn., Internat. Inst. Republican. Home: 4420 Old Colony Dr Flint MI 48507

DYER, ROBERT LEE, psychologist; b. Terre Haute, Ind., Sept. 16, 1947; s. Ora and Mary Ethel (Mullen) D.; m. Jane Ellen Martin, Feb. 20, 1971; children—Jason Martin, Joshua Reed, Brody Lee. B.S., Ind. State U., 1969, M.S., 1970, Ph.D., 1978. Correctional diagnostic specialist Johnston Youth Community Ctr., Terre Haute, 1972-73; staff psychologist Hamilton Ctr., Terre Haute, 1973-81; dep. dir. So. Hills Mental Health Ctr., Jasper, Ind., 1981-84; exec. dir. Quinco Cons. Ctr., Columbus, Ind., 1984—; pres. Pro-Care, Inc.; bd. dirs. Associated Core Systems Ind. Served with U.S. Army, 1970-72. Mem. Am. Psychol. Assn., Ind. Psychol. Assn., Ind. Council Community Mental Health Ctrs. (pres., bd. dirs.), Assn. Mental Health Adminstrs., Am. Mgmt. Assn., Mental Health Corp. Am. Contbr. articles to profl. jours. Office: 2075 Lincoln Park Dr Columbus IN 47201

DYER, WILLIAM ALLAN, JR., newspaper executive; b. Providence, Oct. 23, 1902; s. William Allan and Clara (Spink) D.; m. Marian Elizabeth Blumer, Aug. 9, 1934; children: Allan H., William E. B.Ph., Brown U., 1924, LL.D., 1984; LL.D. (hon.), Ind. U., 1977; H.L.D. (hon.), Butler U., 1983, U. Indpls., 1986. Reporter Syracuse (N.Y.) Jour., 1923; various advt. positions Syracuse Post-Standard, 1925-41; v.p., gen. mgr. Star Pub. Co., Indpls., 1944-49; v.p., gen. mgr. Indpls. Newspapers, Inc., 1949-74, pres., 1975—; pres. Muncie Newspapers, Inc., 1975—; dir. Central Newspapers, Inc., Indpls., 1949—, exec. v.p., 1964-73; N.Y.C. dir Met. Sunday Newspapers, 1951-75, pres., 1969-75; pres. Central Newspapers Found. Indpls., 1969—. Mem. exec. com. United Fund Indpls., 1954-77, pres., 1970, chmn. bd., 1971; v.p. Community Service Council, Indpls., 1967-68; trustee Brown U., 1952-59; pres. Indpls. Community Hosp. Found., 1976-83, hon. bd. dirs., 1983—; pres. Goodwill Industries Found., 1980-86; bd. dirs., v.p. Ind. Symphony Soc., 1977-86. Served to lt. comdr. USNR, 1941-44. Recipient Brown Bear award Brown U., 1968; Torch of Truth award Advt. Club, 1975; Silver medal Am. Advt. Fedn., 1971. Mem. Better Bus. Bur. Indpls. (dir. 1950—, pres. 1958, 65), Nat. Better Bus. Bur. (dir. 1950-70), Council Better Bus. Burs. (dir. 1970-78, 80-86), Indpls. C. of C. (dir. 1967—, v.p. 1970-73), Am. Newspaper Pubs. Assn. (labor relations com. 1953-63, bd. dirs., bur. advt. 1963-69, Research Inst. 1955-64, pres. 1963-64), Indpls. Advt. Club (dir. 1952-54, pres. 1952-53), Indpls. Community Hosp. (dir. 1952-54, 66-69, v.p. 1954). Club: Brown U. Ind. (sec. 1946-52, pres. 1952-54). Home: 401 Buckingham Dr Indianapolis IN 46208 Office: The Indpls Star Indpls Newspaper Inc 307 N Pennsylvania St Indianapolis IN 46204

DYKES, DIANA NOVACEK, dentist; b. Benkelman, Nebr., Oct. 14, 1947; d. Frederick Stanley and Evelyn LaVern (Scott) Novacek; m. Calvin R. Dykes, Aug. 21, 1966 (div. Sept. 1983); children: Stephanie R., Brian P. BS, U. Iowa, 1970, MS in Dental Hygiene Edn., 1972, DDS, 1979. Lic. dentist, Iowa. Dental hygienist J.D. McPike, DDS, Muscatine, Iowa, 1970-71; teaching asst. U. Iowa, Iowa City, 1971-72, asst. prof. dental hygiene, 1972-74; gen. practice dentistry Wapello, Iowa, 1979—, Plaza Pl. Dental, Muscatine, Iowa, 1985—. Community cons. Muscatine Sch. Bd., 1985—; bd. dirs. Great River Bend Mental Health Assn., Muscatine, 1986—. Mem. ADA (county dental health com.), Iowa State Dental Assn., Davenport Dist. Dental Soc. Democrat. Avocations: swimming, boating, sports cars, dancing, skiing. Home: 812 Marquette St Muscatine IA 52761 Office: Plaza Pl Dental 1612 Plaza Pl Muscatine IA 52761

DYKSTRA, DAVID ALLEN, business executive; b. Kalamazoo, Feb. 5, 1938; s. Alle and Elizabeth (VanderHorst) D. m. Kathryn Ann DeNio, Aug. 4, 1962 (div. Nov. 1985); children: Brian Thayer, Kristen Lee, Holly Beth. BBA, Western Mich. U., 1966. Pres. Allied Waste Inc., Portage, Mich., 1970-80, Dykert Enterprises, Portage, 1981—; cons. Waste Industry, Mich., 1976-82. Bd. dirs. Portage C. of C., 1980-83; alt. del. Rep. Conv., Mich., 1984. Mem. Safari Club Internat., Lakes Area Conservation Club. Republican. Methodist. Club: Beacon. Lodge: Sertoma (pres. Kalamazoo club 1978). Avocations: big game hunting, racquetball. Home: 7221 W VW Ave Schoolcraft MI 49087 Office: The Windjammer 275 Romence Ave Portage MI 49081

DYMACEK, ROSALIE MARIE, educator; b. Laurel, Nebr., June 4, 1940; d. Robert R. and Mildred H. (Anderson) Stone; m. Myles W. Dymacek, Jr., Dec. 22, 1962; children—Myla, Dawn, Dana. B.S., U. Nebr., 1966, M.S., 1975. Tchr. Spanish, English pub. schs., Lincoln, Nebr., 1966-67, 68-70, 75-76, tchr. presch. handicapped program, 1980-86, tchr. elementary sch., 1986—; coordinator day care in-service tng. program Southeast Community Coll., Lincoln, 1977-80. Bd. dirs., mem. child care com. YWCA, 1980-83. Mem. Nat. Assn. for Edn. of Young Children, Council for Exceptional Children.

DYRDA, ROBERT JOSEPH, electrical engineer; b. Chgo., Apr. 20, 1954; s. Joseph Edward and Eleanor Therese (Leganski) D. B.S., No. Ill. U., 1976; B.S., Elmhurst Coll., 1981; M.B.A., Loyola U., 1984. Elec. engr. Rockwell Internat., Chgo., 1976-79; project engr. Goodman Equipment Corp., Chgo., 1979-84; project engr. Nabisco Brands, Inc., Chgo., 1984—. Roman Catholic. Avocations: racquetball, vintage automobiles. Office: Nabisco Brands Inc 7300 S Kedzie Ave Chicago IL 60629

DYREKS, RAYMOND RICHARD, JR., accountant; b. St. Louis, June 2, 1956; s. Raymond Richard Sr. and Vernamae (Branson) D.; m. Elizabeth Ann Woods, July 14, 1979 (div. Oct. 1985). CPA, Mo., Fla. Staff acct. Fox and Placht, CPA's, St. Louis, 1974-79; sr. acct. Huber Ring & Co., St. Louis, 1980-81; pvt. practice acctg. St. Louis, 1981—; sr. acct. Korljan & Frogge, St. Louis, 1983-85; sr. auditor St. John & Mersmann, Inc., Chesterfield, Mo., 1985—; controller Am. Athletic Clubs, St. Louis, 1983-84. Mem. Am. Inst. CPA's, Mo. Soc. CPA's, Fla. Soc. CPA's, Chesterfield Jaycees. Republican. Roman Catholic. Lodge: Optimists. Avocations: bodybuilding, fitness, computers, model trains, remote control airplanes. Home and Office: 8971 S Swan Circle Saint Louis MO 63144-1717

DYRENFURTH, MICHAEL JOHN, vocational technical and industrial arts educator, consultant; b. Schlitz, Fed. Republic Germany, June 16, 1946; came to U.S., 1970; m. Mary Belle Gullekson, June, 1967; children: Walter John, Michelle Lee, Grant Michael. EdB, U. Alta., Can., 1968, MEd, 1970; PhD, Bowling Green (Ohio) State U., 1973. Cert. tchr., Alta. Tchr. indsl. arts pub. schs., Alta., 1967-69; asst. prof., chmn. dept. indsl. edn. Valley City (N.D.) State Coll., 1972-75; assoc. prof. indsl. edn. Montclair (N.J.) State Coll., 1975-78; prof. indsl. practical arts, vocat. tech. edn. U. Mo., Columbia, 1978—; pres. Applied Expertise Assocs. Contbr. articles to profl. jours. Mem. Internat. Tech. Edn. Assn. (Outstanding Young Leader award 1985), Internat. Vocat. Edn. and Tng. Assn., Am. Vocat. Assn. (Service award 1983, IAD Profl. Leadership award 1986), Council Tech. Tchr. Edn., Nat. Assn. Indsl. and Tech. Tchr. Edn., Indsl. Tech. Edn. Assn. Mo., Mo. Vocat. Assn. (Outstanding Service award 1985), Phi Delta Kappa, Kappa Delta Phi, Epsilon Pi Tau. Office: U Mo Dept PAVTE 103 Indsl Edn Bldg Columbia MO 65211

DZIURMAN, JOHN JOSEPH, architect planner, educator; b. Hamtramck, Mich., July 5, 1941; s. John Leonard and Helen (Sklarski) D.; m. Katherine G. Rasegan, Oct. 3, 1964; children—Kimberly, Tiffany. Student U. Detroit, 1959-61; BArch Lawrence Inst. Tech., 1970; postgrad. Internat. Art Inst., 1974-76. Registered architect, Mich. Architect, Meathe Kessler Assocs., Grosse Pointe, Mich., 1964-70; project designer Giffels Assocs., Detroit, 1970-74; v.p. Straub, VanDine, Dziurman Architects, Troy, Mich., 1974-79; pres. John Dziurman Assocs., Inc., Rochester, Mich., 1979—; v.p., bd. dirs. Wade Trim Group, Plymouth, Mich., 1980—; adj. instr. Mich. State U., East Lansing, 1983—; lectr. in design Lawrence Inst. Tech., Southfield, Mich., 1970-75. Prin. works include Tarralinga Homes, 1972; patentee in field. Mem. Downtown Devel. Authority, City of Rochester, 1983—. Recipient Alumni Achievement award Lawrence Inst. Tech., 1980. Mem. Engring. Soc. Detroit (Outstanding Young Engr. 1975), AIA (housing com. 1981—, treas. Detroit chpt. 1976-78, sec. 1980), Rochester C. of C., Rochester-Avon Hist. Soc. Club: University (Detroit). Avocations: sketching, golfing, squash, carpentry, travel. Office: 155 Romeo Rd Rochester MI 48063

DZURAK, STEVEN J., lawyer; b. Brookfield, Wis., Jan. 27, 1955; s. Stephen J. and Irene D. (Hage) D. BS, Marquette U., 1977; MA, U. Chgo., 1978; JD, U. Wis., 1981. Bar: Wis. 1981, U.S. Dist. Ct. (we. dist.) Wis. 1981, U.S. Dist. Ct. (ea. dist.) Wis. 1983, U.S. Tax Ct. 1983, Minn. 1985. Tax acct. Arthur Young, Milw., 1981-83; assoc. Petrie, Stocking, Milw., 1983-85, O'Connor & Hannar, Mpls., 1985—. Editor: Wis. TAXNEWS, 1983—, Milw. Lawyer, 1984-86. Mem. ABA, Wis. Bar Assn., Am. Inst. CPA's, Minn. Soc. CPA's, Am. Swedish Inst. Lutheran. Club: Nordic Ski (Milw.) (bd. dirs. 1984-85). Lodge: Sons of Norway. Avocation: cross country skiing. Office: O'Connor & Hannan 80 S 8th St Minneapolis MN 55402

EADES, EDWIN O., marketing executive; b. Bloomington, Ill., Dec. 19, 1947; s. Dale T. and Betty T. (Stearn) E.; m. Connie Jo Manahan, May 11, 1968; children: Damon Todd, Jennifer Jo, Jaime Jo, Andrew Jason. Student, Western Ill. U., Macomb, 1966-67; BS in Animal Sci., Ill. State U., 1970. Sales mgr. Roberts Labs, Inc., Rockford, Ill., 1973-79; product mgr. Hopkins Agrl. Chem. Co., Madison, Wis., 1979-82; mktg. mgr. Ceva Labs, Inc., Overland Park, Kans., 1982—. Coach Johnson County Football, Cheerleaders Youth Program, 1982—. Mem. Nat. Agrl. Mktg. Assn. (mem. chmn. 1984-85), Am. Mktg. Assn. Republican. Methodist. Avocations: football coach, antique auto restoration. Home: 10243 Hauser Dr Lenexa KS 66215 Office: Ceva Labs Inc 10551 Barkley Suite 500 Overland Park KS 66212

EAGLEMAN, PATRICIA JOAN, psychiatric social worker; b. Wichita, Kans., July 5, 1945; d. Everett Wayman and Adelaide June (Meyers) Bass; m. Donald Roy Eagleman, Sept. 19, 1970; 1 child, Patrick Shane. BE, Okla. Christian Coll., 1967; MSW, Kans. U., 1983. Lic. master social worker, Kans., sch. social worker, Kans.; cert. tchr., Kans. Tchr. Dallas Ind. Schs., 1967-68; elem. tchr. Wichita Pub. Schs., 1968-71; contract counselor Luth. Social Services, Wichita, 1984-86; psychiat. social worker Sedgwick County Mental Health Ctr. N., Wichita, 1986—. Crisis counselor Women's Crisis Ctr., Wichita, 1980-81; victim adv. Wichita Area Rape Ctr., 1981; vol. community support services Horizons Mental Health Ctr., Hutchinson, Kans., 1985. Mem. Nat. Assn. Social Workers, Mental Health Assn. (Wichita), Acad. Cert. Social Workers (cert.). Republican. Mem. Ch. Christ. Avocations: tennis, racquetball, writing poetry, gardening. Home: 9308 Briarwood Ct Wichita KS 67212 Office: Sedgwick County Mental Health Ctr North 1801 E 10th Wichita KS 67214

EAGLETON, BETH B., nurse, educator; b. El Dorado, Kans., Sept. 8, 1950; d. Bobbie Nell (Hall) Bouchard; m. Larry Allan Eagleton, June 6, 1970; 1 child, Kelly Nicole. BS in Nursing magna cum laude, Wichita State U., 1976, M in Nursing, 1980; PhD in Adult and Continuing Edn., Kans. State U., 1984. Cert. critical care nurse. Dir. nursing Prairie Homestead, Wichita, Kans., 1974-80; coordinator of continuing edn. U. Kans. Sch. Med., Wichita, 1980-81; critical care instr. HCA/Wesley Med. Ctr., Wichita, 1981-83, quality assessment coordinator, 1983, critical care educator, mgr., 1983-84, dir. allied health and nursing edn., 1984-87, asst. dir. nursing, med. services, 1987—; asst. prof. Kans. State U., 1986; adj. nursing faculty Wichita State U., 1982—. Manuscript reviewer Critical Care Nurse Mag., 1985—. CPR instr. Am. Heart Assn., Wichita, 1980—. Mem. Am. Assn. of Critical Care (pres. greater Wichita chpt. 1986—), Kans. Hosp. Assn. of Edn. Coordinators, Phi Kappa Phi, Sigma Theta Tau. Democrat. Seventh Day Adventist. Avocations: golf, acting. Home: 1652 Tamarisk Ct Wichita KS 67230 Office: Wesley Med Ctr 550 N Hillside Wichita KS 67214

EAGLETON, THOMAS FRANCIS, senator; b. St. Louis, Sept. 4, 1929; s. Mark David and Zitta Louise (Swanson) E.; m. Barbara Ann Smith, Jan. 20, 1956; children: Terence, Christin. B.A. cum laude, Amherst Coll., 1950; LL.B. cum laude, Harvard U., 1953. Bar: Mo. bar 1953. Since practiced in St. Louis; partner firm Eagleton & Eagleton; circuit atty. St. Louis, 1957-60; Atty. gen. State of Mo., 1960, lt. gov., 1964-68; mem. U.S. Senate from Mo., 1968-86; mem. law firm Thompson & Mitchell, St. Louis, MO., 1987—. Served with USNR, 1948-49. Office: Thompson & Mitchell Suite 3400 One Mercantile Center Saint Louis MO 63101 *

EAKIN, THOMAS CAPPER, sports promotion executive; b. New Castle, Pa., Dec. 16, 1933; s. Frederick William and Beatrice (Capper) E.; m. Brenda Lee Andrews, Oct. 21, 1961; children: Thomas Andrews, Scott Frederick. B.A. in History, Denison U., 1956. Life ins. cons. Northwestern Mut. Life Ins. Co., Cleve., 1959-67; dist. mgr. Putman Pub. Co., Cleve., 1968-69; regional bus. mgr. Chilton Pub. Co., Cleve., 1969-70; dist. mgr. Hitchcock Pub. Co., Cleve., 1970-72; founder, pres. Golf Internat. 100 Club, Shaker Heights, Ohio, 1970—; founder, pres., dir. Cy Young Mus., 1975-80; pres. TCE Enterprises, Shaker Heights, Ohio, 1973—; founder, pres. Ohio Baseball Hall of Fame, 1976—, Ohio Baseball Hall of Fame Celebration, 1977-79, Ohio Baseball Hall of Fame and Mus., 1980—, Ohio Sports Hall of Fame, 1985—, Ohio Assn. of Sports Hall of Fame, 1985—, Ohio Sports Council, 1985—; founder, chmn. Ohio Baseball Hall of Fame Golf Invitational, 1980—, Ohio Baseball Hall of Fame media award, 1981; bd. dir. New Hope Records, Greater Toledo Sports Hall of Fame; trustee Newcomerstown Sports Corp., 1975-80; Founder, nat. chmn. Cy Young Centennial, 1967; founder, nat. chmn. Cy Young Golf Invitational, 1967-79, (champion 1967, 1969-72, 1979); mem. adv. bd. Cleve. Indian Old Timers Com., 1966-67, Portage County Sports Hall of Fame (Ohio), 1983—, Sportsbeat, 19856 ; hon. dir. Tuscarawas County (Ohio) Old Timers Baseball Assn., 1972—, commendation, 1970; Ohio exec. sponsor chmn. World Golf Hall of Fame, Pinehurst, N.C., 1979—; founder, pres. Toledo Baseball Bluecoats, 1984—, Tuscarawas County Sports Hall of Fame, 1980—; adv. bd. Sportsbeat, 1985—; mem. adv. bd. Damascus Steel Casting Co., 1987—; founder, chmn. Ohio Baseball Hall of Fame Lifetime Achievement award, 1987—; mem. disting. citizens adv. bd. Am. Police Hall of Fame & Mus., 1987—. Feature story in Amateur Athletics World, 1982. Fund drive rep. Boy Scouts Am., Cleve., 1959-60, United Appeal, 1959-63, Heart Fund, 1963-64; mem. Cleve. Council Corrections, 1971-73; mem. adv. bd. Cuyahoga Hills Boys Sch., Warrensville Heights, Ohio, 1971—, Camp Hope, Warrrensville Twp., 1973—, Fitness Evaluation Services, Inc., 1977-79, Interact Club of Twinsburg (Ohio), 1981—, The Old Time Ball Players Assn. of Wis., Greater Youngstown Old Timers Baseball Assn.; founder, bd. dirs. TRY (Target/Reach Youth), 1971—, Interact Club Shaker Heights, 1971—; mem. exec. com. Tuscarawas County Am. Revolution Bicentennial Commn., 1974-76; trustee Tuscarawas County Hist. Soc., 1978-81; bd. dirs. Shaker Hts. Youth Center, 1975, Tuscarawas Valley Tourist Assn., 1979-81, Buckeye Tourist Assn., 1979-80; mem. adv. bd. Ohio Racquetball Assn., 1981-82; bd. trustees Nat. Jr. Tennis League, 1985-87; mem. adv. bd. Middlefield Hist. Soc., 1986—. Served with AUS, 1956-58. Recipient commendation awards Cy Young Centennial Com., 1967, commendation awards Tuscarawas County C. of C., 1967, commendation awards Sporting News, 1968, commendation awards Gov. James A. Rhodes, Ohio, 1968, 75, 78, commendation awards Gov. John J. Gilligan, Ohio, 1972, commendation awards Newcomerstown (Ohio) C. of C., 1967, commendation award N.C. Senate, 1984, commendation award State of Pa.Senate, 1984, Disting. Service award, Hubbard, Ohio, 1986— ; Outstanding Contbn. to Baseball award baseball commr. William Eckert, 1967; Sport Service award Sport mag., 1969, Feature Cover Story Personality award Amateur Athlete's World mag., 1982; Civic Service award Cuyahoga Hills Boys Sch., 1970; citation of merit La. Stadium and Expn. Dist., 1972; Presdl. commendations Nixon, Ford, Reagan; Disting. Service award Camp Hope, 1974; Founder's award Interact Club Shaker Heights, 1974; Gov.'s award for community action State of Ohio, 1974; award of achievement Ohio Assn. Hist. Socs., 1975; named to Order of Long Leaf Pine, State of N.C., 1984; Chief Newawatowes award Newcomerstown C. of C., 1975; Proclamation award, Thomas C. Eakin Day City of Cleve., 1974, and in numerous Ohio cities 1984-86; Outstanding Alumnus award Phi Delta Theta Alumni Club, Cleve., 1975; commendation states of La., N.C., Ohio Senate, House of Rep.; certificate of merit Tuscarawas County Am. Revolution Bicentennial Commn., 1976; Appreciation award Am. Revolution Bicentennial Adminstrn., 1977; Cert. of Merit State of La., 1978; Gov.'s award State of Ohio, 1978; named Hon. Citizen City of New Orleans, 1978, City of Memphis, 1986, City of Little Rock, 1986, numerous Ohio cities; Founder's award TRY, Target/Reach Youth 1979; inducted into Chautauqua Sports Hall of Fame (N.Y.), 1983; hon. bd. dirs. Chautauqua Sports Hall of Fame (N.Y.), 1982—; Commissioners' award Trumbull County Ohio, 1985; presdl. tributes presidents Nixon, Ford, Reagan; honor resolution New Orleans City Council, 1984; Commendation, N.C. Senate, 1984, Pa. Senate, 1984; recipient various honors resolutions, tributes and commendations; named to hon. order Ky. Cols., 1986. Fellow Intercontinental Biog. Assn.; fellow Am. Biog. Inst.; mem. Tuscarawas County Hist. Soc. (trustee 1978-81), Shaker Hist. Soc. (trustee 1980-82), Internat. Platform Assn., English Speaking Union, Denison U. Cleve. Men's Club (v.p. 1964-65), Phi Delta Theta (pres. Cleve. alumni club 1970, Appreciation award 1971, dir. 1971-75, exec. com. nat. Lou Gehrig award com. 1975—, trustee Ohio Iota chpt. 1979-82). Baptist (mem. bd. 1966-69). Clubs: Rotary (pres. Shaker Heights 1970-71, founder and chmn. club's internat. student exchange program U.S. and Can. 1965-70, Outstanding Young Rotarian award 1962, founder, chmn. Henry G. Duchscherer Meml. award com. 1971, trustee V. Blakeman Qua Scholarship Fund 1972-73), Wahoo (dir. 1975-77); Executive (Woodmere, Ohio); PGA Nat. Golf (Palm Beach Gardens, Fla.) (internat. mem.); Legend Lake Golf (Chardon, Ohio); Univ. Sch. Tennis (Shaker Heights). Address: 2729 Shelley Rd Shaker Heights OH 44122

EARHART, MICHAEL JON, pharmacist; b. Wichita, Kans., Nov. 29, 1945; s. Harold Wilson and Dorothy Lee (Yeager) E. B.S. in Pharmacy, U. Mo.-Kansas City, 1972; M.A. in Health Services Mgmt., Webster U., 1983. Registered pharmacist, Mo., Tex. Pharmacist Deaconess Hosp., St. Louis, 1973-75, 76, asst. dir. pharmacy, 1976-77, dir. pharmacy, 1977-81, div. mgr.-pharmacy/IV therapy, 1981-85, dir. physician practice services, 1985—; pharmacist Valley Bapt. Hosp., Harlingen, Tex., 1975-76; dir. Network, St. Louis, 1984-85; adj. clin. instr. pharmacy St. Louis Coll. Pharmacy, 1980-85. Treas. Shaw/Garden/Central, Inc. Neighborhood Assn., St. Louis, 1984—; sec. bd. trustees Oak Woods Inc. Land Owners Assn., 1985—. Served to USN, 1963-66. Mem. Am. Soc. Hosp. Pharmacists, St. Louis Soc. Hosp. Pharmacists, U. Mo.-Kansas City Alumni Assn. (life), Webster U. Alumni Assn. Republican. Lutheran. Avocations: art glass, camping. Home: 3857 Shaw Blvd Saint Louis MO 63110 Office: Deaconess Hosp 6150 Oakland Ave Saint Louis MO 63139

EARL, ANTHONY SCULLY, former governor of Wisconsin; b. Lansing, Mich., Apr. 12, 1936; s. Russell K. and Ethlynne Julia (Scully) E.; m. Sheila Rose Coyle, Aug. 11, 1962; children: Julia, Anne, Mary, Catherine. B.S., Mich. State U.; J.D., U. Chgo. Bar: Wis., Minn. Asst. dist. atty. Marathon County, Wausau, Wis., 1965-66; city atty. City of Wausau, 1966-69; mem. Wis. Assembly, Madison, 1969-74; mem. firm Crooks, Low & Earl, 1969-74; sec. Wis. Dept. Adminstrn., Madison, 1974-75, Dept. Nat. Resources, Madison, 1975-80; v.p. firm Foley & Lardner, Madison, 1980-82; gov. State of Wis., Madison, 1983-87; ptnr. Quarles and Brady, Madison, 1987—. Served as lt. USN, 1962-65. Democrat. Roman Catholic. Office: Quarles and Brady 1 S Pinckney St Madison WI 53701

EARL, JOSEPH HENRY, engineer; b. Winslow, Wash., Nov. 28, 1953; s. Joseph L. and Alice (Lidburg) E.; m. Joann Elizabeth Kinsey, July 12, 1975; children: Elizabeth, Joseph L., Allison, Kevin, Tanya. BSE, Purdue U., 1980; M in Engring Mgmt., Northwestern U., 1986. Registered profl. engr., Ill. Project engr. U.S. Gypsum, Ft. Dodge, Iowa, 1980-84; facilities mgr. USG Corp. Research, Libertyville, Ill., 1984—. Mem. Am. Inst. Plant Engrs., Soc. Profl. Engrs., Soc. Mfg. Engrs. Avocations: sailing, camping, hiking, swimming. Office: USG Corp 700 N Highway 45 Libertyville IL 60048

EARLE, ARTHUR SCOTT, plastic surgeon; b. Lexington, Mass., Dec. 13, 1924; s. Arthur Hinkley Earle and Mildred (Scott) Oliver; m. Constance Earle (div.); children: Wendy, Victoria, Scott; m. Barbara Milici; children: Christopher, Alison, David. AB in Biology cum laude, Harvard U., 1948, MD, 1953. Diplomate Am. Bd. Surgery, Am. Bd. Plastic and Reconstructive Surgery. Instr. in biology Boston U. Gen. Coll., 1948-49; intern Peter Bent Brigham Hosp., Boston, 1953-54, resident, 1954-55, 56-58, Harvey Cushing research fellow, 1955-56; instr. in anatomy Harvard Med. Sch., 1955-56; chief resident surgeon Peter Bent Brigham Hosp., Boston, 1958-59; surgeon Moritz Community Hosp., Sun Valley, Idaho, 1959-70; resident in plastic surgery U. Hosps. Cleve., 1970-72, asst. plastic surgeon, 1972—; dir. plastic surgery div. Cleve. Met. Gen. Hosp., 1972—; asst. prof. Case Western Res. U. Sch. Medicine, Cleve., 1972-76, assoc. prof., 1976-86, prof., 1986—. Contbr. articles to profl. publs. Mem. bd. dirs. Idaho div. Am. Cancer Soc., 1965-70, Idaho Blue Cross, 1967-70. Fellow Am. Coll. Surgeons; mem. Ohio State Med. Assn., Am. Assn. History Medicine, Am. Soc. for Plastic and Reconstructive Surgery, Am. Assn. for Plastic and Reconstructive Surgery, Ohio Valley Soc. for Plastic and Reconstructive Surgery, Am. Soc. for Reconstructive Microsurgery, Am. Soc. for Surgery of Hand, Cleve. Surg. Soc., Am. Burn Assn. Office: 3395 Scranton Rd Cleveland OH 44109

EARLY, BERT HYLTON, lawyer, legal search consultant; b. Kimball, W.Va., July 17, 1922; s. Robert Terry and Sue Keister (Hylton) E.; m. Elizabeth Henry, June 24, 1950; children—Bert Hylton, Robert Christian, Mark Randolph, Philip Henry, Peter St. Clair. Student, Marshall U., 1940-42; A.B., Duke U., 1946; J.D., Harvard U., 1949. Bar: W.Va. 1949, Ill. 1963, Fla. 1981. Assoc. Fitzpatrick, Marshall, Huddleston & Bolen, Huntington, W.Va., 1949-57; asst. counsel Island Creek Coal Co., Huntington, W.Va., 1957-60, assoc. gen. counsel, 1960-62; dep. exec. dir. ABA, Chgo., 1962-64, exec. dir., 1964-81; sr. v.p. Wells Internat., Chgo., 1981-83, pres., 1983-85; pres. Bert H. Early Assocs. Inc., Chgo., 1985—; Instr., Marshall U., 1950-53; cons. and lectr. in field. Bd. dirs. Morris Meml. Hosp. Crippled Children, 1954-60, Huntington Pub. Library, 1951-60, W.Va. Tax Inst., 1961-62, Huntington Galleries, 1961-62; mem. W.Va. Jud. Council, 1960-62, Huntington City Council, 1961-62; bd. dirs. Community Renewal Soc., Chgo., 1965-76, United Charities Chgo., 1972-80, Am. Bar Endowment, 1983—, sec. 1987—, Hinsdale Hosp. Found., 1987—; mem. vis. com. U. Chgo. Law Sch., 1975-78; trustee David and Elkins Coll., 1960-63. mem., Hinsdale Plan Commn., Ill., 1982-85. Served to 1st lt. AC, U.S. Army, 1943-45. Life Fellow Am. Bar Found., Ill. State Bar Found. (charter); mem. Am. Law Inst. (life), Internat. Bar Assn. (asst. sec. gen. 1967-82), ABA (Ho. of Dels. 1958-59, 84—, chmn. Young Lawyers div. 1957-58, Disting. Service award Young Lawyers div. 1983), Nat. Legal Aid and Defender Assn., Am. Jud. Soc. (bd. dirs. 1981-84), Fla. Bar, W.Va. State Bar, Chgo. Bar Assn. Presbyterian. Clubs: Harvard (N.Y.C.); Metropolitan (Washington); University, Economic (Chgo.); Hinsdale Golf (Ill.). Office: Bert Early Assocs 111 W Washington St Suite 1421 Chicago IL 60602

EARLY, GERALD LEE, cardiovascular and thoracic surgeon, educator; b. St. Joseph, Mo., June 10, 1947; s. Abram Lee and Arline Joyce (Stein) E.; 1 dau., Jennifer Lynn. B.A., Central Methodist Coll., Fayette, Mo., 1969; M.D., U. Mo.-Kansas City, 1973; M.A., U. Mo.-Columbia, 1975. Diplomate Nat. Bd. Med. Examiners, 1974, Am. Bd. Surgery, 1980, Am. Bd. Thoracic Surgery, 1983. Intern, Kansas City Gen. Hosp. and Med. Ctr., 1973-74; resident in internal medicine Pensacola Ednl. Program, 1974-75; resident in surgery U. Mo.-Kansas City, 1976-79, in thoracic surgery Ohio State U., 1979-81; dir. dept. emergency medicine Pensacola (Fla.) Ednl. Program, 1975-76; dir. cardiovascular and thoracic surgery Truman Med. Ctr., Kansas City, Mo., 1982-83; clin. asst. prof. surgery U. Mo.-Kansas City, 1982—. Recipient Meritorious Service award West Fla. Heart Assn., 1976; named Surgery Resident of Yr., Truman Med. Ctr., 1978, 79; USPHS Reproductive Biology Tng. grantee, 1970-71. Fellow Am. Coll. Surgeons, Am. Coll. Chest Physicians; mem. Jackson County Med. Soc., Mo. Med. Assn., AMA, Assn. Acad. Surgery, Kansas City Pulmonary Round Table. Methodist. Contbr. articles sci. jours. Office: 6700 Troost St 348 Rockhill Med Bldg Kansas City MO 64131

EARNEST, SANDRA FLORENCE, nurse, administrator; b. Grosse Pointe, Mich., Apr. 12, 1938; d. Waldo T. and Alice G. (Upton) Cooper; children: Robin, Ruth, Jill. Diploma in Nursing, Evangelical Deaconess Hosp., Detroit, 1959; BS in Nursing, Case Western Reserve U., 1965; MS in Nursing, Ohio State U., 1976. RN, Ohio, Ind. Dir. nursing Shriners Hosp., Cin., 1978-80; dir. sch. practical nursing Marion (Ohio) Gen. Hosp., 1974-76; asst. adminstr. Our Lady Mercy Hosp., Mariemonte, Ohio, 1977-78; dir. staff devel. Meml. Hosp., South Bend, Ind., 1980—; instr. nursing Marion Tech. Coll., 1974; adj. asst. prof. Ind. U.; adj. prof. Andrews U., Berrien Springs, Mich., 1984—. Author: (with others) Nursing Care of Burn Patients, 1982; contbr. articles to profl. jours. Mem. Am. Hosp. Assn., Am. Soc. Healthcare Edn. and Tng., Internat. Assn. Quality Circles. Club: Toastmasters. Home: 5027 E Blackford Dr South Bend IN 46614 Office: Meml Hosp 615 N Michigan St South Bend IN 46601-9986

EASLEY, JIMMY PARKER, utility executive; b. Calhoun City, Miss., Aug. 26, 1939; s. Edgar Smith and Dora Idell (Parker) E.; m. Donna J. McKee, June 2, 1964; children: Stephen Michael, Jodi Michelle. BSEE, Miss. State U., 1963. Registered engr., Ohio. Various engring, mtkg. positions Ohio Edison Co., Akron, 1963-83, dir. bus. devel., 1983—. Dist. chmn. Boy Scouts Am., SPringfield, 1980-82. Mem. Indsl. Devel. Research Council (assoc.), Ohio Econ. Devel. Council (chmn. 1986-87), Ohio Devel. Assn., Soc. Indsl. Office Realtors (assoc.). Republican. Methodist. Lodge: Lions (pres. Springfield 1975-76). Avocations: golf, house and garden work. Office: Ohio Edison 76 S Main St 18th Floor Akron OH 44308

EAST, F. HOWARD, paper company executive; b. Muncie, Ind., Dec. 25, 1937; s. F. Harold and Esther (Hall) E.; m. Lynn A. Haskett; children: Kim L., Kathy A. B.S., Ball State U., 1960, M.S., 1960. C.P.A., Ind. Mgmt. cons. Ernst & Whinney, Indpls., 1960-65; controller, v.p. fin. Bell Fibre Products, Marion, Ind., 1965-78, exec. v.p., 1978-80, pres., 1980—; dir. Am. Bank and Trust Co., Marion; c.p., dir. Marion Nat. Corp., 1972—; v.p., dir. Menominee Paper Co., Mich., 1973—. Mem. adv. com. Marion Coll., 1979—; pres. Marion Easter Pageant, 1981-85; treas., bd. dirs. Marion Gen. Hosp., 1978-83; bd. dirs. YMCA, Marion, 1978-80, Jr. Achievement, 1972—; mem. Marion Redevel. Com., 1978-80. Mem. Am. Inst. C.P.A.s, Ind. C.P.A. Soc., Pres.'s Assn., Fin. Execs. Inst., Am. Mgmt. Assn., Nat. Assn. Accts., Marion C. of C. Republican. Clubs: Mecca; Mesingomesia Country (Marion). Lodges: Masons; Shriners. Home: 916 W Sydney Ln Marion IN 46952 Office: Bell Fibre Products Corp 3102 S Boots St Marion IN 46952

EASTBURN, RICHARD A., consulting firm executive; b. West Chester, Pa., Jan. 16, 1934; s. Louis W. and Alma S. (Shellin) E.; B.A., Shelton Coll., 1956; M.S.T., N.Y. Theol. Sem., 1959; M.Ed., Temple U., 1970; M.B.A., Columbia U., 1979; m. Heidi Fritz, June 15, 1963; children—Karin J., R. Marc. Ordained to ministry Am. Baptist Conv., 1959; minister, Laurelton, N.J., 1959-61; dir adult programs Central YMCA, Phila., 1961-65; dir. Opportunities Industrialization Ctr., Phila., 1965-67; mgr. tng. and devel. Missile & Surface Radar div. RCA, Moorestown, N.J., 1967-68, mgr. mgmt. devel. govt. and comml. systems group, dir. mgmt. devel., 1969-71; group mgr. personnel for internat. field ops. Digital Equipment, Maynard, Mass., 1971-75; corp. dir. orgn. and productivity devel. Am. Standard, Inc., N.Y.C., 1975-79; corp. dir. mgmt. devel. edn. and staffing TRW, Inc., Cleve., 1979-85; pres. Retirement Community Concepts, 1981—, founder Laurel Lake Retirement Community, Hudson, Ohio, 1985; mng. ptnr. Benoit-Eastburn, Hudson, 1986-87; sr. v.p. Strategic Mgmt. Group of Phila., Chagrin Falls, Ohio, 1987—; producer, moderator Ask the Clergy, Sta. WIP, Phila., 1965-67. Bd. dirs. exec. program adv. bd. U. Ind.; bd. dirs. Burlington County (N.J.) Community Com., 1967-69. Recipient Disting. Community Service award Shelton Coll. Alumni, 1956; Dedicated Service award Phila. March of Progress, 1967. Mem. Am. Soc. Tng. and Devel. (dir., 1979-80), Orgn. Devel. Network. Mem. United Ch. Christ. Clubs: Chagrin Valley Athletic, A & A Sportsman. Home: 170 Pheasant Run Chagrin Falls OH 44022 Office: PO Box 224 Chagrin Falls OH 44022

EASTEP, PHILLIP BEN, dentist; b. Wichita, Kans., July 25, 1944; s. Joseph Ben and Nelda (Capps) E.; m. Margret Karen Crowe, July 1, 1966 (div. July 1970); m. Sharon Lee Polster, Nov. 28, 1970; children: Ben, Melissa. Student, U. Kans., 1962-64; DMD, U. Ky., 1968. Intern USPHS, S.I., N.Y., 1968-69; dental cons. USPHS, Phila., 1969-70; sr. dental cons. USPHS, Denver, 1970-71; instr. U. B.C., Vancouver, 1971-74; gen. practice dentistry Cherryvale, Kans., 1976—; pres. Montgomery County Crude, CHerryvale, 1979—; bd. dirs. City State Bank, Ft. Scott, Kans., Gardner (Kans.) Nat. Bank, Radiant Electric Corp.; chmn. bd. Community Nat. Bank, Chanute, Kans., Edna (Kans.) State Bank. Chmn. bd. Rural Water Dist. 6, Neodesha, Kans., 1976-80, Class Ltd., Columbus, 1984—; area rep. Youth for Understanding, Washington, 1985—. Mem. ADA, Kans. Dental Assn., Southeast Kans. Dental Assn., Am. Acad. Oral Medicine (cert. of merit 1968), Am. Assn. Endodontics (cert. of merit 1968), Neosho Valley Study Club (pres. 1978-79), Sunflower Study Club (pres. 1986—). Republican. Avocation: reading.

EASTERBROOK, FRANK HOOVER, judge; b. Buffalo, Sept. 3, 1948; s. George Edmund and Vimy (Hoover) E. B.A., Swarthmore Coll., 1970; J.D., U. Chgo., 1973. Bar: D.C. Law clk. to judge U.S. Ct. Appeals, Boston, 1973-74; asst. to solicitor gen. U.S. Dept. Justice, Washington, 1974-77, dep. solicitor gen. of U.S., 1978-79; asst. prof. law U. Chgo., 1979-81, prof. law, 1981-84, Lee & Brena Freeman prof., 1984-85; prin. employee Lexecon Inc., Chgo., 1980-85; judge U.S. Ct. Appeals (7th cir.), Chgo., 1985—; mem. adv. com. on tender offers SEC, Washington, 1983. Author: Antitrust, 1981; editor Jour of Law and Econs., Chgo., 1982—; contbr. articles to profl. jours. Recipient Prize for Disting. scholarship Emory U., Atlanta, 1981. Mem. Am. Law Inst., Phi Beta Kappa, Order of Coif. Home: 1648 E 54th St Chicago IL 60615 Office: U S Ct of Appeals 219 S Dearborn St Chicago IL 60604

EASTLUND, MARVIN EUGENE, physician; b. Breman, Ind., Apr. 25, 1944; s. Allen Edward and Ruth Mae (Barden) E.; m. Phyllis Diane Brower, June 4, 1966; children: Shelly Lynn, Kimberly Diane, Darcy Kay, John Bradley. AB, Manchester Coll., 1966; MD, Ind. U., 1970. Diplomate Am. Bd. Ob-Gyn. Intern St. Vincent Hosp., Indpls., 1970-71, resident in ob-gyn, 1971-74; practice medicine specializing in ob-gyn Ft. Wayne, Ind., 1976—; mem. staff Ft. Wayne Ob-Gyn Inc. 1976—, pres. 1979-80; mem. staff Parkview Meml. Hosp., Ft. Wayne. Bd. dirs., sec. Blackhawk Christian Sch.; bd. dirs. Ft. Wayne Area Youth for Christ. Served with M.C., USN, 1974-76. Named Outstanding Young Man of Am., 1978. Fellow Am. Coll. Obstetricians and Gynecologists; mem. AMA, Ind. Med. Assn., Ft. Wayne Med. Soc., Ft. Wayne Acad. Medicine and Surgery, Ft. Wayne Ob-Gyn Soc., Ind. Ob-Gyn Soc., Am. Assn. Gynecologic Laparoscopists. Baptist. Home: 5431 Vance Ave Fort Wayne IN 46815 Office: 3124 E State Blvd Fort Wayne IN 46805

EASTMAN, JAMES THOMAS, dentist; b. South Bend, Ind., Nov. 10, 1923; s. Arthur Andrews and Lydia Georgina (Dittman) E.; m. Daisy Louise Lovejoy, July 17, 1948; children: Gail, Janet, James Jr., Patricia, William. Student, Northwestern U., 1941, 45, Ind. U., 1942-43; DDS, Loyola U. Sch. Dentistry, Chgo., 1949. Gen. practice pediatric dentistry Elkhart, Ind., 1949—; chmn. dental adv. com. Dept. Pub. Welfare Elkhart County, 1954-80, Ind. U. at South Bend, 1970-74. Served with USN, 1943-45, to 1st lt. U.S. Army, 1952-53. Recipient Disting. Service award Elkhart County Assn. for the Retarded, 1969, Benefactor award, 1975. Fellow Am. Acad. Pediatric Dentistry; mem. ADA, Ind. Dental Assn. (pres. north cen. dist. 1968-69, trustee 1976-79, Service Recognition award 1979), Am. Soc. Dentistry for children (pres. Ind. chpt. 1973-74), Ind. Soc. Pediatric Dentistry (pres. 1970-71). Republican. Presbyterian. Clubs: Elcona Country (Elkhart), East Lake Woodlands Golf and Racquet (Palm Harbor, Fla.). Lodge: Elks. Avocations: golf, swimming, reading. Home: 1755 Crabtree Ln Elkhart IN 46514 Office: 1300 Johnson St Elkhart IN 46514

EASTMAN, LYNN ALFRED, social services administrator; b. Flint, Mich., Nov. 2, 1948; s. Dale K. and V. Bernice Eastman; m. Jeanne Ann; 1 child, Stephanie Ann. BA, U. Mich., Flint, 1970, Cen. Bible Coll., Springfield, Mo., 1971; MA, U. Mich., 1977. Cert. social worker. Youth and edn. dir. 1st Assembly of God, Lawrence, Kans., 1971-72; dir. youth guidance Youth for Christ, Flint, 1972-73, exec. dir., 1973-81; exec. dir. Diversion, Inc., Flint, 1981—; guest lectr. U. Mich., 1975-77. Contbr. articles to profl. jour. Bd. dirs. Heart Beat, Flint, 1982-84; Rep. candidate for Ho. of Reps., 1980; mem. Rep. Presdl. Task Force, 1984—. Mem. Mich. Assn. Children' Agy., U. Mich. Hist. Soc. (pres. 1969-70). Presbyterian. Club: Flushing Valley Golf and Country. Avocations: golf, tennis., racquetball, jogging. Home: 1260 Woodkrest Dr Flint MI 48504

EASTMAN, SUZANNE KATHLEEN, psychologist; b. Saginaw, Mich., Sept. 22, 1944; d. Douglas C. and Betty Jean (Loomis) E.; m. Gerald Peter Esmer, Sept. 18, 1964 (div. Oct. 1978); children: Rand, Robert, Gregory. BS, Eastern Mich. U., 1978, MS, 1980. Nurse, therapist Univ. Ctr., Ann Arbor, Mich., 1979-80; psychologist Plymouth Ctr., Northville, Mich., 1980-83, Forensic Ctr., Ypsilanti, Mich., 1983—; cons. Clinical Resources, Brighton, Mich., 1981-82. Mem. Am. Psychol. Assn., Mich. Psychol. Assn. Unitarian. Club: New Dimensions. Lodge: Dream Circle. Avocations: painting, windsurfing, tennis, golf. Office: Ctr for Forensic Psychiatry 3501 Willis Rd Ypsilanti MI 48197

EASTRIDGE, HARRY E., school superintendent; b. Bryant's Store, Ky., Aug. 30, 1940; s. Lowell B. Eastridge and Nannie M. (Golden) Lane; m. Shirley A. Edwards, Feb. 16, 1963; children: Christine Noelle, Jennifer Ann. BA, Defiance Coll., 1963; MA in History, Miami U., Oxford, Ohio, 1966; MEd, Wright State U., 1975; PhD, U. Cin., 1983. Cert. tchr., Ohio. Tchr. Vandalia (Ohio)-Butler High Sch., 1970-73; asst. prin. Brookville (Ohio) High Sch., 1973-76; prin. Westbrook Sch., Brookville, 1976-78; supt. Franklin Monroe Schs., Pitsburg, Ohio, 1978-82, Ravenna (Ohio) City Schs., 1982—; adv. mem. U. Akron Adminstrv. Council, 1985-86; mem. Kent State U. Tchr. Edn. Council, 1984-86; bd. dirs. Mid-East Ohio Spl. Edn. Resource Ctr., 1984-86. Contbr. articles to profl jours. Mem. Portage County Child Council, Ravenna, 1983-86; bd. dirs.Children"s Trust Fund, Ravenna and Columbus, 1985-86; chmn. missions bd. 1st Ch. of God, Ravenna, 1984-85. NSF scholar, 1972; Inst. Devel. Ednl. Activities fellow, Kettering Found., 1982-86; named to Hon. Order Ky. Cols., 1981. Mem. Am. Assn. Sch. Adminstrs., Ohio Assn. Local Sch. Adminstrs. (program chmn. 1978-86, NE Ohio Supt. Assn. (program chmn. 1984-86), Buckeye Assn. Sch. Adminstrs. (speaker State Supt. Group 1984, various coms. 1978-86), Ravenna C. of C., Ravenna Heritage Assn., Phi Delta Kappa. Democrat. Lodge: Lions (Ravenna and Pitsburg Jr. Citizenship chmn. 1978-86). Avocations: reading, family activities. Home: 554 E Riddle Ave Ravenna OH 44266 Office: Ravenna Bd Edn 507 E Main St Ravenna OH 44266

EATON, CHARLES MILLER, osteopathic physician; b. Quincy, Ill., Jan. 21, 1921; s. Charles Miller and Frances Elizabeth (Channon) E.; m. Kathleen Hanks, Apr. 12, 1944; children: Charles III, James, Douglas, John, Susan. DO, Osteopathic Coll., 1951. Pvt. practice osteopathic medicine Quincy, 1951. Mem. ch. choir, Quincy, 1951—; active Boy Scouts Am., Quincy, 1956-68. Served to lt. USNR, 1942-45. Congregationalist. Lodge: Rotary. Avocations: fishing, canoeing, square dancing. Home: 1845 S 24th Quincy IL 62301 Office: 1932 State St Quincy IL 62301

EATON, GORDON PRYOR, university president, geologist; b. Dayton, Ohio, Mar. 9, 1929; s. Colman and Dorothy (Pryor) E.; m. Virginia Anne Gregory, June 12, 1951; children: Gretchen Maria, Gregory Mathieu. B.A., Wesleyan U., 1951; M.S. (Standard Oil fellow), Calif. Inst. Tech., 1953, Ph.D., 1957. Instr. geology Wesleyan U., Middletown, Conn., 1955-57, asst. prof., 1957-59; asst. prof. U. Calif.-Riverside, 1959-63, assoc. prof., 1963-67, chmn. dept. geol. sci., 1965-67; with U.S. Geol. Survey, 1963-65, 67-81; dep. chief Office Geochemistry Geophysics, Washington, 1972-74; project chief geothermal geophysics Office Geochemistry Geophysics, Denver, 1974-76; scientist-in-charge Hawaiian Volcano Obs., 1976-78; assoc. chief geologist Reston, Va., 1978-81; dean Coll. Geoscis. Tex. A&M U., 1981-83, provost, v.p. acad. affairs, 1983-86; pres. Iowa State U., Ames, 1986—; bd. dirs. Iowa Resources Inc., Bankers Trust. Mem. editorial bd.: Jour. Volcanology and Geothermal Research, 1976-78; contbr. articles to profl. jours. NSF grantee, 1955-59. Fellow Geol. Soc. Am.; mem. AAAS, Am. Geophys. Union, Hawaii Natural History Assn. (dir. 1976-78). Club: Rotary. Home: The Knoll Ames IA 50010 Office: Office of the Pres Iowa State U Ames IA 50011

EATON, MARCIA MAY, philosophy professor; b. Galesburg, Ill., Oct. 5, 1938; d. Hermann Richard and Annie Verneice (Richmond) Mueller; m. Morris LeRoy Eaton, Aug. 13, 1964; 1 child, Dennis Owen. BA, Knox Coll., 1960; PhD, Stanford U., 1969. Asst. prof. philosophy U. Ill., Chgo., 1966-70; from asst. to prof. philosophy U. Minn., Mpls., 1971—, also chmn. dept., 1986—. Author: Art and Nonart, 1983, Basic Issues in Aesthetics, 1987; contbr. articles to profl. jours. Minn. Humanities Commission grantee, 1983-84; Bush Found. fellow, 1984-85. Mem. Am. Philos. Soc. (exec. com. 1981-84), Am. Soc. Aesthetics (trustee 1976-78), British Soc. Aesthetics. Home: 33 Park Ln Minneapolis MN 55416 Office: U Minn Philosophy Dept 224 Church St SE Minneapolis MN 55455

EBBERS, JAMES PAUL, minister, religious organization administrator; b. Oostburg, Wis., Oct. 6, 1926; s. Chester Lewis and Lavina Loretta (Zehms) E.; m. Dorothy Jean DeHaan, Dec. 28, 1949; children: Michael A., Susan K., Christopher E., Steven M. BA, Cen. Coll., Pella, Iowa, 1948; MDiv, New Brunswick (N.J.) Theol. Sem., 1951. Ordained to ministry Reformed Ch. in Am., 1951. Pastor Reformed Ch., Philmont and Mellenville, N.Y., 1951-58, Walden, N.Y., 1959-62; exec. sec. Reformed Ch. Am. Bd. World Missions, N.Y.C., 1962-69, Council of Chs., Akron, Ohio, 1969-78; pastor United Ch. of Christ, Akron, 1978-85; exec. sec. Ill. Conf. Chs., Springfield, 1985—. Home: 44 Marquette Ln Springfield IL 62707 Office: Ill Conf of Chs 615 S 5th St Springfield IL 62703

EBELING, CHARLES EDWIN, public relations executive; b. Green Bay, Wis., July 1, 1943; s. John Altman and Mary (Hennick) E.; m. Victoria Pawling Edelston, May 13, 1978. Student, U. Chgo., 1963; BJ, Bradley U., 1966. Pub. affairs rep. Allstate Ins. Co., Northbrook, Ill., 1969-71; pub. relations mgr. Amco Industries, Inc., Franklin Park, Ill., 1971-73; account exec. Burson Marsteller, Inc., Chgo., 1973-74; from account exec. to sr. v.p. Golin/Harris Communications, Chgo., 1974-81; dir. corp. communications Baxter Travenol Labs., Deerfield, Ill., 1981-85, McDonald's Corp., Oak Brook, Ill., 1985—. Mem. nat. adv. bd. Children's Oncology Services, Chgo., 1976-81. Served to 1st lt. U.S. Army, 1966-69, Vietnam. Recipient Golden Trumpet award Publicity Club Chgo., 1970. Mem. Pub. Relations Soc. Am. (accredited, Silver Anvil award 1980). Club: Internat. Home: 1440 N State Pkwy Chicago IL 60610 Office: McDonald's Corp 1 McDonald Plaza Oak Brook IL 60521

EBENSTEINER, KENNETH BERNARD, accountant; b. Little Falls, Minn., Sept. 16, 1951; s. Ernest Joseph and Elverna (Athmann) E.; m. Diane Carol Roth, May 24, 1974. BS, St. Cloud State U., 1973. CPA, Minn., N.D. Auditor Legis. Audit Commn., St. Paul, 1973-76, Ness, Waller, Nygaard and Co., Alexandria, Minn., 1976-80; controller H. Boyd Nelson, Inc., Alexandria, 1980-82; dir. fin. analysis services Farm Credit Services, Fargo, N.D., 1982—. Mem. Am. Inst. CPA's, Minn. Soc. CPA's, N.D. Soc. CPA's. Roman Catholic. Avocations: golf, fishing, basketball. Office: Farm Credit Services 1749 38th St SW Fargo ND 58103

EBERBACH, STEVEN JOHN, consumer electronics company executive; b. Ann Arbor, Mich., Apr. 30, 1943; s. Robert Ottmar and Marie (Eichelberger) E.; m. Mary Jean Head, Oct. 15, 1983; 1 child, Amy Elizabeth. BSEE, MIT, 1965; MBA, U. Mich., 1967. Engr. U. Mich. Space Physics Research Lab., Ann Arbor, 1967-73; founder, owner, engr., v.p. and chmn. DCM Corp., Ann Arbor, 1974—. Inventor in field of loudspeaker design, 1979—. Mem. IEEE, Audio Engring. Soc. Club: Mac Technics (Ann Arbor). Avocations: sailing, photography, cross country skiing, computer sci. and programming. Home: 4455 Loch Alpine Dr E Ann Arbor MI 48103 Office: DCM Corp 670 Airport Blvd Ann Arbor MI 48104

EBERHARD, WILLIAM THOMAS, architect; b. St. Louis, Apr. 11, 1952; s. George Walter and Bettie Alma (Seilkop) E.; m. Cynthia Ann Hardy, Aug. 20, 1977 (div. 1981); m. Linda W. Bayer, Dec. 5, 1986. B. Arch., U. Cin., 1976; postgrad. Archtl. Assn., London, 1974. Registered architect Ohio, Mich., Pa., Fla., D.C. Vice pres. Visnapuu & Assocs. Inc., Cleve., 1972-82; prin.-in-charge Oliver Design Group, Cleve., 1983—. Profl. team leader Inst. Urban Design, Cleve., 1983. Mem. AIA (chpt. sec. 1982-84), Nat. Trust for Hist. Preservation, Inst. Urban Design Am. Soc. Interior Designers (assoc.), Seminotic Soc. Am. (founding). Club: Shaker Heights Country. Avocations: drawing; photography; tennis; snowmobiling; golf. Home: 3256 Glencairn Rd Shaker Heights OH 44122 Office: Oliver Design Group 1920 Huntington Bldg Cleveland OH 44115

EBERHART, JAMES WILLIAM, computer systems specialist; b. Angola, Ind., Jan. 30, 1960; s. William Don and Margie (Libke) E.; m. Jennifer J. Klika, Mar. 2, 1985; 1 child, Jessica. Student, DePauw U., 1978-80; BS in Chemistry, Ind. U., 1982, MS in Computer Sci., 1983. Research analyst A.C. Nielsen Co., Northbrook, Ill., 1983-85, assoc. mgr. systems, 1985-87; computer scientist DuPont Critical Care, Waukegan, Ill., 1987—. Software developer, Sitesearch, 1986. Mem. Chgo. Assn. Microcomputer Profls., Chgo. Computer Soc. Avocations: sailing, camping. Home: 33070 Indian Ln Wildwood IL 60030 Office: DuPont Critical Care 1600 Waukegan Rd Waukegan IL 60085

EBERHART, STEVEN W., psychologist; b. St. Louis, Oct. 12, 1952; s. Carl A. and Cora H. (Kruckeberg) E. BA in Psychology, So. Ill. U., 1974; MS in Psychology, Western Ill. U., 1980; EdS in Sch. Psychology, U. Iowa, 1984, PhD in Sch. Psychology, 1986. Lic. psychologist, Minn.; cert. sch. psychologist, Minn., Iowa; cert. clin. psychologist, Ky. Mental health technician Anna (Ill.) State Hosp., 1974-78; clin. psychologist Barren River Comprehensive Care, Bowling Green, Ky., 1980-82; sch. psychologist Meeker and Wright Spl. Edn. Co-op, Cokato, Minn., 1985—. Contbr. article to profl. jours. Ill. State scholar. Mem. Nat. Assn. Sch. Psychologists, Am. Psychol. Assn., Mensa. Avocations: running, karate, traveling, juggling. Home: 10453 295th St Saint Joseph MN 56374

EBERHART-WRIGHT, ALICE MARIE, family therapist, researcher; b. Orange, Calif., Nov. 10, 1942; s. Charles William and Gertrude Spencer (Geer) Eberhart; m. Merrill Lee Wright, Apr. 30, 1936; stepchildren: Karla, Marci. BA, Mills Coll., 1964; MA, Tufts U., 1968. Chief Child devel. Ctr. Topeka State Hosp., 1967-76; family therapist Counseling and Consultation Services, Topeka, 1976-83; pvt. practice family therapy Topeka, 1983—; researcher Menninger Found., Topeka, 1982—; workshop faculty Emporia State U., Kans., 1979—; speaker on mental health and edn. issues. Author, composer: Swinging On a Tune, 1976; co-producer (film) Adolescent Pregnancy, 1986—. Bd. dirs. YWCA, Topeka, 1984-85; co-chairperson Family Fair, Topeka, 1983-85; pres. bd. dirs. St. Vincent Children's Home, Topeka, 1981-82. Mem. Am. Assn Marriage and Family Therapy. Democrat. Avocations: playing harp, swimming, composing, reading, photography. Home: 841 Anderson Terr Topeka KS 66606 Office: 3600 Burlingame Suite 1A Topeka KS 66611

EBERIUS, KLAUS OTTO, machine tool executive; b. Koethen, Germany, Feb. 13, 1940; s. Otto and Gertrud (Marx) E.; came to U.S., 1972; engring. degree Akademie of Engring., Cologne, Germany, 1967; m. Amei Brauns, Apr. 17, 1964; children—Edda, Susanne. Asst. plant mgr. Anton Piller Kg., Osterode, Germany, 1967-68; mgr. tng. center VDF Corp., Hannover, Germany, 1968-72; tech. services mgr. Upton, Bradeen & James, Sterling Heights, Mich., 1972-73, mgr. metal cutting div., 1973-76; v.p., gen. mgr. Unitec Nat. Co., Broadview, Ill., 1976-79; pres., dir. Uni-Sig Corp., 1979-82; corp. v.p. Oerlikon Motch Corp., 1983-84, corp. exec. v.p., 1984-85, pres., chief exec. officer, dir., 1985—; instr. programming night sch., Hannover. Recipient award NC-Research, 1969. Mem. Soc. Mfg. Engrs. Home: 7545 Muirwood Ct Chagrin Falls OH 44022 Office: 1250 E 222d St Cleveland OH 44117

EBERLE, CHARLES EDWARD, retired consumer products company executive, consultant; b. St. Louis, Mar. 20, 1928; s. Charles Edward and Hazel (Williams) E.; m. Nancy Ellen Paddock, Aug. 1, 1953; children: Charles Edward, Richard Clay, Julia Lee. B.S. in Chem. Engring., Washington U., St. Louis, 1949. Prodn. mgr. Procter & Gamble, St. Louis, 1949-55; plant mgr. Procter & Gamble, Lexington, Ky., 1955-57, St. Louis, 1957-60, Sacramento, 1960-64; mgr. mfg. Procter & Gamble, Cin., 1964-79, v.p. mfg., 1979-84, v.p. engring., 1984-85; pres. CEE Enterprises, Cin., 1985—, Thomas & Eberle Assocs., Inc., Cin., 1986—; Mem. mfg. studies bd. NRC/Nat. Acad. Scis. Vice pres. bd. trustees Children's Hosp. Med. Ctr., Cin., 1975—; mem. Cin. Council on World Affairs, 1979—; v.p. Dan Beard council Boy Scouts Am. Served with U.S. Army, 1951-52. Recipient Engring. Alumni Achievement award Washington U., 1977. Clubs: Queen City, Indian Hill. Home: 1055 Catawba Valley Ln Cincinnati OH 45226 Office: Thomas & Eberle Assocs Inc 455 Delta Ave Cincinnati OH 45226

EBERLEY, HELEN KAY MARIE, opera singer, classical record company executive; b. Sterling, Ill., Aug. 3, 1947; d. William Elliot and Catherine P. (Conneely) E.; m. Vincent P. Skowronski, July 15, 1972. MusB, Northwestern U., 1970, MusM, 1971. Pres. Eberley-Skowronski, Inc., Evanston, Ill., 1973—; Artisitic coordinator Eberley-Skowronski, Inc., 1973; founder Eberley-SkowronskiProdns., 1976, tchr.-coach, 1976; exec. dir., performance cons. Eberley-Skowronski Mgmt., 1985; participating artist Honors Concert Northwestern U., 1970. Operatic debut Peter Grimes Lyric Opera, Chgo., 1974; appeared in: Cosi Fan Tutte, Le Nozze Di Figaro, Dido and Aeneas, La Boehme, Faust, Don Giovanni, Brigadoon, others; performing artist Oglebay Opera Inst., Wheeling, W.Va., 1968, WTTW TV/Pub. Broadcasting System, Chgo., 1968, Continental Bank Concerts, United Airlines-Schumann WFMT Radio, Chgo., 1982, 86; producer/annotator Gentleman Gypsy, 1978, Skowronski: Strauss & Szymanowski, 1979, One Sonata Each: Franck & Szymankowski, 1982; artist/ exec. producer Separate But Equal, 1976, Opera Lady, 1978, Eberley Sings Strauss, 1980, Helen-Kay Eberley: An American Girl, 1983, Helen- Kay Eberley: Opera Lady II; performed Am. and Can Nat. Anthems for Chgo. Cubs Baseball Team, 1977-83. Mem. Mayor's founding com. Evanston Arts Council, 1974-75; judge Ice-skating Competition Wilmette (Ill.) Park Dist., 1985-86; fin. chmn. Chgo. Youth Orchestra, 1974-77, bd. dirs. 1973-77. Recipient Creative and Performing Arts award Ind. Jr. Miss, 1965, Louis Sundler award Northwestern U., 1966, Frederic Chramer award Northwestern U., 1967, F.K. Weyerhauser Scholar award Met. Opera, 1967, Milton J. Cross award Met. Opera Guild, 1968; prizewinner Met. Opera Nat. Auditions, Lincoln Ctr., N.Y., 1968. Mem. Am. Guild Musical Artists. Clubs: St. Mary's Acad. Alumnae Assn., Delta Gamma. Office: EB-SKO Prodns 1726 1/2 Sherman Ave Evanston IL 60201

EBERLY, CHARLES GEORGE, university administrator, educator; b. McComb, Ohio, Sept. 8, 1941; s. George Willis and Herma Elizabeth (Sower) E.; m. Sharon Rosalee Newcomer, June 21, 1964; children—Mary Barbara, Judith Elizabeth, Michael Charles. B.S. in Chemistry, Bowling Green State U., 1963; M.S. in Edn., Syracuse U., 1966; Ph.D. in Edn., Mich. State U., 1970. Acting asst. dean students Wilmington Coll., Ohio, summer 1964; instr. student personnel U. Wis.-Oshkosh, 1966-69; asst. prof. evaluation services Mich. State U., East Lansing, 1970-74, assoc. prof. undergrad. univ. div., 1974—, asst. to dir. admissions, 1981—; asst. prof. educational psychology, coordinator grad. program coll. student personnel work Ea. Ill. U., 1987—; vis. instr. Mie U., Tsu, Japan, 1977-78. Author: Building and Maintaing the Chapter Library, 1970. Mem. zoning bd., Mason, Mich., 1970-71. Recipient Carter Ashton Jenkens award Sigma Phi Epsilon, 1964. Mem. Assn. for Measurement and Evalution in Counseling and Devel. (newsletter editor 1979-84, treas. 1984—), Mich. ACT Council (exec. council 1981-86), Mich. Assn. for Measurement and Evaluation in Guidance (pres. 1984-85, Outstanding Profl. Service award 1985-86), Mich. Assn. for Counseling and Devel. (chmn. adminstrv. asst. evaluation com. 1984-85, editor jour. 1985-87), Am. Coll. Personnel Assn. (founder Commn. XVI 1979, dir. Commn. XVI 1979-82, profl. standards com. 1980-83), Am. Assn. Counseling and Devel., Nat. Council on Measurement in Edn., Am. Ednl. Research Assn., Nat. Assn. Acad. Affairs Adminstrs., Mich. Coll. Personnel Assn. (mem.-at-large exec. com. 1986-87), Phi Delta Kappa, Sigma Phi Epsilon, Alpha Phi Omega, Phi Kappa Phi. Republican. Methodist. Avocations: racquetball; cycling; woodworking; music; little theatre. Home: 2609 6th St Circle Charleston IL 61920 Office: Eastern Ill U Dept Educational Psychology Buzzard Bldg Charleston IL 61920

EBERLY, WILLIAM ROBERT, biology educator; b. North Manchester, Ind., Oct. 4, 1926; s. John H. and Ollie M. (Heaston) E.; m. Eloise L. Whitehead, June 30, 1946; children—Diana Sue, Brenda Kay, Sandra Jo. B.A., Manchester Coll., 1948; M.S., Ind. U., 1955, Ph.D., 1958. Tchr. music and sci. Laketon and Somerset pub. schs., Wabash County, Ind., 1947-52; teaching asst. dept. zoology Ind. U., Bloomington, 1952-55; asst. prof. Manchester Coll., North Manchester, 1955-60, assoc. prof., 1960-67, prof. biology, 1967—, dir. Environ. Studies, 1971—, chmn. biology dept., 1986—, chmn. natural sci. div., 1986—; cons. Ind. Dept. Natural Resources, Indpls., 1968, 76-82; vis. scientist U. Uppsala Inst. Limnology, Sweden, 1963-64. Author: History of Church of the Brethren in Northwestern Ohio, 1982. Contbr. articles to profl. jours. Mem. Ind. Pesticide Rev. Com., Indpls., 1971-83. Named Sagamore of Wabash, Ind. Gov., 1983; Ind. scholar Indpls. Star newspaper, 1984. Fellow Ind. Acad. Sci. (founder/editor spl. monograph series of publs. 1968—, chmn. publs. com. 1977-80, pres. 1982, chmn. constn. rev. com. 1983—); mem. Am. Soc. Limnology and Oceanography, Am. Inst. Biol. Scis., Internat. Assn. Theoretical and Applied Limnology, Nat. Assn. Biology Tchrs., Beta Beta Beta. Republican. Mem. Ch. of Brethren. Avocations: fishing; historical and genealogical research. Home: 304 Sunset Ct North Manchester IN 46962 Office: Dept Biology Manchester College North Manchester IN 46962

EBERSOLE, FREDERICK LEVI, SR., insurance executive; b. Shelby, Ohio, July 23, 1939; s. Elmer Raymond and Jessie Myrl (Huggins) E.; m. Joy Sondra Hatfield, Jan. 27, 1968; children: Robert Wayne, Frederick Levi. Grad high sch., Shelby, Ohio. Salesman Home State Ins., Columbus, Ohio, 1964-68; dist. mgr. Home State-Harvest, Columbus, 1968-81; dist. mgr. Walker & Assoc. Ins., Mansfield, Ohio, 1981-83, state sales mgr., 1983-84; gen. agt., chief exec. officer Ebersole Agy., Rock Creek, Ohio, 1984—; instr. Zig Zigler course, Mansfield, 1984; bd. dirs. Ohio Mktg Co. Inc. Lexington, Ohio, 1983-86. Designer file system, 1963. Served as cpl. USMC, 1960-64. Mem. Nat. Assn. Life Underwriters, Nat. Assn. Health Underwriters, Am. Legion. Republican. Methodist. Lodges: Shriners (unit dir. 1984), Masons (pres. 1977, cert. achievment 1980). Avocations: water skiing, fishing, swimming, hunting. Home: 1851 Morning Star Dr Rock Creek OH 44084

EBERSOLE, GEORGE DAVID, manufacturing executive; b. Plattsmouth, Nebr., July 11, 1936; s. George Benjamin and Wilma (Shepard) N.; m. Beverly F. Sullivan, Nov. 28, 1957; children: Karen, Kent, Kyle. BSME, Milw. Sch. Engring., 1961; MSME, U. Wis., 1963; PhD, U. Tulsa, 1971. Registered profl. engr., Okla. Cons. engr. Madison, Wis., 1963; sr. group leader Phillips Petroleum, Bartlesville, Okla., 1963-73; asst. v.p. research and devel. Frito Lay Inc., Irving Tex., 1973-74; gen. div. mgr. Hoover Universal, Ann Arbor, Mich., 1974-80; pres. Energy Absorption Systems subs. Quixote Corp. of Chgo., Sacramento, Calif., 1980—, Spincast Plastics subs. Quixote Corp. of Chgo., South Bend, Ind., 1980—; Contbr. articles to profl. jours.; patentee in field. Mem. ASME. Home: 7831 Forest Hill Ln Palos Heights IL 60463 Office: Energy Absorption Systems 1 E Wacker Dr Chicago IL 60601

EBERSOLE, JO ANN, dietitian; b. Corpus Christi, Tex., Feb. 13, 1945; d. Ronald A. and Ruth A. (White) E. BS in Dietetics, Mich. State U., 1967. Dietitian St. Lawrenc Hosp., Lansing, Mich., 1968-69; asst. chief dietitian Children's Meml. Hosp., Chgo., 1972-78; dir. food services Walther Meml. Hosp., Chgo., 1972-78, Forkosh Meml. Hosp./ Lincoln West Med. Ctr., Chgo., 1979-86, Our Lady of Mercy Hosp., Dyer, Ind., 1987—; cre; lectr. in field. Mem. Am. Dietetic Assn., Am. Soc. Hosp. Food Service Adminstrs. (nat. membership com., awards com. 1985, bd. dirs. Chgo. chpt. 1984-85, pres. elect 1986, pres. 1987), Ill. Dietetic Assn. (chmn. peer rev. com. 1978-80), Chgo. Dietetic Assn. (treas. 1980).

EBERSOLE, RONALD OTIS, hospital administrator; b. Wichita, Kans., June 25, 1943; s. Harvey Orrison and Dortha (Otis) E.; m. Rhoda Beth Bartz, Sept. 9, 1972; children—Catherine Emily, Jay William. A.B., Wichita State U., 1966; M.H.A., Washington U., St. Louis, 1969. Asst. adminstr. M.D. Anderson Hosp. and Tumor Inst., Houston, 1969-75; assoc. adminstr. St. Joseph Hosp., Mo., 1975-82; adminstr. Johnson County Meml. Hosp., Warrensburg, Mo., 1982-84; exec. dir. North Iowa Med. Ctr., Mason City, 1984—; mem. accreditation com. Mo. Hosp. Assn., 1982-84. Pres. bd. dirs. Northwest Mo. Health Edn. Ctr., St. Joseph, 1980-82; bd. dirs. Warrensburg unit Am. Heart Assn., 1982-84. Named Boss of Yr., Am. Bus. Women's Assn., Warrensburg, 1983. Mem. Am. Coll. Hosp. Adminstrs., Mason City C. of C. (mem. leadership devel. com. 1984, bd. dirs. 1985, divisional v.p. 1986), Iowa Hosp. Assn. Council Profl. Affairs. Republican. Lutheran. Lodge: Rotary. Avocations: gardening; fishing; cooking. Home: 181 Parkridge Dr Mason City IA 50401 Office: North Iowa Med Ctr 910 N Eisenhower Ave Mason City IA 50401

EBLE, DEBORAH ANN, pharmaceutical company administrator; b. St. Louis, Oct. 5, 1954; d. Walter Harry and Lucille Catherine (Daniel) E. BS in Mktg., U. Mo., 1976, MBA, 1978. Adminstrv. trainee Emerson Electric, St. Louis, 1976-77; mktg. requirements analyst NCR, Dayton, Ohio, 1978-80; client accounts mgr. Distbn. Scis., Des Plaines, Ill., 1980-83; customer service supr. Pfizer, Hoffman Estates, Ill., 1983-84, ops. control supr., 1984—. Mem. Woman's Transp. Seminar. Roman Catholic. Avocations: bowling, volleyball. Home: 847 Chasefield Ln #4 Crystal Lake IL 60014 Office: Pfizer Inc 2400 W Central Rd Hoffman Estates IL 60196

EBRIGHT, JAMES R., computer company executive; b. Columbus, Ohio, Apr. 27, 1947; s. Robert Louis and Dorothy Maxine (Swift) E.; m. Jane Loughead, May 6, 1978 (div. July 1985); children: Robert L. II, Samantha Jane, Erik Bertrand. BS in Urban Studies, MIT, 1971. Programmer State of Ohio, Columbus, 1972, Worthington Industries, Columbus, 1972-73, Accuray Corp., Columbus, 1973; applications developer Compu-Serv Inc., Columbus, 1973-75; chmn., chief exec. officer Software Results Corp., Columbus, 1985—. Editor: (newsletters) Networds, 1983-85, Pageswapper, 1979-83. Mem. Columbus Bd. Edn., 1984-85, Exec. Com. Franklin County Dems., Columbus, 1984-85; del. Ohio Dems. Mem. Assn. for Computing Machinery Digital Equipment Users Soc. Avocations: chess, reading, politics. Office: Software Results Corp 2887 Silver Dr Columbus OH 43211-1081

EBY, MARTIN KELLER, JR., construction company executive; b. Wichita Falls, Tex., Apr. 19, 1934; s. Martin and A. Pauline (Kimbell) E.; children: Stanley, Suzanna, David; m. Susan Sheldon, Dec. 27, 1985. B.S. in Civil Engring, Kans. State U., 1956. Registered profl. engr., Kan. With Martin K. Eby Constrn. Co., Inc., Wichita, Kan., 1956—; engr., project mgr., v.p. Martin K. Eby Constrn. Co., Inc., 1956-67, pres., 1967—, chmn., 1979—; dir. First Nat. Bank in Wichita, Kans. Assoc. Gen. Contractors, Topeka, 1965-68; mem. engring. adv. council Kans. State U., Maanhattan, 1970—. Bd. dirs. Veritas Found., Wichita, 1981—; mem. Wichita Mayor's Econ. Analysis Panel, 1982-83; chmn. Constrn. Industry Polit. Action Com. of Kans., Topeka, 1978. Mem. Kans. Engring. Soc., Nat. Soc. Profl. Engrs., ASCE, Wichita Profl. Engring. Soc., Chief Execs. Orgn., Inc. Methodist. Home: 1401 W River Blvd Apt 4B Wichita KS 67203 Office: Martin Eby Constrn Co Inc 610 N Main Wichita KS 67203

ECKARDT, ROBERT EDWARD, gerontologist, foundation official; b. N.Y.C., June 29, 1951; s. Robert Edward and Mary Lenore (Harvey) E.; m. Virginia A. Sheehan, Feb. 18, 1983; children: Allison Lenore, Megan Ann. B.A. with honors, Grinnell (Iowa) Coll., 1973; Thomas J. Watson fellow, Spain and Denmark, 1973-75; M.P.H. (Klare Meml. fellow 1976-77), U. Mich., 1977, cert. aging, 1977, D in Pub. Health, 1986. Research asst. Mich. Dept. Pub. Health, 1976-77; planning asso. Fedn. Community Planning, Cleve., 1977-82; coordinator Long Term Care Gerontology Center, Cleve., 1979-82; program officer Cleve. Found., 1982—. Pew Meml. fellow in health policy U. Mich., 1984—. Mem. Am. Public Health Assn., Gerontol. Soc. Am., Grantmakers in Health, Grantmakers in Aging (exec. com.), Cleve. Orch. Pub. Relations Adv. Council, Phi Beta Kappa. Author monograph in field. Home: 26700 Midland Rd Bay Village OH 44140 Office: 1400 Hanna Bldg Cleveland OH 44115

ECKART, DENNIS EDWARD, congressman; b. Cleve., Apr. 6, 1950; s. Edward Joseph and Mary Eckart; m. Sandra Jean Pestotnik; 1 son, Edward John. B.S., Xavier U., 1971; LL.B., Cleveland John Marshall Law Sch., 1974. Mem. Ohio Ho. of Reps., 1975-80; chmn. Cuyahoga County del., 1979-80; mem. 97th Congress 22d Ohio dist. and 98th-100th Congress 11th Ohio dist., 1981—. Office: 1210 Longworth Bldg Washington DC 20515 also: 5970 Heisley Rd #220 Mentor OH 44060

ECKERSON, RAYMOND GROVER, data processing executive; b. Cobleskill, N.Y., May 11, 1926; s. Grover Cleveland and Lucinda (Hadsell) E.; m. Mary Kay Lee, Sept. 4, 1964 (div. June 1984); children: Julie Rae, Darcy Kay; m. Nancy Fiedler, July 27, 1984. BBA, Wichita (Kans.) Coll. Bus. Adminstrn., 1964. Dir. data processing Wichita Coll. Bus. Adminstrn., 1964-66; sr. programmer Wesley Med. Ctr., Wichita, 1966-67, maintenance programmer, 1967-68, ops. mgr., 1968-72; asst. dir. data processing St. Joseph's Hosp., Denver, 1972-73; med. cons. PSI Systems Corp., Baton Rouge, 1973-74, sr. cons., 1974-75; sr. systems engr. McDonnell Douglas Corp., St. Louis, 1975-78; dir. data processing Ingalls Meml. Hosp., Harvey, Ill., 1978—. Served to capt. USAF, 1958-63. Mem. Data Processing Mgmt. Assn., Am. Cons. League, Am. Legion, VFW. Republican. Lodge: Moose. Avocations: woodworking, gardening. Home: 2424 Heather Rd Homewood IL 60430

ECKHARDT, BRUCE N., financial executive; b. Balt., Jan. 17, 1949. BS in Acctg., U. Md., 1971; MBA, Loyola U., Balt., 1977. CPA. Plant controller Black & Decker, Fayetteville, N.C., 1975-78; controller Black & Decker, Towson, Md., 1978-84, Emerson Electric, Sidney, Ohio, 1984—. Mem. Fin. Execs. Inst., Am. Inst. CPA's.

ECKHARDT, CRAIG JON, chemistry educator; b. Rapid City, S.D., June 26, 1940; s. Reuben H. and Hilda W. (Craig) E. B.A. magna cum laude, U. Colo., 1962; M.S., Yale U., 1964, Ph.D., 1967. Asst. prof. chemistry U. Nebr., Lincoln, 1967-72, assoc. prof., 1972-78, prof., 1978—, interim chmn. dept. chemistry, 1986-87; cons., mem. adv. panel, condensed matter scis. div. materials research NSF, 1976-79. NIH predoctoral fellow, 1964-67; Yale predoctoral fellow, 1967; John Simon Guggenheim fellow, 1979-80; German Acad. Exchange fellow; NSF grantee, 1974—; Dept. Energy grantee, 1979-82; Petroleum Research Fund-Am. Chem. Soc. grantee, 1968-72; Research Corp. grantee, 1971-74. Mem. Am. Phys. Soc., Am. Assn. Physics Tchrs., Optical Soc. Am., Am. Chem. Soc., Royal Chemistry Soc., Phi Beta Kappa, Sigma Xi. Office: Dept Chemistry U Nebr Lincoln NE 68588

ECKHARDT, WILLIAM E., manufacturing company executive; b. 1933. Student, Ill. Inst. Tech., 1954. With Tex. Instrument Co., Dallas, 1956-66; with Bundy Corp., Warren, Mich., 1966—, v.p. planning, 1973—, exec. v.p., 1974-78, pres., chief op. officer, from 1978, also bd. dirs. Office: Bundy Corp 12345 E Nine Mile Rd Warren MI 48090 *

ECKLAR, LAURA RUTH, public relations executive; b. Berea, Ohio, Dec. 19, 1950; d. Lawrence Paul and Ruth Ann (Bebenroth) Stelter; m. George Patrick Ecklar, Sept. 2, 1972; 1 son, Trent Edward. B.S. in Journalism, Ohio U., 1972. Advt. saleswoman, feature writer, Cable TV Program mag., Worthington, Ohio, 1976-77; asst. pub. info. adminstr. Mid-Ohio Regional Planning Commn., Columbus, 1977-79, pub. info. adminstr., 1979-82; pub. info. officer Columbus pub. schs., 1982—. Publicity chmn. Snyder for Council com., 1981; trustee Columbus Area Leadership Program, 1981-87; active YWCA, Met. Women's Ctr., Mt. Carmel Hosp. Aux. Recipient Outstanding Employee award Mid-Ohio Regional Planning Commn., 1979. Mem. Pub. Relations Soc. Am., Central Ohio Pub. Relations Soc., Nat. Sch. Pub. Relations Assn. (pres. Ohio chpt. 1983-84), Nat. Assn. Regional Councils (award of excellence, 1980, 81), Nat. Sch. Pub. Relations Assn. (Gold Medallion award 1983). Club: Met. (Columbus). Office: Columbus Public Schools 270 East State St Columbus OH 43215

ECKRICH, DONALD P., food company executive; b. Fort Wayne, Ind., Sept. 6, 1924; m. Barbara Eckrich; children: Emily, George, Joseph, Ellen, James, Eleanor, Louise, Diane. B.B.A., U. Mich., 1948. Plant mgr. Peter Eckrich & Sons, Inc., Kalamazoo, 1948-62; corp. gen. mgr. ops. Peter Eckrich & Sons, Inc., Fort Wayne, 1962-65, dir. ops., 1965-66, exec. v.p., 1966-69, pres., 1969-72, chmn. bd., chief exec. officer, 1972-75; exec. v.p. Beatrice Foods, Chgo., 1975-77, vice chmn., 1977-79, pres., chief operating officer, 1979-82; pres., chief exec. officer Central Soya Co., Inc., Fort Wayne, 1985—, dir., 1982—; dir. Gen. Telephone of Ind., Micro Data Base Systems, Lafayette, Ind., Harris-Kayot, Fort Wayne, Kanppen Milling Co., Augusta, Mich., Pioneer Hi-Bred Internat., Inc., Des Moines. Bd. dirs. St. Joseph Hosp., Fort Wayne, Fort Wayne Fine Arts, Cath. Social Services, Ft. Wayne, Jr. Achievement, Fort Wayne. Served with U.S. Army, 1943-45. Office: Central Soya Co Inc 1300 Fort Wayne Nat Bank Bldg Fort Wayne IN 46802 *

EDDY, ARTHUR RICHARD, JR., chemist, chemical engineer; b. Buffalo, Oct. 15, 1944; s. Arthur Richard and Ethel Aurellia (Stemler) E.; m. Judith Jean Kane, Oct. 4, 1969; children: Amy Renee, Jennifer Alison, Arthur Richard III. Student, Canisius Coll., 1962-65; BS in Chemistry, SUNY, Buffalo, 1969. Asst. scientist Ortho Diagnostics, Raritan, N.J., 1973-74; area supr. Buffalo Gen. Hosp., 1974-78; sr. assoc. research scientist Miles Labs., Elkhart, Ind., 1978-81; sr. chemist Graphic Controls, Buffalo, 1981-83, engr. quality assurance, reliability, 1983-86; sr. engr. Bard Critical Care, Lombard, Ill., 1986—; Faculty Sch. Med. Tech. Buffalo Gen. Hosp., 1974-78. Inventor in field. Vol. United Way, Buffalo, 1983-84. Mem. Am. Chem. Soc., Am. Assn. for Clin. Chemistry, Assn. for Advancement of Med. Instrumentation. Republican. Roman Catholic. Avocations: tennis, softball, chess, pinochle, paleontology. Home: 1301 Galena Ct Naperville IL 60565 Office: Bard Critical Care 331 S Eisenhower Ln Lombard IL 60148

EDELEN, MARY BEATY, state legislator; b. Vermillion, S.D., Dec. 9, 1944; d. Donald William and Marjorie (Heckel) Beaty; m. Joseph Ruey Edelen, Jr., June 8, 1968; children: Audra Angelica, Anthony Callaghan, Jarrod Arthur. Student Cottey Coll., Nevada, Mo., 1963-64; BA, U. S.D., 1967; MA, Trinity U., San Antonio, 1971. Asst. med. librarian U. S.D., Vermillion, 1965-67; lectr. U. S.D., Vermillion, 1969-70, Yankton (S.D.) Coll., 1973-74; mem. S.D. Ho. of Reps., 1972-80, 82—. Vice chmn. Clay County Reps., Vermillion, 1982—; mem. exec. com. Southeastern Council of Govts.; mem. U. S.D. Community Edn. Adv. Council; mem. S.D. Safety Council's Restraint Coalition, S.D. Autocap Panel. Recipient Burgess Book award U. S.D., 1966; S.D. Safety Council award, 1984, Friends of Library award S.D. Library Assn., 1986, Legis. Leadership award Mountain Plains Library Assn., 1986. Mem. Nat. Order Women Legislators (v.p. 1983-84, pres. 1985-86), Nat. Conf. State Legislators (com. children and youth 1983—), AAUW (life), U. S.D. Alumni Assn. (recorder), Vermillion C. of C., Zeta Phi Eta. Mem. United Ch. of Christ. Lodges: Order Eastern Star (worthy matron), PEO. Avocations: running, camping, snowmobiling. Home: 311 Canby St Vermillion SD 57069

EDELMAN, DIANE LYNN, human resource consultant,infosystems specialist; b. Chgo., Aug. 11, 1956; d. Donald R. and Harriette P. (Duncan) E. B.S. in Math., Chgo. State U., 1977. Systems analyst Zurich Am., Chgo., 1978-80; account mgr. Cyborg Systems, Chgo., 1980-83; sr. systems analyst Marsh & McLennan, Chgo., 1983; mgmt. info. systems mgr. Saxon Paint, Chgo., 1983-85; account mgr., cons. ISI, Downers Grove, Ill., 1985-86; pres. Edelman & Assocs., Ltd., Hinsdale, Ill., 1986—. Vol. Starlight Found. Mem. Micronet Computer Cons., U.S. Polo Assn., Hinsdale C. of C., Kappa Delta Pi. Episcopalian. Club: Oak Brook Polo (Ill.) (mem. ladies com., membership com.). Avocations: polo, architectural art.

EDEN, REBECCA PLOTKIN, nursing educator; b. Youngstown, Ohio, June 22, 1922; d. Benjamin L. and Frieda (Schwartz) Plotkin; children—Samuel W., David N., Sheryl R., Diane H. R.N., St. Luke's Hosp. Sch. Nursing, 1943; B.S.N., Case Western Res. U., 1949. Staff, head nurse St. Luke's Hosp., Cleve., 1943-44; staff nurse Mt. Sinai Hosp., Cleve., part-time 1944-46; instr. St. John's Hosp. Nursing, Cleve., 1949-50, Jane Addams Sch. Practical Nursing, Cleve., 1959-71, dir., 1971-85; ret., 1985; mem. Ohio Bd. Nursing Edn. and Nurse Registration, 1976-80, 81-85, pres., 1978-80; mem. com. Nat. Council State Bds. Nursing. Served with Nurse Corps, U.S. Army, 1944-46. Mem. Am. Vocat. Edn. Assn., Ohio Vocat. Edn. Assn., Nat. League Nursing, Ohio Student Fin. Aid Adminstrs., Midwest Student Fin. Aid Adminstrs., Nat. Assn. Practical Nurse Edn., Ohio Practical Nurse Educators Assn., Jewish War Vets Aux. (pres. 1962-64, 69-70). Democrat. Jewish. Club: ORT. Home: 3271 Warrensville Center Rd Apt 17D Shaker Heights OH 44122

EDENS, DAVID, educator; b. Sumter, S.C., Feb. 11, 1926; s. Henry Timmons and Lila Mae E.; m. Virginia Deane Buckner, July 7, 1950; children: Deena, Debra. AA, Mars Hill Coll., 1948; BA, Wake Forest U., 1950; M Div, So. Bapt. Theol Sem., 1953, ThM, 1954; postgrad., Merrill Palmer Inst., 1954-55; EdD, Columbia U., 1957. Dir. counseling Trinity Bapt. Ch., San Antonio, 1957-67; prof. family life edn., dir. marriage and family program Stephens Coll., Columbia, Mo., 1967—. Author: Sexual Understanding Among Young Adults, 1959, Teen Sense, 1971, The Changing Me, 1973; (with Virginia Buckner Edens) Why God Gave Children Parents, 1966, Making the Most of Family Worship, 1968. Contbr. articles to profl. jours. Pres. San Antonio Mental Health Assn., 1960-61, Mo. Council on Family Relations, 1968-69, Planned Parenthood Cen. Mo., 1969-70. Served with USNR, 1944-46. Fellow Am. Assn. Marriage and Family Counselors. Home: 817 Colgate St Columbia MO 65201 Office: Stephens Coll 1200 E Broadway Columbia MO 65201

EDFORS, HUGH TERRANCE, real estate consultant, lawyer; b. Saginaw, Mich., Nov. 7, 1946; s. Hugh Wayne and Gertrude May (Forbes) E. BA, Northwestern U., 1969; MS, U. Wis., 1974; MBA, U. Chgo., 1975; JD, DePaul U., 1979. Appraiser, constrn. insp. Home Fed. Savs. and Loan Assn., Chgo., 1970-72; real estate cons. Real Estate Research Corp., Chgo., 1975-80; assoc. Roan & Grossman, Chgo., 1980-82; pvt. practice real estate cons., sole practice law Chgo., 1982—; co-founder Sheffield Equities, Inc., Chgo., 1982-84. Mem. ABA, Chgo. Bar Assn., Ill. State Bar Assn., Internat. Real Estate Fedn., Real Estate Securities and Syndication Inst., Appraisers, Chgo. Real Estate Bd. Republican. Lutheran. Avocations: antique and classic automobiles, travel. Home and Office: 1150 N Lake Shore Dr 18K Chicago IL 60611

EDGAR, IRVING ISKOWITZ, psychiatrist; b. Rozwadow, Poland, Austria-Hungary, July 4, 1902; Came to U.S., 1910; s. Asher Laser and Bella Gitel (Schlussel) Itzkowitz; m. Gertrude Forman, Nov. 6, 1971; children: Joy Vronsky, David L., Richard S. MB, Wayne State U., 1926, BA, 1927, MD, 1927, MA, 1933. Diplomate Am. Bd. Neurology and Psychiatry. Intern Grace Hosp., Detroit, 1926-27; pvt. practice medicine specializing in psychiatry Detroit, 1927-86; med. dir. Island View Adolescent Ctr., Detroit, 1971-74; cons. various hosps., Detroit. Author: Shakespeare, Medicine and Psychiatry, 1970, Essays in English Literature and History, 1971, Origins of the Healing Art, 1978, Meditations in an Anatomy Laboratory and Other Poems, 1979, A History of Early Jewish Physicians in the State of Michigan, 1982. Mem. exec. council Am. Jewish Hist. Soc., 1975; mem. Jewish Hist. Soc. Mich. Fellow Am. Coll. Physicians, Am. Psychiat. Assn. (diplomate). Home: 29233 Wellington Ct #61 Southfield MI 48034

EDGAR, JAMES, secretary of state Illinois; b. Vinita, Okla., July 22, 1946; m. Brenda Smith; children: Brad, Elizabeth. Grad., Eastern Ill. U., 1968;

postgrad., U. Ill., Sangamon State U., 1971-74. Legis. intern pres. pro tem Ill. Senate, 1968; key asst. to speaker ho. Ill. Ho. of Reps., 1972-73; aide to pres. Ill. Senate, 1974, to Ho. minority leader, 1976; mem. Ill. Ho. of Reps., from 1977; dir. legis. affairs Ill. Gov., 1979-80; sec. state State of Ill., 1981—. Precinct committeeman, treas. Coles County Republican Com., 1974; dir. state service Nat. Conf. State Legislatures, 1975, 76; mem. Ill. Ho. Rep. Campaign Com., 1977-79. Mem. Coles County Hist. Soc. (pres. 1976-79). Baptist. Office: State House Room 213 Springfield IL 62756 *

EDGAR, KEITH ARMON, accountant; b. Royal Oak, Mich., Mar. 5, 1956; s. Phillip Thomas and Betty Jane (Snyder) E.; m. Joanne Valarie Newberry, Sept. 18, 1977; children: Joshua Keith, Jordan Lee. Student, Cen. State U., Edmond, Okla., 1977-78; BS in Acctg., Andrews U., 1979. CPA, Mich. Staff acct. Maner, Costerisan & Ellis, P.C., Lansing, Mich., 1979-80, in-charge acct., 1980-82, audit supr., 1982—. Mem. Am. Inst. CPA's, Mich. Assn. CPA's, Lansing Accts. Assn., Delta Mu Delta, Alpha Chi. Republican. Adventist. Avocations: camping, sports, softball, ice hockey. Home: Quiet Cove 31 Laingsburg MI 48848 Office: Maner Costerisan & Ellis PC 6105 W St Joseph Suite 202 Lansing MI 48917

EDGELL, GEORGE PAUL, lawyer; b. Dallas, Mar. 9, 1937; s. George Paul and Sarah Elizabeth (McDonald) E.; B.S. in Aero. Engring., U. Ill., 1960; J.D., Georgetown U., 1967; M.B.A., Roosevelt U., 1983, B.G.S. in Computer Sci., 1986; m. Karin Jane Williams; 1 son, Scott Rickard. Admitted to Va. bar, 1967, D.C. bar, 1968, Ill. bar, 1980; patent examiner U.S. Patent Office, Washington, 1963-65; ptnr. firm Schuyler, Birch, McKie & Beckett, Washington, 1969-80, assoc., 1965-69; group patent counsel Gould Inc., Rolling Meadows, Ill., 1980-86, asst. chief patent counsel, 1986—. Vol. tutor Hopkins Ho., 1968-69; officer St. Stephen's Dads' Club, 1975-77. Served with USMC, 1960-63. Mem. ABA, D.C., Ill., Va. bar assns., Am. Intellectual Property Law Assn., Licensing Execs. Soc. Republican. Presbyterian. Clubs: Army Navy Country, Meadow. Home: 5403 Chateau Dr Rolling Meadows IL 60008 Office: Gould Inc Intellectual Property Law Dept 1 Gould Center Rolling Meadows IL 60008

EDGERTON, F(REDRICK) VAN, college administrator; b. Allegan, Mich., Nov. 27, 1947; s. Fredrick G. and Gertrude (VandeBunte) E.; B.A., Alma Coll., 1974; M.S.A., Central Mich. U., 1982; m. Elizabeth Mary Boylon, Dec. 28, 1985. Asst dir. placement Alma (Mich.) Coll., 1975, coordinator practicums, 1975-83, dir. placement, 1977-86, asst. to v.p. for student life and career programs, 1982-86, dir. corp. and found. relations, 1986—. Bd. dirs. Alma Highland Festival and Games, 1979-83, pres., 1981-82; pres. bd. dirs. Mid-Mich. Community Action Council, 1982-84; mem. Greater Gratiot Devel., Inc., 1982-84, CAPC Pvt. Industry Council, 1983-86. Served with AUS, 1969-72. Decorated Bronze Star. Recipient Disting. Service award Jaycees, 1983. Presbyterian. Home: 522 River Ave Apt. #1 Alma MI 48801 Office: Alma Coll Reid-Knox Bldg Alma MI 48801-1599

EDIDIN, ANSEL HOWARD, accountant; b. Chgo., Apr. 2, 1939; s. Louis and Dorothy (Rosen) E.; m. Audrey Johns, July 26, 1964; children: Laura, Eric. AB, U. Chgo., 1960, MBA, 1963. Acct. mgr. J.K. Lasser & Co., Chgo., 1961-75; ptnr. B. L. Resenberg & Co., Chgo., 1975-83, Abrams & Singer Ltd., Chgo., 1983-87, Maller, Edidin & Co., Northbrook, Ill., 1987—. Served as sgt. U.S. Army, 1962. Mem. Am. Inst. CPA's, Inst. CPA's. Jewish. Club: East Bank (Chgo.). Lodge: B'Nai Brith. Avocation: horseback riding. Home: 356 Anjou Dr Northbrook IL 60062 Office: Maller Edidin & Co 555 Skokie Blvd Northbrook IL 60062

EDISON, BERNARD ALAN, retail apparel company executive; b. Atlanta, 1928; s. Irving and Beatrice (Chanin) E.; m. Marilyn S. Wewers, Apr. 26, 1975. B.A., Harvard U., 1949, M.B.A., 1951. With Edison Bros. Stores Inc., St. Louis, 1951—; asst. v.p. Edison Bros. Stores Inc., 1957-58, v.p. leased depts., 1958-67, v.p., asst. treas., 1967-68, pres., 1968-87, chmn. fin. com., 1987—, also dir.; dir. Gen. Am. Life Ins. Co., Mercantile Bank, N.A., Mercantile Bancorp, Anheuser-Busch Cos., Inc. Office: Edison Bros Stores Inc 501 N Broadway Saint Louis MO 63102

EDISON, JULIAN I., retail company executive; b. St. Louis, May 12, 1929; s. Mark A. and Ida (Edison) E.; m. Hope Rabb, Jan. 4, 1959; children: Mark, Aaron. A.B., Harvard U., 1951, M.B.A., 1953. With Edison Bros. Stores, Inc., St. Louis, 1955—, v.p., 1964-74, exec. v.p., 1974, chmn. bd., 1974—; chmn. bd. Edison Bros. Shoe Stores, Inc., St. Louis, 1983—, pres., 1963-83; dir. Boatmen's Bancshares, Inc., Boatmen's Nat. Bank St. Louis, The Stop and Shop Cos., Inc., Boston. Pres. Assoc. of St. Louis U. Libraries, Inc., 1967-69; bd. dirs. Barnes Hosp., St. Louis, Jewish Fedn., St. Louis, 1967-76, 78-80, John Burroughs Sch., 1978-84; mem. Pres.'s Council, St. Louis U., 1967—; co-chmn. Interracial Council for Bus. Opportunity of St. Louis, 1969-72; bd. trustees St. Louis Art Mus., 1969-75, KETC-TV, 1977-84. Served with U.S. Army, 1953-55. Mem. Footwear Retailers Am. (pres. 1976-77), Am. Retail Fedn. (dir.). Clubs: Westwood Country, Mo. Athletic. Home: 16 Dromara Rd Saint Louis MO 63124 Office: Edison Bros Stores Inc 501 N Broadway Saint Louis MO 63102 *

EDISON, STEPHEN WILLIAM, jewelry manufacturing financial executive; b. Grand Rapids, Mich., Jan. 4, 1958; s. William Haynes and Patricia (Hannagan) E. BS, U. Va., 1980. CPA, Mich. Staff acct. Arthur Andersen & Co., Grand Rapids, 1980-83; controller Petco, Inc., Grand Rapids, 1983-86; fin. officer Terryberry Co., Grand Rapids, 1986—. Commr. City of East Grand Rapids, 1985—; football coach East Grand Rapids Sch. System, 1980—. Mem. Am. Inst. CPA's, Mich. Assn. CPA's. Republican. Episcopalian. Office: Terryberry Co 2033 Oak Industrial Dr Grand Rapids MI 49505

EDLAND, ROBERT WILLIAM, radiation oncologist; b. Madison, Wis., Feb. 14, 1932; s. Alfred O. and Ella W. (Freund) E.; m. Carole F.McGinley, Sept. 17, 1955; children: Christopher, Anne, Christina, David. BS, U. Wis., 1953, MD, 1956. Diplomate Am. Bd. Radiology. Chmn. radiation oncology dept. Gundersen Clinic, La Crosse, Wis.; clin. prof. radiation oncology U. Wis., Madison, 1978-86, radiation oncology Med. Coll. Wis., 1983-86. Contbr. articles to profl. jour. Served to lt. col. USMC, 1956-67. Fellow Am. Coll. Radiology (mem. steering com. 1985-87); mem. Am. soc. Therapeutic Radiology and Oncology (pres. 1986-87). Home: 2200 Hickory Ln La Crosse WI 54601 Office: Gundersen Clinic 1836 S Ave La Crosse WI 54601

EDLEBECK, MARY JEAN, small business owner; b. Oconto Falls, Wis., Oct. 15, 1934; d. Magnus and Hazel Rose (George) Peterson; m. Edward Edlebeck, July 28, 1956; children: Anton, Linda, Cynthia, Dean, Sharon, Dennis. Grad. high sch., Oconto Falls, 1953. Receptionist, sec. Engman Taylor Co., Milw., 1954-56; typist Pleuss and Pleuss Pub. Acct., Milw., 1959-61; dietician Falls Nursing Home, Oconto Falls, 1973-75, Community Meml. Hosp., Oconto Falls, 1978-79; prin. Kiddie Korner Day-Care, Oconto Falls, 1981—. sec., treas. Boy Scouts Am., Milw., 1969-72; pres., tchr. single parent group, Oconto County, 1973-75; founder Youth Ctr., Oconto Falls, 1979-81. Republican. Roman Catholic. Avocations: crossword puzzles, walking, spectator sports.

EDMUNDS, GAIL RICHARD, surgical sales representative; b. Decatur, Ill., July 9, 1951; s. Russell and Eunice Evelyn (Weerts) E.; m. Karla Lynn Potrafka, Aug. 19, 1972 (div. Sept. 1978); m. Ann Marie Biddy, July 5, 1986. BS, Ill. State U., 1973; postgrad., Washington U., St. Louis, 1980-81. Gen. sales rep. The Upjohn Co., Kalamazoo, 1977-81, hosp. sales rep., 1981-85, surg. sales rep., 1985-87; rep. Health Scis. Assoc., 1987—. Mem. St. Louis Arthroscopy Soc., St. Louis. Orthopaedic Assts. Assn., St. Louis Soc. Hosp. Pharmacists, St. Louis Triumph Owners Assn. Home: 3405 A Pestalozzi Saint Louis MO 63118 Office: The Upjohn Co 11710 Borman Dr Saint Louis MO 63141

EDNEY, WILLIAM MILTON, retail executive; b. Cozad, Nebr., Dec. 20, 1925; s. Fred and Ferne (Lippincott) E.; m. Olga Schaffer, Apr. 30, 1950; children: Douglas, Cynthia, Debra. BA, Chadron (Nebr.) State Coll., 1950. Acct. Anderson's, Inc., Pickstonw, S.D., 1950-53; sales rep. Edney Distbg. Co., Inc., Huron, S.D., 1955-60; pres., gen. mgr. Edney Distbg. Co., Inc., Huron, 1960—. Served with USN, 1943-46, PTO. Mem. Farm Equipment Wholesalers Assn., Nat. Assn. Wholesalers, Am. Legion. Democrat. Methodist. Lodges: Masons, Shriners (local pres. 1972), Elks. Home: Rural Rt 1 Box 147C Huron SD 57350 Office: Edney Distbg Co Inc Hwy 14 E Huron SD 57350

EDSALL, JOHN FREDERICK, landscape architect, land planner; b. Albany, N.Y., Feb. 6, 1941; s. Leslie and Esther Lulu (Blood) E.; m. Deborah Christine Rose, June 21, 1964; 1 child, Scott Christopher. BS, Mich. State U., 1963, M in Landscape Architecture, 1965. Registered landscape architect, Ohio, W.Va., Mass. City planner I Columbus (Ohio) Div. City Planning, 1965; asst. landscape architect Ohio State U., Columbus, 1965-66; assoc. Carroll V. Hill Assocs., Columbus, 1966-68, Parkins, Rogers & Assocs., Columbus, 1968-70, Schooley Cornelius Assocs., Columbus, 1970-73; ptnr. Edsall & Assocs., Columbus, 1973—; vis. lectr. Columbus Tech. Inst., 1979, Ohio State U., Columbus, 1980, Mich. State U., East Lansing, 1984; planner-in-charge Ohio Dept. Devel., Columbus, 1969. cons. Godman Guild Assn., Columbus, 1974-80, Players Theater Columbus, 1980, Victorian Village Soc./Hunter House, Columbus, 1982; speaker Columbus Pub. Library, 1979. Recipient project design awards various orgns., 1975—. Mem. AIA, Am. Soc. Landscape Architects (pres. Buckeye sect. Ohio chpt. 1967-68), Am. Planning Assn., Nat. Recreation and Park Assn., Nat. Assn. Indsl. and Office Parks, Ohio Planning Conf., Ohio Soc. Cons. Planners, Ohio Parks and Recreation Assn., Southside Bus. and Indls. Assn., Sigma Lambda Alpha. Republican. Methodist. Avocations: photography, woodworking, automobile restoration, travel. Home and Office: 754 Neil Ave Columbus OH 43215

EDSON, WAYNE E., dentist, consultant; b. Marinette, Wis., July 4, 1947; s. E.J. Edson and Anita (Pearson) Edson Sebero; m. Linda Mary Hullison, Apr. 3, 1971; children: William Earl, Erin Hullison Edson. B.S., U. Wis.-Madison/Milw., 1973; D.D.S., Northwestern U., 1977. Pvt. dentist, Winnetka, Ill., 1982—. Pres. Kenilworth United Fund, 1983-84, bd. dirs., 1981—; com. mem. Kenilworth Baseball, 1978-83. Served with USN, 1965-72. Mem. Chgo. Dental Soc., Ill. State Dental Soc., ADA. Roman Catholic. Avocations: hunting; fishing. Clubs: John Evans of Northwestern U., G.V. Black Soc. of Northwestern U., Kenilworth. Home: 624 Exmoor Rd Kenilworth IL 60043 Office: 22 Greenbay Rd Winnetka IL 60093

EDWARDS, ANDREW WALLACE, social worker, educator, clergyman; b. Danville, Ill., Dec. 16, 1946; s. Simeon and Edna (Henderson) E.; m. Anna Bell, Aug. 2, 1980; children—Andrew Wallace, Mark, Gregory. B.A. in Sociology, William Jewell Coll., 1969; M.S.W., U. Kans., 1971; Ph.D., Kans. State U., 1978; postgrad. Central Bapt. Theol. Sem., 1981; M.Div., Ashland Theol. Sem., 1987. Social worker Jackson County (Mo.) Juvenile Ct. Services, 1971-72; asst. prof. social work and sociology Park Coll., Mo., 1972-75, U. Kans., 1975-77; assoc. prof. child, family and community services Sangamon State (Ill.) U., 1978-81, U. Nebr., Omaha, 1980-81; faculty Cleve. State U., 1982—, prof. social work, 1985—. Project dir., co-founder Project Second Chance; bd. dirs. Lindwood Community YMCA, Kansas City, Mo., 1973-76, Black Adoptions Program and Services, Kansas City, Kans., 1974-77, Opportunities Industrialization Ctrs. Am., Mo., 1974-76, Sangamon Family Services Ctr., 1979-81, Good Samaritan Youth Ctr., Cleve., 1983-85. Served to capt. M.C., USAR, 1970-76. Recipient civic community service awards. Mem Nat. Assn. Christian Social Workers, NAACP, Nat. Assn. Black Social Workers, Assn. Social and Behavioral Scientists, Nat. Acad. Counselors and Family Therapists, Phi Delta Kappa. Baptist. Contbr. articles to profl. jours. Office: Cleve State U Dept Social Services Cleveland OH 44115

EDWARDS, BENJAMIN FRANKLIN, III, investment banker; b. St. Louis, Oct. 26, 1931; s. Presley William and Virginia (Barker) E.; m. Joan Moberly, June 13, 1953; children: Scott P., Benjamin Franklin IV, Pamela M. Edwards Bunn, Susan B. B.A., Princeton U., 1953. With A.G. Edwards & Sons, Inc., St. Louis, 1956—; pres. A.G. Edwards & Sons, Inc., 1967—, chmn., 1983—, also chief exec. officer; bd. dirs. Jefferson Bank and Trust Co., Psychol. Assocs., Helig-Meyers, Inc., N.Y. Stock Exchange, Washington U., St. Louis Art Mus., Mo. Hist. Soc. Mem. Mo. Hist. Soc. Served with USNR, 1953-56. Mem. Investment Bankers Assn. (gov. 1968—), Securities Industry Assn. (gov. 1974-81, chmn. 1980—). Presbyterian. Clubs: Old Warson Country (St. Louis); Bogey. Office: AG Edwards & Sons Inc 1 N Jefferson Ave Saint Louis MO 63103

EDWARDS, BROOKS RICHARD, cement manufacturing company executive; b. Easton, Pa., Apr. 29, 1930; s. Warren D. and Florence M. (Crout) E.; m. Ruth Richter, Sept. 29, 1956; children: Lori Jean, Kevin Brooks. Student, Muhlenberg Coll., 1948-50; BS in Commerce, Rider Coll., 1956. Sales rep. NCR, Allentown, Pa., 1956-60; mgr. data processing Alpha Portland Cement Co., Easton, 1960-67, asst v.p. mktg., 1968-72; v.p. Alpha Portland Cement Co., Frederick, Md., 1972-82; sr. analyst Ingersoll-Rand Co., Phillipsburg, N.J., 1967-68; sales mgr. Coplay Cement Co., Frederick, 1983-85; v.p. mktg. and sales Coplay Cement Co., Speed, Ind., 1985—; mem. Frederick County adv. bd. Md. Nat. Bank, 1980-85. V.p. Evang. Luth. Ch., Frederick, 1977-79; bd. dirs. United Way, 1977; bd. assocs. Hood Coll., Frederick, 1980-82; trustee Frederick Meml. Hosp., 1980-85; mem. exec. council Boy Scouts Am., 1986. Served with USAF, 1951-53. Mem. Md. C. of C. (v.p. 1978-80, dir. 1977-80), Frederick County C. of C. (pres. 1976, dir. 1974-76), So. Ind. C. of C. (bd. dirs. 1985—, v.p. 1986—). Republican. Lodges: Rotary (pres. Frederick club 1979-80, bd. dirs. 1977-80), Elks, Masons. Office: Coplay Cement Co Hwy 31 Speed IN 47172

EDWARDS, BRUCE RANDY, bank executive; b. Vandalia, Ill., July 2, 1954; s. Bruce R. and Helen D. (Walker) E.; m. Cheryl L. Henderson, May 29, 1974 (div. July 1978); m. Karolyn K. Kelley, May 10, 1980; children: Joe, Tim, Amy. AA, Lake Land Coll., 1974; degree, Ill. Bankers Sch., 1979, Prochnow Sch. Banking, 1983. Asst. v.p. 1st Nat. Bank of Vandalia, 1978-84, v.p., 1984—. Treas. Vandalia Retail Merchants, 1983-86, treas. Vandalia Youth Orgn., 1986; commr. Vandalia Park Dist., 1978-86; bd. dirs. Family YMCA of Fayette County, 1982-86; mem. Vandalia Vol. Fire Dept., 1980-86. Mem. Ind. Community Banks Ill. (mem. pub. relations com 1984-86), Vandalia C. of C. (treas. 1986), Jaycees (pres. 1979-80). Democrat. Methodist. Lodges: Lions (bd. dirs. 1982-83), Masons, Moose. Home: 1409 W Jefferson Vandalia IL 62471 Office: 1st Nat Bank Vandalia 432 W Gallatin Vandalia IL 62471

EDWARDS, CHARLES ARTHUR, fund raising consultant; b. Chgo., May 7, 1940; s. Arthur Lewis and Kathleen (McGinnis) E.; m. Sandra Rae Hughes, July 14, 1984; children by previous marriage—Valerie Kathleen, Jennifer Anne. A.B., U. Chgo., 1965. Asst. dir. devel. Smith Coll., Northampton, Mass., 1966-69, Conn. Coll., New London, 1969-71; dir. devel. and pub. affairs Wadsworth Atheneum, Hartford, Conn., 1971-78; dir. devel. Barnard Coll., N.Y.C., 1979-81; v.p. Charles R. Feldstein & Co., Chgo., 1982-84; pres. The Edwards Group, Hinsdale, Ill., 1984—. Contbr. articles to profl. jours. Mem. exec. com. Nat. Alumni Fund Bd., U. Chgo., 1975-77, Conn. Gov.'s Com. on Arts and Tourism, 1973-75; mem. Nat. Alumni Cabinet, U. Chgo., 1969-72; chmn. New Eng. Conf. Devel. Group, Am. Assn. Mus., 1977-78. Served with U.S. Army, 1958-62. Decorated Chevalier Order of Polonia Restituta (London). Mem. Nat. Soc. Fund Raising Execs. (cert., bd. dirs. 1986—), Am. Assn. Mus., Art Mus. Devel. Assn. (pres. 1976-77), Intelligence Corps Assn. (hon. life), Newport Artillery Co. (hon.). Congregationalist. Clubs: DuPage; Princeton of N.Y. Office: Edwards Group PO Box 153 Hinsdale IL 60521

EDWARDS, CHARLES C., JR., newspaper publisher; b. Denver, Jan. 5, 1947; s. Charles C. and Sue Cowles (Kruidenier) E.; m. Harriet Hubbell, June 24, 1979; children—Hayley, Emily. B.A. in History, U. Colo., 1970; postgrad. Drake U., 1973. Advt. salesman Des Moines Register, 1970-74, news reporter, 1974-79, circulation dir., 1979-82, advt. dir., 1982-84, mktg. dir., 1984—. V.p. Des Moines Art Ctr., 1985; trustee Gardner Cowles Found., Inc., Des Moines; bd. dirs. Iowa Coll. Found., Des Moines. Republican. Congregationalist. Avocations: running; tennis; golf. Office: The Des Moines Register Des Moines Register & Tribune Co 715 Locust St PO Box 957 Des Moines IA 50309

EDWARDS, DORIS STECK, nursing educator; b. Montgomery County, Ohio, Dec. 27, 1944; d. Russell Luther and Elsie Elizabeth (Schumaker) Steck; m. Neil Kenneth Edwards, Sept. 17, 1966; children: Jeffrey Kenneth, Steven Donald. Diploma, Miami Valley Hosp. Sch. Nursing, 1965; BSN summa cum laude, U. Cin., 1976, EdD, 1984; MS, Wright State U., 1980. RN. Head nurse Dayton State Hosp. (Ohio), 1965-66; clinic nurse Hamilton County Ct., Cin., 1967-68; nursing instr. Jewish Hosp. Sch. Nursing, Cin., 1976-80; nursing instr. U. Cin., 1980-82, asst. prof. nursing, 1982-86,assoc. prof. nursing, 1986-87, sophomore dept. chmn., 1983-87, exec. com. women's studies faculty, 1983-87; prof., dean Capital U., Columbus, Ohio, 1987—. Mem. Southwestern Ohio Nurses Assn. (bd. dirs. 1979-82, pres. 1982-84, legis. liaison 1982-83), Am. Nurses Assn., Council Nurse Researchers, Ohio Nurses Assn. (bd. dirs. 1983—, Mary/Hamer Greenwood award), Assembly of Nurse Educators (chmn.), Assembly of Nurse Researchers, Assn. Women Faculty U. Cin. (bd. dirs.), Sigma Theta Tau, Kappa Delta Pi, Phi Delta Kappa. Lutheran. Home: 5731 Rushwood Dr Dublin OH 43017 Office: Capital Univ Columbus OH 43209

EDWARDS, GEORGE CLIFTON, JR., judge; b. Dallas, Aug. 6, 1914; s. George Clifton and Octavia (Nichols) E.; m. Margaret McConnell, Apr. 10, 1939; children: George Clifton III, James McConnell. B.A., So. Meth. U., 1933; M.A., Harvard U., 1934; J.D., Detroit Coll. Law, 1949. Bar: Mich. 1944. Coll. sec. League Indsl. Democracy, 1934-35; prodn. worker Kelsey Hayes Wheel Co., 1936; rep. UAW-CIO, 1937, dir. welfare dept., 1938-39; dir., sec. Detroit Housing Commn., 1940-41; mem. Detroit Common Council, 1941-49, pres., 1945-49; with firm Edwards & Bohn, Detroit, 1946-50, Rothe, Marston, Edwards and Bohn, 1950-51; probate judge charge Wayne County Juvenile Ct., 1951-54; judge Jud. Circuit, Wayne County, 1954-56; justice Supreme Ct., Mich., 1956-62; commr. of police City Detroit, 1962-63; judge U.S. Ct. Appeals 6th Circuit, 1963—, chief judge, 1979-83; chmn. com. adminstrn. criminal laws Jud. Conf. U.S., 1966-70; mem. Nat. Com. Reform of Fed. Criminal Laws, 1967-71. Author: The Police on the Urban Frontier, 1968, (with others) The Law of Criminal Correction, 1963, Pioneer-at-Law, 1974; also articles on crime and delinquency. Chmn. S.E. Mich. Cancer Crusade, 1950-51; chmn. 13th Congressional Dist. Democratic party Wayne County, 1950-51. Served from pvt. to lt., inf. AUS, 1943-46. Recipient award for community work for social progress Workmen's Circle, 1949; award for community work for civil rights St. Cyprian's Episcopal Ch., 1950; Americanism award Jewish War Vets., 1953; award for outstanding achievement juvenile rehab. VFW, 1953; St. Peter's medal for outstanding service to youth St. Peter's Episcopal Ch., Detroit, 1956; August Vollmer award Am. Soc. Criminology, 1966; Judiciary award Assn. Fed. Investigators, 1971. Mem. VFW, Am. Legion, Am., Mich., Detroit bar assns., Nat. Council Judges, Nat. Council Crime and Delinquency, Am. Law Inst., Phi Beta Kappa, Kappa Sigma. Democrat. Episcopalian. Club: Masons. Home: 4057 Egbert Cincinnati OH 45220 Office: US Courthouse Cincinnati OH 45202

EDWARDS, HARRY LESTER, real estate broker; b. Kansas City, Kans., Apr. 30, 1948; s. Erma (Montgomery) E.; m. Franchester Smith. BA, Ottawa U., 1971. Cert. real estate broker; cert. property mgr. Pres. H.L. Edwards Realty, 1973—. Bd. dirs. Rehab. Loan Corp., Kansas City, Mo., East Meyer Community Assn., Kansas City, Mo. Recipient Good Neighbor award East Meyer Community Assn., 1985. Mem. Nat. Assn. Realtors, Inst. Real Estate Mgmt. Avocations: swimming, reading, computer programming. Office: 7225 Prospect Kansas City MO 64132

EDWARDS, HENRY DEXTER, hospital and homes administrator; b. San Francisco, Aug. 2, 1938; s. Roy Waldrup and Ruby (Lee) E.; m. Beverlee Jean Salts, Oct. 10, 1964; children—Tara, Jason. B.A., San Francisco State Coll., 1964; M.A., Chico State Coll., 1970; Ed.D., Calif. Coast U., 1983. Teaching and adminstrv. credentials, Calif., N.D. Tchr., South San Francisco Unified Sch. Dist., 1964-66, Yuba City (Calif.) Unified Sch. Dist., 1966-70, prin., 1971-75; supt. Manzanita Sch. Dist., Gridley, Calif., 1970-71; prin. Western Placer Unified Sch. Dist., Lincoln, Calif., 1975-81; adminstr. Anne Carlsen Sch., Lutheran Hosps. and Homes Soc., Jamestown, N.D., 1981—; recreation dir. Brisbane Sch. Dist. (Calif.), 1958-62; chief negotiator Western Placer Unified Sch. Dist., 1981; state coop. dir. State of Calif., 1979-81; mem. curriculum and instrn. com. Assn. Calif. Sch. Adminstrs., 1971-75. Mem. Greater N.D. Assn.: State C. of C. (bd. dirs.). Author: History of Brisbane School District, 1970, Anne Carlsen School, 1983. Served with USN, 1962-64. Mem. Nat. Assn. Pvt. Schs. for Exceptional Children (1st v.p., bd. dirs. 1987—). Republican. Lodges: Lions, Elks, Masons, Rotary, Shriners (pres. Central Sacramento Valley 1972). Home: 1021 Eighth Ave NW Jamestown ND 58401 Office: Lutheran Hosps and Homes Soc Anne Carlsen Sch 301 7th Ave NW Jamestown ND 58401

EDWARDS, HOMER FLOYD, JR., educator; b. Forsyth, Ga., June 25, 1918; s. Homer Floyd and Mary Beulah (Jay) E.; B.A., Emory U., 1947, M.A., 1948, Ph.D., 1964; m. Marjorie H. Duncan, Apr. 29, 1967; 1 son, Christopher B. Instr. classics Emory U., Atlanta, 1954-55, instr. French and German, Emory-at-Oxford, 1955-57; asst. prof. humanities Morehouse Coll., Atlanta, 1959-63, Wayne State U., Detroit, 1963-65; faculty, head dept. theoretical studies Cranbrook Acad. Art, Bloomfield Hills, Mich., 1967-75; asso. prof. humanities Wayne State U., 1965-80, prof., 1980—, chmn. dept. humanities, 1964-75; adj. prof. history U. Windsor (Ont., Can.), 1977-79; music critic Detroit Monitor, 1968—; dir. Passau-Augsburg program Mich. Consortium Medieval and Early Modern Studies, Detroit, 1977-82; dir. Consortium for Austro-Bavarian Studies, 1982—; asso. fellow U. Mich., 1978—. Served with AUS, 1941-45. Univ. fellow Emory U., 1958-59. Mem. AAUP, Am. Musicol. Soc., Am., Brit. socs. aesthetics, Assn. Gen. Studies, Coll. Art Assn., Mind Assn. (Eng.), Modern Lang. Assn., Am. Hist. Assn., Hist. Assn. (Eng.), Mich. Acad., Nat. Assn. Humanities Edn. Episcopalian. Clubs: Scarab; Faculty of Wayne State U. Home: 201 E Kirby St Apt 904 Detroit MI 48202

EDWARDS, IAN KEITH, obstetrician, gynecologist; b. Spartanburg, S.C., Mar. 2, 1926; s. James Smiley and Georgina (Waters) E.; m. Glenda Melissa Joselyn, Dec. 27, 1968; children—Darien, Jennifer, Carol, Terry. A.B., Duke U., 1949, M.D., 1953. Diplomate Am. Bd. Ob-Gyn. Spl. study pediatrics St. Bartholomew's Hosp., London, 1952; resident in ob-gyn Grady Meml. Hosp., Atlanta, 1955-58; chief ob-gyn Valley Forge Army Hosp., Pa., 1958-61; practice medicine specializing in ob-gyn Olney, Ill., 1969—; prnr. Trover Clinic, Madisonville, Ky., 1961-68, Weber Med. Clinic, Olney, 1969—; dir. dept. ob-gyn Weber Med. Clinic, 1970-74, 78-83, chmn. bd. dirs., 1983—, med. dir., 1987—; chief of staff Hopkins County Hosp., Ky., 1967-68, Richland Meml. Hosp., Olney, 1974-76; clin. instr. ob-gyn U. Ky. Med. Ctr., Lexington, 1965-68; cons. Childbirth Edn. League. Contbr. articles to med. jours. Mem. Found. com. Olney Central Coll. Served to capt. M.C., U.S. Army, 1954-55; Korea. Fellow Am. Coll. Obstetricians and Gynecologists (exec. com. Ill. sect.); mem. AMA, Phila. Obstet. Soc., S.E. Ill. Consortium Maternal and Fetal Welfare, Ill. Assn. Maternal and Child Health, N.Y. Acad. Scis., Am. Acad. Med. Dirs., Am. Group Practice Assn. (nat. mktg. com., clin. editorial cons.), Ill. Med. Soc., Hopkins County Med. Soc. (pres. 1968), Richland Med. Soc. (pres. 1974-76), Ill. Soc. Ob-Gyn., Am. Soc. Colposcopist and Cervical Pathologists., Am. Assn. Gynecol. Laparoscopists, Am. Legion, VFW. Democrat. Methodist. Office: Weber Med Clinic 1200 N East St Olney IL 62450

EDWARDS, JOSEPH CASTRO, physician; b. Springfield, Mo., Dec. 24, 1909; s. Lyman Paul and Lela (Bedell) E.; m. Virginia Anne Moser, Jan. 8, 1942; children: Virginia Lee, Joseph Byron, Jonathan Paul. A.B., U. Okla., 1930; M.D., Harvard, 1934. Diplomate Am. Bd. Internal Medicine. Tutorial fellow cardiology Dr. Paul D. White Mass. Gen. Hosp., 1934; intern Springfield (Mass.) Hosp., 1935; house physician med. service Barnes Hosp., St. Louis, 1936-37; Stroud fellow, resident Pa. Hosp., Phila., 1937-38; Eli Lilly fellow on pneumonia research Washington U. Med. Sch., St. Louis, 1939, Smith Kline and French fellow in hypertension, 1940, instr. clin. medicine, 1939-60, asst. prof. clin. medicine, 1960—, cons. clinics and div. gerontology; pres. Barnes Hosp.; vis. physician St. Louis City Hosp.; mem. staff Deaconess Hosp.; mem. cons. staff St. Joseph Hosp., St. Louis; cardiologist, dir. high blood pressure clinic St. Luke's Hosp.; area med. cons. hearings and appeals div. U.S. Social Security Adminstrn.; med. cons. R.R. Retirement Bd.; cardiovascular cons. div. gerontology Washington U. Sch. Medicine, St. Louis.; med. cons. Fifth Army U.S.A., Chgo. Author: Hypertensive Disease and Clinical Management, 1959, Management of Hypertensive Disease, 1960; also chpt. in Drugs of Choice, 1959, others; Cons. bd.: also chpt. in Folia Clinica Internacional, Barcelona, Spain.; Contbr. articles to profl. Jours. Bd. dirs. Boys Town, Mo.; former bd. dirs. Speech and Hearing Soc. St. Louis; pres. Doctors Med. Found., St. Louis,

1964; mem. steering com. U.S. Senatorial Bus. Adv. Bd., 1981—. Served as lt. col., M.C. AUS. Decorated Legion of Merit. Fellow A.C.P., Am. Coll. Cardiology (gov. Mo. 1962-65), Royal Soc. Medicine (London); mem. Miss. Valley Med. Soc. (pres. 1958), St. Louis Med. Soc. (pres. 1970), Am. Heart Assn., Mo. Heart Assn. (dir.), St. Louis Heart Assn., St. Louis Cardiac Club (dir.), Central Soc. Clin. Research, A.M.A. (cons. council on drugs), So. Med. Assn., Am. Diabetes Assn., Endocrine Soc., Am. Therapeutic Soc. (v.p. 1961, treas. 1962), Constantinian Soc. (pres. 1978), Paul Dudley White Soc., Soc. for Acad. Achievement (mem. adv. and editorial bd.), S.A.R., Phi Beta Kappa, Alpha Omega Alpha. Methodist (ofcl. bd.). Clubs: Skeet and Trap (St. Louis), Internists (St. Louis), University (St. Louis); Marshland Duck. Home: 610 W Polo Dr Clayton MO 63105 Office: 2107 Queeny Tower 4989 Barnes Hospital Plaza Saint Louis MO 63110

EDWARDS, LOUIS WARD, financial planner; b. Roanoke Rapids, N.C., Jan. 3, 1907; s. Walter Coker and Sarah Louise (Ward) E.; m. Saddie Tryke, Oct. 1932 (div. May 1945); children: Louis Ward, Barbara Jean, Carolyn Louis; m. Elizabeth Kipp Stahl, July 31, 1952; children: Becky Kipp, Stephen Allen, LuAnne. BA in Edn., U. S.C., 1928, degree in Internat. Acctg., 1933; postgrad., Western Mich. U., 1969—. CPA; registered fin. planner; registered geneologist. Ptnr. Price Waterhouse, Battle Creek, Mich., 1932-68; pvt. practice photography Edwards Photography, Richland, Mich., 1968-76; pvt. practice geneology and fin. planning Edwards Enterprises, Richland, 1977—. Author: History of My Lifetime, 1986; co-author: Ancestors of F. Kate Ely, 1984, Halladay Family, 1985. Mem. Am. Inst. CPA's, Inst. Cert. Fin. Planners, Mich. Assn. CPA, Soc. Colonial Wars, Huguenot Soc. Am., SAR, Alpha Tau Omega. Club: Exec. (Battle Creek) (pres. 1961-62); Gull Lake Country (Richland); Beacon (Kalamazoo). Lodge: Rotary (pres. Gull Lake 1970-79). Avocations: photography, research, study, writing, botany. Home and Office: 9876 W Gull Lake Dr Richland MI 49083

EDWARDS, MARK A., broadcasting executive; b. Chgo., Oct. 18, 1959; s. Irving and Arline Joyce (Lufman) Edelstein. Student, U. Evansville, Ind., 1980. Announcer Sta. WIKY-AM-FM, Evansville, 1978; announcer, producer Sta. WIBC, Indpls., 1980-84; program dir. Sta. WTPI, Indpls., 1984—; producer radio network Indpls. Motor Speedway, 1985—; cons. programming various radio stations, 1983—; freelance segment producer CBS Radio, N.Y.C., 1985—. Publicity advisor Commn. for Downtown, Indpls., 1983-85; walkamerica chmn. March of Dimes, Indpls., 1985. Recipient Best Sports Reporting award Ind. Associated Press, 1982, Addi award Advt. Club Indpls., 1985; named Best Undiscovered Talent of Yr., Indpls. mag. 1984, Person to Watch in 1985, Indpls. Monthly mag., 1985. Mem. Ind. Broadcasters Assn., Indpls. C. of C. (communications chmn. 1985). Clubs: Indpls. Press, Columbia, Skyline (Indpls.). Home: 863 A Indigo Ln Indianapolis IN 46260 Office: Sta WTPI 20 N Meridian St Suite 800 Indianapolis IN 46204

EDWARDS, MICHAEL DAVID, real estate developer; b. Cape Girardeau, Mo., Mar. 29, 1955; s. Ralph Leon and Phyllis Marie (Rupp) E. BS in Bus. Mgmt., Tex. Christian U., 1977. V.p. Ralph Edwards Sportswear, Cape Girardeau, 1977-80; pres. Buckskin & Leathers, Cape Girardeau, 1979—, Ralph Edwards Sportwear, Cape Girardeau, 1980—. Mem. Menswear Retailers Am., Nat. Retail Merchts. Assn., Cape Girardeau C. of C. Home: 1903 Weissinger Ln Cape Girardeau MO 63701 Office: Ralph Edwards Sportswear 250 Silver Springs Rd Cape Girardeau MO 63701

EDWARDS, MICHAEL PAUL, electrical engineer; b. Lemay, Mo., Apr. 13, 1950; s. William Riley and Mary Lena (Curry) E.; m. Joyce Jeanette Reich, Apr. 14, 1973. BEE, U. Mo., Rolla, 1973; MBA, Wash. U., St. Louis, 1986. Elect. engr. McDonnell-Douglas, St. Louis, 1973-75, 1977-79; mgr. engring. Autocontrol, Inc., St. Louis, 1974-77; mgr. computer services Anheuser-Busch Cos., St. Louis, 1979—. Social issues com. First Congl. Ch., St. Louis, 1986. Mem. IEEE (sr.), Mem. Soc. Mfgr. Engrs., Eta Kappa Nu, Beta Gamma Sigma. Republican. Club: Engineers. Avocations: Woodworking, travel. Home: 135 Hammel Ave Saint Louis MO 63119 Office: Anheuser Busch Cos One Busch Pl 202-3 Saint Louis MO 63118

EDWARDS, RICHARD ALAN, bank executive; b. Minot, N.D., Apr. 26, 1957; s. Duane LaVoy Sr. and Virginia Ione (Lyson) E. BBA, Minot State Coll., 1979. Bank teller Norwest Bancorp., Minot, 1977-80; bank examiner N.D. Dept. Banking, Fargo, 1980-85; loan adminstrn. officer Banks of Iowa, Inc., Des Moines, 1985—. Mem. Am. Inst. Banking. Lutheran. Lodge: Elks. Avocations: bowling, jogging, softball, waterskiing. Home: 1006 66th St Des Moines IA 50311

EDWARDS, RICHARD GAROLD, optometrist; b. Rock Island, Ill., Dec. 28, 1928; s. Willard Garold and Cora (Graves) E.; m. Iris L. Holmes, Aug. 6, 1955; children: Garold Loren, David Loyd; stepchildren: Gregory Klema, Terry Klema. BS, Ill. Coll. Optometry, 1952, DO, 1953. Pvt. practice optometry Rock Island, Ill., 1953—. Served with U.S. Army, 1953-55. Mem. Ill. Optometric Assn. Lodges: Kiwanis, Masons. Home: 2328 40th St Ct Rock Island IL 61201 Office: Rock Island Optometric Ctr Ltd 2501 24th St Rock Island IL 61201

EDWARDS, SANDRA JEAN, graphic artist; b. Detroit, Sept. 6, 1960; d. Donald and Nancy Elaine (Heinrich) Begg; m. Lyle Edward Edwards, Mar. 14, 1981. Student, Macomb Community Coll., 1978-79. Graphic artist Esquire Products, Fla., 1979-83; copy technician Meteor Photo Co., Troy, Mich., 1983—. Recipient Peak Performance award Meteor Photo Co., 1986. Mem. Am. Rose Soc., Detroit Rose Soc., Harley Owners Group. Avocation: motorcycling. Office: Meteor Photo Co 1099 Chicago Rd Troy MI 48084

EDWARDS, VERNON THOMAS (BUD), construction executive; b. Cleve., June 22, 1946; s. Vernon Lafell and Lois (Erney) E.; m. Patricia Colleen Cooney, Oct. 1, 1983; 1 child, Brian. BS in Chemistry, Cleve. State U., 1971, MS in Environ. Sci., 1975. Lic. tugboat capt. USCG. Research chemist Ferro Corp., Cleve., 1970-73; mgr. environ. sect. City of Cleve., 1973-76; engring. mgr. Pollutronics, Inc., Cleve., 1977-80; pres. Shoreline Contractors, Inc., Cleve., 1980—; instr. YMCA Scuba Program, Cleve., 1970-80, U.S Power Squadrons, Cleve., 1986. Patentee water sampler. Mem. Underwater Soc. Am. (com. chmn. 1972), Ohio Council of Scuba Clubs (v.p. 1975), Shipmaster's Assn. Republican. Roman Catholic. Club: Aqua Amigos Scuba (Cleve.)(pres. 1970-73). Home: 3598 W 139th St Cleveland OH 44111 Office: Shoreline Contractors Inc PO Box 10088 Cleveland OH 44110

EDWARDS, WARREN PRATT, psychologist; b. Charleston, W.Va., May 19, 1937; s. Warren Pratt and Mary Elizabeth (Roll) E.; m. Laura Lynne Boyers, June 16, 1962; children: Jason Warren, Jennifer Lynne. BA, W.Va. U., 1961; MS, Ohio U., 1964, PhD, 1968. Staff psychologist Community Mental Health Ctr., Marquette, Mich., 1968-72; staff psychologist VA Med. Ctr., Iowa City, 1972-75, chief psychologist, 1975—. Served with U.S. Army, 1957-59. Office: Psychology Service VA Med Ctr Iowa City IA 52240

EDWARDS, WILBUR SHIELDS, communications company executive; b. Charlotte, N.C., July 25, 1916; s. William James and Amy (Shields) E.; m. Jane Holman, Mar. 16, 1940; children: Ashton S., William J., Alisa Carroll. B.A., Davidson Coll., 1937; postgrad, Yale U. Div. Sch., 1938. With CBS, 1938-56; account exec. WBT, Charlotte, N.C., 1938-40; account exec. WCBS, N.Y., 1940-42, CBS radio sales, 1942-45; western sales mgr. CBS Radio Sales, Chgo., 1945-48; asst. gen mgr. WEEI, Boston, 1948-50; dir. KNX, Los Angeles, 1950-51; gen mgr. KNXT, Los Angeles, 1951-52; gen. sales mgr. CBS Films, N.Y.C., 1952-56; v.p. Ency. Brit. Films, Inc., 1956-62; exec. v.p. Ency. Brit. Ednl. Corp., 1965-71; pres., dir. F.E. Compton & Co., 1962-65, chmn., chief exec. officer, 1971-73; pres., dir. Electronic Pub. Inc., 1974-77; pres., chief exec. officer, dir. Magna Systems Inc., 1978—. Bd. dirs. Presbyn. Home, Evanston, Ill., David C. Cook Found. Presbyn. (elder, stated clk.). Club: Barrington Hills Country. Home: Route 2 Box 95 Barrington IL 60010

EDWARDS, WILLIAM B., retail discount drug store chain executive; b. 1940; married. BS, U. R.I., 1963. V.p. merchandising W.T. Grant Co., 1963-74; v.p. sales mktg. J.T. Kiernan Co., 1974-76; v.p. Mattel Co., 1976-78; exec. v.p. F&M Distbrs., Inc., 1978-82, pres., 1982-85; pres., chief operating officer Revco D.S., Inc., 1985—, also dir. Office: Revco DS Inc 1925 Enterprise Pkwy Twinsburg OH 44087 *

EELLS, WILLIAM HASTINGS, automobile company executive; b. Princeton, N.J., Mar. 30, 1924; s. Hastings and Amy (Titus) E.; 1 child, Jonathan William; B.A., Ohio Wesleyan U., 1946; M.A., Ohio State U., 1950; D.H.L. (hon.), Kent State U., 1983 D.Pub. Service, Bowling Green State U., 1983. Asst. to dir. Inst. Practical Politics, Ohio Wesleyan U., 1948-50, asst. dir., 1952-53, dir., 1953-57; instr. dept. polit. sci., 1952-59; instr. polit. sci. Mt. Union Coll., 1950-51; coordinator Atomic Devel. Activities, State of Ohio, 1957-59; Midwest regional mgr. civic and govtl. affairs Ford Motor Co., Columbus, 1959—. Mem. Ohio Gov.'s Cabinet, 1957-59; chmn. bd. Blue Cross of Northeast Ohio, 1967-72, Blossom Music Center, Cleve., 1968-76; chmn. bd. govs. Gov.'s Council on Rehab., 1966-68; mem. exec. com. Met. Opera's Nat. Council, 1967-81; pres. Nat. Council High Blood Pressure Research, 1974-79; chmn. Ohio Pub. Expenditure Council, 1981-84 , Ohio Adv. Council Coll. Prep. Edn., 1981-84 , Gov.'s Task Force on State Ops., 1984-85; vice chmn. Ohio Bicentennial Com., 1987—; mem. Nat. Council on Arts, Nat. Endowment for Arts, 1976-82; bd. dirs. Am. Heart Assn., 1974-79, award for disting. service, 1979; trustee Cleve. Orch., 1964—, Ednl. TV, Cleve., 1965-75, Cleve. Playhouse, 1965—, Cleve. Ballet, Cleve. Zoo, Columbus Arts Council, Columbus Symphony, Cleve. Luth. Hosp., Columbus Assn. Performing Arts, 1980—, vice chmn., 1980—; bd. mem. Nat. Council French Am. Scholarship Found., 1985—; bd. dirs. Columbus Mus. Art, 1982—, Opera/Columbus, 1984-86, Columbus Ballet, 1985-86 . Recipient awards including USCG Distinguished award, 1965, Silver medal Royal Life Saving Soc., Ohio State U. Devel. award, 1967, Alumni Citizenship award Ohio State U., 1987, Silver medal Japanese Red Cross Soc., award Ohio Arts Council, 1979, Ohio Theatre Alliance, 1981. Mem. SAR, Ohio C. of C. (v.p., chmn., 1987—), Ohio Mfrs. Assn. (trustee), N.J. Hist. Soc. (trustee 1983-86), Soc. Cin., Pi Sigma Alpha, Pi Gamma Mu, Omicron Delta Kappa, Delta Tau Delta. Republican. Presbyn. Clubs: Princeton (N.Y.); Columbus, U. Columbus (pres.); Union (Cleve.); F Street (Washington). Author: Your Ohio Government, 1953, 6th edit., 1967. Contbr. articles to profl. publs. Home: Honeystone 54 Elmwood Dr Delaware OH 43015 Office: 37 W Broad St Columbus OH 43215

EFFINGER, KATHARINA VIOLA, hospital executive; b. Milw., June 15, 1941; d. Charles William and Eleanora (Hauer) E.; student Ft. Wayne (Ind.) Luth. Sch. Nursing, 1959-61; B.A. in Behavior Scis., Nat. Coll. Edn., Evanston, Ill., 1981. Reservation supr. Braniff Internat., 1961-69; sales rep. United Gasket Corp., 1969-70; admitting mgr. MacNeal Meml. Hosp., Berwyn, Ill., 1970-73; bus. office mgr. Lake Forest (Ill.) Hosp., 1974-77; asst. v.p. fin. Victory Meml. Hosp., Waukegan, Ill., 1978—; adv. bd. Lake County Vocat. Center. Mem. Hosp. Fin. Mgmt. Assn., Nat. Assn. Patient Accounts Mgrs. Office: 1324 N Sheridan Rd Waukegan IL 60085

EFTEKHAR, KAMBIZ, international management consultant; b. Tehran, Iran, Nov. 4, 1944; came to U.S., 1963; s. H.E. Amireddin Eftekhar and Vageeheh (Meghnot) Steele; m. Judith Laura Pashby, Dec. 7, 1970; children—Darius, Damien. B.S.E. in Aerospace Engring., U. Mich., 1968, M.S.E. in Fluid Dynamics, 1970, M.M. in Gen. Mgmt., 1976. Mktg. coordinator Reynold's Aluminum Co., Richmond, Va., 1970-73; product devel. engr. Ford Motor Co., Dearborn, Mich., 1973-76; sr. cons. Arthur Andersen & Co., Chgo., 1976-78; mgr. Kearney Mgmt. Cons. (A. T. Kearney Inc.), Chgo., 1978—. Mem. Am. Mgmt. Assn. Office: A T Kearney Inc. 222 S Riverside Plaza Chicago IL 60606

EFTIMOFF, ANITA KENDALL, educational consultant; b. Granite City, Ill., May 3, 1927; d. David Harlow and Ollie Lorena (Galloway) Kendall; m. Vasil Eftimoff, June 14, 1959; 1 child, James Kendall. BA, Washington U., St. Louis, 1949; MA, So. Ill. U., Edwardsville, 1978, EdD, 1983. Cert. in multiple gen. edn., spl. edn., Ill. Spl. edn. instr. Community Unit 9, Granite City, 1968-83; ednl. cons. Efti Enterprises, Granite City, 1982—; program dir. At-Risk Presch. Grant, Granite City, 1986—; del. NDEA Conf. Eastern Mich. U., Ypsilanti, 1968, Gifted Edn. Conf. Ill. Office of Edn., Springfield, 1975-77; adminstrv. intern Ill. State Bd. Edn., Springfield, 1981. Bd. dirs. Gov.'s Adv. Council on Women's Affairs, Springfield, Ill., Rape Crisis and Sexual Abuse Ctr., So. Ill. U., 1978-82; chmn. Adopt-A-Friend, St. Louis Ambassadors, 1982-84, co-chmn. Vet.'s Day, 1984-86; chmn. St. Louis Symphony Youth Orch., 1985-87; aux. St. Louis Children's Hosp., 1980. At-Risk Preschool grantee Ill. State Bd. Edn., 1986—. Mem. World Council for Gifted and Talented Children, Nat. Assn. for Gifted Children, Assn. for the Gifted, Ill. Council for the Gifted, Women's Assn. (bd. dirs. 1961—), St. Louis Symphony Women's Assn., WAAUW, Delta Kappa Gamma, Phi Delta Kappa. Lodges: Daus. of Nile, Rotary-Anns. Avocations: performing arts, classical music. Home: 2800 Michigan Ave Granite City IL 62040 Office: At-Risk Presch Program 2300 W 25th St Granite City IL 62040

EFTINK, JEFFREY JOSEPH, accountant; b. Cape Girardeau, Mo., Oct. 31, 1956; s. August Joseph and Majorica Ann (Peters) E.; m. Mary Louise Holifield, Oct. 13, 1984; 1 child, Toni Marie. BS Bus Adminstrn., AAS in Computer Sci., Southeast Mo. State U., 1979. CPA, Mo. Staff acct. Vernon E. Heck, CPA, Perryville, Mo., 1979-83; ptnr. Dewilde & Eftink, CPA's, PC, Lutesville, Mo., 1983—. Vice chmn. Lutesville-Marble Hill Consolidation Com., 1985. Mem. Am. Inst. CPAs, Mo. Soc. CPAs. Republican. Roman Catholic. Lodge : KC (treas. Leopold, Mo. 1977—, Knight of Yr. 1977, 86). Avocations: hunting and fishing, softball, camping, floating. Home: PO Box 408 Lutesville MO 63762 Office: Dewilde and Eftink CPAs Inc PO Box 408 Lutesville MO 63762

EGAN, FRANK BOLAND, insurance agent; b. Nov. 26, 1913; s. Frank B. Sr. and Agnes N. (Duffy) E.; 1 child, Mary Theresa. BA, Regis Coll., 1935; BLS, U. Denver, 1940, MA in English Lit., 1941. Assoc. editor Catholic Register, Denver, 1935-39; reference librarian U. Nebr., Lincoln, 1940-41; pres. Percy Jones Jr. Coll., Battle Creek, Mich., 1944-46; dist. agt. Nat. Life Ins. Co., Battle Creek, 1948—. Author: Tax Sheltered Annnuity Plans. Served to capt. U.S. Army, 1943-46. Mem. Battle Creek Life Underwriters Assn. (past. pres.), Life Leders Assn. Mich. (past. pres.). Republican. Roman Catholic. Avocations: cartooning, collect and play folk songs. Office: Nat Life Ins Co 702 Comerica Bldg Battle Creek MI 49016

EGAN, RAYMOND C., pharmaceutical comapny executive. Exec. v.p. Bristol Meyers U.S. Pharm. and Nutritional Group, Evansville, Ind. Office: Bristol-Myers US Pharm & Nutritional Group 2400 W Pennsylvania St Evansville IN 47721 *

EGGER, JOSEPH PATRICK, data processing executive; b. Deadwood, S.D., July 9, 1948; s. Joseph Patrick and Hazel Marie (Robley) E.; m. Cherie Lorraine Thompson, July 19, 1970; children: Patrick Joseph, Matthew David. BA, U. S.D., 1970. Lead programmer Mutual of Omaha, 1970-73; programmer analyst Assocs. Corp. of N.Am., South Bend, Ind., 1973-75; system programmer analyst Omaha Nat. Bank, 1975-76, sr. system programmer analyst, 1976-80; mgr. tech. planning and support Firstier Data Service, Omaha, 1980-86, Firstier Data Service/EDS, Omaha, 1986—. mem. telecommunications adv. bd. Coll. St. Mary, Omaha, 1983—. Served to 2d lt. Army, 1969-72. Mem. Mo. Valley Communications Assn. Republican. Lutheran. Office: Firstier Data Service/EDS 17th & Farnam Omaha NE 68102

EGGERT, GENE, architect; b. Chgo., Nov. 13, 1958; s. Gene Winfred and Sandra Rae (Robinson) E.; m. Robin Heidi Biedermann, June 11, 1982. BArch, U. Wis., 1983. Facilities planner AIGI Properties, Inc., Milw., 1983-84; project architect Heike/Design Assocs., Brookfield, Wis., 1984—; pvt. practice residential architect, Milw., 1986—. Mem. AIA (minuteman), Wis. Soc. Architects. Lutheran. Avocations: constructing architectural ideas, skiing, travel, softball. Home: 1029 E Colfax Pl Milwaukee WI 53217 Office: Heike/Design Assocs Bishops Woods E Suite 201 13255 W Bluemound Rd Brookfield WI 53005

EGGLESON, ROBERT AAKER, public relations executive; b. Stoughton, Wis., Nov. 18, 1928; s. Anon Odegard and Caroline (Aaker) E.; m. Barbara Ann Krupnick, June 25, 1960; 1 dau., Karen Jean. B.A. in English, Luther Coll., 1950. Newspaper reporter, Iowa and Minn., 1950-57; pub. relations rep. Northwestern U., Evanston, Ill., 1957-59; div. publicist 3M Co., 1959-61; pub. relations asst. Internat. Minerals & Chem. Co., 1961-62; asst. to dir. pub. affairs Champion Papers Inc., 1962-66; pub. relations mgr. Welch Foods Inc., 1966-72; mfg. communications mgr. Internat. Harvester Co., 1972-83; pres. Robert Eggleson/Communications, 1983; dir. pub. affairs Black Hawk Coll., Moline, Ill., 1984—. Mem. long range task force United Way of Rock Island-Scott Counties. Served with U.S. Army, 1950-52. Mem. Iowa-Ill. Pub. Relations Council, Rock Island C. of C. (past dir.). Republican. Home: 9 Hawthorne Rd Rock Island IL 61201 Office: 6600 34th Ave Moline IL 61265

EHLERS, LARRY LEE, mechanical engineer; b. Kansas City, Mo., Mar. 10, 1953; s. Rufus Arndt and Wanda Marie (Pickett) E.; m. Teresa Ann Gunter, Jan. 24, 1981; children: Megan Ann, Austin Lee. MS, Purdue U., 1976; BME, Gen. Motors Inst., 1977. Lic. profl. engr., Kans. Environ. engr. Gen. Motors Corp., Kansas City, Kans., 1976-79; corp. plant engr. Bendix/King div. Allied-Signal, Inc., Olathe, Kans., 1979—. Mem. Internat. Communications Assn. (voting), DBX Users Assn. (bd. dirs. 1985—, pres. 1987), Assn. Energy Engrs., Am. Inst. Plant Engrs., MidAm. Telecommunications Assn. Libertarian. Lutheran. Avocation: aircraft building. Home: 11512 W 108th St Overland Park KS 66210 Office: Bendix/King div Allied-Signal 400 N Rogers Rd Olathe KS 66062

EHLERS, THOMAS MARTIN, investments and retail consultant; b. Worthington, Minn., Feb. 6, 1937; s. Martin Andrew and Genevieve Ellen (Rust) E.; m. Sandra Joan McCartney, Apr. 12, 1964; children—Joseph, Genevieve, T. Michael. B.A., Hamline U., 1959; M.S.R., NYU, 1960. Exec. trainee Daytons, Mpls., 1960; v.p. Ehlers of Redwood Falls (Minn.), 1961-70, pres., 1971—, also bd. dirs.; bd. dirs. Ehlers Apparel, Inc., 1987—; pres. Boxrud Bldg. Corp., 1985—; v.p. MGT Investment Corp. Home: 595 N Lake Spicer MN 56288 Office: 219 S Washington St Redwood Falls MN 56283

EHLERS, WILLIAM FREDERICK, accountant; b. St. Louis, Oct. 21, 1957; s. Fred T. and Ruth E. (Taylor) E.; m. Vicki L. Grubbs, June 24, 1978. BSBA, Washington U., St. Louis, 1980, MBA, 1981. CPA, Mo. Audit mgr. Arthur Andersen & Co., St. Louis, 1981—. Mem. Am. Inst. CPA's, Mo. Soc. CPA's. Avocations: softball, waterskiing. Home: 916 Camargo Ballwin MO 63011 Office: Arthur Andersen & Co 1010 Market St Saint Louis MO 63101

EHRENKRANZ, DOUGLAS WILLIAM, marketing professional; b. Hudson, N.Y., Nov. 4, 1957; s. Ted Eugene and Margaret (Andrews) E. BBA, U. Ariz., 1979. Sales rep. Procter & Gamble, 1979-81, dist. field rep., 1981-82, unit sales mgr., 1982-85, regional mktg. mgr., 1985-87, dist. mgr. beverage sales, 1987—. Mem. U. Ariz. Alumni Assn. (bd. dirs. 1980-81), Sigma Chi. Democrat. Club: Active 20-30 (v.p. membership 1982-84). Avocations: bicycling, skiing, tennis, golf. Home: 478 Bolero Donville CA 94526 Office: Beverage Sales Proctor & Gamble 2 Proctor & Gamble Plaza Cincinnati OH 45201

EHRENSAFT, MORRIS, industrial supply executive; b. Chgo., June 18, 1917; s. Joseph Benjamin and Dora (Karlins) E.; m. Edith Hoyt, June 15, 1940; children: Philip, Diane, Richard. Grad. high sch., Chgo. Purchasing agt. Garcy Corp., Chgo., 1937-44; sales rep. Triangle Supply Co., Chgo., 1944-46; v.p. Marklin Supply Co., Chgo., 1946-72, pres., 1972—, also bd. dirs. Treas. N. Cen. Homeowners Assn., Skokie, Ill., 1956, v.p., 1957-60; v.p. Skokie Caucus Party, 1958-64, pres. 1965-68. Recipient Civic Appreciation award, Skokie Village Bd., 1968. Mem. Chgo. Audubon Soc. Lodge: Masons. Avocations: gardening, literature, music. Office: Marklin Supply Co 3060 N Elston Ave Chicago IL 60618

EHRLICH, BURTON STANLEY, lawyer; b. Chgo., July 21, 1953; s. Sam A. and Tobie (Schwartz) E. BA with high honors, Northeastern Ill. U., 1974; M.B.A. with distinction, DePaul U., 1975; J.D. with high honors, IIT-Chicago-Kent, 1978; postgrad. LL.M. John Marshall Law Sch., 1978—. Bar: Ill. 1978, U.S. Dist. Ct. (no. dist.) Ill. 1978, U.S. Ct. Appeals (7th cir.) 1979, U.S. Ct. Customs and Patent Appeals 1980, U.S. Supreme Ct. 1980. Law clk. Burton R. Rosenberg, Chgo., 1975-78; assoc. Brezina & Lund, Chgo., 1979, Brezina & Buckingham, Chgo., 1979-87, ptnr. Myers & Ehrlich, Ltd., 1987—; dir. various corps. Contbr. articles to profl. publs. Active Congl. elections. Mem. ABA, Ill. Bar Assn., Chgo. Bar Assn., Am. Judicature Soc., Delta Mu Delta (award Eta chpt.), B'nai Brith (various chpt. offices, awards), Econs. Club (award). Home: 1116 W 187th St Homewood IL 60430 Office: Myers & Ehrlich Ltd 1516 Monadnock Block 53 W Jackson Blvd Chicago IL 60604

EHRLICH, CLARENCE EUGENE, physician, educator; b. Rosenberg, Tex., Oct. 19, 1938; s. Oscar Lee and Gertrude Gene (Walzel) E.; children—Tracey Janet, Bradley Scott, Suzanne Margaret. B.A., U. Tex., 1961; M.D., Baylor Coll. Medicine, 1965. Diplomate Am. Bd. Ob-Gyn (mem. div. gynec. oncology 1982—, dir. 1985—). Intern Phila. Gen. Hosp., 1965-66; resident Charity Hosp.-Tulane U., New Orleans, 1966-69; asst. prof. Ind. U., Indpls., 1973-77, assoc. prof., 1977-81, prof., chmn. ob/gyn dept., 1981—. Contbr. articles to profl. publs., chpts. in books. Served to major USAF, 1969-71. Grantee USPHS, 1975-78, Upjohn Co., 1976-81, Gynecol. Group, 1978-80, 80-84, Eli Lilly & Co., 1982-85. Mem. AAAS, Am. Assn. Cancer Research, Am. Coll. Obstetricians and Gynecologists, ACS, AMA, Am. Radium Soc., Am. Soc. Clin. Pharmacology and Therapeutics, Am. Soc. Parental and Enteral Nutrition, Am. Soc. Clin. Oncology, Am. Soc. Colposcopists and Colpomicroscopists, Assn. Profs. Gynecology and Obstetrics, Sigma Xi, others. Office: Ind U Med Ctr 926 W Michigan St Indianapolis IN 46223

EHRLICH, KINGSTON W., real estate developer; b. Racine, Wis., Jan. 18, 1914; s. Arthur and Nellie Cecile (Kingston) E.; m. Phydele Jane Gourley, Mar. 25, 1940; children: Susan Elizabeth Smith, Robin Jane Eastham. PhB, U. Wis., 1936. Pres. King Ehrlich Co., Inc., Racine, Wis., 1946—; bd. dirs. Heritage Bank, Racine. Served to lt. col. U.S. Army, 1940-46. Mem. Soc. Real Estate Counselors, Nat. Assn. Realtors (v.p. 1972), Wis. Realtors Assn. (pres. 1968). Clubs: Univ. (Milw.); Racine Country (bd. dirs. 1979-82), Racine Yacht. Home: 5447 Crown Chase Racine WI 53405 Office: King Ehrlich Co Inc 4101 Washington Ave Racine WI 53405

EHRLICH, THOMAS, university administrator, law educator; b. Cambridge, Mass., Mar. 4, 1934; s. William and Evelyn (Seltzer) E.; m. Ellen Rome, June 18, 1957; children—David, Elizabeth, Paul. AB, Harvard U., 1956, LLB, 1959; LLD (hon.), Villanova U., 1979, Notre Dame U., 1980, U. Pa., 1987. Bar: Wis. bar 1959. Law clk. Judge Learned Hand U.S. Ct. Appeals 2d Circuit, 1959-60; spl. asst. to legal adviser Dept. State, 1962-64; spl. asst. to under-sec. U.S. Dept. State, 1964-65; assoc. prof. law Stanford (Calif.) U., 1965-68, prof., 1968-75, also dean, 1971-75, Richard E. Lang dean and prof., 1973-75; pres. Legal Services Corp., Washington, 1976-79; dir. Internat. Devel. Coop. Agy., Washington, 1979-81; provost, prof. law U. Pa., Phila., 1981-87; pres., prof. law Ind. U., Bloomington and Indpls., 1987—. Author: (with Abram Chayes and Andreas F. Lowenfeld) The International Legal Process, 3 vols, 1968, (with Herbert L. Packer) New Directions in Legal Education, 1972, International Crises and the Role of Law, Cyprus, 1958-67, 1974; Editor: (with Geoffrey C. Hazard, Jr.) Going to Law School?, 1975. Office: Ind Univ Office of President Bryan Hall Bloomington IN 47405

EHRMAN, CHAIM MEYER, marketing educator; b. Scranton, Pa., Sept. 3, 1947; s. Gaston and Esther (Horowitz) E.; m. Eva Darcy Glick, May 19, 1973; children—Rivka Laya Gitl, Deetsa Mindl, Sara Hadassa, Yaakov Zev. Student, Yeshiva S.R. Hirsch, N.Y.C., 1966-70; B.B.A., Baruch Coll., CUNY, 1970, M.B.A., 1973; M.S., Temple U., 1981; Ph.D. in Mktg. U. Pa., 1984. Ordained rabbi, 1970. Cert. tchr. math., N.Y. Analyst market research Editor and Pub., 1972-74; instr. Queensborough Community Coll., CUNY, Bayside, N.Y., 1974-75, Rutgers U., Camden, N.J., 1975-78, Pa. State U., Lima, 1978-81; grad. faculty Wharton Sch., U. Pa., 1981-83; prof. dept. mktg. U. Ill.-Chgo., 1983-86; prof. Loyola U., Chgo., 1986—; vis. asst. prof. U. Chgo., summer 1986; vis. scholar Argonne Nat. Lab, 1986. Contbr. articles on internat. mktg., bus. stats. in profl. journs. Grantee Ctr. Internat. Bus. Studies, U. Pa., 1981-83, Pepsico-Mktg. Dept., 1982-83; recipient

Community Service award Young Israel Wynnefield, Phila., 1983. Mem. Am. Mktg. Assn., Am. Statis. Assn., Inst. Mgmt. Sci., Ops. research Soc. Am. Republican. Jewish. Avocations: playing violin; sailing; swimming. Home: 6735 N Richmond Chicago IL 60645 Office: Loyola U 10 E Pearson St Chicago IL 60611

EHRMANN, FRANK A., hospital supply manufacturing and distributing company executive. Pres., chief operating officer Am. Hosp. Supply Corp., Evanston, Ill. Office: Am Hosp Supply Corp 1 American Plaza Evanston IL 60201 *

EICHACKER, GEORGE L.D., savings and loan association executive, accountant; b. Homestead, Iowa, Mar. 9, 1930; s. Charles A. and Marie (Geiger) E.; m. Lois A. Harper, Apr. 27, 1969; chidlren: Milton, Lois, Virginia. BA, U. Iowa, 1951, MA, 1952. CPA, Iowa. Acct. Amana (Iowa) Soc., 1954-55, McGladrey, Hansen and Dunn, Keokuk, Iowa, 1955-58; prin. George Eichacker, CPA, Keokuk, 1958—; sec.-treas. Keokuk Fed. Savings, 1962-81, pres., 1982—; v.p. Keokuk Venture Capital, 1987—, bd. dirs. Chmn. Urban Devel. Commn., Keokuk, 1966-69; pres. Keokuk Area Hosp., 1983-84; exec. dir. United Way Keokuk, 1958-64; bd. dirs. Keokuk Indsl. Devel. Corp., 1985—. Served to sgt. U.S. Army, 1952-54. Mem. U.S. League Savings Insts., Am. Soc. CPA's, Iowa Soc. CPA's, Iowa Jaycees (Disting. Service award 1963), Keokuk Jaycees (pres. 1957-58), Phi Beta Kappa. Episcopalian. Club: Keokuk Country. Lodge: Rotary (pres. Keokuk club 1969-70). Avocations: golf, gardening. Home: Rural Rt 2 Box 44 Fort Madison IA 52627 Office: Keokuk Fed Savings 320 Concert St Keokuk IA 52632

EICHHOLZ, JERRY RAYMOND, educational professional; b. St. Louis, Mo., Mar. 5, 1942; s. Joseph H. and Christeen J. (Gross) E.; m. Faye Ellen Schaedlich, June 25, 1966; children: Dawn M., Jeffrey R. BA in Edn., Harris Tchrs. Coll., 1971; MA in Edn., Washington U., 1974; EdD, St. Louis U., 1984. Fellow Am. Bd. Master Educators; cert. sch. supt., Mo.; cert. tchr., Mo.; cert. prin., Mo., Ill. Ednl. profl. Ferguson-Florissant (Mo.) Schs., 1971—; adminstrv. cons. United Community in Christ Sch., St. Louis, 1980-86. Served with U.S. Army, 1966-69. Mem. Nat. Assn. for Elementary Sch. Prins., Assn. for Supervision and Curriculum Devel., Pi Lambda Theta (bd. dirs. 1985-86), Phi Delta Kappa, Kappa Delta Pi (treas. 1972-76). Avocations: investing, gardening, reading. Home: 12774 Partridge Run Dr Florrisant MO 63033 Office: Ferguson-Floressant Sch Dist 1005 Waterford Dr Florissant MO 63033

EICHHORN, ARTHUR DAVID, music director; b. St. Louis, Oct. 13, 1953; s. Arthur Louis and Adele (Stankunas) E. BA, Concordia Coll., River Forest, Ill., 1975, MA, 1976; MA, Webster U., 1986. Cert. elem. tchr., Ill. Dir. music St. John Luth. Ch., Mt. Prospect, Ill., 1974-76, Our Savior Luth. Ch., Springfield, Ill., 1976-81, Holy Cross Luth. Ch., St. Louis, 1981—. Mem. Choristers Guild. Music Educators Nat. Conf., Mo. Music Educators Assn. Republican. Home: 7116 Mardel Ave Saint Louis MO 63109-1123 Office: Holy Cross Luth Ch 2650 Miami St Saint Louis MO 63118

EICHHORN, BRADFORD REESE, infosystems specialist; b. Cleve., Jan. 24, 1954; s. Charles Albert Jr. and Jeanne Yvonne (Reese) E.; m. Dawn Lynette Mattern, Feb. 25, 1980; children: Serena Ruth, Reese Aaron. BS in Computer Sci. magna cum laude, Cleve. State U., 1975, MS in Operations Research summa cum laude, 1977. Mgr. applications devel. Control Data Corp., Lakewood, Ohio, 1976-83; sr. cons. Coppers & Lybrand, Cleve., 1983-84; mgr. bus. systems Ferro Corp., Independence, Ohio, 1984—; treas. Blossom Property Devel., Cleve., 1985—. Chmn. fin. com. All Saints Luth. Ch., Olmsted Falls, Ohio, 1984-85; steward, sec. fin. com. Our Saviour Luth. Ch., Hinckley, Ohio, 1986—. Home: 149 Salem Ct Hinckley OH 44233-9620 Office: Ferro Corp 7500 E Pleasant Valley Rd Independence OH 44131

EICHHORN, JACOB, chemical company executive; b. Sheboygan, Wis., Sept. 14, 1924; s. Jacob and Elizabeth (Strauch) E.; m. Mary Kay Winn, Dec. 27, 1959; children—Kurt, Eric, Karen. B.S. in Chem. Engring., U. Mich., 1946, M.S., 1947, Ph.D., 1950; P.M.D., Harvard U., 1968. Research engr. Dow Chem. Co., Midland, Mich., 1950-61, mgr. flex packaging tech. service and devel., 1961-66, mgr. spl. projects, packaging, 1966-71, ventures mgr. plastics, 1971-80, lab. dir., 1980-82, sr. project mgr., corp. research and devel., 1982-86, devel. scientist, 1986—; grad. lectr. U. Mich., Ann Arbor, 1952-54; v.p., dir. Dolco Packaging Corp., Los Angeles, 1968-74. Contbr. articles to profl. jours. Contbr. chpt. to Industrial and Specialty Papers, 1968. Patentee in field. Mem. Am. Chem. Soc., Am. Inst. Chem. Engrs. (pres. local sect. 1957), TAPPI, Instrument Soc. Am. Republican. Mem. United Ch. of Christ. Clubs: U. Mich. (v.p. 1963), Midland Country (Midland). Avocations: photography; golf; skiing. Home: 4501 Arbor Dr Midland MI 48640 Office: Dow Chemical Co Bldg 1776 Midland MI 48674

EICHSTAEDT, DONALD WATSON, automotive mechanical engineer; b. Warsaw, Ind., Mar. 16, 1933; s. Roy Lewis and Natalie Fern (Watson) E.; m. Nancy Judd Merritt, Dec. 11, 1977. BSME, Gen. Motors Inst., Flint, Mich., 1962. Parts mgr. Unity Chevrolet, North Judson, Ind., 1958; devel. engr. Chevrolet Engring., Warren, Mich., 1962-65; supr. test lab. McCord Corp., Detroit, 1965-66; proj. engr. Kar Kraft, Inc., Dearborn, Mich., 1966-71; devel. engr. Ford Motor Co., Dearborn, 1971—. Served with U.S. Army, 1954-57, Japan. Mem. Soc. Automotive Engrs., Oakland County Road Racing Assn. (bd. dirs. 1969). Clubs: Corvette (Detroit) (v.p. 1959). Avocation: automobile racing. Home: 18222 Redwood Ave Lathrup Village MI 48076

EICHTEN, BEATRICE MARY, pastoral psychotherapist; b. Wanda, Minn., Sept. 15, 1943; s. Everett Peter and Mary Eugenia (Beert) E. BS in Edn., BS in Home Econs., Coll. St. Teresa, 1969; M in Pastoral Studies, Loyola U., Chgo., 1983. Tchr. St. Francis High Sch., Little Falls, Minn., 1971-73; counselor, adminstr. Hope Community, Little Falls, 1973-76; v.p. Franciscan Sisters, Little Falls, 1976-80; dir., counselor Pastoral Counseling Service, Niles, Ill., 1983-85; tng. intern Pastoral Psychotherapy Inst., Park Ridge, Ill., 1982-85, sr. staff mem., 1985—. Mem. Am. Assn. Pastoral Counseling, Assn. Psychol. Type. Democrat. Roman Catholic. Avocations: gardening, pottery, knitting, crocheting, drawing. Home: 929 Lakeside Pl Chicago IL 60640 Office: Pastoral Psychotherapy Inst 1875 Dempster Ave Park Ridge IL 60048

EICK, ARNOLD ROBERT, electrical engineer; b. Flint, Mich., Jan. 16, 1938; s. Albert R. and Mildred R. (Hillier) E.; m. Sharon K. Brown (div.); m. Fay C. Murphy (div.); children: Deborah, Carol. ASE, Flint Jr. Coll., 1961; BSE EE, U. Mich., 1964. Engr. Space Guidance Ctr. IBM, Owego, N.Y., 1964-66, AC Electronics div. Gen. Motors, Milw., 1966-70, AC Spark Plug div. Gen. Motors, Flint, Mich., 1970-86, Delco Electronics div. Gen. Motors, Flint, Mich., 1986—. Patentee Colored Liquid Crystal Display. Served with USAF, 1955-59. Avocations: tennis, golf, cross country ski. Home: 11733 Hazel Ave Grand Blanc MI 48439 Office: Delco Electronics 1300 N Dort Hwy Flint MI 48556

EICKHOLT, JOHN LEWIS, neurologist; b. Toledo, Aug. 29, 1952; s. John Lewis Eickholt and Jean Neilson; m. Sandra Lou Oelker, June 30, 1981; children: Jessica, Ashley. BA, U. Toledo, 1974; MD, Ohio State U., 1977. Diplomate Am. Bd. Psychiatry and Neurology. Resident in neurology Wake Forest Hosp., Winston-Salem, N.C., 1981; staff neurologist, dir. neurolognostic lab. Grandy Meml. Hosp., Delaware, Ohio, 1981—; pres. Del. (Ohio) Neurol. Assocs. Inc., 1982—; cons. staff Mary Rutan Hosp., Belfountain, Ohio, 1981—, Marion Gen. Hosp., Marion, Ohio, 1981—. Mem. Am. Acad. Neurology, Am. Electroencephalographic Soc., Am. Med. Electroencephalographic Soc. Home: 8432 Kilbirnie Ct Dublin OH 43017 Office: Del Neurol Assocs 561 W Central Ave Delaware OH 43015

EICKMAN, JENNIFER LYNN, conference center manager, writer, artist; b. Urbana, Ill., Nov. 7, 1946; d. Marvin A. and Emma L. (Hartrick) Smith; B.F.A., U. Ill., 1967, postgrad. in Art History, 1967-70; m. Gary Edwin Eickman, June 9, 1968. Tchr., Univ. High Sch., Urbana, 1968, Champaign (Ill.) Public Schs., 1969-70; mem. faculty U. Ill., 1968-77, Richland Coll., Decatur, Ill., 1975-77; asst. to dir. of extension in visual arts U. Ill., 1969-70, asst. dir. Allerton House Conf. Center, 1974—; dir. Allerton Art Inst., 1984—; bd. dirs. Monticello Design and Mfg.; guest lectr., tchr. art workshops. Mem. Pacific Tropical Bot. Gardens, Defenders of Wildlife, Nat. Trust Hist. Preservation, Internat. Platform Assn., Kappa Alpha Theta. Staff writer Champaign-Urbana mag.; author articles on art history, music, edn. and natural history. Home: Gate House Allerton Park Monticello IL 61856 Office: Allerton House Allerton Park Monticello IL 61856

EID, PATRICIA ANN, nurse; b. West Bend, Wis., Nov. 18, 1947; d. William Joseph and Kathleen (Kelly) Dooley; m. Malford Collin Eid, Aug. 9, 1969; children: Eric Collin, Erin Patricia, Evan Patrick. BS, Coll. St. Catherine, 1969; MPH, U. Minn., 1981. Nurse supr. Abbott/N.W. Hosp., Mpls., 1970-81; nurse practitioner Brainerd (Minn.) Internal Medicine, 1981-84, Fosston (Minn.) Clinic, 1984-86, Bagley (Minn.) Med. Ctr., 1987—; prof. psychology Northland Community Coll., Thief River Falls, Minn., 1986—; cons. fitness Good Samaritan Nursing Home, Brainerd, 1982-83, Woman's Females for Fitness, Fosston, 1986—, Women's Fit for Life, Clearbrook, Minn., 1986—; cons. quality assurance Good Samaritan Nursing Home, Clearbrook, 1986. Columnist Fosston Newspaper, 1984—. Chairperson pub. edn. Caner Soc., Polk County. Mem. Am. Nurses Assn., Minn. Nurses Assn., Sigma Theta Tau. Mem. Democratic Farm Labor party. Lutheran. Club: Community (v.p.) (CLearbrook). Avocation: running. Home: 300 Hospital St Clearbrook MN 56634 Office: Bagley Medical Center Bagley MN 56634

EIFF, SHARON LEE DOROTHY, designer; b. Wauwatosa, Wis., Feb. 7, 1951; s. Frederick John Henkel and Bernice Emily (Wirth) Lasky; m. Gerald Charles Eiff, Oct. 12, 1974; children: James Frederick, Jordon Christopher. Student, Marquette U., 1970-73; diploma interior and environ. design, Layton Sch. Art & Design, 1973; student, U. Wis., 1981-82. Sr. interior designer Zimmerman Design Group, Milw., 1973-82; designer, owner Sharon Lee Eiff Design, Wauwatosa, 1982—; instr. Milw. Inst. Art & Design, 1978-84, Milw. Area Tech. Coll., 1984—; bd. dirs. Multi-Fab Products Corp., Brookfield, Wis., 1980—. Designer various interior projects for offices, hosps., schs., restaurants, 1975—; designer prototype neon lights series for Lights of Am. show, U. Wis.-Milw., 1985. Recipient various design awards Wis. chpt. AIA. Mem. United Ch. Christ. Avocations: painting, drawing, gardening, photography, collecting antique carousel horses. Home and Office: 1417 Lombard Ct Wauwatosa WI 53213

EIGEL, JOHN ROHAN, investment consultant, political activist; b. St. Louis, Feb. 26, 1944; s. Edwin George and Catherine Christina (Rohan) E.; m. Sue Ellen Walker, Feb. 6, 1970; 1 child, John Rohan Jr. BA, St. Louis U., 1966. Pension adminstr. Marsh & McLennan, Inc., St. Louis, 1969-72, pension cons., 1973-77; pension mgr. Consolidated Aluminum Corp., St. Louis, 1977-80; pres., owner JRE Investors, St. Louis, 1980-82, Meramec Fin. Services, Inc., St. Louis, 1982—; state adv. U.S. Congl. Adv. Bd., Washington, 1984. Author: The American Eigels, 1984, The Am. Rohans, 1985. Mem. Rep. Presdl. Task Force, Washington, 1984—, Nat. Rep. Congl. Com., Washington, 1984—. Served to sgt. USAF, 1966-69. Mem. Am. Assoc. Individual Investors, Nat. Assn. Investors Corp., Am. Security Council Found., Permanently and Totally DAV, St. Louis Geneal. Assn., Nat. Rifle Assn. Roman Catholic. Avocations: genealogy, numismathist. Home and Office: 1304 Tahiti Dr Crestwood MO 63126

EIGEL, ROBERT LOUIS, computer services company executive; b. St. Louis, Jan. 10, 1937; s. Edwin George and Catherine (Rohan) E.; m. Charlotte Ross, Aug. 31, 1968; children: Karen, Robert Jr., Deborah, William. BEE, St. Louis U., 1959; MS in Indsl. Engring., Ga. Inst. Tech., 1968. Program mgr. Cin. Electronics, 1982-84; v.p., gen. mgr. Dayton div. RJO Enterprises, Inc., Lanham, Md., 1984—. chmn. activities com. Alter High Sch. Edn. Commn., Kettering, Ohio, 1986—; mem. Rep. Bus. Com., Dayton, 1986. Served to col. USAF, 1959-82. Mem. Inst. Indsl. Engrs. (sr.), Air Force Assn., Nat. Security Indsl. Assn. Roman Catholic. Avocations: golf, classical music. Home: 2111 Old Vienna Dr Dayton OH 45459 Office: RJO Enterprises Inc 101 Woodman Dr Dayton OH 45431

EIGENFELD, ROGER CONRAD, clergyman; b. Milw., July 24, 1940; s. Otto Paul and Dorothy Anna (Wiedoff) E.; m. Carolyn Jeanne Vermazen, June 15, 1963; children: Peter, Whitney, Kirsten, Jacqueline, Lauri. BA, Carthage Coll., 1962; BD, Northwestern Luth. Theol. Sem., 1966. Developer mission Christus Victor Luth. Ch., Apple Valley, Minn., 1966-67; youth pastor Richfield Luth. Ch., Mpls., 1967-70; assoc. pastor Holy Trinity Luth. Ch., Mpls., 1970-72; sr. pastor St. Andrew's Luth. Ch., Mahtomedi, Minn., 1972—; mem. exec. bd. Minn. Synod, Mpls., 1978-80. Author: Decisions About Death, 1981. Bd. dirs. Camp Du Nord YMCA, St. Paul, 1977-80, gen. bd., St. Paul, 1980. Avocations: camping, canoeing, writing. Office: St Andrews Luth Ch 900 Stillwater Rd Mahtomedi MN 55115

EIGHMEY, DARRYL LYNN, dentist; b. Monroe, Mich., July 14, 1947; s. Raymond Gilbert and Doris Marie (Lazette) E.; m. Patricia Jean O'Keefe, Oct. 22, 1972 (div. Apr. 1975); m. Rebecca Joyce Evans, Oct. 21, 1984; 1 child, Austin Evans. AA, Monroe Community Coll., 1972; BA, Eastern Mich. U., 1974; DDS, U. Mich., 1978. Lic. dentist, Mich. Dir. dentistry Monroe County Health Dept., 1978-81; gen. practice dentistry Monroe, 1981—. Councilman 2d precinct Monroe City Council, 1986—. Served with USN, 1966-70. Mem. Monroe County Dental Soc. Lodge: Kiwanis. Avocations: music, books, computers, gambling, golf. Home: 515 Hollywood Dr Monroe MI 48161 Office: 115 W Front St Monroe MI 48161

EIGHMEY, DOUGLAS JOSEPH, JR., hospital official; b. Cambridge, N.Y., Dec. 19, 1946; s. Douglas Joseph and Theresa E. (McGuire) E.; m. Karen S. Rife, Apr. 27, 1973; 1 child, Sarah Elizabeth. BS in Biology, SUNY, Cortland, 1968; MPH, U. Tenn., 1971. Public health cons. Ohio Dept. Health, Columbus, 1971-76, supr. cert. of need program Ohio Dept. Health, 1976-78; v.p. Cen. Ohio River Valley Assn., Cin., 1978-79, St. Francis-St. George Hosp., Inc., Cin., 1979-82; v.p., adminstr. Huber Heights Health Services Inc. (Ohio), 1982-84; pres., v.p. Children's Med. Ctr., Dayton, Ohio; mem. Montgomery County Mental Health Bd., 1986—. Recipient award USPHS, 1970. Mem. Am. Hosp. Assn., Ohio Hosp. Assn., Am. Coll. Hosp. Adminstrs., Ohio Hosp. Planning Assn. (dir.-at-large 1980-82, pres. elect 1985, pres. 1986), Am. Soc. Hosp. Planning, Ohio Pub. Health Assn., Nat. Assn. Clock and Watch Collectors, St. Vincent DePaul Soc. Roman Catholic. Lodges: Rotary, Elks. Office: One Children's Plaza Dayton OH 45404

EIKELBERNER, IKE K., manufacturing company executive; b. Logansport, Ind., July 20, 1947; s. Joseph Edwin and Ercil Amy (Neff) E.; m. Lora Gail Taulman, July 30, 1967; children: Jeffrey I., Joseph E. BS in Bus., Ind. U., 1969. Sr. acct. Price Waterhouse & Co., South Bend, Ind., 1969-73; controller, asst. treas. Adams Engring., Inc., South Bend, Ind., 1973-76; controller Excel Industries, Inc., Elkhart, Ind., 1976-81; v.p., controller Weldun Internat., Inc., Bridgman, Mich., 1981—. Mem. Am. Inst. CPA's, Ind. Soc. CPA's. Republican. Club: Am. Turners (South Bend). Avocations: golf, water skiing, boating. Home: 18100 Chipstead Dr South Bend IN 46637 Office: Weldun Internat Inc 9850 Red Arrow Hwy Bridgman MI 49106

EIKENS, RONALD OWEN, media executive; b. Mpls., Dec. 13, 1945; s. Owen Henry and Lois (Hager) E.; m. Susan Margaret Theis, Aug. 27, 1971; children: Eric, Nicole. AA, U. Minn., 1967; BS, St. Cloud State U., 1969, MBA, 1970. Materials mgr. Medalist Industries, Milw., 1974-79; gen. mgr. Gilbert Freeman Fabrics, Boston, 1979-80; exec. v.p. Earth Shelter Corp., Berlin, Wis., 1980-83; pres. System 7 Corp., Mpls., 1983-85; v.p. Hal Pubs., N.Y.C., 1985-87; gen. mgr., v.p., chief exec. officer KXLI/KXLT TV Broadcasting Inc., St. Clovo, Minn., 1987—. Republican. Roman Catholic. Home: 5379 Brooks Circle SE Prior Lake MN 55372 Office: 800 St Germain Saint Cloud MN 56302

EINERSON, RICHARD JOHN, church official; b. Montevideo, Minn., July 21, 1935; s. Raymond O. and Grace Elaine (Hegstrom) E.; m. Carolyn Jeanne Smothers, June 4, 1955; children: Stephanie, Sonia, Andrea. AB, Warner Pacific Coll., 1957; BDiv, Pacific Sch. Religion, 1961; D of Ministry, Andover Newton Theol. Sch., 1972. Intern Vandberbilt U., Nashville, 1959-60; pastor First Congl. Ch., Pelican Rapids, Minn., 1961-65, United Protestant Ch., Silver Bay, Minn., 1965-68, Sayles Meml. Ch., Lincoln, R.I., 1968-76; chaplain St. Luke's Hosp., Fargo, N.D., 1977—; supr. New Bedford (Mass.) Council of Chs., 1974-76. Author audio-visual counseling programs, 1983, 85. Fellow Am. Assn. Pastoral Counselors (supr. mems.-in-tng. 1974—), Coll. of Chaplains; mem. Assn. Clin. Pastoral Edn. (clin.), Mental Health Assn. Democrat. Mem. United Ch. of Christ. Avocations: photography, golf, carpentry, fishing. Home: 3250 15th Ave SW #18 Fargo ND 58103 Office: St Lukes Hosps 5th at Mills Fargo ND 58122

EINHORN, EDWARD (EDDIE) MARTIN, professional baseball team executive; b. Paterson, N.J., Jan. 3, 1936; s. Harold Benjamin and Mae (Lippman) E.; m. Ann Magdelene Pelachik, Apr. 24, 1962; children: Jennifer, Jeffrey. A.B., U. Pa., 1957; J.D., Northwestern U., 1960. Radio sports announcer Sta.-WXPN, Phila., 1954-57; founder, pres. Midwestern Sports Network, Chgo., 1957-61; founder, pres. TV sports Inc. (name changed to TVS 1968, became subs. Corinthian Broadcasting Corp. 1973), N.Y.C., 1961-65, pres., chief exec. officer, 1965-78; exec. producer CBS Sports, N.Y.C., from 1978; pres. Chgo. White Sox, 1981—; dir. Corinthian Broadcasting Corp., 1973-77. Editor-in-chief: Jour. Air Law and Sci., 1959-60, Northwestern Jour. Criminal Law Sci., 1958-60. Recipient Honor award Namismith Basketball Hall of Fame, 1973; recipient Merit award Nat. Assn. Basketball Coaches, 1973, Victor award City of Hope, 1974. Mem. Nat. Acad. Radio, TV Arts and Scis., Internat. Radio, TV Soc., Nat. Assn. TV Program Execs., Nat. Assn. Coll. Dirs., Nat. Assn. Basketball Coaches. Home: 160 E Pearson Chicago IL 60611 Office: care Chgo White Sox 324 W 35th St Chicago IL 60616

EINODER, CAMILLE ELIZABETH, educator; b. Chgo., June 15, 1937; d. Isadore and Elizabeth T. (Czerwinski) Popowski; student Fox Bus. Coll., 1954; B.Ed. in Biology, Chgo. Tchrs. Coll., 1964; M.A. in Analytical Chemistry, Gov.'s State U., 1977; MA in Adminstrn. and Supervision, Roosevelt U., 1986; postgrad. m. Joseph X. Einoder, Aug. 5, 1978; children—Carl Frank, Mark Frank, Vivian Einoder, Joe Einoder, Tim Einoder, Sheila Einoder, Jude Einoder. Secretarial positions, Chgo., 1955-64; tchr. biology Chgo. Bd. Edn., 1964—, tchr. biology and agr., 1975-81, tchr. biology, agr. and chemistry, 1981—; human relations coordinator Morgan Park High Sch., Chgo., 1980—, tchr. biology Internat. Studies Sch., 1983—; career devel. cons. for agr. related curriculum. Bds. dirs., founding mem., author constn. Community Council, 1970—; bd. dirs., edn. cons. Neighborhood Council, 1974; rep. Chgo. Tchrs. Union, 1969. Mem. Phi Delta Kappa. Home: 10637 S Claremont St Chicago IL 60643 Office: 1744 W Pryor St Chicago IL 60643

EIS, LORYANN MALVINA, educator; b. Muscatine, Iowa, Apr. 3, 1938; d. Chester N. and Anna M. (Lenz) E. A.B., Augustana Coll., 1960; M.Ed., U. Ill., 1963; postgrad. Montclair State Coll., 1965-67, Indiana U. of Pa., 1968, U. Iowa, 1970, Western Ill. U., 1978-80. Circuit analysis engr. Automatic Electric Co., Northlake, Ill., 1960-61; math. tchr. Orion (Ill.) Community Sch. Dist., 1961-63; math. tchr., dept. chmn. United Twp. High Sch., East Moline, Ill., 1963—; lectr. Augustana Coll., Rock Island, Ill., 1982—. Chmn. Math Task Force, Edn. Service Ctr. #8, 1986-87;. Bd. sec. Citizens to Preserve Black Hawk Park Found., 1977—; v.p. council Salem Lutheran Ch.; bd. dirs. Augustana Coll. Hist. Soc.; mem. Moline YWCA. Mem. NEA, Ill. Edn. Assn., Nat. Council Tchrs. of Math., Ill. Council Tchrs. of Math., Classroom Tchrs. Assn., Assn. Supervision and Curriculum Devel., Rock Island Scott Counties Sci. and Math. Tchrs. Assn., Women in Ednl. Adminstrn., AAUW (past state pres.; grantee 1975-76), Delta Kappa Gamma (state treas.), Am. Philatelic Soc., TransMiss. Philatelic Soc., Quad City Stamp Club. Republican. Cons. General Mathematics Textbook, 1978-79. Home: 2037 15th St Moline IL 61265 Office: 42nd Ave and Archer Dr East Moline IL 61244

EISENBERG, DEAN STEVEN, dentist, pharmacist; b. Cleve., May 4, 1949; s. Harold M. and Selma I. (Miller) E.; m. Faith Irene Dorris, June27, 1972; children: Leah Beth, Aaron Lee. BS in Biology, U. Akron, 1972; BS in Pharmacy, Ohio No. U., 1975; DDS, Case Western Res. U., 1983. Pharmacist Northfield Drug, Northfield Ctr., Ohio, 1975-80, Revco Drug Stores Inc., Cleve., 1980-85; gen. practice dentistry Cleve. and South Euclid, Ohio, 1983—. Recipient Rexall award Rexall Drug Co., 1975. Mem. Hillcrest Dental Study Club, Ohio State Pharm. Assn., Alpha Zeta Omega (Outstanding Mem., 1975). Jewish. Avocations: auto mechanics, bicycle mechanics, lawnmower mechanics, softball. Home: 4125 Linnell South Euclid OH 44121 Office: 3216 Payne Ave Cleveland OH 44114 Office: 1500 S Green Rd South Euclid OH 44114

EISENBERG, EARL, management and financial consulting company executive; b. Cleve., Mar. 30, 1953; s. Harold and Selma (Miller) E.; m. Janice Wolf, Nov. 4, 1979. BBA, U. Cin., 1975. Loan officer SBA, Cleve., 1975; controller Simmonds Design Builders, Valley City, Ohio, 1975-78; pres. Eisenberg & Assocs., Cleve., 1978—; com. mem. Geauga County Revolving Loan Fund, Chardon, Ohio, 1984—; bd. dirs. Cleve. Area Fin. Devel. Corp., 1986—. Dem. committeeman, Geauga County, 1986. Mem. Nat. Assn. Accts. (dir. mem. retention 1983-84, dir. mem. acquistions 1984-85). Office: Eisenberg & Assocs Inc PO Box 22631 Cleveland OH 44122

EISENBERG, JAMES, beef processing company executive; b. Chgo., Apr. 17, 1930; s. Sam and Celia (Hackner) E.; m. Nancy Elin Ladany, Aug. 5, 1955; 1 son, Steven Jamie. B.A., Carleton Coll., 1952. Western sales mgr. Eisenberg Originals, Chgo., 1952-55; with Vienna Sausage Mfg. Co., Chgo., 1956—; v.p., sec. Vienna Sausage Mfg. Co., 1964-73, exec. v.p., 1973-78, pres., chief exec. officer, 1979-86, chmn. bd., chief exec. officer, 1986—; dir. Food Internat. Japan, Tokyo. Clubs: Northmoor Country, Standard. Avocations: welding, fishing, golf. Office: Vienna Sausage Mfg Co 2501 N Damen Ave Chicago IL 60647

EISENHUT, RICHARD JEAN, pharmacist, owner pharmacy; b. Indpls., Dec. 8, 1929; s. George Robert and Dorothy Mae (Weber) E.; m. Donna Lee Kinney, May 5, 1956; children: Richard Jr., Timothy, Robert, Theresa. BA, Butler U., 1950; PhD (hon.), Ind. Pharm. Assn., 1980. Pharmacist, owner Eisenhut Drugs, Indpls., 1950-86; with Peoples Pharmacy, Indpls., 1987—. Served as cpl. U.S. Army, 1952-54. Mem. Ind. Pharm. Assn. Home: 1327 N Hawthorne Ln Indianapolis IN 46219 Office: Eisenhut Drugs Inc 5353 English Ave Indianapolis IN 46219

EISENSCHENK, MARK GERARD, accountant; b. Cold Spring, Min., Aug. 31, 1957; s. Elmer John and Donna Mae (Feneis) E.; Janet Annamay Hommerding, Aug. 9, 1980. BS in Acctg., St. Cloud (Minn.) State U., 1981. CPA, Minn. Sr. auditor Arthur Andersen & Co., Mpls., 1980-86; mgr. acctg., fin. reporting Sinclair & Valentine, St. Paul, 1986—. Exec. advisor Jr. Achievement, Mpls., 1981-86. Mem. Am. Inst. CPA's, Minn. State Soc. CPA's. Avocations: investing, international travel. Home: 7881 Xerxes Ct N Brooklyn Park MN 55444 Office: Sinclair & Valentine 2520 Pilot Knob Rd Suite 250 Saint Paul MN 55120

EISERMANN, ECKEHARD HERMANN, corporate executive; b. Munich, Jan. 13, 1943; came to U.S., 1980; s. Gunter Ludwig and Lisa (Klusmann) E.; m. Karin Ursula Pfeiffer, May 8, 1968; children: Philip Okken, Lukas Georg. BS, Tech. U., Clausthal, Fed. Republic of Germany, 1964; MS in Engring., Tech. U., Berlin, 1967, PhD in Engring., 1969. Application mgr. M&P, Cologne, Fed. Republic of Germany, 1975-77, sales mgr., 1977-80; gen. mgr. M&P, Lorain, Ohio, 1980-87; pres. M&P, Inc., Lorain, 1987—. Home: 4499 Mapleview Dr Vermilion OH 44089

EISMAN, ESTHER, international sales director; b. Linz, Austria, June 10, 1950; came to U.S., 1951; d. Hilel and Gusta (Rosenberg) E. BA, Butler U., 1972; MBA, Ind. U., 1979. Assoc. editor Hardware Retailing Mag., Indpls., 1972-76; dir. mktg. Blue Lustre Home Care Products, Inc., Indpls., 1976-84; dir. advt., pub. relations Howard W. Sams & Co., Indpls., 1984-85, dir. internat. sales, 1985—. Mem. Am. Mktg. Assn., Ind. U. Sch. Bus. Alumni Assn. Avocations: reading, dancing, aerobics. Home: 5847 N Rural Indianapolis IN 46220 Office: Howard W Sams & Co 4300 W 62d St Indianapolis IN 46268

EISNER, DIANA JOCELYN, financial broker; b. Forest Hills, N.Y., Aug. 17, 1959; d. Bruno Henry and Patricia Ellen (McQuaid) E. BA, Ohio State U., 1981. Registered commodity trading rep. With Contifin. Services, Chgo., 1981-82; rep. Drexel Burnham, Chgo., 1982-85; broker Merrill Lynch,

Chgo., 1985—. Mem. The Art Inst. Chgo., 1982—, Friends Chgo. City Ballet, 1985—; mem. Chgo. Council on Fgn. Relations. Mem. Chgo. Bd. Trade. Presbyterian. Avocations: long distance cycling, dance, cinema, primitive art, languages. Home: 1414 N LaSalle Chicago IL 60610

EKHOLM, BRUCE PETER, biostatistician; b. Mpls., Nov. 1, 1956; s. Richard Ernest and Beverly Maxine (Carlson) E.; m. Julie Kay Hunnicutt, Sept. 14, 1985. B.A., St. Olaf Coll., 1978; M.S., U. Minn., 1980. Advanced biostatistician 3M/Riker Labs., Inc., St. Paul, 1981-84, sr. biostatistician, 1984—. Mem. Am. Statis. Assn. (chpt. sec.-treas. 1984-86, pres. 1987-88), Biometrics Soc., Sigma Pi Sigma. Lutheran. Avocations: cross-country skiing; softball. Home: 4511 Audrey Ave E Inver Grove Heights MN 55075

EKSTROM, NORRIS KENNETH, machinery company executive; b. Kiron, Iowa, Nov. 4, 1927; s. John Edwin and Anna Catherine (Ogren) E.; m. Genevieve Lydia Schwartz, May 25, 1963. B.A., Gustavus Adolphus Coll., St. Peter, Minn., 1949; C.P.A., Northwestern U., Chgo., 1958; postgrad., U. Chgo., 1958-59. Accountant, internal auditor, plant controller Link-Belt Co., Chgo., 1949-61; asst. to v.p., controller Bucyrus-Erie Co., South Milwaukee, Wis., 1961; plant mgr. Bucyrus-Erie Co., Erie, Pa., 1961-62; controller Bucyrus-Erie Co., South Milwaukee, 1962-66; v.p., controller Bucyrus-Erie Co., 1966-68, v.p. fin., treas., controller, dir., 1968-75, v.p. fin., treas., dir., 1975-78; chmn., dir., chief exec. officer Bucyrus-Erie Co. (now Becor-Western Corp.), 1978—; chmn. bd., pres., dir. Bucyrus Disc, Inc.; chmn. bd., dir. Bucyrus-Erie Co. of Can., Ltd., Bucyrus (Africa) Proprietary, Ltd., Bucyrus (Australia) Proprietary, Ltd., Brad Foote Gear Works, Inc., Pitts. Gear Co., Bucyrus Internat., Inc.; pres., dir. Bucyrus-Erie Found.; dir. Ruston-Bucyrus, Lincoln, Eng., W.H. Brady Co., Milw. Mem. Greater Milw. Com. on Community Devel.; mem. adv. council U. Wis. Sch. Bus. Adminstrn., Milw. Recipient Disting. Alumni citation Gustavus Adolphus Coll., 1978. Clubs: Milwaukee, Milw. Country, University of Milw.; Knollwood Country (Lake Forest, Ill.); University (N.Y.C.); Bent Pine (Vero Beach, Fla.). Office: Becor Western Inc 1100 Milwaukee Ave South Milwaukee WI 53172 *

EKSTROM, ROBERT CARL, music educator, singer, choral director; b. Duluth, Minn., Mar. 26, 1917; s. Hans Birger and Hilda Sophia (Nelson) E.; m. Charlotte Virginia Tuttle, Dec. 28, 1940; children: Robert, Virginia, Carol, Richard, Lorrie, Cheryl. Diploma, Duluth Jr. Coll., 1937; BS in Music Edn., U. Minn., 1940, MEd in Music Edn., 1946; EdD in Music Edn., UCLA, 1959. Cert. tchr., Minn., Calif., Ill. Head vocal dept. Sherburn (Minn.) Bd. Edn., 1940-41; instr. music Duluth Pub. Schs., 1941-52, 54-64; prof. music Pasadena (Calif.) City Coll., 1952-54; head music dept. Lindblom Tech. High Sch., chgo., 1964—; dir. and soloist Chgo. Choral Soc., 1970—; mem., oratorio dir. Chgo. Swedish Choral and Symphony Orch., 1964-74; mem., dir. Am. Union Swedish Singers, 1958—; choir dir. and soloist various chs. Minn., Calif., Ill., 1941—; music dir. Calif. Bur. Music, Los Angeles, 1951-59, Mayor's Cultural Com., Chgo., 1972-79, State St. Council, Chgo., 1975-79, various musical groups, 1949—; tenor soloist and singer radio, television, stage, others; recorded with Capitol Records; sang at coronation festivities Coronation of Queen Elizabeth II, London, 1953; gave command performance for King of Sweden, Stockholm, 1980. Author: The Male Voice, 1945, Correlation of Music Talent With Intelligence, 1946, Development of the Madrigal, 1947, Comparison of the Male Voice, 1959, Boys Life in Minnesota, 1986. Recipient Singers medal of Merit, Am. Union Swedish Singers, 1974. Mem. Am. Choral Dirs. Assn., Music Educators Nat. Conf., Associated Male Choruses Am. (dir. upper midwest dist., pres. 1949-52). Club: Ill. Athletic (Chgo.). Lodge: Masons (music dir. 1969—, Meritorious Service award 1980). Home: 2321 W 110th Pl Chicago IL 60643 Office: Chgo Choral Soc 12 S Michigan Ave Chicago IL 60603

EKVALL, BERNT, dentist; b. Nora, Sweden, June 25, 1915; s. Johan Alexis and Elin Karolina (Persson) E.; L.D.S., U. Stockholm, 1944; D.D.S., U. Mich., 1951; m. Margit Andersson, June 23, 1940 (div. 1982); 1 dau., Lucie Margita. Came to U.S., 1949, naturalized, 1954. With Swedish Govt. Dental Services, 1943-45; pvt. practice dentistry Sweden, 1945-49, Clinton, Mich., 1951-52, Dearborn, 1952-55, 57-58, Detroit, 1958-81, 87—, St. Clair, Mich., 1981-87; v.p. Scandinavian Am. Republican Club, 1960-68, pres., 1968-72; treas. Rep. State Nationalities Council, 1971-73; Bd. dirs. Scandinavian Symphony Soc., 1961-72; bd. mgrs. Hannan br. YMCA, 1962—, chmn. Eastside br., 1976. Served to capt. AUS, 1955-57. Fellow Royal Soc. Health, Internat. Acad. Dentistry, Acad. Gen. Dentistry, Internat. Coll. Dentists, Am. Coll. Dentists; mem. Am., Mich. Dental Assns., Detroit Dist. Dental Soc., Detroit Dental Clinic Club (membership sec. 1972-73, sec. 1973-74, pres. 1975-76), Bunting Periodontal Study Club, Mich. Acad. Gen. Dentistry (sec. 1975-76, v.p. 1976-78, pres. 1978-80). Clubs: Prismatic Renaissance (Detroit); Grosse Pointe Hunt. Home: 1063 Woodbridge E Saint Clair Shores MI 48080 Office: 11110 Morang Detroit MI 48224

ELAM, ALBERT GARLAND, II, military officer; b. Akron, Ohio, June 21, 1955; s. Albert Garland and Anne Marie (Brown) E.; m. Lillian Cruz Mercado, June 24, 1978; children: Natalie Anne, Albert Garland III. BBA, Ohio U., 1977; MBA, Oklahoma City U., 1981. Commd. 2d lt. USAF, 1977, advanced through grades to capt., 1981; cost and mgmt. analysis officer 93 Bomb Wing, Castle AFB, Calif., 1978; chief cost and mgmt. analysis br. 552 Airborne Warning and Control Wing, Tinker AFB, Okla., 1978-80; budget officer 553 Airborne Warning and Control Wing, Tinker AFB, Okla., 1980-82; budget officer Hdqrs. Air Force Communications Command, Scott AFB, ILL., 1982-84, exec. officer, 1985-86, dir. plans and programs, 1986—; comptroller 1012 Air Base Group, Thule Air Base, Greenland, 1984-85; cons. Dept. of Treasury, 1983. Contbr. articles to profl. jours. Decorated Meritorious Service Medal with one oak leaf cluster. Mem. Inst. Cost Analysis (cert., pres. local chpt. 1982-84, 85—), Am. Soc. Mil. Comptrollers (newsletter editor local chpt. 1986—), Am. Assn. Budget and Program Analysis, Air Force Assn., Phi Beta Sigma. Roman Catholic. Avocations: playing and listening to jazz, playing chess. Home: 110 Red Pine Ave O'Fallon IL 62269 Office: Hdqrs AFCC/ACE Scott AFB IL 62221-6001

ELAMAN, MICHAEL O'NEIL, accounting company exeucutive; b. Pontiac, Mich., Apr. 14, 1947; s. Wesley O'Neil and Mary Ellen (Varble) E.; m. Darlene Kaye Bottoms, Oct. 15, 1971; children: Jennifer Lynn, Joshua O'Neil. BS in Acctg., Oakland City (Ind.) Coll., 1973; MBA in Bus., U. Evansville, 1976. CPA, Ind. Ptnr. Wyatt & Elaman Assocs., Tell City, Ind., 1981-86; ptnr., mgr. Harding, Shymanski, & Co., Tell City, Ind., 1986—. Trustee Tell City Ch. of Christ, 1973—; pres. and trustee Tell City Pub. Library, 1981—; pres. Maple Manor Christian Homes, Sellersburg, Ind., 1986—. Served with USN, 1966-69, Vietnam. Mem. Am. Inst. CPA's, Ind. Soc. CPA's. Republican.Lodge: Kiwanis. Avocations: running, tennis. Home: 1146 21st St Tell City IN 47586

ELBERSON, ROBERT EVANS, food industry executive; b. Winston-Salem, N.C., Nov. 9, 1928; m. Helen Hanes; children: Nancy Ann, Charles Evans II. Grad., Choate Sch., 1946; B.S. in Engring, Princeton U., 1950; M.B.A., Harvard U., 1952. Mgmt. trainee Hanes Hosiery Mills Co., Winston-Salem, 1954-56; office mgr. Hanes Hosiery Mills Co., 1956-62, sec., 1959-62, v.p. mfg., 1962-65, mem. exec. com., dir., 1963-65; v.p. planning Hanes Corp. Hanes Hosiery Mills Co. (merger Hanes Hosiery Mills Co. and P.H. Hanes Knitting Co.), 1965-68, pres. hosiery div., v.p. corp., 1968-72, pres., chief exec. officer, 1972-79, dir., 1972-79; dir. Sara Lee Corp. (formerly Consol. Foods Corp.), 1979—, exec. v.p., 1979-82, vice chmn., 1982-83, pres., chief operating officer, 1983-86, vice chmn., 1986—; dir. W.W. Grainger Co., Skokie, Ill., CBI Industries, Oak Brook, Ill., No. Trust Corp., Chgo., Sonoco Products Co., Hartsville, S.C. Bd. visitors Babcock Grad. Sch. Mgmt., Wake Forest U., 1977-83; trustee Salem Acad. and Coll., Winston-Salem, 1980—, Mus. Sci. and Industry, Chgo., 1984—. Served as lt. USAF, 1952-54. Office: Sara Lee Corp Three First National Plaza Chicago IL 60602

ELCONIN, MICHAEL HENRY, computer company executive; b. Cleve., June 20, 1953; s. Arnold N. and Jane R. (Rose) E.; m. Jolene E. Kiefer, Aug. 31, 1986. BA, U. Wis., Milw., 1984. Del. Wis. Ho. of Reps., Milw., 1973-77; chief of staff Govs. Office, Madison, Wis., 1977-78; dir. Assembly Dem. Caucus, Madison, 1978-79, Milw. Sch. Bd., 1979-83; pres. Software Banc, Inc., Milw., 1981—; bd. dirs. Jewish Vocat. Service, Milw. Avocations: politics, cross-country skiing. Office: Software Banc Inc 3121 W Wisconsin Ave Milwaukee WI 53208

EL DEEB, MOHAMED EL SAYED NASSER, oral and maxillofacial surgeon, educator; b. Cairo, May 19, 1950; came to U.S., 1976; s. El Sayed Nasser El Deeb and Olaft Mohamed Riad; m. Margaret Mary El Deeb, June 30, 1983; 1 child from previous marriage, Ahmed. Grad., Coll. Sci., Cairo, 1972; MS, U. Minn., 1979. Instr. oral surgery Azhar U., Cairo, 1973-76; asst. prof. Dept. Oral and Maxillofacial Surgery, U. Minn., Mpls., 1980-85, assoc. prof., dir. research, 1985—; staff U. Minn. Hosp., Fairview Hosp., St. Mary's Hosp., Cook Clinic. Contbr. numerous book chapters, research papers, and abstracts to profl. jours. and sci. publs. Instr., trainer basic and advanced cardiac life support Am. Heart Assn., Mpls., 1981—; bd. dirs. Union Gospel Mission Dental Clinic, St. Paul, 1983—. Fellow Am. Assn. Hosp. Dentists, Am. Coll. Dentists, Am. Coll. Oral and Maxillofacial Surgeons, Internat. Coll. Dentists; mem. ADA, Am. Assn. Dental Schs., Am. Assn. Oral and Maxillofacial Surgeons, Am. Assn. Oral and Maxillofacial Surgeons, Am. Assn. Oral and Maxillofacial Surgeons Ednl. Found., Am. Cleft Palate Assn., Am. Dental Soc. Anesthesiology (pres. elect 1986—), Egyptian Dental Assn., Internat. Assn. for Dental Research, Internat. Congress Oral Implantologists, Minn. Dental Assn., Minn. Soc. Oral and Maxillofacial Surgeons, Soc. Educators in Oral and Maxillofacial Surgery, Omicron Kappa Epsilon, Beta Beta. Home: 4413 Ellsworth Dr Edina MN 55432 Office: Sch Dentistry U Minn 515 Delaware St SE Minneapolis MN 55455

ELDER, DOUGLAS PAUL, manufacturing company financial executive; b. Scottsbluff, Nebr., Feb. 1, 1951; s. Paul Russell and Doris Madelyn (Thompson) E.; m. Wendy Sue Weaver, May 26, 1973; children: Tyler Paul, Spencer Douglas, Andrew Graham. BS in Computer Sci., U. Nebr., 1973; postgrad. studies in exec. program, U. Chgo., 1986—. CPA, Ill. Staff auditor, mgr. Peat Marwick Mitchell, Chgo., 1973-81; sr. mgr. Peat Marwick Mitchell, Chgo, 1982-84, Adelaide, Australia, 1981-82; mgr. corp. fin. reporting Motorola, Inc., Schaumburg, Ill., 1984—. Mem. Am. Inst. CPA's. Republican. Home: 359 W Peregrine Dr Palatine IL 60067 Office: Motorola Inc 1303 E Algonquin Rd Schaumburg IL 60196

ELDER, WYATT NORRIS, JR., food products executive; b. Bryan Mawr, Pa., Dec. 12, 1959; s. Wyatt Norris and Barbara Ann (Ackroyd) E.; m. Mary Newby, Apr. 11, 1987. BS, U. Colo., 1983. Quality control chemist Cargill, Inc., Gainesville, Ga., 1983-85; lab. mgr. Cargill, Inc., Hartsville, S.C., 1985-86; tech. service rep. Cargill, Inc., Mpls., 1986—. Mem. Am. Oil Chemists Soc. (pres. club 1986), Assn. Dressings and Sauces. Republican. Episcopalian. Avocations: photography, reading, snow skiing. Home: 8324 Abbott Ave N Brooklyn Park MN 55443 Office: Cargill Inc PO Box 9300 PRG-2 Minneapolis MN 55443

ELDRED, DONALD FRED, computer company executive; b. Ft. Madison, Iowa, Apr. 8, 1941; s. Wesley Eugene and Frances Catherine (Freesmeier) E.; m. Marilou Denbo, July 13, 1974; 1 child, Sarah Elizabeth. BA, St. Ambrose Coll., 1963; MA in Theology, Aquinas Inst., 1967; MA in Music, U. Iowa, 1971; MBA, St. Thomas Coll., 1978. Ordained priest Roman Catholic Ch., 1967. Priest Diocese of Davneport, Iowa, 1967-74; asst. prof. music St. Ambrose Coll., Davenport, 1969-74; mgr. programming Brown & Bigelow, St. Paul, 1975-79; systems mgr. Proform, Mpls., 1979-82; info. ctr. mgr. Onan Corp., Mpls., 1982—. Pres. Summit Hill Assn., St. Paul, 1980. Mem. Assn. Systems Mgrs. (bd. dirs. 1985—). Democrat. Avocations: art, music, reading. Home: 946 Fairmount Saint Paul MN 55105 Office: Onan Corp 1400-73 Rd Ave NE Minneapolis MN 55432

ELEGANT, LAWRENCE DAVID, allergist; b. Bklyn., May 26, 1923; s. Maurice and Sarah (Horowitz) E.; m. Joan Marjorie Sherman, Dec. 21, 1946; children: Linda-Faye, Bruce Michael, Jeffrey Lee, Michelle Sue. BS, Western Res. U., 1943; MD, U. Health Sci., Chgo. Med. Sch., 1950. Diplomate Am. Bd. Pediatrics, Am. Bd. Allergy and Immunology. Intern Michael Reese Hosp. and Med. Ctr., Chgo., 1950-51, resident in basic sci., 1951-52, resident in pediatrics, 1952-54, clin. asst. dept. pediatrics, 1954-57, adj. clin. asst. dept. pediatrics, 1957-61, assoc. attending physician dept. pediatrics, 1961-66, physician-in-charge pediatric allergy clinic, 1969-71, acting chmn. dept. pediatrics, 1971-73, attending physician dept. pediatrics, 1966—; assoc. attending physician dept. pediatrics Cook County Hosp., Chgo., 1962-64; practice medicine specializing in pediatrics Chgo., 1954-68; practice medicine specializing in allergy and immunology Mt. Prospect, Ill., 1968—; courtesy staff Chgo. Lying-in Hosp., 1960; mem. various coms. Michael Reese Hosp., 1954-66; instr. pediatric medicine U. Ill., Chgo., 1953-54, Chgo. Med. Sch., 1960-63, clin. asst. div. pediatrics, 1963-64, clin. assoc., 1964-65, clin. asst. prof., 1965-69. cons. Chgo. Bd. Health, 1966—. Adv. pediatrician Hyde Park Neighborhood Club, Chgo., 1965-66. Served with MC, U.S. Army, 1943-46. Fellow Am. Acad. Pediatrics (mem. youth commn. Ill. chpt.), Am. Pub. Health Assn., Am. Acad. Allergy, Chgo. Med. Soc., Inst. Medicine Chgo., Chgo. Allergy Soc. (pres. 1971); mem. AMA, Ill. State Med. Soc., Ill. Pediatric Soc. (com. on adolescence 1965-66, youth com. 1966, chmn. sports com. 1985—), Ill. State Soc. Allergy and Clin. Immunology (pres. 1971-72), Chgo. Pediatric Soc., , Chgo. Maternal and Child Care Adv. Com., 1973—. Office: 221 W Prospect Mount Prospect IL 60056

ELEK, LOUIS A., bank administrator; b. Pitts., Aug. 3, 1952; s. Louis and Dorothy (Lengyel) E.; m. Barbara Hall, May 20, 1972; children: Jennifer Renee, Melanie Lynn. Student, Robert Morris Coll., 1979. CPA, Pa., Ohio. Br. mgr. Norwest, Pitts., 1976-79; staff acct. Snodgrass & Co., Pitts., 1979-80; mgr. loan acctg. Equibank, Pitts., 1980-84; mgr. cost acctg. Bank One, Columbus, Ohio, 1984-87; mgr. internal reporting Huntington Nat. Bank, Columbus, 1987—; cons. Bank One Summit Software, Dallas, 1985-86. Served with USAF, 1972-76. Mem. Am. Inst. CPAs, Nat. Assn. Bank Cost and Mgmt. Acctg., Ohio Soc. CPAs, Am. Legion. Republican. Presbyterian. Avocation: sports. Home: 4400 Bitter Root Dr Westerville OH 43081 Office: Huntington Nat Bank 41 S High St Columbus OH 43287

ELESH, RICHARD HENRY, obstetrician, gynecologist; b. Chgo., Feb. 18, 1935; s. Solomon A. and Miriam B. (Reddell) E.; m. Betty B., June 29, 1957; children: Carolyn, Herbert, Ronald. BA, Northwestern U., 1956, MD, 1959. Diplomate Am. Bd. Ob-Gyn. Intern Wesley Meml. Hosp., Chgo., 1959-60, resident obstetrician, 1960-62, 63-64; resident obstetrician Chgo. Maternity Ctr., 1962-63; sr. attending physician Wesley Hosp., Chgo., 1965-73, Evanston (Ill.) Hosp., 1973—; asst. clin. prof. Northwestern U. Med. Sch., Chgo., 1964—. Contbr. articles to profl. jours. Fellow Am. Coll. Ob-Gyn, Chgo. Gynecol. Soc., Cen. Assn. Obstetrics and Gynecology; mem. AMA, Am. Soc. Cytology, Chgo. Med. Soc. Jewish. Club: Sheridan Shore Yacht (Wilmette). Home: 2131 Elmwood Ave Wilmette IL 60091 Office: North Suburban Gyn-Ob Ltd 2530 Ridge Ave Evanston IL 60201

ELGER, WILLIAM ROBERT, JR., accountant; b. Chgo., Mar. 20, 1950; s. William Robert and Grace G. (LaVaque) E.; m. Kathryn Michele Johnson, July 10, 1971; children: Kimberly, William, Kristin, Joseph. AS in Applied Sci., Coll. of DuPage, Glen Ellyn, Ill., 1970; BS magna cum laude, U. Ill.-Chgo., 1972. CPA, Ill. Staff acct. Ernst & Whinney, Chgo., 1973, in-charge acct., 1973-74, sr. acct., 1974-78, mgr., 1978-82, sr. mgr., 1982—; presenter various confs. in field Ernst & Whinney, Chgo., 1980—. Author, developer: (tng. course) Auditing Third Party Reimbursement, 1986. Mem. Union League Civic and Arts Found., Chgo., 1982—, Union League Found. for Boy's Clubs, Chgo., 1982—; treas. Newport Assn., Carol Stream, Ill., 1982-83; coach Tri-City Soccer Assn., St. Charles, Ill., 1984, 87. Mem. Healthcare Fin. Mgmt. Assn. (acctg. and reimbursement com. 1982-86, chpt. task force com. 1986, auditing com. 1986, Spl. Recognition award 1986), Ill. Soc. CPA's (mem. long-term healthcare com. 1983), Am. Inst. CPA's, Chgo. Health Execs. Forum. Methodist. Club: Union League (Chgo.). Avocations: golf, tennis. Home: 1505 Madison Ave Saint Charles IL 60174 Office: Ernst & Whinney 150 S Wacker Dr Chicago IL 60606

ELGIN, MARY LOUISE, pollution control operator; b. Clarksdale, Ariz., Nov. 1, 1944; d. Sallie M. (Jones) Martin; m. Robert Elgin Jr., June 20, 1968 (div. Sept. 1972); children: Lori A., Steven F. Hunter. Student, Ind. U., Bloomington, 1963-65, Calumet Coll., 1967-68, 80-82, Ind. U., Gary, 1979-84. Sec. Amoco Oil Co., Chgo., 1966-70; pollution control operator Inland Steel Co., East Chicago, Ind., 1972—. Mem. com. Precient Orgn., Gary, 1984-86, Gary commn. Status of Women, 1987-91; local chmn. Katie Hall for Ind. Congress 1st Dist., 1982, 86. Mem. NAACP, Coalition of Black Trade Unionists (regional v.p., pres. 1984), United Steel Workers Am. (founding, co-chair dist. 31 women's caucus 1976-85, bd. dir. dist. 31 black caucus 1979-86, sec. 1977—), Coalition Labor Union for Women (nat. bd. dir. 1984-86, Northwest Ind. chpt. pres., state v.p.). Home: 572 Mount St Gary IN 46406

ELIAS, HOUGHTON F., surgeon; b. Wymore, Nebr., Dec. 22, 1911; s. Francis L. and Olive (Todd) E.; m. Ruth Eleanor Bronson, Sept. 15, 1934 (div. 1948); children: Sharon L., Houghton F. Jr.; m. Jane Virginia Sutton, Dec. 10, 1949; children: Jane F. Elliott, Julie Ann, John H. BS, U. Nebr., 1933; MD, U. Nebr., Omaha, 1936. Diplomate Am. Bd. Surgery. Asst. instr. physiology U. Nebr., Omaha, 1933-34; resident in surgery U. Rochester, N.Y., 1936-37; chief resident Cleve. Clinic, 1939-40; chief surg. service Ft. Crook Hosp., Rochester, Minn., 1941-42; med. dir. Civil Def. Gage County, 1945-55; chmn. pub. relations Nebr. State Med. Assn., 1954-64; founder Hall of Health, 1955; cons. VA Hosp., Lincoln; asst. prof. surgery Creighton U. Originated Cleve. Clinic newsletter; inventor crash cart. Bd. dirs. Nebr. Blue Shield; chmn. Cancer Task Force Nebr., S.D. Served to lt. col. U.S. Army, 1941-46, ETO. Decorated six battle stars; named to Soc. of Fellows, Cleve. Clinic, 1985. Fellow ACS (mem. Southwestern Surg. Congress 1962—, mem. credentials com., pres. Nebr. chapt.); mem. Nebr. State Med. Assn.(chmn. pub. relations com.), Pan-Pacific Surg. Soc., Southwestern Surg. Soc., Nebr. (founder), Cleve. Clinic Alumni Assn. (pres.), Gage County Hist. Soc. (life). Republican. Methodist. Club: Manhattan Country (Kans.). Lodge: Elks. Avocations: hunting, skiing, sports cars, golfing, Am. quarter horses. Home: Rural Rt 1 Box 23 G Randolph KS 66554 Office: Med Arts Bldg PO Box 728 Beatrice NE 68310

ELIASON, PHYLLIS MARIE, missionary, educator; b. Greenacres, Fla., Dec. 21, 1925; d. John Sylvester Underhill and Catherine (Graef) Males; m. Albert Eliason, Aug. 22 (dec. Nov. 1955); children: PHyllis, James, Nancy, Albert Jr. BA in Psychology, U. Guam, 1971, MEd, 1974. Cert. guidance counselor. Missionary dir. Child Evangelism Fellowship, Inc., Palm Beach County, Fla., 1957-62; missionary serving Guam and Micronesia Child Evangelism Fellowship, Inc., Warrenton, Mo., 1962-85; counselor Marshalls Christian High Sch., Majuro, Marshall Islands, 1976-77; mission recruiter, tchr. trainer Child Evangelism Fellowship, 1985—. Pres., v.p. Girls Scouts Guam, 1963-75; Bd. dirs. Guam Scout Council, 1967, 79-82, Simpson Bible Coll. Extension Sch., Guam. Named Hon. Citizen of Huntsville, Ala., City Council, 1966. Mem. Am. Profl. Guidance Assn. Avocations: collecting stamps, collecting shells. Office: Child Evangelism Fellowship Inc Box 348 Warrenton MO 63383

ELICK, RONALD LEE, electrical engineer; b. Lancaster, Ohio, Aug. 3, 1953; s. Jerry Lester and Shirley Louise (Thomas) E.; m. Mary Ann Kearns, Sept. 18, 1976; children—Michelle, Amanda. B.S. in Elec. Engring., U. Cin., 1977. Sales engr. Gen. Electric Co., Cin., 1977-84; sr. sales engr. ITRAN Corp., Cin., 1984—. Mem. Soc. Mfg. Engrs. Home: 5692 Lake Michigan Dr Fairfield OH 45014 Office: 270 Northland Blvd Suite 225 Cincinnati OH 45246

ELISEO, THOMAS STEPHEN, psychologist; b. Bklyn., Apr. 9, 1932; s. Frank and Leonarda (Caruso) E.; m. Dolores G. Eliseo, Nov. 11, 1955 (dec.); children: Stephen, Matthew; m. Nancy Tesmer McNamara, Apr. 28, 1984. BA, CUNY, Queens, 1953; MS, Purdue U., 1959, PhD, 1960. Diplomate Am. Bd. Profl. Psychology. Clin. psychologist VA Hosp., Lebanon, Pa., 1960-63, Psychiat. Service, Knoxville, Tenn., 1963-64; pvt. practice psychology Rockford, Ill., 1964—; dir. adult programs Swedish-Am. Hosp., Rockford, 1984—; asst. prof. psychiatry U. Ill. Med. Sch., Rockford, 1985—. Trustee Unitarian Ch., Rockford, 1986—. Served in U.S. Army, 1953-55. Mem. Am. Psychol. Assn., Ill. Psychol. Assn., Soc. for Clin. and Exptl. Hypnosis. Democrat. Avocations: music, history, swimming. Home: 5331 Regency Way Rockford IL 61111 Office: Alpine Psychiat Ctr 1301 N Alpine Rd Rockford IL 61107

ELKHANIALY, HEKMAT ABDUL RAZEK, demographic cons.; b. Egypt, Dec. 17, 1935; came to U.S., 1961, naturalized, 1975; d. Abdul Razek Hussein and Nabiha Mursi (Kutb) E.; B. Commerce/Econs., Cairo U., 1959; Ph.D. in Sociology, U. Chgo., 1968; m. Chandra Kant Jha, Dec. 20, 1969; 1 dau., Lakshmi. Mem. faculty Roosevelt U., Chgo., 1968-75, asso. prof. sociology, 1973-75; demographic cons., Chgo., 1975—; research assoc. Population Research Ctr., U. Chgo., 1977-80; v.p. PSM Internat. Mem. Population Assn. Am., Am. Sociol. Assn., Chgo. Council Fgn. Relations. Contbr. articles to profl. jours. Home: 2800 N Lake Shore Dr Chicago IL 60657 Office: PSM Internat 446 E Ontario Suite 1000 Chicago IL 60611

ELKINS, JAMES PAUL, physician; b. Lincoln, Nebr., Mar. 20, 1924; s. James Hill and Antonia (Wohler) E.; M.D., U. Va., 1947; m. May Hollingsworth Reynolds, June 15, 1946; children—Patricia May Elkins Riggs, Paulette Frances Elkins Phillips, James Barrington. Cert. Emergency Med. Services Commn. Intern, DePaul Hosp., Norfolk, Va., 1947-48; resident in ob-gyn Alexandria (Va.) Hosp., 1948-49, Franklin Sq. Hosp., Balt., 1949-50, St. Rita's Hosp., Lima, Ohio, 1950, Tripler Army Hosp., Honolulu, 1953-54; practice medicine specializing in ob-gyn, Indpls., 1954-73; chief ob-gyn St. Francis Hosp., Beech Grove, Ind., 1965-66; mem. teaching staff Gen. Hosp., Indpls., 1954-73; dep. coroner Marion County, 1965-74; med. cons. disability determination div. Ind. Rehab. Services; examining physician Plasma Alliance Ctr.; ringside physician Ind. State Boxing Commn., Indpls. Pal Club, Ind. Golden Gloves.Mem. World Med. Adv. Bd. World Boxing Council. Served with AUS, 1949-54. Recipient Fred Deborde Award Ind. Golden Gloves, 1985. Mem. Am. Coll. Ob-Gyn, AMA, Ind. State Med. Assn., Marion County Med. Soc., Indpls. Press Club (hon. life), Police League Ind., Fraternal Order Police, Nat. Sojourners, 500 Festival Assos., Police League Ind., Ind. Sports Corp. (charter gold mem.), U.S. Auto Club (life), Phi Chi. Clubs: Ind. Pacers Booster (charter), Thundering Herd Booster Indpls. Colts (charter mem.). Lodges: Masons, Shriners (life). Home: 2045 Lick Creek Dr Indianapolis IN 46203 Office: 6th Floor Illinois Bldg 17 W Market St PO Box 7069 Indianapolis IN 46207

ELKINS, STEVENS JAMES, musician; b. Oklahoma City, May 21, 1958; s. Brewster Rush and Mary Ila (Stevens) E. MusB, Northwestern U., 1980. Free-lance performer, composer, writer Kapture, The Loop Group, The New Art Ensemble, The Pitzen Brass Ensemble, Light Opera Works, others, Chgo. area, 1980—. Composer various musical compositions, 1980—; author articles. Mem. New Music Chgo. (founding bd. mem. 1982-86, treas. 1982-84, pres. 1984-86, festival dir. 1986), Chgo. Fedn. Musicians, Percussive Arts Soc.

ELLEFSON, TIMOTHY HAROLD, real estate appraiser; b. Hampton, Iowa, Jan. 2, 1953; s. Harold William and Anne Sofia (Stoffer) E.; m. Peggee Ann Leonard, June 14, 1975; 1 child, Cassandra Marie. BS, Iowa State U., 1975. Broker Leonard Realty, Eldora, Iowa, 1977—; abstractor, sec., treas. Hardin County Abstract Co., Eldora, 1977—; pres. T.H.E. Appraisers, Eldora, 1979—. Mem. Am. Inst. Real Estate Appraisers (chmn. edn. com, 1984-86, Residential Mem. designation 1984), Nat. Assn. Realtors (Grad. Realtor Inst. 1978), Heart of Iowa Bd. Realtors (pres. 1979, Grad. Realtor Inst. designation 1978), Iowa Land Title Assn. Republican. Lodge: Rotary (bd. dirs. Eldora 1986—). Avocations: sailing, golf, woodworking. Home: Rural Rt #3 Eldora IA 50627 Office: The Appraisers 1300 Edgington Ave Eldora IA 50627

ELLEN, MARTIN M., financial services executive; b. Chgo., Dec. 28, 1953. BS in Acctg., U. Ill., 1975; postgrad in mgmt., Northwestern U., 1987. CPA, Ill. Auditor Price Waterhouse, Chgo., 1975-78, sr. auditor, 1978-81, mgr. auditing, 1981-84, sr. mgr. auditor, 1984; controller D&K Fin., Chgo., 1984-86, v.p. fin., 1986—. Mem. Fin. Exec. Inst., Am. Inst. CPA's, Ill. CPA Soc. Office: D&K Fin Corp 200 Tri-State International Lincolnshire IL 60015

ELLENS, J(AY) HAROLD, theologian, educator; b. McBain, Mich., July 16, 1932; s. John S. and Grace (Kortmann) E.; m. Mary Jo Lewis, Sept. 7, 1954; children: Debra, Jackie, Dan, Beckie, Rocky, Brenda. AB, Calvin Coll., 1953; BD, Calvin Sem., 1956; ThM, Princeton Sem., 1965; PhD,

Wayne State U., 1970; M in Divinity, Calvin Seminary, 1986. Ordained to ministry Christian Reformed Ch., 1956. Pastor Newton (N.J.) Christian Reformed Ch., 1961-65, North Hills Ch., Troy, Mich., 1965-68, Univ. Hills Ch., Farmington Hills, Mich., 1968-79; pvt. practice psychotherapy Farmington Hills, 1967—; religious broadcaster TV, weekly, 1970-74, periodically to date; lectr. humanities, classicsWayne State U., John Wesley Coll., 1970—;vis. lectr. Princeton U., 1978—; lectr. U.S. and abroad. Author: History of TV Format Development, 1970, Models of Religious Broadcasting, 1974, Chaplain (Major General) Gerhart W. Hyatt: An Oral History, 1977, Psychology in Worship, 1984, (with others) Baker's Encyclopedia of Psychology, 1984; editor Ethical Reflections, 1977, Eternal Vigilance, 1980, God's Grace and Human Health, 1982, Life and Laughter, 1983, Jour. Psychology and Christianity; contbr. articles to profl. jours. Served to col. AUS, 1956-61, now Res. Created knight, Queen Juliana, The Netherlands, 1974. Mem. Christian Assn. Psychol. Studies (now exec. dir.), AAUP, Am. Psychol. Assn., Soc. Bibl. Lit. and Exegesis, Speech Communication Assn., Mil. Chaplain Assn., Res. Officers Assn., Archeol. Inst. Am., Am. Personnel and Guidance Assn., Mil. Order World Wars, Am. Sci. Assn., World Assn. Christian Communicators. Home and Office: 26705 Farmington Rd Farmington Hills MI 48018

ELLER, CARL, chemical dependency center administrator; b. Winston-Salem, N.C., Jan. 25, 1942; m. Mahogany Jaclynne Fasnacht, Dec. 21, 1979; children: Regis Hubert, Holiday Elizabeth. Grad., U. Minn., 1964. Cert. chemical dependency counselor. Defensive end Minn. Vikings, Mpls., 1964-78, Seattle Seahawks, 1979-80; search cons. Eller, Brunsvold, Mpls., 1980-82; color analyst Sta. NBC-TV, N.Y.C., 1981-82; exec. dir. Nat. Inst. Health and Humanities, Mpls., 1981-85, Triumph Life Ctrs., Mpls., 1985—; cons. NFL, N.Y.C., 1981—. Author: Beating the Odds, Game Plan II; Winning Families, Life Planning and Decision Making. Active Citizens Adv. Council. Mem. Minn. Council Chem. Dependency, U.S. Athletes Assn. (bd. dirs. 1984—). Office: Triumph Life Ctr 555 Simpson St Saint Paul MN 55104

ELLERBROOK, NIEL COCHRAN, gas company executive; b. Rensselaer, Ind., Dec. 26, 1948; s. James Harry and Margaret (Cochran) E.; m. Susan Lynne Stamper, Mar. 8, 1969; children—Jennifer, Jeffrey, Jayma. BS, Ball State U., 1970. CPA, Ind. Staff acct. audit Arthur Andersen & Co., Indpls., 1970-72, audit sr., 1972-75, audit mgr., 1975-80; asst. to sr. v.p. adminstrn. and fin. Ind. Gas Co., Inc., Indpls., 1980-81, v.p. fin., 1981-84, v.p. fin., chief fin. officer, 1984-87, sr. v.p. fin., chief fin. officer, 1987—. Bd. dirs. Ctr. Grove Little League, Greenwood, Ind., 1983—. Mem. Am. Inst. CPAs, Ind. CPA Soc. (bd. dirs. Indpls. chpt., past pres. 1977-83, state bd. dirs. 1984—), Fin. Execs. Inst., Ind. Fiscal Policy Inst. (bd. dirs. 1985—), Ind. State C. of C. (taxation com. 1982-87, chmn. 1987). Methodist. Office: Ind Gas Co Inc 1630 N Meridian St Indianapolis IN 46202

ELLERY, DALE RAPHAEL, accountant; b. Alpena, Mich., Dec. 1, 1939; s. Raphael H. and Mary (Minton) E.; m. Marguerite Santarossa, Feb. 15, 1963; children: Lisa, Rick. BBA, U. Mich., 1963; MS in Taxation with highest honors, Walsh Coll., 1978. CPA, Mich. Acct. Ford Motor Co., Mich., 1961-65; tax supr. Touche Ross & Co., Mich., 1965-69; tax mgr. Am. Motors Corp., Mich., 1969-76; dir. tax and customs Volkswagen of Am., Mich., 1977—; bd. dirs. Penrickton Ctr., Taylor, Mich. Chmn. Internat. Bus. Forum, Detroit, 1984. Mem. Nat. Assn. Accts., Nat. Assn. of Fgn. Trade Zones (bd. dirs. 1982-83), Tax Execs. Inst. (treas. 1982), Detroit C. of C. (bd. dirs. 1987—). Club: World Trade (pres. 1987). Avocations: real estate, genealogy. Home: 14721 Williamsburg Ct Riverview MI 48192 Office: Volkswagen of Am 888 Big Beaver Troy MI 48007

ELLFELDT, HOWARD JAMES, orthopedic surgeon; b. Kansas City, Mo., Feb. 11, 1937; s. Howard James and Peggy Maude (Bowen) E.; m. Dee Anne Park, June 18, 1960; children: Kimberly, Jeffrey, Kamela, Kent. AB, U. Kans., 1959, MD, 1963. Cert. Am. Bd. Orthopedic Surgery. Practice medicine specializing in orthopedic surgery Kansas City, Mo., 1970—; team physician Kansas City King's Basketball Club, 1972-84, Kansas City Chief's Football Club, 1973—; chief of staff Research Med. Ctr., Kansas City, 1984-85, bd. dirs. 1986; bd. dirs. Research Health Services, Kansas City, 1985—; pres. Research Comprehensive Health Care, Inc., 1986. Mem. adv. council Cholly Fund for Injured Atheltes, Lee's Summit, Mo., 1982; bd. dirs. K-Life, Shawnee Mission, Kans., 1983-86. Served to maj. U.S. Army, 1968-70, Vietnam. Fellow Am. Acad. Orthopedic Surgeons; mem. ACS (diplomate), Am. Orthopedic Soc. for Sports Medicine, Am. Coll. Sports Medicine, Alpha Omega Alpha. Republican. Episcopalian. Club: Mission Hills (Kans.) Country. Avocations: hunting, fishing. Home: 8544 Roe Blvd Prairie Village KS 66207 Office: Kansas City Bone Clinic 6420 Prospect Suite T207 Kansas City MO 64132

ELLINGER, RUDOLPH HENRY, food industry consultant; b. Grand Rapids, Mich., Aug. 18, 1920; s. Waldo G. and Gertrude (Waechter) E.; m. Julia R. Simpson, Sept. 1, 1950; children: Debra Lee Fournier, Steven Simpson. BS, Mich. State U., 1950; MS, Iowa State U., 1953, PhD, 1954. Tech. dir. product improvement Pillsbury Co., Mpls., 1954-59; dir. research and quality J.D. Jewell Inc., Gainesville, Ga., 1959-61; tech. service Durkee Famous Foods, Chgo., 1961-64; food product devel. Stauffer Chem., Dobbs Ferry, N.Y., 1964-69; dir. tech. services Stouffer Foods, Solon, Ohio, 1969-71; dir. quality assurance Kraft Inc., Glenview, Ill., 1971-81; owner, cons. Dr. R.H. Ellinger & Assocs., Ltd., Northbrook, Ill., 1981—. Author: Phosphates as Food Ingredients, 1972. Mem. Inst. Food Technologists (vice chmn. 1985), Assn. Cereal Chemists, Assn. Food and Drug Ofcls., Internat. Dairy Fedn., Nat. Cheese Inst. Republican. Avocations: gardening, photography, Christmas tree farming. Home and Office: 3946 Dundee Rd Northbrook IL 60062

ELLINGSON, DAVID ALAN, accountant; b. Plainview, Nebr., Sept. 22, 1950; s. Paul William and Alyce (Hilkemeier) E.; m. Patricia Lynn Gillilan, Jan. 31, 1970 (div. 1979); m. Emilie Marie Brown, Feb. 13, 1982; children: Christopher, Carrie, Lauren. BS, U. Nebr., 1972. CPA. Ptnr. Dana F. Cole & Co., Lincoln, Nebr., 1972—; treas. ARC, Lincoln, 1984—, Sr. Ctrs. Found., Lincoln, 1984—, Lincolnfest, Inc., 1985—. Vol. United Way, YMCA, Lincoln, 1987. Mem. Am. Inst. CPAs, Nebr. Soc. CPAs. Republican. Methodist. Club: Otoe Creek Hunt (pres. 1985-87). Avocations: hunting, fishing, outdoor recreation, carpentry. Home: 3645 Holmes Park Rd Lincoln NE 68506 Office: Dana F Cole & Co 200 NBC Ctr Lincoln NE 68508

ELLIOTT, ARLENE MAY EDWARDS, club manager; b. Chgo., Feb. 15, 1929; d. Clayton Arlin and Adelina Petronilla (Lovreglio) Edwards; divorced; children: Seth Edwards, Phillip Clarke, Mead Crispin. BS in Home Econs., Ill. Inst. Tech., 1951. Cert. elem. and secondary tchr., Ill. Researcher Swift & Co., Chgo., 1951; lectr., stylist Gimbel Bros., N.Y.C., 1952-56; tchr. Darien (Ill.) Sch. Dist., 1967-79; substitute high sch. tchr. Palos Park (Ill.) and Palos Heights (Ill.) Sch. Dist., 1981-85; pres., gen. ptnr. A.S.E. Services, La Grange, Ill., 1978—; mgr. Woman's Club of Great Neck, N.Y., 1985-86; founder, dir. Edwards Inst., Palos Park, 1984—. Author: (reading card games) Roots and Stems, Look-Alikes, 1978; composer: (art song) Morning Melody, 1969; drama critic Worth-Palos Reporter, 1983-84. Mem. Nat. Exec. Housekeeper's Assn. (cert.), Sigma Kappa. Republican. Avocation: auctioneering. Home: HCR3 Box 3575 Shell Knob MO 65747

ELLIOTT, BARBARA JEAN, librarian; b. Bluffton, Ind., Oct. 2, 1927; d. Dale A. and Gwendolyn I. (Long); m. Robert J. Elliott, June 13, 1949; 1 son, Michael Roger. B.S. with honors, Ind. U., 1949, M.L.S., 1979. Dir. tech. info. services uranium div. Mallinckrodt Chems., St. Louis, 1949-59; research librarian Petrolite Corp., Webster Groves, Mo., 1961-63; head tech. services St. Frances Coll., Ft. Wayne, Ind., 1974-76; asst. dir. Bluffton-Wells County Pub. Library, 1976—. Publicity chmn. TRIALSA Library Coop., Ft. Wayne, 1983—, mem. long range planning com., 1985-86.. Mem. ALA, Ind. Library Assn. (fed. legis. coordinator), LWV of Ind. (state sec. 1981-83, chmn. health care 1983—, 3d vice pres. 1985—), Ind. Bus. and Profl. Women (pres.). Club: Bluffton Garden (v.p. 1983—). Home: 6831 SE State Rd 116 Bluffton IN 46714 Office: Bluffton Wells County Pub Library 223 W Washington St Bluffton IN 46714

ELLIOTT, CHARLES STEWART, continuing education educator; b. Portland, Tenn., July 18, 1941; s. Edwin Simon and Rhoda Mae (Stewart) E.; m. M. Elaine Rose, Sept. 18, 1965; children: Marsha, Barry. BME, Gen. Motors Inst., 1964; MS, Ind. U., 1965; PhD, Mich. State U., 1972. Engr. Allison div. Gen. Motors Corp., Indpls., 1959-65; assoc. dean Gen. Motors Inst., Flint, Mich., 1965-74; coordinator extension programs Wayne State U., Detroit, 1974-79; dir. continuing engring. edn. Purdue U., West Lafayette, Ind., 1979-85, dir. continuing edn., 1985—. cubmaster Boy Scouts Am., Troy, 1975-77. Mem. Inst. Indsl. Engrs. (sr., pres. Cen. Ind. chpt.), Nat. Univ. Continuing Edn. Assn. (profl.), Am. Assn. Higher Edn., Am. Soc. Mechl. Engrs., Assn. for Continuing Higher Edn., Assn. Media-Based Continuing Edn. (chmn. bd.), Am. Soc. Engring. Edn. (chmn. CPD div. 1982-83, Disting. Service award 1984), Gen. Motors Inst. Alumni Assn. (treas. 1971-74). Lodge: Rotary. Home: 725 Kent Ave West Lafayette IN 47906 Office: Purdue U 116 Stewart Ctr West Lafayette IN 47907

ELLIOTT, EDDIE MAYES, college president; b. Grain Valley, Mo., Sept. 12, 1938; s. Franklin E. and Edna Mae (Rowe) E.; m. Sandra Temple, Nov. 23, 1960; children: Glenn, Gregg, Grant. A.B., William Jewell Coll., 1960; M.A., Columbia U., 1964; Ed.D., U. No. Colo., 1969. Tchr. Harrisonville High Sch., Mo., 1960-61, Excelsior Springs Pub. Schs., Mo., 1961-63, The Trinity Sch., N.Y.C., 1963-64; mem. faculty dept. phys. edn. CUNY, 1964-65; chmn. athletics, coach Mo. Valley Coll., Marshall, 1965-71, dean spl. studies, 1973-75; dir. grad. studies Wayne State Coll., Nebr., 1971-73, v.p., 1975-82, pres., 1982-85; pres. Central Mo. State U., Warrensburg, 1985—; assoc. Ctr. for Planned Change, 1975-82; mem. adv. bd., bd. dirs. Nebr. Council on Econ. Edn., 1977-83; bd. incorporators Higher Edn. Strategic Planning Inst., 1981—; mem. Council Pub. Higher Edn. Mo. Named outstanding faculty mem. Wayne State Coll., 1973, recipient Disting. Service award, 1986; recipient Cecil R. Martin award William Jewell Coll., 1960, citation for achievement, 1986, Disting. Alumni award, 1986. Mem. Am. Assn. Higher Edn., AAUP, Am. Coll. Sports Medicine, Assn. Health, Phys. Edn. and Recreation, N. Central Assn. Evaluation Teams, Nat. Council Accreditation of Tchrs., Am. Assn. State Colls. and Univs., Warrensburg C. of C., Phi Kappa Phi. Lodge: Rotary. Home: 518 S Holden St Warrensburg MO 64093 Office: Cen Mo State Univ Office of the Pres Warrensburg MO 64093

ELLIOTT, KAREN CASEY, publishing company executive; b. LaFayette, Ind., July 18, 1939; d. James Orlando and Thelma Bernice (Kirkpatrick) E.; m. William Joseph Hilty, Jan. 28, 1961 (divorced Apr. 1973); m. Joseph Mathew Casey, Oct. 2, 1982. B.S., Purdue U., 1962; M.A., U. Minn., 1975, Ph.D., 1979. Cert. elem. tchr., Ind., Minn. Elem. tchr. LaFayette Pub. Schs., Ind., 1962-64, St. Paul Pub. Schs., 1964-69; instr. U. Minn., Mpls., 1971-76; mng. editor Hazelden Found., Center City, Minn., 1979-80, mktg. mgr., 1981-83, div. dir., 1984—; cons. Minn. State Depts. Edn., St. Paul, 1977-79. Author: Each Day A New Beginning, 1982, The Promise of a New Day, 1983; The Love Book, 1985, If Only I Could Quit, 1987. Mem. Nat. Women's Polit. Caucus, 1984—, NOW, 1984—, Soc. Against Nuclear Expansion, 1984—, Am. Friends Soc., 1984—, Alcohol and Drug Problems Assn. Mem. Am. Booksellers Assn., Upper Midwest Booksellers Assn., Minn. Roundtable Assn. (v.p. 1984). Democrat. Roman Catholic. Avocations: participatory sports; cooking; reading.

ELLIOTT, MICHAEL F., bank executive; b. Lafayette, Ind., Oct. 5, 1951; s. Shirley and Winifred (Dorsey) E.; m. Suzanne R. Sutton, May 1979 (div. 1981); 1 child, Bradley S. BS in Bus., U. Evansville, 1973. Bank examiner Comptroller of Currency, Cleve., 1973-74; exec. v.p. Spurgeon (Ind.) State Bank, 1974-82; pres., chief exec. officer State Bancorp., Inc., Washington, Ind., 1982—, State Bank Washington, 1982—; pres. Bank of Mitchell, Ind., 1986—; bd. dirs. Spurgeon Fin. Corp., Spurgeon State Bank, Pike County Bank, State Bancorp, Inc., The State Bank of Washington, Bank of Mitchell. Lodge: Elks. Home: 23 Green Acres Washington IN 47501 Office: State Bank Washington 300 E Main Washington IN 47501

ELLIOTT, PEGGY GORDON, university chancellor; b. Matewan, W.Va., May 27, 1937; d. Herbert Hunt and Mary Ann (Renfro) Gordon; m. Scott Vandling Elliott, Jr., June 17, 1961; children—Scott Vandling III, Anne Gordon. B.A., Transylvania Coll., 1959; M.A., Northwestern U., 1964; Ed.D., Ind. U., 1975. Tchr. Horace Mann High Sch., Gary, Ind., 1959-64; instr. English Ind. U. N.W., Gary, 1965-69, 71-73, lectr. edn., 1973-74, asst. prof. edn., 1975-78, assoc. prof., 1978-80, supr. secondary student teaching, 1973-74, dir. secondary student teaching, 1974-75, dir. student teaching, 1975-77, dir. Office Field Experiences, 1977-78, dir. profl. devel., 1978-80, spl. asst. to chancellor, 1981-83, asst. to chancellor, acting chancellor, 1983-84, chancellor, 1984—; instr. English Am. Inst. Banking, Gary, 1969-70; faculty devel. cons. City of Hammond, Ind., 1976-77; profl. devel. cons. N.W. Ind. Pub. Sch. Supt.'s Assn., 1978-81; vis. prof. U. Ark., 1979-80, U. Alaska, 1982; ptnr. Ind. Research Assocs., 1980—; dir. Gainer Nat. Bank and Corp. Author: Handbook for Secondary Student Teaching, 1975, 3d edit., 1977; (with C. Smith) Reading Activities for Middle and Secondary Schools: A Handbook for Teachers, 1979, Reading Instruction for Secondary Schools, 1985, How to Improve Your Scores on Reading Competency Tests, 1981; (with C. Smith and G. Ingersoll) Trends in Educational Materials: Traditionals and the New Technologies, 1983; also numerous articles. Mem. adv. com. Lake County Community Devel. Com., 1983—; bd. dirs. N.W. Ind. Symphony, Mental Health Assn. Lake County, N.W. Ind. World Affairs Council, Methodist Hosp., Inc., Gainer Corp. Recipient numerous grants; Am. Council on Edn. fellow in acad. adminstrn. Ind. U., Bloomington, 1980-81. Mem. Assn. Tchr. Educators (nat. pres. 1984-85), Nat. Acad. Tchr. Edn. (dir. 1983—), Ind. Assn. Tchr. Educators (past pres.), N.W. Ind. Forum and Assn. Commerce and Industry (bd. dirs.), Internat. Reading Assn., Phi Delta Kappa (Outstanding Young Educator award), Delta Kappa Gamma (Leadership/Mgmt. fellow 1980), Pi Lamda Theta, P.E.O., Chi Omega. Republican. Episcopalian. Avocations: music; writing; poetry. Home: 1350 Orchard Dr Merrillville IN 46410 Office: Ind Univ NW 3400 Broadway Gary IN 46408

ELLIOTT, ROBERT BETZEL, physician; b. Ada, Ohio, Dec. 8, 1926; s. Floyd Milton and Rose Marguerite (Betzel) E.; m. Margaret Mary Robichaux, Aug. 26, 1954; children: Howard A., Michael D., Robert Bruce, Douglas J., John C., Joan O. BA, Ohio No. U., 1949; MD, U. Cin., 1953. Diplomate Am. Bd. Family Practice. Intern Charity Hosp., New Orleans, 1953-54; resident in pathology Bapt. Meml. Hosp., Memphis, 1958-59; practice medicine specializing in family practice Ada, 1959—; mem. staff Ohio No. U. Health Service, Ada, 1960-70; Coroner Hardin County, 1973—. Served with U.S. Army, 1945-46, PTO. Mem. Ada Exempted Village Sch. Bd., 1960—, pres., 1966-69, 72—, v.p. 1971—. Named Ohio Family Physician of Yr., 1985. Mem. AMA, Ohio State Med. Assn., Hardin County Med. Soc. (pres. 1964), Am. Acad. Family Physicians, Ohio Acad. Family Physicians, Lima Acad. Family Physicians, Am. Coll. Health Assn. Democrat. Presbyterian. Lodges: Masons, Elks. Home: 4429 State Rt 235 Ada OH 45810 Office: 302 N Main St Ada OH 45810

ELLIOTT, RONALD ALLEN, human resources and financial executive; b. Beatrice, Nebr., Oct. 21, 1945; s. Donald Roy and Catherine Redner (McDonald) E.; m. Joanne Kay Lamp, Dec. 23, 1968; children: Gregory Mark, Jill Catherine. BA, Creighton U., 1967, MBA, 1974. Dir. human resources, fin. Wilson & Co., Engrs. & Architects, Salina, Kans., 1980—. Mem. exec. com. Salina Human Relations Commn., 1985-86, Salina Child Care Assn., 1985-86. Mem. Am. Soc. Personnel Adminstrn. (program chmn. 1986, treas. 1987), Fin. Mgrs. Group. Club: Toastmasters (pres. Salinas chpt. 1985-86). Avocations: collecting clocks, sailing. Home: 720 Colonial Place Salina KS 67401

ELLIOTT, SANDRA LLOYD, civic worker; b. Indpls., Aug. 9, 1940; m. George Charles Elliott, Aug. 26, 1961; children: John, Mollianne, Jane, LIsa, David. BS, Ind. U., 1983. Service rep. Ind. Bell Tel. Co., Indpls., 1960-62; book keeper Elliott Rentals, Noblesville, Ind., 1975-85; sec.-treas. Art, by George!, Noblesville, 1978-85. V.p. parent-faculty council Novlesville High Sch., 1986—, community adv. council, 1984-85, title I reading parent adv. council, 1980-81, textbook adoption com., 1985, vol. tutor, 1984—; bd. dirs. Hamilton County Hist. Soc., 1982—; mem. Internat. Ctr. Indpls., Noblesville Boys Club, Hist. Landmarks Found. of Ind.; mayoral appointee Human Relations Commn., Noblesville, 1977-79; vol. Probation task force, Noblesville, 1981; sec. Community Awareness Program, Noblesville, 1979-80. Mem. Ind. U. Alumni Assn. (life), Classic Car Club, Blatchley Nature Club, Kappa Delta (chmn. redecoration com. 1985—, chmn. alumni com. 1986). Republican. Avocations: tng. for pvt. pilot, internat. travel, reading. Home: 399 N 10th St Noblesville IN 46060

ELLIOTT, WILLIAM DOUGLAS, English educator, writer, academic administrator; b. Bemidji, Minn., Jan. 13, 1938; s. Alfred Marlyn and Lulu (Maynard) E.; m. Gwendolyn Warren, July 19, 1960; children—Sharon Elizabeth, Douglas Warren. B.A., Miami U., Oxford, Ohio, 1960; M.A., U. Mich., 1961, Ed.D. in English, 1967; M.F.A. in Creative Writing, U. Iowa, 1962. Teaching asst. in English, U. Mich., Ann Arbor, 1960-61, 63-64, teaching fellow in English, 1962-63; scholar in writing U. Iowa, 1961-62; instr. Muskingum Coll., New Concord, Ohio, 1964-65; instr. Washtenaw Community Coll., Ypsilanti, Mich., 1966-67; asst. prof. English Bemidji State U., 1967-68, assoc. prof., 1969-79, prof., 1980—, chmn. dept. English, 1983-86; author: (criticism) Henry Handel Richardson, 1975, (novel) Blue River, 1978, (poetry) Fishing the Offshore Island, 1980, To Middle River, 1984; dir. Can. Studies Com.; dir. Upper Midwest Writers' Conf. Recipient Hopwood award in creative writing U. Mich., 1959-62, award in short fiction McKnight Found., 1968, award for distinction Best Am. Fiction, 1969, Research award Am. Philos. Soc., 1974; fellow Miami U., 1959-60, Minn. State Arts Bd., 1975; Can. embassy grantee, 1981, 83. Mem. MLA, Midwestern MLA, Associated Writing Programs, Internat. Council Can. Studies, Assn. Can. Studies, Assn. Commonwealth Studies in Can., Am. Assn. Can. Studies, World Lit. Written in English. Democrat. Methodist. Contbr. to lit. jours.

ELLIS, ANGLES LISA, small business owner, consultant; b. Detroit, Apr. 21, 1956; d. Thornell Law and Mozella (Epps) Banks; m. Reginald Christopher Ellis, June 30, 1979; 1 child, Reginald Robert II. Cert. in word processing, Wayne State U., 1983, cert. in fundamentals of speaking, 1984; cert. in grammar and communication, Marygrove Coll., 1985. Owner Helpmate Services, Detroit, 1982—; instr. Marygrove Coll., Detroit, 1985—. Campaign vol. mayoral candidate, Detroit, 1985. Mem. Nat. Alliance Homebase Bus. Women, Assn. Mcpl. Profl. Women, Nat. Assn. Advancement of Colored People, Detroit C. of C. (exhibitor 1986—), Am. Soc. Tng. Devel. Democrat. Baptist. Avocation: reading. Office: Helpmate Services PO Box 4475 Detroit MI 48204

ELLIS, ARTHUR E., university official. Pres. Cen. Mich. U., Mt. Pleasant. Office: Central Mich Univ Office of the President Mount Pleasant MI 48859 *

ELLIS, GUY ERIC, hydrologist, administrator; b. Fairbury, Nebr., July 20, 1947; s. Charles William and Dollie (Reynolds) E.; m. Kay Lorraine Skalla, May 22, 1971; 1 child, Mark. BS in Agr., Kans. State U., 1973; M in Pub. Adminstrn., U. Kans., 1986. Hydrologist I Div. Water Resources Kans. State Bd. Agr., Topeka, 1973-74, hydrologist II, 1974-84, hydrologist III, 1984—. Served with USAF, 1966-69. Mem. Am. Soc. Pub. Adminstrn., Nat. Speleological Soc., Kans. Speleological Soc., Kans. Canoe Assn. Republican. Methodist. Avocations: caveing, canoeing, snow skiing, hiking, hunting. Home: 1339 NW Glick Rd Topeka KS 66615 Office: Kans Bd Agr Div Water Resources 109 SW 9th St Topeka KS 66612

ELLIS, JACK GRAVES, university administrator; b. Frankfort, Ky., May 14, 1934; s. Earl Graves and Sally Mae (True) E.; m. Dewana Sue Mathis, Jan. 16, 1960; children: Sallie Renee Ellis Stephens, Rebecca Suzanne, Patricia Leah Ellis Kraus, Joel Mathew. Student Miami U., Oxford, Ohio, 1952-54; BS, Ohio U., 1957. Credit analyst Atlantic Richfield Co., Los Angeles, 1957-58; systems analyst Remington Rand Corp., Los Angeles, 1958-59; dist. mgr. Speery Rand Corp., Pomona, Calif., 1959-60; mfg. rep. Pacific Bus. Interiors, Los Angeles, 1961-67; exec. dir. Ohio U. Alumni Assn., Athens, 1967-70, dir. devel., 1970-85, v.p. devel., 1985—; exec. dir. Ohio Univ. Fund, Inc., 1973—. Bd. dirs. Athens Concerned Citizens Against Drug Abuse, 1980—. Mem. Council Advancement and Support Edn. (dist. program chmn.), Ohio Council Instl. Advancement Officers (chmn. 1986-87), Ohio Assn. Devel. Officers, Athens C. of C. Republican. Methodist. Lodge: Rotary. Home: 17 Mulligan Rd Athens OH 45701 Office: Ohio Univ 305 McGuffey Hall Athens OH 45701

ELLIS, JAMES DEAN, mechanical engineer; b. Marietta, OH, Dec. 17, 1959; s. Dean Edwin and Rosemary (Rauch) E.; m. Monica DeAnne Komar, Apr. 12, 1986. BSMechE, Ohio State U., 1983. Jr. ops. engr. Cleve. Electric Illuminating Co., 1983-85, assoc. ops. engr., 1985—. Mem. Am. Nuclear Soc. (grade), ASME, Ohio State U. Alumni Club. Republican. Roman Catholic. Avocations: racquetball, basketball, jogging. Home: 8366 Findley Dr Mentor OH 44060

ELLIS, JAMES EDWARD, brokerage house executive, real estate appraiser; b. Cin., Aug. 5, 1936; s. Hillman E. and Jewell (Taylor) E.; m. Kaye Ellis, Sept. 3, 1962 (div. Nov. 1979); children: Rusty, Randy, Roddy, Rich, Mike, Mark; m. Fran Ellis, Dec. 19, 1981. Student, N.Am. Coll., Rome, 1954, Xavier U., 1957. V.p. Merril Lynch & Co., Virginia Beach, Va., 1967-81; pres., cheif exec. officer Ellis, Nislly Assocs. Inc., Cin., 1981—. Mayor City of Erlanger, Ky., 1978; chmn. crime commn., Erlanger, 1976; mem. exec. com. state crime commn., 1975, 76, 77. Served to capt. USAF, 1954-59. Mem. Internat. Inst. Bus. Broker, Internat. Orgn. Real Estate Appraisers. Republican. Roman Catholic. Home: 6608 Pleasant Cincinnati OH 45227 Office: Ellis Nisly Assocs Inc 1802 Triangle Park Dr Cincinnati OH 45246

ELLIS, JEFFREY WARREN, medical administrator; b. Chgo., May 14, 1947; s. Edward F. Lis and Sonne N. (Kowalsen) Ellis; m. Marla Swanson, June 29, 1974; children: Courtney, Christopher. AB, Grinnell Coll., 1969; MD, U. Ill., 1973. Diplomate Am. Bd. Obstetrics and Gynecology. Ob-gyn intern U. Ill. Hosp., Chgo., 1973-74; gen. surgery resident U. Ark. Med. Ctr., Little Rock, 1974; asst. prof., attending physician Rush Med. Coll., Chgo., 1978-80; dir. Northwestern Found. Research and Edn., Chgo., 1981-84; med. dir. Planned Parenthood Chgo., 1984-86; Med. dir. Matrix Cos., Chgo., 1984-85. Author: Clinical Manual of Obstetrics, Clinical Manual of Gynecology; editor: Medical Symptoms and Treatment, 1982, Family Medical Guide, 1983. Recipient Hoffman-LaRoche award Roche Pharms., 1973. Mem. Am. Coll. Obstetricians and Gynecologists, Assn. Profs. of Gynecology and Obstetrics, Cen. Assn. Obstetricians and Gynecologists. Roman Catholic. Avocations: writing, fishing.

ELLIS, JOSEPH N., distribution company executive; b. Tenn., Oct. 19, 1928; s. Richard M. and Pearl A. (Fuqua) E.; m. Barbara Harpster, Sept. 17, 1955; 1 child, Patricia Anne. B.S., Northwestern U., 1954. Co-founder LaSalle-Deitch Co., Inc., Elkhart, Ind., 1963; exec. v.p. LaSalle-Deitch Co., Inc., 1969-72, pres., chief exec. officer, 1972—. Served with U.S. Army, 1950-52. Home: 54400 Old Bedford Trail Mishawaka IN 46545 Office: LaSalle-Deitch Co Inc 640 Industrial Pkwy PO Box 2347 Elkhart IN 46515

ELLIS, LUCILLE LORRAINE LAUGHLIN (MRS. WALLACE IVERSON ELLIS), realtor; b. Solsberry, Ind., Sept. 22, 1914; d. Rutherford and Mabel (Ingles) Laughlin; student Ind. U., 1930-31, 60-61, Danville Central Normal, 1931-32; m. Wallace Iverson Ellis, July 28, 1931; children—Betty Lucille (Mrs. Timothy Wininger), Charles Robert, Mary (Mrs. Hane), Rebecca (Mrs. Maxwell-Slingsby-Davies). Tchr., LaCrosse Sch., Martinsville, Ind., 1932-33; partner Ellis Gen. Store, Springville, Ind., 1933-44; partner, mgr. Ellis Super Market, Bloomington, Ind., 1945-59; founder, owner Ellis Real Estate, Bloomington, 1960—; owner Bloomington Downtown Motel, 1973—. Den Mother White River council Boy Scouts Am., 1948-50; brownie leader Tulip Trace council Girl Scouts U.S.A., 1954-56. Patron Hoosier Art Salon, Indpls. Mem. Bloomington Bd. Realtors (sec.-treas. 1963-65), Ind. Real Estate Assn., Nat. Assn. Real Estate Bds., Bloomington C. of C. (bd. dirs., sec. exec. com. 1969-70), Ind. U. Alumni Assn. (life), Internat. Platform Assn., Motel Assn. Am., Nat. Brokers Council, Ind. U. Woodburn Guild (charter), Delta Sigma Kappa (life mem.; nat. treas. 1965-67, nat. v.p. 1967-69, nat. pres. 1969-71, chmn. bd. 1971-73). Clubs: Arganaut, Women's Dept. (Bloomington). Republican. Presbyn. Home: 835 Sheridan Rd Bloomington IN 47401 Office: 408 S Walnut St Bloomington IN 47401

ELLIS, ROBERT GRISWOLD, engineering company executive; b. Kokomo, Ind., Dec. 28, 1908; s. Ernest Eli and Ethel (Griswold) E.; A.B.,

Ind. U., 1934; m. Rachel O. Burckey, Oct. 27, 1984. Mem. staff Ind. U., Bloomington, 1930-34; researcher Blackett-Sample-Hummert Inc., Chgo., 1934, asst. mgr. merchandising, 1935-36; prodn. mgr. Harvey & Howe, Inc., Chgo., 1936-37; Chgo./Midwest dist. mgr. L.F. Grammes & Sons, Inc., Allentown, Pa., 1937-45; with Ellis & Co., Chgo. and Park Ridge, Ill., 1945—, pres., chief engr., 1948—, mng. dir., chief engr. Ellis Internat. Co., Chgo. and Park Ridge, Ill., 1965—, chief engr. Ellis Engring. Co., Park Ridge, 1969—. Chmn. Citizens Com. for Cleaner and More Beautiful Park Ridge, 1957-60; trustee, treas. bd. dirs. 1st United Methodist Ch., Park Ridge, 1974-77. Recipient Civic Achievement award City of Park Ridge, 1959. Mem. Soc. Automotive Engrs., Armed Forces Communications and Electronics Assn. (life), Ind. U. Alumni Assn. (life), Quartermaster Assn. (pres. Chgo. chpt. 1957-58), Ind. Acad. Sci., Am. Powder Metallurgy Inst., Ill. Acad. Sci., Mfrs. Agts. Assn. Gt. Britain and Ireland,Internat. Union Comml. Agts. and Brokers, Am. Logistics Assn., Am. Soc. Metals, Indiana Soc. of Chgo. Republican. Clubs: Union League, Varsity (pres. Chgo. 1957), Ind. U. Alumni (pres. Chgo. 1956-57), Emeritus of Ind. U., Internat. Trade. Home: 643 Parkwood St Park Ridge IL 60068 Office: Box 344 306 Busse Hwy Park Ridge IL 60068-0344

ELLIS, ROBERT KEITH, orthopedic surgeon; b. Kingston, Jamaica, Mar. 19, 1942; s. Keith B. and Mavis (Glave) E.; m. Mary E. Escoffery; children: Sara, Juliet, Robert. BS, MB, U. West Indies, 1969. Practice medicine specializing in orthopedic surgery Orthopedic Surgeons of Elkhart, Ind., 1974—; chief of staff Elkhart Gen. Hosp., 1984. Fellow Royal Coll. Surgeons Can., ACS; mem. Am. Soc. Surgery of the Hand, Internat. Coll. Surgeons, Am. Acad. Orthopedic Surgeons, Am. Bd. Orthopedic Surgery, Mid-Am. Orthopedic Assn., Ind. Orthopedic Soc. Avocations: reading, music, tennis, photography.

ELLIS, WALTER DEAN, communications educator; b. Gary, Ind., Oct. 20, 1930; s. Arthur and Iris Blanch (Seward) E.; m. Darlene Nell, Mar. 21, 1953; children: Derek, David. AA in Communication and Union Leadership, U. Chgo., 1964. Mgmt. trainee Ill. Bell Telephone, Gary, Ind., 1953-80; mgmt. installation and repair Ill. Bell Telephone, Hinsdale, Ill., 1964-71; instructional technologist Ill. Bell Telephone, Chgo., 1972-80; mgr. personnel Ind. Bell Telephone, Indpls., 1980-81, mgr. instructional tech. computer-based tng., 1981—. Served to sgt. U.S. Army, 1953-55. Mem. Am Soc. Tng. and Devel. Lodge: Masons. Home: 9331 Melissa Ann Dr Indianapolis IN 46234 Office: Ind Bell Telephone 5737 E Washington St Indianapolis IN 46219

ELLIS, WILLIAM CHARLES, accountant; b. LeRoy, Kans., Nov. 3, 1944; s. Charles Allen and Dorothy Aileen (Birk) E.; m. Sharyl Lynne Young, Aug. 7, 1965; children: Ronald Allen, Dennis Evan, Teresa Ann. BS in Bus.-Acctg., Emporia State U., 1966. CPA. Ptnr. Schulte, Klein, Gaeddert & Agler, Emporia, Kans., 1965-72, Pettengill & Co., Waukegan, Ill., 1972-81; mng. ptnr. Ellis & Co., Waukegan, 1981—; instr. acctg. Nat. Found. Funeral Service, Evanston, Ill., 1981—; cons. Nat. Selected Morticians, Evanston, 1972—. Contbr. articles to profl. jours. Mem. Victory Meml. Hosp. Devel. Com., Waukegan, 1983—; bd. dirs.Lake County Family YMCA, Waukegan, 1982—. Mem. Am. Inst. CPA's, Ill. CPA Soc. (chpt. pres. 1978-79, MAS com. 1974-78). Republican. Methodist. Lodge: Rotary. Home: 9937 W Michigan Blvd Zion IL 60099 Office: Ellis & Co 2744 Grand Ave Waukegan IL 60085

ELLIS, WILLIAM GRENVILLE, educational administrator, management consultant; b. Teaneck, N.J., Nov. 29, 1940; s. Grenville Brigham and Vivian Lilian (Breeze) E.; m. Nancy Elizabeth Kempton, 1963; children—William Grenville, Bradford Graham. B.S. in Bus. Adminstrn., Babson Coll., 1962; M.B.A., Suffolk U., 1963; Ed.M., Westfield State Coll., 1965; Ed.D., Pa. State U., 1968; MLE (Sears Roebuck Found. scholar), Harvard U., 1980; IAL, MIT, 1984. Asst. prof. bus. Rider Coll., 1968-69; div. dir., assoc. prof. Castleton State Coll., 1969-72; exec. v.p., prof. Coll. of St. Joseph the Provider, Rutland, Vt., 1972-73; acad. v.p., dean grad. sch. Thomas Coll., Waterville, Maine, 1973-82; pres. Wayland Acad., Beaver Dam, Wis., 1982—; corporator 1st Consumers Savs., 1974-81, Maine Savs., 1981-83; dir. Marine Bank. Auditor, Town of Castleton (Vt.), 1969-71; pres. Kennebee Valley Youth Hockey, Augusta, Maine, 1975-77; sec., bd. dirs. Beaver Dam Community Hosp. Named Cons. of Yr., SBA, 1975, 77; recipient Community Service award Rutland C. of C., 1973. Mem. Am. Psychol. Assn., Nat. Assn. Ind. Schs., Nat. Assn. Intercollegiate Athletics (cert. of merit 1979), North Central Assn. Colls. and Secondary Schs., Wis. Assn. Ind. Schs. (pres. 1984-86), Ind. Schs. Assn. Central States, Beaver Dam C. of C. (pres.-elect 1985, pres. 1986), Cum Laude Soc., Alpha Chi, Pi Omega Pi, Alpha Delta Sigma, Delta Pi Epsilon, Phi Delta Kappa Clubs: Madison, Natanis, Old Hickory. Lodge: Rotary. Author: The Analysis and Attainment of Economic Stability, 1963; The Relationship of Related Work Experience to the Teaching Success of Beginning Teachers, 1968; contbr. numerous articles, abstracts to profl. publs. Home: 101 N University Ave Beaver Dam WI 53916 Office: Wayland Acad PO Box 398 Beaver Dam WI 53916

ELLISON, GERALD (GARY) L., advertising executive, entertainer; b. San Francisco, May 24, 1943; s. Olyn G. and Margaret (Gracey) E.; m. Janet A. Wulkan, July 26, 1969; children: Shannon, Mark. BS, S.W. Mo. State U., 1966. Nightclub entertainer, U.S.A., 1965-72, concert entertainer, 1972—; pres. Gary Ellison Prodns. Inc., Springfield, Mo., 1972—. Cinematographer film: ECCO (Addy award), 1980; TV comml.: Ozark Mountain Country (Addy award), 1981. Pres., Friends of the Zoo, 1978-82, host and exec. producer Telethon, 1984; host Telethon, United Cerebral Palsy S.W. Mo., Springfield, 1980-86; pres. Mus. of Ozarks History, 1986—. Named Mo.'s Ofcl. Ragtime Piano Player, 1973; Gary Ellison Day proclaimed by Gov. Mo., Mar. 3, 1984; recipient 1st Friend of the Sch. award, Springfield Sch. Bd., 1978; Entertainment citation Dept. Def., 1967. Mem. Springfield Assn. Musicians, Am. Advt. Fedn. (nat. govt. relations 1982, chmn. govt. relations 9th dist. 1981), Springfield Advt. Club (Ad Man of Yr., Silver medal 1980, pres. 1978-80, bd. dirs. 1987—). Presbyterian (elder). Clubs: Twin Oaks Country (Springfield); Stockton Yacht (Mo.). Home: 4554 S Roanoke Springfield MO 65807 Office: Gary Ellison Prodns Inc 5337 D South Campbell Springfield MO 65807

ELLMANN, SHEILA FRENKEL, investment co. exec.; b. Detroit, June 8, 1931; d. Joseph and Rose (Neback) Frenkel; B.A. in English, U. Mich., 1953; m. William M. Ellmann, Nov. 1, 1953; children—Douglas Stanley, Carol Elizabeth, Robert Lawrence. Dir. Advance Glove Mfg. Co., Detroit, 1954-78; v.p. Frome Investment Co., Detroit, 1980—. Mem. U. Mich. Alumni Assn., Nat. Trust of Historic Preservation. Home: 28000 Weymouth St Farmington Hills MI 48018

ELLORANDO, FRANK L., medical social worker; b. Samar, Philippines, June 4, 1926; came to U.S., 1968; s. Cocopate Ellorando and Rosa Lenalcozo; 1 child, Nepthali Jun. BBA, U. of East, Manila, 1952; MSW, Philippine Sch. Social Work, Manila, 1961. Registered social worker, Ill. Dir. boys work YMCA, Manila, 1954-68; acct. II Cook County Hosp., Chgo., 1968-70, med. social worker, 1970—. Democrat. Presbyterian. Lodges: Masons, Royal Arch. Avocations: camping, fishing, hiking, swimming. Home: 3921 S Artesian Ave Chicago IL 60632 Office: Cook County Hosp 1835 W Harrison St Chicago IL 60612

ELLS, RALPH EUGENE, financial firm executive; b. Aknon, Ohio, June 11, 1941; s. Rlaph Webster and Margaret (Balsiger) E.; m. Madeline Louise, Aug. 22, 1964; children: Jennifer, David, Meg. AB, Harvard U., 1963; MBA, U. Chgo., 1965. CPA, Wis. With audit staff Arthur Young & Co., Milw., 1965-69, cons., mgr., ptnr., 1970-83, ptnr. entrepreneurial services, 1983—; pres. Wis. Venture Network, Milw., 1987—. Treas. Citizens Govtl. Research Bur., Milw., 1975—, North Shore Congl. Ch., Milw., 1980—, Future Milw., 1984-87. Mem. Wis. Inst. CPA's (chmn. mgmt. adv. services com. 1976, chmn. econ. devel. com. 1987—), Am. Inst. CPA's. Clubs: Milw Country, University. Avocations: golfing, fishing, canoeing, furniture building. Home: 714 W McIntosh Ln Mequon WI 53092 Office: Arthur Young & Co 777 E Wisconsin Ave Suite 2100 Milwaukee WI 53092

ELLSON, STEVEN KENT, healthcare educator; b. Indpls., Apr. 3, 1951; s. Lloyd Wesley Ellson and Norma Jane (Hill) Jesse; m. Patricia Ann Murphy, Nov. 23, 1984. BA, Ind. U., 1973, MS, 1979, M in Pub. Adminstrn., 1987. Edn. coordinator Vis. Nurse Home Care, Indpls., 1981-84; edn. services mgr. Meml. Hosp., South Bend, Ind., 1984—; lectr. Ind. U., Indpls., 1977, Ind. State U., Terre Haute, 1977, Ind. Dietary Mgrs. Assn., South Bend, Ind., 1985, Ind. Soc. Med. Techs. State Assn. Program, South Bend, 1985. Contbr. articles to profl. jours. Tchr. Community Ch. Greenwood, Ind., 1980-83, co-chmn. singles group, 1980-83; mem. steering com. Cable TV Consortium, Indpls., 1980-81. Mem. Cen. Ind. Am. Soc. Tng. and Devel. (co-chair region conf. 1982), Ind. Soc. for Healthcare Edn. and Tng., Inc. (lectr. state conv. 1983, 85, bd. dirs. 1985-86, pres.-elect 1987). Avocations: running, youth work, photography. Home: 4252 Irish Hills Dr Apt 2C South Bend IN 46614 Office: Meml Hosp South Bend 615 N Michigan St South Bend IN 46601

ELLSTROM-CALDER, ANNETTE, social worker; b. Duluth, Minn., Dec. 19, 1952; d. Raymond Charles Ellstrom and Ruth Elaine (Bloomquist) Larson; m. Jeffrey Ellstrom Calder, July 30, 1982. BA in Social Work, Psychology, Sociology, Concordia Coll., 1974; MSW, U. Wis., 1978. Group therapist N.D. State Indsl. Sch., 1973; social worker Fergus Falls (Minn.) State Hosp., 1974, Jackson County Dept. Social Services, Black River Falls, Wis., 1975-77; clin. social worker U. Wis. Hosp., Madison, 1979—; cons. Waupun (Wis.) Meml. Hosp., 1979-84; lectr. grad. sch. social work U. Wis., Madison, 1979—, lectr. U. Wis. med. sch., Madison, 1979-82, prin. investigator in research U. Wis. Hosp., Madison, 1985-86. Editor: A Guide to Patients and Families, 1984; contbr. articles to profl. jours. Del. trustee, bd. dirs. Nat. Kidney Found., Milw., 1985—, chmn. bd. dirs., Milw., 1985—, vice chmn. 1983-85, sec. 1982-83, chmn. patient services com. 1981-82, bd. dirs. 1981—; bd. dirs. Madison chpt., 1979—. Recipient Health Advancement award Nat. Kidney Found. Wis., 1985, Vol. Yr. award Nat. Kidney Found. Wis., 1983, Vol. Service award Nat. Kidney Found. Wis., 1984; hon. adoptee Winnebago Indian Tribe, 1978. Mem. Council Nephrology Social Workers (nat. v.p. 1984-86, nat. exec. com. 1984-86), Nat. Assn. Social Workers, Pi Gamma Mu. Democrat. Avocations: travel, camping, skiing, gardening, swimming. Home: 3538 Topping Rd Madison WI 53705 Office: U Wis Hosp 600 Highland Ave E5/620 Madison WI 53792

ELLSWORTH, CYNTHIA ANN, teacher, financial consultant; b. Springfield, Ohio, Jan. 19, 1950; d. Donald Harry and Jeanne Marie (Glover) E. BE, Western Conn. State U., 1972; M in Spl. Edn., Ohio U., 1976; Postgrad., Ohio State U., 1985-86; postgrad., U. Dayton, 1986—. Tchr. LBD Fed. Hocking Schs., Stewart, Ohio, 1972-76, Southwestern City Schs., Grove City, Ohio, 1977—; supr. elmr. LBD Vinton County Schs., McArthur, Ohio, 1976-77; registered rep. Chubb Securities, W.L. Walker & Assocs., Columbus, Ohio, 1981—. Named one of Outstanding Young Women Am., 1980. Mem. Council Exceptional Children, Phi Delta Kappa. Avocations: gardening, bicycling. Home: 421 E Whittier St Columbus OH 43206 Office: W L Walker & Assocs 3677 Karl Rd Columbus OH 43224

ELLSWORTH, JAMES RICHARD, steel service center executive; b. Kenosha, Wis., Oct. 31, 1952; s. Richard and Ruth (McDonald) E.; m. Debra D. Congdon, Jan. 25, 1975; children: Jacqueline, Matthew. BA in Econs., U. Wis., Parkside, 1974. Inside salesperson J.T. Ryerson & Son, Chgo., 1975-76; outside salesperson J.T. Ryerson & Son, Milw., 1977-79, credit rep., 1979-82, credit, office mgr., 1983-87, inside sales mgr., 1987—. Tchr. Jr. Achievement "Project Bus.," Milw., 1981-82. Mem. Nat. Assn. Credit Mgrs. (bd. dirs. 1984—), Adminstrv. Mgmt. Soc. (1983—). Home: 1262 School Dr Waukesha WI 53186 Office: PO Box 534 Milwaukee WI 53201

ELMENDORF, HENRY J., auto agency executive; b. Sept. 28, 1922; m. Ethel, June 16, 1951; children—Donna Elmendorf Hutchison, Nancy Elmendorf Calvert. Student, St Louis U. Sch. Commerce and Fin. With Jim Meagher Chevolet-Oldsmobile of St. Charles, Mo., sec.-treas.; dir. Mercantile Bank of St. Peters, Mo. Chmn. bd. St. Charles Visitor Info. Ctr., Crossroads Econ. Devel. Corp. of St. Charles County, Inc., Mo.-St. Louis Met. Airport Authority, Devel. Council St. Joseph Health Ctr. of St. Charles; bd. dirs. Lindenwood Coll., St. Charles; past bd. dirs. St. Louis Symphony, St. Louis Regional Commerce and Growth Assn.; vice chmn. devel. council Archdiocese of St. Louis, Indsl. Devel. Authority of St. Charles County. Named Knight of Malta and Knight of Holy Sepulchre of Jerusalem, Roman Catholic Ch. Mem. St. Charles C. of C. (Man of Yr. 1964, 66, 81). Lodge: Kiwanis (pres. 1963). Address: 902 Hawthorne Saint Charles MO 63301

ELMETS, CHARLOTTE, small business owner, social and business function consultant; b. N.Y.C.; d. Lejser and Hilda (Kaminkowitz) Musin; m. Harry Barnard Elmets, Dec. 9, 1945; children: Craig Alan, Steven Kent, Douglas Gregory. Student, U. Nebr., 1943-45. Owner, cons. Charlotte Elmets Ltd., Des Moines, 1980—; v.p. Gen. Inns, Des Moines, 1984—. Chmn. mem. council Des Moines Art Ctr.; bd. dirs. Temple B'Nai Jeshurun, 1970-76, Iowa Jewish Home, 1976-82, Des Moines Ballet, 1981-83, Des Moines Opera, 1985 88. Home and Office: 4238 Park Hill Dr Des Moines IA 50312

ELMETS, HARRY BARNARD, osteopath, dermatologist; b. Des Moines, Apr. 22, 1920; s. William and Sara Charlotte (Ginsberg) E.; m. Charlotte Irene Musin, Dec. 9, 1945; children—Craig Allan, Steven Kent, Douglas Gregory. B.A., U. Iowa, 1942; D.O. with distinction, Coll. Osteo. Medicine and Surgery, Des Moines, 1946. Intern Des Moines Gen. Hosp., 1946-47; resident in dermatology Coll. Osteo. Medicine, Des Moines, 1947-52; practice osteo. medicine specializing in dermatology Des Moines, 1952—; mem. staff Iowa Methodist Med. Ctr., Iowa Lutheran Hosp., Broadlawns Polk County Med. Ctr., Mercy Hosp. Med. Ctr.; clin. prof. dermatology U. Osteo. Medicine and Health Scis., 1947—; vis. prof. dermatology Kirksville Coll. Osteo. Medicine; guest lectr. Coll. Medicine U. Iowa; cons. dermatology VA Med. Ctr., Knoxville, Iowa; mem. Iowa Task Force Venereal Disease. Editorial referee Jour. Am. Osteo. Assn.; editorial bd. CUTIS, 1982—. Trustee, bd. dirs. Coll. Osteo. Medicine and Surgery; co-chmn. Des Moines-Polk County Immunization Program; bd. dirs. Des Moines Ctr. Sci. and Industry. Named Alumnus of Yr., Coll. Osteo. Medicine and Surgery, 1980. Fellow Am. Osteo. Coll. Dermatology; mem. Am. Osteo. Coll. Dermatology (pres. 1963, 71), Am. Osteo. Bd. Dermatology (chmn. 1962—), Am. Osteo. Assn., Iowa Soc. Osteo. Physicians and Surgeons, Polk County Osteo. Assn. (past pres.), Iowa Acad. Sci., Am. Social Health Assn. (bd. dirs. 1968-77), Am. Venereal Disease Soc., Am. Acad. Dermatology, Iowa Dermatol. Soc., Missouri Valley Dermatol. Soc., Minn. Dermatol. Soc., Nat. Assn. VA Dermatologists (charter). Republican. Jewish. Clubs: Wakonda Country, Embassy (Des Moines). Lodges: Masons, Shriners. Home: 4238 Park Hill Dr Des Moines IA 50312 Office: 1010 Midland Financial Bldg Des Moines IA 50309

EL'MOHAMMED, ALI MALIK BELL, psychotherapist; b. Monroe, La., Mar. 12, 1944; s. Ali Malik and Lucille (Culpepper) eL-M.; m. Musette Bell, Mar. 23, 1974; children: Angela, Chris, Aliah, Ali IV. AAS in Social Work, NYU, 1971, BS in Secondary Edn., 1972, MS in Black Studies, 1973, MSW, 1975; PhD, Columbia Pacific U., 1982. Cert. permanent tchr., N.Y.; cert. social worker, N.Y., Mich. Project dir. Congress Racial Equality, N.Y.C., 1964-65; mental health worker Albert Einstein Coll. Medicine-Lincoln Community Mental Health Services, Bronx, N.Y., 1966-68, supr. community orgn., 1968-69, dir. community orgn., 1969-71, assoc. dir. dept. cons. and edn., 1971-75, clin. supr., 1975-77; clin. supr. Misericordia Hosp. Med. Ctr., Bronx, 1977-79; clin. social worker Mich. Inst. Mental Health, Diamondale, 1979-80; program supr. Riverwood Community Mental Health Services, St. Joseph, Mich., 1983-84; psychotherapist Genesee Psychiat. Ctr., Kalamazoo, Mich., 1980—, Kalamazoo Community Counselling, 1981—; mgr. assertive community treatment program Douglass Community Assn., Kalamazoo, 1985—; Adminstr. Cannan Counseling Service, Harlem, N.Y., 1978-79; mem. Council Against Domestic Assault, East Lansing, 1979-80; mem. steering com. Community Support Systems, Mich., 1984; mem. numerous community programs, N.Y.C., 1966-79. Trustee Kalamazoo Acad. Bd., 1985-86; chmn. Kalamazoo Civic Black Theatre, 1984-85; mem. Northside Task Force on Housing, Kalamazoo, 1986, Mich. Steering Com. on Community Support Systems, 1984, St. Martin's Episcopal Adv. Bd., 1984-85; mem. admission com. Mich. State U. Med. Sch., 1980-82. Recipient Outstanding Contribution award Island of Curacag, 1978, S. Bronx Action award, 1968. Fellow Am. Orthopsychiat. Assn.; mem. Nat. Assn. Black Social Workers, Nat. Assn. Social Workers, Am. Group Psychotherapy Assn. Muslim. Avocations: collecting books by Black authors, stamps, volleyball. Home: 1167 Mount Royal Dr Kalamazoo MI 49009 Office: Afram Cons Service G3300 Miller Rd #125 Flint MI 48507

EL-NAGGAR, AHMED SAMI, civil engineering educator, laboratory and global engineering executive; b. Egypt, Dec. 18, 1926; s. Ahmed Mohammad and Sanya (Hefny) El-N.; m. Janet Eileen Spinn, May 26, 1956; children: Tarik, Rhonda, Jilanne, Kareem. BSCE, U. Cairo, Egypt, 1948; MSCE, U. Calif., Berkeley, 1951; PhD in Environ. Engring., Purdue U., 1956. Registered profl. engr. Egypt, Ind., Ill. Asst. lectr. Engring. Coll., Cairo, 1949-50; teaching asst. U. Calif., Berkeley, 1951-53; constrn. engr. C.E., U.S. Army, San Francisco, 1952-56; asst. prof. environ. engring. U. Alexandria, 1956-56; research assoc. Purdue U., 1956-59; design engr. Clyde E. Williams & Assocs., 1959-60; prof. environ. and civil engring. Valparaiso (Ind.) U., 1960—, also pres. No. Labs. and Engring., Inc., 1978—, Global Engring. & Testing Services, Inc., 1981—; cons. Met. San. Dist. Greater Chgo.; vis. prof. High Inst. Pub. Health, Alexandria, 1957-58, Ains Shams U., Cairo, 1958. WHO fellow in san. engring., 1958; recipient Egyptian Govt. award, 1948; NSF grantee, 1962-64, 66-68, 74, 77-79. Mem. ASCE, AAAS, Am. Soc. Engring. Edn., Am. Water Works Assn., Am. Pub. Works Assn., Water Pollution Control Fedn., Ind. Water Pollution Control Assn. (pres. 1970-71, award for outstanding paper 1965), Am. Water Resources Assn., Valparaiso C. of C., Sigma Xi, Chi Epsilon, Mu San, Tau Beta Pi. Lodge: Kiwanis (pres. Valparaiso 1969-70). Contbr. articles profl. jours.; patentee biol. reactor. Office: Valparaiso University Valparaiso IN 46383 Office: 2400 Cumberland Dr Valparaiso IN 46383

ELORANTA, NANCY JO, architect; b. Ft. Wayne, Ind., Dec. 16, 1955; d. Walter Gunnar and Grace Olive (Sprunger) E. BArch, B in Environ. Sci., Ball State U., 1980. Registered architect, Ind. Grad. architect Schenkel & Schultz, Inc., Ft. Wayne, 1979-83; architect Cole-Matott-Riley, Ft. Wayne, 1983-84, LeRoy Troyer & Assocs., Goshen, Ind., 1984-86, Nat. Enterprises, Inc., Lafayette, Ind., 1986—. Mem. Goshen Housing Task Force, 1985—; v.p., bd. dirs. Habitat for Humanity of Elkhart County, 1986—. Mem. AIA (bd. dirs. No. Ind. chpt., 1986—), Goshen Hist. Soc. Democrat. Evangelical Mennonite. Avocations: calligraphy, music, photography. Home: 3101 New London Ct #507 Lafayette IN 47905 Office: Nat Enterprises Inc 401 S Earl Ave Lafayette IN 47903

ELROD, ROBERT GRANT, lawyer; b. Indpls., Feb. 24, 1940; s. French McElroy and B. Burrlene (Holland) E.; m. Beverly Anne Wahl, Aug. 23, 1964; children: Franklin Matthew, Benjamin Grant, Jeremiah French, Jonathan Robert. BA with honors, DePauw U., 1962; JD cum laude, Harvard U., 1965. Bar: Ind. 1965. Assoc. Elrod, Taylor & Williams, Indpls., 1965-66; ptnr. Elrod & Elrod, Indpls., 1967-79, Elrod, Elrod & Mascher, Indpls., 1980—, Elrod, Rees, Mascher & Whitham, Indpls., 1986—; asst. county atty. Marion County, Indpls., 1967-68; county atty. Marion County, 1969, asst. atty. city-council legal div., 1970-71, gen. counsel, city-county, 1972—. Treas., Young Reps. Marion County, 1968-69, sr. v.p., 1969-71, pres., 1971-73; 11th dist. chmn. Ind. Young Rep. Fedn., 1971-74, nat. committeeman, 1975-77; del. Rep. State Conv., 1968, 70, 72, 74, 76, 78; precinct committeeman 1970-78, 84—, ward chmn., 1977-80. Recipient Outstanding Male Young Rep. award Ind. Young Rep. Fedn., 1972, Marion County, 1974. Mem. ABA, Ind. State Bar Assn., Johnson County Bar Assn., Indpls. Bar Assn., Am. Judicature Soc., Comml. Law League Am., Am. Hosp. Attys. Methodist. Club: Columbia (Indpls.). Lodge: Masons. Home: 6730 S Arlington Ave Indianapolis IN 46237 also: 6960 S Gray Rd Suite A Indianapolis IN 46237

EL SAFFAR, RUTH SNODGRASS, Spanish language educator; b. N.Y.C., June 12, 1941; d. John Tabb and Ruth (Wheelwright) Snodgrass; m. Zuhair M. El Saffar, Apr. 11, 1965; children: Ali, Dena, Amir. B.A., Colo. Coll., 1962; Ph.D., Johns Hopkins U., 1966. Instr. Spanish, Johns Hopkins U., Balt., 1963-65; instr. English, Univ. Coll. Baghdad, 1966-67; asst. prof. Spanish, U. Md.-Baltimore County, 1967-68; asst. prof. U. Ill.-Chgo., 1968-73; asso. prof. U. Ill., 1973-78, prof., 1978-83, research prof. Spanish, 1983—; dir. summer seminar on Spanish Golden Age lit. NEH, 1979, 82. Author: Novel to Romance: A Study of Cervantes's Novelas Ejemplares, 1974, Distance and Control in Don Quixote, 1975, Cervantes's Casamiento engañoso and Coloquio de los perros, 1976, Beyond Fiction, 1984, Critical Essays on Cervantes, 1986; adv. bd. PMLA; editorial bd. Cervantes. Woodrow Wilson fellow, 1962; NEH fellow, 1970-71; Guggenheim fellow, 1975-76; Danforth assoc., 1973-79; Am. Council Learned Socs. grantee, 1978; Newberry Library fellow, 1982; U. Ill. Inst. Humanities fellow, 1985-86; sr. univ. scholar U. Ill., 1986—. Mem. MLA (exec. council 1974-78, commn. on future of the profession 1980-82, exec. com. div. on Spanish Golden Age poetry and prose 1977-82), Am. Assn. Tchrs. Spanish and Portuguese, Midwest MLA, Cervantes Soc. Am. (exec. com. 1979-82, 86—). Home: 7811 Greenfield River Forest IL 60305 Office: Univ Ill Dept Spanish Chicago IL 60680

ELSBERND, HELEN AGNES, college dean; b. Calmar, Iowa, Jan. 15, 1938; d. Alois and Loretta (Kuennen) E.; B.A., Viterbo Coll., 1965; M.S., U. Ill., 1967, Ph.D., 1969; postgrad. Harvard U., 1979. Tchr., Sacred Heart Sch., Eau Claire, Wis., 1959-62; tchr. sci. and math. St. Francis High Sch., Provo, Utah, 1963-65; research fellow U. Ill., Urbana, 1966-69, summer 70-72, tchg. asst., 1968-69; mem. chemistry faculty Viterbo Coll., LaCrosse, Wis., 1969-75, dept. chairperson, 1970-75, acad. dean, 1976—, Title III Coordinator, 1975-76; vis. prof. U. Wis., Madison, 1975; cons. Regional Sem. Project, Milw., 1981. Bd. dirs. Franciscan Health System, 1984—, St. Francis Med. Ctr., 1984—. Contbr. articles to profl. jours. NIH, fellow, 1967-69; Bush Found. fellow, 1979; named Woman of Yr. Bus. and Profl. Women, 1984. Mem. Am. Assn. Higher Edn., Nat. Assn. Women Deans, Adminstrs., and Counselors, North Central Assn. Acad. Deans, Soc. Higher Edn., Greater LaCrosse C. of C. (bd. dirs. 1984—, ambassador 1982—, com. chmn. 1983—). Office: Viterbo Coll 815 S 9th St LaCrosse WI 54601

ELSON, JOEL DUERING, radiologist; b. Grand Island, Nebr., Dec. 16, 1953; s. Kenneth Hamilton and Josephine (Duering) E.; m. Brenda Scott Russell, Nov. 14, 1982. BS, Kearney State Coll., 1974; MD with distinction, U. Nebr., 1977, cert. radiology, 1981. Fellow in angiography and interventional radiography U. Va. Med. Ctr., Charlottesville, 1981-82; staff radiologist, angiographer Radiology Nuclear Medicine, Inc., Bishop Clarkson Meml. Hosp., Omaha, 1982—; asst. prof. radiology U. Nebr. Med. Ctr., Omaha, 1982—. Author: (jour.) Radiology, 1982. Mem. AMA, Am. Coll. Radiology, Radiology Soc. N. Am., Soc. Cardiovascular and Interventional Radiology, Alpha Omega Alpha. Office: Radiology Nuclear Medicine Inc 622 Doctors Bldg Omaha NE 68105

ELSTER, TOBY, petroleum geologist, oil company executive, planning and financial consultant; b. Calipatria, Calif., Feb. 15, 1923; s. Jack and Pauline (Gelles) E.; m. Mary M. Benest, 1949 (div. 1975); children—Marc, Louis, Paulette; m. T. Alayne Corbell, Jan. 28, 1979. B.S. in Bus. Adminstrn., Wichita State U., 1948, B.A. in Geology, 1950. Staff geologist, Nat. Coop. Refining Assn., Wichita, 1953-55, Petroleum, Inc., Wichita, 1955-56; cons., Wichita, 1956-68, 70—; sr. v.p. exploration Acme Oil Corp., Wichita, 1968-70. Author articles. Wing comdr CAP, Wichita, 1968-70, mem. CAP, 1965—. Served to capt. USAFR, 1942-83. Mem. Soc. Ind. Profl. Earth Scientists (service award 1970, 72, chmn. Wichita chpt. 1970, nat. dir. 1971-72), Am. Assn. Petroleum Geologists, Kans. Geol. Soc., Soc. Exploration Geophysicists, Soc. Econ. Paleontologists & Mineralogists, Rocky Mountain Geol. Soc., Am. Arbitration Assn., Alumni Assn. Wichita State U. (life), VFW (life). Clubs: Petroleum, Cosmopolitan (Wichita). Lodges: Moose, Elks. Home: PO Box 78068 Wichita KS 67278-0628 Office: Pan-Western Petroleum Inc Board of Trade Ctr Suite 501 Wichita KS 67202

ELSWICK, JERRY CLARENCE, poet, pharmacist; b. Pike County, Ky., Oct. 19, 1931; s. John Robert and Carmen Forest (Maynard) E. B.S. in Pharmacy, Ohio State U., 1963. Registered pharmacist, Ohio. Pharmacist Gray Drug Fair div. of Rite Aid Corp., Columbus, Ohio, 1963—. Author numerous poems. Patentee billiard cue with guide member, 1970. Served with U.S. Army, 1953-55. Mem. Am. Pharm. Assn., Ohio State Pharm. Assn., Acad. Am. Poets, Delta Phi Alpha. Democrat. Avocations: boating, swimming. Office: Rite Aid Pharmacy 3834 E Broad St Columbus OH 43213

ELTO, PATRICK WILLIAM, sales executive; b. Detroit, July 30, 1947; s. Edwin Edward and Alice L. (Gallagher) E.; m. Leatrice Lyle Webb, Sept. 29, 1973. BS in Bus. Edn., Ferris State U., 1971; MEd, Western Mich. U., 1982. Dist. mgr. J. Lewis Cooper Co., Detroit, 1974; field mktg. mgr. Mogen David Wine, No. Ohio, 1974-76; state mgr. wine group Mogen David Wine,

Grand Rapids, Mich., 1976-81, area mktg. mgr. wine group, 1981-83; sales mgr. beer div., mktg. mgr. wine div. Henry A. Fox Sales, Kentwood, Mich., 1983—. Mem. Rep. Nat. Com. Served with U.S. Marines, 1966-67. Mem. Grand Rapids Retail Assn., Nat. Rifle Assn., Pi Omega Pi. Roman Catholic. Lodge: Elks. Home: 6310 W Encantado Ct Rockford MI 49341 Office: Henry A Fox Sales Co 4494 36th SE Kentwood MI 49341

ELWIN, JAMES WILLIAM, JR., university dean, lawyer; b. Everett, Wash., June 28, 1950; s. James William Elwin and Jeannette Georgette (Zichy-Litscheff) Sherman; m. Regina K. McCabe, Oct. 25, 1986. B.A., U. Denver, 1971, M.A., 1972; J.D., Northwestern U., 1975. Bar: Ill. 1975, U.S. Dist. Ct. (no. dist.) Ill. 1975, U.S. Ct. Appeals (7th cir.) 1977, U.S. Supreme Ct. 1980. Trial atty. antitrust div. U.S. Dept. Justice, Chgo., 1975-77; asst. dean Northwestern U. Sch. Law, Chgo., 1977-82, assoc. dean, 1982—, exec. dir. Corp. Counsel Ctr. Northwestern U., 1984—; planning dir. Corp. Counsel Inst., Chgo., 1983—; dir. Short Course for Pros. Attys., Chgo., 1981—, Short Course for Def. Lawyers in Criminal Cases, Chgo., 1979—. Bd. dirs. Legal Assistance Found. of Chgo., 1985—; vice chmn. Gov.'s Adv. Council on Criminal Justice Legislation, 1986—. Fellow German Academic Exchange Service, 1986. Mem. Chgo. Bar Assn. (bd. mgrs. 1983-85), Chgo. Bar Found. (bd. dirs. 1985—), Ill. Inst. Continuing Legal Edn. (chmn. 1987-88), Assn. Am. Law Schs. (chmn. sect. Instl. Advancement 1985), Phi Beta Kappa, Pi Gamma Mu. Clubs: Legal, Univ. (Chgo.). Office: Northwestern Univ Sch Law 357 E Chicago Ave Chicago IL 60611

ELWOOD, BRIAN CLAY, purchasing agent; b. Akron, Iowa, May 10, 1958; s. William Clay and Mathilda (Middle) E.; m. Roxie Jewel Rexilius, Aug. 29, 1980. BBA, Nebr. Wesleyan U., 1980. Cert. purchasing mgr., adminstrv. mgr. Assoc. purchasing mgr. R.L. White Co., Lincoln, Nebr., 1980-81, asst. purchasing mgr., 1981-82, purchasing mgr., 1982-84; purchasing agt. Southeast Community Coll., Lincoln, 1984—; tax preparer, cons., Lincoln, 1981—; instr. computers, Southeast Community Coll., Lincoln, 1986—. Bd. dirs. Central Alliance Daycare Ctr., Lincoln, 1986—; music dir. Central Alliance Ch., Lincoln, 1983-85, head deacon, fin. sec. 1983—. Mem. Nat. Assn. Purchasing Mgmt., Adminstrv. Mgmt. Soc. (chmn. profl. devel. com. 1984-86), Nat. Assn. Ednl. Buyers, Nebr. Wesleyan U. Letter Club, Omicron Delta Epsilon. Republican. Avocations: vocal and instrumental performance and composition, coin collecting, computers. Office: Southeast Community Coll 8800 O St Lincoln NE 68520

ELY, WAYNE HARRISON, broadcast engr.; b. Alliance, Ohio, Aug. 31, 1933; s. Dwight Harrison and Mable Evellen (Jones) E.; student Mount Union Coll., 1955-56, Ohio U., 1956-62; m. Roslyn Rose Ambrose, June 14, 1964 (div. Nov. 2, 1981); children—Eric (dec.), Kevin, Gayle, Mitchell. Transmitter engr. Sta. WOUB-AM-FM, Ohio U., Athens, 1958-62; studio field engr. ABC, N.Y.C., 1962-66, 67-72; studio engr. CBS, N.Y.C., 1966-67; transmitter supr. Sta. WOUC-TV, Ohio U., Quaker City, 1972—; tchr. radio tech. Ohio U., Zanesville. Served with C.E., U.S. Army, 1952-54. Mem. Soc. Broadcast Engrs. (sr. broadcast engrs. cert.). Home: 3705 Woodland Dr Zanesville OH 43701 Office: WOUC-TV Route 3 Quaker City OH 43773

EMAL, JAMES G., biometry educator; b. Minden, Nebr., Dec. 13, 1947; s. Marvin C. Emal and Glendola L. (Deeds) Kraft; m. LeAnn K. Rogers, Apr. 5, 1969; 1 child, Cory. Extension agt. chmn. Cooperative Extension Service, Wilber, Nebr., 1972-82; extension computer specialist Cooperative Extension Service, Lincoln, Nebr., 1982—. Editor Inst. Agr. and Natural Resources Computing News, 1982—. Bd. dirs. Wilber Housing Authority, 1980-85. Mem. Nebr. Cooperative Extension Agts. Assn. (bd. dirs. 1987—), Nebr. Range Soc. (pres. 1980-81), Gamma Sigma Delta, Epsilon Sigma Phi, Sigma Xi, Alpha Zeta. Methodist. Lodge: Lions (pres. Wilber). Avocations: woodworking, outdoors, automotive work, local history. Home: Rt 1 Box 174 Wilber NE 68465 Office: Univ Nebr 205 Miller Hall Lincoln NE 68583-0712

EMBAR, INDRANI MABBU, information services administrator, consultant; b. Bangalore, Mysore, India, Dec. 4, 1934; came to U.S., 1958; d. Parthasarathy and Rukmini Mabbu; children: Mohan Embar, Maya Embar. BS, Maharani's Coll., Bangalore, India, 1958; MLS, Rosary Coll., 1960. Asst. librarian World Book, Inc., Chgo., 1960-65, sr. researcher, 1965-77, head librarian, 1977-81; pres. Embar Info. Cons., Wheaton, Ill., 1982—; dir. info. services Boston Cons. Group, Chgo., 1982—. Mem. Am. Soc. Info. Sci., Spl. Libraries Assn., Online (chmn. sects. ITE, SLA 1986). Avocations: travel, hiking, music. Office: Boston Cons Group 200 S Wacker Chicago IL 60606

EMBERT, PAUL SYLVESTER, JR., criminal justice educator; b. Portland, Maine, June 4, 1936; s. Paul S. and Beatrice Mae (Dunham) E.; m. Leanora Ann Skeldon, July 19, 1958; 1 child, Robin Ann. BS, Mich. State U., 1965, MS, 1969; M in Mil. Art and Sci., Army Command and Gen. Staff Coll., 1978. Enlisted USAF, 1955, advanced through ranks to sgt., 1962, commd. 2d lt., 1965, advanced through grades to lt. col., 1980, retired, 1983; asst. prof. aerospace studies Mich. State U., East Lansing, 1980-83, tng. specialist criminal justice, 1983—; instr. Montcalm Community Coll., Sidney, Mich., 1984—; mng. assoc. KER & Assocs.Cons., East Lansing, 1985—. Contbr. articles to profl. jours. Mem. Acad. Criminal Justice Scis., Air Force Assn. (past state program chmn.), Am. Correction Assn., Am. Jail Assn., Am. Soc. Indsl. Security (co-editor Lansing chpt. newsletter), Internat. Assn. Chiefs of Police, Mich. Corrections Assn., Midwest Criminal Justice Assn. Republican. Roman Catholic. Avocation: collecting antiques. Office: Mich State U Sch Criminal Justice 560 Baker Hall East Lansing MI 48824-1118

EMBRY, WAYNE RICHARD, basketball executive; b. Springfield, Ohio, Mar. 26, 1937; s. Floyd and Anna Elizabeth (Gardner) E.; m. Theresa Jackson, June 6, 1959; children: Deborah, Jill, Wayne Richard. B.S., Miami U., 1958. Profl. basketball player Cin. Royals, 1958-66, Boston Celtics, 1966-68; basketball player Milw. Bucks, 1968-69, gen. mgr., 1972-77, v.p., cons., 1977-85; v.p., cons. Ind. Pacers, Indpls., 1985-86; v.p., g.m. Cleveland Cavaliers, Cleveland, 1986—; dir. recreation City Boston, 1969-70. Trustee Basketball Hall of Fame. Office: care Cleveland Cavaliers The Coliseum 2923 Streetsboro Rd Richfield OH 44286 *

EMDE, RICHARD K., insurance agent; b. Indpls., Sept. 21, 1938; s. Herman C. and Kathren (Devaney) E.; m. Doris Thompson, Sept. 9, 1961; children—Christine Louise, Gregg Alan. B.Sc., Ohio U., 1960. Chartered fin. cons. Agt., Union Central Life, Dayton, Ohio, 1962-71; asst. gen. agt. New Eng. Life, Dayton, 1971-72, gen. agt., St. Louis, 1972—, exec. com. gen. agts., 1984-85; bd. dirs. Nelesco. Mem. Life Underwriters (bd. dirs. 1978-81), Chartered Life Underwriters, Million Dollar Round Table (life, gen. agts. mgmt. award), Gen. Agents Assn. (bd. dirs. 1981-83). Republican. Presbyterian. Club: Melrose (Hilton Head, S.C.). Office: New England Fin Services 12400 Olive Blvd Suite 102 St Louis MO 63141

EMELANDER, RONALD LEE, accountant; b. Grand Rapids, Mich., Sept. 8, 1961; s. Sherwyn Jay and Marilyn Jeanne (Vanden Berg) E.; m. Lorie Marie Hamming, Oct. 13, 1984. AAS, Davenport Coll.ll., 1981; BS, Ferris State Coll., 1983. CPA, Mich. Asst. auditor gen. Office of Auditor Gen., Lansing, Mich., 1983-86; supr. EDP audit programmers Seidman and Seidman, Grand Rapids, 1986—. Mem. Am. Inst. CPA's, EDP Auditors Assn. (cert. info. systems auditor). Office: Seidman & Seidman BDO 99 Monroe NW Suite 300 Grand Rapids MI 49503

EMERICK, DAVID ALAN, accountant; b. Harlan, Iowa, Sept. 1, 1961; s. Tyron David and Margaret Ann (Propst) E. BS in Acctg. and Polit. Sci., William Jewell Coll., Liberty, Mo., 1984. CPA, Mo. Br. acct. Carpentours, Inc., Libery, Mo., 1982-83; sr. acct. Coopers & Lybrand, Kansas City, Mo., 1984—. Trustee Restoration Br., Independence, Mo., 1986-87. Mem. Am. inst. CPA's, Mo. Soc. CPA's, Phi Gamma Mu (pres. 1983-84), Delta Mu Delta. Reorganized Ch. of Jesus Christ of Latter-day Saints. Avocations: running, traveling, pub. affairs. Office: Coopers & Lybrand 12th & Baltimore Suite 900 City Ctr Sq Kansas City MO 64105-2175

EMERING, EDWARD JOHN, employee benefits consulting executive, actuary; b. N.Y.C., June 14, 1945; s. Edward John and Antoinette (Imperato) E.; m. Sandra Ann Troutmann, July 11, 1981; children—Whitney, Scott, Eric, Daniel. B.A. in Econs., Seton Hall U., 1967; M.B.A. in Fin., U. Utah, 1970; M. Taxation, DePaul U., 1986. Enrolled actuary. Mgmt. trainee Prudential, Newark, 1970-72; sr. cons. Becker Co., East Orange, N.J., 1972-75; sr. actuary William Mercer Co., Detroit, 1976-77; mgr. Coopers & Lybrand, Chgo., 1977-79; ptnr. Touche Ross & Co., Chgo., 1979-85; sr. v.p. Johnson & Higgins, ins. and human resource cons., 1985-86; pres., chief exec. officer Noble Lowndes, Inc., Chgo., 1986—. Contbr. articles to publs. in field. Served to lt. USN, 1967-70. Decorated Navy Cross, Nat. Order (Republic of Vietnam); recipient hon. sci. award Bausch & Lomb, 1964. Fellow Am. Soc. Pension Actuaries; mem. Am. Acad. Actuaries, Internat. Actuarial Assn., Am. Mgmt. Assn., Chgo. Assn. Commerce and Industry. Clubs: East Bank, Monroe (Chgo.). Office: Noble Lowndes Inc 525 W Monroe Suite 2405 Chicago IL 60606

EMERSON, MARK FORBUSH, restaurant company executive; b. Boston, July 26, 1947; s. Leon Kingman and Eleanor (Peterson) E. BS in Hotel Adminstrn., Cornell U., 1969. Gen. mgr. Mnorx Inc., Ithaca, N.Y., 1969-71; asst. mgr. Steak and Ale, Houston, 1971-73; v.p. Mason Jar Restaurant, Houston, 1973-75; dir. ops. Red Bull Inns, Carnegie, Pa., 1976-80; v.p. Max and Erma's, Columbus, Ohio, 1980—, also bd. dirs.; guest lectr. U. Houston, 1973-75; cons. Nat. Food Service Panel, Escondido, Calif., 1983—. Mem. Cornell Alumni Assn. (sec., vice chmn., pres. sch. com. 1982—), Cornell Club of Cen. Ohio, Sigma Chi. Republican. Avocations: travelling, golfing, collecting sports memorabilia. Home: 5757 Shannon Pl Ln Columbus OH 43220 Office: Max & Erma's Inc PO Box 03325 Columbus OH 43203

EMERSON, ROGER DALE, automotive engineer, lawyer; b. Akron, Ohio, July 22, 1958; s. John Ludwig and Patsy Louise (Ayers) E.; m. Deborah Reneé Schwarz, June 26, 1982. BSME, U. Akron, 1981, JD, 1987. Mech. engr. Goodyear Tire, Akron, 1981-82, staff engr., 1982-85, sr. engr., 1985-87; assoc. Fay, Sharpe, Fagan, Minnich & McKee, 1987—. Inventor tire reinforcement. Mem. ABA. Republican.

EMERSON, WILLIAM, congressman; b. St. Louis, Jan. 1, 1938; s. Norvell Preston and Marie (Reinemer) E.; m. Jo Ann Hermann, June 21, 1975; children: Victoria Marie, Katharine; children by previous marriage: Elizabeth, Abigail. B.A., Westminster Coll., 1959; LL.B., U. Balt., 1964. Mem. congressional staffs 1961-70; dir. govt. relations Fairchild Industries, Germantown, Md., 1970-74; dir. public affairs INGAA, Washington, 1974-75; exec. asst. to chmn. Fed. Election Commn., 1975; dir. fed. relations TRW, Inc., Washington, 1975-79; public affairs cons. 1980; mem. 94th congress from 10th Dist. Mo., 1975-77, 98th-100th congresses from 8th Dist. Mo., 1983—; mem. Ho. Agr. Com., Com. on Interior and Insular Affairs, Select Com. on Hunger. Served to capt. USAF. Republican. Presbyterian. Home: Cape Girardeau MO 63020 Office: US House of Reps 418 Cannon House Office Bldg Washington DC 20515

EMERSON-NELSON, DIANE MARIE, marketing executive; b. Superior, Wis., Oct. 6, 1953; d. Robert Leroy and Imogene Augusta (Sayers) Emerson; m. Bradley Jon Nelson, Apr. 15, 1978. BS, U. Minn., 1981, MBA, 1983. Dir. The Kingman Cons. Group, St. Paul, 1983-84; mgr. corp. mktg. research H.B. Fuller Co., St. Paul, 1984—. Mem. planning group Minn. Women's Press, St. Paul, 1984—. Mem. planning adv. com. Como Conservatory planning adv., 1985—, fundraising steering com. 1986; chmn. landscaping task force Hubert Humphrey Job Corps, St. Paul, 1986. Mem. Chem. Mktg. Research Assn., Am. Mktg. Assn., Minn. Hort. Soc. (bd. dirs. 1985—, 2d v.p. 1987—). Mem. Dem. Farm Labor Party. Club: Garden (St. Paul) (pres. 1985). Avocations: landscaping, photography. Office: HB Fuller Co 3530 N Lexington Ave Saint Paul MN 55126

EMIG, RICHARD CARL, jeweler; b. Detroit, Oct. 13, 1956; s. Robert Carl and Ellie Lee (Black) E. Grad. in gemology, Gemological Inst. Am., 1976, Gemological City Coll., 1978. Pres. W.M. Spaman Jewelers, Kalamazoo, Mich., 1976—. Contbr. articles on jewelry to profl. jours. Mem. Mich. Jewelers Assn., Retail Jewelers Assn. (bd. dirs.), Kalamazoo C. of C.(bd. dirs.), Nat. Assn. Jewelry Appraisers. Republican. Methodist. Avocations: swimming, boating, horseback riding, sports. Home: 6721 Kingswood S Kalamazoo MI 49007 Office: W M Spaman Jewelers 112 W South Kalamazoo MI 49007

EMILEY, STEPHEN FRANK, psychologist, educator; b. Chgo., July 20, 1947; s. Harold L. and Ruth (Miller) E.; m. Nancy K. Gannon, Aug. 23, 1969; children: Jamie, Mark, David. BS, Loyola U., Chgo., 1969; MA in Clin. Psychology, DePaul U., 1971, PhD, 1974. Cert. clin. psychologist, Ill., Wis.; cert. sch. psychologist, Ill. Staff psychologist Ctr. for Child and Family Studies, Arlington Park, Ill., 1974-76; cons. psychologist Milw. Devel. Ctr., 1976-85, Homestead Family Therapy Services, Cedarburg, Wis., 1985—; grad. faculty Cardinal Stritch Coll., Milw., 1977-83; clin. asst. prof. U. Wis., Milw., 1983—. Bd. dirs. Ozaukee County (Wis.) Mental Health Assn., 1978-86. Named Wis. Mental Health Assn. Man of Yr., 1986. Mem. Am. Psychol. Assn., Soc. Clin. Cons. Psychologists, Wis. Biofeedback Soc. (bd. dirs. 1984-85), Cedarburg Jaycees (bd. dirs. 1982—, v.p. 1983-84, outstanding v.p. award 1983-84, outstanding 1st yr. Jaycee award 1982-83). Avocations: camping, rafting. Home: W65N772 Washington Ave Cedarburg WI 53012 Office: Homestead Family Therapy Services 4922 Columbia Rd Cedarburg WI 53012

EMM, DEBORAH LYNN, psychologist; b. Dayton, Ohio, June 4, 1947; d. Louis G. and Delphine (Ostrowski) E. BA, Ohio State U., 1969, PhD, 1985; MA, W. Ga. Coll., 1972. Lic. psychologist, Ohio. Social worker City and State Agencies, Columbus, Ohio, 1969-72; psychologist, supr. Ohio Dept. Corrections, Columbus, 1983-84; pvt. practice psychology Columbus, 1976—; dir. Survivors of Crime, Columbus, 1985—; cons. FBI, U.S.Dept. of State, 1984-85; researcher on cohabitation and sexual assault. Mem. adv. council League Against Child Abuse, Columbus, 1986, Incest Program, Columbus, 1986. Mem. Ohio Psychol. Assn., Nat. Orgn. Victim Assistance, Ohio Victim Witness Assn. (v.p. 1986). Democrat. Avocations: tennis, golf, karate, sewing, travel. Office: Survivors of Crime 1555 Bryden Rd Columbus OH 43205

EMMERICH, JAMES CHARLES, athletic trainer, coach; b. New Ulm, Minn., Mar. 18, 1911; s. Charles and Bertha (Keckeisen) E. BS, S.D. State Coll., 1940. Assoc. prof. phys. edn., coach off track and field, cross country trainer S.D. State Coll., Brookings, 1940-60; coach track and field, trainer, adminstrv. asst. Amateur Athletic Union USA, U.S. Olympic Com., 1956—; phys. therapist Dr. Dooley Clinic, Pomona, Calif., 1962; vic. lectr. Eastern Mich. U., Ypsilanti, 1966, Calif. Western U., San Diego, 1968. Named Coach of Yr. S.D. Coll., 1954; elected to Helms Hall Track and Field Coaches Hall of Fame, S.D. State U. Athletic Hall of Fame, S.D. Sports Hall of Fame, S.D. Cowboy and Western Heritage Hall of Fame; recipietn Disting. Service award S.D. State U. Jackrabbit Club, 1977. State leader Pres.'s Council Phys. Fitness. Served with AUS, 1942-46. Mem. Nat. Athletic Trainers Assn., Internat. Track Coaches Assn., U.S. Track Coaches Assn., U.S. Olympic Soc., Assn. U.S. Army, Am. Legion (life), DAV (life), Brookings C. of C., (Community Service award 1981), S.D. State U. Alumni Assn., S.D. High Sch. Activities Assn. (Disting. Service award 1982), Am. Turners, Blue Key, Phi KappaPhi, Alpha Zeta, PiGamma Mu. Congregationalist. Lodges: Elks (life, Elk of Yr. award 1977), Lions. Address: 517 2d Ave Brookings SD 57005

EMMONS, RANDALL WAYNE, physics educator; b. St. Louis, Aug. 23, 1952; s. Robert Guy and Ruth (Thomas) E. BS in Physics, U. Mo., Rolla, 1974, MS in Physics, 1976, PhD in Physics, 1981. Asst. prof. N.E. Mo. State U., Kirksville, 1982—; instr. Mo. Scholars Acad., Columbia, 1985; cons. gifted edn. Kirksville Sch. Dist., 1984-86; asst. dir. N.E. Mo. Regional Sci. Fair, 1983—. Contbr. articles to profl. jours. Pres. Friends of the Gifted, Kirksville, 1984-86; bd. dirs. N.E. Mo. Jr. Acad. Sci., 1984—. Named one of Outstanding Young Men in Am., 1984-86; Coordinating Bd. for Higher Edn. grantee, 1986. Avocations: woodworking, hiking, biking. Home: 1104 S Boundry Kirksville MO 63501 Office: Northeast Mo State U Sci Dept Kirksville MO 63501

EMOND, SUE ELLEN, education educator; b. Evansville, Ind., Sept. 24, 1943; d. Preston Earle and Nell (Carson) Bethel; m. John A. Emond, July 21, 1978; children: Joseph John, Robert Earle. BS, Ind. State U., 1965, MS, 1968; EdD, U. Fla., 1978. Tchr. Wayne Twp. Elem. Sch., Indpls., 1965-67; elem. sch. tchr. Unit #5, Normal, Ill., 1967-70; reading specialist Gadsden County Schs., Gretna, Fla., 1970-72; elem. tchr., researcher P.K. Yonge Lab Sch., Gainesville, Fla., 1972-77; teaching asst. U. Fla., Gainesville, 1977-78; prof. edn. Saginaw (Mich.) Valley State Coll., 1978—; cons. various sch. dists. throughout Mich., 1978—. Contbr. articles to profl. jours. Recipient Franc A. Landee award for Teaching Excellence Saginaw Valley State Coll., 1985; named Disting. Mem. Faculty Mich. Assn. Governing Bds., 1986. Mem. Internat. Reading Assn., Mich. Reading Council, Saginaw Area Reading Council, Phi Delta Kappa, Delta Gamma (v.p. 1963-64). Episcopalian. Avocations: reading, skiing, camping. Home: 5511 Cathedral Dr Saginaw MI 48603 Office: Saginaw Valley State Coll 229 Brown Hall Saginaw MI 48710

EMRICK, CHARLES ROBERT, JR., lawyer; b. Lakewood, Ohio, Dec. 19, 1929; s. Charles R. and Mildred (Hart) E.; m. Lizabeth Keating; children—Charles R. III, Caroline K. B.S., Ohio U., 1951, M.S., 1952; J.D., Cleve. State U., 1958. Bar: Ohio 1958. Ptnr. Calfee, Halter & Griswold, Cleve., 1965—; lectr. U. Services Bus. Ctr., John Carroll U., 1970—; dir. Best Sand Co., Gt. Lakes Lithograph, Clamco Corp., Hunter Mfg. Co., Ken-Mac Metals, S & H Industries, Somerset Techs., Inc., Wedron-Silica Sand Co. Former trustee, br. bd. chmn. YMCA; former officer, trustee Lake Erie Jr. Nature and Sci. Ctr.; former adj. prof. Baldwin Wallace U.; lectr. Chartered Life Underwriters Assn.; former adj. lectr. Case Western Res. U.; trustee Rocky River Pub. Library; trustee, treas. Cleve. Area Devel. Fin. Corp.; trustee Fairview Gen. Hosp., Cleve. Zool. Soc., Lake Ridge Acad.; prin. Enterprise bd., former mem. nat. policy adv. com. New Eng. Mut. Life Ins. Co.; mem. vis. com. Cleve. State Law Sch.; bd. dirs. N.E. chpt. Am. Cancer Soc. Methodist. Clubs: Westwood Country (former sec., legal counsel), Union, Cleveland Yachting, The Clifton. Office: Calfee Halter & Griswold 1800 Society Nat Bank Bldg Cleveland OH 44114

EMRICK, DONALD DAY, chemist; b. Waynesfield, Ohio, Apr. 3, 1929; s. Ernest Harold and Nellie (Day) E.; B.S. cum laude, Miami U., Oxford, Ohio, 1951; M.S., Purdue U., 1954, Ph.D., 1956 Grad. teaching asst. Purdue U., Lafayette, Ind., 1951-55; with chem. and phys. research div. Standard Oil Co. Ohio, 1955-64, research assoc., 1961-64; cons., sr. research chemist research dept. Nat. Cash Register Co., Dayton, Ohio, 1965-72, chem. cons., 1972—. Mem. AAAS, Am. Chem. Soc., Phi Beta Kappa, Sigma Xi. Patentee in Field. Contbr. articles to profl. jours. Home: 4240 Lesher Dr Kettering OH 45429

EMSWILER, TOM NEUFER, minister; b. Overland Park, Kans., Apr. 18, 1941; s. Thomas Clair and Velva Mae (Allmand) E.; m. Sharon Elaine Neufer; children: Evan, Elaine. BA, Emporia (Kans.) State Coll., 1963; BD, So. Meth. U., 1966; MA, Northwestern U., 1967. Pastor Trinity United Meth. Ch., Lawrence, Kans., 1967-70; assoc. pastor First United Meth. Ch., Wichita, Kans., 1970-72; co-dir. The Wesley Found. Ill. State U., Normal, 1972-86; free-lance writer Springfield, Ill., 1986—; Prof. Garrett Evang. Seminary, Evanston, 1978, Iliff Sch. Theology, Denver, 1978; cons. in field, Springfield, 1986—. Co-author Women and Worship: A Guide to Non-Sexist Hymns, Prayers and Liturgies, 1974; (cassette and guide) It's Your Wedding: A Practical Guide to Planning Contemporary Ceremonies, 1975, Wholeness in Worship, 1980; co-editor Sisters and Brothers, Sing!, 1977; author Love is a Magic Penny, 1977, The Click in the Clock, 1981, Money for your Campus Ministry, Church, or Other Non-profit Organization-How to Get It, 1981, A Complete Guide to Making the Most of Video in Religious Settings, 1985; author, producer The Beautitudes, 1985. Guy Maier scholar Nat. Assn. Piano Tchrs., 1960; recipient Rockefeller Found. Trial Yr. in Seminary award, 1963, 1st Nat. Meth. Fellowship in Preaching award, 1966. Mem. Nat. Assn. Campus Ministers, Cen. Ill. Conf. United Meth. Ministers. Democrat. Avocations: video, coins, stamps. Home and Office: 1121 S Walnut St Springfield IL 62704-2852

ENDICOTT, WAYNE ALLEN, writer, photographer; b. Chgo., Dec. 6, 1939; s. John Girard and Edith Margaret (Wolf) E.; m. Holly Evelyn Skreko, Sept. 2, 1961; children: Mark Allen, Karen Denise. Student, U. Wis., 1957-59. Mng. editor Profl. Builder, Chgo., 1966-68; editor-in-chief Automation in Housing, Chgo., 1968-74; exec. editor Constrn. Equipment, Chgo., 1974-81; editor-in-chief Brick & Clay Record, Chgo., 1981-86; owner, operator Comm Con, Palatine, Ill., 1986—. Deacon St. John United Ch. Christ, Arlington Heights, Ill., 1976-78. Mem. Soc. Profl. Journalists, Am. Soc. Bus. Press (Jesse H. Neal award 1970), Constrn. Writers Assn. (bd. dirs. 1980-81), Athletic Ofcls. Am. (pres. 1980-82), Nat. Assn. Athletic Ofcls., Ill. High Sch. Assn., Jaycees (pres. Arlington Heights 1975). Avocations: racquetball, golf, reading. Office: Comm Con PO Box 1074 Palatine IL 60078-1074

ENDLICH, LEATRICE ANN, therapist; b. Topeka, Aug. 27, 1928; d. Harry and Roselle (Dauer) E.; m. Howard L. Swartzman, June 27, 1950 (div. Aug. 1984); children: Susan Swartzman Freeman, Steven Swartzman, Julie Swartzman. BA, Mills Coll., 1950; MSW, U. Kans., 1963. Social worker Jewish Family and Children's Services, Kansas City, Mo., 1968-73, dir. family life edn., 1973-77; pvt. practice clin. social work Prairie Village, 1977-78; teaching assoc. dept. child psychiatry U. Kans. Med. Ctr., Kansas City, 1978-84; day treatment therapist Gillis Ctr., Kansas City, 1984-86; pvt. practice Leawood, Kans., 1986—; Bd. dirs. Johnson County Mental Health Ctr., Overland Park, Kans., Crittenden Ctr., Kansas City. Mem. adv. com. Kans. Behavioral Scis. Regulatory Bd., 1983; mem. Menorah Med. Ctr. Auxiliary (life), Kansas City, Friends of Art, Kansas City, Lyric Opera Guild, Kansas City, William Jewell Coll. Fine Arts Guild. Mem. Am. Assn. Marriage and Family Therapy (clin.), Nat. Assn. Social Workers, Acad. Cert. Social Workers (cert.), Nat. Council Jewish Women (life mem. Mo. chpt.). Democrat. Club: Oakwood Country (Kansas City), Overland Park Racquet. Avocations: photography, arts, travel, poetry. Home: 8725 Catalina Dr Shawnee Mission KS 66207 Office: 3700 W 83d St Leawood KS 66206

ENDSLEY, GREGORY HOWARD, computer executive; b. Wichita, Kans., Mar. 13, 1949; s. Howard Milton and Helen Maxine (Jewell) E.; m. Linda Marie Stephens, Aug. 28, 1971; 1 child, Sarah. BS in Physics, U. Kans., 1971. V.p. Integrated Tech., Inc., Kansas City, Mo., 1979-82; customer service mgr. Colorgraphics Systems, Madison, Wis., 1982-85; pres. White Oak Enterprises, Oregon, Wis., 1985—. Avocations: piano, photography.

ENENBACH, DAVID EDWARD, accountant, councilman; b. Columbia, Mo., May 20, 1959. BS in Bus. Acctg., U. Kans., 1981. CPA, Mo. Audit mgr. Donnelly, Meiners & Jordan, Kansas City, Mo., 1981—. Councilman City of Westwood, Kans., 1986—; v.p., treas. Westwood Found., 1986—; treas. Kans. Teke Alumni Bd., 1986—. Mem. Am. Inst. CPAs, Kans. Soc. CPAs, Mo. Soc. CPAs (tech. com. 1985—), Greater Kansas City Orgn. Service and Tng. Roman Catholic. Home: 2500 W 51 Terrace Westwood KS 66205 Office: Donnelly Meiners & Jordan 9215 Ward Pkwy Kansas City MO 64114

ENGBER, DIANE, communications specialist; b. Staten Island, N.Y., Feb. 12, 1952; s. Jacob J. and Bettie Samuels (Loeb) E.; m. Leslie Frank Chard II, Dec. 21, 1980; 1 child, Joseph Samuels Chard. BA in English, Oakland U., 1973; MA in Modern Brit. Lit., U. Cin., 1978. Pub. relations coordinator Women Helping Women, Cin., 1978-79; devel. officer Legal Aid Soc. of Cin., 1982-84; communications specialist Cin. Pub. Schs., 1984—; lectr. English U. Cin., 1978—; assoc. bus. and tech. communications Thomas Sant and Assocs., 1980-82; assoc. editor Wapora Inc., 1979-80. Mem. jud. candidate rating com. Cin. Bar Assn., 1986—, Alice Paul House Com. on Adminstrn., YWCA Bd., 1985—; travel chair grant sub-com. U. Cin. Women's Studies Exec. Com., 1985—; mem. mental health allocations com. Community Chest, 1984—, chair, 1986—; career advisor U. Cin. Alumni Assn., Career Resource Ctr., 1983—; chair personnel com. U-Kids Coop., 1982. Recipient various pub. relations awards for Etcetera newsletter, 1985-86. Mem. Nat. Womens Studies Assn., Ohio Assn. Adminstrs. of State and Federal Edn. Programs, Womans City Club. Democrat. Jewish. Avocations: swimming, reading, knitting.

ENGBERG, KEN, mining company executive. Chmn. Baukol-Noonan, Inc., Minot, N.D. Office: Baukol-Noonan Inc Box 879 Minot ND 58702 Address: Baukol-Noonan Inc 26 N Main Crosby ND 58730 *

ENGBLOM, ERIC ALBIN, engineering company executive; b. Detroit, Dec. 10, 1922; s. Eric Gunnar and Edith (Wiirtanen) E.; m. Georgina Elizabeth Reich, Apr. 10, 1943; children: Suzanne, Eric Jr., Edith. BSME, Wayne State U., 1953. Registered profl. engr., Mich. Sr. staff engr. Gen. Motors Corp., Warren, Mich., 1959-81; pvt. practice engrng. cons. Bloomfield Hills, Mich., 1981—. Pres. bd. dirs. Christian Family Services, Southfield, Mich., 1977—. Served with U.S. Army, 1944-46, ETO. Decorated Purple Heart, Bronze Star. Baptist. Avocation: golf. Home: 2621 Brady Dr Bloomfield Hills MI 48013

ENGEBRETSON, JAMES DENNIS, sales executive; b. Beloit, Wis., Feb. 10, 1939; s. Lyman Everett and Mary Cecelia (Hayes) E.; m. Julia Alice Sheahan, Jan. 15, 1966; children: Peter, Marcy, Becky, Eric. BS, No. Ill. U., 1965. From asst. sales mgr. to mgr. project devel. Amoco Fabrics Co., Chgo., 1968-83; gen. sales mgr. Bennett Industries, Peotone, Ill., 1983—. V.p. Lake Charlotte Homeowners Assn., St. Charles, Ill., 1980, treas., 1981. Served as pvt. U.S. Army, 1958-60. Republican. Roman Catholic. Avocations: tennis, jogging. Home: 410 E Nebraska St Frankfort IL 60423 Office: Bennett Industries 515 1st St Peotone IL 60468

ENGEL, ALBERT JOSEPH, judge; b. Lake City, Mich., Mar. 21, 1924; s. Albert Joseph and Bertha (Bielby) E.; m. Eloise Ruth Bull, Oct. 18, 1952; children: Albert Joseph, Katherine Ann, James Robert, Mary Elizabeth. Student, U. Md., 1941-42; A.B., U. Mich., 1948, LL.B., 1950. Bar: Mich. 1951. Ptnr. firm Engle & Engel, Muskegon, Mich., 1952-67; judge Mich. Circuit Ct., 1967-71; judge U.S. Dist. Ct. Western Dist. Mich., 1971-74; circuit judge U.S. Ct. Appeals, 6th Circuit, Grand Rapids, Mich., 1974—. Served with AUS, 1943-46, ETO. Fellow Am. Bar Found.; mem. Am., Fed., Cin., Grand Rapids bar assns., Am. Judicature Soc., Am. Legion, Phi Sigma Kappa, Phi Delta Phi. Episcopalian. Club: Grand Rapids Torch. Home: 7287 Denison Dr SE Grand Rapids MI 49506 Office: 640 Fed Bldg Grand Rapids MI 49503

ENGEL, GEOFFREY RICHARD, accountant, consultant; b. Cleve., Apr. 12, 1956; s. Earl Daniel and Rosemary Ann (Petunia) E.; m. Joanne Renee Nicolosi, June 21, 1980; children: Stephanie, Joseph. BBA in Acctg., Cleve. State U., 1979. CPA, Ohio. Staff acct. Gangloff, Kemme & Supelak CPA's, Cleve., 1979-85; acctg. supr. McManamon, Gilbert, Doeringer CPA's, Rocky River, Ohio, 1985—. Contbg. photographer Cleve. State U. publs., 1979. Instr. Jr. Achievement, Cleve. 1986. Mem. Am. Inst. CPA's, Ohio Soc. CPA's, Westlake C. of C. Avocations: photography, personal computing. Home: 5953 Pearl Rd Parma Heights OH 44130

ENGEL, SUSAN LEE, pharmaceutical industry executive, physician; b. Chgo., Oct. 7, 1954; d. Ted S. Dziengiel and Marian L. (Carpenter) Kasper. B Arts and Scis., Northwestern U., 1975; MD, Chgo. Med. Sch., 1982. Med. technician G.D. Searle, Skokie, Ill., 1972, 73, assoc. dir., 1983-84, dir., 1984-86; research editorial asst. U. Chgo., 1974; research assoc. Loyola U., Maywood, Ill., 1977-78; mgr. Hosp. Products div. Abbott Labs, Abbott Park, Ill., 1986—; Vis. prof. Rush Presbyn.-St. Luke's Hosp., Chgo., 1985, faculty assoc., 1985—; assoc. investigator, asst. prof. King Drew Med. Ctr., UCLA, 1985—, asst. prof. medicine, 1985—. Contbr. articles to profl. and scholarly jours. Bd. govs. Art Inst. of Chgo., 1985—, mem. multiple benefit coms., 1984—, vice chmn. capital campaign, 1984-85; mem. pres. com. Landmark Preservation Council, Chgo., 1984—, chmn. multiple coms. polit. candidates, 1986; bd. dirs. Marshall unit Chgo. Boys Clubs, 1984—. Internat. Coll. Surgeons fellow, 1982. Mem. AMA, Am. Coll. Physicians, Am. Fedn. for Clin. Research, So. Med. Assn., Ill. State Med. Soc., Chgo. Med. Soc., Am. Acad. Med. Dirs., Anchor Cross Soc., Nat. Acad. Arts & Scis. Avocations: German lang., swimming, organ playing, composing music.

ENGELBRECHT, DALE ROBERT, lawyer; b. Neosho, Mo., Apr. 3, 1959; s. Carl H. and Carol Ann (Schneider) E. BS in Acctg. magna cum laude, Southwest Mo. State U., 1981; JD, U. Mo., Kansas City, 1984. Bar: Mo. 1984, U.S. Dist. Ct. (we. dist.) Mo. 1984. Law clk. to sr. judge U.S. Dist. Ct., Springfield, Mo., 1984, 1986; assoc. Miller & Sanford, Springfield, 1986—; auditor Mo. State Auditor's Office, Neosho, 1980. Mem. Dem. Alliance, Springfield, 1986. Named one of Outstanding Young Men Am., 1985. Mem. ABA, Assoc. Trial Lawyers Am., Mo. Bar Assn., Greene County Bar Assn., Phi Kappa Phi, Ducks Unltd. Lutheran. Avocations: softball, golf, basketball, travel. Home: 2217 S Maryland Springfield MO 65807 Office: Miller & Sanford PO Box 1097 Springfield MO 65805

ENGELHARDT, MARK DOUGLAS, secondary school principal; b. Cape Cirardeau, Mo., Nov. 5, 1952; s. W. Gene and Delba Aletha (Hartle) E.; m. Gelina Lee Ann Bridges, July 27, 1975; 1 child, Douglas Lee. EdB summa cum laude, S.E. Mo. State U., 1974, MEd, 1981; postgrad., St. Louis U., 1981—. Cert. secondary sch. tchr., Mo.; cert. secondary sch. prin., Mo. Tchr. social studies Hazelwood Sch. Dist., Florissant, Mo., 1974-86, asst. dir. adult edn., 1979-86; prin. Maplewood (Mo.)-Richmond Heights Sch. Dist., 1986—; adj. prof. psychology St. Louis U., 1979—; dir. St. Louis econ. edn. program U. Mo., St. Louis, 1976; mem. tchrs. work learn program Ryerson Steel Co., St. Louis, 1978; coordinator workshop on Reflective Teaching. Tech. dir. Hazelwood Cen. Theatre, Florissant, 1979-86. Mem. Am. Psychol. Assn., Assn. Supervision and Curriculum Devel., Nat. Assn. Secondary Sch. Prins., Imperial Dance Club, Phi Delta Kappa (pres. 1984, regional and nat. del. 1981, Internat. Service Key, 1985), Pi Lambda Theta. Unitarian-Universalist. Avocations: tech. theatre, backpacking, karate, swimming, sailing. Home: 2135 Somerset Dr Florissant MO 63033 Office: Valley Grade Ctr 2801 Oakland Maplewood MO 63143

ENGELKES, JAMES RICHARD, psychologist; b. Aplington, Iowa, Nov. 15, 1942; s. Bernard Melvin and Leona (Sherman) E.; m. Marcia N. Hopp, Aug. 15, 1964; children: Traci L., Ross J. BA, Cen. Coll., Pella, Iowa, 1964; MA, U. Iowa, 1966, PhD, 1969. From asst. prof. to prof. psychology Mich. State U., East Lansing, 1969-85; pres., psychologist Lansing Psychol. Assocs., East Lansing, 1976—; commr. Commn. on Rehab., Chgo., 1975-81, Council on Rehab. Edn., 1978-81; vocat. expert witness Social Security Adminstrn., 1977—. Steering com. mem. 6th Dist. Congl. Race, Mich., 1980. Mem. Am. Psychol. Assn., Am. Assn. Counseling and Devel., Mich. Vocat. Guidance Assn. (pres. 1976). Republican. Presbyterian. Avocations: walking, reading, music, theater. Home: 6343 Skyline Dr East Lansing MI 48823 Office: Lansing Psychol Assocs 2500 Kerry St Lansing MI 48912

ENGELKING, ELLEN MELINDA, foundry pattern company executive, real estate broker; b. Columbus, Ind., May 12, 1942; d. Lowell Eugene and Marcella (Brane) E.; children: Melissa Claire Prohaska, John David Prohaska, Ellen Margaret Prohaska. Student Sullins Coll., 1961, Franklin Coll., 1961-62, Ind. U., 1963. Vice chmn., pres., chief exec. officer Engelking Patterns, Inc., Columbus, Ind., 1980—, dir., treas., chief exec. officer Engelking Properties, Inc., Columbus, 1980—; guest speaker Bus. Sch., Ind. U., Bloomington, 1985-86, Ball State U., Muncie, Ind., 1986. Campaign chmn. Am. Heart Assn., Bartholomew County, 1980-81; chmn. Mothers March of Dimes, Bartholomew County, 1967; sec. Bartholomew County Republican Party, 1976-80; bd. dirs. Found. for Youth, 1975-78, Quinco Found., 1978-79; protocol hostess Pan Am. Games X, Inpls., 1987. Mem. U.S. C. of C., Ind. C. of C., Ind. Mfg. Assn., Am. Foundrymens Soc., Acad. of Model Aeronautics, Delta Delta Delta. Roman Catholic. Avocations: study and present adaptation of Shaker work ethic, remote-controlled aircrafts, literature, oil painting. Office: Engelking Patterns Inc PO Box 607 Columbus IN 47202

ENGELS, PATRICIA LOUISE, lawyer; b. Joliet, Ill., July 2, 1926; d. Fred Adolph and Loretta Mae (Fisk) B.; m. Henry William Engels, Feb. 1, 1947; children: Patrick Henry, Michael Bruce, Timothy William. BE, Olivet Nazarene Coll., 1970, MEd, 1971; JD, John Marshall Law Sch., 1979. Bar: Ill. 1979, Ind. 1979; cert. elem. and high sch. tchr., edn. adminstrn., Ill. Tchr. Bourbonnais (Ill.) and Momence (Ill.) Unit Schs., 1970-76; instr. Kankakee (Ill.) Community Coll., 1975; sole practice Ind. and Ill., 1979—. Active Lake Village (Ind.) Civic Assn., 1980—; edn. coordinator St. Augusta Ch., Lake Village, 1985—. Mem. ABA, Ind. Bar Assn., Ill. Bar Assn., Pub. Defender Bar Assn., Theta Chi Sigma, Kappa Delta Pi. Roman Catholic. Avocations: exercise, swimming, sewing, square dancing, reading. Home: Rt 1 Box 448 Momence IL 60954 Office: Engels Law Office PO Box 103 Lake Village IN 46349

ENGLAND, JAMES E., management consultant; b. Plestenburg, Ky., Dec. 16, 1938; s. George E.; children: Brian, Russell. BA, U. Calif., Fresno, 1970, MA, 1970, fin. and indsl. mgmt. degree, 1982. Cert. secondary and coll. tchr. Pres. James & Assoc., Monterey, Calif., 1968—; br. mgr. USA Fin. Services Inc., Warsaw, Ind., 1986; pres. England Inc., Warsaw, 1986—. Contbr. articles on outdoor life to mags. Served to cpl. USMC, 1958-61. Mem. Am. Bankers, ASTA, Monterey Bd. Realtors (pres. 1980-81). Lodge: Moose (sec. 1978). Avocations: golf, hunting, music, reading, writing. Office: England Inc 500 E Lincoln Way Valparaiso IN 46383

ENGLAND, ROBERT CLEYTON, optometrist, contact lens accessory manufacturer; b. Columbus, Ohio, Jan. 30, 1941; s. Dennis Cleyton and Louella May (Rush) E.; m. Anne-Marie Baker, Sept. 18, 1964; children—Kirk Alan, Keith Andrew, Kristen Elaine. B.S. in Optometry, Ohio State U., Dr. Optometry, 1967. Diplomate Am. Bd. Optometry. Gen. practice optometry, Bellevue, Ohio, 1967-78, Zanesville, Ohio, 1978—; owner, mgr. Ophthalmic Arts Lab., Bellevue, 1972-74; pres. DMV Corp., Zanesville, 1977—; clin. instr. Ohio State U., Columbus, 1975-78. Patentee in field. Bd. dirs. St. John's Luth. Zanesville, 1980-86; bd. dirs. Goodwill Industries, 1982—, pres. bd. dirs., 1985-86; sec. bd. dirs. YMCA, 1984—; pres. Samaritan Counseling Ctr., Zanesville, 1982-84; bd. dirs. Bethesda Hosp., Zanesville, 1985—, trustee, 1985—; mem. Careone (parent of Bethesda), 1987—. Mem. Ohio Optometric Assn. (sec. zone 5 1979—), Contact Lens Mfrs. Assn., Am. Optometric Assn. Republican. Lodges: Kiwanis (pres. Bellevue 1972), Rotary (pres. Zanesville 1983). Avocations: photography, flying, graphic art, canoeing, computer programming.

ENGLE, ALBERT LEE, manufacturing company executive; b. Abilene, Kans., Oct. 1, 1938; s. Raymond Earl and Pauline Gertrude (Long) E.; m. Elizabeth Ann Miser, Feb. 23, 1963; children: Albert Christopher, Mark Edward, Gregory Michael. BSEE, Kans. State U., 1962. Sales engr. Reliance Electric Co., Lubbock, Tex., Memphis and Milw., 1964-72; dist. mgr. Reliance Electric Co., Youngstown, Ohio, 1972-74; sales and mktg. mgr. Cleve. Machine Controls, 1974-1980; v.p. Unico, Inc., Franksville, Wis., 1980—; bd. dirs. Unico Inc. Pres. Nordonia Hills Band Parents, Northfield, Ohio, 1979; bd. dirs., pres. Nordonia Hills Athletic Assn., Northfield, 1974-80, Christ the Redeemer Lutheran Ch., Brecksville, Ohio, 1975-80; chmn. Boy Scouts Am. Cub Pack, Northfield, 1974-80; v.p. Southeastern Wis. council Boy Scouts Am., Racine, 1985—. Mem. TAPPI. Republican. Lutheran. Club: Racine Country. Avocations: golf, tennis. Home: 7007 Hoods Creek Rd Franksville WI 53126 Office: Unico Inc 3725 Nicholson Rd Franksville WI 53126

ENGLER, JOHN MATHIAS, state senator; b. Mt. Pleasant, Mich., Oct. 12, 1948; s. Mathias John and Agnes Marie (Neyer) E.; B.S. in Agrl. Econs., Mich. State U., 1971; J.D., Thomas M. Cooley Law Sch., 1981; Mem. Mich. Ho. of Reps., 1971-78; mem. Mich. Senate, 1979—, Republican leader, 1983, majority leader, 1984—. Bd. dirs. Mich. State U. Agr. and Natural Resources Alumna; del. White House Conf. on Youth, 1972. Recipient Disting. Service to Agr. award Mich. Agr. Conf., 1974; named Legislator of Yr., Police Officers Assn. Mich., 1981; One of 5 Outstanding Young Men of Mich., Mich. Jaycees, 1983. Mem. Nat. Conf. State Legislators. Republican. Roman Catholic. Club: Detroit Economic. Office: Box 30036 State Capitol Lansing MI 48909

ENGLER, PHILIP, materials scientist; b. N.Y.C., Jan. 5, 1949; s. Samuel and Selma (Cohen) E.; m. Shelley Falb, July 7, 1973; children—Daniel, Seth. B.S., Cornell U., 1970; M.S., Northwestern U., 1972, Ph.D., 1978. Tech. service scientist Johnson & Johnson, Chgo., 1972-74; analytical scis. project leader Standard Oil Co. Ohio, Cleve., 1978-83, analytical scis. group leader, 1983—. Served to capt. USAR. Mem. Am. Chem. Soc., Soc. Plastics Engrs. (dir. engrng. properties and structures div. 1980-83), Sigma Xi, Tau Beta Pi, Acacia. Contbr. articles to tech. lit. Office: Standard Oil Research and Devel 4440 Warrensville Ctr Rd Cleveland OH 44128

ENGLERT, MARK ALLAN, lawyer, real estate executive; b. Jasper, Ind., Sept. 3, 1955; s. Earl L. and Betty J. (Rowekamp) E.; m. Nancy L. Marshall, Apr. 30, 1983. BA in Econs., Wabash Coll., 1977; JD, Ind. U., 1981. Bar: Ind. 1981, U.S. Dist. Ct. (so. dist.) Ind. 1981. Assoc. Helmer & Nelson, P.C., Indpls., 1981; ptnr. Harlow, Wright & Englert, Indpls., 1981-82; assoc. Bayh, Tabbert & Capehart, Indpls., 1983-85; v.p., counsel Sycamore Group, Inc., Indpls., 1985-87, pres., 1987—. Mem. Ind. Bar Assn., Indpls. Bar Assn., Real Estate Securities and Syndication Inst. Republican. Roman Catholic. Home: 65 Lexington Dr Zionsville IN 46077 Office: Sycamore Group Inc 9000 Keystone Crossing #510 Indianapolis IN 46240

ENGLISH, FLOYD LEROY, telecommunications company executive; b. Nicholas, Calif., June 10, 1934; s. Elvan L. and Louise (Corliss) E.; m. Wanda Parton, Sept. 8, 1955 (div. 1980); children: Roxane, Darryl; m. Elaine Ewell, July 3, 1981; 1 child, Christine. A.B. in Physics, Calif. State U.-Chico, 1959; M.S. in Physics, Ariz. State U., 1962, Ph.D. in Physics, 1965. Div. supr. Sandia Labs., Albuquerque, 1965-73; gen. mgr. Rockwell Internat.-Collins, Newport Beach, Calif., 1973-75; pres. Darcom, Albuquerque, 1975-79; cons in energy mgmt. and acquisitions Albuquerque, 1979-80; v.p. U.S. ops. Andrew Corp., Orland Park, Ill., 1980-82; pres., chief operating officer Andrew Corp., 1982-83, pres., chief exec. officer, 1983—, dir., 1982—. Contbr. articles to profl. jours. Served to 1st lt. U.S. Army, 1954-57; served to capt. USAR, until 1969. Mem. IEEE. Republican. Presbyterian. Office: Andrew Corp 10500 W 153d St Orland Park IL 60462

ENGLISH, LAURA JEAN, medical administrator; b. Chgo., Feb. 15, 1960; d. Ronald Roy and Francine Lois (Savan) Burklund; m. Leo Gerald English, May 16, 1981. Assoc. applied sci., Sauk Valley Coll., 1980. Registered radiologic technologist. X-ray technologist Drs. Maylah and Drennan, Evanston, Ill., 1980-, Medcheck/Wesley, Wichita, Kans., -85; med. mgr. Wesley Med. Ctr., Wichita, 1985—. Republican. Lutheran. Avocations: painting, softball. Home: 999 Silver Springs Apt 2007 Wichita KS 67212 Office: Wesley Med Ctr 550 N Hillside Wichita KS 67214

ENGLISH, MARLANDA, manufacturing engring; b. Chgo., Apr. 14, 1962; d. Benjamin and Lavelma (Gaddis) E. BS in Indsl. Engrng., Northwestern U., 1983, M in Mfg. Engrng., 1986. Indsl. engr. Ethicon Inc. sub. Johnson and John, Chgo., 1983-85; mfg. engr. Borg-Warner Automotive, Bellwood, Ill., 1985—. C.H. Mason Found. scholar, Memphis, 1979. Mem. Am. Inst. Indsl. Engrs. Democrat. Mem. Ch. of God in Christ. Avocations: music, reading, skating, softball. Office: Borg-Warner Automotive 700 S 25th Ave Bellwood IL 60104

ENNIS, ROBERT LEON, oral surgeon; b. St. Louis, Oct. 18, 1945; s. Herbert Leon and Gladys Fern (Carrens) E.; m. Sharon Kay Lewellen, Nov. 24, 1968; 1 child, Gregory Scott. Student pre-dentistry, U. Mo., Columbia, 1963-66; DDS, U. Mo., Kansas City, 1970; cert. oral and maxillofacial surgery, U. Mo. Gen. Hosp., Kansas City, 1973. Diplomate Am. Bd. Oral and Maxillofacial Surgery. Pvt. practice dentistry Kansas City and Independence, Mo., 1973—; assoc. prof. oral and maxillofacial surgery U. Mo. Kansas City, 1973—; mem. office anesthesia com. Mo. Dental Bd., Jefferson City, 1983—; bd. dirs. Blue Cross Blue Shield, Kansas City, 1981—; lectr. local study clubs and profl. orgns. Mem. adminstrv. bd. Blue Ridge United Meth. Ch., Kansas City, 1980-83. Fellow Am. Assn. Oral and Maxillofacial Surgeons (Mo. del. 1980—); mem. ADA, Jackson County Med. Soc., Midwestern Soc. Oral and Maxillofacial Surgeons (sec/-treas. 1983), Am. Dental Soc. Anesthesiology, Eastern Jackson County Dental Study Group. Avocations: waterskiing, snow skiing, bird hunting, fishing, softball. Home: 211 Aspen Lees Summit MO 64063 Office: Burk Ennis Wendelburg Allen 1010 Carondelet Kansas City MO 64114

ENSLEN, RICHARD ALAN, judge; b. Kalamazoo, May 28, 1931; s. Ehrman Thrasher and Pauline Mabel (Dragoo) E.; m. Pamela Gayle Chapman, Nov. 2, 1985; children—David, Susan, Sandra, Thomas, Janet, Joseph. Student, Kalamazoo Coll., 1949-51, Western Mich. U., 1955; LL.B., Wayne State U., 1958; LL.M., U. Va., 1986. Bar: Mich. 1958, U.S. Dist. Ct. (we. dist.) Mich. 1960, U.S. Ct. Appeals (6th cir.) 1971, U.S. Ct. Appeals (4th cir.) 1975, U.S. Supreme Ct 1975. Mem. firm Stratton, Wise, Early & Starbuck, Kalamazoo, 1958-60, Bauckham & Enslen, Kalamazoo, 1960-64, Howard & Howard, Kalamazoo, 1970-76, Enslen & Schma, Kalamazoo, 1977-79; dir. Peace Corps. Costa Rica, 1965-67; judge Mich. Dist. Ct., 1968-70; U.S. dist. judge Kalamazoo, 1979—; mem. faculty Western Mich. U., 1961-62, Nazareth Coll., 1974-75; adj. prof. polit. sci. Western Mich. U., 1982—. Co-author: The Constitution Law Dictionary: Volume One, Individual Rights, 1985; Volume Two, Governmental Powers, 1987, Constitutional Deskbook: Individual Rights, 1987. Served with USAF, 1951-54. Recipient Disting. Alumni award Wayne State Law Sch., 1980, Disting. Alumni award Western Mich. U., 1982; Outstanding Practical Achievement award Ctr. Pub. Resources, 1984; award for Excellence and Innovation in Alternative Dispute Resolution and Dispute Mgmt., Legal Program; Jewel Corp. scholar, 1956-57; Lampson McElhorne scholar, 1957. Mem. ABA (spl. com. on dispute resolution 1983—), Am. Judicature Soc. (bd. dirs. 1983-85), Mich. Bar Assn. Office: U S Dist Ct 410 W Michigan Ave Kalamazoo MI 49005

ENTNER, PAUL DWIGHT, psychologist; b. Connersville, Ind., Apr. 9, 1947; s. Charles Leroy and Lenora Frances (Hirschy) E.; m. Ruth Elizabeth Kauffold, Aug. 23, 1968; 1 child, James. BS, Cedarville Coll., 1969; MEd, Wright State U., 1972; MA, Rosemead Grad. Sch. Profl. Psychology, 1974, PhD, 1976. Lic. psychologist, Ohio. Dir. children services Voorman Psychiat. Med. Clinic, Upland, Calif., 1976; psychologist, founder Agape Counseling Ctr., Dayton, Ohio, 1976—; ednl. cons. Kettering (Ohio) City Schs., 1978-80; supervision cons. Kettering Med. Ctr., 1985-86; indsl. cons. Manville Corp., Richmond, Ind., 1986; speaker in field. Speaker, Pastor Forum Serices, Centerville, Ohio, 1981-86; pres.'s assoc. Cedarville Coll., 1983-86; mem. pres.'s circle Biola U., La Mirada, Calif., 1984-86; advisor Support Group for Children of Divorced Families, Kettering, 1986. Mem. Am. Psychol. Assn., Ohio Psychol. Assn., Miami Valley Psychol. Assn., Christian Assn. Psychologists. Evangelical. Avocations: tennis, snow skiing, photography. Home: 705 W Stroop Rd Kettering OH 45429 Office: Agape Counseling Ctr 175 S Main St Centerville OH 45459

ENTRIKEN, ROBERT KERSEY, JR., newspaper editor, motorsport writer; b. Houston, Feb. 13, 1941; s. Robert and Jean (Finch) (stepmother) E.; married, 1972; div., 1982; 1 child, Jean Louise. Student Sch. Journalism, U. Kans., 1961-69. Gen. assignment reporter Salina Jour., Kans., 1969-71, motorsport columnist, 1970-83, courts reporter, 1971-82, Sunday editor, 1972-75, spl. sects. editor, 1975—; sr. editor Sports Car Mag., Santa Ana, Calif., 1972—; motorsport columnist Motorsports Monthly, Tulsa, Okla., 1983-85; operator Ikke så Hurtig Racing. Served with USN, 1969-71, Guam. Mem. Am. Auto Racing Writers and Broadcasters Assn. (gen. v.p. 1982-86, Midwest v.p. 1980-82, chmn. All-Am. Team selections 1983—), Sigma Delta Chi, Sports Car Club Am. (Best Story award 1972, 73, 76, 77, 78, 83-86; Solo Cup nat. award 1981, Nat. Solo I champion 1986; Solo Driver of Yr. Wichita region 1976, 1982, Solo II Champion, Kans. 1978, 84, Midwest div. 1984). Club: Tri-Rivers Running. Avocations: sports car racing; autocrossing; running; skiing. Home: 1513 Pershing Salina KS 67401 Office: The Salina Journal 333 S 4th PO Box 740 Salina KS 67402

ENTZEROTH, ROBERT ELLEARD, architect; b. St. Louis, Jan. 24, 1926; s. Elleard Colburn and Erma (Braun) E.; m. Barbara Elizabeth Ingold, Aug. 18, 1950; children—Lee Catherine, Lyn Suzanne, Julie Ann. B.Arch., Washington U., St. Louis, 1951. Architect Harris Armstrong (Architect), St. Louis, 1949-51, Murphy & Mackey, St. Louis, 1951-52, 53-54; partner in charge design Smith-Entzeroth, St. Louis, 1955-86; dir. design SMP/Smith-Entzeroth, St. Louis, 1986—; vis. prof. archtl. design Washington U. Sch. Architecture; mem. Mo. Bd. Architects, Profl. Engrs. and Land Surveyors. Prin. works include Pierre Laclede Center, Clayton, Mo., Coll. Center of Principia Coll, University City Pub. Library, Washington U. Chemistry and Engrng. Labs, Safeco Ins. Co. Offices, St. Louis, Nashville, Chgo., Mo. State Office Bldg, St. Louis, Alumni House Principia Coll, AAA Hdqrs. Bldg, St. Louis County, Interco Corp. Tower. Served with USNR, 1944-46. Recipient numerous archtl. design awards including Archtl. Forum, 1961, numerous archtl. design awards including Am. Fedn. Arts, 1968, numerous archtl. design awards including 40 under 40 Exhbn. of Architects' Works, 1968; LeBrun Traveling scholar, 1952. Fellow AIA. Mem. United Ch. Christ. Club: St. Louis. Home: 106 Mason Ave Saint Louis MO 63119 Office: SMP/Smith-Entzeroth 101 S Hanley Suite 400 Saint Louis MO 63105

ENZER, CHARLES HART, psychiatrist; b. Schenectady, N.Y., June 29, 1935; s. Milton M. and Esther E. (Markman) E.; m. Laura Pearl Ceasar; children: Yehoash Rahm, Yael Radha, Daphna Genai. AB in Social Philosophy, Union Coll., 1957; MD, N.Y. Med. Coll., 1964. Diplomate Am. Bd. Psychiatry and Neurology. Rotating intern Albany (N.Y.) Med. Ctr., 1964-65; resident in gen. psychiatry U. Cin. Med. Ctr., 1967-69, fellow in child psychiatry, 1969-72; gen. psychiatrist Alcoholism Clinic, City of Cin., 1967-72; practice medicine specializing in child, adolescent, adult and family psychiatry Cin., 1971—; cons. child psychiatry Hamilton County Diagnostic Ctr., 1970-72; cons. psychiatry Model City Law Office, Cin., 1972, Comprehend Inc., Maysville, Ky., 1972, VA Hosp., Cin., 1972—, Warren County Mental Health and Mental Retardation Bd., 1972-77, Hamilton County Ct. of Common Pleas, Cin. 1973—, Gen. Motors, Norwood, Ohio, 1979—, and others. Co-editor The Newsletter of the Am. Acad. of Child and Adolescent Psychiatry, 1982—; contbr. quarterly column in Newsletter, numerous articles and book revs. to profl. jours. Speaker B'nai Tzedak Synagogue, 1972—; bd. dirs. Yavneh Day Sch., Cin., 1976-79, mem. com. Faculty Council on Jewish Affairs, Cin., 1978—. Served with USPHSH, 1965-67. Fellow Am. Acad. Child Adolescent Psychiatry (peer rev. com. 1977—, council liaison to ins. com. 1974-80, liaison to psychiat. dimensions of infancy com. 1980-81, consumer issues Ad Hoc com. 1982, work group consumer issues 1982—, assoc. editor jour. 1982—); mem. Acad. Medicine Cin. (ins. com. 1978—, legis. com. 1980—, health legis. subcom. 1980—), Am. Assn. Profl. Standards Rev. Orgns., Am. Psychiat. Assn. (appeals reviewer, CHAMPUS psychiat. peer rev. project. 1981—), Am. Soc. Adolescent Psychiatry, 1979—, Cin. Mental Health Assn. (speaker 1969—). Jewish. Office: 2820 Vernon Pl Cincinnati OH 45219

EPICH, RICHARD PATRICK, industrial engineer; b. Chgo., Oct. 25, 1958; s. Raymond Joseph and Patricia Ann (Alford) E. BS in Indsl. Engrng., Bradley U., 1980. Indsl. engr. Rockwell div. Wescom, Downers Grove, Ill., 1980-81; sr. engr. GTE Communications Systems Corp., Northlake, Ill., 1981—. Fellow Am. Inst. Indsl. Engrs. Republican. Roman Catholic. Avocations: auto restoration, boating, fishing. Home: 18102 A Kingery Quarter Hinsdale IL 60521 Office: GTE Communications Systems Corp 400 N Wolf Rd Northlake IL 60164

EPNER, PAUL LAWRENCE, marketing professional; b. Buffalo, Mar. 9, 1950; s. Robert and Rosann Shirley (Krohn) E.; m. Cheryl Irene Stein, Feb. 10, 1973; children: Jack William, Jamie Michelle. BS, U. Ill., 1972, MEd, 1978; MBA, U. Chgo., 1986. Cert. secondary tchr., Ill. Tchr. sci. Antioch (Ill.) Grade Sch., 1972-77; GMP tng. coordinator Abbott Diagnostics, Abbott Park, Ill., 1977-79, supr. mfg., 1980-81, sect. mgr. mfg., 1981-83, mgr. mfg. ops., 1983-85, strategic market planner, 1985-86, product mktg. mgr., 1986-87, project mgr. joint venture, 1987—; regulatory conformance specialist Abbott Hosp. Products, Abbott Park, 1979-80. Mentor, Career Guidance Consortium, Grayslake, Ill., 1985—; mem. campaign adv. bd. Project D/ART (Depression, Awareness, Recognition, Treatment) NIMH, Bethesda, Md., 1986—; co-founder, chmn. Citizen's Recreation Com., Lindenhurst, Ill., 1975-77; elected to sch. bd. Millburn (Ill.) Sch. Dist. 24, 1983—; nat. v.p. Nat. Found. Ileitis & Colitis Inc., N.Y.C., 1984—; founder Lake County Chpt. Ileitis & Colitis, Libertyville, Ill., v.p. 1986—, past pres.; founder Greater Milw. Chpt. Ileitis & Colitis, chmn. bd. dirs. 1982—, past pres.; confirmation tchr. Congregation Am Echod, Waukegan, Ill., 1985—, bd. dirs. 1985-86; mem. governing bd. Spl. Edn. Dist. Lake County, Ill., 1983—. Named one of Outstanding Young Men of Am., 1978; recipient Pres.'s award Abbott Labs., 1983. Mem. Soc. Mfg. Engrng. (sr.). Jewish. Avocations: tennis, fishing, photography, cross-country skiing. Home: 2514 Timber Ln Lindenhurst IL 60046 Office: Abbott Labs D-924 AP-6C Abbott Park IL 60064

EPP, MARY ELIZABETH, software engineer, consultant; b. Buffalo, Aug. 7, 1941; d. John Conrad and Gertrude Marie (Murphy) Winkelman; m. Harry Francis Epp, Aug. 31, 1963. BA in Math., D'Youville Coll., 1963; MS in Math., Xavier U., 1974, MBA in Fin., 1981. Systems analyst Gen. Electric, Evendale, Ohio, 1965-71; techniques and ops. mgr. Palm Beach Co., Cin., 1972-73; hardware systems engr. Procter & Gamble, Cin., 1973-76;

systems engr. CalComp Inc., Anaheim, Calif., 1980-84; software engr. SDRC Inc., Cin., 1984-86; sr. software engr. SAMI/Burke Mktg., Cin., 1986—; cons. Shelley & Sands, Zanesville, Ohio, 1983-85. Contbr. articles to profl. jours. Mem. Fairfield Charter Rev. Commn., 1981-83. Mem. AAUW (br. treas. 1975-79, state women's chair 1979-80, state treas. 1980-82), Nat. Assn. Female Execs., Nat. Fedn. Music (Ohio fedn. music parade chair 1979-81.). Republican. Roman Catholic. Clubs: Mercy Hosp. Aux. (treas. 1978-79), Musical Arts. Avocations: bridge, skiing, music, fishing, travel. Home: 4900 Pleasant Ave Fairfield OH 45014 Office: SAMI/Burke Mktg 800 Broadway Cincinnati OH 45202

EPP, TELFER L., church official. Reverand Mid-Am. Bapt. Ch., Des Moines. Office: Mid Am Bapt Chs PO Box 7508 Des Moines IA 50322 *

EPPERSON, CLAUDIA MARIE, business management consultant; b. Chgo., Aug. 4, 1952; d. George Fred and Dorcas Irma (Seeman) Bollnow; m. Steven Frank Francisco, May 24, 1975; (div. Sept. 1983); m. John Robert Epperson, June 15, 1985 (div. 1987). BS in Fashion Merchandising, Mich. State U., 1973; MBA, Western Mich. U., Kalamazoo, 1983. Asst. chem. supr. Consumers Power Co., Covert, Mich., 1981-82, nuclear tng. instr., 1982-84, nuclear chemistry supr., 1982-84; nuclear cons. Radiation controls, Inc., Little Silver, N.J., 1984-85; cons. bus. nuclear South Haven, Mich., 1985—; ptnr. Country Petals and Particulars, South Haven, 1986. Mem. Am. Mgmt. Assn., Western Mich U. Alumni Assn., 1979, South Haven C. of C., Beta Gamma Sigma. Republican. Avocation: Aerobic Dancing, modeling.

EPPERT, JOHN WAYNE, veterinarian; b. Brazil, Ind., Feb. 1, 1933; s. John Wayne and Mildred Ester (Loughmiller) E.; m. Stella Louise Rogers, Feb. 9, 1974; m. Charlotte Ruth Loftstom, June 15, 1952 (div. July 1973); children: John, Michelle, Cindy, Patricia, Sandra. DVM, Mich. State U., 1956. Owner Seelyville (Ind.) Vet. Clinic, 1959—. Mem. Seelyville Town Bd., 1964-72, pres. 1966; mem. Seelyville Vol. Fire Dept., 1958—, chief, 1980—, emergency med. technician 1977—. Named 6th Dist Firefighter of Yr. Am. Legion, 1986. Mem. AVMA, Ind. Vet. Med. Assn., Ind. Vol. Fireman's Assn., Ind. Fire Instrs. Assn. (bd. dirs.) Nat. Rifle Assn. Republican. Methodist. Lodge: Masons. Avocations: hunting, fishing. Home and Office: PO Box 1933 Seelyville IN 47878

EPPICH, KENNETH LOUIS, chemical manufacturing company executive; b. Cleve., Sept. 17, 1941; s. John E. and Dorothy (Terepka) E. BS in Bus. Adminstrn., Ohio State U., 1963. Sales order supr. Gen. Mills Chems., Mpls., 1969-72, acctg. analyst, 1972-74, research controller, 1974-77; asst. treas. Henkel of Am., Mpls., 1977-78, treas., 1978-86, v.p. fin., treas., 1986—. Mem. Fin. Execs. Inst., Nat. Assn. Accts. Avocations: scuba diving, jogging, reading. Home: 2248 Drew Ave S Saint Louis Park MN 55416 Office: Henkel of Am 7900 W 78th St Minneapolis MN 55435

EPPLEY, ROBERT JAMES, JR., municipal administrator; b. Youngstown, Ohio, Jan. 26, 1921; s. Robert J. and Louise Maguerite (Rose) E.; m. Joan Elaine Fortney, Dec. 27, 1942; children—Robert J. III, William L., Elaine L. Hand, John L. B.A., Ohio State U., 1942. City mgr. City Washington (Ohio), 1946-47; village mgr. Village of Greendale (Wis.), 1947-50; purchasing agt. Johnson Rubber Co., Middlefield, Ohio, 1951-57; village mgr. Village of Palatine, Ill., 1957-60; city mgr. City of Northlake, Ill., 1960-61; village mgr. Village of Lombard, Ill., 1961-63; exec. v.p. Homebuilders Assn. Chicagoland, Oak Brook, Ill., 1963-65; city mgr. City of Wheaton, Ill., 1965-71; village mgr. Village of Mt. Prospect, Ill., 1971-78, Village of Skokie, Ill., 1979-87; council pres. City of Middlefield, 1951, mayor, 1952-54. Served to 1st lt. AUS, 1942-45; ETO. Mem. Ill. City Mgmt. Assn. (pres. 1970-71). Methodist. Lodges: Rotary (pres. Middlefield 1951-52), Shriners. Home: 8214 Laramie Ave Skokie IL 60077

EPPS, DAVID CURTIS, insurance association executive; b. Oklahoma City, Mar. 26, 1945; s. Curtis Howard and Marie (Jones) E.; m. Bonnie J. Clark, Feb. 23, 1980. BA in Bus. Adminstrn., Cen. Meth. Coll., 1967. Underwriter Fireman's Fund Ins. Co., St. Louis, 1970-75, loss control rep., 1975-78; risk mgmt. supr. City of Columbia (Mo.), 1978-81; exec. dir. Mo. Intergovtl. Risk Mgmt. Assn., Columbia, 1981—, v.p. Pub. Risk Insurance Mgmt. Assn. 1982-84, pres. pooling sect., 1983-84, bd. dirs. pooling sect., 1983-87, v.p. pooling sect., 1986-87; mem. resolutions com. Mo. Mcpl. League, 1985—. Contbr. articles to profl. jours. Served to sgt. U.S. Army, 1968-70. Decorated Bronze Star, Air medal, Army Commendation medal; recipient Disting. Service award City of Columbia Fin. Dept., 1981. Mem. Am. Soc. Safety Engrs., Am. Pub. Power Assn. (risk mgmt. and ins. com. 1982—), Pub. Risk Ins. Mgmt. Assn. (bd. dirs.), Nat. Rifle Assn. (mem. inst. for legis. action). Club: Columbia Ski. (bd. dirs. 1984-86). Office: Mo Intergovtl Risk Mgmt Assn 2409 W Ash Columbia MO 65203

EPPS, ROBERT LYLE, government agency administrator; b. Harrisonville, Mo., Oct. 14, 1941; s. Robert Lyle and Charlotte Mary (Ely) E.; m. Anita Maxine Johnson; children—Renee Christine, Benjamin Robert. B.A., Washburn U., 1965; M.P.A., U. Kans., 1970; cert. health care adminstrn., U. Ala., 1972. Bus. mgr. Kans. Neurol. Inst., Topeka, 1972-74; sr. fiscal analyst Kans. State Legislature, Topeka, 1974-79; dir. planning Div. State Planning, Topeka, 1979-80; prin. budget analyst Div. Budget, State of Kans., Topeka, 1980-83, dir. adminstrn. dept. health and environment, Topeka, 1980-83 ; cons. Nebr. Dept. Adminstrn., Lincoln, 1979-80. Author: (govt. report) Budget in Brief, 1982-83. Editor (govt. report) Kansas State Investment Practices, 1980. Treas., sec. Shawnee County Mental Health Ctr., Topeka, 1983—; sec. Kans. Advocacy and Protective Services Inc., Manhattan, 1980—; chmn. Essex County Planning Commn., Westport, N.Y., 1971-72; bd. dirs. Adirondack Found., Westport, 1970-71. Mem. Am. Assn. Pub. Adminstrn. Republican. Episcopalian. Home: 1825 Webster Ave Topeka KS 66604 Office: Kans Dept Health and Environment Forbes Field Topeka KS 66620

EPSTEIN, DIANA TRIPLETT, brokerage house executive; b. Boston, Mar. 22, 1946; d. Travis Riley and Beulah Grey (Taylor) Triplett; m. Richard Lewis Epstein, June 7, 1986 (dec.). BA, Hartwick Coll., 1968; MA, St. John's U., 1970; PhD, U. Wis., 1980. Program evaluator State of Wis., Madison, 1975-79, programmer, systems analyst, 1979-83, data processing area mgr., 1983; supr. info. planning Chgo. Bd. Options Exchange, 1983-84, project mgr., 1984-85, dir. corp. planning, 1985—. Named one of Outstanding Young Women in Am., 1980. Mem. Nat. Rehab. Assn., Psi Chi, Pi Lamda Theta. Unitarian. Avocations: jogging, reading, music, horseback riding, canoeing. Office: Chgo Bd Options Exchange LaSalle at Van Buren Chicago IL 60605

EPSTEIN, LAURA, social work educator, consultant; b. Chgo., Oct. 31, 1914; d. Ellik and Rose (Kwatnez) E. A.M., U. Chgo., 1936. Cert. Acad. Cert. Social Workers. Field instr. social work U. Chgo., 1967-70, asst. prof., 1970-72, assoc. prof., 1972-76, prof., 1976—; vis. prof. Wilfred Laurier U., Waterloo, Ont., Can., 1980-82; cons. W.Va. Dept. Social Welfare, Charleston, 1982, Villemarie Community Service, Montreal, Que., Can., 1982. Author: Helping People: The Task Centered Approach, 1980, 2d rev. edit., 1987, (with William J. Reid) Task Centered Casework, 1972, Talking and Listening: guide to the Helping Interview, 1985; editor: (with William J. Reid) Task Centered Practice, 1977. Mem. Council on Social Work Edn. (del. 1980-83), Nat. Assn. Social Workers. Jewish. Home: 5530 S Shore Dr Chicago IL 60637 Office: U Chgo 969 E 60th St Chicago IL 60637

EPSTEIN, PHILIP BARRY, clinical psychologist; b. Washington, July 26, 1947; s. Julius and Shirley Frances (Zinkow) E.; children: Ariella, Joshua. BA, George Washington U., 1968, MA in Edn., 1970; PhD, U. Cin., 1976. Lic. psychologist, Ohio. Staff psychologist Cin. Ctr. for Devel. Disorders, 1974-77, Hadassah Hosp., Jerusalem, Israel, 1977-78; sr. psychologist Jerusalem Ctr. for Child Devel., 1977-78; clin. dir. Diagnostic Clinic, Youngstown, Ohio, 1979-85; mng. ptnr. Inst. for Motivational Devel., Cleve., 1985—; ltd. faculty Youngstown State U., 1981-82; cons. Children's Service Bd., Youngstown, 1984-85; lectr. U. Cin., 1987. Mem. Am. Psychol. Assn., Ohio Psychol. Assn., Cleve. Psychol. Assn., Am. Assn. on Mental Deficiency, Soc. Pediatric Psychology, Phi Delta Kappa. Office: Inst Motivational Devel 3793 S Green Rd Beachwood OH 44122

EPSTEIN, SIDNEY, moving and storage company executive; b. Stamford, Conn., Jan. 26, 1923; s. Max and Rae Epstein; m. Paula Goldenberg, Feb. 18, 1951; children—Ellen, Julie. Student, pub. schs., Stamford. Vice pres. Neptune WorldWide Moving, Inc., New Rochelle, N.Y., until 1978; sr. v.p. Allied Van Lines, Broadview, Ill., 1978-79; pres., chief operating officer Allied Van Lines, 1979—. Served with USAF, 1942-46. Mem. Conn. Warehousemen's Assn. (pres.), Household Goods Carriers' Bur. (pres.), Am. Movers Conf. (exec. com., vice chmn. 1984, Exec. of Yr. award 1984). Office: Allied Van Lines Inc 25th Ave and Roosevelt Rd Broadview IL 60153 *

ERAMO, JOHN JEFFREY, marketing executive; b. Bridgeport, Conn., July 30, 1954; s. Joseph Charles and Isabel (Sancibrian) E.; m. Lynne Rosenberg, June 16, 1978. BA, Princeton U., 1976; MBA, U. Mich., 1978. CPA, Ill. Sr. acct. Arthur Andersen & Co., Chgo., 1978-80; v.p. Baldwin Cooke Co., Deerfield, Ill., 1980—. Plan commr. Lincolnshire (Ill.) Planning Commn., 1987—. Mem. Am. Inst. CPA's, Ill. CPA Soc., Direct Mktg. Assn. Republican. Roman Catholic. Avocations: golf, tennis. Home: 53 Cedar Ln Lincolnshire IL 60015 Office: Baldwin Cooke Co 2401 Waukegan Rd Deerfield IL 60015

ERB, RICHARD LOUIS LUNDIN, resort and hotel executive; b. Chgo., Dec. 23, 1929; s. Louis Henry and Miriam (Lundin) E.; m. Jean Elizabeth Easton, Mar. 14, 1959; children: John Richard, Elizabeth Anne, James Easton, Richard Louis. BA, U. Calif.-Berkeley, 1951, postgrad., 1952; student San Francisco Art Inst., 1956. Cert. hotel adminstr. Asst. gen. mgr. Grand Teton Lodge Co., Jackson Hole, Wyo., 1954-62; mgr. Colter Bay Village, Grand Teton Nat. Park, Wyo., 1962-64, Mauna Kea Beach Hotel, Hawaii, 1964-66; v.p., gen. mgr. Caneel Bay Plantation, Inc., St. John, V.I., 1966-75; gen. mgr. Williamsburg (Va.) Inn, 1975-78; exec. v.p., gen. mgr. Seabrook Island Co., Johns Island, S.C., 1978-80; v.p., dir. hotels Sands Hotel and Casino, Inc., Atlantic City, 1980-81; v.p., gen. mgr. Disneyland Hotel, Anaheim, Calif., 1981-82; chief operating officer Grand Traverse Resort, Grand Traverse Village, Mich., 1982—; v.p. Spruce Devel. Co., 1986—. Contbr. articles to trade jours. V.p. V.I. Montessori Sch., 1969-71, bd. dirs., 1968-76; bd. dirs. Coll. of V.I., 1976-79; mem. adv. bd. U. S.C., 1978-82, Calif. State Poly. Inst., 1981-82, Orange Coast Community Coll., 1981-82, Northwestern Mich. Coll., 1983—; trustee Munson Med. Ctr., Traverse City, 1985—; vice chmn. Charleston (S.C.) Tourism Council, 1979-81; bd. dirs. Anaheim Visitors and Conv. Bur., 1981-82, Grand Traverse Conv. and Visitors Bur., 1985—, US 131 Area Devel. Assn., 1983—, Traverse Symphony Orch., 1984—, N.A. Vasa, 1987—; mem. adv. panel Mich. Communities of Econ. Excellence Program, 1984—. Served to lt., arty. U.S. Army, 1952-54. Mem. Am. Hotel and Motel Assn. (dir. 1975-77, Service Merit award 1976; trustee Ednl. Inst. 1977-83, mktg. com., exec. com. 1978-83, chmn. projects and programs com. 1982-83, AH & MA resort com. 1986—, AH & MA condominium com., Ambassador award 1986), Caribbean Hotel Assn. (1st v.p. 1972-74, dir. 1970-76, hon. life mem., Extraordinary Service Merit award 1974), V.I. Hotel Assn. (pres. chmn. bd. 1971-76, Merit award 1973), Calif. Hotel Assn. (dir. 1981-82), Caribbean Travel Assn. (dir. 1972-74), Internat. Hotel Assn. (dir. 1971-73), S.C. Hotel Assn. (dir. 1978-82), Va. Hotel Assn., Williamsburg Hotel Assn. (dir. 1975-78), Atlantic City Hotel Assn. (v.p. 1981-82), Mich. Lodging Assn. (dir. 1983—, treas. 1986—, mktg. com. 1986—, govtl. affairs com. 1986—, chmn. edn. com. 1983-84), Mich. Gov.'s Task Force on Tourism, 1986—, Grand Traverse C. of C. (bd. dirs. 1984—), Nat. Restaurant Assn., Beta Theta Pi. Congregationalist. Clubs: Tavern, Golden Horseshoe, German, Greate Bay, Seabrook Island, Kiawah Island, Grand Traverse Resort. Lodge: Rotary. Address: Grand Traverse Resort Grand Traverse Village MI 49610-0404

ERBES, WILLIAM TRACY, oral surgeon; b. Milw., July 29, 1948; s. John and Maraleen (Bates) E.; m. Margaret Mary Buck, Dec. 15, 1973; children: Alexandra Kathleen, Tracy Elspeth, Robert Philip. BS, U. Wis., 1971; DDS, Marquette U., 1976. Diplomate Am. Bd. Oral and Maxillofacial Surgery. Gen. practice dentistry Milw., 1976-78; resident in oral and maxillofacial surgery U. Pa., Phila., 1978-81; practice dentistry specializing oral and maxillofacial surgery Mpls., 1981-83; practice dentistry specializing oral and maxillofacial surgery Grafton, Wis., 1983—; clin. instr. Marquette U., 1976-78; cons. Wis. Peer Rev. Orgn., Milw., 1985—; active various profl., hosp. coms. Fellow Internat. Assn. Oral and Maxillofacial Surgeons, Am. Assn. Oral and Maxillofacial Surgeons, Am. Coll. Oral and Maxillofacial Surgeons, Am. Dental Soc. Anesthesiology; mem. ADA, Wis. Dental Assn., Washington-Ozaukee County Dental Soc. (sec., treas. 1986, v.p. 1987), Del. Valley Assn. Oral Surgery Residents (pres. Phila. chpt. 1980-81). Office: 101 Falls Rd Suite 500 Grafton WI 53024

ERDMAN, LOWELL PAUL, civil engineer, land surveyor; b. Wesley, Iowa, Aug. 11, 1926; s. Paul William and Olive Jane (Stillwell) E.; m. Audrey Lucille Stephenson, Aug. 18, 1956; children—Lindsay, Paul, Jeffrey. B.S. in Civil Engring., Iowa State U., 1950. Profl. engr., Iowa, Minn., Wis.; registered land surveyor, Iowa, Wis. Inspector Iowa Hwy. Commn., Jefferson, 1950-52; field engr. Phillip Petroleum Co., Bartlesville, Okla., 1952-55; cons. engr. Erdman Engring., P.C., Decorah, Iowa, 1955—, pres., 1955—; city engr., Decorah, 1955—; mem. delegation environ. engrs. to People's Republic of China, 1986. Co-chmn. Brandstad for Gov. Com., Winneshiek County, 1982. Served with USAAF, 1945-46. Fellow ASCE; mem. Nat. Soc. Profl. Engrs., Iowa Engring Soc., Soc. Land Surveyors of Iowa. Republican. Lutheran. Club: Oneota Golf and Country. Avocations: Golf; bowling; fishing; fly tying. Home: 1303 Skyline Dr Decorah IA 52101 Office: Erdman Engring P C 405 College Dr Decorah IA 52101

ERDMAN, ROBERT J., marketing professional, electrical engineer; b. Washington, Sept. 20, 1938; s. Milton R. and Helen K. (Kreider) E.; m. Carole F. Maley, June 27, 1964 (div. 1978); children: Michael, David, Kristen. BEE, Ohio State U., 1962; MA in Physics, John Carroll U., 1970. Sr. project engr. Keithley Instrument Inc., Solon, Ohio, 1966-76, project mgr., 1976-78, market planning mgr., 1978-82, mgr. bus. area, 1982-86; mktg. mgr. Keithley Instrument Inc., Solon, Ohio, 1986—. Author: Low Level Measurements, 1984; mem. edit. rev. bd. Rev. Sci. Instruments, 1986—; contbr. articles to profl. jours. Served with U.S. Army, 1957-63. Mem. Precision Instrument Assn., Am. Phys. Soc., Assn. Sales and Mktg. Execs. Mem. Unitarian Ch. Avocation: playing piano in jazz band. Home: 2068 Stoney Hill Hudson OH 44236 Office: Keithley Instruments Inc 28775 Aurora Solon OH 44139

ERDMANN, TODD A., biochemist; b. Milw., June 28, 1957; s. Ken Allen and Elizabeth (Prokop) E.; m. Shelley Lynn Shillingstad, Oct. 12, 1978; children: Shannon Lynn, Chad Allen. Student, U. Wis., Racine, 1978. Sales rep. Mennen Med., Milw., 1978-80; field mgr. Siemens Med. Systems, Milw., 1980—. Named Salesman of Yr., Mennen Med., 1980, Salesman of Yr., Siemens Med. Systems, 1984, 85, Multi Million Dollar Producer, Siemens Med. Systems, 1982, 83. Mem. Midwest Biomed. Assn., Ferrari Club, Beachcraft Aero Club. Office: Siemens Med Systems 12040 W Feerick Milwaukee WI 53222

ERENBERG, GERALD, neurologist; b. Chgo., June 5, 1938; s. Harry and Lucy (Singerman) E.; m. Shulamith Sylvia Ehrlich, June 11, 1961; children: Francine, Helene, Steven. Student, U. Ill., 1956-58, MD, 1962. Intern Michael Reese Hosp., Chgo., 1963-65; fellow in neurology Albert Eistein Coll. Medicine, Bronx, 1968-71, from asst. to assoc. prof. neurology and pediatrics, 1971-76; child neurologist Cleve. Clinic, 1976—; dir. Morrisania Ctr. Child Devel., Bronx, Cleve. Clinic Learning Disabilities Clinic. Contbr. articles to prof. jours. Bd. dirs. Cuyahoga United Cerebral Palsy, Cleve., 1981—, Northeast Ohio Epilepsy Found., Cleve., 1980-82. Served to capt. USAF, 1965-67. Fellow Am. Acad. Pediatrics (chmn. neurology 1983-85), Am. Acad. Neurology; mem. Am. Epilepsy Soc., Am. Acad. Cerebral Palsy, Child Neurology Soc. Avocation: gardening. Office: Cleve Clinic A120 9500 Euclid Ave Cleveland OH 44106

ERICKSON, BARBARA ANN, nurse, educator; b. Fairmont, W.Va., Dec. 28, 1936; d. John Joseph and Addie May (Carr) E. BSN cum laude, St. John Coll. of Cleve., 1962; MSN, Cath. U. Am., 1971; postgrad., Union Grad. Sch. Staff nurse, head nurse, supr. St. Elizabeth Hosp., Youngstown, Ohio, 1962-65, nurse clinician, 1972-75; asst. head nurse Villa Maria Infirmary (Pa.), 1965-66, dir. nursing service, 1966-67; head nurse, supr. CCU, St. Joseph Hosp., Lorain, Ohio, 1967-69; instr. nursing Youngstown State U., 1971-76, asst. prof., 1976-78; cardiovascular clin. specialist Frank Tiberio, M.D., Inc., Youngstown, 1975—; clin. specialist Family Medicine Ctr. of St. Elizabeth Hosp. Med. Ctr., Youngstown, 1979-81; co-dir. Clin. Edn. Assocs., 1979—; clin. specialist Youngstown Hosp. Assn., 1981-84; asst. prof. nursing Youngstown State U., 1984—; cons. to film "Cardiac Auscultation," 1978. Author: (with others) Problem Oriented Medical Record, 1973, Cardiac Auscultation, 1975; mem. editorial staff Dimensions of Critical Care Nursing, 1981-82, Heart and Lung-Jour. Critical Care, 1973-76; also articles. Mem. Ohio Nurses Assn. (bd. dirs. dist. 3), Am. Assn. Critical Care Nurses (cert.), Sigma Theta Tau, Phi Kappa Phi. Democrat. Roman Catholic. Office: Youngstown State U Youngstown OH 44555

ERICKSON, DOROTHY LOUISE, counselor, secondary school teacher; b. Kansas City, Mo., Dec. 8, 1932; d. Knute Emanuel and Agnes Victoria (Bergsten) Swanson; m. Richard Harold Erickson, Aug. 30, 1953; children: Victoria Helen, Richard Edward. BA in Edn., U. Mo., Kansas City, 1968, MA in Edn. Counseling, 1971. Tchr. home econs. Cen. Jr. High, Kansas City, 1970-86, counselor, 1983—; counselor Red Bridge Elem. Sch., Kansas City, 1986—. Mem. Nat. Edn. Assn. (Mo. chpt.), Mo. Sch. Counseling Assn., Greater Kansas City Home Econs. Assn., Greater Kansas City Sch. Counselors Assn., Center Edn. Assn. Home: 10230 Locust Ave Kansas City MO 64131 Office: Cen Jr High Sch 326 E 103rd St Kansas City MO 64114 also: Red Bridge Elem Sch 10781 Oak St Kansas City MO 64114

ERICKSON, ELAINE FRANCES, utility company executive; b. Dickinson, N.D., July 5, 1940; d. Ralph Ben and Pauline Mary (Miller) Hatzenbuhler; m. Wesly Fredrick Erickson, Dec. 29, 1962; children: Twila Marie, LeNita Kaye. BS, U. Mary, 1985. Operator NW Bell Telephone Co., Dickinson, N.D., 1957-60, service rep., 1960-68; office clerical supr. Piper, Jaffrey, Hopwood, Bismark, N.D., 1968-72; asst. chief documentary Basin Electric Power, Bismark, 1972-85; records mgr. Basin Electric Power Cooperative, Bismark, 1985—; Newsletter editor, 1984. Co-founder, sec. Utility Industry Action Com., 1984-86; mem. N.D. Right to Life, 1983-87. Mem. Am. Record Mgmt. Assn. (fouder Bismarck-Mandan chpt., pres., chmn. bd. 1984-1985, speaker confs. 1985-86, Mem. of Yr. award 1985). Democrat. Roman Catholic. Office: Basin Electric Power Cooperative 1717 E Interstate Ave Bismarck ND 58501

ERICKSON, GARWOOD ELLIOTT, manufacturing company official; b. Little Silver, N.J., Jan. 8, 1946; s. Gustaf Walter and Martha Lake (Adams) E.; m. Carol Wyborski, July 21, 1973; 1 son, Christopher Lake. AB, Dartmouth Coll., 1967; BE, Thayer Sch. Engring., 1968, ME, 1969; MBA, U. Mich., 1974. Systems analyst Ford Motor Co., Dearborn, Mich., 1969-72, unit supr., 1972-76, cons., 1976-78, sect. supr., 1978-82, mgr., 1982-83; corp. dir. mgmt. info. services Hoover Universal, Ann Arbor, Mich., 1983-86, Vickers, Inc., Troy, Mich., 1986—. Sec. Trayer Lakes Community Assn., Ann Arbor, Mich., 1977. Advanced Research Projects Agy. fellow, 1967-69. Republican. Club: Dartmouth (pres. Ann Arbor 1982-86). Office: Vickers Inc 1401 Crooks Rd Troy MI 48084

ERICKSON, GEORGE EVERETT, JR., lawyer; b. Ft. Scott, Kans., July 20, 1937; s. George Everett Sr. and Cora Kathleen (Hayden) E.; m. Carrol Ann Guthridge, Dec. 23, 1966; children: Ingrid Ann, Karin Ruth. BS, U.S. Naval Acad., 1959; JD, Washburn U., 1966. Bar: Kans. 1966, Okla. 1966, U.S. Dist. Ct. Kans. 1966, U.S. Ct. Appeals (10th cir.) 1967, U.S. Supreme Ct. 1972, D.C. 1985. Commd. ensign USN, 1959, advanced through grades to lt., 1963, resigned, 1963; atty. Amerada-Hess Corp., Tulsa, 1966-69; ptnr. Cosgrove, Webb & Oman, Topeka, 1969-73; sole practice Topeka, 1973-84; ptnr. Erickson & Hall, Topeka, 1984—; prof. Washburn U. Law Sch., Topeka, 1973-74; bd. dirs. The Am. Cos., Topeka, 1973—; atty. City of Auburn, Kans., 1976-82. Mem. Auburn-Washburn Rural Sch. Bd., Topeka, 1977-79. Mem. ABA, Fed. Bar Assn., D.C. Bar Assn., Kans. Bar Assn., Judge Advocates Assn, Nat. Lawyers Club. Republican. Clubs: Army, Navy (Washington); Shawnee Country (Topeka). Home: 6000 Urish Rd Topeka KS 66604 Office: Erickson & Hall 3320 Harrison Topeka KS 66611

ERICKSON, JAMES HUSTON, clergyman, physician; b. Omaha, Sept. 7, 1931; s. Paul Ferdinand and Naomi Marie (Berglund) E.; m. Shirley Arlene Nordling, Dec. 26, 1959; children: Jonathan, Sonja, Ingrid. AA, North Park Coll., 1950; AB, Stanford U., 1952; MD, U. Colo., 1959; MPH, U. Minn., 1975; MS, Loyola Coll., Balt., 1982. Ordained to ministry Evang. Covenant Ch. Asst. minister Bethel Covenant Ch., Orange, Calif., 1960-61; med. missionary Christian Med. Coll., Ludhiana, India, 1965; supply pastor Covenant and Presbyn. Chs., various locations, 1965-81; commd. USPHS, 1970—, advanced through grades to asst. surgeon gen.; chaplain Boy Scouts Am., Laurel, Md., 1977-81; dir. health services, prof. community health No. Ill. U., DeKalb, Ill., 1981—; assoc. minister Hillcrest Covenant Ch., DeKalb, 1982-85, interim minister, 1985—; bd. dirs. The Holmstad, Batavia, Ill.; mem. commn. Christian action Evang. Covenant Ch., Chgo., 1984—. Fellow Am. Coll. Preventive Medicine, Royal Soc. Health; mem. Aerospace Med. Soc., Am. Acad. Family Physicians, Am. Assn. Counseling and Devel., N.Y. Acad. Scis., DeKalb County Epilepsy Assn. (bd. dirs. 1981—), DeKalb Ministerial Assn. Avocations: reading, running, bicycling. Office: No Ill U Univ Health Ctr Wirtz Dr W DeKalb IL 60115

ERICKSON, JOHN ARTHUR, dentist; b. Mpls., Apr. 17, 1953; s. Paul Reynold and Reita Marie (Davids) E.; m. Janet Ann Soderling, Dec. 27, 1975; children: Jacob Thomas, Sarah Elaine. BS, U. Minn., 1976, DDS, 1978. Assoc. dentist Family Dental Clinic, P.A., Mpls., 1981—. Chmn. bd. Woodlake Children's Ctr., Richfield, Minn., 1984-87. Served to capt. U.S. Army, 1978-81. Mem. ADA. Republican. Lutheran. Avocations: camping, hunting, fishing, cross-country skiing. Office: Family Dental Clinic PA 4454 Chicago Ave S Minneapolis MN 55407

ERICKSON, JOHN DUFF, mining engineering educator; b. Crawford, Nebr., Apr. 1, 1933; s. Harold Edward and Ruth Isabel (Duff) E.; m. Janet Eileen Lind, Dec. 28, 1955; children: Gregory Duff, Sheryl Ann. B.S. in Mining Engring., S.D. Sch. Mines and Tech., 1955; M.S. in Indsl. Mgmt., MIT, 1965. Mine planning engr. Kennecott Copper Corp., Salt Lake City, 1965-67, truck ops. supt., 1968-69; mine mgr. Bougainville Copper Ltd., Bougainville, Papua, New Guinea, 1970-72, exec. mgr. tech. services, 1973-75, asst. gen. mgr., 1976-77; head dept. mining engring. S.D. Sch. Mines and Tech., Rapid City, S.D., 1978—; mining cons. Bechtel Civil and Minerals, San Francisco, 1979—, Fluor Engrs., Redwood City, Calif., 1983—; dir. So. Hills Mining Co., Rapid City, S.D., 1982—. Served to capt. AUS, 1961-62. Sloan Fellow awardee, 1964-65. Mem. AIME (chmn. Black Hills sect. 1983—), Black Hills Mining Assn., S.D. Sch. Mines and Tech. Alumni Assn. (exec. dir.). Republican. Clubs: Arrowhead Country, Elks. Home: 2958 Tomahawk Dr Rapid City SD 57702 Office: SD Sch Mines and Tech 501 E St Joseph St Rapid City SD 57701

ERICKSON, KENNETH RICHARD, consumer goods company executive; b. Elgin, Ill., May 25, 1952; s. Richard Eugene and Laverne M. (Kucera) E.; m. Karen Kay Butenscheon, Sept. 12, 1973 (div. Aug. 1981); 1 child, Lukas Paul; m. Linda Joan Milbrandt, Oct. 27, 1984. Student, Inst. Engring. Tech., Morrison, Ill., 1970-71. Mgr. ops. Erickson's Inc., Palatine, Ill., 1971-76; dist. mgr. Snap-On Tools, Kenosha, Wis., 1976-80; nat. accounts mgr. Makita U.S.A., Cerritos, Calif., 1980-83; v.p. Ryobi Am., Bensenville, Ill., 1983-87; pres. Atec, Roselle, Ill., 1987—. Named one of Top 100 Best and Brightest Young Mktg. Execs., Advt. Age mag., 1986. Mem. Power Tool Inst. (bd. dirs. 1984-87). Republican. Methodist. Home: 110 Reston Ct Roselle IL 60172

ERICKSON, KIM L., maxillofacial surgeon; b. Fort Atkinson, Wis., Oct. 1, 1951; s. LaVerne Vincent and Gwendolyn Ardell (Beuchler) E.; m. Veronica Meriel Cottom, Dec. 18, 1982. BA in Econs., Kalamazoo Coll., 1973; DDS, U. Mich., 1977. Diplomate Am. Bd. Oral and Maxillofacial Surgery. Resident Mt. Sinai Med. Ctr., N.Y.C., 1978-81; staff oral and maxillofacial surgery Glan Clwyd Hosp., North Wales, Wales, 1981; gen. practice specializing in oral and maxillofacial surgery Scarsdale, N.Y., 1982-86, Grand Rapids, Mich., 1986—; oral surgeon Blodgett Meml. Med. Ctr., Butterworth Hosp., Grand Rapids, 1986—; surgeon White Plains (N.Y.) Hosp. Med. Ctr.; instr. dept. oral and maxillofacial surgery Montefiore Hsop. Med. Ctr., Bronx, N.Y., 1982-85; lectr. in field, 1982—. Contbr. articles to profl. jours. Fellow Am. Assn. Oral and Maxillofacial Surgeons, Am. Dental Soc. Anesthesia; mem. ADA, Am. Cleft Palate Assn., Am. Heart Assn. (instr.). Avocations: summer and winter sports, astronomy. Office: 1900 Wealthy St #395 Grand Rapids MI 49506

ERICKSON, NANCY JANE, music educator; b. Grand Rapids, Mich., June 5, 1939; d. Herman and Arletta K. (Blough) Lindhout; m. Robert Victor Erickson, June 19, 1957; children: Brenda Kay Erickson Anderson, Robert Victor II, Nicole Ann. Cert. in teaching, Sherwood Music Sch., 1955. Second v.p. St. Cecilia Music Soc., Grand Rapids, 1974-78, first v.p., 1981-83, gold cup chmn., 1981—, jr. coordinator, 1984-86. Head organist St. Paul Luth. Ch., Caledonia, Mich., 1955—; pres. Piano Tchrs. Forum of Grand Rapids, 1982-86. Mem. Nat. Music Tchrs. Assn., Mich. Music Tchrs. Assn. (cert.), Nat. Guild Piano Tchrs. (Hall of Fame award 1985), St. Cecilia Music Soc., Am. Guild Organists. Home and Office: 2461 Okemos Dr SE Grand Rapids MI 49506

ERICKSON, PAUL E., bishop. Synodical bishop Luth. Ch. Am., Chgo. Office: Luth Ch 18 S Michigan Ave Room 800 Chicago IL 60603 *

ERICKSON, ROLF HERBERT, librarian, historian; b. Green Bay, Wis., Nov. 18, 1940; s. Herbert Stanley and Ethel Helena (Ramseth) E. BA, St. Olaf Coll., 1962; MA in Library Sci., U. Wis., 1966. Tchr., librarian Luth. Mission, Lae, Terr. of Papua, New Guinea, 1962-64; librarian Random Lake (Wis.) High Sch., 1964-65; asst. reference librarian Northwestern U. Library, Evanston, Ill., 1966-67; adminstrv. asst. Northwestern U. Library, Evanston, 1967-70, head circulation services dept., 1970—. Co-editor: From Fjord to Prairie, 1976, Our Norwegian Immigrants, 1978. Chmn. Chgo. History Com., 1981—; trustee, mem. exec. com. Vesterheim Norwegian-Am. Mus., Decorah, Iowa, 1977; mem. exec. com. Religion and Ethics Inst., Evanston, 1984—; bd. dirs. Ctr. for Scandinavian Studies, North Park Coll., Chgo., 1987—. Grantee U.S. State Dept., 1984, Am. Scandinavian Found., 1986; recipient St. Olav medal H.M. King Olav V of Norway, 1985. Mem. Norwegian-Am. Hist. Assn. (exec. com. 1981—, v.p. 1984—), Swedish Am. Hist. Soc. (bd. dirs. archives 1983—), Nordmanns Forbundet (pres. Chgo. chpt. 1984-86), Chgo. Caxton Club (editorial com. 1983—), Chgo. Academic Library Council Circulation Group, Soc. for Advancement of Scandanavian Studies, Midwest Archives Conf., Northwestern Univ. Library Council. Lodges: Sons of Norway, Valdres Samband. Home: 1116 Davis St Evanston IL 60201 Office: Northwestern U Library 1935 Sheridan Rd Evanston IL 60208

ERICKSON, ROY FREDERICK, JR., hospital administrator; b. Chgo., Aug. 16, 1928; s. Roy Frederick and Irene Elsa (Jacobson) E.; m. Julia Ellen Raffington, Oct. 18, 1958; children: Elizabeth, Peter, Stephen. B.S., Northwestern U., 1950, M.S., 1956. Asst. adminstr. Decatur (Ill.) Meml. Hosp., 1956-60; adminstr. Passavant Meml. Area Hosp., Jacksonville, Ill., 1960-64, Blessing Hosp., Quincy, Ill., 1964-72; pres. Ball Meml. Hosp., Muncie, Ind., 1972—; adj. prof. physiology and health sci. Ball State U., Muncie, 1979—; bd. dirs. Bi-State Regional Med. Program, 1969-72; mem. assoc. faculty Muncie Center for Med. Edn.; mem. adv. council Health Systems Agy., Area II. Bd. dirs. Cancer Soc.; div. chmn. United Fund; mem. Citizens Adv. Council for Vocat. Edn. Served with USAF, 1950-54. Mem. Am. Hosp. Assn., Ill. Hosp. Assn. (trustee 1968-70), Ind. Hosp. Assn. (dir. 1976-82), Am. Mgmt. Assn., Am. Coll. Hosp. Adminstrs. Methodist. Club: Rotary. Home: 4201 University Ave Muncie IN 47304 Office: 2401 University Ave Muncie IN 47303

ERICKSTAD, RALPH JOHN, state supreme ct. justice; b. Starkweather, N.D., Aug. 15, 1922; s. John T. and Anna Louisa (Myklebust) E.; m. Lois Katherine Jacobson, July 30, 1949; children: John Albert, Mark Anders. Student, U. N.D., 1940-43; B.Sc. in Law, U. Minn., 1947, LL.B., 1949. Bar: N.D. bar 1949. Practiced in Devils Lake, 1949-62; State's atty. Ramsey County, 1953-57; mem. N.D. Senate from, Ramsey County, 1957-62; asst. majority floor leader N.D. Senate from, 1959, 61; asso. justice Supreme Ct. N.D., 1963-73, chief justice, 1973—; Treas. N.D. States Attys. Assn., 1955, v.p., 1956; mem. N.D. Legislative Research Com., 1957-59, N.D. Budget Bd., 1961-63, Gov. N.D. Spl. Com. Labor, 1960. Past mem. exec. com. Mo. Valley council Boy Scouts Am.; chmn. bd. trustees Mo. Valley Family YMCA, 1966-77. Served with USAAF, 1943-45, ETO. Recipient Silver Beaver award Boy Scouts Am., 1967; Sioux award U. N.D., 1973; 1st Disting. Service award Missouri Valley Family YMCA, 1978. Mem. Am., N.D., Burleigh County bar assns., Nat. Conf. Chief Justices (exec. council), Am. Judicature Soc., Am. Law Inst. Lutheran (del. 1st biennial conv., mem. nominating com.). Clubs: Am. Legion, VFW, Kiwanian. Office: Supreme Ct North Dakota State Capitol Bismarck ND 58505 *

ERICSON, HURON LESLIE, orthopaedic surgeon; b. Milw., Apr. 30, 1939; s. Pierce Albert and LaVaughn Chenawah (Smith) E.; m. Mary Margaret Hoye, Sept. 21, 1963; children: Julie Anne, Emily Elizabeth, Katherine Louise. BA, DePauw U., 1961; MD, Northwestern U., 1965. Diplomate Am. Bd. Orthopaedic Surgery. Resident Loyola U., Maywood, Ill., 1966-70; practice medicine specializing in orthopaedic surgery Racine, Wis., 1972-84, Kurten Med. Group, Racine, 1984—. Bd. dirs. Goodwill Industries, Racine, 1975-82, Societies Assets, 1979-83; mem. vestry St. Lukes Episcopal Ch., Racine, 1974-77. Served to maj. U.S. Army, 1970-72, Vietnam. Fellow Am. Acad. Orthopaedic Surgeons, ACS; mem. Mid-Am. Orthopaedic Soc., AMA, Wis. Med. Soc. (bd. dirs. 1986). Avocations: tennis, stamp collecting. Home: 12 Raven Turn Racine WI 53402 Office: 2405 Northwestern Ave Racine WI 53404

ERICSON, RICHARD CHARLES, social service agency executive, consultant; b. St. Paul, June 21, 1933; s. Rolph Christopher and Sonia Margaret (Carlson) E.; m. Carol Joy Turnwall, Jan. 1, 1955; children—Lynn Ericson Starr, David Alan. B.A., Roosevelt U., 1959; M.A., U. Chgo., 1961. U.S. probation officer U.S. Probation Office, Chgo., 1960-61; juvenile probation officer Hennepin County Ct. Services, Mpls., 1961-62; asst. supr. Hennepin County Juvenile Detention Center, Mpls., 1962-63; asst. dir. Pres.'s Com. on Youth Crime, Charleston, W.Va., 1963-64; project coordinator parolee rehab. project Mpls. Rehab. Center, 1964-67; pres. Minn. Citizens Council on Crime and Justice, 1967—; trustee Klingberg Family Centers, New Britain, Conn., Sunny Ridge Family Center, Wheaton, Ill.; mem. Minn. Crime Victim and Witness Adv. Council; pres. Ericson Properties, Inc. Active Mpls. Soc. Fine Arts, Walker Art Center. Served with C.E., U.S. Army, 1954-56. Grantee in field. Mem. Nat. Council on Crime and Delinquency, Am. Correctional Assn. Presbyterian. Lodge: Rotary of Mpls. Contbr. articles on crime and justice to profl. jours. Office: 822 3rd St S #101 Minneapolis MN 55415

ERIKSMOEN, DUANE ALAN, agriculturist; b. Minnewaukan, N.D., Mar. 31, 1934; s. Ole and Beatrice (Olson) E.; m. Bonnie LaVonne Ose, Oct. 21, 1956; children: Patti Jain Eriksmoen Matsalia, Eric Duane, Kris Alan. BS, N.D. State U., 1957; student, U. Nev., 1962, U. Wis., River Falls, 1963, Calif. Poly., 1967, U. Minn., 1986. Cert. tchr., N.D.; cert. spl. tchr., Calif. High sch. tchr. Napoleon, N.D., Yerington, Nev., Manteca, Calif., 1957-63; soil cons. U.S. Dept. Agriculture, Napa and King City, Calif., 1963-68; irrigation officer Near East Found., Dar es Salaam, Tanzania, 1968-70; mgr. project farm Experience, Inc., Arusha, Tanzania, 1970-78; project adminstr. Experience, Inc., Mpls., 1978-83, 85—; project agronomist Experience, Inc., Damazin, Sudan, 1983-85; cons. Internat. Fin. Corp., Cairo, Egypt, 1982, SYLICO, Damascus, Syria, 1983. Scout master Boy Scouts Am., Leeds, N.D., 1970. Recipient Genetics in Agriculture award NSF, 1963. Mem. Am. Soc. Agriculture Cons. Republican. Lutheran. Lodge: Rotary. Avocation: travel. Home: 1117 Marquette Ave #806 Minneapolis MN 55403 Office: Experience Inc 2000 Dain Tower Minneapolis MN 55402

ERKIS, RONALD SHELDON, orthodontist, educator; b. Columbus, Ohio, July 10, 1942; s. Donald and Sylvia (Hartman) E.; m. Joyce L. Mulford, Dec. 18, 1976; children—Todd, Andy, Brad. Student Ohio State U., 1960-63; D.D.S., Case Western Res. U., 1967; M.S. in Orthodontics, U. Pitts., 1974. Gen. practice dentistry, Columbus, Ohio, 1969-72; practice dentistry specializing in orthodontics, Columbus, 1974—; tchr. Ohio State U., Columbus Children's Hosp. Bd. dirs. Columbus Jewish Ctr.; past bd. dirs. Jewish Family Services. Served with Dental Corps, US Army, 1967-69. Recipient Koach leadership award Jewish Ctr., 1982. Mem. Columbus Dental Assn., Ohio Dental Soc., ADA, Am. Assn. Orthodontists, Central Ohio Orthodontic Study Club (pres.), Alpha Omega (past pres.). Home: 50 Ashbourne Columbus OH 43209 Office: 5350 E Main St Columbus OH 43213

ERNEST, JUDITH ELLEN, secondary teacher; b. Hammond, Ind., Nov. 6, 1938; d. Gerhardt Herman and Hazel Bertha (Weseloh) Busch; m. Raymond Harry Ernest, Dec. 21, 1963; children: Gregory, Patricia. BA, Valparaiso U., 1960; MA, Northwestern U., 1966. Cert. secondary tchr., Ind. Tchr. social studies Portage (Ind.) Schs., 1961, Hammond Schs., 1961-67; tchr. computer sci. Gary (Ind.) Schs., 1974—. Mem. park bd. Town of Cedar Lake, Ind., 1985—; trustee Lake County Pub. Library System, Merrillville, Ind., 1979—, bd. pres., 1985—. Mem. ALA, Am. Library Trustee Assn. (intellectual freedom com. 1979—), Ind. Library Trustee Assn. (personnel com 1982-83), No. Ind. Library Bd. Assn. (pres. 1981), NEA. Lutheran. Avocations: reading, baking, camping, fishing. Office: Lake County Pub Library 1919 W Lincoln Hwy Merrillville IN 46410

ERNSBERGER, DAVID JACQUES, psychologist, clergyman; b. Rochester, N.Y., Apr. 8, 1930; s. Paul Edgar and Helen (Jacques) E.; m. Deborah Scott, Aug. 29, 1953; children—Paul, Daniel, Gail. B.A., Wesleyan U., 1952; M.Div., Yale U., 1955; S.T.M., Union Theol. Sem., 1957; Ph.D., U. Tex.-Austin, 1976. Lic. cons. psychologist, Minn., 1980; ordained to ministry, Presbyn. Ch., 1956. Organizing minister Countryside Presbyn. Ch., Saginaw, Mich., 1955-62; minister Greenhills Community Ch., Cin., 1962-68, Covenant Presbyn. Ch., Springfield, Ohio, 1968-72; vis. prof. Austin Presbyn. Sem., 1972-75; minister Grace Presbyn. Ch., Mpls., 1975-83; staff psychologist Inst. for Psychol. Therapies, Mpls., 1977-84; dir., cons. Neighborhood Involvement Program, Mpls., 1976—; dir. Kiel Clin. of Mpls., 1985—. Mem. Am. Psychol. Assn., Minn. Psychol. Assn. Democrat. Presbyterian. Author: A Philosophy of Adult Christian Education, 1959; Education for Renewal, 1965. Home: 3921 Xerxes Ave S Minneapolis MN 55410 Office: 1111 Third Ave Minneapolis MN 55404

ERNST, CHESTER NELSON, manufacturing company executive; b. Harrisburg, Pa., Apr. 6, 1948; s. H. Nelson and Blanche E. (Stillwell) E.; m. Norma Marie DeGhetto, Feb. 21, 1971; children: Patrick, Terence, Douglas, Katherine. BS, U.S. Mil. Acad., 1970; MBA, U. Chgo., 1984. Commd. 2d lt. U.S. Army, 1970, advanced through grades to capt., 1973, resigned, 1975; prodn. planner Masonite Corp., Towanda, Pa., 1975-76; mgr. prodn., inventory control Masonite Corp., Chgo., 1976-79; mgr. prodn., inventory control indsl. sealing div. EG&G Sealol, Elmhurst, Ill., 1979-82, materials mgr. indsl. sealing div., 1982-83, ops. mgr. indsl sealing div., 1983—. Fellow Am. Prodn. and Inventory Control Soc. Republican. Roman Catholic. Home: 516 Irvington Ct Bartlett IL 60103 Office: EG&G Sealol Indsl Sealing div 442 W Fullerton Ave Elmhurst IL 60126

ERNST, JOSEPH RICHARD, pastor; b. Sloan, Iowa, Mar. 11, 1934; s. George John and Doris Beatrice (Miquelon) E.; m. Sara Ellen Lee, June 30, 1955; children: Joy Denise Ernst Rowland, John Richard, Jerald Lynn. AA, Miltonvale Wesleyan U., 1954, BA in Religion, 1956; BA in Philosophy, Phillips U., 1958. Ordained elder Wesleyan Ch., 1957. Asst. minister 1st Wesleyan Ch., Enid, Okla., 1956-58; sr. pastor Wesleyan Ch., Ponca City, Okla., 1958-62, Guymon, Okla., 1962-66; sr. pastor Hillside Wesleyan Ch., Cedar Rapids, Iowa, 1966—; youth pres. Okla. dist. Wesleyan Ch., 1956-60, sec. 1958-64, sec. Iowa dist., 1971-73, bd. dirs., 1971—. Editor Dist. Jour., 1958-64, 71-73. Bd. dirs., vice chmn. Keys to Living, Cedar Rapids, 1982-85; bd. dirs. Linn County Jail Chaplaincy, Cedar Rapids, 1985—. Recipient Letter of Commendation, Gov. Iowa, 1986, Congressman Tom Tauke, Senator Tom Harkin. Mem. Ministerial Assn. (pres. Ponca City 1960-61, Guymon, 1963-64, Cedar Rapids, 1967, 74, 80), Iowa Assn. Evangelicals. Republican. Club: Toastmasters. Lodge: Kiwanis (pres. Cedar Rapids 1974-76). Avocations: golfing, photography, gardening. Home: 110 31st St NW Cedar Rapids IA 52405 Office: Hillside Wesleyan Ch 2600 First Ave NW Cedar Rapids IA 52405

ERNST, TERRY OTTO, architect; b. Chgo., June 20, 1942; s. Otto A.C. and Marcella A. (Wolfe) E.; m. Carol K. Fane, June 4, 1966; children: Terry J., Brian E. BArch, U. Ill., Champaign, 1965. Registered architect, Ill., Wis., Ind. Commd. 2d lt. U.S. Army, 1966, advanced through grades to capt., 1974, resigned, 1974; draftsman Millin, Ewald, Proctor, Crystal Lake, Ill., 1968-72; project mgr. The Meland Assn., Mundelein, Ill., 1972-76, office mgr., 1976-79, owner, operator, 1979-80; owner, operator Ernst, Marn & Burger, Mundelein, 1980-82; prin. Terry O. Ernst, Architects, Crystal Lake, 1982—. Bd. dirs. Crystal Lake Zoning Bd., 1981-84. Mem AIA (Northeastern chpt.), Constrn. Specifications Inst., Nat. Council Archtl. Registration Bds. (cert.). Republican. Lutheran. Clubs: Midwest Javelin Sailing (Lake Geneva, Wis.), Catalina Sailing 22 (Chgo.). Avocations: sailing, stained glass, photography, golf, archeology. Home: 167 Edgewater Dr Crystal Lake IL 60014 Office: PO Box 646 Crystal Lake IL 60014

ERON, LEONARD DAVID, psychology educator; b. Newark, Apr. 22, 1920; s. Joseph I. and Sarah (Hilfman) E.; m. Madeline Marcus, Mar. 21, 1950; children—Joan Hobson, Don, Barbara. B.S., CCNY, 1941; M.A., Columbia U., 1946; Ph.D., U. Wis., 1949. Diplomate Am. Bd. Profl. Psychology. Asst. prof. psychology and psychiatry Yale U., New Haven, 1948-55; dir. research Rip Van Winkle Found., 1955-62; prof. psychology U. Iowa, Iowa City, 1962-69; research prof. U. Ill.-Chgo., 1969—. Author 7 books; editor Jour. Abnormal Psychology, 1973-80; assoc. editor Am. Psychologist, 1986—; contbr. numerous articles to profl. jours. Served to 1st lt. AUS, 1942-45. Fulbright lectr., U. Amsterdam, 1967-68; recipient Fulbright Sr. Scholar award, Queensland U., Australia, 1976-77, James McKeen Cattell Sabbatical award, U. Rome, 1984-85. Fellow Am. Psychol. Assn. (Disting. Contbns. to Knowledge award 1980), Am. Orthopsychiat. Assn., AAAS; mem. Midwestern Psychol. Assn. (pres. 1985-86), Internat. Soc. for Research in Aggression (pres.-elect 1988—). Home: 1616 Sheridan Rd Wilmette IL 60091 Office: U Ill Dept Psychology Chicago IL 60680

ERON, MADELINE MARCUS, psychologist; b. New Brunswick, N.J., Sept. 8, 1919; d. Israel and Rae (Becker) Marcus; m. Leonard David Eron, May 21, 1950; children: Joni Eron Hobson, Don Marcus, Barbara Faye. Student, U. Mich., 1937-39; BA, NYU, 1941; MA, Columbia U., 1942. Cert. sch. and clin. psychologist, Ill., N.Y. Intern in psychology Phila. State Hosp., 1942-43; psychology extern Neurol. Inst. Columbia Presbyn. Med. Ctr., N.Y.C., 1943-44; sr. clin. psychologist Inst. Crippled and Disabled, N.Y.C., 1944-51; cons. psychologist New Haven, 1951-55; clin. psychologist Rip Van Winkle Clinic and Found., Hudson, N.Y., 1958-62; chief psychologist Berkshire Farm for Boys, Canaan, N.Y., 1961-62; pvt. practice psychology specializing in retng. the brain injured Iowa City, 1962-63; cons. Cedar Rapids (Iowa) Community Sch. Dist., 1963-67; dir. psychol. services U. Iowa Comprehensive Evaluation and Rehab. Ctr., Iowa City, 1968-69; sch. psychologist Winnetka, Glencoe and Skokie (Ill.) Elem. Sch. Dists., 1969-72, Evanston (Ill.) Twp. High Sch., 1972—; bd. dirs. Lincoln Ctr. Clin. Services, Highland Park, Ill. Mem. Am. Psychol. Assn. (div. sch. psychology, rehab. psychology, child and youth service), Iowa Psychol. Assn. (sec. 1965-67), Midwestern Psychol. Assn., Nat. Assn. Sch. Psychologists (charter), Ill. Sch. Psychologists Assn. (charter), Assn. Advancement Psychology, N.Y. State Psychol. Assn., Psi Chi. Home: 1616 Sheridan Rd Wilmette IL 60091 Office: Evanston Twp High Sch 1600 Dodge Ave Evanston IL 60204

ERONDU, JOSEPH ONYENOWE, dentist; b. Aba, Imo, Nigeria, Jan. 25, 1954. Home: 4109 Begg Blvd Saint Louis MO 63121 Office: 6830 Natural Bridge Rd Saint Louis MO 63121

EROS, ALAN GORDON, meterorologist; b. Detroit, Oct. 1, 1937; s. Louis Thomas Eros and Ellen Taylor (Beauvais) Gilpin; m. Friedel Lussman Hansen, Sept. 30, 1967; children: Angela Gay, Anne-Lise, Justin David. Grad., High Sch., Ypsilanti, Mich., 1959. Enlisted USAF, 1960, advanced through grades to, retired; weather forecaster Nat. Weather Service, 1982—. Mem. Nat. Weather Assn. Republican. Mormon. Home: 6336 W Granner Dr Indianapolis IN 46241-9313 Office: Nat Weather Service Forecast Office PO Box 51526 Indianapolis IN 46251-0526

ERSKINE, DWIGHT R., II, brokerage house executive; b. Centralia, Ill., Feb. 6, 1945; s. Dwight R. and Helen L. (Gillette) E.; m. Karen S. Stone, Oct. 12, 1983; children: Dwight R. III, James S., Andrew H. BA, Northwestern U., 1973. Cons. Chgo. Title and Trust Co., 1973; v.p., mktg. Ben Franklin Savs. and Loan, Oak Brook, Ill., 1974; mgr. bond sales First Nat. Bank Chgo., 1974-75; rep. Edward D. Jones and Co., Effingham, Ill., 1975-78, ptnr., 1979—; bd. dirs. Aerie Corp., Effingham; instr. Lakeland Coll., Mattoon and Effingham, Ill., 1977—; mktg. cons. in field, Ill., Ind., Fla., N.Y., 1985—. Campaign cons., mgr. 21st, 48th ward Reps., Chgo., 1971-72; pres. Effingham YMCA, 1981-83; chmn. planning commn., Effingham, 1978—; bd. dirs. exec. com. Indsl. Commn., Effingham, 1981—. Mem. ABA (gov. 7th cir. 1971), Internat. Soc. Registered Reps. (charter), Internat. Assn. Fin. Planners, Alpha Sigma Lambda. Republican. Presbyterian. Clubs: Municipal Bond Chgo., Effingham Country (bd. dirs. 1980), John Evans (Evanston, Ill.). Avocations: golf, flying, photography, automobiles, art. Home: 1021 Cardinal Dr Effingham IL 62401 Office: Edward D Jones & Co 212 E Jefferson PO Box 1136 Effingham IL 62401

ERTEL, GARY ARTHUR, accountant; b. Racine, Wis., Feb. 16, 1954; s. Arthur and Jean Ann (Potterville) E.; m. Judith Marie Vasy, Aug. 9, 1975; 1 child, James Arthur. BSBA in Acctg. cum laude, Drake U., 1975; MBA, Marquette U., 1984. CPA, Wis. Mem. staff Arthur Andersen & Co., Milw., 1975-77; mgr. Jezzo, Deppisch & Co., Cedarburg, Wis., 1978; gen. acctg. mgr., budget control analyst, fin. analyst, asst. to the treas., asst. treas. Grede Foundries, Inc., Milw., 1978—. Mem. Amateur Radio Emergency Service, Milw., 1984—; bd. dirs. Grace Evang. Luth. Ch., Milw., 1984—. Mem. Am. Inst. CPA's, Wis. Inst. CPA's (chmn. acctg. careers com. 1979—, Service award 1987), Nat. Cash Mgmt. Assn., Wis. Cash Mgmt. Assn. (program com. 1985—), Risk and Ins. Mgmt. Assn. Avocations: skiing, tennis, amateur radio, golf. Home: 780 Garvens Ave Brookfield WI 53005 Office: Grede Foundries Inc 9898 W Bluemound Rd Milwaukee WI 53226

ERTEL, GEORGE EDWARD, financial services executive; b. Dayton, Ohio, Dec. 7, 1946; s. Edward G. and Frances M. (George) E.; m. Rowena M. Poock, July 1, 1967; children: Lisa R., Tracy C., Erica N. BBA, Ohio State U., 1968; M in Mgmt., Northwestern U., 1976. Corp. planner Blue Cross/Blue Shield Assn., Chgo., 1976-80; sr. bus. analyst GATX Corp., Chgo., 1980-84; mktg. mgr. The Paxall Group, Inc., Chgo., 1984-85; asst. v.p. stategic planning and mktg. Heller Fin., Inc., Chgo., 1985—. Contbr. articles to The Am. Spectator. Served to 1st lt. U.S. Army, 1968-70, Vietnam. Mem. Am. Mktg. Assn. Republican. Home: 1295 Pembrook Circle Roselle IL 60172 Office: Heller Fin Inc 105 W Adams Chicago IL 60603

ERTZ, CAROL ANN RYAN, human resources administrator; b. Framingham, Mass., Aug. 24, 1955; d. Edward Joseph and Mary Constance (Brennan) Ryan; m. David Brian Ertz, Sept. 20, 1986. BS in Elem. Edn., U. Maine, Orono, 1977; MS Edn., Boston U., 1986. Cert. elem. and spl. edn. tchr., Maine, Mich. Tchr. Title I Sch. Union #90, Bradley, Maine, 1977-78; tchr. spl. edn. Gray-New Gloucester (Maine) Jr. and Sr. High Sch., 1978-85, coordinator, tchr. gifted edn., 1980-85; intern Continuing Edn. for Bus./Industry U. So. Maine, Portland, 1984; tng. program specialist Enrollment Services Boston U., 1985-86; intern Human Resource Devel. Ctr. Wang Labs., Lowell, Mass., 1986; tng. adminstrn. coordinator Mt. Carmel Mercy Hosp., Detroit, 1987—; Contbg. author curriculum Maine Resources for Gifted Education, 1983. Mem. NEA, Am. Soc. for Tng. and Devel. (membership com. Detroit 1986-87), Mich. Soc. Instructional Technologists, Bus. and Profl. Women's Assn., Profl. Women's Network, Maine Assn. for Gifted/Talented Edn. (exec. com. 1983-84). Avocations: downhill and cross-country skiing, tennis, racquetball, jazz dance, travel. Office: Mt Carmel Mercy Hosp Tng and Devel 6071 W Outer Dr Detroit MI 48235

ERWIN, CHESLEY PARA, JR., utility co. exec.; b. Milw., Apr. 6, 1953; s. Chesley Para and Constance June (Raab) E.; student Occidental Coll., 1971-72; A.B., Stanford U., 1974; M.A. in Public Policy and Adminstrn., U. Wis., Madison, 1976, M.S. in Bus., 1976, J.D./M.B.A., U. Wis., 1987; m. Karen Jane Leonard, Dec. 27, 1974. Intern, Bur. Fiscal Policy Planning and Analysis, Wis. Dept. Revenue, 1976; energy researcher energy systems and policy research group Inst. Environ. Studies, U. Wis., Madison, 1974-76; health planning analyst Wis. Dept. Health and Social Services, Madison, 1976-77; energy analyst Office State Planning and Energy, Wis. Dept. Adminstrn., Madison, 1977-78; govt. relations specialist Wis. Power & Light Co., Madison, 1978-81; regulatory affairs advisor, 1981-85, coordinator environ. regulation, 1985—. Mem. New Republican Conf. Wis., 1976—; coordinator Anderson for Pres., Dane County, Wis., 1979-80; moderator, pres. First Congl. United Ch. of Christ, Oconomowoc, Wis., 1986; alt. del. Rep. Nat. Conv., 1980; mem. Waukesha County Solid Waste Mgmt. Bd., 1982-85. Mem. Am. Econs. Assn., ABA (student div.), Am. Soc. Public Adminstrn., Chgo. Council Fgn. Relations. Republican. Home: 820 Old Tower Rd Oconomowoc WI 53066 Office: PO Box 192 222 W Washington Ave Madison WI 53701

ERWIN, SHARON PRESS, telecommunications engineer; b. Little Falls, Minn., Nov. 25, 1949; d. Herman Bernard and Leona Frances (McGuire) P.; m. Phillip Wayne Erwin, Sept. 24, 1977. BA summa cum laude, U. Minn., Duluth, 1970; MA, U. Minn., 1972. Account exec. Northwestern Bell, Mpls., 1979-80; dir. instl. mktg. Ellerbe Inc., Mpls., 1980-81; nat. account exec. AT&T, Mpls., 1981-83; devel. specialist No. Telecom, Mpls., 1983-85; voice network analyst Honeywell Inc., Mpls., 1985, sr. network engr., 1986—; cons. subject matter expert, tech. writer Golle & Holmes, Mpls., 1985—; speaker on integrated technol. and high-capacity long distance services, various orgns., 1983—. telecommunications sales and mktg. tng. courseware developer, 1984—. James Wright Hunt scholar U. Minn., Duluth, 1967-70. Mem. Minn. Telecommunications Assn., Mensa. Home: 3158 Kentucky Ave N Minneapolis MN 55427

ERWINE, STAN(FORD) WRIGHT, advertising executive; b. Waco, Tex., Apr. 6, 1956; s. Wright Hartwell and Anna Jean (Rasmussen) E.; m. Paula Lyn Gatzoulis, Mar. 3, 1979. BA in Journalism and Mass Communications, Kansas State U., 1978. Advt. sales rep. Nebr. Farmer Mag., Lincoln, 1978-81; sr. account exec. Miller, Friendt, Ludemann Advt., Lincoln, 1981-84; account exec. Fletcher Mayo Assocs., St. Joseph, Mo., 1984-86, Christenson, Barclay and Shaw, Overland Park, Kans., 1987, Nicholson, Kovac, Huntley & Welsh, 1987—; lectr. advt. Kans. State U., U. Nebr., 1984-87. Tech. writer irrigation brochures, Farm Forum Mag., 1984-86; photographer agrl., indsl., sport and travel advt., Farm Forum Mag. (best cover awards Nebr. Farm Mag., 1984,85); exhibitor Cornhusker Internat. Photo Expo., 1983. Mem. Lincoln Clean Community Com., 1983, City of Lincoln Regenerative Funding Com., 1984. Recipient Addy award, 1983, 84. Mem. Nat. Agrl. Mktg. Assn. (bd. dirs. 1982-84, careers chmn. 1984-86, Kans. State U. student chpt. advisor, Mo./Kans. chpt. 1985-87, bd. dirs. Midlands chpt. 1983-84, U. Nebr. student chpt. advisor, 1983-84, 4 regional advt. awards, Midlands, Midwest and Mo./Kans. chpts., 1982-86, 2 nat. awards 1985, 86, Mokan Careers chmn. 1987), Am. Advt. Fedn. (Addy awards 1985-86). Republican. Presbyterian. Club: Lincoln Camera, Kansas City Ad. Avocations: art, photography, sports, music, World War and mil. history. Office: Nicholson Kovac Huntley & Welsh 301 E Armour Kansas City KS 64141

ESCHBACH, JESSE ERNEST, judge; b. Warsaw, Ind., Oct. 26, 1920; s. Jesse Ernest and Mary W. (Stout) E.; m. Sara Ann Walker, Mar. 15, 1947; children: Jesse Ernest III, Virginia. BS, Ind. U., 1943, JD with distinction, 1949, LLD (hon.), 1986. Bar: Ind. 1949. Ptnr. Graham, Rasor, Eschbach & Harris, Warsaw, 1949-62; city atty. Warsaw, 1952-53; dep. pros. atty. 54th Jud. Circuit Ct. Ind., 1952-1954; judge U.S. Dist. Ct. Ind., 1962-81; chief judge judge U.S. Dist. Ct. Ind., 1974-81; judge U.S. Ct. Appeals (7th cir.), Chgo., 1981-85, sr. judge, 1985—; Pres. Endicott Church Furniture, Inc., 1960-62; sec., gen. counsel Dalton Foundries, Inc., 1957-62. Editorial staff: Ind. Law Jour, 1947-49. Trustee Ind. U., 1965-70. Served with USNR, 1943-46. Hastings scholar, 1949; Recipient U.S. Law Week award, 1949. Mem. U.S. C. of C. (labor relations com. 1960-62), Warsaw C. of C. (pres. 1955-56), Nat. Assn. Furniture Mfrs. (dir. 1962), Ind. Mfrs. Assn. (dir. 1962), ABA, Ind. Bar Assn. (bd. mgrs. 1953-54, ho. dels. 1950-60), Fed. Bar Assn., Am. Judicature Soc., Order of Coif. Presbyn. Club: Rotarian (pres. Warsaw 1956-57).

ESCHMANN, JOEL EDWARD, equipment manufacturing corporation executive; b. Racine, Wis., Aug. 6, 1942; s. Edward and Lydia (Pribyl) E.;

children—Joellen, Sara.; m. Linda Ann Scharpf, Dec. 28, 1985; 1 stepchild, Charles Christopherson. Assoc. in Math. and Physics, Gateway Inst., 1968. Mech. engr. Gould/Gettys Mfg. Co., Racine, 1963-80, Graham Co., Milw., 1980-83, Allen Bradley Co., Brown Deer, Wis., 1983—; instr. Milw. Sch. Engring., 1981-83. Mem. Internat. Electronics Packaging Soc., Am. Soc. Metals. Lutheran. Club: Lakeshore Repeater Assn. (Racine) (pres. 1976-79). Avocations: amateur radio; sailing; fishing. Home: 6964 Meadowdale Dr Hartford WI 53027 Office: Allen Bradley Co 8949 N Deerbrook Trail Brown Deer WI 53223

ESHELBRENNER, ROBERT JACK, insurance company executive; b. Ft. Scott, Kans., Nov. 1, 1947; s. Jack Leitz and Sarah (Handly) E.; m. Nancy Wogan, June 7, 1969; children: Erin Beth, Kate Handly. BS in Bus. Administrn., Pittsburg (Kans.) State U., 1969. CPCU. Systems coordinator The Western Ins. Cos., Ft. Scott, 1972-77, supr. systems, 1977-85, asst. corp. sec. systems, 1982, mgr. systems, 1986—. Chmn. Ft. Scott Planning Commn., 1973-77; mem. U243 Sch. Bd., Ft. Scott., 1978-86. Served to 1st lt. U.S. Army, 1969-72. Mem. Soc. CPCU's. Republican. Presbyterian. Home: 402 S Main Fort Scott KS 66701 Office: The Western Ins Cos 14 E First St Fort Scott KS 66701

ESHELMAN, RAYMOND HARRY, telephone directory advertising executive; b. Dayton, Ohio, July 10, 1925; s. Harry and Winifred Ann (LeJeune) E.; m. Alice Joyce McMullen, Sept. 20, 1952; children: Peter, Julie, Timothy. Student, U. Nebr., 1945-46. Account exec. Pat Patrick Advt. Agy., Glendale, Calif., 1946; with L.M. Berry and Co., Dayton, 1947—; gen. sales mgr. L.M. Berry and Co., 1963, v.p. sales, 1965, exec. v.p. ops., 1973-80, pres., chief operating officer, 1980—, pres., chief exec. officer, 1986—, also bd. dirs.; pres., dir. L.M. Berry and Co.-NYPS, 1977, L.M. Berry Services Inc., 1980—; dir. ITT World Directories, ITT World Directories (U.K.), Intermedia, Inc. Trustee Loren M. Berry Found., 1979—, Wright State Found., Dayton Performing Arts Fund, 1982—, Dayton Art Inst., 1984—; bd. dirs. Jr. Achievement. Served with USNR, 1943-46. Mem. Nat. Yellow Pages Services Assn. (pres. 1976-77, bd. dirs. 1976—), Dayton C. of C. Republican. Roman Catholic. Clubs: Moraine Country (Dayton) (dir.), Racquet (Dayton), Bicycle (Dayton), The Hundred (Dayton); Wilderness Country (Naples, Fla.); Seaview Country (Absecon, N.J.). Office: LM Berry & Co 3170 Kettering Blvd PO Box 6000 Dayton OH 45401

ESHETU, FISSEHA, teacher; b. Dessie, Wollo, Ethiopia, June 10, 1947; came to U.S., 1978; s. Ayele Eshetu and Taitu (Wolde) Mariam; m. Gwendelbert Lewis, Feb. 17, 1984. BEd, Haile Sellassie U., Addis Ababa, Ethiopia, 1969; diploma in Edn., U. London, 1973, MA, 1974; PhD, U. Wis., Milw., 1986. Cert. tchr., prin., Wis. Tchr. Ministry of Edn., Jimma, Ethiopia, 1962-64; prin. Ministry of Edn., Axum, Ethiopia, 1969-71; trainer Swedish Internat. Devel. Agy., Stockholm, Sweden, 1972-73; ednl. planner Planning Commn., Addis Ababa, Ethiopia, 1975-77; tchr. Milw. Pub. Schs., 1984—. Mem. Comparative and Internat. Soc., Am. Ednl. Research Assn., Am. Ednl. Studies Assn., African Studies Assn., Phi Delta Kappa. Avocation: shortwave radio. Home: 3019 N 55th St Milwaukee WI 53210

ESHETU, GWENDELBERT LEWIS, social worker; b. Cairo, Ill., Mar. 22, 1940; d. Rassie A. and Naomi (Briggs) Lewis; m. Frederick O. Carr (div. Nov. 1976); 1 child, Melisande Caprice; m. Fisseha Eshetu, Feb. 17, 1984. BA, U. Wis., Milw., 1966, MS, 1972. Caseworker Milw. County Dept. Social Services, 1966-70; social worker Ill. Dept. Children and Family Services, Cairo, 1971, Milw. Pub. Schs., 1972—; instr. field placement for grad. students, Milw. Pub. Schs. and U. Wis., Milw., 1973-75. Mem. Nat. Assn. Social Workers, Nat. Assn. Black Social Workers, Milw. Sch. Social Workers Assn., Wis. Assn. Black Social Workers (office holder), Acad. Cert. Social Workers, NAACP, Mensa, Eta Phi Beta. Democrat. Club: North Cen. Service (Milw.). Avocation: writing fiction. Home: 3019 N 55th St Milwaukee WI 53210 Office: Milwaukee Public Schools 5225 W Vliet St Milwaukee WI 53208

ESMER, GERALD PETER, engineering executive; b. Chgo., Apr. 28, 1943; s. Peter and Lottie (Wojciechowski) E.; m. Suzanne K. Eastman, Sept. 16, 1964 (div. Oct. 1978); children—Rand M., Robert G., Gregory J. B.S.E.E. with honors, Mich. State U., 1965; M.S.E.E., Stanford U., 1966; postgrad. in systems engring. U. Pa., 1968-69; M.B.A. with distinction, U. Mich., 1981; student in Spanish U. Mich.-Dearborn, 1983-84; postgrad. in statistics Eastern Mich. U., 1985-86. Asst. elec. engr. Gen. Motors Corp., Saginaw, Mich., summers 1963, 64; mem. tech. staff Bell Telephone Labs., Whippany, N.J., summer 1965; chief engr.'s staff Gen. Electric Co., Missiles & Space Div., Valley Forge, Pa., 1966-70; project engr. Systems Div., Bendix Corp., Ann Arbor, Mich., 1970-72; supr. Transport Systems Ops., Ford Motor Co., Dearborn, Mich., 1972-77, supr. Elec. and Electronics Div., 1977—; rep. Soc. Automotive Engrs. and Ford Motor Co. at meetings of Internat. Standards Orgn., various European cities. Patentee in field; author tech. papers. Chmn. Green Oak Twp., South Lyon, Mich., 1974; bd. dirs. Georgetown Commons S. Condominium Assn., 1984-85. NSF fellow, 1965-66. Mem. Soc. Automotive Engrs., Eta Kappa Nu, Tau Beta Pi, Beta Gamma Sigma. Club: Ann Arbor Ski. Avocations: skiing, tennis, computers, racquetball, reading, travel. Home: 2832 Bombridge Ct Ann Arbor MI 48104 Office: Ford Motor Co Elec and Electronics Div C275 DPTC 17000 Rotunda Dr Dearborn MI 48121

ESPESETH, DONALD WILLIAM, hospital radiology administrator; b. Rice Lake, Wis., May 4, 1932; s. Robert E. and Mary (Willemssen) E.; m. Kathryn Ann Stafford, Sept. 7, 1957 (div.); children—Brady D., Lori Kay. Cert. Lawton Sch. Radiologic Tech., Beverly Hills, Calif., 1951. with Waukesha (Wis.) Meml. Hosp., 1955—, chief radiologic technologist until 1970, radiology adminstr., 1970—; mem. Waukesha County Health Systems Com.; corp. mem. Southeastern Wis. Health Systems Agy.; mem. Wis. Adv. Com. for Para-Med. Health Occupations, Wis. Bd. Vocat. Tech. Adult Edn.; chmn. radiology adminstrs. adv. com., mem. shared services com. Wis. Hosp. Purchasing, Inc.; mem. health-care team working with refugees in Indo-China, 1980; mem. China-U.S. Sci. Exchange (radiation adminstrn.). Served with USAF, 1951-55. Mem. Am. Soc. Radiologic Technologists, Wis. Soc. Radiologic Technologists (pres. 1975-76), Am. Hosp. Radiology Adminstrs., Radiology Adminstrs. Southeastern Wis. Home: 207 Coolidge Ave Waukesha WI 53186 Office: 725 American Ave Waukesha WI 53186

ESPING, EDWARD D., wholesale food distribution company executive. Pres. Cardinal Foods Inc., Columbus, Ohio. Office: Cardinal Foods Inc (Subs Cardinal Distribution Inc) 315 Phillipi Rd Columbus OH 43228 *

ESPY, CARROLL JOHN, psychotherapist; b. Dayton, Ohio, Sept. 16, 1952; s. Everett Joseph and Florence Mary (Pelphrey) E.; m. Donna Darlene Bennett, Apr. 22, 1972; 1 child, Matthew John. BS, Wright State U., 1977; MSW, PhD, Ohio State U., 1980. Lic. psychotherapist. Mgr. neurotoxicology toxic hazards br. U. Calif., Wright Patterson AFB, Dayton, Ohio, 1973-80; clin. supr. South Community, Inc., Dayton, 1980-83; clin. supr., asst. dept. dir. Good Samaritan Hosp., Dayton, 1983—; exec. dir., clin. dir. Character Disorders Inst./Kettering (Ohio) Psychotherapy Assn., 1980—. Contbr. chpt. to book and papers in field. Mem. Am. Acad. Psychotherapists, Internat. Soc. for the Study of Multiple Personality and Dissociation, Alpha Delta Mu. Avocations: chess, classicist music. Home: 2245 S Patterson Blvd Kettering OH 45409 Office: Character Disorders Inst Kettering Psychotherapy Assn 3104 Wilmington Pl Kettering OH 45429

ESREY, WILLIAM TODD, telecommunications company executive; b. Phila., Jan. 17, 1940; s. Alexander J. and Dorothy (B.) E.; m. Julie L. Campbell, June 13, 1964; children: William Todd, John Campbell. B.A., Denison U., Granville, Ohio, 1961; M.B.A., Harvard U., 1964. With Am. Tel & Tel. Co., also N.Y. Telephone Co., 1964-69; pres. Empire City Subway Ltd., N.Y.C., 1969-70; mng. dir. Dillon, Read & Co. Inc., N.Y.C., 1970-80; exec. v.p., chief fin. officer United Telecommunications, Inc., Kansas City, Kans., 1980-81, 84-85; pres. United Telecommunications, Inc., Kansas City, Kans., 1985—, United Telecom Communications, Inc., Kansas City, Mo., 1982-85; bd. dirs. The Equitable Life Assurance Soc. U.S., Panhandle Eastern Corp. Bd. dirs. U. Kansas City, Greater Kansas City Community Found.;trustee Pembroke Hill Sch., Denison U., Midwest Research Com. for Econ. Devel. Mem. Phi Beta Kappa. Clubs: Mission Hills Country, River, Links. Home: 2302 W 69th Terr Shawnee Mission KS 66208 Office: United Communications Inc PO Box 11315 Kansas City MO 64112

ESSER, GEORGE FRANCIS, architect; b. Sedalia, Mo., July 28, 1955; s. Richard Charles and Mary Ellen (Butcher) E.; m. Victorial Lynn Viebrock, Dec. 18, 1976; children: Joseph Andrew, Alan Charles. Student, State Fair Community Coll., 1973-74, U. Kans., Lawrence, 1974-76; BArch, U. Okla., 1979. Registered architect, Mo. Project architect Graves Assocs., Oklahoma City, Okla., 1977-79, Casey and Assocs., Springfield, Mo., 1979-80, State of Mo., Jefferson City, 1980-84; prin. JCA Architects Inc., Columbia, Mo., 1984—. Mem. AIA, Mo. Council Architects, Nat. Trust for Hist. Preservation, Jaycees, Jefferson City C. of C. Republican. Roman Catholic. Office: JCA Architects Inc 809 Slate Ln Jefferson City MO 65101

ESSEX, CHARLES KINNISON, telecommunications company executive; b. Kirkersville, Ohio, July 6, 1923; s. Charles Emerson and Anna Eleanor (Kinnison) E.; m. Helen Rose Holcomb, June 12, 1948; children: Charles Raymond, Susan Marie Essex Elliot. BS, Ohio State U., 1949. Dist. sales mgr. Marion Power Shovel Co., Ohio, Pa., N.Y., 1950-54; indsl. sales Crane Co., Columbus, Ohio, 1954-57; sales engr. Yale & Town, Columbus, 1957-58; sales A. Stanley Tuck Orgn., Columbus, 1959; engr., supr. engr. dept. E.I. DuPont, various, 1958, 60-63; pres. Executone of Columbus, Inc., 1963—, bd. dirs.; bd. dirs. SureCom Corp., Inc., Columbus, 1985—. Served U.S. Army, 1943-45, ETO. Decorated Purple Heart, Bronze Star. Republican. Methodist. Club: Capitol (Columbus). Lodge: Masons. Avocations: travel. Home: 4484 Loos Circle E Columbus OH 43214 Office: Executone of Columbus Inc 3930 Indianola Ave Box 14845 Columbus OH 43214

ESSIG, RICHARD HENRY, physician; b. Cleve., Apr. 28, 1950; m. Barbara Jo Halahan, Sept. 8, 1973; children: Jeremy G., Jenna L. BA in Chemistry, Case Western Reserve U., 1971; MD, Ohio State U., 1975. Intern. Akron (Ohio) City Hosp., 1975-76, resident in ob-gyn, 1976-79; ptnr. Fairview West Ob-Gyn Assocs., Cleve., 1979-86; practice medicine specializing in ob-gyn Zanesville, Ohio, 1986—; vice-chmn Dept ob-gyn Fairview Gen. Hosp., Cleve., 1985-86. Fellow Am. Coll. Obstetrician Gynecologists; mem. AMA, Ohio State Med. Assn., Muskingum County Acad. of Medicine. Office: Physician's Office 830 Bethesda Dr Doctors Park Bldg #1 Zanesville OH 43701

ESSMAN, ALYN, photographic studios company executive. Chmn. CPI Corp., St. Louis. Office: CPI Corp 1706 Washington Ave Saint Louis MO 63103 *

ESSMAN, DENISE IRENE, marketing educator; b. Greenfield, Iowa, Mar. 31, 1948; d. Harold William and Eleanor Irene (Johnson) Bricker; m. Allen Kent Essman, June 1, 1968; children: Bradly Allen, Brady Kent, Barrett William. B.S., Iowa State U., 1973, postgrad., 1977-78; M.B.A., Drake U., 1980. Mktg. trainee The Bankers Life, Des Moines, 1975-76; v.p. mktg. Essman & Assocs., 1977—; instr. mktg. Iowa State U., Ames, 1978-79, 81-84; cons. Small Bus. Devel. Ctr., 1984—, instr. mktg. Drake U., Des Moines, 1984—; manuscript reviewer. Com. mem. Des Moines Art Ctr., 1975—. Mem. AAUP, Am. Mktg. Assn. (dir. 1983—, v.p. midwestern region 1983—85), Iowa Mktg. Assn. (dir. 1982-85, treas. 1979-80, v.p. 1980-81, pres. 1981-82), Life Office Mgmt. Assn., Alpha Mu Alpha (advisor). Democrat. Lutheran. Home: 3008 SW Thornton Ave Des Moines IA 50321

ESSMAN, DOUGLAS JAY, aerospace engineer; b. St. Louis, June 26, 1956; m. Peggy Sue Cooper, July 4, 1981. AS in Aircraft Maintenance Engring. Tech., Parks Coll., 1976, BS in Aeros., 1977; MSME, U. Dayton, 1984. Aerospace engr. Wright Aero. Labs., Dayton, Ohio, 1977-80, test and evaluation engr. and designer for advance gas turbine engines, 1981—. Contbr. articles on advance turbine engine propulsion to profl. jours. Mem. ASME, Am. Inst. Aeros. and Astronautics, Pi Mu Epsilon.

ESTEP, ERNEST ROBERT, obstetrician and gynecologist; b. Tiffin, Ohio, Sept. 6, 1941; s. Wade Louis and Margaret C. (Wetzel) E.; m. Bonnie Lynn Cline, Aug. 9, 1964. B.S., Heidelberg Coll., 1963; M.D., Ohio State U., 1967. Intern, Akron (Ohio) City Hosp., 1967, resident in ob-gyn, 1970-74, chief resident, 1974; practice medicine specializing in ob-gyn, Greeley, Colo., 1974-76, Akron, Ohio, 1976—; active teaching staff Akron City Hosp. Served with Div. Indian Health, USPHS, 1968-70. Named Resident of Yr., Akron City Hosp., 1974. Fellow Am. Coll. Ob-Gyn.; mem. Am. Assn. Gynecologic Laparoscopists, AMA, Ohio State Med. Assn., Summit County Med. Assn. Republican. Lutheran. Club: Heidelberg Fellows (pres.). Contbr. article to profl. publ. Office: 733 W Market St Akron OH 44303

ESTES, DOUGLAS LEE, motel owner; b. Oakland, Calif., Sept. 12, 1944; s. Elmer Leroy and Patricia Lillian (Hansen) E.; Justine Nell Pinard, Mar. 5, 1977; children: Jordan, Aaron, Natasha, Allison. BS in Bus. Adminstrn., U. S.D., 1966; MS, U. Wyo., 1971. Teaching asst. U. Wyo., 1969-70; devel. dir. Yankon Sioux Tribe, Wagner, S.D., 1970-71; price analyst Cost of Living Council, Washington, 1972-74; fin. analyst Fed. Energy Office, Washington, 1974-75; owner, mgr. Sands Motel, Wall Motel, Wall, S.D., 1975—; mem. S.D. Tourism Adv. Bd., Pierre, 1980—; chmn. S.D. Mktg. Task Force, 1986—. Bd. dirs. S.D. Bldg. Authority, Pierre, 1983—; Rep. committeeman, Pennington County, 1978-86; mem. Black Hills Badlands Lakes Assn., Rapid City, 1976—. Served with U.S. Army, 1967-69. Mem. Am. Legion (post comdr. 1980-81), Wall C. of C. (bd. dirs. 1984—), Wall Hospitality Assn. (v.p. 1986), Beta Gamma Sigma. Methodist. Avocations: jazz music, community theatre. Office: Sands Motel 804 Glenn St Wall SD 57790

ESTES, ELAINE ROSE GRAHAM, librarian; b. Springfield, Mo., Nov. 24, 1931; d. James McKinley and Zelma Mae (Smith) Graham; m. John Melvin Estes, Dec. 29, 1953. B.S. in Bus. Adminstrn., Drake U., 1953, teaching cert., 1956; M.S. in L.S, U. Ill., 1960. With Public Library, Des Moines, 1956—; coordinator extension services Public Library, 1977-78, dir., 1978—; lectr. antiques, hist. architecture, libraries; mem. conservation planning com. for disaster preparedness for libraries. Author bibliographies of books on antiques; contbr. articles to profl. jours. Mem. State of Iowa Cultural Affairs Adv. Council, 1986—; chmn. Des Moines Mayor's Hist. Dist. Commn.; bd. dirs. Des Moines Art Center, 1972—; mem. bd. Friends of Library USA, 1986—; mem. nominations rev. com. Iowa State Nat. Hist. Register. Recipient recognition for outstanding working women—leadership in econ. and civic life of Greater Des Moines YWCA, 1975, Disting. Alumni award Drake U., 1979. Mem. ALA, Iowa Library Assn. (pres. 1978-79), Iowa Urban Pub. Library Assn., Library Assn. Greater Des Moines Metro Area (pres.), Iowa Soc. Preservation Hist. Landmarks. Clubs: Links, Quester's, Inc. (pres. 1982, state 2d v.p. 1984-86). Office: Pub Library of Des Moines 100 Locust St Des Moines IA 50308-1791

ESTOW, EMILY BARBARA, social service agency administrator; b. Bronx, N.Y., Nov. 24, 1942; d. Sidney and Sophie (Cohen) E; m. Robert B. Carroll, Aug. 1, 1987. BA, Smith Coll., 1964; MA, U. Chgo., 1966. Dir. emergency housing program Northwestern Meml. Hosp. Inst. Psychiatry, Chgo., 1985—; sec. mem. exec. bd. Inst. Autonomous Living Chgo., 1984-86. Mem. Nat. Assn. Social Workers. Home: 2930 N Sheridan Rd Chicago IL 60657 Office: Emergency Housing Program 30 W Chicago Chicago IL 60610

ETCHELECU, ALBERT DOMINIC, energy company executive; b. Santa Barbara, Calif., Sept. 30, 1937; s. John and Etiennette E.; m. Judith Ann Matthews, June 7, 1975; children: Steven, Scott, Cheri, Michael, David. Student, U. Calif., Santa Barbara, 1957; student program for mgmt. devel., Harvard U. Bus. Sch., 1972. Prodn. mgr. East Tex. Sun Co., 1972-79; v.p., gen. mgr. Sun Info. Services, Phila., 1979-80; pres., chmn. bd. Sperry-Sun, Inc., Houston, 1980; pres., chief exec. officer Minnegasco, Inc., Mpls., 1980-84, chmn., chief exec. officer, 1984—, also bd. dirs.; pres., chief exec. officer Diversified Energies, Inc., Mpls., 1984—; bd. dirs. Lane Mgmt. Co. State chmn. Am. Cancer Soc., 1981-82. Mem. Am. Gas Assn. Club: Mpls. Office: Diversified Energies Inc 201 S 7th Ave Minneapolis MN 55402 *

ETHEREDGE, FOREST DEROYCE, state senator, former community college president; b. Dallas, Oct. 21, 1929; s. Gilbert Wybert and Theta Erlene (Tate) E.; m. Joan Mary Horan, Apr. 30, 1955; children: Forest William, John Bede, Mary Faith, Brian Thomas, Regina Ann. BS, Va. Poly. Inst. and State U., 1951; MS, U. Ill., 1953; postgrad., Northwestern U., 1953-55; PhD, Loyola U., Chgo., 1968. Mem. faculty City Colls. Chgo., 1955-65, chmn. phys. sci. dept., 1963-65; dean instrn. Rock Valley Coll., 1965-67, v.p., 1966-67; pres. McHenry County Coll., 1967-70, Waubonsee Community Coll., 1970-81; U.S. senator from Ill. 1981—, higher edn. com., 1981—, mem. intergovtl. coop. commn., 1982—, co-chmn. legis. info. system, 1983—, minority spokesman appropriations I com., 1986—. Bd. dirs. Mercy Ctr. for Health Care Services, Aurora, Ill.; mem. citizens' adv. council Dept. Alcoholism and Substance Abuse; mem. Sci. Adv. Council. Mem. Ill. Council Pub. Community Coll. Pres. (chmn. 1971-72), Chgo. Met. Higher Edn. Council (bd. dirs.), No. Ill. Pub. TV Consortium (bd. dirs.), Suburban Community Coll. TV Consortium (bd. dirs.). Republican. Roman Catholic. Lodge: Rotary (pres. Aurora chpt. 1978-79). Home: 843 W Hardin Ave Aurora IL 60506 Office: 52 W Downer St Aurora IL 60506 also: State House Room 309H Springfield IL 62706

ETHERIDGE, MARGARET DWYER, medical center administrator; b. Atlanta, Jan. 5, 1938; d. Philip Fitzgerald and Mary Catharine (Dwyer) E.; m. Roy Charles McCracken, May 5, 1975; m. William Bertram Smitheram, Aug. 17, 1985. BA, Emory U., 1960; M Hosp. Adminstrn., Washington U., St. Louis, 1973. Registered record adminstr. Spl. asst. to dir. VA Med. Ctr., Roseburg, Oreg., 1973-74; hosp. adminstrn. specialist VA Central Office, Washington, 1974-76; asst. dir. trainee VA Med. Ctr., Phila., 1976; assoc. dir. VA Med. Ctr., Hampton, Va., 1976-80, Buffalo, N.Y., 1980-81; Presdl. exchange exec. Kimberly Clark Corp., Neenah, Wis. and Roswell, Ga., 1981-82; dir. VA Med. Ctr., Grand Island, Nebr., 1982—; instr. Cerritos Coll., Calif., 1969-70. Bd. dirs. Project 2M Coordinating Council, Inc., Grand Island, 1985—, Community Concert Assn., 1987—, Grand Island Area United Way, 1987—, Goodwill Industries, 1987—; mem. rev. bd. State of Nebr. Foster Care. Fellow Am. Coll. Healthcare Execs.; mem. Am. Hosp. Assn., Fed. Exec. Assn. (pres.), Nebr. Hosp. Assn., Grand Island C. of C. (legis. affairs com. 1984-85, priorities com. 1984-85). Democrat. Roman Catholic. Club: Riverside Golf (Grand Island). Home: 2508 Apache Rd Grand Island NE 68801 Office: VA Med Ctr 2201 N Broadwell Ave Grand Island NE 68803

ETHRIDGE, DAVID ALLAN, mental health facility administrator; b. Canton, Ill., Oct. 12, 1933; s. Joseph Wesley and Freida Marie (Wright) E.; m. JoAnn Lee Lawhead, May 19, 1956; children: Barry, Deborah, Todd. BS, Western Mich. U., 1956; MA, Wayne State U., 1964; PhD, Mich. State U., 1974. Registered occupational therapist, master therapeutic recreation therapist; cert. rehab. counselor. Rehab. counselor Northville (Mich.) State Hosp., 1962-66; cons. Mich. Dept. of Mental Health, Lansing, 1966-70, bur. chief, 1970-74; dir. Riverside Ctr., Ionia, Mich., 1974-76, Oakdale Regional Ctr., Lapeer, Mich., 1976—; cons. NIMH, Chgo., 1971-78; bd. mem. Accreditation Council for Services for Mentally Retarded and other Developmentally Disabled Persons, Boston, 1986-88. Author: Research in Occupational Therapy, 1971; contbr. articles to profl. jours. Served to capt. USAF, 1956-58. Recipient Mich. Minuteman award Greater Mich. Found., Lansing, 1969, Ernest Blohm award Mich. Activity Therapy Conf., Sugarloaf Mountain, 1983. Fellow Am. Occupational Therapy Assn. (accreditation council, Rockville, Md. 1979-86); mem. Mich. Occupational Therapy Assn. (pres. 1976-72, Pres. award 1972), Nat. Assn. of Supt. Pub. Residential Facilities. Lodge: Rotary (v.p. Lapeer 1986—). Avocations: golf, wine study, travel. Home: 2775 W Genesee Lapeer MI 48446

ETLING, DAVID RICHARD, computer services executive; b. Benton Harbor, Mich., Sept. 21, 1952; s. Forest Richard and Mary Francis (Bowlus) E.; m. Jeanne Marie Grimmer; children: Melissa Megan, Michael David. BS in Polit. Sci., No. Ill. U., 1974. Computer programmer IRS, Washington, 1974-79, computer analyst, 1979-80, computer specialist, team leader, 1980-83; program analyst IRS, Chgo., 1983-86, dist. chief computer services, 1986—. Chmn. election com. Burke (Va.) Ctr. Conservancy, 1980-82; mem. Palatine (Ill.) Library Friends, 1985—; bd. dirs. Linmar Homeowners Assn., Alexandria, Va., 1978-80, pres. 1978-79, treas., 1979-80. Mem. Data Processing Mgmt. Assn. Avocations: geneological research, woodworking. Office: IRS Computer Services Staff 230 S Dearborn St Chicago IL 60604

ETTER, EDITH FRANCES, educator; b. Plummer, Minn., Aug. 7, 1932; d. Fred Eugene and A. Katherine (Polson) Mykleby; m. Wallace Herman Etter, Aug. 28, 1954; 1 son, David Fred. B.S., Bemidji State U., 1963, postgrad. Elem. tchr. Aurora (Minn.) Public Schs., 1952-54, Mounds View (Minn.) Pub. Schs., 1954-55, St. Peter (Minn.) Pub. Schs., 1956-57, Pipestone (Minn.) Pub. Schs., 1957-61, Thief River Falls (Minn.) Pub. Schs., Minn., 1961—. Sunday Sch. tchr. Trinity Luth. Ch., 1962-69; den mother Cub Scouts, 1964-66; chmn. youth bd. Trinity Luth. Ch., 1967-69; youth bd. Thief River Falls Conf., 1967-79, No. Minn. Dist. Youth, 1968-79; Sunday sch. supt. Trinity Luth. Ch., 1972-75; human relations com. Thief River Falls Schs., 1972-73; city planning commn. Thief River Falls, 1980—. Recipient, Honor Roll Tchr. Yr. Minn., 1973; Outstanding Woman educator, 1978; commendation Outstanding Reading Council Activities, 1981. Mem. Thief River Falls Edn. Assn., Kramer-Brown Uniserv (chairperson 1980-81, chairperson Instrn. and Profl. Devel. Council 1975-81), Thief River Falls Edn. Assn. (TEPS chmn., 1962-63, v.p., 1964-66, program chmn., 1964-68, salary com., 1967-68, negotiating council, 1967-68, 69-70, 70-71, 74, 75, 79—, chmn. Improvement Instrn., 1967-69), Minn. Edn. Assn. (sec. resolutions com., 1973—, state instrn. and profl. devel. council, 1975—, chmn. tchr. ctr. instrn., 1978-81, chairperson women's caucus, 1979-81), NEA (del., 1967-69, 71-72, 76—, resolution com., 1976-80), AAUW, Assn. Supervision and Curriculum Devel., Thief River Falls Concert Assn., Internat. Reading Assn., Educators Exceptional Children, Assn. Classroom Tchrs. (div. pres. 1967-71, state pres., 1972-74, del., 1967-69, 71-72. Democrat. Lutheran. Lodge: Modern Woodmen. Home: 416 S Maple Thief River Falls MN 56701 Office: 1424 E Gulf Thief River Falls MN 56701

ETTERS, MICHAEL, restaurant owner; b. Berlin, Fed. Republic Germany, Jan. 1, 1956; came to U.S., 1959; s. William Johnson and Helga Margarita Herta (Schäl) E.; m. Sandra Denise Junkin, May 4, 1977; children: Kevin Michael, Denise Michele. BS in Mktg. and Bus. Adminstrn., Cen. Mo. State U., 1978. Owner, operator Uchie's Fine Foods, Clinton, Mo., 1978—. Mem. Park and Recreation Bd., Clinton, 1985—. Mem. Restaurant Bus. Assn. (research adv. panel 1986—), Mo. Restaurant Assn. (bd. dirs. 1985-86). Republican. Lodge: Optimist. Avocations: softball, canoeing, coaching youth sports. Home: 2202 Arcadia Clinton MO 64735 Office: Uchies Fine Foods 127 W Franklin Clinton MO 64735

ETTINGER, JOSEPH ALAN, lawyer, educator; b. N.Y.C., July 21, 1931; s. Max and Frances E.; B.A., Tulane U., 1954, J.D. with honors, 1956; m. Julie Ann Ettinger; children—Amy Beth, Ellen Jane, Alex William. Admitted to La. bar, 1956, Ill. bar, 1959; asst. corp. counsel City of Chgo., 1959-62; practiced in Chgo., 1962-73, 76—; sr. partner firm Ettinger & Schoenfield, Chgo., 1980—; asso. prof. law Chgo.-Kent Coll., 1973-76; chmn. Village of Olympia Fields (Ill.) Zoning Bd. Appeals, 1969-76; chmn. panel on corrections Welfare Council Met. Chgo., 1969-76. Served to capt., Judge Adv. Gen. Corps, U.S. Army, 1956-59. Recipient Service award Village of Olympia Fields, 1976. Mem. Chgo. Bar Assn., Assn. Criminal Def. Lawyers (gov. 1970-72). Clubs: Ravisloe Country, Carlton Club, Contbr. articles to profl. publs. Office: 415 N LaSalle St Chicago IL 60610

ETZEL, BARBARA COLEMAN, psychologist, educator; b. Pitts., Sept. 19, 1926; d. Walter T. and Ruth (Coleman) E. A.A., Stephens Coll., 1946; B.S. in Psychology, Denison U., 1948; M.S., U. Miami, Fla., 1950; Ph.D. in Exptl. Child Psychology, State U. Iowa, 1953. Staff psychologist Ohio State Bur. Juvenile Research, Columbus, 1953-54; asst. prof. psychology Fla. State U., Tallahassee, 1954-56; chief psychologist, child psychiatry U. Wash. Med. Sch., Seattle, 1956-61; assoc. prof. psychology Western Wash. State U., Bellingham, 1961-65, dir. grad. program in psychology, 1963-65; spl. fellow sect. early learning and devel. NIMH, Bethesda, Md., 1965-66; assoc. prof. dept. human devel. U. Kans., Lawrence, 1965-69, mem. grad. faculty, 1965—, prof. human devel., 1969—, dir. Edna A. Hill Child Devel. Lab., 1965-72, dir. Kans. Ctr. for Research in Early Childhood Edn., 1968-71, assoc. dean Office of Research Adminstrn. and Grad. Sch., 1972-74, dir. John T. Stewart Children's Ctr., 1975-85; vis. prof. Universidad Central de Venezuela, Caracas, 1981-82; cons. Manchester Sch. Presch. Program, U. Mex., Mexico City, 1973-75, George Peabody Tchrs. Coll., 1978, St. Luke's Hosp., Kansas City, Mo., 1981-83, Anne Sullivan Sch. for Handicapped Children, Lima, Peru, 1982-85. Author: (with J.M. LeBlanc and D.M. Baer) New Developments in Behavioral Research, 1977; contbr. articles to profl. jours.; mem. editorial bd. Behavior Analyst, 1979-83. Bd. dirs. Community Children's Ctr., Inc., 1968-71; trustee Ctr. for Research, Inc., U. Kans., 1975-78.

Elected to U. Kans. Women's Hall of Fame, 1975; Japan Soc. Promotion for Sci. fellow, 1981. Fellow Am. Psychol. Assn.; mem. Assn. Behavior Analysis (pres. 1987—, pres.-elect 1986-87), Soc. Research in Child Devel., Midwestern Psychol. Assn., Am. Ednl. Research Assn., AAAS, AAUP, Southwestern Soc. Research in Human Devel., Sigma Xi, Psi Chi, Pi Lambda Theta. Home: Woodsong at JB Ranch Route 1 PO Box 82-E Oskaloosa KS 66066 Office: U Kans Dept Human Devel Lawrence KS 66045

ETZEL, JOHN MARVID, toy company executive; b. Ft. Dodge, Iowa, Oct. 2, 1930; s. William Fred and Pearl L. (Carlson) E.; divorced; children: Gregory, Mark, Kathy, Scott, Cheryl. BS, U. Iowa, 1957, postgrad., 1969-70. Sales mgr. NW Iowa Toy Co., Ft. Dodge, 1958-65; prin., mgr. Midwest Toy Co., Ft. Dodge, 1965—; tchr., coach Lineville (Iowa) High Sch., 1970-72, Coon Rapids (Iowa) High Sch., 1973-74. Office: Midwest Toy Co 510 N 7th St Fort Dodge IA 50501

ETZENBACH, JOHN WILLIAM, periodontist; b. Spring Valley, Ill., Apr. 7, 1957; s. William L. and Gerry H. (Hicks) E. AS, Ill. Valley Community Coll., 1977; BS in Dentistry, U. Ill., 1980, DDS, 1982, Cert. in periodontics, 1984. Practice dentistry specializing in periodontics Peru, Ill., 1984—. Bd. dirs. LaSalle-Peru Twp. High Sch. Bd. Edn., 1985—; fundraiser, health sect. chmn. United Way of Ill. Valley, LaSalle-Peru, 1986. Mem. ADA, Am. Acad. Periodontology, Midwest Soc. Periodontology, Ill. Valley Dental Soc., Western Soc. Periodontology, U. Ill. Dental Alumni Assn. (bd. dirs. 1983—). Club: Ill. Valley Wine (co-dir. 1985—). Avocations: tennis, bicycling, skiing. Home: Rural Rt #1 Oglesby IL 61348 Office: 2200 Marquette Rd Suite 112 Peru IL 61354

EUANS, ROBERT EARL, architect; b. Columbus, Ohio, July 6, 1941; s. William Weldon Euans and Hilda Aurelia (Daugherty) Roberts; m. Carol May Chamberlain, Dec. 18, 1964; children: Bradley James, Lori Ellen, Bryant Scott, Bruce Allen. BArch, Ohio State U., 1967. Registered architect, Ohio, Mich., Pa., Ind., Ill., Minn, Mo., Ky., Fla. Draftsman Blaw-Knox Corp., Pitts., 1967-68; chief draftsman Schofield & Assocs., Columbus, Ohio, 1968-70; project architect Karlsberger & Assocs., Columbus, 1970-74, dir. tech., 1974-77; pvt. practice architecture Columbus, 1977—. Mem. AIA (bd. dirs. Columbus chpt. 1984-86), Architects Soc. Ohio, Constrn. specification Inst. Lutheran. Avocations: camping, sports, swimming. Office: 6770 Lauffer Rd Columbus OH 43229

EUCHNER, EVERETT BRUCE, chemical company executive; b. Chgo., Jan. 9, 1924; s. Charles Andrew and Joan (Dienert) E.; B.S. in Chem. Engring., Purdue U., 1948; M.S. in Organic Chemistry, Case-Western Res. U., 1952; m. Patricia Enz, Aug. 21, 1948; children—Renee, Jenee, Elaine, Eric. With Glidden Coating and Resin, Cleve., 1948—, dir. polymer research, 1961-64, mgr. regional labs., 1964-65, dir. research center, 1965-75, v.p., dir. research and devel., 1976—. Bd. dirs. Community Chest, 1962-64; mem. Zoning Bd. Appeals, Avon Lake, Ohio, 1962-68; mem. Bldg. Code Bd. Appeals, Avon Lake, 1962-68. Served with USAAF, 1942-45. Decorated D.F.C. Mem. Am. Chem. Soc., Cleve. Engring. Soc., Soc. Plastics Industry, Fedn. Socs. Paint Tech., Indsl. Research Inst., AAAS, Sigma Xi. Office: 16651 Sprague Rd Strongsville OH 44136

EULL, JOEL ROY, concrete company executive, consultant; b. Mpls., Sept. 5, 1956; s. Earl Arnold and Clarine Jeanette (Roy) E.; m. Kim M. Kjellberg, June 14, 1980. Student North Hennepin Community Coll., 1981-83. Prodn. mgr. Eull Concrete Products, Monticello, Minn., 1974-79; v.p. Eull Concrete Products, Inc., Albertville, Minn., 1979-84, pres., 1984—; cons. concrete prodn. machinery Zenith Block Co., Mpls., 1985, Acme Brick, Dallas, 1985, Fleming Mfg., Cuba, Mo., 1982-84. Designer, fabricator automated precast concrete system, 1978, automated material storage and handling system, 1984. Campaign vol. Congressman Vin Weber, Wright County, Minn., 1980. Mem. Associated Gen. Contractors, Minn. Utility Contractors Assn. (directory com. 1985, membership com. 1985). Republican. Roman Catholic. Avocations: travel; golf; photography. Home: Route 3 Box 136 Monticello MN 55362 Office: Eull Concrete Products Inc 5836 Large Ave NE Albertville MN 55301

EUTSLER, STEVE DWIGHT, pastor; b. Springfield, Mo., Jan. 8, 1958; s. Dallas Wayne and Paula June (Crabb) E.; m. Jacqueline Gene Plumlee, Jan. 10, 1977. BA, Cen. Bible Coll., 1982. Ordained to ministry Assemblies of God. Asst. pastor Galena (Mo.) Assembly of God, 1979; interim pastor KirbyVille (Mo.) Community Ch., 1981; sr. pastor West Grand Assembly of God, Springfield, Mo., 1982—; sect. treas. Springfield Sect. Assemblies of God, 1983—, youth rep. 1984. Contbr. book revs. to profl. pub. Named one of Outstanding Young Men Am., 1983. Republican. Avocations: gardening, genealogy. Home: 1145 N Dury Springfield MO 65802 Office: West Grand Assembly of God 3144 W Grand Springfield MO 65802

EVA, JOHN ARNOLD, tax executive; b. Jackson, Mich., Feb. 2, 1953. BBA in Acctg., Adrian Coll., 1982. Staff acct. Bond and Co., Jackson, 1983; tax sr. Pannell, Kerr, Forster, Detroit, 1984-85; tax mgr. Patrick Petroleum, Jackson, 1986—. Mem. Am. Inst. CPA's, Mich. Assn. CPAs. Avocations: athletics. Office: Patrick Petroleum Co 301 W Mich Ave Jackson MI 49201

EVANEGA, GEORGE RONALD, medical company executive; b. Cementon, Pa., Feb. 6, 1936; s. George and Helen A. (Cesanek) E.; m. Anne V. Kabat, Oct. 12, 1963; children: George C., Veronica A. BS in Engring., Lehigh U., 1957; MS, Yale U., 1958, PhD in Organic Chemistry, 1961. Research scientist Union Carbide, Tarrytown, N.Y., 1962-69; mgr. Pfizer Cen. Research, Groton, Conn., 1969-75; dir. Biodynamics, Indpls., 1975-78; hauptabteilungsleiter Boehringer Mannheim, Tutzing, Fed. Republic Germany, 1978-79; v.p. Boehringer Mannheim Diagnostics, Indpls., 1979—. NIH fellow, 1961. Mem. Am. Assn. Clin. Chemists, Am. Chem. Soc., N.Y. Acad. Sci. Avocations: tennis, golf, oenology. Home: 3705 Carmel Dr Carmel IN 46032 Office: Boehringer Mannheim Diagnostics 9150 Hague Rd Indianapolis IN 46250

EVANS, CHARLES DAVID, service executive; b. Marion, Va., Aug. 31, 1946; s. Charles Elmer and Irene Bessie (Russell) E.; m. Teresa Catherine Mercer, Dec. 11, 1976; children: Carlee Elizabeth, Chalee Angela. Assoc. Applied Sci., Ohio U., 1965, BS, 1976; MA, Cen. Mich. U., 1978. Adminstrv. asst. Paint Valley Mental Health Ctr., Chillicothe, Ohio, 1975-76, assoc. dir., 1975-79; exec. dir. Tusc and Carroll Mental Health Bd., New Philadelphia, Ohio, 1979-85, Western Stark County Mental Health Ctr., Massillon, Ohio, 1985—; mem. faculty Ohio U., Chillicothe, 1976-79. Acting exec. dir. Belmont Mental Health Bd., St. Clairsville, Ohio, 1983-84. Served to sgt. USMC, 1964-72, Vietnam. Democrat. Methodist. Lodge: Masons (jr. warden 1983-84). Home: 846 S Haueter Sq Bolivar OH 44612 Office: Western Stark County Mental Health Ctr 111 Tremont Ave SW Massillon OH 44646

EVANS, CHARLES SAMUEL, psychologist; b. Feb. 8, 1949; s. D.P. and Lois Evans; m. Judith Ann Hobson. BA in Psychology, Drake U., 1971, MA in Exptl. Psychology, 1975; PhD in Clin. Psychology, The Fielding Inst., 1985—. Lic. psychologist, Minn. Dir. diagnosis, evaluation and treatment ctr. Rochester (Minn.) State Hosp., 1974-81; dir. residential services Harley and Nelson Clinic, 1981-82; co-dir. Associated Clinic Psychology, Mpls., 1982—. Recipient Achievement award State of Minn., 1977, 79. Mem. Am. Assn. on Mental Deficiency, Assn. Behavior Analysts, Minn. Assn. of Behavior Analysts, Prader-Willi Syndrome Assn., Assn. for Alzheimers Disease and Related Disorders. Home: 9604 Brighton Ln Eden Prairie MN 55344 Office: Associated Clinic Psychology 1730 Clifton Place Suite 106 Minneapolis MN 55403

EVANS, CLYDE MERRILL, academic administrator; b. Gallipolis, Ohio, June 26, 1938; s. Owen Wade and Reva Belle (Hutchinson) E.; m. Rosemary Salser, Aug. 26, 1961; children: Mary Margaret, Sarah Leigh, Nancy Jane, Dylan Owen Wade. BA, Union Coll., 1960; MA, Eastern Ky. State U., 1962; PhD, U. So. Miss., 1972; cert. in adminstrn., Ohio U., Athens, 1967. Cert. secondary tchr., Ohio; cert. counselor, Ohio; cert. prin., Ohio. V.p. student devel. Rio Grande (Ohio) Coll., 1972-77, provost, 1977-84; project dir., assoc. prof. sports mgmt. U.S. Sports Acad., Mobile, Ala., 1984-86; dir. guidance and counseling Vinton County Schs., McArthur, Ohio, 1986—. Author short stories. Pres. Rio Grande Village Council, 1968-70, O.O. McIntyre Park Dist., Gallipolis, 1973-84; bd. dirs., treas. Southeastern Ohio Emergency Med. Service, Gallipolis, 1977-80. Named one of Outstanding Young Men of Am., Outstanding Ams. Found., 1970. Mem. Ohio Sch. Counselors Assn. Republican. Baptist. Avocations: reading, sports. Home: Box 36 Rio Grande OH 45674 Office: Vinton County Schs 302 Main St McArthur OH 45674

EVANS, DANIEL E., sausage manufacturing and restaurant chain company executive; b. 1936. With Bob Evans Farms Inc., Columbus, Ohio, 1957—, chmn. bd., sec. and chief exec. officer, also dir. Office: Bob Evans Farms Inc 3776 S High St Box 07863 Sta G Columbus OH 43207 *

EVANS, DAVID LYNN, farm equipment manufacturing company executive; b. Red Oak, Iowa, June 26, 1941; s. John Louis and Margaret Alice (Young) E.; m. Mary Susan Ricke, Aug. 4, 1963; children—John Louis, Mary Lynn, Sarah Leigh, Michael Ricke. BS, Iowa State U., 1964; MBA, U. Pa., 1966. With Deere and Co., Moline, Ill., 1964—, various positions fin. div., indsl. equipment div., corp. staff depts., 1966-77, mgr. mktg. assets, 1977-83; mgr. John Deere Info. Systems, 1983-87, dir. fin. Deere & Co., 1987—; v.p. John Deere Leasing Co., Deere Mktg. Services, Inc.; bd. dirs., chmn. audit com. Mut. Selection Fund, Inc.; bd. dirs. Dataline, Inc. Bd. dirs. World Federalists Assn., 1980-86, v.p. Midwest Region, 1977-82; dir. Campaign for UN Reform, 1979-82, sec., 1980-81, treas., 1982—; trustee John Deere Dealer Group Ins. Trust, 1981-85; elder Presbyn. Ch. Mem. Quad Cities World Affairs Council (pres. 1984), Am. Econ. Assn., UN Assn., Iowa Mfrs. Assn. (chmn. econ. edn. com., 1979-81). Republican. Club: Constitution. Lodge: Elks. Home: 33 Oakbrook Dr Bettendorf IA 52722 Office: John Deere Info Systems 501 Third Ave Moline IL 61265

EVANS, DENNIS EDWARD, banker; b. N.Y.C., Aug. 3, 1938; s. Robert Thomas and Ellen (Martin) E.; m. Mary Jayne Boeger; children: Thomas, James, Robert, David. B.S., Ind. U., 1960, M.B.A., 1961. Vice pres. Glore Forgan William R. Staats Co., investment bankers, N.Y.C., 1969-72; v.p., dir. research, then exec. v.p. resources mgmt. and planning group First Nat. Bank Mpls., 1972-80, pres., 1980-82, chmn., chief exec. officer, 1982-85; pres., chief operating officer First Bank System, Inc., Mpls., 1985—; also dir. First Bank System, Inc.; bd. dirs. Minn. Mut. Life Ins. Co., Minn. Power & Light, Duluth. Bd. dirs. Walker Art Ctr. Mem. Fin. Analysts Fedn., Twin Cities Soc. Cert. Fin. Analysts. Clubs: Minneapolis; Wayzata (Minn.) Country, Minikahda Country. Office: First Bank System Inc 1200 First Bank Place East Minneapolis MN 55480

EVANS, DONALD LEROY, real estate company executive; b. Madison, Wis., Apr. 22, 1933; s. LeRoy E. and Pearl U. Evans. BS, U. Wis., 1959, MS, 1964. Staff appraiser Am. Appraisal Group, Milw., 1959-64; founder, pres. D.L. Evans, Inc., Madison, 1964—. Served as sgt. U.S. Army, 1953-55, Korea. Recipient appreciation award, U. Wis. Real Estate Alumni Assn., 1979. Mem. Am. Soc. Appraisers (sr.; pres. 1968; Appreciation award 1968), Am. Soc. Real Estate Counselors, Am. Inst. Real Estate Appraisers (pres. 1972; Appreciation award 1972), Madison Bd. Realtors (bd. dirs. 1974-76; Appreciation award 1976). Republican. Lutheran. Club: Madison. Lodge: Rotary. Office: D L Evans Co Inc 6409 Odana Rd Madison WI 53719

EVANS, EDWARD WILLIAM, JR., restauranteur; b. Waterbury, Conn., Mar. 5, 1950; s. Edward William and Loribel (Simpson) E.; m. Linda Nell Davis, May, 30, 1983; children: William, Edward III. BBA, Babson Coll., 1972. Asst. mgr. Stouffer's Restaurants, N.Y.C., Phila., 1972-76; food and beverage dir. Holly's Inc., Grand Rapids, Mich., 1976-81; F&B dir. Stouffer's Hotels, Ft. Lauderdale, Fla. and Dayton, Ohio, 1981-84; owner The Fireplace Inn, Dayton, 1984—, Steak Internat., Dayton, 1984—. Republican. Congregationalist. Lodge: Kiwanis. Avocation: pvt. pilot. Office: Fireplace Inn 1818 Woodman Dr Dayton OH 45420

EVANS, EILEEN BEARY, university program director; b. Elk Twp., Pa., May 13, 1946; d. Virgil Robert and Blanche Eleanor (Fulton) Beary; m. Oliver Houston Evans, Sept. 10, 1971; children: Rachel, Ethan. BS magna cum laude, Clarion (Pa.) State Coll., 1968; MA, Purdue U., 1970, PhD, 1976. Tchr. Franklin (Pa.) Area Sch. Dist., 1968; asst. prof. writing S.D. State U., Brookings, 1973-80, supr. of composition, 1978-80, assoc. prof. writing, 1980; asst. prof. bus. writing Western Mich. U., Kalamazoo, 1981-84, coordinator writing lab., 1984—; reviewer Wadsworth Pub. Co., Belmont, Calif., 1978—, Harcourt Brace Jovanovich, San Diego, 1980—, Random House Pub. Co., N.Y.C., 1982—. Author: The Whole Composition, 9th edit., 1982, Instructor's Guide: Harbrace College Handbook, 9th edit., 1982, The Harbrace Test Package: Diagnostic and Achievement Tests, 1982. Mem. Am. Assn. Higher Edn., Nat. Council Tchrs. of English (v.p., pres. elect S.D. chpt. 1979-80), Intellectual Skills Assn. (adv. bd. jour.), Conf. Coll. Composition and Communication, C. of C. (bd. dirs.), World Bus. Council, Chief Exec. Orgn., Phi Kappa Phi, Sigma Tau Delta, Kappa Delta Pi, Alpha Mu Gamma. Lodges: Soroptimist (v.p. Kalamazoo chpt. 1985-86, pres. 1986-87), Spertus Coll. of Judaica (bd. dirs.). Home: 420 Southland Ave Portage MI 49002 Office: Western Mich U Academic Skills Ctr 1044 Moore Hall Kalamazoo MI 49008-5031

EVANS, GARY LEE, communications educator; b. Davison, Mich., June 26, 1938; s. Joe Howard and Annie Annette (Colden) E.; children: Gary James, Aimee Lynn. BA, Wayne State U., 1962; MA, U. Mich., 1965, PhD, 1977. Prof. Eastern Mich. U., Ypsilanti, 1964—; bd. dirs. wilderness edn. program Eastern Mich. U., 1984-86; dir. Summer Inst. for Talented and Gifted Students, Mich. State Bd. Edn., 1984, 85, 86; cons. Med. Data Systems, Medtronic, Ann Arbor, Mich., 1980-84, Mich. Pub. Schs., 1982—, Volvo Automated Systems, Sterling Heights, Mich., 1985—, NSK-Hoover, Inc., Ann Arbor, 1985—. Editor Communication Jour., 1979. Sec. bd. edn. Pinckney Community Schs., 1980-84. Mem. Internat. Communication Assn., Speech Communication assn., Mich. Acad. Sci., Arts and Letters (communication chmn. 1982), Mich. Speech Communication Assn. (communication chmn. 1978—), Phi Kappa Phi, Delta Sigma Rho. Home: 8775 Coyle Dr Pinckney MI 48169 Office: Eastern Mich U 121 Quirk Bldg Ypsilanti MI 48197

EVANS, GERALDINE ANN, academic administrator; b. Zumbrota, Minn., Feb. 24, 1939; d. Wallace William and Elda Ida (Tiedemann) Whipple; m. John Lyle Evans, June 21, 1963; children: John David, Paul William. AA, Rochester Community Coll., 1958; BS, U. Minn., 1960, MA, 1963, PhD, 1968. Cert. tchr., counselor, prin. and supt., Minn. Tchr. Hopkins (Minn.) Pub. Schs., 1960-63; counselor Anoka (Minn.) Pub. Schs., 1963-66; cons. in edn. Mpls., 1966-78; policy analyst Minn. Dept. Edn., St. Paul, 1978-79; dir. personnel Minn. Community Coll. System, St. Paul, 1979-82; pres. Rochester (Minn.) Community Coll., 1982—; bd. dirs. Marquette Bank, Rochester, Minn., 1983—. Vice chair, bd. dirs. Wayzata (Minn.) Sch. Bd., 1980-83; moderator Mizpah United Ch. Christ, Hopkins, 1982; mem. Gov.'s Job Tng. Council, St. Paul, 1983—. Inst. Ednl. Leadership fellow, Washington, 1978-79. Mem. Am. Assn. Community Jr. Colls. (bd. dirs. 1984-87), North Cen. Assn. Community and Jr. Colls. (evaluator). Congregationalist. Avocations: travel, gradening.

EVANS, H. DEAN, state superintendent of public instruction; b. Indpls., Sept. 1, 1929; m. Veronica Evans. AB, Franklin (Ind.) Coll., 1951, LittD (hon.), 1986; MEd, U. Ill., 1952; postgrad., Butler U., Indpls., 1954-64; EdD, Ind. U., 1966. Prin. Eastwood Jr. High Sch., Indpls., 1963-65; asst. supt. Washington Twp. Schs., Indpls., 1965-70, supt. designate, 1970-71, supt., 1971-76; sr. program officer Lilly Endowment, Inc., Indpls., 1976-85; supt. pub. instrn. State of Ind., Indpls., 1985—; founder Ind. Congress on Edn., 1983—; mem. Ind. Edn. Council, 1985—, N. Cen. Regional Edn. Lab., 1985—; chmn. State of Ind. Bd. of Edn., 1985—; bd. dirs. State of Ind. Vocat. and Tech. Edn. Bd., 1985—. Mem. Ind. Econ. Devel. Council, 1985—, Corp. Sci. and Tech., 1985—; chmn. Ind. Computer Consortium, 1985—; bd. visitors Ind. U., 1985—; trustee Franklin Coll.; bd. dirs. Interdepartmental Bd. for Coordination of Human Services, 1985—. Named Educator of Yr., Ind. Assn. Ednl. Secs., 1987; recipient Am. Educator award Eisenhower Meml. Scholarship Found., 1987. Mem. Ind. Assn. Pub. Sch. Supts. (Outstanding Educator award 1982), Nat. Sch. Pub. Relations Assn. (Ind. chpt., Friends of Schs. award 1984), Ind. U. Coll. Edn. Alumni Assn. (Alumni award 1986). Office: Ind Dept Edn State House Bldg Room 229 Indianapolis IN 46204

EVANS, HAROLD EDWARD, banker; b. Detroit, Apr. 23, 1927; s. Harold J. and Mary Esther (Keenoy) E.; m. Margaret A. Reinke, Oct. 28, 1957 (div. Aug. 1968); children: D'lorah Ann, M'liss Lorraine, David Keenoy, Craig Edward; m. Patricia Mae Persons Willy, Mar. 28, 1982. BBA, U. Mich., 1950; cert., Bank Adminstrn. Inst., U. Wis., 1968, Stonier Grad. Sch. Banking, Rutgers U., 1975. Auditor Second Nat. Bank Saginaw, Mich., 1952-61, controller, 1961-73, v.p., cashier, sec., chief fin. officer, 1973—; treas., sec. 2d Nat. Corp., also bd. dirs; treas. Century Life Ins. Co., Mich. 1973; also bd. dirs. Mem. Greater Saginaw Area Health Facilities Planning Council, Saginaw Citizens Council for Cen. Bus. Dist., 1970—; mem. adv. bd. Urban Renewal, chmn. econ. base study com., 1954-55; chmn. Downtown Saginaw Beautificaton Commn., 1968-83; chmn. Greater Saginaw Beautification Residential Com., 1965-68; sec., trustee Saginaw Osteo. Hosp., 1960-84; treas., trustee Saginaw Symphony Orch., 1965-72; past trustee Saginaw Hist. Mus.; treas., dir. United Rehab. Services, 1954-64, Temple Theater Arts Assn., 1980—; fin. officer Saginaw CAP, 1978-84; trustee, treas. Saginaw Valley Dancers, 1977—; v.p. Citizens Banking Corp., Flint, Mich., 1986—. Served with USNR, 1945-46. Mem. Saginaw C. of C., Bank Adminstrn. Inst. (pres. Eastern Mich. conf. 1955-56, v.p. Mich. 1958-59, life mem.), Econ. Club Detroit. Republican. Mem. Unity Ch. Clubs: Breakfast Optimist (dir. 1960—, treas. 1961-63, pres. 1970-72), Univ. Mich. Alumni (Saginaw). Lodge: Elks. Home: 1710 N Charles Saginaw MI 48602 Office: 2d Nat Bank Saginaw 101 N Washington St Saginaw MI 48607

EVANS, JAMES FORREST, agricultural educator; b. Monmouth, Ill., Sept. 3, 1932; s. Walker Hamilton and Ruth Marie (Carden) E.; m. Marlene Mae Cornwell, June 13, 1954; children: Dena Elaine, Lynn Douglas, Loren Eric. BS, Iowa State U., 1954; MBA, U. Chgo., 1961; PhD, U. Ill., 1968. Farm editor Sta. WBAY-radio and TV, Green Bay, Wis., 1954; asst. account exec. Aubrey, Finlay, Marley & Hodgson, Inc., Chgo., 1957-60; mgr. teaching, reaearch and agrl. communications U. Ill., Urbana, 1962-85, chief agrl. communications and extension edn., 1985—; internat. communications devel. council. Midwest Univs. Consortium for Internat. Activities, Lansing, Mich., 1968-71; cons. office communications USDA, Washington, 1972; Thomas Pawlett visiting scholar U. Sydney, Australia, 1979-80. Author: Prairie Farmer and WLS: The Burridge D. Butler Years, 1969, Communications In Agriculture: The American Farm Press, 1974. Served to 2d lt. USAF, 1955-56. Mem. Agrl. Communicators in Edn. (Teaching and Research Excellence award 1979), Assn. Edn. in Journalism and Mass Communication, AAAS, Alpha Zeta. Presbyterian. Avocation: photography. Home: Rural Rt 1 Box 68 Philo IL 61864 Office: U Ill 67 Mumford Hall 1301 W Gregory Urbana IL 61801

EVANS, JANET ANN, music educator; b. Muskegon, Mich., Aug. 26, 1936; d. Burt and Mildred (Gervers) Ruffner; 1 child, Eric Alan. BMus., U. Mich., 1958, MusM, 1959. Permanent secondary teaching cert., Mich. Vocal dir. South Redford (Mich.) Schs., 1959-63, orch., band and vocal dir., 1966-79; band dir. Detroit Pub. Schs., 1979—; band dir. Fine Arts Honor Bands, Detroit Pub. Schs., 1980-82, 84, 86, co-coordinator Fine Arts Festival, 1986. Author: (manual) Build Leadership NOW, 1983, Mich. NOW Policies and Guidelines, 1986; also articles. Mem. legis. liasion Older Women's League, Farmington Hills, Mich., 1981-86; del. Mich. Women's Assembly, Jackson, 1984, 86; precinct del. Mich. Dem. Party, 1984-88; state chair, treas. Mich. Women's Polit. Caucus, Roseville, 1985—. Recipient Band Scholarship award, U. Mich., 1957, 58, Cert. Achievement, Metro-Detroit YWCA, 1985, Cert. Spl. Recognition, Detroit Pub. Schs., 1985, Cert. Appreciation, Mich. Dem. Party, 1986. Member NOW (pres., N.W. Wayne County chpt., 1980-82, developer Mich. State chpt. 1982-84, adminstrv. v.p. 1984-86, Mich. Leadership award 1981, 82, Leadership plaque N.W. Wayne County 1982, Mich. Conf. 1984, 86), ACLU (state bd. dirs. 1985—), Coalition of Labor Union Women (Metro Detroit chpt.), Mich. Women's Studies Assn., Women Band Dirs. Nat. Assn. (nat. historian 1985—), Am. Fedn. Tchrs., Mich. Fedn. Tchrs., Detroit Fedn. Tchrs., Women in the Arts, Inc. (charter), Martha Cook Bldg. Detroit Alumnae Assn. (bd. dirs. 1968-70, 86—), Bus. and Profl. Women's Club (sec. Farmington Hills chpt. 1981-82, Leadership award pin 1982), Alpha Delta Kappa (chpt. pres. 1978-80, pres. dist. II 1980-82, Pres. award pin 1980), Tau Beta Sigma (life), Sigma Alpha Iota. Democrat. Presbyterian. Avocations: reading, swimming, travel. Office: Clinton Sch 8145 Chalfonte Detroit MI 48238

EVANS, JERRY J., pediatrician; b. Hammond, Ind., July 23, 1937; s. George Thomas and Marion Ruth (Gruen) E.; m. Linda Ann Simmance, Sept. 1, 1962 (div. 1983); children: Jeffrey, Gregory, Jennifer; m. Barbara Ann Wellman, June 30, 1984; 1 child, Janelle. BA, Depauw U., 1959; MD, Northwestern U., 1963. Diplomate Am. Bd. Pediatrics, Am. Bd. Perinatal-Neonatal Medicine. Commd. lt. USN, 1962, advanced through grades to lt. comdr., 1969; intern U.S. Naval Hosp., Chelsea, Mass., 1963-64; naval officer U.S. Naval Hosp., Naples, Italy, 1964-67; residentin pediatrics U.S. Naval Hosp., Chelsea, 1967-69; chief of pediatrics U.S. Naval Hosp., Pensacola, Fla., 1969-71; resigned U.S. Naval Hosp., 1971; practice medicine specializing in pediatrics and neonatology Saginaw, Mich., 1971—. Fellow Am. Acad. Pediatrics; mem. N.E. Mich. Pediatric Soc., Saginaw County Med. Soc., Mich. State Med. Soc., Am. Med. Assn. Home: 1754 Brockway Saginaw MI 48602 Office: 4855 Berl Dr Saginaw MI 48604

EVANS, LANE, congressman; b. Rock Island, Ill., Aug. 4, 1951; s. Lee Herbert and Joycelene (Saylor) E. B.A., Augustana Coll., 1974; J.D., Georgetown U., 1978. Bar: Ill. 1978. Mng. atty. Western Ill. Legal Assistance Found., Rock Island, 1978-79; mem. nat. staff Kennedy for Pres., Washington, 1978-80; atty., ptnr. Community Legal Clinic, Rock Island, Ill., 1981-82; mem. 96th, 98th-100th congresses from 17th Ill. Dist., 1979-81, 83—. Served with USMC, 1969-71. Mem. AmVets, Am. Legion, Marine Corps League, Vietnam Vets Ill. Democrat. Roman Catholic. Office: US House of Representatives 328 Cannon House Office Bldg Washington DC 20515 *

EVANS, MALINDA MURPHEY, librarian; b. Bloomington, Ill., Sept. 11, 1935; d. Earl C. and Imogene (Swigart) Murphey; B.S. in L.S., Ill. State U., Normal, 1973; m. Donald Lee Evans, Apr. 25, 1976; children by previous marriage—Melanie, Laurie, Patrick. Librarian, Vespasian Warner Pub. Library, Clinton, Ill., 1973—; author weekly column Bookmarks, Clinton Daily Jour.; pub. sec. Jr. Mens Round Table, 1977. Sec. Central Ill. Tourism Council, 1986-87. Mem. Am., Ill. (dir.-at-large jr. mems. round table), Am. Bus. Women's Assn. (sec. 1976, pres. 1977, Woman of Yr. 1977), Clinton C. of C. (pres. 1985). Methodist. Home: 40 Park Ln Clinton IL 61727 Office: 120 W Johnson St Clinton IL 61727

EVANS, MARK IRA, obstetrician, geneticist; b. Bklyn., May 14, 1952; s. Robert Bernard and Sonia Beatrice (Silverstein) E.; m. Wendy JoAnne Greenwood, Sept. 5, 1981. BS in Psychology, Tufts U., 1973; MD, SUNY, Bklyn., 1978. Diplomate Am. Bd. Ob-Gyn, Am. Bd. Med. Genetics. Resident in ob-gyn U. Chgo., 1978-82; med. genetics fellow NIH, Bethesda, Md., 1982-84; dir. reproductive genetics Hutzel Hosp. Wayne State U., Detroit, 1984—; mem. med. adv. bd. Ehlors Danlos Found., Southgate, Mich., 1986—; mem. ethics com. Am. Coll. Ob-Gyn., Washington, 1987—. Author texts: Pretest: Obstetrics and Gynecology, 3d edit., 1984, 4th edit., 1987, (with Linco) Intrauterine Growth Retardation, 1984, (with several others) Fetal Diagnosis Therapy: Science, Ethics, and the Law, 1988; contbr. numerous articles to sci. jours. Mem. Internat. Fetal Medicine Surgery Soc. (pres. 1986—), Am. Soc. Human Genetics. Jewish. Home: 4734 Rolling Ridge West Bloomfield MI 48033 Office: Hutzel Hosp Dept Reproductive Genetics 4707 Saint Antoine Detroit MI 48201

EVANS, MARTHA MACCHESNEY, educator; b. Chgo., Nov. 2, 1941; d. Luther Johnson and Harriet (MacChesney) E.; A.A., Kendall Jr. Coll., 1961; B.A., Roosevelt U., 1964; M.A., Northeastern Ill. U., 1974; cert. advanced study Nat. Coll. Edn., 1981; Ed.D., Vanderbilt U., 1986. Cert. master tchr., Ill. Tchr. lang. arts East Maine Jr. High Sch., Des Plaines, Ill., 1965-66; caseworker Cook County Dept. Public Aid, Chgo., 1966-67; tchr. English coordinated basic English program Farragut High Sch., Chgo., 1968-73, reading lab. dir., 1973-74, reading clinician Wells High Sch., Chgo., 1974-83, learning disabled tchr., 1983—; instr. continuing edn. dept. Roosevelt U., 1987—; content area reading coordinator, 1984, lead tchr. degrees of reading power, 1984-85 mem. reading clinic adv. bd. Chgo. Bd. Edn., 1976-78; part time instr. Roosevelt U., Chgo., 1987. Chmn. membership com. 2d Unitarian Ch. Chgo., 1978-79, pres. Womans Group, 1979-80, chmn. involvement com., 1984-85 mem. adv. bd. Nat. Hydrocephalus Found., 1984—. Mem. Internat. Reading Assn. (presenter St. Louis regional conv. 1984, Minn. regional conv. 1985), Chgo. Area Reading Assn., Assn. Curriculum Devel., Assn. Children with Learning Disabilities, Phi Delta Kappa. Home: 1029 S Westmore #103 Lombard IL 60148 Office: Wells High School 936 N Ashland Ave Chicago IL 60622

EVANS, MAX WELLINGTON, educator; b. Norwich, Ohio, Mar. 26, 1927; s. John Sherman and Mary Janette (Hoon) E.; m. Kathleen May Briggs, June 4, 1955; children—Eric, Maureen, John. B.Sc., Ohio U., 1951; M.A., Ohio State U., 1956, Ph.D., 1961. Elem. tchr., prin., pub. schs., Bremen, Ohio, 1951-53; exec. head Clinton-Liberty Sch. Dist., Mt. Vernon, Ohio, 1953-55; prin., super. Mt. Vernon City Schs., 1955-58; asst. supt. Marietta (Ohio) City Schs., 1961-64, supt., 1964-67; assoc. prof. edn. adminstrn. Ohio U., Athens, 1967-79, prof., 1980—; chief-of-party Ohio U/US AID team in Botswana; head primary edn. dept. U. Botswana, 1984—; cons. in field. Served with USN, 1945-46. Recipient Bd. Dirs. award Appalachina Ednl. Lab., 1982; Danforth/Nat. Acad. for Sch. Execs. fellow, 1975. Mem. Am. Assn. Sch. Adminstrs., Am. Assn. Sch. Personnel Adminstrs., Nat. Conf. Profs. Ednl. Adminstrn. (pres. 1980), Buckeye Assn. Sch. Adminstrs., AAUP, Internat. Platform Assn., Phi Delta Kappa. Methodist. Clubs: Kiwanis, Rotary. Author: Standards for School Personnel Administrators, 1978; Selecting and Evaluating the School Superintendent, 1981. Office: Ohio Univ McCracken Hall Athens OH 45701

EVANS, PATRICK JOSEPH, marketing company executive; b. Evergreen Park, Ill., Nov. 7, 1951; s. David James and Eileen Ann (Quinn) E.; m. Josephine Anne Cismoski, Nov. 27, 1976; children: Shenade, Lauren, Brett. BS in Biology, No. Ill. U., 1973. Sales mgr. Friden Mailing Equipment, Schiller Park, Ill., 1973-77; leasing broker 1st United Leasing, Northbrook, Ill., 1977-79; pres. Evcor Systems, Inc., Downers Grove, Ill., 1979—; cons., distributor Evcor Distributorships, Downers Grove, 1982—; speaker on future of mailing and shipping industry, 1986—. Patentee in field. Mem. Assn. Ind. Mailing Equipment Dealers, Chgo. Barter Corp. Republican. Roman Catholic. Avocation: sailboat racing. Home: 1608 Mirror Lake Dr Naperville IL 60540 Office: Evcor 4728 Yender Lisle IL 60532

EVANS, ROBERT EDWARD, recording company executive; b. Little Rock, Dec. 2, 1943; s. Robert Edward and Ida Vera (Thomas) E.; m. Doris, Dec. 23, 1972; children—April, Kim. Writer/singer Trevia Record Co., Detroit, 1972-73, Big Star Records, Detroit, 1973-75, D.T. Records, 1975-81, Liberty Records; owner, pres. April Records, 1981—, Funnwagon Music Co., 1983—; pub. relations dir. Renaissance Contemporary Music, Inc., 1980-81. Jehovah's Witness. Recorded album Shades of Love/Gold, 1981; recs. include: You Can't Stop Me From Loving You (included in Blues Archives, U. Miss. Ctr. Cultural Study 1983), The Ingredient of Love.

EVANS, ROBERT L., restaurant executive; b. Sugar Ridge, Ohio, May 30, 1918; s. Stan and Elizabeth E.; m. Jewell Waters, 1940; children: Stanley, Robin, Gwen, Debbie, Steve, Bobbie. Grad., Ohio State U. Engaged in restaurant bus. 1944—; now pres. Bob Evans Farms, Inc., Columbus, Ohio.; mem. Vet. Medicine Adv. Com. Ohio, Dept. Agr. Meat Adv. Bd.; dir. council Food Industries Ctr. Fund raising chmn. Ohio Soc. Prevention Blindness, 1977; hon. chmn. Heart Fund Drive, 1979; state chmn. Easter Seal Campaign; mem. exec. bd. Rio Grande Coll.; sponsor Ohio 4-H Conservation Camp; trustee Ohio Forestry Assn. Served with AUS, 1944-45. Named Ohio Soil Conservationist of Year, 1969, Ohio Wildlife Habitat Conservationist of Year, 1972, 80; named Ohio Ambassador Natural Resources, 1981; named to Hall of Fame Ohio State Fair, 1976, Hall of Fame Ohio 4-H, 1982; recipient Bus. Tourism award, 1973, Gov. Ohio award, 1978, Meritorious Service award Ohio State U. Coll. Agr., 1978, Ohio Conservation Achievement award, 1978, Wildlife Council Service award, 1978, 79, Meritorius Service award Ohio State U. Coll. Agr. Alumni, 1983, Hon. award Furture Farmers Am., Disting. Service award Gallia County Soil and Water Conservation Dist., Nat. Charolais Congress Breeders award. Mem. Am. Charolais Assn. (past dir.), 4-H Club (adv. bd. Ohio), Ohio Charolais Assn. (dir.), Ohio Wildlife Council, Ohio C. of C. (dir.); mem. Spanish-Barb Mustang Breeders Assn. (founding mem.). Home: Route 2 Mt Zion Rd Bidwell OH 45614 Office: Bob Evans Farms Inc 3776 S High St Columbus OH 43207 *

EVANS, ROBERT OWEN, English language educator, administrator; b. Chgo., Sept. 19, 1919; s. Franklin Bachelder and Arline Henrietta (Brown) E.; m. Margery Brooks, Aug. 2, 1941; children—Robert Jr., Michele Chosney, Douglas Brooks. A.B., U. Chgo., 1941; M.A., U. Fla., 1950, Ph.D., 1954; postgrad., Harvard U., 1950-51. Instr., U. Fla., Gainesville, 1948-54; instr. to prof. U. Ky., Lexington, 1954-80, dir. honors program, 1966-78; prof, English, dir. gen. honors U. N.Mex., Albuquerque, 1980-86, prof. emeritus, 1986—; vis. prof., U. Helsinki, Finland, 1958-59; U. des Saarlands, Saarbrucken, Germany, 1963-64, Lincoln Coll., Oxford U., England, 1963, U. Wis., Madison, 1967-68, Am. Coll., Paris, 1970-71; dir. Nat. Collegiate Honors Council, 1975—, pres. 1978. Author: Osier Cage, 1966; Metrical Elision, 1966. Editor: Style/Rhetoric/Rhythm, 1966; Graham Greene-Critical Considerations, 1964; Wm. Golding Critical Considerations, 1976. Contbr. articles to profl. jours. Bd. dirs. Macatawa Cottagers Assn., Mich., 1954-80. Mem. MLA (USA & Finland), Internat. Assn. Univ. Profs. English, Nat. Collegiate Honors Council (pres. 1978), Internat. Comparative Lit. Assn., Western Regional Honors Council, Phi Beta Kappa, Phi Kappa Phi, Psi Upsilon. Democrat. Episcopalian. Home: PO Box 4 Macatawa MI 49434

EVANS, TERENCE THOMAS, judge; b. Milw., Mar. 25, 1940; s. Robert Hansen and Jeanett (Walters) E.; m. Joan Marie Witte, July 24, 1965; children: Kelly Elizabeth, Christine Marie, David Rourke. B.A., Marquette U., 1962, J.D., 1967. Bar: Wis. 1967. Law clk. to justice Wis. Supreme Ct., 1967-68; dist. atty. Milw. County, 1968-70; pvt. practice Milw., 1970-74; circuit judge State of Wis., 1974-80; judge U.S. Dist. Ct. Eastern Dist. Wis., Milw., 1980—. Mem. ABA, State Bar Wis., Milw. Bar Assn. Roman Catholic. Office: U S Dist Ct 371 U S Courthouse 517 E Wisconsin Ave Milwaukee WI 53202 *

EVANS, TIMOTHY RICHARD, architect; b. Bay City, Mich., Aug. 6, 1946; s. Donald M. and Florence E. (Smith) E.; m. Linda Kay Dice, May 7, 1967; children: Cindy Lee, Kelly Jean. Student, Delta Coll., 1964-66; BArch, U. Mich., 1970. Registered architect, Mich. Architect Alden Dow, Architect, Midland, Mich., 1970-76, Wm. Prine, Arch., Saginaw, Mich., 1977-82; pvt. practice architecture Sanford, 1982—. Contbr. articles to profl. jours. Served to 2d lt. USNG, 1970-76. Mem. AIA (pres., bd. dirs. Saginaw chpt. 1982-86), Mich. Soc. Architects, Energy Resource Group. Republican. Club: Nature Ctr. (Midland, Mich.). Avocations: sailing, boating, swimming, photography, camping. Home and Office: 2365 N Meridian Sanford MI 48657

EVENBECK, SCOTT EDWARD, university official, psychologist; b. Findlay, Ohio, Aug. 14, 1946; s. Benjamin F. and Norma H. (Kelley) E.; m. Elizabeth Ann Jones, Aug. 14, 1970; 1 child, Benjamin F. III. AB, Ind. U., 1968; MA, U. N.C., Chapel Hill, 1971, PhD, 1972. Asst. prof. psychology Ind. U.-Purdue U., Indpls., 1972-76, asst. dean Purdue U. Sch. Sci., 1977-79, assoc. dean, 1979-80, assoc. dir. adminstrv. affairs, assoc. prof. psychology, 1976—, assoc. dir. adminstrv. affairs, 1980-85, dir. continuing studies, 1985—, also assoc. dean Ind. U. Sch. Continuing Studies, 1985—; bd. dirs. Parent Info. Resource Center, 1977-85. Contbr. articles in field to profl. jours. Mem. exec. com., asst. treas., v.p., pres. Am. Lung Assn. Central Ind., bd. dirs., 1985—, v.p. 1986; pres.-elect Am. Lung Assn. Ind., 1987; bd. dirs. Christamore House, 1985—; sec. Indpls.-Searborough Peace Games, 1977-80. USPHS trainee, 1968-72; Arthur R. Metz scholar Ind. U., 1964-68. Mem. Am. Psychol. Assn., Nat. Council Univ. Research Adminstrs. (mem. exec. com. 1979-80), Indpls. C. of C. (mem. exec. com. speaker's bur.). Republican. Episcopalian. Clubs: Kiwanis, Masons. Home: 1630 E 83d St Indianapolis IN 46240 Office: 620 Union Dr Indianapolis IN 46202

EVENS, RONALD GENE, radiologist; b. St. Louis, Sept. 24, 1939; s. Robert and Dorothy (Lupkey) E.; m. Hanna Blunk, Sept. 3, 1960; children: Ronald Gene, Christine, Amanda. BA, Washington U., 1960, MD, 1964, postgrad. in bus. and edn., 1970-71. Intern Barnes Hosp., St. Louis, 1964-65; resident Mallinckrodt Inst. Radiology, St. Louis, 1965-66, 68-70, prof., head dept. radiology, dir., 1971-72; Elizabeth Mallinckrodt prof., head radiology dept., dir. Mallinckrodt Inst. Radiology, 1972—; research assoc. Nat. Heart Inst., 1966-68; asst. prof. radiology, v.p. Washington U. Med. Sch., 1970-71, prof., head dept. radiology, dir., 1971-72, Elizabeth Mallinckrodt prof., head radiology dept., 1972—; radiologist-in-chief Barnes Hosp., St. Louis, 1971—, Children's Hosp., 1971—; mem. adv. com. on specialty and geog. distbn. of physicians Inst. Medicine, Nat. Acad. Scis., 1974-76, Hickey lectr., 1976, Carmen lectr., 1983; Hampton lectr. Harvard U., 1984.; ann. orator Can. Radiol. Soc., 1984; dir. City Bank St. Louis; chmn. bd. Med. Care Group St. Louis, 1980—. Contbr. over 120 articles to profl. jours. Active Boy Scouts Am., 1975-81; bd. dirs. St. Louis Comprehensive Neighborhood Health Ctr., OEO, 1970-74; elder Glendale Presbyn. Ch., 1971-74, Kirkwood Presbyn. Ch., 1983—. Served with USPHS, 1966-68. Advance Acad. fellow James Picker Found, 1970; recipient Disting. Serviced award. St. Louis C. of C., 1972. Fellow Am. Coll. Radiology; mem. AMA, Mo. Radiol. Soc. (pres. 1977-78), Soc. Nuclear Medicine (trustee 1971-75), St. Louis Med. Soc., Mo. State Med. Assn., Soc. Chmn. Acad. Radiology Depts. (pres. 1979), Radiol. Soc. N.Am., Assn. Univ. Radiologists, Am. Roentgen Ray Soc. (v.p. 1982, treas. 1983—), Phi Beta Kappa, AlphaOmega Alpha (Sheard-Sanford award). Office: 510 S Kingshighway Saint Louis MO 63110 Office: Washington U Dept of Radiology Saint Louis MO 63130

EVENSTAD, KENNETH L., pharmaceutical manufacturing executive; b. Baudette, Minn., July 9, 1943; s. O.M. and Sophie (Mickelson) E.; m. Grace Gregory, Dec. 17, 1966; children: Serene, Mark. BS in Pharmacy, U. Minn., 1967. Pres., chief exec. officer Upsher-Smith Labs., Mpls., 1969—. Patentee in field, 1982. Mem. Am. Pharm. Assn., Minn. State Pharm. Assn., Young Pres. Orgn. Republican. Episcopalian. Clubs: Chevaliers du Tastevin (Mpls.); Wayzata.

EVEREST, GORDON C., business educator; b. Red Deer, Alta., Can., July 19, 1940; came to U.S., 1963; s. Charles J. and Olive (Lefenko) E.; m. Martha V. Watt, Oct. 21, 1967; children: James, Robert, Mary, Sarah, Peter. B Commerce, U. Alta., 1962; SM, MIT, 1965; PhD in Bus., U. Pa., 1974. Tech. cons. Auerbach Corp., Phila., 1967-70; asst. prof. bus. computing U. Minn., Mpls., 1971-76, assoc. prof., 1976—; cons. Minn. Dept. Transportation, St. Paul, 1984—. Author: (book) Database Management, 1986; editor: Readings in Mgmt. Info. Systems, 1976. Vice chmn. computer adv. com. Roseville Sch. Dist. PTA, 1983—. Named Boss of Yr., Am. Bus. Women's Assn., 1978. Mem. Am. Fedn. Info. Processing (spl. com. right to privacy 1975-82), Assn. Computing Machinery, Am. Nat. Standards Inst., Common Data Model Task Group, Codasyl Systems Com. Lutheran. Avocation: badminton. Office: U Minn Sch Mgmt Minneapolis MN 55455

EVERETT, JONATHAN JUBAL, lawyer; b. Bellingham, Wash., Sept. 10, 1950; s. John Thomas and Dawn Irene (Speirs) E.; m. Mary Kathryn Penar, May 27, 1973. BA, U. Chgo., 1972; MA, Harvard U., 1975, JD, 1979. Bar: Calif. 1981, Ill. 1982. Law clk. presiding judge U.S. Ct. Appeals (5th cir.), Baton Rouge, 1979-80; assoc. O'Melveny and Myers, Los Angeles, 1980-81, Mayer, Brown and Platt, Chgo., 1982-84, Skadden, Arps, Slate, Meagher and Flom, Chgo., 1984-87; ptnr. Skadden, Arps, Slate, Meagher and Flom, 1987—. Office: Skadden Arps et al 333 W Wacker Dr Chicago IL 60606

EVERETT, RONALD EMERSON, government official; b. Columbus, Ohio, Jan. 4, 1937; s. John Carmen and Hermione Alicia (Lensner) E.; B.A., Ohio U., 1959; postgrad. Baldwin-Wallace Coll., 1962-63; grad. U.S. Army Command and Gen. Staff Coll., 1978, U.S. Army War Coll., 1984; cert. Inst. Cost Analysis, 1982; m. Nancy Helen Leibersberger, Aug. 10, 1963; children—Darryl William, Darlene Anne, John Lee. Reporter, Dun & Bradstreet, Cleve., 1960-66; program analyst Lewis Research Center, NASA, Cleve., 1967-70, contract price analyst and negotiator, 1970-85, chief contract support br., 1985-86; chief space systems br., 1986—. Served with inf. U.S. Army, 1960; now col. USAR. Decorated Meritorious Service medal with two oak leaf clusters, Army Commendation medal with oak leaf cluster; recipient NASA Group Achievement awards, Sustained Superior Performance award, 1974, 80; cert. cost analyst. Mem. Assn. Govt. Accts., Res. Officer Assn., Internat. Platform Assn., Am. Def. Preparedness Assn., Assn. U.S. Army, Am. Security Council, Nat. Estimating Soc., Army War Coll. Found. Republican. Mem. Reformed Ch. in Am. Home: 27904 Blossom Blvd North Olmsted OH 44070 Office: 21000 Brookpark Rd Cleveland OH 44135

EVERHART, ROBERT (BOBBY WILLIAMS), entertainer, songwriter, recording artist; b. St. Edward, Nebr., June 16, 1936; s. Phillip McClelland and Martha Matilda (Meyer) Everhart. Student U. Nebr., 1959-62, Iowa Western Coll., 1976-78, U. Iowa, 1979-80. Pres., Royal Flair Music, BMI Pub., Council Bluffs, Iowa, 1974—; rec. artist Folkways Records, N.Y.C., Westwood Records, G.B., Folk Variety Records, Europe, Allied Records, Philippines, RCA Records, N.Z., internat. concert artist performing traditional Am. country and folk music; festival promoter Old-Time Country Music Contest and Pioneer Exposition, 1976—; pres. Nat. Traditional Country Music Assn., Inc., 1982—; regular performer La. Hayride, 1985—. Served with USN, 1954-59. Mem. Great Plains Old Time Music Assn., Kans. Bluegrass Assn., Mo. Area Blue Grass Assn., Minn. Old Time Music Assn., Heart of the Ozarks Assn., Acad. Country Music, Nat. Bluegrass Assn., Ill. Traditional Country Music Assn., Tri-State Bluegrass Assn., Internat. Bluegrass Music Assn., Swallow Hill Music Assn., Ind. Friends of Country Music, Profl. Musicians Club of Iowa. Democrat. Lutheran. Club: Carribean. Editor, Tradition Country Music Mag., 1980—; author: Clara Bell, 1976; Hart's Bluff, 1977; (poetry) Silver Bullets, 1979; Savage Trumpet, 1980; Prairie Sunrise, 1982; Snoopy Goes to Mexico, 1983; (TV scripts) The Life of Jimmie Rodgers, 1984, Matecombe Treasure, 1984; recordings include: Let's Go, Dream Angel, She Sings Sad Songs, Love to Make Love, Bad Woman Blues. Address: 106 Navajo Lake Manawa Council Bluffs IA 51501

EVERINGHAM, LYLE J., grocery chain executive; b. Flint, Mich., May 5, 1926; s. Kenneth L. and Christine (Everingham) E.; m. Rlene Lajiness, Mar. 31, 1929; children: Nancy, Mark, Christine. Student, U. Toledo, 1956-63. With Kroger Co., 1946—; v.p. Kroger Co. (Dayton div.), Ohio, 1963-64; v.p. produce merchandising Kroger Co. (Dayton div.), Cin., 1964-65; successively v.p. Kroger Co. (Dayton div.), from 1966. Active Mt. Lookout Civic Club; Mem. Cin. Bus. Com. Served with cav. AUS, 1943-46. Roman Catholic. Clubs: Cin. Country (Cin.), Queen City (Cin.), Comml. (Cin.). Office: The Kroger Co 1014 Vine St Cincinnati OH 45202-1119

EVERINGHAM, MARILYN MARIE, computer educator; b. Lansing, Mich., Nov. 5, 1952; d. Donald Rex and Norma June (Lippincott) Sidel. BA, Mich. State U., 1977. Cert. high sch. tchr., Mich. Tchr. Olivet (Mich.) High Sch., 1978-80; ednl. programs coordinator Mich. State U., E. Lansing, 1982—. Mem. Soc. Tech. Communication (Achievement award 1985, Merit award 1987), Assn. for Computing Machinery (mem. spl. interest group on univ. and coll. computing services, award 1985). Home: 26 University Dr East Lansing MI 48823 Office: Mich State U 515 Computer Ctr East Lansing MI 48824-1042

EVERMAN, CYNDEE E., data processing educator; b. Portsmouth, Ohio, Aug. 12, 1959; s. Douglas Earl and Wilma Jean (Stroth) E. Assoc. in Applied Bus., Shawnee State Community Coll., 1977-79. Sr. data processing instr. Delaware City County Joint Vocat. Sch., Ohio, 1979-80; sr. programmer/analyst State of Ohio, Columbus, 1980-81; tng. adminstr. Warner Cable Communications, Columbus, 1981-86, project mgr., 1986—. Mem. Am. Youth Hostels. Mem. Assn. System Mgrs., Am. Soc. Tng. and Devel., Data Processing Mgrs. Assn. Republican. Avocations: bicycling, volleyball, racquetball, tennis. Office: Warner Cable Communications 2222 Dividend Dr Columbus OH 43228

EVERS, LA FONDA A., library director; b. Randalia, Iowa, Feb. 13, 1931; d. William Donald and Loretta Caroline (Treager) Bronn; m. Wayne Leonard Evers, Mar. 22, 1949; children—Keith Wayne, Cheri Lynn. B.S., Eastern Ill. U., 1981; studied music with Allen Hancock, Santa Maria, Calif., 1968-70. Cert. social rehab. activity dir., social services dir. Social rehab. dir. Wil-Care Home, Wilmington, Ill., 1971-74; workshop tchr. Assn. Health Care, Chgo., 1974; social rehab. dir. Ill. Knights Templar, Paxton, 1975-79; activity therapist Ford County Home, Paxton, 1979-81; coordinator Ford County Task Force on Early Childhood Devel.; ednl. advocate for State Ill. Children's Family Service; dir. Paxton Carnegie Library, 1981—. Bd. dirs. Paxton Nursery Sch., 1983—; mem. welfare services com. and personnel adv. bd. Ford County (Ill.) Dept. Pub. Aid, 1984—. Mem. Lincoln Trails Library Assn. (sec. 1981-82, v.p. 1982-83, pres. elect 1985). Lutheran. Lodge: Order Eastern Star (officer Paxton 1978-81). Home: 1001 Park Terr Paxton IL 60957 Office: Paxton Carnegie Library 154 S Market Paxton IL 60957

EVERSON, DIANE LOUISE, publishing executive; b. Edgerton, Wis., Mar. 27, 1953; s. Harland Everett and Helen Viola (Oliver) E. BS, Carroll Coll., 1975. Advt. mgr. Edgerton (Wis.) Reporter, 1976—; pres. Silk Screen Customs 1981—. Pub. Directions Mag., 1981. Trustee Carroll Coll., 1987—. Democrat. Lutheran. Home: 114 Kellogg Rd Edgerton WI 53534 Office: Directions Pub 21 N Henry Edgerton WI 53534

EVERY, RUSSEL B., business executive; b. Bridgewater, Mich., Oct. 13, 1924; s. William Ward and Ola M. (Bennet) E.; m. Marion J. Olson, May 12, 1945; children—Gloria, David, William. Student, Cleary Coll. With Midland-Ross Corp., 1969-76, v.p., gen. mgr. frame div., group v.p. automotive, until 1976; an organizer Midland Steel Products Co., Cleve., 1976; with Midsco, Inc. (merged into Lamson & Sessions Co.), Lakewood, Ohio; chmn., pres. Midsco, Inc. (merged into Lamson & Sessions Co.), 1979—; pres., chief operating officer, dir. Lamsom & Sessions Co., 1980-84, chmn., pres., chief exec. officer, 1984—. Served with USN. Mem. Am. Mgmt. Assn., Ohio Mfrs. Assn., Ohio C. of C., Greater Cleveland Growth Assn., Presidents Assn., Soc. Automotive Engrs., U.S. C. of C. Clubs: Lakewood Country, Detroit Athletic, Mid-Day, Union, Pepper Pike (Ohio) Country. Office: Lamson & Sessions Co 25701 Science Park Dr Cleveland OH 44122

EWALD, CHRISTOPHER JOHN, architect; b. Toledo, Mar. 16, 1952; s. Alvin E. and Ruth (Thorton) E.; m. Vicki Lynn Whitescarver, Apr. 1, 1978; children—Katrina Renee, Melinda Anne. B.Arch., Kent State U., 1975. Student architect Bauer, Stark and Lashbrook, Toledo, 1971-75, architect-in-tng., 1975-78, architect, 1978, assoc., 1979-80, sr. assoc., 1980-83, prodn. dir., 1981-83; project mgr. SSOE, Inc., Toledo, 1983-85, assoc., 1985—. Mem. AIA (sec. Toledo chpt. 1982-83, v.p. 1984, pres. 1985, bd. dirs. 1986—), Architects Soc. Ohio (alt. dir. 1984-85, bd. dirs. 1986—). Lodge: Kiwanis (dir. 1984-85). Home: 3232 River Rd Toledo OH 43614

EWALD, HENRY THEODORE, JR., foundation executive; b. Detroit, Sept. 29, 1924; s. Henry T. and Oleta (Stiles) E.; m. Carolyn Davison Taylor, June 24, 1950; children: Wendy, Holly, Henry, John, Tracey, Kristi. BA, Yale U., 1947; LLB, Detroit Coll. Law, 1950. Bar: Mich. 1951. Pres. Ted Ewald Chevrolet Co., Detroit, 1958—; pres. H.T. Ewald Found., Grosse Pointe, Mich., 1954—. Bd. dirs. Franklin Wright Settlement, Detroit Ednl. TV-PBS. Recipient Northwood Inst. Dealer Edn. award 1973; named Michiganian of Yr., Detroit News, 1984, One of Five Unsung Sports Heroes of Met. Detroit, Police Athletic League, 1985. Bd. dirs. Detroit Pistons, Hutzel Hosp. Clubs: University, Country of Detroit. Office: 15175 E Jefferson Grosse Pointe MI 48230

EWBANK, ROBERT CHAPMAN, JR., dentist; b. Chgo., July 19, 1941; s. Robert Chapman and Grace (White) E.; m. Mary Daisy Read, June 16, 1962; children: Michael Andrew, Robert Charles. Student, Milligan Coll., 1959-61; DDS, Northwestern U., 1965. Dentist USAF, 1965-67; pvt. practice gen. dentistry Johnson City, Tenn., 1967-71; pvt. practicegen. dentistry Springfield, Ohio, 1972—; mem. teaching staff Mashoko Christian Hosp., Zimbabwe, 1984; mem. staff Mercy Med. Ctr., Springfield, 1972—; pres. Global Missionary Radio Ministries, Inc., 1985—. Bd. dirs. Mt. Healthy Christian Home, Cin., 1979—. Served to capt. USAF, 1965-67. Mem. Mad River Valley Dental Soc. (treas. 1976-78, v.p. 1979, pres.-elect 1980, pres. 1981), ADA, Ohio Dental Assn. (del. 1982-84), Acad. Gen. Dentistry, Am. Orthopedic Soc., Clinical Straight Wire Found., Christian Benevolent Assn. (bd. dirs. 1975—), Am. Orthodontic Soc. Avocations: ch. activities, boating, golf, racquetball, basketball and soccer. Home: 110 Brighton Rd Springfield OH 45504 Office: 914 N Limestone St Springfield OH 45503

EWBANK, THOMAS PETERS, banker, lawyer; b. Indpls., Dec. 29, 1943; s. William Curtis and Maxine Stuart (Peters) E.; m. Alice Ann Shelton, June 8, 1968; children—William Curtis, Ann Shelton. Student Stanford U., 1961-62; A.B., Ind. U., 1965, J.D., 1969. Bar: Ind. 1969, U.S. Tax Ct., 1969, U.S. Dist. Ct. (so. dist.) Ind. 1969, U.S. Supreme Ct. 1974. Legis. asst. Ind. Legis. Council, 1966-67; estate and inheritance tax adminstr. Mchts. Nat. Bank, Indpls., 1967-69; assoc. Hilgedag, Johnson, Secrest and Murphy, Indpls., 1969-71; asst. gen. counsel Everett I. Brown Co., Indpls., 1971-72; with Mchts. Nat. Bank & Trust Co., Indpls., 1972—, successively probate adminstr., head probate div., head personal account adminstrn. group in trust div., v.p. and sr. trust officer, sr. v.p., head trust and investment div. Asst. treas. Ruckelshaus for U.S. Senator Com., 1970; candidate for Ind. Legislature, 1970, 74. Fellow Ind. Bar Found. (patron); mem. Estate Planning Council Indpls. (pres. 1982-83), Indpls. Bar Assn., Ind. Bar Assn., Indpls. Bar Found. (treas. 1976-81), Blue Key. Republican. Baptist. Clubs: Meridian Hills Country, Broadmoor Country, Riviera, Masons (Indpls.); Kiwanis Circle K Internat. (internat. trustee 1963-65, pres. 1964-65, George Hixson Diamond fellow), Kiwanis of Indpls. (treas. 1980-81, 84-85 designated a maj. builder 1983). Contbr. articles to profl. jours. Home: 4516 Sylvan Rd Indianapolis IN 46208 Office: One Merchants Plaza Suite 600E Indianapolis IN 46255

EWEN, DALE EDWARD, mathematics educator; b. Kampsville, Ill., June 10, 1941; s. Edward Joseph and Letha Marie (Calvey) E.; m. Carol Joyce Shaw, Jan. 28, 1967; children: Kurt, Amy. BS, U. Ill., 1963, MEd, 1966; postgrad., U. Minn., 1966. Math. tchr., dept. chairperson Rantoul (Ill.) Twp. High Sch., 1963-69, Parkland Coll., Champaign, Ill., 1969—. Author: Mathematics for Career Education, 1972, Physics for Career Education, 1974, Mathematics for Technical Education, 1976, Technical Calculus, 1977, Physics for Technical Education, 1981, Trigonometry with Applications, 1984, Scientific Calculator Handbook, 1984, Elementary Technical Mathematics, 1987. Mem. Am. Math. Assn. Two-Year Colls. (Midwest v.p. 1983-87), Ill. Math. Assn. Community Colls. (pres. 1980-81), Ill. Council Tchrs. Math. (chairperson bd. dirs. 1978-81), Math. Assn. Am., Nat. Council Tchrs. Math. Home: Rt 3 Box 142 Champaign IL 61821 Office: Parkland College 2400 W Bradley Ave Champaign IL 61821

EWERT, RUSSELL HOWARD, bank executive; b. St. Paul, Mar. 7, 1935; s. Russell Howard Ewert and Josephine (Conger) Ewert Murphy; m. Marilyn Norgard, Aug. 30, 1957 (div. 1980); children: Russell III, Ann Brenan, Stephen David; m. Pat. Guyer, Aug. 10, 1985. BSL, U. Minn., 1958, BBA with honors, 1960, JD, 1960. Bar: Minn. 1960, Ill. 1980. Asst. v.p., asst. sec. First Capital Corp., Chgo., 1961-64; asst. cashier First Nat. Bank, Chgo., 1964-68, v.p., loan div. head, 1968-74, v.p., sr. lending officer, 1978-80; v.p., regional mgr. First Nat. Bank, Kansas City, Mo., 1974-78; pres., chief exec. officer Drexel Nat. Bank, Chgo., 1980—; dir. Suburban Trust and Savs. Bank, Oak Park, Ill. Co-author: Obtaining Unsecured Loans, 1976. Gen. chmn. Fighting Fund for Freedom dinner Chgo. Southside NAACP, 1984; Ill. state treas. Jesse Jackson for Pres. Com.; bd. advisors Mercy Hosp. and Med. Ctr., Chgo.; active Chgo. Crime Commn., Cosmopolitan C. of C., Chgo. Recipient Cosmopolitan C. of C. and U.S. SBA award of merit, 1968; Talent Assistant Program cert. of appreciation, 1970; Am. Inst. Banking award for outstanding contbns., 1972; Malcolm X Ednl. Found. award for outstanding contbns., 1974; Am. Legion citation of appreciation, 1982; Chgo. South End Jaycees Bus. Person of Month award, 1982; Black Contractors United Spl. award, 1982; Abraham Lincoln Centre Select Four Community Leadership award, 1982; Mt. Olive African Meth. Episc. Ch., Inc. award of honor, 1983; City Colls. of Chgo. cert. of appreciation, 1983. Mem. ABA, Chgo. Bar Assn. Home: 2106 N Magnolia Chicago IL 60614 Office: Drexel Nat Bank 3401 S King Dr Chicago IL 60616

EWING, DONNA MARIE, business educator; b. McLean, Ill., Apr. 16, 1936; m. Nathaniel H. Ewing, Dec. 24, 1954; children: Nathaniel H. Jr., Cindy Marie. BS in Bus. Edn., Ill. State U., 1971, MS in Bus., 1975; postgrad., U. Ill., 1985—. Acctg. clk., exec. sec. Ill. Agrl. Assn., Bloomington, 1971-75; instr. secretarial sci. Ill. Cen. Coll., East Peoria, 1975—; cons. econ. edn. book Caterpillar. Mem. Nat. Bus. Edn. Assn., Assn. Records Mgrs. and Adminstrs. (chmn. scholarship com.), Ill. Bus. Edn. Assn., Ill. Vocat. Assn., Cen. Ill. Word Processing Assn., Peoria Area Bus.

Edn. Assn., Faculty Forum, Kappa Omicron Phi, Kappa Delta Pi, Delta Pi Epsilon (v.p.), Pi Omega Pi. Republican. Methodist. Club: Home Extension (Armington, Ill.). Avocation: painting. Home: Box 34 Armington IL 61721 Office: Ill Cen Coll East Peoria IL 61635

EWING, RAYMOND PEYTON, educator, management consultant; b. Hannibal, Mo., July 31, 1925; s. Larama Angelo and Winona Fern (Adams) E.; A.A., Hannibal La-Grange Coll., 1948; B.A., William Jewell Coll., 1949; M.A. in Humanities, U. Chgo., 1950; m. Audrey Jane Schulze, May 7, 1949; 1 dau., Jane Ann. Marketing mgmt. trainee Montgomery-Wards, Chgo., 1951-52; sr. editor Commerce Clearing House, Chgo., 1952-60; corp. communications dir. Allstate Ins. Cos. & Allstate Enterprises, Northbrook, Ill., 1960-85, issues mgmt. dir., 1979-85, pres. Issues Mgmt. Cons. Group, 1985—; assoc. prof., dir. corp. pub. relations program Medill Sch. Journalism Northwestern U., Evanston, Ill., 1986—; pub. relations dir. Chicago Mag., 1966-67, book columnist, 1968-70; staff Book News Commentator, Sta. WRSV, Skokie, Ill., 1962-70; dir., assoc. prof. master's program in corp. pub. relations, Medill Sch. Journalism, Northwestern U., 1986—. Mem. Winnetka (Ill.) Library Bd., 1969-70; pres. Skokie Valley United Crusade, 1964-65; bd. dirs. Suburban Community Chest Council, Onward Neighborhood House, Chgo., Kenilworth Inst.; mem. Pvt. Sector Foresight Task Force, 1982-83. Served with AUS, 1943-46; ETO. Mem. Pub. Relations Soc. of Am. (accredited; Silver Anvil awards for pub. affairs, 1970, 72, for fin. relations 1970, for bus. spl. events 1976, chmn. nat. pub. affairs sect. 1984), Publicity Club of Chgo. (v.p. 1967, bd. dirs. 1966-68; Golden Trumpet award for pub. affairs, 1969, 70, 72, 79, for fin. relations 1970), Insurers Public Relations Council (pres. 1980-81), Issues Mgmt. Assn. (founder, pres. 1981-83, chmn. 1983-84), Mensa, World Future Soc., U.S. Assn. for Club of Rome, Chgo. Poets and Writers Found. (pub. relations dir. 1966-67), Club: Union League (Chgo.). Author: Mark Twain's Steamboat Years, 1981, Managing the New Botom Line, 1987; contbr. articles to mags. Office: 1813 Hinman Ave Evanston IL 60201

EWING, ROGER LON, health care company executive; b. Lawrence, Kans., Oct. 5, 1927; s. Alonzo Byron and Sally Mae (Winsby) E.; m. Margaret Lavonne, Mar. 30, 1947 (div. June 1979); children: C. Craig, Cynthia A., Kent B., Bart A.; m. Clarice Innes, Jan. 31, 1981; stepchildren: Scott Alan, Matthew Reed. BS, U. Kans., 1950. CPA, Mo., Kans. Sr. acct. Peat, Marwick, Mitchell & Co., Kansas City, Mo., 1950-55; pres. The Home of Tile, Inc., Kansas City, 1956-86, St. Luke's Health Ventures, Inc., Kansas City, 1986—. Treas. Episc. Diocese of Western Mo., Kansas City, 1964-80; treas bd. dirs. St. Luke's Hosp. of Kansas City, 1966-86. Served as sgt. U.S. Army, 1946-47. Mem. Am. Inst. CPA's. Republican. Club: Saddle & Sirloin (Kansas City). Home: Rt 6 PO Box 316 Warrensburg MO 64093 Office: St Luke's Health Ventures Inc 801 W 47th St Suite 200 Kansas City MO 64112

EWING, STEPHEN E., natural gas company executive; b. 1944; married. B.A., DePauw U., 1965; M.B.A., Mich. State U., 1971, Harvard U., 1982. With Gen. Electric Co., 1965-66; with Mich. Consolidated Gas. Co., 1971—, coordinator mgmt. orgn. devel., 1972-73, mgr. adminstr. planning devel. services, 1973, dir. customer service, 1973-75, v.p. personnel, 1975-79, v.p. personnel and adminstrn., 1979-81, v.p. customer service, 1981-84, exec. v.p., 1984—, chief operating officer, pres., pres., 1985—. Served with USAF, 1966-70. Office: Mich Consol Gas Co 500 Griswold St Detroit MI 48226

EWING, THOMAS GENE, real estate developer; b. Avon, Ill., Aug. 21, 1951; s. W. Vernon and Ethel (Hinckley) Ewing; m. Cathy L. Beacher, June 21, 1975; children: Laura Elizabeth, Andrew Thomas. Student, Carl Sandburg Coll., 1970-72, Rock Valley Coll., 1970-82; BS in Bus. Adminstrn., Ill. State U., 1974. Lic. real estate broker, Ill.; lic. ins. broker, Ill. Pres. Ewing Contractors, Bloomington, Ill., 1974-75; loan rep. Lyons (Ill.) Bank, 1975-76; with bus. devel. dept. United Bank, Rockford, Ill., 1976-79; v.p. United Realty Corp., Rockford, 1979—. Mem. Inst. Real Estate Mgmt., Bldg. Onwers and Mgrs. Inst. Internat., Nat. Assn. Corp. Real Estate Execs., Rockford Apt. Assn. Republican. Lutheran. Lodge: Rotary. Avocations: family-time, golf. Office: United Realty Corp PO Box 7327 Rockford IL 61126

EWING, WAYNE TURNER, coal company executive; b. Beech Creek, Ky., Dec. 1, 1933; s. O.E. and Elizabeth E.; m. Jane Gray, June 3, 1960; children—Allyson, Sally. B.A., Georgetown Coll.; M.A., Western Ky. U. With Peabody Coal Co., 1963-85; pres. Peabody Coal Co., St. Louis, 1983-85, Peabody Devel. Co., St. Louis, 1985—; dir. Magna Group, Inc., First Nat. Bank of Belleville, Ill., 1981—. Mem. bd. assos. Georgetown Coll., 1980-82. Served with U.S. Army, 1955-57. Mem. Nat. Coal Assn., Ill. Coal Assn. Methodist. Clubs: Mason, St. Clair Country, Mo. Athletic. Office: Peabody Devel Co 200 N Broadway Saint Louis MO 63102

EWING, WILLIAM HAROLD, design engineer; b. Atlanta, Mar. 16, 1949; s. Harold Theodore and Mary (Brooks) E.; divorced; children: Andrew William, Scott Thomas. BS in Gen. Engring., U.S. Mil. Acad., 1971. Commd. 2d lt. U.S. Army, 1971, advanced through ranks to capt., resigned, 1977; detail project engr. Pontiac (Mich.) Motors div. Gen. Motors Co., 1977-78, project engr., 1978-79; sr. project engr. Pontiac (Mich.) Motors div. Gen. Motors Co., Pontiac and Warren, Mich., 1979-85; devel. engr. Chevrolet Pontiac Can. group Gen. Motors Co., Warren, 1985—. Mem. Soc. Automotive Engrs. Episcopalian. Avocations: golf, jogging, woodworking, oil painting. Home: 215 Pine St Rochester MI 48063 Office: CPC Group of GM 30003 Van Dyke Warren MI 48090

EXE, DAVID ALLEN, electrical engineer; b. Brookings, S.D., Jan. 29, 1942; s. Oscar Melvin and Irene Marie (Mattis) E.; m. Lynn Rae Roberts; children: Doreen Lea, Raena Lynn. BSEE, S.D. State U., 1968; MBA, U. S.D., 1980; postgrad. Iowa State U., 1969-70, U. Idaho, 1978-80. Registered profl. engr., Idaho, Oreg., Minn., S.D., Wash., Wyo., Utah. Applications engr. Collins Radio, Cedar Rapids, Iowa, 1969-70; dist. engr. Bonneville Power Adminstrn., Idaho Falls, Idaho, 1970-77; instr. math U. S.D., Vermillion, 1977-78; chief exec. officer EXE Assocs., Idaho Falls, Idaho, 1978-83; agys. mgr. CPT Corp., Eden Prairie, Minn., 1983-85; owner, chief exec. officer Exe Inc., Eden Prairie, 1983—; chmn. bd. Applied Techs. Idaho, Idaho Falls, 1979—; chmn., chief exec. officer Azimuth Cons., Idaho Falls, 1979-81; v.p. D & B Constrn. Co., Idaho Falls, 1980-83. Mem. Eastern Idaho Council on Industry and Energy, 1979—. Served with USN, 1960-64. Mem. Am. Cons. Engrs., IEEE, Nat. Soc. Profl. Engrs., Nat. Contrcts Mgrs. Assn., IEEE Computer Soc., Mensa, Am. Legion. Lodges: Masons, Elks. Office: 80 W 78th St Chanhassen MN 55317

EXLEY, CHARLES ERROL, JR., manufacturing company executive; b. Detroit, Dec. 14, 1929; s. Charles Errol and Helen Margaret (Greenizen) E.; m. Sara Elizabeth Yates, Feb. 1, 1952; children: Sarah Helen, Evelyn Victoria, Thomas Yates. B.A., Wesleyan U., Middletown, Conn., 1952; M.B.A., Columbia U., 1954. With Burroughs Corp., Detroit, 1954-76; controller Burroughs Corp. (Todd div.), 1960-63, corp. controller, 1963-66, v.p., group exec. office products group, 1966-71, v.p. fin., 1971-73, exec. v.p. fin., 1973-76; also dir.; pres. NCR Corp., Dayton, Ohio, 1976—, chief exec. officer, 1983—, chmn. bd., 1984—; also dir., mem. exec. com. NCR Corp. Clubs: Grosse Pointe (Grosse Pointe Farms, Mich.); Moraine Country (Dayton); Dayton Racquet; The Brook (N.Y.C.). Home: 3720 Ridgeleigh Rd Dayton OH 45429 Office: NCR Corp 1700 S Patterson Blvd Dayton OH 45479

EXON, JOHN JAMES, senator; b. Geddes, S.D., Aug. 9, 1921; s. John James and Luella (Johns) E.; m. Patricia Ann Pros, Sept. 18, 1943; children: Stephen James, Pamela Ann, Candace Lee. Student, U. Omaha, 1939-41. Mgr. Universal Finance Corp., Nebr., 1946-53; pres. Exon's, Inc., Lincoln, Nebr., 1954-71; gov. Nebr., 1971-79; mem. U.S. Senate from Nebr., 1979—. Active state, local, nat. Democratic coms., 1952—; del. Dem. Nat. Conv., 1964-74, Dem. nat. committeeman, 1968—. Served with Signal Corps AUS, 1942-45. Mem. Am. Legion, VFW. Clubs: Masons (32 deg.), Shriners, Elks, Eagles, Optimist Internat. Office: US Senate 340 Dirksen Senate Office Bldg Washington DC 20510 *

EXON, ROBERT ALLEN, dentist; b. Pickstown, S.D., Mar. 15, 1952; s. Robert Allen and Onalee (Parker) E.; m. Karen Hunt, Aug. 10, 1974; children: Michael, Jamie. BA, Washburn U., 1974; DDS, U. Mo., Kansas City, 1979. Gen. practice resident VA Med. Ctr., Topeka, 1979-80; gen. practice dentistry Topeka, 1980—. Mem. ADA. Democrat. Episcopalian. Club: Shawnee Yacht (Topeka) (Commodore 1985-86). Avocations: sailboat racing, softball. Home: 3000 SW 33d St Topeka KS 66614 Office: 1919 W 10th Topeka KS 66604

EYBERG, DONALD THEODORE, JR., architect; b. Mpls., July 8, 1944; s. Donald Theodore and Helen Irene (Young) E.; m. Sally Jo Birch, Dec. 30, 1967; children: Jon, Erin. Student, Mankato State U., 1962-64; BArch, U. Minn., 1968. Registered architect, Minn., Fla. Planner Midwest Planning and Research, Mpls., 1966-67; designer Matson-Wegleitner, Mpls., 1967-68; architect Ellerbe Assocs., Mpls., 1968-76, exec. architect, 1977-82, v.p., 1983—. Prin. works include Providence (R.I.) Civic Ctr., 1971, Dahlgren Hall U.S. Naval Acad., Annapolis, Md., 1973 (numerous awards), Rupp Arena/Hyatt Regency Hotel, Lexington, Ky., 1975 (numerous awards), Huntington (W.Va.) Civic Ctr., 1977, Charleston (W.Va.) Civic Ctr., 1980 (Merit award Athletic Bus., 1981), Hartford (Conn.) Coliseum, 1981 (numerous awards), Mpls. Coll. Art and Design, 1982, Children's Theater Co., Mpls., 1983, Mpls. Inst. Arts, 1984, Ocean Ctr., Daytona Beach, Fla., 1985, Manatee Ctr., Bradenton, Fla., 1985, Thirteen Hundred Biscayne Blvd. Study, Miami, 1985 (Minn. Paper Architect award AIA), Santa Clara (Calif.) Conv. Ctr., 1986, Mayo Civic Ctr., Rochester, Minn., 1986. Mem. AIA, Urban Land Inst., Minn. Soc. Architects (Merit award 1977), Nat. Council Archtl. Registration Bd., Mpls. Soc. Fine Arts., Nat. Fire Protection Assn. Home: 6600 Dakota Trail Minneapolis MN 55435 Office: Ellerbe Assocs Inc One Appletree Sq Minneapolis MN 55420

EYHUSEN, EDWARD ALLEN, lawyer; b. Springfield, Ohio, June 25, 1951; s. George R. and Elinore A. (Evans) E.; m. Cathy S. Johnson, Aug. 25, 1974 (div. Dec. 1983); m. Deidra D. Dixon, Apr. 11, 1985. B.A., Wittenberg U., 1973; J.D., Yale U., 1976. Bar: N.Y. 1977, Ohio 1985. Assoc. Chadbourne, Parke, Whiteside & Wolff, N.Y.C., 1976-83, Baker & Hostetler, Cleve., 1984—. Mem. ABA, Ohio Bar Assn., Cleve. Bar Assn. Avocations: record collecting; guitar. Home: 25275 Shaker Blvd Beachwood OH 44122 Office: Baker & Hostetler 3200 Nat City Ctr Cleveland OH 44114

EYNON, THOMAS GRANT, sociology educator; b. Evanston, Ill. Aug. 10, 1926; s. John and Ruth (Deal) E.; m. Janet Arstingstall, Nov. 24, 1956; children—James Walter, John Robert, Sarah Carolyn. B.Sc. in Psychology, Ohio State U., 1953, M.A. in Anthropology (Scott fellow), 1955, Ph.D. in Criminology and Sociology, 1959. Asst. prof. to assoc. prof. Ohio State U., 1959-68; prof. sociology So. Ill. U., 1968—; vis. prof. U. Stockholm, 1972, Nat. U. Ireland, Galway and Dublin, Queens U. Belfast, Oxford U., London Sch. Econs., U. Leeds, 1973, St. Lawrence U., 1962-70, U. Minn., 1970-75, Ill. Inst. Tech. Research Inst., 1974; dir. Social Sci. Research Bur., 1977-79; commr. Ill. Juvenile Justice Commn., 1983—; mem. Task Force on Prison Crowding, 1983-84. Chmn. adv. bd. Ill. Dept. Corrections, 1979—; chmn. Reading Is Fundamental Program, 1978—; mem. Gov.'s Task Force Mental Health, 1970-72. Served as naval aviator USNR, 1944-51, PTO, Korea. Decorated Silver Star, Purple Heart, D.F.C. Methodist. Author: Offender Classification in the United States, 1976. Editor Sociol. Quar., 1981-84. Contbr. numerous articles and revs. to profl. jours., chpts. in books. Office: Dept of Sociology So Ill U Carbondale IL 62901

EZOP, PHYLLIS PEGGY, marketing and business planning executive; b. Chgo., Sept. 27, 1950; d. Frank J. and Helen (Rocen) Panno; m. Richard V. Ezop, July 4,1970. BS in Math., U. Ill., 1971; MBA, U. Chgo., 1977. Analyst First Fed. of Chgo., 1971-73; analyst Allied Van Lines, Broadview, Ill., 1974-77, dir. mktg. support, 1981-82; planning analyst U.S. Gypsum, Chgo., 1978-79; product cons. Western Electric div. AT&T, Warrenville, Ill., 1979-81; prin. Ezop and Assocs., LaGrange Park, Ill., 1982—. Mem. Am. Mktg. Assn. (chairperson research roundtable conf. 1987, bd. dirs., v.p. elect services and mktg. div. 1987—), U. Chgo. Women's Bus. Group (bd. dirs. 1982-83, contbr. to newsletter 1985-86). Club: Toastmasters (ednl. v.p. Hinsdale (Ill.) chpt. 1984-85, pres. 1986). Home and Office: 321 N Catherine LaGrange Park IL 60525

EZZAT, HAZEM A(HMED), research executive; b. Cairo, July 12, 1942; came to U.S., 1966, naturalized, 1978; s. Ahmed M. and Hanya A. (Safwat) E.; m. Shaza Abdelghaffar, Aug. 2, 1972; children—Jeneen H., Waleed H. B.Sc., U. Cairo, 1963; M.S., U. Wis., 1967, Ph.D., 1971. Project engr. Suez Canal Authority, Egypt, 1963-65; instr. faculty engring. Cairo U., 1965-66; research asst. U. Wis., Madison, 1966-70; with Gen. Motors Research Labs., Warren, Mich., 1970—, asst. head engring. mechanics dept., 1981-84, head power systems research dept., 1984—. Mem. ASME (Henry Hess award 1973), Soc. Automotive Engrs., Am. Acad. Mechanics, Engring. Soc. Detroit, Sigma Xi. Contbr. articles to profl. jours. Office: Gen Motors Research Labs Warren MI 48090

FABER, WILLIAM JOSEPH, osteopath; b. Des Moines, Mar. 21, 1950; s. Albert P. and Dorothy L. (Hoefer) F.; m. Barbara Havey, Nov. 18, 1983. BA, Drake U., 1972; Doctor Osteopathic, U. Health Sci., 1976. Diplomate Am. Bd. Osteopathic Med. Examiners. Med. dir. Milw. Pain Clinic, Milw., 1981—. Active Pub. Edn. Com. Med. Soc., Milw., 1984-86. Mem. Am. Acad. Sclerotherapy (bd. dirs. 1984-86), Am. Osteopathic Assn. Home: 404 W Wisconsin Oconomowol WI 53066 Office: Milw Pain Clinic 6529 W Fond Du Lac Ave Milwaukee WI 53218-4920

FABIN, FRANK JOSEPH, engineer, entrepreneur; b. Lucisboro, Pa., Sept. 1, 1948; s. Frank Louis and Mathilda J. (Prebish) F.; m. Louise Johanna Trow, July 10, 1971. BS in Eng., U. Md., 1970; MBA, Coll. St. Thomas, St. Paul, 1979. Registered profl. engr., Calif. Engr. Md. Fire Underwriters, Balt., 1970-71; engr. 3M Co., St. Paul, 1971-80, engring. supr., 1980—; pres. Grand Mining Co., St. Paul, 1986—. Recipient Excalibur award 3M Co., 1986. Mem. Nat. Fire Protection Assn., ASME. Republican. Roman Catholic. Club: West End Gun (Rosemont, Minn.) (trap chmn. 1976-79). Lodge: Masons. Avocations: trap shooting, hunting, collecting sports cars. Home: 613 S Greenleaf Dr Eagan MN 55123

FACE, PHILIP JON, financial planner; b. Duluth, Minn., Apr. 29, 1961; s. Knolen J. and Anna Elizabeth (Nielsen) F. Student, Moorhead State U., 1980-81, William Patterson Coll., 1981-82; BS in Mgmt., U. Minn., 1983. Sales adminstr. The Creamette Co., Mpls., 1983-84; fin. planner IDS Fin. Services/Am. Express Inc., St. Paul, 1984—. Republican. Lutheran. Avocations: photography, running marathons. Home: 3050 Old Hwy 8 #314 Roseville MN 55113

FAESSLER, EDWIN JOSEPH, management consultant; b. Cin., Nov. 27, 1944; s. Edwin C. and Rosemarie (Schlie) F.; B.A. in Psychology, U. Cin., 1967; M.S.W., Ohio State U., 1969; m. Deborah Braun, Nov. 25, 1978; children by previous marriage—Joseph Michael, Robert James. Clin. instr. psychiat. social work U. Cin., 1971-72; dir. therapeutic foster home project Children's Home of Cin., 1972-75; asst. prof. Edgecliff Coll., Cin., 1974-78, program dir. social work, 1975—; founder, pres. Interpersonal Communication Assoc., Inc., Cin., 1975—; adj. asst. prof. dept. social work U. Cin., 1978-79; dir. social service Jewish Hosp. Cin., 1977-79; cons. to various schs., ch. groups and hosps., Cin. area, 1974—. Pres. Norwood Bd. Health, 1977-83; bd. dirs. Norwood Service League; mem. Bd. Mental Health Services of N. Central Hamilton County, 1981-83. Mem. Cin. C. of C., Cin. Inst. Small Enterprise. Home: 621 Mehring Way #711 Cincinnati OH 45202

FAETH, GERARD MICHAEL, aerospace engineering educator, researcher; b. N.Y.C., July 5, 1936; s. Joseph and Helen (Wagner) F.; m. Mary Ann Kordich, Dec. 27, 1959; children: Christine Louise, Lorraine Vera, Elinor Jean. BME, Union Coll., 1958; MS, Pa. State U., 1961, PhD, 1964. Instr. mech. engring. Pa. State U., University Park, 1958-59, research asst., 1959-64, asst. prof., 1964-68, assoc. prof., 1968-74, prof., 1974-85, prof. emeritus, 1985—; Modine prof. U. Mich., Ann Arbor, 1985—; vis. prof. Air Force Office Sci. Research, Washington, 1983-84; cons. Gen. Motors Corp., Warren, Mich., 1977-87, applied research lab. Pa. State U., 1964-85; prof. in residence Gen. Motors Corp., Detroit, 1983. Mem. editorial bd. (jour) Combustion Sci. and Tech., 1979—; contbr. numerous articles to profl. jours. Rep. Precinct Chmn., Centre County, Pa., 1977-84; bd. dirs. Eagles Mere (Pa.) Assn., 1982—, Eagles Mere Park Assn., 1978-85. Recipient Research award Pa. State U., 1979; Frank Bailey scholar Union Coll., 1954-58. Fellow ASME (tech. editor 1981-85, sr. tech. editor 1985—), AIAA (assoc.); mem. AAAS, Combustion Inst., Sigma Xi. Episcopalian. Home: 2665 Overridge Dr Ann Arbor MI 48104-4039 Office: U Mich 218 Aerospace Engring Bldg Ann Arbor MI 48109-2140

FAGEL, SORREL, physician; b. Chgo., July 31, 1943; s. Maurice Fagel and Roze (Rappaport) F.; m. Rochelle Miriam Fagel, Nov. 26, 1970; children: Jeffrey, Todd. AB, U. Ill., 1965; MS, Roosevelt U., Chgo., 1966; MD, Chgo. Med. Sch., 1970. Diplomate Am. Bd. Otolaryngology. Intern U. Ill. Hosp., Chgo., 1970-72; gen. surgeon U. Ill. Coll. Medicine, Chgo., 1970-72; resident Wadsworth Va. and UCLA Hosps., 1974-77; practice medicine specializing in otolaryngology Elk Grove Village, Ill., 1977—. Served to maj. USAF, 1972-74. Recipient Sama-Squibb Scientific award, 1969. Mem. AMA, Am. Acad. Otolaryngology, Ill. State Med. Soc., Chgo. Med. Soc. Republican. Jewish. Office: 850 W Biesterfield Elk Grove Village IL 60007

FAGERBERG, ROGER RICHARD, lawyer; b. Chgo., Dec. 11, 1935; s. Richard Emil and Evelyn (Thor) F.; m. Virginia Fuller Vaughan, June 20, 1959; children: Steven Roger, Susan Vaughan, James Thor, Laura Craft. B.S. in Bus. Adminstrn., Washington U., St. Louis, 1958, J.D., 1961, postgrad., 1961-62. Bar: Mo. 1961. Grad. teaching asst. Washington U., St. Louis, 1961-62; assoc. firm Rassieur, Long & Yawitz, St. Louis, 1962-64; ptnr. Rassieur, Long, Yawitz & Schneider and predecessor firms, St. Louis, 1965—. Mem. exec. com. Citizens' Adv. Council Pkwy. Sch. Dist., 1974—, pres.-elect, 1976-77, pres., 1977-78; bd. dirs. Parkway Residents Orgn., 1969—, v.p., 1970-73, pres., 1973—; scoutmaster Boy Scouts Am., 1979-83; Presbyn. elder, 1976—, pres. three local congs. 1968-70, 77-78, 83-84. Mem. ABA, Mo. Bar Assn., St. Louis Bar Assn., Christian Bus. Men's Com. (bd. dirs. 1975-78, 87—), Full Gospel Bus. Men's Fellowship, Order of Coif, Omicron Delta Kappa, Beta Gamma Sigma, Pi Sigma Alpha, Phi Eta Sigma, Phi Delta Phi, Kappa Sigma. Republican. Lodges: Kiwanis (past bd. dirs.), Masons, Shriners. Home: 13812 Clayton Rd Town and Country MO 63011 Office: Rassieur Long Yawitz & Schneider 1150 Boatmen's Tower Saint Louis MO 63102

FAGG, GEORGE GARDNER, judge; b. Eldora, Iowa, Apr. 30, 1934; s. Ned and Arleene (Gardner) F.; m. Jane E. Wood, Aug. 19, 1956; children: Martha, Thomas, Ned, Susan, George, Sarah. B.S. in Bus. Adminstrn., Drake U., 1965, J.D., 1956. Bar: Iowa 1958. Ptnr. Cartwright, Druker, Ryden & Fagg, Marshalltown, Iowa, 1958-72; judge Iowa Dist. Ct., 1972-82, U.S. Ct. Appeals (8th cir.), 1982—; mem. faculty Nat. Jud. Coll., 1979. Mem. Am. Judicature Soc., ABA, Iowa Bar Assn., Order of Coif. Office: 301 US Courthouse E 1st and Walnut Sts Des Moines IA 50309

FAGG, MARTHA A., lawyer; b. Marshalltown, Iowa, Mar. 22, 1957; d. George G. and Jane (Wood) F. BA, Iowa State U., 1979; JD, Drake U., 1985. Assoc. Law office of Alvin D. Shapiro, Kansas City, Mo., 1985—; law instr. Avila Coll., Kansas City, 1986. Mem. ABA, Mo. Bar Assn., Kansas City Bar Assn. Office: Law office Alvin D Shapiro 911 Main 2830 Commerce Tower Kansas City MO 64105

FAHEY, DENNIS JOHN, dentist, dental educator; b. Madison, Wis., Sept. 18, 1951; s. William John and Pauline Katherine (Schrepfer) F.; m. Jane Ingwell, Aug. 23, 1975; children: Meredith, Meghan, Martin. BBS, U. Wis., 1974; DDS, Marquette U., 1978. Practice gen. dentistry Kenosha, Wis., 1979—; asst. prof. Marquette U. Dental Sch., Milw., 1979—. Founded and maintain dental clinic in Port-au-Prince, Haiti, 1983—. Grantee Omicron Kappa Upsilon, 1987. Fellow Am. Acad. Gen. Dentistry; mem. ADA, Wis. Acad. Gen. Dentistry (bd. dirs. 1984—), Phi Kappa Phi. Roman Catholic. Avocations: golf, sailing, learning Creole. Home: 7022 3d Ave Kenosha WI 53140 Office: 6121 7th Ave Kenosha WI 53140

FAHLGREN, JAMES WHITCOMB, manufacturing company executive, lawyer; b. Rochester, Minn., June 27, 1938; s. Nels Oscar and Mary Cynthia (Whitcomb) F. B.A., Macalester Coll., 1960; LL.B. cum laude, U. Minn., 1963. Bar: Minn. 1963; U.S. Supreme Ct. 1978. Law clk. to justice Minn. Supreme Ct., St. Paul, 1963-64; trial atty. NLRB, Mpls., 1964-66; assoc. Maun, Hazel, & Green, St. Paul, 1966-71; ptnr. Fahlgren & Hartfeldt, St. Paul, 1971-78; pres. Dura-Process Co., Mpls., 1971—, Twin Cities Industries, Inc., Mpls., 1973—, Graphic Metals, Inc., Bay City Mich., 1986—; adj. instr. law U. Minn., Mpls., 1968-73. Mem. editorial bd. Minn. Law Rev., 1961-63. Vol. atty. Ramsey County Legal Aid, St. Paul, 1969-78; mem. planning com. Minn. Zoo, St. Paul, 1968; class agt. Macalester Coll., 1986—. Mem. ABA, Minn. Bar. Assn., Am. Mgmt. Assn. Methodist. Clubs: Minnesota, University, Town and Country (St. Paul). Home: 32 N Mississippi River Blvd Saint Paul MN 55104 Office: Dura-Process Co 4000 Winnetka Ave N Minneapolis MN 55427

FAHNER, TYRONE CLARENCE, lawyer, former state attorney general; b. Detroit, Nov. 18, 1942; s. Warren George and Alma Fahner; B.A., U. Mich., 1965; J.D., Wayne State U., 1965; LL.M., Northwestern U., 1971; m. Anne Beauchamp, July 2, 1966; children—Margaret, Daniel, Molly. Admitted to Mich. bar, 1968, Ill. bar, 1969, Tex. bar 1984; mem. criminal def. litigation unit Northwestern U., 1969-71; asst. U.S. atty. for No. Dist. Ill., Chgo., 1971-75, dep. chief consumer fraud and civil rights, 1973-74, chief ofcl. corruption, 1974-75; mem. firm Freeman, Rothe, Freeman & Salzman, Chgo., 1975-77; dir. Ill. Dept. Law Enforcement, 1977-79; partner firm Mayer, Brown & Platt, Chgo., 1979-80, 83—; atty. gen. State of Ill., Springfield, 1980-83; instr. John Marshall Law Sch., 1973—. Ford Found. fellow, 1969-71. Mem. Am. Bar Assn., Ill. Bar Assn., Mich. Bar Assn., Chgo. Bar Assn., Tex. Bar Assn., Am. Judicature Soc., Nat. Assn. Attys. Gen. Republican. Lutheran. Office: Mayer Brown & Platt 190 S LaSalle St Chicago IL 60603

FAHRENWALD, WILLIAM EDWARD, editor; b. Chgo., Aug. 12, 1955; s. Francis Merrick and Joan (Brautigan) F.; m. Martha Anderson, July 5, 1977. BA, Columbia Coll., Chgo., 1976. Assoc. editor PSA Jour., Chgo., 1976-78; freelance writer, photographer Chgo., 1978-81; assoc. editor Railway Age, N.Y.C., 1981—; editor Intermodal Age Internat., Chgo., 1985—; Founder, exec. dir. 20th Century Railroad Club, Chgo., 1983-85. Editor Uptown People's Law Ctr., Chgo., 1979; contbg. author: Kids Guide to Chicago. Avocations: reading, gardening, photography, bicycle, travel.

FAIBVRE, LAMONT, real estate appraiser; b. Chgo., June 27, 1944. Pvt. practice real estate appraisal Chgo., 1966—. Mem. Art. Inst. Chgo. (life), Chgo. Acad. Scis. (life). Served with USN, 1961-65. Mem. Northside Real Estate Bd., Nat. Assn. Real Estate Appraisers (cert. Real Estate Appraiser), Internat. Real Estate Inst. (sr. cert valuer). Republican. Roman Catholic. Home and Office: 2434 N Albany Ave Chicago IL 60647

FAIN, SHARON LEE, academic administrator; b. Cin., May 21, 1957; d. Norval and Leecola (Sullins) F.; m. Bradley W. Kibbel, May 14, 1983 (div. Jan. 1987). BAgr, Ohio State U., 1979. Indsl. appraiser Cole-Layer-Trumble Co., Columbus, Ohio, 1980; tech. writer, editor Ohio State U., Columbus, 1981-83; dir. mgmt. devel. programs Case Western Res. U., Cleve., 1984-86; adminstrv. dir. Weatherhead Sch. Mgmt. Case Western Res. U., Cleve., 1986—. Editor ednl. newsletters, 1981-83. Democrat. Avocations: antique restoration, archery, riflery, tennis, music. Home: 2850 E 128th St Cleveland OH 44120 Office: Ctr Mgmt Devel Case Western Res U 406 Sears Library Cleveland OH 44106

FAIR, DOUGLAS MONTAGUE, chiropractor. Student, Kans. Wesleyan U., 1958-60; D in Chiropractic Medicine cum laude, Nat. Chiropractic Coll., 1964; BA in Nutrition, Columbia (Mo.) Coll., 1977; M in Nutrition, U. Bridgeport, 1983. Cert. Diagnostic Roentgenology, Applied Kinesiology, Acupuncture, Acupressure and Acutherapy. Practice chiropractic medicine specializing in wholistic health care St. Francis, Kans., 1964—, Oberlin, Kans., 1986—. Mem. Am. Chiropractic Assn. (council on nutrition 1980—, council on roentgenology 1968—), Kans. Chiropractic Assn. (pres. 1969-70, council of roentgenology and orthopedics 1968—, bd. dirs. 1970-79, pres. N.W. dist. 1965, 66, 81, 82, dir. 1967). Office: 504 N Penn Oberlin KS 67749 also: 120 N Scott Saint Francis KS 67756

FAIR, JAMES RICHARD, architect; b. Bloomington, Ill., July 18, 1950; s. Edmund Parker and Dorothy Alice (Graves) F. BArch, Oklahoma State U., 1973. Registered architect, Ill. Architect Neuhaus & Taylor, Houston, 1973-74, Skidmore, Owings & Merrill, Chgo., 1974-84, Larson Assocs., Inc., Chgo., 1984-86, Kober & Belluschi Assocs., Chgo., 1986—. Mem. AIA, Constrn. Specifications Inst., Nat. Fire Protection Assn., Bldg. Ofcl. and Code Adminstrs. Internat. Democrat. Presbyterian. Avocations: music, baseball. Office: Kober & Belluschi Assocs 30 W Monroe Suite 500 Chicago IL 60603

FAIRWEATHER, HELEN LOUISE, bookkeeper; b. Boston, Dec. 20, 1946; d. Charles Arthur and Edna Ann (Kimbrough) Parraway; m. Arthur George Fairweather, Dec. 20, 1984. AA, Essex County Coll., 1966. Asst. controller Sheraton Catalina Inn, Orlando, Fla., 1970-72; controller Mid-Fla. Harvesting, Orlando, 1972-79; full charge bookkeeper Tiremasters, Miami, Fla., 1979-80; controller Sanderson Industries, Chgo., 1980-82; fin. adminstr. Rockland County YMCA, Nyack, N.Y., 1983-86; pvt. practice bookkeeper Grand Junction, Mich., 1986—. Mem. Nat. Assn. Female Execs., Smithsonian Inst. Assocs. Republican. Avocations: oil painting, sewing, crafts. Home and Office: 4991 106th Ave Grand Junction MI 49056

FALCONER, BARBARA JOAN, architect; b. Birmingham, Mich., Feb. 10, 1953; s. Harry W. and Elaine D. (Johnson) Carlson; m. Robert P. Falconer, Aug. 12, 1978. BS in Archtl. Studies, U. Ill., 1976. Architect Skidmore, Owings and Merrill, Chgo., 1976-84; asst. dir. devel. Chgo. Housing Authority, 1984-86; sr. project mgr. Archtl. Interiors, Inc., Chgo., 1986—. Pres. Condominium Assn., Chgo., 1985-86. Mem. AIA, Art Inst. Chgo. Club: Chgo. Yacht. Avocations: sailing, skiing, running, drawing. Office: Archtl Interiors 600 W Fulton Chicago IL 60606

FALK, LAWRENCE ADDNESS, JR., virologist; b. Houston, May 5, 1938; s. Lawrence A. and Lorraine Oletha (Wilson) F. A.A. Lon Morris Coll., 1958; B.A., Centenary Coll., La., 1962; M.A., U. Houston, 1966; Ph.D., U. Ark., 1970. Research asst. Baylor Med. sch., 1963-65; postdoctoral fellow Presbyterian-St. Luke's Med. Ctr., Chgo., 1969-71, asst. prof., assoc. prof. Rush-Presbyn.-St. Luke's Med. Ctr., 1971-78; asst. prof. assoc. prof. U. Ill. Med. Sch., 1974-78; chmn. div. microbiology New Eng. Regional Primate Research Ctr., Southboro, Mass., 1978-83; assoc. prof. micro and molecular genetics Harvard Med. Sch., assoc. prof. microbiology Harvard Sch. Pub. Health, 1978-83; sr. virologist Abbott Labs., North Chicago, Ill., 1983—; vis. scientist Karolinska Inst., 1976-77; cons. U.S. Govt. Leukemia Soc. NIH fellow, 1970; Am. scholar, 1975-80. Mem. Am. Assn. Immunologists, AAAS, Am. Soc. Microbiology, Tissue Culture Assn., Am. Assn. Research on Cancer. Contbr. articles to profl. jours. Office: Abbott Labs, North Chicago, IL 60064

FALK, MARSHALL ALLEN, physician, university dean and official; b. Chgo., May 23, 1929; s. Ben and Frances (Kamins) F.; m. Marilyn Joyce Levoff, June 15, 1952; children: Gayle Debra, Ben Scott. B.S., Bradley U., 1950; M.S., U. Ill., 1952; M.D., Chgo. Med. Sch., 1956. Diplomate: Am. Bd. Psychiatry. Intern Cook County Hosp., Chgo., 1956-57; resident Mt. Sinai Hosp., Chgo., 1964-67; gen. practice medicine Chgo., 1959-64; resident in psychiatry, faculty dept. psychiatry Chgo. Med. Sch., 1964-67, prof., acting chmn. dept. psychiatry, 1973-74, dean, 1974—, v.p. med. affairs, 1981-82, exec. v.p., 1982—; med. dir. London Meml. Hosp., 1964-74; mem. cons. com. commr. health, City of Chgo., 1972-82 ; mem. Gov.'s Commn. to Revise Mental Health Code Ill., 1973-77, Chgo. Northside Commn. on Health Planning, 1970-74, Ill. Hosp. Licensing Bd., 1981—. Contbr. articles to profl. jours. Served to capt. AUS, 1957-59. Recipient Bd. Trustees award for research Chgo. Med. Sch., 1963; Distinguished Alumni award Chgo. Med. Sch., 1976. Fellow Am. Psychiat. Assn., Am. Coll. Psychiatrists, Ill. Council Deans (pres. 1981-83), Waukegan/Lake County (Ill.) C. of C., 1984—, Sigma Xi, Alpha Omega Alpha. Home: 3860 Mission Hills Rd Northbrook IL 60062 Office: 3333 Green Bay Rd North Chicago IL 60064

FALK, WILLIAM JOHN, actuary; b. Elmhurst, Ill., Sept. 29, 1949; s. William Ernest and Maisie Phyllis (Johnson) F.; m. Lydia Ann, Wilson, May 4, 1969; children: Erik, Audrey, Roger. BA with honors, Mich. State U., 1970. Actuary CNA, Chgo., 1972-76; cons. Towers, Perrin, Forster & Crosby Inc., Los Angeles, 1976-77, Chgo., 1977-84; prin. Towers, Perrin, Forster & Crosby, Inc., Chgo., 1985—. Served with U.S. Army, 1971-72. Fellow Soc. Actuaries; mem. Am. Acad. Actuaries, Cons. Actuaries in Pub. Practice. Lutheran. Office: Towers Perrin Forster & Crosby Inc 200 W Madison Chicago IL 60606

FALLIS, JAMES EDWARD, II, professional sports team manager; b. Darmstadt, Germany, Nov. 28, 1952; s. Archie Thomas and Karin Marie (Driver) F.; m. Anna Marie Czap, Aug. 28, 1976; children—Thomas Edward, Natalie Marie. B.A., Lake Superior State Coll., 1974; M.Ed., No. Mich. U., 1977. Cert. level III defensive tactics instr., Mich. Instr. Lake Superior State Coll., Sault Ste. Marie, Mich., 1974-81, asst. prof. recreation and phys. edn., 1981-86, head wrestling coach, 1974-86; developer wellness program for city police and U.S. Forest Service, Sault St. Marie, 1982. Dir. Eastern Upper Peninsula Spl. Olympics, 1982. Named to Nat. Assn. Intercollegiate Athletics Hall of Fame, 1980; Gt. Lakes Intercollegiate Athletic Conf. Coach of Year, 1986; travelled to USSR for study in field, 1978. Mem. AAHPERD (life), Assn. Advancement of Health Edn., Assn. for Research, Adminstrn., Profl. Councils and Socs., Nat. Assn. Sport and Phys. Edn., Nat. Wrestling Coaches Assn. Roman Catholic. Club: Lions. Coached two teams to top ten place finishes. nat. competition, 1978, 82; coached 11 individual Nat. Collegiate All-Americans including 1 nat. champion. Office: Norris Center Lake Superior State Coll Sault Saint Marie MI 49783

FALLON, RICHARD HENRY, physician, health care administrator; b. Boston, Mar. 4, 1931; s. William T. and Mary V. (O'Donoughue) F.; m. Ann Giessow, June 28, 1957; children—Lynn, Brian, Malcolm, Duncan, Lara. B.S. in Biology, Boston Coll., 1952; M.D., Harvard U., 1956; M.A. in History, Washington U., 1974. Diplomate Am. Bd. Surgery. Intern, Barnes Hosp., St. Louis, 1956-57, resident, 1959-62; resident Boston City Hosp., 1957-59; practice medicine, St. Louis, 1964-79; pres. Physicians Multisplty. Group, St. Louis, 1979—, Maxicare Health Plan Mo., St. Louis, 1983—; asst. prof. Washington U. Med. Sch., St. Louis, 1964—; pres. St. Louis PSRO, 1973. Served to capt. USAF, 1962-64. Fellow Am. Coll. Surgeons; mem. Group Health Assn. (med. dirs. div.), St. Louis Met. Med. Soc. (councilor 1971-73, v.p. 1973), Mo. State Med. Soc. (councilor 1978-85), AMA, So. Med. Soc. Republican. Clubs: Univ. Racquet (St. Louis). Avocations: squash; sailing; Russian history. Home: 57 Berkshire St Louis MO 63117 Office: Physicians Multispecialty Group 3908 S Grand St Louis MO 63118

FALLS, ARTHUR GRANDPRÉ, physician, surgeon; b. Chgo., Dec. 25, 1901; s. William Arthur and Santalia Angelica (de GrandPré) F.; m. Lillian Steele Proctor, Dec. 1928; 1 child, Arthur GrandPré. Student Crane Jr. Coll., 1918-20; B.S. in Medicine, Northwestern U., 1924, M.D., 1925; postgrad. U. Chgo., U. Ill.-Chgo., Cook County Postgrad. Sch., NYU. Intern Kansas City Gen. Hosp., Mo., 1924-25; gen. practice surgery, Chgo., 1925—; mem. staff Provident Hosp.; faculty Postgrad. Sch. Tb, Chgo., 1939-44, Sch. Nursing, Provident Hosp., Chgo., 1960-65; founder, pres. Com. to End Discrimination in Chgo.'s Med. Instns.; founder, exec. vice chmn. Council for Equal Med. Opportunity; founder, pres. Council for Bio-Med. Careers; founder, chmn. Chgo. chpt. Med. Com. for Human Rights; mem. pub. health com. Commn. on Human Relations, City of Chgo.; mem. health com. Welfare Council Met. Chgo.; chmn. ann. health campaign Nat. Negro Bus. League. Editor Bull. Cook County Physicians Assn., 1930-32, 35-36; assoc. editor Interracial Rev., 1931-34, Bull. Interracial Commn. of Chgo., 1933-36; Chgo. editor Catholic Worker, 1935-38. Contbr. articles to various publs. Mem. exec. bd. Nat. Cath. Interracial Fedn., 1931-36, pres. Chgo. br., 1933-34; founder Chgo. Cath. Workers Credit Union, 1937, bd. dirs., 1950-53, pres., 1952-53; founder, chmn. Progress Devel. Corp., 1959. Recipient award for service in civil rights and liberties Kenwood-Ellis Community Ctr., 1957, Good Am. award Chgo. Com. of 100, 1963. Fellow Am. Coll. Chest Physicians, Am. Geriatrics Soc.; mem. ACLU, Chgo. Urban League, Nat. Urban League, NAACP, Ams. for Democratic Action, Am. Cath. Sociol. Soc. Roman Catholic. Avocations: gardening; traveling; photography; stamp collecting; coin collecting. Home: 4812 Fair Elms Ave Western Springs IL 60558 Office: 5050 S State St Chicago IL 60009

FALLS, KATHLEENE JOYCE, photographer; b. Detroit, July 3, 1949; s. Edgar John and Acelia Olive (Young) Haley; m. Donald David Falls, June 15, 1974; children: Daniel John, David James. Student, Oakland Community Coll., 1969-73, Winona Sch. Profl. Photography, 1973-80. Printer Guardian Photo, Novi, Mich., 1967-69; printer, supr. quality control N.Am. Photo, Livonia, Mich., 1969-76; free lance photographer Livonia, 1969-76; owner, pres. Kathy Falls, Inc., Carleton, Mich., 1976—; instr. Monroe County Community Coll. Continuing Edn., 1981-83; judge Congl. Art Competition, 1985, 1986; owner Picture Perfect, Carleton, 1987. Contbr. articles to profl. jours. Represented in spl. categories in the Nat. Loan Collection, Profl. Photographers Am., 1980, 81, 83; represented in permanent Collections Monroe County Hist. Mus., Archives Notre Dame. Catechist St. Patrick's Ch., Carleton, 1984-87; active Big Bros. and Big Sisters, Monore, 1986-87; corr. sec. Monroe Women's Ctr, 1986—. Recipient numerous awards granted by profl. photographic orgns. Mem. Detroit Profl. Photographers Assn. (bd. dirs., artisan chmn. 1981-82, Best of Show award 1981, 83), Profl. Photographers Mich. (artisian chairperson 1982-83, Best of Show award 1976, 81, Artist of Yr. 1980), Profl. Photographers Am. (cert. profl. photog. specialist), Am. Photographic Artisans Guild (council mem., bd. dirs. 1986-87), Monroe C. of C. (chmn. council women bus. owners), Nat. Orgn. Women Bus. Owners. Democrat. Roman Catholic. Club: Monroe Camera. Lodge: Women of the Moose. Avocations: guitar, piano, drawing, travel, camping. Home and Office: 14554 Grafton Carleton MI 48117

FALLS, ROBERT ARTHUR, theater director; b. Springfield, Ill., Mar. 2, 1954; s. Arthur Joseph and Nancy (Stribling) F. BFA, U. Ill., 1976. Artistic dir. Wisdom Bridge Theatre, Chgo., 1977-86, Goodman Theatre, Chgo., 1987—. Office: Goodman Theatre 200 S Columbus Dr Chicago IL 60603 *

FALTER, DAVID ALBERT, marketing executive; b. Cin., Mar. 20, 1961; s. James Wherle and Suasn Martha (Mayer) F.;. AB in English, Miami U., Ohio, 1983; M in English, U. Va., 1984. Creative dir. Franklin Creation Group, Dayton, 1984-85; sales mgr. Barbizon Internat. Modeling, Dayton, 1985; mktg. mgr. CAD CAM, Inc., Dayton, 1985-87; nat. account mgr. Intergraph Corp. and Ford Motor Co., Farmington Hills, Mich., 1987—. Vol. Dayton Art Inst., 1986; usher St. Paul's Ch., Dayton, 1985—. Miami U. fellow, 1983. Mem. Omicron Delta Kappa. Democrat. Episcopalian. Home: 22601 Braeside Circle Apt 20301 Farmington Hills MI 48024 Office: Intergraph Corp 30555 Northwestern Hwy Suite 300 Farmington Hills MI 48018

FALVO, ANTHONY J., wood products manufacturing executive. With L&W Supply Corp., 1974-80; regional ops. mgr. East 1974-75, dir. planning and devel., 1975-76, pres., 1976-80; with USG Corp., Chgo., 1955-74, 1980-85; sales corr. 1955-56, sales rep., 1956-62, mgr. large jobs, 1962-64, dist. mgr. Hudson Valley, 1964-67, dist. mgr. Washington, 1967-70, area sales mgr., 1970-74, dir. gypsum group services, 1980-82, v.p. mktg., 1982-84, group v.p. consumer products, 1984-85; with Masonite Corp., Chgo., 1985—, pres., chief exec. officer, 1986—. Office: Masonite Corp 1 S Wacker Dr Chicago IL 60606 *

FANCHER, PAMELA TORRE, personnel director; b. Ottawa, Kans., June 19, 1951; d. George Gingerich Jr. and Naomi (Adams) Heidner; m. Thomas P. Torre, Aug. 11, 1973 (div. Jan. 1982); 1 child, Trisha Blythe; m. Thomas D. Fancher, Dec. 23, 1985; 1 child, Jon. BBA, Emporia State U., 1972, MS in Counseling, 1973. Cert. in Employee Relations Law, Inst. Applied Mgmt. and Law; realtor. Spl. agt. Prudential Ins. Co., Springfield, N.J., 1973-74; career counselor Independence (Kans.) Community Coll., 1975-77; acct. Arco Pipeline Co., Independence, 1977-79; asst. to pres. Cornbelt Chem. Co., McCook, Nebr., 1979-82; personnel dir. Emporia (Kans.) State U., 1982—; cons. Cornbelt Chem. Co., 1982-83; dir. statewide program for supervisory mgmt. for all univs., 1984. Author: Performance Enhancement, 1985; author in house program (employee suggestion award 1985). Bd. dirs. Big Bros./Big Sisters, Independence, 1977-78, Emporia Day Care Assn., 1983-84, Hornet Athletic Club, Emporia, 1986-87; edn. chmn. Lyon County (Kans.) United Way, 1985. Mem. AAUW (v.p. Independence 1979), Bus. and Profl. Women Assn. (pres. McCook 1982), Coll. and U. Personnel Assn., Nat. Assn. Coll. and U. Bus. Officers. Republican. Roman Catholic. Club: Osage City (Kans.) Country. Avocations: golf, swimming, antiques. Home: 610 Sunset Dr Osage City KS 66523 Office: Emporia State U 1200 Commercial Emporia KS 66801

FANCHER, ROBERT BURNEY, electric utility executive; b. Wharton, Ark., Dec. 13, 1940; s. Robert Burney and Lillian Olga (Steele) F.; m. Patricia Elizabeth Donahae, Mar. 25, 1967; children: Terri Michele, John Robert, Samuel Joseph. BSEE, Okla. State U., 1966; MSEE, U. Ark., 1971. Registered profl. engr., Mo. Enlisted as airman USAF, 1960, commd. 2d lt., 1966, advanced through grades to capt., 1969; electronics officer USAF, Ft. Mead, Md., 1967-70; resigned USAF, 1970; engr. Empire Dist. Electric Co., Joplin, Mo., 1972-75, rate engr., 1975-76, dir. computer services, 1976-77, dir. corp. services, 1977-84, v.p. corp. services, 1984—. Deacon Villa Heights Christian Ch., Joplin, 1975-86. Named Young Engr. of Yr., Southwest Chpt. Mo. Soc. Profl. Engrs., 1976. Mem. IEEE, Soc. Profl. Engrs. (S.W. Mo. chpt. pres. 1978-79), Edison Electric Inst. (rate com., strategic planning com.), Mo. Valley Electric Assn. Republican. Lodge: Rotary. Avocations: photography, golf, fishing. Home: 2519 S Kingsdale Joplin MO 64804 Office: Empire Dist Electric Co PO Box 127 Joplin MO 64802

FANELLA, ROBERT JOSEPH, high technology company executive; b. Chgo., July 3, 1950; m. Sandra Ellen Fleege, Oct. 13, 1973; children: Corinne, Christopher, Patrick, Anne. BS, No. Ill. U., 1972; MBA, U. Chgo., 1978. CPA, Ill. Mgr. fin. analysis Motorola, Inc., Schaumberg, Ill., 1972-80; dir. ops. analysis Am. Internat., Chgo., 1980-81; v.p. fin. C.D.I., Addison, Ill., 1981-83; chief fin. officer MicroEnergy, Inc., Carol Stream, Ill., 1983—. Roman Catholic. Home: 220 Regent Glen Ellyn IL 60137 Office: MicroEnergy Inc 350 Randy Rd Carol Stream IL 60188

FANG, JEFFREY MING-SHAN, research economist; b. Tainan, Taiwan, Sept. 15, 1940; came to U.S. 1963, naturalized 1975; s. Nau Sou and Tau Tsai F.; m. Yu-Mei Lu, Jan. 1, 1970; children: Eric Y., Karen Y., Gary Y. BA in Econs., Nat. Taiwan U. 1962, MA U. Wash. 1965, PhD 1969. Lectr. econs. Western Wash. U., Bellingham 1968-69, asst. prof. 1969-75; staff economist Dept. Energy State of Oreg., Salem 1975-79; sr. research economist Battelle Pacific N.W. Labs., Richland, Wash. 1979-86; dir. energy conservation program Ill. Commerce Commn., Springfield, Ill., 1987—. Served with Republic of China Army 1962-63. Mem. Am. Econ. Assn., Western Econ. Assn. Republican. Contbr. in field. Home: 706 N Bruns Ln Apt B Springfield IL 62702 Office: Ill Commerce Commn 527 E Capitol Ave Springfield IL 62794-9280

FANGER, JOHN BARRY, manufacturing engineer; b. Kalida, Ohio, Aug. 3, 1939; s. Louis J. and Geraldine M. (Sheibley) F.; m. Linda Sue Zeller, June 23, 1962; children: John R., Mark L. BEE, U. Cin., 1962; MSEE, U. Pitts., 1966; MBA, U. Dayton, 1977. Registered profl. engr., Ohio. Engring. supr. Westinghouse Electrical Co., Lima, Ohio, 1967-69, program mgr., 1969-73, mgmt. systems mgr., 1970-73, mfg. unit mgr., 1973-79, 81-84, materials mgr., 1984—. Founder, dir. Shawnee Youth Soccer, Lima, 1970-77, Shawnee Basketball Assn., Lima, 1977-83; mem. adv. com. Shawnee Schs., 1975-77; cons. Jr. Achievement, 1979-80. Mem. Am. Prodn. and Inventory Control Soc., Soc. Mfg. Engrs., Lima Soc. Profl. Engrs. (pres.).

FANIA, MARJIE LEE, employment manager; b. St. Louis, Oct. 19, 1932; d. William Oscar and Dorothy Elizabeth (Stuart) Barlow; m. Robert Walmsley Fania, Aug. 29, 1949. Student, Washington U., 1961-70. Various positions Laclede Gas, St. Louis, 1965-75, personnel asst., 1975-76, employment mgr., 1976—. Mem. Personnel Assn. St. Louis, St. Louis Artists Guild (chmn. hospitality 1984). Home: 132 W Cedar Webster Groves MO 63119

FARBER, EVAN IRA, librarian; b. N.Y.C., June 30, 1922; s. Meyer M. and Estelle H. (Shapiro) F.; m. Hope Wells Nagle, June 13, 1966; children: Cynthia, Amy, Jo Anna, May Beth; stepchildren: David Nagle, Jeffrey Nagle, Lisa Nagle. AB, U. N.C., 1944, MA, 1953, BLS, 1953; DHL, St. Lawrence U., 1980. Instr. polit. sci. U. Mass., Amherst, 1948-49; asst. documents dept. U. N.C. Library, 1951-53; librarian State Tchrs. Coll., Livingston, Ala., 1953-55; chief serials and binding div. Emory U. Library, Ga., 1955-62; head librarian Earlham Coll., Richmond, Ind., 1962—; dir. seminar on non-Western studies for coll. librarians Columbia U. Sch. Library Ser., summers, 1966, 68-69; cons. Eckerd Coll., Asbury Theol. Sem., Malone Coll., Macalester Coll., Maryville Coll., Knox Coll., Ill. Coll., Messiah Coll., Hiram Coll., Convenant Theol. Sem., Colby Coll., Ga. State U., Ripon Coll., Hampshire Coll., Rockhurst Coll., Nat. Endowment for Humanities, Lilly Endowment, North Central Assn. Author: (with Andreano and Reynolds) Student Economists Handbook, 1967, Classified List of Periodicals for the College Library, 5th edit., 1972; assoc. editor: Southeastern Librarian, 1959-62; asst. editor: Explorations in Entrepreneurial History, 1964-66; co-editor: Earlham Rev., 1965-72; editor: Combined Retrospective Index to Book Revs. in Scholarly Jours., 1886-1974, 1979-83, Combined Retrospective Index to Revs. in Humanities Jours., 1802-1974, 1983-85, (with Ruth Walling) Essays in Honor of Guy R. Lyle; columnist: Choice Mag., 1974-80, Library Issues, 1982—. Recipient Librarian of Yr. award, 1980, Miriam Dudley award, 1987, B.I. Librarian of Yr award, 1987. Mem. Assn. Coll. and Research Libraries (pres. 1978-79), ALA (council 1969-71, 79-83), Assn. Am. Colls. Home: 304 SW H St Richmond IN 47374 Office: Lilly Library Earlham College Richmond IN 47374

FARBER, IRVING ALBERT, business consultant; b. Chgo., Nov. 19, 1927; s. Benjamin and Esther (Axelrod) F.; m. Naomi Karlin, Dec. 19, 1948; children: Susan Pechter, Janet Goldman, Phillip. BS, Roosevelt U., 1950; MBA, Loyola U., 1976. V.p., dir. Frigidments, Inc., Chgo., 1953-78; treas., dir. Gits Cos., Chgo., 1978-82; pres. B.I.M., Inc., Lincolnwood, Ill., 1983—; cons. in field, Lincolnwood, Ill., 1981—; lectr. U. Ill., Chgo., 1984—. Served to sgt. USAF, 1946-47. Mem. Midwest Soc. Profl. Cons. (sec., dir. 1983-84).

FARE, CHARLEY EUGENE, construction company executive; b. Sheridan, Mich., June 1, 1948; s. Charles Fred and Geraldine Dorothey (Thompson) F.; student Montcalm Community Coll., 1967-68, Lansing Community Coll., 1982-83; children: Mark John, Steven Matthew. Owner, pres. Gene Fare Inc., Stanton, Mich., 1973-84, Fare Investment Co., 1975-84; mentor, advocate Mentally Ill and Crises Intervention Dwelling Place, Inc., 1985; advisor Govt. Am. Samoa Pub. Works, 1986—. Served with AUS, 1968-69. Home: 1117 Holland Rd Stanton MI 48888 Office: care Am Samoa Govt Pub Works Pago Pago AS 96799

FAREED, AHMED ALI, university dean; b. Cairo, Sept. 27, 1932, came to U.S. 1961; s. Ali E. and Fayka M. (Yousef) F.; m. Houreya A. Abul-Kheir, Sept. 26, 1957, children—Dahlia, Tony-Khalid. B.A. with honors, Cairo U., 1953; gen. diploma Ein Shams U., Cairo, 1954, spl. diploma, 1959; Ph.D., U. Chgo., 1969. Tchr. Kobba Model Sch., Cairo, 1954-56; curriculum expert Ministry of Edn., Cairo, 1956-61; diagnostician U. Chgo., 1965-68; vis. prof. Northwestern U., Evanston, Ill., 1969; prof., chmn. Northeastern Ill. U., Chgo., 1968-79, dean Coll. Edn., 1979—; cons. sch. dists., Ill., 1967—; speaker, panelist profl. orgns., 1965—; ednl. planning expert Kuwait U., 1978; trustee Am. Islamic Coll., Chgo., 1983—; vice chmn. governing bd. Ednl. Service Ctr., Chgo., 1986. Author standardized silent reading tests, instructional resource units, resource units for elem. tchrs. Contbr. articles to profl. jours. Recipient Outstanding Dissertations in Reading award Internat. Reading Assn., 1970, Outstanding Contbn. Field of Vision award Coll. Optometrists in Vision Devel., 1974, Outstanding Educator Am. award Outstanding Educators of Am., Washington, 1975, Internat. Understanding in Edn. award Ameer Khusra Soc. Am., 1986, Appreciation award dist. 4 Chgo. Bd. Edn., 1987. Mem. Ill. Assn. Deans of Pub. Colls. Edn. (pres. 1983-84), Am. Assn. Colls. of Tchr. Edn., Am. Ednl. Research Assn., Tchr. Edn. Council State Colls. & Univs., Ill. Assn. Colls. of Tchr. Edn., Internat. Reading Assn. (commendation for excellent service 1981), Assn. Egyptian Am. Scholars, Phi Delta Kappa. Avocations: classical music; poetry. Office: Dean Coll Edn Northeastern Ill U 5500 N St Louis Ave Chicago IL 60625

FARES, EDWARD NICHOLAS, data processing executive; b. Chicago Heights, Ill., Dec. 19, 1948; s. Albert Anthony and Lena (Granno) F.; m. Kathleen Ann Camaioni, Apr. 25, 1970; children: Renee Lynn, Edward Jr. BBA, U. Chgo., 1977, BS in Computer Sci., 1979. Programming mgr. Time Inc., Chgo., 1970-78; tech. dir. Beatrice Foods, Chgo., 1978-81; v.p. Information Resources, Chgo., 1981-86, First Options of Chgo., 1986—. Mem. Concerned Citizens, Chicago Heights, 1980; asst. to commr. Chgo. Heights Park Dist., 1982. Mem. Data Processing Mgmt. Assn., IBM Guide. Roman Catholic. Lodge: Kiwanis. Home: 805 Bradoc St Chicago Heights IL 60411 Office: First Options Chgo 440 S La Salle Chicago IL 60605

FARHA, ZACK, food company executive; b. Kansas City, Mo., Oct. 9, 1928; s. Zack Abraham and Jennie M. (Monsour) F.; m. Jeannette Leilah Naifeh, Feb. 11, 1961; children: Vincent, Christopher. BS in Mktg., U. Kans., 1951. Gen. mgr. Pioneer Foods Co., Hutchinson, Kans., 1951-56; owner Pioneer Sales Co., Wichita, Kans., 1956-59; co-founder, exec. v.p. Swiss Chalet Food Products, Wichita, 1970-73, sales cons., 1974—, owner, 1981—; chmn. bd. dirs. Pioneer Properties, Inc., Wichita and Toronto, Can. Contbr.: (textbook) Dynamics in Marketing, 1951. Active local Boy Scouts Am.; bd. dirs. St. Jude's Hosp., Memphis, Aid to Lukemia Stricken Am. Children. Served with AUS, 1951-53. Mem. Kans. U. Alumni Assn., Sigma Phi Epsilon, Order St. Ignatius. Republican. Eastern Orthodox. Lodges: Masons, Shriners, Elks, Lions (past internat. bd. dirs.). Home: 509 Tallyrand Wichita KS 67206 Office: 622 E 3d St PO Box 800 Wichita KS 67201

FARISON, JAMES BLAIR, electrical engineer, educator; b. McClure, Ohio, May 26, 1938; s. Blair Albert and Marie Lucille (Ballard) F.; m. Gail Donahue, Mar. 30, 1961; children: Jeffrey James, Mark Donahue. B.S. summa cum laude in Elec. Engring, U. Toledo, 1960; M.S., Stanford U., 1961, Ph.D., 1964. Registered profl. engr., Ohio. Asst. prof. elec. engring. U. Toledo, 1964-67, assoc. prof., 1967-74, prof., 1974—, asst. dean engring., 1969-71, dean engring., 1971-80. Contbr. tech. articles to profl. jours. Recipient Outstanding Young Man of 1971 award Toledo Jr. C. of C., 1972, Boss of Year award Limestone chpt. Am. Bus. Women's Assn., 1973, Toledo's Engr. Yr. award, 1984, Outstanding Tchr. award U. Toledo, 1986; named Disting. Alumnus, U. Toledo, 1983. Fellow Ohio Acad. Sci.; mem. Nat. Soc. Profl. Engrs, Ohio Soc. Profl. Engrs. (Young Engr. of Year award 1973, citation 1983, Outstanding Engring. Educator award 1984), Toledo Soc. Profl. Engrs. (Young Engr. of Year award 1973), IEEE (Toledo Elec. Engr. of Year awards 1972, 74, 76), Instrument Soc. Am., Am. Soc. Engring. Edn., Tech. Soc. Toledo, Soc. of Mfg. Engrs., Area Council for Tech., Blue Key, Sigma Xi, Tau Beta Pi, Pi Mu Epsilon, Phi Kappa Phi, Eta Kappa Nu (Outstanding Young Elec. Engr. award 1971). Home: 2314 Secor Rd Toledo OH 43606 Office: U Toledo 2801 W Bancroft St Toledo OH 43606

FARLEY, D. STEPHEN, banker; b. Chgo., Jan. 15, 1928; s. Donald Stephen and Alice (Duncan) F.; m. Georgia Mae Bank, Jan. 15, 1955; children: Thomas, Patricia, Sarah, Mary, Ann., Stephen. BS, U.S. Merchant Marine Acad., 1949; LLD, U. Wis., 1952. Trust officer First Nat. Bank Chgo., 1954-1963; v.p., dir. First Nat. Bank Neenah, Wis., 1963-69; sr. v.p. Norwest Bank St. Paul, 1970-80; v.p. Norwest Corp., Mpls., 1980—. Bd. dirs. Mpls. Zoological Found., 1980-86. Served to comdr. USNR. Mem. Am. Bankers Assn. (pres. trust div. 1983), Minn. Bar Assn. Republican. Roman Catholic. Clubs: Town Country (bd. dirs. 1983), Mpls. Athletic. Home: 480 S Mississippi River Blvd Saint Paul MN 55105 Office: Norwest Corp 1200 Peavey Bldg Minneapolis MN 55479

FARLEY, DEANE M., obstetrician-gynecologist; b. Fullerton, Nebr., Aug. 12, 1916; s. Hiram C. and Mary Emma (Maffett) F.; m. Ruth E. Epp, June 13, 1942; children: Sarah Jane, David James, Martha Sue. BA, North Cen. U., Naperville, Ill., 1939; MD, Northwestern U., 1943. Cert. Am. Bd. Ob-Gyns. Obstetrician-gynecologist Suburban Ob-Gyn., S.C., Berwyn, Ill., 1946—; chmn. dept. ob-gyn. MacNeal Meml. Hosp., Berwyn, Ill., 1960, pres. med. staff 1961, attending physician 1950—; assoc. staff Cook County Hosp., Chgo., 1953-57; assoc. prof. dept. ob-gyn. U. Ill. Med. Sch., Chgo., 1950—. Served to major U.S. Army, 1944-46, ETO. Fellow Am. Coll. Ob-Gyn., Cen. Assn. Ob-Gyn.; mem. Ill. Ob-Gyn. Soc. Republican. Avocations: photography, gardening, travel. Home: 128 Riverside Rd Riverside IL 60546 Office: Suburban Ob-Gyn SC 3231 Euclid Berwyn IL 60402

FARLEY, DONNA, research scientist; b. Cascade, Iowa, Dec. 11, 1943; d. Orland J. and Irma Laura (Becker) Boyle; m. Donald Thomas Farley, June 11, 1967; children: Nadine, Alissa. BA, Clarke Coll., 1966. Project asst. in pharmacology U. Wis., Madison, 1966-67; research asst. in internal medicine U. Iowa, Iowa City, 1967-69, research asst. in pharmacology, 1970-73, sr. research asst. in pharmacology, 1973-78, sr. resident asst. ob-gyn, 1978—; instr. biology Mt. Mercy Coll., Cedar Rapids, Iowa, 1969-71, sr. research asst. ob-gyn, 1978—. Contbr. articles to profl. jours. Bd. dirs. Montessori Sch. Cedar Rapids, 1971-73. Mem. Iowa City Tennis Assn. (sec. 1982-83, pres. 1983—), U.S. Tennis Assn. Democrat. Roman Catholic. Club: Univ. Book (sec. 1981, pres. 1982-83). Avocations: children, sports, tennis, scuba diving, nature appreciation. Home: Rt 2 Box 243 North Liberty IA 52317 Office: U Iowa Dept Ob-Gyn 463 MFR Iowa City IA 52240

FARLEY, DONNA OETJEN, health adminstrator; b. Westfield, N.J., Sept. 28, 1943; d. Donald V. and Grace S. Oetjen; m. David P. Farley, Apr. 29, 1967 (div. June 1978); children: Kristina Lynn, William David. BA, Coe Coll., 1965; MPH, U. Ill., Chgo., 1975, MS, 1976. Tech. asst. Ill. Pollution Control Bd., Chgo., 1976-77; assoc. dir. Suburban HSA, Oak Park, Ill., 1977-80; exec. dir. Dental Assisting Nat. Bd., Chgo., 1980-83; v.p. Alexian Bros. Med. Ctr., Elk Grove Village, Ill., 1983-85; sr. v.p. Ancilla Systems, Inc., Elk Grove Village, 1985-87; pres. PKR Assocs., Inc., Elk Grove Village, 1987—; trustee, past. chmn. Alexian Bros. Med. Ctr., 1973-82; past. chmn. Elk Grove Health Bd., 1970-76. Bd. dirs. Girl Scouts USA Council, Elk Grove, 1980-82, United Way of Elk Grove 1984—. Named Citizen of Month Voice Newspaper, 1977. Mem. Soc. Hosp. Planning, Am. Pub. Health Assn., Greater O'Hare Assn. of Industry and Commerce (bd. dirs. 1983-85), Elk Grove Jaycees (Citizen of Yr. 1972). Avocations: travel, art, theater. Home & Office: 700 D Bordeaux Ct Elk Grove Village IL 60007

FARLEY, JOHN MICHAEL, steel company executive; b. Bklyn., July 10, 1930; s. John F. and Lucile J. Farley; m. Dorothy O. Stacy, Nov. 29, 1959; children: Anne L., Joan E., John O. B.C.E. magna cum laude, Syracuse U., 1952; M.S., U. Ill., 1954. Registered prof. engr., Ohio, Pa. Project mgr. Cleve. works Jones & Laughlin Steel Corp., 1957-64; mem. engrng. staff Jones & Laughlin Steel Corp., Pitts., 1964-72, v.p. research and engrng., 1972-75, v.p. raw materials, 1975-77; pres. raw materials div. Jones & Laughlin Steel Corp., 1977-82, v.p. raw materials, purchasing, traffic, 1982-85; v.p. research, engrng. and traffic LTV Steel Co., 1985—. Served with USN, 1954-57. Mem. Am. Iron and Steel Inst., AIME, Iron and Steel Soc., Assn. Iron and Steel Engrs., Sigma Xi, Tau Beta Pi. Clubs: Duquesne (Pitts.); Union (Cleve.).

FARLEY, LLOYD EDWARD, educator; b. Nebr. Sand Hills nr. Broken Bow, Nebr., June 20, 1915; s. Arthur L. and Effie (Tyson) F.; A.B., Kearney State Coll., 1945; M.A., Stanford U., 1947, Ed.D., 1950; postgrad. U. Hawaii, U. Oreg., Princeton U.; Litt.D., William Woods Coll., 1982. Tchr. elem. and secondary schs., also adminstr., 1937-41, 47-51; ednl. specialist U.S. Govt., Washington, Anchorage, Edwards AFB, Calif., 1952-60; prof. edn. U. Alaska, Anchorage, 1960-64; Louis D. Beaumont Distinguished prof. edn., head div. social sci., Marshall faculty William Woods Coll., Fulton, Mo.; chmn. dept. edn. Westminster and William Woods Colls., Fulton, 1964-80, prof. edn. emeritus, 1980—; vis. prof. St. Cloud State U., summers 1968-72, Aeromed. Inst., FAA, 1980—. Served to maj. AUS, 1941-46. Named Hon. Tchr. Korea; recipient Centennial medal William Woods Coll. Mem. Mo. Tchrs. Assn., Nat. Assn. Tchr. Educators, Internat. Council on Edn. for Teaching, Phi Delta Kappa, Kappa Delta Pi (hon. mem., named Outstanding Educator). Methodist. Address: 12 Tucker Ln Fulton MO 65251

FARLEY, RAYMOND FRANCIS, wax and chemical specialty manufacturing executive; b. Montclair, N.J., Nov. 27, 1924; s. John A. and Mabel B. (Kinsey) F.; B.S. in Bus., Northwestern U., 1951; m. Mary Miller, Nov. 27, 1954; 1 dau., Gwen Elizabeth. With S.C. Johnson & Son, Inc., Racine, Wis., 1951—, beginning as indsl. products salesman, successively indsl. products regional sales supr., field sales mgr. indsl. products, Porelon products enterprise mgr., regional dir. Japan and Far East, v.p. and regional dir. Japan and Far East, v.p. corp. planning, exec. v.p. U.S. ops., exec. v.p. overseas consumer products, 1951-80, pres., chief operating officer, 1980—; dir. Hart Schaffner & Marx, Chgo., Heritage Bank & Trust Co., Racine. Bd. dirs. St. Mary's Med. Ctr., trustee Northwestern U.; mem. adv. council J.L. Kellogg Grad. Sch. Mgmt. of Northwestern U.; adv. council Ctr. Study of U.S.-Japan Relations of Northwestern U. Served with AUS, World War II. Decorated Bronze Star; named Man of Yr., Internat. Advt. Assn., 1981. Mem. Pvt. Industry Council S.E. Wis. (chmn.), Nat. Alliance Bus. (dir. S.E. Wis.), Racine Area Mfrs. and Commerce, Inc. (dir.), U.S. C. of C., Conf. Bd. (internat. council). Club: Racine Country (past pres.). Office: S C Johnson & Son Inc 1525 Howe St Racine WI 53403 *

FARLEY, ROBERT HUGH, police detective, child abuse consultant; b. Chgo., Sept. 12, 1950; s. Hugh John and Dorothy Marie (Kennedy) F.; m. Diane Lunn Ody, July 5, 1981. BS in Edn., Chgo. State U., 1970; cert., Northwestern U., 1979, U. So. Calif., 1983, U. Louisville, 1979, 84, FBI, 1985. Cert. tchr., Ill. Patrolman Cook County Sheriff's Police Dept., Chgo., 1973-74, tactical officer, 1974-75, detective crimes against children, 1975—; instr., cons. office of deliquency prevention U.S. Dept. Justice, 1986—; instr. Ill. Local Law Enforcement Tng. Bd., Springfield, 1984—, Ill. State Police Tng. Acad., Springfield, 1985—, Fed. Law Enforcement Tng. Ctr., Glynco, Ga., 1986—; faculty Nat. Coll. Edn., Evanston, Ill., 1986—, Moraine Valley Coll., Palos Hills, Ill., 1985—. Contbr. articles to profl. jours. Mem. Ill. State Senate Com. on Teen Suicide Prevention, Cook County States Atty.'s Task Force on Sexual Molestation. Recipient Law Enforcement award U. So. Calif., 1985, Superior Pub. Service award City of Chgo., 1986. Mem. Ill. Police Assn. (state exec. bd. 1983—, chmn. 1985—, Law Enforcement award for Bravery 1986), Ill. Juvenile Officer Assn., South Suburban Juvenile Officers Assn., Fedn. of Police, Emerald Soc. of Ill. Office: Cook County Sheriffs Police Dept 1401 S Maybrook Dr Maywood IL 60153

FARLING, ROBERT J., utility company executive; b. 1936; married. BSEE, Case Inst. of Tech., 1958; MBA, Case Western Res. U., 1965. With Cleve. Elec. Illuminating Co., 1959—, mgr. mktg., services dept., 1971-74, mgr. residential energy application dept., 1974-76, mgr. consumer services dept., 1976-77, mgr. systems ops. and test dept., 1977-80, v.p. adminstrn. services, from 1980, now pres., operating officer, dir. Office: Cleve Elec Illuminating Co 55 Public Sq Cleveland OH 44113

FARMER, WALTER INGS, interior designer; b. Alliance, Ohio, July 7, 1911; s. Fred Eilbu and Alice Matilda (Putland) F.; m. Renate M. Wichelmann, June 15, 1947 (div. 1966); 1 child, Margaret C. BA, BArch, Miami U., Oxford, Ohio, 1935; LHD (hon.), Miami U., Ohio, 1973. Designer A.B. Closson, Jr. Co., Cin., 1935-42; style coordinator Foley's, Houston, 1946-49; designer, owner Greenwich House Interiors, Cin., 1949—; lectr. Cin. Art Mus., 1936-70, Columbus (Ohio) Art Mus., 1949-60; instr. U. Cin., 1950-67; designer, trustee Martin D'Arcy Art Gallery Loyola U., Chgo. Author: In America Since 1607, 1987; author numerous papers. Founder, 1st pres. bd. Contemporary Art Mus., Houston, 1945-49; founder Walter I. Farmer Mus., Miami U., 1978; chairperson O'Byronville Bus. Assn., 1971-73; mem. spl. com. for Park Bd. City of Cin. Served to capt., U.S. Army, 1942-45, ETO, ret. col. res. Recipient S.M. Hexter award, 1963, Factory's Top Plants of Yr. award, 1967, Designer's Choice award F. Schumacher and Co., 1972; Disting. Alumni award Alliance High Sch., 1987. Mem. AIA (affiliate), Am. Soc. Interior Design (state bd. govs., pres.), Inst. Practicing Designers, Soc. Archtl. Historian, Soc. Colonial Wars, Cin. Art Mus. (life), Taft Mus. (life), Mil. Order World Wars, Print and Drawing Circle (pres.), Literary Club (trustee, v.p., pres.), Delta Phi Delta, Phi Mu Alpha. Republican. Episcopalian. Avocation: collecting art, gardening, music, genealogy. Home: 3457 Observatory Pl Cincinnati OH 45208

FARNAN, WILLIAM THORNTON, architect, educator; b. Mason City, Iowa, Nov. 29, 1947; s. Thornton James and Geraldine Mary (Bassler) F.; divorced; children: Michael, Timothy. Student, St. John's U., 1966-68; BA, Iowa State U., 1970. Registered architect, Minn. Mem. staff planning div. City of Bloomington, Minn., 1971-73; v.p. Eldon Morrison Architects, White Bear Lake, Minn., 1973-80; project coordinator U. Minn., Mpls., 1981-82; prin. Farnan Architects, White Bear Lake, 1982—; educator Tech. Inst., St. Paul, 1986—. Author: Earth Sheltered Residential Design Manual. Mem. adv. bd. Met. Council Housing and Redevel., St. Paul, 1980-83; mem. parish council St. Mary of the Lake, White Bear Lake, 1979—. Nat. Merit Scholar. Mem. AIA, Minn. Soc. Architects. Roman Catholic. Home and Office: 4713 Stewart Ave White Bear Lake MN 55110

FARNELL, ALAN STUART, lawyer; b. Hartford, Conn., Mar. 14, 1948; s. Denis Frank and Katherine Dorothy (Dettenborn) F.; m. Roberta Ann Arquilla, May 21, 1983; children: Thomas Alan, Jeffrey Stuart. B.A. with honors, Trinity Coll., 1970; J.D., Georgetown U., 1973. Bar: D.C. 1973, N.Y. 1975, Ill. 1980, U.S. Dist. Ct. (no. dist.) Ill. 1980, U.S. Ct. Appeals (7th cir.) 1980. Assoc. Kaye, Scholer, Fierman, Hayes & Handler, N.Y.C., 1973-79; assoc. Isham, Lincoln & Beale, Chgo., 1979-83, ptnr., 1983—; gen. counsel 1550 N. State Pkwy. Condominium Assn., Chgo., 1984—; gen. counsel, bd. govs. Ginger Creek Community Assn., Oak Brook, Ill., 1984—. Editor Georgetown Law Jour., 1972-73. Mem. ABA. Club: Butterfield Country (Oak Brook). Home: 31 Baybrook Ln Oak Brook IL 60521 Office: Isham Lincoln & Beale Three First Nat Plaza Chicago IL 60602

FARNER, PETER WORDEN, entrepreneur; b. South Bend, Ind., Apr. 21, 1954; s. James Edward and Maryanne (Worden) F.; m. Betsy J. Meyers, Oct. 18, 1980. B.A., Duke U., 1976; M.B.A., U. Mich., 1980. Pricing analyst Stroh Brewery Co., Detroit, 1977-79, corp. planning assoc. mgr., 1980-81, asst. to pres., 1981-82, brand dir., 1982-84; pres. Peter Worden & Co., 1984—, Worden Traditional Neon Display Co., Inc.; chmn. Worden Sign & Signal, Inc. Republican. Clubs: Country of Detroit (Grosse Pointe, Mich.); Detroit. Home: 16899 Village Ln Grosse Pointe MI 48230 Office: Peter Worden & Co 345 Fisher Rd Grosse Pointe MI 48230

FARNSWORTH, NILE WELDON, accountant, tax consultant; b. Parkersburg, W.Va., Aug. 29, 1928; s. Carroll and Lelah Gertrude (Gorrell) F.; m. Hope Harney, Apr. 7, 1956 (div. May 1970); children: Paula Hope, Jeffrey John; m. Maria Lea Paley, June 19, 1970; children: William Carroll, Robin Elisabeth; stepchildren: Philip Graham Wolfe, John Bennett Wolfe. BSBA, W. Va. U., 1953. CPA, Mich., Mo., Ill. Ptnr. Touche, Ross & Co., Detroit, N.Y.C. and St. Louis, 1953-74; asst. treas. Bank Bldg. Corp., St. Louis, 1975-76; ptnr. Fin. Service Assn., San Francisco, 1977, KMG Main Hurdman, Tulsa, Chgo. and St. Louis, 1978-87; with Baird, Kurtz & Dobson, St. Louis, 1987—. Treas., bd. dirs. St. Louis Nat. Charity Horse Show, 1985; mem. St. Louis Ambassadors, 1985. Served with USN, 1946-49. Mem. Am. Inst. CPAs, Mo. Soc. CPAs. Republican. Episcopalian. Clubs: Media (St. Louis); Forest Hills Country (Chesterfield, Mo.) Lodges: Masons, Rotary. Avocations: golf, tennis, bowling. Home: 646 Clovertrail Dr Chesterfield MO 63017 Office: Baird Kurtz & Dobson 200 N Broadway Saint Louis MO 63102

FARQUHAR, ROBERT NICHOLS, lawyer; b. Dayton, Ohio, Apr. 23, 1936; s. Robert Lawrence and Mary Frances (Nichols) F.; A.B., Kenyon Coll., 1958; J.D., Cornell, 1961; m. Elizabeth Lynn Bryan, Aug. 29, 1959 (div. 1971); children—Robert Nichols, Laura Ann; m. 2d, Carol A. Smith, Dec. 27, 1975. Bar: Ohio 1961, U.S. Dist. Ct. 1962, U.S. Ct. Appeals 1966, U.S. Supreme Ct. 1978. Assoc. Altick & McDaniel, Dayton, 1961-69; ptnr. Gould, Bailey & Farquhar, and predecessor firms, Dayton, 1969-78, Brumbaugh, Corwin & Gould, Dayton, 1978-80, Altick & Corwin, 1981—; dir. ACB Am., Inc., Dayton. City atty., Centerville, Ohio, 1969—. Mem. Montgomery County Rep. Central Com., 1965-69, Exec. Com., 1968-69. Bd. dirs. Centerville Hist. Soc., 1971-75, pres., 1973-74; trustee Montgomery County Legal Aid Soc., 1972-76; trustee Dayton Law Library Assn., 1972—, pres., 1980-86; mem. congressional screening com. U.S. Naval Acad., 1979-83. Mem. ABA, Ohio Bar Assn. (chmn. legal ethics and profl. conduct com. 1982-86), Dayton Bar Assn. (pres. 1984-85), Delta Phi, Phi Delta Phi. Episcopalian. Clubs: Dayton Bicycle, Dayton Lawyers. Home: 32 Williamsburg Ln Centerville OH 45459 Office: 1300 Talbott Tower Dayton OH 45402

FARRA, CHARLES RAYMOND, physician; b. Alexandria, Egypt, Nov. 29, 1929; came to U.S., 1962; s. Fadlalla and Chafika (Wakim) F.; m. Nadia Toutounji, Feb. 28, 1958; children—Charles, George, David. M.B., B.Ch., Ein Shams U., Cairo, 1953, D.L.O., 1955, D.S., 1959. Diplomate Am. Bd. Internal Medicine. Intern, resident Demerdash U. Hosp., Cairo, 1953-55, Cook County Hosp., Chgo., 1962-67; practice medicine, Riverside, Ill.; attending physician McNeal Meml. Hosp., Berwyn, Ill., 1967—; attending physician Hinsdale Sanitarium Hosp., Ill., 1977—, Community Meml. Hosp., La Grange; asst. prof. clinical medicine Rush Presbyn.-St. Luke's Med. Sch. ; clin. asst. prof. Abraham Lincoln Sch. Medicine, U. Ill.-Chgo., 1970—. Bd. dirs. Am. Lebanese League, Washington, 1978—. Mem. AMA, Chgo. Med. Soc., Ill. State Med. Soc. Republican. Avocations: history, classical music, travel, languages. Office: 3722 S Harlem Ave Riverside IL 60546

FARRAR, LYNDA FAIVRE, optometrist; b. Reedsburg, Wis., Sept. 22, 1947; d. Everett Ernest and Kathleen (Page) F.; m. Dennis Edwin Farrar, Aug. 25, 1968; children: Erin, Erik, Elin. BS, Ill. Coll. Optometry, 1971, OD, 1971. Instr. Ill. Coll. Optometry, Chgo., 1971; optometrist Drs. Farrar & James, Oregon, Wis., 1971—; practice optometry Jackson Clinic, Madison, Wis., 1984—; instr. Madison Area Tech. Sch., 1978-82; mem. dept. licensing and regulation Wis. Optometry Examining Bd., Madison, 1984—; bd. dirs. Valley Bank of Oregon. Pres. Oregon Preschool Inc., 1980-81, 82-83. Mem. Am. Optometric Assn., Wis. Optometric Assn., Madison Area Optometric Soc., Epsilon Sigma Alpha. Methodist. Avocations: reading, swimming. Home: 298 Waterman Oregon WI 53575 Office: 287 Dewey St Oregon WI 53575

FARRELL, DAVID COAKLEY, department store executive; b. Chgo., June 14, 1933; s. Daniel A. and Anne D. (O'Malley) F.; m. Betty J. Ross, July 9, 1955; children: Mark, Lisa, David. B.A., Antioch Coll., Yellow Springs, Ohio, 1956. Asst. buyer, buyer, br. store gen. mgr., mdse. mgr. Kaufmann's, Pitts., 1956-66, v.p., gen. mdse. mgr., 1966-69, pres., 1969-74; v.p. May Dept. Stores Co., St. Louis, 1969-75, dir., 1974—, chief operating officer, 1975-79, pres., 1975-85, chief exec. officer, 1979—, chmn., 1985—; dir. 1st Nat. Bank, St. Louis. Bd. dirs. St. Louis Symphony Soc., St. Louis Area council Boy Scouts Am., Arts and Edn. Fund Greater St. Louis; trustee Com. for Econ. Devel., St. Louis Children's Hosp., Washington U., St. Louis; active Salvation Army; mem. Bus. Com. for Arts, Civic Progress. Mem. Nat. Retail Mchts. Assn. (dir.). Roman Catholic. Clubs: University (N.Y.C.); Duquesne (Pitts.); Bogey (St. Louis), Mo. Athletic (St. Louis), Noonday (St. Louis), St. Louis (St. Louis), St. Louis Country (St. Louis). Office: May Dept Stores 6th and Olive Sts Saint Louis MO 63101 *

FARRELL, JEREMIAH EDWARD, automotive company executive; b. Albany, N.Y., Aug. 11, 1937; s. Joseph Courtney and Margaret Mary (Burns) F.; m. Joan Marie Cregan, Dec. 27, 1958; children: Michael, Daniel, Kathleen, Margaret, Maura. Student, Siena Coll., 1955-56, Wayne State U., 1973-74. Br. mgr. Assoc. Investment Co., South Bend, Ind., 1958-67; staff exec. Chrysler Fin. Corp., Detroit, 1967-69; regional mgr. Chrysler Fin. Corp., Atlanta, 1969-75; v.p. central U.S. Chrysler Fin. Corp., Troy, Mich., 1975-81; v.p. ops. Chrysler Fin. Corp., 1981-85, pres., 1985—. Served with USMC, 1956-58. Office: Chrysler Financial Corp 901 Wilshire Dr Troy MI 48084 *

FARRELL, M. PATRICIA, clinical psychologist; b. Sioux Falls, S.D., Nov. 8, 1950; d. John Maurice Williams and Doris Mae (Devine) Williams Rhody; m. John Leo Farrell, Aug. 11, 1974 (div. Oct. 1982). BS, Loyola U., Chgo., 1973; MS, Ill. Inst. Tech., 1976, PhD, 1981. Lic. psychologist, Ill. Staff psychologist Chgo. Bd. of Health, 1977-83; adjunct prof. Ill. Inst. Tech., Chgo., 1983; grant dir. City Colls. of Chgo., 1984-85; staff psychologist Anchor Health Maintenance Orgn., Chgo., 1985—; asst. prof. Rush Med. Sch., Chgo., 1986—; cons. City Colls. of Chgo., 1985—. Recipient Cert. Recognition Citizens for Parents and Children Under Stress, 1982. Mem. Am. Psychol. Assn. Roman Catholic. Home: 13020 Cornell Ln Palos Park IL 60464 Office: Anchor HMO 10436 SW Hwy Chicago Ridge IL 60415

FARRELL, MARY LOU, business educator; b. Whittemore, Iowa, Aug. 20, 1947; d. Orville John and Alvina (Reding) Wagner; m. Dennis Michael Farrell, July 3, 1970; children—Janelle, Nicolle, Ian. B.S., Mt. Mercy Coll., 1969; M.A., U. Iowa, 1977. Educator/coordinator Clear Creek Community Schs., High Sch. Center, Tiffin, Iowa, 1969—. Mem. Nat. Bus. Edn. Assn., Iowa Bus. Edn. Assn., Am. Vocat. Assn., Multi-Occupations Coop. Coordinators of Iowa. Democrat. Roman Catholic. Home: 1511 Derwen St Iowa City IA 52244 Office: Clear Creek Community Schs Tiffin IA 52340

FARRELL, MICHAEL THOMAS, industrial psychologist; b. Cin., Mar. 23, 1954; s. Harvey Joseph and Elva Estell (Gunlack) F.; m. Deborah Eileen Day, Aug. 20, 1976; children: Stephanie Nicole, Andrew Michael, Amanda Christine. BA, Thomas More Coll., 1976; MS, Eastern Ky. U., 1979; PhD, Ill. Inst. Tech., 1983. Lic. psychologist, Ohio, Ky. Intern, staff psychologist Richmond (Ky.) Comprehensive Care, 1978-79; asst. dir. Inst. Psychol. Services, Chgo., 1980-83; v.p., psychologist Midwest Assessment & Cons., Cin., 1984—; adj. faculty mem. U. Cin., 1987. Contbr. articles to profl. jours. Mem. Greater Cin. Assn. Counseling and Devel. (bd. dirs. 1985-86, editor newsletter 1986), Cin. Psychol. Assn., Am. Psychol. Assn., Ohio Psychol. Assn., Acad. Mgmt. Assn., Cin. Acad. Medicine, South Western Ohio Rehab. Assn. Roman Catholic. Home: 2342 Mt Vernon Fairfield OH 45014 Office: 8228 Winton Cincinnati OH 45231

FARRELL, NEAL JOSEPH, banker; b. Bklyn., Aug. 31, 1932; s. Joseph D. and Gertrude B. (Behan) F.; m. Joan Pendergast, Aug. 13, 1955; children—Michael J., Daniel S., Patrick J., Nancy E. B.A., Dartmouth Coll., 1954; grad. Advanced Mgmt. Program, Harvard U., 1970. With Chase Manhattan Bank, N.Y.C., 1956-78; sr. v.p. Chase Manhattan Bank, 1971-78; pres., dir. Mercantile Bank (N.A.), St. Louis, 1978—; vice chmn., dir. Mercantile Bancorp. Inc. Bd. dirs. United Way St. Louis, Arts and Edn. Fund Greater St. Louis, St. Louis Regional Commerce and Growth Assn., Washington U. Med. Ctr.; trustee St. Louis U., St. Louis Children's Hosp., Hawthorn Found. Served to lt. (j.g.) USNR, 1954-56. Mem. Am. Bankers Assn., Assn. Rev. City Bankers. Clubs: Old Warson Country (St. Louis), St. Louis (St. Louis); Log Cabin. Office: Mercantile Bank NA Mercantile Tower Saint Louis MO 63166

FARRELL, THOMAS NEELY, engineering corporation executive, pollution control consultant; b. Memphis, Tenn., Aug. 11, 1930; s. Edwin Thomas and Lois (Neely) F.; m. Mary Mathis, June 22, 1962; children—Michael Geren, John Neely. Student U. Tenn., 1952-55. Photographic technician U.S. Forest Service, 1955-58; mil. analyst U.S. Army Photo Interpretation Ctr., 1958-63; sr. intelligence analyst Nat. Photog. Interpretation Ctr., 1963-77; pres. DeVansco Inc., Fenton, Mich., 1977-79; gen. mgr. Vander Velden, Inc., Grand Blanc, Mich., 1979-80; pres. Xebex Engring. Corp., Fenton, 1980—; pres. Farrell Enterprises, Fenton, 1980—; cons. pollution control Gen. Motors, 1980—. Asst. scout master Tall Pines council Boy Scouts Am., Fenton, 1978-81; chmn. adminstrv. bd. Fenton United Meth. Ch., 1982-84; del. Mich. Republican. Conv., 1982-83. Served with USAF, 1948-52. Recipient Spl. Service award Def. Intelligence Agy., 1965, Outstanding Performance awards, 1965, 68. Mem. Am. Soc. Photogrammetry, Air Pollution Control Assn., Sigma Nu. Lodge: Lions (sec. Fenton 1980-82, pres. 1985-86). Home: 337 W Caroline St Fenton MI 48430 Office: PO Box 189 Fenton MI 48430

FARRINGTON, HELEN AGNES, utility company executive; b. Queens, N.Y., Dec. 1, 1945; d. Joseph Christopher and Therese Marie (Breazzano) F. A.S., Interboro Inst., N.Y.C., 1965; A.A., Ohio State U., 1983, B.S. in Human Resource Mgmt., 1986. Mgmt. cert. U. Mich., 1980. With Ohio Power div. Am. Electric Power Co., Newark, Ohio, 1979—, now personnel mgr. Mem. Licking County Personnel Mgmt. Assn., Safety Council. Mem. adv. bd. Central Ohio Tech. Coll., Licking County Joint Vocat. Sch., Newark High Sch.; mem. Presdl. Task Force, 1983-84. Mem. Am. Soc. Profl. Female Execs., Nat. Assn. Female Execs., Licking County C. of C. Home: 1380 Londondale Pky C-1 Newark OH 43055

FARRIS, WILLIAM PETER, computer/sensors company executive; b. Chgo., May 9, 1952; s. Rolland F. and Mary Anne (Diemer) F.; m. Robbyn Lee Howell, Aug. 9, 1975; children—Michael William, Andrew Timothy. B.S. Mech. Engring., in Ind. Inst. Tech., 1974; M.B.A., Xavier U., 1981. Sales engr. Gen. Electric Co., 1974-77, sales specialist, Schenectady, 1977-78, generation sales engr., Cin., 1978-79; mgr. product devel. FMC Link-Belt, Lexington, Ky., 1979-80, mgr. mktg. devel., 1980-82, mgr. mktg. planning, Cedar Rapids, Iowa, 1982, mgr. product and resource planning, 1982; mgr. nat. accounts Combustion Engring. Accu-Ray, Columbus, Ohio, 1983—. Mem. Sigma Phi Epsilon (alumni bd. 1978-79). Democrat. Roman Catholic. Home: 792 McCall Ct Worthington OH 43085 Office: 650 Ackerman Rd Columbus OH 43202

FARRUG, EUGENE JOSEPH, lawyer; b. Detroit, May 22, 1928; s. Michael and Bridget Mary (Foley) F.; m. Dolores Marie Augustine, Apr. 14, 1951; children—Elizabeth Marie Streit, Eugene Joseph Jr., Matthew Augustine, Pamela Ann, Bridget Louise, Donna Michele. B.B.A., U. Mich., 1950, J.D., 1958. Bar: Ill. 1958, U.S. Dist. Ct. (no. dist.) Ill. 1958; U.S. Supreme Ct. 1980. With Lincoln-Mercury div. Ford Motor Co., Dearborn, Mich., 1950, Aircraft Engine div., Chgo., 1951; assoc. McKenna, Storer, Rowe, White & Farrug, Chgo., 1958-62, ptnr., 1962—. Mem. Citizens of Greater Chgo., 1970-80, pres., 1976-79. Served with USN, 1951-55. McGreggor Fund scholar, 1946; Mich. Bd. Realtors scholar, 1949. Mem. ABA, Ill. Bar Assn., Chgo. Bar Assn., DuPage County Bar Assn., Am. Judicature Soc., Cath. Lawyers Guild, Soc. Trial Lawyers, Trial Lawyers Club Chgo., Fedn. Ins. and Corp. Counsel, Phi Alpha Delta. Lodge: Kiwanis (pres. 1964). Home: 206 N Lincoln St Hinsdale IL 60521

FARUKI, CHARLES JOSEPH, JR., lawyer; b. Bay Shore, N.Y., July 3, 1949; s. Mahmud Taji and Rita (Trownsell) F.; m. Nancy Louise Glock, June 5, 1971; children—Brian Andrew, Jason Allen, Charles Joseph. B.A. summa cum laude, U. Cin., 1971; J.D. cum laude, Ohio State U., 1973. Bar: Ohio 1974, U.S. Dist. Ct. (no. and so. dists.) Ohio 1975, U.S. Ct. Appeals (9th cir.) 1977, U.S. Tax Ct. 1977, U.S. Supreme Ct. 1977, U.S. Ct. Appeals (6th cir.) 1978, U.S. Dist. Ct. (no. dist.) Tex. 1979, U.S. Dist. Ct. (ea. dist.) Ky. 1982, U.S. Ct. Appeals (D.C. cir.) 1982, U.S. Ct. Customs and Patent Appeals 1982, U.S. Ct. Appeals (4th cir.) 1986. Assoc. Smith & Schnacke, Dayton, Ohio, 1974-78, ptnr., 1979—, also dir.; lectr. various continuing legal edn. programs. Contbr. articles in field. Served to capt. U.S. Army Res., 1971-79. Mem. ABA, Fed. Bar Assn. Ohio Bar Assn., Dayton Bar Assn. Avocation: numismatics. Home: 238 Greenmount Blvd Oakwood OH 45419 Office: Smith & Schnacke PO Box 1817 2000 Courthouse Plaza NE Dayton OH 45401-1817

FARVER, MARY JOAN, building products company executive; b. Nov. 17, 1919; d. Peter Herman and Emma Lucile Kuyper; m. Paul V. Farver, Oct. 12, 1945 (div. 1979); children—Mary Farver Griffith, Charles S., Suzanne. B.A., Grinnell Coll., 1941. Sec. Central Nat. Bank, Des Moines, 1941-43; sec. TWA Exec. Office, Washington, 1943-45; chmn. bd. Pella Rolscreen Co., Pella, Iowa, 1980—. Bd. dirs., mem. exec. com. Central Coll., Pella, 1978—; mem. bd. Iowa Coll. Found., Des Moines, 1984—, Iowa Pub. TV Found., Des Moines, 1983—. Republican. Mem. Reformed Ch. of Am. Clubs: Pella Garden (pres. 1961). Lodge: P.E.O. Sisterhood (pres. 1962-64). Home: 2609 Spring Grove Terr Colorado Springs CO 80906 Office: Pella Rolscreen Co 102 Main St Pella IA 50219

FARWELL, MARGARET JOHN, medical foundation/medical center executive; b. Chgo., Sept. 8, 1947; d. John Howland and Carol (Bowers) F. Student U. Exeter, Devon, Eng., 1968; BA, Baker U., 1969; postgrad. U. Kans., 1974-76. Jr. account exec. Biddle Advt. Agy., Kansas City, Mo., 1970-72; admissions officer Baker U., Baldwin, Kans., 1972-74, Benedictine Coll., Atchison, Kans., 1974-76; asst. dir. devel. Rush-Presbyn.-St. Luke's Med. Ctr., Chgo., 1978-81; devel. assoc. Mus. Sci. and Industry, Chgo., 1981-83; exec. v.p./dir. fund devel. Columbus-Cuneo-Cabrini Med. Found./Med. Ctr., Chgo., 1984—; program speaker Chgo. Planned Giving Officers Roundtable, 1984, 86. Bd. dirs., sec. women's bd. Travelers and Immigrants Aid, Chgo., 1982—. Mem. Nat. Soc. Fundraising Execs. (membership com. Chgo. chpt. 1981-83, cert. com. 1982-83, co-chmn. nat. conf. com. 1985-86), Nat. Assn. Hosp. Devel. (regional conf. speaker Chgo. 1984), Nat. Cath. Devel. Conf., 1200 Club of Ill. (bd. dirs. Chgo. chpt. 1983-85). Republican. Episcopalian. Office: Columbus-Cuneo-Cabrini Med Found 676 N St Clair Suite 1900 Chicago IL 60611

FASHING, EDWARD MICHAEL, ranch owner, physical sciences educator; b. Chgo., Jan. 27, 1936; s. Michael George and Leontine (LeClercq)

F.; m. Annette Louise Lubker, Jan. 29, 1959; children: Anita Fashing Kiska, Mary Fashing Schillig, Edward Jr., James, John. BS in Chemistry, Loyola U., Chgo., 1960; MS in Chemistry, DePaul U., 1968; postgrad., U. Mo., 1982-84. Cert. jr. coll. chemistry tchr., Ill. Instr. geology Triton Coll., River Grove, Ill., 1969-81; cattle rancher Cedar Ln. Farm, Sturgeon, Mo., 1974—; asst. prof. N.E. Mo. State U., Kirksville, 1981-82; chemistry asst. U. Mo., Columbia, 1982-84; instr. physics Columbia (Mo.) Coll., 1986. Leader 4H, Sturgeon, 1974-84; news commentator, show moderator and producer KOPN-Radio, 1985—; poster maker Mo. Crisis Ctr., Columbia, 1986—. NSF grantee, 1976. Mem. Am. Assn. Physics Tchrs., Mo. Acad. Sci., Am. Agrl. Movement (publicity dir. 1985, demonstrator 1985, spokesman 1984-86), Farm Alliance of Rural Mo., N.Am. Farm Alliance, United Farmer and Rancher Congress, Phi Delta Kappa (treas. 1978). Democrat. Roman Catholic. Avocations: beekeeping, rockhounding, gardening, clowning, entomology. Home and Farm: Cedar Ln Farm Rt 1 Box 286 Sturgeon MO 65284

FASS, FRED WILLIAM ROBERT, geologist, consultant; b. Milw., Oct. 30, 1951; s. Fred William and Barbara Ann (Schwerdtmann) F. B.S., Mich. Tech. Univ., 1975; M.S. (grad. research asst.), Univ. Mo., Rolla, 1981. Geol. technician Coastal Mining Co., St. Louis, 1977; temp. geologist Amoco Minerals Co., Englewood, Colo., 1978, Asarco, Inc., Knoxville, Tenn., 1979; geologist I Cities Service Co. Tulsa, 1981, geologist II, Oklahoma City, 1981-83; jr. processing geophysicist Digicon Geophys. Corp., Oklahoma City, 1984; cons. geology, Milw., 1984—. Mem. AIME, Am. Assn. Petroleum Geologists, Oklahoma City Geol. Soc., Sigma Xi, Sigma Gamma Epsilon. Avocations: Rock and mineral collecting; singing; camping; canoeing; hiking. Home: 1654 E Newton Ave Milwaukee WI 53211

FASSAK, GARY THOMAS, marketing and advertising executive; b. Paterson, N.J., Apr. 4, 1954; s. John Jr. and Lucy Marie (Di Bon) F. BA, Cornell U., 1976, MBA, 1978. Brand asst. Procter and Gamble Co., Cin., 1978-79, asst. brand mgr., 1979-82, brand mgr., 1982-86, assoc. advt. mgr., 1986—; pres. Cornell U. Radio Guild, Inc. 1975-76; gen. mgr. Sta. WVBR-FM Radio, Ithaca, 1975-76. Mem. Am. Mktg. Assn. Home: 3397 Erie Ave #218 Cincinnati OH 45208

FASSER, WALTER BLANCHARD, JR., consulting company executive, marketing executive; b. Springfield, Mass., June 27, 1937; s. Walter B. and Pauline A. (Marceau) F.; m. Cheryl Lynn Biskup, Dec. 20, 1980; 1 child, David Joseph; 1 child by previous marriage, Cynthia Ann. Cert. mfg. engr. Ops. mgr. Gen. Electric Co., 1955-69; salesman Bellows Internat., Peoria, Ill., 1969-73; sales mgr. Parker Hannifin Co., Cleve., 1973-79; gen. mgr. Alloy Engring., Berea, Ohio, 1979-82; v.p., gen. mgr. MacLean-Fogg-Flodar, Cleve., 1982-85; pres. I.C. Cons. Inc., Euclid, Ohio, 1985—; cons., Ill., Ohio, Ind., Pa., 1971—. Mem. Soc. Mfg. Engrs., Sliva Internat. Grads. Assn. (pres. 1983-84). Republican. Home: 13126 Tradewinds Dr Strongsville OH 44136 Office: IC Cons PO Box 17423 Euclid OH 44117

FASSLER, CRYSTAL G., marketing consultant; b. Marion, Ohio, Mar. 15, 1942; d. Lloyd C. and Iola M. (Runkle) Mahaffey; student public schs., Prospect, Ohio; m. Donald D. Fassler, May 6, 1960; 1 son, Curtis A. Media buyer H. Swink Advt., Marion, 1968-73; media buyer and planner Tracey Locke Advt., Columbus, Ohio, 1973-74, Lord, Sullivan & Yoder Advt., Marion, 1974-82; youth conselor State of Ohio Employment Services, Marion, 1982-83; nat. mktg. consultant WMRN-AM and FM, Marion, 1983-84, asst. gen. mgr., 1985; gen. sales mgr. WRFD Radio, Columbus, 1986—. Home: 1846 Smeltzer Rd Marion OH 43302 Office: 1330 N Main St Marion OH 43302

FAUBER, BERNARD M., retail executive; b. 1922; married. With K Mart Corp., Troy, Mich., 1942—; from jr. asst. to mgr. K-Mart Corp., 1946-59, dist. mgr., 1959-61, asst. regional mgr. South, 1961-65, asst. to pres., 1965-66, Western regional mgr., 1966-68, v.p., 1968-77; sr. exec. v.p., chief adminstrv. officer K Mart Corp., 1977-80, chmn. bd., chief exec. officer, 1980—, also dir.; dir. K Mart Can. Ltd., K Mart Apparel Corp. Served with USN, 1941-45. Office: K Mart Corp 3100 W Big Beaver Rd Troy MI 48084 *

FAUCHALD, THOMAS HARLAN, accounting educator; b. Fargo, N.D., Mar. 15, 1954; s. Melvin J. and Margret (Thomas) F.; m. Rita Ann Jewell, Aug. 11, 1984. BS, Regis Coll., 1976; MS, U. No. Colo., 1978. CPA, N.D. Internal revenue agt. IRS, Denver, 1975-76; prof. acctg. Valley City (N.D.) State Coll., 1978-82, Bemidji (Minn.) State U., 1982—; cons. SBA, Bemidji, 1982—. Mem. Am. Inst. CPA's, North Oak Soc. CPA's, Delta Pi Epsilon. Lutheran. Office: Bemidji State U Dept Bus Adminstrn Bemidji MN 56601

FAULCONER, JAMES GAYLE, mental health administrator, counselor; b. Jackson, Miss., July 1, 1928; s. James N. and Viola (Brock) F.; m. Marilyn Brondell, July 9, 1954; children: Walter, Laura, Julie, Marsha. BA, Transylvania U., 1950; MDiv, Lexington Theol. Sem., 1953; MS in Counseling, Wright State U., 1971. Pastor First Christian Ch., Cambridge, Ohio, 1956-62, Kettering, Ohio, 1962-70; pastoral counselor Miami County Mental Health Clinic, Troy, Ohio, 1971-75, Daymont West Mental Health Clinic, Dayton, Ohio, 1975-77; dir. Shelby County Mental Health Clinic, Sidney, Ohio, 1977—. Mem. Assn. Mental Health Adminstrs., Am. Assn. Marriage & Family Therapists, Am. Assn. Pastoral Counselors. Lodge: Kiwanis. Avocations: genealogy, woodworking, photography. Home: 199 S Dorset Rd Troy OH 45373 Office: Shelby County Mental Health Clinic 500 E Court St Sidney OH 45365

FAULKNER, CHARLES BRIXEY, government official; lawyer; b. Springfield, Mo., Feb. 11, 1934; s. Charles Franklin and Josephine Frances (Brixey) F.; B.S., U. Ark., 1956; LL.B., U. Mo., 1960; m. Noralee Phariss, Dec. 29, 1956; children—Charlesa, Charles Byron. Admitted to Mo. bar, 1960, Fed. bar, 1962; partner Ratican & Faulkner, Aurora, Mo., 1960-71; legal adviser U.S. Bur. Prisons, U.S. Med. Center, Springfield, Mo., 1972; regional atty U.S. Bur. Prisons, Kansas City, Mo., 1974—; pros. and county atty., Lawrence County, Mo., 1961-70; city atty. Aurora, 1970-72, Marionville, Mo., 1961-72. Chmn. bd. dirs. A.R.C., Lawrence County, 1963-65. Served with 1st div., 26th Inf., AUS, 1956-57. Recipient Kansas City Trust award in estate planning, 1960. Mem. 39th Jud. Circuit Bar Assn. (v.p. 1966-70), Scabbard and Blade, Beta Gamma Sigma. Rotarian (dir. 1961-72). Editorial bd. Mo. Law Rev., 1958-60. Home: 312 S Elliott St Aurora MO 65605 Office: Air World Ctr 10920 Ambassador Dr Suite 2 Kansas City MO 64151

FAULKNER, EDWIN JEROME, insurance company executive; b. Lincoln, Nebr., July 5, 1911; s. Edwin Jerome and Leah (Meyer) F.; m. Jean Rathburn, Sept. 27, 1933. B.A., U. Nebr., 1932; M.B.A., U. Pa., 1934. With Woodmen Accident & Life Co., Lincoln, 1934—; successively claim auditor, v.p. Woodmen Accident & Life Co., 1934-38, pres., dir., 1938-77, chmn. bd., chief exec. officer, 1977-83, hon. chmn., exec. counsel, 1983—; pres., dir. Comml. Mut. Surety Co., 1938—; dir. Lincoln Telecommunications Inc., Universal Surety Co., Inland Ins. Co.; past dir. 1st Nat. Bank & Trust Co., Lincoln; chmn. Health Ins. Council, 1959-60; mem. adv. council on social security HEW, 1974-75. Author: Accident and Health Insurance, 1940, Health Insurance, 1960; Editor: Man's Quest for Security, 1966. Chmn. Lincoln-Lancaster County Plan Commn., 1948-67; mem. medicare adv. com. Dept. Def., 1957-70; Neb. Republican State Finance chmn., 1968-73; Chmn., trustee Bryan Meml. Hosp.; trustee Doane Coll., 1961-70, Lincoln Found., Am. Coll. Life Underwriters, Cooper Found., Newcomen Soc. N.Am.; chmn. bd. trustees U. Nebr. Found.; bd. dirs. Nebraskans for Pub. TV., Bus. Industry Polit. Action Com., Washington. Served from 2d lt. to lt. col. USAAF, 1942-45. Decorated Legion of Merit; recipient Disting. Service award U. Nebr., 1957; Harold R. Gordon Meml. award Internat. Assn. Health Ins. Underwriters, 1955, Ins. Man of Year award Ins. Field, 1958; Dist. Service award Nebr. Council on Econ. Edn., 1986, Exec. of Yr. award Am. Coll. Hosp. Adminstrs., 1971; Nebr. Builders award, 1979; Disting. Service award Lincoln Kiwanis Club, 1980. Mem. Health Ins. Assn. Am. (1st pres. 1956), Am. Legion, Am. Life Conv. (exec. com. 1961-70, pres. 1966-67), Ins. Econs. Soc. (chmn. 1971-73), Nebr. Hist. Soc. (pres. 1982-84), Ins. Fedn. Nebr. (pres.), Phi Beta Kappa, Phi Kappa Psi, Alpha Kappa Psi (hon.). Republican. Presbyn. Lodges: Masons, Elks. Home: 4100 South St Lincoln NE 68506 Office: 1526 K St Lincoln NE 68508

FAULKNER, JAMES CHARLES, electrical contractor; b. Fairfax, Mo., Oct. 21, 1951; s. James Gerald and Eva Gertrude (McClaskey) F.; m. Katherine Dell Martin, Dec. 15, 1973; children—Joshua James, Renee Elizabeth. Student Universal Trade Sch., Omaha, 1969-70, Southwest Mo. State U., 1979. Electrician, B & N Cooling and Heating, Fairfax, Mo., 1970-71; electrician Polk County Elec. Co., Bolivar, Mo., 1971-79, ptnr., 1979—. Chmn. dept. church men Ozark Lakes Area Christian Ch. Mid.-Am. Mem. Nat. Fedn. Ind. Bus., Bolivar C. of C. Mem. Christian Ch. Lodges: Optimists (Bolivar, Mo.); Masons (sec.). Home: Rt 3 Box 132 Bolivar MO 65613 Office: 116 S Market St Bolivar MO 65613

FAUMAN, BEVERLY JOYCE, psychiatrist, educator; b. Detroit, Jan. 18, 1943; d. Jack Walter and Irene Sonia (Neiman) Freedman; m. Michael Arthur Fauman; children: Eric, Susan, Karen, Lisa. BA in Math., Fla. State U., 1962; MD, Tufts U., 1968. Diplomate Am. Bd. Psychiatry and Neurology. Intern Boston VA Hosp., Jamaica Plain, Mass., 1968-69, fellow in internal medicine, 1967-70; resident in psychiatry U. Chgo. Hosp., 1970-73; dir. psychiat. emergency service U. Chgo., 1973-78, from instr. to asst. prof., 1973-78; dir. psychiat. emergency service Henry Ford Hosp., Detroit, 1978-81; asst. prof. U. Mich., Ann Arbor, 1979-82; dir. psychiat. edn. Sinai Hosp., Detroit, 1981—; asst. prof. Wayne State U., Detroit, 1981-86, assoc. prof., 1986—. Author: Emergency Psychiatry for the House Officer, 1981; contbr. articles to profl. jours. Fellow Am. Psychiat. Assn., Mich. Psychiat. Soc. (chair program com. 1982-85), Mich. Psychiat. Soc. (counselor, Pres. award 1984), Am. Coll. Emergency Physicians (Pres. award 1981). Avocations: music, crafts, needlework, children. Office: Sinai Hosp 6767 W Outer Dr Detroit MI 48235

FAUSAK, WILLIAM ARTHUR, writing paper company executive; b. Jersey City, N.J., Oct. 31, 1938; s. William Otto and Eleanore Louise (Carnie) F.; B.S., U. Pa., 1961; m. Carol Jean Davis, Sept. 16, 1967; 1 son, Erik Davis. Auditor, Uniroyal, Inc., N.Y.C., 1963-66; sr. internal auditor GAF Corp., N.Y.C., 1966-68; fin. controls supr. Random House, Inc., N.Y.C., 1968-70; sr. auditor, supr. audits, mgr. audits The Singer Co., N.Y.C., 1970-75, dir. trade relations, 1975-77; dir. corp. internal auditing Parker Pen Co., Janesville, Wis., 1977-86; dir. internal audit Appleton (Wis.) Papers Inc., 1986—. Served with USNR, 1961-63. Cert. internal auditor. Mem. Inst. Internal Auditors. Clubs: Janesville Country, Blackhawk Curling. Home: 3135 N Peach Tree Ln Appleton WI 54911 Office: Appleton Papers Inc 825 E Wisconsin Ave Appleton WI 54912

FAUST, THOMAS EUGENE, accountant; b. Brazil, Ind., Nov. 21, 1954; s. Leland Woodrow and Jean Marie (Applegate) F.; m. Judith Irene Molina, Nov. 20, 1976; children: Brianne, Jonathan. BS Acctg., Ball State U., 1976. CPA, Ind. Supr. acctg. services Smith, Thompson, Wihebrink & Co., Lafayette, Ind., 1976—. Mem. budget com. Greater Lafayette United Way, 1984-87. Mem. Ind. CPA Soc., Lafayette CPA Chpt. (pres. 1985). Methodist. Clubs: Lafayette Lotus Users, Lafayette Ski. Home: 174 Coldbrook Dr Lafayette IN 47905 Office: Smith Thompson Wiltebrink & Co Inc. 427 N Sixth Lafayette IN 47901

FAUVER, VERNON ARTHUR, chemical engineer; b. Hammond, Ind., Mar. 25, 1928; s. Gale Vernon and Charlotte Irene (Guss) F.; m. Dorothy Ruth Faulstich, Dec. 23, 1947; children—John Vernon, Gayle Ellyn. B.S. in Chem. Engring., Purdue U., 1952, M.S. in Chem. Engring, 1953. Registered profl. engr., Mich. Chem. engr. Eastman Kodak Co., Rochester, N.Y., 1953, Dow Chem. U.S.A., Midland, Mich., 1954—. Bd. dirs. Chippewa Nature Ctr., Midland, Mich. 1981—, pres., 1985-86. Served with USN, 1946-48. Mem. Am. Inst. Chem. Engrs. (chmn. mid-Mich. sect. 1980), Am. Chem. Soc. (editorial adv. panel CHEMTECH 1975-83, chmn. div. indsl. and engring. chemistry, 1973, Disting. Service award, 1974) Nat. Soc. Profl. Engrs. Avocations: nature study; photography. Office: Dow Chem USA Bldg 1131 Midland MI 48667

FAVA, CHRISTOPHER ROBERT, controller; b. St. Louis, Mar. 23, 1958; s. Clyde John and Alice Marie (Booth) F.; m. Mary Walsh Murphy, June 2, 1984; 1 child, Christopher Jr. BSBA, St. Louis U., 1979. CPA, Mo. Sr. acct. Fox & Co., CPA, St. Louis, 1980-82, Robert Berri, CPA, Clayton, Mo., 1982-84; controller Paric Corp., St. Louis, 1984—. Mem. alumni bd. dirs. St. Louis U. High, 1976—. Mem. Am. Inst. CPA's, Mo. Soc. CPA's. Roman Catholic. Home: 4954 Sutherland Saint Louis MO 63109 Office: Paric Corp 689 Craig Rd Saint Louis MO 63141

FAVAZZA, ARMANDO RICCARDO, psychiatrist, educator; b. N.Y.C., Apr. 14, 1941; s. Armando G. and Estelle (Barra) F.; m. Barbara Starks, 1967; children: Terence, Laura. BA, Columbia U., 1962; MD, U. Va., 1966; MPH, U. Mich., 1971. Intern Bon Secours Hosp., Grosse Pointe, Mich., 1966-67; resident U. Mich., Ann Arbor, 1967-71; prof., assoc. chmn. psychiatry dept. U. Mo., Columbia, 1973—. Author: Anthropological Themes in Mental Health, 1977, Themes in Cultural Psychiatry, 1982, Bodies Under Siege, 1987; editor in chief Dept. Psychiatry Jour., 1973—. Served to lt. USNR, 1971-73. Recipient George B. Kunkel award Harrisburg Hosp., 1987. Fellow Am. Psychiat. Assn., Am. Coll. Psychiatrists, Am. Assn. for Social Psychiatry; mem. Mo. Psychiat. Soc. (pres. 1981-82). Avocation: tennis. Home: 2710 Malibu Ct Columbia MO 65203 Office: U Mo Dept Psychiatry 3 Hospital Dr Columbia MO 65201

FAVERMAN, GERALD ALDEN, management consultant; b. Boston, Nov. 21, 1935; s. Irving J. and Sarah (Alden) F.; m. Frances Labatt, July 30, 1961; children: David Gregory, Paul Alan. BS, Boston Coll., 1957; MA, Boston U., 1960; PhD, Mich. State U., 1975. Fiscal cons. Legis. Fiscal Agy., Lansing, Mich., 1968-71; asst. dean. Coll. of Osteo. Medicine Mich. State U., East Lansing, Mich., 1971-75; founding dean Coll. of Osteopathic Medicine Ohio U., Athens, 1975-77, vice provost planning, 1977-78; project dir. Am. Osteo. Assn., Chgo., 1978-80; founder, chmn. Pub. Sector Cons., Inc., Lansing, 1980—. Author: Mesopotamia, First Light, 1966, Kellogg Report: Graduate Osteopathic Medical Education, 1981. Bd. dirs. Impression V Mus., Lansing, 1981—; pres. Mid-Mich. Opera Co., 1983-85; bd. dirs. Friends of Turner-Dodge House, Lansing, 1986—; mem. Mich. Commn. on Bicentennial of U.S. Constn., 1986—. Jewish. Clubs: Lansing City, University. Avocations: archaeology, military history, travel, opera, reading. Home: 1374 Lakeside Dr East Lansing MI 48823 Office: Pub Sector Cons Inc 300 S Washington Sq Lansing MI 48933

FAWCETT, JAMES DAVIDSON, herpetologist, educator; b. New Plymouth, N.Z., Jan. 10, 1933; s. James and Edna Lola (Catterick) F.; B.Sc., U. N.Z., 1960; M.Sc., U. Auckland (N.Z.), 1964; Ph.D., U. Colo., 1975; m. Georgene Ellen Tyler, Dec. 21, 1968. Head dept. biology Kings Coll., Auckland, 1960; grad. demonstrator dept. zoology U. Auckland, 1961-62, sr. demonstrator, 1963-64; grad. asst. U. Colo., 1969-72; instr. biology U. Nebr., Omaha, 1972-75, asst. prof., 1975-81, asso. prof., 1981—. Recipient Great Tchr. award U. Nebr., 1981. Mem. Royal Soc. N.Z., N.Z. Assn. Scientists, Am. Soc. Zoologists, Soc. Systematic Zoology, Herpetologists League, Brit. Soc. Herpetologists, AAAS, Nebr. Herpetological Soc. (pres. 1979-80), Sigma Xi (pres. Omaha chpt. 1980-81), Phi Sigma. Contbr. articles to profl. jours. Home: 309 S 56th St Omaha NE 68134 Office: Biology Dept U Nebr Omaha NE 68182

FAWCETT, RICHARD STEVEN, agriculture educator; b. Iowa City, Apr. 26, 1948; s. Alfred Walter and Helen Marie (Hodgen) F.; m. Linda Carol Ryan, Mar. 25, 1972; children: Jennifer Malissa, Lindsay Marium. BS in Agronomy, Iowa State U., 1970; PhD in Agronomy, U. Ill., 1974. Asst. prof. U. Wis., Madison, 1974-76; asst. to assoc. prof. Iowa State U., Ames, 1976-81, prof., 1981—. Contbr. articles to profl. jours. Mem. Weed Sci. Soc. Am. (bd. dirs. 1982-85, Outstanding Extension 1985), N. Cen. Weed Control Conf. (bd. dirs. 1977-80), Am. Soc. Agronomy, Crop Sci. Soc. Am., Iowa Fertilizer and Chem. Soc. (bd. dirs. 1981—), Am. Soybean Assn. (Recognition award 1981). Quaker. Avocations: guitar, singing, hiking. Office: Iowa State U Dept Agronomy Ames IA 50011

FAWCETT, SHERWOOD LUTHER, research laboratory executive; b. Youngstown, Ohio, Dec. 25, 1919; s. Luther T. and Clara (Sherwood) F.; m. Martha L. Simcox, Feb. 28, 1953; children: Paul, Judith, Tom. BS, Ohio State U., 1941; MS, Case Inst. Tech., 1948, PhD, 1950; hon. degrees, Ohio State U., Gonzaga U., Whitman Coll., Otterbein Coll., Detroit Inst. Tech., Ohio Dominican Coll. Registered profl. engr., Ohio. Mem. staff Columbus Labs. Battelle Meml. Inst., 1950-64, mgr. physics dept., 1959-64; dir. Pacific Northwest Labs., Richland, Wash., 1964-67; exec. v.p. Battelle Meml. Inst., Columbus, Ohio, 1967-68; pres., chief exec. officer Battelle Meml. Inst., 1968-80, chmn., chief exec. officer, 1981-84, chmn. bd. trustees, 1984—; bd. dirs. Columbia Gas Systems, Inc. Served with the USNR, 1941-46. Decorated Bronze Star. Mem. Am. Phys. Soc., Am. Nuclear Soc., Nat. Soc. Profl. Engrs., Am. Inst. Metall. Engrs., Sigma Xi, Delta Chi, Sigma Pi Sigma, Tau Beta Pi. Home: 2820 Margate Rd Columbus OH 43221 Office: Battelle Meml Inst 505 King Ave Columbus OH 43201

FAWELL, HARRIS W., congressman; b. West Chicago, Ill., Mar. 25, 1929; m. Ruth Johnson, 1954; children: Richard, Jane, John. Student, Naperville North Central Coll., 1949; LL.D., Chgo.-Kent Coll. Law, 1952. Ptnr. Fawell, James & Brooks, Naperville, Ill., 1954-84; mem. Ill. Senate, Springfield, 1963-77; gen. counsel Ill. Assn. Park Dists., 1977-84; mem. 99th-100th Congresses from 13th Ill. dist., Washington, 1985—. Office: Ho of Reps Office House Members Washington DC 20515 *

FAY, DOUGLAS PAUL, chemist; b. Fayette, Iowa, Aug. 14, 1943; s. John D. and Opal F. (Dumermuth) F.; m. Deanna M. Powell, June 4, 1966; children: Brian E., Jeffery E., John D. (dec.), Christopher J. BS, Upper Iowa U., 1965; PhD, Okla. State U., 1969. V.p. research and devl. Alva (Okla.) Research Corp., 1971-74; mgr. Alva Concrete, 1974-78; salesman Dearborn div. W.R. Grace, Cedar Rapids, Iowa, 1978-79; dist. mgr. Dearborn div. W.R. Grace, Chgo., 1979-81, nat. accts. mgr., 1981—. Mem. Alva City Council, 1976-78. Mem. Am. Chem. Soc., Nat. Assn. Corrosion Engrs. Republican. Methodist. Home: 2512 Yellowstar St Woodridge IL 60517

FAY, MARGARET F., computer analyst; b. Cin., June 5, 1949; s. James Joseph and Martha C. (Vogel) F.; m. Samuel H. Feder, Oct. 12, 1975. AS summa cum laude, U. Cin., 1974, BS summa cum laude, 1975. Computer technician Procter & Gamble, Cin., 1968-86, computer analyst, 1986-87, systems analyst, 1987—. Tutor Labach Literacy Council, Cin., 1986—. Mem. Assn. Computing Machinery, Cat Fanciers Fedn. (all breed judge 1980—), Mensa. Jewish.

FAY, PETER CARLYLE, mechanical engineer; b. Pitts., Nov. 2, 1958; s. Carlyle Waldie and Marjorie Ann (Sundquist) F.; m. Laura Elizabeth Coerper, Nov. 27, 1981. BSME, U. Wis., 1981. Field engr. Schlumberger Wells Services, Laurel, Miss., 1981-83; tech. engr. Commonwealth Edison, Braidwood, Ill., 1983-84, startup test engr., 1984-85, hot functional dir., 1985-86, fuel load coordinator, 1986, startup test coordinator, 1986—. Mem. ASME, Am. Nuclear Soc. Republican. Lutheran. Avocations: airplane and balloon flying, home restoration. Home: 201 S 1st St Wilmington IL 60481 Office: Commonwealth Edison Rt 1 Box 84 Braceville IL 60407

FAZIO, ANTHONY LEE, investment company executive; b. Wheeling, W.Va., Jan. 27, 1937; s. Frank G. and Julia Louise (DeFillipo) F.; m. Faye Elizabeth Kelly, Sept. 3, 1964; children: Tracey Lee, Kelly Ann. BSEE, W.Va. U., 1959. Registered investment advisor, real estate syndicator; cert. fin. planner. With computer div. RCA, 1964-72, mgr. product mktg., 1970-71, mgr. systems planning, 1971-72; dir. bus. and product planning Univac, 1972-73, dir. product mktg. and bus./product planning N.Am., 1973-75, regional mgr., 1975-77; v.p. sales Sycor, Inc., Ann Arbor, Mich., 1977-78; v.p. sales No. Telecom Systems Corp., 1978-79, v.p. mktg., 1979-80; pres. Gibbs Irwin Investments Co., 1981-83; product procurement and due diligence officer Midland Mgmt. Corp., 1983-86; regional dir. Fin. Network Investment Corp., 1986—; mktg. dir. NIDA, Inc., 1986—. Served with Signal Corps, U.S. Army, 1959-61. Mem. Internat. Assn. Fin. Planners, Data Processing Mgmt. Assn. (cert. in data processing), Tau Beta Pi, Eta Kappa Nu. Republican. Methodist. Home: 4770 Regents Walk Shorewood MN 55331 Office: 6120 Earle Brown Dr Suite 600 Minneapolis MN 55430

FAZIO, PETER VICTOR, JR., lawyer; b. Chgo., Jan. 22, 1940; s. Peter Victor and Marie Rose (LaMantia) F.; m. Patti Ann Campbell, Jan. 3, 1966; children—Patti-Marie, Catherine, Peter. A.B., Holy Cross Coll., Worcester, Mass., 1961; J.D., U. Mich., 1964. Bar: Ill. 1964, U.S. Dist. Ct. (no. dist.) Ill. 1965, U.S. Ct. Appeals (7th cir.) 1972, U.S. Ct. Appeals (D.C. cir.) 1981, U.S. Supreme Ct. 1977. Assoc. Schiff, Hardin & Waite, Chgo., 1964-70, ptnr., 1970-82, 84—; exec. v.p. Internat. Capital Equipment, Chgo., 1982-83, also dir., 1982-84, sec., 1982-87; dir. Planmetrics Inc., Chgo., 1984—, Chgo. Lawyers Commn. for Civil Rights Under Law, 1976-82, co-chmn., 1978-80, Seton Health Corp. Northern Ill., 1986—. Trustee Barat Coll., Lake Forest, Ill., 1977-82; mem. exec. adv. bd. St. Joseph's Hosp., Chgo., 1984—, chmn., 1986—. Mem. ABA, Ill. State Bar Assn., Chgo. Bar Assn., Am. Soc. Corp. Secs. Clubs: Saddle & Cycle (sec. 1983-86), Tavern, Metropolitan. (Chgo.). Office: Schiff Hardin & Waite 7200 Sears Tower Chicago IL 60606

FEARING, SANDRA DOSCH, accountant; b. Bismarck, N.D., Aug. 5, 1960; d. Jacob Phillip and Lucille (Braun) Dosch; m. Mitchell Ray Fearing, May 20, 1983. Student, Valley City State Coll., 1978-80; BBA in Acctg., U. N.D., 1980-82. CPA, Oreg., N.D. Staff auditor Touche Ross & Co., Mpls., 1982; auditor Touche Ross & Co., Portland, Oreg., 1983-85; tax acct., auditor Zine, Hoover & Voller, Williston, N.D., 1985—. Reader, money counter, mem. choir St. Joseph's Cath. Ch., Williston. Mem. AAUW (chmn. publicity com., annual book bazaar), Am. Inst. CPA's, N.D. Soc. CPA's (govtl. com., sec. treas. Williston chpt.), Am. Women's Soc. CPA's (active various coms.). Avocations: tennis, music, golfing, bike riding, reading. Office: Zine Hoover & Voller 111 E Broadway Williston ND 58801

FEATHERSTONAUGH, HENRY GORDON, psychologist; b. San Diego, Nov. 11, 1917; s. Henry Stuart and Evelyn (Borrow) F.; B.S., U. Calif., Berkeley, 1939; M.S., Lehigh U., 1974; Ph.D., U. Mo., 1978; m. Nancy Ellen Couper, July 28, 1946; children—Wendy, Rusby. Chemist, H.J. Heinz Co., Berkeley, Calif., 1938-40; dist. mgr. Union Carbide Corp., N.Y.C., 1945-73; geriatric services coordinator The Center for Mental Health, Anderson, Ind., 1979-82; v.p., sec. Living Skills Inst., Inc., Indpls., 1982—; lectr. in field. Exec. bd. Madison County Council on Aging, 1979—. Served with U.S. Army, 1941-43, USAAF, 1943-45; ATO, CBI. Decorated Air medal with oak leaf cluster, D.F.C.; Lehigh U. teaching asst. and tuition grantee, 1972-73; U. Mo. research grantee, 1974-78; diplomate in profl. psychotherapy Internat. Acad. Profl. Counseling and Psychotherapy. Mem. Am. Psychol. Assn., Ind. Psychol. Assn., Gerontol. Soc. Am., Internat. Assn. Applied Psychology, Am. Assn. Sex Educators, Counselors and Therapists, Am. Chem. Soc., Internat. Platform Assn., Psi Chi, Phi Kappa Phi. Contbr. articles to profl. jours. Office: 8204 Westfield Blvd Indianapolis IN 46240

FEDELL, JEAN MARIE, gemologist, jewelry appraiser, consultant; b. Neenah, Wis., Sept. 22, 1956; d. John Randolph and Arlene Ross (Jenzen) F. BA, U. Wis., Madison, 1979; postgrad. Gemol. Inst. Am., 1980, Gemological Assn. Gt. Britain, 1986. Gemologist, colored stone buyer Ball Co., Chgo., 1980, ind. auditor of jewelry, 1981; gemologist appraiser Bailey Banks and Biddle div. of Zale Corp., Schaumburg, Ill., 1980-87; pres. r. Jaimeson Brown Evaluation Cons.'s, Inc., Schaumburg, 1987—. Leader Blackhawk council Girl Scouts U.S., 1978.Mem. Gemol. Inst. Am., Smithsonian Assocs. Avocations: photography, needlework. Office: R Jamieson Brown Evaluation Cons Inc J308 Woodfield Mall Schaumburg IL 60173

FEDERER, JOSEPH HERMAN, systems analyst; b. Columbus, Ohio, Feb. 4, 1960; s. John Leo and Jeanne Elizabeth (Rogers) F.; m. Cathy Joan Schnabel, Nov. 27, 1982. BS, Miami U., Oxford, Ohio, 1982. Programmer, analyst NCR Corp., Dayton, Ohio, 1982-85, sr. analyst, 1985-86, mgr. fin. systems CDISS, 1987—. Mem. Dayton Info. Ctr. Profl. Orgn., CONSCO User Assn. (bd. dirs., sec.). Republican. Roman Catholic. Avocations: soccer, softball, basketball. Office: NCR Corp World Hdqrs 1700 S Patterson Blvd Dayton OH 45479

FEDI, PETER FRANCIS, dentistry educator; b. East Hampton, N.Y., Feb. 16, 1924; s. Peter and Rose (Sorce) F.; m. Ann Agnes Donnelly, Oct. 1, 1944; children—Bonnie, Peter F. III, Robert. D.D.S., U. Pa., 1946; M.Sc., Ohio State U., 1956. Diplomate Am. Bd. Periodontology. Practice dentistry, Southampton, N.Y., 1946-52; commd. lt. Dental Corps, U.S. Navy, 1952, advanced through grades to capt., 1963; chmn. dept. dentistry USS

Yorktown, 1958-60; chmn. dept. periodontics U.S. Navy Dental Sch., Bethesda, Md., 1962-69; chmn. dental services U.S. Navy Hosp., Orlando, 1970-72; ret., 1972; Rinehart prof. U. Mo.-Kansas City Sch. Dentistry, 1972—, chmn. dept. periodontics, 1976-82, dir. clin. spltys. advanced edn. programs, 1982—; cons. periodontics VA Hosp., Leavenworth, Kans., 1972—. Author: The Periodontics Syllabus, 1985. Fellow Am. Coll. Dentists; mem. ADA (cons. Council on Dental Edn. 1982—), Am. Acad. Periodontology (chmn. subcom. on predoctoral edn. 1981—, mem. exec. council 1981-84), Midwest Soc. Periodontology, Am. Assn. Dental Schs. Republican. Roman Catholic. Home: 455 E Lakeshore Dr Lake Quivira KS 66106 Office: Univ Mo Sch Dentistry 650 E 25th St Kansas City KS 64108

FEE, CHESTER FRANKLIN, orthopaedic surgeon; b. Cunningham, Kans., Sept. 21, 1925; s. Charles John and Winefred Elizabeth (Thompson) F.; m. Ardyce Lorraine Pearson, Aug. 28, 1955; children: Suzanne, Carolyn, Michael, Janet. AB, U. Kans., 1951, MA Bacteriology, 1952, MD, 1956. Diploma Am. Bd. Orthopaedic Surgeons; licensed aircraft engine mechanic. Gen. practice medicine Overland Park, Kans., 1957-60, Prairie Village, Kans., 1960-64; fellow Cleve. Clinic, 1964-68; orthopaedic surgeon Drisko, Fee & Parkins, Inc., Kansas City, Mo., 1968—; chief of surgery Trnity Luth. Hosp., 1973-76, chief orthopaedic surgery, 1976-84, bd. dirs. Author Cleve. Clin. Quarterly, 1968, Minn. State Med. Jour., 1968. Served to corp. USAAF, 1943-46. Mem. AMA, Mo. State Med. Assn., Jackson County (Mo.) Med. Soc., Am. Acad. Orthopaedic Surgery, Mo. State Orthopaedic Soc., Kansas City Orthopaedic Soc. (v.p., sec., treas. 1968). Republican. Lutheran. Avocations: woodworking, hunting, fishing, boating. Home: 16960 South Metcalf Stilwell KS 66085 Office: Drisko Fee & Parkins Inc 2929 Baltimore Kansas City MO 64108

FEE, GERARD WAYNE COWLE, professional association executive; b. North Fairfield, Ohio, Feb. 12, 1933; s. Cleland Randolph and Helen Marcella (Cole) F. BA, Washington & Lee U., 1955; LittB, Oxford U., 1959; postgrad., U. Madrid, 1955, 1959-60. Asst. to pres. Lake Erie Coll., Painesville, Ohio, 1964-74; exec. dir. Ohio State Pharm. Assn., Columbus, Ohio, 1974-79; exec. sec. Ohio State Bd. Optometry, Columbus, 1979-80; exec. dir. The Inst. Internal Auditors, Altamonte Springs, Fla., 1980-81; dir. adminstrv. services The Lexington (Ky.) Sch., 1982-84; exec. dir. EDP Auditors Assn., Carol Stream, Ill., 1984—; lectr. various univs. and assns. Editor Ohio Pharmacist jour., 1975-79, EDP Auditor Update, 1984—. Reading clk. Ohio Ho. of Reps., 1961-63, rules clk., 1962-63; sec. treas. Ohio Pharmacy Polit. Action Com., 1975-79; vestry mem. Christ Ch. Anglican, 1979, 82; founder, pres. Blue Grass Assn. Ind. Schs., 1982-84. Fulbright scholar, 1955-57. Mem. Oxford Soc., Am. Soc. Assn. Execs., Wheaton (Ill.) C. of C., Conf. Computer Audit, Phi Beta Kappa, Pi Sigma Alpha. Republican. Clubs: United Oxford & Cambridge (London); Athletic of Columbus. Avocations: antiques, athletics, biographical studies, music, mystery stories. Home: One Wheaton Ctr #211 Wheaton IL 60187 Office: EDP Auditors Assn Found 455 Kehoe Blvd PO Box 88180 Carol Stream IL 60188-0180

FEELEY, SHARON DENISE, marketing and management consultant; b. Chgo., Sept. 17, 1949; d. Darrell Ford and Florence Marsha (Gregorek) F. Student, SUNY. Coll. mgr. Sara Beattie Secretarial Coll., Hong Kong, 1976-77; bus. mgr. Transplex Inc., Oak Park, Ill., 1977-79, gen. mgr., 1981-84; trade officer far east State of Ill., Hong Kong, 1979-81; purchase agt., sales aide Honeywell Inc., Bensenville, Ill., 1984-86; now internat. bus. mktg. and mgmt. cons. Lake Zurich, Ill., 1986—. Editor: Tai Chi Classics, 1978. Mem. Asian Women's Mgmt. Assn. (vice chmn., founding mem. 1979-81), Mensa Club. Lodge: Rosicrucians. Avocations: power volleyball, Chinese cultural studies. Home: 1183 Betty Dr Lake Zurich IL 60047

FEELY, RICHARD ALAN, physician, surgeon; b. Berwyn, Ill., Jan. 4, 1952; s. Daniel Richard and Donna Jean (LaCount) F.; m. Carol Anne Frieders, June 29, 1974; 1 son, Brad Richard. B.S., N.E. Mo. State U., 1974; D.O., Kirksville Coll. Osteo. Medicine, 1978. Diplomate Nat. Bd. Examiners Osteo. Physicians and Surgeons; cert. Am. Osteopathic Bd. Gen. Practice, 1986. Nat. Assn. Disability Evaluating Physicians. Dir. osteo. manipulative medicine Good Samaritan Hosp., Tampa, Fla., 1979-80; physician Mauer Clinic, Zion, Ill., 1980-81; instr. Chgo. Coll. Osteo. Medicine, 1980-82, asst. prof., 1982-83, clin. asst. prof. osteo. medicine, 1983-86; clin. assoc. prof. family medicine, 1986—; pres. Rhema Med. Assocs. Ltd., Chgo., 1985—. Sci. editor Cranial Acad. Newsletter, 1983—. Mem. Sutherland Cranial Found. (faculty mem. 1982—), Cranial Acad. (trustee 1983—), Christian Med. Found. (regional v.,p.), Am. Osteo. Assn., Am. Osteo. Acad. Sports Medicine, North Am. Acad. Manipulative Medicine, Am. Acad. Orthopedic Medicine (trustee 1987—). Republican. Roman Catholic. Office: Rhema Med Assocs Ltd 46 E Oak St Suite 401 Chicago IL 60611

FEENEY, DON JOSEPH, JR., psychologist; b. Greenville, N.C., Jan. 17, 1948; s. Don Joseph Sr. and Louise (Saieed) F.; m. Ruth Ann Kalemba, Aug. 16, 1986; 1 child, Kelly Lynn. BA, Colgate U., 1971; MA, Gov.'s State U., 1973; PhD, Loyola U., Chgo., 1979, fellow, 1976. Registered psychologist, Ill., Ind.; cert. additions counselor. Clin. dir. Champaign (Ill.) Council on Alcoholism, 1976-79; pvt. practice psychology, hypnotherapy, family services Downers Grove, Ill., 1979—; team chief Dangerous Drugs Com., Chgo., 1979-80; psychologist Tri-City Mental Health Ctr., East Chicago, Ind., 1980-82; psychologist alcohol treatment program Christ Hosp., Oak Lawn, Ill., 1982—; chmn. adv. council on alcoholism Gov.'s State U., University Park, Ill., 1979-82; cons. Psychol. Cons. Services, Downers Grove, 1985—. Contbr. articles to profl. jours. Mem. Am. Psychol. Assn., Ill. Psychol. Assn. Roman Catholic. Avocations: chess, tennis, weightlifting, jogging, reading. Home: 326 Pine Hill Rd Frankfort IL 60423 Office: Psychol Cons Services 6800 S Main St Suite 12 Downers Grove IL 60516

FEHR, PETER EILERT, obstetrician/ gynecologist; b. East Grand Forks, Minn., Jan. 9, 1932; s. Eilert Peter and Clara (Luithle) F.; m. Doris Alvina Adam, Sept. 11, 1954; children: Diana Jean, David John, Douglas Peter, Doreen Ruth. BS, U. Minn., 1954, MD, 1957. Diplomate Am. Bd. Ob-Gyn. Med. missionary N.AM. Bapt. Ch., Oakbrook Terrace, Ill., 1958-68; resident in ob-gyn U. Minn., Mpls., 1969-72; practice medicine specializing in ob-gyn Mpls., 1972-84, St. Paul, 1984—; dir. maternal-fetal medicine United Hosp., St. Paul, 1984—. Contbr. articles to profl. jours. Fellow Am. Coll. Ob-Gyn; mem. AMA, Minn. State Med. Soc., Hennepin County Med. Soc., Ramsey County Med. Soc., Minn. Ob-Gyn Soc., Cen. Assn. Ob-Gyn, Soc. Perinatal Obstetricians, Minn. Perinatal Orgn. Baptist. Avocations: canoeing, gardening. Office: 333 Smith Ave N Saint Paul MN 55102

FEHRENBACH, ROBERT JAMES, medical electronics company executive; b. St. Mary's, Pa., Oct. 27, 1937; s. George J. and Margaret (Lynch) F.; m. Nancy Klatman, July 9, 1960; children: Ann, John, James, Kurt, Molly, George, Frank. BSEE, MIT, 1959; MSEE, Purdue U., 1960. Chief engr. Fiatron Systems, Glendale, Wis., 1980-81, Amtronix, Germantown, Wis., 1981-83; chief engr. Biochem Internat., Inc., Waukesha, Wis., 1983-84, v.p., 1984—. Roman Catholic. Avocations: swimming, amateur sports with family. Home: 1460 Church St Wauwatosa WI 53213 Office: Biochem Internat Inc W238N1650 Rockwood Dr Waukesha WI 53188-1149

FEHRING, LAWRENCE JOSEPH, lawyer; b. Milw., Aug. 7, 1958; s. Jerome John and Loretta M. (Kaltenbach) F.; m. Elizabeth Anne Hanlon, July 4, 1981; Heidi Leigh, Margaret Ann, Charles Hanlon. Student, University Coll., Cork, Ireland, 1977-78; BA, Marquette U., 1980, JD, 1983. Bar: Wis. 1983, U.S. Dist. Ct. (ea. and we. dists.) Wis. 1983. Assoc. Kasdorf, Lewis and Swietlik, Milw., 1983-85; assoc. Habush, Habush and Davis, Milw., 1985-87, ptnr., 1987—; guest lectr. Marquette U. Coll. Nursing, Milw., 1984—. Mem. Assn. Trial Lawyers Am., Wis. Acad. Trial Lawyers, Wis. Bar Assn. Roman Catholic. Avocation: bicycling. Office: Habush Habush and Davis 777 E Wisconsin Ave Suite 2200 Milwaukee WI 53202

FEIG, THEODORE QUENTIN, business consultant; b. Mpls., Apr. 18, 1928; s. Theodore Henry and Dorothy (Samd) F.; m. Patricia Cosgrove, Sept. 9, 1949 (div. Sept. 1974); children: Steven, Kristine; m. Judith Peterson, Nov. 2, 1979. BBA, U. Minn., 1951, postgrad., 1972. CPA, Minn.; CLU. Sr. auditor Peat, Marwick, Mitchell & Co., Mpls., 1951-56; chief acct. The Toro Co., Mpls., 1956-58; sr. v.p., treas. Luth. Brotherhood, Mpls., 1958-86. Bd. dirs. Ebenezer Soc., Mpls., 1981—, bd. chmn., 1986—. Served with U.S. Army, 1946-47. Mem. Am. Inst. CPA's, Minn. Soc. CPA's, Am. Coll. Underwriters, Fin. Exec. Inst. Home: 629 N Ferndale Rd Wayzata MN 55391 Office: Luth Brotherhood 625 Fourth Ave S Minneapolis MN 55415

FEIGELSON, HOWARD HARVEY, radiologist, educator; b. N.Y.C., May 4, 1924; s. Albert George and Estelle (Stein) F.; m. Marilyn Rose Tunick, June 1, 1946; children: Marsha Jean, Margaret Jane, Judith Ann, Geri, Shelley B., Daniel J., Bruce J. MD, U Cin., 1950. Cert. Am. Bd. Radiology, Am. Bd. Nuclear Medicine. Radiologist Sinai Hosp. Detroit, 1954-68; asst. prof. radiology Wayne State U., Detroit, 1954-68; radiologist St. Francis-St. George Hosp., Cin., 1968—; asst. prof. radiology U. Cin., 1968—; Radiologist Project HOPE, Washington, 1964-65. Pres. Am. Cancer Soc., Detroit, 1965. Served to sgt. U.S. Army, 1942-46, ETO. Fellow Am. Coll. Radiology; mem. AMA, Radiol. Soc. N.Am., Soc. Nuclear Medicine, Ohio State Med. Assn. Home: 297 Ritchie Ave Wyoming OH 45215 Office: Western Hills Radiology 5049 Crookshank Cincinnati OH 45238

FEIGHAN, EDWARD FARRELL, congressman, lawyer; b. Lakewood, Ohio, Oct. 22, 1947; s. Francis X. and Rosemary (Ling) F.; m. Nadine Hopwood, Apr. 24, 1976; children: Lauren, David, Farrell. B.A., Loyola U., New Orleans, 1969; J.D., Cleve.-Marshall Coll. Law, 1978. Bar: Ohio 1978. Tchr. Cleve., 1969-72; mem. Ohio Ho. of Reps., 1973-78; county commr. Cuyahoga County, Cleve., 1979-82; mem. Carney, Rains & Feighan, now Carney & Rains, Cleve., from 1982, 97th-99th Congresses from 19th Ohio Dist. Contbr. to anthology, 1983. Mem. Ohio Bar Assn., Cleve. Bar Assn., LWV, Citizen League, City Club. Democrat. Roman Catholic. Office: 1124 Longworth House Office Bldg Washington DC 20515

FEIKENS, JOHN, judge; b. Clifton, N.J., Dec. 3, 1917; s. Sipke and Corine (Wisse) F.; m. Henriette Dorothy Schulthouse, Nov. 4, 1939; children: Jon, Susan Corine, Barbara Edith, Julie Anne, Robert H. A.B., Calvin Coll., Grand Rapids, Mich., 1939; J.D., U. Mich., 1941; LL.D., U. Detroit, 1979, Detroit Coll. Law, 1981. Bar: Mich. 1942. Gen. practice law Detroit; dist. judge Ea. Dist. Mich., Detroit, 1960-61, 70-79, chief judge, 1979-86, sr. judge, 1986—; past co-chmn. Mich. Civil Rights Commn.; past chmn. Rep. State Central Com.; past mem. Rep. Nat. Com. Past bd. trustees Calvin Coll. Fellow Am. Coll. Trial Lawyers; mem. ABA, Detroit Bar Assn. (dir. 1962, past pres.), State Bar Mich. (commr. 1965-71). Club: University of Michigan. Home: 1574 Brookfield Dr Ann Arbor MI 48103 Office: Fed Bldg 231 W Lafayette Blvd 7th Floor Detroit MI 48226

FEIL, LINDA JEAN, human resource director; b. Peoria, Ill., Feb. 22, 1949; d. William Wesley and Erma Mae (Largent) McVicker; m. Edward Joseph Feil, Apr. 28, 1984. BA, Eureka Coll., 1971; MA, Northeastern Ill. U., 1981. Spl. asst. Office of State's Atty., Chgo., 1973-74; adminstrv. support specialist Blue Cross Assn., Chgo., 1974-78; asst. to dir. human resources Sheridan Rd. Hosp. of Rush Presbyn. St. Luke's Hosp., Chgo., 1978-81; compensation and personnel specialist United Way, Chgo., 1981-83; human resource dir. Chgo. Lighthouse for the Blind, 1983—; bd. dirs. personnel cons. Metro-Help Chgo., 1986—. Mem. Am. Soc. Personnel Adminstrn., Am. Compensation Assn. Lodge: Zonta. Home: 5518 S Kimbark Chicago IL 60637

FEIL, NAOMI WEIL, script writer, gerontologist; b. Munich, Germany, July 22, 1932; came to U.S., 1937, naturalized, 1944; d. Julius and Helen (Kahn) Weil; m. Edward Feil, Dec. 29, 1963; children: Edward G., Kenneth J.; children by previous marriage: Victoria, Beth. Student Oberlin Coll., 1950-51, Western Res. U., 1950-51; BS cum laude, Columbia U., 1954, MSW, 1956. Dir. group work William Hodson Ctr., 1960-62, Bird S. Coler Hosp., Welfare Island, N.Y., 1962-63, Montefiore Home for Aged, 1963-80; script writer, actress documentary films Edward Feil Prodns., 1963—; exec. dir. Validation Tng. Inst., Inc., 1983; cons. Case Western Res. U., also adj. field instr.; workshop leader; group worker, cons. Amasa Stone. Author: Validation: The Feil Method, 1982, Resolution: The Final Life Task, 1985, also books on gerontology, documentary films; films include: Where Life Still Means Living, 1965, The Inner World of Aphasia, 1967, Looking for Yesterday: 100 Years to Live, 1981 (various internat. awards); contbr. articles to Gerontology mag., Humanistic Jour., Pilgrimmage mag. Recipient award for Human Relations in Pub. Service, Cleve., 1974, Cine award for Documentary Films, 1965, 68, 82, Disting. Service award Assn. Ohio Philanthropic Homes and Housing for Aging, 1986. Mem. Nat. Assn. Social Workers, Transpersonal Psychology Assn., Humanistic Psychology Assn., Univ. Film Assn., Gerontology Assn. Democrat. Jewish. Founder validation theory for restoring dignity to the aged. Home: 21987 Byron Rd Cleveland OH 44122 Office: 4614 Prospect Ave Cleveland OH 44103

FEIN, ROGER G., lawyer; b. St. Louis, Mar. 12, 1940; s. Albert and Fanny (Levinson) F.; m. Susanne M. Cohen, Dec. 18, 1965; children—David I., Lisa J. Student Washington U., St. Louis, 1959, NYU, 1960; B.S., UCLA, 1962; J.D., Northwestern U., 1965; M.B.A., Am. U., 1967. Bar: Ill. 1965, U.S. Dist. Ct. (no. dist.) Ill. 1968, U.S. Ct. Appeals (7th cir.) 1968, U.S. Supreme Ct. 1970. Atty. div. corp. fin. SEC, Washington, 1965-67; ptnr. Arvey, Hodes, Costello & Burman, Chgo., 1967—, mem. exec. com., 1977—; mem. Securities Adv. Com. to Sec. State Ill., 1973—, chmn., 1973-79, 87—, vice chmn., 1983-87; spl. asst. atty. gen. State of Ill., 1974-83, 85—; mem. Appeal Bd., Ill. Law Enforcement Commn., 1980-83; mem. lawyer's adv. bd. So. Ill. Law Jour., 1980-83; mem. adv. bd. securities regulation and law report Bur. Nat. Affairs Inc., 1985—; lectr., author. Mem. Bd. Edn., Sch. Dist. No. 29, Northfield, Ill., 1977-83, pres., 1981-83; vice-chmn. Chgo. regional bd. Anti-Defamation League of B'nai B'rith, 1980—; chmn. lawyers' com. for ann. telethon Muscular Dystrophy Assn., 1983; past bd. dirs. Jewish Nat. Fund., Am. Friends Hebrew U., Northfield Community Fund. Recipient Sec. State Ill. Pub. Service award, 1976, Citation of Merit, WAIT Radio, 1976, Sunset Ridge Sch. Community Service award, 1984; City of Chgo. Citizen's award 1986. Fellow Am. Bar Found., Ill. Bar Found. (bd. dirs. 1978—, v.p. 1982-84, pres. 1984-86, chmn. Fellows 1983-84, Cert. of Appreciation 1985, 86), Chgo. Bar Found.; mem. Fed. Bar Assn., Am. Judicature Soc., Decalogue Soc. Lawyers, Attys. Title Guaranty Fund, ABA (state regulation of securities com. 1982—, Ill. liaison of com.), ho. of dels. 1981-85), Ill. State Bar Assn. (bd. govs. 1976-80, del. assembly 1976—, sec. 1977-78, cert. of appreciation 1980, chmn. Bench and Bar com. 1982-83, sect. council 1983-84, chmn. bar elections supervision com. 1986-87, chmn. assembly com. on hearings 1987—, mem. standing com. on fed., jud. and related appointments 1987—), Chgo. Bar Assn. (mem. task force delivery legal services 1978-80, cert. of appreciation 1976, chmn. land trusts com. 1978-79, chmn. consumer credit com. 1977-78, chmn. state securities law subcom. 1977-79), Legal Club Chgo., Tau Epsilon Phi, Alpha Kappa Psi, Phi Delta Phi. Clubs: Standard, Legal (Chgo.). Office: Arvey Hodes Costello & Burman 180 N LaSalle St Suite 3800 Chicago IL 60601

FEIN, THOMAS PAUL, data security administrator; b. Cin., Jan. 13, 1946; s. Harold Robert and Virginia May (Gray) F.; m. Linda Ann Stofle, Dec. 11, 1971. Student, Ohio State U., 1964-67, BBA, 1976. Programmer The Ohio Casualty Group, Hamilton, 1976, Am. Laundry Machinery, Cin., 1976; programmer/analyst Automated Data Systems, Cin., 1976-78, Savs. and Loan Data Corp., Cin., 1978-81; programmer/analyst Champion Internat. Corp., Hamilton, 1981-85, data security adminstr., 1985—. Served with USN, 1967-73. Mem. ACF2 Nat. Users Group, Ohio-Ky.-Ind.-Tenn. ACF2 Users Group, Cin. Kaypro Users Group, Ohio State U. Alumni Assn. (life). Republican. Methodist. Lodges: Masons (local trustee 1982—, sec.-treas. 1982—, chmn. scholarship com. 1983-86), Order of Eastern Star. Avocations: sports, electronics, antiques, gardening. Home: 650 History Bridge Ln Hamilton OH 45013 Office: Champion Internat Corp 101 Knightsbridge Dr Hamilton OH 45020

FEINBERG, ELEANOR KEMLER, psychotherapist; b. Winthrop, Mass., July 26, 1938; d. Mathew and Ann Kemler; m. Walter Feinberg, June 21, 1964; children: Deborah, Jill. BA, Boston U., 1960; MEd, State Coll. at Boston, 1963; PhD, U. Ill., 1974. Registered psychologist, Ill. Lectr. U. Ill., Champaign, 1974-79; psychotherapist Champaign County Mental Health Ctr., 1979-85, psychotherapist part time, 1985—; practice psychotherapy Champaign, 1983—; adj. prof. U. Ill., 1986—; workshop leader Ctr. for Health Info., 1982—; guest speaker on psychol. issues area orgn., radio and TV programs, 1983—. Author: (monograph with Walter Feinberg) The Invisible and Lost Community of Work and Education, 1979; local radio and tv guest. Mem. Am. Psychol. Assn., Ill. Psychol. Assn. Club: Executive of Champaign County. Home and Office: 1704 Henry St Champaign IL 61821

FEINBERG, HARVEY DAVID, advertising agency executive, public relations consultant, copy writer; b. Cleve., Mar. 3, 1922; s. Alfred Joseph and Mary F.; m. Audrey Lois Friedman, June 25, 1950; children—Steven Richard, Rachel Ann, Amy Marcia, Barbara Rose. B.B.A., Case Western Res. U., 1949. Exec. asst. to pres. of clothing mfg., 1950-52; advt. account exec. Robert Silverman Agy., Cleve., 1953-64; founder Ad-Vantages, Inc., Cleve., 1964—; co-founder, sec.-treas. Seven-Step, Inc., Cleve., 1985; pub. relations cons. City of Cleveland Heights, 1967-68, City of Cleve., 1970; producer audio/visual material for Cleve. Poison Ctr., 1967; pub. relations cons. Cleve. Mental Health Assn., 1968, Karamu Settlement House, 1968. Mem. bd. Edn. Cleveland Heights, 1972-80, pres., 1973, 74, 77, 79, negotiator affirmative action policy, author human relations policy; dist. chmn. University Heights Neighbors Watch; chmn. Save Our Schs. com., 1984; candidate University Heights city council race, 1987. Served with USAAF, 1942-45. Named to Cleveland Heights High Sch. Disting. Alumni Hall of Fame, 1984; Citizen of Yr., University Heights, 1984. Mem. Cleve. Advt. Club, Ohio Sch. Bd. Assn., Nat. Sch. Bd. Assn. Lodge: Masons. Creator several audio/visual programs dealing with drugs and alcohol control. Home and office: 14449 E Carroll Blvd University Heights OH 44118

FEINBERG, RICHARD ALAN, consumer science educator, consultant; b. N.Y.C., June 12, 1950; s. Irving and Belle (Kolkowitz) F.; m. Fran Susan Jaffe, Jan. 21, 1973; 1 son, Seth Jason. B.A., SUNY-Buffalo, 1972; M.S., SUNY-Cortland, 1974; Ph.D., U. Okla., 1976. Asst. prof. psychology Ohio State U., 1976-78, Juniata Coll., Huntington, Pa., 1978-80; asst. prof. consumer scis., retailing and environ. analysis Purdue U., West Lafayette, Ind., 1980-85, assoc. prof. consumer and retailing, 1985—, dir. retail mgmt. internship program; research assoc. Purdue Retail Inst., 1980—. David Ross fellow, 1980; NIMH fellow, 1975; Purdue Agrl. Expt. Sta. grantee, 1981. Mem. Am. Psychol. Assn., AAAS, Assn. Coll. Profs. Textiles and Clothing. Contbr. articles in field to profl. jours. Office: Dept Consumer Scis and Retailing Purdue U West Lafayette IN 47907

FEINSILVER, DONALD LEE, psychiatrist; b. Bklyn., July 24, 1947; s. Albert and Mildred (Weissman) F. B.A., Alfred U., 1968; M.D., Autonomous U.-Guadalajara, Mexico, 1974. Diplomate Am. Bd. Psychiatry and Neurology. Intern in medicine L.I. Coll. Hosp., Bklyn., 1975-76; resident in psychiatry SUNY-Bklyn., 1977-78, chief resident, 1979; asst. prof. psychiatry and surgery Med. Coll. Wis., Milw., 1980-85, assoc. prof., 1985—; dir. psychiat. emergency service Milw. County Mental Health and Med. Complexes, 1980—. Contbr. articles to profl. jours.; editor: Crisis Psychiatry: Pros and Cons, 1982; mem. editorial bd. Psychiat. Medicine Jour., 1983—. Mem. Am. Psychiat. Assn., AMA, Am. Acad. Psychiatry and the Law, AAAS, Acad. Psychosomatic Medicine. Office: Med Coll Wis 8700 W Wisconsin Ave Milwaukee WI 53226

FEINSTEIN, JEFFREY MITCHELL, radiation oncologist; b. N.Y.C., June 5, 1946; s. Jerome and May (Wolpin) F.; m. Linda Louise Musso, Apr. 27, 1974; children: Trevor M., Joscelynne M., Whitney I., Alexander P., Koren E., Casselyn L. AB cum laude, NYU, 1967, MD, 1971. Diplomate Am. Bd. Radiology. Intern NYU Med. Ctr., N.Y.C., 1971-72, resident in radiation oncology, 1972-75; head radiation oncology Naval Regional Med. Ctr., Phila., 1975-77; dir. radiation oncology Hinsdale (Ill.) Hosp., 1977—; cons. Good Samaritan Hosp., Downers Grove, Ill., 1977—, Edward Hosp., Naperville, Ill., 1981—, Suburban Hosp., Hinsdale, 1985—, Hines VA Hosp. Radiation Technol. Sch., Maywood, Ill., 1985—. Pres. PTO, Oak Elementary Sch., Hinsdale, 1986-87; bd. dirs. v.p. DuPage unit Am. Cancer Soc., Glen Ellyn, Ill., 1980—. Served to lt. comdr. USNR, 1975-77. Mem. Am. Med. Soc., Pan Am. Med. Soc., Am. Coll. Radiology, Am. Soc. Clin. Oncology, Am. Soc. Therapeutic Radiology and Oncology, Am. Endocurietherapy Soc., Phi Beta Kappa. Office: Hinsdale Hosp Div Radiation Oncology 120 N Oak St Hinsdale IL 60521

FEIOCK, JOHN PAUL, academic administrator; b. Waukegan, Ill., Jan. 11, 1944; s. Paul Edward and Lillian Pauline (Ellis) F.; m. Carol Moody; children: Kristin, Holly. BS, Georgetown Coll., Ky., 1967; MS, Ind. U., 1971; MA, Webster U., 1987. Cert. tchr., Ind. Tchr., coach South Harrison Sch. Corp., Laconia, Ind., 1969-79; supr. Contel of Ind., Scottsburg, 1979-80; coordinator Webster U., St. Louis, 1980-86, sr. program dir. grad. ctr., educator econs. and bus. adminstrn., 1986—; adj. instr. Vincennes U., Ind., 1974-79, U. Ky., 1981-86, McKendree Coll., Louisville, 1985. Mem. Leadership Clark County, Ind., 1984. Named Ky. Colonel, Gov. State Ky., 1982, Hon. Sec. State, State Ind., 1982, Commodore of Port, Mayor City of Jeffersonville, Ind., 1983, Jerusalem Pilgrim, Mayor Jerusalem, 1984. Mem. Am. Soc. Tng. and Devel., Clark County C. of C., Floyd County C. of C., So. Ind. C. of C. Baptist. Lodges: Elks, Rotary. Avocation: golf. Office: Webster U Grad Ctr 321 E Court Ave Jeffersonville IN 47130

FEIOCK, RAY EDWARD, financial data processing executive; b. McLeansboro, Ill., July 28, 1944; s. Forest Thruman and Dorothy Vivian (Compton) F.; m. Christine Madeline Wallbank, Aug. 3, 1965 (div. June 1969); m. Marilyn Jean Milli, Mar. 29, 1975; children: Howard Nikos, Kimberly Reneé, Michael Hans, Dennis Charles. BS, U. Toledo, 1965; MS, Case Inst. Tech., 1967; PhD, Case Western Res. U., 1969. Asst. prof. U. Toledo, 1969-71, Case Western Res. U., 1971-72, Ind. Nat. Bank, Indpls., 1972-75; software programmer Lane Bryant Stores, Indpls., 1975-76, Am. States Ins., Indpls., 1976-77; data adminstr. Ind. Nat. Bank, Indpls., 1977—, asst. v.p., 1983-85, v.p., 1985-87. Mem. Ind. Nat. Officer Polit. Action Com., Indpls., 1980-87. Democrat. Baptist. Avocations: golfing, bowling, camping, pocket billiards. Home: 4415 Radnor Rd Indianapolis IN 46226 Office: Ind Nat Bank Suite M830 Indianapolis IN 46266

FEIT, ARLINE FAY, auditor, accountant; b. St. Louis, June 28, 1958; d. Sidney and Dorothy (Kolker) F. Student, Webster U., 1976-78; BSBA in Acctg., Washington U., St. Louis, 1980. CPA, Mo. Field auditor, reimbursement acct. Blue Cross, St. Louis, 1983-85; acct., auditor Deloitte, Haskins & Sells, St. Louis, 1985; asst. auditor Farm Credit Banks of St. Louis, 1987—. Mem. Am. Inst. CPA's, Mo. Soc. CPA's, Young Profls. Orgn. (music and planning dir. 1983—), Flute Soc. St. Louis. Jewish. Avocations: music, photography, art, theater, tennis. Home: 20 Nassau Circle Saint Louis MO 63146

FEIT, LAWRENCE ANTHONY, small business owner; b. Evanston, Ill., Jan. 28, 1961; s. Jerome A. and Genevieve (Trella) F.; m. Georgia Louise Rossmann, Sept. 22, 1985; 1 child, Branden Nicole. BS in Bus. and Acctg., Ind. U., Bloomington, 1983. Acct. Borg Warner, Chgo., 1982; electronic service technician Ind. U., Bloomington, 1983; acct. Parkside Med. Services, Park Ridge, Ill., 1984-85; fin. mgr. Luth. Gen. Hosp., Park Ridge, Ill., 1985-86; pres. Chgo. Computer & Light Inc., Chgo., 1986—. Mem. Alpha Tau Omega. Office: Chgo Computer & Light Inc 5001 N Lowell Ave Chicago IL 60630

FEITLER, ROBERT, shoe company executive; b. Chgo., Nov. 19, 1930; s. Irwin and Bernice (Gombrig) F.; m. Joan Elden, May 30, 1957; children: Pamela, Robert, Richard, Dana. B.S., U. Pa., 1951; LL.B., Harvard U., 1954. Pres., treas. Weyenberg Shoe Mfg. Co., Milw., 1964-72; pres. Weyenberg Shoe Mfg. Co., 1972—; chmn. Hynite Corp., 1975—; dir. Assoc. Commerce Bank, Champion Parts Rebuilders, Inc., Kelley Co., TC Mfg. Co. Pres. Smart Family Found.; pres. Milw. Art Mus.; v.p. Milw. Repertory Theater. Served with U.S. Army, 1954-56. Jewish. Clubs: University (Milw.), Milwaukee, Milw. Athletic; Harvard (N.Y.C.). Home: 1712 E Cumberland Blvd Whitefish Bay WI 53211 Office: Weyenberg Shoe Mfg Co 234 E Reservoir St Milwaukee WI 53212

FEJÉR, PAUL HARALYI, design engineer; b. Gyoma, Hungary, Feb. 27, 1921; s. Lajos Haralyi Fejer and Laura (Varasdi) Persaits F.; B.S., Ludovica Academia, Budapest, Hungary, 1944; m. Maria Shylo-Wasylchenko, Nov. 16, 1946; children—Paul Haralyi, Alexandra Martha, Douglas Kay. Came to U.S., 1949, naturalized, 1955. Sr. product analyst Chrysler Corp., Highland Park, Mich., 1962-68; sr. design engr. Ford Motor Co., Mt. Clemens, Mich., 1968-83. Served to 2d lt. Hungarian Army, 1944-45. Recipient Gold medal Hungarian Arpad Acad. Scis., 1984. Mem. Macomb Electronics Assn. (treas. 1958), Indsl. Math. Soc. (treas. 1970-73, pres. 1985-86), Soc. Automotive Engrs., Soc. Plastic Engrs., Soc. Mfg. Engrs., Soc. Exptl. Stress Analysis, Hungarian Arpad Acad., Engring. Soc. Detroit and Affiliate Council (treas.). Author: Measuring Numbers System, 1975; Fundamentals of Dynamic Geometry: The Fejer Vector System, 1980; Time in Dynamic Geometry (founder), 1984; Originator measuring numbers system for measuring continuous magnitudes, dynamic geometry, Fejer Vector system; pioneer new universal time theory. Home: 1472 Timberview Trail Bloomfield Hills MI 48013

FELBER, RICHARD JAMES, design firm executive; b. Cleve., Oct. 12, 1928; s. Tobias L. and Mina (Liebenthal) K.; m. Ann Wasserman, Dec. 27, 1953 (div. 1971); children: Andrew t., Carolyn Bankhurst, Linda Wirtshafter; m. Judith Sammon, Aug. 25, 1979. BS in Mktg., U. Ill., 1950. Exec. v.p. S.M. Hexter Co., Cleve., 1957-86; pres. Richard Felber Designs, Inc., Cleve., 1986—. Author: (wallcovering and fabric collections) Greenfield Village, Crosswinds, Fair Winds, Village Gallery, Countryside, Heather Hill, East Winds, Colors Provence. Mem. Mens Com. Cleve. Play House, 1972—. Home: 18000 Parkland Dr Shaker Heights OH 44122 Office: 2800 Superior Ave Cleveland OH 44114

FELDBUSCH, MICHAEL FARRELL, engineering company executive; b. Evansville, Ind., Aug. 26, 1951; s. Ronald Farrell and Rita Carolyn (Snodgrass) F.; m. Lisa Ann McDowell, Feb. 14, 1986. AAS in architecture, ITT Tech. Inst., Indpls., 1971. Cert. profl. land surveyor, Ind., Ky. Engr. Lake States Engrng., Chgo., 1974, Mayfair Constrn., Detroit, 1975; surveyor Warrick County Planning Commn., Boonville, Ind., 1976, Warrick County, Boonville, 1977-85; pres., owner AES/Warrick Engrng., Newburgh, Ind., 1978—; pres. Warrick County Planning Commn., 1978, 85; chief surveyor Warrick County, 1985—. Del. Ind. Dems., Indpls., 1978, 82, 86; sec. Newburgh Youth Sports Assn., 1980-81. Served with USAR, 1971-77. Recipient Edward Gesser Jr. Meml. award Newburgh Youth Sports Assn., 1986; named one of Outstanding Young Men Am., 1980, 81, 83-85. Mem. NSPE, Ind. Soc. Prof. Land Surveyors, County Surveyors Assn., Am. Congress on Surveying, Nat. Soc. Prof. Surveyors, Ind. Jaycees (Top 40 award, 1979). Lodge: Lions. Avocations: boating, camping. Home: 7111 Woods Dr Newburgh IN 47630 Office: AES/Warrick Engring Inc 605 State St Newburgh IN 47630

FELDE, MARTIN LEE, accountant; b. Milw., Feb. 26, 1951; s. Walter Henry and Arline B. (Bergman) F.; m. Virginia Rose Schlesing, Aug. 9, 1975; children—Erin, David. B.B.A., U. Wis., 1972. C.P.A., Wis. Staff auditor Arthur Andersen & Co., Milw., 1972-74; controller Page-Schwessinger, Milw., 1974-78; fin. adminstr. Bozell & Jacobs, Milw., 1978-79; controller Hoffman York, Milw., 1979-82, v.p., controller, 1982-83, v.p. fin., 1983—. Mem. Am. Inst. C.P.A.s, Wis. Inst. C.P.A.s. Home: 17550 Senlac Ln Brookfield WI 53005 Office: Hoffman York & Compton Inc 330 E Kilbourn Ave Milwaukee WI 53202

FELDER, JAMES, microbiologist; b. Orangeburg, S.C., Dec. 15, 1930; s. Harry and Simmie (Darby) F.; m. Betty Thomas, July 30, 1955; children: Gregory Gawaine, Kevin Lawrence. BS, Claflin Coll., 1951; postgrad., Ohio State U., 1957-58; MS, Wright State U., 1973. Microbiologist St. Elizabeth Hosp., Dayton, Ohio, 1959-60, Middletown (Ohio) Hosp., 1960—; v.p., bd. dirs. M.F. Industries, Centerville, 1983—; bd. dirs. Miami Valley Regional Small Bus. Incubator, Inc.; pres., chief exec. officer Britfelbow, Inc., Yellow Springs, Ohio, 1984—. Served to major USAF, 1951-56. Mem. Am. Soc. for Microbiology, South Cen. Assn. Microbiology. Presbyterian. Avocations: acting, singing, racquetball. Home: 659 Omar Circle Yellow Springs OH 45387 Office: Middletown Regional Hosp 105 McKnight Dr Middletown OH 45044

FELDEWERT, CHARLES FRANCIS, financial executive; b. St. Charles, Mo., Jan. 25, 1939; s. Alex C. and Leona A. (Sommer) F.; m. Rosalie C. Wehde, Nov. 26, 1962; children: Michael, Edward, Michelle, Juliet. BBA, U. Mo., 1963. CPA, Mo.; cert. real property adminstr., Mo. Dept. mgr. Peat, Marwick & Mitchell, St. Louis, 1969; pres. Westgate Mgmt., St. Louis, 1973, Turley Martin Co., St. Louis, 1972; bd. dirs. Mo. Growth Assn., St. Louis, 1986—. Founding dir. Regional Sewer Dist., St. Charles, 1972-74; bd. dirs. Gov's. Com. on Energy Conservation., Mo., 1976-77. Served with U.S. Army, 1957-58. Mem. Am. Inst. CPA's, Soc. Real Property Adminstrs. (founding), Bldg. Owner's and Mgrs. Assn. Internat. (pres. St. Louis 1980-81, nat. officer 1984—, Disting. Service award 1983). Democrat. Roman Catholic. Clubs: Media, Clayton (St. Louis). Avocations: skiing, ranching, wine. Home: 848 Guthrie Rd Wentzville MO 63385 Office: Turley Martin Co 131 S Bemiston Ave Saint Louis MO 63105

FELDMAN, BERNARD JOSEPH, physics educator, consultant; b. San Francisco, July 20, 1946; s. David H. and Ena G. (Paster) G.; m. Marjorie A. Braham, July 16, 1970; children: Joshua, Aaron. AA, City Coll. San Francisco, 1965; AB, U. Calif., Berkeley, 1967; AM, Harvard U., 1968, PhD, 1972. Research assoc. U. Calif., Berkeley, 1972-74; asst. prof. physics U. Mo., St. Louis, 1974-80, assoc. prof. physics, 1980-85, prof. physics, 1985—; cons. McDonnell Douglas, St. Louis, 1980—. Author 40 articles. U. Mo. grantee, 1974—. Mem. Am. Physical Soc., Am. Assoc. Physics Tchrs., Materials Research Soc., Phi Beta Kappa. Democrat. Jewish. Home: 466 Fourwynd Dr Saint Louis MO 63141 Office: U Mo Dept Physics Saint Louis MO 63121

FELDMAN, CARY STEPHEN, optometrist; b. Hibbing, Minn., Feb. 7, 1952; s. Herman and Cecille (Margolis) F.; m. B. Sue Boerger, Dec. 28, 1983. BS, Ind. U., 1976, OD, 1977. Lic. optometrist, S.D. Optometrist, owner 20/20 Vision Ctr., Sioux Falls, S.D., 1977—. Mem. Am. Optometric Assn., S.D. Optometric Soc., Sioux Falls C. of C. Club: Sioux Falls Bridge (pres. 1984-86). Lodge: B'nai B'rith (v.p. 1986—). Avocations: video photography, fishing, bridge. Office: 1918 S Minnesota Ave Sioux Falls SD 57105

FELDMAN, HARRIS JOSEPH, radiologist, educator; b. Balt., Mar. 4, 1942; s. Charles William and Ruth (Emanuel) F. AB, Western Md. Coll., 1963; MD, U. Md., 1967. Diplomate Am. Bd. Radiology. Intern, Mercy Hosp., Balt., 1967-68; resident in radiology George Washington U. Hosp., Washington, 1968-71; staff radiologist U. Ill. Hosp., Chgo., 1973-77, Bethany Meth. Hosp., Chgo., 1977-87, Walther Meml. Hosp., Chgo., 1977-87, Weiss Meml. Hosp., Chgo., 1987—, Lincoln West Hosp., Chgo., 1987—; cons. radiologist Langley AFB Hosp., 1972-73; asst. prof. Abraham Lincoln Sch. Medicine, U. Ill., Chgo., 1974-77, clin. asst. prof., 1977—. Served with M.C., USN, 1971-73. Mem. AMA, Ill. Med. Soc., Chgo. Med. Soc., Am. Coll. Radiology, Ill. Radiol. Soc., Chgo. Radiol. Soc., Radiol. Soc. N.Am. Home: 1339 N Dearborn Pkwy Chicago IL 60610 Office: Louis D Weiss Meml Hosp Dept Radiology 4646 N Marine Dr Chicago IL 60640

FELDMAN, HY, retail company executive; b. Chgo., May 21, 1932; s. Abraham and Liza (Radawolsky) F.; m. Virginia Audino, Jan. 22, 1955 (dec. Aug. 1961); children: Bruce, Brian, Gail, Elizabeth, Daniel; m. Diane Joseph, Feb. 14, 1979. Student, Wright Jr. Coll., U. Ill., 1954; grad. gemologist, Gemological Inst. Am., 1982-83. Sale rep. Fortune Sales, Chgo., 1957-60, Plough, Inc., Memphis, 1960-71, Gunst Kanow Gassin, Inc., Skokie, Ill., 1971-79; pres. Ultra Custom Services, Inc., Skokie, 1979-82, Allied Gem Appraisers, Ltd., Chgo., 1982—. Mem. Gemological Inst. Am. Alumni Assn. (charter), Nat. Assn. Jewelry Appraisers (charter), Aububon Soc., Cousteau Soc., ACLU, Simon Wiesgnthal Ctr., Chgo. Jewelry Salesman Alliance, Am. Gem Soc. (Chgo. chpt.). Avocations: arts, music, theatre, conservation. Home: 2201 Crestview Ln Wilmette IL 60091 Office: Allied Gem Appraisers Ltd 55 E Washington St Suite 807 Chicago IL 60602

FELDMAN, MARVIN MEYER, accountant, consultant; b. St. Louis, June 27, 1919; s. Sam and Sadie (Hirschfeld) F.; m. Charlotte Siegel, Oct. 26, 1946; children: Ira Frederick Leslie, Nancy Lyn, Victoria Susan, William Mark. BSBA, Washington U., St. Louis, 1941, MBA, 1959. CPA, Calif., Mo.; cert. real estate broker, Calif., Mo. Auditor Defense Contract Audit Agy., U.S. Dept. Defense, St. Louis, 1951-80; prin. Marvin M. Feldman CPA Co., St. Louis, 1981—; cons. on defense contracting, St. Louis, 1980—; real estate broker, St. Louis, 1980—; panel mem. 9th U.S. civil service region, Bd. U.S. Civil Service Examiners, St. Louis, 1962—. Served to sgt. USAF, 1942-45. Mem. Accts. Emergency Assistance Assn., Washington U. Alumni Assn. Republican. Lodges: Aleph Zadek Aleph (life mem. St. Louis chpt.), Jr. Order B'nai B'rith. Avocation: chess. Home and Office: 809 Bitterfield Dr Ballwin MO 63011

FELDPAUSCH, CORINNE MARY, social worker; b. Fowler, Mich., Nov. 4, 1917; d. Joseph Frank and Regina E. (Wieber) F. BS in Bus. Edn., Nazareth Coll., 1952. Lic. social worker, Mich. Tchr. Sisters of St. Joseph, Kalamazoo, 1943-55; acct. St. Joseph Hosp., Flint, Mich., 1955-66; bus. mgr. Lee Meml. Hosp., Dowagiac, Mich., 1966-70; social worker Sisters of St. Joseph, Detroit, 1970-77, 85—; adminstr. Marian Oakland West, Farmington Hills, Mich., 1977-84; patient relations hostess Borgess Hosp., Kalamazoo, 1985—. Mem. Daughters of Isabella, Dearborn, Mich., 1975—, Cath. Interracial Council, Detroit, 1975—. Mem. Nat. Right to Life, Am. Assn. Retired Persons. Roman Catholic. Clubs: East Side, Mothers' (Detroit). Avocation: foreign and domestic travel. Home and Office: Sisters of St Joseph Nazareth Ctr Nazareth MI 49074-9999

FELGER, RALPH WILLIAM, retired military officer, educator; b. Hamilton, Ohio, Oct. 14, 1919; s. Edward Lewis and Blanche Esther (House) F.; m. Bernice Regina Moeller, Dec. 28, 1944; 1 child, Mary Karen. BA, Whitworth Coll., 1951; MBA, U. Denver, 1952; MS, Trinity U., 1954. Cert. instr. bus. and psychology, Calif. Commd. 2d lt. U.S. Army, 1942, personnel tng. officer, 1941-46, relieved from active duty, 1946; commd. 1st lt. USAF, 1951, advanced through grades to lt. col., edn. and personnel officer, 1951-67, retired, 1967; asst. prof. Bakersfield (Calif.) Coll., 1967-68; dean continuing edn. Lincoln Land Community Coll., Springfield, Ill., 1968-72; dir. corp. tng. Sangamo Electric Co., West Union, S.C., 1972-74; asst. campus dir. Ohio State U., Marion, 1974-79; asst. to v.p. Ohio State U., Columbus, 1979-83; exec. v.p. Internat. Mgmt. Inst., Westerville, Ohio, 1983-84; dir. continuing edn. N.Mex. Inst. Mining and Tech., Socorro, 1984-85; cons. edn. and mktg. Midwest Human Resource Systems, Columbus, 1985-87. Div. chmn. United Way, Springfield, 1973; mem. Police Human Relations Com., Springfield, 1970-72; bd. dirs. ARC, Oconee, S.C., 1973; edn. chmn. Marion econ. council, edn. chmn. Marion County chpt. Am. Heart Assn. Decorated Legion of Merit. Mem. Personnel Mgrs. Club (v.p. 1972-74), Delta Sigma Pi (life). Republican. Lodges: Lions (chmn. edn. com. Waterville, Maine club. 1958-61). Avocations: hunting, fishing, camping, travelling, cooking. Home and Office: 2153 Olde Sawmill Blvd Dublin OH 43017

FELICI, ANTHONY ALBERT, controller; b. Cleve., Oct. 26, 1955; s. Albert Frank and Audrey Elizabeth F. BS, Ohio State U., 1978; MBA, Cleve. State U., 1987. CPA, Ohio. Audit staff G., K. & S., CPA's, Cleve., 1978-80; staff acct. Oster Electric Co., Cleve., 1980-82; controller Med. Cons., Cleve., 1982—; bd. dirs. Ohio Telephone Systems, Cleve. Notary pub., Ohio, 1979—. Mem. Am. Inst. CPA's, Ohio Soc. CPA's. Republican. Roman Catholic. Club: Edgewater Yacht (Cleve.) (mem. planning and audit coms. 1987—). Home: 18029 Ponciana Cleveland OH 44135 Office: Med Cons 2609 Franklin Blvd Cleveland OH 44113

FELKNER, JOSEPH GEORGE, health care executive, accountant; b. Columbus, Ohio, Mar. 16, 1957; s. George Joseph and Thelma Cecelia (Sauer) F.; m. Cinda Ann Wartluft, Dec. 13, 1980; 1 child, Allison Marie. BSBA, Ohio State U., 1979, MHA, 1981. CPA, Ohio. Mgmt. cons. Ernst & Whinney, Columbus, 1981-85; sr. fin. analyst U.S. Health Corp., Columbus, 1985—. Bd. dirs. Choices for Victims of Domestic Violence, Columbus, 1985—. Mem. Am. Inst. CPA's, Am. Coll. Healthcare Execs., Am. Hosp. Assn., Healthcare Fin. Mgmt. Assn. (sec., treas. 1985-87), Cen. Ohio Healthcare Execs. (sec. 1986-87). Roman Catholic. Avocations: racquetball, golf, gardening. Home: 106 Spring Valley Rd Westerville OH 43081 Office: US Health Corp 3555 Olentangy River Rd Columbus OH 43214

FELL, DIANA DICKSON, computer consultant; b. Glens Falls, N.Y., Dec. 13, 1946; d. Louis Thomas and June (Voyles) Dickson; m. S. Kennedy Fell, May 8, 1965; children: Melissa Ann, Michael Kennedy. Student, U. Del., 1970-72, Oakland U., 1972, Pontiac Bus. Inst., 1973; student in bus., Thomas Edison State Coll. Proprietor, pres. Plato Enterprises, Norman, Okla., 1983-84, Boulder, Colo., 1984-85, Cleve., 1985—; tech. service mgr. Renaissance Technologies, Hudson, Ohio, 1986; mgr. adminstrv. services Progressive Communications Techs. Inc., Cleve., 1987—. Mem. Nat. Assn. Female Execs. Office: Progressive Communications Techs Inc 29525 Chagrin Blvd Cleveland OH 44122

FELL, LEON WILLIAM, auditor; b. Flint, Mich., June 20, 1956; John L. and Shirley (Fowler) F. BBA, Cen. Mich. U., 1980; MBA, U. Mich., 1986. CPA. Mich.; cert. internal auditor; cert. mgmt. acct. Auditor Schilling, Werner & Brilinski, Bay City, Mich., 1980-82, State of Mich., Lansing, 1983-87, Exxon, Houston, 1987—. Mem. Am. Inst. CPA's, Inst. Internal Auditors, Inst. Mgmt. Accts., Mich. Assn. CPA's. Home: 1615 Genesee Lapeer MI 48446

FELL, ROBERT B., chemical company executive. Pres. Standard Oil Chem. Co., Cleve. Office: Standard Oil Chem Co 200 Public Sq Cleveland OH 44114 *

FELL, SAMUEL KENNEDY, infosystems executive; b. Wilmington, Del., Oct. 6, 1944; s. S. Kennedy and Anna Elizabeth (Alford) F.; m. Diana Marie Dickson, May 8, 1965; children: Melissa Ann, Michael Kennedy. BSBA, Oklahoma City U., 1983; postgrad. in bus., John F. Kennedy U. Mgmt. and data processing trainer, programming and system design Gen. Motors Corp., Wilmington, Del., 1967-69; system adminstr., staff asst. in material control Gen. Motors Corp. Tech. Ctr., Warren, Mich., 1970-78; system adminstr. in material control Gen. Motors Corp., Oklahoma City, 1978-80; mgr. prodn. and material control Gen. Motors Corp., Shreveport, La., 1980-81; dir. mgmt. info. systems Tech. Oil Tool div. Baker Internat., Norman, Okla., 1981-84, Miniscribe Corp., Longmont, Colo., 1984-85; v.p. computer info. services Cleve. Pneumatic Co. subs. Pneumo-Abex Corp. div. IC Industries, 1985—; mem. exec. systems steering com. Pneumo-Abex Corp., Boston, 1985—. Mem. Data Processing Mgrs. Assn., Am. Prodn. and Inventory Control Soc., Digital Equipment Corp. Users Group, Soc. Info. Mgrs. Office: Cleveland Pneumatic Co 3781 E 77th St Cleveland OH 44105

FELLAND, BRUCE GODFRED, investment company executive, mortgage broker, consultant; b. Madison, Wis., Dec. 30, 1942; s. Godfred Carl and Evelyn Elda (Kerlinski) F.; m. Inger Johanna Tjomsaas, July 7, 1968; children—James, Ruthann, Jason. Student AG Aviation Acad., 1967. Lic. real estate broker, Wis. Real estate broker, developer Exec. Mgmt., Inc., Madison, 1974-79; pres. Global Investors, Inc., Madison, 1979—; bd. dirs. Nordic Capital Corp., Glenview, Ill. Named hon. lt. col. Ala. State Militia; former treas. Wis. Epilepsy Assn. Served with U.S. Army, 1963-64. Democrat. Lutheran. Home: 148 E Prospect St Stoughton WI 53589

FELLER, JOHN DOUGLAS, lawyer; b. West Point, Nebr., Apr. 5, 1951; s. Douglas John and Bonnie Claire (Fleming) F.; m. Beth Ann Heineman, June 22, 1974; 1 child, Matthew William. BA, U. Nebr., 1973, JD, 1976. Bar: Nebr. 1976, U.S. Dist. Ct. Nebr. 1976. Sole practice Dodge, Nebr., 1976-79; ptnr. Feller & Giese, Beemer, Nebr., 1979-81, Beckenhauer, Feller & Giese, Beemer and West Point, 1981-86; sole practice Beemer, 1986—; atty. Cuming County, Nebr., 1979—. Com. mem. St. Joseph's Home Devel. Com., West Point, 1986. Mem. Nebr. Bar Assn. Democrat. Lodge: Optimists (Beemer) (bd. dirs.). Home: 409 Lambrecht St Beemer NE 68716 Office: 212 Main St Beemer NE 68716

FELLERS, JANET ROSALIE WALSH, small business owner; b. Columbus, Ohio, Sept. 26, 1938; d. John Henry and Alice Mae (Reinstetle) Ball; m. Richard Lee Smales, Apr. 8, 1961 (div.); 1 child, Kim Marlene; m. Lawrence Leonard Walsh, Aug. 9, 1979 (dec. 19, 1980); m. Elmer Lee Fellers, Dec. 23, 1985. Grad. high sch., Groveport, Ohio, 1956. With various orgns. FDIC, Counter Intelligence Corp., The Ohio Dept. Taxation, The Ohio Bell Telephone Co., Columbus; legal sec. various corps. Columbus, Tulsa, Okla., Miami (Fla.) and San Diego, 1961-80; owner Jan-A-Lee's Restaurant, Anna, Ohio, 1980—, Walsh (Deckers) Restaurant, Cridersville, Ohio, 1980-85. Democrat. Lutheran. Avocations: dancing, piano, sewing, boating, fishing. Home: 502 W Main PO Box 77 Anna OH 45302 Office: Jan-A-Lee's Restaurant 14499 SR 119 Anna OH 45302

FELSENTHAL, STEVEN ALTUS, lawyer; b. Chgo., May 21, 1949; s. Jerome and Eve (Altus) F.; m. Carol Judith Greenberg, June 14, 1970; children—Rebecca Elizabeth, Julia Alison. A.B., U. Ill., 1971; J.D., Harvard U., 1974. Bar: Ill. 1974, U.S. Dist. Ct. (no. dist.) Ill. 1974, U.S. Ct. Claims 1975, U.S. Tax Ct. 1975, U.S. Ct. Appeals (7th cir.) 1981. Assoc. Levenfeld & Kanter, Chgo., 1974-78, ptnr., 1978-80; sr. ptnr. Levenfeld, Eisenberg, Janger, Glassberg & Lippitz, Chgo., 1980-84, Sugar, Friedberg & Felsenthal, Chgo., 1984—; lectr. Kent Coll. Law, Ill. Inst. Tech., Chgo., 1978-80. Mem. ABA, Ill. State Bar Assn., Chgo. Bar Assn., Harvard Law Soc. Ill., Phi Beta Kappa. Clubs: Standard, Harvard (Chgo.). Office: Sugar Friedberg & Felsenthal 200 W Madison St Suite 3550 Chicago IL 60606

FELTEN, EDWARD JOSEPH, business executive, accountant; b. Manitowoc, Wis., July 7, 1938; s. Peter N. and Adela A. (Stein) F.; m. Catherine A. Poehling, June 16, 1962; children—Edward W., Anne C., Peter G., Mark D. B.A. magna cum laude in Acctg., U. Wis., 1960. Acct., Armour & Co., Sheboygan, Wis., 1960-65, controller div. sheepskin leather subs. Armour Leather Co., Boston, 1962-65; with Wis. Supply Corp., Madison, 1965—, pres., gen. mgr., 1977—; dir. Community Banks Inc., Madison, Bank of Shorewood Hills (Wis.), La Crosse Plumbing Supply Co., Eau Claire Plumbing Supply Co.; lectr. in field. Pres. adv. bd. Edgewood High Sch., Madison, 1981-82. Recipient Man of Achievement award State of Wis., 1976. Mem. Am. Supply Assn. (bd. dirs. 1980-81, 85-86), Mid. Am. Supply Assn. (pres. 1984-85), Plumbing Heating Cooling Council U.S.A. (bd. dirs. 1979-86). Roman Catholic. Club: Nakena. Home: 5205 Whitcomb Dr Madison WI 53711 Office: 630 W Mifflin St PO Box 8124 Madison WI 53708

FELTHOUSE, TIMOTHY ROY, research chemist; b. Berkeley, Calif., Sept. 25, 1951; s. James Whitman and Patricia Mae (Avrit) F. B.S. magna cum laude, U. Pacific, 1973; Ph.D., U. Ill., 1978. NSF research participant Wash. State U., Pullman, 1972; research asst. U. Pacific, Stockton, Calif., 1973; grad. teaching, research asst. U. Ill., Urbana, 1973-78; research assoc. Tex. A&M U., College Station, 1978-80; sr. research chemist Monsanto Co., St. Louis, 1980-83, research specialist, 1983-87, sr. research specialist, 1987—. Contbr. articles on chemistry to profl. jours. Calif. State scholar, 1969-73. Mem. Am. Chem. Soc. (news editor St. Louis 1981-82, analytical div. undergrad. award 1972), Am. Inst. Chemists, N.Y. Acad. Scis., Catalysis Soc., Phi Kappa Phi, Sigma Xi, Phi Lambda Upsilon. Republican. Methodist. Club: Monsanto-Catalysis (chmn. 1982-83). Office: Monsanto Co 800 N Lindbergh Blvd QHA Saint Louis MO 63167

FELTMAN, ELVIN CRANE, dentist; b. Shiloh, N.J., July 22, 1925; s. Elvin C. Sr. and Ruth Ann (Watson) F.; m. Lillian Elliott, Sept. 15, 1946 (div. 1983); children: David John Donald; m. Icyle Craig, Nov. 26, 1983. BA, Columbia Union Coll., Takoma Park, Md., 1948; DDS, Case Western Res. U., 1962. Gen. practice dentistry Milan, Ohio; cons. Erie-Huron-Ottawa Joint Vocat. Sch., Milan, 1970-80. Parade chair Milan Melon Festival, 1965-78; pres. Milan C. of C., 1978-79. Fellow Internat. Coll. Miami, 1976. Fellow Nat. Acad. Gen. Dentistry (del., council mem. 1976-86), Am. Coll. Dentistry; mem. Ohio Acad. Gen. Dentistry (pres., bd. mem. 1971-86), Ohio Dental Assn. (del., council mem. 1980-86), North Cen. Ohio Dental Soc. (bd. dirs. 1979-86). Avocations: camping, boating, hiking. Home: 2690 Ridge Rd Norwalk OH 44857 Office: Public Sq Milan OH 44846

FELTMANN, JOHN MEINRAD, former advt. and radio exec.; b. St. Louis, Jan. 30, 1910; s. Henry Conrad and Catherine (Lake) F.; certificate in commerce and finance St. Louis U., 1938; m. Adeline A. Fiedler, Nov. 25, 1944; children—John Thomas, Mary Anne Kenney, Robert Joseph, James Anthony (dec.). Clk., Nat. Telephone Directory Co., St. Louis, 1924-36, auditor, 1936-60; sec., dir. Von Hoffmann Corp., Union, N.J., 1947-60, treas., dir., 1960-67, v.p., treas., dir., 1967-69; dir. Von Hoffmann Press, Inc., St. Louis, 1947-69, treas., dir., 1960-69; treas. dir. Publishers Lithographers, Inc., St. Louis, 1959-69; sec., treas. von Hoffmann Realty and Mortgage Corp., 1954-59; v.p., treas., dir. Victory Broadcasting Corp., Jacksonville, Fla., 1968-78, ret., 1978; v.p. treas. Nat. Telephone Directory Corp., Union, N.J., 1968-72, dir., 1968-83, exec. v.p., 1972-78, also cons.; dir. Mid-State Printing Co., Jefferson City, Mo., 1947-54. Sec., treas. George Von Hoffmann Found., 1954-59. Mem. Delta Sigma Pi, Roman Catholic. Club: Mo. Athletic. Home: 7250 Christopher Dr Saint Louis MO 63129

FENIGER, JUDITH A., public relations executive; b. Cleve., Oct. 29, 1951; d. Russell A. and Leona (Chesnick) Magid. BA, Notre Dame Coll., 1983. Copywriter Brown & Richie, Hollywood, Fla., 1978-79; communications asst. Master Builders, Cleve., 1979-83; acct. exec. pub. relations Publicom, Cleve., 1983-85, 1985-86, 1986—; lectr. various groups, Cleve. Author: (newsletter) The Master Builder, 1978 (Bd. Report award of merit, 1982); contbr. articles to profl. jours. Pres. Leeland Condo bd. dirs., Cleve., 1985-86. Mem. Sales & Mktg. Execs. (dir. pub. relations, assoc. bd. dirs. 1985—). Office: Publicom 23200 Chagrin Blvd Beachwood OH 44122

FENING, WALTER EDWARD, obstetrician-gynecologist; b. Covington, Ky., Apr. 21, 1920; s. Aloysius Oscar and Rose Anna (Diephaus) F.; m. Wanda Lee Lewis, Dec. 31, 1949; children: Sharon, Christopher, Diane, Timothy, Mike, Edward, Tracy, Brady, Lara. BA, Miami U., Oxford, Ohio, 1941; MD, U. Cin., 1944. Diplomate Am. Bd. Ob-gyn. Practice medicine specializing on ob-gyn Middletown, Ohio, 1951-60, 1963—, Lake Worth, Fla., 1960-63. Contbr. articles to profl. jours. Served to lt. (j.g.) USN 1942-44, with Res. 1945-46, 50-51. Roman Catholic. Avocation: working with stained glass. Home: 4129 Rosedale Rd Middletown OH 45042 Office: 2101 Central Ave Middletown OH 45042

FENNEDY, DENNIS LEE, controller; b. Troy, Mo., Aug. 25, 1950; s. Edwin Albert and Georgia Lee (Westerman) F.; m. Mildred Mary Zakrzewski, Oct. 1, 1971; children: Christina, Susan. Student, U. Mo., 1969-71. Controller Hilton Hotel, St. Louis, 1971—. Republican. Roman Catholic. Avocations: photography, fishing. Office: Hilton Hotel 10330 Natural Bridge Saint Louis MO 63134

FENNER, JACK RALPH, JR., sales manager; b. Dayton, Ohio, June 14, 1947; s. Jack Ralph Sr. and Mary Joan (Sarber) F.; m. Deborah Jo Hazelbaker, Nov. 7, 1970; children: Derek Jack, Matthew Lee. BBA, U. Cin., 1970. Territory mgr. Gen. Tire, Cin., 1970-74; store mgr. Gen. Tire, Lexington, Ky., 1974-76; product mgr. Gen. Tire, Akron, Ohio, 1976-82; zone rep. Gen. Tire, Akron, 1982-84, off-road reg. mgr., 1985-86, nat. mgr. of sales, 1986—. Chmn. Arrive Alive Com., Owensboro, Ky., 1982; co-chmn. Am. Heart Assn. Fund-raising, Owensboro, 1982. Named one of Outstanding Young Men Am., 1983. Mem. Owensboro Jaycees (bd. dirs. 1980-84, treas. 1984-85, pres.'s award 1982, dir. quarter 1982, officer yr. 1983). Lutheran. Lodge: Elks (lecturing knight 1978-79, leading knight 1979-80). Avocations: golf, reading, baseball. Home: 4306 Larchwood Canton OH 44718 Office: Gen Tire Inc One General St Akron OH 44329

FENSTERMAKER, JAMES P., utilities company executive; b. 1924. BS, Ohio State U., 1949. With Columbus & Southern Ohio Electric Co., Columbus, 1948—; plant supr. 1953-64, asst. mgr., 1964-71, v.p., 1971-73, sr. v.p., 1973-84, pres., chief operating officer, 1984—, also bd. dirs. Office: Columbus & So Ohio Electric Co 215 N Front St Columbus OH 43215 *

FERG, PATRICK DAVID, provincial judge; b. Glenboro, Man., Can., Nov. 2, 1927; s. Francis Milton and Helen Fleming (Paterson) F.; children: Allison, Michael, John. BA, U. Man., 1948, LLB, 1959. Ptnr. Wright, Ferg and Ferg, Flin Flon, Man., 1960-67, Ferg and Singh, Flin Flon, Man., 1967-73; sr. ptnr. Ferg, Cameron, Ginnell and Drapack, Flin Flon and Thompson, Man., 1973-75; judge Ct. of Queen's Bench, Man., 1984—. Office: Court of Queen's Bench, Law Courts Bldg, Winnipeg, MB Canada R3C 0V8 *

FERGER, LAWRENCE A., gas distribution utility executive; b. Des Moines, May 3, 1934; s. Cleon A. and Helen K. (Jacobs) F.; m. LaVon Stark, Oct. 20, 1957; children: Kirsten A., Jane S. B.S. in Bus. Adminstrn., Simpson Coll., Indianola, Iowa, 1956. Auditor Arthur Andersen & Co., Chgo., 1956-64; dir. data processing Ind. Gas Co., Inc., Indpls., 1964-74, v.p. planning, 1974-79, v.p., treas., 1979-80, sr. v.p. fin., 1980-81, exec. v.p., 1981-84, pres., 1984—, also bd. dirs.; bd. dirs. Entrade Corp., Ind. Energy, Inc. Served with U.S. Army, 1957-59. Mem. Ind. Gas Assn. (treas. 1966-80, sec. 1966-70, dir. 1980—). Office: Indiana Gas Co Inc 1630 N Meridian St Indianapolis IN 46202

FERGUS, TERRENCE PATRICK, accountant; b. Cleve., Sept. 10, 1954; s. Donald Francis and Betty Ann (Distefan) F.; m. Mary Dolores Cook, July 16, 1977; children: Nathan Patrick, Meredith Rose, Caitlin Marie, Kristen Michelle. Student, John Carroll U., 1972-76; BAcctg., Cleve. State U., 1982. CPA, Ohio. Prin. T.F.S. Cons., Cleve., 1975-82; tax mgr. Peat, Marwick, Main & Co., Cleve., 1982—. Football coach St. James 7th and 8th grade boys, Lakewood, Ohio, 1978—; cons. Lakewood Nursery Sch., 1985—. Mem. Am. Inst. CPA's (personnel fin. planning div.), Ohio Soc. CPA's. Republican. Roman Catholic. Club: Cleve. Athletic. Avocations: coaching football, bowling, golf, computers.

FERGUSON, ADLAI CLEVELAND, broadcasting executive; b. Arthur, Ill., Jan. 14, 1919; s. Adlai Cleveland and Arlena (Jones) F.; m. Marjorie Virginia Weber, Oct. 6, 1942; children—Sandra L. Ferguson Wheeler, Karen A., Jan D. Ferguson Lange. Grad. Terre Haute Comml. Coll., 1938. Chmn. bd. Paris Broadcasting Corp., Stas. WPRS-WACF-FM, Paris, Ill., 1951—. Served as lt. USAAF, 1942-45. Mem. Nat. Assn. Broadcasters, Nat. Radio Broadcaster's Assn., Ill. Broadcasters Assn., Ill. C. of C. Club: Paris. Lodge: Rotary. Home: 9 Janice Ave Paris IL 61944 Office: PO Box 396 Paris IL 61944

FERGUSON, ARDALE WESLEY, former industrial supply executive; b. Cedar Springs, Mich., Aug. 6, 1908; s. George Ardale and Alice Lucina (Andrus) F.; student pub. schs.; m. Hazel Frances Lokker, Oct. 28, 1931; children: Constance Ann Ferguson Klaasen, Mary Alice Ferguson Ritsema, Judy Kaye Furguson Ruffino; m. 2d G. Dolores Laker, Aug. 1976. Sales exec. John Deere Plow Co., Lansing, Mich., 1935-50; exec.-treas., mgr. Ferguson Welding Supply Co., Benton Harbor, Mich., 1950-76; sec.-treas. Lape Steel Stores, Inc., Benton Harbor, 1955-85; dir. Modern Light Metals, Inc. Mem. Benton Twp. Bd. Rev., 1963, Mich. Econ. Advancement Council, 1963-64; chmn. Mich. Hwy. Commn., 1964-68; pres. Twin Cities Community Chest, 1956. Treas. Mich. Republican Central Com., 1957-61; del. to Rep. Nat. Conv., 1960. Recipient award of spl. merit, Twin Cities Community Chest, 1956; named to Mich. Transp. Hall of Honor, 1984. Methodist. Clubs: Mountain Shadows Country, Peninsular. Lodge: Rotary (Cedar Springs chpt. master, 1933, pres. St. Joseph-Benton Harbor chpt. 1960). Home: 2609 Golfview Dr Apt 105 Troy MI 48084

FERGUSON, CHARLES SIBLEY, III, bank executive; b. Chgo., Mar. 6, 1942; s. Charles Sibley Jr. and Jane (Melchert) F.; m. Sandra Louise Rykoff, Nov. 22, 1975; children: Rebecca Jane, Charles Sibley IV. BA, U. Colo., 1966. Personnel mgr. Procon, Inc., Des Plaines, Ill., 1972-74; dir. human resources U.S. League Savs. Instns., Chgo., 1974-81; asst. v.p. adminstrn. Freedom Fed. Savs. Bank, Oakbrook, Ill., 1981—; v.p. Inst. Fin. Edn., Chgo., 1984-85, pres. 1985-86. Served to chief petty officer USCG, 1966-71. Mem. Bus. Forms Mgmt. Assn., Assn. Record Mgrs. and Adminstrs. Republican. Congregationalist. Avocations: model railroading, home remodeling. Home: 460 Shady Ln Barrington IL 60010

FERGUSON, DONALD JOHN, orthodontist, educator; b. Scotia, Calif., May 25, 1945; s. John Charles and Agnes Bregeta (Dahlberg) E.; m. Janet Ethyl Schmiege, July 30, 1977; children—Jon, Dana, Zachary. Student Humboldt State U., 1963-66; D.M.D., U. Oreg., 1970; cert. of residency Oakland Naval Hosp., 1971; cert. of orthodontics U. Pacific, 1976. Diplomate Am. Bd. Orthodontists. Clin. instr. endodontics U. Pacific Sch. Dentistry, San Francisco, 1974, lectr. anatomy, orthodontics, 1976-77, research assoc., 1976-77; orthodontic dir. Mt. Zion Hosp., San Francisco, 1976-80, co-dir. craniofacial deformities team, 1976-80; assoc. dir. gen. practice residency program Highland Gen. Hosp., Oakland, Calif., 1980-82; orthodontic dir. Ctr. for Correction Dentofacial Deformities, San Francisco, 1980-82; assoc. prof. orthodontics Ind. U., Indpls., 1982-85; chmn. orthodontics Marquette U.-Sch. Dentistry, Milw., 1985—, dir. grad. tng. program, 1985—; asst. clin. prof. Med. Coll. Wis., 1986—; cons. craniofacial anomalies team Ind. U. Med. Ctr., 1982-85; dir. surg. orthodontics Ind. U. Sch. Dentistry, 1982-85; cons. Wishard Mem. Hosp., Indpls., 1983-85, Milwaukee County Hosps., 1986—, Froedtert Meml. Luth. Hosp., 1986—, VA Hosp., San Francisco, 1980-82, Ctr. for Correction of Dentofacial Deformities, Milw. County Med. Complex, 1986—. Author: Craniofacial Growth and Development, 1984; contbr. Dentistry for the Child and Adolescent, 1986. Served to lt. USN, 1970-73, Vietnam. Recipient Ann. Teaching award Mount Zion Hosp., 1978, Outstanding Achievement award in orthodontics and periodontics U. Oreg. Sch. Dentistry, 1970. Mem. Am. Assn. Dental Schs., ADA, Am. Assn. Orthodontists, Wis. Dental Assn., Waukesha County Dental Soc., Midwest Soc. Orthodontists, Wis. Soc. Orthodontists, Edward H. Angle Soc. Orthodontists. Republican. Presbyterian. Avocations: sculpture, photography, horticulture, scuba diving, skiing. Office: Dept Orthodontics Marquette U Sch Dentistry 604 N 16th St Milwaukee WI 53233

FERGUSON, EDWARD AUGUSTUS, JR., office equipment executive, service manager; b. N.Y.C., July 21, 1942; s. Edward A. Sr and Oletha (Higgs) F.; m. Cynthia Henderson, May 4, 1968; children: Edward Augustus III, Candace Patrice, Derek Anzy. BBA in Fin., Iona Coll., 1965; MBA in Exec. Mgmt., St. John's U., Jamaica, N.Y., 1970-74; postgrad., NYU, 1975-78. V.p. personnel and adminstrn. Bedford Stuyvesant Restoration Corp., Blkyn., 1970-74; mgr. br. control Xerox Corp., N.Y.C., 1974-78; mgr. sales commn. adminstrn Xerox Corp., Rochester, N.Y., 1978-80, service cons., 1980-84; support mgr. dist. ops. Xerox Corp., Columbus, 1984-85; dist. mgr. customer service Xerox Corp., Akron, Ohio, 1985—. Bd. dirs. Berkshire Youth Services Bd., Caanan, N.Y., 1976—; Rochester Cath. Youth Orgn. Bd., 1980-84. Served to lt. col. USAR. Roman Catholic. Avocations: golf, racquetball, tennis. Office: Xerox Corp 3250 W Market St Akron OH 44313

FERGUSON, EDWIN EARLE, JR., physician; b. Alexandria, Va., Nov. 8, 1944; s. Edwin Earle Sr. and Alice Adonna (Jewell) F.; m. Margaret Both, May 10, 1986. BS in Chemistry, U. Rochester, 1966; MD, George Washington U., 1974. Diplomate Am. Bd. Internal Medicine. Intern U. Wis. Hosps., Madison, 1974-75, resident physician, 1975-77; practice medicine specializing in internal medicine and geriatrics Physicians Plus, Waunakee, Wis., 1980—, Quisling Clinic, Waunakee, 1980—; asst. clin. prof. dept. medicine U. Wis., Madison, 1983—. Contbr. articles to profl. jours. Fellow Am. Coll. Physicians; mem. Alpha Omega Alpha, Waunakee Soc. Model Railroaders (pres. 1982-84). Home and Office: 208 S Century Ave Waunakee WI 53597

FERGUSON, EVA DREIKURS, psychologist, educator, researcher; b. Vienna, Austria, Aug. 28, 1929; d. Rudolf and Sadie (Ellis) Dreikurs; m. John A. Ferguson, Jan. 28, 1950 (div. 1969); children: Rodney, Beth, Bruce, Linda. BA with honors, U. Ill., 1950; MA with honors, Melbourne U., Australia, 1953; PhD, Northwestern U., 1956. Sociologist Lady Gowrie Child Ctr., Melbourne, 1951-52; intern in psychology Ill. Neuropsychiat. Hosp., Chgo., 1954-55; postdoctoral fellow Western Psychiat. Inst., Pitts., 1956-58; psychologist Craig House for Children, Pitts., 1959-62; asst. prof. psychology Melbourne U., 1962-65; assoc. prof. psychology So. Ill. U., Edwardsville, 1965-69, prof., 1969—; staff mem. Alfred Adler Inst., Chgo., 1965—; vis. prof. U. Vt., 1970-71, Northwestern U., 1979; chairperson Com. for Adlerian Summer Schs. and Insts., 1978—; vis. scholar U. Calif, Berkeley, 1985-86. Author: Motivation: An Experimental Approach, 1976, 82, Adlerian Theory: An Introduction, 1984; cons. editor Psychology of Women Quar., Jour. Individual Psychology; contbr. articles to profl. jours. Recipient award in sociology Chi Omega, 1950. Fellow Am. Psychol. Assn.; mem. AAAS (life), Sigma Xi, Psychonomic Soc. Office: So Ill U Dept Psychology PO Box 1121 Edwardsville IL 62026

FERGUSON, JOHN ALLEN, music educator; b. Cleve., Jan. 27, 1941; s. Allen Bebee and Nancy Sophie (Carlson) F.; m. Ruth Ann Hofstad, Aug. 28, 1971; 1 child, Christopher. B in Music, Oberlin Coll., 1963; MA, Kent State U., 1965; D in Musical Arts, Eastman Sch. Music, 1976. From instr to prof. music Kent (Ohio) State U., 1965-78; organist, choirmaster United Ch. Christ, Kent, 1963-78; music dir., organist Cen. Luth. Ch., Mpls., 1978-83; prof. organ and ch. music St. Olaf Coll., Northfield, Minn., 1983—; endowed chair in ch. music St. Olaf Coll., 1986; vis. prof. U. Notre Dame, Ind.; organ cons. Coll. St. Thomas, St. Paul, 1985—, Luth. Northwestern Seminary, St. Paul, 1985—; ch. music cons. 1st Luth., Sioux Falls, S.D., 1986, Augustana Luth., Denver, 1986—; lectr. in field; active various hymn festivals. Author: Walter Holtkamp Organ Builder, 1979, Guide to Planning for Workship Music, 1983; co-author: Musician's Guide to Church Music, 1981; editor: Hymnal-United Ch. Christ., 1975; contbr. articles to profl. jours.; composer ch. music. Named one of Outstanding Young Men of Am., Jaycees, 1976; Ford Found. Venture Fun grantee 1974, Am. Luth. Ch. grantee 1986. Mem. Am. Guild Organists (sec. com. profl. edn. 1980—, gen. chmn. nat. conv. 1974), Nat. Assn. Pastoral Musicians, Hymn Soc. Am. Avocations: stamp collecting, restoration antique vehicles. Home: 820 Ivanhoe Dr Northfield MN 55057 Office: St Olaf Coll Northfield MN 55057

FERGUSON, JOHN BOWIE, professional hockey team executive; b. Vancouver, B.C., Can., Sept. 5, 1938; m. Joan Ferguson; children: Christine, Cathy, John, Joanne. Player Montreal Canadiens, NHL, 1963-72; asst. coach Team Can., 1972; coach, gen. mgr. N.Y. Rangers, NHL, 1976-78; v.p., gen. mgr. Winnipeg Jets, NHL (formerly with World Hockey Assn.), 1978—, coach, 1985-86. Mem. B.C. Sports HALL Of Fame. Mem. Stanley Cup Championship Team, 1965, 66, 68, 69, 71; player NHL All-Star Game, 1965, 67. Office: Winnipeg Jets, 15-1430 Maroons Rd, Winnipeg, MB Canada R3G 0L5 *

FERGUSON, JOHN WAYNE, librarian; b. Ash Grove, Mo., Nov. 4, 1936; s. John William and Eula M. Ferguson; m. Nancy C. Southerland, Sept. 25, 1939; children—John Wayne, Mark, Steven. B.S., S.W. Mo. State Coll., Springfield, 1958; M.S. in Library Sci., Okla. U., 1962. Librarian, Springfield Pub. Library, 1952-64; asst. dir. Mid-Continent Pub. Library, Independence, Mo., 1964-81, dir. libraries, 1981—. Past pres. Independence YMCA; bd. dirs. Independence Hosp. and Sanitarium. Served to capt. F.A., U.S. Army, 1959-65. Mem. ALA, Mo. Library Assn. Lodge: Rotary (past pres., dist. gov. 1986-87). Home: 3820 Stonewall Ct Independence MO 64055 Office: 14505 E 43d St Independence MO 64055

FERGUSON, MARY ROSALIE, utilities company executive; b. Indpls., Jan. 1, 1939; d. Francis John and Catherine Marie (Osterman) Schmidt; m. Kenneth H. Ferguson, Jr. (div. July 1969); 1 child, Kimberlie Marie. Student in English, Butler U., 1957-73; student in mgmt., Ind. U. Purdue U. at Indpls., 1982—. Staff supr. mktg. Ind. Bell. Telephone Co., Indpls., 1967-72, evaluator assessment ctr., 1972-73, accounts mgr. mktg., 1973-82, specialist bus. services, 1982, mgr. spl. services, 1982—; cons. mgmt., Indpls., 1986—. Mem. exec. com. 2d Quadrennial Internat. Violin Competition of Indpls., 1986; performance site chairperson Pan Am. Music Festival of Champions, Indpls., 1987; bd. dirs. Cathedral Arts, Inc., Indpls., 1987, Fine Arts Soc., Inc., Indpls., 1987. Named Nat. Am. Businesswoman Yr. Am. Businesswomen's Assn., 1973. Mem. Women's Bus. Initiative, Inc., The Network of Women in Bus., Inc. (charter mem. Exec. Club 1985-87, pres., bd. dirs. 1981-85, Networker of Yr., 1984), Telephone Pioneers Am. Republican. Roman Catholic. Club: Business (Indpls.) (pres. 1983). Avocations: music, opera, scripture study. Office: Ind Bell Telephone Co Inc 220 N Meridian Room 795 Indianapolis IN 46250

FERGUSON, RICHARD LEE, protective services official; b. Kokomo, Ind., Jan. 20, 1938; s. Elza Curtiss and Mabel Lavanne (Blacklidge) F.; m. Glenda Marlene Murphy, June 28, 1958; children: Richard Allen, Michelle Lynn Johnson. AS, Ind. U., Kokomo, 1974, BA, 1976. Chief dep. Howard County Police Dept., Kokomo, 1967-72; capt. Kokomo Police Dept., 1974-77, inspector patrol div., 1979-80, lt., 1981—. Pres. Common Ground Clinic, Kokomo, 1977. Mem. Ind. U. Alumni Assn. (pres. 1979-80), Fraternal Order Police. Republican. Mem. Nazarene Ch. Lodges: Elks, Shriners. Avocations: distance running, fishing. Home: 2408 S Berkley Rd Kokomo IN 46902 Office: Kokomo Police Dept 100 S Union St Kokomo IN 46901

FERGUSON, ROBERT ERNEST, educator; b. Rochester, Minn., Sept. 13, 1937; s. Victor Burnett and Josephine Irene (Anderson) F.; m. Karen Marie Swanson, July 25, 1964; 1 child, Kari Josephine. BA, Bemidji (Minn.) State U., 1963, MA, 1969; EdS, St. Thomas Coll., 1982. Cert. tchr., adminstr., Minn. Tchr. Rosemount (Minn.) Dist. 196, 1963-65, prin., 1966—; speaker Nat. Elem. Sch. Prins., Anaheim, Calif., 1974, State Elem. Prin. Conv., Columbus, Ohio, 1975, Minn. Elem. Schs. Prin. Conv., St. Paul, 1976. Bd. dirs. Minn. Zoo Bd., 1976-81, Rural Electric Assn., Dakota County, Minn., 1980-85; mem. Higher Edn. Coordinating Bd. (bd. dirs. 1983-87, pres. 1985-86); active Minn. Edn. Council, 1971-76. Mem. Higher Edn. Coordinating Bd. (bd. dirs. 1983-87, pres. 1985-86). Democrat. Methodist. Club: West End Gun (St. Paul) (bd. dirs. 1978-85). Lodges: Masons, Shriners (clown pres. St. Paul chpt. 1977, circus dir. 1985-86). Avocations: hunting, traveling. Home: 855 Cliff Rd Eagan MN 55123 Office: Rosemount Sch Dist #196 14445 Diamond Path Rosemount MN 55068

FERGUSON, ROBERT LEE, computer programmer, educator; b. Scottsbluff, Nebr., Aug. 24, 1944; s. Robert Elmer and Majorie Jane (Echle) F.; m. Glenda I. Irvine, Sept. 29, 1968; children: Robert L. III, Shannone R. AA, Nebr. Western Jr. Coll., 1971; postgrad., U. Wis., Green Bay, 1985—. Asst. mgr. Nebr. Western Computer Ctr., Scottsbluff, 1970-74; sr. analyst, programmer Lockwood Corp., Gering, Nebr., 1974-81; sr. systems programmer Schreiber Foods, Inc., Green Bay, 1981—; instr. Northeastern Wis. Tech. Inst., Green Bay, 1984—. Mem. Northeastern Wis. Data Processing Mgrs. Assn. Republican. Avocations: amateur, radio, camping. Home: 2131 S Ridge Rd Green Bay WI 54304 Office: Schreiber Foods Inc PO Box 19010 Green Bay WI 54307-9010

FERINO, CHRISTOPHER KENNETH, computer information scientist; b. Chgo., May 25, 1961; s. Natale Ferino and Carol Marie (Anderson) Huckeby; m. Anita Louise Vanderhoof, Oct. 19, 1985. Cons. Lachman Assn., Inc., Wesmont, Ill., 1979-80; AS/RS operator W.W. Grainger, Niles, Ill., 1980-82; mem. computer staff Paddock Publs., Arlington Heights, Ill., 1982-84; data processing coordinator Power Systems, Schaumburg, Ill., 1984-85; tech. specialist Follett Software Co., Crystal Lake, Ill., 1985—. Mem. Boston Computer Soc. Avocations: computers, numismatics, personal finance.

FERLIS, NICHOLAS WILLIAM, investment executive; b. Kankakee, Ill., Sept. 17, 1947; s. William Nicholas and Magdeline Gail (Bogordos) F.; m. Sally Phillippi, Sept. 18, 1982. B.B.A., Loyola U., Chgo., 1970; M.B.A., Northwestern U., 1972. C.P.A., Ill.; registered investment advisors Registry Fin. Planning Practitioners; registered securities broker dealer; cert. fin. planner. Internal auditor Consol. Packaging Co., Chgo., 1968-70; sr. staff acct. Arthur Andersen & Co., Chgo., 1970-74; group controller Apeco Corp., Evanston, Ill., 1974-75; v.p. Splty. Fin. Services, Glenview, Ill., 1975-79; pres. Ferlis & Assocs., Des Plaines, Ill., 1979-82; pres. Equity Advisors, Inc., Northfield, Ill., 1982—. Mem. Am. Mgmt. Assn. (pres. club 1979—), Internat. Assn. Fin. Planners (nat. rev. com. 1983—), Am.Inst. C.P.A.s, Ill. Soc. C.P.A.s, N.Am. Assn. Securities Dealers. Republican. Greek Orthodox. Office: Equity Advisors Inc 790 Frontage Rd Northfield IL 60093

FERNANDES, BRISTON JOSEPH, social services administrator; b. Bombay, India, Nov. 4, 1941; came to U.S., 1973; s. John J. and Basilia (Pereira) F.; m. Melanie Bernadette Kirthisinghe, July 18, 1981; 1 dau., Melissa Bernadine. B.E., Tilak Coll., Pune, India, 1968; M.Ph., Colegio San Francisco de Borja, Barcelona, Spain, 1965; Th.M., Pontifical Athenaeum, Pune, 1972; M.A. in Couseling Psychology, Loyola U., Chgo., 1973-75. Tchr., St. Xavier's High Sch., Bombay, 1965-66; counselor St. Peter's Parish, Bombay, 1972-73; counseling psychologist Elgin Catholic Social Service (Ill.), 1976-80; exec. dir. McHenry County Cath. Social Service, Woodstock, Ill., 1980-83, Cath. Social Service Elgin, 1983—. Mem. Commn. for Justice and Peace, Cath. Diocese of Rockford (Ill.). Author articles, poetry. Democrat. Roman Catholic. Home: 8858 E Dee Rd Des Plaines IL 60016 Office: 566 Dundee Ave Elgin IL 60120

FERNANDEZ, JOHN VICTOR, pyschiatrist; b. Bangalore City, India, Sept. 7, 1950; came to U.S., 1975; s. Felix G. and Clara (Mascarenhas) F.; m. Maria Castelino, May 9, 1975; children: Maya C., Binoy D., Rajiv J. Student, St. Xavier's Coll., Bombay, India, 1966-67; MD, St. John's Med. Coll., Bangalore City, 1973. Cert. Am. Bd. Psychiatry. Intern B.Y.L. Nair Hosp., Bombay, 1973-74; resident Holy Spirit Hosp., Bombay, 1974-75; resident in psychiatry Nebr. Psychiat. Inst., Omaha, 1975-78; gen. practice medicine specializing in psychiatry Council Bluffs, Iowa, 1978—; active staff Mercy Hosp., Council Bluffs, Iowa, 1978—, Jennie Edmundson Meml. Hosp., Council Bluffs, Iowa, 1978—. Mem. AMA, Iowa Med. Soc., Pottawattomie-Mills County Med. Soc., Am. Psychiat. Assn., Iowa Psychiat. Soc. Office: Bluffs Psychiat Assocs PC 105 Doctors Bldg Council Bluffs IA 51501

FERNBACH, JOHN STEVEN, obstetrician, gynecologist; b. Subotica, Yugoslavia, Sept. 2, 1943; came to U.S., 1969; s. John and Charlotte (Birkas) F.; m. Arla Ann Kotila, May 13, 1972; children: Laura, Nerine, Michael. MD, U. Zagreb, Yugoslavia, 1967. Diplomate Am. Bd. Obs. and Gyns. Intern Fairview Gen. Hosp., Cleve., 1970-71, staff mem. dept. obgyn., 1974; resident Cleve. Clinic, Fairview Gen. Hosp., 1971-74; ptnr. Fairview West Ob-Gyn., North Olmsted, Ohio, 1974—; chancellor exec. council ob-gyn. dept. Fairview Gen. Hosp., Cleve., 1985-86. Served to lt. USAF, 1968, Yugoslavia. Fellow Am. Coll. Ob-Gyn; mem. Am. Fertility Soc., Cleve. Acad. Medicine. Avocations: hunting, soccer, skiing, photography. Home: 2350 Pebblebrook Westlake OH 44145 Office: Fairview West Ob/Gyn 24700 Lorain Rd North Olmsted OH 44070

FERNG, DOUGLAS MING-HAW, infosystems executive; b. Anshan, Peoples Republic of China, Feb. 27, 1945; came to U.S., 1968; s. Jau-Tarng and Hwei-In (Chu) F.; m. Gloria K. Chao, Oct. 28, 1972; children: Jennifer, Albert. BS, Nat. Taiwan U., Taipei, 1967; M in Forestry, Yale U., 1970; MBA, U. Wash., Seattle, 1979. Scientific programmer Weyerhaeuser Co., Federal Way, Wash., 1970-72, computer analyst, 1972-77, forest economist, 1977-79; mgr. silvicultural econs. Champion Internat., Stamford, Conn., 1979-80, mgr. resource econs., 1980-83; mgr. bus. systems Champion Internat., Hamilton, Ohio, 1983—. Served as lt. Taiwan Army, 1967-68. Fellow Yale Univ., 1968-70. Mem. Paper Industry Mgmt. Assn., Cin. Chinese Assn., Chinese Assn. of Fairfield County (v.p. 1981-83). Club: cin. Yale. Avocation: photography. Office: Champion Internat 101 Knightsbridge Dr Hamilton OH 45020

FERO, DAVID DALE, clinical psychologist; b. Youngstown, Ohio, Feb. 8, 1947; s. Glen Chester and Helen (Puccine) F.; m. Jane Bernadette Merklinger, Jan. 1, 1969 (div. Oct. 1980); 1 child, Adam Matthew; m. Eugenia Moskova, Dec. 22, 1985; 1 stepson, Andrean Moskov. BS magna cum laude, Bowling Green (Ohio) State U., 1969, MA, 1972, PhD, 1975. Staff psychologist and coordinator day hosp. Cleve. VA Med. Ctr., 1975-79, staff psychologist DDTP, 1979-80, staff psychologist and coordinator psychological substance abuse, 1980-86, staff psychologist and coordinator neorotraining, 1986—. Contbr. articles to profl. jours. Vol. Big Bros. and Big Sisters of Akron, Ohio, 1983-86; bd. dirs. Unity of Akron, 1984-86. Served to capt. USAR, 1969-74. Mem. Am. Psychol. Assn., Ohio Psychol. Assn., Psychologists for Social Responsibilty, Sierra Club. Avocations: running, personal fitness, computers, outdoor activities. Home: 610 Prior Park Cuyahoga Falls OH 44223 Office: Cleve VA Med Ctr Brecksville Div 116(B) 10000 Brecksville Rd Brecksville OH 44141

FERRARI, RICHARD MARION, real estate executive; b. Chgo., May 3, 1955; s. Philip and Mollie Lucy (Salerno) F.; B.B.A. magna cum laude, Loyola U., Chgo., 1977; M.B.A. in Fin., DePaul U., 1982. Mgmt. intern IRS, Chgo., 1975-77, agt., 1977-79; sr. exec. v.p., controller Ferrari Builders, Inc., Bensenville, Ill., 1979—; cons. AMD Cons., Inc., Bensenville Coin Wash. Bd. dirs. St. Charles Homeowners Assn., 1979-81, Tudor on the Greens Homeowners Assn., 1982—. C.P.A., registered real estate broker, Ill. Mem. Am. Inst. C.P.A.s, Ill. Soc. C.P.A.s, Nat. Assn. Realtors, DuPage Bd. Realtors, Fin. Mgmt. Assn., Beta Gamma Sigma, Beta Alpha Psi, Alpha Sigma Nu. Roman Catholic. Office: 1090-98 W Irving Park Rd Bensenville IL 60106

FERRARO, CHARLES DOMENIC, psychologist, educator; b. Cleve., Apr. 12, 1913; s. Ross and Mary (Cundra) F.; m. Alice Carolyn Nimrichter, Dec. 30, 1939 (div. Dec. 1965); children: Diane, Linda; m. Donna Joan Gamble, Apr. 12, 1966. AB, Ohio U., 1936; BS, Case Western Res. U., 1938, MA, 1953, PhD, 1957. Lic. psychologist, Ohio. Chief counselor John Carroll U., University Heights, Ohio, 1949-51, lectr. psychology, 1951-70, 81-86, assoc. prof., 1970-74, prof., chmn. psychology dept., 1974-78; placement officer NASA-Lewis Research Ctr., Cleve., 1951-70; pvt. practice counseling psychologist Lakewood, Ohio, 1953—. Bd. dirs., chmn., governance com. Far W. Mental Health Ctr., Westlake, Ohio, 1979-85. Recipient Career Service award Cleve. Fed. Exec. Bd., 1969, Fed. Service award Am. Soc. Pub. Adminstrn., 1969, Commendation cert. Pres. Nixon, 1970. Mem. Am. Psychol. Assn. (life), Ohio Psychol. Assn. (life). Avocations: swimming, reading, travel. Home: 1550 Cedarwood Dr Westlake OH 44145 Office: 14213 Detroit Ave Lakewood OH 44107

FERRARO, JOSEPH CARMELO, dentist; b. Hartford, Conn., Nov. 6, 1956; s. Joseph John and Rebecca Sarah (Gentile) F.; m. Cynthia Kay Gittins, June 7, 1980; children: Joseph John, Aubrey Cathleen, Ashley Rebecca. BA in Biology, Taylor U., 1978; postgrad., Creighton U., 1978-80; DDS, Marquette U., 1984. Practice dentistry Menasha, Wis., 1984—. Bd. dirs. Menasha Action Council. Mem. Menasha Bus. Assn. (pres.), ADA, Acad. Gen. Dentistry, Wis. Dental Assn., Menasha C. of C. (govt. affairs com.). Avocations: sports, gardening, woodworking. Home: 944 Grove St Menasha WI 54952 Office: 419 First St Menasha WI 54952

FERRENDELLI, JAMES ANTHONY, neurologist, educator; b. Trinidad, Colo., Dec. 5, 1936; s. Alex and Edna Ferrendelli; children—Elisabeth, Cynthia, Michael. AB cum laude in Chemistry, U. Colo., Boulder, 1958; M.D., U. Colo., Denver, 1962. Diplomate Am. Bd. Psychiatry and Neurology. Intern U. Ky. Med. Ctr., 1962-63; resident in neurology Cleve. Met. Gen. Hosp., 1965-68; research fellow in neurochemistry Washington U. Sch. Medicine, St. Louis, 1968-70; asst. prof. neurology and pharmacology Washington U. Sch. Medicine, 1970-74; assoc. prof. Sch. Medicine, Washington U., 1974-77, prof., 1977—, Seay prof. clin. neuropharmacology in neurology, 1977—. Contbr. numerous articles to profl. jours. Served to capt. M.C., U.S. Army, 1963-65. Recipient research career devel. award USPHS, 1971-76; Founders Day award Washington U., 1981; NIH grantee, 1971—. Mem. Am. Acad. Neurology, Am. Neurol. Assn., Am. Soc. for Pharmacology and Exptl. Therapeutics (Epilepsy award 1981), Am. Epilepsy Soc. Avocation: fly-fishing. Office: Washington U Med Sch Dept Neurology 660 S Euclid Ave Saint Louis MO 63110

FERRIER, RUBY JANE, healthcare executive; b. Bryant, Va.; s. Rufus Mulford Dodd and Alice Eva (Falls) Hailey; m. Waymon Ferrier; children: Gregory, Deborah. Student, Leicester Coll., 1973-74, St. Louis Community Coll., 1976-77. Adminstr. Oak Hill Nursing Home, Middleboro, Mass., 1972-75, Friendship Village, St. Louise, 1975-78; adminstr. Beverly Enterprises, Owensville, Mo., 1979-82, Brookville, Ohio, 1982-84, Columbus, Ohio, 1984-86; regional mgr. Beverly Enterprises, Peoria, Ill., 1986—. Mem. Am. Coll. Healthcare Adminstrs. (chpt. sec. 1978-79, regional sec. 1980-82), United Healthcare Assocs. (sec. 1973-75). Avocations: swimming, reading, music. Home: 10308 Forrest Terr N Peoria IL 61615 Office: Beverly Enterprises 907 Clocktower Springfield IL 62704

FERRILL, JOHN WESLEY, infosystems specialist; b. Taylorville, Ill., Feb. 6, 1947; s. Kenneth Ray and Mary Jean (Cummins) F.; m. Alma Rose Fleigle, June 15, 1968; children: Don Michael, Doug Wesley. AA, Lincolnland Community Coll., 1975; BA, Sangamon State U., 1979. Computer operator Ill. Dept. Pub. Aid, Springfield, 1970-80; sr. system analyst Ill. Dept. Transp., Springfield, 1980—; instr. pt. time Lincoln Land Community Coll., Springfield, 1982—. Pres. Palmer Morrisonville Recreation Assn., Inc., 1980-86, Village of Morrisonville, 1981—, trustee, 1981-83, mayor 1982—. Served to staff sgt. USAF, 1966-70. Mem. Am. Legion (comdr. 1983-84), Morrisonville Area C. of C. (pres. 1984, 86). Office: Ill Dept Transp 126 E Ash Springfield IL 62704-4766

FERRINI, JOSEPH PHILIP, dentist; b. Cleve., Apr. 8, 1953; s. Vincent Frank and Josephine Ferrini; m. Cynthia Marie Chmelik, Aug. 24, 1979; children: Joseph Philip Jr., Kristina Elizabeth. BS in Biology magna cum laude, Baldwin-Wallace Coll., 1975; DDS, Ohio State U., 1978. Gen. practice dentistry Middleburg Heights, Ohio, 1978—; mem. staff Am. Dental Ctrs., Brookpark, Ohio, 1978-79, Southwest Gen. Hosp., Middleburg Heights, 1979—; cons. Willowwood Nursing Home, Brunswick, Ohio, 1979. Lectr. Youth for Christ, Cleve., 1979, Christian Bus. Men Com., Cleve.,

1981—; mem Grace Christian and Missionary Alliance, trustee 1981-82, Shepherding Ministry, 1981-84. Named one of Outstanding Young Men Am., Jaycees, 1981. Mem. ADA, Ohio Dental Assn., Cleve. Dental Assn., Ohio State Alumni Assn., Delta Sigma Delta (Man of Yr. 1978). Republican. Avocations: bible study, golf, fishing. Office: 18660 Bagley Rd Suite 304 Middleburg Heights OH 44130

FERRIS, DAN GEORGE, advertising executive, radio commentator; b. Waukegan, Ill., Sept. 20, 1958; s. Donald L. and Susan M. (Whalen) F. Grad. high sch., Arlington Heights, Ill. Sales rep. Midwest Outdoors, Hinsdale, Ill., 1980-84; advt. dir. Midwest Outdoors, Hinsdale, 1984—; radio show host Sta. WMAQ, Chgo., 1985—; narrator Sta. WCIU-TV, Chgo., 1985—; announcer Midwest Outdoors, 1982-83, sports show coordinator, 1984—; cons. Shadowbox Prodns., Oak Park, Ill., 1985—. Author articles; theme music songwriter. Rep. campaign booster, Highland Park, Ill., 1980-84. Recipient mayor's commendation Village of Arlington Heights, 1980, Appreciation award Lake Gogebic (Mich.) C. of C., 1986. Avocations: music, sports, literature, etymology. Home: 2 Hawthorne Prospect Heights IL 60070 Office: Midwest Outdoors 111 Shore Dr Hinsdale IL 60521

FERRIS, JOSEPH EDWARD, electrical engineer; b. Jackson, Mich., Apr. 27, 1929; s. Harry R. and Caroline J. (Davis) F.; m. Jean Marie Kleps, Jan. 20, 1951; children: Noreen L., Wolcott, Cynthia E. Smith, Joseph E. Jr. BEEE, George Washington U., 1961. Engr. Melpar Inc., Falls Church, Va., 1955-61; sr. engr. Bendix Systems Div., Ann Arbor, Mich., 1961-63; research engr. U. Mich., Ann Arbor, 1963-84; pres. JEF Cons. Inc., Saline, Mich., 1984—, engr., 1979-84. Patentee broadband high gain antenna, millimeter wave microstrip antenna. Served to sgt. U.S. Army, 1952-55. Mem. IEEE (Antenna Propagation Group spl. recognition award 1969). Avocation: woodworking. Home and Office: 3544 Weber Rd Saline MI 48176

FERRIS, RICHARD J., former airline company executive; b. Sacramento, Aug. 31, 1936; married. B.S., Cornell U., 1962; postgrad. in Bus., U. Wash. Former staff analyst, restaurant mgr. Olympic Hotel; former gen. mgr. Carlton Hotel; with Western Internat. Hotels, 1962-66; gen. mgr. Continental Plaza Hotel, Chgo., 1966-71; pres. carrier's food service div. United Air Lines, Inc., Chgo., 1971-74, corp. sr. v.p. mktg., 1974, pres., 1974-85, chief exec. officer, 1976-85, chmn., 1978-87; also dir. United Air Lines, Inc.; chief exec. officer UAL, Inc. (name changed to Allegis Corp., 1987) parent co., Chgo., 1979-87, chmn., pres., 1982-87, also dir.; dir. Western Internat. Hotels, Westin Hotel Co., Amoco Corp. Office: United Air Lines PO Box 66100 Chicago IL 60666 *

FERRIS, THOMAS JOHN, accountant, auditor; b. Janesville, Wis., Nov. 22, 1950; s. William Harold Sr. and Margaret Arlene (Parkin) F.; m. Aileen Marie Schmitz, Aug. 28, 1971; children: Robert John, Michael William, Patricia Marie. BA in Economics, U. Wis., 1972, BBA in Acctg., 1974. CPA, Wis. Audit section chief Bur. Mcpl. Audit, Wis. Dept. Revenue, Madison, 1974-82; dir. fin. City of Manitowoc, Wis., 1982; supr. audit Wis. Pub. Service Commn., Madison, 1982—. Vol., auditor Madison Area Adult Day Ctrs., Inc., 1980—. Mem. Am. Inst. CPA's, Wis. Inst. CPA's (mem. profl. conduct com.). Congregationalist. Avocations: bicycling, golf. Home: 13 Star Fire Court Madison WI 53719 Office: Wis Pub Service Commn PO 7854 Madison WI 53711

FERRISS, DAVID PLATT, advertising consultant; b. St. Louis, Jan. 27, 1919; s. Henry Theodore and Edith (Platt) F.; m. Marion Harris Ford, July 9, 1942 (div. July 1951); children: Carol (dec. 1967), Marion Ferriss Wilson; m. Elizabeth Lashly States, May 17, 1952 (div. July 1963); m. Jean O. Browne, Jan 18, 1964 (div. Mar. 1976); m. Ruth Knight Schneider, Sept. 2, 1976. BA, Yale U., 1940. Reporter St. Louis Star-Times, 1940-41; v.p. Gardner Advt. Co., Inc., St. Louis, N.Y.C., 1946-70; pres. Ralph Jones Advt., Inc., Cin., 1970-75; chmn. Fahlgren & Ferriss Advt., 1975-78; pub. Cin. Mag., 1979-80; v.p. The Angus Group, 1980-85; pres. The Ferriss Co., Cin., 1985—; Assoc. lectr. English, Washington U., 1947-51, George Washington U., 1951-52; lectr. bus. communications U. Cin. Served to capt. CIC, AUS, 1941-45; capt. CIA, 1951-52. Mem. Am. Mktg. Assn. (chpt. pres. 1982-83), Advt. Club Cin. (pres. 1979), Gyro Internat. (pres. Cin. chpt. 1987—). Republican. Episcopalian. Clubs: Cin. Country, Queen City. Home: 3649 Traskwood Circle Cincinnati OH 45208

FERRITTO, JERAULD DAMIAN, podiatrist; b. Cleve., May 2, 1950; s. Jerauld Dominic and Rose Ida (Violante) F.; m. Susan Elaine Long; 1 child, Elaine Marie. BS, Ohio State U., 1972; D in Podiatric Medicine, Ohio Coll. Podiatric Medicine, 1976. Diplomate Am. Bd. Podiatric Orthopedics. Resident in podiatric medicine and surgery Cleve. Foot Clinic, 1976-77; pvt. practice podiatry Columbus, Ohio, 1977-81, Grove City, Ohio, 1981—; cons. in podiatry Columbus Devel. Ctr., 1979—, Ohio Dept. Human Services, 1980—, Med. Plan, 1986—; adj. clin. faculty mem. Ohio Coll. Podiatric Medicine, 1981—; mem. surg. staff Grant Hosp., 1980—, Doctor's Hosp., 1984—; St. Anthony Med. Ctr., 1985—, Mount Carmel Med. Ctr., 1986—; mem. adv. council Hilltop Neighborhood Health Ctr., 1978-81. Mem. steering com. Greater Hilltop Area Commn., 1979-80, Hilltop Bus. Assn., 1979-81. Named one of Outstanding Young Men of Am., 1984. Fellow Am. Coll. Foot Orthopedists; mem. Ohio Podiatric Med. Assn. (profl. standards rev. orgn. 1977-79, continuing med. edn. com. 1978—, alt. del. to Am. Podiatry Assn. 1981—), Am. Podiatric Med. Assn., Am. Pub. Health Assn., Cen. Acad. of Ohio Podiatric Med. Assn. (pres. 1983-84, pres.-elect 1982-83, v.p. 1981-82, sec. 1979-81, chmn. externship program 1978-79, chmn. grand rounds 1978-79, alt. trustee to Ohio Podiatric Med. Assn. Bd. 1979-86, del. to Ohio Podiatric Med. Assn. 1978—), Am. Assn. Hosp. Podiatrists, Ohio State U. Alumni Assn., Grove City Area C. of C., Beta Nu, Sigma Nu (social chmn. 1969-70, v.p. 1970-71, others). Democrat. Roman Catholic. Lodge: Kiwanis (bd. dirs. Hilltop of Columbus club 1978-81). Avocations: music, audio-video, automobiles. Office: 3873 Broadway Grove City OH 43123

FERRY, MICHAEL JAMES, health care executive; b. South Bend, Ind., June 30, 1957; s. Daniel Joseph and Doris May (Robertson) F.; m. Anne Marie Eslinger, July 17, 1982; 1 child, Michael James Jr. BS, Cen MIch. U., Mt. Pleasant, 1979; M Pub. Adminstrn., Ind. U., South Bend, 1983. Cert. in health care pub. mgmt. Employment specialist St. Joseph's Med. Ctr., South Bend, 1981, mgmt. devel. specialist, 1981-82, mgr. employee relations, 1982-85, dir. human resources, 1985-86; dir. managed care plans St. Joseph's Care Group, Inc., South Bend, 1986—; co-chmn. Ind. State Employer Job Service Com., South Bend, 1982-83; mem. personnel com. of bd. Notre Dame Credit Union, South Bend, 1984-86; cons. corp. systems Images, South Bend, 1986. Mem. advisory council Holy Cross Health System, South Bend, 1983-86; rep. United Religious Communities, South Bend, 1983—; facilitator Madison Ctr. Dislocated Worker Program, South Bend, 1983-84; mem. Ind. U. Sch. Pub. Environ. Affairs Alumni Council, South Bend, 1984—; v.p. bd. Sagamore Preferred Provider Orgn., 1987. Mem. Am. Soc. Personnel Adminstrs., Ind. Soc. for Hosp. Personnel Adminstrs. (legis. editor State Newsheet 1983-84), N. Cen. Ind. Hosp. Personnel Adminstrs., South Bend and Mishawaka C. of C. Avocations: golf, cross country skiing, backpacking, raising family. Home: 1748 N Adams South Bend IN 46628 Office: St Joseph's Care Group Inc 707 E Cedar South Bend IN 46617

FERSHTMAN, JULIE ILENE, lawyer; b. Detroit, Apr. 3, 1961; d. Sidney and Judith Joyce (Stoll) F. Student, Mich. State U., 1979-81; BA in Philosophy and Polit. Sci., Emory U., 1983, JD, 1986. Bar: Mich. 1986. Summer assoc. Kitch, Saurbier et al, Detroit, 1985; assoc. Miller, Canfield, Paddock and Stone, Detroit, 1986—. Mem. ABA, Am. Trial Lawyers Assn., Common Cause, Women Lawyers Assn. Mich., Nat. Mus. Women and Arts, Phi Alpha Delta, Omicron Delta Kappa, Pi Sigma Tau, Phi Sigma Alpha. Avocations: horseback riding, writing, music, art. Home: 28490 Franklin River Dr Apt 302 Southfield MI 48034-1659 Office: Miller Canfield Paddock & Stone 2500 Comerica Bldg Detroit MI 48226

FERSTENFELD, JULIAN ERWIN, internist, educator; b. Des Moines, Sept. 5, 1941; m. Sharon Rukas, Mar. 8, 1975; children—Megan Ann, Adam Justin. B.A., U. Iowa, 1963, M.D., 1966. Intern Milwaukee County Gen. Hosp., Milw., 1966-67, resident in internal medicine, 1969-71, fellow in infectious diseases, 1972-73; instr. internal medicine Med. Coll. Wis., Milw., 1974-75, asst. prof. medicine, 1975-78, asst. clin. prof. medicine and family practice, 1978-83, assoc. clin. prof. family practice and medicine, 1983—, internal medicine dir. Waukesha family practice residency, 1978—; practice medicine specializing in infectious diseases, Milw., 1974—; mem. staff Waukesha Meml. Hosp. (Wis.), West Allis Meml. Hosp. (Wis.), Elmbrook Meml. Hosp., Brookfield, Wis., Froedtert Meml. Hosp., Milw. Served as capt. M.C., U.S. Army, 1967-69; Korea. Fellow ACP; mem. Wis. Thoracic Soc., Am. Fedn. Clin. Research, Phi Beta Kappa. Contbr. articles, abstracts to profl. jours.

FESLER, VIRGINIA LORRAINE, real estate developer; b. Hutchinson, Kans., Sept. 15, 1930; d. George W. and Audrey G. (Brown) Ebeling; m. Dennis R. Christopher, Mar. 23, 1948 (div. Aug. 1948); children: Timothy, Peggy, Christopher; m. Delton R. Fesler, Aug. 7, 1985; children: Dalene, Janet, Carol, Judy. Co-owner Fesler Investment Rentals & Property Mgmt., Hutchinson, 1971—; budget counselor KPL & Gas Service, Hutchinson, 1982—, Salvation Army, Hutchinson, 1982—; real estate investment counselor Hutchinson, 1984—. City commr. City of Hutchinson, 1982-85; mem. transportation commn. Nat. League Municipalities, Hutchinson, Kans. Advocacy and Protective Services for Developmentally Disabled, Inc., Manhatten, Kans., legis. comm. Kans. League Municipalities, Hutchinson Planning Commn., Reno Co. sub-division, Hutchinson. Mem. Assn. Landlords Kans. (bd. dirs. 1985—), Cen. Kans. Landlords Assn. (pres. Hutchinson chpt. 1976—), Kans. Bd. Realtors, Hutchinson Bd. Realtors, Am. Bus. Womens Assn. Democrat. Club: ABWA (pres. 1985—). Lodge: Moose. Home and Office: 609 N Walnut Hutchinson KS 67501

FESS, MARILYNN ELAINE EWING, occupational therapist; b. Casper, Wyo., June 20, 1944; d. Frederick Eugene and Norma Wagner (Jarrett Pence) Ewing; m. Stephen W. Fess, Nov. 26, 1966. BS, Ind. U., 1967, MS, 1977. Staff occupational therapist Marion County Gen. Hosp., Indpls., 1966-70; supr. phys. dysfunction unit, 1970-72; supr. adult occupational therapy Ind. U. Med. Ctr., Indpls., 1972-74, instr. occupational therapy curriculum, 1974-76; hand therapist Strickland & Steichen, M.D.'s, Inc., 1974-79; designer, developer, dir. hand therapy Hand Rehab. Ctr. Ind., 1976-79; cons. hand rehab. and hand research, 1979—; cons. to hand surgeons various hosps. and nursing homes. Author: (with others) Hand Splinting Principles and Methods, 1980, 2d edit., 1987; mem. editorial rev. bd. Occupational Therapy Jour. Research, 1983-84, Am. Jour. Occupational Therapy, 1985-87, Jour. Hand Therapy, 1987—, also articles. Mem. exec. bd. Ind. Cerebral Vascular Accident Com., 1973-76. Mem. Am. Occupational Therapy Assn. (roster of fellows 1983, sec. orgn. affiliate pres. 1976-78), Am. Soc. Hand Therapists (founding, mem. at large exec. bd. 1978-79, sec. 1980-82), Ind. Occupational Therapy Assn. (sec. 1969-71, v.p. 1972-73, pres. 1974-76, hand therapy liaison to exec. bd. 1978—). Office: 635 Eagle Creek Ct Zionsville IN 46077

FESSLER, DENIS EUGENE, utilities executive; b. Kansas City, Mo., Oct. 25, 1949; s. Everett John and Rita (Knapp) F.; m. Rita Terese Heitman, May 29, 1976; children: Michael Benjamin, Jennifer Christine. BSEE, U. Mo., 1971, MSEE, 1972; MBA, St. Louis U., 1977. Registered profl. engr., Mo., Ill., Iowa. Asst. engr. system planning Union Electric Co., St. Louis, 1972-75, engr. corp. planning, 1975-77, supervising engr. system planning, 1977-85, dist. mgr., 1985—. Cubmaster Boy Scouts Am., Ellisville, Mo., 1987; subcom. chmn. U. Mo. Continuing Engring. Edn. Div., Columbia, 1978—, St. Louis adv. com., 1978—, indsl. adv. council Elec. Engring. Dept., Columbia, 1978—. Mem. Mo. Soc. Profl. Engrs. (treas. St. Louis chpt. 1986-87, named Young Engr. of the Year 1984, bd. dirs.), U. Mo. Alumni Assn. (mem. electrical bd. St. Louis chpt.). Republican. Roman Catholic. Avocations: music, photography, hunting, fishing. Home: 404 Nottingham Ballwin MO 63011 Office: Union Electric Co PO Box 149 Saint Louis MO 63166

FESSLER, KENNETH WAYNE, accountant; b. Alton, Ill., Feb. 8, 1948; s. William Laverne and Evelyn Maxine (Voumard) F.; m. Bonnie Kay Brown, Feb. 4, 1967; children: Barbara, Kenny, Matthew, John. BA, So. Ill. U., Edwardsville, 1972. CPA, Ill. Staff acct. John R. Sutter, St. Louis, 1971-75; sr. acct. Scheffel & Co., Alton, Ill., 1975-78, mgr., 1978-80, ptnr., 1980—; lectr. various seminars on taxation and bus. mgmt. Mem. Twin Rivers Growth Assn., 1981—; bd. dirs. Mississippi Valley Christian Sch., Alton, 1977-84. Served to staff sgt. USAF, 1966-70. Mem. Am. Inst. CPA's, Ill. CPA Soc., Jersey C. of C. Republican. Baptist. Lodge: Lions (Alton bd. dirs. 1982—, Lion of Yr. 1984-85). Home: 5218 Brian Dr Godfrey IL 62035 Office: Scheffel & Co State and Wall Sts Alton IL 62002

FEST, STEPHEN GIBSON, farmer; b. Spencer, Iowa, Nov. 1, 1936; s. Thorrel Brooks and C. Lucille (Etzler) F.; m. Cynthia P. Eiler, Oct. 1, 1960; children: Dawn, Bradley, Michelle. BS in Agrl. Econs. and Farm Mgmt., U. Wis., 1959; cert. in mgmt. and credit analysis, Am. Inst. Banking, 1966; graduate, U. Wis. Grad. Sch. Banking, 1971. Asst. v.p. Comml. State Bank, Madison, Wis., 1968-70; pres., investor West Kenosha (Wis.) State Bank, 1970-73, Heritage Bank of West Bend, Wis., 1973-76; pres. Fest Farms, Inc., West Bend, 1976—; pres., cons. to Agrl., West Bend, 1976—; instr. Am. Inst. Banking, 1968-69. Named one of Wis. Men of Achievement, 1976. Mem. Wis. Farm Mgrs. and Rural Appraisers. Avocations: skiing, camping, travel. Home and Office: Fest Farms Inc 3484 Paradise Dr West Bend WI 53095

FESTA, ROGER REGINALD, chemist, educator; b. Norwalk, Conn., Sept. 6, 1950; s. Reginald and Rosemary (Chappa) F. BA in Biology and Chemistry magna cum laude, St. Michael's Coll., 1972; MA in Agr., U. Vt., 1979; cert. in Adminstrn., Fairfield U., 1981; PhD in Edn., U. Conn., 1982. Tchr. Cen. Cath. High Sch., Norwalk, 1975-79, Brien McMahon High Sch., Norwalk, 1979-82; asst. prof. chemistry Northeast Mo. State U., Kirksville, 1983—, dir. chem. communication devel. ctr., 1984—; adj. prof. U. Conn., 1983. Mem. Kirksville Community Betterment Council, 1984—; sec. Diocese Bridgeport (Conn.) Edn. Assn., 1978-79, sci. cons. schs. office, 1979, exec. adminstr., 1979; bd. dirs. Norwalk Community Services Agy., 1980-81. Fellow Am. Inst. Chemists (bd. dirs. 1982—, chmn. nat. meetings com. 1982—, archivist 1983—, history com. 1982—, edn. editor The Chemist 1981—, editorial bd. 1981-86, pub. edn. com. 1980-82); mem. Am. Chem. Soc. (founding editor The Fairfield Chemist 1978-79, assoc. editor Jour. Chem. Edn. 1980—, vice chmn. edn. com. We. Conn. sect. 1979-81, chmn. com. high sch. chemistry 1979-81, exec. bd. Western Conn. sect. 1979-81, chmn. elect Quincy, Ill.-Keokuk, Iowa sect. 1985, chmn. 1986, exec. bd. 1984—, program chair 1984—), Royal Soc. Chemistry (contbg. editor, U.S. agt. Edn. in Chemistry Jour. 1983—), Chem. Inst. Can. (cons. Can. Chem. News 1983—), St. Louis Inst. Chemists (founder 1984, pres. 1985-87), N.Y. Acad. Scis. (edn. adv. com. 1982-84), Mo. Acad. Sci., Soc. Scholarly Pub., Phi Delta Kappa, Alpha Chi Sigma (assoc. editor The Hexagon 1984—), Kirksville Jaycees (bd. dirs. 1983-86, sec. 1984-85, chair retired sr. vol. com. 1985-87). Home: 114 E McPherson St Kirksville MO 63501 Office: NE Mo State U Dept Chemistry Kirksville MO 63501

FETEN, DOUGLAS LEROY, farmer, agricultural consultant; b. Clear Lake, S.D., Aug. 6, 1951; s. Orven Johannas and Helen Lenore (Anderson) F. BS in Agr., S.D. State U., 1973. Farmer Feten Farms, Clear Lake, 1966-73, ptnr., 1973-79, owner, mgr., 1979—. Bd. dirs. Brookings Deuel Rural Water, Toronto, S.D., 1979—; mem. com. Deuel County Farmers Home Adminstrn., 1976-79; S.D. State Rural Water Assn., Sioux Falls, 1982-86; sec. Rural Water Service Ctr., Brookings, S.D., 1982-86, Aid Assn. for Luths., Brandt, S.D., 1983—; Sunday sch. tchr. Highland Luth. Ch., Brandt, 1971-74, pres., 1977-79, 86—, deacon, 1982-84. Mem. S.D. Farmers Union, Clear Lake Jaycees (Outstanding Young Religious Leader 1982, Outstanding Young Farmer 984, 85). Republican. Avocations: snowmobiling, traveling. Home and Office: Feten Farms Rural Rt 1 Box 153 Clear Lake SD 57226

FETERL, RONALD JOSEPH, sales professional; b. Salem, S.D., Feb. 19, 1935; s. Louis Edward and Mary Julia (Huls) F.; m. Mary Alice Jenneman, Aug. 21, 1956; children: Gayle, Kevin, Rhonda. V.p. sales Feterl Mfg. Co., Salem, S.D.; bd. dirs. McCook County Nat. Bank; proprietor Feterl Farms, Salem, 1969—. Pres. Colonial Manor Nursing Home, Salem, 1966-71, Salem Community Devel. Corp., Salem, 1975-80. Served with U.S. Army, 1954-56, Korea. Mem. Am. Legion. Democrat. Roman Catholic. Lodge: Elks. Avocation: hunting. Home: 429 N Peck Salem SD 57058 Office: Feterl Mfg Co Box 398 Salem SD 57058

FETNER, R. SCOTT, bank holding company executive; b. 1928. With Nat. Bank Waterloo, Iowa, 1976—; now pres., dir. Iowa Nat. Bankshares Corp., Waterloo. Office: Iowa Nat Bankshares Corp 100 E Park Ave Waterloo IA 50703 *

FETRIDGE, BONNIE-JEAN CLARK (MRS. WILLIAM HARRISON FETRIDGE), civic worker; b. Chgo., Feb. 3, 1915; d. Sheldon and Bonnie (Carrington) Clark; student Girls Latin Sch., Chgo., The Masters Sch., Dobbs Ferry, N.Y., Finch Coll., N.Y.C.; m. William Harrison Fetridge, June 27, 1941; children—Blakely (Mrs. Harvey H. Bundy III), Clark Worthington. Bd. dirs. region VII com. Girl Scouts U.S.A., 1939-43, mem. nat. program com., 1966-69, mem. nat. adv. council, 1972-85, mem. internat. commr.'s adv. panel, 1973-76, mem. Nat. Juliette Low Birthplace Com., 1966-69, region IV selections com., 1968-70; bd. dirs. Girl Scouts Chgo., 1936-51, 59-69, sec., 1936-38, v.p., 1946-49, 61-65, chmn. Juliette Low world friendship com., 1959-67, 71-72; mem. Friends of Our Cabana Com. World Assn. Girl Guides and Girl Scouts, Cuernavaca, Mexico, 1969—, vice chmn., 1982-87; founding mem., pres. Olave Baden-Powell Soc. of World Assn. Girl Guides and Girl Scouts, London, 1984—; asst. sec. Dartnell Corp., Chgo., 1981—; bd. dirs. Jr. League of Chgo., 1937-40, Vis. Nurse Assn. of Chgo., 1951-58, 61-63, asst. treas., 1962-63; women's bd. dirs. Children's Meml. Hosp., 1946-50. Staff aide, ARC and Motor Corps, World War II. Vice pres. Latin Sch. Parents Council, 1952-54; bd. dirs. Latin Sch. Alumni Assn. 1964-69, Fidelitas Soc., 1979; women's bd. U.S.O., 1965-75, treas., 1969-71, v.p., 1971-73; women's service bd. Chgo. Area council Boy Scouts Am., 1964-70, mem.-at-large Nat. council, 1973-76, mem. nat. Exploring com., 1973-76; governing mem. Anti-Cruelty Soc. of Chgo. . Recipient Citation of Merit Sta. WAIT, Chgo., 1971; Baden-Powell fellow World Scout Found., Geneva, 1983. Mem. Nat. Soc. Colonial Dames Am. (Ill. bd. mgrs. 1962-65, 69-76, 78-82, v.p. 1970-72, corr. sec. 1978-80, 1st v.p. 1980-84, state chmn. geneal. info. services com. 1972-76, hist. activities com. 1979-83, mus. house com. 1980-83, house gov. 1981-82), Youth for Understanding (couriers bicentennial project), English-Speaking Union, Chgo. Dobbs Alumnae Assn. (past pres.), Nat. Soc. DAR, Chgo. Geneal. Soc., Conn. Soc. Genealogists, New Eng. Historic Geneal. Soc., N.Y. Geneal. and Biog. Soc., Newberry Library Assos., Chgo. Hist. Soc. Guild. Republican. Episcopalian. Clubs: Casino, Saddle and Cycle. Home: 2430 Lakeview Ave Chicago IL 60614

FETRIDGE, WILLIAM HARRISON, corporate executive; b. Chgo., Aug. 2, 1906; s. Matthew and Clara (Hall) F.; m. Bonnie Jean Clark, June 27, 1941; children: Blakely (Mrs. Harvey H. Bundy III), Clark Worthington. B.S., Northwestern U., 1929; LL.D., Central Mich. U., 1954. Asst. to dean Northwestern U., 1929-30; editor Trade Periodical Co., 1930-31, Chgo. Tribune, 1931-34, H. W. Kastor & Son, 1934-35, Roche, Williams & Cleary, Inc., 1935-42; mng. editor Republican mag., 1939-42; asst. to pres. Popular Mechanics mag., 1945-46, v.p., 1946, exec. v.p., 1953-59; v.p. Diamond T Motor Truck Co., Chgo., 1959-61; exec. v.p. Diamond T div. White Motor Co., 1961-65; pres. Dartnell Corp., Chgo., 1965-77, chmn. bd., 1977—; dir. Bank of Ravenswood, Chgo. Author: With Warm Regards, 1976; editor: The Navy Reader, 1943, The Second Navy Reader, 1944, American Political Almanac, 1950, The Republican Precinct Workers Manual, 1968. Trustee Greater North Michigan Ave. Assn., 1949-58; chmn. Ill. Tollway Dedication com., 1958; pres. United Republican Fund of Ill., 1968-73, 79-80; fin. chmn. Ill. Rep. Party, 1968-73; alt. del.-at-large Rep. Nat. Conv., 1956, del.-at-large, 1968, hon. del.-at-large, 1972; mem. Rep. Nat. Finance Com.; chmn. Midwest Vols. Nixon, 1960, Rep. Forum, 1958-60, Nixon Recount Com.; trustee Jacques Holinger Meml. Assn., Am. Humanics Found.; mem. nat. exec. bd., nat. v.p. Boy Scouts Am., 1958-76, chmn. nat. adv. bd., 1976-77; vice chmn. World Scout Found., Geneva, 1977—; trustee Lake Forest Coll., 1969-77; pres. U.S. Found. for Internat. Scouting, 1971-79, hon. chmn., 1979—; past pres. trustees Latin Sch. Chgo.; chmn. bd. dirs. Johnston Scout Mus., North Brunswick, N.J.; mem. Am. com. Westminster Abbey Appeal; elected lauriate Lincoln Acad. of Ill., 1985. Served as lt. comdr. USNR, 1942-45. Decorated chevalier Grand Priory of Malta, chevalier Order St. John of Jerusalem; recipient Abraham Lincoln award United Republican Fund, 1980; Silver Antelope, Silver Beaver, Silver Buffalo Boy Scouts Am., 1956, Bronze Wolf award World Scout Conf., 1973, Distinguished Eagle award, 1976. Mem. Navy League U.S. (past regional pres.), Ill. C. of C., Ill. St. Andrew Soc. (Disting. Citizen award 1980), Newcomen Soc., Soc. Midland Authors, Beta Theta Pi. Clubs: The Casino, Chicago, Union League, Saddle and Cycle (Chgo.); Capitol Hill (Washington); Chikaming Country (Lakeside, Mich.). Lodge: Rotary. Office: 4660 Ravenswood Ave Chicago IL 60640

FETTE, VIRGINIA WRAY, finance executive; b. Royal Oak, Mich., Oct. 28, 1944; d. Raymond Anthony and Kathleen Eleanore (Shea) Wiegand; m. Thomas Patrick Fette, Apr. 4, 1964; children: Bruce A., Annette M., Brenda L. Student, Detroit Bus. Inst., 1963; A in Acctg., Macomb County Community Coll., 1977; B of Accountancy, Walsh Coll., 1980. CPA, Mich. Staff acct. Gerald Langwerowski, CPA, Troy, Mich., 1979-80, Sznewajs, Spacht & Baka, P.C., Troy, 1980-83; asst. v.p. Standard Fed. Bank, Troy, 1983-85; fin. dir. City of Sterling Heights, Mich., 1985—; pension trustee Gen. Employees Pension, Sterling Heights, 1986. Mem. Am. Inst. CPA's, Mich. Assn. CPA's, Govtl. Fin. Officers Assn., Pub. Risk Ins. Mgmt. Assn. Club: Exchange (Sterling Heights) (fin. chmn. 1986—). Home: 11203 Mandale Sterling Heights MI 48077 Office: City of Sterling Heights 40555 Utica Rd Sterling Heights MI 48078

FETZER, JOHN EARL, broadcasting and professional baseball team executive, charitable foundation executive; b. Decatur, Ind., Mar. 25, 1901; s. John Adam and Della Frances (Winger) F.; m. Rhea Maude Yeager, July 19, 1926. Student, Purdue U., 1921; A.B., Andrews U., 1927; student, U. Mich., 1929; LL.D., Western Mich. U., 1958, Kalamazoo Coll., 1972, Andrews U., 1980; Litt.D., Elizabethtown Coll., 1972; D.Eng., Lawrence Inst., 1972; LLD (hon.), Purdue U., 1986. Owner Fetzer Broadcasting Service, Mich., 1970-85, chmn. bd., 1979-85; owner, chmn. bd. Cornhusker TV Corp., Lincoln, Nebr., 1953-85; owner Detroit Tigers Am. League Baseball Club, 1956-83; chmn. bd. John E. Fetzer, Inc., 1968—; chmn. Pro Am Sports Systems, Inc., 1983—; bd. dirs. Domino's Pizza, Inc., 1983—; chmn. Maj. League TV Com., 1963-71; U.S. Censor of radio, 1944-45; reporting to Gen. Eisenhower (engaged in ETO radio studies in), Eng., France, Russia, Germany, Italy and other European countries, 1945; fgn. corr. radio-TV-newspaper mission, Europe and Middle East, 1952; mem. mission Radio Free Europe, Munich, Germany, and Austrian-Hungarian border, 1956; mem. Broadcasters Mission to Latin-Am., Dept. State, 1962; Detroit Tiger Baseball tour of Japan, Okinawa, Korea, under auspices Dept. State, 1962; mem. A.P. tour, Europe, 1966; Dept. State del. Japanese-U.S. TV Treaty, 1972; mem. adv. bd. N.Am. Service, Radio Diffusion Française, Paris, 1946-47. Author: One Man's Family, 1964, The Men from Wengen and America's Agony, 1972; Contbr.: Radio and Television Project, Columbia, 1953. Trustee Kalamazoo Coll., 1954—. Recipient Broadcast Pioneers award, 1968; Distinguished service award Nat. Assn. Broadcasters, 1969; Mich. Frontiersman award, 1969; Fourth Estate award Am. Legion, 1972; citation Mich. Legislature, 1972; Tiger 75th Anniv. award, 1976; Mich. Legis. citation, 1976; Nebr. Pub. TV citation, 1976; Abe Lincoln Railsplitter award, 1979. Fellow Royal Soc. Arts London; mem. Nat. Assn. Broadcasters (chmn. TV bd. 1952), C. of C. (past pres., Summit award 1977), Nat. Geneal. Soc., Acad. Polit. Sci., Am. Soc. Mil. Engrs., I.E.E.E. (life mem.), Internat. Radio and TV Execs. Soc., Broadcast Pioneers (19th Mike award 1981), Alpha Kappa Psi. Presbyn. Clubs: Mason (Kalamazoo) (33 deg., Shriner), Elk. (Kalamazoo), Park (Kalamazoo), Kalamazoo Country (Kalamazoo); Economic (Detroit), Detroit Athletic (Detroit), Press (Detroit), Detroit (Detroit); Tucson Country. Office: Fetzer Broadcasting Corp Kalamazoo MI 49008 also: Tiger Stadium Detroit MI 48216

FEUERSTEIN, LARRY ROBERT, information systems executive; b. Ilion, N.Y., July 4, 1946; s. Robert Edwin and Irene Annette (Loopman); m. Marianne Elaine Kurkowski, Aug. 14, 1976; children: Erin, Kristin, Tracy. BSBA, Syracuse U., 1974; MS in Mgmt., Rensselaer Poly. Inst., 1981. Corp. budget mgr. Mohawk Data Scis. Corp., Parsippany, N.J., 1974-76; mgr. adminstrn. and fin. Data Systems div. Gen. Dynamics, Norwich, Conn., 1976-81, mgr. bus. mgmt., 1981-82; dir. planning and fin. control Data Systems div. Gen. Dynamics, St. Louis, 1982-85, dir. planning and mgmt. systems, 1986—. Team capt. Jr. Achievement Fund Dr., St. Louis, 1986; pres. Norwich Indsl. Park Assn., 1980-82. Mem. Am. Mgmt. Assn., Planning Forum, So. Ill. U. Info. Systems Roundtable. Republican. Avocations: sports, reading bus. publ., travel. Office: Gen Dynamics Data Systems div 12101 Woodcrest Exec Dr Saint Louis MO 63141

FEURER, KAY ANNE, arts administrator; b. Chgo., Mar. 19, 1935; d. Thomas and Mary (McInerney) Morley; m. William E. Feurer, Dec. 16, 1961 (div. 1987); children: Timothy, Jeffrey. Acctg. clk. Illinois Bell Telephone, Chgo., 1954-57; pvt. sec. Illinois Bell Telephone, Springfield, Ill., 1957-61, bus. office supr., 1961-63, asst. mgr., 1963-64; co. mgr. Springfield Ballet Co., 1981-85; exec. dir. Springfield Area Arts Council, 1985—. Pub. relations dir. Aid to Retarded Citizens, Springfield, 1983-85; allocation panel mem. United Way, Springfield, 1984-86; com. mem. Lincoln Acad., State of Ill., 1981-85. Recipient Pres.'s award for Volunteerism, Aid to Retarded Citizens, Springfield, 1981. Mem. Am. Symphony Orch. League, Ill. Arts Alliance (bd. dirs.), Ill. Alliance for Arts Edn., Nat. Assn. Female Execs. Office: Springfield Area Arts Council 510 E Monroe St Springfield IL 62701

FIALA, BRIAN DONALD, human resources executive; b. Waukegan, Ill., Jan. 28, 1950; s. Don and Audrey Pearl (Bordeau) F.; m. Theresa Marie Lombardo, Sept. 3, 1971; children: Heather Ann, Anne Marie. BS in Mgmt., No. Ill. U., 1972; MS in Indsl. Mgmt., Loyola U., Chgo., 1986. Employment mgr. Great Lakes Screw div. U.S. Industries, Chgo., 1973-74; corp. dir. human resources Schwinn Bicycle Co., Chgo., 1975—. Mem. Am. Soc. Personnel Adminstrs., Midwest Personnel Mgmt. Assn. (v.p. 1986—). Republican. Avocations: cycling, fishing. Office: Schwinn Bicycle Co 217 N Jefferson Chicago IL 60606

FIALA, DAVID MARCUS, lawyer; b. Cleve., Aug. 1, 1946; s. Frank J. and Anna Mae (Phillips) F.; m. Maryanne E. McGowan, Jan. 4, 1969 (div. Mar. 1986); 1 child, D. Michael; m. Lyn McDonald Jones, May 31, 1986. B.B.A., U. Cin., 1969; J.D., Chase Coll., No. Ky. State U., 1974. Bar: Ohio 1974, U.S. Dist. Ct. (so. dist.) Ohio 1974, U.S. Tax Ct. 1974. Assoc., Walker, Chatfield & Doan, Cin., 1974-78, ptnr., 1979—; lectr. Southwestern Ohio Tax Inst., 1978-79; bd. dirs. Elkhorn Collieries, Cin. Trustee, sec. Sta. WCET-TV, Cin., 1983—, auction chmn., 1979; trustee Jr. Achievement Greater Cin., 1979—, Mental Health Services West, 1974-83, Contemporary Dance theatre, 1974-80. Mem. ABA, Ohio State Bar Assn., Cin. Bar Assn., Les Chefs de Cuisine Assn. (trustee Cin. chpt. 1985—). Home: 3718 Mt Carmel Rd Cincinnati OH 45244 Office: Walker Chatfield & Doan 1900 Carew Tower Cincinnati OH 45202

FIALA, KENNETH RICHARD, savings and loan officer; b. Mar. 15, 1932; m. Joan Armbruster; children—Dick, Gretchen Ann. B.S.B.A., U. Mo.-Columbia, 1954. With Cornell & Co., C. I.A., St. Louis, Peat, Marwick, Mitchell & Co., St. Louis; with Community Fed. Savs. and Loan Assn., St. Louis, chmn. bd., chief exec. officer, 1984—; dir. Bank Bldg. Corp., Fed. Home Loan Bank Bd. of Des Moines; chmn. bd. Community Agy., Inc., Money Matic, Inc.. Pres. Am. Field Service, Ritenour Community chpt.; bd. dirs. Northwest br. St. Louis YMCA; mem. Met. bd. dirs. YMCA of Greater St. Louis; bd. trustees William Woods Coll., Fulton, Mo.; exec. bd. St. Louis Area council Boy Scouts Am.; bd. dirs. St. Louis Regional Commerce and Growth Assn., Better Bus. Bur.; adv. bd. Salvation Army; mem. St. Louis County Bus. and Indsl. Devel. Commn. Mem. Fin. Mgrs. Soc. of Savs. Instns. (chpt. pres., nat. bd. govs.), St. Louis Savs. and Loan League (past pres.), Mo. Soc. C.P.A.'s, Am. Inst. C.P.A.'s, Kappa Sigma. Lodges: Rotary (past pres.), Masons, Shriner. Address: Community Federal Savs and Loan Assn #1 Community Federal Center Saint Louis MO 63131

FICEK, KENNETH JOHN, chemical marketing executive; b. La Salle, Ill., Oct. 10, 1939; s. Leo Thomas and Josephine Agnes (Krolak) F.; m. Barbara Jean Miglia, Aug. 11, 1962; children: Karen, Mark, Mary, Kevin. AA, St. Bede Coll., 1959. Lab. tech. Carus Chem. Co., Inc., La Salle, Ill., 1960-64, tech. rep., 1964-66, dist. mgr., 1966-69, tech. service mgr., 1969-80, dir. mktg. services, 1981—. Contbr. articles to profl. jours. Commr. City of Oglesby, Ill., 1971-83. Served with USAR, 1963-69. Mem. Am. Water Works Assn. (exec. com., bd. dirs., chmn. mfrs. com. 1986-87, chmn. Ill. sect. 1981-82), Water Pollution Control Assn., Am. Wire Producers Assn. Republican. Roman Catholic. Home: 109 Jordan St Oglesby IL 61348 Office: Carus Chem Co PO Box 1500 La Salle IL 61301

FICK, BRADLEY NORMAN, computer sales; b. Spencer, Iowa, June 12, 1959; s. Norman Ray and Ruth Ann (Ficken) F. AA and AAS in Retail Mktg. Mgmt. with honors, Ellsworth Community Coll., Iowa Falls, Iowa, 1981; BA in Mktg. with honors, U. No. Iowa, 1983. Dept. mgr. Donaldsons, Mpls., 1984-85; account mgr. NCR Corp., Mpls., 1985—. Avocations: traveling, skiing, water skiing, running, reading. Home: 2446 Colfax Ave S Apt #108 Minneapolis MN 55405 Office: NCR Corp 2523 Wayzata Blvd Minneapolis MN 55405

FICK, STEVEN CHARLES, data processing executive; b. Postville, Iowa, Sept. 15, 1954; s. Charles Bentien and Catherine (Grady) F.; m. Janet Marie Garringer, Oct. 3, 1981; 1 child, Mitchell Charles. Grad. high sch., Monona, Iowa, 1972. Draftsman Amana (Iowa) Refrigeration Inc., 1974-84, computer aided design trainer, 1984—. Republican. Roman Catholic. Avocations: hunting, fishing, baseball, football, basketball. Home: 300 Shetland Dr NW Cedar Rapids IA 52405 Office: Amana Refrigeration Inc Main St Middle IA 52203

FICKLE, WILLIAM DICK, lawyer; b. Kansas City, Mo., Oct. 29, 1943; s. William and Elvarea (Dick) F.; children: Tara Elizabeth, William Dick. BA, Westminster Coll., 1965, JD, U. Mo., 1969. Bar: Mo. 1968. Assoc. James, McFarland, Trimble, Austin, North Kansas City, Mo., 1971-72; pros. atty. Platte County, Mo., 1973-74; ptnr. Fickle & Hull, Platte City, Mo., 1973-74, Clevenger, Fickle & McGinness, Platte City, 1975—; chmn. bar ethics com. 6th Jud. Cir. Mem. Mo. Ho. of Reps., 1974-79; bd. dirs. Eyebank of Kansas City, Mo., Home Health Services Clay-Platte and Jackson Counties. Served with U.S. Army, 1969-70. Decorated Legion of Honor; named Outstanding Young Man of Platte County, 1973. Mem. Mo. Bar Ass., Platte County Bar Assn. (pres.). Democrat. Episcopalian. Lodges: Masons, Shriners, Jesters. Home: 7708 NW Mastern Kansas City MO 64152 Office: 204 Marshall Rd Platte City MO 64079

FIDDLER, JEFFREY EDWARD, infosystems specialist; b. N.Y.C., Sept. 25, 1941; s. Charles Norman and Hannah (Cantor) F.; m. Sally Rohs-Emmel, May 15, 1969. AB, Lafayette Coll., 1963; BD, Harvard U., 1967; postgrad., U. Chgo., 1968-72. Systems analyst City of Chgo., 1975-79, Blue Cross/Blue Shield, Chgo., 1979-80, Interstate Nat., Chgo., 1980-81, CNA Ins., Chgo., 1981—. Contbr. articles on religion in Am. history to profl. jours. Fellow Life Mgmt. Inst. Democrat. Unitarian. Avocation: military history. Home: 1113 W Wellington Chicago IL 60657 Office: CNA Ins CNA Plaza Chicago IL 60685

FIDLER, ROBERT GORDON, podiatrist; b. Fairmont, W.Va., Jan. 9, 1934; s. Millard Gordie and Madge Hazel (Woofter) F.; m. Gloria Ann Fidler, June 16, 1956; children: Robert G. Jr., Pamela Lynn. D, Ohio Coll. Podiatric Medicine, 1957. Pvt. practice podiatry Sandusky, Ohio, 1959—. Fellow Acad. Ambulatory Foot Surgeons; mem. Am. Podiatric Medicine Assn., Northwest Ohio Acad. Podiatric Medicine (pres. 1970-72), Ohio Podiatric Medicine Assn. (chmn. ethics com. 1976). Presbyterian. Club: Exchange (pres. 1976-77). Lodge: Elks. Avocation: golf. Office: 2309 Columbus Ave Sandusky OH 44870

FIEDELMAN, HOWARD WILLIAM, mining consultant; b. Sheboygan, Wis., Apr. 23, 1916; s. Sam and Esther (Berg) F.; m. Eleanor Jane Holman, Mar. 23, 1947; children: Charlene Rose Fiedelman Morrow, David Lawrence. BS in ChemE, U. Wis., 1938. Dir. research Morton Salt Co., Woodstock, Ill., 1939-77; exec. dir. Solution Mining Research Inst., Woodstock, 1979—. Patentee pure salt production, 1964, 75, 77. Pres. Easter Seal Soc., Woodstock, 1970-72. Served to capt. USAF, 1942-46, PTO. Decorated Bronze Star. Mem. Phi Lamda Upsilon, Tau Beta Pi. Avocations: tennis, swimming, bridge. Home and Office: 812 Muriel St Woodstock IL 60098

FIEDLER, LEIGH ALLAN, mathematics and computer science educator; b. Moline, Ill., July 22, 1930; s. Leroy Charles and Blanche Emma (Curran) F.; m. Andree Mery Golaz, Nov. 15, 1958; children—Mark, Luc, Daniel, Stephan. A.A., Moline Community Coll., 1950; B.S., U. Ariz., 1952, M.A., 1959; Ph.D., U. Okla., 1969; postgrad. U. Colo., summer 1955, U. Geneva, Switzerland, 1971-72, Augustana Coll., fall 1984. Tchr. Marana High Sch., Ariz., 1955-57; mathematician, computer analyst Shell Oil Co., Los Angeles, 1958, Ctr. European Nuclear Research, Meryn, Switzerland, 1959-60; mathematician, computer cons. Deere and Co., Moline, 1963, 64, 65, 66; dean univ. parallel programs Black Hawk Coll., Moline, 1969-77, prof. math., 1960-69, 77—. Contbr. articles to profl. jours. Allocations com. United Way, Rock Island, Ill., 1972-73, 78; coach Moline Dads Club Baseball, 1968-81; ch. diaconate First Covenant Ch., Moline, 1968-71, 78-83; long range curriculum planning com. Moline Sch. Dist. 40, 1974-75. Ford Found. fellow, 1959-60; NSF fellow, 1965-66. Mem. Math. Assn. Am., Nat. Council Tchrs. Math., AAUP, Pi Mu Epsilon, Phi Delta Kappa (pres. 1979-80). Avocations: golf; travel; softball. Home: 3200 26th Ave Ct Moline IL 61265 Office: Black Hawk Coll 6600 34th Ave Moline IL 61265

FIEGENSCHUH, KARL FRANK, JR., retail jewelry executive; b. Alliance, Ohio, Dec. 17, 1917; s. Karl Frank and Sara B. (Franklin) F.; m. Paula Reed, Nov. 6, 1946; children: Karl Frank III, Paula Wendell. BA, Mount Union Coll., Alliance, 1940; postgrad., Kent State U., 1942. V.p. Fiegenschuh Jewelers Inc., Alliance, from 1945, now pres. Served with USAF, 1944-46. Mem. Am. Gem Soc. (cert. gemologist), Alliance C. of C. (past pres. retail div.), Air Force Assn. Republican. Lutheran. Lodges: Masons, Shriners, Kiwanis. Home: 840 W Milton St Alliance OH 44601 Office: Fiegenschuh Jewelers Inc 248 E Main St PO Box 2358 Alliance OH 44601

FIELD, CHARLES STEVEN, gynecologist, obstetrician; b. Portland, Oreg., Oct. 16, 1945; s. Charles Arthur and Laverna Marie (Travis) F.; m. Susan Creighton Sauer, Aug. 18, 1968; children: Jessica, Joshua, Kristin. BS, Cornell Coll., Mt. Vernon, Iowa, 1968; MD, U. Minn., 1972. Intern U. Oreg. Med. Sch., Portland, 1972-73; resident in ob-gyn Mayo Clinic, Rochester, Minn., 1973-77, staff physician ob-gyn, 1977—, section head obstetrics, 1985—; med. adv. bd. Planned Parenthood Minn., Mpls., 1978—; bd. dirs. Profl. Services Quality Control Southeast Minn., 1978-86. Contbr. articles to profl. jours. Fellow Am. Coll. Ob-Gyn (v.p. Minn. chpt. 1986—); mem. Minn. State Ob-Gyn Soc., Am. Assn. Gynecol. Laparoscopists, Am. Fertility Soc. Presbyterian. Avocations: reading, skiing, golf, tennis, fishing. Office: Mayo Clinic 200 1st St SW Rochester MN 55905

FIELD, CLARK GABRIEL, human relations specialist; b. Owensboro, Ky., Nov. 16, 1936; s. Robert Edwin and Helen Rose (Booth) F.; m. Alice Bernadette Serr, July 9, 1983. PhB, St. Mary's Seminary, 1958, BTh, 1960; M in Pub. Service, Western Ky. U., 1974; cert., Iona Coll., New Rochell, N.Y. Priest, tchr., adminstr. Catholic Diocese, Owensboro, Ky., 1962-73; priest, chaplain Catholic Diocese, Evansville, Ind., 1973-81; field mgr. Citizens Action Coalition, Evansville, Ind., 1983-84; human relations specialist City of Evansville, 1984—; cons. in field; v.p. Evansville Mediation Services, 1986—; pres. Branching Out Counseling, Evansville. Columnist: Evansville Courier, Evansville Press, Times Newspaper, Other Side Mag., 1975—; pub. American Poetry Anthology, vol. VI, 1986; editor: Old Power Plays and New. Pres. Evansville Pub. Action in Correctional Effort, 1974, 77; co-founder House of Bread and Peace, Evansville, 1982; mem. Evansville Project Equality, 1984—; candidate for U.S. Ho. Reps., 1976. Democrat. Roman Catholic. Avocation: tennis. Home: 741 B E Powell Ave Evansville IN 47713 Office: Human Relations Comm Rm 133 Civic Ctr Evansville IN 47708

FIELD, KAREN ANN, real estate broker; b. New Haven, Conn., Jan. 27, 1936; d. Abraham Terry and Ida (Smith) Rogovin; m. Barry S. Crown, June 29, 1954 (div. 1969); children—Laurie Jayne Gulick, Donna Lynn, Bruce Alan, Bradley David; m. 2d Michael Lehmann Field, Aug. 10, 1969 (div. 1977). Student Vassar Coll., 1953-54, Harrington Inst. Interior Design, 1973-74, Roosevelt U., 1987—. Owner Karen Field Interiors, Chgo., 1970—, Karen Field & Assocs., Chgo., 1980-81; now dir. sales La Thomus Realty Group div. La Thomus & Co., Chgo.; pres., ptnr. Field Pels & Assocs., Chgo., 1981-86. Mem. women's council Camp Henry Horner, Chgo., 1960; bd. dirs., treas. Winnetka Pub. Sch. Nursery (Ill.), 1961-63; mem. exec. com. woman's bd. U. Chgo. Cancer Research Found., 1965-66, pres. jr. aux., 1960-66; bd. dirs., sec. United Charities, Chgo., 1966-68, Victory Gardens Theatre, Chgo., 1979; co-founder, pres. Re-Entry Ctr., Wilmette, Ill., 1978-80; mem. br. Parental Stress Services, Chgo., 1981—. Recipient Servian award Jr. Aux. of U. Chgo. Cancer Research Found., 1966, Margarite Wolf award Women's Bd., U. Chgo. Cancer Research Found., 1967. Mem. Chgo. Real Estate Bd., North Side Real Estate Bd. Condex, Chgo. Council Fgn. Relations, English Speaking Union (jr. bd. 1958-59). Office: La Thomus Realty Group div La Thomus & Co 2768 N Lincoln Chicago IL 60614

FIELD, KAY, academic program director; b. Chgo., Oct. 12, 1914; d. Arthur E. and Anna (Goldstein) Huebsch; m. Edmund Field, June 1936; children: Robert Warren, Lawrence Jay. BA, Northwestern U., 1935, MS, 1936. Cert. tchr. and psychologist, Ill. Psychoednl. cons. Ridge Farm for Emotional Disturbed Children, Lake Forest, Ill., 1959-64, Psychiat. and Psychosomatic Inst., Michael Reese Hosp., Chgo., 1965-66, Lakeside Children's Ctr., Milw., 1966-74; cons., psychotherapist Evanston (Ill.) Children's Home, 1961-79; dir. tchr. edn. program Inst. for Psychoanalysis, Chgo., 1965—, mem. postgrad. edn. council and com.; pvt. practice psychotherapy Chgo.; cons. Inst. for Therapy through Arts, 1981—; adj. instr. Nat. Coll. Edn., Northeastern Ill. U.; former positions include lectr. Sch. Social Service Adminstrn. U. Chgo.; cons. Children's Home and Aid Soc. Ill., Roberto Clemente High Sch. Clin. Services and Tng. Program; psychologist Children's Bur. Phila., Phila. Bur. for Colored Children; diagnostician and remedial reading specialist Ill. Inst. Tech. Psychol. Services; parent educator Chgo. Assn. Family Living; ednl. therapist Neuropsychiat. Inst. of U. Ill.; guidance counselor Wilmington (Del.) Pub. Schs.; tchr. Ethical Culture Sch., N.Y.C.; mem. com. emotionally disturbed children Ill. Commn. on Children; mem. task force on treatment of emotionally disturbed children Assn. Children's Residential Ctr., 1967-68; mem. task force for evaluation of Hawthorne Cedar Knolls Residential Ctr. of Jewish Bd. of Guardians, N.Y.C.; mem. task force on interdisciplinary tng. in mental health Am. Assn. Psychiat. Services to Children, 1973-76; speaker various profl. groups in U.S. and abroad; conductor various workshops and seminars. Contbr. papers to confs., articles to profl. jours., chpts. to books; author book revs. Recipient Disting. Alumni award Northwestern U. Mem. Phi Beta Kappa, Sigma Xi. Home: 5719 S Kenwood Ave Chicago IL 60637 Office: Inst for Psychoanalysis 180 N Michigan Ave Chicago IL 60601

FIELD, LARRY FRANCIS, lawyer, county prosecutor; b. Phila., June 15, 1942; s. Frank Sylvester and Lucille (Ward) F.; m. Tamara Myers, June 20, 1964; children: Sean, Nicholas. BA, Georgetown U., 1964; MA, Tufts U., 1965; PhD, Johns Hopkins U., 1968; JD, U. Detroit, 1977. Bar: Mich. 1977. Tchr. Latin U. Liggett's Sch. and Grosse Pointe, 1971-77; assoc. Casanova and Schwedler, Crystal Falls, Mich., 1978-82; county prosecutor County of Iron (Mich.), 1982—; instr. Gogebic Community Coll. Extension Program, Iron River, Mich., 1978-82. Bd. dir. Hiawathaland council Boy Scouts Am.; mem. Timberland Chamber Players. Served to capt. U.S. Army, 1968-71, Vietnam. Woodrow Wilson fellow, 1964-65, Dissertation fellow, 1967-68. Mem. Mich. Bar Assn., VFW, Am. Legion. Democrat. Lodge: Kiwanis. Home: 730 Harrison Crystal Falls MI 49920 Office: Courthouse Crystal Falls MI 49920

FIELD, MICHAEL JAY, university educator; b. N.Y.C., May 1, 1943; s. Nathan H. and Sylvia (Froman) F.; m. Diane Patricia Hoffman, June 28, 1964; children: Valerie, Carolyn, Joshua. BA, SUNY, Stony Brook, 1964; MA, Cornell U., 1965, PhD, 1970. Asst. prof. Temple U., Phila., 1968-72; asst. prof. Bemidji (Minn.) State U., 1972-78, assoc. prof., 1978-81, prof., 1981—; dir. honors program Bemidji State U., 1974—, ctr. profl. devel., 1986—; asst. examiner Internat. Baccalaureate N.Am., 1984—. Contbr. articles to profl. jours. NEH fellow, 1979-80. Fellow Soc. Values Higher Edn.; mem. Assn. Intergrative Studies (bd. dirs. 1985—), Nat. Council Tchrs. English (bd. dirs. 1979-81). Office: Bemidji State U Bemidji MN 56601

FIELD, ROBERT STEVEN, financial planner, accountant; b. Chgo., July 30, 1949; s. Marshall Harvey and Rita (Stock) F.; m. Ruth Ellen Teplinsky, Aug. 7, 1971; children: Lisa, David. BS in Acctg., Ind. U., 1971. CPA, Ill.; registered fin. planner. Acct. Lester White & Co., Chgo., 1971-76; pres., chief exec. officer Atlantic Corp. Cons., Inc., Palatine, Ill., 1976—. Mem. Am. Inst. CPA's, Ill. Soc. CPA's, Internat. Assn. Fin. Planning (bd. dirs. North Shore chpt. 1985—, pres. elect 1987—), Internat. Assn. Registered Fin. Planners. Lodges: Kiwanis (bd. dirs. 1985-86), B'nai B'rith (pres. 1984-85). Avocations: golf, bowling. Home: 812 Downing St Northbrook IL 60062 Office: Atlantic Corp Cons Inc 800 E Northwest Hwy Suite 500 Palatine IL 60067

FIELD, STEVEN DAVID, psychiatrist; b. Chgo., Jan. 21, 1951; s. Irwin and Eileen (Ginsburg) F.; m. Faith Ann Greengoss, July 7, 1973; children: Jamie Lynn, Jessica Sara. BS, U. Ill., Urbana, 1972; MD, U. Ill., Chgo., 1977. Intern in psychiatry Northwestern U. Hosp., Evanston, Ill., 1977-78; resident in psychiatry Evanston Hosp., 1978-81, coordinator psychiatry clerkship, 1981-83, assoc. attending psychiatrist, 1981—; co-dir. psychiatry liaison Glenbrook (Ill.) Hosp., 1981-83; practice medicine specializing in psychiatry Northbrook, Ill.; active staff Highland Park (Ill.) Hosp., 1986—; assoc. prof. Northwestern U., Evanston, 1980—. Contbr. articles to profl. jours. Mem. Am. Psychiat. Assn., Ill. Psychiat. Soc., Am. Assn. Geriatric Psychiatry, Phi Beta Kappa. Avocations: exercise, tennis, photography.

FIELD, THOMAS C., paint equipment and related products company executive; b. Minn., Feb. 14, 1942; s. Cyrus and Helen (Bowen) F.; m. Mary Bittle; children: Brian, Amanda. BA, Hamiline U., 1964; JD, U. Minn., 1967; MBA, U. Chgo., 1973. Gen. counsel Graco, Inc., Mpls., 1968-70, gen. mgr. finishing div., dir. corp. devel., 1970-75, v.p. corp. devel. and mktg., 1975-78, v.p. internat., 1978-84; pres. The DeVilbiss Co., Toledo, 1984—; bd. dirs. Toledo Trust Co. Mng. trustee Toledo Hosp., 1986—; co-chmn. Toledo United Way, 1985-87; steering com. Grace Community Ctr., Toledo, 1986; exec. com. Arts Commn. Greater Toledo, 1987. Mem. Am. Mgmt. Assn. Republican. Clubs: Toledo, Inverness (Toledo). Avocations: golf, squash, tennis. Office: DeVilbiss Co Civ 300 Phillips Ave PO Box 913 Toledo OH 43692

FIELDING, RANDALL JON, architect; b. Huntington, N.Y., Sept. 23, 1953; s. Maxwell H. and Wilma Joy (Guth) F.; m. Kristina Boyce Larson, June 24, 1979. BA in Architecture, Washington U., St. Louis, 1975; MArch, U. Ill., 1981. Registered architect, Ill. Architect, project designer Skidmore, Owings, Merril, Chgo., 1979-81; architect, sr. designer Loewenberg/Fitch, Chgo., 1981-83; pres., design dir. Fielding Inc., Chgo., 1983—. Editor U. Ill. Grad. Jour. Architecture, 1980-82. Mem. AIA, Chgo. Bd. Realtors. Office: Fielding Inc 1954 W Irving Park Rd Chicago IL 60613

FIELDS, CURTIS GREY, public utility executive; b. Goldsboro, N.C., Oct. 23, 1933; s. C.F. and Ethel B. Fields; m. Apr. 5, 1953; children—Curtis Grey, Dwayne L. B.S. in Math. and Physics, East Carolina U., 1955; postgrad. U.N.C., 1967. U. Richmond, 1969. Mktg. and dist. comml. mgr. Carolina Tel. & Tel. Co., Tarboro, N.C., 1955-65, gen. directory mgr., 1965-69, div. comml. mgr., 1969-72; div. comml. mgr. United Telephone Co., Ohio, Mansfield, 1971-72, gen. comml. mgr., 1972-74, v.p. adminstrn., 1974-79, pres., 1979—, chmn. bd., 1978—; mem. Utilities Exec. Steering Com., Columbus, Ohio, bd. dirs. Toledo Trust Corp, Inc., Mansfield. Trustee, bd. dirs., mem. exec. com. Richland Econ. Devel. Corp., Mansfield, 1981—; trustee Mansfield Gen. Hosp., 1985—, Richland County Found., 1985-86; head Richland County Pacesetter, 1986. Mem. Ohio Telephone Assn. (bd. dirs. 1979—, exec. com. 1980-81), Mansfield C. of C. (bd. dirs. 1979—). Episcopalian. Office: United Telephone Co of Ohio 665 Lexington Ave PO Box 3555 Mansfield OH 44907

FIELDS, DARCEY AMES, computer technician; b. South Bend, Ind., Jan. 1, 1950; s. Chester Earl Fields and Marian Louise (Reeves) Bartuska; m. Rita Marie Gapinski; 1 child, James Michael. Cert. in computer electronics, USAF, 1969; cert. home entertainment electronics, Devry Inst., 1973; cert. system electronics, IBM, 1974. Customer engr. IBM Corp., Chgo., 1973-80; customer engr. IBM Corp., South Bend, Ind., 1980-86, systems mgmt. specialist, 1986—; pres. Cousins Family Campground Inc., Lakeville, Ind., 1987—; cons. Computer Techniques, South Bend, 1985—. Served with USAF, 1968-72. Republican. Roman Catholic. Avocations: photography, magic, electronics. Home: 1426 Quincy Mishawaka IN 46544 Office: IBM Corp 215 S Saint Joe South Bend IN 46601

FIELDS, FLOYD EUGENE, industrial engineer; b. Baywood, Va., Mar. 5, 1934; s. Myrah Branson and Mary Lou (Choate) F.; m. Mary Jane Woodard, July 11, 1959; children: Cynthia Ann, Beverly Jean, Stephen Michael, David Andrew. BS, Va. Polytechnic Inst. and State U., 1956; postgrad., Temple U., 1957-60; post grad in bus. adminstrn., Ind. U., 1964-67. Plant indsl. engr. Continental Can Co., Wilmington, Del. and Elkhart, Ind., 1960-67; mgr. indsl. engring. Western Rubber Co., Goshen, Ind., 1967-71; indsl. engr. Beaunit Fibers, Research Triangle Park, N.C., 1971-72; engr. indsl. div. Thiokol Fibers, Waynesboro, Va., 1972-74; indsl. engr. Reynolds Metals, Grand Rapids, Mich., 1974-76; supt. indsl. engring. Ind. Army Ammunition Plant ICI Americas, Inc., Charlestown, 1976—. Scoutmaster Boy Scouts Am., Crandall, Ind., 1980-86; advisor Jr. Achievement, Elkhardt, 1962-64, Grand Rapids, 1974-75; rep. precinct committeeman, 1968-69; trustee New Crandall (Ind.) United Meth. Ch., 1982-85. Recipient Scouter Tng. award Boy Scouts Am., 1982, Scouters Key, 1983. Mem. Inst. Indsl. Engrs. (sr. mem., sec., bd. dirs. South Bend Ind. chpt. 1964-66, 67-70, chmn. membership com., v.p. Shenandoah Valley, Va. chpt. 1972-74, bd. dirs., v.p. Grand Rapids chpt. 1974-76, bd. dirs., treas. v.p., pres. Louisville, Ky., chpt. 1977—), U.S. Jaycees (Outstanding Young Man of Am. 1969), Elkhart Jaycees (Jaycee of Yr. 1968, sen. jr. chamber internat., 1969), Alpha Phi Omega. Lodge: Elks. Avocations: hiking, camping, woodworking, historic crafts, computers. Home: PO Box 9 Crandall IN 47114 Office: ICI America Inc Charlestown IN 47111

FIELDS, HOWARD M., lawyer, accountant; b. Highland Park, Ill., June 7, 1956; s. Milton and Sophy (Trachtenberg) F.; m. Pennie Dee Grusin, May 20, 1979; children: Lauren, Caryn. BS in Fin., U. Ill., 1977; JD, Wash. U., 1980. Bar: Ill. 1980, U.S. Dist. Ct. (no. dist.) Ill. 1980. Supr. sr. tax acct. Peat Marwick, Chgo., 1980-83; tax mgr. Deloitte, Haskins & Sells, Chgo., 1983-85, Allstate Ins. Co., Northbrook, Ill., 1985—. Contbr. articles to profl. jours. Mem. ABA, Am. Inst. CPAs, Ill. CPA Soc., Chgo. Bar Assn. Home: 1144 Devonshire Rd Buffalo Grove IL 60089 Office: Allstate Ins Co Allstate Plaza N B-6 Northbrook IL 60062

FIELY, LAWRENCE FREDERICK, II, sales executive; b. Canton, Ohio, Jan. 16, 1953; s. Donald Earl and Irene Guendolyn (Massie) F.; m. Mary Ann Osgood, Aug. 20, 1977; children: Lawrence F. 111, Melissa Ann. BSBA, John Carroll U., 1975. Sales exec. Philip Morris Inc., N.Y.C., 1977—. Named one of Outstanding Young Men of Am., 1983-86. Mem. Ohio Jaycees (exec. bd. 1986-87, met. dir. 1986, Augustine award 1984-85, Outstanding Local Pres. 1985-86), Canton Jaycees (v.p. 1984, pres. 1985, chmn. bd. dirs. 1986-87, Outstanding Bd. Mem. 1983-84), Canton Palace Theatre Assn. Republican. Roman Catholic. Clubs: St. Michael's Men's (Canton); University, Rugby (University Heights). Home: 6218 Constance Circle NW Canton OH 44718 Office: Philip Morris Inc York Exec Bldg Pearl Rd Parma Heights OH 44130

FIETSAM, ROBERT CHARLES, accountant; b. Belleville, Ill., Oct. 18, 1927; s. Celsus J. and Viola (Ehret) F.; B.S., U. Ill., 1955; m. Miriam Runkwitz, Apr. 12, 1952; children—Robert C., Guy P., Nancy A., Lisa R. C.P.A., Mo., Ill. Claims adjuster Ely & Walker Dry Goods, St. Louis, 1947-48; accountant Price Waterhouse & Co., 1949-54; staff accountant J.W. Boyle & Co., East St. Louis, 1955-59; owner R.C. Fietsam, C.P.A., Belleville, Ill., 1959-68; mng. ptnr. R.C. Fietsam & Co. C.P.A.s, 1969—. Mem. Belle-Scott Com., 1979—; bd. dirs., pres. Belleville Center, Inc., 1980-81; mem. adv. bd. Masterworks Chorale, 1984—; bd. dirs. Meml. Found., Inc., 1986—, Bellville Hosp. Golf Classic, mem., 1983—. Served with USAF, 1951-53. Mem. Ill. Soc. C.P.A. (pres. so. chpt. 1972-73, Mr. So. Chpt. award 1976, bd. dirs. Chgo. chpt. 1979-81, sr. v.p. 1987-88, Pub. Service award 1982-83), Mo. Soc. C.P.A.s, Am. Inst. C.P.A.s (council 1981—), U. Ill. Greater Belleville Illini Club (past pres.), Belleville C. of C. (pres. 1973-74), Belleville Jr. C. of C. (life, Key Man award 1959-60, Outstanding Citizen award 1976), Lambda Chi Alpha Alumnae Assn. Mem. United Ch. of Christ (pres. 1972-73). Elk, Moose. Clubs: St. Clair Country; Belleville Optimists (pres. 1979-80, disting. pres. award internat. orgn. 1979-80, Optimist of Yr., Belleville 1977, Ill. dist. 1980). Home: 23 Persimmon Ridge Dr Belleville IL 62223 Office: 325 W Main Belleville IL 62220

FIFER, RUBY ESTELLE, dentist; b. Toledo, Sept. 21, 1951; d. Newell Eugene and Audrey LaVerne (Hillyer) F.; m. Ian Alexander Miners, July 7, 1986. DDS, Ohio State U., 1976; EdM, M in Guidance and Counseling, U. Toledo, 1984. Gen. practice dentistry Toledo, 1976—; staff mem. Toledo Hosp., 1984-85. Pres. Alice Circle Club, United Meth. Ch., Toledo, 1983-85. Served to capt. U.S. Army, 1976-78. Mem. Toledo Dental Soc., Acad. Gen. Dentistry, Am. Equilibration Soc., Toledo Dental Forum (program chmn. 1985-86, sec. 1986-87), Toledo C. of C. Avocations: dancing, tennis, skiing, travel, people. Office: 5640 Southwyck #262 Toledo OH 43614

FIGGE, FREDERICK H., JR., publishing executive; b. Chgo., Apr. 8, 1934; s. Frederick H. and Theodora M. (Hosto) F.; m. Beverly J. Menz, June 20, 1956; children: Dora, Ann, Jane, Fred C. B.S., U. Ill., 1956. CPA, Ill. With Arthur Young & Co. (C.P.A.s), Chgo., 1958-64; controller Ency. Brit., Inc., Chgo., 1964-74, v.p., treas., 1974-85, sr. vp., 1985-86, exec. v.p., 1986—. Treas. Direct Selling Ednl. Found., bd. dirs.; bd. dirs. Coll. Commerce, U. Ill., Plymouth Pl. Retirement Home, La Grange, Ill. Served with USNR, 1956-58. Mem. Beta Theta Pi, Beta Gamma Sigma. Democrat. Congregationalist. Clubs: LaGrange Country; Chgo. Athletic. Home: 221 S Blackstone St LaGrange IL 60525 Office: Ency Brit Inc 310 S Michigan Ave Chicago IL 60604

FIGLER, ALAN ANTHONY, software engineering manager; b. Rockville Ctr., N.Y., Sept. 17, 1948; s. Edward Leon and Mildred (Aubel) F.; m. Kathleen Backor, June 12, 1971; children: Laura, Brian, Erik. BEE, Rensselaer Poly. Inst., 1970, M in Engring., 1971. Engr. GTE Automatic Electric, Northlake, Ill., 1971-76; group leader Telemed, Inc., Hoffman Estates, Ill., 1976-77; sr. software engr. Gould Labs, Rolling Meadows, Ill., 1979-81; software engring. mgr. Travenol Labs, Round Lake, Ill., 1981—. Patentee in field. Recipient award for Outstanding Technical Achievement, Baxter-Travenol Labs., 1986. Mem. Digital Equipment Corp. Users Group, IEEE (chmn. sub com. med. info. bus. Std. #1073 1986). Lutheran. Avocations: running, railroads. Home: 3709 Live Oak Rd Crystal Lake IL 60012 Office: Travenol Labs PO Box 490 RLT 10 Round Lake IL 60073

FIGUEROA, EDDUYNN ARIEL, child psychiatrist; b. Guatemala, Aug. 1, 1945; came to U.S. 1971; s. Eduardo and Concha (Gracias) F.; m. Margarita Lewin, Apr. 24, 1971; children: Bryan, Gretel. MD, U. San Carlos, Guatemala, 1970. Diplomate Am. Bd. Psychiatry and Neurology. Intern Omaha Univ. Hosp., 1971-72; resident Nebr. Psychiat. Inst., 1971-74; dir. children's outpatient clinic Malcolm Bliss Mental Health Clinic, St. Louis, 1967-78, 1980-81; sec. med. adminstrn. com. Weldon Spring Hosp., St. Charles, Mo., 1982; child psychiatrist St. Louis County Mental Health Clinic, 1980-82; pvt. practice psychiatry St. Louis, 1982—; med. dir. Christian Northwest Hosp. Adolescent Unit, St. Louis, 1986—; cons. Marygrove, St. Louis, 1984—. Mem. Coll. Physicians and Surgeons Guatemala, Am. Psychiat. Assn., Am. Acad, Child Psychiatry, Eastern Mo. Psychiat. Soc., St. Louis County Med. Soc., Can. Psychiat. Assn. Roman Catholic. Home: 431 Greenstone Dr Chesterfield MO 63017 Office: 1245 Graham Rd Florissant MO 63031

FILA, CHERIE LYNN, social worker; b. Norway, Mich., June 19, 1958; d. James Merral and Eileen Jean (Welch) Zeugner; m. Richard Lee Fila, Oct. 10, 1981; 1 child, Brittany Lee. AS in Social Scis., Ferris State Coll., 1978, BS in Social Scis., 1979. Lic. social worker, Mich. Client services coordinator Genesee County Mental Health, Flint, Mich., 1979-81; exec. dir. Big Bros./ Big Sisters., Petoskey, Mich., 1981-84; chmn. progam com. Big Bros./ Big Sisters., Iron Mountain, Mich., 1984—; client services mgr. Dick-Iron County Mental Health, Iron Mountain, 1984-86, program supr., 1986—; social worker Dickinson Counseling Ctr., Kingsford, Mich.; adoptions caseworker Americans for Internat. Aid and Adoptions, Birmingham, Mich., 1985—. Norway, Mich., 1986—. Mem. Mich. Residential Care Assn., Phi Eta Sigma. Methodist. Home: HC Box 95 Norway MI 49870 Office: Dickinson Counseling Ctr 701 Pyle Dr Kingsford MI 49801

FILIPPINE, EDWARD L., fed. judge; b. 1930. A.B., St. Louis U., 1951, J.D., 1957. Bar: Mo. 1957. Sole practice law St. Louis, 1957-77; spl. asst. atty. gen. State of Mo., 1963-64; judge U.S. Dist. Ct., Eastern Dist. Mo., St. Louis, 1977—. Served with USAF, 1951-53. Mem. ABA, Mo. Bar Assn., Bar Assn. Met. St. Louis, St. Louis County Bar Assn. Office: U S Dist Ct 1114 Market St Saint Louis MO 63101 *

FILIPPIS, EUGENE DOMINIC, prosthetist, orthotist; b. Detroit, Oct. 29, 1937; s. Anthony and Frances (Lemma) F.; m. Marilyn Louise Johnson, Aug. 13, 1979; children from previous marriage: Pamala Lupo, Deborah Fagan, Steven, Eugene Anthony. AS in Bus. Adminstrn., Ferris State Coll., 1959; cert. prosthetist, Northwestern U., 1963; cert. orthotist, UCLA, 1965. Prosthetist Wright & Filippis, Inc., Detroit, 1963-75, v.p., 1975-81; pres., chief exec. officer Wright & Filippis, Inc., Rochester, Mich., 1981—; durable med. cons. Blue Cross/Blue Shield, Detroit; bd. dirs. Rehab. Research Ctr., Rochester; mem. Wayne State U. Indsl. Adv. Com., 1985—. Mem. Am. Acad. Orthotists and Prosthetists, Mich. Orthotic and Prosthetic Assn., Am. Bd. Cert. for Orthotists and Prosthetists. Club: Great Oaks Country. Lodge: Elks. Avocations: fishing, woodworking, golfing. Office: Wright & Filippis Inc 2845 Crooks Rd Rochester Hills MI 48063

FILLMAN, LEONARD NOEL, health care executive; b. Vinita, Okla., Feb. 13, 1941; s. Gettis I. and Charlotte M. (Parsons) F.; m. Jinnie Vee Wilson, Jan. 3, 1942; children: Kenneth, Terry, Sharon. BS, So. Coll., 1963; MBA in Health Services Mgmt., Century U., 1981. Adminstrv. dir. blood bank/ immunology Hinsdale (Ill.) Med. Ctr., 1964-74; adminstrv. dir. lab. services Berrien Gen. Hosp., Berrien Center, Mich., 1974—, weekend hosp. adminstr.; univ. lectr. active planning, participant local health fairs. Mem. Am. Coll. Hosp. Adminstrs., Am. Soc. Med. Tech., Clin. Lab. Mgmt. Assn. Seventh-Day Adventist. Home: 6330 Deans Hill Rd Berrien Center MI 49102 Office: Berrien Gen Hosp 1250 Deans Hill Rd Berrien Center MI 49102

FILTER, TERRANCE ANDERSON, clinical psychologist; b. Celina, Ohio, Aug. 15, 1950; s. Donald Francis and Elizabeth Jane (Anderson) F.; m. Patricia Ann Green, Aug. 21, 1971. BA, Ohio State U., 1972; MA, U. Mich., 1976, PhD, 1978. Lic. psychologist, Mich. Fellow psychol. clinic U. Mich., Ann Arbor, 1975-78, research assoc. med. ctr.; pvt. practice clin. psychology Birmingham and Ann Arbor, Mich., 1979—; dir. psychol. services Detroit Psychiat. Inst., 1982-86; program dir. Woodside Med. Ctr., Pontiac, Mich., 1986—; cons. Detroit Osteo. Hosp., Highland Park, Mich., 1982-83, Wyandotte (Mich.) Gen. Hosp., 1984—, Bloomfield Inst. Sleep Disorders, Pontiac, 1986—; dir., v.p. and treas. edn. and research fund Detroit Psychiat. Inst., 1983—. Mem. Am. Psychol. Assn., Mich. Psychol. Assn. (pub. service com. 1986), Mich. Soc. Psychoanalytic Psychologists, Alliance for Mental Health Services. Office: 555 S Woodward #614 Birmingham MI 48011

FINCH, DAVID S., banker; b. Des Moines, Dec. 9, 1941; s. Lindley and Fannie (Hook) F.; m. Veta K. Finch, May 9, 1980; children—David L., Michael S. Student, U. Iowa, 1960-61, Iowa State U., 1965; M.B.A., U. Chgo., 1967. Comml. trainee, credit analyst Harris Trust and Savs. Bank, Chgo., 1967-68, comml. banking rep. personnel div., 1968, mng. coll. recruitment personnel div., 1968-70, comml. banking officer banking dept., 1970-71, asst. v.p., sect. mgr. corp. fin. service, 1973, v.p., div. adminstr. personnel, 1973-78, sr. v.p., group exec. personal trust group, 1978-80, sr. v.p., group exec, instl. trust adminstrn., 1980-81, exec. v.p. trust dept., 1981-86, exec. v.p. investment dept., 1986—; chief fin. officer Internat. Farm Systems, 1971-73; chmn. bd. Harris Trust Co. of Ariz., Scottsdale, 1981-86; bd. dirs. Derivative Markets Mgmt., Inc., Harris Futures Corp, Harris Brokerage Services, Inc. Mem. Corp. Fiduciaries Assn. Ill. (sec.-treas. 1985-86), Midwest Securities Trust Co. (bd. dirs. 1985—). Clubs: St. Charles Country (Ill.); Monroe (Chgo.). Avocations: golf; tennis; fishing. Office: Harris Trust and Savs Bank 111 W Monroe St Chicago IL 60690

FINCH, HAROLD BERTRAM, JR., wholesale grocery company executive; b. Grand Forks, N.D., Oct. 13, 1927; s. Harold Bertram and Ruth M. F.; m. Catherine E. Cole, Sept. 6, 1950; children: Mark, James, Sarah, Martha, David. BBA, U. Minn., 1952, BChemE, 1952. Div. mgr. Archer-Daniels-Midland Co., Mpls., 1960-66; dir. long-range planning, then v.p. sales and ops. Nash Finch Co., Mpls., 1966-78, pres., 1978-85, chief exec. officer, 1982—, chmn., 1985—. Bd. dirs. Jr. Achievement Mpls., 1977-84, Mpls. YMCA, 1965-80. Served with U.S. Maritime Service, 1945-47. Mem. Nat. Assn. Wholesale Grocers Am. (bd. govs.), Food Mktg. Inst. Presbyterian. Office: Nash-Finch Co 3381 Gorham Ave Minneapolis MN 55426

FINCH, JUNE JOHNSON, educator; b. Chgo., June 6, 1927; d. Willard Thomas and Lucile Sarah (Adams) Johnson; m. William Hayes Finch, July 3, 1948; children—Lisa Lynnette, Tina Stephanie. Student Northwestern U., 1944; B.E., Chgo. State U., 1948; postgrad. DePaul U., 1953; M.A., Governors State U., 1977. Tchr., Hayes Sch., Chgo., 1948-53, Lewis Champlain Sch., Chgo., 1957-59, Dixon Sch., Chgo., 1959-70, Powell Sch., Chgo., 1973-76; math. lab. resource tchr., elem. math. tchr. tng. centers Chgo. Public Schs., 1970-73, coordinator living metric environment program, 1976-77, coordinator intensive math. improvement program, 1977-84; coordinator bur. math., 1984-87, instructional coordinator, dist. 14, 1987—; instr. Loyola U., Chgo., summer 1972; cons. in field. Mem. Chatham-Avalon Community Council, Chgo.; vestryperson, Social Service Guild, St. Monica's Guild Episc. Diocese Chgo. Named Tchr. of Yr., Dixon Sch., 1965, Outstanding Tchr., Powell Sch., 1978. Mem. Nat. Council Tchrs. of Math., Ill. Council Tchrs. of Math., Nat. Council Suprs. of Math., Chgo. Elem. Tchrs. of Math., Assn. for Supervision and Curriculum Devel., Ill. Assn. Supervision and Curriculum Devel., Met. Math. Club, Phi Delta Kappa, Delta Sigma Theta. Episcopalian. Clubs: Les Plus Belles, Paragons. Home: 8215 Saint Lawrence Ave Chicago IL 60619 Office: Chgo Pub Schs 1819 W Pershing Rd 6 Center SE Chicago IL 60609

FINE, ARCHIE, retired physiology, radiology educator; b. Toronto, Ont., Can., May 1, 1906; s. Louis and Esther (Freeman) F.; m. Ann Hoffman, Aug. 15, 1932; children: John S., Edward J., Robert L. BA, U. Coll. of U. Toronto, 1927, MA, 1928; MD, U. Toronto, 1931. Instr. physiology U. Toronto, 1927-28; instr. pathology La. State Med. Sch., New Orleans, 1931-34; intern U. Ill. Research and Ednl. Hosp., Chgo., 1934-35; resident in radiology Jewish Hosp., Cin., 1935-38, attending radiologist, 1938-50; assoc. Oncology Assocs., 1978—; dir. radiology Jewish Hosp., Cin., 1950-52, radiation therapy, 1966-81; assoc. clin. prof., 1956-71. Contbr. articles to profl. jours. Served to lt. col. USAF, 1942-46. Fellow Am. Coll. Radiology; mem. Acad. Medicine, Radiol. Soc. N.Am., Ohio State Radiol. Soc. (Spl. award 1982), Am. Soc. Therapeutic Radiol., Radiol. Soc. Cin. (pres. 1947-48), Alpha Omega Alpha. Jewish. Avocations: stamp collecting, golf. Home: 2324 Madison Rd Apt 809 Cincinnati OH 45208 Office: Oncology Assocs 3120 Burnet Ave Cincinnati OH 45229

FINE, GARY MARTIN, dentist; b. Mpls., Nov. 8, 1950; s. Ralph Irving and Beverlee Lois (Rockler) F.; m. Wendy Susan Weisberg, June 19, 1975; children: Rebecca, Mirra, Jenny. BSD, U. Minn., Mpls., 1973, DDS, 1975. Lifeguard, mgr. Mpls. Park Bd., 1969-73; pvt. practice gen. dentistry Mpls., 1977—; Judaic artist Yannai, Yannai art; artist Yannai Art, Mpls., 1969—; dental cons. peer review Blue Cross, Blue Shield, Mpls., 1984—. Mem. bd. nominating com. Adath Jeshuron Synagogue, Mpls., 1986. Served to capt. USAF, 1975-77. Recipient award for Meritorious Service to the People of Israel, ADA, 1985. Mem. Alpha Omega (pres. 1982-84). Jewish. Home: 4037 Upton S Minneapolis MN 55410 Office: 1046 Medical Arts Bldg Minneapolis MN 55402

FINE, PAUL MORRIS, psychiatrist, educator; b. N.Y.C., June 18, 1933; s. Barney and Anna (Cohen) F.; m. Susan Kurz, Dec. 15, 1954 (div. 1968); children: Steven, Kathryn; m. Janet Foster, June 30, 1980. BA, Alfred U., 1958; MD, SUNY, Syracuse, 1958. Diplomate Am. Bd. Psychiatry and Neurology. Intern Maimonides Med. Ctr., N.Y.C., 1958-59; resident in psychiatry Michael Reese Med. Ctr., Chgo., 1959-61, fellow in child psychiatry, 1961-63, staff psychiatrist, 1966-68; asst. prof. psychiatry U. Pa., Phila., 1968-70; assoc. prof. Creighton U., Omaha, 1972—, dir. div. child psychiatry and child psychiatry tng. program, 1972—; clin. assoc. prof. psychiatry U. Nebr., Omaha, 1970—. Contbr. articles to profl. jours. Bd. dirs. Nebr. chpt. Nat. Soc. Autistic Children and Adults, Omaha, 1977—. Served to capt. USAF, 1964-66. Grantee Edna McConnel Clark Found., 1980-84. Fellow Am. Psychiat. Assn., Am. Acad. Child Psychiatry, Am. Orthopsychiat. Assn. Avocations: gardening, racquetball. Home: 2516 Garden Rd Omaha NE 68124 Office: Creighton U 819 Dorcas St Omaha NE 68108

FINEDORE, WILLIAM FRANCIS, SR., manufacturing company executive; b. Grand Rapids, Mich., Apr. 11, 1923; s. William and Clara Finedore; m. Grace M. Brush, Apr. 28, 1952; children—William F., Thomas E., James G., Nancy C., Jeffrey P. Student pub. schs., Chgo. With mech. div. Kraft Foods, Morton Grove, Ill., 1945-62; from apprentice sheetmetal layout to leadman Dover div. Groen Mfg. Co., Elk Grove, Ill., 1962-72; from foreman to supt. custom div. Leedal Inc., Chgo., 1972-77; plant mgr. Bloomfield Indsl. div. Beatrice Foods, Chgo., 1977-78; dir. mfg., supt. custom div. Elkay Mfg. Co., Broadview, Ill., 1978—. Served with USMC, 1942-45. Recipient Ill. Swimming Assn. Swimming and Diving Ofcls. award, 1981; North Suburban YMCA Swim Coach award, 1973. Mem. Nat. Skeet Shooting Assn., Nat. Rifle Assn., Boat Owners Assn. U.S., Mfg. Mgrs. Assn. (past pres.), Republican. Roman Catholic. Clubs: Northbrook Sports, Gt. Lakes Cruising, Harbor Lite Yacht, Keymen's (pres. execs. Elkay Mfg. Co.). Home: 1850 Beechnut Rd Northbrook IL 60062 Office: Elkay Mfg Co 2700 S 17th Ave Broadview IL 60153

FINEFROCK, LAWRENCE CHARLES, retail furniture executive; b. Massillon, Ohio, May 31, 1947; s. Charles Raymond and Mary Elizabeth (Henrich) F.; m. Joan Elizabeth Forney, Mar. 20, 1971; children—Douglas, Kevin, Lauren. B.S. in Bus. Adminstrn., Georgetown U., 1969. Pres., C.O. Finefrock Co., Massillon, 1972—; dir. 1st Savs. and Loan Co., Massillon. Chmn. United Way Western Stark County, 1978; pres. bd. YMCA, Massillon, 1981-83; trustee Massillon Area Community Civic Trust Fund; chmn. bd. Better Bus. Bur. Stark County, 1984-86. Served to lt. (j.g.) USNR, 1970-72. Mem. Interior Design Soc. (sec. local chpt. 1980-82), Nat. Home Furnishings Assn., Ohio Home Furnishings Assn. (bd. dirs.), Massillon Devel. Found. (sec.), Massillon C. of C. (pres. bd. 1976, J.S. Sanders award 1984). Republican. Roman Catholic. Avocations: tennis; volleyball.

FINESMITH, STEPHEN HARRIS, scientist, psychologist; b. N.Y.C., Nov. 7, 1934; s. Murray and Cele (Lerner) F.; B.B.A., Coll. City N.Y., 1955; postgrad. State U. N.Y. at Buffalo, 1955-59, 71-74, U. Wis., 1976-77, Wis. Sch. Profl. Psychology; m. Barbara Kaden, Aug. 28, 1955 (div. June 1977); children—Terri, Robin; m. Cher Halliday, Aug. 3, 1979 (div. Sept. 1979). Asso. scientist Systems Devel. Corp., Santa Monica, Cal., 1959-60; asst. prof. Rutgers U., New Brunswick, N.J., 1960-62; systems analyst Internat. Tel. & Tel. Co., Paramus, N.J., 1962-63; prin. systems design engr., head new techniques and systems group Univac div. Sperry Rand Corp., St. Paul, 1963-67; assoc. prof. U. So. Miss., Hattiesburg, 1967-68; assoc. prof. Mankato (Minn.) State Coll., 1968-71; prof. Governors State U., Park Forest South, Ill., 1971-72; pres., Serendipity Systems, Inc., Janesville, Wis., 1973-75, now chmn. bd.; prof., chmn. psychology dept. Milton (Wis.) Coll., 1972-76; asst. dir. Bur. Systems and Data Processing, Wis. Dept. Revenue, Madison, 1976-79; psychotherapist, communications therapist. Cons. In Mental Health, Janesville, 1973-74. Research scientist, human relations lab. cons., 1960—. Mem. Am. Psychol. Assn. (asso.), AAAS, Assn. Humanistic Psychology, Assn. for Computing Machinery. Club: Country (Lake Windsor, Wis.). Inventor bionic evolutionary adaptive stock trading system, 1964. Home: 222 Randolph Dr Apt 312A Madison WI 53717

FINFROCK, BRUCE DANIEL, religious educator; b. Upland, Calif., Oct. 24, 1950; s. Rex Marvel and Jessie Orliva (Bishop) F.; m. Sandra Jean Book, June 16, 1972; children: Candice Paige, Andrew Paul, Nathan Daniel. BA in Religious Edn., Biola U., 1972; MA in Religious Edn., Talbot Theol. Sem., 1976; postgrad. in Div., North Park Sem. Ordained to ministry Evang. Ch., 1978. Youth pastor First Bapt. Ch., Pomona, Calif., 1971-76, Rolling Hills Covenant Ch., Rolling Hills Estate, Calif., 1976-78; minister Christian edn. Peninsula Covenant Ch., Redwood City, Calif., 1978-83; interim pastor Brethern in Christ Ch., Upland, Calif., 1983-85; minister Christian edn. North Park Covenant Ch., Chgo., 1985—. Mem. Nat. Assn. Dir.'s Christian Edn., Kappa Tau Epsilon. Avocations: snow skiing, bicycling, gardening, travelling, reading. Home: 5905 N St Louis Chicago IL 60659 Office: North Park Covenant Ch 5250 N Christiana Ave Chicago IL 60625

FINK, JON KENNEDY, restauranteur; b. Evansville, Ind., Feb. 27, 1959; s. George Henry and Verna Maxine (Gary) F. Owner Sir Beef Inc., Evansville, 1982—. Home: 9120 Petersburg Rd Evansville IN 47711 Office: Sir Beef Inc 900 W Buena Vista Evansville IN 47710

FINK, REGINALD HEDGES, music educator; b. York, Pa., June 20, 1931; s. Augustus Reginald and Hazel Geraldine (Holcombe) F.; m. Lorraine Julie Friedrichsen, Aug. 29, 1955; children: Carl Peter, Kristine Rebecca. MusB, Eastman Sch. Music, 1953; M in Music Edn., U. Okla., 1957, PhD, 1967. Bass trombone Okla. City Symphony, 1953-55, prin. trombone, 1955-62; asst. prof. W. Va. U., Morgantown, 1962-67, Ithaca (N.Y.) Coll., 1967-70; prof. Ohio U., Athens, 1970—; instr. Okla City U., 1957-62; pres. Accura Music, Inc., Athens, 1968—, Ability Development Assocs., Inc. Athens, 1978—. Author: 36 Studies for F Attachment Trombone, 1962, Introducing the Tenor Clef, 1968, Studies in Legato, 1969, Introducing the Alto Clef, 1969; From Treble Clef to Bass Clef, 1972, The Trombonist's Handbook, 1977. Bd. advisors The Salvation Army, Athens, 1981—. Mem. Am. String Tchrs. Assn., Nat. Assn. Coll. Wind and Percussion Instrs., Music Educators Nat. Conference, Internat. Trombone Assn. (bd. advisors 1984—). Lodge: Rotary. Office: PO Box 520 Athens OH 45701

FINK, RICHARD ALAN, orthopedic surgeon; b. Chgo., Mar. 3, 1942; s. James Russell and Alice Haldis (Gabrielson) F.; m. Donna Jane Emberson, June 5, 1965; children: Stephen Curtis, Gregory Thomas. BA, N. Cen. Coll., Naperville, Ill., 1964; MD, Tulane U., 1968. Diplomate Am. Bd. Med. Examiners; cert. Am. Bd. Orthopaedic Surgery. Intern St. Mary's Hosp., Duluth, Minn., 1968-69; resident in orthopaedic surgery Mayo Grad. Sch. Medicine, Rochester, Minn., 1969-73; orthopaedic surgeon Gundersen Clinic, Ltd., LaCrosse, Wis., 1973—. Mem. AMA, Am. Acad. Orthopaedic Surgeons, Am. Soc. Surgery of the Hand, Am. Assn. Hand Surgery, MidAm. Orthopaedic Assn. Lutheran. Avocations: canoeing, camping, sailing. Home: W5232 Boma Rd LaCrosse WI 54601 Office: Gundersen Clinic 1836 South Ave LaCrosse WI 54601

FINKE, BEVERLY JEANNE, accountant; b. St. Louis, Aug. 19, 1952. BSBA, U. Mo., St. Louis, 1983. CPA, Mo. Acct. Korljan and Frogge Inc., St. Louis, 1981-86; mgr. Baird, Kurtz and Dobson, St. Louis, 1986-87; v.p. Mgmt. Info. Solutions, Inc., Belleville, Ill., 1987—. Mem. Am. Inst. CPA's, Mo. Soc. CPA's, Independent Computer Cons. Assn. Office: MIS Inc Rt 4 Box 148 Belleville IL 62223

FINKEL, BERNARD, public relations, fund-raising, and resource development executive, radio show host; b. Chgo., Nov. 12, 1926; s. Isadore and Sarah (Goldzweig) F.; m. Muriel Horwitz, Dec. 23, 1951; children—Phillip Stuart, Calvin Mandel, Norman Terry. Student Hebrew Theol. Coll., Chgo., 1939-44, Lewis Inst. Arts and Scis., Ill. Inst. Tech., Chgo., 1944-45, U. Ill.-Chgo., 1947-48; B.S. in Journalism, U. Ill., 1951. Reporter, rewriter Peacock Newspapers, Chgo., 1949, Defender Newspapers, Chgo., 1951, Chgo. North Side Newspapers, 1952; asst. dir. pub. relations Combined Jewish Appeal-Jewish Fedn. Met. Chgo., 1953; mng. editor Electric Appliance Service News, Chgo., 1954-57; asst. account exec. Burlingame-Grossman Advt., Chgo., 1957; account exec. Glassner & Assocs., Pub. Relations, Chgo., 1958-61; pub. relations cons. Bernard Finkel Assocs., Chgo., 1961—; dir. devel. and pub. relations Japanese Am. Service Com., Chgo., 1981—; owner, producer, host weekly radio show Jewish Community Hour, Sta. WONX-AM, Evanston, Ill. Author: Life and the World, 1947. Mem. pub. relations and youth commns. Village of Skokie, 1964-65; v.p., coach Boys Baseball, Skokie, 1963-67; mem. adv. bd., chmn. pub. relations Chgo. Area Career Conf., 1961-62; pres. Acad. Assocs. of Ida Crown Jewish Acad., Chgo., 1973-75; v.p. Hillel Torah North Suburban Day Sch., 1965-66, Congregation Or Torah, Skokie, 1970-71. Served with U.S. Army, 1945-46. Recipient awards for pub. service Jewish Community Hour, 1978, Chgo. Rabbinical Council, Chgo. Bd. Rabbis, Council Traditional and Orthodox Synagogues of Greater Chgo., Midwest Region of Nat. Fedn. Jewish Men's Clubs, Israel Aliyah Ctr. of World Zionist Orgn., Religious Zionists of Chgo., B'nai B'rith Lodge of Survivors of Nazi Holocaust, others. Mem. Nat. Soc. Fund-Raising Execs., Fund-Raising Execs., Pub. Relations Soc. Am., Publicity Club of Chgo. (profl. achievement awards). Home: 3300 Capitol St Skokie IL 60076 Office: Bernard Finkel Assocs 4427 N Clark St Chicago IL 60640

FINKEL, WARREN EDWARD, architect; b. Elyria, Ohio, Nov. 2, 1920; s. Edward Raymond and Hzel (Allen) F.; m. Doris Croyle, Nov. 4, 1977. Grad., Case Western Res. U., 1950. Registered architect Ohio, Mich., Fla., N.C. Architect Dalton-Dalton, Cleve., 1950, R.G. Wheeler, San Diego, 1951-52, Weinberg & Teare, Cleve., 1953—; pres. Finkel & Finkel, Inc.; treas. Lorain Community Broadcasting Co., bd. dirs. Cen. Security Nat. Bank. Prin. works include: Oak Hills Country Club, Lorain, 1960, 1st Ch. of Christ, Scientist, Lorain, 1960, Lorain Community Hosp., 1962, Firelands Retirement Community Coll., 1965, Lorain County Red Cross Hdqrs., 1966, Lorain County Sch. for Retarded Children, 1967, Lorain Family YMCA, 1968, Lorain Community Hosp., 1969, Lorain County Community Coll., 1970, Lorain City Hall, 1971, Learning Resource Ctr., 1974, Elyria Savs. and Trust Bank, 1976, Fine Arts Ctr., 1977, Stark Tech., Coll., 1979, St. Joseph Hosp., 1981, Harshaw Chem. Co., 1981, Boy Scouts Am. Ctr., 1982, Fine Arts Ctr., 1980, Advanced Tech. Ctr., 1984, TRW Nelson Div., 1986, R.W. Beckett Corp., 1987. Mem. Lorain Community Devel., capital improvement com. Lorain United Appeal; Urban Renewal Community Devel. Com. Served with USN, 1938-45. Mem. AIA, Architects Soc. Ohio, Lorain C. of C. (pres. 1967). Lodge: Masons. Home: PO Box 382 Lorain OH 44052

FINKELMEIER, PHILIP RENNER, lawyer; b. Cin., Sept. 5, 1914; s. Louis Philip and Lena (Renner) F.; m. Marion A. Oberling, June 24, 1936; children—Phyllis Ruth Finkelmeier Head, Robert Louis. Student, U. Cin., 1931-33; J.D., Salmon P. Chase Law Sch., 1940. Bar: Ohio 1940, U.S. Dist. Ct. (so. dist.) Ohio 1949, U.S. Ct. Appeals (6th cir.) 1967, U.S. Supreme Ct. 1968. Dep. Indsl. Commn., Ohio, 1941-48; ptnr. Hoover, Beall & Eichel, Cin., 1948-58; sole practice Cin., 1958-68; ptnr. Louis J. Finkelmeier Jr., Cin., 1968—. Ruling elder Immanuel Presbyterian Ch. Mem. Ohio Bar Assn. (workers' compensation com.), ABA, Ohio Acad. Trial Lawyers, Assn. Trial Lawyers Am., Cin. Bar Assn. (workers' compensation com.). Club: Cincinnati. Lodges: Masons, Shriners. Home: 5300 Hamilton Ave #1700 Cincinnati OH 45224 Office: 524 Walnut St #808 Cincinnati OH 45202

FINKLANG, KURT WALTER, optometrist; b. Butte, Mont., July 21, 1955; s. John Walter and Jane Ellen (Becker) F.; m. Lynne Marie Hizer, July 27, 1979; 1 child, David Matthew. BA in Biology, U. Mo., 1976; OD, SUNY Coll. Optometry, N.Y.C., 1981. Pvt. practice optometry B.C. Jander & Assocs., House Springs, Mo., 1981-83, Iverson Jehling Eye Clinic, Warrenton and Troy, Mo., 1981-83, Warrenton and Troy, 1984—; adj. asst. prof. U. Mo. Coll. Optometry, St. Louis, 1983-85. Mem. Am. Optometric Assn., Am. Optometric Found., Mo. Optometric Assn. (Continuing Edn. award 1985, 86), St. Louis Optometric Soc., Better Vision Inst., Contact Lens sect. Am. Optometric Assn. (charter), Heart of Am. Contact Lens Soc. Lodge: Rotary. Office: 101 W College Troy MO 63379

FINLAYSON, ALISTER IAN, retired neurological surgeon; b. Omaha, Feb. 3, 1914; s. John Kelly and Annie (MacLeod) F.; m. Ruth Susan Brodbeck, June 24, 1938; children: John David, Judith Louise Watson, Julie Ann Brandon, Jay Kenneth. BS, U. Omaha, 1935; MD, U. Nebr., 1937, MA, 1939. Diplomate Am. Bd. Neurol. Surgery. Postdoctoral fellow Montreal (Que., Can.) Neurol. Inst., 1939-40, Mayo Found., Rochester, Minn., 1940-41; from instr. to prof. U. Nebr. Med. Coll., Omaha, 1946—; practice medicine specializing in neurosurgery Omaha, 1946-80. Contbr. articles to sci. jours. Disability evaluator Soc. Security Adminstrn., Omaha, 1980-86. Served to capt. M.C., U.S. Army, 1941-45. Mem. Neurosurg. Soc. Am., Am. Assn. Neurol. Surgeons, AMA, Rocky Mountain Neurosurg. Soc. Republican. Lutheran. Avocation: vol. mus. docent. Home: 456 S 89 St Omaha NE 68114

FINLEY, JOHN DOUGLAS, social worker; b. Atwood, Kans., Mar. 10, 1955; s. John Dale and Doris Estella (Luedke) F.; m. Donna Jean Phelps, June 5, 1976; 1 child, Christopher Neil. BSW, U. Kans., 1979, MSW, 1983. Lic. social worker. Social worker Kans. Dept. Social Rehab. Services, Great Bend, 1979-81; social services supr. Kans. Dept. Social Rehab. Services, Colby, 1983-84; sch. social worker Northwest Kans. Ednl. Service Ctr.,

Colby, 1984—; protective service rep. Kans. Dept. Social and Rehab. Services, Topeka, 1980-81. Pres. Child Adv. Com., Great Bend, 1980-81, v.p. Child Abuse Coalition, Colby, 1986—. Named Child Adv. of Month, Child Abuse Com., 1982; Outstanding Social Worker Leadership, Kans. Dept. Social and Rehab. Services, 1981. Mem. Nat. Assn. Social Workers, Kans. Nat. Assn. Social Workers (grad. bd. rep. 1982-83), Kans. Assn. Sch. Social Workers (v.p. 1986—). Democrat. Lodge: Lions. Avocations: snow skiing, water skiing, tennis, basketball, music. Home: 422 Smith Dr Colby KS 67701 Office: Northwest Kans Ednl Service Ctr 210 S Range Colby KS 67701

FINN, CATHERINE L., public relations executive; b. Portland, Oreg., June 22, 1960; d. Norman D. Jr. and Gloria M. (Torlai) Starrett. BA, U. Nevada, 1983, postgrad., 1983—. Instr. speech communication U. Nevada, Reno, 1984-85; communications specialist Nat. Judicial Coll., Reno, 1980—, faculty, 1985; communications coordinator J.C. Penney Ins. Co., Westerville, Ohio, 1987—; communications specialist Nat. Jud. Coll., Reno, 1980-86; asst. dir. communications Ohio Bar Title Ins. Co., Columbus, Ohio, 1986-87. Publicity and press relations coordinator Columbus Marathon, 1986—. Mem. Pub. Relations Soc. Am. (coms.), Phi Kappa Phi, Kappa Tau Alpha. Democrat. Office: JC Penney Ins Co Brooksedge Blvd Westerville OH 43081

FINN, MARY MURPHY, orchestra administrator; b. Phila., June 27, 1939; d. Albert Vincent and Mary Catherine (Martin) Murphy; B.A. in Art, Duchesne Coll., 1961; B.A. in Music, St. Mary's Coll., Omaha, 1962; children by previous marriage—Thomas Jerard, Mary Catherine. Tchr. instrumental music Council Bluffs (Iowa) Public Schs., 1961-63; asst. mgr. Omaha Symphony Orch., 1969-75; mgr. Nebr. Chamber Orch., Lincoln, 1975-77; exec. dir. Omaha Pops Orch., 1977—; free-lance comml. artist, 1957—; cons. computer programming, 1977—; systems analyst Automation Inc., 1979-86, Doane Coll., 1986—; bus. mgr. Manresa, Inc., 1983—; violinist Omaha Symphony Orch., Lincoln Symphony, Sioux City Symphony. Bd. dirs. Voices of Omaha; music contractor for Labor Unions' Septemberfest. Recipient Service awards Omaha Musicians Assn., 1977 through 1984; numerous scholarships. Mem. Am. Fedn. Musicians, Am. Symphony Orch. League, Chamber Music Players Am. Democrat. Roman Catholic. Author/editor Orchestral Excerpts for the Second Violin Player. Contbr. articles to various pubs. Home and Office: 5167 Jackson St Omaha NE 68106

FINN, MICHAEL MARTIN, accountant; b. St. Louis, Dec. 12, 1953; s. Jewell Martin and Audrey Lena (Aubuchon) F. BS in Acctg., N.E. Mo. State U., 1981. CPA, Mo. Mem. staff McGladrey Hendrickson & Co., Burlington, Iowa, 1980-81; auditor Peabody Coal Co., St. Louis, 1981-84; controller Lark Refrigeration, Inc., St. Louis, 1984-87; sr. cons. Mitchell Humphrey & Co., St. Louis, 1987—; pres. Michael Martin Devels., St. Louis, 1984—; speaker in field, St. Louis, 1985. Served as sgt. USAF, 1972-76. Mem. Am. Inst. CPA's, Mo. Soc. CPA's, Alpha Kappa Lambda. Roman Catholic. Avocations: personal computing, travel. Home: 12745 Woodward Way Saint Louis MO 63044 Office: Mitchell Humphrey & Co 2029 Woodland Pkwy Saint Louis MO 63146

FINN, RICHARD HAROLD, bank executive; b. St. Paul, Oct. 9, 1947; s. Richard Harold and Elsie Marie (St. Pierre) F.; m. Susan Marie Kirby, July 9, 1971; children: Sean Michael, Ian Peter, Erin Patricia. BEE, U. Minn., 1971; MBA, No. Ill. U., 1979. Elec. engr. Univac, St. Paul, 1971-72; staff engr. GTE Automatic Elec., Northlake, Ill., 1972-74; sr. analyst Motorola, Schaumberg, Ill., 1974-76; officer First Nat. Bank Chgo., 1976—; lectr. Roosevelt U., Chgo., 1982—. Cubmaster Boy Scouts Am., Western Springs, Ill. 1984-86, scoutmaster handicapped troop, Western Springs, 1986—. Mem. Data Processing Mgmt. Assn. Avocations: personal computers, furniture design. Home: 4616 S Johnson Ave Western Springs IL 60558 Office: First Nat Bank Chgo 1 First National Plaza Chicago IL 60670

FINNARN, THEODORE ORA, lawyer; b. Greenville, Ohio, Aug. 20, 1949; s. Theodore Lincoln and Jeannie (Kelman) F.; B.Ed., Miami U., 1972; J.D. cum laude, U. Toledo, 1976; m. Holly C. Bankson, Sept. 15, 1973; children—Shawn April, Theodore O., Thomas A., Alexander H. Bar: Ohio 1976, U.S. Dist. Ct. (so. dist.) Ohio 1978. Acting dir. Preble County Community Action Com., 1973, program developer, 1972-73; chief agrl. engr. Finnarn Farms, Greenville, Ohio, 1976—; individual practice law, Greenville, 1976—; sec.-treas. Finnarn Devel. Corp., 1977—. Bd. dirs. Darke County Center for Arts; active Greenville Friends of the Library, 1977—; sec.-treas. Greenville Boys Clubs, Inc., 1977—. Mem. Assn. Trial Lawyers Am., Ohio Acad. Trial Lawyers, Am., Ohio, Darke County bar assns., Ohio Farmers Union, Darke County Farmers Union (sec.-treas.), Scribes, Phi Alpha Delta. Democrat. Presbyterian. Editor articles in legal jours. Home: 3060 US Rt 127S Greenville OH 45331 Office: 127 W 5th St Greenville OH 45331

FINN-BONEKEMPER, LAWRE, market researcher; b. Cin., July 26, 1958; d. Howard Leonard and Mary (Leininger) Finn; m. William Whayne Bonekemper, May 4, 1985. BA, Sweet Briar (Va.) Coll., 1980. Cons. supr. Datatel Minicomputer Co., Alexandria, Va., 1981-84; data processing cons. Deloitte Haskins & Sells, Cin., 1984; systems analyst Access Corp., Cin., 1985; project dir. Info. Resources, Inc., Cin., 1986-87, account exec., 1987—. Sec. Young Friends of Zoo, Cin., 1986. Home: 11649 Enyart Rd Symmes Township OH 45140

FINNEY, FREDERICK MARSHALL, cost analyst, writer, educator, editor; b. Troy, Ala., Nov. 18, 1941; s. Marshall and Lucille (Curtis) F.; m. Gladys Turner, July 1, 1972. BA in History, Wilberforce U., 1967; MA, Antioch Coll., 1969; MS in Econs., Wright State U., 1973; postgrad., U. Cin., 1973-80, adv. profl. designation in logistics mgmt., Air Force Inst. Tech., 1986 Intern supr., asst. prof. edn. Antioch Grad. Sch., 1968-70; program analyst City of Dayton, Ohio, 1969-70, evaluation dir., 1970-76; numismatic writer, 1972—; prof. econs., bus. and polit. sci. U. Cin., Capital U., and Sinclair Community Coll., 1976-82; cost analyst U.S. Air Force, 1983; founder Econ. Research Ctr., Inc. and Confrontation/Change Rev.; authority on paper money of U.S. Editor and pub. Econ. Research Ctr. Revs., 1973; contbr. over 350 articles to profl. pubs. Served with USAF, 1958-66, Ohio Air NG, 1966-70. Mem. NAACP,Soc. Logistics Engrs. Lodge: Masons, Shriner. Office: Air Force Logistics Command Wright-Patterson AFB OH 45433

FINNEY, JOAN MARIE MCINROY, state official; b. Topeka, Feb. 12, 1925; d. Leonard L. and Mary M. (Sands) McInroy; m. Spencer W. Finney, Jr., July 24, 1957; children: Sally, Dick, Mary. B.A., Washburn U., 1974. Mem. staff U.S. Senator Frank Carlson, Topeka and Washington, 1953-69; commr. elections Shawnee County, Kans., 1970-72; adminstrv. asst. to mayor of Topeka 1973-74; treas. State of Kans., Topeka, 1974—. Bd. dirs. Hayden High Sch. Alumni Assn., Washburn Alumni Assn., Kans. Community Service orgns., St. Francis Hosp. and Med. Ctr. Aux., Mended Hearts Inc. Mem. Nat. Assn. State Auditors (pres. 1987—), Comptrollers and Treas. , Nat. Assn. State Treas., Nat. Unclaimed Property Assn., Kans. Fedn. Women's Democratic Clubs, Reinisch Rose Garden Soc., Santa Fe Railroad Ret. Employers Club, Am. Legion Aux., Sigma Alpha Iota. Catholic. Office: Office of State Treasurer 700 Harrison Topeka KS 66601

FINNEY, JOHN EDWARD, accountant; b. Louisville, Oct. 17, 1928; s. Henry Middleton and Cecilia Blanche (Veeneman) F.; m. Rosemary Faulkner, June 18, 1949; children: Carolyn Marie, Michael Joseph, Mary Ann, Patricia Jean, Rosanne Catherine. BS in Acctg., U. Louisville, 1949. CPA, Ohio; cert. mgmt. acct. Acct. The J.W. Ford Co., Louisville, 1949-53; asst. br. mgr. The J.W. Ford Co., Atlanta, 1953-61; sales and system rep. Service Bur. Corp., Atlanta, 1961-65; mgr. Ernst & Whinney, Atlanta, 1965-73; mgr. Ernst & Whinney, Cleve., 1973-75, sr. mgr., 1975—. Contbr. articles to profl. jours. Served to lt. USNR, 1949-60. Mem. Am. Inst. CPA's, Nat. Assn. Accts. (chpt. pres. 1984-85, bd. dirs.), Assn. For Systems Mgmt. (chpt. pres. 1971-72), Inst. Mgmt. Acctg., Ohio Soc. CPA's. Republican. Roman Catholic. Clubs: Cleve. Athletic, Georgetown Recreation (Atlanta) (pres. 1970-71).

FINSILVER, SHARI ELAINE, consulting company executive; b. Detroit, May 28, 1950; d. Robert Lee Alper and Lenore Faye (Seltzer) Solomon; m. Stanley Harris Finsilver, Sept. 12, 1971; children: Amy, Brett. BS in Math, U. Mich., 1971, MS in Indsl. and Ops. Engring., 1978. Computer programmer/operator Market Opinion Research, Detroit, 1971-72; project engr. William Beaumont Hosp., Royal Oak, Mich., 1978-81, mgmt. engr., 1981-86; pres. Productivity Plus, Inc., West Bloomfield, Mich., 1986—. Author: Beaumont Patient Classification System, 1983. Mem. future planning com. Temple Israel, West Bloomfield, 1985—; chairperson Mother's March March of Dimes, Oakland County, Mich., 1973-77. Mem. Am. Hosp. Assn., Healthcare Info. Mgmt. Systems Soc. Office: Productivity Plus Inc 33020 Northwestern Hwy West Bloomfield MI 48322

FINTEL, DAN JAMES, cardiologist; b. Petach Tikvah, Israel, Apr. 10, 1953; came to U.S., 1956; s. Mark and Slava (Zimmer) F.; m. Robin Randall, June 18, 1978; children: Bara Carrie, Joshua Seth. BS magna cum laude, Yale U., 1979; MD magna cum laude, Harvard U., 1979. Intern, then resident Mt. Sinai Hosp., N.Y.C., 1979-82; fellow cardiology Johns Hopkins U., Balt., 1982-85; assoc. dir. med. intensive care Northwestern U. Med. Ctr., Chgo., 1985—, assoc. prof. medicine, 1985-87, asst. prof. medicine, 1987—. Contbr. articles to profl. jours. Fellow Am. Coll. Cardiology; mem. ACP, Am. Heart Assn., Am. Fedn. Clin. Research, Phi Beta Kappa, Sigma Xi. Democrat. Jewish. Avocations: tennis, snorkeling, bicycling, skiing. Home: 1082 Oak Ridge Dr Glencoe IL 60022 Office: Northwestern Meml Hosp 239 E Chicago Suite 628 Chicago IL 60611

FIRENZE, LOUIS JOHN, business educator; b. Englewood, N.J., Apr. 17, 1948; s. Carmine Louis and Freda Ida (Hess) F.; m. Judith Suzanne Williams, Feb. 15, 1952; children—Michael Carmine, Beth Marie. B.S., Central Mich. U., 1970; M.B.A., 1972; Ph.D., Mich. State U., 1982. Time study mgmt. staff Ferro Mfg. Co., Mt. Pleasant, Mich., 1971-72; purchasing agt. Delta Strapping Industries, N.Y.C., 1973-74; assoc. prof. bus. Northwood Inst., Midland, Mich., 1974—, dir. bus. div., 1984—; cons. in external plans of study. Chmn. Isabella County Republican Com., 1981-82. Mem. Acad. Mgmt., Council Advancement Experiential Learning, Phi Delta Kappa, Sigma Iota Epsilon. Roman Catholic. Home: 468 W Remus Rd Mount Pleasant MI 48858 Office: Northwood Inst Midland MI 48640

FIRMILIAN, bishop. Bishop Serbian Orthodox Ch. of Midwestern Am., Libertyville, Ill. Office: Serbian Orthodox Ch P O Box 519 Libertyville IL 60048 *

FISCHER, BERT, construction company executive; b. 1940. Student, U. Hanover, Federal Republic Germany. Pres., dir. Fru-Con Corp., Ballwin, Mo., 1984—. Office: Fru-Con Corp 1299 Clayton Rd W Ballwin MO 63011 *

FISCHER, BRUCE ELWOOD, JR., psychologist; b. Breckenridge, Minn., Sept. 17, 1951; s. Bruce Elwood and Sally (Anderson) F. BA, U. Minn., 1973, MA, 1976. Lic. psychologist, Minn.; cert. sex counselor, Minn. Pvt. practice psychotherapy Mpls., 1976—; instr. sch. pub. health U. Minn., Mpls., 1976-85, dir. continuing edn. for alcohol and drug abuse profl., 1980-86; instr. dept. family social sci. U. Minn., St. Paul, 1985—; cons. program on human sexuality U. Minn., Mpls., 1978—; pres. Fieri Systems, Mpls., 1985—. Contbr. articles to profl. jours. Mem. Am. Assn. Marriage and Family Therapists, Am. Assn. Sex Educators, Counselors and Therapists. Avocations: skiing, backpacking. Home: 2840 Humbolt Ave S Minneapolis MN 55408

FISCHER, CALVIN HOWARD, physician; b. Pitts., Sept. 9, 1943; s. Herbert George and Anna Violet (Woefel) F. Student, Thiel Coll., 1963, Ill. Inst. Tech., 1963-64; DO, Chgo. coll. Osteopathic Medicine, 1969. Intern Detroit Osteopathic Hosp., Highland Park, Mich., 1969-70; practice osteopathy Chgo., 1970—; chmn. dept. family practice Humana Hosp., Hoffman Estates, Ill., 1982-84, pres. med. and dental staff, 1986—; bd. dirs. Ill. Acad. Family Physicians. Host Health Mag. cable TV show, 1986. Fellow Am. Acad. Family Physicians, Am. Coll. Utilization Rev. Avocations: running, golfing, fishing. Office: 1575 N Barrington Rd Hoffman Estates IL 60194

FISCHER, CARL GARY, food products executive; b. Grafton, N.D., Jan. 1, 1941; s. Carl Fredrich and Isabelle Henrietta (Pokrzywinski) F.; m. Anna Marie Almen, June 25, 1966; children: Jill, Ryan. BA in Chemistry, Concordia Coll., Moorhead, Minn., 1963. Asst. chief chemist Am. Crystal Sugar Co., Rocky Ford, Colo. and Moorhead, 1963-65; chief chemist, supt. Drayton, N.D., 1965-75, plant mgr., 1975-80; ops. mgr. Crookston and Moorhead, Minn., 1980—. Alderman City of Drayton, 1974, 76-80. Served with USNG, 1966-72. Mem. Am. Soc. Sugar Beet Technologists (instr. 1987). Lutheran. Lodge: Rotary. Avocations: amateur radio, fishing, bowling, golf. Home: 3708 Fairway Rd Fargo ND 58102 Office: Am Crystal Sugar Co 2500 N 11th St Moorhead MN 56560

FISCHER, DONALD THOMAS, dentist; b. Cin., Oct. 4, 1957; s. Thomas H. and Leona M. (Havlis) F.; m. Beth Ann Viellieu, Apr. 27, 1985. AB in Chemistry, Ind. U., 1980, DDS, 1984. Gen. practice dentistry Donald T. Fischer & Assocs., Mooresville, Ind., 1984—. Mem. ADA, Ind. Dental Assn., Ind. Dist. Dental Soc., Mooresville C. of C., Ind. W. Side Study Club, Alpha Tau Omega. Lodge: Kiwanis. Avocations: biking, jogging, yard work. Home: 5411 Washington Blvd Indianapolis IN 46220 Office: 124 N Indiana Mooresville IN 46158

FISCHER, JACK LEE, architect; b. Appleton, Wis., Oct. 31, 1953; s. Milton J. and Erma I. (Springstroh) F.; m. Karen R. Adler, Jan. 2, 1982. Student U. Wis.-Stout, 1972-73; B.S., U. Wis.-Milw., 1976, M. Arch., 1978. Pres. Jack L. Fischer Constrn. Co., Appleton, 1970-75, Contemporary Dwellings, Inc., Appleton, 1976-81, Fischer Schutte & Jensen, Inc., Appleton, 1978-82; v.p., dir. Marathon Engrs., Architects, Planners, Inc., Menasha, Wis., 1982—. Prin. works include Earth Shelter Residence, Appleton (Nat. Design award 1979), Tenterasol I Residential Design, Mpls. (Nat. Design award 1979), Earth Shelter Residences, St. Paul (Earth Shelters award 1980).Bd. dirs. Outagamie Mus. Mem. Am. Planning Assn. (charter 1978), AIA, Wis. Soc. Architects, Fox Cities C. of C., (planning com. 1980-83, bd. dirs.), Fox Cities U. Wis. Milw. Alumni Group (chmn.). Lutheran. Lodge: Elks, Rotary. Avocations: scuba diving, skiing, nature study, drawing, boating. Home: 1008 Woodcrest Dr Appleton WI 54915

FISCHER, LYNN HELEN, writer; b. Red Wing, Minn., June 2, 1943; d. Reinhart Henry and Marie Katherine (Olson) F. Student, U. Wis., River Falls, U. Wis., Madison, U. Minn. Free-lance writer Madison and Mpls., 1971—. Author: The 1,2,4, Theory: A Synthesis, 1971, Sexual Equations of Electricity, Magnetism, and Gravitation, 1971, Middle Concept Theory, 1972, A Revised Meaning of Paradox, 1972, Human Sexual Evolution, 1972, Unitary Theory, 1973, An Introduction to Circular of Fischerian Geometry, 1976, Two, Four, Eight Theory, 1977, Fischer's Brief Dictionary of Sound Meanings, 1977, Introducing the Magnetic Sleeve: A Novel Sexual Organ, 1983, The Expansion of Duality, 1984, The Inger Poems, 1985; (cassette tapes) Country Wit, 1986, The Inger Poems and Early Poems, 1986, Letters of the Poet Lynn, 1987. Avocations: playing the piano forte, singing. Home: 1415 E 22d St Apt 1108 Minneapolis MN 55404

FISCHER, MARGARET JANE, liturgical artist, educator; b. Chgo., Apr. 25, 1946; d. Paul Joseph and Jane Caroline (Shriver) F. Diploma, Cleve. Inst. Art, 1968, BFA, 1969; MA, Case Western Res. U., 1977. Sacristan St. Dominic Ch., Shaker Heights, Ohio, 1965-72; tchr. art Jewish Community Ctr., Cleveland Heights, Ohio, 1970—; lectr. Case Western Res. U., Cleve., 1971—; chmn. liturgical arts Art and Architecture Commn. Cath. Diocese Cleve., 1978—; mem. exec. com. Office Pastoral Liturgy, Cleve., 1978—; Cleve. rep. Liturgical Art Guild Ohio, Columbus, 1980—; chmn. liturgy commn. St. Dominic Ch., 1983—. Works include (eucharistic vessels) St. Joseph Cathedral, 1979, St. Mary Sem., 1981; (eucharistic vessel, processional cross) Ch. of Resurrection, 1979, 84; (tabernacle sanctuary lamp) St. Francis St. George Hosp., Inc., 1982. Recipient Juror's award Liturgical Art Guild Ohio, 1975, 77, Juror's award McFall Gallery, 1981, Honorable Mention, Newman Art Show, 1977, 78. Mem. Ohio Designer Craftsmen (sec., 1979-81, N.E. Ohio trustee, 1975-79,Purchase award 1981), Am. Crafts Council, Enamel Guild of Western Res. Club: Dominican Chorale (pres. 1985—) (Shaker Heights). Avocations: singing, kite flying, reading. Home: 3475 Avalon Rd Shaker Heights OH 44120 Office: Case Western Res U Wickenden Bldg Cleveland OH 44106

FISCHER, PHYLLIS LENORE, animal rights activist, beauty shop executive; b. Parkersburg, W.Va., June 24, 1951; d. Robert Paul and June (Fultz) F.; m. Richard Morgan, May 1975; 1 son, R.G. B.S. summa cum laude, Ohio U., 1973. Founder, Writers for Animal Rights, Jonesboro, Tenn., 1978-83; founder, dir. Mobilization for Animals, Columbus, Ohio, 1981-84; founder Protect Our Earth's Treasures, Columbus, 1984-85; founder, pres. Care about the Strays, New Albany, Ohio, 1985—; speaker, media cons. several orgns., 1985—; mng. dir. Topcuts, Inc., Columbus, 1983—. Author numerous published poems. Editor Black Cat jour., 1975—. Avocations: writing; lecturing; rescuing stray animals. Home: PO Box 474 New Albany OH 43054

FISCHER, ROBBINS WARREN, oilseed industry consulting company executive; b. Turin, Iowa, Mar. 31, 1919; s. Lewis Warren and Edith (Robbins) F.; m. Jean Noreen Greenawalt, Apr. 10, 1943; children: Barbara Jean, Martha Lou, Dorothy Ellen. BA, U. Colo., 1942, postgrad. law, 1944-45; postgrad., Rutgers U., 1954. Co-owner, operator Fischer Farms, Turin, 1947-53; sales promotion mgr. Payway Feed Mills, Kansas City, Mo., 1953-55; regional sales mgr. Bristol Myers Co., Kansas City, 1956-58; campaign dir. Burrell, Inc., Kansas City, 1958-59; asst. to pres. Soybean Council Am., Waterloo, Iowa, 1960-63; pres. Soypro Internat., Inc., Cedar Falls, 1963—, Soypro of Iowa, Cedar Falls, 1973—, Internat. Bus. Assocs., Cedar Falls, 1965—, Miller Farms Food Co., Cedar Falls, 1985—; v.p. Continental Soya, Manning, Iowa, 1973-81; chmn. bd., chief exec. officer Burst Products, Denison, Iowa, 1979-82; vice chmn. Iowa Farm Council, 1950-53; mem. Pres. Kennedy's Task Force on Internat. Trade in Agrl. Products, 1962, Pres. Reagan's Task Force on Internat. Agrl. Devel., 1982—; chmn. food and agr. com. Pres. Regan's Task Force on Internat. Pvt. Enterprise, 1983-84; mem. Agribus. Prom. Council, 1982—, Agri-Tech. Com. on Oilseeds and Products, 1982—, Dist. Export Council, 1978—. Mem. Cedar Falls C. of C. (bd. dirs.), Inst. Food Technologists, Monona Harrison Flood Control Assn. (pres. 1951-54), Phi Beta Kappa, Delta Sigma Rho, Pi Gamma Mu. Congregationalist. Club: Des Moines. Lodges: Rotary, Masons. Home: 5614 University Ave Cedar Falls IA 50613 Office: 314 Main St Cedar Falls IA 50613

FISCHER, ROBERT H., retired church history educator; b. Williamsport, Pa., Apr. 26, 1918; s. M. Hadwin and M. Alice (Gortner) F.; m. Edna Mae Black, Sept. 5, 1942; 1 child, Susan K. Fischer Wade. AB, Gettysburg Coll., 1939; BD, Luth. Theol. Sem., Gettysburg, Pa., 1942; PhD, Yale U., 1947. Pastor Community Parish, Hartland, Vt., 1944-45; asst. pastor Zion Luth. Ch., Sunbury, Pa., 1947-49; prof. ch. history Luth. Sch. Theol., Chgo., 1949-86; established Luth. tutorship Mansfield Coll., Oxford U., 1957-58; participant Internat. Congresses for Luth. Research; guest prof. Theologische Hochschule, Berlin, 1973, Japan Luth. Sem., Tokyo, 1980. Author: Luther, 1966; editor: Luther's Works, Vol. 37, 1961, Franklin Clark Fry, 1972, A Tribute to Arthur Vööbus, 1977. Sterling doctoral research fellow Yale U., 1945-46; Assn. Theol. Schs. fellow 1964-65. Mem. Soc. for Reformation Research (pres. 1954), Am. Theol. Soc. (pres. midwest div. 1961-62, sec.-treas. 1964-86), Luth. Historical Conf. (v.p. 1972-76, bd. dirs. 1984—). Republican. Clubs: Sub. Vets. Chorus (accompanist, assoc. dir. 1949-85) (LaGrange). Avocations: music, sports, handicrafts. Home: 5324 Central Ave Western Springs IL 60558 Office: Luth Sch Theology 1100 E 55th St Chicago IL 60615

FISCHER, WILLIAM FRANK, military officer; b. Grand Rapids, Mich., July 12, 1940; s. Charles Frank and Marion Virginia (Stiles) F.; m. Barbara Louise Riordan, June 9, 1962; children: Cynthia, Pamela, Charles, William, James. BS in Physics, The Citadel, 1962; MSEE, U. Tex., El Paso, 1969. Commd. 2d lt. U.S. Army, 1962, advanced through grades to col., 1983; battery comdr. U.S. Army, Fed. Republic of Germany, 1962-65; ops. officer U.S. Army, Republic of Vietnam, 1966-67; personnel officer U.S. Army, Washington, 1969-72; test control officer U.S. Army, Ft. Ord, Calif., 1977-79; NATO staff officer U.S. Army, Shape, Belgium, 1980-83; ops. research U.S. Army, Ft. Sheridan, Ill., 1983—; staff officer four party joint mil. commn., Saigon, Republic of Vietnam. Editor: Recruiting Jour. Decorated Legion of Merit; Vietnamese Cross of Gallantry. Roman Catholic. Avocations: flying, bowling, fishing, hunting, boating. Home: 0-308 Lake Michigan Dr Grand Rapids MI 49504 Office: HQ USAREC Bldg 48C Fort Sheridan IL 60037

FISCHESSER, DONALD JOSEPH, merger and acquisition executive; b. Cin., Aug. 26, 1943; s. Alvin Leo and Mary Elizabeth (Macke) F.; m. Elisa Anne Mennucci, July 15, 1972; children Brian, Susan, Anne. BBA in Acctg., U. Cin., 1966. Staff acct. Alexander Grant & Co., Cin., 1966-68; mgr. corp. acctg. Philips Industries, Dayton, Ohio, 1969-73; v.p. fin., treas. Burcliff Industries, Mishawaka, Ind., 1973-76, Fairmont Homes, Nappanee, Ind., 1977-79; ptnr. Gorton, Fischesser & Assocs., South Bend, Ind., 1979—; bd. dirs. Bromwell Corp., Michigan City, Ind., 1984—, Lake City Van Conversions, Warsaw, Ind., 1986—. Chmn. fin. com. St. Judes Ch., South Bend, 1985—; bd. dirs. Southeast Little League, South Bend, 1985-86. Mem. Corp. Acquisition and Merger Affiliates, South Bend C. of C., Fraternal Order Police. Lodges: Sertoma (pres., bd. dirs. South Bend 1982), Rotary (athletic com. South Bend 1982-86). Avocations: bridge, tennis. Office: Gorton Fischesser & Assocs 224 W Jefferson South Bend IN 46601

FISCHLER, BARBARA BRAND, librarian; b. Pitts., May 24, 1930; d. Carl Frederick and Emma Georgia (Piltz) Brand; m. Drake Anthony Fischler, June 3, 1961; 1 child, Owen Wesley. AB cum laude, Wilson Coll., Chambersburg, Pa., 1952; MM with distinction, Ind. U., 1954, AMLS, 1964. Asst. reference librarian Ind. U., Bloomington, 1958-61, asst. librarian undergrad. library, 1961-63, acting librarian, 1963; circulation librarian Ind. U.-Purdue U., Indpls., 1970-76, pub. services librarian Univ. Library, sci., engring. and tech. unit, 1976-81, acting dir. univ. libraries, 1981-82, dir. univ. libraries, 1982—; vis. and assoc. prof. (part-time) Sch. Library and Info. Sci., Ind. U., Bloomington, 1972—, counselor/coordinator, Indpls., 1974-82; resource aide adv. com. Ind. Voc. Tech. Coll., Indpls., 1974-86; adv. com. Area Library Services Authority, Indpls., 1976-79; mem. core com., chmn. program com. Ind. Gov.'s Conf. on Libraries and Info. Services, Indpls., 1976-78; cons. in field. Contbr. articles to profl. jours. Fund raiser Indpls. Mus. Art, 1971, Am. Cancer Soc., Indpls., 1975; vol. tchr. St. Thomas Aquinas Sch., Indpls., 1974-75; fund raiser Am. Heart Assn., Indpls., 1985; bd. dirs., treas. Historic Amusement Found., Inc., Indpls., 1984—; bd. advisors N.Am. Wildlife Park Found., Inc., Battle Ground, Ind., 1985—. Recipient Outstanding Service award Cen. Ind. Area Library Service Authority, 1979. Mem. ALA, Midwest Fedn. Library Assns. (chmn. local arrangements for conf. 1986-87), Ind. Library Assn. (chmn. coll. and univ. div. 1977-78, chmn. library edn. div. 1981-82, treas. 1984-86)., German Shepherd Dog Club of Cen. Ind. (pres. 1978-79), Wabash Valley German Shepherd Dog Club (pres. 1982-83), Cen. Ind. Kennel Club (bd. dirs.), Pi Kappa Lambda, Beta Phi Mu. Republican. Presbyterian. Avocations: breeder and exhibitor of German Shepherd dogs; ethology. Home: 4255 Cooper Rd Indianapolis IN 46208 Office: Ind-Purdue U 815 W Michigan St Indianapolis IN 46202

FISCHMAR, RICHARD MAYER, controller, consultant; b. N.Y.C., Apr. 11, 1938; s. John B. and Sylvia (Moosnick) F.; m. Sandra P. Fensin, July 3, 1967; children: Brian, Laura. BS, U. Ill., 1959, MA, 1962. CPA, Ill. Sr. auditor L.K.H.&H., Chgo., 1962-66; controller Lake States Engr., Park Ridge, Ill., 1966-68, New Communities Enterprises, Park Forest South, Ill., 1968-73, Ill. Dept. Labor, Chgo., 1973-78, D.L. Pattis Real Estate, Lincolnwood, Ill., 1978-86, Goodman Realty Group, Inc., Chgo., 1986—. Author booklet Bibliography of Management Services, 1972. Mem. Ill. Soc. CPA's. Office: Goodman Realty Group Inc 6160 N Cicero Chicago IL 60646

FISEL, LYLE LEE, financial planner; b. South Bend, Ind., Feb. 12, 1950; s. Kenneth L. and Gertrude (Klingaman) F.; m. Linda S. Smith, May 20, 1972; children: Matthew, Sara. BS, Ball State U., Ind., 1972. Tchr. Rossville (Ind.) Schs., 1972-73; ins. agt. Nat. Guardian, South Bend, Ind., 1974-78, Healy Co., South Bend, 1978-84; co-founder Sticker Store Corp., Portland, Oregon, 1984-85; fin. planner Richard Groff Assocs., Elkhart, Ind., 1985—; owner Capital Resources, Elkhart, 1985—. Contbr. articles to profl. jours.

Past pres. Family Time Community Orgn., South Bend, 1979, First United Meth. Ch. Family Counseling Ctr., South Bend, 1981. Served with USN, 1973. Named Outstanding Com. Chmn., Ind. State Assn. Life Underwriters, 1980. Mem. Nat. Assn. Health Underwriters (cert.). Lodge: Rotary. Avocations: hunting, swimming, racquetball. Home: 11132 Wildwood Dr Osceola IN 46561 Office: Richard Groff Assocs 419 S Main St Elkhart IN 46516

FISH, CARLTON THOMAS, architect; b. Decatur, Ill., Nov. 24, 1945; s. Russel Allen and Mary Edith (Allen) F.; m. Merrilyn Kay Campbell, Aug. 20, 1966; children—Edith Lynn, Jason Lee. A.Arch., So. Ill. U., 1965; B.Arch., U. Okla., 1977, B.S. in Environ. Design, 1977. Registered architect Okla., Mo., Tenn., Tex., Ga., Ohio, Nat. Council Archtl. Registration Bds. Assoc. architect Locke Wright Foster, Architects, Oklahoma City, 1971-78; corp. architect Silver Dollar City, Inc., Marvel Cave Park, Mo., 1978—. Served with U.S. Army, 1967-71. Mem. AIA, Mo. Council Architects. Republican. Baptist. Architect of record for WhiteWater amusement parks, Branson, Mo., Oklahoma City, Grand Prairie, Tex., Garland, Tex., Marietta, Ga.

FISH, CHARLES RUSSELL, gynecologist, obstetrician; b. Wheatland, Wyo., Jan. 9, 1934; s. Arthur Russell and Elizabeth Elberta (Tschiffely) F.; m. Meellee Wanawake Luton, Oct. 2, 1957; children: Howard Tilghman, William Russell, Julia Lacey, Airley Elizabeth, Katherine Nichole. Student, Grinnell (Iowa) Coll., 1952-54; BS, U. Wyo., 1956; MD, McGill U., Montreal, Can., 1961; postgrad., Mayo Grad. Sch., Rochester, Minn., 1965-68. Intern Akron (Ohio) Gen. Hosp., 1961-62; resident St. Mary's Hosp., Rochester, Rochester Meth. Hosp.; resident Mayo Clinic, Rochester, 1965-68, cons. ob-gyn, 1969—. Bd. dirs. Am. Cancer Soc., Olmsted County, Minn., 1970-74. Served to lt. comdr. USNR, 1963-65. Fellow Am. Coll. Obstetricians and Gynecologists (chmn. Minn. chpt. 1980-83); mem. AMA, Minn. Med. Assn., Zumbro Valley Med. Soc., Minn. Ob-Gyn Soc. (sec.-treas. 1973-76, v.p. 1977, pres. 1978), Cen. Assn. Obstetricians and Gynecologists, Am. Soc. Colposcopy and Colpomicroscopy, Am. Fertility Soc. Avocations: gardening, fishing.

FISH, SHIRLEY WILSON, investment executive; b. Worthington, Minn., Mar. 15, 1936; d. Cecil Lloyd and Ruth Irene (Shore) Wilson; m. Merton Raymond Fish, June 7, 1964. B.B.A., U. Minn., 1958. Chartered fin. analyst. Economics research asst. Harris Trust & Savs. Bank, Chgo., 1958-64, security analysis research asst., 1966-77, investment portfolio mgr., v.p., 1977—. Mem. The Investment Analysts Soc. Chgo., D.A.R. Avocations: photography, bridge. Office: Harris Trust and Savs Bank 111 W Monroe St Chicago IL 60690

FISHBURN, KAY MAURINE, nurse; b. Kearney, Nebr., Nov. 1, 1939; d. Kenneth Charles and Maurine Estelle (Neustrom) Kauer; m. Charles Wylie Fishburn, Nov. 21, 1962; children: Jeffrey Scott, Ann Charlotte. Diploma in nursing, Henry Ford Hosp., 1960; BSN with honors, U. Wis., Milw., 1974. Nurse Henry Ford Hosp., Detroit, 1960-61, U. Colo. Med. Ctr., Denver, 1961-63, Wayne County Gen. Hosp., Eloise, Mich., 1964; faculty asst. U. Wis., Milw., 1974-75; pvt. practice occupational health nursing New Berlin, Wis., 1974—. Founder, nat. coordinator Citizens for Debt-Free Am., New Berlin, 1983—. Mem. Am. Nurse's Assn., Am. Assn. Occupational Nurses., Milw. Dist. Nurses Assn. (Nursing Service award 1984). Methodist. Home: 2550 S Sunny Slope Rd New Berlin WI 53151 Office: 17125 W Cleveland Ave New Berlin WI 53151

FISHEL, JAMES DEAN, telecommunications executive; b. Bedford, Ind., Aug. 30, 1953; s. Dale Fishel and Marilyn (Pruitt) Conrad. Student, Ball State U., 1972, Ivy Tech. Coll., 1977. Lic. real estate broker. Builder Fishel Builders, Jeffersonville, Ind., 1973-78; real estate broker Lamping Real Estate Broker, Clarksville, Ind., 1978-82; dir. east coast property TMC, Inc., Louisville, 1982-83; territorial mgr. TMC of Northwest Ind., Munster, 1983—; telecommunications cons. in field. Inventor IN-WATS service for resale carriers, 1985. Dir. Better Bus. Bur., Gary, Ind., 1987. Mem. Ind. C. of C., Hammond C. of C., South Bend C. of C., Chgo. C. of C. Republican. Home: 1464 River Dr Munster IN 46321 Office: TMC of Northwest Ind 900 Ridge Rd Suite T Munster IN 46321

FISHER, ALAN WASHBURN, historian, educator; b. Columbus, Ohio, Nov. 23, 1939; s. Sydney Nettleton and Elizabeth E. (Scipio) F.; m. Carol L. Garrett, Aug. 24, 1963; children: Elizabeth, Ann Christy, Garrett. B.A., DePauw U., 1961; M.A., Columbia U., 1964, Ph.D., 1967. Instr. history Mich. State U., East Lansing, 1966-67; asst. prof. Mich. State U., 1967-70, asso. prof., 1970-78, prof. Russian and Turkish history, assoc. dean for grad. studies and research, coll. arts and letters, 1978—, assoc. dean grad. studies and research, 1987—. Author: Russian Annexation of the Crimea, 1772-1783, 1970, The Crimean Tatars, 1978, revised edit., 1987, Ottoman Studies Directory, I, 1979, II, 1981, III, 1983. Am. Research Inst. in Turkey fellow, 1969, 73, 76; Am. Council Learned Socs. grantee, 1976-77. Fellow Royal Hist. Soc.; Mem. Middle East Studies Assn., Turkish Studies Assn. (pres. 1982-84, editor bull. 1984-87), Inst. Turkish Studies (dir.). Office: Dept History Mich State U East Lansing MI 48824

FISHER, CHARLES THOMAS, III, banker; b. Detroit, Nov. 22, 1929; s. Charles Thomas, Jr. and Elizabeth Jane (Briggs) F.; m. Margaret Elizabeth Keegin, June 18, 1952; children: Margaret Elizabeth (Mrs. F. Macy Jones), Charles Thomas IV, Curtis William, Lawrence Peter II, Mary Florence. A.B. in Econs, Georgetown U., 1951; M.B.A., Harvard U., 1953. C.P.A., Mich. With Touche, Ross, Bailey & Smart, Detroit, 1953-58; asst. v.p. Nat. Bank Detroit, 1958-61, v.p., 1961-66, sr. v.p., 1966-69, exec. v.p., 1969-72, pres., chief adminstrv. officer, 1972—, also dir.; pres., dir. NBD Bancorp, Inc., 1973—, chmn., 1982—; dir. Internat. Bank of Detroit, Nat. Intergroup, Inc., Gen. Motors Corp., Am. Airlines. Civilian aide to sec. army for State of Mich., 1974-77; Chmn. Mackinac Bridge Authority.; Bd. dirs. Greater Detroit Area Hosp. Council. Named Detroit Young Man of Year Detroit Jr. Bd. Commerce, 1961. Mem. Assn. Res. City Bankers, Am. Inst. C.P.A.s, Mich. Assn. C.P.A.s. Clubs: Bloomfield Hills (Mich.) Country; Country of Detroit (Grosse Pointe), Grosse Pointe; Detroit Athletic (Detroit), Detroit (Detroit), Yondotega (Detroit); Links (N.Y.C.); Metropolitan (Washington). Home: Grosse Pointe Farms MI 48236 Office: N B D Bancorp Inc 611 Woodward Ave Detroit MI 48226

FISHER, DONALD, public relations executive; b. Oklahoma City, Okla., Jan. 22, 1949; s. Dawes and Velma Pauline (Johnson) F.; m. Zandra Rue Holaday, June 13, 1970; children: Tammy Renee, Robert Alan. BA in Journalism, Advt., U. Okla., 1970. Reporter, photographer, asst. city editor Okla. Pub. Co., Oklahoma City, 1970-75; spl. agt. Prudential Ins. Co., Oklahoma City, 1975-78; asst. staff mgr. pub. relations dept. Southwestern Bell Telephone Co., Dallas, 1978-80; staff specialist pub. relations dept. Southwestern Bell Telephone Co., Corpus Christi, Tex., St. Louis, 1980-84; staff mgr. pub. relations dept. Southwestern Bell Publs., St. Louis, 1984—. Mem. Southwestern Bell Co. Community Relation Teams, Tex. (outstanding service award 1981). Recipient Katie award Dallas Press Club, 1978, 79. Mem. Internat. Assn. Bus. Communicators (best corp. newspaper award 1979, best corp. newspaper photography 1979, corp. newspaper graphics hon. mention 1979). Democrat. Avocations: photography, swimming, Nautilus workouts. Home: 2336 Sportsmen Hill Dr Chesterfield MO 63017 Office: Southwestern Bell Publs 12800 Publications Dr Suite 400 Saint Louis MO 63131

FISHER, ERMAN CALDWELL, corporate executive; b. Mt. Sterling, Ky., Oct. 10, 1923; s. Cato and Mattalean W. (Tyler) F.; cert. Highland Park Jr. Coll., 1947, Wayne State U., 1965, B.E. in Archtl. Engring., Detroit Inst. Tech., 1954; m. Ruby Nelson, June 28, 1947; children—Paul Cato, Nancy Carol. With Aero. Products, Inc., Detroit, 1943, Great Lakes Mut. Life Ins. Co., Detroit, 1946-48; prin. constrn. insp. City of Detroit Water Dept., 1948-68, supt. bldg. and grounds maintenance, 1968-74, supt. plant and mech. maintenance, 1974-75, mgr. plant, bldg. and mech. maintenance, 1975-77; dep. dir. Detroit Water and Sewage Dept., 1977-80, asst. dir. tech. support, 1980-81; dir. phys. plant Wayne State U., Detroit, 1980-83; gen. mgr. Central Installation Co., Fraser, Mich., 1984—. Bd. dirs. Shaw Coll., 1970-73; del. state conv. Republican party, 1954-55; now mem. Democratic State Central Com. Served with U.S. Army, 1943-46. Recipient Edward Dunbar Rich Service award, 1974. Mem. Am. Pub. Works Assn. (past pres. Inst. Bldgs. and Grounds 1977—, pres. Detroit Met. br., pres. Mich. State chpt. 1986-87, Samuel A. Greeley award 1985), Assn. Phys. Plant Adminstrs. Univs. and Colls., Phylon Soc. Wayne State U., NAACP (life), Am. Water Works Assn., Water Pollution Control Fedn., Engring. Soc. Detroit, Soc. Municipal Engrs., Mich. Assn. Phys. Plant Adminstrs., Detroit Retired City Employees Assn. (assoc. dir. 1980-87), DAV, Alpha Phi Alpha. Club: Lions. Office: 16505 Thirteen Mile Rd Fraser MI 48026

FISHER, EUGENE, marketing executive; b. Chgo., Sept. 30, 1927; s. Morris and Sarah (Edelstein) F.; m. Joline Cobb, July 28, 1956; children—Robin Downing, Amy Homer, Douglas. Ph.B., U. Chgo., 1945, M.B.A., 1948. Product mgr. Brunswick Corp., Skokie, Ill., 1955-59, group product mgr., 1959-63, product mktg. mgr., 1963-67, dir. mktg. planning, 1965-72, dir. corp. mktg. research, 1972-87, corp. mktg. dir., 1987—; mem. mktg. com. Nat. Bowling Council, 1975—; pres. Fisher Mktg. Intelligence, Inc., 1983—; guest lectr. in field Mem. Am. Mktg. Assn., Conf. Bd. (research council), Phi Sigma Delta. Home: 1233 Elder Rd Homewood IL 60430 Office: Brunswick Corp One Brunswick Plaza Skokie IL 60077

FISHER, EVELYN CAROL, construction executive; b. Bedford, Iowa, Sept. 28, 1938; d. H.K. William Jr. and Anita Yvonne (Osburn) Russell; m. Thomas F. Fisher, Dec. 26, 1969; children: Deanna Lynn Poyfair, Sheryl Anne Roth. Student, Iowa State U., 1956-57. Catering asst. Aristo Foods, Des Moines, Iowa, 1968-70; personal banker Iowa Des Moines Nat. Bank, 1970-72; v.p., corp. exec. West Des Moines (Iowa) Sand Co., 1972—. Mem. Am. Bus. Women Am. (pres. 1973-74, Woman of Yr. 1976), Nat. Assn. Homebuilders Auxiliary (nat. conv. chmn. 1980-86), Home Builders Assn. Greater Des Moines (Iowa conv. chmn. 1986-87). Republican. Presbyterian. Avocations: sewing, painting, cross stitch, knitting. Office: West Des Moines Sand Co PO Box 65730 West Des Moines IA 50265

FISHER, GARY LEE, information services executive; b. Akron, Ohio, Mar. 17, 1949; s. Harry Raymond and Elaine Marie (Hall) F.; m. Virginia Leigh Murphy, June 21, 1968; children: Michael William, Lisa Marie. AS in Data Processing, U. Akron, 1973. Lead analyst Bellows Internat., Akron, 1974-76; assoc. programmer tire div. B.F. Goodrich, Akron, Ohio and Thomaston, Ga., 1976-80; sr. analyst EPG div. B.F. Goodrich, Akron, 1980-84, mgr. mgmt. info. services aerospace div., 1984—. Mem. N.E. Ohio Mapics User Group. Democrat. Lodge: Sertoma (v.p. membership Thomaston club 1979). Avocations: swimming, softball, bowling, gardening. Home: 2322 Sesame St Mogadore OH 44260 Office: BF Goodrich 500 S Main St Akron OH 44318

FISHER, GARY WAYNE, optometrist; b. Monticello, Iowa, Sept. 21, 1951; s. Gerald Max Mildred Louise (Lucas) F.; m. Marcia Diane Oltrogge, Aug. 16, 1975; children: Nichole, Cory. BS, Upper Iowa U., 1972; OD, Ill. Coll. Optometry, 1976. Practice optometry Monticello, 1976—; lectr. U. Osteo. Medicine, Des Moines, 1983—; mem. staff John McDonald Hosp., Monticello, 1978—. Contbr. articles to optometry jours. Bd. dirs. Ambulance Bd., Monticello, 1980-85; fin. chmn. for Congressman Tom Tauke, Jones County, 1986; mem. ch. choir, Jones County, 1978—. Named One of Outstanding Young Men of Am. Fellow Am. Coll. Optometric Physicians; mem. Am. Optometric Assn., Iowa Optometric Assn. (trustee), Monticello Jaycees. Republican. Methodist. Lodge: Rotary (pres. Monticello club 1984). Avocations: collecting automobiles, skiing, triathlons. Home and Office: PO Box 228 Monticello IA 52310

FISHER, GENE LAWRENCE, financial executive; b. Chillicothe, Ill., Nov. 15, 1929; s. Lawrence Hubert and Alyce Anne (Neigemeyer) F.; m. Sandra Kay Burns, Sept. 19, 1959; children—Kyle Butler, Kelley Anne. B.S., U. Ill., 1957. Staff acct. Inland Container Corp., Indpls., 1957-63, mgr. corp. acctg., 1964-65, asst. corp. controller, 1966-78, dir. fin. systems, 1979—. Chmn. fin. com.-exec. com. Winona Meml. Hosp., Indpls., 1979-81, chmn. bd. dirs., 1982-83. Served wtih U.S. Army, 1951-53. Mem. Beta Alpha Psi, Sigma Iota Epsilon. Republican. Avocations: fishing, swimming. Home: 5427 Washington Blvd Indianapolis IN 46220 Office: Inland Container Corp 151 N Delaware St Indianapolis IN 46206

FISHER, JOHN EDWIN, insurance company executive; b. Portsmouth, Ohio, Oct. 26, 1929; s. Charles Hall and Bess (Swearingin) F.; m. Eloise Lyon, Apr. 25, 1949. Student, U. Colo., 1947-48, Ohio U., 1948-49, Franklin U., Columbus, Ohio, 1950-51. With Nationwide Mut. Ins. Co., Columbus, 1951—, v.p., office gen. chmn., 1970-72, pres., gen. mgr., dir., 1972-81, gen. chmn., chief exec. officer, 1981—, also dir.; gen. chmn., chief exec. officer, dir. Nationwide Gen. Ins. Co., Nationwide Mut. Fire Ins. Co., Nationwide Property & Casualty Ins. Co., Nationwide Life Ins. Co., Nationwide Variable Life Ins. Co.; dir. Neckura Versicherungs A.G., Oberursel, Germany, 1976—; gen. chmn., dir. Employers Ins. of Wausau, 1985—, Farmland Ins. Cos., 1985—; trustee Ohio Cener Co. Chmn. bd. Nationwide Found., 1981—; pres. bd. trustees Children's Hosp., 1984-87. Mem. Chartered Property and Casualty Underwriters Assn., Chartered Life Underwriters Soc., Assn. Ohio Life Ins. Cos. (past pres.), Ohio Ins. Inst. (pres. 1975-77), Nat. Assn. Ind. Insurers, Am. Risk and Ins. Assn., Griffith Ins. Found. (chmn. 1981), Property-Casualty Ins. Council (chmn. 1981-82), Property and Liability Underwriters, Ins. Inst. Am., Am. Inst. Property-Liability Insurers (chmn. 1985—), Am. Inst. Property and Liability Underwriters, Ins. Inst. Am., Internat. Coop. Ins. Fedn. (chmn. 1984—), Columbus C. of C. (chmn. 1981-82). Office: Nationwide Mutual Ins Co One Nationwide Plaza Columbus OH 43216

FISHER, MARJORIE HELEN, librarian; b. Losantville, Ind., Nov. 27, 1924; d. James Cleo and Isie May (Sutton) Hardwick; student Olivet Nazarene Coll., 1943-45; A.B., Ball State U., 1947; postgrad Ariz. State Tchrs. Coll., 1949, Ind. U., 1955, Ind. State U., 1957, Butler U., 1958; m. Delmar Fisher, Sept. 29, 1950; children—Deljon Ray, Madge Denise Fisher Gaines. Tchr., Superior (Ariz.) Elem. Schs., 1947-48, Yuma (Ariz.) schs., 1949-51; tchr. English, librarian Hamlet (Ind.) High Sch., 1952-56; dir. library services Plymouth (Ind.) Community Sch. Corp., 1957—; organizer Divine Heart Sem. Library, Donaldson, Ind., 1960. Mem. AAUW (sec. Plymouth br. 1979-80), NEA, Ind. State Tchrs. Assn., Assn. Ind. Media Educators. Co-author computer software program; contbr. articles to profl. jours. Home: 917 N Walnut St Plymouth IN 46563 Office: 810 N Randolph Plymouth IN 46563

FISHER, MICHEAL DUANE, data processing executive; b. Ft. Wayne, Ind., Dec. 9, 1952; m. Mary Jo Emerson, Aug. 26, 1978; 1 child, Christopher. Cert. systems profl. (CSP); cert. info. systems auditor (CISA). Programmer trainee Midwestern United Life, Ft. Wayne, 1970-71; computer operator Peoples Trust Bank, 1971-72; ops. support mem. Essex Internat., 1972-74; supr. systems devel. Ft. Wayne Schs., 1974-82; mgr. computer audit assistance group Coopers & Lybrand, Ft. Wayne, 1982—; mem. IV Tech. Programming Curriculum Adv. Com., 1982-86. Mem. Ft. Wayne Schs. Bus. Curriculum Adv. Com., 1982-84, Pleasant Twp. Adv. Com., 1979; pres. Branning Hills Community Assn., 1982, Pheasant Run Community Assn., 1978. Mem. Assn. Systems Mgmt. (pres. 1984-85, div. dir. 1987—), EDP Auditors Assn. Avocations: golfing, sailing, skiing, reading. Home: 2238 Rosita Ct Fort Wayne IN 46815 Office: Coopers & Lybrand 490 Lincoln Bank Tower Fort Wayne IN 46802

FISHER, NEAL SAMUEL, accountant; b. Chgo., Aug. 5, 1948; s. Herman and Marian Rose (Feldstein) F.; m. Diane Paula Dick, Aug. 8, 1971; children: Macre, Scott. BS in Acctg., DePaul U., 1970, MS in Taxation, 1974. CPA, Ill. Tax acct. Price Waterhouse, Chgo., 1971-72; tax ptnr. Wolf and Co., Chgo., 1972-79; v.p. fin. services Lloyd, Thomas, Coats and Burchard, Niles, Ill., 1979-85; tax ptnr. Miller, Cooper & Co., Skokie, Ill., 1985—. Mem. Am. Inst. CPA's (hon. mention 1970), Ill. CPA Soc. (Silver medal 1970), Am. Soc. Appraisers, N.W. Suburban Jewish Community Ctr. (sec. 1986—, bd. dirs. 1985—). Jewish. Avocations: tennis, golf, reading. Home: 960 Providence Ct Buffalo Grove IL 60089 Office: Miller Cooper & Co 9440 N Kenton Skokie IL 60076

FISHER, PHILIP ALAN, advertising executive; b. Shelbyville, Ind., Apr. 14, 1946; s. E. Emerson and Helen Anna (Scholer) F. BS, Purdue U., Indpls., 1969; postgrad., U. Wis., Milw., 1972-74; MA, Wayne State U., 1976. Research analyst R.L. Polk Co., Taylor, Mich., 1979-80; advt. mgr. Harnischfeger Corp., Milw., 1980—. Author: Milwaukee's East Side, 1986. Mem. Am. Mktg. Assn., Chgo. Assn. Direct Mktg. Democrat. Home: 1934 N Oakland Ave Milwaukee WI 53202 Office: Harnischfeger Corp 13400 Bishops Ln Brookfield WI 53005

FISHER, ROBERT WARREN, accountant; b. Springfield, Ohio, Sept. 17, 1952; s. Carl Arthur and Frances (Runyan) F.; m. Elizabeth Ann Davies, Dec. 11, 1982; 1 child, Katherine Marie. BA, Wittenberg U., 1974; MBA, U. Toledo, 1975. CPA; registered investment advisor. Mgr., acct. Price Waterhouse, Battle Creek, Mich., 1975-83, Deloitte, Haskins & Sells, Appleton, Wis., 1983-84; ptnr., acct. Wojahn & Fisher, S.C., Appleton, 1984-85, Schumaker, Romenesko & Assocs., Appleton, 1985—; treas. Wis. Bus. Devel. Fin. Corp., Madison, 1983—. Mem. fin. com. St. Mary's Ch., 1986—, Appleton Cath. Edn. System, 1986—. Mem. Nat. Assn. Accts. (v.p. 1982), Am. Inst. CPA's, Wis. Inst. CPA's, Appleton C. of C. (small bus. com. 1984—). Club: Riverview Country. Lodges: KC, Rotary (membership dir. 1986). Home: 1621 Homestead Dr Appleton WI 54914 Office: Schumaker, Romenesko & Assoc S C 555 N Lynndale Dr Box 2459 Appleton WI 54913

FISHER-MCPEAK, JANET, language educator; b. Midland, Mich., Sept. 17, 1953; d. Arthur J. and Bettie L. (Graves) Fisher; m. John David McPeak, Sept. 5, 1976. M.A. in French, Middlebury Coll., 1976, M.A. in German, 1979, postgrad., 1987—. Instr. French, German, Delta Coll., University Center, Mich., 1977—; instr. German, Saginaw Valley State Coll., University Center, 1981—; asst. dir. Internat. Lang. Sch., Midland, Mich., 1983-85; tech. German cons. Brown & Wilson Machine Co. Author: En Garde! Street Survival in France. Mem. Am. Assn. Tchrs. German. German Cultural Service grantee, 1983, 84. Office: Delta Coll Dept Romance Languages University Center MI 48710

FISHMAN, MADELINE DOTTI, management consulting company executive, consultant; b. Chgo., Oct. 7, 1942; d. Martin and Anne (Sweet) Binder; m. Norton Lee Fishman, Apr. 7, 1963; children: Mark Nathan, Marla Susan. BEd, Nat. Coll. Edn., 1964, MS, 1972. Tchr., Rochester Schs. (Minn.), 1963-64, Orange County Schs., Orlando, Fla., 1967-68; reading cons. Palatine Schs. (Ill.), 1972-73; instr. Parent Effective Tng., Wilmette, Ill., 1974-76, tchr. Effectiveness Tng., 1974-76; pres. Profls. Diversified, Wilmette, Ill., 1976—; remedial and enrichment reading tchr. Waukegan (Ill.) Pub. Schs., 1986—; mgmt. cons. World Wide Diamonds Assn., Schaumburg, Ill., 1979—, Artistic Color, Dallas, 1983—; Pearl direct distbr. Amway Corp., Ada, Mich., 1976—. Author: Organic Gardening, 1975, The Go-Getters Planner, 1986. Leader, Camp Fire Girls, Evanston, Ill., 1963, 75. Recipient Ednl. Scholarship, Nat. Coll. Edn., 1971. Mem. Kappa Delta Pi. Republican. Jewish.

FISHMAN, MARK ALAN, foodservice equipment distributing company executive; b. Cleve., Feb. 15, 1954; s. Howard H. and Pearl A. (Schwartz) F.; m. Terri Ann Oster, Aug. 16, 1986. BA, U. Rochester, 1976; MBA, Ohio State U., 1978. CPA, Ohio. Acct. Price Waterhouse & Co., Columbus, Ohio, 1978-79; sec.-treas. S.S. Kemp & Co., Cleve., 1979—; pres. Supply Purchasing Corp., Chgo., 1986—. Mem. Am. Inst. CPA's, Ohio Soc. CPA's, Internat. Foodservice Equipment Distbrs., Inc. Avocations: scuba diving, boating, fishing, camping, skiing. Office: SS Kemp & Co 4301 Perkins Ave Cleveland OH 44103

FISHMAN, STAN DAVID, packaging company executive; b. Ft. Wayne, July 8, 1951; s. Stan H. and Mary A. (Houlihan) F.; m. Elizabeth Ann White, Apr. 2, 1977; children: Jamie Rose, Jeffrey Joseph. BBA, Bucknell U., 1973. Purchasing agt. Federated, Los Angeles, 1973-75; v.p. mktg. Van Laws, Decatur, Ill., 1975-77; pres. Fishmans, Ft. Wayne, Ind., 1978-83, Webco Packaging, Inc., Ft. Wayne, Ind., 1984—. Republican. Clubs: Ft. Wayne Country, Summit Bus. Lodge: Rotary (fellow, com. chmn. 1986). Avocation: golf. Office: Webco Packaging Inc 5812 Covington Rd Fort Wayne IN 46804

FITCHETT, VERNON HAROLD, physician, surgeon, educator; b. Grover, Colo., May 14, 1927; s. Harold Leroy and Mazie (Bengston) F.; m. Kathryn Hellen Mullin, Aug. 3, 1963; children—Michael, Elizabeth, Benjamin. B.S., Buena Vista Coll., 1949; M.D., U. Iowa, 1953. Diplomate Am. Bd. Surgery. Commd. officer U.S. Navy, 1956, advanced through grades to capt., intern U.S. Naval Hosp., Bremerton, Wash., 1953-54; resident VA Hosp., Portland, Oreg., 1955-56, U.S. Naval Hosp., St. Albans, N.Y., 1956-59; med. officer-in-charge USPHS, DaNang, Vietnam, 1964-65; chief surgery U.S. Navy, DaNang, 1968-69; chmn. dept. surgery Naval Hosp., Oakland, Calif., 1970-76; ret., 1976; mem. staff Jamestown Hosp., N.D., 1976—; asst. clin. prof. surgery N.D. Med. Sch., 1982-87, clin. assoc. prof. surgery, 1987—; chmn. bd. Jamestown Clinic, 1979-85; surg. cons. State Hosp., Jamestown, Ann Carlson Sch., 1976—. Author: War Surgery, 1971. Contbr. articles to profl. jours. Mem. exec. com. N.D. chpt. Am. Cancer Soc., 1979-84. Decorated Legion of Merit with Combat V. Fellow ACS (past pres N.D. chpt.); mem. AMA, Pan Pacific Surg. Soc., Assn. Mil. Surgeons. Roman Catholic. Lodges: Eagles, Elks, K.C. Office: Dakota Clinic-Jamestown Box 1980 Jamestown ND 58402

FITES, DONALD VESTER, tractor company executive; b. Tippecanoe, Ind., Jan. 20, 1934; s. Rex E. and Mary Irene (Sackville) F.; m. Sylvia Dempsey, June 25, 1960; children: Linda Marie. B.S. in Civil Engring., Valparaiso U., 1956; M.S., M.I.T, 1971. With Caterpillar Overseas S.A., Peoria, Ill., 1956-66; dir. internat. customer div. Caterpillar Overseas S.A., Geneva, 1966-67; asst. mgr. market devel. Caterpillar Tractor Co., Peoria, 1967-70; dir. Caterpillar Mitsubishi Ltd., Tokyo, 1971-75; dir. engine capacity expansion program Caterpillar Tractor Co., Peoria, 1975-76, mgr. products control dept., 1976-79; pres. Caterpillar Brasil S.A., 1979-81; v.p. products Caterpillar Tractor Co., Peoria, 1981-85, exec. v.p., 1985—, also bd. dirs.; bd. dirs. Farm and Indsl. Equipment Inst., First Nat. Bank of Peoria. Trustee Farm Found., 1985—, Meth. Med. Ctr., 1985—, Knox Coll., 1986—; mem. adv. bd. Salvation Army, 1985—, admintrv. bd. First United Meth. Ch., 1986—. Mem. Agrl. Roundtable (chmn. 1985-87), SAE. Republican. Clubs: Mt. Hawley Country, Creve Coeur. Home: 7614 N Edgewild Dr Peoria IL 61614 Office: Caterpillar Inc 100 NE Adams St Peoria IL 61629

FITT, MICHAEL GEORGE, reinsurance company executive; b. Whitstable, Kent, Eng., May 16, 1931; came to U.S., 1976; s. Walter H. and Dorothy A. (Young) F.; m. Doreen Elizabeth Leitch, Oct. 1, 1955; children: Colin, Anne, Ian. Student, Brit. schs. Jr. clk. Can. Underwriters Assn., 1953; with Royal Exchange Assurance Ltd., 1953-69; br. mgr. Royal Exchange Assurance Ltd., Montreal, Que., Can.; with Employers Reins. Corp., 1969—; exec. v.p. Employers Reins. Corp., Overland Park, Kans., 1977-79; vice chmn. bd. Employers Reins. Corp., 1979-81, chmn. bd., 1981—, also dir., pres., chief exec. officer, 1983—; chmn. bd. dirs. First Excess and Reins. Corp., Overland Park, Bates Turner, Inc., Employers Reins. Ltd., London; bd. dirs. Boatmen's First Nat. Bank Kansas City, Mo., Boatmen's Bancshares, St. Louis, Gen. Electric Credit Corp., Stamford, Conn., Gen. Electric Fin. Services, Inc., Stamford, Kansas City So. Industries, Inc. Served with Brit. Navy, 1948-53. Fellow Ins. Inst. Can. Episcopalian. Clubs: Kansas City, Mission Hills Country.

FITZGERALD, JAMES FRANCIS, cable TV executive; b. Janesville, Wis., Mar. 27, 1926; s. Michael Henry and Chloris Helen (Beiter) F.; m. Marilyn Field Cullen, Aug. 1, 1950; children: Michael Dennis, Brian Nicholas, Marcia O'Loughlin, James Francis, Carolyn Jane, Ellen Putnam. B.S., Notre Dame U., 1947. With Standard Oil Co. (Ind.), Milw., 1947-48; pres. F.-W. Oil Co., Janesville, 1950—, Total TV, Inc. (cable TV Systems), Wis., 1965—; bd dirs. Milw. Ins. Co. and Vintage Club; Marine First Nat. Bank; chmn. bd. Golden State Warriors-Oakland, Calif., 1986—. Bd. govs., chmn. TV com. NBA; chmn. Greater Milw. Open (PGA Tournament), 1985. Served to lt. (j.g.) USNR, 1944-45, 51-52. Mem. Chief Execs. Forum, World Bus. Council, Wis. Petroleum Assn. (pres. 1961-62). Roman Catholic. Clubs: Janesville Country, Castle Pines Golf, Milw. Athletic; Vintage (Indian Wells, Calif.). Home: PO Box 348 Janesville WI 53547 Office: PO Box 348 Janesville WI 53547

FITZGERALD, JOY BEVERLY, business executive, lawyer; b. Zearing, Iowa, Apr. 22, 1917; d. Seymour Robert and Jennie Blanche (Stevens) Hix;

m. Craig William Fitzgerald, June 17, 1963. B.A., Morningside Coll., Sioux City, 1938; J.D., Drake U., 1941. Bar: Iowa 1941. Atty. Hers, Nevada, Iowa, 1941-44; spl. agent U.S. Dept. Agr., Chgo., 1944-49; interviewer Iowa Employment Security Commn., Amex, 1950-54, mgr., 1954-58; exec. sec. Iowa State Reciprocity Bd., Des Moines, 1958-71; pres. Joy B. Fitzgerald, Inc., Altoona, Iowa, 1971—; pres. Joy B. Fitzgerald Resident Agts., Inc., Altoona, 1983—; broadcaster Sta. WMAQ, Chgo., 1975—, Sta. WHO, Des Moines, 1987— . Mem. motor carrier adv. com. U.S. Dept. Transp., 1982—. Name Iowa Lawyer Advocate of Yr. SBA, 1983. Mem. ABA, Ind. Trucker's Assn. (sec. Iowa div. 1975, nat. sec. 1972—). Democrat. Author: Overdrive Magazine, 1971—. Home: Rural Route Collins IA 50055

FITZGERALD, MICHAEL LEE, state official; b. Marshalltown, Iowa, Nov. 29, 1951; s. James Martin and Clara Francis (Dankbar) F.; m. Sharon Lynn Wildman, Dec. 15, 1979; children: Ryan William, Erin Elizabeth. B.B.A., U. Iowa, 1974. Campaign mgr. Fitzgerald for Treas., Colo., Iowa, 1974; market analyst Massey Ferguson, Inc., Des Moines, 1975-83; treas. State of Iowa, Des Moines, 1983—. Democrat. Roman Catholic. Home: 211 SW Caulder St Des Moines IA 50315 Office: Treasurer of State State Capitol Des Moines IA 50319 *

FITZGERALD, ROBERT DRAKE, financial executive; b. Milw., Dec. 12, 1932; s. Robert Drake Fitzgerald and Virginia (Barker) Ilsley; m. Patricia Louise O'Riley, May 25, 1962; children: Virginia Louise, Robert Ilsley. AB, Brown U., 1955; MBA, U. Chgo., 1960. V.p., div. adminstr. Harris Trust & Savs. Bank, Chgo., 1955-80; corp. treas. Fiat Allis N.Am., Inc., Deerfield, Ill., 1980-84; pres., treas. Drake Meadow Corp., Lake Forest, Ill., 1981—, also bd. dirs. Active Chgo. Crime Commn., 1972—. Mem. Bus. Evaluation Assn. Republican. Presbyterian. Clubs: Chgo., Economic (Chgo.). Office: PO Box 726 Lake Forest IL 60045

FITZGERALD, ROBERT HANNON, JR., orthopedic surgeon; b. Denver, Aug. 25, 1942; s. Robert Hannon and Alyene (Webber) Fitzgerald Anderson; m. Lynda Lee Lang, Apr. 27, 1968 (div. 1984); children—Robert III, Shannon, Dennis, Katherine, Kelly; m. Jamie Kathleen Dent, Mar. 9, 1985; children—Brian, Steven. B.S., U. Notre Dame, 1963; M.D., U. Kans., 1967; M.S., U. Minn., 1974. Instr. orthopedic surgery Mayo Med. Sch., Rochester, Minn., 1974-77, cons. orthopedic surgery, 1974—, assoc. prof., 1982-86 , prof., 1986—; cons. Ctr. Disease Control, Atlanta, 1981—, NIH, 1987—, chief adult reconstructive surgery, 1987—. Assoc. editor Jour. Orthopedic and Traumatology, 1978—, Jour. Bone Joint Surgery, 1982—. Mem. bd. edn. St. John's Grade Sch./Jr. High Sch., Rochester, 1983—; mem. Bd. Devel. Mayo Clinic, 1984—; trustee Lourdes High Sch. Devel. Bd., Rochester, 1982—. Served to capt. USAF, 1968-70. Decorated Air Commendation medal; recipient Kappa Delta award for musculoskeletal research, 1983. Fellow Am. Acad. Orthopedic Surgeons; mem. Orthopedic Research Soc., AMA, Zumbro County Med. Soc., Min-Da-Man Orthopedic Soc., Minn. Orthopedic Soc., Am. Soc. Microbiology, N.Y. Acad. Scis., Hip Soc. (Stinchfield award 1985, Charnley award 1986), Am. Orthopeduic Assn., Surg. Infection Soc., Clin. Orthopaedic Soc., Internat. Soc. Orthopaedic spl. Surgery and Traumatology, Sigma Xi, Kappa Delta, Alpha Epsilon Delta. Republican. Roman Catholic. Avocations: cross-country and downhill skiing; swimming; coaching children's sports. Home: 706 4th St SW Rochester MN 55902 Office: Mayo Clinic 200 1st St SW Rochester MN 55905

FITZGERALD, ROBERT JAMES, civil engineer; b. Massillon, Ohio, Apr. 25, 1922; s. James Dennis and Mayne Ann (McGovern) F.; m. June B. Gilbert, Sept. 13, 1952; children: James, Michael, Dennis, Sue. BSCE, U. Detroit, 1953; MBA, Case Western Res. U., 1978. Registered profl. engr., Ohio, Mich; registered surveyor, Ohio; cert. property mgr. Construction engr. Fed. Govt., Chgo., 1954-60; chief construction engr. Cuyahoga Met. Housing, Cleve., 1960-71, dir., 1971-83; v.p. Lake Mgmt. Co., Cleve., 1983-85; project mgr. Snavely-Burks Project Mgrs., Cleve., 1985—. Bd. Dirs. Catholic Charities Conf., Cleve., 1980—; chmn. civil div. United Way Cleve. Mem. Profl. Engrs. Soc. (Profl. Engr. of Yr., 1972), Inst. Real Estate Mgmt. (pres. Cleve. 1980—, Nat. Acad. Authors, 1972, Property Mgr. of Yr. 1982), Am. Congress on Surveying, Northeast Ohio Apartment and Home Owners Assn. (Property Mgr. of Yr., 1980). Roman Catholic. Lodge: Lions (pres. Northfield, Ohio, 1971-73). Avocations: carving and painting wood duck decoys. Home: 9175 Cherokee Run Macedonia OH 44056 Office: Snavely-Burks Project Mgrs E 107th and Euclid Ave Cleveland OH 44106

FITZGERALD, THOMAS JOE, psychologist; b. Wichita, Kans., July 8, 1941; s. Thomas Michael and Pauline Gladys (Zink) F.; B.A., San Francisco State U., 1965; M.A., U. Utah, 1969, Ph.D., 1971. Dir. behavioral services programs VA Hosp., Topeka, 1971-73; pvt. practice as psychologist, Topeka, 1973-74, Prairie Village, Kans., 1974—; clin. instr. Menninger Sch. Psychiatry, Topeka, 1972-74; v.p. Preferred Mental Health Care, Inc., 1986—; sec.-treas. Kans. Bd. Psychologist Examiners, 1976-79, 79-80, chmn., 1980—, chmn. psychology examining com.; mem. Behavioral Scis. Regulatory Bd., 1980-82; pres. Psychol. Services Corp., Prairie Village, 1974—. Mem. Gov.'s Commn. on Criminal Adminstrn., 1974-76; vice-chmn. Gov.'s Com. on Med. Assistance, 1978-80; mem. Mid-Am. Health Systems Agy., 1979-82. Served with USMCR, 1958-60. Mem. Kans. Psychol. Assn. (pres. 1980-81), Kans. Assn. Profl. Psychologists (pres. 1981-82, Outstanding Psychologist award 1979, 80, 81, 82), Greater Kansas City Soc. Clin. Hypnosis (pres. 1978—). Office: 2108 W 75th St Suite 400 Prairie Village KS 66208

FITZGERALD, TIMOTHY RICHARD, accounting company executive; b. St. Louis, Aug. 24, 1956; s. Timothy G. and Suzanne M. (Frederick) FitzG. BS, St. Louis U., 1976. CPA, Ill. Sr. mgr. Peat Marwick & Co., Decatur, Ill., 1977-83; ptnr. FitzGerald & FitzGerald, St. Louis, 1983—. Basketball coach St. Clare Athletic Assn., St. Louis, 1983—. Mem. Am. Inst. CPA's, Mo. Soc. CPA's. Roman Catholic. Avocation: basketball. Home: 143 B Log Trail Dr Ballwin MO 63011 Office: FitzGerald & FitzGerald 152 Clarkson Executive Park Ellisville MO 63011

FITZGERALD, WILLIAM ALLINGHAM, savings and loan association executive; b. Omaha, Nov. 18, 1937; s. William Frances and Mary (Allingham) F.; m. Barbara Ann Miskell, Aug. 20, 1960; children—Mary Colleen, Katherine Kara, William Tate. B.S.B.A. in Fin., Creighton U., 1959; grad. Savs. and Loan League exec. tng. program U. Ga., 1962, U. Ind., 1969. With Comml. Fed. Savs. & Loan Assn., Omaha, 1959—, v.p., asst. sec., 1963-68, exec. v.p., 1968-73, pres., 1974—; bd. dirs. Fed. Home Loan Bank Topeka; Trustee Ind. Coll. Found.; vice chmn. bd. dirs. Creighton U.; bd. dirs. Coll. of St. Mary, United Way of Midlands; trustee Archbishop's com. for ednl. devel. Roman Catholic Ch. Served to lt. Fin. Corps, U.S. Army. Clubs: Omaha Country, Kiewit Plaza. Lodge: Knights of Ak-Sar-Ben (gov.). Office: Comml Fed Savs & Loan Assn PO Box 1103 DTS Omaha NE 68101

FITZGERALD, WILLIAM FRANCIS, savings and loan association executive; b. Omaha, Jan. 20, 1908; s. James J. and Katherine (O'Rourke) F.; m. Mary Allingham, Sept. 29, 1934; children: Mary Frances (Mrs. J. Emmet Root), William A., Katherine A. (Mrs. A. R. Grandsaert, Jr.). Student, Creighton U., 1926-27, LL.D. (hon.), 1979; B.S. in Mech. Engring., Iowa State Coll., 1931. With Comml. Fed. Savs. & Loan Assn., Omaha, 1932—; sec. Comml. Fed. Savs. & Loan Assn., 1942-50, pres., 1950—, chmn. bd., 1975—, also dir.; dir. Wynn Co., Hannon Co.; vice chmn., dir. Fed. Home Loan Bank, Topeka, 1960-64; Mem. Fed. Savs. and Loan Adv. Council, Washington, 1962-63. Chmn. Creighton U. Alumni Fund drive, 1960-61; Bd. dirs. United Community Fund, Omaha, 1958-61; bd. regents Creighton U., 1961-68; mem. pres.'s research council, 1967-72. Mem. U.S. Savs. and Loan League (dir. 1955-57), Omaha C. of C. (dir. 1958-61), Beta Gamma Sigma (hon.). Clubs: Omaha Country, Omaha, Plaza (Omaha); Ak-Sar-Ben (king 1976-77). Lodge: Kiwanis (charter, bd. dirs., past pres. South Omaha). Home: 685 N 57th St Omaha NE 68132 Office: Comml Fed Savs and Loan Assn 4501 Dodge St Omaha NE 68101

FITZGIBBON, DANIEL HARVEY, lawyer; b. Columbus, Ind., July 7, 1942; s. Joseph Bales and Margaret Lenore (Harvey) FitzG.; m. Joan Helen Meltzer, Aug. 12, 1973; children: Katherine Lenore, Thomas Bernard. BS in Engring., U.S. Mil. Acad., 1964; JD cum laude, Harvard U., 1972. Bar: Ind. 1972; U.S. Dist. Ct. (so. dist.) Ind. 1972, U.S. Tax Ct. 1977. Commd. 2d lt. U.S. Army, 1964, advanced through grades to capt., 1967; served with inf. U.S. Army, West Berlin, Vietnam; resigned U.S. Army, 1969; assoc. Barnes & Thornburg, Indpls., 1972-79, ptnr., 1979—; adminstr. tax and estate depts., 1981—, Barnes and Thornburg, mgmt. com., 1983—, compensation com., 1984-87, exec. com. 1987—; chmn. legal personnel com., 1983-85, exec. com. 1987—; mgmt. com. Barnes and Thornburg Bldg. Co., 1981-84; speaker various insts. Served to capt. U.S. Army, 1964-69, Vietnam. Mem. ABA (tax, corp. bus. and bank law sects.), Ind. State Bar Assn. (chmn. scholarship com. of tax sect. 1983—), Indpls. Bar Assn. (chmn. tax sect. 1982-83, council 1982—). Clubs: Indpls. Athletic, Woodstock. Home: 5833 Eastview Ct Indianapolis IN 46250 Office: Barnes & Thornburg 11 S Meridian St Indianapolis IN 46204

FITZGIBBONS, JAMES JOSEPH, biomedical engineer; b. Chgo., Nov. 26, 1958; s. James Patrick and Rita Ann (Fisher) F. BS in Biology, Tulane U., 1980; postgrad., U. Ill., Chgo., 1981—. Asst. foreman Safeway Steel Co., Chgo., 1978-79; freelance actor, model Shirley Hamilton, Inc., Chgo., 1981—; real estate salesperson Orrington Realty, Evanston, Ill., 1985—; pres. La Bonne Vie Enterprises, Inc. (doing bus. as Fantastik Sam's), Morton Grove, Ill., 1985—; biomed. engr. eye and ear infirmary U. Ill., Chgo., 1983—. Co-adminstr. Marty F. Leoni scholarship fund, Evanston, 1985—. Roman Catholic. Club: Hash House Harriers. Avocations: athletics, electronics. Office: La Bonne Vie Enterprises Inc 6753 W Dempster St Morton Grove IL 60053

FITZHARRIS, JOSEPH CHARLES, history educator; b. Mpls., Oct. 12, 1946; s. Maurice E. and Gertrude I. (McBride) F.; m. Mary Helen Schreiner, Aug. 30, 1969; children—Scott J., Keith R. B.A., Coll. St. Thomas, 1968; M.A., U. Minn., 1969; Ph.D., U. Wis., 1975. Instr. history Coll. St. Thomas, St. Paul, part-time 1971-72, full-time 1972-75, asst. prof., 1975-81, assoc. prof., 1981—, acting chmn. history dept., 1982; research fellow in agrl. and applied econs. U. Minn., part-time 1972-75, research assoc., 1975-79, part-time 1979-80; project evaluator Minn. Humanities Com., 1979-80; reader advance placement Ednl. Testing Service; cons. Ramsey County Hist. Soc.; bd. dirs. St. Thomas Coll. Fed. Credit Union. Mem. Mpls. Aquatennial Parades Com., 1972—; mem. coordinating com. St. Paul Campus Ministry, 1975-77, vice chmn., 1977; vol scouter Indianhead council Boy Scouts Am., 1984. Recipient Certs. Appreciation, Coll. St. Thomas, 1977, 81, medallion, 1982, grantee, 1982; Ford Found. fellow, 1970-71; grantee Rockefeller Found., 1972-75, U. Minn. Agrl. Expt. Sta., 1975-79; recipient Tng. Award medal Boy Scouts Am., 1987. Mem. Orgn. Am. Historians, Econ. History Assn., Am. Econ. Assn. Roman Catholic. Contbr. articles to profl. jours. Home: 13645 Elkwood Dr Apple Valley MN 55124 Office: 434 O'Shaughnessy Edn Ctr Coll St Thomas 2115 Summit Ave Saint Paul MN 55105

FITZPATRICK, CHRISTINE MORRIS, former television executive; b. Steubenville, Ohio, June 10, 1920; d. Roy Elwood and Ruby Lorena (Mason) Morris; student U. Chgo., 1943-44, U. Ga., 1945-46; B.A., Roosevelt U., 1947; postgrad. Trinity Coll., Hartford, Conn., 1970; m. T. Mallary Fitzpatrick, Jr., Dec. 19, 1942; 1 son, Thomas Mallary III. Asso. dir. Joint Human Relations Project, City of Chgo., 1965-66; tchr. English, Austin Sch. for Girls, Hartford, 1966-70; promotion coordinator Conn. Pub. TV, Hartford, 1971-72, dir. community relations, 1972-73, v.p., 1973-77; pub. relations/pub. affairs cons. Commonwealth Edison Co., Chgo., 1977-79; dir. spl. events Chgo. Public TV, 1979-84; v.p. Fitzpatrick Group, Inc., Chgo., 1986—; v.p. Pub. Relations Clinic Chgo., 1980-81. Bd. advisers Greater Hartford Mag., 1975-77; bd. dirs. World Affairs Ctr., Hartford, 1975-77; mem. adv. council Am. Revolution Bicentennial Commn. Conn., 1975-77. Mem. Pub. Relations Soc. Am. (dir. Conn. Valley chpt. 1976-77), Am. Women in Radio and TV (New Eng. chpt. pres. 1976-77), Chgo. Council Fgn. Relations, LWV (Chgo. chpt. pres. 1962-64, Hartford chpt. 1971-73), Chgo. Architecture Found. Mem. United Ch. Christ. Home: 5462 S Cornell Ave Chicago IL 60615

FITZPATRICK, SEAN KEVIN, advertising agency executive, motion picture developer; b. Atlanta, Sept. 28, 1941; s. J.J. and Roxane (Athanassiades) F.; m. Sue Ellen House; children—Seamus McGee, Elizabeth Christina, Samantha Louise. A.B., Hamilton Coll., 1964. Reporter Bloomington (Ind.) Daily Herald, 1963, Hearst Newspaper, Albany, N.Y., 1964; v.p., exec. creative dir. J. Walter Thompson Co., N.Y.C., Toronto and Los Angeles, 1965-75; v.p. creative dir. Bing Crosby Prodns., Hollywood, Calif., 1976-77; creative dir. Columbia Pictures, Burbank, Calif., 1977-78; sr. v.p. creative dir. Dancer Fitzgerald Sample, Torrance, Calif., 1978-83; exec. v.p. creative dir. Campbell-Ewald Co., Warren, Mich., 1983—. Developer movies Final Chpt. Walking Tall, 1976, Mean Dog Blues, 1976, The Great Santini, 1976-77; producer for TV Buford Pusser, Tennessee Sheriff, 1976. Recipient Healy award Interpub., Effies, grand prizes Internat. Film and TV Festival N.Y., Clio awards, numerous other advt. awards. Mem. Motion Picture Acad. Arts and Scis., ASCAP, Detroit Adcraft, Delta Kappa Epsilon. Clubs: Orchard Lake Country (Mich.); Yale (N.Y.C.).

FITZSIMMONS, KEITH ROBERTS, accounting administrator; b. Washington, May 28, 1952; s. Willard Allen and Nancy Elizabeth (Greenwood) F.; m. Pamela Sue Kneisley, Jan. 26, 1971 (div. May 1985); 1 child, Erin Lynzee; m. Laura Jean Maros-Varney, May 24, 1986. AA, U. Md., Heidelburg, Fed. Republic Germany, 1977; student, U. Tex., El Paso, 1977-78; BS, Kans. State U., 1984; postgrad., U. Kans., 1987. Enlisted U.S. Army, 1971, advanced through ranks to sgt., resigned, 1981; asst. acct. Kans. Farm Bur., Manhattan, 1981-84; tax acct. Arthur Young & Co., Kansas City, 1984-86; dir. student acctg. U. Kans. Med. Ctr., Kansas City, Kans., 1986—. Mem. Phi Kappa Phi. Republican. Methodist. Avocation: outdoor sports. Home: 11802 Oakmont Overland Park KS 66210 Office: U Kans Med Ctr-Student Acctg 39th & Rainbow Kansas City KS 66103

FITZSIMONS, GEORGE K., bishop; b. Kansas City, Mo., Sept. 4, 1928. Student, Rockhurst Coll., Immaculate Conception Sem. Ordained prist, Roman Cath. Ch., 1961. Bishop Salina, Kans., 1984—. Address: PO Box 980 Salina KS 67402 *

FIVECOAT, MARTHA HODGE, systems analyst; b. Kansas City, Mo., Aug. 11, 1944; d. Campbell and Harriet (Woodbury) Hodge; m. Gary L. Fivecoat, Aug. 5, 1967; children: David Gary, Jeffrey Campbell. BA, Ohio Wesleyan U., 1966. Programmer Chemical Abstracts Service, Columbus, 1966-68; tchr. Delaware (Ohio) City Schs., 1971-80; programmer, analyst Ohio Wesleyan U., Delaware, 1968-71, 80-84; systems analyst OCLC, Inc., Dublin, Ohio, 1984-87, sect. mgr., 1987—. Den leader Cen. Ohio Council Boy Scouts Am., 1978-82; bd. dirs. Am. Red Cross, Delaware, 1983-85; pres. Smith Sch. PTA, 1979. Mem. Ohio Mayflower Soc., Kappa Alpha Theta (alumnae sec. 1983—). Republican. Methodist. Home: 49 Forest Ave Delaware OH 43015 Office: OCLC Inc 6565 Frantz Rd Dublin OH 43017

FIVELSON, BERTRAM B., dentist; b. Chgo., Nov. 17, 1930; s. Michael and ada (Simon) F.; m. Eleanor G. Wasserman, may 30, 1968; children: Ilene, Janet, Charles. BS, U. Ill., 1953; DDS, U. Ill., Chgo., 1955. Gen. practice dentistry Skokie, Ill., 1957—; pres. Dental Health Plan, Skokie, 1985—. Served to capt. U.S. Army, 1955-57. Fellow Ill. State Dental Soc.; mem. ADA, Chgo. Dental Soc., Acad. Dental Edn. (pres. and bd. dirs. 1984—), Skokie Valley Dental Study Club (sec., treas. 1975—). Club: Men's Garden of N. Shore (Highland Park, Ill.) (bd. dirs. 1985—). Avocation: gardening. Home: 1652 Linden Ave Highland Park IL 60035 Office: 3319 W Main St Skokie IL 60076

FIZZELL, JAMES ALFRED, horticultural consultant; b. Chgo., Nov. 5, 1935; s. James Albert and Gladys Muriel (Blankley) F.; m. Adrienne Jane Ashbaugh, Aug. 30, 1975; children—Michael D., Lori J., Susan E., John W. Lucas. B.S., U. Ill.-Urbana, 1957, M.S., 1962. Farm adviser U. Ill.-Champaign, 1957-64; hort. service mgr. Tectrol div. Whirlpool Corp., St. Joseph, Mich., 1964-65; pres., mgr. Lakeland Greenhouses, Berrien Center, Mich., 1965-66; developmental mgr. Monterey Greenhouse, Salinas, Calif., 1966-69; developmental mgr., dir. Colorado Roses, Inc. div., LaFayette, Colo., 1969-71; sr. extension adviser horticulture U. Ill.-Rolling Meadows, 1971—; sec. Ill. Arborist Certifying Bd., 1985—; guest appearances radio and TV shows. Mem. Am. Soc. Hort. Sci., Ill. Arborist Assn., Midwest Assn. Golfcourse Supts., Garden Writers Assn. Am., Nat. Assn. County Agrl. Agts. (Disting Service award 1984), Sigma Xi, Pi Alpha Xi, Epsilon Sigma Phi, Gamma Sigma Delta. Contbr. numerous articles to mags. Home: 1124 Garden St Park Ridge IL 60068 Office: Univ Ill Agrl Extension 4200 W Euclid Ave Rolling Meadows IL 60008

FLAGG, WALTER VARTKES, dentist; b. Bronx, N.Y., June 28, 1941; s. Benjamin Flagg and Marian Jane (Hartanian) Mouradian; m. Michaelene Helen Sivak, Apr. 27, 1969; children: Christopher M., Darren M. BS, Eastern Mich. U., 1962; DDS, U. Detroit, 1966. Gen. practice dentistry Ferndale, Mich., 1966—; vis. cons. staff BiCounty Hosp., Warren, Mich., 1978-82, Detroit Osteo. Hosp., Highland Park, Mich., 1978-82; forensic dentist Mich. State Police Crime Lab, 1982, Royal Oak (Mich.) Police Dept., 1982. Contbr. articles on wrestling for local and nat. publs. Vol. probation officer Ferndale Mcpl. Ct. System, 1967-71; pres. Pleasant Ridge (Mich.) Soccer Club, 1979-80; pres. pro-tempore South Oakland (County, Mich.) Soccer Assn., 1981; chmn. jr. olympic wrestling Mich. State Wrestling Assn., 1982-84. Recipient Crime Prevention award Ferndale Mcpl. Cts., 1969-70. Mem. ADA, Mich. Dental Assn., Oakland County Dental Soc., Amateur Athletic Union (pres. Mich. chpt. 1985-87, chmn. nat. masters wrestling 1986—, mem. nat. wrestling com. 1986-87), Delta Sigma Delta (life). Mem. Armenian Apostolic Ch. Club: Ferndale Exchange. Avocations: sports, coaching soccer and wrestling. Home: 11 Cambridge Rd Pleasant Ridge MI 48069 Office: 1725 Pinecrest Ferndale MI 48220

FLAGLER, CHRISTINE ELIZABETH FLEISCHER, social worker; b. Madison, Wis., Dec. 9, 1943; d. Herbert Oswald and Dorothy Viola (Groth) Fleischer; m. David Girard Flagler, Aug. 29, 1964; children: James Holland, Amanda Elizabeth, Miriam Tae-soon, Daniel Sung-sik. Student, U. Wis., 1963-64; BA, U. Houston, 1965; MSW, Western Mich. U., 1979. Coordinator of respite care coop. Family and Children's Services, Kalamazoo, 1980-83; dir. Council Internat. Programs, Kalamazoo, 1980-84; adoption specialist Bethany Christian Service, Grand Rapids, Mich., 1983—; founder Heal the Children, Kalamazoo, 1986, cons. 1986—; chmn. bd. Council of Internat. Programs. Active Christian Med. Soc., Honduras and Dominican Republic, 1982, 84. Mem. Concerned Citizens For Internat. Adoption (pres., newsletter editor 1974-80). Avocations: walking, reading. Home: 1510 Academy Kalamazoo MI 49007 Office: Bethany Christian Services 901 Eastern Ave NE Grand Rapids MI 49503

FLAHERTY, JOHN PRESTON, JR., manufacturing company executive; b. Newcastle, Pa., Mar. 20, 1942; s. John Preston Sr. and Lilyan (Richards) F.; m. Sue Ann Branscome, Mar. 17, 1960; children: John P. III, Tammy Sue, Patricia Lynn. BBA, Youngstown (Ohio) U., 1965. Pres. J. Flaherty & Co., New Castle, Pa., 1966-69, Bronze & Metal Inc., Marion, Ohio, 1969—, Copper Alloys Inc., Tiffin, Ohio, 1972-81, Bearing Bronze Co., Cleve., 1986—. Roman Catholic. Home: 5795 Marion Waldo Rd Marion OH 43302 Office: PO Box 749 881 W Center St Marion OH 43302

FLAHIVE, ROBERT FRANCIS, academic administrator; b. Oak Park, Ill., Nov. 3, 1925; s. Thomas Joseph and Helen Margaret (McKenna) F.; m. Corinne Mary Spitz, Nov. 28, 1946; children: Michael, Timothy, Kathleen, Patricia, Margaret, Terrance. PhB, Marquette U., 1949, MA, 1952, EdD, 1973. Cert. high sch. tchr., Wis., lic. sch. supt. From tchr. to asst. supt. pub. schs. Milw., 1951-69; v.p. Cardinal Stritch Coll., Milw., 1969—; instr. various colls., Milw., 1951-60; lectr. various univs., Milw. and Wis., 1953-65. Author: Civics Textbook, 1959, Saints for Scouts, 1960, Saints for Servers, 1961; contbr. numerous articles to profl. jours. Past pres. Milw. Research Clearinghouse, Wis. Diabetes Assn.; former chmn. County Citizenship Commn.; past v.p. Nat. Soc. Fund Raising Execs.; mem. bd. Wis. Council Econ. Edn. Served to master sgt. U.S. Army, 1943-46, ETO. Recipient Merit award Archdiocesan Council Cath. Men, 1966, Archdiocesan Bd. Edn., 1980, Community Service award Marquette U., 1981, Educator Alumnus of Yr. award Marquette U., 1984. Mem. Schoolmasters Club Wis. (pres. 1960-61), Nat. Cath. Ednl. Assn., Am. Assn. Sch. Adminstrn., Wis. Council on Econ. Edn., Phi Delta Kappa, Alpha Sigma Nu. Republican. Roman Catholic. Avocations: sports spectating, sports, reading, writing, ch. activities. Home: 470 E Fox Dale Ct Milwaukee WI 53217 Office: Cardinal Stritch Coll 6801 N Yates Rd Milwaukee WI 53217

FLAIG, PAUL EDWARD, electronics executive; b. Cin., Jan. 27, 1949; s. Paul Edward and Beatrice Mary (Klei) F.; m. Margaret Mary Brausch, Sept. 20, 1980; children: Pamela, Patricia. BSME, U. Cin., 1972, MBA, 1974; JD, No. Ky. U., 1981. Bar: Ohio 1981, Fla. 1981, Ky. 1982, W.Va. 1982; registered profl. engr. Ohio, W.Va., Ky., Ind.; CPA, Ill. W. Va. Staff asst. Bendix, Southfield, Mich., 1974-75; sales engr. Worthington, Cin., 1975-77; sales mgr. Ohio Transmission, Monroe, Ohio, 1977-81; pres., gen. mgr. Wil-Jar div. ITT Corp., Summersville, W.Va., 1981-84, Alco Standard Corp., Chgo. Ind. Rubber, Elmhurst, Ill., 1984-85; mgr. ops. Pittway-BRK Electronics, Aurora, Ill., 1985—. Home: 1134 Blue Larkspur Ln Naperville IL 60540 Office: BRK Electronics 780 McClure Aurora IL 60504

FLAKE, WILLIAM HAROLD, JR., automobile manufacturing executive; b. Indpls., Aug. 5, 1932; s. William Harold Sr. and Nadine Cecil (Furnish) F.; m. Mary Jane Lockhart; children: Denise Ann, William Michael, William Anthony. MBA, Mich. State U., 1975. With various divs. Chrysler Corp., Detroit, 1966-79; mfg. mgr. Perrysburg (Ohio) Machinery div. Chrysler Corp., 1979-82; v.p. mfg. Hercules Engines, Inc. (White Engines, Inc.), Canton, Ohio, 1982—. Mem. Soc. Automotive Engrs., Am. Def. Preparedness Assn., Soc. Mfg. Engrs. Republican. Mem. Christian Ch. Avocation: old car restoration. Home: 9692 Pondera NW Massillon OH 44646 Office: Hercules Engines Inc 101 11th St SE Canton OH 44707-3802

FLANAGAN, HARRY PAUL, publishing executive; b. Columbus, Ohio, Dec. 8, 1933; s. Hugh Anthony and Kathryn Marie (Sutherly) F.; m. Joan Dickas, June 23, 1956; children: Mary Beth, Kevin Hugh, Megan Joan. BS in Mktg., Ohio State U., 1956; Cert. in Mgmt., Capital U., Columbus, 1982; Adv. Mgmt. Cert., Capitol U., Columbus, 1983. Personnel trainer For Lazarus Co., Columbus, 1960-61; supr. Wesleyan Press Co., Columbus, 1961-65; mgr. Xerox Ednl. Publs., Columbus, 1965-84, Field Publs., Columbus, 1984—. Chmn. Christ the King Sch. Bd., Columbus, 1975-80; bd. dirs. Multiple Schlerosis Soc., Franklin County, Ohio, 1980-83. Served to capt. USAF, 1956-60. Recipient citation from Jr. Achievement, Columbus, 1966, Vol. award Ohio Ho. of Reps. Mem. Fulfillment Mgrs. Assn. Roman Catholic. Avocations: golf, tennis, photography. Home: 1236 Haddon Rd Columbus OH 43209 Office: Field Publs 4343 Equity Dr Columbus OH 43228

FLANAGAN, JAMES JOHN, realtor, appraiser; b. Kansas City, Mo., July 22, 1920; s. James Patrick and Catherine F. (Nangle) F.; m. Dorothy Ellen Duffy, Sept. 23, 1950; children: Maureen, James Patrick, Terence Duffy. BS in Econ. and Bus. Adminstrn., U. Mo., Kansas City, 1943, JD, 1949. Bar: Mo. 1949. Pres. Flanagan/Summers and Assocs., Inc., Kansas City, Mo., 1946—; mem. Mo. Real Estate Commn., 1966-75, chmn. Fin. com. Cath. Diocese Kansas City-St. Joseph, Mo., 1979-87; bd. councilors Avila Coll., Kansas City, 1970-87. Served to lt. USN, 1943-46, ETO. Mem. Nat. Assn. Realtors (Omega Tau award 1975), Am. Inst. Real Estate Appraisers (Kansas City chpt. pres. 1959, v.p. 1986), Mo. Real Estate Assn. (Realtor of Yr. 1978), Met. Bd. Realtors (Realtor of Yr. 1977), Soc. Real Estate Appraisers (Kansas City chpt. pres. 1957). Avocations: reading, fishing, photography, stamp collecting. Home: 1212 W 69th Terr Kansas City MO 64113 Office: Flanagan/Summers & Assoc 8080 Ward Pkwy Suite 320 Kansas City MO 64114

FLANAGAN, JOSEPH PATRICK, advertising executive; b. Chgo., Jan. 6, 1938; s. Charles Larkin and Helen Mary (Sullivan) F.; m. Charlotte Mary Stepan, Sept 9, 1961; children—Charlotte, Joseph P. Jr., Michael S., Larkin S., Brian A. B.A., Mich. State U., 1959; M.B.A., U. Chgo., 1961. Dist. sales mgr. Time mag., Pitts. and Chgo., 1961-69; gen. mgr. Ctr. Advanced Research in Design, Chgo., 1969-75; v.p., dir. client services Cohen and Greenbaum Advt., Chgo., 1975-77; sr. v.p., dir. Impact, The Promotion and Design Co., Foote, Cone & Belding, Chgo., 1977-85, pres., dir., 1985—; pres., corp. dir. sales promotion Council Sales Promotion Agys., 1986—. Mem. governing bd. Chgo. Symphony Orch., 1974—; v.p. Lyric Opera Guild, Chgo., 1974. Roman Catholic. Club: Exmoor Country (Highland Park, Ill.). Avocation: classical music. Home: 136 Chestnut St Winnetka IL 60093 Office: Impact FCB Ctr 101 E Erie Chicago IL 60611

FLANAGAN, PATRICK EDWIN, dentist; b. St. Petersburg, Fla., Sept. 25, 1956; s. Albert Elroy and Anita Christine (Ott) F. BA, U. Calif., Berkeley, 1978; DMD, Washington U., St. Louis, 1983. Prin. Doctors DentaHealth, Ballwin, Mo., 1985—. Editor Xi Psi Phi Frat. mag. 1979-81. Republican.

Lutheran. Avocations: gardening, water skiing, travel. Home: 9211 Ladue Rd Saint Louis MO 63124 Office: Doctors Dental Health 15360 Machester Rd Ballwin MO 63011

FLANDERS, DWIGHT PRESCOTT, economist; b. Rockford, Ill., Mar. 14, 1909; s. Daniel Bailey and Lulu Iona (Nichol) F.; m. Mildred Margaret Hutchison, Aug. 27, 1939 (dec. Dec. 1978); children—James Prescott, Thomas Addison. BA, U. Ill., 1931, MA, 1937; teaching cert., Beloit (Wis.) Coll., 1934; PhD in Econs., Yale U., 1939. With McLeish, Baxter & Flanders (realtors), Rockford, 1931-33; instr. U.S. history and sci. in secondary schs. Rockford, 1934-36; asst. prof. econs. Coll. Liberal Arts and Scis.; also statistics Maxwell Grad. Sch., Syracuse (N.Y.) U., 1939-42; acad. staff econs. dept. social sci. U.S. Mil. Acad., West Point, N.Y., 1942-46; mem. faculty U. Ill., Urbana, 1946—; prof. econs. U. Ill., 1953-77; prof. emeritus dept. econs. Coll. Commerce and Bus. Adminstrn., 1977—; prof. emeritus dept. family and consumer econs. Coll. Agr., 1980—; chmn. masters research seminar, 1947-74, cons. in field. Author: Science and Social Science, 2d edit, 1962, Status of Military Personnel as Voters, 1942, Collection Rural Real Property Taxes in Illinois, 1938; co-author: Contemporary Foreign Governments, 1946, The Conceptual Framework for a Science of Marketing, 1964; contbr. numerous articles to profl. jours. Pres. Three Lakes (Wis.) Waterfront Homeowners Assn., 1969-71, dir., 1971-75, ofcl. bd., 1975—. Served to lt. col. AUS, 1942-46. Univ. fellow U. Ill., 1936-37; Univ. fellow Yale U., 1937-39; recipient Bronze tablet U. Ill., 1931, Excellence in Teaching award, 1977. Mem. Am., Midwest econs. assns., Royal Econ. Soc., Econometric Soc., Phi Beta Kappa, Beta Gamma Sigma (chpt. pres. 1959-61), Phi Kappa Phi, Alpha Kappa Psi. Methodist (ofcl. bd.). Club: Yale (Chgo.). Home: 719 S Foley Ave Champaign IL 61820

FLANDERS, RAYMOND ALAN, governmental health agency administrator; b. Bangor, Maine, Jan. 4, 1929; s. Carroll Benjamin and Mary (Watson) F.; m. Anne-Liss Teisen; children: Molly Olivia and Michael Benjamin (twins). Student, Colgate U., 1948-50; BS, U. Miami, Fla., 1955; DDS, U. Md., 1959; MPH, U. Mich., 1979. Mem. faculty W.Va. U., Morgantown, 1964-65; program dir. Project Hope, Brazil, 1976-78; regional dental dir. Va. State Health Dept., Richmond, 1970-76, 79-85; mem. faculty Med. Coll. Va., Richmond, 1980-85; state dental dir. Ill. Dept. Health, Springfield, 1985—; mem. faculty Coll. Dental Medicine So. Ill. U., Alton, 1985—; cons. Project Esperanca, Amazon River, Brazil, 1981, Project HOPE/U.S.A.I.D., Grenada, West Indies, 1984, Project HOPE, Honduras, 1986. Contbr. articles to profl. jours. Served to capt. U.S. Army, 1946-47, 50-51, 60-63. USPHS fellow, 1978-79. Mem. ADA (Preventive Dentistry award 1983), Ill. Dental Assn., Am. Pub. Health Assn., Assn. State Territorial Dental Dirs., Am. Assn. Pub. Health Dentists, Ill. Pub. Health Assn. Office: 535 W Jefferson St Springfield IL 62761

FLANNERY, ARTHUR DANIEL, actor; b. Webster, S.D., Mar. 10, 1944; s. Arthur James and Marcella Margaret (Koenig) F.; m. Maureen Tolman, Dec. 27, 1969; children: Tolman, Brendan, Brian, Caitlan. BBA, Creighton U., 1967. Tchr. Blessed Sacrament Sch., Omaha, 1968-71; area supr. Santa Cruz Imports, Chgo., 1972-75, owner, 1975-81; freelance actor, model Chgo., 1981—. Mem. Am. Fedn. TV and Radio Artists, Screen Actors Guild. Avocations: all sports, theater. Home: 1108 Cleveland Evanston IL 60202

FLANNERY, EDWARD JOSEPH, manufacturing executive; b. Chgo., July 16, 1926; s. Edward J. and Ella (Brennan) F.; m. Dorothy Marie Johnson, May 30, 1953; children: Ann, Kathleen, Michael, Maureen, James, Julie. BSEE, U. Ill., 1950; MBA, U. Chgo., 1959; MSEE, Northwestern U., 1961. Chief engr. Vap Air div. Vapor Corp., Niles, Ill., 1962-69, asst. gen. mgr., 1969-75; v.p., gen. mgr. Raymond Controls, St. Charles, Ill., 1976-83, Brunswick Valve and Control, Morton Grove, Ill., 1983—; cons. Sundstrand Corp., Rockford, Ill., 1976; bd. dirs. Nireco Corp., Tokyo, , NB Inst. Co., San Francisco. Served with USN, 1944-46. Mem. Instrument Soc. Am. (pres. adv. council 1983—), Valve Mfrs. Assn. Roman Catholic. Office: Brunswick Valve & Control 6511 Oakton St Morton Grove IL 60053

FLANNERY, ROBERT GENE, railroad executive; b. Washington, Ind., Sept. 14, 1924; s. Allen H. and Nellie Jane (White) F.; m. Barbara Ann Angell, Feb. 23, 1952; children: Julia Ann, Jennifer Ann, Amy Lynn. B.S. in Civil Engring, Purdue U., 1948. With N.Y.C. R.R., 1948-68; gen. mgr. N.Y.C. R.R., Syracuse, N.Y., 1965; asst. v.p. transp. N.Y.C. R.R., N.Y.C., 1965; v.p. systems devel. N.Y.C. R.R., 1967-68, Penn Central Co., 1968-69; v.p. ops. Penn Central Co., Phila., 1969-70; exec. v.p. Penn Central Transp. Co., 1970, v.p. operations, 1970; exec. v.p. Western Pacific R.R. Co., San Francisco, 1971-72, pres., 1973—, chief exec. officer, from 1975; pres., chief operating officer Union Pacific/Mo. Pacific RRs, 1982—. Served with USNR, 1943-45. Mem. U.S. Ry. Assn. (dir.), Pi Kappa Alpha. Democrat. Club: Mason. Office: Union Pacific Railroad 1416 Dodge St Omaha NE 68179

FLATHOM, GLORIA JEAN, nurse, consultant; b. Beloit, Wis., June 3, 1945; d. Jesse Drell and Jennie (Hynek) Perkins; m. Daniel Flathom; children—Julie, Jill, Jason. A.A.S., Moraine Valley Community Coll., 1980; B.A., Trinity Christian Coll., Palos Heights, Ill., 1985. R.N. Adminstrv. asst. Gen. Telephone Co., Madison, 1967-68; nurse Christ Hosp., Oak Lawn, Ill., 1980—; nurse cons. Johnson & Johnson, Boston, 1983; research nurse Rush-Presbyn.-St. Lukes Med. Ctr., Chgo., 1983; office nurse, 1984-85; asst. adminstr. Women's Health Cons., S.C., Rush-Presbyn. Med. Ctr., 1985-87. Vice pres. Am. Lutheran Ch. Women, Chgo., 1970-72, McKay Sch. PTA, Chgo., 1972-74; patron chmn. cotillion Christ Hosp. Aux., 1982. Ill. state scholar, 1983-85. Mem. Am. Mgrs. of OB/GYN, Nurses Assn. Am. Coll. Ob-Gyn., Trinity Christian Coll. Alumni Assn.

FLATTER, JOHN CLINTON, psychologist; b. Fairborn, Ohio, Nov. 1, 1944; s. Levi Howard and Dorothy (Walther) F.; m. Mary Louise McDonald, June 13, 1970; children: Sean, Brian, Jamie. BS, Bowling Green U., 1967; MS, U. Dayton, 1969; EdD, Wayne State U., 1975. Lic. psychologist, Mich. Tchr. Kettering (Ohio) City Schs., 1968-71; counselor Wayne State U., Detroit, 1971-76; staff psychologist Sinai Hosp., Detroit, 1976-86, asst. dir. outpatient clinic, 1986—; cons. Walsh Coll. Bus., Troy, Mich., 1981—, Birmingham (Mich.) Schs., 1985—, Youth Assistance Oakland County, Mich., 1986—. Mem. Am. Psychol. Assn. Avocations: running, tennis. Office: Problems of Daily Living Clinic 6450 Farmington Rd West Bloomfield MI 48033

FLAUGHER, JEANINE KAREN SUE, mathematics educator; b. Belleville, Ill., Apr. 15; d. Conrad Hugo and Anna Emma (Stroebel) Holle; m. John Wesley Flaugher, Aug. 9, 1968; 1 stepchild, Bobbie Ann Flaugher Nothdurft. AA, Belleville Jr. Coll., 1959; BS in Math. and Secondary Edn., So. Ill. U., 1961, MS in Math. and Secondary Edn., 1964. Cert. high sch. tchr., Ill., cert. jr. coll. tchr. Tchr. math. West dist. Belleville (Ill.) Twp. High Sch., 1961-66, tchr. math. East dist., 1966—; dir. plays, East and West dists. Belleville Twp. High Sch., 1960-70. State of Ill. scholar, Am. Fed. Tchrs. Local 434 scholar, Bus. and Profl. Women's Orgn. scholar, 1957. Avocations: travel, bowling, swimming, macramé, theatre. Office: Belleville Twp High Sch East 2555 W Boulevard Belleville IL 62221

FLAUM, JOEL MARTIN, judge; b. Hudson, N.Y., Nov. 26, 1936; s. Louis and Sally (Berger) F.; m. Thea Kharasch, July 3, 1960; children: Jonathan, Alison. B.A., Union Coll., Schenectady, 1958; J.D., Northwestern U., 1963, LL.M., 1964. Bar: Ill. 1963. Asst. state's atty. Cook County, Ill., 1965-69; 1st asst. atty. gen. Ill., 1969-72; 1st asst. U.S. atty. No. Dist. Ill., Chgo., 1972-75; judge U.S. Dist. Ct. No. Dist. Ill., Chgo., 1975-83, U.S. Ct. Appeals 7th Cir., 1983—; lectr. Northwestern U. Sch. Law, 1967-69, DePaul U. Sch. of Law, 1987—; mem. Ill. Law Enforcement Commn., 1970-72; cons. U.S. Dept. Justice, Law Enforcement Assistance Adminstrn. Mem.: Northwestern U. Law Rev., 1962-63; contbr. articles to legal jours. Mem. adv. bd. Loyola U. Sch. Law, 1978—; mem. vis. com. U. Chgo. Law Sch., 1983-86, Northwestern U. Sch. Law; hon. trustee Congregation Anshe Emet, Chgo., 1978—. Served to lt. JAGC, USNR. Ford Found. fellow, 1963-64; Am. Bar Found. fellow, 1984. Mem. Fed. Bar Assn., ABA, Bar Assn. 7th Circuit, Ill. Bar Assn., Chgo. Bar Assn., Legal Club Chgo., Maritime Law Assn., Law Club Chgo., Judge Advs. Assn., Am. Judicature Soc. Jewish. Office: U S Ct of Appeals 219 S Dearborn St Room 2602 Chicago IL 60604

FLAVIN, GLENNON P., bishop; b. St. Louis, Mar. 2, 1916. Grad., St. Louis Prep. Sem., Kendrick Sem. Ordained priest Roman Catholic Ch., 1941; sec. to archbishop St. Louis, 1949-57; consecrated bishop 1957; ordained titular bishop of Joannina and aux. bishop St. Louis, 1957-67; bishop Diocese of Lincoln, Nebr., 1967—. Office: Chancery Office 3400 Sheridan Blvd PO Box 80328 Lincoln NE 68501 *

FLEENER, CHARLES JOSEPH, history educator; b. New Orleans, Nov. 22, 1938; s. J. Edwin and Marguerite Louise (Borda) F.; m. Mary Denise Cleary, Aug. 26, 1967; children—Cristina Borda, Margarita Cleary. B.S., Georgetown U., 1960; Ph.D., U. Fla., 1969. Instr., St. Louis U., 1966-69; asst. prof. dept. history, 1969-74, assoc. prof. Latin Am. history, 1974—, chmn. dept., 1980-85, dir. pre-law program, 1985—. Mem. Am. Hist. Assn., Am. Cath. Hist. Assn., Conf. Latin Am. History, Latin Am. Studies Assn., Midwest Assn. Pre-Law Advisors (bd. dirs. 1987—). Roman Catholic. Author: The Guide to Latin American Paperback Literature, 1966; Religious and Cultural Factors in Latin America, 1970; Fidel Castro and Revolution in Latin America, 1986. Home: 6363 Waterman University City MO 63130 Office: St Louis U Dept History XH-357 Saint Louis MO 63103

FLEISCHACKER, PAUL REECE, actuarial consultant; b. Des Moines, July 15, 1942; s. Henry J. and Mary M. (Haworth) F.; m. Brenda Lee Lavent, May 30, 1964; children—David, Michael, Melissa, Anita. B.S., Drake U., 1965. Cons. actuary George V. Stennes & Assocs., Mpls., 1965-70, v.p. and treas., 1973-78; actuary Western Life Ins. Co., St. Paul, 1970-73; v.p. Towers, Perrin, Forster & Crosby, Mpls., 1978—. Cubmaster, Boy Scouts Am., Mpls., 1975; mem. bus. adminstrn. com. St. John the Baptist Ch., New Brighton, Minn., 1984—. Fellow Soc. Actuaries; mem. Am. Acad. Actuaries, Twin Cities Actuarial Club. Roman Catholic. Lodge: KC. Avocations: fishing; boating; skiing. Home: 2157 Lakebrook Dr New Brighton MN 55112 Office: 8300 Norman Center Dr Suite 600 Bloomington MN 55437

FLEISHER, NORMA JEAN, accountant; b. Grand Island, Nebr., Oct. 21, 1926; d. Duward Arthur Bodenhamer andMyrtle May (Bouchard) Fricke; m. Niles H. Searls, May 8, 1945 (div. 1954); children: Nancy Kail, Janet Davis; m. Emmett C. Fleisher, Oct. 19, 1957 (dec. July 1981); children: Laura, William. CPA, Nebr. Bookkeeper various firms, Lincoln, Nebr., 1952-61; staff acct. Dana F. Cole & Co., Lincoln, Nebr., 1961-72; controller Sunflower Beef Packers, Inc., York, Nebr., 1972—; pvt. practice tax acctg. Seward and Lincoln, Nebr., 1972—; sr. acct. tax Lincoln (Nebr.) Telecommunications Co., 1980—. Contbr. tax articles to prof. jours. Fin., calling/caring com. Grace United Meth. Ch., 1984—; active Boosalis for Gov., Nebr., 1986; mem. bd. Camp Fire, Lincoln, 1986—. Mem. Am. Inst. CPA's, Nebr. Soc. CPA's (chmn. com. 1968-69, 1983), Assn. Better Mgmt. (treas.), Lincoln C. of C. (com. mem.), Lincoln Women's C. of C. (chmn.). Avocations: gardening, writing, traveling. Home: 261 Sycamore Dr Lincoln NE 68510 Office: Lincoln Telecommunications Co 1440 M St Lincoln NE 68510

FLEISHOUR, BRUCE ALBERT, light manufacturing executive; b. Canton, Ohio, Mar. 5, 1945; s. Albert Fred and Dorothy Florence (Hoopes) F.; m. Susan Kay Hines, May 8, 1967; children: Shelly Sue, Kristen Kay. BS, Walsh Coll., 1967. Owner Economy Mkt., Canton, 1967-70; pres., owner Canton Door Corp., 1970—, Columbus (Ohio) Door Corp., 1984—, Watermaster, Inc., 1985—. Sr. warden St. Mark's Ch., Canton, 1980. Served to maj. USAR, 1966-72. Republican. Lodge: Masons. Avocations: pvt. pilot, boating. Office: Canton Door Corp 1324 Waynesburg Rd SE Canton OH 44707

FLEMING, CHISNA HENRY, utility company executive; b. Hot Springs, S.D., July 23, 1927; s. Henry and Margaret Elizabeth (Hannan) F.; m. Helen Louise Davison, Dec. 24, 1951; children: Kevin Chisna, Martin Kharis, Giselle Marguerite, Rachel Beatrice. BScEE, U. Nebr., 1951; postgrad., U. Akron, 1970, Gen. Electric Power System Engring., Schenectady, N.Y., 1970-71. Registered profl. engr., Ohio. Assoc. engr. Union Carbide Nuclear Corp., Oak Ridge (Tenn.) and Paducah (Ky.), 1951-55; engr. Ohio Edison Co., Akron, 1955-64, sr. engr., 1964-70, gen. planning engr., 1970-80, mgr. advanced engring. and planning dept., 1980—; industry advisor Electric Power Research Inst., 1987—; mem. N.Am. Electric Reliability Council Interregional Rev. Subcom., 1986—. Bd. dirs. Metro Regional Transit Authority, Akron, 1973—, pres., 1979-81; bd. trustees Weathervane Community Playhouse, Akron, 1958-85, pres., 1971-73, 76-77; troop committeeman Boy Scouts Am. Akron council, 1966-74, scoutmaster and asst., Paducah, Akron, 1954-57. Mem. IEEE (sr. rotating mem. machinery com. 1968-71), Power Engring Soc. of IEEE, Sigma Tau. Republican. Roman Catholic. Office: Ohio Edison Co 76 S Main St Akron OH 44308-1890

FLEMING, DENISE PARK, art director; b. Detroit, Jan. 22, 1956; s. Donald B. and Ilene M. (Didsbury) Park; m. William R. Fleming, Apr. 4, 1981. BFA, Miami U., 1978. Art dir. replacement parts div. TRW, Inc., Cleve., 1982—. Mem. Am. Inst. Graphic Arts (edn. com. 1986—), Nat. Assn. for Female Execs. Republican. Methodist. Avocations: collecting antiques, aerobics, drawing. Office: TRW Inc Replacement Parts div 8001 E Pleasant Valley Rd Cleveland OH 44131

FLEMING, DOUGLAS G., agribusiness and food processing company executive; b. Harvey, Ill., Apr. 28, 1930; s. Harold L. and Genevieve (Hodges) F.; m. Sara L. Waters, May 25, 1952; children: Christine J., James C. B.S., Mich. State U., 1954. With Central Soya Co., Inc., Ft. Wayne, Ind., 1954—, asst. mgr. field ops., 1963-65, v.p., dir. mktg., 1965-70, exec. v.p., 1970-76, pres., 1976-85, chief exec. officer, 1979-85, chmn., 1979—, also bd. dirs.; bd. dirs. Ft. Wayne Nat. Bank, Midwestern United Life Ins. Co., Tokheim Corp., Arvin Industries. Bd. dirs. United Way Allen County. Served to 2d lt. AUS, 1951-53. Mem. Am. Feed Mfrs. Assn. Clubs: Ft. Wayne Country, Summit (Ft. Wayne). Home: 16817 Tonkel Rd Leo IN 46765 Office: Central Soya Co Inc 1300 Fort Wayne Nat Bank Bldg Fort Wayne IN 46802 *

FLEMING, FREDERICK HAROLD, computer information scientist; b. Barberton, Ohio, Oct. 13, 1938; s. Warren Austin and Francis Louise (McQuesten) F.; m. Marjorie Evelyn MacKay, July 22, 1961; children: Christy Ann, Glenn Richard, Daniel Warren, Jonathan Paul. Student, Northeastern U., Boston, 1963, Stark Tech. Coll., 1973. Cert. systems profl. computer operator Converse Rubber, Co., Malden, 1962-65; computer programmer Gorton, Corp., Gloucester, Mass., 1965-68; analyst, programmer B.F. Goodrich, Co., Akron, Ohio, 1968-69; asst. data processing mgr. Reiter Foods, Inc., Barberton, 1969-78; sr. systems analyst Lawson Milk, Co., Cuyahoga Falls, Ohio, 1978-79, Diebold, Inc., Canton, Ohio, 1979—. Advisor Wadsworth (Ohio) Rainbow for Girls, 1978-79. Served with USNR. Mem. Data Processing Mgmt. Assn. (pres. 1977-78), Assn. Inst. for Cert. of Computer Profls. Lodge: Masons. Home: 737 Tamwood Dr Canal Fulton OH 44614 Office: Diebold Inc 818 Mulberry Rd Se Canton OH 44711

FLEMING, GEORGE ROBERT, psychologist; b. New Haven, July 24, 1947; s. George Robert and Susie Mae F.; B.A., Hillsdale Coll., 1969; M.A., Mich. State U., 1972, Ph.D., 1975; 1 child, Maisha Amirz. Dir., East N.Y. Mental Health Clinic Adult Day Treatment Program, N.Y.C., 1973-77; chmn. psychology dept. Malcolm-King Harlem Coll. Extension, N.Y.C., 1979, adj. prof., 1977-79; staff psychologist Bedford-Stuyvesant Community Mental Health Center, N.Y.C., 1977-79; cons. Detroit Public Schs., 1981-82, Centrax Diversified Services, 1977—, City of Detroit Comprehensive Youth Services Program, 1980-81; dir. Cen. City br. Children's Ctr., Detroit, 1979-81, Sacred Heart Women's Day Treatment Ctr., 1981-84, Total Health Care, Inc., 1982-86; chief psychologist Southwest Detroit Hosp., 1986— , Greater Detroit Life Consultation Ctr., 1982-84, Detroit Osteo. Hosp., 1984—. NIMH fellow, 1974-75. Mem. Nat. Black Child Devel. Inst. (mem. steering com. met. Detroit 1981), Nat. Register Health Service Providers in Psychology, Am. Psychol. Assn., Assn. Black Psychologists, Am. Orthopsychiat. Assn., Internat. Neuropsychol. Soc., Mich. Psychol. Assn., Mich. Assn. Black Psychologists (chmn. 1981-82), Mich. Soc. Clin. Psychologists, Omicron Delta Kappa. Home and Office: 5019 1/2 Woodward Ave Detroit MI 48202

FLEMING, MILO JOSEPH, lawyer; b. Roscoe, Ill., Jan. 4, 1911; s. John E. and Elizabeth (Shafer) F.; m. Dorothea H. Kunze, Aug. 15, 1942 (dec. 1944); m. Lucy Anna Russell, June 30, 1948; stepchildren: Michael Russell, Jo Ann Russell (Mrs. Clemens); 1 child, Elizabeth Fleming Weber. AB, U. of Ill., 1933, LLB, 1936. Bar: Ill. 1936, U.S. Dist. Ct. (cen. dist.) Ill. 1936, 53, U.S. Tax Ct. 1936, 84, U.S. Ct. Appeals (7th cir.) 1936, 85, U.S. Supreme Ct. 1986. Sole practice law, 1936-42, 58-59; ptnr. Pallissard and Fleming, Watseka, Ill., 1942-46, Pallissard, Fleming & Oram, 1946-58, Fleming & McGrew, 1960-77, Fleming, McGrew and Boyer, 1977, Fleming & Boyer, 1977-79, Fleming, Boyer & Strough, 1980-82, Fleming & Strough, 1982—; master in chancery, Iroquois County, Ill., 1943-44; asst. atty. gen. Ill. for Iroquois County, 1964-69; city atty., Watseka, 1949-57, 61—, Gilman, Ill., 1966-69; village atty. Milford, Ill., 1942-70, Wellington, 1962-72, Woodland, 1958-79, Danforth, 1961-78, Crescent City, Martinton, Sheldon, 1946-79, Onarga, Cissna Park, 1977-82, Beaverville, Papineau; atty. Lake Iroquois Lot Owners Assn. and Cen. San. Dist.; asst. atty. gen. Iroquois County, 1964-69; pres. Iroquois County Devel. Corp., 1961-68; bd. dirs. Belmont Water Co., 1963-81, pres., 1976-81. Chmn. Iroquois County Universities Bond Issues Campaign, 1960; mem. State Employees Group Ins. Adv. Commn., Ill., 1975-78; trustee Welles Sch. Fund, Watseka, 1978—; candidate state rep., Apr. 1940; life mem. U. Ill. Pres.'s Council, 1979—. Recipient Merit award for indsl. relations Watseka Area C. of C., 1983. Mem. ABA (vice chmn. com. ordnances and adminstrv. regulations 1968-69, 73-75, chmn. 1969-72, 75-78, mem. council local govt. sect. 1976-79, mem. council sect. urban, state and local govt. law 1979-80), Ill. Bar Assn., Iroquois County Bar Assn. (pres. 1966-67), Internat. Platform Assn., Smithsonian Instn., Phi Eta Sigma, Sigma Delta Kappa. Democrat. Methodist. Lodges: Masons (32 deg.), Shriners, Odd Fellows (mem. jud. and appeals com. Ill. 1960-62, grand warden Ill. 1962, dep. grand master 1963, grand master 1964-65; grand rep. 1966; trustee Old Folks Home, Mattoon, Ill., 1966-71, sec. bd. 1966-68, vice chmn. bd. 1970—, atty. 1966—; 2d v.p. No. Assn. Odd Fellows and Rebekahs Ill. 1981, 1st v.p., 1982, pres. 1983; Meritorious Service jewel, Grand Encampment of Ill. 1980, elected Grand Sr. Warden Grand Encampment of Ill. 1984, Grand Patriarch Grand Encampment of Ill. 1986). Prepared Municipal Code for City of Watseka, 1953, 80, Milford, 1957, Martinton, 1960, Crescent City, 1960, 66, Woodland, 1961, Cissna Park, 1961, Papineau, 1978. Home: 120 W Jefferson Ave Watseka IL 60970 Office: Fleming & Strough Odd Fellows Bldg PO Box 297 216 E Walnut St Watseka IL 60970

FLEMING, RICHARD WILLIAM, food company executive; b. Evanston, Ill., Jan. 14, 1944; s. James Richard and Henrietta Louise (Koellmann) F.; m. Amber Yarde, Feb. 20, 1971. B.S., Bradley U., 1965; M.B.A., DePaul U., 1975. Mgmt. trainee Campbell Soup Co., Chgo., 1969-70, planning mgr., 1970-74; mgr. fin. planning Am. Hosp. Supply Corp., Evanston, Ill., 1974-76, mgr. comml. devel., 1976-78; dir. corp. planning Stokely-Van Camp, Inc., Indpls., 1978-80; dir. corp. planning Libby, McNeill & Libby, Inc., Chgo., 1980-82, v.p. fin. and planning, 1982—, also dir., mem. exec. com.; mem. fin. com. Nestle Enterprises, Inc. Served with USN, 1967-69. Mem. Nat. Assn. Food Processors, Fin. Execs. Inst., Beta Gamma Sigma, Delta Mu Delta. Republican. Home: 1052 W Inverlieth Rd Lake Forest IL 60045 Office: Libby McNeill & Libby Inc 200 S Michigan Ave Chicago IL 60604

FLEMING, SHEILA MAXINE, bank internal consultant; b. Kansas City, Mo., Aug. 5, 1959; d. Earl Darr and Virginia Lorraine (Walker) H.; m. Douglas A. Fleming, Oct. 9, 1982. BS in Interior Design, William Woods Coll., 1981. Facilities planner Fed. Res. Bank, Kansas City, Mo., 1981-82; internal cons. United Mo. Bank, Kansas City, 1984—. Mem. ch. worship com. St. Luke's United Meth. Ch., Kansas City, Mo., 1981-83; team capt. Parks and Recreation Volleyball League, Lee's Summit, Mo., 1985—. Named a Disting. Scholar, William Woods Coll., Fulton, Mo. 1981. Mem. William Woods Coll. Alumnae Assn. (officer, mem. adv. bd. 1984—), Chi Omega Alumnae Assn. Republican. Methodist. Office: United Mo Bank KC NA 10th and Grand PO Box 226 Kansas City MO 64141

FLEMING, WILLIAM HARE, surgeon; b. Columbus, Ohio, May 1, 1935; s. William Bush and Charlote (Hare) F.; m. Carolyn Etta Swift, June 25, 1959 (div. May 1978); children: Alice Fleming Guzick, William Swift, Edgar Hare. BA, Yale U., 1957; MD, Columbia U., 1961. Diplomate Am. Bd. Surgery, Am. Bd. Thoracic Surgery. Intern in surgery Presbyn. Hosp., N.Y.C., 1961-62; resident in thoracic surgery Manhattan VA Hosp., N.Y.C., 1967, Harlem Hosp., N.Y.C., 1967, Presbyn. Hosp., N.Y.C., 1968; asst. prof. Emory U., Atlanta, 1971-76; chief thoracic surgery VA Hosp., Atlanta, 1971-76; adj. sr. research scientist Ga. Inst. Tech., Atlanta, 1974-76; assoc. prof. surgery U. Nebr. Med. Ctr., Omaha, 1976-80, prof. surgery, 1980—, chief thoracic surgery, 1980—; pres. bd. dirs. Profl. Fees Office Nebr. Clinicians Group, Omaha, 1985—; pres. Coordinated Med. Services, Inc., Omaha, 1986—. Contbr. articles over 65 articles to profl. jours. Served to maj. U.S. Army, 1969-70, Vietnam. Decorated Bronze Star. Fellow ACS, Am. Coll. Cardiology, Am. Acad. Pediatrics; mem. AMA (Physicians Recognition award 1985), Am. Assn. Thoracic Surgery, Soc. Thoracic Surgeons. Republican. Presbyterian. Club: The Omaha. Avocations: tennis, sailing, windsurfing, waterskiing. Home: 2039 S 85th Ave Omaha NE 68124

FLESCH, ROBERT DONALD, quality assurance specialist; b. Dubuque, Iowa, Feb. 11, 1946; s. Donald George and Margaret Elizabeth (Maiden) F.; m. Sally Jane Winckler, June 11, 1971; children: David, Christopher. BA, St. Ambrose Coll., 1968. Rep. Travelers Ins. Co., Davenport, Iowa, 1971-75; interviewer Job Service of Iowa, Davenport, 1975-78; quality assurance specialist Rock Island (Ill.) Arsenal, 1978—. Mem. Bettendorf (Iowa) Park Band, 1973—. Served to staff sgt. USAR, 1968-72, Vietnam. Mem. Am. Soc. Quality Control., Lionel Collectors. Republican. Avocations: computers, trains. Office: SMCRI-QAA Rock Island Arsenal Rock Island IL 61299

FLESHER, ROBERT DANA, gas company official; b. Columbus, Ohio, Dec. 4, 1945; s. John Harvey and Virginia A. (Jackson) F.; m. Sondra K. Arkley, Oct. 16, 1976; 1 dau., Angela Lynn. Student Ohio State U., 1964-67. Sales, Central Ohio Welding (Airco), Columbus, 1971-74; distbn. mgr. Chemetron Corp., Columbus, 1974, Toledo, 1974-78; gen. mgr. fleet maintenance AGA Gas, Inc., Cleve., 1978—. Served in USNR, 1966-70. Recipient numerous awards in field. Mem. Am. Trucking Assn. (bd. dirs. maintenance council 1987), Soc. Automotive Engrs., ASTM, Pvt. Truck Council, Pvt. Carrier Conf., Ohio Trucking Assn., Am. Mgmt. Assn. Roman Catholic. Club: Literary Guild. Home: 7440 Midland Rd Independence OH 44131 Office: 6225 Oaktree Blvd Cleveland OH 44101

FLESSNER, BRUCE WILLIAM, management consultant; b. Lansing, Mich., July 14, 1953; s. Lloyd William and Winifred Marie (Beeman) F.; m. Melanie Vlaich, Aug. 10, 1975; children: Lauren Blair Vlaich, Robert Jason Vlaich. BS, Central Mich. U., 1976; MPA, Western Mich. U., 1978; postgrad. U. Minn., 1978-84. Dir. ann. giving Kalamazoo Coll., 1975-78; devel. officer U. Minn., Mpls., 1978-80, v.p., assoc. dir. U. Minn. Found., 1980-83; prin. Bentz, Whaley, Flessner & Assocs., Inc., Mpls., 1983—. Bd. dirs. Kalamazoo Alcohol and Drug Abuse Council, 1976-78, Mac Phail Ctr. for Arts, 1983—, Family Networks, 1983-85; vice chmn. Kalamazoo County Dem. Party, 1976-78. Recipient key to City of Bay City, Mich., 1972. Mem. Nat. Soc. Fundraising Execs. (bd. dirs. Minn. chpt.), Pub. Relations Soc. Am., Council Advancement and Support of Edn. Presbyterian. Home: 4115 Balsam Lane Plymouth MN 55441 Office: 5001 W 80th St Suite 201 Minneapolis MN 55435

FLETCHER, WALTER EUGENE, purchasing agent; b. Detroit, Mar. 23, 1942; s. Eugene Reed and Marguerite K. (Bibbens) F.; m. Sue Ann Tickner, June 14, 1968; 1 son, Andrew Reed. A.S., McHenry County Coll., Crystal Lake, Ill., 1982. Cert. purchasing mgr. Asst. buyer Acme Mfg. Co., Ferndale, Mich., 1972-73; buyer Ex-Cell-O Corp., Howell, Mich., 1974-79, purchasing agt., Mundelein, Ill., 1980-86; purchasing agent Continental Can Co., West Chicago, Ill., 1986—. Cir. dir. Howell Jr. Achievement, 1975-79. Served to sgt. U.S. Army, 1964-70. Republican. Methodist. Lodge: Elks. Avocations: personal computers, golf, woodworking. Home: 702 S 12th Ave Saint Charles IL 60174 Office: Continental Can Co 1700 Harvester Rd West Chicago IL 60185

FLETCHER, WILLIAM WALLACE, JR., computer software company executive; b. Chgo., Mar. 19, 1947; s. William Wallace Sr. and Velma Lorene (Curry) F.; m. Judith Ann Johnson, Aug. 23, 1969; children: Kristin

Elizabeth, Kari Lynne, Kelly Katherine. BA, Gustavus Adolphus Coll., 1969; MBA, U. Wis., 1970. Mktg. research analyst Investors Diversified Services Inc., Mpls., 1971-73; supr. market research Iowa Power and Light, Des Moines, 1973-76, mgr. budget/corp. model, 1976-79, dir. corp. planning, 1979-83; v.p., gen. mgr. Iowa Computer Resources Inc., Des Moines, 1983—. Pres. bd. dirs. Family Counseling Ctr., Des Moines, 1979-81; pres. council St. Mark Luth. Ch., West Des Moines, Iowa, 1980-81. Served as sgt. USMCR, 1970-76. Mem. Am. Mktg. Assn. (pres. Iowa chpt. 1976-77), Data Entry Mgmt. Assn., Des Moines C. of C. Republican. Home: 4806 Aspen Dr West Des Moines IA 50265 Office: Iowa Computer Resources Inc 500 E Court Ave Des Moines IA 50309

FLICK, KENT RODERICK, merchant marine officer; b. Pontiac, Mich., Mar. 9, 1953; s. Kenneth R. and Ilene H. (Konkel) F.; m. Gina M. Dreussi, July 19, 1980; children: Lydia Ilene, Kenneth Regis. BS in Marine Transp., U.S. Mcht. Marine Acad., 1975, BS in Marine Engring., 1976; MBA, Kent State U., 1981. Diesel engr. Zapata Marine Service, Houston, 1976; deck officer Master, Mates & Pilots Union, Linthicum Heights, Md., 1977—. Served to lt. USNR, 1976—. Roman Catholic. Lodge: Elks. Avocations: sports, classic cars. Home: 1372 Whittier St NE North Canton OH 44721

FLICK, MICHAEL RAYMOND, psychology and education educator; b. Chgo., Oct. 24, 1942; s. Michael A. and Frances S. (Sreboth) F.; m. Jacklyn M. Tucker, June 22, 1968; children: Nicole Lee, Michael R., Jeannine E. AA, Thornton Jr. Coll., 1962; BA, No. Ill. U., 1964, MS in Edn., 1967. Registered psychologist, Ill.; cert. tchr. educationally mentally handicapped, learning disabled, behaviorally disordered. Counseling psychologist Jo Daviess County Edn. Ctr., Elizabeth, Ill., 1967-69; guidance dir. Leaf River (Ill.) Schs., 1970-72; spl. edn. tchr. Oregon (Ill.) Schs., 1972-73; guidance dir. Byron (Ill.) Schs., 1973-79; spl. needs coordinator Harlem Consol., Rockford, Ill., 1980—; psychologist Fairchild & Assocs., Rockford, 1981—; summer dir. Harlem Community Ctr., Rockford, 1984—; ins. advisor Harlem Fedn. Tchrs., 1986. Tax assessor Leaf River (Ill.) Twp., 1972-76; ins. advisor Harlem Fedn. Tchrs., 1985. Recipient Rehab. Worker Service award Internat. Rehab. Assn., 1985. Mem. Ogle County Mental Health Assn. (v.p. 1972-76). Roman Catholic. Lodge: KC. Avocations: golf, carpentry, chess, music. Home: 210 E 2d Leaf River IL 61047 Office: Harlem Consolidated Sch Dist 9229 N Alpine Rockford IL 61111

FLICK, THOMAS MICHAEL, mathematics educator; b. Covington, Ky., July 14, 1954; s. Thomas Lawrence and Crystel (Moore) F. BS, No. Ky. U., 1976, MA, 1981; MEd, Xavier U., 1977; PhD, Southeastern U., 1979. Assoc. vice prin., dean, chmn. math., prin. summer sch. Purcell Marian High Sch., Cin., 1977—; lectr. astronomy Wilmington Coll., Ohio, 1977-78, math. U. Cin., 1979—. Author: Guidelines for Astronomy Courses, 1976, 78; contbr. articles to profl. jours. Vol. Cin. Nature Ctr., Milford, 1976—; chmn. edn. Astron. League, Washington; tchr. Super Saturday Program for Gifted and Talented., Cin., 1983. Recipient Presdl. Award for Excellence in Math. Edn., 1986; Greater Cin. Found./Gen. Electric Corp. grantee, 1987. Mem. Ohio Council Tchrs. Math. (contest coordinator 1983—, Outstanding Math. Tchr. award 1982), Nat. Astron. League (v.p. 1980-82), Nat. Council Tchrs. Math, Math Assn. Am., Ohio Acad. Sci. (Jerry Acker Outstanding Math. Tchr. award 1986-87), Sigma Xi (Outstanding Math. Tchr. award 1985), Pi Mu Epsilon. Roman Catholic. Club: Midwestern Astronomers. Avocations: golf, tennis, bicycling. Home: 1643 Elder Ct Fort Wright KY 41011 Office: Purcell Marian High Sch 2935 Hackberry St Cincinnati OH 45206

FLICKINGER, ROBERT GUY, veterinary company executive; b. Hope, N.D., Feb. 8, 1924; s. Guy Gaylord and May (Glass) F.; m. Elise Elizabeth Devlin, Jan. 9, 1945; children: Joan, Janice, Elise, Guy. DVM, Iowa State Coll., 1949. Ptnr. Valley Veterinary Clinic, Fargo, N.D., 1949-61; owner, pres. Midwest VeterinarySupply, Fargo and Mpls., 1961—; also bd. dirs. Midwest VeterinarySupply; pres. PennwoodLabs, Burnsville, Minn., 1962—, also bd. dirs. Served with USN, 1944-46. Recipient Immnuology award Tech. Assn. Am, 1964. Mem. Am. Legion. Republican. Methodist.Lodge: Elks. Avocation: farming. Office: Midwest Veterinary Supply 12012 12th Ave S Burnsville MN 55337

FLIEGEL, FREDERICK CHRISTIAN, sociology educator; b. Edmonton, Alta., Can., Apr. 3, 1925; came to U.S., 1928, naturalized, 1935; s. John Carl and Ruth Friedeborg (Aastrup) F.; m. Thellyn Ruth Haller, Aug. 25, 1955; children: Frederick M., Ruth E., David C., Johanna C. Student, Moravian Coll., 1942-43; B.A., U. Wis., 1949, M.A., 1952, Ph.D., 1955. Asst. prof. to assoc. prof. Pa. State U., 1955-65; assoc. prof. Mich. State U., 1966-67; prof. sociology U. Ill., 1968—, head dept., 1970-73; vis. prof. U. Wis., summer 1963, Tamil Nadu Agrl. U., Coimbatore, India, spring 1977; Fulbright sr research scholar CEPEC/CEPLAC, Brazil, spring 1985. Author: (with Roy, Sen and Kivlin) Agricultural Innovations in Indian Villages, 1968, Agricultural Innovation Among Indian Farmers, 1968, Communication in India: Experiments in Introducing Change, 1968; Editor: Rural Sociology, 1970-72. Served with USMC, 1943-46. Fellow Am. Sociol. Assn.; mem. Rural Sociol. Soc. (pres. 1975-76), Midwest Sociol. Soc., AAAS, AAUP. Home: 606 W Church St Champaign IL 61820 Office: Mumford Hall Univ Illinois Urbana IL 61821

FLIEGEL, FREDERICK MARTIN, electrical engineer; b. Bellefonte, Pa., Sept. 14, 1956; s. Frederick Christian and Ruth (Haller) F.; m. Hui Lang Wang, Jan. 1, 1982 (div. Jan. 1984). BEE, U. Ill., 1979, MEE, 1982, PhD in Elec. Engring., 1987. Technician, engr. Hal Communications, Urbana, Ill., 1972-79; mem. tech. staff Tex. Instruments, Dallas, 1982-84; mem. tech staff Electronic Decisions, Urbana, 1984-85, project leader, 1985—; research asst. U. Ill., Urbana, 1979-82, 84-86. Contbr. articles to profl. jours. Mem. IEEE, Assn Old Crows. Office: Electronic Decisions Inc 1114 W Springfield Urbana IL 61801

FLIGIEL, ALAN, dermatologist; b. N.Y.C.; 1 child, Helene. BS, CCNY, 1966; MD, SUNY, 1970. Diplomate Am. Bd. Otolaryngology, Am. Bd. Dermatology. Served to lt. comdr. USNR, 1975-77. Fellow Am. Acad. Dermatology, Am. Acad. Otolaryngology (head and neck surgery).

FLING, ANN LESLIE, real estate leasing professional; b. Ypsilanti, Mich., Jan. 24, 1956; d. Kenneth Alger and Viola Marie (Meagher) Raupp; m. Richard Allen Fling, Apr. 13, 1974; children: Rachel Marie, Carrie Ann. Broker Beale Group, Southfield, Mich., 1979-81, Cushman Wakefield, Southfield, 1981-82; retail leasing specialist Schostak Bros., Southfield, 1982-84, Ramco Gershenson, Southfield, 1984—. Office: Ramco Gershenson 31313 Northwestern Hwy 201 Farmington MI 48018

FLINN, LARRY EARL, military research analyst; b. Kenton, Ohio, Jan. 28, 1938; s. Parl Thomas and Lois Avanelle (Musgrave) F.; m. Lillian Louise Brooks, June 30, 1962; children: Lori, Eric, Jeffrey, Erin. BS in Math., Ohio State U., 1962. Math. educator Goshen Local Schs., Midvale, Ohio, 1962-63; chemist Ohio State U. Research Found., Columbus, 1962-63; sr. analyst Dept. Army Comptroller, Ft. Harrison, Ind., 1976-84; computer specialist Air Force Logistics Command, Wright Patterson AFB, Ohio, 1963-76, ops. researcher, 1984—. Home: 462 Crawford Dr Beavercreek OH 45385 Office: USAF AFLC/ACCCE Wright Patterson AFB OH 45433-5001

FLISS, RAPHAEL M., bishop; b. Milw., Oct. 25, 1930. Student, St. Francis Sem., Houston, Cath. U., Washington. Ordained priest, Roman Cath. Ch., 1956. Bishop Superior, Wis., 1985—. Office: Chancery Office 1201 Hughitt Ave Superior WI 54880 *

FLISS, WILLIAM MICHAEL, financial executive; b. Milw., 1951; s. Alfred Michael Fliss and Evelyn Augusta (Grams) Beyer; m. Patricia Ann Ligman, Oct. 28, 1972; children—Jeremy Scot, Noel Michael, Bryan Christopher. B.B.A., U. Wis. 1973. Fin. planning analyst Walker Mfg. Tenneco Automotive, Racine, Wis., 1979-80; mgr. Gen. Acctg. Perfex div. McQuay, Inc., Milw., 1980-81, asst. div. controller, 1981-82, div. controller, 1982-83; div. controller energy Systems and Services div., 1983-85; mgr. adminstrn. McQuay Services, Plymouth, Minn., 1985—; cons. small bus. systems, Milw., 1984—. Adv. Jr. Achievement, Racine, 1976-79; cubmaster Milwaukee County council Boy Scouts Am., Milw., 1983-85. Mem. Nat. Assn. Accts., Am. Mgmt. Assn. Republican. Roman Catholic. Designer and implementer state of the art service mgmt. computer system. Avocations: camping; golf; baseball coach. Home: 15620 49th Ave N Plymouth MN 55446 Office: McQuay Inc 13600 Industrial Park Blvd Plymouth MN 55441

FLOHR, CHARLES EDWIN, radiologist; b. Scottsbluff, Nebr., Dec. 18, 1950; s. Emanuel and Bertha (Wagner) F.; m. Diane Sue Dirkschneider; children: Dana Marie, Jamie Katherine. BS in Zoology, U. Nebr., Lincoln, 1973; MD, U. Nebr., Omaha, 1977. Diplomate Am. Bd. Radiology. Resident in radiology U. Nebr. Med. Ctr. and affiliated hosps., Omaha, 1977-81; chief of staff St. Joseph's Hosp., Mitchell, S.D., 1985; radiologist Dakota Imaging Assocs., Mitchell, 1981-86; chief of staff Meth. Hosp., Mitchell, 1986. Mem. AMA, Am. Coll. Radiology, Radiol. Soc. N. Am., Internat. Assn. Med. Specialists. Methodist. Avocations: hunting, reading, gardening, boating. Home: 1050 Chalkstone Dr Mitchell SD 57301 Office: Dakota Imaging Assocs 5th & Foster Mitchell SD 57301

FLOHRE, ANTONETTE LUCENTE, trade association administrator; b. Dayton, Ohio, Oct. 30, 1952; d. Anthony Joseph and Eileen Rose (Feltz) Lucente; m. Christopher Robert Flohre, Aug. 9, 1975; 1 child, Ryan Christopher. AA, Sinclair Community Coll., 1977. Legal asst. Turner, Granzow & Hollenkamp, Dayton, 1973-82; dir. small bus. devel. ctr. Dayton C. of C., 1982—. Editor: Small Street Journal. Mem. steering com. YWCA, 1986—, exec. com. Women's Entrepreneurial Conf., Dayton. Mem. Miami Valley Internat. Trade Assn. (sec. 1986). Democrat. Roman Catholic. Avocations: politics, researching history of Dayton. Office: Dayton Area C of C 40 N Main St Dayton OH 54523-1980

FLOOD, HOWARD L., banker; b. N.Y.C., 1934; married. With Assoc. Investments Co., 1958-63; pres., chief exec. officer 1st Nat. Bank Akron, Ohio, 1963—; also dir. 1st Nat. Bank Akron. Served with U.S. Army, 1952-58. Office: First Nat Bank of Akron 106 S Main St Akron OH 44308 *

FLORA, KENT ALLEN, farmer; b. Urbana, Ill., Jan. 7, 1944; s. Loyal Lee and Ercel Hannah (Puzey) F.; m. Sharon Jean Bray, Dec. 31, 1974; children: Donald William, William Christopher, Brent Allyn. BS, U. Ill., 1966. Prodn. mgr. Flora Farms, Fairmount, Ill., 1961-70, owner, operator, 1970—; bd. dirs. Vermilion County Agrl. Extension Adv. Council, 1967-69. V.p. Jamaica Unit Dist. #12 Bd. Edn., Sidell, Ill., 1981—, pres. citizen's adv. council, 1978-82; trustee Vance Twp., Fairmount, 1967-75, mem. Park Bd., 1977-81; mem. exec. com. Vermilion County Rep. Cen. Com., 1986—; v.p. Vermilion County Merit Commn. for Law Enforcement, 1986—; pres. Vermilion County Unit Am. Cancer Soc., 1972-73; Vermilion County campaign coordinator Mike Houston for Ill. State Treas., 1986. Served to sgt. USAR. Named Outstanding Young Farmer Jaycees, Danville, Ill., 1972, Hon. Chpt. Farmer Jamaica Future Farmers Assn., 1985; recipient Centennial Farm award State of Ill., 1970. Mem. Ill. Assn. Sch. Bds., Vermilion County Farm Bur., U. Ill. Alumni Assn., Chi Phi. Presbyterian. Lodges: Masons, Shriners. Avocations: family geneology, collecting Abraham Lincoln memorabilia, travel. Home and Office: Rural Rt 1 PO Box 278 Fairmount IL 61841

FLORELL, ROBERT JAMES, agriculture educator; b. Jamestown, Kans., May 3, 1925; s. Carl A. and Myrtle I. Florell; m. Idonna J. Burkhart, Aug. 1, 1954; children: David J., Brenda L., Scott R. BS, U. Nebr., 1949, MS, 1956, EdD, 1966. Vocat. agr. instr. Stanton (Nebr.) High Sch., 1949-53, David City (Nebr.) High Sch., 1953-58; chief wheat div. Nebr. State Dept. Agr., Lincoln, 1958-62; program coordinator U. Nebr., Lincoln, 1962-66, from asst. prof. to prof. vocat. agr., 1966—. Contbr. articles to profl. jours. Served to sgt. U.S. Army, 1945-47, Korea. Mem. Am. Evaluation Assn., Missouri Valley Adult Edn. Assn. Republican. Methodist. Office: U Nebr 217 Ag Hall 35th St and Holdrege Lincoln NE 68583-0703

FLORES, JHONSON EDER, anesthesiologist; b. Cochabamba, Bolivia, Sept. 8, 1947; came to U.S., 1974; s. Teofanes and Neiza (Arteaga) F.; m. Elizabeth Herrera, July 7, 1973; children: Eliana, Esther. BS, U. Mayor de San Simon, Cochabamba, 1974. Diplomate Am. Bd. Anesthesiology. Intern Somerset Med. Ctr., Somerville, N.J., 1975; resident in anesthesiology Barnes Hosp. Washington U., St. Louis, 1976-78; head ob-gyn anesthesia St. Luke's Hosp. West, Chesterfield, Mo., 1979—. Fellow Am. Coll. Anesthesiology; mem. Am. Soc. Anesthesiology. Republican. Avocations: music, gardening. Home: 442 Cheshire Farm Ct Saint Louis MO 63141

FLORES, LUIS GILBERTO, management educator; b. Lima, Peru, Oct. 29, 1943; came to U.S., 1978; s. Enrique Bartolome and Maria Delfina Flores; m. Maria Teresa Espejo, Oct. 13, 1973; children: Luis Fernando, Jose Antonio, Claudia Maria, Natalia Maria. BS in Agrl. Engring., Nat. Agrarian U., Lima, 1967; Magister in Bus. Adminstrn., ESAN Grad. Sch. Bus. Adminstrn., Lima, 1967; PhD in Bus. Adminstrn., Tex. Tech U., 1976. Dir. ESAN Grad. Sch. Bus. Adminstrn., 1971-72, dir. grad. programs, assoc. prof. mgmt., bus. policy, internat. bus., 1976-78; assoc. prof. mgmt., bus. policy, ops. mgmt. U. No. Ala., Florence, 1978-80; assoc. prof. mgmt., dir. internat. exec. banking No. Ill. U., DeKalb, 1981—; adj. instr. mgmt. and bus. policy Tex. Tech U., Lubbock, 1972-76; cons. Household Fin. Services, Prospect Heights, Ill., 1986-87. Author: (with others) Organizational Goals In The Peruvian Co-Determination and The Yugoslav Self-Determination Systems, 1978; contbr. articles to profl. jours. Fulbright scholar, 1972-76; Ford Found. grantee, 1975, Fed. Inst. Tech. Cooperation grantee, 1975. Mem. Acad. of Mgmt., Acad. Internat. Bus., Midwest Acad. Mgmt., Strategic Mgmt. Soc., Bus. Assn. Latin Am. Studies, Associacion de Graduados de ESAN. Home: 1709 Cedarbrook St Sycamore IL 60178 Office: No Ill U Dept of Mgmt DeKalb IL 60115

FLORESTANO, DANA JOSEPH, architect; b. Indpls., May 2, 1945; s. Herbert Joseph and Myrtle Mae (Futch) F.; m. Peggy Joy Larsen, June 6, 1969. BArch, U. Notre Dame, 1968. Designer, draftsman Kennedy, Brown & Trueblood, architects, Indpls., 1965-69, Evans Woolen Assn., architects, Indpls., 1966; designer, project capt. James Assos., architects and engrs., Indpls., 1969-71; architect, v.p. comml. projects Multi-Planners Inc., architects and engrs., 1972-73; pvt. practice architecture, Indpls., 1973—; pres. Florestano Corp., constrn. mgmt., Indpls., 1973—; co-founder, pres. Solargenics Natural Energy Corp., Indpls., 1975—; prof. archtl. and constrn. tech. Ind. U.-Purdue U. at Indpls.; instr. in field. Tech. adviser hist. architecture Indpls. Model Cities program, 1969-70; mem. Hist. Landmarks Found. Ind., 1970-72; chmn. Com. to Save Union Sta., 1970-71, founder, pres. Union Sta. Found. Inc., Indpls., 1971—. Dep. commr. and tournament dir. archery Pan-Am. Games, Indpls., 1987. Recipient 2d design award Marble Inst. Am., 1967, 1st design award 19th Ann. Progressive Architecture Design awards, 1972; Design award for excellence in devel. Marriott Inn, Indpls., Met. Devel. Commn.-Office of Mayor, 1977; 1st place award design competition for Visitor's Info. Center, Cave Run, Lake, Ky., 1978; 2d design award 1st Ann. Qualified Remodeler, Nat. Competition for Best Rehab. Existing Structures in Am., 1979. Mem. U. Notre Dame Alumni Assn., Notre Dame Club Indpls., AIA (nat. com. historic resources 1974—, commn. on community services, Speakers Bur. Indpls. chpt. 1976—), Ind. Soc. Architects (chmn. historic architecture com. 1970—), Ind. Archery Assn. (founder, pres. 1986—), No. Archery Assn. (bd. dirs., v.p. 1987—), Constrn. Specifications Inst., Constrn. Mgrs. Assn. Ind. (incorporator, dir. 1976—), World Archery Ctr. Home: 5697 N Broadway St Indianapolis IN 46220 Office: 6214 N Carrollton Ave Indianapolis IN 46220

FLORETH, FREDERICK DENNIS, lawyer; b. Litchfield, Ill., Mar. 24, 1956; s. Nelson Keiser and Victoria Jane (Swartz) F.; m. Lauren Jean Pashayan, Sept. 3, 1983. BS, So. Ill. U., Edwardsville, 1979; JD, St. Louis U., 1982. Bar: Ill. 1982, U.S. Dist. Ct. (cen. dist.) Ill. 1983. Sole practice Litchfield, 1983; sr. ptnr. Floreth & Pashayan, Litchfield, 1983—. Pub. adminstr., guardian Montgomery County, Ill., 1984—; Rep. precinct committeeman Montgomery County, 1984—. Mem. ABA, Ill. Bar Assn., Montgomery County Bar Assn. (pres. 1985-86). Home: 803 N Jefferson Litchfield IL 62056 Office: Floreth & Pashayan PO Box 246 Litchfield IL 62056

FLORIAN, MARIANNA BOLOGNESI, civic leader; b. Chgo.; d. Giulio and Rose (Garibaldi) Bolognesi; B.A. cum laude, Barat Coll., 1940; postgrad. Moser Bus. Sch., 1941-42; m. Paul A. Florian III, June 4, 1949; children—Paul, Marina, Peter, Mark. Asst. credit mgr. Stella Cheese Co., Chgo., 1942-45; With ARC ETO Clubmobile Unit, 1945-47; mgr. Passavant Hosp. Gift Shop, 1947-49; pres., Jr. League Chgo., Inc., 1957-59; pres. woman's bd. Passavant Hosp., 1966-68; bd. dirs. Northwestern Meml. Hosp., 1974-81, mem. exec. com., 1974-79; pres. Women's Assn., Chgo. Symphony Orch., 1974-77, founder WFMT radio marathon, 1976; chmn., trustee Guild Chgo. Hist. Soc., 1981-84; trustee Orchestral Assn., 1977—, v.p. 1978-82, vice chmn. 1982-86, mem. exec. com. 1978—; mem. women's bd. Northwestern U.; mem. vis. com. dept. music U. Chgo., 1980—; mem. bd. Antiquarian Soc. Art Inst. Chgo., 1986—. Recipient Citizen Fellowship, Inst. Medicine Chgo., 1975. Clubs: Friday (pres. 1972-74), Contemporary; Winnetka Garden.

FLORIAN, SONIA ATZEFF, radio station manager; b. Oak Park, Ill., Sept. 22, 1935; d. Nicola and Olga (Laftery) Atzeff; m. William Chad Florian, June 22, 1967. BA, Roosevelt U., 1960. Mgr. radio sta. WNIB, Chgo., 1958—. Home: 3100 N Sheridan Rd Chicago IL 60657 Office: Sta WNIB 1140 W Erie Chicago IL 60622

FLORINE, GRANT EDWARD, dentist; b. Red Wing, Minn., Apr. 3, 1954; s. Donald Curtis and Dolores Emma (Sass) F.; m. Ruby Jane Muetzel, June 4, 1983. DDS, U. Minn., 1980. Republican. Lutheran. Avocations: reading, golf, boating, cross-country skiing. Office: 913 3d Ave SE Rochester MN 55904

FLORJANCIC, RONALD MERK, manufacturing company executive; b. Cleve., Apr. 24, 1936; s. Merko S. and Jane (Milavec) F.; m. Dorothy M. Maciokas, Apr. 23, 1966; children: Ronald K., Robert S. BBA, John Carroll U., 1970. Market analyst Standard Oil of Ohio, Cleve., 1958-60; dir. fin. analysis and pricing Gould, Cleve., 1966-73; staff controller White Consol. Industries, Cleve., 1973-77; v.p. mfg. Hupp Co. div. White Consol. Industries, Cleve., 1977—. Home: 7060 Bently Pl Concord OH 44077 Office: Hupp Co 1135 Ivanhoe Rd Cleveland OH 44110

FLORQUIST, PAUL ANTHONY, nursing home administrator; b. Denver, Oct. 25, 1946; s. Bernt Iver and Helen Josephine (Hanson) F.; m. Evelyn Ruth Woods, July 28, 1973; children: Christopher, Lane, Travis. BBA, Phillips U., Enid, Okla., 1970. Cert. nursing home adminstr., Colo., Ind., Kans. Adminstr. Alpine Meadows, Stemaboat Springs, Colo., 1973-75, Grandview Manor, Berthoud, Colo., 1975-76, Pueblo Manor, Colo., 1976-77, Villa Pueblo Towers, Pueblo, 1977-81, Meadowood Retirement Community, Bloomington, Ind., 1981-82, Western Prairie Care Home, Ulysses, Kans., 1982—; adv. com. mem. U. So. Colo. LPN Sch., Pueblo, 1976-77. Mem. Kans. Assn. Homes for Aging (bd. dirs., community service com. 1987—), Kans. Health Care Assn. (peer assistance com. 1984-85), Kans. Profl. Nursing Home Adminstrs. Assn. Republican. Baptist. Lodges: Kiwanis, Rotary (Internat. Service award 1983-84, Community Service award 1984-86, Outstanding Community Service award 1985-86, bd. dirs. Ulysses chpt. 1985—). Avocations: skiing, bicycling, classic and fgn. cars. Home: 819 N Cheyenne Ulysses KS 67880 Office: Western Prairie Care Home 300 E Maize Ulysses KS 67880

FLORSHEIM, THOMAS W., shoe manufacturing company executive; b. 1930. BA, Wabash Coll.; MA, U. Chgo., 1955. Mgr. sales, v.p. Florsheim div. Internat. Shoe Co.; with Weyenberg Shoe Mfg. Co., Milw., 1964—, pres., 1964-68, chmn. bd. dirs., chief exec. officer, 1968—. Office: Weyenberg Shoe Mfg Co 234 E Reservoir Ave Milwaukee WI 53201 *

FLORY, ELDON RAY, savings and loan association executive, computer software executive; b. Lawrence, Kans., Jan. 7, 1948; s. Harold Kenneth and Mary Ellen (Kinzie) F.; m. Cheryl Ann Dodder, July 26, 1969; children: Trenton Harold, Tara Lynn. AS, Emporia (Kans.) State U., 1968. Computer programmer Lawrence Pub. Schs., 1968-72; systems analyst Capitol Fed. Savs., Topeka, 1972-82, dir. mgmt. info. systems, 1982—; cons. City of Lawrence, 1972-73, Kustom Electronics, Chanute, Kans., 1970-72; lectr. Am. Water Works Assn., Denver, 1986—, Nat. Fin. Exec. Conf., Palm Springs, Calif., 1986—. Mem. EDP adv. com. Topeka United Way, 1986; mem. curriculum adv. bd. Emporia State U., 1984—; active Free Meth. Ch., Lawrence, 1980—. Mem. Kans. Rural Water Assn., lectr. Kans. Rural Water Assn., Seneca, 1984—. Republican. Methodist. Avocations: photography, skiing. Home: 3122 W 26th Lawrence KS 66046 Office: Capitol Fed Savs 700 Kansas Ave Topeka KS 66603

FLOYD, THOMAS ALAN, oil company executive; b. Racine, Wis., Nov. 25, 1941; s. Lyal William and Mildred Viola (Wemmert) F.; m. Margaret Johanna Kearney, June 17, 1967; children: Thomas, Meg, Kathryn, Kevin, Brendan. BBA, U. Notre Dame, 1963. CPA, Ill. Staff acct. Touche, Ross & Co., Chgo., 1963-74, ptnr., 1974-79; ptnr. Kirkby, Fitzgerald, Rynell, Floyd & Burkett, Bloomingdale, Ill., 1980-82; v.p. fin., treas. Martin Exploration Mgmt. Co. and Martin Oil Marketing Ltd., Alsip, Ill., 1983—; pres., bd. dirs. Fin. Assocs. Inc., Alsip, 1984—; sec., treas., bd. dirs. Colo. Energy Corp., Alsip, 1983—. Commr. Bartlett (Ill.) Park Dist., 1983—, treas., 1984-88. Mem. Am. Inst. CPA's, Ill. Soc. CPA's, Tax Execs. Inst. Roman Catholic. Club: Notre Dame Alumni (Chgo.). Lodge: Rotary (treas. Bartlett 1982-83). Avocations: golf, bridge. Home: 150 Shady Ln Bartlett IL 60103 Office: Martin Exploration Mgmt Co PO Box 298 Blue Island IL 60406

FLUEHR, DARRELL KRELLE, systems analyst; b. Omaha, May 18, 1958; s. John James and Mary Ardys (Krelle) F. BS in Computer Sci., Mich. State U., 1980. Systems analyst Enron, Omaha, 1980-83; sr. systems analyst Henningson, Durham and Richardson, Omaha, 1983-85; systems analyst U. Nebr., Lincoln, 1985—. Mem. Assn. for Computing Machinery, Jaycees (Bronze Key 1982-83), Am. Guild of Organists. Congregational. Home: 2800 Pub Ct #17 Lincoln NE 68516 Office: U Nebr 29 WSEC Lincoln NE 68588

FLUM, JEROME MICHAEL, restoration architect; b. Detroit, Sept. 30, 1950; s. Lawrence John and Mildred Mary (Selensky) F.; m. Rosa Josefine Pischem, Dec. 24, 1976. BArch, U. Detroit, 1972. Field coordinator Greimel, Malcomson et al, Detroit, 1972-75; constrn. mgr. Area Constrn., Detroit, 1977-80; supr. Belvedere Constrn. Co., Detroit, 1977-80; v.p. F. Lax Inc., Ferndale, Mich., 1980-84; sales dir. Guaranteed Constrn., Farmington Hills, Mich., 1984—; Inventor fireplace/kachelofen, 1983; patentee in field. Assoc. Detroit Symphony Orch., 1983; mem. Founders Soc. Detroit Symphony Orch., Ditroit Hist. Soc.; patron Save Orch. Hall. Mem. Internat. Platform Assn. Home & Office: 29800 Stockton Farmington Hills MI 48024

FLUNO, JERE DAVID, business executive; b. Wisconsin Rapids, Wis., June 3, 1941; s. Rexford Hollis and Irma Dell (Wells) F.; m. Anne Marie Derezinski, Aug. 10, 1963; children: Debra, Julie, Mary Beth, Brian. B.B.A., U. Wis., 1963. C.P.A., Ill. Audit supr. Grant Thornton, Chgo., 1963-69; controller W.W. Grainger, Inc., Skokie, Ill., 1969-74, v.p., controller, 1974-75, v.p. fin., 1975-81, sr. v.p., chief fin. officer, 1981-84, vice chmn., 1984—, dir., 1975—; v.p., asst. treas., dir. W.W. Grainger, Internat., Skokie, Ill., 1977—; v.p. , dir. Grainger FSC, Inc.; v.p., dir., asst. treas. Dayton Electric Mfg. Co., Chgo., 1981—. Bd. dirs. Econ. Club Chgo., 1979; mem. Bascom Hill Soc. U. Wis., Madison, 1979; trustee, chmn. Glenkirk Found., Northbrook, Ill., 1981; bd. dirs. U. Wis. Found. Mem. Am. Inst. C.P.A.s, Fin. Execs. Inst., Ill. C.P.A. Soc., U. Wis. Alumni Assn. (bd. dirs.). Republican. Roman Catholic. Clubs: Knollwood (Lake Forest, Ill.); U. Wis. (Chgo.); Island Country (Marco Island, Fla.). Office: W W Grainger Inc 5500 W Howard St Skokie IL 60077

FLYNN, DONALD EDWARD, diversified investment company executive; b. Lincoln, Nebr., May 7, 1940; s. James Raphael and Marjorie L. (Rosenbaum) F.; m. Janice Marie Obereuter, Aug. 25, 1962; children: Ann M., Michael J., Patricia A. BA, U. Iowa, 1962; MBA, San Diego State U., 1970. Investment analyst San Diego Trust & Savs., 1969-70; portfolio mgr. Security Pacific Nat. Bank, Los Angeles, 1970-71; v.p. investments Life Investors Inc., Cedar Rapids, 1971-80; v.p. Moram. Capital Corp., Cedar Rapids, 1980-85; pres. Investam. Venture Group, Inc., Cedar Rapids, 1985—; bd. dirs. Teleconnect Co., Cedar Rapids, Kilborn Photo Products, Cedar Rapids; chmn. bd. Electronic Technology Corp., Cedar Rapids. Served to capt. USAF, 1962-68, Vietnam. Decorated Air medal. Mem. Nat. Assn. Small Bus. Investment Cos., Des Moines Soc. Fin. Analysts. Roman

Catholic. Club: Cedar Rapids Country. Avocations: tennis, golf. Home: 3018 Terry Dr SE Cedar Rapids IA 52403 Office: InvestAm Venture Group Inc 800 American Bldg Cedar Rapids IA 52403

FLYNN, JAMES ARTHUR, marketing executive; b. Potsdam, N.Y., May 7, 1939; s. Francis John and Signa Virginia (Harvey) F.; m. Linda Ann Barfield, July 29, 1961; children: Shelia D., Lisa M., Laura E. BS in Engrng. and Math., U.S. Naval Acad., 1961; MBA in Fin., Harvard U., 1969. Commd. ensign USN, 1961, advanced through grades to lt., 1965, resigned, 1967; sr. engagement mgr. McKinsey & Co., Dallas, 1969-76; pres. Trident Mgmt. Corp., Dallas, 1976-78; v.p. Heidrich & Struggles, Dallas, 1978-80; corp. v.p. Brown Group, Inc., St. Louis, 1980-83; sr. v.p. Brown Shoe Co., St. Louis, 1983-84, exec. v.p., 1984—. Republican. Roman Catholic. Clubs: University (St. Louis), Harvard, Harvard Bus. Sch. Avocation: running.

FLYNN, KEVIN MICHAEL, architect; b. Little Falls, Minn., Sept. 20, 1961; s. Robert Joseph and Patricia Marie (Hayes) F.; m. Jane Mjolsness, Sept. 29, 1984. Student, Moorhead (Minn.) State U., 1979-81; BS, BArch, N.D. State U., 1984. Jr. architect Ackerberg & Assocs., Mpls., 1984-85; architect Sieger-Svedberg, Mpls., 1985-86, Leonard Parker Architects, Mpls., 1986—. Mem. Gov.'s Design Team, Minn., 1985—. Mem. AIA (Paper Architecture award 1987), Nat. Soc. Architects, Minn. Soc. Architects (assoc.), N.D. Soc. Architects (Gold medal 1984). Avocations: sculpture, running.

FLYNN, MARK ANDREW, real estate investment executive; b. St. Louis, Oct. 6, 1945; s. Francis Andrew and Estelle Emily (Myerscough) F.; m. Ann Frances O'Shaughnessy, June 24, 1967; children: Padraic Andrew, Robert Francis, Molly (dec.). BA, St. Louis U., 1967, MA, 1972; postgrad., U. Mo., 1967-78. V.p. Midwest Mgmt. Corp., Kansas City, Mo., 1972-81; chief operating officer Mitchell Energy Co., Kansas City, 1981-82; v.p. The Kansas City Corp., Prairie Village, Kans., 1982-85; pres. Remcor Inc., Prairie Village, 1985—. Pres. Maitland (Mo.) Housing Corp., 1974-78. Mem. Nat. Assn. Realtors. Democrat. Roman Catholic. Avocation: soccer referee. Office: Remcor Inc 7600 Stateline Prairie Village KS 66208

FLYNN, ROBERT ANTHONY, business executive; b. Chgo., May 20, 1931; s. Mortimer G. and Helen M. (Fisherkeller) F.; m. Mary Lou Ladley, June 23, 1962. B.S., U. Ill., 1957. Zone sales mgr. Top Value Enterprises, Dayton, Ohio, 1957-69; v.p. sales Nat. Research, Chgo., 1969-76; pres. M.L. Flynn & Assocs., Naperville, Ill., 1976—. Served with USN, 1950-54. Roman Catholic. Clubs: O'Leary's Upside-Down (Chgo.)(v.p. 1982-84), Town & Country Equestrian Assn. (Chgo.)(pres. 1969-70). Lodges: KC, Elks. Avocations: golf, woodworking. Home: 1 Canterbury Ct South Barrington IL 60010 Office: ML Flynn & Assocs 319 S Washington St Naperville IL 60540

FLYNN, ROBERT EMMETT, process controls equipment company executive; b. Montreal, Que., Can., Sept. 10, 1933; came to U.S., 1957; s. Emmett Joseph and Pauline Perrier (Lupien) F.; m. Irene P. Kantor, July 28, 1960; children: Donna, Darren, Diane. B.S. in Physics, Loyola Coll., Montreal, 1955; B.E. in Engring, McGill U., 1957; M.B.A., Rutgers U., 1962. Vice pres. Carborundum Co., Niagara Falls, N.Y., 1973-76, group v.p., 1976-79, sr. v.p. carborundum, 1979-81; exec. v.p. Fisher Controls Internat. Inc., St. Louis, 1981-82; pres., chief exec. officer Fisher Control Internat. Inc., St. Louis, 1982-85; chmn. bd., chief exec. officer Fisher Control Internat. Inc., 1985—; dir. Nutra Sweet Co. Trustee Foundry Edn. Found., Chgo., 1977-80; bd. dirs. United Way, Niagara Falls, 1972-81, campaign chmn., 1978; mem. pres.'s council St. Louis U., 1984—; bd. dirs. St. Louis Regional Commerce and Growth Assn, 1985—, mem. exec. com., 1985—, chmn. tech. task force, 1985—; bus. devel. com. City of Clayton, Mo.; mem. adv. com. Fontbonne Coll., 1986—; mem. adv. bd. Gateway Mid-Am., St. Louis Tech. Ctr. Served with USMCR, 1958. Republican. Roman Catholic. Clubs: St. Louis (Clayton, Mo.); Old Warson Country (St. Louis). Home: 2 Barclay Woods Saint Louis MO 63124 Office: Fisher Controls Internat Inc 8000 Maryland Ave Clayton MO 63105

FOERSTER, BERND, architecture educator; b. Danzig, Dec. 5, 1923; came to U.S., 1947, naturalized, 1954; s. Joseph and Martha (Brumm) F.; m. Enell Dowling, May 13, 1950; children: Kent, Mark (dec.). Student, Columbia U., 1948-49; B.S. in Architecture, U. Cin., 1954; M.Arch., Rensselaer Poly. Inst., 1957. Worked for Govt. Netherlands, 1945-47; with various engrs. and architects offices 1950-59, ch. bldg. cons., design cons., 1954—; instr. architecture U. Cin., 1954, Rensselaer Poly. Inst., Troy, N.Y., 1954-56; asst. prof. Rensselaer Poly. Inst., 1956-62, assoc. prof., 1962-65, prof., 1965-71; dean Kans. State U., Manhattan, 1971-84; prof. Kans. State U., 1971—; cons. archtl. and community surveys N.Y. State Council on Arts, 1962-71; chmn. Gov.'s Adv. Com. on Historic Preservation in N.Y. State, 1968-71; cons. Albany Hist. Sites Commn., 1967-71, Independence (Mo.) Heritage Commn., 1975-77; leader U.S. del. on preservation planning to People's Republic of China, 1982. Author: Man and Masonry, 1960, Pattern and Texture, 1961, Architecture Worth Saving in Rensselaer County, N.Y, 1965, (with others) Independence, Missouri, 1978; films Man and Masonry, 1961 (Am. Film Festival selection); films What Do You Tear Down Next?, 1964, Earth and Fire, 1964, Assault on the Wynantskill, 1967. Dir. Mohawk-Hudson Council on Ednl. TV, 1968-71, v.p., 1970-71; co-chmn. Conf. on Rensselaer County, 1966; pres. Rensselaer County Council for Arts, 1963-64, 66-67; Bd. dirs. Albany Inst. History and Art, 1967-71; trustee Olana Historic Site, 1969-71; pres. bd. trustees Riley County Hist. Mus., 1977; chmn. Manhattan Downtown Redevel. Adv. Bd., 1979-85; mem. State Bldg. Adv. Commn., 1980-82; mem. Council Drayton Hall, Nat. Historic Landmark, Charleston, S.C., 1985—. Mem. AIA (com. historic resources 1977—, vice chmn. 1986, chmn. 1987, state preservation coordinator 1979—); mem. AIA Coll. Fellows; Mem. Kans. Soc. Architects (sec. 1975, exec. com. 1975-80, pres.-elect 1978, pres. 1979), Nat. Trust Hist. Preservation (bd. advs. 1979-81, trustee 1981—), Nature Conservancy, AAUP (past chpt. pres.), Assn. Collegiate Schs. Architecture, The Land Inst. (dir. 1976-87), Manhattan Arts Council (dir. 1973-78, pres. 1976-77), Kans. Preservation Alliance (dir. 1979-85), Nat. Council Preservation Edn. (dir. 1980—, vice-chmn. 1981-85), Sierra Club, Audubon Soc., Scarab, Tau Sigma Delta., Phi Kappa Phi. Home: 920 Ratone Street Manhattan KS 66502

FOGARTY, DANIEL PATRICK, graphic arts manufacturing executive; b. Kansas City, Mo., Apr. 4, 1961; s. John Francis and Mary Louise (Ernst) F. BA in Journalism, Kansas U., Lawrence, 1984. Asst. account exec. Barickman Advt., Kansas City, 1984-85; account exec. Fletcher Mayo Assocs., Kansas City, 1985-86; dir. mktg. Solna, Inc., Kansas City, 1986—. Republican. Roman Catholic. Avocations: photography, skiing, travel, hiking. Office: Solna Inc 6050 Connecticut St Kansas City MO 64120

FOGEL, ARNOLD DAVID, manufacturing executive; b. Chgo., Aug. 12, 1935; s. Morris and Bessie (Abrams) F.; m. Geraldine Aronov, Oct. 27, 1963; children: Denise Allyn, Kenneth Edward. Student, Roosevelt U., 1957, Harvard U., 1975. Various positions Brunswick Corp., Skokie, Ill., 1956-79, dir. acquisitions, 1979-80, dir. planning, 1981-82, v.p. mktg. BRC, 1982-84, pres. BRC, 1984—; pres. Nat. Bowling Council, Washington, 1985-86; v.p. MDA, N.Y.C., 1984—. Mem. Bowling Proprietors Assn. Am. (promotion com. 1986—). Jewish. Clubs: Muirfield Golf (Dublin, Ohio); Highland Park Country (Ill.). Home: 601 Warbler Ct Highland Park IL 60035 Office: Brunswick Corp One Brunswick Pl Skokie IL 60077

FOGEL, HENRY, orchestra administrator; b. N.Y.C., Sept. 23, 1942; s. Julius and Dorothy (Levine) F.; m. Frances Sylvia Polner, June 12, 1965; children—Karl Franz, Holly Dana. Student, Syracuse U., 1960-63. Program dir., v.p. Sta. WONO, Syracuse, N.Y., 1963-78; orch. mgr. N.Y. Philharm., N.Y.C., 1978-81; exec. dir. Nat. Symphony Orch., Washington, 1981-86; exec. v.p. Chgo. Symphony Orch., 1986—. Record reviewer Fanfare Mag., 1979—. Mem. Am. Symphony Orch. League, Nat. Acad. Rec. Arts and Scis., Assn. Recorded Sound Collections (record reviewer jour. 1978—). Home: 1123 N Oak Park Ave Oak Park IL 60302 Office: Chgo Symphony Orch 220 S Michigan Ave Chicago IL 60604 *

FOGEL, SIDNEY ALLEN, radiologist; b. Phila, Apr. 18, 1931; s. Albert David and Gussie (Garbeil) F.; m. Sarah Anne Millian, June 24, 1954 (dec. June 1976); m. Kristine Serre Merrill, May 28, 1977 (div. Sept. 1980); children: David J., Daniel N., Benjamin, Susan L., Carole, Michael H. BS, Temple U., Phila., 1951; DO, Phil. Coll. Osteo. Medicine, 1955; PhD, Inst. Advanced Study of Human Sex, San Francisco, 1986. Diplomate Am. Bd. Radiology. Gen. practice radiology Mich., 1956-65; radiology resident Pontiac (Mich.) Osteo. Hosp., 1965-68; chmn. radiology Jackson (Mich.) Osteo. Hosp., 1968-71; assoc. prof. radiology Chgo. Coll. Osteo. Medicine, 1971-73; radiologist spl. procedures Northwest Gen. Hsop., Milw., 1973-76; chmn. dept. radiology Mary Rutan Hosp., Bellefontaine, Ohio, 1977—; sex therapist Springfield, Ohio, 1987—. Buddhist. Home: 7798 Country Rd 144 East Liberty OH 45319 Office: Mary Rutan Hosp 205 Palmer Bellefontaine OH 43311

FOGEL, STEVEN TEDD, physician; b. St. Louis, July 7, 1950; s. Harry Y. and Evelyn F.; m. Connie Jean Eller, Dec. 21, 1973 (div. Mar. 1980); 1 dau., Melissa Shawn. AB, Washington U., St. Louis, 1973; MD, U. Mo., 1976. Diplomate Am. Bd. Ob-Gyn., Nat. Bd. Med. Examiners. Intern, Kansas City (Mo.) Gen. Hosp., 1976-77; resident dept. ob-gyn U. Mo., Kansas City, 1976-79, chief resident, 1979-80, asst. clin. prof. dept. ob-gyn; practice medicine specializing in ob-gyn, Kansas City, 1980—; coordinator resident physician teaching program in ob-gyn Menorah Med. Ctr., Kansas City. Mem. AMA, Mo. State Med. Assn., Jackson County Med. Soc., Kansas City Gynecol. Soc., Am. Coll. Obstetricians and Gynecologists, Phi Beta Kappa. Jewish. Clubs: K.C. Racquet. Lodge: B'nai B'rith. Home: 5304 Mission Woods Terr Mission Woods KS 66205 Office: Plaza Medical Bldg 1000 E 50th St Suite 300 Kansas City MO 64110

FOGELMAN, AVRON B., real estate executive; b. Mar. 1, 1940; s. Morris F.; grad. Tulane U., Memphis State U. Law Sch.; m. Wendy Mimeles, Dec. 24, 1961; children—Hal David, Richard Louis, Mark Alan. Pres., Fogelman Properties; co-owner Kansas City Royals; owner Memphis Chick's Baseball Team; chmn. bd. Wendy's of New Orleans. Former chmn. bd. Mud Island Park, Memphis; mem. Pres.'s exec. bd. Tulane U.; chmn. Memphis and Shelby County Land Use Control Bd., 1978-79; chmn. bus. adv. council Memphis State U., 1978; bd. dirs. Tenn. Sports Hall of Fame; vice chmn. bd. Future Memphis; chmn. awards banquet NCCJ, 1981; mem. bd. adminstrn. Tulane U.; bd. dirs. Gov.'s Tech. Found. for Tenn.; bd. dirs. Memphis Jobs Conf., Tenn. Gov.'s Residence Found.; mem. president's council Southwestern Coll.; mem. Gov.'s Adv. Council on Better Schs. Recipient Outstanding Citizen award East Memphis Civitan Club; Liberty Bell award Memphis Bar Assn.; Best Ten of a Decade award Comml. Appeal; Outstanding Community Salesman of Yr. award Sales and Mktg. Execs. Memphis, Inc.; Disting. Service award Memphis State U.; Memphis State U. Bus. Sch. named Fogelman Coll. Bus. and Econs. in his honor; entrepreurial fellow Memphis State U., 1980. Mem. Memphis C. of C. (pres.). Home: 5491 Shady Grove Rd Memphis TN 38117 Office: 1000 Brookfield Memphis TN 38119 *

FOGELSON, GERALD WARREN, real estate developer; b. Dover, N.J., Sept. 10, 1933; s. Harry David and Henrietta Rose (Kurtz) F.; m. Ellen Borde (div.); m. Georgia Jean Bender, July 1, 1984; children: Bruce Alan, Bari Lynn, Douglas, Molly Bender. BS cum laude, LeHigh U., Bethlehem, Pa., 1955. Pvt. practice real estate developer Morris and Sussex Counties, N.J., 1955-58; pres. The Fogelson Co's, Inc., Chgo., 1958—; v.p. Perine Devel. Corp. Indpls., 1960-61; founder, pres. Fogelson Devel. Corp. and Mid-Am. Devel. Corp., 1961; ptnr. Norfold and Western R.R., 1967; chmn. The Fogelson Found.; also mem. adv. bd. numerous others. Developer: Kingston Green Projects, Ind. and Ill., Mansards Projects, Elkhart, Ind., Northbrook Apts., Hammond, Ind., Tiberon Trails, Merrillville, Ind., Briar East Shopping Ctr., Hammond, Pine Island Plaza, Schererville, Ind., Boonton(N.J.) Shopping Ctr., Northbrook Offices, Elkhart, Greenbrier Offices, Indpls., Wrigley-Olfield Mansion, Chgo., Patterson-McCormick Mansion Chgo.; numerous others. Served to cpl. U.S. Army, 1956-58. Office: The Fogelson Co's Inc 867 N Dearborn Chicago IL 60610

FOGERTY, JAMES EDWARD, archivist, state official; b. Mpls., Jan. 26, 1945; s. Robert P. and Ralpha Chamberlain (James) F. B.A., Coll. St. Thomas, 1968; M.L.S., U. Minn., 1972. Regional ctrs. dir. Minn. Hist. Soc., St. Paul, 1972-76, field dir., 1976-79, dep. state archivist, 1979-86, head aquisitions and curatorial dept., 1986—; sec.-treas. Midwest Archives Conf., Chgo., 1977-81, pres., 1983-85. Editor: Oral History Collections of the Minnesota Historical Society, 1984; contbr. articles to Am. Archivist, Midwestern Archivist, History News, others. Mem. Soc. Am. Archivists, Oral History Assn., Midwest Archives Conf., Am. Assn. For State and Local History, Phi Alpha Theta. Avocations: hiking, canoeing, thoroughbred bloodlines research. Office: Minn Hist Soc 690 Cedar St Saint Paul MN 55101

FOGERTY, ROBERT PAUL, historian; b. Elwood, Ind., Sept. 12, 1905; s. Michael Joseph and Antoinette Genevieve (Hueper) F.; A.B., U. Notre Dame, 1928; LL.B., St. Thomas Law Sch., 1933; M.A., U. Minn., 1936, Ph.D., 1942; D.H.L. (hon.), Coll. St. Thomas, 1983; m. Ralpha Chamberlain James, June 22, 1943; children—James Edward, Mary Curran. Admitted to Minn. bar, 1934; instr., Coll. St. Thomas, 1928-36, asst. prof., 1936-42, prof. history, 1946-75, prof. emeritus, 1975—, dir. Div. Social Scis., 1957-75, chmn. dept. history, 1970-75; vis. prof. U. Minn., 1950, Macalester Coll., 1969; mem. Minn. State Rev. Bd. Nat. Register of Historic Places, 1970-83, participating mem. emeritus, 1983—, chmn., 1974-75; reviewer Div. Research Grants, NEH, 1976—. Mem. Gov.'s Commn. on Constl. Revision, Minn., 1950-51. Served to maj. USAAF, 1942-46. Mem. Am. Assn. Colls. for Tchr. Edn. (instl. rep. 1960-72), Am. Hist. Assn., Orgn. Am. Historians, Minn. Hist. Soc., Nat. Trust for Historic Preservation, Upper Midwest History Conf. (chmn. 1953-54, 62-63, sec. 1960-61), Coll. St. Thomas Alumni Assn., Notre Dame Alumni Assn. Roman Catholic. Author: The Law of Contracts in Colonial Massachusetts and Maryland Compared with English Common Law, 1936; An Institutional Study of the Territorial Courts in the Old Northwest, 1788-1848, 1942. Home: 1780 Hampshire Ave Saint Paul MN 55116 Office: Coll St Thomas Box 4158 Saint Paul MN 55105

FOGLAND, DANIEL WILLIAM, city official; b. North Platte, Nebr., May 13, 1953; s. Max Norman and Fern Pauline (Forsberg) F.; m. Christine Ann Cohagan, Aug. 28, 1976; children—Chad, Kylie. A.A., North Platte Jr. Coll., 1973; A.G.S., Mid-Plains Community Coll., 1977. Bldg. insp. City of North Platte (Nebr.), 1972-77; mgr. W.T. Krvelberg Co., North Platte, 1977-78; bldg. insp. City of Rapid City (S.D.), 1978-80; chief bldg. ofcl. City of Grand Island (Nebr.), 1980-84; pres. Copycat Instant Print, 1985—. Mem. Internat. Conf. Bldg. Ofcls., Nebraskaland Conf. Bldg. Ofcls. and Inspectors, City of Grand Island Hall County Regional Planning Commn. Methodist. Home: 1519 W Division Grand Island NE 68801 Office: 1212 W 2d St Grand Island NE 68801

FOGLE, KENNETH JAMES, architect; b. Ridgewood, N.J., Aug. 23, 1951; s. Howard Daniel Jr. and Roberta May (Ashe) F.; ml Janet May Ferguson, Apr. 18, 1970; children: Kenneth J. Jr., Megan Leigh. BS in Architecture, Kent State U., 1973, MA in Architecture, 1975. Registered architect, Ohio. Architect Toguchi & Assoc., Cleve., 1973-78; exec. asst. Cuyahoga County Bd. Mental Retardation, Cleve., 1978-83; assoc. Collins, Rimer & Gordon, Cleve., 1983-86; pres. Fogle/Stenzel Architects, Cleve., 1986—. Chmn. Gov.'s Long Term Care Task Force, Columbus, 1984. T.C. scholar, 1973; Teaching fellow, 1973-75. Mem. AIA (bd. dirs. Cleve. chpt. 1980-85), Architecture Soc. Ohio (treas. 1986—). Presbyterian. Lodge: Rotary. Avocations: golf, skiing. Home: 2869 Hampshire Rd Cleveland Heights OH 44418 Office: Fogle/Stenzel Architects Inc 2044 Euclid Ave Suite 202 Cleveland OH 44115

FOGLESONG, JAMES HAROLD, bank executive; b. Des Moines, Aug. 18, 1945; s. Harold B. and Margaret L. Foglesong; m. Janet A. Guffin, Nov. 8, 1969; children: Amy E., Mark T., Jonathan P. BS, Drake U., 1967. Sr. staff acct. Ernst & Whinney, CPAs, Des Moines, 1967-73; asst. controller Iowa-Des Moines Nat. Bank, 1973-77; exec. v.p. First of Am. Bank-La LaPorte (Ind.) N.A., 1977—; bd. dirs. Ind. Benefit Life Ins. Co., 1984—; instr. Am. Inst. Banking Continuing Edn. Program. Bd. dirs. LaPorte YMCA, 1980—, LaPorte Hosp., 1981-85; v.p. congregation Trinity Luth. Ch., LaPorte, 1981, treas., 1982-86. Served with U.S. Army, 1968-69. Mem. Am. Inst. CPA's. Lodges: Lions, Elks. Office: First of Am Bank LaPorte NA 800 Lincolnway PO Box 5050 LaPorte IN 46350

FOK, THOMAS DSO YUN, civil engineer, educator; b. Canton, China, July 1, 1921; came to U.S., 1947, naturalized, 1956; s D. H. and C. (Tse) F.; m. Maria M.L. Liang, Sept. 18, 1949. B.Eng., Nat. Tung-Chi U., Szechuan, China, 1945; M.S., U. Ill., 1948; M.B.A. Dr. Nadler Money Marketeer scholar, NYU, 1950; Ph.D., Carnegie-Mellon U., 1956. Registered profl. engr., N.Y., Pa., Ohio, Ill., Ky., W.Va., Ind., Md., Fla. Structural designer Lummus Co., N.Y.C., 1951-53; design engr. Richardson, Gordon & Assocs., cons. engrs., Pitts., 1956-58; assoc. prof. engring. Youngstown U., Ohio, 1958-67, dir. computing ctr., 1963-67; ptnr. Cernica, Fok & Assocs., cons. engrs., Youngstown, Ohio, 1958-64; prin. Thomas Fok & Assocs., cons. engrs., Youngstown, Ohio, 1964-65; ptnr. Mosure-Fok & Syrakis Co., Ltd., cons. Engrs., Youngstown, Ohio, 1965-76; cons. engr. to Mahoning County Engr. Ohio, 1960-65; pres. Computing Systems & Tech., Youngstown, Ohio, 1967-72; chmn. Thomas Fok and Assocs., Ltd., cons. engrs., Youngstown, Ohio, 1977—. Contbr. articles to profl. jours. Trustee Pub. Library of Youngstown and Mahoning County, 1973—; trustee Youngstown State U. Found, 1975—; trustee Youngstown State U., 1975-84, chmn., 1981-83. Recipient Walter E. and Caroline H. Watson Found. Disting. Prof.'s award Youngstown U., 1966, Outstanding Person award Mahoning Valley Tech. Socs. Council, 1987. Fellow ASCE; mem. Am. Concrete Inst., Internat. Assn. for Bridge and Structural Engring., Am. Soc. Engring. Edn., Nat. Soc. Profl. Engrs., AAAS, Soc. Am. Mil. Engrs., Ohio Acad. Sci., N.Y. Acad. Sci., Sigma Xi, Beta Gamma Sigma, Sigma Tau, Delta Pi Sigma. Lodge: Rotary. Home: 325 S Canfield-Niles Rd Youngstown OH 44515 Office: 3896 Mahoning Ave Youngstown OH 44515

FOLEY, DANIEL PATRICK, psychology educator; b. Cin., Oct. 15, 1920; s. Daniel Patrick and Mildred Dowell (Lamborn) F. LittB in Greek, Xavier U., 1945; Licentiate in Philosophy, West Baden (Ind.) Coll., 1948, Licentiate in Sacred Theology, 1955; MA in Exptl. Psychology, Loyola U., Chgo., 1951; PhD in Clin. Psychology, Ottawa U., Ontario, Can., 1962. Lic. clin. psychologist, Ohio. Tchr. St. Ignatius High Sch., Cleve., 1950-51; dir. pub. relations St. Xavier Sch., Cin., 1957-58; prof. psychology Xavier U., Cin., 1958—. Contbr. articles to profl. jours. Mem. Am. Psychol. Assn., Cin. Psychol. Assn. (bd. govs. 1966-67). Home: Jesuit Residence 3800 Victory Pkwy Cincinatti OH 45207 Office: Xavier U Elet Hall 2800 Victory Pkwy Cincinatti OH 45207

FOLEY, EDMOND WILLIAM, lawyer, accountant; b. Lebanon, Mo., Nov. 19, 1951; s. Edmond Ignatius and Rosemary Margaret (Guber) F.; m. Barbara Sue Bauer, June 22, 1974; children: Heather, Eileen, Faith, James. BBA in Acctg., U. Notre Dame, 1974, JD cum laude, 1979. Bar: U.S. Dist. Ct. (no. dist.) Ind. 1982; CPA, Ill. Acct. Touche Ross & Co., Chgo., 1974-77; law clerk to presiding justice U.S. Dist. Ct., South Bend, Ind., 1978-79; assoc. Jacobs, Williams, Montgomery, Chgo., 1979-82, Law Offices of R. Kent Rowe, South Bend, 1982—; prof. law, bd. dirs. Michiana Coll., South Bend, 1985—. Recipient Leadership award SAR, 1966. Mem. Am. Inst. CPA's, Ind. State Bar Assn., St. Joseph County Bar Assn. Lodge: KC. Avocations: jogging, racquetball, antiques. Home: 405 Wakewa South Bend IN 46617 Office: Law Offices of R Kent Rowe St Joseph Bank Bldg Suite 900 South Bend IN 46601

FOLEY, JOHN CHARLES, accountant; b. Detroit, Mar. 29, 1931; s. La Vergne C. and La Verne C. (Croteau) F.; m. Elizabeth M. Insell, Nov. 9, 1957; children: John C. Jr., Kevin P., Kathleen M. MacCaffrey, Paul E., Maribeth. BBA, U. Detroit, 1956. Supr. Rutten, Wellin & Co. CPA's, Detroit, 1954-63; treas., controller Ray White Electric Products Co., Mt. Clemens, Mich., 1963-67; mng. ptnr. Balamucki, Foley & Swiger, CPA's, Detroit, 1967-72; mng. dir. Baditoi, Segroves & Co. P.C., Southfield, Mich., 1972—. Usher St. Irenaeus Ch., Rochester, Mich., 1972—, bd. dirs., 1973-75, chmn. adminstrv. commn., 1975—, mem. parish council, 1981-82. Recipient Ed Crowe award Cath. Youth Orgn., Detroit, 1974. Mem. Am. Inst. CPA's (chmn. mgmt. adv. services small bus. cons. practices subcom. 1981—), Mich. Assn. CPA's (past chmn., mem. mgmt. acctg. practice com. 1978—, chmn. pvt. cos. practice sect. coordination com. 1982-87). Roman Catholic. Lodge: KC. Home: 550 Lake Forest Rd Rochester Hills MI 48309 Office: Baditoi Segroves & Co PC 25901 W 10 Mile Rd Southfield MI 48034

FOLEY, KATHLEEN K., nursing administrator, consultant; b. Evanston, Ill., July 30, 1945; d. Norman C. and Evangeline V. (Mowrer) Kend.; m. Fenton James Foley Jr., June 4, 1983; children from previous marriage: Kelly A., Leon G. III. AA, Oakton Community Coll., Morton Grove, Ill., 1975; BS, North Park Coll., 1978; postgrad., Keller Sch. Grad. Mgmt., 1978—. Cert. rehab. nurse. Supr. nursing Regency Nursing Ctr., Niles, Ill., 1978-79; dir. nursing service Warren Barr Pavilion, Ill. Masonic Hosp., Chgo., 1979-81; dir. PM and R St. Joseph Hosp., Chgo., 1981-82; unit coordinator Children's Meml. Hosp., Chgo., 1982—; nursing cons. to legal firms throughout the Chgo. area, 1983—. Developer External Ventricular Drain for Medex Corp., 1986. Mem. Am. Assn. Neurosurgical Nursing, Am. Nurses Assn. Avocations: travel to fgn. countries, photography. Home: 2970 N Lake Shore Dr Chicago IL 60657 Office: Children's Meml Hosp 2300 Children's Plaza Chicago IL 60614

FOLEY, L. MICHAEL, real estate executive; b. Detroit, Nov. 30, 1938; s. Raymond B. and Mabel (White) F.; m. Pamela Wagner, June 16, 1962; children: Michael D., Kimberly B., Robin E. BS, U. Mich., 1960; MBA, Harvard U., 1964. Lic. real estate broker. Pres. Econ. Devel. Corp., Detroit, 1969-71; v.p. Chrysler Realty Corp., Troy, Mich., 1972-77; exec. v.p. Bell and Howell Video Group, Chgo., 1977-80; v.p. fin., chief fin. officer Bell and Howell Corp., Chgo., 1977-80; sr. v.p. Homart Devel. Co., Chgo., 1981-84, exec. v.p., 1984—; sr. exec. v.p. Coldwell Banker Real Estate Group Inc., Chgo., 1986—, also bd. dirs.; bd. dirs. Homart Devel. Co., Chgo. Author: Management of Racial Integration in Business, 1965. Mem. Internat. Council Shopping Ctrs. (trustee), Sigma Alpha Epsilon. Episcopalian. Club: Mich. Shores (Wilmette, Ill.). Home: 822 Central Wilmette IL 60091 Office: Coldwell Banker Real Estate Group 55 W Monroe Suite 3100 Chicago IL 60603

FOLEY, MICHAEL THOMAS, broadcast corporation executive; b. Piedmont, S.D., July 21, 1945; s. Peter Francis and Mary Kathryn (Brockhoff) F.; m. Marilyn Kathryn Etten, July 9, 1977; children—Michelle Kathryn, Matthew John. B.A. in Math. and Sociology, Black Hills State Coll., Spearfish, S.D., 1967; B.S. in Computer Sci., Nat. Coll. Bus., Rapid City, S.D., 1971. Instr. data processing Gates Coll., Waterloo, Iowa, 1971-72; systems analyst Blackhawk Broadcast Corp., Waterloo, 1973; systems engr. NCR Corp., Dayton, Ohio, 1974-78; dir. data processing Forward Communications Corp., Wausau, Wis., 1978-80, v.p. data communications, 1980—; cons. in field. Served with U.S. Army, 1969-70. Decorated Vietnam Cross Gallentry, Bronze Star, Air medals, and numerous commendations; recipient Letter of Commendation, NCR, 1976. Mem. Fedn. Computer Users, Computer User Group, Nat. Computer Graphics Assn, Nat. Assn. Investors Corp. Roman Catholic. Designer, installer computerized broadcast systems, info. systems, and music libraries for various radio and TV stas. Home: 3707 Powers St Schofield WI 54476 Office: 1114 Grand Ave Wausau WI 54401

FOLK, ROGER MAURICE, laboratory director; b. Junction City, Ohio, May 10, 1936; s. Howard Mendelson and Helen Marie (Saffell) F.; m. Marilyn Irene Cannon, June 24, 1956; children: Mark Leslie, Michael Roger, Diana Lynn. BS, Ohio State U., 1962, MS, 1965, PhD, 1971. Technician Battelle Columbus (Ohio) Lab., 1957-62, research biologist, 1962-71, mgr. toxicology, 1972-79; dir. environ. health lab. Monsanto Co., St. Louis, 1979—; adj. asst. prof. Ohio State U., 1973-79; mem. Mo. Safe Drinking Water Council. Contbr. articles to profl. jours.; reviewer Cancer Treatment Reports, 1975-79. Mem. AAAS, Am. Assn. for Lab. Animal Sci., Am. Coll. Toxicology, Soc. Toxicology, Sigma Xi, Phi Eta Sigma. Methodist. Home: 750 Muir View Manchester MO 63011 Office: Monsanto Environ Health Lab 645 S Newstead Ave Saint Louis MO 63110

FOLKEMER, DONALD ARLEN, advertising executive; b. St. Louis, June 6, 1942; s. Anthony Joseph and Norma (Neubauer) F.; m. M. Pamela Kuegele; children: Matthew, Nathan. BJ, U. Mo., 1966, BA, 1966. With advt. dept. Hussmann, St. Louis, 1969-74; advt. mgr. Watlow, St. Louis, 1974-83; acct. exec. BHN Advt., St. Louis, 1983-84; gen. mgr. advt. and sales promotion Graybar, Clayton, Mo., 1984—. Mem. St. John's Bd. Edn., Ellisville, Mo., 1978-85, pres., 1981; pres. West County Athletic Assn., St. Louis, 1980-81, coach, 1982—; bd. dirs. task force Luth. High Sch. West, St.

Louis, 1982—. Served with U.S. Army, 1966-69. Mem. Bus. and Profl. Advt. Assn. Avocations: tennis, outdoors. Home: 805 Bromfield Terr Manchester MO 63021 Office: Graybar 34 N Meramec Clayton MO 63105

FOLKERS, SIGRID ELLEN, advertising account executive; b. Waverly, Iowa, Apr. 7, 1961; d. James Russell and Betty Lou (Voss) A.; m. David John Folkers, Mar. 7, 1987. BA, U. No. Iowa, 1983. Asst. account exec. Colle & McVoy, Inc., Waterloo, Iowa, 1982-86; sales rep. Orent Graphics, Omaha, 1987—. Co-chmn. kickoff com. Cedar Valley United Way, Waterloo, 1986. Mem. Omaha Fedn. Advt. Avocations: snow skiing, tennis, crafts. Office: Orent Graphics 4805 G St Omaha NE 68117

FOLKERTS, BYRON LEE, manufacturing company executive; b. Great Bend, Kans., Dec. 6, 1953; s. Doyle Dean and Ina Lea (Minson) F.; student Barton County Community Coll., 1972-73. With Great Bend Mfg. Co. (Kans.), 1973-82, purchasing agt., 1979-80, dir. purchasing, 1980-82; dir. purchasing Great Bend Industries, 1982—. Home: 1715 Van Buren Great Bend KS 67530 Office: Rural Route 1 Box 106 Great Bend KS 67530

FOLKINS, LARRY DUANE, school administrator; b. Niangua, Mo., Apr. 14, 1934; m. Georgeanne J. Prewitt, 1958; children—Margery Ann, Mark Alexander, Michael Alan, Mary Allison. B.S. in Edn., Southwest Mo. State U., 1957; M.S., Central Mo. State U., 1960; Ph.D. in Edn., U. Mo., 1976; JD (hon.) Lincoln U., 1985. Cert. tchr., adminstr., Mo. Student minister Springfield (Mo.) dist. Methodist Ch., 1955-56; field rep. Southwest Mo. State U., Springfield, 1956-57; tchr. Raytown (Mo.) High Sch., 1958-60; counselor South Jr. High Sch., Raytown, 1960-61, asst. prin., 1961-65; prin. Pittman Hills Jr. High Sch., Raytown, 1965-68; dir. personnel services Springfield (Mo.) Pub. Schs., 1968-72, dir. secondary edn., 1972-77; supt. schs. Jefferson City (Mo.) Pub. Schs., 1977—. Mem. adminstrv. bd. Jefferson City First United Methodist Ch., 1979-80; bd. dirs. Jefferson City YMCA, 1978-83; bd. govs. Meml. Hosp., 1980-83; bd. dirs. United Way, 1978—, pres., 1982-83; bd. dirs. Lincoln U. Found., 1981-83, Mo. Council Econ. Edn., 1980. Mem. Mo. State Tchrs. Assn., Nat. Assn. Secondary Sch. Prins., Mo. Assn. Sch. Adminstrs., Am. Assn. Sch. Personnel Adminstrs., Am. Assn. Sch. Adminstrs., C. of C. (Springfield and Jefferson City sect. chmn.), Phi Delta Kappa Lodge: Rotary (pres. 1986-87). Home: 615 Crest Dr Jefferson City MO 65101 Office: 315 E Dunkin Jefferson City MO 65101

FOLKMAN, MICHAEL STEPHEN, real estate executive; b. Cleve., July 22, 1950; s. Lloyd K. and Louise C. (Levy) F.; m. Claudia Weinstein, June 25, 1972; children: Theodore, Alison, Mollie. BA, Rutgers U., 1972. Sales rep. Herbert Laronge, Inc., Cleve., 1972-75, Premier Barnes and Assocs., Cleve., 1976-77; v.p., appraiser Charles M. Ritley Assoc. Inc., Cleve., 1977-85; pres. appraiser Michael S. Folkman & Assocs. Inc., Beachwood, Ohio, 1985—. Mem. Soc. Real Estate Appraiser (bd. dirs. chpt. 15, 1985, sec. 1987). Jewish. Home: 22275 E Byron Rd Shaker Heights OH 44122 Office: 3690 Orange Pl #12 Beachwood OH 44122

FOLLETT, MARY VIERLING, artist, art conservator, appraiser; b. Chgo., Feb. 9, 1917; d. Arthur Garfield and Grace May (Cummings) Vierling; student U. Southern Calif., 1932-34, grad. Acad. Profl. Art Conservators, 1975, Masters, 1978; m. Garth Benepe Follett, Feb. 16, 1945; 1 dau., Dawn Goshorn; 3 stepchildren. Exhibited in group shows Palette and Chisel Acad. Fine Arts, 1975, 76, 77, 78, Municipal Art League, 1972-78, others; represented in permanent collection Fla., Calif., Italy, others; owner, operator Paintin' Place, gallery, Oak Park, Ill., 1973—; dir. Palette and Chisel Acad. Fine Arts, Chgo., 1975-76. Vice pres. Oak Park LWV, 1952-54, welfare chmn., 1956-58; treas. Oak Park Council Internat. Affairs, 1962-74. Recipient Gold medal Palette and Chisel Acad. Fine Arts, 1976-77, 1st award Civics and Art Found. Union League Chgo., 1977. Mem. Oak Park River Forest Art League (v.p., dir. 1981-82), Pen Women Am., Municipal Art League Chgo., Art Inst. Assos. Oak Park and River Forest (women's bd. 1967—), Oak Park River Forest Hist. Soc. Club: 19th Century Women's. Home: 1440 Park Ave River Forest IL 60305 Office: 820 North Blvd Oak Park IL 60301

FOLLIS, ELAINE RUSSELL, Biblical studies educator, Christian Science practitioner; b. Quincy, Mass., Jan. 28, 1944; d. George Stanley and Celia Russell (Joy) F. A.B. summa cum laude, Tufts U., 1965, B.D., 1968; Ph.D., Boston U., 1976. Asst. prof. religion Principia Coll., Elsah, Ill., 1974-79, assoc. prof., chmn. dept. religion, 1979-83, assoc. prof., chmn. div. humanities, 1983-85, prof., chmn. div. humanities, 1985-86; editorial cons. Christian Sci. Pub. Soc., Boston, 1973—; vis. scholar Harvard Div. Sch., Cambridge, Mass., 1979; reviewer NEH, Washington, 1978-82; lectr. Bibl. studies Principia Coll. Patrons Assn., Elsah, Ill., St. Louis, 1978—. Author: David King of Israel, 1979; Convenant-A Biblical Guide, 1985. Editor: Directions in Biblical Hebrew Poetry, 1987. Contbr. articles to profl. jours. Second reader First Ch. of Christ, Scientist, Elsah, Ill., 1983-85, trustee, 1975-78. Mem. Soc. Bibl. Lit. (Bibl. Hebrew poetry sect. chmn. 1983—), Phi Beta Kappa. Clubs: Nat. Early Am. Glass (Boston); Lockhaven Country (Alton, Ill.). Lodge: Order Eastern Star (worthy matron 1974). Office: Principia Coll Dept Religion Elsah IL 62028

FOLTS, JOHN DAVID, medical educator; b. LaCrosse, Wis., Dec. 11, 1938; s. David Karl and Marie E. (Johnson) F. B.S. in Elec. Engring., U. Wis., 1964, M.S. in Physiology, 1968, Ph.D. in Cardiovascular Physiology and Pathology, 1972. Asst. prof. medicine cardiovascular research lab. U. Wis.-Madison, 1972-78, assoc. prof., 1978-83, prof., 1984—; mem. research com. NIH, 1983-87. Grantee NIH, 1973-79, 83—, Am. Heart Assn., 1977-79, Wis. Heart Assn., 1975-76, 76-77, 81-82. Fellow Am. Coll. Cardiology, Am. Heart Assn. Council on Circulation; mem. Wis. Heart Assn. (research com. 1980—), IEEE (Bioengring. Group 1969—), Am. Physiol. Soc. (circulation group 1977—), Central Soc. Clin. Research, Internat. Cardiac Systems Dynamics Soc. (charter), Internat. Soc. Heart Research, Internat. Soc. Hemostasis and Thrombosis, N.Y. Acad. Scis., Sigma Xi. Lutheran. Contbr. numerous articles to profl. jours. Home: 2537 Chamberlain Ave Madison WI 53705 Office: Clin Scis Center Cardiology U Wis Med Sch H6 Room 379 600 Highland Ave Madison WI 33792

FOLTZ, THOMAS JAMES, computer company executive; b. Indpls., May 18, 1946; s. James Gerald and Barbara Alice (Dickey) F.; B.S., Rose Hulman Inst. Tech., 1968, M.S., 1971; m. Evelyn Rebecca Wilkinson, Dec. 22, 1979. With NASA, Cape Canaveral, Fla., 1968; numerical analyst Gen. Motors, Indpls., 1969-70; sr. systems analyst Ind. Blue-Cross-Blue Shield, Indpls., 1970-77; sr. ops. cons. Ind. Bell Telephone, Indpls., 1977-79; pres., chief exec. officer Total Systems, Inc., Indpls., 1979—. Exec. dir. United Conservatives of Ind., 1977—; exec. bd. Christian Freedom Council, 1974-77; deacon E. 91st St. Christian Ch., Indpls., 1977—; campaign coordinator various candidates U.S. Senate and state office. Named Hon. Sec. of State, Ind., 1980. Mem. Creation Research Soc. Republican. Contbr. articles to profl. jours. Office: 7007 N Graham Rd Box 50159 Indianapolis IN 46250

FONDILLER, SHIRLEY HOPE ALPERIN, nurse, journalist, educator; b. Holyoke, Mass.; d. Samuel and Rose (Sobiloff) Alperin; grad. Beth Israel Hosp. Sch. Nursing, Boston; B.S., Tchrs. Coll. Columbia U., 1962, M.A., 1963, M.Ed., 1971, Ed.D., 1979; m. Harvey V. Fondiller, Dec. 27, 1957 (div. June 1984); 1 son, David Stewart. Staff asst. Am. Nurses Assn., N.Y.C., 1963-64, dir. ednl. adminstrs., cons. and tchrs. sect., 1964-66, coordinator Am. Nurses Assn.-Nat. League for Nursing careers program, 1967-70; coordinator clin. sessions Am. Nurses Assn., 1971-72, editor Am. Nurse, Kansas City, Mo., 1975-78; asso. prof., asst. to dean for spl. projects Rush-Presbyn.-St. Luke's Med. Ctr., 1979-86; exec. dir. Mid-Atlantic regional Nursery Assn., N.Y.C., 1986—. Mem. Kappa Delta Pi, Sigma Theta Tau. Contbg. editor Am. Jour. Nursing, 1971-75; also books and articles. Office: 1753 W Congress Pkwy Chicago IL 60612

FONSECA, EMMA HIDEE, histotechnologist; b. Oriente, Cuba, Dec. 31, 1917; came to U.S., 1964, naturalized, 1971; d. Dalmiro Abel and Ana Marie (Zayas) Sanchez; B.A., B.S., Immaculada Coll., Havana, Cuba, 1936; D.Pharmacy, Havana U., 1939; m. German E. Fonseca, Dec. 25, 1939; children—Emma Julia, Enid. Asst. dir., then tech. dir. Linner Labs., Inc., Havana, 1939-62; with Miles Labs., Inc., Elkhart, Ind., 1964-82, asso. research toxicologist, 1970-75, supr. histology and toxicology dept., 1975-82. Mem. AAUW, Nat. Assn. Female Execs., Nat. Soc. Histotechnologists, Am. Soc. Med. Technologists. Roman Catholic. Home: 54637 Michael Dr Elkhart IN 46516

FONTS, PATRICIA DIANNE, educator; b. Chgo.; d. Alfred Allen Crisler and Ida Lee (Brown) Crisler Thorpe; m. Brigido Castillo Fonts, III, June 24, 1973 (div.); 1 child, Brigido Castillo IV. B.S. in Edn., Chgo. State U., 1975; postgrad. Roosevelt U. Tchr. pub. schs., Chgo., 1975-80, Archdiocese of Chgo., 1985—; tng. specialist Mayor's Office of Employment Tng., 1980-84. Mem. Nat. Cath. Edn. Assn., NEA, Nat. Assn. Female Execs., Nat. Bus. Edn. Assn. Exec. Females, Alpha Kappa Alpha. Avocations: horticulture, cooking, music.

FOOS, RAYMOND ANTHONY, metallurgical company executive; b. Bowling Green, Ohio, Sept. 30, 1928; s. Clarence Herman and Clara Agnes (Neiling) F.; m. Rita Catherine Corcoran, July 11, 1953; children: Catherine, Thomas, Elisa, David, Karen, Stephanie, Michele, Renee, Brian, Andrea, Kevin. BS, Xavier U., Cin., 1946-50; MS, Xavier U., 1950-51; PhD, Iowa State U., Ames, 1954. Group leader Union Carbide Corp., Niagra Falls, N.Y., 1954-57; supr. reserach and devel. Nat. Distillers, Cin., 1957-60; mgr. ore extraction dept. The Brush Beryllium Co., Elmore, Ohio, 1960-65, gen. metal oxide div., 1965-69; dir. corp. research and devel. The Brush Beryllium Co., Cleve., 1969-70, v.p. research and devel., 1970-72, v.p. proudct devel. and research, 1972-74; sr. v.p. Brush Wellman Inc. (formerly The Brush Beryllium Co.), Cleve., 1974-76, sr. v.p. friction and crystal products, 1976-79; sr. v.p. Beryllium Products Group, Cleve., 1979-86; pres. beryllium products group Brush Wellman Inc. (formerly The Brush Beryllium Co.), Cleve., 1984—, exec. v.p., pres., 1986—, pres., chief operating officer, 1986—, also bd. dirs.; bd. dirs. Am. Colloid Co., Arlington Heights. patented over 20 U.S. patents in field. Mem. AIME, Am. Chem. Soc. Roman Catholic. Home: 7376 Bladwin Creek Dr Middleburg Heights OH 44130 Office: Brush Wellman Inc 1200 Hanna Bldg Cleveland OH 44115

FOOTE, DENNIS JOHN, podiatrist; b. Grosse Pointe, Mich., Jan. 19, 1952; s. Lyle Everette and Gladys Mat (Boyer) F.; m. Barbara Argene Bowen, Oct. 25, 1975; children: Jeffrey John-Paul, Katathrine Emily-Anne. BS, Fla. So. Coll., 1976; DPM, Ohio Coll. Podiatric Medicine, 1980. Diplomate Nat. Bd. Podiatry Examiners. Med. lab. technician Cleve. Clinic Found., 1978-80, 83-84; podiatrist Will. Beaumont Army Med. Ctr., El Paso, Tex., 1980-82; chief podiatry Will. Beaumont A.M.C., El Paso, Tex., 1982-83; pvt. practice podiatry Bay Village, Ohio, 1983—; adj. prof. Ohio Coll. Podiatric Medicine, 1980-83; podiatrics staff St. John's Westshore Hosp., Westlake, Ohio, 1984—, St. John's Hosp., Cleve., 1984—, Luth. Home for Aged, Westlake, 1983—. Served with USN, 1972-76, served to capt., U.S. Army, 80-83. Mem. Am. Podiatric Med. Assn., Ohio Podiatric Med. Assn., Northeast Ohio Acad. Podiatric Medicine. Avocations: writing, jogging. Home: 522 Oakmoor Bay Village OH 44140 Office: 551 Dover Ctr Rd Bay Village OH 44140

FORAN, DAVID JOHN, public relations executive, consultant; b. Milw., July 15, 1937; s. George Robert and Kathleen Terese (Melchior) F.; m. Donna Rae Skovira, June 11, 1960; children—Christopher G., Patrick D., Anne K., Mary E., Timothy. B.S. in Journalism, Marquette U., 1959, postgrad. 1966-68. Reporter Catholic Herald Citizen, Milw., 1960, Milw. Jour., 1960-66; dir. news bur. Marquette U., Milw., 1966-74, assoc. dir. pub. relations, 1974-81, exec. dir., 1981—, instr. journalism, 1975-81; moderator TV program Sta. WTMJ, Milw., 1982-83. Past mem. bd. dirs. Wis. Heart Assn., past chmn. pub. relations com.; chmn. adv. com. Walnut Improvement Council ; v.p., mem. Human Relations Radio and TV Council of Milw. Served with U.S. Army, 1959, 61-62. Mem. Soc. Profl. Journalists-Sigma Delta Chi (past pres., chmn., dir. Milw. chpt.), Council for Advancement and Support of Edn., Edn. Writers Assn., Milw. Pen and Mike Club (v.p.). Roman Catholic. Club: Milw. Press. Home: 209 W Lexington Blvd Glendale WI 53217 Office: 1212 W Wisconsin Ave Milwaukee WI 53233

FORBES, FRED WILLIAM, architect, engineer; b. East Liverpool, Ohio, Aug. 21, 1936; s. Kenneth S. and Phylis C. F.; B.S. in Architecture, U. Cin., 1960, postgrad.; m. Carolyn Lee Eleyet, Dec. 27, 1969; children—Tallerie Bliss, Kendall Robert. Material research engr. U.S. Air Force Materials Lab., 1960-61, structural research engr. Flight Accessories Lab., 1961-63, tech. area mgr. Aero Propulsion Lab., 1964-67; prin. Fred W. Forbes, Architect, Xenia, Ohio, 1966-68; br. chief U.S. Air Force Aero Propulsion Lab., Wright Patterson AFB, Ohio, 1967-72, pres. Forbes and Huie, Xenia, 1968-73; pres. Forbes, Huie & Assos., Inc., Xenia, 1973-76; pres. Fred W. Forbes & Assos., Inc., Xenia, 1976—; instr. U. Dayton, 1963-64. Past pres. Xenia Area Living Arts Council. Recipient Exceptional Civilian Service award U.S. Air Force, 1966; Archtl. Award of Excellence for Moraine Civic Center, Masonry Inst., 1976, Archtl. Award of Merit for Xenia br. of 3d Nat. Bank, 1981 Excellence in Masonry, Spl. award for renovation Dayton Area Red Cross Bldg., 1982; Dayton City Beautiful award for Martin Electric Co., 1977; award of merit Greene County Mental Health Facility 1983. Fellow Brit. Interplanetary Soc.; mem. Greene County Profl. Engrs. Soc. (past pres.), Am. Astron. Soc. (past nat. dir.), AIA, Ohio Soc. Profl. Engrs. (Young Engrs. award 1970), Nat. Soc. Profl. Engrs. (top 5 Outstanding Young Engr. award 1972), Nat. Asbestos Contractors Assn. (assoc.), Xenia Area C. of C. (v.p. econ. devel. 1985-86, pres. 1986-87), Theta Chi. Republican. Methodist. Contbr. 24 articles to profl. jours.; patentee in field. Office: 158 E Main St Xenia OH 45385

FORBES, GLENN S., neuroradiologist; b. Chgo., Apr. 16, 1947; s. Sherman R. and Grace (Kochan) F.; Celeste S. Schuck, June 28, 1969; children: Shannon, Ryan. BS, U. Notre Dame, 1969; MD, Yale U., 1973. Diplomate Am. Bd. Radiologists. Fellow in Neuroradiology Mayo Clinic, Rochester, Minn., 1976-77, asst. prof. Radiology, 1977-82, neuroradiology spokesman, 1979-83, assoc. prof. neurology, 1982—; Lectr., vis. prof. various internat. and nat. orgns. Contbr. articles to med. and sci. jours. Mem. Am. Coll. Radiology, Minn. Radiology Soc. (chmn. MRI activities com.) Am. Soc. Neuroradiology (chmn. exhibits com. 1982—), Radiol. Soc. N.Am. Avocations: astronomy, sailing, golf. Office: Mayo Clinic Rochester MN 55905

FORBES, JOHN KENNETH, accountant; b. Cleve., July 31, 1956; s. Kenneth Earl and Athanasia (Gialamas) F.; m. Cheryl Lynn Guest, Sept. 27, 1980; children: Christina Elaine, Shannon Marie, Brian Kenneth. BSBA in Acctg., Bowling Green State U., 1979. CPA, Ohio. Staff acct. Peat, Marwick, Mitchell & Co., Cleve., 1979-81, sr. acct., 1981-84, mgr., 1984-87; sr. mgr. Peat, Marwick, Main & Co., Cleve., 1987—. Active Cystic Fibrosis Found. Mem. Am. Inst. CPA's, Ohio Soc. CPA's, Constrn. Fin. Mgrs. Assn., (program com. 1985—), Associated Gen. Contractors (Ohio Bldg. Chpt.), Wickliffe Jaycees, Phi Eta Sigma, Beta Alpha Psi, Beta Gamma Sigma. Greek Orthodox. Avocations: traveling, softball, weight lifting, sailing. Office: Peat Marwick Main & Co 1600 National City Ctr Cleveland OH 44114

FORBIS, BRYAN LESTER, state agency administrator; b. Jefferson City, Mo., Aug. 14, 1957; s. Lewis Wagner and Thelma Rose (Thompson) F. BA in Polit. Sci. with honors, U. Mo., 1979, MA in Polit. Sci., 1981. Research asst. Mo. Office of Lt. Gov., Jefferson City, 1980; teaching asst. U. Mo., Columbia, 1980-81; legal intern Mo. Office of Atty. Gen., Jefferson City, 1980-81; mgmt. analysis specialist I, Mo. Div. Family Services, Jefferson City, 1981-83; mgmt. analysis specialist II, Mo. Div. Med. Services, Jefferson City, 1983-85; asst. to dir. Mo. Div. of Aging, Jefferson City, 1985—; bd. dirs. Silver Haired Found., Jefferson City. Mem. Capital City Council on Arts, Jefferson City, 1985—, Mo. Mansion Preservation Inc., Jefferson City, 1985—; steering com. March of Dimes, Jefferson City, 1986. Named One of Outstanding Young Men of Am., 1985, 86; curator scholar U. Mo., 1975, 77, 78, William Bradshaw scholar U. Mo., 1979. Mem. Am. Soc. Pub. Adminstrn., Mo. Inst. Pub. Adminstrn., Acad. Polit. Sci., Pi Sigma Alpha, Omicron Delta Kappa, Phi Beta Kappa. Republican. Lutheran. Club: Pachyderms (Jefferson City). Avocations: chess, collecting polit. campaign buttons, football. Home: 935 Fairmount Jefferson City MO 65101 Office: Mo Div of Aging PO Box 1337 Jefferson City MO 65102

FORCE, RONALD CLARENCE, psychologist; b. Toledo, Apr. 10, 1917; s. Rockwell C. and Anna E. (Briner) F.; married, 1941; children: Eric R., Hugh B., Bryan P., Gregory M. BA, Heidelberg Coll., 1940; MA, Miami U., Oxford, Ohio, 1941; postgrad., U. Calif., Berkeley, 1948-50, U. Tex., 1951-52. Commd. 2d lt. USAF, 1941, advanced through grades to lt. col., 1961; clin. research psychologist 3320 retraining group USAF, Amarillo AFB, Tex., 1951-56, dir. clin. services 3320 retraining group, 1961-64; dir. clin. services, psychology dept. mental hygiene USAF, Lackland AFB, Tex., 1957-60; resigned USAF, 1964; clin. coordinator St. Francis Homes, Inc., Salina, Kans., 1966-81, dir. research, 1982-83, cons. research, 1983—; bd. dirs. Test Systems Internat., Wichita, Kans., 1972—. Co-author, developer (test) Biog. and Personality Inventory, 1959, 86; contbr. articles to profl. jours. Mem. Ctr. for Peace Concerns, Salina, 1984—. Fellow AAAS; mem. Am. Psychol. Assn., Union of Concerned Scientists, Fedn. Am. Scientists. Democrat. Presbyterian. Avocation: bicycling. Home: 2811 Melanie Ln Salina KS 67401 Office: St Francis Homes Inc 509 E Elm St Salina KS 67402-1430

FORD, DAVID CLAYTON, lawyer; b. Hartford City, Ind., Mar. 3, 1949; s. Clayton I. and Barbara J. (McVicker) F.; m. Joyce Ann Bonjour, Aug. 22, 1970; children—Jeffrey David, Andrew Clayton. B.A. in Polit. Sci., Ind. U., 1973; J.D., Ind. U.-Indpls., 1976. Bar: Ind. 1975, U.S. Dist. Ct. (no. dist.) Ind. 1977, U.S. Dist. Ct. (so. dist.) Ind. 1976, U.S. Supreme Ct. 1983. City atty. City of Montpelier, Ind., 1977-79; town atty. Town of Shamrock Lakes, Ind., 1977—; chief dep. prosecutor, Blackford County, 1979; pros. atty. 71st Jud. Cir., Blackford County, Hartford City, Ind., 1983—. Republican nominee for 19th Dist. Ind. State Sen., 1986; dir. Blackford County Young Republicans, 1977-82, pres., 1977-78; chmn. Town of Shamrock Lakes Republican Com., 1983; vice-chmn. Blackford County Rep. Central Com., 1978-82; precinct committeeman Blackford County, Licking 7, 1980—; mem. Ind. 10th Congl. Dist. Rep. Caucus, 1978-82; U.S. Edn. Appeals Bd. mem. U.S. Dept. Edn., 1982—; Nat. Def. Execs. Res. 1983—; mem. bus. adv. com. to Congressman Dan Burton; chmn. bus., industries and devel. com. Ptnrs. of Ams., Ind. chpt., 1983—; mem. Blackford County Bd. Aviation Commrs., 1977-83, pres., 1979-83; bd. dirs. Dollars of Scholars, Blackford County, 1977—, v.p., 1977—; mem. St. John's-Riedman Meml. Sch. Bd., 1978-82, pres., 1978-82; mem. Blackford County Sheriff's Merit Bd., 1981-82. Named Man of Yr., Hartford City C. of C., 1978; Sagamore of the Wabash, Gov. Otis Bowen, 1978; Hon. Sec. of State, Edwin J. Simcox, 1981; participant Rotary group study exchange to São Paulo, Brazil, 1981; named Outstanding Young Man of Am., U.S. Jaycees, 1982. Mem. ABA, Assn. Trial Lawyers' Am., Ind. State Bar Assn., Blackford County Bar Assn., World Trade Club Ind., Mensa, Sigma Iota Epsilon. Home: 2776 S Angling Park Hartford City IN 47348 Office: Ford & Young 210 W Main St Hartford City IN 47348

FORD, HARRIETT LEE, English educator, writer; b. Seminole, Tex., July 10, 1946; d. Jones Clifford and Christine (Inness) Barnett; m. John William Ford, Aug. 19, 1966; children: Johnnell, Danae. BA in Edn. magna cum laude, Southwestern State Coll., 1969. Cert. tchr., Okla., Kans., Ill. Tchr. English McAlester (Okla.) High Sch., 1969-71, Bethel Life Sch., Wichita, Kans., 1981-83, Word of Faith Acad., Dallas, 1983-84, Christian Life Ctr., Rockford, Ill., 1985-86; free lance writer Rockford, 1986—; Chmn. discipline com. Bethel Life Sch., Wichita, 1982—. Columnist Rockford Labor News, 1986. Fellow Christian Writers Guild, Okla. Writers Guild (Poetry award 1972). Democrat. Mem. Assembly of God Ch. Avocations: reading, writing. Home: 4110 Martina Dr Rockford IL 61111

FORD, JAMES WILLIAM, finance company executive; b. Alameda, Calif., Feb. 1, 1923; s. Shelton C. and Eunice (George) F.; m. Anne Farley, June 30, 1945; children: Julian, Amy Milkovich, Carol. A.B., Oberlin Coll., 1947; M.A. in Econs, Harvard U., 1949, Ph.D. in Econs, 1954; postgrad. (Fulbright scholar), 1949-51; postgrad. (fellow), U. Chgo., 1958-59. Instr. econs. Columbia U., 1951-53; asst. prof econs. Vanderbilt U., 1953-57; asso. prof. econs. Ohio State U., 1957-59; economist to bd. govs. FRS, 1959-61; various positions including dir. Econs. Office, asst. controller fin. staff Ford Motor Co., 1961-75, v.p., 1980—; exec. v.p. ins. and spl. fin. ops. Ford Motor Credit Co., Dearborn, Mich., 1975-77; pres. Ford Motor Credit Co., 1977-80, chmn., 1980—. Bd. dirs. Youth Living Centers, Inc., 1970-83. Served with USAAF, 1943-46. Office: Ford Motor Credit Co American Rd Dearborn MI 48121

FORD, LEE ELLEN, scientist, educator, lawyer; b. Auburn, Ind., June 16, 1917; d. Arthur W. and Geneva (Muhn) Ford, B.A., Wittenberg Coll., 1947; M.S., U. Minn., 1949; Ph.D., Iowa State Coll., 1952; J.D., U. Notre Dame, 1972. CPA auditing, 1934-44; assoc. prof. biology Gustavus Adolphus Coll., 1950-51, Anderson (Ind.) Coll., 1952-55; vis. prof. biology U. Alta. (Can.), Calgary, 1955-56; asso. prof. biology Pacific Luth. U., Parkland, Wash., 1956-62; prof. biology and cytogenetics Miss. State Coll. for Women, 1962-64; chief cytogeneticist Pacific N.W. Research Found., Seattle, 1964-65; dir. Canine Genetics Cons. Service, Parkland, 1963-69. Sponsor Companion Collies for the Adult, Jr. Blind, 1955-65; dir. Genetics Research Lab., Butler, Ind., 1955-75, cons. cytogenetics, 1969-75; legis. cons., 1970-79; dir. chromosome lab. Inst. Basic Research in Mental Retardation, S.I., 1968-69; exec. dir. Legis. Bur. U. Notre Dame Law Sch., also editor New Dimensions in Legislation, 1969-72; editor Butler Record Herald, 1972-76; bd. dirs. Ind. Interreligious Com. on Human Equality, 1976-80; exec. asst. to Gov. Otis R. Bowen, Ind., 1973-75; dir. Ind. Commn. on Status Women, 1973-74; bd. dirs. Ind. Council Chs.; editor Ford Assos. pubs., 1972-86; mem. Pres.'s Adv. Council on Drug Abuse, 1976-77. Admitted to Ind. bar, 1972. Adult counselor Girl Scouts U.S.A., 1934-40; bd. dirs. Ind. Task Force Women's Health, 1976-80; mem. exec. bd., bd. dirs. Ind.-Ky. Synod Lutheran Ch., 1972-78; bd. dirs., mem. council St. Marks Lutheran Ch., Butler, 1970-76; mem. social services personnel bd.; mem. DeKalb County (Ind.) Sheriff's Merit Bd., 1983-87; founder, dir., pres. Ind. Caucus for Animal Legislation and Leadership, 1984-87. Mem. or ex-mem. AAUW, AAAS, Genetics Soc. Am., Am. Human Genetics Soc., Am. Genetic Assn., Am. Inst. Biol. Scis., Am. Soc. Zoologists, La., Miss., Ind., Iowa acads. sci., Bot. Soc. Am., Ecol. Soc. Am., Am. (dir.), Ind. (dir.), DeKalb County (dir.) bar assns., Humane Soc. U.S. (dir. 1970-88), DeKalb County Humane Soc. (founder, dir. 1970-86), Ind. Fedn. Humane Socs. (dir. 1970-84), Nat. Assn. Women Lawyers (dir.), Bus. and Profl. Women's Club, Nat. Assn. Republican Women (dir.), Women's Equity Action League (dir.), Assn. So. Biologists, Phi Kappa Phi. Club: Altrusa. Editor: Breeder's Jour., 1958-63; numerous vols. on dog genetics and breeding, guide dogs for the blind. Contbr. over 2000 sci. and popular publs. on cytogenetics, dog breeding and legal topics; contbr. Am. Kennel Club Gazette, 1970-81, also others. Researcher in field. Home and Office: 824 E 7th St Auburn IN 46706

FORD, MICHAEL JOHN, JR., financial services executive; b. Phila., Feb. 8, 1936; s. Michael John and Margaret Mary (Brooks) F.; m. Stephanie Marie Smishko, June 14, 1980. BA in English, Villanova U., 1958; MBA in Fin., U. Pa., 1963. Mktg. mgr. IBM Corp., various cities, 1963-73; account mgr. CIGNA Corp., Columbus, Ohio, 1973-80; founder, chief exec. officer Ford Fin. Corp., Worthington, Ohio, 1980—; CLU, chartered fin. cons. Mem. Franklin County Rep. Cen. Com., Columbus, 1980—. Mem. Nat. Assn. Securities Dealers, Am. Soc. CLU. Roman Catholic. Club: Capital (founder), Hickory Hills Country (Columbus). Avocations: golf, football spectator, motor racing. Home: 223 Jackson St Columbus OH 43206 Office: Ford Fin Corp 7650 Rivers Edge Dr Worthington OH 43085

FORD, SAMUEL GEORGE, sales executive; b. Newton, Iowa, Jan. 22, 1927; s. Samuel Hall and Marie (Miner) F.; m. Pauline VanAuken, Oct. 20, 1951; children: James M., Paul N., Janet L. BS in Mech. Engring., Iowa State U., 1951. Design engr. B-O-P div. Gen. Motors Corp., Kansas City, Kans., 1951-52, Detroit Transp. div. Gen. Motors Corp., 1952-54, design engr. sales Eagle Iron Works, Des Moines, Iowa, 1954—. Served with USAF, 1945. Mem. Nat. Sand and Gravel Assn. (engring. com. 1973—, chmn. mfrs. div. 1973-74), Nat. Stone Assn. (chmn. mfrs. div. 1985-87), Assn. Equipment Distbrs. (industry round table). Republican. Mem. Christian Ch. Avocations: church choir, golf, racquetball, auto racing, traveling.

Home: 3201 36th St Des Moines IA 50310 Office: Eagle Iron Works 129 Holcomb Ave Des Moines IA 50313

FORD, TERRY ALAN, data processing executive; b. El Paso, Tex., Nov. 25, 1958; s. Edsel Dallas and Barbara Louise (Feierabend) F. BBA in Computer Sci., Augustana Coll., 1982. Programmer City of Rock Island, Ill., 1982-84, dir. data processing, 1984—. Sunday sch. tchr. First Bapt. Ch. Moline, Ill., 1984—; youth chmn. Bd. Christian Edn., 1985—. Fellow Data Processing Mgmt. Assn. Republican. Baptist. Avocations: basketball, fastpitch softball, weightlifting. Home: 2535 15th St Ct Rock Island IL 61201 Office: City of Rock Island 1528 3d Ave Rock Island IL 61201

FORD, WILLIAM CLAY, automotive company executive; b. Detroit, Mar. 14, 1925; s. Edsel Bryant and Eleanor (Clay) F.; m. Martha Firestone, June 21, 1947; children: Martha, Sheila, William Clay, Elizabeth. B.S., Yale U., 1949. Sales and advt. staff Ford Motor Co., 1949; indsl. relations, labor negotiations with UAW, 1949; quality control mgr. gas turbine engines Lincoln-Mercury div., Dearborn, Mich., 1951; mgr. spl. product ops. Lincoln-Mercury div., 1952, v.p., 1953; gen. mgr. Lincoln-Mercury div. (Continental div.), 1954; group v.p. Lincoln and Continental divs., 1955, v.p. product design, 1956-80, dir., 1948—, chmn. exec. com., 1978—, vice chmn. bd., 1980—; pres., owner Detroit Lions Profl. Football Club. Chmn. Edison Inst.; trustee Eisenhower Med. Center, Thomas A. Edison Found.; bd. dirs. Nat. Tennis Hall of Fame, Boys Clubs Am. Mem. Soc. Automotive Engrs. (asso.), Automobile Old Timers, Phelps Assn., Psi Upsilon. Club: Econ. of Detroit (dir.). Lodges: Masons, K.T. Office: Ford Motor Co The American Rd Dearborn MI 48121

FORD, WILLIAM DAVID, lawyer, congressman; b. Detroit, Aug. 6, 1927; s. Robert Henderson and Jean Bowie (McGhee) F.; children: William David, Margaret, John P. Student, Nebr. Tchrs. Coll., Peru, 1946, Wayne State U., 1947-48; B.S., U. Denver, 1949, LL.B., 1951; L.H.D., Westfield State Coll., 1970; Ph.D. (hon.), Eastern Mich. U., 1976, Grand Valley State Coll. of Mich., 1979, Wayne State U., 1979, Mich. State U., 1980, No. Mich. U., 1980, Central Mich. U., 1981, U. Detroit, 1981, U. Mich., 1982, Cleary Coll., 1984, Northeastern U., 1985, L.I. U., 1986, Columbia Coll., Chgo., 1986. Bar: Mich. bar 1951. Practice law 1951—; justice of peace Taylor, Mich., 1955-57; twp. atty. 1957-64; city atty. Melvindale, Mich., 1957-59; del. Mich. Constl. Conv., 1961-62; mem. Mich. Senate from 21st Dist., 1962-64, 89th to 100th Congresses from 15th Mich. Dist., Washington, 1965—; mem. steering and policy com., edn. and labor com., Dem. nat. whip-at-large 89th to 97th Congresses from 15th Mich. dist., Washington, 1965-81; congressional adviser to UNESCO, 1971-74; vice-chmn. Conf. Great Lake Congressmen. Served with USNR, 1944-46. Recipient Distinguished Service award; Outstanding Young Man of Year award Taylor, 1962. Mem. ABA, Mich. Bar Assn., Downriver Bar Assn. (pres. 1961-62), Am. Legion. Clubs: Masons, Shriners, Eagles, Elks, Moose, Rotary (pres. 1961-62). Home: Taylor MI 48180 Office: 239 House Office Bldg Washington DC 20515

FOREHAND, LARRY WAYNE, dentist; b. Hannibal, Mo., Mar. 15, 1947; s. Rannie and Maxine (Paulus) F.; m. Catherine Forehand, Oct. 31, 1979; 1 child, Tyler Park. AA, Hannibal LaGrange Coll., 1967; BA, U. Mo., 1970; DDS, U. Mo., Kansas City, 1974. Gen. practice dentistry Aurora, Mo., 1974—; cons. Aurora Nursing Ctr., 1975—, Crane (Mo.) Health Care Ctr., 1981—, Mo. Rehab. Ctr., Mt. Vernon, 1980—. Mem. ADA, Mo. Dental Assn. (del.), Springfield Dental Soc. Avocation: farming. Home: Rt 2 Box 217A Aurora MO 65605 Office: 1402 S Elliot Aurora MO 65605

FOREMAN, JAMES LOUIS, judge; b. Metropolis, Ill., May 12, 1927; s. James C. and Anna Elizabeth (Henne) F.; m. Mabel Inez Dunn, June 16, 1948; children: Beth Foreman Banks, Rhonda Foreman Riepe, Nanette. B.S., U. Ill., 1950, J.D., 1952. Bar: Ill. bar. Individual practice law Metropolis, Ill.; partner firm Chase and Foreman, Metropolis, until 1972; Ill. state's atty. Massac County; asst. atty. gen. State of Ill.; chief judge So. Dist. of Ill. East St. Louis, 1972—. Pres. Bd. of Edn., Metropolis. Served with USNR, 1945-46. Mem. Am. Bar Assn., Ill. State Bar Assn., Metropolis C. of C. (past pres.). Republican. Home: PO Box 866 Metropolis IL 62960 Office: US Dist Ct PO Box 186 East St Louis IL 62202

FOREMAN, JANET RAE, accounting educator; b. Johnstown, Pa., Nov. 13, 1943; d. Irvin W. and Marian (Miller) Harbaugh; m. Michael William Foreman, Oct, 20. 1962; children: Matthew Craig, Robert Michael. BS in Bus., Ind. U., 1979, MBA, 1982. CPA, Ind. Acct. Dahms & Yarian CPA's, Warsaw, Ind., 1979-81; asst. prof. Goshen (Ind.) Coll., 1982-84; lectr. Ind. U., Ft. Wayne, 1984-85; asst. prof. Grace Coll., Winona Lake, Ind., 1985—. treas., bd. dirs. New Frontiers, Inc., Warsaw, 1986—; treas. Community Grace Brethern Ch., Warsaw, 1984-86. Mem. Am. Inst. CPA's, Am. Soc. Women CPA's, Ind. CPA Soc., Lakeside User Group (treas. 1986). Republican. Avocations: crochet, sewing, reading, camping. Home: Rural Rt 7 Box 192 Warsaw IN 46580 Office: Grace Coll 200 Seminary Dr Winona Lake IN 46590

FORGET, VERDAYLE MARIE, artist, poet; b. Alliance, Nebr., Oct. 29, 1942; d. Walter Dale O'Neal and AlVerda Mae (Shigley) Brosz; m. Francois Leon Forget, Dec. 18, 1964. Cert. recognition, Famous Artists Sch., 1973; study, Dennis Ramsay Studio, Deal, Eng., 1973. One-woman shows include Bon Nat. Gallery, Seattle, 1977, Merchants Nat. Bank Plaza Gallery, Indpls., 1982, The Glass Chimney, Carmel, Ind., 1983, Cystic Fybrosis Found., Anderson, Ind., 1985, The Honeywell Found., Wabash, Ind., 1985; exhibited in group shows at Olde Main Gallery, Bellevue, Wash., 1971-73, Hoosier Salon, Indpls., 1982-86, Indpls. Mus. Art, 1985-86; work includes Ind. Pacers posters, 1985-86, commemorative painting and poster of Julius "Dr.J." Erving of Phila. 76ers playing his final game against Ind. Pacers, 1987; writer poetry, 1987, Football Centennial poster. Named Most Popular Artist Burien (Wash.) Arts Festival, 1971. Mem. Hoosier Salon. Republican. Protestant. Avocations: tennis, music, psychology, Am. Indian history, travel. Home and Studio: 1990 Picadilly Pl #C Indianapolis IN 46260

FORGEY, JOE EDWARD, pediatric dentist; b. Logansport, Ind., Dec. 27, 1947; s. Morris Wayne and Helen (Martin) F.; m. Jennifer Jacob, June 22, 1974 (div. Dec. 1984); children: Jill Suzanne, Jordan Suzanne. BS, Butler U., Indpls., 1970; DDS, Ind. U., Indpls., 1975, Cert. in Pediatric Dentistry, 1977. Practice dentistry specializing in pediatrics Nobelsville, Ind., 1977—; asst. prof. dentistry Ind. U., Indpls., 1977—; cons. dentist Arendin (Ind.) Children's Home, 1977—, Walston Children's Home, Cicero, Ind., 1977—. Mem. ADA, Ind. Dental Assn., Indpls. Dist. Dental Soc., Am. Acad. Pediatric Dentistry, Ind. Soc. Pediatric Dentistry (pres. 1985). Avocation: exercise. Office: 110 Lakeview Noblesville IN 46060

FORISHA, BILLIE EDWARD, family studies educator, therapist; b. Denison, Tex., Aug. 15, 1942; s. Billie Murry Forisha and Mary Willie (Edens) Mage. BA in History, U. Tex., 1963; MA in History, San Francisco State U., 1968; PhD in Human Devel., U. Md., 1976. Lic. cons. psychologist, Minn.; lic. profl. counselor, Ohio. Faculty Bowling Green (Ohio) State U., 1974—, assoc. prof. human devel. and family studies, 1977—; pvt. practice marriage and family therapy, N.W. Ohio, 1979—; mem., officer numerous coms. Bowling Green U., 1973—; profl. cons. various pub. and pvt. insts. and agys., 1972—; guest speaker various colls., U.S. and abroad, 1975-83. Author: (with Barbara E. Forisha) Moral Development and Education, 1976; (with Frank Milhollan) From Skinner to Rogers: Contrasting Approaches to Education, 1976. Recipient numerous grants for research on moral devel. and androgyny, 1978—. Mem. Am. Psychol. Assn., Am. Assn. Marriage and Family Therapy (clin. 1979, supr. 1985), Nat. Council on Family Relations, Ohio Assn. Marriage and Family Therapy, Ohio Council on Family Relations (pres. 1978, chmn. exec. com. for planning ann. meeting, 1979, Disting. Service to Families award 1980), Assn. for Humanistic Psychology. Democrat. Avocations: skiing, dancing. Office: Bowling Green State U Dept Home Econs Bowling Green OH 43403

FORLINI, FRANK JOHN, JR., cardiologist; b. Newark, Mar. 30, 1941; s. Frank Sr. and Rose Theresa (Parussini) F.; m. Joanne Marie Horch, July 19, 1969; children: Anne Marie, Victoria, Frank III, Anthony. BS in Biology, Villanova (Pa.) U., 1963; MD, George Washington U., 1967. Diplomate Am. Bd. Internal Medicine, Am. Bd. Cardiovascular Disease. Intern Bklyn.-Cumberland Med. Ctr., N.Y., 1967-68, resident in internal medicine, 1968-70; fellow in cardiology Cardiology Inst. Med. Sci. Pacific Med. Ctr., San Francisco, 1970-72; practice medicine specializing in cardiology Rock Island, Ill., 1974—; sr. ptnr. Forlini Med. Speciality Clinic, Rock Island, 1974—; owner Forlini Farm and Forlini Devel. Enterprises; adj. prof. pharmacy L.I. U., Bklyn., 1970; pres., chief exec. officer U.S. Oil and Transp. Co., Inc., 1966—; pres. Profl. and Execs. Ins. Assocs., 1973—, Profl. Assocs., 1973—; med. and exec. dir. Cardiovascular Inst. Northwestern Ill., 1984—. Contbr. articles to profl jours. Chmn. D.C. Young Reps., 1965-66; mem. exec. com. Rep. Cen. Com., Washington, 1965-66; vice chmn. Rock Island Reps., 1985—, precinct committeeman, 1985; dep. registrar County of Rock Island, Ill., 1985—; trustee South Rock Island Twp., Rock Island County, 1987—. Served to maj. USAF, 1972-74. Nat. Inst. heart Disease NIH-USPHS grantee, 1964-66, 70-72. Fellow Am. Coll. Cardiology, N.Am. Soc. Pacing and Electrophysiology. Roman Catholic. Office: 2701 17th St Rock Island IL 61201

FORMAN, FRANKLIN WOLD, fastener company executive; b. Sublette, Ill., Jan. 4, 1923; s. Frank Xavier and Gertrude Ethel (Wold) F.; m. Dorothy Louise Seiter, Apr. 10, 1970; m. Charlotte Mae Moser, May 12, 1944 (dec.); children—Charlyn, Franklin W., Eric, Konrad. Student Wheaton Coll., 1941-42; B.S.M.E., Tri-State U., 1946. Project methods and maintenance engr. Reynolds Wire Div., Dixon, Ill., 1950-57; mgr. plant engring. Barber-Colman Co., Rockford, Ill., 1957-74; mgr. plant engring. Am. Hoist, St. Paul, 1974-76; mgr. facilities and plant engring. Nat. Metalcrafters (formerly Nat. Lock Fasteners), Rockford, Ill., 1976—. Mem. Ill. Gov.'s Bd. Vocat. Edn., 1970-73; mem. Ill. State Grievance Bd., 1970-73. Precinct committeeman Republican party; advisor County Welfare Services; pres. PTA; chmn. Vocat. Sch. Adv. Bd.; trustee Rock Valley Coll. Served with USNR, 1942-45. Named Disting. Alumnus of Year, Tri-State U., 1968. Mem. Nat. Inst. Plant Engrs., C. of C. (edn. com.). Republican. Mem. Evangel. Free Ch. Am. Clubs: Masons. Home: 2212 Silverthorn Dr Rockford IL 61107 Office: 4500 Kishwaukee St Rockford IL 61101

FORMAN, LINDA HELAINE, accountant; b. Chgo., July 15, 1943; d. Hymen and Rose (Klapman) Davis; divorced; children: David, Rachel. BSBA, Loyola U., Chgo., 1969. CPA, Ill. Ptnr., dir. pension and profit sharing cons. dept. Gleeson, Sklar & Sawyers, Chgo., 1972—. Mem. budget com. La Leche League Internat., Franklin Park, Ill., 1984-87, State treas., 1974-76. Mem. Am. Inst. CPA's, Ill. CPA Soc. (chmn. film subcom. 1984-86, chmn. speakers bur. 1986—), Fin. Planning Network (program cochmn. 1986—), Nat. Assn. Women Bus. Owners (bd. dirs. 1986—). Jewish. Avocations: aerobics, cross country skiing. Office: Gleeson Sklar & Sawyers CPA's 7250 N Cicero Ave Chicago IL 60646

FORMAN, LOUIS HYMAN, psychiatrist; b. Kansas City, Mo., July 28, 1912; s. Solomon Oscar and Rose (Seidenman) F.; m. Phyllis Veta, Nov. 9, 1941; children: Ruth Allyne, Maurice Earl. AA, Kansas City Jr. Coll., 1932; AB, U. Kans., 1937; MD, Kans. U., 1939. Diplomate Am. Bd. Psychiatry and Neurology. Pvt. practice psychiatry Kansas City, 1950—; chmn. psychiatry Menorah Hosp., Kansas City, 1951-55; clin. prof. Kans. U., U. Mo., Kansas City until 1984; cons. Family Service, Kansas City, 1952-54, Jewish Family Children, Kansas City, 1950-56, Traveler's Aid, Kansas City, 1957-58. Co-author Hello Sigmund This is Eric, 1978; contbr. articles to profl. jours. Mem. Mayor's Commn. for United Nations, Kansas City, 1983-84. Served to capt. U.S. Army, 1940-45, ETO. Fellow Am. Psychiat. Assn. (life); mem. AMA, Acad. Psychosomatic Medicine, Cen. Neuropsychiat. Assn., Internat. Transactional Analysis Assn. (clin. teacher, Innovative Teaching citation 1981), Am. Group Psychotherapy Assn. Avocations: music, trumpet, photography. Office: 4320 Wornall Rd Kansas City KS 64111

FORMANEK, LUELLA HELEN, civic worker, homemaker; b. Mpls., Aug. 11, 1924; d. Peter Paul and Mary (Stepanek) F. Student, U. Minn. Model N.Y.C., 1946-55; traffic expert Ill. Cen. R.R., Mpls., 1957-64; govt. employee U.S. Govt., Mpls., 1967—. Vol. United Services Overseas, 1943-45, Community Chest, 1945-46; chmn. Greenwich Hosp., 1952-54, ARC, Multiple Sclerosis, Cerebral Palsy, Leukemia, Muscular Dystrophy, Mental Health; mem. aux. St. Mary's Hosp., Mpls., 1963; vol. tutor Women in Service to Edn., 1974—, Nat. Council of Cath. Women, 1974—; mem. March of Dimes, 1974—, Cath. Jr. League, 1964—; trustee a program for the aged, 1975—, Am. Heart Assn., 1974—, Kidney Found. Upper Midwest, 1978—, Epilepsy Found. and Leukemia, The City of Hope, 1978—, Cancer Fund, 1984, Normandale Choral Soc., 1986. Home: 44052 Portland Ave S Minneapolis MN 55407

FORMELL, LESLIE EDWIN, architect; b. Frederic, Wis., Jan. 21, 1938; s. Leslie Edwin and Bertha Esther Josephine (Andreen) F.; m. Marlys Jean Anderson, June 26, 1960; 1 child, Ross Carey. BA, U. Minn., 1960, BArch, 1962. Registered architect, Mpls., Minn., Wis., Okla. Drafsman Roger T. Johnson Architects, Mpls., 1962-64; assoc. architect Horty Elving & Assoc., Mpls., 1964-76; pres., architect Centrum AIA, Mpls., 1976-79, Hills Gilbertson AIA, 1979—; pres. Medici Constrn. Mng. Inc., Mpls., 1981—, Centrum Coordinators Inc., Mpls., 1986—, Engring. Services Inc., Mpls., 1980—; ptnr. Franklin Properties, Mpls., 1983—. Mem. AIA (com. on architect for healthcare, treas. Minn. Soc. 1983-86), Am. Assn. Hosp. Planners. Republican. Lutheran. Lodge: Kiwanis. Avocations: travel, skiing, swimming. Home: 1746 Canyon Ln New Brighton MN 55112 Office: Hills Gilbertson Architects Inc 104 W Franklin Ave Minneapolis MN 55404

FORNACIARI, GILBERT MARTIN, sociologist, management consultant; b. Chgo., July 22, 1946; s. Martin Frank and Josephine Bernadette (Ricci) F.; m. Linda Susan McAlister, May 6, 1978; children: Liza Maree, Marc Dante. BA, George Williams Coll., 1969; MA, Ball State U., 1970; PhD, Ohio State U., 1978. Instr. U. Dayton, Ohio, 1970-72; research assoc. Ohio State U., Columbus, Ohio, 1972-78; area coordinator Young Men's Jewish Council, Chgo., 1978-79; mgmt. cons. Fornaciari Cons., McHenry, Ill., 1980—; grad. instr. George William Coll., Downers Grove, Ill, 1984-85, Nat. Coll. Edn., Evanston, Ill., 1985—; instr. Am. Mgmt. Assn. Inst., Grays Lake, Ill., 1983—. Contbr. articles to profl. jours. Mem. McHenry C. of C., 1983-84. Mem. Ill. Sociol. Assn. (session chmn.), Midwest Sociol. Assn., Am. Soc. Tng. and Devel. (session chmn.), Organ. Devel. Network. Democrat. Episcopalian. Home: 5420 W Sherman Dr McHenry IL 60050 Office: Fornaciari Cons Whispering Point Ctr 4318-D Crystal Lake Rd McHenry IL 60050

FORNATTO, ELIO JOSEPH, otolaryngologist, educator; b. Turin, Italy, July 2, 1928; came to U.S., 1953; s. Mario G. and Julia (Stabio) F.; m. Mary Elizabeth Pearson, Dec. 17, 1960; children: Susan, Robert, Daniel. MD, U. Turin, Italy, 1952. Diplomate Am. Bd. Otolaryngology. Intern Edgewater Hosp., Chgo., 1956-57; resident U. Ill., Chgo., 1953-56; chief otolaryngologist Elmhurst (Ill.) Clinic, 1958—; sr. otolaryngologist Elmhurst (Ill.) Meml. Hosp., 1964—; med. dir. Chgo. Eye Ear Nose Throat Hosp., 1966-69; clin. asst. prof. Loyola U., Chgo., 1967—; dir. laryngectomy program Du Page County Am. Cancer Soc., 1977—; chmn. Elmhurst Clinic, 1980—. Founder Centurion Club, Deafness Research Found., N.Y.C., 1960—. Mem. AMA, Ill. Med. Soc., Am. Acad. Facial Plastic and Reconstructive Surgery, Am. Acad. Otolaryngologic Allergy, Am. Acad. Otolaryngology and Head and Neck Surgery. Roman Catholic. Avocations: music, bicycling. Home: 200 W Jackson St Elmhurst IL 60126 Office: Elmhurst Clinic 172 Schiller St Elmhurst IL 60126

FORNSHELL, DAVE LEE, educational broadcasting executive; b. Bluffton, Ind., July 9, 1937; s. Harold Christman and Mary Ann Elizabeth (Fox) F.; m. Elizabeth Slagle Clinger, Nov. 11, 1978; 1 son, John David. B.A., Ohio State U., 1959. Continuity dir. Sta. WTVN-TV, Columbus, Ohio, 1959-61; traffic dir., asst. program mgr. Sta. WOSU-TV, Columbus, 1961-69; ops. mgr. Md. Center for Pub. Broadcasting, Balt., 1969-70; exec. dir. Ohio Ednl. TV Network Commn., Columbus, 1970—; pres. Ohio Radio Reading Services; dir., mem. exec. com. Central Ednl. Network, 1972—, chmn. bd. dirs., 1986—; mem. exec. com., chmn. Postsecondary Edn. Council of Central Ednl. Network; chmn. Ohio Postsecondary Telecommunications Council; mem. adv. com. Ohio State Awards. Pres. Landings Residents Assn., 1973; active March of Dimes, 4-H. Served with USAF, 1961-62. Recipient award Dayton Fedn. Women's Clubs, 1974. Mem. N.G. Assn., Ohio State U. Alumni Assn., Nat. Acad. TV Arts and Scis. (bd. govs. Columbus chpt. 1970—), Nat. Assn. Ednl. Broadcasters (chmn. state adminstrs. council), Broadcast Pioneers, Health Scis. Communications Assn., Nat. Assn. TV Program Execs., Am. Assn. Higher Edn., Alpha Epsilon Rho, Alpha Delta Sigma, Sigma Delta Chi. Clubs: University, Athletic (Columbus). Lodge: Kiwanis. Home: 240 Larrimer Ave Worthington OH 43085 Office: Ohio Educational Broadcasting 2470 N Star Rd Columbus OH 43221

FORRER, GORDON RANDOLPH, physician; b. Balt., Apr. 1, 1922; s. William Gordon and Blanche (Shules) F.; m. Carol Lucille Hanke, May 26, 1951; children—Jane Elizabeth, Susan Ellen, John Jerritt. Student, State Tchrs. Coll., Towson, Md., 1939-41, Johns Hopkins, 1941-42; B.A., U. Md., 1945, M.D., 1947. Diplomate Am. Bd. Psychiatry and Neurology. Intern U.S. Marine Hosp., Balt., 1947-48; psychiat. resident Ypsilanti State Hosp., Mich., 1948-50, Wayne County (Mich.) Mental Health Clinic, 1950-51; clin. dir. Northville (Mich.) State Hosp., 1954-60; pvt. practice psychiatry Detroit, 1960—; chief psychiatry Mt. Carmel Mercy Hosp.; mem. staff St. Mary Hosp., Livonia, Mich., Detroit Rehab. Inst.; clin. asst. prof. Wayne U. Med. Sch., 1955-68. Author: Weaning and Human Development, 1969, Psychiatric Self-Help, 1973, The Technique of Psychiatric Self-Help, 1975, also articles in field. Trustee Schoolcraft Coll., Livonia, 1963-67. Served to capt. M.C. AUS, 1952-54. Mem. Mich., Wayne County med. socs., Mich. Soc. Psychiatry and Neurology (Research award 1953), Am., Pan-Am. med. assns., Am. Psychiat. Assn. Introduced atropine coma therapy for treatment of psychoses, 1950; devel. psychoanalytic theory of hallucination, psychoanalytic theory of placebo. Home: 46995 W Main St Northville MI 48167 Office: 20141 James Couzens Hwy Detroit MI 48235

FORRESTER, LARRY LEE, trade association executive; b. Bluffton, Ind., Aug. 7, 1944; s. Russell and Frances L. (Teagle) F.; m. Diana Lynn Prince, July 10, 1974; children: Larry Thomas, Eric Lee. BS, Purdue U., 1967. Rep. mem. services Nat. Assn. of Mutual Ins. Cos., Indpls., 1970-72, dir. edn., 1972-74, v.p. mem. services, 1974-80, sr. v.p., 1980-86, exec. v.p., 1986—; pres. Crop Ins. Research Bur., Indpls., 1980-87, sec.-treas., 1987—. Served with U.S. Army, 1967-69, Vietnam. Mem. Am. Soc. Assn. Execs., Ind. Soc. Assn. Execs. (sec. 1987—). Republican. Lodge: Kiwanis. Avocations: golf, fishing, tennis. Office: Nat Assn Mutual Ins Cos 3707 Woodview Trace Indianapolis IN 46268

FORRETTE, JOHN ELMER, podiatrist; b. Chgo., Sept. 4, 1952; s. John E. and Mary L. (Lanoce) F.; m. Marcine Jean Heger, May 24, 1980. BA, St. Mary's Coll., 1974; BS, Ill. Coll. Podiatric Medicine, 1980, DPM, 1980. Diplomate Am. Bd. Podiatry Examiners, Am. Bd. Podiatric Orthopaedics. Podiatrist Winona, Minn., 1981-85, Skemp-Grandview-LaCrosse (Wis.) Clinic, 1985—. Served to capt. USAR, 1982—. Ill. State scholar, 1970; recipient Internat. Youth in Achievement award 1982; named Young Community Leader, 1982. Fellow Am. Coll. Podiatric Radiology; mem. Am. Podiatric Med. Assn., Wis. Soc. Podiatric Medicine, Am. Assn. Hosp. Podiatrists, Ill. Coll. Podiatric Medicine Alumni Assn. (bd. dirs.). Club: Exchange (treas. 1982-85). Office: Skemp Grandview LaCrosse Clinic 212 S 11th St LaCrosse WI 54601

FORSBERG, CRAIG JAMES, dentist; b. Melrose Park, Ill., Aug. 23, 1956; s. Harold Ernst and Dorothy Lorane (Overhaurse) F.; m. Darlene Jane Van Ripor, Aug. 24, 1985. BS, U. Wis., Whitewater, 1978; DDS, Marquette U., 1982. Dentist La Clinica de Los Camposinos, Wild Rose, Wis., 1982, Blado Dental Ctr., Tomah, Wis., 1982-85; pvt. practice gen. dentistry West Salem, Wis., 1985—. Mem. Wis. Dental Assn. (del. 1986—), ADA, Wis. Dental Assn., LaCrosse Dental Soc., Am. Soc. Forensic Odontology. Lodge: Lions. Avocations: golfing, fishing. Office: 215 N Rose St West Salem WI 54669

FORSLUND, ROBERT LEE, food company executive; b. Harcourt, Iowa, Apr. 9, 1938; s. Monrad William and Elsie Maye (Swanlund) F.; student Drake U., 1960; m. Mary Kay Wingert, June 2, 1962; children—Robert Lee, Kristen Kay. With George A. Hormel & Co., Austin, Minn., 1961—, mgr. licensing and joint venture ops., internat. div., 1979—; dir. Stefanutti/Hormel, Santo Domingo, Dominican Republic, Pure Foods Corp., Manila, Philippines, Hormel Ltd. (Japan), Vista Internat. Packaging, Kenosha, Wis. Served with U.S. Army, 1960-62. Republican. Presbyterian. Club: Austin Country. Home: 101 22d St NW Austin MN 55912 Office: 501 16th Ave NE Austin MN 55912

FORSTER, CHARLES WILLIAM, bank executive; b. Durand, Wis., Feb. 23, 1949; s. Harry Joseph and Edna Veronica (Schlosser) F.; m. Jo Ann Peterson, Aug. 19, 1978; 1 child, Lindsey Ann. BBS, U. Wis., Eau Claire, 1971. Agt. N.Am. Life and Casualty, Eau Claire, 1971-73; v.p. First Wis. Nat. Bank, Eau Claire, 1973—; instr. Am. Inst. Banking, Eau Claire, 1982-86. Chmn. Samaritan Club membership com. Luther Hosp., 1986—. Mem. Am. Inst. Banking (bd. dirs. 1985—), Wis. Bankers Assn., Ducks Unltd. (mem. exec. com.). Lodge: Kiwanis, Wis. Indian Head Country Found. (sec., treas.). Avocations: hunting, fishing. Office: First Wis Nat Bank PO Box 7 Eau Claire WI 54702

FORSTER, PETER H., utility company executive; b. Berlin, Germany, May 28, 1942; s. Jerome and Margaret Hanson; m. Susan E. Forster. B.S., U. Wis., 1964; postgrad., Bklyn. Law Sch., Columbia U., 1972. Engr. trainee Wis. Electric Power Co., 1960-64; head regional planning Am. Electric Power Service Corp., 1964-73; atty. Dayton Power & Light Co., Ohio, from 1973; v.p. adminstrn., treas. Dayton Power & Light Co., 1977, v.p. fin. and adminstrn., 1977-78, v.p. energy resources, 1978-79, exec. v.p., 1980-81, exec. v.p., chief operating officer, 1981-82, pres., chief operating officer, 1982-84, pres., chief exec. officer, 1984—, also dir.; bd. dirs. C.H. Gosiger Machinery Co., Edison Electric Inst., Bank One, Dayton, Ohio. Bd. dirs. Bank One, Dayton, F.M. Tait Found., Miami (Ohio) Valley Hosp., United Negro Coll. Fund, Pub. Edn. Fund Governing Bd.; trustee Com. for Econ. Devel. Mem. Am. Bar Assn., Ohio Bar Assn., Dayton Bar Assn., Dayton Area C. of C. (trustee). Club: Dayton Engrs. Office: Dayton Power and Light Co PO Box 1247 Dayton OH 45401

FORSYTHE, ALLAN LEE, consulting and import/export company executive; b. Cleve., Mar. 5, 1937; s. Lee King and Florence King (Bosehart) F.; m. Carol Edna Mathisen, Nov. 28, 1959; children: Scott Allan Zafer, Charles Stuart Dogan. BSCE, Case Inst. Tech., 1958; MS in Chemistry, Case Western Res. U., 1961; MBA, Northeastern U., 1983. Chmn. physics dept. Mercersburg (Pa.) Acad., 1966-67; dir. spl. projects St. Albans Sch., Washington, 1967-75; headmaster Carroll Sch., Lincoln, Mass., 1975-82, Marburn Acad., Columbus, Ohio, 1982-86; pres. ALCA Enterprises, Inc., Columbus, 1986—; cons. Telecomputations, Washington, 1970, NETV, Fairfax, Va., 1972, Concern, Inc., Washington, 1973, Lab Sch., Washington, 1974-75. Contbr. articles to profl. jours. Co-chmn. Gov.'s Commn. on Learning Disabilities, Columbus, 1984; pres. bd. dirs. Parentheses Foster Care Agy., Columbus, 1986—; chmn. publicity Promet Ballet Support Group, Columbus, 1987—. Fellow Washington Acad. Sci., 1974. Mem. Columbus C. of C. (govt. affairs), Beta Gamma Sigma. Republican. Lodge: Rotary. Avocations: backpacking, golf, oceanography. Home: 404 S Spring Rd Westerville OH 43081 Office: ALCA Enterprises 5027 Pine Creek Dr Westerville OH 43081

FORSYTHE, JAMES LEE, historian, university dean; b. Bransford, Tex., Dec. 18, 1934; s. Roy Theodore and Irma May (Smith) F.; B.S., N. Tex. State U., 1960, M.A., 1962; Ph.D. (fellow), U. N.Mex., 1971; m. Sherrill Kay Zartman, Aug. 10, 1956; children—James Lee, Garen David, Dana Sean. Transp. agt. Delta Air Lines, Dallas, 1952-62; asst. prof. history Ft. Hays (Kans.) State Coll. (now Ft. Hays State U.), 1963-68, assoc. prof. history, 1968-71, prof., 1971—, chmn. dept. history, 1975-81, dean of grad. sch., 1981—; mem. Kans. Hist. Records Adv. Bd., 1976—; mem. Kans. State Historic Sites Bd. of Rev., 1980—; dir. Kans. Oral History Project, 1969—. Treas., Ellis County Young Democrats, 1966-70; Dem. precinct committeeman, 1974—. Served with Air N.G., 1953-55; U.S. Army, 1955-57. Recipient Disting. Alumni award Grapevine (Tex.) High Sch., 1970, named to Hall of Fame, 1983; Harry S. Truman Library Inst. Nat. and Internat. Affairs grantee, 1967, 72. Mem. Rocky Mountain Social Sci. Assn. (exec. council 1971-74), Western Social Sci. Assn. (pres. 1976-77), AAUP (pres. Kans. 1972-73), Kans. State Hist. Soc. (dir. 1977—, v.p. 1980-81, pres. 1982-83, exec. com. 1985—), Kans. Com. Humanities (exec. com. 1975-82, chmn. 1981-82), Agrl. History (exec. com. 1986—) Assn., Orgn. Am. Historians, So., N.Mex., Western hist. assns., Phi Alpha Theta (Sigma Chpt. pres. 1962-63), Pi Sigma Alpha, Phi Kappa Phi (pres. Ft. Hays Chpt. 1984), Phi Delta

Kappa. Baptist. Author: The First 75 Years: A History of Fort Hays State University, 1902-1977, 1977; contbr. articles to profl. jours. Home: 2927 Walnut St Hays KS 67601 Office: Grad Sch Fort Hays State U 600 Park St Hays KS 67601

FORSYTHE, PATRICIA HAYS, foundation executive; b. Curtis, Ark.; d. John Chambers and Flora Jane (Eby) Hays; m. Kurt G. Pahl, Dec. 15, 1962 (div. Dec. 1980); children: Thomas Walter, Susan Clara; m. Robert E. Forsythe, June 20, 1981. BA, Calif. State U., Los Angeles, 1974; MSLS, U. So. Calif., 1976. Asst. to dir. devel. office The Assocs., Calif. Inst. Tech., Pasadena, 1978-81; exec. dir. Iowa City Pub. Library Found., 1982—. Mem. LWV (editor 1985-87), Eastern Iowa Nat. Soc. for Fund Raising Execs. (v.p., pres. elect 1987). Congregationalist. Club: Hancher Guild (Iowa City) (audience devel. 1981-85, pres. 1985-86). Avocations: travel, writing, cooking, drama. Home: 1806 E Court St Iowa City IA 52240 Office: Iowa City Pub Library Found 123 S Linn Iowa City IA 52240

FORSYTHE, STANLEY LAWRENCE, computer information analyst; b. Williamston, Ky., June 17, 1950; s. Harold Lee and Mildred Louise (Simpson) F.; m. Barbara Ann Budke, Aug. 5, 1972; children: Sarah Elizabeth, Stanley Lawrence II. BS in Electronic Tech., Eastern Ky. U., 1972. Computer programmer U. Cin., 1975-78; computer analyst Cin. Bell Info. Systems, 1978—. Served with U.S. Army, 1972-74. Democrat. Baptist. Avocations: military miniatures, reading, coach instructional soccer and baseball. Office: Cin Bell Info Systems 116-1300 600 Vine St Cincinnati OH 45202

FORT, GERALD MARSHALL, psychologist, consultant; b. Mitchell, S.D., Mar. 16, 1919; s. Lyman Marion and Mildred May (Dunsworth) F.; m. Pearl Marie Maki, Feb. 6, 1943; children: Michael Lyman, Sandra Mae. BA, Grinnell Coll., 1941; MA, U. Minn., 1948, PhD, 1960. Lic. psychologist, Wis., Minn. Assoc. prof. S.D. State U., Brookings, 1949-59; psychol. cons. Humber, Mundie & McClary, Milw., 1959-72; ptnr., mgr. Humber, Mundie & McClary, Mpls., 1972-84; bd. dirs. N. Cen. Career Devel. Ctr. Contbr. articles to profl. jours. Ch. council member Mt. Zion Luth. Ch., Wauwatosa, Wis., 1966-72, Normandale Luth. Ch., Edina, Minn., 1974-80; chmn. Commn. Profl. Leadership, Minn. Synod, Mpls., 1976-82; bd. dirs. Samaritan Counseling Ctr., New Brighton, Minn., 1982-84. Served to master sgt. USAAF, 1941-45. Recipient Disting. Service award Greater Mpls. C. of C., 1984. Mem. Minn. Psychol. Assn. (life). Republican. Club: Edina Country (sec., bd. dirs. 1972-84). Lodge: Kiwanis, Elks. Avocations: golf, fly fishing, travelling, puzzles. Home and Office: Box 1310 HC 37 Lead SD 57754

FORT, TIMOTHY LYMAN, lawyer, political science educator; b. Burlington, Iowa, Aug. 29, 1958; s. Lyman Rankin and Mildred Lucille (Gibb) F. BA in Govt., U. Notre Dame, 1980, MA in Theology, 1984; JD, Northwestern U., 1983. Bar: Ill. 1983. Ptnr. Fort, Fort & Hennenfent, Stronghurst, Ill., 1983—; prof. polit. sci. Monmouth (Ill.) Coll., 1986—. Author: Law and Religion, 1986, Making It Back, 1986. V.p. A.J. Fort Recreation Co., Stronghurst, 1979—; bd. dirs. Henderson County Retirement Ctr., Stronghurst, 1985—; rep. Young Reps., 17th Congl. dist. 1985—; atty. Warren County Rep. Cen. Com., 1985—; mem. Monmouth Economic Devel. Council, 1985—, Henderson County Young Reps. (pres. 1985—), Knox County Young Reps. (sec. 1985—); local campaign coordinator Gov. James Thompson, Sec. State James Edgar, Henderson and Warren Counties, 1985—. Co-recipient Young Rep. Yr. award Ill. Young Reps. Orgn., 1986. Mem. ABA, Ill. Bar Assn., Henderson County Bar Assn., Warren County Bar Assn. Presbyterian. Home: 902 E Euclid Monmouth IL 61462 Office: Fort Fort & Hennenfent 108 S Broadway Stronghurst IL 61480

FORTIN, DARYL GILBERT, industrial engineer, educator; b. Sioux City, Iowa, Jan. 13, 1952; s. Gilbert Oliver and Elizabeth Ann (Christianson) F.; m. Patricia Ann Capers, Sept. 4, 1971; children: Jennifer, Sean. BS in Indsl. Engring., Columbia U., 1975; MBA, U. No. Iowa, 1982. Indsl. engr. John Deere Component Works, Waterloo, Iowa, 1975-78, sr. indsl. engr., 1978-82, project mgr., 1982-85, sr. value engr., 1985-86, sr. process engr., 1986—; adj. instr. U. No. Iowa, Cedar Falls, 1985—, Upper Iowa U., Fayette, 1986—. Mem. Inst. Indsl. Engrs. (treas. 1983-84, sec. 1984-85). Roman Catholic. Avocations: softball, tennis. Home: 2102 Minnetonka Dr Cedar Falls IA 50613 Office: John Deere Component Works 400 Westfield Ave Waterloo IA 50701

FORTNAM, LINDA LANGS, video production company executive; b. Hillsdale, Mich., Mar. 1, 1953; d. Francis Marion and Virginia (Olsen) Langs; m. Steven Gilbert Fortnam, Aug. 11, 1984; 1 child, Renee Ashleigh. BA with honors, Mich. State U., 1976. Tchr. communications Harry Hill High Sch., Lansing, Mich., 1977; free lance writer Hollywood, Calif., Chgo. and Detroit, 1978-82; assoc. producer After-Image Productions, Grand Rapids, Mich., 1982-83; pres., exec. producer Cable Ads Am. Inc./All Media Productions, Grand Rapids, 1983—. Author: (musical) The Change of Life, 1978; (video prodn.) Impact, 1983, All Eyes on You, 1984; exec. producer (video prodn.) AIDS: Learn For Your Life. Pres. Assault Crisis Team, Hillsdale, Mich, 1980-82. Mem. Alliance Women Entrepreneurs, Bus. and Profl. Women (Outstanding Young Careerist 1982). Republican. Home: 4108-11 Crooked Tree Wyoming MI 49509 Mailing: PO Box K Grand Rapids MI 49501 Office: All Media Prodns 1424 Lake Dr Suite 222-49506 Grand Rapids MI 49501

FORTNER, CARL DAVID, lawyer; b. Chgo., 1958; s. Carl L. and Esther M. (Kaetzel) F.; m. Patti J. Luedtke, 1982. BBA with distinction, U. Wis., 1980, MS in Taxation, 1986, JD cum laude, 1986. CPA, Wis. Tax sr. Arthur Andersen & Co., Milw., 1980-83; teaching asst. U. Wis., Madison, 1984-86; tax atty. Foley & Lardner, Milw., 1986—. Contbr. articles to profl. jours. Mem. ABA, Wis. Inst. CPA's, State Bar Wis., Order of Coif. Avocations: outdoorsman. Office: Foley & Lardner 777 E Wisconsin Ave Milwaukee WI 53202

FORTNER, MICHAEL JAMES, entrepreneur; b. Cleve., Nov. 7, 1956; s. Douglas M. Fortner and Mary Ann (Goodrich) Simpson; m. Patricia Ann Procaccini, Sept. 3, 1982; 1 child, Angela M. Student, Miami U., Oxford, Ohio, 1975-80. Tech. writer Predicasts Inc., Cleve., 1980-81; div. mgr. R.L. Bowen & Assocs., Cleve., 1982-83; bus. broker VR Bus. Brokers, Beachwood, Ohio, 1983-84; owner Prodigy Products Co., Cleve., 1982—; cons. M.J. Fortner & Assocs., Cleve., 1986—. Mem. Cleve. Inventors Connection. Republican. Avocations: writing, juggling, hypnosis. Home and Office: 14152 Superior Rd Suite 4 Cleveland Heights OH 44118

FORTUNATO, PATRICK THOMAS, accountant; b. Brightwaters, N.Y., Feb. 23, 1959; s. Frank and Roberta Ann (Sulig) F.; m. Marcia Mae Groshong, Jan. 2, 1982. BS in Mgmt., Case Western Res. U., 1981, MS in Acctg., 1982. CPA, Ohio. Sr. tax acct. Deloitte, Haskins & Sells, Cleve., 1982-85; tax analyst Acme Cleveland Corp., Pepper Pike, Ohio, 1985-86; tax analyst Agy. Rent-a-Car, Inc., Solon, Ohio, 1986-87, supr. acctg., 1987—. Mem. Am. Inst. CPA's, Ohio Soc. CPA's, Delta Tau Delta. Mem. Assembly of God Ch. Avocations: skiing, volleyball. Home: 167 Woodrow Ave Bedford OH 44146 Office: Agy Rent-a-Car Inc 30000 Aurora Rd Solon OH 44139

FORTUNE, FREDDIE CECIL, architectural engineer; b. Florence, S.C., Aug. 3, 1929; s. Herbert and Thelma (Cooper) F.; m. Givendoline Alpha Young, Jan. 21, 1951; children: Frederic Andre, Phillip Alan, Roger Gerard. BArch Engring., S.C. State Coll., 1950; postgrad., Ill. Inst. Tech., 1954, DePaul U., 1954-56; Cert., U. Ill., Chgo., 1965, U. Ill., 1967; Diploma, Command and Gen. Staff Coll., Ft. Leavenworth, Kans., 1970-73, Nat. Def. U., Washington, 1975-76; MS in Mgmt. and Devel. Human Resources, Nat. Coll. Edn., Evanston, Ill., 1984. Sole practice in archtl. design Florence, 1953-54; engr., designer Gold Bros., Chgo., 1954; archtl. designer Ill. Bronze Co., Chgo., 1954-55; engr. designer Compco Corp., Chgo., 1955-56; sr. engr. AT&T, Skokie, Ill., 1956—; shelter analyst U.S. Dept. Def., Washington, 1965—; instr. Oakton Community Coll., Des Plaine, Ill., 1981—; cons. in field, 1981—. Author: (book) Contamination Control, 1967, Organization and Management Change, 1984; (manual) AT&T Safety Manual, 1970, MOS Maintenance, 1972. Admissions rep. U.S. Mil. Acad., Chgo., 1986; trustee 1st Presby. Ch. Chgo., 1980; bd. dirs. Human Relations Council, Skokie. Served to col. U.S. Army, 1950-53. Decorated Bronze Star, Air medal with three oak leaf clusters; UN medal. Mem. Inst. Environmental Sci. (sr.), Chgo. Assn. Commerce and Industry (rep., Cert. of Merit 1967-80), Reserve Officers Assn. Lodges: Lions, Masons. Avocations: golf, skiing, tennis, softball, swimming. Home: 9150 N Kilbourn Ave Skokie IL 60076 Office: AT&T 5555 Touhy Ave Skokie IL 60077

FORWARD, THEODORE CLAUDE, psychologist; b. Ashtabula, Ohio, June 28, 1931; s. Donald DeKlyn and Constance (Newcomb) F.; m. Patricia Anne Grishkat, July 21, 1956; children: Tracy, Brad, Kyle. BS, Kent (Ohio) State U., 1953, MEd, 1955; PhD, Case Western Res. U., 1959. Lic. psychologist; cert. sch. pyschologist. Counselor Canfield (Ohio) Local Schs., 1959-61, Warren (Ohio) City Schs., 1961-63; psychologist Trumbull County Bd. Edn., Warren, 1963-86; pvt. practice psychology Niles, Ohio, 1968—; instr. Youngstown (Ohio) State U., 1964—; bd. dirs. Child Achievement, Warren, 1967-80; cons. Fairhaven Sch., Niles, 1962-70, Children's Rehab., Warren, 1963-75. Mem. Am. Soc. Clin. Hypnosis, Profl. Hynotherapy Soc., Assn. Psychosomatic Medicine, Ohio Psychol. Assn. Avocation: Western square dancing. Home: 487 N Rhodes Niles OH 44446 Office: Family Med Clinic 1150 Niles-Cortland Rd Niles OH 44446

FOSHER, DONALD H., advertising company executive, inventor; b. St. Louis Mo., Jan. 6, 1935; s. Hobart L. and Alby U. (Andrews) F.; m. Charlotte B. Reich, Oct. 6, 1956 (div. Dec. 1976); 1 child, Carey B.; Janet L. Leiber, Dec. 31, 1977. B.S., in Bus. Adminstrn., Washington U., St. Louis Mo., 1956. Copywriter Gen. Am., St. Louis, Mo., 1956-59; art dir. Artcraft, St. Louis, 1959-67; creative dir. Frank Block Assocs., St. Louis, 1967-69; account exec. Vangard/Wells, Rich, Green, St. Louis, 1969-74; ptnr., v.p. Vinyard & Lee, St. Louis, 1974-77; sr. v.p., creative dir. Hughes Advt., St. Louis, 1977—; pres., owner Don Fosher, Inc., St. Louis, 1974—; co-owner Freelance Studios, Clayton, Mo., 1979—, BrandBank div. Don Fosher Inc., 1986—. Author: Art for Secondary Education, 1962. Contbr. articles on cuisine to popular mags. Patentee sports, medicine, mech. design. Advisor, St. Louis County Spl. Sch. Dist., 1966-76; bd. dirs. Vocat. Schs., St. Louis, 1969—; campaign designer St. Louis Better Bus. Bur., 1975, St. Louis Arts & Edn. Fund, 1984. Recipient Art Dir. of Yr. award Soc. Communications Arts, 1967; Venice Biennial, Internat. Congress Designers, 1966, Package Design award Am. Fishing Tackle Mfrs. Assn., 1981, numerous Creative awards Art Directors, 1959-1987. Mem. Internat. Congress Designers, Soc. Communications Arts (pres. 1966-67), Direct Mail Mktg. Assn., SAR. Mem. Christian Ch. Club: Glen Echo Country. Avocations: inventing, cooking, collecting primative art. Home: 7266 Creveling Dr University City MO 63130 Office: Hughes Advt Inc 130 S Bemiston Clayton MO 63105

FOSS, CHARLES R., government agency buyer; b. Chgo., Nov. 1, 1945; s. Raymond C. and Marilyn (Halas) F. Assoc. in Transp., Davenport Coll., 1973, B in Mktg., 1985, postgrad., 1985-87. Yardmaster Chesapeake and Ohio Ry., Benton Harbor, Mich., 1963-66; ticket agt. Chesapeake and Ohio Ry., Holland, Mich., 1969-71; freight agt., train dispatcher Penn Cen. Ry., Ft. Wayne, Ind., 1971-76; sales rep. Foss Police Equipment and Communications, Battle Creek, Mich., 1976-85; customer service rep. Superior Brand Produce, Hudsonville, Mich., 1985; purchasing buyer U.S. Dept. Def., Dayton, Ohio, 1986—. Author: Evening Before The Diesel, 1980. Coordinator Susquicentennial Commemorative Winchester Carbine, Byron Twp., Byron Ctr., Mich., 1985. Served with U.S. Army, 1966-69, Vietnam. Mem. R.R. Mus. (hon. life), Chgo. and Northwestern Hist. Soc. (contbr.), So. Mich. R.R. Soc. Inc. (contbr.), Am. Truck Hist. Soc. (life), Nat. Rifle Assn. (life). Republican. Avocations: firearms collection, antique cars and trucks, transp. art works collector.

FOSS, KARL ROBERT, income tax auditor; b. Madison, Wis., Aug. 26, 1938; s. Robert Henry and Ethel Caroline (Huston) F.; student U. Wis., 1956-59, 62; B.S., Madison Bus. Coll., 1961. Auditor Wis. Dept. Revenue, Madison, 1962—; owner, mgr. LIST, Middleton, Wis., 1968-76. Bd. dirs. Middleton Hist. Soc., 1976—, v.p., 1980; legis. adv. Old Car Hobby, 1971—. Co-recipient Spl. Interest Autos Appreciation award, 1971. Mem. Wis. Automobile Clubs in Assn. Inc. (co-founder 1971, pres. 1972-74, 77, 78, 80, 86, 87, v.p. 1975-76, 79, 85), Oldsmobile Club Am. (nat. dir. 1973-85 , treas. 1981-85), Acctg. and Mgmt. Assn. (treas. 1981-87), Contemporary Hist. Vehicle Assn., Studebaker Drivers Club, Nash Car Club Am., Crosley Car Club, Antique Automobile Club Am., Model T Ford Am. Publisher: Suppliers List, 1968, Suppliers List Directory, 1969. Home: 1619 Middleton St Middleton WI 53562

FOSS, LUKAS, composer, conductor, pianist; b. Berlin, Germany, Aug. 15, 1922; came to U.S. from Paris, 1937, naturalized, 1942; s. Martin and Hilde (Schindler) F.; (m); 2 children. Student, Paris Lycée Pasteur, 1932-37; grad., Curtis Inst. Music, 1940; spl. study, Yale, 1940-41; pupil of, Paul Hindemith, Julius Herford, Serge Koussevitzky, Fritz Reiner, Isabelle Vengerova; recipient of 4 hon. doctorates. Former prof. UCLA (in charge orch. and advanced composition); faculty Harvard U., 1970-71; Founder Center Creative and Performing Arts, Buffalo U.; vis. prof. Carnegie Mellon U., Pitts., 1987-88. Former condr., music dir., Buffalo Philharmonic, mus. dir., condr., Bklyn. Philharmonic, 1971—, music dir., condr., Milw. Symphony Orch., 1981-86, condr. laureate, 1986—; orchestral compositions performed by many major orchs.; best known works include (opera) Griffelkin, Baroque Variations (orch.), Echoi (4 instruments); orch., chamber music, ballets, works commd. by, League of Composers, Nat. Endowment for Arts, N.Y. Arts Council, NBC opera on TV, Am. Choral Condrs. Assn., Ind. U., 1979 Olympics, others.; (recipient N.Y. Critic Circle citation for Prairie 1944, Soc. for Pub. Am. Music award for String Quartet in G 1948, Rome prize 1950, Horblit award for Piano concerto No. 2 1951, Naumburg Rec. award for Song of Songs 1957, Creative Music grant Inst. Arts and Letters 1957, N.Y. Music Critics Circle award for Time-Cycle orch. songs 1961, for Echoi 1963, Ditson award for condr. who has done the most for Am. music 1973, N.Y.C. award for spl. contbn. to arts 1976, ASCAP award for adventurous programming 1979, CRI rec. award for Thirteen Ways of Looking at a Blackbird 1979). Guggenheim fellow, 1945; Creative arts award Brandeis U., 1983; Laurel leaf award Am. Composers Alliance, 1983. Mem. Nat. Acad. and Inst. Arts and Letters. Address: 17 E 96th St New York NY 10128 Office: co Nat Orch Assn 111 W 57th St Suite 1400 New York NY 10019

FOSS, RICHARD JOHN, minister; b. Wauwatosa, Wis., Dec. 27, 1944; s. Harlan Funston and Beatrice Naomi (Lindaas) F.; m. Nancy Elizabeth Martin, June 21, 1969; children: Susan, John, Naomi, Elizabeth, Peter, Andrew. BA, St. Olaf Coll., 1966; MDiv, Luther Theol. Seminary, 1971; ThM, Luther N.W. Theol. Seminary, 1984. Ordained to ministry Luth. Ch., 1971. Pastor St. Andrews Ch. and Ch. of Christ the Redeemer, Mpls., 1971-77; assoc. pastor First Luth., Fargo, N.D., 1977-79; sr. pastor Prince of Peace Luth., Seattle, 1979-86, Trinity Luth., Moorhead, Minn., 1986—. Soloist F-M Opera Co., Fargo, 1979; coach St. James Girls' Basketball Team, Seattle, 1982-84; vol. Wash. State Patrol Crisis Chaplaincy, Seattle, 1983-86; bd. dirs. Discovery, Inc., Mpls., 1972-77, Highline Boys' and Girls' Club, Burien, Wash., 1980-81, Luth. Compass Ctr., Seattle, 1983-86, v.p., 1985-86. Avocations: racquetball, golf, reading, travel, vocal performance. Home: 1510 S 2d St Moorhead MN 56560 Office: Trinity Lutheran Moorhead MN 56560

FOSTER, BARBARA ANNE, motion picture producer, screenplay writer; b. Cin., Jan. 22, 1955; d. Walter Norman and Rhea Mae (Baumann) F. BS in Communication Arts, Xavier U., Cin., 1977. With positive assembly MGM Labs, Los Angeles, 1977; edit. asst. Burbank (Calif.) Editorial, 1978; film insp. Four Star Internat., Beverly Hills, Calif., 1979-80; owner Horizan Unlimited Prodn. Co., Burbank, Calif., 1980; pres. Sunburst Pictures Inc., Los Angeles, 1981—. Author: (screenplay) Lady Lightning, 1986. Mem. Antique Auto Club Am., Plymouth 4th Cylinder Club. Avocations: racing, sailing, skiing, boating.

FOSTER, BARBARA MAY, teacher; b. Keokuk, Iowa, Aug. 17, 1942; d. Harry Guilford and Gladys Iantha (Baxter) Hanson: M. Richard John Mohr, June 11, 1966 (div. June 1972); 1 child, Troy Leigh; m. Glenn Delmar Foster, Feb. 14, 1981. BS, NE Mo. State U., 1974, MS in Edn., 1979. Cert. life tchr., Mo., Iowa. Tchr. Hawthorne Elem. Sch., Keokuk, 1974-79, Keokuk Middle Sch., 1979-82; tchr. Mollie B. Hoover Sch. Crawfordsville (Ind.) Sch. Corp., 1984—; rep. Prime Time program Ind. State Dept. Edn. Mem. Crawfordsville Edn. Assn., Delta Kappa Gamma (pres. 1984-86), Beta Sigma Phi, Psi Iota Xi. Republican. Lodge: P.E.O. Sisterhood (pres. 1987-89, Continuing Edn. Fund award 1979). Avocations: swimming, sewing, gardening, choir singing. Home: 26 McCormick Dr Crawfordsville IN 47933 Office: Mollie B Hoover Elem Sch 1301 S Elm Crawfordsville IN 47933

FOSTER, HOLMES, bank executive; b. 1927. Dep. supt. State Dept. Banking, Des Moines, 1940-70; pres. Banks of Iowa, Des Moines, 1970—. Office: Banks of Iowa Inc 520 Walnut Des Moines IA 50306 *

FOSTER, JAMES FRANKLIN, sports management and marketing executive; b. Iowa M. (Egerer) F.; m. Susan Jane Salsi, July 19, 1976. B.G.S., U. Iowa, 1972; postgrad. U. Pa., 1982. Retail advt. specialist Maytag Co., Newton, Iowa, 1972-78; founder, gen. mgr. Iowa Nite Hawks AAA Pro Football Club, 1974-78; founder, dir. Am. Pro Football Tour of Europe, 1977, 79; promotion mgr. Nat. Football League Properties, Inc., N.Y.C., 1979-82; asst. gen. mgr. Ariz. Wranglers Pro Football Club, U.S. Football League, Phoenix, 1982-83; exec. v.p. Chgo. Blitz Pro Football Club, U.S. Football League, Chgo., 1983-84; v.p. Chgo. Sting soccer promotions Burke Promo Mktg. Inc., 1984-85; founder, pres. Arena Football, Chgo., 1985—; cons. Minor Pro Football Assn., Elmhurst, Ill., 1982—. Recipient Golden Helmet Excellence awards Nat. Football League Properties, Inc., 1981, 82; named Minor Pro Football Exec. of Yr., Pro Football Weekly, 1976, No. States League Gen. Mgr. of Yr., AAA Football, 1976; named to Minor Pro Football Hall of Fame, 1982. Mem. Iowa State Hist. Soc., Chgo. Jazz Inst., Antique and Classic Boat Soc., Boat Owners Assn. of U.S., Am. Mktg. Assn., Aircraft Owners and Pilots Assn. Democrat. Methodist. Clubs: Nat. Iowa Lettermans; Illiana Traditional Jazz. Home: 3614 Walters Ave Northbrook IL 60062

FOSTER, JAMES NORTON, JR., lawyer; b. St. Louis, Mar. 19, 1954; s. James N. and Virginia (Andretto) F.; m. Elizabeth J. Head; 1 child, Virginia. BA in Polit. Scis. magna cum laude, St. Louis U., 1976, JD cum laude, 1979. Bar: Mo. 1979. Law clerk to presiding justice Mo. Ct. Appeals, St. Louis, 1977-78; trial atty. Nat. Labor Relations Bd., St. Louis, 1979-80; assoc. McMahon, Berger, Hanna, Linihan and Cody, St. Louis, 1980-86, ptnr., 1986—; instr. youth and law program St. Louis Pub. Sch. System; adj. prof. Webster U. Assoc. editor, contbr. St. Louis U. Law Jour. Danforth Found. Me. Leadership fellow, 1974-76; named one of Outstanding Young Men Am., 1976. Mem. ABA, Mo. Bar Assn., Met. Bar Assn. St. Louis, Phi Beta Kappa, Phi Sigma Alpha, Alpha Sigma Nu, Phi Delta Phi. Home: 1218 Arch Terr Richmond Heights MO 63117 Office: McMahon et al 2730 N Ballas Rd Suite 200 Saint Louis MO 63131

FOSTER, JOHN B., steel company executive; b. 1928; married. B.A., Dartmouth Coll., 1952; M.B.A., U. Chgo., 1970. With Joseph T. Ryerson & Son, Inc., Chgo., 1952—; asst. mgr. gen. order dept. Joseph T. Ryerson & Son, Inc., 1957-58, mgr. gen. order dept., 1958-61, gen. line salesman, 1961-62, sales mgr., 1962-67, nat. mktg. mgr. gen. office, 1967-70, gen. mgr. N.Y., 1970-75, gen. mgr. N. Central region and Milw. plant, 1975-77, v.p. adminstrn., 1977-80, pres., 1980—, also dir. Office: Joseph T Ryerson & Son Inc 2621 W 15th Pl Chicago IL 60608

FOSTER, JOHN WILLARD, optometrist; b. Black River Falls, Wis., Sept. 5, 1925; s. Leo W. and Martha (Dietsche) F.; student U. Minn., 1943-48; B.S., Pacific U., 1951, O.D., 1953; m. Dolores Schlaeger, Sept. 3, 1949; children—John, Jeffrey, Gregory, Gary, Mark. Practice optometry, Thorp, Wis., 1953-64, Owen, Wis., 1957-64, Neillsville, Wis., 1964—. Mem. Am. Optometric Found., Optometric Extension program. Mem. Am., Wis. optometric assns., Illuminating Engring. Soc. (asso.), Minn. Fedn. Engring. Socs., Blue Key, Omega Delta, Beta Sigma Kappa, K.C., Lion (pres., dir., chmn. visually handicapped children com.). Address: Box 31 Neillsville WI 54456

FOSTER, LEIGH CURTIS, electronics executive; b. Montreal, Aug. 24, 1925; came to U.S., 1943; s. John Stuart and Flora Marion (Curtis) F.; m. Anne Elizabeth Starke, Jan. 23, 1948; children—Karen Anne, John Curtis. B.Sc., McGill U., 1950; Ph.D., McGill U., 1956. Exec. v.p., gen. mgr. Zenith Radio Research Corp., Menlo Park, Calif., 1956-72; v.p., gen. mgr. Applied Tech., Sunnyvale, Calif., 1972-74; v.p. engring. Motorola, Inc., Schaumburg, Ill., 1974—; dir. Tegal Corp., Novato, Calif., 1977—. Patentee in field; contbr. articles to profl. jours. Mem. Gov.'s Sci. Adv. Bd., State of Ill., 1983—. Mem. IEEE, Am. Phys. Soc. Office: Motorola Corp 1303 E Algonquin Rd Schaumburg IL 60196

FOSTER, MARK JOSEPH, infosystems specialist; b. Oak Park, Ill., Nov. 18, 1960; s. Thomas Warren and Joyce Diane (Anderson) F.; m. JoAnne Gustafson, July 1, 1981. Student, Siena Heights Coll. Devel. programmer Standard Register, Dayton, Ohio, 1979-80; software engr. DAYCOM, Dayton, 1980-82, sr. software engr., 1982-83; sr. software engr. Zenith Data Systems, St. Joseph, Mich., 1983-84, sr. project mgr., 1984-85, chief systems architect, 1985—; pres. Foster Software Co., Stevensville, Mich., 1982—; referee Nat. Computer Conf., 1984. Author computer software programs; contbr. articles to profl. jours.; patentee in field. Mem. Assn. Computing Machinery, AAAS, Heath Mgmt. Assn., Am. Radio Relay League, Exptl. Aircraft Assn., Aircraft Owners and Pilots Assn., Acad. Model Aeronautics, Heath Repeater Club, Atari Nat. Users' Group, Heath Users' Group, Mensa. Democrat. Avocations: microcomputer design, flying, amateur radio, astronomy, reading. Home: 3800 Peach St Stevensville MI 49127 Office: Zenith Data Systems Hilltop Rd Saint Joseph MI 49085

FOSTER, MERRILL WHITE, geology and marine biology educator; b. South Gate, Calif., Mar. 18, 1939; s. Samuel Merrill and Ruth Duval (Johnson) F.; m. Patricia Leigh Blodgett, Sept. 1963 (div. Aug. 1971); children: Warren Duval, Alden Lowell; m. Wilma Marie Rinsch, Aug. 1, 1976 (div. Sept. 1984); 1 child, Jonathan David. AA, Pasadena City Coll., 1959; BA, U. Calif., Berkeley, 1961, MA, 1964; PhD, Harvard U., 1970. Grad. research asst. U. Calif., Berkeley, 1962, teaching asst., 1962-64; teaching fellow Harvard U., Cambridge, Mass., 1964-66; asst. investigator Harvard U., NSF, Cambridge, 1966-69; instr., asst. prof., assoc. prof. dept. geol. scis. Bradley U., Peoria, Ill., 1969-78; prof. chmn. dept. geol. scis. Bradley U., Peoria, 1978—; lead tchr. NSD Field Sci., Peoria, 1979, 80, 81; cons. in research. Author: Antarctic and Subantarctic Brachiopods, 1974; contbr. articles to sci. jours. and books. Mem. AAAS, Peoria Acad. Sci., Internat. Paleontol. Assn., Paleontol. Soc., Soc. Econs. Paleontol. and Minerals, Mid-Am. Paleontol. Soc., Sigma Xi (pres. local group), Phi Beta Kappa. Avocations: body surfing, skiing, hiking, folk dancing, philately. Home: 1114 N Maplewood Ave Peoria IL 61606 Office: Dept Geol Sci Bradley U Peoria IL 61625

FOSTER, MILO GEORGE, manufacturing company executive; b. San Diego, Aug. 2, 1957; s. Milo Hughes and Kathryn G. (Sevastos) F. BS, U. Mo., Rolla, 1979; MBA, Harvard U., 1983. Prodn. team mgr. Procter & Gamble, Cape Girardeau, Mo., 1979-81; strategic planner Hitchiner Mfg., Milford, N.H., 1982; tissue mfg. staff asst. Kimberly-Clark Corp., New Milford, Conn., 1983-84; tissue mfg. supt. Kimberly-Clark Corp., Memphis, 1984-86; mgr. mfg. projects Kimberly-Clark Corp., Neenah, Wis., 1986-87; feminine care plant mgr. Kimberly-Clark Corp., Neenah, 1987—. Avocations: aerobics, backpacking, cross-country skiing, cycling, cooking. Office: Kimberly-Clark Lakeview Mill PO Box 1000 Neenah WI 54956-0057

FOSTER, RONALD G., automotive parts company executive; b. Punxsutawney, Pa., Aug. 15, 1941; s. Wade Hampton and Cecile Alice (Hileman) F.; m. Roberta Lee DeVries, Aug. 22, 1964; children: Kristen Lee, Tawnya

Shawn, Mindan Johanna. BBA, Lakeland Coll., 1964. Corp. ontroller Walker Mfg., Racine, Wis., 1976-77, v.p. fin. adminstrn., 1977-81; v.p. planning and devel. Tenneco Automotive, Bannockburn, Ill., 1981-83, v.p. planning and tech. service, 1983; sr. v.p., gen. mgr. Monroe Auto Equipment Co., Monroe, Mich., 1983—. Served to U.S. Army, 1960-62. Mem. Soc. Automotive Engrs., Nat. Assn. Accts., Monroe County C. of C. (bd. dirs.). Republican. Lutheran. Avocations: running, tennis. Office: Monroe Auto Equipment Co 1 International Dr Monroe MI 48161

FOUCH, LARRY DALE, university administrator, tax consultant; b. Muncie, Ind., July 31, 1948; s. Roscoe B. and Wilma Dean (Terry) F.; m. Donna Marie Yoakum, July 5, 1969; 1 child, Neal. BS, Ball State U., 1975. Registered radiologic technologist; CPA, Ind. Radiologic technologist Ball Meml. Hosp., Muncie, 1969-75; sr. acct. G.S. Olive & Co., Muncie, 1975-78; pvt. practice tax cons. Muncie, 1978—; mgr. acctg. Ball State U., Muncie, 1978—. Treas. Planned Parenthood, Muncie, 1979; treas. Neighborhood Assn., Muncie, 1981-82, v.p., then pres., 1983-85; sec. Metro Football League, Muncie, 1985-86. Mem. Am. Inst. CPA's, Ind. Soc. CPA's. Republican. Baptist. Avocations: fishing, hunting. Home: 5304 Leslie Dr Muncie IN 47304 Office: Ball State U 2000 University Ave Muncie IN 47306

FOUDREE, CHARLES M., accountant, financial executive; b. Macon, Mo., June 29, 1944; s. L. Winifred and Lois H. (Malone) F.; m. Colleen Patton, Aug. 9, 1963; children: Mark, Melanie. BS in Acctg., Northeast Mo. State U., 1966. CPA, Kans., Mo. Acct. Peat Marwick Mitchell & Co., Kansas City, Mo., 1966-72; from controller to chief fin. officer and exec. v.p. Harmon Industries, Inc., Blue Springs, Mo., 1972—; also sec., treas. amd bd. dirs. Harmon Industries, Inc., Grain Valley, Mo.; bd. dirs. Mark Twain Independence Bank, Vale-Harmon Enterprises, Ltd., Electro Pneumatic Corp., Inc., Modern Industries, Inc., Louisville, Harmon Electronics, Inc., Grain Valley, Mo. bd. assocs. St. Mary's Hosp, Blue Springs. Mo. Mem. Am. Inst. CPA's, Nat. Assn. Accts., Mo. Soc. CPA's, Fin. Execs. Inst. (sec., bd. dirs. Kansas City chpt.), Nat. Assn. Corp. Treas., Independence C. of C., Jaycees (pres. 1973, JCI senator), Blue Key, Sigma Tau Gamma. Home: 1110 Porter Ct Blue Springs MO 64015 Office: Harmon Industries Inc PO Box 1570 1900 Corporate Centre Blue Springs MO 64015

FOURNIER, RONALD LESTER, chemical engineering educator; b. Toledo, Mar. 19, 1954; s. Lester Robert and Maude Clare (Van Koughnet) F.; m. Lynn Marie Pioterek, May 22, 1976; children: Joshua Adam, Ryan Michael. BSChemE cum laude, U. Toledo, 1976, MSChemE, 1978, PhD, 1981. Registered profl. engr., Ohio. Chem. engr. Stauffer Chem. Co., Adrian, Mich., 1976-78; asst. prof. chem. engring. U. Toledo, 1985—; cons. Energy Technics, Inc., Chgo., 1979-86, Maumee Research and Engring., U.S. Army. Contbr. articles to profl. jours. Served to capt. U.S. Army, 1981-85. U.S. Army ROTC scholar, 1972-76; recipient award for profl. engr. exam Ohio Soc. Profl. Engrs., 1983. Mem. Am. Inst. Chem. Engrs. (Toledo Young Chem. Engr. of Yr. 1987), Am. Chem. Soc., Am. Soc. Engring. Educators, Sigma Xi. Roman Catholic. Avocations: running, sailing. Home: 3752 Dewlawn Dr Toledo OH 43514 Office: U Toledo Dept Chem Engring 2801 W Bancroft St Toledo OH 43606

FOUTS, KENNETH ALLEN, JR., television producer; b. Ida Grove, Iowa, Feb. 14, 1941; s. Kenneth Allen and Feryle Beverly (Conard) F.; m. Meta Sue Knapp, May 14, 1960; children: Kenneth III, Kathryn, Elizabeth, Timothy. BS, U. Nebr., 1964. Dir., producer TV sta. WLW, Cin., 1966-72, NBC Sports, N.Y.C., 1972-81, ABC Sports, N.Y.C., 1981-85; sr. producer Turner Broadcasting, Atlanta, 1985-86; free lance producer Cin., 1986—; tchr. U. Cin., 1980-81; limousin cattle breeder. Served with USMCR, 1960-66. Recipient Emmy award Nat. Acad. Arts and Scis., 1986. Mem. Dirs. Guild of Am., N. Am. Limousin Found., Eastern Limousin Breeders Assn. Roman Catholic. Avocations: skiing, horseback riding. Home and Office: 5499 Belfast Owensville Rd Batavia OH 45103

FOVENESI, JOHN C., business executive; b. Detroit, Aug. 23, 1951; s. Alix and Lorna (Polzin) F.; m. Debra Susan Fovenesi, Nov. 22, 1974; children: Adam, Kim, Erica, Raquel. BBA, Eastern Mich. U., 1973. Mem. audit staff Touche Ross, Detroit, 1973-77; supr. audit dept. Touche Ross, 1977-79, mgr. audit dept., 1979-82; mgr. nat. office Touche Ross, N.Y.C., 1982-84; mgr. enterprise group Touche Ross, Detroit, 1984-85; ptnr. enterprise group Touche Ross, 1985—. Mem. Detroit Zool. Soc., 1984—, Detroit Inst. Art, 1984—, Leadership Detroit VIII; mem. adv. bd. Coll. Bus. Eastern Mich. U., Detroit, 1987, mem. alumni bd., 1986—; bd. dirs. allocation com., fin. rev. com. United Found., Detroit, 1985—. Named Outstanding Alum Coll. Bus. Eastern Mich. U., 1984, Outstanding Young Alum Eastern Mich. U., 1986. Mem. Am. Inst. CPA's, Mich. Assn. CPA's, Southeastern Mich. Venture Capital Group, Nat. Assn. Credit Mgrs., Jaycees (Key Man award 1984), Greater Rochester C. of C., Detroit C. of C., Beta Alpha Psi (Outstanding Achievement award 1982). Republican. Roman Catholic. Clubs: Detroit Athletic, Econ. of Detroit; Great Oaks Country (Rochester, Mich.). Avocaitons: golf, yacht racing, running 10Ks, softball, football. Office: Touche Ross 200 Renaissance Ctr Detroit MI 48243

FOWLER, ANN TALBOT, teacher; b. Merrill, Wis., Oct. 23, 1956; d. James Melvin and Mary Janice (Finucan) Talbot; m. James Stevens Fowler, Jan. 26, 1980; 1 child, James Stevens Jr. BS, U. Wis., Eau Claire, 1979. Tchr. bus. Random Lake (Wis.) High Sch., 1980—; group facilitator alcohol and other drug abuse program Random Lake High Sch., 1984—, instr./counselor job tng. ptnrship. act., 1986—. Mem. Wis. Bus. Edn. Assn., Nat. Bus. Edn. Assn., Sheboygan Falls Jaycees (sec. 1985-86) Sheboygan Falls Jaycee Women (sec. 1983-84, treas. 1984-85). Roman Catholic. Home: 319 Pine St Sheboygan Falls WI 53085

FOWLER, BERNARD JOHN, small business owner; b. Roscommon, Mich., Dec. 8, 1925; s. William John and Ella Leona F.; m. Patricia Arlene Stephan, June 28, 1952; children—Jeffrey William, Gail Ann Ney, Stuart John. Sales clk., grain mill operator Ohio Farm Bur., 1941-44; cloth cutter Wolverine Knitting Mills, Bay City, Mich., 1950-52; lodge caretaker McLouth Steel Corp., Trenton, Mich., 1952-55; owner, operator Edgewater on the AuSable, Grayling, Mich., 1955—; AuSable River fishing and hunting guide, 1946—; Mich. Dept. Natural Resources Forest Fire Keyman, 1954—; Alaska canoeing and fishing guide, 1982—; supr. Grayling Twp., Mich., 1961-84. Mem. Republican Party Task Force. Served with USMC, 1944-46. Mem. Am. Legion, Mich. Twp. Assn. (pres. 1971, dir.), Mich. Assessors Assn. (dir.). Republican. Mem. Reorganized Ch. Jesus Christ of Latter-day Saints. Club: Booster (Grayling). Inducted to Internat. Canoe Racing Hall of Fame, 1986. Home: Route 2 Box 2333 Grayling MI 49738 Office: PO Box 521 Grayling MI 49738

FOWLER, DEBORAH LYNN, marketing executive; b. Lake Forest, Ill., Mar. 21, 1952; s. Eugene Thurman and Claire (Melchiorre) F.; m. John Miller Schenk, June 14, 1980; 1 child, Rachel Anna. BA in Liberal Arts, U. Ill., 1975, MA in Edl. Psych., 1978, PhD in Edl. Psych., 1980. Lic. cons. psychologist, Minn. Research assoc. U. Ill., Champaign, 1979-80, Alverno Coll., Milw., 1981-82; research assoc. Wilson Learning Corp., Eden Prairie, Minn., 1982-83, mgr. mktg. research, 1984-85; mtkg. mgr. Nat. Computer Systems, Minnetonka, Minn., 1985—; mktg. cons., Mpls., 1985—. Named one of Outstanding Young Women of the Yr., 1983. Mem. Am. Psychol. Assn.

FOWLER, DONA J., biology educator; b. Muncie, Ind., May 8, 1928; d. Cleo E. and Thelma (Broman) Wilson; married; children: Ann L. Mastenbrook, James Sheldon. BS, Purdue U., 1955, MS, 1962, PhD, 1965. RN Ball Meml. Hosp., Muncie, Ind., 1950-52; research asst. Purdue U., West Lafayette, Ind., 1954-57, teaching asst., 1960-62, research asst., 1962-65; assoc. research analytical chemist Eli Lilly Co., Indpls., 1957-60; asst. prof. Western Mich. U., Kalamazoo, 1965-70, assoc. prof., 1970-78, prof., 1978—; disting. vis. prof. dept. biology U. Ariz., Tuscon, 1980-81, 87-88; vis. scientist Argonne (Ill.) Nat. Lab., 1983, continuing assoc., 1984—; vis. scientist Centre Nationale Recherche Scientifique, Gif-sur-Yvette, France; participant in Gordon Conf. on Chronobiology, 1983; research dir. NSF, 1968-70, NIH, 1977-79. Contbr. articles to profl. jours. Dir. neighborhood program, nat. and state elections Dem. Party, 1974—; swim team meet dir., bd. pres. AAU Masters Swim Program, 1978—. Mem. Am. Soc. Chronobiology, Int. Soc. Chronobiology, Am. Soc. Biometerology, Soc. Photobiology and Photochemistry, Am. Inst. Biol. Scis., Assn. Mondiale Zootechnie. Democrat. Unitarian. Club: PEO (Kalamazoo) (program dir. 1970—). Home: 722 Grand Pre Kalamazoo MI 49007 Office: Western Mich U Dept Biology and Biomed Scis Kalamazoo MI 49008

FOWLER, DONN NORMAN, dentist; b. Denver, June 7, 1922; s. Roy Eugene and Vera Louise (Alderson) F.; B.S., Northwestern U., 1945, D.D.S., 1953; m. Charlotte Jean Goff, Mar. 18, 1944; children—Donna Jean (Mrs. Donald J. McLoughlin), Linda (Mrs. Malcolm Cardy), Charles R., Peter N., Paul R. Gen. practice dentistry, Glenview, Ill., 1953—; instr. Coll. Dentistry, Northwestern U., Chgo., 1953-55. Trustee, Kendall Coll., Evanston, Ill. Served to lt. (j.g.) USNR, 1943-46; PTO. Mem. Pierre Fauchard Acad., Acad. Gen. Dentistry, Am. Dental Assn., Chgo. Dental Soc., North Suburban Acad. Dental Research (past pres.), G.V. Black Soc., Glenview C. of C., Wis. Dental Study Club, Pi Kappa Alpha. Methodist (mem. annual conf. com.). Lodge: Kiwanis. Home: 1548 Maple Ave Northbrook IL 60062 Office: 1765 River Dr Glenview IL 60025

FOWLER, EARLE CLINTON, III, data processing executive, computer systems consultant; b. New Haven, May 5, 1954; s. Earle Clinton and Clair (Kilcoyne) F.; m. Michelle Rossman, May 29, 1982. BS in Computer Engring., Case Western Res. Univ., 1987. Programmer, analyst Richman Co., Cleve., 1978-80; dir. EDP Predicasts, Inc., Cleve., 1980—. Mem. Internat. Tandem Users Group. Republican. Home: 30380 Bridle Path Trail Wickliffe OH 44092 Office: Predicasts Inc 11001 Cedar Ave Cleveland OH 44106

FOWLER, GEORGE SELTON, JR., architect, writer, inventor; b. Chgo., Jan. 20, 1920; s. George Selton and Mabel Helena (Overton) F.; m. Yvonne Fern Grammer, Nov. 25, 1945; 1 child, Kim Ellyn. Cert. Hamilton Coll., 1944; B.S., Ill. Inst. Tech., 1949, postgrad. 1968; cert. Elec. Assn. Ill., 1976. Registered architect, Ill., Ohio. Urban planner Chgo. Land Clearance Commn., 1949-50; liaison architect Chgo. Housing Authority, 1950-68, chief design-tech. div., 1968-80, dir. dept. engring., 1980-84; prin. George S. Fowler, Architect, Chgo., 1984—; co-founder, pres. The Modern Arts Press, Chgo., 1946; treas., bd. dirs. Chgo. Housing Authority Credit Union, 1963-65; architect, planner and cons. Interconco., 1965-66; instr. archtl. and related engring. Am. Sch., Am. Technical Soc., Chgo., 1948-65; cons. in field. Author: (text book study guide) Reinforced Concrete Design, 1959. Patentee. Mem. Mayor's Adv. Commn. to Revise the Bldg. Code, 1986—. Served with C.E., U.S. Army, 1942-46. Recipient Citation for Residential Devel., Mayor Richard J. Daley, Chgo., 1960, Black Achievers of Industry Recognition award YMCA, Chgo., 1977; Kappa Alpha Psi grantee, 1936. Mem. Architects in Industry, Nat. Assn. Housing and Redevelopment Officials, Inventors Council of Chgo. Avocations: classic cars; classical music; jazz. Home and Office: 8209 S Rhodes Ave Chicago IL 60619

FOWLER, GLORIA R., medical management consultant; b. Muskegon, Mich., Feb. 20, 1933; d. Harry and Dena (Kuiper) Bultema; student Muskegon Community Coll., 1978; m. William H. Fowler, June 26, 1982; children—Robert Vriesman, Scott Vriesman, Laurie Hodgson, Lynn Caraway, William Fowler, Robert Fowler, James Fowler, Barbara Rector. Gen. practice med. asst. Muskegon, Mich., 1952-69; with Muskegon Surg. Assocs., P.C., 1969—, adminstr., 1972-87; pvt. practice cons., 1987—; guest instr. Muskegon Bus. Coll., 1978, 81. Fellow Am. Coll. Med. Group Adminstrs. (cert.), Med. Group Mgmt. Assn., Mich. Med. Group Mgmt. Assn. (sec. 1981-83, pres.-elect 1984-86, pres. 1986-87), Am. Mgmt. Assn. mem. Berean Ch. Home and Office: 17554-B Parkwood Dr Spring Lake MI 49456

FOWLER, JAMES D., JR., manufacturing company financial executive; b. Washington, Apr. 24, 1944; s. James D. and Romay (Lucas) F.; m. Linda Marie Raiford, May 25, 1968; children—Scott, Kimberly. Student, Howard U., Washington, 1962-63; B.S., U.S. Mil. Acad., West Point, N.Y., 1967; M.B.A., Rochester Inst. Tech., 1975. Coordinator grad. relations Xerox Corp., Rochester, N.Y., 1971-74, mgr. personnel adminstrn., 1974-75; sr. cons. D.P. Parker & Assocs., Inc., Wellesley, Mass., 1975-76; mgr. staffing ITT World Hdqrs., N.Y.C., 1976-78; v.p. dir. of adminstrn. ITT Aetna, Denver, 1978; sr. v.p., dir. adminstrn. ITT Consumer Fin. Corp., Mpls., 1978-84, sr. v.p., dir. adminstrn. and mktg., 1984—. Trustee U.S. Mil. Acad., West Point, 1977-86, 87—. Served to capt. U.S. Army, 1967-71, Vietnam. Decorated Bronze Star (2); recipient Black Achiever award ITT, N.Y.C., 1979. Mem. Assn. M.B.A. Execs., Am. Mgmt. Assn., Nat. Consumer Fin. Assn., Twin Cities Personnel Assn., Exec. Leadership Council (charter, fin. com. 1986—). Office: ITT Consumer Financial Corp 400 S County Rd 18 Suite 800 Minneapolis MN 55440

FOWLER, JOHN RUSSELL, retail executive; b. Pontiac, Mich., Apr. 4, 1918; s. John Tasker and Amy (Hurlburt) F.; m. Dorthalene Borthwick, Oct. 5, 1924; children—John Russell, James Borthwick. B.A., Amherst Coll., 1940. With Jacobson Stores Inc., Jackson, Mich., 1946—; exec. v.p. Jacobson Stores Inc., 1962-68, pres., 1966-82, chmn., chief exec. officer, 1982—; dir. Nat. Bank of Jackson, Tecumseh Products Co., Mich.; Camp Realty Co., Jackson, Gerber Co., Fremont, Mich. Chmn. Torch drive, Jackson, 1956, Community Chest, 1957, City Planning Commn., 1970; Chmn. citizens com. Bd. Edn., Jackson, 1960-61; Bd. dirs. Mercy Hosp., Jackson. Served to lt. comdr. USNR, 1941-45. Decorated D.F.C., Air medal. Clubs: Town (Jackson), Country of (Jackson); Otsego (Gaylord). Home: 1115 S Higby St Jackson MI 49203 Office: Jacobson Stores Inc 1200 N West Ave Jackson MI 49202

FOWLER, ROBERT EDWARD, JR., plastic housewares company executive; b. Camden, Tenn., Oct. 7, 1935; s. Robert Edward and Rebecca (Watson) F.; m. Margaret Caroline Armstrong, Dec. 28, 1957; children: Robert, William, Margaret. B.Engring., Vanderbilt U., 1957. With Gen. Electric Co., Louisville, 1957-78, v.p., 1978-81; pres., chief operating officer Rubbermaid, Inc., Wooster, Ohio, 1981—, dir., 1981—. Office: Rubbermaid Inc 1147 Akron Rd Wooster OH 44691 *

FOX, BONNIE LEA, college program director; b. Dubuque, Iowa, Aug. 16, 1942; s. LuVern William and Jane Alma (Mohrman) Klinkenberg; m. Marion Melvin Fox, June 21, 1964; children: Bradley, Betsy. BA, Marycrest Coll., 1978; MSW, U. Iowa, 1982. Mem. staff Outreach Commn. on Aging, Davenport, Iowa, 1979-81; intern in social work Vera French Mental Health Ctr., Davenport, 1981-82; career counselor Black Hawk Coll., Moline, Ill., 1982-85, dir. dislocated workers program, 1985—. Recipient Job Tng. Ptnrship Act State award Dept. Commerce and Community Affairs, Springfield, Ill., 1986. Mem. Nat. Assn. Social Workers, Ill. Assn. Employment and Tng., Ill. Assn. Continuing Edn., Econ. Devel. Assn. Ill. Lutheran. Avocations: water skiing, boating, tennis, walking. Office: Black Hawk Coll 3430 23d Ave Moline IA 61265

FOX, COTTRELL, insurance company executive; b. St. Louis, Apr. 16, 1946; s. A. Cottrell and Dorothy (Vernon) F.; m. Virginia Kay Hebeler, Sept. 15, 1979; B. Journalism, U. Mo., 1971, M. Journalism, 1972. Sr. mktg. rep. Aetna Casualty & Surety Co., St. Louis, 1973-76; mktg. mgr. J.W. Terrill, Inc., St. Louis, 1976-78, v.p., 1978—, prin., 1981—, exec. v.p., 1984—; regional rep. Aetna Life & Casualty Co. Gt. Performers Exec. Council, 1984-86. Mem. fin. com. City of Creve Coeur, Mo., 1987-88. Served to sgt. USMC, 1966-68; S. Vietnam. Decorated three Purple Hearts, Navy Commendation medal; two Vietnamese Crosses Gallantry (Republic South Vietnam). Mem. St. Paul Ins. Co. Agts. Adv. Council (chmn. 1980-81), Comml. Union Ins. Cos. (chmn. 1983—, producer adv. panel), Ind. Ins. Agts. St. Louis Inc. (v.p. 1981-82, pres. 1983-84). Republican. Home: 217 New Salem Dr Creve Coeur MO 63141 Office: J W Terrill Inc 1982 Concourse Dr Saint Louis MO 63146

FOX, HOWARD TALL, JR., professional baseball team executive; b. Emporia, Va., Sept. 4, 1920; s. Howard Tall Sr. and Erma (Peebles) F.; m. Yvonne Grabow, Jan. 24, 1962; children: Mark, Peter, Thomas, Kirk. Student, Va. Poly. Inst. Pub. relations mgr. Washington Senators, 1952-54, treas. and sec., 1954-61; treas. and sec. Minn. Twins, Mpls., 1961-80, exec. v.p., 1980-84, pres., 1984—. Served to capt. U.S. Army, 1942-46. Episcopalian. Office: Minn Twins Hubert H Humphrey Metrodome 501 Chicago Ave S Minneapolis MN 55415

FOX, JOHN, marketing research executive; b. Cin., Dec. 10, 1951; s. Frank Milford and Marjorie Sally (Kiefer) F.; m. Lisa Susan West, June 20, 1976; children: Marjorie Dara, Richard West. BS in Econs., U. Pa., 1974. Brand mgr. Procter & Gamble, Cin., 1975-81; sr. v.p. mktg. Stockton West Burkhart, Cin., 1981-86; sr. v.p. ADI Research, Inc., Cin., 1986—. Contbr. Cin. Bus. Courier. Chmn., founder Alan R. Mack Parents Ctr., Cin., 1983-85. Mem. Am. Mktg. Assn. Club: Losantiville Country (pres. ltd. bd. 1985) (Cin.). Leader of The 4 Hubcaps musical group, Cin., 1975—. Avocations: golf, writing, softball. Home: 593 Tohatchi Dr Cincinnati OH 45215 Office: ADI Research Inc 9406 Main St Cincinnati OH 45242

FOX, JOHN NELSON, orthodontist; b. St. Louis, July 25, 1952; s. Robert Edward and Laura Louise (Bergdoll) F.; m. Georganne Claire Gayou, Nov. 27, 1981; 1 child, Daniel. BS, John Carroll U., 1974; DDS, U. Mo., Kansas City, 1978; MS, St. Louis U., 1980. Diplomate Am. Bd. Orthodontics. Practice dentistry specializing in orthodontics, Poplar Bluff, Mo., 1980—. Mem. ADA, Am. Assn. Orthodontists, Orthodontic Edn. and Research Found., Mo. Dental Assn., Southeast Mo. Dental Soc., Three Rivers Dental Club (sec. 1980—). Roman Catholic. Home: 1489 Atkins Rd Poplar Bluff MO 63901 Office: 1520 Highland Pl Poplar Bluff MO 63901

FOX, MATTHEW CYRIL, real estate developer; b. N.Y.C., Apr. 18, 1934; s. Frederick R. and Frances (Amster) F.; m. Amanda Clark Fox, June 3, 1972. B in Mgmt. Engring., Rensselaer Poly. U., 1955, B in Civil Engring., 1958; MBA, NYU, 1961. Registered profl. engr., Calif.; lic. real estate broker, Ill. Ptnr. Coopers & Lybrand, N.Y.C., 1961-71; exec. v.p. Brucarla Corp., N.Y.C., 1971-74; chief exec. officer Burnham Cos., Chgo., 1974-83; real estate developer Chgo., 1983—. Contbr. articles to profl. jours. mem. adv. bd. Jr. League of Chgo., 1985—; chmn. Landmarks com. Ill. Assn. Realtors, Chgo., 1980-82; bd. dirs. Landmarks Preservation Council, 1978-82, Chgo. Lyric Opera Guild, Chgo., 1982-84. Served to lt. USNR, 1955-58. Recipient James Lincoln Design award, 1959. Mem. Chgo. Bd. Realtors, Nat. Assn. Realtors, Inst. Real Estate Mgmt., Nat. Assn. Securities Dealers, Sigma Xi, Tau Beta Pi, Beta Gamma Sigma. Episcopalian. Avocations: collecting rare books. Home: 1210 N Astor Chicago IL 60610

FOX, PHILIP CALBREATH, business planning manager; b. Kalamazoo, Mar. 19, 1942; s. Raymond W. and Margaret (Calbreath) F.; m. Andi C. Mitchell, May 28, 1971; children: Jennifer A., Kristen K., Hope A. BA in Econs., Cornell U., 1964, MBA in Fin., 1965. Various positions Ford Motor Co., Dearborn, Mich., 1965-71, Philco-Ford Corp., Bluebell, Pa., 1971-73; cons. Royersford, Pa., 1973-75; various positions RCA, N.Y.C. and Indpls., 1975-80; company planning mgr. The Andersons, Maumee, Ohio, 1980—. Mem. Am. Horse Show Assn., Hunter and Jumper Assn. Mich. Republican. Baptist. Avocations: foxhunting, horse showing, breeder of thoroughbred horses. Office: The Andersons PO Box 119 Maumee OH 43537

FOX, RICHARD K., manufacturing company executive; b. Celina, Ohio, Aug. 7, 1940; s. Reed F. and Mildred F. (Krugh) F.; m. Linda Lou Wiley, Sept. 16, 1961; children: Richard K., Douglas E. A.B.S. in Bus. Adminstrn., Internat. Coll., Ft. Wayne, Ind., 1960; cert. in accountancy and fin. adminstrn., Walsh Inst. Accountancy, Detroit, 1965. Acct. Kent-Moore Corp., Warren, Mich., 1960-65, corp. controller, 1973-75, treas., 1976-78, v.p., treas., asst. sec., 1978-80; pres. Robinair div. Sealed Power Corp., Montpelier, Ohio, 1980—; staff acct. R.J. Clark C.P.A., Farmington, Mich., 1965; vice chairperson valves and assessories div. Air Conditioning and Refrigeration Inst., Arlington, Va., 1982-85, bd. dirs., 1984, chmn., 1986—, vice chmn. edn. and fng. com., 1985—; trustee, sec., treas. Kent-Moore Found., Warren, 1977-80. Pres. Parent-Tchr. Orgn., Jackson, Mich., 1970. Mem. Nat. Assn. Accts. (dir. Jackson-Lansing chpt.), Internat. Inst. Refrigeration (assoc. mem.). Club: Orchard Hills Country (Bryan, Ohio). Lodges: Moose, Rotary. Home: 414 W South St Bryan OH 43506 Office: Robinair Div Sealed Power Corp 1 Robinair Way Montpelier OH 43543

FOX, ROBERT ALAN, psychology educator; b. Marshfield, Wis., Nov. 10, 1951; s. Lawrence George and Barbara Jane (Dern) F.; m. Theresa Ann Blaskowski, Aug. 2, 1975; children: Jennifer Mary, Thomas Lawrence, Benjamin Leo. BS, U. Wis., 1973, MA, 1974, PhD, 1978. Asst. prof. psychology Western Ill. U., Macomb, 1978-80, Ohio State U., Columbus, 1980-82; asst. prof. ednl. psychology Marquette U., Milw., 1982-85, assoc. prof., 1985—; cons. psychologist Milestone Inc., Rockford, Ill., 1982—; program evaluator Teen Pregnancy Service Milw. County Med. Complex, 1985—. Author: Behaviroal Weight Reduction, 1981, Counseling Exceptional Students, 1986; editor: Assessing Handicapped Individuals, 1985; contbr. numerous articles to profl. jours. Mem. Am. Psychology Assn. (editor newsletter), Am. Assn. Mental Deficiency, Wis. Psychology Assn. Roman Catholic. Avocations: fishing, golfing. Home: 1684 Alvin Ln Brookfield WI 53005 Office: Marquette U Schroeder Complex Milwaukee WI 53233

FOX, ROBERT GLENN, dentist; b. Springfield, Mo., Nov. 18, 1948; s. James Adrian Fox and Betty June (McBride) Hoppe; m. Connie Ann Patterson; children: R. Steven, James L. BS in Zoology, Southeast Mo. State U., 1970; DDS, U. Mo., Kansas City, 1975. Gen. practice dentistry Cape Girardeau, Mo., 1975—; mem. governing body Mo. Area V Health Systems Agy. Council, Inc., 1980-82. Fundraiser Am. Cancer Soc., Cape Girardeau, 1977-82, Boy Scouts Am., Cape Girardeau, 1984-85; coach Cape Youth Soccer League, Cape Girardeau, 1980-81, 85-86, Cape Girardeau Ch. Youth Softball League, 1984—. Named one of Outstanding Young Men Am., 1984; recipient Merit award Southeast Mo. State U., 1980. Fellow Internat. Coll. Dentists; mem. ADA, Am. Assn. Forensic Dentists, Mo. Dental Assn. (chmn. Nat. Childrens Dental Health Month local chpt. 1984), Southeast Mo. Dental Soc., Christian Med. Soc., Cape Dental Study Group (past pres., past v.p., past sec.), Pi Kappa Alpha. Republican. Methodist. Lodge: Optimists (pres. local chpt. 1983-84, Optimist of Yr. 1983-84). Avocations: golf, fishing, boating, reading, photography. Home: 2025 Beth Cape Girardeau MO 63701 Office: 832 N Kingshighway Cape Girardeau MO 63701

FOX, SAM, business executive; b. Desloge, Mo., May 9, 1929; s. Max and Fanny (Gold) F.; m. Marilyn Rae Widman, Oct. 25, 1953; children: Cheryl, Pamela, Jeffrey, Gregory, Steven. BBA, Washington U., 1951. Pres., chief exec. officer Fox Industries, Madison, Ill., 1952-72; chief exec. officer Diversified Industries, St. Louis, 1972-75; chmn. bd. Synthetic Industries Ltd., Chickamauga, Ga., 1975-86, Newry, No. Ireland, 1976-86, Clara, Rep. Ireland, 1984-86; chmn. bd., chief exec. officer Harbour Group, Ltd., St. Louis, 1980—; chief exec. officer Allied Healthcare, 1985—, Prosser/Enpo Industries, 1985—, Greenfield Industries, 1986—, Rogers Tool Works, 1986—, KB Alloys, 1986—, Meade Instruments, 1986—, Burks Pump Co., 1986—; bd. dirs. Centerre Bank of Ladue, St. Louis, 1985—. Nat. Gov. Am. Jewish Com., St. Louis, N.Y.C., 1985—; trustee NJC for Immunology and Respiratory Medicine, Denve, 1981—; bd. dirs. Opera Theatre of St. Louis, 1984—. Recipient St. Louis Bus. Jour. Enterprise award, 1986. Mem. Washington U. Bus. Sch. Alumni Assn. (pres. 1983-84, Disting. Alumni award 1986). Jewish. Clubs: Westwood Country, Mo. Athletic, Clayton, St. Louis, Washington U. Century. Avocations: fishing, hunting, skiing. Home: 60 Villa Coublay Saint Louis MO 63131 Office: Harbour Group Ltd 7701 Forsyth Suite 550 Clayton MO 63105

FOX, SHEILA RUDZKI, social worker; b. Auburn, N.Y., July 21, 1939; d. Dalton P. and Sylvia (Wheeler) F.; divorced; children: Kristin, Kathleen, Marie, Carrie. BSEd, U. Detroit, 1961; MA, U. Mich., 1967; MSW, Wayne State U., 1981. Tchr. Detroit Schs., 1961-63, Alexandria (Va.) Schs., 1963-64; psychotherapist North East Guidance, Detroit, 1981-82, Eastwood Clinic, Troy, Mich., 1982—, Macomb County Mental Health, Mt. Clemens, Mich., 1983—. Leader 4-H Club, Rochester, 1975-80. Recipient Am. Assn. Counties award, 1985. Mem. Nat. Assn. Social Workers (cert., clin. diplomat), Acad. Cert. Social Workers, Nat. Assn. Social Workers Register of Clin. Workers, Mich. Assn. Social Workers, Transactional Assn. Social Workers, New Directions in Edn. and Psychotherapy (treas.). Roman Catholic. Avocations: minature doll house furniture making. Home: 1234 Gettysburg Rochester Hills MI 48064 Office: Macomb County Mental Health Ctr 25401 Harper Saint Clair Shores MI 48081

FOX, SUSAN VALERIE, marketing professional, futures researcher, model; b. Waukegan, Ill., Aug. 13, 1948; d. Raymond James and Dorothy Evelyn (Chisholm) Proctor; m. Richard Kent Fox, Apr. 1, 1946; children—Michael Darin, Laura Evelyn. Profl. modeling cert. John Robert Powers, Chgo.,

1983; student Coll. Lake County, Grayslake, Ill., 1973-81. Service mgr./ bookkeeper National Co., Chgo., 1965-76; service mgr. A&P, Chgo., 1978-82; futures researcher MBH Commodities, Winnetka, Ill., 1980—; dir. mktg., cons., spl. events coordinator Extract, Inc., Miami, Fla., 1984; vis. tchr.; dir. numerous cosmetic and skincare seminars; profl. model, 1983—; cons. Futures Symposium, Tucson, 1983—; aerobic instr. Karcher Retirement Home, Waukegan, Ill. Recipient Tennis award Libertyville Park Dist. (Ill.), 1973; various Blue Ribbon/1st Place awards Libertyville Men's Garden Club, 1982, various rose growers awards, 1983. Mem. Am. Rose Soc. (Best Climber nat. trophy 1985), Northeastern Ill. Rose Growers (treas.), No. Ill. Rose Growers Assn., Am. Running and Fitness Assn. Republican.

FOX, THEODORE ALBERT, orthopaedic surgeon; b. Chgo., Feb. 16, 1913; s. Albert and Jennie (Friedman) F.; m. Marcella G. Schaeffer, June 14, 1936; children: Susan, Nancy. BS, U. Chgo., 1933, MD, 1937. Diplomate Am. Bd. Orthopaedic Surgery. Intern Cook County Hosp., Chgo., 1937-39, resident in fractures, 1940-41; resident in gen. surgery Mt. Sinai Hosp., N.Y.C., 1940; resident in orthopedic surgery U. Ill., 1946-47; practice medicine specializing in orthopaedic surgery Chgo., 1947—; from instr. to assoc. prof. orthopaedic surgery U. Ill., Chgo., 1946. Served to comdr. USNR, 1941-46. Fellow Am. Acad. Orthopaedic Surgery, ACS. Clubs: Briarwood Country (Deerfield, Ill.), Presdl. Country (West Palm Beach, Fla.). Avocation: photography. Home: 1170 Oak St Winnetka IL 60093 Office: Lakeview Orthopaedic Assocs Ltd 836 Wellington Ave Chicago IL 60657

FOX, WILLIAM KEITH DONALDSON, management consultant; b. Washington, Dec. 29, 1939; s. John Donaldson and Louise (Hancock) F.; m. Erika Schwenn, Feb. 12, 1962; children—Myles, Alison, Jennifer. B.A., Williams Coll., 1964; M.B.A., Rockhurst Coll., 1983. Mgmt. trainee, asst. br. mgr. C. V. Starr Co., N.Y.C., 1964-68; mktg. mgr. John Hancock Mut., Boston, 1968-71; sales and product mgr. Standard Havens, Inc., Kansas City, Mo., 1971-76, sr. v.p., 1976-82; pres. Standard Havens Research Corp., Kansas City, 1982-85; bus. cons. Aero Transp. Products, Kansas City, Mo., 1985—; adj. prof. mktg. Ottawa U., Kansas City, 1983—; adj. prof. mgmt. Rockhurst Coll., Kansas City, 1986—. Patentee in field. Pres., Bryant Sch. Fathers Club, Kansas City, 1976; chmn. Standard Havens United Fund Campaign, Kansas City, 1978; fund raiser Unitarian Ch., Kansas City, 1979. Recipient Cert. of Achievement, Kansas City Sch. Dist., 1979; Honorarium, McGraw-Hill, Inc., 1983; Cert. of Achievement, Stanford U., 1983. Mem. Phi Gamma Delta. Unitarian. Clubs: Woodside Racquet, Kansas City Blues Rugby (pres. 1976-77) (Kansas City, Mo.). Home: 214 W Concord Ave Kansas City MO 64112 Office: Aero Transportation Products 3711 Gardner Ave Kansas City MO 64120

FOXEN, GENE LOUIS, insurance executive; b. Chgo., Mar. 28, 1936; adopted son Henry and Mary Foxen; student public schs.; m. Diane E. Young, 1986; children from previous marriage: Dan, Kathleen, Michael, Patricia, James, Karen, Ellen. With New Eng. Life Ins. Co., 1957—, assoc. gen. agt., 1970-73, gen. agt., Chgo., 1973—. Cubmaster DuPage council Boy Scouts Am., 1963; Midwest regional dir. Adoptees Liberty Movement Assn. Served with USMC, 1954-57. Recipient life membership award Gen. Agents and Mgrs. Conf.; named as life mem. Hall of Fame, New Eng. Life Ins. Co., 1972, life mem. Million Dollar Round Table. C.L.U. Mem. Nat. Assn. Life Underwriters, Execs. Club Chgo., Gen. Agents and Mgrs. Assn., Am. Soc. C.L.U.'s (pres. Chgo. chpt. 1977-78, v.p. Midwest region 1981-82), Chgo. Estate Planning Council (pres. 1981-82), Am. Soc. Life Underwriters. Republican. Roman Catholic. Club: Metropolitan. Home: 2247 Hidden Creek Ct Lisle IL 60532 Office: Foxen Fin 120 S Riverside Plaza Chicago IL 60606

FOXMAN, CHARLES, textile executive; b. N.Y.C., Jan. 18, 1942; s. Paul and Betty (Rosen) F.; m. Joyce V. Daniels, June 11, 1972; 1 child, Samuel. BBA, Bronx Community Coll., 1962. Mgr. Howard Clothes, N.Y.C., 1959-69; dir. merchandising Kellwood Co., St. Louis, 1969-75; dir. bus. devel. Western Textile, St. Louis, 1975-84; pres. Medtex Products, Inc., St. Louis, 1984—; bd. dirs. Continental Textile, St. Louis. Served with U.S. Army, 1963-69. Avocation: black belt karate. Home: 1525 Timberlake Manor Dr Chesterfield MO 63017 Office: Medtex Products Inc 15 Progress Pkwy Maryland Heights MO 63043

FOXMAN, LORETTA DOROTHY, human resource consultant; b. Los Angeles, Sept. 4, 1939; d. Frederick and Helen (Goldberg) F.; m. Walter L. Polsky, Aug. 9, 1964; children—Michael William, Susan Jennifer. B.A., Calif. State U.-Los Angeles, 1963; M.A., Columbia U., 1964. Tchr., Culver City Unified Sch. Dist. (Calif.), 1964-68; asst. dir. St. Christopher Acad., Westfield, N.J., 1971-75; curriculum cons. Middlesex Community Coll. Daycare Ctr., Edison, N.J., 1973, Lakeview Montessori Acad., Summit, N.J., 1975; instr. Northwestern U., Evanston, Ill., 1982—; prin. Jack Dill Assocs., Chgo., 1976-81; exec. v.p. CAMBRIDGE Human Resource Group, Inc., Chgo., 1981—. Chmn. various coms. LWV, Cranford, N.J. and Glencoe, Ill., 1971—; mem. Ad Hoc Rent Control Com., 1973; chair adv. bd. Northwestern U. Program on Women, 1982—. Author: Resumes That Work: How to Sell Yourself on Paper, 1984; contbg. editor Personnel Jour.; contbr. several articles to profl. jours. Mem. AAUW, Am. Soc. Human Resource Profls. (Woman of Achievement award), Women in Mgmt. Office: Cambridge Human Resource Group Inc 20 N Clark St Suite 2300 Chicago IL 60602

FOY, EDWARD LEO, accountant; b. Enid, Okla., Oct. 19, 1953; s. Leo J. and Geraldine (Corbeil) F.; m. Judith Koskey, Feb. 14, 1976; 1 child, Pamela. BBA in Acctg., Mich. Tech. U., 1975. CPA, Mich., Wis. Accountant Talaska & Sharpe, Ironwood, Mich., 1975-79; ptnr. Huberty & Assocs., Fond du Lac, Wis., 1979-86, Sondergard & Foy S.C., Fond du Lac, 1986—. Commr. housing authority City of Fond du Lac, 1984—. Mem. Am. Inst. CPA's, Wis. Inst. CPA's, Mich. Assn. CPA's. Roman Catholic. Clubs: South Hill Country (treas. 1986—), Exchange (pres. 1986-87) (Fond du Lac). Lodge: Elks. Avocations: corvettes, golf. Home: 864 Kings Ct Fond du Lac WI 54935 Office: Sondergard & Foy SC 21 E 2d St Fond du Lac WI 54935

FRAASCH, DOUGLAS ROGER, savings and loan association executive; b. Madison, Minn., Sept. 25, 1946; s. Elmer Ewald William and Inez Eldora (Bjorgan) F.; m. LaVonne Rae Dockter, June 5, 1966; children: Penny Marie, Jason Douglas, Wayde Alan. Student, U. Minn., 1965-66, Mpls. Sch. Bus., 1966. Mail clerk Archer Daniels Midland Co., Mpls., 1965-66; office clerk Willmar (Minn.) Poultry, Mpls., 1966; personnel supt. Minn. Air N.G., Mpls., 1966-77; asst. v.p. Washington Fed. Savs., Ortonville, Minn., 1977—. Pres. Ortonville United Appeal, 1980; mem. Citizens for Big Stone Lake, 1977—. Served as sgt. USAF, Air N.G., 1966—. Mem. Am. Legion, Minn. N.G. Enlisted Assn. (state treas. 1971-78), Ortonville Civic & Commerce Assn. (pres. 1982), Ducks Unlimited, Jaycees (v.p., treas. Ortonville chpt. 1977-86). Republican. Lutheran. Lodges: Lions (treas. Ortonville chpt. 1985—), Masons (treas. Ortonville chpt. 1985—). Home: Rural Rt 2 Box 170 Ortonville MN 56278 Office: Washington Fed Savs Bank 121 NW 2d St Ortonville MN 56278

FRADE, PETER DANIEL, chemist; b. Highland Park, Mich., Sept. 3, 1946; s. Peter Nunes and Dorathea Grace (Gehrke) F. B.S. in Chemistry, Wayne State U., 1968, M.S., 1971, Ph.D., 1978. Chemist Henry Ford Hosp., Detroit, 1968-75; analytical chemist, toxicologist dept. pathology, div. pharmacology and toxicology Henry Ford Hosp., 1975-86, clin. lab. scientist dept. pathology div. clin. chemistry and pharmacology, 1987—; research assoc. in chemistry Wayne State U., Detroit, 1978-79; vis. scholar U. Mich., Ann Arbor, 1980—; vis. scientist dept. Hypertension Research, Henry Ford Hosp., Detroit, 1986-87. Contbr. sci. articles to profl. jours. Mem. Republican Presdl. Task Force, 1984—. Recipient David F. Boltz Meml. award Wayne State U., 1977. Fellow Am. Inst. Chemists, Nat. Acad. Clin. Biochemistry, Assn. Clin. Scientists; mem. European Acad. Arts, Scis. and Humanities, Fedn. Am. Scientists, Am. Chem. Soc., AAAS, IntraSci. Research Found., Soc. Applied Spectroscopy, Am. Assn. Clin. Chemistry, Assn. Analytical Chemists, N.Y. Acad. Scis., Detroit Hist. Soc., Mich. Humane Soc., Am. Coll. Toxicology, Royal Soc. Chemistry (London), Titanic Hist. Soc., Bibl. Archaeology Soc., Virgil Fox Soc., Founders Soc., Detroit Inst. Arts, Sigma Xi, Phi Lambda Upsilon, Alpha Chi Sigma. Lutheran. Club: U.S. Senatorial (Washington). Home: 20200 Orleans Detroit MI 48203 Office: Henry Ford Hosp 2799 W Grand Blvd Detroit MI 48202

FRADKIN, HOWARD ROSS, psychologist; b. Balt., Oct. 3, 1952; s. Calvin and Frances Sylvia (Meyers) F. BS in Recreation and Leisure Studies, Temple U., 1974, MS in Therapeutic Recreation, 1978; PhD in Counseling Psychology, U. N.C., 1980. Lic. psychologist, Ohio. Psychology intern Ohio State U. Counseling and Consultation Service, Columbus, Ohio, 1979-80; sr. counselor SUNY, Fredonia, 1980-81; clin. counselor S.E. Community Mental Health Ctr., Columbus, 1981-82, psychologist, 1982-83; pres., psychologist Affirmations Psychol. Services, Inc., Columbus, 1982—; adminstrv. dir. support services Columbus AIDS Task Force, 1984-87. Columnist News of the Gay and Lesbian Community, 1984-86, Good Times, 1987—. Mem. Am. Psychol. Assn., Soc. Psychol. Study of Gay/Lesbian Issues, Ohio Psychol. Assn., Assn. Gay and Lesbian Psychologists, Nat. Gay and Lesbian Task Force. Democrat. Jewish. Avocations: sailing, travel,tropical fish, hiking, gardening. Office: Affirmations Psychol Services Inc 918 S Front St Columbus OH 43206

FRAHER, GAIL MARIE, interior designer; b. Chgo., Apr. 17, 1960; d. Ransom Frances Gay and Barbara (Jamrock) Romans; m. Larry Allen Fraher, Nov. 2, 1985. B in Human Resources, So. Ill. U., 1982. Showroom mgr. in-house designer Roseland Draperies Inc., South Holland, Ill., 1983—; freelance comml. residential designs, Ill. Republican. Lutheran. Avocations: reading, drawing, golfing, aerobics, swimming. Home: 17719 Oakley Lansing IL 60438

FRAHM, GEORGE STUART, welding engineer; b. Saginaw, Mich., Sept. 6, 1949; s. Stuart Harold and Lorine Esther (Weiss) F.; m. Sharolyn Marie Deike, Aug. 28, 1971; children: Trephina Lorine, Anika Marie, Seriah Joseph. BSME, Gen. Motors Inst., Flint, Mich., 1972; MS in Welding Engring., Ohio State U., Flint, Mich., 1973. Process engr. Saginaw div. Gen. Motors, 1972-74, research engr., 1974-78, welding engr., 1978-84, simulation analyst, 1984-87, value analyst, 1987—. Mem. Am. Welding Soc. Lutheran. Home: 12565 E Washington Reese MI 98757 Office: Gen Motors Saginaw Div 3900 Holland Rd Saginaw MI 48601

FRAHM, PAUL HANS, psychologist; b. Sioux Falls, S.D., Jan. 22, 1932; s. Hans Jacob and Agnes Isabelle (Langley) F.; m. Cleova Ardella Clark, June 1, 1950 (div. Mar. 1962); children: David, Kathleen, Steven, Timothy; m. Ella Cowan, June 2, 1967; stepchildren: Patricia, Julie, Elva. BA, Drake U., 1953, MDiv, 1956, MA, 1963; PhD, U. Iowa, 1966. Lic. psychologist, Iowa; cert. health service provider, Iowa. Chief psychologist Vera French Community Mental Health Ctr., Davenport, Iowa, 1967-87; cons. Family Resources, Davenport, 1967-87, Davenport Law Enforcement and Jail, 1978-87. Mem. Am. Psychol. Assn., Iowa Psychol. Assn., Scott County Psychol. Assn. Republican. Mem. Christian Ch. Lodges: Lions, Moose. Avocations: photography, hunting, fishing, cross-country skiing, travel. Home: 2439 E 46th St Davenport IA 52807 Office: Psychology Assocs 4645 Brady St Davenport IA 52806

FRAIN, JAMES L., personnel administrator; b. Logansport, Ind., Jan. 27, 1953; s. Maxwell C. and Nila J. (Clark) F.; m. Terrell J. Gustafson, July 14, 1984. BSBA, Ball State U., 1975; M in Pub. Administrn., Ind. U., South Bend, 1986. Cert. human resources profl. Dir. personnel Pulaski Meml. Hosp., Winamac, Ind., 1975-76, South Bend Osteo. Hosp., 1976-80; asst. dir. personnel Elkhart (Ind.) Gen. Hosp., 1980-84, dir. personnel, 1984-86; asst. dir. personnel U. Notre Dame, Ind., 1986—; instr. Ind. U., South Bend, 1987. Mem. Am. Soc. Personnel Administrn. (pres. Michiana chpt. 1985), Coll. and Univ. Personnel Assn. Republican. Mem. Christian Ch. Lodge: Masons. Avocations: racquetball, water sports. Home: 1355 Matthews Ln South Bend IN 46614 Office: U Notre Dame Personnel Dept Notre Dame IN 46556

FRALEIGH, JOHN WALTER, psychotherapist, social worker; b. Grand Rapids, Mich., Oct. 21, 1945; s. John Duncan and Marie Cecilia (Furlong) F. BA, Mich. State U., 1968; MSW, Grand Valley State Coll., 1984. Registered social worker, Mich. With prodn. staff Sat. WZZM-TV, Grand Rapids, 1969-72, asst. film dir., 1973-76, pub. service producer, 1975-77, with gen. prodn. staff, 1979-84; social work intern Kent Oaks Psychiatric Unit, Grand Rapids, 1980-81; psychotherapist, grad. level practicum Diversities Counseling, Grand Rapids, 1981-86; crisis counselor Dwelling Place Inc., Grand Rapids, 1986—; media cons. Grand Rapids Humane Soc., 1974-75; media producer West Mich. Burn Unit, 1975-76, Kent County Spay & Neuter Clinic; vol. Transitions Adult Aftercare Ctr., Grand Rapids, 1982. Calligrapher book frontispiece, centennial commemorative and Grant Art Exhbn. (best of show 1978). Media cons. Grand Rapids Jaycees, 1975-77, recipient spl. award, 1977; pres. Mon. Night Rap Group, Grand Rapids, 1977-80; policy council mem. Mich. Orgn. Human Rights, Detroit, 1977, media producer, meetings coordinator, 1978, 82, v.p., 1982-84; mem. Human Sexuality Task Force for Mich. Ho. of Reps.; coordinator Midwest planning session Lesbian-Gay March on Washington, 1979; asst. in founding many lesbian-gay orgns. in West Mich. and Grand Rapids area; sec. Grand Rapids AIDS Task Force, 1986; part-time choir dir. Chapel Hill United Meth. Ch., Casnovia, Mich, 1974-79; adult edn. instr. Hackley Mus. Art, Muskegon, Mich., 1979. Recipient Appreciation award Chapel Hill United Meth. Ch., 1979. Avocations: music, choral performance, conducting. Home: 24 Burton SE Grand Rapids MI 49507

FRAME, VELMA ANITA WILLIAMS, retired counselor; b. Decatur County, Ind.; d. Frederick Virgil and Emma Flora (Robbins) Williams; B.S., Ball State U., 1935, M.A., 1949, postgrad., 1973; m. David C. Frame, June 29, 1946. Tchr. high sch., Yorktown, Ind., 1935-42, Daleville, Ind., 1951-59; counselor Central High Sch., Marion, Ind., 1959-62, Muncie (Ind.) Southside High Sch., 1962-71; counselor, dir. guidance high sch., Daleville, Ind., 1971-79. Mem. Am., Ind. (pres.) sch. counselors assns., Am., Ind., E. Central (pres.) personnel and guidance assns., Nat. Vocat. Guidance Assn., Ladies Golf Assn. of Valley View Golf Club (treas.). Democrat. Home: 307 Arch St Yorktown IN 47396

FRANANO, SUSAN MARGARET KETTEMAN, orchestra administrator, soprano; b. Kansas City, Mo., Sept. 30, 1946; d. Charley Gilbert and Mary Elizabeth (Bredehoeft) Ketteman; m. Frank Salvatore Franano, Sept. 30, 1946; 1 child, Domenico Frank. AA, Stephens Coll., Columbia, Mo., 1966, BFA, 1967; postgrad., U. Mo., Kansas City, 1967-68; MusM, So. Ill. U., Edwardsville, 1969. Mgr. Kansas City (Mo.) Symphony Orch., Lyric Opera Group, Kansas City, 1976-82; tour coordinator Lyric Opera Kansas City, 1978-85; dir. outreach Kansas City Symphony, 1982-84, asst. mgr., 1984-85, ops. mgr., 1985-86, mgr., 1986—. Nat. v.p. Stephens Coll. Alumnae Assn., Columbia, 1974-76; regional liaison Mo. Citizens for Arts, St. Louis, 1984-86; regional rep. Am. Guild Musical Artists, Kansas City, 1977-81; mem. Kansas City Consensus, 1987. Mem. Am. Symphony Orch. League, Mo. Citizens for Arts, Symphony Women's Assn., Jr. Women's Symphony Alliance, Friends of Symphony. Democrat. Roman Catholic. Clubs: Cen. Exchange (Kansas City); Kansas City Racquet (Shawnee Mission). Avocations: tennis, cooking, travel. Office: Kansas City Symphony Orch 1029 Central Kansas City MO 64105 *

FRANCE, JAMES STUART, hotel administrator; b. Glasgow, Scotland, Dec. 15, 1940; came to U.S., 1965; s. Charles and Alison (Black) F.; m. Dayle Ellen Davies, Sept. 14, 1974; 1 child, Charles. Diploma, Ecole Hoteliere, Lausanne, Switzerland, 1961; cert. in fin. interpretation, Cornell Hotel Schs., 1977. Gen. mgr. Westin Hotels, various locations, U.S. and Abroad, 1969-80; mgr. Four Seasons Hotels, Seattle, 1980-82; gen. mgr. Interstate Hotels, Cambridge, Mass., 1982-85; pres. James France and Assocs., Sarasota, Fla., 1985-86; mng. dir. CPS Hotel Mgmt. Services, Chgo., 1986—; dir. Greater Woodfield Conv. and Visitors Bur., Chgo., 1986—. Contbr. articles to jours. Mem. Am. Hotel Assn., Chaine Des Rotisseurs (maitre de table 1977). Republican. Club: Wash. Athletic (Seattle). Avocations: tennis, skiing, reading, theater, auto racing. Office: CPS Hotel Mgmt Services 250 W Schick Rd Bloomingdale IL 60108

FRANCIS, DAVID WILLIAM, advertising agency executive; b. Cleve., Dec. 24, 1947; s. Walter S. and Jessie (Hammerstrom) F.; m. Diane Marie DeMali, Oct. 16, 1981; 1 child, Georgia Lee. B.A., Baldwin-Wallace Coll., 1969; Grad., Memphis State U., 1970. Group service dir. The Coliseum, Richfield, Ohio, 1974-76; v.p. Chippewa Lake Properties, Inc., Ohio, 1976-78, Loos-Edwards & Sexauer, Inc., Akron, Ohio, 1978—; cons. Keating & Assocs., Cleve., 1977-78, Sea World, Inc., 1978. Contbr. articles to profl. jours. Mem. Cleve. Advt. Club, Canton Advt. Club. Methodist. Club: Great Lake High Sch., Cleve. Grays. Office: Loos Edwards & Sexauer Inc 1225 W Market St Akron OH 44313

FRANCIS, ELIZABETH ANNE, marketing executive; b. Kansas City, Mo., Feb. 18, 1938; d. Charles Arthur and Lillian Eva (Wagner) Sagerser; m. Terence Eugene Beucher, Nov. 24, 1957 (div. Jan. 1966); children: Gregory Alan, Todd Montgomery; m. Jack Dennis Francis, Nov. 17, 1973; stepchildren: Mike, Alan, John, Jodi. Clk., typist Sunflower Ordinance Works, DeSoto, Kans., 1957; secretary Lawrence (Kans.) Paper Co., 1957-59; legal sec. Harlan L. Long, Overland Park, Kans., 1967-70; sec. Young and Rubicam, Overland Park, 1970-71, Shell Chem. Co., Overland Park, 1971-73; mktg. services coordinator Bill Barr & Co., Inc., Overland Park, 1972-85; sec. The Royal Suite, Johnson County, Kans., 1985—. Pres. Luth. Ch. Women, Shawnee, Kans., 1974-75: mem. council Luth. Ch. Mem. Johnson County Bus. Women (pres. 1984-85). Avocations: running, skiing, travel. Home: 6814 Acuff Shawnee KS 66216 Office: The Royal Suite 8600 Farley Overland Park KS 66212

FRANCIS, LEROY ANDREW, lawyer; b. Terre Haute, Ind., June 14, 1910; s. Nathan I. and Flora I. (Campbell) F.; m. Mary Kathryn Reveal, Oct. 4, 1935; children: Richard L., Mary Kay, William Jay, Sharon Rose. BS, Ind. U., 1948, JD, 1949. Bar: Ind. 1949. Ptnr. Hilleary, Shafer & Francis, Terre Haute, 1949-73, Francis, Brames & Cook, Terre Haute, 1973-79, Francis, Cook & Rider, Terre Haute, 1979—; judge Vigo County Ind. Superior Ct., 1958; pres. Sunset Harbor, Inc., 1965-73. Served to lt. col. AUS, 1941-45. Decorated Bronze Star. Mem. ABA, Ind. Bar Assn., Terre Haute Bar Assn., Ind. U. Alumni Assn., Terre Haute C. of C., Delta Tau Delta, Sigma Delta Kappa, Delta Sigma Pi. Club: Terre haute Country. Lodges: Masons (33 degree), Shriners, Elks. Home: 2220 N 10th St Terre Haute IN 47804 Office: 101 Sycamore Bldg Terre Haute IN 47807

FRANCIS, PHILIP HAMILTON, mechanical and manufacturing engineer; b. San Diego, Apr. 13, 1938; s. William Samuel and Ruth Kathryn (Allison) F.; m. Regina Elizabeth Kirk, June 10, 1961 (div. May 1971); m. Diana Maria Villarreal, July 15, 1972; children: Philip Scott, Edward Philip, Mary Allison, Kenneth Joseph. BSME, Calif. Poly. State U., 1959; MS Mech. Engring., U. Iowa, 1960, PhD in Engring. Mechanics, 1965; MBA in Mgmt., St. Mary's U., San Antonio, 1972. Registered profl. engr., Tex. Stress analyst Douglas Aircraft Co., Santa Monica, Calif., 1960-62; sr. research engr. S.W. Research Inst., San Antonio, 1965-79; prof., chmn. dept. mech. and aerospace engring. Ill. Inst. Tech., Chgo., 1979-84; dir. flexible inspection and assembly lab. Indsl. Tech. Inst., Ann Arbor, Mich., 1984-86; dir. advanced mfg. tech. Gen. Systems Group, Motorola Inc., Schaumburg, Ill., 1986—; cons. U.S. Gypsum Co., Chgo., 1983—, Internat. Harvester Co., Chgo., 1979-82. Author: Principles of R & D Management, 1977; editor: Dynamic Problems of Thermoelasticity, 1975, Advanced Experimental Techniques in the Mechanics of Solids, 1973; editor-in-chief Mfg. Rev.; contbr. more than 50 articles on engring. to profl. jours. Mem. Leon Valley City Council (Tex.), 1976-79. Recipient Gustas Larson award ASME and Pi Tau Sigma, 1978. Fellow ASME (dir. mfg. sci. and tech. program); mem. Am. Acad. Mechanics (founding mem.), Army Sci. Bd., Soc. Mfg. Engrs., Sigma Xi, Tau Beta Pi, Pi Tau Sigma. Roman Catholic. Avocations: writing, tennis. Home: 52 Ridge Rd Barrington Hills IL 60010 Office: Motorola Inc Gen Systems Group 1301 E Algonquin Rd Schaumburg IL 60196

FRANCIS, ROY HERBERT, teacher; b. Perryton, Tex., Sept. 10, 1935; s. Ralph Harvey and Vesper Fay (Horan) F.; m. Lois Marie Eickelberg, May 7, 1960; children: Robert Henry, Cynthia Marie. Student, St. John's Coll., 1955-56, Concordia Theol. Sem., 1956-57, 58-60; BA, West Tex. State U., 1961-63; postgrad., N. Tex. State U., 1969-70. Cert. tchr., Tex., Mo. Tchr. Silverton (Tex.) High Sch., 1964-67, Stratford (Tex.) High Sch., 1967-69; tchr., librarian Gunter (Tex.) High Sch., 1970-73, J. Earl Selz High Sch., Pilot Point, Tex., 1973-75; tchr. East Carter High Sch., Ellsinore, Mo., 1976—. Pres. Immanuel Luth. Ch. Van Buren, 1984-85. Served to U.S. Army, 1957. Mem. Nat. Farmers Orgn. Redford (sec. 1975-80), Nat. Council of Tchrs of English, Tex. State Tchrs. Assn, Mo. State Tchrs. Assn., Community TChrs. Assn. (sec. 1979, v.p. 1980, pres. 1981). Lodge: Lions, Order of the DeMolay. Avocations: pro-football fan, gardening, fishing. Home: Rt 2 Box 266 Ellington MO 63638 Office: East Carter County Sch Dist Ellsinore MO 63937

FRANCISCO, RONALD ALAN, political science educator; b. Chgo., Mar. 29, 1948; s. Kenneth Christopher and Helen Louise (Ekstrom) F.; m. Deborah Shaye, June 6, 1970; 1 child, Christopher Alan. Student, U. Vienna, Austria, 1968-69; BA, U. Wis., 1970; AM, U. Ill., 1972, PhD, 1977; student, Free U. of Berlin, Fed. Republic of Germany, 1972-73. Asst prof. U. Kans., Lawrence, 1974-80, assoc. prof., 1981—. Editor: (with R.L. Merritt) Berlin Between Two Worlds, 1986; co-editor Political Economy of Collective Agriculture, 1979, Agricultural Policies in the USSR and Eastern Europe, 1980. Mem. Am. Polit. Sci. Assn., Midwest Polit. Sci. Assn., Internat. Studies Assn. (midwest v.p. 1987—), Conf. Group on German Politics. Home: 2701 Westdale Rd Lawrence KS 66044 Office: U Kans Dept Polit Sci Lawrence KS 66045

FRANCISCO, THURMAN OLIVER, data processing executive; b. Midland, Mich., Apr. 20, 1948; s. Donald Milan and Betty Ezoa (Clay) F.; m. Anne Ruth Shcmidt, Oct. 4, 1969; children: Adam, Joshua, Benjamin, Joel, Matthew (dec.). Student, U. Center, Saginaw, Mich., 1966-68; BS, Western Mich. U., 1971. Fin. analyst Del E. Webb Devel. Co., Sun City, Ariz., 1972-74; ops. auditor Del E. Webb Corp., Phoenix, 1975-77; sr. systems analyst Luth. Ch. Mo. Synod, St. Louis, 1977-81, mgr. systems analysts, 1982-83, mgr. info. services internat. ctr., 1984—; acct. exec. Luth. Ch. Extension Fund, Condordia Pub. House, St. Louis, 1983. Editor: A Standard Accounting System for Lutheran Congregation, 1981, Lutheran Congregational Information System, 1983, A Study of the Role of Computer Enhanced Instruction in Christian Educations within Congregations, 1985. Mem. Aid Assn. Luths. (pres. br. #3409 St. Louis 1986-87), Internat. Soc. Wang Users. Avocations: remodeling homes, water sports. Office: Luth Ch Mo Synod Internat Ctr 1333 S Kirkwood Rd Saint Louis MO 63122

FRANCISCO, W. DAVID, orthopedic surgeon, educator; b. Kansas City, Kans., Apr. 17, 1921; s. Clarence Benjamin and Ethel Brydon (Duke) F.; m. Jean Knablen, Aug. 9, 1947; children: Barbara Jean, Marcia Ann, David Duke. AB, U. Kans., 1941, MD, 1944; Cert. in Orthopedic Surgery, U. Pa., 1948. Intern USN Hosp., Treasure Island, Calif., 1944; resident Children's Mercy Hosp., Kansas City, Mo., 1948-49, U. Kans. Med. Ctr., 1949-51; practice medicine specializing in orthopedic surgery Kansas City, Kans., 1951-85; prof. surgery U. Kans., Kansas City, 1985—; attending orthopedic surgeon Children's Mercy Hosp., Kansas City, Mo., 1952-85; dir. cerebral palsy clinic U. Kans. Med. Ctr., Kansas City, 1951—. Elder Village Presby. Ch., Prairie Village, Kans., 1956; mem. soc. fellow Nelson Gallery Art, Kansas City, Mo., 1970—. Served as lt. (j.g.) M.C., USN, 1943-47, PTO. Mem. Am. Acad. Orthopaedic Surgeons, Clin. Orthopaedic Soc., Mid Cen. Orthopaedic Soc., Wyandotte County Med. Soc. (pres. 1968-69), Am. Acad. Cerebral Palsy. Avocation: travel. Home: 8121 Fontana Prairie Village KS 66208 Office: U Kans Med Ctr Orthopedic Sect 39th and Rainbow Kansas City KS 66103

FRANCK, ARDATH AMOND, educator, school psychologist; b. Wehrum, Pa., May 5, 1925; d. Arthur and Helen Lucille (Sharp) Amond; m. Frederick M. Franck, Mar. 18, 1945; children—Sheldon, Candace. B.S. in Edn., Kent State U., 1946, M.A., 1947; Ph.D., Western Res. U., 1956. Cert. high sch. tchr., elem. supr., sch. psychologist, speech and hearing therapist. Instr., Western Res. U., Cleve., summer 1953, U. Akron, 1947-50; sch. psychologist Summit County Schs., Ohio, 1950-60; cons. psychologist Wadsworth Pub. Schs., Ohio, 1946—; dir. Akron Speech & Reading Ctr., Ohio, 1950—. Author: Your Child Learns, 1976. Bd. dirs., pres. Twirling Unltd., 1982—. Mem. Am. Speech and Hearing Assn., Internat. Reading Assn., Ohio Psychol. Assn. Club: Soroptomist (Akron). Home: 631 Ghent Akron OH

44313 Office: Akron Speech & Reading Assn 700 Ghent Rd Akron OH 44313

FRANCK, MICHAEL, lawyer, association executive; b. Berlin, Oct. 6, 1932; came to U.S., 1941, naturalized, 1950; s. Wolf and Marga (Oppenheimer) F.; m. Carol E. Eichert, May 29, 1965; children: Michele, Lauren, Rebecca, Jennifer. B.A., Columbia U., 1954, J.D., 1958. Bar: N.Y. 1958, Mich. 1970. Trial counsel Liberty Mut. Ins. Co., Bklyn., 1958-60; chief litigator com. on grievances Assn. Bar City N.Y., 1960-70; cons. spl. com. on disciplinary procedures, bd. governance Pa. Supreme Ct., 1969-72; spl. counsel Phila. Ct. Common Pleas, 1970-73; exec. dir. State Bar Mich., Lansing, 1970—; mem. Commn. on Uniform State Laws, 1975—, Mich. Malpractice Arbitration Adv. Com., 1975—; mem. coordinating council on lawyer competence Conf. Chief Justices, 1981-87. Contbr. articles to bar jours. Served with U.S. Army, 1954-56. Mem. ABA (com. on nat. coordination disciplinary enforcement 1970-73, reporter spl. com. on evaluation of disciplinary enforcement 1968-70, chmn. sect. bar activities 1975-76, mem. long-range planning council 1979-81, mem. council sect. on individual rights and responsibilities 1982—, mem. com. on ethics and profl. responsibility 1982—, chmn. com. to implement model rules of profl. conduct 1983—, del. 1976-78, 82—, mem. ALI-ABA adv. com. on model peer rev. 1978-79, liaison to Commn. on Evaluation Profl. Standards 1977-83, chmn. com. profl. discipline 1979-82, mem. task force on lawyer advt. 1973-79), State Bar Mich., Ingham County Bar Assn. Home: 1211 N College Rd Mason MI 48854 Office: 306 Townsend St Lansing MI 48933

FRANCKA, IRENE ANN, business educator; b. Bolivar, Mo., Sept. 18, 1948; d. Procop John and Mary Ann (Ruzicka) F. BS in Edn., Southwest Mo. State U., 1970, MS in Edn., 1975; EdS, U. Ark., 1978. Cert. secondary tchr., Mo. Bus. edn. instr. Humansville (Mo.) R-IV Schs., 1970-76; asst. prof. bus. Southwest Mo. State U., Springfield, 1976—; presenter SW Bus. Symposium., 1985-86. Editor Bus. Edn. Forum Jour., 1985. Mem. Nat. Bus. Edn. Assn., Mo. Bus. Edn. Assn., Info. Processing Assn. (bd. dirs. 1982-83), Delta Sigma Pi, Pi Omega Pi, Kappa Delta Pi. Avocations: horseshoes, golf, softball, basketball, billiards. Office: Southwest Mo State U 901 S National Springfield MO 65804

FRANCO, DAVID MICHAEL, religious organization administrator; b. Detroit, Mar. 14, 1948; s. Frank and Ann (Demaestri) F. BS in Commerce, Niagara U., 1971; MDiv, St. Michael's Coll., 1975; MS in Adminstrn., U. Notre Dame, 1980. Joined Oblates of St. Francis de Sales, 1966, ordained priest Roman Cath. Ch., 1976. Tchr. Bishop Duffy High Sch., Niagara Falls, N.Y., 1971-75; adminstr. Aquinas High Sch., Southgate, Mich., 1976-77, St. Francis de Sales High Sch., Toledo, 1977-81; cons. planning and devel. dept. edn. Archdiocese of Detroit, 1982-84, interim supt. schs., 1985; sec. edn. and supt. schs. Diocese of Joliet, Ill., 1986—. Mem. Nat. Cath. Ednl. Assn., U.S. Cath. Conf., Nat. Assn. Elem. Sch. Prins. Office: 425 Summit St Joliet IL 60435

FRANCO, JOSEPH VINCENT, JR., dentist; b. Omaha, Sept. 26, 1958; s. Joseph Vincent and Peggy Jane (Dearduff) F.; m. Rosemary Anne Laughlin, July 31, 1981; children: Anthony, Christopher, Marie. BA, Creighton U., 1980, DDS, 1984; cert., VA M.C., 1985. Lic. dentist, Nebr. Resident VA Med. Ctr., Omaha, 1984-85; gen. practice dentistry Omaha, 1985—; mem. staff Florence Nursing Home, Omaha, 1985—; clin. instr. Creighton Dental Sch., Omaha, 1985—; cons. Immanuel Med. Ctr., 1986—. Chmn. adminstrn. com. St. Pius X and St. Leo's Bd. Edn., 1986. Mem. ADA, Acad. Gen. Dentistry, Nebr. Dental Assn., Omaha Dist. Dental. Soc. Republican. Roman Catholic. Club: River City Regents (Omaha). Lodge: Kiwanis (chmn. attendance com. Omaha 1986). Avocations: sports, family activities. Home: 7622 Windsor Dr Omaha NE 68114 Office: Physicians Clinic Bldg 10060 Regency Circle Omaha NE 68114

FRANDSEN, TODD ALAN, mechanical engineer; b. LaGrange, Ill., Nov. 22, 1961; s. Richard Russell and Carolyn Louise (Samonds) F.; m. JoAnn Mounts, May 25, 1986. BS in Mech. Engring., Purdue U., 1984. Coop. engr. Danly Machine Corp., Chgo., 1980-83; mech. engr. Andrew Corp., Orland Park, Ill., 1984—. Mem. ASME. Republican. Avocations: restoring automobiles, softball, jazz. Home: 502 Redondo Dr Unit 212 Downers Grove IL 60516 Office: Andrew Corp 10500 W 153d Orland Park IL 60462

FRANK, ALVIN R., psychoanalyst, educator; b. Chgo., Oct. 29, 1927; s. Seymour Jerome and Edith Ida (Benjamin) F.; m. Marlene Podell, Aug. 23, 1952 (dec. Jan. 1980); children: Cathy D., Thomas S., Susan A.; m. Roxanne Harris, Feb. 7, 1981. BS, Purdue U., 1949; MD, U. Ill., Chgo., 1953; postgrad., Chgo. Inst. Psycholanalysis, 1963-68. Diplomate Am. Bd. Psychiatry and Neurology. Intern U. Ill. Coll. Medicine, 1953-54; resident U. Cin., 1956-59, instr., 1959-60; asst. dir. to assoc. dir. dept. psychiatry Jewish Hosp., St. Louis, 1960-63; practice medicine specializing in psychiatry St. Louis, 1963-68, practice medicine specializing in psychoanalysis, 1968—; clin. prof. psychiatry St. Louis U., 1979—; cons. Family and Children's Services St. Louis, 1963-71, Youth Counseling Service St. Louis, 1964-71, Youth Care and Counseling St. Louis, 1975-79, Luth. Family and Children's Service St. Louis, 1968-74, VA Hosp., St. Louis, 1971-76; mem. faculty Chgo. Inst. Psychoanalysis, 1970-71; mem. workshop on reconstrn. and psychoanalytic research, N.Y.C, Ctr. Advanced Pscyhoanalytic Studies, Princeton, N.J., 1970—; Contbr. articles on psychoanalysis to profl. jours.; mem. editorial bd. Internat. Jour. Psychoanalytic Psychotherapy, 1973-79, Psychoanalytic Compendium, 1982—, Psychoanalytic Glossary, 1982—; mem. N.Am. editorial bd. Internat. Jour. Psychoanalysis, 1984—, Internat. Rev. Psychoanalysis, 1984—. Mem Suicide Prevention, Inc. of St. Louis, treas. 1970-71, pres. 1971-72. Served to capt. USAF, 1954-56. Mem. Psychoanalytic Research and Devel. Fund, Am. Psychoanalytic Assn. (com. on devel. resources 1981-84, com. on scientific activities 1986—, council on psycholanalytic edn. study group on tng. analysis 1985—, edit. bd. jour. 1978-81), Mental Health Assn. St. Louis (bd. dirs. 1971-73), St. Louis Psychoanalytic Soc., Chgo. Psychoanalytic Soc., Alpha Omega Alpha, Omega Beta Pi, Alpha Epsilon Delta. Club: Westwood Country (St. Louis). Office: 4524 Forest Park Suite 210 Saint Louis MO 63108

FRANK, DARIO, marketing communications specialist; b. Chgo., Dec. 21, 1954; s. Claudio and Paolina (Fioretti) F.; m. Sandra Ptaszek, Oct. 14, 1978. Student, Oakton Coll., 1972-74; BS in Bus. & Mgmt., Northeastern Ill. U., 1977; BS in Mktg., Roosevelt U., 1986. Asst. advt. mgr. Crane Packing Co., Morton Grove, Ill., 1975-79; mktg. communications specialist A.O. Smith, Arlington Heights, Ill., 1979-85; sr. mktg. communications specialist Omron Bus. Systems, Schaumberg, Ill., 1985—; mktg. communication cons. Ross Plastics, Franklin Park, Ill., 1980—. Author, editor: Getting Your Message Across in Advertising, 1976, Management for Success, 1985. Mem. Am. Bowling Congress. Avocations: bowling, golf. Home: 410 Lamont Buffalo Grove IL 60089 Office: Omron Bus Systems 1717 Penny Ln Schaumburg IL 60173

FRANK, GEOFFREY EDWARD, public relations and personnel specialist; b. Ft. Wayne, Ind., Oct. 23, 1955; s. John L. and Patricia Ann (Drussell) F.; m. Mary Lynn Johnson, Feb. 25, 1984; 1 child, John Edward. Student, Purdue U., Ft. Wayne, 1974-76; BS, Ball State U., 1978, MA, 1985. City editor Bluffton (Ind.) News-Banner, 1978-81; ins. agt. Equitable Life, Ft. Wayne, 1981; auditor Wells County, Bluffton, 1981-85; pub. affairs and human resources coordinator Ft. Wayne Area Job Tng. Program, 1985—. Mem. admissions and rev. com. Wells County United Way, Bluffton, 1980—, Gold award, 1981; mem. Small Cities Econ. Devel. Com., 4th dist., Ind., 1983-85, Pub. Info. and Mktg. Com., 1986-87; city co-chairperson Wells County Dem. Politics, Bluffton, 1982-83; v.p. Wells County Found., Bluffton, 1985-86. Journalism scholar, 1977, 78; recipient 1st place investigative reporting UPI-Ind., 1981. Mem. Internat. Assn. Bus. Communicators, Pub. Info. and Mktg. Coordinating Com. Roman Catholic. Lodge: Optimists (sec. Bluffton 1981-83, bd. dirs. Bluffton 1983-84). Avocations: politics, bowling, bridge, coin collecting. Home: 207 Ridgeview Pl Bluffton IN 46714 Office: Ft Wayne Area Job Tng Program 203 W Wayne St Fort Wayne IN 46802

FRANK, J. LOUIS, oil company executive; b. Santa Barbara, Calif., May 1, 1936; s. Jacob Louis and Ernestine (Andreatta) F.; m. Bobbie Jean Long, July 6, 1957; children: James Louis and Debora Susan. BS, Tex. A&M U., 1958. Registered profl. engr., Tex. Dist. ops. mgr. Marathon Oil Co., Lafayette, La., 1973-77; coordinating mgr. Marathon Oil Co., Findlay, Ohio, 1978; ops. mgr., project dir. Marathon Oil U.K. Ltd., London, 1978-83, pres., 1984; v.p. prodn. Marathon Internat. Oil Co., 1984; pres. Marathon Petroleum Co., Findlay, 1985—; also bd. dirs. Marathon Oil Co., Findlay. Lead organizer United Way Hancock County, Findlay, 1985; trustee Blanchard Valley Hosp., Findlay, 1985—. Mem. Am Petroleum Inst. (bd. dirs.), Soc. Petroleum Engrs. Republican. Presbyterian. Avocations: golf, tennis, racquetball, hunting. Office: Marathon Petroleum Co 539 S Main St Findlay OH 45840

FRANK, JAMES CHARLES, dentist; b. Dayton, Ohio, May 8, 1941; s. Stanley Abraham and Anne R. (Trenner) F.; m. Jacqueline Dee Freidman, May 28, 1975; children: Jeffrey, Jared. Student, Ind. U., 1959-62, Butler U., 1961; DDS, Case Western Res., 1966. Gen. practice dentistry Peru, Ind., 1969—. Served to capt. USAF, 1966-68. Mem. ADA, Ind. Dental Assn., Miami County Dental Assn., Grant County Dental Assn. Jewish. Lodge: Masons. Avocations: fishing, boating. Home: 70 N Hood St Peru IN 46970 Office: 400 N Broadway Peru IN 46970

FRANK, JOHN NICHOLAS, journalist; b. Bklyn., June 4, 1953; s. Salvatore and Faye (Smaldone) F.; m. Mary Louise Osterberg, May 21, 1977; 1 child, Matthew John. BJ, Marquette U., 1975; MS, Northwestern U., 1976. Bus. editor Paddock Publs., Arlington Heights, Ill., 1976-79; mng. editor Pickwick Newspaper, Park Ridge, Ill., 1979; assoc. editor Savs. and Loan News, Chgo., 1979-83; fin. reporter Reuters News Service, Chgo., 1983-84; corr. Bus. Week, Chgo., 1984—; chmn. SF Communications, 1987—; instr. Roosevelt U., Chgo., 1986—. Pub. The Fin. Futures Analyst. Co-founder St. Anthanasius Young Parents Group, Evanston, Ill., 1986; panelist Insurers Pub. Realtions Council, 1986. Mem. Soc. Profl. Journalists (v.p. Marquette U. chpt. 1974-75, Mark of Excellence award 1974-75), Futures Industry Assn., Chgo. Headline Club. Democrat. Roman Catholic. Avocations: soccer, mil. history, journalism edn. Home: 2119 Payne St Evanston IL 60201 Office: Bus Week 645 N Michigan Chicago IL 60611

FRANK, JOHN V., investment advisor; b. Cleve., Oct. 14, 1936; s. Paul A. and Frances (Halbert) F. Student Babson Coll., 1956-57; B.B.A., U. Miami-Fla., 1960. Mgmt. trainee Nat. City Bank, Cleve., 1960-62; investment analyst officer First Nat. Bank, Akron, 1962-70, asst. trust officer, 1970-73, trust officer, 1973-80, v.p., trust officer, 1980-81; pres. Summit Capital Mgmt. Co., Akron, 1982—. Treas., Fairlawn Heights Assn., Inc., Akron, 1971—; pres. Ohio Ballet, 1973-74; trustee Howland Meml. Fund, Akron, 1974—; pres. Burton D. Morgan Found., Akron, 1977—; councilman City of Akron, 1978—; trustee Akron Art Mus., 1976-83, pres., 1979-81; trustee Akron City Hosp. Found., 1980-83. Served to 1st lt. USAR, 1963-69. Mem. Cleve. Soc. Security Analysts. Republican. Episcopalian. Clubs: Portage Country, Akron City; Hillsboro (Pompano Beach, Fla.). Avocation: art collecting. Office: Summit Capital Mgmt Co 2080 Stockbridge Rd Akron OH 44313

FRANK, ROBERT GEORGE, clinical psychologist; b. Paris, Mar. 25, 1952; came to U.S., 1954; s. Fred J. and Dorothea V. (Plaut) F.; m. Janet Susan Askuvich, Jan. 6, 1985; 1 child, Daniel. BS, U. N.Mex., 1974, MA, 1977, PhD, 1979. Diplomate (clinical) Am. Bd. Profl. Psychology. Asst. prof. psychology U. Mo., Columbia, 1979-86; assoc. prof., vice chmn. dept. physical medicine and rehab. Sch. Medicine U. Mo., Columbia, 1986—; surveyor Commn. Accreditation of Rehab. Facilities, Tucson, 1985—; Govs. Head Injury Adv. Council, Jefferson City, Mo., 1985—. Contbr. numerous articles to profl. jours. Bd. dirs. Cen. States A.K. Rice Inst., 1984—. Research grantee Nat. Inst. Health, Washington, 1984—. Mem. Am. Psychol. Assn., Soc. Behavioral Medicine. Roman Catholic. Club: Columbia Masters Swim Team (coach 1979—). Home: 2306 Fairmont Columbia MO 65203 Office: Dept Physical Medicine and Rehab 1 Hospital Dr Columbia MO 65212

FRANK, ROBERT NEIL, opthalmologist, vision research scientist, educator; b. Pitts., May 14, 1939; s. Stanton Harvey and Helen Ruth (Rosenbach) F.; m. Karni Warda Spitz; children—Stephen Emanuel, Ariel Ruth, Dale Michael, Gitta Naomi. A.B. summa cum laude, Harvard U., 1961; M.D., Yale U., 1966. Diplomate Am. Bd. Ophthalmology. Intern Grady Meml. Hosp., Altanta, 1966-67; fellow and resident in ophthalmology Johns Hopkins U., Balt., 1967-72; sr. staff ophthalmologist Nat. Eye Inst., NIH, Bethesda, Md., 1972-76; assoc. prof. ophthalmology Wayne State U., Detroit, 1976-80, prof., 1980—; cons. NIH, Nat. Eye Inst., Nat. Inst. Arthritis, Diabetes and Digestive Diseases and Kidney, Nat. Cancer Inst., VA; mem. adv. bd. Med. Sci. Juvenile Diabetes Found.; mem. steering com. Nat. Diabetes Research Interchange; cons. Nat. Diabetes Adv. Bd.; bd. dirs. Mich. Diabetes Assn. NIH grantee, 1976—. Mem. Am. Diabetes Assn., AMA, Am. Acad. Ophthalmology, AAAS, Assn. Research in Vision and Ophthalmology (Fight for Sight award 1977), So. Med. Assn., Mich. Med. Soc., Wayne County Med. Soc., Mich. Ophthal. Soc. Contbr. articles to profl. jours. Office: 3994 John R St Detroit MI 48201

FRANK, RONALD EDWARD, marketing educator; b. Chgo., Sept. 15, 1933; s. Raymond and Ethel (Lundquist) F.; m. Iris Donner, June 18, 1958; children: Linda, Lauren, Kimberly. B.S. in Bus. Adminstrn, Northwestern U., 1955, M.B.A., 1957; Ph.D., U. Chgo., 1960. Instr. bus. statistics Northwestern U., Evanston, Ill., 1956-57; asst. prof. bus. adminstrn. Harvard U., Boston, 1960-63, Stanford U., 1963-65; assoc. prof. mktg. Wharton Sch., U. Pa., 1965-68, prof., 1968-84, chmn. dept. mktg., 1971-74, vice dean, dir. research and Ph.D. programs, 1974-76, assoc. dean, 1981-83; dean, prof. mktg. Krannert Grad. Sch. Mgmt., Purdue U., 1984—; bd. dirs. Lafayette Life Ins. Co., The MAC Group, Home Hosp. Lafayette (Ind.); cons. to industry. Author: (with Massy and Kuehn) Quantitative Techniques in Marketing Analysis, 1962, (with Matthews, Buzzell and Levitt) Marketing: an Introductory Analysis, 1964, (with William Massy) Computer Programs for the Analysis of Consumer Panel Data, 1964, An Econometric Approach to a Marketing Decision Model, 1971, (with Paul Green) Manager's Guide to Marketing Research, 1967, Quantative Methods in Marketing, 1967, (with Massy and Lodahl) Purchasing Behavior and Personal Attributes, 1968, (with Massy and Wind) Market Segmentation, 1972, (with Marshall Greenberg) Audience Segmentation Analysis for Public Television Program Development, Evaluation and Promotion, 1976, The Public's Use of Television, 1980, Audiences for Public Television, 1982. Bd. dirs., fin. com. Home Hosp. of Lafayette, 1985—. Recipient pub. TV research grants John and Mary R. Markle Found., 1975-82. Mem. Am. Mktg. Assn. (dir. 1968-70, v.p. mktg. edn. 1972-73), Inst. Mgmt. Sci., Assn. Consumer Research, Am. Assn. Pub. Opinion Research. Home: 144 Creighton Rd West Lafayette IN 47906 Office: Purdue U Krannert Grad Sch Mgmt Krannert West Lafayette IN 47907

FRANK, RUBY MERINDA, employment agency executive; b. McClusky, N.D., June 28, 1920; d. John J. and Olise (Stromme) Hanson; student coll., Mankato, Minn., also Aurora (Ill.) Coll.; m. Robert G. Frank, Jan. 14, 1944 (dec. 1973); children—Gary Frank, Craig. Exec. sec., office mgr. Nat. Container Corp., Chgo., 1943-50; owner, operator Frank's Office & Employment Service, St. Charles, Ill., 1957—; bd. dirs. St. Charles Savs. & Loan Assn., Sta. WFXW-FM, Geneva. Sec. bd. trustees Delnor Hosp., St. Charles, 1959-78, chmn. bd., 1985—, also life mem. Women's aux.; vice chmn. Kane County (Ill.) Republican Com., 1968-77; pres. Women's Rep. Club, 1969-77; local bd. Am. Cancer Soc.; adv. council Dellora A. Norris Cultural Arts Center; bd. govs. Luth. Social Service Baker Hotel; adv. bd. Aurora U.; chmn. bd. Delnor Hosp.; co-vice chmn. Delnor Community Health System. Recipient Exec. of Yr. award Fox Valley PSI; Charlemagne award for community service, 1982; bd. dirs. Aurora Found. Mem. St. Charles C. of C. (pres., bd. dirs. 1976-82, ambassador), Kane-DuPage Personnel Assn. (v.p. 1971—), Nat., Ill. employment assns., Ill. Assn. Personnel Cons. (dir.), Women in Mgmt. Lutheran. Clubs: St. Charles Country; Execs. of Chgo. Contbr. weekly broadcast Sta. WGSB, 1970-80, WFXW weekly interview program. Home: 534 Longmeadow Circle Saint Charles IL 60174 Office: Arcada Theater Bldg S 1st Ave Saint Charles IL 60174

FRANK, SANDRA KAYE, mathematics educator; b. Springfield Twp., Mich., June 11, 1941; d. Virgil Euleas and Dorothy Arliene (Wells) Noble; m. Joseph Frederic Frank, Aug. 1, 1970; 1 child, Joseph Lindbergh. B.A., Central Mich. U., 1963; M.A., U. Mont., 1967. Tchr. math. Dearborn Pub. Sch., Mich., 1963—, Edsel Ford High Sch., 1978—. Mem. Mich. Council Tchrs. Math., Mich. Assn. Computer Users and Learners, Nat. Council Teachers of Math., Math. Assn. Am. Clubs: Mich. Flyers, Ninety-Nines. Home: 21222 Audette St Dearborn MI 48124

FRANKE, GLENNA CAROLYN, general practioner; b. Ewing, Ill., Jan. 25, 1936; d. Carl Walter William and Lillian (Midyette) F.; m. James Timothy Williamson, Oct. 8, 1971; 1 child, Heather. BS in Biology and Chemistry, Ill. Wesleyan U., 1957; DO, Kirksville (Mo.) Coll., 1963. Cert. gen. practitioner. Intern Mass. Osteo. Hosp., Boston, 1963-64; gen. practice medicine St. Louis, 1965—. Office: 3394 McKelvey Saint Louis MO 63044

FRANKE, KATHI JANE, cytotechnologist; b. West Bend, Wis., Nov. 17, 1958; d. Ira W. and Betty J. Weber; m. Mark A. Franke, Aug. 24, 1985. BS, Marian Coll., 1976-80; cert. cytology, State Lab Hygiene, Madison, Wis., 1981. Cytologist Columbia Hosp., Milw., 1982-84, Gundersen Clinic, LaCrosse, Wis., 1984—. Mem. Wis. Soc. Cytology (sec. 1987—). Lutheran. Avocations: reading, music. Office: Gundersen Clinic 1836 South Ave LaCrosse WI 54601

FRANKE, MICHAEL WOLFGANG, railroad executive; b. Herford, Westphalia, Fed. Republic Germany, July 31, 1948; came to U.S., 1955; s. Robert Wolfgang and Helena (Holak) F.; m. Jean Davis, Jan. 17, 1975; 1 child, Laura Ann. BSCE, Washington U., St. Louis, 1970; MS, U. Ill., 1971. Registered profl. engr., N.C., Mo. V.p., gen. mgr. WSS Railroad, Winston-Salem, N.C., 1976-78; gen. mgr. NFD Railroad, Suffolk, Va., 1978-79; asst. regional engr. Norfolk & Western Ry., Roanoke, Va., 1981-83; regional engr. Norfolk & Western Ry., St. Louis, 1983-85; gen. mgr. engring. Chgo. South Shore and South Bend Railroad, Michigan City, Ind., 1985-86, v.p. ops., 1986—, bd. dirs.; bd dirs. Chgo. South Shore & South Bend R.R., Chgo., Mo. & Westrern Rwy. Co. Recipient Wayne A. Johnston award Ill. Cen. Railroad, 1970. Mem. Am. Ry. Engring. Assn. (vice-chmn. com.), ASCE, Ry. Tie Assn. Lutheran. Lodge: Rotary. Avocations: reading, model railroading, travelling. Home: 3526 Pottawattomie Trail Michigan City IN 46360 Office: Chgo South Shore and South Bend Railroad N Carroll Ave Michigan City IN 46360

FRANKEN, JAMES LESLIE, electrical contractor; b. Sioux Center, Iowa, Aug. 13, 1953; s. John A. and Darlene Faye (Sandbulte) F.; m. Nancy Ann Vanden Brink, July 20, 1974; children—Jaymi Noelle, Gabriel James. B.S., Northwestern Coll., Orange City, Iowa, 1975. Electrician, Interstates Electric & Engring. Co., Inc., Sioux Center, Iowa, 1966-76, v.p., 1976—, pres. IEEC Internat., Ltd., 1983—; mgr. Franken Manor, Sioux Center, 1974-78. Sec., 1st Reformed Ch., Sioux Center, 1980-82; mem. N.W. Iowa Tech. Coll. Found. Bd. Mem. Associated Builders and Contractors (2d v.p.), Sioux Center C. of C., Northwestern Coll. Alumni, Republican. Office: 1520 Industrial Park Sioux Center IA 51250

FRANKENBERG, BRUCE LIND, investment banker; b. Medina, Ohio, Feb. 21, 1955; s. Robert Curtis and Marjorie (Lind) F.; m. Kari Severson, Sept. 9, 1978; children: Robert Reid, Katharine Lind. BA, Vanderbilt U., 1977; MBA, U. Chgo., 1982. Account exec. Marsh & McLennan, Chgo., 1977-81, A.G. Becker Paribas, Chgo., 1982-84, Morgan Stanley, Chgo., 1984—; instr. Ins. Sch. Chgo., 1980-82. Pres. Shorely Woods Assn., 1980-81. Republican. Presbyterian. Clubs: Barrington Hills Country (Barrington); Univ. (Chgo.). Home: 815 Fairfax Ct Barrington IL 60010 Office: Morgan Stanley & Co 440 S LaSalle St Chicago IL 60605

FRANKER, STEPHEN GRANT, savings and loan executive; b. Spencer, Iowa, July 29, 1949; s. Oscar Grant and Betty Jean (Greenwaldt) F.; m. Dianne Alice Russell, Aug. 24, 1970; children: Derek, Leah. BA, U. No. Iowa, 1971. CPA, Iowa. Staff acct. McGladrey, Hansen, Dunn & Co., CPA's, Mason City, Iowa, 1971-75; audit supr. Clinton, Iowa, 1975-76; controller 1st Fed. Savs. & Loan Assn., Spirit Lake, Iowa, 1976-82, pres., 1982-83; sr. v.p. NW Fed. Savs. & Loan, Spencer, 1983—; Bd. dirs. Midwest Savings Conf. of U.S. League Savings Insts., Chgo., 1985—. Treas. Good Neighbor Fund, Spirit Lake, 1976-80; fund drive chmn. Dickinson County Heart Assn., Spirit Lake, 1981. Mem. Am. Inst. CPA's, Iowa Soc. CPA's. Republican. Lutheran. Lodge: Kiwanis. Avocations: reading, sailing. Home: 503 9th St Spirit Lake IA 51360 Office: NW Fed Savings & Loan Assn 101 W 5th St Spencer IA 51301

FRANKLIN, BENJAMIN BARNUM, dinner club executive; b. Topeka, Kans., Nov. 7, 1944; s. Charles Benjamin and Margaret Lavona (Barnum) F. B.A. in Speech, U. Colo., 1967. With Associated Clubs, Inc., Topeka, 1967—, v.p., 1972-83, pres., 1983—. Honoree, Benjamin Barnum Franklin Day, Lima, Ohio, June 11, 1983. Mem. Kans. Soc. Assn. Execs., Nat. Speakers Assn. (chmn. chpt. 1982-83), Internat. Platform Assn. (gov. 1975—), Am. Polar Soc., Topeka Sales and Mktg. Execs., Explorers Club. Republican. Presbyterian. Lodge: Rotary (bd. dirs. 1975-78). Contbr. articles to profl. publs. Office: One Townsite Plaza Suite 315 Topeka KS 66603

FRANKLIN, BRUCE WALTER, lawyer; b. Ellendale, N.D., Feb. 26, 1936; s. Wallace Henry and Frances (Webb) F.; m. Kristy Ann Jones, Feb. 7, 1944; children—Kevin, Monica, Taylor. Student. U. Mich., 1954-56; grad. Eastern Mich. U., 1957; LL.B., Detroit Coll. Law, 1962. Bar: Mich. 1963. Sole practice, Troy, Mich., from 1962; now mng. ptnr. Franklin, Bigler, Berry & Johnston, P.C., Troy. Past chmn. Mich. Young Republicans. Served with U.S. Army. Office: 14th Floor 900 Tower Dr Troy MI 48098

FRANKLIN, CAROL SUSAN, anthropologist, educational administrator; b. Cleve., Feb. 5, 1953; d. Grant Lafayette and Frances (Mason) F. BA magna cum laude, Hiram Coll., Ohio, 1974; MA in Anthropology, U. Calif., Berkeley, 1975, PhD, 1979. Research assoc. Coll. Urban Affairs, Cleve. State U., 1979-82, adj. prof. urban studies, 1980-82, vis. asst. prof., 1982; asst. dir. devel. edn. Cuyahoga Community Coll., Cleve., 1983—; cons., facilitator Cuyahoga Met. Housing Authority, Cleve., 1980-82; speaker in field. Contbr. in field. Mem. planning commn. Episcopal Diocese of Ohio, chmn. future planning sub-com., 1987—; vice chmn. hunger task force Shaker Heights Community Ch., 1987—. Nat. Fellowships Fund for Black Americans fellow, 1974-79, U. Calif. at Berkeley Inst. Race and Ethnic Relations fellow, 1977-78. Mem. Soc. Urban Anthropology, Am. Anthrop. Assn., Ohio Assn. Devel. Edn., Am. Ethnol. Soc., Soc. Applied Anthropology, Pi Gamma Nu, Alpha Kappa Alpha (1st v.p. chpt. 1985-86, parliamentarian chpt. 1987—). Home: 3676 Avalon Rd Shaker Heights OH 44120

FRANKLIN, CHARLES CURTIS, business consultant; b. Colorado Springs, Colo., Mar. 16, 1932; s. William R. and Lilian P. (Jones) F.; m. Sandra Sue Smith, June 17, 1967; children—Bevin Duane, Brian Aaron. B.S.M.E., U. Wis., Madison, 1964; M.B.A., St. Ambrose Coll., 1982. Field service engr. The Marley Pump Co., Mission, Kans., 1964-66, product engring. mgr., 1966-69, quality control mgr., 1969-73, sales mgr. petroleum products, 1973-79, v.p. mktg., 1979-85. Served with USN, 1950-55. Mem. Petroleum Equipment Inst. Republican. Lutheran. Club: Davenport. Lodges: Masons, Shriners.

FRANKLIN, FREDERICK RUSSELL, legal association executive; b. Berlin, Germany, Mar. 20, 1929; s. Ernest James and Frances (Price) F.; A.B., Ind. U., 1951, J.D. with high distinction, 1956; m. Barbara Ann Donovan, Jan. 26, 1952; children—Katherine Elizabeth, Frederick Russell. Bar: Ind. 1956. Trial atty. criminal div. and ct. of claims sect., civil div. U.S. Dept. Justice, Washington, 1956-60; gen. counsel Ind. State Bar Assn., Indpls., 1960-67; dir. continuing legal edn. for Ind., adj. prof. law Ind. U., Indpls., 1965-68; staff dir. profl. standards Am. Bar Assn., Chgo., 1968-70; exec. v.p. Nat. Attys. Title Assurance Fund, Inc., Indpls., 1970-72; staff dir. legal edn. and admissions to the bar Am. Bar Assn., Chgo., 1972—. Trustee, Olympia Fields (Ill.) United Methodist Ch., 1980-84; treas. bd. dirs. Olympia Fields Pub. Library, 1984—; mem. Olympia Fields Police Bd., 1983—. Served to capt. USAF, 1951-53. Mem. Am., Ind., Ill. bar assns., Fed. Bar Assn. (officer, found. bd. dirs. 1974—, historian 1979—, nat. council 1965—, nat. v.p. 1967-69, chpt. pres. 1965-66, chmn. admission to practice and recert. com. 1980-82, bd. dirs. Chgo. chpt. 1984—), Nat. Orgn. Bar Counsel (pres. 1967), Order of Coif, Phi Delta Phi. Kiwanian, Elk. Home: 3617 Parthenon Way Olympia Fields IL 60461 Office: 750 N Lake Shore Dr Chicago IL 60611

FRANKLIN, MARGARET LAVONA BARNUM (MRS. C. BENJAMIN FRANKLIN), civic leader; b. Caldwell, Kans., June 19, 1905; d. LeGrand Husted and Elva (Biddinger) Barnum; B.A., Washburn U., 1952; student Iowa State Tchrs. Coll., 1923-25, U. Iowa, 1937-38; m. C. Benjamin Franklin, Jan. 20, 1940 (dec. 1983); children—Margaret Lee (Mrs. Michael J. Felso), Benjamin Barnum. Tchr. pub. schs., Union, Iowa, 1925-27, Kearney, Nebr., 1927-28, Marshalltown, Iowa, 1928-40; advance rep. Chautauqua, summers 1926-30. Mem. Citizens Adv. Com., 1965-69; mem. Starmont-Vail Regional Ctr. Hosp. Aux.; bd. dirs. Topeka Pub. Library Found., 1984—. Recipient Waldo B. Heywood award Topeka Civic Theatre, 1967; named Outstanding Alpha Delta Pi Mother of Kans., 1971; Topeka Public Library award, 1977. Mem. DAR (state chmn. Museum 1968-71), AAUW (mem. 50 yrs.), Gemini Group of Topeka, Topeka Geneal. Soc., Topeka Art Guild, Topeka Civic Symphony Soc. (dir. 1952-57, Service Honor citation 1960), Doll Collectors Am., Marshalltown Community Theatre (pres. 1938-40), Topeka Pub. Library Bd. (trustee 1961-70, treas., 1962-65, chmn. 1965-67), Shawnee County Hist. Soc. (dir. 1963-75, sec. 1964-66), Nat. Multiple Sclerosis Soc. (dir. Kans. chpt. 1963-66), Stevengraph Collectors Assn., Friends of Topeka Public Library (dir. 1970-79, Disting. Service award 1980), P.E.O. (pres. chpt. 1956-57, coop. bd. pres. 1964-65, chpt. honoree 1969), Native Sons and Daus. Kans. (life), Topeka Stamp Club, Alpha Beta Gamma, Nonoso. Republican. Mem. Christian Ch. Clubs: Western Sorosis (pres. 1960-61), Minerva (2d v.p. 1984-85), Woman's (1st v.p. 1952-54), Knife and Fork.

FRANKLIN, MARVIN AUGUSTUS, III, manufacturing company executive; b. New Haven, Jan. 22, 1948; s. Marvin A. Jr. and Mary Ellen (Cunningham) F.; m. Elizabeth Anne Keck, Aug. 28, 1971; children: Robert, Elizabeth. AB, Duke U., 1970; MBA, U. R.I., 1975. Mgmt. trainee Dana Corp., Ft. Wayne, Ind., 1975-76, asst. to chief exec. officer, 1977-78, plant mgr., 1979-80, gen. mgr., v.p. spicer heavy axle div., 1981—. Served to lt. USN, 1970-74. Mem. Heavy Duty Mfrs. Assn. (sec. 1987—). Republican. Methodist. Club: Orchard Ridge Country (Ft. Wayne). Avocation: golf.

FRANKLIN, ROBERT CHARLES, dentist; b. East St. Louis, Ill., July 14, 1952; s. Charles Albert and Dolores Maxine (Benson) F.; m. Theresa Jean Wassmer, June 20, 1978; children: Jonathan Adam, Matthew David. BS in Biology, U. Ill., Chgo., 1974, BS in Dentistry, 1977, DDS, 1979. Lic. dentist, Ill. Assoc. dentist Chester (Ill.) Dental Clinic, 1979-80, ptnr., 1980—; gen. dentist Menard (Ill.) Correctional Ctr., 1979085, dental dir., 1985—; asst. officer in charge #932 USAF Clinic Assn., Scott AFB, Ill., 1985—. Mem. ADA, Ill. Dental Assn., So. Ill. Dental Assn., Acad. Gen. Dentistry, Chester Jaycees, Chester C. of C.. Nat. Rifle Assn., U. Ill. Alumni Assn. (life), Res. Officer Assn., Air Force Assn., Alpha Tau Omega, Delta Sigma Delta. Avocations: jogging, scuba diving, amateur radio, hunting. Home: 6 Greenbriar Ln Chester IL 62233 Office: 1654 State St Chester IL 62233

FRANKLIN, WILLIAM HENRY, JR., electronics executive; b. Peoria, Ill., Nov. 12, 1941; s. William H. and Mary (Haas) F.; m. Gloria J. Jacobs, Sept. 29, 1962; 1 child, William Henry III. BSEE, U. Iowa, 1973. Sr. engr. Gilbarco, Greensboro, N.C., 1977-79, Conco-Tellus, Mendota, Ill., 1979-81; pres. B&B Electronics Mfg. Co., Ottawa, Ill., 1981—. Served with USAF, 1961-65. Roman Catholic. Avocation: amateur radio. Office: B&B Electronics Mfg Co 1500 Boyce Meml Dr Ottawa IL 61350

FRANKS, JULIUS, JR., dentist; b. Macon, Ga., Sept. 5, 1922; s. Julius and Nellie (Solomon) F.; children: Darryl, Cheryl, Bobby, Beverly, Fredrick. BS, U. Mich., 1947, DDS, 1951. Gen. practice dentistry Grand Rapids, Mich., 1951—. Trustee emeritus Western Mich. U., Kalamazoo, 1964-82; bd. dirs. Grand Rapids Urban League, 1954-56, United Community Services, Grand Rapids, 1958-67, Am. Red Cross, Grand Rapids, 1964-67, Adv. Ctr. for Teens, Grand Rapids, 1966-69, Blodgett Meml. Med. Ctr., East Grand Rapids, Mich., 1974-86; mem. Afro-Am. Lay Cath. Caucus, Grand Rapids, 1980-85, exec. com. Kent County council Boy Scouts of Am., 1966-68. Named All Am. football player, 1942; named to Mich. Hall of Honor U. Mich., 1983. Mem. ADA, Mich. Dental Soc., Western Mich. Dental Soc. (pres., v.p. 1971-72, Disting. Service award, 1985), Kent County Dental Soc., Grand Rapids Jaycees, Sigma Pi Phi. Republican. Episcopalian. Club: Tawa-si Athletic (pres. 1958-63). Lodge: Rotary (local bd. dirs. 1978-81). Avocations: sports, reading. Home: 1919 Meadow Field NE Grand Rapids MI 49505 Office: 26 Sheldon SE Grand Rapids MI 49503

FRANKUM, DEMRIE DEAN, insurance company executive; b. Wellington, Kans., July 29, 1928; s. Homer Lynderman and Opal Marie (Osborne) F.; m. Patricia Ann Beard, June 30, 1956; children: Demrie Mark, Rebecca Lynn. BS, Kans. State U., 1951. Mgr. group dept. Pacific Mut. Life Ins. Co., Los Angeles, 1954-57; owner Frankum Ins. Agy., Indpls., 1957-71; v.p. agy. dept. Vernon Gen. Ins. Co., Indpls., 1961-71; pres. Group Adminstrn. Services, Inc., Indpls., 1971—, Hoosier Dental Plans, Inc., Indpls., 1982—. Mem. Sel Ins. Inst. Am., Nat. Assn. Health Underwriters. Republican. Lodges: Kiwanis, Masons, Shriners. Avocations: guitar, singing, country music. Office: Hoosier Dental Plans Inc 2940 E 56th St Indianapolis IN 46220

FRANTA, WILLIAM ROY, former computer science educator, investment executive; b. St. Paul, May 21, 1942; s. Roy Andrew and Helen Aleta (Nicholson) F.; B.S., U. Minn., 1964, M.S., 1966, Ph.D., 1970. Asst. prof. computer sci. U. Minn., Mpls., 1970-76, assoc. prof., 1976-81, prof., 1981-84, assoc. dir. Univ. Computer Center, 1976-80, co-dir. Microelectronic and Info. Scis. Center, 1980-81, assoc. dir., 1981-82; mem. computer adv. com. Sci. Mus. Minn., 1981—; mem. tech. adv. com. 1st Midwest Capital Corp., 1981, v.p., 1980-83, pres., 1983-85; treas. ADC Telecommunications, 1985-86; v.p. Network Systems Corp., 1986—; v.p., gen. mgr. Network Cons. Services. NSF grantee, 1979-81. Mem. IEEE, Inst. Mgmt. Scis., Assn. Computing Machinery. Author: The Process View of Simulation, 1977; (with I. Chlamtac) Local Networks: Motivation, Technology, Performance, 1981; (with others) Formal Methods of Program Verification and Specification, 1981; contbr. over 80 research papers in field. Office: ADC Telecommunications Inc 5501 Green Valley Dr Minneapolis MN 55437

FRANTEL, EDWARD WILLIAM, soft drink company executive; b. Wauwatosa, Wis., Mar. 18, 1925; s. Edward S. Frantl and Myrtle E. (Fischer) Frantl) Hollmann; m. Sherry Lieg, Aug. 24, 1946; 1 son, Scott. B.S. in Bus. Adminstrn, Marquette U., 1948. Field sales supr. H. J. Heinz Co., Milw., 1948-53; with Miller Brewing Co., Milw., 1953-79; dir. sales Miller Brewing Co., 1972-74, v.p. sales, 1974-79; pres., chief exec. officer Seven-Up Co., Clayton, Mo., 1979—; v.p. Philip Morris, Inc.; dir. and officer Dixi Cola, Inc., Seven-Up U.S.A., Inc.; dir. Mission Viejo, Cheer Up Co., Marbert, Inc., Seven-Up Bottling of Phoenix, Inc., Seven-Up Bottling Co. of Norfolk, Inc., Seven-Up Can. Ltd., Ventura Coastal Corp., Warner-Jenkinson Co., Inc., Warner-Jenkinson Co. of Calif., Warner-Jenkinson East, Inc., Golden Crown Citrus Corp. Pres. Council of Fitness, Council of St. Louis U.; active Nat. Fitness Found., United Fund. Served with paratroops U.S. Army, World War II. Decorated Bronze Star with oak leaf cluster, Purple Heart with oak leaf cluster; recipient Gold Ring award Philip Morris, Inc., 1979. Mem. Sales and Mktg. Execs. of Milw., Bus. Adminstrn. Alumni Assn. of Marquette U. (Man of Yr. 1978), Confrerie de la Chaine des Rotisseurs. Clubs: St. Louis, Milw. Athletic. Office: The Seven-Up Co 121 S Meramec Clayton MO 63105 *

FRANTSVE, DENNIS JOHN, graphics company executive, educator, columnist; b. Chgo., Mar. 14, 1938; s. Carl Henning and Elizabeth Dorothy (Waldock) F.; m. Julieta Maria Chacon, Oct. 26, 1967; children—Lisa, Julie, Dennis. B.S. in Commerce, DePaul U., 1969. Cost acct. R.R. Donnelley & Sons Inc. Chgo., 1956-60; supr. Gregg Moore Co., Chgo., 1965-69; prodn. coordinator Regensteiner Press, Chgo., 1969-70; supr. Acme Press, Chgo., 1970-72; print buyer Beslow Assocs., Inc., Chgo., 1972-74; exec. v.p. Darby Graphics, Chgo., 1974—. Tchr., Printing Industry Ill. Assn., 1973—. Served with USAR, 1957-63. Honored at testimonial Internat. San. Supply Assn., 1979; recipient cert. of appreciation Printing Industry Ill. Assn., 1980. Mem. Internat. Assn. Bus. Communicators, Publ. Prodn. Club Chgo., Soc. Nat. Assn. Publs., Pan Am. Council, Park Ridge C. of C. (dir. 1980—; cert. of appreciation 1981). Clubs: Toastmasters (treas.) (Des Plaines, Ill.); N.W. Press (Chgo.). Author: Printing Production Management, 1983; columnist Am. Printer mag., 1976—. Home: 215 N Chester Ave Park Ridge IL 60068 Office: 4015 N Rockwell St Chicago IL 60618

FRANZ, JOHN E., bio-organic chemist, researcher; b. Springfield, Ill., Dec. 21, 1929; m. Elinor Thielken, Aug. 7, 1951; children—Judith, Mary, John, Gary. B.S., U. Ill., 1951; Ph.D., U. Minn., 1955. Sr. research chemist Monsanto Agrl. Co., St. Louis, 1955-60, research group leader, 1960-63, Monsanto fellow, 1963-70, sr. fellow, 1970-80, disting. fellow, 1980—. Inventor roundup herbicide. Patentee in field. Contbr. articles to sci. publs. Recipient IR-100 award Indsl. Research Mag., 1977; Indsl. Research Inst. Achievement award, Washington, 1985; J.F. Queeny award Monsanto Co., 1981; Inventor of Yr. award St. Louis Bar Assn., 1986; The nat. Medal of Tech., Washington, 1987; Outstanding Achievement award, U. Minn., 1987. Mem. Am. Chem. Soc. Office: Monsanto Agrl Co 800 N Lindbergh Blvd Saint Louis MO 63167

FRANZ, JOSEPH ALBERT, III, food products executive, accountant; b. Springfield, Ill., June 20, 1947; s. Joseph A. Jr. and Betty (Deerwester) F.; m. Janice E. Botterbusch, Aug. 31, 1968; children: Sherri Y., Jill Marie. M of Acctg. Sci. with honors, BS, U. Ill., 1970. CPA, Ill. Staff, sr. acct. Price Waterhouse, Peoria, Ill., 1970-75; pres., treas., chief exec. officer, controller Heritage House Restaurants Inc., Springfield, Ill., 1975-85; chief exec. officer Arena Distbg. Co., Springfield, 1985—, also bd. dirs.; owner Arena Food Service, Springfield, 1985—, also bd. dirs. Treas. Conv. and Visitors Bus., Springfield, 1983—. Mem. Am. Inst. CPA's, Ill. Soc. CPA's. Republican. Roman Catholic. Lodge: Kiwanis (treas. downtown chpt. 1978-83). Home: 2812 Brandywine Rd Springfield IL 62704 Office: Arena Distbn Co 3750 Winchester Rd Springfield IL 62707

FRANZ, RICHARD WILLIAM, manufacturing executive; b. Chgo., Sept. 9, 1936; s. Walter William and Gladys Mary (Patterson) F.; m. Carol Ann Rohde, Sept. 16, 1967; 1 child, Richard Todd. Buyer Yeomans Bros., Melrose Park, Ill., 1958-66; purchasing agt. Stanadyne, Inc., Bellwood, Ill., 1967-71; v.p. ops. Mfg. Bolt and Nut, Chgo., 1972-75; pres. Windy City Fasteners, Downers Grove, Ill., 1976—. Pres. Lisle (Ill.) Baseball League, 1984-85. Served with U.S. Army, 1956-58. Mem. Chgo. Bolt, Nut and Screw Assn. (pres. 1981-82), Purchasing Agts. Assn. Democrat. Clubs: DuPage, Hundred Club of DuPage. Lodges: Moose, Lions (pres. Lisle chpt. 1986, Super Lion award 1982, 83, 84, 85). Avocations: tennis, golf, sports. Office: Windy City Fasteners 2717 Curtis St Downers Grove IL 60515

FRANZ, ROGER LEE, audio industry executive, musician, composer; b. Omaha, Nebr., Jan. 19, 1949; s. Henry A. and Virginia G. (Christensen) F.; m. Nancy Lynne Zolecke, Sept. 19, 1981; 1 child, Heather. BA, Grinnell (Iowa) Coll., 1971; MS, Northwestern U., 1975. Technician U. Chgo., 1971-73, sr. research technician, 1975-78; engr. Shure Bros., Inc., Evanston, Ill., 1978-82, mgr. quality assurance, 1982—. Author, owner copyrights to original music and recordings; contbr. articles to profl. jours. Research fellow Northwestern U., 1974-75; named one of Outstanding Young Men of Am., 1982. Mem. Am. Soc. for Quality Control. Avocations: old radios, home entertainment, family activities, playing music. Office: Shure Bros Inc 222 Hartrey Ave Evanston IL 60202-3696

FRANZEN, RUSSELL BERNARD, news director; b. Joliet, Ill., May 18, 1955; s. Walter Edrich and Fae Rae (Hughes) F.; m. Roberta Cogswell OAkes, May 25, 1980; 1 child, Emily Claire. BS, So. Ill. U., 1985. Pres. Franzen Radio Prodns., Springfield, Ill., 1978-80; dir. gospel music Sta. WFMB, Springfield, 1980-81; program dir. Sta. WMPC, Lapeer, Mich., 1981-85; news dir. Sta. WMPC, Lapeer, 1985—; pres. Franzen Radio Prodns., Lapeer, 1984—. Author: Improving Media Relations, 1986, Lapeer County Sesquicentennial Reader, 1987; spl. writer The Detroit News, 1985—; columnist Lapeer County Press, 1985—. Mem. exec. com. Reps. Lapeer County, 1986. Mem. Lapeer Jaycees (v.p. community devel. 1986). Office: Franzen Radio Prodns 1840 Brookfield Lapeer MI 48446

FRAPPIER, CARA MUNSHAW, school social worker; b. Grand Rapids, Mich., Feb. 13, 1942; d. Carroll Lambert and Ruth (Switzer) Munshaw; m. Calvin Leslie Frappier, July 30, 1966; 1 child, Arielle. BA, Mich. State U., 1963, MA, 1966, MSW, 1973. Lic. social worker, marriage and family counselor, Mich. Elem. tchr. Lansing (Mich.) Pub. Schs., 1963-65; sch. social worker Ingham Intermediate Sch. Dist., Mason, Mich., 1965—; bd. dirs. profl. staff assn. Ingham Intermediate Pub. Schs., 1981-85. Mem. Nat. Assn. Social Workers, Am. Assn. Marriage and Family Counselors, Am. Orthopsychiat. Assn., Mich. Sch. Social Workers Assn. Democrat. Avocations: downhill skiing, sailing. Home: 11219 Stoney Brook Dr Grand Ledge MI 48837 Office: Ingham Intermediate Sch Dist 2630 W Howell Rd Mason MI 48854

FRASCA, NEIL DONALD, pharmacist; b. Youngstown, Ohio, Oct. 17, 1942; s. Andrew Dan and Lucy (Nigro) F.; m. Angelina Marsilio, Nov. 5, 1966; children—Neil Daniel, Theresa Marie, Christine Louise. B.S. in Pharmacy, Ohio No. U., 1965; postgrad. bus. studies Youngstown State U., 1970-77. Asst. mgr. Thrift Drug Store, Canfield, Ohio, 1965-66, Niles, Ohio, 1966-67; pharmacist Youngstown Hosp., 1967-74; chief pharmacist Youngstown Hosp. Assn. North, 1974-78; pharmacist Youngstown Hosp. Assn. South, 1978—. Fin. sec. Austintown Band Parent Assn., Ohio, 1983-85, treas., 1985-87, fin. sec., 1987—. Mem. Ohio Pharm. Assn., Eastern Ohio Pharm. Assn., Soc. for Preservation and Encouragement of Barbershop Singing in Am. (treas. 1980—). Democrat. Roman Catholic. Avocations: piano; singing. Home: 2613 Birchwood Dr Youngstown OH 44515 Office: Youngstown Hosp Assn South Oak Hill Ave Youngstown OH 44501

FRASER, CAROLYN BONDY, financial analyst; b. Garland, Tex., July 27, 1956; d. Douglas Edward and Betty Marie (Ross) Bondy. BS, Oral Robert U., 1978; M, Am. Grad. Sch. Internat. Mgmt., 1981. CPA, Ill. Collector Bank of Oklahoma, Tulsa, 1978-79; bus. analyst Dun & Bradstreet, Tulsa, 1979-80; staff acountant Ericsson, Inc., Greenwich, Conn., 1982-84; fin. analyst Service Master Industries, Downers Grove, Ill., 1984-86, Ameritech Mobile, Schaumburg, Ill., 1986—. Avocations: reading, traveling. Home: 2950 Juniper Ct Aurora IL 60504 Office: Ameritech Mobile 1515 Woodfield Rd Schaumburg IL 60195

FRASER, DONALD MACKAY, mayor, former congressman; b. Mpls., Feb. 20, 1924; s. Everett and Lois (MacKay) F.; m. Arvonne Skelton, June 30, 1950; children: Thomas Skelton, Mary MacKay, John DuFrene, Lois MacKay, Anne T. (dec.), Jean Skelton. B.A. cum laude, U. Minn., 1944, LL.B., 1948. Bar: Minn. 1948. Practiced in Mpls., 1948-62; partner firm Lindquist, Fraser & Magnuson (and predecessors), 1950-62; mem. Minn. Senate, 1954-62; sec. Senate Liberal Caucus, 1955-62; mem. 88th-95th congresses from 5th Dist. Minn.; mem. internat. relations com., chmn. subcom. on internat. orgn., mem. budget com.; mayor of 88th-95th congresses from 5th Dist. Minn., Mpls., 1980—; mem. study and rev. com. Democratic Caucus; mem. Commn. on Role and Future Presdl. Primaries, 1976—; Vice chmn., dir. Mpls. Citizens Com. on Pub. Edn., 1950-54; Sec. Minn. del. Democratic Nat. Conv., 1960; chmn. Minn. Citizens for Kennedy, 1960; mem. platform com. Dem. Nat. Conv., 1964, mem. rules com., 1972, 76; chmn. Nat. Com. Tithing in Investment, 1964-72; vice chmn. Com. Dem. Selection Presdl. Nominees, 1968; chmn. Democratic Study Group Congress, 1969-71, Commn. on Party Structure and Del. Selection Dem. Party, 1971-72; 1st Am. co-chmn. Anglo-Am. Parliamentary Conf. on Africa, 1964; mem. U.S. del. 7th spl. session and 30th session UN Gen. Assembly, 1975; Congl. adviser to U.S. del. to UN Conf. on Disarmament, 1967-73, to U.S. del. to 3d Law of Sea Conf., 1972, to UN Commn. on Human Rights, 1974. Served as lt. (j.g.) USNR, 1944-46. Mem. Mpls. Fgn. Policy Assn. (pres. 1952-53), Citizens League Greater Mpls. (sec. 1951-54), Minn., Hennepin County bar assns., Ams. for Dem. Action (nat. chmn. 1973-76), Dem. Conf. (nat. chmn. 1976—), U. Minn. Law Alumni Assn. (dir. 1958-61), Univ. Dist. Improvement Assn. (pres.). Office: Office of Mayor City Hall Minneapolis MN 55415 *

FRASER, GEORGE C., auto dealer; b. Bklyn., May 1, 1945; s. Walter F. and Ida F.; m. Nora J. Spencer, Sept. 7, 1973; children—George II, Scott. Student NYU, 1963-66. Sales mgr. Ency. Brittannica Co., Cleve., 1968-70; pres. Black Ednl. Devel Co., Cleve., 1970-72; unit sales mgr. Procter & Gamble Co., Westlake, Ohio, 1972-84; dir. mktg. United Way of Cleve., 1984-87; dealer devel. Ford Motor Co., Mayfield Heights, Ohio, 1987—. Exec. chmn. United Negro Coll. Fund Telethon, 1982-83; pres. The Leader Source Group; trustee Goodwill Industries, Great Lakes Theatre Festival, Clean Land, Ohio, Nat. Jr. Tennis League; bd. dirs. Operation Alert; active Freedom Fund com., NAACP, Urban League Luncheon Com.; past bd. dirs. Ohio Jr. Olympics, Ohio Domestic Registry, Karamm Theatre; mem. Leadership Cleve. '83. Named Nat. Telethon Vol. of Yr., United Negro Coll. Fund, 1982, 83, One of Most Interesting People in Cleve., Cleve. Mag., 1984, 87, One of Outstanding Young Men Am., 1982. Mem. Black Profl. Assn. (trustee). Club: Racqueteers Racquetball (pres.). Home: 31201 Ainsworth Dr Pepper Pike OH 44124 Office: Ford Motor Co 6200 Mayfield Rd Mayfield Heights OH 44124

FRASER, JOHN FOSTER, management company executive; b. Saskatoon, Sask., Sept. 19, 1930; s. John Black and Florence May (Foster) F.; m. Valerie Georgina Ryder, June 21, 1952; children: John Foster Jr., Lisa Ann. B.Commerce, U. Sask., 1952. Pres. Empire Freightways Ltd., Saskatoon, Sask., 1952-60, Empire Oil Ltd., Saskatoon, 1960-62, Hanford Drewitt Ltd., Winnipeg, 1962-69, Norcom Homes Ltd., Mississauga, Ont., 1969-78; pres., chief exec. officer Fed. Industries Ltd., Winnipeg, 1978—, also bd. dirs.; bd. dirs. Bank of Montreal, Investors Group, Inc., Inter-City Gas Corp., Greater Winnipeg Gas Co., Thomson Newspapers Ltd., Can. Motorways Ltd., Thunder Bay Terminals Ltd., Standard Aero, Ltd., Can. Corp. Mgmt. Co., Ltd., Bus. Council Nat. Issues, The Conf. Bd. Can., Wirth Ltd.; chmn. bd. dirs. White Pass and Yukon Corp., Ltd., Russelsteel, Inc., Drummond-McCall Inc. Bd. dirs. Winnipeg Symphony Orch.; chmn. bd. Council for Bus. and Arts in Can.; bd. dirs., founding chmn. Assocs. Faculty of Mgmt. Studies U. Man.; bd. dirs. Can. Council for Native Bus., Council for Can. Unity; past pres. Man. Theatre Centre, Can. Manfuctered Housing Inst.; past bd. govs. St. John's Ravenscourt Sch., Winnipeg; mem. cultural rev. policy com. Province of Man., 1979. Recipient Peter D. Curry award U. Man., 1984, Outstanding Bus. Achievement award as Citizen of Yr. Man. C. of C., 1984. Mem. Am. Mgmt. Assn. (pres.'s assn.). Progressive Conservative. Presbyterian. Clubs: Manitoba, Royal Lake of the Woods Yacht, York, Toronto. Avocations: boating, reading. Home: 900-237 Wellington Crescent, Winnipeg, MB Canada R3M 0A1 Office: Fed Industries Ltd, 1 Lombard Pl, Winnipeg, MB Canada R3B 0X3

FRASIER, RALPH KENNEDY, banker, lawyer; b. Winston-Salem, N.C., Sept. 16, 1938; s. LeRoy Benjamin and Kathryn O. (Kennedy) F.; m. Jeannine Quick, Aug. 1981; children: Karen D. Frasier-Money, Gail S. Frasier Griffin, Ralph Kennedy Jr., Keith L., Marie K., Rochelle D. B.S., N.C. Central U., Durham, 1962, J.D., 1965. Bar: N.C. 1965, Ohio 1976. With Wachovia Bank and Trust Co., N.A., Winston-Salem, 1965-70; v.p., counsel Wachovia Bank and Trust Co., N.A., 1969-70; asst. counsel, v.p. parent co. Wachovia Corp., 1970-75; v.p., gen. counsel Huntington Nat. Bank, Columbus, Ohio, 1975—; sr. v.p. Huntington Nat. Bank, 1976-83, sec., 1981—, exec. v.p., 1983—, cashier, 1983—; v.p., gen. counsel Huntington Bancshares Inc., 1976—, sec., 1981—; sec., dir. Huntington Mortgage Co., Huntington State Bank, Huntington Leasing Co., Huntington Bancshares Fin. Corp., Huntington Investment Mgmt. Co., Scioto Life Ins. Co., Huntington Co., 1976—; v.p., asst. sec. Huntington Bank N.E. Ohio, 1982-84. Bd. dirs. Family Services Winston-Salem, 1966-74, sec., 1966-71, 74, v.p., 1974; chmn. Winston-Salem Transit Authority, 1974-75; bd. dirs. Research for Advancement of Personalities, 1968-71, Winston-Salem Citizens for Fair Housing, 1970-74, N.C. United Community Services, 1970-74; treas. Forsyth County (N.C.) Citizens Com. Adequate Justice Bldg., 1968; trustee Appalachian State U., Boone, N.C., 1973-83, trustee endowment fund, 1973—; trustee, vice chmn. Employment and Edn. Commn. Franklin County, 1981-85; mem. Winston-Salem. Forsyth County Sch. Bd. Adv. Council, 1973-74, Atty. Gen. Ohio Task Force Minorities in Bus., 1977-78; bd. dirs. Inroads Columbus, Inc., 1986—, Greater Columbus Arts Council, 1986—. Served with AUS, 1958-60. Mem. ABA, Nat. Bar Assn., Ohio Bar Assn., Columbus Bar Assn., Columbus Urgan League. Address: Huntington Bancshares Inc 41 S High St PO Box 1558 Columbus OH 43260

FRAUENHOFFER, JOHN ANTON, structural engineer; b. Highland Park, Ill., Mar. 2, 1953; s. Anton Peter and Helen Irene (Dowse) F.; m. Elizabeth Sue Meier, Aug. 15, 1976 (dec. Nov. 1977); 1 child, Jamie; m. Patricia Ann Busick, Feb. 12, 1983; children: Matthew, Gant, Jamie. BSCE, U. Ill., 1975, MS in Structural Engring., 1979. Registered profl. structural engr., Ill. Structural engr. Clark Dietz Inc., Urbana, Ill., 1974-80; pres. John Frauenhoffer and Assocs., Champaign, Ill., 1980—. Trustee First Presbyn. Ch., Champaign. Recipient Young Engrs. Achievement award U. Ill., 1985. Mem. Am. Soc. Civil Engrs. (chmn. 1985—), Ill. Soc. Profl. Engrs. (v.p. 1987), Ill. Soc. Civil Engrs. (Young Engr. Yr. award 1985), Am. Concrete Inst. Presbyterian. Office: Frauenhoffer and Assocs 702 Bloomington Rd Champaign IL 61820

FRAZER, MARILEE HELEN, pathologist; b. Wilmington, Del., Nov. 20, 1953; d. August Henry and Christine (Hoover) F. BA in Biol. Scis., U. Del., 1975; MD, Jefferson Med. Coll., 1978. Diplomate Am. Bd. Anatomic Pathology, Am. Bd. Forensic Pathology. Dep. coroner Cuyahoga County Coroner's Office, Cleve., 1983-84; asst. med. examiner Wayne County Med. Examiner's Office, Detroit, 1984—. Fellow Am. Coll. Pathology; mem. Nat. Assn. Med. Examiners, Am. Acad. Forensic Scis. Office: Wayne County Med Examiners Office 400 E Lafayette Detroit MI 48226

FRAZER, WENDY, nurse, physician's assistant; b. Steubenville, Ohio, June 3, 1943; d. Richard William and Mary Elizabeth (Sliday) F. RN, Beaver Valley Gen. Hosp., New Brighton, Pa., 1964; AAS, Cuyahoga Community Coll., 1983. RN, Ohio, Pa. Pediatrics nurse Cleve. Clinic Found., 1962-65; asst. head nurse Cardiovascular Lab., 1965-73; surg. nurse clinician cardiothoracic surgery Cleve. Clinic Found., 1978—, nurse clinician gen. thoracic surgery, 1986—; admissions officer Lakewood Hosp., 1984-85; mem. steering com. Master's Group of Phoenix Ctr., 1986; physician asst. membership com. Alumnus Assn., 1986. Assoc. founder, counselor Inst. Creative Living, 1976-80. Mem. Nat. Acad. Physician Assts., Nat. Assn. Cardiovascular Physician Assts., Ohio Assn. Physician Assts., Cleve. Zool. Soc., Cleve. Mus. Art, Holden Arboretum, Nat. Geog. Soc., Smithsonian Soc. Republican. Baptist. Office: Cleveland Clinic Foundation 9500 Euclid Ave Cleveland OH 44106

FRAZIER, THOMAS P., dentist; b. Portsmouth, Ohio, Aug. 21, 1933; s. James Hamilton and Louise Marion (Kreger) F.; m. Martha Jane Farry, Sept. 27, 1958; children: Diane, Paula, David. Student, Wilmington Coll., 1951-53; DDS, Ohio State U., 1958. Practice dentistry Centerville, Ohio, 1962—. Mem. Centerville Charter Commn., 1967. Served to capt. USAF, 1958-62. Named Citizen of South Suburbs, Keys Realty, 1978, Layman of Yr., YMCA, 1979. Mem. ADA, Ohio Dental Assn. (del. 1982—, dist. rep. 1986—), Dayton Dental Soc. (pres. 1981-82), Pierre Fauchard Acad. Republican. Presbyterian. Lodge: Optimist (gov. 1975-76, v.p. 1981-82, named disting. and outstanding gov. 1976). Avocations: music, golf, bridge. Home: 5540 Woodbridge Ln Dayton OH 45429

FREAS, GUY JAMES, teacher; b. Amherst, Ohio, Mar. 14, 1962; s. Brian Gilbert Freas and Donna Maxine (Griffin) McKinney; m. Rebecca Lynn Masters, July 16, 1983. BE, U. Akron, 1984. Cert. spl. edn. tchr., Ohio. Tchr. spl. edn. Galion (Ohio) City Schs., 1984—, home instr., 1984—. Community chmn. Muscular Dystrophy Assn., Toledo, 1985; mem. adv. council Sara Beegle Child Day Care Ctr., 1985—, Independent Living Services Program, 1987; v.p. Galion Edn. Assn., 1987—; coach Ohio Spl. Olympics Devel. Sports, 1987. Mem. Nat. Assn. Physically Handicapped (pres. Crawford Tri-County chpt. 1985). Democrat. Home: 216 S Columbus St Galion OH 44833 Office: Renschville Elem Sch 969 Winchester Rd Galion OH 44833

FRECH, ROBERT ADOLPH, banker; b. Chgo., July 24, 1924; s. Robert L.D. and Adolphina (Umbricht) F.; Anna Mae Behrens, June 25, 1949; children: Roger W., William R. BS in Mgmt. with honors, U. Ill., 1949. Mgr. charge accounts Marshall Field & Co., Chgo., 1949-80; chmn. bd. Carpentersville (Ill.) Savs. Bank, 1980-83, First Comml. Bank of Rolling Meadows, Ill., 1983—; pres. Marshall Field & Co. Employee's Credit Union, 1963-64; v.p., bd. dirs. McIntosh Ltd., Rolling Meadows, 1986; chmn., pres. McIntosh Ltd.-Leisure, Crystal Lake, Ill., 1986; v.p., bd. dirs. Plum Grove Bancorp., Rolling Meadows, 1986—. Bd. govs. Northwest Community

Health Services Found., Arlington Heights, Ill., past bd. dirs. Lutheran Gen. Hosp. Men's Assn., Park Ridge, Ill., Dir. 1973-76. Mem. Ill. Bankers Assn. (chmn., bank dirs. commn. 1987), Midwest Assn. of Credit Unions (past mem. exec. com., past bd. dirs.), Rolling Meadows C. of C. (bd. dirs. 1983—), Econ. Devel. Council of Chgo., Kappa Delta Rho. Clubs. Chgo. Farmers (bd. dirs. 1981-83); Meadows (Rolling Meadows); Turnberry Country (Lakewood, Ill.). Home: 1479 Shire Circle Inverness IL 60067 Office: First Comml Bank 2801 Algonquin Rd Rolling Meadows IL 60008

FRECKA, JOHN ALLISON, corporation executive; b. Ironton, Ohio, Jan. 12, 1929; s. James Harold and Margaret Helena (Fowler) F.; m. Lois Joann Williams, Sept. 23, 1950; children—Deborah, David, John, Mary Anne. B.S., Marshall U., 1950; J.D., Wayne State U., 1967. Bar: Mich. 1967. With personnel mgmt. dept. Detroit Strip div. Cyclops Corp., 1951-64, turn supt., 1964-68, gen. supt., 1969-73, gen. mgr., 1974-76; v.p. Empire-Detroit Steel div. Cyclops Corp., Mansfield, Ohio, 1976-78; pres. Cyclops Corp., 1979—, pres. Detroit Strip div., 1986—; bd. dirs. Plymouth Locomotive, Bank I Mansfield. Mem. adv. bd. Mansfield Gen. Hosp.; mem. exec. council Boy Scouts Am. Trustee Richland Found., Mansfield, 1985—. Mem. Mich. Bar Assn., Mansfield C. of C. (bd. dirs. 1984—). Club: Westbrook Country. Home: 2065 Matthes Dr Mansfield OH 44906 Office: Empire-Detroit Steel Div Bowman St Mansfield OH 44906

FREDERICK, JOSEPH BRUCE, banker; b. Louisville, Ky., Apr. 14, 1955; s. George Leonard and Darlene Marjorie (Beeler) F.; m. Jase Ann Greenquist, July 31, 1986. BA, U. Wis., 1977; grad., Agr. Lending Sch., 1979, Prochnow Graduate Sch. Banking, 1983. Asst. v.p. Citizen's First State Bank, Walnut, Ill., 1977-80; v.p. Bank of Plover, Wis., 1980-86, 1st Nat. Bank of LaGrange, Ill., 1986—; bd. dirs. Citizens Bankshares, Walnut, Frederick Farms Inc., Walnut. Bd. dirs. Stevens Point (Wis.) Area Wellness Commn., 1984-86. Mem. Plover Area Bus Assn. (pres. 1985), Portage County Bankers Assn. (pres. 1986), Cen. Wis. C.of C. (treas. 1986). Lodge: Lions. Avocation: jogging. Home: 632 S 8th Ave LaGrange IL 60525-6710 Office: 1st Nat Bank LaGrange 620 W Burlington LaGrange IL 60525

FREDERICK, LARRY J., savings and loan executive; b. Norman, Okla., Oct. 1, 1943; s. William Allan and Pauline L. (Sheen) F.; m. Betty J. Jensen, Aug. 22, 1965; children: Kera K., Matthew J. BA, Kearney (Nebr.) State Coll., 1966; grad. sch. cert., Ind. U., 1977. CPA, Nebr. Acct. Philip G. Johnson and Co., Lincoln, Nebr., 1966-73; sr. v.p. Am. Charter Fed. Savs. and Loan, Beatrice and Lincoln, Nebr., 1973-81; exec. v.p. Am. Charter Fed. Savs. and Loan, Lincoln, 1982—. Bd. dirs. YMCA, Lincoln, 1980—; pres. Nebr. Basketball Boosters, Lincoln, 1984—; v.p. Nebr. Aquatics, Lincoln, 1984. Mem. Am. Inst. CPA's, Nebr. Soc. CPA's, Midwest Savs. Conf. (bd. dirs. 1986—), Nebr. League of Savs. Insts. (bd. dirs. 1981-84), Lincoln C. of C. Lodge: Elks.

FREDERICK, MICHAEL ALAN, veterinarian; b. Cin., June 9, 1952; s. Cloyd and Ruth Frederick; m. Ann Louise Kluesener, Mar. 5, 1983. DVM, Ohio State U., 1976. Veterinarian Agri Pet Vet Service, Hamilton, Ohio, 1976-78, Monfort Heights Animal Clinic, Cin., 1978-85; house-call veterinarian Mobile Vet Service, Cleves, Ohio, 1985-86; owner Miamitown (Ohio) Pet Hosp., 1986—. Mem. Ohio Vet. Med. Assn., Cin. Vet. Med. Assn., Am. Assn. Bovine Practitioners, Am. Assn. Equine Practitioners, Phi Zeta. Avocations: scuba diving, flying, woodworking. Office: Miamitown Pet Hosp 5990 Rt 128 Cleves OH 45002

FREDERICK, THOMAS EDWARD, national athletic association executive; b. Milw., May 15, 1924; s. Roland Hubbard and Kathern (Fleming) F.; m. Betty Jane Haggard, Sept. 4, 1943; children: Thomas, David, Bonnie. BS, U. Wis., 1948, MS, 1951. Tchr., coach Waterloo (Wis.) High Sch., 1948-50; athletic dir., coach Barrington (Ill.) High Sch., 1950-63; asst. exec. sec. Ill. High Sch. Assn., Chgo., 1963-67; assoc. dir. Nat. Fedn. State High Sch. Assns., Kansas City, Mo., 1967—; v.p. U.S. Track and Field Fedn., Tucson, 1969-81; bd. dirs. Nat. Track and Filed Hall of Fame, Charleston, W.Va., 1975-79. Editor, publisher Ill. Coaches Directory, 1957-63. Commr. Barrington Park Dist., 1961-67; pres. Liberty (Mo.) Hills Homeowners Assn., 1983-85. Served to sgt. U.S. Army, 1943-45, ETO. Recipient Sports award Nat. Fedn. Football Rules Com., 1977; inducted into Ill. Football Coaches' Hall of Fame, Ill. Football Coaches Assn., 1981. Mem. Am. Soc. Assn. Execs., Nat. Interscholastic Athletic Adminstrs. Assn. (exec. sec. 1967—, bd. dirs. 1986—, Merit award 1980). Roman Catholic. Club: Liberty Hills Country. Avocation: golf. Office: Nat Fedn State High Sch Assns 11724 Plaza Circle PO Box 20626 Kansas City MO 64195

FREDERICKS, HENRY JACOB, lawyer; b. St. Louis, Dec. 1, 1925; s. Henry Jacob III and Mary Elizabeth (Pieron) F.; m. Marjorie Helen Kiely, 1951 (div. 1962); children: Joseph Henry, James Andrew, Elizabeth Ann.; m. Susan Kay Brennecke, 1971; 1 child, William Michael. JD, St. Louis U., 1950; postgrad., Sch. Commerce and Fin., 1945-47. Bar: Mo. 1950, U.S. Dist. Ct. (ea. dist.) Mo., U.S. Dist. Ct. (so. dist.) Fla., U.S. Ct. Appeals (8th cir.), U.S. Supreme Ct. Sole practice St. Louis County, 1950—; assoc. Mark D. Eagleton, St. Louis, 1960, Goldenhersh Fredericks & Newman, St. Louis, 1961-69, Friedman and Fredericks, St. Louis, 1969-81; chief trial atty for cir. atty. St. Louis, 1955, 1st asst. to cir. atty., 1957, spl. asst to cir. atts., 1960-81; asst. atty. U.S. Dist. Ct. (ea. dist.) Mo.; lectr. in field. Mem. Mo. Athletic Commn., 1974-76, boxing chmn. Mo. Athletic Commn. and AAU, 1977. Served with USAAF, 1943-46, ETO. Decorated Air medal with 4 battle stars. Mem. ABA, Mo. Bar Assn., St. Louis County Bar Assn., Am. Trial Lawyers Assn., Internat. Platform Assn., Delta Theta Phi. Home: 2243 Whitby Rd Clarkson Valley MO 63017 Office: US Ct and Custom House Office US Atty Saint Louis MO 63101

FREDERICKS, MARSHALL MAYNARD, sculptor; b. Rock Island, Ill., Jan. 31, 1908; s. Frank A. and Frances Margaret (Bragg) F.; m. Rosalind Bell Cooke, Sept. 9, 1943; children: Carl Marshall and Christopher Matzen (twins), Frances Karen Bell, Rosalind Cooke, Suzanne Pelletreau. Student, John Huntington Poly. Inst., Cleve.; grad., Cleve. Sch. Art, 1930; student, Heimann Schule, Schwegerle Schule, Munich, Germany, Academie Scandinav, Paris, France; pvt. studies, Copenhagen, Rome and London, Carl Milles' Studio, Stockholm, Sweden; student, Cranbrook Acad. Art; 3 hon. doctorate degrees in fine arts. Faculty Cleve. Sch. Art, 1931, Cranbrook Sch., Bloomfield Hills, Mich., 1932-38; Kingswood Sch., Cranbrook, 1932-42, Cranbrook Acad. Art, Bloomfield Hills, Mich., 1932-42; Royal Danish consul. for, Mich. Local, nat., internat. exhbns. art since 1928 include, Carnegie Inst., Pitts., Cleve. Mus., Pa. Acad., Chgo. Art Inst., Whitney Mus. Am. Art Nat. Invitational, Detroit Art Inst., Denver Mus., Phila. Internat. Invitational, N.Y. World's Fair Am. art exhbn., Modern Sculpture Internat. Exhbn. Detroit, Internat. Sculpture Show Cranbrook Mus., AIA, Nat. Sculpture Soc., Archtl. League of N. Y., Mich. Acad., Brussels, Belgium, others; commns. include Vets. Meml. Bldg, Detroit, adminstrn. bldg. war meml., U. Mich., Louisville Courier-Jour. Bldg, Jefferson Sch., Wyandotte, Mich., Holy Ghost Sem., Ann Arbor, Mich.; State Dept. Fountain, Washington, Cleve. War Meml. Fountain, Milw. Pub. Mus. Sculpture, N.Y. World's Fair permanent sculpture, Fed. Bldg. sculpture, Cin., Community Nat. Bank, Pontiac, Mich., Sir Winston Churchill Meml., Freeport, Bahamas; union bldg., Freeport, Bahamas; J.L. Hudson's Eastland, Northland, and Flint (Mich.) Mall, Two Sister fountain, Cranbrook, Michigan, Dallas Library sculpture, Henry Ford Meml., Dearborn, Mich., Oakland U., Saints and Sinners Fountain, Midland Center for Arts, Crittenton Hosp., Rochester, Fgn. Ministry Copenhagen, Freedom of the Human Spirit, Shain Park, Birmingham, Mich., 1986, Wings of the Morning, Kirk-in-the-Hills, Bloomfield Hills, Mich., 1986, many others; portrait commns. include Willard Dow, Midland, Mich., George G. Booth Meml., Cranbrook, Mrs. Horace Rackham Meml, Pres. John F. Kennedy, Yoshita, others; works included numerous museums, pvt., civic collections. Mem. Pres.'s Com. for Employment of Handicapped; mem. Gov.'s State Capitol Com.; co-founder, dir. DIADEM Program for Internat. Exchange of Handicapped.; Trustee Am.-Scandinavian Found., People-to-People Program, Inc. Served with C.E. U.S. Army, 1942-44; lt. col. 20th bomber command; 8th Air Force 1944-45, Okinawa. Decorated knight Order of Dannebrog, also officer 1st class, comdr. Order Dannebrog (Denmark); knights cross 1st class Order of St. Olav (Norway); recipient of 1st prize Cleve. Mus. Art, 1931; Anna Scripps Whitcomb prize Detroit Inst. Arts, 1938; 1st prize internat. exhbn. Dance Internat., Rockefeller Center, N.Y.C.; 1st prize Barbour Meml. nat. competition; medal Mich. Inst. Architects; gold medal Achtl. League of N.Y.; Golden Plate award Am. Acad. Achievement; citation Mich. Assn. Professions; citation Nat. Soc. Interior Designers; citation Internat. Com. of Internat. Ctr. Disabled; citation U. Detroit; President's Cabinet award U. Detroit, 1973, 1st prize NAD 160th Ann. Exhbn., 1985, Am. Soc. Landscape Architects award, 1987; other Am. and fgn. awards and decorations. Fellow Internat. Inst. Arts and Letters, Royal Soc. Arts, Nat. Sculpture Soc. (Henry Heriog medal, Herbert Adams Medal, Medal of Honor 1985, bd. dirs., 1st v.p. Brookgreen Gardens); mem. Mich. Soc. Architects (hon.), Federation Internationale de la Medaille, AIA (fine arts gold medal 1952, Gold Medal), St. Dunstans Dramatic Guild, Mich. Acad. Sci., Arts and Letters (gold medal honor 1953), Nat. Acad. Design (academician, Agop Agopoff award 1987), C. of C., Am. Soc. Interior Designers, Mich. Assn. Professions, Nat. Soc. Interior Designers, Beta Sigma Phi, Alpha Beta Delta. Clubs: Royal Swedish Yacht, Orchard Lake Country; Architectural League N.Y. (N.Y.C.); Prismatic (Detroit); Royal Norwegian Yacht, Royal Danish Yacht. Studio: 4113 N Woodward Ave Royal Oak MI 48053 also: East Long Lake Road Bloomfield Hills MI 48013

FREDERICKS, NORMAN JOHN, bank executive; b. Detroit, Feb. 12, 1914; s. George John and Mayme (Koenig) F.; m. Lois Foley, Apr. 15, 1939; children: Norman J. Jr., Lois F. Thornbury, Marcia F. McGratty, J. Richard, Anne G., Peter G. AB, U. Notre Dame, 1935; JD, U. Mich., 1938. Bar: Mich. 1938. Dir. Bank of Commerce, Hamtramck, Mich., 1952—, chmn., 1977—; chmn. Commerce Bancorp, Hamtramck, 1983—; sec.-treas. Koenig Fuel and Supply Co., 1942-57, pres., 1957-80, chmn. bd. dirs., 1980-83, also bd. dirs.; bd. dirs. State Bank of Fraser (Mich.), Security Bancorp. Mem. Nat. Ready Mixed Concrete Assn. (bd. dirs. exec. com., past pres.). Roman Catholic. Clubs: Detroit Athletic (bd. dirs. 1957-63, pres. 1963-64); Bloomfield Hills Country (bd. dirs. 1954-61). Avocation: sports. Home: 4219 Lahser Rd Bloomfield Hills MI 48013 Office: Commerce Bancorp Inc 11300 Jos Campau Ave Hamtramck MI 48212

FREDERICKS, NORMAN JOHN, JR., oil and gravel mining executive; b. Detroit, Feb. 15, 1940; s. Norman J. Sr. and Lois (Foley) F.; m. Marjorie E. Toth, Feb. 6, 1965; children: Norman III, Jill, Susan. BSBA, Georgetown U., 1962. Pres. Koenig Fuel and Supply, Detroit, 1962—; bd. dirs. Bank of Commerce, Hamtramck, Mich. Mem. Nat. Ready Mixed Concrete Assn. (officer, bd. dirs., pres. 1972). Republican. Roman Catholic. Club: Detroit Athletic (dir. 1980-86). Avocation: sports. Home: 319 Puritan Birmingham MI 48009 Office: Koenig Fuel and Supply Co 500 E 7 Mile Rd Detroit MI 48203

FREDERICKSON, DENNIS RUSSEL, state legislator, farmer; b. Morgan, Minn., July 27, 1939; s. Louis Bernard and Mary (Kragh) F.; m. Marjorie Davidson, July 15, 1961; children: Kari, Karl, Disa. BS, U. Minn., 1961. Farmer Morgan, 1967—; commr. Redwood County, Minn., 1973-80; mem. Minn. State Senate, St. Paul, 1981—; bd. dirs. Redwood Electric Coop. Author: (with others) The Fairy Tale Grim of Prince Perp, 1986. Served to lt. comdr. USN, 1962-67. Mem. Farm Bur., S.W. Farm Mgmt. Assn., Council for Agr. Sci. and Tech. Republican. Presbyterian. Lodge: Lions (pres. Morgan chpt. 1977). Avocation: running. Home: Rural Rt 1 Box 49 Morgan MN 56266 Office: Minn Senate State Office Bldg Room 143 Saint Paul MN 55155

FREDERIKSEN, BJARNE, product and graphic design company executive; b. Copenhagen, Aug. 27, 1954; Came to U.S., 1966; s. Peter Torben and Annette (Jensen) F.; m. Christine Diane Haworth, May 15, 1982. BA in Indsl. Design, U. Ill., Chgo., 1979. Pres. Frederiksen Design, Inc., Villa Park, Ill., 1980—; v.p., chmn. bd. Inotek, Inc., Glen EL1yn, Ill. Patentee in field. Grantee Fredrik Law Olmstead Soc., Riverside, Ill., 1973-74. Avocations: bicycling, model making, travel. Office: Frederiksen Design Inc 609 S Riverside Dr Villa Park IL 60181

FREDERIKSEN, MARILYNN ELIZABETH CONNERS, physician; b. Chgo., Sept. 12, 1949; d. Paul H. and Susanne (Ostergren) Conners; m. James W. Frederiksen, July 11, 1971; children: John Karl, Paul S., Britt L. BA, Cornell Coll., 1970; MD, Boston U., 1974. cert. subspecialist maternal fetal medicine, 1983. Instr. ob-gyn. Northwestern U., Chgo., 1981-83, asst. prof. ob-gyn., assoc. clin. pharmacology, 1983—; Mem. Ob-gyn. adv. panel 1985-90 USP Com. of Revision, Rockville, Md., 1986—. Contbr. numerous articles to profl. jours. Bd. dirs. Cornell Coll. Alumni Assn., Mt. Vernon, Iowa, 1986—. Recipient Pharm. Mfrs. Assn. Found. Faculty Devel. award, 1984-86; grantee NIH. Fellow Am. Coll. Ob-Gyn. (cert.); mem. Soc. Perinatal Obstericians, Cen. Assn. Obstetricians and Gynecologists, Chgo. Gynecologic Soc., Phi Beta Kappa. Republican. Episcopalian. Avocations: gardening, needlework. Home: 2002 Devon Park Ridge IL 60068 Office: Northwestern U 333 E Superior Chicago IL 60611

FREDETTE, DIANE KAUFMAN, architect; b. Middletown, Ohio, Apr. 13, 1956; d. John Michael and Betty (Reddington) Kaufman; m. Russel John Fredette, June 10, 1978. Student, Oxford U., Eng., 1975; BS in Architecture, Ohio State U., 1978. Registered architect, Ohio. Architect Prindle & Patrick, Columbus, Ohio, 1978-79; project co-ordinator Karlsberger & Assoc., Inc., Columbus, 1979-85; project architect Bohm-NBBJ, Inc., Columbus, 1985—. Mem. nat. register com. Upper Arlington Hist. Soc., Columbus, 1983—, Sr. Concert Alumni Choir, Upper Arlington. Mem. AIA, Architect's Soc. Ohio, Nat. Council Archtl. Registration Bd. Clubs: Northam Tennis (Columbus), Olympic Indoor Tennis. Avocations: hist. renovation, tennis, travel, piano. Home: 1800 Cambridge Blvd Columbus OH 43212 Office: Bohm-NBBJ Inc 55 Nationwide Blvd Columbus OH 43215

FREDETTE, RUSSELL JOHN, architect; b. Saratoga Springs, N.Y., July 6, 1953; s. Duane Russell and Grace Katherin (Scully) F.; m. Diane Kaufman, June 10, 1978. AAS, Hudson Valley Coll., 1974; BS in Architecture, Ohio State U., 1978. Registered architect, Ohio, N.Y.; cert. architect Nat. Council Archtl. Registration Bd. Project coordinator Karlsberger & Assocs., Columbus, Ohio, 1978-83; project mgr. URS Dalton Inc, Columbus, 1983—, assoc., 1984—. Mem. AIA, Architects Soc. Ohio. Avocations: carpentry, music, history, sports, home restoration. Office: URS Dalton Inc 33 N High St Columbus OH 43215

FREDETTE, THOMAS STARK, oil company executive; b. Blue Island, Ill., May 15, 1944; s. Clarence Irwin and Irma Murial (Punt) F.; m. Sharon Jean Miller, May 7, 1966; 1 child, Renee. BS in Chemistry, Millikin U., 1963. Dir. employee relations Clark Oil and Refining Co., Blue Island, 1963—; cons. various labor groups, 1970-79; pres. CKO Ind. Union, Blue Island, 1970-76. Mem. sch. bd. Dist. 200U, Beecher, Ill., 1985—; bd. dirs. Great Lakes Refining Credit Union, Blue Island, 1972-78. Mem. Phi Mu Alpha. Lodge: Lions (sec. Beecher chpt. 1983-84).

FREDMAN-ZITLIN, SUSAN MIRIAM, interior designer; b. Chgo., Nov. 14, 1950; d. David Wolfe Fredman and Selma (Lobelson) Florio; m. Martin Zitlin, Jan. 28, 1984; 1 child, Amanda Beth. BS, Ill. State U., 1973. Display asst. Lane Bryant, Chgo., 1972-73, Lyttons, Chgo., 1973; asst. head visual merchandising Goldblatt's, Chgo., 1973-76; designer Advance Design Assocs., Chgo., 1976; prin. Susan Fredman & Assocs., Chgo., 1976—, Interior Accents Ltd., Highland Park, Ill., 1985—; bd. dirs. Seven-Thirty Network, 1980-85. Mem. steering com. women in professions and trades Jewish United Fund, 1984-85; mem. Hunger Project, Chgo., 1983; vol. Children's Meml. Hosp., Chgo., 1983; exec. com. audience devel. bd. Victory Gardens Theatre; team leader Auction for Prison Possibilities, Inc., 1987. Mem. Internat. Soc. Interior Designers (profl. mem., bd. dirs. 1984-85), "Material Girls" Investment Club. Club: East Bank (Chgo.).

FREDRICHSEN, RICHARD FREDRICK, marketing executive; b. Chgo., Mar. 4, 1934; s. Fredrick Wiliam and Mildred Willamina (Spruth) F.; m. Marilyn Ruth Schaffer, Dec. 26, 1956; children: Kris, Drew. BS in Edn., So. Ill. U., 1956. Cert. pub. communicator. Edcl. dir. Advance Trade Sch., Chgo., 1958-60; product mgr. Bear Brand Hosiery, Chgo., 1960-66; v.p. ops. Neumode Hosiery, Chgo., 1966-69; v.p. mktg. Wigwam Mills, Inc., Sheboygan, Wis., 1969—; curriculum advisor Lakeshore Tech. Inst., Cleve., 1975-80; publicity dir. Road Am., Run, Elkhart Lake, Wis., 1978—. Contbr. articles to profl. jours. Sustaining mem. Republican. Orgn., Wis., 1969—; mem. Am. Cancer Soc., Madison, 1978—. Served with U.S. Army, 1956-58. Recipient award of appreciation Nat. Collegiat Athletic Assn., 1978, U.S. Olympic Com., 1973-76, award for Participation, U.S. Collegiate Sports Council, 1979. Mem. Sheboygan C. of C. (promotional advisor), Bus. Profl. Advt. Assn. (award for Excellence 1983), Milw. Advt. Club (first award 1983), Printing Industries Am. (cert.), Nat. Sporting Goods Assn. (chmn. trade show commn. 1969—), Sporting Goods Mfrs. Assn., Iota Lambda Sigma. Republican. Club: Sheboygan Yacht (vice and rear commodore). Avocation: sailing. Office: Wigwam Mills Inc 3402 Crocker Ave Sheboygan WI 53082

FREDRICK, JAMES WALKER, architect; b. Alliance, Ohio, July 17, 1950; s. Delbert Glen and Vivian Pearl (Walker) F.; m. Elizabeth Ann Sprunger, Sept. 13, 1980; 1 child, James Walker Jr. BArch, Kent State U., 1974. Registered architect, Ohio, Pa., N.J. Ptnr. Graham Fredrick Group, Chagrin Falls, Ohio, 1977-79, Cohen Fredrick Architects, Akron, 1979-83; prin. James Fredrick Architect, Cleve., 1983—. Mem. City Archtl. Rev. Bd., Broadview Heights, Ohio, 1984—. Mem. AIA, Architects Soc. Ohio. Baptist. Club: BMW Am. (Cambridge, Mass.). Lodge: Order of DeMolay (life). Avocations: reading, performance auto enthusiast, softball. Office: 3425 Russett Dr Cleveland OH 44147

FREDRICK, ROBERT FRANK, manufacturing company representative; b. Chgo., Apr. 28, 1948; s. Frank Victor Fredrick and Ardelle Estelle (Black) Block; m. Kathleen Ann Westbrook, Dec. 18, 1971; 1 child, Jason. BA, No. Ill. U., 1969. Asst. store mgr. Lee Wards, Taylor, Mich., 1974-77; chief night crew Jewel Food Stores, Melrose Park, Ill., 1976-77; sales agt. Montgomery Ward, Yorkville, Ill., 1978-82; gen. mgr. Krueger & Krueger, Yorkville, 1981—. Mem. C. of C., Yorkville, 1979-81; bd. dirs. Countryside Mchts. Assn., Yorkville, 1981-82. Served with U.S. Army, 1970-72, Vietnam, with USAR, 1986—. Mem. Refrigeration Service Engrs. Soc. Republican. Baptist. Avocations: photography, woodworking. Home: Rural Rt 1 PO Box 3A Somonauk IL 60552 Office: Krueger & Krueger PO Box 206 Yorkville IL 60560

FREDRICKSON, GEORGE, retail store executive. Chmn. Lewis Drug Store, Sioux Falls, S.D. Office: Lewis Drug Store 309 S Phillips Ave Sioux Falls SD 57102 *

FREEBERSYVER, CRAIG JOSEPH, marketing executive; b. St. Louis, Dec. 22, 1960; s. Ronald Charles and Joan Minette (Zingg) F.; m. Janice Maureen Tierney, Oct. 27, 1984. BSBA in Mktg., U. Mo., St. Louis, 1983, MBA, 1984—. Mktg. research mgr. McDonnell Douglas Electronics Co., St. Charles, Mo., 1984—; cons. Jr. Achievement program Ft. Zumwalt High Sch., 1986. Mem. Am. Mktg. Assn., Alpha Mu Alpha. Republican. Mem. United Ch. Christ. Avocations: tennis, golf. Home: 1203 Mendoza Saint Peters MO 63376

FREEBORN, MICHAEL D., lawyer; b. Mpls., June 30, 1946; s. Andrew W. and Verena M. (Keller) F.; m. Nancie L. Siebel, Oct. 19, 1947; children—Christopher A., Nathan M., Joel C., Paul K. B.S., U.S. Air Force Acad., 1968; M.B.A., U. Chgo., 1975; J.D., Ind. U., 1972. Bar: Ill. 1972, Ind. 1972, Wis. 1983. Assoc., ptnr. Rooks, Pitts & Poust, Chgo., 1972-83; ptnr. Freeborn & Peters, Chgo., 1983—. Gen. editor: O.S.H.A. Law, 1981. Assoc. editor Ind. Law Rev., 1970-71. Contbr. articles to profl. jours. Chmn. citizens adv. council Ill. Coastal Zone Mgmt. Program, Chgo., 1979. Served as capt. USAF, 1968-72. Recipient Founders Day award Ind. U. Law Sch., 1972. Fellow Am. Coll. Environ. Lawyers; mem. Ill. Bar Assn., Ind. Bar Assn., Wis. Bar Assn. Republican. Lutheran. Clubs: Union League, Legal (Chgo.). Home: 122 S Kaspar Ave Arlington Heights IL 60005 Office: 11 S LaSalle St Suite 1500 Chicago IL 60603

FREED, ALAN DAVID, research scientist; b. Elkhorn, Wis., Mar. 18, 1954; s. David Adolph and Marian Helen (Schuchardt) F.; m. Sally Ann Wheelock, Sept. 4, 1974 (div. 1978); 1 child, Jennifer; m. Karen Louise Bradford, Sept. 6, 1980; children: Lee, Nickie. BS, U. Wis., 1978, MS, 1980, PhD, 1985. Asst. prof. U. N.H., Durham, 1984-85; reseach scientist NASA Lewis Research Ctr., Cleve., 1985—. Mem. ASME (assoc.), ASTM, Soc. Exptl. Mechanics, Tau Beta Pi, Sigma Xi. Republican. Morman. Home: 410 Front St Berea OH 44017 Office: NASA Lewis Research Ctr Box 49-7 Cleveland OH 44135

FREEDHEIM, DONALD KOPERLIK, psychology educator, clinical psychologist; b. Cleve., Aug. 31, 1932; s. Eugene H. and Mina K. Freedheim; m. Gerda Irene Kilian, Aug. 31, 1958; children—Amy Jean, Julie Kay, Sara Beth. A.B., Miami U., Oxford, Ohio, 1954; Ph.D., Duke U., 1960. Lic. psychologist, Ohio. Pvt. practice psychology, Cleve., 1963—; asst. prof. psychology Case Western Res. U., Cleve., 1965-69, assoc. prof., 1969—, clin. psychologist Mental Devel. Ctr., 1970-72, acting chmn. dept. psychology, 1970-72; staff psychologist Sonoma (Calif.) State Hosp., summer 1968; vis. assoc. prof. Tel Aviv U., 1974-75; mem. devel. behavioral scis. study sect. NIH, 1970-74; cons. in field. Trustee Montefiore Home, Cleveland Heights, 1964-69, 76—, Jewish Community Fedn., Cleve., 1971-74, 80—, Cleve. Jewish News, 1980—, Cleve. Internat. Program, 1979—; pres. Sheltered Adult Workshops, Inc., Cleve., 1980-83; vice chmn. child and youth panel United Way Services, Cleve., 1980—. Fellow Am. Psychol. Assn. (pres. psychotherapy div.), Am. Orthopsychiat. Assn.; mem. Am. Assn. on Mental Deficiency, Sigma Xi, Psi Chi, Omicron Delta Kappa. Democrat. Jewish. Club: City (Cleve.). Contbr. chpt., articles to profl. publs.; producer films on retardation, 1962, 66, 77; editor: Handbook for Volunteers for Mental Retarded (ARC), 1968; (with E. Walker) Newsletter Editors Manual (Am. Psychol. Assn.), 1974; editor Clin. Psychologist, 1966-69, Profl. Psychology, 1969-77, Psychotherapy, 1983—. Office: Dept Psychology Case Western Res U Cleveland OH 44106

FREEDMAN, ARTHUR ALLEN, accountant; b. Chgo., Dec. 27, 1949; s. Carl and Lillian (Weingart) F.; m. Lynn Hope Rosen, Dec. 18, 1971; children: Stacy, Michael. BS, U. Ill., Chgo., 1971; MBA, Northwestern U., 1973. CPA, Ill. With tax dept. Touche Ross, Chgo., 1973-81; with tax dept. Friedman, Eisenstein, Raemer & Schwartz, Chgo., 1981-82, ptnr., 1983—, head of personal fin. planning, 1985-86, head of tax dept., 1986—. Served with USNG, 1970-76. Mem. Am. Inst. CPA's, Ill. CPA Soc., Internat. Assn. Fin. Planners. Jewish. Avocations: sports, bridge. Office: Friedman Eisenstein Raemer & Schwartz 401 N Michigan Ave Chicago IL 60611

FREEDMAN, DAVID NOEL, educator; b. N.Y.C., May 12, 1922; s. David and Beatrice (Goodman) F.; m. Cornelia Anne Pryor, May 16, 1944; children: Meredith Anne, Nadezhda, David, Jonathan. Student, CCNY, 1935-38; A.B., UCLA, 1939; B.Th., Princeton Theol. Sem., 1944; Ph.D., Johns Hopkins U., 1948; Litt.D., U. Pacific, 1973; Sc.D., Davis and Elkins Coll., 1974. Ordained to ministry Presbyn. Ch., 1944; supply pastor in Acme and Deming, Wash., 1944-45; teaching fellow, then asst. instr. Johns Hopkins U., 1946-48; asst. prof., then prof. Hebrew and O.T. lit. Western Theol. Sem., Pitts., 1948-60; prof. Hebrew and O.T. lit. Pitts. Theol. Sem., 1960-61, James A. Kelso prof., 1961-64; prof. O.T. San Francisco Theol. Sem., 1964-70, Gray prof. Hebrew exegesis, 1970-71, dean of faculty, 1966-70, acting dean of sem., 1970-71; prof. O.T. Grad. Theol. Union, Berkeley, Calif., 1964-71; prof. dept. Near Eastern studies U. Mich., Ann Arbor, 1971—; dir. program on studies in religion U. Mich., 1971—, Thurnau prof. Bibl. studies, 1984—; prof. endowed chmn in Hebrew studies U. Calif., San Diego, 1987—; Danforth vis. prof. Internat. Christian U., Tokyo, 1967; vis. prof. Hebrew U., Jerusalem, 1977, Macquarie U., N.S.W., Australia, 1980, U. Queensland (Australia), 1982, 84, U. Calif., San Diego, 1985-87; Green vis. prof. Tex. Christian U., Fort Worth, 1981; dir. Albright Inst. Archeol. Research, 1969-70, dir., 76-77; centennial lectr. Johns Hopkins U., 1976; Dahood lectr. Loyola U., 1983; Soc. Bibl. Lit. meml. lectr., 1983, Smithsonian lectr., 1984. Author: (with J.D. Smart) God Has Spoken, 1949, (with F.M. Cross, Jr.) Early Hebrew Orthography, 1952, (with John M. Allegro) The People of the Dead Sea Scrolls, 1958, (with R.M. Grant) The Secret Sayings of Jesus, 1960, (with F.M. Cross, Jr.) Ancient Yahwistic Poetry, 1964, rev. edit., 1975, (with M. Dothan) Ashdod I, 1967, The Published Works of W.F. Albright, 1975, (with L.G. Running) William F. Albright: Twentieth Century Genius, 1975, (with B. Mazar, G. Cornfeld) The Mountain of the Lord, 1975, (with W. Phillips) An Explorer's Life of Jesus, 1975, (with G. Cornfeld) Archaeology of the Bible: Book by Book, 1976, Pottery, Poetry and Prophecy, 1980, (with K.A. Mathews) The Paleo-Hebrew Leviticus Scroll, 1985; others; co-author, editor: (with F. Andersen) Anchor Bible Series Hosea, 1980; editor: (with

G.E. Wright) The Biblical Archaeologist, Reader I, 1961, (with E.F. Campbell, Jr.) The Biblical Archaeologist, Reader 2, 1964, Reader 3, 1970, (with W.F. Albright) The Anchor Bible, 1964—, including, Genesis, 1964, James, Peter and Jude, 1964, Jeremiah, 1965, Job, 1965, 2d edit., 1973, Proverbs and Ecclesiastes, 1965, I Chronicles, II Chronicles, Ezra-Nehemiah, 1965, Psalms I, 1966, John I, 1966, Acts of the Apostles, 1967, II Isaiah, 1968, Psalms II, 1968, John II, 1970, Psalms III, 1970, Esther, 1971, Matthew, 1971, Lamentations, 1972, To the Hebrews, 1972, Ephesians 1-3, 4-6, 1974, I and II Esdras, 1974, Judges, 1975, Revelation, 1975, Ruth, 1975, I Maccabees, 1976, I Corinthians, 1976, Additions, 1977, Song of Songs, 1977, Daniel, 1978, Wisdom of Solomon, 1979, I Samuel, 1980, Hosea, 1980, Luke I, 1981, Joshua, 1982, Epistles of John, 1983, II Maccabees, 1983, II Samuel, 1984, II Corinthians, 1984, Luke II, 1985, Judith, 1985, Mark, 1986, Haggai-Zechariah 1-8, 1987, Ecclesiasticus, 1987, 2 Kings, 1988, Amos, 1988, (with J. Greenfield) New Directions in Biblical Archaeology, 1969, (with J.A. Baird) The Computer Bible, A Critical Concordance to the Synoptic Gospels, 1971, An Analytic Linguistic Concordance to the Book of Isaiah, 1971, I, II, III John: Forward and Reverse Concordance and Index, 1971, A Critical Concordance to Hosea, Amos, Micah, 1972, A Critical Concordance of Haggai, Zechariah, Malachi, 1973, A Critical Concordance to the Gospel of John, 1974, A Synoptic Concordance of Aramaic Inscriptions, 1975, A Linguistic Concordance of Ruth and Jonah, 1976, A Linguistic Concordance of Jeremiah, 1978, (with T. Kachel) Religion and the Academic Scene, 1975, Anchor Bible Series, 1981, 82; also, Computer Bible Series publs, Am. Schs. Oriental Research publs; co-editor: (with T. Kachel) Scrolls from Qumran Cave I, 1972, Jesus: The Four Gospels, 1973; assoc. editor: (with T. Kachel) Jour. Bibl. Lit, 1952-54; editor (with T. Kachel), 1955-59; cons. editor: (with T. Kachel) Interpreter's Dictionary of the Bible, 1957-60, Theologisches Wörterbuch des Alten Testaments, 1970—; contbr. (with T. Kachel) numerous articles to profl. jours. Recipient prize in N.T. exegesis Princeton Theol. Sem., 1943, Carey-Thomas award for Anchor Bible, 1965, Layman's Nat. Bible Com. award, 1978, William H. Green fellow O.T., 1944, William S. Rayner fellow Johns Hopkins, 1946, 47; Guggenheim fellow, 1959; Am. Assn. Theol. Schs. fellow, 1963; Am. Council Learned Socs. grant-in-aid, 1967, 76. Fellow Explorers Club, U. Mich. Soc. Fellows (sr., chmn. 1980-82); mem. Soc. Bibl. Lit. (pres. 1975-76), Am. Oriental Soc., Am. Schs. Oriental Research (v.p. 1970-82, editor bull. 1974-78, editor Bibl. Archeologist 1976-82, dir. publs. 1974-82), Archaeol. Inst. Am., Am. Acad. Religion, Bibl. Colloquium. Home: PO Box 7434 Ann Arbor MI 48107 Office: U Mich Studies in Religion 445 W Engineering Hall Ann Arbor MI 48109

FREEDMAN, JAMES OLIVER, university president; b. Manchester, N.H., Sept. 21, 1935; s. Louis A. and Sophie (Gottesman) F. AB, Harvard U., 1957; LLB, Yale U., 1962; LLD, Cornell Coll., 1982. Bar: N.H. 1962, Pa. 1971, Iowa 1982. Prof. law U. Pa., 1964-82, assoc. provost, 1978, dean, 1979-82, also univ. ombudsman, 1973-76; pres., disting. prof. law and polit. sci. U. Iowa, 1982-87; pres. Dartmouth Coll., Hanover, 1987—. Author: Crisis and Legitimacy: The Administrative Process and American Government, 1978; Editorial bd.: U. Pa. Press, 1974-81; chmn., 1979—; contbr. articles to profl. jours. Pres. bd. dirs. Mental Health Assn., SE Pa., 31972, bd. dirs., Pa., 1970-78; mem. Phila. Bd. Ethics, 1981-82; chmn. Pa. Legis. Reapportionment Commn., 1981; chmn. Iowa Gov.'s Task Force on Fgn. Lang. Studies and Internat. Edn., 1982-83; trustee Jewish Pub. soc., 1979—; mem. Salzburg Seminar Am. Studies, 1979, 83; bd. dirs. Am. Council on Edn.; vice-chair Midwest Univs. Consortium for Internat. Activities, 1985—; chmn. govs. task force on Fgn. Langs. and Internat. Study, 1982-83;. Recipient Scholarship award Pa. chpt. Order of the Coif, 1981; NEH fellow and research vis. fellow Clare Hall Cambridge (Eng.) U., 1976-77; 8th ann. Roy R. Ray lectr. So. Meth. U. Sch. Law, 1985. Mem. Am. Law Inst. Office: Dartmouth Coll Office of Pres 207 Pinehurst Hall Hanover NH 03755

FREEDMAN, JOYCE BETH, academic administrator; b. Bklyn., Jan. 17, 1945; d. Nathan and Sarah (Minsky) Shlechter; m. Stuart Jay Freedman, Dec. 16, 1968; 1 child, Paul-Michael. BA in Psychology, UCLA, 1967. Various adminstrv. positions U. Calif., Berkeley, 1969-72; office coordinator Princeton (N.J.) U., 1972-75, dir. grad. admissions, 1975-76; various adminstrv. positions Stanford (Calif.) U., 1977-82; assoc. comptroller U. Chgo., 1982-86, asst. v.p. research, 1986—. Mem. Soc. Research Adminstrs., Council on Govt. Relations. Democrat. Jewish. Club: Quadrangle (Chgo.). Avocations: cross country skiing, handy-crafts, tennis. Home: 5946 Greenview Rd Lisle IL 60532 Office: U Chgo 970 E 58th St Chicago IL 60637

FREEDOM, JOHN, obstetrician-gynecologist; b. Hamadan, Iran, July 12, 1922; came to U.S., 1952; s. David Fredoun and Anna Khoshaba; m. Mary Fleming; children: Thomas, David, John C., Martin, Joseph E., Mary Maragaret. BS, Am. Coll., Hamadan, 1944; MD, Birmingham (Eng.) Med. Sch., 1950; postgrad., Wayne State U., Detroit, 1953-57. Intern Michael Reese Hosp., Chgo., 1950-51; resident in ob-gyn Hartzel Hosp., Detroit, 1953-57; practice medicine specializing in ob-gyn and infertility treatment Tinley Park, Ill., 1962—; attending physician St. Francis Hosp., Blue Island, Ill., 1962—, Palos Hosp., Palos Heights, Ill., 1976—; lectr. ob-gyn, Loyola Hosp., Maywood, Ill., 1981-85; asst. prof., U. Ill., 1980-84. Inventor Fertile Day Finder (merit award World Fedn. Contraception and Health). Served to capt. med. corps Royal Army, Iran, 1950-52. Fellow Internat. Coll. Surgeons, Am. Coll. Surgeons, Am. Coll. Ob-gyn, Am. Soc. Abdominal Surgeons; mem. AMA, Ill. Med. Soc., Chgo. Med. Soc., Am. Fertility Soc. Home: 12800 S 84th Ave Palos Park IL 60464 Office: 17100 S Harlem Ave Tinley Park IL 60477 Office: 1049 E Lincoln Hwy New Lenox IL 60451

FREEMAN, DANIEL JON, accountant; b. Austin, Minn., Aug. 27, 1956; s. Darrell Kenneth and June Jeanette (Fox) F.; m. Barbara E. Scharrer, May 30, 1981. BSBA, Drake U., 1979. Staff acct. Peat Marwick Mitchell & Co., Des Moines, Iowa, 1979-81, Haugen Edson Co., Rochester, Minn., 1981-83; treas., controller Eakin & Assoc., Rochester, 1984-86; acct. Blanski, Peter Kronlage & Zoch, Mpls., 1986—. Mem. Am. Inst. CPA's, Minn. Soc. CPA's, Apple Valley C. of C. Home: 6401 Winsdale St N Golden Valley MN 55427

FREEMAN, DENNIS LESTER, insurance company executive; b. Paton, Iowa, Mar. 2, 1939; s. Lester M. and Leona (Fredrickson) F.; m. Mary Lou Hawkinson, June 10, 1962; children: Mark, Sara, Cary, Maret. BS, Gustavus Adolphus Coll., 1961. CLU; chartered fin. cons. Pres. Freeman Ins. Services, Storm Lake, Iowa, 1970—; dollar plan instr. Nat. Ctr. of Edn., Inc. Mem. Iowa Ho. of Reps., Des Moines, 1969-75; bd. dirs. Indsl. Found., Storm Lake, Iowa, 1975-79; pres. Citizens Scholarship of Storm Lake, 1985-87; dir. Arrowhead Area Edn. Agy., 1985-87. Served with USN, 1962-63. Named one of Outstanding Citizens of Yr., Storm Lake Jaycees, 1972. Mem. Nat. Assn. Life Underwriters, Ind. Ins. Agts. Am., Northwest Cen. Assn. Life Underwriters, Nat. Ctr. for Fin. Edn. (cert. dollar plan instr.). Republican. Lutheran. Lodge: Kiwanis. Home: 311 W Lakeshore Dr Storm Lake IA 50588 Office: 711 Lake Ave Storm Lake IA 50588

FREEMAN, DENNIS MERTON, dentist; b. Detroit, Mar. 8, 1937; s. Ronald and Gertrude (Wallach) F.; m. Barbara Lee Wilner, Dec. 23, 1956; children: Steven, Robert, Gary, Shari. DDS, U. Mich., 1960. Assoc. to Dr. Robert Waltz Inkster, Mich., 1960-61; gen. practice dentistry specializing in TMS therapy, cosmetic bonding, crown and bridge reconstructive work Livonia, Mich., 1964—. Served to capt. U.S. Army, 1962-64. Recipient Frances Vetter Soc. award 1960; research grantee Am. Inst. Dental Research, Ann Arbor, 1959. Mem. Am. Equilibration Soc., Detroit Dist. Dental Soc. (del. 1962-63, ethics and profl. relations com. 1972-73), Western Dental Soc. (pres. 1961-62). Republican. Jewish. Avocations: travel, photography, woodworking, gardening. Home: 3222 Shadydale Ln West Bloomfield MI 48033 Office: 32280 Five Mile Rd Suite 1 Livonia MI 48154

FREEMAN, FRANK GEORGE, social history educator, research consultant; b. Ladysmith, Wis., Mar. 23, 1938; s. Francis G. and Eunice M. (Brand) F.; m. Theresa M. Schneider, Nov. 21, 1980; children—Mary, Ann Marie, Patrick, James, Margaret, Matthew. Prof. Am. history St. John's U., 1967; tchr. church history Sacred Heart Jr. High Sch., McAllen, Tex., 1967-70; tchr. local and Am. history St. Francis High Sch., St. Francis, S.D., 1970-78; research and labor studies United Auto Workers, Mishawaka, Ind., 1979-84; dir. Ednl. Programs and Services, South Bend, 1978—; cons. in field. Recipient Diocese of Ft. Wayne-South Bend, Ind. award 1980; St. George award, 1981. Mem. Am. Assn. Counseling and Devel., Am. Assn. State and Local History, Am. Personnel and Guidance Assn., Nat. Trust for Hist. Preservation, Nat. Mus. Assn., Catholic Coms. on Scouting. Democrat. Roman Catholic. Author: Modern Indian Psychology, 1969; Social Research and Urban Politics, 1970; Strength in Bargaining, 1977; A Short History of American Labor, 1980. Office: PO Box 1917 South Bend IN 46634

FREEMAN, HAROLD WAYNE, sales executive, consultant; b. Mpls., July 13, 1929; s. Harold Phillip and Eileen Marie (Stans) F.; m. Sharon Etta Secor, June 7, 1952; children: Mark, Wendy, Brian. Sales rep. 3M Co., Mpls., 1950-52, IBM Corp., Mpls., 1952-58; sales specialist Honeywell Inc., Mpls., 1958-60; v.p. D.C. Hey Co., Mpls., 1960-65; area sales mgr., br. planning mgr. Xerox Corp., Mpls., 1965-72; v.p. Golle and Holmes, Mpls., 1972-78; pres. S.E.T. Inc., Mpls., 1978—; adv. com. tchr. curriculum U. Minn., Mpls., 1975-78; adv. com. profl. sales, So. Hennepin Vocat. Tech., Mpls., 1974-79. Author: (sales tng. program.) The Sales Process, 1978, 84, Spanish version, 1985. Chmn. Job Transition Support Group Colonial Ch. Edina, Minn., 1981—; chmn. bd. Retrain Twin Cities, 1983-85; founder and exec. dir. Job Transition Ctr., Inc., 1987—. Mem. Sales and Mktg. Execs. (adv. coms., Charles W. Bronstein Youth Edn. award 1971). Republican. Congregational. Avocations: golf, music. Home: 8871 Basswood Rd Eden Prairie MN 55344 Office: SET Inc 5620 Smetana Dr Suite 130 Minnetonka MN 55343

FREEMAN, JACK LEROY, prosthodontist; b. Mansfield, Ohio, May 21, 1935; s. William Alexander and Viola Elizabeth (Bailey) F.; m. Joyce Rae Moody, Nov. 4, 1960; children: Tracy Lynn, Laura Jean. Grad., Ohio State U., 1955, DDS, 1959. Gen. practice dentistry Mansfield, 1961-79, practice dentistry specializing in prosthodontics, 1979—. Elected mem. Mansfield Charter Commn., 1983-84. Served to lt. USN, 1959-61. Proclamation of Appreciation award City of Mansfield, 1976. Mem. ADA, Cen. Ohio Dental Soc., Mansfield Dental Soc. (pres. 1969-70), Amvets, Ohio State U. Alumnae Assn., Psi Omega, Kappa Sigma. Republican. Congregationalist. Lodge: Elks. Avocations: sailing, gourmet cooking. Home: 669 Woodhill Rd Mansfield OH 44907 Office: 260 Park Ave W Mansfield OH 44902

FREEMAN, MICHAEL JAMES, manufacturing executive; b. Grove City, Pa., June 20, 1959; s. Joseph Montleone and Dorothy Louise (Curran) Freeman. B in Adminstrv. Mgmt., Pa. State U., 1982. Supr. quality control Autex Fibers Inc., Meadville, Pa., 1982-83; mgr. quality control Continental Can Co., Chgo., 1983-87, Racine, Wis., 1987—. Republican. Home: 1445 Siemmerston Rd #202 Racine WI 53406 Office: Continental Can Co 1901 Chickory Rd Racine WI 53403

FREEMAN, NED LAVON, organization executive; b. Pittsfield, Ill., Dec. 12, 1942; s. Troy Manard and Grace Marie (Hendrickson) F.; m. Marjorie Ann Hayn, Aug. 31, 1963 (dec. 1977); 1 child, Debbra; m. Shirley Mae Worthington, Nov. 22, 1980; children—Lloyd Weber, Sarah. B.S., So. Ill. U., 1965; M.B.A., So. Ill. U.-Edwardsville, 1973. High sch. tchr. St. Louis County, Melville, Mo., 1965-67; tech. writer Universal Match Corp., Inc., St. Louis, 1967-75; dist. scout exec. Boy Scouts Am., Granite City, Ill., 1975-80, Hannibal, Mo., 1980-87, sr. dist. exec., Columbia, Mo., 1987—; cons. United Way, Hannibal, 1981-84; cons. to youth com. Mark Twain Sesquicentennial Commn., Hannibal, 1984—. Youth advisor Granite City C. of C., 1979-80; staff Boy Scouts Am. Nat. Camp Sch., 1982, 84, World Jamboree U.S. rep., Can., 1983. Recipient Eagle Scout award Boy Scouts Am., 1958, Vigil honor award Boy Scouts Am., 1961, hon. key to city Granite City, 1980; named Disting. Exec., Boy Scouts Am., 1978, 82, 84, 85, 86. Baptist. Lodge: Rotary (youth chmn. 1981-84). Avocations: photography, tropical fish. Home: 7560 Southern Dr Columbia MO 65201 Office: Great Rivers Council Boy Scouts Am 1203 Fay St Columbia MO 65205

FREEMAN, RALPH MCKENZIE, U.S. dist. judge; b. Flushing, Mich., May 5, 1902; s. Horace B. and Laura D. (McKenzie) F.; m. Emmalyn E. Ellis, Aug. 13, 1938. LL.B., U. Mich., 1926. Bar: Mich. bar 1926. Pvt. practice law Flint, 1926-27, 33-54; mem. Freeman, Bellairs & Dean, 1953-54; pros. atty. Genesee County, Mich., 1930-32; U.S. dist. judge Eastern Dist. Mich., 1954—. Mem. Flint (Mich.) Bd. Edn., 1933-49, pres., 1938-39, 48-49. Fellow Am. Bar Found.; mem. Am. Bar Assn., State Bar Mich., Phi Kappa Tau, Sigma Delta Kappa. Clubs: Circumnavigators; Economic (Detroit); Birmingham Country. Office: U S Dist Ct U S Courthouse 231 W Lafayette Blvd Room 718 Detroit MI 48226

FREEMAN, RICHARD BOYD, otolaryngologist; b. Cleve., May 25, 1947; s. Marvin Stanley and Yolanda Clare (Dilgard) F.; m. Barbara Wynne, Sept. 1, 1978; children: Richard Wayne, Ellen Clare. BS, Ohio U., 1969; MD, PhD, Case Western Res. U., 1975. Diplomate Am. Bd. Otolaryngology. Resident in surgery Jewish Hosp. of St. Louis, 1975-76; resident in otolaryngology Washington U. Barnes Hosp., St. Louis, 1976-80; practice medicine specializing in otolaryngol. surgery Cleve., 1980—; clin. instr. dept. otolaryngology Case Western Res. U., Cleve., 1980—. Contbr. articles to profl. jours. Trustee Cleve. Montessori Assn., 1982—, Rulling Montessori Sch., 1986. Fellow ACS, Am. Acad. Otolaryngology; mem. AMA. Home: 17450 Edgewater Dr Lakewood OH 44107 Office: 14601 Detroit Ave Lakewood OH 44107

FREEMAN, ROBERT ARNOLD, laboratory executive, consultant blood banking; b. Denver, Nov. 15, 1927; s. Siler Freeman and Ruth (Campbell) F.; m. Louise Marie Goetz, Oct. 30, 1982; children: Paul, Mark, Sally. B.S., Alma Coll., 1948; M.T., Wayne U., 1950, postgrad., 1951. Registered med. technologist. With ARC, St. Louis, 1955-66, asst. regional mgr., 1966; dep. adminstrv. dir. blood program ARC, Washington, 1967-72; sr. clin. research coordinator Travenol Labs., Deerfield, Ill., 1972-73, mgr. govt. ops., 1973-83, mgr. contract adminstrn. govt. ops. 1984—. Chmn. community health services ARC, Chgo., 1982-86; commr. Deerfield Youth Baseball Assn., 1976-77. Editor: Camp Safety and Health Management, 1982. Pres., Holy Cross Ch. Parish, Deerfield, 1977; vice chmn. United Fund, 1964; vice chmn. St. Louis Archdiocese, 1963; Named Umpire of Yr., Deerfield Youth Baseball, 1979. Mem. Am. Assn. Blood Banks, Ill. Assn. Blood Banks (Merit award 1976). Home: 1305 Mulford St Evanston IL 60202 Office: Travenol Labs One Baxter Pkwy Deerfield IL 60015

FREEMAN, RONALD RAY, engineer; b. Lincoln, Ill., Aug. 19, 1940; s. Raymond L. and Mary E. (Conley) F.; m. Barbara A. Lueke, Sept. 19, 1964; children—Aimee, Michelle. Student Mich. Tech. U., 1964-66, U. Nebr., 1968, Met. Tech. Community Coll., 1983-84. Mgr. Northwestern Bell, Omaha, 1969-77; staff mgr. AT&T Corp. Hdqrs., Basking Ridge, N.J., 1977-79; sr. engr. Northwestern Bell Corp. Staff, Omaha, 1979-86, mgr. network planning, Omaha, 1986— cons. Personal Computer Support Group, Omaha, 1983—. Served with USAF, 1963-67. Mem. Telephone Pioneers Am., Am. Radio Relay League (life). Roman Catholic. Avocations: amateur radio; antique radio collecting. Office: Northwestern Bell Telephone Co 1314 Douglas on the Mall Omaha NE 68102

FREEMAN, SCOT LEWIS, comptroller; b. Salzbury, Md., June 8, 1958; s. Lewis Henry and Margaret (Crumbacker) F.; m. Susan Rae Furry, May 6, 1980; children: Stephanie, Timothy. BBA in Acctg., Shippensburg (Pa.) State U., 1980. CPA, Md., Ohio. Acct. Smith, Elliott, Kearns & Co., Hagerstown, Md., 1980-83; bus. mgr. Sta. WHAG-TV, Hagerstown, 1983-86; comptroller Gt. Trails Broadcasting, Inc., Dayton, Ohio, 1986—. Mem. Am. Inst. CPA's, Pa. Inst. CPA's, Broadcast Fin. Mgmt. Assn. Lutheran. Office: Gt Trails Broadcasting Inc 717 E David Rd Dayton OH 45429

FREESEN, O(SCAR) ROBERT, JR., construction executive; b. Naples, Ill., Sept. 2, 1925; s. Oscar Robert and Opal Mae (Haus) F.; m. Alice Jane Albright, Dec. 12, 1948; children—Oscar Robert III, Kerry Stuart, Matthew Sinclair, Guy Anthony. Student pub. schs., Bluffs, Ill. Ptnr. Freesen Bros., Inc., Bluffs, Ill., 1946-57, pres., 1957-72; ptnr. Heavy Equipment Hauling Co., Bluffs, 1965-70; chmn. bd. Freesen, Inc., Bluffs, 1972—; owner, operator live-stock and grain farms, 1962—; dir. Bank of Bluffs. Trustee McMurray Coll., Jacksonville, Ill., Grace United Methodist Ch., Jacksonville; bd. dirs. Salvation Army, Jacksonville, YMCA, Jacksonville, United Way Morgan County, Sch. Dist. 117, Jacksonville; exec. bd. Boy Scouts Am. Served with U.S. Army, 1944-45. Decorated Bronze Star (3), Purple Heart; recipient Silver Beaver award Boy Scouts Am., 1975; Service to Mankind award Sertoma Club, 1978; named Layman of Yr., Jacksonville YMCA 1977. Mem. Associated Gen. Contractors Ill., Jacksonville C. of C., Am. Legion. Republican. Lodges: Jacksonville Lions, Masons. Office: PO Box 277 Pearl St Bluffs IL 62621

FREGEAU, SUSAN LYNN, controller, accountant; b. Charleston, Ill., July 4, 1960; d. James Bruce and Marijayne (Mason) Gillespie; m. Wayne Fregeau, May 9, 1981. BA with honors, Northeastern Ill. U., 1982. CPA, Ill. Acct. Wm F. Gurrie & Co., Ltd, Oakbrook, Ill., 1983-84; controller WCKG/Cox Enterprises, Chgo., 1984—; acct. Wetlands Research, Chgo., 1986—. Mem. Am. Inst. CPA's, Ill. CPA Soc., Inst. Broadcast Fin. Mgrs., Chgo. Midwest Credit Mgrs. Assn. Avocations: furniture restoration, sewing, gardening. Office: WCKG Inc/Cox Enterprises 150 N Michigan Chicago IL 60601

FREGETTO, EUGENE FLETCHER, transportation engineer; b. Milw., Oct. 18, 1947; s. Fletcher Eugene and Eva Mary F.; m. Judith Ann Shafel, Dec. 26, 1969; children: Katherine Ann, Julie Lynn. Student, Mich. State U., 1965-67; BA in Journalism, Marquette U., 1970; AS in Architecture and Structural Engring., Milw. Sch. Engring., 1972; MBA in Mktg., De Paul U., 1983; postgrad., U. Ill., Chgo., 1986—. Tech. writer Chemetron Corp., Chgo., 1972-73; specification engr. Chgo. Transit Authority, 1973-83, procurement engr., 1983-84, sr. procurement engr., 1984—; lectr. in mgmt. De Paul U., Chgo., 1983—, co-developer grad. entrepreneurship program; lectr. in mktg. U. Ill., Chgo., 1983—. Chmn. publicity St. Mary's Ch., Des Plaines, Ill., 1984, 85; project leader North Cook County 4-H, Rolling Meadows, Ill., 1985-86. Scholar Milw. Sch. Engring., 1970-72. Mem. U.S. Assn. for Small Bus. and Entrepreneurship (v.p. fin. 1983—), Purchasing Mgrs. Assn. of Chgo. (chmn. 1986—), Small Bus. Inst. Dir. Assn., Nat. Assn. Purchasing Mgrs. (cert.). Avocations: photography, fishing, hunting, camping. Home: 800 Laurel Ave Des Plaines IL 60016 Office: Chgo Transit Authority Merchandise Mart Chicago IL 60654

FREGOSI, JAMES LOUIS, professional baseball team manager; b. San Francisco, Apr. 4, 1942; m. Joni Fregosi; children: Jim Jr., Jennifer. Student, Menlo Coll. Profl. baseball player Los Angeles Dodgers, 1961-64, Calif. Angels, 1965-71, N.Y. Mets, 1972-73, Tex. Rangers, 1973-77, Pitts. Pirates, 1977-78; mgr. Calif. Angels, 1978-81, Louisville Redbirds (Am. Assn.), 1983-86, Chgo. White Sox, 1986—; player Am. League All-Star Team, 1964, 66-70. Office: Chgo White Sox Comiskey Park Dan Ryan at 35th St Chicago IL 60616 *

FREHE, DONALD JOSEPH, broadcasting company executive; b. Chgo., Jan. 31, 1945; s. Daniel Joseph and Mary Alice (Tammone) F.; student Wright Jr. Coll.; m. Barbara Jean Ianello, Sept. 18, 1965; 1 son, Joseph James. Accountant, Sahara Coal Co., Chgo., 1964-67; Zenith Radio-Rauland Div., Melrose Park, Ill., 1967-68; v.p., treas. Bing Crosby Productions, Chgo., 1968-71; pres. Vipro Program Services, Chgo., 1971-83; v.p. Orion Pictures, Chgo., 1983—. Mem. River Grove and Elmwood Park (Ill.) Youth Commns., 1971—. Mem. Nat. Acad. TV Arts and Scis., Nat. Assn. TV Program Execs. Roman Catholic. Office: Orion Pictures 625 N Michigan Ave Chicago IL 60611

FREID, MICHAEL ALAN, controller, accountant; b. Chgo., June 5, 1952; s. Paul August and Helen Josephine (Matula) F.; m. 1974 (div. Oct. 1981); m. Doreen Lynn Halinski, Dec. 30, 1983; children: Madelyn, James, Jennifer Irwin, Jessica Irwin. BBA, Western Ill. U., 1974. CPA, Ill. Staff acct. Amphenol div. Bunker-Ramo Corp., Cicero, Ill., 1974-75; plant acct. Amphenol div. Bunker-Ramo Corp., York, Pa., 1975-77; sr. ops. auditor Bunker-Ramo Corp., Oak Brook, Ill., 1977-78; mgr. internal audit Borg Warner Corp., Chgo., 1978-80; plant controller Borg Warner Automotive, Frankfort, Ill., 1980-84; div. controller Borg Warner Automotive, Bellwood, Ill., 1984—. Treas. Brook Crossing Homeowners Assn., Naperville, Ill., 1987. Mem. Am. Inst. CPA's, Ill. CPA Soc., Nat. Assn. Accts. Avocations: golf, hunting, fishing, repairs. Office: Borg Warner Automotive Inc 700 S 25th Ave Bellwood IL 60104

FREIDHEIM, CYRUS F., JR., management consultant; b. Chgo., June 14, 1935; s. Cyrus F. and Eleanor Freidheim; B.S.Ch.E., U. Notre Dame, 1957; M.S.I.A., Carnegie Mellon U., 1963; m. Marguerite VandenBosch; children—Marguerite Lynn, Stephen Cyrus, Scott Jn. Plant mgr. Union Carbide Corp., Whiting, Ind., 1961; cons. Price Waterhouse, Chgo., 1962; fin. analyst Ford Motor Co., Dearborn, Mich., 1963-66; asso. Booz, Allen & Hamilton, Chgo., 1966-69, v.p., 1969-71, v.p. and mng. dir. S.Am., Sao Paulo, Brazil, 1971-74, exec. v.p. internat., Paris, 1974-79, pres. internat., N.Y.C., 1979-80, sr. v.p. and mng. dir., Chgo., 1980—, dir., 1976-85. Trustee, Rush-Presbyn.-St. Luke's Med. Center, 1981—; mem. vis. com. Grad. Sch. Bus., U. Chgo., 1981—, also univ. vis. com. on public policy, 1982—; assoc. Northwestern U., 1981—; trustee Chgo. Symphony Orch.; bd. dirs. Chgo. Central Area Com., Northwestern Library Council. Served as officer USN, 1957-61. Mem. Chgo. Council Fgn. Relations (bd. dirs.), Mid-Am. Com. Clubs: Chicago; Mid Day, Econ., Comml. (Chgo.); Stanwich (Greenwich, Conn.); Metropolitan (N.Y.C.). Home: 45 Indian Hill Rd Winnetka IL 60093 Office: Three First National Plaza Chicago IL 60602

FREINKEL, NORBERT, physician, educator, researcher; b. Mannheim, Germany, Jan. 26, 1926; s. Adolf and Veronika (Kahn) F.; m. Ruth Kimmelstiel, June 19, 1955; children: Susan Elizabeth, Andrew Jonathan, Lisa Ann. A.B., Princeton U., 1947; M.D., NYU, 1949; M.D. honoris causa, Uppsala U., Sweden, 1981, Umea U., Sweden, 1985. Postdoctoral tng. in medicine, endocrinology and metabolism Bellevue Hosp., N.Y.C., Boston City Hosp., Thorndike Meml. Lab., Harvard U. Med. Sch., ARC Inst. Animal Physiology, Cambridge, Eng., 1949-56; from research fellow to assoc. prof. medicine Harvard Med. Sch. and Thorndike Meml. Lab., Boston City Hosp., 1952-66, chief metabolism div., 1957-66; Kettering prof. medicine, chief sect. endocrinology, metabolism and nutrition, dir. Endocrine Clinics, Northwestern U. Med. Sch., 1966—, prof. biochemistry, 1969—, prof. molecular biology, 1981—, dir. Center for Endocrinology, Metabolism and Nutrition, 1973—; mem. metabolism study sect. NIH, 1967-69, chmn. designate, 1970; mem. adv. com. on alcoholism NIMH, 1967-70; mem. subcom. on diabetes Fogarty Internat. Center, NIH, 1972—; mem. com. on renal and metabolic effects Space Flight Space Sci. Bd., Nat. Acad. Sci., 1973-74; mem. nat. diabetes adv. bd. HEW, 1986—; cons. surg. gen. U.S. Army, 1962-79; mem. endocrinology and metabolism adv. com. Bur. Drugs, FDA, 1973-76, cons., 1976—; mem. career devel. com. VA, Washington, 1975-77; mem. sci. adv. com. Solomon A. Berson Fund for Med. Research, Inc., 1976—; mem. spl. study sect. DRTC NIAMDD, 1976-77; mem. nutrition coordinating com. NIH, 1978-80; dir. BioTechnica Internat. Inc., 1981-87; mem. nat. Diabetes adv. bd. HEW, 1986—. Co-editor: Handbook of Physiology Series, Am. Phys. Soc.; Editorial bd.: Endocrinology, Jour. Developmental Physiology, Ann. Rev. Medicine, Jour. Clin. Investigation, Jour. Clin. Endocrinology, Jour. Lab. Clin. Medicine, Bull. Internat. Diabetes Fedn. Hippocrates; editor-in-chief: The Year in Metabolism, 1975-79, Contemporary Metabolism, 1979—; Contbr. articles to profl. jours., chpts. in textbooks. Dir. WHO Reference Ctr. Diabetes in Pregnancy, 1985—; co-convenor steering com. maternal and child health Internat. Diabetes Fedn., 1986—. Served with USNR 1943-45; Served with USNR AUS, 1950-52. Recipient Lilly award and medal Am. Diabetes Assn., 1966; Woodyatt award No. Ill. Diabetes Assn., 1976; Mosenthal award N.Y. Diabetes Assn., 1978; Banting Meml. medal Am. Diabetes Assn., 1978, Banting Meml. award, 1980; Joslin medal New Eng. Diabetes Assn., 1978; Kellion medal Australian Diabetes Assn., 1981; Am. Cancer Soc. fellow, 1953-55; Nat. Found. fellow, 1955-56, First Priscilla White Lectr. award Harvard Med. Sch., 1985, Solomon A. Berson Clin. Sci. award, NYU Med. Sch., 1986. Fellow A.C.P., AAAS, Diabetes Assn. of India (hon.); mem. Assn. Am. Physicians, Am. Soc. Clin. Investigation (editorial com. 1971-76), Am. Physiol. Soc., World Med. Assn. (mem. med. bd. advisers 1975—), Endocrine Soc. (council 1969-72, chmn. meetings com. 1980-83, postgrad. program com. 1983—), Am. Thyroid Assn. (chmn. Van Meter award com. 1977-78), Am. Diabetes Assn. (dir. 1968-79, chmn. com. sci. programs 1971-75, v.p. profl. sect. 1975-76, pres. 1977-78, exec. com. 1975-79), Am. Soc. Clin. Nutrition (council 1984-87, McCollum award 1986), Soc. Exptl. Biology and Medicine, AAAS (mem. at large sect. med. scis.), Alpha Omega Alpha, Phi Beta Kappa, Sigma Xi; hon. mem. High Table, King's Coll., Cambridge, Eng. Home: 938 Edgemere Ct Evanston IL 60202 Office: Northwestern U Med Sch 303 E Chicago Ave Chicago IL 60611

FREITAG, FREDERICK GERALD, osteopathic physician; b. Milw., Feb. 12, 1952; s. Frederick August and Shirley June (Siewert) F.; m. Lynn Nadene Stegner, Sept. 10, 1977. BS in Biochemistry, U. Wis., 1974; DO, Chgo. Coll. Osteopathic Medicine, 1979. Intern Brentwood Hosp., Warrensville Heights, Ohio, 1979-80, resident in family practice, 1980-81; dir., physician Twinsburg (Ohio) Family Clinic, 1981-83; mem. staff Diamond Headache Clinic, Chgo., 1983-86, assoc. dir., 1986—; mem. Janssen Research Council; assoc. prof. family medicine Ohio U. Coll. Osteopathic Medicine, Warrensville Heights, 1982-83; vis. lectr. dept. family medicine Chgo. Coll. Osteopathic Medicine, 1985—; assoc. staff mem. Louis A. Weiss Meml. Hosp., Chgo., 1983—. Contbr. articles to profl. jours. Mem. AMA, Am. Assn. Study Headache, Am. Coll. Gen. Practitioners in Osteopathic Medicine, Am. Osteopathic Assn., Am. Soc. Clin. Pharmacology and Therapeutics, Am. Assn. Osteopathic Specialists, Ill. Assn. Osteopathic Physicians and Surgeons, Ill. Med. Soc., Internat. Assn. Study Pain, Nat. Headache Found, Chgo. Med. Soc. (speaker's bur.), German Wine Soc., U. Wis. Alumni Assn. Lutheran. Avocations: German oenophile, goldfish raising and breeding, model railroading, home carpentry. Home: 920 W Carmen Unit 2E Chicago IL 60640 Office: The Diamond Headache Clinic 5252 N Western Ave Chicago IL 60625

FREITAS, JOHN EUGENE, nuclear medicine physician, internist; b. Detroit, June 1, 1945; s. Eugene Leo and Mary Elaine (Moriarty) F.; m. Mary Elizabeth Marra, June 27, 1970; children—Christopher, David. B.S., U. Notre Dame, 1967; M.D., U. Mich., 1971. Diplomate Am. Bd. Internal Medicine, Am. Bd. Nuclear Medicine. Intern then resident University Hosps., Ann Arbor, Mich., 1971-74; staff physician William Beaumont Hosp., Royal Oak, Mich., 1978—; pres. Mich. Coll. Nuclear Medicine Physicians, Royal Oak, 1983-84; clin. assoc. prof. U. Mich. Med. Sch., Ann Arbor, 1979—, Wayne State U. Med. Sch., Detroit, 1982—. Contbr. articles to profl. jours. Mem. Commn. Edn. St. Thomas Sch., Ann Arbor, 1982—; Served to lt. comdr. USNR, 1974-76. Univ. Hosps. fellow, 1976-78. Fellow ACP; mem. Soc. Nuclear Medicine (bd. trustees 1987—), AMA, Am. Coll. Nuclear Physicians, Am. Thyroid Assn.; Sigma Xi, Alpha Omega Alpha, Alpha Epsilon Delta. Republican. Roman Catholic. Club: Notre Dame (bd. dirs. 1982—). Lodge: KC (grand knight 1983-85). Advocations: aviation sports. Home: 1459 Burgundy Ann Arbor MI 48105 Office: 3601 W 13 Mile Rd Royal Oak MI 48072

FREIVALDS, JOHN, marketing executive; b. Skujene, Latvia, Mar. 12, 1944; s. Evalds and Margarita (Dzenis) F.; m. Susan Lynn Alexander, Jan. 21, 1967; children: Jill, Karla, Maija. BS in Fgn. Service, Georgetown U., 1966, MA in Internat. Affairs, 1967. Economist Devel. Resources Corp., Sacramento, 1970-73; v.p. I.S. Joseph Co., Mpls., 1973-76, 80-83, Experience, Mpls., 1976-80; pres. John Freivalds & Assocs., Mpls., 1983—; dir. Experience, Inc., Mpls., Fgn. Trade, Inc., Mpls. Author: Grain Trade, 1976, Family Plot, 1978, Successful Agribusiness, 1985, McWorld, 1987; founder Jour. Agribus. Worldwide, 1979, Jour. Fgn. Trade, 1984. Vol. Peace Corps., Republic of Panama, Columbia, 1967-71. Mem. Internat. Advt. Assn. (pres. 1985—), Min.. Press Club, Fraternities Rusticana. Unitarian. Avocations: basketball, hiking. Home: 8208 W Franklin Minneapolis MN 55426 Office: Euramerica 701 4th Ave Minneapolis MN 55415

FRELAND, JAMES ISAAC, police chief; b. Cin., Mar. 19, 1950; s. Isaac T. and Martha L. (Blackwell) F.; m. Marianne Snider, Jan. 1977; children—Ann Marie, James Adam. Cert. FBI Nat. Acad., 1982; B.A. summa cum laude, Wilmington Coll., 1983; M in Pub. Adminstrn., Xavier U., 1986; cert. paralegal studies Am. Inst. Paralegal Studies, 1987. Police officer Woodlawn Police, Ohio, 1973-74, Springdale Police, Ohio, 1974-77, Police sgt., 1977-84, col., chief police, 1984—; adj. faculty mem. Wilmington Coll., Ohio, 1983. Served to sgt. USMC, 1969-71. Named one of Outstanding Young Men of Am., 1987. Mem. FBI, Ohio Chief's Assn., Internat. City Mgrs. Assn., Internat. Assn. Chief's Police, Buckeye State Sheriff's Assn., Nat. Assn. Bunco Invest, Order of Ky. Cols. Baptist. Office: Springdale Police Dept 12105 Lawnview Ave Springdale OH 45246

FREMON, MICHAEL WARD, professional recruiting executive; b. Fargo, N.D., Aug. 18, 1941; s. William Joe and Irene (McGoldrich) F.; m. Ann Valerie Adams, Oct. 31, 1964; children: H. Sean, Matthew Wade, Ward Patrick. BA Econs., Beloit Coll., 1964; postgrad., Stanford U., 1959-61. Mktg. coordinator and sales engr. Goodyear Chem. Div., Akron, Ohio, 1964-68; sales engr. Fellows Corp., Springfield, Utah, 1968-70; sr. sales engr. Borden Chem., Leominster, Mass., 1970-73; mgr. sales and adminstrn. E F Hauserman, Cleve., 1973-77; dept. mgr., assoc. Meta Corp., Cleve., 1977-81; pres., mng. ptnr. Western Res. Assocs., Bath, Ohio, 1981—. V.p. Richfield (Ohio) Civic Improvement Assn., 1976-78; new bus. subcom., ambassadors program Akron Regional Devel. Bd., 1983—. Mem. Soc. Plastics Engrs., Am. Soc. Personnel Adninmstrn. Republican. Avocations: canoeing, backpacking, reading, jogging. Home: 3357 Revere Rd Richfield OH 44286 Office: Western Res Assocs 843 Ghent Sq Bath OH 44210

FRENCH, FLOYD RICHARD, research and development executive, consultant; b. Ludington, Mich., Jan. 8, 1937; s. Desmer Lee and Anna Sophia (Johnson) French; m. Mary Louis Slocum, Dec. 4, 1963; children: Jamie Rae, Renée Jane, Eric Richard. Student, Ferris State U., 1957-59, Mich. State U., 1959-61, Cen. Mich. U., 1969-70. Resin chemist Guardsmon Chem. Coatings, Grand Rapids, Mich., 1963-64; sr. research chemist Dow Chem. Co., Midland, Mich., 1964-76; sr. aerosal chemist Amway Corp., Ada, Mich., 1976-78; dir. research and devel. Clayton Corp., St. Louis, Mo., 1978—. Patentee in field. Active Diabetes Assn., St. Louis. Served with USNG, 1962-68. Mem. AAAS, Am. Chem. Soc., Chem. Specialist Mfg. Assn. Avocations: fishing, hunting, canoeing, chess, cards. Home: 700 Shallowford Manchester MO 63021 Office: Clayton Corp 4205 Forest Park Saint Louis MI 63108

FRENCH, GERALD EDGAR, dentist; b. Lebanon, Ind., June 26, 1932; s. Floyd Edgar and Minnie May (McCoy) F.; m. Jacquelyn Anne Muehlbauer, Dec. 28, 1957; children: Geffry Eric, Leslie Ann, Todd Anthony. BS, Ind. U., 1954; DDS, Ind. U., Indpls., 1957. Gen practice dentistry Lebanon, Ind., 1959—. Pres. Lebanon Bd. of Health, Ill. U. Sch. Dentistry, Indpls., 1978-79. Served to capt. U. S. Army, 1957-79. Club: Ulen Country (Lebanon). Lodges: Kiwanis (pres. 1969), Elks. Avocations: golf, travel, fishing, spectator sports. Office: 1602 N Lebanon Lebanon IN 46052

FRENCH, JANET BEIGHLE, editor, reporter; b. Tacoma, Wash., May 19, 1933; d. Dan and Anne (Murray) Beighle; m. Robert French, June 2, 1973. BS in Home Econs., Oreg. State U., 1955; MS in Home Econs., Journalism, U. Wis., 1956. Editor cook books Better Homes and Gardens, Des Moines, 1956-63; editor food sect., food reporter Plain Dealer, Cleve., 1963—. Author: Thrifty Meals for Hearty Appetites, 1975, Plain Dealer Holiday Cook Book, 1978, Measure for Measure, 1983; contbg. author: The Best Places to Eat in America, 1987. Recipient 1st Place Food Writing award Am. Meat Inst., 1964, 74, 1st Place Appliance Article award Am. Home Appliance Mfrs., 1967, 71, 1st Place Nutrition Writing award Carnation Co., 1972, 84. Mem. Newspaper Food Editors and Writers Assn., Inst. Food Technologists, Am. Home Econs. Assn., Northeastern Ohio Home Economists in Bus., Sigma Delta Chi. Office: Plain Dealer 1801 Superior Ave Cleveland OH 44114

FRENCH, PHILLIP LORENZO, psychologist; b. Grafton, N.D., Apr. 14, 1947; s. Lorenzo Amada and Agnes (Kouba) F.; m. Rosalinda Rodriguez, Nov. 21, 1970; children: Phillip Jr., Erica Lea, Estella Rose. BA in Psychology, Moorhead (Minn.) State U., 1975; MS in Psychology, Tex. A&I U., 1978. Cert. psychol. assoc., Tex.; lic. psychologist, Minn. Behavioral therapist Gillette Ctr., Houston, 1978-79; psychologist Richmond (Tex.) State Sch., 1979-80; sch. psychologist N.W. Regional Dist. Council, Newfolden, Minn., 1980-81; therapist Gilfillan Ctr., Bemidji, Minn., 1981; behavior analyst supr. Fergus Falls (Minn.) Regional Treatment Ctr., 1981-82, psychologist, 1982—; pvt. practice psychology, cons., Fergus Falls, 1984—; adv. bd. mem. Assessment Project, St. Paul, 1984—; psychol. cons. Wilderness Treatment Ctr., Marion, Mont., July 1986—; bd. dirs. Region IV Council of Domestic Violence, Fergus Falls, 1986—. Served with USAF, 1966-70. Democrat. Avocations: hunting, auto mechanics, reading, camping. Office: Larson Ctr 1415 College Way Fergus Falls MN 56537

FRENCH, ROBERT LEE, management consultant; b. Middletown, Mo., Dec. 18, 1929; s. Lee and Pearl Marie F.; B.S., U. Mo., 1951, M.S. in Bus. Adminstrn., 1951; m. Barbara Gail Burks, Sept. 17, 1950; children—Carol Jean, Cynthia Ann, James Robert, John Richard. Sr. indsl. engr. Chrysler Corp., Detroit, 1951-60; chief mng. engr. Boats div. Brunswick Corp., Warsaw, Ind., 1960-63; chief indsl. engr. Arnold Engring. div. Allegheny-Ludlum, Marengo, Ill., 1963-66; v.p., dir. Mfg. Household div. Hamilton-Cosco Inc., Columbus, Ind., 1966-70; v.p., gen. mgr. Buckeye Plastics div. Buckeye Internat., Columbus, Ohio, 1970-72; v.p., gen. mgr. Buckeye Ware Inc., Regal Ware Inc., Wooster, Ohio, 1972-74; pres. R.L. French & Co., Inc., South Bend, Ind., 1974—; chmn., chief exec. officer On-Line Data Inc., Mishawaka, Ind.; Pres. Bartholomew County (Ind.) chpt. ARC, 1969. Found. for Youth, Wooster, Ohio, 1973. Served with USAF, 1950-51. Mem. Assn. Mgmt. Cons., Soc. Profl. Mgmt. Cons. Republican. Mem. Christian Ch. (Disciples of Christ). Home: 1617 B N Riverside South Bend IN 46616 Office: 226 N Ironwood Mishawaka IN 46544

FRENCH, ROBERT RAYMOND, small business owner; b. Toledo, Jan. 30, 1924; s. Raymond French and Florence Bernice (Vogt) Brown; m. Leila Josephine Johnson, Aug. 15, 1953; children: Lynnette Rae, Suzanne Lee, Daniel Robert, Jeannine Mae. BS in Secondary Edn., U. Toledo, 1955; MS in Biology, Syracuse U., 1961, postgrad. in edn., 1961—. Cert. sci. and biology tchr., N.Y.; cert. social studies and sci. tchr., Mich. Tchr. Euclid (Ohio) Cen. Schs., 1955-58; tchr., adminstr. Liverpool (N.Y.) Cen. Schs., 1959-79; tchr. L'Anse (Mich.) Area Schs., 1980-84; owner Nite Owl Cafe, L'Anse, 1984—; dir. adult edn. and prin. Liverpool (N.Y.) Cen. Schs., 1968-79. Commr. Dept. Recreation and Human Resources, Clay, N.Y., 1975-77; v.p. St. Paul s Luth. Ch., Liverpool, 1974, pres., Skanee, Mich. Served with USN, 1943-46, ETO. Mem. NEA (del. 1955—, life), N.Y. Assn. Continuing, Community Edn. (pres. 1975-76, hon. life), Liverpool Faculty Assn. (Past Pres. award 1967-69). Republican. Lutheran. Lodge: Kiwanis (1st v.p. 1986—). Home: Rt 1 Box 861 Skanee MI 49962

FRENDT, RICHARD JOSEPH, construction company executive; b. Mt. Clemens, Mich., June 13, 1942; s. Arthur J. and Dorothy M. (Edgette) F.; m. Mary Lou Vollstead, Oct. 12, 1963; children: Richard M., Bethany A. Student, Port Huron (Mich.) Jr. Coll., 1962; BS in Civil Engring., Internat. Corr. Sch., 1967. Field engr. Townsend and Bottom, Ann Arbor, Mich., 1966-76, project mgr., 1976-81, mgr. estimating, 1981-84, v.p., 1984-86; v.p. Kokosing Constrn., Fredricktown, Ohio, 1986—; instr. Eastern Mich. U., Ypsilanti, 1986—. Author : (book) Who We Are, 1979;(play) Perfect Peers, 1986. Chmn. First Christian Ch., Sylvania, Ohio, 1982-83. Mem. Assn. Energy Engrs. Avocations: writing, leaded glass work, travel. Home: 7837 Stonehedge Valley Dr Gregory MI 48137

FRENZEL, BILL, Congressman; b. St. Paul, July 31, 1928; s. Paul and Paula (Schlegel) F.; m. Ruth Purdy, June 9, 1951; children: Deborah, Pamela, Melissa. B.A., Dartmouth, 1950, M.B.A., 1951. Pres. Mpls. Terminal Warehouse Co., 1966-70, No. Waterway Terminals Corp., 1965-70; mem. 92d-100th Congresses from 3d Dist. Minn., 1971—; Mem. Minn. Ho. Reps., 1962-70. Served to lt. USNR, 1951-54, Korea. Republican. Clubs: Rotarian, Minneapolis. Office: Longworth House Office Bldg Washington DC 20515 *

FRENZEL, OTTO N., III, bank executive; b. 1930. BS, U. Pa., 1954. With Mcths. Nat. Bank, Indpls., 1956—, exec. v.p., 1965-70, pres., 1970-73, chmn bd. dirs., 1973—, chief exec. officer, 1979—. Served to 1st lt. USAF, 1954-56. Office: Merchants Nat Corp One Merchants Plaza Suite 415 E Indianapolis IN 46255 *

FREUDENBERGER, JOHN EDWARD, manufacturing company executive; b. Chgo., Apr. 23, 1941; s. Joseph Edward and Mildred (Neilsen) F.; m. Terri Joy Weiland, Sept. 8, 1962; children—Tifinni J. (dec.), Tricia J., John Jr., Justin. B.S. in Mech. Engring., So. Ill. U., 1966. Process engr. Ford Motor Co., Indpls., 1966-68, design engr., Dearborn, Mich., 1968-70; chief engr. Powers and Sons, Montpelier, Ohio, 1970-80; pres., owner Indsl. Steering Products, Inc., Bryan, Ohio, 1980—, R.J. Flohr Co., 1985—. Pres., co-founder Nat. Reye's Syndrome Found., Bryan, 1974—. Served with USAR, 1963-73. Mem. Soc. Automobile Engrs., ASME, Methodist. Club: Rotary. Home: 924 Mayer St Bryan OH 43506 Office: 426 N Lewis Bryan OH 43506

FREUDENBURG, WILLIAM R., sociology educator; b. Norfolk, Nebr., Nov. 2, 1951; s. Eldon G. and Betty M. Freudenburg. BA, U. Nebr., 1974; MA, Yale U., 1976, M in Philosphy, 1977, PdD, 1979. Research assoc. Yale U., New Haven, 1975-77; asst. prof. sociology and rural sociology Wash. State U., Pullman, 1978-83; assoc. prof. rural sociology Wash. State U., 1983-86, U. Wis., Madison, 1986—; researcher, cons. in field. Author: Public Reactions to Nuclear Power: Are There Critical Masses? 1984, Paradoxes of Western Energy Development, 1984; contbr. articles to profl. jours. Hawksworth scholar, 1970-72, Nat. Merit scholar, 1970-74; NSF grad. fellow, 1975-79. Mem. Am. Sociol. Assn. (fellow 1983-84, council, sect. on environ. sociology 1980-83, chair-elect 1987—), Internat. Assn. for Impact Assessment, Rural Sociol. Soc. (chmn. natural resources research group 1982-83, program chmn. 1983-84, mem. various com.), AAAS (Rural Sociol. Soc. rep. 1979-86, sect. on social, econ. and polit. scis. 1986—), Soc. for Risk Analysts, Soc. for Applied Anthropology, Wash. State Sociol. Assn., Phi Beta Kappa, Phi Eta Sigma. Office: Univ Wis Dept Rural Sociology 350 Agriculture Hall 1450 Linden Dr Madison WI 53706

FREUND, MICHAEL HENRY, retail executive; b. St. Louis, Oct. 30, 1939; s. Henry Louis and Natalie Elaine (Edison) F.; m. Barbara Goldstein, June 12, 1965; children: Nancy, William, Candace. BBA, Tulane U., 1962. Plant mgr. Freund Baking Co., St. Louis, 1963-68; with sales dept. Edison Bros. Stores, St. Louis, 1969-70, buyer/controller accessories, 1971-82, v.p., 1980, assoc. dir. accessories, 1981-82, v.p. adminstrn., 1982—, also bd. dirs. Past pres., bd. dirs. Cen. Inst. Deaf, St. Louis; sec., bd. dirs. Jr. Achievement, St. Louis, 1977—; bd. dirs. The Magic House, St. Louis, 1977—, Washington U. Med. Ctr., St. Louis, Chancellor's Council U. Mo., St. Louis. Served with U.S. Army, 1962-63. Jewish. Clubs: Westwood Country (treas. 1984-85, v.p. 1986-87), Noonday. Home: Two Ladue Acres Saint Louis MO 63124 Office: Edison Bros Stores Inc 501 N Broadway Saint Louis MO 63102

FREY, DAVID GARDNER, banker; b. Grand Rapids, Mich., Jan. 12, 1942; s. Edward J. and Frances (Taliaferro) F.; m. Judith G. Campbell Spindle, May 20, 1978; children: David Gardner Jr., Campbell Woodward; stepchildren: William K. Spindle, Robert K. Spindle, David K. Spindle, Jennifer L. Spindle. B.A., U. N.C., 1964, J.D., 1967. Chmn., chief exec. officer, dir. Union Bank & Trust Co., Grand Rapids, 1984—; pres., chief exec. officer dir. Union Bancorp, Grand Rapids, 1985—; chmn. Foremost Corp., Grand Rapids, 1986—. Trustee Aquinas Coll., Grand Rapids, Kendall Sch. Design; bd. dirs. United Way, Kent County. Served to lt. (j.g.) USNR, 1967-71. Republican. Episcopalian. Clubs: Peninsular; Kent Country (Grand Rapids); Indian (Irons, Mich.); River (N.Y.C.). Home: 2011 San Lu Rae SE Grand Rapids MI 49506 Office: Union Bancorp Inc 200 Ottawa NW Grand Rapids MI 49503

FREY, DONALD NELSON, manufacturing company executive, engineer; b. St. Louis, Mar. 13, 1923; s. Muir Luken and Margaret Bryden (Nelson) F.; m. Mary Elizabeth Glynn, June 30, 1971; children by previous marriage: Donald Nelson, Judith Kingsley, Margaret Bente, Catherine, Christopher, Elizabeth. Student, Mich. State Coll., 1940-42; BS, U. Mich., 1947, MS, 1949, PhD, 1950, DS (hon.), 1965; DS, U. Mo., Rolla, 1966. Instr. metall. engring. U. Mich., 1949-50, asst. prof. chem. and metall. engring., 1950-51; research engr. Babcock & Wilcox Tube Co., Beaver Falls, Pa., 1951; various research positions Ford Motor Co. (Ford div.), 1951-57, various engring. positions, 1958-61, product planning mgr., 1961-62, asst. gen. mgr., 1962-65, gen. mgr., 1965-68, co. v.p., 1965-67, v.p. for product devel., 1967-68; pres. Gen. Cable Corp., N.Y.C., 1968-71; chmn., chief exec. officer Bell & Howell Co., Chgo., 1971—, pres., 1973-81; bd. dirs. Clark Equipment Co., Cin. Milicron, Spring Mills. Mem. devel. council U. Mich., 1963—; bd. dirs. Lyric Opera, Chgo. Served with AUS, 1943-46. Named Young Engr. of Yr., Engring. Soc. Detroit, 1953, Outstanding Alumni, U. Mich. Coll. Engring., 1957, Outstanding Young Man of Yr., Detroit Jr. Bd. Commerce, 1958. Mem. Am. Inst. Mining Metall. and Petroleum Engrs. (chmn. Detroit chpt. 1954, chmn., editor Nat Symposium on Sheet Steels 1956), Am. Soc. Metals, Nat. Acad. Engring. (mem. council 1972), ASME, Soc. Automotive Engrs. (vice chmn. Detroit 1958, Russell Springer award 1956), Detroit Engring. Soc. (bd. dirs. 1962—), Elec. Mfrs. Club, Council on Fgn. Relations, Sigma Xi, Phi Kappa Phi, Tau Beta Pi, Phi Delta Theta. Clubs: Chgo., Saddle and Cycle, Tavern (Chgo.); Ocean, Little (Gulfstream, Fla.). Home: 1500 Lake Shore Dr Chicago IL 60610 Office: Bell and Howell Co 5215 Old Orchard Rd Skokie IL 60077 *

FREY, GLENDA JOYCE, educator; b. Indpls., June 29, 1947; d. Oscar M. and Mary D. Butcher; m. Garry L. Frey, June 25, 1966; children: Laura Catherine, Mary Elizabeth. BA, Purdue U., 1969; MS, Ind. U., 1972; adminstrv. cert., Butler U., 1978. With Frankfort (Ind.) Sch. Bd., now prin. South Side Elem. Sch. Mem. Nat. Assn. Elem. Sch. Prins., Ind. Assn. Elem. Sch. Prins. (dist. II by-laws rep.), Ind. Prin. Leadership Acad., Ind. Council Talented and Gifted Children, Ind. Council Internat. Reading Assn., Soc. for Hist. Preservation, Am. Assn. Univ. Women (v.p. membership), Nat. Wildlife Found., Delta Kappa Gamma, Kappa Delta Pi, Kappa Kappa Kappa. Mem. United Ch. of Christ. Clubs: Frankfort Country Purdue of Clinton County (bd. dirs.). Lodge: Zonta. Home: RR4 Box 193 Frankfort IN 46041 Office: South Side Elementary School 1007 Alhambra Ave Frankfort IN 46041

FREY, H. GARRETT, stock broker; b. Cin., Dec. 2, 1938; s. John H. and Mary G. (Grever) F.; student U. Detroit, 1956-57, U. Cin., 1957-59, U. Miami, 1960-61; m. Mary Knollman, July 23, 1960; children—John, Robert, Meg, Amy, Brad, Julie. Salesman, Verkamp Corp., Cin., 1958-60, Formica Corp., Cin., Miami, Fla., and Hartford, Conn., 1960-62; stockbroker Wertheimer & Hayden Stone, Cin., 1962-64; stockbroker Harrison & Co., 1964-66, gen. partner, 1966-73, mng. partner, 1972-77; v.p. Bache Halsey Stuart Shields Inc., Cin., 1977-79; chmn. bd. Queen City Securities Corp., Cin., 1979—; dir. Broadcast Mgmt. Corp. Mem. investment com. Sisters of Charity, Cin., 1970; chmn. Ursuline Acad., 1986—; pres. Springer Ednl. Found.; v.p. Cath. Social Services of SW Ohio. Served with AUS, 1959. Named Big Brother of the Year, 1968. Mem. Cin. (v.p. 1970-72, trustee 1979—), N.Y., Am. stock exchanges, Purcell High Sch. Alumni (pres. 1972-73), Chgo. Bd. Options Exchange, Cath. Big Bros. Cin. (pres. 1966-67). Roman Catholic (council pres. 1971-72). Clubs: Cincinnati Stock and Bond (pres. 1969), Buckeye (pres. 1968-69). Home: 3660 Kroger Ave Cincinnati OH 45226 Office: 1500 Merc Ctr Cincinnati OH 45202

FREY, RONALD JAMES, motel executive; b. Minnesota City, Minn., Nov. 17, 1934; s. Felix Henry and Helen Marguerite (Strupp) F.; m. Melody Margaret Kafora, May 21, 1982; children by previous marriage—Susan, Michael; children—Laura, Karen. Student U. Ala., 1956-57, Upper Iowa U., 1974-75. Cert. property mgr. With Capri Motel, Niles, Ill., 1958-59; mgr. Niles Motel, 1959-61; gen. mgr. Adm. Oasis Motel, Morton Grove, Ill., 1961-65, MGM Motel, Morton Grove, 1965-73, Presdl. Inn, Lyons, Ill., 1973—. Mem. Morton Grove Aux. Police, 1963-67. Served to sgt., USAF, 1954-58. Mem. Motel Greeters of Am., Morton Grove C. of C. (pres. 1965-66, dir. 1963-65), Am. Legion, Frat. Order Police. Club: Yorktown Sertoma (dir.). Office: 3922 S Harlem Ave Lyons IL 60534

FREY, THOMAS F., accountant; b. Grand Rapids, Mich., July 23, 1927; s. Otto J. and May H. (Cox) F.; m. Sherley L. Haskins, Aug. 3, 1946 (div. July 1970); children: Thomas F. Jr., Richard C., Susan E. Padalik, Karen L. Doering, Julia A. Lipsey; m. Barbara J. Davis, Dec. 2, 1972. Student, U. Pa., 1945-47; BBA, Northwestern U. (hon.), 1949. CPA, Ill., Fla. With Arthur Andersen & Co., Chgo., 1949—, mgr., 1954-61, ptnr., 1961—. Bd. dirs. Better Bus. Bur. Chgo., 1980—. Mem. Am. Inst. CPA's, Ill. CPA Soc., French-Am. C. of C. (pres. bd. dirs. 1984-86), Alliance Francaise Chgo. (bd. dirs. 1984—). Clubs: Chgo. Athletic, Hinsdale Golf. Avocations: golf, squash, bridge. Home: 155 N Harbor Dr Chicago IL 60601 Office: Arthur Andersen & Co 33 W Monroe St Chicago IL 60603

FREY, YVONNE AMAR, librarian; b. Chgo., Nov. 23, 1945; d. Wesley Francis and Yvonne Adele (Van Lent) Amar; m. Charles Jerry Frey, Sept. 20, 1975; 1 son, Benedict Francis Charles. A.B. with honors, Loyola U., Chgo., 1967; M.A., Johns Hopkins U., 1969; M.A. in Library Sci., Rosary Coll., 1981. Cert. tchr., Ill. Grad. asst. tchr. Johns Hopkins U., Balt., 1968-69; tchr. English, Montini High Sch., Lombard, Ill., 1970-73; instr. Western Ill. U., Macomb, 1973-78; antique dealer Frey's Tory Peddler, 1978—; instr. Bradley U. Peoria, Ill., 1981-82; supr. reference Ill. Valley Library System, Peoria, 1982-84; head children's room Peoria Pub. Library, 1985—; instr. children's lit. Ill. Cen. Coll., 1987—. Contbr. articles and revs. to profl. jours. Woodrow Wilson scholar, 1967, Johns Hopkins U. scholar, 1968. Mem. ALA, Ill. Library Assn., Peoria Hist. Soc. (docent 1981—), Beta Phi Mu. Roman Catholic. Home: 6523 N Imperial Peoria IL 61614

FREYINGER, KLAUS CHRISTOPH, architect; b. AUgsburg, Fed. Republic Germany, July 9, 1933; came to U.S., 1980; s. Johann Jakob Freyinger and Magdalene Hermine (Amann) Kositz; m. Eva Maria Wilczek, Dec. 16, 1959; children: Claus Christoph, Benjamin Patrick. BArch, Technische Hochschule, Munich, 1956, MArch, 1963. Registered architect, Fed. Republic Germany and Common Mkt. Assoc. architect Scheidle Wörner, Calw, Württemberg, Fed. Republic Germany, 1963-64; pvt. practice architecture Augsburg, 1964-80; pvt. practice real estate investor, developer St. Paul, 1980—; consulting architect Beier/Kraus, Augsburg, 1976-80; real estate cons., St. Paul, 1986; mgmt. cons. K.C.S. Mgmt., Mpls., 1985-86, real estate refinancing cons., 1985-86. Lifeguard Rotes Kreuz, Augsburg, 1974-80. Recipient award for rescuing a swimmer, City of Augsburg, 1959; numerous awards for archtl. competitions in Fed. Republic Germany. Mem. Minn. Soc. of AIA, Bavarian Chamber of Architects. Republican. Presbyterian. Clubs: Town and Country (St. Paul). Avocations: downhill skiing (Nat. Standard Race gold medal), tennis, sailing, golf.

FRICK, JAMES WILLIAM, university administrator, consultant; b. New Bern, N.C., Aug. 5, 1924; s. Odo Aloysius and Mary Elizabeth (Cox) F.; m. Bonita Charlotte Torbert, Mar. 26, 1951 (div. 1984); children—Michael, Terence, Thomas, Theresa, Kathleen; m. Karen Ann Fogle, Oct. 13, 1984. B.S. in Commerce, U. Notre Dame, 1951, Ph.D. in Edn., 1973, LL.D., 1983. Project dir. U. Notre Dame, Ind., 1951-56, regional dir., 1956-61, exec. dir., 1961-65, v.p., 1965-83, asst. to pres., 1983-87, v.p. emeritus, 1987—; pres. James W. Frick Assocs., Inc., South Bend, Ind., 1983—; chmn. exec. com. St. Joseph Bank and Trust, South Bend, 1968—; dir. W.R. Grace Co., Inc., N.Y.C., Magic Circle Energy Corp., Oklahoma City. Contbr. chpts. to books, articles to profl. jours. Chmn. United Way St. Joseph County, 1970, Project Future, South Bend, 1982; exec. com. Fin. Devel. Council Nat. Urban Coalition, Washington, 1975; nat. devel. council Assn. Am. Colls., Washington, 1978. Served to lt. (j.g.) USN, 1942-46. Recipient James E. Armstrong award U. Notre Dame, 1978; named Knight of Malta, Cath. Ch., 1981. Mem. Council Advancement and Support Edn. (pres. 1971-72, Ashmore award 1982), Assn. Governing Bds. (devel. adv. council 1982—), Phi Delta Kappa. Roman Catholic. Clubs: Marco Polo (N.Y.C.); Pith Helmet (Pomona, Calif.). Avocations: operas; symphonies; reading; historical novels; walking. Office: James W Frick Assocs Inc 888 St Joseph Bank Bldg South Bend IN 46601

FRIDHOLM, ROGER THEODORE, beverage company executive; b. Blue Island, Ill., Mar. 18, 1941; s. Theodore William and Bernice (Ver Hulst) F.; m. Bonnie Sylvester, Feb. 23, 1963 (div. Feb. 1981) children: Michael, Hilary, Holly; m. Henrietta Barlow, Apr. 16, 1983. BA, U. Wis., 1963; MBA with distinction, U. Mich., 1964. Account mgr. Benton & Bowles Advt., N.Y.C., 1964-69; cons. McKinsey and Co., N.Y.C., 1969-75; div. v.p. Heublein, Inc., Farmington, Conn., 1975-78; pres. Stroh Brewery Co., Detroit, 1978—, also bd. dirs.; bd. dirs. Comerica, Inc., Detroit. Mem. vis. com. U. Mich. Grad. Sch. Bus., Ann Arbor, 1983-87; exec. com. Detroit Symphony Orch., 1984-87; trustee Henry Ford Health Corp., Detroit, 1987—. Clubs: Detroit Athletic (bd. dirs. 1985-87); Yondotega (Detroit); Country of Detroit (Grosse Point, Mich.). Avocations: golf, sailing. Office: The Stroh Brewery Co 100 River Pl Detroit MI 48207

FRIDRICH, ROBERT E., podiatrist; b. Fort Sill, Okla., July 1, 1945; s. Harry E. and Florence (Kravitt) F.; m. Sandra Jeanne Goldstein, June 20, 1971; children: David Samuel, Julie Elizabeth. BA, Rutgers U., 1967; D Podiatric Medicine, Ohio Coll. Podiatric Med., 1972. Intern St. Luke's Hosp., Phila., 1972-73; assoc. Dr. H. Burton Levine, Paterson, N.J., 1973-74;

gen. practice podiatric medicine Shaker Heights, 1974—, Fairview Park, 1974—; adj. clin. instr. Ohio Coll.Podiatric Medicine, 1975—; cons. Westlake Bd. Edn., 1983—. Contbr. articles to profl. jours. Jewish. Avocations: tennis, jogging. Home: 25 Lochspur Ln Moreland Hills OH 44022

FRIEBERGER, M. DAVID, architect; b. St. Louis, June 5, 1945; s. Gordon August and Miriam Arnette (Colvin) F.; m. Susan Marylyn Schwartz, Aug. 16, 1969; children: Sara Rachel, Lisa Joy. Student U. Mo., 1963-64, U. Mo., St. Louis, 1965-68; student Washington U., St. Louis, 1964-65, BArch, 1985. Registered architect, Mo., Ill. Cub draftsman, team draftsman, then asst. project architect various firms, St. Louis, 1964-74; project architect HBE Corp., St. Louis, 1974—; land developer Olivette Exec. Office Park, 1981. Mem., past vice-chmn. Olivette Planning and Zoning Commn., Mo., 1977—, Olivette Design and Rev. Bd., 1984—. Jewish. Office: HBE Corp 11330 Olive St Rd Saint Louis MO 63141

FRIED, STEVEN J., cardiovascular specialist, health service administrator; b. Youngstown, Ohio, Aug. 23, 1960; s. Edward Bernard and Edna (Heyman) F.; m. Christine Ann Dobozy, Aug. 22, 1981; children: David, Benjamin. BS, Ohio State U., 1982. Cert. circulation technologist. Cardiovascular perfusion techician Perfusion Services, Inc., Brighton, Mich., 1981-82, cirulation technologist, 1982-83; staff circulation technologist Grant Med. Ctr., Columbus, Ohio, 1983—, dir. cardiovascular services, 1985—; trauma cons. C.R. Bard, Inc., Billerica, Mass., 1985—. Patentee in field; contbr. articles to profl. jours. Mem. Am. Soc. Extracorporeal Techs. Office: Grant Med Ctr Cardiovascular Services 111 S Grant Ave Columbus OH 43215

FRIEDEL, MICHAEL GERALD, investment company executive; b. Des Moines, Feb. 28, 1948; s. Lawrence Joseph and Norma Jean (Morrissey) F.; m. Janice Ann Nahra, June 2, 1973; children: Matthew Nahra, Patrick Joseph. Student, U. Iowa, 1967-69; BA, Parsons Coll., 1971. Cert. fin. planner. Asst. sec.-treas. Citizens Fed. Savs. and Loan, Davenport, Iowa, 1972-75; account exec. Merrill Lynch, Davenport, 1975-79; fin. services rep. E.F. Hutton, Bettendorf, Iowa, 1979-81; br. mgr. Fin. Planners Equity Corp., Bettendorf, 1982-84, Titan Capital Corp., Bettendorf, 1984—; mem. adj. faculty Coll. for Fin. Planning, Denver, 1980-85, adv. com., 1984. Mem. Internat. Assn. Fin. Planning (bd. dirs. 1984—), Internat. Assn. of Registered Fin. Planners (bd. dirs. 1985—), Bettendorf C. of C. (bd. dirs. 1985—), Theta Chi (Alumni award 1986), Alpha Phi Omega. Republican. Roman Catholic. Club: Davenport. Lodges: KC, Moose. Avocation: genealogy. Home: 2930 Windsor Dr Bettendorf IA 52722

FRIEDERICHS, NORMAN PAUL, lawyer; b. Ft. Dodge, Iowa, Sept. 13, 1936; s. Norman Paul and Dorothy Mae (Vinsant) F.; m. Marjorie Darlene Farrand, Aug. 23, 1959; children—Laurie Lynne, Norman Paul, Stacie Lynne. A.A., Ft. Dodge Community Coll., 1956; B.A., Wartburg Coll., 1959, J.D., U. Iowa, 1966. Bar: Iowa 1966, Mich. 1968, Minn. 1974, U.S. Ct. Appeals (7th, 8th and fed. cirs.) 1978. Tchr. chemistry Janesville Sch. Dist., Iowa, 1960-63; mem. Woodhams, Blanchaud & Flynn, Kalamazoo, 1966-68; atty. PPG Industries, Pitts., 1968-69, Gen. Mills, Inc., Mpls., 1969-76; mem. Merchant, Gould, Smith, Edell, Welter & Schmidt, Mpls., 1976—. Editor: (booklet) Report of Economic Survey, 1983. Mem. Minn. Rep. Cen. Com.; chmn. St. Louis Park Sch. Dist., Minn., 1973; mem. Suburban Hennepin Vocat.-Tech. Bd., 1980-84, chmn. 1982-84. Mem. Eden Prairie C. of C. (bd. dirs.), Am. Patent Law Assn. (com. chmn. 1980-84), Minn. Patent Law Assn.(chmn. small bus. com.), ABA. Baptist. Clubs: Optimist (pres. 1971-72, lt. gov. 1976-77). Lodge: Masons. Home: 6421 Kurtz Ln Eden Prairie MN 55344 Office: Merchant Gould Smith Edell Welter & Schmidt PA 1600 Midwest Plaza Bldg Minneapolis MN 55402

FRIEDHEIM, STEVEN MARK, television executive; b. N.Y.C., Dec. 22, 1946; s. Philip and Bess (Gutzeit) F.; m. Diane Brown, May 5, 1979 (div. Feb. 1984). BBA, U. Miami, Fla., 1964; M in Internat. Mgmt., Am. Grad. Sch. Internat. Mgmt., 1965. Nat. sales mgr. Sta. WCIX-TV, Miami, 1973-75; gen. sales mgr. Sta. WDCA-TV, Washington, 1975-77; nat. sales mgr. Sta. KCOP-TV, Los Angeles, 1977-82; v.p., gen. ptnr. Sta. WTVU-TV, New Haven, 1982-83; v.p., dir. sales Sta. WNOL-TV, New Orleans, 1983-84; vp., gen. mgr. Sta. KZKC-TV, Kansas City, Mo., 1984—. Republican. Jewish. Avocations: golf, tennis. Home: 4618 Warwick Kansas City MO 64113 Office: Sta KZKC-TV Television Pl Kansas City MO 64126

FRIEDLAENDER, ALEX SEYMOUR, allergist; b. Schenectady, N.Y., Oct. 31, 1911; s. Leo Isadore and Frances (Levine) F.; m. Eileen Berman, Feb. 6, 1942; children: Gary F., Linda Friedlaender Goss, Howard E. BA, Wayne U., 1932, MD, 1936, MS in Pathology, 1938. Diplomate Am. Bd. Allergy and Immunology. Attending staff Sinai Hosp. of Detroit, 1954—; gen. practice medicine specializing in allergies West Bloomfield, Mich.; clin. asst. prof. internal med. Wayne U. Coll. Med. 1945-76. Contbr. articles to profl. jours. Fellow Am. Acad. Allergy, Am. Coll. Allergists, Am. Assn. Clin. Immunology and Allergy (pres. 1971, exec. sec. 1975-77, Disting. Clinician award 1983), Am. Coll. Physicians (subspecialty council 1976-85); Life mem. AMA, Am. Acad. Dermatology, Mich. Allergy Soc. (pres. 1961-62), Am. Soc. Internal Medicine, Mich. Med. Soc., Wayne County Med. Soc., Oakland County Med. Soc. Lodge: Masons. Avocations: swimming, computer science. Home: 8530 Lincoln Dr Huntington Woods MI 48070 Office: Friedlaender Allergy Clinic PC 6450 Farmington Rd Suite 205 West Bloomfield MI 48033

FRIEDLAENDER, SIDNEY, internist, allergist, immunologist; b. Schenectady, N.Y., June 5, 1915; s. Leo I. And Frances (Levin) F.; m. Dorothy Blum, Apr. 20, 1940; children: Roslyn F. Friedlaender Levy, Mitchell H., Robert P. BA, Wayne State U., 1935, MD, 1939; MS in Medicine, Northwestern U., 1946. Diplomate Am. Bd. Internal Medicine, Am. Bd. Allergy and Immunology. Intern Detroit Receiving Hosp.; resident Sinai Hosp., Balt.; practice medicine specializing in internal medicine, allergy and immunology. West Bloomfield, Mich.; dir. occupational and environ. asthma and allergic disease ctr. Sinai Hosp., Detroit; clin. prof. medicine Wayne State U., Detroit, 1948. Editor-in-chief Immunology and Allergy Practice, 1981; contbr. articles to profl. jours. Served to capt. U.S. Army. Fellow ACP, Am. Assn. Clin. Immunology and Allergy (Disting. Physician award), Am. Acad. Allergy and Immunology (Disting. Service award). Home: 22672 Nottingham Ln Southfield MI 48034

FRIEDLAND, BRADLEY NEAL, physician, osteopath; b. Los Angeles, Dec. 27, 1944; s. Dennis and Bernice Gladys (Shore) F.; m. Jeanie Elaine Bundock, Mar. 25, 1972; children: Lisa Danielle, Jeremy. AB, Stanford U., 1966; MA, UCLA, 1972; DO, Coll. Osteopathic Medicine and Surgery, 1977; MPH in Occupational Medicine, U. Mich., 1987. Intern Grand Rapids (Mich.) Osteo. Hosp., 1977-78; gen. practice medicine Grand Rapids, 1979-81; staff physician Grand Rapids Indsl. Clinic, 1981—. Occupational Medicine fellow Dow Chem. co., 1986. Mem. Am. Occupational Medicine Assn., Am. Osteopathic Assn., Mich. Assn. Osteopathic Physicians and Surgeons. Democrat. Jewish. Avocation: gardening. Home: 2428 Lake Dr SE Grand Rapids MI 49506 Office: Grand Rapids Indsl Clinic 436 44th St Kentwood MI 49503

FRIEDLANDER, RICHARD JAY, mathematics educator; b. Los Angeles, Mar. 26, 1944; s. David and Adeline (Cane) F.; m. Lindy Jo Chase, Dec. 30, 1972 (div. Aug. 1977); 1 child, Stan; m. Un Sun Haueisen, Aug. 15, 1982; 1 child, Paul. BA with highest honors, UCLA, 1966, MA, 1968, PhD, 1972; MEd, Wash. State U., 1976. Prof. math. and math. edn. U. Mo., St. Louis, 1972—; assoc. chmn. Dept. Math. Scis., U. Mo., St. Louis, 1983—; exec. com., bd. dirs. St. Louis Maths. & Sci. Edn. Ctr., St. Louis, 1985-87; cons. St. Louis Pub. Sch. Dist., 1985-86. Contbr. articles and research papers on math. and math. edn. Mem. Am. Math. Soc., Math. Assn. Am., Nat. Council Tchrs. Math., Mo. Council Tchrs. Math., Math. Club Greater St. Louis (bd. dirs. 1984-86). Clubs: Gateway Athletics, St. Louis Track (runner of yr. 1984). Avocation: competitive running. Office: U Mo Dept Math Scis Saint Louis MO 63121

FRIEDLANDER, WALTER J., medical educator; b. Los Angeles, June 6, 1919; s. Jacob and Gussie (Gold) F.; married; children: John, Jessie, Joseph. AB in Zoology, U. Calif., Berkeley, 1941; MD, U. Calif., San Francisco, 1945. Rotating intern Mt. Zion Hosp., San Francisco, 1945-46, resident in internal medicine, 1946-47; resident psychiatry Cushing VA Hosp., Framington, Mass., 1947-48, resident in neurology, 1948; resident neurology VA Hosp., San Francisco, 1949-50, staff neurologist, 1950, chief neurology service, 1953-56; dir. Nat. Vets. Epilepsy Ctr. VA Hosp., Boston, 1956-61; dir. sub-dept. EEG Albany (N.Y.) Med. Coll., 1961-66; chmn. dept. neurology U. Nebr. Med. Ctr., Omaha, 1966-73, dir. Clin. Neurology Info. Ctr., NIH, 1972-80; prof. neurology Creighton U., Omaha, 1972—; prof. neurology U. Nebr. Coll. Medicine, 1966—, prof. med. jurisprudence and humanities, 1980—. Contbr. articlea to profl. jours. Fellow ACP; mem. Am. Acad. Neurology (sr.), Am. Assn. History of Medicine, Acad. Aphasia. Office: U Nebr Med Ctr Omaha NE 68105

FRIEDMAN, ALLAN DAVID, pediatrics educator; b. N.Y.C., Dec. 8, 1950; s. Jack William and Irene (Konigsberg) F. BA, Brandeis U., 1972; MD, U. Maryland, 1976. Diplamate Am. Bd. Pediatrics, Nat. Bd. Med. Examiners. Intern Case Western Res. Hosp., Cleve., 1976-77, resident in pediatrics, 1977-79; fellow in pediatric infectious disease U. Pa., Phila., 1979-81; adj. asst. prof. U. Ariz., Tucson, 1981-83; asst. prof. pediatrics St. Louis U., 1983—; co-dir. residency tng. program Cardinal Glennon Children's Hosp., St. Louis U., 1986—. Author: Handbook Pediatric Infectious Diseases, 1987; contbr. articles to profl. jours. Bd. dirs. Operation Liftoff, St. Louis, 1985—. Recipient Upjohn Spl. Achievement award Upjohn and U. Maryland, 1976. Fellow Am. Acad. Pediatrics; mem. Am. Soc. Microbiology, N.Y. Acad. Sci., Physicians for Social Responsibility. Office: St Louis U Cardinal Glennon Children's Hosp 1465 S Grand Blvd Saint Louis MO 63104

FRIEDMAN, BARRY S., accountant; b. Detroit, Oct. 10, 1956; s. Alex and Marilyn Rae (Weinbaum) F.; m. Carol Jean Lindquist, June 22, 1979; children: Amanda Jean, Brian Scott. BBA, U. Mich., Dearborn, 1978. CPA, Mich. Staff acct. Broder, Feinberg & Sukenic, Birmingham, Mich., 1979; acct. Leon Belin, CPA, Southfield, Mich., 1979-82, Frank & Co., Birmingham, 1982-83; controller Waste Mgmt., Inc., Wayne, Mich., 1983-84; supr. Ameritech Publ., Inc., Troy, Mich., 1984-86, mgr. acctg., 1986. Mem. Am. Inst. CPAs, Mich. Assn. CPAs. Jewish.

FRIEDMAN, CHAD ISAAC, obstetrician, gynecologist; b. Chgo., July 31, 1951; s. Alan H. and Beatrice S. (Cohen) F.; m. Charlotte Ann Myer, Apr. 20, 1979; children: Luke, Jonathan. BA, U. Chgo., 1971, MD, 1975. Cert. Am. Bd. Reproductive Endocrinology and Infertility. Resident Ohio State U. Hosp., Columbus, 1975-79, fellow, 1979-81, asst. prof. ob-gyn, 1981—, grad. advisor, 1985—; co-dir. Departmental Area Health Edn. Ctr., Columbus, 1981-85; dir. Reproductive Hormone and Andrology Labs., Columbus, 1982—; liaison Ind. Study Program, Columbus, 1985—. Contbr. numerous articles to profl. jours.; chpts. to books. Grantee Weight Watchers Found., 1980. Fellow Am. Coll. Ob-Gyn; mem. Endocrine Soc., Am. Fertility Soc., Am. Soc. Immunology of Reproduction, Soc. Reproductive Endocrinology, Columbus Obstetric and Gynecology Soc. Jewish. Home: 38 W Beechwold Columbus OH 43214 Office: Ohio State U Hosp 1654 Upham Dr MH-529 Columbus OH 43210

FRIEDMAN, CHARLES STUART, chemical co. exec.; b. Cleve., May 12, 1943; s. Armin Sam and Miriam F.; B.S., John Carroll U., 1965; M.S., Xavier U., 1969; m. Gail Rene Horwitz, July 23, 1967; 1 son, David. With Monsanto Research Corp., Miamisburg, Ohio, 1967-80, research group leader environ. analysis, Dayton, Ohio, 1980-82, environ. mgr., Miamisburg, 1983—. Vice chmn. environ. adv. bd. City of Dayton, 1986—. Recipient Cert. Merit City of Dayton, Ohio, 1987, Fed. Lab. Consortium Spl. award City of Miamisburg. Mem. Am. Chem. Soc. (chmn. public relations com. Dayton), DECUS Computer Soc., Dayton C. of C. (water resources com. 1986—). Appeared in Chem. Mfrs. Assn. accident tng. film; contbr. articles to profl. jours. Office: Mound Rd Miamisburg OH 45342

FRIEDMAN, ERNEST HARVEY, physician, psychiatrist; b. Cleve., Jan. 8, 1931; s. Sol and Ann (Nittskoff) F.; m. Anita Rose Bogdanow, Oct. 26, 1962; children: Rachel Samantha, Sarah Ann, Eric Daniel, Jessica Emily. BS, Case Western Res. U., 1952; MD, Ohio State U., 1956. Diplomate Am. Bd. Psychiatry and Neurology. Intern U. Ill. Hosps., Chgo., 1956-57; psychiat. resident U. Hosps. of Cleve., 1957-60; clin. instr. Case Western Res. U., Cleve., 1974-86, asst. clin. prof., 1983—; vis. psychiatrist Mt. Sinai Hosp., Cleve., 1963-70, sr. vis. psychiatrist, 1970—; med. staff Huron Rd. Hosp., Cleveland Heights, Ohio, 1971—; pvt. practice psychiatry, medicine Cleve., 1962—; owner, computer mfr. Voxaflex Co., East Cleveland, Ohio, 1986—; chmn. ad hoc com. on stress Am. Heart Assn., Cleve., 1977; cons. psychiatrist Nat. Exercise and Heart Disease Study, Washington, 1972-75. Mem. editorial bd. Heart and Lung, 1974-80; patentee computer software and hardware. Served as lt. comdr. M.C., USNR, 1960-62. Grantee-in-aid Am. Heart Assn., Cleve., 1964, 65, 75. Fellow Am. Psychiat. Assn., Am. Coll. Cardiology. Democrat. Jewish. Avocations: tennis, photography, bicycling. Office: Voxaflex Co 1831 Forest Hills Blvd East Cleveland OH 44112-4313

FRIEDMAN, JEROME, pharmacist; b. Columbus, Ohio, Oct. 10, 1943; s. Max Jack and Marjorie Lois (Grundstein) F.; m. Cheryl Ilene Lando, June 30, 1968; 1 child, Julie Beth. B.A. in Zoology, Ohio State U., 1965; B.S. in Pharmacy, 1969. Pharmacist, Ohio State U. Hosp., Columbus, 1969-72, Eastmoor Pharmacy, 1972-73; pharmacist, Westland Med. Pharmacy, Columbus, 1973—, pres., owner, 1979—. Trustee, Nat. Kidney Found Central Ohio, Columbus, 1981-84; bd. govs. Internat. B'nai B'rith Bowling Assn., 1982—, v.p., 1985—. Fellow Am. Coll. Apothecaries; mem. Nat. Assn. Retail Druggists, Ohio State Pharm. Assn., Central Ohio Acad. Pharmacy. Lodge: B'nai B'rith (pres. 1982-83). Avocations: Bowling, tennis, gardening, reading. Home: 345 S Cassingham Rd Columbus OH 43209 Office: Westland Med Pharmacy 455 Industrial Mile Rd Columbus OH 43228

FRIEDMAN, JOHN ARTHUR, psychologist; b. N.Y.C., Apr. 7, 1952; s. Leon Jerome and Rita (Staal) F.; m. Brenda Ruth Van Halsema, July 10, 1982; 1 child, Nicholas Jay. BA, Bucknell U., 1974; MA, U. Chgo., 1976, PhD, 1982. Lic. psychologist, Ill. Chief psychologist Oak Therapeutic Sch., Chgo., 1984-85; dir. mental health George Williams Coll., Downers Grove, Ill., 1985-86; pvt. practice psychology Chgo., 1984—; cons. Perspectives, Chgo., 1985—, Oak Therapeutic Sch., 1986—. Contbr. articles to profl. jours. Mem. Am. Psychol. Assn. Avocations: tennis, golf, reading.

FRIEDMAN, MITCHELL BERTON, photographer; b. Clarksdale, Miss., Jan. 25, 1948; s. Robert S. and Joyce A. (Agrus) F.; m. Sandra Applebaum, Oct. 9, 1969; children: Eric, Stacey. Student, Tex. A&M U., 1966-69. Owner, operator Friedman Film Enterprises, Jackson, Miss., 1971-73; dir. photography Houstin Oilers, 1973-75; dir. video, photography Chgo. Bears Football Club, Lake Forest, Ill., 1976—. Bd. dirs. Vernon Hills (Ill.) Cable Com., 1984—. Mem. Mid States Ind. Photographers, Soc. Motion Picture and TV Engrs. Jewish. Lodge: B'nai Brith (pres. Vernon Hills club 1979-81). Avocations: bowling, golfing. Home: 6 Mayflower Rd Vernon Hills IL 60061 Office: Chgo Bears Football Club 250 N Washington Lake Forest IL 60045

FRIEDMAN, NORMA SHEILA, social science and business educator; b. Springfield, Mass., May 17, 1954; d. Henry and Gladys May (Reiter) F. BS magna cum laude, U. Mass., 1976; MEd, Antioch U., 1978; MA, Columbia U., 1985, postgrad., 1985—. Exec. dir. Kulturama, Holyoke Arts Council (Mass.), 1976; asst. community rep. Mass. Office for Children, 1977; instr. continuing edn. div. U. Mass., Amherst, 1977-79; assoc. prof. social scis. and bus. Ind. Inst. Tech., Ft. Wayne, 1979—; assoc. faculty Ind. U., Purdue U., Ft. Wayne, 1981—; cons. to social and cultural orgns. Recipient study award Project Adolescent Services, Ind. State U., 1979. Mem. Nat. Women's Studies Assn., Ind. Acad. Social Scis., Phi Kappa Phi, Alpha Lambda Delta. Democrat. Jewish. Office: 1600 E Washington St Suite 363A Fort Wayne IN 46803

FRIEDMAN, PHILIP SCOTT, real estate developer, lawyer; b. Lawton, Okla., Oct. 11, 1954; s. Irvin Aaron and Sue (Lerner) F.; m. Linda Ellen Kruhmin, Mar. 11, 1984; 1 child, Jeremy. BA, Northwestern U., 1975, MA in History, 1976, JD, 1979. Bar: Ill., 1980. Cert. real estate broker. Assoc. Reuben & Proctor, Chgo., 1979-81, Goldberg & Kohn, Chgo, 1981-84; pres. Lake Shore Properties, Ltd., Chgo., 1984—. George Marshall Found. fellow, Copenhagen, 1977-79. Mem. Ill. Bar Assn. Office: Lake Shore Properties Ltd 3550 N Lake Shore Dr #100 Chicago IL 60657

FRIEDMAN, SHARON DIANE, computer company recruiting executive; b. Chgo., Jan. 12, 1955; d. Seymour and Ruth Lee (Spiegel) F.; m. David M. Castlewitz, Jan. 5, 1984. BA, U. Ill., Chgo., 1976. Booking agt. Willard Alexander, Inc., Chgo., 1977-78, 79-84, Associated Booking Corp., Chgo., 1978-79; exec. recruiter Associated Data Group, Chgo., 1984, Computer Futures Exchange, Chgo., 1986. Editor Jazz Inst. of Chgo. Newsletter, 1979. promoter Birdhouse Jazz Club, Chgo., 1978-79. Grantee Clement Stone Found., 1973. Mem. Jazz Inst. Chgo. (bd. dirs.), Art Inst. Chgo., Mus. Contemporary Art. Democrat. Jewish. Avocation: quilting. Home: 201 E Walton Pl Chicago IL 60611 Office: Computer Futures Exchange 727 N Hudson Chicago IL 60610

FRIEDMAN, SHELLY ARNOLD, physician, cosmetic surgeon; b. Providence, Jan. 1, 1949; s. Saul and Estelle (Moverman) F.; m. Andrea Leslie Falchook, Aug. 30, 1975; children: Bethany Erin, Kimberly Rebecca. BA, Providence Coll., 1971; DO, Mich. State U., 1982. Diplomat Nat. Bd. Med. Examiners. Intern Pontiac (Mich.) Hosp., 1982-83, resident in dermatology, 1983-86; assoc. clin. prof. dept. internal med. Mich. State U., 1984—; med. dir. Inst. Cosmetic Dermatology, Scottsdale, Ariz., 1986—. Contbr. aritcles to profl. jours. Mem. B'nai B'rith Men's Council, 1973, Jewish Welfare Fund, 1973. Am. Physicians fellow for medicine, 1982. Mem. AMA, Am. osteopathic Assn., Am. Assn. Cosmetic Surgeons, Am. Acad. Cosmetic Surgery, Internat. Soc. Dermatologic Surgery, Internat. Acad. Cosmetic Surgery, Am. Acad. Dermatology, Am. Soc. Dermatol. Surgery, Frat. Order Police, Sigma Sigma Phi. Jewish. Avocations: karate, horseback riding.

FRIEDMAN, STEVEN LEE, podiatrist; b. Cleve., Feb. 4, 1952; s. Harry and Helen (Hammer) F.; m. Heidi Dee Boxerbaum, Mar. 3, 1985. BS, Cleve. State U., 1975; doctorate, Ohio Coll. Podiatric Medicine, Cleve., 1979. Resident in podiatric medicine and surgery Cleve. Foot Clinic, 1979-80; practice podiatric medicine Cleve., 1980—; asst. prof. Ohio Coll. Podiatric Medicine, Cleve., 1980—; faculty advisor Kappa Tau Epsilon Podiatric Fraternity, Cleve., 1981—. Mem. Am. Podiatric Med. Assn., Ohio Podiatric Med. Assn., Northeast Ohio Podiatric Med. Assn. (treas. 1981-83, sec. 1983-84). Home: 4063 Wilmington Rd South Euclid OH 44121 Office: Heights Foot Ctr 2225 Noble Rd Cleveland Heights OH 44112

FRIEDMAN, SYLVAN HAROLD, author, publisher; b. Chgo., July 9, 1918; s. Meyer and Rebecca Beatrice (Finkel) F.; m. Sara Robbin, June 18, 1939 (dec. Aug. 1964); children: David, Robert, Barbara; m. Mary Marjorie Peck Steinberg, July 31, 1966; stepchildren: Michael, Martha. Grad. high sch., Chgo. Gen. mgr. Leterstone Sales Co., Chgo., 1936-47; owner, operator Am. Bearing Co., Chgo., 1947-49, Mpls., 1953-66; sales mgr. Am. Ball Bearing Corp., Bklyn., 1949-50, United Bearing Co., Mpls., 1950-53; owner, operator Interchange Inc., St. Louis Park, Minn., 1966—, also bd. dirs.; cons. in field, Mpls., 1966-74. Author/pub. (cross-reference guides) Internat. Bearing Interchange, 1966, Internat. Seal Interchange, 1975, Internat. Drive Belt Interchange, 1979, Internat. Drive Line Interchange, 1986. Bd. dirs. Big Bros. Inc., Mpls., 1951-65; vol. Amicus, Mpls., 1966-74; pres. Crossroads, Mpls., 1984. Served with USAR, 1944-46. Democrat. Jewish. Avocations: travelling, photo albums, radio and TV talk shows. Office: Interchange Inc 4915 W 35th St Saint Louis Park MN 55416

FRIEDRICH, CHARLES WILLIAM, industrial relations executive; b. Elgin, Ill., Aug. 30, 1943; s. Charles Kenneth and Veronica Elizabeth (Sharpe) F.; B.A., Parsons Coll., 1967; student Loras Coll., 1961-63; m. Janet Lee West, June 20, 1970; children—Joan Elizabeth, Charles Kenneth II. Salesman, Bendix Corp., South Bend, Ind., 1967; safety dir., asst. personnel mgr. Nat. Castings div. Midland Ross, Cicero, Ill., 1968-69; personnel mgr. Continental Tube Co. div. Hofmann Industries, Bellwood, Ill., 1969, asst. indsl. relations mgr., 1970, Midwest dir. indsl. relations Hofmann Industries, 1971-73; dir. indsl. relations, gen. mgr. Lemont Shipbuilding and Repair Co. (Ill.), 1973-75; indsl. relations exec. Modern Mgmt. Methods, Inc., Deerfield, Ill., 1975-77; pres. Standard Cons. Services Co., Inc., Hinsdale, Ill., 1977—3; bd. dirs. G.F. Marchant Co., Chgo., T. & H. Service Co., Oak Park; chmn. Brulé Incinerator Mfg. Co.; past Ill. Pres., Burr Ridge (Ill.) Park Dist. Bd.; scoutmaster Boy Scouts Am., 1982—; past treas. Palisades Sch. Dist. Mem. Packard Automobile Classics Club (regent), Alpha Phi Omega. Club: K.C. (grand knight Mayslake council). Home: 10S431 Glenn Dr Burr Ridge IL 60521 Office: 13920 S Western Blue Island IL 60406

FRIEDRICH, MARILYN DALE, educator; b. Chgo., June 12, 1932; d. Arnold Alfred and Ruth Maria Johnson; m. Jerome William Friedrich, Feb. 14, 1952 (div.); children—Rochelle, Denise, Steven. Student Purdue U., 1951-52; B.A.E., U. Nev., 1955; postgrad. Ind. U., 1958-60, 82-84; M.A.E., Ball State U., 1962. Life cert. tchr., Ind. Recreation dir. Reno City Parks (Nev.), summer 1954; secondary tchr. Kokomo High Sch. (Ind.), 1956-65, cheerleader, block sponsor, 1956-65, 84—, Girls' Athletic Assn. sponsor, 1956-61, curriculum chmn., writer, 1966; recreation dir. Kokomo City Parks (Ind.), summers 1960-62; secondary tchr. Haworth High Sch., Kokomo, Ind., 1968-84, cheerleader, block sponsor, 1968-73, girls' tennis coach, 1975-84, swim meet dir., 1973-82; recreation dir. Crystal Beach Cottagers' Assn., Frankfort, Mich., summers 1963-82; dir., writer synchronized swim shows Internat. Aquatic Art Festival, 1959-68; mem. computer core com. Kokomo-Center Schs., 1983—. Mem. NEA, Ind. State Teachers' Assn., Kokomo Tchrs. Assn., Internat. Order Foresters, Delta Kappa Gamma, Psi Iota Xi. Mem. Disciples of Christ Ch. Club: Interracial. Office: Kokomo High Sch Downtown Campus 303 E Superior Kokomo IN 46901

FRIEDRICH, ROSE MARIE, travel agency executive; b. Chgo., May 17, 1941; d. Theodore A. and Ann Catherine (Coppoth) Dlugosz; m. Gerhard K. Friedrich, Apr. 18, 1964; 1 child, Alan C. Student, Roosevelt U., 1986—. Cert. travel agt. Travel cons. Chgo. Motor Club, 1959, Drake Travel, Chgo., 1960-65; mgr. 1st Nat. Travel, Arlington Heights, Ill., 1969-71, Total Travel, Palatine, Ill., 1971-76; owner, mgr. Travel Bug Ltd., Lake Zurich, Ill., 1977—; advisor Coll. Lake County, Grayslake, Ill., 1985—. Author: (books) Travel Career Textbook, 1980, Guide to Tour Organizing, 1984, Build Profits Through Group Travel, 1984, Independent Travel Agent, 1986. Recipient Shalom award Israel Govt., 1984. Mem. Inst. Cert. Travel Cons. (chmn. edn. forum 1981-84, appreciation award 1984), Soc. Travel and Tourism Educators, State of Ill. Council Vocat. Edn. (mem. Career Guidance Consortium, Appreciation award 1986), Lake Zurich C. of C. (pres. 1984-85). Republican. Roman Catholic. Avocations: writing, travel. Home: 407 E Knob Hill Dr Arlington Heights IL 60004 Office: Travel Bug Ltd 15 S Old Rand Rd Lake Zurich IL 60047

FRIEDRICHS, NIELS GEORG, association executive; b. Luebeck, West Germany, Dec. 22, 1929; s. Peter H. and Gertrud (Hahn) F.; came to U.S., 1958; ed. Katharineum, Luebeck, 1949; m. Ilona Grund, Dec. 18, 1957; children—Kirsten, Dirk. Printer, Flint, Mich., 1959-61; salesman Lufthansa Airlines, Chgo., 1961-63; mng. dir. German Am. C. of C., Chgo., 1963—; lectr. in field. Recipient Order of Merit (Fed. Republic Germany), 1978. Mem. Internat. Bus. Council Midam., Chgo. Assn. Commerce and Industry, Assn. German Fgn. Chamber Mgrs. (Bonn, Germany), Chgo. Fgn. Trade Commn. Group. Lutheran. Clubs: Chgo. Athletic Assn., Executives. Home: 515 Linden Ave Wilmette IL 60091 Office: 104 S Michigan Ave Suite 604 Chicago IL 60603-5978

FRIEDRICHSEN, CAROLE JEAN, accountant, university administrator; b. Cherokee, Iowa, Sept. 6, 1955; d. Clifford Henry and Florence Ellen (Clausen) F. BS in Acctg., Mankato (Minn.) State U., 1976. CPA, Minn. Staff acct. Alexander Grant and Co., LaCrosse, Wis., 1976-81; mgr. McGladrey, Hendrickson & Pullen, LaCrosse, 1981-84, Mpls., Minn., 1984-86; assoc. dir. acctg. U. Minn., St. Paul, 1986—. Treas. LaCrosse Crimestoppers, 1984. Mem. Minn. Soc. CPA's, Am. Inst. CPA's. Office: U Minn 1919 University Ave Saint Paul MN 55104

FRIELING, GARRY DEAN, engineering administrator; b. Holdrege, Nebr., Jan. 2, 1939; s. Lawrence Arnold and Bernice Erma (Aldinger) F.; m. Sandra

Jean Haimerl, June 2, 1979; 1 child, Alicia. BSChemE, U. Nebr., 1961. Registered profl. engr., Wis. Test engr. Wis. Electric Power Co., Milw., 1961-66, sr. project engr., 1973-82, supt. system engring., 1982—; radiochem. engr. Wis. Mich. Power Co., Milw., 1967-73. Contbr. tech. articles to profl. jours. Mem. ASME (mem. com. 1977-80), Am. Nuclear Soc. (participant standards group 1971—), Elec. Power Research Inst. (mem. com. 1977—). Republican. Lutheran. Avocations: reading, history, photography, golf, gardening. Office: Wis Electric Co 231 W Michigan Milwaukee WI 53201

FRIELING, GERALD HARVEY, JR., specialty steel company executive; b. Kansas City, Mo., Apr. 29, 1930; s. Gerald Harvey and Mary Ann (Coons) F.; m. Joan Lee Bigham, June 14, 1952; children: John, Robert, Nancy. B.S. in Mech. Engring, U. Kans., 1951. Application engr. Westinghouse Elec. Corp., Pitts., 1951-53; mfg. mgr. Madison-Faessler Tool Co., Moberly, Mo., 1956-60; gen. mgr. wire and tubing Tex. Instruments Inc., Attleboro, Mass., 1960-69; v.p. Air Products & Chems. Co., Allentown, Pa., 1969-79; pres., chief exec. officer, chmn. bd. dirs. Nat.-Standard Co., Niles, Mich., 1979—; dir. Old Kent Bank & Trust Co.-S.W., Niles, Brockway Glass, CTS, Protection Mut. Ins. Co.; adv. bd. Liberty Mut. Ins. Co.; instr. Brown U., 1965-68. Author. Served to lt. USNR, 1953-56, Korea. Recipient Wire Assn. medal, 1966, Disting. Engring. Service award U. Kans., 1986. Republican. Presbyterian. Clubs: Union League (Chgo.); Point O' Woods, Signal Point Country, Pickwick, Summit. Patentee in field. Office: Nat-Standard Co 1618 Terminal Rd Niles MI 49120

FRIELING, GILBERT ADOLPH, farmer; b. Athol, Kans., Apr. 9, 1934; s. Adolph J. and Anna S. (Zabel) F.; m. Karen Faye Devlin, June 22, 1958; children: Tranda, Kent. Grad. high sch., Gaylord, Kans., 1952. Mgr. Gaylord Implement Co., 1952-60; farmer Gaylord, 1960—; v.p. Frieling Grain Co., Inc., Gaylord, 1964-76; mem. Kans. chpt. USDA Agrl., Stabilization and Conservation Service, chmn. bd. dirs. Smith County chpt., 1981—; bd. dirs. Smith County Farmers Home Adminstrn., Smith Ctr., Kans., 1976-79; bd. dirs. First Nat. Bank, Smith Ctr. Treas. City of Gaylord, 1955-60; clk. of bd. dirs. Harlan Twp., Smith County, Kans., 1965—. Recipient Bankers award Kans. Bankers Assn., 1972. Republican. Lutheran. Avocation: traveling. Home and Office: Rural Rt 1 Box 26 Gaylord KS 67638

FRIEND, D(AVID) DOUGLAS, optometrist; b. Troy, Ohio, May 4, 1957; s. Harold C. and Sue A. (Barger) F.; m. Rebecca Reigh Burnett, Oct. 30, 1982. Student, Ohio State U., 1975-78, OD, 1982. Assoc. Donald A. Bergmann, OD, Cin., 1982-84; pvt. practice optometry Troy, 1984—; cons. optometrist Cin. Eye Inst., 1983—. Named one of Outstanding Young Men of Am., 1982. Mem. Am. Optometric Assn., Ohio Optometric Assn., Miami Valley Soc. Optometrists (treas. 1986), Optometric Extension Program, Am. Radio Relay League, Troy Area C. of C., Beta Sigma Kappa. Republican. Lodge: Kiwanis. Avocations: amature radio, sports. Officw: 1354 W Main St Troy OH 45373

FRIEND, GARY JAY, podiatrist; b. N.Y.C., June 20, 1951; s. Morris B. and Rita E (Rosenfeld) F.; m. Lois Barbara Wolff, May 25, 1975; 1 child, Bonnie. BA, SUNY, Buffalo, 1973; D in Podiatric Medicine, Pa. Coll. Podiatric Medicine, 1977. Diplomate Am. Bd. Podiatric Surgery. Pvt. practice North Shore Podiatry, Deerfield, Ill., 1978—; med. dir. Lake County, Ill. Marathon. Contbr. articles to profl. jours. Fellow Am. Coll. Foot Surgeons. Avocation: photography. Office: North Shore Podiatry 459 Lake Cook Rd Deerfield IL 60015

FRIEND, ROBERT NATHAN, fin. counselor, economist; b. Chgo., Feb. 2, 1930; s. Karl D. and Marion (Wollenberger) F.; A.B., Grinnell Coll., 1951; M.S., Ill. Inst. Tech., 1953; m. Lee Baer, Aug. 12, 1979; children—Karen, Alan. With K. Friend & Co., Chgo., 1953—, v.p., early 1960's, 1st v.p., 1964—, dir. merger activities with Standard Oil Co. (Ind.), trustee employees' benefit trust, 1958—; pres. Twelve Nine Corp., active Friend Finl. Services. Admissions cons. Grinnell Coll., Ill. Inst. Tech., 1968-70; Alumni career counselor Ill. Inst. Tech.; bd. dirs. Nat. Anorexia Nervosa & Associated Disorders Assn. Fellow Econ. Edn. and Research Forum; Am. Finance Assn., So. Finance Assn., Southwestern Fin. Assn., Acad. Internat. Bus., Am. Acad. Polit. and Social Sci., Am. Assn. Individual Investors (dir., Am. Assn. Commodity Traders, Vintage Soc., Renaissance Soc., Sarah Siddons Soc., Art Inst. Chgo. (life), Newcomen Soc. N. Am., Chgo. Council Fgn. Relations, Am. Econ. Assn., Acad. Polit. Sci., Found. for Study of Cycles, Phi Kappa Phi. Clubs: Carlton, Yale. Home: 1209 N Astor St Chicago IL 60610 Office: 222 W Adams St Chicago IL 60606

FRIES, JOHN WILLIAM, radiologist, educator; b. St. Louis, July 7, 1925; s. Arthur John and Anna (Clyde) F.; m. Marilyn Ann Leopold, Jan. 29, 1970; children: Nancy Murphy, John William Jr., Marilyn Crowley. Student, Washington U., St. Louis, 1942-43, Miami U., Oxford, Ohio, 1943-44; MD, La. State U., 1948. Diplomate Am. Bd. Radiology. Commd. ensign USN, 1946, advanced through grades to lt., 1953; chief radiologist USN Hosp., Nat. Naval Med. Ctr., Bethesda, Md., 1954, resigned, 1954; chief radiologist St. Anthony's Med. Ctr., St. Louis, 1956—; radiologist Monsanto Co., St. Louis, 1956—; clin. prof. radiology St. Louis U. Sch. Medicine, 1956—. Painter watercolors. Mem. adv. com. St. Louis Jr. Coll., 1968—. Recipient Disting. Service award St. Louis U. Sch. Medicine, 1981. Fellow Am. Coll. Radiology; mem. Radiol. Soc. N.Am., Am. Roentgen Ray Soc. Republican. Presbyterian. Club: Mo. Athletic (St. Louis). Avocations: jogging, photography. Home: 9002 Sedgwick Pl Saint Louis MO 63124 Office: St Anthonys Med Ctr 10010 Kennerly Rd Saint Louis MO 63128

FRIES, PETER HOWARD, English educator; b. Ann Arbor, Mich., June 18, 1937; s. Charles Carpenter and Agnes (Carswell) F.; m. Nan McDowell, May 16, 1964. BA, U. Mich., 1959; PhD, U. Pa., 1964. Asst. prof. U. Wis., 1965-71; prof. Cen. Mich. U., Mount Pleasant, 1971—; guest lectr. U. Sydney, Australia, 1978, Columbia U., 1981; vis. prof. U. Arizona, 1986-87; internat. linguistics advisor Summer Inst. Linguistics, Dallas, 1977—; researcher, cons. Info. Sci. Inst., U. So. Calif., Marina del Rey, 1983—; N.Am. rep. Internat. Systemics Steering Com., 1983—. Author: Tagmeme Sequences in the English Noun Phrase, 1970; author, editor: Towards an Understanding of Language, 1985; contbr. numerous articles to profl. jours. Fulbright Research grantee, 1965; Am. Council of Learned Socs. fellow, 1962, 63. Mem. Nat. Council Tchrs. of English (bd. dirs. Commn. on English Lang. 1983-84, ESL Assembly 1984-85, chmn. Joint Council/Tchrs. English to Speakers of Other Langs. liaison com. 1984—). Avocations: photography, diving, sailing, canoeing, bird watching. Home: Box 310 Mount Pleasant MI 48858 Office: Cen Mich U Dept English Mount Pleasant MI 48859

FRIES, VERNON JOHN, management consultant; b. Lorain, Ohio, Dec. 3, 1946; s. Vernon C. and Dolores A. (Ziegler) F.; m. Charlyn Vera Taylor, Aug. 28, 1970; children—Bryan James, Cynthia Maria, Susan Michelle. A.B., Lorain County Community Coll., 1970. Systems analyst Ohio Bell Telephone Co., Cleve., 1970-79; sr. cons. McDonnell Douglas, Cleve., 1979-83; mgmt. cons. Arthur Young & Co., Kansas City, Mo., 1983—. Served with USAF, 1964-68. Mem. Assn. Systems Mgmt., Phi Theta Kappa. Republican. Roman Catholic. Office: Arthur Young & Co 920 Main St Kansas City MO 64105

FRIGGLE, MELANIE RENÉ, elementary teacher; b. Jefferson City, Mo., Sept. 16, 1958; d. Paul Henry and Carmen Lee (Yancey) Kolb; m. Mark Eugene Friggle, July 28, 1984. BS in Elem. Edn., Southwest Mo. State U., Springfield, 1981, M in Elem. Edn., 1983. Tchr. 2d grade Bissett Sch., Springfield, 1981-84, York Sch., Springfield, 1984—. Mem. Springfield Edu. Assn. Roman Catholic. Home: 928 S Coachlight Springfield MO 65802 Office: York Sch West Nichols Springfield MO 65802

FRISCH, KURT CHARLES, educator, administrator; b. Vienna, Austria, Jan. 15, 1918; came to U.S., 1939; s. Jacob J. and Clara F. (Spondre) F.; m. Sally Sisson, Sept. 14, 1946; children—Leslie Frisch Nickerson, Kurt C. Jr., Robert J. M.A., U. Vienna, 1938; candidate Sc. Chim., U. Brussels (Belgium), 1939; M.A., Columbia U., 1941, Ph.D., 1944. Project leader Gen. Electric Co., Pittsfield, Mass., 1944-52; acting mgr. research E.F. Houghton & Co., Phila., 1952-56; dir. polymer research and devel. Wyandotte Chems. Corp., Mich., 1956-68; prof., dir. Polymer Inst., U. Detroit, 1968—; v.p., dir. research Polymer Technologies subs. U. Detroit, 1986—; pres. Kurt C. Frisch, Inc., Grosse Ile, Mich., 1982—; cons. various corps. Patentee in field. (50); author, co-author, editor 24 books. Contbr. articles to profl. jours. Recipient medal of merit German Foam Soc., 1981, medal of merit Brit. Rubber and Plastics Group, 1982; named to Polyurethane Hall of Fame, 1984; IR-100 award Indsl. Research Inst. Fellow Am. Inst. Chemists; mem. Soc. Plastics Industry (div. chmn.), Soc. Plastics Engrs.(Outstanding Achievement award 1986), Am. Chem. Soc., Soc. Coating Tech. Republican. Episcopalian. Home: 17986 Parke Ln Grosse Ile MI 48138

FRISCHBERG BAKKER, TAMARA, psychiatrist; b. Kiev, USSR, Mar. 5, 1938; came to U.S., 1975; d. Evsey and Cherna (Feldman) Bakker; m. Antoly Frishberg, Mar. 15, 1961; 1 child, Alexander. MD, Pirogovmedical Sch., Vinnitza, USSR, 1961. Cert. Am. Bd. Psychiatry and Neurology. Physician Kiev Regional Hosp., 1961-74; resident in psychiatry Washington U. Sch. Medicine, 1978; psychiatrist Malcolm Bliss Hosp., St. Louis, 1980-83; staff psychiatrist VA Med. Ctr., St. Louis, 1983—. Mem. Eastern Mo. Psychiat. Assn., Am. Psychiat. Assn. Office: VA Med Ctr Saint Louis MO 63125

FRISCO, JOHN ANTHONY, psychotherapist; b. Alessandria della Rocca, Italy, May 30, 1945; came to U.S., 1956; s. Frank and Carmela (Mangione) F.; m. Shirley Ann McLandrich, July 10, 1971; 1 child, Mara. BA, Youngstown State U., 1969; MSW, Boston Coll., 1973. Youth counselor, supr. Youth Devel. Ctr., New Castle, Pa., 1969-75; dir. social services Columbiana County Mental Health Ctr., Lisbon, Ohio, 1975—; pvt. practice psychotherapy, Sharon, Pa., 1975-79; trainer in communication skills, 1980—; instr. Youngstown (Ohio) State U., 1977-79, U. Pitts., 1982-83, St. Francis Coll., Loredo Pa., 1974-75. Bd. dirs. Salem (Ohio) Childbirth Inc., 1984—. Mem. Nat. Assn. Social Workers (cert.), Soc. Neurolinguistic Programming, Youngstown Soc. Clin. Hypnosis (sec. 1984-85). Democrat. Roman Catholic. Avocations: tennis, bicycling. Office: Columbiana County Mental Health Ctr 40722 State Rt 154 Lisbon OH 44432

FRITCH, WAYNE ALAN, minister; b. Valley City, N.D., Apr. 22, 1962; s. Dean A. and Marlene F. (Wolff) F. BA in Religious Edn. summa cum laude, Mid-Am. Nazarene Coll., 1984. Children's minister 1st Ch. of the Nazarene, Cedar Rapids, Iowa, 1984—. Named one of Outstanding Young Men Am., 1985. Mem. Linn County Evang. Assn., Child Evangelism Fellowship. Home: 2707 Willow St SW Cedar Rapids IA 52404 Office: 1st Ch of the Nazarene 3113 1st Ave SW Cedar Rapids IA 52404

FRITSCHLER, LAWRENCE JOHN, industrial engineer, plant engineer; b. Wisconsin Rapids, Wis., Nov. 29, 1950; s. LeRoy Henry and Loretta Marie (Jaworski) F.; m. Gail Elenore Goska, Feb. 3, 1973; children: Jeffrey Lawrence, Timothy John. BS in Indsl. Tech., U. Wis., Menomenee, 1972. Asst. plant engr. Preway Inc., Wisconsin Rapids, 1972-74, prodn. engr., 1974-77; process engr. Preway Inc., Wisconsin Rapids, Wis., 1977-80, plant engr., 1980—; bd. dirs. Preway Credit Union, Wisconsin Rapids, 1973-74. Chmn. United Way, Wisconsin Rapids, 1974. Mem. Am. Water-ski Assn. Republican. Roman Catholic. Home: 1120 15th St S Wisconsin Rapids WI 54494 Office: Preway Inc 1430 2d St N Wisconsin Rapids WI 54494

FRITZ, CECIL MORGAN, investment company executive; b. Modoc, Ind., July 30, 1921; s. Kenneth M. and Ruby (Howell) F.; m. Lucile Johnson, June 9, 1946; children: John, Susan, Marcia. B.S., Ind. U., 1948, M.B.A., 1949. With City Securities Corp., Indpls., 1949—, now pres., also bd. dirs.; bd. dirs. Eagle Magnetic Co. Inc. Served to capt. USAAF, 1940-46. Mem. Indpls. Soc. Fin. Analysts, Indpls. Bond Club. Republican. Methodist. Club: Columbia (Indpls.). Lodge: Masons (32 degree). Home: 8510 JIB Ct Indianapolis IN 46236 Office: City Securities Corp 400 Circle Tower Indianapolis IN 46204

FRITZ, EDWARD LANE, dentist; b. Evansville, Ind., Dec. 15, 1932; s. Edward E. and Virginia B. (Lane) F.; m. Bettye J. Samples, July 31, 1954; children: Mary Ann, Sarah Jane. AB, Ind. U., 1954, DDS, 1957; BS, U. Evansville, 1975, MBA, 1978. Pvt. practice dentistry Evansville, 1959—; pres., chmn. bd. Health Resources, Inc., 1986—; corp. bd. dirs. Va. Corp., Evansville, 1962-72, Dynatron, Inc., 1980-87. Editor: The Bulletin of the Am. Assn. of Dental Examiners, 1981-85. Served to capt. U.S. Army, 1957-59. Fellow Am. Coll. Dentists, Acad. Gen. Dentistry, Acad. Dentistry Internat., Internat. Coll. Dentists; mem. ADA (continuing edn. com. 1981-83, cons./evaluator 1980), Ind. Dental Assn. (trustee 1983—), Vanderburgh County Dental Soc. (pres. 1967, v.p. 1966, sec.-treas. 1965), First Dist. Dental Soc. (various offices), AM. Assn. Dental Examiners (various offices), Ind. Bd. Dental Examiners (pres. 1982-83, sec. 1980-82), Acad. Operative Dentistry, Internat./Am. Assn. Dental Research, Am. Assn. Dental Editors, Acad. Gen. Dentistry, Am. Soc. Dentistry of Children, Pierre Fauchard Acad., Phi Kappa Phi. Home and Office: 320 W Buena Vista Evansville IN 47710

FRITZ, MARVIN FRANCIS, farmer; b. Tilden, Nebr., May 29, 1954; s. Francis Jerome and Mildred Ann (Beckman) F.; m. Patricia Marie Morgan, Sept. 1, 1973; children: Jeremy, Julie, Jeffrey. Cert. in Bus. Adminstrn., Lincoln Sch. Commerce, 1973. Ptnr. K & F Farming, Bartlett, Nebr., 1977-78; farmer Bartlett, Nebr., 1979—. Sec. Wheeler Cen. Sch. Bd., Bartlett, Nebr., 1982-86. Named Wheeler County Outstanding Young Farmer-Rancher of Yr., Wheeler County Agr. Soc., 1983. Mem. Wheeler County Farm Bur. (treas. 1982-85, v.p. 1984). Republican. Roman Catholic. Lodge: Lions. Home and Office: Star Rt Box 2 Bartlett NE 68622

FRIZEN, EDWIN LEONARD, JR., association executive; b. Chgo., Mar. 9, 1925; s. Edwin Leonard and Hannah (Sweiberg) F.; m. Grace Elizabeth Howell, Aug. 3, 1950. BA, Wheaton Coll., 1949; MA, Columbia Grad. Sch. Bible and Missions, 1954; MS, Fla. State U., 1963; D of Missiology, Trinity Evang. Div. Sch., 1981. Trustee Far Eastern Gospel Crusade, Farmington, Mich., 1949-54, home sec. and treas., 1951-54, Philippine bus. mgr. and treas., 1954-62; exec. dir. Interdenominational Fgn. Mission Assn., Wheaton, Ill., 1963—; v.p. Evang. Lit. Overseas, Wheaton, 1981-86; treas. and editorial com. Evang. Missions Info. Service, Wheaton, 1964—; mem. missions commn. World Evang. Fellowship, Wheaton, 1977—, N.Am. Council, 1987—; bd. dirs. Tyndale House Found., Wheaton, 1964—, pres., 1982—; trustee Henry Parsons Crowell Trust, Chgo., 1977—, sec./treas., 1984—. Editor: (with others) Evangelical Missions Tomorrow, 1977, Christ and Caesar in Christian Missions, 1979, Reaching Our Generation, 1982. Mem. Nat. Assn Evangs. (mem. adminstrn. bd. 1984—, Layman-of-Yr. award 1976), Wheaton Coll. Alumni Assn. (bd. dirs. 1983—, pres. 1986-87). Home: PO Box 1032 Wheaton IL 60189-1032 Office: Interdenominational Fgn Mission Assn PO Box 395 Wheaton IL 60189-0395

FROEHLICH, CLIFFORD WAYNE, editor; b. St. Louis, July 6, 1956; s. Wilbert Walter and Marcella M. (Baeumker) F.; m. Elise Ann VanKavage, Aug. 6, 1983. BA in Polit. Sci. summa cum laude, St. Louis U., 1978; MA in Journalism, U. Mo., 1982. Manuscript editor The C.V. Mosby Co., St. Louis, 1983-84, copywriter, 1984-86; film reviewer The Riverfront Times, St. Louis, 1983—; adj. faculty mem. Webster Univ., St. Louis, 1986—; mng. editor, pub. relations Mallinckrodt Inst. of Radiology, St. Louis, 1986—; film reviewer (radio) Sta. WMRY-FM/KATZ-FM, St. Louis, 1985-86; freelance manuscript editor Cracom Corp., St. Louis, 1986; freelance copywriter RK Communications, St. Louis, 1985-86; freelance reporter St. Louis Globe-Democrat, 1983. Bd. dirs. Madison County Humane Soc., Edwardsville, Ill., 1986-87. Mem. Kappa Tau Alpha, Pi Sigma Alpha. Democrat. Avocations: filmgoing, reading, baseball. Home: 51 Odom Collinsville IL 62234 Office: Mallinckrodt Inst Radiology 510 S Kings Hwy Saint Louis MO 63110

FROEHLICH, ROBERT JOSEPH, management consultant; b. Pitts., Apr. 28, 1953; s. Robert Joseph Froehlich Sr. and Elizabeth Anne Rooney; m. Cheryl Ann André Froehlich, Oct. 15, 1977; children: Marianne Elizabeth, Stephanie Marie. BA, U. Dayton, 1975, M in Pub. Adminstrn., 1976; MA, Cen. Mich. U., 1977; PhD, Calif. Western U., 1979. Budget analyst City of Dayton, 1975-78; supt. adminstrn. Montgomery County, Dayton, 1978-81; city mgr. City of Beavercreek (Ohio), 1981-85; sr. mgr. Ernst & Whinney, Cin., 1985—. Author: A Guide to Understanding County Government, 1981; contbr. articles to profl. jours. bd. dirs. Bergamo Ctr., Dayton. Named one of Outstanding Young Men Am., 1983. Mem. Am. Soc. Pub. Adminstrn. (com. chmn.), Internat. City Mgr. Assn., Am. Water Works Assn., Govt. Fin. Officer Assn. Democrat. Roman Catholic. Avocations: tennis, bicycling, art. Home: 6529 Timberwolf Ct West Chester OH 45069

FROEHLICH, VIRGIL, food products company executive. Pres., gen. mgr. Affiliated Foods Coop, Inc., Norfolk, Nebr. Office: Affiliated Foods Coop Inc 13th St & Omaha Ave Norfolk NE 68701 *

FROIMSON, AVRUM ISAIAH, Orthopedist; b. Beaver Falls, Pa., Mar. 6, 1931; s. David and Annette (Unatin) F.; m. Phyllis Peltz, June 14, 1953; children: Lisa, Eric, Mark, Karen. BS, Case Western Res., 1951; MD, Tulane U., 1955. Diplomate Am. Bd. Orthopaedic Surgery (examiner 1980). Intern Phila. Gen. Hosp., 1955-56; resident St. Lukes, Cleve., 1958-61, Columbia-Presbyn., N.Y.C., 1961-62; chief hand clinic Metro Hosp., Cleve., 1962-78; orthopaedic surgeon St. Luke's Hosp., Cleve., 1962-80; dir. orthopaedics Mt. Sinai Med. Ctr., Cleve., 1980—; clinical prof. orthopaedic surgery Case Western Res. U. Med. Sch., Cleve., 1982—. Contbr. articles, papers, and book chpts. to sci. jour. Served to lt. USN, 1956-58. Fellow ACS, Am. Acad. Orthopaedic Surgeons; mem. Am. Soc. Surgery of Hand. Jewish. Clubs: Union (Cleve.); Racquet (Pepper Pike, Ohio). Avocations: sail yacht racing, running, skiing, tennis. Office: 26900 Cedar Rd Cleveland OH 44122

FROLICHSTEIN, SEYMOUR REES, architect; b. Chgo., May 3, 1936; s. Melvin Wolff and Judith (Rees) F.; m. Susan Heyman, June 28, 1964; children: Rita, Michael. BArch, U. Ill., Champaign, 1960. Mem. tech. staff Harry Weese Assocs., Chgo., 1963-65, Gorden Levin & Assocs., Chgo., 1965-67; job capt. Loebl, Schlossman & Hackl Inc., Chgo., 1967-69; prin. Stowell Cook Frolichstein Inc., Chgo., 1969—. Cons. Albany Park Community Bd., Chgo., 1982—; pres. Devel. Corp. Evanston, Ill., 1980-82. Served to lt. (j.g.) USNR, 1960-63. Mem. AIA (com. chmn. 1982-84). Democrat. Jewish. Home: 916 Lee St Evanston IL 60202 Home: Office Stowell Cook Frolichstein Inc 70 E Lake St Chgo. IL 60601

FROME, VICTOR JOSEPH, JR., data processing executive; b. Milw., Dec. 31, 1943; s. Victor Joseph Sr. and Julia Mary (Neticki) F.; m. Brigitte Margarette Weidendach, Oct. 29, 1965 (div. Apr. 1986); children: Thomas, Christopher. BA cum laude, Golden Gate U., 1971; MA, Cen. Mich. U., 1976. Enlisted U.S. Army, 1962, commd., 1967, advanced through ranks to maj., 1977; adminstr. U.S. Army, San Francisco, 1968-71; project officer U.S. Army, Washington, 1971-76; adminstrn. computer systems command U.S. Army, Zweibrucken, Fed. Republic Germany, 1976-79; sr. exec. U.S.A. Pub. Ctr. U.S. Army, St. Louis, 1979-83; retired U.S. Army, 1983; data processing mgr. Assoc. Equipment Corp., St. Louis, 1983-86. Mem. Assn. Prodn. and Inventory Control, Internat. Assn. Quality Control, St. Louis Met. NCR Computer Users Group (pres. 1986-87). Democrat. Roman Catholic. Avocations: home renovation, electronics. Home: 631 N Geyer Saint Louis MO 63122 Office: Assoc Equipment Corp 5043 Farlin Saint Louis MO 63115

FROMELL-THEIS, ANN INGA-LILL, dentist; b. Stockholm, Sweden, Feb. 8, 1946; came to U.S., 1972; d. Carl Rune and Inga-lill Dorrit Svea (Ahlgreen) Tromell; m. Dennis Clarence Theis, Oct. 9, 1971. Student, Hoögre Allm Laäroverket, 1966; DDS, Sch. of Dentistry, Minn., 1976. Lic. dentist, Faculty of Odontology, Gothenburg, Sweden, 1972. Assoc. dentist Dr. Rymond Eckles, New Hope, Minn., 1976-80, Dr. James Perry, Shakopee, Minn., 1978-80; practice dentistry Rockford (Minn.) Dental Care, 1980—. Liaison Project Minn.-Leon, Rockford, 1986—. Mem. AMA, Minn. Dental Soc., Mpls. Dist Dental Soc. (examiner, mem. peer rev. bd. 1986—), Soc. for Clin. Hypnosis. Avocations: gardening, cross country skiing. Home: PO Box 193 Excelsior MN 55331 Office: Rockford Dental Care Ctr Box 236 900 Walnut St Rockford MN 55373

FROMM, ERIKA (MRS. PAUL FROMM), clinical psychologist; b. Frankfurt, Germany, Dec. 23, 1910; came to U.S., 1938, naturalized, 1944; d. Siegfried and Clementine (Stern) Oppenheimer; m. Paul Fromm, July 20, 1938; 1 child, Joan (Mrs. Greenstone). Ph.D. magna cum laude, U. Frankfurt, 1933; postgrad. child care program, Chgo. Inst. for Psychoanalysis, 1949-51. Diplomate: Am. Bd. Examiners in Profl. Psychology, Am. Bd. Examiners Clin. Hypnosis. Chief psychologist Apeldoorn State Hosp., Holland, 1935-38; chief psychologist Francis W. Parker Sch., 1944-51; supervising psychologist Inst. for Juvenile Research, 1951-53; asst. prof. to assoc. prof. Northwestern U. Med. Sch., 1954-61; prof. U. Chgo., 1961-76, prof. emeritus, 1976—. Author: (with L.D. Hartman) Intelligence-A Dynamic Approach; (with Thomas M. French) Dream Interpretation: A New Approach, 1964, 2d edit., 1986; (with Ronald E. Shor) Hypnosis: Developments in Research and New Perspectives, 1972, 2d edit., 1979; (with Daniel P. Brown) Hypnotherapy and Hypnoanalysis, 1986; (with Daniel Brown) Hypnosis and Behavioral Medicine, 1987; also numerous articles in profl. jours.; mem. editorial bd. Jour. Clin. and Exptl. Psychopathology, 1951-59; clin. editor: Internat. Jour. Clin. and Exptl. Hypnosis, 1968—; assoc. editor Bull. Brit. Soc. Exptl. and Clin. Hypnosis, 1982—; mem. bd. cons. editors Psychoanalytic Psychology, 1982—; mem. adv. bd. editors Imagination, Cognition and Personality: Sci. study of Consciousness, 1981—. Fellow Am. Psychol. Assn. (pres. div. 30 1972-73), Am. Orthopsychiat. Assn. (dir. 1961-63), AAAS, Soc. Clin. Exptl. Hypnosis (sec. 1965-67,v.p. 1971-75, pres. 1975-77); mem. Am. Bd. Psychol. Hypnosis (pres. 1971-74), Ill. Psychol. Assn. (council 1951-53, 55-57, bd. examiners 1959-62, v.p. bd. examiners 1960-61), Soc. Projective Techniques, Sigma Xi. Home: 5715 S Kenwood Ave Chicago IL 60637 Office: Dept Behavioral Sciences U Chicago Chicago IL 60637

FROMM, JOSEPH L., automobile company executive; b. Detroit, May 22, 1930; s. Charles and Elizabeth F.; A.B. cum laude, Princeton U., 1953; M.B.A., Harvard U., 1958; m. Beverly C. Booth, June 18, 1960; children—Charles, Laurence, Kenneth, Lisa, Brian. Research asst. Harvard Bus. Sch., 1959; asst. to pres. Gen. Electronic Labs., Cambridge, Mass., 1960-62; with Chrysler Corp., Highland Park, Mich., 1963-68; treas. Marantette & Co., Detroit, 1969; asst. treas. Am. Motors Corp., Southfield, Mich., 1970—; dir. United Wis. Ins. Co., Grosse Pointe Cable, Inc.; instr. U. Detroit Evening Div., 1964-65. Councilman, City of Grosse Pointe Farms, 1973-86, mayor, 1986—; trustee, Bon Secours Hosp., Grosse Pointe, 1975—. Served with AUS, 1954-56. Mem. Sentinel Pension Inst., Midwest Pension Conf. Republican. Roman Catholic. Club: Grosse Pointe Indoor Tennis, Country of Detroit. Office: Am Motors Corp 27777 Franklin Rd Southfield MI 48034

FROMSTEIN, MITCHELL S., temporary office services company executive; b. 1928. Grad., U. Wis., 1947. With Krueger Homes Inc., 1948-49; account exec. Mautner Advt. Agy., 1949-53; former pres. TV Parts Inc.; ptnr. Fromstein Assocs.; pres., chief exec. officer, dir. The Parker Pen Co., Janesville, Wis., 1985-86; pres., chief exec. officer Manpower, Inc., Milw., 1976—, also dir. Office: Manpower Inc 5301 N Ironwood Rd Box 2053 Milwaukee WI 53201 *

FROSS, ROGER RAYMOND, lawyer; b. Rockford, Ill., Mar. 8, 1940; s. Hollis H. and Dorothy (George) F.; m. Madelon R. Rose, Feb. 14, 1970; 1 child, Oliver. AB, DePauw U., 1962; JD, U. Chgo., 1965. Bar: Ill. 1965. Assoc. Norman and Billick, Chgo., 1965-70; ptnr. Lord, Bissell & Brook, Chgo., 1970—, mng. pntr., 1982—; bd. dirs. Hyde Park Bank and Trust Co., Chgo., 1975—. Bd. dirs. Hyde Park Neighborhood Club, Chgo., 1970—, pres. 1972-73; bd. dirs., mem. exec. com. South East Chgo. Commn., 1978; bd. dirs. Citizens Com. on Juvenile Ct.; mem. Community Conservation Council, Chgo., 1980—; v.p., sec. Hyde Park-Kenwood Local Devel. Corp., Chgo., 1975—. Rector schlor DePauw U., Greencastle, Ind., 1958-62. Mem. ABA, Ill. Bar Assn., Chgo. Bar Assn. (chmn. com. juvenile delinquents 1972). Office: Lord Bissell & Brook 115 S LaSalle St Chicago IL 60603

FROST, ALFRIEDA MARY, school administrator; b. Williamston, Mich., Jan. 12, 1935; d. Rowland Brazil and Emily F. (Bourns) F. BA, Asbury Coll., 1956; MA, Western Mich. U., Kalamazoo, 1961; EdS., Mich. State U., 1974, PhD, 1975. Cert. teacher, Mich. Tchr. jr. high Jefferson County Schs., Louisville, 1956-58; elem. tchr. South Haven (Mich.) Pub. Schs., 1958-66, elem. prin., 1966-74; elem. prin. Grosse Pointe (Mich.) Pub. Schs., 1974-77, dir. elem. curriculum, 1977—; Instr. Mich. State U., 1975. Mem.

AAUW, Mich. Elem. and Middle Sch Prin. Assn. (pres. 1977), Nat. Assn. Elem. Sch. Prins., internat. Reading Assn., Phi Delta Kappa. Office: The Grosse Pointe Pub Sch System 389 Saint Clair Grosse Pointe MI 48230

FROST, BRIAN REGINALD THOMAS, materials scientist; b. London, Sept. 6, 1926; s. Reginald E. and Beatrice A.E. (Cope) F.; m. Pamela C. Heath, June 5, 1954; children: Carol M., Timothy J. BS, U. Birmingham, Eng., 1947, PhD, 1949; MBA, U. Chgo., 1974. Chartered engr., U.K. Scientist A.E.R.E Harwell, Eng., 1947-69; assoc. dir. materials sci. div. Argonne (Ill.) Nat. Lab., 1969-73, dir. materials sci. div., 1973-84, dir. tech. transfer ctr., 1985—; bd. dirs. Materials Reliability Inc, Naperville, Ill.; mem. National Materials Adv. Bd., 1982—. Author: Nuclear Fuel Elements, 1982; co-author: Nuclear Reactor Materials, 1959. Fellow Brit. Inst. Metals, Am. Nuclear Soc., Am. Soc. for Metals. Avocations: sailing, walking. Home: 1311 Marcey Ave Wheaton IL 60187 Office: Argonne Nat Lab 9700 S Cass Ave Argonne IL 60439

FROST, JOHN JARED, JR., manufacturing company executive; b. Kenosha, Wis., Feb. 5, 1954; s. John Jared Sr. and H. Nancy (Philipp) F.; m. Caprice Michelle Hohler, Aug. 10, 1974 (div. Oct. 1976). BS in Indsl. Engring., U. Wis., Madison, 1976; BS in Labor Econs., U. Wis., Kenosha, 1978. Engr. Frost Co., Kenosha, 1976-79, plant mgr., 1979-81, v.p., 1981-87, exec. v.p., 1987—, also bd. dirs. Mem. Kenosha Pretreatment Adv. Council; commr. Kenosha Transit Commn., 1982-86; fin. chmn. Salvation Army, Kenosha, 1983-86. Mem. Kenosha Mfg.'s Assn. (chmn. engrs. group 1983), Amateur Trapshooting Assn. Republican. Congregationalist. Clubs: Conservation of Kenosha County (pres. 1983-84), Silver Dollar (sec. 1985—), Case Gun. Lodge: Elks. Home: 606 72d St Kenosha WI 53141 Office: Frost Co 6523 14th Ave Kenosha WI 53141

FROST, MARY KATHERINE, clinic executive; b. Windsor, Ont., Can., Nov. 13, 1928; came to U.S., 1951, naturalized, 1967; d. Philip Francis and Elizabeth Eppert; cert. in acctg. Windsor Bus. Coll., 1946; student Toronto Conservatory Music, 1946-47, Am. Inst. Banking, 1954-57; A.S., Wayne State U., 1967; m. William Max Frost, July 17, 1948; Teller, bookkeeper, asst. acct. Toronto Dominion Bank, Windsor, 1947-51; with Nat. Bank Detroit, 1951-54; mgr., customer relations officer City Nat. Bank Detroit, 1954-62; psychobiology research supr., adminstrv. asst. dept. mental health Lafayette Clinic, Detroit, 1964—; co-founder, coordinator, polysomnographer Lafayette Clinic Sleep Center, 1975—, lectr., 1978—. Mem. citizens adv. council Lafayette Clinic, chmn. membership, 1979-82, vice chmn., 1982—; bd. dirs. Travelers Aid Soc., 1973—, Casa Maria, 1974-81, Casgrain Hall, 1974—; trustee League Catholic Women, 1974—, mem. adv. bd., 1982—; co-founder Windsor Light Opera Co., 1948; mem. Institutional Animal Care and Use Com., 1974—. Named Disting. Employee of 1981, Lafayette Clinic, 1982. Mem. Mich. State Employees Assn. (pres. mental health dept. Lafayette Clinic chpt. 1975-81), Assn. Polysomnography Technologists, Assn. Profl. Sleep Socs., Am. Narcolepsy Assn., Midwest Inst. Alumni, Nat. Assn. Female Execs., Mich. Assn. Govt. Employees, Econ. Club Detroit, Internat. Platform Assn., Mich. Mental Health Soc., Project Hope League, Smithsonian Assocs. Republican. Clubs: Five o'Clock Forum, U. Detroit, U.S. Senatorial. Contbr. articles to profl. jours. Home: 1 Lafayette Plaisance Suite 2115 Detroit MI 48207 Office: Dept Psychobiology Lafayette Clinic 951 E Lafayette St Detroit MI 48207

FRUCHTER, SCOTT JOSEPH, health care delivery systems consultant; b. Reading, Pa., June 2, 1951; s. Samuel Burns and Margaret Helen (Kremser) F.; m. KeriLyn Christine Burrows, Aug. 4, 1979; children: Chauncey Collier. BA cum laude, Muhlenberg Coll., 1972; MDiv, Yale U., 1976; MBA with distinction, U. Mich., 1983. Field agent Mich. Dept. Corrections, Ann Arbor, 1977-83; product mgr. alternative delivery systems CIGNA, Hartford, 1983-85, asst. dir. alternative delivery systems, 1985; cons. Johnson & Higgins, Cleve., 1985—. Treas. Ctr. for Occupational & Personalized Edn., Ann Arbor, 1978-83; chmn. Conn. Spay/Neuter Program, Hartford, 1984-86; mem. Gov.'s Council for Agriculture, Hartford, 1985-86; chmn. Conn. Agriculture Mktg. Com., 1985. Mem. Group Health Assn. Am.. Nat. Assn. Employers for Health Care Alternatives (adv. bd.). Lutheran. Club: Yale (NYC). Avocations: real estate investments, woodworking, computers. Home: 3481 Dogwood Ln Bath OH 44210 Office: Johnson & Higgins of Ohio 2600 National City Ctr Cleveland OH 44114

FRUIN, ALAN HARTMAN, physician; b. Normal, Ill., Nov. 22, 1941; s. Leon Thomas and Virginia (Ziegler) F.; m. Carolyn Clara Cousins, June 17, 1967; children: Alex Brent, Candace Dawn. BA, Vanderbilt U., 1964, MD, 1967. Diplomate Nat. Bd. Med. Examiners; Cert. Am. Bd. Neurol. Surgery. Intern Vanderbilt U. Hosp., Nashville, 1967-68; asst. resident in surgery Vanderbilt U. Hosp., Omaha, 1968-69; asst. resident in neurosurgery Vanderbilt U. Hosp., Nashville, 1969-72, chief resident in neurosurgery, 1972-73; asst. prof. neurol. surgery Sch. Med. Creighton U., Omaha, 1975-81, assoc. prof., 1981—, acting chmn. surgery, 1982-83, assoc. dean, 1986—; lectr. in field. Contbr. articles to profl. jours. Fellow ACS; mem. Omaha Midwest Clin. Soc., Iowa-Midwest Neurol. Soc., Nebr. Acad. Neurologists and Neurosurgeons, Meacham Neurosurgical Soc., Douglas County Med. Soc., Nebr. Med. Assn., Alpha Omega Alpha. Home: 2906 S 97th Ave Omaha NE 68124 Office: Neurological Surgery 601 N 30th St Omaha NE 68124

FRUIN, ROBERT EDWARD, productivity director; b. Chgo., Mar. 7, 1930; s. Robert Edward Jr. and Mildred Martha (Travis) F.; m. Monica Gisela Brodbeck, Feb. 5, 1955; children: Robert S., Michael T., Mary E., Paul A., John K. BS, U. Notre Dame, 1952; MS, Loyola U., Chgo., 1954. Chemist Standard Oil of Ind. (later Amoco), Whiting, 1956-61; plant mgr. Dielectric Materials, Chgo., 1961-65, United Techs.-Essex, Tiffin, Ohio and Chgo., 1965-74; div. mgr. mfg. United Techs.-Essex, Decatur, Ill., 1975-80; dir. productivity Unitec Techs. Co.-Essex, Decatur, Ill., 1980—. Served with U.S. Army, 1954-56. Republican. Roman Catholic. Avocations: golfing, tennis, music. Home: Rural Rt 1 Box 172F Oreana IL 62554 Office: United Techs-Essex 800 E Garfield Ave Decatur IL 62525

FRUTH, BERYL ROSE, family practice physician; b. Carey, Ohio, Mar. 27, 1952; d. Oscar W. and Alice (Arnett) Fruth. BA in Chemistry magna cum laude, Asbury Coll., 1973; MD, Ohio State U., 1977. Diplomate Am. Acad. Family Practice. Intern Grant Hosp., Columbus, Ohio, 1977-78, resident, 1978-79, chief resident, 1979-80; practice medicine specializing in family practice, Columbus, 1980—; asst. dir. family practice residency Grant Hosp., 1980-81; med. dir. Columbus Dispatch, St. Anthony Breast Evaluation Ctr., 1986—; lectr. Columbus Cancer Clinic, 1984. Contbr. Ohio State U. Med. Sch. Learning Module in Alcoholism, 1983-84. Named Alumna of Yr., Vanlue Sch., Ohio. Mem. AMA, Am. Med. Women's Assn. Methodist. Office: 20 Governors Pl Columbus OH 43203

FRY, JAMES HAROLD, personnel executive; b. St. Joseph, Mo., Aug. 31, 1955; s. Thomas Leo and Phyllis Marie (Fields) F.; m. Denise Louise Grasso, June 23, 1973 (div. Apr. 1982); children: Kevin James, Nicholas Thomas, Mitchell Paul; m. Tracy Lee Thomas, May 4, 1985. BS, Pittsburg (Kans.) State U., 1978, MS, 1980. Machine specialist McNally Pittsburg Inc., Pittsburg, 1973-80, supr. foundry div., 1980, employment mgr., 1980-84, personnel mgr., 1984—; chmn. Personnel Com. Pittsburg, 1986—. Lobbyist Kans. for Liquor by the Drink, Topeka, 1985; adv. Right-to-Know Legislation, Topeka, 1986; chmn. bd. Leadership Pittsburg, 1985—; mem. adv. bd. Blue Cross/Blue Shield, Topeka, 1985—, Reducing Delinquency in Mid-Am., 1984. Mem. Indsl. Mgmt. Council (treas. 1985—), Assoc. Metals Industries, S.E. Kans. Personnel Assn., Tri-State Personnel Assn. Republican. Roman Catholic. Lodge: KC. Avocations: camping, golf, hunting. Office: McNally Pittsburg Inc 315 W 3d Pittsburg KS 66762

FRY, JAMES WILSON, state librarian; b. Canton, Ohio, May 8, 1939; s. Oris Wilson and Cora (Harmon) F.; m. Mary Kociban, June 21, 1986; 1 child, Christine Lee. B.A., Milligan Coll., 1966; M.L.S., Ind. U., 1969; M.A., Ohio State U., 1971, postgrad., 1971-75. Reference librarian Ohio State U., Columbus, 1969-70; head regional campuses, tech. services div. Ohio State U., 1970-75; dep. asst. state librarian State Library of Ohio, 1975-83, dep. state librarian, 1983-84; state librarian Library of Mich., Lansing, 1984—; cons. Columbus Pub. Schs., 1977; editorial cons. Mags. for Libraries, Columbus, 1978; sec. bd. OHIONET, Columbus, 1978-79; exec. council Mich. Library Consortium, Lansing, 1984. Author historic guide: Ohio State U. Library, 1972; contbr. articles to profl. jours. Mem. exec. bd. Mich. Ctr. for the Book, 1986—. Mem. Chief Officers of State Library Agencies (Network devel. com.), ALA (resources and tech. services div.), Assn. Specialized and Coop. Library Agys. Home: 2110 Barritt St Lansing MI 48909 Office: Library of Mich 735 E Michigan Ave Lansing MI 48909

FRY, ROBERT WILLIAM, orthodontist; b. Independence, Mo., Apr. 23, 1948; s. Stanton and Marie (Jorgensen) F.; m. Mary Louise Stowell, Aug. 15, 1970; children—Jeremy Randall, Mary Whitney. B.S./A.A., Graceland Coll., Lamoni, Iowa, 1970; D.D.S., U. Mo.-Kansas City, 1973; M.S., U. N.C., 1977. Cert. fin. planner Coll. Fin. Planning, Denver, 1979. Gen. practice dentistry, U.S. Army, Fort Hood, Tex., 1973-75; practice dentistry specializing in orthodontics, Overland Park, Kans., 1977—. Mem. Parks and Recreation Bd., Lenexa, Kans., 1979-80; vice chmn. Planning Commn., Lenexa, 1980-84; chmn. Leffel for Congress, Kans., 1984; trustee Johnson County Community Coll., 1987—. Served to capt. USAR, 1973-75. Recipient Leadership Kans. award Kans. Assn. Commerce and Industry, 1984. Mem. ADA (del. 1983-84), Kans. Dental Assn. (del. 1979-82, chmn. publs. 1980-82, treas. 1982-85, pres. 1987—), Am. Assn. Orthodontics, Kans. Orthodontics Soc. (assoc. editor jour. 1982-83), Assn. Fin. Planners, Lenexa C. of C. (pres. 1982). Republican. Mem. Reorganized Ch. Jesus Christ of Latterday Saints. Lodge: Toastmasters. Home: 12340 Pflumm Rd Olathe KS 66062 Office: 5600 W 95th Overland Park KS 66207

FRY, ROY H(ENRY), librarian, educator; b. Seattle, June 16, 1931; s. Ray Edward and Fern Mildred (Harmon) F.; m. Joanne Mae Van de Guchte, Sept. 12, 1970; 1 dau., Andrea Joy. B.A. in Asian Studies, U. Wash., 1959, B.A. in Anthropology, 1959; M.A. in Library Sci., Western Mich. U., 1965; M.A. in Polit. Sci., Northeastern Ill. U., 1977; archives cert. U. Denver, 1970. Cert. tchr., Wash.; cert. pub. librarian, N.Y.; cert. Med. Library Assn. Librarian and audio-visual coordinator Zillah (Wash.) Pub. Schs., (Wash.), 1960-61; librarian Mark Morris High Sch., Longview, Wash., 1961-64; evening reference librarian Loyola U. of Chgo., 1965-67, head reference librarian, 1967-73, bibliog. services librarian, 1973-74, head circulation librarian, 1974-76, coordinator pub. services, 1976-85, gov. documents librarian, 1985—, teaching asst. in anthropology, 1966-67, instr. library sci. program for disadvantaged students, 1967, 68, univ. archivist, 1976-78, bibliographer for polit. sci., 1973—, instr. corr. study div., 1975-85. Mem. Niles Twp. Regular Republican Orgn., Skokie, Ill., 1982—, sec. 1986—; mem. Skokie Caucus Party, 1981—; vol. Deputy Registration Officer, 1986; mem. Skokie Traffic Safety Commn., 1984—, Skokie 4th July Parade com., 1986—; election judge, Niles Twp., 1983—. Served with USNR, 1951-52. Mem. Nat. Librarians Assn. (founding mem., bd. dirs. 1975-76), Asian/Pacific Am. Librarians Assn. (founding mem.), Chgo. Area Theol. Librarians Assn., Pacific N.W. Library Assn., Chgo. Area Archivists (founding mem.), Midwest Archives Conf. (founding mem.), ALA, Assn. Coll. and Research Libraries, Ill. Prairie Path Assn., Royal Can. Geog. Soc., Skokie Hist. Soc. (recording sec. 1986—), Nat. Cathedral Assn., Am. Legion, VFW, Korean War Vets. Assn., Pi Sigma Alpha. Republican. Episcopalian. Home: 10059 D Frontage Rd Skokie IL 60077 Office: Loyola Univ E M Cudahy Meml Library 6525 N Sheridan Rd Chicago IL 60626

FRYDENLUND, ARTHUR JORGEN, motel executive; b. nr. Buffalo, S.D., Aug. 16, 1907; s. Olaf and Ella (Halvorson) F.; student pub. schs.; m. Elaine A. Eyler, June 25, 1934; children—Gerald, John, Karen (Mrs. Gerald Bouzek), Jane (Mrs. Elliott Moore), Eric. Barber, Prairie du Chien, Wis., 1932-51; owner Motel Brisbois, Prairie du Chien, 1951—, Moto-Miter Co., Prairie du Chien, 1959—; dir. Hidden Valley-Nine County Tourist Promotion. City chmn. Heart Fund, Prairie du Chien, 1962; mem. adv. bd. Campion Jesuit High Sch., 1970—; mem. Father Marquette Tercentenary Com., 1972—; pres. Blackhawk Com., 1974—. Mem. County Bd. Suprs., chmn. health com., 1974—, mem. social services com. Bd. dirs. Indsl. Devel., 1952-63, pres., 1963—; trustee Meml. Hosp., 1957—; commr. transit com. Milw. R.R.; dir. 9 county tourist promotion Hidden Valley, 1979; mem. Gov's. Tourism Council, 1985-86. Mem. Wis. Innkeepers (v.p. 1974—, bd. dirs.), Prairie du Chien C. of C. (pres. 1959, dir. 1952—, named Man of Yr. 1978), Gt. Fire Engine Race Am. (dir. 1972—). Methodist. Patentee in field. Home: 533 N Marquette Rd Prairie du Chien WI 53821

FRYDENLUND, MARVIN MILTON, safety lecturer and administrator, writer; b. Cashton, Wis., July 7, 1924; s. Martin Adolph and Mabel (Dahlen) F.; m. Evonell Corrine Nestingen, Aug. 9, 1947; children: Bona Leigh, Valerie Ann, Tara Therese. BA in Journalism, San Jose State U., 1950. News editor Daily Record-Herald, Wausau, Wis., 1950-54; bldg. editor Small Homes Guide, Chgo., 1954-56; mng. editor Bldg. Supply News, Chgo., 1956-61; mng. dir., chmn. Lightning Protection Inst., Chgo., then Harvard, Ill., 1962—; dir., owner, cons. Sch. Lightning Protection Tech., Harvard, 1978—; editor Spartan Daily, San Jose; speaker in field. Author: (book) Land Development, 1961; editor: Harvard:1929-1976, 1976; contbr. articles to mags. and jours. Mem. Harvard Bicentennial Commn., 1976; founding chmn. Harvard Area HIst. Soc., 1977. Served with AC, U.S. Army, 1943-45. Mem. Chgo. Soc. Assn. Execs., Am. Legion, Harvard C. of C. (pres. 1978). Republican. Lutheran. Lodge: Rotary, Moose. Avocations: skiing, archery, woodworking. Home: 402 Marawood Dr Woodstock IL 60098 Office: Lightning Protection Inst 48 N Ayer St Harvard IL 60033

FRYE, DELLA MAE, portrait artist; b. Roanoke, Va., Feb. 16, 1926; d. Henry Vetchel and Helen Lavinia Theradosia (Eardley) Pearcy; m. James Frederick Frye, Nov. 1, 1944; children: Linda Jeanne Frye Chaikin, James Marvin, David Scott. Student, Hope Coll., 1968, Grand Valley State Coll., 1969-71. Asst. med. records librarian Bapt. Hosp., Little Rock, 1944; receptionist, sec. Stephens Coll., Columbia, Mo., 1945-46; art tchr. Jenison (Mich.) Christian Sch., 1965-67, pvt. classes, 1964-74; realtor 1978-80; with Diversified Fin., 1979-82; portrait artist 1967—; cons. World Traders, Grand Rapids, Mich., 1986—. Author various poems; exhbns. include Salon Des Nations (cert. honor), 1984, Ann Arbor (Mich.) Art Guild, Kalamazoo Artists, Internat. Art Gallery, Hawaii, La Mandragore Gallery Internationale D'Art Contemporain. Pres. mother's club Jenison Christian Sch., 1965-66; treas. Band Boosters, Jenison, 1966. Recipient awards for nat. contests in portrait painting. Republican. Baptist. Avocations: songwriting, swimming. Home: 7677 Steele Ave Jenison MI 49428 Mailing Address: PO Box 2484 Grand Rapids MI 49501

FRYE, KRISTOFER DOBY, architect; b. Muncie, Ind., May 16, 1962; s. James Joseph and Roberta May (Reynolds) F. BS in Archtl. Engring., Purdue U., 1985. Architect James Assocs., Indpls., 1985-86, Browning Day Mullins, Dierdorf, Indpls., 1986—. Mem. AIA (assoc.), Sigma Tau Gamma. Democrat. Avocation: collecting music.

FRYE, LARRY ROBERT, trade association administrator; b. Logansport, Ind., Aug. 15, 1938; s. Bailey and Retta Mae (Lee) F.; m. Mary Lee Woodruff, Aug. 19, 1961; children: Nelson Bailey, Christina Marie. BS in Forestry, Purdue U., 1963. Forester Ind. Div. of Forestry, Indpls., 1963-65; timber buyer Pike Lumber Co., Akron, Ind., 1965-66; extension forester Purdue U., Lafayette, Ind., 1966-67; dir. forestry programs fine hardwoods div. Am. Walnut Assn., Indpls., 1967-78, exec. dir. fine hardwoods div., 1978—. Author: (booklet) Hardwood Dollars and Sense, 1967, Fine Hardwoods Selectorama, 1978; editor Wood Unlimited newsletter, 1982. Served to 2d lt. U.S. Army, 1960. Lodge: Masons (sr. warden 1987). Home: 35 Village Ct Zionsville IN 46077 Office: Fine Hardwood Veneer Assn and Am Walnut Mfrs Assn 5603 W Raymond St Suite O Indianapolis IN 46241

FRYKBERG, W. RANDOLPH, government services agency executive; b. Hackensack, N.J., Mar. 19, 1947; s. William Samual and Virginia Ann (Walker) F.; m. Diane Kay Rollins, June 21, 1970; 1 child, Andrew Timothy. AA, U. Fla., 1967; BA, Western Mich. U., 1968, MA, 1973, Specialist of Arts in Sci. Edn., 1974, PhD, 1976; MS, U. Mich., 1972. Research biologist Parke-Davis & Co., Ann Arbor, Mich., 1969-71; project dir. EPA and Muskegon County (Mich.) Dept. Pub. Works Muskegon County Wastewater Mgmt. System, 1974-76; asst. dir. environ. programs mgr. N.E. Mich. Council Govts., Gaylord, 1976-79, exec. dir., 1979-83; city mgr. City of Boyne City, Mich., 1983—; mem. Pub. Involvement Work Group, Great Lakes Basin Commn, 1977-80, Toxic Sites Assessment Model Review Com., 1986—; tech. advisor Dept. of Energy; commr. Mich. Air Pollution Control Commn., 1982-85; facilitator 2d World Conf. on Large Lakes, Mackinac Island, Mich., 1986. Tng. advisor No. Mich. Nat. Ski Patrol System, Inc., 1970-80. HEW fellow, 1972-74; EPA grantee, 1974-76; recipient commendation Resource Conservation and Devel. Program, 1979. Mem. Water Pollution Control Fedn., Mich. Water Pollution Control Fedn., Am. Water Resources Assn., N.Am. Benthological Soc., N.Am. Lake Mgmt. Soc., Mich. Soc. Planning Ofcls., Micro-Computers in Planning, Charlevoix County Growth Alliance (pres. 1985-87, treas. 1987—). Clubs: Charlevoix (Mich.) Yacht, Boyne City Yacht. Home: 1249 Lakeshore Dr Boyne City MI 49712 Office: City of Boyne City PO Box 68 Boyne City MI 49712

FRYSTAK, LEO, dental laboratory owner; b. Park Ridge, Ill., Mar. 21, 1960; s. Richard and Mary Jane Frances (Pedi) F. AS, Triton Coll., 1982. Cert. dental technician. Intern Hines VA Hosp., Chgo., 1981-82; dept. head removeable prosthodontics Midland Haynes Dental Lab., Niles, Ill., 1981-84, intern dental technician, 1982-84; owner Frystak Prosthetics Inc., Park Ridge, 1984—; tech. advisor W.W. Granger, Niles, 1984-85. Served with USAF, 1978-79. Mem. Nat. Assn. Dental Labs. Republican. Club: Marvin Healy Study of Greater Chgo. Avocations: fishing, hunting.

FUCHIK, DAVID JOHN, manufacturing company executive; b. Columbus, Ohio, Feb. 13, 1951; s. John F. and Velma Rose (Winko) F.; m. Anne M. Weber, May 5, 1979. B in Indsl. and Systems Engring., Ohio State U., 1973; MBA, U. Dayton, 1980. Indsl. engr. Inland Div. Gen. Motors Corp., Dayton, Ohio, 1973-75; mgr. indsl. engring. Jeffrey Mining Machinery Div. Dresser Industries, Columbus, 1975-84; dir. mfg. Big Drum Div. Alco Standard Corp., Columbus, 1984—. Mem. Inst. Indsl. Engrs. (sr. mem., sec. 1979-80, v.p. 1980-81, pres. 1981-82, dir. govt. affairs region VI 1983-86, Excellence award 1982). Republican. Roman Catholic. Avocations: golf, woodworking. Office: Big Drum div Alco Standard Corp 1740 Joyce Ave Columbus OH 43216

FUCHS, DONALD JAMES, JR., dentist; b. St. Louis, Feb. 5, 1949; s. Donald James and Mary Virginia (Eckert) F.; m. Carol Marie Bushey, Nov. 25, 1978; children: Michelle, Donald James III, Timothy. AB Biology, St. Louis U., 1971; DDS, U. Mo., 1975. Resident in gen. practice Letterman Med. Ctr., San Francisco, 1975-76; asst. clinic chief Dunham Health Clinic, Carlisle, Pa., 1976-78; gen. practice dentistry Cuba, Mo., 1978—. Mem. ADA, Mo. Dental Assn. (del. 1984—), Greater St. Louis Dental Assn. (bd. dirs.), Acad. Gen. Dentistry, Ozark Dental Soc., Cuba C. of C. (pres. 1982-84). Lodge: Lions (pres. Cuba 1982-84). Avocations: flying, snow skiing, running, drums, karate. Home: HCR 80 Box 114 Cuba MO 65453 Office: 405 W Washington Cuba MO 65453

FUCHS, KATHLEEN F., psychologist, educator; b. Chgo., May 24, 1946; d. Frank T. and Dorothy E. (Mills) Fitzgerald; m. Raymond P. Fuchs, June 27, 1970; children: Brian C., Laura E. BA cum laude, Barat Coll., 1968; MS, St. Louis U., 1971, PhD, 1975. Lic. psychologist, Wis. Psychologist II S.C. State Hosp., Columbia, 1973-74; cons. Richland Sch. Dist., Columbia, 1974; clin. psychologist Lansdowne Mental Health Ctr., Ashland, Ky., 1976-77, Lawrence U., Appleton, Wis., 1977—; vis. assoc. prof. Lawrence U., Appleton, 1985-86, 87—. Mem. bd. edn. St. Pius Parish, Appleton, 1979-82. St. Louis U. fellow, 1968-69, NIMH fellow, 1969-70. Mem. Am. Psychol. Assn., Kappa Gamma Pi, Delta Epsilon Sigma. Roman Catholic. Avocations: gardening, cross-country skiing. Home: 2412 N Division St Appleton WI 54911 Office: Lawrence U Counseling Ctr Box 599 Appleton WI 54912

FUCHS, MICHAEL ALVIN, orthodontist; b. Hastings, Minn., Jan. 16, 1949; s. Conrad Albert and Elizabeth Ann (Leifeld) F.; m. Mary Elizabeth Swanson, Aug. 28, 1971; children: Ryan, Rick, Ann Marie. BA, St. John's U., Collegeville, Minn., 1971; DDS, U. Minn., 1974. Diplomate Am. Bd. Orthodontics. Practice dentistry specializing in orthodontics Huron, S.D., 1976—. Mem. Huron Bd. Edn., 1982—, pres. 1985—; bd. dirs. Greater Huron Devel. Corp., 1986—; bd. dirs., pres. Our Home Inc., 1977-78. Named Outstanding Young Citizen, Huron Jaycees, 1985. Mem. ADA, S.D. Dental Assn. (trustee 1981—), Am. Assn. Orthodontists, S.D. Orthodontic Soc. (pres. 1982-83), Minn. Orthodontic Soc. (affiliate). Lutheran. Lodge: Kiwanis (pres. Huron 1982-83). Avocations: hunting, fishing, jogging, gardening, canoeing. Home: 1860 Robin Ct Huron SD 57350 Office: Profl Arts Bldg 530 Iowa SE Huron SD 57350

FUCHSTEINER, JUDITH AGNES, accountant; b. La Crosse, Wis., Dec. 29, 1947; d. Joseph Herman and Irene Marie (Banasik) Steidl; m. Steven Joseph Fuchsteiner, Jan. 11, 1969; children: Amy, Ellyn, Christopher. BS in Math. and Fin., U. Wis., La Crosse, 1969, BS in Acctg., 1974. CPA, Wis. Staff acct. HUD Hawkins Ash Baptie & Co., La Crosse, 1969-74, staff acct. audit and acctg., 1974-77, sr. acct., 1977-80, mgr., 1980-83, ptnr. designate, 1983-85, ptnr., 1985—. Mem. St. James Sch. Bd., La Crosse, St. James Parish Council, La Crosse; chmn. St. James Parish Fin. Council, La Crosse, 1983—; treas. Aquinas Music Assn., La Crosse, 1985—. Mem. Am. Inst. CPA's, Wis. Inst. CPA's (treas. La Crosse area chpt. 1980), Nat. Assn. Accts. Roman Catholic. Club: Coulee Region Bus. and Profl. Women (treas. 1983-84) (La Crosse). Avocations: counted cross stitch, reading. Office: Hawkins Ash Baptie & Co PO Box 1508 La Crosse WI 54602-1508

FUERSTE, FREDERICK, physician, ophthalmologist; b. St. Louis, Dec. 9, 1921; s. Frederick and June (Brown) F.; m. Marion Skagen, Dec. 28, 1948; children—Nanette, Gretchen, Hunter, Rommel, Madelin, Garth. B.A., U. Iowa, 1953, M.D., 1945. Diplomate Am. Bd. Ophthalmology. Intern, Cook County Hosp., Chgo., 1945-46; resident Northwestern U. Med. Sch., Chgo., 1948-49, Milwaukee County Hosp., Wis., 1949-51; practice medicine specializing in ophthalmology, Dubuque, Iowa, 1953—; asst. in clin. ophthalmology eye dept. St. Louis City Hosp., 1952-53; asst. in clin. ophthalmology Washington U. Med. Sch., eye dept. McMillan Hosp., St. Louis, 1951-53. Served to lt. (j.g.) USNR, 1946-48. Mem. Dubuque County Med. Assn., Iowa Med. Assn., AMA, ACS, Am. Acad. Ophthalmology, Phi Beta Kappa, Alpha Omega Alpha. Home: 130 S Booth St Dubuque IA 52001 Office: 1400 Dodge St Dubuque IA 52001

FUESTON, SYLVESTER HENRY, teacher; b. Lebanon, Ohio; s. Sylvester Henry and Etta Mae (Doughman) F.; m. Patricia Susanah Sautter, June 30, 1963; children: John Christopher, Robert Nelson, Jill Alison. Home: 1644 Helena Dr Mansfield OH 44904 Office: Madison Jr High Sch 690 Ashland Rd Mansfield OH 44905

FUGATE, EDWARD, minister; b. Springfield, Ohio, Aug. 22, 1956; s. Claude and Arminda (Noble) F.; m. Adina Sue Campbell, Oct. 6, 1979; children: Malinda Renee, Rebecca Ellen. BA, Berea Coll., 1978; MDiv, United Tehol. Seminary, 1986. Ordained to ministry Meth. Ch. as deacon, 1984. Sales agt. Commonwealth Ins. Co., Springfield, Ohio, 1979-80; sales mgr. Commonwealth Ins. Co., Piqua, Ohio, 1980-82; pastor New Paris (Ohio) United Meth. Ch., 1982-86, Seaman (Ohio) United Meth. Ch., 1986-87, Piketon-Jasper United Meth. Ch., Piketon, Ohio, 1987—. Named an Outstanding Young Man of Am. 1985, 86. Methodist. Lodge: Kiwanis (bd. dirs. New Paris 1983-85, com. chmn. 1984-86). Home and Office: Piketon-Jasper United Meth Ch 530 Marple Box 397 Piketon OH 45661

FUGO, DENISE MARIE, small business executive; b. Cleve., Apr. 4, 1953; d. William Anthony and Mary Magdelene (Madar) F.; m. Ralph Thomas Di Orio, Nov. 25, 1977; children: Dena J., Michael P. (dec.). BS in Communication, Ohio U., 1975; MBA, U. Chgo., 1977. Stockbroker Goldman, Sachs & Co., Chgo., 1977-79; fin. analyst Standard Oil Co., Cleve., 1979-81; pres. City Life Inc. (Sammy's, Tenth St. Mkt., Tenth St. Cafe and Wine Bar), Cleve., 1980—. Bd. dir. Clev. Council Smaller Enterprises, 1986-89; mem. mktg. com. Convention and Visitor's Bur., Cleve., 1984—, bd. dirs. 1986—; mem. Downtown Bus. Council, Clev., 1984—, United Way Investment Com., 1980-85. Recipient Chivas Regal Young Entrepreneur award 375 Spirits Co., N.Y., 1986. Roman Catholic. Club: One Fitness Ctr. Office: City Life Inc 1400 W 10th St Cleveland OH 44113

FUHRER, LARRY, investment banker; b. Ft. Wayne, Ind., Sept. 23, 1939; s. Henry Roland and Wilhelmine Ellen (Kopp) F.; A.B., Taylor U., 1961; postgrad. No. Ill. U., 1965—; m. Linda Larsen, Dec. 31, 1962; 1 son, Lance. Exec. club dir. Youth for Christ, Miami, Fla., 1961; publs. mgr. Campus Life mag. Wheaton, Ill., 1962-65; asst. to pres. then v.p. Youth for Christ Internat., Wheaton, 1965-66; asso. dir. devel. Ill. Inst. Tech., 1966-68; exec. asst. to pres., The Robert Johnston Corp., Los Angeles, Chgo., N.Y.C.,

1968; pres. Compro, Inc. now Presdl. Services, Inc., Glen Ellyn, Ill., 1973-85; chmn., pres. The Centre Capital Group Inc., Wheaton; pres. Killian Assocs. Inc., Wheaton, 1973-75; chmn. Family Programming Inc., Rockford Equities Ltd., Rockford Prodns. Inc., Fin. Services Group Ltd., Equity Realty Group Inc., Internat. Telemedia Ltd., Quadrus Media Ministry, Inc.; pres. Presdl. Services, Inc., Travel Equities and Mgmt. Co. (Teamco), Chgo Sports Prodns. Inc., Royal Travel Services Inc., ednl. mgmt. cons. numerous pvt. colls. and sems. Bd. dirs. Chicagoland Youth for Christ. Mem. Am. Mgmt. Assn., Am. Inst. Mgmt. Cons.'s, DuPage Bd. Realtors, Nat., Ill. assns. realtors, Am. Mktg. Assn., Mortgage Bankers Assn. Presbyterian. Club: Union League (Chgo.). Home: 521 Iroquois Naperville IL 60540 Office: Box 1077 Lisle IL 60532

FUJITA, SHIRO, otolaryngologist; b. Tokyo, Apr. 5, 1929; came to U.S., 1959; s. Masao and Shizu (Otake) F.; m. Marie Louise Josephine Kulpanowski; children: Kenji Gordon, Joey Brian, Michelle Miyoko, Jeffrey Michael. Premed. grad., Tokyo Met. U., 1949; MD, U. Tokyo, 1955, postgrad. in otolaryngology, 1959; postgrad., Harvard U., 1962. Fellow in otology Henry Ford Hosp., Detroit, 1962-65, sr. otolaryngologist, 1967—, dir. neuro-otology; instr. otology U. Tokyo, 1965-66, asst. prof., 1966-67; clin. instr. otolaryngology U. Mich., 1976-80, clin. asst. prof. 1980-84, clin. assoc. prof. 1984—. Author: Snoring & Sleep Apnea, 1986. Fellow Am. Acad Otolaryngology, Head and Neck Surgery (mem. subcom. sleep disorders); mem. AMA, Mich. Otolaryn. Soc., Mich. State Med. Soc., Wayne County Med. Soc., Am. Med. Writers' Assn., Southeastern Mich. Surg. Soc. Diplomate Am. Bd. Otolaryngology, Head and Neck Surgery. Avocations: reading, photography, art, painting. Home: 32075 Waltham Birmingham MI 48009 Office: Henry Ford Hosp 2799 W Grand Blvd Detroit MI 48202

FUKUMORI, TOSHIRO, psychiatrist; b. Nabarishi, Mei-ken, Japan, Feb. 8, 1931; came to U.S., 1965; s. Jiro and Kinuko Fukumori; m. Mutsuko Hayami, Mar. 10, 1960; children: Ichiro, Toshiko, Naomi. MD, Kyoto Prefectural U. Med., 1955. Diplomate Am. Bd. Psychiatry and Neurology. Resident in psychiatry Kings Park (N.Y.) State Hosp., 1967-70; chief pediatrician Kawanishi City Hosp., Japan, 1970-71; fellow in child psychiatry U. Iowa, Iowa City, 1972-74; child psychiatrist Cherokee (Iowa) Mental Health Inst., 1974-76; staff psychiatrist Hastings (Nebr.) Regional Ctr., 1976-87, Osawatomie (Kans.) State Hosp., 1987—. Mem. Nebr. Med. Assn. Avocation: studying Shakespeare. Home: 632 North Shore Dr Hastings NE 68901 Office: Osawatomie State Hosp Osawatomie KS 66064

FULANI, ANIL VANMALI, engineer, construction company president; b. Kosamba, India, Mar. 23, 1950; came to U.S., 1971; s. Vanmali K. and Revaben V. Patel; m. Ashvina Anil Patel, May 6, 1979; children: Sonya, Daniel. BS, U. Baroda, India, 1970; BSCE, Lamar U., 1974; MCE, U. Houston, 1977. Structural engr. Stone & Webster, Boston, 1979-80; stress engr. Duke Power Co., Charlotte, N.C., 1980; stress analyst Sargent & Lundy, Chgo., 1980-83; pres. Fulani Motel Corp., Springfield, Mo., 1981—. Republican. Hindu. Avocations: traveling, stock market technician, reading. Office: 2555 N Glenstone Ave Springfield MO 65803

FULCOMER, VIRGINIA ANN, psychologist; b. Greeley, Minn., Oct. 11, 1916; s. Louis John and Viola Florence (Sybrant) Rohlf; m. Charles Frederick Fulcomer, Sept. 1, 1938; children: Judith Fulcomer Willour, Mark Charles, Cheryl Fulcomer Kriska. BA, UCLA, 1956; MS in Edn., Westminster Coll., 1959; PhD, Case Western Res. U., 1963. Lic. psychologist, Ohio. Psychologist Child Guidance Ctr., Youngstown, Ohio, 1962-69, dir., 1964-69; dir. Child and Adult Mental Health Ctr., Youngtown, 1971-77; pvt. practice psychology Youngstown, 1969-71, 77—, Scioto Paint Mental Health Ctr., Chillicothe, Ohio, 1984-87. Mack fellow Westminster Coll., New Wilmington, 1960. Mem. Am. Psychol. Assn., Ohio Psychol. Assn., Psi Chi, Kappa Delta Pi. Republican. Presbyterian. Avocation: travel. Home: 708 3d St Waverly OH 45690

FULGENZI, BENJAMIN, data processing company owner, consultant; b. Arkansas City, Kans., Oct. 27, 1925; s. Benjamin and Daisy June (Logan) F.; m. Betty Jean Ehman, Sept. 24, 1943 (dec. Nov. 1982); children: Sheila Ann, Benjamin III; m. Susan Anne Power, May 29, 1985. Student, Okla. A&M Coll., 1946-47, U. Miami, 1947-51. Internat. lic. coordinator ACF Industries, Houston, 1961-64; mgr. export sales Comml. Filters Div. Carborundum Co., Lebanon, Ind., 1964-71; v.p., chief exec. officer Systems Mfg. Corp., Indpls., 1972-76, also bd. dirs.; v.p., chief exec. officer SMC Pneumatics, Inc., Indpls., 1977-86, also bd. dirs.; pres. B. Fulgenzi & Co., Inc., Indpls., 1972—. Served with USN, 1941-46, PTO. Mem. Adminstrv. Mgmt. Assn., Data Processing Mgmt. Assn., Fluid Power Soc., Sales Exec. Internat., World Trade Club Ind., Ind. C. of C., Internat. Wang Users Group, Am. Legion. Republican. Avocation: oil painting. Home: 8461 Westport Ln Indianapolis IN 46234 Office: B Fulgenzi & Co Inc 7457 W 10th St Indianapolis IN 46224

FULGHUM, DAVID ARLIN, truck manufacturing company executive; b. Mason City, Iowa, Oct. 9, 1945; s. Willard S. and Dorothy M. (Murren) F.; m. Brigid Murphy, Nov. 23, 1984; children—Katherine Brigid, Margaret Rebecca. B.S.A.E., Iowa State U., 1969; M.B.A., U. Chgo., 1974; P.M.D., Harvard U., 1981. Registered profl. engr., Ill.; C.P.A., Ill. Engr., Internat. Harvester Co., Chgo., 1969-77 (now Navistar Internat. Corp.), controller strategic bus. unit, 1978-79, adminstrv. asst. to pres., 1980, mgr. agrl. tractors, 1981, mgr. worldwide prodn. programming, 1982-83, dir. prodn. programming and asset mgmt., 1983-85, mgr. market research and scheduling, 1985-86; with Navistar Internat. Corp., Chgo., 1986—; mem. engr. sub-com. Am. Nat. Standards Inst.; mem. safety standards devel. Consumer Product Safety Comm. Mem. Zoning Bd. Appeal, Indian Head Park. Mem. Am. Soc. Agrl. Engrs. Republican. Patentee in field. Home: 4131 Johnson Ave Western Springs IL 60558 Office: Navistar Internat Corp 401 N Michigan Ave Chicago IL 60611

FULKES, JEAN ASTON, author, musician; b. Chattanooga Tenn., Mar. 21; d. Isaac David and Inez (Elder) Aston; m. James Sherman Fulkes, Jr. (dec.1972); children-David, Duane, Marilyn. Student, So. Ill. U.; A.B., U. Tenn.; postgrad. Advanced French Inst., 1961, U. Mo.-Columbia, 1960-81. Tchr. French, English, creative writing Mexico High Sch., 1959-78; dir. vocal music and chapel activities Mo. Mil. Acad., 1978-82; speaker writers confs. St. Louis U. and U. Mo., free-lance writer, speaker, antique, dealer, interior designer, composer performer. Author: Forever, Forever; A Lovely Thing; New Road New Song; others. Contbr. articles, poetry to mags. Mem. com. Republican Party, Mo., 1950-60. Shakespeare fellow Yale U., 1961; recipient French award City of Centralia, Mo., 1985, U. Mo. Fgn. Lang. Inst. Mem. Mo. State Tchr.'s Assn. (conv. speaker 1982), Presbyn. Women's Assn., Old Books and New Assn. (pres. 1973-), Delta Kappa Gamma (officer 1970's). Club: Silent Unity (Unity Village, Mo.). Avocations: travel, oil painting, music, gardening Home: 1605 Pollack Rd Mexico MO 65265 Office: Old Books and New Assn Route 4 White Birch 1605 Mexico MO 65265

FULLER, BETTY WINN HAMILTON, editor; b. Covington, Ky., Feb. 23, 1926; d. Jefferson Ogden and Elizabeth Ann (Winn) Hamilton; m. Samuel Ashby Fuller, June 10, 1948; children—Mary Cheryl Fuller Hargrove, Karen Elizabeth Fuller Wolfe, Deborah Ruth. B.S., U. Cin., 1948; M.S., Butler U., 1977. Children's library asst. Carmel Pub. Library, Ind., 1973-79; free-lance writer, Indpls.; editor: (health and edn.) Children's Better Health Inst., Benjamin Franklin Library and Med. Soc., Inc., 1979-87, Jack and Jill Mag., Humpty Dumpty Mag., Turtle Mag., Child Life Mag., Children's Digest Mag., Children's Playmate Mag. Contbr. articles, poems, stories, book revs. to childrens' mags. Sec. Childrens. Bur. Aux., Indpls., 1960, Boys Club Aux., Indpls., 1964; pres. Ladywood Mothers Club, Indpls., 1966, St. Pius X Womens Club, Indpls., 1958; former bd. dirs. Indpls. Pub. Sch. Adv. council, Friends of Carmel Library, St. Luke Catholic Sch. Bd. Recipient Ednl. Journalism award EdPress, 1982. Mem. DAR (regent 1976-78, sec. 1984—), Soc. Profl. Journalists, Ednl. Press Assn. Am. Republican. Club: Harbour Trees Golf.

FULLER, CHARLES ARTHUR, auditor; b. Salt Lake City, Oct. 28, 1946; s. Duane E. and Lillian M. (Tong) F.; m. Joan E. Ankeney; children: Nathan C., Nolan K. MS in Acctg., U. Utah, 1969; MBA, George Mason U., 1977. CPA, Va. Auditor-in-charge Naval Area Audit Service, San Diego, 1968-73; project mgr. Office of Insp. Gen. Dept. of Def., Rosslyn, Va., 1973-82; program mgr. Air Force Audit Agy., Wright Patterson AFB, Ohio, 1982—. Mgr. Fairfax Little League Assn., 1980-81, Wright Patterson AFB Youth Baseball Program, 1982-87; pres. Wright Patterson AFB Major League, 1984-85. Served to sgt. U.S. Army, 1964-70. Mem. Am. Inst. CPA's, Am. Soc. Mil. Comptrollers. Democrat. Lutheran. Avocation: basketball, softball, golf. Home: 1862 Fairground Rd Xenia OH 45385 Office: AFAA/QLW Wright Patterson AFB Fairborn OH 45433-5000

FULLER, LEE DENNISON, nursing educator, therapist; b. Oceana County, Mich., June 7, 1910; s. Arthur Oglethorpe and Georgiana Katrina (Dennison) F. BS, N.Y.U., 1949, MA, 1950; EdD, Ind. U., 1970. Registered nurse, Mass. Staff nurse N.Y. State Psychiat. Inst., N.Y.C., 1944-52; dir. in-service edn. Jacksonville (Ill.) State Hosp., 1953-55; edn. cons. Ind. Dept. Mental Health, Indpls., 1955-60; prof. nursing Ind. U., Indpls., 1955-80, prof. emeritus, 1980—; pvt. practice psychotherapy Bloomington, Ind., 1982—; cons. Reid Meml. Hosp., Richmond, Ind., 1973-74, 77, Ind. State Prison, Mich. City., Ind., 1973, Psychodrama Ind. Meth. Ch., 1979-81, Marion (Ind.) Vets. Hosp., 1977-83; adj. staff therapist South Cen. Community Mental Health Ctr., Bloomington, 1975-85. Leader Boy Scouts U.S., Belmont, Mass., 1932-36, N.Y.C., 1944-48; layreader Trinity Epsicopal Ch., N.Y.C., 1943-52, Jacksonville, 1953-54, Bloomington, 1956-65. Mem. Am. Nurses Assn. (pres. dist. 16 1968-72, Lit. award, cert.), Am. Group Psychotherapy Assn., Am. Soc. Group Psychotherapy and Psychodrama, Am. Assn. Marriage and Family Therapy, Tri-State Group Psychotherapy Assn. (pres. 1978-79), Oceana County Hist. Soc. Club: Ruby Creek Conservation (Mich.). Home: 600 E 2d St Bloomington IN 47401

FULLER, LISA MARIE, purchasing agent; b. Mpls., Sept. 8, 1958; d. Goodrich Allen and Margaret Del (Roscoe) Peterson; m. Frank Michael Fuller; Apr. 9, 1983; children: Amber Marie, Chelsea Elizabeth. BS, St. Cloud (Minn.) State U., 1981. Personnel rep. J.L. Marsh, Golden Valley, Minn., 1977-79; dir. publs. AME Corp., Minnetonka, Minn., 1981-82; purchasing agent TITN Inc., Edina, Minn., 1982—. Avocations: bowling, golf, cooking, horseback riding. Office: TITN Inc 5591 W 78th St Edina MN 55435

FULLER, MICHAEL LYNN, school psychologist; b. Bellaire, Ohio, Feb. 11, 1951; s. Forest Dana and Barbara (Fuller) Greenlee; m. Terri Lindsey, Sept. 19, 1974; children: Stacy Anne, Geoffrey Michael. BA summa cum laude, Ohio U., 1977, MS, 1980. Lic. sch. psychologist, Ohio. Guest lectr. Muskingum Area Tech. Coll., Zanesville, Ohio, 1982-84; psychologist Cambridge (Ohio) Devel. Ctr., 1984-86; sch. psychologist Muskingum County Bd. Edn., Zanesville, 1980—. Mem. Muskingum County Head Start Policy Council, Zanesville, 1983-85; v.p. bd. trustees Child Care Resources Inc., Columbus, 1984-85; mem. Appalachian Consortium for Treatment/Tng. for Women and Children, Zanesville, 1986. Served to sgt. USAF, 1970-74. Mem. Assn. for Counseling and Devel., Phi Beta Kappa, Phi Kappa Phi. Democrat. Avocations: running, motorcycles, carpentry, reading. Home: 2233 Dresden Rd Zanesville OH 43701

FULLER, ROBERT HAROLD, mechanical engineer, consultant; b. Columbus, Ohio, July 1, 1941; s. Raymond Harold and Rhoda May (Hewitt) F.; m. Barbara Susan Steiner, May 1, 1965; children—James, Amy. B.S. in Mech. Engring., Ohio State U., 1964. Registered profl. engr., Ohio, N.Y. Engr. quality control Eastman Kodak Co., Rochester, N.Y., 1965-68; v.p. W.E. Monks & Co., Columbus, 1968-74; asst. dir. energy conservation Ohio State U., Columbus, 1974-79; pres. R.H. Fuller & Assocs. Inc., Columbus, 1979—; pres. Facility Mgmt. Services, Inc., Columbus, 1983—. Author: Energy Conservation Manual, 1975. Contbng. author Conserving Energy in Mechanical Systems, 1981. Contbr. articles to profl. jours. Recipient Disting. Service award Council Edn. Facility Planners Internat., 1978, 86. Mem. ASME, ASHRAE, Nat. Soc. Profl. Engrs., Am. Cons. Engrs. Council. Lutheran. Avocations: jogging, tennis, skiing. Home: 187 Riverview Park Dr Columbus OH 43214 Office: 2901 N High St Columbus OH 43202-1196

FULLER T., HEYWOOD, lawyer, health care administrator, nurse; b. Montgomery, Ala., Aug. 17, 1944; s. Havert and Addie B. (Thornton) F.; m. Ingrid Shenita Britton, Apr., 1983. ASD, Long Beach City Coll., 1976; BA, Concordia Coll., 1977; MBA, U. Chgo., 1979; JD, Georgetown U., 1984; postdoctoral, U. Ill., Chgo., 1985—. Bar: Ill. 1984, D.C. 1985, U.S. Dist. Ct. (no. dist.) Ill. 1985. Fin./budget analyst Def. Logistics Agy., Chgo. and Alexandria, Va., 1982-84; asst. adminstr. Jackson Park Hosp., Chgo., 1984; adminstr. Friedell Clinic, Chgo., 1984-85; atty. Neighborhood Lawyers Ctrs., Chgo., 1985—; pres. Neighborhoods Internat., Inc., Chgo., 1985-86; staff relief registered nurse Myerscough Med. Ctr., Chgo., 1978-79, 84-86, S.R.T. Med. Ctr., Alexandria, 1980-83; v.p. The Nurse Assocs., Inc., Chgo., 1986—; bd. dirs. C.O.H.E.R.E., Inc., Chgo. V.p., bd. dirs. Lake Terr. Condominium Assn., Chgo., 1985—. Council Opportunity Grad. Mgmt. Edn. fellow U. Chgo., 1978. Mem. ABA, Assn. Trial Lawyers Am., Chgo. Bar Assn., Nat. Black Nurse's Assn., Am. Coll. Healthcare Execs., Am. Assn. Nurse Attys., Am. Acad. Hosp. Attys., Nat. Assn. Hosp. Lawyers. Avocations: chess, family, econs., world affairs. Office: Neighborhood Lawyers Ctrs 2459 E 75th St Chicago IL 60649-3731

FULTON, ELAINE, association executive, parliamentarian; b. Hunnewell, Mo., Apr. 12, 1928; d. Dennis Jefferson and Flora Opal (Barnes) Bailey; m. Irving Gerard Fulton, May 28, 1949; children—Nancy Elizabeth Fulton Beachner, Robert Dennis. Student in Acctg., Chillicothe Coll., Mo., 1946, Penn Valley Coll., Kansas City, Mo., 1975. Registered parliamentarian. Exec. sec. Nat. Assn. Parliamentarians, Kansas City, 1973—; parliamentarian Nat. Rural Elec. Assn., Washington, 1979—, Nat. Bds. Pharmacy, Chgo., 1979—, Nat. Pork Producers Council, Des Moines, 1980—. Author: (booklet) Sharpen Your Meeting Skills, 1983. Parliamentarian ch. groups, PTA, other local orgns., Kansas City area. Mem. Am. Soc. Assn. Execs. Republican. Clubs: Heart Am. Parliamentary (Kansas City) (pres. 1972-74); Santa Fe Trail Parliamentary (Independence, Mo.) (pres. 1971-73). Lodge: Eastern Star. Home: 4309 Crisp Ave Kansas City MO 64133 Office: Nat Assn Parliamentarians 6301 James A Reed Rd Suite 114 Kansas City MO 64133

FULTON, JOHN FREDERICK, gynecologist; b. Pitts., Dec. 7, 1930; s. John Dickson and Louise (Mueller) F.; m. Jeanne Pudney, Dec. 27, 1952; children: Lucinda, Janis, Diane, David. BS, U. Pitts., 1952, MD, 1955. Diplomate Am. Bd. Ob-Gyn. Commd. 1st lt. USAF, 1955; intern Shadyside Hosp., Pitts., 1955-56; resident Elizabeth Steel Magee Hosp., Pitts., 1956-59; advanced through grades to capt. USAF, 1964, resigned, 1964; pvt. practice specializing in ob-gyn. Chateauroux, France, 1959-62, Wichita Falls, Tex., 1962-64; practice medicine specializing in gynecology Kent, Ohio, 1964—. Lodge: Rotary (pres. 1984-85). Avocations: photography, enology, travel, graphic arts. Home: 1374 Mockingbird Dr Kent OH 44240 Office: 136 N Water St Kent OH 44240

FULTON, ROBERT D., meat packing company executive. Chmn. Rath Packing Co., Waterloo, Iowa. Office: Rath Packing Co Elm & Sycamore Waterloo IA 50703 *

FULTZ, CLAIR ERVIN, former banker; b. nr. Jeffersonville, Ohio, Nov. 23, 1911; s. Roy Bertis and Addis (Ervin) F.; m. Isabelle Eichelberger, Aug. 18, 1935; children: Robert Edward, Karen Lynn, Pamela Jane. B.S., Ohio State U., 1934; grad., Rutgers U. Grad Sch. Banking, 1946. With Huntington Nat. Bank, Columbus, Ohio, 1934-72; v.p. Huntington Nat. Bank, 1953-57, dir., 1956-77, pres., 1958-67, chmn., chief exec. officer, 1967-72; pres. Huntington Bancshares, Inc., 1966-73, chmn., 1973-83; Mem. fed. adv. council Fed. Res. System, 1973-75. Trustee Battelle Meml. Inst., 1963—, former chmn.; past pres. Children's Hosp.; Past chmn. Devel. Com. Greater Columbus. Mem. Ohio Bankers Assn. (past pres.), SAR, Soc. Mayflower Descs., Ohio State Med. Assn. (hon. mem.), Ohio State U. Pace Setters (hon.), Newcomen Soc. N.Am., Beta Gamma Sigma, Alpha Kappa Psi, Phi Alpha Kappa. Clubs: Washington Country, Presidents of Ohio State U. Home: 15726 SR 729 NW Jeffersonville OH 43128-9725

FUNDINGSLAND, KIM A., reporter, sportscaster; b. Minot, N.D., May 24, 1952; s. Dale G. And Mable N. (Rasmussen) F.; 1 child, Jaime. Sports dir. Sta. KMOT-TV, Minot, 1970-76; assignment editor Sta. KXMC-TV, Minot, 1977-85; outdoor reporter Meyer TV Network, various locations, N.D., 1986—; play-byplay reporter Sta. KRRZ-AM, Minot, 1986—; presenter slide programs to civic orgns. Author, editor: The Witchery of Archery, 1986; pub. N.D. Nature Calendar, 1985-86; contbr. articles to sports jours. Chmn. Minot's Community Halloween Party, 1986; hon. chmn. N.W. N.D. March-of Dimes, 1986. Recipient Friend of Nat. Wildlife Service Refuge System award U.S. Fish and Wildlife Service, 1983, Spl. Media Conservation award N.D. chpt. Wildlife Soc., 1984, 3d place N.C. Assoc. Press, 1983, 84; named Minot's Eagle of Month, 1975, Communicator of Yr., N.D. Wildlife Fedn., 1983. Mem. Minot Exchange Club (bd. dirs. 1986), N.D. Wildlife Fedn. (Communicator of Yr., 1983), Pheasants Forever (co-chmn. Minot chpt.), Minot's Town and Country Sportsmen, Minot State Coll. Beaver Boosters, 7th Cavalry Co. M. (pres.), Outdoor Writer's Assn. Am. Lodge: Elks. Avocation: photography. Home: 1825 15 1/2 St SW Minot ND 58701

FUNK, DAVID ALBERT, law educator; b. Wooster, Ohio, Apr. 22, 1927; s. Daniel Coyle and Elizabeth Mary (Reese) F.; children—Beverly Joan, Susan Elizabeth, John Ross, Carolyn Louise; m. Sandra Nadine Henselmeier, Oct. 2, 1976. Student, U. Mo., 1945-46, Harvard Coll., 1946; B.A. in Econs., Coll. of Wooster, 1949; M.A., Ohio State U., 1968; J.D., Case Western Res. U., 1951, LL.M., 1972; LL.M., Columbia U., 1973. Bar: Ohio 1951, U.S. Dist. Ct. (no. dist.) Ohio 1962, U.S. Tax Ct. 1963, U.S. Ct. Appeals (6th cir.) 1970, U.S. Supreme Ct. 1971. Ptnr. Funk, Funk & Eberhart, Wooster, Ohio, 1951-72; assoc. prof. law Ind. U. Sch. Law, Indpls., 1973-76, prof., 1976—; vis. lectr. Coll. of Wooster, 1962-63; dir. Juridical Sci. Inst., Indpls., 1982—. Author: Oriental Jurisprudence, 1974, Group Dynamic Law, 1982; (with others) Rechtsgeschichte und Rechtssoziologie, 1985; contbr. articles to profl. jours. Chmn. bd. trustees Wayne County Law Library Assn., 1956-71; mem. Permanent Jud. Commn., Synod of Ohio, United Presbyn. Ch. in the U.S., 1968. Served to seaman 1st class USNR, 1945-46. Harlan Fiske Stone fellow Columbia U., 1973; recipient Am. Jurisprudence award in Comparative Law, Case Western Res. U., 1970. Mem. Assn. Am. Law Schs. (sec. comparative law sect. 1977-79, chmn. law and religion sect. 1977-81, sec., treas. law and soc. sci. sect. 1983-86), Japanese-Am. Soc. Legal Studies, Law and Soc. Assn., Am. Soc. for Legal History, Pi Sigma Alpha. Republican. Office: Ind U Sch Law 735 W New York St Indianapolis IN 46202

FUNK, JAMES WILLIAM, JR., insurance agency administrator; b. Vincennes, Ind., May 31, 1947; s. James William and Elizabeth (Bauer) F.; B.A., Butler U., Indpls., 1969; m. Janis Burrell, Aug. 11, 1973; children—Christopher James, Kelly Elizabeth. Mem. campaign staff U.S. Senator Birch Bayh, Indpls., 1968; bus. cons. Dun & Bradstreet, Inc., Indpls., 1969-71; dir. ops. Terry Properties Inc., Springfield, Ill., 1971-72; personnel mgr. Am. Underwriters, Inc., Indpls., 1972-73, adminstrv. asst. to pres., 1973-75, asst. sec., 1975-78, v.p. public relations, 1978-79; adminstrv. mgr. Affiliated Agys., Inc., Indpls., 1979—; bd. dirs. Am. Underwriters Group, Inc. Sec., treas. Central N. Civic Assn., Indpls., 1976, pres., 1977-78. Mem. Ind. Soc. Chgo., Independent Ins. Agts. Ind. (mem. agy.-co. relations com.), Profl. Ins. Agts. Ind. (v.p., 1984-85, pres. 1986-87, chmn. legis. com., treas. polit. action com., bd. dirs. 1982-83), Indpls. Children's Mus., Indpls. Zool. Soc. Roman Catholic. Clubs: Preussian Benefit Soc., Heimaths Benefit Soc., Butler Univ. President's, K.C. Home: 6445 Spring Mill Rd Indianapolis IN 46260 Office: 8802 N Meridian St Suite 201 Indianapolis IN 46240

FUNK, JOHN WILLIAM, electronics manufacturing company executive restaurant company executive, paper converting company executive, lawyer, packaging company executive; b. Detroit, Apr. 6, 1937; s. Wilson S. and Myrtle M. (Johnston) F.; m. Carol E. Sutton, June 14, 1958; children—Michael John, Steven John, David John, Susan Elizabeth; m. Helen Rebecca Dutko, July 5, 1980. Student, Gen. Motors Inst., Flint, Mich., 1955-57; B.B.A., U. Mich, 1959, M.B.A., J.D., 1962. Bar: N.Y. 1962. Assoc. Hodgson, Russ, Andrews, Woods & Goodyear, Buffalo, 1962-66; staff atty. Kroger Co., Cin., 1966-68; counsel Litton Industries, Milw. and Hartford, Conn., 1969-72; gen. counsel, v.p. internat. Jeffrey Galion, Columbus, Ohio, 1972-77; gen. counsel, sec. Wendy's Internat., Inc., Columbus, 1977-80, exec. v.p., chief adminstrv. officer, sec., 1980-86; dir. Wendy's Internat., Inc., 1981—; pres., dir. Vanner, Inc., Columbus, 1986—, Pressware Internat., Inc., Columbus, 1987—. Mem. N.Y. State Bar Assn., Phi Kappa Phi. Roman Catholic. Club: University. Avocations: tennis; golf; skiing. Home: 2111 Cheltenham Rd Columbus OH 43220 Office: Pressware Internat Inc 2120 Westbelt Dr Columbus OH 43228 also: Vanner Inc 745 Harrison Dr Columbus OH 43204

FUNK, LINDA LOUISE, marketing professional; b. Janesville, Wis., July 4, 1954; d. Wayne William and Ruth Mary (Diehls) F. BS in Home Econ. Edn., U. Wis.-Stout, Menomonie, 1976. Extension home economist extention service U. Wis., Juneau, 1976-77; elderly nutrition dir. Commn. on Aging, Juneau, 1977-79; in-store home economist Jewel Food Store, Milw., 1979-80; consumer advisor Wis. Gas Co., Milw., 1979-81; dir. home econs. Ambrosia Chocolate, Milw., 1981-82, asst. to pres., 1982-83, mktg. and advt. mgr., 1983-87; mktg. and advt. mgr. Pepsi-Cola Bottling Group, Troy, Mich., 1987—. Mem. Internat. Foodservice Editorial Council, Home Economist in Bus. (pres. 1984-85, Outstanding Young Profl. award), Tempo Young Profls., Jr. League, Alpha Phi Alumni. Methodist. Avocations; reading, traveling. Home: 3905 Crooks Rd Apt 33 Royal Oaks MI 48073

FUNKEY, MARY ANN, retail executive, realtor; b. Evergreen Park, Ill., Nov. 7, 1955; s. William Anthony and Virginia Mary (Gavin); m. Corey Donovan, Oct. 1, 1978. BA in Communication Arts, Loyola U., Chgo. Store mgr. Joy's Clock Shop, Chgo., 1981—, Brooks Clothing, North Riverside, Ill., 1981—, Jean Nicole, Chgo., 1981—, Allison's, Chgo., 1981—; dist. mgr. Gateway Apparel, St. Louis, Mo., 1985—; trainer mgmt. of human resources-retail supervisory, 1986—; pvt. practice fashion cons.; modern dance instr. various Chgo. studios. Mem. women's adv. council Misericordia Home for Retarded Children, Chgo., 1986—. Mem. Council Cath. Women. Democrat. Roman Catholic. Avocations: golf, skiing, dancing, travel. Home: 14521 Mustang Dr Lockport IL 60441 Office: Gateway Apparel 128 Ogden Ave Downers Grove IL 60515

FUNT, RICHARD CLAIR, horticulturist; b. Gettysburg, Pa., Feb. 13, 1946; s. Sterling Samuel and Dorothy Mildred (Guise) F.; m. Shirley May Fox, Sept. 6, 1969; children—Elizabeth Anne, Caroline Claire. B.S., Delaware Valley Coll., 1968; M.S., Pa. State U., 1971, Ph.D., 1974; postgrad., Wye Coll., Kent, Eng., 1985. Asst. prof., extension pomologist U. Md.-College Park, 1974-78, assoc. prof., extension pomologist, 1978-86; prof., extension horticulturist Ohio State U., Columbus, 1986—. Mem. adminstrv. bd. United Meth. Ch., 1976-77, 81-83, pres. Men's Club, 1976-77, mem. council ministries, 1976-77, com. pastor-parish relations, 1985-87. Served with U.S. Army, 1968-70. Decorated Bronze Star; recipient Shepard award Am. Pomological Soc., 1977, Goadling Meml. Lectures award, 1986; C. K. Bay grantee, 1979-83, 84, 85, Kellogg grantee, 1985-87. Mem. Sigma Xi, Gamma Sigma Delta, Phi Sigma, Phi Epsilon Phi, Epsilon Sigma Phi. Home: 1877 Stockwell Dr Columbus OH 43220 Office: 2001 Fyffe Ct Ohio State U Columbus OH 43210

FURCON, JOHN EDWARD, management and organizational consultant; b. Chgo., Mar. 17, 1942; s. John F. and Lottie (Janik) F.; m. Carolyn Ann Warden, Aug. 15, 1964; children: Juliana, Annalisa, Diana. BA, DePaul U., 1963, MA, 1965; MBA, U. Chgo., 1970. With Human Resources Ctr. (name formerly Indsl. Relations Ctr.), U. Chgo., 1963-81, project dir., 1966-70, research psychologist, div. dir., 1970-81; with Chgo. div. Harbridge House, Inc., Northbrook, Ill., 1981—, v.p., 1987—; mem. faculty Traffic Inst., Northwestern U., 1969-84, DePaul U. Sch. for New Learning, 1974-82; cons. bus., ednl. and govt. orgns.; lectr. in field. Contbr. articles on personnel mgmt. and human resources planning to profl. jours. Served to lt. AUS, 1963-65. Mem. Am. Psychol. Assn., Indsl. Psychology Assn. Chgo. (chmn. 1973-75), Internat. Assn. Chiefs of Police. Office: Chgo Div Harbridge House Inc 2875 Milwaukee Ave Northbrook IL 60062

FUREY, MICHAEL WAYNE, dentist; b. St. Paul, Minn., July 12, 1953; s. Versal Wayne and Norma (Gorman) F.; m. Kathleen Joy Ekdahl, Sept. 18, 1976; 1 child, Erin Elizabeth. BS, U. Minn., 1979, DDS, 1981. Assoc. dentist William Papp DDS, PA, St. Paul, 1981-82, Brent Martin DDS, PA, St. Paul, 1982-83, Gregory Sheehan DDS, PA, Shoreview, Minn., 1981—; practice dentistry Shoreview, 1986—; dental dir. ACR Home, Shoreview, 1981—. Mem. ADA, Minn. Dental Assn., St. Paul Dist. Dental Soc., Omnicron Kappa Upsilon. Roman Catholic. Club: North Star Study (St.

Paul). Avocations: avocations, golf, racquetball, guitar, bicycling. Home: 1845 Dayton Ave Saint Paul MN 55104 Office: North Suburban Dental 404 West Hwy 96 Shoreview MN 55126

FURGASON, ROBERT ROY, university official, chemical engineering educator; b. Spokane, Wash., Aug. 2, 1935; s. Roy Elliott and Margaret (O'Halloran) F.; m. Gloria L. Althouse, June 14, 1964; children: Steven Scott, Brian Alan. BSCE, U. Idaho, 1956, MSCE, 1958; PhD in Chem. Engring., Northwestern U., 1961; postdoctoral, U. Wis., 1961. Registered profl. engr., Idaho. Design engr. Phillips Petroleum Co., Bartlesville, Okla., 1956; research engr. Martin Marietta Co., Denver, 1958; instr. chem. engring. U. Idaho, Moscow, 1957-59, asst. prof., 1961-63, assoc. prof., 1963-67, acting head dept. chem. engring., 1964-65, chmn. dept. chem. engring., 1965-74, prof., 1967-84, dean Coll. Engring., 1974-78, v.p. acad. affairs and research, 1978-84; prof. U. Nebr., Lincoln, 1984—, vice chancellor acad. affairs, 1984—; cons. in field; NSF advisor scientists and engrs. in econ. devel. program Escuela Politecnica Nacional, Quito, Ecuador, 1973-74, 76; proposals reviewer NSF, 1965—; program reviewer Clearwater Econ. Devel. Assn., 1978-84; mem. long range planning commn. Idaho State Bd. Edn., 1978-80, Gov.'s Com. Faculty Salary Equity, 1980, State of Idaho Energy Policy Bd., 1980-84, adv. com. Northwest Power Policy Council, 1982-84, engring. accreditation commn. Accreditation Bd. Engring. and Tech., 1981—, exec. bd. 1984—, vice chmn., 1985-87, chmn., 1987—; bd. dirs. Leesburg Land and Mining Corp. Contbr. articles to profl. jours. Chmn. Idaho-Ecuador Ptnrs. of Ams., 1975-77; commr. Moscow Parks and Recreation Commn., 1977-81; bd. dirs. Southwest Moscow Community Assn., 1977-84, Am. Festival Ballet, 1978-80. Recipient Pub. Service award Idaho State Library Assn., 1978; Citizen of Yr., Kappa Sigma Frat., 1980; Walter P. Murphy fellow. Mem. Am. Inst. Chem. Engrs. (chmn. nat. tech. sessions 1967, sec. dept. heads forum 1971-72, chmn. 1981, nat. vis. lectr. 1977-79, edn. and accreditation com. 1981—, accreditation visitation group 1977—), Am. Chem. Soc., Am. Soc. Engring. Edn. (Pacific Northwest coordinator effective teaching 1962-64, bd. dirs. chem. engring. div. 1974-77), Nat. Soc. Profl. Engrs., Idaho Soc. Profl. Engrs. (No. Idaho chpt. pres. 1970, state pres. 1980, Idaho's Young Engr. of Yr. 1967), Northwest Coll. and Univ. Assn. Scis. (exec. com. bd. dirs. 1976-80, 81-84, chmn. bd. dirs. 1979-80), Sigma Xi, Phi Kappa Phi, Phi Eta Sigma, Sigma Tau. Clubs: Crucible (Lincoln); Wranglers. Lodge: Lions (program chmn., corr. sec., bd. dirs.). Avocations: piloting, skiing, camping, woodworking. Home: 1241 Evergreen Dr Lincoln NE 68510 Office: U Nebr Dept Chem Engring Administration Bldg 309 Lincoln NE 68588-0420

FURGISON, CLIFFORD FREDRIC, psychologist; b. Chgo., Dec. 4, 1948; s. Jack Warren and Vernie Florence (Snyder) F.; m. Zoe Ann Grace Keros, Apr. 4, 1983; 1 child, Tracie Michelle. B Mus. Edn., Ea. Mich. U., 1971, MA, 1975; PhD, Union Grad. Sch., 1982. Lic. psychologist. Educator Manchester (Mich.) Pub. Schs., 1971-73; substance abuse therapist Providence Hosp., Southfield, Mich., 1975-76, substance abuse program dir., 1976—, chief psychologist, 1982—; pvt. practice clin. psychology Southfield, 1976—; adj. asst. prof. Mercy Coll., Detroit, 1984-86. Mem. Am. Psychol. Assn., Mich. Psychol. Assn., Mich. Alcohol and Addict Assn. Office: Providence Hosp 16001 W Nine Mile Southfield MI 48037

FURLONG, GREGORY WILLIAM, marketing executive; b. Piqua, Ohio, Dec. 11, 1947; s. William Jesse and Mary (Swift) F.; m. Susan Leigh Wright, Mar. 21, 1970; children: Lucas Gregory, Anthony Paul. BA, Wittenberg U., Springfield, Ohio, 1970; MBA, Wright State U., Dayton, Ohio, 1980. Social worker Miami County Chidren's Sch., Troy, Ohio, 1970-72; sales correspondent Joyce/Dayton (Ohio) Corp., 1972-74, mgr. customer service, 1974-78, mgr. field sales, 1978-85, mktg. mgr., 1985—. Bd. dirs. Big Bros. of Miami County, Troy, 1972-74, Tipp Youth Soccer, Inc., Tipp City, Ohio, 1980. Mem. U.S. Inst. Theater Tech., Power Transmissions Reps. Assn. Republican. Club: Tipp Players (Tipp City). Avocations: golf, carpentry. Home: 4756 S Peters Rd Troy OH 45373 Office: Joyce/Dayton Corp PO Box 1630 Dayton OH 45401

FURLONG, PATRICK DAVID, educator; b. Cleve., Sept. 27, 1948; s. Harold Joseph and Jean Ann (Blair) F.; B.A. magna cum laude, Lake Erie Coll., Painesville, Ohio, 1975. Staff psychometrist VA Med. Center, North Chicago, Ill., 1975-78; psychometrist Northwestern U. Med. Sch., Chgo., 1978-80; counselor/coordinator vets. affairs Columbia Coll., Chgo., 1980-81; assoc. coordinator internat. edn. Roosevelt U., Chgo., 1981-84; dir. accreditation Nat. Commn. on Correctional Health Care, Chgo., 1984-85; coordinator student support services, Airco Tech. Inst., Chgo., 1985—. Served with USN, 1967-71; Vietnam. Decorated Navy Achievement medal with combat V. Mem. N.Y. Acad. Scis., Am. Assn. for Counseling and Devel., Ill. Psychol. Assn., Psi Chi. Home: 1233 W Winnemac Chicago IL 60640

FURMAN, ANDREW RICHARD, sports executive; b. Bklyn., Dec. 16, 1949; s. Bernard and Ruth (Vilinsky) F.; m. Wendy Loney, Sept. 6, 1984. B.A., Hunter Coll., 1972. With sports dept. N.Y. Post, N.Y.C., 1972-73; sports pub. relations exec. St. Francis Coll., Bklyn., 1976-77, Oral Roberts U., Tulsa, 1978-79; dir. pub. relations Buffalo Raceway, Monticello Raceway, Lake Region Greyhound Park, Belmont, N.H., Latonia Race Course, Florence, Ky., 1981—; sports dir. Sta. WLW, Cin., 1987—. Mem. Baseball, Football, Basketball Writers' Assn., Turf Publicists. Lodges: Rotary, Lions. Office: 700 WLW Radio 3 E 4th St Cincinnati OH 45202

FURMAN, DALE FLEMING, safety engineer; b. Royal Oak, Mich., Dec. 13, 1935; s. Dale and Alice (Michalson) F.; m. Yvonne Patricia Gourgues, mar. 29, 1968; children: Stephanie, Sean. BS, U.S. Naval Acad., 1961; postgrad. in Meteorology, USN Postgrad. Sch., 1966-67. Cert. safety profl. Commissioned ensign USN, 1961, advanced through grades to lt., 1971, resigned, 1971; indsl engr. Mobil Oil, Trenton, Mich., 1971-72; mfg. engr. Fedral Mogul, Southfield, Mich., 1972-73; maintenance supr. Kelsey Hay's, Romulus, Mich., 1973-75; safety engr. Travelers Ins., Southfield, 1975—. Cubmaster Boy Scouts Am., Southfield, 1985—; soccer coach. Decorated Air medal with gold star. Mem. Am. Soc. Safety Engr. (sec. Detroit 1986—), VFW. Home: Alexandria Towne #6 Southfield MI 48075

FURMAN, ROBERT HOWARD, pharmaceutical company consultant; b. Schenectady, N.Y., Oct. 23, 1918; s. Howard Blackall and Jane Blessing (MacChesney) F.; m. Mary Frances Kilpatrick, Feb. 10, 1945; children: Carol K. Furman Friedman, Jane C. Furman Dougherty, Robert Howard, Hugh Patrick. AB (Allison prize 1939), Union Coll., Schenectady, 1940; MD, Yale U., 1943. Diplomate Am. Bd. Internal Medicine. Intern, then asst. resident in medicine New Haven Hosp., 1944-45; asst. in medicine Yale U. Med. Sch., 1944-45; asst. resident physician, then resident physician Vanderbilt U. Hosp., 1948-50; from research asst. in medicine to asst. prof. Vanderbilt U. Med. Sch., 1946-52; assoc. prof., then prof. research medicine U. Okla. Med. Sch., 1952-70; prof. medicine Ind. U. Med. Sch., 1970—; head cardiovascular sect. Okla. Med. Research Found. and Hosp., 1952-70, assoc. dir. found., 1957-70; exec. dir. clin. research Eli Lilly and Co., Indpls., 1970-73, v.p. corp. med. affairs, 1976-83; v.p. Lilly Research Labs., 1973-76; clin. research cons. Walker Clin. Research, Indpls.; mem. vis. staff Wishard Meml. Hosp., Indpls., 1971; pres. Okla. Heart Assn., 1967-68; mem. cardiovascular study sect. Nat. Heart Inst., NIH, 1960-63, heart spl. projects com., 1963-66; bd. mgrs., sci. adv. com. Wistar Inst., 1972-78; sci. adv. com. Hormel Inst., Austin, Minn., 1973-83; mem. clin. scis. panel NRC, 1978-83; mem. clin. pharmacology adv. com. PMAF, 1977-83. Contbr. to med. jours.; mem. editorial bds. jours. Mem. council Inst. Adminstrn. and Mgmt.; mem. adv. bd. Union Coll., trustee, 1982; bd. dirs. Cathedral Arts, Indpls.; assoc. trustee U. Pa.; bd. dirs., exec. com. Indpls. Symphony Orch. Served to comdr., M.C. USNR, 1945-46, 55-57. Fellow Am. Coll. Cardiology, A.C.P., N.Y. Acad. Scis., Royal Soc. Medicine; mem. Am. Assn. World Health (dir. 1974-83), AAAS, Am. Clin. and Climatol. Assn., Am. Fedn. Clin. Research, Am. (fellow council arteriosclerosis, nat. bd. dirs., exec. and central coms.; chmn. research com. 1964-65), Ind. (dir.), Marion County heart assns.), Am. Physiol. Soc., Am. Soc. Clin. Pharmacology and Therapeutics, Am. Soc. Internal Medicine, Assn. Yale Alumni in Medicine, Central Soc. Clin. Research (council 1963-66), Endocrine Soc., Ind., Marion County med. assns., Soc. Exptl. Biology and Medicine, So. Soc. Clin. Research, Southwestern Soc. Naturalists, Wilson Ornithol. Soc., Nat. Audubon Soc., Sigma Xi, Alpha Omega Alpha, Delta Upsilon. Clubs: Cosmos, Capitol Hill (Washington); Confrerie des Chevaliers du Tastevin; Mohawk (Schenectady); Garden of the Gods, Colorado Springs Country, Plaza (Colorado Springs).

FURMANSKI, PATRICIA HANES, systems analyst, administrator, counselor; b. Warsaw, Ind., July 5, 1951; d. Charles E. and E. Kathleen (Kirby) Hanes; m. Louis S. Furmanski, Nov. 5, 1977; children: Taya Kathleen, Jessica Ann. BA in Edn. and Spanish, Purdue U., 1973, MS in Counseling and Student Personnel Services, 1975; postgrad., Va. Poly Inst., 1984. Tchr. Purdue U., West Lafayette, Ind. and Lebanon (Ind.) schs., 1973-77; asst. dir. Placement Services Purdue U., 1975-77; acting dir. career planning and placement Union Coll., Schenectady, N.Y., 1977-78; recruitment dir. placement services Va. Poly. Inst., Blacksburg, 1978-84, programmer analyst systems devel., 1984-85; system analystComputing Ctr. Ft. Hays State U., Hays, Kans., 1986—; mem. Pres.' Commn. on Status of Women. 1977-78; mem. task force on computing Coll. Placement Council, Va. Poly. Inst., 1983, communication computing com., 1983, instr. career/life planning course, presentor confs., workshops, 1981-84. Contbr. articles to Coll. Placement Jour. Named one of Outstanding Young Women Am. Mem. Kappa Delta Pi, Mortar Bd., Zeta Tau Alpha. Avocations: travel. sports, decorating.

FURRER, ALLEN PAUL, transportation company owner; b. Rensselaer, Ind., Nov. 7, 1956; s. John F. and Marcille J. (Kyburz) F.; m. Karen A. Talman, June 30, 1979 (div. Dec. 1979); m. Margret J. Schuster, Dec. 31, 1982; children: James V., Shara J., Blair E., Blaine A. Grad. high sch., Wolcott, Ind., 1974. Owner, operator Curve Inn, Wolcott, Ind., 1975-76; gen. mgr. Sam Young, Inc., Wolcott, 1977-84, pres., owner, 1984-86; pres. Sam Young, Inc., Remington, Ind., 1986-87; v.p. adminstrn. Schilli Transp. Srervices, Inc., 1987—. Club: Hazelden Country (Brook, Ind.) (bd. dirs. 1985—); Lafayette (Ind.) Country; Cub Master (Remington). Lodge: Masons. Avocation: golf. Home: Rural Rt 1 Box 138-B Remington IN 47977 Office: Schilli Transp Services Inc PO Box 351 Remington IN 47977

FURRER, JOHN RUDOLF, business executive; b. Milw., Dec. 2, 1927; s. Rudolph and Leona (Peters) F.; m. Annie Louise Waldo, Apr. 24, 1954; children: Blake Waldo, Kimberly Louise. B.A., Harvard U., 1949. Spl. rep. ACF Industries, Madrid, 1949-51; asst. supr. Thermo nuclear Devel. and Test-Los Alamos, Eniwetok Atoll, 1952-53; dir. product devel. ACF Industries, N.Y.C., 1954-59; dir. machinery, systems group, central engring. labs. FMC Corp., San Jose, Calif., 1959-68; gen. mgr. engineered systems div. FMC Corp., San Jose, 1968-70; v.p. in charge planning dept., central engring. labs. an engineered systems div. FMC Corp., Chgo., 1970-71, v.p. material handling group, 1971-77, v.p. corp. devel., 1977—; bd. dirs. Centocor, Teknowledge, Inc. Patentee in field. Trustee Ravinia Festival, 1986—. Served with USN, 1945-46. Mem. ASME, Council of Planning Execs. (chmn. conference bd. 1986-87). Clubs: Harvard (N.Y.C. and Chgo.); Glen View Country (Golf, Ill.); Economic, Mid-America, Chgo. Yacht Club. Home: 1242 N Lake Shore Dr Chicago IL 60610 Office: FMC Corp 200 E Randolph St Chicago IL 60601

FURST, FRANK EVERETT, diversified products company executive; b. Freeport, Ill., May 1, 1939; s. Charles Wilkins and Jeanne Margaret (Whitman) F.; m. Harriet Edith Eaton, Sept. 24, 1960; children: Martha Whitman, Susan Webster, Elisabeth Harriet. BA, Yale U., 1960; MBA with high distinction, U. Mich., 1963. CPA, Mich., Ill. Acct. Arthur Andersen & Co., Detroit, 1963-66; with Furst-McNess Co., Freeport, 1966—, pres., chief exec. officer, 1970—; bd. dirs. Northwest Ill. Bancorp/State Bank of Freeport, Vermont Am. Corp., Louisville, The First Nat. Co., Storm Lake, Iowa. Mem. Stephenson County Bd., Freeport, 1972-78, Freeport Dist. Sch. Bd., 1978-85; chmn. bd. dirs. Freeport Meml. Hosp., 1979-81. Mem. Am. Inst. CPA's, Ill. Soc. CPA's, Ill. State C. of C. Republican. Episcopalian. Clubs: Union League (Chgo.); Freeport Country. Lodge: Rotary. Office: Furst-McNess Co 120 E Clark St Freeport IL 61032

FURSTE, WESLEY LEONARD, II, surgeon, educator; b. Cin., Apr. 19, 1915; s. Wesley Leonard and Alma (Deckebach) F.; m. Leona James, Mar. 28, 1942; children—Nancy Dianne, Susan Deanne, Wesley Leonard III. A.B. cum laude (Julius Dexter scholar 1934-35); Harvard Club scholar 1933-35), Harvard U., 1937, M.D., 1941. Diplomate: Am. Bd. Surgery. Intern Ohio State U. Hosp., Columbus, 1941-42; fellow surgery U. Cin., 1945-46; asst. surg. resident Cin. Gen. Hosp., 1946-49; sr. asst. surg. resident Ohio State U. Hosps., 1949-50, chief surg. resident, 1950-51; limited practice medicine specializing in surgery Columbus, 1951—; instr. Ohio State U., 1951-54, clin. asst. prof. surgery, 1954-66, clin. assoc. prof., 1966-74, clin. prof. surgery, 1974-85, clin. prof. emeritus, 1985—; mem. surg. staff Mt. Carmel Med. Center, chmn. dept. surgery, 1981-85, dir. surgery program, 1981-82; mem. surg. staff Children's, Grant Med. Ctr., Univ., Riverside, Meth. hosps., St. Anthony Med. Ctr. (all Columbus); surg. cons. Dayton (Ohio) VA Hosp., Columbus State Sch., Ohio State Penitentiary, Mercy Hosp., Benjamin Franklin Hosp., Columbus; regional adv. com. nat. blood program ARC, 1951-68, chmn., 1958-68; invited participant 2d Internat. Conf. on Tetanus, WHO, Bern, Switzerland, 1966, 3d, São, Paulo, Brazil, 1970, 5th, Ronneby Brunn, Sweden, 1978, 6th, Lyon, France, 1981, 7th, Copanello, Italy, 1984, 8th, Leningrad, USSR, 1987; invited guest signing of health services extension amendments act Pres. Johnson, 1965; invited rapporteur 4th Internat. Conf., Dakar, Sénégal, 1975; mem. med. adv. com. Medic Alert Found. Internat., 1971-73, 76—, bd. dirs., 1973-76; Douglas lectr. Med. Coll. of Ohio, Toledo; founder Digestive Disease Found. Prime author: Tétanos; Tetanus: A Team Disease; contbg. author: Advances in Military Medicine, 1948, Management of the Injured Patient, Immediate Care of the Acutely Ill and Injured, 1978; editor Surgical Monthly Review; contbr. articles to profl. jours. Mem. Ohio Motor Vehicle Med. Rev. Bd., 1965-67; bd. dirs. Am. Cancer Soc. Franklin County, pres., 1964-66. Served to maj., M.C. AUS, 1942-46, CBI. Recipient 2 commendations for surg. service in China U.S. Army; cert. of merit Am. Cancer Soc.; award for outstanding achievement in field clostridial infection dept. surgery Ohio State U. Coll. Medicine, 1984, Outstanding Service award, 1985; award for outstanding and dedicated service Mt. Carmel Med. Ctr., 1985; award for over 25 yrs. service St. Anthony Med. Ctr. Mem. Cen. Surg. Assn., Surgical Infection Soc., Internat. Biliary Assn., Shock Soc., Soc. Am. Gastrointestinal Endoscopic Surgeons (com. on standards of practice and on resident and fellow edn.), Soc. Surgery of Alimentary Tract, AAAS, A.C.S. (gov.-at-large, chmn. Ohio com. trauma; nat. subcom. prophylaxis against tetanus in wound mgmt., Ohio chapter Disting. Service award 1987; Ohio adv. com.), Am. Assn. Surgery of Trauma, Ohio Surg. Assn., Columbus Surg. Assn. (hon. mem.; pres. 1983), AMA, Am. Trauma Soc. (founding mem., dir.), Ohio Med. Assn., Acad. Medicine Columbus and Franklin County (Award of Merit for 17 yrs. service), Acad. Medicine Cin., Am. Public Health Assn., Am. Med. Writers Assn., Grad. Surg. Soc. U. Cin., Robert M. Zollinger Club, Mont Reid Grad. Surg. Soc., Am. Geriatrics Soc., N.Y. Acad. Scis., Assn. Program Dirs. in Surgery, Assn. Physicians State of Ohio, Collegium Internationale Chirurgiae Digestivae, Assn. Am. Med. Colls., Internat. Soc. Colon and Rectal Surgeons, Soc. Internat. de Chirurgie, Am. Med. Golfing Assn., Internat. Brotherhood Magicians, Soc. Am. Magicians, N.Y. Cen. System Hist. Soc. Presbyterian. Clubs: Scioto Country, Ohio State U. Golf, Ohio State Faculty (Columbus); University (Cin.); Harvard (Boston). Invited White House guest of Pres. Johnson for signing of Community Health Services Extension Amendments Act, 1965. Home: 3125 Bembridge Rd Columbus OH 43221 Office: 3545 Olentangy River Rd Columbus OH 43214-3955

FURSTENAU, BURNELL WILLIAM, information services executive; b. Scripner, Nebr., Nov. 6, 1925; s. Harry and Agnes Anne (Ries) F.; m. Anne Virginia Puerner, July 26, 1952; children: Stephen, Michael, Charles, Anne, Thomas, Karen. BEE, U. Nebr., 1949; MEE, U. Ill., 1952. Account mgr. Medicus, Cin., 1973-75; program dir. tech. data systems NIH, Bethesda, Md., 1975-80; v.p. info. systems Michael Reese Hosp., Chgo., 1980-84; v.p. info. services Ingalls Hosp., Harvey, Ill., 1984—. Served with USN, 1944-46. Mem. Sigma Tau, Eta Kappa Nu. Republican. Avocations: tennis, boating. Office: Ingalls Meml Hosp Info Services 1 Ingalls Dr Harvey IL 60426

FURTADO, ROBERT, plastic surgeon; b. Anabally, Karnataka, India, Apr. 30, 1936; came to U.S., 1963; s. Victor and Bridgette (Bothello) F.; married, 1962; 2 children. B in Medicine, Sugrery, Govt. Med. Coll., Mysore, Karnataka, 1961. Diplomate Am. Plastic Surgery, Am. Bd. Surgery. Practice medicine specializing in plastic surgery Ft. Wayne, Ind., 1972—. Mem. Am. Soc. Plastic and Reconstructive Surgeons, Ohio Valley Soc. of Plastic Surgeons. Home: 6406 Covington Rd B-1 Fort Wayne IN 46804 Office: 800 Broadway Fort Wayne IN 46802

FUSCO, SAMUEL ANTHONY, military officer; b. Buffalo, June 15, 1959; s. Anthony Matthew and Ida Mary (Cianfrone) F. BS, USAF Acad., 1981; MA, SUNY, Buffalo, 1982. Commd. 2d lt. USAF, 1981, advanced through grades to capt., 1985; with B-52G electronic warfare USAF, Castle AFB, Calif., 1984; officer electronic warfare USAF, Wurtsmith AFB, Mich., 1985—; officer squadron awards and decorations 524th Bomb Squadron, 1985—, officer squadron tactics, 1986—. Franklin C. Wolfe fellow, 1981. Mem. Assn. Old Crows, French Exchange Union. Roman Catholic. Home and Office: PSC Box 836 Wurtsmith AFB MI 48753

FYANS, LESLIE J., JR., clinical psychologist, researcher; b. Salt Lake City, Sept. 6, 1952; s. Leslie J. and Antoinette Marie (Picco) F.; m. Paula M. Peterson, May 18, 1974. B.A.Concordia Coll., Ann Arbor, Mich., 1973; M.A. in Psychology, U. Ill., 1975, Ph.D. in Psychology and Psychometrics, 1977. Cert. psychologist, Ill. Research fellow Inst. Child Behavior and Devel. U. Ill., Champaign; dir. testing program, research psychometrician Ill. Dept. Edn., Springfield, 1977-83; dir. Market Studies Ltd; chief exec. officer, cons. clin. psychologist Clin. Counseling Ltd., Springfield, 1983—; cons. in polit. polling to numerous polit. coms. Author: Achievement Motivation, 1980; Generalizability Theory, 1983; nat. exec. editor Measurement mag.; contbr. articles to profl. jours. Nat. Inst. Edn. grantee, 1975, 77, 80; U.S. Dept. Edn. grantee, 1979. Mem. Am. Bus. Club, Roman Cultural Soc. Lutheran. Clubs: Sangamo, Illini Country (Springfield). Home: 1638 S Mac Arthur Blvd Springfield IL 62704

FYLER, CARL JOHN, dentist; b. Spearville, Kans., May 14, 1921; s. John Henry and Helen Elsie (Parthie) F.; m. Marguerite E. Burris, Feb. 14, 1946. DDS, U. Mo., 1950. Practice dentistry Topeka, Kans., 1950—. Served to maj. USAF, 1942-46, ETO. Decorated Purple Heart, 5 Air Medals, Distinguished Flying Cross. Mem. ADA (life), Kans. Dental Assn., Shawnee County Dental Assn., Internat. Fedn. Dentists, Am. Ex-Prisoners of War (nat. dir. 1974-85, nat. jr. vice comdr. 1984-85), Kans. Ex-Prisoners of War (Gov.'s adv. com. 1978-86). Republican. Presbyterian. Avocations: flying, lapidary, rock hunting. Home: 300 Yorkshire Rd Topeka KS 66603 Office: 612 Kansas Ave Suite A Topeka KS 66603

GAAR, NORMAN EDWARD, lawyer, former state senator; b. Kansas City, Mo., Sept. 29, 1929; s. William Edward and Lola Eugene (McKain) G.; student Baker U., 1947-49; A.B., U. Mich., 1955, J.D., 1956; children—Anne, James, William, John; m. Marilyn A. Wiegraffe, Apr. 12, 1986. Bar: Mo. 1957, Kans. 1962, U.S. Supreme Ct. 1969. Assoc. Stinson, Mag, Thomson, McEvers & Fizzell, Kansas City, 1956-59; ptnr. Stinson, Mag & Fizzell, Kansas City, 1959-79; mng. ptnr. Gaar & Bell, Kansas City and St. Louis, Mo., Overland Park and Wichita, Kans., 1979—; mem. Kans. Senate, 1965-84, majority leader, 1976-80; mem. faculty N.Y. Practising Law Inst., 1969-74; adv. dir. Panel Pubs., Inc., N.Y.C. Mcpl. judge City of Westwood, Kans., 1959-63, mayor, 1963-65. Served with U.S. Navy, 1949-53. Decorated Air medal (2); named State of Kans. Disting. Citizen, 1962. Mem. Am. Bar Assn., Am. Judicature Assn., Nat. Conf. State Legislatures, Am. Radio Relay League, Antique Airplane Assn., Exptl. Aircraft Assn. Republican. Episcopalian. Clubs: Woodside Racquet, Brookridge Country. Office: Gaar & Bell 8717 W 110th Suite 640 Overland Park KS 66210

GABBARD, GLEN OWENS, psychiatrist, psychoanalyst; b. Charleston, Ill., Aug. 8, 1949; s. Earnest Glendon and Lucina Mildred (Paquet) G.; children: Matthew, Abigail, Amanda, Allison; m. Joyce Eileen Davidson, June 14, 1985. BS, Eastern Ill. U., 1972; MD, Rush Med. Coll., 1975; degree in psychoanalytic tng., Topeka Inst. for Psychoanalysis, 1984. Diplomate Am. Bd. Psychiatry and Neurology. Resident in psychiatry Menninger Sch. Psychiatry, Topeka, Kans., 1975-78; staff psychiatrist C.F. Menninger Hosp., Topeka, 1978-83, sect. chief, 1984—; staff psychoanalyst The Menninger Found., Topeka, 1984—; mem. faculty Menninger Sch. Psychiatry, 1978—, Topeka Inst. for Psychoanalysis, 1984—; clinician-researcher The Menninger Found., 1985—. Author: With the Eyes of the Mind, 1984, Psychiatry and the Cinema, 1987; contbr. articles to profl. jours.; mem. editorial bd. Bull. Menninger Clinic, 1984—. V.p. Topeka Civic Theatre, 1981-82, pres. 1982-83, bd. dirs. 1981-83. Named one of Outstanding Young Men in Am. U.S. Jaycees, 1984. Mem. AAAS, Am. Psychoanaltyic Assn., Am. Psychiat. Assn. (Falk fellow 1976), Soc. Psychotherapy Research, Menninger Sch. Psychiatry Alumni Assn. (pres. 1982-83), Alpha Omega Alpha. Avocations: theater, music, bird-taming. Home: 5410 SW Mission Topeka KS 66610 Office: Menninger Found PO Box 829 Topeka KS 66601

GABBAY, ALAN, lawyer; b. Oceanside, N.Y., Apr. 23, 1953; s. Maurice and Violet (Shashou) G. BA, Yale U., 1975; JD, Harvard U., 1978. Bar: N.Y. 1979, Ill. 1984. Assoc. Webster & Sheffield, N.Y.C., 1978-83, Sidley & Austin, Chgo., 1983—. Editor in chief, founder Harvard Environ. Law Rev., 1976-77. Mem. ABA, Ill. State Bar Assn., Chgo. Bar Assn. Avocation: bicycle riding. Home: 30 E Elm St Apt 7A Chicago IL 60611 Office: Sidley & Austin One First Nat Plaza Chicago IL 60603

GABBERT, DANIEL FRANKLIN, videographer, producer; b. Detroit, June 9, 1952; s. Daniel Birchell and Shirley June (Sollars) G. BS, Cen. Mich. U., 1975; cert., Am. Film Inst., 1981. Pvt. practice film/video producer Dearborn Heights, Mich., 1976—; photographer WBKB TV, Alpena, Mich., 1979-80; prodn. mgr. L&W Prodns., Dearborn, Mich., 1981-83; videographer, producer WJBK TV, Detroit, 1983—. Prodn. coordinator (film) Miss Lonelyhearts, 1981; producer, dir., writer, videographer (TV documentary) Noble Odyssey, 1983. Mem. Am. Film Inst. Alumni Assn., Alpha Epsilon Rho. Avocations: scuba diving, photography. Home: 5961 Colonial Dearborn Heights MI 48127 Office: WJBK TV Box 2000 Southfield MI 48037

GABE, JANICE ELAINE, chemical dependency treatment center director; b. Forsyth, Mont., Mar. 12, 1957; d. Henry Stanberry and Sharon Essie (Kennedy) Ewart; m. Steven Lee Gabe, July 1, 1978. BA in Sociology, No. Ill. U., 1979; MSW, U. Ill., 1987. Cert. addictions counselor; registered social worker. Youth supr. Rosecrance Ctr., Rockford, Ill., 1979-80, group therapist, 1980-81, team supr., 1981-82, clin. supr., 1982-86; program dir. Life Works Adolescent Chem. Dependency Ctr., Bolingbrook, Ill., 1985—. Vol. Ill. Teen Inst., Springfield, Ill., 1985—; mem. Bolingbrook Substance Com., 1986; Regional Prevention Group, Joliet, Ill., 1986. Mem. Juvenile Officers Assn., Cen. Service Team, Ill. Alcoholism and Drug Dependence Assn. Avocation: porcelain doll making. Office: Life Works Adolescent Chem Dependency Ctr 420 Med Ctr Dr Suite 230 Bolingbrook IL 60439

GABEL, ALAN DENNIS, lawyer; b. Portsmouth, Ohio, Mar. 26, 1949; s. Jerome and Grace Gabel; m. Roberta Patricia Melcher; children: David, Courtney, Ryan. BA, U. Cin., 1971, M in Pub. Adminstrn., 1973; postgrad., Ga. Inst. Tech., 1972-74; JD, U. Dayton, 1983. Bar: Ohio 1984, U.S. Dist. Ct. (so. dist.) Ohio 1984. Mgr. City of Alpharetta, Ga., 1974-75; dir. Atlanta C. of C., 1975-77; asst. mgr. City of Portsmouth, 1977-78; dir. Nat. League of Cities, Washington, 1979-80, cons. housing rehab. program, 1980-81; legal intern Office Staff Judge Advocate Hdqrs. Air Force Logistics Command, Wright-Patterson AFB, Ohio, 1980-83; prosecutor Montgomery County, Dayton, Ohio, 1984—. Vol. presdl. election for Jimmy Carter, 1975-76; dir. community devel. City of Portsmouth, Ohio, 1979. Andrew Mellow trust scholar Ga. Inst. Tech., 1972-74; scholar Woman's Auxilary Dayton Bar Assn., 1982; grad. scholar U. Cin., 1971. Mem. ABA, Nat. Trial Lawyers Assn. Jewish. Avocations: volunteer coach, religious teacher. Home: 8 Spirea Dayton OH 45419 Office: Montgomery County Prosecutor 41 N Perry St Dayton OH 45402

GABELMAN, RICHARD JOHN, marketing professional, technical writer; b. Rochester, N.Y., Dec. 17, 1945; s. Richard Jacob and Catherine Ellen (McPhillips) G.; m. Katherine Helen Adams, Nov. 19, 1971; 1 child, Richard Patrick. BSBA in Mktg., Xavier U., 1968, MBA in Mgmt., 1974. Media mgr. Burke & Co. Inc., Cin., 1968-71; group spl. agt. CNA Ins., Cin., 1971-73; sr. tech. writer Cin. Milacron, Inc., 1973-75; pres. Consultamark, Inc., Cin., 1975—; bd. dirs. Aquasurvey and Instrument, Inc., Cedarville, Ohio,

1976—. Mem. Mt. Washington Civic Assn., Cin., 1979—. Recipient Found. award E.W. Scripps Co., Inc., 1971. Mem. Am. Mgmt. Assn. Republican. Club: Ohio Skindivers (Cedarville) (v.p. 1986—). Avocations: woodworking, numismatics, book collecting. Home and Office: 2560 Meadowmar Ln Cincinnati OH 45230

GABOVITCH, EDWARD ROBERT, internist; b. Hammond, Ind., Jan. 3, 1934; s. Carl and Rea (Shlensky) G.; m. Phyllis Stein, Oct. 16, 1955; children: Ellen, David, Michael, Bill, Jane. BA, Ind. U., Bloomington, 1954; MD, Ind. U., Indpls., 1957. Intern Marion County Gen. Hosp., Indpls., 1957-58, resident in internal medicine, 1958-61; fellow in rheumatology Ind. U. Sch. Medicine, Indpls., 1961-62; practice medicine specializing in internal medicine Indpls., 1962—; clin. prof. medicine Ind. U., Indpls., 1962—; cons. VA Hosp., Indpls, 1962—; bd. dirs. Meth. Hosp. Ind. Pres. Jewish Community Ctr. Assn. Indpls., 1969-72, Ind. Chpt. Arthritis Found., Indpls., 1976-78, Beth-El Zedeck Synagogue, Indpls., 1977-80, Indpls. Jewish Welfare Fedn., Indpls., 1984-86; bd. dirs. Meth. Hosp. Ind., 1986—. Fellow Am. Rheumatism Assn.; mem. AMA, Ind. State Med. Assn., Marion County Med. Assn. Democrat. Home: 595 Holliday Ln Indianapolis IN 46260 Office: 1801 N Senate Blvd Suite 315 Indianapolis IN 46202

GABRICK, ROBERT WILLIAM, American history educator; b. Mpls., Nov. 11, 1940; s. Michael Jr. and Helen Marie (Lendt) G.; m. Lorretta Jean Miller, Oct. 27, 1962; children: Brad William, Ross Michael. BS, U. Minn., 1962, postgrad., 1962, 63; MEd, Macalester Coll., 1969; postgrad., U. Wis., River Falls, 1968-69, 71, 84. Cert. social studies tchr. Tchr. River Falls, Wis., 1962-70, White Bear Lake, Minn., 1970-84, 87—; tchr. Blaine (Minn.) Sr. High Sch., 1984-87; cons., teaching Ednl. Growth, 1974—. Advisor Apple River Risers 4-H Club, Somerset, Wis., 1979-84; council mem. Christ Luth. Ch., Somerset, 1978-84, council mem. Ezekiel Luth. Ch., River Falls, 1973-76. Scholar Am. Studies Inst., COE Found., 1965, NDEA Foreign Policy Inst., U. Wis., 1968, Inst. for Staff Devel., White Bear Lake Schs., 1972, 73, Minn. History Teaching Alliance, 1987—; Allen J. Ellander fellow Close-Up Program, 1973. Mem. Assn. Tchr. Educators, Assn. Supervision and Curriculum Devel., Orgn. Am. Historians, Wis. Assn. Tchr. Educators (exec. bd. 1984—), St. Croix Valley Assn. Tchr. Educators (pres. 1984-86), Phi Delta Kappa (chpt. pres. 1986—). Home: Rt 2 Box 265J Somerset WI 54025 Office: White Bear Lake Pub Schs White Bear Lake MN 55110

GABRIELSEN, TRYGVE OLAV, neuroradiologist; b. Vest-Agder, Norway, Mar. 27, 1930; came to U.S., 1949; s. Frank and Marie Viktoria (Andreasen) G.; m. Irene Kielland, Mar. 3, 1955 (dec. Aug. 1974); children: Jan Trygve, Claire Anne, Stein Erik, Dag Norman; m. Ragnhild Vatne, Sept. 30, 1976. BS, U. Wash., Seattle, 1953, MD, 1956. Diplomate Am. Bd. Radiology. Intern U. Tex. Med. Branch, Galveston, 1956; resident in radiology U. Mich., 1957-60, from instr. to prof. radiology, 1962—, dir. div. neuroradiology, 1965—; cons. VA Med. Ctr., Ann Arbor, Mich., 1965—. Served to capt. U.S. Army, 1960-62. Mem. Assn. Univ. Radiologists (travel grant 1968), Am. Soc. Neuroradiology (chmn. bylaws com. 1984-85; nominating com. 1984-85; exec. com. 1984-85), Radiol. Soc. N.Am., Fred J. Hodges Radiol. Soc., Am. Assn. Neurol. Surgeons, Am. Soc. Head and Neck Radiology, Mich. State Med. Soc., Washtenaw County Med. Soc. Avocations: jogging, skiing, sailing, wind surfing, music. Office: U Mich Dept Radiology 1500 E Med Ctr Dr B1D530-0030 Ann Arbor MI 48109-0030

GADD, JOHN LAWRENCE, real estate appraiser, consultant; b. Chgo., Oct. 21, 1933; s. John Joseph and Marcella Signe (Hedin) G.; m. Yvonne Hershey, Oct. 4, 1958; children: John P., Mary, Scott, Cathy. Student, Loyola U., Chgo., 1952-54, DePaul U., 1959-60. V.p. Lloyd Thomas/Coats & Burchard Co., Niles, Ill., 1952-84; sr. real estate cons. Arthur Andersen & Co., Chgo., 1984—. Contbr. articles to profl. jours. Pres. Scarsdale Estates Homeowners Assn., Arlington Heights, Ill., 1973; mem. indsl./comml. devel. com. Village of Arlington Heights, 1982—. Served as cpl. U.S. Army, 1956-58. Fellow Am. Soc. Appraisers (exec. com. 1978-85, internat. pres. 1982), Inc. Soc. Valuers and Auctioneers of Eng.; mem. Am. Inst. Real Estate Appraisers (sr.), Am. Soc. Real Estate Counselors, Appraisal Inst. Can. (sr.), Soc. Real Estate Appraisers (sr., chmn. internat. relations com. 1983), Chgo. Real Estate Bd. (bd. govs. appraisers div. 1986—), Lambda Alpha Land Econs. Frat. Republican. Roman Catholic. Avocations: collecting military memorabilia. Home: 843 S Burton Pl Arlington Heights IL 60005 Office: Arthur Andersen & Co. 33 W Monroe St Chicago IL 60603

GADDES, RICHARD, opera company administrator; b. Wallsend, Northumberland, Eng., May 23, 1942; s. Thomas and Emilie Jane (Rickard) G. L.T.C.L. in piano, L.T.C.L. for sch. music; G.T.C.L., Trinity Coll. Music, London, 1964; D. Mus. Arts (hon.), St. Louis Conservatory, 1983; D.F.A. (hon.), U. Mo.-St. Louis, 1984; D.Arts (hon.), Webster U., 1986. Founder, mgr. Wigmore Hall Lunchtime Concerts, 1965; dir. Christopher Hunt and Richard Gaddes Artists Mgmt., London, 1965-66; bookings mgr. Artists Internat. Mgmt., London, 1967-69; artistic adminstr. Santa Fe Opera, 1969-78; gen. dir. Opera Theatre of St. Louis, 1975-85, bd. dirs., 1985—; bd. dirs. Am. Inst. Mus. Studies; cons. William Mathews Sullivan Found., Nat. Inst. for Music Theatre. Recipient Lamplighter award, 1982, Mo. Arts award, 1983, St. Louis award, 1983, Human Relations award Jewish-Am. Com., St. Louis, 1985, Nat. Inst. for Music Theatre award, 1986, Cultural Achievement award Young Audiences, 1987. Office: Opera Theatre of St Louis PO Box 13148 Saint Louis MO 63119

GADOMSKI, NINA MARIE, advertising executive; b. Chgo., Nov. 18, 1960; d. Zbigniew Andrew and Stella (Telesz) B. BS in Advt., U. Ill., 1982. Account executive Bernard Hodes Advt., Chgo., 1982—. Roman Catholic. Home: 2141 N 74th Ave Elmwood Park IL 60635

GAEBE, ROBERT JOHN, dairy farmer; b. New Salem, N.D., May 28, 1938; s. Theodore William and Edith Helen (Kunkel) G.; m. Mary Alice Dewitz, Oct. 3, 1964; children: Lance Dewitt, Randall John, Dirk Robert, Marla Allison, Andrea Sue. Student, Dickinson State Coll., 1956-58. Owner, operator Gaebe Dairy, New Salem, 1960—; bd. dirs. Land O' Lakes, Mpls., Farmers Union Oil Co., New Salem, 1986; pres. Morton Oliver DHIA, New Salem, 1978-83, Land O' Lakes Dist. 18, N.D., 1970-82. Chmn. Engelter Twp., New Salem, N.D., 1976—; pres. New Salem Jaycees, 1972-73, Peace United Ch. of Christ, New Salem, 1986; sec. Land O' Lakes Resolution Com., Mpls., 1976-82; mem. New Salem Centennial Singers. Named an Outstanding Young Farmer, New Salem, 1972. Mem. N.D. Dairy Herd Improvement Assn., Morton-Oliver Dairy Herd Improvement Assn. (pres. 1978-83), N.D. Assn. Coops. (v.p.). Lodges: Lions, Elks. Address: RR 2 PO Box 92 New Salem ND 58563

GAEBLER, ROBERT (ADAMS), psychologist; b. Cleve., Jan. 4, 1932; s. Herman Ernest and Ruth (Adams) G.; m. Carol Rose Armin, Mar. 26, 1961; children: David, Kenneth, Michael. BA with honors, Ohio U., 1955; MS in Clin. Psychology, Northwestern U., 1959. Trainee clinical psychology VA Mental Health Clinic, Chgo., 1958-60; USPHS fellow Conn. State Hosp., Middletown, 1957-58; clin. psychologist Inst. Juvenile Research, Chgo., 1960-63; sch. psychologist Proviso Spl. Edn., Maywood, Ill., 1963-65, Niles West High Sch., Skokie, Ill., 1965-66; state psychology supr. No. Ill. Ill. Office Supt. Pub. Instrn., Chgo., 1967-71; pvt. practice psychology specializing in sch. children Chgo. and suburbs, 1971—; diagnostic cons. Head Start, various locations, 1965-67. Editor: newsletter Chgo. Psychol. Assn., 1984—; contbr. articles to profl. jours. Nat. sec. SCI Internat. Voluntary Service, 1962-63, 69-71, also mem. nat. com., 1961-85. USPHS fellow Northwestern U. Mem. Am. Psychol. Assn. (chmn. com. ethical practice div. sch. psychology, 1969-71), Midwest Psychol. Assn., Ill. Psychol. Assn. (treas. sect. 1969-71, mem. council 1974-76), Chgo. Psychol. Assn. (mem. council 1970-72, pres. 1974-75, 85-86), Nat. Assn. Sch. Psychologists (sec. Ill. sect. 1968-69, Ill. del. 1969-71).

GAERTNER, DONELL J., librarian; b. St. Louis, Sept. 30, 1932; s. Elmer Henry and Norine Helen (Colomb) G.; m. Darlene Gaertner, Mar. 17, 1956; children—Karen Elaine, Keith Alan. A.B. in Econs., Washington U., 1954; M.L.S., U. Ill., 1955. Adminstrv. asst. St. Louis County Library, 1957-64, asst. dir., 1964-68, dir., 1968—. Served to 1st lt. U.S. Army, 1955-57. Mem. ALA, Mo. Library Assn., Spl. Library Assn., Phi Beta Mu, Omicron Delta Gamma. Mem. United Church of Christ. Lodges: Masons, Order Eastern Star. Office: St Louis County Library 1640 S Lindbergh Blvd Saint Louis MO 63131-3598

GAFF, JERRY GENE, academic administrator; b. DeKalb County, Ind., Feb. 5, 1936; s. Kenneth E. and Mona F. (Traxler) G.; chidlren: David B., Amy E. AB, DePauw U., 1958; PhD, Syracuse U., 1965. Asst. research prof. U. Calif., Berkeley, 1967-72; project dir., vis. prof. Calif. State U.'s and Colls., 1972-75; project dir. Soc. Values in Higher Edn., Washington, 1975-81; dir. curriculum devel. Assn. Am. Colls., Washington, 1981-83; dean coll. liberal arts Hamline U., St. Paul, 1983-87, acting pres., 1987—; mem. task force on acad. workplace Council of Ind. Colls., 1985; cons. in higher edn., 1970—. Author: The Cluster College, 1970, Toward Faculty Renewal, 1975, Professional Development, 1978, General Education Today, 1983. Grantee Exxon Edn. Found., 1972-74, 78-81, U.S. Govt. 1975-78. Mem. Am. Assn. for Higher Edn. (trustee 1985—), Assn. Am. Colls. (instl. rep.), Am. Council on Edn. (instl. rep.). Avocations: fishing, jogging, sports, theatre, walking. Home: 1151 Benton Way Arden Hills MN 55112 Office: Hamline U Office of Pres Saint Paul MN 55104

GAFFIGAN, TERRANCE CHARLES, infosystems specialist; b. Springfield, Ill., May 26, 1942; s. Joseph Patrick and Cecelia (Gardiner) G. AA, Springfield Coll., 1962; BA, Ill. Coll., 1964. MIS system liaison mgr. Gov.'s Office of Manpower and Human Devel., Springfield, 1978-84; internal MIS audit mgr. State of Ill. Dept. Commerce and Community Affairs, Springfield, 1984—. Sustainer Rutledge Youth Found., Springfield, 1983—. Mem. Inst. Internal Auditors Assn., Am. Film Inst. Republican. Roman Catholic. Avocations: painting, scuplture, films, travel, writing fiction. Office: State of Ill Dept Commerce and Community Affairs 620 E Adams St Springfield IL 62701

GAFFNEY, DEBRA ELIZABETH, social worker; b. Monroe, Mich., Aug. 4, 1953; d. Thomas F. and Betty J. (Smith) G.; m. Gary N. Gershon, Sept. 30, 1978; 1 child, Amelia. BA, Western Mich. U., 1975, MSW, 1982. Social worker Blodgett Homes for Children, Grand Rapids, Mich., 1979-84, Mary Free Bed Hosp., Grand Rapids, 1984—; bd. dirs. Foster Care Rev. Bd., Grand Rapids, 1985, Women's Resource Ctr., Grand Rapids, 1986, Kent County Council for Prevention of Child Abuse and Neglect, 1987; mem. adv. bd. Nurses Unltd., 1986. Mem. Nat. Assn. Social Workers. Home: 444 College SE Grand Rapids MI 49503 Office: Mary Free Bed Rehab Ctr 235 Wealthy SE Grand Rapids MI 49503

GAFFNEY, DENNIS JOHN, accounting educator, consultant; b. Milw., Dec. 27, 1944; s. Nicholas Thomas and Ann Marcella (Jestrab) G.; m. Maureen H. Smith, Oct. 25, 1985; 1 child, Michael Nicholas. B.S.B.A., Marquette U., 1966; M.A.S., U. Ill., 1969, Ph.D., 1973. C.P.A., Wis., Ill. Asst. prof. No. Ill. U., DeKalb, Ill, 1969-72, assoc. prof., 1975-77; asst. prof. Fla. Atlantic U., Boca Raton, 1972-75; prof. Mich. State U., East Lansing, 1977-86; prof., dir. grad. tax program F.E. Seidman Sch. Bus., Grand Valley State Coll., Grand Rapids, Mich., 1985—; prof. in residence, cons. IRS, Washington, 1983-84; cons. Arthur Anderson & Co., Chgo., McGladrey, Hendrickson & Pullen, Davenport, Iowa., U.S. Treasury Dept., Washington, 1986. Author: Principles of Federal Income Taxation, 1982, 83, 84, 85, 86; Accelerated Cost Recovery, 1981-87. Contbr. articles to profl. jours. Grantee U. Ill., Marathon Oil, Mich. State U., C.P.A. firms. Mem. Am. Inst. C.P.A.s, Wis. Inst. C.P.A.s, Am. Taxation Assn., Am. Acctg. Assn. Roman Catholic. Home: 2079 Ashland Ave Okemos MI 48864

GAFFNEY, DONNA LEE MARIE, nurse, educator; b. Appleton, Wis., Jan. 22, 1946; d. Harley Daniel and Theresa Lena (Jackson) Gottfried; m. Thomas Francis Gaffney, Apr. 17, 1971; 1 child, Cory Gottfried. BS in Nursing, Alverno Coll., Milw., 1968; MS in Nursing, U. Ill., Chgo., 1976. RN, Ill., Wis. Staff nurse Milw. Visiting Nurse's Assn., 1968; staff nurse Visiting Nurse Assn. Chgo., 1968-70, asst. supr., 1970-72; nursing cons. Div. Services for Crippled Children U. Ill., Chgo., 1972-74; clin. faculty Wayne Stat U., Detroit, 1976-78, Madonna Coll., Livonia, Mich., 1978-82, 1985; lectr. in nursing Oakland U., Rochester, Mich., 1985—. Mem. Detroit Zool. Soc., Cranbrook Sci. Inst. Friends. Mem. Am. Pub. Health Assn., Mich. Pub. Health Assn., Kappa Gamma Pi, Sigma Theta Tau. Republican. Roman Catholic. Avocations: travel, skiing. Home: 4279 Echo Rd Bloomfield Hills MI 48013 Office: Oakland U O'Dowd Hall Rochester MI 48963

GAGE, EDWIN C. (SKIP), III, travel, hospitality, sales company executive; b. Evanston, Ill., Nov. 1, 1940; s. Edwin Cutting and Margaret (Stackhouse) G.; m. Barbara Ann Carlson, June 26, 1965; children—Geoff, Scott, Christine, Richard. B.S. in Bus. Adminstrn., Northwestern U., 1963, M.S. in Journalism, 1965. Vice pres. direct mktg. Carlson Mktg. Group of Carlson Cos., Mpls., 1970-75, exec. v.p., 1975-77, pres., 1977-83; exec. v.p. Carlson Cos. Inc., Mpls., 1983, pres., chief operation officer, 1984—; now also pres. Carlson Mktg. Group, Inc., Mpls. Served to lt. U.S. Navy. Mem. Young Pres. Orgn. Avocations: music folk and popular; tennis. Office: Carlson Marketing Group Inc 12755 State Hwy 55 Minneapolis MN 55441

GAGE, J. P., chemical company executive. Pres., chief exec. officer Liquid Carbonic Corp., Chgo. Office: Liquid Carbonic Corp 135 S La Salle St Chicago IL 60603 Also: CBI Industries Inc 800 Jorie Blvd Oak Brook IL 60522 *

GAGE, JOHN, opera company executive; b. Grand Rapids, Mich., Nov. 25, 1937; s. John McKay and Frances Charlotte (Hulswit) Criner. B.A., Wayne State U., 1965, M.A., 1969. Instr. speech and theatre Heidelberg Coll., 1966-70; mem. faculty speech and theatre Hamline U., 1971-73; gen. mgr. Friar's Theatre, Mpls., 1971-72; artistic dir. Chimera Theatre Co., St. Paul, 1971-73; stage mgr. St. Paul Opera, 1972-74; gen. mgr. Theatrical Rigging Systems, Mpls., 1974-77; prodn. stage mgr. Dallas Civic Opera, also Miami Opera, 1977-80; gen. mgr. Florentine Opera Co., Milw., 1980—, Opera America. Served with USAF, 1956-60. Office: Florentin Opera Co 750 N Lincoln Memorial Dr Milwaukee WI 53202

GAGE, MICHAEL JAY, accountant; b. Vermillion, S.D., Feb. 4, 1952; s. Dale Jesse and Darleen Elsie (Noteboom) G.; m. Susan Marie Whetzel, Dec. 10, 1977; 1 child, Daniel Jacob. BBA, U. S.D., 1980. CPA, S.D., Minn. Mem. staff Peat Marwick Mitchell, Mpls., 1980-82, sr. staff mem., 1982-83; supr. sr. staff mem. Peat, Marwick, Mitchell, Mpls., 1983-85, mgr., 1985-87, sr. mgr., 1987—. Vol. Children's Home Soc., St. Paul, 1983—. Mem. Am. Inst. CPA's, Minn. Soc. CPA's, Nat. Soc. Accts. for Cooperatives. Presbyterian. Home: 2134 Perry Ave N Golden Valley MN 55422 Office: Peat Marwick Main & Co 1700 IDS Ctr Minneapolis MN 55402

GAGE, STEVEN K., energy management engineer; b. Milw., Nov. 13, 1959; s. Kenneth E. and Barbara A. (Kentowski) G.; m. Mary P. Beaty, July 3, 1982; children: Steven K. II, Bradley J. BSEE, Marquette U., 1982, postgrad. in bus. adminstrn., 1983—. Mktg. engr. Utility Power Corp., West Allis, Wis., 1978-79; applications support engr. Utility Power Corp., Brookfield, Wis., 1979-80; planning engr. Wis. Electric Power Co., West Allis, 1980-81; applications engr. Wis. Electric Power Co., Milw., 1982-84, distbn. system design engr., 1984-86, energy mgmt. engr., 1986—. Judge freshmen design project competition, Marquette U. Coll. Engring., Milw., 1985-86; alumni asst. high sch. adv. group Marquette U. Office Admissions, Milw., 1985-86. Mem. NSPE, Triangle Frat. (v.p. alumni bd. dirs. Marquette chpt.) Tau Beta Pi, Eta Kappa Nu. Avocations: golf, racquetball, softball, photography, swimming, reading. Home: 3920 S 53d St Milwaukee WI 53220 Office: Wis Electric Power Co 10708 W Janesville Rd Hales Corners WI 53130

GAGE, THEODORE JUSTIN, journalist; b. Evanston, Ill., July 3, 1956; s. Edwin C. and Frances I. (Grange) G. m. Anissa Nedzel, 1984. B.S. in Journalism, Northwestern U., 1978, M.S. in Journalism, 1979. prin. FLW Enterprises, 1986—; cons. Cole Taylor Fin. Group, Inc., 1987—. Sr. editor Cashflow mag.; feature articles in nat. and internat. newspapers and mags. including: Advt. Age, N.Y. Times, McGraw Hill World News, Time Inc. Publs., Chgo. Mag.; author monthly column: Capital Ideas, Cashflow mag., 1980—; contbr. short stories to publs., 1983—. Recipient Peter J. Lisagor award Soc. Profl. Journalists, 1978; Outstanding Sports Reporting award Ill. Gymnastic Coaches, 1980; Excellence in Writing award Am. Soc. Bus. Press Editors, 1983. Mem. Chgo. Classical Guitar Soc. (v.p., bd. dirs. 1986—), Soc. Light Opera Works, Evanston Hist. Soc. Avocation: hist. renovation and decorating cons.

GAGLANI, RAJESH DHIRAJLAL, cardiologist; b. Mombasa, Kenya, Oct. 28, 1952; came to U.S., 1977; s. Dhirajlal Amritlal and Saroj Dhirajlal (Sheth) G.; m. Rajendrakumari Patel, Jan. 16, 1978; children: Meera, Jay. MB, BS, Baroda (India) Med. Coll., 1977. Diplomate Am. Bd. Internal Medicine. Resident New Brunswick (N.J.) Hosp., 1978-81; fellow in cardiology Mt. Carmel Med. Ctr., Columbus, Ohio, 1982-84, attending cardiologist, 1984—. Mem. AMA. Hindu. Avocation: photography. Home: 4181 Lyon Dr Columbus OH 43220 Office: Columbus Cardiology Clinic 777 W State St Columbus OH 43222

GAGNON, ROGER JOSEPH, business adminstration educator; b. Worcester, Mass., Nov. 4, 1946; s. Ernest Joseph and Rita Theresa (Morin) G.; m. Christine Claire, July 5, 1974; children: Denise Michele, Russell Joseph. BS, Boston U., 1968; MBA, Clark U., 1971; PhD in Bus. Adminstrn., U. Cin., 1982. Indsl. engr. Johnson Steel & Wire Co., Worcester, Mass., 1968-73; asst. prof. ops. mgmt. U. Ga., Athens, 1979-83, Ohio State U., Columbus, Ohio, 1983—. Contbr. articles to profl. jours. Judge State of Ga. Sci. and Engring. Fair, Athens, 1982; active St. Peter's Cath. Ch., Worthington, Ohio. Winner 1985 Decision Scis. Inst. Instl. Innovation award Competition; U. Cin. Fellow, 1973, grantee 1978, 86. Mem. Inst. Indsl. Engrs. (sr., pres. NE Ga. chpt. 1982-83, bd. dirs. 1980-83), Am. Prodn. and Inventory Control Soc. (bd. dirs. Columbus 1985-86), Inst. Mgmt. Scis., Decision Scis. Inst. (Alpha Iota Delta 1985), Ops. Mgmt. Assn., Soc. Mfg. Engrs., Engring. Mgmt. Soc., Acad. Mgmt., Beta Gamma Sigma, Sigma Iota Epsilon, Delta Tau Kappa. Democrat. Roman Catholic. Avocations: woodworking, piano, weightlifting, jogging, swimming. Home: 1644 Crusoe Dr Worthington OH 43085 Office: Ohio State U Coll Bus Columbus OH 43210

GAGOSZ, BERNARD ARTHUR, diplomat; b. Val d'Or, Que., Can., Apr. 4, 1940; s. John and Emilia (Kostek) G.; came to U.S., 1983; m. Mary-Lou T. Wanamaker, May 9, 1964; children—Natalie Monique, Christopher B. Degree in Bus. Adminstrn. with honors, Sir Wilfred Laurier U., Waterloo, Ont., 1964; diploma Banff Sch. Advanced Mgmt., 1974. First sec. Can. Embassy, Brussels, Belgium, 1965-69, consul/sr. trade commr., Manila, Philippines, 1969-71, counsellor, Athens, Greece, 1971-76; dir. personnel Trade Commn. Service, Ottawa, Ont., Can., 1976-79; consul gen. Can. Consulate, Melbourne, Australia, 1979-83, Mpls., 1983—. Contbr. articles to internat. trade jours. Mem. Profl. Assn. Fgn. Service Officers. Clubs: Mpls., Minikahda (Mpls.). Avocations: sailing, scuba diving, skiing, tennis, golf. Office: Canadian Consulate General 15 S 5th St Minneapolis MN 55402

GAHAGAN, HAYES EDWARD, corporate executive; b. Presque Isle, Maine, Nov. 6, 1947; s. John Edward and Chrystal Hazel (Smith) G.; m. Linda Diane Stone, Jan. 13, 1973; children: Erin, Ryan, Adam, Joseph, Sarah. Diploma, Oxford U., 1968-70; BA, U. Maine, 1971, M in Pub. Adminstrn., 1972. Rep. Maine State Legislature, Augusta, 1972-74, senator, 1974-76; pres. U.S. Devel. Corp., Maine, Ind., Calif., 1978—. Republican. Avocation: running. Office: US Devel Corp One Airport Rd West Lafayette IN 47906

GAINES, ROBERT DARRYL, lawyer, food services executive; b. Kansas City, Mo., May 27, 1951; s. Ralph Robert and Betty June (Crawford) G.; m. Shanette Carrol Kirch, Aug. 14, 1977; 1 child, Ariel Kirch. BA, U. Ariz., 1972; MBA, Mich. State U., 1973; JD, U. Mo., Kansas City, 1983. Bar: Mo. 1983, Ariz. 1983. Sole practice Kansas City, 1983—; pres. Colony Lobster Pot Co., Kansas City, 1984—, Colony Plaza Co., Kansas City, 1985—, GCB Corp., 1987—. Mem. ABA, Mo. Bar Assn., Ariz. Bar Assn., Kans. City Bar Assn., Nat. Restaurant Assn., Mo. Restaurant Assn., Phi Delta Phi (treas. 1982-83). Avocations: flying, racquetball. Home: 9819 Mercier Kansas City MO 64114 Office: Colony Lobster Pot Corp 30 W Pershing Rd Kansas City MO 64108

GAJDA, JAMES EDWARD, accountant; b. Munster, Ind., July 14, 1947; s. Edward Joseph and Stephany Ann (Pogorzelski) G.; m. Christine Mary Czapla, Sept. 28, 1974; 1 child, Ashley Marie. BS in Computer Sci. and Econs., Purdue U., 1969; MBA, U. Chgo., 1972, MS in Computer Sci., 1973; JD, Ill. Inst. Tech., 1978; LLM in Taxation, DePaul U., 1981. Bar: Ill. 1979, Ind. 1979; CPA, Ill.; Cert. Mgmt. Acct. Asst. to v.p. Masonite Corp., Chgo., 1973-74; sr. fin. analyst Standard Oil Co., Chgo., 1974-75; prof. Ind. U., Gary, 1971—; acct. supr., asst. to v.p., controller Natural Gas Pipeline, Lombard, Ill., 1975—; pvt. practice tax cons. Munster, Ind., 1980—. General Motors scholar, 1969; NDEA fellow U. Chgo., 1973. Mem. ABA, Am. Inst. CPA's, Ind. Bar Assn., Ill. Bar Assn., Ill. CPA Soc., Chgo. Bar Assn., Inst. Mgmt. Acctg. Republican. Roman Catholic. Avocations: foreign travel, reading, collecting objets d'art, aerobics.

GALANTE, LOUIS, municipal official. Fire chief, City of Chgo. Office: Office of the Fire Chief City Hall Room 105 121 N LaSalle St Chicago IL 60602 *

GALARIA, IBRAHIM RAJAK, abdominal surgeon; b. Jasdan, Gujarat, India, Oct. 4, 1943; s. R. and H. Galaria; m. Zarina Ibrahim; children: Irfan, Alzena. MD, N.H.L. Mcpl. Med. Coll., Gujarat, 1968. Diplomate Am. Bd. Surgery, Am. Bd. Abdominal Surgery. Intern V.S. Hosp., Ahmedabad County, India, 1968-69; intern Harlem Hosp., N.Y.C., 1970-71, resident in abdominal surgery, 1971-72; resident in abdominal surgery Highland Park (Mich.) Gen. Hosp., 1972-75; practice medicine specializing in abdominal surgery Warren, Mich., 1975—. Mem. Mich. State Med. Soc., Wayne County Med. Soc., Detroit Surg. Assn. Office: 28666 Ryan Warren MI 48092

GALARNYK, TIMOTHY GERARD, safety engineer; b. Madison, Wis., July 19, 1958; s. Ihor Anton and Jennifer Stephan (Lechman) G.; m. Toni Lee Epple, Oct. 11, 1986. AS in Emergency Med. Scis., U. Ark., Little Rock, 1981; BS in Occupation and Indsl. Safety, U. Wis., Platteville, 1982. Cert. safety specialist; cert. safety exec. Corp. safety engr., risk mgr. Lunda Constrn., Black River Falls, Wis., 1981—; risk mgr. Phoenix Steel, Inc., Eau Claire, Wis., 1981—, also cons. Mem. World Safety Orgn., Am. Soc. Safety Engrs. (named Safety Profl. of Yr. 1986), Nat. Safety Council (Award of Hon. 1985-86), Am. Trauma Soc. (bd. dirs. 1983—, sec. 1985—), Associated Gen. Contractors (H.B. Alexander award 1986). Republican. Ukranian Catholic. Home: 868 Kari Dr Eau Claire WI 54701 Office: Lunda Constrn Co 620 Gebhardt Rd Black River Falls WI 54615

GALASK, RUDOLPH PETER, obstetrician-gynecologist; b. Fort Dodge, Iowa, Dec. 23, 1935; s. Peter Otto and Adeline Amelia (Maranesi) G.; m. Gloria Jean Vasti, June 19, 1965. B.S., Drake U., 1959; M.D., U. Iowa, 1964, M.S., 1967. Diplomate Am. Bd. Ob-Gyn. Research fellow in microbiology U. Iowa, Iowa City, 1965-67, resident in ob-gyn, 1967-70, asst. prof., 1970-74, asst. prof. microbiology, 1973-74, assoc. prof. ob-gyn microbiology, 1974-78, prof., 1978—; cons. various pharm. and diagnostic cos. Editor: Infectious Diseases in the Female Patient, 1986; contbr. numerous articles to profl. jours.; mem. editorial bd. Jour. Reproductive Immunology and Microbiology, 1985. Served to staff sgt. USNG, 1954-64. Recipient numerous grants to study the efficacy of various antibiotics and chemotherapeutics. Fellow Am. Gynecological and Obstetrical Soc., Am. Coll. Ob-Gyn., Infectious Disease Am.; mem. Central Assn. for Obstetricians and Gynecologists, Infectious Disease Soc. for Ob-Gyn. (pres. 1982-84, founding mem.), Soc. Gynecol. Investigation, Am. Soc. Microbiology, Izaac Walton League Sigma Xi. Roman Catholic. Club: Ducks Unltd. (sponsor). Office: Univ Iowa Hosps Dept Ob-Gyn Iowa City IA 52242

GALATI, ANASTASIA MARIE, communications executive; b. Athens, Greece, Apr. 17, 1941; d. Louis George and Evanthia (Galati) Pappas; m. Ervin Arthur Wolff, Dec. 27, 1964 (div. July 1976); 1 child, Adam Arthur; m. Brain Eugene Sprunck, May 21, 1982. BS, Iowa State U., 1964; PhD, U. Oreg., Eugene, 1973. Reading instr. Welch Jr. High Sch., Ames, 1964-65; teaching asst. U. Oreg., 1970-71; asst. prof. English Dept. Hamline U., St. Paul, 1972-76, dir. counseling, 1976-78; pres. Practical Communications Inc., St. Paul, 1979—; cons. in field. Author, producer (viedotapes, text and workbook) Writing for the Information Age, 1986; contbr. articles to profl. jour. Mem. Am. soc. Tng. and Devel., Soc. Tech. Communications, Assn. Bus. Communications, Nat. Council Teachers of English, Am. Bus. Communication Assn. Democrat. Home and Office: 482 Holly Ave Saint Paul MN 55102

GALAWAY, BURTON ROBERT, social work educator; b. York, Nebr., May 15, 1937; s. Robert Henry and Armintie Ursula (Reisinger) G.; m. Natalie Ann Wigandt, Aug. 12, 1962; children: Karla Ruth, Andrew Lauritz. BA in Sociology with high distinction, Nebr. Wesleyan U., 1959; MSW, Columbia U., 1961; PhD in Social Work, U. Minn., 1980. Caseworker foster care unit Nebr. Dept. Pub. Welfare, Lincoln, 1961-64; dist. supr. juvenile parole service Iowa Dept. Corrections, Cedar Rapids, 1964-67; instr. Mt. Mercy Coll., Cedar Rapids, 1967-68, asst. prof., 1968-70; instr. U. Minn., Mpls., 1970-73; prof., chmn. doctoral program U. Minn. Sch. Social Devel., Mpls., 1984—, dir. grad. studies, 1984-87; dir. restitution ctr. Minn. Dept. Corrections, 1973-74; instr. social work U. Minn. Sch. Social Devel., Duluth, 1974-80, asst. prof., 1981-83, acting dean, assoc. prof., 1983-85; sr. research fellow New Zealand Dept. Justice, 1982-83; incorporator, sec. bd. dirs. Social Devel. Assocs., Inc., 1978—; incorporator, bd. dirs. Human Service Assocs., Inc., past pres. and treas.; bd. dirs. Twin City Internat. Program for Social Workers and other Human Service Profls., 1985—; co-dir. German-Am. Juvenile Justice Inst., 1982-84; mem. planning com. Am. Pub. Welfare Assn. Cen. States Regional Meeting, 1983; cons. and lectr. in field; tchr. various extension courses. Author: (with B. Compton) Social Work Processes, 1975, 2d edit., 1979, 3d edit., 1984; (with Joe Hudson) Considering the Victim: Selected Readings in Victim Compensation and Restitution, 1975, Community Corrections: A Reader, 1976, Restitution in Criminal Justice: A Critical Assessment, 1977, 2d edit., 1980, Offender Restitution in Theory and Action, 1978, 2d edit., 1980, Perspectives on Crime Victims, 1980, Victims, Offenders, and Alternative Sanctions, 1980; cons. editor, referee Social Work jour., 1983—; editor Minn. Assn. for Crime Victims newsletter, 1984-86; contbr. articles to profl. jours., monographs, and book revs. Incorporator, sec. bd. dirs. Social Devel. Assocs., Inc., 1978—; incorporator, bd. dirs. Human Service Assocs., Inc., 1980—, past pres. and treas. Recipient numerous grants for research projects, 1974-80. Mem. Am. Soc. Criminology, Nat. Assn. Social Workers (bd. dirs. 1975-78, trustee legal def. service 1977-82, del. assembly rep. 1977), Nat. Conf. Social Welfare, Nat. Orgn. for Victim Assistance (mem. research bd. 1981, bd. dirs. 1984-86), Minn. Social Services Assn., Minn. Assn. for Crime Victims (bd. dirs., editor newsletter 1984—), Minn. Foster Parents Assn. (bd. dirs., v.p. 1973), World Soc. Victimology, Internat. Assn. Schs. Social Work, Acad. Cert. Social Workers. Methodist. Home: 155 Windsor Ct New Brighton MN 55112 Office: U Minn Sch Social Work 400 Ford Hall 224 Church St SE Minneapolis MN 55455

GALBREATH, DANIEL MAUCK, real estate executive; b. June 15, 1928; children: Laurie Galbreath Nichols, Lizanne Galbreath Megrue, John Wilmer II. BA, Amherst Coll., 1950; MBA, Ohio State U., 1952. Pres. Pitts. Pirates, 1971-79; chmn. bd. dirs. Galbreath-Ruffin Corp., Columbus, Pitts., N.Y.C., 1979—; pres. John W. Galbreath & Co., Columbus, Ohio, 1983—; pres. Grand Cen. Art Galleries, N.Y.C., also bd. dirs.; bd. dirs. Fed. Bank Cleve., Ohio Bell Telephone Co., Ohio Ctr. Co., Churchill Downs Inc., Koppers Co., Inc. Trustee Rollins Coll., Winter Park, Fla.; bd. dirs. Boys Club Columbus, Columbus chpt. ARC, Cleve. Zool. Soc., Columbus Zool. Park Assn., Nat. Football Found. and Hall of Fame; former chmn. governing bd. Columbus Found., First Community Ch. Recipient Ohio Govs. award, 1980; named Sportsman of Yr., Ohio League of Sportsmen and Nat. Wildlife Fedn., 1973. Mem. Ohio C. of C., Columbus Area C. of C. (bd. dirs., past chmn.), Ohio Thoroughbred Breeders and Owners Assn., Ducks Unltd. (nat. trustee), Atlantic Salmon Fedn. (trustee). Club: Grand Slam, Jockey, Explorers, Coaching. Lodges: Rotary (past pres.), Masons. Avocations: hunting, fishing, conservation activities. Home: 925 Darby Creek Dr Galloway OH 43119

GALBREATH, THEODORE RALPH, insurance sales executive; b. Natrona, Pa., June 23, 1953; s. Ralph T. and Helen P. (Reesman) G.; m. Amy Elizabeth Tuttle, Oct. 2, 1976; children: Benjamin Christopher, Joellen Marie, Bethany Dawn. BA, Cedarville Coll., 1975; cert., Ins. Inst. Am., 1983, assoc. in claims, 1984. Announcer Sta. WOLC-Radio, Princess Ann, Md., 1976-77; account rep. Miami Valley Pub., Fairborn, Ohio, 1977-78, Applied Communications, Dayton, Ohio, 1978-79; property claims adjuster GAB Bus. Services, Columbus, Ohio, 1979-81; br. mgr. GAB Bus. Services, Springfield, Ohio, 1981-83; nat. sales rep. Credit Gen. Ins. Co., Springfield, 1983—. Author: (brochures) Collateral Protection Blanket Mortgage, 1985; video producer : Blanket Mortgage Protection, 1985, co-authored manual, 1986. Pack com. chmn. Cub Scouts Am., Springfield, 1986; choir mem. Southgate Bapt. Ch., Springfield, 1981-86, christian edn. and hospitality com., 1983-86, men's quartet, 1984-86, Sunday sch. supt., 1986; pres. Moorefield Twp. Fire Dept., 1986-87, lt. 1985—. Named one of Outstanding Young Men. Am., Montgomery, Ala., 1985. Mem. Springfield Claims Club (pres. 1982-83), Mortgage Bankers Assn. (nat. ins. com. 1985—). Republican. Avocations: hunting, fishing, sports, fire fighting. Home: 4910 Tulane Rd Springfield OH 45503 Office: Credit Gen Ins Co One S Limestone St Springfield OH 45502

GALDIANO, JOSE M., educator, credit executive; b. Victoria, Tex., Oct. 6, 1925; s. Jose M. and Antonia (Lopez) G.; m. Betty Jane Reinwald, Oct. 30, 1948; children—David, Denise. B.A., U. Colo., 1961. Commd. Enlisted U.S. Air Force, 1943; advanced through grades to sr. master sgt., 1964; instr., 1943-59, edn. coordinator, Latin Am., 1959-61, Iran, 1962-63, sch. supt., Amarillo AFB, Tex., 1963-67; ret., 1967; dir. edn., research and pub. relations Am. Collectors Assn., Mpls., 1968-79; instr. mktg. Normandale Community Coll., Bloomington, Minn., 1973—; Owner Credit Humanics, Mpls., 1975—, seminar instr., 1975—, mgmt. cons., 1979—; owner, pres. Comml. Adjustment Corp., Mpls., 1982—. Contbr. articles to profl. jours. Decorated Air medal with 5 oak leaf clusters; recipient Silver Beaver award Boy Scouts Am., 1973. Mem. Sales and Mktg. Execs., Minn. Edn. Assn., NEA. Republican. Congregationalist. Lodge: Toastmasters. Home: 4617 York Ave S Minneapolis MN 55410 Office: Normandale Community Coll 9700 France Ave S Bloomington MN 55431

GALE, PATRICIA SUZANNE, tax practitioner, financial planner, stock broker; b. Detroit, Mar. 17, 1950; d. Charles Jack and Julia Celine (Vidal) Lefler; m. Vern Walter Gale, Sept. 9, 1972; children: Kristopher W., Michael C., Julia P., Patrick S. BS, Mich. State U., 1972. Owner, mgr. H&R Block, Grayling, Mich., 1976-85, Pat Gale Agy., Grayling, 1986—; br. mgr. Southmark Fin. Service, Grayling, 1985—, Office of Supervisory Jurisdiction, Grayling, 1986—. Mem. Nat. Assn. Tax Practitioners, Enrolled Agts. Assn., Grayling C. of C. Republican. Roman Catholic. Lodges: Rebekahs, Eagles. Avocations: golf, travel. Home: 3251 Nina Gaylord MI 49735 Office: Pat Gale Agy 308 Cedar Grayling MI 49738

GALE, ROBERT HARRISON, JR., lawyer; b. Syracuse, Kans., Feb. 21, 1953; s. Robert H. and Avonne (Gould) G.; m. Linda C. Reitz, June 18, 1978; children: Joshua Robert, Zachary Tyler. B.S., U. Kans., 1975, J.D., 1978. Bar: Kans. 1978, U.S. Dist. Ct. Kans. 1978, U.S. Ct. Appeals (10th cir.) 1978. Asst. dist. atty. Johnson County, Olathe, Kans., 1978-79; Hamilton County atty. Syracuse, Kans., 1979-85; ptnr. Gale & Gale, Syracuse, 1983—; dir. First Nat. Bank, Syracuse, 1980-82; dir., pres. S.C.A.T., Inc., Syracuse, 1982-84. Precinct committeeman Democratic Party, Johnson County, Kans., 1978; elder First Presbyterian Ch., Syracuse, 1982-86. Mem. Kans. Bar Assn., Kans. County and Dist. Attys. Assn., Nat. Dist. Attys. Assn., ABA, Hamilton C. of C. (bd. dirs. 1983-84). Lodges: Rotary, Moose. Home: 55 High Syracuse KS 67878 Office: Gale & Gale Box 906 Syracuse KS 67878

GALE, STEVEN HERSHEL, college director; b. San Diego, Aug. 18, 1940; s. Norman Arthur and Mary Louise (Wilder) G.; m. Kathy L. L. Johnson, May 20, 1973; children—Shannon Erin, Ashley Alyssa, Kristin Heather. B.A., Duke U., 1963; M.A., UCLA, 1965; Ph.D., U. So. Calif., 1970. Reading asst. English, Los Angeles Met. Coll., 1965-66; teaching asst. U. So. Calif., 1966, instr., 1967-68; assoc. UCLA, 1968-70; asst. prof. U. P.R., Rio Piedras, 1970-73; Fulbright prof. U. Liberia, Monrovia, 1973-74; assoc. prof. U. Fla., Gainesville, 1974-80; prof., head dept. English, Mo. So. State Coll., Joplin, 1980-84, dir. coll. honors program, 1984—; dir. Univ. Players, Monrovia Players; author lecture series Am. Film History for USIS, Liberia, 1974, Assn. Depts. English Ann. Salary Survey, 1984—; spl. advisor Liberian Ministry Edn., 1973-74; cons. NEH, Fla. Fine Arts Council; participant confs., convs., seminars, also NEH Humanities Perspectives on Professions, USIS cultural exchange tour, India, 1964. Author: Butter's Going Up, 1977; Harold Pinter: An Annotated Bibliography, 1978; S. J. Perelman: An Annotated Bibliography, 1985; Harold Pinter: Critical Approaches, 1986, S.J. Perelman: A Critical Study, 1987, Ency. of Am. Humorists, 1987; also short stories, dramas, poetry. Abstractor ann. Internat. Bibliography of the Theatre, Abstracts of English Studies. Series editor: Contemporary American and British Drama and Film. Pacific film editor RIMU. Editor: Reading for Today's Writers, 1980; co-editor: The Pinter Rev.; contbr. articles to profl. jours. Reviewer, Garland Press, John Wiley & Sons, St. Martin's Press, Modern Drama, Pacific Quar., Harcourt, Brace, Jovanovich, Little-Brown, Prentice-Hall, William C. Brown. Referee, Theatre Jour., Publs. of Mo. Philol. Assn., Studies in Am. Humor. Mem. alumni admissions com. Duke U.; judge Joplin Globe Regional Spelling Bee; sideline ofcl. Joplin Boys' Club Girls' Soccer; v.p. Great Plains Regional Honors Council, 1986; pres., adv. bd. dirs. Joplin-Nat. Affiliation for Literacy Advance, 1982—. Grantee NEH, 1987, U. P.R., 1971, 72, U. Fla. Humanities Council, 1975, 77, Mo. So. State Coll., 1980, 81, 82, 83, 84, 85, 86, 87; Danforth assoc., 1976—, grantee, 1982. Mem. MLA (dir. session grad. program and curriculum devel., Del. Assembly 1981-83, co-chmn. Assn. Depts. English Job Seekers Workshop 1981), Am. Theatre Assn. regional del. Univ. and Coll. Theatre Assn.), African Studies Ctr. (U. Fla.), AAUP, Am. Film Inst., So. Assn. Africanists, Fulbright Alumni Assn., Nat. Ret. Tchrs. Assn., Con. on Coll. Composition, Coll. Eng. Assn., Nat. Collegiate Honors Council, Beckett Soc., Harold Pinter Soc. (founder, pres. 1986—), Fla. Track Ofcls. Assn., Mid-Fla. Ofcls. Assn., Fla. High Sch. Activities Assn., Mo. State Tchrs. Assn., Am. Soc. Theatre Research, Chi Delta Pi. Home: Route 5 Box 510 Joplin MO 64804 Office: Dept English Mo So State Coll Joplin MO 64801

GALICH, LORNA DOIG, personnel training specialist; b. Evanston, Ill., May 21, 1934; d. James and Frances (Devere) Doig; m. Jerome J. Galich, May 23, 1956; children: Gay Catherine Galich Magura, Gavin, Abigail. BA in Elem. Edn. and Art Edn., Nat. Coll. Edn., Evanston, Ill., 1974, MS, 1984. Cert. tchr., Ill. Tchr. Sch. Dist. 65, Evanston, 1975-77; tng. writer, instr. Allstate Ins. Co., Northbrook, Ill., 1978-80; tng. specialist Washington Nat. Ins. Co., Evanston, 1980—; adj. faculty Nat. Coll. Edn., 1985—; speaker various orgns., Chgo. area, 1980—. Author: On-The-Job Training, 1984. Vol. chair PTA, Evanston and Wilmette, Ill., 1971-74; leader Girl Scouts U.S., Wilmette and Evanston, 1970-75, Boy Scouts Am., Wilmette and Evanston, 1970-75; womens wellness counselor YMCA, Evanston, 1986; pres. Art Encounter, Evanston, 1985—; facilitator Community Bds., suburban Chgo. area, 1980—. Mem. Ill. Tng. and Devel. Assn. (edn. com.), Kappa Delta Pi. Unitarian. Home: 2409 Hartzell Evanston IL 60201 Office: Washington Nat Ins Co 1630 Chicago Ave Evanston IL 60201

GALIMI, JOSEPH JOHN, therapist; b. Bklyn., Mar. 23, 1943; s. Vincent and Lucy Catherine (Catanzaro) G.; m. Mary E. Grant, Oct. 10, 1965 (div.); children: Christa, Lily, Joseph. AA, State Island Community Coll., 1963; BA, David Lipscomb Coll., 1968; MA, Christian Theol. Sem., 1974, MDiv, 1975. Pastor Christ Ch. Disciples, New Palestine, Ind., 1971-75; family therapist Comprehensive Psychological Ctr., Indpls., 1975-80; chaplain, therapist Koala Ctrs., Lebanon, Ind., 1980-83; private practice specializing in family therapy Indpls. and Lebanon, 1983—; pres. Boone County Ministerial Assn., Lebanon, 1986—; bd. dirs., pres. Boone County Mental Health Assn., Lebanon, 1986—. Bd. dirs. Orton Dyslexia Soc., Indpls., 1986—, Project Help, Lebanon, 1986—. Mem. Am. Assn. Marriage and Family Therapists, Am. Assn. Counseling and Devel., Mental Health Assn. Ind. (citation recognition 1983, 84), Theta Phi. Republican. Avocations: gardening, farming, fishing, reading. Home: Rural Rt 2 Box 17 Thorntown IN 46071 Office: 2002 E 62d St Indianapolis IN 46220

GALINDO, PETER ADON, insurance company executive; b. Rock Rapids, Iowa, May 18, 1945; s. Pete and Elizabeth Jean (Myhra) G.; m. Cathy Jo Ulven, Oct. 15, 1966; 1 son, Jason Peter. Student U. Calif.-Berkeley, 1967. Claims supr. S.D. Blueshield, Sioux Falls, 1968-70, mgr., 1971-74, dir., 1975-77, v.p., 1978-84, sr. v.p., 1984-85, exec. v.p., 1985—; lobbyist S.D. Blue Cross-Blue Shield, Pierre, 1973—; chmn. adv. com. Dakota State Coll. Bus. Sch., Madison, S.D., 1979-80. Chmn. Boy Scouts Scout-O-Rama, Sioux Falls, 1971; loaned exec. United Way, Sioux Falls, 1978; coach VFW Teenage Baseball, Sioux Falls, 1981-82; pres. Edison Jr. High PTA, Sioux Falls, 1982-83; bd. dirs. Food Service Ctr., 1984-86, vice chmn., 1985-86; chmn. Holiday Festival of Trees, S.D. Chpt. Am. Diabetes Assn., 1985; bd. dirs. S.D. Easter Seals Soc., 1986—. Recipient Outstanding Service award Boy Scouts Am., 1971; Best TV campaign awards S.D. Advt. Fedn., 1974, 75; Spl. Vol. award United Way, 1978. Mem. S.D. Advt. Fedn., S.D. Press Assn. Republican. Roman Catholic. Lodge: Lions. Home: 5501 W 52d St Sioux Falls SD 57106 Office: SD Blue Shield 1601 W Madison St Sioux Falls SD 57104

GALIP, RONALD GEORGE, lawyer; b. Youngstown, Ohio, Feb. 28, 1934; s. George A. and Agnes A. (Ellis) G.; m. Eileen E. Bott, 1955; children: Rochelle D., Kathleen A. Galip Mootz. BA, Youngstown (Ohio) State U., 1955; JD, Ohio State U., 1957. Gen. counsel Cafaro Co., Youngstown, 1957-78; ptnr. Galip & Manos, Youngstown, 1978-83; sole practice Youngstown, 1983—; pres. Youngstown Title Agy., 1986; counsel, bd. dirs. Youngstown Devel. Co., 1986. Bd. dirs. Ohio Heart Inst.; trustee Easter Seal Soc., Youngstown. Mem. ABA, Ohio Bar Assn., Mahoning County Bar Assn., Internat. Council Shopping Ctrs., Am. Arbitration Assn. Roman Catholic. Avocations: golf, tennis, travel. Home: 3445 Logan Way Youngstown OH 44505 Office: 422 City Center One Youngstown OH 44503

GALITZA, LOUIS EDWARD, small business owner, amusement consultant; b. Bucyrus, Ohio, Apr. 27, 1937; s. Louis Joseph and Pearl Elizabeth (Keckler) G. Student, Bowling Green (Ohio) State U., 1956, Ohio State U, 1957. Assoc. editor Archeol. Soc. Ohio, Columbus, 1956-58; owner Ghost Town Mus. Park, Findlay, Ohio, 1959—. Com. mem. Findlay Area C. of C.; pres. Hancock County (Ohio) Hist. Preservation Guild, 1971. Served as sgt. USNG. Democrat. Roman Catholic. Home and Office: 10936 CR 40 Findlay OH 45840

GALL, ELIZABETH BENSON, dating service executive; b. Williamson, W.Va., June 11, 1944; d. Thomas Jefferson Bluebaum and Ollie Mae (Moore) Bluebaum Walker; stepdau. Charles B. Walker; 1 child, Thomas Kontoleon. Ptnr., dir. Chicagoland Register, dating service, Chgo., 1974-84; cooking instr. Elizabeth Benson Internat. Cooking Lessons, 1978-84; owner Ethnic Party People Catering, 1981—, Phone-A-Friend Dating Service, Chgo., 1984—. Home and Office: 6314 N Troy St Chicago IL 60659

GALL, RANDALL JAY, orthopaedic surgeon; b. Sheboygan, Wis., Nov. 28, 1942; s. Harold George and Esther Lillian (Lohr) G.; m. Patricia Ellen Hoffmann, Oct. 1, 1977. BS, U. Wis., 1965, MD, 1968. Intern Parkland Meml. Hosp., Dallas, 1968-69, resident in gen. surgery, 1969; resident in orthopaedic surgery Mayo Clinic, Rochester, Minn., 1972-76; resident in gen. surgery Gunderson Clinic, LaCrosse, Wis., 1971-72, orthopaedic surgeon, 1976—. Served to capt. U.S. Army, 1969-71, Vietnam. Decorated Bronze Star. Mem. AMA, Wis. State Med. Soc., LaCrosse County Med. Soc., Am. Acad. Orthopedic Surgeons, Am. Foot and Ankle Soc., Mid-Am. Orthopedic Assn. Home: W5095 CTH B LaCrosse WI 54601 Office: Gundersen Clinic Ltd 1836 South Ave LaCrosse WI 54601

GALL, STANLEY ADOLPH, physician, immunology researcher; b. Bismarck, N.D., May 31, 1936; s. Adolph and Wilma Thelma (Nickisch) G.; m. Florence Marie Ketterling, Aug. 17, 1958; children—Stanley, Kathryn Louise, Mark Allan, Thomas Andrew. B.A., U. Minn., 1958, M.D., 1962. Diplomate Am. Bd. Ob-Gyn. Intern, U. Oreg. Hosp., Portland, 1962-63; resident in ob-gyn U. Minn. Hosp., Mpls., 1963-66; asst. prof. ob-gyn U. Miami, 1968-73; assoc. prof. ob-gyn Duke U. Med. Center, Durham, N.C., 1973-78, prof., 1978—, dir. div. perinatal medicine; prof. ob-gyn, assoc. head dept. ob-gyn U. Ill. Coll. Medicine, 1985—. Served to capt. U.S. Army Med. Corps, 1966-68. Fellow Am. Coll. Obstetricians and Gynecologists; mem. Soc. Gynecol. Oncology, Soc. Gynecol. Investigations, Infectious Diseases Soc. Ob-Gyn, Cen. Assn. Obstetricians and Gynecologists, Soc. Perinatal Obstetricians. Contbr. articles to profl. jours. Lutheran. Home: 7537 Ridgewood Lane Burr Ridge IL 60525 Office: 840 S Wood St Chicago IL 60612

GALLAGHER, DENNIS HUGH, TV, film and multi-media writer/producer/director; b. Chgo., May 2, 1936; s. Frederick Hugh and Mildred Agnes (Buescher) G.; student Wright Coll., 1954-56, Ill. Inst. Tech., 1956-57; B.Sc. in Physics, U. Ariz., 1966. Dir., Noble Planetarium and Obs., Ft. Worth Mus. Sci. and History, 1960-64; planetarium dir. Man. Mus. Man and Nature, Winnipeg, Can., 1966-70; pres. Omnitheatre Ltd., Winnipeg, 1970-72; pres. Gallagher & Assocs., Chgo., 1972-78, Internat. Travel Theatres, Chgo., 1978-81, Galaxy Prodns. Ltd., Chgo., 1981—; mem. faculty in astronomy and civil engring. U. Man., 1967-68; cons. edn., theater, 1967—. Served with USAR, 1959-65. Mem. Planetarium Assn. Can. (founding pres. 1968-69), Internat. Council Planetarium Execs., Am. Astron. Soc., Nat. Acad. TV Arts and Scis., Am. Soc. Tng. and Devel., Internat. TV Assn., Assn. Multi-Image, Chgo. Film Council. Author: North American Planetariums, 1966; Planetariums of the World, 1969; contbr. articles to profl. jours.; writer, producer, dir. multi-media road show: The Beginning & End of the World, 1972. Office: 5820 N Oriole St Chicago IL 60631

GALLAGHER, FRANCIS WEBSTER, obstetrician, gynecologist; b. Columbus, Ohio, May 22, 1914; s. Francis Mankopf and Mary Edith (Webster) G.; m. Doris Elaine Clickenger, July 8, 1941; children: James Francis, Thomas Franklin, Elaine Louise. Student, Ohio State U., 1933-35, MD, 1940; student, Ohio No. U., 1935-36. Diplomate Am. Bd. Ob-gyn. Intern Mercy Hosp., Pitts., 1940-41; gen. practice medicine Columbus, Ohio, 1941-49; resident in ob-gyn. L.I. Coll. Hosp., Bklyn., 1949-53; practice medicine specializing in ob-gyn. Columbus, 1953-77, practice medicine specializing in gynecology, 1977—; chmn. dept. gynecology St. Ann's Hosp., Columbus, 1953-77; clin. assoc. prof. dept. ob-byn. Ohio State U. Coll. Medicine. Med. dir. Planned Parenthood Assn. of Columbus, 1954-56; past trustee Cen. Ohio Chtp. Am. Cancer Soc. Fellow Am. Coll. Obstetricians and Gynecologists (life); mem. Ohio State Med. Assn., Columbus Ob-gyn Soc. (hon., past pres.), Acad. Medicine of Columbus and Franklin County. Republican. Methodist. Clubs: The Athletic, Ohio State U. Faculty (Columbus). Avocations: reading, fishing, traveling. Home: 343 S Columbia Ave Columbus OH 43209 Office: 2719 E Main St Columbus OH 43209

GALLAGHER, IDELLA JANE SMITH (MRS. DONALD A. GALLAGHER), foundation executive, author; b. Union City, N.J., Jan. 1, 1917; d. Fred J. and Louise (Stewart) S.; Ph.B., Marquette U., 1941, M.A., 1943, Ph.D., 1963; postgrad. U. Louvain, Belgium, U. Paris; m. Donald A. Gallagher, June 29, 1938; children—Paul B., Maria Noel. Lectr. philosophy Marquette U., 1943-52, 54-56; instr. philosophy Alverno Coll., Milw., 1956-58; asst. prof. philosophy Villanova U., 1958-62; asst. prof. philosophy Boston Coll., 1962-68, asso. prof., 1968-69; assoc. prof. philosophy U. Ottawa, 1969-71, prof., 1971-73; projects adminstr. DeRance Found., Milw., 1973-80, v.p., 1981—; vis. prof. philosophy Niagara U., 1976-81. Mem. Sudbury (Mass.) Com. for Human Rights, 1963-69; trustee Mt. Senario Coll., Ladysmith, Wis., 1976—. Recipient Sword and Shield award St. Louis U., Baguio City, Philippines, 1975. Mem. Metaphys. Soc. Am., Am. Cath. Philos. Assn. (exec. council 1967-69), Am. Soc. Aesthetics, Assn. Realistic Philosophy, AAUP, Brit. Soc. Aesthetics, Canadian Philos. Assn., Canadian Assn. U. Tchrs., Phi Alpha Theta, Phi Delta Gamma. Author: (with D. A. Gallagher) The Achievement of Jacques and Raissa Maritain, 1962; The Education of Man, 1962; (with D. A. Gallagher) A Maritain Reader, 1966; (with D.A. Gallagher) St. Augustine—The Catholic and Manichaean Ways of Life, 1966. Morality in Evolution: The Moral Philosophy of Henri Bergson, 1970. Gen. editor: Christian Culture and Philosophy Series, Bruce Pub. Co., 1965-68. Contbr. to New Cath. Ency., also articles to profl. jours. Home: 7714 W Wisconsin Ave Wauwatosa WI 53213 Office: DeRance Found 7700 W Bluemound Rd Milwaukee WI 53213

GALLAGHER, JANET FRANCES, interior designer; b. Buffalo, June 6, 1951; d. Richard Oliver and Mary Bernice (Hillenbrand) Merrick; m. Michael D. Gallagher, Aug. 19, 1972; children: Robyn, Kelly, Matthew. BS in Psychology, U. Evansville, 1977. Interior designer Gallagher Niemeier Interiors, Evansville, Ind., 1984. Pres. Newburgh (Ind.) Welcome Wagon, 1978-79. Clubs: Newburgh Women's (pres. 1984-85), Tri-State Petroleum Wives (pres. 1975-76) (Evansville, Ind.). Avocations: boating, skiing, tennis, bridge, reading. Home: 1515 Audubon Ct Evansville IN 47715 Office: 1324 N Fares Ave Evansville IN 47711

GALLAGHER, NORA ELIZABETH, foundation administrator; b. Garfield Heights, Ohio, May 25, 1951; d. Karl David and Virginia Berneice (Berjenski) Naffin; m. William Thomas Gallagher, Aug. 22, 1975; children: Katie, Ryan, Cullen. BA, Coll. of Mt. St. Joseph on the Ohio, 1973; MEd, Miami U., Ohio, 1976. Tchr. Oak Hills Local Sch. Dist., Cin., 1974-78, St. Bernard's, Green Bay, Wis., 1978-79, Cath. Cen. Grade Sch., Green Bay, 1979-80; dir. The Providence Fund, Sandusky, Ohio, 1986—. Pub. relations worker Green Bay Symphony Guild, 1985-86. Mem. AAUW (pub. relations worker), Nat. Assn. for Hosp. Devel., Nat. Soc. Fund-Raising Execs., Phi Delta Kappa. Roman Catholic. Avocations: sailing, skiing, reading. Office: The Providence Fund 1912 Hayes Ave Sandusky OH 44870

GALLAGHER, R.C., bank executive. Pres. Kellogg-Citizens Nat. Bank, Green Bay, Wis. Office: Kellogg-Citizens Nat Bank 200 N Adams St Green Bay WI 54301 *

GALLAGHER, RICHARD FRANCIS, psychiatrist; b. Chgo., July 8, 1937; s. Frank R. Gallagher and Catherine K. (Shortall) Albee; m. Beverly J. Euler; Karl Gregory, Jeffrey Andrew, Kevin Richard. B, MD, Loyola U., Chgo., 1964. Diplomate Am. Bd. Psychiatry and Neurology. Regional dir. Ill. Dept. Mental Health, Maywood, 1968-70; founder, dir. Suburban Psychiat. Assn., DuPage County, Ill., 1971-83; practice medicine specializing in adult and exec. psychiatry Oak Brook, Ill., 1974—; asst. prof. psychiatry Loyola U., 1971—; founder, chmn. bd. TW3 Corp., Oak Brook, 1980—; founder Human Edge Software Corp., Palo Alto, Calif., 1982—; founder, pres. Market Edge Ptnrs., Oakbrook, 1984—; cons. in applied intelligence FBI hostage negotiations, Chgo., 1980—; cons. applied psychiatry numerous Fortune 500 cos., 1982—. Author: The Mind Prober, 1984, Mind over Minors, 1985; author, inventor bus. strategy software. Served to capt. USAFR, 1965-70. Mem. Am. Psychiat. Assn., AMA, Am. Mgmt. Assn., Am. Entrepreneurs Assn., Assembly Bank Dirs. Republican. Roman Catholic. Avocations: research and teaching of creativity, applied intelligence; pioneered use of automated psychol. testing and psychol. skill transfer tech. using expert systems. Office: 1200 Harger Rd Suite 511 Oakbrook IL 60521

GALLAGHER, STANLEY CARSON, physician, pharmacist; b. Wheaton, Minn., May 9, 1947; s. Harold Carson and Julia Adila (Carlson) G.; m. Joyce Marie Hilfer, Dec. 20, 1969; children: Kristin Joy, Bradley Carson. BS in Pharmacy, N.D. State U., 1970; DO with hon., Coll. Osteo. Surgery and Medicine, Des Moines, 1976. Intern Des Moines Gen. Hosp., 1976-77; practice osteo. medicine specializing in family practice Wheaton, Minn., 1977—; mem. staff Wheaton Community Hosp. Sec. bd. dirs. Wheaton Community Hosp., 1980-86; mem. Wheaton Pub. Health Task Force. Served to lt. USPHS, 1970-73. Mem. Minn. State Osteo. Physician Assn. (bd. dirs. 1980-84), Am. Legion. Roman Catholic. Lodge: Lions. Avocations: sports, body surfing, travel. Home: 1111 5th Ave N Wheaton MN 56296 Office: Wheaton Clinic 12th St and 5th Ave Wheaton MN 56296

GALLANIS, THOMAS CONSTANTINE, obstetrician and gynecologist; b. Chgo., Mar. 6, 1927; s. Constantine A. and Kathryn (Koclanes) G.; m. Jeanette Andria Nassos, Apr. 2, 1979; children: Kathryn Ann, Craig. Student, U. Ill., 1945-48; BS, Northwestern U., 1949, MD, 1952. Diplomate Am. Bd. Ob-Gyn. Intern Passavant Meml. Hosp., Chgo., 1952-53, resident in ob-gyn, 1953-56; practice medicine specializing in ob-gyn Evanston, Ill., 1956—; mem. staff Evanston Hosp., Glenbrook Hosp.; faculty dept. ob-gyn Northwestern U. Med. Sch., 1956—. Fellow Am. Coll. Ob-Gyn.; mem. AMA, Ill. Med. Soc., Chgo. Med. Soc., Chgo. Gynecologic Soc., Chgo. Civil Round Table, Phi Rho Sigma. Home: 1346 Somerset Dr Glenview IL 60025 Office: 2500 Ridge Ave Evanston IL 60201

GALLANT, JENNIFER JUNG, media center administrator; b. Cleve., Sept. 26, 1951; d. Gan Lam and Helen Jung; m. Stephen Laurie Gallant, Apr. 23, 1983. B.A. in English, Case Western Res. U., 1973, M.L.S., 1974. Librarian, Rocky River High Sch. (Ohio), 1975-78, Cuyahoga County Pub. Library, Cleve., 1978—; dir. library Bay View Hosp., Bay Village, Ohio, 1979-81; dir.

media ctr. St. John and West Shore Hosp., Westlake, Ohio, 1981—. Contbr. articles to Med. Newsletter Update, 1982-83. Chairperson alumni fund drive and telethon Case Western Res. U. Matthew A. Baxter Sch. of Info. Sci., Cleve., 1983-84, chairperson telethon drive, 1982-83. Recipient August Alpers award Case Western Res. U., 1974; H.W. Wilson scholar, 1974. Mem. ALA, Med. Library Assn., Med. Library Assn. of Northeast Ohio (v.p. 1983, pres. 1984), Ohio Ednl. Library Media Assn. (award 1974), Cleve. Area Met. Library Assn. (trustee 1985-87), Ohio Health Info. Orgn. (treas. 1986—), Phi Beta Kappa. Office: St John and West Shore Hosp 29000 Center Ridge Rd Westlake OH 44145

GALLAS, DANIEL O., oil pipeline company executive. BS, U. Okla., 1954. With Atlantic Richfield Co., 1954—; sr. v.p. ops. Arco Pipeline Co., Independence, Kans., 1985-86, pres., 1987—, also bd. dirs. Served to 1st lt. AUS. Office: ARCO Pipeline Co ARCO Bldg Independence KS 67301 *

GALLE, WILLIAM JACOB, consultant; b. Dodge City, Kans., Sept. 29, 1921; s. Kurt R. and Louisa M. (Epp) G.; m. Geraldine M. Sey-Burgauer; children—Patricia, Carol, William K., Deborah, Robert E., Alan J. B.S. in Chem. Engring., Kans. State U., 1943; M.S., Purdue U., 1950. Registered profl. engr., Calif. Jr. chem. engr. Aluminum Co. Am., East St. Louis, Ill., 1943-44, 46-48; quality engr., statistician Armour & Co., Chgo., 1950-64; ops. research analyst Brunswick Corp., Chgo., 1964-69, John Morrell & Co., Chgo., 1969-75; tech. cons. W.A. Golomski & Assocs., Chgo., 1976—. Served to lt. (j.g.) USN, 1944-46, PTO. Mem. Am. Soc. Quality Control (sr. mem., div. chmn. 1984—), Am. Statis. Assn., Am. Prodn. and Inventory Control Soc. Presbyterian. Club: Toastmaster Internat. (pres. Park Forest, Ill. 1973). Avocations: music, pub. speaking, bridge. Home: 216 Washington St Park Forest IL 60466 Office: W A Golomski & Assocs 59 East Van Buren St Chicago IL 60605

GALLERO, JEFFERY ALAN, athletic coach; b. Pontiac, Mich., July 31, 1954; s. Florentine and Patricia Louise (Cooper) G.; m. Kellie Marie Klefman, May 24, 1987. Student Eastern Mich. U., 1972-73, Oakland Community Coll., 1974, U. Nev.-Reno, 1985. Lic. pvt. and comml. pilot.; cert. flight instr. Asst. track coach Pontiac No. High Sch., 1973-77; head coach women's cross country, men's track, women's basketball Roeper City Country Sch., Bloomfield Hills, Mich., 1978-81; football coach Larson Middle Sch., Troy, Mich., 1982; head coach men and women track and field Rochester (Mich.) Adams High Sch., 1983; asst. track and cross country coach Southwestern Mich. Coll., Dowagiac, 1983-84; asst. coach Mich. Track Club; asst. meet dir. Nat. Jr. Coll. Marathon Championships, 1984; law clk. Harrison Law Offices, Dowagiac, 1983-84; asst. coach men's track and cross country U. Nev.-Reno, 1985-86. Campaign vol. Waterford Democratic Club, 1983; mem. Pontiac PTA. Bd. regents scholar Eastern Mich. U., 1972-73. Mem. Track Athletics Congress, Nat. Jr. Coll. Coaches Assn., Mich. Interscholastic Track Coaches Assn. Home: 506 Jordon St Pontiac MI 48058

GALLIGAN, FRANK DANIEL, automotive parts company executive; b. Bronx, N.Y., Apr. 15, 1938; s. Frank A. and Mary G. (Moran) G.; B.S., U. Scranton, 1960; grad. exec. devel. program U. Ill., 1975; m. M. Elizabeth Jordan, Oct. 14, 1961; children—Michael F., Eileen M., Paul F. Vice pres. mktg. Toledo Tools Co., 1971-74; nat. sales mgr. AP Parts Co., Toledo, 1974-77; v.p. McQuay-Norris, Inc., St. Louis, 1977-84; exec. v.p., dir. Delta Inc. of Ark., Jonesboro, 1984-87 ; v.p., dir. Delta Group Inc., 1984-87, World Motor Cons., Inc., 1987—. Pres., Brightwaters Acres Civic Assn., 1965-66; mem. bus. adv. com. Lucas County Port Authority, 1976-77. Mem. Automotive Parts and Accessories Assn., Automotive Service Industries Assn. (mem. young exec. nat. bd. dirs. 1977-78). Republican. Roman Catholic. Club: Glen Echo Country (bd. govs.) (St. Louis). Office: PO Box 601 Saint Louis MO 63006-0601

GALLINOT, RUTH MAXINE, educational consultant, educator; b. Carlinville, Ill., Feb. 16, 1925; d. Martin Mike and Augusta (Kumpus) G. BS, Roosevelt U., Chgo., 1971, MA with honors, 1974; PhD, Union for Experimenting Colls. and Univs., Cin., 1978. Adminstrv. asst., exec. sec. Karoll's Inc., Chgo., 1952-66; asst. dean Cen. YMCA Community Coll., Chgo., 1966-81, dir. life planning inst., 1979-80; pres. Gallinot & Assocs., Chgo. and St. Louis, 1980—; mem. criteria and guidelines com. Council on Continuing Edn. Unit, 1983-86, survey and research com., 1984-86; mem. nat. adv. council bus. edn. div. Am. Vocat. Assn., 1980-84, sec., 1982-84. Editor: Certified Professional Secretaries Review, 1983; contbr. articles to profl. jours and mags.; show host Sta. WGCI-FM, Chgo., 1975-81. Chmn. Commn. Status of Women in State of Ill., 1963-68; del. City of Chgo. White House Conf. on Info. and Library, 1976, del. State of Ill. White House Conf. Info. Services and Library Services, 1977; pub. mem. Fgn. Service Selection Bd. U.S. Dept. State, 1984. Recipient Leadership in Civic, Cultural and Econ. Life of the City award YWCA, Chgo., 1972, Achievement in FieldEdn. award Operation P.U.S.H., Chgo., 1975. Mem. Profl. Secs. Internat. (pres. 1961, 62, ednl. cons. 1980-84), Edn. Network Older Adults (v.p., sec. 1979-86), Nat. Assn. Parliamentarians (Ill. chpt., Chgo. chpt.), Literacy Council Chgo. (bd. dirs. 1979-86). Club: Zonta of Chgo. (treas. 1965-66). Home and Office: Gallinot & Assocs 11161 Estrada Dr #9 Spanish Lake Saint Louis MO 63138

GALLIVAN, CLARIBELL LOU, educational administrator; b. Bolivar, Mo., Sept. 29, 1934; d. Roscoe Bowen and Eulah May (Lafferty) G.; m. Ralph C. Webb, Mar 25, 1961 (div. Jan. 1983): 1 child, Cara Glynn Morgan. BS in Home Econs., U. Mo., 1956. Home agt. various extension services 1961-77; substitute tchr. various locations, 1976-82; office mgr. U. Mo., Columbia, 1982—. Vol. Meth. Ch. in Cuba, Costa Rica, 1956-60. Avocations: study of psychology, occult. Home: 2106 Ammonette Box 7048 Columbia MO 65205 Office: U Mo 102 Whitten Hall Columbia MO 65211

GALLMEYER, CHARLES CHRISTIAN, manufacturing executive; b. Grand Rapids, Mich., Aug. 1, 1948; s. William Christian and Barbara Alice (Wykes) G.; m. Jane Ellen Chamberlin, May 5, 1984; children: Alice Follett, William Chamberlin. BA, Lawrence U., Appleton, Wis., 1970; MA, UCLA, 1973, postgrad., 1974; MBA, U. Mich., 1976. Asst. trainee Carl Fischer of Chgo., 1976-77; br. controller Carl Fischer, Inc., N.Y.C., 1977-79; purchasing mgr. Gallmeyer & Livingston, Grand Rapids, 1979-86, pres., 1986—. Account exec. United Way, Grand Rapids, 1986. Avocation: fly fishing. Office: Gallmeyer & Livingston Co 336 Straight Ave SW Grand Rapids MI 49504

GALLOWAY, FRANKLYN ALLEN, computer manufacturing company executive; b. Canon City, Colo., Nov. 9, 1946; s. Charles Franklyn and Phoebe Jane (Glover) G.; m. Linda Kay Parrott, Nov. 14, 1971; children: Scott Allen, Sarah Elizabeth. AA, Coffeyville Jr. Coll., 1966; BBA, Wichita Sate U., 1978. Mgr. recreational vehicle warranty dept. Coleman Co., Inc., Wichita, Kans., 1969-78; mgr. spl. projects Communication Arts Assn., Wichita, 1978-81; v.p. adminstrn. Mycro-Tek, Inc., Wichita, 1981—. Mem. budget com. United Way, Wichita, 1987. Mem. Disciples of Christ Ch. Avocations: golf, camping, fishing. Office: Mycro-Tek Inc 9229 E 37th N Wichita KS 67002

GALLOWAY, JODY LYNN, accountant; b. Grinnell, Iowa, Sept. 1, 1960; s. Denton Eugene and Judy Kaye (Evans) G.; m. Bobette Parker, Aug. 21, 1982; 1 child, Logan Parker. BA in Acctg. summa cum laude, Simpson Coll., 1982; postgrad., Drake U., 1982—. CPA, Iowa. Tax acct. Peat, Marwick and Mitchell, Des Moines, 1982-85; corp. tax mgr. Allied Group Ins., Des Moines, 1985—; adj. instr. acctg. Simpson Coll., Indianola, Iowa, 1985—. Mem. Am. Inst. CPA's, Iowa Soc. CPA's. Methodist. Club: Des Moines Golf and Country. Lodge: Masons. Avocation: golf. Home: 1109 58th St West Des Moines IA 50265 Office: Allied Group Ins Des Moines IA 50309

GALOFRE, ALBERTO, medical educator; b. Santiago, Chile, Dec. 10, 1937; came to U.S., 1973; naturalized, 1982; s. Estanislao and Margarita (Terrasa) G.; m. Nancy Kay Evert, June 23, 1968; children—Ana Margarita, Christine Elizabeth, Mary Kay. B.Sc., Catholic U. Chile, 1959; M.D. summa cum laude, U. Chile, 1962; M.Ed., U. Ill.-Urbana, 1974. Instr. pediatrics Catholic U., Santiago, 1963-70, asst. prof. pediatrics, 1970-73; asst. prof. pediatrics and human devel. Mich. State U., East Lansing, 1974-78; asst. prof. internal medicine St. Louis U., 1978-85, assoc. prof., 1985—, asst. dean curriculum Med. Sch., 1979-85, assoc. dean, 1985—; mem. adv. panel WHO, Geneva, 1980—; cons. med. edn. Panam. Health Orgn., Washington, 1975—; dir. pediatric research U. Chile, Santiago, 1964-72; mem. sci. adv. com. Latin Am. Ctr. Ednl. Tech. for Health Scis., Mexico City, 1979-81, Rio de Janeiro, Brazil, 1980-83. Contbr. chpts. to books, articles to med. jours. Nat. Fund Med. Edn. grantee, 1982-84; W.K. Kellogg fellow, 1967-68; USPHS fellow, 1974-75. Mem. ACP, Am. Ednl. Research Assn., Nat. Council Measurement in Edn., AAAS, Am. Pub. Health Assn., Am. Assn. Higher Edn. Avocations: nature photography; tennis; scuba; jogging. Office: Saint Louis U Sch Med 1402 S Grand LRC101 Saint Louis MO 63104

GALUSZKA, MARY HELENE, nun, financial analyst; b. Chgo., Aug. 19, 1945; d. Jospeh Frank and Adeline Frances (Les) G. BS, Coll. of St. Francis, Joliet, Ill., 1969; MS, St. Mary's Coll., 1974; MBA, St. Louis U., 1986. Cert. tchr., Ill. Elementary tchr., asst. prin. Franciscan Sisters of Chgo., 1966-74; tchr. Madonna High Sch., Chgo., 1974-84; dir. fiscal services, mem. planning com. Franciscan Sisters of Chgo. Home Office, 1986—; research sponser Ill. Jr. Acad. Sci., Chgo., 1967-84; instr. City Colls. of Chgo., 1983-84; dir. sec. bd. Madonna High Sch., Inc., Chgo., 1980—, dept. chmn., 1982-84; dir. sec. bd. St. Joseph Home, Inc., Chgo., 1984—. NSF grantee, 1970-74; Diedrich scholar St. Louis U., 1984-85. Mem. Healthcare Fin. Mgmt. Assn. Avocation: needlework. Home and Office: Franciscan Sisters of Chgo 1220 Main St Lemont IL 60439

GALVIN, ROBERT W., electronics executive; b. Marshfield, Wis., Oct. 9, 1922. Student, U. Notre Dame, U. Chgo.; LL.D. (hon.), Quincy Coll., St. Ambrose Coll., DePaul U., Ariz. State U. With Motorola, Inc., Chgo., 1940—, exec. v.p., 1948-56, pres., from 1956, chmn. bd., 1964—, chief exec. officer, 1964-86, also dir. Former mem. Pres.'s Commn. on Internat. Trade and Investment.; chmn. industry policy adv. com. to U.S. Trade Rep.; mem. Pres.'s Pvt. Sector Survey; chmn. Pres.'s Adv. Council on Pvt. Sector Initiatives; chmn. Ill. Inst. Tech., U. Notre Dame; bd. dirs. Jr. Achievement Chgo. Served with Signal Corps, AUS, World War II. Named Decision Maker of Yr. Chgo. Assn. Commerce and Industry-Am. Statis. Assn., 1973; Sword of Loyola award Loyola U., Chgo.; Washington award Western Soc. Engrs., 1984. Mem. Electronic Industries Assn. (pres. 1966, dir., Medal of Honor 1970, Golden Omega award 1981). Office: Motorola Inc 1303 E Algonquin Rd Schaumburg IL 60196 *

GAMBILL, BETHANY LUELLA, telephone company official; b. Painesville, Ohio, Oct. 12, 1953; s. Garfield and Shirley Mae (Jones) Johns; A.S. in Computer Programming, Inst. Computer Mgmt., Cleve., 1973; student Cuyahoga Community Coll., 1974, U. Akron, 1983, Kent State U., 1985; m. Stephen Carl Gambill, May 21, 1977. Bookkeeper, asst. to art dir. Revere Chem. Corp./Monroe Co., Solon, Ohio, 1973-75; with Alltel Corp., Twinsburg, Ohio, 1975—, transmission coordinator, 1976, toll coordinator, 1977-85, programmer, 1985—. Vol. ARC. Mem. Nat. Assn. Female Execs., Nat. Fedn. Bus. and Profl. Women (2d v.p. Tallmadge chpt. 1982-84, 1st v.p. 1984-86). Home: 95 N River Rd Munroe Falls OH 44262 Office: 2000 Highland Rd Twinsburg OH 44087

GAMBILL, JOHN RANDOLPH, physician, mental health adminstr.; b. Harrisonburg, Va., Apr. 21, 1918; s. John Randolph and Alice (Filler) G.; m. Wilmer Peters, Apr. 26, 1946; children—John David, Sarah Frances, Martha Sue, Paul William. B.A., Bridgewater Coll., 1940; Th.B., So. Bapt. Theol. Sem., Louisville, 1943; M.D., U. Louisville, 1946; LL.B., Blackstone Sch. Law, Chgo., 1958. Diplomate: Am. Bd. Psychiatry and Neurology. Intern Louisville Gen. Hosp., 1946-47; sr. physician, chief female service Taunton (Mass.) Hosp., 1948-51; clin. dir., dir. tng. Norwich (Conn.) State Hosp., 1951-59; clin. dir., dir. tng. and research Madison (Ind.) State Hosp., 1959-62; dep. commr. Ind. Dept. Mental Health., Indpls., 1962-67; acting commr. Ind. Dept. Mental Health., 1966-67; supt. Mental Health Inst., Clarinda, Iowa, 1967-76; staff psychiatrist VA Hosp., Des Moines, 1976—; chief psychiatry Broadlawns Med. Ctr., Des Moines, 1984—; clin. instr. psychiatry Yale Med. Sch., 1957-59; asst. prof. psychiatry Med. Center Ind. U., 1962-67. Served with USPHS, 1947-48. Named Sagamore of Wabash. Fellow Am. Psychiat. Assn., Am. Geriatrics Soc.; mem. AMA, AAAS, Iowa Psychiat. Soc. (pres. 1977), Assn. Mil. Surgeons U.S. Baptist (deacon). Clubs: Mason, Rotarian, Sycamores (past dir.). Address: 4118 Lynner Dr Des Moines IA 50310

GAMBLE, JAMES CALVIN, landscape architect; b. Grand Rapids, Mich., Dec. 18, 1944; s. Arthur Earl and Elizabeth (Wiltzer) G.; m. Donna Kay Staton; children: Angela, Alison, Amanda, Andrew. B Landscape Architecture, U. Mich., 1968. Registered landscape architect, Ohio, Tex. Landscape architect assoc. Bircher, Bonnell Assocs., Inc., N. Canton, Ohio, 1968-72; sr. assoc. Barton Aschman Assoc. Inc., Evanston, Ill., 1972-83; v.p. Teska Assoc., Inc., Evanston, 1983-86; ptnr. Land Design Collaboration, Evanston, 1987—; mem. Design Profls. Adv. Com. Sculpture Chgo., 1988. V.p. Design Evanston, 1985; pres. Keep Evanston Beautiful, Inc., 1986-87; mem. adv. com. Skokie (Ill.) Park Dist., 1986. Mem. Am. Soc. Landscape Architects (sec., treas. Ill. chpt. 1979-82, v.p. 1982-84, pres. 1984-86, Design Merit award 1983), (mem. adv. com. Nat. Trust for Hist. Preservation. Avocations: camping, antique furniture restoration.

GAMBLE, JAMES EDWARD, surgeon; b. Earlington, Ky., July 3, 1935; s. Paul Eugene and Hazel Marie (Harris) G.; m. Virginia Nell Allsbrook, June 14, 1956; children: Cynthia Beth, James Barton. BA, Murray State U., 1956; MD, U. Louisville, 1960. Diplomate Am. Bd. Otoloryngology. Resident in otolaryngolic surgery U. Miami, Fla., 1961-62; clin. and research fellow Harvard U., 1969-70; practice medicine specializing in otolaryngology E. W. T. Assocs., Pom Pano Beach, Fla., 1971-78, Tri State Head and Neck Surgery, Evansville, Ind., 1978—. Contbr. articles to tech. and med. publs. Served to capt. U.S. Army, 1962-64. Fellow ACS, Am. Acad. Otolaryngology, Am. Soc. for Head and Neck Surgery, Am. Acad. Facial Plastic and Reconstructive Surgery. Avocations: tennis, fishing, skiing. Mailing Address: 350 W Columbia St Evansville IN 47710

GAMBLE, KEITH LEWIS, industrial trade show and graphic designer; b. Cleve., Feb. 23, 1953; s. Donald H. and Wilma J. (Lewis) G.; m. Robbyn F. Shamis, Sept. 11, 1983. Student, Cuyahoga Community Coll., 1971-73; BFA, Bowling Green State U., 1975. Graphic designer Downing Displays, Cleve., 1976-78, design dir., 1979-81; designer Universal Exhibit Builders, Cleve., 1978-79; v.p. design Contemporary Exhibit & Design, Lorain, Ohio, 1981-83; sr. designer Gallo Displays, Inc., Cleve., 1983—. Designer, art dir. Budweiser- Cleve. Grand Prix Poster, 1987. Republican. Jewish. Avocations: woodworking, skiing, racquetball. Office: Gallo Displays Inc 1260 E 38th St Cleveland OH 44114

GAMBLIN, LAWRENCE RODGERS, chemical company executive; b. Princeton, N.J., June 10, 1959; s. Rodger Lotus Gamblin and Elizabeth Bidwell (Bates) Zenowich. BA, U. Calif., Santa Barbara, 1981. Asst. to pres. Dayton (Ohio) Tinker, 1981-82; pres. Saranda Corp., Dayton, 1985—, also bd. dirs.; pres. Bradford Chem. Co., Dayton, 1982—, also bd. dirs.; bd. dirs. Universal Ink Jet, Dayton. Home: 5824 Millshire 2D Dayton OH 45440 Office: Bradford Chem Co 55 Compark Rd Dayton OH 45459

GAMBOW, NEIL EDWARD, JR., manufacturing company executive; b. Cleve., Oct. 16, 1945; s. Neil Edward and Lucille Marie (Wunderle) G.; m. Margaret Ann Sanders, Sept. 2, 1967; children: Jennifer A., Dennis M. BSME, U. Dayton, 1967. Plant mgr. B.F. Goodrich, Fenwick, W.Va., 1979-82; dir. engring. B.F. Goodrich, Akron, Ohio, 1982-83, gen. mgr., 1983-85, group gen. mgr., 1985-87, group v.p., 1987—. Pres. Summersville (W.Va) Little League, 1980-82, league commr. Wadworth (Ohio) Little League, 1984-86; bd. dirs. Nicholas County Sheltered Workshop, Summersville, 1981. Mem. Tipp City (Ohio) Jaycees (pres. 1978). Republican. Roman Catholic. Avocations: antique cars. Home: 369 Amy Way Wadsworth OH 44281 Office: BF Goodrich 250 N Cleveland Massillon Rd Akron OH 44313

GAMMAS, MAMON A., plastic surgeon, otolaryngologist; b. Damascus, Syrian Arab Republic, Mar. 26, 1946; came to U.S., 1972; s. Abdulkader and Norria (Mussa) G.; m. Hanan Fayad, July 22, 1978; children: Iham, Nader, Danyo. PCB, Coll. Sci., Damascus, 1965; MD, Damascus U., 1971. Diplomate Am. Bd. Otolaryngology, Am. Bd. Plastic and Reconstructive Surgery. Intern Damascus U. Hosp., 1969-71, resident in anesthesiology, 1971-72; resident in gen. surgery United Hosp. Newark, 1973-74; resident in otolaryngology Johnson Med. Sch., Piscataway, N.J., 1974-77; with emergency medicine dept. surgery Mennonite Hosp., Bloomington, Ill., 1977-78; practice medicine specializing in otolaryngology Mattoon, Ill., 1978, 79-80; preceptor head and neck surgery, plastic surgery Sacred Hosp. affiliated Jefferson Med. Coll., Norristown, Pa., 1978-79; resident in plastic surgery Wilmington (Del.) Med. Ctr. affiliated Jefferson Med. Coll., 1980-82; multi-specialty group practice Weber Med. Clinic Ltd. affiliated Richland Meml. Hosp., Olney, Ill., 1982—; chief surgery Richland Meml. Hocp., Olney, 1985-87; clin. instr. otolaryngology N.J. Coll. Medicine, 1974-77. Contbr. articles to profl. jours. Mem. AMA, ACS, Am. Soc. Plastic and Reconstructive Surgeons, Am. Acad. Facial Plastic and Reconstructive Surgery, Am. Acad. Otolaryngology Head and Neck Surgery, Am. Council Otolaryngology, Ill. State Med. Soc., Richland County Med. Soc. Lodge: Rotary. Avocations: painting, reading, sports. Office: Weber Med Clinic Ltd 1200 N East St Olney IL 62450

GAMMELL, WAYNE WILLIAM, title company executive; b. Dayton, Ohio, Mar. 2, 1940; s. Willard DeWitt and Violet Gay (McNew) G.; m. Gail Louise Martin, Apr. 28, 1962; children: Jeffrey Wayne and Susanne Louise. Engring. student, U. Dayton, 1958-61. Lic. title ins. agt., real estate agt. Escrow officer, title examiner Lawyers Title Ins., Dayton, 1961-67; escrow officer Ohio Title Corp., Dayton, 1967-69; v.p., mgr. Louisville Title, Dayton, 1969-73; owner, pres., chmn. bd. Gammell Land Title Agy., Inc., Dayton, 1973—; bd. dirs. Olympic Title Ins. Co., Dayton. Asst. treas. Centerville (Ohio) Schs. Levy Renewal, 1975. Served with Air NG, 1962-68. Mem. Dayton Area Bd. Realtors, Mortgage Bankers Assn. (sec., bd. dirs. 1980-84 Dayton Title Underwriters (pres. 1982-83), South Dayton C. of C., Nat. C. of C. Republican. Lutheran. Club: Am. Bus. Home: 6311 Marshall Rd Centerville OH 45459 Office: Gammell Land Title Agy Inc 7918 Kingsridge Dr Dayton OH 45459

GAMON, ADAM EDWARD, internist; b. Hillside, N.J., Sept. 6, 1918; s. Adam Edward and Mary (Yanick) G.; m. Lottie Irene Snyder, Sept. 8, 1939; children: Judith Diane, Robert Edward. BS, Alfred U., 1939; MD, Temple U., 1943. Diplomate Am. Bd. Internal Medicine. Intern N.Y.C. Hosp., 1944, resident in pathology, 1946, asst. med. resident, 1947-47, chief med. resident, 1948-49; resident internal medicine Saginaw (Mich.) Gen. Hosp., 1946-47; gen. practice internal medicine Saginaw, 1950-69; with Mich. State Disability Determination Service Lansing, 1969-71; med. dir. Malleable Iron div. Gen. Motors, Saginaw, 1971-73, Dow Corning Corp., Midland, Mich., 1973—; chief medicine St. Luke's Hosp., Saginaw, 1953-67; cons. St. Mary's Hosp., Gen. Hosp., St. Luke's Hosp., Saginaw Midland Hosp. Inventor disposable tracheotomy set, portable bed chair. Dep. coroner Saginaw County, 1973—; cons. Social Security Adminstrn., HEW, Saginaw, 1973-77. Served to capt., M.C., U.S. Army, 1944-46. Mem. ACP (life), Am. Coll. Angiology, Am. Soc. Internal Medicine, Mich., Midland County Med. Socs., AMA, Mich. Soc. Internal Medicine, Indsl. Med. Assn., Pan Am. Med. Assn., Am. Radio Relay League. Home: 15317 W Brant Rd PO Box 97 Brant MI 48614 Office: Dow Corming Corp S Saginaw Rd Midland MI 48640

GAMORAN, ABRAHAM CARMI, mgmt. cons., real estate broker; b. Cin., Mar. 15, 1926; s. Emanuel and Mamie (Goldsmith) G.; m. Ruth Kump, Apr. 14, 1973; children: Shirley, Mary Samuel, Benjamin, Joseph. BBA, U. Cin., 1948; MBA, NYU, 1950. CPA, N.Y.; lic. real estate broker, N.Y., Ohio. Mem. staff Harris, Kerr Forster & Co., N.Y.C., 1949-52, supr. mgmt. services div., 1962-67; mgmt. cons. Burke, Landsberg & Gerber, Balt., 1953-54; v.p. Helmsley-Spear, Inc., N.Y.C., 1969-81; v.p. Helmsley-Spear, Inc., Cleve., 1981—; lectr. Cornell U., Mich. State U., Okla. State U., Am. Hotel and Motel Assn., others; vis. prof. U. Nev., Las Vegas, Coll. Hotel Adminstrn., 1985-87. Author articles in field, also real estate rev. portfolios. Recipient medal Wall St. Jour., 1948; Benjamin Franklin award, 1982. Mem. Am. Inst. CPA's, Am. Soc. Real Estate Counselors, Am. Soc. Appraisers (sr.), N.Y. State Soc. CPA's, Ohio Realtors Assn., Nat. Assn. Corp. Real Estate Execs., Cleve. Area Bd. Realtors. Democrat. Jewish. Home: 1 Bratenahl Pl Bratenahl OH 44108 Office: 1310 Terminal Tower Cleveland OH 44113

GAMPETRO, JAMES ALAN, real estate and construction executive; b. Bellvue, Ohio, May 9, 1947; s. John Anthony and Marrianne (Artino) G.; m. Joan Elaine Gresser, Apr. 14, 1979; children: John Anthony, Jennifer Ann, James Robert. BS in Mgmt. Scis., Case Inst. of Tech., 1970; MBA, Case Western Res. U., 1972. Mkt. research analyst Glidden-Durkee div. SCM, Cleve., 1972-74; dir. mkt. research and planning Cen. Nat. Bank, Cleve., 1974-78; v.p. mktg. Women's Fed. Savs. and Loan, Cleve., 1978-79; dir. bus. planning and devel. Sherwin Williams, Cleve., 1979-82, region dir. sales and ops., 1982-86, v.p. real estate and constn. and engring., 1986—; pres. Sherwin Williams Devel. Corp., Cleve., 1986—. Mem. Nat. Assn. Corp. Real Estate Execs., Internat. Council Shoppints Ctrs. Roman Catholic. Club: Ohio Gun Collectors. Avocations: running, hunting, astronomy. Office: Sherwin Williams 101 Prospect Ave Cleveland OH 44115

GAMSKY, NEAL RICHARD, university administrator, psychology educator; b. Menasha, Wis., Feb. 17, 1931; s. Andrew P. and Lillian G.; m. Irene Janet Jimos, Aug. 16, 1956; children—Elizabeth, Patricia. B.S., U. Wis.-Madison, 1954, M.S., 1959, Ph.D., 1965. Counselor, Appleton Pub. Schs. (Wis.), 1959-62; ednl. and counseling cons. Wis. Div. Mental Hygiene, 1967. dir. ednl. services Wis. Diagnostic Center, Madison, 1962-67; dir. research pupil personnel services Coop. Edn. Service Agy., Waupan, Wis., 1967-70; dir. student counseling center Ill. State U., Normal, 1970-73, v.p. student affairs, prof. psychology, 1973—; Served with U.S. Army, 1954-56. Mem. Am. Psychol. Assn., Am. Assn. Counseling and Devel., Nat. Assn. Student Personnel Adminstrs., Am. Assn. Higher Edn., Am. Coll. Personnel Assn., Am. Orthopsychiat. Assn. Author: (with G.F. Farwell and B. Mathieu-Coughlan) The Counselor's Handbook, 1974; contbr. 26 articles in field to profl. jours. Office: 506 DeGarmo Hall Normal IL 61761

GANDHI, ASHVIN HIRALAL, real estate corporation officer; b. Rajpipla, Gujarat, India; came to U.S., 1964; s. Hiralal N. and Lalita (Ben) G.; m. Ushaben Ambalal, Aug. 15, 1969; children: Sonia, Ashish. BSME, Birla Engring. Coll., Vidyaivagar, India, 1961; M of Indsl. Engring., W.Va. U., 1966. Registered profl. engr., Mass., N.J., Ohio. From mgr. engring. to asst. to pres. Am. Optical, Southbridge, Mass., 1971-79; dir. materials Wilkinson Sword Co., Basking Ridge, N.J., 1979-81; pres. Book Serve, Inc., Westfield, N.J., 1981-83; chief exec. officer, bd. dirs., chmn. Dava, Inc., Cin., 1983—; cons. Profit Protection Systems, Westfield, N.J., 1982-83. Pres. Worcester (Mass.) India Soc., 1975; founder Greenville (S.C.) India Soc., 1978. Home: 937 Finney Trail Cincinnati OH 45231 Office: Dava Inc 7759 Reading Rd Cincinnati OH 45237

GANDHI, BHARAT R., construction company executive; b. India, Oct. 16, 1942; came to U.S., 1971; naturalized, 1979; s. Ramanlal and Shardaben (Sura) G.; m. Purnima Bharat, Dec. 25, 1966; children—Manish, Nisha. B.S. in Civil/Sanitary Engring., V.J.J. Inst., Bombay, India, 1964; postgrad. constrn. engring. U. Wis., 1971-72. Ptnr., v.p. constrn. co. in India; project mgr. Corbetta Constrn. Co. Des Plaines, Ill., 1972-75; project mgr. Pepper Constrn. Co., Schaumburg, Ill., 1975—, v.p. healthcare div., 1981-84, exec. v.p., 1984—. Contbg. author articles in field to profl. publs. Home: 2333 Sussex St Northbrook IL 60062 Office: Pepper Constrn Co 643 N Orleans St Chicago IL 60610

GANDHI, KANTI, chemical company executive; b. Bombay, India, Nov. 18, 1940; came to U.S., 1964; s. Vithaldas and Ambaben Gandhi; m. Renu Gandhi, Apr. 27, 1969; children: Bela, Ravin. BS, U. Bombay, 1962, MS, 1964; postgrad., U. Detroit, 1964-66. Chemist Bishop & Babcock Corp., Birmingham, Mich., 1966-68; sr. chemistr Midland div. Dexter Corp., Waukegan, Ill., 1968-83; v.p., tech. dir. Coatings & chems. Corp., Chgo., 1983—; gen. mgr. R.K. Labs., Chgo., 1983—. Mem. Soc. Mfg. Engrs., Chgo. Paint and Coatings Assn. Hindu. Home: 3308 Lakewood Ct Glenview IL 60025 Office: Coatings and Chems Co 3067 N Elston Ave Chicago IL 60618

GANESH, OREKONDE, physician; b. Davangere, Mysore, India, Oct. 19, 1941; came to U.S., 1967; d. Bakkappa and Muppama Orekonde; m. Dakshayeni Ganesh, Dec. 8, 1967; children: Nisha, Nina, Nitya. MD, U. Mysore, 1964. Diplomate Am. Bd. Psychiatry and Neurology. Intern K.R. Hosp. U. Mysore, 1964-65, Meml. Hosp., R.I., 1965-67; resident in internal medicine V.S. Gen. Hosp., Gujarat, India, 1965-67; resident in psychiatry Northville (Mich.) State Hosp., 1968-71; pres. Comprehensive Med. Clinics, P.C., Southfield, Mich., 1977—. Mem. Nat. Geno Scis. (pres. 1980—), Am. Psychiatric Assn., Am. Sch. Health Assn., Oakland County Med. Soc., Mich. State Med. Soc., AMA, Am. Sch. Tropical Medicine, Am. Coll. Internat. Physicians, Am. Diabetes Assn. Home: 2003 Wickford Ct Bloomfield Hills MI 48013 Office: 28165 Greenfield Rd Southfield MI 48076

GANNON, RICHARD GALEN, state senator, rancher, farmer; b. Goodland, Kans., July 29, 1950; s. Bill Elmer and Geraldine Francis (Veselik) G.; m. Martha Ellen Wall, Nov. 26, 1976; children: Jessica Michelle, Elizabeth Ashley. A.A., Colby Community Coll., 1970; B.S. in Edn., Kansas U., 1973. Vice-pres. Rocking Chair Farms Inc., Goodland, 1973—; mem. Kans. Senate, 1976—, minority whip, 1985—. Active 4-H, 1980—. Recipient citation Meritorious Service, Kans. Vets. World War I, 1978. Mem. Nat. Conf. State Legislatures, Midwestern Conf.-Council State Govts. (vice chmn. agr., food policy and nutrition com.), First Congressional Dist. Democrats, Acacia Frat. (dir. Kans. U. chpt. 1978—, pres. 1981—), Kans. U. Alumni Assn. (life). Democrat. Roman Catholic. Clubs: KC, Elks. Home: Route 3 Box 68 Goodland KS 67735 Office: State Capitol Topeka KS 66612

GANS, ERNA IRENE, printing co. exec.; b. Bielsko, Poland; d. Adolf and Rosa (Pelzman) Reicher; came to U.S., 1948, naturalized, 1953; B.A., Roosevelt U., 1971; M.A., Loyola U., Chgo., 1974; m. Henry Gans, Apr. 16, 1947; children—Alan, Howard. Asst. prof. dept. sociology Loyola U., Chgo., 1976; pres. Internat. Label & Printing Co., Bensenville, Ill., 1972—. Chmn., Skokie (Ill.) Youth Commn., 1968—; bd. govs. Israel Bond Orgn.; founder, chmn. Holocaust Meml. Found. Ill.; mem. U.S. Holocaust Meml. Council. Recipient Edward S. Sparling award Roosevelt U., 1987. Mem. Am. Sociol. Assn., Nat. Fedn. Ind. Bus., Am. Acad. Polit. and Social Sci. Republican. Jewish. Clubs: B'nai B'rith (pres. 1976—). Home: 2812 Woodland Dr Northbrook IL 60062 Office: 810 Maple Lane Bensenville IL 60106

GANSZ, FRANK, professional football coach; b. Altoona, Pa., Nov. 22, 1938. Grad., U.S. Naval Acad. Comd. 2d lt. USN, 1961, advanced through grades to capt., resigned, 1966; asst. football coach USAF Acad., Colorado Springs, Colo., 1964-66, Colgate U., Hamilton, N.Y., 1968, U.S. Naval Acad., Annapolis, Md., 1969-72, Okla. State U., Stillwater, 1973, 75, U.S. Mil. Acad., West Point, N.Y., 1974, UCLA, 1976-77, San Francisco 49ers, NFL, 1978, Cin. Bengals, NFL, 1979-80; asst. football coach Kansas City (Mo.) Chiefs, NFL, 1981-82, 86, head coach, 1987—; asst. coach Phila. Eagles, NFL, 1983-85. Office: Kansas City Chiefs One Arrowhead Drive Kansas City MO 64129 *

GANTZ, BRUCE JAY, otolaryngologist, educator; b. N.Y.C., May 18, 1946; m. Mary Katherine DeJong; children: Ellen Katherine, Jessica Rose, Jay Alexander. BS in Gen. Sci., U. Iowa, 1968, MD, 1974, MS in Otolaryngology, 1980; fellow neurotology, U. Zürich, 1981-82. Asst. prof. dept otolaryngology U. Iowa Coll. Medicine, Iowa City, 1980-84, assoc. prof., 1984-87, prof., 1987—. Contbr. articles to profl. jours. Recipient Tchr.-Investigator Devel. award Pub. Health Service, 1981-86, program project award NIH, 1985—. Mem. AMA, Assn. for Research in Otolaryngology, Deafness Research Found. (state chmn. 1985—), Am. Acad. Otolaryngology-Head and Neck Surgery, Soc. Univ. Otolaryngologists, Am. Neurotology Soc., Am. Otological Soc. Office: U Iowa Hosps and Clinics Dept Otolaryngology Iowa City IA 52242

GANTZ, LOUIS ESTES, accountant; b. Chgo., Mar. 16, 1955; s. Henry and Sally (Estes) G.; m. Susan G. Grahn, July 11, 1976; children: Christopher, Joshua. BS Gen. Engring., U. Ill., 1976; postgrad. in law, Loyola U., Chgo., 1976-78. CPA, Ill. Staff acct. Warady & Davis, Lincolnwood, Ill., 1978-81; mgr. mgmt. adv. services Warady & Davis, Lincolnwood, 1981-86; fin. mgr. Combined Metals, Bellwood, Ill., 1986-87; pres. Louis Estes Gantz, P.C., Northbrook, Ill., 1987—. Mem. Am. Inst. CPA's, Ill. CPA Soc. Office: Louis Estes Gantz PC PO Box 4225 Northbrook IL 60065-4225

GANZARAIN, RAMON CAJIAO, psychoanalyst; b. Iquique, Chile, Apr. 18, 1923; s. Eusebio Gastanaga and Maria Gonzalez G.; m. Matilde Vidal Soto, Oct. 10, 1953; children: Ramon, Mirentxu, Alejandro. BS, St. Ignacio Coll., Santiago, Chile, 1939; MD, U. Chile, Santiago, 1947; postgrad., Chilean Psychoanalytic Inst., 1947-50, cert. tng. analyst, 1953. Med. Diplomate. Asst. prof. psychiatry U. Chile, Santiago, 1955-68, dir. dept. med. edn., 1962-68; prof. depth psychology, sch. psychology Cath. U., Santiago, 1962-68; dir. Chilean Psychoanalytic Inst., Santiago, 1967-68; tng. analyst Topeka Inst. Psychoanalysis, 1968-87; dir. group psychotherapy services The Menninger Found., Topeka, 1978-87. Author: Fugitives of Incest, 1987; contbr. articles to profl. jours. Fellow Am. Group Psychotherapy Assn.; mem. Internat. Assn. Group Psychotherapy (bd. dirs., exec. counselor 1986), Am. Group Psychotherapy Assn. (bd. dirs. 1984-87), Internat. Psychoanalytic Assn., Am. Psychoanalytic Assn., AMA, Kans. Med. Soc., Topeka Psychoanalytic Soc. (pres. 1985-87). Roman Catholic. Avocations: music, swimming, photography, writing, collecting Antarctic stamps. Office: The Menninger Found PO Box 829 Topeka KS 66601

GAPCO, BRIAN ELLIOTT, engineer; b. N.Y.C., Oct. 7, 1951. BSME, Rensselaer Poly. Inst., 1973; MBA, U. Mich., 1983. Staff engr. mil. vehicles operation Gen. Motors, Troy, Mich., 1983—. Served to 1st lt. USMC, 1973-77. Mem. Soc. Automotive Engrs. Avocation: flying, cert. flight instr.

GAPEN, DELORES KAYE, librarian, educator; b. Mitchell, S.D., July 1, 1943; d. Lester S. and Lena F. G. B.A., U. Wash., 1970, M.L.S., 1971. Gen. cataloger Coll. William and Mary, Williamsburg, Va., 1971-72; instr., asst. head Quick Editing Ohio State U., Columbus, 1972-74; head Ohio State U., 1974-77; asst. dir. tech. services Iowa State U., Ames, 1977-81; dean, prof. univ. libraries U. ALa., University, 1981-84; dir. gen. library system U. Wis., Madison, 1984—; exec. com. Council U. Wis. Libraries; cons. Northeast Mo. State U., 1980, Assn. Research Libraries task force on bibliog. control, 1981, Pa. State U., 1982, Conn. Coll., 1982; vice chmn. exec. com. of bd. trustees U. Wis. Online Computer Library Ctr., Madison, 1984-86, also mem. research libraries adv. com. (chair task force on Future of Research Library Coop. in Changing Techs. Environment, 1986, chmn. com. short cataloging records, 1983-84); cons. Bryn Mawr Coll. Online System Planning, 1983, Council Library Resources Edn. Task Force on Future of Library Sch. Edn., 1983, Tex. A&I U. reaffirmation team cons. for So. Assn. Colls. and Schs., 1984, Dickinson Coll. Library Autocat System, 1987; chair Assn. of Research Libraries Task Force for Govt. Info. in Electronic Form, 1986-87; mem. Assn. of Research Libraries Task Force on Scholarly Communication, 1983-87; mem. exec. com. Council of Wis. Libraries, 1986-87, vice chmn. and chmn. elect, 1987—. Contbr (articles to profl. publs.). Mem. AAUP, ALA, Southeastern Library Assn., Ala. Library Assn., Assn. Research Libraries (chmn. task force govt. info. in electronic form 1986-87), Bus. and Profl. Women's Assn., Beta Phi Mu, Alpha Lamba Delta. Democrat. Roman Catholic. Home: 702 Seneca Pl Madison WI 53711 Office: Meml Library 728 State St Madison WI 53706

GAPPA, BOB, university administrator; b. Colorado Springs, Colo., Dec. 22, 1954; s. Robert Gregory and Naomi Ruth (Hann) G. BA magna cum laude, Bethany Nazarene Coll., 1975; MA in Theol. Studies, McCormick Sem., 1980; MS in Indsl. Relations, Loyola U., Chgo., 1984. Human resources systems analyst U. Chgo., 1978-85; human resources system adminstr. Loyola U., Chgo., 1985—. Vol. Howard Brown Meml. Clinic, Chgo., 1979-82; vice moderator Good Shepherd Parish, Chgo., 1984; mem. Chgo. Gay Mens Chorus, 1985. Mem. Am. Compensation Assn., Human Resource System Profls. Avocations: music, bicycling, body building. Home: 3763 N Wilton Chicago IL 60613 Office: Loyola U Chgo 840 N Wabash Chicago IL 60611

GARAFOLO, JOSEPH, real estate executive; b. Bklyn., Aug. 31, 1940; s. Alfred James and Sadie Lilian (Marchiano) G.; m. Laura Jean St. Peter, Dec. 15, 1984; children: Tracy Sue, Jill, Joseph. BSEE, Manhattan Coll., 1961; MBA, NYU, 1967. Engr. IBM, Poughkeepsie, N.Y., 1961-62; adminstrv. dir. Fairchild Camera, Syosset, N.Y., 1962-68; cons. Fantus Co., South Orange, N.J., 1968-72; exec. dir. Citicorp Realty Cons., N.Y.C., 1972-75; v.p. Real Estate Research Corp., N.Y.C., Chgo., 1975-78; asst. v.p. Baird & Warner, Chgo., 1978-82; pres. Equest Real Estate and Fin. Corp., Lincolnwood, Ill., 1982—. Contbr. articles to profl. jours. Mem. Nat. Assn. Securities Dealers, Nat. Assn. Realtors, Chgo. Real Estate Bd. (chmn. sales council 1985-86). Republican. Presbyterian. Office: Equest Real Estate and Fin Corp 7337 N Lincoln Lincolnwood IL 60646

GARAMELLA, TODD JONATHAN, broadcasting company owner; b. Mpls., June 19, 1955; s. Joseph John and Christine Irene (Bouchard) G.; m. Barbara Ann Rock, June 2, 1972; children: Jessica Tatum, Jasmine Ann. Student, U. Minn. Gen. mgr. Hennepin Broadcasting, Mpls., 1975-82; owner Sta. KBMO-AM-FM, Benson, Minn., 1982—, Sta. KMSR-FM, Sauk Centre, Minn., 1983—; pres. Garamella Broadcasting Co., Mpls., 1983—; owner KBJJ-FM, Marshall, Minn., 1985—; bd. dirs. Dollars for Scholars, Sauk Centre. Mem. Minn. Broadcasters Assn. Republican. Roman Catholic. Clubs: Interlachen Country, Decathalon. Avocations: golf, boating, swimming. Home: 7 Meadow Hill Rd Hopkins MN 55343 Office: Garamella Broadcasting Co 508 S Main St Sauk Centre MN 55378

GARAVELLI, JOHN STEPHEN, research scientist; b. Memphis, Sept. 7, 1947; s. Daniel and Frances Louise (Chambers) G. BS, Duke U., 1969; PhD, Wash. U., St. Louis, 1975. Postdoctoral fellow Duke Marine Lab., Beaufort, N.C., 1975-76; postdoctoral fellow, lectr. U. Del., Newark, 1976-80; research assoc., lectr. Tex. A&M U., College Station, 1980-83; sr. research fellow NASA Ames Research Ctr., Moffett Field, Calif., 1983-85; research assoc., dir. computer ops. Agouron Inst., La Jolla, Calif., 1986; dir. computer ops., biomolecular analysis facilities U. Ill., Chgo., 1986—. Contbr. articles to profl. jours. Candidate Tenn. Ho. of Reps., Shelby County 13th Dist., 1970. Served with U.S. Amry, 1970-72. Proctor & Gamble Acad. scholar, 1965-68; grantee Tenn. Acad. Sci. Research, 1964-65, NSF Undergrad. Research Tng., 1968-69, NIH Predoctoral Trainee, 1969-70, 71-75, NASA Research Assoc., 1982-83; fellow NASA, summers 1982, 83, NRC Sr. Research, 1983-85. Mem. AAAS, Am. Chem. Soc., Am. Philatelic Soc., Am. Soc. Gravitational and Space Biology, Internat. Soc. Study of Origin of Life, Internat. Union of Pure and Applied Chemistry, Am. Uniform Assn. Democrat. Home: Box 804675 Chicago IL 60680 Office: U Ill Coll Pharmacy Dept Med Chem (MC781) Biomolecular Analysis Facility Chicago IL 60612

GARBACZEWSKI, DANIEL FRANK, restaurateur; b. Chgo., Sept. 4, 1950; s. Daniel Jacob and Sophie Evelen (Kurranty) G.; m. Dawn Marie Ciciora, May 7, 1983. AA, No. Ill. U., 1970; cert. recording engr., Inst. Audio Research, 1974. V.p. Garbaczewski Corp., Chgo., 1979—, Am. Video Corp., Chgo., 1983—; pres. Fantasy Food Corp., Chgo., 1985—. Republican. Roman Catholic. Lodge: Lions (v.p. Chgo. chpt.). Avocations: music, racquetball, photography. Home: 15800 S 86th Ave Orland Park IL 60462 Office: Chesdan Restaurant 4465 S Archer Chicago IL 60632

GARBER, SAMUEL B., lawyer, retail company executive; b. Chgo., Aug. 16, 1934; s. Morris and Yetta (Cohen) G.; children—Debra Lee, Diane Lori. J.D., U. Ill., 1958; M.B.A., U. Chgo., 1968. Bar: Ill., 1958; mem. firm Brown, Dashow and Langluttig, Chgo., 1960-62; corporate counsel Walgreen Co., 1962-69; v.p., gen. counsel, exec. asst. to the pres. Jewel Box Stores Corp., 1969-73; dir. legal affairs Stop & Shop Co., Inc., 1973-74; gen. counsel Goldblatt Bros., Inc., 1974-76; v.p., sec., gen. counsel Evans, Inc., 1976—; prof. bus. law DePaul U., 1975—. Served with U.S. Army, 1958-60. Mem. ABA, Nat. Retail Mchts. Assn., Ill. Retail Mchts. Assn. Clubs: Carlton, East Bank. Home: 320 Oakdale Chicago IL 60657 Office: Evans Inc 36 S State St Chicago IL 60603

GARBER, SHELDON, hospital executive; b. Mpls., July 21, 1920; s. Mitchell and Esther (Amdur) G.; B.A., U. Minn., 1942; postgrad. U. Chgo., 1952-53; m. Elizabeth Sargent Mason, May 16, 1949 (div. May 1983); children—Robert Michael, Daniel Mason, Sarah Sargent; m. Joellen Palmer Prullage, July 21, 1985. Reporter, editor U.P.I., Mpls., Chgo., Springfield, Ill., 1938-58; dir. media services U. Chgo., 1958-64; asso. dir. communication Blue Cross Assn., Chgo., 1964-69; exec. v.p. Charles R. Feldstein & Co., 1969-73; v.p. philanthropy and communication Rush-Presbyn.-St. Luke's Med. Center, Chgo., 1973—, sec. bd. trustees, 1976—; cons. Orthopaedic Research and Edn. Found., Chgo. Zool. Soc. (Brookfield Zoo), Dermatology Found., Commn. on Drug Safety, Great Books Found., Am. Assn. U. Programs in Hosp. Adminstrn., Am. Nurses Found., Am. Acad. Pediatrics, Sigma Theta Tau; mem. faculty Inst. on Indsl. and Tech. Communications, Colo. State U., Fort Collins, 1970. Adv. bd. Internat. Inst. Edn.; trustee Citizens Information Service, Northlight Theater, Evanston, Ill.; mem. bd. Nat. Soc. Fund Raisers, 1974-77. Served to 1st lt. C.E., AUS, 1942-46, 50-52. Fellow Royal Soc. Health (London); mem. Pub. Relations Soc. Am., Publicity Club Chgo., Am. Soc. Hosp. Pub. Relations Dirs., Am. Pub. Health Assn., AAAS, Nat. Assn. Sci. Writers, Am. Med. Writers Assn., Am. Acad.Pediatrics, Inst. Medicine Chgo., Chgo. Zoological Soc., Sigma Delta Chi. Club: Union League (Chgo.). Office: 1725 W Harrison Chicago IL 60612

GARBER, STANLEY LEE, physician, obstetrician-gynecologist; b. Dayton, Ohio, May 3, 1933; s. Paul Solomon and Edith Alvertia (Baker) G. B.S., U. Cin., 1955, M.D., 1959. Diplomate Am. Bd. Obstetricians and Gynecologists. Vice pres. South Dayton Ob-Gyn Assn., Ohio, 1964-82, pres., 1982—; assoc. clin. prof. Wright State Coll. Medicine, Dayton, 1975—. Fellow Am. College Obstetricians and Gynecologists. Republican. Mem. Ch. of Brethren. Avocations: concert piano playing; opera coaching; baseball. Home: 3119 Windingway Dayton OH 45419 Office: South Dayton Ob-Gyn Assn 529 E Stroop Rd Dayton OH 45429

GARCIA, EMMANUEL BAUTISTA, JR., actuarial software company executive; b. Nampicuan, Philippines, Jan. 23, 1946; s. Emmanuel S. and Fe (Bautista) G.; m. M. Teresa Locsin, Feb. 1, 1969; children: Ana Fe, Maria Elena, Isabel Linda, Emmanuel Benjamin III. BS in Gen. Engring., Ateneo de Manila U., Quezon City, Philippines, 1967; M in Mgmt. Sci., Stevens Inst. Tech., 1969. Pension cons. Westley & Co. Cons. Inc., N.Y.C., 1967-70; mgr. pensions U.S. Life Ins. Co., N.Y.C., 1970-74; dir. pensions Sun Life of Am., Balt., 1974-75; v.p. product devel. Datair Systems, Chgo., 1976-78; pres. EBG & Assocs. Inc., Chgo., 1978—; enrolled actuary Joint Bd. for Enrollment of Actuaries, 1976. Author: Detailed Solutions to the Joint Board Exam, 1975. Fellow Am. Soc. Pension Actuaries; mem. Am. Acad. Actuaries. Club: Ateneans USA (Chgo.) (pres. 1981-83). Avocation: golf. Home: 3950 N Lake Shore Dr #2310 Chicago IL 60613 Office: EBG & Assocs Inc 70 E Lake St Suite 1400 Chicago IL 60601

GARCIA, FERNANDO SALCEDO, financial planner; b. Manila, July 3, 1960; Came to U.S., 1970; s. Dionicio Castillo and Nenita Baquir (Salcedo) G. BBA, Loyola U., Chgo., 1983. Cert. ins. producer, real estate agt., Ill. Dept. mgr. Carson Pirie Scott and Co., Chgo., 1983-84; computer operator Comml. Nat. Bank, Chgo., 1984-85; fin. planner IDS Fin. Services, Des Plaines, Ill., 1985-86, Southmark Fin. Services, Northbrook, Ill., 1986—; pres., owner First Am. Securities Corp., Northbrook, Ill., 1987—. Mem. Internat. Assn. Fin. Planning, Nat. Futures Assn., Nat. Assn. Securities Dealers (series 3, 7, 8, 24, 27, and 63), Ill. Dept. Ins. (producer), Theta Xi (athletic coordinator 1979-80). Republican. Roman Catholic. Clubs: KAPWA (Chgo.) (pres. 1980-82), Invesment (Chgo.) (pres. 1985—). Avocations: chess, racquetball, swimming, tennis, dancing. Home: 1055 Brentwood Ln Wheaton IL 60187 Office: Southmark Fin Services Inc 633 Skokie Blvd Suite 304 Northbrook IL 60062-2817

GARCIA, JOSEPH ANTONIO, lawyer, legislative consultant; b. Highland Park, Mich., Oct. 14, 1947; s. Joseph and Zena (Fesik) G.; m. Mary Christine Fredericks, June 19, 1970; children: Joseph Jr., Mark, Anthony, Jennifer. BA in Econs., Wayne State U., 1969; JD with distinction, Thomas M. Cooley Coll., 1978. Bar: Mich. 1979, U.S. Dist. Ct. (ea. dist.) Mich. 1980. Tchr., coach Pontiac (Mich.) Cath. High Sch., 1969-73; assoc. pub. affairs Mich. Cath. Conf., Lansing, 1973-78; legis. counsel Mich. Food Dealers Assn., Lansing, 1978-70; legis. cons. Karoub Assn., Lansing, 1980—; gen. counsel Mich. Racing Assn., Lansing, 1980—; gen. counsel Northville (Mich.) Driving Club, 1984—. Mem. ABA, Mich. Bar Assn. Roman Catholic. Lodge: KC. Office: Karoub Assocs 200 N Capitol Suite 500 Lansing MI 48933

GARCIA, JOSEPH E., accountant; b. Caibarien, Cuba, Mar. 1, 1945; came to U.S., 1958, naturalized, 1966; s. Enrique and Mirta (Gonzalez) G.; B.S., DePaul U., 1969; M.B.A. in Acctg., U. Miami, 1974. Reservation agt. TWA, Chgo., 1966-68; acctg. mgr. Burger King Corp., 1968-73, Mondex, Inc., 1973-77; asst. controller William M. Mercer, Inc., 1978-84. Mem. Nat. Assn. Accountants. Office: Allstate Ins Co Allstate Plaza Northbrook IL 60062

GARCIA, JOSEPH EVERETT, public library director; b. Savanna, Ill., Jan. 2, 1937; s. John Augustine and Gertrude J. (Randall) G.; m. Ramona Joyce Sartwell, Jan. 29, 1965; children: Kevin Joseph, Lance Randall. BA, Ill. Coll., Jacksonville, 1960; MLS, Rutgers U., 1970; MBA, Winthrop Coll., Rock Hill, S.C, 1977. Dir. York County Library, Rock Hill, 1973-77, Ocean County Library, Toms River, N.J., 1977-80; sales mgr. Clover Indsl. Pipe, Toms River, 1980-82; dir. McDowell Pub. Library, Welch, W.Va., 1982-83, Kent County Library, Grand Rapids, Mich., 1983—; mem. adv. bd. Tri-State Regional Telecommunications, N.Y.C., 1978. Pres. Coll./Community Arts Council, Celina, Ohio, 1972; active Kent County United Way, Grand Rapids, 1984—. Mem. ALA, Mich. Library Assn. Lodges: Moose, Elks, Rotary (pres. Rock Hill chpt. 1974-75). Home: 1241 Cricklewood SW Wyoming MI 49509 Office: Kent County Library System 775 Ball Ave NE Grand Rapids MI 49503

GARCIA, LUIS ARTURO, otolaryngologist; b. Fajardo, P.R., Dec. 30, 1944; s. Federico Luis and Juanita (Martinez) G.; m. Patricia Ellen Cross, Aug. 13, 1966; children: Anne, David, Matthew, Patrick, Mary. BS, U. Dayton, 1965; MD, Marquette U., 1969. Diplomate Am. Bd. Otalaryngology, Nat. Bd. Med. Examiners. Intern Stamford (Conn.) Hosp., 1969-70, resident, 1970-71; resident otolaryngology Tulane Med. Sch., New Orleans, 1974-77; staff Mercy Hosp., Mason City, Iowa, 1977—, also bd. dirs. Bd. dirs. Interparish bd. edn., Mason City, 1978-80, Newman High Sch., 1985—. Served to maj. U.S. Army, 1971-74. Recipient Cert. Honor, City New Orleans, 1976. Fellow ACS, Am. Acad. Otolaryngology and Head and Neck Surgery, Am. Acad. Facial Plastic and Reconstructive Surgery; mem. AMA, Iowa Med. Soc. Roman Cathlolic. Avocations: music, reading, golf. Home: 3 Hawthorn Mason City IA 50401 Office: Surg Assocs 300 Eisenhower Ave Mason City IA 50401

GARD, WILLIAM YOUNG, tooling manufacturing company executive; b. Detroit, June 10, 1927; s. Paul D. and Martha P. (Young) G.; B.S., Yale U., 1949; m. Nancy Frazer Pierson, Feb. 2, 1952; children—Elizabeth, Paul, Martha. Motor products salesman Sun Oil Co., Detroit, 1949-51; sales rep. Dura Corp., Detroit, 1952-67; pres. D & F Corp., Sterling Heights, Mich., 1968-85; chmn. bd. D&F Corp., Sterling Heights, 1986—. Bds. dirs. Univ.-Liggett Sch., 1971-77, Friends of Grosse Pointe Public Library, 1963-73, Grosse Pointe War Meml. Assn., 1970-73, Detroit Community Music Sch., 1982—; vestryman Christ Episcopal Ch., Grosse Pointe, 1970-73, 76-79. Served with USNR, 1945-46. Mem. Soc. Automotive Engrs., Econ. Club Detroit, Mich. Mfrs. Assn., Nat. Assn. Mfrs., Mich. Model Mfrs. Assn. Clubs: Detroit Athletic, County Club of Detroit. Home: 238 Dean Ln Grosse Pointe Farms MI 48236 Office: 42455 Merrill Rd Sterling Heights MI 48078

GARDINE, RICHARD PAYTON, osteopath; b. Des Moines, Nov. 21, 1939; s. Leroy Ernest Gardine and Mary Ann (Miller) Thompson; m. Kristin Helen Skingley, Mar. 7, 1970; children: Jennifer, Hilary, Tyler. AB, U. Mo., 1962; DO, Kirksville (Mo.) Coll. Osteo. Medicine and Surgery, 1967. Diplomate Bd. Osteo. Examiners,. Intern Doctors Hosp., Columbus, Ohio, 1967-68; gen. practice osteo. medicine Viburnum, Ohio; emergency room physician Bi County Community Hosp., Warren, Mich., 1970-74; osteopath Metro Indsl. Clinic, Romulus, Mich., 1980-82, Mich. Osteo. Med. Ctr., Detroit, 1983-86; assoc. dir. chem. dependency unit Health Alliance Plan, Detroit, 1986—. Mem. Am. Coll. Emergency Physicians (charter), Am. Assn. Osteo. Occupational Health, Am. Coll. Neuropsychiatry, Am. Osteo. Assn., Am. Med. Soc. Addiction, Alcoholism and Alcoholics Anonymous, Internat. Doctors in Alcoholics Anonymous, Alpha Phi Omega, Beta Theta Pi, Theta Psi. Republican. Club: Bachelor's. Avocations: travel, reading, sports. Home: 21430 Summerside Ln Northville MI 48167 Office: Oak Creek Med Ctr Livonia MI 48105

GARDINER, JOHN WILLIAM, insurance company executive; b. Newark, Feb. 16, 1931; s. Frank and Alice G.; m. C. Joan Matthews, Sept. 15, 1951; children—Timothy, Glenn, Nancy, Jacquelynn. Student pub. and pvt. schs. Agt. John Hancock Mut. Life Ins. Co., 1954-58, agency mgr., 1958-60, gen. agt., 1960-66, v.p. gen. agencies, 1966-67, sr. v.p. field mgmt. and marketing, 1967-70; pres., chief exec. officer, dir. All Am. Life & Casualty Co., Chgo., 1970-77; pres. Holding Corp. Am., Denver, 1977—; pres., dir. ICH Corp., 1981—, Great Southern Life Ins. Co., 1983—, Bankers Life And Casualty Co., 1984—; chmn. bd. dir. Mass. Gen. Life Ins. Co., 1981—, Bankers Union Life Ins. Co. 1981—; bd. dirs. All. Am. Assurance Co., Bankers Multiple Line Ins. Co., Cert. Life Ins. Co., Chase Nat. Life Ins. Co., Facilities Mgmt. Installation, Marquette Nat. Life Ins. Co., Modern Am. Life Ins. Co., Nat. Am. Life Ins. Co.; pres. Phila. Life Ins. Co., 1987, Southwestern Life Ins. Co., 1987, SWL Re Life Ins. Co., 1987. Served with U.S. Army, 1949-50, 51-54.

GARDNER, CLIFFORD JAMES, JR., banker; b. Chgo., June 25, 1944; s. Clifford James and Mary Elizabeth (Hurley) G.; m. Renell Siemione, July 3, 1965; children—Lorraine, Brian. Student DePaul U., 1964-69. With Continental Ill. Nat. Bank, Chgo., 1962-86, ops. mgr. Taipei br. (Taiwan), 1972-76, Paris br., 1976-79, mgr. letter of credit ops. div., Chgo., 1979-81, product mgr. trade fin. div., 1981-86, v.p., 1984-86; banking specialist Internet Systems Corp., Chgo., 1986—. Lay zone minister United Methodist Ch., 1983-86 . Mem. Mid-Am. Council Internat. Banking (planning bd., 1982-86, chmn. letter of credit com. 1982-85, sec. 1985-86). Home: 2018 Crown Point St Woodridge IL 60517 Office: Internet Systems Corp 200 W Madison St Suite 1700 Chicago IL 60606

GARDNER, DON CHARLES, dentist; b. Kempton, Ill., Mar. 22, 1931; S. Charles H. and Ila F. (Malone) G. BS, U. Ill., Chgo., 1953, DDS, 1955. Gen. practice dentistry Mason City, Ill., 1962-86; vol. dentist Agy. for Internat. Devel. Ptnrs., Mexico, Honduras, Columbia, 1972-85;. Mem., pres. Mason City (Ill.) Library Bd., 1969-81; Served to capt. U.S. Army, 1955-61. Mem. The Nature Conservancy (life). Avocations: prairie restoration and preservation. Home: Rt 2 Box 110 Kempton IL 60946

GARDNER, DONNA K., dentist; b. Joplin, Mo., Feb. 21, 1952; s. Donald Calvin and Norma Jean (Thompson) Keeter; m. Jimmie Charles Davidson, June 5, 1970 (div. 1979); m. Johnny Lee Gardner, Feb. 17, 1982; children: Erin Keeter, Kyle Leah, Sean Christopher. BS, U. Mo., 1976, DDS, 1980. Dentist Independence, Mo., 1980-83, Overland Park, Kans., 1983—; cons. Optimist Club Girls Home, Overland Park. Mem. Am. Dental Assn., Nat. Assn. Women Bus. Owners, Am. Bus. Women Assn., Dimensions Unltd. Home: 10743 Oakmont Overland Park KS 66210 Office: 11011 King St Room 115 Shawnee Mission KS 66210

GARDNER, JAMES RAYMOND, business executive, county official; b. Indpls., Dec. 24, 1920; s. Raymond and Flora (Eberhardt) G.; B.S., Purdue U., 1950; m. Viola M. Chandler, Sept. 7, 1952; 1 son, John S. Personnel rep., labor relations rep. Western Electric Co., 1952-64; clk.-treas. City of Lawrence, Ind., 1956-60; dep. commr. Ind. Revenue Dept., Indpls., 1964-68; pres. G & H Enterprises, Inc., Indpls., 1957-71, Gardner & Guidone, Inc., Indpls., 1965—; adminstr. Gov.'s Wage Stblzn. Bd.; treas., controller Marion County Health and Hosp. Corp., 1970-77; chief fin. officer Marion County Health Dept., 1978—; sec. Betatek, Inc., Indpls., 1981—. Pres. Lawrence Twp. Civic Assn., 1955-56; dist. commr. Boy Scouts Am., 1951-54; pres. Marion County Fair, 1976-79. Served with USMC, 1943-46. Mem. Ind. Soc. Pub. Accountants, Pi Kappa Alpha Home Assn. (pres. 1964-69, dir. 1960-75), Sagamore of Wabash, Pi Kappa Alpha, Alpha Phi Omega. Methodist (chmn. ofcl. bd.). Lodges: Masons, Rotary. Home: 7625 E 51st St Indianapolis IN 46226 Office: 222 E Ohio St Indianapolis IN 46204

GARDNER, JAY KENT, data processing executive; b. Davenport, Iowa, Mar. 29, 1947; s. Lowell Edmund and Louise Elizabeth (Eden) G.; m. Constance Jane Moe, July 23, 1973; children—Adam Jay, Joseph Paul, Anne Elizabeth, John Michael. A.S., Scott Community Coll., 1969; B.A., Govs.

State U., Park Forest, Ill., 1983. Cert. data processing. Systems analyst Nat. Cash Register Corp., Davenport, Iowa, 1968-70, Northwest Bank, Davenport, 1970-75; ops. mgr. Fin. Industry Systems, Rock Island, Ill., 1975-79; v.p. data processing Microdata, Kankakee, Ill., 1979-83, Midwest Fin. Group, Peoria, Ill., 1984—; part-time instr. Kankakee Community Coll., 1980. Chmn., United Way Kankakee, 1981, 82; sustaining membership chmn. Kankakee Trails council Boy Scouts Am., 1983. Mem. Data Processing Mgmt. Assn. (v.p. 1978-80). Republican. Roman Catholic. Lodge: Kiwanis. Home: 1118 W Sleepy Hollow Ct Peoria IL 61615 Office: MFG Info Systems 1318 S Johanson Rd Bartonville IL 61607

GARDNER, JOHN CRAWFORD, newspaper publisher; b. Atlanta, Ga., Apr. 19, 1935; s. James Watts and Mary Jane (McCoy) G.; m. Ann S. Lindsay, Mar. 24, 1956; children: Ellen, Elizabeth, Paul, John, Matthew. B.J., Northwestern U., 1956; postgrad., Columbia, 1956-57. Writer A.P., N.Y.C., 1956-57; reporter Charlotte (N.C.) Observer, 1957-59, So. Illinoisan, Carbondale, 1959-61; city editor So. Illinoisan, 1961-62, mng. editor, 1962-64, editor, gen. mgr., 1964-76, pub., 1977-84; pres. So. Illinoisan Inc., 1966-79; pub. Quad City Times, Davenport, Iowa, 1984—; lectr. journalism Medill Sch. Journalism, Northwestern U., 1972-79; vis. lectr. Sch. Journalism, So. Ill. U., Carbondale, 1977-84. Mem. Am. Soc. Newspaper Editors, Ill. A.P. Editors Assn. (pres. 1974-75), Inland Daily Press Assn. (chmn. edn. com. 1975-80), Sigma Delta Chi. Episcopalian. Office: Quad-City Times 124 E 2d PO Box 3828 Davenport IA 52808

GARDNER, JOSEPH HENRY, engineer; b. Princeton, Ind., Nov. 19, 1935; s. Joseph Franklin and Lillie Ellen (Wolfe) G.; m. Judith Lee Casebier, June 24, 1956; children: Brett Alan, Gary Joseph. AS in Mech. Engring., U. Evansville, 1972, BBA, 1975, AS in Acctg., 1976, A in Elect. Engring., 1980, BS in Engring. Mgmt., 1982, BS in Indsl. Engring., 1986. Registered profl. engr., Ind. Design engr. Hansen Mfg. Co., Inc., Princeton, Ind., 1962-68, project engr., 1968-73, asst. chief engring., 1973—. Treas. Princeton Community High Sch. Band Boosters, 1981-82. Mem. IEEE, NSPE, Am. Soc. Mech. Engrs., Am. Soc. Quality Control (cert. reliability engr., cert. quality engr.), Soc. Mfg. Engrs. (cert., chmn. bd. 1984-85). Republican. Mem. Ch. of Nazarene. Avocations: shooting, fishing, spectator sports. Home: Rural Rt 4 Box 179 Princeton IN 47670 Office: Hansen Mfg Co Inc 901 S First St Princeton IN 47670

GARDNER, KIM LAMARR, dentist; b. Cambridge, Ohio, Feb. 17, 1955; s. Wilbur Arndt and Betty Eileen, (Tucker) G.; m. Susan Elaine Herman, July 9, 1977; children: Paul William, John Andrew. BS cum laude, U. Pitts., 1977; DDS, Case Western Res. U., 1981. Gen. practice dentistry Chardon, Ohio, 1981—; staff dentist Hattie Larlham Found., Mantua, Ohio, 1982—; cons. dentistry Geauga Community Hosp., Chardon, 1981—. Scout coordinator Boy Scouts Am., Chesterland, Ohio, 1983—; chmn. profl. edn. Am. Cancer Soc, 1985—, also bd. dirs.; mem. choir Chesterland Bapt. Ch., 1981—, sec., treas., bd. deacons, 1984—, Sunday sch. tchr., 1986. Mem. ADA, Northeastern Ohio Dental Soc. (Geauga County rep., 1985—, com. chmn., 1985—), Ohio Dental Assn., Acad. Gen. Dentistry. Republican. Avocations: golf, gardening, reading.

GARDNER, MARSHALL ALLEN, office products distribution company executive; b. Chgo., Feb. 15, 1940; s. Sol Gardner and Sylvia (Edelheit) Fischman; m. Paulette Adler, Apr. 7, 1960; children: Robert Philip, Deborah Renee. BSBA, Roosevelt U., 1962, MS in Acctg., 1965, cert. in data processing, 1967. CPA, Ill. Asst. controller Maremont Corp., Chgo., 1962-71; group v.p. Whitaker Corp., Chgo., 1971-74; prof. DePaul U., Chgo., 1974—; sr. v.p. fin. and adminstrn., chief fin. officer United Stationers, Chgo., 1975—; speaker in field. Pres. Homeowners Assn., Niles, Ill., 1970. Mem. Am. Inst. CPA's, Ill. Soc. CPA's, Fin. Exec. Inst., Wholesale Stationers Assn. (chmn. trade stats. com. 1982—). Clubs: Ravina Green Country (Riverwoods, Ill.); Met. (Chgo.). Lodge: B'nai B'rith. Office: United Stationers 2200 E Golf Rd Des Plaines IL 60016

GARDNER, PAUL ALLEN, manufacturing executive; b. Chgo., Feb. 23, 1947; s. Anton Allen and Estelle Elaine Gardner; m. Carol Ann Klimaszewski, Sept. 9, 1972. BSIndslE, U. Ill., Chgo., 1970; MBA, Loyola U., Chgo., 1975; cert. matls. mgmt., Harper Coll., Palatine, Ill., 1978. Cert. Fellow Prodn. and Inventory Mgmt. Gen. supr. material control ElectroMotive div. Gen. Motors Corp., La Grange, Ill., 1976-78, br. coordinator rebuild mfg., 1978-81, supt. prodn. control, 1981-83, adminstr. strategic mgmt., 1984-85, supt. indsl. engring., 1985-86, mgr. prodn. and matl. control, 1986-87, mgr. prodn. and matl. control and indsl. engring., 1987—; mem. MBA faculty Loyola U., Chgo., 1981-85, Ill. Benedictine Coll., Lisle, 1985—. Mem. strategy devel. subcom. INROADS, Chgo., 1986. Served with U.S. Army, 1971-77. Fellow Am. Prodn. and Inventory Control Soc.; mem. Soc. Automotive Engrs. Roman Catholic. Avocations: sailing, bicycling. Home: 124 Carriage Way Burr Ridge IL 60521 Office: Electro Motive div Gen Motors Corp 9100 W 55th St La Grange IL 60525

GARDNER, ROBERT MEADE, building contractor; b. Portsmouth, Ohio, Aug. 12, 1927; s. David Edward and Mary Petrea (Gableman) G.; m. Ruth Sieker, Aug. 8, 1952; children: Leslie, Robert Jr., Stephen, Lorianne. BA, Ohio Wesleyan U., 1951. Engr. J.A. Jones, Charlotte, N.C., 1944; v.p. D.E. Gardner Co., Columbus, Ohio, 1951-55; pres. The Gardner Co., Columbus, Ohio, 1955—; Dir. Builders Exchange, Columbus, 1959-60; officer Young Pres.' Orgn. Cen. Ohio, 1969-79. Mem. alumni bd. Ohio Wesleyan U., Delaware, 1969—, Columbus Bldg. Code Commn., 1974, World Bus. Council, Columbus, 1980—; officer Upper Arlington (Ohio) Booster Assn., 1974; pres. Vision Ctr. Cen. Ohio, Columbus, 1981. Named to Ohio Wesleyan U. Athletic Hall of Fame; recipient Disting. award Phi Gamma Delta. Clubs: Scioto Country (bd. dirs.), Athletic, Capitol, Racquet (all Columbus). Home: 4500 Dublin Rd Columbus OH 43220 Office: The Gardner Co 4588 Kenny Rd Columbus OH 43220

GARDNER, WILLIAM MICHAEL, library adminstr.; b. Cleve., Dec. 16, 1932; s. William Michael and Rosemary (Jansing) G.; m. Betty Jane Krug, July 23, 1960; children—Amy, Daniel, Robert. B.S., John Carroll U., 1955; M.S. in Library Sci, Case Western Res. U., 1960. Asst. librarian Albert R. Mann Library, Cornell U., 1960-64; agr. librarian U. Ky., 1965-66; asst. dir. U. Ky. Libraries, 1966-74; dir. libraries Marquette U., Milw., 1975—. Served with Security Agy. AUS, 1955-57. Mem. ALA. Home: 13380 W Graham St New Berlin WI 53151 Office: Marquette U Meml Library 1415 W Wisconsin Ave Milwaukee WI 53233

GARDON, JOHN LESLIE, paint company research executive; b. Budapest, Hungary, June 5, 1928; came to U.S., 1958; s. Louis and Clara (Popper) G.; m. Berta Rost, Dec. 26, 1951; children: Jessica Joan, Frederic Paul. B.S., Swiss Fed. Inst. Tech., 1951; Ph.D., McGill U., 1955. Chemist Can. Internat. Paper Co., Hawkesbury, Ont., Can., 1955-58; sr. chemist, group leader, research assoc., mgr. Rohm and Haas Co., Springhouse, Pa., 1958-68; dir. research and devel. M & T Chems., Southfield (Mich.) and Rahway (N.J.), 1969-80; v.p. corp. research and devel. Sherwin Williams Co., Chgo., 1981-85; v.p. research and devel. Akzo Coatings Am., Inc., Troy, Mich., 1985—; trustee Paint Research Inst., Kent, Ohio, 1972-81; chmn. Gordon Research Conf. of Adhesion, New Hampton, N.H., 1976. Editor Non-Polluting Coatings and Processes, 1973, Emulsion Polymerization, 1976; contbr. articles to profl. jours., patentee in field. Mem. Am. Chem. Soc. (chem. organic coatings and plastics div. 1980), Fedn. of Soc. for Paint Tech. (Roon award 1966), Chem. Inst. Can., Soc. Plastics Engrs., Soc. Mfg. Engrs., N.Y. Acad. Scis., Sigma Xi. Office: Akzo Coatings Am Inc 650 Stephenson Hwy Troy MI 48083

GARFIELD, JOAN BARBARA, mathematics/statistics educator; b. Milw., May 4, 1950; d. Sol. L. and Amy L. (Nusbaum) G.; m. Michael G. Luxenberg, Aug. 17, 1980; children—Harlan Ross and Rebecca Ellen (twins). Student, U. Chgo., 1968; B.S., U. Wis., 1972; M.A., U. Minn., 1978, Ph.D., 1981. Asst. prof. math./stats. The Gen. Coll., U. Minn., Mpls., 1981—, coordinator research and evaluation, 1984—; created various tables on evaluations of coll. retention programs, 1979-82, 85. Mem. Am. Statis. Assn., Am. Assn. Higher Edn., Am. Ednl. Research Assn., Internat. Assn. for Statis. Computing. Jewish. Club: Mpls. Twins Topics (research chmn. 1984—). Avocations: violinist/violist; participant in lit. group. Office: U Minn Gen Coll Div Sci Bus Math 216 Pillsbury Ave SE 106 Nicholson Hall Minneapolis MN 55455

GARFIELD, JOEL FRANKLIN, life and health insurance agent; b. Detroit, May 15, 1944; s. Jack and Alyce H. (Pliss) G.; m. Linda Joyce Ferst, Aug. 11, 1969; children—Jennifer M., Marla L., Stephanie M., Lauren Andrea. Student U. Detroit, 1962-64, Mich. State U., 1964-65; B.A. in History, Grand Valley State Coll., Mich., 1967; M.A. in History, U. Detroit, 1969. Registered health underwriter; C.L.U.; lic. life ins. counselor. Sales rep. IBM Corp., 1969; ins. salesman Mass. Indemnity Ins. Co., 1970-72, Mass. Mut. Life Ins. Co., 1972-82; life and health ins. agt. Conn. Mut. Life Ins. Co., Southfield, Mich., 1982—; tchr. life underwriter tng. course; spl. cons. to Mich. Ins. Bur., 1982—. Vice pres. Met. Detroit B'nai B'rith Council, 1979-82, charge youth services appeal fundraising, 1980-81. Named Agt. of Month, Mass. Mut. Life Ins. Co., 1980; life and qualifying mem. Million Dollar Round Table, 1973—; fellow in history U. Detroit, 1968-69. Mem. Am. Soc. CLUs, Oakland County Estate Planning Council, Greater Detroit Assn. Life Underwriters (v.p.), Mich. Assn. Life Underwriters, Nat. Assn. Life Underwriters, Mich. Assn. Life Ins. Counselors. Lodge: Ivan S. Bloch B'nai B'rith. Home: 2935 Woodland Ridge Dr West Bloomfield MI 48033 Office: 3000 Town Center Suite 2400 Southfield MI 48075

GARFIELD, NANCY ELLEN, marketing and advertising professional; b. Cin., Sept. 18, 1954; d. M. Robert and Pegge (Gerber) G. BA in Econs., Rollins Coll., 1976; MBA, Xavier U., 1980. Mktg. specialist Am. Standard, Cin., 1977-81; mktg. services specialist F.H. Lawson, Cin., 1982-83; dir. mktg. Talsol Corp./Mar-Hyde subs. RPM Inc., Cin., 1983—. Mgmt. advisor Cin. Jr. Achievement, 1978-81. Mem. Losantiville C. of C. (ltd. bd. dirs. 1986-87), Cin. Indsl. Advertisers, Chi Omega. Office: Talsol Corp/Mar-Hyde 4677 Devitt Dr PO Box 46465 Cincinnati OH 45246-0465

GARFIELD, ROBERT EARL, lawyer; b. Cleve., Sept. 23, 1937; s. Irwin Charles Garfield and Mathilda Rose; m. Joan Susan Ross, Mar. 24, 1963; children—Mark Clayton, Steven Matthew, Patricia Faith. B.A., Western Res. U., 1959; LL.B., Cornell U., 1962; LL.M., Georgetown U., 1969. Bar: Ohio 1962. Trial atty. Office Chief Counsel, IRS, Washington, 1963-68; assoc. Arter & Hadden, Cleve., 1968-69; ptnr. Hertz & Kates, Cleve., 1969-72, Chattman, Garfield, Friedlander & Paul, Cleve., 1973—. Bd. dirs., counsel Cleve. Childrens Mus., 1981; chmn. bd. of trustees The Singing Angels; bd. dirs., gen. counsel Commerce Exchange Bank, ATI, Inc. Served to capt. USAR, 1966-68. Mem. ABA, Ohio State Bar Assn., Cleve. Bar Assn., Cuyahoga Bar Assn. Democrat. Jewish. Club: Oakwood (Cleve. Heights). Avocations: golf; music; travel; history of WWII. Office: Chattman Garfield Friedlander & Paul 400 Engineers Bldg Cleveland OH 44114

GARG, OM PRAKASH, mining executive; b. Narnaul, India, June 25, 1943; s. Chhanga Mal and Surji (Goel) G.; m. Veena Goel, Jan. 26, 1972; children: Priyanka, Nalini, Amit. BS, MS in Geology, Panjab U., India, 1966; MS in Rock Mechanics, U. Saskatchewan, Can., 1969. Engr. Iron Ore Co. Can. affiliate M.A. Hanna Co., Schefferville, Que., Can., 1970-75; supr. mining and devel. Iron Ore Co. Can. affiliate M.A. Hanna Co., Labrador City, Nfld., Can., 1975-77; supr. engring. Iron Ore Co. Can. affiliate M.A. Hanna Co., Labeadore City, Nfld., Can., 1977-80, chief long range planning, 1980-81; dir. mine planning and research Iron Ore Co. Can. affiliate M.A. Hanna Co., Cleve., 1981—; guest lectr. U. Queens, U. McGill, U. Toronto. Contbr. articles to profl. jours. Mem. Soc. Mining Engrs. (chmn. NE Ohio sect. 1984-85, 86-87, program chmn. open pit mining unit 1985), Can. Inst. Mining (dist. councillor 1980-82, lectr.), Soc. Exploration Geophysics, Nat. Soc. Profl. Engrs., Order Engrs. of Quebec, Assn. Profl. Engrs. Saskatchewan, Assn. Geologists for Internat. Devel., Internat. Soc. Rock Mechanics. Avocations: hiking, swimming, world affairs. Home: 3732 Middle Post Ln Rocky River OH 44116 Office: MA Hanna Co 100 Erieview Plaza Cleveland OH 44114

GARL, TIM C., athletic trainer, nonprofessional athletics; b. South Bend, Ind., July 9, 1956; s. Thomas Edward and Charlotte Mary (Plummer) G. BS in Edn., U. Ala., 1978; MS in Adminstrn., U. Miss., 1979; postgrad., Ind. U., 1981—. Asst. trainer U. Miss., Oxford, 1979-81; head basketball trainer Ind. U., Bloomington, 1981—; head trainer U.S.A. Nat. Basketball Team 1982 World Championship, Cali, Columbia, 1986 World Championshipsm, Madrid, U.S.A. Elite Basketball Team, Asian Tournament Tour, 1983, U.S.A. Olympic Basketball Team, Los Angeles, 1984. Author Conditioning for Indiana Basketball, 1983; contbr. articles to profl. jours. Vol. ARC, Bloomington. Named Outstanding Young Man of Am., 1985. Mem. Nat. Athletic Trainers Assn., Am. Coll. Sportsmedicine, Nat. Strength and Conditioning Assn. (research com. 1979—). Home: 136 Parkridge Rd Bloomington IN 47401 Office: Ind U Basketball Office Assembly Hall Bloomington IN 47405

GARLINGHOUSE, RICHARD EARL, retired physician, gynecologist, obstetrician; b. Iola, Kans., Mar. 5, 1910; s. Orestes Lucian and Pearl Amy (Clark) G.; m. Miriam Esther Thoroman, June 17, 1934; children: Richard Earl Jr., Gretchen Ann Huddleston. AB, U. Kans., 1930; MD, U. Pa., 1934. Diplomate Am. Bd. Ob-Gyn. Intern, then resident ob-gyn St. Louis City Hosp., 1934-37; practice medicine specializing in ob-gyn Lincoln, Nebr., 1937-83; mem. staff Lincoln Gen. Hosp., 1937-83, Bryan Meml. Hosp., 1937-83, St. Elisabeth Hosp., 1937-86, VA Hosp., Lincoln, 1946-86. Contbr. several articles to Nebr. State Med. Jours. Served as commdr. USNR, 1942-46. Fellow ACS (gov. 1955-57), Am. Coll. Ob-Gyn (state chmn. 1961-63); mem. AMA, Nebr. State Med. Assn., Am. Legion. Clubs: Lincoln Country, Lincoln Univ. Lodge: Elks. Avocations: travel, golf, photography. Home: 3500 S 28th St Lincoln NE 68502

GARLO, OLGIERD CASIMIR, physician; b. Nowe Swieciany, Poland, Jan. 26, 1919; came to U.S., 1949; s. Michal and Maria (Skersinis) G.; m. Maria Petraskevicius, Aug. 7, 1943; children: Alexander, Alma, Dolores. MD, Vytanto Didziojo U., Kaunas, Lithuania, 1943. Intern County Hosp., Panevezys, Lithuania, 1943-44; surg. tng. Hubertus Krankenhaus, Berlin, Germany, 1944-45; surg. tng. Polish VA Hosp., Luebeck, Fed. Republic of Germany, 1945-46, Schleswig, Fed. Republic of Germany, 1947-48; ship surgeon U.S. Army transport Gen. Stewart, 1948-49; intern Helen Fould Hosp., Trenton, N.J., 1949-51, resident psychiatry, 1952-55; supervising psychiatrist Pilgrim State Hosp., West Brentwood, N.Y., 1955-57; dir. Mental Health Ctr., Tiffin, Ohio, 1957-60; practice medicine specializing in psychiatry, surgery, emergency medicine, obstetrics Tiffin, 1960-86; practice medicine specializing in emergency medicine Freemont and Tiffin, Ohio, 1976—; county coroner Seneca County, Tiffin, Ohio, 1972-85. Mem. Ohio Med. Soc., Ohio and Am. Psychiat. Assn. (chmn. ethics and membership com. 1975-76). Republican. Home and Office: 53 Clay St Tiffin OH 44883

GARLOVSKY, IRVING SAMUEL, urologist; b. Miami Beach, Fla., Dec. 13, 1938; s. Jack S. and Mildred (Cohen) G.; m. Marsha A. Palmer, Oct. 3, 1965; children: Lauren, Elizabeth, Jonathan. BS in Zoology, U. Ill., Urbana, 1960; MD, U. Ill., Chgo., 1965. Diplomate Am. Bd. Urology. Intern Cook County Hosp., Chgo., 1965-66, resident in urology, 1969-73; practice medicine specializing in urology Chgo., 1973—. Served to capt. USAF, 1966-69. Fellow: ACS; mem. AMA, Chgo. Med. Soc., Am. Urol. Assn., N. Cen. Sect. Am. Urol. Assn., Chgo. Urol. Assn. (exec. com. 1986-87). Home: 2012 Burr Oaks Ln Highland Park IL 60035 Office: 2320 W Peterson Chicago IL 60659

GARMEZY, NORMAN, psychologist; b. N.Y.C., June 18, 1918; s. Isadore and Laura (Weiss) G.; m. Edith Linick, Aug. 8, 1945; children: Kathy, Andrew, Lawrence. B.B.A., CCNY, 1939; M.A., Columbia U., 1940; Ph.D. in Clin. Psychology, State U. Iowa, 1950. From asst. prof. to prof. psychology Duke U., Durham, N.C., 1950-60; tng. specialist in psychology NIMH, Bethesda, Md., 1956-57; sr. research psychologist Worcester State Hosp., 1948-50; prof. U. Minn., Mpls., 1961—; clin. prof. psychiatry dept. U. Rochester (N.Y.) Sch. Medicine, 1969-79; vis. prof. U. Copenhagen, 1965-66, Cornell U., 1969-70; vis. colleague Inst. Psychiatry, Maudsley Hosp., London, 1975-76; vis. prof. psychiatry Stanford U. Med. Sch., 1979—; mem. com. on schizophrenia research Scottish Rite, Boston, 1968-82; cons. NIMH, also past mem. grants com.; mem. task force on research Presdl. Commn. on Mental Health, 1977-78; bd. dirs. Founds. Fund for Research in Psychiatry, 1976-82; mem. overall sci. adv. com. to health program McArthur Found., chmn. research network on risk and protective factors in major mental disorders. Author: (with G. Kimble and E. Zigler) Principles of General Psychology, 6th edit, 1984; editor: (with Rutter) Stress, Coping and Development in Children, 1983; mem. internat. adv. editorial bd.: Schizophrenia Bull, 1974—, Psychol. Medicine, 1976—; corr. editor: Jour. Child Psychology and Psychiatry, 1975-85, editorial bd., 1986— ; adv. editor, MCGraw-Hill Book Co., 1969-85; Ann. Rev. Psychology, 1982-86. Served with U.S. Army, 1943-45. Recipient Lifetime Research Career award NIMH, 1962—, Disting. Grad. award in Psychology, U. Iowa, 1986; co-recipient Stanley Dean award for basic research in schizophrenia, 1967; fellow Center for Advanced Studies in Behavioral Scis., Palo Alto, Calif., 1979-80. Fellow AAAS, Am. Psychol. Assn. (Disting. Scientist award sect. 3 1974, pres. div. clin. psychology 1977-78), Am. Psychopath. Assn., Am. Acad. Arts and Scis.; mem. AAUP, Psychonomic Soc., Soc. Research in Child Devel., Assn. Advancement Psychology (chmn. bd. trustees 1977-78), Nat. Acad. Sci. (Inst. of Medicine, 1986), Am. Orthopsy Assn. (Ittelson Rsch award 1986). Club: Cosmos (Washington). Home: 5115 Lake Ridge Rd Edina MN 55436 Office: N419 Elliott Hall Univ Minn Minneapolis MN 55455

GARNER, DON EUGENE, accounting educator; b. Bucyrus, Ohio, Aug. 10, 1935; s. Alonzo Arista and Elizabeth Rachel (Patton) G. BS in Acctg., Ohio State U., 1962; MS in Bus. Adminstrn., Sacramento State U., 1968; D in Bus. Adminstrn., U. So. Calif., 1972. CPA, Ohio, Ill.; cert. internal auditor. Acct. Gen. Motors Corp., Columbus, Ohio, 1954-62; auditor USAF Audit Agy., 1962-68; asst. prof. acctg. Calif. State U., Los Angeles, 1968-72; prof. Kent (Ohio) State U., 1972-74, 79-81; prof., dean Ill. Inst. Tech., Chgo., 1974-79; prof. John Carroll U, Cleve., 1981—. Author: Degree Titles of AACSB Schools, 1978, Corporate Audit Costs and Staffing, Vol. I, 1980, Vol. II, 1982, Vol. III , 1984; editor: The Nature and Purpose of Accounting; contbr. articles to profl. jours. Served with U.S. Army, 1958-60. Mem. Am. Inst. CPA's, Ohio Soc. CPA's, Am. Acctg. Assn., Inst. Internal Auditors. Home: 912 Faustina Ave Bucyrus OH 44820 Office: John Carroll U Sch Business Cleveland OH 44118

GARNER, JEFFREY HOERATH, real estate company executive; b. Everett, Wash., Mar. 9, 1955; s. Johnnie Lemar and Tillie Noreen (Hoerath) G.; m. Mary Lynn Gorman, June 29, 1985. BA in History, U. Wash., 1978. Instr. swimming Jeff Garner Enterprises, Edmonds, Wash., 1970-73; chief exec. officer Garner Enterprises, Junction City, Kans., 1985—. Served to capt. U.S. Army, 1978-85. Republican. Episcopalian. Avocations: collecting coins, running. Home: PO Box 637 Junction City KS 66441

GARNER, LAFORREST DEAN, dental educator; b. Muskogee, Okla., Aug. 20, 1933; s. Sanford G. and Fannie (Thompson) G.; m. Alfreida Thomas, July 18, 1964; children—Deana Y., Thomas L., Sanford E. D.D.S., Ind. U., 1957, M.S.D., 1959; cert. orthodontics Ind. U., 1961. Diplomate Am. Bd. Orthodontics. Mem. faculty Sch. Dentistry Ind. U., Indpls., 1959—, assoc. prof. dentistry, 1967-70, prof., chmn. orthodontics dept., 1970—; assoc. dean minority student services, 1987. Fellow Am. Coll. Dentists; mem. Am. Assn. Orthodontists, E.H. Angle Soc., Great Lakes Soc. Orthodontists, Internat. Assn. Dental Research, Am. Cleft Palate Assn., Ind. Dental Assn., Indpls. Dist. Dental Soc. Democrat. Presbyterian. Club: Nat. Boule (Indpls.). Contbr. articles to profl. jours. Home: 6245 Riverview Dr Indianapolis IN 46260 Office: 1121 W Michigan St Indianapolis IN 46202 Office: 2416 Capitol Ave N Indianapolis IN 46208

GARNER, ROYAL STANLEY, physician, flight surgeon; b. St. Louis, Mar. 11, 1940; s. Lynn Mason and Esther Vivian (Smith) G.; m. Mary Ellen Arrington, Mar. 30, 1968 (div. 1977) 1 dau., Darcy Paige; m. Karen Elizabeth Long, Feb. 11, 1977. A.B., Mo. U., 1963, M.D., 1968. Diplomate Am. Acad. Family Physicians. Intern U.S. Air Force, Wright-Patterson AFB, Ohio; commd. capt. U.S. Army, 1969, advanced through grades to lt. col., 1985; gen. practice medicine, Jefferson City, Mo., 1971—; med. dir. Westinghouse Electric, Jefferson City, 1972—; med. cons. Social Security Disability, Jefferson City, 1972—. Decorated Bronze Star, Air medal. Fellow Am. Acad. Family Physicians. Republican. Baptist. Avocations: railroading; fishing; flying. Home: 2025 Wendemere Ct Jefferson City MO 65101 Office: 1804 Southwest Blvd Jefferson City MO 65101

GAROFOLA, ANTHONY CHARLES, dentist; b. Detroit, Apr. 5, 1954; s. Charles Joseph and Virginia (Russo) G.; m. Debra Jean Fracassa, Aug. 17, 1974; children: Kathryn Sara, Anthony Charles Jr. BS in Biology summa cum laude, U. Detroit, 1976, DDS, 1980. Practice dentistry Harper Woods, Mich., 1980-82, Kalamazoo, Mich., 1982—; mem. staff Bronson Meth. Hosp., Kalamazoo; assoc. Emergency Dental Referral Service, Kalamazoo. Mem. ADA, Acad. Gen. Dentistry, Am. Endodontic Soc., Am. Acad. Gnathologic Orthopedics, Kalamazoo Valley Dist. Dental Soc., Nat. Right to Life Assn., Mich. Right to Life Assn., Functional Jaw Orthopedic Study Club, Kalamazoo Crozat Study Club. Roman Catholic. Avocations: photography, baseball, hockey, woodworking, reading. Home: 7208 Starbrook Portage MI 49081 Office: 516 Whites Rd Kalamazoo MI 49008

GAROUFALIS, MATTHEW GEORGE, podiatrist; b. Chgo., Sept. 30, 1955; s. Byron L. and Irene Garoufalis; m. Marcia Tzakis, Sept. 3, 1983. BS in Biology, Econs., Heidelberg Coll., 1974-78; DPM, Ill. Coll. Podiatric Medicine, 1978-82. Diplomate Nat. Bd. Podiatric Examiners, Internat. Coll. Podiatrist Laser Surgery. Surg. resident Westside VA Med. Ctr., Chgo., 1982-83; assoc. podiatrist Surg. and Orthopedic Podiatrics, Chgo., 1983-85; pvt. practice Preferred Podiatry Services, Chgo., 1985—; clin. asst. prof. podiatry U. Osteo. Medicine and Health Scis., Des Moines; adj. clin. asst. prof. Dr. William M. Scholl Coll. Podiatric Med.; adj. clin. prof. Pa. Coll. Podiatric Medicine; adj. faculty clinician Ohio Coll. Podiatric Medicine; attending staff Westside VA Med. Ctr., Chgo., South Shore Hosp., Chgo., Wenske Laser Inst. Ravenswood Hosp. Med. Ctr., Chgo.; dir. Podiatry Sports Med. Ctr., Chgo.; pres. Preferred Podiatry Services, Ltd.; bd. dirs. Northwest Suburban Home Care, Inc., Arlington Heights, Ill., Stretch-Nastics/Tan-er-Cise, Inc., Chgo., In Home Health Care N.E. Chgo., Inc. Fellow Am. Coll. Foot Surgery (assoc.), Am. Soc. Podiatric Med.; mem. Am. Podiatric Med. Assn. (Podiatrist's Recognition award 1986), Ill. Podiatric Med. Assn. (zone 1 del. to bd. dirs.), Assn. Hosp. Podiatrists, Am. Podiatric Med. Writers Assn. (charter), Am. Coll. Sports Medicine, Assn. Mil. Surgeons, Nat. Athletic Trainers Assn., Hellenic Profl. Soc. Ill. Avocations: skiing, racquetball, travel, photography. Home: 1230 N State Parkway Chicago IL 60810 Office: Preferred Podiatry Services Ltd 4527 N Pulaski Rd Chicago IL 60630

GARPOW, JAMES EDWARD, financial executive; b. Detroit, July 30, 1944; s. Roy Joseph and Jeanne Beechner (Brader) G.; B.B.A., U. Mich., 1968; m. Elizabeth Marie Conte, Aug. 30, 1969; children—Barbara Jean, Susan Marie. Audit mgr. Ernst & Ernst, Detroit, 1966-73; mgr. corp. acctg. Fed. Mogul Corp., Detroit, 1973-79; corp. controller LOF Plastics, Inc., Detroit, 1979-80; treas. chief fin. officer KMS Industries, Inc., Ann Arbor, Mich., 1980-83; corp. controller Simpson Industries, Inc., Birmingham, Mich., 1983—; audit mgr. Ernst & Whinney. C.P.A., Mich. Mem. Am. Inst. C.P.A.s, Nat. Assn. Accts., Mich. Assn. C.P.A.s, Fin. Execs. Inst., Beta Alpha Psi, Alpha Kappa Psi. Office: care of Simpson Industries Inc 32100 Telegraph Rd Suite 120 Birmingham MI 48010

GARRETT, BETTY LOU, accountant; b. Nampa, Idaho, June 18, 1930; d. William B. and Mildred (Reinhardt) Corn; m. George Garrett, May 3, 1956 (dec. July 1971); children: Raymond E., Paul K. BS, DePaul U., Chgo., 1978, MBA, 1981. CPA, Ill. Audit sr. J.K. Lasser & Co., Chgo., 1974-79; various assignments Laventhol & Horwath, Chgo., 1979-81, audit mgr., 1981-84; asst. controller property Homart Devel. Co., Chgo., 1985-86, sr. mgr. corp. receivables, 1986—. Active Democratic Orgn., Evanston, Ill., 1985-86. Mem. Ill. CPA Soc. (real estate com. 1985-87, audit procedures com. 1979-85, bus. counseling and edn. com. 1987—). Episcopalian. Office: Homart Devel Co 55 W Monroe Chicago IL 60603

GARRETT, CHARLES WESLEY, therapist and counselor; b. Gainesville, Tex., Apr. 17, 1923; s. Charles Ballard and Opal (Shaver) G.; B.A., So. Meth. U., 1943, B.D., 1946, M.A., 1948; Ph.D., N.Y. U., 1953; m. Avis Devon Bedford, Sept. 24, 1979; children—Susanna Wesley, Charles Davidson, Alice Frances, Thomas Ruston. Pvt. practice therapy, Kansas City, Mo., 1970—; cons. Johnson County Dist. Cts., 1970—. Author: Anniversaring, 1987. Mem. Am. Psychol. Assn., Kans. Psychol. Assn. Research in geriatrics, conceptual models of health.

GARRETT, LORRAINE MAE, elementary school teacher; b. Detroit, Aug. 28, 1928; d. Clifford Emanuel and Zelma (Ford) Wilkes; m. Nathaniel Garrett (dec.), July 21, 1951; children: Victoria, Raymond, Ellen, Denise, Erin, Tameria. BS in Edn., Wayne State U., 1976, MEd, 1983. Cert. social worker. Tchr. asst. Office of Econ. Devel., Sumpter, Mich., 1968-71; assoc. tchr. Inkster (Mich.) Pub. Schs., 1971-76, tchr., 1976—; vol. tutor Belleville-Milan, Mich. 1971—. Co-author: Handbook for the Homecare of CHildren, 1971. Recipient Parent-Involvement award Out Wayne County Head Start, 1973, Service award, 1977. Mem. Mich. Reading Assn., Phi Delta Kappa. Democrat. Baptist. Avocations: reading, sewing. Office: Inkster Pub Schs 29115 Carlysle Ave Inkster MI 48141

GARRETT, ROBERT DEAN, insurance company executive; b. Fairfield, Ill., Apr. 13, 1933; s. Roy Smith and Halene (Pickett) G.; student Eastern Ill. U., 1986—; m. Peggy Jean Spence, Dec. 8, 1955; children—Daniel Bryant, Evelyn, Brenda, Ronald. With U.S. Post Office, Chgo., 1954-60, Gen. Telephone Co., So. Ill., 1960-67; agt. MFA Ins. Co., Mt. Carmel, Ill., 1967-70; with Fed. Kemper Ins. Co., Decatur, Ill., 1970—, v.p. adminstrn., 1977-86, v.p. adminstrn., sec., 1986—. Bd. Commrs. Decatur Housing Authority, 1987—; bd. dirs. Jr. Achievement, Decatur, 1978-81, Council of Community Services, Decatur, 1978—, pres., 1983-84; bd. dirs. Decatur Boys Club, 1979, pres., 1981-83; bd. dirs. United Way Decatur and Macon Counties, 1985—; trustee Richland Community Coll., 1985—. Served with USAF, 1950-54. Recipient Cert. in Gen. Ins., Ins. Inst. Am., 1975. Mem. Pvt. Industry Council (chmn. 1983-84), C. of C. Presbyterian. Office: 2001 E Mound Rd Decatur IL 62526

GARRETT, WILLIAM J., steel company executive; b. Muncie, Ind., July 7, 1936; s. Cletus Loren Garrett and Martha Sue (Turner) Stahl; m. Judith Ann Creviston, Aug. 3, 1955; children—Barbara, Beth, Bruce, Julie. Grad. Ironworker's Union, Indpls., 1959; student Ind. Bus. Co., Muncie, Ind., 1962-63, Ball State U., 1965-68. Steel fabricator, painter Creviston Steel Co., Inc., Cowan, Ind., 1955-57, steel fabricator, 1958-60, foreman erection crew, 1960-61, job supt., 1960-69, glass furnace rebuilder, 1969-70, gen. field supr., from 1970; now co-owner, pres. H.A.G. Steel Contractors, Inc., Muncie, Ind. Pres. Cowan Athletic Booster Club, Cowan Sch., 1975; pres. Monroe Community Sch. Bd., 1982-84, v.p., 1983. Republican. Methodist. Club: Murat Temple (Indpls.). Lodge: Masons. Avocation: private pilot. Home: RR #4 Box 272 Muncie IN 47302

GARRIGAN, RICHARD THOMAS, finance educator, consultant; b. Cleve., Mar. 4, 1938; s. Walter John and Priscilla Marie (Hill) G.; m. Kristine Ottesen, Dec. 26, 1962; 1 child, Matthew Osborne. BS summa cum laude, Ohio State U., 1961, MA, 1963; MS, U. Wis., 1966, PhD, 1973. Asst. prof. fin. U. Wis., Whitewater, 1974-76, assoc. prof., 1976-77; v.p. research Real Estate Research Corp., Madison, 1975-76; presdl. exchange exec. Fed. Home Loan Bank Bd., Washington, 1977-78; assoc. prof. DePaul U., Chgo., 1978-83, prof., 1983—; pres. Richard T. Garrigan & Assocs., Inc., Chgo., 1982—; bd. dirs. Hinsdale (Ill.) Fed. Savs. and Loan Assn. Co-editor: The Handbook of Mortgage Banking, 1985; contbr. articles to profl. jours. Served with U.S. Army, 1955-58. Alfred P. Sloan scholar, 1959-61; recipient Excellence award Haskins and Sells, 1960, Achievement award Pres.'s of U.S. Commn. on Exec. Exchange, 1978; fellow Mershon Nat. Security, Ohio State U., 1961-62, urban studies Ford Found., 1964-65, bus. Ford Found., 1965-66. Mem. Am. Real Estate and Urban Econs. Assn., Ill. Mortgage Bankers Assn. (bd. dirs. 1985—), Lambda Alpha Internat. (Ely chpt. sec. 1984, v.p. 1985, pres. 1986), Beta Gamma Sigma, Phi Kappa Phi, Phi Eta Sigma, Sphinx. Office: DePaul U Fin Dept 25 E Jackson Blvd Chicago IL 60604

GARRIOTT, TAMI LEA, systems analyst; b. Cin., Nov. 1, 1958; d. George H. and E. Lois (Phelps) Van Pelt; m. Robert Edward Garriott, June 21, 1986. BBA in Acctg., Eastern Ky. U., 1981. Computer programmer Western-Southern Life, Cin., 1981-83, programmer analyst, 1983-85, asst. systems analyst, 1985-86, tech. systems researcher, 1986-87. Youth counselor United Meth. Ch., Lakeside Park, Ky., 1986—. Mem. Am. Mgmt. Assn., Eastern Ky. U. Alumni Assn. Democrat. Avocations: weight tng., aerobics, scuba diving, reading, cooking. Office: Western-Southern Life 400 Broadway Cincinnati OH 45202

GARRISON, CHARLES EUGENE, fleet manager; b. New London, Conn., Apr. 9, 1943; s. Charles Westel and Thelma Rae (Coleman) G.; m. Trudy Elisabeth Thorburn, Aug. 26, 1967 (div.); children: Matthew Charles, Mark Andrew. BA, Mich. State U., 1965, MBA, 1966. Supr. service garage and motor pool Mich. State U., East Lansing, 1972, mgr. automotive services dept., 1972—; Co-owner The Latest Scoop, 1980-85; fleet mgmt. instr. various agys., 1985—; cons. in field, 1985— Elder Holt Presbyn. Ch., 1975-77, mem. various coms. 1977-85; div. coordinator United Way, 1972-73; mem. E. Lansing Mass Transit Com., 1972-75; judge Ingham County Fair, 1977-80. Served to capt. USAF, 1967-72. Recipient Vol. Achievement award United Way, 1984, 85, Cost Reduction Incentive award Nat. Assn. Coll. and Univ. Bus. Officers. Mem. Nat. Assn. Fleet Adminstr., Big Ten Transp. Assn. Lodge: Kiwanis (Internat. Diamond Single Service award 1982, Mich. dist. Disting. Pres. award 1982, Outstanding Bulletin Editor 1983). Avocations: golf, bowling, bridge, softball, spectator sports. Home: 625 Peachtree Mason MI 48854 Office: Mich State U Automotive Services Stadium Rd East Lansing MI 48824

GARRISON, LARRY PAUL, international trade executive; b. San Angelo, Tex., July 31, 1945; s. Robert Allen Garrison and Dorothy Mae (Kelsall) Heitkotter; m. Carolyn Jean West, Apr. 2, 1977; children—Brianne, Kerry, Andrew. B.B.A., U. Minn., 1985. Asst. mgr. Moritani Am. Corp., Chgo., 1968-69; mgr. traffic and imports Reliance Trading Corp., Chgo., 1969-74; mgr. customs adminstrn. Control Data Corp., Mpls., 1974-79; pres. North Star World Trade Services, Mpls., 1979-84, Internat. Pursuits, Ltd., Mpls., 1985—; cons. Minn. Dept. Vocationsl Edn., St. Paul, 1984—; instr. St. Paul Tech. Vocational Inst., 1983-84. Mem. Econ. Devel. Commn., Burnsville, Minn., 1983—. Recipient Appreciation award City of Burnsville, 1984. Mem. Minn. World Trade Assn. (bd. dirs. 1984—, v.p. 1985), Nat. Customhouse Broker and Freight Assn. Am. Republican. Methodist. Avocations: music; travel; children. Office: International Pursuits Ltd 1408 Northland Ave Suite 306 Mendota Heights MN 55120

GARRISON, LARRY RICHARD, accounting educator; b. Kansas City, Mo., Jan. 10, 1951; s. Robert Milton and Virginia Claire (Huntington) G.; m. Sheila Caroline Murry, Aug. 10, 1973. BBA, Cen. Mo. State U., 1973; MS in Acctg., U. Mo., 1982; PhD, U. Nebr., 1986. CPA, Mo. Mgr. Garrison & Co., CPA's, Kansas City, 1973-79; controller G.F. & F. Enterprises, Kansas City, 1979-82; instr. U. Nebr., Lincoln, 1983-86; asst. prof. U. Mo., Kansas City, 1986—. Contbr. articles to profl. jours. Recipient Disting. Teaching award U. Nebr., 1984-85. Mem. Am. Inst. CPA's, Am. Taxation Assn., Mo. Soc. CPA's, Am. Acctg. Assn., Beta Alpha Psi, Beta Gamma Sigma. Office: U Mo 5100 Rockhill Rd Kansas City MO 64110

GARRISON, ROBERT DAVID, programmer; b. Oct. 18, 1947; s. Virgil Garrison and Florence (Schleeper) Erwin; m. Linda S. Massara, July 19, 1969 (div. Nov. 1972); chidlren: Lisa, Stacey; m. Sue A. Taylor, June 12, 1982. BS, So. Ill. U., 1982. Acct. AT&T, Ballwin, Mo., 1970-87; programmer Profl. Mgmt. Systems, Alton, Ill., 1987—. Treas., trustee Fosterburg Fire Protection Dist., Alton, Ill., 1985. Home: Rural Rt 1 Box 404 Alton IL 62002 Office: Profl Mgmt Systems 2850 Homer Adams Pkwy Suite A Alton IL 62002

GARRISON, TED BEAMAN, communications executive; b. Paden City, W.Va., Dec. 20, 1936; s. Ted B. and Brenda E. (McCurdy) G.; m. Brenda E. McCurdy, Aug. 15, 1964; children: Merle T., Theodore S. BS, Miami U., Oxford, Ohio, 1961. Various positions Ohio Bell Telephone Co., Cleve., 1965-74; dist. traffic mgr. Ohio Bell Telephone Co., Akron, 1974-76; dist. mgr. Ohio Bell Telephone Co., Cleve., 1976-77, AT&T, N.Y.C., 1977-79; gen. mgr. 216 residence services Ohio Bell Telephone Co., Cleve., 1979-80, gen. mgr. statewide RSC, 1981-84, asst. v.p., 1984—. Mem. Better Bus. Bur., Bldg. Owners and Mgrs. Assn., Urban League, NAACP, Bus. Roundtable, Greater Cleve. Roundtable, Teen-Father Program. Methodist. Home: 1820 Miles Standish Ln Hudson OH 44236 Office: Ohio Bell Telephone Co 45 Erieview Plaza Room 741 Cleveland OH 44114

GARRISON, WILLIAM LLOYD, social worker; b. Ridgway, Pa., Dec. 26, 1939; s. Lloyd and Mary Rebecca (Morrow) G.; m. Mary Jo Florio, May 30, 1964; children: David, Mark. BA in Psychology, Ohio Wesleyan U., 1962; postgrad, Garrett Theol. Sem., 1962-63; MSW, Fla. State U., 1967; MS in Mgmt., Case Western Res. U., 1976. Caseworker Mpls. Ct. Chgo., 1963-64, United Cerebral Palsy Assn., Phila., 1964-65; psychiat. social worker Bellefaire, Shaker Heights, Ohio, 1967-74; dir. personnel and tng. Ctr. Human Services, Cleve., 1974-81, dir. resource devel., 1981-83; exec. dir. Cleve. Soc. for the Blind, 1983-85, Cleve. Eye Bank, 1983-85; exec. v.p. Lake View Cemetery Assn., Cleve., 1985—; adj. prof. Sch. Applied Social Sci., Case Western Res. U., 1974-80; v.p. E.A. Mabry Inc., Akron, Ohio, 1970—. Dist. Chmn. Cub Scouts, 1978-81, dist. chmn. Boy Scouts Am., 1981-84, scoutmaster, 1983-87, mem. exec. bd. council, 1981—, asst. council commr., 1984—; v.p. Boy Scouting, 1987—; active personnel com. Lake Erie council Girl Scouts U.S.; mem. Big Bros. Cleve., 1968-73; pres. Mayfield Heights Homeowners Assn., 1974-84; bd. dirs. Garfield Meml. United Meth. Ch., 1979-81; bd. dirs. Cuyahoga County Reach Out Services, 1977—. Recipient Merit award Boy Scouts Am., 1980, Silver Beaver award, 1984; Menniinger Found. fellow. Mem. Acad Cert. Social Workers, Nat. Assn. Social Workers, Am. Soc. Personnel Administrs., Personnel Accreditation Inst., Am. Cemetery Assn., Ohio Assn. Cemetery Supts. and Ofcls., Greater Cleve. Cemetery Assn. (pres. 1987—), Nat. Eagle Scout Assn., Greater Cleve. Personnel Council, Delta Tau Delta, Phi Mu Alpha. Clubs: Cleveland, Univ. Circle Inc., Am. Field Service, Cleve. Playhouse. Office: Lake View Cemetery Assn 12316 Euclid Ave Cleveland OH 44106

GARROW, DERINDA KYLE, nurse; b. Highland Park, Mich., Aug. 13, 1954; d. John Paul and Dorothy Marcellee (Wilkinson) Day; m. Donald Howard Garrow, Aug. 26, 1979; children—Heather Elayne, Joshua Donald John. A.A.S. in Nursing with honors Delta Coll., 1982. R.N.; Mich. Asst. supr. Day's Adult Foster Care Home, Linwood, Mich., 1970-79; meter officer Bay City Police Dept., Mich., 1977-78; third shift charge nurse St. Mary's Hosp., Saginaw, Mich., 1982; ICU-CCU staff nurse Bay Med. Ctr., Bay City, 1982—, emergency rm. staff nurse, 1984—. Twp. chmn. Com. to Elect Kevin Green Sheriff, Beaver Twp., Mich., 1980, Com. to Elect James Miner, Cir. Ct. Judge, Beaver Twp., 1980, Com. to Re-elect Kevin Green, Beaver Twp., 1984. Mem. Nat. Union Hosp. and Health Care Employees, Delta Coll. Student Nurses Assn. (v.p. 1980-81, pres. 1981-82), Phi Theta Kappa. Seventh-day Adventist. Home: 1835 S Eleven Mile Rd Auburn MI 48611 Office: Bay Med Ctr Emergency Rm 1900 Columbus Ave Bay City MI 48706

GARRY, MICHAEL JOSEPH, dentist; b. Terre Haute, Ind., Sept. 29, 1953; s. Robert Francis and Betty Lou (Lagemann) G.; m. Patricia Lynn Baker, May 18, 1975; children: Jennifer Lynn, Sarah Marie, Joseph Ryan. BS cum laude, Ind. State U., 1975; DDS, Ind. U., Indpls., 1979. Gen. practice dentistry Terre Haute, Ind., 1979—; teaching clinician extramural programs Ind. U. Dental Sch., Indpls., 1979—; mem. dental audit com. Union Hosp., Terre Haute, 1980-86. Vol. dentist Indigent Care Program, Vigo County, Ind., 1979—, League of Terre Haute, 1979—. Mem. ADA, Western Ind. Dental Soc. (bd. dirs. 1985—), Ind. Dental Assn., Wabash Valley Arabian Horse Club. Democrat. Baptist. Lodge: Elks. Avocations: golfing, tennis, horse show jumping. Home: Rural Rt #52 Box 112 Terre Haute IN 47805 Office: 1024 Lafayette Terre Haute IN 47804

GARSON, ARNOLD HUGH, newspaper editor; b. Lincoln, Nebr., May 29, 1941; s. Sam B. and Celia (Stine) G.; m. Marilyn Grace Baird, Aug. 15, 1964; children—Scott Arnold, Christopher Baird, Gillian Grace, Megan Jane. B.A., U. Nebr., 1964; M.S., UCLA, 1965. Reporter Omaha World-Herald, 1965-69; reporter Des Moines Tribune, 1969-72, city editor, 1972-75; reporter Des Moines Register, 1975-83, mng. editor, 1983—. Recipient John Hancock award for excellence in bus. and fin. journalism, 1979; Disting. Pub. Affairs Reporting award Am. Polit. Sci. Assn., 1969. Mem. Am. Soc. Newspaper Editors, Assoc. Press. Mng. Editors. Jewish. Home: 2815 Ridge Rd Des Moines IA 50312 Office: The Des Moines Register 715 Locust St PO Box 957 Des Moines IA 50304

GARSON, WILLIAM J., writer, editor, historian; b. Hammond, Ind., May 1, 1917; s. John Soteriou and Helen Glenn (McKennan) G.; B.A., Milton Coll., 1939; postgrad. Grad. Sch. Bank Mktg., Northwestern U., 1968; m. Florence Rebecca Penstone, Sept. 21, 1974; children—Geneva Garson Swing, Gary William. Mng. editor, reporter, columnist Rockford (Ill.) Register-Republic, 1939-55; pub. relations dir. Sundstrand Corp., Rockford, 1956-65; community info. officer Rockford C. of C., 1965-66; mktg. dir. City Nat. Bank & Trust Co. Rockford, 1966-82; pub. relations cons. imagination plus, Rockford, 1955—. Bd. dirs. Tb Assn., Heart Assn., ARC, 1952-54; Recipient George Washington Honor medals Freedoms Found., 1965-66. Mem. Am. Interprofl. Inst. (local pres.), Rockford C. of C. (Community Service award 1952, dir.), Am. Inst. Banking, Bank Mktg. Assn., Internat. Assn. Bus. Communicators, Internat. Word Processing Assn., Rockford Hist. Soc. (pres., treas.). Methodist. Author: Daddy Wore An Apron, 1974; Brother Earth, 1975; The Knight on Broadway, 1978; Rockford-The Pet Food Story, 1923-87 (One Chapter in the History of the Quaker Oats Company), 1987; also numerous short stories and articles; co-author: Political Primer, 1960; We The People..., 1976; Forest City Firelog, 1982; hist. cons. Wordprints in the Sands of Time, 1984—. Home: 3516 Meadow Ln Rockford IL 61107 Office: Box 3126 Rockford IL 61106

GARTEN, EDWARD DALE, academic library administrator; b. Hinton, W.Va., Feb. 19, 1948; s. Paul M. and Hazel (Holland) G.; m. Fran Guenther, Apr. 3, 1971; 1 child, Noah. BS, Concord Coll., Athens, W.Va., 1968; MA and MDiv, Meth. Theol. Sem., Delaware, Ohio, 1972; MLS, Kent (Ohio) State U., 1974; PhD, U. Toledo, 1977. Asst. dir. libraries Moorhead (Minn.) State U., 1977-79; dir. libraries No. State Coll., Aberdeen, S.D., 1979-81, Tenn. Tech. U., Cookeville, 1981-85, U. Dayton, Ohio, 1985—. Recipient Disting. Alumnus award Kent State U., 1984. Mem. ALA, Library Adminstrn. and Mgmt. Assn. (editor newsletter 1981-86, editorial bd. jour. 1982—), Assn. Coll. and Research Libraries, Am. Soc. Info. Sci. Democrat. Methodist. Home: 6185 Millbank Centerville OH 45459 Office: U of Dayton Roesch Library 300 College Park Dayton OH 45469

GARTLEY, CHERYLE BLUMBERG, foundation administrator; b. Ottawa, Ill., Mar. 18, 1947; d. Herman S. and Lucille (Flood) Blumberg. BS, No. Ill. U., 1969; postgrad., U. Chgo., 1976-80. Advt. mgr. State Nat. Bank, Evanston, Ill., 1973-78; pres. Simon Found., Wilmette, Ill., 1983—. Author, editor: (book) Managing Incontinence, 1983. Founder Evanston Vet's. Day, 1974; co-chmn com. Bicentennial Festival, Evanston, 1976; bd. dirs. North Shore Am. Cancer Soc., bd. dirs. Srs. Action Services, Evanston, 1976-77. Mem. Internat. Continence Soc., Assn. Continence Advisors. Office: Simon Found Box 815 Wilmette IL 60091

GARTNER, DANIEL LEE, computer information executive; b. Newark, Ohio, Jan. 24, 1945; s. Harold Jerome and Hazel Marie (Wright) G.; m. Patsy Lee Kerns, June 22, 1968. Student, Ohio State U., 1967-74; BA, Park Coll., 1978; MS, Air Force Inst. Tech., 1985. Computer programmer USAF, Newark AFB, 1974-78, computer systems analyst, 1978-82, chief info. ctr., 1981-82; adj. prof. logistics and computers Park Coll., Newark, Ohio, 1986—; cons. pvt. sector, Newark, 1983—. Designer 1st broadband local area network, 1st info. ctr. Air Force Logistics Command. Adv. Boy Scouts Am., Newark AFB, 1984-86; active Big Bro. and Big Sister, Newark AFB, 1986. Mem. Newark C. of C. (mem. leadership tomorrow 1986). Avocation: computers. Home: 6500 Horns Hill Rd Saint Louisville OH 43071 Office: AGMC/SIC Newark AFB OH 43057

GARTNER, JACK ISSIE, manufacturing company executive; b. Montreal, Quebec, Can., Oct. 20, 1942; s. William and Lisa (Smith) G.; m. Sandra Gail Altman, May 27, 1967; children: Lara, Steven. BEE, McGill U., Montreal, 1965. Registered prof. engr. Various project engr. positions 1967-72; chief engr. tire plant Firestone Tire & Rubber, Nashville, 1972-77; project engring. mgr. Firestone Tire & Rubber, Akron, Ohio, 1977-82, dir. design and constrn., 1982—. Served to capt. Canadian Army, 1960-65. Home: 2063 Brookshire Rd Akron OH 44313 Office: Firestone Tire & Rubber Co PO Box 81073 AMF Cleveland OH 44181

GARTNER, LAWRENCE MITCHEL, pediatrician, medical college administrator; b. Bklyn., Apr. 24, 1933; s. Samuel and Bertha (Brimberg) G.; m. Carol Sue Blicker, Aug. 12, 1956; children— Alex David, Madeline Hallie. A.B., Columbia U., 1954; M.D., Johns Hopkins U., 1958. Intern pediatrics Johns Hopkins Hosp., 1958-59; resident pediatrics Albert Einstein Coll. Medicine, 1959-60, chief resident, 1960-61, instr. pediatrics, 1962-64, asst. prof., 1964-69, asso. prof., 1969-74, prof., 1974-80, dir. div. neonatology, 1967-80, dir. div. pediatric hepatology, 1967-80; dir. clin. research unit Rose F. Kennedy Center, 1972-80; attending physician Hosp. of Albert Einstein Coll. Medicine; prof., chmn. dept. pediatrics U. Chgo. Pritzker Sch. Medicine Michael Reese Hosp., 1980—; dir. Wyler Children's Hosp., U. Chgo. Med. Center, 1980—; chmn. dept. pediatrics Michael Reese Hosps., Chgo., 1986—. Contbr. articles to med. jours. and textbooks. Mem. adv. bd. Children's Liver Found.; Trustee Internat. Pediatric Reseach Found. Recipient award NIH, 1967-74; Appleton Century Crofts prize, 1956; Mosby book award, 1958; NIH grantee, 1967—. Mem. Am. Pediatric Soc., Soc. Pediatric Research, Perinatal Research Soc., Am. Assn. Study Liver Disease, Chgo. Pediatric Soc., Am. Acad. Pediatrics, AAAS, N.Am. Soc. Pediatric Gastroenterology (pres. 1974- 75), LaLeche League Internat., Chgo. Pediatric Soc., Phi Beta Kappa, Alpha Omega Alpha. Office: U Chgo Pritzker Sch Medicine 5841 S Maryland Ave Chicago IL 60637

GARTON, ROBERT DEAN, state senator; b. Chariton, Iowa, Aug. 18, 1933; s. Jesse Glenn and Ruth Irene (Wright) G.; B.S., Iowa State U., 1955; M.S., Cornell U., 1959; m. Barbara Hicks, June 17, 1955; children—Bradford, Brenda. Personnel rep. Cummins Engine Co., Columbus, Ind., 1959-61; owner Garton Assocs., mgmt. cons., Columbus, 1961—; mem. Ind. Senate, 1970—, minority caucus chmn., 1976—, 79, majority caucus chmn., 1979-81, pres. pro tempore, 1981—; chmn. Mid-West Conf. State Legislatures, Council State Govts., 1984-85. Bd. dirs. Ind. Pub. Health Found., 1976—; chmn. Ind. Civil Rights Commn., 1969-70; mem. exec. com. Nat. Fedn. Young Republicans, 1966; bd. dirs. Ind. Econ. Devel. Council, Rural Water System, Columbus, 1969—. Served with USMCR, 1955-57. Named Hon. Citizen Iowa, 1962, Tenn., 1977; winner internat. speech contest Toastmasters, 1962; recipient Disting. Service award Jr. C. of C. Columbus, 1968, One of 5 Outstanding Young Men in Ind., 1968. Mem. Beta Theta Pi. Lodge: Rotary Office: 530 Franklin St Columbus IN 47201

GARVENS, KEITH RONALD, electrical engineer; b. Waukesha, Wis., Feb. 19, 1959; s. Ronald Alfred and Arlene Katherine (Christison) G.; m. Marcia Weller Harrington, Aug. 27, 1983; 1 child, Daniel Christopher. BEE, U. Wis., 1980. Staff engr. IBM Corp, Rochester, Minn., 1980—. Methodist. Avocations: camping, outdoor sports, jogging. Home: 2536 Crestwood Ct SE Rochester MN 55904 Office: IBM Corp Highway 52 N Rochester MN 55901

GARVER, FREDERICK MERRILL, industrial engineering executive; b. Indpls., Mar. 25, 1945; s. Clyde Louis and Elizabeth Kemp (Finch) G.; m. Ruth Sikkema, Nov. 8, 1969. BS, Western Mich. U., 1967; postgrad., Grand Valley State Coll., 1976-77. Cert. mfg. engr. Methods analyst Boeing Co., Seattle, 1968-69; indsl. engr. Wolverine World Wide, Inc., Rockford, Mich., 1969-72; mgr. indsl. engring. Leigh Products Inc., Coopersville, Mich., 1972-77; dir. indsl. engring. Integrated Metal Techs., Spring Lake, Mich., 1977-79; mgr. plant engring. Haworth Inc., Holland, Mich., 1979—; cons. Mich. Engring. Systems, Grand Rapids, 1984—. Mem. Inst. Indsl. Engrs. (sr.), Soc. Mfg. Engrs. (sr., ad hoc govt. relations com.), Chem. Coaters Assn., Assn. Bus. Advocating Tariff Equity, Assn. Finishing Processes, Jaycees (treas. Ithaca, Mich. chpt. 1971-72). Republican. Mem. Reformed Church of America. Avocations: computers, skiing, tennis. Home: 7039 Magnolia Dr Jenison MI 49428 Office: Haworth Inc 1 Haworth Ctr Holland MI 49423

GARVER, ROBERT CHARLES, metallurgical engineer; b. Massillon, Ohio, Oct. 2, 1937; s. Lloyd Christian and Layonette Geneva (Monbarren) G.; m. Nancy M. Hartman, Feb. 26, 1961; children: Jonathan (dec.), Diahann E. BSMetE, Case Inst. Tech., 1959; postgrad., Alexander Hamilton Inst., Akron U., 1961-63. Mgr. quality engring. then mgr. indsl. engring. Hoover Co., North Canton, Ohio, 1959-67; product metallurgist Republic Steel, Canton, 1968-76, chief metallurgist, 1976-84; mgr. quality control LTV Steel, Canton, 1984—; v.p. Massillon Ednl. Loan Found., 1984—. Served with USAF, 1960-68. Mem. Am. Soc. Quality Control (directory chmn. 1976-77), Am. Iron and Steel Engrs., Am. Soc. for Metals. Republican. Mem. United Ch. of Christ. Avocations: biking, tennis, hiking, car restoration, house restoration. Home: 1825 Jackson NW Massillon OH 44646 Office: LTV Steel 2633 8th St NE Canton OH 44708

GARVER, THOMAS K., industrial and research psychologist; b. Marion, Ohio, Dec. 29, 1938; s. Albert Asa and Dorothy Mae (Conklin) G.; m. Loretta E. Roloson, Jan. 9, 1966 (div. 1979); children—Lucreda E., Robin C. B.S. in Indsl. Psychology, Ohio State U., 1965; M.S., San Jose State Coll., 1967; postgrad. U. Akron, 1968-72, Ed.D. in ednl. adminstrn, 1978. Fireman, Erie Lackawanna R.R., Marion, 1960-65; research asst. Advanced System Design Devel. Lab., IBM, Los Gatos, Calif., 1966; asst. project dir. personnel research, U.S. Navy, San Diego, 1968; cons. program eval. and research, Akron, 1972-73; personnel analyst Akron CSC, 1973-75; assoc. coordinator, personnel devel., Firestone Tire and Rubber Co., 1979—. Served with USN, 1956-59. Mem. Am. Psychol. Assn., Am. Ednl. Research Assn., Phi Delta Kappa. Home: 144 7th St NE North Canton OH 44720 Office: 1200 Firestone Pkwy Personnel Devel Akron OH 44317

GARVEY, JOHN KINDEL, petroleum exploration company executive; b. Wichita, Kans., June 11, 1947; s. Willard White and Jean (Kindel) G.; m. Joan Ann Mirandy, Oct. 2, 1976 (div. 1980); m. Jane Mary O'Connor, Nov. 3, 1982; children: John Robert, William James Kindel, Timothy Joseph O'Connor. B.A., U. Kans., 1969; M.S.W., U. Denver, 1975, M. Pub. Adminstrn., 1976; M. in Pub. and Pvt. Mgmt., Yale U., 1979. Tchr., vol. VISTA, Peace Corps, Salt Lake City and Morocco, 1970-71; intern-analyst Congl. Budget Office, Washington, 1978; fin. analyst Overseas Pvt. Investment Corp., Washington, 1979-80; v.p. Amortibanc Investment Co., Wichita, 1981-82; pres. Global Resources, Wichita, 1982—, Spines-Garvey Exploration, Wichita, 1985—; pres., broker J.K. Garvey & Sun, Wichita, 1984—; audit chmn. Garvey Industries, Wichita, 1983—, also mng. dir.; project mgr. Kansas Showcase of Solar Homes, Wichita, 1983—; vice chmn. Petroleu, Inc., 1987; pres. Amortibanc Investment Co., Inc., 1987. Del. White House Conf. on Youth, Estes Park, Colo., 1971; bd. dirs. Wichita Community Theater, 1982—; trustee Garvey Kans. Found., Wichita, 1982—; mem. Leadership Kans., 1982-83; trustee Plymouth Congl. Ch., Wichita, 1982—; mem. Gov.'s Task Force on Pre-sch. Handicapped Children, Kans., 1983-84; exec. com. Wichita Com. on Fgn. Relations, 1984—. Mem. Kans. Ind. Oil and Gas Assn., Nat. Assn. Realtors, Nat. Assn. Home Builders, Am. Solar Energy Soc., Beta Gamma Sigma, Sigma Iota Epsilon, Delta Upsilon. Lodge: Rotary. Home: 808 Brookfield Wichita KS 67206 Office: Global Resources/ Garvey Industries 300 W Douglas #1000 Wichita KS 67202

GARVIN, ALFRED DARRAGH, education educator; b. Chgo., Mar. 14, 1920; s. Frank Hunt and Catherine Elizabeth (MacDonough) G.; m. Myrna Morse Macklin, July 12, 1943 (dec. Sept. 1983); children: Virginia Morse, Patricia Garvin Held; m. Mary Ann Dameron, June 9, 1984. BS, U.S. Naval Acad., 1941; MA, U. Md., 1964, PhD, 1968. Commd. ensign USN, 1941, advanced through grades to commdr., 1954, retired, 1965; prof. edn. U. Cin., 1968-85, prof. emeritus, 1985—; research cons. Cin. Pub. Schs., 1968-85. Author: Shortcuts in Mathematics, 1973, Discovery Problems, 1975, Applied Statistics, 1977, Probability in Your Life, 1979. Decorated Bronze Star with two oak leaf clusters, Legion of Merit. Republican. Avocation: flying. Home: 1504 Hollywood Ave Cincinnati OH 45224

GARVIN, CHARLES DAVID, social work educator, researcher, consultant, therapist; b. Chgo., June 17, 1929; s. Hyman and Etta (Raphaelson) G.; m. Janet Louise Tuft, Jan. 27, 1957; children: David, Amy, Tony. AM, U. Chgo., 1951, PhD, 1968. Cert. social worker. Social worker Henry Booth House, Chgo., 1948-56, Jewish Community Ctrs., Chgo., 1956-64; research assoc. U. Chgo., 1964-65; prof. U. Mich., Ann Arbor, 1965—; chmn. Com. for the Advancement of Social Work with Groups, N.Y.C., 1982-86. Author: The Work Incentive Experience, 1974, Contemporary Group Work, 1981, Interpersonal Practice in Social Work, 1985, Contemporary Group Work (second edition), 1987; also over 50 articles. Active Model Cities Policy Bd., Ann Arbor, 1970-73. Served to capt. U.S. Army, 1952-54. Grantee U.S. Dept. Labor, 1969-73, U.S. Health Service NIMH, 1986-89; fellow U.S. State Dept., Pakistan, 1973-74. Fellow Am. Orthpsychiat. Assn.;

mem. Am. Sociol. Assn., Nat. Assn. Social Workers, Council on Social Work Edn., Brit. Assn. Social Workers. Jewish. Home: 2925 Park Ridge Dr Ann Arbor MI 48103 Office: Univ Mich 1065 Frieze Bldg Ann Arbor MI 48109

GARVIN, GREGORY LLOYD, osteopathic physician; b. Davenport, Iowa, June 29, 1949; s. I. J. and Doris Juanita (Caulk) G.; m. Donna M. Norman, Dec. 28, 1973; children—Gregory, II, Gretchen, Andrew. Student St. Ambrose Coll., 1968; B.S., Tulane U., 1971; D.O., Kirksville Coll. Osteo. Medicine. Intern, Davenport (Iowa) Osteo. Hosp., 1976-78; resident in gen. pediatrics Normandy Osteo. Hosp., St. Louis, 1978; postdoctoral fellow in gen. and acute care pediatrics Cardinal Glennon Meml Hosp., St. Louis, 1979; practice osteo. medicine specializing in pediatrics, Davenport, 1979—; dir. Neonatal Intensive Care Nursery, St. Luke's Hosp., 1982-83; chmn. pediatrics Davenport Med. Ctr., 1979—; mem. staff Mercy Hosp., chief pediatrics, 1986—. Mem. med. care evaluation com. Iowa Found. for Med. Care; past pres., bd. dirs. Community Health Care; past bd. dirs. Am. Cancer Soc. Recipient 1st place award Pediatric Residents Writing Contest, 1979. Mem. Scott County Med. Soc. (exec. com.), Scott County Osteo. Soc., Iowa Soc. Osteo. Physicians and Surgeons (membership chmn. 1981, trustee, mem. ho. of dels. 1981, 82, 83), Am. Osteo. Assn., Iowa Osteo. Med. Assn., Davenport Osteo. Hosp. Assn. (bd. dirs.), Miss. Valley Ind. Physicians Assn. (past pres., now chmn. utilization, bd. dirs.), Davenport C. of C. (human resources com.), Soc. for Preservation of Barbershop Quartet Singing in Am. (membership v.p.), Davenport Chordbusters (baritone, tenor), Tri Beta, Sigma Chi. Republican. Methodist. Lodges: Kiwanis (Bettendorf), Masons. Mem. editorial bd. Hawkeye Osteo. Jour.

GARVIN, JOAN LA VONNE, educational administrator, educator; b. St. Peter, Minn., Mar. 6, 1936; d. Harold John and Pearl Verna (Wendelschafer) G. BS, Mankato State U., 1958, MS, 1968.Cert. elem. tchr., Minn. Tchr., program adminstr. pub. schs., Minn. and Calif., 1958-72; project dir. Bloomington (Minn.) Pub. Schs., 1972-76, instructional generalist, elem. schs., 1976-80, coordinator staff devel. programs, 1980—; cons. in health edn. field. Bd. dirs. Am. Lung Assn. Minn., 1983-86; state rep. Trans-Nat. Golf Assn., 1975-86. Recipient several state golf titles and awards, 1966—, Paul Schmidt award Minn. Assn. for Health, Phys. Edn., Recreation and Dance, 1978, Disting. Alumna Service award Mankato State U., 1983, Community Service award Am. Lung Assn. Minn., 1985; Joan Garvin Sports Classic award named in her honor Mankato State U., 1977; inducted into Athletic Hall of Fame, Mankato State U., 1980. Mem. Minn. Assn. for Supervision and Curriculum Devel. (bd. dirs. 1978-79), Nat. Staff Devel. Council, Am. Fedn. Tchrs., Minn. Fedn. Tchrs., Minn. Women's Golf Assn., Mankato State U. Alumni Assn. (alumni bd. dirs. 1985-86), Delta Kappa Gamma, Phi Delta Kappa, Pi Lambda Theta. Home: 8569 Dunkirk Ln Maple Grove MN 55369 Office: Bloomington Pub Schs 8900 Portland Ave S Bloomington MN 55420

GARVIN, THOMAS MICHAEL, food products company executive; b. Chgo., 1935; married. BSC, Loyola U., 1957, MBA, 1969. CPA. With Lybrand Ross Bros. & Montgomery, 1957-61; controller Ekco Products Co., 1962-65; group controller Am. Home Products Co., 1966-69; controller Keebler Co., Elmhurst, Ill., 1969-70, v.p. fin. and treas., from 1970, then exec. v.p. ops., now pres., chief exec. officer, also bd. dirs. Office: Keebler Co One Hollow Tree Ln Elmhurst IL 60126 *

GARVIN, WILLIAM FRANCIS, orthopaedic surgeon; b. Boston, July 8, 1946; s. William Henry and Catherine Frances (Curley) G.; m. Jeanne Marie Murphy, June 3, 1972; children: Brian Patrick, Paul Francis. BS, Boston Coll., 1968; MD, Boston U., 1972. Diplomate Am. Bd. Orthopaedic Surgery. Surg. intern Albany Med. Ctr. Hosp., N.Y.C., 1972-74; resident in orthopaedic surgery Carney and Affiliated Hosps., Boston, 1975-77; fellow in hand surgery U. Miami, Fla., 1980, Tufts U., Boston, 1978; practice medicine specializing in orthopaedic surgery Lincoln, Nebr., 1981—; bd. dirs. Lincoln Med. Edn. Found., 1985—; chmn. dept. orthopaedic surgery St. Elizabeth's Hosp., Lincoln, 1986. Served to maj. USAF, 1978-80. Fellow Am. Acad. Orthopaedic Surgeons; mem. AMA, Nebr. Med. Assn., Am. Assn. Hand Surgery, Mid Cen. States Orthopaedic Soc. Clubs: University, Hillcrest Country (Lincoln). Avocations: jogging, skiing, skating. Home: 1640 Buckingham Dr Lincoln NE 68506 Office: 600 N Cotner Blvd Lincoln NE 68505

GARY, EUGENE LEE, real estate company executive, consultant; b. Cleve., Apr. 6, 1929; s. David B. and Ruth I. (Levine) G.; m. Gerry Horowitz, Mar. 18, 1951 (div. 1977); children—Joel, H., Jamie S.; m. Joan Gary, 1986. BCS, Ohio State U., 1951. Owner, pres. Ohio Motor Sales, Lorain, 1951-78; sec.-treas. Shiff-Gary Inc., Lorain, 1979—; cons., officer Wedgewood Inc., G & S Inc., SSS & G Inc., Gary Enterprises. Active, Lorain Jewish Welfare. Mem. Lorain C. of C., Phi Sigma Delta (founder). Jewish. Clubs: Oak Hill Country (Lorain), Elks (Lorain), A.B.I. Men's.

GARY, JAMES FRANCIS, mental health counselor, educational counselor; b. Chgo., Feb. 22, 1943; m. Sylvia A. Gary; children: Marc, Daniel. BA, Lewis U., 1965; MS, No. Ill. U., 1967. Cert. mental health counselor, Ill. Counselor Maine Twp. High Sch., Des Plaines, Ill., 1966—, Maryville Acad., Des Plaines, 1967-82; clin. mental health counselor J.F. Gary, Ltd., Elk Grove, Ill., 1976—. Mem. Am. Assn. Counseling and Devel., Ill. Edn. Assn., Nat. Assn. Cert. Clin. Mental Health Counselors. Office: 100 Turner Ave Elk Grove Village IL 60007

GASKIN, KATHLEEN ALICE, real estate brokerage executive; b. Lansing, Mich., Nov. 29, 1941; d. Roger J. and Mary A. (Lilly) Small; m. Karl A. H. Bohnhoff, Oct. 7, 1961 (div. 1970); children—Karl A., Kandice A.; m. Keith L. Gaskin, May 23, 1970; Student Grace Brethern coll., 1959-60, Mich. State U., 1961-62. Lic. broker, Mich. Customer rep. Xerox Corp., Buffalo, 1963-65; vehicle scheduler Ford Motor Co., Lansing, 1965-66; customer rep. Xerox Corp., Lansing, 1966-68; sales rep. Simon Real Estate, Lansing, 1968-77; pres. Century 21 Gaskin Realty, Lansing, 1977—; instr. in real estate sales Lansing Community Coll., 1975-82; dir. Capitol Nat. Bank, Lansing. Recipient Centurion award Century 21 Internat., 1983, 84, 85, 86; Gold Medallion award Century 21 Internat., 1983, 84. Mem. Lansing C. of C., Lansing Bd. Realtors (bd. dirs. 1978-80, sec. 1979, Life Mem. Million Dollar Club, First Woman to obtain Million Dollar Club). Republican. Club: Walnut Hills Country (Lansing). Avocation: golf. Home: 1424 Somerset Close East Lansing MI 48823 Office: Century 21 Gaskin Realty 1601 E Grand River St Lansing MI 48906

GASPAR, TIMOTHY MICHAEL, nurse, educator, consultant; b. Sioux Falls, S.D., Aug. 27, 1955; s. Michael Phillip and Madelyn Alice Gaspar; B.S. in Nursing, S.D. State U., 1977; M.S.N., U. Nebr., 1981. Asst. in nursing S.D. State U., Brookings, 1978-79, instr., 1981-84, asst. prof., 1984—; research assoc. U. Nebr., Omaha, 1980-81; nursing cons. Crowell Meml. Home, Blair, Nebr., 1980-81. Mem. Am. Nurses Assn., S.D. Nurses Assn., Midwest Nursing Research Soc., Oncology Nursing Soc., Western Soc. for Nursing Research, NEA, Sigma Theta Tau. Home: 2256 Foothill Dr Apt F118 Salt Lake City UT 84109 Office: South Dakota State U Coll Nursing PO Box 2275 Brookings SD 57007

GASSER, BRENT PADLEY, resort camp executive; b. Baraboo, Wis., June 23, 1956; s. David Lloyd and Elinore Doris Gasser. B.A., U. Wis., 1978. Ops. mgr. Yogi Bear's Jellystone Park, Wisconsin Dells, Wis., 1978—; supr., purchasing agt. Bear & Co., 1981-82; supr., retailer Happy Acres Grocery, 1981-82. Elder, United Presbyterian Ch., 1983—. Mem. Wis. Assn. Campground Owners (sec., dir. 1983-85), Wisconsin Dells C. of C. Home: PO Box 610 One Gasser Rd Lake Delton WI 53940 Office: Yogi Bear's Jellystone Park PO Box 510 Wisconsin Dells WI 53965

GASSER, RANDALL WILLIAM, accountant; b. Wadsworth, Ohio, May 20, 1958; s. William Carl and Doris Elizabeth (Marty) G.; m. Susan Kaye Stieglitz, Aug. 1, 1982; children: Brady Randall, Alexis Suzanne. BSBA with honors, Bowling Green State U., 1980. CPA, Ohio, Mich. Sr. acct. Ernst & Whinney, Akron, Ohio, 1980-84; mgr. fin. Homecare Resource Mgmt., Inc., Akron, 1984-86; adminstr. Apostolic Christian Woodhaven, Livonia, Mich., 1986—; bd. dirs. MED/PRO Fed. Credit Union, Akron, 1985-86. Crisis counselor SUPPORT, Inc., Akron, 1984-86; cert. emergency med. tech. City of Rittman, Ohio, 1984-86. Mem. Am. Coll. Health Care Adminstrs., Healthcare Fin. Mgmgt. Assn., Am. Inst. CPA's, Ohio Soc. CPA's. Republican. Apostolic Christian. Avocations: jogging, music, traveling. Home: 14900 Arcola Livonia MI 48154-3926 Office: Apostolic Christian Woodhaven 29667 Wentworth Ave Livonia MI 48154-3256

GASSMAN, MAX PAUL, mechanical engineer; b. Bonesteel, S.D., Sept. 1, 1930; s. Walter Ernest and Elizabeth (Schibli) G.; B.S. in Mech. Engring., S.D. Sch. Mines and Tech., 1956; M. Mech. Engring., Iowa State U., 1963; m. Gail Elizabeth Evans, Aug. 5, 1955; children—Paul Michael, Philip Walter. With John Deere Co., Waterloo, Iowa, 1956-85, sr. design engr., 1965-68, sr. design analyst, 1968-79, diagnostic coordinator, 1979-83; prof. mech. engring. Iowa State U., 1985—; v.p. John C. Rider & Assos., Inc., 1976-79. Cubmaster, Winnebago Council Boy Scouts Am., 1967-70, scoutmaster, 1970-74. Pres. bd. dirs. Splash Inc., 1970; pres. Lord of Life Luth. Ch., Waterloo. Served with USAF, 1948-52. Registered profl. engr., Iowa. Mem. Nat. Soc. Profl. Engrs. (chmn. Iowa sect. profl. engrs. in industry group), Iowa Engring. Soc. (pres. bd. dirs. N.E. Iowa 1971-72, Anson Marston award 1972), ASME (dir. 1971-72, 85-87), Waterloo Tech. Soc. (chmn. tech. student activity com. 1970-71), Am. Soc. Agrl. Engrs. (vice chmn. T-5 computer com. 1983-84), Soc. Automotive Engrs. Club: John Deere Supervisors (Waterloo). Patentee in field. Home: 4105 Phoenix St Ames IA 50010 Office: Iowa State U Ames IA 50011

GASSMANN, HENRY, insurance company executive; b. Olney, Ill., Nov. 8, 1927; s. Zean Goudy and Gertrude (Weber) G.; m. Patricia Louise Zuber, Feb. 11, 1956; children—Louis, Mary, Zean, James, John, Frank, Neal. B.S., U. Ill., 1949; M.B.A., U. Mich., 1950. With Zean Gassmann Co., Olney, Ill., 1950—, owner, 1981—; dir. Olney Trust Bank, Rich Land Bancorp. Mem. adv. bd. Ill. Dept. Ins., 1981-86; mem. citizens com. U. Ill., 1958—; chmn. Richland County Republican Central Com., 1976—; chmn. 54th Rep. Legis. Dist., 1982—; chmn. 107th Rep. Rep. Dist., 1982—; v.p. Ill. Rep. County Chmns. Assn., 1982—; pres. Richland Heritage Found., 1984-85. Served with USN, 1945-47. Mem. Ind. Ins. Agts. Am., Ind. Ins. Agts. Ill., Am. Legion. Republican. Roman Catholic. Club: Petroleum. Lodges: Rotary, Elks. Home: 316 N Elliott St Olney IL 62450 Office: 313 Whittle Ave Olney IL 62450

GAST, MARK ANTHONY, tax administrator; b. Kansas City, Kans., July 5, 1954; s. Edward and Edith Louise (Stumpff) G.; m. Glenda Ann Jones, June 2, 1984. BSBA, Rockhurst Coll., 1976; MBA, U. Kansas, 1977; MS in Taxation, U. Mo., Kansas City, 1987. CPA, Kans., Mo. Instr. U. Kans., Lawrence, 1976-77; tax specialist Peat, Marwick, Mitchell & Co., Kansas City, Mo., 1978-81; tax mgr. Panhandle Eastern Pipe Line Co., Kansas City, 1981—. Mem. Am. Inst. CPA's, Mo. Soc. CPA's, Alpha Sigma Nu, Beta Gamma Sigma. Democrat. Roman Catholic. Avocation: sports. Home and Office: 11421 W 106th St Overland Park KS 66214

GASTA, WILLIAM LEONARD, gas company executive; b. Bay City, Mich., Mar. 4, 1940; s. Chester Carl and Romaine (Stasinski) G.; m. Sara Catherine Lyman, May 19, 1962; children: Maria, Steven, Thomas, Rebecca. AA in Gen. Studies, Bay City Jr. Coll., 1961; BS in Indsl. Engring., Ea. Mich. U., 1969. Registered landscape architect, Ind.; lic. pilot FAA. Designer Johnson, Johnson & Roy, Ann Arbor, Mich., 1967-69; supr. Inland div. Gen. Motors, Dayton, Ohio, 1969-78; project engr. GMAD div. Gen. Motors, Arlington, Tex., 1978-80; supt. Detroit Diesel Allison, Indpls., 1980—; mem. City-Wide Devel. Corp., Dayton, 1974-75; cons., prin. BG & Assocs., Indpls., 1982—. Chmn. project devel. com. Model Cities Program, Dayton, 1975. Recipient Cert. Appreciation Mayor James McGee, Dayton, 1974; Eastern Mich. U. scholar, 1968. Mem. Am. Soc. Landscape Architects (assoc.). Roman Catholic. Lodge: Kiwanis (bd. dirs. N.W. Indpls. 1985-86), Elks. Home: 3212 Babson Ct Indianapolis IN 46268 Office: Detroit Diesel Allison PO Box 894 M-36 Indianapolis IN 46206

GASTMAN, IRVIN JOSEPH, physician, bio-medical physicist, consultant computer applications to medicine; b. N.Y.C., June 5, 1944; s. Adolph A. and Anna R. (Karp) G.; m. Eda Halpern, July 3, 1967; children—Brian Reuben, Rebecca Rachael, Michelle Ann. M.S. in Elec. Engring., CCNY, 1967; Ph.D. in Bio-Med. Physics, U. Mich., 1974; D.O., Mich. State U., 1977. Diplomate Nat. Bd. Med. Examiners; registered profl. engr., N.Y. Family practice medicine, Pontiac, Mich., 1976—; mem. faculty Mich. State U., 1974—; cons. various ins. groups. Bd. dirs. Jewish Community Center Mich.; trustee Holocost Meml. Center. NDEA fellow, 1966-68. Mem. Am. Osteo. Assn., Mich. Assn. Physicians & Surgeons, Oakland Osteo. Physicians & Surgeons. Contbr. articles to profl. jours. Patentee ultrasound field. Home: 1710 Morningside Way Bloomfield Hills MI 48013 Office: 3560 Pontiac Lake Rd Pontiac MI 48054

GASTON, GREGG STEVEN, accountant; b. Steubenille, Ohio, Oct. 12, 1959; s. Stanley Allan and Carole Terry (Willis) G. BS in Acctg., U. Akron, 1983. CPA, Ohio. Staff acct. Bruner, Cox, Lotz, Syler & Graves, Canton, Ohio, 1983-86; internal auditor GenCorp, Akron, Ohio, 1986—. Bd. dirs. Canton Jaycees, 1986—. Mem. Am. Inst. CPA's, Ohio Soc. CPA's, Canton C. of C. (hall of fame grand parade com. 1986). Republican. Avocations: swimming, water skiing, reading, golf. Home: 740 Manor Ave SW Canton OH 44701 Office: Bruner Cox Lotz Syler Grave 500 Ameritrust Bldg Canton OH 44702

GASTON, HUGH PHILIP, marriage counselor, educator; b. St. Paul, Sept. 12, 1910; s. Hugh Philander and Gertrude (Heine) G.; B.A., U. Mich., 1937, M.A., 1941; postgrad. summers Northwestern U., 1938, Yale U., 1959; m. Charlotte E. Clarke, Oct. 1, 1945 (dec. 1960); children—Gertrude E. Gaston Crippen, George Hugh. Counselor, U. Mich., Ann Arbor, 1936; tchr., counselor W. K. Kellogg Found., Battle Creek, Mich., 1937-41; tchr. spl. edn., Detroit, 1941; instr. airplane wing constrn. Briggs Mfrs. Co., Detroit, 1942; psychologist VA, 1946-51; sr. staff asso. Sci. Research Asso., Chgo., 1951-55; marriage counselor Circuit Ct., Ann Arbor, 1955-60; pvt. practice marriage counseling, Ann Arbor, 1955—; former chief Guidance Center, U. Mich. and Mich. State U.; lectr., Eastern Mich. U., Ypsilanti, 1964-67, asst. prof., 1967-81; mem. Study Group for Health Care of Elderly, China, USSR, 1983, Profl. Study Group on Family Affairs, USSR, 1986. Acting postmaster, Ann Arbor, 1960-61. Chmn. Wolverine Boys State, Am. Legion, 1957-86; chmn. com. on Christian marriage Presbyn. So. Mich., 1962-69; mem. exec. com., legis. agt., chmn. legis. com. Mich. Council Family Relations, 1972-74; bd. dirs. Internat. Parents Without Partners, 1968-69, 1st pres. Mich. chpt., 1961; bd. dirs. Ann Arbor Sr. Citizens, 1982-85, Washtenaw County Council Alcoholism, 1982-84. Served with U.S. Army, 1943-46. Decorated Purple Heart (2), Bronze Star; Medallion of Nice (France); named Citizen of Year, Am. Legion, 1968, Single Parent of Yr., 1978. Mem. Am. Assn. Marriage Counselors, Circumnavigators Club, Am. Personnel and Guidance Assn., Nat. Vocat. Guidance Assn., D.A.V. (past comdr.), Am. Soc. Tng. Dirs., Mich. Indsl. Tng. Council (charter), SAR (past pres.), U. Mich. Band Alumni Assn. (pres. 1957-58), Mil. Order Purple Heart (nat. exec. com. 1977-82, 1st comdr. chpt. 459 Mich., state comdr. Mich. 1984-85, nat. historian 1981-85), Phi Delta Kappa (past pres. U. Mich.). Lodge: Rotary. Address: 1404 Cambridge Rd Ann Arbor MI 48104

GASTWIRTH, BART WAYNE, podiatrist; b. Mineola, N.Y., Feb. 11, 1953; s. Milton and Janette (Wasserman) G.; m. Gwen Kaufman, Nov. 2, 1954; children: Seth, Jennifer. Student, U. Hartford, 1971-73; D of Podiatric Medicine, Ill. Coll. Podiatric Medicine, 1977. Diplomate Am. Bd. Podiatric Othopedics. Gen. practice podiatric medicine Arlington Heights, Ill., 1977—; instr. dept. med. sci. Ill. Coll. Podiatric Medicine, Chgo., 1979-80, asst. prof. podiatric medicine, 1980-81; assoc. prof., chmn. dept. orthopedic scis. Scholl Coll. Podiatric Medicine, Chgo., 1981—; med. dir. Langer Biomechanics Lab., Chgo., 1986—. Contbg. editor Jour. Foot Surgery, 1981—. Mem. Am. Coll. Foot Surgeons, Am. Podiatric Med. Assn. (Appreciation award Am. Podiatric Med. Students Assn. 1986), Am. Pub. Health Assn. (sec. 1973, Podiatric Health Sect. award 1977), Ill. Podiatric Med. Assn. (treas. 1985-86, sec. 1986-87). Office: Northpoint Podiatry Ctr 348 E Rand Rd Arlington Heights IL 60004

GASTWIRTH, CRAIG MARSHALL, podiatrist; b. Mineola, N.Y., Mar. 1, 1950; s. Milton and Jeannette Gastwirth; m. Cheryl Zeltzer, June 23, 1973; children: Stacy Michelle, Andrew Jay. BA, Rutgers U., 1972; D Podiatric Medicine, N.Y.C. Coll. Podiatric Medicine, 1976. Diplomate Am. Bd. Podiatric Surgery. Practice medicine specializing in podiatrics Detroit, 1977—; clin. supr. Kern Hosp., Warren, Mich., 1980-85; chief podiatry sect. Westland Med. Ctr., Westland, Mich., 1985—; specialty advisor Mich. Peer Rev. Orgn.; disability evaluation specialist Aetna Ins. Co.; adj. faculty Ohio Coll. Podiatric Medicine. Assoc. editor Jour. Foot Surgery, 1981—. Cert. of Appreciation, Midwest Podiatry Conf., 1980, 84. Fellow Am. Coll. Foot Surgeons, Am. Soc. Podiatric Dermatology; mem. Am. Podiatric Med. Assn., Am. Pub. Health Assn. (chmn. podiatric sect. 1982-84, Disting. Service award 1976, 84), Mich Podiatric Med. Assn. (pres. southeast div. 1981-82), Mich. Health Council, Greater Detroit Area Health Council, Met. Detroit Health Edn. Council. Jewish. Avocations: racquetball, basketball, softball. Home: 6648 Aldersley Way West Bloomfield MI 48033 Office: 3800 Woodward Ave Suite 318 Detroit MI 48201

GATENBEE, ROBERT JAMES, aeronautical engineer; b. Louisville, Nov. 9, 1937; s. Robert James and Mary Elizabeth (Robbins) G.; m. Sara Frances Hart, Oct. 19, 1968; Elizabeth Kathryn, Robert Andrews. B in Mech. Engring., U. Louisville, 1961, M in Mech. Engring., 1974. Gen. engr. Wright Patterson AFB, Ohio, 1960-75; dep. dir. Multinational Programs, Wright Patterson AFB, 1975-82; asst. div. chief Brussels, 1982-83, tech. advisor, 1983-85; supr., mgr. aquisition F-16 SPO, Wright-Patterson AFB, Ohio, 1985—. Mem. Am. Inst. Astronautics and Aeronautics, Am. Rocket Soc. (pres. 1959-60), Soc. Space Freefloaters, Admirals Club, Nat. Model Railroad Assn. Republican. Episcopalian. Home: 7281 Candlewyck Ct Centerville OH 45459 Office: ASD/YPLF Wright Patterson AFB OH 45433

GATES, CHARLES ALBERT, JR., manufacturing executive; b. Peoria, Ill., Aug. 28, 1945; s. Charles Albert and Dorothy Marie (Crowley) G.; m. Sara Ann Brettner, July 11, 1964; children: Timothy, Thomas, Tedmund. AAS in Mfg. Tech., Ill. Cen. Coll., 1976; BA in Mgmt., Sangamon State U., 1980; MS in Indsl. Tech., Purdue U., 1984. cert. mfg. engr. Mgr. mgmt. devel., edn. and tng. Caterpillar Tractor Co., Lafayette, Ind., 1980-83, mgr. planning and tooling, 1983-85, mgr. tech. services, 1985—. Mem. Lafayette Sch. Corp. Challenge Program, 1986; chmn. firm campaign Lafayette United Way, 1981. Mem. Soc. Mfr. Engrs. (chmn. edn. com.), Lafayette C. of C., Pvt. Industry Council, Ind. High Sch. Athletic Assn., Western Ind. Officials Assn. (scheduling chmn.). Avocations: football and basketball officiating, writing. Home: 40 Joye Ct Lafayette IN 47905 Office: Caterpillar Inc 3701 SR 26 E Lafayette IN 47905

GATES, CHARLES CASSIUS, rubber company executive; b. Morrison, Colo., May 27, 1921; s. Charles Cassius and Hazel LaDora (Rhoads) G.; m. June Scowcroft Swaner, Nov. 26, 1943; children: Diane, John Swaner. Student, MIT, 1939-41; B.S., Stanford U., 1943; D.Eng. (hon.), Mich. Tech. U., 1975, Colo. Sch. of Mines, 1985. With Copolymer Corp., Baton Rouge, 1943-46; with Gates Rubber Co., Denver, 1946—, v.p., 1951-58, exec. v.p., 1958-61, chmn. bd., 1961—; chmn. bd., chief exec. officer The Gates Corp., 1982—; chmn. bd. Gates Learjet Corp., Wichita, Kans.; dir. Hamilton Bros. Petroleum Corp., Denver, Robinson Brick Co., Denver. Pres., trustee Gates Found.; pres. bd. trustees Denver Mus. Natural History. Recipient Community Leadership and Service award Nat. Jewish Hosp., 1974; Mgmt. Man of Year award Nat. Mgmt. Assn., 1965; named March of Dimes Citizen of the West, 1987. Mem. Conf. Bd. (dir.), Conquistadores del Cielo. Clubs: Denver Country, Cherry Hills Country, Denver, Outrigger Canoe, Waialae Country, Boone and Crockett, Club Ltd, Country Club of Colo, Roundup Riders of Rockies, Shikar-Safari Club Internat. (dir.), Augusta Nat. Golf, Castle Pines Golf.

GATES, CRAWFORD MARION, conductor, composer; b. San Francisco, Dec. 29, 1921; s. Gilbert Marion and Leila (Adair) G.; m. Georgia Lauper, Dec. 19, 1952; children: Stephen Randall, Kathryn, Elizabeth, David Wendell. B.A., San Jose State Coll., 1944; M.A., Brigham Young U., 1948; Ph.D., Eastman Sch. Music, 1954. Grad. asst. music theory Eastman Sch. Music, 1948-50; faculty Brigham Young U., 1950-66, prof. music, chmn. dept., 1960-66; artist-in-residence Beloit (Wis.) Coll., 1966—, chmn. dept. music, 1982-87; owner Pacific Publs. (music pubs.), Provo, Beloit, 1948—. Free-lance orchestrator, 1946—, orchestrator radio, Sta. KSL, Salt Lake City, 1946-47, music dir., condr., Beloit-Janesville Symphony Orch., 1963-64, 66—, music dir., Quincy (Ill.) Symphony Orch., 1969-70, Rockford (Ill.) Symphony Orch., 1970-86; asst. to music dir. Broadway prodn. Redhead, 1958; guest condr., Utah Symphony, numerous others; composer: Utah Centennial mus. play Promised Valley, 1947; Hill Cumorah Pageant, Palmyra, N.Y., 1957,, commns. for religious ednl. films and Utah Symphony, U. Utah, numerous others; author: Catalog of Published American Choral Music, rev. edit. Mem. gen. bd. Mut. Improvement Assn., Ch. Jesus Christ of Latter-day Saints, 1949-66, mem. gen. music com., 1960-73. Served with USNR, World War II, PTO. Recipient Max Wald Meml. Fund award N.Y.C., 1955; ASCAP standard award annually, 1965—. Mem. Nat. Fedn. Music Clubs (nat. choral chmn. 1951-53, 69-71), ASCAP. Club: Timpanogos (Salt Lake City). Home: 911 Park Ave Beloit WI 53511 Office: Miles Music Ctr Beloit Coll Beloit WI 53511

GATES, MARTINA MARIE, food products company executive; b. Mpls., Mar. 19, 1957; d. John Thomas and Colette Clara (Luetmer) G. BSBA in Mktg. Mgmt. cum laude, Coll. St. Thomas, 1979, postgrad., 1984—. Tchrs. asst. Mpls. Area Vocat. Tech. Inst., Mpls., 1978-79; sec., regional sales mgr. Internat. Multifoods, Mpls., 1979, sec. bakery mix, mktg. mgr., 1979-80, sec., v.p. sales and new bus. devel., 1980, customer service rep. regional accounts, 1980-81, customer service rep. nat. accounts, 1981-82, credit coordinator indsl. foods div., 1982-85, asst. credit mgr. consumer foods div., 1985, advt./sales promotion mgr. indsl. foods div., 1985-86, asst. credit mgr. fast food and restaurant div., 1986—. Vol. seamstress Guthrie Theater Costume Shop, Mpls., 1975—; alumni mem. New Coll. Student Adv. Council St. Thomas, St. Paul, 1984—; vol. Mpls. Aquatennial, 1987. Mem. Omicron Delta Epsilon. Avocations: golf, music, sewing, tennis, biking.

GATES-JOHNSON, KRISTIN MARIE, psychologist; b. Northfield, Minn., Apr. 18, 1958; d. Frank Dale and Evelyn Rosetta (Barsness) Gates; m. Jon Bradley Johnson, June 4, 1983. BS, U. Minn., 1980; MA, Western Mich. U., 1985. Lic. classroom tchr. Minn., Mich. Mgr. retail store Mulberry Bush Inc., Winona, Minn., 1980-81; tchr. grade 4 Ind. Sch. dist. #659, Northfield, 1981-82, tchr. grade 3, 1982-83; psychologist Battle Creek (Mich.) Adventist Hosp., 1985-86; research psychologist U.S. Army, Ft. Riley, Kansas, 1986—; tutor Northfield Pub. Schs., 1981-82; crisis worker Victim Support, Northfield, Minn., 1981-82, Western Mich. U., Kalamazoo, 1985; vol. day treatment Borgess Hosp. Mental Health Kalamazoo, 1984. Republican. Lutheran. Avocations: running, fishing, water sports, downhill skiing, painting. Home: 1837 Concord Ln Manhattan KS 66442 Office: US Army Correctional Activity Research & Evaluation Div Bldg 1970 Camp Funston Fort Riley KS 66442

GATHERUM, PATRICIA BRANDLEY, public relations executive; b. Salt Lake City, Oct. 2, 1926; d. Ralph Canton and Nellie Emeline (Sutton) Brandley; m. Gordon Elwood Gatherum, July 31, 1947; children—Laurie Patricia, Mark Gordon, Kristin Lee. B.A., U. Utah, 1947; M.A., Ohio State U., 1980. Editorial asst. Miller Freeman Pubs., Seattle, 1947-49; librarian Ames Pub. Library, Iowa, 1964-69; chief reference librarian Ohio Hist. Soc., Columbus, 1969-74, devel./membership officer, 1974-79; community services mgr. Nationwide Ins., Columbus, Ohio, 1979—. Contbr. articles to profl. jours. Bd. dirs. Epilepsy Assn. Central Ohio. Democrat. Club: Columbus Met. (bd. dirs.). Avocations: reading; walking; cross-country skiing; jazz and classical music. Home: 5710 Strathmore Ln Dublin OH 43017 Office: Nationwide Ins Cos One Nationwide Plaza Columbus OH 43216

GATHMAN, JAMES DENIS, real estate investment company executive; b. Chgo., Dec. 23, 1941; s. James Arthur and Helen Mary (Konkolitz) B.; m. Julianne Clare Thompson; children—Alaina, Joseph, Matthew, Michael, Justin, Christopher. B.B.A. in Fin., Loyola u., 1963. Real estate appraiser Talman Fed. Savs. and Loan, Chgo., 1963-74; v.p., dir. Real Estate Research Corp., Chgo., 1974-83; sr. v.p. VMS Realty, Inc., Chgo., 1983—. Contbr. articles to profl. publs., chpts. to books. Mem. Am. Inst. Real Estate Appraisers, Soc. Real Estate Appraisers, Am. Arbitration Assn., Lambda

Alpha. Roman Catholic. Home: 509 S Patton St Arlington Heights IL 60005 Office: VMS Realty Inc 8700 W Bryn Mawr St Chicago IL 60631

GATTOZZI, ANGELO LUCIANO, electrical company executive; b. Matrice, Italy, Dec. 12, 1947; s. Domenico Germano and Angiolina (Appugliese) G.; m. Marianna Storto, Dec. 27, 1984. BS, Case Western U., 1971, MS, 1975, PhD, 1978; cert. acctg., John Carroll U., 1976. CPA, Ohio. Elec. engr. Reliance Electric, Cleve., 1974-77, project mgr., 1977-80; pres. Tyler Power Systems Inc., Mentor, Ohio, 1980—. Contbr. articles to tech. jours. Mem. IEEE, ASTM, Am. Mathematical Assn., Am. Inst. CPA's, Ohio Soc. CPA's, Am. Soc. Quality Control, N.Y. Acad. Sci. Roman Catholic. Home: 2110 Apple Dr Euclid OH 44143 Office: Tyler Power Systems Inc 8648 Tyler Blvd Mentor OH 44060

GATYAS, NANCY CAROL, education educator; b. Green Bay, Wis., Aug. 27, 1933; d. Bernard Charles and Leonora Petra (Jorgensen) Sleger; m. Frank Gatyas, Nov. 4, 1950; children: Frank, Kenton. Grad., Sheboygan County Tchrs. Coll., 1971; BA, Lakeland Coll., 1979; MA in Reading, Cardinal Stritch Coll., 1983. Cert. tchr., Wis. Tchr. elem. schs. Plymouth, 1970-84; instr. speed reading U. Wis., Sheboyhan, Wis., 1984; reading specialist Riverview Middle Sch., Plymouth, 1982-84, Middleton-Cross Plains Schs., Wis., 1984—. Chmn. Plymouth Conservation Drives, 1974-81; active Dept. Agr. Mem. Wis. State Reading Assn. Republican. Lutheran. Clubs: Monroe Woman's, (program chmn. 1987—), Plymouth Woman's (pres. 1970-72), Sheboygan County Woman's (pres. 1972-74). Avocation: swimming. Home: 2618 22nd Ave Monroe WI 53566

GATZ, STEPHEN EDWARD, engineer, consultant; b. Sterling, Ill., Sept. 20, 1960; s. Russell Wayne and Carleen Edna (Leno) G.; m. Laura Bernice Thetard, June 19, 1982; children: Charles Wayne, Lawrence Edward. BS, Valparaiso U., 1982. Assoc. engr. Underwriters Labs, Northbrook, Ill., 1982-85; product engr. Wahl Clipper Corp., Sterling, 1985—; cons. Sterling Engring. Cons. Services, 1986—. Inventor stubble device. Mem. IEEE. Lutheran. Avocation: competive cyclist. Home: 5206 Spruce St PO Box 22 Galt IL 61037 Office: Sterling Engring Cons Services PO Box 193 Sterling IL 61081

GAUCI, LOUIS EMMANUEL, architect, cultural organization executive; b. Mtarfa, Malta, Mar. 24, 1948; came to U.S., 1950; s. Anthony Paul and Phyllis (Sammut) G.; m. Maureen Grace O'Connell, June 16, 1973; children: Gianina, Maria. Student, Lawrence Inst. Tech., 1966-69; BArch, U. Detroit, 1973. Project architect Muchow and Ptnrs., Denver, 1976-79, Hoover Berg Desmond, Denver, 1979-80; dir. of design John Hilberry and Assocs., Detroit, 1980-84; chief designer Founders Soc. Detroit Inst. Arts, 1984-85, group dir., exhibitions and design, 1985—; instr. Met. State Coll., Denver, 1976, Wayne State U., 1980, U. Detroit, 1982-84. Archtl. designer Crystal Gallery, Detroit, 1982, DeSalle Gallery, Detroit, 1983, Dutch, German and English Galleries, 1986, Poplack Gallery, Detroit, 1986. Com. mem. Children's Ctr. Wayne County, Detroit, 1984, 85, 86. Mem. AIA, Mich. Soc. Architects.

GAUGER, OTTILIE ERNSTINE, typesetting, graphic arts and computer services company executive, researcher, consultant; b. Milw., Sept. 8, 1917; d. William and Pauline (Krueger) Heinz; m. Charles Paul Gauger, May 31, 1941; children—Lynn, Charla Gauger Becker. Student various courses in bus. mgmt., behavioral sci. Milw. Area Vocat. Sch., 1959-60, Marquette U., 1961-62. Sec. purchasing agt. Blatz Brewery, Milw., 1936-39; sec. Riverside High Sch., Milw., 1939-43; sec., sales mgr. Wis. Motor Corp., Milw., 1943-45; v.p. research Litho Compositors, Milw., 1950-60; v.p. prodn. C.P. Gauger Co., Milw., 1960-80; v.p., cons. Dataplex Services, Milw., 1980—, also dir.; tchr. typesetting various schs., Wis., 1954-80, Wis. Sch. for Deaf, Goodwill Industries. Pres. Alpha Phi Mothers Aux., Milw., 1970; sec.-treas. Christ Lutheran Ch., Mequon, Wis., 1970-72, Wolf River Lakes Assn., White Lake, Wis., 1984—. Mem. Nat. Cold Type Assn. (charter), Nat. Composition Assn. (charter). Republican. Lodge: Shriners Aux. Avocations: needlework, bicycling, golf, fishing, world travel. Home and Office: 8450 W Forest Home Ave Milwaukee WI 53228

GAUGHAN, JOHN JAMES, radiation oncologist; b. Leetonia, Ohio, May 14, 1922; s. Michael Joseph and Jessie J. (Gallagher) G.; m. Alma Marie; children: Marcia, Sharon, Patricia, Kathleen, Maureen. BS, Adelbert Coll. of Case Western Res. U., Cleve., 1943; MD, St. Louis U., 1946. Diplomate Am. Bd. Radiology. Intern St. John's Hosp., Cleve., 1946-47; resident Chile VA Hosp., Cleve., 1949-52; radiologist Lakewood (Ohio) Hosp., 1952-57, St. John Hosp., 1957-81; radiation oncologist Med. Ctr. Radiologists Luth. Med. Ctr., Cleve., 1981—; chmn. bd. dirs. Physician Ins. Co. Ohio and subs. cos., Pickerington; bd. dirs. Fla. Physician Ins. Co., Jacksonville, Fla. Physician Ins. Co., Indpls. Served to capt. AUS, 1947-49, PTO. Fellow Am. Coll. Radiology; mem. AMA (del.), Am. Soc. Radiation Oncologists, Radiol. Soc. N.Am., Eastern Radiol. Soc., Ohio State Med. Assn. (pres. 1978-79), Acad. Medicine of Cuyahoga County, Acad. Medicine of Cleve. (pres. 1973-74). Club: Westwood Country (Rocky River, Ohio). Avocations: golf, bridge. Home: 4498 W 214th St Fairview Park OH 44126 Office: Med Ctr Radiologists 2609 Franklin Ave Cleveland OH 44113

GAUGHAN, NORBERT F., bishop; b. Pitts., May 30, 1921; s. Thomas L. and Martha (Paczkowska) G. M.A., St. Vincent Coll., Latrobe, Pa., 1944; Ph.D., U. Pitts., 1963; LL.D., Seton Hill Coll., 1963; D.D. (hon.), Lebanon Valley Coll., 1980. Ordained priest Roman Catholic Ch., 1945. Chancellor Diocese of Greensburg, Pa., 1960-75, vicar gen., 1970-75, aux. bishop, 1975-84; bishop Diocese of Gary, Ind., 1984—. Author: Shepherd's Pie, 1978. Bd. dirs. Westmoreland Mus. Art, Greensburg, v.p., 1979—. Avocations: photography; silkscreens. Home: 180 W Joliet Rd Valparaiso IN 46383 Office: Diocese of Gary 9494 Broadway Merrillville IN 46402 *

GAULT, STANLEY CARLETON, manufacturing executive; b. Wooster, Ohio, Jan. 6, 1926; s. Clyde Carleton and Aseneth Briton (Stanley) G.; m. Flo Lucille Kurtz, June 11, 1949; children: Stephen, Christopher, Jennifer. B.A., Coll. of Wooster, 1948. With Gen. Electric Co. (and subs.), 1948-79; v.p. and group exec. maj. appliance bus. group Gen. Electric Co. (and subs.), Louisville, 1970-77; v.p. and sector exec. consumer products and services sector Gen. Electric Co. (and subs.), Fairfield, Conn., 1977; sr. v.p., sector exec. Gen. Electric Co. (Indsl. Products and Components sector), 1977-79; vice chmn. bd. Rubbermaid Inc., Wooster, Ohio, 1980; chmn. bd., chief exec. officer Rubbermaid Inc., 1980—; dir. Avon Products, Inc., Internat. Paper Co., PPG Industries, Inc.; chmn. Nat. Assn. Mfrs.; mem. exec. bd. Nat. Bus. Council for Consumer Affairs, from 1972, vice chmn. subcouncil for product safety, 1972. Trustee Coll. of Wooster. Served with USAAF, 1944-46. Mem. NAM (bd. dirs., chmn. bd. 1986-87). Republican. Methodist. Office: Rubbermaid Inc 1147 Akron Rd Wooster OH 44691

GAUNT, SANDRA L.L., zoology educator; b. St. Charles, Ill., June 16, 1942; s. John M. and E. Louise (Soverign) Lovett; m. Abbot S. Gaunt, Aug. 1963. Student, Middlebury Coll., 1963-64; BA, Kans. U., 1964; student, SUNY, Buffalo, 1967-68; MS, U. Vt., 1968. Teaching asst. Middlebury (Vt.) Coll., 1964-65, U. Vt., Burling, 1966-67; research asst. SUNY, Buffalo, 1967-69; asst. prof. Capital U., Columbus, Ohio, 1973-78; adj. asst. prof. zoology Ohio State U., Columbus, 1978—; curator Borror Lab. Bioacoustics Ohio State U., 1985—. Contbg. author and artist: (textbook) Ornithology in Laboratory and Field, 1985; author: (directory) The Flock, 1985; co-author (jour.) Zoomorphology, 1985. NSF grantee. Mem. Am. Ornithologists' Union (elective), Cooper Ornithol. Soc., Wilson Ornithol. Soc., Am. Soc. Zoologists (edn. com. 1980-82), Ornithol. Soc. N.Am. (bd. dirs. 1979-82, 84—), Sigma Xi. Avocations: gardening, photography, ballet, running. Home: 4795 Hayden Blvd Columbus OH 43220 Office: Borror Lab Bioacoustics Ohio State U Dept Zoology 1735 Neil Ave Columbus OH 43210

GAUTHIER, CLARENCE JOSEPH, utility executive, retired; b. Houghton, Mich., Mar. 16, 1922; s. Clarence A. and Muriel V. (Beesley) G.; m. Grayce N. Wicall, July 25, 1941; children: Joseph H., Nancy M. B.S. in Mech. Engring. U. Ill., 1943; M.B.A., U. Chgo., 1960. Registered profl. engr., Ill. With Pub. Service Co. No. Ill., 1945-54; with No. Ill. Gas Co., 1954-86, v.p. finance, 1960-62, v.p. ops., 1962-64, exec. v.p., 1965-69, pres., 1969-76, chmn., 1971-86, chief exec. officer, 1971-81, dir., 1965-86; chmn., pres., chief exec. officer, dir. NICOR Inc., 1976-86, chief exec. officer, chmn. and dir. subs.; dir. GDC, Inc., Bank of Yorktown, Lombard, Ill., 1968-84, GATX Corp., Nalco Chem. Co., Sun Electric Corp., Chgo. and NorthWestern Transp. Co.; vice chmn., dir. AEGIS, Ltd., 1978—; bd. dirs. Acme Steel Corp., CNW Corp., Cole Taylor Fin. Group, Aegis Ins. Services, Inc., DOLI, Ltd. Contbr. articles to profl. jours. Trustee Council Energy Studies, 1977—; bd. dirs. Gas Research Inst., 1977-82; mem. Northwestern U. Assos., 1977-85; citizens bd. U. Chgo., 1972—; chmn. devel. campaign Good Samaritan Hosp., Downers Grove, Ill., 1974-77; trustee George Williams Coll., Downers Grove, 1968-77, Ill. Inst. Tech., 1976-86, IIT Research Inst., 1976-80; bd. dirs. Mid-Am. chpt. ARC, 1962-78; trustee Met. Crusade of Mercy, Chgo., 1965-77; mem. Ill. Savs. Bond Com., 1975-85, U. Ill. Presidents Council, 1978—, U. Ill. Adv. Council, 1981-86, U. Ill. Found.; bd. sponsors Evangel. Hosp. Assn., Oak Brook, Ill., 1977-85. Served to capt. C.E. AUS, World War II, PTO. Decorated Silver Star, Bronze Star with V; recipient Distinguished Alumnus award, 1971, Alumni Honor award U. Ill., 1974, Loyalty award, 1977. Mem. Internat. Gas Union (council 1970-75, chmn. Com. Gas Utilization 1970-73), Am. Gas Assn. (dir. 1970-76, chmn. bd. 1975, Disting. Service award 1976), Midwest Gas Assn. (dir. 1964-67), So. Gas Assn. (dir. 1966-69), Ind. Natural Gas Assn. Am. (dir. 1972-73), Inst. Gas Tech. (trustee 1964-70, 71-78, chmn. bd. trustees 1976-78), AAAS, Am. Finance Assn., U. Chgo. Grad. Sch. Bus. Alumni Assn. (pres. 1964-65), Ill. C. of C., Chgo. Council on Fgn. Relations (Chgo. com. 1974-86), Chgo. Assn. Commerce and Industry (dir. 1966-71, 73-79), ME-IE Alumni Assn. U. Ill. (pres. 1976-77, dir. 1973—), Sigma Pi, Pi Tau Sigma, Tau Beta Pi, Beta Gamma Sigma, Tau Nu Tau. Clubs: Comml. (Chgo.), Economic (Chgo.). Home: 15 Lochinvar Ln Oak Brook IL 60521 Office: 477 E Butterfield Rd Suite 206 Lombard IL 60148

GAVIN, JAMES JOHN, JR., diversified company executive; b. Phila., July 18, 1922; s. James John and Mary E (Ludlow) G.; m. Zita C. Kabeschat, Aug. 23, 1952; children—William, James, Kevin, Steven, Peter. B.S. in Econs, U. Pa., 1949. Sr. accountant Peat, Marwick, Mitchell & Co. (C.P.A.'s), Phila., 1949-53; chief accountant Indian Head Mills, Inc. (name changed to Indian Head Inc.), N.Y.C., 1953; asst. treas. Indian Head Mills, Inc. (name changed to Indian Head Inc.), 1953-56, controller, 1956-61, treas., v.p., 1961-66, v.p. finance, 1966-68; v.p. finance, controller Borg-Warner Corp., Chgo., 1968-75; sr. v.p. finance Borg-Warner Corp., 1975-85, vice-chmn., 1985—. Served with USNR, 1943-46. Mem. Pa. Inst. C.P.A.'s, Delta Sigma Pi, Beta Alpha Psi, Beta Gamma Sigma. Home: 161 Thorn Tree Ln Winnetka IL 60093 Office: Borg-Warner Corp 200 S Michigan Ave Chicago IL 60604 *

GAVIN, LAWRENCE RICHARD, retail executive; b. Chgo., May 13, 1927; s. Frederick Richard and Ruth (Brauner) G.; m. Rita Grace Wolcott, Aug. 4, 1974; children: Richard, Ronald, John. Warehouse mgr. Ace Hardware Corp., Oak Brook, Ill., 1958-73; v.p. ops. Ace Hardware Corp., Oak Brook, 1973-82, exec. v.p., 1982, pres., 1983—; also bd. dirs. Ace Hardware Corp. Served with U.S. Army, 1945-47. Clubs: Ruth Lake Country (Hinsdale, Ill.); Central States Hardware. Home: 8473 Kimberly Ct Burr Ridge IL 60521 Office: Ace Hardware Corp 2200 Kensington Ct Oak Brook IL 60521 *

GAVIN, MICHAEL JAMES, accountant; b. Reedsburg, Wis., Jan. 10, 1952; s. James Francis and Mary Catherine (Doyle) G.; m. Julie Alayne Gustafson, May 24, 1980; children: Brooke Elizabeth, Robert Michael. BBA in Acctg., St. Norbert Coll., 1974; MBA in Acctg., U. Wis., Oshkosh, 1975; MS in Taxation, U. Wis., Milw., 1985. CPA, Wis. Sr. acct. Wippli Ullrich and Co., Wausau, Wis., 1970-79; tax. mgr. Sentry Ins., Stevens Point, Wis., 1979-82; tax surp. Touche Ross and Co., Milw., 1982-86; tax mgr. Jannsen and Co. S.C., Milw., 1986—; guest lectr. U. Wis., Stevens Point, 1979-82. Editor: Multistate Corporate Tax Alumnae, 1987. Mem. Am. Inst. CPA's, Wis. Inst. CPA's (com. fed. taxation 1987—), U. Wis. Tax Assn. Republican. Roman Catholic. Avocations: golf, hunting, fishing. Office: Jannsen & Co SC PO Box 13647 Milwaukee WI 53213

GAW, EDWARD RICHARD, manufacturing executive; b. N.Y.C., Aug. 13, 1936; s. John and Cecilia G.; m. Isabel O'Brien, June 11, 1960; children: Edward, John, Christopher, Daniel, Kevin. BBA, Iona Coll., 1958; MBA, U. Mich., 1959. CPA, N.Y., N.J. Auditor Arthur Young & Co., N.Y.C., 1959-65; mgr. acctg. Mobil Chem., Plainfield, N.J., 1965-68; internat. controller C.R. Bard, Murray Hill, N.J., 1968-77; treas., controller Clopay Corp., Cin., 1977-80, pres. mfr. div., 1980—. Mem. Am. Inst. CPA's, Fin. Exec. Inst. Office: Clopay Corp 101 E 4th St Cincinnati OH 45202

GAWECKI, FREDERICK, medical educator; b. Toledo, July 18, 1936; m. Mary C. McCoy, 1977. BS, U. Toledo, 1958; MD, Boston U., 1962. Intern, pres. St. Luke's Hosp., Chgo., 1962-64, 66-68.; asst. in obstetrics U. Ill., Chgo., 1963-64; commd. M.C. USAF, 1964, advanced through grades to lt. col., 1971; chief ob-gyn USAF Hosp., Azores, Portugal, 1964-66, Pacific Air Force Hosp., Clark AFB, Philippines, 1968-70; chief ob-gyn Ehrling Bergquist Hosp., Offutt AFB, Neb., 1970-72, chief surg. services, flight med. officer, 1971-72; resigned USAF, 1974; asst. prof. ob-gyn Creighton U. Sch. Medicine, Omaha, 1972-74, assoc. prof., 1974-77, assoc. clin. prof. family practice and ob-gyn, 1977—, practice medicine specializing in ob-gyn, 1977; assoc. staff Archbishop Bergan Mercy Hosp., Omaha, 1972, active staff, 1973-86, mem. surg. records com., ob-gyn rep., 1973, courtesy staff, 1987—; assoc. staff ob-gyn Creighton Meml. St. Joseph Hosp., Omaha, 1972, active staff, 1973—, mem. med. records com., 1973, mem. utilization com., 1976; active staff Midlands Community Hosp., Papillion, Neb., 1976—; chief ob-gyn services Midlands Community Hosp., Papillion, 1978-81, pres. med. staff, 1982. Creator: (display) The Technique of Amniocentesis, 1976 (Hon. mention Omaha Mid-West Clin. Soc. Annual Meeting 1976); contbr. articles to profl. jours. Mem. Nebr. State Med. Assn., Neb. State Ob-Gyn Soc. (pres. elect 1976-77, pres. 1977-78), Nebr. Med. Assn. (mem. standing com. on edn. and preventive medicine 1977, ad hoc com. for med. malpractice 1987), Omaha-Douglas Med. Soc., Omaha Mid-West Clin. Soc. (ob-gyn sect. chmn. 1974-78, mem. exec. com. 1978-79), Sarpy County Med. Soc. (pres. 1985-86). Home: 5801 Mark St Papillion NE 68133-2428 Office: 1414 S 84th St Papillion NE 68046

GAWLIK, THOMAS JAMES, controller, finance executive; b. Chgo., July 25, 1955; s. Edward Stanley and Irene Ann (Pajak) G.; m. Judith Ann Krelberg, Aug. 5, 1978; children: Thomas James II. BS, Ill. State U., 1977; MBA, U. Chgo., 1982. CPA, Ill., Mich. Sr. acct. Price Waterhouse, Chgo., 1977-80; controller Baldwin-Gregg Inc., Countryside, Ill., 1980-81; sr. fin. analyst Bendix Corp. Allied Auto, Southfield, Mich., 1983; mgr. fin. analysis Bendix Corp. Allied Auto, Southfield, 1983-85; controller, chief fin. officer Prestolite Wire Corp., Farmington Hills, Mich., 1985—. Bd. dirs., chmn. fin. com. Big Bros./Big Sisters, Southfield, 1985—. Named one of Outstanding Young Men Am., 1986. Mem. Am. Inst. CPA's, Mich. Assn. CPA', Soc. Automotive Engrs., Soc. Mfg. Engrs. Avocations: baseball, hockey, skiing. Home: 1095 Dewey Plymouth MI 48170 Office: Prestolite Wire Corp 32781 Middlebelt Rd Farmington Hills MI 48018

GAY, JOHN WILLIAM, II, management executive; b. Peoria, Ill., May 22, 1944; s. John W. and Verla L. (Dunkel) G.; m. Drew Velde, Feb. 28, 1972; children: Andrea, John W. III. BS, Western Ill. U., Macomb, 1969; cert. in mgmt., Bradley U., 1980. Pres. Gaystar Enterprises, Peoria, 1972—, John Gay and Assocs., Peoria, 1972—, Preferred Eyecare Ctrs. Ins., Colorado Spring, Colo., 1986, Eyecare Mgmt. Inst., Colorado Spring, Colo., 1986, Profl. Mgmt. Cons., Inc., Colorado Spring, Colo., 1986; agt., rep. Prudential Ins., Peoria, 1983—; agt. of record IOA, Chgo. 1983—. Contbr. numerous review to optometric monthly jour. Ambassador Eureka Coll., 1978—; dir., v.p. Dirksen Cons. Research Ctr., Pekin, 1973—; mem. Dirksen Endowment Fund; adminstrv. aid U.S. Senator, Pekin, 1967-69; del. White House Conf. on Small Bus., 1980-86. Named one of Outstanding Young Men Am., U.S. Jaycees, 1977, 78, 80.; recipient Dirksen Service award, Dirksen Ctr., Pekin, 1975. Mem. Internat. Assn. Fin. Planning, Million Dollar Round Table, Life Underwriters Assn. Club: Mt. Hawley Country (Peoria). Lodge: Masons. Avocations: music, cycling, fishing, hunting, , skiing. Home: 11110 Quail Ln Peoria IL 61615 Office: John Gay & Assocs 1000 Community Nat Bank Bldg Peoria IL 61602

GAYLORD, EDSON I., manufacturing company executive. Chmn., pres. Ingersoll Milling Machine Co., Rockford, Ill. Office: Ingersoll Milling Machine Co 707 Fulton St Rockford IL 61103 *

GAYLORD, THOMAS GEORGE, obstetrician, gynecologist; b. Detroit, Oct. 1, 1949; s. Howard Wesley and Erdin Elizabeth (Chittick) G.; m. Lou Ann Fischer, May 15, 1976; children: Christopher, Erin. BS, Mich. State U., 1971; MD, U. Mich., 1975. Diplomate Am. Bd. Ob-Gyn. Intern then resident in ob-gyn Ind. U. Hosp., 1975-78; head dept. ob-gyn Morgan County Hosp., Martinsville, Ind., 1980—, chief of staff, 1983-85. Mem. Morgan County Med. Soc. (pres. 1980). Presbyterian. Avocations: scuba diving, marathons, triathalons, golf. Home: 1918 Foxcliff N Martinsville IN 46151 Office: So Ind Ob-Gyn 2200 Wooden Dr #106 Martinsville IN 46151

GAYNOR, TIMOTHY MICHAEL, automotive hand tool company executive; b. Milw., May 16, 1943; s. Thomas E. and Irene Mary (Gendrich) G.; m. Elizabeth Anne Drehfal, June 20, 1975; children: Claire Marie, Anne Marie. BA, St. Francis Sem. Coll., 1965; MS, U. Wis., Milw., 1975. Program dir. Kenosha (Wis.) Youth Devel. Services, 1974-77; mgr. tng. and devel. Snap-On Tools Corp., Kenosha, 1977—; founder Midwest Tng. Mgrs. Network, 1983-86. Mem. Am. Soc. Tng. and Devel., Am. Soc. of Personnel Adminstrs. (chmn. Milw. tng. and devel. com., 1983-84). Avocations: skiing, cycling, walking. Office: Snap-On Tools Corp 2801-80th St Kenosha WI 53140

GEAKE, RAYMOND ROBERT, state senator; b. Detroit, Oct. 26, 1936; s. Harry Nevill and Phyllis Rae (Fox) G.; B.S. in Spl. Edn., U. Mich., 1958, M.A. in Guidance and Counseling, 1959, Ph.D. in Edn. and Psychology, 1963; m. Carol Lynne Rens, June 9, 1962; children—Roger Rens, Tamara Lynne, William Rens. Coordinator child devel. research Edison Inst., Dearborn, Mich., 1962-66; dir. psychology dept. Plymouth (Mich.) State Home and Tng. Sch., Mich. Dept. Mental Health, 1966-69; pvt. practice ednl. psychology, Northville, Mich., 1969-72; mem. Mich. Ho. of Reps., 1973-76, Mich. Senate, 1977—; adj. asst. prof. edn./psychology dept. Madonna Coll., Livonia, Mich., 1984—. Trustee-at-large Schoolcraft Community Coll., 1969-72, chmn. bd. trustees, 1971-72; vice chmn. nat. adv. com. on mental health and illness of elderly HEW, 1976-77. Mem. N.E.A. (life), Mich. Soc. Geneal. Research. Republican. Rotarian. Co-author: Visual Tracking, a Self-instruction Workbook for Perceptual Skills in Reading, 1962. Office: Mich Senate PO Box 30036 Lansing MI 48909

GEARHART, KEVIN JOHN, accountant; b. Iowa City, July 3, 1960; s. John Darwin and Marylis JoAnne (Gardner) G.; m. Marcia Coleen Sellegren, June 14, 1986. BA in Acctg., Cen. U. of Iowa, 1982. CPA, Iowa. Jr. acct. Pollard Plate and Co., Grinnell, Iowa, 1983-84; sr. acct. Pollard and Co., Des Moines, 1984—. Mem. Am. Inst. CPA's, Iowa Soc. CPA's. Republican. Methodist. Club: Toastmasters. Home: 824 19th St West Des Moines IA 50265 Office: Pollard and Co 508 10th St Des Moines IA 50309

GEDALECIA, DAVID, history educator; b. N.Y.C., June 8, 1942; s. Ben and Edith (Marks) G.; m. Pei-hsin Chia, Sept. 9, 1967; children: Derek, Julie. BA, Queens Coll., 1965; MA, Harvard U., 1967, PhD, 1971. Research asst. Ben Gedalecia Assocs., N.Y.C., 1966; advt. asst. J. Walter Thompson, N.Y.C., 1967; teaching fellow Harvard U., 1969-70; prof. history Coll. of Wooster, Ohio, 1971—, chmn. internat. edn. com., 1974-76, 80-81, chmn. history dept., 1984—; assoc. U. Seminar in Neo-Confucianism, Columbia U., 1980—. Fellow NDEA Title VI in Chinese, 1965-71, fellow East-West Philospher's Conf., 1982. Mem. Phi Beta Kappa. Democrat. Jewish. Avocations: guitar, five-string banjo. Office: Coll Wooster Wooster OH 44691

GEDDES, EARL RUSSELL, acoustical engineer, physics educator; b. Detroit, Mar. 21, 1951; s. Andrew Eric and Dorothy Louise (Russell) G.; m. Ruth Ann Wright, June 6, 1981. BS, Eastern Mich. U., 1975, MS, 1978; PhD, Penn. State U., 1982. Recording engr. Earl Klugh, Detroit, 1978-80; design engr. Ford Motor Co., Dearborn, Mich., 1978-80; tech. specialist Ford Motor Co., Dearborn, 1982—; prof. physics Eastern Mich. U., Ypsilanti, 1987—. Contbr. articles to profl. jours. Mem. Audio Engring. Soc. (v.p. 1985-87), Soc. Automotive Engrs., Acoustical Soc. Am., Inst. Noise Control Engrs. Home: 16183 Southampton Livonia MI 48154

GEDGAUDAS, EUGENE, radiologist, educator; b. Lithuania, Oct. 7, 1924; came to U.S., 1963, naturalized, 1968; children—Kristina, Nora, Sandra. M.D., U. Munich, 1948. Diplomate: Am. Bd. Radiology. Intern St. Boniface Hosp., Winnipeg, Man., Can.; resident in radiology St. Boniface Hosp., Winnipeg, U. Minn. Hosp., Mpls.; chmn. cardiac unit, asso. radiologist St. Boniface Gen. Hosp., Winnipeg, 1958-63; also dir. dept. radiology Mericordia Gen. Hosp., Winnipeg; asst. prof. radiology U. Minn., Mpls., 1963-67; assoc. prof. U. Minn., 1967-69, prof., 1969—, prof. emeritus, 1986—, head radiology dept., 1969-73; chmn. council clin. scis. Med. Sch. Med. Sch., 1973-82, mem. dean's adv. council, 1973-83. Contbr. articles to profl. jours. Fellow Royal Coll. Physicians and Surgeons Can., Am. Coll. Radiology, Royal Soc. Medicine, Royal Soc. Medicine; mem. AMA, Radiol. Soc. N.Am., Am. Roetgen Ray Soc. (pres. 1985-86), Minn. Radiology Soc., Minn. Acad. Medicine, Assn. Univ. Radiologists; Soc. Chmn. Acad. Radiology Depts. Home: 26 Evergreen Rd North Oaks St Paul MN 55127 Office: Box 292 Radiology 420 Delaware St SE Minneapolis MN 55455

GEDO, JOHN EMERIC, psychoanalyst, author, lecturer; b. Lucenec, Czechoslovakia, Nov. 19, 1927; came to U.S., 1941; s. Mathaas Stephen and Anna (Mandl) G.; m. Mary Lucille Mathews, Apr. 17, 1953; children: Paul Mathews, Andrew Lloyd, Nicholas McGuigan. BA, NYU, 1946, MD, 1951. Diplomate Am. Bd. Psychiatry and Neurology. Clin. prof. U. Ill., Chgo., 1970—; tng. and supervising analyst Chgo. Inst. Psycholanalysis, 1971—; ind. psychoanalyst Chgo., 1956—. Author: Models of the Mind, 1973, Beyond Interpretation, 1979, Portraits of the Artist, 1983, Psychoanalysis and its Discontents, 1984, Conceptual Issues in Psychoanalysis, 1986; contbr. over one hundered articles and book reviews to profl. jours. Served with U.S. Army, 1946-47. Fellow Am Psychiatric Assn.; mem. Am. Psychoanalytic Assn., Chgo. Psychoanalytic Soc. (pres. 1981-82), Ill. Psychiatric Soc. Avocation: art collecting. Home: 666 N Lake Shore Dr Chicago IL 60611 Office: 400 E Randolph Dr Chicago IL 60601

GEDULD, HERBERT HASKELL, chemical company executive; b. Cleve., May 25, 1931; s. Jacob and Florence Anna (Paley) G.; m. Toby Gail Wolf; children: Elissa, Elana, David. BA, Wayne State U., 1957. Dist. mgr. R.O. Hull & Co., Detroit, 1949-62; internat. v.p. R.O. Hull & Co., Cleve., 1967-75; materials mgr. Israel Aircraft, Lod, 1964-67; chmn. bd. Columbia Chem., Macedonia, Ohio, 1975—. Author: Israel Inside Out, 1972; contbr. articles to profl. jours. Served with USMC, 1950-51. Mem. Am. Electroplaters Soc. Jewish. Avocations: picture framing, woodworking, gardening. Home: 2192 S Belnoir University Heights OH 44118 Office: Columbia Chem Corp 837 E Highland Rd Macedonia OH 44056

GEE, JOHN C., systems analyst; b. Watertown, N.Y., Jan. 8, 1955; s. Chuck Y. and Kam Oy (Hom) G.; m. Anne Lee, Sept. 23, 1981. BS, Washington U., St. Louis, 1977. Assoc. analyst Control Data Corp., St. Louis, 1977-79, analyst, 1979-82, sr. analyst, 1982-85; tech. cons. ETA Systems, Inc., St. Louis, 1985—. Designer software. Avocations: skiing, golf. Office: ETA Systems Inc 425 N New Ballas Rd Suite 101 Saint Louis MO 63141

GEE, ROBERT LEROY, agriculturist, dairy farmer; b. Oakport Twp., Minn., May 25, 1926; s. Milton William and Hertha Elizabeth (Paschke) G.; m. Mae Valentine Erickson, June 18, 1953. B.S. in Agronomy, N.D. State U., 1951, postgrad., 1955; postgrad., Colo. A&M U., 1954. Farm labor controller Minn. Extension Service, Clay County, 1944-45, county 4-H agt., 1951-57; rural mail carrier U.S. Postal Service, Moorhead, Minn., 1946-47; breeder registered shorthorn cattle and registered southdown sheep Moorhead, Minn., 1950-63; owner, operator Gee Dairy Farm (Oak Grove Farm), Moorhead, Minn., 1957—; asst. prof. status U. Minn., 1951-57; bd. dirs. Red River Valley Fair, West Fargo, N.D., 1960-86, Minn. Dairy Promotion Bd., St. Paul, 1968-69, Red River Valley Devel. Assn., Crookston, Minn., 1973—; bd. dirs. Red River Milk Producers Pool, Minn. and N.D., 1963-78, treas., 1968-78; dir. Cass Clay Creamery Inc., Fargo, N.D., 1969—, chmn. bd., 1982-85; mem. U.S. Meat Animal Research Ctr., Clay Center, Nebr., 1970; mem. Nat. Dairy Promotion Bd., Washington, 1984—. Treas. Oakport Twp., Minn., 1974-82, elected supr., 1986—, v.p., 1987. Served to seaman 1st class USN, 1945-46; PTO. Recipient Grand Champion Farm Flock award

Man. Expn., 1960; named Clay County King Agassiz, Red River Valley Winter Shows, 1966, Grand Champion forage exhibit Red River Valley Winter shows, 1979, 82; co-recipient Clay County Dairy Farm Family of Yr. award Red River Valley Dairymen's Assn., 1979. Mem. Minn. Milk Producers Assn. (bd. dirs. and treas. 1978—), Minn. Assn. Coops. (bd. dirs. 1984—), State Coop. Assn. (dairy council 1975—), Am. Farm Bur. Fedn., Nat. Farmers Union, Kragnes Farmers Elevator Assn., Red River Valley Livestock Assn., Am. Shorthorn Breeders Assn., Am. Southdown Breeders Assn., Holstein-Friesian Assn. Am. Republican. Mem. United Ch. of Christ. Club: Agassiz (v.p. 1979-81, pres. 1981-82) (Moorhead). Avocations: hunting; fishing; skiing. Home and Office: Rural Rt 1 Box 118 Moorhead MN 56560

GEEDING, PHILLIP WARREN, technical services veterinarian; b. Joplin, Mo., Dec. 19, 1949; s. George W. and Margery K. (Bushner) G.; m. Ginger E. Shoemaker, Aug. 7, 1976; children: Amy Antonia, Phillip Eugene. Student Mo. So. State Coll., 1972; DVM, U. Mo., 1976. Herd health veterinarian Great Plains Ova Transplant, Ada, Okla., summer 1976; veterinarian Atchison Vet. Clinic, Kans., 1976; veterinarian, owner Larson Vet. Clinic, Pittsburg, Kans., 1976-79; relief veterinarian Vet. Relief Services, Atchison, 1979-80; veterinarian, owner Hillside Vet. Clinic, Atchison, 1980-81; tech. services staff veterinarian Boehringer-Ingelheim U.S.A. Animal Health Div., St. Joseph, Mo., 1981—. Mem. Am. Vet. Med. Assn., Am. Assn. Indsl. Veterinarians, Am. Assn. Bovine Practitioners, Kans. Vet. Med. Assn. Office: Boehringer Ingelheim USA 2621 N Belt Hwy Saint Joseph MO 64502

GEERDES, HAROLD PAUL, writer, acoustical consultant, educator; b. Chgo., Sept. 5, 1916; s. Lubbertus K. and Kathrine (Dering) G.; m. Gladys Van Haitsma, Nov. 22, 1939; children: Paul H., Richard M., Judith A. AB, Calvin Coll., 1937; MEd, Chgo. State U., 1940; studied conducting Nicolai Malko, Chgo., 1942-46; postgrad., Mich. State U., 1943-45, U. Mich., 1956. Music tchr. high schs. Wyoming, Trufant and Zeeland, Mich., 1937-46; organizer, dir. city-wide program instrumental music Grand Rapids (Mich.) Christian Schs., 1947-55; assoc. prof. music Calvin Coll., Grand Rapids, 1955-79; exec. dir. St. Cecilia Music Soc., Grand Rapids, 1979—; condr. concert band Calvin Coll., 1955-69, condr. symphony orch., 1955-77, oratorio soc., 1967-81, mgr. Fine Arts Ctr., 1966-78; violinist Grand Rapids Symphony, 1935-39, 42-53; condr. Zeeland Civic Chorus, 1942-46; active as guest condr., adjudicator, 1950—; lectr., cons. on acoustics Olivet Coll. Conservatory, Taylor U. Music Bldg., Upland, Ind., Forest Hills (Mich.) Pub. Schs., Gerald Ford Presdl. Mus., Macomb Community Coll., Mt. Clemens, Mich., numerous others; mem. long-range planning com. Mich. Council for the Arts, design com. for new Grand Rapids Performing Arts Ctr.; mem. Music Adv. Panel Mich. Council For the Arts. Author: Planning and Equipping Educational Music Facilities, 1975, Music Buildings and Equipment, 1987; editor: Bicentennial Music Handbook for Michigan Teachers, 1975; contbr. articles on music and acoustics to mags. Trustee Grand Rapids Symphonic Band Bd., 1982—; active Round Table Service Club, Grand Rapids. Mem. Mich. Sch. Band and Orch. Assn. (hon.), Am. Symphony Orch. League, Acoustical Soc. Am., Music Educators Nat. Conf. (Mich. bicentennial chmn.), Mich. Music Edn. Assn. (Award of Merit 1986), Am. String Tchrs. Assn., Nat. Orch. Assn., Christian Instrumental Dirs. Assn. (adv. bd. 1986—), Audio Engrs. Soc. (life), Am. Fedn. Musicians (life). Mem. Christian Reformed Ch. Avocation: travel. Home and Office: 2210 Woodlawn Ave SE Grand Rapids MI 49506

GEETHA, RANGASWAMI, biostatistician; b. Manamadurai, Tamilnadu, India, Nov. 19, 1949; came to U.S., 1975; d. Agrapet Srinivasa and Thangam (Anantharamakrishnan) Rangaswami. B.A. with honors in Math., Lady Shri Ram Coll., New Delhi, 1969, M.A. in Math., 1971; M.Sc. in Stats., U. Alta., Edmonton, 1975; M.S. in Ops. Research, Mich. State U., 1979, Ph.D. in Stats., 1981. Grad. teaching asst. Mich. State U., East Lansing, 1975-81; asst. prof. Bowling Green State U., Ohio, 1981-84; research scientist, biostatistician Bristol-Myers, Evansville, Ind., 1984—; statis. cons. Computer Lab., Mich. State U., East Lansing, 1980-81; research project advisor Bowling Green State U., Ohio, 1982-83. Vol. Nat. ARC, Lansing, Mich., 1977-81, Friend A Friend Program, Evansville, Ind., 1984-85, Youth Crisis Bur., Evansville, 1984-85. Jr. research fellow Delhi U., India, 1972-73. Mem. Am. Statis. Assn., Biometrics Soc., Soc. for Clinical Trials. Avocations: tennis, chess, volunteer work, travel, photography. Home: 5599 Kenwood Dr Newburgh IN 47630 Office: Bristol Myers Pennsylvania Ave Evansville IN 47721

GEHL, RENÉ JOSEPH, industrial advertising executive; b. New Holstein, Wis., Mar. 18, 1919; m. Betty Lee Bruens, Nov. 13, 1948; children: Mary, Bill, Anne, Maragaret, Tom. BSME, U. Wis., 1943. Copywriter R.M. Young Co., Milw., 1947-69; exec. v.p. Ind. Pub. Services, Milw., 1969-83; pres. R.J. Gehl and Assocs., New Berlin, Wis., 1983—. Served to lt. (j.g.) USN, 1944-46. Office: RJ Gehl & Assocs 15975 W National Ave New Berlin WI 53151

GEHLEN, JOSEPH PETER, accountant, management consultant; b. St. Paul, July 6, 1955; s. Donald Joseph and Helen Mary (Feyerson) G.; m. Pamela Jean Welter, Dec. 29, 1979. BS in Bus., U. Minn., 1978. Lic. pub. acct., Minn. Acct., mgmt. cons. Mansco Corp., Mpls., 1977-81; v.p., cofounder ABConsulting, Mpls., 1981-85; owner, mgr. Joseph P. Gehlen, LPA, Mpls., 1985-86; pres. Joseph P. Gehlen, Ltd., Mpls., 1986—. Mem. Assn. Minn. Pub. Accts. Avocations: hunting, fishing, collecting wildlife art. Home: 4816 Overlook Dr Bloomington MN 55437 Office: 140 W 98th St Suite 100 Bloomington MN 55420

GEHLING, J. A., refrigerator manufacturing company executive. Pres. Greenville (Mich.) Products Co. Office: Greenville Products Co 635 W Charles St Greenville MI 48838 *

GEHLING, JOHN ADAM, manufacturing company executive; b. Cambridge, Mass., July 23, 1920; s. Daniel C. and Hazel A. (Dyson) G.; m. Madelyn Virginia Brown, July 25, 1943; children: Nancy, Martha, Jack, Bill, Jim, Tim, Virginia, Jane. BSME magna cum laude, Tufts U., 1943; MBA, Harvard U., 1947. V.p. mfg. WCI Kelvinator, Grand Rapids, Mich., 1969-70; exec. v.p. WCI Greenville (Mich.) Prodns., 1970-72, pres., group v.p., 1972-83, corp. v.p., pres., 1983-86; group v.p., gen. mgr. WCI Refrigerator Div., Greenville, 1986—. Past mem. Sch. Bd., Cold Springs Harbor, N.Y., Planning Commn., South Russell, Ohio, City Council, South Russell. Served to lt. USN, 1943-46. Mem. Assn. Home Appliance Mfrs. (past chmn. refrigerator freezer exec. bd.). Club: Cascade Hills Country (Grand Rapids). Home: 7314 Cascade Rd Grand Rapids MI 49508 Office: WCI Major Appliance Group 635 W Charles St Greenville MI 48838

GEHM, DAVID EUGENE, contruction management company executive; b. St. Louis, Nov. 15, 1952; s. John Francis and Rosemary Helen (Krupp) G.; m. Cynthia Louise Rosson, Sept. 10, 1978 (div. Dec. 1980). Cert. civil engrng. tech., St. Louis Community Coll. Florissant Valley, 1973. Quality control inspector Fla. Testing and Engr., Ft. Lauderdale, 1973-76; surveyor Wunderlich Co., Union, Mo., 1976-77; quality control inspector The Binkley Co., Warrenton, Mo., 1977-78, Daniel Internat., Fulton, Mo., 1978-79; project mgr. Booker Assocs., Inc., St. Louis, 1979-86; pres. Gehm Constrn. Mgmt. Inc., Florissant, Mo., 1986—. Mem. Nat. Inst. Cert. Engrng. Techs., Inst. Cert. Engr. Techs., Tau Alpha Pi, Sons of the Am. Legion. Roman Catholic. Avocations: hunting, fishing. Home and Office: 849 N Lafayette St Florissant MO 63031

GEHR, THOMAS YEATS, JR., railway industry executive; b. Michigan City, Ind., Nov. 23, 1953; s. Thomas Yeats and Marie V. Gehr; m. Joan Valentine Miller, Sept. 4, 1982; 1 child, Samantha Kientzy. Student Purdue U., Research Inst. Am. Operator, Automation Industries/Sperry Rail Service, Danbury, Conn., 1974-75; sales rep. Esco Equipment Service Co., Palatine, Ill., 1975-81, v.p. sales, 1981—, treas., 1986—; also asst. sec., dir. Mem. Am. Ry. Engrng. Assn., Roadmaster and Maintenance of Way Assn., New Eng. Ry. Assn., Am. Short Line Ry Assn. Met. Ry. Assn. (exec. com. 1984—). Office: 909 Wilmette Rd Palatine IL 60067

GEHRING, BENJAMIN ROBERT, management consultant; b. Chillicothe, Ohio, Feb. 26, 1915; s. Louis C. and Jennie (Rector) G.; m. Ellen R. Payne, Nov. 6, 1937; children: Julie, Barbara Lee, Susan Jane. Student, Ohio State U., 1936. CPA, Ohio. With Kent & Rector, 1940-49; pres. Andre Wood Products, Inc., 1949-59; pres., dir. Kilgore, Inc., Westerville, Ohio, 1951-56; pres. Am. Gen. Corp., Columbus, 1961-84; dir., sec. Timmons Metal Products Co., Stardust Lanes, Inc., Eastern Enterprises Corp., Columbus, Ohio, Zip Lock Co.; mgmt. cons. Mem. Am. Inst. CPAs, Am. Acctg. Assn., Am. Mgmt. Assn., Ohio Soc. CPAs. Clubs: Scioto Country, Athletic. Lodges: Masons, Rotary. Home and Office: 4090 Bayberry Ct Columbus OH 43220

GEIER, GREGORY FRANCIS, pharmacist; b. Kansas City, Kans., May 28, 1958; s. Rupert Rudolph and Mary Helen (Sneller) G. B.S. in Pharmacy, U. Kans., 1981. Registered pharmacist, Kans., Mo. Pharmacist, asst. mgr. Treasury Drug, Olathe, Kans., 1981-85, pharmacist-in-charge, Rene Ryan Prescription Shop, Kansas City, 1985—; cons. pharmacist Keystone Treatment Ctr., Kansas City, 1985—, Regency Health Care Ctr., 1984-85. Kappa Psi scholar, 1979. Mem. Kans. Pharmacists Assn., Phi Kappa Theta Alumni Assn. (Theta chpt. v.p. 1985—, sec., 1982-85, bd. dirs.). Republican. Roman Catholic. Avocations: golf; weightlifting; reading.

GEIER, JAMES AYLWARD DEVELIN, manufacturing executive; b. Cin., Dec. 29, 1925; s. Frederick V. and Amey (Develin) G.; children: Deborah Anne, James Develin, Aylward Whittier. Attended, Williams Coll., 1947-50. With Cin. Milacron Inc., 1951—, became v.p., 1964, dir., 1966, exec. v.p., 1969, pres., chief exec. officer, 1970, also chmn.; dir. Clark Equipment Co., Central Bancorp., USX Corp. Trustee Cin. Museum Natural History; mem. adv. bd. Cin. Council on World Affairs; mem. Kenton County Airport Bd.; trustee Children's Home of Cin., Rensselaer Poly. Inst., 1987—; bd. dirs. Cin. chpt. ARC.; adv. council Cin. Zoo. Served with USAAF, 1944-46. Mem. NMTBA, Conf. Bd., Machinery and Allied Products Inst. (exec. com.), Mgmt. Execs. Soc. (exec. com.). Republican. Clubs: Commercial, Commonwealth, Queen City, Camargo. Office: Cin Milacron Inc 4701 Marburg Ave Cincinnati OH 45209

GEIGER, RONALD RAY, accountant, financial executive; b. Omaha, Dec. 2, 1949; s. Raymond A. and Twyla J. (Olson) G.; m. Wendy L. Wilson, Mar. 20, 1976; children—Matthew R., Laura L. B.S.B.A., U. Nebr., 1978. C.P.A., Nebr., Iowa. Auditor, Coopers and Lybrand, Omaha, 1978-81; controller Harker's Inc., LeMars, Iowa, 1981-84, treas., 1984-86, v.p. fin., treas., 1986—. Bd. dirs. Plymouth County Work Activity Ctr. (pres. 1987), LeMars, 1984. Served to petty officer 5 USN, 1970-75. Mem. Nebr. Soc. C.P.A.'s, Nat. Assn. Accts. (v.p. 1982-85, pres. 1986, north cen. regional council v.p. 1987), Iowa Cash Mgmt. Assn. (sec. 1984-85), LeMars C. of C. (v.p. 1984, pres. 1986), Fin. Execs. Inst. Lodge: Lions (pres. 1986). Avocations: golf, softball, volleyball. Home: 530 1st Ave SW LeMars IA 51031 Office: Harker's Inc 527 8th Ave SW LeMars IA 51031

GEILMAN, HAROLD, architect; b. Pitts., June 24, 1918; s. Joseph and Pauline (Hoffman) G.; m. Ruth B. Waldron, Aug. 4, 1945; children: Susan, Douglas, Gregory. Cert. in architecture, Carnegie Mellon U., 1941. Registered architect, Ill., Pa., Ind. Architect Schmidt, Garden & Erickson, Chgo., 1951-56; assoc. Cone & Dornbush, Chgo., 1956-58; prin. Loebl, Schlossman & Hackl, Chgo., 1958—. Chmn. zoning bd. appeals City of Park Forest, Ill., 1954-56; mem. bldg. bd. appeals City of Deerfield, Ill., 1963-70, mem. caucus for village mgr. 1972, mem. caucus for sch. bd., 1974. Served to lt. USN, 1943-46, PTO. Mem. AIA. Republican. Avocation: tennis. Home: 1665 Cranshire Ct Deerfield IL 60015 Office: Loebl Schlossman & Hackl 845 N Michigan Ave Chicago IL 60611

GEIMAN, J. ROBERT, lawyer; b. Evanston, Ill., Mar. 5, 1931; s. Louis H. and Nancy O'Connell-Crowe G.; m. Ann L. Fitzgerald, July 29, 1972; children: J. Robert, William Patrick, Timothy Michael. BS, Northwestern U., 1953; JD, Notre Dame U., 1956. Bar: Ill. 1956, U.S. Ct. Appeals (7th cir.) 1956, U.S. Supreme Ct. 1969. Assoc. Eckert & Peterson, Chgo., 1956-65; ptnr. Peterson, Ross, Schloerb & Seidel, Chgo., 1965—; mem. com. on civil jury instructions Ill. Supreme Ct., 1979-81. Case editor Notre Dame Lawyer, 1956. Bd. advisors Cath. Charities of Archdiocese of Chgo., 1973—. Fellow Am. Coll. Trial Lawyers, Ill. Bar Found.; mem. ABA (aviation com., tort and ins. practice sect. 1980—), Ill. Bar Assn. (sec. 1969-70, sec. bd. govs. 1969-71), Chgo. Bar Assn. (aviation law com. 1970-73), Bar Assn. of 7th Fed. Ct. (meetings com. 1968-70, vice chmn. membership com. 1973-75), Soc. Trial Lawyers, Cath. Lawyers Guild of Chgo. (bd. advisors 1973—), Law Club Chgo. Republican. Clubs: Chgo. Athletic Assn. (pres. 1973), Mid-Am.; Exmoor Country (Highland Park, Ill.); Mich. Shore (Wilmette). Home: 1034 Seminole Rd Wilmette IL 60091 Office: Peterson Ross Schloerb & Seidel 200 E Randolph Dr #7300 Chicago IL 60601

GEIS, PENNINGTON (PENNY), mediator, consultant; b. Melrose, Mass., Jan. 26, 1942; d. Charles Pennington and Marian Thomas (Soule) Leonard; children: Stephen, Genevieve, Nelson, Heidi. Student, Am. U., 1962; BA, Kans. Wesleyan Ill., 1963. Area instr. human relations LaLeche League Internat., Salina, Kans., 1971-81; internat. instr. human relations LaLeche League Internat., Chgo., 1981-83, dir. human relations, 1984; pres. Conflict Resolution, Salina, 1985-87; dir. Kans. Farmer/Creditor Mediation Service, 1987—. Chmn. Planning and Zoning Commn, Salina., 1978; vice chmn. sch. facilities Salina Bd. Edn., 1985, Salina County Commr., 1986—. Mem. Assn. Family and Conciliation Cts., Domestic Violence Assn. Cen. Kans. (planning chmn. 1983—), Acad. Family Mediators, Soc. Profls. Dispute Resolution, Heartland Mediators Assn. (pres. 1987—), Nat. Assn. Counties, Nat. Assn. Dem. County Ofcls. (exec. com. 1987), Salina C. of C. (goals steering com. 1986). Home: 1831 E Iron Salina KS 67401 Office: Kans Farmer/Creditor Mediation 1901 E 1st St Newton KS 67114-0467 Office: County Commn 300 W Ash Salina KS 67401 Office: Conflict Resolution 227 N Santa Fe Salina KS 67401

GEISBERGER, GEORGE BAHR, educator; b. Freeport, Ill., Jan. 21, 1935; s. August and Rose Anna (Bahr) G.; B.A., Rockford Coll., 1956, M.A., 1962; postgrad. U. Wis. Tchr., Harlem Jr. High Sch., Rockford, Ill., 1956, Union (Ill.) Sch., 1957-62; head tchr. Argyle Sch., Rockford, 1962-64; chmn. sociology dept., dir. field work placement program Milton (Wis.) Coll., 1964-70; program coordinator U. Wis. Extension, Madison, 1972-77; dir. Dept. Edn., Beloit (Wis.) Meml. Hosp., 1977-85; faculty, Cardinal Stritch Coll., Milw., 1985—. title search/cons. recreational devels., 1970-76. Sec.-treas. chpt. Muscular Dystrophy Assns. Am.; bd. dirs. Abaris Ctr. for the Chemically Dependent. Mem. AAUP, Am. Judicature Soc., Wis. Soc. for Health Manpower Edn. and Tng., Phi Delta Kappa. Home: PO Box 704 Rockford IL 61105

GEISENDORFER, JAMES VERNON, author; b. Brewster, Minn., Apr. 22, 1929; s. Victor H. and Anne B. (Johnson) G.; student Augustana Coll., 1950-51, Augsburg Coll., 1951-54, Orthodox Luth. Sem., 1954-55; B.A., U. Minn., 1960; LL.D., Burton Coll. and Sem., 1961; m. Esther Lillian Walker, Sept. 23, 1949; children—Jane, Karen, Lois. Grain buyer Pillsbury Mills, Inc., Worthington, Minn., 1947-48; hatchery acct., Worthington, 1949-50; night supr. Strutwear, Inc., Mpls., 1951-52; dispatcher Chgo. and North Western Ry., 1953-54; office mgr. Froedtert Malt Corp., Mpls., 1955-56, Nat. Automotive Parts Assn., 1957-60; sr. creative writer Brown & Bigelow, St. Paul, 1960-72; religious researcher, writer, 1972—; research cons. Inst. for the Study of Am. Religion; mem. panel of reference Chelston Bible Coll., New Milton, Eng.; mem. U.S. Congl. Adv. Bd., 1985. Recipient Amicus Poloniae medal Polish Ministry of Culture and Edn., 1969. Mem. Am. Acad. Religion, Acad. Ind. Scholars, Wis. Evang. Luth. Synod Hist. Inst., Augustana Hist. Soc., Wis. Acad. Scis., Arts and Letters, Can. Soc. Study of Religion, Aristotelian Soc., Hegel Soc. Am., Acad. Polit. Sci. Lutheran. Author: (with J. Gordon Melton) A Directory of Religious Bodies in the United States, 1977; Religion in America, 1983; mem. editorial bd. Biog. Dictionary of American Cult and Sect Leaders; contbr. articles to books and periodicals; cons. editor Directory of Religious Organizations in the United States, 1977. Address: 1001 Shawano Ave Green Bay WI 54303

GEISER, ROBERT NEIL, computer scientist; b. Cleve., Jan. 20, 1961; s. Roger Neal and Betty Lou (Keiner) G.; m. Laura Jane Burkholder, June 18, 1983; 1 child, Jessika Christen. BS in Acctg., AS in Data Processing, U. Akron, 1982. CPA, Ohio; cert. data processor, Ohio. Acct., programmer G&S Titanium, Inc., Wooster, Ohio, 1979-83, cons., 1983—; computer specialist, acct. Hall, Kistler & Co., Canton, Ohio, 1983—; cons. G&S Titanium, Inc., 1983—. Group leader Appalachia Service Project Home Repair, various locations, 1984-87. Mem. Am. Inst. CPA's, Ohio Soc. CPA's (chmn. local computers in practice 1987—, mem. statewide computers in practice panel 1987—), Nat. Assn. Accts. (assoc. dir. mem. attendance 1986—, Mem. of Yr. award 1984-85), Assn. of the Inst. for Cert. of Computer Profls. Republican. Mennonite. Avocations: golfing, swimming, studying computer-related topics, reading and studying the Bible. Home: 4748 Fredericksburg Rd Wooster OH 44691 Office: Hall Kistler & Co 900 Central Trust Tower Canton OH 44702-1498

GEISLER, HANS EMANUEL, gynecologic oncologist; b. Ratibor, Fed. Republic of Germany, Apr. 5, 1935; came to U.S., 1938; s. Harry and Marianne C. (Barthel) G.; m. Margaret Ann Colglazier; children: Dorothy Marianne, Kathleen Marie, Stephan Harry, Suzanne Joan, John Patrick. HAB, Xavier U., 1955; MD, Loyola U., Chgo., 1959. Cert. Am. Bd. Ob-Gyn., Gynecologic Oncology. Practice medicine specializing in gynecology and oncology Indpls., 1965—; asst. prof. ob-gyn. Ind. U. Med. Ctr., Indpls. 1967-84, dir. gynecol. tumor service 1967-70, clin. assoc prof. ob-gyn. 1984—; dir. gynecol. oncology Meth. Hosp., Indpls., 1970-72, 85—; dir. gynecol. oncology div. St. Vincent Hosp., Indpls., 1972—, chmn. cancer com., 1985—, dir. oncology program, 1985—, chmn. dept. ob-gyn., 1987—. Contbr. articles to profl. jours. Mem. Marion County Cancer Soc., Indpls., profl. edn. com. Am. Cancer Soc., Ind., Fire Merit Bd. Indpls., Com. to Select Police Chief, Indpls., 1975. Mem. AMA, Ind. Med. Soc., Marion County Med. Assn., Am. Coll. Ob-Gyns., Soc. Gynecol. Oncologists, Cen. Assn. Ob-Gyns., Continental Gynecol. Soc. (pres.), Soc. Meml. Gynecol. Oncologists (pres.), Midwest Soc. Gynecol. Oncologists, Am. Assn. Pro-Life Ob-Gyns. Republican. Roman Catholic. Avocations: golf, tennis. Home: 10609 Winterwood Carmel IN 46032 Office: 1311 N Arlington Indianapolis IN 46219

GEISLER, HERBERT GEORGE, JR., music educator; b. N.Y.C., May 29, 1949; s. Herbert George and Gladys (Robertson) G. BA, Concordia Coll., River Forest, Ill., 1971; MEd, Concordia Coll., 1974; postgrad., U. Mich., 1978. Cert. elem. and secondary tchr., Mich. Tchr. music, English Concordia Middle Sch., Hong Kong, 1971-75; teaching asst. U. Mich., Ann Arbor, 1976-78; substitute tchr. Ann Arbor Pub. Schs., 1976-78; dir. choral music Luth. High Sch. West, Detroit, 1978-79; asst. prof. music Concordia Coll., Ann Arbor, 1979—; dir. music Univ. Luth Chapel, Ann Arbor, 1975-81, St. Luke's Luth. Ch., Ann Arbor, 1981—. Contbr. articles to Mich. Music Educator and Luth. Edn. Grantee Aid Assn. for Luths., 1983-84. Mem. Mich. Music Educators Assn. (chmn. pub. relations com. 1984—, bus. mgr. 1986—), Soc. Ethnomusicology (life, edn. com.), Am. Choral Dirs. Assn. (life), Am. Guild of English Handbell Ringers. Lutheran. Home: 2905 Carlton Dr Ann Arbor MI 48108 Office: Concordia Coll 4090 Geddes Rd Ann Arbor MI 48105

GEISLER, JOHN P., convention bureau executive; b. Aberdeen, S.D., Nov. 21, 1921; s. Louis Benjamin and Amelia Grace Geisler; m. Anne Marie Knaub, July 12, 1952; children: John E., Gregory Louis, Julie. BS, No. Coll., 1943. Exec. sec. Jaycees, Aberdeen, 1946-52; mng. dir. St. Paul Winter Carnival, 1952-70; v.p. pub. affairs Hamm Brewery, St. Paul, 1970-75; exec. dir. St. Paul Convention Bur., 1976-87. Recipient Founder award Internat. Festival Assn., 1956, State Tourism of Yr. award Minn. Tourism Dept., 1986. Avocation: hunting. Home: 1129 Edgcombe Saint Paul MN 55105

GEISMAN, RAYMOND AUGUST, chemical engineer; b. St. Louis, Oct. 14, 1921; s. William Henry and Mary CeCelia (Schuengel) G.; m. Mary Patricia Abels, Apr. 26, 1952; children: Barbara Ann, Raymond August, Richard Abels. BSChemE, Washington U., St. Louis, 1943, MSChemE, 1944, MS in Engrng. Adminstrn., 1954. Profl. engr., Mo. Prodn. supr. Monsanto Co., St. Louis, 1946-53, sales engr., 1953-55, chief chemist, 1955-77, prin. engr., 1977—. Served to lt. USN, 1944-46, ATO. Mem. Am. Inst. Chem. Engrs., Am. Chem. Soc., Inst. Soc. Am., Sigma Xi, Tau Beta Pi. Roman Catholic. Avocations: fishing, hunting, reading, auto and home repairs. Home: 6231 Delor Saint Louis MO 63109 Office: Monsanto Corp 800 N Lindbergh Blvd Saint Louis MO 63167

GEISTFELD, RONALD ELWOOD, dental educator; b. St. James, Minn., Nov. 9, 1933; s. Victor E. and Viola (Becker) G.; m. Lois N. Tolzman Wilkens, June 15, 1955 (div. June 1974); m. Annette L. Swenson, Jan. 14, 1977; children: Shari, Mark, Steven, Ann, Leah, Erik. AA, Bethany Jr. Coll., 1952; BS, U. Minn., 1954, DDS, 1957. Gen. practice dentistry Northfield, Minn., 1959-72; clin. asst. prof. dentistry U. Minn. Sch. Dentistry, Mpls., 1969-72, assoc. prof., 1972-77, chmn. dept. operative dentistry, 1978-87, prof., 1982—; dental cons. Hennepin County Med. Ctr., Mpls., 1975—, Vets. Hosp., Mpls., 1977—, Vets. Hosp., St. Cloud, Minn., 1978—. Pres. PTA, Northfield, 1965, Arts Guild, Northfield, 1968; bd. dirs., chairperson Rice County Health and Sanitation Bd., Faribault, Minn., 1966-74; bd. dirs. Northfield Bd. Edn., 1969-74. Served to capt. U.S. Army, 1957-59. Am. Coll. Dentists fellow, 1972. Mem. Am. Dental Assn. (chairperson operative dentistry sect. 1979-80, curriculum cons. 1981—), Minn. Dental Assn. (ethics com. 1969-76, chairperson sci. and ann. sessions com. 1984-86), Mpls. Dist. Dental Soc. (program chairperson 1978-79), Minn. Acad. Restorative Dentistry (pres. 1979-80), Minn. Acad. Gnathological Research (pres. 1986-87), Am. Assn. Dental Schs. (chairperson operative dentistry sect. 1984-85, edit. rev. bd. 1984—), Acad. Operative Dentistry (exec. council 1978 81, research com. 1987—), Am. Acad. Gold Foil Operators, Northfield C. of C. (treas. and chairperson 1968-70), Delta Sigma Delta, Omicron Kappa Upsilon (Theta chpt.). Lutheran. Lodge: Rotary (pres. Northfield 1972-73). Home: 2173 Folwell Ave Saint Paul MN 55108 Office: U Minn Sch Dentistry 515 Delaware St SE 8-450 Moos Tower Minneapolis MN 55455

GEKAS, ALEXANDRA, health care association administrator; b. Chgo., Nov. 14, 1942; d. Peter Basica and Nada (Govedarica) Wudell; divorced; 1 child, Haralambos. BS, Loyola U., Chgo., 1967. Dir. Nat. Soc. Patient Reps. of Am. Hosp. Assn., Chgo., 1977—. Coauthor: (booklet) Development and Implementation of a Patient's Bill of Rights, 1979, Customer Oriented Mgmt. for Hospitals, 1987. Mem. Soc. Consumer Affairs, Profls. in Bus.

GELDERLOOS, PAUL, psychology educator, researcher; b. Hilversum, North-Holland, The Netherlands, Mar. 28, 1953; Came to U.S., 1983; s. Harm Derk and Margaretha Alida (Oord) G.; m. Garance Catherine Jaquet, Oct. 23, 1981. Candidate, Vrije Universiteit, Amsterdam, 1973, Doctorandus, 1977; Doctor, Katholieke Universiteit, Nijmegen, The Netherlands, 1987. Bar: N.Y. 1977. Dir., researcher Maharishi European Research U., Seelisberg, Switzerland, 1979-80; instr. Maharishi European Research U., Bangalore, India, 1981-82; tchr. Academie voor Bewustzijnsontwikkeling, Laag Soeren, The Netherlands, 1981-82, Stichting Onderwijs WCI, The Hague, The Netherlands, 1982-83; asst. prof. Maharishi Internat. U., Fairfield, Iowa, 1983—; cons. Stichting Fobie Club Nederland, Woerden, The Netherlands, 1980-81; pres. Infinite Fin. Resources, Inc., Fairfield, Iowa, 1984—. Author: Valuation and Transcendental Meditation, 1987; articles to profl. jours. Served to 2d lt. Supply, 1977-79, The Netherlands. Mem. Netherlands Inst. Psychologists, Midwestern Psychol. Assn., Am. Psychol. Assn. (fgn. affiliate, 1987). Avocations: meditation, sailing, windsurfing. Home and Office: Maharishi Internat U Faculty Residences Fairfield IA 52556

GELEHRTER, ANN GORRIS, educational specialist; b. Cleve., Aug. 2, 1949; d. William Eugene and Marian (Stropko) Gorris; m. George Ludwig Gelehrter, June 30, 1972; children: Thomas Aaron, David Andrew. BA, Georgian Ct. Coll., 1971; MEd, John Carroll U., 1986. Cert. specialist in learning disabled, behavior disordered and gifted and talented, Ohio. Tchr. Gesu Sch., University Heights, Ohio, 1971-80; ednl. specialist, office dir. Townsend Learning Ctr., Cleveland Heights, Ohio, 1986—. Editor: (book) Rave Reviews, 1983. Founder Children's Mus., Cleve., 1985-86; exec. bd. dirs. The Cleve. Play House, 1982—. Mem. Ohio Assn. for Gifted Children, Consortium Ohio Coordinators for the Gifted. Democrat. Roman Catholic. Avocations: car rallying, car racing, judging automobile shows, swimming, tennis. Home: 2733 Leighton Rd Shaker Heights OH 44120 Office: Townsend Learning Ctr 2460 Fairmount Blvd Cleveland Heights OH 44106

GELFAND, IVAN, investment advisor, columnist; b. Cleve., Mar. 29, 1927; s. Samuel and Sarah (Kruglin) G.; m. Suzanne Frank, Sept. 23, 1956; children: Dennis Scott, Andrew Steven. B.S., Miami U., Oxford, Ohio, 1950; postgrad., Case-Western Res. U., 1951; grad., Columbia U. Bank Mgmt. Program, 1968; certs., Am. Inst. Banking, 1952-57. Acct. Central Nat. Bank Cleve., 1950-53, v.p., mgr. bank and corp. investments, 1957-75; chief acct. Stars & Stripes newspaper, Darmstadt, Germany, 1953-55; account exec. Merrill, Lynch, Pierce, Fenner & Smith, Inc., Cleve., 1955-57; chmn., chief exec. officer Gelfand, Quinn & Assos., Inc., Cleve., 1975-83; v.p., mng. dir. Prudential-Bache Securities, Inc., 1983-85; pres. Lindow, Gelfand and Quinn, Inc., 1976-83; co-editor Gelfand-Quinn/Liquidity Portfolio Mgr. Newsletter, 1978-81, Gelfand-Quinn Analysis/Money Market Techniques, 1981-84; money market columnist Nat. Thrift News, 1976-78, guest money market columnist, 1982-85; pres. Ivan Gelfand & Assocs., Inc., 1985—; sr. v.p. Prescott, Ball & Turben, Inc., 1986—; instr. investments adult div. Cleve. Bd. Edn., 1956-58, Am. Inst. Banking, 1958-68; guest lectr., speaker nat. and local TV and radio stas.; lectr. in econs., fin. instn. portfolio mgmt., cash mgmt., 1972—. Mem. investment com. United Torch Cleve., 1972-74; study-rev. team capt. Lake Erie Regional Transp. Authority, 1973-77; trustee Mt. Sinai Med. Ctr., Cleve., 1983—, treas., 1986—, trustee Jewish Community Fedn., 1986—; mem. bond com. Jewish Community Fedn., Cleve., 1979—, mem. fin. com., 1981-85; mem. Cuyahoga County Republican Fin. Com., 1978-82; mem. exec. com. Cuyahoga County Rep. Orgn., 1982—. Served with AUS, 1945-47. Mem. Greater Cleve. Growth Assn., Cleve. Soc. Security Analysts, Les Politiques. Republican. Clubs: Mid-day (Cleve.), Commerce (Cleve.), Oakwood, Union. Lodge: Masons. Home: 2900 Alvord Pl Pepper Pike OH 44124 Office: 390 Statler Office Tower Cleveland OH 44115

GELFIUS, LARRY WILLIAM, librarian; b. Columbus, Ind., Aug. 6, 1946; s. Albert Lee and Anna Marie (Dietrich) G. Student, Earlham Coll., 1964-65; BS, Ind. U., 1968, MLS, 1968-71. Library coordinator Edinburgh (Ind.) Schs., 1968-71; dir. instructional materials ctr. Harrison High Sch., West Lafayette, Ind., 1971-73; adminstrv. librarian Markham (Ill.) Pub. Library, 1973-76, Homewood (Ill.) Pub. Library, 1976—; IMT coordinator Prairie State Coll., Chicago Heights, Ill., 1977-84. Mem. ALA, Ill. Library Assn., Library Adminstrs. No. Ill., South Suburban Library Assn. (pres. 1978-80), Alpha Sigma Phi. Office: Homewood Pub Library Dist 17900 Dixie Hwy Homewood IL 60430

GELLER, ROBERT DENNIS, internist; b. N.Y.C., Apr. 5, 1941; s. Martin Max and Elvira Joan (Reich) G.; B.Met.E. cum laude, N.Y. U., 1962; M.D., Cornell U., 1966; m. Karen Hannk Greshes, Feb. 7, 1974; children—Meredith Anne, Evan Scott. Intern, Bellevue Hosp., N.Y.C., 1966-67, resident in medicine, 1967-68; resident in medicine North Shore U. Hosp., 1968-70; practice medicine specializing in internal medicine, cons. infectious disease, Manhasset, N.Y., 1972-77; practice medicine specializing in internal medicine, cons. infectious disease Freeport (Ill.) Clinic, S.C., 1977—, pres., chmn. bd., 1981—; cons. infectious disease. Theda Clark Regional Med. Ctr., Neenah, Wis., 1980—; pres. med. staff Freeport Meml. Hosp., 1982—, chief medicine, 1986—; clin. asst. prof. medicine Cornell U., U. Ill., 1986—; mem. med. malpractice panel N.Y. State Supreme Ct., Mineola, 1976; peer rev. com., bd. dirs. No. Ill. Profl. Standards Rev. Orgn., Rockford, 1978; mem. Freeport Bd. Health, 1984—. Served with USPHS, 1970-72. Diplomate Am. Bd. Internal Medicine. Fellow A.C.P.; mem. Am. Heart Assn., Am. Soc. Microbiology, Am. Fedn. Clin. Research, AMA, Ill., Stephenson County med. socs. Contbr. articles on Coccidioidin skin test sensitivity to Am. Rev. Respiratory Diseases, 1972-73. Office: 1036 W Stephenson St Freeport IL 61032

GELLERSTEDT, MARIE ADA, manufacturing company executive; b. Davenport, Iowa, Oct. 19, 1926; d. Charles Beecher and Marie Elizabeth (Pasvogel) Kaufmann; m. Keith Orval Gellerstedt, Mar. 16, 1957; children—Lori Beth Doroba, Keith Todd, Jon Erik, Cory Andrew. B.A. in Bus. Adminstrn., Augustana Coll., 1950. Gen. mgr., pres. Nixalite Co. Am., East Moline, Ill., 1957—. Life mem. Moline St. High Sch. PTA, dir., 1973-76. Mem. Ill. Mfrs. Assn., Nat. Trade Show Exhibitors Assn., Internat. Exhibitors Assn., Nat. Pest Control Assn., Nat. Animal Damage Control Assn., Nat. Assn. Women Bus. Owners, Nat. Assn. Ind. Bus. Republican. Lutheran. Clubs: Zonta, Daus. of Mokanna, Zal Caldron, Daus. of the Nile.

GELLNER, CAROL ANN, educator; b. Wheeling, W.Va., June 19, 1950; d. Charles Herman and Helen June (Gantzer) G. BA, West Liberty State Coll., 1971; MEd, Kent State U., 1975; postgrad., Miami U., Oxford, Ohio. Cert. vocat. educator and supr., supt., Ohio. Bus. edn. tchr. Yorkville (Ohio) High Sch., 1972; bus. edn. tchr. Wheeling Cen. High Sch., 1972-74; bus. edn. tchr. Belmont (Ohio) County Vocat. Sch., 1974-78; adj. faculty W.Va. No. Community Coll., Wheeling, 1974-78; CETA coordinator Belmont Vocat. Sch., 1978; ESEA project dir. Stark (Ohio) County Schs., 1978-79; instructional supr. Upper Valley Joint Vocat. Sch. Dis., Piqua, Ohio, 1979-83, equal employment opportunity, Title IX officer, 1979-83; vocat. dir. Greene Vocat. Sch., Xenia, Ohio, 1983—; cons. and lectr. in field. Author: (manual) Vocational Education for Exceptional Students, 1979; contbr. to profl. newsletter in field. Vol. Am. Cancer Soc., 1981—. Mem. AAUW, Am. Vocat. Assn., Ohio Vocat. Assn., Nat. Council Local Adminstrs., Ohio Vocat. Dirs. Assn., Phi Delta Kappa. Presbyterian. Office: 2960 W Enon Dr Xenia OH 45385

GELPI, MICHAEL ANTHONY, corporate executive; b. Columbus, Ohio, Dec. 28, 1940; s. Andre and Eleanor (Amorose) G. A.B., Georgetown U., 1962. Store mgr. Swan Cleaners, Columbus, 1964-65, dist. supr., 1965-68, v.p., 1968-76, exec. v.p., treas., 1976-81, also dir.; v.p. Rainbow Properties, Columbus, 1971-83, pres., 1983-85, chmn. bd. The Neoprobe Corp., Columbus; bd. dirs. Health Options. Trustee Am. Cancer Soc., 1978—, crusade chmn., 1979-84, 1st v.p., 1981-84, pres., 1984-85, chmn., 1985—, trustee Ohio div., 1984—, state spl. gifts chmn., 1984—, recipient Vol. of Yr. award, 1981; trustee Players Theatre of Columbus, 1981—, v.p., 1985-86, pres. 1986—; trustee German Village Hist. Soc., 1980-81; trustee Cen. Ohio Radio Reading Service, 1982—, pres., 1983-85; mem. Republican Fin. com., 1981—; trustee Town-Franklin Hist. Neighborhood Assn., 1979-85, v.p., 1983-85; chmn. advance gifts Bishops Ann. Appeal, 1981—; bd. dirs. Human Rights Campaign Fund, 1985—. Served to 1st lt. U.S. Army, 1962-64. Roman Catholic. Clubs: Columbus, Athletic (Columbus). Office: The Neoprobe Corp 2219 Summit St Columbus OH 43201

GENDE, JOSEPH J(AMES), food service company executive, inventor; b. Rock Island, Ill., July 28, 1934; s. Joseph and Eva Theodora (Bawiec) G.; m. Irene Susan Most, July 21, 1962; children—Susan K., Theresa A., Joseph A., Mary M., Paul E. Student U. Ill., 1952-57, UCLA Extension, 1960-63. Mech. designer E. J. Kelly & Assocs., Los Angeles, 1959-61; project engr. Whittaker Corp., Los Angeles, 1961-70; pres. Sagemark Ltd., Moline, Ill., 1970—. Served with U.S. Army, 1957-59. Patentee spring mechanism, aerosol replacement; v.p. Western Ill. Inventors Council, 1986. Mem. Nat. Restaurant Assn., Mississippi Valley Restaurant Assn., Nat. Assn. Ind. Businessmen, U.S. C. of C., Rock Island County C. of C. Roman Catholic. Club: Alleman Boosters (treas. 1976-77, v.p. 1980-81) (Rock Island, Ill.). Lodge: K.C. Home: 4311 7th Ave Moline IL 61265 Office: Hungry Hobo Div Sagemark Ltd 5306 23d Ave Moline IL 61265

GENIS, ALAN PAUL, electrical engineering educator; b. Chgo., Apr. 13, 1951; s. Peter Paul and Mary Ann (Nemeth) G.; m. Carol Ann Van Der Marel, May 24, 1980; 1 child, Laura Jean. Lab. asst. Sherwin Williams Labs., Chgo., 1968-69; grad. research asst. No. Ill. U., DeKalb, 1973-77, instr., 1975-77, mem. faculty dept. industry and tech., 1981-85, assoc. prof. dept. elec. engring., 1985—, dir. labs. Coll. Engring. and Engring. Tech., 1985—; grad. research asst. Colo. State U., Ft. Collins, 1977-81; cons. Colo. Crystal Corp., 1979-80. Contbr. articles to profl. jours. Mem. IEEE, Internat. Soc. for Hybrid Microelectronics, Electron Device Soc. Republican. Office: Northern Illinios U Coll Engineering Dir Labs DeKalb IL 60115

GENOVA, JAMES RUSSELL, newspaper entrepreneur; b. Detroit, Jan. 15, 1950; s. Harry Isodore and Christine Marion (Stocking) G.; m. Leslie Anne Hirth, Nov. 5, 1971; children: Natalie Anne, Nathan James. Student, Eastern Mich. U., 1969-71. Gen. mgr. Waghtenaw News, Ann Arbor, Mich., 1971-72, div. mgr., 1973-79; v.p. Genova News Co. Inc., Lansing, Mich., 1979-85, owner, 1985—, also trustee, bd. dirs. Sponsor Red Cedar Recreation, Williamston, Mich., 1979—. Republican. Presbyterian. Clubs: Pentwater Yacht, Capital City Rifle. Avocations: sailing, travel, coin collecting, coaching, trap-shooting. Home: 1174 Wild Cherry Dr Williamston MI 48895 Office: Genova News Co Inc 589 W Grand River Okemos MI 48864

GENOVA, LESLIE ANNE, news company executive; b. Ann Arbor, Mich., Apr. 5, 1952; d. Edwin William and Norma Jean (Upchurch) Hirth; m. James Russell Genova, Nov. 5, 1971; children: Natalie Anne, Nathan James. Student, Eastern Mich. U., 1970-72. Sec. Washtenaw News, Ann Arbor, 1972-73; sec. Genova News Co. Inc., Lansing, Mich., 1973-84, treas., 1984-85, pres., 1985—. Room mother Williamston (Mich.) Elem. Sch., 1983, active in sch. functions, fund raisers, 1979—. Republican. Lutheran. Club: Pentwater Yacht. Avocations: sailing, decorating, racquetball, caligraphy, interior design.

GENOVESE, GASPER, computer information scientist; b. Detroit, Mar. 24, 1957; s. Nicola and Theresa (Girlanda) G.; m. Laura Ann Williamson, May 23, 1980; 1 child, Anthony Robert. BBA, Eastern Mich. U., 1979; MA, Cen. Mich. U., 1986. Programmer, analyst The Detroit News, 1979-81, computer systems mgr., 1985—, bus. systems mgr., 1981-84; cons. Resource Plus, Inc., Troy, Mich., 1984-85. Rep. precinct del., Warren, Mich., 1986—. Avocation: golf. Office: The Detroit News 6200 Metro Pkwy Sterling Heights MI 48077

GENSHAFT, JUDY LYNN, psychologist, educator; b. Canton, Ohio, Jan. 7, 1948; d. Arthur I. and Leona (Caghan) G. BA, U. Wis., 1969; MA, Kent State U., 1973, PhD, 1975. Lic. psychologist, Ohio. Sch. psychologist Canton (Ohio) City Schs., 1972-75; asst. prof. Ohio State U., 1976-81, assoc. prof., asst. chmn., 1981-85, prof., 1985—, asst. chair, 1985-86, chair, 1987—, presdl. intern, acting assoc. provost, 1986-87; psychiat. social worker Canton Mental Health Clinic, 1970-72; vis. prof. U. British Columbia, Vancouver, Can., 1976-81. Contbr. numerous articles and book chpts. to profl. publ. Mem. Ballet Met., Columbus, 1986; cons. League Against Child Abuse, Columbus, 1978—, Bur. Vocat. Edn., Columbus, 1980—; mem. adv. bd. Support for Talented Students, Columbus, 1985—. Nat. Research grantee, 1984-85; recipient Kathryn Schoen Endowment award, 1986, Hon. award Ohio Dept. Edn., 1984. Mem. Am. Psychol. Assn., Nat. Assn. Sch. Psychologist, (sec. 1983-85, Presl. award 1982, 85), Am. Assn. Counseling and Devel., Internat. Assn. Sch. Psychologists, Ohio Sch. Psychologist Assn. (ethics chmn. 1985-86), Sigma Xi. Avocations: sports, reading. Home: 3451 W Henderson Rd Columbus OH 43220 Office: Ohio State U 356 ARPS Hall Columbus OH 43210

GENSHAFT, NEIL, meat packing company executive; b. 1943. M.B.A., U. Chgo., 1968. With Superior's Brand Meats Inc., Massillon, Ohio, 1968—, asst. sec., 1969-71, adminstrv. v.p., 1971-79, pres., 1979—, chief exec. officer, treas., 1982—, dir.; chmn., past pres. Sugardale Food Inc. (subs.), Canton, Ohio. Office: Superior's Brand Meats Inc PO Box 571 Massillon OH 44648 *

GENSKOW, JACK KUENNE, psychology educator; b. Milw., Mar. 19, 1936. BS, U. Wis.-Milw., 1961; MA, U. Ill., 1962, PhD, 1967. Psychologist, dir. Decatur (Ill.) Evaluation Ctr., 1965-77; research utility specialist Ill. D.V.R., Springfield, 1977-78; assoc. prof. Sangamon State U., Springfield, 1978—; psychol. cons. Goodwill Industries, Springfield, 1978—. Harold Scharper Achievement fellow U. Ill. Delta Sigma Omicron, 1967, World Rehab. Fund fellow, 1986; recipient Marlene Nelson Service award Ill. Rehab. Assn., 1977. Mem. Am. Psychol. Assn. Nat. Rehab. Assn., Am. Assn. Counseling and Devel. Home: 1916 Claremont Rd Springfield IL 62703 Office: Sangamon State U Brookens 348 Springfield IL 62708

GENTILE, CHARLES R., lawyer; b. Omaha, Mar. 9, 1955; s. Samuel Richard and Rosemary (Traynor) G. B.A., U. Nebr., 1977; J.D., Creighton U., 1980. Bar: Nebr. 1980, U.S. Dist. Ct. Nebr. 1980, U.S. Ct. Appeals (8th cir.) 1980, U.S. Tax Ct. 1982. Assoc., Byrne & Randall, P.C., Omaha, 1980-83; prin. Byrne Rothery, Gentile & Blazek, P.C., Omaha, 1983; exec dir. Nebr. Commn. of Indsl. Relations, Lincoln, 1983-85; sole practice, Omaha, 1983—; atty. Farm Credit Banks Omaha, 1985—;lectr. Nebr. Coll. Bus., Omaha 1980-84, U. Nebr., Omaha, 1981—. Mem. editorial staff Creighton Law Rev., 1979. Mem. ABA, Nebr. Bar Assn., Omaha Bar Assn., Phi Alpha Theta, Pi Sigma Theta. Republican. Office: Farm Credit Banks Omaha 206 S 19th St Omaha NE 68102

GENTILE, RICHARD JOSEPH, geology educator, researcher; b. St. Louis, June 25, 1929; s. Richard and Anne L. (Kreji) G. B.A. in Geology, U. Mo.-Columbia, 1956, M.A. in Geology, 1958; Ph.D., U. Mo.-Rolla, 1965. Geologist Mo. Geol. Survey, Rolla, 1958-65, chief geologist (coal), 1965-66; asst. prof. U. Mo., Kansas City, 1966-70, assoc. prof., 1970-75, prof. geology, 1975—; cons. non-metallic mineral resources; faculty adv. U. Mo. student chpt. Am. Assn. Petroleum Geologists; lectr. various amateur geology clubs, Kansas City area. Author: Geology of the Belton Quadrangle, 1984. Contbr. articles on geology to profl. jours. Fellow Geol. Soc. Am.; mem. Nat. Assn. Geology Tchrs. (pres. Central sect. 1984-85), Soc. Engring. Geologists (pres. Kansas City/Omaha sect. 1979-81), Sigma Xi (sec., treas. Kansas City chpt. 1970-85; Cert. Recognition award 1981). Avocation: hiking. Home: 5401 Brookside Blvd Apt 300 Kansas City MO 64112 Office: Univ Mo Dept Geoscis 5100 Rockhill Rd Kansas City MO 64110

GENTINE, LEE MICHAEL, marketing professional; b. Plymouth, Wis., Feb. 18, 1952; s. Leonard ALvin and Dolores Ann (Becker) G.; m. Debra Ann Skemnicht, Dec. 29, 1973; children: Amanda, Joshua, Jonathan. BBA, U. Notre Dame, 1974; MBA, DePaul U., 1977. Acct. Hurdman & Cranston, Chgo., 1974-75; sales rep. Sargento Cheese Inc., Plymouth, 1975-78, mktg. mgr., 1978-81, sr. v.p. mktg., 1981-85, exec. v.p. mktg., 1985—. Pres. Plymouth Softball Assn., 1980-85, Plymouth Indsl. Devel. Corp., 1981—. Mem. Am. Mktg. Assn., Sheboygan County C. of C. (bd. dirs. 1987), Beta Gamma Sigma. Roman Catholic. Avocations: softball, golf, woodworking.

GENTRY, JILL JONES, dentist; b. Logansport, Ind., Sept. 30, 1953; d. W. Max and Patricia Maxine (Harner) Jones; m. Philip Arthur Gentry, July 24, 1982; 1 child, Peter Daniel. BS, Purdue U., 1975, MS, 1977; DDS, Ind. Sch. Dentistry, 1982. Acad. advisor Purdue U., West Lafayette, Ind., 1976-78; gen. practice dentistry VA Hosp., Indpls., 1983—; staff dentist Millers Merry Manor Nursing Home, Logansport, 1983—. Mem. Y-Bd., Cass County Family YMCA, Logansport, 1985; mem. adminstrn. bd., trustee 1st United Meth. Ch., Logansport, 1984—. Mem. ADA, Am. Gen. Dentistry, Ind. Dental Assn., Kappa Kappa Kappa. Republican. Avocations: camping, canoeing, piano, gardening. Home: 3011 Greenhills Dr Logansport IN 46947 Office: 1107 E Broadway PO Box 76 Logansport IN 46947

GENTRY, JOSEPH WESLEY, personnel manager; b. Alpena, Mich., Sept. 26, 1951; s. Joseph Wesley and Dorothy Mae (Haglund) G. AA, Alpena Community Coll., 1971; BS, Mich. State U., 1973. Cert. CPR, advanced first aid and water safety instr. Mixed control chemist Huron div. Nat. Gypsum, Alpena, 1973; safety and tng. Besser Co., Alpena, 1973-87, mgr. personnel, 1987—; cross country coach Alpena Community Coll., 1984—, evening bus. instr., 1985—; indsl. advisor Thunder Bay Watershed Council, Alpena, 1981—; bd. dirs. adv. com. health and fitness Alpena Community Coll. , 1984—. Pres., bd. dirs. Big Bros./Big Sisters, Alpena, 1980-84; bd. dirs. Northeast Mich. United Way, Alpena, 1984—, v.p., 1987—; pres. Grace Luth. Ch., Alpena, 1979-82, 87—. Mem. Am. Soc. Safety Engrs., Nat. Jr. Coll. Coaches Assn., N.E. Mich. Personnel Assn. (trustee 1985-86). Republican. Avocations: running, hiking, reading, mountain biking. Home: 7398 N Point Shores Alpena MI 49707 Office: Besser Co 801 Johnson Alpena MI 49707

GEOGA, DOUGLAS GERARD, real estate development company executive; b. Detroit, Aug. 13, 1955; s. Christ and Virginia M. (Juras) G.; m. Carol A. Huber, Mar. 11, 1977. AB, Harvard U., 1977, JD, 1980. Bar: Mich. 1980. Assoc. Miller, Canfield, Paddock and Stone, Detroit, 1980-83; devel. counsel Hyatt Devel. Corp., Chgo., 1983-85, gen. counsel, 1985-86, v.p., gen. counsel, 1986—. Mem. ABA, Urban Land Inst. (assoc.). Democrat. Roman Catholic. Office: Hyatt Devel Corp 200 W Madison Chicago IL 60606

GEOGHEGAN, JOSEPH ALOYSIUS, JR., architect; b. Evergreen Park, Ill., Apr. 18, 1957; S. Joseph Aloysius and Patricia Marie (Scotty) G.; m. Joan Marie Kaiser, Aug. 8, 1981; children: Marisa Lynn, Maureen Therese. BArch, Ill. Inst. Tech., 1980. Registered architect, Ill., Calif., Ariz., Mont. Intern architect Robert G. Lyon Assocs., Chgo., 1979-82, architect, 1982—. Mem. Nat. Council of Archtl. Registration Bds., Alpha Sigma Phi. Home: 1044 S East Ave Oak Park IL 60304 Office: Robert G Lyon Assocs Inc 470 N Milwaukee Chicago IL 60610

GEORGE, DONALD ELIAS, lawyer; b. Akron, Ohio, July 8, 1950; s. George John and Thelma Beatrice (Goforth) G.; m. Christine Kaderle Cirignano, May 1, 1982; children: Michelle, Michael. B.A., U. Akron, 1972, J.D., 1975. Bar: Ohio 1975, U.S. Dist. Ct (no. dist.) Ohio 1975, U.S. Supreme Ct. 1979, U.S. Ct. Appeals (6th cir.) 1985. Sole practice, Akron, 1975—; bankruptcy trustee, U.S. Bankruptcy Ct., Akron, 1975-78; arbitrator Am. Arbitration Assn., Cleve., 1976-79. Author: Israeli Occupation: International Law and Political Realities, 1979. Mem. Akron Regional Devel. Bd., 1984—, guest speaker Sta. WHLO, Steve Fullerton Show, Akron, 1979-80; mem. adv. coms. for judicial candidates, 1979, 86; choir dir. St. George Orthodox Ch., 1969-75. Mem. ABA, Ohio State Bar Assn., Akron Bar Assn., Summit County Humane Soc., Akron Law Library Assn., Democrat. Avocation: piano playing. Office: 572 W Market St Suite 11 Akron OH 44303

GEORGE, MUMTAZ, physician; b. Baghdad, Iraq, Sept. 22, 1942; came to U.S., 1950, naturalized, 1955; s. John and Nora (Sharrak) G.; children—Jennifer, Matthew. Student Detroit Inst. Tech., 1960-61; B.S., Wayne State U., 1967; M.D., U. Granada, Spain, 1975. Resident in internal medicine Providence Hosp., Southfield, Mich., 1976-79, fellow in critical care, 1979-80; fellow in residence Rocky Mountain Poison Ctr., Denver, 1980; practice medicine specializing in internal medicine, 1980—; owner, dir. Farmington Urgent Care Ctr., Farmington Hills, Mich., 1982—; ptnr., owner Kingswood Urgent Med. Ctr., Bloomfield Hills, Mich., 1983—; emergency room physician Pontiac Gen. Hosp., Mich., 1981—, St. Mary's Hosp., Livonia, Mich., 1982—. Mem. AMA, Oakland County Med. Assn., Am. Coll. Emergency Physicians, Soc. Critical Care Medicine, Mich. State Med. Soc. Home: 34010 Ramble Hills Dr Farmington Hills MI 48018

GEORGE, RICHARD G., drug store company executive; b. 1939. BS, U. Ill., 1961, MBA, 1962. With Jewel Cos., Inc., 1961-73; with Osco Drugs, Inc., Hinsdale, Ill., 1978—, pres., chief exec. officer, 1979—. Office: Osco Drug Inc 1818 Swift Dr Oak Brook IL 60521 *

GEORGE, RICHARD JOSEPH, accountant; b. Trenton, N.J., Sept. 18, 1961; s. Robert Joseph and E. Elaine (Andrews) G.; m. Susan Kay Kingston, Aug. 3, 1985. BS in Accountancy, U. Ill., 1983. CPA, Ill. Staff acct. Arthur Andersen & Co., Chgo., 1983-84, Clifton, Gunderson & Co., Champaign, Ill., 1984—. Mem. Am. Inst. CPA's, Ill. CPA Soc. Avocations: racquetball, travel, reading. Home: 145 Paddock Dr E Savoy IL 61874 Office: Clifton Gunderson & Co 203 W Clark St Champaign IL 61820

GEORGE, SHARON LYNN, academic administrator; b. Detroit, June 5, 1951; s. Gerald Stanley and Esther (Dietsch) G. BA in Sociology, Western Mich. U., 1974, MA in Counseling, 1976; MS in Adminstrn., Cen. Mich. U., 1985. Proceedings officer, asst. dean students Cen. Mich. U., Mt. Pleasant, 1976-77, coordinator student activities, 1977-86, asst. dir. Office of Student Life, 1987—. Trustee Mich. Women's Found., Detroit, 1986. Mem. Nat. Assn. Campus Activities, Nat. Assn. Women Deans, Adminstrs., Counselors, Am. Coll. Personnel Assn., Assn. Frat. Advisors, Nat. Assn. Student Personal Adminstrs., Assn. Coll. Unions-Internat., Phi Chi Theta, Sigma Sigma Sigma. Home: 1429 Lake Shore Dr Weidman MI 48893 Office: Cen Mich U Office Student Life 251 Foust Hall Mount Pleasant MI 48859

GEORGE, WILLIAM WALLACE, manufacturing company executive; b. Muskegon, Mich., Sept. 14, 1942; s. Wallace Edwin and Kathryn Jean (Dinkeloo) G.; m. Ann Tonnlier Pilgram, Sept. 6, 1969; children: Jeffrey, Jonathan. BS in Indsl. Engring. with honors, Ga. Inst. Tech., 1964; MBA with high distinction, Harvard U., 1966. Asst. to asst. sec. Dept. Def., Washington, 1966-68; spl. civilian asst. to sec. Navy, Washington, 1968-69; with Litton Industries, 1969-78; dir. long-range planning Litton Industries, Cleve., 1969-70; v.p. Litton Industries, 1976—; with Litton Microwave Cooking Products, 1970-78; v.p. Litton Microwave Cooking Products, Mpls., 1970-71; exec. v.p. Litton Microwave Cooking Products, 1971-73, pres., 1973-78; v.p. corp. devel. Honeywell, Mpls., 1978-80, exec. v.p., 1983-87; pres. Honeywell Europe (S.A.), 1980-82, Indsl. Automation, 1987—; bd. dirs. Valspar Corp. Bd. dirs. Minn. Symphony Orch., 1976-80, United Way, 1976-79, nat. chmn., Belgium, 1982-83; bd. dirs., pres., treas. Guthrie Theater, 1977— ; vice chmn. United Theol. Sem., 1977-80, fin. com. Abbott-Northwestern Hosp., 1984—; trustee MacCalaster Coll., 1987—. Recipient Meritorious Civilian Service Award Sec. Navy, 1969. Sigma Chi (Internat. Balfour award 1964); (trustee 1971-77). Episcopalian. Clubs: Minneapolis, Minikahda. Home: 2284 W Lake of Isles Blvd Minneapolis MN 55405 Office: Honeywell Inc Honeywell Plaza Minneapolis MN 55408

GEORGIA, KENNETH LEE, management consultant; b. Toledo, Nov. 6, 1953; s. Wayman Edward and Vern Agnes (Riley) G.; m. Sherry Irene Day, Aug. 22, 1980; children: Gary Brock, Heather Louise, Michelle Lee. BS, U. Toledo, 1976. Programmer Whirlpool Corp., Findlay, Ohio, 1977-79; lead analyst, programmer Owens Corning Fiberglas, Toledo, 1979-82; sr. analyst, programmer Libbey-Owens-Ford, Toledo, 1982-85, bus. systems cons., 1985—. Sponsoring mem. Internat. Shooting Team Olympic Tng. Ctr., Boulder, Colo., 1985. Democrat. Roman Catholic. Avocations: competition rifle shooting, golf, bowling, model rocketry. Home: 4680 Ventura Dr Toledo OH 43615 Office: Libbey Owens Ford 811 Madison Ave Toledo OH 43695

GEPHARDT, RICHARD ANDREW, congressman; b. St. Louis, Jan. 31, 1941; s. Louis Andrew and Loreen Estelle (Cassell) G.; m. Jane Ann Byrnes, Aug. 13, 1966; children: Matthew, Christine, Katherine. B.S., Northwestern U., 1962; J.D., U. Mich., 1965. Bar: Mo. bar 1965. Partner firm Thompson & Mitchell, St. Louis, 1965-76; alderman 14th ward, St. Louis, 1971-76; mem. 96th-100th Congress from 3d Mo. Dist., 1979—; possible candidate for Dem. nomination for Pres. of U.S. 1987-88; Pres. Children's Hematology Research Assn., St. Louis Children's Hosp., 1973-76; Democratic committeeman 14th ward St. Louis, 1968-71. Mem. Mo., St. Louis bar assns., Am. Legion, Young Lawyer's Soc. (chmn. 1972-73). Club: Mid-Town (St. Louis). Lodge: Kiwanis. Office: US House of Representatives 218 Cannon House Office Bldg Washington DC 20515 *

GERADS, RODERICK BERNARD, operations manager; b. Grey Eagle, Minn., July 25, 1944; s. William H. and Erma Linda (Bueckers) G.; m. Irene L. Douvier, May 21, 1966; children: Timothy, Jeffrey, Kimberly, Bradley. Cert. data processing, Minn. Sch. Bus., 1963. Ops. mgr. St. Cloud (Minn.) State U., 1976—; mapper coordinator St. Cloud State U., 1985—. Chmn. bd. Upsala (Minn.) Sch. Bd., 1984-86; chmn. St. Francis Ch. Parish Council, 1986, lector, 1975-86. Republican. Roman Catholic. Avocations: reading, fishing. Home: Rt 2 PO Box 59AA Freeport MN 56331 Office: St Cloud State U CH 43 B Saint Cloud MN 56331

GERARD, PASCAL ANTHONY, mechanical engineer; b. Elmwood Park, Ill., Jan. 6, 1931; s. Jerry and Bridget (Petrone) G.; m. Aglaea Kaludis, July 16, 1955; children: Pascal Jr., Michael, Gregory, Teresa, Mary, Carole. BSME, U. Ill., 1953; MBA, U. Chgo., 1959. Quality control engr. AT & T Teletype, Skokie, Ill., 1959-64, factory supr. mfg., 1964-66, engring. dept. chief, 1966-69, chief engring. dept., 1969-81, mfg. mgr., 1981-84, engring. mgr., 1984—. Mem. Norridge (Ill.) Youth Activity, 1965-75; pres. Norridge Little League, 1965-75; v.p. St. Eugene Sch. Bd., Norridge, 1979-80; worker Dem. Party, Norridge, 1974-75. Mem. Am. Soc. for Quality Control (sr., membership chmn. 1965-66), Am. Soc. Mechl. Engrs. Roman Catholic. Lodge: KC. Avocations: reading, jogging, sports. Office: AT & T Teletype 5555 N Touhy Ave Skokie IL 60077

GERARDI, JOHN EUGENE, state agency official; b. Columbus, Ohio, Apr. 10, 1950; s. John Salvatore and Stella Gloria (D'Angelo) G. BA, Ohio State U., 1972; MBA, Capital U., 1980. Bailiff Franklin County Mcpl. Ct.,

Columbus, 1972-82, bailiff domestic relations, 1983-86, adminstrv. analyst, 1986—. Republican. Roman Catholic. Home: 1462 S James Rd Columbus OH 43227 Office: Franklin County Mcpl Ct 375 S High St Columbus OH 43215

GERBER, CARL JOSEPH, hospital administrator, psychiatrist; b. Detroit, Feb. 15, 1934; s. William J. and Signe (Wallin) G.; m. LaVora R. Sartain, Oct. 28, 1932. BS, U. Detroit, 1956; PhD, Washington U., St. Louis, 1960; MD, Duke U., 1967. Diplomate Am. Bd. Psychiatry and Neurology. Assoc. prof. med. Duke U., Durham, N.C., 1961-72; chief consultation, liaison psychiatrist Wash. U., Seattle, 1972-74; chief of staff V.A. Med. Ctr., Tacoma, Washington, 1974-82, Des Moines, 1982-86; dir. V.A. Med. Ctr., Ft. Meade, S.D., 1986—. Contbr. sci. articles to profl. jours. Served to lt. col. USAR, 1986—. Mem. Am. Psychiat. Assn., Am. Coll. Health Care Execs. Avocations: golfing, bowling. Office: VA Med Ctr Fort Meade SD 57741

GERBER, JEFFRY CHRISTOPHER, lawyer; b. Glen Gardner, N.J., Oct. 4, 1943; s. Edwin Louis and Claire (Martin) G.; children—Eric, Adam. B.S. in Mech. Engring., Stevens Inst. Tech., 1965; J.D., Boston U., 1972. Bar: Ohio 1972, D.C. 1983. Registered profl. engr., Mass. Engr., Stone & Webster Corp., Boston, 1965-69; engr., computer analyst C.T. Main Corp., Boston, 1969-72; trial atty. Gallagher, Sharp et al, Cleve., 1972-76; sr. atty. Bendix Corp., Cleve., 1976-81; house counsel Donn Corp., Cleve., 1981-83; sole practice, Cleve., 1983—. Mem. Ohio Bar Assn., Mensa. Presbyterian. Avocations: skiing, sailing. Home: 5010 Mayfield Rd Cleveland OH 44124

GERBER, RANDALL ERIC, TV writer and producer; b. Millersburg, Ohio, Nov. 20, 1947; s. Adrian Andrew and Mary Alice (Blosser) G.; m. Karel Curtis, June 21, 1969 (div. Oct. 1973); 1 child, Ticia Louise; m. Christine Louise Stanley, Dec. 24, 1985. BS summa cum laude, Kent (Ohio) State U., 1969. Announcer Sta. WJER, Dover, Ohio, 1963-69; news dir. Sta. WJAN-TV, Canton, Ohio, 1969-72, WKBN-TV, Youngstown, Ohio, 1972-76; exec. producer pub. TV Youngstown State U., 1976-78; pres. The Image Producers, Youngstown, 1978—; columnist Warren (Ohio) Tribune, 1979-82; columnist/reviewer Tng. News mad., 1982-85. Served as pvt. U.S. Army, 1969-73. Mem. Internat. TV Assn., Am. Soc. Tng. and Devel. Democrat. Methodist. Avocations: racquet sports, painting, music. Office: Image Producers/Gerber Group 3119 Market St Youngstown OH 44507

GERBER, WILLIAM ROBERT, obstetrician, gynecologist; b. St. Louis, June 17, 1945; s. Rudolph Vogt and Isabel (Bauer) G.; m. Joan Elizabeth Vielhaber, June 3, 1967 (div. Jan. 1982); children: Joseph R., Elizabeth M.; m. Cheryl Lynn Tenney, Aug. 22, 1986. BSEE, St. Louis U., 1967; MSEE, Syracuse U., 1971; MD, St. Louis U., 1976. Diplomate Am. Bd. Ob-Gyn. Commd. 2d lt. USAF, 1967, advanced through grades to col., 1985; electronics engr. Rome Air Devel. Ctr., Griffiss AFB, N.Y., 1967-72; resident in ob-gyn. Walter Reed Hosp., Washington, 1976-80; staff obstetrician-gynecologist Scott Med. Ctr., Scott AFB, Ill., 1980-82, chmn. Ob-Gyn, 1982—; medico-legal cons. Staff Judge Advocate, Scott AFB, 1980—; cons. Surgeon Gen. Dept., Scott AFB, 1982—; asst. clin. prof., St. Louis U., 1985—. Fellow Am. Coll. Ob-Gyn, Soc. Air Force Clin. Surgeons (sr. mem.), Alpha Sigma Nu. Roman Catholic. Avocations: bicycling, photography. Home: 6450 Devonshire Saint Louis MO 63109 Office: Scott Med Ctr Dept Ob-Gyn Scott AFB IL 62225

GERDE, PRISCILLA MURPHY, audiovisual and graphics specialist; b. Indpls., Dec. 5, 1949; d. Moris Leon and Josephine (Clark) Murphy; B.A., Purdue U., 1972; postgrad. Ind.-Purdue U., Indpls., 1978; m. Carlyle Noyes Gerde, July 4, 1976. Dir. publs. Ind. Dept. Commerce, 1972-73; coordinator editorial services Eli Lilly & Co., 1973-76, dept. head employee communications, 1983-86; sec. Eli Lilly & Co., Found., Indpls., 1976-83; Lilly sales rep., Pittsfield, Mass., 1979. Bd. dirs. Eli Lilly Fed. Credit Union, sec., 1980—; bd. dirs. Indpls. Civic Theatre, 1982—, pres., 1986—; bd. dirs. Christanore House, 1984—, Ind. Soc. to Prevent Blindness, 1983—, v.p.,pres. elect, 1986—. Named Outstanding Woman in Lafayette, Lafayette (Ind.) Bus. and Profl. Women, 1978. Home: Lakehurst Battle Ground IN 47920 Office: Lilly Corp Ctr Indianapolis IN 46285

GERDENER, JOHN GERHARD, accountant; b. Appleton, Wis., Feb. 27, 1949; s. Gerhard William and Dorothy Esther (Suelflow) G. BBA, U. Wis., Oshkosh, 1971, MBA, 1979. CPA, Wis. Auditor Wis. Dept. Revenue, Madison, 1971-72; staff acct. Schenck & Assocs. S.C., Appleton, 1972-74; sr. acct. Schewck & Assocs. S.C., Appleton, 1974-78, mgr., 1978—; lectr. CPA rev. course, Wis., 1982-83. Mem. adv. com. Appleton Area Sch. Dist., 1982; treas. Rep. Party, Eight Congl. Dist., Wis., 1983-85. Fellow Wis. Inst. CPA's (lectr. 1982, com. chmn. 1985-86, bd. dirs., chpt. pres. 1987-88), The Planning Forum (chpt. pres. 1987-88), Nat. Assn. Accts. (v.p. 1985-88), Cercle West 1 Owner's Assn. (v.p. 1981-86), Fox Cities C. of C. (very important person council 1985-87), Alpha Phi Omega, Phi Eta Sigma, Beta Gamma Sigma. Lutheran. Avocations: swimming, racquetball, traveling, meeting people.

GERDES, NEIL WAYNE, library director; b. Moline, Ill., Oct. 19, 1943; s. John Edward and Della Marie (Ferguson) G. A.B., U. Ill., 1965; B.D., Harvard U., 1968; M.A., Columbia U., 1971; M.A. in L.S., U. Chgo., 1975. Diplomate: Ordained to ministry Unitarian Universalist Assn., 1975. Copy chief Little, Brown, 1968-69; instr. Tuskegee Inst., 1969-71; library asst. Augustana Coll., 1972-73; editorial asst. Library Quar., 1973-74; librarian, prof. Meadville Theol. Schs., Chgo., 1973—; library program dir. Chgo. Cluster Theol. Schs., 1977-80; dir. Hammond Library, 1980—; prof. Chgo. Theol Sem., 1980—. Mem. ALA, Am. Theol. Library Assn., Chgo Area Theol. Library Assn., Phi Beta Kappa. Office: Hammond Library Chgo Theol Seminary 5757 S University Ave Chicago IL 60637

GERDES, RALPH DONALD, fire safety consultant; b. Cin., Aug. 11, 1951; s. Paul Donald and Jo Ann Dorothy (Meyer) G. BArch, Ill. Inst. Tech., 1975. Registered architect, Ill. Architect Schiller & Frank, Wheeling, Ill., 1976; sr. assoc. Rolf Jensen & Assocs., Inc., Chgo., 1976-84; pres. Ralph Gerdes & Assocs., Inc., Indpls., 1986—; Lectr. Purdue U., Ind. U., Ill. Inst. Tech., Butler U. Co-author: Planning and Designing the Office Environment, 1981. Mem. Soc. of Fire Protection Engring. (assoc.), Nat. Fire Protection Assn., AIA, Internat. Conf. of Bldg. Officials, Ind. Fire Safety Assn. (exec. com. 1986). Roman Catholic. Club: Columbia (Indpls.). Home: 556 Lockerbie Circle N Indianapolis IN 46202 Office: 127 E Michigan St Indianapolis IN 46204

GEREND, JOHN B., training and development executive; b. Sheboygan, Wis., May 30, 1947; s. Raymond Mathias and Gertrude Mary (Reinl) G.; m. Elizabeth Schott, June 7, 1969; children: Timothy John, Peter Jacob, Thomas Raymond. BS in Psychology, St. John's U., Collegeville, Min., 1969. Prodn. supr. Corning Glass Works, Bluffton, Ind., 1972-75, prodn. mgr., 1975-80, tng. mgr., 1980-83; mgr. tng. and devel. Barber-Colman Co., Rockford, Ill., 1983—; instr. Rockford (Ill.) Coll., 1986. Mem. edn. adv. com. U. Ill., Rockford, 1985-86; mem. allocations com. United Way, Rockford, 1985-86; bd. dirs. Rockford Regional Acad. Ctr., 1984-86, Rockford Boys Club, 1985-86, Promised Land Employment Service, Rockford, 1986. Served to 1st lt. U.S. Army, 1969-72, Vietnam. Decorated Bronze Star. Mem. Am. Soc. Tng. and Devel., Rockford Area Personnel Assn. Republican. Presbyterian. Club: Y's Men (bd. dirs. 1985-86) (Rockford). Lodge: Elks. Home: 911 Tamarack Ln Rockford IL 61107 Office: Barber-Colman Co 1354 Clifford Ave Loves Park IL 61132

GERING, DONALD VERN, photographer; b. Sioux Falls, S.D., Mar. 6, 1947; s. Vernon Walter and Irene J. (Graber) G.; m. Susan Marie Culp, May 30, 1977; 1 child, Shannon Elaine. AA, Freeman Coll., 1971. Printer Pine Hill Printery, Freeman, S.D., 1969-72, Mennonite Press, North Newton, Kans., 1972-79; prin. Picture Place, Henderson, Nebr., 1979; advt. mgr. Hesston (Kans.) Record, 1980-84; prin. The Photographer, Hesston, 1980—. Pub. Hesston Coloring Book, 1985. Mem. Profl. Photographers Am., Kans. Profl. Photographers Assn., Greater Wichita Profl. Photographers Assn. (bd. dirs.). Republican. Mem. Mennonite Ch. Home and Office: 116 W Vesper Hesston KS 67062

GERLACH, FRANKLIN THEODORE, lawyer; b. Portsmouth, Ohio, Apr. 11, 1935; s. Albert T. and Nora Alice (Hayes), G.; m. Cynthia Ann Koehler, Aug. 1, 1958; children—Valarie, Philipp. B.B.A., U. Cin., 1958; M.P.A., Syracuse U., 1959; J.D., U. Cin., 1961. Bar: Ohio 1961, U.S. Dist. Ct. (so. dist.) Ohio 1969, U.S. Supreme Ct. 1971. Dir. Purchasing, Planning and Renewal, City of Portsmouth, 1961-62; city mgr., 1962-66; asst. dir. Ohio U., Portsmouth, 1966-68; sole practice, Portsmouth, 1968—; solicitor Village New Boston, Ohio, 1968-70; trustee Ohio Acad. Trial Lawyers, Columbus, Ohio, 1984-85. Recipient Outstanding Young Man of Ohio award (1 of 5) Portsmouth Jaycees, 1968, Ohio Jaycees, 1969. Mem. Portsmouth Bar and Law Library Assn. (pres. 1986), Ohio Acad. Trial Lawyers. Democrat. Lodges: Rotary. Avocation: antiques. Home: 1221 20th St Portsmouth OH 45662 Office: 1030 Kinneys Ln Portsmouth OH 45662

GERLACH, GARY GENE, newspaper publisher; b. Osage, Iowa, June 8, 1941; s. Gene Wayne and Norma Linda (Rosel) G.; m. Karen Ann Conner, June 21, 1980. B.A., U. Iowa, 1964; M.S., Columbia U., 1965; J.D., Harvard U., 1970, M.P.A., 1972. Reporter copy editor Miami Herald, 1964; staff writer Nat. Observer, Washington, 1965-67; legal asst. Commr. Nicholas Johnson, FCC, Washington, 1970-71; atty. Arnold & Porter, Washington, 1972-74; exec. v.p., gen. counsel dir. Des Moines Register and Tribune Co., 1974-82, exec. v.p., dir., 1982-86; pres., pub. Des Moines Newspapers, 1982-86; bd. editors Nat. Media Law Reporter, Washington, 1978—; pres., dir. Midwest Newspapers, Inc., Des Moines, 1986—. Pres. Des Moines Met. Opera, 1981; pres. Iowa Freedom of Info. Council, 1978; v.p. Des Moines Met. YMCA, 1979-81; trustee Civic Center Greater Des Moines, 1975-86; bd. dirs. U. Iowa Found., Iowa City, 1978—. Mem. ABA, Am. Newspaper Pub. Assn. (dir. press-bar com.), Bar Commonwealth Mass., D.C. Bar, Iowa State Bar, Phi Beta Kappa. Lutheran. Clubs: Des Moines; Prairie (Des Moines); Harvard (N.Y.C.). Office: Midwest Newspapers Inc 317 Fifth St Ames IA 50010

GERLACH, JOHN B., business executive; b. Columbus, Ohio, Jan. 28, 1927; s. John Joseph and Pauline (Pollitt) G.; m. Dareth Axene, Sept. 30, 1949; children: John B., David P., Susan. Student, Ohio State U., 1945-47, Ohio U., 1947-49. Ptnr. John Gerlach & Co., Columbus, 1949—; pres. Lancaster Glass Corp. (Ohio), 1958—, dir.; pres. Ind. Glass Co., Dunkirk, 1952—, dir.; pres. Lancaster Colony Corp., Columbus, Ohio, 1963—, dir.; sec.-treas., dir. Pretty Products Inc., Coshocton, Ohio, Nat. Glove Inc., Coshocton, Ohio; dir. Columbus Dental Mfg. Co., Mills Inc., Columbus, Jackson Corp. (Ohio), Beverage Mgmt. Inc., Columbus. Trustee Columbus Gallery Fine Arts. Clubs: Univ, Columbus, Sciotto Country, Coshocton Country. Home: 2320 Onandaga Dr Columbus OH 43215 Office: Lancaster Colony Corp 37 W Broad St Columbus OH 43215 *

GERLACH, JOHN J., diversified company executive; b. Columbus, Ohio, 1902. Grad., Ohio State U., 1923. Ptnr. John Gerlach & Co., Columbus; chmn., sec. Lancaster Colony Corp., Columbus, Ohio, N.Y. Frozen Foods, Molded Products Inc.; v.p., sec., dir. Lancaster Glass Co., Ind. Glass Co.; sec., dir. Am. Mat. Co., August Barr Inc., Candle Lite Inc., Enterprise Aluminum Co., Loma Corp., Nelson McCoy Pottery Co., Nat. Glove Inc., Jackson Corp., I. Marzetti Co., Barr Inc., Koneta Rubber Co. Office: Lancaster Colony Corp 37 W Broad St Columbus OH 43215 *

GERLACH, WILLIAM EMBER, printing executive; b. Bay City, Mich., May 10, 1927; s. George Clayton and Lillian Mae (Sawden) G.; m. L. Eugenia Bowling, Oct. 28, 1946; children—Thomas Eugene, John William, James Walter, B.A., Mich. State U., 1949. Mgr. Aldrich Market, Lansing, Mich., 1950-53; ind. retail grocer, 1953-63; founder Check Reporting Services, Inc., Lansing, 1960—; founder, owner P&F Printing Co., Lansing, 1987—; condr. check cashing seminars Mich. Bankers Assn., Lansing Community Coll. Chmn. Caravan Circus, 1983, 84. Served with U.S. Army, 1946. Mem. Mich. Assn. Check Investigators, Nat. Fedn. Ind. Bus., Greater Lansing C. of C., Greater Lansing UN Assn., Lansing Council for the Arts, Circus Fans Assn. Am. Baptist. Club: Mich. Conservation. Lodges: Elks, Masons, Shriners. Office: Check Reporting Services Inc 5217 Lansing Rd Lansing MI 48917

GERLING, PAUL JOSEPH, manufacturing executive; b. N.Y.C., Feb. 5, 1947; s. Ross L. and Louise G. (Tremmel) G.; m. Kerry A. Masef, Jan 20, 1973; 1 child, Jason P. BBA, St. Bonaventure U., Olean, N.Y., 1969. Sales rep. Am. Laundry Machinery, Inc., Cin., 1969-77, mgr. sales, 1977-80, v.p. mktg., 1980-86, pres., chief operating officer, 1986—. Served with U.S. Army, 1969-70. Mem. Textile Care Allied Trades Assn. (bd. dirs. 1984-86, v.p. 1986-88). Club: Harpers Point (Cin.). Avocations: tennis, skiing, swimming. Home: 10806 Stockbridge Ln Cincinnati OH 45249 Office: Am Laundry Machinery Inc 5050 Section Ave Cincinnati OH 45212

GERLITZ, FRANK EDWARD, biomedical engineer; b. Phila., May 31, 1948; s. Frank Edward and LaNieta Vivian (Souden) G. BS, Bucknell U., 1970, U. Wis., 1973; MS, U. Wis., 1977. Biomed. engr. Otto Hiller Co., Madison, Wis., 1973—, U. Wis., Madison, 1973—, Madison Area Tech. Coll., 1975-76. Mem. ASCE, ASME, Am. Engring. Model Soc., Biomed. Engring. Soc. Home: 1933 N Hudson Chicago IL 60614 Office: AEC Inc 850 Pratt Blvd Elk Grove Village IL 60007

GERM, JOHN A., management consulting firm executive; b. Cleve., May 8, 1930; s. John A. and Doris Elizabeth (Taylor) G.; m. Shirley J. Oertel, June 30, 1956; children—Karen Brian, Lynn Walker. B.A., Case Western Res. U., 1956; M.B.A., U. Chgo., 1972. With mktg. dept. Standard Products, Cleve., 1955-60, Nalco Co., Chgo., 1960-67; dir. personnel Velsicol Chem. Co., 1967-69; prin. Cresap, McCormack & Paget, Chgo., 1969-75; v.p. Chi Systems, Ann Arbor, Mich., 1975-77, A.T. Kearney, Inc., Chgo., 1977-81; pres., dir. JNS Assocs., Inc., Naperville, Ill., 1981—; lectr. in field; dir. JNS Aviation; cons. Network Ltd. Served to sgt. USAF, 1949-53. Mem. Am. Mgmt. Assn., Am. Hosp. Assn., Am. Compensation Assn. Developed applied mgmt. programs. Office: JNS Assocs Inc 549 S Washington Naperville IL 60540

GERMANN, DOUGLAS DEAN, SR., lawyer, accountant; b. South Bend, Ind., Oct. 23, 1946; s. Harold F. and LaVerne (Kepschull) G.; m. Linda Jo Schlundt, Dec. 21, 1968; children: Douglas Jr., Michael J. BSBA, Valparaiso U., 1969, JD, 1973. Bar: Ind. 1973, U.S. Dist. Ct. (no. and so. dists.) Ind. 1973, Mich. 1974, U.S. Tax Ct. 1974, U.S. Dist. Ct. (we. dist.) Mich. 1976. Tax atty. Clark Equipment Co., Buchanan, Mich., 1973-75; sole practice Manistique, Mich., 1975-77, Mishawaka, Ind., 1980—; assoc. Bingham, Loughlin, Means & Mick, Mishawaka, 1977-80; pres. St. Joseph County Estate Planning Council, South Bend, 1980-81. Bd. dirs. St. Peter Luth. Ch., Inc., Mishawaka, 1979—, pres. 1980-85. Mem. ABA, Mich. Bar Assn., Ind. Bar Assn., St. Joseph County Bar Assn., Am. Inst. CPA's, Ind. CPA Soc., Nat. Speakers Assn. Club: Toastmasters (South Bend). Avocation: fishing. Office: 415 Lincoln Way W Mishawaka IN 46544

GERMANN, JACK LEONARD, investor, entrepreneur; b. Springfield, Ill., Dec. 5, 1956; s. Victor Kenneth and Marie Margaret (Hensey) G. BA in Mgmt., Sangamon State U., spring 1981, MA in Bus. Adminstrn., winter 1981, MBA, 1985. Petroleum lab. analyst F.S. Services, Springfield, 1972-78; distbr., merchandiser Pepperidge Farms Inc., Springfield, 1978—; owner Essex Investments, Springfield, 1983—; ptnr., co-developer Megasigns, Springfield, 1986—. Mem. GOP Victory Fund, Nat. Rep. Congl. Com., Washington, 1985. Recipient Golden Laurel award Springfield Inter-Civic Club Council, 1975. Mem. Am. Entrepreneurs Assn. Club: The Jones-Janusweski-Germann Group (Springfield) (bd. dirs. 1985—). Avocations: collecting antique books and carvings, bicycling, tennis. Home: 3037 S 14th St Springfield IL 62703 Office: Essex Investments 1405 Stevenson Dr Suite 3-660 Springfield IL 62703

GERMANN, RICHARD P(AUL), chemist, business executive; b. Ithaca, N.Y., Apr. 3, 1918; s. Frank E.E. and Martha Mina Marie (Knechtel) G.; m. Malinda Jane Plietz, Dec. 11, 1942; 1 child, Cheranne Lee. B.A., Colo. U., 1939; student, Western Res. U. (Naval Research fellow), 1941-43, Brown U., 1954. Chief analytical chemist Taylor Refining Co., Corpus Christi, 1943-44; research devel. chemist Calco Chem. div. Am. Cyanamid Co., 1944-52; devel. chemist charge pilot plant Alrose Chem. Co. div. Geigy Chem. Corp., 1952-55; new product devel. chemist, research div. W.R. Grace & Co., Clarkesville, Md., 1955-60; chief chemist soap-cosmetic div. G.H. Packwood Mfg. Co., St. Louis, 1960-61; coordinator, promoter chem. product devel. Abbott Labs., North Chicago, Ill., 1961-71; internat. chem. cons. to mgmt. 1971-73; pres. Germann Internat. Ltd., 1973-82, Ramtek Internat. Ltd., 1973—; real estate broker, 1972—. Author: Science's Ultimate Challenge—The Re-Evaluation of Ancient Occult Knowledge; patentee in U.S. and fgn. countries on sulfonamides, vitamins, detergent-softeners and biocides. Rep. Am. Inst. Chemists to Joint Com. on Employment Practices, 1969-72; vestryman St. Paul's Episcopal Ch., Norwalk, Ohio, 1978-81, also chmn. adminstrn. and long-range planning commn., 1980-81; trustee Services for the Aging, Inc., 1982—; chmn. nutritional council Ohio Dist. Five Area Agy. on Aging, 1983-84; sr. adv. Ohio Assn. Ctrs. for Sr. Citizens, Inc., 1982—; bd. dirs. Christie Lane Workshop, 1981—. Fellow AAAS, Am. Inst. Chemists (chmn. com. employment relations 1969-72), Chem. Soc. (London), AAAS, Am. Assn. Ret. Persons; mem. Am. Chem. Soc. (councilor 1971-73, chmn. membership com. chem. mktg. and econs. div. 1966-68, chmn. program com. 1968-69, del. at large for local sects. 1970-71, chmn. 1972-73, chmn. Chgo. program com. 1966-67, chmn. Chgo. endowment com. 1967-68, dir. Chgo. sect. 1968-72, chmn. awards com. 1972-73, sec. chem. mktg. and econs. group Chgo. sect. 1964-66, chmn. 1967-68), Internat. Sci. Found., Sci. Research Soc. Am., Comml. Chem. Devel. Assn. (chmn. program com. Chgo. conv. 1966, mem. fin. com. 1966-67, ad hoc com. of Comml. Chem. Devel. Assn.-Chem. Market Research Assn. 1968-69, co-chmn. pub. relations Denver conv. 1968, chmn. membership com. 1969-70), Chem. Market Research Assn. (mem. directory com. 1967-68, employment com. 1969-70), Midwest Planning Assn., Nat. Security Indsl. Assn. (com. rep. ocean sci. tech. com., maintenance adv. com., tng. ad. com. 1962-70), Midwest Fedn., Midwest Planning Assn., Am. Assn. Textile Chemists and Colorists, Am. Pharm. Assn., Midwest Chem. Mktg. Assn., Am. Pharm. Assn., Am. Assn. Textile Chemists and Colorists, N.Y. Acad. Scis., Internat. Platform Assn., Water Pollution Control Fedn., Lake County Bd. Realtors, World Future Soc., Midwest Planning Assn. Am., Sigma Xi, Alpha Chi Sigma (chmn. profl. activities com. 1968-70, pres. Chgo. chpt. 1968-70). Clubs: Chemists (N.Y.C., Chgo.); Torch. Lodges: Lions (sec. Allview, Md. 1956-57), Kiwanis, Masons (32 degree), Knights Templar, Rotary. Home and Office: 6 Vinewood Dr Norwalk OH 44857

GERNHARDT, KAREN KAY, kindergarten teacher; b. Crawfordsville, Ind., May 6, 1949; d. Jamie Mervyn and Virginia Louise (Hiner) Cunningham; m. Walter John Gernhardt II, Oct. 7, 1972. BS, Purdue U., 1971; MS, Butler U., 1975. Cert. nursery/kindergarten tchr., Ind. Kindergarten tchr. Noblesville (Ind.) Schs., 1971-77, 80—; elem. tchr. Am. Coop. Sch., Monrovia, Liberia, 1977-78, kindergarten tchr., 1978-80; sec. elem. sch. self-study project Am. Coop. Sch., 1979-80. Recipient Outstanding Tchr. award Community of Noblesville, 1986. Mem. Ind. Assn. Edn. Young Children, Purdue Alumni Assn., Kappa Kappa Kappa. Republican. Avocations: reading, bridge, swimming, traveling. Home: 170 Wellington Pkwy Noblesville IN 46060

GERSHBEIN, LEON LEE, chemist; b. Chgo., Dec. 22, 1917; s. Meyer and Ida (Shutman) G.; m. Ruth Zelman, Sept. 30, 1956; children—Joel Dan, Marcia Renee, Carla Ann. S.B., U. Chgo., 1938, S.M., 1939; Ph.D.; Northwestern U., 1944. Research assoc. Northwestern U., Evanston, Ill., 1944-47; asst. prof. biochemistry U. Ill. Med. Sch., Chgo., 1947-53; assoc. prof. biology Ill. Inst. Tech., Chgo., 1953-57, adj. prof., 1957—; pres., dir. Northwest Inst. Med. Research, Chgo., 1957—; dir. labs. Northwest Hosp., Chgo., 1957—. U. Chgo. scholar, 1936-38; recipient Merit award Chgo. Chromatography Discussion Group, 1978; citations Ill. State Acad. Scis., 1975-79. Mem. Am. Chem. Soc., Am. Inst. Chemists, Am. Oil Chemists Soc., AAAS, Ill. Acad. Sci., Soc. Exptl. Biol. Medicine, Soc. Applied Spectroscopy, Am. Phys. Soc., Am. Fedn. Clin. Research, Am. Assn. Cancer Research, Contbr. numerous articles to profl. jours. Home: 2836 Birchwood Ave Wilmette IL 60091 Office: Northwest Inst 5636 W Eddy Chicago IL 60634

GERSHON, WILLIAM I., writer, communications company executive; b. Chgo., Apr. 12, 1934; s. Irving and Ruth (Gershbein) G.; m. Matilda (Marion) K. May, June 29, 1957. Grad., Wright Jr. Coll., Chgo., 1954; BA in Speech and English, Roosevelt U., 1956. Writer H. Epstein Advt., Chgo., 1956-59; asst. to copy chief Walgreen Co., Deerfield, Ill., 1959-61; advt. mgr. Lyon & Healy, Inc., Chgo., 1961-63; writer/account mgr. Garfield-Linn & Co., Chgo., 1963-78, v.p., 1978-82; sr. writer Abelson-Taylor, Inc., Chgo., 1983-84; owner Bill Gershon/Persuasive Communications, Skokie, Ill., 1982—. Mem. Independent Writers of Chgo. Avocations: reading, photography, language study, short-wave radio. Home and Office: Bill Gershon/Persuasive Communications 9828 Crawford Ave Skokie IL 60076

GERSHOW, SUSAN JANE, marketing and public relations executive; b. Dayton, Ohio, Mar. 10, 1952; d. Herman Maurice and Fanny Belle (Saul) G. BA in Communications, U. Wis., 1974. Asst. news bur. dept. Dayton's, Mpls., 1975-80; dir. pub. relations Girl Scouts U.S., Mpls., 1981-84; mktg. dir. City Ctr., Mpls., 1984—; with pub. info. dept. Am. Cancer Soc., Mpls., 1981-83; mem. mktg. com. Downtown Council, Mpls., 1984—, Christmas chairperson; active 75th anniversary Girl Scouts U.S., Mpls., 1985—; bd. dirs. Kaiser Roll Found. Named Exemplary Vol. Am. Cancer Soc., 1984, Minn. Woman of Month, Skyway News, Aug. 1986. Mem. Internat. Council Shopping Ctrs. Democrat. Jewish. Avocations: running, tennis, reading, career counseling.

GERSON, CAROL ROBERTS, pediatric otolaryngologist; b. Phila., Jan. 28, 1948; s. Milton and Lillian (Becket) Roberts; m. Gary Gerson, Oct. 12, 1969; children: Jordana, Jessica. BA, U. Pa., 1969, MD, 1976. Diplomate Am. Bd. Otolaryngology. Tchr. deaf children Bet Shemesh Sch., Israel, 1969-70; counselor retarded children Wood Sch., Langhorne, Pa., 1970; instr. dept. otolaryngology Northwestern U. Med. Sch., Chgo., 1982-84, assoc. prof. otolaryngology, 1984; provisional attending surgeon Children's Meml. Hosp., Chgo., 1982-83, attending surgeon otolaryngology, 1983-84, active assoc., 1984—; cons. Parenthesis Child-Parent Ctr., Oak Park, Ill. Contbr. articles to profl. jours. Recipient Cancer Bioassay fellowship U. Pa. Med. Coll., 1974-75, Academic Excellence award Am. Women's Med. Assn., 1976. Fellow Am. Acad. Pediatrics (mem. com. early childhood, adoption and dependent care 1984—, program chmn. 1986); mem. AMA, Am. Bronchesophological Assn., Am. Acad. Otolaryngology, Head and Neck Surgery, Am. Soc. Pediatric Otolaryngology, Soc. Univ. Otolaryngologists, Head and Neck Surgeons. Jewish.

GERSON, ROBERT MITCHELL, plastic and reconstructive surgeon; b. N.Y.C., Apr. 7, 1953; s. Julius H. and Pearl (Jacoff) G.; m. Sally Jacinto, Mar. 10, 1980; children: Suzanne Marie, Amy Elizabeth. BA maga cum laude, Adelphi U., 1975; MD, Loyola U., Maywood, Ill., 1979. Diplomate Am. Bd. Otolaryngology, Am. Bd. Plastic Surgery. Intern Long Island Jewish Hillside Med. Ctr., New Hyde Park, N.Y., 1979-80; resident in gen. surgery Monmouth Med. Ctr., Sloan-Kettering Meml. Hosp., Long Branch New Jersey and N.Y.C., 1980-81; chief resident in otolaryngology Northwestern U., Chgo., 1981-84; resident in plastic and reconstructive surgery U. Ill., Chgo., 1984-86, chief resident in plastic and reconstructive surgery, 1985-86; practice medicine specializing in plastic and reconstructive surgery Chgo., 1986—; instr. surgery U. Ill., 1986—. Contbr. articles to profl. jours. Mem. AMA, ACS, Am. Soc. Plastic and Reconstructive Surgery, Chgo. Plastic Surgery Soc. Avocations: skiing, running, fine arts. Office: 70 E Walton St Chicago IL 60611

GERSTEIN, KENNETH ALLAN, periodontist; b. Chgo., July 24, 1946; s. Kenneth Irwin Gerstein and Muriel June (Doonan) Welsh; m. Martha June Miller, June 22, 1971; children—Kimberly Inge, Kendra Leigh. B.S./D.D.S., U. Ill.-Chgo., cert. periodontics. Practice dentistry, specializing in periodontics, Champaign, Ill., 1978—; instr. Parkland Coll., Champaign, 1979—. Contbr. articles to profl. jours. Served to lt. comdr. USN, 1971-76. Recipient award Odontographic Soc. Chgo., 1971; Stanley D. Tylman award, Univ. award of Merit, Capt. Simon Kessler Meml. award U. Ill., 1971. Mem. ADA, Am. Acad. Periodontology, Midwest Soc. Periodontology, Western Soc. Periodontology, Ill. State Dental Soc., Illini Dist. Dental Soc., Omicron Kappa Upsilon. Avocations: golf; tennis; woodworking. Home: 1846 Maynard Lake Dr Champaign IL 61821 Office: 303 W Springfield Champaign IL 61821

GERSTEIN, RONALD JAY, clinical psychologist; b. Chgo., July 13, 1945; s. Abe and Ida (Glass) G.; m. Joy Patricia Hawkes, June 26, 1976; step-daus. Kathy, Nicole. B.A., U. Ill.-Chgo., 1967; M.A., Roosevelt U., 1970. Staff psychologist/instr. Mt. Sinai Hosp./Chgo. Med. Sch., 1969-70; psychologist II, Inst. for Juvenile Research, Chgo., 1970; staff psychologist St. Francis Hosp., Evanston, Ill., 1970-76; pvt. practice clin. psychology, Morton Grove, Ill., 1976-77; staff psychologist/supr. Proviso Family Services, Melrose Park, Ill., 1977-83; staff psychotherapist, office mgr. Inst. for Motivational Devel., Lombard, Ill., 1984—. Mem. Chgo. Musicians Union. Home: 9354 Shermer Rd Morton Grove IL 60053

GERSTNER, ROBERT WILLIAM, structural engineering educator; b. Chgo., Nov. 10, 1934; s. Robert Berty and Martha (Tuchelt) G.; m. Elizabeth Willard, Feb. 8, 1958; children: Charles Willard, William Mark. B.S., Northwestern U., 1956, M.S., 1957, Ph.D., 1960. Registered structural and profl. engr., Ill. Instr. Northwestern U., Evanston, Ill., 1957-59; research fellow Northwestern U., 1959-60; asst. prof. U. Ill., Chgo., 1960-63; asso. prof. U. Ill., 1963-69, prof. structural engring., architecture, 1969—; structural engr. cons., 1959—. Contbr. articles to profl. jours. Pres. Riverside Improvement Assn., 1973-77, 79-82. Fellow ASCE; Mem. Am. Concrete Inst., Am. Soc. for Engring. Edn., AAAS, AAUP, ACLU. Home: 2628 Agatite Ave Chicago IL 60625

GERWERT, PHILIP EDWARD, automotive executive; b. Pittsburg, Kans., Jan. 1, 1936; s. Victor John and Nelle Evelyn (Amrein) G.; m. Patricia Ann Vitzthum, June 9, 1957; 1 child, Vicki Lynn. AS, Joplin Jr. Coll., 1955; BS in Chem. Engring., U. Mo., Rolla, 1958; cert. Exec. Mgmt., Pa. State U., 1985. Foreman in prodn. Gen. Motors Corp., St. Louis, 1959-62; process engr. Gen. Motors Corp., Detroit, 1962-64; gen. foreman prodn. Gen. Motors Corp., Tarrytown, N.Y., 1964-65, supr. work standards, 1965-70, mfg. planner, 1969-70, sr. process engr., 1970-71, environ. engr., 1971-73; staff engr. Gen. Motors Corp., Warren, Mich., 1973-74, sr. staff engr., 1974-84, mgr. water pollution control, 1983-86, exec. dir. chemical emergency task force, 1986-87, mgr. indsl. wastes, 1987—. Served with U.S. Army, 1958. Mem. Water Pollution Control Fedn. (reviewer, contbr. Manual of Practice, 1981,chmn. indsl. waste com. 1981-85, bd. dirs. 1985—), Nat. Acad. Engring. (roundtable on engring. contributions to the Clean Water Act 1982), Engring. Soc. Detroit. Republican. Presbyterian. Lodge: Kiwanis (bd. dirs. Rochester 1977-79, pres. 1982-83). Avocations: golf, bridge, yard work, woodworking. Home: 971 Hemlock Rochester MI 48063 Office: Gen Motors Environ Activities Staff Bldg 30400 Mound Rd Warren MI 48090-9015

GESIORSKI, STANLEY LOUIS, accountant; b. Chgo., Sept. 10, 1951; s. Stanley and Katharine (Nowak) G.; m. Julie Graham, Sept. 24, 1983. BS in Acctg., U. Ill., Chgo., 1973. CPA., Ill. Revenue agt. IRS, Chgo., 1973-77; pvt. practice acctg. Addison, Ill., 1978—. Mem. Am. Inst. CPA's, Ill. CPA Soc. Roman Catholic. Avocations: sports, camping, travel. Office: 256 W Fullerton Addison IL 60101

GESSLEY, GLEN ROYAL, park planning administrator; b. Hannibal, Mo., Mar. 9, 1951; s. Norman and Annabel Scott (Teeter) G.; m. Kristin Wassmuth, Feb. 14, 1981. B.S., Colo. State U., 1973. Long-range planner Mo. Dept. Natural Resources, Jefferson City, 1973-79, planning dir., 1979—; mem. Mo. Natural Areas com., Jefferson City, 1977—. Chmn. Holts Summit Planning and Zoning Comn., Mo., 1982; active Boy Scouts Am. Mem. Mo. Parks Assn. Mem. Disciples of Christ Ch. Lodges: Masons, Shriners. Avocations: making stained-glass windows; photography; woodworking. Home: 243 Pheasant Ln Holts Summit MO 65043 Office: Dept Natural Resources PO Box 176 Jefferson City MO 65102

GETMAN, BURRILL MYERS, JR., small business consultant; b. Phila., May 27, 1931; s. Burrill M. and Virginia B. Getman; m. Elizabeth S. Sweeting, Jan. 18, 1958; children: George, Linda, Brian. AB in Econs., Haverford (Pa.) Coll., 1952; MBA in Mktg., U. Mich., 1954. Salesman Chicopee Mills, Inc., N.Y.C., 1954-58, product mgr., 1958-63, distbn. mgr., 1963-65; pres. Jelco Labs., Ltd., Toronto, Ont., Can., 1965-67; v.p. mktg. Felters Co., Millbury, Mich., 1967-76, Berkeley & Co., Spirit Lake, Iowa, 1976-80; cons. Gen. Bus. Services, Spirit Lake, 1980—. Pres., bd. dirs. Camp Foster YMCA, Spirit Lake, 1985-86; bd. dirs. Iowa Great Lakes Indsl. Devel. Bd., Spirit Lake, 1985-86; adv. bd. Small Bus. Devel. Ctr., Spencer, Iowa, 1986—, Small Bus. Adminstrn., Des Moines, 1986—. Mem. Inst. Cert. Fin. Planners, Iowa Great Lakes C. of C. (bd. dirs. 1980-86). Republican. Presbyterian. Lodge: Kiwanis. Avocations: golf, gardening. Home and Office: Rural Rt 7214 Spirit Lake IA 51360

GETTA, THOMAS JUDE, obstetrician-gynecologist; b. Cedar Rapids, Iowa, Sept. 4, 1955; s. Leo Edward and Helen Elizabeth (Schmitt) G.; m. Janet Patricia Haskins, July 30, 1977; children: Jeremy, Dustin. BS, U. Iowa, 1977, MD, 1980. Intern Med. Coll. Va., Richmond, 1980-81, resident in ob-gyn, 1983-84; practice medicine specializing in ob-gyn Cedar Rapids, 1984—; med. dir. Linn County Planned Parenthood, Cedar Rapids, 1984—; cons. high risk obstetrics. Fellow Am. Coll. Ob-gyn. Roman Catholic. Avocation: tennis. Office: 712 5th Ave SE Cedar Rapids IA 50403

GETTEL, JAMES JOSEPH, lawyer; b. Evanston, Ill., June 22, 1959; s. James Robert and Mary Ellen (Davis) G.; m. Jennifer Anne Vogel, Aug. 13, 1983. BA in Philosophy, Northwestern U., 1980; MBA, JD, U. Ill., 1984. Bar: Wis. 1984, U.S. Dist. Ct. Wis. 1984, U.S. Ct. Appeals (7th cir.) 1984. Assoc. Minahan & Peterson S.C., Milw., 1984—. Author: Fundamental Reform of Philosophy, 1987; assoc. editor U. Ill. Law Rev., 1982-84. Legal counsel Neurofibromatosis Found., Milw., 1985—; mem. Brotherhood of St. Andrew, Whitefish Bay, Wis., 1985—; mem. vestry Christ Ch., Whitefish Bay, 1987—, bd. dirs. endowment trust, 1987—. Harno scholar U. Ill.; recipient Rickert award U. Ill. Mem. ABA (taxation and corps. sect.), Wis. Bar Assn., Federalist Soc. Republican. Episcopalian. Avocation: pvt. pilot. Home: 10120 W Heather Dr Mequon WI 53092 Office: Minahan & Peterson SC 411 E Wisconsin Ave Suite 2200 Milwaukee WI 53202-4499

GETTLEMAN, ROBERT WILLIAM, lawyer; b. Atlantic City, May 5, 1943; s. Charles Edward and Beulah (Oppenheim) G.; m. Joyce Reinitz, Dec. 23, 1964; children: Lynn Katheryn, Jeffrey Alan. BSBA, Boston U., 1965; JD, Northwestern U., 1968. Bar: Ill. 1968, U.S. Dist. Ct. (no. dist.) Ill. 1968, U.S. Ct. Appeals (7th cir.) 1968, U.S. Dist. Ct. (ea. dist.) Wis. 1972, U.S. Supreme Ct. 1973. Law clk. to presiding justice U.S. Ct. Appeals, Chgo., 1968-70; assoc. D'Ancoma & Pflaum, Chgo., 1970-74, ptnr., 1974—; bd. dirs. John Howard Assn., Chgo., 1973—, pres., 1978-81, chmn. legal and policy coms.; commr., chmn. devel. disabilities and individual rights coms. Gov.'s Commn. to Revise Mental Health Code of Ill., 1973-77; chmn. steering com. Chgo. Project on Residential Alternatives, 1984-85; mem. Cook County State's Atty.'s Profl. Adv. Com., 1984—; treas. Ill. Guardianship and Advocacy Commn., 1984, vice chmn., 1985, chmn., 1986; bd. dirs., chmn. legal com. Pact, Inc., 1985—; mem. mcpl. officers election bd. Village of Lyons, Ill., 1985. Contbr. articles to law revs. Bd. dirs. Ill. div. ACLU, 1973-78. Fellow Am. Bar Found.; mem. Ill. Bar Assn., Chgo. Bar Assn., 7th Fed. Cir. Bar Assn., Chgo. Council Lawyers. Office: D'Ancoma & Pflaum 30 N LaSalle St Room 3100 Chicago IL 60602

GETTLESON, FRANKLIN DAVID, lawyer; b. Mich., Nov. 30, 1936; s. Benjamin and Helen Gettleson; m. Gail Marilynn Cohen, Aug. 15, 1969; children: Michelle L., Scott M., Robin A. BBA, Wayne State U., 1961; JD, Detroit Coll. Law, 1969. Bar: Mich., 1969; CPA, Mich. Sole practice Birmingham, Mich., 1969—; chmn. Unauthorized Practice Commn., Pontiac, Mich., 1982-83, Cir. Ct. Judges Liaison, Pontiac, 1986-87. Treas. Met. Detroit Cystic Fibrosis Found. Mem. Am. Inst. CPA's, Mich. Trial Lawyers Assn., Mich. Bar Assn. (assembly rep. 1986-87), Oakland County (Mich.) Bar Assn. (chmn. coms.), Southfield (Mich.) Bar Assn. (pres. 1984-85). Home: 4786 Pickering Rd Birmingham MI 48010 Office: 6735 Telegraph Suite 320 Birmingham MI 48010

GETZENDANNER, SUSAN, U.S. dist. ct. judge; b. Chgo., July 24, 1939; d. William B. and Carole S. (Muehling) O'Meara; children—Alexandra, Paul. B.B.A., Loyola U., 1966, J.D., 1966. Bar: Ill. bar 1966. Law clk. to presiding justice U.S. Dist. Ct., 1966-68; assoc. Mayer, Brown & Platt, Chgo., 1968-74; ptnr. Mayer, Brown & Platt, 1974-80; judge U.S. Dist. Ct., Chgo., 1980—. Recipient medal of excellence Loyola U. Law Alumni Assn., 1981. Mem. Chgo. Council Lawyers. Office: US Dist Ct 219 S Dearborn St Chicago IL 60604

GEURINK, TERRY LEE, agricultural credit services executive; b. Wausau, Wis., July 16, 1959; s. Roger Arthur and Betty Jane (Fremming) G.; m. Colleen Kay Brooks, Aug. 25, 1984. BS, U. Wis., River Falls, 1981. Asst. credit analyst Farm Credit Services, St. Paul, Minn., 1982-83, credit analyst, 1983-84, bus. analyst, 1984-85, sr. bus. analyst, 1985-86; mgr. Farm Credit Services, Wausau, Wis., 1986—. Mem. Alpha Gamma Rho (bd. dirs. 1984-87), Alpha Zeta. Republican. Presbyterian. Avocations: football, baseball, coin collecting, running, reading. Home: 1001 Yawkey Ave Rothschild WI 54471 Office: Farm Credit Services Cooperative Credit 611 S 32d Ave Wausau WI 54401

GEVERS, MARCIA BONITA, lawyer, lecturer, consultant; b. Mpls., Oct. 11, 1946; d. Sam and Bessie (Gottlieb) Fleisher; m. Michael A. Gevers, Sept. 13, 1970; children—Sarah Nichole, David Seth. B.A. Nat. Coll. Edn., 1968; M.A., N.E. Ill. U., 1973; J.D., DePaul U., 1980. Bar: Ill. 1980. Tchr., Chgo. Bd. Edn., Harris Sch., North Suburban Spl. Edn. Dist., Highland Park, Ill., 1968-73; legis. asst., campaign mgr. Ill. State Rep., Dolton, 1974-79; sole practice, Park Forest and Dolton, Ill., 1980-83, Park Forest, 1987—; cons. LWV, Chgo., 1978; ptnr. Getty and Gevers, Dolton, 1983—. Producer, host cable TV show The Law and You, 1982-83. Bd. dirs. Park Forest Zoning Bd. Appeals, Fair Housing Rev. Bd., Housing Bd. Appeals, Equal Employment Opportunity Rev. Bd., 1975—; pres., bd. dirs. South Suburban Community Hebrew Day Sch., Olympia Fields, Ill., 1982-86; bd. dirs. Congregation Beth Sholom Ch., Park Forest, 1980-82; pres. Ill. Women Polit. Caucus; mem. steering com. Nat. Women's Polit. Caucus, Washington; pres., founder Metro South Women's Polit. Caucus, Chgo. suburbs; alt. del. Dem. Nat. Conv., N.Y.C., 1980. Mem. ABA, Ill. State Bar Assn., South Suburban Bar Assn. (unauthorized practices com.), Chgo. Bar Assn., Am. Arbitration Assn. (arbitrator), Decalogue Soc. Lawyers, LWV. Lodges: Hadassah, B'nai B'rith Women. Office: Getty and Gevers 15000 Dorchester Ave PO Box 603 Dolton IL 60419

GEYER, SIDNA GAYE, educational administrator; b. Anderson, Ind., Dec. 9, 1943; d. James Dale and Lavada Belle (Lantz) Priest; m. James Eugene Geyer, Aug. 29, 1965; children: Jonathan Andrew, Susan Leigh. BSEd, Ball State U., 1969; MSEd, U. Wis., Oshkosh, 1975; EdS, U. Wis., Stout, 1980. Cert. secondary tchr., Wis.; lic. counselor, Wis.; cert. tchr. post-secondary Bd. Vocat., Tech. and Adult Edn., Wis.; cert. counselor, supr./coordinator, Wis. Tchr. sixth grade St. Mary's Sch., Charlotte, Mich., 1966-67; tchr. bus. edn. Oak Hill High Sch., Converse, Ind., 1969-70, Stockbridge (Wis.) High Sch., 1970-72; tchr. bus., counselor Fox Valley Tech. Inst., Appleton, Wis., 1972-83, bus. coordinator, 1983—; evaluator bus. edn. U. Wis., Stout, 1981, N.E. Wis. Tech. Sch., Green Bay, 1985; mem. bus. adv. com. Brillion (Wis.) High Sch., 1983—; mem. state-wide task force to develop curriculum for a sex equity course VTAE staff, 1983. Mem. Wis. Vocat. Assn. (awards com.), Wis. East Cen. Assn. Vocat. Edn. (treas.), Bus. and Profl. Women Assn. (treas. 1984), Women In Mgmt. (edn. com.), Am. Inst. Banking (edn. com.), Am. Soc. Tng. and Devel., AAUW (bd. dirs. 1971-75), North Cen. Assn. (bus. edn. evaluator 1984, 87—). Methodist. Avocations: reading, playing bridge, bowling. Home: 1911 Draper St Baraboo WI 53913 Office: Fox Valley Tech Inst 1825 N Bluemound Dr Appleton WI 54913

GEYER, WAYNE ALLAN, forester, researcher; b. Oak Park, Ill., Nov. 24, 1933; s. Herman M. and Alice J. (Miller) G.; m. Patricia J. Wheeler, Aug. 20, 1960; children: Keith A., Kewin W. BS, Iowa State U., 1955; MF, Purdue U., 1966; PhD, U. Minn., 1971. Field forester Ga. Kraff Paper Co., Macon, 1956-58; research forester U. Ill., Simpson, 1962-65; prof. forestry Kans. State U., Manhattan, 1966—; owner Geyer Forestry Cons., Manhattan, 1971—. Contbr. numerous forestry research articles to various profl. jours. Served to lt. USNR. Mem. Soc. Am. Foresters, Kans. Acad. Scientists, Sigma Xi, Gamma Sigma Delta, Xi Sigma Pi. Avocations: fishing, hiking. Home: 905 Ivy Corner Manhattan KS 66502 Office: Dept Forestry Call Hall Kans State U Manhattan KS 66506

GHETTI, BERNARDINO FRANCESCO, neuropathologist, neurobiology researcher; b. Pisa, Italy, Mar. 28, 1941; s. Getulio and Iris (Mugnetti) G.; m. Caterina Genovese, Oct. 8, 1966; children—Chiara, Simone. M.D. cum laude, U. Pisa, 1966, specialist in mental and nervous diseases, 1969. Lic. physician, Italy; cert. Edn. Council for Fgn. Med. Grads.; diplomate Am. Bd. Pathology. Postdoctoral fellow U. Pisa, 1966-70; research fellow in neuropathology Albert Einstein Coll. Medicine, Bronx, N.Y., 1970-73, resident, clin. fellow in pathology, 1973-75, resident in neuropathology, 1975-76; asst. prof. pathology Ind. U., Indpls., 1976-77, asst. prof. pathology and psychiatry, 1977-78, assoc. prof. pathology and psychiatry, 1978-83, prof., 1983—; mem. Nat. Inst. Neurol. and Communicative Disorders and Stroke rev. com. NIH, 1985—. Contbr. articles and abstracts to profl. jours. Mem. Am. Assn. Neuropathologists, Soc. Neurosci., Assn. Research in Nervous and Mental Diseases, Am. Soc. Cell Biology, Italian Soc. Psychiatry, Italian Soc. Neurology, Sigma Xi. Roman Catholic. Home: 1124 Frederick Dr S Indianapolis IN 46260 Office: Ind U 635 Barnhill Dr Room 157 Indianapolis IN 46223

GHILONI, VINCENT JEROME, building contractor; b. Newark, Ohio, Feb. 8, 1958; s. Arthur Karl and Easter Bertha G. (Denz) G.; m. Debora Jean Mitchell, June 18, 1977 (div. Dec. 1984); 1 child, Sarah Nichole; m. Marijane Anderson, Oct. 11, 1986. Grad. high sch., Newark, 1976. Carpenter R. E. Morrison, Granville, Ohio, 1976-77; owner, pres. Ghiloni Woodwork Constrn. Co., Newark, 1977—. Chmn. adv. bd. joint vocat. schs., Newark, 1982—. Recipient 2d place Nat. Young Entrepreuneurial award, 1986. Mem. Nat. Assn. Self Employed, Ohio Home Builders Assn., Woodworkers Assn. N.Am., Order Sons of Italy Am. Roman Catholic. Avocation(s) fishing, reading, ethnic cooking. Home and Office: 114 N Buena Vista #6 Newark OH 43055

GHOLSON, DAN J., periodontist; b. Peoria, Ill., Nov. 8, 1951; s. Samuel David and Sharon Rose (Hardesty) G.; m. Kathleen Sue Daschler, June 15, 1974; children: Lee Michael, Benjamin Brian, Alexandra Lauren. BA, Millikin U., 1973; DDS, Loyola U., Chgo., 1977, Cert. in Periodontics, 1979. Assoc. Endodontics & Periodontics Assocs., Ltd., Homewood, Ill., 1979-81; practice dentistry specializing in periodontics LaCrosse, Wis., 1981—; assoc. clin. prof. Loyola U., Chgo., 1979-81; bd. dirs. St. Francis Med. Ctr., LaCrosse, 1984—. Mem. adminstrv. council Wesley United Meth. Ch., LaCrosse, 1981—. Named one of Outstanding Young Men of Am., U.S. Jaycees, 1983. Mem. ADA, Am. Acad. Periodontology, N. Am. Soc. Periodontists, Midwest Soc. Peridontists, Wis. Soc. Peridontists, LaCrosse Area C. of C. (mem. health care task force 1984—). Avocations: sailing, sports, reading, watercolors. Home: N2015 Stonecrest Rd LaCrosse WI 54601 Office: 615 S 10th St LaCrosse WI 54601

GHOSH, SATYENDRA KUMAR, structural engineer, educator; b. Berhampore, W. Bengal, India, Sept. 17, 1945; came to U.S., 1975; s. Santosh Kumar and Sadhana (Bose) G.; m. Sumita Majumdar, July 4, 1973; children—Elka, Sourish. B.E., U. Calcutta, India, 1966; M.A.Sc., U. Waterloo (Ont., Can.), 1969, Ph.D., 1972. Structural engr. Kuljian Corp., Calcutta, India, 1966-67; research and teaching asst. U. Waterloo, 1967-69; 70-72, postdoctoral fellow, 1973, research assoc., 1973, adj. prof., 1973-74; research and teaching asst. U. Pitts., 1969-70; structural engr. Portland Cement Assn., Skokie, Ill., 1974-75, sr. structural engr., 1975-80, prin. structural engr., 1980-83; assoc. prof. civil engring. U. Ill.-Chgo., 1984—; cons. Portland Cement Assn., Skokie, Ill., 1984—; ptnr. Elan Assocs., Waterloo, 1972-73; vis. lectr. dept. Materials Engring. U. Ill., Chgo., 1980, 82, 83. Treas. Ill. chpt. Assn. of Indians in Am., 1981-82, v.p., 1983-84. Recipient U. Calcutta Gold medal, 1966. Fellow Inst. of Engrs. India (Engring. Congress prize 1982); mem. Am. Concrete Inst., ASCE. Contbr. articles in field to profl. jours. Home: 1811 Cree Ln Mount Prospect IL 60056 Office: U Ill-Chgo Chicago IL 60680

GIALDE, STEVE THOMAS, family physician; b. Kansas City, Mo.; s. Thomas Joseph and Angeline C. (Cicero) G.; m. Joanne Teresa Abbott, June 29, 1968; children: Angela Louise, Marianne, Stephanie. BS in Physiology, U. Mo., Kansas City, 1968; DO, Univ. Hosp., Kansas City, 1972. Gen. practice medicine Oak Grove (Mo.) Med. Clinic, 1976—; asst. clin. prof. medicine Univ. Hosp., Kansas City, 1976—. Co-inventor White Pulmonary Resuscitator, 1981. Mem. planning and zoning com. City of Oak Grove, 1977-80; mem. City of Oak Grove Sch. Bd. RV1, 1980-83. Fellow Am. Coll. Osteo. Gen. Practice; mem. Am. Osteo. Assn., Mo. Assn. Osteo. Physicians, Jackson County Osteo. Assn., S.W. Clin. Soc. Office: Oak Grove Med Clinic 1900 Broadway Oak Grove MO 64075

GIANNANGELO, EMIL FRANK, dentist; b. Monongahela, Pa., Oct. 5, 1918; s. Frank Giannangelo and Maria Schenna; m. Dorothea Jean Gray, Jan. 26, 1947; 1 child, Maria. DDS, U. Mo., Kansas City, 1944. Gen. practice dentistry Pratt, Kans., 1944-81, Giannangelo-Shinkle Dental Clinic, Pratt, 1981—. Served to capt. U.S. Army, 1954. Fellow Acad. Gen. Dentistry; mem. ADA, Kans. State Dental Assn., Pratt County Dental Assn., Pierre Fauchard Acad., Kans. State Jaycees (pres. 1954-55), Am. Legion. Lodge: Elks. Home: 205 Stout Pratt KS 67124 Office: Giannangelo-Shinkle Dental Clinic 610 E 2d St Pratt KS 67124

GIANNELLA, RALPH AROUNE, internist; b. Paterson, N.J., Oct. 23, 1939; s. Mario P. and Josephine (Rossi) G.; m. Patricia Ann Barker, May 3, 1970; children: Andrew, Christopher. AB, Cornell U., 1961; MD, Albany Med. Coll., 1965. Diplomate Am. Bd. Internal Medicine, Am. Bd. Gastroenterology. Intern and jr. resident Boston City Hosp., 1965-67; sr. resident Boston VA Hosp., 1967-68; fellow in gastroenterology Thorndike-Mallory Lab., Boston City Hosp., 1968-71; from asst. to prof. U. Ken. Coll. Medicine, Lexington, 1974-80; prof. medicine, dir. digestive diseases div. U. Cin. Coll. Medicine, 1980—. Contbr. articles to profl. jours. Served with USMC, 1971-74. Vets. Adminstrn. grantee, 1974—; World Health Orgn. grantee, 1983-86; NIH grantee, 1984—, 1986—. Fellow Am. Coll. Physicians; mem. Am. Soc. Clin. Investigation, Am. Gastroent. Assn. (chmn. research com. 1970). Roman Catholic. Avocations: history, opera. Home: 615 Stanley Ave Cincinnati OH 45226 Office: U Cin Coll Med 231 Bethesda Ave Cincinnati OH 45267

GIANNINI, ANGELO ANTHONY, industrial engineer, business educator; b. Youngstown, Ohio, Mar. 9, 1950; s. Anthony and Theresa Rose (Tassile) G.; m. Kathleen Marie MeLe, Aug. 7, 1976; children: Allison, Meghan. BA, Youngstown (Ohio) State U., 1973, MBA, 1983. Indsl. engr. GF Furniture Systems, Youngstown, 1973-77, value analysis mgr., 1977-79; sr. indsl. engr. Universal-Rundle Corp., New Castle, Pa., 1979-85; mgr. indsl. engring. Midland Steel Products, Cleve., 1985—; prof. bus. Pa. State U., Sharon, 1984—. Mem. Am. Inst. Indsl. Engrs., Assn. MBA Execs., Automotive Industry Action Group, Mahoning Valley Indsl. Mgmt. Assn., Tau Kappa Epsilon. Roman Catholic. Avocations: chinese cooking, golf, racquetball, tennis, travel. Home: 218 S Main Youngstown OH 44515 Office: Midland Steel Products 10615 Madison Ave Cleveland OH 44101

GIANNINI, EVELYN LOUISE, library consultant; b. Evanston, Ill., June 19, 1924; d. Bernard Peter and Thelma Thay (Wescoat) Smith; m. Aldo Joseph Giannini, Mar. 23, 1946; children: Michael, John. Student, Northwestern U. Sch. Commerce, 1942-43. Library clk. Kemper Group, Chgo., 1959-64, acquisitions librarian, 1964-70; asst. librarian Kemper Group, Long Grove, Ill., 1970-77, corp. librarian, 1977-87; exec. v.p. Arlington Group, Inc., Arlington Heights, Ill., 1987—. Mem. Am. Assn. Law Libraries, Chgo. Assn. Law Libraries, Spl. Libraries Assn., N.W. Suburban Spl. Libraries (co-founder). Republican. Episcopalian. Home: 1330 S Harvard Ave Arlington Heights IL 60005 Office: Arlington Group Inc PO Box 502 Arlington Heights IL 60006

GIANOLI, LOUIS FRANCIS, retired county official, law enforcement consultant; b. Genoa, Wis., Nov. 10, 1920; s. Frank E. and Agnes M. (Penchi) G.; m. Cora M. Gruny, Aug. 24, 1946; children: Sandra L. Gianoli Smith, Linda M. Gianoli Krogwold. Diploma, Wis. Tech. Sch., 1942. Ry. telegrapher Milw. Rd. Services, Wausau, Wis., 1946-47; police officer Wausau Police Dept., 1947-50; hwy. patrolman Wis. County Hwy. Patrol, Wausau, 1950-56; undersheriff Marathon County Sheriff's Dept., Wausau, 1957-60, sheriff, 1961-86; cons., pub. speaker on law enforcement and corrections 1986—. Contbr. articles to profl. jours. Life mem. adv. bd. Salvation Army, Wausau, 1984—. Served to sgt. U.S. Army 1942-45, with Res., 1945-80. Mem. Nat. Sheriff's Assn. (exec. bd. 1961—, pres. 1984-85, life), Am. Jail Assn. (bd. dirs. 1973-86), Midwest Crime Conf. (treas. 1968-86), Wis. Sheriff's Assn. (pres. 1975), VFW (dist. comdr., life), Am. Legion, United Comml. Travelers, Marathon County Agr. Soc. (life). Republican. Roman Catholic. Lodges: Moose, Optimists (pres. Wausau 1987—), KC, Chef De Gare of 40 & 8. Avocations: playing guitar, fishing. Home: 602 Cedar St Wausau WI 54401

GIBANS, JAMES DAVID, architect; b. Akron, Ohio, Feb. 10, 1930; s. Myer Jacob and Sylva (Hirsch) G.; m. Nina Freedlander, July 16, 1955; children: David Myer, Jonathan Samuel, Amy, Elisabeth. BA, Yale U., 1951, BArch, 1954, MArch, 1954. Architect George K. Raad & Assocs. et al, San Francisco, 1958-63; project architect Ward and Schneider, Cleve., 1964-68; sr. assoc. William A. Gould and Assocs., Cleve., 1968-74, Don M. Hisaka and Assoc., Cleve., 1974-76; pvt. practice architecture Cleve., 1976-81; v.p. Teare Herman & Gibans, Inc., Cleve., 1981—; faculty Edn. for Aesthetic Awareness Cleve. State U., 1977-79. Trustee, mem. exec. com., 1st v.p. Cleve. Chamber Music Soc., 1970-78; mem. adv. bd. Environ. Resource Ctr. Cleve. Pub. Library, 1973-76; bd. dirs. Cleve. Soc. Contemporary Art, 1985—. Served with U.S. Army, 1955-57. Fulbright grantee, 1954-55. Mem. AIA, Cleve. Chpt. AIA (sec. 1973-74, 2d v.p. 1976, bd. dirs., com. chmn. 1986—), Architects Soc. Ohio (trustee 1975-76, bd. dirs. 1986—). Democrat. Jewish. Club: Cleve. City. Avocations: music, art, jogging, cross-country skiing. Home: 13800 Shaker Blvd Cleveland OH 44120 Office: Teare Herman & Gibans Inc 1120 Terminal Tower Cleveland OH 44113

GIBB, CLARK RAYMOND, retired mfrs. rep. co. exec.; b. Cottonwood, Minn., Sept. 5, 1914; s. Raymond J. and Huldah (Pettersen) G.; B.B.A., U. Minn., 1940; m. Margaret L. Foucault, June 30, 1954. Sales engr. Despatch Oven Co., Mpls., 1941; mem. prodn. control staff Gen. Mills, Mpls., 1941-42; owner Aurex Minn. Co., Mpls., 1946-51; partner A & G Chip Steak Co., Mankato, Minn., 1947-61; v.p. Chip Steak & Provision Co., Mankato, 1961-65, pres., owner, 1965-81; pres. Clark R. Gibb Co., Mpls., 1952-79, GIBBCO Sci., Inc., 1974-79; owner Wooddale Farms, Yellow Medicine County, Minn.; developer ClarMar Woods, Washburn County, Wis., 1975—. Served with AUS, 1942-46, 51-52. Mem. U. Minn. Alumni Assn., Electronic Reps. Assn. (chmn. bd., past pres.), Am. Legion, VFW. Republican. Presbyn. Elk. Clubs: Electronic VIP (past pres.), Mpls. Athletic, Minikahda (Mpls.). Home: 2020 Cedar Lake Pkwy Minneapolis MN 55416 Office: 11100 Bren Rd W Minnetonka MN 55343

GIBBONS, CHARLES CREW, management consultant; b. Lost Springs, Wyo., June 21, 1916; s. Frank Eli and Alice Kathleen (Crew) G.; m. Wilma Ruth Householder, Sept. 13, 1949; children—Betsy Gibbons Lindland, Jennifer Anne Lindland. B.S., Ohio U., 1937, M.A., 1938; Ph.D., Ohio State U., 1942. Dir. personnel research Owens Ill. Glass Co., Toledo, 1942-45; indsl. program dir. Upjohn Inst. for Employment Research, Kalamazoo, Mich., 1945-56, now vice chmn., adminstrv. cons. Upjohn Co., 1956-81, ret.; cons., speaker in field. Fellow Am. Psychol. Assn. Methodist. Home: 223 E Ellis St PO Box 459 DeGraff OH 43318

GIBBONS, CHARLES THOMAS, manufacturing engineer; b. Knoxville, Iowa, Sept. 5, 1955; s. Tommy Alven and Patrica Eileen (Taylor) G.; m. Lynn Kay Redmond, Aug. 7, 1976; children: Eric Andrew, Jeffrey Adam, Daniel Alan, Kristin Anne, Kathleen Ann. BA in Mgmt., U. No. Iowa, 1977. Standards analyst Rolscreen Co., Pella, Iowa, 1977-79, supr. methods and standards, 1979-81, indsl. engr., 1981-84; project mgr. fire reconstrn. Caradco Corp., Rantoul, Ill., 1986, sr. mfg. engr., 1984—; bd. dirs. Baker-Scott Industries, Fayette, Iowa. Mem. Inst. Indsl. Engrs. (v.p. 1979-80, pres. 1980-82, bd. dirs. 1982-84, Nat. Award of Excellence 1982, Outstanding member 1982, Disting. Service award 1984). Republican. Presbyterian. Avocations: sports, home remodeling, woodworking. Home: 1074 Pinecrest Dr Rantoul IL 61866 Office: Caradco Corp 201 Evans Dr Rantoul IL 61866

GIBBONS, KELLEY SUE, educator, coach; b. Ottawa, Kans., May 21, 1955; d. Charles Elmer and Sue (Gatlin) Gillette; m. Johnnie Ray Gibbons, May 19, 1974. BA, Cameron U., 1977; MEd, Southwestern Okla. State U.,

1982. Cert. tchr. secondary edn. Tchr. Altus (Okla.) Schs., 1978-81, Olathe (Kans.) Sch. Dist., 1981—; cons. writing Greater Kansas City (Mo.) Writing Project, 1984—. Mem. NEA, Nat. Council for the Social Studies, Phi Delta Kappa (sec. Johnson County chpt.). Avocations: reading, golf, jogging. Home: 16031 W 143d Terr Olathe KS 66062 Office: Oregon Trail Jr High Sch 1800 W Dennis Olathe KS 66061

GIBBONS, MARY CATHERINE, nursing education director; b. St. Louis, Aug. 7, 1944; d. John Patrick and Effie C. (Weber) G. B.S. in Nursing, St. Louis U., 1966, M.S. in Nursing of Children, 1971. Staff nurse St. Mary's Health Ctr., St. Louis, 1966-70, head nurse, 1970-71; instr. obstetrics nursing Jewish Hosp. Sch. Nursing, St. Louis, 1971-72; maternity coordinator Luth. Med. Ctr. Sch. Nursing, St. Louis, 1972-82, dir. nursing edn., 1982—; instr. continuing edn. programs. Bd. dirs. YWCA, St. Louis, 1984—. Recipient Humanitian award Hosp. Assn. St. Louis, 1983. Mem. Nat. League Nursing, Am. Nurses Assn., Nurses Assn. of Am. Coll. Obstetricians and Gynecologists (chmn. Dist. VII 1982-83, Mo. sect. 1978-79), Assn. Female Execs., Sigma Theta Tau. Home: 10123 Mullally Dr Saint Louis MO 63123 Office: Luth Med Ctr Sch Nursing 3547 S Jefferson Ave Saint Louis MO 63118

GIBBONS, MICHAEL RANDOLPH, lawyer; b. Kirkwood, Mo., Mar. 24, 1959; s. Michael and Folsta Sara (Bailey) G. BA, Westminster Coll., 1981; JD, St. Louis U., 1984. Bar: Mo. 1984. Assoc. Michael Gibbons, Kirkwood, 1984-86; ptnr. Gibbons and Gibbons, Kirkwood, 1986—. Councilman City of Kirkwood, 1986—; mem. Bonhomme Township Rep. Club, v.p., 1985-87, bd. dirs.; vestry mem. Grace Episcopal Ch., Kirkwood, 1986. Mem. Bar Assn. of Met. St. Louis, St. Louis County Bar Assn., Kirkwood C. of C. (bd. dirs. 1986). Republican. Lodge: Kiwanis (pres. Kirkwood club 1986-87). Avocations: sports. Home: 512 N Kirkwood Rd Kirkwood MO 63122 Office: Gibbons & Gibbons 214 N Clay Kirkwood MO 63122

GIBBONS, ROBERT J., insurance company executive; b. Niagara Falls, N.Y., Apr. 22, 1933; s. Richard Lawrence and Madeleine Elizabeth (Schultz) G.; m. Rita Marie Rychlik, July 4, 1952; children: Kathleen Marie, Karen Susan. Cert. estate bus. and fin. advisor. Sales rep. Met. Life, Batavia, N.Y., 1959-62; sales rep., supr., gen. agent Aetna Life and Casualty, Columbus, Ohio and Buffalo, 1962-76; regional dir. Ky. Cen. Life, Columbus, 1980—. Contbr. articles to ins. pubs. Served to cpl. U.S. Army, 1953-55. Mem. Nat. Assn. Life Underwriters (polit. action com., nat. del.), Nat. Execs. Inst., Am. Legion, V.F.W. Republican. Roman Catholic. Club: Worthington Hills Country (membership chmn. 1974-75). Avocations: golf, tennis, swimming, reading, writing. Home: 830 Mission Hills Ln Worthington OH 43085

GIBBS, BARBARA JILL, art therapist; b. Dayton, Ohio, Apr. 5, 1955; d. Joshua Stokes and Barbara Anne (Clawson) G.; m. Allen Joe Doepel, Aug. 17, 1984. B in Art Edn., Ohio State U., 1979; M in Art Therapy, Wright State U., 1985. Cert. art tchr., Ohio. Recreation asst. Ohio State U. Hosp., Columbus, 1979-80; art therapist Westview Sch., Dayton, 1981-82, Samaritan Ctr. for Youth Resources, Dayton, 1982—; part-time faculty Sinclair Community Coll., Dayton, 1986-87; supr. art therapy interns Wright State U., Dayton, 1983—; cons. on art therapy Good Samaritan Hosp., Dayton, 1986-87. Camp leader Seal of Ohio council Girl Scouts US, Galloway, Ohio, 1978. Mem. Am. Art Therapy Assn. (profl.), Buckeye Art Therapy Assn. (chmn. membership 1985—), Sierra Club, Soc. for Improvement of Conditions for Stray Animals, World Wildlife Fund, Cousteau Soc. Avocations: art, bicycling, reading, dance, tennis. Office: Samaritan Ctr for Youth Resources 5670 Philadelphia Dr Dayton OH 45415

GIBBS, DORSIE JOE, botanist, executive; b. Ashland, Ky., Feb. 19, 1940; s. Dorsie Wilson and Frances Susan (Simpson) G.; m. Madalyn Jeanne Wiegman, Mar. 23, 1963; children: Kayla Dawn, April Renae. BS in Biology, Bethany Nazarene Coll., 1965. Ops. mgr. Stemen Labs., Visalia, Calif., 1965-67; botanist Internat. Biologicals Inc., Oklahoma City, 1967-72; owner, founder Aero-Allergen Labs., Carthage, Mo., 1972-80, exec. v.p., chief ops. officer Allergon Inc., subs. Pharmaç ia Diagnostics, Uppsala, Sweden, 1980-85; owner, founder Interstate Flor-All, Joplin, Mo., 1985-87. Recipient Outstanding Alumni award Bethany Nazarene Coll., 1981. Republican. Inventor field vacuum for collecting pollens in large quantities; inventor methods for particle sizing and separation of pollens. Home: PO Box 1113 Joplin MO 64802

GIBBS, JOHN CLARK, psychology educator, consultant; b. Paterson, N.J., June 7, 1946; s. John Lowell and Ila Louise (Burns) G.; m. Valerie Viereck, Nov. 18, 1972; children: Valerie Sophia, Stephanie Anne, Jonathan Lowell. BA, Princeton U., 1968; MA, Harvard U., 1971, PhD, 1972. Instr. psychology dept. McMaster U., Hamilton, Ont., Can., 1973-75; research faculty mem. Harvard U. Grad. Sch. Edn., Cambridge, Mass., 1975-79; asst. prof. psychology Ohio State U., Columbus, 1979-84, assoc. prof., 1984—; mem. adv. bd. Assn. for Moral Edn., 1982-86. Author: Social Intelligence, 1982; contbr. numerous chpts. to books, articles to profl. jours.; mem. editorial bd. Child Devel., 1982-83. Served to capt. USAF, 1973. Can. Council Humanities and Social Scis. research grantee, 1974-75, NIMH grantee, 1980, 81-82; recipient William F. Milton Meml. Fund award Harvard U., 1976-77. Mem. Am. Psychol. Assn., Jean Piaget Soc., Soc. for Research in Child Devel., Common Cause.

GIBBS, SHELDON ARNOLD, accountant; b. Chgo., Mar. 13, 1939; s. Milton and Lillian (Adelman) G.; m. Leah Sharron Green, June 10, 1962; children: David, Daniel, Mitchell. MBA, U. Chgo., 1971. CPA, Ill. Controller, treas. Sciaky Bros., Bedford Park, Ill., 1972-75; controller Am. Soc. Clin. Pathology, Chgo., 1975-81; dir. fin. A.L.P. Lighting, Chgo., 1981-85, Sonicraft Inc., Chgo., 1985-86; gen. mgr. Elco Sales Inc., University Park, Ill., 1986—. Mem. Am. Inst. CPA's, Ill. CPA Soc. Avocations: photography, microcomputers, travel.

GIBIAN, THOMAS GEORGE, chemical executive; b. Prague, Czechoslovakia, Mar. 20, 1922; came to U.S., 1940, naturalized, 1951; s. Richard and Vera (Sindelar) G.; m. Laura Cynthia Sutherland, Feb. 19, 1949; children: Barbara Mary, Janet Cynthia, Thomas Richard, David George. B.S., U. N.C., 1942; Ph.D., Carnegie Mellon U., 1948. Research chemist Atlantic Refining Co., 1948-51; with W.R. Grace & Co., 1951-74; devel. engr. Dewey & Almy (Chem. div.); plant mgr., gen. mgr. battery separators, v.p., gen. mgr. organic chems. div., tech. group exec., corporate v.p.; pres. Chem. Constrn. Corp., N.Y.C., 1974-76; chmn., pres., dir. TGI Corp., Inc., 1976-80; dir., exec. v.p., chief operating officer Henkel of Am., Inc.; also pres., chief exec. officer dir. Henkel Corp.; pres., dir. Amchem Products, Inc., 1980-85; ptnr. Arosa Devel. Ltd., 1986—. Bd. dirs. Sandy Spring Friends Sch., Montgomery Gen. Hosp., Friends House; trustee Carnegie-Mellon U., mem. vis. com. chemistry dept. Served with RAF, 1942-46. Recipient Merit award Carnegie-Mellon U., 1975, Internat. Palladium medal, 1983. Mem. Am. Chem. Soc., Indsl. Research Inst. Clubs: Cosmos (Washington); Univ. (Pitts.); RAF (London).

GIBLER, MYRANA LOIS, auditor, state administrator; b. Washington, Mo., Oct. 22, 1957; d. Eddie Frederick and Thelma Adell (Nicks) Weller; m. Dale Frederick Gibler, Oct. 27, 1984. BS in Acctg. and Bus. Adminstrn., Lincoln U., Jefferson City, Mo., 1980. CPA, Mo. Audit asst. Mo. State Auditor's Office, Jefferson City, 1980-81; auditor then sr. auditor Mo. State Auditor's office, Jefferson City, 1981-85, research and tng. auditor mgr., 1985—, audit mgr., 1985—. Mem. Am. Inst. CPA's, Assn. Govt. Accts. (treas. Mid-Mo. chpt. 1986— officer recognition and 5 yr. mem. recognition award 1987). Republican. Baptist. Avocations: reading, crafts. Office: Mo State Auditor's Office 301 West High St PO Box 869 Jefferson City MO 65102

GIBLIN, LEONARD JOHN, mortgage company executive; b. Chgo., Sept. 2, 1934; s. John Thomas and Lucille G. (Villwock) G.; m. Jean C. Berthold, Aug. 13, 1955 (div. May 1975); children: Michael Scott, Deborah Jean, Markham Scott; m. Barbara Ann Young, Jan. 24, 1976; 1 child, Matthew Scott. BA, U. Chgo., 1953, MBA, 1956; cert. in mortgage banking, Northwestern U., 1958. V.p. Great Lakes Mortgage Corp., Chgo., 1956-79, also bd. dirs.; pres., chief exec. officer Midwest Mortgage Services, Inc., Oakbrook Terr., 1980—. Author: (book) FHA/VA Foreclosure Procedures, 1974; contbr. articles to profl. jours. Mem. Fed. Nat. Mortgage Assn. (Midwest adv. council), Mortgage Bankers Assn. Am. (chmn. mortgage servicing com. 1971-72, bd. govs. 1977-80, Housing Urban Devel. shared task force 1978-79), Ill. Mortgage Bankers Assn. (pres. 1975, exec. com. and bd. dirs. 1982—, chmn. various coms., Disting. Service award 1971). Avocations: community theater director and set designer. Home: 26 W 175 Wiesbrook Rd Wheaton IL 60187 Office: Midwest Mortgage Services Inc 1901 S Meyers Rd Suite 300 Oakbrook Terrace IL 60148

GIBSON, BENJAMIN F., judge; b. Safford, Ala., July 13, 1931; s. Eddie and Pearl Ethel (Richardson) G.; m. Lucille Nelson, June 23, 1951; children: Charlotte, Linda, Gerald, Gail, Carol, Laura. B.S., Wayne State U., 1955; J.D. with distinction, Detroit Coll. Law, 1960. Bar: Mich. 1960. Acct. City of Detroit, 1955-56, Detroit Edison Co., 1956-61; asst. atty. gen. Mich., 1961-63; asst. pros. atty. Ingham County, Mich., 1963-64; pvt. practice law Lansing, Mich., from 1964; judge U.S. Dist. Ct. Western Dist. Mich., Grand Rapids, 1979—. Hearing officer, East Lansing; bd. dirs. Lansing Jr. Achievement, Greater Lansing Legal Aid Bur. Mem. Am. Trial Lawyers Assn., Am. Bar Assn., Ingham County Bar Assn., State Bar Mich. (grievance bd. hearing panel 1971), Sigma Pi Phi. Club: Rotary. Office: U S Dist Ct 616 Fed Bldg 110 Michigan St NW Grand Rapids MI 49503 *

GIBSON, DANIEL NATHAN, educator; b. Louisville, Oct. 30, 1950; s. Wallace and Margaret Geisinger (Noss) G.; m. Karen Lynn Stanley, Aug. 19, 1972; children: Stacey Kay, Kristen Lynette. BS in Math. Edn., Ferris State U., 1973; MA in Edn. Adminstrn., Cen. Mich. U., 1982. Resident asst. Ferris State U., Big Rapids, Mich., 1969-72; tchr. Lanse Cruse Sch., Mt. Clemens, Mich., 1970— (summers); wrecker driver Frost Standard, Kalamazoo, Mich., 1973-74; tchr., coach basketball, track Hillman (Mich.) Schs., 1974—; Editor, advisor (high sch. yearbook), 1980-85. Pres. Hillman Edn. Assn., 1979—; area rep. Youth for Understanding, Hillman, 1984—; adminstrv. bd. mem. United Meth. Ch., Hillman, 1983—; sponsor United Meth. Youth Fellowship, Hillman, 1984—. Mem. NEA, Mich. Edn. Assn., Northern Mich. Edn. Assn., Mich. Council Math. Tchrs. Avocations: stamps, camping, hunting, shooting, carpentry. Home: PO Box 41 Hillman MI 49746 Office: Hillman Community Schs 245 Third St Hillman MI 49746

GIBSON, FLOYD ROBERT, judge; b. Prescott, Ariz., Mar. 3, 1910; s. Van Robert and Katheryn Ida G.; m. Gertrude Lee Walker, Apr. 23, 1935; children: Charles R., John M., Catherine L. Gibson Jobst. A.B., U. Mo., 1931, LL.B., 1933. Bar: Mo. 1932. Practiced law Independence, 1933-37, Kansas City, 1937-61; mem. firm Johnson, Lucas, Bush & Gibson (and predecessor), 1954-61; county counselor Jackson County, 1943-44; judge U.S. Dist. Ct. (we. dist.) Mo., 1961-65, chief judge, until 1965; judge U.S. Ct. Appeals (8th cir.), Kansas City, Mo., 1965—, chief judge, 1974-80; former chmn. bd. Mfrs. & Mechanics Bank, Kansas City, Mo., Blue Valley Fed. Savs. & Loan Assn.; mem. Nat. Conf. Commrs. Uniform State Laws, 1957—, Jud. Conf. U.S., 1974-80; chmn. Chief Judges Conf., 1977-78; bd. mgrs. Council State Govts., 1960-61; pres. Nat. Legis. Conf., 1960-61. Mem. Mo. Gen. Assembly from 7th Dist., 1940-46; mem. Mo. Senate, 1946-61, majority floor leader, 1952-56, pres. pro tem, 1956-60; del. Nat. Democratic Conv., 1956, 60; Mem. Mo. N.G. Named 2d most valuable mem. Mo. Legislature Globe Democrat, 1958, most valuable, 1960; recipient Faculty-Alumni award U. Mo., 1968; citation of merit Mo. Law Sch. Alumni, 1975; Spurgeon Smithson award Mo. Bar Found., 1978. Fellow ABA (adv. bd. editors Jour., chmn. jud. adminstrn. div. 1979-80, chmn. conf. sect. 1980-81, chmn. appellate judges conf. 1973-74, mem. ho. of dels.); mem. Fed. Bar Assn., Mo. Bar, Kansas City Bar Assn. (Ann. Achievement award 1980), Lawyers Assn. Kansas City (past v.p., Charles Evans Whittaker award 1985), Mo. Law Sch. Found. (life), Mo. Acad. Squires, Order of Coif, Phi Delta Phi, Phi Kappa Psi (Man of Yr. 1974). Clubs: University (Kansas City, Mo.), Carriage (Kansas City, Mo.), Mercury (Kansas City, Mo.). Home: 2102 3 San Francisco Tower 2510 Grand Kansas City MO 64108 Office: US Ct of Appeals 837 US Courthouse 811 Grand Ave Kansas City MO 64106

GIBSON, GARY WAYNE, manufacturing company marketing executive; b. Mexico, Mo., Oct. 28, 1949; s. Lawrence William Gibson and Martha Lorraine (Sims) Riggs; m. Constance Ann Queen, May 11, 1974 (div. Mar. 1982); 1 child, Amanda McKay; m. Jonna Lou Carter, Mar. 7, 1987. BA in Polit. Sci., Southwest Mo. State U., 1972, MBA, 1977. Asst. personnel mgr. Fasco Industries, Ozark, Mo., 1973-75, personnel mgr., 1975-78, div. mgr. mktg. and personnel, 1978-85, product sales mgr., 1985—; bd. dirs. Associated Industries Mo., Jefferson City, 1983—; cons. EDCO Microfilming, Springfield, Mo., 1984—. Contbr. articles to trade publs. Chmn. bd. Salvation Army, Springfield, 1982-85; com. chmn. United Way of the Ozarks, Springfield, 1983—; vol. Am. Cancer Soc., Springfield, 1986. Served to sgt. U.S. Army, 1968-70, Korea. Republican. Roman Catholic. Avocation: softball. Home: 2345 E Grand Springfield MO 65807 Office: Fasco Industries 1600 W Jackson Ozark MO 65721

GIBSON, JOHN ROBERT, judge; b. Springfield, Mo., Dec. 20, 1925; s. Harry B. and Edna (Kerr) G.; m. Mary Elizabeth Vaughn, Sept. 20, 1952 (dec. Aug. 1985); children: Jeanne, John Robert; m. Diane Allen Larrison, Oct. 1, 1986; stepchildren: Holly, Catherine. AB, U. Mo., 1949, JD, 1952. Bar: Mo. 1952. Assoc. Morrison, Hecker, Curtis, Kuder & Parrish, Kansas City, Mo., 1952-58, ptnr., 1958-81; judge U.S. Dist. Ct. (we. dist.) Mo., 1981-82, U.S. Ct. Appeals (8th cir.), Kansas City, 1982—; mem. Mo. Press-Bar Commn., 1979-81. Vice chmn. Jackson County Charter Transition Com., 1971-72; mem. Jackson County Charter Commn., 1970; v.p. Police Commrs. Bd., Kansas City, 1973-77. Served with AUS, 1944-46. Fellow Am. Bar Found.; mem. ABA, Mo. State Bar (gov. 1972-79, pres. 1977-78; Pres.'s award 1974, Smithson award 1984), Kansas City Bar Assn. (pres. 1970-71), Lawyers Assn. of Kansas City (Charles Evan Whittaker award 1980), Phi Beta Kappa, Omicron Delta Kappa. Presbyterian. Home: 801 W 57th St Kansas City MO 64113 Office: US Ct of Appeals 851 US Courthouse 811 Grand Ave Kansas City MO 64106

GIBSON, LENORA JANE SPRINGER, occupational health nurse; b. Brownsvalley, Ind., Nov. 18, 1930; d. Ralph Leon and Helen Elnora (West) Springer; m. Kenton Glenn Gibson, Oct. 29, 1952; children: Kent Glenn, Dean Allen. Student Waynetown Sch., 1936-48; diploma, Home Hosp. Sch. Nursing, 1951. Cert. occupational health nurse. Surg. nurse Montgomery County Culver Union Hosp., Crawfordsville, Ind., 1951-52; occupational health nurse R.R. Donnelley & Sons, Crawfordsville, 1952-55; head nurse nursery Meth. Hosp., Indpls., 1958-59; staff Detroit Diesel Allison div. Gen. Motors Corp., Indpls., 1959-80, supr. nurses, 1981—. Recipient Occupational Health Nurse award Schering Corp., 1982. Fellow Ind. Acad. Occupational Health Nurses; mem. Mid-Ind. Assn. Occupational Health Nurses, Ind. Assn. Occupational Health Nurses (treas., pres.), Am. Assn. Occupational Health Nurses. Baptist. Home: 3302 Shadow Brook Dr Indianapolis IN 46224 Office: General Motors Corp PO Box 894 Indianapolis IN 46206

GIBSON, LEONA (LEE) RUTH, medical society administrator; b. Columbia, Mo., Aug. 11, 1929; d. Raymon Henry and Mabel Virginia (Barnes) Keel; m. Willian Oscar Gibson, Jr., May 8, 1948 (div.); children—Linda Nadine Gibson Phillips, George William. Student U. Mo., 1947-48. Cert. profl. sec. Sec. to gen. mgr. Gen. Telephone Co. of Mid-West, Columbia, 1948-63; devel., owner, mgr. Lee Gibson Business Service, Columbia, 1963-84; owner, mgr. Office Plaza I Service Center, Columbia, 1984; exec. dir. Boone County Med. Soc., Columbia, 1984—; cons., tchr. adult edn. Chmn. fund raising Columbia Coll.; chmn. Bus. License Commn. City of Columbia. Mem. Profl. Assn. Secretarial Services, Cen. Mo. Psychiat. Soc. (exec. dir. 1986—), Columbia Northside Bus. Assn. (pres.), Profl. Secretaries Assn. (pres. chpt.), Columbia C. of C. (dir.). Republican. Lutheran. Club: Mo. State Genealogical Assn. (bd. dirs.). Office: 2100 I-70 Dr SW Columbia MO 65205

GIBSON, PAUL ROBERT, chemical and metallurgical engineer; b. Mpls., May 4, 1950; s. Robert Blake and Evelyn Fannie (Klein) G.; m. Debra Ann Lee, Nov. 11, 1978; children: Nicole Lee, Jonathan David, Michael Paul. BA in Biology with honors, U. No. Iowa, 1977. Cert. secondary tchr., Iowa. Tchr. sci. Logan Jr. High Sch., Waterloo, Iowa, 1977-78; instr. teaching lab. sci. U. No. Iowa, Cedar Falls, 1978-80; metall. technician Waterloo works John Deere, Waterloo, 1980-86, chem. and metall. engr., 1986—. Area Edn. Agy. 7 Tchr. Ctr. grantee, 1979. Mem. Am. Welding Soc., Am. Soc. Metals. Avocations: sports, computers, reading. Office: John Deere Tractor Works 3500 E Donald PO Box 3500 Waterloo IA 50704

GIBSON, ROBERT PETER, hospital administrator; b. Pawtucket, R.I., Sept. 6, 1945; s. Foster Forrest and Laura Susan (Zakowski) G.; m. Jo Anne Passaggio, Jan. 6, 1968; children—Peter Scott, Amy Elizabeth, Matthew Patrick. B.A., U. Conn., 1967; M.H.A., Xavier U., 1975. Resident St. Francis Hosp., Cin., 1974-75; pres., adminstr. Fort Wayne State Hosp. and Tng. Center (Ind.), after 1975, now asst. supt. adminstr. Chmn. adult edn. Am. Cancer Soc.; bd. dirs. Health Systems Agy. Served to capt. USAF, 1967-72. Decorated Air Medals with clusters (4). Recipient Boss of Yr. award Am. Bus. Women's Assn., 1982. Mem. Am. Coll. Hosp. Adminstrs., Hosp. Fin. Mgmt. Assn., Am. Pub. Health Assn. Roman Catholic. Clubs: Kiwanis, Elks (Fort Wayne). Author: Relocation of Long Term Care Facility, microfilm, 1975. Home: 9108 Seawind Pl Fort Wayne IN 46804 Office: 4900 St Joe Rd Fort Wayne IN 46815

GIBSON, SCOTT WILBERT, agronomist; b. St. Charles, Ill., Feb. 27, 1948; s. Wilbert and Dorothy Elaine (Kemp) G.; 1 child, Jessica Sekhet. MS in Plant and Soil Sci., So. Ill. U., 1978. Area field mgr., agronomist Velsicol Chem. Co., Princeton, Ill., 1978-80; agrl. research scientist 3M Co., Princeton, 1980-84; research and devel. rep. BASF Chem. Corp., Princeton, 1984-86; pres. Mo. Agrl. Mgmt., Jefferson City, Mo., 1984—. Contbr. articles to profl jours. Mem. Plant Growth Regulator Working Group, Weed Sci. Soc. Am., Internat. Plant Protection Congress, Am. Soc. Agronomy, Council Agrl. Sci. and Tech., Internat. Grassland Crongress, North Cen. Weed Control Soc., Ill. Acad. Sci. Methodist. Home and Office: 2411A Beasley Ct Jefferson City MO 65101

GIBSON, WILLIAM CHARLES, county government parks and recreation official; b. Midland, Mich., July 26, 1944; s. Harold David Gibson and Erma Elizabeth (Emmrich) Westfall; m. Karen Marie Jarmol, Oct. 5, 1974. Student Mich. Technol. U., 1962-63, U. Mich., 1963-65; B.S. with high honors, Mich. State U., 1972. Registered parks and recreation profl., Mich. Dir. parks and recreation City of Mason, Mich., 1972-74; supt. parks County of Midland, Midland, 1974-78, dept. dir. parks and recreation, 1978-83, dir. parks and recreation, 1983—. Chmn., County of Midland Employees Safety Com., 1983, 84; mem. Midland Found., 1984—, chmn. coms., 1985, 86, 87. Mich. Recreation and Parks Assn. scholar, 1971, 72; trustee Midland Found., 1987. Mem. Nat. Recreation and Parks Assn. (cert. profl.), Mich. Assn. County Park and Recreation Ofcls., Mich. Recreation and Parks Assn. (park resources com. 1980—, chmn. 1982-83, bd. dirs. 1982-83, long-range planning com. 1983-86), Midland Area C. of C., Mich. State U. Coll. Agr. and Natural Resources Alumni Assn. (bd. dirs. 1985—), Alpha Zeta. Presbyterian. Lodge: Elks. Avocations: golf, scuba diving, tennis, listening to music, woodworking. Home: 5708 Drake St Midland MI 48640 Office: Midland County Dept County Devel 1270 James Savage Rd Midland MI 48640

GIEBNER, CARA RAE, trade association adminstrator; b. Cleve., Sept. 29, 1940; children: Catherine, Elaine, Christopher. BS, Ohio U., 1960. Exec. sec. Marcus Advt., Cleve., 1969-75; with personnel dept. Van Dorn Plastics, Strongsville, Ohio, 1975-80; exec. v.p. Spring Service Assn., Medina, Ohio, 1980—; exec. sec. Heavy Duty Reps. Assn., Medina, 1986—. Newsletter editor Van Dorn Plastics Press, 1975-80, Spring Service Assn., 1981—, Gerspacher, 1981-85. Mem. Sales and Mktg. Execs. Cleve., Cleve. Area Meeting Planners, Fleet Maintenance Council of N.E. Ohio, Greater Cleve. Soc. Assn. Execs., Medina County Bd. Realtors. Home and Office: 4015 Marks Rd Suite 2B Medina OH 44256

GIECK, JACK EDGAR, chemical engineer, filmmaker; b. Milw., Feb. 19, 1923; s. Edgar Fred And Lydia Louise (Abel) G.; m. Victoria Louise Voelker, June 14, 1947; children: Anne, John. BSChemE, Iowa State U., 1947. Registered profl. engr., Ohio. Various positions Firestone Indsl. Products, various locations, 1947-66; dir. mktg. Firestone Diversified Products, Akron, Ohio, 1966-72, dir. new product div., 1972-80; asst. dir. research Firestone T&R, Akron, 1980-82; pres. CINEMARK, Inc., Akron, 1982—; cons. ARNCO, La Palma, Calif., 1981—. Writer, producer: (film) City at the Summit, 1976, many other historic and technical documentary films, 1954—; author: A Photo Album of Ohio's Canal Era, 1825-1913, 1987; contbr. articles to profl. jours. pres., trustee Canal Soc. Ohio, Akron, 1966—; v.p., trustee Summit County Hist. Soc., Akron, 1976—. Served 1st lt. U.S. Army, 1943-47, ETO. Grantee NSF, Washington, 1968. Mem. Soc. Automotive Engrs., Soc. Motion Picture and TV engrs. Clubs: Akron Torch (pres. 1980). Avocation: writing. Home and Office: 1761 Karg Dr Akron OH 44313

GIELEN, MICHAEL ANDREAS, conductor; b. Dresden, Germany, July 20, 1927; s. Josef and Rose (Steuermann) G.; m. Helga Augsten, May 20, 1957; children: Claudia, Lucas. Student, U. Dresden, 1936, U. Berlin, 1937, U. Vienna, 1940, Buenos Aires U., 1950. Coach, Teatro Colón, Buenos Aires, 1947-50, condr., Vienna State Opera, 1950-60, Stockholm Royal Opera, 1960-65, free lance condr., Cologne, Germany, 1965-68, mus. dir., Belgian Nat. Orch., Brussels, 1969-73, chief comdr., Netherlands Opera, 1973-75, music dir., gen. mgr., Frankfurt (Germany) Opera House, from 1977, music dir., Cin. Symphony Orch., 1980—, prin. guest condr., BBC Symphony Orch., London, guest condr., Washington Nat. Symphony, Chgo. Symphony, Pitts. Symphony, Minn. Orch., Detroit Symphony, others.; Composer: 4 Gedichte von Stefan George, 1958, Variations for 40 Instruments, 1959, Un dia Sobresale, 1963, die glocken sind auffalscher spur, 1969, Mitbestimmunes Modell, 1974. Office: Cin Symphony Orch 1241 Elm St Cincinnati OH 45210 *

GIENAPP, KATIE ANN, psychologist; b. Danville, Ill., Mar. 21, 1939; d. William Robert and June Aileen (Buckelew) Berg; m. John Charles Gienapp, Aug. 22, 1964; children: Anne A., John W. BS, Concordia Coll., River Forest, Ill., 1961; MS, U. Kans., Lawrence, 1968; PhD, U. Ill., 1980. Lic. psychologist, Ill. Psychologist Incentives, Inc., Des Plaines, Ill., 1980-82, Cheryl Caliendo Peacout and Assocs., Libertyville, Ill., 1982-83; ptnr., psychologist Lindquist, Gienapp, Strauss and Assocs., Lake Bluff, Ill., 1983—; dir. homebased program for mothers and children Lutheran Social Services, Ft. Wayne, 1974-76. Dir. Allen County (Ind.) Community Coordinated Child Care, 1974-76; vol. Allen County Child Abuse Task Force, 1974-76. HEW fellow U. Kans., 1967-68. Mem. Am. Psychol. Assn., Ill. Psychol. Assn. Lutheran. Avocations: music, literature, drama. Home: 1018 11th St Wilmette IL 60091 Office: Lindquist Gienapp Strauss Assocs 49-51-P Sherwood Terr Lake Bluff IL 60044

GIERING, RICHARD HERBERT, computerized information systems co. exec.; b. Emmaus, Pa., Nov. 27, 1929; s. Harold Augustus and Marguerite (Bruder) G.; B.S. in Engring. and Math., U. Ariz., 1962; m. Carol Alice Scott, Aug. 16, 1959; children—Richard Herbert, Scott K. Enlisted U.S. Army, 1947, commd. 2d lt., 1963, advanced through grades to capt., 1965; sect. chief data processing Def. Intelligence Agy., Washington, 1965-67; ret., 1967; with Data Corp. (name changed to Mead Tech. Labs. 1968), Dayton, Ohio, 1967-77, v.p. tech. ops., 1970-71, dir. info. systems, 1971-77; pres., chief exec. officer DG Assos., Inc., 1974—; pres. Infotex Assos., 1977-86, mgr. Product Systems, Commerce Clearing House, Inc., 1986—; instr. data processing U. Ariz., Tucson, 1962-63. Mem. Assn. Computing Machinery, Am. Soc. Info. Scis. Inventor Data/Central (used to establish electronic newspaper libraries). Home: 906 Red Top Dr Libertyville IL 60048 Office: Box 2151 Dayton OH 45429

GIERKE, HERMAN FREDRICK, III, state supreme court justice; b. Williston, N.D., Mar. 13, 1943; s. Herman Fredrick, Jr. and Mary (Kelly) G.; m. Judith Lynn Olson, June 12, 1965; children—Todd H.F., Scott H.F., Craig H.F., Michelle Lynn. B.A., U. N.D., 1964, J.D., 1966; attended, JAG Sch., U. Va., 1967, 69. Bar: N.D. 1966, U.S. Dist. Ct. N.D., U.S. Supreme Ct. Practice law Watford City, N.D., 1971-83; state's atty. McKenzie County, 1974-82; city atty. City of Watford, 1974-83; justice N.D. Supreme Ct., Bismarck, 1983—. Served as capt. JAGC, U.S. Army, 1967-71. Recipient Outstanding Service award Gov. of N.D., 1984. Fellow Am. Coll. Probate Counsel; mem. N.D. Trial Lawyers Assn. (bd. govs. 1977-83), N.D. State Attys. Assn. (pres. 1979-80), N.D. Council Sch. Attys. (charter), NW Jud. Dist. Bar Assn. (pres. 1977-79), State Bar Assn. N.D. (pres. 1982-83), Am. Judicature Soc., Assn. Trial Lawyers Am., Nat. Dist. Attys. Assn.,

Aircraft Owners and Pilots Assn., Am. Legion (N.D. comdr. 1984, judge adv. state assn., nat. vice comdr. 1985—), ABA, Blue Key, Phi Delta Phi. Lutheran. Lodge: Elks. Avocations: racquetball; golf; tennis; raising horses. Office: ND State Supreme Ct Judicial Wing 1st Floor State Capitol Bismarck ND 58505

GIERTZ, ROBERT WILLIAM, heavy equipment manufacturing company executive; b. Clifton, Ill., Mar. 24, 1925; s. William Chris and Emma Louise (Meyer) G.; m. Vera Rosalie Herrmann, Nov. 30, 1946; children: Deborah Giertz Staack, Nancy Giertz Natvig, Norman, James, Julie Giertz Elias. BS, U. Ill., 1950; postgrad. MIT, 1964. Registered profl. engr., Ill. Mech. engr. John Deere Waterloo Tractor Works of Deere & Co., Waterloo, Iowa, 1950-64, chief engr., 1964-67, gen. mgr., 1967-74, dir. mfg., Moline, Ill., 1974-86; pres. Giertz Enterprises, Ltd., Bettendorf, Iowa, 1986—. Mem. Dist. Jud. Nominating Commn., 1969-75; mem. Waterloo Indsl. Devel. Assn., 1968-75; past mem. United Services of Black Hawk County. Trustee Schoitz Meml. Hosp., 1968-74, Mt. Mercy Coll., Cedar Rapids, Iowa, 1979-82; bd. govs. Iowa Coll. Found., vice chmn., 1976, chmn., 1977; bd. govs. U. No. Iowa Found., pres. 1973-75; past bd. dirs. Waterloo Civic Found.; bd. dirs. Quad City World Affairs Council, pres., 1980-81. Served with USAF, 1946-47. Mem. Soc. Automotive Engrs., Am. Soc. Agrl. Engrs., Assn. Mgmt. Cons., Ops. Mgmt. Assn., U. Ill. Alumni Assn. (bd. dirs. 1987—). Republican. Lutheran. Clubs: Crow Valley Golf, Symposium. Home and Office: 2410 Eagle Circle Bettendorf IA 52722

GIES, CAROL J., public relations and marketing executive; b. Detroit, Jan. 20, 1947; m. Craig M. Gies, Mar. 31, 1966. BS, Wayne State U., 1971, MA, 1972; MBA, Mich. State U., 1985. Pub. relations dir. Met. Detroit Conv. and Visitors Bur., 1973-78, v.p. civic affairs, 1979; exec. dir. host com. Rep. Nat. Conv., 1980; exec. dir. Mich. Host Com. for Super Bowl XVI, 1982; sr. v.p. Anthony M. Franco, Inc., Detroit, 1982-87; v.p. Ketchum Pub. Relations, Chgo., 1987—; ptnr. Root Photographers, Inc., Chgo., 1987—. Recipient Gold Quill, Internat. Assn. Bus. Communicators, 1975; Mich. Embassy of Tourism award; named Woman of Wayne Headliner, 1980. Mem. Pub. Relations Soc. of Am. (Nat. Silver Anvil award, 3 dist. awards), Women in Communications (Clarion award). Office: Root Photographers Inc 1131 W Sheridan Rd Chicago IL 60660 also: Ketchum Pub Relations 142 E Ontario Chicago IL 60611

GIESEKE, WILLIAM DAVID, psychotherapist; b. Oak Park, Ill., Oct. 21, 1947; s. Harvey A. and Lenice (Meyer) G.; m. Gaylord Andersen, Aug. 2, 1975; stepchildren: Kyle A. Thomas, Carson H. Thomas. BS, Valparaiso U., 1971; MS, Ill. Inst. Tech., 1975; postgrad., Inst. Psychoanalysis, Chgo., 1980-86. Exec. dir. Glencoe (Ill.) Youth Services, 1972-77; pvt. practice psychotherapy Winnetka, Ill., 1976—; psychotherapist Irene Josselyn Clinic, Northfield, Ill., 1977—; Mem. New Trier Twp. Mental Health Com., 1975-77. Mem. AAAS, Assn. Child Psychotherapists (treas. 1984-86, pres. 1986-87), N. Network Coalition (pres. 1974-77). Office: 723 Elm St Winnetka IL 60093

GIFFELS, ANNE MARIE, accountant; b. Akron, Ohio, Nov. 16, 1958; d. William Charles and Lorena Anne (Buehrle) G. BBA in Accountancy, U. Notre Dame, 1981. CPA, Ill. Tax preparer Pennaco Resources, Chgo., 1982; mgmt. cons. Deloitte Haskins & Sells, Chgo., 1982-86; sr. tax analyst Marmon Group, Inc., Chgo., 1986—. Mem. Am. Inst. CPA's, Ill. CPA Soc. Republican. Roman Catholic. Avocations: bicycling, golf, reading. Office: Marmon Group Inc 39 S LaSalle St Suite 520 Chicago IL 60603

GIFFEN, DANIEL HARRIS, lawyer, educator; b. Zanesville, Ohio, Feb. 11, 1938; s. Harris Macartor and Anne Louise (Crawford) G.; m. Jane Louise Cayford, Nov. 23, 1963 (div. 1970); children—Sarah Louise, Thomas Harris; m. Linda Eastin, Aug. 19, 1972. A.B., Coll. of William and Mary, 1960; M.A., U. Pa., 1962, U. Pa., 1967; J.D., Case Western Res. U., 1973. Bar: Ohio 1973. Corp. asst. Lippincott Library U. Pa., Phila., 1961-63; assoc. curator La. State Mus., New Orleans, 1963-64; sec., dir. N.H. Hist. Soc., Concord, 1964-69; asst. dir. Arents Research Library Syracuse U., N.Y., 1969-70; sole practice Cleve., 1973—; asst. prof. law Cleve. State U. Ohio, 1976-79, Kent State U., Ohio, 1980—; v.p. Village Press, Inc., Concord, 1969-74; editor Walter Drane Co., Cleve., 1974-76; lectr. Monadnock Community Coll., Peterborough, N.H., 1968-69. Author: Adventures in Vermont, 1969, Adventures in Maine, 1969, New Hampshire Colony, 1970. Contbr. articles to profl. jours. Sec. Cleve. Restoration Soc., 1974-79; bd. dirs. Soc. of Collectors, Cleve., 1975-78; v.p. N.H. Antiquarian Soc., Concord, 1966-68; bd. dirs. N.H. Assn. Hist. Socs., Concord, 1967; life mem. (hon.) Pres.'s Council Coll. of William and Mary, 1980. Recipient Kenyon English Prize scholarship, 1956; fellow Heritage Found., 1959, 60, Nat. Trust, 1959, 60, 61, 67, 73. Mem. Ohio Bar Assn., Cleve. Bar Assn., ABA, Am. Soc. Interior Design, Am. Assn. Museums, Am. Assn. State and Local Historians, Nat. Trust, Soc. Am. Archivists, Soc. Archtl. Historians, Pewter Collectors' Club, United Faculty Profs. Assn. (bd. dirs. 1983—). Episcopalian. Lodges: Masons, Shriners. Home: 2067 Ridgewood Rd Fairlawn Heights OH 44313 Office: Kent State U 100 Nixson Hall Kent OH 44242

GIFFEN, LAWRENCE EVERETT, SR., family physician, anesthesiologist; b. Jefferson City, Mo., Jan. 30, 1923; s. Fred Lemon and Angeline Henrietta (Patterson) G.; m. Mary Opal McKnight, Oct. 15, 1947 (div. Mar. 1950); 1 child, Lawrence Everett Jr.; m. Jerena East, June 17, 1955; children: Michael Gregory, Jerena Ann. DO, Kirksville Coll. Osteo Medicine, 1945; BS in Biology, Lincoln U., 1960; BA in History, U. Md., 1981; MS in Criminal Justice, Cen. Mo. State U., 1980; MA in History, Lincoln U., 1987. Diplomate Am. Osteo. Bd. Anesthesiology, Am. Bd. Family Practice. Intern Osteo. Hosp. Maine, Portland, 1945-46; practice gen. medicine Chamois, Mo., 1946-50; resident in anesthesiology Art Ctr. Hosp., Detroit, 1950-51; practice gen. medicine and anesthesiology Jefferson City, Mo., 1951-80, 83—; med. examiner Jefferson City, 1968-80. Contbr. articles to profl. jour. Served to comdr. USNR, 1980-83. Fellow Am. Osteo. Coll. Anesthesiologists (pres. 1962), Am. Osteo. Coll. Surgeons (hon.), Am. Acad. Family Physicians; mem. AMA, Mo. State Med. Soc., U.S. Naval Inst., Am. Assn. Mil. Surgeons, Am. Assn. History Medicine. Republican. Presbyterian. Lodge: Masons, Shriners. Avocation: history studies. Home: 1915 Hayselton Dr Jefferson City MO 65101 Office: 420 E High St Jefferson City MO 65101

GIFFEY, DONALD F., agricultural cooperative executive. b. Minot, N.D., Oct. 4, 1920; s. Ernest Andrew and Marvelle (Larson) G.; m. Avis C. Giffey, Feb. 27, 1944; children: Donald C., Nancy Giffey Renhowe. Pres., chief operating officer, chmn., dir. Harvest States Coops., St. Paul, Minn.; vice chmn. N.D. Rural Rehabilitation Corp., Bismarck, 1965—. State rep. N.D. Ho. of Reps., Bismarck, 1960-72. Home: HC 1 PO Box 26 Roseglen ND 58775 Office: Harvest States Cooperatives 1667 N Snelling Ave Saint Paul MN 55164

GIFFIN, MARY, psychiatrist, educator; b. Rochester, Minn., Mar. 30, 1919; d. Herbert Ziegler and Mary Elizabeth (Nace) G. BA, Smith Coll., Northampton, Mass., 1939; MD, Johns Hopkins, 1943; MS, U. Minn., 1948. Diplomate Am. Bd. Psychiatry and Neurology. Cons. in neurology and psychiatry Mayo Clinic, Rochester, 1949-58; med. dir. Josselyn Clinic, Northfield, Ill., 1948—; mem. faculty Inst. for Psychoanalysis, Chgo., 1963—. Contbr. numerous articles to profl. jour. Fellow Am. Psychiat. Assn.; mem. Ill. Psychiat. Soc., Am. Acad. Child Psychiatry. Republican. Am. Baptist. Avocation: creative writing. Home: 1190 Hamptondale Rd Winnetka IL 60093 Office: Irene Josselyn Clinic 405 Central Northfield IL 60093

GIFFORD, FRANK, JR., real estate developer; b. Marion, Ohio, Feb. 21, 1953; s. Frank and Marjorie Dorothy (Rothman) G.; m. Donna Mary Madlener, June 12, 1981; children: Sarah Elizabeth, John Franklin. BBA, Ohio State U., 1978. Field analyst Kenneth Danter & Co., Columbus, Ohio, 1978-81; leasing agt. Ohio Equities, Inc., Columbus, 1981-82; pres. realty div. Continental Real Estate Co., Columbus, 1982—. Recipient Life Saving Heroism award ARC, 1971, Dirs. award Small Bus. Adminstrn., 1979. Mem. Nat. Assn. Realtors, Internat. Assn Corp. Real Estate Execs., Urban Land Inst. Avocations: golf, fitness, reading, economics, skiing. Office: Continental Real Estate Cos 1070 Morse Rd Columbus OH 43229

GIFFORD, RICKY LEE, municipal electrical inspector; b. Kokomo, Ind., Mar. 19, 1947; s. William Benjamin and Barbara Lou (Bailey) G.; m. Linda Lou Atkisson, Aug. 20, 1966 (div. Oct. 1978); children: Melissa L., Tonya L., Cathy L.; m. Loren Louise Crume, Feb. 14, 1979. Student, Ind. U., Kokomo, 1971-75. Corp. sec., bus. mgr. Circle City Electric Co., Indpls., 1972-74; v.p., bus. mgr. Intra-State Electric Co., Kokomo, 1974-78; owner, operator Gifford Electric Co., Kokomo, 1978-80; chief elec. inspector City of Kokomo, 1980—. Mem. adv. council Ind. Vocat. Tech., Kokomo, 1982—. Served with USN, 1965-69. Mem. Internat. Assn. Elec. Inspectors (Western sect. rep. 1985—, chmn. Ind. chpt. 1984-85), Disabled Am. Vets., Howard County Vietnam Vets. Democrat. Baptist. Lodges: Masons, Elks. Avocations: golf, travel, building, woodworking. Home: 315 Walnut St E Kokomo IN 46901 Office: City of Kokomo 100 N Union St Kokomo IN 46901

GILB, CORINNE LATHROP, history educator; b. Lethbridge, Alta., Can., Feb. 19, 1925; d. Glen Hutchison and Vera (Passey) Lathrop; m. Tyrell Thompson Gilb, Aug. 19, 1945; children: Lesley, Tyra. BA, U. Wash., 1946; MA, U. Calif., Berkeley, 1951, law student, 1950-53; PhD, Harvard U., 1957. History lectr. Mills Coll., Oakland, 1957-61; prof. humanities U. San Francisco, 1964-68; research assoc. U. Calif., Berkeley, 1953-68; prof. history Wayne State U., Detroit, 1968—; dir. planning City of Detroit, 1979-85; special cons. Calif. Legis., 1963, 64. Author: Conformity of State to Federal Income Tax, 1964, Hidden Hierarchies. 1966; contbr. articles to profl. jours. Recipient Guggenheim fellowship, 1957; grantee Social Sci. Research Council, various others. Mem. Internat. Soc. Comparative Study of Civilizations (governing council 1985—), No. Calif. World Affairs Council, various acad. assns. Presbyterian.

GILBERG, STEVEN MICHAEL, marketing professional; b. Chgo., Apr. 22, 1962; s. Barry Paul and Judith Marsha (Frank) G. BBA, U. Iowa, 1984. Mktg. rep. Xerox Corp., Omaha, 1984-85; major accounts rep. Xerox Corp., Des Moines, 1985-87; acct. mgr. Knoll Internat., Chgo., 1987—; career cons. U. Iowa, 1984—. Named one of Outstanding Young Men of Am., 1984. Mem. Am. Mktg. Assn. Republican. Jewish. Home: 440 W Barry #305 Chicago IL 60654 Office: Knoll Internat 1111 Merchandise Chicago IL 60654

GILBERT, BARTON, environmental science executive; b. Cleve., Jan. 13, 1936; s. Bernard and Rose (Richman) G.; m. Elaine Judith Weiss, July 3, 1966; children: Brian, Haley. BS in Commerce, Ohio U., 1960. Gen. mgr. Signal Chem. Co., Bedford Heights, Ohio, 1960-66; pres. Duron Corp., Cleve., 1966-74, Gen. Environ. Sci., Cleve., 1974—; nat. com. chmn. Water Pollution Control, Washington, 1984-87. Patentee in field. Corp. fund raiser Cleve. Opera, 1983-86; div. chmn. Jewish Welfare Fund, Cleve., 1985-86. Served with U.S. Army, 1957-59. Jewish. Club: Hawthorne Valley Country (Solon, Ohio) (pres. 1985-87). Avocations: golf, tennis, reading. Home: 31899 Chestnut Ln Pepper Pike OH 44124 Office: Gen Environ Sci PO Box 22294 Cleveland OH 44122

GILBERT, CHARLES NELSON, management information services executive; b. Elmira, N.Y., Mar. 31, 1951; s. Donald L. and Virginia (Kipp) G.; m. Lisa P. Dupont, Aug. 23, 1975; children: Christopher, Brian, Mark. BBA, Elmira Coll., 1976; MS in Info. Services, SUNY, Binghamton, 1978. Mgr. fin. analysis Masonite Corp., Towanda, Pa., 1978-78, mgr. mgmt. info. services div., 1980-83, mgr. fin. services, 1983-84; dir. mgmt. info. services group Masonite Corp., Chgo., 1984—; ptnr. CBM Enterprises, Elmira, 1984—. Mem. Data Processing Mgmt. Assn., Internat. Mgmt. Consul. Home: 102 Bridgeport Ln Geneva IL 60134 Office: Masonite Corp 1 S Wacker Dr Chicago IL 60606

GILBERT, CLARENCE HARVEY, JR., writer, former educational administrator; b. San Diego, Mar. 3, 1947; s. Clarence Harvey and Ardith Corine (King) G.; m. Kathryn Jeanne Hogue, June 14, 1969 (div. Mar. 1985); children—Cori, Chris, Keri. A.A., Pratt Community Coll., 1967; B.A. in English and Journalism, Fort Hays State U., 1970; M.S. in Ednl. Adminstrn., Emporia State U., 1981: post grad. Okla. State U., 1984. Tchr. English and journalism, coach Iola High Sch., Kans., 1972-73; tchr. journalism, coach Hutchinson High Sch., Kans., 1973-78; tchr. English, coach F.L. Schlagle High Sch., Kansas City, Kans., 1978-81; bldg. prin. W. Elk Jr. Sr. High Sch., Howard, Kans., 1981-82, Udall Jr.-Sr. High Sch., Kans., 1983-86; bldg. prin., acting supt. Unified Sch. Dest. 463, Udall, Kans., 1984-85; radio commentator Sta. KWHK, Hutchinson, Kans., 1976-78. Author: (with others) Raymond Berry's Complete Guide to Coaching Pass Receivers, 1982; Raymond Berry's Complete Guide for Pass Receivers, 1982. Mem. Nat. Assn. Secondary Sch Prins., Kans. Assn. Secondary Sch. Prins., Assn. Supervision and Curriculum Devel., Kans. Assn. Sch. Adminstrs. Avocations: reading; writing; sports participation. Home and Office: 424 Lauber Ln Derby KS 67037

GILBERT, DARREN ROBERT, chemical engineer; b. Jersey City, July 11, 1960; s. Frederick Anton Gilbert and Barbara Ann (Milano) Ernest. BSChemE, Northwestern U., 1983. Lab. technician Colgate-Palmolive, Jersey City, 1980-83; with product devel. Stepan Co., Northfield, Ill., 1983—. Named one of Outstanding Young Men Am., Jaycees of Am., 1984. Mem. ASTM (com. chmn. 1983-84), Am. Chem. Soc., Chem. Industries Council, Soc. Plastics Industries, Am. Assn. Individual Investors, Am. Mgmt. Assn. Roman Catholic. Lodge: KC. Avocations: basketball, volleyball. Home: 8912 Skokie Blvd Skokie IL 60076 Office: Stepan Co 22 W Frontage Rd Northfield IL 60093

GILBERT, GERALD WAYNE, manufacturing company executive; b. Gladewater, Tex., Mar. 22, 1933; s. Charles Marlin Gilbert and Elsie Pauline (Bohannon) Pruett; m. Elaine Joan Hushagen, Sept. 20, 1953; children: Terence, Shawn, Erin, Shelley. AA, Lower Columbia Coll., 1953; BS, U. Wash., 1962. Tech.r ep. Boeing Co., Seattle, 1951-62; reliability mgr. Litton Ind., Blacksburg, Va., 1962-67; dir. quality assurance Control Data Corp., Mpls., 1967-69, dir. ops., 1969-71, gen. mgr. mfg., 1971-73, gen. mgr. div., 1973-74, v.p. group exec., 1974-75, v.p. engring systems, 1983-86; exec. v.p. Magnetic Peripherals Inc., Mpls., 1975-77, pres., chief ops. officer, 1977-83; pres., chief exec. officer Winnebago Industries, Forest City, Iowa, 1986—, also bd. dirs. Lodge: Rotary. Avocations: golfing, boating. Home: 102 Knollwood Dr Forest City IA 50436

GILBERT, JAMES DEFOREST, orthopedic surgeon; b. Greenville, Mich., Dec. 8, 1946; s. William Theodore and June Elizabeth (Barlow) G.; m. Barbara Howard, June 20, 1969; children: Eric William, Mary Kathleen, Margaret Howard, Elizabeth Jane, Mary Ellen. BS with honors, Mich. State U., 1969, MD, 1973. Cert. Mich. Bd. Medicine. Orthopedic surgeon Kalamazoo Orthopedic Clinic, 1978-81; orthopedic surgeon, founder Midwest Orthopedic Surgery P.C., Kalamazoo, 1981—; cons. Western Mich. U. Sports Clinic; assoc. clin. prof. surgery Mich. State U., 1978—. Contbr. articles to med. jours. Chmn. med. staff annual fund drive Bronson Health Found., 1986—. Mem. Am. Acad. Orthopedic Surgeons, Mich. Orthopedic Soc., Kalamazoo Acad. Medicine. Club: Gull Lake Country (Richland, Mich.). Home: 4304 Old Colony Rd Kalamazoo MI 49008 Office: Midwest Orthopedic Surgery PC 502 Bronson Med Ctr Kalamazoo MI 49007

GILBERT, MARTIN, marketing professional; b. Madison, Wis., May 2, 1954; s. Jerome Marvin and Rose (Zunamon) G. BS in Bus., Miami (Ohio) U., 1976; MBA in Internat. Bus., Loyola U., Chgo., 1981. Copywriter Bernard Hodes Advt., Chgo., 1977-78; internat. copywriter Dentsu Advt., Inc., Tokyo, 1978-80; internat. product planner Motorola, Schaumburg, Ill., 1981-83, sr. internat. promotions planner, 1983-86, market planning mgr.-Asia Pacific, 1986—; cons., v.p. Japan Am. Mktg. Group, Chgo., 1982-84; guest lectr. internat. mktg. DePaul U., Chgo., 1986—. Recipient Grand Prize award Japan's Internat. Advt. Show, 1979. Avocations: sports (selected all-star Tokyo Internat. Softball League, 1979), photography, jazz, travel, oriental art. Home: 2225 N Halsted St #25 Chicago IL 60614 Office: Motorola Inc 1301 E Algonquin Rd Schaumburg IL 60196

GILBERT, PHYLLIS JO, dental assistant, consultant; b. Mpls., Jan. 25, 1944; d. Philip Rod and Josephine Elsie (Korinek) Wicklund; m. Richard Earl Gilbert, Sept. 17, 1966; children—Scott Richard, Nicole Susan. Cert. dental assisting, U. Minn., 1963; B.S. cum laude in Dental Assisting Edn., 1981. Cert. Dental Assisting Nat. Bd.; registered dental asst., Minn. Office dental asst., mgr. Ralph R. Nielson, Mpls., 1963-71; dental assisting instr. North Suburban Hennepin County Vocat. Sch., Mpls., 1971-73, Normandale Community Coll., Mpls., 1976-78; ops. asst. Park Dental Health Ctrs. and freelance dental assisting instr., Mpls., 1981-85; ops. asst. Park Dental Health Ctrs., 1985—; dir. Mpls. Vocat. Tech. Inst., China-U.S. Sci. Exchanges. Leader 1st dental assts. del. to China, 1982, 2d del., 1984. Mem. Mpls. Dental Soc., Minn. Dental Assts. Assn. (pres. 1984-86, achievement award 1981, 84), Am. Dental Assts. Assn. (outstanding article, most valuable state mem. 1982), Minn. Educators Dental Assts., Am. Needlepoint Guild, Minn. Alumni Club. Republican. Lutheran. Lodge: Order Eastern Star. Author curriculum for Mpls. Tech. Inst., 1982; contbr. articles to profl. jours. Home: 3309 W 55th St Edina MN 55410 Office: 6415 Brooklyn Blvd Minneapolis MN 55429

GILBERT, STEPHEN JOHN, chemical executive; b. Detroit, Dec. 15, 1956; s. Ellwyn Araunah and Johanna Melanie (Wachtler) G. BS in Med. Tech., Grand Valley State Coll., Allendale, Mich., 1979, BS in Chemistry, 1980; BSChemE, Wayne State U., 1982. Chemist Light Metal Corp., Wyoming, Mich., 1978-81; tchrs. aid Wayne State U., Detroit, 1981-82; sr. chemist Viking Chemical, Pontiac, Mich., 1982-84; tech. dir. Clayton Industries, El Monte, Calif., 1984—; sr. cons. Midwest Chem., Detroit, 1985—, cons. Great Lakes Assocs., Youngstown, Ohio, 1983—, chemistry tutor Grosse Pointe (Mich.) Schs., 1980-86; bd. dirs. Rojes U., Detroit, 1986—. Contbr. articles to profl. jours. Vol. fund raiser Detroit Symphony Orch., 1982—, Granbrook (Mich.) Inst. Sci., 1986—; coach Grosse Point Red Baron's Football, 1983—; mem. adv. council toxic waste State of Mich., 1984-86. Recipient Bronze medal Water Conf. Bd. Mich., 1985. Mem. Am. Inst. Chemists, AAAS, Am. Chem. Soc., Phi Kappa Phi. Lutheran. Avocations: restoring older Jaguars, racquetball, weightlifting. Home: 5071 Grayton Detroit MI 48224 Office: Clayton Industries 24750 Swanson Rd Southfield MI 48037

GILBERT, VINCENT NEWTON, publisher; b. Chgo., Dec. 7, 1955; s. Herman Cromwell and Ivy Newton (McAlpine) G.; m. Denise Sharon Rawlings, Aug. 15, 1982; 1 child, Diona Vinise. B.A. in Polit. Sci., Ind. U., 1978; J.D., John Marshall Law Sch., 1983. Dir., Maple Park Strong Ctr., Chgo., 1976; terr. mgr. Carnation Co., Chgo., 1978-81; sales dir. Path Press, Chgo., 1982—; exec. v.p. CDM Transp. Service, Inc., Chgo., 1984-86; dir. consumer edn. dept. of consumer services, Chgo., 1987—. Speech writer Savage for Alderman campaign, Chgo., 1983; area coordinator Savage for Congress campaign, Chgo., 1982, Washington for Mayor campaign, Chgo., 1983. Mem. Student Bar Assn., Black Am. Law Student Assn. Methodist. Office: Dept of Consumer Services 121 N LaSalle St Chicago IL 60602

GILBERT, WILLIAM CECIL, medical equipment company executive; b. Cloverport, Ky., May 17, 1945; s. William Earl and Margaret (Weatherholt) G.; B.A., Wayne State U., 1971; cert. in respiratory therapy U. Chgo., 1972; m. Joan Esche, Dec. 20, 1969; children—Kristopher, Nickolas. Supr. respiratory therapy Detroit Osteo. Hosp., 1966-71; dir. respiratory care service Mercy Hosp., Cadillac, Mich., 1971-75; chief exec. officer Pneumatology Assocs., Inc., Cadillac, 1975-83; chief exec. officer Gilbert Healthcare Service, 1983—; mem. Respiratory Therapy Nat. Bd., 1972—. Pres. N.W. chpt. Mich. Lung Assn., 1972, trustee, 1975—. Served with USAF, 1963-67. Registered respiratory therapist; cert. respiratory therapy technician. Mem. Am. Assn. Respiratory Therapy, Mich. Soc. Respiratory Therapy, Nat. Assn. Med. Equipment Suppliers. Republican. Episcopalian. Home: 210 Stimson St Cadillac MI 49601 Office: Box 283 Stimson St Cadillac MI 49601

GILBERTSON, ALAN DALE, psychologist; b. Cleve., Feb. 20, 1953; s. Ewald Raymond and Esther Viola (Johnson) G.; m. Susan Long, Oct. 6, 1979. BA, Mt. Union Coll., 1975; MA, U. Akron, 1978; PhD, Ohio State U., 1981. Lic. psychologist, Ohio; cert. chem. dependency counselor, Ohio. Coordinator of psychol. services Townhall II, Kent, Ohio, 1980-82; dir. psychology tng. Fallsview Hosp., Akron, 1982—; pvt. practice Kent, 1980—; assoc. prof. psychology Northeastern Ohio U. Coll. Medicine, Rootstown, Ohio, 1983—; cons. Edwin Shaw Hosp., Akron, 1982—. Contbr. articles to profl. jours. Mem. exec. council psychology section Northeastern U. Sch. Medicine. Recipient Faculty Recognition award Northeastern U. Coll. Medicine, 1986. Mem. Am. Psychol. Assn., Ohio Psychol. Assn., Psychol. Soc. Western Res., Am. Soc. Clinical Hypnosis. Avocations: travel, gardening, art. Home: 3460 Kent Rd Stow OH 44224 Office: Kevin Coleman Mental Health Ctr Martinel Dr Kent OH 44224

GILBERTSON, ERIC E., management information systems manager; b. Menomonie, Wis., Mar. 31, 1931; s. Elmer and Margaret Ann (Burkart) G.; m. Donna H. Hoffe, Aug. 22, 1954; children: Amy, Jay, Kurt. BS, Beloit Coll., 1953. Mgr. mgmt. info. systems Uniroyal Goodrich Tire Co., Inc., Eau Claire, Wis., 1964-74, controller, 1974-81; mgr. mgmt. info. systems Uniroyal Goodrich Tire Co., Inc., Eau Claire, 1981—; bd. dirs. Blue Cross Blue Shield Wis. Bd. dirs. Wis. Mfg. and Commerce, Madison, 1975-78; bd. dirs., treas. Luth. Hosp., Eau Claire, 1976-86; bd. dirs., treas. Wis. Council Safety, Madison, 1978-82. Served as col. U.S. Army Counter Intelligence, 1953-55. Mem. Eau Claire C. of C. (bd. dirs., pres. 1978-80), Nat. Rifle Assn. Republican. Avocations: hunting, fishing, flying. Office: Uniroyal Goodrich Tire Co Inc Box 127 Eau Claire WI 54702

GILBO, GERY OCTAVIUS, clinical therapist; b. Chgo., Aug. 4, 1950; s. James O. and Bette (Dennie) G.; B.A., Quincy Coll., 1972; M.A., Roosevelt U., 1976. Cert. Neuro-linguistic programming, cert. master programmer. Orderly, Little Co. of Mary Hosp., Evergreen Park, Ill., 1974-75, mental health technician/intern, 1975-77; assoc., cons. Palos Center for Individual and Family Counseling, Palos Heights, Ill., 1975-77; sr. staff mem., clin. coordinator Palos Neuropsychiatric Inst., Inc., Palos Heights, 1977—. Mem. Am. Psychol. Assn. (assoc.), Coordinating Council for Handicapped Children. Home: 14505 Central Ct Apt G2 Oak Forest IL 60452 Office: Palos Neuropsychiatric Institute Inc 7600 W College Dr Palos Heights IL 60463

GILCHREST, THORNTON CHARLES, association executive; b. Chgo., Sept. 1, 1931; s. Charles Jewett Gilchrest and Patricia (Thornton) Thornton; m. Barbara Dibbern, June 8, 1952; children: Margaret Mary, James Thornton. B.S. in Journalism, U. Ill., 1953. Cert. tchr., Ill. Tchr. pub. high sch. West Chicago, Ill., 1957; exec. dir. Plumbing-Heating-Cooling Info. Bur., Chgo., 1958-64; asst. to pres. A.Y. McDonald Mfg. Co., Dubuque, Iowa, 1964-68; exec. dir. Am. Supply Assn., Chgo., 1968-77, exec. v.p., 1977-82; exec. v.p. Nat. Safety Council, Chgo., 1982-83, pres., 1983—. Served with USN, 1953-55. Mem. Am. Soc. Assn. Execs., Chgo. Soc. Assn. Execs. Methodist. Club: University (Chgo.). Office: Nat Safety Council 444 N Michigan Ave Chicago IL 60611

GILCHRIST, DON KARL, orthopaedic surgeon; b. Iowa Falls, Iowa, Dec. 21, 1928; s. Leo Karl and Fae Ailene (Mossman) G.; m. Barbara Jean Patterson, Aug. 21, 1954; children: Richard, Ann, Patti, John. BA, Ill. Coll., 1951; BS, U. Ill., Chgo., 1953, MD, 1955. Diplomate Am. Bd. Orthopaedic Surgery. Intern St. Francis Hosp., Peoria, Ill., 1955-56; resident U.S. Naval Hosp., Portsmouth, Va., 1957-60, Orange Meml. Hosp., Orlando, Fla., 1961-62; orthopaedic surgeon U.S. Naval Hosp., Jacksonville, Fla., 1962-67, The Quincy (Ill.) Clinic, 1967—; clin. assoc. in family practice and surgery So. Ill. U. Med. Sch., Springfield and Quincy, Ill., 1981—; staff Blessing Hosp., St. Mary Hosp. Served to commdr. USN, 1956-67. Fellow Am. Acad. Orthopaedic Surgeons; mem. Ill. Orthopaedic Soc., Cen. Ill. Orthopaedic Club. Home: 1862 Kentucky St Quincy IL 62301 Office: The Quincy Clinic 1400 Maine St Quincy IL 62301

GILCHRIST, DONNA ANN, librarian; b. Ames, Iowa, Jan. 28, 1955; d. Donald Merton and Angelyn Rosaland (Braland) G. AA, Des Moines Area Community Coll., 1975; student, U. Iowa, 1975-76; cert. library technician, Kirkwood Community Coll., 1979; BS in Secondary Edn., Library Sci., N.W. Mo. State U., 1983. Librarian NESCO Community Schs., McCallsburg, Iowa, 1983—. Sec. NESCO Sch. Edn. Assn., 1984-85, pres., 1987—. Mem. Alpha Beta Alpha (pres. 1981-82, sec.-treas. 1980-81). Lutheran. Home: 218 Ash Zearing IA 50278 Office: NESCO Community Schs Box B McCallsburg IA 50154

GILCHRIST, JAN SPIVEY, artist, educator; b. Chgo., Feb. 15, 1949; s. Charles and Arthric (Jones) Spivey; m. Arthur Van Johnson, Aug. 1, 1970 (div. Aug. 1980); 1 child, Ronké Diarra; m. Kelvin Keith Gilchrist, Sept. 5, 1983; 1 child, William Kelvin. Student, Hartwick Coll., 1985; BS in Art Edn., Ea. Ill. U., 1973; MA in Painting, U. No. Iowa, 1979. Tchr. Chgo. Bd. Edn., Chgo., 1973-75; art tchr. Dist. 147, Harvey (Ill.) Schs., 1976-79, Cambridge (Mass.) Sch. Dept., 1980-81, Joliet (Ill.) Pub. Schs., 1982-83; free-lance artist Glenwood, Ill., 1983—; illustrator for Putnam Pub., N.Y.C., Ill. State Dept. Represented in permanent collections Isabelle Neal Gallery, Evanston Art Ctr. Co-op Gallery; artist: commd. Ea. Ill. U., 1974, State of Ill. Families With A Future campaign, 1986-87, Putnam Pub. to illustrate Children of Long Ago, 1987. Recipient Purchase awards Dusable Mus., Chgo., 1983-85; Purchase award Varied Treasures, Ill. Benedictine Coll., Lisle, Ill., 1985. Mem. Ill. Artisans Shop, Art. Inst. Chgo. Sales and Rental Gallery, Chgo. Artists Coalition, Phi Delta Kappa. Democrat. Home: 304 Ingleside Glenwood IL 60425 Office: Evanston Art Coop Gallery 2603 Sheridan Rd Evanston IL 60202

GILDEHAUS, GERALD CLEMENS, restauranteur; b. Washington, Mo., July 22, 1943; s. Leo George and Naomi Barbara (Buhr) G.; m. Oma Louise Bradley, Mar. 22, 1975; children: Gerald Jr., Glenda, Gina, Gayle, Geralynn, Marynell, Thomas, Ashley. Grad. high sch., Washington, 1961. Indusl. engr. Kellwood Co., New Haven, Mo., 1962-79; owner Cowan's Restuarant, Washington, 1977—; sec., treas. Granny's Attic Gifts, Washington, 1984—. Mem. Nat. Restaurant Assn., Mo. Resuarant Assn., Fedn. Ind. Bus., Washington C. of C., Downtown Washington Merchants. (pres. 1986-87, bd. dirs. 1983-87). Roman Catholic. Home: #4 Elmwood Estates Dr Washington MO 63090 Office: Cowan's Restaurant 106-114 Elm st Washington MO 63090

GILDEHAUS, THOMAS ARTHUR, manufacturing company executive; b. Little Rock, Sept. 29, 1940; s. Arthur Frederick and Susanna (Packham) G.; m. Barbara Lee Quimby, Oct. 29, 1960; children: Elizabeth, Thomas Arthur, Charles, Christopher, Allen. B.A. in History, Yale U., 1963; M.B.A. with distinction, Harvard U., 1970. With Citibank, N.Y.C. and P.R., 1963-70; v.p. Temple, Barker and Sloane, Inc., Lexington, Mass., 1970-80; sr. v.p. Deere & Co., Moline, Ill., 1980-82; exec. v.p. Deere & Co., 1982—, also dir.; dir. Davenport Bank and Trust Co., Iowa. Trustee Nat. 4-H Council, 1983—. Address: Deere & Co John Deere Rd Moline IL 61265

GILDNER, RICHARD EUGENE, purchasing company executive; b. Dubuque, Iowa, Aug. 30, 1930; s. Fred and Ethel (Ball) G.; m. Jane E. Olson, Nov. 15, 1952; children: David, Mary. Grad., Moody Bible Inst., 1950. Exec. v.p. Allied Purchasing Co., Mason City, Iowa, 1953—. Trustee Moody Bible Inst., Chgo., 1973—; pres. Meals on Wheels, Mason City, 1977—. Served to staff sgt. U.S. Army, 1951-53, Korea. Republican. Baptist. Home: 80 Granada Dr Mason City IA 50401 Office: Allied Purchasing Co PO Box 1249 Mason City IA 50401

GILES, CONRAD LESLIE, ophthalmic surgeon; b. N.Y.C., July 14, 1934; s. Irving Samuel Giles and Victoria Ampole; m. Marilyn Toby Schwartz, June 20, 1955 (div. 1978); children—Keith Martin, Suzanne Speer, Kevin William, Brian Alan; m. Lynda Fern Schenk, Nov. 26, 1978; stepchildren—Jared Schenk, Jamie Schenk. M.D., U. Mich., 1957, M.S., 1961. Diplomate Am. Bd. Ophthalmology. Clin. assoc. NIH, Bethesda, Md., 1961-63; clin. asst. prof. Wayne State U. Sch. Medicine, Detroit, 1965-72, clin. assoc. prof. ophthalmology, 1973—. Contbr. articles to med. jours. Vice Pres. Jewish Welfare Fedn., Detroit, 1981-86, pres. 1986—. Fellow Am. Acad. Ophthalmology; mem. AMA, Mich. State Ophthal. Soc. Avocations: golf; tennis. Home: 6300 Westmoor St Birmingham MI 48010 Office: 4400 Town Ctr Southfield MI 48075

GILES, DUANE WALLACE, accountant; b. Kankakee, Ill., Apr. 24, 1943; s. Wallace Chester Giles and Anna Louise (Johnson) Cann; m. Judy Harriet Lentz, July 17, 1965; children: Melissa, Timothy. BA, Knox Coll., 1965; postgrad., Lewis U., 1979-80. CPA, Ill. Auditor Union Nat. Bank, Joliet, Ill., 1965-68; v.p., cashier Peotone (Ill.) Bank & Trust, 1968-79; acct. Wilkes Besterfield, Olympia Fields, Ill., 1979-85, asst. dept. mgr., 1985-87, mgr., 1987—. Bd. dirs. Peotone Village Bd., 1970-75; elder Immanuel United Ch. Christ, Peotone, 1987, supt. Sunday sch., 1974-86. Mem. Am. Inst. CPA's, Ill. CPA Soc. (career opportunities com. 1986-87). Office: Wilkes Besterfield Co Ltd 20280 Governors Hwy Olympia Fields IL 60442

GILES, EUGENE, anthropology educator; b. Salt Lake City, June 30, 1933; s. George Eugene and Eleanor (Clark) G.; m. Inga Valborg Wikman, Sept. 9, 1964; children: Eric George, Edward Eugene. AB, Harvard U., 1955, AM, 1960, PhD, 1966; MA, U. Calif., Berkeley, 1956. Diplomate Am. Bd. Forensic Anthropology. Instr. in anthropology U. Ill., Urbana, 1964-66, assoc. prof., 1970-73, prof., 1973—, head dept. anthropology, 1975-80, 82-83; asst. prof. Harvard U., Cambridge, Mass., 1966-70; assoc. dean Grad. Coll. U. Ill., 1986—. Editor: (with J.S. Friedlaender, jr. editor) The Measures of Man: Methodologies in Biological Anthropology, 1976. Served with U.S. Army, 1956-58. NSF postdoctoral fellow, 1967-68; NSF grantee, 1970-72, NIH grantee, 1965-68. Fellow Am. Anthropol. Assn., AAAS, Am. Acad. Forensic Scis.; mem. Am. Assn. Phys. Anthropologists (exec. com. 1973-76, v.p. 1979-80, pres. 1981-83), Human Biology Council (exec. com. 1974-77), Phi Beta Kappa, Sigma Xi. Forensic anthropology research in Papua New Guinea and Australia. Home: 1106 S Lynn St Champaign IL 61820 Office: U Ill Dept Anthropology 607 S Mathews Urbana IL 61801

GILES, HOMER WAYNE, lawyer; b. Noble, Ohio, Nov. 9, 1919; s. Edwin Jay and Nola Blanche (Tillison) G.; m. Zola Ione Parke, Sept. 8, 1948; children: Jay, Janice, Keith, Tim, Gregory. A.B., Adelbert Coll., 1940; LL.B., Western Res. Law Sch., 1943, LL.M., 1959. Bar: Ohio bar 1943. Mem. firm Davis & Young, Cleve., 1942-43, William I. Moon, Port Clinton, Ohio, 1946-48; pres. Strabley Baking Co., Cleve., 1948-53; v.p. French Baking Co., Cleve., 1953-55; law clk. 8th Dist Ct. Appeals, Cleve., 1955-58; ptnr. Kuth & Giles, Cleve., 1958-68, Walter, Haverfield, Buescher & Chockley, Cleve., 1968—; pres. Clinton Franklin Realty Co., Cleve., 1958—, Concepts Devel., Inc., 1980—; sec. Holiday Designs, Inc., Sebring, Ohio, 1964—; trustee Teamster Local 52 Health and Welfare Fund, 1950-53; mem. Bakers Negotiating Exec. Com., 1951-53. Contbr. articles to profl. publs.; editor: Banks Baldwin Ohio Legal Forms, 1962. Troop com. chmn. Skyline council Boy Scouts Am., 1961-63; adviser Am. Security Council; trustee Hiram House Camp, Florence Crittenton Home, 1965; chmn. bd. trustees Am. Econ. Found., N.Y.C., 1973-80, chmn. exec. com., 1973-80. Served with AUS, 1943-46, ETO. Mem. Am. Bar Assn., World Law Assn. (founding), Am. Arbitration Assn. (nat. panel), Com. on Econ. Reform and Edn. (life), Inst. Money and Inflation, Speakers Bur. Cleve. Sch. Levy, Citizens League, Pacific Inst., Phila. Soc., Aircraft Owners and Pilots Assn., Cleve. Hist. Soc., Mus. Modern Art, Met. Mus., Mercantile Library, Delta Tau Delta, Delta Theta Phi. Club: The City. Unitarian. Clubs: Cleve. Skating, Harvard Bus., The City. Home: 2588 S Green Rd University Heights OH 44122 Office: Walter Haverfield et al 1215 Terminal Tower Cleveland OH 44113

GILES, LYNDA SCHENK, social worker; b. Detroit, May 18, 1943; s. Samuel and Shirley (Finkelstein) S.; m. David Reuven Schenk, Sept. 5, 1965 (div. July 1975); children: Jared, Jamie; m. Conrad Leslie Giles, Nov. 26, 1978. BA, U. Mich., 1965; MSW, Wayne State U., 1977. Clinical social worker Counseling Assocs. Inc., Southfield, Mich., 1977—. Mem. com. identity and affiliation Jewish Welfare Fedn., Detroit, 1985—. Mem. Nat. Assn. Social Workers, Counseling Assocs. (chmn. Southfield gifted and talented program 1979-81), Mich. Soc. Clin. Social Workers. Democrat. Club: Franklin Country. Avocations: tennis, skiing. Home: 6300 Westmoor Birmingham MI 48010 Office: Counseling Assocs Inc 25835 Southfield Rd Southfield MI 48075

GILFERT, JAMES CLARE, engineering educator, consultant; b. Tamaqua, Pa., June 21, 1927; s. Charles A. and Leah M. (Bensinger) G.; m. Sara Louise McCalmont, June 23, 1949; children—Susan, Ted, Charles. B.S., Antioch Coll., 1950; M.Sc., Ohio State U., 1951, Ph.D., 1957. Registered profl. engr., Ohio. Assoc. prof. dept. elec. engring. Ohio State U., 1957-67; cons., tech. specialist N.Am. Rockwell, 1961-67; faculty dept. elec. engring. Ohio U., Athens, 1967—, prof. elec. engring., 1969—; research contractor to Ohio Dept. Transp., 1975—; cons. Nat. Semiconductor Corp., 1977-78, Static Handling, Inc., 1982—; founder Athens Tech. Specialists, 1982—; vis. prof. Chubu Inst. Tech., Japan, 1973, 80. Served with USNR, 1945-46. Kettering fellow, 1950-51; Am. Council Edn. fellow, 1971-72; Japan Soc. Promotion Sci. vis. sr. researcher, 1980. Mem. IEEE, Sigma Xi, Sigma Pi Sigma, Eta Kappa Nu. Contbr. articles in field to profl. jours.; patentee in field. Home: 16101 S Canaan Rd Athens OH 45701 Office: Ohio U Dept Elec and Computer Engring Athens OH 45701

GILGEN, ALBERT RUDOLPH, psychologist, educator; b. Akron, Ohio, Sept. 19, 1930; s. Albert and Jeannette (Rufer) G.; m. Carol E. Keyes, 1954; children: James D., Jeanne Elizabeth, Albert P. AB in Chemistry, Princeton U., 1952; MA in Psychology, Kent State U., 1963; PhD in Psychology, Mich. State U., 1965. Lic. psychologist, Wis. Asst. then assoc. prof. Beloit (Wis.) Coll., 1965-73; prof., head of dept. U. No. Iowa, Cedar Falls, 1973—. Author: American Psychology Since World War II; editor: Contemporary Scientific Psychology, 1970; co-editor: International Handbook of Psychology, 1987; contbr. numerous articles to profl. jours. Served with USN, 1952-55. Fulbright Exchange student U. Coll. Galway, Ireland, 1971-72. Fellow Am. Psychol. Assn., Am. Psychol. Assn.; mem. AAAS, Fulbright Alumni Assn. Avocations: reading, helping son with antique bus. Home: 1107 Washington St Cedar Falls IA 50613 Office: Dept Psychology Univ No Iowa Cedar Falls IA 50614

GILKERSON-DAEHNKE, CYNTHIA ALEXANDRA, public relations consultant, real estate investor; b. Del Rio, Tex., Apr. 3, 1959; d. H.R. and Mary Alexandra (Sakovich-Rule) Gilkerson; m. Keith Arthur Daehnke, Dec. 12, 1980 (div. Oct. 1982); 1 child, Jeremiah Arthur. BA in Journalism and Pub. Relations, Ohio State U., 1982; student, Miami U., Oxford, Ohio, Va. Poly Inst. Adminstrv. asst. media relations Acad. of Medicine Franklin County, Columbus, Ohio, 1982-83; prodn. supr. Sattlemeyer Filmworks, Columbus, 1983-84; free-lance cons. pub. relations, advt., mktg. various orgns., Columbus, 1984-85; dir. pub. relations Patriot Life Ins., Columbus, 1985-86; owner, pres. CD Communications, Johnstown, Ohio, 1986—; owner Jeremiah Investments; owner, pres. Neat As A Pin, Inc., 1987—. Editor, copywriter numerous newsletters, 1983—. Richard Piergallini Meml. scholar, Ohio State U., 1982. Mem. Pub. Relations Soc. Am. (scholar 1980), Women in Communications, Advt. Fedn., Internat. Assn. Bus. Communicators. Republican. Episcopalian. Lodge: Eagles. Avocations: travel, writing, composing music, family. Home and Office: 11161 Woodhaven Rd Johnstown OH 43031

GILL, GORDON THOMAS, manufacturing executive; b. Stambaugh, Mich., Nov. 30, 1952; s. John Lawrence and Anna Pauline (Bennett) G.; m. Mary Beth Myers, July 29, 1972; children: Jennifer Lynn, Sarah Elizabeth. BS in Info. Processing, U. Toledo, 1979, MBA in Fin., 1983. Programmer U. Toledo, 1975; sr. programmer N.W. Ohio Data Ctr., Toledo, 1975-78, St. Vincent Hosp., Toledo, 1977-78; sr. systems analyst Gen. Motors, Sandusky, Ohio, 1978-85; mfg. systems mgr. Electronic Data Systems, Sandusky, 1985—. Chmn. missions Trinity United Meth. Ch., Port Clinton, Ohio, 1983-86. Served with U.S. Army, 1971-74. Mem. Phi Kappa Phi. Home: 731 E Second St Port Clinton OH 43452

GILL, HERBERT H., food services company executive; b. 1908. Mgr. Ace Box Lunch Co., Inc., 1930-65; with ABC Consol. Corp., 1965-69; with Gladieux Corp., Washington, 1969—, v.p., 1969-73; pres., chief op. officer Gladieux Corp., Toledo, 1973—, also bd. dirs. Office: Gladieux Corp 2630 W Laskey Rd Toledo OH 43697 *

GILL, LINDA TRACY, accountant; b. Cin., Oct. 20, 1951; d. George William and Helen Mary (Lauber) Tracy; m. Robert D. Gill, June 29, 1979; children: Dennis, Brian. BS summa cum laude in acctg., U. Cin., 1976, MBA in Taxation, Xavier U., 1982. CPA, Ohio. Media clk. Procter & Gamble, Cin., 1970-74, media staff asst., 1974-76; staff auditor Arthur Young & Co., Cin., 1976-78, mem. tax staff, 1978-81, tax mgr., 1981-84; mgr. tax dept. Aronowitz, Chaiken & Hardesty, Cin., 1984—; founder Women Entrepreneurs' Conf., 1984. Mem. Am. Inst. CPAs, Ohio Soc. CPAs, Cin. Women CPAs, Bus. and Profl. Women's Club. Office: Aronowitz Chaiken & Hardesty PO Box 5367 Cincinnati OH 45201

GILL, LYLE BENNETT, lawyer; b. Lincoln, Nebr., May 11, 1916; s. George Orville and Ruth (Bennett) G.; B.A., Swarthmore Coll., 1937; LL.B., Nebr. Coll. Law, 1940; m. Rita M. Cronin, Aug. 28, 1975; children by previous marriage—George, Valerie, Marguerite. Admitted to Nebr. bar, 1940; practice law, Fremont, 1945—; city atty. Fremont, 1959-62, 67—. Vice chmn. A.R.C., Dodge County, 1953-59. Chmn., Dodge County Republican Com., 1945-51. Served with USNR, 1942-45, 1951-52; lt. comdr. (ret.). Mem. Am., Nebr., Dodge County (pres. 1962) bar assns., Trial Lawyers Assn., V.F.W., Am. Legion. Episcopalian. Home: PO Box 642 Fremont NE 68025 Office: 505 Bldg Fremont NE 68025

GILL, SUZANNE, software publisher; b. Quincy, Ill., June 30, 1941; s. Harry J. and Anne (McDonnell) Lutz; m. James H. Gill, June 25, 1966; children: Michael, Brian, Molly. BS, Fontbonne Coll., St. Louis, 1963; MS, U. Mich., 1967. Tchr., librarian Parkway Sch. Dist., St. Louis, 1963-66; coordinator LTA Program U. Toledo, Cuyahogha Community Coll. (Cleve.), St. Louis Community Coll., 1967-84; pres. Info. Resources Cons., St. Louis, 1977—. Author: File Management and Information Retrieval Systems, 1981; contbr. numerous mag. articles; developed numerous software programs, 1984-86. Mem. Mo. Sch. Library Assn., Am. Legion Aux. Republican. Roman Catholic. Home: 11920 Hargrove Des Peres MO 63131 Office: Info Resources Cons 12015 Manchester #150 Saint Louis MO 63131

GILLAHAN, ROBERT DUGAN, dentistry educator; b. Lawson, Mo., Sept. 25, 1926; s. William and Georgia (Roper) G.; m. Marjorie Louise Mossman, June 1, 1953; children—Sally, Sara, Susan. D.D.S., U. Mo.-Kansas City, 1952; diploma U. Mex., 1977, U. Paraguay, 1979. Licensed dentist, Kans., Mo. Gen. practice dentistry Lawrence, Kans., 1952-74; assoc. prof. U. Mo., Kansas City, 1974—, chmn. dept. occlusion, co-chmn. Tempro Mandibular Joint Clinic, 1979-85, dir. occlusion, 1979-85; lectr. U. Mex. Ptnrs. Am., Mexico City, Pueblo and Guadalahara, Mex., 1977-78, Paraguay, 1979, 81, 83; cons. Truman Hosp., Kansas City, 1980-85, Mercy Hosp., Kansas City, 1981-85. Author manual on occlusion, 1981. Contbr. articles to profl. jours. Chmn. bd. dirs. Achievement Place for Boys, Lawrence, 1966. Served with USAAF, 1944-46. Mem. Ortho-occlusal Study Club (lectr., sec. 1979-80), 1st Dist. Dental Soc. (pres. 1961), Lawrence Dental Study Club (pres.), Oku (pres. 1982-83, Tchr. of Yr. 1962), Am. Equilibration Soc. (life). Republican. Clubs: Lawrence Country (pres. 1956-57), Kansas U. Downtown Quarterback (pres. 1960-61) (Lawrence), Cosmopolitan (v.p. 1964-65). Avocations: woodworking, fishing, shooting, swimming.

GILLAM, HEATHER LEE, burial vault company executive; b. Youngstown, Ohio, Jan. 19, 1955; d. Robert James and Rejena Pearl (McKinney) Fithian; Russell W. Gillam Jr., Nov. 5, 1985; stepchildren: Russell W. III, Robert Christopher, Elizabeth Rae. AS in Police Sci., Youngstown State U., 1972, grad. Ohio Peace Officers Sch., 1974, BS in Law Enforcement Adminstrn., 1976. Dep. sheriff Mahoning County Sheriff's Dept., Youngstown, 1972-77; photographer Photo Corp. Am., Boardman, Ohio, 1977-79; office mgr. Fithian-Wilbert Burial Vault Co., Boardman, 1979-84, exec. mgr., 1984—; dispatcher Canfield (Ohio) Police Dept., 1987—; founder Heather's Koala Tees. Big sister Big Bros./Big Sisters, Youngstown, 1984—. Mem. Wilbert Mfg. Assn., Ohio Funeral Dirs., Women's and Men's Softball Assn., Canfield Hist. Soc. Republican. Lodge: Order Eastern Star (worthy matron 1986—), Shriners (worthy high priestess, 1985-86), Eagles. Avocations: bowling, counted cross stitch, softball. Office: Fithian-Wilbert Burial Vault Co 6234 Market St Youngstown OH 44512

GILLANI, NOOR VELSHI, mechanical engineering and atmospheric sciences educator, researcher; b. Arusha, Tanzania, Mar. 8, 1944; came to U.S., 1963, naturalized, 1976; s. Noormohamed Velshi and Sherbanu (Kassam) G.; m. Mira Teresa Pershe, Aug. 13, 1971; children: Michael, Michelle, Nicole. GCE (Advanced Level), U. London, 1963; AB cum laude, Harvard U., 1967; MS in Mech. Engring., Washington U., St. Louis, 1969, DSc, 1974. Vis. scientist Stockholm U., 1977; research assoc. Washington U., 1975-76, research scientist, 1976-77, asst. prof., 1977-80, assoc. prof. 1981-84, prof. mech. engring., 1985—, faculty assoc. CAPITA, 1979—, dir. air quality spl. studies data ctr., 1981—; organizer NATO CCMS 15th internat. tech. meeting on air pollution modeling and its applications, St. Louis, Apr. 1985; mem. Sci. Bd. NATO/CCMS Air Pollution Pilot Study, 1986-94. Author 2 chpts. in EPA Critical Assessment Document on Acid Deposition, 1984; editor: Air Pollution Modeling and Its Applications V, vol. 10, 1986; contbr. articles on superconductivity, bioengring., atmospheric scis. and air pollution to nat. and internat. profl. jours. Mem. H.H. Prince Aga Khan Ismailia Bd. Edn. for U.S.A. Aga Khan scholar and travel grantee, 1961-63; Harvard Coll. scholar, 1963-67; Washington U. Grad. Engring. fellow, 1967-69; research assistantships NIH, EPA, 1971-74; EPA Research grantee, 1978—. Mem. N.Y. Acad. Scis., Air Pollution Control Assn., Am. Meteorol. Soc., Am. Chem. Soc., ASME. Club: Harvard (St. Louis). Avocations: music, racquetball, tennis. Home: 1455 Sycamore Manor Dr Chesterfield MO 63017 Office: Dept Mech Engring Washington U Box 1185 Saint Louis MO 63130

GILLER, THOMAS MARSHALL, lawyer; b. Milw., June 10, 1955; s. Herbert and Ruth (Lessin) G.; m. Jessica Diane Radolf, Nov. 20, 1983. BA, Haverford Coll., 1977; JD, U. Calif., Hastings Coll. Law, 1983; MA in Energy and Resources, U. Calif., Berkeley, 1983. Bar: Calif. 1983, Wis. 1984, Ill. 1986. Atty. Shute, Mihaly & Weinberger, San Francisco, 1983-84; law clk. to presiding justice U.S. Dist. Ct. (ea. dist.) Wis., 1984-86; assoc. environ. atty. Gessler, Wexler, Flynn, Loswell & Fleishmann, Chgo., 1986—; research assoc. Ctr. Renewable Resources, Washington, 1981; energy cons. Environ. Def. Fund, Berkeley, 1981, Future Resource Assocs., 1983-84. Pres. Hastings Pub. Interest Law Found., San Francisco, 1981-82. Frederica de LaGuna award Bryn Mawr Coll. Anthropology Dept., 1977. Mem. ABA, Calif. Bar Assn., Wis. Bar Assn., Ill. Bar Assn., Chgo. Bar Assn., Order of Coif. Jewish. Avocations: jazz, bird watching, bicycling. Home: 654 W Aldine Ave Apt 1 Chicago IL 60657 Office: Gessler Wexler Flynn Laswell & Fleischmann 3 1st Nat Plaza Suite 2300 Chicago IL 60602

GILLESPIE, ESTHER HOLBROOK, nursing care director; b. Madison County, Ill., Mar. 29, 1934; d. Orville and Ertrie E. (Fallin) Holbrook; m. Frank E. Gillespie, Aug. 26, 1956; children—Frank, Cassandra Funkhouser. Diploma, Alton Meml. Sch. Nursing, 1955; student Lewis and Clark Community Coll., 1975, Florissant Valley Community Coll., 1981; student St. Louis U., 1983, BS in Nursing, 1985. R.N., Ill. cert. nurse adminstr. Staff nurse Alton (Ill.) Mem. Hosp., 1955-56; nurse St. Joseph's Hosp., Alton, 1966-67, head nurse med. unit, 1967-68, inservice instr., 1968, asst. dir. nursing, 1968-78, dir. nursing care, 1978—; bd. dirs. Affiliated Home Health Services, St. Louis. Mem. Ill. Soc. for Nurse Adminstrs. Office: Affiliated Home Health Services 1129 Macklind Saint Louis MO 62002

GILLESPIE, HOUSTON OLIVER, JR., broadcasting executive; b. Nashville, Jan. 13, 1941; s. Houston Oliver and Mary Elizabeth (Haley) G.; m. Patricia Kirkland; children—David, Elizabeth. B.S., Western Ky. U., 1966; M.S., George Williams Coll., 1973. Dir. urban programs Nat. Park Service, U.S. Dept. Interior, Washington, 1965-74; exec. dir. Living History Farms Found., Des Moines, 1974-81; pres., gen. mgr. Quad-Cities Communications Corp., WQAD-TV, Moline, Ill., 1981—; adj. prof. Iowa State U., U. Minn. Pres. Iowa Travel Council; dir. Boy Scouts Am. Council, United Way, Quad Cities. Recipient Superior Performance Award, Nat. Park Service, 1970, Quad Cities Outstanding Citizen Award, Bethany Found., 1982. Mem. Iowa and Ill. Broadcasters Assn., Nat. Assn. Broadcasters, Assn. Broadcast Execs., NEA. Lutheran. Clubs: Minneapolis, Crow Valley Golf, Davenport. Contbr. numerous articles to nat. publs. Home: 901 Mississippi Ave Davenport IA 52803 Office: 3003 Park 16th St Moline IL 61265

GILLESPIE, J. MARTIN, sales and distribution company executive; b. Detroit, Sept. 27, 1949; s. John Martin and Shirley Ann (Rees) G.; BBA, Xavier U., 1971; MBA, U. Mich., 1973; m. Jeannette Downes, Sept. 27, 1975; children: Heather, Tara. Account exec. Foote Cone & Belding, Chgo., 1973-76; account supr., 1976-77; mktg. mgr. Hansen Corp., Walled Lake, Mich., 1977-80, gen. mgr., 1980-82; chmn., chief exec. officer Hansen Mktg. Services, Inc., Walled Lake, 1982—. Recipient Merit award Nat. Alliance Businessmen, 1973. Mem. Assn. MBA Execs., Am. Mgmt. Assn., Nat. Acad. TV Arts and Scis., Nat. Assn. Credit Mgmt., Nat. Bldg. Materials Distbn. Assn., Alpha Kappa Psi. Home: 3792 W Pemberton Bloomfield Hills MI 48013 Office: Hansen Corp 1000 Decker Rd PO Box 638 Walled Lake MI 48088

GILLESPIE, JAMES LAURENCE, historian; b. Cleve., Apr. 5, 1946; s. James Joseph and Elizabeth A. M. (Koch) G.; A.B., Kenyon Coll., 1968; B.S. in Edn., Kent State U., 1973; M.A. (fellow), Princeton U., 1970, Ph.D. (fellow), 1973. Lectr., St. Mary's Coll. of Queen's U., Belfast, No. Ireland, 1971-72; asst. prof. Appalachian State U., Boone, N.C. 1974-75, Lakeland Community Coll., Mentor, Ohio, 1975-76, U. Minn., Duluth, 1976-77, Catawba Coll., Salisbury, N.C., 1977-81; vis. prof. U. Minn., Duluth, 1983-84; legal writer Squire, Sanders & Dempsey, Cleve., 1980-83; adj. prof. Ursuline Coll., 1985—; dean Griswold Inst., 1984-86; chmn. dept. social scis. Notre Dame Coll. Ohio, Cleve., 1986—; reader on medieval English history for Albion publ., 1975—; mem. organizing com. Ohio Conf. Medieval Studies, 1975-76. Vestryman St. Paul's Episcopal Ch., Cleve., 1976-79; mem. exec. bd. Carolinas Symposium on Brit. Studies. Mem. Am., So. hist. assns., Cleve. Medieval Soc., Phi Beta Kappa, Kappa Delta Pi, Phi Alpha Theta. Author: A Series of Commentaries on the Sacraments, 1977; also articles. Home: 956 Roanoke Rd Cleveland Heights OH 44121 Office: Notre Dame Coll Ohio 4545 College Rd Cleveland OH 44121

GILLESPIE, KENNETH WAYNE, physical property administrator, construction representative, energy auditor; b. Independence, Mo., Dec. 7, 1941; s. Carl Early and Mildred Lorene (O'Dell) G.; m. Marija Nijole Gavelis, Aug. 21, 1971; children: Brigette, Kenneth. BBA, Cen. Mo. State U., 1967, MS in Indsl. Mgmt., 1977. Adminstrv. asst. Standard Brands Inc., Kansas City, Mo., 1969-71; facilities devel. specialist The Met. Community Colls., Kansas City, 1971-73, physical plant coordinator, 1973-79, physical plant dir., 1979—; energy auditor State of Mo., 1979—; cons. Denver Community Colls., 1979, Electronic Computer Programming, Kansas City, 1985; mem. evaluation team Md. State Bd. Edn., Annapolis, 1985. Mem. Independence Neighborhood Council, 1977. Served with U.S. Army, 1967-69. Mem. Assn. Physical Plant Adminstrs., Cen. States Assn. Physical Plant Adminstrs. Republican. Baptist. Avocations: boating, sailing, automobile restoration, reading. Home: 224 Locust Lee's Summit MO 64063 Office: Met Community Colls 3200 Broadway Kansas City MO 64111

GILLESPIE, NEAL ROBERT, insurance company executive; b. Hugoton, Kans., Oct. 3, 1953; s. Glenn Ernest and Laura Virginia (Wilson) G. Chartered life underwriters degree, The Am. Coll., 1978. Spl. agent Kans. Farm Bur. Ins., Hugoton, Kans., 1971-81, agy. mgr., 1981—. Named Outstanding Young Man of Am., 1978. Mem. Nat. Assn. Life Underwriters (7 Nat. Quality awards), Am. Soc. CLU, Pres.-Agent Assn., Hugoton C. of C. (pres. 1981). Republican. Mem. Christian Ch. Lodge: Rotary. Avocation: water sports. Home: 109 W 8yh Hugoton KS 67951 Office: Kans Farm Bur Ins PO Box 610 Hugoton KS 67951

GILLESPIE, WILLIAM TYRONE, judge; b. Great Falls, Mont., Mar. 7, 1916; s. William G. and Alma (McBride) G.; A.B., J.D., D.C.L., Willamette U., 1939; LL.D., Hillsdale Coll., 1957; m. Eleanor Johnson, Aug. 31, 1941; 1 son, William Tyrone. Admitted to Oreg., Wash. bars, 1939, Mich. bar, 1948; spl. agt. FBI, 1939-42; partner Pope & Gillespie, Salem, Oreg., 1946-48; mem. legal dept. Dow Chem. Co., Midland, Mich., 1948-54, asst. to pres., 1954-66; partner firm Gillespie, Riecker & George, Midland, Mich., 1966-76; judge Mich. 42d Jud. Circuit, 1977—. Trustee Hillsdale Coll., 1957-72, chmn., 1972-75, chmn. emeritus, 1975—. Served from 2d lt. to lt. col. AUS, 1942-46. Mem. State Bar Mich., Oreg., Wash., Midland County (past pres.) bar assns., Am. Legion, Michigan C. of C. (v.p.), 40 and 8, Blue Key, Beta Theta Pi. Republican. Methodist. Clubs: Masons (33 deg.), Rotary. Home: 1200 W Sugnet Rd Midland MI 48640 Office: Courthouse Midland MI 48640

GILLET, ANDRE, food processing company executive; b. Paris, 1926. Grad., U. Paris, 1944. With Internat. Multifoods Corp., 1951—, div. v.p., gen. mgr. internat. div., 1968-79, exec. v.p. internat. div., 1979-83, pres., chief operating officer, 1983-84, pres., chief exec. officer, 1984-85, chmn., chief exec. officer, 1985—. Office: Internat Multifoods Corp Box 2942 Minneapolis MN 55402

GILLETT, GEORGE N., meat packing company executive. Chmn., pres., treas. Packerland Packing Co., Inc., Green Bay, Wis. Office: Packerland Packing Co Inc PO Box 1184 Green Bay WI 54305 *

GILLETT, RICHARD M., banker; b. Grand Rapids, Mich., 1923. Grad. U. Mich., 1944. With trust dept. Old Kent Fin. Corp., Grand Rapids, 1958-62, pres., 1962-72, chief exec. officer from 1972, chmn., 1972—, also bd. dirs.; owner Windsor Furniture Co.; dir. Steketee Dept. Store, Ameritech Inc., Consumers Power Co., Fed. Res. of Chgo., Ball Corp. Office: Old Kent Fin Corp 1 Vandenberg Ctr Grand Rapids MI 49503 *

GILLETTE, CAROL MAY, medical technologist; b. Cleve., Nov. 30, 1940; d. Henry Blair and Grayce Phare (Davidson) Hubble; m. Donald Alfred Gillette, Feb. 26, 1958; children—Catherine A., Anthony J., Lucia M., David G., Carroll D., Andrea J., Lisa M., Daniel A., Rosemary J. Assoc. in Sci., Flint Jr. Coll., 1960; B.A. in Biology with honors, U. Mich.-Flint, 1963. With Fed. Dept. Store, 1958; lab. aide Flint Osteo. Hosp., 1960-61; intern in med. tech. St. Joseph Hosp., Flint, 1961-62, 62-63, staff med. technologist, 1963—; staff lab. technologist Flint Gen. Hosp., 1961-62, 65-66; staff technologist Ballenger Hwy. Med. Lab. Clinic, Flint, part-time 1965-66; chief med. technologist Flint Med. X-Ray & Lab. Clinic, 1976-87, microbiology technologist Flint Med. Clinic, 1984—; tutor students in field; tchr. piano. Vol. collector Cystic Fibrosis. Recipient 20 yr. service pin St. Joseph Hosp., 1983, Employee Suggestion award, 1983; nat. dean's list, 1985-86. Mem. Am. Soc. Clin. Pathologists (cert.), Mensa. Roman Catholic. Home: 9174 N Irish Rd Mount Morris MI 48458 Office: St Joseph Hosp 302 Kensington Ave Flint MI 48502

GILLEY, BARBARA KAY, optometrist; b. Kansas City, Mo., Dec. 22, 1955; d. Burl H. and Anna Sue (Horn) Gilley; m. Scott E. Foster, Jan. 12, 1979. Student Univ. Ark., Fayetteville, 1973-75; B.S. in Optometry, So. Coll. Optometry, Memphis, 1979. Registered optometrist, Mo., Tenn. Optometrist, Drs. Stringer, Friedman and Burke, Memphis, 1979-80, Dr. Charles Ingram, Memphis, 1980-82; pvt. practice, Raytown, Mo., 1984—. Mem. Tenn. Optometric Assn., Mo. Optometric Assn., Am. Optometric Assn. Republican. Mem. Assemblies of God. Avocations: Racquetball. Office: 5600 E Bannister Kansas City MO 64137

GILLFILLAN, NANCY MILES, librarian; b. Robinson, Ill., Jan. 8, 1942; d. Halsey Lincoln Miles and Betty (Ingram) Miles Davenport; m. Richard Allen Gillfillan, June 9, 1963; 1 son: David Miles. B.A., U. Ill., 1964, M.S., 1966; student U. Denver, 1980. Reference librarian Kansas City Pub. Library (Mo.), 1964-66; instr., extended services librarian Ind. State U., Terre Haute, 1966-69; part-time instr. Ill. Valley Community Coll., Oglesby, Ill., 1977-80, reference librarian, 1985-86; owner, mgr. Book Barn, Walnut, Ill., 1980—; library dir. Dixon (Ill.) Pub. Library, 1986—. Contbr. articles to profl. jours.; author: Pocket Guide to Bureau County Authors, 1983. Vice pres. Bur. County Home Health Services Bd., 1979—, pres., 1984-86. Mem. Ill. Homemakers Extension Fedn. (bd. dirs., editor newsletter 1977-80, state sec. exec. com. 1982—), Adult Edn. Assn. Ind. (exec. bd., co-editor newsletter), Assn. for Field Services in Tchr. Edn. (exec. bd. 1968-69), ALA, Ill. Library Assn. Republican. Methodist. Clubs: United Meth. Women, Ill. Fedn. Women's, Order Eastern Star. Address: Rural Route 1 Walnut IL 61376

GILLIES, ROBERT WILLIAM, radiation oncologist; b. Muskegon, Mich., Sept. 15, 1933; s. William Kinrade and Jeanette (Drewes) G.; m. Delorna Berghnis, June 20, 1956 (div. Oct. 1975); children: Robert, Laura; Charlence Dara Burton, July 1, 1976; stepchildren: Michael, Mark, Matthew, Mahacek. AB, Calvin Coll., 1955; MD, U. Mich., 1959. Diplomate Am. Bd. Radiology. Resident in radiology U. Mich., Ann Arbor, 1959-63; radiologist Saint Joseph Hosp., Ann Arbor, 1963-64; gen. practice radiotherapy Grand Rapids, 1964-67; assoc. radiotherapist U. Iowa, Iowa City, 1967-68; radiotherapist Butterworth Hosp., Grand Rapids, 1968—. Mem. Am. Coll. Radiology, Am. Bd. Radiology, Am. Med. Assn., Am. Soc. Theapeutic Radiology, Southwest Oncology Group. Republican. Episcopalian. Avocations: archeology, anthropology, skiing, boating, hiking. Home: 2568 Hottman NE Grand Rapids MI 49505 Office: Butterworth Hosp 100 Michigan NE Grand Rapids MI 49503

GILLIGAN, MICHAEL CHARLES, application systems development manager; b. Columbus, Ohio, July 29, 1953; s. Charles Martin and Virginia Ann (Core) G.; m. Mary Elizabeth Scarborough, May 4, 1974; children: Shaun, Katherine, Erin, Colin. BS in Computer and Info. Sci., Ohio State U., 1974. Cert. systems profl., Ohio; CPCU, Ohio. Sr. programmer JC Penney Casualty Ins., Westerville, Ohio, 1975, programmer analyst, 1975-76, sr. programmer analyst, 1976-78, systems and programmer mgr., 1978-80, systems and programmer sr. mgr., 1980-83; program devel. mgr. JC Penney Co., Inc., Westerville, Ohio, 1984—. project mgr. cons. bus. div. Jr. Achievement, Franklin County, Ohio, 1980-86. Mem. Assn. for Systems Mgmt. (treas. Cen. Ohio chpt. 1984-85, v.p. 1985-86, pres. 1986, Cert. of Recognition 1983-84, chpt. Service award 1986-87), Soc. CPCU. Roman Catholic. Avocations: reading, gardening, fishing, tennis, racquetball. Home: 223 Storington Rd Westerville OH 43081 Office: JC Penney Co Inc 800 Brooksedge Blvd Westerville OH 43081

GILLIKIN, RICHARD CHARLES, accountant; b. Detroit, Feb. 13, 1952; s. Gerald Joseph and Liselotte (Klumpp) G.; m. Susan T. Truesdale, May 21, 1977. BS in Bus. Sci., Ea. Mich. U., 1974. CPA, Mich. Auditor MCUL, Southfield, Mich., 1974-76; sr. acct. Skillman, Zielesch & Co., Southfield, 1976-77, David & Bradish, CPA, Southfield, 1977-79; jr. ptnr. G.W. Smith & Co., P.C., Southfield, 1979-82; pvt. practice acctg. Livonia, Mich., 1982—. Mem. Am. Inst. CPA's (tax div.), Mich. Assn. CPA's, Northville (Mich.) C. of C., Plymouth C. of C. Office: 29200 Vassar Suite 724 Livonia MI 48152

GILLILAND, ROBERT EUGENE, consumers club executive; b. Van Wert, Ohio, Jan. 15, 1940; s. Eugene Joseph and Mary Evelyn (Nogel) G.; m. Carol Sue Baxter, July 11, 1959; children—Cynthia Sue, Brent Eugene. Student pub. schs., Van Wert. Agt., Western & So. Life Ins., Van Wert, 1964-66; state mgr. Nat. Heritage Mgmt. Corp., Cleve., 1967-76; gen. mgr. Jeffrey Martin Inc. DBA United Consumers Club, Country Club Hills, Ill., 1976-82, owner, chief exec. officer, 1982—; cons. United Consumers Club Miami, 1984-85, United COnsumers Club Chgo., 1984-86. Served with USAF, 1958-64. Mem. United Consumers Club Dirs. Assn. (Dir. of Yr. 1979, Founders award 1983). Republican. Lodge: Kiwanis (charter mem. Countryside club). Office: Jeffrey Martin Inc 40 Countryside Plaza Countryside IL 60525

GILLIOM, BONNIE LEE, arts professor, consultant; b. Mansfield, Ohio, Mar. 1, 1933; s. Gregor Leonard and Rella Hildegard (Jacobs) Cherp; m. Morris Eugene Gilliom, Dec. 27, 1956; children: Gregor William, Julia Lee. BA, Heidelberg Coll., 1955; MA, Ohio State U., 1961, PhD, 1971; postdoctoral, Tucson Creative Dance Ctr., 1976, Chelsea (Eng.) Sch. of Human Movement, 1978. Cert. tchr., Ohio. TV tchr., writer Stas. WOSU, WVIZ. NIT, KPIX, Columbus, Ohio, Cleve. and San Francisco, 1959-68; asst. prof. Ohio State U., Columbus, 1971-76; dir./developer Meanings, Modes and Moods of Movement Program, Ohio, 1979-82; assoc. dir. Inst. for the Advancement of the Arts Edn. Ohio State U., Columbus, 1982—; lectr. San Francisco State U., 1962-65; cons. 4M program 48 schs., Ohio, W.Va., Utah and Mex., 1973—; project dir. elem. sec. edn. action Columbus Pub. Schs., 1971-73. Co-author: ITV: Promise into Practice, 1972; author: Basic Movement Education for Children, 1970, Hebrew edit., 1977. Mem. Columbus Council on World Affairs, Friends of WOSU; mem. adv. council Ohio Dept. Edn., Columbus, 1980-86; patron Upper Arlington Performing Arts; bd. dirs. Ohio Very Spl. Arts Network, Columbus, 1980-86, Upper Arlington Arts Council. Grantee Ohio Edn. Deans Task Force, 1983, 84, 85, Ohio State U., 1984, 85, 86, 87, Ohio Arts Council, 1985, 86, 87; recipient 1st Place award Inst. for Instruction by Radio and TV, 1962, Meritorious award, Ohio Assn. of Health, Physical Edn. and Dance. Mem. Am. Alliance Health, Physical Edn., and Recreation; Nat. Dance Assn., Heidelberg Fellow, Kappa Delta Pi, Pi Delta Epsilon, Pi Lambda Theta. Democrat. Methodist. Avocations: travel, art, music, skiing, snorkeling. Home: 2495 Haverford Rd Columbus OH 43220 Office: Ohio State U 345C Larkins Hall Columbus OH 43210

GILLIS, ALLEN DEAN, osteopathic physician; b. St. Joseph, Mo., Jan. 19, 1944; s. Dean Robert and Helen Marie (Browning) G.; m. Antoinette Finnell, Dec. 13, 1969; children—Heather Elizabeth, Paul David, Erica Mae, William Spencer. B.S. in Pharmacy, U. Mo., 1968; D.O., Kansas City Coll. Osteo. Medicine, 1976. Practice osteo. medicine Coffeyville Family Practice Clinic, P.A., Coffeyville, Kans., 1977—; chief of staff Coffeyville Meml. Hosp., 1983—. Bd. dirs. Kans. Found. for Med. Care, Topeka. Served with USAR, 1968-73. Mem. Am. Osteo. Assn., Kansas Osteo. Assn., Southeastern Kans. Osteo. Assn. (pres. 1982-83), Am. Diabetes Assn., Am. Heart Assn. Club: Mallard (Coffeyville). Lodge: Rotary. Home: 1404 Columbus Coffeyville KS 67337 Office: 209 7th St Coffeyville KS 67337

GILL-JACOBSON, ROSEANN, director student center; b. Youngstown, Ohio, May 14, 1957. BS, Ohio U., 1982, MeD, 1983. Asst. tchr. Mahoning County Sch. for Retarded, Youngstown, 1975-79; bookeeper Logan Coll. Book Store, Athens, Ohio, 1979-82; grad. assoc. student life programs Ohio U., 1982-83; coordinator co-curricular activities Marietta (Ohio) Coll., 1983-84, dir. student ctr., summer confs., 1984—, chair High Sch. Leadership Conf., 1986; advisor Marietta Coll., 1983—. Mem. Am. Assn. Counseling and Devel., Ohio Coll. Personnel Assn. (awards com. 1983—, exec. bd. 1986-87, chair Fall Young Profls. Conf.), Marietta C. of C. (leadership com 1986—). Democrat. Roman Catholic. Avocations: jogging, reading, arts and crafts. Home: 509 8th St Marietta OH 45701 Office: Marietta Coll Gilam Center Marietta OH 45750

GILLUM, SANDRA SUE, real estate management company executive; b. Indpls., May 25, 1940; d. Hugh Knox and Mary Lou (Briles) Thatcher; m. Donald C. Gillum, Nov. 28, 1964; children: Bradford Thatcher, Jane Bowie. AB, Miami U., Oxford, Ohio, 1962. Lic. real estate broker, Ill. Research microbiologist Abbott Labs., North Chicago, Ill., 1962-67; microbiologist Cos Corp., Evanston, Ill., 1967; pres. Cambridge Mgmt., Ltd., Wilmette, Ill., 1981—; assoc. Tighe Realty Co., Inc., Wilmette, 1984—. Pres. Wilmette PTA, 1978; treas. Jr. League Evanston, 1978-80;. Mem. North Shore Bd. Realtors. Avocations: Nordic skiing, sailing.

GILMAN, LEIGHTON CURTIS, communications executive; b. Cambridge, Mass., Apr. 15, 1931; s. George P. B. and Karen E. (Theller) G.; m. Audrey Knowles Gilman, Oct. 13, 1956; children—Scott, Gregg, Diane. B.A., U. N.H., 1954. News corr. AP, Boston Globe, Manchester Union-Leader, N.H., 1948-54; pub. relations mgr. AT&T, N.Y.C., 1964-73; asst. v.p. pub. relations New Eng. Telephone, Boston, 1973-77; v.p. pub. relations Ohio Bell, Cleve., 1977-83; v.p. corp. communications Ameritech, Chgo., 1983-87; v.p. pub. relations & pub. affairs Ohio Bell, Cleve., 1987—. Pres. Ameritech Found. Mem. Pub. Relations Soc. Am., Arthur W. Page Soc. (trustee). Club: Nat. Press (adv. council). Office: Ohio Bell 45 Erieview Plaza Cleveland OH 44114

GILMAN, RICHARD JAY, accountant; b. Chgo., July 9, 1952; s. Marvin and Joyce Susan (Hoffman) G.; m. Helene Renee Rieger, Aug. 18, 1974; children—Jason Stuart, Jordan Elliott, Rachel Cari. A.A., Oakton Community Coll., 1972; B.S. in Mgmt., DePaul U., 1975, B.S. in Acctg., 1976. C.P.A., Ill. Acctg. ptnr. Kupferberg, Goldberg and Neimark, Chgo., 1976—. Exec. mem. Jewish United Fund. Mem. Ill. C.P.A. Soc., Am. Inst. C.P.A.s, Am. Mgmt. Assn., Am. Israeli C. of C. Democrat. Jewish. Home: 2517 Greenwood Glenview IL 60025

GILMAN, SID, neurologist; b. Los Angeles, Oct. 19, 1932; s. Morris and Sarah Rose (Cooper) G.; m. Carol. G. Barbour. B.A., UCLA, 1954; M.D., 1957. Intern UCLA Hosp., 1957-58; resident in neurology Boston City Hosp., 1960-63; from instr. to assoc. in neurology Harvard Med. Sch., 1965-68; from asst. prof. to prof. neurology Columbia U., N.Y.C., 1968-76; H. Houston Merritt prof. neurology 1976-77; prof., chmn. dept. neurology U. Mich., Ann Arbor, 1977—; cons. VA Hosp., Ann Arbor; adj. attending neurologist Henry Ford Hosp., Detroit. Author: (with J.R. Bloedel and R. Lechtenberg) Disorders of the Cerebellum, 1981, (with Sarah S. Winans Newman) Manter and Gatz's Essentials of Clinical Neuroanatomy and Neurophysiology, 1987; mem. editorial bd. Annals of Neurology, Exptl. Neurology; contbr. articles to profl. jours. Mem. research adv. council United Cerebral Palsy Found.; mem. research adv. com. Nat. Multiple Sclerosis Soc.; mem. sci. adv. council Nat. Ataxia Found. Served with USPHS, 1958-60. Recipient Weinstein Goldenson award United Cerebral Palsy Assn., 1981; Lucy G. Moses prize Columbia U., 1973. Mem. Am. Neurol. Assn.(1st v.p. 1985-86, pres. elect 1987-88, pres. 1988-89), Mich. Neurological Assn. (pres. 1987—), Soc. Clin. Investigation, Am. Physiol. Soc., Am. Assn. Neuropathologists, Soc. Neurosci., Am. Acad. Neurology, Am. Epilepsy Soc., Assn. Research and Nervous and Mental Disease, AAAS. Home: 3411 Geddes Rd Ann Arbor MI 48105 Office: Dept Neurology U Mich Ann Arbor MI 48109

GILMER, ARDEN E., church official. Moderator Brethren Ch., Ashland, Ohio. Office: Brethren Ch 619 Park St Ashland OH 44805 *

GILMORE, HELEN CAROL, computer specialist; b. Trenton, N.J.; d. Louis Alfred and Catherine (Peto) Fennimore; m. Lester Wayne Gilmore, Oct. 18, 1963; 1 child, Matthew Todd; 1 child from previous marriage, Warren Jeffrey Russell. Student, Rider Coll., 1969, Purdue U., 1977-78, St. Mary-of-the-Woods Coll., 1980-85. Stenographer USAF, McGuire AFB, N.J., 1958-63; investigative recorder USAF, McGuire AFB, 1963-65; assoc. realtor Faherty Real Estate, Bordentown, N.J., 1969-74; asst. terminal mgr. G&G Tank Terminal Co., Inc., Columbus, N.J., 1974-76; adminstrv. asst. to assoc. dean Krannert Grad. Sch. Mgmt., Purdue U., West Lafayette, Ind., 1976-78; cons. Secs., Inc., Oak Brook, Ill., 1979; adminstrv. asst. to dir. materials Amphenol N.Am., Bunker Ramo Corp., Broadview, Ill., 1979-80; inventory specialist, product planner Amphenol N.Am., Bunker Ramo Corp., Broadview, 1980-81; system analyst Eastman Kodak Co., Oak Brook, Ill., 1981-85; applications engr. Eastman Kodak Co., Oak Brook, 1985-87; sr. system engr. NBI, Inc., 1987—. Recipient Kiwanis Acad. Excellence award, 1958. Mem. N.J. Assn. Realtors, Am. Bus. Women's Assn. (chpt. v.p. 1979), Nat. Assn. Female Execs., Soc. Office Automation Profls. (charter), Am. Prodn. and Inventory Control Soc. Office: 1901 W 22d St Oak Brook IL 60521

GILMORE, HORACE WELDON, U.S. dist. judge; b. Columbus, Ohio, Apr. 4, 1918; s. Charles Thomas and Lucille (Weldon) G.; m. Mary Hays, June 20, 1942; children—Lindsay Gilmore Lasser, Frances Gilmore Hayward. A.B., U. Mich., 1939, J.D., 1942. Bar: Mich. bar 1946. Law clk. U.S. Ct. Appeals, 1946-47; practiced in Detroit, 1947-51; spl. asst. U.S. atty., Detroit, 1951-52; mem. Mich. Bd. Tax Appeals, 1954; dep. atty. gen. State of Mich., 1955-56; circuit judge 3d Jud. Circuit, Detroit, 1956-80; judge U.S. Dist. Ct., 1980—; adj. prof. law Wayne State U. Law Sch., 1966—; lectr. law U. Mich. Law Sch., 1969—; faculty Nat. Coll. State Judiciary, 1966—; mem. Mich. Jud. Tenure Commn., 1969-76; chmn. Mich. Com. To Revise Criminal Code, 1965—, Mich. Com. To Revise Criminal Procedure, 1971-79; trustee Inst. for Ct. Mgmt. Author: Michigan Civil Procedure Before Trial, 2d edit, 1975; contbr. numerous articles to legal jours. Served with USNR, 1942-46. Mem. Am. Bar Assn., State Bar Mich., Am. Judicature Soc., Am. Law Inst., Nat. Conf. State Trial Judges. Office: US Dist Ct US Courthouse 231 W Lafayette Blvd Room 802 Detroit MI 48226

GILMORE, JAMES STANLEY, JR., broadcasting company executive; b. Kalamazoo, June 14, 1926; s. James Stanley and Ruth (McNair) G.; m. Diana Holdenreide Fell, May 21, 1949 (dec.); children: Bethany, Sydney, James Stanley III, Elizabeth, Ruth; m. Susan Chitty Maggio, Sept. 13, 1980. Student, Culver Mil. Acad., Western Mich. U., Kalamazoo Coll., 1945; Litt.D. (hon.), Nazareth Coll. Owner, chmn., pres., chief exec. officer Jim Gilmore Enterprises, Kalamazoo, 1960—; chmn., chief exec. officer Gilmore Broadcasting Corp.; v.p. Jim Gilmore Cadillac-Pontiac Nissan Inc.; pres. Gilmore Racing Team, Inc. (A.J. Foyt, driver); v.p., dir. Continental Corp. Mich.; asst. sec., dir. Fabri-Kal Plastics Corp., Kalamazoo; partner Hotel Investment Realty Corp., Greater Kalamazoo Sports, Inc. (hockey franchise); owner Anthony Abraham Chevrolet, Miami, Fla., GEC Life Ins. Co., Miami, Anthony Abraham Lincoln Mercury, Hialeah, Fla.; ptnr. Kalamazoo Stadium Co.; dir., mem. trust com. First Am. Bank-Mich. N.A.; dir. First Am. Bank Corp.; presdl. advisor Republic Airlines.; Mem. Pres.' Citizens Adv. Com. on Environ. Quality; former dir. Fed. Home Loan Bank Bd., Indpls.; mem., past chmn. Mich. Water Resources Commn.; mem. Mich. Gov.'s Forum, Alexander Graham Bell Bd., Washington, Pres.'s Commn. Health Phys. Edn. Sports; mem. nat. adv. cancer council HEW; mem. Nat. Assn. Broadcasters' adv. com. to Corp. for Pub. Broadcasting.; pres. Kalamazoo County Young Rep. Club, 1947-49; mayor Kalamazoo, 1959-61; past mem. Kalamazoo County Bd. Suprs.; past chmn. Kalamazoo County Rep. Exec. Com.; del. Rep. Nat. Conv. Asso. bd. dirs. Boys Clubs Am.; bd. dirs., past chmn. Kalamazoo County chpt. A.R.C.; former chmn. bd. trustees Nazareth Coll.; trustee, mem. finance com. Greater Mich. Devel. Found.; mem., chmn. bldg. com. fund dr. Constance Brown Speech and Hearing Center; past trustee Kalamazoo Coll.; mem. adv. group Center Urban Studies and Community Services; trustee past vice chmn. Kalamazoo Nature Center; mem. bldg. and exec. coms. Bronson Hosp., also chmn. ad hoc legis. com.; past trustee, past v.p. Mich. Found. for Arts, Detroit; founder bd. dirs. Martin Luther King Meml. Fund; life dir. Family Service Center Kalamazoo; mem. Mich. bd. dirs. Radio Free Europe, Novi Motorsports Mus.; nat. sponsor Ducks Unltd.; life mem. March Dimes; chmn. spl. reorganizational com. United Fund; mem. fund raising com. Pres. Ford Library/Mus.; mem. Pres.'s Council Phys. Fitness and Sports; hon. trustee Mich. Alvin Bentley Charitable Found. Served with USAAF, 1943-46. Named Kalamazoo Young Man of 1960, One of Mich.'s 5 Young Men of 1960, hon. citizen of Houston and Indpls.; recipient Ann. Service to Mankind award Sertoma Club, Man of Yr. award Mich. Auto Racing Fan Club, Auto Racing Found. Frat., honors Hoosier Racing Assn., Auto Racing Frat. Found., Inc., Milw. Mem. Kalamazoo County C. of C. (past pres., past dir., mem. exec. com. of indsl. devel. com.), Mich. C. of C. (mem. law and order com.), N.A.M., Mich. Acad. Sci., Arts and Letters. Episcopalian (mem. bd. diocese Western Mich., chmn. cathedral drive, mem. com. Bishop Whittemore Found.). Clubs: Capitol Hill (Washington); Park (Richland, Mich.) (past dir.); Mid-America (Chgo.); Otsego Ski (Gaylord, Mich.); Ocean Reef (Key Largo, Fla.). Home: 1550 Long Rd Kalamazoo MI 49008 also: 5040 Woodlawn Beach Gull Lake Hickory Corners MI 49060 : 25 Card Sound Ocean Reef Club Key Largo FL Office: Jim Gilmore Enterprises 202 Mich Bldg Kalamazoo MI 49007

GILMORE, JUNE ELLEN, psychologist; b. Middletown, Ohio, Oct. 22, 1927. BS, Miami U., Oxford, 1961; MS, Miami U., 1964. Lic. psychologist, Ohio. Intern in psychology Hamilton (Ohio) City Schs., 1963-64; psychologist Talawanda, Shiloh, Trenton Schs., Butler County, Ohio, 1964-66, Franklin (Ohio) City Schs., 1966-72, Wapakoneta (Ohio) City Schs., 1972-76, Cin. City Schs., 1978-86; pvt. practice psychology 1975—; planner, evaluator Warren/Clinton Counties Mental Health Bd., Ohio, 1986—. Co-author: Summer Children-Ready or not for School, 1986. Sec. Tri County Drug Council, Lima, Ohio, 1974; chmn. Auglaize County Social Services, Wapakoneta, Ohio, 1973-75. Mem. Ohio Sch. Psychologists Assn. (exec. bd. 1982-86), Southwestern Ohio Sch. Psychologist Assn. (pres.), Southwest Council Exceptional Children (Pres.), Nat. Assn. Sch. Psychologists, Ohio Psychol. Assn., Butler County 648 Mental Health Bd. (bd. dirs., pres. 1978-86, pres. 1983-84). Republican. United Methodist. Home and Office: 6120 Michael Rd Middletown OH 45042

GILMORE, ROBERT CURRIE, rail company executive; b. Vancouver, B.C., Can., Aug. 22, 1926; s. Robert H. and Isabel M. (Currie) G.; m. Shelagh M. Rowlette, Mar. 9, 1957; children: Katherine, Claudia, Robin, Jennifer. B. Comm., U. B.C., 1954. With Can. Pacific Rail, 1961—; asst. to gen. mgr. and mgr. mktg. Can. Pacific Rail, Montreal, Que., Can., 1961-66, systems mgr. market planning, 1966-70; regional mgr. mktg. and sales Can. Pacific Rail, Toronto, Ont., Can., 1970-71, gen. mgr. mktg. and sales, 1972-74; asst. v.p. mktg. and sales Can. Pacific Rail, Montreal, Que., Can., 1974-75, 77, v.p. mktg. and sales, 1977-84; exec. v.p. Can. Pacific Rail, 1984-86; pres., chief operating officer Soo Line Railroad Co., 1986—; dir. Aroostook River R.R. Co., Can. Pacific Steamships Ltd., CanPac Terminals Ltd., Houlton Br. R.R. Co., Incan Ships Ltd., Incan Superior Ltd., Internat. R.R. Co. of Maine, Soo Line R.R. Co., Thunder Bay Terminals Ltd.; apptd to coal industry adv. bd. Internat. Energy Agy., Paris, 1980. Mem. Nat. Freight Transp. Assn., Montreal Bd. Trade. Clubs: Whitlock Golf (Hudson, Que.); Can. Ry, Traffic of Montreal. Home: 630 Main Rd, Hudson Heights, PQ Canada J0P 1J0 Office: Soo Line RR Co Soo Line Bldg Box 530 Minneapolis MN 55440

GILMORE, ROGER, educational administrator; b. Phila., Oct. 11, 1932; s. Wheeler and Edith Seal (Thompson) G.; m. Beatrice Reynolds, Sept. 17, 1952; children: Christopher, Jennifer E., Lesley Margaret. A.B., Dartmouth Coll., 1954; postgrad., U. Chgo. Div. Sch., 1958-63. Social worker N.H. Dept. Pub. Welfare, Woodsville, 1954-55; adminstrv. asst. Furn Corp. Lisbon (N.H.), 1955-56; office mgr., asst. to pres. Cole's Mill Inc., Littleton, N.H., 1956-58; accountant, office supr. U. Chgo., 1958-61, asst. dir. fin. aid, 1961-63; asst. to dean Sch. Art Inst. Chgo., 1963-65, acting dean, 1965-68, dean, 1968—; Dir. commn. accreditation and membership Nat. Assn. Schs. of Art, 1975 78; mem. Joint Commn. on Dance and Theatre Accreditation, 1978-82; bd. dirs. Internat. Council Fine Arts Deans, 1986—; pres. Ox-Bow Summer Sch. and Artists Colony, 1987—. Fellow Nat. Assn. Schs. Art and Design (life mem., v.p. 1984—); mem. Soc. Archtl. Historians, Nat. Trust for Historic Preservation, Advs. for Arts, Am. Assn. Higher Edn., Internat. Council Fine Arts Deans (bd. dirs. 1986—), Coll. Art Assn., Landmarks Preservation Council, Nat. Art Edn. Assn.. Democrat. Episcopalian. Home: 4371 Central Ave Western Springs IL 60558 Office: Sch of Art Inst Chgo Columbus Dr and Jackson Blvd Chicago IL 60603

GILMORE, STEPHEN VINCENT, actuary; b. Fremont, Ohio, June 23, 1952; s. Harold Stanley and Florence Katherine (Ramseyer) G.; m. Sharon Ann Conkle, June 21, 1986. BS, Miami U., Oxford, Ohio, 1974, MS in Stats., 1975. With Cowan Actuarial Co., Cin., 1975-82; assoc. actuary Maccabees Mut. Life Ins. Co., Southfield, Mich., 1982-86; sr. cons. Peat Marwick Mitchell & Co., Cleve., 1986-87; sr. actuarial cons. Compensation Systems, Inc. Am., 1987—. Mem. Soc. Actuaries (assoc., cert.), Am. Acad. Actuaries, Pi Mu Epsilon. Avocations: traveling, photography, bicycling, classical music. Home: 4213 Circle Dr Flint MI 48507 Office: Compensation Systems Inc Am G-5054 W Bristol Rd Flint MI 48507

GILMOUR, ALLAN DANA, automotive company executive; b. Burke, Vt., June 17, 1934; s. Albert Davis and Marjorie Bessie (Fyler) G. A.B. cum laude, Harvard Coll., 1956, M.B.A., U. Mich., 1959. Financial analyst, sect. supr., dept. mgr., asst. to exec. v.p. Ford Motor Co., Dearborn, Mich., 1960-72; exec. v.p. adminstrn. Ford Motor Credit Co., Dearborn, 1972-73; exec. v.p. adminstrn. and spl. financing ops. Ford Motor Credit Co., 1973-75, pres., 1975-77; exec. dir. Ford Motor Co., 1977-79, v.p., controller, 1979-84, v.p. external and personnel affairs, 1984-85, exec. v.p., chief fin. officer, dir., 1986—. Mem. vis. com. U. Mich. Grad. Sch. Bus. Adminstrn.; trustee U. Detroit, Henry Ford Hosp. Mem. Phi Kappa Phi, Beta Gamma Sigma. Clubs: Fairlane (Dearborn); Econ. (Detroit). Home: 36 Blair Ln Dearborn MI 48120 Office: Ford Motor Co The American Rd Dearborn MI 48121

GILPIN, JOHN STEPHEN, veterinarian; b. Kalamazoo, Aug. 30, 1941; s. Gerald Merle and Mildred Elaine (Davidson) G.; D.V.M., Purdue U., 1966. Veterinarian, Gateway Animal Hosp., Glendale, Calif., 1966-67. County Line Animal Hosp., La Habra, Calif., 1970-71, specializing in small animal practice, Highland Animal Hosp., Ind., 1971-85, Wabash Vet. Hosp., Ind., 1985—. Served to capt. U.S. Army, 1967-69; Vietnam. Deocrated Bronze Star. Mem. AVMA, Ind. (dir. 1982-85), Calumet Area (pres. 1981) vet. med. assns., Ind. Acad. Vet. Medicine, Delta Sigma Phi. Republican. Episcopalian. Club: Kiwanis Internat. (bd. dirs. Wabash club 1986—). Home: RR 5 Box 193 Wabash IN 46992 Office: 1721 S Wabash St Wabash IN 46992

GILSON, M. DESALES, consultant, writer; b. Fremont, Ohio, Aug. 16, 1945; d. Richard C. and Mercedes C. (Ziebold) Grachek; student Bowling Green State U., 1964-66, Ursuline Coll., 1976-78, St. Mary-of-the-Woods Coll., 1978-79, Antioch Sch. Law, 1981; m. J. Richard Gilson, Jan. 31, 1970. Customer service rep. Toledo Edison Co., 1963-67; programmer Standard Oil Co. Ohio, Cleve., 1967-70, successively analyst, tng. coordinator, mgr. personnel devel. corp. adminstrn. employee relations, mgr. retail systems, from 1971, retail credit and info systems, 1984-85; prin. Daedalean Assocs.; owner Ampersand & Friends, typesetters; Sumi painter; lectr. Trustee, Light; vice chmn. The Bart Brooks Ctr. for Ethics and Human Values. Recipient Woman of Achievement award YWCA, 1976. Mem. Assn. Humanistic Psychology, Am. Soc. Tng. and Devel. Home: 3400 Wooster Rd Rocky River OH 44116 Office: PO Box 16056 Rocky River OH 44116

GILTNER, F. P., bank executive. Pres. First Nat. Bank Nebr., Omaha. Office: First Nat Bank of Nebraska Inc 1 First National Center Omaha NE 68103 *

GILZOW, HOMER FLOYD, JR., state government official; b. Springfield, Mo., Aug. 15, 1950; s. Homer Floyd Sr. and Elizabeth Jeane (Moseley) G.; m. Becky L. Goodwin, June 7, 1969; children: Paul F., Joshua F., Timothy A. Grad. in theology, Bapt. Bible Coll., 1971. News dir. KWFC Radio, Springfield, Mo., 1969-71, news editor, 1974-79; minister of youth Calvary Bapt. Ch., Bellflower, Calif., 1971-74; purchasing dir. Greene County, Springfield, 1979-81, dep. clk., 1981-85; dep. sec. State of Mo., Jefferson City, 1985—. Bd. dirs. Jefferson City United Way, 1985—, Mo. Music Makers, Jefferson City, 1986—; cubmaster Boy Scouts Am., Springfield, 1981-84; chmn. Envirn. Adv. Bd., Springfield, 1977-79; committeeman Greene County Reps., Springfield, 1980-85; program chmn. PTA, Springfield, 1980-85. Named one of Outstanding Young Men Am., 1985; recipient First Place Coverage award Assoc. Press, Kansas City, 1970. Avocations: woodworking, camping, bicycling, canoeing. Home: 110 Forest Hill Jefferson City MO 65101 Office: Sec of State PO Box 778 Jefferson City MO 65102

GIMPELSON, RICHARD JOEL, physician; b. St. Louis, May 26, 1946; s. Hymen and Alice (Pernikoff) G.; m. Nancy Lee Aleshire, Oct. 26, 1975; children: Joshua Michael, Jonathan Adam. BSEE, Washington U., 1968; MD, U. Mo., columbia, 1973. Diplomate Am. Bd. Ob-Gyn. Gynecologist Wash. U. Student Health Ctr., St. Louis, 1977-79; clinical instr. Mo. Bapt. Hosp., St. Louis, 1978-79; med. dir. St. Charles (Mo.) Family Planning Ctr., 1977—, Woodson Terrace (Mo.) Family Planning Ctr., 1984-85; pvt. practice ob-gyn Chesterfield, Mo., 1977—. Prin. Investigator Ovabloc, Chesterfield, 1983—; clinical investigator Nd:YAG laser endometrial ablation Cooper LaserSonics, Calif., 1986; inventor med. instrument, 1986; contbr. articles to Jour. Reproductive Medicine. Rep. candidate for U.S. Senate, Mo., 1986. Fellow Am. Coll. Ob-Gyn, Am. Assn. Gynecol. Laparoscopists, Am. Soc. Colposcopy and Cervical Pathology, Am. Fertility Soc.; mem. Matt Weiss Soc. (sec. 1982-84), St. Louis Met. Med. Soc., AMA, Mo. State Med. Assn. Republican. Jewish. Office: 222 S Woods Mill Rd Suite 400 Chesterfield MO 63017

GIN, JACKSON, architect; b. Chgo., June 11, 1934; s. Frank Tsue and Jennie Shee (Pang) G.; m. Jayne Ping Kan, Oct. 5, 1963; children: Paul L., Michael F., Daniel. BA, U. Ill., 1958. Designer Milton M. Schwartz, Architects, Chgo., 1958-60; project architect Greenberg & Finfer, Architects, Chgo., 1960-62, Hausner & Macsai, Architects, Chgo., 1962-67; project architect, ptnr. Dubin, Dubin, Black & Moutoussamy, Architects, Chgo., 1967-77; prin., pres. Mann, Gin, Ebel & Frazier, Ltd., Architects-Engrs., Chgo., 1977—. Trustee Chinese Christian Union Ch., 1968-70; bd. dirs. Neighborhood Redevel. Assistance, 1972-74; mem. Euclid-Lake Assn., Mount Prospect, Ill. Mem. AIA, Chinese Am. Civic Fedn. Club: Builders of Chgo. Home: 1332 Peachtree Ln Mount Prospect IL 60056 Office: Mann Gin Ebel & Frazier Ltd 30 S Michigan Ave Chicago IL 60603

GINDER, JON CHRISTIAN, corporation executive; b. Flint, Mich., Jan. 9, 1943; s. Christ and Anneabelle Shirley (Becton) G.; m. Elaine Margaret VanDeveire, June 24, 1966; children: Christopher, Josh. Student, Waubonsee Jr. Coll., 1973. V.P. J. L. Manta Inc., Chgo., 1968-81; chief exec. officer The Delcon Group, Carol Stream, Ill., 1981—. Chmn. bd. Metro Chgo. Youth for Christ, Wheaton, Ill., 1985-86; chmn. Jurisdictional Disputes Com., Falls Church, Va., 1982-83. Served with U.S. Army, 1961-62. Republican. Mem. Christian Ch. Club: Medinah Country. Avocations: golf, artist. Home: 1308 Clifden Ct Wheaton IL 60187 Office: The Delcon Group 538 Randy Rd Carol Stream IL 60188

GINDER, MICHAEL FRANCIS, osteopath, cardiovascular thoracic surgeon; b. Trenton, N.J., Sept. 26, 1936; s. Michael and Caroline (Duacsek) G.; m. Bonnie Braff, Dec. 16, 1964 (div. Dec. 1976); m. Gwendolyn Irene Sopris, Mar. 6, 1977; children: Heather Oona, Heidi Oona, Elizabeth. BA, Seton Hall U., South Orange, N.J., 1958; DO, Phila. Coll. Osteo. Medicine, 1964. Diplomate Am. Bd. Osteopathic Surgery. Intern Flint (Mich.) Osteo. Hosp., 1964-65; resident in gen. surgery Phila. Coll. Osteo. Medicine, 1965-67, Met. Hosp., Phila., 1966-68; resident in thoracic and cardiovascular surgery Detroit Osteo. Hosp., 1970-71, Chgo. Osteo. Hosp., 1971-72; surgeon Tucson Gen. Hosp., 1971-77, Met. Hosp., Grand Rapids, Mich., 1977—; practice medicine specializing in cardiovascular thoracic surgery Grand Rapids, 1977—; sec. dept. surgery Met. Hosp., 1982-83, program chmn. surgical update, 1983-86. Mem. Am. Osteo. Assn., Mich. Assn. Osteo. Physicians and Surgeons, Kent County Assn. Osteo. Physicians and Surgeons, Am. Coll. Osteo. Surgeons (program chmn. thoracic cardiovascular sect. 1985). Mem. Disciples of Christ. Avocations: swimming, gardening. Home: 2814 Burrwick SE Grand Rapids MI 49506 Office: 2355 E Paris SE Grand Rapids MI 49506

GINDHART, MARY ELIZABETH, educational administrator; b. Phila., Nov. 7, 1937; d. Joseph Eugene and Beatrice Margaret (Mitchell) G. B.A., Holy Family Coll., 1959; M.A., Ind. U., 1967; M.A. in Religion, Athenaeum of Ohio, 1978. Tchr. Abraham Lincoln High Sch., Phila., 1959-61, Thomas Edison High Sch., Phila., 1963-64; adminstr. Grailville Ctr., Loveland, Ohio, 1966-72, 75-76, dir. career edn. project, 1977-81, devel. officer, 1982-87; devel. assoc. The Salvation Army, 1987—; tutor, research officer James Cook U., Townsville, Australia, 1973-75; lay pastoral minister Archdiocese of Cin., 1978—; project dir., coordinator books on edn., history. Bd. dirs. Human Involvement Project, Inc., Cin., 1983—; chmn. allocations com. Community Chest, Cin., 1980-81; trustee Chatfield Coll., St. Martin, Ohio, 1975-77; sec. Townsville Welfare Council, 1973-74. Mem. Nat. Soc. Fund Raising Execs., The Grail, NOW. Office: The Salvation Army 114 E Central Pkwy Cincinnati OH 45210 Home: Grailville 932 O'Bannonville Rd Loveland OH 45140

GINDIN, R. ARTHUR, neurosurgeon; b. Perth Amboy, N.J., Sept. 10, 1934; m. Margaret Forsyth, Apr. 11, 1960 (dec.). Undergrad., U. Richmond, 1955; MD, Va. Commonwealth U., Richmond, 1959. Diplomate Am. Bd. Neurological Surgery. Intern U. Okla. Hosp., Oklahoma City, 1959-60; resident Montreal (Can.) Neurol. Inst., 1963-65, Med. Coll. Va., 1965-67; assoc. prof. neurological surgery Med. Coll. Ga., Augusta, 1967-78; practice medicine specializing in neurological surgery Monroe, Wis., 1985—. Mem. Am. Assn. Neurol. Surgery. Avocation: photography. Office: 1515 10th St Monroe WI 53566

GINGOLD, WILLIAM, psychologist, social services administrator; b. Warsaw, Poland, Sept. 20, 1939; s. David and Lilliam (Weintal) G.; m. Phyllis Kay Shapiro, Aug. 22, 1964; children: Steven, Shara, Tamara, Jason. BS, U. Wis., Milw., 1963; MS, U. Wis., Madison, 1966, PhD, 1971; MHA, U. Minn., Mpls., 1974; post doctorate, UCLA, 1976, 77. Lic. psychologist; cert. sch. supt., tchr., spl. edn. dir. Tchr. regular and spl. edn. Milw. and Madison Pub. Schs., 1963-67; dir. spl. edn. CESA #3, Gillett, Wis., 1967-70; chmn. dept. spl. edn. Moorhead (Minn.) State U., 1971-72; exec. dir. Severely Mentally Handicapped and Retarded Ctr., Fargo, N.D., 1972-81; chief exec. officer, dir. Devel. Services Ctr., Champaign, Ill., 1981—; asst. clinical prof. U. N.D. Med. Sch., Fargo, 1975-81; pres., chief exec. officer Disabled Children's Found., Champaign, 1982—, v.p. and sec. Champaign Chem. Corp., 1985—; adjunct prof. U. Ill., Urbana, 1982—. Author: (tests) Magic Kingdom, 1976, (tng. materials) Individualizing of Instruction, 1972, Geriatric Curriculum, 1981, Watch Me Grow, 1985; editor Am. Assn. Mental Deficiency jour., 1985. Mem. Pres. Commn. for Children's Mental Health, Washington, 1979; chairperson Minn. State Adv. Council on Child Care, Mpls., 1971; trustee The neuropsychiatric Inst. and Hosp., Fargo, 1978-81. Served with USAR, 1958-66. Recipient honor scholarship U. Wis., 1958, project asstship. OE/HEW, 1970; grad. fellow RSA/HEW, 1965. Mem. Am. Assn. on mental Deficiency (tres. 1985—), Am. Assn. on Healthcare Execs., Council for Exceptional Children (pres. 1969-70, Northeast Wis. award 1970), Am. Edn. Research Assn. Jewish. Lodge: Kiwanis. Avocations: handball, Racquetball, stamp collecting. Office: Devel Services Ctr 1304 W Bradley Ave Champaign IL 61821

GINGRASS, RUEDI PETER, plastic surgeon; b. Milw., May 10, 1932; s. Rudolph Peter and Colette (Host) G.; m. Katherine Carol Sundberg, June 14, 1958 (div. Dec. 1982); children: David, Mary, Charles, Sarah, Amy; m. Julie Marie Welu, Aug. 27, 1983. AB, U. Mich., 1954, MD, 1958; MS, Marquette U., 1963. Intern Mpls. Gen. Hosp., 1958-59; resident gen. surgery Marquette U. Affiliated Medicine Program, Milw., 1959-63; resident plastic surgery Duke U. Med. Ctr., Durham, N.C., 1963-66; chmn. dept. plastic surgery Med. Coll. Wis., Milw., 1969-83; practice medicine specializing in plastic surgery Milw., 1983—. Contbr. articles to profl. jours. Bd. dirs. Chgo. Symphony Orgn., Milw., 1979-83; chmn. Suburb Redevel. Planning, Wauwatosa, Wis., 1975-76. Mem. Plastic Surgery Edn. Found. (pres. 1982-83). Home: 7130 Wellauer Dr Wauwatosa WI 53213 Office: 9800 W Bluemound Rd Milwaukee WI 53226

GINN, ROBERT MARTIN, utility company executive; b. Detroit, Jan. 13, 1924; s. Lloyd T. and Edna S. (Martin) G.; m. Barbara R. Force, 1948; children: Anne, Martha, Thomas. B.S. in Elec. Engring., U. Mich., 1948, M.S. in Elec. Engring., 1948. With Cleve. Electric Illuminating Co., 1948—, controller, 1959-62, v.p. gen. services, 1963-70, exec. v.p., 1970-77, pres., 1977-83, chmn., 1983-86, chief exec. officer, 1979-86, dir.; chmn., chief exec. officer, dir. Centerior Energy Corp., Toledo Edison Co., 1986—; dir. Soc. Corp., Soc. Nat. Bank Cleve., Ferro Corp. Mem. Shaker Heights Bd. Edn., (Ohio), 1968-75, pres., 1973-74; pres. Welfare Fedn. Cleve., 1968-69; chmn. Cleve. Commn. on Higher Edn., 1983-86; trustee John Carroll U., Martha Holden Jennings Found., 1983—. Served with USAAF, 1943-46. Office: Centerior Energy Corp PO Box 94661 Cleveland OH 44101-4661

GINSBURG, SCOTT MICHAEL, financial analyst; b. Pitts., May 28, 1960; s. Jerome Jack and Geraldine (Siegel) G.; m. Cindy Lee Satterfield, May 19, 1985. BS, Pa. State U., 1981. CPA, Ohio. Sr. auditor Ernst & Whinney, Cleve., 1982-85; fin. analyst Cragin, Lang, Free & Smythe, Inc., Cleve., 1985—. Mem. Am Inst. CPA's, Ohio Soc. CPA's. Democrat. Jewish. Lodge: KP (fin. com. local chpt. 1987—). Home: 4198 Hinsdale Rd South Euclid OH 44121 Office: Cragin Lang Free & Smythe Inc 1215 Superior NE Cleveland OH 44114

GINSBURG, SHELDON HARVEY, accountant; b. Chgo., Mar. 22, 1938; s. Max L. and Sophie L. (Schwimmer) G.; m. Rosemaree Vass Ginsburg; children: Howard, Linda, Steven. BS, DePaul U., 1959. CPA, Ill., Fla. Pres. Shell Devel. Corp., Northbrook, Ill., 1969—; cons. Laventhol & Horwath, Northbrook, 1986—; chmn. bd. Pick Fisheries, Inc.; pres. Internat. Found. for Time-Sharing; trustee UFCW Local 546 Food Handlers Health and Welfare Fund. Mem. Am. Inst. CPA's, Ill. Soc. CPA's, Fla. Soc. CPA's, Beta Gamma Sigma, Pi Gamma Mu, Beta Alpha Psi. Office: 40 Skokie Blvd Suite 350 Northbrook IL 60062

GINTZ, ALAN FREDERICK, military officer; b. Dover, Ohio, Apr. 17, 1953; s. Robert Gilgen and Marjorie Geraldine (Diefenbach) G. BS in Nautical Sci., U.S. Merchant Marine Acad., 1975. With U.S. Merchant Marines, 1976—, capt. Great Lakes Steamship div. Bethlehem Steel Corp., 1984—. Avocations: boating, boat building, hunting, camping, travel. Home: Rt 9 Box 142B Lowell OH 45744

GIOIOSO, JOSEPH VINCENT, psychologist; b. Chgo., Mar. 6, 1939; s. Vincent James and Mary (Bonadonna) G.; B.A., DePaul U., 1962, M.A., 1963; Ph.D. summa cum laude, Ill. Inst. Tech., 1971; m. Gay Powers, Dec. 28, 1963; children—Joseph, Randy Marie, Danielle. Psychologist, Sch. Assn. for Spl. Edn. in DuPage County, Wheaton, Ill., 1964-67; pvt. practice as clin. psychologist, Chgo. and Downers Grove, Ill., 1966—; clin. psychologist J.J. McLaughlin, M.D., Profl. Corp., Chgo., 1970—. Founder dept. psychology Ill. Benedictine Coll., Lisle, 1968, chmn. dept. psychology, prof., dir. testing, 1968-71; cons. psychologist Chicago Ridge (Ill.) Sch. Dist. 127 1/2, 1973-76, Cath. Charities Counseling Service, Chgo., 1963-66, St. Laurence High Sch., Oak Lawn, Ill., 1963-64, Oak Lawn-Hometown Sch. Dist. No. 123, 1967-68, Addison (Ill.) Sch. Dist. 4, 1969-72; vis. prof. psychology Inst. Mgmt., Lisle, 1968-69, George Williams Coll., Downers Grove, 1970-71; chief psychologist Valley View Sch. Dist. 365U, Bolingbrook, Ill., 1971-73; dir. Pub. Program for Exceptional Children, Lisle, 1969-71; mem. Nat. Register Health Service Providers in Psychology, 1975—. Bd. dirs. Ray Graham Assn. for Handicapped, DuPage County, Ill., 1970-73; adv. bd. Care and Counseling Center DuPage County, 1977—. DePaul U. publ. grantee, 1959-61, Fitzgerald Bros. Found. grantee, 1969-71. Mem. Am., Midwestern, Ill. psychol. assns., Soc. Pediatric Psychology, AAAS, Alpha Phi Delta. Clubs: Lakeside Country (Downers Grove); Racquet (Hinsdale, Ill.). Author: Completion Intelligence Test, 1963; Children's Emotional Symptoms Inventory, 1979. Contbr. articles to profl. jours. Home and Office: 6800 S Main St Downers Grove IL 60516

GIORGIANNI, NICHOLAS THOMAS, oil company executive; b. Cleve., Jan. 28, 1934; s. Frank and Mary (Gliozzo) G.; m. Alda Palmerini, Aug. 24, 1963; children: Paul, Lisa, Mark. BS in Bus. and Econs., Kent State U., 1956. Various sales and adminstrv. positions. Standard Oil Co., Cleve., 1958-72, mgr. allocations, 1973-75, mgr. adminstrn. and mktg., 1975-78, project dir. hdqrs. bldg. constrn., 1982-85, dir. corp. services, 1985—; mgr. wholesale sales Be Oil Inc., Wilmington, Del. and Cleve., 1978-82. Served to 1st lt. U.S. Army, 1956-58. Republican. Roman Catholic. Avocations: opera, photography, literature, tennis, travel. Home: 8335 Belle Vernon Dr Novelty OH 44072 Office: Standard Oil Co 200 Public Sq Cleveland OH 44072

GIORGINI, ALDO, civil engineering educator; b. Voghera, Italy, Mar. 15, 1934; came to U.S. 1962; s. Adelmo and Pierina (Salvadeo) G.; m. Elena Belotti, June 21, 1964 (dec. Oct. 1977); children—Massimiliano, Flaviano. Dr.Ing., Politecnico di Torino (Italy), 1959; Ph.D., Colo. State U., 1966. Assoc. prof. hydraulics Politecnico di Torino, 1959-61; NATO researcher CISE, Segrate, Italy, 1961-62; fellow Nat. Ctr. for Atmospheric Research, Boulder, Colo., 1966-67; asst. prof. Sch. Civil Engring, Purdue U., West Lafayette, Ind., 1967-70, assoc. prof., 1970—. Bd. dirs. Lafayette Art Ctr., 1976-79; Opera De Lafayette, 1981. Recipient 1st place award Internat. Competition of Computer Art, Augsburgh, Germany, 1982; Purdue Research Found. grantee, 1968, 69, 71, 72; Office of Water Research and Tech. grantee, 1973-74, 83; Apple Found. grantee, 1981; Dept. Agr. grantee, 1980-83. Mem. AAAS, Soc. Indsl. and Applied Math. Contbr. articles to profl. jours.; art work exhibited in U.S., Europe, Japan. Home: 1137 Berkley Rd Lafayette IN 47904 Office: Purdue U Sch Civil Engring West Lafayette IN 47907

GIOVANETTI, MICHAEL LOUIS, optometrist; b. Cin., Dec. 1, 1953; s. Armando and Margaret L. (Beller) G.; m. Paula Marie Lytis, Apr. 22, 1979; children: Paul A., Lynne Marie. Student, Xavier U., 1975; OD cum laude, Ill. Coll. Optometry, 1979. Gen. practice optometry Cin., 1979—. Mem. Am. Optometric Assn., Ohio Optometric Assn., Cin. Optometric Assn. (pres. 1985—), Western Hills Jaycees (treas. 1982-83). Roman Catholic. Lodge: Lions. Avocations: radio control aviation, stamp collecting, computers. Home: 4037 Ebenezer Rd Cincinnati OH 45248 Office: 5547 Bridgetown Rd Cincinnati OH 45248

GIOVANNONI, ROBERT NICHOLAS, principal; b. Chgo., Sept. 14, 1947; s. Bruno C. and Angeline M. (Lucchesi) G. A.B. magna cum laude, Loyola U., Chgo., 1969, M.Ed., 1973; C.A.S., Harvard U., 1981. Cert. tchr. and adminstr., Ill., sch. adminstr., Chgo. Cath. Sch. Bd. Tchr., program dir. St. Patrick High Sch., Chgo., 1969-74; asst. gen. mgr. Grady Co., Chgo., 1974-75; asst. prin. and curriculum dir. Notre Dame High Sch., Chgo., 1975-80; prin. Harvard-St. George Sch., Chgo., 1981-83; prin. Immaculate Conception High Sch., Elmhurst, Ill., 1983—; ednl. and organizational cons. NSF fellow in comparative govt., 1969; NDEA fellow in govt., 1969. Mem. Assn. for Supervision and Curriculum Devel., Nat. Cath. Edn. Assn., Nat. Assn. Secondary Sch. Principals, Phi Delta Kappa. Roman Catholic. Club: Harvard (Chgo.) Co-author, I-Project: A Prospectus (monograph). Home: 1551 Monroe River Forest IL 60305 Office: 217 Cottage Hill Ave Elmhurst IL 60126

GIOVINGO, THOMAS PETER, marketing professional; b. Rockford, Ill., Aug. 11, 1956; s. Vito D. and Marian E. (Cacciatore) G.; m. Kathleen M. Keller, May 27, 1978; children: Gina, Thomas. BA in Bus. cum laude, Loras Coll., 1978. Customer service mgr. GC Electronics, Rockford, 1978-79, mgr. mktg. services, 1979-82, dir. retail sales, 1983—. Bd. dirs. Family Advocate Inc., Rockford, 1983—. Mem. Loras Alumni Club Rockford (pres. 1979—). Roman Catholic. Avocations: skiing, golf, gardening. Office: GC Electronics 1801 Morgan St Rockford IL 61102

GIRDNER, LINDA KATHLEEN, anthropologist, family mediator; b. Santa Ana, Calif., Oct. 20, 1950; d. Ted Dock and Elfriede Maria (Weber) G.; m. Fred C. Hyman, Aug. 2, 1986; 2 stepsons. BA in German, Ohio Wesleyan U., 1972; PhD in Anthropology, Am. U., 1981. Teaching fellow anthropology Am. U., Washington, 1974-77; coordinator mediation services Divorce and Marital Stress Clinic, Arlington, Va., 1979-81; asst. trainer Family Mediation Assn., 1979-81; asst. prof. human devel. and family ecology Inst. Child Behavior and Devel. U. Ill., Urbana-Champaign, 1981-87; cons., tng. in family mediation. Contbr. articles to profl. jours. Recipient Doctoral Dissertation award, 1978, NIMH Research Service award, 1978; Nothman scholar, 1979, D.C. Community Council Humanities scholar, 1980. Mem. Acad. Family Mediators (bd. dirs. 1987—), Am. Anthrop. Assn. (Congl. fellow 1987-88), Ill. Council on Family Relations, Champaign County Mediation Task Force, Phi Beta Kappa. Democrat. Office: U Ill Inst Child Behavior Devel 51 Gerty Dr Champaign IL 61820

GISH, EDWARD RUTLEDGE, physician; b. St. Louis, Sept. 5, 1908; s. Edward C. and Bessie (Rutledge) G.; A.B., Westminster Coll., 1930; M.D., St. Louis U., 1935, M.S., 1939; m. Miriam Schlicker, July 8, 1938; children—Ann Rutledge, Mary Priscilla. Intern, St. Louis U. Hosps., 1935-36; resident in surgery St. Mary's Group Hosps., St. Louis, 1936-39; pvt. practice medicine specializing in surgery, Fulton, Mo., 1946—; staff mem. Callaway Meml. Hosp., Fulton. Bd. dirs. Mo. Symphony Soc., pres., 1981; med. dir. Callaway County CD. Served from maj. to lt. col., AUS, 1943-46; lt. col. ret. Res. Hon. col. Gov.'s Staff Mo. Fellow ACS; mem. Royal Soc. London (affiliate), Internat. Coll. Surgeons, AMA, Mo., Callaway County med. socs., Mo. Red Poll Breeders Assn. (pres.), Am. Law Enforcement Officers Assn., Delta Tau Delta, Alpha Omega Alpha. Contbr. articles to profl. jours. Co-capt. U.S. team World Masters Cross-Country Ski Assn., 1985. Home: 7 W 10th St Fulton MO 65251 Office: 5 E 5th St Fulton MO 65251

GISSLER, SIGVARD GUNNAR, JR., newspaper editor; b. Chgo., July 2, 1935; s. Sigvard Gunnar Sr. and Louisa (Anderson) G.; m. Mary Catherine Engman, Oct. 23, 1954; children—Gary, Glenn, Gregory. B.A. in Am. Civilization, Lake Forest Coll., 1956; Student, Northwestern U., 1958-61. News editor Independent Register, Libertyville, Ill., 1958-59; exec. editor News-Sun, Waukegan, Ill., 1963-67; editorial writer Milw. Jour., 1967-77, editorial page editor, 1977-84, assoc. editor, 1984-85, editor, 1985—; v.p. Jour. Communications, Milw., 1987—, also bd. dirs.; sr. v.p. Jour./Sentinel Inc., Milw., 1987—, also bd. dirs.; journalism fellow Stanford U., Calif., 1975. Recipient Disting. Service citation Lake Forest Coll., 1977. Mem. Am. Soc. Newspaper Editors, Press Inst. Home: 6021 N Kent St Whitefish Bay WI 53217 Office: The Milw Journal Div of Journal Communications Inc PO Box 661 Milwaukee WI 53203

GITCHELL, ROBERT GRAHAM, orthopedic surgeon; b. Cresco, Iowa, Dec. 14, 1941; s. Lester Graham and Josephine June (Flower) G.; m. Deborah Rae Ziffren, June 3, 1965; children: Joseph Graham, Sarah Lynn. BA, U. Iowa, 1963, MD, 1967. Diplomate Am. Bd. Orthopedic Surgery. Intern Los Angeles County Gen. Hosp., 1967-68; resident U. Iowa, Iowa City, 1968-72; staff McFarland Clinic, Ames, Iowa, 1974—, dir. HMO devel., 1984—, also bd. dirs.; chief of surgery Mary Greeley Med. Ctr., Ames, 1978-79. Served to maj. USAF, 1972-74. Fellow Am. Acad. Orthopedic Surgeons; mem. Iowa Orthopedic Soc. (pres. 1986). Avocation: golf. Home: 2513 Northwood Ames IA 50010

GIVAN, RICHARD MARTIN, associate justice state supreme court; b. Indpls., June 7, 1921; s. Clinton Hodell and Glee (Bowen) G.; m. Pauline Marie Haggart, Feb. 28, 1945; children: Madalyn Givan Hesson, Sandra Givan Chenoweth, Patricia Givan Siwek, Elizabeth Givan Whipple. LL.B., Ind. U., 1951. Bar: Ind. bar 1952. Partner firm Bowen, Myers, Northam & Givan, 1960-69; justice Ind. Supreme Ct., 1969-74, chief justice., 1974-87, assoc. justice, 1987—; dep. pub. defender Ind., 1952-53, dep. atty. gen., 1953-64; dep. pros. atty. Marion County, 1965-66; mem. Ind. Ho. Reps., 1967-68. Served to 2d lt. USAAF, 1942-45. Mem. ABA, Ind. Bar Assn., Indpls. Bar Assn., Ind. Soc. Chicago, Newcomen Soc. N.Am., Internat. Arabian Horse Assn. (past dir., chmn. ethical practices rev. bd.), Ind. Arabian Horse Club (pres. 1971-72), Sigma Delta Kappa. Mem. Soc. of Friends. Lodge: Lions. Office: Supreme Ct Ind 324 State House Indianapolis IN 46204

GIVENS, DAVID W., banker; b. Gary, Ind., Mar. 18, 1932; s. James M. Givens; m. Betty J. Davis, July 3, 1955; children: Kathryn D., David W. Jr. AB, Wabash Coll., 1956; JD, Ind. U., 1960. Ptnr. Krieg, DeVault, Alexander & Capehart, Indpls., 1960-74; v.p., gen. counsel Ind. Nat. Bank, Indpls., 1974-76, sr. v.p., gen. counsel, 1976-79, exec. v.p., 1979—; vice chmn. Ind. Nat. Corp., Indpls., 1979-85, pres., 1985—. Pres. 500 Festival Assocs., 1982; mem. devel. council Ind. U. Sch. Law; vice chmn. adv. council Corner Prairie Settlement, chmn. capital devel com. 1986; chmn. William Conner Soc.; bd. dirs., mem. exec. com. Indpls. Holiday Com., Inc.; bd. dirs., mem. tour service and fin. coms. Hist. Landmarks Found. Ind.; chmn. corp. fund drive Ind. Sports Corp.; chmn. corp. sect. Indpls. Symphony Orch. Fund Drive, 1986; bd. dirs., asst. treas., exec. com., human services com. Greater Indpls. Progress Com.; trustee Krannert Charitable Trust, Wabash Coll.; exec. com., sec. bd. dirs., chmn. safety and security com. Commn. for Downtown, Inc.; bd. dirs. The Beethoven Found.; mem. program com. Community Service Council. Served to sgt. U.S. Army, 1953-54. Mem. ABA, Ind. Bar Assn., Indpls. Bar Assn., Indpls. Bar Found., Ind. Legal Found. Inc. (bd. dirs.), Assn. Bank Holding Cos., Assn. Res. City Bankers, Govtl. Affairs Soc. Ind., State Ind. Bd. Law Examiners, Bank Capital Markets Assn. (com. competitive securities markets), Am. Bankers Assn. Avocation: tennis. Office: Ind Nat Corp 1 Indiana Sq #501 Indianapolis IN 46266

GIVHAN, STEVEN ALLEN, engineering company executive; b. Chgo.; s. Claude Raymond and Christine E. (Jackson) G.; m. Octavia Walker, Jan. 3, 1982; children—Khaliah, Kevin. B.S. in Mech. Engring., U. Calif.-Santa Barbara, 1974; M.S., U. Hawaii, 1976; M.B.A. (hon.) Oxford U., Eng., 1981. Registered profl. engr., Ill., Calif., D.C. Mech. designer Sonicraft Inc., Chgo., 1980-82; pres. NDT 1 Inc., Chgo., 1982—; dir. Auburn Park Engelwood Local Devel. Corp. Patentee in field. Bd. dirs. Kennedy King Coll., Chgo., 1984; mem. Congl. Task Force, Chgo., 1984—. Served to lt. comdr. USN, 1973-79. Mem. ASME, Nat. Assn. Profl. Engrs., AAAS, Vietnam Vets. Roman Catholic. Avocations: golf, swimming, tennis, model railroading.

GIVOT, STEVEN IRA, foreign exchange and commodities trader, corporate executive; b. Chgo., Feb. 18, 1950; s. Martin Lionel and Elyse Sue (Abrams) G.; children: Brian Lamond, Susan Elizabeth, Sarah Elyse. SB, MIT, 1971; MS with distinction, London Sch. Econs., 1973; MBA with honors, U. Chgo., 1974. Pres. Tech. Enterprises Inc., Barrington Hills, Ill., 1975-86; head market maker, J. Aron & Co., 1986—; mem. Chgo. Bd. Options Exchange, 1974-87, chmn. facilities com., 1979-83, chmn. securities and new product com., 1979-80, mem. exec. com., 1980-82, 84-86, chmn. systems com., 1985-86; mem. Chgo. Bd. Trade, 1977-87, Midwest Stock Exchange, 1978-81, N.Y. Futures Exchange, 1980-82, Chgo. Merc. Exchange, 1986—; head market maker J. Aron & Co., Chgo., 1986—; dir. Chgo. Options Exchange Bldg. Corp., 1980-86. Treas. campaign Armstrong-Libertarian for gov. of Ill. 1982; Libertarian Party candidate for U.S. Senate from Ill., 1984, for Ill. sec. state, 1986; mem. nat. com. Libertarian Party, 1985-86. Mem. Smithsonian Instn. Jewish. Home and Office: Rt 2 1 Middlebury Rd Barrington Hills IL 60010

GIZYNSKI, MARTHA NOBLE, educator; b. Malden, Mass., Jan. 18, 1928; d. Royce Jennings and Ruth Lunt (Moulton) Noble; m. Waldemar Edmund Gizynski, Aug. 26, 1949; children—Elizabeth, Susan. B.A., Radcliffe Coll., 1949; M.S.W., U. Mich., 1967, Ph.D., 1971. Lectr. social work U. Mich., Ann Arbor, 1969-74, asst. prof., 1974-78, assoc. prof., 1978—; pvt. practice psychotherapy, Ann Arbor, 1980—. Mem. Nat. Assn. Social Workers, Am. Psychol. Assn. Home: 6478 Clark Lake Rd Jackson MI 49201 Office: U Mich 4060 Frieze Bldg Ann Arbor MI 49105

GLABE, ELMER FREDERICK, food scientist; b. Chgo., Apr. 3, 1911; s. Fred John and Holdina (Jennrich) G.; m. Marjorie Browne; children: John E., Lynne Glabe Mueller, David H. BS in Chemistry, Ill. Inst. Tech., 1942. Analytical chemist W.E. Long Co., Chgo., 1929-38; research chemist, tech. dir. Stein Hall and Co., Chgo., 1938-45; founder, pres. Food Tech., Inc, Chgo., 1946—, Food Tech. Lab. and Food Tech. Products, Chgo. Author numerous tech. papers in food sci.; patentee (110) in field. Recipient Outstanding Service award Am. Council Indsl. Labs. Mem. Inst. Food Technologists, Am. Chem. Soc., Am. Assn. Cereal Chemists, Am. Soc. Bakery Engrs. Lutheran. Office: 3000 Dundee Rd #204 Northbrook IL 60062

GLADDEN, DEAN ROBERT, arts administrator, educator, consultant; b. Columbus, Ohio, Dec. 27, 1953; s. Cyril Robert and Eileen (Faulkner) G.; m. Jane Frances Tellers, Aug. 27, 1953; children: John Dean, Catherine Eileen. B in Music Edn., Miami U., Oxford, Ohio, 1976; MS in Urban Arts Mgmt., Drexel U., 1978. Exec. dir. Council for Arts of Greater Lima, Ohio, 1977-80, Arts Comm. Greater Toledo, 1980-82; dir. devel. and adminstrn. Great Lakes Theater Festival, Cleve., 1982-86; assoc. mng. dir. The Cleve. Play House, 1986, mng. dir., 1987—; cons., Ohio Arts Council, Cleve., 1977—, chmn. sponsor/touring panel, 1981-83; adj. assoc. prof. U. Akron, Ohio, 1984—. Author booklets on the arts in Ohio, 1983, 85. Mem. Nat. Soc. Fund Raising Execs., Assn. Coll. Univ. and Community Arts Adminstrs., Ohio Soc. Fund Raising Execs., Ohio Regional Assn. Concert and Lecture Enterprises. Episcopalian. Avocations: piano, drums. Home: 3605 Ingleside Rd Shaker Heights OH 44122 Office: The Cleve Play House 8500 Euclid Ave Cleveland OH 44106

GLADUE, BRIAN ANTHONY, psychologist, researcher; b. Norwich, Conn., Nov. 30, 1950; s. William Raymond and Julia (Boako) G.; m. Lynn D. Jordan, Jan. 7, 1984; 1 child, Garrett William. BA, Northeastern U., 1973; PhD, Mich. State U., 1979; postdoctoral studies psychiatry, SUNY, Stony Brook, 1979-81. Research assoc. L.I. Research Inst. of SUNY, Stony Brook, N.Y., 1981-84; asst. prof. psychiatry SUNY, Stony Brook, 1982-84; asst. prof. N.D. State U., Fargo, 1984—, dir. human sexuality program, 1985—; chairperson instnl. rev. bd. N.D. State U., 1985—; vis. lectr. Rutgers U., New Brunswick, N.J., 1983-84. Contbr. chpts. to book, Human Sexuality, 1983-86; also articles (over 20) to profl. jours. Grantee NSF, 1986; recipient Nat. Research Service award Nat. Inst. Mental Health, 1979, 80, 81. Mem. Internat. Soc. for Human Ethology, N.Y. Acad. Scis., Internat. Acad. Sex Research, Endocrine Soc., Sigma Xi. Club: Valley Wine Soc. (Fargo). Avocations: cross-country skiing, military games, collecting comics. Home: Rural Rt 1 237 Forest River Fargo ND 58103 Office: ND State Univ Dept Psychology Fargo ND 58105

GLANCY, ALFRED ROBINSON, III, public utility company executive; b. Detroit, Mar. 14, 1938; s. Alfred Robinson and Elizabeth A. (Tant) G.; m. Ruth Mary Roby, Sept. 15, 1962; children—Joan Courts, Alfred R. IV, Douglas Roby, Andrew Roby. B.A., Princeton U., 1960; M.A., Harvard Bus. Sch., 1962. Vice pres. corp. planning Am. Nat. Gas Service, Detroit, 1976-79; econ. and fin. planning staff Mich. Consol. Gas Co., Detroit, 1962-64, supr. econ. studies and rates, 1965-67, mgr. econ. and fin. planning dept., 1967-68, treas., 1969-72, v.p., treas., 1972-73, v.p. customer and mktg. services, 1976-79, v.p. mktg./dist. ops., 1979-81, sr. v.p. mktg./customer services, 1981-83, sr. v.p. utility ops., 1983-84, chmn., pres., chief exec. officer, 1984—; dir., exec. com. UNICO Properties, Inc., Seattle; dir. Primark Corp., McLean, Va., First Fed. Mich., Detroit, MLX Corp., Detroit. Bd. dirs. Detroit Symphony Orch.; vice chmn. Rehab. Inst. Detroit; chmn. New Detroit, Inc., 1981-88. Republican. Clubs: Princeton of Mich., Country of Detroit, Detroit. Office: Mich Consol Gas Co 500 Griswold St Detroit MI 48226

GLANERT, KAREN LOUISE, educator; b. Sheboygan, Wis., July 21, 1954; d. Alvin H. and Laverne E. (Haun) G. B.S. summa cum laude in Edn., U. Wis.-Whitewater, 1976, postgrad. Tchr., Lakeland (Wis.) Mfg. Co., 1972-76; instr. Sheboygan Pub. Schs., 1978—; counselor emotionally disturbed children; coach. Mem. Council Exceptional Children, Nat. Ret. Tchrs. Assn., Wis. Edn. Assn., Sheboygan Edn. Assn., PTA, Assn. Supervision and Curriculum Devel., Council Basic Edn., Luth. Women's League, Beta Sigma Phi. Lutheran. Home: 2427 Camelot Blvd Apt A Sheboygan WI 53081 Office: Farmsworth Middle Sch 1017 Union Sheboygan WI 53081

GLASER, DAVID STERLING, accounting firm executive; b. St. Louis, Mar. 25, 1957; s. Sterling Raymond and Virginia Rose (Bergesch) G.; m. Karen Marie Prichard, Sept. 20, 1985. BSBA, Southeast Mo. State U., 1978; MBA, U. Mo., 1984. CPA, Mo. Auditor Ronnie D. Hopper, CPA, St. Louis, 1978-81; fin. analyst Container Corp. of Am., St. Louis, 1981-83; audit sr. Price Waterhouse, St. Louis, 1983-84, audit mgr., 1984-85, tax mgr., 1985—. Deacon Westminster Presbyn. Ch., Ballwin, Mo., 1985—. Mem. Chesterfield (Mo.) C. of C., Am. Inst. CPA's, Mo. Soc. CPA's, Nat. Assn. Accts. Republican. Presbyterian. Avocations: tennis, bicycling. Home: 18746 Petra Ct Glencoe MO 63038 Office: Price Waterhouse 55 W Port Plaza Saint Louis MO 63146

GLASER, WILLIAM PHILIP, accountant; b. Cin., Nov. 16, 1955; s. Albert Bernard and Esther Helen (Hoffman) G. BA with honors, U. Chgo., 1977; M Mgmt., Northwestern U., 1982. CPA, Ill. Mem. audit staff Deloitte Haskins & Sells, Chgo., 1982-84; instr. Ill. Inst. Tech., Chgo., 1985-86; staff acct. SEC, Chgo., 1986—. Mem. Aldine Block Club, Chgo., 1979—. Mem. Am. Inst. CPA's, Ill. CPA Soc. Avocations: running, skiing, aerobics. Home: 622 W Aldine Chicago IL 60657

GLASGOW, JAMES FREDRICK, infosystems specialist; b. Paducah, Ky., Jan. 14, 1957; s. Jake Harbine and Dorothy Maxine (Roberts) G.; m. Doreen Marie Almer, July 17, 1982; 1 child, James William. A in Applied Sci, U. Akron, 1977, BS in Tech. Edn., 1981; postgrad., Kent State U., 1983; MS in Tech. Edn., U. Akron, 1987. Computer operator Vis. Nurse Service, Akron, Ohio, 1977-79, programmer, analyst, 1979-84; systems cons. Profl. Software Systems, Cuyahoga Falls, Ohio, 1984—; tech. tng. Digital Equipment Corp., Bedford, Mass., 1979; asst. to prof. U. Akron, 1981, 87; seminar software engr. Battelle, Columbus, 1982. Recipient Eagle Scout award Boy Scouts Am., 1973. Mem. Data Processing Mgmt. Assn., Assn. Computing Machinery, Ky. Hist. Soc., Lyon County Hist. Soc. (life). Home: 1348 Hammel St Akron OH 44306 Office: Profl Software Systems Inc 141 Broad Blvd Cuyahoga Falls OH 44221

GLASS, EDWARD LEE, coach, secondary school educator; b. Alliance, Ohio, Dec. 7, 1937; s. John Maurice and Florence Angeline (Shriver) G.; m. Dixie P. Baucum, Mar. 25, 1961; 1 child, Jason Anthony. BA in History, Mt. Union Coll., 1965; MS in Edn., Youngstown (Ohio) State U., 1976. Permanent cert. tchr.; cert. secondary prin., supt. Asst. football coach W. Br. High Sch., Beloit, Ohio, 1965-66, head football coach, 1967-70; asst. football coach Mt. Union Coll., Alliance, 1966-67; asst. football coach Harding High Sch., Warren, Ohio, 1970-73, head football coach, 1973-75; head football coach Hubbard (Ohio) High Sch., 1975-81, Hoover High Sch. North Canton, Ohio, 1981—. Served with U.S. Army. Recipient numerous coaching awards, 1974—. Mem. Ohio High Sch. Football Coaches Assn. (bd. dirs. 1974-77, v.p. 1978, pres. 1979), Am. Football Coaches Assn. (allied), Nat. High Sch. Coaches Assn., Stark County Coaches Assn., NEA, Ohio Edn. Assn., North Canton Edn. Assn. Democrat. Roman Catholic. Home: 820 Harmon SW North Canton OH 44720 Office: Hoover High Sch 605 Fair Oaks SW North Canton OH 44720

GLASS, GUNTER MCKEMIE, human resources administrator; b. Oklahoma City, Aug. 16, 1944; s. Theodore Gunter and Florence Joy (McKemie) G.; m. Salley Owens, Sept. 6, 1965 (div. Apr. 1967); m. Kathleen Louise Topczewski, Oct. 12, 1985. BS in Mgmt., So. Ill. U., 1969. Claims adjuster Liberty Mut. Ins. Co., Milw., 1969-73; mgr. personnel Continental Baking Co., Milw. and Mpls. and St. Louis, 1973-79; dir. personnel div. Continental Baking Co., Los Angeles, 1979-85; dir. field personnel Continental Baking Co., St. Louis, 1985—. Republican. Episcopalian. Avocations: sailing, woodworking, astronomy. Home: 6346 Highland Estate Dr Saint Louis MO 63129 Office: Continental Baking Co Checkerboard Sq Saint Louis MO 63164

GLASS, JAMES RICHARD, retired tire and rubber manufacturing company executive; b. Springfield, Ohio, Jan. 10, 1923; s. Stewart Burdette and Mary Catherine (Brunner) G.; m. Frieda Berta Hess, June 12, 1946; children: Michael Andrew, Timothy Joseph, James Thomas, John Edward. B.S. in Bus. Adminstrn., Ohio State U., 1948. Diplomate: C.P.A., Ohio, N.Y. Pres. Companhia Goodyear do Brasil, 1975-79, Motor Wheel Corp., Lansing, Mich., 1979-81; asst. to group exec. v.p. fin. Goodyear Tire & Rubber Co., Akron, 1982, v.p., comptroller, 1982, group exec. v.p., 1982, dir. group exec. v.p. fin. and planning, 1983-84, exec. v.p. fin. and planning, 1984-87; bd. dirs. Libbey-Owens Ford Co. Bd. dirs. YMCA, Akron, 1982—; bd. dirs. Akron Priority Corp., 1983-87, pres., 1985. Served with U.S. Army, 1943-45. Mem. Nat. Assn. Accts., Am. Inst. CPA's, Ohio Soc. CPA's. Roman Catholic. Club: Fairlawn Country. Lodge: K.C. Home: 1019 Bunker Dr Akron OH 44313

GLASS, JAMES WILLIAM, theatre pipe organ installer; b. Oak Park, Ill., Dec. 13, 1946; s. Louis James and Grace Marie (Whaples) G.; B.S. in Elec. Engring., Ill. Inst. Tech., 1968. Electronic design engr. in data communications Gen. Telephone & Electronic Automatic Electric Labs., Inc., Northlake, Ill., 1968-72; self-employed as theatre pipe organ installer, Hinsdale, Ill., 1972—. Mem. Audio Engring. Soc., Am. Theatre Organ Soc., Owl Cinema Organ Guild (pres., chmn. bd. 1971—), Soc. Motion Picture and TV Engrs., Eta Kappa Nu. Home: 7823 Eleanor Clarendon Hills IL 60514 Office: 29 E 1st St Hinsdale IL 60521

GLASS, KENNETH EDWARD, management consultant; b. Ft. Thomas, Ky., Sept. 28, 1940; s. Clarence E. and Lucille (Garrison) G.; m. Nancy Romanek, May 9, 1964; children—Ryan, Lara. M.E., U. Cin., 1963, M.S., 1965, grad. student, 1967. With Allis Chalmers Mfg. Co., Cin. and Eng., 1963-73; v.p. mfg. Fiat Allis Contrn. Machinery, Inc., Chgo., 1973-75; pres. Perkins Diesel Corp., Canton, Ohio, 1975-77; pres., chief exec. officer Massey-Ferguson, Inc., Des Moines, 1978, v.p., gen. mgr. N. Am. ops. Massey Ferguson Ltd., Des Moines, 1978; chmn., pres., chief exec. officer Union Metal Mfg. Co., Canton, Ohio, 1979-85; pres. K.E. Glass, Inc., 1985—; dir. Belden & Blake Oil Prodn., Inc. Trustee, Aultman Hosp. Mem. Young President's Orgn., ASME, Soc. Automotive Engrs. Patentee in field.

GLASS, RICHARD MCLEAN, psychiatry educator; b. Phoenix, Sept. 25, 1943; s. Richard Kirkpatrick and Harriet Margaret (Bradshaw) G.; m. Rita Mae Catherine Denk, Mar. 4, 1967; children: Kathryn, Brendan Neil. BA, Northwestern U., 1965, MD, 1968. Diplomate Am. Bd. Psychiatry and Neurology. Asst. prof. psychiatry U. Chgo., 1975-82, assoc. prof., 1982—; dir. adult psychiatry clinic U. Chgo., 1985—. Mem. editorial bd. Archives of Gen. Psychiatry, 1984—; contbr. numerous articles to profl. jours. Served to major U.S. Army, 1970-72. Mem. AAAS, AMA, Am. Psychiat. Assn. Presbyterian. Avocations: tennis, music, trombone. Office: U Chgo Dept Psychiatry Box 411 5841 S Maryland Chicago IL 60637

GLASS, ROB ROY, SR., manufacturing company executive; b. New London, Conn., Jan. 1, 1941; s. Thomas Eldred and Annabel (Montgomery) G.; m. Janet Elaine Wasson, Mar. 8, 1959 (div. Oct. 1981); children: Rob Roy Jr., Thomas Montgomery. Grad. high sch., Rome City, Ind., 1958. Owner Scotch Design & Mfg., Clearwater, Fla., 1969-74; chief engr. Autojectors, Inc., Albion, Ind., 1974-81; gen. mgr. Insert Molders, Inc., Brimfield, Ind., 1978-81; v.p. Union Products Internat., Cromwell, Ind., 1981—; insert molding cons. Teledyne Aerospace, Ford Aereospace, Gen. Motors Corp., 1974-80. Patentee refrigeration lampholders. Home and Office: 1246 Pleasant Point Rome City IN 46784

GLASSER, JAMES J., leasing company executive; b. Chgo., June 5, 1934; s. Daniel D. and Sylvia G.; m. Louise D. Rosenthal, Apr. 19, 1964; children: Mary, Emily, Daniel. A.B., Yale U., 1955; J.D., Harvard U., 1958. Bar: Ill. 1958. Asst. states atty. Cook County, Ill., 1958-61; mem. exec. staff GATX Corp., Chgo., 1961-69; pres. GATX Corp., 1974—, chmn. bd., chief exec. officer, 1978—, also dir.; gen. mgr. Infilco Products Co., 1969-70; v.p. GATX Leasing Corp., San Francisco, 1970-71, pres., 1971-74; dir. Harris Bankcorp, Inc., Harris Trust & Savs. Bank, Mut. Trust Life Ins. Co., Oak Brook, Ill., B.F. Goodrich Co., Stone Container Corp. Bd. dirs. Northwestern Meml. Hosp., Chgo., Michael Reese Hosp. and Med. Center.; trustee Chgo. Zool. Soc. Mem. Econ. Club Chgo., Chi Psi. Clubs: Casino (Chgo.), Chicago (Chgo.), Racquet (Chgo.), Tavern (Chgo.), Commercial (Chgo.); Onwentsia (Lake Forest, Ill.), Winter (Lake Forest, Ill.); Lake Shore Country (Glencoe, Ill.). Home: 644 E Spruce Ave Lake Forest IL 60045 Office: 120 S Riverside Plaza Chicago IL 60606

GLASSOCK, DANIEL LEWIS, computer programmer; b. St. Louis, Feb. 11, 1964; s. Roy VanDivere and Bonnie Karen (Adams) G. Lead data control clk. St. Louis U. Hosp., 1982-84, programmer analyst, 1984—; assoc. v.p. Prog. Systems Inc., St. Louis, 1985—. Designer computer programs on billing and marketing. Asst. scoutmaster Boy Scouts Am., St. Louis, 1985-87; choir mem. Tower Grove Bapt. Ch., St. Louis, 1985—, jr. choir tchr., 1986—. Recipient Worldwide Conservation award Boy Scouts Am., 1980; Brotherhood mem. Order of Arrow, Boy Scouts Am., 1979. Republican. Baptist. Office: St Louis U Hosp 1325 S Grand Saint Louis MO 63104

GLAUBER, ROBERT HASKELL, curator, author; b. N.Y.C., July 28, 1920; s. Lester and Lillian (Green) G. Student pub. schs. Editor, Alfred A. Knopf, Inc., N.Y.C., 1946-49, Decker Press, Prairie City, Ill., 1949-50; dir. pub. relations Nat. Assn. Bedding Mfrs., Chgo., 1951-58; writer pub. relations dept. Ill. Bell Telephone Co., Chgo., 1958-78, curator, 1958-78; curator AT&T, 1972-77; editor Beloit Poetry Jour., Wis., 1953-84; curator Union League Club, Chgo., 1982-84, First Ill. Bank, Evanston, 1981—, Sonnenschein Gallery, Lake Forest Coll., 1984—, Arthur Andersens' Co., Chgo., 1984—; writer art lit., lang. China and Japan, Ency. Brit. Jr., Chgo., 1965—; art critic Skyline, Art Scene, Chgo., 1967-75; instr. lit. Columbia Coll., Chgo., 1967-70; guest dir. Violence in Recent Am. Art, Mus. Contemporary Art, Chgo., 1968. Served with AUS, 1942-45. Recipient Chris award for documentary films Film Council Columbus, Ohio, 1962; writer Emmy-award- winning TV spls. Giants and the Common Man, 1968, From the Ashes, 1976. Contbr. articles to newspapers and lit. mags. Home: 424 W Melrose Chicago IL 60640

GLAUBERMAN, LIONEL, chemical company executive; b. Bklyn., June 5, 1930; s. Abe and Jean Glauberman; m. Bee Gilman, May 25, 1952; children: Susan, Steven. BS, Northeastern U., Boston, 1953. Div. mgr. Assembly Products Inc., Chesterland, Ohio, 1954-60; chmn. bd. Malco Products, Inc., Barberton, Ohio, 1960-82; pres. Lionel Industries, Akron, Ohio, 1982—; cons. Active Corp. Execs., Akron, 1982—; bd. dirs. Fixture Services, Cleve. Jewish. Avocation: golf. Office: 2035 Burlington Rd Akron OH 44313

GLAUCH, ALDEN GLENWOOD, retired air force officer; b. Traverse City, Mich., Nov. 14, 1919; s. Harold E. and Edna M. (Ebel) G.; m. Rhea E. Forton, Oct. 1, 1940; children: Alden W., Grant E., Cheri L. Student, Coll. Mines, El Paso, Tex., 1937-38, U. Md., Rhein Main AB, Fed. Republic Germany, 1950-51, U. Md., Washington, 1960-62. Commd. 2d lt. USAF, 1943, advanced through grades to maj. gen., 1973; squadron comdr., dep. comdr. Air Transport Group USAF, McGuire AFB, 1955-56; comdr. 55th Air Rescue Squadron USAF, Greenland, 1959; ops. officer in Pentagon USAF, 1960-65, dir. current ops. 22d Air Force, 1965; dir. ops. 834 Air div. USAF, Vietnam, 1968-69; chief staff ops. 21st Airforce USAF, McGuire AFB, 1969; comdr. 435th mil airlift support wing USAF, Rhein Main Air Base, Feb. Republic Germany, 1970; chief staff ops. mil. airlift command USAF, Scott AFB, Ill., 1971-75; comdr. 21st air force USAF, McGuire AFB, 1975-77; retired USAF; Pres. Whittler's Inc.; v.p. Port Traverse Constrn. Inc. Decorated DSM, DFC, Air Medal, Armed Forces Honor medal (Rep. Vietnam); recipient Silver Beaver award Boy Scouts Am. Mem. Nat. Def. Transp. Assn. (exec. com.), Air Force Assn., Nat. Fed. Post Office Clks. (v.p. Mich. 1946), Airlift Assn., VFW. Lutheran. Lodges: Daedalians, Rotary. Home: 414 Washington St Traverse City MI 49684

GLAZER, STANFORD PAUL FRANK, restauranteur; b. Kansas City, Mo., Jan. 1, 1932; s. Jack and Ella (Gitterman) G.; m. Rita Ann Studna, July 1, 1951 (div. June 1968); children—Craig, Jeffery, Jack; m. Cheryl Anne Hurley Sheehan, Feb. 12, 1978. Grad. Kemper Mil. Sch., 1949. Pres., Royal Automotive Parts Co., 1958-61, Sav-On Stores, Inc., 1960-62, Mid-West Automobile Auction Corp., 1962-65; exec. v.p. Allied Material Equipment Corp., 1965-70; pres. Kansas City Arena, Ltd., 1970-74, Stanford Glazer & Assocs., 1978-81; chief exec. officer Stanford & Sons, Inc., Kansas City, Mo., 1976—, Stanford & Sons of St. Louis. Fellow Harry S. Truman Library. Served with M.C., U.S. Army, 1952-54. Recipient Epicurean award Carte Blanche, 1976, 77; Good Dining award Am. Diners Soc., 1977, 78; Mobil Fine Dining award; Silver Spoon award Outlook Mag., 1980; rated "Top 1200 Restaurants in Am." in Jacques Pepin book. Mem. Nat. Restaurant Assn., Mo. Restaurant Assn. Jewish. Lodges: Masons, Shriners. Office: 504 Westport Rd Kansas City MO 64111

GLAZIER-WERNER, LESLIE ANN, advertising executive; b. Detroit, Feb. 9, 1953; d. Douglas Albert and Dolores Mary (Potter) Glazier; m. Allen Harvey Werner. BA in Psychology, U. Mich., 1978; MBA, U. Houston, 1983. Co-owner Aurora Solar Heating adn Insulation, Inc., Riverview, Mich., 1977-81; asst. acct. exec. Point Communications, Houston, 1981-82, account exec., 1982-83; asst. account exec. Ogilvy & Mather, Houston, 1984; advt. mgr. Zenith Data Systems, Glenview, Ill., 1985—. Home: 1217 S Wilke #104 Arlington Heights IL 60005 Office: Zenith Data Systems 1000 Milwaukee Ave Glenview IL 60025

GLAZZARD, CHARLES DONALDSON, psychiatrist; b. Cleve., Apr. 10, 1928; s. Charles Earl and Kathleen Hazel (Donaldson) G.; m. Margaret Hughes Leoni, Aug. 2, 1974; children by previous marriage—Charles F., Eric D., Kim E., Teri L.; stepchildren—Dan, Linda and Bill Leoni. Student, U. Miami, 1946-48; A.B., U. Mich., 1951, postgrad., 1951-52; M.D., Wayne State U., 1956. Diplomate Am. Bd. Psychiatry and Neurology. Comml. pilot, flight instr. Intern St. Vincents Hosp., Toledo, 1956-57; gen. practice medicine El Cajon, Calif., 1960-61; resident Menninger Sch. Psychiatry, Topeka, 1961-64; practice medicine specializing in psychiatry Kansas City, Mo., 1971-72, Olathe, Kans., 1974—; clin. asst. prof. psychiatry U. Kans. Med. Ctr., 1980—; med. dir. Midcontinent Psychiat. Hosp., 1972-74, Kans. Inst., Olathe, 1984-87; mem. staffs various hosps.; asst. sect. chief VA Hosp., Topeka, 1964-67; psychiatrist Forbes AFB, Topeka, 1967-71; acting med. dir. Johnson County Mental Health Ctr., Olathe, 1974-75, bd. dirs., 1976-79; dir. Psychiat. and Edn. Ctr. Olathe; mem. adv. com. Family Ct. of Johnson County, 1980. Mem. Olathe Human Relations Commn., 1974-77; bd. dirs. Cedar House, 1980. Served with USNR, 1958-60; qualified submarine med. officer. Fellow Am. Psychiat. Assn.; mem. Kans Psychiat. Soc. (pres. 1986-88), Mid Continent Psychiat. Assn., Pan Am. Med. Assn., World Med. Assn., AAAS, Royal Soc. Health, Am. Assn. Adminstrv. Psychiatry, Johnson County Med. Soc., Flying Physicians Assn., Airplane Owners and Pilots Assn. Lodge: Rotary. Home: 14301 Locust St Olathe KS 66062 Office: 407 Clairborne St Olathe KS 66062

GLEASON, DARLENE HARRIETTE, personnel staffing specialist; b. Wichita, Kans., Apr. 18, 1933; d. John Wilbur and Mildred Catherine (Zogleman) Garnett; m. Orval Lee Gleason, Nov. 22, 1953; children: Michael Lee, Michelle Catherine Gleason Wolf. AA in Elem. Edn., Wichita State U., 1952. Tchr. Ellsworth (Kans.) Elem. Sch., 1952-53; bookkeeper Wichita (Kans.) Fin. & Thrift, 1953-56; with payroll Coleman Co., Wichita, 1957-58, Aircapitol Mfg., Wichita, 1961-62; acctg. technician Dept. Air Force, Wichita, 1964-67; staffing asst. U.S. Office Personnel Mgmt., Wichita, 1967-76, personnel staffing specialist, 1976—. Fin. sec. Southwest Presbyn. Ch., Wichita, 1963-81, elder, 1970, trustee 1971-73, 1980-82, chmn. bd. trustees, 1973, 81, 82. Avocations: sewing, swimming, walking. Office: US Office Personnel Mgmt 120 S Market Wichita KS 67202

GLEASON, STEPHEN CHARLES, physician; b. Leon, Iowa, June 30, 1946; s. Charles Gerald and Ferne Louise (Pollard) G.; B.S., Iowa State U., 1971; D.Osteopathy, Coll. Osteo. Medicine and Surgery, 1974; m. Lisa Ann Corcoran, Aug. 22, 1981; children—Michael John, Timothy Charles, Christian Kelly, Sean Patrick, Keriann Louise. Resident in family practice, Meml. Med. Center, Corpus Christi, Tex., 1974-75; family practice medicine, West Des Moines, Iowa, 1975—; chmn. dept. family practice Mercy Hosp. Med. Center, Des Moines, 1979-82, dir. Mercy Health and Human Services, chief med. officer Mercy Clinic System, 1984; med. dir. West Suburban Center, West Des Moines; chief med. officer Mercy Clinic System; dep. med. examiner, Polk County, Des Moines, 1976-77; adj. clin. prof. family practice Coll. Osteo. Medicine and Surgery, Des Moines, 1979-86; regional med. adv. Emergency Med. Tng. Program Central Iowa, 1975-76; physician adv. Iowa Found. Med. Care, Profl. Standards Review Orgn., West Des Moines, 1978—; toxicology cons. Adolescent Detoxification Ctr., Mercy Hosp. Med. Ctr., 1986; dir. Our Primary Purpose, Inc., Family Health Plan; chmn. bd., pres. Valley Med. Services P.C. faculty instr. Iowa Heart Assn., Des Moines, 1978—; mem. papal med. security team Pope John Paul's Am. Pilgrimage, 1979. Chmn. Iowa CARES Med. Project, 1985, Dem. Nat. Health Policy Conf., 1987, Iowa Dem. Health Legislation Com., 1987; bd. dirs. Family Health Plan, Health Maintenance Orgn., 1985. Diplomate Am. Bd. Family Practice. Mem. Am. Acad. Med. Dirs., Am. Acad. Clin. Toxicology, Assn. Med. Educators and Researchers in Abuse, Am. Coll. Emergency Physicians, AMA, Am. Acad. Med. Dirs., Am. Acad. Clin. Toxicology, Assn. Med. Educators and Researchers in Substance Abuse, Iowa Acad. Sci., Iowa Med. Soc., Polk County Med. Soc., Sigma Alpha Epsilon, Sigma Sigma Phi. Democrat. Office: Valley West Mall Suite 106 West Des Moines IA 50265

GLEASON, THOMAS DAUES, shoe company executive; b. St. Louis, Jan. 24, 1936; s. Thomas J. and Hermine (Daues) G.; m. Sarah M. Santen, Feb. 6, 1960; children: Margaret E., Thomas Daues, J. Andrew, Anthony L. A.B., Holy Cross Coll., 1957; M.B.A., Harvard U., 1959. Co-founder, pres. Talent Assistance Program, Chgo., 1968-70; v.p. Wolverine World Wide, Inc., Rockford, Mich., 1970-72; pres. Wolverine World Wide, Inc., 1972-87, chief exec. officer, 1972—, chmn., 1980—. Bd. dirs. Grand Rapids Symphony Soc., 1974-83. Mem. Am. Footwear Industries Assn. (dir. 1973—), Harvard Bus. Sch. Assn. Chgo. (past v.p.). Clubs: Kent Country, Penisular (Grand Rapids). Office: Wolverine World Wide Inc 9341 Courtland Dr Rockford MI 49351

GLEASON, WALTER JAMES, psychologist; b. Chgo., Mar. 29, 1923; s. Walter James and Ethel Winifred (Beckman) G.; m. Josephine Colletti, June 13, 1949; children: Brian, Lydia, Laura. BS, Roosevelt U., 1949; MA, Northwestern U., 1951, PhD, 1953. Dir. Lakeland Counseling Ctr., Elkhorn, Wis., 1960-81; pvt. practice psychology Delavan, Wis., 1981—; vice chmn. Psychology Examining Bd., Madison, Wis., 1983-86. Served to capt. U.S. Army, 1951-59. Mem. Am. Psychol. Assn., Wis. Psychol. Assn. (pres. 1981-83). Home: Rt 3 Box 429 Delavan WI 53115 Office: PO Box 250 607 E Walworth Delavan WI 53115

GLEAVES, EARL WILLIAM, animal science educator; b. Miami, Okla., Apr. 3, 1930; s. Orville and Mattie L. (Able) G.; m. Lois D. Price, Dec. 30, 1950; children—Aloah, Kenneth, Dale. B.S., Okla. State U., 1953, M.S., 1961, Ph.D., 1965. Mgr., Williams Ranch, Santa Fe, 1953-56, Moneka Farm Stores, Parsons and Oswego, Kans., 1956-57; mem. faculty Okla. State U., Stillwater, 1962-63; mem. faculty U. Nebr., Lincoln, 1964—, prof. animal sci., poultry nutrition, 1973—. 4-H Club leader, 1965-75; active Partners of the Americas, 1979—. Ralston Purina Co. fellow, 1961; recipient Poultryman of Yr. award Nebr. Poultry Industries, 1971, Excellence in Programming award Nebr. Coop. Extension Service, 1979, Livestock Service award Walnut Grove Products, 1980. Mem. Poultry Sci. Assn. (Pfizer Extension award 1984), World Poultry Sci. Assn., Nebr. Coop. Extension Assn., Epsilon Sigma Phi, Gamma Sigma Delta (Extension award 1984). Democrat. Methodist. Contbr. numerous articles to profl. jours. Office: U Nebr Dept Animal Sci 105 Mussehl Hall East Lincoln NE 68583

GLEICH, GERALD JOSEPH, medical scientist; b. Escanaba, Mich., May 14, 1931; s. Gordon Joseph and Agnes (Ederer) G.; m. Elizabeth Louise Hearn, Aug. 16, 1955 (div. 1976); children: Elizabeth Genevieve, Martin Christopher, Julia Katherine; m. Kristin Marie Leiferman, Sept. 26, 1976; children: Stephen Joseph, David Francis, Caroline Louise. B.A., U. Mich., 1953, M.D., 1956. Diplomate: Am. Bd. Internal Medicine. Intern Phila. Gen. Hosp., 1956-57; resident Jackson Meml. Hosp., Miami, Fla., 1959-61; instr. in medicine and microbiology U. Rochester, N.Y., 1961-65; cons. in medicine, prof. immunology and medicine Mayo Clinic-Med. Sch., Rochester, Minn., 1965—; chmn. dept. immunology Mayo Clinic, Rochester, Minn., 1982—; mem. bd. sci. counselors Nat. Inst. Allergy and Infectious Disease, 1981-83; chmn. subcom. on standardization allergens WHO,

Geneva, 1974-75; lectr. Am. Acad. Allergy, 1976, 82; mem., chmn. immunological scis. study sect. NIH, 1984—. Contbr. articles on eosinophilic leukocyte to profl. jours. Served to capt. USAF, 1957-59. Grantee Nat. Inst. Allergy and Infectious Disease, 1970-86. Fellow ACP, Am. Acad. Allergy and Immunology; mem. Am. Soc. Clin. Investigation, Am. Assn. Immunologists, Assn. Am. Physicians, Phi Beta Kappa, Phi Kappa Phi, Alpha Omega Alpha. Roman Catholic. Home: 799 SW 3d St Rochester MN 55902 Office: Mayo Clinic Mayo Found 200 1st St SW Rochester MN 55905

GLEICHMAN, JOHN ALAN, safety and security executive; b. Anthoney, Kans., Feb. 11, 1944; s. Charles William and Caroline Elizabeth (Emch) G.; m. Martha Jean Cannon, July 1, 1966; 1 son, John Alan Jr. B.S. in Bus. Mgmt., Kans. State Tchrs. Coll., 1966. Cert. hazard control mgr.; cert. safety profl.; cert. safety exec. Office mgr. to asst. supt. Barton-Malow Co., Detroit, 1967-72, safety coordinator, 1972-76, corp. mgr. safety and security, 1976—; instr. U. Mich., Wayne State U., 1977-81; mem. constrn. safety standards commn. adv. com. for concrete constrn. and steel erection Bur. of Safety and Regulations, Mich. Dept. Labor, 1977—. Instr. multi media first aid ARC, 1976—; past trustee Apostolic Christian Ch., Livonia, Mich. Recipient Safety Achievement awards Mich. Mut. Ins. Co., 1979-83; Cameron award Constrn. sect. Indsl. div. Nat. Safety Conf., 1982. Mem. Mich. Safety Council (pres. 1984-85), Am. Soc. Safety Engrs. (pres. Detroit chpt. 1982, nat. adminstr.-elect constrn div. 1987, Safety Prof. of Yr. chpt. 1984) Nat. Safety Council (chmn. tech. rev. constrn. sect. indsl. div. 1980-84, chmn. standards com. indsl. div. 1983-85, chmn. assn. com. indsl. div. 1985-86, dir. tech. support com. indsl. div. 1986-87, bd. dirs. 1987-88, rep. Am. Nat. Standards Inst.), Am. Arbitration Assn. (panel arbitrators 1985). Author: (with others) You, The National Safety Council, and Voluntary Standards, 1981. Office: PO Box 5200 Detroit MI 48235

GLEICHMAN, KENTON CHARLES, dentist; b. Chelsae, Mass., Mar. 3, 1957; s. Richard Arthur and Patricia Ann (Meyers) G.; m. Cathy Lynn Cobb, Aug. 4, 1979; 1 child, Allison Lynn. BS, U. Iowa, 1979, DDS, 1983. Gen. gractice dentistry West Des Moines, 1983—. Basketball coach Sacred Heart Sch., West Des Moines, 1984, 85. Mem. ADA, Iowa Dental Assn., Des Moines Dist. Dental Soc. Roman Catholic. Club: G.U. Black Study. Avocations: golf, tennis, wood refinishing, gardening, photography. Office: 1300 37th St West Des Moines IA 50265

GLEISS, HENRY WESTON, lawyer; b. Detroit, Nov. 22, 1928; s. George Herman and Mary Elizabeth (Weston) G.; m. Joan Bette Christopher, July 23, 1955; children—Kent G., Keith W. B.A., Denison U., 1951; J.D., U. Mich., 1954. Bar: Mich. 1955, U.S. Dist. Ct. (ea. dist.) Mich. 1955, U.S. Dist. Ct. (we. dist.) Mich. 1960, U.S. Ct. Appeals (6th cir.) 1964, U.S. Supreme Ct. 1967. Sole practice, Benton Harbor, Mich., 1957-61; ptnr. Globensky, Gleiss & Bittner, St. Joseph, 1961—; spl. asst. atty. gen. Mich., 1960—. Officer Jaycees, Mich.; bd. dirs. United Fund. Served with U.S. Army, 1955-57. Mem. ABA, Mich. Bar Assn., Berrien County Bar Assn. (pres. 1974), Assn. Trial Lawyers Am., Twin Cities C. of C. (v.p. 1975). Congregationalist. Clubs: Kiwanis, Moose (Benton Harbor); Economic of S.W. Mich.; Elks (St. Joseph). Home: 1224 Miami Benton Harbor MI 49022 Office: 610 Ship St PO Box 290 Saint Joseph MI 49085

GLEN, JEFFREY DAVID, dentist, inventor; b. Boston, June 22, 1958; s. Lester Nathaniel and Eileen (Rosenson) G.; m. Robin Sue Goldberg, June 23, 1985. BA, Boston U., 1980; DDS, Northwestern U., 1984. Gen. practice dentistry Chgo., 1984-86; staff dentist Chgo. Osteo. Hosp., 1986—; dental dir. geriatric outreach Chgo. Osteo. Hosp., 1986—; cons., lectr. med. assistance tng. program Ill. Dept. Pub. Aid U. Chgo., 1985—; dentist Headstart, Chgo., 1984—. Patentee in field. Mem. Simon Wiesenthal Ctr., 1984. Mem. ADA, Chgo. Dental Soc., Am.-Israel Pub. Affairs Com. Jewish. Avocations: reading, fishing, tennis, skiing, camping. Home: 1380 E Hyde Park Blvd #620 Chicago IL 60615 Office: Chgo Osteo Hosp 5200 S Ellis Chicago IL 60615

GLENN, JOHN HERSCHEL, JR., U.S. Senator; b. Cambridge, Ohio, July 18, 1921; s. John Herschel and Clara (Sproat) G.; m. Anna Margaret Castor, Apr. 1943; children: Carolyn Ann, John David. Student, Muskingum Coll., 1939-42, B.Sc., 1962; naval aviation cadet, U. Iowa, 1942; grad. flight sch., Naval Air Tng. Center, Corpus Christi, Tex., 1943, Navy Test Pilot Tng. Sch., Patuxent River, Md., 1954. Commd. 2d lt. USMC, 1943, assigned 4th Marine Aircraft Wing, Marshall Islands campaign, 1944, assigned 9th Marine Aircraft Wing, 1945-46; with 1st Marine Aircraft Wing, North China Patrol, also Guam, 1947-48; flight instr. advanced flight tng. Corpus Christi, 1949-51; asst. G-2/G-3 Amphibious Warfare Sch., Quantico, Va., 1951; with Marine Fighter Squadron 311, exchange pilot 25th Fighter Squadron USAF, Korea, 1953; project officer fighter design br. Navy Bur. Aero. Washington, 1956-69; astronaut Project Mercury, Manned Spacecraft Center NASA, 1959-64; pilot Mercury-Atlas 6 orbital space flight launched from Cape Canaveral, Fla., Feb., 1962; ret. as col. 1964; v.p. corp. devel. and dir. Royal Crown Cola Co., 1966-74; U.S. Senator from, Ohio, 1975—. Co-author: We Seven, 1962; Author: P.S., I Listened to Your Heart Beat. Trustee Muskingum Coll. Decorated D.F.C. (five), Air medal (18), Astronaut medal USMC, Navy unit commendation; Korean Presidential unit citation; Distinguished Merit award Muskingum Coll.; Medal of Honor N.Y.C.; Congl. Space Medal of Honor, 1978. Mem. Soc. Exptl. Test Pilots, Internat. Acad. of Astronautics (hon.). Democrat. Presbyn. First supersonic transcontinental Flight, July 16, 1957. Office: US Senate 503 Hart Senate Bldg Washington DC 20510

GLENNEN, ROBERT EUGENE, JR., university president; b. Omaha, Mar. 31, 1933; s. Robert E. and La Verda (Elledge) G.; m. Mary C. O'Brien, Apr. 17, 1958; children: Maureen, Bobby, Colleen, Billy, Barry, Katie, Molly, Kerry. A.B., U. Portland, 1955, M.Ed., 1957; Ph.D., U. Notre Dame, 1962. Asst. prof. U. Portland, 1956-60; asst. prof., assoc. prof. Eastern Mont. Coll., Billings, 1962-65; assoc. dean U. Notre Dame, South Bend, Ind., 1965-72; dean, v.p. U. Nev.-Las Vegas, 1972-80; pres. Western N.Mex. U., Silver City, 1980-84, Emporia State U., Kans, 1984—; cons. HEW, Washington, 1964-84. Author: Guidance: An Orientation, 1966. Contbr. articles to profl. jours. Pres. PTA, South Bend, Ind., 1970-71; bd. trustees Am. Coll. Testing Corp., Iowa City, 1977-80; chmn. Kans. Regents Council of Presidents. Named Coach of Yr. Coach & Athletic Mag., 1958; Ford Found. fellow, 1961-62. Mem. Kans. C. of C. (bd. dirs.), Emporia C. of C. (bd. dirs.), Am. Personnel and Guidance Assn., Am. Assn. State Colls. and Univs., Am. Assn. Higher Edn., Nev. Personnel and Guidance Assn., Assn. Counselor Educators and Suprs., Am. Assn. Counseling and Devel., Nat. Assn. Student Personnel Adminstrs.,. Republican. Roman Catholic. Avocations: racketball, walking, reading; hiking. Office: Emporia State U Pres Office Emporia KS 66801

GLENNER, RICHARD ALLEN, dentist, dental historian; b. Chgo., Apr. 14, 1934; s. Robert Joseph and Vivian (Prosk) G.; B.S., Roosevelt U., 1955; B.S. in Dentistry, U. Ill., 1958, D.D.S., 1959; m. Dorothy Chapman, July 13, 1957; children—Mark Steven, Alison. Gen. practice dentistry, Chgo., 1962—; cons. on dental history to Smithsonian Instn., ADA, various corps., libraries, univs., museums, dental jours.; lectr. in field. Served to capt. AUS, 1960-62. Mem. Am., Ill. dental assns., Chgo. Dental Soc., Assn. Mil. Surgeons U.S., Am. Acad. History of Dentistry (historian 1984, chmn. Smithsonian Instn. adv. group 1987, Hayden-Harris award 1983), Fed. Dentaire Internationale, Am. Med. Writers Assn., Sci. Instrument Soc., Alpha Omega. Author: The Dental Office: A Pictorial History; cons. editor A Bicentennial Salute to Am. Dentistry, 1976; contbr. articles on dental history to profl. jours. Home: 6715 N Lawndale Ave Lincolnwood IL 60645 Office: 3414 W Peterson Ave Chicago IL 60659

GLENNER, ROBERT JOSEPH, obstetrician, gynecologist; b. Chgo., July 3, 1909; s. Jacob and Sarah Mary (Joseph) G.; m. Vivian Prosk, June 14, 1931 (dec. Jan. 1979); children: Richard Allen, Gary Marvin, Stuart Michael, Jeanne Frances Glenner Adis. BS, U. Ill., Chgo., 1929, MD, 1931. Diplomate Am. Bd. Ob-Gyn. Intern Binghamton (N.Y.) City Hosp., 1931-32, Los Angeles County Gen. Hosp., 1932-33; residency in obstetrics Chgo. Lying-In Hosp., 1933-46; attending staff Cook County Hosp., Chgo., 1946-60; chmn., dept. chief ob-gyn Edgewater Hosp., Chgo., 1947-53; assoc. prof. dept. ob-gyn U. Ill., Chgo., 1943-77; clin. cons. ob-gyn Chgo. Bd. Health, 1976—; cons. ob-gyn Edgewater Hosp, Chgo., 1933-74, Am. Hosp., Chgo., 1933-74; clin. researcher U. Ill. Hosp., 1943-74. Inventor, patentee hysterectomy forceps and retractors, 1951; produced early electronic fetal heart monitor, 1958. Served to capt. M.C. 2d inf., U.S. Army, 1944-46. Founding fellow Am. Coll. Ob-Gyn (life); fellow Internat. Coll. Surgeons, Am. Soc. Abdominal Surgeons; mem. AMA (fifty yr. club, Cert. Merit), Ill. State Med. Soc., Chgo. Med. Soc. Avocations: stamp and coin collecting, autographed first-edition book collecting. Home: 3180 N Lake Shore Dr 21C Chicago IL 60657 Office: Chgo Bd Health 845 W Wilson Ave Chicago IL 60640

GLENSKI, JOSEPH WILLIAM, computer company executive; b. Kansas City, Mo., 1961; s. James L. and Mary H. Glenski. BA magna cum laude, St. Mary's Coll., Winona, Minn., 1983; postgrad., Coll. St. Thomas, St. Paul, 1984—. Network engr. NCR Comten, St. Paul, 1983-87; performance analyst Cray Research, St. Paul, 1987—. Scoutmaster, dist. com. Boy Scouts Am., St. Paul, 1980—; instr. first-aid ARC, 1981—. Avocations: canoeing, camping, reading.

GLESNE, RONALD LEE, marketing executive; b. Elkader, Iowa, Mar. 29, 1935; s. Raymond Oliver and Myrtle (Josephine) G.; m. Gloria Elaine Lenning, Feb. 10, 1968; 1 dau., Michelle Marie. BS, U. Iowa, 1957. Sales rep. Mobil Oil Co., Mpls., 1957-62; dist. sales mgr. Velie Sales Inc., Mpls., 1962-65; v.p., ptnr. G & D Sales, Inc., Mpls., 1965-71; v.p. Midwest Mktg., Inc., Mpls., 1971-75; pres. Glesne Sales Inc., Mpls., 1975—. Served with AUS, 1958-60. Mem. Sales & Mktg. Execs. (dir. 1979-80 Mpls.), Auto Booster Club, Auto Affiliated Reps. (dir. 1982-84), Auto Parts and Accessories Assn., N.W. Hardware Housewares Club. Republican. Lutheran. Lodges: Masons, Shriners. Home: 1470 Cherry Pl Orono MN 55364 Office: Glesne Sales Inc 6121 Baker Rd Minnetonka MN 55345

GLESSNER, JAMES ROGER, III, insurance broker; b. Phila., Mar. 1, 1947; s. Jame Roger Jr. and Wilhelmina (Schaefe) G.; m. Mary Katherine DeVries, Oct. 22, 1966 (div. June 1976); 1 child, James Robert. BBA, U. Ark., 1971. Pvt. investigator Myers and Assocs., Little Rock, 1973-74; ins. adjuster Aetna Casualty, Grand Rapids, 1974-76, INA, Grand Rapids, 1976-78, Glessner Agy., Grand Rapids, 1979-81; broker Glessner Group Inc., Grand Rapids, 1984—, also bd. dirs.; cons. Talsma and Assocs., Grand Rapids, 1984. Vol. Pine Rest Christian Hosp., Grand Rapids, 1980,81, Bloogett Meml. Hosp., Grand Rapids, 1964. Served with U.S. Army, 1976-68, Vietnam. Decorated Cross of Gallantry. Mem. Life Underwriters, VFW, Am. Legion, Nat. Wildlife Fedn. Republican. Club Chess (Grad Rapids) (pres. 1965). Avocations: fishing, volleyball, sketching.

GLEUE, LORINE ANNA, teacher; b. Lucas, Kans., Feb. 12, 1926; d. Otto Martin and Bertha Marie (Luker) Becker; m. Fred Christoph Gleue, June 12, 1947; children: David Jean, Steven Randolph, Paul Frederick. BS in Edn., Ft. Hays (Kans.) State U., 1971; MS in Elementary Edn., Ft. Hays State U., 1977; reading specialist degree, Kans. State U., 1984. Cert. tchr., Kans. Elementary tchr. Coffey County, Kans., 1944-47; librarian Belleville (Kans.) Pub. Library, 1960-67, Carnegie Free Pub. Library, Concordia, Kans., 1967-68; elementary tchr. Chester, Nebr., 1971-72, Washington (Kans.) Unified Sch. Dist. #222, 1972-75; Chpt. I program instr. Washington, Kans., 1975—. Published poet; contbr. articles to profl. jours. Mem. book selection com. Kans. State Reading Circle, Topeka, 1979-80. Recipient Golden Poet award 3d Ann. Poetry Conv., Las Vegas, Nev., for poem Long Distance, 1987. Mem. PTO (Kans. Govs. Leadership Commendation 1979, 81), NEA, Kans. Edn. Assn., Kans. Tchrs. Assn. (pres. Washington chpt. 1977-81, Citation of Appreciation 1979, 80), Internat. Reading Assn. (Kans. div.). Avocations: reading, travel, originating scripts for 35mm slide presentation.

GLICK, CYNTHIA SUSAN, lawyer; b. Sturgis, Mich., Aug. 6, 1950; d. Elmer Joseph and Ruth Edna (McCally) G. A.B., Ind. U., 1972; J.D., Ind. U.-Inpls., 1978. Bar: Ind. 1978, U.S. Dist. Ct. (so. dist.) Ind. 1978, U.S. Dist. Ct. (no. dist.) Ind. 1981. Adminstrv. asst. Gov. Otis R. Bowen, Ind., 1973-76; law clk. Ind. Ct. Appeals, 1976-79; dep. pros. atty. 35th Jud. Cir., LaGrange County, Ind., 1980-82, pros. atty., 1983—. Campaign aide Ind. Rep. State Cen. Com., Indpls., 1972-73. Named Hon. Speaker, Ind. Ho. of Reps., 1972, Sagamore of the Wabash, Gov. Ind., 1974. Fellow Ind. Bar Found.; mem. ABA, Am. Judicature Soc., Ind. State Bar Assn., LaGrange County Bar Assn. (pres. 1983-86), DAR, Delta Zeta. Republican. Methodist. Lodge: Eastern Star. Home: 113 W Spring St LaGrange IN 46761 Office: Office of Prosecuting Atty LaGrange County Ct House LaGrange IN 46761

GLICK, MILTON DON, chemist, university administrator; b. Memphis, July 30, 1937; s. Lewis S. and Sylvia (Kleinman) G.; m. Peggy M., June 21, 1965; children—David, Sander. A.B. cum laude, Augustana Coll., 1959; Ph.D., U. Wis., 1965. Fellow, dept. chemistry Cornell U., Ithaca, N.Y., 1964-66; asst. prof. chemistry Wayne State U., Detroit, 1966-70, asso. prof., 1970-74, prof., 1974-83, chmn. dept., 1978-83; dean arts and sci. U. Mo.-Columbia, 1983—. Co-founder, pres. Congregation T'Chiyah, 1977-79. Mem. Am. Chem. Soc., Am. Crystallographic Assn. Contbr. articles in structural inorganic chemistry to profl. jours. Office: Univ of Mo Coll of Arts & Scis 210 Jesse Hall Columbia MO 65211

GLICK, PHILLIP RAY, animal health products company executive, veterinarian; b. Columbus, Ohio, June 17, 1940; s. Phil D. and and Bernice Grace (Shasteen) G.; m. Pam. C. Calderone, Oct. 10, 1983 (div. June 1982); children: Kathryn, Julia, Phillip. DVM, Ohio State U., 1964; postgrad. in pathology, U. Ill., 1968-69. Pvt. practice vet. medicine Quakertown, Pa., 1964-67; staff vet. 3M Co., 1968-71; mgr. new products Pitman-Moore, Washington Crossing, N.J., 1971-74, v.p. devel. mktg., 1974-79; gen. mgr. Pitman-Moore Can., Scarborough, Ont., 1979-81; gen. mgr. animal health Boehringer Ingelheim Animal Health, Inc., Ridgefield, Conn., 1981; exec. v.p. comml. affairs Boehringer Ingelheim Animal Health, Inc., St. Joseph, Mo., 1981—, also bd. dirs.; pub. relations com. Animal Health Inst., Washington. Author various articles on animal care, vet. edn. Patron Performing Arts, St. Joseph; bd. dirs. St. Joseph C. of C.; sec./treas. Donovan Downs Homeowners Assn., St. Joseph; chmn. leadership com. United Way. Mem. Am. Vet. Med. Assn., Mo. Vet. Assn. of Indsl. Veterinarians, Nat. Indsl. Veterinarians Assn., St. Joseph C. of C. (agriculture com. 1984—), Am. Vet. Distbrs. Assn. (continuing edn. com. 1984—). Republican. Presbyterian. Club: St. Joseph Ad, St. Joseph Country. Home: 8 Donovan Dr Saint Joseph MO 64505 Office: Boehringer Ingelheim Inc 2621 N Belt Hwy Saint Joseph MO 64502

GLICKFIELD, BARNETT WEIL, computer science educator; b. N.Y.C., Sept. 29, 1939; s. Henry Louis and Celia (Rich) G. BA, Cornell U., 1959; MA in Math., Columbia U., 1960, PhD, 1964; JD, U. Wash., 1976. Bar: Wash. 1977, U.S. Ct. Appeals (9th cir.) 1977. Benjamin Pierce instr. math. Harvard U., Cambridge, Mass., 1964-67; asst. prof. Rockefeller U., N.Y.C., 1969-72, U. Wash., Seattle, 1967-76; staff atty. King County Pub. Defender, Seattle, 1977-80; sr. computer analyst Control Data Corp., Seattle, 1981-84; assoc. prof. computer sci. No. Ill. U., DeKalb, 1985—; invited lectr. Stanford U., Palo Alto, Calif., 1978, Boalt Hall, Berkeley, Calif., 1978. Contbr. articles to profl. jours. Mem. ABA, Wash. State Bar. Assn. (sect. on sci. and tech.). Jewish. Office: No Ill U Dept Computer Sci DeKalb IL 60115

GLICKMAN, DANIEL ROBERT, congressman; b. Wichita, Kans., Nov. 24, 1944; s. Milton and Gladys Anne (Kopelman) G.; m. Rhoda Joyce Yura, Aug. 21, 1966; children: Jonathan, Amy. B.A., U. Mich., Ann Arbor, 1966; J.D., George Washington U., Washington, 1969. Bar: Kans. 1969, Mich. 1970. Trial atty. SEC, 1969-70; assoc., then ptnr. Sargent, Klenda & Glickman, Wichita, 1971-76; mem. 95th-100th Congresses from 4th Kans. Dist.; chmn. subcom. on wheat, soybeans and feed grains, Com. Agricultur, mem. Judiciary, Sci. Space and Tech. coms. Mem. Wichita Bd. Edn., 1973-76, pres., 1975-76. Mem. Order of Coif, Phi Delta Phi, Sigma Alpha Mu. Democrat. Jewish. Office: 1212 Longworth Washington DC 20515

GLICKMAN, LOUIS, industrial sewing equipment manufacturing company executive; b. Chgo., June 7, 1933; s. Michael C. and Florence (Leibov) G.; m. Donna B. Horwitz, Mar. 18, 1962; children: Steven L., Daniel B. B.S., U. Ill., 1955; LL.B., John Marshall Law Sch., 1961. Bar: Ill. 1962. Acct. Inland Steel Co., Chgo., 1955-63; tax mgr. Helene Curtis Industries, Inc., Chgo., 1963-67; treas. J.I. Case Co., Racine, Wis., 1967-85, Union Spl. Corp., Chgo., 1985—; dir. First Am. Nat. Bank, Wausaw, Wis. Mem. adv. com. Pub. Expenditure Survey of Wis., 1977-83. Mem. Ill. Bar Assn., Chgo. Bar Assn., Nat. Assn. Corp. Treas. Home: 310 Sumac Rd Highland Park IL 60035 Office: 400 N Franklin St Chicago IL 60610

GLIEBERMAN, HERBERT ALLEN, lawyer; b. Chgo., Dec. 6, 1930; s. Elmer and Jean (Gerber) G.; m. Evelyn Eraci; children—Ronald, Gale, Joel. Student, U. Ill., 1947, Roosevelt U., 1948-50; J.D., Chgo. Kent Coll. Law, 1953. Bar: Ill. 1954. Pvt. practice Chgo., 1954—; lectr. Chgo. Kent. Coll. Law, Ill. Inst. Continuing Legal Edn. Author: Some Syndromes of Love, 1965; Know Your Legal Rights, 1974; Confessions of A Divorce Lawyer, 1975; Closed Marriage, 1978; Four Weekends to an Ideal Marriage, 1981. Trustee Chgo. Kent. Coll. Law; bd. dirs. Chgo. Council on Alcoholism. Mem. Am. Acad. Matrimonial Lawyers (cert. of appreciation 1967), Decologue Soc. Lawyers (cert. of appreciation 1965, 66, 68), Assn. Trial Lawyers Am. (cert. of appreciation 1973), Ill. Trial Lawyers Assn. (cert. of appreciation 1974), ABA, Ill. State Bar Assn., Chgo. Bar Assn. Jewish (bd. dirs., pres. Temple). Home: 180 E Pearson St Chicago IL 60611 Office: 19 S LaSalle St Chicago IL 60603

GLISAN, ELLEN MCPEEK, publishing executive; b. Freeport, Ill., June 27, 1955; d. Kenneth Anthony and Manie Ellen (Spencer) McPeek; m. Roger Mason Glisan, Jan. 29, 1977; children: Abigail Lane, Rebecca Jane. BEd, Ill. State U., 1976; MA in Learning Disabilities, No. Ill. U., 1981. Cert. elem., secondary spl. edn. tchr., Ill. Spl. edn. tchr. Orangeville (Ill.) High Sch., 1977-80, Freeport (Ill.) High Sch., 1980-82; endl. pub. Peekan Pubs. Inc., Freeport, 1980—. Author workbooks, texts, kits for special edn. Mem. N.W. Ill. chpt. Women in Mgmt., Freeport Mgmt. Assn., Freeport C. of C. Office: Peekan Pubs Inc PO Box 513 Freeport IL 61032

GLOBOKE, JOSEPH RAYMOND, accountant; b. Kansas City, Kans., Mar. 9, 1955; s. Anthony Joseph and Loretta Margaret (Bartkoski) G.; m. Debra Ruth Neumann, Nov. 13, 1982; 1 child, Theresa Renee. BSBA, Rockhurst Coll., 1977. CPA, Mo. Intern Ernst & Whinney, Kansas City, Mo., 1976-77; mgr. Troupe Kehoe Whiteaker & Kent, Kansas City, 1977—. Mem. Mo. Soc. CPA's, Am. Inst. CPA's,. Roman Catholic. Club: Victory Hills Country, Kansas City, Kans. Avocations: reading, fishing, working in yard, woodworking, golf. Home: 16 N 80th Pl Kansas City KS 66111 Office: Troupe Kehoe Whiteaker & Kent 900 Penntower Office Ctr 3100 Broadway Kansas City MO 64111

GLODNY, HENRY FELIX, computer programmer, analyst; b. Chgo., Dec. 24, 1959; s. Felix T. and Bernice Barbara (Majerowicz) G. BS in Engring. Mgmt., U. Ill., Chgo., 1982, MBA, 1984; postgrad. in info. systems, Roosevelt U., 1987—. Programmer, analyst Motorola, Inc., Schaumburg, Ill., 1984—, data security analyst, 1985-86. Mem. Beta Gamma Sigma. Republican. Roman Catholic. Avocations: radio communications monitoring, mystery literature. Office: Motorola Inc 1301 E Algonquin Rd Schaumburg IL 60196

GLOMMEN, HARVEY HAMILTON, social work consultant, counselor; b. Suttons Bay, Mich., Mar. 25, 1928; s. Lars Louis and Serena Sadie (Rorem) G.; B.A., Concordia Coll., 1953; postgrad. U. Minn., 1953-54, 60, 61, 62, U. Chgo., summer 1959; M.S.W., U. Mich., 1964; m. Ina Mae Wollertson, June 24, 1951; children—Brent, Barbara, Beth, Brenda. Social worker Hennepin and Anoka counties (Minn.) Welfare Bds., 1954-58; county welfare dir. Cottonwood County (Minn.) Welfare Dept., Windom, 1959-60; dir. Aitkin County (Minn.) Welfare Dept., Aitkin, 1960-63; tng. cons. for exec., supervisory tng. Minn. Dept. Pub. Welfare, St. Paul, 1964-65, supr. adoptions, 1965-66; dir. foster grandparents program Adminstrn. Aging, HEW, Washington, 1966-67; exec. dir. Minn. Assn. Retarded Citizens, Mpls., 1967-69; practice marriage and family counseling, cons. in human service, Mpls., 1972—; foster parent for mentally ill adults, 1975—; incorporator, pres. Our Place, emotionally disturbed facility, Blaine, 1977—; owner Circus Candy Co., Mpls., 1972-85, 1048 87th Ave NE, Blaine, Minn., 1968—; instr. clock repair, St. Paul, 1981—. Mem. city charter commn., Blaine, 1974-82; chmn. Blaine City Charter Commn., 1976-79; mem. constn. commn. Minn. Dem.-Farmer-Labor Party, 1976-78, fin. dir. Minn. Senate Dist. 47, 1975-78, chmn., 1978-80; treas. Anoka County Assn. for Retarded Citizens, 1969-71, bd. dirs., 1969-72; bd. dirs., incorporator Anoka County Family Service Assn., 1970-72; incorporator, pres. Anoka County Mental Health Advocates Coalitions, 1982-84; mem. Anoka County Health and Human Services Bd., 1983—; mem. Anoka County Mc Knight Mental Health Consortium, 1983—, chmn. residential services com., 1983-85; v.p. Care Van Doon-la-Doon Transp., 1985—; bd. dirs. Care Bus, 1986—. Served to 1st lt. AUS, 1946-50; Germany. Minn. Tng. fellow, 1963. Mem. Nat. Assn. Watch and Clock Collectors, Minn. Watchmakers Assn. (bd. dirs. 1985—), Minn. Clockmakers (chmn. examining com. 1985—) Phi Kappa Phi. Democrat. Lutheran (youth bd. 1970-73, ch. council 1970-73, pres. congregation 1982-84). Home: 1048 87th Ave NE Blaine MN 55434 Office: 915 Hwy 10 Blaine MN 55434

GLOMP, JOSEPH LOUIS, electronics executive; b. Chgo., Apr. 6, 1946; s. Louis and Mary Victoria (Lagowski) G.; m. Donna Lenore Tong, July 30, 1967; children: David, Dawn. Student, Wright Jr. Coll., Chgo., 1965-66; AA, Coll. DuPage, Glen Ellyn, Ill., 1973; student, Elmhurst Coll., 1974. Customer service rep., draftsman Watrous, Inc., Bensenville, Ill., 1964-66; prodn. mgr. Reed Devices, Inc., Carol Stream, Ill., 1970-80; v.p. mfg. Augat/Reed Devices, Carol Stream, 1980—; instr. Midwest Indsl. Mgmt. Assn., Westchester, Ill., 1979-80. Served with USN, 1967-70. Mem. Mfg. Mgrs. Assn., Soc. Mfg. Engrs. Avocation: gardening.

GLORIOSO, SALVATORE JOSEPH, optometrist; b. Chgo., Feb. 16, 1915; s. Pasquale and Theresa (Cernglia) G.; children: Charles, Raymond, Theo, Regina. OD, No. Ill. Coll. Optometry, 1937. Pvt. practice optometry Northlake, Ill., 1937—. Served with USMC, 1941-44. Office: 40 E North Ave Northlake IL 60164

GLOSSBERG, JOSEPH BERKSON, investment counsellor; b. Chgo., Apr. 2, 1941; s. J. William and Pearl (Berkson) G.; children: Jonathon William, David Louis. BS in Econs., U. Pa., 1963, MBA in Fin., 1965. Charted fin. analyst, investment counselor. Pres. med. research inst. council Michael Reese Hosp. and Med. Ctr., Chgo., 1972-74, bd. dirs., 1977—. Mem. investment bd. U. Pa., chmn. pres.' council midwest devel. com., bd. dirs. alumni council on admission, 1977-78, trustee, 1979-84; trustee Chgo. Found. Hearing and Speech Rehab. Mem. Fin. Analysts Fedn. Am., Investment Counsel Assn. Am., Investment Analysts Soc. Chgo., U. pa. Alumni Assn. Chgo. (pres. 1974-79). Republican. Clubs: Standard (bd. dirs.), City, Lake Shore Country (Glencoe, Ill.); New Buffalo Rod and Gun; Princeton N.Y.; Penn Football (bd. dirs.). Home: 1303 N Sutton Pl Chicago IL 60610 Office: 401 N Michigan Ave Chicago IL 60611

GLOVER, ERIC FRANKLIN, financial executive; b. Miami, Okla., Jan. 17, 1961; s. Robert F. and Anna Lue (Anderson) G.; m. Tina M. Helmig, Aug. 21, 1981; 1 child: Zachary Ryan. AA, Northeastern Okla. A&M Coll., 1981; BBA, Mo. So. State U., 1983. CPA, Mo. Staff acct. Baird, Kurtz & Dobson, Joplin, Mo., 1983-86; v.p. fin. Able Body Corp., Joplin, 1986—. Mem. Am. Inst. CPA's, Mo. Soc. CPA's, Nat. Assn. Accts., Am. Mgmt. Assn., Nat. Truck Equipment Assn., Mo. Motor Carriers Assn., U.S. Jaycees, Omicron Delta Epsilon (v.p. 1983). Republican. Baptist. Club: Diplomats (Joplin). Avocations: golf, hunting, fishing, skiing. Home: 2414 Molly Ln Miami MO 74354 Office: Able Body Corp 3400 W 7th St Joplin MO 64801

GLOVER, JAY (JULIANNE) CLEMENS, controller; b. Brighton, Mich.; d. William James Clemens and Jane Stella (Swiatowski) Swiatek; m. David Earl Glover, Apr. 2, 1962 (div. Mar. 1981); children: Matthew, Marjorie, Mark, Brett, Marcia. BA, Wayne State U., 1963, MBA, 1980. Cost acct. Gen Motors Corp., Detroit, 1979-83; fin. analyst Uniroyal Tire Co., Troy, Mich., 1984-86; asst. controller Gale Research, Detroit, 1986—; pvt. fin. cons., Livonia, Mich., 1983—. Pres. Livonia Rep. Women, 1975-77; vice chmn. Livonia Rep. Party, 1977-79, 83-85; bd. dirs. Friends of the Livonia Pub. Library, 1982-84. Mem. Fin. Mgmt. Assn., Nat. Assn. Accts., Women's Econ. Club (pub. relations com. 1986—), Livonia C. of C. (com. mem.), Beta Gamma Sigma, Alpha Lamba Delta. Avocations: aerobics, cross-country skiing, gardening, golfing, sailing. Home: 32292 Auburn Birmingham MI 48009

GLOVER, REBECCA NEWBERRY, accountant; b. Northville, Mich., Mar. 21, 1953; d. Marvin Henry and Clara Lorene (Cannady) Newberry; m. Harry James Glover, June 11, 1977; children: Phillip Braden, Luke Benjamin, Candace Rene. AA, Mich. Christian Coll., 1973; BA in Acctg., Walsh Coll., 1980. CPA, Mich. Bookkeeper Mich. Christian Coll., Rochester, 1973-77; sr. acct. Gross, Bornstein, Grey & Co. P.C., Birmingham, Mich., 1978—. Mem. Am. Inst. CPA's, Mich. Assn. CPA's, Am. Women's Soc. CPA's. Mem. Ch. of Christ. Avocations: reading, knitting, bowling. Office: Gross Bornstein Grey & Co PC 30100 Telegraph #420 Birmingham MI 48010

GLOWACKI, T. M., provincial judge. Judge Ct. of Queen's Bench, Winnipeg, Man., Can. Office: Court of Queen's Bench, Law Courts Bldg, Winnipeg, MB Canada R3C 0V8 *

GLOWER, DONALD DUANE, university dean, mechanical engineer; b. Shelby, Ohio, July 29, 1926; s. Raymond W.W. and Irva (Scheerer) G.; m. Betty Stahl, June 18, 1953; children: Donald, Michel, Leilani, Jacob. B.S., U.S. Mcht. Marine Acad., 1946, Antioch Coll., 1953; M.S., Iowa State U., 1958, Ph.D. (NSF fellow), 1960. Engring. officer Grace Lines, Inc., San Francisco, 1947-49; research engr. Battelle Meml. Inst., Columbus, Ohio, 1953-54; asst. prof. Coll. Engring., Iowa State U., 1954-58, 60-61; mem. research staff Sandia Corp., Albuquerque, 1961-63; head radiation effects dept. Gen. Motors Corp., Milw., 1963-64; prof., chmn. dept. mech. and nuclear engring. Ohio State U., 1964-76, dean Coll. Engring., 1976—; also dir. Engring. Expt. Sta.; cons. to industry, 1964—; bd. dirs. Internat. Techne Group Inc. Author: Graphical Theory and Application, 1957, Basic Drawing and Projection, 1957, Working Drawings and Applied Graphics, 1957, Experimental Reactor Analysis and Radiation Measurements, 1965. Bd. dirs. Ohio Transp. Research Center, Indsl. Tech. Enterprise Bd. Ohio, Orton Found., Nat. Regulatory Research Inst. Recipient Outstanding Bus. Achievement award U.S. Mcht. Marine Acad., 1961; Outstanding Profl. Achievement award Iowa State U., 1979; spl. citation Ohio Senate and Ho. of Reps., 1985; named Tech. Person of Yr., Columbus Tech. Council, 1986. Fellow Am. Nuclear Soc.; fellow ASME; mem. Am. Soc. Engring. Edn. (Donald E. Marlowe award 1987), Ohio Acad. Sci., Argonne Univs. Assn., Ohio Energy Task Force, Sigma Xi, Tau Beta Pi, Texnikoi. Office: Ohio State U Coll Engring 2070 Neil Ave Columbus OH 43210

GLOYD, LAWRENCE EUGENE, diversified manufacturing company executive; b. Milan, Ind., Nov. 5, 1932; s. Oran C. and Ruth (Baylor) G.; m. Delma Lear, Sept. 10, 1955; children—Sheryl, Julia, Susan. B.A., Hanover Coll., 1954. Salesman, Shapleigh-How, St. Louis, 1956-60, W. Bingham Co., Cleve., 1960-61, Amerock Corp., Rockford, Ill., 1961-68, regional sales mgr., 1968-69, dir. consumer products mktg., 1969-71, dir. merchandising, 1971-72, dir. mktg. and sales, 1972-73, v.p. mktg. and sales, 1973-81, exec. v.p., 1981-82, pres., gen. mgr., 1982-86; v.p. Hardware Products Group, Anchor Hocking Corp., Lancaster, Ohio, 1983-86; pres., chief operating officer J.L. Clark Mfg. Co., Rockford, Ill., 1986—, also bd. dirs.; bd. dirs. AMcore Fin. Inc., Rockford; mem. Middle West adv. bd. Liberty Mut. Ins. Co. Bd. dirs. Council of 100; trustee SwedishAmerican Corp. Served with AUS, 1954-56. Mem. Am. Hardware Mfrs. Assn. (bd. dirs.), Presidents Assn. Republican. Lodge: Masons. Home: 4979 Crofton Dr Rockford IL 61111 Office: JL Clark Mfg Co 2300 Sixth St PO Box 7000 Rockford IL 61125 also: Amerock Corp 4000 Auburn St Rockford IL 61125

GLOYER, STEWART WAYNE, chemical company executive; b. Milw., May 22, 1910; s. Otto W. and Edith A. (Stewart) G.; m. Dorothy A. Johnson, Sept. 16, 1939; children: Stewart E., Richard A., Donald M. BS, Beloit Coll., 1932; PhD in Chemistry, U. Wis., 1939. Research chemist Coating and Resins div. PPG Industries, Inc., Milw., 1939-44, group leader, 1944-52, asst. dir. research, 1952-54; asst. dir. Coating and Resins div. PPG Industries, Inc., Pitts., 1954-59, assoc. dir. research and devel., 1959-64, div. dir. coating devel., 1964-67, div. dir. indsl. product, 1967-75; pvt. practice cons. mgmt. and tech. Pitts. and Waukesha (Wis.), 1975—. Contbr. papers to profl. jour.; patentee in field. Dir. Richland Youth Found., Gibsonia, Pa., 1960-73; council mem., pres. Trinity Luth. Ch., Gibson, 1955-65. Chemistry fellow U. Wis., 1938-39. Fellow Am. Ins. Chemist; mem. Am. Chem. Soc., Fedn. Paint Soc.,. Republican. Clubs: University (Pitts.); Merrill Hills (Waukesha). Avocations: reading, fishing. Home and Office: 3145 Madison St Waukesha WI 53188

GLUECKERT, ROBERT STEPHEN, manufacturing executive; b. Chgo., Sept. 3, 1960; s. Robert Carl and Gail Rae (Williams) G. BA, N. Cen. Coll., Naperville, Ill., 1982. Gen. mgr. Coated Marine Product, Waukegan, Ill., 1982-85; exec. v.p. Win-Tec, Inc., Park Ridge, Ill., 1985—. Mem. Nat. Assn. Credit Mgrs., Thermal Insulation Mfrs. Assn. Avocations: skiing, tennis, golf, racquetball. Office: Win-Tec Inc 1460 Renaissance Dr #403 Park Ridge IL 60068

GNAT, RAYMOND EARL, librarian; b. Milw., Jan. 15, 1932; s. John and Emily (Syperko) G.; m. Jean Helen Monday, June 19, 1954; children—Cynthia, Barbara, Richard. B.B.A., U. Wis., 1954, postgrad., 1959; M.S., U. Ill., 1958; M.P.A., Ind. U., Indpls., 1981. Page Milw. Pub. Library, 1950-53, jr. librarian, 1954, librarian, 1958-63; circulation asst. U. Ill., 1956-57, serials cataloger, 1957-58; asst. dir. Indpls.-Marion County Pub. Library, 1963-71, dir., 1972—; Exec. dir. Ind. Nat. Library Week, 1965. Served with AUS, 1954-56. Mem. ALA, Ind. Library Assn. (pres. 1980), Bibliog. Soc. Am. Clubs: Literary, The Portfolio. Home: 8246 Shadow Circle Indianapolis IN 46260 Office: Indpls-Marion County Pub Library 40 E St Clair St PO Box 211 Indianapolis IN 46204

GOALEY, DONALD JOSEPH, insurance company executive, accountant; b. Albia, Iowa, Nov. 20, 1935; m. Shirlee Van Scoy, June 28, 1958; 6 children. Student, St. Ambrose Coll., 1953-54; BBA in Acctg., Creighton U., 1957. CPA, Nebr. Ptnr. Arthur Andersen & Co., Omaha, 1957-72; v.p. acctg. Mut. of Omaha Ins. Co., 1972-74, chief comptroller, assoc. coordinator of affiliates, 1974-80, exec. v.p., assoc. coordinator of affiliates, 1980-82, sr. exec. v.p. internal ops., assoc. coordinator of affiliates, 1982-86, sr. exec. v.p., dir. of affiliates, 1986—; bd. dirs. Omaha Indemnity Co., Tele-Trip Co., Inc., Mut. of Omaha Internat. Ltd., United World Ins. Co., Omaha Property & Casualty Co., Omaha Fin. Life Ins. Co., Kirkpatrick, Pettis, Smith & Polian, Inc. Bd. advisors Creighton Preparatory Sch.; trustee Omaha Pub. Library. Mem. Am. Inst. CPA's, Nebr. Soc. CPA's. Home: 10101 Blondo St Omaha NE 68134 Office: Mut of Omaha Ins Co Mutual of Omaha Plaza Omaha NE 68175

GOBLIRSCH, DEAN EDMUND, otolaryngologist; b. Little Falls, Minn., Nov. 14, 1934; s. Edmund Conrad and Hyacinthe Evangeline (Felix) G.; m. Leila Joyce Kissel, Dec. 29, 1956; children: David, Cynthia, Dean II, Constance. BS, St. John's U., Collegeville, Minn., 1955; DO, Kirksville Coll. Osteo. Medicine, 1959. Practice osteo. medicine specializing in otolaryngology Milw.; mem. staff Lakeview Hosp., Milw., chmn. dept. otolaryngology, 1979—, chmn. dept. surgery, 1982-87; mem. staff NW Gen. Hosp., Milw., chmn. dept. otolaryngology, 1981-86. Fellow Am. Acad. Otolaryngology (cert.), Osteo. Coll. Otolaryngology (mem. Bd. Examiners 1982—); mem. Am. Osteo. Assn. (hosp. insp. residency in otolaryngology 1980—), Wis. Osteo. Assn., Milw. Osteo. Assn., Milw. Head and Neck Soc. Roman Catholic. Avocations: golf, bowling, camping. Home: 830 Shadow Lawn Dr Elm Grove WI 53122 Office: 9900 W Bluemound Rd Milwaukee WI 53226

GODAR-MYERS, GRETCHEN HARDY, lawyer; b. Webb City, Mo., Dec. 6, 1958; d. William Claude Jr. and Carlyn (Merryman) Myers; m. Daniel Joseph Godar, Oct. 11, 1985. BA with honors, U. Mo., 1981, JD, 1984. Bar: Mo. 1984, U.S. Dist. Ct. (we. dist.) Mo. 1984, Calif. 1985, U.S. Dist. Ct. (ea. dist.) Mo. 1985, Ill. 1986. Law clk. to presiding justice U.S. Dist. Ct. Mo., St. Louis, 1984-85; assoc. Hullverson, Hullverson & Frank, St. Louis, 1985—; mem. spl. com. alternative dispute resolution Mo. Bar. Contbg. author: Antitrust Textbook, 1982. Mem. ABA, Bar Assn. Met. St. Louis, Assn. Trial Lawyers Am. (treas. student div. 1982-83, pres. 1983-84), Mo. Assn. Trial Attys., Lawyers Assn., St. Louis. Home: 7130 Maryland Saint Louis MO 63130 Office: Hullverson Hullverson & Frank 1010 Market St Suite 1550 Saint Louis MO 63101

GODDARD, JEREMY PAUL, automotive executive; b. Cambridge, Eng., Apr. 1, 1951; came to U.S., 1973; s. Frederick Paul Preston and Mary Ruth (MacPherson) G.; m. Jean Mary Hudspeth, July 21, 1973; children: Joanna, Lucy, Nicholas. BA in English, Coll. of William and Mary, 1973; BSc in Biology, Auburn U., 1975. Research asst. Johnson Environ. and Energy Ctr., Huntsville, Ala., 1976-78; service dir. Chrysler Electronics, Paris, 1978-83; original equipment mfr. sales mgr. Chrysler Corp., London, 1983-86; strategic planning exec. Chrysler Corp., Detroit, 1986-87, sales mgr. 4 wheel drive systems group, 1987—. Draper's scholar Coll. of William and Mary, 1970-73. Mem. Soc. Automotive Engrs. Clubs: Ferrari Owners, AC Owners (London). Avocations: motor sports, skiing, yachting, sky diving, hot air ballooning. Office: Chrysler Corp Acustar Div 6565 E 8 Mile Warren MI 48091

GODDARD, JESSIE GRAY, school administrator, freelance writer; b. Bremerton, Wash., Dec. 19, 1913; d. Christian Carlos Breiland and Josie Amanda (Gray) B.; m. Cephas Jason Goddard, Aug. 17, 1942; children—Cephas Christian, Jeffrey Olaf, David Gray. Student U. Wash., 1930-34; B.S. in Edn., Minot State Coll., 1963-65; postgrad. Regis Coll. 1969, U. Minn., 1970, U. N.D., 1968-70. Reporter, writer for various newspapers, Wash., N.D., 1930—; tchr. Mandaree High Sch., N.D., 1965-67; grad. teaching asst. U. N.D., Grand Forks, 1968-71, instr. U. N.D.-Williston Ctr., 1972-75; mem. N.D. Humanities Council, 1979-84; county supt. schs. McKenzie County, Watford City, N.D., 1981—. Contbr. articles to profl. jours. Editor Jour. Flickertales, 1960s, Type Hi, 1960s; columnist Williston Daily Herald, 1976—. Fund solicitor Cancer Fund, McKenzie County; chmn. bd. McKenzie County Rural Library, Watford City, 1981—; sec. Helen Gough Scholarship Found., Watford City, 1981—, Tri-County Sch. Bds. Assn., 1981—. Recipient Outstanding Tchr. award Assn. Depts. English and MLA, 1969-70; Groundbreaking award Trenton Housing Project, N.D., 1976; 3d place award for book rev. N.D. Press Women, 1982, 2d place award for personal column, 1983. Mem. N.D. Council Sch. Administrs., Young Citizens League (state bd. dirs. 1982—), State Dept. Pub. Instrn. (regional coordinator Chpt. I monitoring 1983—), N.D. Assn. County Supts. Republican. Presbyterian. Clubs: Nat. CowBelles, N.D. Press Women (dir. 1980-82), OX5 Aviation Pioneers. Lodge: Order Eastern Star (Worthy Matron 1965-66). Avocations: freelance writing and research; reading; travel. Office: McKenzie County Supt of Schs County Courthouse Watford City ND 58854

GODERSKY, JOHN CARL, neurosurgeon; b. Indpls., Mar. 6, 1949; s. George Edwin and Lois Garnet (Shoff) G.; m. Barbara Janet Covey, June 26, 1982. Student, Boston Coll., 1967-68; BA, Ind. U., 1971, MD, 1975. Diplomate Am. Bd. Neurol. Surgery. Resident in surgery U. Tex., Dallas, 1976-77; resident in neurosurgery U. Minn., Mpls., 1977-82; asst. prof. U. Iowa, Iowa City, 1982—. Contbr. articles to profl. jours. Physicians Recognition award, AMA, 1982, 86. Mem. Am. Assn. Neurol. Surgeons, Congress Neurol. Surgeons, Iowa-Midwest Neurosurgical Soc. (sec. 1982-84), Soc. Neuroscience, Research Soc. Neurosurgeons. Home: 1762 Winston Dr Iowa City IA 52240 Office: U Iowa Hosps Div Neurosurgery Iowa City IA 52242

GODFREY, OLLIN, oil and banking executive; b. Cin., Dec. 10, 1930; s. Ollin and Mattie (Clemmons) G.; student Edward Waters Jr. Coll., Jacksonville, Fla., 1949, Malcolm-King Coll., N.Y.C., 1968-71; Master's degree, U. Nigeria, 1974, Ph.D. in Polit. Sci., 1976; m. Joan Jarboe, June 10, 1953; children—Ollin, Mark, David. Vice pres. East Harlem Community Corp., N.Y.C., 1969-71; pres. United Leadership Consultant Services, Inc., N.Y.C., 1972—; now exec. cons., Cin.; cons. Massive Neighborhood Devel. Corp., 1970-72; mem. Republican Presdl. Task Force, 1984, Presdl. Commn., 1985. Past bd. dirs. Malcolm King Coll.; founder Am. Eagle Party, 1984. Served with U.S. Navy, 1950-53. Recipient cert. of appreciation Republican Nat. Com., 1977. Mem. Am. Security Council (adv. bd.), Nat. Rep. Congressional Com. (sponsor), Nat. Rep. Senatorial Com. Baptist. Host radio show Minorities, Sta. WNYC, N.Y.C., 1970-73.

GODFREY, ROBERT FREDRICK, insurance company executive, accountant; b. Detroit, Nov. 12, 1953; s. Robert Edward and Marian Irene (Spicer) G.; m. Janeen Kay Gore, Aug. 24, 1974; children: David, Jenna. BA in Acctg., Mich. State U., 1975. CPA, Mich. Acct. Doeren, Mayhew, CPA, Coldwater, Mich., 1975-76; sr. acct. Hall & Hines, CPA's, Albion, Mich., 1976-77; acctng. mgr. Wick Bldg. System, Coldwater, 1977-80; pvt. practice as CPA Coldwater, 1977-84; audit mgr. Fed. Home Life Ins. Co., Battle Creek, Mich., 1980-84; dir. internal audit Mutual Security Life Ins. Co., Ft. Wayne, Ind., 1984—; v.p. ops. parent co. Great Fidelity Life Ins. Co., Ft. Wayne, 1986—; bd. dirs. Illumicomp, Inc., Ann Arbor, Golden Hare, Inc., Ann Arbor. Mem. Am. Inst. CPA's, Mich. Assn. CPA's, Inst. of Internal Auditors (bd. gov.s), Coldwater Jaycees. Republican. Methodist. Avocations: chess, numismatics, tennis. Home: 3115 Kenaston Dr Fort Wayne IN 46815 Office: Great Fidelity Life Ins Co 1615 Vance Ave Fort Wayne IN 46805

GODING, CHARLES ARTHUR, chemical company executive; b. Aurora, Ill., Aug. 13, 1934; s. Arthur Walter and Lillian (Berg) G.; m. Corinne Doris Dau, Aug. 31, 1957; children: Charles Arthur Jr., Craig Jon, Cynthia Lynn. BA, U. Ill., 1956. Copywriter J. Walter Thompson Co., Chgo., 1956-61, Campbell-Mithun, Inc., Chgo., 1961-64; acct. exec., supr. Marsteller Inc., Chgo., 1964-70; dir. pub. affairs Nalco Chem. Co., Naperville, Ill., 1970—; bd. chmn. Tng. Inc. DuPage County, Lombard, Ill. Mem. task force Sch. Dist. 205, Elmhurst, Ill., 1975; mem. Racket Sports Adv. Com., 1977; pres. Oak Brook (Ill.) Ridesharing Coop., Oak Brook, 1977; mem. Zoning and Planning Commn., Elmhurst, 1986. Mem. Bus. Profls. Adv. Assn. (life, Chgo. pres. 1975-76, internat. pres. 1980-81), Oak Brook Assn. Commerce and Industries (pres. 1981-83), Naperville C. of C. (pub. relations com. 1986), Chem. Mfg. Assn. (communications 1987), Delta Upsilon. Home: 259 Cottage Hill Elmhurst IL 60125 Office: Nalco Chem Co One Nalco Ctr Naperville IL 60566-1024

GODING, THOMAS LEE, bank executive; b. Hastings, Nebr., Aug. 26, 1955; s. Luther and Frances Louise (Teaford) G.; m. Jane C. Matthies, May 5, 1984. BS, U. Nebr., 1977, MBA, 1986. V.p. Fed. Land Bank Assn., North Platte, Nebr., 1977-81, Lincoln, Nebr., 1981-84; asst. v.p. Farm Credit Banks of Omaha, 1984-85; credit and mgmt. supr. R.D. Mgmt., Papillion, Nebr., 1985—; bd. dirs. Gretna (Nebr.) State Bank, Bank of Papillion. Chmn. com. Farm Mgr. and Rural Appraisers, Lincoln. Mem. Lincoln Jaycees (bd. dirs. 1982-83), U. Nebr. Alumni Bd. (bd. dirs. 1985-86). Home: 13518 Atwood Ave Omaha NE 68144 Office: Bank of Papillion 1200 Golden Gate Dr Papillion NE 68046

GODLEW, CAROL LYNN, middle school administrator; b. Highland Park, Mich., Dec. 17, 1942; d. Leslie Kopplow and Elanora Katherine (Pfeffer) Walker; m. Dennis Allan Godlew, Dec. 16, 1961; children—Scott Allan, Cheryl Lynn. B.A., Western Mich. U., 1965, M.Edn. Leadership, 1980, M in Counselor Edn. and Counseling Psychology, 1986. Cert. secondary tchr., Mich. Tchr., Lawrence Pub. Schs., Mich., 1965-66, Bangor Pub. Schs., Mich., 1966-81; prin. Hartford Pub. Schs., Mich., 1981—. Recipient Freedoms Found. award Am. Legion Aux., Bangor, 1978. Mem. Mich. Assn. Secondary Sch. Prins., Prins. (Outstanding Secondary Sch. Prin. Center 7, 1984-85, Middle Level chairperson for state exec. bd. 1986—), Am. Soc. Curriculum Devel., Assn. Career Edn., Mich. Assn. Middle Sch. Educators. Republican. Congregationalist. Avocations: camping, travel, hand bells. Office: Hartford Middle Sch PO Box 158 Hartford MI 49057

GODSEY, C. WAYNE, broadcasting executive; b. Lynchburg, Va., Aug. 5, 1946; s. Carl Dodge and Frances Anna (Keesee) G.; m. Anne Marie Ruzicka, Oct., 1979; children: Rebecca Susan, Patricia Anne, Thomas Lawrence. BA in English, Lynchburg Coll., 1968. Reporter Sta. WSOC-TV, Charlotte, N.C., 1969-71, news dir., 1971-74; reporter, producer Newsweek Broadcasting, N.Y.C., 1974-77; news dir. Stas. WTMJ-TV and Radio, Milw., 1977-82; v.p., gen. mgr. Sta. WTMJ-TV, Milw., 1982-84, Sta. WISN-TV, Milw., 1984—. Bd. dirs. Easter Seal Soc., Milw., 1984—, Better Bus. Bur., Milw., 1984—, Big Bros./Big Sisters, Milw., 1985—, Centurions of St. Joseph Hosp., Milw., 1985—, Children's Hosp. Wis., 1987—. Served with USNG, 1968-74. Mem. Nat. Assn. Broadcasters (task force on drug and alcohol abuse 1984-86), Radio-TV News Dir.'s Assn. (nat. pres. 1981-82, found. pres. 1982-83), Wis. Broadcaster's Assn. (pres.-elect). Republican. Roman Catholic. Clubs: Westmoor Country (Brookfield, Wis.); Milw. Athletic. Lodge: Rotary. Avocations: golf, skeet shooting. Home: 20800 Tennyson Dr Brookfield WI 53005 Office: Sta WISN-TV 759 N 19th St Milwaukee WI 53201

GOEBEL, JOAN MARY, physician, consultant; b. Marietta, Ohio, June 24, 1906; d. Joseph Sylvester and Augusta (Ryan) G. A.B., Trinity Coll., Washington, 1927; M.D., U. Mich., 1932. Diplomate Am. Bd. Anesthesiology. Intern, Hosp. for Women and Children, San Francisco, 1932-33; resident Inst. of Pa. Hosp., Phila., 1933-35; gen. practice medicine, 1935-40; resident in anesthesiology N.Y. Postgrad. Hosp., 1940-42; dir. dept. anesthesiology Deaconess Hosp., Evansville, Ind., 1943-45, St. Anthony's Hosp., St. Louis, 1945-62, dept. dir., 1951-60; with dept. anesthesia Lutheran Hosp. of St. Louis, 1962-72; med. cons. for natural family planning AWARE Ctr. of St. Louis, 1973—; instr., cons. Billings ovulation method of natural family planning. Recipient First Athena award Alumnae Council U. Mich., 1973. Mem. AMA, Am. Soc. Anesthesiologists, Mo. State Med. Soc., St. Louis Met. Med. Soc., LWV. Republican. Roman Catholic. Contbr. sect. to book in field. Home: 5128 Jamieson Ave Saint Louis MO 63109

GOEBEL, MARISTELLA, clinical psychologist, psychology educator; b. Racine, Wis., Sept. 10, 1915; d. James Nicholas and Henrietta Marie (Rademacher) Goebel. B.S., Edgewood Coll., 1944; M.A., Cath. U. Am., 1946, Ph.D., 1966. Diplomate in clin. biofeedback Am. Bd. Clin. Biofeedback. Mem. Dominican Sisters; tchr. English Cathedral High Sch., Sioux Falls, S.D., 1946-47, Heart of Mary High Sch., Mobile, Ala., 1947-49; assoc. prof. edn. Rosary Coll., River Forest, Ill., 1949-61, prof. psychology, 1966—; clin. psychologist Hines VA Hosp., Ill., 1970—; cons. Sinsinawa Dominican Sisters, Wis., 1966—. Author, editor tchr. guides Southeastern Curriculum Com., vols. Kindergarten-grade 8. Mem. editorial bd. Clin. Biofeedback and Health, Am. Assn. Biofeedback Clinics, Des Plaines, 1980—. Contbr. numerous articles to profl. jours. Mem. task force ch. related project Chgo. Heart Assn., 1979—, NHLBI Hypertension Investigation Pooled Project, 1982—, Citizens Ambassador Del. to China, 1987 . Recipient NIH awards, 1962-33, 65-66, 82-84, Outstanding Achievement in Psychol. Research, Ill. Psychol. Assn., 1982; Performance award Hines VA Hosp., 1983. Clin. fellow Am. Assn. Biofeedback Clinicians, Des Plaines, Ill., 1983. Mem. Am. Psychol. Assn., Soc. Clin. and Exptl. Hypnosis, Biofeedback Soc. Am., AAAS, Soc. Behavioral Medicine. Avocations: gardening; knitting, bicycling. Home: 7900 W Division River Forest IL 60305 Office: Hines VA Hosp Hines IL 60141

GOEBEL, PAUL GORDON, insurance executive; b. Grand Rapids, Mich., Mar. 27, 1933; s. Paul Gordon and Margaret Elizabeth (Callam) G.; m. Marjorie Beth Mihlethaler, Aug. 21, 1955; children: Margaret Elizabeth, Paul Gordon III, James Keith. BA, U. Mich., 1954. Supr. Aetna Life Ins. Co., Grand Rpaids, 1957-62; pres. Paul Goebel Group, Grand Rapids, 1962—. Rep. candidate U.S. Congress, 1974; commr. Kent County, Mich., 1972-74; pres. United Way of Kent County, 1975; trustee Alvin M. Bentley Found., Owosso, Mich., 1971—. Named Young Man of Yr. Grand Rapids Jaycees, 1968;. Mem. United Way of Kent County (life). Republican. Home: 7565 Conservation Rd NE Ada MI 49301 Office: 511-F Waters Bldg Grand Rapids MI 49503

GOEBEL, RICHARD ALAN, veterinarian; b. Wabash, Ind., Mar. 16, 1944; s. Meredith Clair and Lavonne Eileen (Leyman) G.; m. Michele J., June 18, 1966; Heidi C., Ross C., Heather E. DVM, Purdue U., 1968. Ptnr. Hafner Vet. Clinic, Huntington, Ind., 1968-69; dir. Monrovia (Calif.) Animal Hosp., 1970-77, Magrane Animal Hosp., Mishawaka, Ind., 1979—, Maplecrest Animal Hosp., Goshen, Ind., 1984—; veterinarian Potawatami Zoo, South Bend, Ind., 1982-85; chmn. bd. Animal Emergency Clinic, Inc., South Bend, 1983-84. Edit. cons. Jour. Am. Animal Hosp. Assn. Moderator Jefferson Brethren Ch., Goshen, 1983-84, deacon, 1985—. Mem. Am. Animal Hosp. Assn. (area dir. 1985—), Am. Assn. Zoo Veterinarians, Assn. Avian Veterinarians, Vet. Mgmt. Group, Michiani Vet. Med. Assn. (treas. 1984, sec. 1985, v.p. 1986), Ind. Vet. Med. Assn., So. Calif. Vet. Med. Assn. (trustee, treas.), Purdue Alumni Assn., Pres.'s Club, Calif. Vet. Med. Assn., Purdue Vet. Alumni Assn. (pres. 1985-86). Republican. Avocations: horticulture, aviculture. Address: Magrane Animal Hosp 2324 Grape Rd Mishawaka IN 46545 Office: Maplecrest Animal Hosp 1214 N Main St Goshen IN 46526

GOECKEL, WERNER FREDERICK, plastics company executive; b. Darmstadt, Hessen, Fed. Republic of Germany, Nov. 13, 1941; s. Friedrich and Elizabeth (Dotzert) G.; m. Patricia Ann Delp; children: Anne Elizabeth, Karen Patricia. BA in Econs., U. Del., 1964; AA in Transp., Del. Tech., 1968. Econs. analyst Hercules Inc., Wilmington, Del., 1967-69; sales rep. E.I. DuPont Co., Wilmington, 1969-75; product mgr. Consolidated Thermoplastics, Arlington Heights, Ill., 1975-77, Eastern sales mgr., 1977-80; v.p. mktg. Consolidated Thermoplastics, Arlington Heights, 1980-81; v.p. mfg. Consolidated Thermoplastics, Arlington Heights, Ill., 1981-84, pres., 1984—; bd. dirs. El Paso Products, Odessa, Tex. Mem. planning commn. City of Savage, Minn., 1972-73; councilman, 1974. Served to capt. U.S. Army, 1964-67, ETO. Named Sales Contest champion Dale Carnegie, 1974. Mem. Am. Mgmt. Assn., Flexible Packaging Assn. (bd. dirs.), Am. Assn. Hypnotists, C. of C. (treas. 1978-80). Republican. Lutheran. Clubs: Del. Saengerbund (Newark) (treas. 1967-69); Toastmasters (pres. 1983-85). Avocations: running, basketball, tennis, fishing, woodworking. Home: 159 Reseda Pkwy Palatine IL 60067 Office: Consolidated Thermoplastics 115 S Wilke Rd Arlington Heights IL 60005

GOEKLER, MALCOLM L., plastic packaging manufacturing company executive; b. Riverside, Calif., Mar. 7, 1945; s. Lester L. and Elizabeth Mae (Bigelow) G.; m. Kenine Ann Hardt, Dec. 27, 1974. BS in ChemE, U. Ariz., 1968. Prodn. supt. Freeport Sulphur Co., New Orleans, 1968-71; prodn. supr. Lubrizol, Cleve., 1971-73; plant engr. Carlon Products, High Springs, Fla., 1973-74; mgr. prodn. and engring. Celanese Corp., various locations, 1974-82; dir., injection molding Kenner Products, Cin., 1982-86; v.p. mfg. Packaging Resources Inc., New Vienna, Ohio, 1986—. Mem. Soc. Plastic Engrs. (sr.). Avocation: orchid growing. Home: 709 Pine Ridge Rd Milford OH 45150 Office: Packaging Resources Inc 5566 New Vienna Rd New Vienna OH 45159

GOEMANN, RICK WILLIAM, farmer, insurance sales agent; b. Wells, Minn., July 31, 1953; s. Orville William and Alice Margaret (Passer) G.; m. Julie KAy Stiles, Sept. 21, 1985; 1 child, Samuel William. BSgr in Agrl. prodn., Mankato Area Voctional Tech. Inst., 1973. Owner, operator Goemann Farms, Kiester, Minn., 1971—; salesman Kaltenberg Seeds, Waunakee, Wis., 1983—, MSI Ins. Co., Mankato, Minn., 1987—. Pres. United Luth., Walters, Minn., 1981-83, Foster United Fund, Walters, 1985—; v.p. bd. dirs. Kiester Pub. Sch., 1986, 87. Mem. Kiester Jaycees (Outstanding Young Farmer 1986). Democrat. Avocations: aviation, boating, stamp/coin collecting, restoring old Oliver tractors. Home: RR 3 Box 61 Wells MN 56097 Office: MSI Ins Co 226 E Clark Albert Lea MN 56007

GOERGEN, JOHN PETER, data processing specialist; b. Flint, Mich., Jan. 23, 1948; s. George Mathias and Helen Marie (LeSage) G.; m. Carolyn Sue Eickhoff, Feb. 20, 1975; children: Jeffery Michael, Michele Renee. Assoc. in Data Processing, Flint Community Coll., 1968; BA in Gen. Bus., Ea. Mich. U., 1970, postgrad., 1973. Control supr., edn. dir. Manatron, Inc., Kalamazoo, 1974-76; coordinator, dir. data processing West Shore Community Coll., Scottville, Mich., 1977-79; sr. analyst, dir. promis project Pros. Atty. Coordinator Council, Lansing, Mich., 1979-82, dir. tech. services, 1982—; cons. Search Group, Sacramento, 1986—. Served with U.S. Army, 1970-72. Mem. Nat. Assn. Justice Info. Systems (founder, co-chair 1981—). Roman Catholic. Lodge: KC. Avocations: travel, camping, biking. Office: Pros Atty Coordinator Council Michigan Bar Bldg 306 Townsend Lansing MI 48913

GOESSEL, WILLIAM W., heavy equipment manufacturing company executive; b. 1927; married. B.S., Carthage Coll., 1950. Exec. v.p. Beloit Corp., 1950-52; pres., chief operating officer Harnischfeger Corp., Milw., 1982-86, chief exec. officer, 1982—, chmn., 1986—. Office: Harnischfeger Corp PO Box 554 Milwaukee WI 53201 *

GOETZ, ELIZABETH MOREY, psychology educator; b. Cin., Aug. 1, 1927; d. John Frederick and Jean White (McDowell) Morey; m. Raymond Goetz, Apr. 24, 1951; children—Raymond, Sibyl; Thomas, Victoria, Steven, Morey. B.A. in Sociology, Grinnell Coll., 1950; M.A. with honors, U. Kans., 1970, Ph.D. in Psychology, 1977. Teaching asst. dept. human devel. U. Kans., Lawrence, 1968-70, instr., 1969-74, tchr. tng. asst., 1970, asst. prof., 1974-78, assoc. prof., 1978-84, prof., 1985—; research cons., lab. supr., 1970—, dir. child devel. lab. dept. human devel., 1978—; cons. in field; bd. dirs. Ptnrs. with Parents Corp. Day Care Cons. Bd. dirs. U. Kans. Art Mus. Friends of Art, Nelson Gallery Friends of Art, Chgo. Art Inst.; pres. bd. dirs. Children's Learning Ctr., Lawrence, 1978-79. Mem. Internat. Reading Assn., Nat. Assn. Edn. of Young Children, Kans. Assn. Edn. of Young Children, Lawrence Assn. Edn. of Young Children, (pres. 1971-72), Am. Ednl. Research Assn., Nat. Assn. Early Childhood Tchr. Educators (bd. dirs.), Assn. Child Edn. Internat., Soc. Research in Child Devel., Am. Psychol. Assn., Council Exceptional Children, Assn. Behavior Analysis, Soc. Advancement Behavior Analysis. Contbr. chpts. to books and articles to profl. jours.; producer ednl. films. Home: 1500 Learnard Lawrence KS 66044 Office: U Kans Haworth Hall Lawrence KS 66045

GOFF, WILMER SCOTT, photographer; b. Steubenville, Ohio, July 11, 1923; s. Floyd Orville and Ellen Armenia (Funk) G.; m. Mary Elizabeth Fischer, Dec. 7, 1950; children: Carolyn, Christopher. BFA with honors, Ohio U., 1949. Photographer Columbus (Ohio) Dispatch, 1949-52, Warner P. Simpson, Columbus, 1952-53; owner Willy Goff Photo Studio, Grove City, Ohio, 1954-59; photographer N.Am. Rockwell, Columbus, 1953-70; supr. Transp. Research Ctr. Ohio, East Liberty, 1970—; photography instr. Columbus Coll. Art and Design, 1949-71; photography judge Ohio State Fair, 1966-68; judge Greater Columbus Film Festival, 1970-72; photographer John Glenn campaign, 1974. One man shows include 100 print exhibit Southern Hotel, Columbus, 1953. Recipient Public's Choice award Columbus Art Gallery, 1958, Photo-Pictoral 1st Pl. award Dix Newspapers, 1960, Best of Show award Balloon Show Competition, 1985. Mem. Aircraft Camera Club (pres. 1954-55), Grove City Camera CLub (pres. 1959-60). Republican. Roman Catholic. Avocations: stamp collecting, recording, cycling. Home: 6110 Darby Ln Columbus OH 43229 Office: Transp Research Ctr Ohio East Liberty OH 43319

GOGGANS, LOUISE ELIZABETH, dietitian, nutrition consultant; b. Trenton, Ky., Mar. 8, 1934; d. Stonewall and Dorothy (Smith) Tyler; m. Otis Goggans, Jr., May 5, 1963; children—Gregory Tyler, Dorothy Victoria. A.B., Ind. U., 1956, M.S.Ed., 1969, D.M.S., 1982. Staff dietitian Hines (Ill.) VA Hosp., 1957; chief dietitian Highland Park (Ill.) Hosp., 1957-61; head therapeutic dietitian Marion County Gen. Hosp., Indpls., 1961-63; asst. chief dietitian Meth. Hosp., Indpls., 1963-68; nutritionist, adminstrv. asst. Vis. Nurses Assn., Indpls., 1968-73; dir. nutrition services Regenstrief Health Ctr., Wishard Meml. Hosp., Indpls., 1973—; vis. prof. Valparaiso U. Vol. Ind. Women's Prison; mem. parents com. Crossroads of Am. council Boy Scouts Am.; bd. dirs. Meals on Wheels, Alpha Home Inc., Auntie Mame's Child Care Ctr.; mem. vol. action ctr. bd. United Way; mem. Ind. Adv. Council on Aging and Community Services. Recipient Ind. Disting. Citizen award Indpls. Bi-Centennial Com., 1976; Drum Major award Ind. Christian Leadership Council, 1981. Mem. Am. Dietetic Assn. (cert.), Ind. Dietetic Assn. (Lute Troutt fellow 1980), Cen. Dist. Dietetic Assn., Am. Diabetes Assn. (dir. Ind. affiliate, com. on pubs.), Am. Heart Assn. (program vol.), Home Econs. Alumni Ind. U. (dir.), NAACP, Urban League, Nat. Council Negro Women, Coalition 100 Black Women, Ind. Black Expo, Sigma Xi, Alpha Kappa Alpha. Baptist. Contbr. articles to profl. jours. Home: 4545 N Brown Rd Indianapolis IN 46226 Office: Wishard Meml Hosp 1001 W 10th St RHC Indianapolis IN 46202

GOGGIO, ERNEST CHARLES, JR., marketing company executive; b. Balt., Dec. 6, 1954; s. Ernest Charles and LaVigne (McCrady) G.; m. Karen Smrstick; children: Nicole Leigh, Allison McCrady. BA in Communication Arts, U. Wis., Madison, 1978. Internat. salesman Pillar Corp., Milw., 1978-80, advt. mgr., 1980-81; v.p. Basic Concepts Inc., Mequon, Wis., 1981-83; pres. MarkeTrends, Inc., Brookfield, Wis., 1983—. Mem. Milw. Advt. Club., Phi Beta Mu (hon). Avocations: sailing, scuba, music. Office: MarkeTrends Inc 2800 N Brookfield Rd Brookfield WI 53005

GOHIL, PRATAPSINH, podiatric physician and surgeon; b. Tanga, Tanzania, May 26, 1950; B.A., M.S., U. Mo., 1975, 76; D.P.M., Ohio Coll. Podiatric Medicine, 1980. Diplomate Am. Bd. Podiatric Surgery. Instr. biomechanics and orthopedics Ohio Coll. Podiatric Medicine, Cleve., 1977-81, research asst. anatomy, mem. research com., 1980-81; assoc. in podiatric medicine and surgery Ankle and Foot Clinic, Kokomo, Ind., 1981—; staff surgery dept. Univ. Heights Hosp., St. Francis Hosp., Indpls., St. Vincent's Hosp., Winona Hosp., St. Joseph Hosp., Kokomo, Howard Community Hosp., Kokomo. Faculty advisor and clinician Kappa Rho Collective and Alpha Gamma Kappa, City of Cleve. Clinics, 1979-81; active Am. Diabetes Assn., ARC. Recipient Syntex award in dermatology, 1979. Fellow Am. Coll. Foot Surgeons (Dr. Kaplan award 1980); mem. Am. Podiatry Assn., Ind. Pub. Health Assn., Ohio Pub. Health Assn., Am. Pub. Health Assn., Am. Coll. Podopediatrics. Hindu. Author: (with Young and Clarke) Hypertensive Ischemic Ulcers of Legs, 1981; (with Young and Graham) Tension Fibrositis of the Legs, 1981. Office: Ankle & Foot Clinic 209 Corwin Ln PO Box 3098 Kokomo IN 46902

GOLBERGER, NORMA MILLER, health science association administrator; b. Toronto, Ont., Can., Dec. 25, 1945; d. Al and Faye (Shapiro) Miller; m. Stephen Golberger, Apr. 28, 1968; children: David, Joshua, Jessica. BA, U. Toronto, 1966, MA, 1967; postgrad., Boston Coll., 1970-71. Dir. counseling Open Door Clinic, Columbus, Ohio, 1971-72; dir. NW Women's Ctr., Columbus, 1972-76, Akron (Ohio) Women's Clinic, 1976—. Mem. Nat. Abortion Fedn., NOW (treas. Canton chpt. 1985-86). Jewish. Avocations: poetry, music, teaching at religious schs., feminist, reading. Office: Akron Women's Clinic 513 W Market St Akron OH 44303

GOLD, BERNARD LEON, allergist; b. Dallas, Jan. 6, 1950; s. Allen Jay and Donnis Bolin (Fernandez) G.; m. Leslie Harris Arwin, Mar. 26, 1976; children: Benjamin, Courtney. BA, U. Mont., 1973; MD, Baylor U., Houston, 1977. Diplomate Am. Bd. Internal Medicine, Am. Bd. Allergy and Immunology. Resident internal medicine St. Joseph Hosp., Ann Arbor, Mich., 1981; resident allergy and immunology U. Mich., Ann Arbor, 1984; head allergy Toledo Clinic, 1984—; clinical instr. U. Mich., Ann Arbor, Mich., 1986—. Fellow Am. Coll. Allergy, Am. Acad. Allergy; mem. Am. Coll. Phys., Ohio State Med. Soc., Sheldon Soc. Office: Toledo Clinic 4235 Secor Rd Toledo OH 43623

GOLD, CLIFFORD DAVID, marketing executive; b. Pitts., Dec. 27, 1952; s. Harold Alvin and Thelma Ethel (Weinstein) G.; m. Julie Annette Siems, Nov. 8, 1975; 1 son, Jeffrey Joseph. BA in Journalism, Ohio State U., 1971-74. Asst. to pres. univ. relations U. Dubuque (Iowa), 1974-78; mgr. communications Blue Cross & Blue Shield of Iowa, Des Moines, 1978-80, dir. communications, 1980-82, dir. pub. relations, 1982-85, v.p. external services, 1985—. Campaign promotions chmn. United Way of Greater Des Moines; vice chmn. United Way Cen. Iowa, 1985-87. Recipient Award of Excellence, Internat. Assn. Bus. Communicators, 1982, Council for Advancement and Support of Edn., 1977. Mem. Pub. Relations Soc. Am., Internat. Assn. Bus. Communicators. Jewish. Home: 4509 Parkview Dr Des Moines IA 50322 Office: 636 Grand Ave Des Moines IA 50307

GOLD, JAMES SAMUEL, orthodontist; b. Pittsville, Wis., June 25, 1914; s. Harry L. and Bessie (Schneidman) G.; m. Flora Jane Schwartz, Nov. 26, 1942; children: Deborah, Robert, Michael, William. BS, U. Chgo., 1937; DDS, U. Ill., Chgo., 1942, MS, 1946. Diplomate Am. Bd. Orthodontics. Gen. practice dentistry specializing in orthodontics Glencoe and Highland Park, Ill., 1947—. Served to capt. U.S. Air Corp, 1942-45. Mem. ADA, Chgo. Dental Soc., Ill. Dental Soc., Am. Orthodontic Assn., North Shore Congl. Israel Brotherhood. Democrat. Jewish. Club: Mens (Glencoe) (bd. dirs. 1981—). Avocations: photography, gardening, travelling. Home: 895 Oak Dr Glencoe IL 60022 Office: 635 Roger Williams Highland Park IL 60035

GOLD, KENNETH HARRIS, lawyer; b. Boston, Oct. 15, 1942; s. Max and Selma (Harris) G.; m. Betsy Ann Brody, Apr. 7, 1968; children: Darren, Justin. BS, Babson Coll., 1963; JD, NYU, 1967, LLM, 1968. Assoc. Parker Chapin Flattau, N.Y.C., 1969-72; ptnr. Smith Miro Hirsch & Brody, Detroit, 1972-81, Miro Miro & Weiner, Bloomfield Hills, Mich., 1981—. Mem. securities law adv. com. Mich. Corp. and Securities Bur., Lansing, 1979—. Mem. ABA (fed. regulation securities com., com. on commodities regulation, corp. banking and bus. law sect. sect.), Detroit Bar Assn. (securities law com.), N.Y. State Bar Assn., Mich. Bar Assn. (Blue Sky law subcom., corp., fin. and bus. law sect.). Democrat. Jewish. Avocations: jogging, photography. Home: 5981 E Millerway Birmingham MI 48010 Office: Miro Miro & Weiner PC 500 N Woodward Suite 200 PO Box 908 Bloomfield Hills MI 48303

GOLDBERG, ARNOLD IRVING, psychoanalyst; b. Chgo., May 21, 1929; s. Morris Henry and Rose (Auerbach) G.; m. Constance Obenhaus; children: Andrew, Sarah. BS, U. Ill., 1949; MD, U. Ill., Chgo., 1953. Diplomate Am. Bd. Psychiatry and Neurology; cert. psychoanalyst. Attending psychiatrist Michael Reese Hosp., Chgo., 1957—; tng. and supervising analyst Chgo. Inst. for Psychoanalysis, 1970—; assoc. attending psychiatrist Rush Presbyterian St. Lukes Hosp., Chgo., 1982—; prof. psychiatry Rush Med. Coll., Chgo., 1982—. Author: Models of the Mind, 1973; editor: Future of Psychoanalysis: Progress in Self Psychology Vols. 1 & 2, 1976-86; contbr. numerous articles to profl. jours. Served as capt. U.S. Army, 1955-57. Fellow Am. Psychiat. Assn.; mem. Am. Psychoanalytic Assn. Home: 844 W Chalmers Pl Chicago IL 60614 Office: 180 N Michigan Ave Chicago IL 60601

GOLDBERG, DAVID PHILLIP, physician; b. Chgo., Nov. 16, 1939; s. David Charles and Hazel Esther (Gottstein) G.; m. Barbara Rae Roseberg, Aug. 23, 1960 (div. Dec. 1971); children: Robert, Cary; m. Patricia Ann Full, Sept. 23, 1972. BA, Northwestern U., 1961; MD, Chgo. Med. Sch., 1965. Diplomate Am. Bd. Radiology, Am. Bd. Nuclear Medicine. Dir. nuclear medicine Englewood Hosp., Chgo., 1971-76, dir. radiology, 1982-86; dir. nuclear medicine Palos Community Hosp., Palos Heights, 1972-80; dir. radiology Jackson Park Hosp., Chgo., 1986; asst. prof. radiology Chgo. Med. Sch., 1986. Treas. Moraine Valley Community Coll. Found., Palos Hills, 1984-87. Fellow Am. Coll. Radiology; Chgo. Ultrasound Soc. (pres. 1986—). Jewish. Avocation: tng. and riding horses. Office: 12351 S 80th Ave Palos Heights IL 60462

GOLDBERG, EDWARD C., osteopathic radiologist; b. Detroit, Aug. 5, 1941; s. Arthur and Anni Leah (Korn) G.; m. Mariette Zomberg, Aug. 11, 1965; children: Lonnie, David, Jonathan. BS in Psychcology, Wayne State U., 1963; DO, Coll. Osteo. Medicine and Surgery, 1967. Diplomate Am. Bd. Radiology. Staff radiologist North Detroit Gen. Hosp., 1973-82, chief radiologist, 1983—. Mem. Am. Coll. Radiology, Mich. Assn. Osteo. Physicians & Surgeons, Am. Roentgen Ray Soc., Radiol. Soc. N. Am., Mich. Radiol. Soc. Jewish. Avocation: jogging. Home: 5370 Old Pond Way West Bloomfield MI 48033 Office: North Detroit Gen Hosp 3105 Carpenter Detroit MI 48212

GOLDBERG, HERBERT S(AM), academic administrator; b. N.Y.C., July 23, 1926; s. Murray and Bella (Rubin) G.; m. Helen S. Smilowitz, Dec. 26, 1948; children—Jacquelyn, Sheryl. B.S., St. John's U., 1948; M.A., U. Mo., 1950; Ph.D. Ohio State U., 1953. Diplomate Am. Bd. Med. Microbiology. Postdoctoral fellow Ohio State U., Columbus, 1953; from asst. prof. to assoc. prof. microbiology U. Mo., Columbia, 1953-57, prof., 1961-84, asst. dean, 1967-70, assoc. dean, 1970-83, assoc. v.p. research, 1985-86; vis. prof. UCLA, 1984. Author: History of Medicine, 1963; Hippocrates, Father of Medicine, 1964; also numerous articles on microbiology research, 1955-85. Editor: Antibiotics: Their Chemistry and Non-Medical Uses, 1959. Served with USNR, 1944-46. Recipient pre-clin. teaching award Student AMA, U. Mo., 1963, Byler Adminstrv. award U. Mo., 1976; NIH grantee. Fellow Royal Soc. Medicine; mem. AAAS, Am. Soc. Microbiology, Soc. Research Adminstrn. Club: Chemist (N.Y.C.). Avocations: reading; fishing; cycling. Office: U Mo Columbia MO 65212

GOLDBERG, LAWRENCE MICHAEL, advertising executive; b. Chgo., Mar. 28, 1940; divorced; 1 child, Sanford. Chief fin. officer S.R. Knapp Assocs., Arlington Heights, Ill., 1983-86; pres. LMG Pub., Arlington Heights, 1986—; chmn. and chief exec. officer LMG Communications, Arlington Heights, 1986—. Mem. Am. Med. Writers Assn., Biomed. Mktg. Assn., Audobon Soc., Nat. Rifle Assn. (life). Clubs: NISA (Mc Henry, Ill.), Northbrook (Ill.) Sportsman, Kenosha (Wis.) County Conservation. Avocations: competive shooting, hiking, nature photography. Home: 1201 Ranch View Ct Buffalo Grove IL 60089 Office: LMG Communications Inc 1156 Shure Dr Arlington Heights IL 60004

GOLDBERG, MARVIN ELEAZER, radiologist; b. Mpls., Nov. 30, 1926; s. Max Wilbert and Frances Lillian (Halpern) G. BA magna cum laude, U. Minn., 1949, BS, 1950, MB, 1952, MD, 1953. Diplomate Am. Bd. Radiology, Am. Bd. Nuclear Medicine. Radiologist Mt. Sinai Hosp., Mpls., 1957-71; assoc. prof. radiology U. Minn., Mpls., 1971—. Contbr. articles to profl. jours. Served with USN, 1945-46. Fellow Am. Coll. Radiology; mem. Minn. Radiol. Soc. (pres. 1980-81), Radiol. Soc. N.Am., Am. Roentgen Ray Soc., Assn. Univ. Radiologists, Soc. Uroradiology, Soc. Nuclear Medicine, Sigma Xi. Avocation: amateur chamber music. Home: 5049 Abbott Ave S Minneapolis MN 55410 Office: U Hosp Dept Radiology Minneapolis MN 55455

GOLDBERG, RICHARD STUART, psychiatrist; b. Buffalo, Nov. 5, 1951; s. Leonard Edward and Shirley Ruth (Greenberg) G.; m. Jane May Meinhold, Aug. 4, 1979; children: Adam Stuart, Aaron David, Joanna Beth. BA in English magna cum laude, SUNY, Buffalo, 1972; MD, U. Ill., 1977. Diplomate Am. Bd. Psychiatry and Neurology. Med. cons. Substance Abuse Services, Inc., Chgo., 1978-81; med. dir. New Day Youth Program, Chgo., 1981-82, Ctr. for Treatment and Rehab., Chgo., 1984-85, Dualities, Inc., Chgo., 1985—; chief of psychiatry Chgo. Lakeshore Hosp., 1987—; cons. dual diagnosis program Hargrove Hosp., 1985, Wilson Care Home, Chgo., 1981—, Am. Plaza Ctr., Evanston, Ill., 1983—. Recipient Laughlin award for Merit Nat. Psychiat. Endowment Fund, 1981. Mem. AMA, Ill. Med. Soc., Ill. Psychiat. Soc., Chgo. Med. Soc., Am. Psychiat. Assn. Avocations: tennis, golf. Office: 505 N Lake Shore Dr #2317 Chicago IL 60611

GOLDBERG, STEVEN MARK, psychotherapist; b. Milw., Dec. 4, 1948; s. Ben and Syrene C. (Bernstein) G.; m. Janice K. Schroeder, July 11, 1969; children: Matthew Aaron, Elisabeth L. BA, U. Wis., 1971; MSW, Fla. State U., 1973. Cert. clin. social worker; diplomate Nat. Assn. Social Workers. Psychotherapist Family Counseling Ctr., Kenosha, Wis., 1973-77, Kenosha Counseling and Psychiat. Clinic, 1977—; cons. Milw. Mental Health Assn., 1975, 76; psychotherapist Family Counseling Ctr., Kenosha, 1973-77. Crisis counselor St. Catherine's Hosp., Kenosha, 1974-76; bd. dirs., sec. Beth Hillel Temple, Kenosha, 1986-87, Salvation Army, 1986—. Mem. Acad. Cert. Social Workers, Nat. Assn. Social Workers, Wis. Soc. Clin. Soc. Workers, Wis. Assn. Outpatient Mental Health Facilities. Office: Kenosha Counseling & Psychiatric Clinic 6530 Sheridan Rd Kenosha WI 53140

GOLDEN, GARY MICHAEL, corporate lawyer; b. Detroit, Jan. 12, 1951; s. Robert and Corinne Beth (Staffin) G.; m. Susan Jane Sisung, May 19, 1973; 1 child, Geoffrey Scott. BA, U. Mich., 1972; JD, U. Detroit, 1976. Atty. Chrysler Corp., Highland Park, Mich., 1976-81, Dana Corp., Toledo, 1981—; bd. dirs. Diamond Savs. and Loan Co., Findlay, Ohio. Mem. ABA, Mich. Bar Assn., Ohio Bar Assn. Avocation: sports. Home: 6065 Barkwood Ln Sylvania OH 43560 Office: Dana Corp 4500 Dorr St Toledo OH 43560

GOLDEN, ROBERT BENNETT, electric company executive; b. Cleve., Feb. 2, 1948; s. Marvin L. and Claire (Alpern) G.; m. Arda L. Kasson, Aug. 26, 1973; children:Matthew, Mara. BBA, Cleve. State U., 1971; MBA, Case Western Reserve U., 1979. CPA, Ohio. Staff acct. Louis A. Blue & Assoc., Cleve., 1969-71, Baden & Linden, CPA's, Cleve., 1971-73; fin. analyst Addressograph-Multi, Cleve., 1973-75; div. controller Anvil Industries, Cleve., 1975-81; v.p. fin. Mueller Electric, Cleve., 1981—. Mem. Am. Assn. CPA's, Ohio Assn. CPA's, Fin. Exec., Inc. Office: Mueller Electric 1583 E 31st St Cleveland OH 44114

GOLDEN, VALERIE ANN OLSEN, accounting administrator; b. Chgo., June 5, 1957; d. Jerome Christopher and Beverly Ann (Gierow) Olsen; m. Donald Craig Golden, Aug. 17, 1986. BA, De Paul U., 1979; MBA, Keller Grad. Sch. Mgmt., 1982. Tchr. Chgo. Pub. Schs., 1979-81; acct. Rubloff, Inc., Chgo., 1981-84; acct., then mgr. internal reporting Henry Crown & Co., Chgo., 1984—; controller Chgo. City Concert Band, 1986—. Mem. Am. Inst. CPA's, Ill. CPA Soc. Avocations: profl. clarinetist, cycling. Office: Henry Crown & Co 300 W Washington Chicago IL 60602

GOLDENHERSH, JOSEPH HERMAN, justice state supreme court; b. East St. Louis, Ill., Nov. 2, 1914; s. Benjamin and Bertha (Goldenberg) G.; m. Maxyne Zelenka, June 18, 1939; children: Richard, Jerold. LL.B., Washington U., St. Louis, 1935; LL.D. (hon.), John Marshall Law Sch., Chgo., 1972. Bar: Ill. 1936. Pvt. practice law East St. Louis, 1936-64; judge Appellate Ct. Ill., 1964-70; justice Supreme Ct. Ill., 1970-78, 82—, chief justice, 1979-82. Chmn. Initial Gifts United Fund East St. Louis, 1952-53; dir. Mississippi Valley council Boy Scouts Am., 1952-58; pres. Jewish Fedn. So. Ill., 1949-51; Trustee emeritus Christian Welfare Hosp., East St. Louis. Recipient Disting. Alumnus award Washington U. Law Sch., St. Louis, 1985. Mem. Appellate Judges Conf. (exec. com. 1969-70), East St. Louis Bar Assn. (pres. 1962-63), ABA, Ill. Bar Assn. Clubs: Mason (St. Louis) (33 deg., Shriner), Missouri Athletic (St. Louis). Home: 7510 Claymont Ct Belleville IL 62223 Office: Supreme Court Office 6464 W Main St Suite 3A Belleville IL 62223 *

GOLDFARB, BERNARD SANFORD, lawyer; b. Cleve., Apr. 15, 1917; s. Harry and Esther (Lenson) G.; m. Barbara Brofman, Jan. 4, 1966; children—Meredith Stacey, Lauren Beth. A.B., Case Western Res. U., 1938, J.D., 1940. Bar: Ohio bar 1940. Since practiced in Cleve.; sr. partner firm Goldfarb & Reznick, 1967—; spl. counsel to atty. gen. Ohio, 1950, 71-74; mem. Ohio Commn. Uniform Traffic Rules, 1973—. Contbr. legal jours. Served with USAAF, 1942-45. Mem. Am., Ohio, Greater Cleve. bar assns. Home: 39 Pepper Creek Dr Pepper Pike OH 44124 Office: 1800 Illuminating Bldg Cleveland OH 44113

GOLDFARB, CLARE ROSETT, English educator, university administrator; b. N.Y.C., Oct. 12, 1934; d. Leonard and Gertrude M. (Rothman) Rosett; m. Russell M. Goldfarb, Aug. 11, 1957; children: Eric D. and Jennifer L. BA, Smith Coll., 1956; MA, NYU, 1957; PhD, Ind. U., 1964. Prof. Western Mich. U., Kalamazoo, 1960—, chmn. English dept., 1978-82, assoc. dean coll arts ans scis., 1984-86. Author: Spiritualism and Nineteenth Century Letters, 1978; contbr. articles to profl. jours. Office: Western Mich U Kalamazoo MI 49008

GOLDFARB, DAVID B., insurance agent; b. Jackson, Mich., Nov. 11, 1954; s. Stuart A. and Shirley F. (Fryman) G. B in Risk and Ins., Mich. State U., 1976. CLU; cert. life ins. counselor. Agent Mass. Mut., Lansing, Mich., 1976-78; agent, pension specialist Mass. Mut., Jackson, 1978—; cons. Sheldon Assocs., Inc., Okemo, Mich., 1977; officer Estate & Pension Plans, Inc., Jackson, 1978—; mem. Midwest Pension Study Group, Chgo., 1984—. Rec. sec. Temple Beth Israel, Jackson, 1987; bd. dirs. Family Services and Children's Aid, Jackson, 1987; active exec. allocations com. United Way of Jackson County, Jackson, 1987, citizens adv. com. Com. Devel. Block Grants, Jackson, 1987. Recipient Nat. Quality award Nat. Assn. Life Underwriters, Washington, 1984-86. Mem. Jackson Assn. Life Underwriters (officer, bd. dirs. 1978-85, pres. 1984-85), Soc. Chartered Life Underwriters, Million Dollar Round Table (provisional), Mass. Mut. Leaders Club. Clubs: Jackson Ski, Profl. Singles of Jackson (bd. dirs. 1986-87). Lodge: Kiwanis (bd. dirs. Jackson East club 1985—). Avocations: photography, skiing, biking, reading. Office: Mass Mut Life Ins Co 507 W Michigan Ave PO Box 826 Jackson MI 49204

GOLDFEDER, HOWARD, retail executive; b. N.Y.C., Apr. 28, 1926; s. Herman and Betty (Epstein) G.; m. Helen Wiggs; children: Carole, Joan. B.A., Tufts U., 1947. With Bloomingdale's, N.Y.C., 1947-67; exec. v.p. Famous-Barr, St. Louis, 1967-69; pres. May Co., Los Angeles, 1969-71; pres., then chmn. Bullock's, Los Angeles, 1971-77; with Federated Dept. Stores, Inc., Cin., 1977—; pres. Federated Dept. Stores, Inc., 1980—, chief exec. officer, 1981—, chmn., 1982—, also dir.; dir. J.P. Morgan and Morgan Guaranty Trust Co., Conn. Mut. Life Ins. Co. Recipient Nat. Brotherhood award NCCJ, 1981. Mem. Nat. Retail Mchts. Assn. (dir., exec. com.), Bus. Roundtable, Bus. Council, Cin. Inst. of Fine Arts (dir.). Clubs: Commercial (Cin.), Queen City (Cin.), Losantiville Country (Cin.). Office: Federated Dept Stores Inc 7 W 7th St Cincinnati OH 45202

GOLDFUS, DONALD WAYNE, glass company executive; b. Mpls., Feb. 17, 1934; s. Alex Goldfus and Ruby Jane (Elliott) Bolander; m. Therese Marie Smuda, Aug. 22, 1959; children: Karen Goldfus O'Connor, Brian John. Student, U. Minn., 1956-59. Advt. mgr. Harmon Glass Co., Mpls., 1959-61, sales mgr., 1961-63, v.p. sales, 1963-67, pres., 1967-79; sr. v.p. Apogee Enterprises, Mpls., 1979-83, pres., 1983—, chief exec. officer, 1985—. Editor Sporting Goods Jour., Mpls., 1958-59. Mem. adv. bd. Leukemia Research Fund, U. Minn., 1973—. Served with USAF, 1951-55. Named Glass Dealer of Yr. The Glass Digest, 1984; named to Pres. Club U. Minn., 1986. Mem. Nat. Glass Assn. (pres. 1983-84), Sales and Mktg. Exes. of Mpls. (bd. dirs. 1967-71, Man of Yr., 1970, Bus. Exec. of Yr. 1986), Auto Glass Industry Com. (bd. dirs.). Club: Lafayette Country (Mpls.); Excelsior Bay Yacht (Minn.). Lodge: Masons. Office: Apogee Enterprises Inc 7900 Xerxes Ave S Bloomington MN 55431

GOLDMAN, ALLEN SEYMOUR, pediatrician, educator; b. Providence, Oct. 25, 1929. AB in Chemistry cum laude, Brown U., 1951, ScM in Biology, 1953; PhD, Yale U., 1954; MD, SUNY, Syracuse, 1958; MA (hon.), U. Pa., 1971. Instr. dept. pediatrics U. Pa., Phila., 1961-64, assoc. in pediatrics, 1964-66, asst. prof., 1966-69, assoc. prof., 1969-78, research prof. pediatrics and pediatrics in pharmacology, 1978-85; prof. pediatrics, craniofacial anomalies, genetics U. Ill. Coll. Medicine, Chgo., 1986—, dir. Ctr. for Craniofacial Anomalies; asst. physician div. exptl. pathology Children's Hosp. of Phila., 1964-65, assoc. physician, 1965-78, sr. physican sect. of teratology div. child devel. and rehab., 1978-85, assoc. dir., 1965-73, co-dir., 1973-76, dir. sect. of teratology, 1976-82; sr. physician Children's Seashore House, Atlantic City and Phila. Home: 1411 N State Chicago IL 60610

GOLDMAN, CAREN SUSAN, editor; b. Bklyn., Mar. 2, 1947; d. Bernard Goldman and Muriel H. (Rosenstock) Oglesby; m. Robert W. Ritter, June 26, 1982; children: Jamie, Evan Clark. Student, NYU, 1964; BA, Ohio Wesleyan U., 1967; postgrad., Ohio State U., 1967, Cleve. State U., 1975, St. Nicholas Training Centre for Montessori, London, 1975. Reporter Plain Dealer, Cleve., 1967-69; sch. adminstr. Montessori Children, Cleve., 1974-76; asst. editor Cleve. Jewish News, 1986—; freelance writer, 1971—. Contbr. numerous articles to profl. jours. and nat. mags. Recipient Foremost Women in Communications award, 1969, Soc. award Cleve. Communicators, 1976; name one of Outstanding Young Women Am., 1975. Avocations: real estate investing, stained glass artistry, teaching music.

GOLDMAN, CHARLES DAVID, surgeon; b. Flushing, N.Y., Dec. 2, 1955; s. Abraham Moses and Rita Doris (Colby) G.; m. Noreene Eve Silzer, Feb. 19, 1983; 1 child, Hannah Louise. AB, Brandeis U., 1977; MD, Washington U., St. Louis, 1981. Lic. M.D., Mo. Intern in surgery Jewish Hosp. of St. Louis, 1981-82, resident in surgery, 1982-86, chief resident, 1986-87; surgeon USAF Med. Ctr. Scott, Scott AFB, Ill., 1987—; researcher pediatric Children's Hosp., St. Louis, 1985—. Mem. Phi Beta Kappa. Avocations: squash, basketball, bicycling, audiophile. Office: Dept Surgery USAF Med Ctr Scott Scott AFB IL 62225

GOLDMAN, JEFFREY HOWARD, physician; b. Chgo., Dec. 9, 1950; s. Michael Marvin and Esther (Kaleko) G.; m. Birgitte Maria Hagen, June 15, 1930; 1 child, Derek Robert. BS, U. Ill., 1972; MD, U. Ill., Chgo., 1976. Diplomate Am. Bd. Internal Medicine, Am. Bd. Gastroenterology. Physician U. Wis., Madison, 1979-81, N. Suburban Gastroenterology, Park Ridge, Ill., 1981—; attending staff Luth. Gen. Hosp., Park Ridge, 1981—, Resurrection Hosp., Chgo., 1981—; spkr. and clinical investigator Pharmacia, Inc., Piscataway, N.J., 1985—. Mem. adv. bd. Nat. Found. for Ileitis and Colitis, 1985—. Mem. ACP, AMA, Am. Gastroent. Assn., Am. Soc. for Gastrointestinal Endoscopy, Chgo. Soc. of Internal Medicine. Jewish. Avocations: photography, jogging, tennis, reading. Home: 2510 Pick Ln Glenview IL 60025 Office: Northwestern Gastroenterology 950 Northwest Hwy Park Ridge IL 60068

GOLDMAN, JONATHAN LEE, lexicographer, editor; b. Cleve., July 18, 1944; s. Bernard Leonard and Pearl M. (Lieberman) G.; m. Kärstin Elsa Olofsson, Aug. 31, 1974; children: Lina Elsa, Anders Bernard. BA, U. Mich., 1966; MA, Case Western Reserve U., 1980. Editor Webster's New World Dictionary, Cleve., 1966—. Contbr. articles to profl. jours. Mem. Northeast Ohio Jazz Soc. (trustee 1983—). Democrat. Jewish. Avocations: reading, jazz, film. Home: 3117 Washington Blvd Cleveland Heights OH 44118 Office: Prentice Hall Press 850 Euclid Room 306 Cleveland OH 44114

GOLDMAN, PAUL MICHAEL, obstetrician-gynecologist, educator; b. Chgo., June 24, 1944; s. Joseph and Dora G.; m. Barbara Alyse, Aug. 20, 1967; 4 children. BS, U. Ill., 1967, DVM, 1969; MD, U. Ill., Chgo., 1977; MS, Pa. State U., Hershey, 1971. Diplomate Am. Bd. Ob-Gyn. Fellow comparative medicine Pa. State U., Hershey, 1969-71; animal disease investigator NIH, Bethesda, Md., 1971-73; resident ob-gyn Presby.-St. Lukes Med. Ctr., Chgo., 1977-81, chief resident ob-gyn., 1980-81; practice medicine specializing in ob-gyn. Park Ridge, Ill., 1981—; clin. asst. prof. ob-gyn. U. Ill., Chgo., 1981—. Contbr. articles to profl. jours. Served with USPHS, 1971-73. James scholar U. Ill., 1962-65, recipient scholarship key, 1965. Fellow ACS; mem. AMA, Am. Assn. Gyn. Lapanoscopists, Am. Fertility Soc. Jewish. Avocations: history, clarinet. Office: 1875 Dempster Park Ridge IL 60018

GOLDMAN, RACHEL BOK, civic volunteer; b. Phila., Mar. 28, 1937; d. W. Curtis and Nellie Lee (Holt) Bok; m. James Nelson Kise, Dec. 20, 1958 (div. May 1974); children: Jefferson B, C. Curtis; m. Allen S. Goldman, Nov. 28, 1981; stepchildren: Jonathan, Benjamin Allen, Adam Louis. Student, Sweet Briar (Va.) Coll., 1955-57; BA in Art History, U. Pa., 1977. Bd. dirs. Arts Exchange mag., 1977-79, chmn. bd. dirs., 1977-79. Mem. collector's circle Pa. Acad. Fine Arts, 1983-85, exhbn. selection com. Morris Gallery, 1979-82; mem. Rittenhouse Sq. Women's Com. Pa. Orchestra, 1979-85; mem. Indian com. Pa. Yearly Meeting, 1971-75; mem. ladies' com. Powel House, 1965-69; co-founder Friends of Curtis Inst. Music, 1982—, chmn. 1982-85; bd. dirs. Mary Louis Curtis Bok Found., 1982—, The Curtis Inst. Music, 1982—, The Buten Mus., 1982-84, Brady Cancer Research Inst. 1983—, Settlement Music Sch., 1984-87, The Phila. Award, 1970—, Elfreth's Alley Assn., 1962-65, sec. 1963-65; bd. dirs. The Am. Found., 1955-83, sec.-treas., 1980-83; bd. dirs. The Community Sch. of Phila., 1971-74, chmn. bd. dirs., co-founder, adminstr.; bd. dirs. Women in Transition, 1973-78, div. counselor, 1974-76; bd. dirs. Friends of Phila. Mus. Art, 1977-83, sec., 1979-81, program chmn., 1981-82, co-chmn., 1982-83; bd. dirs. Samuel Yellin Found., 1977—, co-founder, sec., 1977-84. Democrat. Clubs: Camden Yacht (Maine), Cosmopolitan of Phila. (house com. 1981-84). Avocations: collecting art, sailing, music.

GOLDSMITH, DAVID HIRSH, English professor; b. Chgo., Aug. 13, 1933; s. Milton and Sue (Fisher) G.; m. Vicki Lynn Keck, Dec. 27, 1967 (div. Nov. 1986); children: Rachel, Jocelyn. BA, Bowling Green U., 1958, MA, 1961, PhD, 1970. Asst. prof. English SUNY, Buffalo, 1964-68, Bowling Green (Ohio) U., 1969-70; prof. English No. Mich. U., Marquette, Mich., 1970—; Pres. AAUP No. Mich. U., Marquette, 1979-80, upper peninsula med. edn. selection com., 1983—, dir. WPE, 1986—; host High Sch. Bowl WNMU-TV, 1977—. Author: Kurt Vonnegut: Fantasist of Fire and Ice, 1972, Mystery Kawbawgam's Grave, 1979; columnist Mpls. Star and Tribune. Mem. Bi-Lingual Adv. Council, Lansing, 1976. Served to cpl. U.S. Army, 1952-55, Korea. Fullbright Hays fellow, 1973-74. Mem. AAUP, Nat. Book Critics Circle, Pop. Culture Assn., Fulbright Aluni Assn. Democrat. Avocations: fishing, hunting, African history, military history. Home: 197 1/2 Old Kiln Rd Marquette MI 49855 Office: English Dept No Mich U Marquette MI 49855

GOLDSMITH, ETHEL FRANK, medical social worker; b. Chgo., May 31, 1919; d. Theodore and Rose (Falk) Frank; m. Julian Royce Goldsmith, Sept. 4, 1940; children: Richard, Susan, John. BA, U. Chgo., 1940. Registered social worker, Ill. Liaison worker psychiat. consultation service U. Chgo. Hosp., 1964-68; med. social worker Wyler Children's Hosp., Chgo., 1968—. Treas. U. Chgo. Service League, 1958-62, chmn. camp Brueckner Farr Aux., 1966—; pres. Bobs Roberts Hosp. Service Commn., 1962; mem. Field Mus. Women's Bd., 1966—; bd. dirs. Hyde Park Art Ctr., 1964-82, Chgo. Commons Assn., 1967-77, Alumni Assn. Sch. Social Service Adminstrn., 1976-80, Self Help Home for Aged, 1985—. Recipient Alumni Citation Pub. Service, U. Chgo., 1972. Mem. Phi Beta Kappa. Home: 5631 S Blackstone Ave Chicago IL 60637 Office: Wyler Hosp Dept Social Service 5841 S Maryland Chicago IL 60637

GOLDSMITH, JEWETT, psychiatrist; b. Balt., Apr. 1, 1919; s. Harry and Charlotte B. (Goldstein) G.; m. Halina Ann Zukowski, Aug. 4, 1956; children: Miriam C., Anthony M., Amy L. BA, John Hopkins U., 1938; MD, U. Md., 1942. Diplomate Am. Bd. Psychiatry and Neurology, 1948. Rotating intern Kings County Hosp., Bklyn., 1942-43; resident in psychiatry Duke U. Hosp., Durham, N.C., 1946-48, dir. psychiatric out-patient dept., 1950-56; attending physician VA Hosp., Durham, N.C., 1953-56, ward physician, 1956-59; service chief Ill. State Psychiat. Inst., Chgo., 1959-72, clin. dir. forensic program, 1973-79, service chief, 1980—; assoc. to asst. prof. Dept. Psychiatry, Duke U. Med. Sch., Durham, 1950-59; asst. prof. psychiatry Northwestern U. Med. Sch., Chgo., 1959-64, assoc. clin. prof., 1964—; mem. criminal law subcom. Gov.'s Commn. for Revision of Mental Health Statutes, Chgo., 1974-75. Served to lt. M.C., USNR, 1943-46, CBI. Fellow Am. Psychiat. Assn. (life); mem. AAAS, Ill. Psychiat. Assn., Am. Acad. Psychiatry and the Law. Democrat. Jewish. Avocations: automobiles, jazz. Office: Ill State Psychiat Inst 1601 W Taylor St Chicago IL 60612

GOLDSON, HARRY ALBERT, financial company executive; b. Chgo., Feb. 27, 1930; s. Albert Rothschild and Rose Eileen (Schaeffer) G.; m. Joan Marie Berendt, May 25, 1956 (div. Oct. 1980); m. Piper Loyce, Feb. 12, 1981; children: Allen, Janice. BS in Acctg. and Bus. Law, Walton Sch. Commerce, 1955. CPA. Comml. loan officer Exchange Nat. Bank, Chgo., 1957-61; v.p., sr. loan officer Union Bank, Los Angeles, 1961-70; exec. v.p., chief exec. officer Fund of West, Beverly Hills, Calif., 1970-72; pvt. practice fin. cons. Los Angeles, Chgo., 1972-80; sr. v.p., comml. loans United of Am. Bank, Chgo., 1980-82; regional dir. corp fin. Wells Fargo Bus., Chgo., 1982-83; v.p. midwest region Lazere Fin. Corp., Chgo., 1983—. Author: The Spirit of Enchantment, 1978. Assoc. chmn. Chgo. chpt., Ill. Fin. Council, City of Hope, 1982; chmn. fund raising Shaare Zedek Hosp., Israel, 1982. Served to 1st lt. U.S. Army, 1950-53. Mem. Am. Inst. CPA's, Ill. Soc. CPA's (industry com. Chgo. chpt., 1982-83, found. com. 1984-85). Mem. Am. Inst. CPA's, Ill. Soc. CPA's (industry com. Chgo. chpt. 1982-83, found. com. 1984-85). Clubs: Cliffdwellers, Carlton (Chgo.). Mem. Chgo. Businessmen's Orch. Avocations: collecting fine art and antiques, philately, music. Office: Lazere Fin Corp 208 S LaSalle St Chicago IL 60604

GOLDSTEIN, ARNOLD S., pediatrician; b. Chgo., June 9, 1942; m. Karyn J. Perkers, June 26, 1966; children: Deborah, Rachel, Benjamin. BS, U. Ill., 1963; MD, U. Ill., Chgo., 1966. Diplomate Am. Bd. Pediatrics. Fellow Stanford (Calif.) U. Sch. Medicine, 1971-73; neonatologist and assoc. dir. high-risk nursery Luth. Gen. Hosp., Park Ridge, Ill., 1973-74; gen. pediatrician Highland Park (Ill.) Pediatric Assocs., 1974—; chmn. dept. pediatrics Highland Park Hosp., 1983-86; asst. prof. clin. pediatrics Northwestern U. Sch. Medicine, Chgo., 1983—. Contbr. articles on neonatology to profl. jours. Served to maj. U.S. Army, 1969-71. Fellow Am. Acad. Pediatrics; mem. AMA, Ill. State Med. Soc., Chgo. Pediatric Soc. (exec. com. 1980—, pres. 1986-87), NYU Pediatric Alumni Assn. Office: Highland Park Pediatric Assocs 1160 Park Ave W Highland Park IL 60035

GOLDSTEIN, LOREN DAVID, general dentist; b. Chgo., July 15, 1955; s. Harold and June Marlene Goldstein; m. René Ann Boyd, Mar. 20, 1982. BA, Drake U., 1977; DDS, U. Ill., Chgo., 1982. Gen. practice dentistry Northbrook, Ill., 1982-83, Glencoe (Ill.) Dental Assocs., 1983—. Staff mem. Highland Park (Ill.) Hosp., 1985—; v.p. Towers Condominium Bd., Chgo., 1983—. Mem. ADA, Acad. Gen. Dentistry, Am. Equilibration Soc., Chgo. Dental Soc. (editor northside br. 1984—, pub. media com. 1985—, mediation com. 1985—). Lodge: Masons. Avocations: photography, computers. Office: Glencoe Dental Assocs 331 Park Ave #300 Glencoe IL 60022

GOLDSTEIN, RICHARD JAY, mechanical engineer, educator; b. N.Y.C., Mar. 27, 1928; s. Henry and Rose (Steierman) G.; m. Anita Nancy Klein, Sept. 5, 1963; children: Arthur Sander, Jonathan Jacob, Benjamin Samuel, Naomi Sarith. BME, Cornell U., 1948; MS in Mech. Engring., U. Minn., 1950, MS in Physics, 1951, PhD in Mech. Engring., 1959. Instr. U. Minn., Mpls., 1948-51, instr., research fellow, 1956-58, mem. faculty, 1961—, prof. mech. engring., 1965—, head dept., 1977—; research engr. Oak Ridge Nat. Lab., 1951-54, Lockheed Aircraft, 1956; asst. prof. Brown U., 1959-61; vis. prof. Imperial Coll., Eng., 1984; cons. in field, 1956—; chmn. Midwest U. Energy Consortium; chmn. Council Energy Engring. Research; NSF sr. postdoctoral fellow, vis. prof. Cambridge (Eng.) U., 1971-72. Served to 1st lt. AUS, 1954-55. NATO fellow Paris, 1960-61; Lady Davis fellow Technion, Israel, 1976; recipient NASA award for tech. innovation, 1977. Fellow ASME (Heat Transfer Meml. award 1978, Centennial medallion 1980, BEG v.p. 1984—, pres. assembly for internat. heat transfer confs. 1986—); mem. AAAS, Am. Phys. Soc., Am. Soc. Engring. Edn., Minn. Acad. Sci., Nat. Acad. Engring., Sigma Xi, Tau Beta Pi, Pi Tau Sigma. Research, publs. in thermodynamics, fluid mechanics, heat transfer, optical measuring techniques. Home: 520 Janalyn Circle Golden Valley MN 55416 Office: U Minn Dept Mech Engring 111 Church St SE Minneapolis MN 55455

GOLDSTEIN, SAMUEL R., oil company executive; b. N.Y.C., Apr. 2, 1918; s. Rubin and Rose (Gluck) G.; m. Gloria Elaine Mintz, June 16, 1945 (dec. Apr. 1975); children—Carol Jean Goldstein Jones, Richard Henry. B.A. in Sci., Bklyn. Coll., 1939. Salesman Liggett & Myers Tobacco Co., N.Y.C., 1939-42; instr. Civil Service, Belleville, Ill., 1942-43; ptnr. Standard Tool & Mfg. Co., St. Louis, 1946-48; salesman Apex Oil Co., St. Louis, 1948-61, chmn. bd., 1961—. Bd. dirs. St. Louis Assn. Retarded Citizens, 1981—, Arts and Edn. Council St. Louis, 1982—, St. Louis Mcpl. Theatre, 1982—, Jewish Fedn. St. Louis, 1980—. Served with USAF, 1943-46. Avocations: golf; snow skiing. Office: Apex Oil Co 8182 Maryland Ave Saint Louis MO 63105

GOLDSTEIN, SANDRA, consumer products importing company executive, designer and importer; b. Chgo., Dec. 7; d. Jack Julius and Esther Judith (Glickman) Gilbert; student U. Wis., U. Ill., Champaign-Urbana; m. Seymour Leo Goldstein, Aug. 12, 1951; 1 child, Jennie S. Co-founder, sr. v.p., sales mgr. Jennie G. Sales Co., Inc., Lincolnwood, Ill., 1961—. Bd. dirs. Ill. Found. Dentistry for Handicapped. Mem. Nat. Assn. Convenience Stores, Nat. Oil Jobbers Assn., Ill. Petroleum Assn., Tex. Oil Marketers Assn., Intermountain Oil Jobbers Assn., Wis. Oil Jobbers Assn., Ind. Oil Jobbers Assn., Mich. Oil Jobbers Assn., Mo. Oil Jobbers Assn., Iowa Oil Jobbers Assn. Clubs: Carleton (Chgo.); Springs Country (Palm Springs, Calif.). Office: 3770 W Pratt Ave Lincolnwood IL 60645

GOLDSTEIN, WALTER ELLIOTT, pharmaceutical company executive; b. Chgo., Nov. 28, 1940; s. Henry H. and Dorothy (Davidson) G.; m. Paula G. Copen, Feb. 18, 1962; children—Susan, Marc. B.S. in Chem. Engring., Ill. Inst. Tech., 1961; M.B.A., Mich. State U., 1968; M.S. in Chem. Engring., U. Notre Dame, 1971, Ph.D., 1973. Registered profl. engr., Ind. Process devel. engr. Linde div. Union Carbide, Tonawanda, N.Y., 1961-64; with Miles Labs., Elkhart, Ind., 1964—, assoc. project engr., 1964-67, assoc. research scientist, 1967-72, research scientist, 1972-73, research supr., 1973-76, mgr. Chem. Engring. Research and Pilot Services, 1976-78, dir., 1978-82, v.p. research and devel., 1982—; adj. asst. prof. chem. engring. U. Notre Dame, 1975-76. Active in fund raising Am. Cancer Soc., Am. Heart Assn. Mem. Am. Inst. Chem. Engrs., Soc. Indsl. Microbiology, AAAS, Sigma Xi. Jewish. Club: B'nai B'rith (v.p.). Inventions and publs. in chem. engring. and biotech. field.

GOLDYN, ROBERT S., corporate controller; b. Chgo., Nov. 25, 1944; s. Matthew and Lottie (Ulanski) G.; m. Rosemarie Helmsdorfer, Aug. 2, 1969; children: Robert, David, Brian. BA in Acctg., St. Joseph's Coll., 1966. Staff auditor Haskind & Sells, Chgo., 1966-70; gen. acct. Continental Coffee, Chgo., 1970-72; controller Byman Co., Calumet City, Ill., 1972-76; corp. controller Flame Mgmt., Oakbrook, Ill., 1976—. Served to sgt. U.S. Army, 1967-69, Vietnam. Avocation: fishing. Office: Flame Mgmt 260 E Kenilworth PO Box 250 Villa Park IL 60477

GOLICZ, LAWRENCE JOHN, real estate appraisal company executive; b. Detroit, Feb. 21, 1944; s. Anthony John Golicz and Estelle Ann (Sikorski) Rogowski; m. Peggy Louise Erickson, Aug. 3, 1968; children: Eric John, Karl Peter, Mark Joseph. AA, Henry Ford Community Coll., 1964; BA, U. Mich., 1966; MA, Wash. State U., 1968; PhD, U. Maine, 1973. Demographer State of Wis., Madison, 1973; pres. Am. Appraisal and Feasibilty Corp., Madison, 1973—, Total Realty Inc., Madison, 1974—; mng. ptnr. Madison Mut. Investors, 1979—; proprietor Protel Games & Amusements, Madison, 1985—; pres., founder Affiliated Funding Corp., Madison, 1986; mng. ptnr. Five Star Enterprises, Madison, 1987—; instr. U. Wis. Bus. Devel., Milw. and Madison, 1986—, Madison Area Tech. Coll., 1976-80; bd. dirs. A&W of Windsor, Inc., Madison, 1985—; cons. appraisal to various city govts., Wis., 1977—. Developer (game): Paroah's Quest, 1985-86 (Parents' Choice award, 1986); host (TV series): Economics: Current Problems, 1982. Mem. Westmoreland Youth Hockey Assn., Madison, 1979-82, 85—. Dean's scholar U. Maine Grad. Sch., 1968-72, regent's scholar U. Mich., 1964-66. Mem. Am. Inst. Real Estate Appraisers (bd. dirs. local chpt. 1978), Madison Bd. Realtors, Wis. Bd. Realtors, Wis. Assn. Assessing Officers, Wis. Towns Assn., Internat. Order Foresters, Phi Alpha Theta. Avocations: tennis, model building, hunting, fishing, photography. Home: 1619 Elderwood Circle Middleton WI 53562 Office: Am Appraisal & Feasibility Corp 6506 Schroeder Rd Madison WI 53711

GOLLINGS, ROBERT HARRY, data processing consultant; b. Pitts., July 4, 1931; s. Chester Lyman and Lorena Elizabeth (Grady) G.; B.B.A., U. Pitts., 1953, M.B.A., 1961; postgrad. U. Ill., Chgo., 1979-80; m. Marilyn Campbell, Sept. 19, 1959 (dec. Apr. 1981); children—Anne, Graham. Systems analyst Westinghouse Electric Corp., Pitts., 1956-65; supr. systems and programming Joy Mfg. Co., Pitts. and Michigan City, Ind., 1965-67; project mgr. Standard Oil Co. (Ind.), 1967-75; project mgr., lead analyst G.D. Searle & Co., Skokie, Ill., 1975-78; sr. mgr. Comsi, Inc., Oak Brook, Ill., 1978-79; coordinator mgmt. systems U. Ill., Chgo., 1979-80; data processing cons., owner RHG Systems, 1981-83; pres. Matrix Techs., Inc., Park Forest, Ill., 1983—; instr. Calumet Coll., Thornton Community Coll. Chmn., Parks and Recreation Bd., Park Forest, Ill., 1978-82; bd. dirs. Community Chest, Park Forest-Richton Park, 1973-82, pres., 1975; bd. dirs. South Suburban Symphony, 1975-78, Park Forest Symphony, 1978-83. Served to 1st lt. USAF, 1953-56; Korea. Mem. Assn. Systems Mgmt., Internat. Computer Consultants Assn., Midwest Soc. Profl. Cons., Am. Arbitration Assn. (computer panel arbitrator) Republican. Presbyterian. Club: Chgo. Bus. Sch. Alumni Club of U. Pitts. (sec.). Home: 19 Dogwood St Park Forest IL 60466

GOLTON, MARGARET APPEL, psychotherapist; b. Cleve., Jan. 12, 1909; m. Eugene G. Golton (dec.). BA, Case Western Res. U., 1931, MSW, 1945, D Social Work, 1964. Lic. ind. social worker, Ohio. Case worker, supr. Office of Pub. Welfare, Cleve., 1933-47; supr. Pvt. Child Welfare, Cleve., 1947-59; pvt. practice social psychotherapist Cleve., 1961—; vice chmn. Internat. Conf. Advancement of Pvt. Practice. Author: Unlock Your Potential, 1982, Your Brain At Work, 1983, Professional Potpourri, 1984; developed brain orgn. neural network theory of personality and behavior (BONN theory) 1982; contbr. articles to profl. jours. Mem. Nat. Assn. Social Workers (various coms.), Nat. Registry Clin. Social Work. Avocations: dress making, poetry, writing. Home: 2628 Whiton Rd University Heights OH 44118 Office: 24700 Chagrin Blvd Beachwood OH 44122

GOLUB, HARVEY, finance company executive. Pres., chief exec. officer IDS Fin. Services, Inc., Mpls. Office: IDS Life Ins Co IDS Tower Minneapolis MN 55402 *

GOLUSIN, MILLARD R., obstetrician/gynecologist; b. Detroit, Feb. 14, 1947; s. Raddie and Joan (Lalich) G.; m. Yvonne Marie Cronovich, Sept. 29, 1974; children: Milan, Marko. BS with honors, Wayne State U., 1968, MS, 1970, MD, 1975. Diplomate Am. Bd. Obstetrics and Gynecology. Intern, then resident William Beaumont Hosp., Royal Oak, Mich., 1975-78; practice medicine specializing in obstetrics and gynecology Village Gynecologic and Obstetric Assocs., P.C., Southfield and Troy, Mich., 1978—; bd. trustees Oakland/Macomb Preferred Providor Orgn., Troy, 1986; mem. quality assurance com., William Beaumont Hosp., Royal Oak, Mich., 1979—, utilization com., Troy, 1978—. Served with U.S. Army, 1969-71. Fellow Am. Coll. Obstetricians and Gynecologists; mem. Am. Fertility Soc., Mich. State Med. Soc., North Am. Yugoslavian Med. Acad. (life, pres. 1985—), Serbian Singing Soc. Ravanica (musical dir. 1967—, pres. 1981-82). Republican. Serbian Eastern Orthodox. Avocations: music, golf. Office: Village Gynecologic and Obstetric Assn 16800 W 12 Mile Rd Southfield MI 48076

GOMEZ, JORGE, plastic surgeon; b. Bucaramanga, Colombia, Feb. 27, 1936; came to U.S., 1961; s. Jorge Gormez and Marina Ortiz; m. C. Ginette paramo, Dec. 10, 1960; children: Diana, Ginette, Anamaria. MD, Javeriana U., Bogota, Colombia, 1954-61. Diplomate Am. Bd. Plastic Surgery, Am. Bd. Surgery. Intern Jefferson Hosp., Roanoke, Va., 1962-63; resident in gen. surgery Henry Ford Hosp., Detroit, 1963-67, staff surgeon, 1970-74, resident in plastic surgery, 1973-76; mem. staff E.W. Sparrow Hosp., Detroit, Ingam Med. Ctr., Detroit, 1971-74; practice medicine specializing in plastic surgery Lansing, Mich., 1976—, St. Lawrence Hosp., Lansing, 1971-74; assoc. clinical prof. Mich. State U., East Lansing, 1977—. Served as comdr. USN, 1967-70, Vietnam, with Res. 1970-76. Fellow ACS; mem. AMA, Am. Soc. Plastic and Reconstructive Surgeons, Am. Soc. Plastic and Reconstructive Surgery, Inc., Am. Soc. Maxillofacial Surgeons, Am. Asssn. Hand Surgery, Am. Cleft Plate Assn., Mich. State Med. Soc., Mich. Acad. Plastic Surgeons (pres.), Ingham County Med. Soc., Roy McClure Alumni Soc. Repbulican. Roman Catholic. Avocations: equestrian sports, dressage. Home: 4106 Meridian Okemos MI 48864 Office: 921 Abbott Rd East Lansing MI 48823

GOMEZ, MANUEL RODRIGUEZ, physician; b. Minaya, Spain, July 4, 1928; came to U.S., 1952, naturalized, 1961; s. Argimiro Rodriguez Herguedas and Isabel Gomez Torrente; m. Joan A. Stormer, Sept. 25, 1954; children: Christopher, Gregory, Douglas, Timothy. M.D., U. Havana, Cuba, 1952; M.S. in Anatomy, U. Mich., 1956. Intern Michael Reese Hosp., 1952-53, asst. resident in pediatrics, 1953-54; resident in neurology U. Mich., 1954-56; fellow in pediatric neurology U. Chgo. Med. Sch., 1956-57; instr. neurology U. Buffalo Med. Sch., 1957-58, 59-60; clin. clk. neurology Inst. Neurology, U. London, 1958-59; asst. prof., then assoc. prof. neurology Wayne State U. Med. Sch., 1960-64; mem. faculty Mayo Med. Sch., Rochester, Minn., 1964—; prof. pediatric neurology Mayo Med. Sch., 1975—; cons. pediatric neurology, head sect. Mayo Clinic, 1964-84. Author: Tuberous Sclerosis, 1979, Neurocutaneous Diseases, 1987; adv. bd.: Brain and Devel., Pedriatrika. Mem. Am. Acad. Neurology, Am. Neurol. Assn., Child Neurology Soc., Philippine Pediatric Soc. (hon.), Sociedad Española de Neuropediatria (hon.), Assn. Research Nervous and Mental Disease, Orton-Dyslexia Soc., Neurology Soc. (adv. bd.), Am. Epilepsy Soc., Internat. Child Neurology Soc., Cen. Soc. Neurol. Research, Nat. Tuberous Sclerosis Assn. Home: 4225 Meadow Ridge Dr SW Rochester MN 55901 Office: Mayo Clinic 200 1st St SW Rochester MN 55901

GOMEZ, ROSE, psychiatrist; b. Havana, Cuba, Jan. 9, 1946; d. Jose Manuel and Maria (Rivera) G. Student, U. Ill., Chgo., 1972-74; MD, Loyola U., Maywood, Ill., 1977. Diplomate Am. Bd. Psychiatry and Neurology. Intern Loyola, Maywood, Ill., 1978; resident in psychiatry Northwestern U., Chgo., 1981; practice medicine specializing in psychiatry Chgo., 1981—; assoc. prof. psychiatry Northwestern U. Med. Sch., 1981—; med. dir. Little Co. Mary Hosp. Chem. Dependency Program, Evergreen Park, Ill., 1982—; med. dir. Palos Community Hosp. Chem. Dependency Program, Palos Hills, Ill., 1984—, chmn. dept. psychiatry, 1985—, med. dir. psychiatric unit, 1985—. James scholar U. Ill., 1973. Mem. Am. Psychiatric Assn., Am. Med. Soc. on Alcoholism and Other Drug Dependencies (cert. addictionologist), Ill. Psychiatric Soc. (chmn. com. on women 1985-86). Roman Catholic. Avocations: tennis, skiing. Home: 260 E Chestnut #4106 Chicago IL 60611 Office: 845 N Michigan Suite 903E Chicago IL 60611 Office: 4700 W 95th St Suite 308 Oaklawn IL 60453

GOMOLL, GEORGE, sales executive; b. Chgo., Aug. 7, 1950; s. George Albert and Dolores Marie (Pokorney) G.; m. Barbara Ann Esser, Aug. 21, 1971; children: Jennifer, Rebecca, Laura. BS in Edn., No. Ill. U., 1972. Tchr. Braceville and Plainfield (Ill.) Sch. Dist., 1973-75; sales rep. Winthrop Labs., N.Y.C., 1975-76; asst. store mgr. Radio Shack, Joliet, Ill., 1976-77; sales rep. 3M Co., Oakbrook, Ill., 1977-82; terr. mgr. Domtar, Schiller Park, Ill., 1982—; Bd. chmn. So. Sub. Elem., Homewood, Ill., 1984—. Mem. Am. Leading Execs. Seventh Day Adventists. Avocations: camping, gardening, woodburning art forms. Home: Rural Rt 1 Polk St Matteson IL 60443

GONANO, AULO IVO, lawyer; b. Detroit, Apr. 2, 1952; s. Vero H. and Annamaria (Solari) G.; m. Patricia Ann Christian, Oct. 30, 1980. BA in Polit. Sci., U. Mich., 1972; JD, Wayne State U., 1976. Bar: Mich. 1976. Assoc. Law Offices of Leonard Jaques, Detroit, 1976-77; city prosecutor City of Southgate, Mich., 1977-80; sole practice Wyandotte, Mich., 1977—; magistrate 28th Dist. Ct., Southgate, 1983—; bd. dirs. Mich. Barber Bd., 1982-86. Nat. del. Mich. Reps., 1984. Mem. ABA, Mich. Bar Assn., Downriver Bar Assn. Home: 20495 Thorofare Grosse Ile MI 48138 Office: 1932 Ford Ave Wyandotte MI 48192

GONDEK, GREGORY WARREN, sales executive; b. LaCrosse, Wis., May 9, 1947; s. Eugene Paul and Evelyn Kristine (Helgeson) G.; m. Pamela R. Jeffers, July 25,1970; children: Jeffrey W., Allison K. BBA, Wright State U., 1972. Project mgr. RNS Construction, Dayton, Ohio, 1972-74; pres. Dayton Indsl. Builders, 1973-74, Ohio Structures, Dayton, 1974-75; project mgr. Sun Construction, Greenville, Ohio, 1975-78; dist. sales mgr. Am. Bldgs. Co., Jamestown, Ohio, 1978—. Served to sgt. USAFR, 1966-72. Mem. Wright State U. Alumni Assn. Republican. Roman Catholic. Home: 111 Tall Hickory Trail Dayton OH 45415 Office: Am Bldgs Co PO Box 129 Jamestown OH 45335

GONDRING, WILLIAM HENRY, orthopedic surgeon; b. St. Joseph, Mo., Jan. 27, 1937; s. William Henry and Wilamina (Ostwald) G.; m. Phyllis Jean Withiam, June 4, 1964; children: Stacy, Christie, Jody. AS, St. Joseph Jr. Coll., 1956; AB, U. Mo., 1958; MD, Washington U., 1962. Orthopedic surgeon Lincoln (Nebr.) Fracture Clinic, 1970-76, St. Joseph Orthopedics, 1976—; adj. prof. mech. engring., U. Nebr., Lincoln, 1975-77; chief of surgery Heartland Hosp. East, Heartland Hosp. West, 1986—. Contbr. articles to profl. jours. Bd. dirs. Buchanan County ARC, internat. del. Recipient Cert. Appreciation Republic Vietnam Ministry Health, 1966, Vietnamese Medal of Honor, Vietnam Civil Action award, Vietnam Campaign Medal, Vietnam Service Medal, Disting. Service award Nat. Arthritis Found., 1983, Vol. Service award U.S. Dept. Health and Human Services, 1984. Mem. AMA (Physician's award), Mem. Soc. Mil. Surgeons, Am. Fracture Assn., Arthroscopy Assn. N.Am., Internat. Arthroscopy Assn., Assn. Mil. Surgeons, Am. Rheumatism Assn., Am. Acad. Orthopedic Surgeons, Soc. Biomaterials, Mo. Orthopedic Assn., Western Mo. Arthritis Assn. (past bd. dirs.), Medland Empire Arthritis Found. (exec. com.), Mo. State Med. Assn., Buchanan County Med. Assn., Am. Legion, Navy League (life), United Naval Inst., U.S. Naval Res. Assn. (sec. Pony Express chpt.) Phi Beta Kappa, Phi Theta Kappa. Lutheran.

GONSER, STEPHEN GEORGE, travelogue film producer, lecturer; b. Marion, Ind., Sept. 30, 1945; s. Ralph Lloyd and Marjorie (Botkin) G.; m. Suzan Jo Scott, Dec. 28, 1968 (div. Sept. 17, 1984); children—Luke Mitchell, Joel Daniel; m. Rookmin Persaud, Nov. 29, 1984; 1 child, Ronnie. B.A. in Edn., Marion Coll., 1967; M.A. in Edn., Ball State U., 1971. Cert. elem. tchr., Ind. Tchr. Mississinewa Community Sch., Gas City, Ind., 1967-77; mgr. presentation services Bell Fibre Products, Marion, 1977-80; film producer, lectr. Windoes Travelogues, Grand Rapids, Mich., 1980—. Producer (film) Costa Rica: Gem of the Americas, 1984, Puerto Rico: Isle of Enchantment, 1986. Mem. Internat. Travel-Adventure Film Guild, Internat. Motion Picture and Lecturers Assn., Internat. Fedn. Travel Writers and Journalists. Republican. Lodge: Kiwanis. Avocations: mountain climbing, hiking, bicycling, golf, metal detecting. Home: 1131 E Taylor St Kokomo IN 46901 Office: Windoes Travelogues McKay Tower Suite 1326 146 Monroe Ctr NW Grand Rapids MI 49503 Home: 4220 E 350 N Marion IN 46952

GONYEA, RONALD FRANCIS, insurance company executive, financial planner; b. Worcester, Mass., Nov. 30, 1947; s. Roland Phillip and Jeanne D'Arc (Routhier) G.; m. Joan Germain StClair, Dec. 30, 1967; children: Nicole, Glenn, Mark. Student, Quinsigamond Community Coll., 1968, Clark U., 1968-72. From underwriter to mgr. policy holder services Paul Revere Ins. Co., Worchester, 1968-79; gen. mgr. Paul Revere Ins. Co., St. Louis, 1981-87; brokerage mgr. Conn. Mut. Life Ins. Co., Mpls., 1979-81, Monarch Life Ins. Co., St. Louis, 1987—; cons. disability ins. Ind. Liberty Life Ins. Co., Grand Rapids, Mich., 1972-74. Vol. St. Richards Sch. Paper Dr., Mpls., 1978-81, Mpls. Reps., 1980; sponsor Fgn. Exchange Student Program, St. Louis, 1984; co-chmn. Howard Ruff Community Forum, St. Louis, 1985-86. Mem. Nat. Assn. Life Underwriters (cert.), Nat. Assn. Health Underwriters (bd. dirs. 1978-80), Internat. Assn. Fin. Planners (cert.), Life Office Mgmt. Assn. (fellow Life Mgmt. Inst., cert.), Chartered Life Underwriters Assn., Gen. Agts. and Mgrs. Assn., Life Underwriter Tng. Council (moderator 1983—, instr. ins. course 1983—). Avocations: woodworking, travelling, teaching. Office: Monarch Life Ins Co 7930 Clayton Rd #402 Saint Louis MO 63117

GONZALEZ, DIANE KATHRYN, social worker; b. Cin., Aug. 20, 1947; d. Joseph Curtis and Kathryn Mary (Diskin) Gonzalez; B.A. in Social Work, U. Dayton, 1969; A.M. in Social Work, U. Chgo., 1973; m. Thomas Connolley Leibig, July 5, 1974; 1 dau., Abigail. Social worker Hamilton County Welfare Dept., Cin., 1969-71; social worker obstetrics dept. and prenatal clinic social service dept. St. Francis Hosp., Evanston, Ill., 1973-78; rap group leader Teen Scene, Planned Parenthood Assn., Chgo., part-time, 1979-80; social worker Chgo. Comprehensive Care Center, 1980—; chmn. adv. com. Evanston Continuing Edn. Center, 1978-80. Mem. landmark dist. com. Old Town Triangle, 1983—; gen. co-chmn. Old Town Art Fair, 1984-85, gen. chmn. 1986-87. Mem. Nat. Assn. Social Workers (cert.). Roman Catholic. Home: 218 W Menomonee St Chicago IL 60614

GONZALEZ, FREDERICK, international trade consultant; b. N.Y.C., Dec. 22, 1916; s. Casimiro and Providencia (Román) G.; m. Alma Agrippa, Mar. 2, 1947 (dec. Jan. 1985); children: Lynn Bullard, Frederick Carl, Nan Burns; m. Faith Samson, June 22, 1985. BS in Social Sci., St. John's U., 1943; MA in Social Sci. and Polit. Sci., Columbia U., 1947. Export mgr. McCall Corp., N.Y.C., 1941-47; export sales mgr. Gerber Baby Foods, Fremont, Mich., 1947-59; v.p., gen. mgr. Gerber Baby Foods, Mexico City, 1959-68; asst. internat. dir. consumer div. Ralston Purina, S.A., Mexico City, 1968-72; dir. accounts Iconic, S.A., Mexico City, 1972-75; exec. dir. Cosmopolitan Internat. Club, Overland Park, Kans., 1975-86; internat. trade cons. Overland Park, 1986—. Bd. dirs. Prime Health HMO, Kansas City, Mo., 1979—. Mem. Mid-Am. Soc. of Assn. Execs., Export Mgr.'s Club of New York (v.p. 1943-47), Cosmopolitan Internat. Club (pres. 1961-63, editor Cosmo Topics, Cosmo Rap Sheet), Am. Soc. of Mex. (bd. dirs., v.p. 1969-72), Club Interamericano (past pres.). Roman Catholic. Avocations: writing, fishing, philately, travel. Home and Office: 6327 W 108 St Overland Park KS 66211

GONZENBACH, JACK EUGENE, electronics company executive; b. St. Louis, Nov. 11, 1950; s. Eugene Ruhl and Ellen Jane (Lienhop) G.; m. Patricia Lynn Bauer, Dec. 18, 1971; children: Catherine, Laura. BSEE, U. Mo., Rolla, 1973; MBA, So. Ill. U., 1985. With Harmon Electronics, Grain Valley, Mo., 1973—, mgr. quality analysis, 1985-86, gen. mgr., 1986—. Mem. Lake St. Louis (Mo.) Archtl. Control Commn., 1979-80, chmn., 1981-82. Mem. IEEE, NSPE, Am. Soc. Quality Control, Assn. for Computing Machinery, Mo. Soc. Profl. Engrs. Avocations: golf, tennis, fishing, computers. Home: 2116 Timberline Blue Springs MO 64015 Office: Harmon Electronics Argo & Dillingham Rds Grain Valley MO 64029

GOO, ABRAHAM MEU SEN, aircraft company executive; b. Honolulu, May 21, 1925; s. Tai Chong and Lily En Wui (Dai) G.; m. Shin Quon Wong, June 12, 1950; children—Marilynn, Steven, Beverly Cardinal. B.S. in Elec. Engring., U. Ill., 1951; postgrad. MIT, 1975. With The Boeing Co., Seattle, 1951-73; B-1 avionics program mgr. Boeing Aerospace Co., Seattle, 1974-75, v.p., gen. mgr. aircraft armament div., 1975-77; v.p. mil. systems Boeing Mil. Airplane Co., Wichita, Kans., 1977-79, exec. v.p., 1979-84, pres., 1984—. Served with USAAF, 1946-47. Recipient Disting. Alumnus award U. Ill., 1984. Mem. Airlift Assn., AIAA, Nat. Aero. Assn., Army Aviation Assn. Am., Assn. for Unmanned Vehicle Systems (hon. trustee), IEEE, Air Force Assn., Am. Security Council, Am. Def. Preparedness Assn., Armed Forces Communication and Electronics Assn., U.S. Naval Inst., Assn. Naval Aviation, The Tailhook Assn. Home: 1507 Blue Sage Circle Wichita KS 67230 Office: Boeing Mil Airplane Co PO Box 7730 Wichita KS 67277

GOOD, ANDREW EVANS, obstetrician; b. Rochester, Minn., May 31, 1943; s. C. Allen and Virginia (McClure) G.; m. Alison Jean Bach, July 8, 1967; children: Susan Erickson, Colin. BA, Williams Coll., 1965; MD, U. Sask., Saskatoon, Can., 1970; MS, U. Minn., 1977. Diplomate Am. Bd. Ob-Gyn. Intern Chas. T. Miller Hosp., St. Paul, 1970-71; resident Mayo Grad. Sch. of Medicine, Rochester, Minn., 1971-72, 74-76; obstetrician Evanston (Ill.) Hosp., 1977—. Contbr. articles on fertility and sterility to profl. jours. Served to maj. U.S. Army, 1972-74. Fellow Am. Coll. Ob-Gyn; mem. Am. Fertility Soc. (bd. dirs. 1975-82, assoc. mems. prize paper 1975), Continental Gynecologic Soc., Inst. Medicine of Chgo., Westmoreland C. of C. Presbyterian. Home: 2144 Greenwood Ave Wilmette IL 60091 Office: Evanston Hosp 2530 Ridge Ave Evanston IL 60201

GOOD, LINDA MARIE, retail store owner; b. Mt. Clemens, Mich., Dec. 19, 1944; d. Arthur William and Isabelle Doreen (Pegelo) Coleman; m. Robert Ray Good, Dec. 19, 1959 (div. 1967); children: Ray Allen, Barbie Lynn, Linda Lee, William Arthur. AA in Gen. Edn., Macomb County Community Coll., 1981. Social worker St. Joseph Hosp., Mt. Clemens, 1971-85; owner U.S.A. Uniforms and Shoes, Port Huron, Mich., 1985—; cons. social worker Rehab. Com., Mt. Clemens, 1972-77. Mem. InterAgency (membership chmn. 1974-76, treas. 1976-77). Served with USNR, 1977-82. Democrat. Roman Catholic. Home and Office: 916 Military Port Huron MI 48060

GOOD, MARILYN BLANCHE, construction company executive; b. Dayton, Ohio, July 25, 1942; d. Clarance Victor and Helen Amelia (Stang) Trame; m. Ronald J. Good, Jan. 5, 1963 (div. Dec. 1974); children: Ronald James, Katrina Ann, Sean Michael. Peace worker N.C.R. Corp., Dayton, 1960-63; secretary Paul Tipps Realtors, Dayton, 1963-65; owner, operator Good Cleaning Service, Dayton, 1965-80; pres. M.B. Good Devel. Inc., Dayton, 1977—, Mari-gold & Silver Inc., Dayton, 1982—. Mem. Home Builders Assn., Am. Bus. Womens Assn. Republican. Roman Catholic. Avocations: swimming, golf, fishing, boating, traveling. Address: PO Box 569 Dayton OH 45459

GOOD, MILTON, physician, neurologist; b. Berwyn, Ill., Mar. 12, 1939; s. Henry Harmon and Mildred Gertrude (Billings) G.; m. Donna Marie DeWitz; children: Jean Marie, Karen Lynn, Amy Beth. BS, Bowling Green State U., 1961; MD, Ind. U., 1965. Diplomate Am. Bd. Psychiatry and Neurology. Intern Bronson Meth. Hosp., Kalamazoo, 1965-66; resident in neurology Cleve. Clinic, 1966-69, staff in neurology dept., 1969-74; staff pres. in neurology dept. Fairview Gen. Hosp., Cleve., 1974—; staff neurology dept. Lakewood (Ohio) Hosp., 1974—. Served to capt. USAR. Mem. Am. Epilepsy Soc., Am. Acad. Neurology, Am. Acad. Clin. Neurophysiology, Am. Electroencephalographic Soc., Am. Assn. Study of Headache. Home: 20638 Morewood Pkwy Rocky River OH 44116 Office: 18099 Lorain Ave Cleveland OH 44111

GOOD, RICHARD HALE, association executive; b. Omaha, Nov. 17, 1927; s. Everett H. and Virginia M. (Chandler) G.; m. Virginia L. Pettit, July 16, 1950; children—Kathleen, Alan, Paul (dec.), Joan. B.S., Iowa State U., 1951. Asst. county extension agt. Dodge County Extension Service, Fremont, Nebr., 1951, Douglas County Extension Service, Omaha, 1951-53, county extension agt., 1953-54; agrl. mgr. C. of C., Omaha, 1954-59; pres., chief exec. officer C. of C., Grand Island, Nebr., 1959—; pres. Grand Island Indsl. Found., 1984—. Chmn. Small Bus. Adv. Council, Omaha, 1972-75, United Meth. Ch., Grand Island, 1974; chmn. adminstrv. bd. Trinity Meth. Ch., Grand Island, 1984, chmn. div. bd. regents for Orgn. Mgmt., U. Colo., 1967-68; v.p. Nebr. Land Found., Lincoln, 1976. Recipient Dist. Service award Nebr. Assn. Soil and Water Conservation Dist., 1958; named Hon. State Farmer, Nebr. Assn. Future Farmers Am., 1959. Mem. Am. C. of C. Execs. (chmn. Washington 1977, trustee fringe benefits 1978—), U.S. C. of C. (agrl. com. 1967-68, Top Chamber Program Cities 25-50,000 1962), Mid-Am. C. of C. Execs. (chmn. Sioux Falls 1974-75), Nebr. C. of C. Execs. (pres. 1959), Nebr. Indsl. Developers Assn. (pres. 1986). Republican. Club: Riverside Golf. Lodges: Elks, Eagles. Avocation: genealogy. Office: Grand Island Indsl Found 309 W 2d St Grand Island NE 68801

GOOD, ROBERT GAYLEN, osteopathic physician; b. Cedar Rapids, Iowa, Jan. 15, 1953; s. Gaylen Adam and Frances Marie (Garbers) G.; m. Brenda Joy Nelson, June 1, 1974; children: Jessica, Leslie, Kara. BA in biology and Chemistry with high honors, U. No. Iowa, 1974; DO with distinction, Coll. Osteopathic Medicine and Surgery, 1977. Diplomate Am. Bd. Gen. Practice. Intern Sun Coast Osteopathic Hosp., Largo, Fla., 1977-78; practice family medicine Valley Community Med. Clinic, Elgin, Iowa, 1978-79, Clark Med. Clinic, Osceola, Iowa, 1979-82; practice medicine Osceola, 1982-83; practice family and emergency medicine Monticello (Iowa) Med. Ctr., 1983—; chief of staff John McDonald Hosp., Monticello, 1984-85, 86—; assoc. staff Anamosa Community Hosp., 1984-87; mem. staff St. Luke's Hosp., Cedar Rapids, 1985, Mercy Hosp., Cedar Rapids, 1986. Contbr. monthly feature It's Your Health, Monticello Express. Bd. dirs. Monticello Ambulance Service, 1985—, med. dir., 1987—; bd. dirs. John McDonald Hosp., 1984-85; med. advisor Jones County Ambulance Assn.; mem. bd. edn. St. John's Luth. Ch. Named One of Outstanding Young Men of Am., 1984. Mem. Am. Osteopathic Assn., Iowa Osteopathic Med. Assn. (dist. II v.p. 1982-83, fin. com. 1981-82, legal and legis. com. 1981-83), Am. Coll. Gen. Practitioners Osteopathic Medicine (pres. Iowa chpt. 1986), Am. Acad. Family Physicians, Am. Coll. Emergency Physicians, Iowa Found. Med. Care, Jones County Med. Soc., Am. Heart Assn. Home: Rural Rt #3 Box 89 Monticello IA 52310 Office: 619 S Main Monticello IA 52310

GOOD, SHELDON FRED, realtor; b. Chgo., June 4, 1933; s. Joseph and Sylvia (Schwartz) G.; student Drake U., 1951; B.B.A., U. Ill., 1955; m. Lois Kroll (dec. July 1985); children—Steven, Todd. Sales mgr. Baird & Warner Real Estate, Chgo., 1957-65; pres. Sheldon F. Good & Co. Realtors, Chgo., 1965—; guest lectr. Northwestern U., U. Chgo., U. Calif., Wharton Grad. Sch., U. Pa., Stanford U., Vanderbilt U., U. Ill.; staff instr. Central YMCA City Coll., Chgo.; cons. in field. Chmn. real estate divs. Chgo. Crusade Mercy, United Settlement Appeal, Chgo., YMCA Edn. Library Drive, Chgo., Chgo. Jewish United Fund. Bd. dirs. Child, Inc.; pres. Gastrointestinal Research Found., U. Chgo., 1979. Served with AUS, 1955-57. Recipient Levi Eshkol Premier medal State Israel, 1967, Crown of A Good Name award Jewish Nat. Fund, 1972; named one of 10 outstanding young men Chgo., 1968. Mem. Chgo. Real Estate Bd. (treas.), Nat. Assn. Real Estate Bds., Chgo. Better Bus. Bur., Chgo. Assn. Commerce and Industry, Alpha Epsilon Pi, Lambda Alpha, Omega Tau Rho. Club: Bryn Mawr Country (pres.), Hundred of Cook County (bd. dirs.). Author: How to Sell Apartment Buildings; Techniques of Investment Property Exchanging; How to Lease Suburban Office Buildings; The Real Estate Auction as a Marketing Tool. Home: 180 E Pearson St Chicago IL 60611 Office: 11 N Wacker Dr Chicago IL 60606

GOOD, TIMOTHY JAY, medical equipment services company executive; b. Lima, Ohio, May 3, 1947; s. Marion Edward and Erma Mae (Sibold) G.; m. Ruth Ann Wray, July 22, 1967; children: Lucinda, Kelley, Ryan, Evan, Andrew. Student, Sinclair Community Coll., Dayton, Ohio, 1976-78, Ohio U., 1976-80, BioSystems Inst., Phoenix, 1982-86. Cert. cardiopulmonary technologist; cert. respiratory therapy technician; cert. pulmonary function technician. Asst. dir. respiratory therapy Bethesda Hosp., Zanesville, Ohio, 1968; dir. respiratory therapy Mount St. Mary Hosp., Nelsonville, Ohio, 1968-75, Hocking Valley Hosp., Logan, Ohio, 1972-81, Med. Ctr. Hosp., Chillicothe, Ohio, 1975-78; pres. Cardiopulmonary Care, Inc., Logan, 1976—, Patient Evaluation Services, Logan, 1986—; cons. respiratory therapy S.E. Ohio Tb Hosp., Nelsonville, 1970-72, Ohio Lung Assn., 1978; adv. com. and clin. faculty Shawnee State Coll., Portsmouth, Ohio, 1976-78. Pres. Hocking County (Ohio) Heart Assn., 1977; trustee Green Twp. (Ohio), 1980-82; chmn. Hocking, Vinton and Athens Counties (Ohio) Mental Health Bd., 1986, Hocking County Regional Planning Commn., 1986. Mem. Am. Assn. Respiratory Care (bd. dirs. 1982-84), Nat. Soc. Cardiopulmonary Technologists, Nat. Assn. Med. Equipment Suppliers, Ohio Soc. Respiratory Care (pres. 1978). Republican. Mennonite. Lodge: Kiwanis (pres. Logan chpt. 1986—). Avocations: reading, politics. Home and Office: 35190 Linton Rd Logan OH 43138

GOODALL, NANCY NORTON, lawyer; b. Miami, July 2, 1952; d. Daniel Joseph Norton and Betty Catherine (Blake) Pond; m. Robert G. Goodall, July 22, 1978. MusB, U. Miami, 1974; JD, Washburn U., 1983; LLM, U. Mo., Kansas City, 1984. Music dir. Ft. Lauderdale (Fla.) High Sch., 1974-78; tchr. McCarter Sch., Topeka, 1979-80; research atty. Supreme Ct. Kans., Topeka, 1984-85; lawyer Fisher, Patterson, Sayler & Smith, Topeka, 1985—; bd. dirs. E&D Enterprises, Inc., Topeka, 1983—. Co-author: Supplement to Closely Held Corporations, 1983-84. Cons. atty. Topeka Parks and Recreation Found., 1985; music dir., conductor Washburn U., Topeka Civic Theater, 1985—; mem. Topeka Festival Singers, 1985—; membership drive Community Concert Assn., 1985—; organist Christ the King Cath. Ch., Topeka, 1985—. Mem. ABA, Kans. Bar Assn. (exec. com., real estate and probate div.), Nebr. Bar Assn., Topeka Bar Assn., Women Attys. Assn. Republican. Roman Catholic. Home: 641 E 35 St Terr Topeka KS 66605 Office: Fisher Patterson Saylor & Smith PO Box 949 Topeka KS 66601

GOODE, BILLY W., senior systems programmer; b. Greenville, Tex., Nov. 20, 1957; s. Lloyd C. and Joyce M. (Robertson) G.; m. Rebecca J. Black, Apr. 25, 1981; children: Matthew, Meghan. AAB in Data Processing, U. Akron, Ohio, 1985. Operator trainee Gencorp., Akron, 1976-77, operator, 1977-78, systems program trainee, 1979-80, assoc. systems programmer, 1980-81, systems programmer, 1981-87, sr. systems programmer, 1987—. Mem. Alpha Sigma Lambda. Mem. Assemblies of God. Avocations: softball, golf, football, bowling. Office: Gencorp Inc 1 General St Akron OH 44329

GOODERUM, GORDON ARNOLD, manufacturing engineer; b. Lengby, Minn., Apr. 27, 1935; s. Wiggo August and Ethel Louise (Gran) G.; m. Jean Marie Nevling, June 20, 1964; children: Mark Patrick, Kevin Jason. Student, U. Minn., 1958-62, Coll. of St. Thomas, St. Paul, 1972, 74, Crosby Quality Coll., 1986. Elec. technician Ramsey Engring. Co., St. Paul, 1962-65; mfg. engr. Univac div. Sperry Corp., St. Paul, 1965-69, Control Data Corp., Mpls., 1969-79; project engr. H.O.N. Co., Muscatine, Iowa, 1979-80; sr. prodn. engr. F.S.I. Corp., Chaska, Minn., 1980—, quality improvement advisor, 1986—. Leader cubscouts St. Paul council Boy Scouts Am., 1976-79, dist. commr. Muscatine council, 1979-80; asst. dist. commr. cubscouts, Chaska council, 1980—; adv. Jr. Achievement, St. Paul, 1967—; com. mem. Summer Soccer League, Chaska, 1981—. Served as sgt. USAF, 1953-57. Mem. Am. Inst. Indsl. Engring. Clubs: Liberty Coin (St. Paul) (pres. 1975-76), Minn. Numismatic (v.p. 1974-75). Avocation: camping. Office: FSI Corp 322 Lake Hazeltine Dr Chaska MN 55318

GOODFELLOW, ROBIN IRENE, surgeon; b. Xenia, Ohio, Apr. 14, 1945; d. Willis Douglas and Irene Linna (Kirkland) G. B.A. summa cum laude, Western Res. U., Cleve., 1967; M.D. cum laude, Harvard U., 1971. Diplomate Am. Bd. Surgery. Intern, resident Peter Bent Brigham Hosp., Boston, 1971-76; staff surgeon Boston U., 1976-80, asst. prof. surgery, 1977-80; practice medicine specializing in surgery, Jonesboro, La., 1980-81, Albion, Mich., 1984-87, Coldwater, Mich., 1987—. Bd. overseers Case Western Res. U., 1977-82. Fellow AAUW, 1970; mem. AMA, Phi Beta Kappa. Republican. Methodist.

GOODGER, JOHN VERNE, specialty materials company executive; b. Milton, Wis., Mar. 25, 1936; s. Harry E. and Elsie (Wachlin) G.; m. Priscilla C. Arnold, Oct. 18, 1958; children—Steven J., Karin. Student, Whitewater State Coll., 1954-56; B.B.A., U. Wis., Milw., 1958. C.P.A., Wis. Staff auditor Price, Waterhouse & Co., Milw., 1958-63; with Bucyrus-Erie Co., Milw., 1963-66; mgr. corp. data processing Bucyrus-Erie Co., 1965-66; mgr. internal auditing Koehring Co., Milw., 1966-69; mgr. corp. accounting Koehring Co., 1969-71, asst. treas., 1971-74; treas. Ferro Corp., Cleve., 1974—; v.p. Ferro Corp., 1984—. Served with U.S. Army, 1959-62. Mem. Fin. Execs. Inst., Am. Inst. CPA's, Ohio Inst. CPA's, Cleve. Treas's. Clubs: Greater Cleve. Growth Assn, Nat. Investor Relations Inst. Home: 2996 Falmouth Rd Shaker Heights OH 44122 Office: Ferro Corp One Erieview Plaza Cleveland OH 44114

GOODHEW, HOWARD RALPH, JR., wholesale executive; b. Manitowoc, Wis., Aug. 28, 1923; m. Marie Goodhew; 5 children. Grad. high sch. Various positions including credit mgr., br. store supr. Ridge Co., Inc., South Bend, Ind., 1940-46, sec., 1946-56, pres., 1956-86, chmn. bd. dirs., 1986—; supt. South Bend Water Works, 1964-84, South Bend Utilities, 1966-68; dir. Nat. Bank & Trust Co., South Bend; sec., dir. H.J. Schrader Co., 1963-69, Grunow Authorized Service, Inc., 1966-69, pres. St. Joe Sales Co., 1949-55, P.B.M. Inc., 1968-79; chmn. bd. St. Joe Distbg. Co., 1984—. Mem. South Bend Crime Commn., 1974—; pres. Better Bus. Bur. South Bend-Mishawaka, 1961-62, 74-75; mem. adv. bd. Adrian Coll. Found., 1958-75; deacon 1st Presbyn. Ch., South Bend, 1963-66, trustee, 1967-76; bd. dirs. United Community Services of St. Joseph County, Inc., 1966-70; mem. bd. mgrs. community planning div. United Community Service, 1965-70; bd. dirs. Meml. Hosp. South Bend, 1969, chmn. bldg. com., 1960-72; bd. dirs. South Bend Community Sch. Corp., 1969-73, pres., 1971-72; mem. Ind. Wage Adjustment Bd., 1969-74; fin. chmn. Ind. Rep. 3d Dist., 1964-70; fin. chmn. South Bend City Rep. Com., 1963, 67, St. Joseph County Rep. Com., 1964, 65, 70; mem. St. Joseph County Rep. Adv. Bd., 1964—; primary candidate for mayor of South Bend, 1963, 71; chmn. Local Property Tax Control Bd. Ind. State, 1982-84; pres. South Bend Middle Schs. Bldg. Corp., 1974-84, South Bend Pub. Library Leasing Corp., 1981-84. Brethern Care South Bend, Inc., 1974-83; numerous other civic activities. Served with U.S. Army, World War II. Decorated Bronze Star. Recipient GEORGE award Mishawaka Enterprise-Record newspaper, 1975; Rotary Community Service award, 1983. Mem. Automotive Service Industries Assn. South Bend-Mishawaka Area C. of C. (dir. 1968-84, v.p. 1970, 82). Club: Summit. Lodges: Rotary Eagles. Home: 2230 Topsfield Rd South Bend IN Office: 1535 S Main St South South Bend IN 46613

GOODKIN, HELEN FAIRBANK, rehabilitation specialist; b. Chgo., Mar. 6, 1945; d. John Young and Laverne L. (Dulfer) Fairbank; m. Michael Goodkin, Oct. 1, 1971; children: Graham Laird, Nathalie Fairbank. AB, Bryn Mawr (Pa.) Coll., 1967; postgrad. in bus., U. Chgo., 1969. Securities analyst Continental Ill. Nat. Bank, Chgo., 1968-72; membership coordinator Better Govt. Assn., Chgo., 1972-73; dir. access Chgo. Rehab. Inst. Chgo., 1973-74; prin. Helen F. Goodkin & Assocs., Chgo., 1975—; mem. Ill. Gov.'s Com. on Employment of Handicapped, 1974-75, transp. com. Mayor's Office for Sr. Citizens and Handicapped, Chgo., 1978; mem. arts and edn. com. Chgo. Planning Council on Aging and Rehab., 1978; spl. asst. on disabled Chgo. Transit Authority, 1980-81; cons. White House Conf. on Handicapped Individuals, 1976-77. Author: A Guide to Community Action for the Handicapped, 1976, Eliminating Transportation Barriers, 1976, (with others) Environmental Aspects of Rehabilitation, 1979, editor: Access Chicago: AGuide to the City, 1973, Architect's And Designer's Handbook of Barrier-Free Design, 1974. Co-chmn. sculpture in the park Art Inst. Chgo., 1974, mem. libraries com., 1977; founder Friends of Ryerson and Burnham Libraries, 1982; mem. vis. com. Oriental Inst. and Dept. Visual Arts U. Chgo., 1983—; bd. dirs. Chgo. Area Project, 1969-71, asst. treas., 1971; bd. dirs. Rec. for the Blind, 1980—, Rehab. Inst. Chgo., 1984—, Chgo. Acad. Scis., 1985—. Episcopalian. Clubs: Racquet, Saddle and Cycle, Casino (gov. 1982—). Office: 537 W Arlington Pl Chicago IL 60614

GOODKIN, MICHAEL JON, publishing company executive; b. N.Y.C., June 10, 1941; s. Harold and Rose (Mostkoff) G.; m. Helen Graham Fairbank, Oct. 1, 1971; children: Graham Laird, Nathalie Fairbank. B.A., Harvard U., 1963; postgrad., U. Chgo. Bus. Sch., 1964. Trainee Random House, N.Y.C., 1964-65; asst. dir. Simulmatics, N.Y.C., 1966-67; account exec. World Book Ency., Inc., Chgo., 1967-70; research dir. World Book Ency., Inc., 1970-73, v.p. mktg., 1973-76, v.p., gen. mgr. mail order div., 1976-78, pres., chief operating officer, 1978, chmn., chief exec. officer, pres., dir., 1983; exec. v.p. World Book Inc., 1978-84, pres., 1984-86, sr. v.p., 1979-80; exec. v.p., corp. dir. mktg., dir. World Book Internat. Inc., 1983-84; pres. World Book Life Ins. Co., 1983; dep. dir. World Book Pty. Ltd. (Australia), 1983-86; prin. Chgo. City Capital Group, 1987—; chmn. Med. Holdings, Inc., 1987—. Bd. dirs. Chgo. Area Project; pres. aux. bd. Art Inst. Chgo., 1975-77, trustee, 1975—, also chmn. mktg. com.; trustee Modern Poetry Assn., Latin Sch. Chgo., 1983—, DMA Edn. Found., 1983—; mem. vis. com. visual arts U. Chgo. Served with Army N.G., 1963-69. Mem. Direct Mktg. Assn. (internat. council steering com. 1983, trustee Ednl. Found. 1983), Direct Selling Assn. (instl. com. 1982-86), Young Presidents' Orgn. Clubs: Racquet, Harvard (N.Y.C.); Harvard (Boston); Met.; Casino, Saddle and Cycle (Chgo.). Office: Sears Tower Suite 9300 Chicago IL 60656

GOODMAN, DAVID WAYNE, accountant; b. Oskaloosa, Iowa, Mar. 17, 1954; s. Rex Ralph and Donna Mae (Brantingham) G.; m. Aprile Jeanette King, Mar. 25, 1972; 1 child, Matthew David. Assoc. of Specialized Bus., Am. Inst. Bus., 1974. CPA, Iowa. Staff acct. Herbert J. Mullins CPA, Des Moines, 1974-76, Anderson Larkin & Co., Ottumwa, Iowa, 1976-79; ptnr. Anderson, Larkin & Co. P.C., Ottumwa, 1979—. Treas. Midwest Little League, Ottumwa, 1984-85. Mem. Am. Inst. CPA's, Iowa Soc. CPA's (sec.-treas. S.E. Iowa chpt. 1982, v.p. 1983, pres. 1984). Avocations: tennis, investing. Home: 2805 Oak Meadow Dr Ottumwa IA 52501 Office: Anderson Larkin & Co PC 226 W Main St PO Box 533 Ottumwa IA 52501

GOODMAN, EARL OWEN, JR., university administrator; b. Louisville, July 2, 1930; s. Earl Owen and Katherine Louise (Poole) G.; m. Pauline Elizabeth Scarborough, July 14, 1957 (div. July 1977); children: Cathryn Elizabeth, David Earl. BA, Baylor U., 1953; EdD, Columbia U., 1962; postdoctoral internship, Merrill-Palmer Inst., 1962-63. Asst. prof. child devel. and family relations U. Conn., Storrs, 1961-62; assoc. prof. U. N.H., Durham, 1963-72; prof. No. Ill. U., DeKalb, 1972-74, assoc. dean Coll. Profl. Studies, 1975—; counselor Portsmouth Mental Health Clinic, 1964-67, Stafford Guidance Clinic, 1965-66; pvt. practice family therapy, 1965-76. Bd. dirs. DeKalb County Heart Assn. (v.p., 1986—). Mem. Am. Assn. Marriage and Family Therapy (approved supr., bd. dirs. 1967-68), Ill. Family Planning Council (bd. dirs. 1981-83, v.p., 1982-83), Ill. Assn. Marriage and Family Counselors (v.p. 1976-78). Home: 115 W Royal DeKalb IL 60115 Office: No Ill U Coll Profl Studies DeKalb IL 60115

GOODMAN, FLOYD GROSVENOR, orthopaedic surgeon; b. Branch County, Mich., Apr. 10, 1934. BS, U. Mich., 1957, MD, 1961. Diplomate Am. Bd. Orthopaedic Surgery. Intern Oakwood Hosp., Dearborn, Mich., 1961-62, resident in gen. surgery, 1962-63; resident in orthopaedics Barnes and Allied Hosps., Washington U. Sch. Medicine, St. Louis, 1963-66; fellow orthopaedic surgery and rehab. Racho Los Amigos Hosp., Downey, Calif., 1966-67; fellow hand and upper extremity surgery Torro Hosp. and Bapt. Hosp., New Orleans, 1967; attending staff White Meml. Hosp., Los Angeles, 1967; practice medicine specializing in orthopaedic surgery East Lansing, Mich., 1969; chief spinal cord injury unit Edward W. Sparrow Hosp., Lansing, 1970-78, staff, 1969—; chmn. sect. orthopaedic surgery Ingham Med. Ctr., Lansing, 1977-79, exec. com., 1978-80, staff, 1969—; staff St. Lawrence Hosp., Lansing, 1969—; cons. in hand and upper extremity surgery Rancho Los Amigos, 1967, cons. spinal cord injury Valley Forge Gen. Hosp., Phoenixville, Pa., 1968-69; asst. clin. prof. Mich. State U., Coll. Human Medicine, 1972-78, assoc. clin. prof., 1978. Author: (book) Questions and Answers in Orthopaedics, 1966; contbr. numerous articles to profl. jours. Served to maj. M.C. U.S. Army, 1967-70. Mem. ACS, Am. Bd. Orthopaedic Surgeons, Am. Acad. Orthopaedic Surgeons, Mich. State Med. Soc., Ingham

County Med. Soc., Riordan Hand Soc. Office: 4528 S Hagadorn Rd East Lansing MI 48823

GOODMAN, GAYLE ANNE, bank executive; b. Chgo., Dec. 19, 1952; d. Karl Eidel and Eleanor Lorraine (Smithwick) G. Student, DePaul U.; MBA, Lake Forest (Ill.) Coll., 1985. Proof operator Mercantile Nat. Bank, Chgo., 1971-73; inquiry clk. Bank of Ravenswood, Chgo., 1973-75; bookkeeper Bank of Northfield, Ill., 1975-76; asst. v.p. Deerbrook State Bank, Deerfield, Ill., 1976-81; corp. v.p. Bank of Highland Park, Ill., 1981—. Bd. dirs. Quincy Park Homeowners Assn., Prospect Heights, Ill., 1979, 81-83, 85—, treas., 1979, 81, 83, v.p. 1983, 86; bd. dirs. Pal-Willow Alliance, Prospect Heights, 1986. Mem. Nat. Assn. Bank Women (state v.p. 1986-87, state pres. 1987—, state conf. chmn. 1987), Assn. MBA Execs. Office: Bank of Highland Park 1835 1st St Highland Park IL 60035

GOODMAN, G.D. WATSON, publisher; b. Cin., Jan. 22, 1920; s. William Preston and Myrtie Viola (Martt) G.; m. Rose Amelia Stair, Aug. 30, 1943; children: Victoria Raye, Donald Watson, Ruth Estelle, Harry Woodrow. ThB, Marion (Ind.) Coll., 1942, BA, 1943. Pastor Friend's Ch., Fiat, Ind., 1941-43, Pilgrim Holiness Ch., Milton, Del., 1944; dist. supr. Pilgrim Holiness Ch., Mt. Frere, Republic of South Africa, 1945-48; pres. Union Bible Coll., Brakpan, South Africa, 1948-50; dir. Gospel Centre Work, Germiston, South Africa, 1951-61; pres., founder World Missionary Press, Inc., New Paris, Ind., 1961-87; chief exec. officer Enterprises for Emmanuel, Elkhart, Ind., 1985—. Author: (booklets) Is Jesus Christ God, What Jesus Said About Divorce, Help From Above, Who Am I That A King Would Die in My Place, Satan vs. Christ, Wings Over Zion, Let's Praise the Lord, The Power Of God; (book) Look-Out Everybody. Avocations: writing, gardening. Home: PO Box 1773 Elkhart IN 46515

GOODMAN, GRANT KOHN, historian, educator; b. Cleve., Oct. 18, 1924; s. Lewis M. and Elaine M. (Kohn) G. BA with honors, Princeton U., 1948; MA, U. Mich., 1949, PhD, 1955. Asst. prof acct. U. Wash., 1955-56; instr. U. Del., Newark, 1956-58; asst. prof. SUNY, Fredonia, 1958-62; prof. U. Kans, Lawrence, 1962—; vis. prof. Japan Found., Hong Kong and Philippines, 1984-85. Author: Four Aspects Philippines, 1967, Davao: A Case Study in Japanese -Philippines Relations, 1967, Japan: The Dutch Experience, 1986, America's Japan 1945-1946, 1986. Served to 1st lt. U.S. Army, 1943-46. Fulbright fellow 1959-60, 1964-65, NIAS fellow, 1976-77. Mem. AAUP (pres. U. Kans. chpt. 1983-84, pres. Kans. State Conf. 1984-85), Assn. Asian Studies (bd. dirs. 1979-82), Am. Hist. Assn. (nominating com. 1983-85), Midwest Conf. Asian Affairs (pres. 1973-74), Conf. Asian History (Chmn. 1977—). Republican. Jewish. Avocations: teaching and research in Asia and Europe. Home: 934 Pamela Ln Lawrence KS 66044 Office: U Kans Dept History 3001 Wescoe Hall Lawrence KS 66045

GOODMAN, IRVIN G., government environmental executive; b. Sterling, Ill., Jan. 25, 1933; s. Irvin G. and Lois L. (Mathis) G.; m. Marilyn Warner Goodman, 1957; children: Virginia, Valerie. BS in Ceramic Engring., U. Ill., 1955; JD, John Marshall Law Sch., 1973. Bar: Ill. 1973. Supt. melting Midland Ross, Melrose Park, Ill., 1957-69; asst. dir. environ. research Bus. and Profl. People, Chgo., 1974-75; vice chmn. Ill. Pollution Control Bd., Chgo., 1975—. Served with U.S. Army. Recipient Presdl. Achievement award Rep. Nat. Com. Mem. Electric Metal Worker's Guild. Republican. Home: 2222 35th St Oak Brook IL 60521

GOODMAN, JERRY ALAN, obstetrician/gynecologist, educator, therapist, consultant; b. Indpls., Jan. 31, 1946; s. Edward Harold and Joan Josephine (Weiss) G.; m. Diana Jane Scott, Aug. 23, 1975; children: Andrea Shawn, Grant Adam, Amy Nicole, Rachel Brooke. BS, Ind. U., Bloomington, 1966; MD, Ind. U., Indpls., 1970. Diplomate Am. Bd. Ob-Gyn. Intern, then resident in ob-gyn Meth. Grad. Med. Ctr., Indpls., 1970-74; practice medicine specializing in ob-gyn Cin., 1974—; instr. Jewish Hosp., Cin., 1974—, U. Cin., 1974—; dir. Cin. Premenstrual Syndrome Ctr. Contbr. articles to profl. jour. Served to capt. USNG, 1970-76. Fellow Am. Coll. Ob-Gyn; mem. Am. Fertility Soc., Am. Assn. Sex Educators, Counselors and Therapists (cert. therapist), Cin. Ob-Gyn Soc., Alpha Omega Alpha. Club: Crest Hills. Avocations: golf, hiking. Office: 2825 Burnet Ave Cincinnati OH 45219

GOODMAN, KENNETH ALLEN, dentist; b. Detroit, June 2, 1952; s. Robert and Betty Ann (Feiler) G.; m. Debra Gayle Tilleman, June 24, 1972; 1 child, Aaron Michael. BS in Zoology, U. Mich., 1974, DDS, 1978. Dental clinic dir. MIC-Prescad (Wayne County Health Dept.), Detroit, 1979; pvt. practice dentistry Kalamazoo, 1979—; cons., lectr. Chronic Pain Outreach, Kalamazoo, 1983-85. Mem. ADA, Mich. Dental Assn., Kalamazoo Valley Dist. Dental Soc., Acad. of Gen. Dentistry. Jewish. Lodge: Kiwanis. Avocations: photography, running, golf. Office: 1821 Whites Rd Kalamazoo MI 49008

GOODMAN, RICHARD M., lawyer; b. Detroit, Sept. 28, 1933; s. Ernest and Freda (Kesler) G.; children—Carlos, Alicia. B.A., U. Mich., 1955; J.D., U. Chgo., 1958. Bar: Mich. 1959, Calif. 1960, Colo. 1976. Atty., ptnr. Goodman, Eden, Millender, Goodman & Bedrosian, Detroit, 1958-76; atty., pres. Richard M. Goodman, P.C., Detroit, 1977—; lectr. Editor U. Chgo. Law Rev., 1957-58; contbr. articles to law jours. Mem. Assn. Trial Lawyers Am., Inner Circle of Advs. Office: Richard M Goodman P C 1394 E Jefferson St Detroit MI 48207

GOODRICH, LOUIS LEE, electrical engineer; b. Wewoka, Okla., July 19, 1937; s. Earl Benjamin and Alpha Omega (Miller) G.; m. Marie Alice Boyce, Aug. 10, 1963; children: Linda, Louis II. Diploma, Okla. State Tech., 1955-57; BS, Eastern Mich. U., 1965-68. Electronic technician Areo Precision Industries, Okla. City, 1957, Boeing Aircraft, Wichita, Kans., 1957-59, Cook Electric, Chgo., 1959; electronic field engr. ITT Fed. Electric, Paramus, N.J., 1959-64; adminstr. engr. Gen. Telephone & Electric Co., Ft. Wayne, 1968—. Pres. Mardego Hills Subdiv. Assn., Ft. Wayne, 1984-86. Methodist. Avocations: fishing, hunting, reading, travel. Home: 325 Marcelle Dr Fort Wayne IN 46825 Office: Gen Telephone & Electric Co 8001 W Jefferson Fort Wayne IN 46804

GOODSON, CHARLES HENRY, JR., data processing executive; b. Hartsville, S.C., June 16, 1944; s. Charles Henry and Dorothy Dean (Swain) G.; m. Sharol Kay Rice, Mar. 15, 1967 (div. Nov. 1969); m. JoAnne Snyder, Dec. 20, 1969; children: Amy Elizabeth, Charles Henry III. Grad. high sch., Hartsville. Tabulating operator BF Goodrich, Akron, Ohio, 1966-67, scheduler, 1967-69, online system coordinator, 1969-74, supr. scheduling, 1974-79, mgr. computer ops., 1979-86; mgr. computer ops. Uniroyal Goodrich Tire Co., Akron, 1986—. Advisor Explorer Scouts, Akron, 1984-85. Served with USN, 1962-66. Democrat. Methodist. Club: Foremen's. Avocations: golf, bowling, music, reading, travel. Home: 350 Crestview Dr Munroe Falls OH 44262 Office: Uniroyal Goodrich Tire Co 600 S Main St Akron OH 44318

GOODSON, R. EUGENE, automotive supply executive; b. Canton, N.C., Apr. 22, 1935; s. Lon R. G. and Ruby M. (Goodson); m. Susie Elisabeth Tweed, Aug. 10, 1957; children: Kathryn, Kenneth. A.B., Duke U., 1957, B.S.M.E., 1959; M.S.M.E., Purdue U., 1961, Ph.D., 1963. Registered profl. engr., Ind. Mem. faculty Purdue U., West Lafayette, Ind., 1963-81; chief scientist U.S. Dept. Transp., Washington, 1973-75; dir. Interdisciplinary Inst., Purdue U., 1975-80, assoc. dean research, 1980-81; pres., chief exec. officer GLN, Lafayette, Ind., 1971-81; corp. v.p., gen. mgr. Automotive Systems group Johnson Controls, Inc., Milw., 1981—, group v.p. Automotive Systems group. Patentee in field; contbr articles to tech. jours. Mem. Soc. Automotive Engrs., ASME (chmn. exec. com. 1965-70). Republican. Presbyterian. Office: 825 Victors Way Ann Arbor MI 48106

GOODSTEIN, SANDERS ABRAHAM, scrap iron company executive; b. N.Y.C., Oct. 3, 1981; s. Samuel G. and Katie (Lipson) G.; m. Rose Laro, June 29, 1942; children: Peter, Esther, Jack, Rachel. Student, Wayne State U., 1934-36; AB, U. Mich., 1938, MBA, 1939, JD, 1946; postgrad., Harvard, 1943. Bar: Mich., 1946. Sec. Laro Coal & Iron Co., Flint, Mich., 1946-60, pres., 1960—; owner, operator Paterson Mfg. Co., Flint, 1953—; gen. ptnr. Indianhead Co., Pontiac, Mich., 1955-70, pres., 1965-70; sec. Amatac Corp., Erie, Pa., until 1969; chmn. bd. Gen. Foundry & Mfg. Co., Flint., Mich., 1968—, pres. 1970—; pres. Lacron Steel Co., Providence, 1975—, ETL Corp., Flint, 1983—; mem. corp. body Mich. Blue Shield, 1970-76. Served to lt. comdr.USNR, 1942-46. Mem. Fed. Bar Assn., Am. Bar Assn., Bar Mich., Am. Pub. Works Assn., Am. Foundrymen's Soc., Order of Coif, Beta Gamma Sigma, Phi Kappa Phi. Jewish. Home: 2602 Parkside Dr Flint MI 48503 Office: G-4296 W Pierson Rd Flint MI 48504

GOODWIN, DELLA MCGRAW, nurse, educator; b. Claremore, Okla., Nov. 21, 1931; d. James Edward and Allie Mae (Meadows) McGraw; m. Jesse F. Goodwin, Dec. 26, 1959; children—Gordon Francis, Paula Therese, Jesse Stephen. M.S. in Nursing, Wayne State U., 1962. R.N., Mich. Dir. nursing Blvd. Gen., Detroit, 1964-69; cons. Paramed., Detroit, 1969-72; dean nursing and health Wayne County Community Coll., Detroit, 1970-86; pres., cons. Della Goodwin & Co., 1986—; chmn. Detroit Substance Abuse Council, 1982—; pres. Health Systems Agy., Southeast Mich., 1979-81; lectr. in field. Author column. Mem. State Health Coordinating Council, Lansing, Mich., 1979; mem. Detroit Health Commn., 1982; mem. Drunk Driving Task Force, Lansing, 1982; dean emeritus Wayne County Community Coll., 1986; mem. Women's Conf. Concerns, Detroit, 1984. Recipient Health Law award Detroit Coll. Law, 1980, Senate Concurrent resolution, Mich., 1982, cert. of recognition Detroit Common Council, 1973, Headliners award Wayne State U., 1973, Spirit of Detroit award Detroit City Council, 1985; testimonial resolution Detroit City Council, 1985. Mem. Am. Nurses Assn. (cabinet nursing edn. 1984—), Mich. Nurses Assn. (congl. dist. coordinator, Bertha Lee Culp Human Rights award 1985), Nat. League Nursing, United Community Services (v.p. 1983—), Delta Sigma Theta, Sigma Theta Tau. Democrat. Roman Catholic. Avocations: swimming, golf, photography. Home: 19214 Appoline St Detroit MI 48235 Office: PO Box 21121 Detroit MI 48221

GOODWIN, GLENN LAVERN, accountant; b. Hayward, Wis., Oct. 2, 1931; s. Vernon Willis and Violet Helen (Markstedt) G.; m. Rosemary Badger, Aug. 29, 1955; children: Mark, Catherine, Ruth, Alysha, Christine. BS, Brigham Young U., 1956. Sr. acct. Arthur Young & Co., Los Angeles, 1959-63; ptnr. Joseph Bentley & Co., Los Angeles, 1963-69, Seidman & Seidman, Grand Rapids, Mich., 1969—. Contbr. articles to profl. jours. Pres. area Boy Scouts Am., Mich., 1984—; stake pres. Ch. Jesus Christ of Latter-day Sts., Grand Rapids, 1975-85. Served to capt. USAF, 1956-59. Recipient Silver Beaver award Boy Scouts Am., 1972, Silver Antelope award Boy Scouts Am. 1982. Mem. Am. Inst. CPA's, Mich. Assn. CPA's, Nat. Assn. Accts. (nat. dir. 1982-84), Gov. Fin. Officers Assn. (spl. rev. com. 1985—), Assn. Govt. Accts., Grand Rapids C. of C. Republican. Mormon. Lodge: Rotary (dist. treas. Grand Rapids club 1984-85). Avocations: genealogy, camping, hiking, gardening. Home: 2510 Lake Dr SE Grand Rapids MI 49503 Office: Seidman & Seidman 99 Monroe NW Suite 800 Grand Rapids MI 49503

GOODWIN, JEAN MCCLUNG, psychiatrist; b. Pueblo, Colo., Mar. 28, 1946; d. Paul Stanley and Geraldine (Smart) McClung; m. James Simeon Goodwin, Aug. 8, 1970; children: Laura (dec.), Amanda Harding Goodwin, Robert Caleb, Paul Joshua, Elizabeth Cronin Goodwin. BA in Anthropology summa cum laude, Radcliffe Coll., 1967; MD, Harvard U., 1971; MPH, UCLA, 1972. Diplomate Am. Bd. Psychiatry and Neurology, Am. Bd. Forensic Psychiatry. Resident in psychiatry Gerogetown U. Hosp., 1972-74, U. N.Mex. Medicine, 1974-76; asst. dir., dir. psychiatric residents tng. U. N.Mex., 1976-85; prof., dir. joint academic program Med. Coll. Wis., Milw. County Mental Health Complex, 1985—; from inst. to assoc. prof. dept. psychiatry U. N.Mex. Sch. Medicine, 1976-85; cons. protective services Dept. Human Services, N.Mex., 1976-84; lectr. profl. groups. Author: (book) Effects of Hight Altitude on Human Birth, 1969, Sexual Abuse: Incest Victims and their Families, 1982; editorial bd. Jour. Psychosocial Stress, 1985—; contbr. numerous articles on child abuse to profl. jours. Chmn. work group on child sexual abuse Surgeon Gen.'s Violence and Pub. Health, Leesburg, Va., 1985. Recipient Saville Prize in Family Planning, UCLA Sch. Pub. Health, 1972; Nat. Cen. Child Abuse and Neglect grantee, 1979-82, Nat. Inst. Aging grantee, 1980-85. Fellow Am. Psychiat. Assn. (dist. br. treas., sec. N.Mex. br. 1980-82, exhibits subcom. 1985—), Internat. Soc. Study Multiple Personality Dissociative Disorders (child abuse liason com. 1984), Am. Profl. Soc. Sexual Abuse Children (bd. dirs. 1986), Am. Med. Women's Assn. (state dir. 1978-80),. Democrat. Roman Catholic. Home: 4015 N Lake Dr Milwaukee WI 53211 Office: Milw County Mental Health Complex 9455 Watertown Plank Rd Milwaukee WI 53226

GOODWIN, NORMAN J., state senator; b. Austin, Minn., Jan. 5, 1913; s. Nels and Nellie G.; B.S., U. Minn., 1936, M.S., 1945; m. Marion Blomgren, 1936; 3 children. Extension dir. Clinton County (Iowa), 1951-78; now mem. Iowa Senate. Recipient Bereford-Quaife award, 1967; Iowa Cattlemen's award, 1969; named hon. master pork producer, 1971; Liberty Bell award, 1975; R. K. Bliss extension citation, 1976. Mem. Iowa Assn. County Extension Service Dirs. (pres. 1965), Nat. Assn. Agrl. Agts. (pres. 1975), Farm Bur., Cattlemen's and Pork Producers Assn. Methodist. Clubs: Lions, Masons, Toastmasters. Office: State Senate Des Moines IA 50319

GOODYEAR, STANLEY DODDS, banker; b. Peoria, Ill., Feb. 25, 1955; s. Leo Dodds and Shirley Mae (Brumhead) G. BS with honors, Ill. State U., 1976, MS in Acctg., 1977; cert. comml. lending, U. Okla., 1984. CPA, Iowa; cert. fin. planner, Iowa. Acct. McGladrey, Hendrickson and Pullen, Davenport, Iowa, 1977-83; v.p., comml. loan dept. mgr. Northwest Bank & Trust Co., Davenport, 1983—. Asst. advisor Boy Scouts Am., Davenport, 1984—, chmn. sustaining membership enrollment Kittan Dist., 1986; treas. Campfire Girls, Davenport, 1981-84, v.p. 1984-85; vice chmn. St. John's United Meth. Ch. Found., Davenport, 1986—, chmn fin. com. 1984-85. Mem. Am. Inst. CPA's, Ill. CPA Soc., Inst. Cert. Fin. Planners, Iowa-Ill. Miss. Valley Group (alt. sr. mem., chmn. 1985—), Robert Morris Assocs. (sec. Mo. Valley chpt. 1983-85). Lodge: Sertoma (v.p. Davenport 1984-85). Home: 2504 Fairhaven Rd Davenport IA 52803-2222 Office: NW Bank and Trust Co 100 E Kimberly Rd Davenport IA 52806-5911

GOOLD, FLORENCE WILSON, occupational therapist; b. Chgo., Aug. 26, 1912; d. Frank Elmer and Marie Louise (Walker) Wilson; m. Robert Charles Goold, Dec. 28, 1938; children: Frances Louise Goold Felty, Nancy Jean, Elizabeth Jane, Robert Charles. Student, U. Wis., 1934; BA, Boston Sch. Occupational Therapy, 1936. Occupational therapist Ypsilanti (Mich.) State Hosp., 1936-40, Michael Reese Hosp., Chgo., 1940-42, DuPage County Easter Seal Ctr., Villa Park, Ill., 1959-62; dir. occupational therapy Hinsdale (Ill.) Sanitarium and Hosp., 1962-71, Marianjoy Rehab. Hosp., Wheaton, Ill., 1971-73, Cen. DuPage Hosp., Winfield, Ill., 1972-73, Royal Oak Convalescent Home, Oak Park, Ill., 1973, Highland House Nursing Home, Downers Grove, Ill., 1973-75, St. Charles Med. Ctr., Aurora, Ill., 1975-78, Westmont (Ill.) Health Ctr., 1978-80, Americana Health Care Ctr., Naperville, Ill., 1981-84, Med. Personnel Pool, Chgo., 1985—, Home Health Care Providers, Westmont, 1986—. Pres. bd. dirs. DuPage County Easter Seal Ctr., Villa Park, 1942-59; bd. dirs. Community Adult Day Care, Downers Grove. Mem. Am. Occupational Therapy Assn., Ill. Occupational Therapy Ass. (past pres.), Phi Mu. Episcopalian. Lodge: PEO. Home: 5604 Middaugh Ave Downers Grove IL 60516

GOOSMAN, EDGAR THOMAS, family therapist; b. Wheeling, W.Va., July 29, 1934; s. Edgar and Clarice Masse (Poliskey) G.; m. Lois Jean Stout, June 2, 1957 (div. 1975); children: Thomas Perry, Vickie Lynn Hicks; m. Linda Jean Smith, July 2, 1979; stepchildren: Todd Alan Mushrush, Tracie Lynn Mushrush. BA, Bethany Coll., 1956; BD, Lexington Theol. Sem., 1963. Social worker Commonwealth of Ky., Lexington, 1958-60; pastoral counselor First Christian Ch., Alliance, Ohio, 1961-65; social worker State of Ohio, Cuyahoga Falls, Ohio, 1966-70; family counselor Family Service Orgn., Alliance, 1966-70; coordinator of outpatient services Community Profl. Service, Dover, Ohio, 1970—; cons. pre-marriage seminars Canton (Ohio) Ecumenical Council, 1965-68; bd. dirs. program for divorcing parents Common Pleas Ct., New Philadelphia, Ohio, 1985—. Recipient Dirs. award Community Mental Health Bd., Tuscarawas County, Ohio, 1981. Mem. Am. Assn. Marital and Family Therapy (pres.-elect, pres. Ohio div. 1981-85, award of Honor 1987), Alpha Sigma Phi (pres. local chpt. 1954-55). Democrat. Avocation: boating. Office: Community Profl Services Inc 201 Hospital Dr Dover OH 44622

GOOTEE, JANE MARIE, lawyer; b. Jasper, Ind., July 5, 1953; d. Thomas H. and Anne M. (Dreifke) G. BA, Ind. U., 1974; JD cum laude, St. Louis U., 1977. Bar: Ind. 1977, Mo. 1978, Mich. 1980, Ohio 1983, U.S. Dist. Ct. (so. dist.) Ind. 1977, U.S. Dist. Ct. (ea. dist.) Mich. 1980, U.S. Ct. Appeals (7th cir.) 1978, U.S. Supreme Ct. 1980, U.S. Ct. Appeals (6th cir.) 1982, U.S. Ct. Appeals (4th cir.) 1986. Dep. atty. gen. Ind., Indpls., 1977-79; corp. atty. Dow Chem. Co., Midland, Mich., 1979-81, ea. div. counsel, 1981-84, sr. atty., 1984-86, Mich. div. counsel, 1986—; mem. issue mgmt. team Dow Chem. Groundwater, 1986—, adv. com. Nat. Chamber Litigation Ctr. Environ. Law, 1985—; chair Dow Epidemiology Instl. Rev. Bd., 1984—; pro-bono def. Midland Cir. Ct., 1980-81; adj. prof. Saginaw Valley State Coll., University Center, Mich., 1979-80. Bd. dirs. Big Sisters Midland, 1979-81, 84-86, Big Bros./Big Sisters Midland, 1986—. Mem. ABA, Mo. Bar, Ohio Bar Assn., Mich. Bar Assn., Bar Assn. Greater Cleve. (corp. sec. gov.'s com. 1983), Assn. Trial Lawyers Am. Republican. Roman Catholic. Home: 1412 Brentwood Dr Midland MI 48640 Office: Dow Chem Legal Dept Michigan Div 47 Bldg Midland MI 48667

GOPALSAMI, NACHAPPA GOUNDER, electrical engineer; b. Karaipalayam, Tamilnadu, India, Apr. 3, 1948; s. K. and Thirumayi (Pappai) Nachappagounder; m. Chellam I. Chitra, Apr. 23, 1982; 1 child, Anand. B.S., Coimbatore Inst. Tech., India, 1970; M.S., P.S.G. Coll. Tech., 1973; Ph.D., U. Ill.-Chgo., 1981. Trainee, Malco, Mettur Dam, India, 1970; research scholar Indian Inst. Sci., 1973-76; research asst. U. Ill.-Chgo., 1976-79, teaching asst., 1979-80; cons. Argonne (Ill.) Nat. Lab., 1979, asst. elec. engr., 1980-84, elec. engr., 1984—. Mem. IEEE, Sigma Xi. Contbr. articles on control theory and instrumentation to sci. jours. Home: 1312 Creighton Ave Naperville IL 60565 Office: Argonne Nat Lab Bldg 308 9700 S Cass Ave Argonne IL 60439

GORCHEFF, NICK A., controller; b. Salem, Ohio, Sept. 20, 1958; s. Albert N. and Jean A. (Felger) G. BS, Youngstown State U., 1981. Acct., computer programmer RE Gibson Contractor Inc., Lisbon, Ohio, 1981-85; controller The Traichal Construction Co., Niles, Ohio, 1985—; cons. in field, 1983—. Home: 724 Notre Dame Ave Austintown OH 44515-4204 Office: The Traichal Construction Co 332 Plant St PO Box 70 Niles OH 44446-0070

GORD, MARY ANN SHERWIN, educator; b. Aurora, Ill., Jan. 20, 1948; d. Norman B. and Daisy Elsie (Miller) Sherwin; m. Robert Perry Stenfelt, Aug. 8, 1970 (dec. 1980); m. 2d, Robert Andrew Gord, July 14, 1983; 1 child, Amelia Matea; stepchildren—Katherine Sue, Timothy Andrew. B.S. in Edn., No. Ill. U., 1970; M.S. in Edn., 1974; postgrad. U. Ill., 1975, U. Wis.-Superior, 1978, Nat. Coll. of Edn., 1982. Tchr. Greenman Sch., West Aurora, Ill., 1970-81, 83-85; reading cons. dist. 129, chpt. 1 dir. West Aurora Pub. Schs., 1985—; lang. arts resource tchr. dist. 129, West Aurora, 1981-82; intermediate team tchr. Smith Sch., West Aurora, 1982-83; condr. in-service workshops on reading and writing edn. Recipient Book of Recognition, life membership, Nat. Council of PTA. Mem. Internat. Reading Assn., Ill. Reading Council, No. Ill. Reading Council, Fox Valley Reading Council (pres.), NEA, Ill. Edn. Assn., Aurora Edn. Assn. (West chpt.), Assn. for Supervision and Curriculum Devel., Nat. Council Tchrs. English, Alpha Delta Kappa (v.p.). Club: Hinckley Jr. Women's (pres.). Home: 321 Maple St Box 776 Hinckley IL 60520 Office: West Aurora Pub Schs 80 S River Aurora IL 60507

GORDEN, NANCY DEE, foundation executive; b. Traverse City, Mich., Apr. 30, 1937; d. Harry L. and Vera V. (Donner) Doty; m. Jerry L. Gorden, June 1, 1958; children: Steven K., Shelly A., Sherry B. AA, Graceland Coll., Lamoni, Iowa, 1957, student, 1958. Sec. Men's Garden Clubs Am., Johnston, Iowa, 1972-78, exec. sec., news editor, 1981—; sec. Nat. Cath. Rural Life, Des Moines, 1979-80. Editor Men's Garden Club Am. Newsletter, The Gardener mag. Elder Reorganized Ch. of Jesus Christ of Latter-day Saints, 1985. Mem. Am. Soc. Assn. Execs., Profl. Secs. Internat. Avocations: music, reading. Office: Men's Garden Clubs of Am PO Box 241 Johnston IA 50131

GORDIN, RICHARD DAVIS, former university athletic director, educator; b. South Charleston, Ohio, July 16, 1928; s. Edwin Ray and Mildred (Davis) G.; m. Paula Alice Egan, July 23, 1949; children: Richard D. Jr., Robert H., Douglas P. BA, Ohio Wesleyan U., 1952; MA, Ohio State U., 1954, PhD, 1967. Dir. recreation United Cerebral Palsy, Columbus, Ohio, 1954; instr. phys. edn. Ohio Wesleyan U., Delaware, 1954-59, asst. prof., 1959-67, asso. prof., 1967-71, prof., 1971—, dir. athletics, 1977-85, emeritus, 1985—; edn. cons. Nat. Golf Found., 1966—. Author: (with others) Golf Fundamentals, 1973; editor: The Golf Coach's Guide, 1975; instruction editor Golfworld mag., 1987. Mem. parks recreation bd. City of Delaware, 1970-77, chmn., 1974. Recipient citation Delaware City Council, 1977; named to Golf Coaches Hall of Fame, 1980. Mem. U.S. Golf Assn. (mus. com. 1981), Golf Coaches Assn. Am. (pres. 1979-80, 81-82). Home: 180 N Franklin St Delaware OH 43015 Office: Ohio Wesleyan Univ Delaware OH 43015

GORDLEY, RICHARD L., savings and loan association executive; b. 1941. BA, Bowling Green State U., 1964. Pres., chief exec. officer Tuscaranas Savs., 1976-79, RR Savs., 1979-81; chief fin. officer, sr. v.p. Diamond Savs. and Loan Co., Findlay, Ohio, 1982-86, pres., chief exec. officer, 1986—. Office: Diamond Savings & Loan Co 500 S Main St Findlay OH 45480 *

GORDMAN, A. DAN, retail store executive; b. 1912. With Richman Stores, Omaha, 1937-64, ptnr., 1937-57, pres., treas., 1957-64, pres., 1964; now pres., chief exec. officer Richman Gordman Stores, Inc., Omaha. Office: Richman Gordman Stores Inc 12100 W Center Rd Omaha NE 68144 *

GORDON, AMY GLASSNER, academic administrator, history educator; b. Bklyn., Feb. 12, 1942; d. Herman M. and Sylvia Lillian (Graff) Glassner; m. Michael D. Gordon, Mar. 22, 1964; children: Nathan Abraham, Joshua David. BA in History, Conn. Coll., 1963; MA in History, U. Chgo., 1964, PhD in History, 1974. Lectr. in history CCNY, 1967-68; instr. Denison U., Granville, Ohio, 1968-69, 70-72, from asst. to assoc. prof., 1975-84, prof., 1984—, dean of coll., 1987—. Contbr. 7 articles to profl. jours. Woodrow Wilson fellow, 1963-64; Woodrow Wilson dissertation fellowship, 1966-67; Newberry Library Research grant, Chgo., 1975. Mem. French Colonial Hist. Soc. (sec.-treas. 1984—), Hakluyt Soc., Phi Beta Kappa. Avocations: jogging, cooking. Home: 113 Chapin Pl Granville OH 43023 Office: Denison U Granville OH 43023

GORDON, BERNARD, management and communications consultant; b. N.Y.C., Apr. 24, 1922; m. Margaret V. Cohn, June 20, 1948; children—Anne J., Jonathan M., Alan D. B.S., Coll. City N.Y., 1943; M.B.A., Harvard U., 1948. With William Filene's Sons Co., Boston, 1948-50; comptroller, chief bus. officer Brandeis U., Waltham, Mass., 1950-58; adminstrv. v.p., dir. foreign operations Wasco Chem. Co., Cambridge, Mass., 1958-60; pres. Chgo. div. Cahners Pub. Co., 1960-68; pres., chief exec. officer Denoyer-Geppert Co., Chgo., 1968-72; gen. mgr. Dun-Donnelley Pub. Co., Chgo., 1972-77; pres. Bernard Gordon and Assocs., Mgmt. and Communications Cons., Glencoe, Ill., 1977—; adj. prof. Medill Sch. Journalism, Northwestern U., 1977—. Pres. Fine Arts Music Found. Chgo., 1978-79. Served with AUS, 1943-46. Mem. Chgo. Bus. Publications Assn. (pres. 1976-77). Home and Office: 1030 Forest Ave Glencoe IL 60022 Office: 655 Fifteenth St Suite 320 NW Washington DC 20005

GORDON, DAVID EDWARD, marketing professional; b. Waterbury, Conn., Apr. 30, 1945; s. Samuel and Shirley (White) G.; m. Ellen C. Harman, July 30, 1972; children: Shari, Richard. BSBA, Bryant Coll., 1967; MBA, Suffolk U., 1968. Mktg. analyst Olin Corp., New Haven, Conn., 1968-71, mgr. mktg. research, 1971-74; account exec. NFO Research, N.Y.C., 1975-76; br. mgr. NFO Research, Chgo., 1976-79; exec. v.p. B. Angell & Assocs., Chgo., 1979—; mktg. adv. council Suffolk U., Boston, 1985—. Mem. Am. Mktg. Assn. (ins. trustee 1983—, mktg. adv. council 1984-85, pres. Chgo. chpt. 1984-85). Home: 1449 Oxford Dr Buffalo Grove IL 60089 Office: B Angell & Assocs Inc 1 E Superior Chicago IL 60611

GORDON, EDWARD, music association executive; b. 1930. D.F.A. (hon.), North Central Coll., Naperville, Ill., 1980. Asso. mgr. Grant Park summer concerts, Chgo. Park Dist., 1958-65; mgr. Grant Park summer concerts, 1965-68; gen. mgr. Ravinia Festival Assn., Chgo., 1968-70; exec. dir. Ravinia

Festival Assn., 1970—, chief operating officer, 1982—; Mem. music adv. panel U.S. Dept. State; mem. recommendation bd. Avery Fisher Artist Award program; judge, mem. adv. bd. Naumburg Award; mem. adv. bd. Van Cliburn Internat. Piano Competition, Internat. Piano Competition, Sydney, Australia; mem. festivals panel Nat. Endowment for Arts.; mem. Music panel Arts Club of Chgo.; mem. vis. com. Sch. Fine Arts Oberlin Coll. Former concert pianist. Adv. trustee to bd. dirs. Chgo. City Ballet; bd. dirs. Chgo. Chamber Musicians; trustee Mozart Soc. Performed age 9 with Chgo. Symphony under Frederick Stock. Office: Ravinia Festival Assn 1575 Oakwood Ave Highland Park IL 60035

GORDON, EZRA, architect, educator; b. Detroit, Apr. 5, 1921; s. Abraham and Rebecca (Reimer) G.; m. Jeanette Greenberg, Oct. 8, 1942; children: Cheryl P. Gordon Van Ausdal, Rana Gordon Oremland, Judith Gordon. Student, Roosevelt Coll., 1946-48; B.S. inArchitecture, U. Ill., 1951. Draftsman Pace Assos. Architects, 1951-53; sr. planner Chgo. Plan Commn., 1953-54; project architect Harry Weese & Assos., 1954-61; ptnr. Gordon-Levin & Assocs., Chgo., 1961-84, Ezra Gordon & Assocs., Chgo., 1984—; cons. Dept. Urban Renewal City Chgo., Council for Jewish Elderly, Chgo. Jewish Fedn.; prof. U. Ill., Chgo.; mem. Mayor's Adv. Council on Bldg. Code Ammendments; master juror Nat. Council Archtl. Registration Bds. Works include South Commons, Chgo., 1968, IBM Office bldgs, Kalamazoo, 1969, Jefferson City, Mo., Omaha, 1971, Wexler Pavilion and Siegel Inst., Michael Reese Hosp., Chgo., 1971, Newberry Plaza, Chgo., 1973, River Plaza, Chgo., 1976, Elm St. Plaza, Chgo., 1976, Dearborn Park, Chgo., 1979, Huron Plaza, Chgo., 1981, 400 Streeterville, Chgo., 1983, East Bank Club, Chgo., 1983, Dearborn-Elm Apts., 1986-87. Bd. dirs. Hyde Park-Kenwood Community Conf.; v.p. Harper Ct. Found. Served with AUS, 1942-45. Decorated Croix de Guerre with palm; recipient Honor award Dept. Housing and Urban Devel., 1967, Honor award AIA-Chgo. C. of C., 1967, award AIA-House & Home Mag., 1967, Distinguished Bldg. award AIA, 1957, 63, 69, 71, 73, 75, award City of Chgo. Beautification, 1969, 75, award of excellence Concrete Post Tensioning Inst., 1984, Silver Circle award for excellence in teaching U. Ill., Chgo., 1985. Fellow AIA (dir. Chgo. chpt.); mem. Labor Zionist Alliance, Am. Profs. for Peace in Middle East, Am. Jewish Congress, Lambda Alpha. Jewish. Club: Cliff Dwellers. Office: 101 E Ontario St Chicago IL 60611

GORDON, GEORGE RICHARD, physician, educator; b. Fairmont, Minn., July 13, 1947; s. George Richard and Rose Ella (Nissen) G.; m. Diane Lynn Iverson, Nov. 15, 1969; children: Peder Jon, Christopher George, Megan Lynn. BS, St. Olaf Coll., Northfield, Minn., 1969; MD, U. Minn., 1973. Diplomate Am. Bd. Family Practice. Practice family medicine Hutchinson (Minn.) Med. Ctr., P.A., 1976—; clin. instr. dept. family practice Peoria (Ill.) Sch. Medicine, 1974-76; asst. med. dir. Stonehenge-Ill. Drug Treatment Program, Peoria, 1973-76; clin. instr. dept. family practice and community health U. Minn., Mpls., 1978-82, assoc. clin. prof., 1982—; chief of staff Hutchinson Community Hosp., 1982-83. Bd. dirs. Ind. Sch. Dist. 423 Bd. Edn., Hutchinson, 1980—, chairperson 1982—; bd. dirs. Hutchinson C. of C., 1979-81, Minn. Lung Assn., 1978-79, Dollars for Scholars, Hutchinson, 1981-86; pres. Hutchinson ABC Montessori Found., 1980. Mem. AMA, Minn. Med. Assn., Am. Acad. Family Physicians, McLeod County Med. Assn. Lutheran. Avocations: camping, travel, snow skiing. Home: 1019 Lewis Hutchinson MN 55350

GORDON, GERALD ARTHUR, research scientist; b. Chgo., Mar. 5, 1934; s. Jacob Norman and Bacia (Manfeld) G.; m. Sandra Lee Lavine, Mar. 31, 1967; children: Jacob Jonathon, Eva Jennifer. BSChemE, Purdue U., 1956; MSChemE, MIT, 1957, ScD in Chem. Engring., 1961. Research chemist Kimberly Clark Co., Munising, Mich., 1961-63; sr. research scientist Continental Can Co., Chgo., 1963-75, adv. scientist, 1975-81; research cons. Continental Fibre Drum Co., Lombard, Ill., 1981—; adj. prof. polymer sci. U. Ill., Chgo., Roosevelt U., Chgo., Ill. Inst. Tech., 1971-81. Contbr. articles to profl. jours.; patentee in field. Mem. AAAS, Am. Chem. Soc., Soc. Plastics Engrs., Fedn. Am. Scientists, Tech. Assn. Pulp and Paper Industry, Inst. Food Technoloigsts, Gymnastics Booster Assn. (co-pres. 1984-86). Club: Circle Pines Ctr. (Delton, Mich.) (bd. dirs. 1961-73, sec. 1962-67, pres. 1967-69, 75-80). Avocations: reading, sailing, camping, skiing, scuba diving. Home: 9150 Keystone Skokie IL 60076 Office: Continental Fibre Drum Inc 245 Eisenhower Ln S Lombard IL 60148

GORDON, IRVING MARTIN, osteopathic physician; b. Canton, Ohio, Aug. 10, 1926; s. Harry and Sarah (Axelrod) G.; m. Roberta Levine, Feb. 12, 1956; children—Ellen, Nina, Bruce, Roger. B.A., Case Western Res. U., 1949; B.S., Kent State U., 1950; D.O., Chgo. Coll. Osteo. Medicine, 1954. Lic. osteo. physician, Ohio, S.C.; cert. in family practice Am. Bd. Gen. Practitioners in Osteo. Medicine and Surgery. Intern, Detroit Osteo. Hosp., 1954-55; locum tenens, Fort Lee, N.J., 1955-56; gen. practice osteo. medicine, Massillon, Ohio, 1957-63, Gordon & Sharkis, 1963-70, Gordon, Sharkis & Larusso, Inc., 1970-71; pres. Perry Family Practice Ctr., Inc., 4 physician group; gen. practice family medicine Perry Family Practice Ctr., Inc., Massillon, 1972-85; clin. asst. prof. family practice Ohio U. Coll. Osteo. Medicine, 1977—; lectr. Chgo. Coll. Osteo. Medicine, 1980, 81; lectr. Howard U. Hosp., Washington, and Grandview Hosp., Dayton, Ohio, Ohio U. Coll. Osteo. Medicine, 1984, Des Moines Gen. Hosp., 1984, Botsford Hosp., Farmington, Mich., 1985. Trustee Wooster Eight County Health Systems Agy. (Ohio), 1975-81; mem. pres.'s adv. bd. Stark Tech. Coll., Canton, 1980—, trustee, 1982; mem. annual fund-raising com. United Jewish Appeal, 1970—, fin. com. Temple Israel, 1979—; founding mem., trustee Doctors Hosp. Stark County (Ohio), 1963—, mem. fin. com., chmn. community affairs com., chmn. edn. com. Served to cpl. USAF, 1945-46. Fellow Am. Coll. Gen. Practice; mem. Am. Osteo. Assn., Akron-Canton Acad. Osteo. Medicine and Surgery (pres. 1974-75), Ohio Soc. Am. Coll. Gen. Practitioners Osteo. Medicine and Surgery (pres. 1981-82). Clubs: Catawba Island (Port Clinton, Ohio); Nat. Amateur Radio Relay League, Med. Amateur Radio Council (founding mem.), Canton, Lodges: Masons, Shriners. Home: 2915 Croydon Dr NW Canton OH 44718 Office: 4125 Lincoln Way E Massillon OH 44646

GORDON, JOAN MAY, communication analyst, career exploration specialist; b. Lancaster, Ohio, Nov. 24, 1946; d. George Leo and Esther May (George) G.; m. James J. Thimmes, Aug. 22, 1970 (div. Nov. 1975). BS in Edn., Capital U., 1969; cert. in profl. edn., Ohio State U., 1975, MA in Communication, 1980, postgrad., 1983—. Cert. tchr., Ohio. Tchr. Upper Arlington Schs., Columbus, Ohio, 1968-80, career edn. program specialist, 1980-81, career edn. exploration analyst, 1982—; communications cons. Ohio Bar Assn., Mich. Bar Assn., Ohio and Mich. ednl. adminstrs., radio and TV broadcast studios, Ohio State U., Capital U., local bus. Co-host Upper Arlington Today TV Show, 1981-83; contbr. articles to profl. jours. Sec. adv. commn. Columbus Area Cable TV. Mem. Internat. Telecommunications Assn., Internat. Assn. Bus. Communicators, Assn. Supervision and Curriculum Devel., Assn. Ednl. Communications and Technology, Am. Assn. Career Edn., Upper Arlington Edn. Assn. (v.p. 1974-75), Capital U. Alumnae Assn., Pi Lambda Theta, Phi Delta Kappa. Republican. Avocations: modern interpretive and jazz dancing, tennis, writing poetry. Home: 662 S Grant Ave Columbus OH 43206 Office: Upper Arlington City Sch Dist 1950 Mallway Columbus OH 43221

GORDON, JULIE STARKMAN, actuary; b. Chgo., Jan. 30, 1957; d. Marvin Harold and Dorothy (White) Starkman; m. Richard Earl Gordon, Mar. 6, 1983; 1 child, Amy Elizabeth. BS in Actuarial Sci., U. Ill., 1978. Assoc., mgr. Hewitt Assocs., Lincolnshire, Ill., 1978—. Fellow Soc. Actuaries; mem. Am. Acad. Actuaries. Jewish. Office: Hewitt Assocs 100 Half Day Rd Lincolnshire IL 60015

GORDON, LANCE DEWEY, auditor; b. Milw., May 24, 1946; s. Royal Leander and Donna Ilene (Randall) G.; m. Ellen Therese DeForno, July 21, 1973; children: Christopher John, Matthew Deforno. BA, Wartburg Coll., 1968; MS in Computer Sci., North Tex. State U., 1981; MS in Taxation, U. Wis., Milw., 1985. CPA, Wis. Prodn. mgr. Linnehan Welding, Milw., 1973; fin. planner Am. United Life, Milw., 1973-74; revenue agt. IRS, Milw., 1974-80, computer audit specialist, 1980—; bd. dirs. Randall Graw, Inc., La Crosse, Wis.; fin. planner, Heil Fin. Group, Milw., 1986—; guest speaker various Assns. Served with USN, 1968-72. Mem. Wis. Inst. CPA's, Am. Inst. CPA's, U. Wis. (Milw.) Tax Assn. Republican. Lutheran. Avocations: tennis, softball, skiing. Home: 715 E Beaumont Ave Whitefish Bay WI 53217 Office: IRS 517 E Wisconsin Ave Milwaukee WI 53201

GORDON, LEWIS ALEXANDER, electronics executive; b. Milw., Aug. 4; s. Lewis Alexander and Verna Alma (Stocker) G.; B.S. in Mech. Engring., Purdue U., 1959; postgrad. RCA Insts., 1962, No. Ill. U., 1967-68; m. Frances Rita Dziadzio, June 4, 1960; children—Robert Alan, Richard Alan, Pamela Ann. Process engr. Ill. Tool Works, Elgin, 1959-63; chief engr. Norcon Electronics, Elgin, 1963-65; v.p. Midland Standard, Inc., Elgin, 1964-78, chmn. bd., 1967-78; pres., chief exec. officer Gt. Lakes Industries, Elgin, 1978—; del. Joint Electronics Industry Conf.; mem. adv. bd. Electronics mag., 1976—. Vice pres. bd. trustees Gail Borden Pub. Library Dist., 1971—, pres., bd. dirs. North Suburban Library System, 1971-74; mem. automation com. Ill. State Library, 1982—; bd. advisers Easter Seal Assn., Elgin, 1971-74; adv. bd. Elgin Community Coll., 1977—. Registered profl. engr., Ill., Mich., Wis. Mem. Ill. C. of C., Elgin Assn. Commerce, ALA, Ill. Library Assn. (automation com. 1975—), Ill. Council Library Systems Presidents (pres.), Ill. Library Trustee Assn. (bd. dirs. 1983—, pres. 1985-87), Future Ill. Libraries Com., Exptl. Aircraft Assn., Future Ill. Libraries Com., Exptl. Soc. Profl. Engrs., Nat. Brit. Horological Inst., Kane County Farm Bur., Ill. Mfrs. Assn., Assn. Watch and Clock Collectors, Mensa, Agent-Aeronca Champion Club, Pi Tau Sigma. Lutheran. Contbr. articles to profl. jours. Patentee in field. Home: 705 Diane Ave Elgin IL 60123 Office: PO Box 783 Elgin IL 60121

GORDON, LONNY JOSEPH, choreographer, dance and fine arts educator; b. Edinburg, Tex.; s. Floyd Charles and Ruth Rebecca (Lee) G. B.F.A., U. Tex., 1965; M.F.A., U. Wis., 1967; D.F.A., Nishikawa Sch. of Classical Japanese Dance, Tokyo, 1980. Numerous teaching positions in the fine arts, 1964—, including: dir. Kinetic Art Theater, N.Y.C., 1970, Tokyo, 1971-72; dir. modern dance Jacobs Pillow, Lee, Mass., 1970; dir. So. Repertory Dance Theater, So. Ill. U., Carbondale, 1972-76; artist-in-residence Smith Coll., Northampton, Mass., 1975; grad. dir. dance U. Wis., Madison, 1976—; choreographer numerous dance works including Fleetings; cons. and lectr. in dance and fine arts to numerous profl. dance cos. and ednl. instns. Contbr. articles to profl. jours.; subject of numerous books and profl. works in dance. One man exhbn. watercolor paintings, collage and mixed media works. Grantee numerous profl. and ednl. instns., fellow Fulbright-Hays, 1967-69, 83, NEA Choreographers, 1982-83; Fulbright researcher, Korea, 1983; Japan Found. profl. fellow, 1979. Mem. Asian Dance Assn. (bd. dirs.), Fulbright Alumni Assn. Club: University Club (U. Wis.). Avocations: painting; writing; swimming; bodybuilding; gardening. Office: U Wis Lathrop Hall 1050 University Ave Madison WI 53706

GORDON, LOUIS EDWARD, hospital administrator; b. Jackson, Mich., Dec. 18, 1930; s. George Edward and Anna A. (Hansmann) G.; m. Shirley Winifred Bishop, Nov. 14, 1954; children: Jan Alyce, Jill Annette, Traci Lynn. BA, Andrews U., 1952; MA, Mich. State U., 1957. Adminstr. Battle Creek (Mich.) Sanitarium, 1961-67; dir. Liberian Nat. Med. Ctr. Project, Liberia, 1967-72; dir. Ind. Regional Med. Program, Indpls., 1972-73; dir. Kino Community Hosp., also dept. hosps. and nursing homes, Pima County, Tucson, 1973-78; adminstr. Bannock Regional Med. Ctr., Pocatello, Idaho, 1978-83; exec. v.p. Shawnee Mission Med. Ctr., Kans., 1983-85, pres. Western Mo. Med. Ctr., 1985—; cons. Health Care Orgn. and Devel., AID; mem. faculty Idaho State U., Pocatello, Cen. Mo. State U. Bd. dirs., v.p. Mountain States Shared Service Corp., 1978-83; city commr. City of Battle Creek; pres., founder, Idaho Health Services Consortium, 1978-83; pres. South Ariz. Hosp. Council, 1976. Served with U.S. Army, 1952-54. Decorated Govt. of Liberia, 1973; recipient Unity for Service award Nat. Exchange Club, 1967, Meritorious Honor award U.S. Dept. State. Mem. Royal Soc. Health, Am. Coll. Hosp. Adminstrs., Am. Hosp. Assn., Am. Pub. Health Assn., Idaho Hosp. Assn. (dir. 1978-83), Idaho Hosp. Research and Edn. Found. (pres.), Internat. Fedn. Hosps. Lodges: Rotary, Masons, Shriners. Home: 21002 Whispering Dr Lenexa KS 66220 Office: Western Mo Med Ctr Warrensburg MO 64093

GORDON, MARSHALL, university president; b. La Center, Ky., Sept. 1, 1937; m. Annette Waters, Mar. 17, 1962; 1 dau., Mary Ann. B.A., Murray State U., 1959; Ph.D., Vanderbilt U., 1963. Teaching asst. dept. chemistry Vanderbilt U., Nashville, 1959-63; assoc. prof. chemistry Vanderbilt, Nashville, summer 1965; research chemist E. I. duPont de Nemours Co., Chattanooga, summer 1961; asst. prof. Murray State U. (Ky.), 1963-65, assoc. prof., 1965-68, prof., 1968-75, dean Coll. Environ. Scis., 1975-77, trustee found., 1977-83, v.p. univ. services, 1977-83; pres. S.W. Mo. State U., Springfield, 1983—; mem. adv. council NSF, Washington, 1978-82; bd. dirs. Purchase Tng. Ctr., Mayfield, Ky., 1981-83, Environ. research, 1981, 82. Bd. dirs. Murray Calloway County Indsl. Found., 1981-82, United Way of the Ozarks, 1987; mem. regional adv. bd. Hammons Heart Inst., Springfield, 1983—; pres. adv. council; bd. dirs. Lester E. Cox Med. Ctr., Springfield, 1985—; pres. The Gateway Collegiate Athletic Conf., 1987—. Mem. Am. Chem. Soc. (sec.-treas. Ky. Lake sect. 1968-70); mem AAAS; mem. Ky. Acad. Sci. (assoc. editor Transactions 1968-73), Internat. Assn. Water Pollution Research, Am. Assn. State Colls. and Univs. (com. on sci. and tech. 1983—, task force on corp./coll. relations 1984—, pres. mid-continent univs. 1987—), Springfield C. of C. (dir. 1983-86), Sigma Xi. Lodge: Rotary (Murray and Springfield). Home: 1515 S Fairway Springfield MO 65804 Office: SW Mo State Univ 901 S National Springfield MO 65804

GORDON, MICHAEL DUANE, optometrist; b. Coffeyville, Kans., Apr. 14, 1949; s. Otho Wayne and Wilma Lea (Hodges) G.; B.S. cum laude, U. Houston, 1973, O.D. magna cum laude, 1973; m. Vicki Jo Baker, May 31, 1969; children—Kimberly Michelle, Ryan Michael, Nicole Tasha. Pvt. practice optometry, Wichita, Kans., 1973—, Derby, Kans., 1977—; optometric cons. VA Hosp., Wichita, 1975-84; v.p. Rota Enterprises, Inc., Derby, 1978-81, pres., 1981—; cons. Winfield State Mental Hosp., 1980—; FDA clin. investigator for Cooper Labs., 1981—, for Bausch & Lomb Soflens, 1981—. Mem. Coll. Optometrists in Vision Devel., Am. Optometric Assn., Optometric Extension Program Found., Inc., Kans. Optometric Assn., Wichita Optometric Soc., Derby C. of C., Derby Jaycees. Republican. Coinventor, patentee motorized revolving visual exam. center; inventor soft contact lens measuring device; co-inventor Rota module. Home: 10225 E 71st S Derby KS 67037 Office: 154 S Rock Rd Wichita KS 67207 Office: 234 Greenway St Derby KS 67037

GORDON, RICHARD LEE, newspaper editor; b. Chgo., Apr. 10, 1948; s. Monnie and Lorraine Elizabeth (Strand) G.; m. Vivian Eleanor Vahlberg, June 26, 1976; children: Brady, Ross, Alexander. BA in History, U. Ill., Chgo., 1969. From reporter to asst. city editor City News Bur., Chgo., 1969-72; reporter Chgo. Tribune, Arlington Heights, Ill., 1972-73; assoc. editor Pensions and Investments, Bus. Ins. mags., Chgo. and Washington, 1973-76, Advt. Age, Washington, 1976-84; mng. editor Advt. Age, Chgo., 1984-87, editorial page editor, 1987—. Mem. Nat. Press Club (chmn. awards com. 1980-84), U.S. House/Senate Periodical Press Galleries. Home: 530 Melrose Kenilworth IL 60043 Office: Advertising Age 740 N Rush St Chicago IL 60611

GORDON, ROBERT M., lawyer; b. Chgo., July 17, 1953; s. Lloyd M. and Betty (Bernstein) G.; m. Alanna Barr, Apr. 16, 1978. AB, U. Ill., Chgo., 1974; JD, Northwestern U., 1983. Bar: Ill. 1983, U.S. Dist. Ct. (no. dist.) Ill. 1983, U.S. Tax Ct. 1985. Editor Argus Communications, Niles, Ill., 1975-78; assoc. editor Follett Pub. Co., Chgo., 1978-80; assoc. Wilson & McIlvaine, Chgo., 1983-87, Winston & Strawn, Chgo., 1987—. Contbr. articles to profl. jours. Vol. atty. Lawyers for the Creative Arts, Chgo. Mem. ABA, Chgo. Bar Assn., Chgo. Council Lawyers. Office: Winston & Strawn One First Nat Plaza Chicago IL 60603

GORDON, VIVIAN HOPP EINSTEIN, law educator; b. Chgo., Feb. 12, 1947; d. Samuel Leonard and Jeanne Ruth (Taub) Hopp; children from a previous marriage: Douglas, Mark, Richard; m. Michael Louis Gordon, June 30, 1985. BA, Northeastern Ill. U., 1968; JD, John Marshall Law Sch., 1980; PhD, Northwestern U., 1983. Bar: Ill. 1980, U.S. Dist. Ct. (no. dist.) Ill., U.S. Ct. Appeals (7th cir.), U.S. Supreme Ct. 1987; cert. tchr., Ill. Tchr. Chgo. Pub. Schs., 1968-80; mem. adj. faculty John Marshall Law Sch., Chgo., 1980-81, instr., 1982-84, asst. prof., 1984—; lectr. in field. Contbr. articles to profl. jours. Recipient Chgo. Vol. Legal Services award, 1982-85, YWCA Leadership award, 1983, UN Internat. Youth award, 1985, Nat. Bar Assn. award, 1985; named one of Outstanding Young Women Am., 1983; Nat. Endowment for the Humanities fellow, 1986. Mem. ABA (negotiations competition com., faculty team advisor), Am. Arbitration Assn. (arbitrator), Ill. Bar Assn., Chgo. Bar Assn. (Outstanding Young Woman Lawyer Yr. 1983, past chmn. community action com.), Phi Alpha Delta, Phi Delta Kappa. Avocation: piano. Home: 1203 Larraway Dr Buffalo Grove IL 60089 Office: John Marshall Law Sch 315 S Plymouth Ct Chicago IL 60604

GORDON, WILLIAM DOUGLAS, mechanical engineer; b. Cin., Sept. 28, 1946; s. A. Cedric and Joyce Margaret (Danenhauer) G.; m. Judy Kay Shaughnessy, July 25, 1981; 1 child, Christopher Scott. BME, Gen. Motors Inst., 1969; MA in Computer and Info. Sci., Oakland U., 1987. Sr. programmer Pontiac Motor div. Gen. Motors Corp., Pontiac, Mich., 1969-77; cons. Digital Equipment Corp., Maynard, Mass., 1977-82; staff engr. GMF Robotics, Troy, Mich., 1982-87; cons. Digital Equipment Corp., 1987—. Mem. IEEE Computer Soc. Republican. Office: Digital Equipment Corp 34119 W 12 Mile Rd Farmington Hills MI 48018

GORDON-LATHROP, SUSAN MARIE, bank executive; b. Pitts., Dec. 13, 1950; d. LeRoy Thrift and June (Spring) Gordon; m. William Lathrop, Nov. 10, 1981. BS in Edn., No. Ill. U., 1972. Tchr. Butterworth Elem. Sch., Moline, Ill., 1972-76; salesperson IBM, Denver, 1976-80, Exxon Office Systems, Denver, 1980-81, Bus. Telephone Systems, Columbus, Ohio, 1981-82; project mgr., conversion specialist BancOhio Nat. Bank, Columbus, 1982—. Mem. Columbus Zoo, 1986—, Cin. Zoo, 1986—, Cin. Nature Ctr., 1986—. Named Young Career Woman of Yr., Bus. and Profl. Women's Assn., Denver, 1978. Mem. Am. Inst. Banking, Am. Running and Fitness Assn. Republican. Congregationalist. Avocations: running, skiing, tennis, piano, reading. Home: 3093 Walden Ravines Columbus OH 43220 Office: BancOhio Nat Bank 4661 E Main Columbus OH 43251

GORE, CATHERINE ANN, social worker; b. Mullens, W.Va., Feb. 2, 1937; d. Bernard Joseph and Agnes Cecilia (Spradling) G.; BA, Thomas More Coll., 1968; MSW, Ohio State U., 1971, MA in Pub. Adminstrn., 1983; PhD in Social Work, 1986. Caseworker, Cath. Charities, Cin., 1967-69, 71-72; psychiat. social worker Mcpl. Ct. Psychiat. Clinic, Cin., 1973; instr. psychiat. social work, social work supr., Ct. Psychiat. Center, U. Cin., 1974-77, asst. prof. psychiat. social work, coordinator consultation services, 1978-80, grad. research and teaching assoc. Ohio State U., Columbus, 1981-85; cons. Hamilton County Welfare Dept.; instr. No. Ky. U. Mem. Nat. Assn. Social Workers, Acad. Cert. Social Workers. Democrat. Roman Catholic. Home: 1545 Northview Ave Cincinnati OH 45223

GORE, DONALD RAY, orthopaedic surgeon; b. Michigan City, Ind., Mar. 13, 1936; s. Clarence Bernard and Susan Leone (Fuller) G.; m. Jacqueline Marie Kraabel, Aug. 25, 1956; children: Donald, Daniel, Jennifer, Elizabeth. BS, U. Ill., 1958, MD, 1960; MS, Marquette U., 1967. Cert. Am. Bd. Orthopaedic Surgery. Intern Milw. County Gen Hosp., 1960-61; resident gen. surgery Marquette U. Sch. Medicine, Milw., 1961-64, resident orthopaedic surgery, 1964-67; fellow Biomechanics Lab U. Calif., San Francisco, 1967-68; practice medicine specializing in orthopaedic surgery Sheboygan (Wis.) Orthopaedic Assocs., S.C., 1968—; clin. prof. dept. orthopaedic surgery Med. Coll. Wis., Milw., 1980—; staff St. Nicholas Hosp., Sheboygan, Sheboygan Meml. Hosp.; cons. surgery Wood (Wis.) VA Hosp., 1970—; asst. instr. dept. surgery Med. Coll. Wis., 1964-68, clin. instr. dept. surgery, 1969-72, asst. clin. prof., 1972-73, assoc. clin. prof., 1973-80; research assoc. VA Med. Ctr., Milw., 1970—, co-investigator kinesiology research lab., 1970-84. Mem. bd. editors Jour. Orthopaedic Surg. Techniques, 1985—; contbr. articles to profl. jours. Served to capt. USAF, 1962-63. Fellow Am. Acad. Orthopaedic Surgeons (bd. councilors 1985—); mem. AMA, Mid-Am. Orthopaedic Soc., Clin. Orthopaedic Soc., Wis. Orthopaedic Soc. (pres. 1982-84), Milw. Orthopaedic Soc., Wis. Arthritis Found. (bd. dirs. 1974-82), Sierra Cascade Trauma Soc., Cervical Spine Research Socs. Republican. Lutheran. Avocations: skiing, fishing, tennis, golf, backpacking. Home: 2528 N 3d St Sheboygan WI 53083 Office: Sheboygan Orthopaedic Assocs SC 1226 N 8th St Sheboygan WI 53081

GORE, RICHARD MICHAEL, radiologist; b. Chicago, July 1, 1953; m. Margaret Dembo. BS in Medicine, Northwestern U., 1975, MD, 1977. Diplomate Am. Bd. Radiology. Resident Northwestern U., Chgo., 1977-81; fellow U. Calif., San Francisco, 1981-82, instr. radiology, 1981-82; asst. prof. radiology Northwestern U. Med. Sch., Chgo., 1982-84, assoc. prof., 1984—; chief abdominal radiology Northwestern Meml. Hosp., Chgo., 1982—. asst. editor Gastrointestinal Radiology, 1984—; contbr. 70 papers and chpts. on radiology; also reviews. Mem. AMA, Am. Coll. Radiology, Assn. Univ. Radiologists, Soc. Gastrointestinal Radiologists, Radiol. Soc. N.Am. Office: Northwestern Meml Hosp Dept Radiology 710 N Fairbanks Ct Chicago IL 60611

GOREN, HERSHEL, physician; b. Detroit, Oct. 9, 1938; s. Phillip and Sylvia (Demb) G. BS, Mich. State U., 1960; MD, Wayne State U., 1964. Cert. Am. Bd. Psychiatry and Neurology. Intern Cleve. Met. Gen. Hosp., 1964-65; resident in neurology Mayo Grad. Sch. Medicine, Rochester, Minn., 1965-68; practice medicine specializing in neurology Cleve. Clinic, 1970—; clin. instr. neurology dept. La. State U. Sch. Medicine, 1970; vis. physician neurology dept. Charity Hosp. La., New Orleans, 1970; asst. clin. prof. neurology dept. Case Western Res. U. Sch. Medicine, Cleve., 1980—. Served to capt. USAF, 1968-70, Vietnam. Fellow Am. Acad. Neurology, Am. Heart Assn. (stroke council); mem. Am. Electroencephalographic Soc., Am. Epilepsy Soc., N.Y. Acad. Scis., AAAS, AMA, Ohio State Med. Assn., Clevel. Acad. of Medicine, Am. Soc. Internal Medicine, Ohio Soc. Internal Medicine. Home: 17100 Van Aken Blvd Shaker Heights OH 44120 Office: Cleve Clinic 9500 Euclid Ave Cleveland OH 44106

GORENCE, PATRICIA JOSETTA, lawyer; b. Sheboygan, Wis., Mar. 16, 1943; d. Joseph and Antonia (Marinsheck) G.; m. John Michael Bach, July 11, 1969; children—Amy Jane Bach, Mara Jo Bach, John Christopher Bach. B.A., Marquette U., 1965; M.A., U. Wis.-Madison, 1968, J.D. cum laude, 1977. Bar: Wis. 1977, U.S. Dist. Ct. (ea. and we. dists.) Wis. 1977, U.S. Ct. Appeals (7th cir.) 1979, U.S. Supreme Ct. 1980. Writer/researcher Alverno Coll., Milw., 1970-71; writer/editor Council on Urban Life, Milw., 1970-73; instr. Carroll Coll., Waukesha, Wis., 1973-74; law clk. U.S. Dist. Ct. (ea. dist.) Wis. 1977-79; asst. U.S. atty. Dept. Justice, Milw., 1979-85, 1st asst. U.S. atty., 1985—; mem. adv. com. on local ct. rules U.S. Dist. Ct. (ea. dist.) Wis. 1982—. Mem. Wis. state com. U.S. Commn. on Civil Rights, 1972—. Mem. ABA, 7th Cir. Bar Assn., State Bar Wis., Milw. Bar Assn., Profl. Dimensions, Assn. Women Lawyers, Slovenian Arts Council. Roman Catholic. Home: 3028 N Hackett Ave Milwaukee WI 53211 Office: US Atty's Office 517 E Wisconsin Milwaukee WI 53202

GORMAN, COLUM ALPHONSUS, endocrinologist; b. Mayobridge, North Ireland, June 27, 1936; came to U.S., 1961; s. James Gorman and Mary (McCollum) G.; m. Una Elizabeth O'Neill, Feb. 9, 1961; children: Kevin, Paul, Fiona, Michael. MB, Bch, BAO, Queens U., Belfast, Ireland, 1959; PhD, U. Minn., 1968. Cons. endocrinology Mayo Clinic, Rochester, Minn., 1966—; asst. prof. Mayo Grad. Sch. Medicine, Rochester, 1971-78, assoc. prof., 1976-81, prof., 1981—; chmn. div. endocrinology Mayo Clinic, Rochester, 1985—. Editor, author The Eye and Orbit in Thyroid Disease, 1984. Recipient Carnwath medal and prize Queens U. 1959, Mayo Staff Meml. award 1966. Fellow ACP; mem. AAAS, Am. Thyroid Assn. (sec. 1984—), Endocrine Soc. Republican. Avocations: reading, cross country skiing, automobile restoration. Office: Mayo Clinic Desk W18 A 200 SW 2d St Rochester MN 55905

GORMAN, CORNELIUS FRANCIS, JR., account manager; b. N.Y.C., Aug. 13, 1952; s. Cornelius Francis and Madonna I. (Riendeau) G.; B.S., Marquette U., 1974; m. Rita Elaine Iris, May 21, 1974; 1 son, Cornelius Francis. Sales rep. Robertson, Inc., Milw., 1975-76, Surg. div. Parke-Davis, Madison, Wis., 1976-77, IPCO Hosp. Supply, Chgo., 1977-78, Medi, Inc., Chgo., 1978-79; regional rep. William Harvey Research Corp., Detroit, 1979-85; account mgr. Laser Sonics, 1985—; system analyst Cordis Corp., 1981—. Roman Catholic. Home: 553 N Riverside Saint Clair MI 48079

GORMAN, GERALD WARNER, lawyer; b. North Kansas City, Mo., May 30, 1933; s. William Shelton and Bessie (Warner) G.; m. Anita Belle McPike,

June 26, 1954; children—Guinevere Eve, Victoria Rose. A.B. cum laude, Harvard U., 1954, LL.B. magna cum laude, 1956. Bar: Mo. 1956. Assoc. firm Dietrich, Davis, Dicus, Rowlands, Schmitt & Gorman, Kansas City, 1956-62; ptnr. Dietrich, Davis, Dicus, Rowlands, Schmitt & Gorman, 1963—; dir. North Kansas City State Bank, 1967-83, Musser-Davis Land Co., 1970—. Bd. govs. Citizens Assn. Kansas City, 1962—; trustee Harvard/Radcliffe Club Kansas City Endowment Fund, chmn. bd., 1977-83, trustee Kansas City Mus., 1967-82, Avondale Meth. Ch., 1969—, Citizens Bond Com. of Kansas City, 1973—, chmn. 7th jud. cir. citizens com., 1983—, chmn. Downtown Council Allis Plaza Reconstrn., 1983-85; bd. dirs. Spofford Home for Children, 1972-77. Served with U.S. Army, 1956-58, capt. USAR, 1958-64. Mem. Lawyers Assn. Kansas City (exec. com. 1968-71), ABA, Mo. Bar Assn., Kansas City Bar Assn., Clay County Bar Assn., Harvard Law Sch. Assn. Mo. (pres. 1973). Republican. Clubs: Harvard (pres. 1966), University (dir. 1983—), Kansas City, 611, Old Pike Country. Home: 917 E Vivion Rd Kansas City MO 64118 Office: 1700 City Center Sq Kansas City MO 64105

GORMAN, JAMES JOSEPH, real estate corporation officer; b. Chgo., July 17, 1937; s. James J. and Tillie (John) G.; m. Sharon E. Gilchrist, Nov. 5, 1978. BS in Social Sci., Loyola U., Chgo., 1960. Regional v.p. Citizens Mfg. Corp., Chgo., 1968-72, CNA Mfg. Investors, Chgo., 1972-76; exec. v.p. Real Estate Research Corp., Chgo., 1976-87, vice chmn., 1987—. Mem. Chgo. Athletic Assn.; bd. dirs. Chgo. City Ballet; CNA Mktg. Investors, Ltd. Mem. Nat. Assn. Corp. Real Estate Execs., Nat. Assn. Indsl. and Office Parks, Urban Land Inst., Pension Real Estate Assn., Mortgage Bankers Assn., Internat. Council Shopping Ctrs. Office: Real Estate Research Corp 72 W Adams St Chicago IL 60603

GORMAN, JOSEPH TOLLE, manufacturing executive; b. Rising Sun, Ind., 1937; m. Bettyann Gorman. B.A., Kent State U., 1959; LL.B., Yale U., 1962. Assoc. Baker, Hostetler & Patterson, Cleve., 1962-67; with legal dept. TRW Inc., Cleve., 1968-69, asst. sec., 1969-70, sec., 1970-72, v.p. sr. counsel automotive worldwide ops., 1972-73, v.p., asst. gen. counsel, 1973-76, v.p., gen. counsel, 1976-80, acting head communications function, 1978, exec. v.p. indsl. and energy sector, 1980-85, asst. pres., 1984-85, pres., chief operating officer, 1985—, mem. policy group, 1975—, also bd. dirs.; bd. dirs. Soc. Corp., Soc. Nat. Bank Cleve., Standard Oil Co. Trustee Univ. Circle, Inc., Govtl. Research Inst., Cleve. Play House, Cleve. Inst. Art, Leadership Cleve., United Way Services, Cleve. Council on World Affairs, Musical Arts Assn.; past trustee Cleve. Fedn. Community Planning; past mem. exec. com. Ctr. of Pub. Resources Project on Dispute Resolution; bd. advisors Yale Law Sch. Urgent Issues Program. Mem. ABA, Assn. Gen. Counsel (emeritus), Ohio Bar Assn., Cleve. Bar Assn., Yale Law Sch. Assn. (exec. com.), Greater Cleve. Growth Assn. (trustee, exec. com.), U.S. C. of C. (past chmn. corp. governance and policy com.), Council on Fgn. Relations. Office: TRW Inc 1900 Richmond Rd Cleveland OH 44124

GORMAN, PAUL JOSEPH, educator; b. Mitchell, S.D., June 29, 1946; s. Elmer E. and Celestine (Turnis) G.; m. Janice Miller, May 25, 1985; children: Carma, Joseph, Cara. B.S. in Agrl. Edn. S.D. State U., 1968; M.S., Mankato State U., 1977. Vocat. agr. instr. Central City, Iowa, 1968-71; farm mgmt. ops. instr. Northwest Iowa Tech. Coll., 1971-74; agri-bus. instr. Mankato (Minn.) Tech. Inst., 1974—; precinct del. Minn. Democratic Farmer-Labor Party county conv.; co-founder, bd. dirs. Minn. Earth Assn.; project dir. MIT State of Minn. Sweet Sorghum Research Project, 1985—. Mem. NEA (del. 1985 conv. Washington), Minn. Vocat. Assn., Am. Vocat. Assn., Minn. Vocat. Agr. Instrs. Assn., Am. Vocat. Assn., Minn. Edn. Assn., North Mankato Police Res. Democrat. Lodge: Lions. Contbr. articles to profl. jours. Developed successful alternative on-farm fuel energy project. Home: 1405 Lor Ray Dr North Mankato MN 56001 Office: 1920 Lee Blvd North Mankato MN 56001

GORNICK, ALAN LEWIS, lawyer; b. Leadville, Colo., Sept. 23, 1908; s. Mark and Anne (Grayhack) G.; m. Ruth L. Willcockson, 1940 (dec. May 1959); children: Alan Lewis, Diana Willcockson (Mrs. Lawrence J. Richard, Jr.), Keith Hardin; m. Pauline Martoi, 1972. AB, Columbia U., 1935, JD, 1937. Bar: N.Y. 1937, Mich. 1948. Assoc. Baldwin, Todd & Young, N.Y.C., 1937-41, Milbank, Tweed, Hope & Hadley, 1941-47; asso. counsel charge tax matters Ford Motor Co., Dearborn, Mich., 1947-49; dir. tax affairs, chmn. tax com., tax counsel Ford Motor Co., 1949-64; lectr. tax matters NYU, Inst. Fed. Taxation, 1947-49, ABA and Practicing Law Inst. (courses on fundamentals in fed. taxation), 1946-55, Am. Law Inst. (courses in continuing legal edn.), 1950; spl. lectr. sch. bus. adminstrn. U. Mich., 1949, 53. Author: Estate Tax Handbook, 1952, Arrangements for Separation or Divorce, Handbook of Tax Techniques, 1952, Taxation of Partnerships, Estates and Trusts, rev. edit, 1952; adv. editor Nat. Tax Jour., 1952-55; contbr. articles on tax matters to profl. jours. Exec. bd. Detroit area council Boy Scouts Am., chmn. fin. com., 1960; pres. Mich. Assn. Emotionally Disturbed Children, 1962-65; v.p. Archives of Am. Art; mem. Mich. Heart Assn., Columbia Coll. council Columbia U., N.Y.C., Founder's Soc. Detroit Inst. Art; trustee Council on World Affairs, Detroit; trustee, past pres. Detroit Hist. Soc.; mem. bd. Zoning Appeals City Bloomfield Hills, 1980—. Recipient Gov.'s Spl. award State Colo., 1952. Mem. ABA (council tax sect. 1957-58), Detroit Bar Assn., N.Y. City Bar Assn. (chmn. subcom. estate and gift taxes 1943-47), Am. Law Inst., Tax Inst. Inc. (pres. 1954-55), U.S. C. of C., Empire State C. of C., Council on Fgn. Relations, Nat. Tax Assn. (exec. com.), Internat. Fiscal Assn. (council, nat. reporter 6th Internat. Congress Fiscal Law, Brussels 1952), Internat. Law Assn., Assn. Ex-Mems. Squadron A, Nat. Fgn. Trade Council (mem. com. taxes 1950), Automobile Mfrs. Assn. (chmn. com. on taxation 1960-62), Tax Execs. Inst. (pres. 1956-57), Fedn. Alumni Columbia (bd. dirs. 1946), Class 1935 Columbia Coll. (pres.), N.Y. Adult Edn. Council (bd. dirs. 1939-45), Detroit Hist. Soc. (trustee, pres. 1083-85), Phi Delta Phi. Clubs: Bloomfield Hills (Mich.) Country, Detroit, Detroit Athletic, Columbia U., Church (N.Y.C.); Lawyers of U. of Mich., Columbia U. Alumni of Mich. (pres. 1950—), Otsego Ski (Gaylord, Mich.); Little (Gulfstream, Fla.). Home: 150 Lowell Ct Bloomfield Hills MI 48013 Office: 1565 Woodward Ave Suite 8 PO Box 957 Bloomfield Hills MI 48013

GOROZYCKI, AMY ANN, social services auditor; b. Detroit, Aug. 22, 1950; d. Bruno W. and Anna M. (Lewandowski) G. BA, Wayne State U., 1972, MBA, 1985. Social worker State of Mich., Detroit, 1974-85; medicare auditor Travelers Ins. Co., Detroit, 1985—. Mem. Phi Beta Kappa, Beta Alpha Psi, Beta Gamma Sigma. Avocations: travel, music. Office: Medicare Auditor Travelers Ins 1000 Travelers Tower Southfield MI 48076

GORR, IVAN WILLIAM, rubber company executive; b. Toledo, Ohio; s. Paul Robert and Edna Louise (Wandt) G.; m. Dorothy J. Brandt, June 21, 1951; children: Louise (Mrs. Gary Stephenson), Jean (Mrs. Donald Jones), Robert C., Amy S., Sally M. B.S. in Bus. Adminstrn., U. Toledo, 1951. C.P.A., Ohio. Prin. Arthur Young & Co., Toledo, Ohio, 1953-72; corp. controller Cooper Tire & Rubber Co., Findlay, Ohio, 1972-75, chief fin. officer, 1975-82, treas., 1976-77, exec. v.p., treas., 1977-82, pres., chief operating officer, 1982—; dir. First Ohio Bancshares Inc., Toledo, Cooper Tire & Rubber Co. Chmn., pres. Blanchard Valley Health Assn., Findlay, 1982-85, bd. dirs., 1974—; chmn. bus. adv. council U. Toledo, 1987—; advisor Findlay Area Arts Council. Served with U.S. Army, 1951-53, Korea. Mem. Nat. Assn. Accountants (pres. Northwestern Ohio chpt. 1977), Ohio Soc. C.P.A.'s (bd. dirs. 1972). Republican. Lutheran. Clubs: Rotary, Findlay Country. Avocations: golf, sailing, bowling. Home: 1705 Windsor Pl Findlay OH 45840 Office: Cooper Tire & Rubber Co Lima & Western Aves Findlay OH 45840

GORSKE, ROBERT HERMAN, lawyer, arbitrator; b. Milw., June 8, 1932; s. Herman Albert and Lorraine (McDermott) G.; m. Antonette Dujick, Aug. 28, 1954; 1 child, Judith Mary (Mrs. Charles H. McMullen). Student, Milw. State Tchrs. Coll., 1949-50; B.A. cum laude, Marquette U., 1953, J.D. magna cum laude, 1955; LL.M. (W.W. Cook fellow), U. Mich., 1959. Bar: Wis. bar 1955, D.C. bar 1968, U.S. Supreme Ct. bar 1970. Assoc. firm Quarles, Spence & Quarles, Milw., 1955-56; atty. Allis-Chalmers Mfg. Co., West Allis, Wis., 1956-62; instr. law U. Mich. Law Sch., Ann Arbor, 1958-59; lectr. law Marquette U. Law Sch., Milw., 1963; assoc. firm Quarles, Herriott & Clemons, Milw., 1962-64; atty. Wis. Electric Power Co., Milw., 1964-67, gen. counsel, 1967—, v.p., 1970-72, 76—; mem. firm Quarles & Brady, Milw., 1972-76; gen. counsel Wis. Energy Corp., 1981—. Contbr. articles to profl. jours.; Editor-in-chief: Marquette Law Rev, 1954-55. Bd. dirs. Guadalupe Children's Med. Dental Clinic, Inc., Milw., 1976-86; trustee Ronald McDonald House, Wauwatosa, Wis., 1987—. Mem. State Bar Wis., Am. Bar Assn., Edison Electric Inst. (vice chmn. legal com. 1975-77, chmn. 1977-79), Am. Arbitration Assn. (panelist comml. arbitrators 1985—). Home: 12700 Stephen Pl Elm Grove WI 53122 Office: Wis Electric Power Co 231 W Michigan St Box 2046 Milwaukee WI 53201

GORSKI, PAMELA LEE, hospital administrator; b. Ancon, Panama Canal Zone, July 27, 1944; came to U.S., 1962; d. Walter Dean and Margaret Evelyn (Rutledge) Johnston; m. Damian John Gorski, Aug. 26, 1967; children—Jeffrey, Justin. B.S., Case Western Res. U., 1966, M.B.A., 1980. Adminstrv. asst. (1st woman) to mayor City of Lakewood, Ohio, 1978-80, personnel asst., 1980-81; planning asst. Lakewood Hosp., 1981-84, dir. planning and devel., 1984-86, dir. aux. services & fund devel., 1986—. Vice pres. Lakewood Mcpl. Employees Fed. Credit Union, 1985-86; commr. Lakewood Youth Softball Commn., 1985—; co-chmn. Lakewood Arts Festival, 1978—. Mem. Nat. Soc. Fund Raising Execs., Lakewood Pub. Relations Officers Assn. Republican. Home: 14519 Detroit Ave Lakewood OH 44107 Office: Lakewood Hosp 14519 Detroit Ave Lakewood OH 44107

GORSUCH, SARAH ELIZABETH, educator, fraternal organization administrator; b. Marietta, Ohio, Feb. 11, 1935; d. Rolland and Alice Elizabeth (Plumer) Rose; m. William H.B. Skaates, June 21, 1959 (div. June 1979); children: Joanna E., C. Calvin; m. Richard Harold Gorsuch, Aug. 16, 1981. BS in Edn., Otterbein Coll., Westerville, Ohio, 1956; MA, Ohio State U., 1982. Tchr. Columbus (Ohio) Schs., 1956-60, Westerville Schs., 1960-61, 78—; coordinator Christian edn. Ch. of Master United Meth., Westerville, 1973-78; exec. sec./treas. Theta Alpha Phi, Westerville, 1980—. Contbr. articles to children's mags. and regional pubs. Mem. St. Ann's Hosp. Guild, Westerville. Mem. NEA, Ohio Edn. Assn., Ohio Council Internat. Reading Assn., AAUW. Republican. Methodist. Avocations: reading, travel, gardening, needlework. Home: 53 Glenwood Dr Westerville OH 43081

GORTNER, ROBERT VANDERBILT, management educator, administrator; b. Davidsville, Pa., Jan. 20, 1930; s. Maurice Rynerson and Ruth Runyan (Vanderbilt) G.; m. Aileen Melva Kraekel, Feb. 15, 1952 (dec. Apr. 1981); children—Deborah, Susan, William, David: m. 2d, Jane Elaine Le Master, May 22, 1982; stepchildren—Ted, Beth. B.S. in Commerce and Engring., M.B.A., Drexel U. Cert. mgmt. cons. Indsl. engr. Eastman Kodak Co. Rochester, N.Y., 1955-59; supt. Hercules, Inc., Rocky Hill, N.J., 1959-65; prodn. mgr. Polymer Corp., Reading, Pa., 1965-68; plant mgr. Thiokol Corp., Trenton, N.J., 1968-70; sr. mgr. (cons.) Price Waterhouse & Co., N.Y.C., 1970-80; assoc. prof., chmn. mgmt. dept. Taylor U., Upland, Ind., 1980—; adj. prof. Drexel U., Phila., 1963-65, Union Community Coll., Westfield, N.J., 1979-80, Rochester Inst. Tech., (N.Y.), 1958. Pres. PTA, Wyomissing Hills, Pa., 1967; supr. twp. Northampton Twp., Bucks County, Pa., 1963-65; coach and mgr. Little League and Babe Ruth Baseball, Lower Makefield, Pa. and Summit, N.J., 1968-80; bd. dirs. Jr. Achievement, Marion, Ind., 1981-83, Leadership/Grant County, Marion, 1983. Served as lt. USNR, 1952-55. Mem. Acad. Mgmt., Inst. Indsl. Engrs., Am. Prodn. and Inventory Control Soc., Inst. Mgmt. Cons., Blue Key, Phi Kappa Phi. Republican. Presbyterian. Lodge: Rotary (Marion, Ind.). Home: 9240 E 700S Upland IN 46989 Office: Taylor U Upland IN 46989

GORYL, KATHLEEN CARMODY, healthcare policy administrator; b. Springfield, Ill., Oct. 19, 1957; d. Robert Walter and Rosemary (Dolan) Carmody; m. Steven Michael Goryl, Nov. 8, 1980. BS, So. Ill. U., 1979; postgrad., Loyola U., Chgo., 1986—. Registered dietitian, Ill. Clin. dietitian Riverside Med. Ctr., Kankakee, Ill., 1980-83; cons. dietitian Hawthorne Lodge, Watseka, Ill., 1982-83; asst. dir. clin. nutrition St. Joseph's Hosp., Elgin, Ill., 1983-85; cons. dietitian Countryside Manor, Elgin, 1984-85; sr. survey report analyst Joint Commn. Accreditation of Hosps., Chgo., 1985-87; cons. dept. ops. Blue Cross and Blue Shield Assn., Chgo., 1987—. Bd. dirs. Am. Diabetic Assn., Kankakee, 1984-85. Mem. Am. Dietetic Assn., W. Suburban Dietetic Assn. (chmn. various coms. 1984—), Am. Hosp. Assn., Am. Coll. Healthcare Execs., Soc. for Ambulatory Care Profls., Nat. Council Against Health Fraud. Avocations: skiing, traveling. Office: Blue Cross and Blue Shield 676 N St Clair St Chicago IL 60611

GOSNELL, THOMAS CHARLES, mayor; b. London, Ont., Can., Apr. 7, 1951; s. James Fredrick and Evelyn Winnifred (Head) G.; m. Laurel Joanne Strople, Apr. 17, 1986. BA in Polit. Sci. and History, U. Western Ont., 1974. Pres. Gosnell Paving Stone, Inc., London, 1978; alderman City of London, 1978-85, mayor, 1985—; chmn. bd. of control City of London; member ex-officio devel. adv. bd. planning com., environment and transp. com., community and protective services com., pub. utilities commn. City of London; bd. commrs. London Police Dept. Mem. diaster and emergency coordinating com., liaison com. City of London/Middlesex County; bd. dirs. London Pub. Library, Western Fair Assn., London; bd. govs. U. Western Ont., Can. Mem. Fedn. Can. Municipalities (big city mayor's caucus), Assn. Municipalities of Ont. Avocations: golf, football. Office: Corp City of London, PO Box 5035, 300 Dufferin Ave, London, ON Canada N6A 4L9

GOSS, DONALD E., accountant; b. Chgo., Feb. 6, 1931; s. Anton J. and Pansy M. (Sanders) G.; m. Kay A. Hesson, Aug. 21, 1954; children—William, Donna, Thomas, Robert, Marilee, Donald E. B.S. in Accountancy, U. Ill., 1953; grad., Advanced Mgmt. Program, Harvard U., 1973. C.P.A., Ill. With Arthur Young & Co. (C.P.A.'s), Chgo., 1953—, prin., 1961-62, ptnr., 1962—, Midwest regional mng. ptnr., 1976-85, vice chmn., 1981-85, Midwest regional sr. ptnr., 1985—; adv. council U. Ill. Coll. Commerce, 1977—. Mem. Chgo. Crime Commn., 1970, U. Ill. Found., 1972. Served with AUS, 1953-54. Mem. Am. Inst. C.P.A.'s, Ill. Soc. C.P.A.'s. Club: Edgewood Valley Country. Home: 4807 Johnson Ave Western Springs IL 60558 Office: Arthur Young & Co 1 IBM Plaza Chicago IL 60611

GOSS, EDWIN J., insurance company executive. Pres. Am. Economy Ins. Co., Indpls. Office: Am Economy Ins Co 500 N Meridian St Indianapolis IN 46207 *

GOSS, ROBERT MITCHELL, manufacturing and construction executive; b. Chgo., Dec. 16, 1956; s. Howard Simon and Roberta (Jacobs) G.; m. Lisa Kay Goldberg, Aug. 4, 1979; children: Danielle, Neal. BS in Econs., U. Pa., 1979, MBA, 1980. CPA, Ill. Cons. Coopers and Lybrand, Chgo., 1980-82; v.p. Hillman's, Inc., Chgo., 1982-83; v.p. Transco, Inc., Chgo., 1983—, also bd. dirs. Mem. N. Suburban Jewish Community Ctrs. (bd. dirs. 1985—, exec. bd. 1986, v.p. 1987). Home: 1091 Elm Ridge Dr Glencoe IL 60022 Office: Transco Inc 55 E Jackson Blvd Chicago IL 60604

GOSSAIN, VED VYAS, medical educator; b. Jhang, India, Mar. 25, 1941; came to U.S., 1967; s. Bhagwan Dass and Rani (Virmani) G.; m. Veena Virmani, May 25, 1970; children—Anuja, Maneesh; m. 2d, Rama Dhamija, Aug. 24, 1979; 1 child, Vineeth. M.B.B.S., Med. Coll. Amritsar (India), 1963; M.D., All India Inst. Med. Scis., 1967. Diplomate Am. Bd. Internal Medicine. Intern V.J. Med. Coll. Hosp., Amritsar, India, 1963-64; clin. resident All India Inst. Med. Scis., New Delhi, 1965-67, vis. prof., 1979, 81; resident Springfield (Mass.) Hosp. Med. Ctr., 1967-70; clin. and research fellow endocrinology and metabolism U. Cin. Med. Ctr., 1970-72; research fellow endocrinology and metabolism Milw. County Gen. Hosp., 1972-73; mem. staff internal medicine VA Hosp., St. Louis, 1973-75, dir. endocrine metabolic clinic, 1973-75; asst. prof. internal medicine St. Louis U., 1973-75; asst. prof. internal medicine Coll. Human Medicine, Mich. State U., East Lansing, 1975-78, assoc. prof., 1978-82, prof., 1982—; vis. prof. Guy Hosp. Sch. Medicine, London, 1981; cons. in field. Fellow Royal Coll. Physicians Can., ACP, All India Inst. Diabetes; mem. AMA, Am. Fedn. Clin. Research, The Endocrine Soc., AAAS, Am. Diabetes Assn., Mich. State Med. Soc., Ingham County Med. Soc., India Cultural Soc. Greater Lansing (pres. 1986—). Hindu. Contbr. articles to profl. jours.

GOSSAN, BRIAN WESLEY, clergyman; b. Escanaba, Mich., Feb. 18, 1954; s. Alfred Anthony and Virginia Anne (Abrahah) G.; m. Janice Diane Phillips, Feb. 5, 1983; children: Brijan Kahla, Kristopher Ryan. AA, Bay De Noc Community Coll., 1978; BS, Andrews U., 1980; postgrad., Grand Valley State Coll. Ordained to ministry United Pentecostal Ch. Internat., 1984. Lay worker and evangelist United Pentecostal Ch., Escanaba, 1975-77; youth minister Bethel Apostolic Tabernacle, Buchanan, Mich., 1978-80; sec. Mich. United Pentecostal Ch. Internat. Conquerors, Holland, Mich., 1979-80, pres., 1979-85; pastor Holland Abundant Life Fellowship, 1980—; dir. Christian edn., youth leader sect. 6 Upper Peninsula United Pentecostal Chs., Mich., 1974-76; camp dir. jr. and sr. high sch. camps, Albion, Mich., 1980—; tchr., evangelist Fishermen's Workshop, Jackson, Miss., 1982—. Contbg. editor Mich. Dist. News, 1980—; contbr. articles to Life, others. Bd. dirs. Cen. Ave. Group Home of the Mich. West Shore chpt. Mich. Soc. for Autistic Children. Recipient Youth Leader Honor award sect. 4 S.W. Mich. United Pentecostal Ch. chs., 1980, sect. 5, 1982, Fishermen's Workshop award Pentecostal Ch. Kingston, Jamaica, 1983, Camp Dir. Honors award Mich. dist. Pentecostal Ch., 1983—, Outstanding Service award World Evangelism Ctr. United Pentecostal Ch. Internat., 1984. Mem Nat. Fedn. Decency, Christian Action Council (promoter, anti-abortion com. 1984—), Travelers Protection Assn., The Attending Clergy Assn. (speaker 1986—), Moral Majority (pubs. com. 1984—). Avocations: fishing, boating, swimming, organ, baritone. Home: 501 Central Ave Holland MI 49423 Office: Holland Abundant Life Fellowship 20th and Central Holland MI 49423

GOSSER, JON WALTER, educator; b. Seattle, May 15, 1941; s. Lawrence and Ellinore (Jones) G.; B.S. cum laude, U. Wash., 1962, M.S., 1964, postgrad., 1964-65; postgrad. U. Kans., 1965-67. Reader in stats. U. Wash., Seattle, fellow research asst. in psychology, 1962-63, USPHS predoctoral research fellow NIMH, 1963-65; predoctoral trainee in ednl. research Bur. Child Research, U. Kans., Kansas City, 1965-66; tchr. psychology, logic and marriage and family relations Kansas City (Kans.) Community Jr. Coll., 1966-67; instr. psychology Delta Coll., University Center, Mich., 1967-69, asst. prof., 1970-75, asso. prof., 1975—, dir. Mid-Mich. Psychologist, Inc., 1973-76, 79—, treas., 1978—; pres. Nat. Ednl. Network, Inc., 1978—, bd. dirs. 1982-83. Mem. Data Processing Mgmt. Assn. (dir. 1971-73; individual performance award 1981), Am. Psychol. Assn., AAAS, AAUP (corr. sec. Delta chpt. 1969), Am. Ednl. Research Assn., Assn. Behavior Analysis, Mich. Acad. Sci., Arts and Letters, Internat. Soc. for Individual Instrn., Sigma Xi. Author: (with Harbans Lal) Research on Teaching Pharmacy: The Role of Student Ratings, 1968; A Computerized Method of Longitudinal Evaluation of Student Performance, 1969; Computerized Test Library, 1974; Longitudinal Evaluation and Improvement of Teaching: An Empirical Approach Based on Analysis of Student Behaviors, 1975; (with Packwood and Walters) The Effect of Repeated Testing on Long Term Retention and Generalization in a General Psychology Course, 1979. Home: 3200 Noeske St Midland MI 48640 Office: Delta Coll University Center MI 48710

GOSSETT, DONALD IRA, real estate company officer; b. Independence, Kans., Apr. 11, 1941; s. Ira Smith and Dorothy Nadine (Swazey) G.; m. Karen Sue Lakin, Apr. 14, 1961; children: Eric Alan, Barry Chadwick. Student, Kansas City (Kans.) Jr. Coll., 1964-65, U. Mo., Kansas City, 1967, 84, Inst. Real Estate Mgmt., 1968-70, Johnson County Community Coll., 1971-72. Cert. real estate broker, Kans., Mo., Nebr.; registered property mgr. Asst. to exec. v.p. Charles F. Curry Real Estate Co., Kansas City, Mo., 1963-68; v.p. commercial real estate div. Oppenheimer Industries, Inc., Kansas City, 1968-74; broker/salesman Fishman and Co., Johnson County, Kans., 1974-75; prin. Gossett & Assocs., Overland Park, Kans., 1975—. Bd. dirs. Bus. Dist. League of Kansas City, 1974, Downtown Inc., Kansas City, 1972-74, Bldg. Owners Mgrs. Assn., 1973-74, Kansas City chpt. Inst. Real Estate Mgmt., 1972-74, comml. investment div. Johnson County Bd. Realtors, 1984-85. Served with USAF, 1959-63. Mem. Nat. Assn. Realtors, Nat. Inst. Real Estate Mgmt. (chpt. pres.), Kans. Real Estate Assn., Johnson County Bd. Realtors Inc., Met. Kansas City Bd. Realtors, Lenexa C. of C., Mission C. of C. Lodge: Masons. Avocations: golf, fishing, photography. Home: 11308 W 71st St Shawnee KS 66203 Office: 7700 W 63d St Overland Park KS 66202

GOSSETT, DONALD LANCE, oral and maxillofacial surgeon; b. Kansas City, Mo., Aug. 16, 1954; s. Donald William and Shirley Gertrude (Lance) G.; m. Sheryl Ann Akers, Aug. 25, 1979; children: Dustin Lance, Lauren Ashley. BS in Biology, U. Mo., Kansas City, 1972-77, DDS, 1981. Diplomate Am. Bd. Oral and Maxillofacial Surgeons. Resident in oral and maxillofacial surgery Carle Found. Hosp., Urbana, Ill., 1981-84; practice dentistry specializing in oral and maxillofacial surgery St. Joseph, Mo., 1984—; asst. prof. oral surgery U. Mo. Dental Sch., Kansas City, 1981; teaching staff Truman Med. Ctr., Kansas City, 1985—. Fellow Am. Assn. Oral and Maxillofacial Surgeons, Am. Coll. Oral and Maxillofacial Surgeons; mem. ADA, Midwest Soc. Oral and Maxillofacial Surgeons, N.W. Mo. Dental Soc. (program dir. 1985—). Lodges: Rotary (internat. rep. St. Joseph 1986—). Avocations: hunting, skeet shooting, tennis, golf. Office: 5301 Faraon St Suite 100 Saint Joseph MO 64506

GOSSETT, GLORIA JEAN, nurse, social worker; b. Urbana, Ohio, Oct. 7, 1953; d. Owen Edward and Goldie (Gardenhire) G.; m. Michael C. Rogan, Apr. 27, 1985. B.S. cum laude, Central State U., 1975; nursing diploma Community Hosp. Sch. Nursing, 1982. R.N., Ohio. Social field worker Greene County Commn. on Aging, Yellow Springs, Ohio, 1975; social worker Ohio Orphans Home, Xenia, 1976-77; staff nurse Community Hosp., Springfield, 1982—. Mem. Alpha Kappa Mu. Home: 2803 Oxford Dr Springfield OH 45506

GOSSETT, JON KEVIN, arts organization administrator; b. Steubenville, Ohio, Sept. 15, 1955; s. Isaac Watson and Frances Jean (Turrentine) G. B in Mcpl. Adminstrn., U. Mich., 1973-77. Gen. mgr. orchestras Univ. Sch. Music, Ann Arbor, Mich., 1975-77; program dir. N.C. Arts Council, Raleigh, 1977-79; asst. dir. Asheville (N.C.) Civic Ctr. Complex, 1979-80; exec. dir. High Point (N.C.) Arts Council, 1980-83; exec. dir. Ft. Wayne (Ind.) Fine Arts Found., 1984-87, pres., 1987—; cons. Community Sch. Arts, Charlotte, N.C., 1985, S.C. Arts Commn., Columbia, 1979. Bd. dirs. Campus Minstry, Inc., Ft. Wayne, 1987—. Mem. Am. Council for Arts, Nat. Assembly Local Arts Agys., Ind. Assembly of Local Arts Agys. (v.p. 1985-87, pres. 1987—), Ind. Advocates for Arts (v.p. legis. 1987—). Lutheran. Club: Quest (Ft. Wayne). Lodge: Rotary. Avocations: weightlifting, music, running, travel. Office: Ft Wayne Fine Arts Found 114 E Superior St Fort Wayne IN 46802-1289

GOSSETT, ROBERT LAMONT, human resources executive; b. Lancaster, Ohio; s. Robert Loyal and Nancy Jean (Upp) G.; m. Tolli Buchanan; children: Erynne Buchanan, Robert Laird. BBA, Ohio U. Indsl. relations mgr. Anchor Hocking Corp., Lancaster, 1975-76, personnel mgr., 1976-77, mgr. compensation, 1977-79, mgr. employee devel., 1979-83, mgr. employee services, 1983-85; div. mgr. human resources Elk Grove Village, Ill., 1985—; Bd. dirs. Glassco Credit Union, Lancaster. Bd. dirs. Alcoholism Counsel, Lancaster, 1977, County Mental Health Assn., Lancaster, 1985. Mem. Am. Mgmt. Assn., Am. Compensation Assn., Regional Personnel Group. Avocations: tennis, handball. Office: Anchor Hocking Corp 1501 W Pratt Blvd Elk Grove Village IL 60007

GOSSMEYER, MELVIN LEON, security services executive; b. Chgo., Oct. 5, 1951; s. Melvin Leon and Marie (Prosser) G.; m. Davina L. Clark, Sept. 18, 1971; children: Monica L., Marcus L. Student, Moraine Valley Coll., 1970—. Lic. pvt. detective, Ill.; lic. security contractor, Ill. Partsman Consol. Freightways, Chgo., 1972-79, supr., 1979—; pres. Ill. Security Services Inc., Chgo., 1984—; mem. Ill. State Police Meml. Com. Coordinator gold star families Chgo. Police Dept.; bd. dirs. Greater Cook County Council Police Chiefs. Served to 2d lt. U.S. Army, 1969-72. Mem. Ill. Trucking Assn. (chmn. cargo theft com., mem. terminal mgmt. sect. com.), Ill. Fedn. Police., Am. Legion. Baptist. Home: PO Box 2058 Bridgeview IL 60455-6058 Office: Ill Security Services Inc 29 S LaSalle St Suite 350 Chicago IL 60603-1502

GOSTICH, CYRIL M., podiatrist; b. Cleve., Mar. 20, 1953; s. Martin and Ivanka (Zagar) G.; m. Joan E. Zupon, June 21, 1975. BA, Cleve. State U., 1975; D in Podiatric Medicine, Ohio Coll. Podiatric Medicine, 1980. Diplomate Am. Bd. Podiatric Surgery. Resident in podiatric surgery New Berlin (Wis.) Meml. Hosp., 1980-81; practice podiatric surgery Euclid, 1981—. Fellow Am. Coll. Foot Surgeons, Am. Podiatric Med. Assn., Ohio Podiatric Med. Assn. Avocations: fishing, travel. Office: 21936 Lakeshore Blvd Euclid OH 44123

GOSTOMSKI, VICTOR GEORGE, JR., engineer; b. Peru, Ill., Nov. 17, 1940; s. Victor George and Ruth Ann (Vrba) G.; m. Sandra Jean Kuhn, Oct. 6, 1962; children: Susanne, Robert, Ruth Ann. BS in Engring., U.S. Merchant Marine Acad., 1962; postgrad., No. Ill. U., 1966-68. Lic. marine engr. USCG. Test engr. U.S. Bur. Ships, Boston, 1962-64; plant engr. Foster Grant Co., Peru, 1964-65; project engr. Sundstrand Corp., La Salle, Ill., 1965-71; sect. mgr. engring. Sundstrand Corp., Ames, Iowa, 1971-84, mgr. engring., 1984—. Patentee in field; contbr. articles to profl. jours. Mem. Peru Sch. Dist. Sch. Bd., 1967-71; co-chmn. Ames United Way, 1985-86. Mem. Soc. Automotive Engrs., Soc. Marine Engrs. and Naval Architects, Sigma Kappa (sec./treas.). Avocations: reading, culturing bonsai trees, gardening, fishing, hunting. Home: 2715 Cleveland Dr Ames IA 50010 Office: Sundstrand Corp 200 E 13th St Ames IA 50010

GOTAAS, DAVID JOHN, construction company executive, accountant; b. Chgo., Mar. 2, 1951; s. David Stanley and Iona Lois (Benson) G.; m. Sally Slingerland, Nov. 18, 1978; children: Anne Elizabeth, Kathryn Joy, Mary Jane. BA, Wheaton Coll., 1972; M Mgmt, Northwestern U., 1974. Staff acct. Arthur Andersen & Co., Chgo., 1974-76; proprietor, acct. D.J. Gotaas & Co., Winnetka, Ill., 1976-85; exec. v.p. Glenn Johnson Contrn., Evanston, Ill., 1985—. Trustee, bd. dirs. Chgo. Gospel Mission, 1980—. Named Paul Harris fellow Rotary Internat., Evanston, 1982. Mem. Am. Inst. CPA's, Ill. CPA Soc., Fla. CPA Soc., Constrn. Fin. Mgmt. Assn. Republican. Presbyterian. Lodge: Rotary (bd. dirs. Winnetka). Avocations: sports, travel. Office: Glenn H Johnson Constrn Co 2521 Gross Point Evanston IL 60201

GOTCH, LOU ANN MEYER, banker; b. Ft. Wayne, Ind., June 23, 1947; d. Donald LeRoy and Marjorie Ruth (Dyer) Meyer; m. John Raymond Gotch, Oct. 7, 1967; 1 child, Andrew John. Student, So. Ill. U., 1965-66, Am. Inst. Banking, 1979-81; cert. Sch. Bank Mktg., 1982. Teller Carbondale Savs. & Loan, Ill., 1974-76; customer service/advt. mgr. State Savs., Bowling Green, Ohio, 1976-78; mktg. asst. Pk. Nat. Bank, Newark, Ohio, 1978-79; dir. mktg. Central Trust Co., Newark, 1979-85; v.p. mktg. United Nat. Bank, Canton; Ohio, 1985—; cons. pub. speaking Bus. and Profl. women, Newark, 19; cons., mktg. Bldg. Better Bds., Newark, 1984. Newspaper columnist 1984-85. Loaned exec. United Way, Licking County, Ohio, 1978; bd. dirs. Am. Cancer Soc., Licking County, 1978-85, Named Outstanding Women of Am., 1983. Mem. Nat. Assn. Bank Women, Ohio Sch. Bank Mktg. Alumni Assn., C. of C. Licking County. Avocations: teaching aerobics, public speaking, music, Sunday Sch. Lit., sewing. Office: United Nat Bank PO Box 190 Canton OH 44701

GOTH, STEPHEN CHARLES, corporate executive; b. Danville, Ill., Jan. 25, 1941; s. Stephen Eldridge and Edna (Smith) G.; m. Suzanne Sutphin, June 6, 1963 (div. Oct. 1980); children: Stephen J., Julianna E. BS, U.S. Mil. Acad., 1963; MBA, Harvard U., 1970. Commd. 2d lt. U.S. Army, 1963, advanced through grades to capt., 1966; served in Vietnam War, resigned, 1968; v.p., gen. mgr. FMC of Can. Ltd., Burlington, Ont., Can., 1970-78; pres. Brown Fintube Co., Tulsa, 1978-80, Chloride Industrial Batteries, Kansas City, Mo., 1980-83, Balco Internat., Inc, Wichita, Kans., 1983—. Republican. Avocations: Wichita Symphony, athletics. Home: 3702 E Second Wichita KS 67208 Office: Balco Internat 2626 S Sheridan Wichita KS 67217

GOTKIN, MICHAEL STANLEY, lawyer; b. Washington, Aug. 15, 1942; s. Charles and Florence (Rosenberg) G.; A.A., Montgomery Community Coll., 1962; B.S., Columbia U., 1964; J.D., Vanderbilt U., 1967; m. Diana Rubin, Aug. 22, 1964; children—Lisa, Steven. Admitted to D.C. bar, 1968, Tenn. bar, 1973; trial atty. Bur. Restraint of Trade, FTC, Washington, 1967-70; atty. H.J. Heinz Co., Pitts., 1970-73; partner firm Moseley & Gotkin, Nashville, 1973; atty. K.F.C. Corp., Louisville, 1974-75; v.p., gen. counsel Farley Candy Co., Skokie, Ill., 1975—, also dir.; v.p., gen. counsel, dir. Taste-T-Sweets, Inc. Mem. ABA, Am. Corp. Counsel Assn. (bd. dirs. Chgo. chpt.), D.C. Bar Assn., Tenn. Bar Assn., Montgomery Community Coll. Assn. (past pres.), Skokie C. of C. (past pres., dir.), Columbia U. Alumni Assn., Candy Prodn. Club, Vanderbilt U. Alumni Assn. Club: Sportsman's Country (Northbrook, Ill.). Lodge: B'nai Brith. Office: 4820 Searle Pkwy Skokie IL 60077

GOTMAN, ABRAHAM GOLDSMID, obstetrician and gynecologist; b. Kolici, Luck, Poland, Mar. 4, 1934; came to U.S., 1960; s. Mordko L. and Lida (Goldszmid) G.; m. Elsa Zands, June 29, 1958; children: Sandra, Miriam, Marsha. BS, Instituto #1, Habana, Cuba, 1951; MD, Havana U., Habana, Cuba, 1960. Diplomate Am. Bd. Ob-Gyn. Practice medicine specializing in ob-gyn Southfield, Mich. Youth advisor, pres. Temple Bethel El. Mem. AMA, Am. Fertility Soc., Coll. Ob-Gyn, Midwest Ob-Gyn, Mich. State Med. Soc., Oakland County Med. Soc. Republican. Jewish. Club: Detroit Tennis and Squash. Avocations: tennis, boating, fishing, singing.

GOTSHALL, MARK EDWARD, substance abuse counselor; b. Cin., Dec. 4, 1960; s. Raymond E. and Delores M. A. (Kuehm) G. AA, William Rainey Harper Coll., Palatine, Ill., 1981; BS, Carroll Coll., Waukesha, Wis., 1984. Cert. substance abuse counselor. Child care worker St. Rose Residence, Milw., 1984; group home counselor DePaul Rehab. Hosp., Milw., 1984; counselor Mercy Health Ctr., Dubuque, Iowa, 1984—. Named one of Outstantding Young Men. Am., 1984. Mem. Nat. Assn. Drug and Alcohol Counselor, Substance Abuse Assn. Iowa. Methodist. Avocations: biking, hiking, cross country skiing. Home: 1319 Mount Pleasant St Dubuque IA 52001

GOTT, WESLEY ATLAS, art educator; b. Buffalo, Mar. 6, 1942; s. Raymond and Rowena (Pettitt) G.; m. Alice Blalock, May 26, 1972; children—Andrew, Deidre. B.S., S.W. Mo. State U., 1965; M.Ch.Music, Southwestern Theol. Sem., 1969; M.F.A., George Washington U., 1975. Tchr. ceramic classes Springfield Art Mus., Mo., 1964-66; minister of music Terrace Acres Bapt. Ch., Ft. Worth, Tex., 1966-70; minister music and youth First Bapt. Ch. Wheaton, Md., 1970-75; asst. prof. art S.W. Bapt. U., Bolivar, Mo., 1975-79, assoc. prof., chmn. dept. art, 1979—; judge art contests, 1978-84. Artist sculpture with lights, 1981-84. Mem. Coll. Art Assn. Am., Mid-Am. Coll. Art Assn., Smithsonian Assocs., Nat. Trust for Historic Preservation, Community Concert Assn., Alpha Gamma Theta, Phi Mu Alpha. Baptist. Avocations: hunting; fishing; boating; tennis; golf. Home: 127 W Maupin Bolivar MO 65613 Office: Southwest Bapt Univ 623 S Pike Bolivar MO 65613

GOTTA, KURT A., life underwriter, financial consultant; b. Ft. Wayne, Ind., June 4, 1956; s. Robert Earl and Margaret Ann (Myers) G.; m. Rooney O'Neil, Oct. 20, 1979. BBA in Fin. and Investments, U. Notre Dame, 1978. CLU. Spl. agt. N.W. Mut., Akron, Ohio, 1978-82; owner Akron, 1982—. Mem. Am. Soc. CLU's/Cert. Fin. Cons., Nat. Assn. Life Underwriters (Nat. Quality award 1984, 85, 86, Nat. Sales Achievement award 1984, 85, 86). Club: Notre Dame (Akron) (pres. 1985-86). Avocations: tennis, basketball. Home: 1222 Sharon Copley Rd Wadsworth OH 44281 Office: 76 S Main St #1612 Akron OH 44308

GOTTFRIED, GLENN EDWARD, utility and management consultant; b. Chgo., Oct. 6, 1956; s. Paul and Kitty (Teruko) G.; m. Gayle Louise Vits, Apr. 6, 1985. BSME cum laude, U. Vt., 1977; MS in Nuclear Engring., Ga. Inst. Tech., 1978; MBA, U. Chgo., 1984. Engr. U.S. NRC, Bethesda, Md., 1977; bus. devel. mgr. Sargent & Lundy, Chgo., 1978-85; client dir. Impell Corp., Bannockburn, Ill., 1985; cons. Cresap, McCormick & Paget, Chgo., 1985—; v.p. Gen. Products Inc., Winooski, Vt., 1980—; speaker U.S. Com. for Energy Awareness, Chgo., 1983-85. Bd. dirs. Council for Energy Independence, Chgo., 1984. Mem. Ctr. Entrepreneurial Mgmt., Ill. Software Assn., U. Vt. Alumnus (coordinator). Avocations: collecting art, glass and wine, cooking, sailing. Office: Cresap McCormick & Paget 200 W Madison St Chicago IL 60606

GOTTFRIED, MARK ELLIS, accountant; b. Toledo, Mar. 12, 1953; s. Max and Barbara Alice (Johnston) G.; m. Linda Jean Perkins, Aug. 7, 1976; 1 child, Christopher Ellis. BA, Northwestern U., 1975; MBA, U. Chgo., 1980. CPA Ill., Ind. Sr. acct. Deloitte Haskins & Sells, Chgo., 1980-84; corp. mktg. mgr. Micro Data Base Systems, Lafayette, Ind., 1984-85; sr. cons. Deloitte Haskins & Sells, Indpls., 1985-86, mgr., 1986—. Editorial bd. Computers in Acctg., 1984—. Bd. dirs. Chgo. Theatre Group, 1984; cons. Jr. Achievement, Indpls., 1986. Mem. Am. Inst. CPA's, Ind. Soc. CPA's, Indpls. C. of C. (govt. com. 1986—). Republican. Episcopalian. Home: 3953 Wind Drift Dr Indianapolis IN 46254 Office: Deloitte Haskins & Sells 1440 Merchants Plaza Indianapolis IN 46204

GOTTI, MARY BETH, research physicist; b. Cleve., Jan. 14, 1953; d. John Romanus and Mary Geraldine (Pavlosky) Abele; m. Howard Charles Gotti, Nov. 17, 1978. BS in Physics, John Carroll U., 1974, MS in Physics, 1976. Engr. quality control Gen. Electric Bus. Engring., Cleve., 1976-77, engr. product devel., 1977-80, design physicist, 1980-85, research physicist, 1985—. Named one of Disting. Women in Sci., Shaw High Sch., East Cleveland, 1987. Mem. Illuminating Engring. Soc. Roman Catholic. Avocations: piano, golf, gardening. Home: 1058 Riverview Dr Macedonia OH 44056 Office: Gen Electric Nela Park East Cleveland OH 44112

GOTTLIEB, MARVIN EMANUEL, psychiatrist; b. Cleve., Aug. 1, 1934; s. Ben Nathan and Sylvia, (Horowitz) G.; m. Judith Balin, June 22, 1958 (div. 1981); children—Joel, Robert; m. Margaret R. Reissig, June 10, 1983. B.A., Case Western Res. U., 1956, M.D., 1961. Diplomate Am. Bd. Psychiatry and Neurology, 1968. Intern, Mt. Sinai Hosp., Cleve., 1961-62; resident in psychiatry U. Rochester (N.Y.), 1962-65; asst. chief outpatient service Fairhill Psychiat. Hosp., Cleve., 1967-68; asst. prof. Med. Coll. Toledo, 1968-70, assoc. prof., 1970—, dir. psychiat. residency, 1970—; pvt. practice, Cleve., 1967-68, Toledo, 1968—. Vice pres. Jewish Family Services Toledo, 1970. Served to lt. comdr. USNR, 1965-67; Viet Nam. Fellow Am. Psychiat. Assn., mem. Ohio Med. Assn., Toledo Lucas County Med. Assn., Am. Coll. Psychiatrists. Jewish. Lodge: B'nai B'rith (dir. 1981—). Co-editor Psychiatry Continuing Edn. Rev., 1973. Home: 5211 Saddle Creek Rd Toledo OH 43623 Office: Med Coll Ohio CS 10008 Toledo OH 43699

GOTTO, RALPH J., computer company executive; b. Bankston, Iowa, June 2, 1940; s. Peter H. and Catherine M. (Meyer) G.; m. Nancy Mary Ann Kramer, Nov. 19, 1963; children: Renee Roechelle, Sara Lynn. BA, Loras Coll., 1962; MBA, St. Thomas Coll., St. Paul, 1976. Controller Control Data, Mpls., 1968-75, ops. controller, 1975-78, gen. mgr. corp. planning/reporting, 1982-84, gen. mgr. fin. and adminstrn., 1984—; dir. fin. Computer Peripherals, Inc., Mpls., 1978-82. Mem. Nat. Assn. Accts. (bd. dirs.), Minn. Acctg. Aid Soc. (bd. dirs.). Republican. Roman Catholic. Avocation: tennis. Home: 312 E 135th St Burnsville MN 55337 Office: Control Data Corp 1101 E 78th St Bloomington MN 55420

GOTTSACKER, PETER, accountant, pharmaceutical executive; b. Sheboygan, Wis., Oct. 6, 1953; s. William Anthony and Evelyn (Parker) G.; m. Elizabeth Ann Shannon, Nov. 24, 1979; children: Erin, Jody. BBA summa cum laude, U. Notre Dame, 1976. CPA, Wis. Staff acct. Arthur Young and Co., Louisville, 1976-77; mgr. Arthur Andersen and Co., Milw., 1977-86; v.p. fin. Kremer-Urban Pharm. Co., Milw., 1986—; bd. dirs. East Side Housing Assn., Milw. Treas. Rod Johnston for Congress, Milw., 1984. Mem. Assn. Ind. CPA's, Wis. Inst. CPA's, St. Joseph's Soc. Republican. Roman Catholic. Avocation: sports. Home: 1348 N 71st Milwaukee WI 53213 Office: Kemer-Urban Pharm 5600 Countyline Rd Meguon WI 53202

GOTTSCHALK, ALFRED, college president; b. Oberwesel, Fed. Republic Germany, Mar. 7, 1930; came to U.S., 1939, naturalized, 1945; s. Max and Erna (Trum-Gerson) G.; m. Deanna Zeff Frank, 1978; children by previous marriage: Marc Hillel, Rachel Lisa. A.B., Bklyn. Coll., 1952; B.H.Lit., Hebrew Union Coll.-Jewish Inst. Religion, 1957, M.A. with honors, 1957; Ph.D., U. So. Calif., 1965, LL.D., 1976, S.T.D. (hon.), 1968, D.H.L., 1971; LL.D. (hon.), U. Judaism, 1976; D.Litt. (hon.), Dropsie U., 1974; D.H.L. (hon.), U. Cin.; D.Religious Edn. (hon.), Loyola-Marymount U., 1977; LL.D. (hon.), Xavier U., 1981; Litt.D. (hon.), St. Thomas Inst.; D.D. (hon.), NYU, 1985; hon. fellow, Hebrew U. Jerusalem. Rabbi 1957; mem. faculty, adminstr. Hebrew Union Coll.-Jewish Inst. Religion, Los Angeles, 1957—; prof. Bible and Jewish religious thought Hebrew Union Coll.-Jewish Inst. Religion, 1965—, pres. coll., 1971—. Author: Your Future as a Rabbi-A Calling that Counts, 1967, The Future of Human Community, 1967, The Man Must be the Message, 1968, Jewish Ecumenism and Jewish Survival, 1968, Ahad Ha-Am, Maimonides and Spinoza, 1969, Ahad Ha-Am as Bible Critic, 1971, A Jubilee of the Spirit, 1972, Israel and the Diaspora: A New Look, 1974, Limits of Ecumenicity, 1979, Israel and Reform Judaism: A Zionist Perspective, 1979, Ahad Ha-Am and Leopold Zunz: Two Perspectives on the Wissenschaft Des Judentums, 1980, Hebrew Union College and Its Impact on World Progressive Judaism, 1980, Diaspora Zionism: Achievements and Problems, 1980, What Ecumenism Means to a Jew, 1981, A Laudatio for Gershom G. Scholem, 1981, Introduction: Religion in a Post-Holocaust World, 1982, Tribute to Judaism, 1982, Some Jewish Perspectives on Ecumenism, 1982, Problematics in the Future of American Jewish Community, 1982, Introduction to The American Synagogue in the Nineteenth Century, 1982, A Strategy for Non-Orthodox Judaism in Israel, Our Problems and Our Future: Jews and America, 1983; translator: Hesed in the Bible, 1967, From the Kingdom of Night to the Kingdom of God: Jewish Christian Relations and the Search for Religious Authenticity after the Holocaust, 1983; contbr. to: Studies in Jewish Bibliography, History, and Literature, 1971, The Yom Kippur War: Israel and the Jewish People, 1974, The Image of Man in Genesis and the Ancient Near East, 1976, The Public Function of the Jewish Scholar, 1978, The Reform Movement and Israel: A New Perspective, 1978, also numerous articles to profl. publs. mem. Pres.'s Com. on Equal Employment Opportunity, 1964-66, Gov.'s Poverty Support Corps Program, 1964-66, Pres.'s Commn. on Holocaust, 1979, U.S. Holocaust Meml. Council, 1980—, co-chmn. exec. com. U.S. Holocaust Meml. Council, 1980—; chmn. N.Am. adv. com. Internat. Center Univ. Teaching of Jewish Civilization, 1982; trustee Cin. United Appeal, 1982, Am. Sch. Oriental Research, 1982; mem. Pres.'s Council Near Eastern Studies N.Y.U., 1983. State Dept. research grantee, 1963; Guggenheim fellow, 1967, 69; recipient award for contbns. to edn. Los Angeles City Council, 1968, 71; Myrtle Wreath award Hadassah, 1977; Brandeis award, 1977; Nat. Brotherhood award NCCJ, 1979; Alfred Gottschalk Chair in Jewish Communal Service Hebrew Union Coll.; Gottschalk Dept. Judaica named in his honor; Kfar Silver Israel, 1979. Mem. Jerusalem (exec. com.), Union Am. Hebrew Congregations and Central Conf. Am-Rabbis (exec. com.), AAUP, NEA, Soc. Study Religion, Am. Acad. Religion, Soc-Bibl. Lit and Exegesis, Internat. Conf. Jewish Communal Service, Israel Exploration Soc., So. Calif. Assn. Liberal Rabbis (past pres.), So. Calif. Jewish Hist. Soc. (hon. pres.), World Union Jewish Studies, Synagogue Council Am. (inst. research and planning), Am. Jewish Com. (exec. com.), World Union Progressive Judaism (v.p.). Home: 17 Belsaw Pl Cincinnati OH 45220

GOTTWALT, THOMAS JOHN, accountant; b. Little Falls, Minn., Jan. 24, 1960; s. Louis M. and Eileen M. (Ryan) G.; m. Maria S. Saja, Oct. 11, 1986. BS, St. John's U., 1982; postgrad. in taxation, U. Minn., 1982—. CPA, Minn. Audit staff B Coopers & Lybrand, Mpls., 1982-83, audit staff A, 1983-84, audit sr., 1984-85, tax assoc., 1985-86, tax specialist, 1986-87, tax supr., 1987—. Vol. Minn. Aid Soc., Mpls., 1986. Mem. Am. Inst. CPA's, Minn. Soc. CPA's (mem. legis. policy com., chmn. subcom. on tort reform). Home: 1912 Dupont Ave S #301 Minneapolis MN 55403 Office: Coopers & Lybrand 1000 TCF Tower Minneapolis MN 55402

GOUDY, JOSEPHINE GRAY, social worker; b. Des Moines, Nov. 30, 1925; d. Gerald William and Myrtle Maria (Brooks) Gray; B.A., State U. Iowa, 1953, M.S.W., 1966; m. John Winston Goudy, June 5, 1948; children: Tracy Jean, Paula Rae. Lic. social worker, Iowa. Child welfare supr. Iowa Dept. Social Services, 1960-68; psychiat. social worker Community Mental Health Center Scott County (Iowa), 1966-71; social work instr. Palmer Jr. Coll., Davenport, Iowa, 1967-70; psychiat. social worker, chief social services Jacksonville (Ill.) State Mental Hosp., 1971-74; coordinator community mental health outpatient services McFarland Mental Health Center, Springfield, Ill., 1974; exec. dir. Macoupin County Mental Health Center, Carlinville, Ill., 1974—; chmn. Human Services Edn. Council, Springfield, 1979-81; past exec. Davenport Community Welfare Council. Mem. Nat. Assn. Social Workers (Social Worker of Yr. Central Ill. area 1983), Acad. Cert. Social Workers, Am. Personnel and Guidance Assn., AAUW (br. pres. 1964-66, mem. state bar 1966-68, br. grantee 1975), Internat. Fedn. U. Women, U. Iowa Alumni Assn., Bus. and Profl. Women (Woman of Yr. 1983), Delta Kappa Gamma, Kappa Delta Pi. Republican. Methodist. Club: Carlinville Women's (pres. 1975-77). Home: 364 W Tremont St Waverly IL 62692 Office: 100 N Side Sq Carlinville IL 62626

GOUGH, RUTH RUUD, educational consultant; b. Long Beach, Calif., Dec. 12, 1952; d. Paul David and Virginia June (Bentley) Ruud; m. William Roger Gough, Aug. 19, 1979; 1 son, Mark Roger. B.A. in Sociology and Elem. Edn., Calif. State U., Long Beach, 1975; M.S. in Counseling and Guidance, Univ. Wis., Madison, 1978, Ph.D. in Edn. Adminstrn., 1981. Lic. tchr., Minn. Tchr., Garfield Elem. Sch., Bell Gardens, Calif., 1976; house fellow, residence halls, U. Wis., Madison, 1976-77; intern Dean of Students Office, 1977-78, student orientation leader for new student services, summer 1979; tchr. adult edn. Madison Area Tech. Coll., 1978-81; cons. human devel., St. Paul, 1981—; substitute tchr. Jean Lyle Childrens' Ctr., St. Paul, 1987—; researcher in field. Leader Air Pollution campaign against local automobile paint plant, 1985-86; campaign worker Mondale/Ferraro Campaign, St. Paul. Villas scholar, 1980; Legis. appointment Univ. Wis. State Senator Krueger, 1976-81. Mem. Am. Coll. Personnel Assn., Am. Assn. Counseling and Devel., Pi Lambda Theta, Phi Kappa Phi. Presbyterian. Club: Mother's (St. Paul). Avocations: travel; sewing; baking; piano playing; painting. Home and Office: 6941 Hillcrest Ln Edina MN 55435

GOUKE, CECIL GRANVILLE, economist, educator; b. Bklyn., Dec. 5, 1928; s. Joseph and Etheline (Grant) G.; m. Mary Noel, June 19, 1964; 1 son, Cecil Granville. B.A., CCNY, 1956; M.A., N.Y. U., 1958, Ph.D., 1967. Instr. econs. Fisk U., 1958-60; asst. prof. Grambling Coll., 1962-64, asso. prof., 1964-67; prof., chmn. Hampton (Va.) Inst., 1967-73; prof. Ohio State U., 1973—; cons. U.S. Treasury Dept., 1973. Author: Amalgamated Clothing Workers of America, 1940-66, 1972, Blacks and the American Economy, 1987; assoc. editor: Jour. Behavioral and Social Scis, 1974-84. Served with U.S. Army, 1947-49, 50-51. Recipient Founders Day award N.Y. U., 1967; sr. Fulbright scholar, 1979-80. Mem. Am. Econ. Assn., Am. Fin. Assn., Am. Statis. Assn., Indsl. Relations Research Assn., Western Econ. Assn., Nat. Econ. Assn., Hampton NAACP (exec. bd. 1968-70), Ohio Assn. Econs. and Polit. Sci. (v.p. 1986-87), Phi Beta Sigma. Democrat. Episcopalian. Home: 1788 Kenwick Rd Columbus OH 43209 Office: Dept Econs Ohio State U Columbus OH 43210

GOULAIT, SHARON IRENE, telecommunications and information services executive; b. Lowell, Mass., July 28, 1946; d. George Walter and Mary Elizabeth (Champagne) Laurila; divorced, 1974; children: James Michael, Mary Elizabeth; remarried Feb. 1987. Regional adminstr. Dymo Bus. Systems, Ferndale, Mich., 1976-77; purchasing sec. U. Detroit, 1977-78, buyer, 1978-79, mgr. purchasing and communications, 1979-81; dir. telecommunications Providence Hosp., Southfield, Mich., 1981—, dir. telecommunications and info. services, 1986—; communications cons. U. Detroit, 1981-82. Mem. Am. Hosp. Assn., Am. Soc. for Hosp. Engring., Mich. Assn. for Telecummunication in Health Care (2d v.p. 1984-85, 1st v.p. 1985-86), U. Detroit Women's Assn. (pres. 1978-79). Roman Catholic. Office: Providence Hosp 16001 W Nine Mile Rd Southfield MI 48075

GOULD, GEORGIA AGATHA, advertising executive; b. Glencoe, Minn., July 29, 1934; d. George Casper and Ruth Agatha (Lippert) G. Student, U. Minn., 1952-56. Jr. editor TV Guide mag., N.Y.C., 1957-58; research writer The Perry Como Show, Roncom Prodns., N.Y.C., 1958-62; creative asst. Marschalk Advt., N.Y.C., 1965-69; creative services mgr. Sta. WTCN-TV, Mpls.and St. Paul, 1970-80; advt., publicity mgr. Sta. KTCA-TV, Mpls.and St. Paul, 1980—; publicity cons. Met. Boy's Choir, Mpls., 1969-72. Author teleplay. Recipient PBS Promotion award, 1982, 86. Mem. Am. Women in Radio and TV. Lodge: Order Eastern Star. Avocations: acting, singing, directing, playwright, children's books. Office: KTCA-TV 1640 Como Ave Saint Paul MN 55108

GOULD, JOHN PHILIP, JR., economist, educator, university dean; b. Chgo., Jan. 19, 1939; s. John Philip and Lillian (Jicka) G.; m. Kathleen J. Hayes, Sept. 14, 1963; children: John Philip III, Jeffrey Hayes. BS with highest distinction, Northwestern U., 1960; PhD, U. Chgo., 1966. Faculty U. Chgo., 1965—, prof. econs., 1974—, disting. service prof. econs., 1984—, dean Grad. Sch. Bus., 1983—; vis. prof. Nat. Taiwan U., 1978; spl. asst. econ. affairs to sec. labor, 1969-70; spl. asst. to dir. Office Mgmt. and Budget, 1970; past chmn. econ. policy adv. com. Dept. Labor; bd. dirs. ARCH Devel. Corp., Chgo. Bd. Trade, DFA Investment Dimensions Group, MidAm. Commodity Exchange. Author: (with C.E. Ferguson) Microeconomic Theory, 5th edit, 1980; contbg. author: Microeconomic Foundations of Employment and Inflation Theory, 1970, Editor Jour. of Bus. , 1976-83, Jour. Fin. Econs., 1976, Jour. Accounting and Econs., 1978; Contbr. articles to profl. jours. Bd. dirs. United Way/Crusade of Mercy, 1986—; trustee First Lakeshore Funds, 1985—. Recipient Wall St. Jour. award, 1960, Am. Marketing Assn. award, 1960; Earhart Found. fellow. Mem. Am. Econ. Assn., Western Econ. Assn., Econometric Soc. (chmn. local arrangements 1968). Home: 5514 S Kenwood Ave Chicago IL 60637

GOULD, TERRY ALLEN, lawyer, financial executive; b. St. Louis, Sept. 30, 1942; s. Courtney A. and Dorothy (Bitker) G.; m. Patricia Ann Wolf, July 21, 1968; children: Kristine Ann, Bradford Allen. BS, Miami U., Oxford, Ohio, 1965; postgrad. in bus. adminstrn., Washington U., St. Louis, 1966; JD cum laude, St. Louis U., 1981. Bar: Mo. 1981, U.S. Dist. Ct. (we. dist.) Mo. 1981, U.S. Dist. Ct. (ea. dist.) Mo. 1983, Wis. 1987, U.S. Supreme Ct. 1987. Security analyst Merc. Trust Co., St. Louis, 1965-66; mgmt. trainee Misco-Shawnee, Inc., St. Louis, 1966-68, br. mgr., 1969-72, v.p., 1972-73, exec. v.p. adminstrn., 1973-78, sec./treas., 1975-78, dir., 1976-79; trustee Misco-Shawnee Profit Sharing Trust, 1975-78; v.p., dir. GORA Investment Co., St. Louis, 1975-78; gen. ptnr. Tera Investment Assocs., 1978—; sole practice law, 1981-85; of counsel Morganstern, Soraghan, Stockenberg, McKitrick & Spoeneman, St. Louis, 1985-86, ptnr., 1986; ptnr. Morganstern, Soraghan, Stockenberg, McKitrick & Gould, 1986—; dir. Tera Mgmt. Corp., 1980—; dir. Suburban Nat. Bank Elk Grove (Ill.), 1972-77. Mem. bd. mgrs., vice chmn. fin. com., mem. membership com., downtown br. Greater St. Louis YMCA, 1976-82; bd. dirs. Wis. Music Network, 1982—, Clef, Inc., 1982—, St. Louis Charitable Found., 1984—. Mem. ABA, Met. St. Louis Bar Assn. (chmn. real estate and devel. com. 1983-84, chmn. bus. law sect. 1985-86), Delta Sigma Pi, Beta Theta Pi. Office: Morganstern Soraghan et al 1750 Interco Corp Tower 101 S Hanley Saint Louis MO 63105

GOULD, THOMAS, department store company executive. Pres. Yonkers, Inc., Des Moines. Office: Yonkers, Inc. 7th & Walnut Sts Des Moines IA 50397*

GOULD, WILLIAM ALLEN, architect; b. Lakewood, Ohio, Mar. 8, 1928; s. Daniel and Esther (Itlaner) G.; m. Harriet Rosenthal, June 23, 1959; children: Philip, David, Rebecca. BArch, U. Mich, 1952; MArch, Cranbrook Acad. Art, 1956; diploma, Fountainbleau (France) Acad. Art, 1957. Sr. planner City of Cleve. Planning Commn., 1953-59; asst. prof. architecture Western Res. U., Cleve., 1958-61; prin. William A. Gould & Assocs., Cleve., 1961—, pres., 1979—; lectr. Case Inst. Tech., 1960-61; vis. asst. prof. architecture and environ. design Kent State U., 1972-73. Works include Cascade Plaza, Akron, Ohio, Hillel Ctr. Case Western Res. U., Wayne Gen. and Tech. Coll. U. Akron, Univ. Circle Research Ctr.; planner Blossom Music Ctr., Cleve.; executed capital improvements program analysis Ohio Bd. Regents, new city plans for Barberton, Shaker Heights, and Youngstown, Ohio; master plan update NASA Lewis Research Ctr., Cleve.; planned communities Greenwood Village, Sagamore Hills, Ohio, Riverbend East, Athens, Ga.; renovation and expansion plans Massillon (Ohio) State Hosp.; Cleve. Warehouse Dist. study (Design award); Ohio City master plan; socio-econ. study Ashtabula County; devel. planner for Borden, Inc., Lakeland, Fla.; designer, rebuilder transit stas. Greater Cleve. Regional Transit Authority (2 Design awards). Mem. City of Cleveland Heights Planning Commn. Served to 1st lt. USAF, 1952. Mem. AIA (bd. dirs. Cleve. chpt. 1967—, pres.), Am. Inst. Planners (pres. Ohio chpt. 1967-69, nat. urban design com.). Home: 2722 Scarborough Rd Cleveland Heights OH 44106 Office: 1404 E 9th St Cleveland OH 44144

GOULD, WILLIAM R., photographic paper and chemistry company executive; m. Marian Gould; 3 children. Student, U. Calif. With DeKalb Ag Research, 1949-56; with Western Litho Plate, exec. v.p.; ptnr. Nat. Graphics, Inc., St. Louis, 1974—, pres. Chmn. Small Bus. Assn. adv. council; founding bd. dirs. Midcontinent Small Bus. United; bd. dirs. Regional Commerce and

Growth Assn., chmn. small bus. council; del. White House Conf. on Sl. Bus., 1980, co-planner, 1983 and 84 for Mo. Conf. on Sml. Bus.; mem. Mo. Dist. Export Council of Commerce Dept. Club: World Trade. Lodge: Rotary. Address: 2711 Miami St Saint Louis MO 63118

GOULDER-ABELSON, ABBY MAUD, rheumatologist; b. Cleve., June 14, 1952; d. Richard Monroe and Lois Marilyn (Freeman) Goulder; m. Tom Isaac Abelson, June 29, 1973; children: Adam, Ben. BA, Kirkland Coll., 1974; MD, Case Western Res. U., 1979. Diplomate Am. Bd. Internal Medicine. Resident Mt. Sinai Hosp., Cleve., 1979-82, chief resident, 1982; fellow in rheumatology Univ. Hosps., Cleve., 1983-86. Mem. Case Western Res. U. Sch. Medicine (bd. trustees 1983). Office: Univ Hosps Dept Rheumatology 2065 Abington Rd Cleveland OH 44106

GOULET, PETER GREGORY, business educator; b. Chgo., Nov. 24, 1944; s. George Alphonse and Sarabel (Williams) G.; m. Lynda Mary Lantz, Mar. 18, 1967; 1 dau., Meridith. B.A. with honors, Denison U., 1966; M.B.A., Ohio State U., 1967, Ph.D., 1970. Asst. prof. So. Ill. U., Edwardsville, 1970-71; asst. to the pres. ILC Products Co., Elkhart, Ind., 1972-74; asst. prof. bus. U. No. Iowa, Cedar Falls, 1974-77, assoc. prof., 1977-87, prof., 1987—, head dept. mgmt., 1981-82; dir. Midwest Soc. for Case Research, 1987—. Author: Real Estate: A Value Approach, 1979; contbr. articles to profl. jours. Mem. Am. Fin. Assn., Fin. Mgmt. Assn., Phi Alpha Kappa. Avocations: electronics; bridge; reading. Home: 2718 Abraham Dr Cedar Falls IA 50613 Office: U No Iowa Sch Bus Cedar Falls IA 50614

GOULET, ROBERT PATRICK, chemical company executive; b. Boston, Aug. 30, 1932; s. Louis William and Sarah Veronica (Noone) G.; m. Barbara Ann Sitarz, Oct. 21, 1961 (div. Oct. 1982); children: Amy, Christopher; m. Elaine Marie Kindlund, Sept. 28, 1985; stepchildren: Steve, Debra. BA, Boston Coll., 1951; BS in Chem. Engring., Lawrence Inst. Tech., 1963; MBA, U. Mich., 1973. Profl. football player N.Y. Giants, N.Y.C., 1954-57, Hamilton (Ont., Can.) Tiger Cats, 1957-62; mgr. sales Ecclestone Chem., Detroit, 1962-70; v.p., gen. mgr. CP Chems., Sewaren, N.J., 1970—. Served to 1st lt. USAF, 1951-54, Korea. Decorated Silver Star, Air medal. Mem. Am. Electronics Soc. (del. 1972—, br. pres. 1981-82, nat. dir. 1983—, service award 1983, award of excellence 1985), Am. electroplaters and Surface Finishers Soc. (chmn. Gt. Lakes regional council 1970-83), Comdrs. of Mich. (bd. dirs. 1983-86, comdr. Naval Militia). Roman Catholic. Avocations: photo designing, golf, fishing. Home: 6130 Nicholas Dr West Bloomfield MI 48033 Office: CP Chemical 42049 Michigan Ave Wayne MI 48184

GOVEKAR, PAUL LOUIS, JR., military officer, writer; b. Waukegan, Ill., Apr. 11, 1945; s. Paul Louis Sr. and Dorothy Leona (Bergstrom) G.; m. Michele Ann Canning, Nov. 4, 1967; children: Christopher Paul, Eileen Michele. BBA, Loyola U., Chgo., 1967; MBA, DePaul U., 1971. Commd. 2d lt. U.S. Army, 1967, advanced through grades to lt. col., 1985; comdr. 101st mil. police co. U.S. Army, Fed. Republic of Vietnam, 1970-71; asst. provost Marshall 3d infantry div. U.S. Army, 1980-81; officer personnel mgmt. 88th USAR Command, 1984—. Contbr. articles to profl. jours. Decorated Bronze Star. Roman Catholic. Home: 1201 E 140th St Burnsville MN 55337 Office: 88th USARCOM DCS PER US Army Bldg 506 Ft Snelling Saint Paul MN 55337

GOVERT, JAY H., criminal investigator, small business owner; b. Griffith, Ind., May 25, 1947; s. Maurice John and Anna (Elman) G.; m. Kathy Ann Frets, May 8, 1954; children: Brian Jay, Melissa Ann, Anthony Jay. Student, Kans. State U., 1967; BS in Criminal Justice, Calumet Coll., 1987. Asst. security mgr. S.S. Kresge & Co., Hammond, Ind., 1968-71; detective sgt., criminal investigations dept. Hammond Police Dept., 1971—; mem. steering and reorganization com. Hammond Police Dept., 1987; com. mem. Hammond Police Employees, 1982; mem. Hammond Investment Co., 1980-83. rep. fund-raiser City of Hammond Ann. Christmas Cheer Fund, 1985. Served as cpl. U.S. Army, 1966-68. Named to hon. commission, atty. gen. staff State of Ala., 1978; grantee Fed. Criminal Investigator's Assn., 1986. Mem. Fraternal Order Police, Am. Legion. Democrat. Roman Catholic. Lodges: Masons. Office: Hammond Police Dept 5925 Calumet Ave Hammond IN 46320

GOVIND, RAKESH, chemical engineering educator; b. Bikaner, Rajasthan, India, Feb. 10, 1953; s. Prakash Govind and Nirmala Mathur; m. Mona Kishore, Jan. 18, 1977; 1 child, Sarika. B of Tech., Indian Inst. Tech., Kanpur, India, 1974; MS, Carnegie-Mellon U., 1977, PhD, 1978. Dir. indsl. control ctr. Mellon Inst., Pitts., 1978-79; sr. scientist Polaroid Corp., Boston, 1979-80; asst. prof. chem. engring. U. Cin., 1980-83, assoc. prof., 1983—, Jr. Morrow Chair, 1983; dir. research Process Research and Devel., Covington, Ky., 1984—; cons. Procter and Gamble, Cin., 1985—. Contbr. articles to profl. jours.; inventor distillation column. Mentor woodward High Sch., Cin., 1981. Mem. Am. Inst. Chem. Engrs. (treas. 1985—). Avocations: painting, gardening. Home: 10409 Stone Ct Cincinnati OH 45242

GOYAL, SATISH CHANDRA, engineering educator, consultant; b. Kasganj, Uttarpradesh, India, Sept. 10, 1921; came to U.S., 1979; s. Bankeylal and Ram Devi (Agrawal) Karariwale; m. Kunti Kumari, Jan. 16, 1941; children—Ashok Kumar, Sushma Rani, Arunkumar, Arvindkumar, Anand Kumar. B.Sc., Agra U., India, 1940; C.E., Thomason Coll. Civil Engring., Roorkee, U.P., India, 1943; M.S. in Civil Engring., U. Calif.-Berkeley, 1961. Engr. Pub. Works Dept. Govt., Agra, Gonda, Basti, U.P., India, 1943-47; lectr., reader Roorkee U., U.P., India, 1947-54; prof. structural engring. M.B.M. Engring. Coll., Jodhpur U., Rajasthan, India, 1954-63, 69-72, 77-79, dean engring., 1963-66, 1972-74; dean engring. Pant U., Pantnagar, U.P., India, 1966-69; vice-chancellor Jodhpur U., Rajasthan, 1974-77; prof. civil engring. Tri-State U., Angola, Ind., 1979—; cons. structural design work, U.S.A., India. Author: (with O.P. Tain) Manual of Estimating, 1954; (with S. Divakaran) Design of Structures in Structural Steel, 1961; (with B. C. Punmia) Theory of Structures and Strength of Materials, 1964; (with M. R. Sethia) Engineering Mechanics, 1977. Dir., chmn. Univ. Centre of Desert Studies, Jodhpur, 1976-77; dir. Rural Housing Wing, Govt. India, Jodhpur, 1977-79. Recipient citation Rajasthan Govt. India, 1962; exchange visitor to U.S.A., AID, 1960. Fellow ASCE, Instn. Engrs. India (chmn. Rajasthan Centre, Citation 1974), Indian Soc. Desert Tech. (pres. 1975-78); mem. ASME. Hindu. Lodge: Rotary. Avocations: yoga; reading; meditation. Home: 42451 Ravina Ct Northville MI 48167 also: 1 Residency Rd, Jodhpur 342001, India Office: Tri State U Dept Civil Engring Angola IN 46703

GOYETTE, BRUCE DONALD, accountant; b. Ripon, Wis., June 25, 1951; s. Donald Charles amd Evelyn Sophia (Brown) G.; m. Constance Marie Remmel, Sept. 24, 1977; children: Amanda, Sara. BS in Econs., U. Wis., Oshkosh, 1973, BBA in Acctg., 1974. CPA, Wis. Gen. acct. Menasha Corp., Neenah, Wis., 1975-77, sr. acct., 1977-80; acctg. mgr. Menasha Corp., Watertown, Wis., 1980—; pvt. practice acctg., Watertown, 1980—. Mem. Wis. Inst. CPA's. Roman Catholic. Avocations: tennis, golf, motorcycling. Home: 921 Liberty Ln Watertown WI 53094 Office: Menasha Corp Lewisystems Div 128 Hospital Dr Watertown WI 53094

GRABIA, HEINZ H., religious organization official. Head Am. Bapt. Chs. of Nebr., Lincoln. Office: Am Bapt Chs of Nebr 6404 Maple St Omaha NE 68104 *

GRABINER, FRED S., obstetrician, gynecologist; b. Chgo., Nov. 19, 1947; s. Syd S. and Mildred (Kasower) G.; m. Enid Ayn Feldman, Aug. 23, 1970; children: Stacy, Brain, Amanda. BS, U. Ill., 1969, MD, 1974. Diplomate Am. Bd. Ob-Gyn. Resident in ob-gyn U. Ill., Chgo., 1974-77; practice medicine specializing in ob-gyn Northwest Ob-Gyn Assocs., Park Ridge, Ill., 1977—; clin. instr. U. Ill., Chgo., 1977—, clin. asst. prof. Loyola U., Maywood, Ill., 1985—. Bd. dirs. North Suburban Jewish Community Ctr., Highland Park, Ill., 1985-86. Fellow Am. Coll. Ob-Gyn; mem. AMA, Am. Assn. Gynecol. Laparoscopists, Am. Soc. Colposcopy and Cervical Pathology, Gynecol. Laser Soc., Ill. State Med. Soc., Cook County Med. Soc. Jewish. Avocations: coaching little league baseball and children's soccer teams, tennis. Office: Northwest Ob Gyn Assn Ltd 2 Talcott Park Ridge IL 60068

GRABINSKI, LAWRENCE AUGUST, electronics executive, designer; b. Chgo., Aug. 10, 1929; s. August Jerome and Pearl Josephine (Wanat) G.; (div.); children—Martin, Thomas. Student U. Md., 1950-52, Ill. Inst. Tech., 1952-54, Morraine Valley Coll., 1980. Quality control engr. Foote Bros., Chgo., 1952-55; designer W.L. Stennsgaard, Chgo., 1955-57; chief draftsman Klemp Corp., Chgo., 1957-65; structural designer Rippel Archt. Metals, Chgo., 1965-74; asst. div. mgr. Pullman Sheet Metal Co., Chgo., 1974-77; computer systems specialist Castle Engring. Co., Chgo., 1977—. Served with USAF, 1948-52, ETO. Mem. Am. Fedn. Musicians. Home: 7801 S Lotus Burbank IL 60459 Office: Castle Engring Co 3579 W Columbus Ave Chicago IL 60652

GRABLE, R(EGINALD) HAROLD, psychologist; b. Putnam County, Ind., Sept. 22, 1917; s. Reginald R. and Cecil Ruth (Jones) G.; A.B., U. Kans., 1938, tchr.'s diploma, 1940; M.A., U. Minn., 1949; m. Elizabeth Hannah Baird, Aug. 17, 1946; children—Celia, Nancy, Daniel. Group leader occupational coders Nat. Roster Sci. and Specialized Personnel, Washington, 1940-42; vocat. counselor U. Minn., Mpls., 1947; clin. psychologist trainee VA Hosp., St. Paul, 1947-49; chief clin. psychologist Willmar (Minn.) State Hosp., 1949-51, Winnebago (Wis.) State Hosp., 1951-61; clin. psychologist West Shore Mental Health Clinic (formerly Hackley Adult Mental Health Clinic), Muskegon, Mich., 1961-82; clin. psychologist Kalamazoo Regional Psychiat. Hosp., 1983-85; pvt. practice psychology, Willmar, Minn., 1949-51, Oshkosh, Wis., 1951-61, Spring Lake, Mich., 1961—; instr. extension div. U. Wis., 1956-61; mem. profl. adv. bd. Wis. Council Mentally Retarded Children, 1956-61. Contbr. articles to profl. jours. First aid instr. ARC, 1963-79; exec. bd. Grand Valley council (name now West Mich. Shores council) Boy Scouts Am., 1966-76, dist. chmn., 1968-70, commr., 1972—; various offices PTA, 1953-78, Vols. in Probation; elder, chmn. bd. Muskegon Christian Ch. (Disciples of Christ), 1970-73. Served with AUS, 1942-46. Recipient Silver Beaver award Boy Scouts Am., 1981, Dist. award of Merit, 1977; lic. psychologist, Mich. Mem. Am. Psychol. Assn., Mich. Assn. Children with Learning Disabilities. Lodge: Rotary. Home and Office: 717 Summer St Spring Lake MI 49456

GRABOW, JACK DAVID, neurologist, educator; b. Hartford, Conn., Dec. 7, 1929. BS, Rutgers U., 1951; postgrad., Columbia U., 1951-52; MD, SUNY, Buffalo, 1956. Diplomate Am. Bd. Neurology. Intern U. Minn. Hosp., Mpls., 1956-57; fellow in internal medicine, neurology and electroencephalography Mayo Found., Rochester, Minn., 1957-64; dir. electroencephalography lab. U. Wis., Madison, 1964-70; cons. section of electroencephalography Mayo Clinic, Rochester, 1970—; assoc. prof. neurology U. Wis., Madison, 1969, prof. neurology, Mayo Med. Sch., 1982. Served with USNR, 1961-63. Fellow Am. Acad. Neurology, Am. EEG Soc. (pres. 1980-81); mem. Am. Neurol. Soc., Cen. Assn. EEG (pres. 1873-74), Soc. Neuroscience, Am. Epilepsy Soc. Office: Mayo Clinic EEG Sect 200 1st St SW Rochester MN 55905

GRABOW, RAYMOND JOHN, mayor; b. Cleve., Jan. 27, 1932; s. Joseph Stanley and Frances (Kalata) G.; B.S. in Bus. Adminstrn., Kent State U., 1953; J.D., Western Res. U., 1958; m. Margaret Jean Knoll, Nov. 27, 1969; children—Rachel Jean, Ryan Joseph. Bar: Ohio 1958. Counsel, No. Ohio Petroleum Retailers Assn., Cleve., 1965—; counsel, trustee Alliance of Poles Fed. Credit Union, 1972, also gen. counsel Alliance of Poles of Am.; councilman City of Warrensville Heights (Ohio), 1962-68, mayor, 1969—; sec. Sam's Investment Inc. Cleve., 1965—, Atlas Sewer & Pipe Cleaning Corp., Cleve., 1962—, Wick Restaurant Inc., Cleve., 1962—, Ohio Awning Co., Space Comfort Co., Wagner Awning & Mfg. Co. Mem. exec. com. Democratic party Cuyahoga County, 1966—, precinct com., 1966-80; trustee Brentwood Hosp.; bd. dirs. Polonia Found. Recipient award Polonia Found., 1970, other groups. Mem. Ohio State, Cuyahoga County, Greater Cleve. bar assns., Nat. Advs. Soc., Am. Judicature Soc., Assn. Trial Lawyers Am., Ohio Trial Lawyers Assn., Am. Legion, PLAV Vets., Cath. War Vets., Cleve. Soc., Warrensville Heights C. of C. (trustee), Nat. League Cities, Ohio Assn. Pub. Safety Dirs., Mcpl. Treas. Assn., Ohio Service Dirs. Assn., Ohio Jud. Conf., Cuyahoga County Safety Dirs. Assn., Ohio Mayors Assn., Ohio Mcpl. League, numerous ethnic orgns. Lodge: Order of Alhambra. Home: 20114 Gladstone Rd Warrensville Heights OH 44122 Office: Suite 815 Superior Bldg Cleveland OH 44114

GRABOWSKI, MARIANNE CECILIA, attorney; b. Oak Park, Ill., Oct. 7, 1958; d. Casimir John and Pearl Alice (Paprocki) G. BA in Econs., Yale U., 1980; JD, Harvard U., 1983. Bar: Ill., 1983. Assoc. Mayer, Brown and Platt, Chgo., 1983-86; assoc. regional counsel Prudential Ins. Co. Am., Chgo., 1986—. Mem. ABA, Chgo. Council Lawyers.

GRACE, J. PETER, business executive; b. Manhasset, N.Y., May 25, 1913; s. Joseph and Janet (Macdonald) G.; m. Margaret Fennelly, May 24, 1941. Student, St. Paul's Sch., Concord, N.H., 1927-32; B.A., Yale U., 1936; LL.D., Mt. St. Mary's Coll., Manhattan Coll., Fordham U., Boston Coll., U. Notre Dame, Belmont Abbey, Stonehill Coll., Christian Bros. Coll., Adelphi U., Furman U., Rider Coll., Mt. St. Vincent Coll.; Dr. Latin Am. Relations, St. Joseph's Coll.; D.Sc., Clarkson Coll.; D.C.S., St. John's U.; L.H.D., Fairleigh Dickinson U. With W.R. Grace & Co., N.Y.C., 1936—, sec., 1942, dir., 1943—, v.p., 1945, pres., chief exec. officer, 1945-81, chmn., chief exec. officer, 1981—, pres., 1987—; chmn., bd. dirs. Chemed Corp., Taco Villa, Inc., Restaurant Enterprises Group, Inc., Centennial Ins. Co.; hon. dir. Brascan Ltd.; dir. emeritus Ingersoll-Rand Co.; dir. Stone & Webster, Inc., Omnicare, Inc., Roto-Rooter, Inc., Universal Furniture Ltd., Milliken & Co.; trustee Atlantic Mut. Ins. Co. Bd. dirs., pres. Cath. Youth Orgn. of Archdiocese of N.Y.; bd. dirs. Boys Clubs Am.; chmn. Radio Free Europe/Radio Liberty Fund, Inc.; pres., trustee Grace Inst.; mem. investment com., mem. pres.'s com. Greater N.Y., Notre Dame U.; chmn. council nat. trustees Nat. Jewish Ctr. for Immunology and Respiratory Medicine, Denver; chmn. Pres.'s Pvt. Sector Survey on Cost Control in Fed. Govt., 1982-84; trustee U.S. Council for Internat. Bus.; bd. govs. Thomas Aquinas Coll.; chmn., dir. Amerishares Found., Inc.; bd. dirs. Americares Found.; trustee emeritus Notre Dame U., mem. investment com. Recipient Knight Grand Cross, Equestrian Order Holy Sepulchre of Jerusalem; decorated by govts. of Colombia, Chile, Ecuador, Panama, Peru. Mem. Newcomen Soc., Council on Fgn. Relations. Clubs: Sovereign Mil. Order of Malta (pres. Am. assn., bd. founders), Racquet and Tennis, Madison Square Garden (gov.), Links, India House (N.Y.C.); Meadow Brook, Pacific Union (San Francisco); Everglades; Lotus. Office: W R Grace & Co Grace Plaza 1114 Ave of Americas New York NY 10036-7794

GRACE, JOHN FRANCIS, accountant; b. Dunkirk, N.Y., Nov. 30, 1953; s. James T. and Frances E. (Schug) G.; m. Marion K. Hardy, June 28, 1975; children: Nathan, Matthew, Brian. BS, SUNY, Buffalo, 1976. CPA, Okla., Mich. Ops. adminstr. St. Anne's Ch., Broken Arrow, Okla., 1975-76; chief acct. ARC, Tulsa, 1976-77; acct. Terra Resources, Tulsa, 1977-78; sr. tax mgr. Seidman & Seidman, Tulsa, 1978-86; tax ptnr. Seidman & Seidman, Traverse City, Mich., 1986—. Contbr. articles to profl. jours. Mem. Munson Hosp. Devel. Council, 1986—. Mem. Am. Inst. CPA's, Mich. Assn. CPA's, Nat. Assn. CPA's (bd. dirs. 1980-83, v.p. 1983-86). Republican. Roman Catholic. Lodges: Rotary, Kiwanis. Avocations: racquetball, emergency medicine, scouting. Office: Seidman & Seidman PO Box 112 Traverse City MI 49685

GRACE, ROBERT MARK, dentist; b. LaPorte, Ind., Dec. 8, 1950; s. Robert Martin and Marjorie Ann (Shroyer) G.; m. Pamela Kaye Hamlett, Aug. 12, 1972; children: Brandon, Kristyn. AB in Zoology, Ind. U., 1973, DDS, 1978. Pvt. practice dentistry Merrillville, Ind., 1978—. Vol. Kiwanis Bike-a-thon for MS, Merrillville, 1980; vol. dental edn. for sch. children Northwest Ind. Dental Soc., Merrillville, Gary, Crown Point, Ind., 1983—. Mem. Acad. Gen. Dentistry, ADA, Am. Endodontic Soc., Ind. Dental Soc., Northwest Ind. Dental Soc. (bd. dirs. 1978), Chgo. Dental Soc. (bd. dirs.). Roman Catholic. Lodge: Kiwanis. (local sec. 1981-82). Avocations: golf, camping, fishing. Home: 534 E 78th Ln Merrillville IN 46410 Office: 7725 Broadway Merrillville IN 46410

GRACILLA, RANULFO V., orthopaedic surgeon; b. Manila, Apr. 20, 1927; s. Lucas Obsum and Feliza (Villareal) G.; m. Mary L. Kavlics, Apr. 4, 1959; children: Tanya Marie, Ranulfo. Rochelle Marie, Nicholas K. Pre-med. degree, U. St. Thomas, Manila, 1948, med. degree, 1953. Demonstrator anatomy Ottawa (Can.) U., 1960-61; research fellow Western Res. U., Cleve., 1961-62; practice medicine specializing in orthopaedics Warren, Ohio, 1979-83; clin. instr. orthopaedics Met. Gen. Hosp., Cleve., 1961-62; chief orthopaedics Trumbull Meml. Hosp., Warren, 1979-83; orthopaedic cons. Hillside Hosp. and Children's Rehab., Warren. Med. dir. Warren Bd. Health, 1985. Mem. Am. Acad. Orthopaedic Surgery, Internat. Coll. Surgeons, Mid-Am. Orthopaedic Assn., Internat. Physician Assn., Ohio Orthopaedic Soc., Warren C. of C. Republican. Roman Catholic. Lodge: Rotary. Avocations: racing and showing horses, farming, tennis, basketball. Home: 2700 Citadel Dr NE Warren OH 44483 Office: 2000 E Market St Warren OH 44483

GRADE, JEFFERY T., manufacturing company executive; b. 1943. BS, Ill. Inst. Tech., 1966; MBA, DePaul U., 1972. With Plasto Mfg. Corp., 1965-66, Motorola Inc., 1966-67, Bell and Howell, 1967-68, Ill. Cen. Gulf R.R., 1968-73; v.p. fin. IC Industries, 1973-83; with Harnischfeger Corp., 1983—, pres., chief operating officer, bd. dirs., 1986—. Served with USN, 1865-66. Office: Harnischfeger Corp PO Box 554 Milwaukee WI 53201 *

GRADE, LORNA JEAN, health science facility administrator; b. Milw., May 7, 1954; d. William H. and Carol A. (Kaczmarowski) Momberg; (div.); 1 child, Aaron D.; m. Scott F. Grade, Aug. 16, 1986. BA in Bus. and Communications, Alverno Coll., 1981. Supr. med. records Mt. Sinai Med. Ctr., Milw., 1974-79; mgr. cardiovascular disease ctr. med. sch. Univ. Physicians Milw. Practice Plan, Inc., Milw., 1980—; mgr. Heart Study Ctr., Winter Park, Fla., 1981—, Mobile Cardiovascular Testing, Milw., 1985—, Mobile Diagnostic Services, Milw., 1987—. Contbr. articles to profl. jours. Mem. AAAS, Am. Heart Assn. Roman Catholic. Avocations: reading, golf, cross country skiing, camping. Home: 413 E Birch Ave Milwaukee WI 53217 Office: Univ Physicians Milw Practice Plan Inc 950 N 12th St Milwaukee WI 53233

GRADELESS, DONALD EUGENE, educator, genealogist; b. Warsaw, Ind., Apr. 17, 1949; s. Harmon Willard and Donna Maxine (Mort) G. BS in Acctg., U. Wis., Stevens Point, 1972; MS in Teaching, U. Wis., Eau Claire, 1975. Cert. in data edn. Tchr. high schs. Racine, Wis., 1972-77; mgr. constrn. Computer Control Corp., Milw., 1977; indsl. engr. Weatherhead div. Dana Corp., Milw., 1977-78; isntr. bus. edn. Elmbrook pub. schs., Brookfield, Wis., 1978—; coordinator instructional data processing Racine Unified Schs., 1973-77. Author geneal. books. Fellow Am. Coll. Genealogists; mem. NEA, SAR (sec., host 1977, registrar 1975-76, publs. chmn. 1975-77, pres. 1976-77, Nat. Soc. Mem. awards 1976-78, Silver Good Citizenship medal 1978, mem. Ind. soc.), S.R. (chmn. 1975-79, pres. 1979-83, registrar 1979-82, 84-87, sec. 1983—, Gen. Pres.'s Spl. Commendation award 1985, Outstanding Service award 1982, mem. various state bds. mgrs.), Nat. Bus. Edn. Assn., Wis. Bus. Edn. Assn, Children Am. Revolution (sr. registrar 1976-77, 80-83, sr. v.p. 1984-86, sr. pres. 1986—), Sons and Daus. of Pilgrims (counselor 1979-80), Soc. Colonial Wars (dep. sec. Wis. chpt. 1978-79), Nat. Genal. Soc., Whitley County Hist. Soc., Soc. Ind. Pioneers, Sons of Union Vets. of Civil War, Delta Phi Epsilon, Phi Delta Kappa. Lodge: Masons (32 degree), K.T. Home: 1721 Edgewood Ave Racine WI 53404 Office: 3305 N Lilly Rd Brookfield WI 53005

GRADISON, WILLIS DAVID, JR., congressman, investment broker; b. Cin., Dec. 28, 1928; s. Willis David and Dorothy (Benas) G.; m. Helen Ann Martin, June 25, 1950 (div. 1974); children: Ellen, Anne, Margaret, Robin, Beth; m. Heather Jane Stirton, Nov. 29, 1980; children: Maile Jo, Benjamin David, Logan Jane. A.B., Yale, 1948; M.B.A., Harvard, 1951, D.C.S., 1954. With W.D. Gradison & Co., Cin., 1949; research asst., also research assoc. Harvard Bus. Sch., 1951-53; asst. to undersec. Dept. Treasury, 1953-55; asst. to sec. HEW, 1955-57; gen. partner W.D. Gradison & Co., from 1958; mem. Cin. City Council, 1961-74, mayor, 1971; mem. 94th-100th Congresses. Office: 2311 Rayburn House Office Bldg Washington DC 20515

GRADOWSKI, STANLEY JOSEPH, JR., publishing company executive; b. Chgo., Nov. 21, 1938; s. Stanley J. Sr. and Mary A. (Wolak) G. AA, Morton Coll., 1958; BS, Northwestern U., 1960, MBA, 1962. CPA, Ill. With Price Waterhouse Co., Chgo., 1961-68, tax mgr., 1968-76; tax mgr. Tribune Co., 1976-79, sec., 1979-82, sec., v.p., 1982—; bd. dirs. Chgo. Equity Fund. Bd. dirs. Chgo. Tribune Found., 1983—, Chgo. Tribune Charities, 1983—, St. Mary on Nazareth Hosp. Ctr., Chgo., 1984—. Served with U.S. Army, 1961-63. Mem. Am. SOc. Corp. Secs., Tax Execs. Inst., Am. Inst. CPA's, Ill. Soc. CPA's. Home: 1420 Willow St Western Springs IL 60558 Office: Chgo Tribune Co 435 N Michigan Ave Chicago IL 60611

GRADY, JAMES JOSEPH, accounting executive; b. Chgo., June 1, 1939; s. James J. and Laurentine C. (Curry) G.; m. Patricia M. Torpy, Apr. 16, 1967; children: James, Robert, Timothy. BS, Marquette U., 1961. CPA, Ill., Iowa, N.C. Ptnr. Ernst & Whinney, Chgo.; speaker to trade groups. Bd. dirs. St. John's Sch., Western Springs, Ill., 1982-85; industry rep. United Way, Chgo., 1984-86. Mem. Am. Inst. CPA's, Ill. Soc. CPA's, Jr. Assn. Commerce and Industry (bd. dirs. 1973). Club: Edgewood Valley Country (Western Springs) (bd. dirs. 1986), Plaza (Chgo.). Avocations: golf, tennis, art. Office: Ernst & Whinney 150 S Wacker Dr Chicago IL 60606

GRADY, JOHN F., federal judge; b. Chgo., May 23, 1929; s. John F. and Lucille F. (Shroder) G.; m. Patsy Grady, Aug. 10, 1968; 1 son, John F. B.S., Northwestern U., 1952, J.D., 1954. Bar: Ill. 1955. Practice law Chgo., 1955; asst. U.S. atty. for no. dist. Ill., 1956-61; practice law Waukegan, Ill., 1967-76; judge U.S. Dist. Ct. (no. dist.) Ill., Chgo., 1976-86, chief judge, 1986—. Assoc. editor: Northwestern U. Law Rev. Mem. Phi Beta Kappa. Office: US Dist Ct 219 S Dearborn St Chicago IL 60604

GRAEBE, ANNETTE MULVANY, college administrator, educator; b. Benton, Ill., Feb. 11, 1943; d. Augusta (Magnabosco) Mulvany; m. William Fredrick Graebe, Jr., Feb. 23, 1974. B.S., So. Ill. U.-Carbondale, 1962, M.A., 1964. Research asst., speech instr. So. Ill. U.-Carbondale, 1962-64; chmn. speech and theater dept. McKendree Coll., Lebanon, Ill., 1964-68; dir. info. center, So. Ill. U., Edwardsville, 1968—, assoc. prof. speech communication, 1968—, mem. faculty bd. govs.; cons. communications, pub. speaker. Coordinator Edwardsville Autumn Festival Children. Recipient Ill. and U.S. Bicentennial Commn. citation, 1976, Council Advancement and Support of Edn. exceptional achievement community relations award, Washington, 1976, 77, 81, Toronto, Can., 1982, Silver Medal for Pub. Relations Projects, Council Advancement and Support of Edn., 1986, Bronze Quill award Internat. Assn. Bus. Communicators, 1986; named Outstanding Faculty Adviser, Pub. Relations Soc. Am., 1982; named one of Outstanding Faculty-Midwest, Pub. Relations Student Soc. Am., 1982; Woman of Year, Bus. and Profl. Women's Club, Edwardsville, 1983. Mem. Pub. Relations Soc. Am. (edn. chmn., chpt. adviser; bd. dirs. St. Louis chpt. 1987-88), Univ. Ambassadors (hon.), Pi Kappa Delta, Kappa Delta Pi, Zeta Phi Eta, Alpha Phi Omega. Contbr. articles to profl. jours.; book reviewer. Office: So Ill U Campus Box 1017 Edwardsville IL 62026

GRAEBEL, WILLIAM PAUL, engineering educator; b. Manitowoc, Wis., July 15, 1932; s. Adolph Fred and Erna Violet (Huhn) G.; m. June Erna Ness, June 12, 1954; children: Jeffrey Paul, Susan Kay. B.S., U. Wis.-Madison, 1954, M.S., 1955; Ph.D., U. Mich., 1959. Registered profl. engr., Mich. Mem. tech. staff Bell Telephone Labs., Whippany, N.J., 1955-56; instr. engring. U. Mich., 1956-59, asst. prof., 1959-62, asso. prof., 1962-67, prof., 1967—; design specialist Douglas Aircraft Co., Santa Monica, Calif., 1962; summer visitor Nat. Center Atmospheric Research, Boulder, Colo., 1963; research collaborator Centre d'Etudes Nucléaires de Grenoble, France, 1979; research scientist Netherlands Ophthalmic Research Inst., Amsterdam, 1979; sr. design analyst Westinghouse Marine Div., 1981; vis. prof. Stanford (Calif.) U., 1987; cons. in field. Contbr. numerous articles to profl. jours. Mem. Am. Phys. Soc., ASME, U. Mich. Research Club, Am. Theatre Organ Soc., Sigma Xi. Unitarian. Home: 1318 Fountain St Ann Arbor MI 48103

GRAEBNER, ROBERT WILLIAM, physician, neurologist; b. Neenah, Wis., Mar. 30, 1943; s. Winfred Henry and Frances (Pike) G.; m. Linda Louise Menke, Dec. 19, 1965; children: Laura Louise, Melissa Emily. BS, U. Wis., 1965, MD, 1968. Diplomate Am. Bd. Psychiatry and Neurology, Am. Bd. Clin. Neurophysiology, Am. Bd. Med. Examiners. Intern U. Oreg., Portland, 1968-69; resident in neurology U. Wis., Madison, 1969-71, U. Wash., Seattle, 1973-74; practice medicine specializing in neurology Madison, 1974—; asst. clin. prof. neurology Med. Coll. Ga., 1971-73; assoc. clin. prof. neurology U. Wis., Madison, 1974—; pres., chmn. Dean Found. Health,

Research and Edn., Madison, 1986—. Contbr. articles to profl. jours., chpt. to book. Fellow ACP, Am. EEG Soc., Am. Assn. Legal and Indsl. Medicine; mem. AMA, Am. Acad. Neurology, Am. Soc. Electromyography and Electrodiagnosis, Wis. Epilepsy Soc. (sec. 1980-86), Am. Epilepsy Soc., N.Y. Acad. Scis., Wis. Neurol. Soc. (sec. 1982-83, v.p. 1986-87), Wisc. Med. Alumni Assn., Wis. Med. Soc., Dane County Med. Soc., Am. Assn. Study of Headaches, Cen. EEG Soc., Western EEG Soc., Clin. Sleep Soc. Presbyterian. Clubs: Madison Print (Wis.); Great Lakes Cruising (Chgo.); Other Other Club. Avocations: sailing, skiing, antique maps, music, natural landscaping. Home: 209 Saratoga Circle Madison WI 53705 Office: Dean Med Ctr 1313 Fish Hatchery Rd Madison WI 53715

GRAEF, LUTHER WILLIAM, consulting civil engineer; b. Milw., Aug. 14, 1931; s. John and Pearl (Luther) G.; B.C.E., Marquette U., 1952; M.C.E., U. Wis., 1961; m. Lorraine Linnerud, Sept. 18, 1954; children—Ronald, Sharon, Gerald. Engr., C.W. Yoder & Assos., cons. engrs., Milw., 1956-61; partner Graef-Anhalt-Schloemer, cons. engrs., Milw., 1961—; chmn. bd., pres. Graef Anhalt Schloemer Assos., Inc., Milw., 1967—; chmn. engr. adv. com. U. Wis., Milw., also U. Wis. extensions. Active Boy Scouts Am. Chmn. bd. assessment, City of Milw., 1962—. Served to 1st lt. AUS, 1953-56. Named Disting Marquette U. alumnus, 1982, Wis. Profl. Engr. of Yr., 1983. Mem. ASCE (sect. pres. 1968), Nat., Wis. socs. profl. engrs., Cons. Engrs. Council Wis. (pres. 1973-75), Engrs. Scientists Milw. (pres. 1975), Marquette U. Alumni Assn., Tau Beta Pi, Pi Mu Epsilon, Chi Epsilon. Lutheran (pres. ch. council 1969). Home: 3788 S Massachusetts St Milwaukee WI 53220 Office: 345 N 95 St Milwaukee WI 53226

GRAESER, MARK RUSSELL, architect; b. Cin., Sept. 4, 1949; s. Russel John and Martha Margaret (Santel) G.; m. Pamela S. Kemp, Aug. 6, 1977; children: Andrea, Patrick. Student, Internat. Sch. Arts, Florence, Italy, 1972; BArch, Kent State U., 1973. Registered architect, Ohio. Designer, draftsman Levin Porter Archs., Dayton, Ohio, 1973; project mgr. Dues Devel., Dayton, 1973-76; v.p. Endeco Assoc. Archs., Dayton, 1976-80, pres., 1980-85; v.p. design services Danis Devel. Corp., Dayton, 1985—; bd. dirs. Hearing Speech Ctr., Dayton, 1985-86, Eastway Properties, Dayton, 1984-86. Archtl. commentator (radio series) Archtl. Preservation, 1982, (television series) Superior House, 1983. Mem. com. United Way, Dayton, 1984, steering com. Boy Scouts Am., Dayton, 1983, 648 Bd. Mental Health of Mont. County, Dayton, 1983; bd. dirs. Leadership Dayton 84. Recipient Honor award Masonry Inst., 1985. Mem. AIA, Architects Soc. Ohio, Epsilon Delta Rho. Roman Catholic. Club: Oakwood (Ohio) Track (bd. dirs. 1985-86) Lodge: Rotary. Avocations: golf, jogging, photography, art. Home: 234 Patterson Rd Oakwood OH 45419 Office: Danis Devel Corp 2 Riverplace PO Box 1510 Dayton OH 45401

GRAF, LAURANCE JAMES, communications executive; b. Elko, Nev., Dec. 11, 1940; s. Philip Edgar and Ethel (Bellinger) G.; m. Kathleen Ann Krueger, Oct. 30, 1960; children: David, Steven, James. Student, Brown Inst., Mpls., 1960. Lic. FCC radiotelephone. Radio announcer Sta. KDUZ, Hutchinson, Minn., 1960-61, radio sales rep., 1961-65, sales mgr., 1966-75, asst. mgr., 1975-82, v.p. gen. mgr., 1983. Active City Recreation Bd., Hutchinson, 1965-73; pres. Hutchinson Youth Hockey Assn., 1984-85, Burns Manor Mcpl. Nursing Home, Hutchinson, 1985; exec. bd. dirs. McLeod County Regional Rail Authority. Baptist. Lodges: Optimists (sec., treas., v.p., pres. Hutchinson club, 1965-69, D.M.M. Dist. Gov's. award 1972-73, Operation Mars award 1969), Ambassadors (sec., treas., v.p., pres. Hutchinson club, 1975-79). Avocations: model railroading, photography. Home: 860 Ash St Hutchinson MN 55350 Office: KDUZ/KKJR Hwy 15 N Box 10 Hutchinson MN 55350

GRAF, ROBERT E., publisher; b. Milw., Jan. 13, 1943; s. Robert E. and Jeanette (Housey) G.; m. Patricia Ann Guarino, Apr. 25, 1969; children: David, Peter. Student, Jesuit Coll., 1961-65; BA in Philosophy & Letters, St. Louis U., 1967; postgrad., Marquette U., 1967-68; MS, U. Wis., Milw., 1972. Tchr., co-founder, adminstr. Ind. Learning Ctr., Milw., 1970-74; community organizer Wilmington, Del., 1974-75, Kennsington Action Now, Phila., 1975-77; sales mgr. Nat. Bus. Services, Green Bay, Wis., 1978-81; pub. Common Sense mag., Madison, Wis., 1981—; part-time tchr. Madison Area Tech. Coll., 1983—; cons. Common Sense-Milw., 1986. Active civil rights and anti-Vietnam movements, Milw., 1967-69; mem. Milw 14; organizer neighborhood groups, Wilmington, 1974-75, Phila., 1975-77; pres. PTO, Frank Allis Sch., Madison, 1983. Democrat. Roman Catholic. Home: 1505 Deerwood Dr Madison WI 53716 Office: Community Savs Mag PO Box 8634 Madison WI 53708

GRAF, STEVEN ALLEN, chief of police; b. Toledo, Ohio, July 31, 1951; s. Richard A. and M. Lucille (Weaver) G.; m. Karen S. Beck, June 28, 1975; children: Linda K., Julie A., Glenn R. Student in acctg., Bowling Green State U., 1969-72. Cert. peace officer, Ohio. Police officer Grand Rapids (Ohio) Police Dept., 1971-73, 74-76, Waterville (Ohio) Police Dept., 1973-74, Archbold (Ohio) Police Dept., 1976; chief of police Weston (Ohio) Police Dept., 1976—; sec.-treas. Weston Improvement Corp., 1984—. Scoutmaster Toledo Area council Boy Scouts Am., Ohio, 1972-76, unit commr., Weston, 1981—; asst. coordinator Wood County Arson Task Force, Bowling Green, 1984. Recipient Commendation award Am. Fedn. Police, 1976, Commendation award FBI, 1978, Commendation award Bowling Green Police, 1983. Mem. Internat. Assn. Chiefs of Police, Ohio Assn. Chiefs of Police (audit com. 1983-86, legis. com. 1986). Lutheran.

GRAF, WILLIAM PAUL, accountant; b. Evanston, Ill., Aug. 24, 1961; s. William Andrew and Nancy Ann (McGraw) G.; 1 child, William Paul. BS in Acctg., U. Ill., 1983. CPA, Ill. Staff auditor Arthur Andersen & Co., Chgo., 1983—. Mem. Am. Inst. CPA's, Ill. CPA Soc. Office: Arthur Andersen & Co 33 W Monroe St Chicago IL 60603

GRAGG, DONALD EDWARD, county official; b. Wichita, Kans., Oct. 5, 1939; s. Farris G. and Velma Iclone (Fuson) G.; m. Rebecca Ann, Jan. 11, 1964; children—Gretchen, Donald Edward II. Student, Wichita State U., 1957-61. Account exec. Wheeler Kelly Hagny Investment Co., Wichita, Kans., 1961-79; county commr. First Dist. Sedgwick County, Wichita, 1979—, chmn. bd., 1981—. Chmn. Tri County Planning Com., 1981-82; bd. dirs. S.E. Kans. Econ. Devel. Commn., 1980—. Mem. Nat. Assn. Counties (vice chair energy policy), Am. Soc. Pub. Adminstrn., Wichita State U. Alumni Assn., Phi Delta Theta. Republican. Mem. Christian Ch. Clubs: Crestview Country, Petroleum, Mason. Home: 926 Lawrence Lane Wichita KS 67206 Office: Sedgwick County Court House 525 W Main Suite 320 Wichita KS 67203

GRAHAM, ALBERT BRUCE, audiologist, speech and language pathologist; b. Oil City, Pa., Aug. 8, 1919; s. Albert Vanderlin and Octavia (Kellogg) G.; m. Mary Margaret Zeller, June 4, 1943; children: Janice, Michael. AB, Colo. State Coll. Edn., 1940; AM, U. Denver, 1949; PhD, Northwestern U., 1953. Tchr. high sch. drama Coolidge, Kans., 1940-42; prin. Schofield High Sch., Schofield Barracks, Hawaii, 1946-48; dir. Speech and Hearing Clinic and Cerebral Palsy Ctr. Bowling Green (Ohio) State U., 1951-52; chief div. audiology, speech and lang. pathology Henry Ford Hosp., Detroit, 1952-78; audiology cons. Blue Cross/Blue Shield, Mich.; clin. assoc. prof. audiology Wayne State U. Sch. Medicine, Detroit, 1979-83. Editor: Sensorineural Hearing Processes and Disorders, 1967. Bd. dirs. Detroit Hearing and Speech Ctr., 1956-70, pres., 1961-62, 66-67; bd. dirs. Mich. Assn. Better Hearing and Speech, 1967—, pres., 1976-77; mem. profl. adv. council United Cerebral Palsy Assn. Mich., 1960—, chmn., 1968-69; bd. dirs. Nat. Assn. Hearing and Speech Agys., 1960-72, 79-81, 1st v.p., 1968-69; mem. speakers bur. United Found., Detroit; survey cons. Commn. on Accreditation Rehab. Facilities, 1970-72. Served with USAAF, 1942-46. Fellow Am. Speech and Hearing Assn. (legis. council 1969-75, 78-81); assoc. fellow Am. Acad. Ophthalmology and Otolaryngology; mem. Acad. Rehab. Audiology, Assn. Research in Otolaryngology, Am. Audiological Soc. (exec. com. 1974-82), Soc. Med. Audiologists, Mich. Speech and Hearing Assn. (pres. 1957), Council Exceptional Children; assoc. mem. Mich. Otol. Soc. Home: 3236 Lincoln St Dearborn MI 48124 Office: Henry Ford Hosp 2799 W Grand Blvd Detroit MI 48202

GRAHAM, BRYAN ALASTER, systems engineer; b. Detroit, Oct. 20, 1962; s. Alex L. and Elizabeth G. (Conley) G.; m. Jayne C. Hanzek, May 26, 1984; 1 child, Adam B. BS in Indsl. and Systems Engring., U. Mich., Dearborn, 1985. Application engr. Lamb Technicon, Warren, Mich., 1985, systems engr., 1986—. Mem. Soc. Mfg. Engrs., Inst. Indsl. Engrs., Computer and Automated Systems Assn. Home: 9255 Melrose Livonia MI 48150 Office: Lamb Technicon 5663 E Nine Mile Rd Warren MI 48091

GRAHAM, COLIN, stage director; b. Hove, Sussex, Eng.; s. Frederick Eaton and Diana Alexandra (Finlay) G. Diploma, Royal Acad. Dramatic Art, 1953, D.Arts, 1985. Dir. prodns. English Opera Group, 1963-75; artistic dir. Aldeburgh Festival, 1969—; artistic dir., founding dir. English Music Theatre, 1975—; dir. prodns. English Nat. Opera, London, 1978-83; assoc. artistic dir., dir. prodns. Opera Theatre of St. Louis, 1978-85; artistic dir. Bantt Festival Opera, 1984—, Opera Theatre of St. Louis, 1985—; artistic dir. prodns. for Met. Opera, N.Y.C., N.Y.C. Opera, Santa Fe Opera, Glyndebourne Opera, Royal Opera Covent Garden, others. Lighting and set designer, librettist: Penny for a Song (Bennett), 1967, Golden Vanity (Britten), 1967, Postman Always Rings Twice (Paulus), 1982, Joruri (Miki), 1985, others. Recipient Orpheus award for War and Peace, 1973; Churchill fellow, 1974. Mem. Brit. Actors Equity, Can. Actors Equity, Am. Guild Mus. Artists. Office: Opera Theatre of St Louis PO Box 13148 Saint Louis MO 63119

GRAHAM, DAVID BOLDEN, food products executive; b. Miami Beach, Fla., Feb. 10, 1927; s. Robert Cabel and Bertha Eugenia (Hack) G.; m. Stuart Hill Smith, Sept. 1, 1956; children: Bird, Ellen, Darnall, Lamar, Lyle, Gerard, Barbara, David Bolden. Student Colegio de san Bartolome, Bogota, Colombia, 1946; BS, Georgetown U., 1949; postgrad. Harvard Bus. Sch., 1950. Chmn. Graham Farms, Inc., Washington, Ind., 1950—, Graham Cheese Corp., Washington, 1950—; sec. Bal Harbour Square (Fla.), 1956-57, Graham Bros., Inc., Washington, 1950-72; chmn. Peoples Nat. Bank, Washington. Pres. Washington planning commn., regional planning commn.; bd. dirs. Hist. Landmarks Found., Ind.; mem. Ind. Agrl. Adv. Council Served to lt. col. USAF Res., 1949-77. Republican. Roman Catholic. Clubs: Columbia (Indpls.); Rotary (past pres.). Lodge: Elks. Contbr. articles on agr., transp., early fur traders to various publs. Home and Office: Graham Farms PO Box 391 Washington IN 47501

GRAHAM, GENE STEVEN, podiatrist; b. Columbus, Ohio, Mar. 2, 1951; s. Lloyd Erwin and Isabelle Helen (Paudicz) G.; m. Cynthia Teachnor, Apr. 8, 1979; children: Heather, Nicholas. Student, U. Miami, Ohio, 1969-70, Ohio State U., 1970-73; postgrad., Ohio State U., 1977; D Podiatric Medicine, Ohio Coll. Podiatric Medicine, 1977, BS in Microbiology, 1977. Lic. podiatrist, Ohio, Calif., W.Va. Staff Columbus Podiatric Group Inc., 1977-83; practice podiatric medicine specializing in sports medicine and surgery Columbus, 1983—; staff Riverside Meth. Hosp., St. Ann's Hosp., St. Anthony Med. Ctr., Columbus, 1977-87; practice podiatric medicine Columbus, 1987—; team physician, cons. cen. Ohio high schs. and athletic clubs; lectr. various med., health, and sports seminars, clinics. Contbr. editor Ohio Runner mag., 1983—; contbr. articles to profl. mags. Mem. Ohio Podiatric Assn., Am. Podiatry Assn., Am. Coll. Sports Medicine, Am. Coll. Podiatric Sports Medicine, Ohio Acad. Podiatric Medicine (v.p. 1982-83, pres. elect 1983-84, pres. 1984-85, mem. various coms.). Roman Catholic. Avocations: basketball, running, raquetball, triathlons, all sports. Home: 962 Dark Shadows Ct Westerville OH 43081 Office: 1495 Morse Rd B-1 Columbus OH 43229

GRAHAM, H. JAMES, restaurant company executive; b. Columbus, Ohio, Sept. 14, 1946; s. Harry Edward and Kathleen (Dietrick) G.; m. Sheila A. Seidel, Nov. 30, 1968; children: Brian, Keith, Michael. BSBA, Xavier U., 1968. Field mgr. Ford Motor Co., Jacksonville, Fla., 1968-72; real estate analyst Deffett Cos., Columbus, 1973-74; dir. real estate Wendy's Internat. Inc., Dublin, Ohio, 1974-78, v.p. real estate, 1978-85, v.p. nat. devel., 1985—; guest lectr. various industries and univs. Named to the Hon. Order Ky. Cols. Mem. Internat. Council Shopping Ctrs., Nat. Assn. Corp. Real Estate Execs. (bd. dirs. 1983-85, pres. restaurant industry council 1981-82), Nat. Assn. Realtors, Nat. Rev. Appraisers. Avocations: reading, swimming, golf. Office: Wendy's Internat Inc PO Box 256 Dublin OH 43017

GRAHAM, HOWARD HOLMES, manufacturing executive; b. Greensburg, Pa., Apr. 24, 1947; s. Howard B. and Dorothy (Holmes) G.; m. Roberta A. Grant, June 8, 1968 (div. Feb. 1984); m. Linda A. Cossarek, Mar. 14, 1987. BS, Carnegie Mellon U., 1968; MBA, U. Chgo., 1973. CPA, Ill. Various positions Zenith Electronics, Glenview, Ill., 1973-81, dir. acctg., 1981-82, v.p. fin. services, 1982-87, v.p. fin., 1987—. Mem. adv. bd. acctg. dept. U. Ill. at Chgo., 1982—. Served to capt. U.S. Army, 1968-71, Vietnam. Decorated Bronze Star; recipient Elijah Watt Sells award Am. Inst. CPA's, 1982. Mem. Beta Gamma Sigma. Club: Chgo. Yacht. Office: Zenith Electronics Corp 1900 N Austin Chicago IL 60639

GRAHAM, JACK W., psychologist, educator; b. Kokomo, Ind., May 11, 1925; s. Ralph Waldo and Christine (Vickery) G.; m. Sofie B. Larson, June 16, 1953; children—Mark, Karen. A.B., DePauw U., 1946; M.A., U. Wis., 1949; Ph.D., Purdue U., 1951. Asst. in math. U. Wis., 1946-47; instr. in math. DePauw U., 1947-49; research asst. Purdue U., 1950-51; asst. prof. guidance So. Ill. U., Carbondale, 1951-54, assoc. prof. guidance and psychology, 1954-63; prof. guidance and ednl. psychology, 1963—, prof. higher edn., 1967—, dir. Counseling and Testing Ctr., 1951-64, dean students, 1964-67, assoc. dean Grad. Sch., 1974-79, chmn. dept. higher edn., 1983-85. Recipient Outstanding Service to Students award So. Ill. U., 1981. Mem. Ill. Coll. Personnel Assn. (pres. 1968-69), Am. Coll. Personnel Assn., Am. Personnel and Guidance Assn (mem. senate 1963-64), Phi Kappa Phi (pres. Carbondale chpt. 1978-79). Methodist. Club: Rotary. Contbr. articles to profl. jours. Home: 25 Hillcrest Dr Carbondale IL 62901 Office: So Ill U Dept Ednl Adminstrn and Higher Edn Carbondale IL 62901

GRAHAM, JAMES LOWELL, federal judge. Judge U.S. District Courtfor Southern Ohio, Columbus, 1986—. Office: 109 US Courthouse 85 Marconi Blvd Columbus OH 43215 *

GRAHAM, JUSTYN LAIR, education educator; b. Hutchinson, Kans., Oct. 7, 1927; s. O.L. and Avis Exalee (Lair) G.; m. Lola Nadine Royston, Nov. 22, 1951; children: Gayla Dawn Graham Strack, Marc Lair. BS in Secondary Edn., Elem. Edn., N.W. Mo. State U., 1950; MEd, U. Colo., 1955; EdD, U. No. Colo., 1965. Cert. Elem. Sch. Tchr., Principal, Secondary Sch. Tchr. Elem. sch. tchr. Atchinson (KAns.) Pub. Schs., 1950-54, Independence (Mo.) Pub. Schs., 1954-55; elem. principal Savannah (Mo.) Pub. Schs., 1955-65, University City (Mo.) Pub. Schs., 1965-67; instr. U. Mo. grad. program N.W. Mo. State U., Maryville, 1967; assoc. prof. edn. Cen. Mo. State U., Warrensburg, 1967—. Served with USN, 1945-51. Mem. NEA (life), Mo. Tchrs. Assn., Community Tchrs. Assn., Phi Delta Kappa (pres. local chpt. 1986—). Methodist. Avocations: travel, photography, farming. Home: Rt 1 W Oake Warrensburg MO 64093 Office: Cen Mo State U Coll Edn Warrensburg MO 64093

GRAHAM, MICHAEL ALAN, advertising executive; b. Flint, Mich., Nov. 14, 1954; s. James Harold and Virginia Mary (Brookshire) G.; m. Kimberly Beth Cleland, May 21, 1977; 1 child, Jordan George. BS, No. Mich. U., 1976. Acct. exec. Darcy, MacManus & Masius, Bloomfield Hills, Mich., 1976-78; acct. exec. J. Walter Thompson, Dearborn, Mich., 1978-80, acct. supr., 1980-82; sr. acct. supr. William Esty, Los Angeles, 1982-83; v.p. acct. supr. BBDO, Southfield, Mich., 1983-86, v.p. mgmt. supr., 1986—. Asst. dist. commr. Detroit Area council Boy Scouts Am., 1985, unit commr. 1984. Mem. Adcraft Club Detroit. Republican. Roman Catholic. Home: 6400 W Surrey Birmingham MI 48010

GRAHAM, MICHAEL DAVID, dentist; b. Bluffton, Ind., Jan. 2, 1953; s. James Robert and Carolyn (Goldsberry) G.; m. Constance Sue Walburn, Apr. 26, 1986. BA in Biol. Scis., Ind. U., Bloomington, 1975; DDS, Ind. U., Indpls., 1979. Practice dentistry Bluffton, 1979-85; dentist Caylor-Nickel Med. Ctr., Bluffton, 1986—. Deacon First United Ch. of Christ, Bluffton, 1984—, pres. softball league, 1983-85. Mem. ADA, Ind. Dental Assn., Am. Straight Wire Orthodontic Soc., Northeast Regional Study Group, Isaac Knopp Dist. Dental Soc. Republican. Lodge: Optimists (pres. Bluffton 1987), Elks. Avocations: golf, softball, basketball, scuba diving. Home: 319 W Central Ave Bluffton IN 46714 Office: Caylor Nickel Med Ctr One Caylor Nickel Square Bluffton IN 46714

GRAHAM, RICHARD BRIAN HILL, financial services executive, consultant; b. N.Y.C., June 29, 1956; s. Philip L. and Louise (Hill) G. B.A. magna cum laude with departmental honors, U. Pa., 1978; M.B.A., U. Chgo., 1981. Accounts analyst Elkins, Stroud Suplee & Co., Phila., 1978-79; assoc. corp. fin. Warburg Paribas Becker, N.Y.C., 1981; assoc. corp. fin. div. Continental Ill. Nat. Bank and Trust Co. of Chgo., 1981-82; v.p. Diversified Fin. Services Corp., Chgo., 1983-85; pres. Washington Square Fin. Cons., Inc., Chgo., 1985—; sr. cons. Deloitte Haskins & Sells, Chgo., 1987—; fin. planner and cons. various profl. and service corps. Club: University. Office: 200 E Randolph Dr 75th Floor Chicago IL 60601

GRAHAM, ROBERT GRANT, business executive; b. Ottawa, Ont., Can., Apr. 8, 1931; s. Wilmer A. and Lylian (Wiltsie) G.; B.Comm., McGill U., 1952; m. Diane K. Wilson, May 28, 1953; children—Susan Diane, Bruce Wilson. Pres., chief exec. officer, dir. Inter-City Gas Corp., Winnipeg, Man., Can., MICC Investments Ltd., Toronto, Ont.; pres. Mortgage Ins. Co. Can.; chmn. bd. Winnipeg Jets Hockey Club, Roam Communications, KeepRite Inc. dir. mem. exec. com. Guaranty Trust Co. Can., Traders Group Ltd., Great-West Life Assurance Co., Can. Gen. Ins. Co.; dir. Fed. Industries Ltd., Moffat Communications Ltd., ICG Scotia Gas Ltd. Bd. dirs. Winnipeg Found. Mem. Conf. Bd. Can. (sr. mem., dir.). Office: Can Hydrocarbons Ltd, 444 St Mary Ave, Winnipeg, MB Canada R3C 3T7 Office: Suite 16, 1 Dundas St W, PO Box 12, Toronto, ON Canada M5G 1Z3 *

GRAHAM, WILLIAM B., pharmaceutical company executive; b. Chgo., July 14, 1911; s. William and Elizabeth (Burden) G.; m. Edna Kanaley, June 15, 1940 (dec.); children: William J., Elizabeth Anne, Margaret, Robert B.; m. Catherine Van Duzer, July 23, 1984. S.B. cum laude, U. Chgo., 1932, J.D. cum laude, 1936; LL.D., Carthage Coll., 1974, Lake Forest Coll., 1983; L.H.D., St. Xavier Coll. and Nat. Coll. Edn., 1983. Bar: Ill. 1936. Patent lawyer Dyrenforth, Lee, Chritton & Wiles, 1936-40; mem. Dawson & Ooms, 1940-45; v.p., mgr. Baxter Travenol Labs., Inc., Deerfield, Ill., 1945-53; pres., chief exec. officer Baxter Travenol Labs., Inc., 1953-71, chmn. bd., chief exec. officer, 1971-80, chmn. bd., 1980-85, sr. chmn., 1985—, also dir.; dir., mem. exec. com. 1st Nat. Bank, Chgo.; dir. Deere & Co.; prof., chairperson Weizmann Inst., 1978. Bd. dirs., pres. Lyric Opera Chgo.; vice chmn. bd. dirs. Nat. Park Fedn.; bd. dirs. Chgo. Hort. Soc., Nat. Council U.S.-China Trade; trustee Orchestral Assn., U. Chgo., Evanston (Ill.) Hosp. Recipient V.I.P. award Lewis Found., 1963; Disting. Citizen award Ill. St. Andrew Soc., 1974; Decision Maker of Yr. award Am. Statis. Assn., 1974; Marketer of Yr. award AMA, 1976; Found. award Kidney Found., 1981; Chicagoan of Yr. Chgo. Boys Club, 1981; Bus. Statesman of Yr. award Harvard Bus. Sch. Club Chgo., 1983; Achievement award Med. Tech. Services, 1983; Disting. Fellows award Internat. Ctr. for Artificial Organs and Transplantations, 1982; Chgo. Civic award DePaul U., 1986; recognized for pioneering work Health Industry Mfrs. Assn., 1981; inductedJr. Achievement Chgo. Bus. Hall of Fame, 1986. Mem. Am. Pharm. Mfrs. Assn. (past pres.), Ill. Mfrs. Assn. (past pres.), Pharm. Mfrs. Assn. (past chmn., award for spl. distinction leadership 1981), Phi Beta Kappa, Sigma Xi, Phi Delta Phi. Clubs: Chicago (past pres.), Commonwealth, Mid-Am., Commercial, Indian Hill, Casino (Chgo.); Old Elm (Lake Forest, Ill.); Seminole, Everglades, Bath & Tennis (Fla.); University, Links (N.Y.C.). Home: 40 Devonshire Ln Kenilworth IL 60043 Office: Baxter Travenol Labs Inc One Baxter Pkwy Deerfield IL 60015

GRAHAM, WILLIAM QUENTIN, computer lessor; b. Ann Arbor, Mich., Jan. 17, 1944; s. William and Marie (MacGregor) G.; B.B.A., Eastern Mich. U., Ypsilanti, 1969; m. Susan H. Scheinker, Sept. 10, 1967; children—David Aaron, Robert Lewis, Alexandra Marie. Research asst. TRW, Los Angeles, 1965; field engr. IBM, Ann Arbor, 1966-69, salesman, Detroit, 1969-73; salesman Cambridge Memories, Inc., 1973-76; large computer specialist CMI Corp., Troy, Mich., 1976-81; lessor Meridian Leasing, Birmingham, Mich., 1981-84, Graham & Assocs., 1984—; data processing cons. and advisor. Mem. Zionist Orgn. Am. Mem. Detroit Soviet Jewry Com., Jewish Welfare Fedn. Clubs: Motor City Striders, Motor City Packards, B'nai B'rith. Home: 5709 Stonington Ct West Bloomington MI 48033 Office: 5600 W Maple Rd Bloomfield MI 48033

GRALLA, EUGENE, natural gas company executive; b. N.Y.C., May 3, 1924; s. Jacob and Anna Ruth (Kleiman) G.; m. Beverly Dorman, Apr. 7, 1946; children: Rhona Gralla Spilka, Steven Stuart. B.S., U.S. Naval Acad., 1945; M.B.A., Harvard U., 1947. Commd. ensign USN, 1945, advanced through grades to comdr., 1961; served sea duty 1947-49, 54-56; control officer (Naval Supply Depot, Guantanamo Bay), Cuba, 1959-61; with (Office Asst. Sec. Def. for Installations and Logistics), 1961-64; ret. 1966; dir. data systems planning Trans World Airlines, N.Y.C., 1966-68; corp. dir. mgmt. info. systems Internat. Paper Co., N.Y.C., 1968; v.p. electronic data processing Columbia Gas System Service Corp., Wilmington, Del., 1969-73; sr. v.p. Columbia Gas Distbn. Cos., Columbus, Ohio, 1973-86, pres., 1986—. Chmn. bd. trustees Ohio Pub. Expenditure Council. Mem. U.S. Naval Inst., Navy League Columbus, Harvard Bus. Sch. Club Columbus, Agonis Club Columbus. Club: Mason. Home: 5850 Forestview Dr Columbus OH 43213 Office: Columbia Gas Distbn Cos 200 Civic Center Dr Columbus OH 43215

GRANDERSON, GEORGE, science teacher; b. Arlington, Tenn., Apr. 25, 1937; s. Willie and Minnie Lee (Davis) G.; m. Marie Nadine Majors, Oct. 2, 1959; children: George, Michael, Gerald, Mark. BS, Tenn. State U., Nashville, 1960, MS, 1965; AS, Lawrence Inst. Tech., 1974; PhD, U. Mich., 1978. Tchr. sci. Durfee Jr. High Sch., Detroit, 1964-68, Cen. High Sch., Detroit, 1968-73; tchr. sci., head dept. Southwestern High Sch., Detroit, 1973—; instr. chemistry Community Coll., Wayne County, Mich., 1978—. Served with U.S. Army, 1960-63, Korea. Recipient Centennial Tchr. award NIH, Bethesda, Mass., 1987, Honor Roll Tchr. award 1987, Prism award Detroit Sci. Ctr., 1987. Fellow AAAS, Nat. Sci. Tchrs. Assn., Am. Chem. Soc., Mich. Sci. Tchrs. Assn., Metro Detroit Sci. Tchrs. Assn., Phi Delta Kappa; mem. Alpha Kappa Mu. Democrat. Home: 607 Susan Ann Arbor MI 48103 Office: Southwestern High Sch 6921 W Fort St Detroit MI 48209

GRANDLE, RALPH WESLEY, manufacturing company executive; b. Chgo., May 28, 1936; s. William Raymond and Jessie Victoria (Anderson) G.; m. June Marlene King, Sept. 24, 1960; children—Patricia, Susan. B.S. in Indsl. Engring., Bradley U., 1958. Exec. v.p. Tricon Industries, Inc., Downers Grove, Ill., 1963—; mem. Ill. Gov.'s Conf. on Small Bus., Springfield, Ill., 1984. Bd. dirs. Indian Boundry YMCA, Downers Grove, 1969-84; pres. bd. dirs. Bradley U. Parents, Peoria, Ill., 1984—; bd. dirs., assoc. trustee Bradley U., 1984—. Recipient Service to Youth award Indian Boundry YMCA, 1974. Mem. Inst. Indsl. Engring., Am. Soc. Quality Control, Downers Grove C. of C. (chmn. 1983-84, bd. dirs. 1980-85). Republican. Baptist. Club: Oakbrook Executive Breakfast (Ill.). Avocations: water and snow skiing, basketball, softball, flying, boating. Home: 906 Central Ave Downers Grove IL 60516

GRANDSTRAND, KAREN LOUISE, lawyer; b. Colorado Springs, Colo., Apr. 14, 1955; d. Kent B. and Mabel L. (Danielson) Quanbeck; m. David Paul Grandstrand, May 29, 1976. BA summa cum laude, Concordia Coll., 1977; JD, Loyola U., Chgo., 1982. Bar: Ill. 1982, U.S. Dist. Ct. (no. dist.) Ill. 1982, Minn. 1984, U.S. Dist. Ct. Minn. 1986. Law clk. Baker & McKenzie, Chgo., 1980-83; assoc. Frankel & McKay, Ltd., Chgo., 1983-85; atty. Fed. Res. Bank Mpls., 1985—; instr. legal writing U. Minn., Mpls., 1986—. Mem. ABA, Minn. Bar Assn. Office: Fed Res Bank Mpls 250 Marquette Ave Minneapolis MN 55480

GRANDY, FRED, U.S. Congressman, actor; b. Sioux City, Iowa; s. William Frederick and Bonnie G.; m. Catherine Mann, 1987. B.A. in English, Harvard U., 1970. Founder improvisational group The Proposition, Harvard U.; mem. 100th Congress from 6th Iowa Dist., 1987—; serves on house com. Agr., Edn. and Labor. Appeared: in play Green Julia, N.Y.C.; collaborator rev.: in play Pretzels; appeared in: in play Joe Papp's In the Boom Boom Room, until, 1974; film appearances include Close Encounters of the Third Kind; television films include The Girl Most Likely To, 1973, Blind Ambition, 1979, Love Boat II, Love Boat III; television series The Love Boat, 1977-86; other television appearances include Welcome Back Kotter. Candidate for U.S. Congress from Iowa, 1986. Office: U S House of Representatives Office of House Members Washington DC 20510

GRANGE, JANET LENORE, tax lawyer; b. Chgo., Sept. 5, 1958; d. Albert Edward and Marie Loretta (Hart) G. BS in Acctg., U. Ill., Chgo., 1980; JD,

U. Ill., 1983. Bar: Ill. 1983; CPA, Ill. Sr. tax cons. Grant Thornton, Chgo., 1983-85, Deloitte, Haskins & Sells, Chgo., 1985-86, Kraft, Inc., Northbrook, Ill., 1986—. Mem. Chgo. Bar Assn. (fed. taxation com.), ABA (fed. taxation sect.), Am. Inst. CPA's, Ill. CPA Soc., U. Ill. Alumni Assn. (bd. dirs. 1987—), Beta Gamma Sigma. Avocations: tennis, aerobics. Office: Kraft Inc 2211 Sanders Rd Northbrook IL 60062

GRANNEMAN, GARY NORMAN, high technology executive, consultant; b. Clinton, Iowa, Oct. 9, 1944; s. Melvin A. and Mary Elizabeth (Rowe) G.; m. Marilyn J. Moore, Nov. 28, 1968; 1 child, Christopher N. Student Ind. U., 1962-66. Pres. Granneman Automotive Co., Indpls., 1973—, Granneman & Assocs., Inc., Indpls., 1973—; chmn. Granneman Internat., Indpls. and London, 1983—; founder, pres. Emerging Technologies Corp.; mktg. cons. internat. high tech. Chmn. Dems. For Lugar, Indpls., 1976; founder Ted Doesn't Either Com., Indpls., 1978, Com. for Multilateral Disarmament, Indpls., 1981, Com. for Soviet Disarmament, Indpls., 1983; mem. Nat. Com. for Prevention Child Abuse; founding mem. Family Support Ctr. Indpls. Mem. Mensa. Republican. Unitarian. Club: Mackinac Family (pres. 1985-87). Home: 7206 Crest Ln Indianapolis IN 46256 Office: Granneman Internat 7340 E 82d St Indianapolis IN 46256

GRANT, ANETT D., communications executive; b. Montreal, Que., Can., May 25, 1950; d. Ralph and Mildred (Gussman) Drabinsky; m. Peter Williams Grant, Aug. 24, 1975. B.E., McGill U., 1971; M.F.A., U. Minn., 1975. Free-lance theater reviewer, nat. feature writer and community theater dir., 1975-79; pres. Exec. Speaking, Inc., Mpls., 1979—. Steel Co. Can. scholar, 1967; recipient Gardner Kneeland Meml. prize in English, McGill U., 1969; Que. Govt. Grad. scholar, 1971-73. Mem. Pub. Relations Soc. Am., Am. Soc. Tng. and Devel. Contbr. articles to profl. jours.; developer Core-Satellite Systems, 1982. Home: 5011 Colonial Dr Minneapolis MN 55416 Office: 960C Butler Sq Minneapolis MN 55416

GRANT, CHARLES TRUMAN, mergers and acquisitions executive; b. Chgo., Oct. 10, 1946; s. Charles H. and Mildred E. (Larrey) G.; B.A., DePaul U., Chgo., 1968, M.B.A. in Fin. and Acctg., 1975; 1 dau., Jordanna Lynne. Dir. internal audit and credit Rand McNally & Co., Skokie, Ill., 1973-75; cost and gen. acctg. mgr. V. Mueller div. Am. Hosp. Supply Corp., Chgo., 1971-73, corp. dir. acctg. and reporting Am. Hosp. Supply Corp., Evanston, 1975-77, officer and controller Am. Hosp. Supply div., McGaw Park, Ill., 1977-78; area v.p. ops. and adminstrn. Mead Corp., Hillside, Ill., 1978-80, pres. Ft. Dearborn Paper Co., Chgo., 1980-83; pres. The Guidance Concept Inc.; exec. v.p. Acquisition Mgmt., Inc., 1983-85; pres. Acquisition Mgmt./MidAm., Inc., 1985-86; v.p. mergers and acquisitions Baird & Warner, Inc., Chgo., 1986—; dir. CEDCO Capital, Inc. Lectr. Merit Youth Employment Council, 1976—; fin. adv. Jr. Achievement, 1971-75. Recipient Disting. Alumni award De Paul U., 1982; named Outstanding M.B.A. of Yr., 1982, Top Ten Bus. Profl. of Yr., 1982. Mem. Nat. Black M.B.A. Assn. (pres. 1981-83). Contbr. career articles to Ebony, Black Enterprise mag., Dollars and Sense mag., Crain's Chgo. Bus., Bus. and Soc. Rev. Avocations: art, travel, horseback riding. Home: 1240 N Lake Shore Dr Apt #6-B Chicago IL 60610

GRANT, J. KIRKLAND, gynecologist/obstetrician; b. Port Arthur, Tex., Dec. 10, 1954; s. Ulysses Jerry and Beatrice Lee (Barnum) G.; m. Carmen Lydia Jimenez, July 6, 1985; 1 stepchild, Rufino Quintin Jimenez. BA, Johns Hopkins U., 1976; MD, U. Tex., Houston, 1979. Diplomate Am. Bd. Ob-Gyn. Resident in ob-gyn U. Ill. Hosp., Chgo., 1979-83; mem. staff Northcare, Schaumberg, Ill., 1983—; instr. U. Ill. Hosp., Chgo., 1983—. Fellow Am. Coll. Ob-Gyn; mem. AMA, Ill. Med. Soc., Chgo. Med. Soc. Baptist. Avocation: photography. Home: 419 W Wellington Apt 1 G Chicago IL 60657 Office: Northcare 1931 Meacham Schaumberg IL 60173

GRANT, JOHN THOMAS, state supreme court justice; b. Omaha, Oct. 25, 1920; s. Thomas J. and Mary Elizabeth (Smith) G.; m. Marian Louise Saner, Dec. 27, 1947; children—Martha Grant Novak, John P., Susan J., Joseph W., Timothy K. LL.B., J.D., Creighton U., 1950. Bar: Nebr. 1950. Sole practice law Omaha, 1950-74; judge State Dist. Ct., Omaha, 1974-83; justice Nebr. Supreme Ct., Lincoln, 1983—. Served with Signal Corps, U.S. Army, 1942-45, PTO. Home: 1640 Twin Ridge Rd Lincoln NE 68506 Office: Nebraska Supreme Court State Capitol Bldg Lincoln NE 68509

GRANT, MICHAEL EUGENE, mortgage banker; b. Chgo., June 25, 1944; s. Joseph S. and Marie E. (Salk) G.; m. Diane Goldenberg, June 15, 1968; children: Scott, Dana. BS, U. Wis., 1966; JD, Loyola U., 1969. Bar: Ill. 1969; lic. real estate broker, Ill. 1st v.p., prin. J.S. Grant Mortgage Co., Chgo., 1969-80; exec. v.p. Salk, Ward & Salk, Chgo., 1980-83; v.p., prin. Mid-North Fin. Services Inc., Chgo., 1983 ; mem. faculty Cen. YMCA Real Estate Inst., 1976-81, Mortgage Bankers Assn. Am., East Lansing, Mich., 1981, Prof. Edn. Systems Inc., 1982-84, Ill. Inst. Continuing Legal Edn., Chgo., 1985-86. Contbr. articles to profl. jours. Bd. dirs. North Shore Congregation Presch., Glencoe, Ill., 1974, North Shore Congl. Israel Sch. Bd., Glencoe, 1982-84; mem. task force Com. to Study Declining Enrollment in Pub. Schs., Glencoe, 1975; coach softball, soccer, hockey Glencoe/Winnetka (Ill.) Park Dists.; chmn. Zoning Bd. Appeals, Glencoe, 1983; chmn. Sch. Bd. Nominating Com., Glencoe, 1977; sec., co-founder Friends of Glencoe Parks, 1977. Mem. Ill. State Bar Assn., Chgo. Bar Assn. (chmn. 1975, real property sub-com. on finance), Ill. Mortgage Bankers Assn. (bd. dirs. 1977-79, 82-84, named Comml. Mortgage Banker of Yr., 1979, chmn. legislation com. 1978, sec.-treas. 1985, v.p. 1986, pres. 1987), Jr. Real Estate Bd. (bd. dirs. 1977, mem. in Perpetuity, 1980), Nat. Assn. Rev. Appraisers, Francis W. Park Sch. Alumni Assn. (bd. dirs. 1986—). Jewish. Avocations: travelling, history, swimming, biking, reading. Home: 720 Appletree Ln Glencoe IL 60022 Office: Mid-North Fin Services 205 W Wacker Chicago IL 60606

GRANT, MICHAEL PETER, electrical engineer; b. Oshkosh, Wis., Feb. 26, 1936; s. Robert J. and Ione (Michelson) G.; m. Mary Susan Corcoran, Sept. 2, 1961; children: James, Steven, Laura. B.S., Purdue U., 1957, M.S., 1958, Ph.D., 1964. With Westinghouse Research Labs., Pitts., summers 1953-57; mem. tech. staff Aerospace Corp., El Segundo, Calif., 1961; instr. elec. engring. Purdue U., West Lafayette, Ind., 1958-64; sr. engr. Combustion Engring. Corp., Columbus, Ohio, 1964-67, mgr. advanced devel. and control systems, 1967-72, mgr. control and info. scis. div., 1972-74, asst. gen. mgr. indsl. systems div., 1974-76; mgr. system design AccuRay Corp., Columbus, Ohio, 1976—. Contbr. articles to profl. jours.; patentee in field of automation. Mem. IEEE, Sigma Xi, Eta Kappa Nu, Pi Mu Epsilon, Tau Beta Pi. Home: 4461 Sussex Dr Columbus OH 43220 Office: AccuRay Corp 650 Ackerman Rd Columbus OH 43202

GRANT, PETER WILLIAMS, psychologist; b. Sewanee, Tenn., Nov. 3, 1945; s. Robert McQueen and Margaret Huntington (Horton) G.; m. Anett D. Grant, Aug. 24, 1975. BA, U. Minn., 1967, PhD, 1982; AM, U. Chgo., 1971. Licensed cons. psychologist. Pvt. practice psychotherapy Mpls., 1975—; cons. Met. Clinic Counseling, Mpls., 1983-85; v.p., bd. dirs. Y.E.S./Neon, Mpls., 1985—. Mem. Am. Psychol. Assn., Nat. Assn. Social Workers, Acad. Cert. Social Workers. Home: 5011 Colonial Dr Minneapolis MN 55416 Office: 747 Med Arts Bldg Minneapolis MN 55416

GRANT, ROBERT ALLEN, judge; b. Marshall County, Ind., July 31, 1905; s. Everett F. and Margaret E. (Hatfield) G.; m. Margaret Anne McLaren, Sept. 17, 1933; children—Robert A., Margaret Ann Soderberg. A.B., U. Notre Dame, 1928, J.D., 1930. Bar: Ind. bar 1930, U.S. Supreme Ct. bar 1940. Practiced in South Bend, Ind.; dep. pros. atty. St. Joseph County, 1935-36; mem. 76th-80th congresses from 3d Ind. Dist.; U.S. dist. judge No. Dist. Ind., 1957—, chief judge, 1961-72, sr. judge, 1972—; apptd. to Temp. Emergency Ct. Appeals U.S., 1976. Trustee U. Indpls., 1976—; mem. nat. council representing No. Ind., Boy Scouts Am., 1967. Mem. Am., Ind. bar assns. SAR. Republican. Methodist. Clubs: Masons (33 deg.), K.T., Shriners, Rotary, Elks, Order DeMolay (internat. supreme council, past grand master), Columbia (Indpls.); Summit (South Bend); Union League (Chgo.). Home: 98 Schellinger St Mishawaka IN 46544 Office: U S Dist Ct 308 Fed Bldg 204 S Main St South Bend IN 46601

GRANT, W. D., insurance company executive; b. 1917. BA, U. Kans., 1939; postgrad., U. Pa., 1950. With Bus. Men's Assurance Co. Am., Kansas City, Mo., 1941—, v.p., 1951-56, exec. v.p., 1956-60, pres., 1960-69, chief exec. officer, 1960—, chmn. bd. dirs., 1969—. Served to lt. comdr. USN, 1940-45. Office: Bus Men's Assurance Co of Am BMA Tower Kansas City MO 64141 *

GRANT, W. THOMAS, II, insurance company executive; b. 1950. BA, U. Kans., 1972; MBA, U. Pa., 1976. With Bus. Men's Assurance Co. Am., Kansas City, Mo., 1976—, dir. planning, 1980-81, v.p., dir. corp. planning, 1981-83, sr. v.p. corp. research, 1983-84, pres., bd. dirs., 1984—. Office: Bus Men's Assurance Co of Am BMA Tower Kansas City MO 64141 *

GRANTER, SHARON SAVOY, restaurant owner; b. Hammond, Ind., Oct. 21, 1940; d. Theodore Grummer and Marie Theresa (Vincent) Kocur; m. John Albert Savoy, Aug. 14, 1959 (div. Nov. 1974); children: Renee Savoy Heuss, Jennifer Lynn Savoy, Elizabeth Anne Savoy; m. Donald Ralph Granter, Feb. 10, 1979. Student, Ohio State U., 1958-59, Lancaster Bus. Coll., 1959. Sec., bookeeper Manpower, Inc., Albany, N.Y., 1960-64; owner, operator, caterer Granter's Deli, Mansfield, Ohio, 1979—. Editor newsletter NCO Rehab. Ctr., 1971-74, New Start Seminar, 1973-79. Vocalist Ohio State U. Jazz Forum Big Band, 1955-59; founder, dir. New Start Seminar, Mansfield, 1973-79; sec. Miss Ohio Scholarship Pageant, Mansfield, 1974-80, traveling companion, 1974-80, judge, 1974-86; mem. procurement com. Mansfield Gen. Hosp., 1973-74; pres. aux. AMA Riverside Hosp., Columbus, 1972. Mem. Nat. Restaurant Assn., Ohio Restaurant Assn. Republican. Home: 536 Chevy Chase Rd Mansfield OH 44907 Office: Granters Deli Catering Div 1354 Park Ave W Mansfield OH 44906

GRANZOW, PAUL H., printing company executive; b. 1927. Student, U. Dayton; LLB, U. Cin, 1950. Ptnr. Turner, Granzow & Hollenkamp; with Standard Register Co., Dayton, Ohio, 1966—, chmn. bd. dirs., 1984—. Served with AUS, 1945-46. Office: The Standard Register Co 600 Albany St Dayton OH 45408 *

GRAPSKI, LADD RAYMOND, accountant; b. Chgo., Nov. 3, 1942; s. Lad Francis and Dorothy (Kuhn) G.; m. Sharon Lee Kennedy, Aug. 31, 1968; children: Lad R., Kevin M. BBA, Loyola U., Chgo., 1969; CPA, U. Ill., 1971. Auditor Arthur Andersen & Co., Chgo., 1969-74; acctg. mgr. Peerless, Chgo., 1974-76; controller Accu Ray Corp., Columbus, Ohio, 1976—. Pres., trustee Knolls Civic Assn., Columbus, 1981-84; treas., trustee North Columbus Sports Assn., 1982—. Served as staff sgt. U.S. Army, 1963-66. Fellow Ohio Soc. CPA's; mem. Am. Soc. CPA's, Fin. Exec. Inst. Home: 626 Lummis Ford Ln N Columbus OH 43214 Office: Accu Ray Corp 650 Ackerman Rd Columbus OH 43202

GRASER, EARL JOHN, industrial designer; b. Toledo, Dec. 27, 1920; s. Ottomar S. and Irene Olga (Frommer) G.; m. Marianne Loveless, Nov. 19, 1942; 1 child, Cathy Ann. B.S., U. Cin., 1950. Assoc. Edwin W. Fuerst Indsl. Design, Toledo, 1947-50; v.p., assoc. Packaging and Product Devel. Inst., Cin., 1958-61; mgr. product devel. Olinkraft Inc. subs. Johns-Manville Corp., West Monroe, La., 1961-75, mgr. packaging systems div., 1975-77, dir. indsl. design, 1977-81, dir. indsl. design Manville Forest Products Corp., 1981-82; pres. Packaging and Product Devel. Assocs., Inc., Cin., 1982—. Contbr. articles to profl. jours. Patentee in field. Set design dir. Miss La. Pageant, 1974; flotilla comdr. USCG Aux., 1958-61; active Monroe Fine Arts Found., CAP, St. Francis Hosp., Bldg. Fund; bd. dirs. Monroe Little Theater. Served with USN, 1942-45. Recipient Inventor of Yr. award Olinkraft, Inc., 1971, Package of Yr. award Food and Drug Packaging mag., 1972, Set Design of Yr. award Strauss Playhouse, 1974. Mem. Packaging Inst. U.S.A., World Packaging Orgn., Am. Mgmt. Assn., Am. Soc. Innovators in Tech. (bd. dirs.), Am. Frozen Food Inst., Nat. Soft Drink Asn., Soc. Indsl. Designers, Nat. Assn. Awareness in Music, Aircraft Owners and Pilots Asn., Soc. Soft Drink Technologists, Alpha Sigma Phi. Republican. Roman Catholic. Club: Aero Nutz, Inc. Home: 6520 Apache Circle Cincinnati OH 45243

GRASLIE, SCOTT ARTHUR, dentist; b. Spearfish, S.D., Mar. 28, 1954; s. Louis Laverne and Anna Kay (Smith) G.; m. Barbara Lee Carlson, Aug. 16, 1980; 1 child, Kirsten Alyssa. BS, Black Hills State Coll., 1976; DDS, Loyola U., Maywood, Ill., 1980. Gen. practice dentistry Spearfish, 1980—. Treas. Yellowjacket Found., 1985—. Named one of Outstanding Young Men of Am., 1985. Mem. ADA, S.D. Dental Assn., Black Hills Dist. Dental Soc. (del. 1985), Spearfish C. of C. (membership com. 1984—). Republican. Roman Catholic. Club: Green and Gold (Spearfish) (pres. 1981-84, Booster of Yr. award 1985). Lodge: Kiwanis (membership com. 1984-85). Office: 825 Main Spearfish SD 57783

GRASSLEY, CHARLES E., U.S. Senator; b. New Hartford, Iowa, Sept. 17, 1933; m. Barbara Ann Speicher; children: Lee, Wendy, Robin Lynn, Michele Marie, Jay Charles. B.A., U. No. Iowa, 1955, M.A., 1956; postgrad., U. Iowa, 1957-58. Farmer; instr. polit. sci. Drake U., 1962, Charles City Community Coll., 1967-68; mem. Iowa Ho. of Reps., 1959-75, 94th-96th Congresses from 3d Iowa Dist., U.S. Senate from Iowa, 1981—. Mem. Am. Farm Bur., Iowa Hist. Soc., Pi Gamma Mu, Kappa Delta Pi. Baptist. Lodges: Masons, Order of Eastern Star. Office: US Senate 135 Hart Senate Bldg Washington DC 20510

GRASSMAN, VICTOR A., economic development consultant, urban planner; b. Lake Forest, Ill., May 20, 1955; s. Robert Irwin and Verneal Martha (Ziemann) G. BS, U. Wis., La Crosse, 1977; M in Urban Planning, U. Wis., Madison, 1982. Cert. real estate broker, Wis. Telemktg. specialist Hatco Corp., Milw., 1980-82; econ. devel. analyst City of Milw., 1982-85; econ. devel. cons. State of Wis., Madison, 1985—. Mem. Am. Econ. Devel. Council, Am. Inst. Cert. Planners, Am. Planning Assn., Wis. Econ. Devel. Assn. Democrat. Club: Capital Investment. Avocations: music, jogging, weight lifting, reading, sailing. Home: 6816 Schroeder Rd #8 Madison WI 53711 Office: Dept Devel State Wis PO Box 7970 123 W Washington Ave Madison WI 53707

GRATZIANNA, JOHN ALBERT, towing and recovery service company executive; b. Chgo., May 6, 1943. Pres. O'Hare Truck Service, Inc., Northlake, Ill., 1971—; leading advocate and spokeman for towing and recovery industry in the Midwest. Founder, contbr. Tow Times Mag.; contbr. articles to trade assns. mags. Recipient numerous awards and honors from trade assns. Mem. Profl. Towing and Recovery Operators Ill. (founder, 1st pres. 1979—), Towing and Recovery Assn. Am. (Ill. dist. rep. 1980-84, membership chmn. 1983-86, cabinet mem. 1985-87), Council of State Towing Assn. (founder, pres. 1982-87), Interstate Towing Assn. (bd. dirs. 1985-86), Wis. Towing Assn., Automobiles Wholesalers Ill., Nat. Fedn. Small Bus. Assns., Midwest Truckers Assn., Northlake C. of C. Republican. Roman Catholic. Home: 3723 Madison Oak Brook IL 60521 Office: O'Hare Truck Service Inc 2039 N Mannheim Rd Northlake IL 60164

GRATZON, FRED, ice cream manufacturing executive; b. Phila., Mar. 25, 1946; s. Edward and Frieda (Honixfeld) G. BA, Rutgers U., 1968; MSci, Maharishi European Research U., Weggis, Switzerland, 1977. Tchr. transcendental meditation World Plan Exec. Council, N.Y., Pa., N.J., R.I., 1970-79; founder, pres. The Great Midwestern Ice Cream Co., Fairfield, Iowa, 1979—. Named Ice Cream Retailer of Yr. Nat. Ice Cream Retailers Assn., 1986. Home: 209 N 16th St Fairfield IA 52556 Office: The Great Midwestern Ice Cream Co Box 1717 Fairfield IA 52556

GRAU, JAMES JOHN, brokerage house executive; b. Cin., July 9, 1949; s. John Conrad Jr. and Gloria Viven (Cowalsh) G.; m. Linda Lee Seats, Mar. 31, 1974 (div. Apr. 13, 1983); children: Jennifer, Christopher. Grad. high sch., Pitts., 1967. Sales mgr. various corps., 1971-74; pres., chief exec. officer Woods Music and Conservatory, Shawnee, Kans., 1975-79, Kope Food Products Inc., Lenexa, Kans., 1980—, Internat. Leasing Co., Lenexa, 1982—, Internat. Fin. Brokerage Inc., Lenexa, 1982—; cons. in field. Served with USN, 1967-73. Republican. Methodist. Avocations: photography, playing guitar. Office: Internat Fin Brokerage Inc PO Box 14631 Lenexa KS 66215

GRAUER, DOUGLAS DALE, pipeline engineer; b. Marysville, Kans., June 27, 1956; s. Norman Wayne and Ruth Ann (Schwindaman) G.; m. Bette Lynn Bohnenblust, Aug. 16, 1980; children: Diana Kathryn, Laura Jaclyn. Student, Baker U., 1976; BSCE, Kans. State U., 1979. Registered profl. engr., Kans., Okla. Pipeline engr. Cities Service Pipeline Co., Shreveport, La., 1979-80; products terminal engr. Cities Service Co., Braintree, Mass., 1980-81; project engr. Cities Service Co., Tulsa, 1981-83; staff engr. Cities Service Oil and Gas Corp., Tulsa, 1983-85; asst. products pipeline and terminal supt. Nat. Coop. Refinery Assn., Blue Rapids, Kans., 1985—. Mem. ASCE, NSPE, Okla. Soc. Profl. Engrs., Kans. Engring. Soc., Chi Epsilon. Republican. Avocations: golf, tennis, fishing, woodworking. Home: 1406 Debbie Ln Marysville KS 66508 Office: Nat Coop Refinery Assn PO Box 158 Blue Rapids KS 66411

GRAVEN, RICHARD DON, data processing executive; b. Akron, Ohio, Aug. 29, 1943; s. Buell Laverell and Florence Gaynel (Schader) G.; m. Bonnie Sue Hoffer, Oct. 5, 1968; children: Laura, Matthew. BSBA, Kent State U., 1965. Programmer Bobbi Brooks, Inc., Cleve., 1968-69; assoc. programmer IBM, Raleigh, N.C., 1969-70; programmer, analyst Neoterics, Cleve., 1970-73; sr. systems analyst Westfield Cos., Westfield Center, Ohio, 1973-79, ops. mgr., 1979—. Served to 1st lt. U.S. Army, 1966-68, Vietnam. Avocations: chess, golf. Home: 280 Montview Dr Medina OH 44256 Office: Westfield Cos 1 Park Circle Westfield Center OH 44251

GRAVEREAU, VICTOR P., marketing cons., ret. educator; b. Thunder Bay, Ont., Can., Mar. 20, 1909; s. James and Malvina (Lemieux) G.; came to U.S., 1910, naturalized, 1934; B.A., Ohio Wesleyan U., 1936; M.A., Kent State U., 1943; M.B.A., Case Western Res. U., 1951; m. Mildred Irene Snyder, Aug. 11, 1934. Salesman, Motorists Mutual Ins. Co., Wooster, Ohio, 1936-37; tchr. of commerce Rittman (Ohio) High Sch., 1937-46; accountant Gerstenslager Co., Wooster, Ohio, 1944; asst. prof. commerce Kent (Ohio) State U., 1946-49, asso. prof. commerce, 1949-51, prof. marketing, 1951-76, prof. marketing emeritus, 1976—, coordinator coll. grad. program, 1957-60, asst. dean, 1960-61; partner Pfeiffer, Gravereau & Assos., Kent, 1954-63; dir., v.p. Clark Zimmerman & Assos., Inc., Cleve., 1971-84. Recipient Pres.'s. medal Kent State U., 1977; Republic Steel Corp. Economics-in-Action fellow Case Western Res. U., 1964. Mem. Am. Mktg. Assn., Am. Acad. Advt., Am. Advt. Fedn., Nat. Assn. of Purchasing Mgmt. (faculty intern fellow 1962), Bus. Profl. Advt. Assn., Advt. Club Akron, Beta Gamma Sigma, Delta Sigma Pi, Delta Tau Delta, Kappa Delta Pi. Clubs: Masons, Kiwanis, Akron City. Author: Purchasing Management: Selected Readings, 1973; contbr. articles in field to profl. publs.; mktg. scholarship Kent State U. established in his name, 1977. Home: 212 Elmwood Dr Kent OH 44240

GRAVES, CAROL DORREANE, construction company executive; b. Boise, Idaho, May 3, 1937; d. Elmer Kenney and M. Elizabeth (Rogers) Kenney Stolquist; m. Philip L. Graves, Aug. 6, 1955; children: Steven P., Kenton L., Cynthia M. Owner Carols, Peoria, Ill., 1975-78; realtor Clifton-Strode E.R.A., Peoria, 1978-83; pres. Little Red Hen Outlets Inc., Peoria, 1983—; sec., treas. Asbestos Enviro-Clean Inc., Pekin, Ill., 1987—. Rep. precinct committeeperson, Peoria, 1983—; funds dir. YWCA, Oconomowoc, Wis., 1965. Mem. Kickapoo Twp. Assn. (bd. dirs. 1984), Downtown Bus. Assn. (bd. dirs., pres. 1987), Heart of Ill. Food Service Assn. Roman Catholic. Avocation: breeding Red Angus cattle. Home: 4121 N Koerner Rd Peoria IL 61615 Office: PO Box 681 Pekin IL 61554

GRAVES, JAMES HENRY, psychiatrist, educator, physician; b. Herrin, Ill., Sept. 29, 1924; s. James Henry and Anna Joyce (Keaster) G.; m. Helen A. Mataya, June 26, 1949 (div. June 1984); children—Christina Adrienne, James Willis, John David Nicholas. B.S., Northwestern U., 1946, M.B., M.S., 1949, M.D., 1950. Diplomate Am. Bd. Psychiatry and Neurology. Intern, Charity Hosp., New Orleans, 1949-50; resident in psychiatry U.S. Air Force Med. Corp., 1950-53; chief women's div. Ypsilanti State Hosp., Mich., 1953-55; chief male service-psychiatry Detroit Receiving Hosp., 1955-58, dir. psychiatry, 1958-64; med. dir. Oakland County Community Mental Health Services Bd., 1985—; clin. assoc. prof. psychiatry Wayne State U. Coll. Medicine, Detroit, 1963—; practice medicine specializing in psychiatry, Ann Arbor, Mich., 1954-55, Detroit, 1955-85, Franklin Village, Mich., 1985—; commr. mental health State of Mich., 1959-63; chmn. Pub. Policy Task Force on Mental Health, 1983-84. Mem. Med. Adv. Com. to Pres. Kennedy, 1960-61, Physicians for Social Responsibility, Detroit, 1983—; v.p. Oakland County Interagency Council on Children and Youth; bd. dirs. Comprehensive Health Planning Council of Southeastern Mich., Alliance for Mental Health Services. Served to capt. USAF, 1950-53. Fellow Am. Psychiat. Assn. (life), Am. Pub. Health Assn., Am. Orthopsychiat. Assn.; mem. AMA, Mich. State Med. Soc., Oakland County Med. Soc., Mich. Psychiat. Soc. (councillor 1960-63, v.p. 1984-85, pres. 1986-87). Club: Cajal (Montreal, Que., Can.). Avocations: tennis; distance swimming; sailing; skiing. Home: 254 Lewiston Grosse Pointe Farms MI 48236 Office: Oakland County Community Mental Health Services Bd 1200 N Telegraph Pontiac MI 48053

GRAVES, JOANNE MARIE, personnel manager; b. Seattle, Aug. 12, 1960; d. Douglas Hall and Betty Marie (Olsen) Ames; m. David L. Graves, Feb. 14, 1987. BS, U. Houston, 1983. Mgmt. trainee Mayflower, Stouffer, Washington, 1983-84; personnel mgr. Stouffer Dayton (Ohio) Plaza, 1984—; cons. Greater Dayton Job Tng., 1985—, Pvt. Industry Council, 1986—. Advisor Jr. Achievement, Dayton, 1984—; leader exploring group Boy Scouts Am., Dayton, 1985; group leader Search Bible Study, Centerville, Ohio, 1985—. Mem. Am. Soc. Personnel Adminstrn., Miami Valley Personnel Assn. Republican. Roman Catholic. Avocations: skiing, bicycling, knitting, hiking. Office: Stouffer Dayton Plaza 5th and Jefferson Dayton OH 45402

GRAVES, WILLIAM PRESTON, Kansas secretary of state; b. Salina, Kans., Jan. 9, 1953; s. William Henry and Helen (Mayo) G. BBA, Kans. Wesleyan U., Salina, 1975; postgrad., U. Kans., 1978-79. Dep. asst. sec. of state State of Kans., Topeka, 1980-85, asst. sec. of state, 1985-87, sec. of state, 1987—. Mem. Kans. Cavalry; trustee Kans. Wesleyan U., 1987—; bd. dirs. Kans. Community Service Orgn., Topeka, 1987—. Named Outstanding Young Alumnus, Kans. Wesleyan U., 1978, to Hall of Fame, 1986; named Outstanding Young Kansan, Salina Jaycees and Kans. Jaycees, 1986. Mem. Nat. Assn. Secs. of State, Greater Topeka C. of C. Republican. Methodist. Lodge: Kiwanis. Avocations: running, reading, traveling. Office: Office of Sec State State Capitol 2d Floor Topeka KS 66612

GRAVES, WILLIAM XAVIER, controller; b. Sioux Falls, S.D., Apr. 29, 1955; s. Joseph John and Darlene Josephine (Thom) G.; m. Linda Marie Wingert, Aug. 14, 1976; children: James, Carrie, Robert. BSBA, U. S.D., 1977, MBA, 1985. CPA, Minn., Iowa. Auditor Touche Ross & Co., Mpls., 1977-79; internal auditor Medtronic, Mpls., 1979-80; controller Terra Internat., Inc., Sioux City, Iowa, 1980—. Chmn. Sioux City March of Dimes, 1986. Mem. Am. Inst. CPAs, Beta Gamma Sigma. Roman Catholic. Lodge: Optimists (local pres. 1986—). Avocations: philately, piano.

GRAVLIN, KIM LINWOOD, systems analyst; b. Selridge AFB, Mich., Aug. 5, 1953; s. William Edward and Beverly Joan (Worthington) G.; m. Beverly Jean Wiltshire, June 22, 1974; children: Shawn Alan, Brandy Jean. Student, Community Coll. of Air Force, 1974-75; grad., DeVry Tech. Inst., 1977. Programmer, analyst Grand Traverse County, Traverse City, Mich., 1978-80; systems analyst Bellin Meml. Hosp., Green Bay, Wis., 1980-82; sr. systems analyst O'Sullivan Inds., Inc., Lamar, Mo., 1982—. Served with USAF, 1974-77. Avocations: photography, flying. Home: Rte 3 Box 330B Lamar MO 64759 Office: O'Sullivan Inds Inc 19th & Gulf Lamar MO 64759

GRAY, ALAN I., financial services company executive; b. Chgo., Sept. 20, 1951; s. Seymour and Rae (Kreda) G.; m. Niki Alexandroff, May 26, 1976; children: Jamie Anna, Suzanne Alyse. BS in Acctg., So. Ill. U., 1973. CPA, Ill.; cert. shopping ctr. mgr. Acct. Drebin, Lindquist & Geruasio, Chgo., 1973-76; v.p. sales The Balcor Co., Skokie, Ill., 1976-86, Shearson, Lehman Bros., Chgo., 1987—. Mem. Am. Inst. CPA's, Internat. Assn. Fin. Planners (v.p. membership 1985—), Internat. Council Shopping Ctrs., Ill. CPA Soc. Avocations: golf, reading. Office: Shearson Lehman Bros 3 First National Bank Plaza Suite 3600 Chicago IL 60602

GRAY, AVRUM, manufacturing company executive; b. Chgo., Sept. 13, 1935; s. Joseph Jacob and Mae (Kalis) G.; m. Joyce Taymor, Aug 12, 1962;

children: Lori, James, Matthew. BS in Engring., Purdue U., 1956; PhD, Spertus Coll. of Judaica, 1983. Pres., chief exec. officer Alloy Mfg. Co., Chgo., 1960—; pres. Omni Capital Corp., Chgo., 1978—; sr. ptnr. G-Bar Partnership, Chgo., 1981—. Chmn. Jewish United Fund, Chgo.; bd. overseers Ill. Inst. Tech. Served to 1st lt. U.S. Army, 1956-58. Mem. ASME, Soc. Automotive Engrs., Motor Equipment Mfrs. Assn., Automotive Pres.'s Council. Clubs: Standard (Chgo.), Northmoore Country. Lodge: Elks, B'nai B'rith (bd. dirs.). Home: 1077 Elm Ridge Glencoe IL 60616 Office: Alloy Mfg Co 3205 S Shields Chicago IL 60616

GRAY, CARL THOMAS, architect; b. Montclair, N.J., June 14, 1943; s. Earl Boone and Mary (Dunlap) G.; m. Janet Ann Rulli, Oct. 23, 1976; children: Randall Joseph, Brian Thomas. BArch, Miami U., Oxford, Ohio, 1967. Registered architect, Minn. Archtl. designer Fisk Rhinehart, Cin., 1971-72, Toltz, King, Douvau & Anderson, St. Paul, 1973-74, Steenberg Constrn. Co., St. Paul, 1975-80, Milo Architects and Engrs., St. Paul, 1980-82; pvt. practice architecture St. Paul, 1983—; architect for renovation of Comstock Hall U. Minn., Mpls., 1986—. Mem. Sci. Mus. St. Paul, Minn. Mus. Art. Served with U.S. Army, 1967-70. Mem. AIA (historic resource com.), Minn. State Assn. Architects. Republican. Roman Catholic. Avocation: drawing. Home: 261 Summit Ave Saint Paul MN 55102 Office: U Minn Shopps Bldg 319 15th Ave S Minneapolis MN 45455

GRAY, COLIN LESTER, insurance executive, accountant; b. Dublin, Ireland, Dec. 24, 1956; came to U.S., 1979; s. George and Phyllis (Connor) Gray; m. Paula Kuhn, Nov. 29, 1979 (div. Dec. 1982); m. Cynthia Ban, Oct. 19, 1985; 1 child, Hilary Joy. BBA, Trinity Coll., Dublin, 1978. CPA, Ill. Accountant Deloitte, Haskins & Sells, Dublin, 1978-79, Chgo., 1979-80; sr. accountant Conticommodity Services, Chgo., 1980-84; asst. v.p. Crum & Forster Mgrs. Corp., Chgo., 1984—; cons. Granum Agy., Chgo., 1984-86. Mem. Am. Inst. CPA's, Ill. Inst. CPA's. Baptist. Home: 4140 N Kostner Ave Chicago IL 60641 Office: Crum & Forster Mgrs Corp 200 S Wacker Ave Chicago IL 60606

GRAY, DAHLI, accounting educator; b. Grand Junction, Colo., Dec. 28, 1948; d. Forrest Walter and Mary (Crockett) G.; m. Paul Victor Konka, Jan. 23, 1981. BS, Ea. Oreg. State U., 1971; MBA, Portland (Oreg.) State U., 1976; D of Bus. Adminstrn., George Washington U., 1984. Instr. acctg. Portland State U., 1976-79, George Mason U., Fairfax, Va., 1980, George Washington U., Washington, 1981-82; asst. prof. Oreg. State U., Corvallis, 1983-86; research fellow U. Notre Dame, South Bend, Ind., 1986—. Contbr. articles to profl. jours. Named Tchr. of Yr., Alpha Lambda Delta, 1986; Peat Marwick Mitchell & Co. fellow, 1986. Mem. Internat. Assn. Acctg. Research and Edn., Am. Inst. CPA's, Nat. Assn. Accts. (Andrew Barr award 1982, 84, Cert. Merit 1982), Am. Acctg. Assn., Inst. Cert. Mgmt. Accts. Democrat. Home: 4340 Wimbleton Ct Apt H South Bend IN 46637 Office: U Notre Dame Coll Bus Notre Dame IN 46556

GRAY, DON NORMAN, chemist; b. Carlyle, Ill., July 28, 1931; s. Garold Norman and Mary Louisa (Shoupe) G.; BS in Chemistry, Colo. State U., 1953; PhD in Chemistry, Colo. U., Boulder, 1956; m. Mary Kelly, Oct. 10, 1959; children: Christy Elizabeth, Andrew Kelly, Jane Moore. Faculty Denver U., staff Denver Research Inst., 1956-63; scientist Martin Marietta Aerospace, Balt., 1963-66; mgr. biotechnology and toxicology Owens-Illinois, Toledo, 1966-85; pres. Anatrace, Maumee, Ohio, 1985—. Mem. Am. Chem. Soc., N.Y. Acad. Scis., Am. Soc. Artificial Internal Organs, Sigma Xi. Inventor Biobland plastics; contbr. writings to profl. publs.; patentee. Home: 5503 Brixton Dr Sylvania OH 43560

GRAY, GEORGIA NEESE, banker; b. Richland, Kans.; d. Albert and Ellen (O'Sullivan) Neese; A.B., Washburn Coll., 1921; D.B.A. (hon.), 1966; student Sargent's, 1921-22; L.H.D. (hon.), Russell Sage Coll., 1950; m. George M. Clark, Jan. 21, 1929; m. 2d, Andrew J. Gray, 1953. Began as actress, 1923; asst. cashier Richland State Bank, 1935-37, pres., 1937—; pres. Capital City State Bank & Trust Co., Topeka, 1964-74; dir. Capital City State Bank and Trust, Topeka; treas. of U.S., 1949-53; mem. Commn. Jud. Qualifications Supreme Ct. Kans. Del.-at-large nat. adv. com. SBA; Democratic nat. committeewoman, 1936-64; hon. chmn. Villages project C. of C. Bd. dirs. Kans. A.A.A., 1950—; bd. dirs., former chmn. Kans. div. Am. Cancer Soc.; mem. bd. exec. campaign and maj. gifts com. Georgetown U.; bd. dirs. Seven Steps Found., Harry S. Truman Library; chmn. Alpha Phi Found., 1962-63; mem. nat. bd. Women's Med. Coll. Pa.; chmn. bd. regents Washburn U., 1975-86; mem. bd., treas. Sex Information and Edn. Council U.S.; mem. White House Com. on Aging. Recipient Disting. Alumni award Washburn U., 1950. Mem. Am. Bus. Women's Assn., Topeka C. of C., Met. Bus. and Profl. Women's Club, Women in Communications, Alpha Phi (nat. trustee), Alpha Phi Upsilon, Alpha Delta Kappa. Clubs: Soroptimist (hon. life), Met. Zonta, Topeka Country. Address: 2709 W 29 St Topeka KS 66614

GRAY, INA TURNER, fraternal organization administrator; b. Eagleville, Mo., July 25, 1926; d. Farris T. and Teloir (Anderson) Turner; m. Wallace G. Gray Jr., Dec. 18, 1948; children: Toni Jo, Tara Joy. BS with high honors, Cen. Meth. Coll., 1948; MA, Scarritt Coll., 1952; postgrad., U. Hawaii, 1969. Tchr. Rutherford-Met. Sch. Bus., Dallas, 1948-49; dir. Christian edn. 1st Meth. Ch., Lawton, Okla., 1953-54, Winfield, Kans., 1957-58; dir. religious life Southwestern Coll., Winfield, 1958-59; dir. commn. on archives and history Kans. West Conf., Winfield, 1960-78; exec. dir. Pi Gamma Mu, Winfield, 1976—; English tchr. JoGakuin Jr. High, Hiroshima, Japan, 1971-72. Mem. editorial bd. Fire on the Prairie, 1961-69. Mem. Winfield Council for the Arts, 1985; chmn. archives and history com. First United Meth. Ch., 1978—. Mem. Assn. Coll. Honor Socs. (del. 1986—), Commn. Archives and History (local Ch. History award 1982—), Faculty Dames (pres. 1981-82). Republican. Avocations: travel, hist. research. Home: 1701 Winfield St Winfield KS 67156 Office: Pi Gamma Mu 1717 Ames Winfield KS 67156

GRAY, JOHN DOUGLAS, investment banking executive; b. Evanston, Ill., Feb. 15, 1945; s. John D. and Ruth (Campbell) G.; m. April Townley, Oct. 9, 1976 (div. Dec. 1980); m. 2d, Karen Zateslo, June 9, 1984. B.A., Miami U., Oxford, Ohio, 1966; postgrad., U.Chgo., 1966-68; D.H.L. (hon.), Huron Coll., S.D., 1985. With Price Waterhouse, Chgo., Ill., 1969-71; fin. and adminstrn. positions Esmark, Inc-Swift & Co., Chgo., 1971-78; exec. v.p. Swift & Co., 1979-80, Swift Ind. Corp., Chgo, 1980-83; pres., chief operating officer Swift Ind. Packing Corp., Chgo., 1983-86; mng. dir. Morgan Stanley & Co., Inc., Chgo., 1986—; v.p. BRK Electronics Div., Aurora, Ill., 1978-79. Trustee Northwestern Meml. Hosp., Chgo., 1982—; bd. dirs. Rehab. Inst. Chgo., 1984-86, chmn. bd., 1986—; bd. dirs. Leadership of Greater Chgo., 1987—. Clubs: Chgo., Commonwealth; The Links (N.Y.C.); Shoreacres (Lake Bluff, Ill.); Glen View (Golf, Ill.); Old Elm. Avocations: golf, hunting, skiing, swimming. Office: Morgan Stanley & Co Inc 440 S LaSalle 37th Floor Chicago IL 60605 Office: Swift Ind Pkg Co PO Box 650206 Dallas TX 75265-0206

GRAY, KENNETH J., U.S. congressman; b. West Frankfort, Ill., Nov. 14, 1924; m. Gwendolyn June Croslin; children: Diann, Rebecca, Jimmy. Student Army Advanced Sch., World War II. Engaged in automobile business; operated air service, Benton, Ill.; mem. 84th-93d Congresses, 1955-75; 99th-100th Congresses from 22d dist. Ill., 1985—; pres. Ken Gray & Assocs., Bus. Cons.; owner Ken Gray's Antique Car Mus. Founder Walking Dog Found. for Blind, 1950; bd. dirs. Nat. Coal Mus. Served with USAAF, World War II. Mem. Am. Legion, Forty and Eight, VFW. Lodges: Elks, Kiwanis. Office: US House of Representatives 2109 Rayburn House Office Bldg Washington DC 20515

GRAY, MELVIN, psychiatry educator; b. Bklyn., Sept. 9, 1925; s. Morris Eli and Esther (Schwartzman) Grablowsky; m. Leona Wahrsinger (div. Dec. 1983); children: Janine, Michael. Student, U. N.C., 1942-44, Med. Coll. Va., 1944-46; MD, U. Louisville, 1949; postgrad., De Paul U., 1980—. Lic. psychiatrist, Ky., Pa., Ill., Fla.; cert. Am. Bd. Psychiatry and Neurology. Rotating intern U. Ill. Research and Ednl. Hosps., 1949-50, resident in psychiatry, 1953-55; resident in internal medicine VA Hosp., Bklyn., 1950; instr. psychiatry U. Ill. Abraham Lincoln Sch. Medicine, 1955-57, asst. prof. psychiatry, 1957-59; assoc. prof., dir. grad. psychiat. edn. Chgo. Med. Sch., 1959-60; clind. prof. psychiatry Chgo. Coll. Osteopathic Medicine, 1955—; pvt. practice psychiatry Chgo., 1955—; lectr. Cook County Grad. Sch. Medicine, Chgo., 1972-84; cons. psychiatrist Dysfunctioning Child Ctr. Michael Reese Hosp. Respite Care Program, Chgo., 1983-85; med. dir. Total Home Health Care, Chgo., cons. psychiatrist Chgo. Coll. Osteopathic Medicine Ctr. on Aging, 1986—; attending staff Michael Reese Hosp., Chgo., 1983—; cons. staff Columbus/Cuneo/Cabrini Hosps., Chgo., 1973—; cons. physician Grant Hosp., Chgo., 1955—; chmn. dept. of psychiatry Chgo. Coll. Osteopathic Medicine, 1987—. Author: Neuroses: A Comprehensive and Critical View, 1979; also chpts. to books and articles to profl. jours. Served to capt. U.S. Army, 1950-52. Mem. Soc. Philosophy and Psychology, Am. Philosophical Assn., Soc. Phenomenology and Existential Philosophy, Inst. Medicine Chgo., Soc. Med. History Chgo.. Jewish. Home: 2440 N Lakeview Ave Chicago IL 60614 Office: 55 E Washington St Chicago IL 60602

GRAY, MOSES WILLIAM, automotive company executive; b. Rock Castle, Va., Apr. 12, 1937; s. Moses and Ida B. Young; m. Ann Marie Powell, Nov. 22, 1962; children: Tamara Ann, William Bernard. BS in Phys. Edn., Ind. U., 1961. Former lineman N.Y. Jets; with Detroit Diesel Allison div. Gen. Motors Corp., Indpls., 1962—, dir. community relations, 1979-83, mgr. mfg. services, 1983—; bd. dirs. Opportunities Industrialization Ctr., Indpls. Bd. dirs. Ind. Vocat. Tech. Coll., Indpls. Urban League, Indpls. United Way, NAACP, Black Expo (adminstrn. minority vol. award), 100 Black Men of Indpls., WFYI PBS TV, Indpls., Children's Bureau of Indpls., Flanner House, Indpls., Washington High Sch. Partners in Edn., Indpls., The Wilma Rudolph Found.; chmn. Negro Coll. Fund Telethon, Indpls. Bus. Devel. Found., Office of Equal Opportunity, Indpls., Black Adoption Com.; mem. planning com., advisory com. MSD Washington Township, life mem. com. NAACP, Nat. Black Child Devel. Inst. Com.; active participant in numerous community activities. Recipient award Homes for Black Children, 1986; named Citizen of Yr., Omega Psi Phi Fraternity, 1986, Pub. Citizen of Yr., Indpls. chpt. Nat. Assn. Social Workers, 1986; Moses Gray award named in his honor, 1986. Mem. Indpls. C. of C. (mem. corp. community affairs discussion group), Ind. Assn. on Adoption and Child Care Services (Loux Mem. award 1976), Bus. Profls. of Indpls. (Outstanding Achievement in Pub. and Community Service 1982), Sigma Pi Phi. Lodge: B'nai B'rith (named Indpls. Man of the Yr. 1974). Home: 1631 Kessler Blvd W Dr Indianapolis IN 46208 Office: Detroit Diesel Allison div Gen Motors Corp 4700 w 10th St Indianapolis IN 46206

GRAY, NANCY JEAN, marketing and communications specialist, consultant; b. Waterbury, Conn., Nov. 29, 1939; d. William Vernon and Mearl Lauretta (Smith) Sigmon; m. Carl L. Gray, Mar. 14, 1976; stepchildren—Steven, Cheryl. B.S., Manchester Coll., 1966; M.A., U. Dayton, 1984. Tchr. Beavercreek Schs., Dayton, Ohio, 1962, New Madison Schs., Ohio, 1965-72; communication specialist Good Samaritan Hosp. and Health Ctr., Dayton, 1972-85, mktg. specialist, 1986—; producer, host Room to Grow cable TV and FM radio show, 1981-85; workshop presenter Samaritan Ctr. for Youth Resources, Dayton, 1972-85; pres., founder Dayton Area Stepfamily Assn. Am., Inc., 1984—, nat. bd. dirs., 1986—. Vol. social service worker Brethren Vol. Services, 1962-64. Mem. Am. Orthopsychiat. Assn., Sigma Phi Gamma (corr. sec. Kappa Beta chpt. 1984, service sec. 1985-87). Democrat. Avocations: travel; photography; entertainment. Home: 405 Westview Pl Englewood OH 45322 Office: Room to Grow 2222 Philadelphia Dr Dayton OH 45406

GRAY, PATRICIA ANNE, film editor, writer; b. Omaha, Mar. 15, 1960; d. Myles Mclure and Marilyn Ida (Osberg) G. BA in Communications, U. Mich., 1982. Prodn. mgr. R.J. Prodns., Ann Arbor, Mich., 1983-85; stage mgr., producer Performance Network Theatre, Ann Arbor, 1985-86; asst. editor Image Express, Southfield, Mich., 1986—; sound editor Monolith Pictures, Ann Arbor, 1986, Weekend Entertainment, Mt. Clemens, Mich., 1986. Coordinator Rep. Phone Bank, Cedar Rapids, Iowa, 1984. Mem. Detroit Producers Assn., Mensa. Avocations: photography, graphic art, nordic mythology, bicycle touring, travel. Address: 4153 Commonwealth Detroit MI 48208 Office: Image Express 15565 Northland Dr Southfield MI 48075

GRAY, RICHARD, art dealer, consultant, holding company executive; b. Chgo., Dec. 30, 1928; s. Edward and Pearl B. Gray; m. Mary Kay Lackritz, Mar. 28, 1953; children—Paul, Jennifer, Harry. B.Arch., U. Ill., 1951. Pres. The Grayline Co.; sec.-treas. The Edward Gray Corp., 1952-63; prin., dir. GrayCor, 1963—; dir. The Richard Gray Gallery, Chgo., 1963—; lectr., juror, panelist Guggenheim Mus., N.Y.C., Art. Inst. Chgo., Harvard U., U. Ill., Mich. State U., Milw. Art Mus., New Sch. for Social Research, N.Y., Colloquium-The Getty Mus., U. Chgo. Contbr. articles to Chgo. Tribune, Chgo. Daily News, Crain's Chgo. Bus., Chgo. Mag., Collector Investor Mag. Bd. dirs. WFMT, Chamber Music Chgo., Chamber Music Live, Sculpture Chgo.; trustee WTTW Channel 11—Chgo. Pub. TV; bd. dirs., mem. exec. com. Goodman Theatre, Chgo.; chmn. internat. adv. com. Chgo. Internat. Art Exposition; vice chmn. bd. Chgo. Internat. Theater Festival; adv. com. Smithsonian Inst.; bd. dirs. Old Masters Soc., Art Inst. Chgo.; mem. steering com. Friends of the Libraries; mem. capital devel. bd. State of Ill., pub. arts adv. com., selection com. Gov.'s Awards for Arts; mem. nat. adv. bd. Ohio State U. Wexner Ctr. for Visual Arts; former dir. Art Dealers Assn. Am.; former pres. Chgo. Art Dealers Assn.; chmn. Navy Pier Task Force, City of Chgo.; mem. vis. com. U. Chgo. Humanities Div., bd. govs. Alfred Smart Gallery. Mem. Chgo. Pub. Schs. Alumni Assn. (chmn. bd.), Chgo. Council Fgn. Relations (Chgo. com.). Clubs: Chicago, Quadrangle (U. Chgo.), Arts of Chgo. (exhibitions com.). Specialist in contemporary, modern and impressionist masters. Office: Richard Gray Gallery 620 N Michigan Ave Chicago IL 60611

GRAY, TAMMY LYNN, marketing executive; b. Chgo., Apr. 7, 1959; d. William Shipp and Marilyn June (Krause) G. BS in Indsl. Engring., Northwestern U., 1981, M in Mgmt. with distinction, 1986. Engr. Chgo. Bridge & Iron, Memphis, 1981; indsl. engr. Union Carbide Corp., Chgo., 1982-85; product planner Ford Motor Co., Dearborn, Mich., 1986—. Mem. Beta Gamma Sigma, Kappa Delta (v.p. 1980-81). Avocations: traveling, photography, skiing, bicycling. Office: Ford Motor Co Product Planning 20000 Rotunda Dr Dearborn MI 48121

GRAY, THOMAS WARREN, purchasing executive; b. Greenville, Miss., Mar. 16, 1948; s. Arthur L. and Fannie M. (Redmond) G.; divorced; children—Keith, Brian. B.S., Tougaloo Coll., 1969; postgrad. Ind. Central U., 1980-82. Analytical chemist Internat. Harvester, Indpls., 1971-72, prodn. supr., 1972-76, process engr., 1976-79, EEO tng. supr., 1979-80, buyer components group, 1980-82, corporate buyer, Schaumburg, Ill., 1982—; sales advisor Jr. Achievement Central Ind., 1970-73; mem. adv. council Center Leadership Devel., Indpls., 1981-82; mgr. employee services, Navistar Internat. Corp., Schaumburg, 1985—; cons. Nat. Alliance Bus., Washington, 1983—. Mem. planning com. Washington Twp. Sch. System, Indpls., 1979-81; mem. child devel. com. Jewish Community Assn., Indpls., 1980-82; loaned exec. United Way of Greater Indpls., 1981; treas. Trinity Ch. Young Adult Task Force, Indpls., 1981-83. Served with U.S. Army, 1969-75. Recipient Acad. Scholarship, Tougaloo Coll., 1969; Disting. award Center for Leadership Devel., 1981. Mem. Am. Foundrymen Soc. (dir. Central Ind. 1978-81), Alpha Phi Alpha (Man of Yr. 1981). Methodist. Home: 205 Regency Dr Bloomingdale IL 60108 Office: Navistar Internat Corp 600 Woodfield Dr Schaumburg IL 60196

GRAYE, GERARD EDWARD, automotive engineer; b. Detroit, Oct. 13, 1952; s. Chester Anthony and Stephanie Julia (Krzywda) Gay; m. M. Christine Gerstenberg, Nov. 16, 1974. BSME, Gen. Motors Inst., 1975; MBA, U. Mich., Flint, 1984. Gen. supr. mfg. Chevrolet Detroit Gear and Axle div. Gen. Motors Corp., 1977-79, coordinator budget and Computer systems, 1979; salaried employee tng. Chevrolet Detroit Gear & Axel div. Gen. Motors Corp., 1980, gen. supr. plant ops., 1980-84; sr. project engr. Advanced Engring. Staff div. Gen. Motors Corp., Warren, Mich., 1982-84, supr. devel. engring., 1984—. Patentee robotic assembly cell. Republican. Roman Catholic. Clubs: Atlas Valley Golf, Rockwell Springs Trout. Avocations: golf, fishing, equestrian sports. Home: 6390 Park Trail Dr Clarkston MI 48016 Office: Gen Motors Corp Advanced Engring Staff 30300 Mound Rd Warren MI 48090-9040

GRAYSON, DAVID S., paper company executive; b. Binghamton, N.Y., Oct. 16, 1943; s. Milton M. and Helen A. (Oretskin) G.; m. Wendy W. Grayson (div. June 1986); children: Natalie, Marc, Dana. BS, Coll. Forestry, Syracuse, N.Y., 1965; MS, Rensselaer Poly., 1967. Various positions Riegel Paper div. James River Co., Milford, N.J., 1967-80; sales mgr. Kerwin Paper, Appleton, Wis., 1980-81; pres., founder Am. Fine Paper, Appleton, 1981—. Mem. Moses Montiflore Temple Bd., Appleton, 1983-86. Republican. Jewish. Home: Willow Creek Apt 48 1401 S Nicolet Rd Appleton WI 54914 Office: Am Fine Paper 103 W College Ave Suite 1125 Appleton WI 54911

GRAYSON, LEONARD DAVID, allergist; b. Bklyn., Aug. 20, 1921; s. Irving and Elizabeth (Maller) G.; m. Rosalin Esther Berman, Dec. 25, 1946; children: Laura Susan Grayson Timmerwilke, Elizabeth, Gail Grayson Leach, Mitchell. BS, Long Island U., 1943; MB, Chgo. Med. Sch., 1950, MD, 1951; postgrad., NYU, 1951-53. Cert. Am. Bd. Dermatology, Am. Bd. Allergy and Immunolgy. Preceptor Dr. Marion Sulzberger, N.Y.C., 1953-55; dermatologist, then allergist Physicians and Surgeons Clinic, Quincy, Ill., 1955—; clin. asst. NYU Coll. Medicine, Bklyn., 1954-55; asst. clin. medicine Washington U. Med. Sch., St. Louis, 1963-70; clin. assoc. So. Ill. U. Med. Sch., Springfield, 1979—; cons. McDonough Dist. Hosp., Macomb, Ill., 1959—, Macon Dist Hosp., Havana, Ill., 1959—, Meml. Hosp., Carthage, Ill., 1959—; lectr. in field, 1956—. Editor Adams County Mental Health Bulletin, 1962; contbr. articles to profl. jours. Pres. Community Little Theatre, Quincy, Ill, 1958; mem. health arts adv. com. John Woods Community Coll., Quincy, 1978-79. Served with U.S. Army, 1943-46, PTO, USPHS, 1950-51. Fellow Am. Coll. Allergists, Am. Acad. Dermatology, Am. Geriatric Soc., Am. Acad. Allergy, Ma. Assn. Clin. Immunology & Allergy, Am. Assn. Cert. Allergists. Republican. Hebrew. Lodge: Optimist (editor Quincy 1960-61). Avocations: computers, tennis, golf. Home: 2109 N Wilmar Dr Quincy IL 62301 Office: Physicians and Surgeons Clinic 1101 Maine St Quincy IL 62301

GRAZIANO, CHARLES DOMINIC, pharmacist; b. Cariati, Italy, June 28, 1920; s. Frank Dominic and Marianna (Bambace) G.; student Dowling Jr. Coll., 1939, 40; B.S. in Pharmacy, Drake U., 1943; m. Corrine Rose Comito, Feb. 5, 1950; children—Craig Frank, Charles Dominic II, Marianne, Kimberly Rose, Mark, Suzanne. Pharamacist Kings Pharmacy, Des Moines, 1946-47; partner Bauder Pharmacy, Des Moines, 1948-61, owner, 1962—. Mem. Des Moines Art Center. Served with AUS, 1943-45; ETO. Decorated Bronze Star. Named Drake U. Parent of the Year, 1983-84. Mem. Des Moines C. of C., Nat. Assn. Retail Druggists, Iowa, Polk County pharm. assns., St. Vincent de Paul Soc., Am. Pharm. Assn., Phi Delta Chi. Roman Catholic. Office: 3802 Ingersoll Ave Des Moines IA 50312

GREATHOUSE, FERN LUCILLE, social worker; b. Garden City, Kans., Nov. 15, 1924; d. Ralph Goodman and Viola Fern (Collins) Greathouse. BA in Edn., Wichita State U., 1957. Lic. social worker, Kans. Tchr. Finney County (Kans.) Rural Schs., 1942-46; sec. 1st United Meth. Ch. Garden City, 1946-51; tchr. Shawnee Mission (Kans.) Pub. Schs., 1955-71; social worker Kans. Dept. Social and Rehab. Services, Garden City, 1971-78; dir. social services St. Catherine Hosp., Garden City, 1978—. Active Garden City Friends of the Zoo. Mem. Nat. Assn. Social Workers, Kans. Conf. on Social Welfare, Kans. Soc. Hosp. Social Work Dirs. (pres. Sunflower chpt. 1985—), Nat. Assn. Hosp. Social Work Dirs., Nat. Com. for Prevention Child Abuse, Kans. Com. for Prevention Child Abuse. Home: 623 Magnolia Box 531 Kansas City KS 67846 Office: 608 N 5th St Garden City KS 67846

GREATON, KAREN MARGUERITE, jewelry store executive; b. St. Paul, Jan. 19, 1948; d. W. Eben and Geraldine Evelyn (Swanson) G.; m. Daniel Michial Hoverman, Nov. 14, 1974 (div. Jan. 1983); m. William Charles Gillespie, Mar. 24, 1984; 1 child, Robert Eben Greaton Gillespie. Student Patricia Stevens Sch. (now Lowthian Coll.), 1966-67, Gemol. Inst. Am. Mgr. Patricia Stevens Sch. (now Lowthian Coll.), Mpls., 1967-70; employment counselor Assoc. Clerical Specialists, Mpls., 1970-72; mgr., counselor Roth Young-Clerical div., Mpls., 1972-74; mgr. Greaton's Jewelers, Inc., New Richmond, Wis., 1975-84, pres., 1984—. Mem. New Richmond C. of C. (chmn. retail com. 1977, bd. dirs. 1977-79, Appreciation award 1979), Hist. Soc. New Richmond. Republican. Methodist. Lodge: Jobs Daus. (hon. queen 1965). Avocations: breeding Old English sheepdogs; aquariums; photography; aerobics; skiing. Home: 454 S Hill Dr New Richmond WI 54017 Office: Greatons Jewelers Inc 224 S Knowles Ave New Richmond WI 54017

GREBENS, GEORGE, executive management consultant; b. June 12, 1943; m. Katherine Panon, Sept. 3, 1972; 1 dau., Alexandra. B.A. in European Studies, U. Montreal (Can.), 1966; M.A. in Internat. Relations Mgmt., Mich. State U., 1968, Ph.D. in Internat. Relations, Bus. and Indsl. Mgmt., 1972. Instr., lectr. Oberlin Coll. (Ohio), 1970; asst. prof. European studies U. Ky., Lexington, 1972-74; asst. prof. Area studies Tex. A&M U., College Station, 1974-78, internat. engring. cons., dir., 1978-80; policies and proceduresmgmt. auditor, internat. clients Daniel/Parsons, 1980-82; directrate staff asst. at internat. airports, exec. planner, Bechtel, Middle East, 1982-84, ABCL-KKIA/KFIA Riyadh and Damman, Saudi Arabia, 1982-84; asst. to dir., planning cons. in industry and airports ATW, 1984-85; exec. indsl. mgmt. cons., exec. dir., indsl. mgmt. and corp. planning Internat. Kensing Cons., 1985—. Author: Theory of Soviet Science, 1978; Before the Beginning, 1979; contbr. articles to profl. jours., 1975-78. Mich. State U. fellow, 1968-70. Mem. AAAS, Am. Mgmt. Assn. Mailing Address: 323 S Franklin Blvd S804/K20 Chicago IL 60606

GREEN, ALLISON ANNE, educator; b. Flint, Mich., Oct. 5, 1936; d. Edwin Stanley and Ruth Allison (Simmons) James; m. Richard Gerring Green, Dec. 23, 1961 (div. Oct. 1969). B.A., Albion Coll., 1959; M.A., U. Mich., 1978. Cert. tchr., Mich. Tchr. phys. edn. Southwestern High Sch., Flint, 1959-62; tchr. math. Harry Hunt Jr. High Sch., Portsmouth, Va., 1962-63; receptionist Tempcon, Inc., Mpls., 1963-64; tchr. phys. edn. and math. Longfellow Jr. High Sch., Flint, 1964-81, tchr. math., 1981-87, tchr. lang. arts and social studies, 1986-87. Mem. Fair Winds council Girl Scouts U.S.A., 1943—, leader Lone Troop, Albion, Mich., 1957, sr. tchr. aide adviser, 1964-67; mem. Big Sisters Genesee and Lapeer Counties, 1964-68; mem. adminstrv. bd. Court St. United Methodist Ch.; treas. edn. work area, mission commn., sec. council on ministries United Meth. Women Soc. Christian Service, also chmn. meml. com. Mem. NEA, Mich. Edn. Assn., Mich. Assn. Mid. Sch. Educators, United Tchrs. Flint (bldg. rep.), Delta Kappa Gamma (treas. 1982—, profl. affairs chmn. 1978-80, legis. chmn. 1980-82), Alpha Xi Delta (pres. Flint, alumnae, v.p., treas., corp. pres. Albion Coll., alumnae dir. province 1972-77, Outstanding Sr. Albion Coll. 1959), Embroiderers Guild Am. (sec. 1977-80, maps rep. 1980-82). Home: 1002 Copeman Blvd Flint MI 48504 Office: 1255 N Chevrolet Ave Flint MI 48504

GREEN, BARBARA CAROL, medical technician, educator; b. Buffalo, Minn., Jan. 19, 1958; d. Leonard Ernest and Dorothy Loraine (Darrow) Rogness; m. Troxel D. Green, Sept. 20, 1980. Student, Northwestern Bible Coll., 1976-77; cert. med. lab. technician, Northwest Inst. Med. Tech., 1979. Head lab. and x-ray dept. Offices of Dr. Williams et al, St. Paul, 1979-83; head lab. Offices of Dr. Ralph Olsen, Brookfield, Wis., 1983-84; chief med. technician Clin. Lab. Cons., Milw., 1984-86; head lab., educatorfamily practice residents in clin. lab. medicine Waukesha (Wis.) Meml. Hosp., 1986—. Singer Elmbrook Ch. Choir, Waukesha, 1987—. Mem. Am. Med. Technologist Assn. Republican. Avocations: calligraphy, biking, embroidery, skiing. Home: 2723 N University Dr #203E Waukesha WI 53188 Office: Waukesha Family Practice Clinic 434 Madison St Waukesha WI 53188

GREEN, DANIEL FRANK, dentist; b. Upper Sandusky, Ohio, July 17, 1953; s. Amel K. and Genelle C. (Levitt) G.; m. Cynthia Ann Scott, Jan. 12, 1979; children: Jill Erin, Elaina Nelle, Chelsea Elizabeth. BS, DDS, Ohio State U., 1977. Pvt. practice dentistry Chillicothe, Ohio, 1977—; co-dir. Frankfort (Ohio) Dental, 1985—. Pres. Burton Stevenson Soc., 1984; bd. dirs., v.p. Speech and Hearing Bd., Ross COunty, 1978-84. Mem. ADA, Rehwinkle Dental Soc., Ohio Dental Assn., Jaycees (pres. 1984). Avocations: tennis, sailing, golf, kids. Home: 41 Timberlane Dr Chillicothe OH 45601 Office: 265 N Woodbridge Ave Chillicothe OH 45601

GREEN, DAVID, manufacturing company executive; b. Chgo., Mar. 22, 1922; s. Harry B. and Carrie (Scheinbaum) G.; m. Mary I. Winton, June 15, 1951; children—Sara Edmond, Howard Benjamin, Jonathan Winton. B.A. in Econs., U. Chgo., 1942, M.A. in Social Scis., 1949. Mgr., Toy Co., Chgo., 1949-54; founder, pres. Quartet Mfg. Co., Skokie, 1954—; pres. Colleague, Inc., Booneville, Miss., 1967—; chmn. bd. and cons. DG Group, Chgo., 1977—; chmn. Quartet Ovonics, 1986—. Spl. cons. to White House-Trade Expansion Act, Washington, 1962; chmn. Winnetka Caucus (Ill.), 1971; chmn. Ill. state Dan Walker for Gov., 1972, 76; spl. asst. to Gov. for intergovtl. relations, Ill., 1973-76. Served with U.S. Army, 1942-45, PTO. Mem. Nat. Office Products Assn., Wholesale Stationers' Assn. Clubs: Metropolitan (Chgo.); Pelican Bay (Naples, Fla.). Home: 969 Tower Manor Dr Winnetka IL 60093 Office: Quartet Mfg Co 5700 Old Orchard Rd Skokie IL 60077

GREEN, DAVID FERRELL, city official; b. Sioux Falls, S.D., Nov. 13, 1935; s. John C. and Mary A. (Meyer) G.; m. Renata M. Kappenman, Apr. 15, 1961; children—Tobin L., Anthony F., Thomas D. B.A. summa cum laude, Augustana Coll., Sioux Falls, 1980; postgrad. U. S.D., 1981—; grad. FBI Nat. Acad., 1972; Juvenile Officers Inst., 1966. Cert. police officer; cert. police firearms instr. Dispatch dept. mgr. Sioux Falls Argus Leader, S.D., 1954-58; with Sioux Falls Police Dept., 1958—, patrol officer, 1958-63, sgt., 1963-68, lt., 1968-71, capt., 1971-82, chief, 1982—; mem. NCIC Policy Bd. Justice Dept., Washington, 1976-78; mem. NCIC North Central Group, 1978—, State Juvenile Task Force; vice chmn. Gov.'s Police Task Force S.D., 1979-81. Bd. dirs. Vol. Nat. Ctr. for Citizen Involvement, Washington, 1978-81, St. Therese Sch. Bd., Sioux Falls, pres., 1973-74; pres. Vol. Action Ctr., Sioux Falls, 1979-80; treas. found. bd. Little Flower Sch. Served with USNR, 1953-61. Recipient J. Edgar Hoover award Justice Dept., 1972; Jaycees Officer Yr. award Sioux Falls Jaycees, 1972; named to Augustana Coll. Honor Soc., 1980. Mem. Fraternal Order of Police (trustee 1971-83, chmn. bd. trustees 1979-83, Outstanding Service award 1983), Am. Soc. Pub. Adminstrs., Internat. Assn. Police Chiefs, S.D. Police Chief's Assn., Tri-State Peace Officers Assn. (v.p. 1972-73), S.D. Peace Officers Assn. Republican, Am. Legion. Roman Catholic. Clubs: Flatlander's Muzzle-Loading (Garretson, S.D. pres. 1980-82); Split-Rock Muzzle-Loading (Baltic, S.D.). Lodges: Elks, K.C. Office: Office of the Police Chief 505 N Dakota Ave Sioux Falls SD 57104

GREEN, DONALD JOSEPH, information systems analyst, programmer, manufacturing consultant; b. O'Neill, Nebr., Jan. 18, 1953; s. Lyle M. and Jennie M. (Neyens) G.; m. Nancy E. Larson, June 14, 1975; children: Thomas Allan, Elizabeth Jennie. BS in Computer Sci., U. Nebr., 1975. Computer cons. U. Nebr., 1973-75; programmer Agrl. Network U. Nebr., 1975, Fed. Land Bank, Omaha, 1976-78; lead analyst and programmer Vickers Inc., Omaha, 1978—. Air Force ROTC scholar U. Nebr., 1972-75. Mem. Am. Prodn. Inventory Control Soc. (treas. and sec. 1978-80, cert. prodn. and inventory mgmt. 1980), U. Nebr. Alumni Assn., Upsilon Pi Epsilon. Republican. Roman Catholic. Club: Big Red Apple (Norfolk, Va.) (contbr. author). Avocations: family, golf, racquetball, coaching youth sports. Home: 3204 S 128th Ave Omaha NE 68144 Office: Vickers Inc 6600 N 72d St Omaha NE 68122

GREEN, GEORGE DALLAS (DALLAS GREEN), professional baseball team executive; b. Newport, Del., Aug. 4, 1934; s. George Dallas and Mayannah Sealy (Jones) G.; m. Sylvia Lowe Taylor, Jan. 31, 1958; children: Dana, John, Kim, Douglas. Student, U. Del., 1952-55, B.B.A., 1981. Former profl. baseball player Phila. Phillies; asst. dir., then dir. minor leagues and scouting Phila. Phillies Profl. Baseball Team, 1969-79, mgr. parent team, 1979-82; exec. v.p., gen. mgr. Chgo. Cubs, 1982-84, pres., gen. mgr., 1984—. Trustee Del. Found. Retarded Children. Office: Chgo Cubs Orgn Wrigley Field Addison at Clark St Chicago IL 60613 *

GREEN, GREGORY ALAN, contracting firm executive, real estate developer; b. Dayton, Ohio, Mar. 3, 1947; s. Birchel Green and Charlotte Elizabeth (Whitman) Farkas; m. Sandra Kay Rossi, Apr. 3, 1971; children: Gregory Michael, Jodi Michelle. BS, Ohio State U., 1970. Regional mgr. McKesson div. Narco Aviation, Toledo, 1970-73; dir. field engring. Acuity Systems Inc., McLean, Va., 1973-75; pres. G.A. Green and Assocs., Columbus, Ohio, 1975—; pres., chief exec. officer A.K. Greg-Sand, Inc., Columbus, 1982-86, Mktg. Connections, Columbus, 1986—; cons. Ohio Atty. Gen, Columbus, 1982—, Ohio Ins. Assn., Columbus, 1980—; consumer advocate Ohio Atty. Gen., Columbus, 1980—. Sponser Big Bros. and Big Sisters, Columbus, 1976. Mem. Am. Chem. Soc., Ohio Plumbing Inspectors Assn., Plumbing, Heating and Cooling Contractors Assn., Nat. Employee Service and Recreation Assn., Mkt. research Assocs, Am. Mktg. Assn, North Columbus Jaycees, Theta Chi. Roman Catholic. Avocations: wilderness camping, private pilot, scuba diving, photography. Home: 5194 Maplewood Court W Columbus OH 43229 Office: PO Box 29613 Columbus OH 43229

GREEN, HARWOOD, quality assurance executive; b. Boston, Feb. 10, 1956; s. Victor J. and Shirley M. Green. BA, Duke U., 1978; postgrad. bus. adminstrn. program Babson Coll., 1978-80. Cert. quality engr. Quality control technologist New Eng. Nuclear, Billerica, Mass., 1974-77, spl. projects engr. quality assurance, 1978-79, process engring. supr., 1980; tech. rep. Gelman Scis., Ann Arbor, Mich., 1981, sr. tech. cons., 1982, mgr. corp. quality assurance, 1983-85, dir. corp. quality assurance, 1985-86, dir. mfg., 1986—. Mem. Am. Mgmt. Assn., Internat. Soc. Pharm. Engrs., Parenteral Drug Assn., Am. Soc. Quality Control. Office: Gelman Scis 600 S Wagner Rd Ann Arbor MI 48106

GREEN, JERRY HOWARD, banker; b. Kansas City, Mo., June 10, 1930; s. Howard Jay and Selma (Stein) G.; B.A., Yale U., 1952; m. Betsy Bozarth, July 18, 1981. Pres., Union Chevrolet, 1955-69, Union Securities, Inc., Kansas City, Mo., 1969—, Union Bancshares, Inc., Kansas City; chmn. Union Bank, Kansas City, 1976—, Budget Rent-A-Car of Mo., Inc., 1961—, Budget Rent-A-Car of Memphis, Inc.; chmn., dir. Security Bank & Trust Co., Branson, Mo., 1979—; pres. Douglas County Bancshares, Kansas City, Taney County Bancorp., Kansas City, 1981—, Pembroke Bancshares, Kansas City, Mo., 1983—; chmn., dir. Citizens Bank, Ava, Mo., 1980—; dir. Century City Artists Corp., Los Angeles, Union Bank, Kansas City, Citizens Nat. Bank, Ft. Scott, Kans. Bd. dirs. Boys' Clubs Kansas City, Jackson County Pension Plan Com. chmn. Yale Class of 1952 Reunion Gift. Served to 1st lt. USAF, 1952-55. Mem. Am. Bankers Assn., Yale Alumni Assn. (bd. dirs.). Republican. Clubs: Kansas City, Oakwood Country, Saddle and Sirloin. Home: 5200 Belleview Kansas City MO 64112 Office: Union Bank 12th and Wyandotte Kansas City MO 64105

GREEN, JOSEPH MARTIN, psychiatrist, educator; b. Mt. Horeb, Wis., July 19, 1925; s. Joseph Marinus and Agnes Helene (Dahle) G.; m. Ruth Mary Fenner, June 17, 1952 (div. Dec. 1975); children: Richard C., Karen S., Jeffrey M. Student, U. Wis., 1946-48; MD, Northwestern U., 1952. Diplomate Am. Bd. Psychiatry and Neurology, Am. Bd. Child Psychiatry. Intern in psychiatry Wesley Meml. Hosp., Chgo., 1952-53; resident and fellow in psychiatry Menninger Found., Topeka, 1953-57; clin. dir. Kans. Treatment Ctr. for Children, Topeka, 1956-59; practice medicine specializing in child psychiatry Tucson, 1961-73; med. dir. for children LaFrontera Ctr., Tucson, 1973-76; dir. of child and adolescent psychiatry U. Wis., Madison, 1976—; mem. gov.'s adv. com. on mental health, Phoenix, Ariz., 1965-66; cons. Arizona Acad., Phoenix, 1968; chief examiner Am. Bd. Psychiatry and Neurology, Evanston, Ill., 1974-82; del. Am. Bd. Med. Specialties, Chgo., 1974-75; councillor psychiatry Joint Commn. Accreditation of Hosps., Chgo., 1977-79; cons. NIMH, Washington, 1977-81; faculty to gov.'s Spouses Seminar, Madison, Wis., 1986. Author: (with others) Basic Handbook of Child Psychiatry, 1979; contbg. author Group for Advancement of Psychiatry pubs., 1972, 73, 82, Internat. Encyclopedia Neurol Psychiatry, Psychoanalysis and Psychology, 1977; reviewer Am. Jour. Psychiatryand Journ. Child Psychiatry, 1971, 75, 76, 78, 79, 80, 82. Founding bd. dirs. Big Bros. Tucson, 1964-67. Served as pvt. U.S. Army, 1943-46, ETO. Fellow Am. Psychiat. Assn. (pres. Ariz. chpt. 1966-67, pres. Wis. chpt. 1981-82), Am. Orthopsychiat. Assn. (v.p. 1973-74), Am. Acad. Child Psychaitry (councillor 1983-86); mem. AMA (residency review com. for psychiatry 1978-82), Soc. Profs. Child Psychiatry (pres. 1986—), Group Advancement Psychiatry (com. chmn. 1972-76). Democrat. Avocations: hiking, canoeing, cross-country skiing, reading. Home: 13 Gray Birch Terr. Madison WI 53717 Office: U Wis Dept Psychiatry 600 Highland Ave Madison WI 53792

GREEN, JOYCE, book publishing company executive; b. Taylorville, Ill., Oct. 22, 1928; d. Lynn and Vivian Coke (Richardson) Reinerd; A.A., Christian Coll., 1946; B.S., MacMurray Coll., 1948; m. Warren H. Green, Oct. 8, 1960. Assoc. editor Warren H. Green, Inc., St. Louis, 1966-78, dir., 1978—; v.p. Visioneering Advt. Agy., 1972—; exec. sec. Affirmative Action Assn. Am., 1977—; pres. InterContinental Industries, Inc., 1980—; asst. to pres. Southeastern U., New Orleans, 1982-86; mem. bd. regents, v.p. adminstrn. No. Utah U., Salt Lake City, 1986—. Mem. Am. Soc. Profl. and Exec. Women, Direct Mktg. Club St. Louis, C. of C. Democrat. Methodist. Clubs: Jr. League, World Trade, Clayton, Media. Home: 12120 Hibler Dr Creve Coeur MO 63141 Office: 8356 Olive Blvd Saint Louis MO 63132

GREEN, KAREN, health executive, consultant; b. Milw., Apr. 18, 1940; d. Nathan and Myn (Apter) Paschen; children—Charles, Roberta; m. Richard Tarney, Oct, 6, 1985. B.S. with honors, U. Wis.-Milw., 1978, M.S. in Nursing, 1982. In-service dir. Colonial Mayor, Milw., 1979; teaching asst. U. Wis.-Milw., 1982, lectr., 1984; v.p. Wis. div., cons., Lifegain, Milw., 1978—; pres. Karen Green & Assocs., Milw., 1979—; instr. Med. Coll. Wis., Milw., 1984—. Wis.; guest speaker, workshop creator-presentor. Reviewer: Applied Nursing Diagnosis, 1985; contbr. articles to profl. jours.; reviewer books. Coordinator Congregation Emanu-El Program on Grief, Loss, Milw., 1979; tng./support group U. Wis. Extension-Grief and Loss, Milw., 1980-81; asst. dir. pub. relations Milw. Jewish Fedn., 1970-71; fundraiser Wis. Kidney Found., Milw. Mem. Am. Nurses Assn., Nat. League Nursing, Women's Welfare Bd., Wis. Nurses Assn., Wis. Speakers Assn. Club: Toastmasters (Milw.) (sec. 1980-81). Avocations: writing; bicycling; walking; swimming; travel. Office: 603 Mulberry Ct PO Box 17705 Milwaukee WI 53217

GREEN, LENNIS HARRIS, psychologist; b. Indpls., July 14, 1940; d. William James and Anna Jane (McLane) Harris; m. Burdette L. Green, Sept. 11, 1965. BS, Ohio State U., 1962, MA, 1966, PhD, 1971. Lic. psychologist, Ohio. Pvt. practice psychology, forensics Columbus, Ohio, 1968—; program dir. Lattie Lazarus Counseling Ctr., Columbus, 1971-72; bd. dirs. North Area Mental Health, Inc., Columbus, 1980-85, clin. cons., 1985—; clin. cons. Midwest Career Ctr., Columbus, 1985—, Worthington Counseling Ctr., Columbus, 1986—; prin. research investigator, Proctor Fund, Honolulu, 1984. Contbr. articles to mags. Del. Nigerian Consultation, Episc. Ch., Geneva, Switzerland, 1983; bd. dirs. Transcultural Family Inst., Columbus, 1983-84. Behavioral and Sci. Inst. fellow, U. Hawaii, Honolulu, 1985. Mem. Internat. Council Psychologists, Internat. Assn. Crosscultural Psychology, Am. Psychol. Assn., Am. Anthropology Assn. Avocations: music, arts. Home: 1899 Greenglen Ct Columbus OH 43229 Office: 6290 Busch Blvd Columbus OH 43229

GREEN, LORETTA ANN JONES, sales executive; b. Kansas City, Kans., June 1, 1946; d. Robert G. and Elizabeth Margaret (Schneider) Jones; m. Richard L. Green; 1 child, Stephanie Leigh Jones. BA, Kans. State U., 1973. Mktg. rep. Service Bur. Corp., Kansas City, Mo., 1973-75; territorial mgr. Prince Matchabelli, Kansas City, 1975-78; life ins. agt., estate planner Mass. Mut., 1978-79; dist. sales mgr. G.A.F. Pictoral Products, Kansas City, 1979-81; ter. sales mgr. Houbigant, Inc., Kansas City, 1981-83, dist. sales mgr., 1983—. Rep. precinct capt. Dallas, 1972; mem. Starlight Adv. Bd. Mem. Am. Bus. Women's Assn. (pres. Carrollton chpt.), Carrollton Jaycettes (sec.-treas.). Roman Catholic. Clubs: Kansas City, Woodside Racquet, Pallateers. Home: 8415 Gillette Lenexa KS 66215

GREEN, PAUL MARVIN, financial executive, management consultant; b. Ravenna, Ohio, Sept. 19, 1943; s. Roy and Gladys Adelaid (Allen) G.; m. Donna Rae King, May 4, 1974. BS in Engring., Case Inst. Tech., 1965, MSEE, 1968; MA in Indsl. Econs., Case Western Res. U., 1973; MBA, Harvard U., 1978. Mgr. Bailey Controls, Wickliffe, Ohio, 1965-76; v.p. corp. devel. Infolink Corp., Northbrook, Ill., 1978-85; sr. ptnr. P.M. Green Assocs., Lake Forest, Ill., 1985—; pres. Decision Tree Enterprises, Inc., Lake Forest, 1987—. Author, editor: Money Master, 1987. Mem. Chgo. Venture Capital Network, Harvard Bus. Sch. Club Chgo. Republican. Avocations: sailing, golf. Home: 795 E Longwood Dr Lake Forest IL 60045 Office: Decision Tree Enterprises Inc PO Box 189 Highland Park IL 60035

GREEN, PHILLIP MICHAEL, neurologist, gerontologist; b. Washington, Apr. 20, 1944; s. Samuel and Ann Jeanette (Ralston) G.; m. Sharon Ann Myers, May 27, 1974; children: Joshua, Adrian, Matthew, Ryan. BS, U. Wis., 1965; MD, U. Md., 1969; postgrad., Western Mich. U., 1985—. Diplomate Am. Bd. Psychiatry and Neurology (examiner 1979—), Am. Bd. Neurophysiology. Rotating intern Washington U. Hosps., St. Louis, 1969-70; resident in psychiatry U. Wis., Madison, 1970-71; resident in neurology Barnes Hosp. Group Washington U., 1971-74; neurologist Marshfield (Wis.) Clinic, 1976-82, EEG fellow, 1978-79, chmn. dept. neurology, 1981-82; neurologist Kalamazoo Neurology, 1982—; chmn. dept. geriatric medicine, dir. geriatric medicine Borgess Med. Ctr., Kalamazoo, 1987—; instr. VA Physician's Asst. Program, St. Louis, 1972-74, Sch. Phys. Therapy and Occupational Therapy, Sch. Medicine Washington U., 1973-74; asst. clin. prof. medicine and neurology Eastern Va. Med. Sch., 1975-76; clin. asst. prof. neurology U. Wis., Madison, 1977-82, clin. assoc. prof., 1982; clin. assoc. prof. medicine Mich. State U., Lansing, 1983—; adj. assoc. prof. gerontology Western Mich. U., 1984—. Contbr. numerous articles to profl. jours. Mem. adv. bd. S.Cen. Mich. Commn. on Aging, Kalamazoo, 1985—; active various coms. Marshfield Med. Found. Served to lt. commdr. USN, 1974-76. Recipient William G. Birch Ednl. Excellence award Physicians Assistance Program, 1984, V.K. Volk award Mich. Soc. Gerontology, 1986. Fellow Am. Acad. Neurology, Am. EEG Soc. (ethics and legal relations com. 1979—,vice chmn. 1980—); mem. Am. Epilepsy Soc., Am. Geriatrics Soc., AMA, Am. Soc. Law and Medicine, Cen. EEG Assn. (membership com. 1981—), Clin. Sleep Soc., Soc. Clin. Neurology, Mich. Neurol. Soc., Mich. State Med. Soc. (com. on aging 1984—), Kalamazoo Acad. Medicine (community relations com. 1984—, aging com. 1987—, chmn. liaison com. legal-med. relations 1984—), Wis. Neurol. Soc. (com. on neurol. practice and peer rev. 1977-79, com. on legis. affairs 1979-82, sec.-treas. 1980-81, v.p. 1981-82, rep. to White Ho. Conf. on Aging 1981), State Med. Soc. Wis. (com. on environ. health 1977-79, alt. del. 1980-82, subcom. on brain death 1979-82, com. on aging and longterm care 1981-82), Alzheimer's Disease and Related Disorders Soc. (bd. dirs. 1986—), Kalamazoo Valley Parkinsons Soc. (bd. dirs. 1985—), Midstate Epilepsy Assn. (v.p., bd. dirs. 1979-82). Democrat. Unitarian. Avocation: antiquarian book collecting. Office: Kalamazoo Neurology 1717 Shaffer Rd Kalamazoo MI 49001

GREEN, RICHARD KENNY, physician; b. Council Bluffs, Iowa, Oct. 4, 1939; s. John Clayton and Dorothy Eva (Kenny) G.; m. Doris Shreve Post, Dec. 29, 1962; children: Robert, Barbara. BS, U. Nebr., 1962, MD, 1964. Diplomate Am. Bd. Obsterics and Gynecology. Intern Wesley Med. Ctr., Wichita, Kans., 1964-65; mem. staff Bluffs Gynecology Assocs., Council Bluffs, 1970—; resident U. Nebr. Hosp., Omaha, 1965-68. Served to capt. USAF, 1968-1970. Fellow Am. Coll. Obstetricians and Gynecol. Republican. Mem. United Ch. Christ. Home: 114 Sleepy Hollow Council Bluffs IA 51501 Office: 201 Ridge St Council Bluffs IA 51501

GREEN, RUTH MILTON, college administrator; b. Sioux City, Iowa, Feb. 29, 1924; d. John and Myrtle Alma (Phipps) Milton; m. Robert Wood Green, Dec. 31, 1943; children: Robert William, Sandra Lou Green Montignani. Student, Morningside Coll., 1943-45. Registrar East High Sch., Sioux City, Iowa, 1943; acct. Buehler Bros., Iowa City, 1947-49; asst. dir. tchr. placement Morningside Coll., Sioux City, 1951-55, mem. staff registrar's office, 1960-65, asst. to registrar, 1965-70, dir. spl. project funding, 1971-81, dir. Title III Strengthening Devel. Institutions program, 1975-84, v.p. instl. research, planning and spl. projects, 1984—. Pres. First Congregational Ch., Sioux City, 1980; bd. dirs. Siouxland Mental Health Agy. Named Woman of Excellence, Woman Working Creatively div., 1986. Mem. Nat. Council Univ. Research Adminstrs., Nat. Council Univ. Bus. Officers, Am. Assn. Higher Edn., Council Advancement and Support of Edn., World Future Soc. Democrat. Home: 3801 6th Ave Sioux City IA 51106 Office: Morningside Coll 1501 Morningside Ave Sioudx City IA 51106

GREEN, RUTH NELDA (CUMMINGS), educator; b. Greenway, Ark., Aug. 25, 1928; d. William Harrison and Opal Lee (Davis) G.; B.S. in Edn., U. Omaha (now U. Nebr., Omaha), 1966, postgrad.; m. Robert C. Green, Jr., Apr. 22, 1951 (dec.); children—Dana Lynn Green Schrad, Lisa Jane Green Noon. Tchr., Public Schs. Greenway, 1948-51, Hancock County (Miss.), 1951-53, Bellevue (Nebr.), 1961-86; sec. Nebr. Ornithologists' Union, 1986—. Vol. tchr./naturalist Fontenelle Forest Nature Ctr., 1968—, bd. govs. edn. com. NSF scholar, 1968-73. Mem. NEA, Greater Nebr. Assn. Tchrs. Sci. (state pres. 1984-85), Nebr. Wildlife Assn., Nat. Audubon Soc. (Edn. award 1975), Omaha Audubon Soc., Bellevue Edn. Assn., Nebr. Edn. Assn., Inland Bird Banding Assn., Am. Birding Assn., Nebr. Ornithologists Union (pres. 1982, v.p. 1983-85, bd. dirs., sec. 1986—), Alpha Delta Kappa. Mem. Ch. of Christ. Columnist for Audubon Soc. Omaha Newsletter, Nebr. Ornithologists Union Newsletter. Home: 506 W 31st Ave Bellevue NE 68005 Office: 700 Galvin Rd Bellevue NE 68005

GREEN, WALTER EDGAR, JR., architect; b. Chgo., Sept. 2, 1930; s. Walter Edgar Sr. and Lucy Josephine (Murdock) G.; m. Norma Jean Pruitt, Mar. 17, 1984. BArch, U. Ill., 1952, MArch, 1956. Registered architect, Ill., Ind., Wis., Mo. Draftsman Ralph C. Harris, Chgo., 1952-56; designer Perkins & Will, Chgo., 1956-59; job capt. Harry Weese & Assocs., Chgo., 1959-61; prin. W. E. Green, Wheaton, Ill., 1961—. Author: (audiovisual show): C. S. Frost, Architect, 1982. Served with U.S. Army, 1952-54. Recipient Award of Merit Chgo. Lighting Inst., 1971. Mem. AIA (v.p. Chgo. chpt. 1973), Archtl. Assn. Ill. (del. 1963-65), Ill. Archtl./Engring. Council (del. 1965-66), West Communities Architects (pres. 1971-72), Soc. Archtl. Historians, Nat. Trust for Hist. Preservation, Constrn. Specifications Inst., Wheaton C. of C. (pres. 1983). Mormon. Lodges: Lions (pres. Wheaton). Avocations: travel, art, skiing, genealogy, history. Home: 712 N Summit St Wheaton IL 60187 Office: 117 W Wesley St Wheaton IL 60187

GREEN, WARREN HAROLD, publisher; b. Auburn, Ill., July 25, 1915; s. John Anderson Logan and Clara Christina (Wortman) G.; m. Joyce Reinerd, Oct. 8, 1960. Student, Presbyn. Theol. Sem., 1933-34, Ill. Wesleyan U., 1934-36; M.B., Southwestern Conservatory, Dallas, 1938; M.M., St. Louis Conservatory, 1940, Ph.D., 1942; H.L.D. (hon.), Southeastern U., New Orleans, 1983; L.L.D. (hon.), Institut de Droit Practique, Limoges, France, 1983; D.D. (hon.), Calif. Theol Sem., 1980; Litt.D. (hon.), Confédération Européenne de L' Ordre Judiciaire, France, 1983. Prof. voice, composition, conducting and aural theory St. Louis Conservatory, 1938-44; program dir. U.S.O., Highland Park, Ill., Brownwood, Tex., Orange, Tex., Waukegan, Ill., 1944-46; community service specialist Rotary Internat., Chgo., 1946-47; editor in chief Charles C. Thomas, Pub., Springfield, Ill., 1947-66; pub., pres. Warren H. Green, Inc., St. Louis, 1966—, Warren H. Green Internat., Inc., 1970—; sec. John R. Davis Assos., Chgo., 1955—; exec. v.p. Visioneering Advt., St. Louis, 1966—; mng. dir. Pubs. Service Center, St. Louis, Chgo. and Longview, Tex., 1967—; mng. dir., v.p. InterContinental Industries, Inc., St. Louis, 1976—; cons. U.S., European pubs., profl. socs.; lectr. med. pubs. Civil War. Contbr. articles to profl. jours., books on Civil War history, writing, editing. Mem. Mayor's Com. on Water Safety, Met. St. Louis Art Mus., Mo. Bot. Gardens; chief exec. officer Affirmative Action, Inc., St. Louis, 1974—; pres. Southwestern U., 1984-85, No. Utah U., 1986—. Recipient Presdl. citation for outstanding contbn. export expansion program U.S., 1973, citation Md. Crime Investating Com., 1962, citation Internat. Preventive Medicine Found., 1977, citation AMA, 1978. Mem. Civil War Round Table (v.p. 1969—), Am. Acad. Criminology, Am. Acad. Polit. and Social Sci., Am. Assn. Med. Book Pubs., Am. Judicature Soc., Great Plains Hist. Soc., Co. Mil. Historians, Am. Soc. Personnel Adminstrs., University City C. of C. (pres. 1978—), Internat. Assn. Chiefs of Police, Mo. Hist. Soc., Ill. Hist. Soc., St. Louis Philharmonic Soc. Clubs: Mo. Athletic, Media, Elks, World Trade, Direct Mktg. (St. Louis); Clayton (Mo.). Home: 12120 Hibler Dr Creve Coeur MO 63141 Office: 8356 Olive Blvd Saint Louis MO 63132

GREENBERG, BEVERLY LEE, zoological society administrator; b. Milw., July 6, 1946; d. Jack and Julia (Reitman) Young; m. Martin J. Greenberg, Mar. 29, 1969; children: Kari, Steven. BS in Secondary Edn., U. Wis., Milw., 1968. Tchr. Brookfield (Wis.) Cen., 1968-72, Shorewood (Wis.) High, 1979-81, MATC, Milw., 1981—; devel. dir. Zool. Soc. Milw. County, Milw., 1984—; cons. Milw. Jewish Fedn., 1981—. Pres. PTO Lake Bluff Sch., Milw., 1978-79, PTA Maple Dale Sch., Milw., 1984-85; bd. dirs. Milw. Jr. Showcase, 1982—, The Theatre Sch. Ltd., Milw., 1983—, Congregation Emanuel B'n Jeshurun, Milw., 1983, Jewish Family-Children's Service, Milw., 1981—. DAR scholar, 1965. Mem. Nat. Soc. Fund Raising Execs., Am. Assn. Zool. Parks and Aquariums, Wis. Tchr. Cert., Nat. Educators Assn., Wis. Communications Assn., Sigma Tau Delta. Avocations: golfing, racquetball, reading. Home: 9429 N Broadmoor Rd M'lwaukee WI 53217 Office: Zool Soc Milw County 10001 W Bluemound Rd Milwaukee WI 53226

GREENBERG, DANIEL ARTHUR, communications educator, writer; b. Detroit, Dec. 21, 1931; s. Israel and Doris (Levin) G.; m. Roslynne Mayer, Dec. 20, 1959; children: Julie Elise, Jonathan Eric, Elizabeth Ann. BA, U. Mich., 1954; MA Theater, Wayne (Mich.) State U., 1962, PhD Mass Communications, 1965. Free-lance theatrical prod. work 1954-55; ct. stenographer Ct. Reporting Service, 1957-61; prof. mass communications dept. Wayne State U., Detroit, 1962-64; bus. mgr. Sta. WTVS-TV, Detroit, 1964-65; prof. Oakland Community Coll., Bloomfield Hills, Mich., 1965—; film critic Observer & Eccentric Newspapers, Detroit area, 1983—, Arts in Rev. OCC-TV, Oakland County, Mich., 1985—; manuscript cons. Macmillan Pub. Co., Random House Inc., Proscenium Pubs., W.C. Brown Co.; programmer and presenter Adat Shalom Ann. Jewish Film Festival, 1983—, programmer and administr. Orchard Ridge Competitive Film Festival. Author: (script) How to Install Your Own Garage Door Opener, documentary commemorating Detroit Sinai Hosp.'s 25th anniversary; contbr. book and theatrical revs. to Film Quar., Choice, others, 1983—. Interviewer U. Mich. Regents-Alumni Scholarship, 1982—. Served with USN, 1955-57. Mem. Am. Film Inst., Soc. Cinema Studies, Univ. Film and Video Assn., Detroit Film Soc. (bd. dirs.), U. Mich. Alumni Assn. (past bd. dirs.). Jewish. Avocations: cycling, reading, photography, carpentry. Home: 32459 Nottingwood Farmington Hills MI 48018 Office: Oakland Community Coll 27055 Orchard Lake Rd Farmington Hills MI 48018

GREENBERG, DAVID BERNARD, engineering educator; b. Norfolk, Va., Nov. 2, 1928; s. Abraham David and Ida (Frenkil) G.; m. Helen Muriel Levine, Aug. 15, 1959 (div. Aug. 1980); children—Lisa, Jan, Jill. B.S. in Chem. Engring., Carnegie Inst. Tech., 1952; M.S. in Chem. Engring., Johns Hopkins U., 1959; Ph.D., La. State U., 1964. Registered profl. engr., La. Process engr. U.S. Indsl. Chem. Co., Balt., 1952-55; project engr. FMC Corp., Balt., 1955-56; asst. prof. U.S. Naval Acad., Annapolis, Md., 1958-61; from instr. to prof. La. State U., Baton Rouge, 1961-74; prof. chem. and nuclear engring. U. Cin., 1974—, head dept., 1974-81; cons. Chem. Systems Lab., Dept. Army, Edgewood, Md., 1981-83, Burk & Assocs., New Orleans, 1970-78; program dir. engring. div. NSF, Washington, 1972-73. Contbr. numerous articles on chem. engring. to profl. jours. Mem. Cin. Mayor's Energy Task Force, 1981—. Served to lt. USNR, 1947-52. Esso research fellow, 1964-65, NSF fellow, 1961. Fellow Am. Soc. for Laser Medicine and Surgery; mem. Am. Inst. Chem. Engrs., Am. Chem. Soc., Am. Soc. for Engring. Edn., Sigma Xi, Tau Beta Pi, Phi Lambda Upsilon. Jewish. Home: 8591 Wyoming Club Dr Cincinnati OH 45215 Office: PO Box 21068 Cincinnati OH 45221

GREENBERG, EVA MUELLER, librarian; b. Vienna, Austria, July 19, 1929; came to U.S., 1939; d. Paul and Greta (Scheuer) Mueller; m. Nathan Abraham Greenberg, June 22, 1952; children—David Stephen, Judith Helen, Lisa Pauline. A.B., Harvard/Radcliffe Coll., 1951; M.L.S., Kent State U., 1975. Head reference McIntire Library, Zanesville, Ohio, 1978; with Lorain Pub. Library, Ohio, 1978-81; head reference Elyria Pub. Library, Ohio, 1981-82; reference librarian adult services Cuyahoga County Pub. Library, Strongsville, Ohio, 1983—. Contbr. articles to profl. jours. Mem. ALA, Ohio Library Assn. (coordinator community info. task force). Home: 34 S Cedar St Oberlin OH 44074 Office: Cuyahoga Public Library 13213 Pearl Rd Strongsville OH 44136

GREENBERG, MARTIN JAY, lawyer, educator, author; b. Milw., Aug. 5, 1945; s. Sol and Phyllis (Schunder) G.; m. Beverly L. Young, Apr. 29, 1969; children—Kari, Steven. B.S., U. Wis., 1967; J.D., Marquette U., 1971. Bar: Wis. 1971. Assoc. Hoyt, Greene & Meissner, Milw., 1971-74, Weiss, Steuer,

Berzowski & Kriger, Milw., 1974-76; ptnr. Greenberg & Boxer, Milw., 1976-78; sole practice, Milw., 1978—; asst. prof. law Marquette U., Milw., 1976-79, adj. prof., 1979—; bd. dirs., pres. Law Projects, Inc.; mem. book revisions com. Wis. Real Estate Examining Bd., 1978—. Mem. brotherhood bd. Congregation Emanu-El B'ne Jeshurun, Milw., 1976-78, treas., 1979—; bd. dirs. Community Coordinated Child Care, Milw., 1976-77, Jewish Nat. Fund, Project Re-Unite; mem. Shorewood (Wis.) Bd. Rev., 1977-81. Served with Wis. N.G., 1968-74. Morris Guten Vets. scholar, 1965; I.E. Goldberg scholar, 1966; Carnegie grantee, 1966; Wis. Student Assn. scholar, 1967; Thomas More scholar, 1969; Francis X. Swietlik scholar, 1971. Mem. ABA, Wis. Bar Assn., Milw. Bar Assn., Wis. Bar Found. (lectr. Project Inquiry 1980-81, Lawyer's Pro Bono Publico award 1978), Marquette U. Law Alumni Assn. (trustee), Jewish Vocat. Service (corp.), Woolsack Soc., Scribes, Tau Epsilon Rho (chancellor grad. chpt. 1972-73). Lodge: Masons. Author: Real Estate Practice, 1976, rev. edit., 1977; Wisconsin Real Estate, 1982; Mortgages and Real Estate Financing, 1982; editor Marquette Law Rev., 1969-71. Home: 9429 N Broadmoor Bayside WI 53217 Office: 1139 E Knapp St Milwaukee WI 53202

GREENBERG, PHILIP ROBERT, accountant, drug wholesaling company executive; b. Chgo., May 12, 1940; s. Max and Lorraine Ruth (Bernberg) G.; m. Barbara Sandra Schulman, June 24, 1962; 1 child, Nancy Tracy. Student, U. Ill., 1958-60; BSBA in Acctg., Roosevelt U., 1960-62. CPA, Ill. Chief acct. Ekco Products, Chgo., 1965-67, Beckley-Cardy, Chgo., 1967-69; controller Ronco Teleproducts, Elk Grove Products, Ill., 1969-77, Jovan Inc., Chgo., 1977-79, Nelson Brothers Furniture, Chgo., 1979-87; fin. officer Dik Drug Co. Inc., Burr Ridge, Ill., 1987—. Treas. Am Shalom, Glencoe, Ill., 1981. Served with U.S. Army, 1962-68. Mem. Am. Inst. CPA's. Avocations: racquetball, softball, basketball, swimming. Home: 695 Lombardy Deerfield IL 60015 Office: Dik Drug Co Inc 160 Tower Rd Burr Ridge IL 60521

GREENBERG, STUART LIONEL, mortgage banker; b. Chgo., Aug. 22, 1941; s. Ralph E. and Hilda Sharon (Stone) G.; m. Marsha Turner, Feb. 17, 1968; children: Jennifer, Jill, Phillip. BA, Roosevelt U., 1965; grad., Northwestern U. Sch. Mortgage Banking, 1975. Cert. mortgage banker, rev. appraiser; lic. real estate broker, Ill. Tchr. Chgo. Pub. Schs., 1965-68; asst. treas. Advance Mortgage Corp., Chgo., 1969-70; loan officer Salk Ward Salk, Chgo., 1971-72; v.p. Republic Mortgage Co., Chgo., 1973-78; exec. v.p. Abacus Group, Chgo., 1978-84; sr. exec. v.p. Focus Real Estate Fin. Co., Chgo., 1984—; also bd. dirs. Focus Real Estate Fin. Co.; mem. faculty real estate dept. Gov.'s State U. Sauk Village, Ill., 1983-84. Contbr. articles to profl. jours. Mem. Ill. Mortgage Bankers Assn. (past pres.), Jr. Real Estate Bd. Chgo.(past pres.), Assn. Indsl. Real Estate Brokers, Chgo. Real Estate Bd., Nat. Assn. Indsl. and Office Parks, Nat. Assn. Corp. Real Estate Execs., Mortgage Bankers Assn. Am., Chgo. Assn. Commerce and Industry, Greater N. Mich. Ave. Assn., Lambda Alpha. Jewish. Clubs: Mid-Day, Monroe, Plaza, Met., River (Chgo.), Meadow (Rolling Meadows, Ill.). Avocations: golf, swimming, cycling, reading, travel. Office: Focus Fin Group Inc 200 W Madison St Chicago IL 60606

GREENBERG, SUZANNE GABRIELLE SCHLICHTMAN, professional recruiting consultant; b. Rockville Ctr., N.Y., May 30, 1961; d. William and Mary (Hynes) Schlichtman; m. Alan Bruce Greenberg, Aug. 12, 1984. BA, John Carroll U., 1983. Employment counselor, service rep. BTR, Inc., Northbrook, Ill., 1983-84; with ITH/Employer's Overload, Midland, Mich., 1984-86; personnel cons. Select Employment Agy., Midland, Mich., 1986—. Eucharistic minister Christian Service Commn. Blessed Sacrament, Midland; mem. Crisis Telephone Service, Big Sister Program. Mem. Am. Soc. for Personnel Adminstrn., Nat. Assn. Personnel Cons., Mich. Assn. Personnel Cons., Valley Soc. Personnel Adminstrs., U.S. Jaycees, Midland Jaycees (bd. dirs. 1985-86, v.p. individual devel. 1986-87, various awards). Roman Catholic. Avocation: softball. Office: Select Employment Agy 415 Jerome St Midland MI 48640

GREENBERGER, NORTON JERALD, physician; b. Cleve., Sept. 13, 1933; s. Sam and Lillian (Frank) G.; m. Joan Narcus, Aug. 10, 1964; children: Sharon, Rachel, Wendy. A.B., Yale U., 1955; M.D., Western Res. U., 1959. Diplomate: Am. Bd. Internal Medicine (sec.-treas. 1980-82). Intern Univ. Hosps., Cleve., 1959-60; resident internal medicine Univ. Hosps., 1960-62; USPHS fellow in gastroenterology Harvard U., 1962-65, Mass. Gen. Hosp., Boston, 1962-65; with Ohio State U., Columbus, 1965-72; dir. div. gastroenterology Ohio State U., 1967-72, prof., 1971-72; prof., chmn. dept. medicine U. Kans., Kansas City, 1972—; mem. Nat. Bd. Med. Examiners, 1971-75; mem. gen. medicine study sect. A, NIH, 1973-76. Author: Gastrointestinal Disorders: A Pathophysiologic Approach, 1976, 3d edit., 1986; (with others) Drug Treatment of Gastrointestinal Disorders; editor: (with others) gastroent. sect. Yearbook of Medicine, 1969—; editor Yearbook for Digestive Diseases, 1984. contbr. articles to med. jours. Recipient Outstanding Teaching award House Staff Dept. Medicine Ohio State U., 1970-71, Outstanding Teaching award Kans. U. Med. Sch. Class of 1978, Outstanding Med. Educator, 1984, 85. Fellow ACP (editorial com. gastroenterology sect. 1975-77, regent 1984—); mem. Am. Fedn. Clin. Research (pres. Midwestern sect. 1973-74), Central Soc. Clin. Research (councilor 1975, pres. 1979-80), N.Y. Acad. Scis., AAAS, Midwestern Gut Club, Am. Gastroent. Assn. (pres.-elect 1983-84, pres. 1984), Am. Soc. Clin. Investigation, Am. Soc. Pharmacology and Exptl. Therapeutics, Assn. Am. Physicians, Assn. Profs. Medicine (pres. 1986-87), Phi Beta Kappa, Sigma Xi, Alpha Omega Alpha. Home: 2611 W 70th Terr Mission Hills KS 66208 Office: U Kans Dept Medicine 39th and Rainbow Sts Kansas City KS 66103

GREENBERGER, PAUL ALLEN, physician, educator; b. Pitts., May 28, 1947; s. Lawrence Fred and Jean (Half) G.; m. Rosalie Simon, Dec. 29, 1974; children: Rachel, Daniel. BS, Purdue U., 1969; MD, Ind. U., 1973. Intern Meth. Hosp., Indpls., 1973; resident in medicine Washington U., St. Louis, 1974-76; allergy, immunology fellow Northwestern U., Chgo., 1976-78, asst. prof. medicine, 1979-83, assoc. prof., 1983—. Contbr. articles to profl. jours. Fellow ACP, Am. Acad. Allergy and Immunology. Office: Northwestern U Dept Medicine 303 E Chicago Ave Chicago IL 60611

GREENBERT, HAROLD C., dentist; b. Detroit, Jan. 25, 1922; s. Max and Clara (Katz) G.; m. Gloria Mae Fox, Aug. 19, 1947; children: Gail Susan, Marcy Ann, Alan Jay. BS, Wayne State U., Detroit, 1939-43; postgrad., U. N.D., 1944; DDS, U. Mich., 1950. Gen. practice dentistry Royal Oak, Mich., 1950-78, Greenbert-Goldin, Troy, Mich., 1978—; also pres. Greenbert-Goldin, Clawson, Mich., 1986—; treas. Foxxivision Inc., Farmington Hills, Mich., 1984-85; cons. Beacon Woods Woodcarvers Assn., Bayonet Point, Fla., 1983-86. Served with inf. AUS, 1943-45, ETO. Decorated Bronze Star (2). Mem. ADA, Mich. Dental Assn., Oakland County Dental Assn., Detroit Dist. Dental Assn., U. Mich. Alumni Assn., Alpha Omega. Club: Tam O'Shanter Country (Orchard Lake, Mich.). Avocation: woodcarving. Home: 33000 Covington Club Dr #50 Farmington Hills MI 48018 Office: 440 S Main St Clawson MI 48017

GREENBLATT, DEANA CHARLENE, educator; b. Chgo., Mar. 13, 1948; d. Walter and Betty (Lamasky) Beisel; B.S. in Edn., Chgo. State U., 1969; M.A. in Guidance and Counseling, Roosevelt U., 1973; m. Mark Greenblatt, June 22, 1975. Tchr., counselor Chgo. Pub. Schs., 1969-75, City Colls. of Chgo. GED-TV, 1976; tchr. Columbus (Ohio) Pub. Schs., 1976—; participant learning exchange, Chgo. Active B'nai B'rith; vol. Right-to-Read, Columbus; mem. Community Learning Exchange, Columbus. Certified tchr. K-9, Ill., Ohio; certified personnel guidance, Ill., Ohio; certified Chgo. Bd. Edn. Mem. Am. Personnel and Guidance Assn., Internat. Platform Assn. Democrat. Club: B'nai B'rith Women (chpt. v.p.). Home: 4083 Vineshire Dr Columbus OH 43227

GREENBLATT, MARK LEO, lawyer, urban planner; b. New Brighton, Pa., Mar. 9, 1947; s. Harry Abraham and Edna Bess (Rosenberg) G.; m. Deana Charlene Beisel, June 22, 1975. B.A., Mich. State U., 1968, postgrad., 1968-69; M.City Planning, U. Pa., 1971; J.D., Capital U., 1985. Bar: Ohio, 1986, U.S. Dist. Ct. (so. dist.) Ohio, 1987. Asst. acct. Harry A. Greenblatt, New Brighton, Pa., 1971-72; planner Village of Arlington Heights (Ill.) Planning Dept., 1972-75; planner Allen L. Kracower & Asso., Des Plaines, Ill., 1975-76; planner Mid-Ohio Regional Planning Commn., Columbus, 1976-84; sole practice, Columbus, 1986—. Served with U.S. Army, 1971, capt. Res. Richard King Mellon fellow, 1968-69. Mem. ABA, Am. Inst. Cert. Planners, Am. Planning Assn., Ohio Planning Conf., Columbus Bar Assn. Jewish. Club: B'nai B'rith. Home: 4083 Vineshire Dr Columbus OH 43227 Office: 761 S Front St Columbus OH 43206

GREENBLATT, MAURICE THEODORE, transportation executive; b. Vineland, N.J., Oct. 2, 1928; s. Benjamin and Emma (Pollock) G.; m. Joan Tobye Bailinger, Apr. 8, 1951; children: David, Daniel. Student, Bucknell U., 1945-48. Pres. Ware's Van and Storage Co., Inc., Vineland, 1958—; chmn., chief exec. officer United Van Lines, Inc., Fenton, Mo., 1984—; vice chmn. Security Savs. and Loan, Vineland, 1977—, also bd. dirs.; bd. dirs. United Van Lines Ltd., Toronto, Can., Am. Movers Conf., Household Goods Carriers Bur. Republican. Jewish. Home: Ocean Plaza #417 Longport NJ 08403 Office: Ware's Van & Storage Co PO Box W Vineland NJ 08360

GREENBLATT, SAMUEL HAROLD, neurosurgery educator; b. Potsdam, N.Y., May 16, 1939; s. Louis and Rose Leah (Clopman) G.; m. Judith Ruth Shapiro, June 23, 1963; children: Rachel Laura, Daniel Edward, Miriam Elizabeth. BA in History with honors, Cornell U., 1961, MD, 1966; MA, Johns Hopkins U., 1964. diplomate Am. Bd. Neurol. Surgery. Intern III Surg. Service Boston City Hosp., 1966-67; resident in neurology Boston VA Hosp., 1967-68; resident in neurol. surgery Dartmouth Affiliated Hosps., Hanover, N.H., 1970-74; instr. neurol. surgery Albert Einstein Coll. Medicine, N.Y.C., 1974-77; asst. prof. neurol. surgery Med. Coll. Ohio, Toledo, 1977-80, assoc. prof. surgery and neurosurgery, 1980—; asst. attending neurol. surgeon Bronx (N.Y.) Mcpl. Hosp. Ctr., Hosp. Albert Einstein Coll. Medicine, Montefiore Hosp. Med. Ctr., N.Y.C., 1974-77; clin. asst. in neurol. surgery St. Barnabas Hosp., N.Y.C., 1975, research asst. in neurol. surgery, 1976-77; staff neurosurgeon Dept. Neurol. Surgery Med. Coll. Ohio Hosp., Toledo, 1977—; assoc. staff neurosurgeon Mercy Hosp., Toledo, 1977-80, courtesy staff neurosurgeon, 1980—; v.p. Associated Physicians of Med. Coll. Ohio, Inc., 1987—, pension com., 1979-81, asst. treas., 1980-83, treas., 1983-87, chmn. fin. com., 1983-87, exec. com., 1980—, bd. dirs., 1980—; trustee Toledo Area Med. Found. , 1986—. Contbr. articles, book revs. to profl. jours., chpts. to books. Mem. house com. Temple T'nai Israel, Toledo, 19778-79, long range planning com., 1985—; bd. govs. Jewish Community Ctr. of Toledo, 1984-85. Served to capt. M.C., USAFR, 1968-70. Fellow Johns Hopkins Inst. History of Medicine, USPHS, 1963-64, Tiffany Blake, Hitchcock Found., 1972-73; grantee Am. Philos. Soc., 1962, Hitchcock Found., 1971-72, Med. Coll. Ohio, 1983-84. Fellow ACS; mem. Am. Assn. History of Medicine, History of Sci. Soc., Internat. Neuropsychol. Soc., Am. Epilepsy Soc., Congress of Neurol. Surgeons, Soc. Neurosci., Acad. Medicine Toledo and Lucas County, Ohio State Med. Assn., Ohio State Neurosurg. Soc. (bd. dirs. 1986—), Am. Assn. Neurol. Surgeons (com. undergrad. edn., jt. com. edn. in neurol. surgery 1980—), Behavioral Neurology Soc., Acad. Aphasia, Phi Beta Kappa. Avocations: book collecting, skiing. Home: 3416 W Bancroft Toledo OH 43606 Office: Med Coll Ohio Dept Neurological Surgery Toledo OH 43699

GREENBURG, DAVID EUGENE, educational association executive; b. Gary, Ind., Mar. 23, 1942; s. Donald Eugene and Martha Ann (Powell) G.; m. Barbara Anne Rice, Aug. 19, 1967; children: Charles Wiston, Mandy Rice, Wendy Lea, Douglas Eugene. BS, Ball State Tchrs. Coll., 1964, MA, 1970; postgrad., Butler U., Indpls., 1974; DEd, Ind. U., 1983. Speech therapist Ind. Sch. Dists., 1964-70; spl. edn. adminstr. Indpls. Pub. Schs., 1970-81; tng. coordinator ind. U., Bloomington, Ind., 1981-82; asst. prof. ind. U., Bloomington, 1984—; project coordinator Ind. Dept. Edn., Indpls., 1982-84; mem. project panel Research Triangle Inst., Research Triangle, N.C., 1984—, futures panel U.S. Dept. Edn., Washington, 1983; del. Ind. Congress on Edn., Indpls., 1983-84. Mem. editoral bd. Spl. Service in the Schs., Piscataway, N.J., 1984—. Bd. dirs. Cen. Ind. United Cerebral Plasy, Indpls., 1981; adv. com. Marion County Assn. for Retarded Citizens, Indpls., 1978; task force chmn. Ind. Council Vol. Orgns.-Handicapped, Indpls, 1980. Mem. Council for Exceptional Children (bd. dirs. 1978-81), Council Adminstrs. of Spl. Edn. (pres. 1982-83, exec. dir.), Ind. Council for Exceptional Children (pres. 1976-77), Am. Assn. Sch. Adminstrs., Nat. Orgn. Legal Problems in Edn. Republican. Methodist. Lodge: Masons. Office: Ind U ES3108 902 W New York St Indianapolis IN 46223

GREENDORFER, SUSAN LOUISE, sociologist; b. San Francisco, Aug. 30, 1940; d. William Benjamin and Justine Louise (Nascimento) G. AB, U. Calif., Berkeley, 1962, MA, 1965; PhD, U. Wis., 1974. Cert. secondary sch. tchr., Calif. Asst. prof. sports psychology U. N.Mex., Albuquerque, 1974-75; asst. prof. U. Ill., Urbana, 1975-80, assoc. prof., 1980—. Editor (book) Sociology of Sport: Diverse Perspectives, 1981, Social Science of Play, Games and Sports, 1982. Fellow Assn. Anthrop. Study of Play; mem. Am. Alliance Health, Phys. Edn. and Recreation, Internat. Com. Sport Sociology, Ill. Sociol. Assn., N.Am. Soc. Sociology of Sport (treas. 1978-86, pres. 1986-87). Avocations: golf, tennis, plants. Home: 2204 Briar Hill Dr Champaign IL 61821 Office: U Ill Dept Phys Edn 906 S Goodwin Urbana IL 61801

GREENE, CHARLES NELSON, business educator; b. Springfield, Ohio, Apr. 28, 1937; s. James Edward Pollard and Founta (Davis) Greene Pollard; m. Margaret Ann Pennell, Dec. 18, 1966; 1 child, Charles N. III. BS, Ohio State U., 1959, MBA, 1961, PhD, 1969. Employee relations supr. Owens-Corning Fiberglas, Toledo, 1961-63; manpower and organizational devel. NCR Corp., Dayton, Ohio, 1963-67; prof. Ind. U. Sch. Bus., Bloomington, 1969-86, U. So. Maine Sch. Bus., Portland, 1986; prin. Mgmt. Cons. and Research Services, 1986. Co-author: Management, 1985; contbr. articles to profl. jours. Mem. Am. Psychol. Assn., Midwest Acad. Mgmt. (pres. 1979-80, Outstanding Service award 1986), Acad. Mgmt. (bd. gov's. 1981-83, Outstanding Service award 1983), Sigma Iota Epsilon, Beta Gamma Sigma. Avocations: stock market analysis, boating.

GREENE, DEBRA LYNN, fund raising executive, financial aids consultant; b. St. Cloud, Minn., Dec. 16, 1958; d. Charles William and Evelyn Darlene (Callewart) G.; m. Prakash Khemchand Adiani, Aug. 4, 1984. News dir. Minn. Pub. Radio Inc., St. Paul, 1981-83; producer Minn. Pub. Radio Inc., Collegeville, Minn., 1985-86; asst. admissions dir. St. John's Preparatory Sch., Collegeville, 1984-85; fund rasing dir. Applied Info. Mktg. Inc., Saint Cloud, Minn., 1985—; lang. educator World Acad., Tokyo, 1983-84; lectr. various organs., 1984—. Author: A Voyage To Nemow, 1980; editor: Prep Life, 1985. Mem. KSJR Regional Bd. Home: 905 Kilian Blvd Saint Cloud MN 56301 Office: Saint Cloud Technical Inst 1540 Northway Dr Saint Cloud MN 56301

GREENE, EDWARD HAMPTON, school psychologist; b. Aurora, Ill., Sept. 20, 1947; s. Robert Spencer and Barbara Louise (Rich) G.; m. Deborah Lee Coffman, Aug. 22, 1970; children: Liberty, Melissa, Madeline. BA, U. Wis., 1969; MA, No. Ill. U., 1972. Cert. sch. psychologist, spl. educator. Tchr. Aurora (Ill.) Pub. Schs., 1969-72, West Bend (Wis.) Sch. Dist., 1972-75; sch. psychologist Beaver Dam (Wis.) Unified Schs., 1976—. Pres. Big Bros. and Big Sisters of Dodge County, Beaver Dam, 1978; bd. dirs. Dodge Group Home, Waupun, Wis., 1980-81, Beaver Dam United Way. Mem. Wis. Sch. Psychologist Assn., Beaver Dam Edn. Assn., Capital Lake Assn. Sch. Psychologists. Lutheran. Club: Astro Investment (sec. 1984-86). Lodge: Optimist (bd. dirs. 1985—). Avocation: playing banjo. Home: 510 West St Beaver Dam WI 53916 Office: Ednl Service Ctr 705 McKinley St Beaver Dam WI 53916

GREENE, ERIC STEWART, televison newscaster and producer; b. Newark, June 24, 1956; s. Richard and Ruth Felice (Brown) G.; m. Susan McVey, July 15, 1979; 1 child, Brandy. BA in History, Tulane U., 1977. Newscaster, govt. reporter Sta. KTBS-TV, Shreveport, La., 1978; newscaster, producer Sta. WNEM-TV, Flint, Mich., 1978-79, Sta. KFDA-TV, Amarillo, Tex., 1979-80; newscaster, producer, talk show host Sta. WEYI-TV, Flint, 1980-83, Sta. WIFR-TV, Rockford, Ill., 1983—. Telethon host Easter Seals Soc., Flint and Rockford, 1980—; walk-a-thon chmn. United Cerebral Palsy, Rockford, 1985-86; pub. relations bd. Big Bros./Big Sisters, Rockford, 1986; media spokesman Animal Outreach, Rockford, 1987. Recipient Best News Anchor award Genesee County Audio-Visual Awards, 1982, Best Feature award Ill. Associated Press, 1983, 84, Best Spot news arard, 1985. Jewish. Avocations: golf, music, animals, writing. Home: 1910 E Riverside Blvd #11 Rockford IL 61111 Office: Sta WIFR-TV 2523 N Meridian Rd Rockford IL 61103

GREENE, GERALD LEE, entomologist; b. Jewell, Kans., July 7, 1937; s. Niles Norman and Mary (Chilcott) G.; m. Phyllis A. Greene; children: Geri A. Coen, Pamela S. Galle. BS in Agrl. Edn., Kans. State U., 1959, MS in Entomology, 1961; PhD in Entomology, Oreg. State U., 1966. Research assoc. U. Ky., Lexington, 1964-66; entomologist U. Fla., Quincy, 1966-76; sta. head Kans. State U., Garden City, 1976-82, livestock entomologist, 1982—; bd. dirs. Southwest Devel. Services Inc., Garden City. Treas. Southwest Kans. Mex. Am. Ministries, Garden City, 1978—, treas., 1984—. Mem. Entomol. Soc. Am., Kans. Entomol. Soc., Fla. Entomol. Soc., Nat. Biocontrol Com. Livestock Insects. Office: Kans State U Southwest Kans Exptl Sta 4500 E Mary Blvd 924 Garden City KS 67846

GREENE, GERALD MICHAEL, clinical psychologist; b. Chgo., May 7, 1940; s. Albert and Ruth (Kaplan) G.; B.A., Carleton Coll., 1961; Candidate I Diplomate Rijksuniversiteit Te Leiden (Netherlands), 1963; M.S., U. Okla., 1966, Ph.D., 1971; children—Erin Kylie, Kegan Ellery, Gavin Gregory. Asst. instr. U. Kans., Lawrence, 1966-68; chief psychologist Head Start Program of East Central Kans., Ottawa, 1967-68; asso. dir. East Central Kans. Supplementary Tng. Program, adj. instr. Emporia State Tchr's. Coll., 1967-68; instr. Rockhurst Coll., 1968-69; staff psychologist Osawatomie (Kans.) State Hosp., 1968-69; coordinator program, asst. prof. edn. and psychology Central State U., Edmond, Okla., 1969-71; mem. staff Okla. Psychol. and Ednl. Center, Oklahoma City, 1970-71; instr. phys. therapy Northwestern U. Med. Sch., 1971-72, postdoctoral fellow and intern in clin. psychology, 1971-72, project coordinator Rehab. services, 1972-73, asso. dept. psychiatry, 1972—, dept. community health and preventive medicine, 1973—, Sch. Dentistry depts. pedodontics and orthodontics, 1972—, intervention dir. Multiple Risk Factor Intervention Trial, 1973-80; pvt. practice clin. psychology, Chgo., 1972—; cons. Chgo. Bd. Mental Health, 1972-78; field supr. U. Ill. Jane Adams Sch. Social Work, 1976-78. OEO grantee, 1967-68; Office Edn. tng. grantee, 1969-71; Social and Rehab. Services grantee, 1972-76; City of Chgo. Head Start-Model Cities grantee, 1972-76; licensed clin. psychologist, Ill. Fellow Am. Assn. Profl. Hypnotherapists, Am. Orthopsychiat. Assn.; mem. Am. Assn. for Counseling and Devel., N.Y. Acad. Scis., Am. Mental Health Couselors Assn., Council Exceptional Children, AAUP, NEA, Assn. Tchr. Educators Emotionally Disturbed Children, Council Children with Behavior Disorders, Assn. Children with Learning Disabilities, Assn. Advancement Behavior Therapy, Midwestern Assn. Advancement Behavior Therapy, Chgo. Psychol. Club, Acad. Psychologists in Marital and Family Counseling, Ill. Biofeedback Soc., Council for Nat. Register Health Service Providers in Psychology, Soc. Behavior Medicine, Council for Advancement of Psychologic Professions and Scis., Assn. for Advancement of Psychology, Soc. Police and Criminal Psychology, Am. Soc. Psychologists in Pvt. Practice, Chgo. Soc. Clin. Hypnosis, Am. Soc. Clin. Hypnosis, Am. Group Psychotherapy Assn., Assn. Advance and Promote Hypnosis, Psychol. Soc. (Republic of Panama; hon. diplomate), Sigma Xi, Psi Chi, Phi Delta Kappa, Kappa Delta Pi. Office: 500 N Michigan Ave Suite 542 Chicago IL 60611

GREENE, HARVEY MITCHELL, lawyer; b. Shelburn, Ind., Jan. 25, 1927; s. Guy Benton and Arslee (Mitchell) G.; student Butler U., 1947-49; LL.B., Ind. U. at Indpls., 1954; m. Charlotte Elizabeth Shook, Dec. 25, 1946 (dec. Nov. 1979); children—Cheryl Greene Palmer, Guy Frederick, Cynthia Diane Greene Dicken, Carole Dawn; m. Theda L. Poole, Oct. 25, 1980. Admitted to Ind. bar, 1954; ordained to ministry Primitive Bapt. Ch., 1959; dep. prosecutor Dearborn County, Ind., 1965-66; city atty., Aurora, Ind., 1960-63, 68-71; county atty. Dearborn County, 1977-80. Pres., Aurora High Sch. Booster's Club, 1964-70. Bd. dirs. Dearborn and Ohio Counties Humane Soc., 1971-72. Served with USAAF, 1945-47. Mem. Am. Bar Assn., Dearborn and Ohio Counties Bar Assn. (pres. 1961), Assn. Trial Lawyers Am., Aurora Bd. Aviation Commrs. (sec. 1977-87). Club: Rotary (past pres.). Home: 110 Dawn Dr Aurora IN 47001 Office: 437 2d St Aurora IN 47001

GREENE, H(ILLIARD) FRANKLIN, SR., industrial manufacturing executive; b. Winfield, Ala., Apr. 28, 1914; s. James Columbus and Lula Florence (Weeks) G.; m. Aileen Riggins, Mar. 2, 1942 (div. June 1971); children: Patti Jo, Bonnie Aileen; m. Sandra Jean Muelver, Aug. 12, 1971; children: Hilliard F., Melissa Anne. Student, U. Ill., Chgo., Gen. Motors Inst., DePaul U., Venard Theol. Seminary. Pres., owner Precision Screw Machine Co., Hillside, Ill., 1948—. Patentee in field. Named Hon. Ky. Col., 1980. Mem. Nat. Assn. and Ctr. for Outlaw and Lawman History (pres., newsletter pub. 1980-81). Clubs: Ridgeman Country, Riviera Racquet and Handball, Westerners Corral (Chgo.); Tournament Players (Jacksonville, Fla.). Home: 400 E Randolph St Chicago IL 60601 Office: Precision Screw Machine Co 4125 W Washington Blvd Hillside IL 60162

GREENE, JEFFREY BRYAN, dentist; b. Chgo., Sept. 21, 1956; s. Melvyn and Bette Greene. BA, U. Ill., 1978; DDS, Loyola U., Maywood, Ill., 1982. Pvt. practice dentistry Schaumburg, Ill., 1982—, Skokie, Ill., 1986; lectr. Loyola U., Maywood, 1982, clin. instr., 1982-86; dentist Friendship Village, Schaumburg, 1982-86. Mem. ADA, Acad. Gen. Dentistry, Ill. State Dental Soc. (speakers bur., service plans com.), Chgo. Dental Soc., Alpha Omega, Skokie C. of C. Avocation: tennis. Office: 650 E Higgins Suite 7E Schaumburg IL 60195

GREENE, MARK ROBERTSON, communications executive; b. Cin., Mar. 9, 1953; s. Doris (Haffner) G.; m. Elisabeth Koch. Pres. Indsl. Tng. Aids, Inc., Cin. Office: Indsl Tng Aids Inc Dana Ave and I-71 Cincinnati OH 45207

GREENE, MARY SNIDER, computer specialist; b. Memphis, Nov. 11, 1929; d. Luther Lonnie and Carolyn Gardner (Peterson) Snider; m. Fredericke Marshall Greene, Nov., 1959 (div.); 1 dau., Jeanie Carolyn Mercer. AA, U. Md., 1975; BS, SUNY, 1984; MA Ball State U., 1987. Cert. data processor. Computer programmer Dept. Army, Washington, 1959-61; comml. pilot flight instr., mgr. Giles County Mcpl. Airport, Pulaski, Tenn., 1961-64; computer specialist, Dept. Army Redstone (Ala.) Arsenal, 1964-69, Zweibruecken, Germany, 1969-75; chief Acad. Computer Facility, U.S. Army Adminstrn. Ctr., 1975-79; dir. U.S. Army automation and info. mgmt. U.S. Army Soldier Support Ctr., Ft. Harrison, Ind., 1979-85; dir. U.S. Army Info. Systems Command-FBH, Ft. Harrison, 1985—. Recipient Dept. Army comdrs. award for civilian service, 1982. Mem. Federal Exec. Assn., Assn. Women in Computing. Presbyterian. Club: Sertoma. Office: US Army Info System Cmd-FBH ASNB-BH Bldg 1 Fort Harrison IN 46249-5101

GREENE, RAYMOND PHILIP, fiberglass structural consultant; b. Bklyn., Jan. 16, 1913; s. Herman Lancelot and Mabel Helene (Pfluger) G.; m. Joanne Greene, Oct. 23, 1945 (div. Nov. 1973); children: Kathy Jan, Kristina Louise, Raymond Karl Lance; m. Dorothy Owen, Aug. 25, 1975. B in Indsl. Engring., Ohio State U., 1937, BSME, 1937. Pres. Ray Greene and Co., Inc., Toledo, 1941-73; owner Ray Greene Industries, Toledo, 1974—; mil. advisor USN, 1962-63. Mem. Boating Industries Assn. (sailboat com. 1962-75), Ohio State U. Alumni Assn. (Disting. Alumni award 1963). Republican. Episcopalian. Lodge: Rotary. Avocation: sailing. Home: 4713 Ryan Rd Toledo OH 43614 Office: 508 S Byrne Rd Toledo OH 43609

GREENE, ROBERT BERNARD, JR. (BOB GREENE), journalist, author; b. Columbus, Ohio, Mar. 10, 1947; s. Robert Bernard and Phyllis Ann (Harmon) G.; m. Susan Bonnet Koebel, Feb. 13, 1971; 1 dau., Amanda Sue. B.S., Northwestern U., 1969. Reporter Chgo. Sun-Times, 1969-71, columnist, 1971-78; syndicated columnist Field Newspaper Syndicate, Irvine, Calif., 1976-81, Tribune Co. Syndicate, N.Y.C., 1981—; contbg. corr. ABC News Nightline, 1981—; columist Chgo. Tribune, 1978—; lectr. fine arts U. Chgo. Contbg. editor: Esquire Mag., 1980—; books include We Didn't Have None of Them Fat Funky Angels on the Wall of Heartbreak Hotel and Other Reports from America, 1971; Running: A Nixon-McGovern Campaign Journal, 1973, Billion Dollar Baby, 1974, Johnny Deadline, Reporter: The Best of Bob Greene, 1976, (with Paul Galloway) Bagtime, 1977, American Beat, 1983, Good Morning, Merry Sunshine, 1984, Cheeseburgers, The Best of Bob Greene, 1985. Recipient Nat. Headliner award for best newspaper column in U.S., 1977, Peter Lisagor award, 1981. Office: Chicago Tribune 435 N Michigan Ave Chicago IL 60611 *

GREENE, WILLIAM E., animator, artist; b. Ravenna, Ohio, Nov. 29, 1949; s. George Merrill and Marie Louise (Kinghorn) G.; m. Catherine Rose

Miller, May 25, 1974; children: Andrew Dustin, Nicholas Evan. BFA, Miami U., Oxford, Ohio, 1972, MFA, 1978. With corp. display dept. Shillito's, Cin., 1978-81; owner Triad Studios, Oxford, 1981-83; asst. art dir. Advanced Animations, Inc., Southbury, Conn., 1983-84; owner Incredible Machine Factory, Oxford, 1985—; free lance writer, 1978—, sculptor, 1984—. Mem. Nat. Assn. Display Industries, Nat. Assn. Self-Employed. Home and Office: Incredible Machine Factory 3191 Shollenbarger Rd Oxford OH 45056

GREENFIELD, ANNE LOUISE, librarian; b. Rochester, N.Y., July 2, 1953; d. Leigh Silburn and Edria (Rathburn) G. BA in Liberal Arts, Bradley U., 1975; MLS, Florida State U., 1977. Legal specialist Baxter Travenol, Deerfield, Ill., 1978-79, asst. librarian, 1979-80; supr. records adminstrn. FMC Corp., Chgo., 1980-82; records analyst Nat. Gas Pipeline, Chgo., 1982-85; supr. library and legal records MidCon Corp., Lombard, Ill., 1985—. Mem. Assn. Records Mgrs. and Adminstrs. (sec. 1986, Chpt. Mem. of Yr. award 1985), Scottish Cultural Soc. Roman Catholic. Home: 7030 Newport Dr #203 Woodridge IL 60517 Office: MidCon Corp 701 E 22d St Lombard IL 60148

GREENFIELD, GEORGE B., physician; b. N.Y.C., May 4, 1928; s. Jacob and Rose (Wolf) G.; m. Barbara Anne O'Driscoll, Mar. 3, 1956; children: Edward James, Sheelagh Anne. B.A., NYU, 1949; M.D., State U. Utrecht, Netherlands, 1956. Diplomate: Am. Bd. Radiology, Am. Bd. Nuclear Medicine. Intern Bridgeport (Conn.) Hosp., 1956-57; resident radiology Presbyn.-St. Lukes Hosp., Chgo., 1957-60; practice medicine, specializing in radiology Chgo., 1960—; radiologist Cook County Hosp., 1961-66, asst. dir. diagnostic radiology, 1966-69; assoc. prof. radiology U. Ill., 1966-69; prof., chmn. dept. radiology Chgo. Med. Sch., 1969-74; prof., chmn. dept. radiology Mt. Sinai Hosp. Med. Center, 1969—, pres. med. staff, 1983-85; prof. diagnostic radiology Rush Med. Coll.; prof. radiology Cook County Grad. Sch. Medicine. Author: Radiology of Bone Diseases, 4th edit., 1986; sr. author: A Manual of Radiographic Positioning, 1973; sr. author: Computers in Radiology, 1985. Contbr. articles to profl. jours. Bd. of trustees Mt. Sinai Hosp., 1986—. Served with U.S. Army, 1951. Fellow Am. Coll. Radiology; mem. AMA, Chgo. Med. Soc., Chgo. Roentgen Soc., Am. Roentgen Ray Soc., Radiol. Soc. N.Am., Inst. Medicine Chgo., Assn. Univ. Radiologists, AAAS, Internat. Skeletal Soc. Office: Mt Sinai Med Ctr 15th St and California Ave Chicago IL 60608

GREENFIELD, ROGER ALAN, restaurant company executive; b. Chgo., Oct. 14, 1951; s. Martin David and Helen Geneva (Solberg) G.; m. Elizabeth Mary Fritz, Mar. 15, 1986. BA, Occidental Coll. Owner American Grill, Glenview, Ill., The Diner, Glenview, Dixie Bar & Grill, Chgo., Coyote Grill, Chgo., Jim McMahon's, Chgo., Cucina Cucina! Chgo. Home: 1200 Lindenwood Dr Winnetka IL 60093 Office: Greenfield Restaurant Group 414 N Orleans Suite 310 Chicago IL 60610

GREENFIELD, RONALD HOWARD, coal company executive; b. Dixon, Ill., May 13, 1944; s. Howard Raymond Carl and Kathryn Ella (Withey) G.; m. Valerie Gay Glessner, Aug. 21, 1966; children: Heather, Heath. BS, U. Ill., 1966, MS, 1971. Chief internal info. USAF Acad., Colorado Springs, Colo., 1968-70, dep. chief pub. info., 1970-71, chief pub. info., 1971-72; mgr. pub. relations Cen. Soya Co., Inc., Ft. Wayne, Ind., 1972-81; dir. pub. affairs Peabody Coal Co., St. Louis, 1981-83, Peabody Holding Co., St. Louis, 1983—. Vice chmn. adminstrn. bd. New Haven (Ind.) United Meth. Ch., 1979, chmn. council ministries, 1980; mem. Adminstrn. Bd. First United Meth. Ch., O'Fallon, Ill., 1987—; bd. dirs. Highland Terr. Community Assn., New Haven, 1975. Served to capt. USAF, 1968-72. Mem. Am. Coal Found. (operating com. 1982—), Am. Mining Congress (communications com. 1983—), Nat. Coal Assn. (pub. relations com. 1982—), Internat. Assn. Bus. Communications, Pub. Relations Soc. Am. (accredited), St. Louis Press club. Club: Media (St. Louis). Avocation: jogging. Home: 315 Donna Dr O'Fallon IL 62269 Office: Peabody Holding Co 301 N Memorial Dr Saint Louis IL 63102

GREENFIELD, STANLEY, laboratory executive; b. Omaha, Mar. 16, 1941; s. Max and Sarah (Fishman) G.; m. Karen Zeinfeld, June 7, 1964; children: Michael, Sharon, Debra. BS, U. Calif., Berkeley, 1963; MS, Ind. U., 1965; PhD, Weizmann Inst., Rehovoth, Israel, 1967; cert., U. Pa., 1970. Sr. chemist Rohm & Haas, Springhouse, Pa., 1967-73; gen. mgr. Polyscis. Inc., Warrington, Pa., 1973-80; mktg. mgr. Vitamins, Inc., Chgo., 1980-82; pres. Custom Chem. Co., Indpls., 1982-83, Q.A. Labs., Inc., Kansas City, Mo., 1983—. Holder 17 patents in chemistry and biology. Mem. Am. Chem. Soc. Jewish. Home: 8115 W 97th St Overland Park KS 66212 Office: QA Labs 404 Admiral Blvd Kansas City MO 64106

GREENGRASS, MARTIN JOSEPH, clinical psychologist; b. N.Y.C., Nov. 8, 1948; s. Isidore and Freda (Warszawska) G.; m. Judith Prizer, Oct. 28, 1973, children—Sara, Rachel. B.A., Brandeis U., 1970; M.A., U. Conn., 1974, Ph.D., 1976. Lic. clin. psychologist, Ind. Clin. psychologist Conn. Correctional Facility, Somers, 1976-77; chmn. dept. of psychology St. Francis Coll., Ft. Wayne, Ind., 1977-79; psychologist Park Center, Inc., 1979-86; dir. clinical supervision Northeastern Ctr., Kendallville, Ind., 1986—; cons. mcpl. govt.; neuropsychology cons. Co-founder Alzheimers group, Ft. Wayne. NIMH fellow U. Conn., 1970. Mem. Am. Psychol. Assn., Ind. Psychol. Assn. (membership chmn. Div. II), Assn. of Children of Holocaust Survivors. Democrat. Jewish. Home: 5613 Albany Ct Fort Wayne IN 46835 Office: Samaritan Ctr 300 W Wayne Fort Wayne IN 46802 2d Office: Northeastern Ctr PO Box 817 Kendallville IN 46755

GREENLAW, ROBERT HIRAM, radiation oncologist; b. Norway, Maine, Dec. 14, 1927; s. Norman U. and Bernice H. (Hood) G.; m. Louise A. Zurovski, Feb. 19, 1955; children: Ann, Mary, Sarah, Paul N. BS, Tufts Coll., 1948; MD, U. Rochester, 1952. Diplomate Am. Bd. Radiology. Prof. radiation medicine U. Ky., Lexington, 1961-70; instr. U. Rochester, N.Y., 1968-70; radiation oncologist Marshfield (Wis.) Clinic, 1970—. Mem. Am. Cancer Soc. Served to capt. USAF, 1955-57. Fellow Am. Coll. Radiology; mem. AMA, Am. Soc. Therapeutic Radiology and Oncology. Home: Rt 4 Marshfield WI 54449 Office: Marshfield Clinic Marshfield WI 54449

GREENLEE, ROBERT L., psychiatrist; b. Akron, Ohio, Mar. 23, 1922; s. Albert Robert and Bessie (Atkinson) G.; m. Louise Jean Toombs, Dec. 22, 1946; children: Kent, Mark, Allen. MD, George Washington U., 1949. Diplomate Am. Bd. Psychiatry and Neurology. Exec. dir. Ft. Wayne Child Guidance Ctr., 1954-67, Mental Health Ctr. at Ft. Wayne, 1967-81; med. dir. Park Ctr., Ft. Wayne, 1981—; cons. psychiatrist Ft. Wayne Devel. Ctr., 1956—. Served to 1st lt. USAF, 1949-50. Fellow Am. Orthopsychiat. Assn.; mem. Am. Psychiat. Assn. (life, assoc.), Am. Assn. Sex Educators, Counselors and Therapists, Allen County Med. Assn. Home: 3344 Sanibel Dr Fort Wayne IN 46815 Office: Park Ctr 909 E State Blvd Fort Wayne IN 46805

GREENLEE, ROGER ALAN, real estate executive; b. Cheyenne, Wyo., Feb. 29, 1944; s. Robert Archie and Florence Irene (Higgins) G.; m. Frances Gwen Turner, Dec. 31, 1967; children: Marilyn Kaye, Michael Roger, Matthew Roy. Grad. high sch., Cheyenne, Wyo. Sta. agt. Frontier Airlines, Inc., Cheyenne, 1963-72; mgr. sales service Frontier Airlines, Inc., Garden City, Kans., 1972-76, Rock Springs, Wyo., 1976-79; station agt. Frontier Airlines, Inc., Rapid City, S.D., 1979-86; pres., chmn. Key Realty, Inc., Rapid City, 1985—. Mgr., coach Canyon Lake Little League, Rapid City, 1982; mgr., coach Black Hills Pony League, 1984-85; deacon 1st Bapt. Ch. Mem. Black Hills Bd. Realtors, C. of C. Club: Mayflower Descendants. Lodges: Kiwanis, DeMolays, Masons, Shriners. Avocations: chess, golfing, fishing, hunting, swimming. Home: 4907 Nonanna St Rapid City SD 57702 Office: Key Realty Inc 821 Jackson Blvd Suite 7 Rapid City SD 57702

GREENLEE, THOMAS WRIGHT, chemist; b. Dayton, Ohio, Mar. 13, 1932; s. John McKinley and Lucia Walker (Wright) G.; m. Joanne Emidy, Oct. 10, 1964; children—Patrick, Kevin, Joel. A.B., U. Chgo., 1953; A.B., Northwestern U., 1955; Ph.D., Stanford U., 1959. Research physicist and assoc. chemist Armour Research Found., Chgo., 1959-60; devel. chemist Aerojet-Gen. Corp., Sacramento, 1960-65, Dow Corning Corp., Midland, Mich., 1966-71; Angestellter in der Tatigkeit eines Studienrats, Schulbehorde der Freien Hansestadt, Bremen, W.Ger., 1971-73; sr. chemist Tremco Inc., Cleve., 1973—. Levehulme vis. fellow Trinity Coll., 1965-66. Mem. Am. Chem. Soc., AAAS, Phi Lambda Upsilon. Anglican Catholic. Lodge: Order of Scottish Clans. Patentee in field. Office: 10701 Shaker Blvd Cleveland OH 44104

GREEN-SAPPINGTON, HARRIETT PAULA, interior designer; b. Mexico, Mo., Mar. 1, 1958; d. Paul Riggs and Elizabeth Ree (Shaw) G.; m. Robert Jay Sappington, May 24, 1980; 1 child, Michael Edward, Erin Elizabeth. BS in Home Econs., Univ. Mo., 1980. Designer Yukon Office Supply, Anchorage, 1981; freelance interior designer Columbia, Mo., 1982, Interiors Unltd., Columbia, 1982-84; coordinator of interior design dept. residential life U. Mo., Columbia, 1984—. Mem. Profl. Design League, Assn. Univ. Interior Designers (sec. 1985—). Office: U Mo Residential Life Facility Ops 8A DeFoe Columbia MO 65201

GREENSLATE, PAMELA SUE, social services administrator; b. Quincy, Ill., Oct. 25, 1946; d. Kendall T. and Mary Frances (Smith) Sprague; m. Roger William Greenslate, Feb. 12, 1947; children: Tad Scott, Jason Travis. BS, Iowa State U., 1970. Cert. social worker; registered clin. social worker. Social worker Childrens Home, Peoria, Ill., 1971-75, coordinator, 1975-79; supr., social worker Luth. Social Services, Peoria, 1979-84; founder, dir. Ctr. Against Sexual Assault, Peoria, 1984—; mem Task Force on Sexual Violence, Peoria, 1985; pres. bd. dirs. WomenStrength, Peoria, 1981-84; bd. dirs. Parents Anonymous, Peoria, 1979-81, Child Care Assn., Peoria, 1972-75; lectr. on clin. treatment of sexual abuse, various seminars and workshops, 1980—. Mem. Sexual Assault Adv. Com., Women Strength, Peoria, 1987. Mem. NOW (Peoria bd. dirs. 1984-85, task force chairperson, 1985), Com. for Prevention of Early Childhood Sexual Abuse (co-founder). Avocations: writing, hiking, wood carving. Office: Ctr Against Sexual Assault 2508 N Sheridan #3 Peoria IL 61604

GREENSPAN, PETER BOGACH, physician; b. Bklyn., Sept. 12, 1954; s. Reynold Solomon and Lenore (Bogach) G.; divorced; children—David Benjamin, Aliya Rebecca. B.A., U. Mo., 1975; D.O., Chgo. Coll. Osteo. Medicine, 1980. Fellow osteo. medicine Chgo. Osteo. Med. Ctr., 1977-80, intern, 1980-81; resident ob-gyn Truman Med. Ctr., Kansas City, Mo., 1981-84, chief resident dept. ob-gyn, 1984-85; practice medicine specializing in ob-gyn, Independence, Mo., 1985—; asst. clin. prof. dept. ob-gyn Truman Med. Ctr., U. Mo. Sch. Medicine; docent dept. ob-gyn U. Mo.-Kansas City Sch. Medicine. Mem. Am. Coll. Obstetricians and Gynecologists. Jewish. Avocations: photography; coin collecting; antique medical books. Office: Hausheer Braby and Assocs 1515 W Truman Rd Suite 306 Independence MO 64050

GREENSPAN, STEVEN BARRY, pediatric optometrist, psychologist; b. Chgo., Oct. 6, 1945; s. Lawrence and Bernice (Katz) G.; m. Barbara Ann Powell, Aug. 18, 1968 (div. 1976); children: Amy, Bradley; m. Caren Lynn Weisz, Sept. 11, 1977; children: Neil, Joshua. Student, U. Wis., 1963-65; BS, OD, Ill. Coll. Optometry, 1968; MS, Ind. U., 1970; PhD in Psychology, Ill. Inst. Tech., 1973. Diplomate in Binocular Vision and Perception. Optometrist Greenspan Optometric Assocs. Profl. Corp., Harvey, Ill., 1970—, Chicago Heights, Ill., 1981—; cons. learning disabilities and mental retardation. Contbr. over 50 articles to profl. jours. Bd. dirs. Congregation Am Echad, 1986-88. Grantee Am. Optometric Found. Fellow Am. Acad. Optometry; mem. Am. Psychol. Assn., Beta Sigma Kappa (Silver Medal 1968), Karate Soc. Shotokan-Ryu., Am. Karate Assn. (Black Belt award 1983). Office: 15437 Broadway Ave Harvey IL 60426

GREENSTREET, ROBERT CHARLES, architect, educator; b. London, June 8, 1952; s. Joseph Philip Henry and Joan (Dean) G.; m. Karen Eloise Holland, Sept. 6, 1975. Diploma in architecture, Oxford Poly. Inst., 1976, PhD in Architecture, 1983. Registered architect, Eng. Vis. asst. prof. Kans. State U., 1978-79; asst. prof. U. Kans., 1979-80; vis. prof. Ball State U., Muncie, 1980-81; assoc. prof. U. Wis., 1981—, asst. vice chancellor, 1985-86, chmn. dept. architecture, 1986—. Contbr. books and 50 articles and papers to profl jour. Fellow Royal Soc. Arts; mem. AIA (assoc.), Royal Inst. Brit. Architects, Wis. Soc. Architects, Chartered Inst. Arbitrators, Faculty, Architects and Surveyors; mem. Am. Abitration Assn. Mem. Ch. of Eng. Office: Dept Architecture U Wis PO Box 413 Milwaukee WI 53201

GREENWALD, GERALD, automotive company executive; b. St. Louis, Sept. 11, 1935; s. Frank and Bertha G.; m. Glenda Lee Gerstein, June 29, 1958; children: Scott, Stacey, Bradley, Joshua. B.A. Cumlaude (Univ. scholar), Princeton U., 1957; M.A., Wayne State U., 1962. With Ford Motor Co., 1957-79; pres. Ford Venezuela; dir. non-automotive ops. Europe; vice chmn. Chrysler Corp., Highland Park, Mich., 1979-85; chmn. Chrysler Motors. Nat. exec. bd. Boy Scouts Am.; bd. dirs. Detroit United Fund, Detroit Renaissance; mem. nat. exec. bd. Boy Scouts of Am. Served with USAF, 1957-60. Mem. U.S. C. of C. (bd. dirs.), Motor Vehicle Mfrs. Assn. (exec. com.), Econ. Club Detroit, Chief Execs. Orgn. Clubs: Princeton, Detroit Athletic.

GREENWOOD, ANITA RURKA, marketing services executive; b. Chgo., July 6, 1956; d. Alexander Roman and Rosalie Eva (Magrowski) Rurka; m. Mark Allen Greenwood, Nov. 19, 1983; 1 child, Lauren Lucille. BA, No. Ill. U., 1978; postgrad., DePaul U., 1981, Marquette U., 1984. Founder, dir. Greenwood & Assocs., Racine, Wis., 1983-86; mgr. mktg. services Harper Grace Hosps., Detroit, 1986—; cons. Grosse Pointe (Mich.) Hist. Soc. Recipient Addy award Racine Advt. Club, 1984. Mem. Am. Mktg. Assn., Sigma Kappa Alumni Assn. Roman Catholic. Club: Grosse Pointe Newcomers. Avocations: piano, art. Home: 886 University Pl Grosse Pointe MI 48230 Office: Harper Hosp Corp Mktg 3990 John R Detroit MI 48202

GREENWOOD, RUSSELL LEE, electrical company executive; b. Peoria, Ill., Aug. 29, 1945; s. Lester Carl and Maxine Virginia (Wood) G.; m. June Audry Getz, Dec. 3, 1984; children—Carl, Angela, Paulette, Loretta. Degree in Bus. magna cum laude, Ill. Central Coll., 1970. Prodn. control supr. Westinghouse, Peoria, Ill., 1964-70; material control mgr. Kiefer Electric, 1970-80; corp. ops. mgr. Kirby Risk, Lafayette, Ind., 1980-83; exec. v.p., gen. mgr. Interstate Electric Supply, Racine, Wis., 1983-86, pres., 1987—. Mem. Internat. Material Mgrs. Soc., Adminstrv. Mgmt. Soc., Electric League of Milw., Nat. Assn. Elec. Distbrs. Republican. Methodist. Avocations: boating; golf; fishing; reading. Home: 4839 Lakeshore Dr Racine WI 53403 Office: Interstate Electric Supply 2601 Lathrop Ave Racine WI 53405

GREER, DANIEL WILLIAM, information services manager; b. Wood River, Ill., Feb. 14, 1949; s. John William and Goldie Violia (Chamberlain) G.; m. Randi Joan McClenahan, Aug. 27, 1977; children: Danielle Kathleen, Jennifer Anne, Matthew William. AS in Bus. Adminstrn., Lewis and Clark Community Coll., 1976, AAS in Data Processing, 1976; BBA, So. Ill. U., Edwardsville, 1980. Computer programmer Pet Inc., St. Louis, 1973-78; project leader Boatmen's Nat. Bank, St. Louis, 1978-80; systems engr. Systematics Inc., St. Louis, 1980-81; cons. Computer Task Group Inc., St. Louis, 1981-85; info. services mgr. Amax Zinc Inc., Sauget, Ill., 1985—. Served with U.S. Army, 1969-72, Vietnam, with Res. 1977—. Mem. Data Processing Mgmt. Assn., U.S. Army Warrent Officers Assn. Republican. Roman Catholic. Avocations: reading, personal computer, children. Office: Amax Zinc Co PO Box 2347 Sauget IL 62202

GREGG, ALVIS FORREST (FORREST GREGG), professional football coach; b. Birthright, Tex., Oct. 18, 1933. B.S. in Phys. Edn., So. Methodist U., 1959. Player Green Bay Packers, NFL, Wis., 1956, 58-70, Dallas Cowboys, NFL, 1971; asst. coach Green Bay Packers, 1969-70, San Diego Chargers, 1972-73; asst. coach, then head coach Cleve. Browns, 1974-77; head coach Toronto Argonauts, CFL, 1979, Cin. Bengals, NFL, 1980-83, Green Bay Packers, NFL, 1984—; played in NFL Pro Bowl, 1960-64, 66-68, NFL Championship Game, 1960-62, 65-67; played in Super Bowl, 1966-67, coach, 1981. Address: care Green Bay Packers 1265 Lombardi Ave Green Bay WI 54303 *

GREGG, DUANE LAWRENCE, publishing company executive; b. Hiawatha, Kans., Dec. 23, 1926; s. Albert Best and Margaret Emily (Lawrence) G.; m. Corinne Elizabeth Holm, June 17, 1951; children—David Lawrence, Kent Steven. B.S. in Engring, Kans. State U., 1950. Tchr. Hamlin (Kans.) pub. schs., 1950-52, Manhattan (Kans.) pub. schs., 1952-63; with Meredith Corp., Des Moines, 1963—; adminstrv. editor mag. div. Meredith Corp., 1973-76, publishing group adminstrv. editor, 1976-80, publishing group editorial services dir., 1980-83, exec. dir. editorial services, 1983—. Served with USN, 1944-46. Mem. Sigma Nu. Republican. Presbyterian. Home: 1501 41st Pl Des Moines IA 50311 Office: 1716 Locust St Des Moines IA 50336

GREGG, STEWART DAVID, lawyer; b. Sioux Falls, S.D., July 27, 1954; s. John Bailey and Pauline Benfer (Snyder) G. BGS, U. Iowa, 1975; JD, U. S.D., 1981; LLM, NYU, 1982. Bar: S.D. 1981, Minn. 1983. Staff atty. Office of Gen. Counsel Securities & Exchange Commn., Washington, 1983-85; assoc. Holmes & Graven Chartered, Bloomington, Minn., 1985-86, Oppenheimer, Wolff & Donnelly, Mpls., 1987—. Episcopalian. Office: Oppenheimer Wolff & Donnelly Suite 4800 IDS Ctr 80 S 8th St Minneapolis MN 55402

GREGOIRE, ERNEST JOSEPH, real estate broker; b. Grand Forks, N.D., Apr. 26, 1938; s. Ernest Joseph and Florence Alice (Henry) G.; m. Carole Marie Pramhus, Dec. 31, 1961; children: Stephanie Monique, Ernest Mitchell, Brent Joseph. PhB, U. N.D., 1963. Broker Gregoire Realty, Grand Forks, 1964, Gregoire Century 21, Grand Forks, 1975-80; v.p. motel devel. Midland Mortgage and Land Corp., Grand Forks, 1968-74, pres., 1975-80; chief ops. officer Thirsty Saloon Inc., Grand Forks, Minn., 1983-86; pres., chief ops. officer Shenanigans Inc., East Grand Forks, Minn., 1983—; bd. dirs. ASP Constrn. Co., Inc; lectr. mgmt. dept. U. N.D., 1985—; commr. Tri State Securites and Syndication Inst., Chgo., 1979-80. Contbr. articles to profl. jours. State advisor U.S. Congl. Adv. Bd., Washington. Recipient Nat. Service award Gov. N.D., Bismark, 1961, Elderly Housing award, HUD, Denver, 1977, Mgmt. Excellance award Century 21 Real Estate, Mpls., 1980. Mem. Real Estate Securities and Syndication Inst. (vice chmn. 1976—), Internat. Council Shopping Ctrs., Nat. Bd. Realtors, Nat. Bd. Home Builders, Builders and Traders Soc., Internat. Fedn. Real Estate (bd. dirs.), N.D. Edn. Found. (bd. dirs. 1976), Alpha Tau Omega (Silver award 1983). Republican. Roman Catholic. Club: Community Theater. Lodge: Lions, Elks. KC. Avocations: model ship builder, curling. Home: 3415 Belmont Rd Grand Forks ND 58201 Office: 1639 24th Ave S Grand Forks ND 58201

GREGONIS, JEROME ALBERT, fleet sales executive, consultant; b. Reading, Pa., Nov. 5, 1942; s. Adam Paul and Helen Anne (Bonkavage) G.; m. Patricia Marie Lawlor. Feb. 8, 1964; children: Michael, Robert, Joelle, Joseph. Grad. high sch., Reading, Pa. Various sales and ops. positions Rollins Leasing Corp., various locations, 1966-78; v.p. adminstrn. Allstate Leasing Corp., Mpls., 1978-80; sales mgr. United Truck Leasing, Mpls., 1980-81; fleet sales mgr. Brookdale Chrysler Plymouth, Mpls., 1981—; pres. Transp. Mgmt. Systems, Mpls., 1986—. coach soccer and baseball Burnsville (Minn.) Athletic Club, 1984—. Served with USN, 1960-63, USNR, 1965—. Recipient Century Club award Chrysler Corp., 1984-85. Mem. Car and Truck Renting and Leasing Assn. (v.p. 1986—), Nat. Assn. Fleet Adminstrs., Delta Nu Alpha. Republican. Roman Catholic. Avocations: Bowling, coaching youngsters. Home: 12100 Allen Dr Burnsville MN 55337 Office: Brookdale Chrysler Plymouth 6121 Brooklyn Blvd Brooklyn Center MN 55429

GREGORCY, JOHN RAYMOND, controls engineer, business executive; b. Rockford, Ill., Dec. 3, 1929; s. Stanley and Evelyn Alice; student in Indsl. Electronics, Memphis State U., 1948-52; m. Willie May Mickey, Aug. 12, 1950; children—Perry, Paul, Patricia, Pamela, Philip. Design engr. W.F. and John Barnes Co., Rockford, 1952-56; chief elec. engr. Ill. Water Treatment Co., Rockford, 1956-72; chief controls engr. Techni-Chem, Inc., Cherry Valley, Ill., 1972—, now v.p. Trustee, Techni-Chem, Inc. Pension Fund. Served with U.S. Navy, 1948-52. Recipient award Foxboro Instrument Sch., 1966. Mem. IEEE, Instrument Soc. Am., Rockford Engring. Soc. Republican. Lutheran. Club: Rockford Hockey. Designer cobolt unit treatment, solid state ion exchange unit. Home: 912 Starview Dr Rockford IL 61108 Office: 6853 Indy Dr Belvidere IL 61008

GREGORIAN, LEON, music educator, conductor; b. Tehran, Iran, Dec. 24, 1943; came to U.S., 1952; s. Rouben and Manoosh (Haroutounian) G.; m. Linda Strandness, Aug. 29, 1971; children: Ara, Ani, Alicia. Student, Berkshire Music Ctr., 1962-63; diploma in piano, New Eng. Conservatory, 1965, MusB, 1966; MusM, Mich. State U., 1968, PhD, 1971. Music dir., conductor Owensboro (Ky.) Symphony Orch., 1971-86; artist in residence Brescia Coll., Owensboro, 1973-83; prof. music, dir. orch. Mich. State U., East Lansing, 1984—; adj. prof. Western Ky. U., Bowling Green, 1975-78; music dir., conductor New Eng. Music Camp, Sidney, Maine, 1985—, Plymouth (Mich.) Symphony Orch., 1986-87, Midland (Mich.) Symphony Orch., 1987—. Guest conductor various orchs. around the world, 1973—. Active Mayor's Com. on the Arts, Owensboro, 1973-75, Summer Festival Com., Owensboro, 1980-85. Recipient cert. Outstanding Service City of Owensboro, 1986, cert. Appreciation USCG, Owensboro, 1986, Service award Kiwanis Club, Owensboro, 1986; named Ky. Col. Gov. Ky., Owensboro, 1981, Hon. Sec. of State, Frankfort, Ky., 1980, Hon. Judge Exec. County Judge Exec., Owensboro, 1986. Mem. Am. Symphony Orch. League, Nat. Music Educators Assn., Mich. Music Educators, Owensboro C. of C. (Ambassador at Large award 1973), Phi Mu Alpha Sinfonia, Phi Kappa Lambda. Mem. Armenian Apostolic Ch. Avocations: gardening, sports, photography. Office: Mich State U Sch Music East Lansing MI 48824

GREGORIO, DANIEL THOMAS, health insurance company executive; b. N.Y.C., Sept. 10, 1946; s. James and Elizabeth (Enders) G.; m. Dallas Lorraine Stout, Apr. 3, 1983; children: Christina Marie, Dawn Marie, Vicki Lynn. BS in Acctg., St. John's U., 1968; M in Pub. Health Adminstrn., L.I. U., 1975; postgrad. in health care, U. Mich., 1975; postgrad. in mgmt., Northwestern U., 1985. CPA, N.Y., Ill. Chief acct. Blue Cross/Blue Shield of Greater N.Y., N.Y.C., 1971-73, mgr. acctg., 1973-74, exec. asst. to pres., 1974-75, dir. profl. reimbursement, 1975-78; dir. audit Blue Cross/Blue Shield of Ill., Chgo., 1978-85, officer hosp. contracts and reimbursement, 1985—. Mem. Am. Inst. CPA's, Healthcare Fin. Mgmt. Assn. (advanced), Am. Coll. Healthcare Execs., Ill. CPA Soc. (chmn. hosp. com.), Ill. Assn. Preferred Provider Orgns. (bd. dirs.). Home. 1560 N Sandburg Terr #3501 Chicago IL 60610 Office: Blue Cross Blue Shield Ill 233 N Michigan Ave Chicago IL 60601

GREGORY, DELLA ARLENE ARLEDGE, educator; b. Martinsville, Ohio, Oct. 6, 1938; d. George and Lucille Irene (Shiverdecker) Arledge; B.A., Ohio State U., 1959, M.A., 1977, doctoral candidate, U., 1979—; student Ohio Wesleyan U., summers 1969, 70, 72, 74, 75, 77, 78; m. James Andrew Gregory, Dec. 20, 1959; children—James Andrew, Julie Ann, Janis Arlene. Tchr., Delaware (Ohio) City Schs., 1960—; part-time communications instr. Marion Tech. Coll.; also ednl. cons. Mem. adv. bd. Help Anonymous, 1974—; adv. 4-H Club, 1969—; adv. Am. Field Service, 1973-79, host mother, 1974-75; mem. edn. com. local Methodist ch., 1977—; publicity coordinator Delaware Arts Festival, 1977-79; vol. family outreach program Juvenile Ct. Annie Webb Blanton scholar Delta Kappa Gamma, 1979—, Louise and Marguerite Morse scholar, 1981, Martha Holden Jennings scholar, 1986-87; Lily Found. grantee, 1972; NEH grantee, 1983, 1987. Mem. Ohio Assn. for Gifted and Talented Edn., Assn. for Curriculum and Devel., United Teaching Profession, Ohio Council Tchrs. of English Lang. Arts (sec. 1973-76), Nat. Council Tchrs. of English (com. on poets in schs. 1974-76, judge writing awards 1975-79), Delaware City Tchrs. Assn. (pres. 1979-81), AAUW (charter pres. Delaware br. 1965-67), Delta Kappa Gamma (pres. Iota chpt.), Pi Lambda Theta. Editor: Hot Air, Ohioans Celebrate Their Teachers. Contbr. articles to profl. jours. Home: 240 Homestead Ln Delaware OH 43015 Office: 289 Euclid Ave Delaware OH 43015

GREGORY, DENNIS LEANDER, controller; b. Belgrade, Minn., Sept. 30, 1956; s. Urban James and Rita Julia (Haider) G.; m. Barbara Eleanor Walz, Apr. 15, 1978; 1 child, Brent. BS summa cum laude, St. Cloud (Minn.) State U., 1981. CPA, Minn. Staff acct. McMahon, Hartman, Amundson & Co., St. Cloud, 1981-83, sr. acct., 1983-86, supr., 1986; controller Hanson Silo Co., Lake Lillian, Minn., 1986—, Shuttlecraft USA, Inc. Pub. info. chairperson Am. Cancer Soc., St. Cloud, 1981-85, pres., 1985—. Mem. Am. Inst. CPA's, Minn. Soc. CPA's. Roman Catholic. Avocations: tennis, softball, collecting.

GREGORY, MARION F., JR., tool manufacturing executive; b. Denison, Tex., Oct. 26, 1933; s. Marion F. and Nannie (Huseman) G.; m. Fay, Dec. 27, 1975; children: Mark, Gary, Vivian, Nicole, Colette. With Snap-on Tools Corp., 1955—; gen. sales mgr. Snap-on Tools Corp., Kenosha, Wis., 1976-81, v.p., 1977-81, sr. v.p. mfg. and product research and devel., 1981-83, exec. v.p., dir., 1983-85, chief operating officer, dir., 1985—, pres., 1986—; dir. Hand Tools Inst., Tarrytown, N.Y. Served with U.S. Navy, 1951-55. Mem. Wis. Mfg. and Commerce Assn. (bd. dirs. 1985—). Office: Snap-on Tools Corp 2801 80th St Kenosha WI 53140

GREGORY, MICHAEL ALFRED, civil engineer; b. Midland, Mich., July 9, 1955; s. Frederick Gregory and Tula (Bitzer) Seidenstucker; m. Roma Ellwood, Dec. 30, 1978; children: Amanda Francis, Thomas James. BSCE, Valparaiso U., 1977; M in Civil Sci. and Environ. Engring., U. Wis., 1979; MBA, De Paul U., 1981. Registered profl. engr., Wis. Engr. U.S. Army C.E., Chgo., 1979-83; engr. U.S. Treasury, Brooklyn Center, Minn., 1983-84, engring. mgr., 1984—. Patentee in field. Bd. dirs. Lowery Hill East Neighborhood Assn., Mpls., 1985—, Hawthorne Neighborhood Assn., Chgo., 1982-83, Lakeview Neighborhood Assn., Chgo., 1982-83. Mem. ASCE, Delta Mu Delta, Chi Epsilon. Office: US Treasury Dept Room 300 6040 Earle Brown Dr Brooklyn Center MN 55430

GREGORY, THOMAS BRADFORD, mathematics educator; b. Traverse City, Mich., Dec. 13, 1944; s. Philip Henry and Rhoda Winslow (Hathaway) G. BA, Oberlin (Ohio) Coll., 1967; MA, Yale U., 1969, M of Philosophy, 1975, PhD, 1977. Lectr. Ohio State U., Mansfield, 1977-78, asst. prof. math., 1978-84, assoc. prof. math., 1984—. Reviewer: Math. Revs., 1984—; contbr. articles to profl. jours. Active Mansfield (Ohio) Symphony Chorus, 1977—, Presbytery Youth Ministries Com., New Philadelphia, Ohio, 1980—, Univ. Singers, Mansfield, 1985—. Served to lt. comdr. USNR, 1969—. Fellow NSF, Washington, 1967; hon. fellow U. Wis., Madison, 1987—. Mem. Am. Math. Soc. (translator 1974-82), Ohio Council Tchrs. Math., Am. Soc. Naval Engrs., Naval Inst., Res. Officers Assn., Naval Res. Assn., Navy League, Phi Beta Kappa, Sigma Xi. Republican. Avocations: classical piano, singing, amateur radio, volleyball, jogging. Home: 930 Maumee Ave Mansfield OH 44906 Office: Ohio State U 0-15 1680 University Dr Mansfield OH 44906

GREIER, DONALD KARL, mechanical engineer; b. Youngstown, Ohio, Sept. 14, 1956; s. Richard and Wilda Mae (Owings) G.; m. Deborah Sue Vestal, May 2, 1981; children: Melissa, Christine. BS in Engring., Youngstown State U., 1980. Stress engr. BF Goodrich, Troy, Ohio, 1980-84; sr. engr. Sheffield Measurement Div., Dayton, Ohio, 1985—. Home: 326 Winnimac Ave Englewood OH 45322 Office: Sheffield Measurement Div 721 Springfield St Dayton OH 45403

GREIN, RICHARD FRANK, bishop, educator; b. Bemidji, Minn., Nov. 29, 1932; s. Lester Edward and LaVina Minnie (Frost) G.; m. Joan Dunwoody Atkinson, Nov. 25, 1961; children: David, Margaret, Mary Leslie, Sara. B.A. in Geology, Carlton Coll., 1955; M. Div., Hashotah House Sem., Wis., 1959; S.T.M., Hashotah House Sem., 1970. Ordained priest Episcopal Ch., 1959; priest-in-charge Elk River mission field, Minn., 1959-64; rector St. Mathew's Ch., Mpls., 1964-69, St. David's Ch., Minnetonka, Minn., 1969-73; prof. pastoral theology Nashotah House House Theol. Sem., 1973-74; rector St. Michael and All Angel Ch., Mission, Kans., after 1974; bishop The Episcopal Ch., Tepeka, kans. Co-author: Preparing Younger Children for First Communion, 1972. Priest assoc. Order Holy Cross; pres. Guardian Angels Found., Elk River, 1963-64. Mem. Councial Assoc. Parishes. Office: Episc Ch Bethany Pl Topeka KS 66612 *

GREIS, JON BRIAN, obstetrician-gynecologist; b. Johannesburg, Republic South Africa, Feb. 11, 1948; came to U.S., 1974; s. Julius and Bertha (Cohen) G.; m. Barbara Gail Malk, Feb. 10, 1974; children: Jason, Justin. BS, U. Witwatersrand, Johannesburg, 1969, MD, 1973. Intern Hines V.A. Hosp., Maywood, Ill., 1974-75; resident Michael Reese Hosp., Chgo., 1975-79; attending physician Lake Forest (Ill.) Hosp., 1979—. Mem. AMA, Lake County Med. Soc., Am. Coll. Ob-Gyn, Ill. State Med. Soc. Avocations: music, art, reading. Home: 395 Carriage Way Deerfield IL 60015 Office: Lake Forest Hosp 700 N Westmoreland Blvd Lake Forest IL 60045

GREIS, WAYNE RAYMOND, data processing executive; b. Chgo., Sept. 24, 1942; s. Raymond Julius and Lorraine Marie (Rietschel) G.; m. Annette Teresa Plata, May 14, 1965 (div. May 1980); children: Jodie Marie, Michele Antonette; m. Deborah Ann Hardesty, Sept. 25, 1982. Student, U. Ill., Chgo., 1960, Bogan Jr. Coll., Chgo., 1961, Loop Jr. Coll., Chgo., 1962, Northwestern U., 1967-68. Computer programmer Martin Brower Corp., Forest View, Ill., 1962-66; mgr. programming Morton Thiokol, Inc., Chgo., 1966-72, mgr. data processing, 1972-78, mgr. information security, 1978—; lectr. various bus. and profl. orgns. Youth coordinator St. Peter's Cath. Ch., Antioch, Ill., 1976-79. Served to staff sgt. U.S. Army, 1963-69. Mem. Computer Security Inst., GUIDE. Republican. Lutheran. Avocation: designing, manufacturing and selling fishing lures. Office: Morton Thiokol Inc 110 N Wacker Dr Chicago IL 60606

GREIWE, JOHN ROBERT, architect; b. Cin., Dec. 31, 1960; s. Robert Leo and Kathleen Cecil (Hadley) G.; m. Rebecca Jean Cardone, Jan. 4, 1986. BArch, U. Cin., 1985. Builder Cin. Environs, 1985; architect, designer Skidmore Owings & Merril, Chgo., 1985-87; Cin. project architect Greiwe Interiors, archtl. designer, Cin., 1987—. Chgo. rep. U. Cin. Admissions Dept., 1985—. Mem. AIA (assoc.), Sigma Sigma (pres. 1985), Sigma Alpha Epsilon Ohio Alumni Assn., Metro Mens Honorary, Omega Greek Honorary, Cincinnatus (pres. 1984). Office: Greiwe Interiors 3979 Eric Ave Cincinnati OH 45211

GREJCZYK, DENNIS FRANCIS, marketing executive; b. Chgo., Oct. 9, 1943; s. Robert I. and Laura (Bawelkiewicz) G.; m. Diane Lynn Dufty, Oct. 21, 1966; children—Deborah Ann, Dennis F., Daniel B. Student Marquette U., 1980-82. Dist. sales mgr. Apeco, Cin., 1972-73; sales rep. W. H. Brady, Milw., 1973-74; regional sales mgr. Kroy, Detroit, 1974-77; br. gen. mgr. Savin, Detroit, 1977-78; gen. mktg. mgr. Sycom, Madison, Wis., 1978-83; v.p. mktg. Barber-Greene Info. Systems, Inc., Downers Grove, Ill., 1983-84; mgr. O.E.M. Mktg. Ryan-McFarland Corp., Chgo., 1984-85; v.p. mktg., sales Voice Computing, Inc., Madison, 1985—. Pres., Parent Tchrs. Orgn., Canton, Mich., 1975. Served with USAF, 1961-65; ETO. Mem. Sales and Mktg. Execs., Am. Mgmt. Assn. Roman Catholic. Home: 1810 Broadway Sun Prairie WI 53590 Office: Voice Computing Inc 1250 Femrite Dr Suite 109 Madison WI 53716

GREMMINGER, ROGER ANTHONY, physician; b. Campbellsport, Wis., Feb. 24, 1947; s. Paul Killian and Frances Josephine (Fox) G. B.S. in Math., Divine Word Coll. Sem., 1969; M.D., Med. Coll. Wis., 1976. Intern, St. Mary's Hosp., Milw., 1976-77, emergency physician, 1978—; staff mem. Brady E. Sexually Transmitted Disease Clinic, Milw., 1978—, med. dir., 1979-84; staff St. Joseph's Hosp., Milw., 1978—, St. Mary's Hosp., Racine, Wis., 1978-83; mem. staff St. Anthony's Hosp., Milw., 1983—, also med. dir. Herpes Health Ctr. Mem. Ad Hoc Task Force for Vaccination Strategies for Sexually Transmitted Hepatitis B, 1981-83. Active Am. Pub. Health Assn., Wis. Pub. Health Assn., Am. Venereal Disease Assn., Nat. Coalition of Gay Sexually Transmitted Disease Services, ACLU, Wis. Civil Liberties Union, Wis. Council of Human Concerns. Mem. AAAS. Democrat. Roman Catholic. Lectr. symposia, workshops.

GRENARD, NANCY CAROLE, data processing executive; b. Lafayette, Ind., July 17, 1946; d. Lawrence Gilbert and Audrey Jane (Lohr) Pitstick; m. Bradley Ray Grenard, Sept. 1, 1972; 1 child, Tammy Lynn Schieler. BS in Mgmt., Purdue U., 1980, MS in Computer Sci., 1985. Asst. dir. personnel info. systems Purdue U., West Lafayette, Ind., 1978-83, mgr. users info. ctr., 1983—. Mem. Coll. and Univ. Personnel Assn. (MIS council), Cen. Ind. Users' Group (program com. 1986), Beta Gamma Sigma. Avocations: rose growing, hiking, reading, crafts. Office: Purdue U UIC/SCCC West Lafayette IN 47907

GRETTUM, JAMES ARNOLD, accounting company executive; b. Fargo, N.D., Mar. 2, 1954; s. Henry W. and Ruby D. (Hellerud) G. BA in Acctg., Moorhead (Minn.) State U., 1976. CPA, N.D. Staff acct. Eide, Helmeke & Co., Bismarck, N.D., 1976-78; supr. Charles Bailly & Co., Fargo, 1978-79, Banco, Inc., Moorhead, 1979-81; mng. dir. Grettum & Co. CPA's, Fargo, 1981—. Mem. Am. Inst. CPA's, N.D. State Soc. CPA's. Home: 1621 S 16 1/2 St Fargo ND 58103 Office: 1323 S 23d St Suite C Fargo ND 58103

GREW, PRISCILLA CROSWELL, state official; b. Glens Falls, N.Y., Oct. 26, 1940; d. James Croswell and Evangeline Pearl (Beougher) Perkins; m. Edward Sturgis Grew, June 14, 1975. BA magna cum laude, Bryn Mawr Coll., 1962; PhD, U. Calif., Berkeley, 1967. Instr. dept. geology Boston Coll., 1967-68, asst. prof., 1968-72; asst. research geologist Inst. Geophysics UCLA, 1972-77, adj. asst. prof. environ. sci. and engring., 1975-76; dir. Calif. Dept. Conservation, 1977-81; commr. Calif. Pub. Utilities Commn., San Francisco, 1981-86; dir. Minn. Geol. Survey, St. Paul, 1986—; prof. dept. geology U. Minn., St. Paul, 1986—; vis. asst. prof. dept. geology U. Calif., Davis, 1973-74; chmn. Calif. State Mining and Geology Bd., Sacramento, 1976-77; exec. sec., editor Lake Powell Research Project, 1971-77; cons., vis. staff mem. Los Alamos (N.Mex.) Nat. Lab., 1972-77; mem. com. minority participation in earth sci. and mineral engring. U.S. Dept. Interior, 1972-75; chmn. Calif. Geothermal Resources Task Force, 1977, Calif. Geothermal Resources Bd., 1977-81; mem. earthquake studies adv. panel U.S. Geol. Survey, 1979-83; mem. adv. com. U.S. Geol. Survey, 1982-86; mem. adv. council Gas Research Inst., 1982-86, research coordination council, 1987—; mem. subcom. earthquake research NRC, 1985—, bd. on mineral and energy resources Nat. Acad. Scis, 1982—. Contbr. articles to profl. jours. Fellow NSF, 1962-66. Fellow AAAS, (chmn. electorate nominating com. sect. E 1980-84, mem. at large 1987—), Geol. Soc. Am. (chmn. com. on geology and pub. policy 1981-84, com. on coms. 1986-87); mem. Am. Geophys. Union (chmn. com. pub. affairs 1984—), Soc. Mayflower Descs., Nat. Parks and Conservation Assn. (trustee 1982-86), Nat. Assn. Regulatory Utility Commrs. (com. on gas 1982-86, exec. com. 1984-86, com. on energy conservation 1983-84), U.S. Nat. Com. Geology (mem. at large 1985—), NSF (com. equal opportunities in sci. and tech. 1985-86). Office: Minn Geol Survey 2642 University Ave Saint Paul MN 55114

GREWELL, JUDITH LYNN, data processing executive; b. New Orleans, Aug. 27, 1945; d. Raymond Walter and Dorothy Marie (Reymann) Potratz; m. John Nolting Grewell, Aug. 28, 1964; children: Patricia Lynn, Amy Elizabeth. BA with honors, Wayne State U., 1972; MA with honors, Oakland U., 1976. Supr. mfg. Chevrolet-Pontiac-div. Gen. Motors of Can., Pontiac, Mich., 1978-80; purchasing agt. Chevrolet-Pontiac Gen. Motors of Can. div., Pontiac, Mich., 1980-82, trainer, organizational cons., 1982-84; supr. systems tng. Electronic Data Systems div. Chevrolet-Pontiac Gen. Motors of Can. div., Troy, Mich., 1985-86, supr. tech. tng. devel., 1986—; head trainer UAW-Gen. Motors Nat. Workshop, Black Lake, Mich., 1983. Contbg. editor Univ. Assocs. Handbook of Structured Experiences, 1985. Vol. Oakland County (Mich.) Rep. Com., 1981, 84; task force mem. Joint Nat. UAW-Gen. Motors Quality of Work Life Com., Detroit, 1983-84. Mem. Pi Lambda, Phi Upsilon Omicron. Republican. Presbyterian. Avocations: art, cross country skiing, fitness, reading, sailing. Home: 806 Aspen Dr Rochester MI 48063 Office: Gen Motors Corp Electronic Data Systems Div 803 W Big Beaver Rd Troy MI 48007

GREY, HENRY, financial executive; b. Chgo., Jan. 6, 1954; s. Eugene and Stella (Trybula) G.; m. Beverly Marie Pilch, Nov. 26, 1983. BS, U. Ill., 1974; MBA, DePaul U., 1976. CPA, Ill. Mgr. Arthur Andersen & Co., Chgo., 1974-86; v.p. fin., treas. UNR Industries, Inc., Chgo., 1986—. Mem. Am. Inst. CPA's, Ill. Inst. CPA's. Office: UNR Industries Inc 332 S Michigan Ave Chicago IL 60604

GRIDER, JEAN CATHERINE, business educator, consultant; b. Leesburg, Ohio, Aug. 1, 1928; d. Frank C. Shope and Ida C. (Redmon) S.; m. Curtis Grider, Apr. 15, 1960 (div.), children—Pamela, Carla, Lisa, Paula. B.S. in Edn., Wilmington Coll., 1950; Ed.M., U. Cin., 1960, Cert., tchr. and supr. vocat. edn., Ohio. Tchr., Anderson Hich Sch., Cin., Xenia City and Western Brown High Schs., Mt. Orab, Ohio, and So. Joint Vocat. Sch., Georgetown, Ohio; adult supr. So. Hills Joint Vocat. Sch.; instr. So. State Community Coll., Sardinia, Ohio, U. Cin.; cons. to industry. Mem. AAUW, Delta Pi Epsilon, Delta Kappa Gamma. Methodist. Club: Order of Eastern Star.

GRIDLER, PAUL THOMAS, electronics executive; b. Latrobe, Pa., Nov. 10, 1944; s. Joseph Edward Gridler and Veronica Elizabeth (Kolman) Siko; m. Judith Suzanne Arnold, Jan. 22, 1966; children: Patrick, Jennifer, Sarah. A in Applied Sci., Purdue U., 1970, BS in Indsl. Engring. Tech., 1972; postgrad., Ball State U., 1985—. Indsl. engr. Flint & Walling, Inc., Kendallville, Ind., 1972-75; mfg. engr. Majestic (Am. Standard), Huntington, Ind., 1976-78; project engr. Magnavox Electronic Systems, Ft. Wayne, Ind., 1978-84, mgr. plant engring., 1984-86, dir. facilities, 1986—. Served with U.S. Army, 1962-65. Mem. Inst. Indsl. Engrs. (sr.), Purdue Alumni Assn. Republican. Lutheran. Club: Magnavox Mgmt. Avocations: photography, golf, computers. Home: 2206 Wawonaissa Trail Fort Wayne IN 46809 Office: Magnavox Electronic Systems 1313 Production Rd Fort Wayne IN 46808

GRIEM, JOHN MICHAEL, management consultant; b. San Francisco, Apr. 29, 1945; s. John Dyrsen and Gwendolyn (Pyeatt) G.; Sc.B.E. magna cum laude, Brown U., 1965, Sc.M.E., 1966; M.B.A., U.Chgo., 1968; m. Peggy Clarke, Sept. 16, 1967; children—John Michael, Marjorie Lynne. Sr. economist USPHS, 1968-70; assoc. to v.p., dir. Cresap, McCormick and Paget, Chgo., 1970-81, mng. partner subs. Cresap, McCormick and Paget do Brasil Servicos Ltda., 1978-81; v.p. A.T. Kearney, Chgo., 1981—, pres. Kearney; Health Services Cons., 1981-87. Gov. Am. Soc. of Sao Paulo (Brazil), 1979-81. NDEA fellow, 1965-66; Ford Found. fellow, 1965, 67-68. Mem. Inst. Mgmt. Cons. (cert.), Sigma Xi, Tau Beta Pi, Beta Gamma Sigma. Republican. Presbyterian. Clubs: Exmoor Country; Brown U. (Chgo.). Home: 120 Indian Rd Lake Bluff IL 60044

GRIES, BRETT EVAN, manufacturing company executive; b. Culver City, Calif., Feb. 26, 1948; s. Harold A. and Ellen L. (Callow) G.; m. Arlene J. Bruch, Apr. 10, 1976; children: Blaze Christopher, Brandi Marie, Sierra Lynn. BBA, U. Wis., Whitewater, 1971; MBA, Bradley U., 1982. CPA, Wis. Tax supr. Congoleum Corp., Milw., 1976-77; tax mgr. Keystone Consol. Industries, Inc., Peoria, Ill., 1977-82; dir. fin. reporting, taxation Newell Co., Freeport, Ill., 1982—. Mem. Am. Inst. CPA's, Midwest Council Sports Car Clubs (Champion Formula V 1974). Republican. Roman Catholic. Office: Newell Co 29 W Stephenson St Freeport IL 61032

GRIESHEIMER, RITA ANN, accountant; b. Washington, Mo., Dec. 11, 1952; d. Robert William and Loretta Francis (Marquart) Maune; m. John Elmer Griesheimer, June 15, 1974; children: Sean, Aaron, Michelle. AA, East Cen. Coll., Union, Mo., 1973; BS, S.W. Mo. State U., 1975. CPA, Mo. Acct. Hochschild, Bloom & Co., Washington, 1975—. Mem. Am. Inst. CPA's, Mo. Soc. CPA's. Roman Catholic. Club: Riverview Civic League (Washington). Home: 33 Oxford Dr Washington MO 63090 Office: Hochschild Bloom & Co 1000 Washington Sq Washington MO 63090

GRIEVE, PIERSON MACDONALD, specialty chemicals and services company executive; b. Flint, Mich., Dec. 5, 1927; s. P.M. and Margaret (Leamy) G.; m. Florence R. Brogan, July 29, 1950; children: Margaret, Scott, Bruce. B.S. in Bus. Adminstrn., Northwestern U., 1950; postgrad., U. Minn., 1955-56. With Caterpillar Tractor Co., Peoria, Ill., 1950-52; staff engr. A.T. Kearney & Co. (mgmt. consultants), Chgo., 1952-55; pres. Rap-in-Wax, Mpls., 1955-62; exec. AP Parts Corp., 1962-67; pres., chief exec. officer Questor Corp., Toledo, 1967-82; chmn. bd., chief exec. officer (NYSE) Ecolab Inc., St. Paul, 1983—; bd. dirs. Diversified Energies, St. Paul Cos. Inc., Norwest Corp., Meredith Corp. Adv. council J.L. Kellogg Grad. Sch. Mgmt., Northwestern U.; bd. overseers Sch. Mgmt., U. Minn.; trustee Macalester Coll.; bd. dirs. Guthrie Theatre, St. Paul United Way. Served with USNR, 1945-46. Mem. Minn. Bus. Partnership (exec. com.), Chevaliers du Tastevin, Beta Gamma Sigma (dirs. table). Episcopalian. Clubs: St. Paul Athletic, Minn. (St. Paul); Mpls., Economic (N.Y.C.). Office: Ecolab Inc Ecolab Ctr Saint Paul MN 55102

GRIFF, FRANKLIN W., cardiologist; b. Phila., Jan. 24, 1944; s. Albert Louis and Lillian Martha G.; m. Merle Dawn Krouse, Dec. 22, 1968; children: Adam Michael, Richard Asher. BA in Classics, U. Pa., 1965; MD, Temple U., 1969. Intern Presbyn. U., Pitts., 1970, resident, 1970-72, cardiology fellow, 1972-74; asst. prof. medicine, asst. dir. cardiac lab. U. Pitts., 1974-76; assoc. prof. N.E. Ohio U., Canton, Ohio, 1979—; attending physician Aultman Hosp., Canton, 1976—. Contbr. articles to profl. jours. Served to capt. USAR. Fellow Am. Coll. Cardiology, Council Clin. Cardiology; mem. Am. Heart Assn. (pres. local chpt. 1979-83). Home and Office: 214 Dartmouth Ave Southwest Canton OH 44710

GRIFFIN, BOB FRANKLIN, lawyer, state legislator; b. Braymer, Mo., Aug. 15, 1935; s. Benjamin Franklin and Mildred Elizabeth (Cowan) G.; m. Linda Charlotte Kemper, Aug. 18, 1957; children: Julie Lynn, Jeffrey Scott. BS, U. Mo., 1957, JD, 1959. Bar: Mo. 1959, U.S. Supreme Ct. 1959. Pros. atty. Clinton County, Plattsburg, Mo., 1963-70; mem. Mo. Ho. of Reps., 1970—; speaker pro tem 1977-80, speaker, 1981—; sole practice Cameron, Mo., 1983—; of counsel Craft, Fridkin, Slatter & Rhyne, Kansas City, Mo., 1987—. Mem. exec. com. Nat. Conf. State Legislators, 1981—; mem. exec. com. Council of State Govts., past chmn. midwestern legis. conf.; mem. Dem. Legis. Leaders Caucus, 1981—. Served to capt. JAGC, USAF, 1959-62. Mem. Mo. Bar Assn., Clinton County Bar Assn., Order of Coif, Phi Alpha Delta. Methodist. Office: 223 E 3d St Cameron MO 64429

GRIFFIN, CARLETON HADLOCK, accountant; b. Richmond Heights, Mo., Oct. 30, 1928; s. Merle Leroy and Bernice Hilder Edwards (Nelson) G.; m. Mary Lou Goodrich, Dec. 26, 1953; children: Julia, Anne. B.B.A., U. Mich., 1950, J.D., 1953, M.B.A., 1953. Mem. audit and tax staff Touche Ross & Co., Detroit, 1955-59; adminstrv. partner Touche Ross & Co., Denver, 1959-71; nat. tax dir. Touche Ross & Co., N.Y.C., 1971-72; nat. dir. ops. and adminstrn. Touche Ross & Co., 1972-74, chmn. bd., 1974-82, sr. ptnr., 1982-85, regional ptnr., 1983-85; prof. acctg. U. Mich., 1985—. Contbr. articles to profl. jours. Sr. warden St. Paul's Episcopal Ch., Darien, Conn., 1979-81. Served with Fin. Corps AUS, 1953-55. Mem. Am. Inst. C.P.A.s, Colo. Soc. C.P.A.s (pres. 1970-71), N.Y. Soc. C.P.A.s, Mich. Soc. C.P.A.s. Republican. Office: Univ Mich Sch Bus Adminstrn Ann Arbor MI 48109

GRIFFIN, JAMES ANTHONY, bishop; b. Fairview Park, Ohio, June 13, 1934; s. Thomas Antohny and Margaret Mary (Hanousek) G. B.A., Borromeo Coll., 1956; J.C.L. magna cum laude, Pontifical Lateran U., Rome, 1963; J.D. summa cum laude, Cleve. State U., 1972. Ordained priest Roman Catholic Ch., 1960, bishop, 1979; asso. pastor St. Jerome Ch., Cleve., 1960-61; sec.-notary Cleve. Diocesan Tribunal, 1963-65; asst. chancellor Diocese of Cleve., 1965-68, vice chancellor, 1968-73, chancellor, 1973-78, vicar gen., 1978-79; pastor St. William Ch., Euclid, Ohio, 1978-79; aux. bishop Diocese of Cleve.; vicar of western region Diocese of Cleve., Lorain, Ohio, 1979-83; bishop of Columbus Diocese of Columbus (Ohio), 1983—; mem. clergy relations bd. Diocese of Cleve., 1972-75, mem. clergy retirement bd., 1973-78, mem. clergy personnel bd., 1979-83. Author: (with A.J. Quinn) Thoughts for Our Times, 1969, Thoughts for Sowing, 1970, (with others) Ashes from the Cathedral, 1974, Sackcloth and Ashes, 1976, The Priestly Heart, 1983. Bd. dirs. Holy Family Cancer Home, 1973-78; trustee St. Mary Sem., 1976-78; bd. dirs., mem. pension com. Cath. Cemeteries Assn., 1978-83; bd. dirs. Meals on Wheels, Euclid, 1978-79; vice-chancellor Pontifical Coll. Josephinum, 1983—; bd. dirs. Franklin County United Way, 1984—; chmn. bd. govs. N.Am. Coll., Rome, Italy, 1984—. Mem. Am. Canon Law Soc., Am. Bar Assn., Ohio Bar Assn., Euclid Ministerial Assn. (pres. 1978-79). Office: 198 E Broad St Columbus OH 43215

GRIFFIN, JOHN E., retail drug company executive. Pres. Lewis Drug Store, Sioux Falls, S.D. Office: Lewis Drug Store 309 S Phillips Ave Sioux Falls SD 57102 *

GRIFFIN, JOSEPH LAWRENCE, transp. exec.; b. Utica, Miss., Sept. 5, 1951; s. Shallie, Jr., and Carrie B. (Lyle) G.; student U. Ill., 1969-71; cert. in transp. and traffic mgmt. Coll. Advanced Traffic, 1978; m. Rhonda Evans, July 28, 1970; children—Joel, Jerl, Rael, Marel. Supr. terminal ops. Consol. Rail Corp., Chgo., 1977-78, asst. terminal mgr., 1978-79; asst. terminal mgr. Pa. Truck Lines, Inc., Chgo., 1979-81; multimodal sales rep. Consol. Rail Corp., Chgo., 1981-83, multimodal sales mgr., Detroit, 1983-84, King of Prussia, Pa., 1984-85; pres. Griffin Transp. Services Inc., Chgo., 1985—; transp. cons., 1981—. Notary public. Mem. Intermodal Operating Com., Am. Mgmt. Assn., Piggyback Assn. Chgo., Detroit Intermodal Assn., Kappa Alpha Psi. Home: 958 Central Park Flossmoor IL 60422 Office: 2000 W 43d St Chicago IL 60609 Office: PO Box 3205 Southfield MI 48075

GRIFFIN, JOYCE MARIE, accounting instructor; b. Kansas City, Kans., May 26, 1955; d. Robert Christian and Elaine Blanche (Mauck) K.; m. Wesley K. Griffin, Aug. 13, 1977; children: Katherine Gail, Jill Marie. BS in Acctg., Kans. State U., 1977; MBA, U. Mo., Kansas City, 1986. Staff auditor Touche Ross & Co., Topeka, 1977-80; internal auditor Kansas City (Mo.) Power & Light, 1980; acctg. instr. Kansas City Kans. Community Coll., 1981—; instr. tax return workshops, Kansas City, Kans., 1986—; acctg. software cons. Tom Little & Co., Kansas City, Kans., 1987—. Com. mem. Kansas City Kans. Community Coll. Endowment Assn., 1986-87. Mem. Am. Inst. CPA's, Beta Gamma Sigma. Democrat. Roman Catholic. Club: Wyandotte County Bar Auxiliary (treas. 1986, sec. 1987) (Kansas City, Kans.). Avocations: reading, needlework. Home: 4132 N 110th St Kansas City KS 66109 Office: Kansas City Kans Community Coll 7250 State Ave Kansas City KS 66112

GRIFFIN, MARY VELMA SHOTWELL (MRS. JAMES LEONARD GRIFFIN), author; b. nr. Carrollton, O., Aug. 11, 1904; d. Winfield Scott and Eva Anaz (Smith) Shotwell; certificate elementary edn., Kent State U., 1925; m. James Leonard Griffin, Oct. 2, 1929. Accordionist, Radio Sta. WTAM, Cleve., 1926, Chatauqua and Lyceum circuits, 1927-28, Accordion Gypsies, 1931-48, Ringling Bros.-Barnum and Bailey Circus, 1935-36; tchr. pub. schs., Ohio, 1922-65; ret., 1965; now free lance writer. Gray lady, ARC, 1967—; bd. dirs. Bell-Herron Scholarship Found., 1965—; pres. Carroll County Hist. Soc., 1965-67, dir., 1963—, curator, 1967—. Recipient Disting. Service award Jaycees, 1979. Mem. NEA, Carroll County Ret. Tchrs. Assn., Ohio, Carroll County (pres. 1964-65) edn. assns., Ohio Hist. Soc., Ohio, Carroll County geneal. socs., Ohioana Library Assn. (county chmn. 1958—). Republican. Presbyterian. Clubs: Rebekah, Order Eastern Star. Author: Fair Prize, 1956; Circus Daze, 1957; Mystery Mansion, 1958; numerous short stories pub. in popular mags. Home: 11 Arch St Dellroy OH 44620

GRIFFIN, MICHAEL JAMES, media design and production company executive; b. Valparaiso, Ind., Feb. 9, 1948; s. Charles F. and Pauline A. (Lungren) G.; m. Janet Kay Yudt, Feb. 12, 1972; children—Heather, Shannon, Shane, Tara, Nathan, Patrick, Eric. B.S. in Edn., Ind. U., 1971. Tchr., Fegley Middle Sch. Portage, Ind., 1971-73; copy dir. Whiteco & Assocs. Advt., 1973-74; founder, pres. Michaeljay Communications, Inc. (name now Griffin Media Design), Chesterton, Ind., 1975—; adj. lectr. Valparaiso U. Pres., bd. trustees Westchester Twp. Library; bd. dirs. Jackson/Liberty Sch. Bldg. Corp. Recipient William Randolph Hearst Journalism award Ind. U., 1970; Golden Drummer award Bldg. Supply News, 1979; U.S. Indsl. Film Festival awards, 1981, 83; Cert. of Craftsmanship, Internat. Film Festival, Salerno, Italy, 1983; Advt. Achievement award Fleet Owner Mag., 1981; Community Improvement award Westchester C. of C., 1981, Nat. Travel Mktg. award, Internat. TV Assn. video award of excellence, Video Award of Merit; Ernie Pyle scholar. Mem. Assn. for Multi-Image, Sigma Delta Chi. Roman Catholic. Writer, producer numerous film and audio-visual prodns. for bus., industry and edn. Home: 313 1300 N Chesterton IN 46304 Office: 802 Wabash Chesterton IN 46304

GRIFFIN, PATRICK JOSEPH, lawyer, accountant; b. Chgo., Apr. 5, 1956; s. James L. and Annamae (Dorney) G.; m. Christina L. Besecker, May 24, 1986. B Bus. Adminstrn., U. Notre Dame, 1978; JD, De Paul U., 1983, postgrad., 1983—. Tax mgr. Coopers & Lybrand, Chgo., 1981-85; ptnr. Griffin & Gallagher, Chgo., 1985—. Mem. ABA, Ill. Bar Assn., Chgo. Bar Assn., Am. Inst. CPA's, Ill. CPA Soc., Young Irish Fellowship, St. Rita Alumni Assn. (v.p.). Democrat. Roman Catholic. Office: Griffin & Gallagher 100 W Monroe Suite 1901 Chicago IL 60603

GRIFFIN, PAUL DENNIS, optometrist; b. Sioux City, Iowa, June 14, 1930; s. John William and Ethel (Styles) G.; m. Frances Christen Phillips,

July 10, 1954 (div. May 1982); children: Paula Dennis Griffin Miller, Kevin Anson. BS, Morningside Coll., 1952, Ill. Coll. Optometry, 1953; DO, Ill. Coll. Optometry, 1954. Lic. optometrist, Ill., Iowa, Minn. Optometry Dr. William R. Dole, Olney, Ill., 1957; optometrist Vent Air Contact Lens Co., Mpls., 1958, Am. Contact Lens Co. Inc., St. Paul, 1958—; pvt. practice optometry St. Paul. ward worker Rep. Party, Mpls., 1965—. Served to 1st lt. U.S. Army, 1955-57. Mem. Am. Optometric Assn., Nat. Eye Research Found., Met. Optometric Dist. Soc., Internat. Shrine Clown Assn. (treas.), Sigma Pi Sigma. Lodge: Eagles, Shriners (bd. control), Masons. Avocations: clowning, hunting, fishing, swimming, wood crafts. Office: 412 Minnesota St Saint Paul MN 55101

GRIFFIN, RICHARD NORMAN, chemist, researcher; b. Winchester, Mass., Nov. 2, 1929; s. Norman Bernard and Helen Victoria (Kiernan) G.; m. Nancy Ann Noren, June 4, 1955; children: Arthur, Janet, Lee. AB, Columbia U., 1951; PhD, MIT, 1958. Research chemist Du Pont, Wilmington, Del., 1957-61; research chemist Gen. Electric Co., King of Prussia, Pa., 1961-78, Schenectady, N.Y., 1978-83; sr. scientist Gen. Electric Co., Cin., 1983—. Contbr. articles to profl. jours.; patentee in field, 1962, 74. Served to lt. (j.g.) USN, 1951-54. Recipient cert. of achievement NASA, 1970. Mem. Am. Chem. Soc., Soc. Advancement Materials and Process Engrs., U.S. Power Squadrons (comdr. 1975-76). Republican. Presbyterian. Avocation: boating. Home: 9821 Tollgate Ln Cincinnati OH 45242 Office: General Electric Co 1 Neumann Way Cincinnati OH 45215

GRIFFIN, ROBERT P., lawyer, former U.S. senator; b. Detroit, Nov. 6, 1923; s. J.A. and Beulah M. G.; m. Marjorie J. Anderson, 1947; children—Paul Robert, Richard Allen, James Anderson, Martha Jill. A.B., B.S., Central Mich. U., 1947, LL.D., 1963; J.D., U. Mich., 1950, LL.D., 1973; LL.D., Eastern Mich. U., 1969, Albion Coll., 1970, Western Mich. U., 1971, Grand Valley State Coll., 1971, Detroit Coll. Bus., 1972, Detroit Coll. Law, 1973; L.H.D., Hillsdale (Mich.) Coll., 1970; J.C.D., Rollins Coll., 1970; Ed.D., No. Mich. U., 1970; D. Pub. Service, Detroit Inst. Tech., 1971. Bar: Mich. Practiced in Traverse City, 1950-56; mem. 85th-89th congresses from 9th Dist. Mich.; U.S. senator from Mich. 1966-79; vis. fellow Am. Enterprise Inst. Public Policy Research, 1979—; counsel Miller, Canfield, Paddock & Stone, Traverse City, 1979-86; assoc. judge Mich. Supreme Ct., Traverse City, 1987—. Trustee Gerald R. Ford Found.; mem. World bd. govs. USO. Served with inf. AUS, World War II, ETO. Named 1 of 10 Outstanding Young Men of Nation U.S. Jaycees, 1959. Mem. Am., Mich., D.C. bar assns. Lodge: Kiwanis. Office: Mich Supreme Ct 13561 W Bay Shore Dr Traverse City MI 49684

GRIFFIN, RONALD CHARLES, law educator; b. Washington, Aug. 17, 1943; s. Roy John and Gwendolyn (Points) G.; m. Vicky Treadway, Nov. 26, 1967; children—David Ronald, Jason Roy, Meg Carrington. B.S., Hampton Inst., 1965; postgrad. Harvard U., summer 1965; J.D., Howard U., 1968; LL.M., U. Va., 1974. Bar: D.C. 1970, U.S. Supreme Ct. 1973. Asst. corp. counsel Govt. of D.C., 1970; asst. prof. law U. Oreg., 1974-78; assoc. prof. law Washburn U., Topeka, 1978-81, prof., 1981—; vis. prof. U. Notre Dame, 1981-82; dir. Council on Legal Ednl. Opportunity, Summer Inst., Great Plains Region, 1983; grievance examiner Midwest region EEOC, 1984-85; arbitrator consumer protection complaints Northeast Kans. Better Bus. Bur., 1986-87. Served to capt. JAGC, U.S. Army, 1970-74. Named William O. Douglas Outstanding Prof. of Yr. 1985-86; Rockefeller Found. grantee Howard U., 1965-68; fellow Parker Sch. Fgn. and Comparative Law, Columbia U., summer 1981; Kline sabbatical research and study, Japan, 1985. Mem. ABA, Cen. States Law Sch. Assn. (pres.-elect 1987—). Contbr. articles to legal jours. Home: 2031 Bowman Ct Topeka KS 66604 Office: Washburn U Sch Law Topeka KS 66621

GRIFFIN, W(ILLIAM) L(ESTER) HADLEY, shoe company executive; b. Edwardsville, Ill., May 17, 1918; s. Ralph D. and Julia (Hadley) G.; m. Phoebe M. Perry, Apr. 1, 1942; children: Dustin H. II, Lockwood Perry, Peter Burley. A.B., Williams Coll., 1940, LLD (hon.), 1987; LL.B., Washington U., 1947. Bar: Mo. 1947. Counsel Wohl Shoe Co., St. Louis, 1947-51; asst. sec. treas. Wohl Shoe Co., 1950-51; sec. Brown Shoe Co. (name changed to Brown Group, Inc. 1972), St. Louis, 1954-64; v.p. Brown Shoe Co. (name changed to Brown Group, Inc. 1972), 1964-66, exec. v.p., 1966-68, pres., 1968-72, chief exec. officer, 1969-72, 79-82, chmn. bd., 1972-85, pres., 1972-79, chmn. exec. com., 1971—, also dir.; chmn. bd. Fed. Res. Bank St. Louis; dir. Gen. Am. Life Ins. Co., Owens-Corning Fiberglas Corp., TW Services Inc., Ralston Purina Co. Chmn. bd. trustees Washington U.; chmn. nat. bd. Smithsonian Assocs., 1983-84; trustee Williams Coll., 1975-80; vice chmn. bd. trustees St. Louis Symphony Soc. Assn., former pres.; pres. United Fund Greater St. Louis, 1973, campaign chmn., 1972; former pres. St. Louis Civic Progress. Served from ensign to lt. USNR, 1941-45; as lt. comdr. 1951-52, Korea. Mem. Am. Footwear Industries Assn. (past chmn.). Republican. Office: Brown Group Inc 8400 Maryland Ave Saint Louis MO 63105

GRIFFITH, B(EZALEEL) HEROLD, physician, educator; b. N.Y.C., Aug. 24, 1925; s. Bezaleel Davies and Henrietta (Herold) G.; m. Jeanne B. Lethbridge, 1948; children: Susan, Nancy. Student, Johns Hopkins U., 1943-44; M.D., Yale U., 1948. Diplomate: Am. Bd. Plastic Surgery (dir. 1976-82, chmn. 1981-82). Intern Grace New Haven Community Hosp.-Yale U., 1948-49; resident in surgery VA Hosp., Newington, Conn., 1949-50; asst. resident in surgery 2d (Cornell) Surg. Div., Bellevue Hosp., N.Y.C., 1952-53; resident in plastic surgery VA Hosp., Bronx, 1953-55, U. Glasgow, Scotland, 1955, N.Y. Hosp. Cornell Med. Center, N.Y.C., 1956; research fellow in plastic surgery Cornell U. Med. Coll., 1956-57; practice medicine specializing in plastic surgery Chgo., 1957—; attending plastic surgeon Northwestern Meml., Children's Meml., VA Lakeside hosps., Rehab. Inst. Chgo.; instr. surgery Northwestern U., 1957-59, asso. in surgery, 1959-62, asst. prof. surgery, 1962-67, asso. prof., 1967-71, prof., 1971—, chief div. plastic surgery, 1970—; cons. plastic surgeon Nantucket (Mass.) Cottage Hosp. Assoc. editor: Plastic and Reconstructive Surgery, 1972-78; contbr. articles to profl. jours. Trustee Roycemore Sch., Evanston, 1966-79. Served to lt., M.C. USNR, 1950-52. Fellow A.C.S., Am. Assn. Plastic Surgeons, Chgo. Surg. Soc., Royal Soc. Medicine; mem. Am. Soc. Plastic and Reconstructive Surgeons (sec. 1972-74), Brit. Assn. Plastic Surgeons, Plastic Surgery Research Council (chmn. 1969), Am. Cleft Palate Assn., N.Y. Acad. Scis., AAAS, AMA, Ill., Chgo. med. socs., Assn. Am. Med. Colls., Midwestern Assn. Plastic Surgeons, Soc. Head and Neck Surgeons, Ill., Chgo. hist. socs., Civil War Round Table, Evanston Hist. Soc. (trustee 1974-78), Sigma Xi (pres. Northwestern U. 1986-87). Club: Yale (Chgo.). Lodge: Masons. Research in transplantation, skin tumors, cleft palate, paraplegia. Office: 251 E Chicago Ave Chicago IL 60611

GRIFFITH, CLEM WITHERS, retired electrical engineer; b. Lodgepole, Nebr., July 8, 1917; s. Louie Eugene and Leola Elsie (Withers) G.; m. Alvina Frank, Oct. 23, 1943; children—Lucille, Louise. B.S.E.E., Colo. State U., 1939. Registered profl. engr., Kans., Okla. Design engr. Boeing Airplane Co., Wichita, Kans., 1942-46, Brink & Dunwoody, Iola, Kans., 1947-52; city engr. Iola, 1952-59; design engr. Brink & Dunwoody, 1959-74; v.p. Shetlar Griffith Shetlar, Iola, 1974-87. Contbr. articles to profl. jours. Elder First Presbyn. Ch., Iola, 1960—. Served wtih USN, 1945-46. Mem. IEEE, Nat. Soc. Profl. Engrs., Kans. Engring. Soc. (sec. 1952-58, pres. 1958-59), Am. Water Works Assn., Kans. Rural Water Assn. Republican. Lodge: Rotary (bd. dirs. 1982—). Home: 209 S Oak St Iola KS 66749 Office: Shetlar Griffith Shetlar 216 N Jefferson Ave Iola KS 66749

GRIFFITH, D. KENDALL, lawyer; b. Aurora, Ill., Feb. 4, 1933; s. Walter George and Mary Elizabeth Griffith; m. Susan Smykal, Aug. 4, 1962; children—Kay, Kendall. B.A., U. Ill., 1955, J.D., 1958. Bar: Ill. 1958, U.S. Supreme Ct. 1973. Assoc. Hinshaw, Culbertson, Moelmann, Hoban & Fuller, Chgo., 1959-65, ptnr., 1965—; spl. asst. atty. gen. Ill., 1970-72; lectr. Ill. Inst. Continuing Legal Edn., 1970—. Trustee, Lawrence Hall Sch. for Boys, 1967—, v.p. for program, 1969-74; bd. dirs. Child Care Assn. Ill., 1970-73; mem. Lake Forest High Sch. Bd. Edn., 1983-84. Served to 2d lt. USAF, 1956. Mem. ABA (chmn. appellate advocacy com. 1983-84), Ill. Bar Assn., Chgo. Bar Assn., Appellate Lawyers Assn. Ill. (pres. 1973-74), Def. Research Inst., Ill. Def. Counsel, Chgo. Trial Lawyers Club. Club: University of Chgo. Mem. editorial bd. Ill. Civil Practice After Trial, 1970; co-editor The Brief, 1975-83; contbr. author Civil Practice After Trial, 1984; contbr. article to legal jour. Office: Hinshaw Culbertson Moelmann et al 69 W Washington St Suite 2700 Chicago IL 60602

GRIFFITH, DONALD NASH, minister; b. Glenwood Springs, Colo., Mar. 1, 1935; s. Paul Donal and Charlestine Louise (Nash) Tedford; m. Marilyn M. Bartlett, Aug. 26, 1956; children: Brenda, Janet, David. BA, U.Evansville, Ind., 1956; MDiv., Drew U., Madison, N.J., 1959; D in Ministry, Christian Theol. Sem., Indpls., 1977. Ordained elder United Meth. Ch., 1959. Minister Cook Meml. United Meth. Ch., Jeffersonville, Ind., 1960-64, Arlington United Meth. Ch., Bloomington, Ind., 1964-68; sr. minister St. Andrew United Meth. Ch., Indpls., 1968-75, Bradley United Meth. Ch., Greenfield, Ind., 1975-84, Irvington United Meth. Ch., Indpls., 1984—; pres. N. Cen. Commn. on Ministry, United Meth. Ch., 1985—; bd. dirs. Bd. Higher Edn., Min. Div. Ordained Ministry United Meth. Ch., Nashville, 1985—. Mem. Indpls. City and County Council, 1972-76. Named Conf. Chairperson of Yr., Bd. Health and Welfare Ministries, United Meth. Ch., 1976; recipient Leadership award Indpls. Ch. Fedn., 1976. Republican. Lodge: Rotary. Avocations: flying, reading, travel. Office: Irvington United Meth Ch 30 N Audubon Rd Indianapolis IN 46219

GRIFFITH, DOUGLAS, research scientist; b. Paterson, N.J., May 6, 1946; s. Fred Gleason and Grace (Nilsson) G.; m. Kisoon Jung, Jan. 3, 1978. B.A. in Psychology with distinction, Ohio State U., 1967; M.S., U. Utah, 1972, Ph.D., 1974. Research asst. dept. psychology U. Utah, 1970-74, teaching assoc., 1974-77; research psychologist Army Research Inst., Ft. Hood, Tex., 1974-81; research scientist Environ. Research Inst. Mich., Ann Arbor, 1981—. Served with U.S. Army, 1968-70. Mem. Psychonomic Soc., Human Factors Soc., Am. Psychol. Assn., Am. Ednl. Research Assn., AAAS. Contbr. articles to profl. jours.

GRIFFITH, MARIELLEN SHELLENBERGER, educator; b. Newton, Kans., Mar. 28, 1935; d. Peter Simon and Mabel Bertha (Deschner) Shellenberger; m. David Scott Griffith, July 15, 1961 (div. 1987); children—Scott Whittier, Jon Peter. Ed.S., Butler U., Indpls., 1973; Ed.D., Ball State U., 1976. Mem. faculty Bluffton Coll., 1959-61; sch. counselor Western Boone Corp., Jamestown, Ind., 1971-74; mem. faculty Butler U., Indpls., 1975—, assoc. prof. marital and family therapy; cons. women and bus., stress mgmt., assertion tng. Mem. Am. Psychol. Assn., Am. Assn. Counseling and Devel., Acad. Psychologists in Family Psychology, AAUW, Am. Assn. Marriage and Family Therapy. Office: Butler U 4600 Sunset Ave Indianapolis IN 46208

GRIFFITHS, MARTHA, lieutenant governor of Michigan; b. Pierce City, Mo., Jan. 29, 1912; m. Hicks G. Griffiths. B.A., U. Mo.; J.D., U. Mich.; postgrad., Wayne State U. Mem. Mich. Ho. of Reps., 1949-52; judge Recorders Ct., Detroit, 1953; mem. ways and means com. U.S. Congress, Washington, 1955-75; lt. gov. State of Mich., 1983—; ptnr. Griffiths & Griffiths, Detroit. Democrat. Office: Lieutenant Gov's Office 77940 McFadden Rd Romeo MI 48605 *

GRIFFITHS, RICHARD REESE, general aviation corporation executive; b. Youngstown, Ohio, July 6, 1931; s. Frank Reese and Louise Mary (Hoffman) G.; m. Alma M. Mackin, June 22, 1957; children: Richard Reese, Gregory, Douglas. B.S., Youngstown U., 1957; M.B.A., Kent State U., 1960. Mgr. personnel Babcock & Wilcox, Barberton, Ohio, 1959-69; indsl. relations mgr. Dresser Industries, Chgo., 1969-77; v.p. human resources Trane Co., La Crosse, Wis., 1977-79; sr. v.p. human resources Geosource Inc., Houston, 1979-85; v.p. indsl. relations Beech Aircraft Corp., Wichita, Kans., 1985—. Served with USMC, 1952-54. Mem. Am. Soc. Personnel Adminstrn., Machinery and Allied Products Inst. (vice-chmn. 1983-84). Republican. Roman Catholic. Clubs: Kingwood (Tex.) Country; Wichita, Wichita Country. Office: Beech Aircraft 9709 E Central Wichita KS 67201

GRIFFITHS, ROBERT PENNELL, banker; b. Chgo., May 6, 1949; s. George Findley and Marion E. (Winterrowd) G.; m. Susan Hillman, Jan. 31, 1976. B.A., Amherst Coll., 1972; M.S. in Mgmt., Northwestern U., 1974. Comml. banking officer No. Trust Co., Chgo., 1978-80, 2d v.p., 1980-83, v.p., 1983-85; sr. v.p. comml. lending UnibancTrust Co., Chgo., 1985—. Clubs: University (Chgo.), Metropolitan. Home: 1100 Waveland Rd Lake Forest IL 60045 Office: UnibancTrust Co Sears Tower Chicago IL 60606

GRIGGS, FRED, facilities planning executive, electrical engineer; b. Weston, W.Va., July 18, 1922; s. Luther Alonzo and Dora Tense (Cooper) G.; m. Betty Mae Samples, Aug. 24, 1946; children: Hildreth Kay Griggs Wright, Reynie Jay Griggs Hughes. BSEE, W.Va. U., 1949; postgrad., W.Va. U., Parkersburg, 1951, 63, Milw. Sch. Engring., 1969, Soc. Mfg. Engrs., 1975. Coal preparation engr. Consol. Coal Co., Fairmont, W.Va., 1949-57; sr. elect. engr. Kaiser Aluminum & Chem. Co., Ravenswood, W.Va., 1957-65; asst. facilities planning Dayton Walther Corp., Dayton, Ohio, 1965-74, mgr. facilities planning, 1974—. Advisor Jackson County (W.Va.) Bd. Edn., 1962-65, sec. adult edn. com., 1964. Served with U.S. Army, 1943-46, ETO. Recipient Grand Cross of Color, Internat. Rainbow Girls, 1964; named to Honorable Order of Ky. Cols., 1971, Ky. Admls., 1971. Republican. Methodist. Lodges: Shriners, Masons. Avocations: gardening, obedience tng. dogs, bridge, walking, reading. Home: 6118 Flemington Rd Dayton OH 45459 Office: Dayton Walther Corp 2800 E River Rd PO Box 1022 Dayton OH 45401

GRIGSBY, JEFFREY DALE, data processing executive; b. Ft. Wayne, Ind., July 18, 1945; s. Dale Adelbert and Joan Katherine (Blum) G.; m. Elizabeth Rose Horton, May 29, 1976; children: Daniel Charles, Bryant Jeffrey. BS in Math, Purdue U., 1969. Programmer analyst Control Data Corp., Arden Hills, Minn., 1967-76; systems analyst, supr., mgr. NCR Comten, Roseville, Minn., 1976—. Co-leader Cub Scout Am., New Brighton, Minn., 1982-86. Mem. NCR Comten Mgmt. Club (program dir. 1985). Club: MCA Rapid Riders (Whitewater Expdn. Coordinator 1986). Avocation: whitewater canoeing, music. Home: 1641 Chatham Ave Arden Hills MN 55112 Office: NCR Comten 2700 Snelling Ave N Roseville MN 55115

GRIGSBY, ROBERT HOPKINS, dentist; b. Greenville, S.C., July 7, 1945; s. Robert Hopkins and Lucretia (Peacock) G.; m. Mary Grace Montalbano, Apr. 20, 1968; 1 child, Rebecca. Student, Pa. State U., 1964-65, U. Wis., Janesville, 1969-72; DDS, Marquette U., 1976. Gen. practice dentistry Beloit, Wis., 1976-85; assoc. dentist Drs. Frey and Grigsby S.C., Beloit, 1985—; cons. bur. identification Rock County Sheriff's Dept., Janesville, 1983—. Served with US Army, 1964-67. Mem. ADA, Wis. Dental Soc., Rock County Dental Soc., Am. Soc. Forensic Odontologists, Nat. Model R.R. Assn. Mem. United Ch. Christ. Club: Ducks Unlimited (Beloit) (sponsor 1985-86). Lodge: Elks (Exalted Ruler 1982). Office: Drs Frey and Grigsby SC 2149 Pioneer Beloit WI 53511

GRILLOT, FRANCIS ALBERT, JR., manufacturing company executive, chemical engineer; b. Parsons, Kans., Feb. 3, 1935; s. Francis Albert Grillot and Eleanor Frances (Hillegas) Evilsizer; m. Mary Ellen Haley, July 20, 1957; children: Timothy J., Tammmy M. Grillot Taylor, Jacqueline Grillot Brown, Janetta L. AA, Parsons Jr. Coll., 1955; BChemE, Kans. State U., 1958; MS in Bus. Adminstrn., Wichita State U., 1965. Process engr. CRA, Inc., Coffeyville, Kans., 1958-60; foreman, supt., mgr. Vulcan Materials, Wichita, Kans., 1960-68, Giesmar, La., 1968-70; v.p. environ. F.C. Schaffer & Assocs., Baton Rouge, 1970-74; v.p. mktg. and devel. Peabody Tec Tank, Parsons, Kans., 1974-78; dir. mktg. A.O. Smith Harvestore Products Inc., DeKalb, Ill., 1978—. Mem. Am. Waterworks Assn., Water and Waste Equipement Mfrs. Assn. (chmn. 1985-86), Nat. Soc. Profl. Engrs., Ill. Soc. Profl. Engrs., NRA. Club: Anvil (Dundee). Lodge: KC (pres. 1955), Lions (officer Parsons 1976-77). Avocations: woodworking, sports officiating, coin collecting, antiques. Home: Ellwood Greens Country Club Rural Route 2 Box 40 Genoa IL 60135 Office: AO Smith Harvestore Products Inc 345 Harvestore Dr DeKalb IL 60115

GRIM, PETER CHRISTOPHER, manufacturing engineer; b. Bryn Mawr, Pa., Mar. 27, 1961; s. George William and Mary Elizabeth (Cordsen) G. BME, Gen. Motors Inst., Flint, Mich., 1984. Prodn. engr. AC Spark Plug div. Gen. Motors Copr., Flint., 1984-85, mfg. system engr., 1985-86; mfg. system engr. Delco Electronic Corp., Flint., 1986—. Mem. Soc. Mfg. Engrs., Machine Vision Assn. Republican. Lutheran. Avocatins: motor sports, carpentry, targetshooting, painting and drawing.

GRIMALDI, ANTHONY MICHAEL, surgeon; b. Detroit, Jan. 30, 1944; s. Ignazio Robert and Eva Laura (Hernandez) G.; m. Alexandra G. Charles, Aug. 12, 1967; children: Anthony Ignazio, John Alexander. BA in Biology, Olivet Coll., 1966; D. Osteo. Medicine, Chog. Coll. Osteo. Medicine, 1971. Intern Detroit Osteo. Hosp., 1971-72, resident in urology, 1972-76; chief sect. urology Chgo. Osteo. Med. Ctr., 1976—, assoc. prof. surgery, 1976—, resident trainer urol. surgery; chief sect. urology Olympia Fields (Ill.) Osteo. Med. Ctr., 1976—; flight examiner FAA, 1978—. Trustee Chgo. Am. Cancer Soc., 1980. Fellow Am. Coll. Osteo. Surgeons; mem. AMA, Am. Osteo. Assn., Ill. Assn. Osteo. Physicians and Surgeons, Ill. State Med. Soc. Club: Olympia Fields Country. Avocations: flying, golf. Office: 5200 S Ellis Ave Chicago IL 60615

GRIMES, CHARLES FRANCIS, II, controller; b. Chicago Heights, Ill., Feb. 2, 1956; s. Charles F. and Laverne V. (Bunte) G.; m. Donna J. Granno, June 20, 1981; 1 child, Jennifer Marie. BS, No. Ill. U., 1978. CPA, Ill. Auditor Ernst & Whinney, Chgo., 1978-79; controller F.H. Ayer Mfg. Co., Chicago Heights, 1979—, also bd. dirs. Mem. Am. Inst. CPA's, Ill. CPA Soc. Roman Catholic. Home: 21912 Main St Richton Park IL 60471 Office: F H Ayer Mfg Co 2015 Halsted St Chicago Heights IL 60411

GRIMES, GEOFFREY C., architect; b. Marshalltown, Iowa, Jan. 8, 1946; s. Lloyd Orville and Irene Genevieve (Peterson) G.; m. Vicki Sue King, Apr. 28, 1973; children: Tiffani Clare, Ryan Matthew. BArch, Iowa State U., 1969. Registered architect, Iowa. Grad. architect Stenson & Warm, Waterloo, Iowa, 1969-73; registered architect and officer Stenson Warm Grimes Port, Architects, Waterloo, 1973—; adj. prof. U. No. Iowa, Cedar Falls, 1975-77;. Pres. Waterloo Community Playhouse, 1978, 79, 84, Cedar Valley United Way, Waterloo, 1982; v.p. Leadership Investment for Tomorrow, Waterloo, 1986; mem. Cedar Falls Planning and Zoning Commn., 1980—. Mem. AIA (architecture in edn. com.), Am. Arbitration Assn. (constrn. arbitrator 1978—), Council Ednl. Facility Planners, Black Hawk County Alumni Club (Service Key award 1986), Waterloo C. of C. (v.p. 1987), Alpha Sigma Phi (Delta Beta Xi award 1978). Republican. Prebsyterian. Lodge: Lions (pres. Waterloo 1979). Home: 1476 Laurel Circle Cedar Falls IA 50613 Office: Stenson Warm Grimes Port 3404 Midway Dr Waterloo IA 50701

GRIMES, HUGH GAVIN, physician; b. Chgo., Aug. 19, 1929; s. Andrew Thomas and Anna (Gavin) G.; m. Rose Anne Leahy, Aug. 21, 1954; children—Hugh Gavin, Paula Anne, Daniel Joseph, Sarah Louise, Nancy Marie, Jennifer Diane. Student, Loyola U., 1947-50; B.S., U. Ill., 1952, M.D., 1954. Diplomate Am. Bd. Ob-Gyn. Intern St. Joseph Hosp., Chgo., 1954-55; resident in ob-gyn St. Joseph Hosp., 1955-58; practice medicine specializing in ob-gyn Chgo., 1960—; lectr., asst. clin. prof. Stritch Sch. Medicine, Loyola U., Chgo.; active staff St. Joseph Hosp., Chgo., also v.p. med. staff, 1977-78, pres. staff, 1979-80; asst. prof. clin. ob-gyn Northwestern U. Med. Sch., 1980—. Contbr. articles to profl. jours. Trustee Regina Dominican High Sch. Served to capt. M.C., AUS, 1958-60. Fellow Am. Coll. Ob-Gyn, Chgo. Gynecol. Soc.; mem. Am. Cancer Soc. (mem. profl. edn. com. Chgo. unit), Am. Fertility Soc., AMA, Ill. Med. Soc., Chgo. Med. Soc., Cath. Physicians Guild, Assn. Am. Physicians and Surgeons, Am. Soc. Colposcopy and Colpomicroscopy, Am. Assn. Gynecologic Laparoscopists, Assn. Art Inst. Chgo., Assn. Field Mus., Assocs. Smithsonian Instn., Pi Kappa Epsilon. Office: 2800 N Sheridan Rd Suite 406 Chicago IL 60657

GRIMLEY, JEFFREY MICHAEL, dentist; b. Alton, Ill., Feb. 3, 1957; s. John Richard and Joyce Imogene (Mallin) G.; m. Julie Ellen Gardner, Aug. 2, 1980; children: Joel Michael, Christopher Mark. BS, U. Iowa, 1979, DDS, 1983; cert., Miami Valley Hosp, Dayton, Ohio, 1984. Gen. practice dentistry Naperville, Ill., 1984—. Mem. ADA, Acad. Gen. Dentistry, Ill. Dental Soc., Chgo. Dental Soc. Methodist. Avocations: sports, photography. Office: 14 S Main Naperville IL 60540

GRIMM, MARY HEIL, dentist; b. St. Louis, Sept. 27, 1950; d. Floyd Willard and Marguerite Ida (Speh) Heil; m. Fred Peter Grimm, Dec. 11, 1982. BS, U. Notre Dame, 1973; DMD, Washington U., 1983. Lab technician, instr. Washington U., St. Louis, 1976-79; gen. practice dentistry St. Louis, 1983—. Active Gateway Devel., St. Louis. Mem. ADA, Assn. Gen. Dentistry, Mo. Dental Soc., Greater St. Louis Dental Soc. Republican. Roman Catholic. Avocations: tennis, golf, piano. Home: 1101 Westmoor Pl Saint Louis MO 63131 Office: Loughborough Dental Group Saint Louis MO 63109

GRIMM, PETER LEROY, meteorologist; b. Morristown, N.J., Jan. 8, 1959; s. Charles Leroy and Rose Patricia (Faramo) G. BS in Meteorology, Lyndon State Coll., 1981; postgrad. in meteorology, U. Wis., 1982-87. Meteorologist I.P Krick Assocs. Inc., Palm Springs, Calif., 1981, Oceanweather Inc., Cos Cobb, Conn., 1981, 84, Space Sci. and Engring. Ctr., Madison, Wis., 1986—. Recipient Rita L. Bole award Lyndon State Coll., 1981. Mem. Am. Meteorol. Soc., Nat. Weather Assn. Avocations: racquet sports, skiing, violin, music. Home: 125 S Brittingham Pl Madison WI 53715 Office: U Wis Dept Meteorology 1225 W Dayton St Madison WI 53706

GRIMM, ROBERT ARTHUR, chemical company executive; b. Two Rivers, Wis., July 25, 1937; s. Arthur Adolph and Lillian Ann (Zimmer) G.; m. Mary Catherine Schwinghamer, June 26, 1965; children—Ann, Therese, Christopher. B.S., U. Wis., 1959; Ph.D., Stanford U., 1963. Research chemist Archer Daniels Midland Co., Mpls., 1963-67, sr. research chemist, 1967-73, mgr. organic chemistry, 1973; sect. mgr. organic chemistry Ashland Chem., Columbus, Ohio, 1973-77, sect. mgr. organic ventures, 1977-80, research mgr. organic ventures, 1980-83, research mgr. new project generation, 1983—. Mem. Am. Chem. Soc., AAAS, Sigma Xi. Contbr. articles to profl. jours. Home: 1810 Ivanhoe Ct Columbus OH 43220 Office: Ashland Chem PO Box 2219 Columbus OH 43216

GRIMMELMANN, KARL WILLIAM JOHN, advertising executive, reserve military officer; b. Teaneck, N.J., Dec. 8, 1947; s. Karl William John and Jean Ruth (Vogt) G.; m. Cynthia Ann Pacini, Feb. 25, 1971; children: Barbara, Erika. BS, Black Hills State Coll., 1973. Sales mgr. Sta. KCHE Radio, Cherokee, Iowa, 1974—. Vice chmn. Cherokee Community Credit Union, 1985—. Served to lt. USNR, 1966—. Mem. Naval Res. Assn., Naval Enlisted Res. Assn., Cherokee C. of C. (rodeo bd. govs.), Meml. Weekend Rodeo. Republican. Lutheran. Lodge: Kiwanis (sec.-treas. Cherokee club 1979-81, pres. 1981-82). Avocation: antique automobile restoration. Home: Church St Larrabee IA 51029 Office: Sta KCHE Radio 201 S Fifth St Cherokee IA 51012

GRIMMER, MARGOT, dancer, choreographer, director; b. Chgo., Apr. 5, 1944; d. Vernon and Ann (Radville) G.; student Lake Forest; 1963, Northwestern U., 1964-68. Dancer, N.Y.C. Ballet prodn. of Nutcracker Chgo., 1956-57, Kansas City Starlight Theatre, 1958, St. Louis Mcpl. Theatre, 1959, Chgo. TentHouse-Music Theater, 1960-61, Lyric Opera Ballet, Chgo., 1961, 63-66, 68, Ballet Russe de Monte Carlo, N.Y.C., 1962, Ruth Page Internat. Ballet, Chgo., 1965-70; dancer-choreographer Am. Dance Co., Chgo., 1972—, artistic dir., 1972—; dancer, choreographer Bob Hope Show, Milw., 1975, Washington Bicentennial Performance, Kennedy Center, 1976, Woody Guthrie Benefit Concerts, 1976-77, Assyrian Cultural Found., Chgo., 1977-78, Iranian Consulate Performance, Chgo., 1978, Israeli Consulate Concert, Chgo., 1980 Chgo. Council Fine Arts Programs, 1978—, U.S. Boating Indsl. Show, 1981—; dir.-tchr. Am. Dance Sch., 1971—; appeared in TV commls. and indsl. films for Libbys Foods, Sears, Gen. Motors, others, 1963—, also in feature film Risky Business, 1982; soloist in ballet Repertory Workshop, CBS-TV, 1964, dance film Statics (Internat. Film award), 1967; soloist in concert Ravinia, 1973. Ill. Arts Council grantee, 1972-74, 78, Nat. Endowment Arts grantee, 1973-74. Mem. Actors Equity Assn., Screen Actors Guild, Am. Guild Mus. Artists. Important works include ballets In-A-Gadda-Da-Vida, 1972, The Waste Land, 1973, Rachmaninoff: Theme and Variations, 1973, Le Baiser de la Fee and Sonata, 1974, Four Quartets, 1974, Am. Export, 1975, Earth, Wind and Fire, 1976, Blood, Sand and Empire, 1977, Disco Fever, 1978, Pax Romana, Xanadu,

1979, Ishmael, 1980, Vertigo, 1982, Eye in the Sky, 1984, Frankie Goes to Hollywood, 1986, Power House African, 1987, others; dance critic Mail-Advertiser Publs., 1980-82; host cable TV show Spotlight, 1984-85, Viewpoints, 1987. Home: 970 Vernon Ave Glencoe IL 60022 Office: 442 Central Ave Highland Park IL 60035

GRIMSRUD, LARS GUDMUND, aerospace executive, association executive; b. Baerum, Norway, Aug. 24, 1956; s. Lars and Randi (Theige) G.; divorced; children: Kristil, Lars Eirik. Student, Brigham Young U., 1974-76; BS in Aviation Mgmt., Metro State Coll., Denver, 1978. Quality control mgr. Parker-Hannifin Aero., Longmont, Colo., 1978-84; sr. quality engr. Martin Marietta Aero., Denver, 1984—; pres., chief exec. officer GTO Assn. Am., Broomfield, Colo., 1982—. Editor: The Legend, GTO Assn. Am., 1985—; contbr. tech. articles to The Legend. Office: GTO Assn Am 1634 Briarson Dr Saginaw MI 48603

GRINDON, HOWARD JAMES, coal company executive, accountant; b. Pipestone, Minn., June 15, 1927; s. Howard A. L. and Geraldine D. (Harger) G.; m. Naomi K. Savoy, June 5, 1951; children: Cheryl N., Russell H. BBA, Case Western Res. U., 1957. CPA, Ohio. Staff acct. Haskins & Sells, CPA's, Cleve., 1954-60; asst. treas. Investment Life Ins. Co., Cleve., 1960-62; acct. Keister, Cerio & Radice, Cleve., 1962-64; asst. treas. N.Am. Coal Co., Cleve., 1964—. Treas. St. Mary's Episc. Ch., Cleve., 1955-62, St. Matthew's Episc. Ch., Brecksville, Ohio, 1963-68. Served as staff sgt. USAF, 1950-54. Recipient De Molay Cross of Honor, Internat. Supreme Council Order of De Molay, 1979. Mem. Am. Inst. CPA's, DAV, Am. Assn. Retired Persons. Lodge: Masons. Home: 7583 Keywest Dr Parma OH 44134 Office: North Am Coal Corp 12800 Shaker Blvd Cleveland OH 44120

GRING, SUSAN DIETRICH, nursing services administrator, nurse; b. Mineola, N.Y., Aug. 21, 1945; d. Rodney Siegfred and Jeanne (Russell) Dietrich; m. David Michael Gring, June 3, 1967; children: Lisa Marie, Christian Nathaniel. Diploma in nursing, Hosp. of the Med. Coll. Pa., Phila., 1966; BA in Health Care Adminstrn. summa cum laude, Concordia Coll., Moorhead, Minn., 1984. Registered nurse, N.D., Minn. Charge nurse Eventide Long Term Care, Moorhead, 1979-83; adminstrv. resident Luth. Hosps. and Homes, Fargo, N.D., 1984; geriatric care coordinator Fargo Clinic, 1985, asst. dir. patient services, 1985-86, dir. nursing services, 1986—. Sunday sch. tchr., mem. Laotian refugee com., Olivet Luth. Ch., Fargo, 1982-85. Luth. Social Service System Ednl. scholar Am. Luth. Ch., 1983-84. Mem. Gerontol. Soc. Am., Alpha Soc. Democrat. Clubs: C-400 Concordia Coll., Concordia Book, E-100 Eventide Home (Moorhead, Minn.). Avocations: gourmet cooking, tennis, skiing, hiking. Home: 2411 S 18th St Moorhead MN 56060 Office: Fargo Clinic 737 Broadway Fargo ND 58123

GRIPP, MIRIAM LUCILLE, medical office administrator, radiology technician; b. Jamestown, N.Y., May 31, 1939; d. Everett Barry and Frances Mildred (Taylor) Eaton; m. William Arthur Gripp, Sept. 30, 1961; children—Cynthia Lane, Richard Eaton. Grad. Mt. Sinai Hosp. Sch. Radiology Technologists, 1959; student Western Res. U., 1958-61. X-ray technician to Drs. Krause, Lubert and Assocs., Inc., Cleveland Heights, 1959, office mgr., 1974, adminstr., University Heights, Ohio, 1979—. Mem. Greater Clev. Growth Assn. Mem. Am. Registry Radiologic Technologists (cert.), Am. Mgmt. Assn. Republican. Presbyterian. Club: Chagrin Valley (Ohio) Athletic. Office: 14100 Cedar Rd 250 University Heights OH 44121

GRISMORE, JOHN RICHARD, jeweler, watchmaker; b. Corydon, Iowa, Oct. 21, 1924; s. John Arthur and Jennie Gertrude (Bussey) G.; m. Virginia Lynn Rice, Dec. 30, 1947; children—John Richard, Jr., Carol Lynn. Student Bradley U., 1946-48. Lic. watchmaker. Ptnr. Grismore Jewelry, Centerville, Iowa, 1963—. Author poetry, short stories, genealogy. Pres. Community Club, Seymour, Iowa, 1956. Served with U.S. Army, 1943-46, ETO. Mem. C. of C. Methodist. Avocations: astronomy; archaeology; physics; anthropology; nature. Home: 1101 S 15th St Centerville IA 52544 Office: Grismore Jewelry 303 N 13th St Box 543 Centerville IA 52544

GRISMORE, MICHAEL ALLEN, electrical engineer; b. Evansville, Ind., Mar. 24, 1941; m. Linda Faye Davis, Nov. 11, 1966; children: Lisa, Eric. BEE, U. Evansville, 1964. Product engr. Potter and Brumfield, Princeton, Ind., 1970-75, mgr. prodn. engring., 1975—. Mem. Soc. Mfg. Engrs., Valley Mgmt. Assn. Club: Princeton Country. Lodge: Elks (trustee Princeton club). Avocations: golfing, bowling, camping. Home: Rural Rt 1 Columbia Estates Princeton IN 47670 Office: Potter & Brumfield 1200 E Broadway Princeton IN 47671

GRISWOLD, KENNETH WALTER, educator; b. Joliet, Ill., Nov. 2, 1937; s. Robert P. and Louise A. (Kaatz) G.; BS, Ill. State U., 1961; MS, No. Ill. U., 1965; EdD, No. Ill. U., 1986; m. Carole Rockwood, Feb. 3, 1962; children—Stephen R., Kent R. Tchr., coach Reed-Custer High Sch., Braidwood, Ill., 1961-64; counselor Lockport (Ill.) Central High Sch., 1964-66, Santa Ana (Calif.) Unified and Jr. Coll. Dist., 1966-67; prof. Rock Valley Coll., Rockford, Ill., 1967—. Mem. Am. Assn. Counseling and Devel., Am. Psychol. Assn., Am. Coll. Personnel Assn., Internat. Soc. Sport Psychology. Republican. Episcopalian. Contbr. articles in field to profl. jours. Home: 3901 Spring Creek Rd Rockford IL 61111 Office: 3301 N Mulford Rd Rockford IL 61111

GRISWOLD, PAUL MICHAEL, clinical psychologist, consultant; b. Milw., Sept. 26, 1945; s. Willard Matthew and Evelyn (Haerle) G.; m. AnnMari Gerardine La Valle, Aug. 2, 1969; children: Matthew Paul, Jennifer Jean. BA, Marquette U., 1967, MS, 1969; PhD, Kent State U., 1972. Sr. staff psychologist Wis. Div. Corrections, Milw., 1972-83; pvt. practice clin. and cons. psychology Menomonee Falls, Wis., 1973—; lectr. Mount Mary Coll., Milw., 1973-78; faculty Wis. Sch. of Profl. Psychology, Milw., 1981—; cons. Ethan Allen Sch. Wis. Div. Corrections, Wales, Wis., 1984—. Contbr. articles to profl. jours. Mem. Am. Psychol. Assn., Wis. Psychol. Assn., Milw. Area Psychol. Assn. Avocations: old cars, sailing, ice boating. Home: 1366 County Hwy J Hubertus WI 53033 Office: Clin Psychology Assocs W156 N8327 Pilgrim Rd Menomonee Falls WI 53051

GRIVNA, HOWARD WALTER, manufacturing executive; b. Mpls., Nov. 16, 1934; s. John J. and Mary (Svec) G.; m. Marlene Veronica Kaeder, May 14, 1955; children: Marybeth, Christine, Michael, Craig. Grad. high sch., Mpls. V.p., gen. mgr. Timesaver Sanders, Mpls., 1959-71; regional sales mgr. Kimwood Corp., Cottage Grove, Oreg., 1977-80; owner, pres. Abrasive Engring. and Mfg. Inc., Mpls., 1971-77; pres. Abrasive Engring. and Mfg. Inc., Olathe, Kans., 1980—; bd. dirs. Woodworking Machinery Mfrs. Am., Phila., 1982-84. Inventor grinding machine, 1959, cross-grain sander, 1973, centering feed system, 1981. Pres. Rice Creek Watershed Assn., Mpls., 1972-75. Roman Catholic. Avocations: hunting, fishing. Home: 12317 King Ave Overland Park KS 66213 Office: Abrasive Engring & Mfg Inc 540 E Hwy 56 Olathe KS 66061

GROBMAN, ARNOLD BRAMS, educator; b. Newark, Apr. 28, 1918; s. Samuel H. and Sophia (Brams) G.; m. Hulda Gross, Feb. 20, 1944; children: Marc Ross, Beth Allison. B.S., U. Mich., 1939; M.S., U. Rochester, 1941, Ph.D., 1943. Instr. zoology U. Rochester, 1943-44; research asso. Manhattan project 1944-46; from asst. prof. to asso. prof. biology U. Fla., 1946-59; research participant Oak Ridge Inst. Nuclear Studies, summer 1950, research specialist, med. center study, 1951-52; dir. Fla. State Mus., 1952-59; dir. biol. scis. curriculum study U. Colo., 1959-65; dean (Coll. Arts and Scis.); prof. zoology Rutgers U., New Brunswick, N.J., 1965-67; dean Rutgers Coll. Rutgers U., prof. zoology Rutgers Coll., 1967-72; vice chancellor for acad. affairs, prof. biol. scis. U. Ill., Chgo., 1973-74; spl. asst. to pres. U. Ill., 1974-75; chancellor U. Mo.-St. Louis, 1975-85, chancellor emeritus, 1985—, prof. biology, 1975—, research prof., 1986—; adj. curator Fla. State Mus., 1982—; vis. lectr. Utah State U., U. So. Ill., Nat. Taiwan Normal U., U. Campinas, Brazil, U. New Delhi, India, U. No. Sumatra, Indonesia, U. Sind, Pakistan, Chulalongkorn U., Bangkok, Thailand, U. Singapore, Sophia U., Japan, Chiang Mia U., Thailand; cons. to govt., industry, founds. and ednl. instns., 1954—; Mem. div. biology and agr. NRC-Nat. Acad. Scis., 1954-58, com. adult edn., 1956-58; sec. U.S. nat. com. Internat. Union Biol. Scis., 1966-69; Chmn. Ednl. Opportunity Center of Met. St. Louis, 1976-78; mem. advisory team sci. soc., Thailand, 1971; fgn. observer Treaty Plebiscite, Gov. Panama, 1977-78; mem. Commn. on Adult Learner. Author: (with others) Island Life: A Study of the Land Vertebrates of Eastern Lake Michigan, 1948, Our Atomic Heritage, 1951, Genetics Effects of Chronic X-irratiation Exposure in Mice, 1960, BSCS Biology Implementation in the Schools, 1964, The Changing Classroom, 1969; Editor: (with others) Social Implications of Biological Education, 1970; contbr. (with others) articles to newspapers, profl. jours., encys. and newspapers. Bd. dirs. in St. Louis United Way, Laumeier Sculpture Park, Narcotics Service Council, Regional Commerce and Growth Assn.; v.p. St. Louis Conf. on Edn., 1980—; bd. dirs. in St. Louis Higher Edn. Ctr., St. Louis Pub. Library. Recipient Fred H. Stoye prize Am. Soc. Ichthyologists and Herpetologists, 1941; A Cressy Morrison prize N.Y. Acad. Scis., 1943; Macalaster award Nat. Assn. Biology Tchrs., 1966; award of merit Urban League, 1984; Commanders Cross, Order of Merit, Fed. Republic Ger., 1985. Mem. Acad. Zoology in India (exec. com. 1967-69), Am. Assn. Higher Edn., AAAS (council 1961-65), Am. Assn. Museums (mus. tng. com. 1960-63), Am. Assn. State Colls. and Univs. (urban affairs com. 1977-85), Am. Ednl. Research Assn., Am. Inst. Biol. Scis. (exec. com. 1958-61, Disting. Service award 1984), Am. Soc. Ichthyologists and Herpetologists (bd. govs. 1952—, pres. 1964), Am. Soc. Naturalists, Am. Soc. Zoologists, Assn. Am. Med. Colls., Assn. Southeastern Biologists, Assn. Supervision and Curriculum Devel., Asian Assn. Biol. Edn., Biol. Scis. Curriculum Study (chmn. steering com. 1965-69), Biol. Soc. China, Biol. Soc. Washington, Council on Fgn. Relations, NEA, Edn. Programs Improvement Corp. (trustee 1970-74), Colo.-Wyo. Acad. Sci., AAUP, Explorers Club, Fla. Acad. Sci., Fla. Found. Future Scientists (chmn. 1957-59), Mo. Council Pub. Higher Edn. (exec. com. 1977-82, v.p. 1978, pres. 1979), Mo. Bot. Garden, Nat. Council Accreditation Tchr. Edn. (chmn. 1970-71), Genetics Soc., Herpetologists League, Philippine Assn. Sci. Tchrs., Nat. Assn. Biology Tchrs. (pres. 1966, editorial bd. 1974-77, dir. 1978-80), Nat. Assn. Research Sci. Teaching, Nat. Assn. State Univs. and Land Grant Colls. (exec. com. 1979-80, council on acad. affairs 1974-76, chmn. div. urban affairs 1978-79), Nat. Sci. Tchrs. Assn., Nature Conservancy, Newcomen Soc., N.J. Acad. Scis., Sci. Soc. Thailand, Soc. Study Amphibians and Reptiles, Soc. Study Evolution, Soc. Systematic Zoology, Soc. Vertebrate Paleontology, Southeastern Museums Conf. (pres. 1955-57), Assn. Tropical Biology, Phi Beta Kappa, Sigma Xi, Phi Kappa Phi, Phi Sigma, Alpha Sigma Lambda, Alpha Epsilon Delta. Office: Univ of Mo-St Louis 429 Marillac Hall 8001 Natural Bridge Rd Saint Louis MO 63121

GRODI, MICHAEL EDWARD, hospital administrator, respiratory therapist; b. Toledo, June 9, 1951; s. Leroy Edward and Laura Marie (Gibson) G.; m. Jacqueline Kay Schultz, May 14, 1974 (div. Apr. 1983); 1 child, Aaron; m. Yvette Marie Zimmerman, Apr. 14, 1984. BS, U. Cin., 1975, MBA, 1986. Registered respiratory therapist. Respiratory therapist Children's Hosp. Med. Ctr., Cin., 1973, The Jewish Hosp., Cin., 1973-75; dir. respiratory therapy C.R. Holmes Hosp., Cin., 1975-78, asst. adminstr., 1978-85, sr. asst. adminstr., 1985-86; sr. asst. adminstr. U. Cin. Hosp., 1986—. Avocations: history, biology, collecting firearms, reading. Office: U Cin Hosp 234 Goodman St Cincinnati OH 45267

GROE, ANTOINETTE (TONI) DIANNE, home economics and adult educator, municipal official; b. Sandstone, Minn., Oct. 12, 1949; d. Charles Raymond and Alice Lara (Goebel) Yaste; m. Daniel Noreen Groe, June 12, 1971; children: Christopher, Erin, Blake. Student, Augsburg Coll., 1967-68; BS in Home Econs. Edn., U. Minn., 1974. Adjustment clk. Fed. Reserve Bank, Mpls., 1969-79; subs. tchr. Anoka (Minn.)-Hennepin Pub. Sch. Dist. #11, 1975; tchr. home econs. Sandstone Pub. Schs., 1976-77, lead tchr. Gen. Equivalency Diploma community edn. program, 1982—; tchr. home econs. Anoka Pub. Schs., 1978-79; asst. mgr. Joann Fabrics, Mpls., 1979-80; v.p. adv. council community edn., Sandstone, 1984-85, pres. 1985-86. Sandstone Twp. treas., 1984—. Mem. Sandstone Homemakers' Club (sec. 1983, pres. 1985). Avocations: selling handicrafts, canoeing, tennis, walking, swimming.

GROESBECK, WAYNE JAY, social worker; b. Albany, N.Y., Jan. 20, 1945; s. Wilbur J. and Ruth Hilda (Williman) G.; m. Sandra Jane Crosier, Aug. 28, 1965; children: Adam Jay, Faith Janette. BA, Hope Coll., 1967. Lic. social worker, Mich. Social worker N.Y. Dept. Social Services, 1971-73, Mich. Dept. Social Services, Muskegon, 1973—. Mem. Sr. Substance Abuse Coalition Muskegon; deacon Covenant Community Ch., Muskegon Heights, 1986; chmn. Mich. State Employees Assn. Constl. Conv., 1981-82. Served with U.S. Army, 1969-71. Democrat. Mem. Reformed Ch. in Am. Club: Muskegon Country Steelheaders. Avocation: fishing. Home: 1308 Calvin Ave Muskegon MI 49442 Office: Mich Dept Social Services PO Box 999 Muskegon MI 49443

GROESCH, JOHN WILLIAM, JR., oil company executive; b. Seattle, Nov. 22, 1923; s. John William and Jeanette Morrison (Gilmur) G.; B.S. in Chem. Engring., U. Wash., 1944; m. Joyce Eugenia Schauble, Apr. 25, 1948; children—Sara, Mary, Andrew. Engr., Union Oil Co., Los Angeles, 1944-48, corp. economist, Los Angeles, 1948-56, chief statistician, 1956-62, mgr., 1962-68, mgr., Schaumburg, Ill., 1968—. Bd. dirs. Arlington Heights (Ill.) Boy Scouts Am., 1977—, v.p., 1979, 82-85; commr. 1980-81, mem. Oak-Brook (Ill.) East Cen. Region, 1984—; treas. Scout Cabin Found., Barrington, 1977—. Served with USN, 1944-47. Mem. West Coast Mktg. Research Council (chmn. 1969), Am. Petroleum Inst. (chmn. com. 1970-72). Lodge: Mason. Home: 17 Shady Ln Deer Park Barrington IL 60010 Office: 1650 E Golf Rd Schaumburg IL 60196

GROETSCH, CHARLES WILLIAM, mathematics educator; b. New Orleans, Feb. 15, 1945; s. Gilbert G. and Lillian (Dooley); m. Sandra Carver, Sept. 3, 1966; children: Kurt, Heidi. BS, La. State U., 1966, MS, 1968, PhD, 1971. Research assoc. USAF Flight Dynamics Lab., 1978; exchange scientist East German Acad. Sci., 1979; asst. prof. U. Cin., 1971-76, assoc. prof., 1976-81, prof., 1981—, head dept. math., 1985—; vis. prof. U. Manchester, Eng., 1980, U. Kaiserlautern, Fed. Republic of Germany, 1983, Australian Nat. U., 1986; cons. NRC, NSF, Mgmt. Decisions Devel. Corp. Author 6 books, 45 research papers. Grantee Air Force Office Scientific Research, Sci. Research Council of Gt. Britain, NSF. Mem. Am. Math. Soc., Math. Assn. Am. Home: 2590 Bonnie Dr Cincinnati OH 45230 Office: U Cin Math 025 Cincinnati OH 45221

GRONAUER, CLIFFORD R., data processing manager; b. Ft. Knox, Ky., July 24, 1958; s. Clifford R. and Sharon E. (Reising) G.; m. Kathleen L. Hanifen, Aug. 10, 1979; children: Andrew Joseph, Amy Suzanne. BA, Columbia Coll., 1981; postgrad., Keller Grad. Sch. Mgmt., 1981—. Programmer analyst Swift Ind., Chgo., 1981-84; sr. analyst Equitable Relocation, Chgo., 1984; systems adminstr. Citicorp, Chgo., 1984-86; sr. analyst Exchange Nat. Bank, Chgo., 1986—. Treas. Citiclub, Chgo., 1986. Served with U.S. Army, 1978-81. Named one of Outstanding Young Men of Am., 1982; Founder's scholar Culver-Stockton Coll., 1976. Republican. Roman Catholic. Avocations: golfing, gardening, photography, woodworking. Home: 4905 Edward Ave Downers Grove IL 60515 Office: Exchange Nat Bank 200 W Monroe Suite 416 Chicago IL 60606

GRONBJERG, KIRSTEN ANDERSEN, sociology educator; b. Sonderborg, Denmark, Mar. 8, 1946; came to U.S., 1965; d. Jens R.M. and Christine (Andersen) G.; m. Gerald D. Suttles, June 20, 1970. BA in Sociology, Pitzer Coll., 1968; MA in Sociology, U. Chgo., 1971, PhD in Sociology, 1974. Lectr. sociology Hofstra U., Hempstead, N.Y., 1971-73; asst. prof. SUNY, Stony Brook, N.Y., 1973-76; asst. prof. Loyola U., Chgo., 1976-78, assoc. prof., 1978-86, prof., 1986—; Chgo. field assoc. The Urban Inst., Washington, 1982-87. Author: Mass Society and Extension of Welfare, 1977; (with others) Poverty and Social Change, 1978; editor Am. Behavioral Sci. Jour., 1983. Mem. United Way Priority Rev. com., Chgo., 1986-87. Mem. Am. Sociol. Assn., Soc. for Study of Social Problems, Midwest Sociol. Soc., Internat. Sociol. Assn. (v.p. research com. on poverty 1979-86). Avocations: reading, cooking, ballet. Office: Loyola Univ Dept Sociology 6525 N Sheridan Chicago IL 60626

GRONEFELD, WILLIAM PAUL, software designer; b. Covington, Ky., May 28, 1943; s. Paul Joseph and Mary Louise (Carrell) G.; m. Barbara Kaye Busse, June 24, 1967; children: Eric Michael, Heidi Marie. BA in Math., Thomas More Coll., 1963; postgrad., U. Cin., 1964-65, Xavier U., 1965-67. Sr. systems programmer Mead Corp., Dayton, Ohio, 1965—. Served with U.S. Army, 1967-69. Mem. SHARE. Republican. Avocations: Karate, Kobudo, architectural design. Home: 54 Benzell Dayton OH 45459 Office: Mead Corp Courthouse Plaza NE Dayton OH 45463

GRONEWOLD, RUSSELL RAY, business educator; b. Beatrice, Nebr., Feb. 9, 1962; s. Roger Kenneth Charlotte Ann (Schmidt) G.; m. Jane Marie Huser, Aug. 16, 1986. BA in Bus. and Acctg., Midland Luth. Coll., 1984. Sr. acct. Arthur Andersen & Co., Omaha, Nebr., 1984-86; instr. bus. Midland Luth. Coll., Freemont, Nebr., 1986—. Active Big Bros. and Sisters of Michllands, Omaha, 1984—; mem., speaker Fellowship Christian Athletes, 1983—. Named one of Outstanding Young Men Am., 1987; Scherer Faculty Devel. grantee Midland Luth. Coll., 1987;. Mem. Am. Inst. CPA's, Nebr. Soc. CPA's. Republican. Mem. Christian Ch. Avocations: skiing, racquetball, piano, singing. Home: 9605 Binney St Omaha NE 68134

GRONLI, JOHN VICTOR, college administrator, pastor; b. Eshowe, South Africa, Sept. 11, 1932; s. John Einar and Marjorie Gellet (Hawker) G.; came to U.S., 1934, naturalized, 1937; B.A., U. Minn., 1953; M.Div., Luther Theol. Sem., 1958, D.Min., 1978; M.A., Pacific Luth. U., 1975; m. Jeanne Louise Ellertson, Sept. 15, 1952; children—Cheryl Marie Mundt, Deborah Raechel Hokanson, John Timothy, Peter Jonas, Daniel Reuben. Ordained to ministry, 1958; pastor Brocket-Lawton Luth. Parish, Brocket, N.D., 1958-61; Harlowton (Mont.) Luth. Parish, 1961-66; sr. pastor St. Luke's Luth. Ch., Shelby, Mont., 1966-75; missionary Paulinum Sem., Otjimbingwe, Namibia, 1975-76; dean, chmn. dept. philosophy and humanities Golden Valley Luth. Coll., Mpls., 1976-85; dir. Summer Inst. Pastoral Ministry, Mpls., 1980-85, sr. pastor Pella Luth. Ch., Sidney, Mont., 1985—. Bd. dirs. Mont. Assn. Chs., 1973-75; sec. bd. for communications and mission support Am. Luth. Ch., 1973-75; mem. dist. council Rocky Mountain Dist., 1963-75, sec., 1963-70, mem. S.African affairs task force SEM Dist., 1978-79; trustee Luth. Bible Inst., Seattle, 1986—. Mem. personnel and guidance assns., Am., Minn. coll. personnel assns. Editor: Rocky Mountain Dist. Yearbook, 1963-70; Rocky Mountain Views, 1973-75; contbr. to Lutheran Standard, 1973-77; contbr. articles to religious jours.

GRONLUND, BRIAN M., controller; b. Sterling, Ill., Sept. 24, 1959; s. Arne A. and Edna M. (Ahonen) G. Student, St. John's Coll., 1977-78; AS, Sauk Valley Coll., 1979; BS in Acctg., No. Ill. U., 1981. CPA, Ill. Staff auditor Roger A. Colmark, CPA, Sterling, 1981-82; controller Riverview Mgmt. Services Group, Inc., Dixon, Ill., 1982—. Instr. Ill. Heart Assn., Dixon, 1985-87. Mem. Am. Inst. CPA's, Ill. CPA Soc., Health Care Fin. Mgmt. Assn. Republican. Lutheran. Avocations: theatre, weightlifting, volleyball. Office: Riverview Mgmt Services Group Inc 403 E First St Dixon IL 61021

GROOVER, CLIFTON REESE, utility company executive; b. Springfield, Mo., Aug. 4, 1941; s. Clifton Reese Jr. and Mildred Maxine (Smith) G.; m. Marilyn Kay Peer, Mar. 30, 1963 (dec. 1969); 1 child, Jennifer Lynn. BS in Acctg., Southwest Mo. State U., Springfield, 1964, postgrad., 1979-80; postgrad., Drury Coll., 1973-75. CPA, Mo. Internal auditor City Utilities of Springfield, 1964-68, sr. systems analyst, 1968-72, asst. mgr. acctg., 1973-79, comptroller, 1979-85; sr. mgr., adminstrv. comptroller City Utilities of Springfield, Springfield, 1985—; dir. cash mgmt. Mid-Am. Dairymen, Springfield, 1972-73. Acct. exec. United Way, Springfield, 1984-86; bd. dirs., tchr. St. Paul Meth. Ch., 1977-82. Mem. Am. Inst. CPA's, Mo. Soc. CPA's, Am. Pub. Power Assn., Am. Gas Assn., S.W. Mo. State U. Alumni Assn., Springfield C. of C. (small bus. com. 1985-86, masters com. 1986-87). Methodist. Clubs: SOS Investment (Springfield) (pres. 1982-83), Ozarks Bass (v.p. 1973-80). Avocations: fishing, water skiing, travel. Home: 1784 E Lafayette Springfield MO 65807 Office: City Utilities Springfield 301 E Central Springfield MO 65802

GROOVER, ROBERT VANN, pediatric neurologist; b. Atlanta, Oct. 1, 1931; s. Vann and Elizabeth (Anderson) G.; m. Ann Mulder; 2 children: Elizabeth Ann, Robert Anderson. BA, Emory U., 1953, MD, 1957. Diplomate Am. Bd. Pediatrics, Am. Bd. Psychiatry & Neurology. Intern Cin. Gen. Hosp., 1957-58; resident pediatrician Children's Hosp., Cin., 1958-60; fellow pediatric neurology Columbia Presbyn. Med. Ctr., N.Y.C., 1962-65; cons. pediatric neurology Mayo Clinic, Rochester, Minn., 1965—; bd. dirs. Hickwatha Children's Home, Rochester, 1971-84, pres. 1983. Served to capt. USMC, 1962-64. Fellow Am. Acad. Pediatrics, Am. Acad. CP Devel. Medicine (pres. 1985, bd. dirs. 1984—), Am. Acad. Neurology; mem. Child Neurology Soc., Profs. Child Neurology (councillor 1983-85). Office: Mayo Clinic 2001 St SW Rochester MN 55905

GROSCH, AUDREY NOISKE, infosystems specialist, consultant; b. Mpls., Jan. 10, 1934; s. Frank and Marie Beatrice (Kalina) Noiske; m. Charles Bernard Grosch, May 31, 1958. BA, U. Minn., 1955, MA, 1956. Asst. librarian Gen. Mills, Inc., Mpls., 1957-62; prof. U. Minn. Libraries, Mpls., 1965—, prof., asst. to librarian for infosystems, 1985—; Cons. NATO, The Hague, Netherlands, 1977, UNESCO, Paris, 1982, 85, UN ESCAP, Bangkok, 1981, 85. Author: Minicomputers in Libraries, 1979-80, 81-82, Distributed Computing and the Electronic Library, 1985. Mem. Am. Soc. for Info. Sci. (bd. dirs. 1976-79, pres. 1978), Spl. Libraries Assn. (rep. to NISO Z-39, SLA Profl. award 1977), Assn. for Computing Machinery, Assn. for Women in Computing, Data Processing Mgmt. Assn., U.S. Shooting Team. Republican. Clubs: Mpls. Gun, Park Gun. 8 world competition medals Internat. Clay Pigeon shooting, 8 time U.S. Ladies Champion Internat. Clay Pigeon Shooting. Home: 17210 Cedarcrest Dr Eden Prairie MN 55344 Office: U Minn Libraries S-98 Wilson Library 309 19th Ave S Minneapolis MN 55455

GROSCHEN, RALPH EDWARD, educator; b. Mpls., Aug. 2, 1945; s. William John and Katherine Julia (Ludwig) G.; m. Sandra Jo Scullen, June 19, 1970; children—Chad, Michelle, Alicia. B.S. in Agronomy, U. Minn., 1968, B.A. in Agr. Edn., 1975. Adult farm bus. mgmt. instr. Sch. Dist. 640, Wabasso, Minn., 1975-78; dist. sales mgr. Standard Chem. Mfg. Co., Omaha, 1978; cons., mgmt. tng. seminar leader Sandy Corp., Southfield, Mich., 1978-80; agr. resource mgmt. coordinator Hennepin Tech. Ctrs., Mpls., 1979-86 ; cons. seminar leader Sandy Corp.; cons. writer Control Data Corp.; Chmn. Minn.-Grown Promotion Group, 1983-85, exec. dir., 1986—; pres. Groschen Inc., Stillwater, Inc. First alt. Nat. Honey Promotion Bd., 1986—; dir. dept. agriculture trade div. Minn. Dept. Agriculture, St. Paul. Served with U.S. Army, 1978-79. Decorated Bronze Star, Army Commendation medal. Mem. Minn. Vocat. Agr. Instr. Assn., Nat. Vocat. Agr. Instr. Assn. Contbr. articles to profl. jours. Home: 9240 Saint Croix Trail North Stillwater MN 55082 Office: 90 W Plato Blvd Saint Paul MN 55107

GROSE, WILLIAM HENRY, industrial engineer; b. Cleve., Feb. 16, 1956; s. William henry and Marian Mae (Kuschel) G.; m. Beth Ann Otfinoski, Oct. 1, 1983. BS in Indsl. Engring., Purdue U., 1978, MS in Indsl. Engring., 1980; MBA, Baldwin-Wallace Coll., 1987. Internat. trainee The Navigators, Tokyo, 1980-83; bus. intern TRW Inc., Cleve., 1984, packaging engr., 1984-85, indsl. engr., 1984-86; capital coordinator TRW Inc./Argo-Tech Corp., Cleve., 1986—; gear cell champion, indsl. engr. Argo-Tech Corp., Cleve., 1986—. Mem. Delta Mu Delta. Republican. Mem. Grace Brethren Ch. Avocations: cycling, skiing, camping. Office: Argo-Tech Corp 23555 Euclid Ave Cleveland OH 44117

GROSHANS, DAVID EDWIN, personnel director, educator; b. Holyoke, Colo., Dec. 15, 1951; s. Edwin Louis and Mary Reva (Vaughn) G.; m. Rhonda Lee Smith, Jan. 6, 1979; children: Nathan, Scott. BA, Chadron (Nebr.) State Coll., 1974; M in Pub. Adminstrn., U. Nebr., Omaha, 1980. Asst. to v.p. Chadron State Coll., 1974-79; personnel dir. Nebr. Western Coll., Scottsbluff, 1981—. Orgnl. designer Scottsbluff United Way, 1984; legis. aide Nebr. Unicameral Legis., Lincoln, 1974; panhandle campaign coordinator Election Com. for Senator James Waldron, Lincoln, 1975; mem. Scottsbluff-Gering Merger Task Force, 1986. Named one of Outstanding Young Men Am., 1977, 82; recipient Outstanding Service award United Way, Scottsbluff, 1982. Mem. Nebr. Personnel Assn. (chmn. 1983-84), Coll. and Univ. Personnel Assn., Am. Soc. Personnel Adminstrn., Am. Soc. Pub. Adminstrn. (treas. local chpt. 1979). Republican. Methodist. Lodges: Kiwanas, Elks. Avocations: skiing, golf, hunting. Home: 2680 Arroyo Rd Gering NE 69341 Office: Nebr Western Coll 1601 E 27th St Scottsbluff NE 69361

GROSS, CYRIL VOGEL, obstetrician/gynecologist; b. Phila., July 9, 1914; s. Samuel and Rosa (Vogel) G.; m. Cecilia Rosenblum, Sept. 1, 1946; children: Rosemary, Catherine, Oscar Benjamin. AB, U. Mich., 1936; MD, Hahnemann Med. Coll., 1940. Diplomate Am. Bd. Ob-Gyn. Resident St. Luke's Hosp. and Children's Med. Ctr., Phila., 1940-41, Margaret Hague Maternity Hosp., Jersey City, 1948, Bellevue Hosp., N.Y.C., 1948-49; resident Aultman Hosp., Canton, Ohio, 1949, mem. med. staff, 1949-80, hon. mem., 1980—. Served to col. M.C., USAR, 1936—, commdg. officer, 1957-61. Decorated Bronze Star. Fellow Am. Coll. Ob-Gyn, Am. Coll. Surgeons, Am. Coll. Emergency Physicians. Avocations: tennis, gardening, woodworking.

GROSS, DAVID DANFORTH, banker; b. Yankton, S.D., Oct. 10, 1949; s. Norman Charles and Marjorie D. (Danforth) G.; m. Sandra A. MacTavish, Aug. 22, 1970; children: Andrew, Sadie. BA, U. S.D., 1971, JD, 1974, MBA, 1975. Bar: S.D. 1974, U.S. Dist. Ct. S.D. 1978, Minn. 1983. Sr. v.p. 1st Dakota Nat. Bank, Yankton, S.D., 1975-82; pres. Rosemount (S.D.) Nat. Bank, 1982-84; v.p. Midway Nat. Bank, St. Paul, 1984—; instr. Freeman (S.D.) Jr. Coll., 1975, Yankton Coll., 1976-80. Chmn. United Fund Campaign, Yankton, 1978; pres. S.D. Easter Seal Soc., Pierre, 1979-81; chmn. bd. dirs. GoodWill Industries, St. Paul, 1987—. Named one of Outstanding Young Men of Am., Jaycees, 1981-84. Mem. Am. Bankers Assn. (cert. comml. lender, cert. fin. services counselor), Minn. Bankers Assn. (mem. Minn. lending com. 1983-84), Minn. Assn. Life Underwriters, S.D. Bankers Assn. (mem. S.D. lending com. 1982), S.D. Assn. Realtors, S.D. Assn. Life Underwriters. Republican. Episcopalian. Lodges: Lions, Elks. Home: 13154 Hannover Ave Apple Valley MN 55124 Office: Midway Nat Bank 1578 University Saint Paul MN 55104

GROSS, HOWARD IRVING, accountant; b. Gary, Ind., Dec. 8, 1951; s. Alex and Frances (Greenbaum) G.; m. Kathy Joan Simon, June 3, 1979; children: Allison Gail, Michelle Anne, Adam Tyler. BS cum laude, U. Ind., 1983. CPA, Ind. Staff acct. Ernst & Whinney, Indpls., 1973-74, sr. acct., 1975-78, mgr., 1979-80; mgr. Peachin Birk Schwartz & Co., PC, Indpls., 1981, ptnr., 1982—. Pres. Indpls. B'nai Brith, 1982-83, state treas. 1983-86; treas. Cen. Ind. Anti-Defamation League, 1986; bd. dirs. Indpls. Hebrew Congregation, 1985-86. Mem. Am. Inst. CPA's, Ind. CPA Soc. (gov. services com. 1983-84, fed. and state taxation com. 1984-86). Home: 8936 Wickham Rd Indianapolis IN 46260 Office: Peachin Birk Schwartz & Co PC 36 S Pennsylvania #640 Indianapolis IN 46204

GROSS, JOHN DONALD, engineering company executive; b. Evansville, Ind., Sept. 28, 1951; s. Donald Robert and Sylvia Estelle (Whobbrey) G.; m. Donna Rae Reuter, June 21, 1975; children: Lauren Michelle, Lisa Marie. BS in Engring., U. Evansville, 1973. Registered profl. engr., Ind. Engr. Ashdee div. George Koch Sons, Evansville, 1973-75, project engr., 1975-79, project mgr., 1979-80, chief engr., 1980-82; v.p. C. Gott & Assocs., Evansville, 1982—; adv. council sci. and engring. U. Evansville, 1984—; adv. com. Ind. Tech. Vocat. Coll., Evansville, 1984—. Mem. Soc. Automotive Engrs., ASME. Republican. Mem. United Ch. Christ. Home: 5806 Twickingham Dr Evansville IN 47711

GROSS, MITCHELL NEAL, ceramic engineer; b. Bklyn., Nov. 27, 1954; s. Isidore and Edna Ann (Goldberg) G. BS in Ceramic Engring., Alfred U., 1975, M in Ceramic Engring., 1977; MBA, Cen. Mich. U., 1986. Research engr. Ford Motor Co., Dearborn, Mich., 1977-79; process engr. Spl. Metals Corp. div. Allegheny Internat., New Hartford, N.Y., 1979-81; ceramic engr. TRW, Cleve., 1981-83; materials engr. Int. Gas Tech., Chgo., May to Dec., 1983; ceramic research specialist Dow Corning Corp., Midland, Mich., 1984—; cons. Wyle, Inc., Cleve., 1983. Contbr. articles to profl. jours. TGIF chairperson Club Mid, Midland, 1986-87. Mem. Nat. Inst. Ceramic Engrs., Am. Ceramic Soc., Soc. Automotive Engrs. Jewish. Avocations: cross-country skiing, racketball, bicycling, sailing, pottery. Home: 3101 Beech St Midland MI 48640 Office: Dow Corning Corp 3901 S Saginaw Rd MS 540 Midland MI 48686

GROSS, MORTIMER DAVID, psychiatrist; b. Newark, Sept. 22, 1922; s. Joseph and Rosalie (Kerner) G.; m. JoAnn Brabenec, Oct. 10, 1952; children: David Joseph, Jonathan Paul. BS, Poly. Inst. Bklyn., 1942; MS U. Akron, 1947; MD, U. Chgo., 1950. Intern U. Ill. Hosps., Chgo., 1951; Resident in Psychiatry Elgin (Ill.) State Hosp., 1952, U. Ill., Chgo., 1953, Michael Reese Hosp., Chgo., 1954; practice medicine specializing psychiatry Highland Park, Ill., 1955—; cons. Ill. State psychiatry Inst., Chgo., 1956-74; chmn. sect. psychiatry Highland Park Hosp., 1960-78; clin. assoc. prof. psychiatry, U. Ill., Chgo., 1962-83; assoc. prof. psychiatry, Univ. Health Scis. Chgo. Med. Sch., 1983—. Author: (with W.C. Wilson) Minimal Brain Dysfunction, 1974, Neurology Primer for Non-Physicians; contbr. textbooks chpts., articles to profl. jours. Chmn. Highland Park Lakefront Commn., 1975-80, 1985—. Fellow Am. Psychiat. Assn., Am. Soc. Social Psychiatry; mem. AMA. Avocations: sailing, music. Home: 205 Sheridan Rd Highland Park IL 60035 Office: 750 Homewood Ave Highland Park IL 60035

GROSS, SHELDON JEFFREY, accounting executive, tax consultant; b. Chgo., Jan. 7, 1960; s. Stuart Marvin and Marlene Faye (Edelman) G.; m. Lauren Davida Goldberg, May 27, 1984. BS, DePaul U., Chgo., 1982. CPA, Ill. Tax mgr. Arthur Andersen & Co., Chgo., 1982-86. Mem. Am. Inst. CPA's, Ill. Soc. CPA's. Republican. Jewish. Avocations: music, sports. Office: Arthur Andersen & Co 33 W Monroe Chicago IL 60603

GROSS, TERRENCE P., advertising executive; b. Oshkosh, Wis., Apr. 1, 1957; s. Donald Edward and Jacqueline Ann (Frieberg) G. BS in Communications, U. Wis., Stevens Point, 1981. Dist. exec. Boy Scouts Am., Muscatine, Iowa, 1981-82; asst. gen. mgr. Paper Valley Hotel, Appleton, Wis., 1982; account exec. Mktg. Group Inc., Milw., 1982—. Mem. Am. Mktg. Assn. Roman Catholic. Avocations: reading, swimming, photography, travel, sportscars. Home: PO Box 93422 Milwaukee WI 53203 Office: Mktg Group Inc 312 E Buffalo Milwaukee WI 53202

GROSS, THOMAS LESTER, obstetrician/gynecologist, researcher; b. Decatur, Ill., Aug. 17, 1945; s. Gilbert Wayne and Anna (Graham) G.; m. Judy Beth Osborn, Dec. 30, 1967; children—Elizabeth, Matthew, Joshua. B.A. in Chemistry, Bluffton (Ohio) Coll., 1967; M.D., U. Ill., 1971. Diplomate Am. Bd. Ob-Gyn, subsplty. maternal/fetal medicine. Intern and resident Akron (Ohio) Gen. Med. Ctr., 1973-77; fellow in maternal/fetal medicine Case Western Res. U., 1977-79; asst. to dir. perinatal clin. research ctr. Cleve. Met. Gen. Hosp., 1982-85, acting dir. Perinatal Clin. Research Ctr., 1985-86; asst. prof. ob-gyn Case Western Res. U., Cleve., 1977-85, assoc. prof., 1985-86; assoc. prof. ob-gyn U. Ill. Coll. Medicine, Peoria, 1986—, chmn. dept., 1986—; instr. Internat. Symposuim Fetal Eval., Lima, Peru, 1983. Mem. Physicians for Social Responsibility. Mem. Am. Coll. Obstetricians and Gynecologists (1st prize research 1984), Central Assn. Obstetricians and Gynecologists (Community Hosp. Research award 1981, Ann. Prize award for Research, 1982), Soc. Perinatal Obstetricians, Soc. Gynecologic Investigation, Perinatal Research Soc., Peoria Ob-Gyn Soc. Contbr. numerous articles to sci. jours. Office: One Illini Dr Box 1649 Peoria IL 61656

GROSS, WILLIS CHARLES, JR., dentist; b. St. Louis, June 3, 1924; s. Willis Charles and Mary Ida (Kelly) G.; A.A., Harris Jr. Coll., 1943; D.D.S., St. Louis U., 1946; postgrad. U. Detroit, 1952-53; m. Rosemarie Dorothy Horak, Feb. 14, 1948 (dec. 1985); 1 son, Alan Charles; m. Verda Nell Politte, Jan. 4, 1986. Commd. 1st lt. Dental Corps, U.S. Army and USAF, 1946, advanced through grades to maj., 1952; ret., 1953; pvt. practice dentistry, Affton, Mo., 1954—; pres. Willis C. Gross Dental Assocs.; v.p. C & W Gross Corp. Served with AUS, 1942-44. Fellow Acad. Gen. Dentistry, Royal Soc. Health (Eng.); mem. Am., Mo. dental assns., St. Louis Dental Soc., Concord Village Bus. Men's Assn., Am. Legion, V.F.W., Alpha Sigma Nu, Omicron Kappa Upsilon, Delta Sigma Delta (past pres., sec.-treas. St. Louis chpt.), Alpha Phi Omega. Republican. Mason (Shriner, chmn. temple med. staff, 32 deg.), Lion (dir. pres. Concord Village 1965-66). Clubs. Liberty Country (dir.) (Horine, Mo.); Big Game Hunters (St. Louis). Home: 20 Dorclin Ln Saint Louis MO 63128 Office: 7 Concord Center Dr Saint Louis MO 63123

GROSSE, SUSAN JANE, educator; b. Milw., Jan. 3, 1946; d. Walter Denton and Theresa Imogene (Hanglin) G. BS, U. Wis., Milw., 1968, MS, 1971. Cert. tchr., Wis. Phys. edn. tchr. Menononee Falls (Wis.) Pub. Sch., 1968-69, Milw. Pub. Schs., 1969—; tchr. cons. Dade County Pub. Schs., Fla., 1980-82; lectr. various colls. and univs. Author: Physical Education for the Uncoordinated Student, 1974; contbr. articles to profl. jours. Vol. ARC, 1964—; instr. canoeing, first aid, life guarding, water safety and adapted aquatics Nat. Aquatic Schs., 1974-76. Recipient Service award ARC, 1981. Mem. Am. Alliance for Health, Phys. Edn., Recreation and Dance (sec. therapeutic council 1976, Mabel Lee award 1982), Wis. Assn. for Health, Phys. End., Recreation and Dance (v.p. gen. div. 1986-87, pres. elect 1987—), Nat. Assn. Sport for Cerebral Palsied, Delta Kappa Gamma (1st pres. 1982-84). Lutheran. Lodges: Order Eastern Star, Shriners. Avocations: sports, photograph, stitchery, camping, travel. Home: 7252 W Wabash Ave Milwaukee WI 53223

GROSSKREUTZ, JOSEPH CHARLES, physicist, engineering researcher; b. Springfield, Mo., Jan. 5, 1922; s. Joseph Charles and Helen (Mobley) G.; m. Mary Catherine Schubel, Sept. 7, 1949; children—Cynthia Lee, Barbara Helen. B.S. in Math., Drury Coll., 1943; postgrad., U. Calif.-Berkeley, 1946-47; M.S., Washington U., St. Louis, 1948, Ph.D. in Physics, 1950. Research physicist Calif. Research Corp., La Habra, 1950-52; asst. prof. physics U. Tex.-Austin, 1952-56; research scientist Nuclear Physics Lab., Austin, 1952-56; sr. physicist Midwest Research Inst., Kansas City, Mo., 1956-59, prin. physicist, 1959-63, sr. adviser, 1963-67; prin. advisor Midwest Research Inst., Kansas City, 1967-71; chief mech. properties sect. Nat. Bur. Standards, Washington, 1971-72; mgr. solar programs Black & Veatch Cons. Engrs., Kansas City, Mo., 1972-77, mgr. advanced tech. projects, 1979—; dir. research Solar Energy Research Inst., Golden, Colo., 1977-79; spl. cons. NATO, 1967. Contbr. physics and energy articles to profl. jours. Served to lt. USN, 1943-46. Recipient Disting. Service award Drury Coll., 1959; Washington U. fellow, 1948-49. Fellow Am. Phys. Soc., ASTM (dir. 1977-80, Merit award 1972); mem. Sigma Xi, Sigma Pi Sigma. Methodist. Home: 4306 W 111th Terr Leawood KS 66211 Office: Black & Veatch PO Box 8405 Kansas City MO 64114

GROSSMAN, ANDREW WILLIAM, data processing executive, consultant, writer; b. Ancon, Ecuador, Sept. 16, 1943; came to U.S., 1946; s. Alexander and Margaret (Fendrich) G.; m. Linda J. Passan, Aug. 27, 1974; children: Daniel, Rachel, Lisa. BA, Case Western Res. U., 1969; M in History, John Carroll U., 1972; M in Communication, Cleve. State U., 1976. Cons. Ohio Bell Telephone Co., Cleve., 1969-78, adminstr., 1979-80, project mgr., 1980, computer analyst, software designer, 1980—. Author: (book) PBX and System Management, 1983. Bd. dirs. Choral Arts Performing Soc., Cleve., 1981—; mem. Citizens League Cleve.,1971-76, Am. Jewish Com., Cleve., 1971-80. Sociology scholar NSF, 1968; recipient Bell Mktg. System, sales award AT&T. Mem. Am. Hist. Soc., Am. Sociol. Assn. Democrat. Lodge: Knights of Pythias. Avocations: reading, chess, classical and jazz music, writing children's stories. Office: Ohio Bell Telephone Co 45 Erieview Plaza Cleveland OH 44114

GROSSMAN, EARL MARTIN, acquisition executive; b. Jan. 8, 1958; s. Gordon William and Mary Ann (Creel) G. BA in Math., Dartmouth Coll., 1980; MBA, U. Chgo., 1985. Mktg. rep. IBM Corp., Westport, Conn., 1980-81; mgmt. cons. The Chgo. Group, 1982-84; prin. Merger & Acquisition Strategies, Inc., Lincolnshire, Ill., 1985-86. Republican. Home: 121 Old McHenry Hawthorn Woods IL 60047 Office: Merger & Acquisition Strategies Inc 111 Barclay Blvd Lincolnshire IL 60069

GROSSMAN, JERROLD WAYNE, mathematics educator; b. St. Louis, Apr. 25, 1948; s. Isadore I. and Florence P. (Kaufman) G.; m. Carol E. Burroughs, June 5, 1971 (div. July 1982); m. R. Suzanne Zeitman, Aug. 15, 1982; 1 child, Pamela Jane. BS, Stanford U., 1970, MS, 1970; PhD, MIT, 1974. Asst. prof. Oakland U., Rochester, Mich., 1974-81; assoc. prof. Oakland U., Rochester, 1981—. Contbr. research articles to math. jours. Mem. Am. Math. Soc., Math. Assn. Am. Avocation: duplicate bridge. Office: Oakland U Math Dept Rochester MI 48309

GROSSMAN, LISA ROBBIN, clinical psychologist, lawyer; b. Chgo., Jan. 22, 1952; d. Samuel R. and Sarah (Kruger) G. B.A. with highest distinction and departmental honors in Psychology, Northwestern U., 1974, J.D. cum laude, 1979, Ph.D., 1982. Bar: Ill. 1981; registered psychologist, Ill. Jud. intern, U.S. Supreme Ct., Washington, 1975; pre-doctoral psychology intern Michael Reese Hosp. and Med. Center, Chgo., 1979-80; therapist Homes for Children, Chgo., 1980-83; psychologist Psychiat. Inst., Cir. Ct. Cook County, Chgo., 1981—; pvt. practice, 1984—; invited participant workshop HHS, Rockville, Md., 1981. Contbr. articles to profl. jours. Mem. Am. Psychol. Assn., Ill. Psychol. Assn., Chgo. Assn. for Psychoanalytic Psychologists (parliamentarian 1982), ABA, Ill. State Bar Assn., Chgo. Bar Assn., Mortar Bd., Phi Beta Kappa, Shi-Ai, Alpha Lambda Delta. Office: Psychiat Inst Circuit Ct Cook County 2650 S California Ave Chicago IL 60608

GROSSMAN, N. BUD, diversified transportation services company executive; b. 1921; married. B.A., U. Minn., 1941. Chmn. bd., chief exec. officer Gelco Corp., Hopkins, Minn., 1957—. Served with USAAF. Office: Gelco Corp One Gelco Dr Eden Prairie MN 55344

GROSSMAN, PAULINE FRIED, clinical social worker; b. Detroit, Sept. 29, 1916; d. Aron and Fani (Goldberger) Fried; m. Sol. C. Grossman, June 20, 1939; children: Marilyn, Nancy G. BA, Wayne State U., 1937, MSW, 1941. Cert. social worker, Mich. Sr. psychiat. social worker Ypsilanti (Mich.) State Hosp., 1937-39; sr. caseworker Jewish Family Services, Detroit, 1939-41; pvt. practice clin. social work Southfield, Mich., 1946—; admissions dir. sch. social work Wayne State U., Detroit, 1966-68; casework supr. Oakland Family Service, Berkley, Mich., 1966—; cons. atty. gen. bd. S.W. Mich., Lansing, 1981—. Scholarship chmn. Nat. Council Jewish Women, 1960-73; pres. Maimonides Med. Auxiliary. Mem. Nat. Assn. Social Workers, Am. Assn. Marriage and Family Therapists, Mich. Assn. Clin. Social Workers, Mich. Assn. Marriage and Family Therapists (bd. dirs. 1971-83, supr. tng. 1980—, Recognition Citation 1981), Mich. Interprofl. Assn. Marriage, Family and Div. (v.p. 1986—). Avocations: reading, travel, swimming. Home and Office: 29614 Farmbrook Villa Ct Southfield MI 48034

GROSSMAN, ROBERT MICHAEL, advertising executive; b. Canton, Ohio, Oct. 10, 1957; s. Morton and Vivienne (Axelrod) G. Student, U. Cin., 1975-76; BS in Bus., Colo. U., 1979. Assoc. product mgr. Automated Mktg. Systems, Detroit, 1979-81; advt. sales rep. Tex. Sport Mag., Dallas, 1981-84, So. Living Mag., Dallas and Chgo., 1984—; dist. advt. mgr. So. Living Mag., Chgo., 1984—; bd. dirs. Festival Ventures Inc., Santa Fe, N.Mex. Contbr. sports report to various publ. Vol. christmas hosp. programs Jewish Welfare Fund, Dallas, 1981-84; recruiter U. Colo., Boulder, 1982—. Democrat. Jewish. Club: Agate (Chgo.). Avocations: cycling, skiing, weightlifting, golf, tennis, squash. Office: Southern Living Mag 10 S Riverside Plaza #1625 Chicago IL 60606

GROSSMAN, STEVEN JAY, state agency administrator; b. N.Y.C., Oct. 4, 1945; s. Mortimer and Doris (Orent) G.; m. JoAnne Dreyfuss, June 15, 1968; children: Marc, Elena. BA, Lehigh U., 1967; MS, MIT, 1969. Mgmt. analyst ACTION, Washington, 1972-77; dir. regional recruitment ACTION, Atlanta, 1977; program mgr. ACTION, Washington, 1978-82; asst. dir. Ohio EPA, Columbus, 1983—. Pres. Woodmoor-Pinecrest Citizens Assn., Silver Spring, Md., 1979-81, Temple Beth Shalom, Columbus, Ohio, 1986—. Democrat. Jewish. Avocations: gardening, running, softball. Office: Ohio EPA 1800 Watermark Dr PO Box 1049 Columbus OH 43266-1049

GROSSMAN, WARREN DELANO, psychologist; b. Cleve., Nov. 6, 1940; s. Morris and Mildred Ruth (Koosed) G.; m. Sylvia Pinkas, Aug. 28, 1961 (div. 1969); 1 child, Joshua; m. Carol Jo Desanto, Jan. 26, 1980;. BA, Cleve. State U., 1971, MA, 1973; PhD, Kent State U., 1980. Psychologist Lake County Mental Health Ctr., Mentor, Ohio, 1973-79; head psychologist Warren D. Grossman and Assocs., Cleve., 1979—. Mem. Am. Psychol. Assn., Internat. Assn. for Bioenergetic Analysis, Gestalt Inst. Cleve. Home: 2605 Ashton Rd Cleveland Heights OH 44118 Office: Warren D Grossman & Assocs 2460 Fairmount Blvd #207 Cleveland Heights OH 44106

GROTBERG, JAMES BERNARD, biomedical engineer, educator; b. Oak Park, Ill., July 22, 1950; s. John Edward and Edith (Henderson) Burchinal; m. Karen Faith Rubner, June 22, 1980; children: Anna Christine, John Christian. Ph.D., Johns Hopkins U., 1978; M.D., U. Chgo., 1980. Lic. physician, Ill. Assoc. prof. Northwestern U., Evanston, Ill., 1980—. Contbr. articles to profl. jours. Recipient Achievement award Johns Hopkins U., 1973, New Investigator, NIH, 1983, Presl. Young Investigator, NSF, 1984, Research Career Devel. award NIH, 1987. Mem. Am. Phys. Soc., Phi Beta Kappa, Tau Beta Pi. Office: Northwestern Univ Technological Inst Dept Biomed Engineering Evanston IL 60201

GROTELUESCHEN, DALE MELVIN, veterinarian; b. Columbus, Nebr., June 11, 1949; s. Melvin Franklin and Loretta Ruth (DeBower) G.; m. Elizabeth Carol Conkling, Aug. 22, 1969; children: Kris Ellen, Sarah Elizabeth. Student, U. Nebr., 1967-70; DVM, U. Mo., 1974. Pvt. practice veterinary medicine Seymour, Wis., 1974-76, Curtis, Nebr., 1976-85; vet. extension, research specialist U. Nebr., Scottsbluff, 1985—. Mem. Am. Vet. Med. Assn., Nebr. Vet. Med. Assn. (chmn. pub. relations com. 1984—), Soc. Theriogenology, Am. Acad. Vet. Nutritionists, Am. Assn. Swine Practitioners. Republican. Lutheran. Avocations: skiing, running, purebred cattle, family. Home: 2520 Valencia Dr Gering NE 69341 Office: U Nebr Panhandle Research and Extension Service 4502 Avenue I Scottsbluff NE 69361

GROTELUSCHEN, MARELLE ELLEN, interior designer; b. Morgantown, Pa., Feb. 27, 1939; s. Naaman Mast and Mary Buckwalter (Weaver) Stoltzfus; m. Jon Kingdon Groteluschen, Sept. 4, 1964; children: Andrea, Inga. BS in Home Econs. Edn., Eastern Mennonite Coll., 1963; postgrad., U. Iowa, 1966. Vol. Peace Corps., Turkey, 1963-65; field advisor Girl Scouts Am., Lexington, Ky., 1966-69; interior designer John Hale Interiors, Elm Grove, Wis., 1973-79; interior designer Marelle Interiors, Elm Grove, 1979-82, Alma, Mich., 1982—; Interior design instr. Waukesha County (Wis.) Tech. Inst., 1972-82; instr. Continuing Edn., Alma, 1982—; mem. women's adv. bd. Heritage Bank, Milw., 1981-83. Editor Country Decorating, 1979—. Mem. AAUW, Altrusa (program chmn. 1980-82). Democrat. Presbyterian. Club: Alma Women's (pres. 1984-85). Avocations: golf, skiing, horseback riding. Home: 590 Faircrest St Alma MI 48801 Office: Marelle Interiors 327 N State St Alma MI 48801

GROTH, LARUE JUNE, academic advisor; b. Carroll, Iowa, June 13, 1949; d. Harvey Frank and Annette (Hoffmeier) Vetter; m. Thomas V. Groth, Sept. 1, 1972; 1 child, Paul. BS, Iowa State U., 1971, postgrad., 1978, 79; MEd, U. Ill., 1973. Tchr. Ar-We-Va Sch., Vail, Iowa, 1971-72; adminstrv. asst. N.Y.U., N.Y.C., 1973-74; tchr. Montessori Family Schs., N.Y.C., 1974-75; case mgr. Polk County Dept. Social Services, Des Moines, 1976-78; guidance counselor West Marshall Sch. Dist., State Ctr., Iowa, 1978-82; coordinator acad. advising Iowa State U., Ames, 1982—. Bd. dirs. Childcare Services of Cen. Iowa, Inc., Ames, 1982-84. Named Outstanding Young Woman of Yr., 1984; recipient Iowa State U. Council Internat., Edn. grantee, 1985. Mem. Iowa Personnel and Guidance Assn., Story County Counseling Assn., Nat. Elem. Guidance Conf. (publicity chairperson 1980), Nat. Acad. Advising Assn. Avocations: travel, reading, gourmet dining, biking, jogging. Home: 900 South Dakota C-3 Ames IA 50010 Office: Iowa State U Dept Elem Edn N131 Lagomarcino Hall Ames IA 50011

GROTY, CHARLES KEITH, personnel director, arbitrator; b. Detroit, Feb. 7, 1939; s. Frederick Reynolds and Clara Helen (Stolpman) Ford; children from previous marriage: Jeffrey Douglas, Christopher Keith; m. Mary Vornholt, May 10, 1975; 1 child, Karyll Marie. BS, U. Mich., 1962, AM, 1964, PhD, 1970. Counselor Royal Oak (Mich.) Schs., 1964-66; personnel dir. Southfield (Mich.) Schs., 1966-68; faculty Mich. State U., East Lansing, 1968—, asst. v.p., 1972—. Contbr. articles to profl. jours. Mem. legis. com. Pub. Employee Relations Act, 1970; bd. dirs. Lansing Area Joint Labor Mgmt. Com., 1983-87. Mem. Am. Soc. Personnel Adminstrn., Am. Arbitration Assn., Indsl. Relations Research Assn. (mem. Detroit, Mid Mich., nat.), Soc. Profls. Dispute Resolution, Coll. Univ. Personnel Assn. (pres. 1984-85), Fedn. Fly Fishers (v.p. ops., treas. 1983-86), Mich. Wildlife Habitat Found. (v.p. 1987). Presbyterian. Avocations: tennis, fishing, hunting, boating. Home: 3496 Josephine Ln Mason MI 48854 Office: Mich State U 140 Nisbet Bldg East Lansing MI 48824

GROTZINGER, LAUREL ANN, university dean; b. Truman, Minn., Apr. 15, 1935; d. Edward F. and Marian Gertrude (Greeley) G. B.A., Carleton Coll., 1957; M.S., U. Ill., 1958, Ph.D., 1964. Instr., asst. librarian Ill. State U., 1958-62; asst. prof. Western Mich. U., Kalamazoo, 1964-66; assoc. prof. Western Mich. U., 1966-68, prof., 1968—, asst. dir. Sch. Librarianship, 1965-72, chief research officer, 1979-86, interim dir. Sch. Library and Info. Sci., 1982-86, dean grad. coll., 1979—. Author: The Power and the Dignity, Scarecrow, 1966; editorial bd.: Jour. Edn. for Librarianship, 1973-77, Dictionary Am. Library Biography, 1975-77; contbr. articles to profl. jours. Mem. AAUW, ALA (sec. treas. Library History Round Table 1973-74, vice chmn., chmn.-elect 1983-84, chmn. 1984-85), Acad. Mgmt., Assn. Library Info. Sci. Edn., Am. Assn. Higher Edn., Council Grad. Schs., Mich. Council Grad. Deans (chmn. 1983-84, 86), Nat. Council Research Adminstrs., Mich. Acad. Sci., Arts and Letters (mem.-at-large, exec. com. 1980-86, pres. 1983-85), Phi Beta Kappa (pres. SW Mich. chpt. 1977-78), Beta Phi Mu, Pi Delta Epsilon, Alpha Beta Alpha, Delta Kappa Gamma. Home: 2729 Mockingbird Dr Kalamazoo MI 49008

GROVE, BARBARA, scientific technologist; b. Evanston, Ill., Oct. 21, 1956; d. William Glenn and Gladys Viola (Johnson) G. BA in Biology, Knox Coll., 1979. Research asst. Knox Coll., Galesburg, Ill., 1979; lab. technician Sara Lee, Deerfield, Ill., 1979-80; cytogeneticist Children's Meml. Hosp., Chgo., 1980; sr. lab. technician Travenol Labs. div. Baxter Travenol, Morton Grove, Ill., 1981-83; research asst. diagnostics research and devel. Abbott Labs., Abbott Park, Ill., 1983—. Co-inventor diagnostic test, 1985. Office: Abbott Labs Dept 571 Abbott Park IL 60064

GROVE, EWART LESTER, chemist; b. Greensburgh, Kans., May 31, 1913; s. William Ewart and Theo Etha (Grove) G.; m. Ethel Lucille Metcalf, June 12, 1944; children: Edward Lester, Ernest William. BEd, St. Cloud State Coll., 1933; MA, Ohio State U., 1945; PhD, Western U., 1951. Tchr., Tyler (Minn.) High Sch., 1938-40, Cuyahoga Heights High Sch., Cleve., 1940-47; instr. Fenn Coll., 1942-44, Minn. State Tchrs. Coll., St. Cloud, 1947-48; research participant Oak Ridge Nat. Lab., summers 1953-54; asso. prof. U. Ala., 1951-59; research chemist, sr. scientist, mgr. analytical chemistry research Ill. Inst. Tech. Research Inst., Chgo., 1960-70; v.p. Freeman Labs., Inc., Rosemont, Ill., 1970-75; sr. scientist Ill. Inst. Tech. Research Inst., Chgo., 1976—. Mem. Am. Chem. Soc., Soc. Applied Spectroscopy, Am. Inst. Chemists, Sigma Xi. Methodist. Co-author math. textbooks; editor: Developments in Applied Spectroscopy; editor, contbr. Analytical Emission Spectroscopy, Vols. I-II, Applied Atomic Spectroscopy, Vols. I-II; contbr. numerous articles to profl. jours. Home: 28 W 074 Gary's Mill Rd Winfield IL 60190 Office: Ill Inst Tech Research Inst Chicago IL 60616

GROVE, HELEN HARRIET, historian, artist; b. South Bend, Ind.; d. Samuel Harold and LaVerne Mae (Drescher) Grove; grad. Bayle Sch. Design, Meinzinger Found., 1937-39, Washington U., 1940-42; spl. studies, Paris, France. Owner studios of historic research and illustration, St. Louis, Chgo., 1943—; dir. archives, bus. history research Sears, Roebuck & Co., 1951-67; commmns. art and research for Northwestern U., Chgo.-Sears Roebuck & Co., art Lawrence U., Appleton, Wis. Home: 6326 N Clark St Chicago IL 60626 Studio: 6328 N Clark St Chicago IL 60626

GROVE, JACK FREDERICK, lawyer, educator; b. Hamilton, Ohio, Aug. 31, 1953; s. James Edward and Eleanor Katherine (Schlichter) G.; m. Susan Kathleen Flick, July 24, 1976; 1 child, Adam Nathaniel. B.S. in Agr., Ohio State U., 1975; J.D., U. Dayton, 1979. Bar: Ohio 1979, U.S. Dist. Ct. (so. dist.) Ohio 1979, U.S. Supreme Ct. 1984. Law clk. to Judge Fred B. Cramer, Hamilton, Ohio, 1979-80; asst. pros. atty. Butler County, Hamilton, 1980-87 instr. fin. Miami U., Oxford, Ohio, 1981-84; ptnr. Grove & Marte, Fairfield, Ohio, 1979—; bd. dir. adv. council Hamilton Tool Co., 1982-86. Mem. exec. com. Butler County Reps., Hamilton, Ohio, 1980-81; propr. Copper Fox Stables, Silverwood Farm. Mem. ABA, Ohio State Bar Assn., Butler County Bar Assn., Cin. Bar Assn., Sierra Club, Nat. Snaffle Bit Assn., Gamma Sigma Delta. Republican. Clubs: New London Hills, Hamilton City; Am.

Quarter Horse Assn., Ohio Quarter Horse Assn., Tex. Quarter Horse Assn. Home: 1093 Davis Rd Hamilton OH 45013 Office: 1251 Nilles Rd Suite 10 Fairfield OH 45014

GROVER, HERBERT JOSEPH, state agency administrator; b. Fond du Lac, Feb. 5, 1937; s. Felix N. and Helen (Hardgrove) G.; m. Caroline Grover; children: John, Mike, Pat, Johanna, Caroline, Kristie, Mary, Herbert. BA, St. Norbert Coll., DePere, Wis., 1959; MA, Am. U., 1963; Cert. in Teaching, U. Wis., Stevens Point, 1967; PhD, U. Wis., Madison, 1974. Cert. tchr., Wis. Mem. Wis. State Assembly, Madison, 1965-74; supt. Niagara (Wis.) Pub. Sch. Dist., 1974-78, Monona (Wis.) Pub. Sch. Dist., 1978-81, Wis. Dept. Pub. Instrn., Madison, 1981—; exec. com. Edn. Commn. of States; bd. dirs. Wis. Higher Ednl. Aids. Mem. nat. adv. bd. March of Dimes Reading Olympics; governing bd. N. Cen. Regional Ednl. Lab; exec. bd. Four Lakes council Boy Scouts Am.; bd. regents U. Wis. System, Madison; bd. dirs. Agy. Instructional TV, Sunburst Youth Homes. Recipient Environ. Edn. award Wis. Assn. Environ. Edn., 1983, St. Norbert Coll. Alma Mater award St. Norbert Coll. Alumni Assn., Spl. Recognition award Am. Assn. Ednl. Service Agys., Friend of Edn. award Wis. Edn. Assn. Council, 1986. Mem. Council Chief State Sch. Officers (bd. dirs.), Phi Delta Kappa (named one of 75 Outstanding Educators in U.S. 1981). Home: 4333 Damascus Trail Cottage Grove WI 53527 Office: Wis Dept Pub Instrn 125 S Webster Box 7841 Madison WI 53707

GROVES, DELORES ELLIS, educational administrator; b. Shelby County, Ky., Jan. 29; d. David Irvin and Mary Eliza (Powell) Ellis; m. Robert Louis Graves, Sept. 29, 1957; children—Angela, Robin; m. Clyde Groves, Dec. 20, 1969. B.S., Spalding Coll., 1966; M.A., John Carroll U., 1972; postgrad. postgrad. Kent State U., Cleve. State U., Akron U. Tchr., pub. schs., Louisville, 1966-69, Cleve., 1970, Shaker Heights, Ohio, 1970-78; adminstr. pub. schs., Shaker Heights, 1978—, prin. elem. sch., 1980—. Mem. Assn. Supervision and Curriculum Devel., NAACP, Ohio Assn. Elem. Sch. Adminstrs., Nat. Assn. Elem. Sch. Prins., Nat. Alliance Black Educators, Ohio Alliance Black Educators, Shaker Heights Interest Group, Phi Delta Kappa, Delta Sigma Theta. Baptist. Democrat. Club: VIPS Social and Civic.

GROWE, JOAN ANDERSON, state official; b. Mpls., Sept. 28, 1935; d. Arthur F. and Lucille M. (Brown) Anderson; children: Michael, Colleen, David, Patrick. B.S., St. Cloud State U., 1956; cert. in spl. edn, U. Minn., 1964; exec. mgmt. program State and local govt., Harvard U., 1979. Tchr. elem. pub. schs. Bloomington, Minn., 1956-58; tchr. for exceptional children elem. pub. schs. St. Paul, 1964-65; spl. edn. tchr. St. Anthony Pub. Schs., Minn., 1965-66; mem. Minn. Ho. of Reps., 1973-74; sec. of state State of Minn., St. Paul, 1975—; mem. Judicial Planning Com.; exec. council Minn. State Bd. Investment; candidate U.S. Senate, 1984; mem. adv. com. Fed. Elections Commn. Active Minn. Nuclear Freeze Campaign; mem. Gov.'s Commn. on Poverty, Women's Campaign Fund; Greater Mpls. council Girl Scouts U.S.A., Minn. Women's Econ. Roundtable. Recipient Minn. Sch. Bell award, 1977, YMCA Outstanding Achievement award, 1978; Disting. Alumni award St. Cloud State U., 1979; Charlotte Striebel Long Distance Runner award Minn. NOW, 1985. Mem. Nat. Assn. Secs. of State (pres. 1979-80), Bus. and Profl. Women, Women's Polit. Caucus, League Women Voters, Common Cause, Women Against Mil. Madness, Citizen's League, Minn. Assn. Retarded Citizens, AAUW, Zonta. Mem. Democratic Farmer Labor Party. Roman Catholic. Office: Sec of State's Office 180 State Office Bldg Saint Paul MN 55155

GRUBA, JOHN ANTHONY, restaurant and resort executive; b. Gilman, Minn., Oct. 24, 1934; s. John Matthew and Salomi (O'Konek) G.; m. Patricia Frances Lepinski, Oct. 17, 1953; children: Rodney John, David Charles, Jeffrey Michael. Student, Dunwoody Inst., 1954, St. Cloud Vocat., 1956-59. Owner Gruba's Cabinets, Sauk Rapids, Minn., 1960-75, Silver Rapids Lodge and Restaurant, Ely, Minn., 1975—. Advisor Ely Lodging Tax Com., 1986—. Mem. Minn. Assn. Campground Operators (pres. 1983—), Minn. Campground Assn. (pres. 1983—). Roman Catholic. Lodge: Lions. Avocations: traveling, meeting people. Home and Office: Star Rt 1 Box 2992 Ely MN 55731

GRUBB, DAVID ALAN, data processing executive; b. Washington, Ohio, June 26, 1950; s. Sheldon Emerson and Edith Irene (Pollard) G.; m. Penny Sue Bartley, June 4, 1977 (div. Oct. 1980); m. Connie Sue McConnaughey, Sept. 4, 1982; children: Joshua David, Adam Michael. Cert. in Advanced Computer Programming, So. Ohio Coll., 1969. Computer operator Ohio Dept. Liquor Control, Columbus, 1970-83; supr. EDP Buckeye Steel div. Worthington Industries, Columbus, 1983—. Mem. Data Processing Mgmt. Assn. Republican. Mem. Ch. of Christ. Avocations: fishing, softball, baseball, basketball, football. Home: 353 Branding Iron Dr Galloway OH 43119 Office: Worthington Industries Buckeye Steel Div 2211 Parsons Ave Columbus OH 43207

GRUBB, LINDA FERN, architect; b. Maryville, Mo., Nov. 22, 1944; d. Earl Jackson and Juanda Fern (Boatwright) Shoemaker; m. Stephen Leslie Grubb, Sept. 3, 1966; children: Cydney Katherine, Jack Christopher. BArch, Kans. State U., 1967. Registered architect, Ill. Intern Coffin & Scherschel, Barrington, Ill., 1969-72, architect, 1972-74; dir. devel. Village of Barrington, 1974; pvt. practice planning cons. Barrington, 1975-77, pvt. practice architect, 1975—; plan commr. Village of Barrington, 1981—; preservation commr. Barrington Area Hist. Soc., 1982—, devel. com., 1986; bd. dirs. United Meth. Ch. Bldg. Commn., Elgin, Ill., 1982—. Bd. dirs. The Elgin (Ill.) Acad., 1985—. Recipient Excellence award Archtl. Woodwork Inst., 1982. Mem. AIA, Assn. Preservation Technology, Soc. Archtl. Historians, Nat. Trust Hist. Preservation. Republican. Avocations: reading, travel, antiques. Office: 102 N Cook St Barrington IL 60010

GRUBB, LINDA SUE, human resources specialist; b. Columbus, Ohio, Nov. 1, 1953; d. John Bruce and Shirley Ann (Parker) Witwer; m. David R. Grubb, Mar. 6, 1971; children: Kareena Marie, Leanna Christine. Student, Ohio U., Zanesville, 1974-77. Adminstrv. asst. Hilliard Lyons, Zanesville, 1978-79; employment counselor Darrow Employment, Zanesville, 1979-80; mgr. adult tng. C.O.R.C., Zanesville, 1980-84; coordinator human resources Mideast Ohio Vocat. Sch. Dist., Zanesville, 1984—; mktg. dir. Witwer & Assocs., St. Louis, 1980—. Trainer United Way, Zanesville, 1986; bd. dirs. Heart Ohio council Girl Scouts USA, Zanesville, 1984-85; bd. dirs. Chataqua Found., McConnelsville, Ohio, 1979. Mem. Muskingeum Valley Personnel Assn. (treas. 1984-85, v.p. 1985-86, pres. 1986-87), Muskingeum Tech. Coll., (placement adv. bd. 1982-86). Home: 2825 Deerpath Dr Duncan Falls OH 43734 Office: Mid East Ohio Vocat Sch 400 Richard Rd Zanesville OH 43701

GRUBB, PATRICIA MITCHELL, travel agent; b. Syracuse, N.Y., Aug. 16, 1937; d. David Thomas and Alberta (Hinton) Mitchell; m. William B. Grubb, Dec. 22, 1956; children: Linda G. Tucker, Jeffrey B. BA, U. Mich., 1964. Co-owner, asst. mgr., pres. Travel Design Ltd., Appleton, Wis., 1960—. Mem. Outagamie County Med. Aux., Appleton, 1966—. Mem. Northeast Wis. Woman in Travel (v.p. 1986—). Republican. Lodge: King's Daus. Avocations: golf, tennis, reading, traveling. Home: 34 River Dr Appleton WI 54915 Office: Travel Design Ltd 309 E Washington Appleton WI 54911

GRUBBS, DAVID HAROLD, tax accountant; b. Miami, Fla., Dec. 3, 1951; s. Harold Eugene and Jean (Anderson) G.; m. Sheila Marie Witmer, July 28, 1973. BA in Sociology, Wheaton Coll., 1973; postgrad. in acctg., Fla. State U., 1978-79. CPA. Tax acct. Ernst & Whinney, Grand Rapids, Mich., 1979-83; stockbroker Thomson McKinnon Securities, Grand Rapids, 1983-85; v.p. fin. Starseal Pacific Corp., Dutton, Mich., 1985-86; dir. personal fin. planning Seidman & Siedman, Grand Rapids, 1986—; incorporator, bd. dirs. Venture Capital Resources, Grand Rapids. Served to capt. U.S. Army, 1973-78. Mem. Am. Inst. CPA's, Internat. Assn. Fin. Planners, Mich. Assn. CPA's, Grand Rapids C. of C. (founder, chmn. venture capital com. 1983-85). Republican. Avocations: weightlifting, karate, bridge, reading, hunting. Home: 1311 Philadelphia SE Grand Rapids MI 49506 Office: Seidman & Seidman 99 Monroe NW Suite 800 Grand Rapids MI 49503

GRUBBS, GARY ARTHUR, electronics executive; b. St. Louis, Jan. 1, 1954; s. Everett Owen and Joyce Jane (Heck) Goessling; m. Donna Lynn Clark, June 18, 1977; children: Kerrie Catherine, Christine Curran, Christopher Clark. BS in Planning and Econs., S.W. Mo. State U., 1976. Account rep. Tamko, Joplin, Mo., 1976-77; account mgr. Johnson & Johnson, New Brunswick, N.J., 1977-79; account rep. Texas Instruments, Dallas, 1979-80, br. mgr., 1980-84; mgr. regional sales Texas Instruments, St. Louis, 1984—. Mem. Sigma Phi Epsilon. Republican. Roman Catholic. Club: Castle Oak Tennis (Chesterfield, Mo.). Home: 15714 Heathercroft Chesterfield MO 63017 Office: Texas Instruments Inc 11618 Borman Dr Saint Louis MO 63146

GRUBER, CARL LAWRENCE, electrical engineer, educator; b. Chgo., Nov. 30, 1938; s. Lawrence Carl and Ingrid Hilda (Fahlén) G.; m. Margaret Louise Geisel, Dec. 26, 1959; children: William Lawrence, Scott Alan. BEE, U. Ill., 1960, MEE, 1962, PhD, 1967. Registered profl. engr., S.D., Minn. Asst. prof. elec. engring. S.D. Sch. Mines and Tech., Rapid City, 1964-77, prof. elec. engring., 1977-81; sr. prin. engr. solid state electronics div. Honeywell, Inc., Plymouth, Minn., 1981-82, mgr. sensor devel. dept. solid state electronics div., 1982-83; prof. elec. engr. Mankato (Minn.) State U., 1983—; founder, cons., Minn. Laser Corp., Roseville, 1980—, also bd. dirs.; cons. Solid State Electronics Div., Honeywell, Inc., Plymouth, 1983—, Physical Scis. Ctr., Honeywell, Inc., Bloomington, Minn., 1983—, Midland-Ross Corp., Mankato, 1986—. Inventor free carrier laser modulator, 1971, RF Co2 laser, 1986. Recipient Significant Tech. Achievement award NASA, 1971. Mem. IEEE, Nat. Soc. Profl. Engrs., Am. Soc. Engring. Edn., Electrochem. Soc., Sigma Xi. Democrat. Avocation: lapidary work. Home: 1201 Janett NE Saint Michael MN 55376 Office: Mankato State U Box 3 Mankato MN 56001

GRUBESICH, MICHAEL PHILLIP, JR., internal revenue officer, accountant, educator; b. St. Louis, Oct. 28, 1943; s. Michael Phillip and Anntonette (Rock) G.; m. Connie Bess Rassas, June 6, 1967 (div. Mar. 1982); m. Sharon Kay Dowdy, Nov. 20, 1982. AA, Harris Stowe State Coll., 1963; BS, U. Mo., 1965; MS, St. Louis U., 1971. CPA, Mo. With systems dept. McDonnall Douglas, St. Louis, 1969-71; with treasury dept. Ralston Purina Co., St. Louis, 1971-73; agt. IRS, St. Louis, 1973—; instr. acctg. Harris Stowe State Coll., St. Louis, 1985-86, Lincoln U., Jefferson City, Mo., 1986—; vita coordinator IRS, Lincoln U., 1987—. Served with U.S. Army, 1967-69, Vietnam. Mem. Am. Inst. CPA's (tax sect.). Avocations: teaching, tax preparation through vita vols. Home: 321 Woodward Ln Jefferson City MO 65101

GRUBIAK, MICHAEL ROBERT, chemist; b. Yonkers, N.Y., Aug. 1, 1934; s. Michael John and Ann (Fenyo) G.; m. Dorothy Ann Nylis, May 12, 1956 (div. Jan 1982); children: Lorraine, Linda, Robert, James, Jeffrey, Christopher; m. Lois Brenda Williamson, Aug. 21, 1982. Student, Bklyn. Community Coll., 1952, Columbia U., 1956-58, Fordham U., 1958-61. Sr. lab. technician Philips Labs., N.Y.C., 1958-66; engring. specialist Ferruxcube Corp., N.Y.C., 1966-84; sr. chemist Tempel Steel Corp., Chgo., 1985—. Served with USN, 1954-56. Mem. AAAS, Am. Chem. Soc., Soc. Applied Scis. Democrat. Lodge: Lions (sec. 1978-80, v.p. 1980-81). Office: Tempel Steel Corp 5990 W Touhy Ave Niles IL 60648

GRUBICH, DONALD NICHOLAS, association administrator; b. Buhl, Minn., Feb. 1, 1934; s. Nick and Sophia (Smilanich) G.; m. Claire Ann DeLano, Oct. 12, 1974; children: Leah, Nicole. AS, Virginia (Minn.) Jr. Coll., 1953; BBA in Indsl. Adminstrn., U. Minn., 1955. Mining engr. Iron Range Resources and Rehab. Bd., Hibbing, Minn., 1956-71; research supr. Iron Range Resources and Rehab. Bd., Eveleth, Minn., 1971—; organizing chmn. 6th Internat. Peat Congress, Duluth, Minn., 1980. Mem. Arrowhead Regional Devel. Commn., Duluth, 1984-86; bd. dirs. Mt. Iron (Minn.) Bd. Edn., 1981-84. Mem. Internat. Peat Soc. (U.S. council mem.), U.S. Nat. Com. Internat. Peat Soc. (sec./treas. 1982—), Minn. Peat Assn. (bd. dirs. 1984—). Democratic Farmer Labor Party. Serbian Orthodox. Lodges: Masons, Shriners, Elks. Avocations: hunting, fishing, curling. Home: 132 Spruce Dr Mountain Iron MN 55768 Office: Iron Range Resources and Rehab Bd PO Box 441 Eveleth MN 55734

GRUENWALD, JAMES HOWARD, association executive, consultant; b. Cin., Aug. 30, 1949; s. Howard Francis and Geraldine Emma (Mueller) G. B.S., Xavier U., 1971. Cert. profl. in recreation and leisure service, Ill. Rep. pub. relations Catholic Youth Orgn., Cin., 1969-72; advtransp. sales rep. Spade Trucking Co., Cin., 1972-73; field rep. Ohio Dept. Transport, Columbus, 1973-76; editorial, sales rep. Cin. Suburban Newspaper, 1976-77; asst. devel. dir. Cin. Art Acad., 1977-79; nat. exec. dir. SAY SOCCER USA, Cin., 1979—; co-founder, exec. dir. U.S. Indoor Soccer Orgn., 1985—; bd. dirs. Buckeye Men's Baseball, Cin., 1982-86, chmn. 1982-86; dir. Amateur Athletic Union, Indpls., 1983-85 ; cert. trainer Am. Coaches Effectiveness Program, Champaign, Ill., 1983—. Author Jour. Nat. Recreation and Parks, 1983; Jour. Ohio Parks and Attractions, 1985. Editor jour. Touchline, 1980—, Parents Guide to Soccer, 1985—. Candidate for city council City of St. Bernard, Ohio, 1977; mem. adv. bd. Church Parish, Cin., 1974-76. Recipient Exec. Dir. Service award SAY SOCCER USA, 1979; State of Mich. Community Service award, 1986. Mem. Cin. Assn. Execs., Nat. Council Youth Sports Dirs., Nat. Recreation and Parks Assn., Mich. Recreation and Parks Assn. (Community Service award 1986), Soc. for Non Profits. Avocations: hiking; reading; writing; teaching; conducting workshops. Home: 610 E Mitchell Ave Cincinnati OH 45217 Office: SAY SOCCER USA 5945 Ridge Rd Cincinnati OH 45213

GRUHN, ROBERT STEPHEN, parole officer; b. N.Y.C., Dec. 9, 1938; s. Jerome and Beatrice (Fuchs) G.; m. Shirley Darlene Brayfield, Sept. 14, 1984. BS, NYU, 1961; MA in Criminology, Sam Houston State U., 1975; AB in Legal Studies, Drury Coll., 1987. Cert. criminal investigator. Collection mgr. Sears, Roebuck & Co., Albuquerque, 1961-64; adjuster Gen. Adjustment Bur., Albuquerque, 1964-65; indsl. engr. LTV Aerospace Corp., Dallas, 1965-66; agy. sec. Am. Nat. Ins., Dallas, 1966-72; parole officer Tex. Bd. Parole, Dallas and Houston, 1974-80, Mo. Bd. Parole, Springfield, 1980—. Author Collision Course, 1984. Bd. dirs. Wayback Halfway House, Dallas, 1977-80. Served with U.S. Army, 1961-64. Recipient Cert. Commendation N.Y. Police Dept., 1961. Mem. Am. Mgmt. Assn. (internat. v.p., 1971-74), Soc. for Advt. Mgmt. (sec. 1968-71, pres. 1971-72), Soc. for Advancement of Mgmt. (Profl. Achievement award 1972), Mo. Corrections Assn., Mu Gamma Tau. Avocation: writing. Home: 2214 E Nora Springfield MO 65803 Office: 149 Park Central Sq Room 232 Springfield MO 65806

GRUMMON, PHYLLIS HAIGHT, management consultant; b. Syracuse, N.Y., Oct. 13, 1951; d. Jay Allen and Polly Elizabeth (Farnsworth) Haight; m. David Swanson Grummon, Sept. 5, 1981; 1 child, Katherine Swanson. AB, Cornell U., 1973; PhD, U. Mich., 1982. Sch. psychologist Yorkwoods Ctr., Ypsilanti, Mich., 1976-78; mental health profl. Washtenaw Community Mental Health, Ann Arbor, Mich., 1977-80; owner, operator Haight Assocs., East Lansing, Mich., 1980—. Contbr. articles to profl. jours. Mem. Am. Soc. Tng. and Devel. (bd. dirs. Ann Arbor chpt. 1982-86, bd. dirs. south cen. Mich. chpt. 1987), Am. Psychol. Assn., Nat. Soc. Performance Instrn., Assn. Life Underwriters, Cornell Alumni Assn. (chmn. 2d schs. com. 1981-85). Office: Haight Assocs 314 Kedzie St East Lansing MI 48823

GRUNDMANIS, JOHN VISVALDIS, architect, educator; b. Liepaja, Curland, Latvia, Aug. 9, 1926; came to U.S., 1951; s. Christopher and Luise (Dobele) G.; m. Ieva M. Metra, June 21, 1955; children: Lauris J., Markus V., Ava B. BArch., U. Minn., 1955; MEd, U. La Verne, 1979; PhD, Walden U., 1985. Registered architect Minn., Calif., Fla., N.Y., Pa., Ill., Mich., Mass., Tex., Ala., Ind., Iowa, Mo., Nebr., Okla., S.D., Wis. Intern designer Magvolo & Quick, Mpls., 1954-58; architect Hills, Gilbertson & Fisher, Mpls., 1958-66; sr. architect 3M Corp., St. Paul, 1966-71; profl. assoc. Ellerbe Architects Inc., Bloomington, Minn., 1971-76; cons. Grundmanis & Assocs., Fridley, Minn., 1976—; tchr. Anoka (Minn.) Tech. Inst., 1976—. Prin. works include Reflective Products Plant, Tex., 1967, Lab. and Office Bldg., Minn., 1968, Printing Plant, Okla., 1969, Decorative Products Plant, Mo., 1979, Irvin Army Hosp., Riley, Kans., 1972, Med. Products Plant, S.D., 1970, Scott and White Clinic and Meml. Hosp., Tex., 1971, St. Luke's Meth. Hosp., Iowa, 1971, Rochester (Minn.) Meth. Hosp., 1972, St. Paul and Ramsey Med. ctr., 1975. Deacon Latvian Evang. Luth. Ch., Mpls.; pres. Minn. chpt. Latvian Acad. Fraternity Lettonia, 1957-60. Mem. AIA, Minn. Soc. Architects., Minn. Edn. Assn., Am. Inst. Design and Drafting. Avocations: photography, travelling, history. Home and Office: 185 NE Hartman Circle Fridley MN 55432

GRUNKE, RICHARD JOHN, otolaryngologist; b. Portage, Wis., Sept. 6, 1951; s. Herbert John and Mary Louise Grunke. BS in Zoology, U. Wis., 1973; MD, Med. Coll. Wis., 1977. Diplomate Am. Bd. Otolaryngology. Internship St. Luke's Hosp., Milw., 1977-78; residency Med. Coll. of Wis. Affiliated Hosps., Milw., 1978-82; practice medicine specializing in otolaryngology Menomonee Falls, Wis., 1982—; asst. clin. prof. otolaryngology Med. Coll. Wis., Milw., 1985—. Office: N 84 W 16889 Menomonee Ave Menomonee Falls WI 53051

GRUNLAN, STEPHEN ARTHUR, clergyman, educator; b. N.Y.C., Feb. 9, 1942; s. Magnus Arthur and Esther (Helliksen) G.; m. Sandra Jean Smits, Oct. 7, 1964; children—Stephen Arthur, Jaime C., Rebecca Sue. B.S., Nyack (N.Y.) Coll., 1970; M.A., Wheaton (Ill.) Coll., 1972; M.A., U. Ill., Chgo., 1976; D.Min., Luther Theol. Sem., St. Paul, 1981. Ordained to ministry Christian and Missionary Alliance, 1978; missionary Missionary Gospel Fellowship, Turlock, Calif., 1972-74; prof. Moody Bible Inst., Chgo., 1974-77, St. Paul Bible Coll., 1977-82; sr. pastor Minnetonka (Minn.) Community Ch., 1983-86, Appleton (Wis.) Alliance Ch., 1986—; prof. Northwestern Coll. and St. Paul Bible Coll., part-time, seminar leader pastoral tng. Served with U.S. Army, 1960-65. Mem. Christian Assn. Psychol. Studies, Christian Sociol. Soc. Author: (with Marvin Mayers) Cultural Anthropology: A Christian Perspective, 1979; (with Milton Reimer) Christian Perspectives on Sociology, 1982; (with Daniel Lambrides) Healing Relationships, 1983; Marriage and the Family: A Christian Perspective, 1984; Serving with Joy, 1985; also numerous articles. Office: 3310 N Durkee St Appleton WI 54911

GRUNST, DAVID GERALD, lawyer; b. Dearborn, Mich., Aug. 12, 1954; s. Gerald James and Arnona J. (Straw) G. BS in Acctg., Ferris State Coll., 1978; JD, Thomas Cooley Law Sch., 1983. Bar: Mich. 1984. Asst. pros. Tuscola County, Caro, Mich., 1985—. Mem. ABA (family and criminal law sects.), Mich. State Bar Assn., Tuscola County Bar Assn. (treas.). Republican. Lutheran. Address: PO Box 313 Caro MI 48723

GRUSENMEYER, JEFFREY ALAN, architect; b. Dayton, Ohio, Nov. 11, 1958; s. Robert J. and Betty J. (Schock) G.; m. Monica A. Mahinske, Aug.6, 1983; 1 child, Andrew R. BArch, U. Detroit, 1981; diploma in Music Theory, Marygrove Coll., Detroit, 1981; student, guest musician, U. Mich., Dearborn, 1977-81. Registered architect, Ohio. Designer King James Group, Westlake, Ohio, 1978; project architect Ventura & Assocs., Detroit, 1979-80; archtl. developer Albert Kahn Assocs., Detroit, 1980; architect T.A. Badowski, Architect, Lakewood, Ohio, 1981, Argentieri Assocs., Wickliffe, Ohio, 1982-84; sole practice architecture Lakewood, 1985—; design cons. T.A. Badowski, Architect, Lakewood. Mem. St. Edward High Sch. Alumni Bd. Nat. Merit Scholar, 1976. Mem. AIA. Avocation: music, performance. Home and Office: 1384 Clarence Lakewood OH 44107

GRUTZMACHER, HAROLD MARTIN, JR., bookstore owner, writer; b. Chgo., Nov. 17, 1930; s. Harold Martin and Irene Evelyn (Kowalski) G.; m. Marjorie Sharlene Andersen, Nov. 5, 1955; children—Stephen, Sharon, Alison. B.A., Beloit Coll., 1952; M.A., Northwestern U., 1953, Ph.D., 1962. Asst. prof. Carthage Coll., Ill., 1958-60, Knox Coll., Galesburg, Ill., 1960-65; chmn. rhetoric Parsons Coll., Fairfield, Iowa, 1965-67; v.p. acad. affairs U. Tampa, Fla., 1967-70; dean students Beloit Coll., Wis., 1970-75; owner, mgr. Passtimes Books, Ephraim and Sister Bay, Wis., 1978—; book reviewer Chgo. Tribune, 1962-73, Tampa Tribune, 1967-70; poetry reviewer Milw. Jour., 1980—. Author: A Giant of My World, 1960; Generations, 1983 (poetry). Editor: A Grace Samuelson Sampler, 1986; Young With Ephraim, 1985. Writer Door County Advocate, 1976-85. Served with U.S. Army, 1956-58. Mem. Peninsula Arts Assn., Wis. Acad. Republican. Avocations: reading; sports reporting. Home: Box 153 Ephraim WI 54211 Office: Passtimes Books Box 153 Ephraim WI 54211

GRUVER, DARYL LEE, business educator; b. Kewanee, Ill., Mar. 18, 1945; s. Herschel Leroy and Mildred (Gingrich) G.; m. Evelena Wilson, June 8, 1974; children: Aaron, Sara. BS in Bus., Campbellsville Coll., 1968; MA in Bus., Cen. Mo. State U., 1972. Asst. prof. bus. Bethel Coll., North Newton, Kans., 1972-76, Mt. Vernon (Ohio) Nazarene Coll., 1976—. Contbr. articles to profl. jours. Pres., treas. Faith Luth. Presch. Bd., Mt. Vernon, 1980-83; exec. bd. mem. State Conv. Bapts. in Ohio, 1987—. Served with U.S. Army, 1968-71. Named one of Outstanding Young Men in Am., 1980. Home: 35 Mansfield Ave Mount Vernon OH 43050 Office: Mt Vernon Nazarene Coll Mount Vernon OH 43050

GRUYS, ROBERT IRVING, physician, surgeon; b. Silver Creek, Minn., Oct. 15, 1917; s. Herman and Dorothy (Vondergon) G.; m. Cornelia Mol, June 30, 1943 (div. 1976); children—Kathy, Robert, William, John. B.S., U. Minn., 1945, B.S. in Medicine, 1946, M.D., 1947. Rotating intern Wayne County Gen. Hosp., Detroit, 1949, Mpls. VA Hosp., 1958, 62; postgrad. Cook County Gen. Hosp., Chgo., 1957, 63, 64, Mayo Clinic, Rochester, Minn., 1949-58, U. Minn., 1958-68, 70-75; physician, surgeon Watkins Clinic, Wells, Minn., 1950-58, 63-67, 70-75, Ganado Presbyn. Hosp., Ariz., 1953-57, Southwest Clinic, Edina, Minn., part time, 1967-68, Chiayi Christian Hosp., Taiwan, 1968-70, Estes Park Med. Clinic, Colo., 1975-79, St. Cloud Va Med. Ctr., 1979—; mem. staff Wells Community Hosp., 1951-75, Meth. Hosp., Mpls., 1967-68, Mt. Sinai Hosp., Mpls., 1967-68, North Meml. Hosp., Mpls., 1967-76, Fairview Southdale Hosp., Mpls., 1967-68, Met. Med. Ctr., Mpls., 1967-76, Elizabeth Knutson Meml. Hosp., Estes Park, Colo., 1975-79, Weld County Gen. Hosp., Greeley, Colo., 1976-79, St. Cloud VA Med. Ctr., 1979—. Mem. Am. Soc. Abdominal Surgeons, Internat. Coll. Surgeons, Christian Med. Soc., AMA, Physicians Serving Physicians in Minn., Stearns-Benton County Med. Soc., Alpha Omega Alpha. Lutheran. Lodge: Masons. Avocations: flying country-western music. Home: PO Box 1817 Saint Cloud MN 56302 Office: St Cloud VA Hosp 8th St Saint Cloud MN 56301

GRYGLAS, STEVEN EUGENE, manufacturing company executive; b. Chgo., July 16, 1943; s. Stephen and Harriet Gryglas; m. Joyce E. Deming, Dec. 16, 1967; children: Any, Nina, Stephen. BS in Indsl. Engr., U. Iowa, 1967. Process engr. 3M Co., St. Paul, 1967-69; engring. cons. Booz, Allen & Hamilton, Los Angeles, 1969-71; mgmt. cons. Booz, Allen & Hamilton, San Francisco, 1972-74; dir. ops. analysis City of Phoenix, 1971-72; pres. Acme Tool & Specialties, Des Plaines, Ill., 1974—; spl. cons. Booz, Allen & Hamilton, Washington, 1974-84. Republican. Methodist. Avocations: big game and bird hunting. Home: 1312 S Fernandez Ct Arlington Heights IL 60005 Office: Acme Tool & Spltys 55 E Bradrock Dr Des Plaines IL 60018

GRYGOTIS, MICHELE M., medical writer; b. Chgo., Sept. 30, 1948; d. Marshall Edward and Margaret Frances (Foley) Neuberg; m. Garry Guy Grygotis, Sept. 16, 1972. BA, Northwestern U., 1970, cert. radiologic technologist, 1972. Adminstrv. asst. dept. surgery Evanston (Ill.) Hosp., 1976-80; freelance med. writer Wilmette, Ill., 1980—. Author: Parent's Guide to Infant Nutrition, 1986; editor: Head & Neck Injuries in Sports, 1984. Mem. Am. Med. Writers Assn. Avocations: swimming, running, cross country skiing, reading. Home and Office: 1051 Cherokee Rd Wilmette IL 60091

GRYTE, ROLF EDWARD, internist; b. Mpls., Mar. 8, 1945; s. Ralph Edward and Irene (Lindquist) G.; m. Barbara Lee Deems, June 8, 1971; children—David, Kirsten, Kristofer. B.A., U. Minn., 1967; D.O., Kirksville Coll. Osteopathic Medicine, 1971. Diplomate Am. Osteopathic Bd. Internal Medicine. Intern Kirksville Osteopathic Hosp., Mo., 1971-72, resident in internal medicine, 1972-75, chief resident, 1974-75, assoc. prof. internal medicine, 1975-79, mem. clin. faculty, 1979—, hosp. epidemiologist, 1977-79; practice medicine specializing in internal medicine, Kirksville, 1979—; med. dir. inhalation therapy dept. Kirksville Osteopathic Hosp., 1975-80, Grim-Smith Hosp., Kirksville, 1979-87, med. dir. pulmonary rehabilitation program, 1983—; black lung examiner Dept. Labor, Denver, 1983-87; social security disability examiner, Jefferson City, Mo., 1975—. Med. dir. Planned Parenthood of Northeast Mo., Kirksville, 1972-82, chmn. med. adv. com., 1972—; mem. Great Lakes Region Med. Adv. Com. Planned Parenthood World Fedn., 1983—. Named Outstanding Prof., Kirksville Coll. Osteopathic Medicine sophomore class, 1979; Nat. Osteopathic Coll. scholar. Mem. Am. Coll. Internal Medicine, Am. Heart Assn., Mo. Thoracic Soc., Mo. Assn. Osteopathic Physicians and Surgeons, Northeast Mo. Osteopathic Assn., Sigma Sigma Phi, Psi Sigma Alpha. Republican. Lutheran. Clubs: Appaloosa Horse (Moscow, Ida.); Central Mo. Appaloosa Horse (Columbia) (pres. 1981-86). Avocations: Appaloosa breeding farm; hunting; fishing. Home: RR 1 Kirksville MO 63501 Office: 1108 E Patterson Ste 2 Kirksville MO 63501

GRZEZINSKI, DENNIS MICHAEL, lawyer; b. Sheboygan, Wis., Jan. 4, 1950; s. Donald Joseph and Elfrieda Elizabeth (Walz) G. AB, Princeton U., 1972; JD, Yale U., 1975. Bar: Wis. 1975. Law clk. to judge U.S. Dist. Ct., Milw., 1975-77; assoc. Frisch, Dudek & Slattery Ltd., Milw., 1977—, also bd. dirs. Sec., treas. Vocat. Edn. Alternative of Milw., Inc., 1985—; pres. bd. dirs. Wis. Civil Liberties Union, Milw., 1983-85, sec. 1985—; bd. dirs. Legal Action Wis., Inc., Milw., 1982—. Named Mem. of Yr., Wis. Civil Liberties Union, 1986. Mem. ABA, Wis. Bar Assn., Assn. Trial Lawyers Am., Wis. Acad. Trial Lawyers. Avocations: photography, hiking, camping, reading, gardening. Home: 3025 N Farwell Ave Milwaukee WI 53211

GRZYBOWSKI, JAMES, manufacturing company executive; b. Detroit, Feb. 4, 1949; s. Gregory Joseph and Rita (Andjewski) G.; m. Voula Katherine Armyros, Apr. 12, 1980. Student, Pacific Western U., 1980-86. Engring. mgr. Martin Engring., Detroit, 1975-79; maintenance engr. ITT, Brighton, Mich., 1979-81; engring. mgr. United Techs., Alma, Mich., 1982-86; mgr. engring. Dott Mfg., Deckerville, Mich., 1986-87, Baylock Mfg. ITT, Leonard, Mich., 1987—. Inventor in field. Served with USMC, 1969-75. Mem. Soc. Plastic Engrs. Orthodox. Lodge: Elks. Avocations: golf, tennis.

GUARDIA, DAVID KING, obstetrics-gynecology educator; b. New Orleans, June 13, 1952; s. Charles Edward and Dorothy (Tangye) G. BA in Biology, Pittsburg (Kans.) State U., 1974; MD, U. Kans., Kansas City, 1977. Diplomate Am. Bd. Ob-Gyn. Intern U. Kans. Sch. Medicine, Kansas City, 1978-79, resident in ob-gyn, 1979-81; asst. prof. ob-gyn U. Kans. Med. Ctr., Kansas City, 1982; div. dir. Ob/Gyn Emergency Services, Kansas City, 1982—; clin. cons. VA Hosp., Kansas City, 1982—; liason dir. Kaiser-Permante, Shawnee Mission, Kans., 1984—; clin. cons. Ayerst Pharms. Fellow Am. Coll. Ob-Gyn (jr.); mem. AMA, Assn. Profs. of Ob-Gyn (undergrad. edn. com. 1983—), Kansas City Round Table Endocrinology, Kermit E. Krantz Soc. Democrat. Episcopalian. Home: 8205 Perry Overland Park KS 66204 Office: U Kans Med Ctr 39th St and Rainbow Blvd Kansas City KS 66103

GUARENDI, RAYMOND NICHOLAS, psychologist; b. Canton, Ohio, June 14, 1952; s. Nicholas Raymond and Amelia (Gialluca) G.; m. Randi Diane Peach, May 19, 1984. BA, MA, Case Western Res. U., 1974; PhD, Kent State U., 1978. Staff psychologist Columbiana County Mental Health Ctr., Lisbon, Ohio, 1976—; clin. psychologist Stark County Head Start, Canton, 1982—; pvt. practice psychology North Canton, 1982—; clin. psychologist Wayne/Medina (Ohio) County Head Start, 1985—, Westcare Mental Health Ctr., Massillon, Ohio, 1986—; speaker in field, 1981—. Author: You're a Better Parent Than You Think!, 1985; also articles. Mem. Am. Psychol. Assn., Ohio Psychol. Assn. (legis. network 1985). Democrat. Roman Catholic. Avocations: weight lifting, softball, antique cars, organ playing. Home: 5630 Cherokee NW North Canton OH 44720 Office: Columbiana County Mental Health Ctr 40722 State Rt 154 Lisbon OH 44432

GUARNIERI, DONALD LEWIS, lawyer; b. Warren, Ohio, May 8, 1934; s. Albert Andrew and Elsie Katherine (McKay) G.; m. Sandra Arlene Alesky, 1970. AB, Hiram Coll., 1956; LLB, Cleveland State U., 1960, LLM, JD. Bar: Ohio 1960, U.S. Supreme Ct. 1968, D.C. 1975. Sole practice Warren, 1960—. Author: Eighth Day of May. Chmn. bd. Warren Civic Music Assn.

GUBBE, MARY PATRICIA, social worker; b. Mendota, Ill., June 8, 1951; d. Robert Paul and Caroline Fidelis (Leonard) G. BA in Sociology, Ill. Benedictine Coll., 1972; MS in Ednl. Counseling, No. Ill. U., 1975. Registered social worker; cert. sch. tchr. Dir. Winn County Juvenile Program, Rockford, Ill., 1974-75, No. Ill. Fedn. for Offenders, Rockford, 1976; program mgr. Goodwill Industries, Rockford, 1976-82; therapist Counseling Assocs., Rockford, 1983-84; program dir. Stepping Stones, Inc., Rockford, 1982—. Coach Am. Youth Soccer Assn., Rockford, 1983-86. Mem. Nat. Rehab. Assn., Ill. Rehab. Assn. (awards chairperson 1976—, treas. to pres. NW chpt. 1976—), Alliance for Mentally Ill. Democrat. Roman Catholic. Avocations: golf, soccer, gardening, theater, travel. Home: 3831 16th Ave Rockford IL 61108 Office: Stepping Stones Inc 1130 E State St Rockford IL 61108

GUBBINS, MICHAEL ANTHONY, corporate executive; b. Chgo., Dec. 6, 1950; s. George Phillip and Eve Ann (Panneck) G.; m. Jeanmarie Delegato, Aug. 24, 1973; children—Jessica, Anna, Kyle, Keith, Marrissa. BS, St. Joseph's Coll., Rensselaer, Ind., 1972; MS, George Williams Coll., Downers Grove, Ill., 1977. Mgr. personnel Midwest region reservation ctr. Holiday Inns, Inc., Oak Brook, Ill., 1975-78; orgn. devel. rep. Zurich Ins. Co., Chgo., 1978-80; dir. compensation G.A.T.X. Corp., Chgo., 1980-86; dir. compensation Swift-Eckrich Co., 1986—. Mem. adv. bd. DuPage Area Vocat. Ednl. Assn., Addison, Ill., 1975-78; co-pres. W. suburban adoptive parent orgn., 1981-82. Mem. Am. compensation Assn., Human Resource Mgmt. Assn. Chgo., Chgo. Compensation Assn. Democrat. Roman Catholic. Avocations: folk music, composing. Home: 1219 Mandel St Westchester IL 60153 Office: GATX Corp 120 S Riverside Plaza Chicago IL 60606

GUBIN, RONALD, farm products company executive. Pres. S.D. Wheat Growers Assn., Aberdeen. Office: SD Wheat Growers Assn PO Box 1460 Aberdeen SD 57401 *

GUBIOTTI, ROSS ANTHONY, information systems specialist; b. Bklyn., Sept. 25, 1948; s. Antonio and Josephine (Montante) G. BS in Chemistry, Manhattan Coll., Bronx, N.Y., 1970; MS in Chemistry, Fordham U., 1972. Projects mgr. Battelle Meml. Inst., Columbus, Ohio, 1978—. Author: (with others) Numeric Databases, 1984; also articles. Served to capt. USAF, 1972-78. Mem. Am. Soc. for Info. Sci. (chmn. spl. interest group numeric data base 1986-87), ASTM (mem. interface studies com. 1986—), Am. Soc. for Metals (mem. materials info. com. 1986-89). Office: Battelle Meml Inst 505 King Ave Columbus OH 43201

GUCKENHEIMER, DANIEL PAUL, banker; b. Tel Aviv, Oct. 10, 1943; s. Ernest and Eva Guckenheimer; came to U.S., 1947, naturalized, 1957; B.B.A. in Fin., U. Houston, 1970; cert. hosp. adminstrn., Trinity U., San Antonio, 1973; m. Helen Sandra Fox, Dec. 21, 1969; children—Debra Ellen, Julie Susan. Asst. adminstr. Harris County Hosp. Dist., Houston, 1970-76; pres. Mid Am. Investments, Kansas City, Kans., 1976; exec. dir. Allen County Hosp., Iola, Kans., 1977-78; comml. loan officer Traders Bank, Kansas City, Mo., 1979; v.p. and mgr. Traders Ward Pkwy. Bank, 1980, v.p., mgr. installment loans, 1981, v.p., comml. loan officer, 1982; sr. v.p., mgr. comml. loans United Mo. Bank South, 1982—. Bd. dirs. United Way, Iola, Kans., 1977-78, Food Distbn., Inc., 1983—; adv. bd. Country Side Estate Nursing Home, Iola, 1977-78; clinic adminstr. 190th USAF Clinic, 1977-84. Served with USAF, 1962-66, maj. Res., retired 1984. Mem. Am. Coll. Hosp. Adminstrs., N.G. Assn., C. of C. Kansas City (Mo.), Am. Bankers Assn., Mo. Bankers Assn., Nat. Assn. Credit Mgmt., Robert Morris Assocs. Clubs: Iola Rotary; Kansas City, B'nai Brith (v.p. 1982-83, pres. 1984-85). Home: 8439 W 113th St Overland Park KS 66210 Office: 9201 Ward Pkwy Kansas City MO 64114

GUEBERT, RICHARD LOUIS, JR., farmer; b. Red Bud, Ill., Aug. 9, 1951; s. Richard Louis Sr. and Twila Ruth (Hannebutt) G.; m. Nancy Kay Muench, Mar. 18, 1972; 1 child, Kyle Alan. BS in Agrl. Edn., So. Ill. U., 1974. Asst. herdsman So. Ill. U., Carbondale, 1972-74; herdsman Indian Farm, Modoc, Ill., 1974-80; owner R-N-K Farms, Ellis Grove, Ill., 1980—. Pres. Randolph Agrl. Council, Sparta, Ill., 1985, sec., 1986; dir. Randolph County Service Com.; vice chmn., sec. Randolph County Rep. Cen. Com., Chester, Ill., 1975-80; mem. Econ. Devel. Southwestern Ill., Ill. Dept. Transp., Springfield, 1986. Republican. Lutheran. Club: Randolph County Corn (sec., treas 1985). Home: Rural Rt 1 Box 248 G Ellis Grove IL 62241

GUENTHER, BRENDA M., accountant; b. Ft. Scott, Kans., Mar. 27, 1960; d. Henry Emmanual and Doris Katherine (Graham) Ericson; m. Eric Jerome Guenther, Sept. 3, 1983; 1 child, Amanda Nicole. BS in Acctg., Kans. State U., 1982. CPA, Kans. Pipeline acct. Koch Industries, Inc., Wichita, Kans., 1982-83; internal/EDP auditor Western Ins. Co., Ft. Scott, 1983-86; fin. administr. Lincoln Nat. Corp., Ft. Scott, 1986—. V.p. Altar Soc., Fulton, Kans., 1986—. Mem. Am. Inst. CPA's, Future Farmers Am. Alumni Assn. (treas Uniontown, Kans. chpt. 1986—, sec. 1985-86). Roman Catholic. Avocations: sewing, gardening. Office: Lincoln Nat Corp 102 S National Fort Scott KS 66701

GUENTHER, JOHN STANLEY, financial executive; b. Detroit, May 28, 1942; m. Christine Guenther, July 1, 1972; children: Elizabeth, Andrew. BBA, U. Mich., 1964. CPA, Ill. Mgr. audit Arthur Andersen & Co., Chgo., 1966-73; v.p. fin. George J. Ball Inc., Chgo., 1973—. Mem. editorial adv. bd. Cashflow mag., 1985—. Served to lt. (j.g.) USN, 1964-66. Mem. Am. Inst. CPA's, Ill. Soc. CPA's, Fin. Execs. Inst.

GUERIN, CHRISTOPHER DAVID, arts administrator; b. Biloxi, Miss., Aug. 22, 1953; s. John Warren and Charlene Wanda (Roovart) G.; m. Ruth M. Diamond, Nov. 26, 1978. BA in English, No. Ill. U., 1975, MA in English, 1977. Publicist DoAll Co., Des Plaines, Ill., 1977-79; publicist Colorado Springs (Colo.) Symphony Orch., 1979-84, asst. mgr., 1984-85; gen. mgr. Ft. Wayne (Ind.) Philharm. Orch., 1985—. Bd. dirs. Springspree Festival, Colorado Springs, 1979-84, Forte Festival, Ft. Wayne, 1985-86. Mem. Am. Symphony Orch. League. Avocations: golf, writing. Office: Ft Wayne Philharm 222 W Berry St Fort Wayne IN 46802

GUERNSEY, WILLIAM ARNOLD, JR., manufacturing company executive; b. Indpls., Dec. 5, 1951; s. William Arnold and Elsie Marie (Cook) G.; m. Georgette Funk, May 20, 1978; children: Felicia Loraine, Adelle Kristin. BSCE, Purdue U., 1974; MBA, Stanford U., 1976. Dir. logistics Cummins Mex., Mexico City, 1978-80; dir. worldwide parts mktg. Cummins Engine Co., Columbus, Ind., 1980, dir. components strategy, 1980-82, dir. internat. planning, 1982-84, dir. internat. distrbn., 1984-86, plant mgr., 1986—; bd. dirs. Internat. Productivity Cons., Columbus. Big Bro. Big Bros. of Barth County, Columbus, 1977-78; deacon First Presbyn. Ch., Columbus, 1983—, chmn. stewardship com., 1985, chmn. bd. deacons, 1986; attach/aide Pan Am Games, Indpls., 1986-87. Named one of Outstanding Young Men of Am., 1981. Republican. Avocations: tennis, golf, woodworking, spectator sports. Home: 1066 Goldfinch Columbus IN 47203 Office: Cummins Engine Co Box 3005 MC 30250 Columbus IN 47202-3005

GUERRA, VERA BELLE, nurse; b. Tyndall, S.D., Feb. 29, 1924; d. Floyd Arthur Ball and Ruth Ella (Kubowitz) Graybill; m. Virgil Benjamin Guerra, Nov. 2, 1942; children—Kathleen, Lawrence, Jill, Jeanine. Lic. practical nurse, Omaha Pub. Sch. Practical Nursing, 1967; A.S., Coll. of St. Mary's, 1982. R.N., Nebr. Practical nurse Archbishop Bergan Mercy Hosp., Omaha, 1967-69, Univ. Med. Ctr., Omaha, 1970-82, staff nurse, 1983—. Recipient Commendation Univ. Med. Ctr. Hosp., 1976. Mem. Am. Nurses Assn., Nebr. Nurses Assn. (del. to conv. 1983-86). Democrat. Roman Catholic. Office: Univ Med Ctr 42d and Emilie Sts Omaha NE 68105

GUEST, H(OWARD) BRANDON, computer information systems specialist; b. Hamel, Minn., Jan. 8, 1959; s. Howard Mathias and Edris Jean (Dorweiler) G.; m. Colleen Marie McCarthy, Sept. 11, 1982. BS with distinction, Northwestern U., 1981; MBA, U. Minn., 1986. Sr. computer systems analyst Control Data Corp., Plymouth, Minn., 1981—; bd. dirs. Farmers State Bank, Hamel. Vol. firefighter Hamel Fire Dept., 1976—. Mem. Tau Beta Pi. Republican. Home: 18335 31st Ave N Plymouth MN 55447-1001 Office: Control Data Corp 2300 Bershire Ln N Plymouth MN 55441

GUETH, THOMAS FRANKLIN, electrical engineer; b. Columbus, Ohio, Jan. 18, 1950; s. Clarence Francis and Jacqueline (Cummins) G. B.S. in Elec. Engring., Ohio State U., 1973; B.S. in Engring. Mgmt., U. Evansville, 1979. Elec. engr. Warrick ops. Alcoa, Newburgh, Ind., 1974-77, sr. elec. engr., 1978-79; mgr. systems dept. Kinetic Systems Corp., Lockport, Ill., 1979-81, indsl. market dir., 1981-82, v.p. indsl. systems, 1982-83, pres. systems. tech. group., 1983-84; dir. computer engring. Multigraphics div. AM Internat., 1983-84, dir. elec. systems engring., 1984-86; dir. devel. engring. Inserter Systems div. Pitney-Bowes Corp., Danbury, Conn., 1987—; evening lectr. U. Evansville, 1979. Mem. IEEE, Instrument Soc. Am., Am. Mgmt. Assn., DECUS, Tau Beta Pi.

GUGEL, PAUL EDWARD, lawyer, accountant; b. Detroit, Sept. 14, 1956; s. Paul Walter Jr. and Patricia Angela (Sullivan) G. BBA with high distinction, U. Mich., 1977; JD with honors, T.M. Cooley Law Sch., 1983; MBA, Mich. State U., 1986. CPA, Mich. 1983, Minn. 1985. Staff acct. Peat, Marwick & Mitchell, CPA's, Detroit, 1977-78, Sallan, Zack, CPA's, Southfield, Mich., 1978-79; asst. tax mgr. Dart Mgmt. Corp., Mason, Mich., 1980-85; staff atty. Kelly Services, Inc., Troy, Mich., 1986—; polit. cons. Part-Time Legislature Com., Brighton, Mich., 1985, Chrysler for Gov., Brighton, 1986. Mem. ABA, State Bar Mich., State Bar Minn., Am. Inst. CPA's, Mich. Assn. CPA's. Republican. Roman Catholic. Avocations: athletics, coin collecting, radio/TV. Home: 842 Yorktown Ct Northville MI 48167 Office: Kelly Services Inc 999 W Big Beaver Rd Troy MI 48084

GUGGENHEIM, RICHARD BENDER, hotel chain company executive; b. Chgo., Apr. 22, 1923; s. Milton S. and Sylvia (Bender) G.; m. Gail Porges; children: Paul, Jenny, Michael, Robert. BA, U. N.C., 1945. With Julius Bender, Inc., 1945-53; mgr. Midwest Terr. Design, Inc., St. Louis, 1953-57; v.p. Americana Congress Hotels, Chgo., 1957-87; pres., chief operating officer Comfort Inns of Elmhurst, Ill., 1987—. Active exec. com. Anti-Defamation League. Served with USMCR, 1943-45. Mem. Am. Hotel and Motel Assn. (pub. relations com.), Hotel Sales Mgmt. Assn. Home: 125 Country Ln Highland Park IL 60035 Office: 370 N Rt 83 Elmhurst IL 60126

GUGLIOTTA, BARBARA MARIE, accounting and finance educator; b. Louisville, May 5, 1948; d. Tony Clement and Ann Louise (Cataldo) G.; m. John Michael Finch, Nov. 25, 1983; children: Don, Robert, Kerry. BS, U. Louisville, 1978; MPA, U. Mo., Kansas City, 1987. CPA. Acct. Athur Young & Co., Louisville, 1978-83; mgr., health care cons. Athur Young & Co., Kansas City, Mo., 1984-86; controller Jewish Hosp., Louisville, 1983-84; instr. Rockhurst Coll., Kansas City, 1986—. Mem. Jr. Women Symphony Alliance, Kansas City. Mem. Am. Inst. CPA's, Mo. Soc. CPA's, Ky. Soc. CPA's, Fin. Execs. Inst. (bd. dirs. 1984—), Kans. Forum for Women Healthcare Execs. (charter, bd. dirs. 1986—), Midwest Bioethics Assn. Republican. Episcopalian. Avocations: needlepoint, sailing, skiing, singing. Home: 13917 Falkirk Circle Grandview MO 64030

GUIDERA, RICHARD THOMAS, real estate company executive, consultant; b. Rockville Center, N.Y., Nov. 11, 1928; s. Thomas Francis and Augusta Loretta (Jenkins) G.; m. Marie Woolaver, Jan. 9, 1954; children: Richard Jr., Ellen, Peter, Paul, Mary, Megan, William. AB, Harvard U., 1950. V.p. real estate Dayton Hudson Co., Mpls., 1977-80; exec. v.p. The Ctr. Co., Mpls., 1980-84; pres. The Guidera Group, Mpls., 1984—; bd. dirs. Pinstripes Petites, Mpls., 1986—. Mem. Internat. Council Shopping Ctrs. (bd. realtors). Republican. Roman Catholic. Club: Harvard (N.Y.C., Mpls.). Home: 173 Ridgeview Dr Wayzata MN 55391 Office: The Guidera Group Inc 1219 Marquette Ave Minneapolis MN 55403

GUILBERT, MARY SENNETT, marketing professional, consultant; b. Coral Gables, Fla., Feb. 17, 1933; d. Maurice Reed and Geraldine (Hawley) Sennett; m. Lucien E. Guilbert, Jan. 7, 1967; 1 child, Catherine Louise. BS in History, Washington U., St. Louis, 1964. Tchr. various locations, 1955-67, pvt. practices communications cons., 1967-80; sr. acct. exec. Ohio Bell Telephone Co., 1980-84; pres. Mktg. Solutions, Inc., Reynoldsburg, Ohio, 1984—. Mem. Nat. Assn. Female Execs. Roman Catholic. Avocations: swimming, camping. Home: 7739 Burkey Dr Reynoldsburg OH 43068 Office: Mktg Solutions Inc 7335 E Livingston Reynoldsburg OH 43068

GUINEY, LAURA ANNE, technical publications specialist; b. Cin., June 3, 1961; d. James Dale and Jean Helene (Marquard) D.; m. Robert Carl Guiney, May 18, 1984; 1 child, William Benjamin. BA in English, Miami U., 1983. Tech. writer Datapoint Corp., San Antonio, 1983-84; tech. publs. specialist NCR Corp., Dayton, Ohio, 1984—. Author, editor co. publs. Republican. Methodist. Avocations: reading, creative stitchery. Home: 40 Peachgrove Ave Centerville OH 45459 Office: NCR Corp SE Retail GMBU 1700 S Patterson Blvd SER 2 Dayton OH 45479

GUINN, STANLEY WILLIS, tax professional; b. Detroit, June 9, 1953; s. Willis Hampton and Virginia Mae (Pierson) G.; m. Patricia Shirley Newgord, June 13, 1981. BBA in Acctg. with high distinction, U. Mich., 1979, MBA in Corp. Fin. with distinction, 1981; MS in Taxation with Distinction, Walsh Coll., 1987. CPA, Mich.; cert. mgmt. acct., Mich. Tax mgr. Coopers & Lybrand, Detroit, 1981—. Served with USN, 1974-77. Mem. Am. Inst. CPA's, Nat. Assn. Accts., Mich. Assn. CPA's, Inst. Mgmt. Acctg., Phi Kappa Phi, Beta Gamma Sigma, Beta Alpha Psi, Delta Mu Delta. Republican. Presbyterian. Avocations: tennis, motorcycling. Home: 2200 W Circle Dr Dearborn MI 48128 Office: Coopers & Lybrand 400 Renaissance Ctr Detroit MI 48243

GUINN, WILLIAM HARRY, city official; b. Joplin, Mo., May 21, 1931; s. William Irene and May Ellen (Campbell) G.; m. Doris Jean Highley, Sept. 30, 1952; children—William Harry, John Robert. Grad. Nat. Hazards Control Inst., 1978, grad. Nat. Fire Acad., 1986. Firefighter Joplin Fire Dept., 1953-57, engr., 1957-59, lt., 1959-63, tng. officer, 1963-71, insp., asst. chief, 1971-81, fire chief, 1981—; cons. Health Tank Testing, Whitefish Bay, Wis., 1983—, Ozark Gateway Fire Chief, Carthage, Mo., 1983—; adviser Fire Protection and Rescue Tech., Crowder Coll., Neosho, Mo., 1984. Author: In Case of Fire, 1983; Hazardous Materials Disaster Operation Plan, 1982. Active Toys for Tots, Joplin, chmn., 1982; officer Civil Def. Joplin, 1959-81; chmn. Mokan council Boy Scouts Am., Joplin, 1957. Recipient Outstanding Service award State of Mo., 1963, 1965. Mem. Ozark Gateway Fire Chief Assn. (v.p. 1983), Internat. Assn. Fire Chiefs, Nat. Fire Protection Assn., Mo. State Fire Chiefs Assn., Mo. Valley Fire Chiefs. Lodge: Masons (master 1975). Avocations: hunting, fishing. Home: 711 Moffet Joplin MO 64801 Office: 303 E 3d St Joplin MO 64801

GUINNUP, DAVID ROBERT, urban and regional planner; b. Marion, Ind., Jan. 4, 1948; s. Robert E. and Doris I. (Campbell) G.; m. Diana Louise Stone, Aug. 29, 1970. B.S. in Urban Planning, Ball State U., 1971; postgrad. Wright State U., 1981—. Planner, Henry-Hancock Community Action Program, Inc., New Castle, Ind., 1972-75; dir. Wyoming County (Pa.) Planning Commn., 1975-78; dir. Shelby County (Ohio) Regional Planning Commn., 1978-83; research grad. asst. dept. econs. Wright State U., 1983-85; econ. and planning cons., 1984—; planning cons. Mem. Am. Planning Assn., Am. Inst. Cert. Planners, Am. Soc. Pub. Adminstrn., Omicron Delta Epsilon, Theta Xi. Democrat. Lodge: Kiwanis (Sidney). Contbr. articles to profl. jours. Home: 1142 Evergreen Dr Sidney OH 45365

GUINTA, JOHN JOSEPH, advertising executive; b. Chgo., July 14, 1930; s. Sam and Josephine (Costa) G.; m. Marie Therese, Aug. 6, 1955; children: John, Michael, Daniel, Thimothy, Cara, Lea, Emily. Student, Morgan Park Jr. Coll., 1948-50, U. Ill., Chgo., 1950-51. Pres. Jonathan & Assocs., Palos Park, Ill., 1961—; cons. in field. Producer, dir., St. Alexander Theater Group, Palos Heights, Ill., 1980—. Served to cpl. U.S. Army, 1951-53, Korea. Roman Catholic. Avocations: theater, jogging.

GUINTER, S. ROBERT, design engineer; b. Chgo., Mar. 27, 1927; s. Seward Haise and Agnes (Uek) G.; m. Betty Ann Welch, Sept. 8, 1951; children: Raymond, Patricia Ann. BS in Mfg. Engring., Ill. Inst. Tech., 1957. Product designer Union Special Machine Co., Chgo., 1949-50; test engr. Sears Roebuck & Co., Chgo., 1956-61; chief engr. Counselor Co., Rockford, Ill., 1961—; mem. charter Conf. of Weights ane Measures, Washington, 1979—. Patentee in field. Advisor Boy Scouts Am., Rockford, 1970—, Jr. Achievement, Rockford, 1964-69; bd. dirs. Wesley Willows Home, Rockford, 1980-86; elder Christ Meth. Ch., Rockford, 1965-80. Served with USN, 1945-46. Mem. Soc. Cert. Mfg. Engrs., Soc. Mfg. Engrs. (cert. mfg. engring.), Nat. Model Railroad Assn. Republican. Avocations: model railroading, photography. Home: 4449 Charles St Rockford IL 61108 Office: Counselor Co 2107 Kishwaukee St Rockford IL 61101

GUIO, MICHAEL VICTOR, Federal Bureau of Investigation agent; b. Indpls., Sept. 11, 1942; s. Victor Milton and Marian (Gearen) G.; m. Jean Marie Julian, Nov. 29, 1969; children—Michael Jason, Julian Matthew. B.A., Butler U., 1964. Spl. agt. FBI, Boston, 1968-69, N.Y.C., 1969-76, Gary, Ind., 1976-78, Indpls., 1978—; mem. organized crime com. FBI, Boston, N.Y.C., Gary, Indpls., 1969-76, organized and white collar crime com., 1976—. Contbr. articles to profl. jours., chpts. to books. Investigator Nat. Grant Child Abuse, Midwest Region, 1980-83. Served to lt. USNR, 1967. Republican. Presbyterian. Clubs: Indpls. Athletic (pres. men's swim 1984-85), Carmel Dads. Avocations: indoor and outdoor sports; creating stained glass windows and lamps. Office: FBI PO Box 1186 Indianapolis IN 46206

GUITHUES, DENISE MICHELE, accounting educator; b. St. Louis, Sept. 28, 1954; d. Henry James and Florence Mary (Meert) G.; 1 child, James Franciscus. BS in Bus. Adminstrn., St. Louis U., 1975, M in Fin., 1977, PhD in Bus. Adminstrn., 1983. CPA, Mo.; lic. real estate agt., Mo. Staff acct. Price Waterhouse, St. Louis, 1975-76; inst. acctg. St. Louis U., 1979-83, Webster U., St. Louis, 1983-84; asst. prof. Fontbonne Coll., St. Louis, 1984—; cons. mgmt., St. Louis, 1976—; adj. asst. prof. Parks Coll., Cahokia, Ill., 1983-84. Author: Innovative Reporting of Foreign Currency Translation, 1985. Recipient Outstanding Student award Fin. Execs. Inst., 1976. Fellow Am. Acctg. Assn. (doctoral consortium); mem. Am. Inst. CPA's, Nat. Assn. Accts., Am. Assn. Individual Investors, Beta Alpha Psi, Beta Gamma Sigma. Roman Catholic. Avocations: equestrian sports, tennis, swimming. Office: Fontbonne Coll 6800 Wydown Saint Louis MO 63105

GUIZZOTTI, CHARLES MICHAEL, dentist; b. Buffalo, Jan. 28, 1958; s. Anthony Joseph and Ann Marie (Mancuso) G.; m. Cheryl Ann Arent, Aug. 8, 1980; children: Jessalyn Brooks, Derek Anthony. BS cum laude, SUNY, Buffalo, 1980; DDS, Case Western Reserve U., 1984; real estate license, John Carroll U., 1984. Pulmonary function technician VA Hosps., Cleve., 1981-84; dentist Family Dental Ctrs., Middleburg Heights, Ohio, 1984-85; pvt. practice dentistry Brooklyn, Ohio, 1985—. Coach Little League Baseball, Strongsville, Ohio, 1986-87. Named Nat. Del. of Yr. Am. Student Dental Assn., 1983. Mem. Acad. Gen. Dentistry, Cleve. Soc. Clin. Hypnosis, Am. Soc. Clin. Hypnosis, Am. Orthodontic Soc., Internat. Assn. of Orthodontics. Republican. Roman Catholic. Home: 17074 Raccoon Trail Strongsville OH 44136

GULATI, VIPIN, accountant; b. New Delhi, India, Nov. 3, 1953; came to U.S., 1982; s. Har Kishan Lal and Shakuntalarani (Sachdeva) G.; m. Ramanjit Bais, July 24, 1986. Diploma hotel mgmt., Inst. Hotel Mgmt., Bombay, India, 1976; BA, U. Delhi, 1979; MBA, U. Ratasthan, Jaipur, India, 1981. CPA, Mich. Gen. mgr. Hotel Kandhari, Vijayawada, India, 1979-81; mgr. food and beverage Holiday Inn, Agra, India, 1981-82; acct. Irving Kaplan, Farmington Hills, Mich., 1983-87, S.B. Malerman P.C., Southfield, Mich., 1987—. Fellow Am. Inst. CPA's, Mich. Assn. CPA's. Club: Centaur (West Bloomfield, Mich.). Avocations: tennis, golf, traveling. Home: 28033 Gettysburg Farmington Hills MI 48018

GULLEDGE, BILLY RAY, aero. engr.; b. Poplar Bluff, Mo., Aug. 25, 1947; s. Twedell Arvil and Virginia Genevieve (Campbell) G.; student Coll. of Sch. of Ozarks, 1965-67; A.A., Austin Peay State U., 1973; B.S., Embry-Riddle U., 19—; m. Brenda Diana Hill, June 2, 1968; children—Brian Dewayne, Piper Diana. Asst. mgr. trainee J.J. Newberry Co., Poplar Bluff, Mo., 1964-67; joined U.S. Army, 1967, advanced through grades to capt., 1971, ret., 1977; asso. Keele Realty, Poplar Bluff, 1977-79; regional mgr. United Nat. Life Ins. Co., Springfield, Ill., 1978; asso. Mattingly Realty, Florissant, Mo., 1979—; engr. product support planning McDonnell Aircraft Co., St. Louis, 1979—; grad. asst. instr. Dale Carnegie course, St. Louis. Vol. fireman Sch. of Ozarks, 1965-67; radiol. monitor instr., 1965-67. Decorated Bronze Star medal with oak leaf cluster, Meritorious Service medal, Air medal with 24 oak leaf clusters, Vietnamese Cross of Gallantry; recipient Flight Safety Achievement award U.S. Army Aviation Sch., 1971, Dale

Carnegie Course Human Relations award, 1978. Travel-Study Club scholar, 1965-67. Licensed real estate and life ins. agt. Mo., radiol. monitoring instr., Mo. Mem. Aircraft Owners and Pilots Assn., AMVETS, Army Aviation Assn. Am. (local treas. 1974-75), Nat. Assn. Realtors, Ret. Officers Assn., Mo. Assn. Realtors, Florissant (Mo.) Jr. C. of C. (Springboard, Speak-up, Regional First-timer awards 1978). Clubs: Business; Library; Reading; United Nat. Presidents; Century. Home: 1950 Forest Haven Imperial MO 63052

GULLEKSON, EDWIN HENRY, JR., physician; b. Flint, Mich., May 14, 1935; s. Edwin Henry and Amy Marcella (Graves) G.; student Flint Community Coll., 1953-56; M.D., U. Mich., 1961; m. Rosemary Evelyn Leppien, May 5, 1968; children—Kathryn Dawn, Hans Edwin, Heidi M. Intern McLaren Gen. Hsop., Flint, 1961-62, resident, 1962-63; gen. practice medicine, Flint, 1963—; chief of staff McLaren Gen. Hosp., 1977-81; mem. staffs Hurley, St. Joseph, Genesee Meml. hosps. (all Flint). Served to capt. M.C., AUS, 1966-67. Upjohn Research grantee, 1958, 59, 60. Diplomate Am. Bd. Family Practice. Mem. Mich. Med. Soc., Genesee County Med. Soc. (pres. 1983-84), AMA, Am. Acad. Family Practice, Mich. Acad. Gen. Practice. Patentee surg. instrument. Home: 1721 Laurel Oak Dr Flint MI 48507 Office: 5031 Villa Linde Pkwy Flint MI 48504

GULLER, HAROLD, company executive; m. Mildred Bekow; 4 children. Student, Washington U. With Essex Industries, Inc., St. Louis, chmn. bd., chief exec. officer; chmn. bd., chief exec. officer Essex Cryogenics of Mo., Inc., Essex Precision Controls, Inc., Essex Screw Products, Propellex Corp., Dolphin Systems Corp., Essex Fluid Controls Div., Del., 1980 White House Conf. on Small Bus.; mem. Spl. Nat. Sml. Bus. and Innovation adv. task force; mem. 1984 Joint Civilian Orientation Conf., Washington, Fed. Res. Bank Adv. Council; chmn. Mo. Agrl. and Sml. Bus. Authority; bd. dirs. Am. Jewish Com., Arts and Edn. Council Greater St. Louis, Central Agy. for Jewish Edn.; exec. com. Jewish Fedn. St. Louis; mem. Solomon Schechter Day Sch. of St. Louis, Herbert Hoover Boys Club, St. Louis Regional Commerce and Growth Assn., Parks Coll. Adv. Com., St. Louis U. Pres.'s Council. Named Mo. Small Businessman of Yr., SBA, 1981, others. Mem. Air Force Assn., Am. Def. Preparedness Assn. (pres. St. Louis chpt.), Soc. Mfg. Engrs., Survival and Flight Equip. Assn., William Elliot Soc. of Washington U. Office: Essex Industries Inc 7700 Gravois Ave Saint Louis MO 63123

GULLICK, THOMAS H., home health care administrator; b. Marshfield, Wis., July 16, 1949; s. Harold T. and Lenice M. (Swenson) G.; m. Susan Joan Fehrenbach, Nov. 25, 1972; 1 dau., Amy Sue. B.S., U. Wis.-LaCrosse, 1971, M.S., 1979; M.B.A., Western Colo. U., Grand Junction, 1983. Personnel adminstr. U.S. Air Force, 1972-76; county adminstr., clk. Juneau County, Mauston, Wis., 1976-80; asst. adminstr. St. Joseph's Hosp., Hillsboro, Wis., 1980-81; adminstr. VNA Home Care, Neenah, Wis., 1981—; VNA rep. Hospice of Neenah-Menasha. Blood chmn. ARC, Mauston, 1976-80; bd. dirs. Parkview Eldercare, Hillsboro, 1980—; loaned exec. United Way, Neenah, 1983. Recipient Meritorious Pub. Service award Am. Legion, 1977-78. Mem. Am. Coll. Health Care Adminstrs., Nat. Home Care Orgn., Wis. Home Care Orgn., U. Wis. Alumni Assn. Lodge: Rotary Internat. (dir. 1982-85, Rotarian of Yr. 1984). Home: 10316 N La Cresta Dr. Mequon WI 53092-6020 Office: Milw Med Clinic 3003 W Good Hosp Rd Milwaukee WI 53217

GULLIKSON, ROBERT CHRIS, computer services director; b. Pueblo, Colo., Dec. 9, 1951; s. Robert C. Gullikson and Nancy Marie (DiPalma) Crain; m. Dolores Jean Vorhies, May 20, 1972; 1 child, Robert Mike. Diploma, Cleve. Inst. Electronics, 1974; student, U. Nebr., Omaha, 1974—. cert. electronic tech. FCC. Regional mgr. Micor Inc., Omaha, 1974-81; dist. mgr. Decision Data, Inc., Omaha, 1981-84; dir. First Data Resources, Omaha, 1984—. Served to staff sgt. USAF, 1970-74. Mem. Assn. Field Service Mgrs. Republican. Roman Catholic. Avocations: golf, bowling, fitness, home projects. Home: 12630 Southdale Dr Omaha NE 68137 Office: First Data Resources 7302 Pacific St Omaha NE 68114

GULMEN, SULEYMAN, dentist; b. Elene, Bulgaria, June 27, 1945; came to U.S., 1969; s. Huseyin and Fatma Gulmen; m. Guner Buyukkus, July 9, 1969; children: Funda, Tolga. DDS, Harettepe U., Ankara, Turkey, 1968; MSD, U. Minn., 1972; DMD, Washington U., St. Louis, 1977; MSD, St. Louis U., 1985. Diplomate Bd. Oral Pathology. Asst. prof. dentistry Washington U., 1974-76, assoc. prof., 1976-82; practice dentistry specializing in orthodontics St. Louis, 1984—; clin. assoc. prof. Southern Ill. U., Alton, 1985—. Contbr. articles to profl. jours. Fellow Am. Acad. Oral Pathology; mem. Am. Assn. Orthodontists (assoc.). Home: 12554 Royal Manor Dr Saint Louis MO 63141 Office: 6500 Chippewa Saint Louis MO 63109

GULSTRAND, RUDOLPH ELMER, JR., chemical company executive; b. Mpls., May 21, 1984; s. Rudolph Elmer and Marian (Clothier) G.; m. Bonnie Gail Nichols, Nov. 7, 1969; children: Julie Ellen, JoAnne Elizabeth, Jennifer Ann. BS in Pharmacy, U. Minn., Mpls., 1963; MBA, Mich. State U., East Lansing, 1970; BS in Strategic Mktg., Harvard U., 1979. Registered pharmacist, Minn. Tech. supr. pharm. products Miles Labs., Elkhart, Ind., 1968-73; prodn. mgr. Miles Labs., West Haven, Conn., 1973-74; plant mgr. Miles Labs., Zeeland, Mich., 1974-77; ops. mgr. Hexcel Corp., Zeeland, Mich., 1977-80; dir. bus. devel. Sherwin Williams Co., Cleve., 1980-82; mng. dir. internat., gen. mgr. polymer additives PMC, Inc., Rocky River, Ohio, 1982-87; v.p., gen mgr. internat. div. PMC, Inc., 1987—. Scoutmaster Boy Scouts Am., Elkhart, 1970-73; v.p. Zeeland C. of C., 1976-78; pres. Rocky River Boosters, 1986—. Served with U.S. Army, 1964-68. Mem. Beta Sigma Phi. Republican. Presbyterian. Avocations: sailing, cross country ski racing, jogging. Home: 2124 Morewood Pkwy Rocky River OH 44116 Office: PMC Specialties Group Inc 20525 Center Ridge Rd Rocky River OH 44116

GUMB, JACKSON JAY, social services administrator; b. Burwell, Nebr., Jan. 26, 1948; s. Clarence Dale and Marjorie (Banks) G.; m. Glenna Marie James, May 24, 1970; children: Misty Marie, Jaimie Lynn. BA in Sociology, Southwestern Coll., 1970. Cert. social worker, adult care home adminstr. Student pastor United Meth. Ch., Atlanta, Kans., 1967-70; income maintenance worker Social and Rehab. Services., Kansas City, Kans., 1971-72, income maintenance supr., 1972-77; income maintenance supr. Social and Rehab. Services., Topeka, Kans., 1977-78, quality control adminstr., 1978-79, dir., 1979—; bd. dirs. Kans. Conf. on Social Welfare, Wichita, pres. 1987—. Recipient Disting. Service in Govt. award Kans. Health Care Assn., 1985. Democrat. Lodge: Optimists (pres. 1978). Avocations: water skiing, wood cutting, restoring old cars. Home: 307 Spruce Ln Topeka KS 66617 Office: Social and Rehab Services Biddle Bldg 2700 W 6th St Topeka KS 66606

GUMBERT, JACK LEE, surgeon; b. Ft. Wayne, Ind., July 14, 1934; s. Martin Fredrick and Beulah Faye (McClain) G.; B.A., Cin. U., 1957, M.D., 1961; m. Lois Irene Scheimann, June 15, 1957; children—Jack, Lori, Brad, Grant, Joseph. Intern, Marion County Gen. Hosp., Indpls., 1961-62, resident 1962-66; practice medicine specializing in surgery, Ft. Wayne, Ind., 1968—; staff surgeon Luth., St. Joseph hosps., Ft. Wayne, 1968—; chmn. surgery service Parkview Hosp., 1977—, also mem. bd. dirs.; asso. faculty mem. Ind. U. Sch. Medicine; chmn. Physicians Health Plan No. Ind. Bd. dirs. Ft. Wayne YMCA, UPD Inc., Dukes Day Inc., Allen County Bd. Health. Served to capt. M.C., U.S. Army, 1966-68. Decorated Bronze Star, Air medal (Vietnam); Army Commendation medal with oak leaf cluster; named to Ind. Basketball Hall of Fame, 1978. Diplomate Am. Bd. Surgery. Fellow ACS (bd. dirs. Ind. chpt.); mem. AMA, Ind. State, Ft. Wayne med. socs., Ind. State, Ft. Wayne (pres. 1978-79) surg. assns. Lutheran. Club: Pine Valley Country (pres. 1976-77). Contbr. articles to med. jours. Home: 10810 Old Colony Rd Fort Wayne IN 46825 Office: 5010 Riviera Ct Fort Wayne IN 46825

GUMBLETON, MICHAEL JAMES, accountant; b. Detroit, Dec. 3, 1954; s. Gerrard Leo and Marian Clare (Knechtges) G.; m. Rebecca Ann Byrnes, June 23, 1979. BSBA, Xavier U., 1977. CPA, Ohio. Staff acct. Ernst & Whinney, Cin., 1977-78, mem. advanced tax staff, 1978-79, sr. tax acct., 1979-81, tax mgr., 1981-83, tax sr. mgr., 1983—. Mem. Am. Inst. CPA's, Ohio Soc. CPA's, Nat. Assn. Accts., Estate Planning Council, Internat. Assn. Fin. Planners, Delta Sigma Pi. Club: Cincinnati. Avocations: tennis, softball. Office: Ernst & Whinney 1300 Columbia Plaza Cincinnati OH 45202

GUNASEKERA, JAY SARATH, mechanical engineer, educator; b. Kalutara, Sri Lanka, July 26, 1946; came to U.S., 1981; s. Don M. and Bonnie M. Gunasekera; m. Kamini Mal Hettiarachchi, Dec. 5, 1952; children: Manisha, Eva. BSE, U. Sri Lanka, 1967; MS, U. London, 1970, PhD, 1972. Registered profl. engr. Head dept. U. Sri Lanka, Peradeniya, 1973-78; sr. lectr. Monash U., Melbourne, Austraila, 1978-81; sr. scientist USAF, Dayton, Ohio, 1981-83; assoc. prof. Ohio U., 1983-85, prof., 1985—; bd. dirs. Super Tech. Internat., Athens. Author: Metal Forming, 1983. Mem. ASME, Soc. Mfg. Engrs., Inst. Mech. Engrs. U.K., Inst. Prodn. Engrs. U.K. Home: 289 Carroll Rd Athens OH 45701 Office: Ohio Univ Stocker Center Athens OH 45941

GUND, GEORGE, III, financier; b. Cleve., May 7, 1937; s. George and Jessica (Roesler) G.; m. Mary Theo Feld, Aug. 13, 1966; children—George, Gregory. Student, Western Res. U., Menlo (Calif.) Sch. Bus. Engaged in personal investments San Francisco, 1967—; cattle ranching Lee, Nev., 1967—; partner Calif. Seals, San Francisco, 1976-77; pres. Ohio Barons, Inc., Richfield, 1977-78; chmn. bd. Northstar Fin. Corp., Bloomington, Minn., 1978—, Minn. North Stars, Bloomington; dir. Ameritrust Cleve.; vice-chmn. Gund Investment Corp., Princeton, N.J.; chmn. North Stars Met Center Mgmt. Corp., Bloomington; v.p. hockey Sun Valley Ice Skating, Inc., Idaho. Chmn. San Francisco Internat. Film Festival, 1973—; mem. sponsors council Project for Population Action; adv. council Sierra Club Found.; mem. internat. council Mus. Modern Art, N.Y.C.; collectors com. Nat. Gallery Art; bd. dirs. Calif. Theatre Found., Bay Area Ednl. TV Assn., San Francisco Mus. Art, Cleve. Health Museum, George Gund Found., Cleve. Internat. Film Festival, Sun Valley Center Arts and Humanities, U. Nev. Reno Found., Sundance Inst. Served with USMCR, 1955-58. Clubs: Calif. Tennis (San Francisco), University (San Francisco), Olympic (San Francisco); Union (Cleve.), Cleve. Athletic (Cleve.), Kirkland Country (Cleve.), Rowfant (Cleve.); Ranier (Seattle). Office: 1821 Union St San Francisco CA 94123

GUND, GORDON, entrepreneur, financier; b. Cleve., Oct. 15, 1939; s. George and Jessica (Roesler) G.; m. Llura Liggett; children—Grant Ambler, Gordon Zachary. B.A., Harvard U., 1961; D.Pub. Service (hon.), U. Maryland, 1980. Pres., chief exec. officer Gund Investment Corp.; gen. ptnr. GUS Enterprises; co-owner Cleve. Cavaliers, NBA, 1983—; co-chmn., chief exec. officer Minn. North Stars, NHL, 1978—; chmn. Nationwide Advt. Service, Inc.; dir. First Fla. Banks, Inc., Kellogg Co.; mem. bd. govs. NHL, NBA. Co-founder Nat. Retinitis Pigmentosa Found. Fighting Blindness, 1971, also chmn.; pres., bd. trustees Groton Sch.; pres., trustee Gund Collection of Western Art; mem. Nat. Adv. Eye Council, 1980-84. Office: Gund Investment Corp 14 Nassau St PO Box 449 Princeton NJ 08542-0449

GUNDERSON, STEVE C., congressman; b. Eau Claire, Wis., May 10, 1951; s. Arthur E. and Adeline C. G. B.A., U. Wis., 1973. Mem. Wis. Assembly, 1974-79; legis. dir. Rep. Toby Roth, 1979; mem. 97th-100th Congresses from Wis. 3d dist.; Dir. spl. projects Wis.'s Gov. Dreyfus campaign, 1978. Republican. Lutheran. Club: Pleasantville Lions. Office: 227 Cannon House Office Bldg Washington DC 20515

GUNDERSON, STEVEN ALAN, anesthesiologist; b. Rockford, Ill., Feb. 9, 1949; s. Donald Hans and Margaret E. (Johanson) G.; m. Tina A. Anstedt, June 29, 1976; children: Kelly, Kimberly, Troy. As, Rock Valley Coll., 1969; BA, Drake U., 1972, postgrad., 1972-74; DO, Coll. Osteopathic Medicine, Des Moines, Iowa, 1977. Diplomate Am. Bd. Anesthesia. Staff anesthesiologist Rockford (Ill.) Anesthesia Assn., 1984—; clin. faculty Rockford Sch. Medicine, 1986—. Served to lt. comdr. USN, 1978-81. Mem. AMA, Internat. Anesthesia Research Soc., Ill. State Med. Soc., Winnebago Med. Soc. Republican. Lutheran. Club: University (Rockford). Avocations: biking, fishing, swimming, wood working, reading. Office: Rockford Anesthesiologists Assn 2929 N Main St Rockford IL 61107

GUNN, GEORGE F., JR., federal judge; b. Ft. Smith, Ark., Oct. 29, 1927. A.B., Westminster Coll., 1950; J.D., Washington U., St. Louis, 1955. Assoc. Gleick & Strauss, St. Louis, 1955-56; atty. Wabash R.R. Co., St. Louis, 1956-58; ptnr. Rebman La Tourette & Gunn, St. Louis, 1958-68; city atty. City of Brentwood (Mo.), 1963-71; counsel Terminal R.R. Assn., St. Louis, 1968-71; county counselor St. Louis County (Mo.), 1971-73; judge Rock Hill (Mo.) Mcpl. Ct., 1971, Eastern Dist. Mo. Ct. Appeals, Clayton, 1973-82; assoc. justice Mo. Supreme Ct., Jefferson City, 1982-85; judge U.S. Dist. Ct. (ea. dist.) Mo., 1985—. Chmn. South County region ARC, St. Louis, 1971-74; bd. mgrs. Mid County YMCA, 1961—; bd. dirs. World Congress Equality and Freedom, 1975. Mem. ABA, Mo. Bar Assn., Met. St. Louis Bar Assn., Washington U. Law Alumni (pres. 1974), Phi Delta Phi. Office: U S Court & Custom House 1114 Market St Room 828 Saint Louis MO 63101

GUNN, HARRY E., psychologist; b. Harvey, Ill., Jan. 3, 1930; s. Harry Elmer and Irma (Zatkalik) G.; m. Violet C. Brilando, June 29, 1964; children: Buddy Stewart, Billy Lee. BA, Beloit Coll., 1952; MS, Purdue U., 1955; PhD, Loyola U., Chgo., 1961. Lic. psychologist, Ill. Research asst. Ill. Neuropsychiat. Inst., Chgo., 1957-59; clin. psychologist Inst. Juvenile Research, Chgo., 1959-72; research asst. Loyola U., 1961-73; instr. Thorton Jr. Coll., Harvey, Ill., 1961-73; supr. psychologist Mental Health Clinic, Chgo., 1962-68; gen. practice psychology Hinsdale, Ill., 1966—; cons. in field. Author: How to Paly Golf with Your Wife, 1980, Manipulation By Guilt, 1982; co-author: The Test Your Self Book, 1981, The Test for Success Book, 1984. Mem. Olympia Fields (Ill.) Village Appeals Bd., 1970—. Mem. Am. Psychol. Assn., Bd. Examiners in Psychology, Ill. Psychol. Assn. Club: Olympia Fields Country. Avocation: golf. Home: 20660 Corinth Olympia Fields IL 60461 Office: 120 E Ogden Ave Hinsdale IL 60521

GUNNING, LAURIE FRÖYDIS, vocational counselor; b. Hollywood, Calif., March 11, 1950; d. Everard Frederick Marsek and Fröydis Lenore (Flint) Deupree; m. William Charles Gunning, Jr., Aug. 11, 1973; children—William C. III, Bryn Taira; B.A. in Sociology, Calif. State U.-Northridge, 1972; M.Ed. in Adult Counseling, U. Mo.-St. Louis, 1980. Vocat. rehab. counselor, St. Louis, 1979-80; mgr. edn. div. Mincomp Corp., Denver, 1980-82; dir. Adult Vocat. Guidance Plus, Denver, 1983-86; field rep. Cons. Psychologists Press, Inc., Chgo., 1987—; pvt. vocat. counseling and mgmt. cons., Chgo. Recipient recognition award U. Denver. Mem. Ill. Assn. Counseling and Devel., Ill. chpt. Am. Soc. Tng. and Devel., Ill. Assn. Measurement and Evaluation in Counseling and Devel. Co-author slide tape presentation, manual and video in profl. field. Home: 949 Peregrine Dr Palatine IL 60067

GUNNING, MICHAEL ANTHONY, state agency adminstrator; b. Los Angeles, Feb. 2, 1958; s. Elon Sammeul and Monica Olwen (Minott) G. BA, Claremont Men's Coll., 1979, postgrad. in Pub. Policy Analysis, 1985—. Oprs. asst. and teller Bank of Am., Claremont, Calif., 1978-79; banking officer First Interstate Bank of Calif., Los Angeles, 1979-83; exec. asst. Mo. State Treasurer, Jefferson City, 1985—. Loan exec. United Way of Los Angeles, 1979, allocations vol., 1981-82. Named Outstanding Young Man of Am., 1981, 85; Coro Found. fellow, 1984. Mem. Nat. Orgn. Black Law Enforcement Execs. (assoc.). Republican. Methodist. Avocations: racquetball, collecting comic books, tropical fish, gourmet cooking. Home: 920 Washington Jefferson City MO 65101 Office: Mo State Treas Office Mo State Capitol Rm 229 Jefferson City MO 65101

GUNTHER, ARTHUR GORDON, restaurant executive; b. Dunkirk, N.Y., Mar. 18, 1936; s. Truman Arthur and Ella Katherine (Kenny) G.; B.A., Gannon U., 1958; m. Rebecca Mae David, June 8, 1960; children: Michael, Lisa, Kathleen. With Marc & Co., Pitts., 1960-63; asst. v.p. mktg. services McDonald's Corp., Oakbrook, Ill., 1973-76; v.p. mktg. Sambo's Restaurants, Inc. Santa Barbara, Calif., 1976-79; sr. v.p. mktg. ops. Long John Silvers, Inc., 1979-80; pres., chief operating officer Pizza Hut, Inc., Wichita, Kans., 1980—, now pres., chief exec. officer, also bd. dirs. Mem. bd. incorporators Gannon U. Served to 1st lt. U.S. Army, 1958-60. Mem. steering com. Crest, Inc., 1978-80. Office: Pizza Hut Inc 9111 E Douglas St Wichita KS 67207 *

GUNYOU, JOHN M., city finance director; b. Columbus, Ohio, Aug. 21, 1948; s. Lyman J. and Shirley (Knight) G.; m. Kathy Arnold, June 13, 1970; children: Nicole, Emily. BS in Econs., USAF Acad., 1970; MA in Econs., UCLA, 1971; MPA in Fin., U. Colo., 1976. Commd. 2d lt. USAF, 1970, advanced through ranks to 1st lt., resigned, 1972; tchr. Boulder/ St. Vrain (Colo.) Sch. Dist., 1972-73; analyst City of Boulder, 1973; econ. analyst Denver Regional COG, 1974-77; ptnr. BBC, Inc., Denver, 1977-84; fin. dir. City of Mpls., 1984—; adj. prof. Hamline U., St. Paul. Mem. Govt. Fin. Officers Assn. (govtl. debt. com., Japanese/European fin. markets task force, conf. spkr. 1983-86, Cert. Excellence 1986), Nat. Council Pub. Works Improvements (fin. task force), Internat. City Mgmt. Assn., Am. Planning Assn. (Outstanding Planning award 1984), Nat. Assn. Counties (Achievement award 1984), Govt. Acctg. Standards Bd. (adv. com.). Home: 5208 James Ave S Minneapolis MN 55419 Office: City of Mpls 331 City Hall Minneapolis MN 55415

GUPTA, BHAGWANDAS, anesthesiologist; b. Hyderabad, India, Jan. 13, 1946; s. Sriram and Badami Bai Gupta; m. Bhagirathi Sanghi, July 10, 1970; children: Rashmi, Rohit, Ruchi. MBBS, Osmania U., Hyderabad, 1970, MD, 1976. Diplomate Am. Bd. Anesthesiology. Resident in anesthesiology NYU Hosp., N.Y.C., 1976-78; fellow in neurolanesthesiology NYU Hosp., Bellevue, N.Y.C., 1978-79, instr., 1979-81; asst. prof. Ohio State U., Columbus, 1981—, dir. neuroanesthesiology, 1981—, assoc. dir. resident edn. dept. anesthesiology, 1983—. Mem. Am. Soc. Anesthesiologists, Ohio Soc. Anesthesiology, Internat. Anesthesiology Res. Core Soc., Soc. Neurosurgical Anesthesiologists and Neurosurgery Support. Hindu. Club: Sawmill Athletic. Avocations: racquetball, tennis, jogging, reading, fin. planning. Home: 4657 Crompton Dr Columbus OH 43220

GUPTA, MADHU SUDAN, electrical engineering educator; b. Lucknow, India, July 13, 1945; came to U.S., 1966; s. Manohar Lal and Premvati Gupta; m. Vijaya Lakshmi Tayal, July 9, 1970; children: Jay Mohan, Vineet Mohan. BS, Allahabad U., India, 1966; MS, Fla. State U., 1967; MA, U. Mich., 1968, PhD, 1972. Registered profl. engr., Ont. Asst. prof. elec. engring. Queen's U., Kingston, Ont., Can., 1972-73; asst. prof. elec. engring. MIT, Cambridge, 1973-78, assoc. prof. elec. engring., 1978-79; assoc. prof. elec. engring. U. Ill., Chgo., 1979-84, prof. elec. engring., 1984—, dir. grad. studies, 1980-83; cons. Lincoln Lab. MIT, Lexington, 1976-79, Hughes Research Labs., Malibu, Calif., 1986-87. Editor: Electrical Noise, 1977, Teaching Engineering, 1987; contbr. articles to profl. jours. Lilly fellow, 1974-75. Mem. IEEE (sr.), IEEE Microwave Soc. Chgo. (vice chmn. 1984-86, chmn. 1986-87). Office: U Ill Dept Elec Engring and Computer Sci Box 4348 Chicago IL 60680

GUPTA, SATYA PRAKASH, economics educator; b. India, July 4, 1931; came to U.S., 1968; s. Atma Ram and Sona Devi G.; m. Bhag Wanti, May 5, 1954; 1 child, Anuj Kumar. B.Sc., Agra (India) U., 1951, M.Sc., 1953; B.Ed., Jamia Millia Islamia, New Delhi, India, 1957; M.S., So. Ill. U., 1970, Ph.D., 1975. Sr. tchr. M.D. High Sch., Faridabad, Delhi, 1953-56; lectr. Bajoria Coll., Saharenpur, U.P., India, 1957-63; sr. tchr., head math. dept. Ministry of Edn., Addis Ababa, Ethiopia, 1964-66; tchr. math. Miller Collegiate, Altona, Man., Can., 1966-68; teaching asst. So. Ill. U., Carbondale, 1969-74; research analyst Ill. Dept. Local Govt. Affairs, Springfield, 1975-76; assoc. prof. econs. Augsburg Coll., Mpls., 1976-87, prof., 1987—. Danforth assoc., 1981—; Danforth Found. grantee, 1982; Am. Luth. Ch. faculty growth awardee, 1983. Mem. Am. Econ. Assn. Hindu. Contbr. articles to local newspaper; author book on solid geometry, 1963. Home: 7533 N Meadowood Ct Brooklyn Park MN 55444 Office: 731 21st Ave S Augsburg Coll Minneapolis MN 55454

GURLEY, VICTORIA IRENE, supervisory systems accountant, educator; b. East St. Louis, Ill., Sept. 15, 1950; d. Walter Oswald and Bernice Virginia (Reiniger) Samoska; m. Richard Allen Gurley, Nov. 27, 1970; 1 child, Amy Marie. BS, So. Ill. U., 1978, MBA, 1984. CPA, Ill. Revenue agt. IRS, East St. Louis, 1979-84; systems acct. Farmers Home Adminstrn., St. Louis, 1984-86, supervisory systems acct., 1986—; tchr. So. Ill. U., Edwardsville, 1983. Recipient Cert. of Merit Farmers Home Adminstrn., 1985. Mem. Am. Inst. CPA's, Ill. Soc. CPA's, Assn. Govt. Accts. (bd. dirs. 1986—, Mem. of Yr., 1986), Beta Gamma Sigma. Home: 545 Crestview East Alton IL 62024 Office: Farmers Home Adminstrn 1520 Market St Saint Louis MO 63103

GURNEY, PAMELA KAY, youth association administrator; b. Joliet, Ill., Sept. 25, 1948; d. Wayne Franklin and Charlotte Marie (Geissler) G. BA, Coll. St. Francis, 1971. Tchr. Joliet (Ill.) Pub. Schs., 1971-73; field dir. Trailways Girl Scout Council, Joliet, 1973-76; dir. adult devel. Mich. Waterways Girl Scout Council, Port Huron, Mich., 1976-80, Irish Hills Girl Scout Council, Jackson, Mich., 1980—. Mem. Am. Soc. Tng. Dirs., AAUW (bd. dirs. publ., v.p. of program), Assn. Girl Scout Exec. Staff, Mich. Girl Scout Edn. Dirs. (chmn. 1976-85). Avocations: outdoor activities, needlework, conf. planning, travel. Home: 902 Gettysburg Jackson MI 49203 Office: Irish Hills Girl Scout Council 729 W Michigan Jackson MI 49201

GURSIN, ALVIN VICTOR, orthodontist; b. Detroit, Dec. 7, 1930; s. Victor Z. and Alice L. (Krogul) G.; m. Doris M. Brien, June 27, 1959; children—Alvin V., Jr., Kevin J., Steve S. D.D.S., U. Detroit, 1956; M.S., Northwestern U., 1963; M.R.S.H. (hon.), Her Majesty, The Queen, London, 1959, F.R.S.H. (hon.), 1973. Practice dentistry specializing in orthodontics, Rochester, Mich. Contbr. articles to profl. jours. Chmn., Selective Service Commn., Mich., 1982—. Served to maj. USAF, 1956-61. Mem. Am. Assn. of Orthodontists, Am. Dental Assn., Great Lakes Soc. of Orthodontists, Mich. Soc. of Orthodontists, Oakland Dental Soc., Delta Sigma Delta, Omicron Kappa Upsilon. Roman Catholic. Lodge: Elks (Rochester). Avocations: fishing; hunting. Home: 1129 Main St Rochester MI 48063 Office: 412 Main St Rochester MI 48063

GUS, MYRON BURTON, dentist; b. Detroit, Sept. 29, 1937; s. Sol and Frances Ilene (Shafer) G.; m. Elaine Shafer (div.); children: Stuart, Pamela. DDS, U. Mich., 1961. Pvt. practice dentistry Southfield, Mich., 1961—. Active Jewish Community Ctr., West Bloomfield, Mich. Served to capt. U.S. Army, 1961-63. Mem. Mich. Dental Assn., Am. Dental Assn., Oakland County Dental Soc., Detroit Dental Soc. Mem. Congregation B'nai Israel. Lodge: B'nai B'rith. Home: 32005 W 12 Mile Rd Farmington Hills MI 48018 Office: 21701 W Eleven Mile Southfield MI 48076

GUSTAFSON, BARBARA ANN HELTON, lawyer; b. Washington, Ill., Apr. 26, 1948; d. Joseph and Marilou (Buckles) Balogh; m. Lee Alan Gustafson, Dec. 20, 1969. B.Music, So. Ill. U., 1969; M.Mus. Edn., Vandercook Coll., 1972; J.D., U. Chgo., 1983. Bar: Ill. 1983. Tchr. music Harrison Sch., Wonderlake, Ill., 1969-72, Cook County Dist. 125, Alsip, Ill., 1972-73; dir. orch. Kankakee Dist. III, Ill., 1973-80; atty. MidCon Corp., Lombard, Ill., 1983—. Asst. dir. Kankakee Youth Symphony (Ill.), 1973-76; violinist Kankakee Orch., 1977-80; musician Kankakee Valley Theater, 1976-80. Mem. Ill. State Bar Assn., Chgo. Bar Assn., AAUW, Mu Phi Epsilon (treas. 1968-69). Lutheran. Home: 176 Hickory Creek Dr Frankfort IL 60423 Office: MidCon Corp 701 E 22nd St Lombard IL 60148

GUSTAFSON, CAROL CHRISTINE, computer programmer, consultant; b. Lansing, Mich., Dec. 23, 1960; d. Robert Lloyd and Mary Margaret (Marshall) G. BA in Econs., Mich. State U., 1983. Programmer Gen. Motors Corp., Lansing, 1983-85; customer engr. Electronic Data Systems, Lansing, 1985; conf. cons. Mich. State U., East Lansing, 1985—. Avocations: computers, fishing, weight lifting, reading, photography. Office: Mich State U 7 Olds Hall East Lansing MI 48824-1047

GUSTAFSON, EVERETTE, gynecologist, obstetrician, consultant; b. Ironwood, Mich., Nov. 17, 1916; s. Charles John and Hilda (Sandquist) G.; m. Georgia Mae Johnson, Dec. 22, 1943; children: Gene, Barbara, Beverly, Gary, Jackie, Gregorie. AA, Ironwood Jr. Coll., Mich., 1934-1936; student, U. Minn., 1934-37, U. Chgo., 1937-41; MD, U. Mich., 1941-1944. Diplomate Am. Bd. Ob-Gyn. Commd. USN, 1943, advanced through grades to lt. comdr., 1958, ret., 1966; with M.C. USNR, 1966-77, ret., 1977; intern U.S. Naval Hosp., Quantico, Va., 1944-45; resident in ob-gyn Pontiac (Mich.) Gen. Hosp., 1947-50, chief of staff, 1962; practice medicine specializing in ob-gyn Grandview Clinic, LaCrosse, Wis., 1951-55, Pontiac, 1955—. Assoc.

editor Oakland Med. Soc., Pontiac, 1960—; contbr. articles to profl. jours. Bd. dirs. YMCA, Pontiac, 1967; candidate for Mich. legislature, Lansing, 1978. Recipient General award Pontiac Gen. Hosp. Boosters, 1985; named Man of Yr., YMCA, Pontiac, 1967, Outstanding Tchr., House Staff Pontiac Gen. Hosp., 1967, 68, 71. Fellow Am. Coll. Ob-Gyn; mem. Physicians for Social Responsibility. Republican. Avocations: writing, reading. Home: 3780 Lakewood Dr Drayton Plains MI 48020 Office: 35 S Johnson Pontiac MI 48053

GUSTAFSON, LINDA CHANEY, educator, administrator; b. Washington, Feb. 7, 1947; d. James Louis and Louise (Bockelman) Chaney; m. Roger William Gustafson, Apr. 15, 1972. BS, U. Md., 1970, MLS, 1973, EdD, 1982. Media specialist Howard County Pub. Schs., Columbia, Md., 1970-80; librarian Dixon (Ill.) Pub. Schs., 1980-84; prin. Neponset (Ill.) High Sch., 1985-87; supt. Dalxell (Ill.) Schs., 1987—. Mem. NEA, Ill. Edn. Assn., Dixon Tchrs. Assn., Sauk Valley Reading Council, Bur. County Adminstrs. Assn., Ill. High Sch. Assn., LWV (treas. 1983—), Alpha Lambda Delta. Home: Hidden Lake Dr Princeton IL 61356

GUSTAFSON, MARY SUSAN, advertising executive; b. St. Paul, Oct. 1, 1955; d. George Eric and Dorothy Mae (Stuart) G. BA in Journalism, U. Minn., 1981. Dir. pub. relations Am. Lung Assn., St. Paul, 1982-84; exec. dir. Advt. Fedn. Minn., Mpls., 1984—. Mem. Am. Women in Radio and TV (state bd. dirs. 1986—), Alpha Delta Sigma. Club: Minn. Barking Spiders (affiliate). Avocations: skiing, flag football. Office: Advt Fedn Minn 600 1st Ave N Minneapolis MN 55403

GUSTOFF, MARY JANE STRANG, teacher; b. Independence, Iowa, Sept. 29, 1932; d. Raymond Peter and Irene Elizabeth (Weber) Strang; m. Edward Eugene Gustoff, June 16, 1956; children: Sandra E., Billy Ray, Stephanie Lynn. Student, Mt. Mercy Jr. Coll., 1950-52; BS, Upper Iowa Coll., 1968. Tchr. 2d and 3d grades Walford (Iowa) Sch., 1952-53; tchr. 5th and 6th grades Troy Mills (Iowa) Sch., 1953-57, 61-65; tchr. 3d and 7th grades Walker (Iowa) Sch., 1957-61; tchr. 3d and 6th grades Central City (Iowa) Sch., 1965-77; tchr. chpt. I Remedial Reading Central City (Iowa) Community Sch., 1977—; tchr. ch. religion classes. Mem. NEA, Iowa State Edn. Assn. (sec., assembly del.), Central City Edn. Assn. (numerous offices and coms.). Democrat. Roman Catholic. Avocations: golf, bowling, cards, basketball. Home: 321 Main St Rural Rt 2 Center Point IA 52213

GUTENBERG, RHONDA LYNN, industrial psychologist, educator; b. Detroit, July 28, 1957; d. Harold and Arlene Dorothy G. B.A. with honors, U. Calif.-Berkeley, 1978; M.A., U. Houston, 1980, Ph.D., 1982. Mgmt. cons. Jeanneret & Assocs., Inc., Houston, 1980-86; vis. prof. U. Minn., Mpls., 1986-87; mgmt. cons. Personnel Decisions Inc., St. paul, 1987—. Mem. Am. Psychol. Assn., Acad. Mgmt. Office: Personnel Decisions Inc Saint Paul MN 55101

GUTERMUTH, SCOTT ALAN, accountant; b. South Bend, Ind., Nov. 24, 1953; s. Richard H. and Barbara Ann (Bracey) G. BS in Bus., Ind. U., 1976. CPA, Ind. With Coopers & Lybrand, Indpls., 1976-83, supervising auditor, 1980-83, audit mgr., 1983; v.p., controller Society Nat. Group, Indpls., 1983—; instr., nat. update analyst Becker CPA Rev. Course, 1980—. Adv., Jr. Achievement; mem. Marion County Republican Com., 1978—, Rep. Nat. Com., 1972—. Fellow Life Mgmt. Inst.; mem. Am. Inst. CPA's, Nat. Assn. Accts., Ins. Acctg. and Statis. Assn., Ind. Assn. CPA's (ins. com. 1984—), Life Mgmt. Inst. (assoc.). Methodist. Home: 3132 Sandpiper S Dr Indianapolis IN 46268 Office: 9101 Wesleyan Rd Indianapolis IN 46268

GUTH, JAMES EDWARD, investment analyst, counsel; b. St. Louis, July 4, 1955; s. John Elias and Mary Jane (Wolf) G. AB, Dartmouth Coll., 1977; M of Mgmt., Northwestern U., 1983. Assoc. corp. fin. Warburg Paribas Becker, Chgo., 1977-78; floor mgr. Pacific Trading, Chgo., 1979; asst. to pres. Thrush and Co., Chgo., 1980-82; investment analyst Miami Corp. Chgo., 1982-87, v.p. investments, 1987—. Mem. Fin. Analyst Fedn., Investment Analysts Soc. Chgo. Club: Racquet (Chgo.). Office: Miami Corp Room 590 410 N Michigan Ave Chicago IL 60611

GUTHIER, JAMES DONALD, hearing aid company executive; b. Huntington, Ind., Nov. 26, 1955; s. Frederick and Virginia (Lantis) G.; m. Diane Marie French, Apr. 23, 1976; children: Christa, James, David. Grad. high sch., Angola, Ind. Electronics technician Qualitone, St. Louis Park, Minn., 1978-79, asst. products mgr., 1979-80; electronics technician Hearing Services, Inc., Hopkins, Minn., 1980-82; prod. mgr. Danavox, Inc., Eden Prairie, Minn., 1982-84, product mgr., 1984-85, mktg.product mgr., 1986—; lectr. Nat. Inst. Hearing Instrument Studies, 1983—. Served with USN, 1974-77. Named Outstanding Citizen Stueben County, Angola Lions Club, 1973. Mem. Robbinsdale Jaycees (community devel. v.p. 1982, pres. 1983, Jaycee of Yr. 1982). Republican. Avocation: softball. Home: 9940 64th Circle Maple Grove MN 55369 Office: Danavox Inc 6400 Flying Cloud Dr Eden Prairie MN 55344

GUTHRIE, FRANK ALBERT, science educator; b. Madison, Ind., Feb. 16, 1927; s. Ned and Gladys (Glick) G.; m. Marcella Glee Farrar, June 12, 1955; children: Mark Alan, Bruce Bradford, Kent Andrew, Lee Farrar. A.B., Hanover Coll., 1950; M.S., Purdue U., 1952; Ph.D., Ind. U., 1962. Mem. faculty Rose-Hulman Inst. Tech., Terre-Haute, Ind., 1952—; asso. prof. Rose-Hulman Inst. Tech., Terre-Haute, 1962-67, prof. chemistry, 1967—, chmn. dept., 1969-72, chief health professions adviser, 1975—; Kettering vis. lectr. U. Ill., Urbana, 1961-62; vis. prof. chemistry U.S. Mil. Acad., West Point, N.Y., 1987—. Mem. exec. bd. Wabash Valley council Boy Scouts Am., 1971—, v.p. for scouting, 1976; selection chmn. Leadership Terre Haute, 1978-80. Served with AUS, 1945-46. Recipient Silver Beaver award Boy Scouts Am., 1980. Fellow Ind. Acad. Sci. (pres. 1970); mem. Am. Chem. Soc. (sec. 1973-77, editor directory 1965-77, chmn. div. analytical chemistry 1979-80, counselor Wabash Valley sect. 1980—), Coblentz Soc., Midwest Univs. Analytical Chemistry Conf., Nat. Assn. Advs. Health Professions, Hanover Coll. Alumni Assn. (pres. 1974, Alumni Achievement award 1977), Sigma Xi, Phi Lambda Upsilon, Phi Gamma Delta, Alpha Chi Sigma. Presbyterian. Club: Masons (32 deg.). Home: 19 S 21st St Terre Haute IN 47803-1819 Office: Rose Hulman Inst Technol 5500 Wabash Ave Terre Haute IN 47803-3999

GUTHRIE, GEORGE RALPH, real estate development corporation executive; b. Phila., Mar. 12, 1928; s. George Ralph and Myrtle (Robertson) G.; m. Shirley B. Remmey; children: Mary Elizabeth, Brenda Ann. B.S. in Econs, U. Pa., 1948. With I-T-E Imperial Corp., Phila., 1948-70; controller, financial planner I-T-E Imperial Corp., 1960-68, treas., 1968-69, v.p. finance, 1969-70; pres. N. K. Winston Corp., N.Y.C., 1970-76; exec. v.p. Urban Investment and Devel. Co., Chgo., 1976-78; pres. Urban Investment and Devel. Co., 1978-82, chmn., 1982—; vice chmn. JMB Institutional Realty Corp., 1987—; dir. Zenith Electronics Corp. Trustee Nat. Coll. Edn.; chmn. Cornerstone Found.; mem. pres.'s council Lutheran Social Services of Ill.; bd. dirs. March of Dimes, Augustana Coll., Jr. Achievement; mem. pres.'s council, assoc. trustee U. Pa.; co-chmn. Chgo. Devel. Council. Mem. Financial Execs. Inst., Urban Land Inst. (trustee), Chgo. Assn. Commerce and Industry (bd. dirs.), Nat. Realty Com. (bd. dir.), Chgo. Council on Fgn. Relations (Chgo. com.), Chgo. Devel. Council (co-chmn.). Republican. Clubs: Glen View, Jupiter Hills, Carlton, Economics, Chicago. Office: 875 N Michigan Ave Suite 3900 Chicago IL 60611

GUTHRIE, MYRNA JEAN, educator; b. Newton, Iowa, June 30, 1929; d. Frank Andrew and Hazel (Dolph) Guthrie; student Central Coll., 1947-49; B.A., Drake U., 1951, M.S., 1963. Child welfare worker State of Iowa, 1951-60; guidance counselor Newton Community Schs., 1960—, counselor Upward Bound, Central Coll., Pella, Iowa, 1967; cons. Jasper County Headstart program, 1968; coordinator Newton Achievement Motivation Project, 1971-72, Futures project Newton Community Sch., 1975; bd. dirs. Jasper County Arts Council, Iowa. Past bd. dirs. Jasper County Community Action; past pres. RMR Soc.; past bd. dirs. Newton Community Orch; past pres. Iowa Future Problem Bd. Recipient Maytag Found. Conv. award, 1965; named Nat. Future Problem Solving Coach of Yr., 1980. Mem. Internat. Platform Assn., Nat., Newton edn. assns., Am., Iowa personnel and guidance assns., Newton Bus. and Profl. Women's Club (past pres.), Jasper County Hist. Soc., Iowa Woman's Polit. Caucus, Newton Community Theater, Questers (past pres.), ITAG, Alpha Xi Delta, Alpha Kappa Delta, Beta Sigma Phi. Republican. Methodist. Clubs: Soroptimist (past pres.) (Newton); Hazel Dell Acad., PEO. Co-pub. series Before the Colors Fade. Home: 326 E 4th St S Newton IA 50208

GUTMAN, ARNOLD AVRAM, allergist, immunologist, internist; b. Phila., July 13, 1927; s. Joseph N. and Frances Gutman; m. Adele Olga Nurock, June 20, 1951; children: Brenda, Steven, Daniel. BA, Johns Hopkins U., 1949; MA, U. Del., 1951; MD, Hahnemann U., 1955. Diplomate Am. Bd. Allergy and Immunology, Am. Bd. Internal Medicine. Intern Hahnemann Hosp., Phila., 1955-56; resident VA Hosp., Phila., 1956-57; fellow Mayo Clinic, Rochester, Minn., 1959-61; practice medicine specializing in allergy Chgo., 1962—; mem. faculty Northwestern U., Chgo., 1965-75; clin. asst. prof. medicine U. Ill Chgo., 1972—. Served to capt. USAF, 1957-59. Fellow Am. Acad. Allergy and Immunology, Am. Coll. Allergists, Ill. Soc. Allergy and Clin. Immunology; mem. AMA, Ill Med. Soc., Chgo. Med. Soc., Amer. Soc. Internal Medicine. Republican. Jewish. Avocations: opera, symphony, theater, motorcycling, phys. fitness. Office: Assoc Allergists Ltd 111 N Wabash Chicago IL 60602

GUTMANN, MAX, department store executive; b. Germany, 1922. Chmn. bd., chief exec. officer Elder-Beerman Stores Corp., dept. store chain; cofounder div. Bee-Gee Shoe Corp., 1953, now chmn. bd.; chmn. bd. div. Spare Change, Margo's women's splty. chain, El-Bee Chargit Corp., Office Outfitters; dir. Bank One of Dayton, Dayco Corp., Frederick Atkins, Inc. Bd. dirs. Good Samaritan Hosp., Dayton Art Inst., Urban League, Jewish Fedn. of Greater Dayton; mem. area progress council Downtown Devel. Council; mem. bus. adv. council U. Dayton; past dir. United Way. Mem. Nat. Retail Mchts. Assn. (bd. dirs.), Ohio Council Retail Mchts. (bd. dirs.), Dayton Area C. of C. (past bd. dirs.). Club: One Hundred. Home: 9556 Bridlewood Trail Spring Valley OH 45370 Office: The Elder-Beerman Stores Corp 3155 El-Bee Rd Dayton OH 45401 *

GUTOF, RICHARD STEWART, lawyer; b. Chgo., July 30, 1940; s. Harry and Rose (Dreebin) G.; m. Anita L. Weiss, June 26, 1964; children—Daniel, Deborah. B.S., U. Ill., 1962; J.D., DePaul U., 1964. Bar: Ill. 1964, U.S. Dist. Ct. (no. dist.) Ill. 1964, U.S. Supreme Ct. 1971. Asst. state's atty. Cook County (Ill.), 1964-69; sole practice, Skokie, Ill., 1970—. Mem. ABA, Ill. Bar Assn., Chgo. Bar Assn., N.W. Suburban Bar Assn., North Suburban Bar Assn., Coalition Suburban Bar Assns. Cook County (past pres.), North Suburban Cook County Bar Assn. (past pres.). Home: 607 Lavergne Ave Wilmette IL 60091 Office: 9933 Lawler Ave #312 Skokie IL 60077

GUTSCHICK, WILLIAM CHARLES, hospital administrator; b. Chgo., Aug. 12, 1945; s. Lester Charles and Eileen May (Williams) G.; m. Nancy Michele Hobgood, June 29, 1968; children—Scott Charles, Brian William. B.S., No. Ill. U., 1967. Material control expediting supr. Zenith Radio Corp., Chgo., 1967-68, prodn. control systems analyst, 1968-69; sr. corp. methods and procedures analyst Walgreen Co., Deerfield, Ill., 1969-78, mgr. corp. methods and forms control, 1978-85; dir. systems Marianjoy Rehab. Ctr., Wheaton, Ill., 1986—. Mem. council adv. bd. Boy Scouts Am., Arlington Heights, Ill., 1984—, dist. advancement chmn., 1982-86, asst. council advancement chmn. N.W. Suburban Area, 1984—. Recipient Silver Tepee award Boy Scouts Am., 1983, Golden Tepee award, 1984, Dist. award of merit, 1985. Mem. Assn. Records Mgrs. and Adminstrs. (chmn. pub. relations, chmn. legis.), Assn. Systems Mgmt. (dir.), Hosp. Mgmt. Systems Soc., Nat. Micrographics Assn. Republican. Lutheran. Club: Grace Lutheran Ch. Young Couples (co-founder, dir. 1978-80). Home: 3 S 115 Burr Oak Rd Glen Ellyn IL 60137

GUTSELL, PHILIP MICHAEL, management consultant; b. Chgo., May 10, 1950; s. Charles Aloysius and Rosalie Estelle (Claxton) G.; m. Yvonne Marie George; 1 child, Philip Charles. BA, DePaul U., 1972. Pvt. practice mgmt. consulting Chgo., 1972—. Mem. Nat. Home Furnishing Assn. Roman Catholic. Avocations: softball, touch football, ice hockey. Office: 3415 W Peterson Chicago IL 60659

GUTSHALL, ARTHUR ROBERT, financial executive; b. Kewanee, Ill., May 6, 1948; s. Robert Reid and Doris (Simon) G.; m. Mariann Elizabeth Babka, Sept. 18, 1971; children: Nicole Marie, Maureen Doris, Emily Ruth. BS Accountancy with high honors, U. Ill., 1970. CPA, Ill. Staff auditor Price Waterhouse, Peoria, Ill., 1972-74, sr. auditor, 1974-77, audit mgr., 1977-81; sr. audit mgr. Price Waterhouse, N.Y.C., 1981-83; asst. controller, dir. audit Hartmarx Corp., Chgo., 1983—; bd. dirs. Peoria Econ. Devel. Assn., Peoria, Ill., 1980-81. Mem., chmn. allocations com. United Way, Peoria, 1979-81. Served as sgt. U.S. Army, 1970-72. Mem. Am. Inst. CPA's, Inst. Internal Auditors. Mem. United Ch. Christ. Avocations: tennis, bridge. Office: HartMarx Corp 101 N Wacker Dr Chicago IL 60606

GUTTADAURO, ANGELO DE, military officer; b. San Francisco, July 5, 1937; s. Nino and Dorothy Rose (Bio) de G.; m. Giuliana Gabriella Revetria, July 16, 1964; children: Andrea Riccardo, Lorenzo Ranieri. BA in Bus. Adminstrn. (hon.), San Jose State U., 1959; cert. Bus. Council for Internat. Understanding, Am. U., 1965; MA in Internat. Relations, U. So. Calif., 1971; student, Army War Coll., 1976-77. Commd. USAR, advanced through grades to col., 1980; instr. USAR Sch., Munich, 1974-76; dir. res. components Ft. Bliss, El Paso, Tex., 1977-81; strategic analyst Strategic Studies Inst., Carlisle, Pa., 1981-83; sr. res. forces adv. to the supreme allied comdr. Supreme Hdqrs. Allied Powers Europe, Casteau, Belgium, 1983-86; spl. asst. comdg. gen. Army Res. Personnel Ctr., St. Louis, 1986—. Contbr. articles to profl. jours. Alt. mem. Exec. Council, Fed. Exec. Bd.; chmn. Joint Work Group, Combined Fed. Campaign, St. Louis, 1987. Decorated M.S.M. with oak leaf cluster, Armed Forces Res. medal with Ten-Year Device, Knight Officer with Swords of the Order for Maltese Merit, Sovereign military Order of Malta, Rome, Medal of Honor, Oslo, Deutsche Sportabzeichen, Degree of Gold. Mem. Interallied Confederation of Res. Officers (internat. sec. gen. 1984-86, U.S. del. to exec. com., 1986—), Res. Officers Assn. (life) (pres. European theatre, Minuteman award 1986).

GUTTING, DAVID EDWARD, controller; b. Kansas City, Kans., Jan. 7, 1958; s. Roscoe A. and Gwendolyn A. (Rodeger) G.; m. Sally A. Borton, Feb. 14, 1987; children: Jacob, Abraham. BS in Acctg., Ind. U., 1980. CPA, Ind. Staff acct. George S. Olive & Co., CPA's, Ft. Wayne, Ind., 1980-84; controller O'Daniel Oldsmobile, Inc., Ft. Wayne, 1984—. Treas. Child Care Allen County, Ft. Wayne, 1986—. Mem. Am. Inst. CPA's, Ind. Inst. CPA's. Republican. Methodist. Lodge: Sertoma (v.p. programs 1987—). Avocations: sports, family, outdoor activities. Home: 1711 Lakewood Dr Fort Wayne IN 46819 Office: O'Daniel Oldsmobile Inc PO Box 517 Fort Wayne IN 46801

GUTTMAN, IRVING ALLEN, opera stage director; b. Chatham, Ont., Can., Oct. 27, 1928; s. Shea and Bernetta (Schaffer) G. Opera student, Royal Conservatory Music, Toronto, Ont., 1947-48. Asst. to Herman Geiger Torel of Can. Opera Co., Toronto, 1948-52; dir., under Pauline Donalda Montreal (Que., Can.) Opera Guild, 1959-68. Founding artistic dir., Vancouver (B.C., Can.) Opera Assn., 1960-74, artistic dir., Edmonton (Alta., Can.) Opera Assn., from 1966, Man. (Can.) Opera Assn., Winnipeg, from 1972; dir. numerous TV productions of opera, including first full-length TV opera for, CBC French Network, 1953, operatic productions for numerous U.S. opera cos., also Can. and European cos.; founding artistic dir., Opera Group, Courtenay Youth Music Camp; author: The Unlikely Pioneer—David Watmough, 1987. Decorated Centennial medal, Queen Elizabeth Jubilee medal. Mem. Canadian Equity, Am. Guild Musical Artists. Office: Manitoba Opera Assn, 555 Main St No 121, Winnipeg, MB Canada R3B 1C3

GUY, ERNEST THOMAS, association executive; b. Detroit, May 12, 1921; s. William G. and Anna (Utas) G.; B.A., Mich. State U., 1943; postgrad. U. Ga., 1946, U. Mich., 1948; m. Bernice Louise Smith, Mar. 8, 1945 (dec.); children—E. Timothy, Cynthia Louise. State coordinator vets. tng. Ga. Dept. Edn., Atlanta, 1946-47; mgr. sta. WATL, Atlanta, 1947-48; program dir. sta. WKNX, Saginaw, Mich., 1948-50; pub. relations dir. Mich. Heart Assn., Detroit, 1950-53, exec. dir., 1953-58; exec. dir. Tex. Heart Assn., Houston, 1958-68, Chgo. Med. Soc., 1968-69, Calif. Dental Assn., San Francisco, 1969-73, So. Calif. Dental Assn., Los Angeles, 1972-73, Unified Calif. Dental Assn., 1973-74; cons. Am. Soc. Clin. Hypnosis, Des Plaines, Ill., 1974-75; dir. meetings Am. Bar Assn., Chgo., 1975—, project dir. ann. and midyr. meetings, 1984—; bd. dirs. Meeting Planners Internat.; mem. industry adv. bd. Meeting World, 1978-80. Mem. adv. com. Tex. Rehab. Assn. Faculty pub. health classes U. Mich., Ann Arbor, 1953-58; del. White House Conf. Edn., 1956; vice chmn. Fed. Service Campaign for Health Agys. in Tex., 1961-62; mem. governing council Soc. Heart Assns. Profl. Staff, 1959-62. Mem. Pres.'s Bicentennial Commn., 1976; Precinct worker Houston Republican Com., 1960-68; mem. fin. com. George Bush for Pres. Campaign, 1978-80. Served to capt. AUS, 1943-46. Co-recipient Blakeslee award, 1953; recipient award of merit Mich. Heart Assn., 1958, Merit award Tex. Heart Assn., 1968, commendation award Calif. Dental Assn., 1974. Certified assn. exec. 1st class, 1973; named one of 5 U.S. Grand Masters of Meeting Planning, Meetings and Conv. Mag., 1986. Mem. Am. Soc. Assn. Execs., Am. Pub. Relations Soc., Nat. Assn. Parliamentarians, Profl. Conv. Mgmt. Assn., Internat. Platform Assn., Am. Assn. Dental Editors, Nat. Pub. Relations Council, Nat. Assn. Exhibit Mgrs., U.S. Parachute Assn. Republican. Episcopalian (lay reader). Contbr. numerous articles to profl. publs. Home: 930 N Northwest Hwy #202 Park Ridge IL 60068 Office: ABA 750 N Lake Shore Dr Chicago IL 60611

GUY, JOHN EDWARD, lawyer; b. Danville, Ill., July 15, 1924; s. John Milton Jr. and Beatrice (Marks) G.; m. Muriel Elaine Becking, Nov. 29, 1947; children—Randall Edward, Scott Evan, Carolyn Elizabeth. Ph.B., U. Chgo., 1947; LL.B., J.D., John Marshall Law Sch., Chgo., 1951. Bar: Ill. 1951, U.S. Supreme Ct., U.S. Dist. Ct. (no. dist.) Ill. Practice law Chgo., 1951—; ptnr. Querrey, Harrow, Gulanick & Kennedy; lectr. continuing legal edn. programs. Contbr. articles, monographs on surviving tort actions, punitive damages, distbn. tort damages, trial strategies to legal jours. Sec. Civic Betterment party Village of Glen Ellyn, Ill., 1976-80; adult leader local Boy Scouts Am., 1971-72. Served with AUS, 1943-46. Recipient Order of Arrow, Boy Scouts Am., 1972. Mem. Soc. Hosp. Attys., Soc. Trial Lawyers, Appellate Lawyers Assn., Am. Judicature Soc., Am. Arbitration Assn., Ill. Bar Assn., Chgo. Bar Assn., Def. Research Inst. (chmn. practice and procedure com. 1983—), Ill. Def. Counsel (dir. 1972—, officer 1979-82, pres. 1982-83), Trial Lawyers Club Chgo. Office: 135 S LaSalle St Chicago IL 60603

GUY, RALPH B., JR., judge; b. Detroit, Aug. 30, 1929; s. Ralph B. and Shirley (Skladd) G. AB, U. Mich., 1950, JD, 1953. Bar: Mich. 1953. Sole practice Dearborn, Mich., 1954-55; asst. corp. counsel City of Dearborn, 1955-58, corp. counsel, 1958-69; chief asst. U.S. Atty.'s Office (ea. dist.), Detroit and Mich., 1969-70, U.S. Atty., 1970-76; judge U.S. Dist. Ct. (ea. dist.) Mich., Ann Arbor, 1976-85, U.S. Ct. Appeals (6th cir.), Ann Arbor, 1985—; treas. Detroit-Wayne County Bldg. Authority, 1966-73; chmn. sch. study com. Dearborn Bd. Edn., 1973; mem. Fed. Exec. Bd., 1970—, bd. dirs., 1971-73. Recipient Civic Achievement award Dearborn Rotary, 1971; Distinguished Alumni award U. Mich., 1972. Mem. ABA (state chmn. sect. local govt. 1965-70), Fed. Bar Assn. (pres. 1974-75), State Bar Mich. (commr. 1975—), Detroit Bar Assn., Dearborn Bar Assn. (pres. 1959-60), Am. Judicature Soc., Nat. Inst. Municipal Law Officers (chmn. Mich. chpt. 1964-69), Mich. Assn. Municipal Attys. (pres. 1962-64), Mich. Municipal League, Out-County Suprs. Assn. (pres. 1965), Phi Alpha Delta, Lambda Chi Alpha. Club: U. Mich. Alumni (local pres. Dearborn 1961-62). Lodge: Rotary (local pres. 1973-74). Office: US Ct House 200 E Liberty Suite 226 Ann Arbor MI 48104

GWIN, FRANCIS B., cooperative executive; b. Morrowville, Kans., Jan. 13, 1921; s. Roy Elmer and Genevieve Anna (Brooks) G.; m. Mary Arlene Mastin, July 11, 1948 (dec. 1959); 1 child, Francene; m. Margaret Ann Widrig, June 6, 1963; 1 child, Brenda. B.S. in Agrl. Econs., Kans. State U., 1947. Asst. to supr. Farmers Home Adminstrn., Clay Center, Kans., 1948-49; farmer Leoti, Kans., 1949-54; fieldman Consumers Coop. Assn., Kansas City, Mo., 1954-59; fieldman Farmway Coop Inc., Beloit, Kans., 1959-62, elevator dept. mgr., 1962-69, gen. mgr., 1969-86; bd. dirs. Farmland Industries, Inc., Kansas City, 1972—, chmn. bd., 1981-86; dir. Nat. Coop. Refinery Assn., McPherson, Kans., 1981—, Farmland Mut. Ins. Co., Des Moines, 1972-81, Far Mar Co., Kansas City, 1977-85, Terra Resources, Tulsa, 1981-83, Coop. League of U.S., Washington, 1974-80, Solomon Valley Feed Lot, Beloit, 1972—, Farmland Industries Inc., Kansas City, chmn. 1981-86; mem. adv. com. Arthur Capper Coop. Ctr. Kans. State U., 1984—; mem. Kans. Grain Commn., Topeka, 1974-80, Nat. Com. Agrl. Trade and Export Policy, Washington, 1984—. Served to lt. USAF, 1943-45. Recipient Disting. Agrl. Econ. Alumni award Kans. State U., 1983, Disting. Service award, 1985; Coop. Statesmanship award Am. Inst. Coops., 1985. Republican. Methodist. Lodge: Rotary (pres. Beloit 1963-64). Avocations: golfing; music. Home: 6 Gill Creek Terr Beloit KS 67420 Office: Farmway Coop Inc 204 E Court St Beloit KS 67420

GWINN, ROBERT B., physician; b. Berkeley, Calif., Nov. 20, 1954; s. William D. and Margaret B. (Boothby) G.; m. Pamela Price, July 31, 1982. BA in Biochemistry, U. Calif., Santa Barbara, 1976; DO, Coll. Osteo. Medicine and Surgery, Des Moines, 1980. Resident in family practice Fairview Gen. Hosp., Cleve., 1980-83, chief resident, 1982-83; practice medicine specializing in family practice Coshocton, Ohio, 1983—. Mem. Am. Acad. Family Practice, Ohio Acad. Family Practice. Mem. Christian Ch. Office: 646 Chestnut St Coshocton OH 43812

GWINN, ROBERT P., electrical appliance manufacturing executive; b. Anderson, Ind., June 30, 1907; s. Marshall and Margaret (Cather) G.; m. Nancy Flanders, Jan. 20, 1942; 1 son, Richard Herbert. Ph.B., U. Chgo., 1929. With Sunbeam Corp., 1936—, gen. sales mgr. elec. appliance div., 1951-52, v.p., dir., 1952, pres., chief exec. officer, 1955-71, chmn. bd., chief exec. officer, 1971-82; pres. Sunbeam Appliance Service Co., 1952-82; chmn. bd., chief exec. officer Ency. Britannica; chmn. bd. Titan Oil Co., Exploration, Inc.; dir. Continental Casualty Co., Continental Assurance Co., CNA Financial Corp. Trustee U. Chgo., U. Chgo. Cancer Research Found. Mem. Elec. Assn. Chgo. (dir.), Ill. C. of C. (dir., v.p.), Brit.-Am. C. of C. in Midwest (dir.), Alpha Sigma Phi. Clubs: Chicago (Chgo.), University (Chgo.); Riverside (Ill.) Country, Commercial, Economic. Office: Ency Brit Inc 310 S Michigan Ave Chicago IL 60604

GWINUP, JOHN HAROLD, industrial engineer; b. Litchfield, Ill., July 5, 1940; s. John Daniel Gwinup and Sarah Elizabeth Fogle; m. Rebecca Ann Kearby, July 25, 1975; children: John Christopher, Jeffrey Allen. BS in Indsl. Tech., Southwest Mo. State U., 1970. Indsl. engring. assoc. Western Electric, Inc., Oklahoma City, 1970-75; methods and standards engr. Fasco Industry, Eldon, Mo., 1975-76, Rival Mfg., Sedalia, Mo., 1976-78, Am. Yearbook, Topeka, 1978-79; mgr. indsl. engring. Midland Brake, Iola, Kans., 1979-83; indsl. engr. Ace Electric, Columbus, Kans., 1983-84; sr. indsl. engr. Becton-Dickinson, Holdrege, Nebr., 1984—. Treas. Kearney pack Cub Scouts of Am., 1986. Served with USAF, 1963-67. Mem. Inst. Indsl. Engrs. (bd. dirs. Nebraskaland chpt. 1985-86, chpt. pres. 1987—), Lotus 1-2-3 Users Group (bd. dirs. 1985-86). Republican. Mem. Ch. of Christ. Avocations: camping, hunting, fishing, woodworking. Office: Becton-Dickinson W Hwy 6 Noldrege NE 68949

GYARFAS, MARY GORMAN, social worker; b. Cheyenne, Wyo., Mar. 24, 1920; d. William Ignatius and Margaret Edna (Colloton) Gorman; m. Kalman Gyarfas, Sept. 12, 1953 (dec. Nov. 1967). BA, Rosary Coll., River Forest, Ill., 1941; MA, U. Chgo., 1949, PhD, 1967. Supr. Child Guidance Cath. Youth Ctr., Chgo., 1949-54; pvt. practice social work Chgo., 1952-72, Evanston, Ill., 1972—; asst. prof. U. Chgo., 1954-58, assoc. prof., 1968-76; cons. Juvenile Protection Assn., Chgo., 1979-80, Cath. Charities, Chgo., 1982, Ill. Children Home Aid, Chgo., 1975, Acorn, Evanston, 1986—. Mem. Nat. Assn. Social Workers (cert.). Roman Catholic.

GYENES, LAWRENCE ANDREW, finance and planning executive; b. Chgo., Sept. 16, 1950. BS in Accountancy, U. Ill., 1972; MBA, U. Chgo. Exec. Program, 1983. CPA, Ill. Staff auditor Touche Ross & Co., Chgo., 1972-76, audit supr., 1977-78; dir. fin. reporting G.D. Searle & Co., Skokie, Ill., 1979-80, asst. corp. controller, 1981-83; v.p. bus. planning and control Searle Pharms. Inc., Skokie, 1984-85; v.p. market devel. Lorex Pharms., Skokie, 1986—. Mem. Am. Inst. CPA's, Ill. CPA Soc., Am. Mgmt. Assn., U. Ill. Alumni Assn. (life), U. Chgo. Grad. Sch. Bus. Alumni Assn. Avocations: personal investing, reading, skiing. Office: Lorex Pharms 4930 W Oakton St Skokie IL 60077

HAACK, RICHARD WILSON, police officer; b. Chgo., July 7, 1935; s. Arthur Frank and Mildred Ann (Meyer) H.; m. Ruth Marie Tietz, May 27, 1972; children—Laura Marie, Karl Richard. Grad., Cook County (Ill.) Sheriff's Police Acad., 1967; A.S., Triton Coll., 1973; cert. Chgo. Police Acad., 1974; B.A., Lewis U., 1975; M.A., Northeastern Ill. U., 1979; B.S. in Bus. Adminstrn., Elmhurst Coll., 1982. Shipping clk. Am. Furniture Mart, Chgo., 1955-60; quality control insp. Nat. Can Co., Chgo., 1961-67; police officer Northlake Police Dept. (Ill.), 1967—, watch comdr. patrol div., 1978-85, dept. chief of police, 1986—; realtor Internat. Realty World-Norton & Assocs., 1984—. Recipient John Edgar Hoover Meml. Gold medal, 1987. Mem. Bill Bruce fundraising com. Aid Assn. Luths., Christ Evangelical Luth. Ch., Northlake, 1981-82, mem. Gala Variety Show, 1982, chmn. evang. bd., 1981-85, ch. rep. Internat. Luth. Laymen's League, 1984—, pub. relations dir., usher, 1973-85, dir. Project Compassion, 1983-85; ombudsman No. Ill. dist. Luth. Ch.-Mo. Synod, 1984-85; choir Apostles Luth. Ch., 1985—; dir., master ceremonies Oktoberfest, 1980—, chmn. entertainment, 1984—. Served with USMC, 1952-55, with res. 1955-60, Korea. Recipient numerous letters of commendation, competitive shooting awards. Mem. Ill. Police Assn., Fraternal Order Police (sec.-treas. Perri-Nagle Meml. Lodge 18, 1977-85), St. Jude Police League, Nat. Police Officers Assn., Internat. Conf. Police Assn., German/Am. Police Assn. (bd. dirs. 1980—, Combined Counties Police Assn., Emerald Soc. Ill. Irish/Am. Police Assn., Northeastern Ill. U. Alumni Assn. (bd. dirs. 1980—), Am. Polit. Sci. Assn., Nat. Rifle Assn., Schwaben Verein, N.W. Real Estate Bd., Leyden Real Estate Bd. (inner circle 1984—), Internat. Platform Assn., Realtors Polit. Action Com. Ill. (Inner Circle 1984—), Am. Legion. Republican. Club: Die Hard Cub Fans. Lodge: Moose. Contbr. law enforcement articles to profl. publs. Home: 244 E Palmer Ave Northlake IL 60164 Office: 55 E North Ave Northlake IL 60164

HAAG, ROBERT LEON, development company executive; b. N.Y.C., Sept. 23, 1926; s. Philip B. and Ida (Roth) H.; m. Sylvia M. Cohn, Dec. 22, 1951; children—Donna J., Philip R. Student Bklyn. Poly. Inst., 1943-44; B.S., NYU, 1950, postgrad., 1950-51. Salesman Jules Montenier & Co., N.Y.C., 1950, dist. sales mgr., Denver and Chgo., 1951; regional sales mgr. Leonard H. Lavin & Co., Chgo., 1951-54; nat. sales mgr. Alberto-Culver Co., Chgo., 1955-60, v.p. sales, 1960-66, group v.p. food div., 1966-70; pres. Robert L. Haag & Co., Chgo., 1970—; pres. Monroe Communications, Chgo., 1981—; co-founder, former dir. Alberto-Culver Co.; dir. Midas Internat., Calif. Dreamers, Inc., Shelby Williams Inc., Sharon Broadcasting, Albany Park Nat. Bank & Trust Co. Bd. dirs. Jewish Community Ctrs., 1972-81, Am. Jewish Com. Served to cpl. USAAF, 1945-46. Mem. Am.-Israel C. of C. (named Man of Yr. 1976, pres. 1977-79, bd. dirs. 1970—). Clubs: Standard (Chgo.), Internat. (Chgo.); Bryn Mawr Country (Lincolnwood, Ill.). Office: Robert L Haag & Co Monroe Communications 201 N Wells St Suite 1520 Chicago IL 60606

HAAKE, DANIEL JOSEPH, accountant; b. Kansas City, Mo., Apr. 6, 1951; s. Robert A. Sr. and Marion C. (Huber) H.; m. Patricia M. Bryant, Aug. 19, 1972; children: Hiatt B., Hogan P., Holly B., Hayden R. BSBA, Rockhurst Coll., 1973. CPA, Mo. Revenue agt. U.S. Treasury, Kansas City, 1973-76; ptnr. Donnelly, Meiners & Jordan, Kansas City, 1976—. Pres. Holy Spirit Parent's Assn., Overland Park, Kans., 1985-87; adv. bd. Hamilton Bus. Coll., Independence, Mo., 1982—; hon. dir. Rockhurst Coll., Kansas City, 1978—. Mem. Internat. Group Acctg. Firms, Am. Inst. CPA's, Mo. Soc. CPA's. Roman Catholic. Lodge: KC (bd. dirs.). Avocations: biking, stock market, reading. Home: 11413 W 104th St Overland Park KS 66214 Office: Donnelly Meiners & Jordan 9215 Ward Pkwy Kansas City MO 64114

HAAKENSON, PHILIP NIEL, pharmacist, educator; b. Hatton, N.D., Apr. 15, 1924; s. Martin Selmer and Theodora H.; m. Eldora Ida Robinson, June 19, 1950; children: Mary Kim, Martin Niel. BS in Pharmacy, N.D. State U., 1950, MS in Pharmacy, 1965; PhD in Pharmacy Adminstrn., U. Wis., 1972. Owner Portland (N.D.) Drug, 1950-60, Hatton Drug, 1956-60; asst. prof. pharmacy adminstrn. N.D. State U., Fargo, 1961-65, assoc. prof., 1965-70, prof., 1970-87, prof. emeritus, 1987—, dean sch. of pharmacy, 1970-80; Dir. Pharmacy Continuing Edn., 1982-87. Editor Nordak Pharmacist, 1962-74, 1982-87. Served with USN, 1942-45. Mem. Am. Assn. colls. of Pharmacy, N.D. Pharm. Assn. (recipient Bowl of Hygiea 1979), Am. Pharm. Assn., Kappa Psi (named Outstanding Alumni 1974, Pharmacist of Yr. 1977), Sigma Xi. Republican. Lutheran. Lodges: Lions, Masons, Shriners. Home: 210 28th Ave N Fargo ND 58102 Office: Sudro Hall 215A ND State U Fargo ND 58105

HAAKENSTAD, DALE L., insurance company executive; b. 1929. With Western States Life Ins. Co., Fargo, N.D., 1951—, now chief exec. officer, chmn. bd. dirs. Office: Western States Life Ins Co PO Box 2907 Fargo ND 58108 *

HAAPANEN, LAWRENCE WILLIAM, communication educator; b. Seattle, Apr. 24, 1945; s. Morris William and Helen Marie (Stearns) H.; m. Beverly Ann Biggi, Aug. 19, 1972; children—Laurell, Holly. B.A. in History, U. Wash., 1967; M.A. in Speech, Wash. State U., 1972, Ph.D. in Speech, 1974. Tchr. Neah-Kah-Nie High Sch., Rockaway, Oreg., 1974-76; asst. prof. Utah State U., Logan, 1976-81; assoc. prof., chmn. dept. communication Baker U., Baldwin City, Kans., 1981—. Contbr. chpt. to textbook. Del. State Democratic Conv., Salt Lake City, 1978. Served to capt. USAF, 1967-71. Decorated Air Force Commendation medal; summer fellow NEH, 1980. Mem. Speech Communication Assn. (chmn. commn. on govt. communication 1984-85), Central States Speech Assn., Am. Forensics Assn. Democrat. Lutheran. Avocation: genealogy. Home: 107 Dearborn St Baldwin City KS 66006 Office: Baker Univ Dept Communication 8th and Grove Sts Baldwin City KS 66006

HAARTZ, DAVID WINSOR, scientist, financial consultant; b. Andover, Mass., Feb. 21, 1937; s. Karl J.C. and Bessie Rose (Carter) H.; m. Janet Kay Carlson, June 18, 1960 (div. Jan 1973); children: Margot Elizabeth, David Bradley. BS ChemE, U. Mich., 1960; MBA, Xavier U., 1968. Staff engr. The Proctor & Gamble Co., Cin., 1960-75; scientist The Drackett Co., Cin., 1975—; founder, owner Hist. Property Reconstrn. Co., Cin., 1977—, David W. Haartz Fin. Services, Cin., 1971—. Founder, pres. Nat. Assn. Investment Clubs Cin.-Dayton (Ohio) Council, 1968-72; mem. Updowntowners, Cin., 1979—. Mem. Am. Inst. Chem. Engrs., Am. Chem. Soc., Nat. Fire Protection Assn. Republican. Home: 2239 Park Ave Cincinnati OH 45206

HAAS, GENE ALAN, life and earth science educator; b. Akron, Ohio, Apr. 23, 1946; s. William Luther and Jean (McLain) H.; m. Denise Annette Stull, July 20, 1979; children: Tara Nicole, Christopher Alan. BA in Secondary Edn., U. Akron, 1968, MA in Secondary Edn., 1979. Cert. sch. tchr. and adminstr., Ohio. Tchr. Thornton Jr. High Sch., Akron, Ohio, 1974—, Jennings Middle Sch., Akron, 1975-86; head sci. dept. Jennings Middle Sch., 1977-84. Served to maj. USAFR, 1968—. Decorated Bronze Star; recipient Excellence in Edn. award U.S. Dept. Edn., 1985. Mem. Akron Edn. Assn. (bdlg. rep. 1981-85). Republican. Presbyterian. Avocations: wargames, gardening, reading, travel. Home: 4479 Hickory Trail Stow OH 44224

HAAS, JAMES WAYNE, accountant; b. Merrill, Wis., Sept. 27, 1944; s. Frank Joseph and Verna Antoinette (Beilke) H.; m. Patrice Marie Will, June 2, 1973; children: Christopher Jon, Scott James. Assoc. in Acctg., N. Central Tech. Inst., 1968. Controller, asst. treas. House of Merrill Inc., Merrill, 1968-72; controller Semling Menke Co., Inc., Merrill, 1968-72; treas., dir. North Star Communications, Ltd., Gleason, Wis., 1971-72; pres., dir. Profl. Accounting Systems, Inc., La Crosse, Wis., 1975—; pres., dir. Haas Enterprises, Inc., 1971-82; pres., treas., dir. Adventure Capital, Ltd., 1971—; treas. Systems, Mgmt., Inc., St. Paul, 1983-84; treas. Gateway Acctg. Services, Inc., Ft. Myers, Fla., 1982-83; v.p., treas. ops. mgr. Accounting Bookkeeping Inc., Wauwatosa, Wis., 1975-76; v.p. Marathon Mining & Mfg. Corp., Wausau, Wis., 1976, pres., 1977-79; treas. controller, prodn. mgr. Moduline Windows, Inc., Wausau, 1977-78; mng. partner Haas Properties, Mosinee Wis., 1979-83; owner Midwest Investments, Winona, Minn., 1980—; pres. Accounting Bookkeeping Cons., Ltd., 1987—; pres., bd. dirs. Jim Haas' Triple Check Income Tax Service, Inc., 1986—, pres., dir. Acctg. Bookkeeping Cons., Ltd., 1987. Mem. Adminstrv. Mgmt. Soc., Inst. Internal Auditors, Nat. Notary Assn., Inst. Record Mgrs. and Adminstrs., Am. Soc. Notaries, Nat. Assn. Accts., Am. Inst. Profl. Numismatists (charter mem.), Am. Acctg. Assn. Nat. Soc. Public Accts. Democrat. Roman Catholic. Lodges: K.C., Kiwanis (New Club Bldg. award), Optimists, Winona Lions. Home: 1253 W Broadway Winona MN 55987 Office: 1400 Homer Rd Winona MN 55987 also: 125 N 40th St La Crosse WI 54601

HAASCH, GARY ROBERT, manufacturing engineer; b. Algoma, Wis., Oct. 31, 1961; s. Keith Robert and Carol Mae (Baudhuin) H. BS in Indsl. Tech., U. Wis., Menomonie, 1984. Cert. Mfg. technologist. Indsl. engr. Warner Electric, South Beloit, Ill., 1984-86, mfg. engr., 1986—. Mem. Soc. Mfg. Engrs., Soc. Automotive Engrs., Assn. Integrated Mfg. Tech. Avocations: recreational sports. Home: 5155 Sunbird Dr Rockford IL 61111 Office: Warner Electric 449 Gardner South Beloit IL 61080

HAASE, VERNICE ESTHER, university director; b. Theresa, Wis., Aug. 19, 1939; d. Reinhold and Esther (Wagner) Wendling; m. Robert A. Haase, June 3, 1962; children: Sandra, John, Steven. Diploma, Columbia Sch. Nursing, Milw., 1960; BS in English magna cum laude, U. Wis., Oshkosh, 1978, postgrad. in bus. adminstrn., 1978. RN, Wis. Staff nurse Univ. Hosps., Madison, Wis., 1960-61, nurse obstetrical dept. Quisling Clinic, 1961-64, medicare claims processor Dean Clinic, 1967; nurse operating room Mercy Med. Ctr., Oshkosh, 1972-74, instr. sch. nursing, 1974-75; grad. asst. fin. aid office U. Wis., Oshkosh, 1978-80, asst. dir. fin. aid, 1980—. Bd. dirs. Oshkosh Symphony Inc., 1979—, co-chmn. corp. fund raising 1985-87, pres. 1983-85, v.p. 1982-83; panalist nat. conf. Am. Symphony Orch. League, 1983; pres. Oshkosh Symphony League, 1980-81, v.p. 1979-80, treas. 1976-77; mem. regional screen com. Am. Field Service, 1975-77, 83-85; mem. choir First Congl. Ch., Oshkosh, 1973—; mem. Legal Aux. Winnebago County, Wis., 1968—, pres. 1973; pres. bd. dirs. Sunshine Nursery Sch., 1971-72; publicity chmn. Oshkosh Newcomers Club, 1969. Mem. Midwestern Assn. Student Employment Adminstrs., Wis. Assn. Fin. Aid Adminstrs. (program chmn. spring conf. 1986). Home: 1330 Cambridge Ave Oshkosh WI 54901 Office: U Wis Fin Aid Office 800 Algoma Blvd Dempsey Hall Room 104 Oshkosh WI 54901

HAASETH, RONALD CARL, chemistry educator; b. Seattle, Sept. 6, 1952; s. Carl Antone Roosevelt Haaseth and Christine Virginia (Stoll) Coulter. BS in Chemistry, U. Puget Sound, 1974; PhD in Organic Chemistry, U. Washington, 1982. Teaching, research asst. U. Puget Sound, Tacoma, 1972-74; lab. technician U.S. Oil and Refining Co., Tacoma, 1973-74; predoctoral instr., research asst. U. Washington, Seattle, 1974-82, research assoc., 1982-83; asst. prof. U. Minn., Morris, 1984-85; sr. research assoc. U. Mich., Ann Arbor, 1986—. Recipient Individual Research award U.S. Pub. Health Service, 1978-81. Mem. Am. Chem. Soc., Sigma Nu, Pi Lambda Theta. Avocations: birdwatching, photography, fishing, hiking. Home: 802 Fuller Apt 34 Ann Arbor MI 48104 Office: U Mich Coll Pharmacy Dept Medicinal Chemistry Ann Arbor MI 48109

HAAYEN, RICHARD JAN, insurance company executive; b. Bklyn., June 30, 1924; s. Cornelius Marius and Cornelia Florence (Muskus) H.; m. Marilyn Jean Messner, Aug. 30, 1946; children—Richard Jan, Peter Wyckoff, James Carell. B.Sc., Ohio State U., 1948. With Allstate Ins. Co., 1950—, v.p. underwriting, 1969-75; exec. v.p. Allstate Ins. Co., Northbrook, Ill., 1975-80; pres. Allstate Ins. Co., 1980-86, chmn., chief exec. officer, 1986—, also dir.; bd. dirs. Sears, Roebuck & Co., Nat. Chamber Found., Washington; dir. Ins. Info. Inst., N.Y.C.; chmn. Ins. Inst. Am., Malvern, Pa. Bd. sponsors Evang. Hosp. Assn.; vice chmn. bus. adv. council U. Ill., Chgo. Mem. Nat. Assn. Ind. Insurers, Property Casualty Ins. Council, Chgo. Assn. Commerce and Industry (bd. dirs.), Phi Delta Theta. Republican. Club: Chgo. Union League. Home: 1410 Lake Shore Dr S Barrington IL 60010 Office: Allstate Ins Co Allstate Plaza Northbrook IL 60062

HABENICHT, HERALD ALLEN, allergist, educator; b. Berrien Springs, Mich., Feb. 23, 1933; s. Herald Ambrose and Kathryn A. (Kilpatrick) H.; m. Donna Jeanne Lugenbeal, May 23, 1954; children: Larry, Nancy Habenicht Schilling. BA, Andrews U., 1954; MD, Loma Linda U., 1958; degree in allergy and immunology, U. Mich., 1982-83. Intern in pediatrics White Meml. Hosp., Los Angeles, 1958-61; missionary Inter-Am. div. Seventh-Day Adventist, Miami, Fla., 1961-70; allergist U. Med. Specialist, Berrien Springs, Mich., 1970—; prof. health edn., Andrews U., Berrien Springs, 1970—, dir. student health 1973-82. Author: Doctor! What Can I Do, 1982; contbr. articles to profl. jours. Mem. AMA, Mich. State Med. Soc., Berrien County Med. Soc., Alpha Omega Alpha. Republican. Lodge: Rotary. Avocations: gardening, stamps. Home: 8321 Kephart Ln Berrien Springs MI 49103 Office: U Med Specialties 1130 St Joseph Ave Berrien Springs MI 49103

HABENICHT, HOWARD EUGENE, manufacturing corporation executive; b. Berwyn, Ill., Dec. 28, 1939; s. Eugene Victor and Emily (Cikanek) H.; m. Janice Elizabeth McMicken, Aug. 4, 1961; children: Scott, Sheri, Hilary, Carrie. BBA, Western Mich. U., 1961. Mgr. Ernst & Whinney, Chgo., 1961-80; sec., controller and chief fin. officer Vibro/Dynamics Corp., Countryside, Ill., 1980—, also bd. dirs., trustee pension trust, 1982—. Fin. commn. Presbyn. Ch. of Western Springs, 1974—, treas., 1978—; troop and post advisor Boy Scouts Am., Western Springs, 1976-79; chmn. Meml. Park Showmobile Fund, LaGrange Park, Ill., 1976; v.p. assoc. bd. LaGrange Meml. Hosp., 1978-81, pres., 1982-83, bd. govs., 1984—; mem. fin. com., community relations com., 1984-85, treas., chmn. fin. com., 1986—; pres. West Suburban Community Band, 1981-82; treas., bd. dirs. West Cook Girl Scout Council, Inc., LaGrange Park, 1984-85; treas. Western Springs Centennial Commn., 1984-86; mem. fin. com. Whispering Oaks Girl Scout Council, Inc., LaGrange Park, 1986—. Recipient Service award Assoc. Bd. of LaGrange Meml. Hosp., 1977. Mem. Ill. CPA Soc., Am. Inst. CPA's, Chgo. Fedn. Musicians, Windjammers Unltd. Lodge: Rotary. Home: 4947 Central Ave Western Springs IL 60558 Office: Vibro/Dynamics Corp 500 E Plainfield Rd Countryside IL 60525

HABER, IRVING AARON, clinical psychologist, mental health administrator; b. Chgo., Feb. 5, 1926; s. Benjamin and Goldie (Kaplan) H.; m. Norma Joslove, July 4, 1962 (div.); 1 dau., Laura G. B.A., Roosevelt U., 1952, M.A., 1955; postgrad. Ill. Inst. Tech., 1956-60; Ph.D., Columbia Pacific U., 1983. Lic. psychologist, Ill., Pa.; registered Mental Health Care Provider; cert. social worker, Ill. Psychology intern Ind. Central State Hosp., 1954-55; sr. psychologist Psychiat. Inst., Circuit Ct. Chgo., 1956-58, instr. Crane Jr. Coll., Chgo., 1958-61; psychologist and adminstrv. dir. inpatient ward, outpatient clinics Ill. Dept. Mental Health, Chgo., 196185; supervising psychologist Ill. Youth Ctr., St. Charles Dept. Correction, 1985—; cons. Circuit Ct. Chgo., 1958-61; indls. cons.; profl. cons. Rogers Park Mental Health Assn.; pvt. practice, Oak Brook, Ill, 1985—. Served with USAF, 1944-46. Mem. Am. Psychol. Assn., Ill. Psychol. Assn., Assn. Mental Health Adminstrs., Ill. Group Psychotherapy Assn., Assn. DuPage Psychologists (bd. dirs.) Office: Ill Youth Ctr St Charles Dept Corrections PO Box 122 Saint Charles IL 60174 also: 2607 W 22d Oak Brook IL 60174

HABERMAN, DAVID ALLEN, artist, educator; b. Worthington, Minn., July 29, 1938; s. Joseph James and Marie (Mathias) H.; m. Mary Ann Perich, Apr. 10, 1971; 1 child, Sarah Mathias. BA, St. John's U., 1960; MFA, U. Iowa, 1962. Asst. prof. art Thomas More Coll., Covington, Ky., 1963-66; assoc. prof. art Cuyahoga Community Coll., Cleve., 1967—; sr. lectr. printmaking Manchester (Eng.) Poly., 1978-79. Exhibited paintings in Harbourfront Gallery, Toronto, Can., 1978, etchings in Hong Kong Sch. Art Design, 1981, Spaces Gallery, Cleve., 1985. Mem. New Orgn. Visual Arts (trustee 1972-73). Democrat. Roman Catholic. Avocation: horticulture. Home: 3010 Overlook Rd Cleveland Heights OH 44118 Office: Cuyahoga Community Coll 2900 Community Coll Dr Cleveland OH 44115

HABERMAN, REX STANLEY, state senator, farm manager; b. Friend, Nebr., Jan. 23, 1924; m. Phyllis Kavan, Aug. 22, 1948; children—Mary Lou, George, Rex II, Phillip. Owner, operator 5 photog. studios, 1945-67; personnel dir. Nebr. Vets. Home, 1968-70; mgr. family farms, Imperial, Nebr., 1970—; mem. Nebr. Legislature, 1979—. Mem. Adams County Bd. Suprs., 1964-68, Imperial City Council, 1974-76; del. Republican Nat. Conv., 1976, 84; former state pres. Nebr. Jaycees; former chmn. Adams County Rep. Party, Chase County Rep. Party; former pres. Greater Nebr. Health Systems Agy.; exec. council Nebr. Episcopal Ch., chmn. Nebr. Retirement Systems com., 1987, (mem. exec. bd., panking, commerce and ins. com., revenue com., com. on coms., reference com.). Mem. Hastings C. of C. (dir.), Am. Legion, VFW. Clubs: Masons, Shriners, Elks, Eagles, Rotary. Office: State Capitol Lincoln NE 68509

HABIG, DOUGLAS ARNOLD, manufacturing company executive; b. Louisville, 1946; s. Arnold F. and Mary Ann (Jahn) H. B.S., St. Louis U., 1968; M.B.A., Ind. U., 1972. Comml. loan officer Ind. Nat. Bank, Indpls., 1972-75; exec. v.p., treas., chief fin. officer Kimball Internat. Inc., Jasper, Ind., 1975-81, pres., dir., 1981—. Office: Kimball Internat Inc 1600 Royal St Jasper IN 47546 *

HABIG, THOMAS LOUIS, piano, organ, furniture manufacturing executive; b. Jasper, Ind., June 18, 1928; s. Arnold Frank and Mary Ann (Jahn) H.; m. C. Roberta Snyder, Jan. 31, 1953; children: Randall, Julia, Brian, Sandra, Paul. B.B.A., Tulane U., 1950. With Kimball Internat., Inc. (predecessor firm), Jasper, Ind., 1952—, exec. v.p., 1960-63, pres., 1963—, chmn., chief exec. officer, 1981—, also dir.; dir. Springs Valley Nat. Bank. Served with AUS, 1950-52. Mem. Am. Legion, Sigma Chi. Roman Catholic. Club: K.C. Office: Kimball Internat Inc 1600 Royal St PO Box 460 Jasper IN 47546 *

HABLUTZEL, NANCY ZIMMERMAN, lawyer, educator; b. Chgo., Mar. 16, 1940; d. Arnold Fred Zimmerman and Maxine (Lewison) Zimmerman Goodman; m. Philip Norman Hablutzel, July 1, 1980; children—Margo Lynn, Robert Paul. B.S., Northwestern U., 1960; M.A., Northeastern Ill. U., 1972; J.D., Ill. Inst. Tech. Chgo.-Kent Coll. Law, 1980; Ph.D., Loyola U., Chgo., 1983. Bar: Ill. 1980, U.S. Dist. Ct. (no. dist.) Ill. 1980. Speech therapist various pub. schs. and hosps., Chgo. and St. Louis, 1960-63, 65-72; audiologist U. Chgo. Hosps., 1963-65; instr. spl. edn. Chgo. State U., 1972-76; asst. prof. Loyola U., Chgo., 1981-87; adj. prof. Ill. Inst. Tech. Chgo.-Kent Coll. Law, 1982—; legal dir. Legal Clinic for Disabled, Chgo., 1984-85, exec. dir., 1985—; of counsel Whitted & Spain P.C., 1987—. Mem. Ill. Gov.'s Com. on Handicapped, 1972-75; exec. mem. Council for Exceptional Children, faculty moderator student div., 1982-87. Loyola-Mellon Found. grantee, 1983. Fellow Chgo. Bar Found.; mem. ABA, Ill. Bar Assn. (sec. standing com. on juvenile justice, 1986—, Inst. Pub. Affairs 1985—), Chgo. Bar Assn. (exec. com. of corp. law com. 1984—), Am. Ednl. Research Assn. Republican. Office: Legal Clinic for Disabled Rehab Inst of Chgo 345 E Superior StRoom 1172 Chicago IL 60611

HABLUTZEL, PHILIP NORMAN, law educator; b. Flagstaff, Ariz., Aug. 23, 1935; s. Charles Edward and Electa Margaret (Cain) H.; m. Nancy Zimmerman, July 1, 1980; children—Margo Lynn, Robert Paul. B.A., La. State U., 1958; postgrad. U. Heidelberg, W.Ger., 1959-60, 60-62; M.A., U. Chgo., 1960, J.D., 1967. Bar: Ill. 1967, U.S. Dist. Ct. (no. dist.) Ill. 1967. Research atty. Am. Bar Found., Chgo., 1967-68, sr. research atty., 1968-71; asst. prof. law Chgo.-Kent Coll. Law, Ill. Inst. Tech., 1971-73, assoc. prof., 1973-79, prof., 1979—, dir. grad. program in fin. services law, 1985—; cons. OEO Legal Services Program, 1967-69; reporter Ill. sec. state's com. on revision of not-for-profit corp. act, 1984-87. Pres., trustee, Chgo. Sch. Profl. Psychology, 1979-83; reporter Ill. Sec. of State's corp. laws adv. com., 1986—. Rotary Found. Advanced Study fellow, 1959-60. Fellow Chgo. Bar Found.; mem. ABA (chmn. subcom. on adoption of Uniform Trade Secrets Act 1984-86), Ill. State Bar Assn., Chgo. Bar Assn. (chmn. com. on sci., tech. and law 1971-72, sec. corp. law com. 1986-87). Republican. Episcopalian. Author: (with R. Garrett, W. Scott) Model Business Corporation Act Annotated, 2d edit., 3 vols., 1971, (with J. Levi) Model Residential Landlord-Tenant Code, 1969. Avocations: travel, sailing, photography. Office: IIT Chgo-Kent Coll Law 77 S Wacker Dr Chicago IL 60606

HACK, JUDITH LYNN, dietitian, educator; b. Chgo., May 27, 1947; s. Melvin Sylvester and Helen Berneice (Hall) H. BA, Clarke Coll., 1969; MS, Purdue U., 1976. Clin. dietitian VA Hosp., Hines, Ill., 1969-71; program mgr. and planning chief VA Hosp., Charleston, S.C., 1971-72; assoc. dir. foods and nutrition Palos Community Hosp., Palos Heights, Ill., 1972-75; dir. dietetics St. Mary Med. Ctr., Gary and Hobart, Ind., 1976-85; asst. prof. restaurant, hotel, Inst. Mgmt. Purdue U. Calumet, Hammond, Ind., 1985—; lectr. in behavioral scis., Purdue U. Calumet, Hammond, Ind., 1981-84, mem. food service adv. com. 1980-84. Pres. Dunewood Property Owners Assn., Bridgman, Mich., 1986—. Named Outstanding Young Woman of Am., 1981. Mem. Am. Dietetic Assn., Am. Soc. for Hosp. Food Services Adminstrs., Internat. Food Service Execs. Assn., Council of Hotel, Restaurant and Inst. Mgmt. Educators, Northwest Ind. Dietetic Assn. (chmn. mgmt. com. 1977-78, 84-85, chmn. edn. com. 1985-86), Purdue Alumni Assn., Clarke Alumni Assn. Avocations: photography, travel. Home: PO Box 132 Bridgman MI 49106 Office: Purdue U Behavioral Scis Dept Hammond IN 46323

HACKENBERG, ALOYSIUS T., financial planner, lawyer; b. Williston, N.D., Sept. 7, 1925; s. Joseph and Susanna (Stepanek) H.; m. Delores C. Lynch, Sept. 5, 1955; children: Therese, Mary Kay, Michael, Thomas, Stephen, Patrick, James, Colleen. BA, U. N.D., 1947, JD, 1949; bus. mgmt. cert., Gen. Motors Inst., 1949. Sole practice Williston, 1953-63; judge Williams County Ct., Williston, 1954-61; ins. agt. KC, Grand Forks, N.D., 1963-69, Northwestern Nat. Life, Grand Forks, 1969-83; fin. planner Hackenberg Agy., Grand Forks, 1983—. Chmn. Rep. Pro-Life Caucus, 1976, 80, 82, 84; parliamentarian Grand Forks Reps., 1976, 80, 82, 84; mem. Mayor's Community Council, 1977-79, Gov.'s Family Conf., 1980. Named Outstanding Young Man Yr., N.D. Jaycees, 1956, Outstanding Handicapped, State N.D., 1976; Outstanding Life Tng. fellow. Mem. CLU (pres. 1985-87), N.D. Life Underwriters (PAC chmn. 1976-80, named Outstanding Life Underwriter 1979, State Pub. Relations chpt., 1986), Chartered Fin. Cons. (pres. 1985-87), Million Dollar Roundtable, Right to Life (v.p. local chpt., v.p. for state mem.), Phi Delta Theta (Named Outstanding Mem. for U.S. and Can. 1977). Republican. Roman Catholic. Lodge: Lions (local pres.), KC (Grand Knight). Home: 3627 9th Ave N Grand Forks ND 58201 Office: Box 1011 Grand Forks ND 58206

HACKER, KENNETH LEE, small business owner; b. Nevada, Mo., May 7, 1955; s. James Daniel and Rita (Dicks) H.; m. Alice Luc, Nov. 20, 1976; 1 child, Sonia Tek-Li. Diploma, Kansas City (Mo.) Sch. Cert. watchmaker, clockmaker, diamond setter. Owner, pres. Hacker's Jewelry Inc, El Dorado Springs. Bd. dirs. Youth Activity Ctr., El Dorado Springs, Mo., 1980-81. Recipient Disting. Service award El Dorado Springs Jr. C. of C., 1983. Mem. Mo. Jewelers Assn., Ind. Jewelers Orgn., Preserve Our Past Soc. (bd. dirs. 1984-85, 86), El Dorado Springs C. of C. (pres. 1983-84, Largest Membership award 1983), Downtown Bus. Assn. (bd. dirs. 1981-82). Club: Alumni (pres. 1981-82). Lodges: Rotary (bd. dirs. 1980-81), Optimists (bd. dirs. El Dorado Springs club 1987, charter mem. Nev. State club 1987). Office: Hackers Jewelry Inc 101 N Main St El Dorado Springs MO 64744 Office: 124 N Walnut Nevada MO 64772

HACKETT, BARBARA K., judge. Judge U.S. Dist. Ct. Mich., Detroit, 1986—. Office: 802 U S Courthouse Detroit MI 48226

HACKL, DONALD JOHN, architect; b. Chgo., May 11, 1934; s. John Frank and Frieda Marie (Weichmann) H.; m. Bernadine Marie Becker, Sept. 29, 1962; children: Jeffrey Scott, Craig Michael, Cristina Lynn. B.Arch., U.

Ill., 1957, M.S. in Architecture, 1958. Project architect Loebl Schlossman & Bennett (architects-engrs.), Chgo., 1962-64; assoc. Loebl, Schlossman Bennett & Dart, Chgo., 1967—; partner Loebl, Schlossman Bennett & Dart, 1970—, exec. v.p., dir., 1974—; pres., dir. Loebl Schlossman & Hackl Inc., 1975—, Dart-Hackl Internat. Ltd., 1975—; mem. Nat. Council Archtl. Registration Bds.; chmn. Midwest Architecture Design Conf., 1983; guest design critic dept. architecture U. Ill., 1975, 76, 81; guest lectr. U. Notre Dame, 1977, 78, 80, 82; cons. Public Service Adminstrn., Washington, 1974-76; v.p. Chgo. Bldg. Congress, 1983-85. Prin. works include Samsonite Corp. Hdqrs., Denver, 1968, Water Tower Place, Chgo., 1976, HFC World Hdqrs., Northbrook, Ill., 1978, Square D Internat. Hdqrs., Palatine, Ill., 1978, Cancer Research Inst., King Faisal Specialist Hosp. and Research Center, Riyadh, Saudi Arabia, 1978, Allstate Ins. Co., Barrington, Ill., 1981, Shriners Hosp. Crippled Children, Chgo., 1979, West Suburban Hosp., Oak Park, Ill., 1981, One Pierce Place, 1985, corp. hdqrs. Commerce Clearing House, 1986, Pepper Cos., 1985One Centry Centre, 1986, One Shaumburg Place, 1986, Physicians Pavillion at Greater Balt. Med. Ctr., 1987, 3200 Highland Office Bldg., 1987, numerous Sears, Roebuck and Co.; Contbr. articles to profl. jours. and trade publs. Mem. Chgo. Met. Cancer Crusade, 1973, Urban Planning Com., 1978—; trustee Chgo. AIA Found., 1981-83; bd. dirs. Chgo. Archtl. Assistance Ctr., 1982—; trustee West Suburban Hosp., Oak Park, Ill., 1983—; mem. adj. faculty Constrn. Law Inst., Kent Coll. Law, 1982—. Fellow AIA (dir. 1982-84, v.p., exec. com. 1985, treas., dir., v.p., pres. Chgo. chpt. 1976-82, dir. Ill. council 1979-81, v.p. 1985 1st v.p., pres. 1987), Royal Archtl. Inst. Can.; mem. Chgo. Bldg. Congress (dir. 1978-79), Nat. Trust Hist. Preservation, Chgo. Assn. Commerce and Industry, Greater North Michigan Ave. Assn., Art Inst. Chgo., Field Mus. Nat. History. Clubs: Tavern, Carlton, Economic, Lake Zurich. Office: 845 N Michigan Ave Chicago IL 60611

HACKLEY, (MARY) SUSAN, insurance company executive; b. Decatur, Ill., May 14, 1949; d. Robert B. and Alice Virginia (Davern) Coble; m. Gary D. Hackley, July 19, 1975; 1 child, Adam. AB, U. Calif., Riverside, 1971; postgrad., Golden Gate U., 1981-83. Claims examiner, asst. claims mgr. State Compensation Ins. Fund, San Francisco, 1971-79; workers' compensation mgr. Transamerica Corp., San Francisco, 1979-83; v.p. claims mgmt. services Fred. S. James & Co., Chgo., 1983-85, sr. v.p. CMS, 1986—; bd. dirs. Workers' Compensation Research Inst., Boston. Mem. Nat. Council Self-Insurers, Calif. Self-Insurers Assn., MENSA. Avocations: computers, reading, writing, nature.

HACKMAN, HELEN ANNA HENRIETTE, home economist; b. New Melle, Mo., Oct. 8, 1908; d. John Henry and Lydia Eliza (Meier) Hackman; A.B., Central Wesleyan Coll., Warrenton, Mo., 1929; B.S., U. Mo., 1942, postgrad., 1942; postgrad. U. Wis., 1934, U. Colo., 1953, 75, U. Ariz., 1975, 77. Prin., Wright City High Sch., 1929; home econs. tchr., Cape Girardeau, Mo., 1930-42; sr. extension adviser home econs. U. Ill., Pittsfield, 1942-78; sec. Pike County Health and Social Services Coordinating Com. Dietitian, buyer Oshkosh Wis. Camp Fire Girls Camp, summers 1935, 36, 37; sec.-treas. Western Ill. 4-H Camp Assn., 1952-54; mem. Western Ill. Fair Bd. Com., Griggsville, 1946—; v.p. Tri-county Assn. for Crippled, 1960—; tech. cons. White House Conf., 1960, 70; pres. Pike County Heart Assn., 1969, organizer Family Planning Centers, Diabetic and Blood Pressure Clinics, Pike County Health Dept., 1971; sec. Illini Hosp. Aux., 1978; Bd. dirs. Pike County Mental Health. Recipient Distinguished Service award Nat. Home Demonstration Agts. Assn., 1952; Meritorious Service award Heart Assn., 1960, 61. Mem. Ill. Home Advisers Assn. (sec. 1948), Nat. Assn. Extension Home Economists (3d v.p. 1951-53, pub. relations chmn. 1951-53), Am. Home Econs. Assn. (sec. Ill. nutrition com. 1967-69), Pittsfield Hist. Soc. Epsilon Sigma Phi (chief 1962), Gamma Sigma Delta. Clubs: Pittsfield Woman's (pres. 1979, 80, 81, 82), Pike County Bus. and Profl. (pres. 1970-71). Home: 230 S Illinois St Pittsfield IL 62363 Office: Hwy 36 and 54th St E Po Box 227 Pittsfield IL 62363

HACKNEY, HOWARD SMITH, county official; b. Clinton County, Ohio, May 20, 1910; s. Volcah Mann and Gusta Anna (Smith) H.; B.S. cum laude, Wilmington Coll., 1932; m. Lucille Morrow, June 28, 1933; children—Albert Morrow, Roderick Allen, Katherine Ann Becker. Farmer, Wilmington, Ohio; farm reporter Agrl. Adjustment Adminstrn., Wilmington, 1934-40, committeeman, 1940-52, office mgr., 1952—, county exec. dir. Agrl. Stblzn. and Conservation Service, 1961—. Treas., dir. Clinton County Community Action Council; treas. Clinton County Council Chs.; trustee mem. agrl. adv. com. Wilmington Coll.; trustee Clinton County Hist. Soc. Named to Ohio State Fair Hall of Fame, 1983, Swine Hall of Fame, 1986. Mem. Nat. Assn. Stblzn. and Conservation Service Office Employees (awards 1970, state, regional legis. cons.), AAAS, Soil Conservation Soc. Am., Farmers Union, Ohio Duroc Breeders Assn. (pres., dir.), Ohio Acad. Sci., Ohio Acad. History, Ohio Hist. Soc., Grange, Ohio Southdown Breeders Assn., Clinton County Farm Bur. (sec., dir.), Clinton County Agrl. Soc. (treas., dir., award 1975), Clinton County Lamb and Fleece Improvement Assn. (dir.), Clinton County Hist. Soc. Republican. Quaker. Lodge: Masons. Home: 2003 Inwood Rd Wilmington OH 45177 Office: 24 Randolph St PO Box 509 Wilmington OH 45177

HACKWORTH, JOHN DENNIS, fund raising, development executive; b. St. Louis, Nov. 9, 1937; s. JOhn Thomas and Pansy Beth (Cole) H.; m. Jeanne Opal Farris, Dec. 26, 1964; children: John Thomas, Jeana Denise. BA, William Jewell Coll., 1959; MA, U. Kans., 1962; MDiv, Midwestern Baptist Sem., 1966; cert., Coll. for Fin. Planning, 1979. Pastor U. Baptist Ch., Wichita, Kans., 1968-69; assoc. prof. Southwest Baptist U., Bolivar, Mo., 1969-73; life underwriter N.Y. Life Ins. Co., Kansas City, 1973-77; assoc. dir. devel. William Jewell Coll., Liberty, Mo., 1977-81; stockbroker Stifel, Nicolaus & Co., Liberty, 1981-85; area dir. Christian Broadcasting Network, Virginia Beach, Va., 1985-87, sr. fin. planning specialist, 1987—. pres. Liberty High Sch. PTA, 1983; campaign mgr. John Ashcroft for Congress, Polk County, Mo., 1972. Mem. Internat. Assn. Fin. Planners (bd. dirs. Kansas City, 1980). Republican. Baptist. Avocations: reading, jogging, church activities. Home and Office: 818 Park Ln Liberty MO 64068

HACKWORTHY, DAVID CHARLES, investment company executive; b. Milw., Aug. 26, 1938; s. Alan Charles and Theresa (Umhoefer) H.; m. Patricia Ann Kelly, May 13, 1961; children—David, Michael, Anne, Jennifer, James. B.A. in Econs., Lawrence U., 1960; postgrad. U. Wis., 1961-62. Security analyst First Nat. Bank, Mpls., 1961-65; with Robert W. Baird and Co., Madison, Wis., 1965—, resident mgr., 1980—, 1st v.p., 1980—, also bd. dirs.; bd. dirs. Randall Bank, Univ. Book Store, chmn., 1987—. Mem. fin. com. Madison Art Center, 1977—, bd. dirs., 1977-80, chmn., 1979-80; v.p. athletic assn. Edgewood High Sch. (Wis.), 1968-72, pres., 1972-75, 84-85, mem. adv. bd., 1972-82. Served with USCG, 1961-66. Republican. Roman Catholic. Mem. Lawrence U. Alumni Assn. (pres. 1981-83). Clubs: Madison (bd. dirs. 77), Nakoma. Lodge: Rotary.

HADAS, JULIA ANN, social services adminstrator; b. Rome, Ga., May 23, 1947; d. Robert Franklin and Myrtle Julia (Patrick) Richmond; m. John R. Hadas, Apr. 22, 1967 (div.); children: Kevin, Brian. BS magna cum laude, No. Mich. U., 1972, MA, 1977. Cert. social worker. Placement worker adult community Mich. Dept. Social Services, Marquette, 1976-80, supr. vol. services, 1980-86, supr. children services, 1986—. Chairperson Parent Adv. Council Marquette Area Pub. Schs., 1984-85; adv. bd. Student Vol. Orgn. No. Mich. U., 1984-85; sec., personnel com. Women's Ctr. Named Outstanding Young Woman Am., 1982. Mem. Assn. Retarded Citizens, Childbirth Edn. Assn. (pres. 1975-76), Mich. Assn. Vol. Adminstrs. Episcopalian. Club: Zonta (pres. 1982-83) (Marquette). Avocations: reading, travel, interior decorating.

HADIPRIONO, FABIAN CHRISTY, engineering educator, researcher; b. Cirebon, Java, Indonesia, Oct. 6, 1947; came to U.S., 1976; s. Robertus Sudarjo and Wertriani (Yoyoh) H. BCE, MCE, Parahyangan U., 1973; MS, U. Calif., Berkeley, 1978, M of Engring., 1980, DEng, 1982. Registered profl. engr., Ohio. Project engr. various design and constrn. cos., SE Asia, 1965-75; project mgr. Phoenix Inc., Jakarta, Indonesia, 1974-75; engr., asst. bd. dirs. Mahkota Group, Indonesia, 1975-77; instr., teaching assoc. U. Calif., Berkeley, 1981-82; asst. prof. civil and constrn. engring. and mgmt. Ohio State U., Columbus, 1982—; Tech. cons. Carlile Patchen Murphy and Allison, Ohio, 1984; advisor Chandra and Assocs. Inc., Indonesia, 1984—; lectr. in field. Contbr. articles to profl. jours. Recipient Dale Carnegie Human Relation award, 1976; Ohio State U. grantee, 1985, 1986, U.S. Army C.E. grantee, 1986; USAF fellow and grantee 1986; Newhouse Found. fellow U. Calif., Berkeley, 1978, Harry H. Hilp fellow U. Calif., Berkeley, 1981, Robert B. Rothchild Jr. fellow U. Calif., Berkeley, 1982. Mem. ASCE, NSPE, ASME, Internat. Assn. Bridge and Structural Engring., Am. Concrete Inst., Archtl. and Engring. Performance Info. Ctr. (research adv. com. 1984), Associated Sch. Constrn. (research adv. com. 1986). Roman Catholic. Avocations: nature, cultural arts, classical music, tennis. Home and Office: Ohio State U 2070 Neil Ave Columbus OH 43210

HADJI, SERGE BASIL, lawyer; b. Salonica, Greece, Sept. 25, 1942; came to U.S., 1961; s. Basil Hadji-Mihaloglou and Katherine Hadji-Toliou; m. Yanna Mariolopoulou, Oct. 29, 1976; children: Alexios, Philip, Andreas. BA, U. Buffalo, 1965; JD, Detroit Coll. Law, 1968; LLM in Internat. Law, NYU, 1970. Bar: Mich. 1968, N.Y. 1970, U.S. Supreme Ct. 1974, Ohio 1980. Assoc. Rogers, Hoge & Hills, N.Y.C., 1970-78; trademark counsel TRW Inc., Cleve., 1978-82, sr. counsel, 1982—; adj. asst. prof. law NYU, 1974-78; vis. prof. Temple U., Athens, Greece, 1981. Trustee Anatolia Coll., Thessaloniki, Greece. Mem. Am. Soc. Internat. Law, Assn. of Bar of City of N.Y., U.S. Trademark Assn., Licensing Execs. Soc., Hellenic U. Grads. Assn. (trustee, counsel). Home: 22149 Westchester Rd Shaker Heights OH 44122 Office: TRW Inc 1900 Richmond Rd Cleveland OH 44124

HADWIGER, KENNETH EUGENE, communication educator; b. Alva, Okla., July 18, 1936; s. Claude Lester and Edith Dorothy (Hamann) H.; children: Michael Eugene, Mark Andrew. BA, Okla. State U., 1958; MA, State U. Iowa, 1959; PhD, Okla. U., 1964. Prof. Ea. Ill. U., Charleston, 1964—, dean arts & scis., 1972-76, dean grad. sch. research, 1976-83; cons. in communications, 1964—. exec. producer ednl. TV, 1977-78; contbr. articles to profl. jours. Commr. Airport Authority, county govts., Ill., 1985—. Mem. Speech Communication Assn. (commr. internat. communication 1980-84), World Communication Assn., Internat. Communication Assn., Ill. Communication Assn., Cen. Communication Assn., Aircraft Owners and Pilots Assn. Roman Catholic. Clubs: Kaskaskia Yacht (Shelbyville, Ill.)(commodore); Charleston Country. Avocations: computers, video productions, real estate. Home: 523 Coolidge Charleston IL 61920 Office: Eastern Ill U 231 B Coleman Charleston IL 61920

HAEBERLE, WARREN KEITH, electronics company executive; b. Milw., Jan. 13, 1956; s. Warren Clarence and Audrey Angeline (Eberle) H.; m. Bernadette Angeline DeMuri, June 28, 1980; 1 child, Michael Warren. B in Biomed. Engring., Marquette U., 1978; MBA, U. Wis., Milw., 1981. Systems analyst A.O. Smith Data Systems, Brown Dees, Wis., 1979-82; pres. Electronic Service Specialists, Menomonee Falls, Wis., 1982-86, Electronic Service Specialists/Bell Atlantic, Phila., 1986—. Mem. IEEE, Assn. Field Service Mgrs., Nat. Computer Service Network. Avocations: racquet ball, jogging, swimming. Home: 14705 W Juneau Blvd Elm Grove WI 53122

HAEBERLE, WILLIAM LEROY, business educator, entrepreneur; b. Marion County, Ind., May 19, 1922; s. Louis Leroy and Marjorie Ellen (Jared) H.; B.S., Ind. U., 1943, M.B.A., 1947, D.B.A., 1952; m. Yvonne Carlton, June 17, 1947; children—Patricia, William C., David C. Faculty, Ind. U., Bloomington, 1946—, prof. mgmt., 1963—; chmn. bd. Gen. Ill. Investment Corp., 1949—, Century Petroleum Corp., 1957—; New Bus. Design, Inc., 1984—; dir. Innovest Group, Inc., Transactions Verifications Systems, Inc. ; pres., dir. Nat. Entrepreneurship Found., 1982—; dir. Ind. Inst. for New Bus. Ventures, Inc., 1983—. Served to capt. U.S. Army, 1943-46; lt. col. USAFR, 1947-82. Mem. Air Force Assn., Res. Officers Assn., Am. Legion, VFW, Sigma Alpha Epsilon. Club: Metropolitan (N.Y.C.). Home: 1213 S High St Bloomington IN 47401 Office: PO Box 5521 Bloomington IN 47402

HAEGER, PHYLLIS MARIANNA, association management company executive; b. Chgo., May 20, 1928; d. Milton O. and Ethel M. B.A., Lawrence U., 1950; M.A., Northwestern U., 1952. Midwest editor TIDE mag., 1952-55; exec. v.p. Smith, Bucklin & Assos., Inc., Chgo., 1955-78; pres. P.M. Haeger & Assos., Inc., Chgo., 1978—. Mem. Am. Soc. Assn. Execs., Chgo. Soc. Assn. Execs., Inst. Assn. Mgmt. Cos., Nat. Assn. Women Bus. Owners, Com. of 200, Chgo. Network, Nat. Assn. Bank Women (exec. v.p.).

HAEMMERLE, JAMES HENRY, orthopedic surgeon; b. Jersey City, Feb. 22, 1947; s. Herman Joseph and Rose Ida (Urscheler) H.; m. Deanna Gail Berry, Dec. 19, 1970; children: Karin, Marcus. BS in Chemistry magna cum laude, Boston Coll., 1968; MD, U. Minn., 1973, MS in Orthopedics, 1978. Resident in orthopedics Mayo Grad. Sch. Medicine, Rochester, Minn., 1978; orthopedic surgeon Red Cedar Clinic, Menomonie, Wis., 1978—; bd. trustees Myrtle Werth Med. Ctr., Menomonie, 1986—; med. dir. Menomonie Ambulance Service, 1986-87. Fellow Am. Acad. Orthopedic Surgeons; mem. Minn. Med. Soc. Roman Catholic. Office: Red Cedar Clinic 2211 Stout Rd Menomonie WI 54751

HAEMMERLE, JOHN MARTIN, nursing home and retirement housing executive; b. Columbus, Ohio, Dec. 6, 1942; s. Carl H. and Mary E. (Langen) H.; m. Diane K. Horstman, Apr. 30, 1966; children—J. Michael, Jill, Jodi, Jeffrey. B.S., U. Dayton, 1965; M.B.A., Ohio State U., 1966. C.P.A., Ohio. Audit supr. Peat Marwick Mitchell, Columbus, 1966-70; ptnr. Haemmerle, Heximor & Harvey, C.P.A.s, Columbus, 1970-78; exec. v.p., chief fin. officer Americare Corp., Columbus, 1978-84, vice chmn., 1984-85; chmn. bd. pres. Liberty Village Sr. Communities, Inc., Dublin, Ohio, 1985—; ptnr. Health Trust Ptnrs., 1985—. Treas., Franklin County for Ronald Reagan, 1980; pres. parish council St. Peter's Roman Catholic Ch., 1983; bd. trustees Columbus Diocese Found. Served with USAR, 1966-72. Mem. Am. Inst. C.P.A.s, Ohio Soc. C.P.A.s, Fin. Execs. Inst. Republican. Clubs: Country of Muirfield Village, Columbus Athletic, Capital. Office: Liberty Village Sr Communities 2867 Cranston Dr Dublin OH 43017

HAENICKE, DIETHER HANS, university president; b. Hagen, Germany, May 19, 1935; came to U.S., 1963, naturalized, 1972; s. Erwin Otto and Helen (Wildfang) H.; m. Carol Ann Colditz, Sept. 29, 1962; children: Jennifer Ruth, Kurt Robert. Student, U. Gottingen, 1955-56, U. Marburg, 1957-59; Ph.D. magna cum laude in German Lit. and Philology, U. Munich, 1962; DHL (hon.), Cen. Mich. U., 1986. Asst. prof. Wayne State U., Detroit, 1963-68; assoc. prof. Wayne State U., 1968-72, prof. German, 1972-78, resident dir. Jr. Year in Freiburg (Ger.), 1965-66, 69-70, dir. Jr. Year Abroad programs, 1970-75, chmn. dept. Romance and Germanic langs. and lits., 1971-72, assoc. dean Coll. Liberal Arts, 1972-75, provost, 1975-77, v.p., provost, 1977-78; dean Coll. Humanities Ohio State U., 1978-82, v.p. acad. affairs, provost, 1982-85; pres. Western Mich. U., Kalamazoo, 1985—; asst. prof. Colby Coll. Summer Sch. of Langs., 1964-65; lectr. Internationale Ferienkurse, U. Freiburg, summers 1961, 66, 67. Author: (with Horst S. Daemmrich) The Challenge of German Literature, 1971, Untersuchungen zum Versepos des 20. Jahrhunderts, 1962; editor: Liebesgeschichte der schonen Magelone, 1969, Der blonde Eckbert und andere Novellen, 1969, Franz Sternbalds Wanderungen, 1970; contbr. articles to acad. and lit. jours. Fulbright scholar, 1963-65. Mem. Modern Lang. Assn. Am., AAUP, Am. Assn. Tchrs. of German, Mich. Acad. Arts and Scis., Internationale Vereinigung fur Germanische Sprach-und Literaturwissenschaft, Hoelderlin Gesellschaft, Phi Beta Kappa. Office: Western Michigan Univ Office of the President Kalamazoo MI 49008-3899

HAESSLER, JOHN F., insurance company executive; b. Fremont, Nebr., Mar. 25, 1936; s. H.P. and Florence (Dunigan) H.; m. Nancy Lee Allen, Aug. 1, 1959; children: Linda, Michele, Marty. BS, U. Nebr., 1957, JD, 1960. Assoc. Cassem, Tierney, Adams & Henatsch, Omaha, 1960-62; pres., chief exec. officer Woodmen Accident and Life Co., Lincoln, Nebr., 1962—, also bd. dirs.; bd. dirs. Comml. Mut. Soc., Lincoln, 1977—, 1985—, Firstier Bank Lincoln N.A. Bd. dirs. U. Nebr. Found., Lincoln, 1985—; bd. trustee, Nebr.-Wesleyan U., 1985—; vice chmn. United Way of Lincoln, 1985—; chmn. United Way of Lincoln, 1987. Mem. Order of Coif, Lincoln Bar Assn. (bd. trustees 1973-81, pres. 1980-81), Nebr. Bar Assn., Health Ins. Assn. Am., (bd. dirs.), Phi Beta Kappa. Democrat. Lutheran. Avocations: sports, reading. Home: 6400 Rogers Circle Lincoln NE 68506 Office: Woodmen Accident and Life Co 1526 K Lincoln NE 68508

HAFER, MARILYN DURHAM, psychologist, consultant; b. Guthrie, Okla., Feb. 10, 1924; d. Walker Phillip and Elizabeth (Gooch) Durham; m. E.M. Hafer, July 4, 1943 (div. July 1955). BA in Psychology, Tex. Women's U., 1966; PhD in Psychology, Tex. Tech. U., 1971. Registered psychologist, Ill. Asst. prof. psychology Ill. Inst. Technology, Chgo., 1971-77; asst. prof. adminstrv. studies ctr. DePaul U., Chgo., 1977-78; psychologist U.S. Office Personnel Mgmt., Chgo., 1977-79; assoc. prof. rehab. inst. So. Ill. U., Carbondale, Ill., 1979-86; prof. emeritus So. Ill. U., Carbondale, 1986—; cons. in field, Carbondale, Commn. on Rehab. Counselor Cert., Chgo., 1981-83; tech. reviewer and panelist, U.S. Dept. Edn., Washington, 1985. Cons. editor Jour. Rehab. Adminstrn., 1981—; mem. editorial bd. Rehab. Counseling Bulletin, 1983—; contbr. articles to profl. jours. NSF fellow, 1966-70. Mem. Am. Psychol. Assn., Nat. Rehab. Assn., Nat. Rehab. Adminstrn. Assn., Southwest Psychol. Assn. (Cert. Scholarly Attainments In Psychology 1977), Psi Chi. Home and Office: 2021 A Woodriver Dr Carbondale IL 62901

HAFFEY, MARYANN SINGER, management systems analyst; b. Highland Park, Mich., Nov. 7, 1955; d. Raymond Leon Singer and Mary Margaret (Pane) S.; 1 child, Erin Leigh. BS in Bus., Am. Tech. U., 1982, MS in Mgmt. Info. Systems, 1985. Computer programmer U.S. Army Civil Service, Killeen, Tex., 1980-82, computer programmer, systems analyst, 1982-84, fin. computer info. specialist, 1984-85; mgmt. systems analyst U.S. Army Mgmt. Engring. Tng. Activity, Rock Island, Ill., 1985—; cons. U.S. Army Material Command, Alexandria, Va., 1985—. Developer Army Info. Mgmt. course, 1986. Mem. Am. Soc. Military Comptrollers, Data Processing Mgmt. Assn. Republican. Lodge: Rotary. Avocations: music, traveling, teaching college computer courses. Office: US Army Mgmt Engring Tng Activity Bldg 90 Rock Island Arsenal IL 61299

HAFFNER, CHARLES CHRISTIAN, III, printing company executive; b. Chgo., May 27, 1928; s. Charles Christian and Clarissa (Donnelley) H.; m. Anne P. Clark, June 19, 1970. B.A., Yale U., 1950. With R.R. Donnelley & Sons Co., Chgo., 1951—; treas. R.R. Donnelley & Sons Co., 1962-68, v.p. and treas., 1968-83, vice-chmn. and treas., 1983-84, vice-chmn., 1984—, also dir.; chmn. bd. dirs. Lakeside Bank, 1970; dir. DuKane Corp., Protection Mut. Ins. Co. Chmn. Morton Arboretum; trustee Sprague Found., Art Inst. of Chgo., Newberry Library, Latin Sch., Chgo., 1978-84, Ill. Cancer Council, 1984—; bd. govs. Nature Conservancy., 1973-84, chmn. Ill. chpt., 1984-87; mem. Chgo. Plan Commn., 1986—. Served to 1st lt. USAF, 1952-54. Clubs: Chicago, Commercial, Commonwealth, Racquet, Caxton, Casino, Saddle and Cycle. Home: 1524 N Astor St Chicago IL 60610 Office: R R Donnelley & Sons Co 2223 S Martin Luther King Dr Chicago IL 60616

HAGBERG, CHARLES A., civil engineer; b. Ironton, Minn., Oct. 14, 1930; s. Harry A. and Esther A. (Gulberg) H.; m. Joan L. Seely, Oct. 21, 1950; children: Marta, Roxanne, Timothy, Wade, Blenda. BS in Civil Engring., N.D. State U., 1952; MS, U. Wis., 1974. Registered profl. engr. Minn., Wis., Mich., Fla. Civil engr. Hallett Constrn. Co., St. Peter, Minn., 1950-55, (civilian) Fifth Army, Savanna, Ill., 1955-57; chief engr. Zalk Josephs Co., Duluth, Minn., 1957-65; chief engr. Wis. Dept. Industry and Labor, Madison, 1965-67, adminstr. safety bldgs., 1967-73; pres. Hagberg & Assocs., Inc., Crosby, Minn., 1973—; cons. in field. Patentee in field. Sec. Gov.'s Task Force on Bldg. and Housing. Mem. Nat. Fire Protection Assn., Wis. Registration Bd. Architects, Engrs. and Land Surveyors, Nat. Conf. States on Bldg. Codes and Standards (chmn. standards and evaluation com. 1968), Wis. Soc. Profl. Engrs. (energy conservation com.). Republican. Mem. Assembly of God Ch. Avocations: private pilot, fishing, hunting, travel. Home and Office: PO Box 126 Crosby MN 56441

HAGE, ROGER ALAN, oil company executive, architect; b. Chgo., Aug. 12, 1942; s. Ralph and Irene Violet (MacCashin) H.; m. Penelope Joyce Beyerau, June 26, 1965; 1 child, Mary MacCashin. BArch, U. Ill., 1965. Registered architect, Ill., Wis., Colo., Tex., Okla. Project mgr. Perkins & Will, Chgo., 1967-71; mgr. archtl. service Standard Oil Co. (name now Amoco Corp.), Chgo., 1971-77; mgr. property ops. Amoco Corp., Chgo., 1977—. Planning commr. Bloomingdale (Ill.) Planning Commn.; mem. Chgo. Com. on High-Rise Bldgs., 1984—. Served to lt. USN, 1965-67. Mem. Bldg. Owners and Mgrs. Assn. Chgo. (bd. dirs. 1984—), Bldg. Owners & Mgrs. Assn. Internat., Nat. Fire Protection Assn. Club: Plaza (Chgo.). Avocations: sports, stamp collecting, woodworking, gardening. Office: Amoco Corp 200 E Randolph Dr Chicago IL 60601

HAGELIN, JOHN SAMUEL, theoretical physicist; b. Pitts., June 9, 1954; s. Carl William and Mary Lee (Stephenson) H.; m. Margaret Cowhig, Nov. 22, 1985. AB summa cum laude, Dartmouth Coll., 1975; MA, Harvard U., 1976, PhD, 1981. Scientific assoc. European Orgn. for Nuclear Research, Geneva, 1981-82; research assoc. Stanford (Calif.) Linear Accelerator Ctr., 1982-83; assoc. prof. physics Maharishi Internat. Univ., Fairfield, Iowa, 1983-84, prof. physics, dir. doctoral physics program, 1984—; mem. faculty Maharishi Internat. U., Fairfield, 1985—. Contbr. numerous articles to scientific jours. Tyndall fellow Harvard U., 1979-80. Mem. Iowa Acad. Scis. Avocation: research. Home and Office: Maharishi Internat U Fairfield IA 52556

HAGELY, JOHN RODGERS, architect; b. Chillicothe, Ohio, Dec. 21, 1929; s. John Elmer and Inez (Margraf) H.; m. Wilma Louise Johnson, Aug. 22, 1954; children: John Todd, James Eric, David Scott. BArch, Ohio State U., 1953; MArch, U. Ill., 1961. Registered architect, Ohio. Architect, designer Kellam & Foley, Architects, Columbus, Ohio, 1955-56; instr. architecture Ohio State U., Columbus, 1955-60; architect Sims, Cornelius, Schooley, Columbus, 1956-60; asst. prof. architecture U. Cin., 1961-62; sr. research architect Battelle, Columbus, 1962-86, mgr. facility planning, 1986—. Developed innovative housing concepts and research programs; Contbr. articles and tech. papers on housing and constrn. research to profl. jours.and Encyclopedia Brittanica. Tech. advisor Mayor's Energy Council, Columbus, Ohio, 1978; chmn. Residential Energy Task Force, 1978; advisor housing task force City of Columbus, 1984-85. Served to 1st lt. USAF, 1953-55. Mem. AIA (Columbus chpt.), Architects Soc. Ohio.. Republican. Methodist. Avocations: family and outdoor activities, photography. Home: 4100 Woodbridge Rd Columbus OH 43220 Office: Battelle Nat. Lab Columbus Div 505 King Ave Columbus OH 43201

HAGEN, NEIL BRUCE, oral and maxillofacial surgeon; b. Chgo., Oct. 26, 1951; s. Earl Bernard and Lola Marie (Belstner) H.; m. Diane Lynn Thomas, May 10, 1986. BS, No. Ill. U., 1973; DDS, Northwestern U., 1977, cert., 1981. Diplomate Am. Bd. Oral and Maxillofacial Surgeons. Practice dentistry specializing in oral and maxillofacial surgery Chgo., 1981—; instr. Northwestern U. Dental Sch., Chgo., 1981-83, asst. prof., 1983—. Fellow Am. Assn. Oral and Maxillofacial Surgeons, ADA. Avocation: sports. Home: 431 N Northwest Hwy Park Ridge IL 60068 Office: 251 E Chicago #1426 Chicago IL 60611

HAGEN, R. E., bank executive; b. 1933. BS, Morningside Coll., 1959; postgrad., U. Wis., 1968. With Security Nar. Bank, Sioux City, Iowa, 1957—, now pres., chief exec. officer. Served with AUS, 1953-55. Office: Security Nat Bank PO Box 147 Sioux City IA 51102 *

HAGENS, MITCHELL ALAN, engineer; b. El Paso, Tex., Aug. 8, 1957; s. Howard Glen and Jolene Ann (Lenz) H.; m. Betsy Lynn Beckman, Sept. 27, 1980; 1 child, Ross Walden. BS in Mech. Engring. with honors, U. Wis., 1979. Registered profl. engr., Wis. Engr. trainee Ohio Med., Madison, Wis., 1979-80; project engr. Arnold and O'Sheridan, Madison, 1980-84; mgr. mech. dept. Jaspal Engr. Services, Madison, 1984—. Mem. ASHRAE (assoc., vice chmn. local chpt.), Tau Beta Phi. Democrat. Methodist. Avocations: reading, running, music. Office: Jaspal Engring Services Inc 410 O'Onofrio Dr Madison WI 53719

HAGER, DOUGLAS EUGENE, healthcare executive; b. Charleston, W.Va., Apr. 2, 1947; s. Arnold Frederick and Thelma Grace (Boggs) H.; m. Linda Vogt, Aug. 22, 1981; children: Jennifer, Joshua. BBA, Ohio State U., 1969; MBA, U. Dayton, 1979. Dir. Ross Planning Assocs., Columbus, Ohio, 1976—. Author, lectr. on neonatal environments and perinatal trends. Councilman Village of Powell, Ohio, 1986-90. Served to 1st lt. U.S. Army,

1970-72. Home: 95 Woodland Dr Powell OH 43065 Office: Ross Labs 625 Cleveland Ave Columbus OH 43216

HAGER, JAMES CLAYTON, JR., marketing professional; b. Bluefield, W.Va., Dec. 8, 1938; s. James C. and Juanita (Smith) H.; m. Mary Ann Wolfe, July 1, 1961; children: Stephanie Lynn, James C. III. BSEE, U. Tenn., 1970. Project mgr. Accuray Inc., Columbus, Ohio, 1971-75; v.p. McFadden Sales, Inc., Columbus, 1976-82, owner, chief exec. officer, 1982—. Served with U.S. Army, 1961-64. Named Layman of Yr., Lane Ave. Bapt. Ch., Columbus, 1975. Republican. Avocations: reading, music, fishing, golfing. Home: 1829 N Devon Rd Columbus OH 43212 Office: McFadden Sales Inc 2939 Donnylane Blvd Columbus OH 43220

HAGER, KENNETH VINCENT, accountant; b. Kansas City, Mo., Jan. 8, 1951; s. George D. and Elaine H. (Boutross) H.; m. Marilyn Jean Ricono, June 28, 1975; children: Christina, Joseph. BS in Bus. Adminstrn. and Acctg., U. Kans., 1972. CPA, Mo., Kans. From mem. audit staff to mgr. Arthur Young, Kansas City, Mo., 1973-82; v.p. fin. Kreeuncy Control Products, Olathe, Kans., 1982; internal audit mgr. Puritan Bennett Corp., Overland Park, Kans., 1982-84; supr. EDP, audit Kansas City (Mo.) So. Ind., 1984-86, internal audit mgr., 1986—. Bd. dirs. Am. Cancer Soc., Kansas City, Mo., 1981—, chmn. pub. edn., 1984—. Mem. Am. Inst. CPA's, Inst. Internal Auditors. Roman Catholic. Avocations: baseball, golf, basketball. Home: 11916 Cherokee Ln Leawood KS 66209 Office: Kansas City So Ind 114 W 11th Kansas City MO 64105

HAGERSON, LAWRENCE JOHN, health agency executive, consultant; b. Lakewood, Ohio, Dec. 30, 1931; s. John Lawrence and Ruth Evelyn (Watson) H.; m. Shirley Lorraine Carter, July 2, 1955; children—Nancy Lynn, Tracy Ann, Laura Jane. B.S. in Econs., U. Pa., 1954, postgrad, in Economics, 1957-59. Cons. John Price Jones Co., N.Y.C., 1960-62, U.S Agy. for Internat. Devel. Southeast Asia, 1970-74; asst. to chancellor U. Calif., Santa Barbara, 1962-63, U. Mo., Kansas City, 1967-70; cons. Asia Found., Singapore, Malaysia, 1964-67; exec. v.p. Mid. Am. Health Edn. Consortium, Kansas City, 1970-78; dir. bus. and devel. Inst. Logopedics, Wichita, Kans., 1978—. Mem., officer Kans. City Civic Orchestra Bd., 1976-78; bd. dirs. Greater Kans. City Urban Coalition, 1969-70. Served to lt. USN, 1954-56. Mem. Nat. Soc. Fund Raising Execs. (nat. bd. dirs. 1984—). Republican. Presbyterian. Lodge: Kiwanis. Avocation: golf. Home: 7115 Chadowes Wichita KS 67206 Office: Inst Logopedics 2400 Jardine Dr Wichita KS 67219

HAGERTY, PAUL JAMES, school superintendent; b. Milw., July 25, 1939; s. Leo Daniel and Margaret (Malherbe) H.; m. Nancy Therese Stefanovic, Aug. 19, 1961; children: Kathleen, Daniel, Timothy, Patrick. BS, Marquette U., 1961, MEd, 1963, MS, 1967; PhD, Fla. State U., 1974. Tchr. Milw. Pub. Schs., 1961-67, 68-77; systems engr. Internat. Bus. Machines, Milw., 1967-68; supt. Bibb County Schs., Macon, Ga., 1977-81, Springfield (Mo.) Pub. Schs., 1981—. Chmn. United Way of Ozarks, Springfield, 1986; bd. dirs. Boy's Club, Springfield, 1986, Boy Scouts Am., Springfield, 1986, Jr. Achievement, Springfield, 1986. Mem. Am. Assn. Sch. Adminstrs., Vanderbilt Advanced Study Group, Phi Delta Kappa. Roman Catholic. Lodge: Rotary. Avocations: reading, traveling, jogging. Home: Rt 9 Box 506-D Springfield MO 65804 Office: Springfield Reorganized Sch Dist 12 940 N Jefferson Springfield MO 65802

HAGGARD, FORREST DELOSS, minister; b. Trumbull, Nebr., Apr. 21, 1925; s. Arthur McClellan and Grace (Hadley) H.; m. Eleanor V. Evans, June 13, 1946; children—Warren A., William D., James A., Katherine A. A.B., Phillips U., 1948; M.Div., 1953, D.D. (hon.), 1967; M.A., U. Mo., 1960. Ordained to ministry Christian Ch., 1948; minister Overland Park (Kans.) Christian Ch., 1953—; pres. Kansas City Area Ministers Assn., 1959, Kans. Christian Ministers Assn., 1960; mem. adminstrn. com., gen. bd. Christian Ch., 1968-72; pres. World Conv. Chs. of Christ (Christian/Disciples of Christ), 1975—; chmn. Grad. Sem. Council, Enid, Okla., 1970; pres. Nat. Evangelistic Assn., 1972. Author: The Clergy and the Craft, 1970, also articles. Pres. Johnson County (Kans.) Mental Health Assn., 1962-63; mem. council Boy Scouts Am., 1964-69; bd. dirs. Kans. Home for Aged, 1960-65, Kans. Children's Service League, 1964-69; pres. bd. dirs. Kans. Masonic Home, 1974-75; mem. bd. dirs. Kans. Masonic Found, 1970—; trustee Nat. Properties Christian Ch., 1987—. Club: Masons (grand master Kans. Chaplain Genl. Grand Chpt. Royal Arch Internat. 1975—). Home: 6816 W 78th Terr Overland Park KS 66204 Office: 7600 W 75th St Overland Park KS 66204

HAGGART, NICKIE SHOEMAKER, social worker; b. N.Y.C., May 16, 1942; d. Samuel Moor and Helen (Smith) Shoemaker; m. Samuel S. Rea., Dec. 28, 1963 (div. 1977); children: Bayard Dodge Rea, Benjamin Shoemaker Rea; m. Virgil J. Haggart Jr., Nov. 17, 1979; stepchildren: Laura, Virgil J. III, Cynthia. BA in Philosophy, Goucher Coll., 1965; MSW, U. Nebr., 1982. Gen. practice social work Creighton Psychiat. Assocs., Omaha, 1982-84, Family Enrichment, Omaha, 1984—; Chairperson Lic. Task Force for Legal Regulation of Social Work, 1982—. Mem. Nat. Assn. Social Workers (named Social Worker of Yr. Nebr. chpt. 1986), Am. Group Psychotherapy Assn., Acad. Cert. Social Workers (cert.). Democrat. Episcopalian. Avocations: bloodhounds, gardening, interior design, singing. Home: 8619 Woolworth Ave Omaha NE 68124 Office: Family Enrichment 5002 Dodge St Omaha NE 68132

HAGGE, JERRY WAYNE, electrical engineer; b. Paton, Iowa, May 8, 1940; s. Harry Detlef and Eliza Jane (Taylor) H.; m. Dora Marie Willits, June 9, 1962; children: Allan Keith, Kathryn Marie. BSEE, Iowa State U., 1962; postgrad., Kearney State Coll., 1986—. Registered profl. engr., Nebr. Relay engr. Nebr. Pub. Power Dist., Columbus, 1962-65, system protection supr., 1965-67, control engring. supr., 1968-76, protection and control engring. mgr., 1976—; organizer IA-NE System Protection Seminar, Omaha, 1977-80; chmn. Elec. Utility Engring. Edn. Adv. Bd., Lincoln, Nebr., 1979-83; mem. MAPP Subcom. on Elec. Effects, Mpls., 1978—, Southeast Community Coll. Adv. Bd., Seward, Nebr., 1976-83. Cable TV adv. bd. City of Columbus, Nebr., 1983-87; bd. dirs. Loup River Fed. Credit Union, Columbus, 1978-80. Mem. IEEE (tech. council power engring. soc. sec. 1986-87, power system communicatins com. chmn. 1983, 84, 86, Disting. Service award 1986, task force on orgn. and procedures chmn. 1984-86). Republican. Presbyterian. Avocations: genealogy, stamp collecting, bridge, golfing. Home: 2367 45th Ave Columbus NE 68601 Office: Nebr Pub Power Dist 1414 15th St Columbus NE 68601

HAGGLUND, CLARANCE EDWARD, lawyer, computer company executive; b. Omaha, Feb. 17, 1927; s. Clarence Andrew and Esther May (Kelle) H.; m. Dorothy S. Hagglund, Mar. 27, 1953; children—Laura, Bret, Katherine; m. Merle Patricia Hagglund, Oct. 28, 1972. B.A., U. S.D., 1949; J.D., William Mitchell Coll. Law, 1953. Bar: Minn. 1955, U.S. Ct. Appeals (8th cir.) 1974, U.S. Supreme Ct. 1963. Diplomate Am. Bd. Profl. Liability Attys. Ptnr. Hagglund & Johnson and predecessor firms, Mpls., 1973—; ptnr. Hagglund, Oskie, Priesz and Jefferson, to present; pres. Internat. Control Systems, Inc., Mpls., 1979—, Hill River Corp., Mpls., 1976—; gen. counsel Minn. Assn. Profl. Ins. Agts., Inc., Mpls., 1965-86. Contbr. articles to profl. jours. Served to lt. comdr. USNR, 1945-46, 50-69. Fellow Internat. Soc. Barristers; mem. Minn. Bar Assn., ABA, Lawyer Pilots Bar Assn., U.S. Maritime Law Assn. (proctor), Acad. Cert. Trial Lawyers Minn. (dean 1983-85), Nat. Bd. Trial Advocacy (cert. in civil trial law). Roman Catholic. Clubs: Ill. Athletic (Chgo.); Edina Country (Minn.); Calhoun Beach (Mpls.). Home: 3719 Xerxes Ave S Minneapolis MN 55410 Office: 4000 Olson Memorial Hwy Suite 501 Golden Valley MN 55422

HAGLE, RICHARD ALLEN, journal editor; b. Chgo., Oct. 29, 1946; s. Richard Vincent and Geraldine Antoinette (Peterson) H.; m. Patricia Ann Condon (div. Jan. 1987); children: Matthew, Mara, Jesse. BA in English, Elmhurst Coll., 1968. Dir., head acquisitions and mktg. devel. Crain Books, Chgo., 1980-83; exec. v.p. Commerce Communications, Chgo., 1983-85; sr. editor Longman Fin. Services Pubs., Chgo., 1985—. Contbr. articles to Sales Promotion Monitor, 1983-85.

HAGMAN, NORM A., orthopedic surgeon; b. Gary, Ind., June 19, 1933; s. Norm A. and Margaret (Bailey) H.; m. Patricia Ann Jeffries, Aug. 20, 1955; children: Lynn Patrice, Allison Ann. AB in Anatomy and Physiology, Ind. U., 1955; MD, Ind. U., Indpls., 1958. Intern Phila. Gen. Hosp., 1958-59; resident in orthopedic surgery Ind. U. Hosp., Indpls., 1959-63; orthopedic surgeon Rockford (Ill.) Orthopedic Assocs., Ltd., 1965—; asst. clin. prof. orthopedic surgery U. Ill., Rockford, 1971—. Advisor Comprehensive Health Planning Winnebago County, Ill., 1974-76; mem. Orgn. Council on Affordable Health Care, Rockford, 1983—. Served to capt. U.S. Army, 1963-65. Mem. AMA, Ill. State Med. Soc., Winnebago County Med. Soc. (pres. 1984-85), Am. Acad. Orthopedic Surgeons, Ill. Orthopedic Soc., Chgo. Orthopedic Soc., Phi Beta Kappa, Alpha Omega Alpha. Club: Rockford Country. Home: 5059 Crofton Dr Rockford IL 61111 Office: Rockford Orthopedic Assocs 5668 E State St Suite 1500 Rockford IL 61108

HAGQUIST, DONALD JOHN, infosystems specialist; b. Aitkin, Minn., Sept. 15, 1937; s. John H. and Anna M. (Bodine) H.; m. Jean Strong, Aug. 8, 1981; stepchildren: Lisa Strong, Trey Strong. BS Econs. and Stats., U. Minn., 1966. Edp analyst Bankers Life, Des Moines, 1970-74, sr. edp analyst, 1974-77, sr. systems analyst, 1977-78, asst. dir., 1978-86; dir. Prin. Fin. Group, Des Moines, 1986—. Served with U.S. Army NG, 1960-66. Fellow Life Office Mgmt. Assn., Data Processing Mgmt. Assn. (pres. 1980-81), Intercomm User Group (pres. 1981-84). Office: The Prin Fin Group 711 High St Des Moines IA 50131

HAGUE, RICHARD NORRIS, architect; b. Chgo., Aug. 4, 1934; s. Howard B. and Harriet (Jones) H.; m. Gail L. Elwell, Mar. 24, 1960; children—Jonathan Norris, Mark Richard. B.A. in Architecture, U. Ill., 1959. Prin., Richard N. Hague, River Forest, Ill., 1961-63; with Hague-Richards Assocs. Ltd., Chgo., 1964—, v.p., 1966-69, pres., dir., 1969—. Mem. Frank Lloyd Wright Home and Studio Adv. Bd., Oak Park, 1983. Mem. Nat. Council Archtl. Registration Bds., AIA (Fall-Out Shelter Design award 1964), Scarab, Alpha Rho Chi. Republican. Presbyterian. Clubs: Tavern, Arts (Chgo.); Oak Park Country. Home: 1310 William St River Forest IL 60305 Office: Hague-Richards Assocs Ltd 153 W Ohio St Chicago IL 60610

HAHLBECK, EDWIN CHARLES, manufacturing company executive; b. Milw., May 24, 1940; s. Edwin J. and Elizabeth (Toll) H.; m. Edith A. Klechowitz, Aug. 8, 1959; children: Elizabeth, Sara, Edwin J., Heidi. Assoc. in Engring., Milw. Tech. Coll., 1968. Registered profl. engr., Wis. Mgr. quality control Milw. Gear Co., 1965-70, dir. engring., 1970-76, v.p. engring., 1976—; v.p. engring Airborne Industries, Milw., 1985—. patentee in field. Mem. Soc. Automotive Engr., Soc. Mfg. Engr. (cert.), Am. Gear Mfg. Assn. Roman Catholic. Office: Milw Gear Co 5150 N Port Rd Milwaukee WI 53217

HAHN, BENJAMIN DANIEL, health care executive; b. Embden, N.D., Oct. 24, 1932; s. Benjamin D. and Laura E. (Martin) H.; m. Eleanor B. Anseth, June 8, 1957; children—Lezlie, Deann Bobette, Lara, Amy. Staff acct. Broeker Hendrickson, Fargo, N.D., 1961-63; asst. adminstrn., controller N.D. State Hosp., Jamestown, 1963-74; pres. the Neuropsychiat. Inst., Fargo, 1974—; faculty Jamestown Coll., part-time, 1963-74. Bd. dirs. Bethany Home, Fargo, 1975-81, S.E. Mental Health Center, 1975-81. Served with U.S. Army, 1954-56. C.P.A., N.D. Am. Coll. Hosp. Adminstrs. fellow, 1976. Mem. Am. Inst. C.P.A.s, Med. Group Mgmt. Assn. Lutheran. Clubs: Elks, Fargo Country. Home: 21 35th Ave NE Fargo ND 58102 also: 700 1st Ave Fargo ND 58102

HAHN, CARL HORST, auto company executive; b. July 1, 1926; m. Marisa Traina, 1960; 4 children. Chmn. bd. Continental GummiWerk AG, 1973-81; chmn. bd. Volkswagen AG, 1981—; chmn. supervisory bd. Gerling-Konzern Speziale Kreditversicherungs-AG, Cologne; dep. chmn. Supervisory bd. AG fur Industrie und Verkehrswesen, Frankfurt am Main, Gerling-Konzern Zentrale Vertriebs-AG, Cologne; mem. supervisory bd. Gerling-Konzern Allgemeine Versicherungs-AG, Cologne, Wilhelm Karmann GmbH, Norddeutsche Landesbank-Girozentrale, Hanover, Uniroyal Englebert Reifen GmbH, Aachen. Mem. Fed. Econs. Ministry (adv. com.), Salk Inst. (internat. adv. com. La Jolla, Calif. chpt.), Founders' Assn. German Sci. (bd. mgmt.), Deutsche Bank AG (group cons.). Address: Volkswagen AG, 3180 Wolfsburg Federal Republic of Germany *

HAHN, COLETTE CAMILLE, accountant; b. Chgo., Dec. 6, 1961; d. Nicholas George and Camille Lybia (Cerveny) H. BS, DePaul U., 1983, M in Acctg., 1984. CPA, Ill. Staff acct. Arthur Young and Co., Chgo., 1984-86; acctg. mgr. Audit Bur. of Circulations, Schaumburg, Ill., 1986—. Tchr. St. Julian Eymard Sch. Religious Edn., Elk Grove Village, Ill., 1984-85. Ledger and Quill scholar, 1979. Mem. Am. Inst. CPA's, Am. Woman's Soc. CPA's, Ill. Soc. CPA's, Chgo. Soc. Women CPA's, Theta Phi Alpha (treas. 1981-82, pres. 1982-83). Avocations: skiing, calligraphy, riding, sailing. Home: 1076 Stonehedge Dr Schaumburg IL 60194 Office: Audit Bur Circulations 900 N Meacham Schaumburg IL 60173

HAHN, DAVID BENNETT, hospital administrator, marketing professional; b. Louisville, Ohio, June 5, 1945; s. Bennett E. and Betty J. (McGaughey) H.; m. Elizabeth Burdine, Nov. 4, 1975; children: Stephen, Sarah, Scott. BS in Agrl. Econs., Ohio State U., 1967; MBA, U. Toledo, 1977. Social worker, supr. Franklin County Welfare, Columbus, Ohio, 1968-71, personnel asst., 1971-73; personnel dir. Mansfield (Ohio) Gen. Hosp., 1973-76; adminstr. Kettering Hosp., Loudonville, Ohio, 1978-81; asst. adminstr. Marietta (Ohio) Hosp., 1981—. Mem. Am. Coll. Health Care Execs., Ohio Hosp. Assn. Com., Am. Mktg. Assn., Ohio Hosp. Soc. for Planning and Mktg., Forum of Health Care Execs., Loudonville C. of C. (pres. bd. dirs. 1981), Pioneer Alumni Ohio State U. (bd. dirs., v.p.), Am. Mktg. Chpt. (local bd. dirs.). Republican. Mem. United Ch. Christ. Lodges: Rotary (bd. dirs. Loudonville 1978-81), Lions, Julliard, Shriners. Avocations: racquetball, reading, gardening, running. Office: Marietta Meml Hosp 401 Mathews Marietta OH 45750

HAHN, EDWARD LESTER, accountant, consultant; b. Reedsburg, Wis., Jan. 9, 1940; s. Lester Edward and Etta Arlene (Krueger) H.; m. Jacqueline Jean Schultz, May 13, 1961; children: Carrie, Suzanne, Mark. BS, Concordia U., 1961. CPA, Wis. Office mgr. Mittco, Inc., Milw., 1959-64; ptnr. Hill, Christensen and Co., Marshfield, Wis., 1964—; mem. adv. council Ins. Commr., Madison, Wis., 1982—; mem. legal, tax and acctg. com. Nat. Council of Farmer Coops., Washington, 1987—. Treas. mayoral candidate, Marshfield, 1981, Immanuel Luth. Ch., 1981—; mem. planning commn. City of Marshfield, 1982-86. Mem. Wis. Inst. CPA's (chmn. agr. com. 1982—), Wis. Inst. CPA's, Mich. Inst. CPA's, Minn. Inst. CPA's. Lodge: Elks, Optimists. Avocations: boating, hunting, fishing, water skiing, reading. Home: 909 W Upham St Marshfield WI 54449 Office: Hill Christensen and Co PO Box 428 Marshfield WI 54449

HAHN, FRED ERICK, advertising company executive; b. Würzburg, Fed. Republic Germany, Aug. 22, 1925; came to U.S., 1935, naturalized, 1945; s. Samson and Anna (Falk) H.; m. Alice Joan Hiraoka, Aug. 25, 1950; children: Frederick Mark, Lisa Cynthia. BA in Philosophy, Roosevelt U., 1951; MA in Comparative Lit., Columbia U., 1953. Advt. mgr. Kroch & Brentano Co., Chgo., 1953-63; dir. edn. info. Roosevelt U., Chgo., 1963-64, lectr. philosophy, 1963-67; advt. mgr. Rand McNally Corp., Chgo., 1965-67; v.p. Holtzman-Kain Advt. Co., Chgo., 1967-70; pres. Hahn, Crane & Assocs. Advt., Chgo., 1970—; instr. advt. Ill. Valley Community Coll., 1986—; cons. Open Ct. Publ. Co. Co-author: The Writer's Manual, 1977. Active Boy Scouts Am., 1969—. Served with AUS, 1945-46. Mem. Roosevelt U. Alumni Assn. (dir. 1970-73). Home: 2035 Hawthorne Ln Evanston IL 60201 Office: Hahn Crane Advt 1718 Sherman Ave Evanston IL 60201

HAHN, GERALD EUGENE, educator; b. Peoria, Ill., July 15, 1942; s. Earl L. and Clarice A. (Briggs) H. BS, U. Ill., 1965, MEd, 1968. Cert. indsl. edn. tchr., Ill. Tchr. Thornton Twp. High Sch., Harvey, Ill., 1965—, chmn. dept. indsl. edn., 1985—. Mem. Holy Name Soc. Queen of Apostles Parish, PTA (life). Mem. NEA, Ill. Edn. Assn., Internat. Tech. Edn. Assn., Kappa Delta Pi. Roman Catholic. Lodge: KC. Avocations: swimming, stained glass crafting, canoeing, travel, music. Home: 14261 Pennsylvania #11 Dolton IL 60419 Office: Thornton Twp High Sch 151st St and Broadway Harvey IL 60426

HAHN, NICHOLAS GEORGE, JR., controller; b. Berwyn, Ill., Sept. 20, 1960; s. Nicholas G. and Camille (Cerveny) H.; m. Paula Jean Coplea, May 31, 1986. BSC, DePaul U., Chgo., 1982. CPA, Ill. Sr. acct. Coopers and Lybrand, Chgo., 1982-85; controller Shatkin Trading Co., Chgo., 1985—; cost, budget mgr. First Options of Chgo., Inc., 1985—. Organizer St. Julian Youth Club, Elk Grove, Ill., 1985—, coach, capt. St. Julian Mens; Basketball Team, 1984—, mem. St. Julian Men's Softball, 1983-84. Recipient Bob Neu Meml. scholarship DePaul U. "D" club, 1976-82. Mem. Ill. Soc. CPA's (program com. 1984-85), Am. Inst. CPA's, Futures Industry Assn. (fin. credit com. 1985—), Blue Key (v.p. 1981), Delta Mu Delta. Republican. Roman Catholic. Avocations: basketball, skiing, tennis, audiophile, weight-lifting.

HAHN, RAYMOND CURTIS, dentist; b. Detroit, June 12, 1958; s. Edwin Earl and Lorraine Marie (Carney) Hahn. BS in Biochemistry, Oakland U., 1980; DDS, U. Detroit, 1984. Gen. dentist Warren (Mich.) Dental, 1984—; gen. practice dentistry Novi, Mich., 1987—. Mem. ADA, Acad. Gen. Dentistry, Mich. Dental Assn., Oakland U. Biol. Soc. Republican. Roman Catholic. Avocations: snow skiing, golf. Home: 27600 Gateway Dr E #D307 Farmington Hills MI 48018 Office: 24520 Meadowbrook Rd Novi MI 48050

HAHN, RICHARD WAYNE, hospital administrator; b. Phillipsburg, N.J., June 12, 1942; s. Albert L. and Irene S. (Nagy) H.; m. Anne Lenora Waugh, Apr. 12, 1969; children—Gregory, Susan. B.S., Trinity U., San Antonio, 1964; M.H.A., U. Minn., 1970. Asst. adminstr. United Hosps., Newark, 1969-73, Mont. Deaconess Hosp., Great Falls, 1973-76; adminstr. Syosset Hosp., N.Y., 1976-78; exec. dir. Dunn Meml. Hosp., Bedford, Ind., 1978—; clinic adminstr. Mont. Air N.G., 1973-76, N.Y. Air N.G., 1976-78, Ind. Air N.G., 1978—. Elder, 1st Presbyn. Ch., Bedford, since 1984—. Served to lt. col. USAFR, 1973—. Decorated Bronze Star. Mem. Am. Coll. Hosp. Adminstrs. Republican. Lodge: Rotary (Bedford). Avocations: hunting, fishing, outdoor activities. Home: 435 Ravine Dr Bedford IN 47421 Office: Dunn Meml Hosp 1600 23d St Bedford IN 47421

HAHN, WILLIAM FRANK, management and technical consultant, mechanical engineer, educator; b. Holyoke, Mass., Nov. 16, 1940; s. Frank J. and Phyllis C. (Smith) H.; m. Marilyn E. Kleiber, Aug. 4, 1962; children: Karla Lyn, Douglas William, Gregory William. BSME, Valparaiso U., 1962; MSME, U. Ill., 1964, PhD, 1969. Instr. Valparaiso U. (Ind.), 1964-66; sr. project engr. Corning Glass Works (N.Y.), 1969-75; prin. Booz Allen & Hamilton, Cleve., 1975-83; owner, pres. Mfg. and Tech. Assocs., Inc., Cleve., 1983—; faculty Gannon U. Coll. Sci. and Engring., Erie, Pa., 1986—. Mem. ASME, Soc. Mfg. Engrs., Robotics Internat., Illumination Engring. Soc. N.Am., Soc. Advancement Materials and Process Engring.

HAILE, GAIL ANNE, nurse; b. Providence; d. Ernest F. and Eleanor (Whittaker) Robillard; m. James S. Haile; 1 child, Cynthia Jane. Nursing Diploma, R.I. Hosp. Sch. Nursing, Providence, 1954; BA in Clin. Counseling Psychology, Stevens Coll., Columbia, Mo., 1983. Staff nurse R.I. Hosp., Providence, VA Hosp., Grand Island, Nebr.; dir. nursing Luth. Med. Ctr., Grand Island; ednl. cons. Bergan Mercy Hosp., Omaha, mgr. ednl. resources; adv. com. allied health Cen. Nebr. Tech. Coll., Hastings, 1974; chmn. profl. and pub. edn. com. Am. Cancer Soc., Grand Island, 1973-74. Cert. of Appreciation, Am. Cancer Soc., 1975; Caring Kind award Nebr. Hosp. Assn., 1978; Cert. of Appreciation, Am. Heart Assn., 1981-84. Mem. Am. Soc. Health Care Edn. and Tng. (chmn. Omaha conf. group Nebr. chpt. 1985, pres. 1986), Am. Soc. Tng. and Devel. Republican. Avocations: reading, golf, skiing. Home: 13963 Frederick Circle Omaha NE 68138 Office: Bergan Mercy Hosp 7500 Mercy Rd Omaha NE 68124

HAINES, GERRY P., optometrist; b. Unionville, Mo., July 13, 1940; s. Aaron W. and Lucille L. (Wells) H.; m. Janet M. Robb, Nov. 12, 1960; children—Beth A., Sheri L. A.A., Moline Community Coll., Ill., 1961; B.S., Ill. Coll. Optometry, Chgo., 1963, O.D., 1965. Optician Quad City Optical, Moline, Ill., 1957-61; pvt. practice optometry, Freeport, Ill., 1965—. Coauthor audio-cassette Wine Appreciation Course, 1984. Mem. Am. Optometric Assn., Ill. Optometric Assn., Soc. Wine Educators. Lodge: Kiwanis. Home: 1615 W Harrison St Freeport IL 61032 Office: 1000 Kiwanis Dr Freeport IL 61032

HAINES, MICHAEL CURTIS, lawyer; b. Batavia, N.Y., Feb. 8, 1949; s. Paul Robert and Dorothy Grace (Ludington) H.; m. Patricia Yvonne Van Dyken, May 22, 1982; children: Daniel Curtis, Mark Timothy. A.B., U. Mich., 1971, J.D., 1974. Bar: Mich. 1974, U.S. Dist. Ct. (we. dist.) Mich. 1974. Assoc., Mika, Meyers, Beckett & Jones, Grand Rapids, Mich., 1974-79, ptnr., 1980—; mem. securities law adv. com. Mich. Corp. and Securities Bur., Lansing, Mich., 1977-85; commr. City of Adrian Gas Rate Commn., Mich., 1983-84, 86; lectr. in field. Mem. Grand Rapids Bar Assn., State Bar Mich., ABA, Mich. Oil and Gas Assn. (chmn. legal and legis. com. 1977—), Order of Coif, Phi Beta Kappa. Republican. Mem. Reformed Ch. Am. Office: Mika Meyers Beckett & Jones 500 Frey Bldg Grand Rapids MI 49503

HAINES, MICHAEL ROBERT, economist, educator; b. Chgo., Nov. 19, 1944; s. James Joshua and Anne Marie (Welch) H.; m. Patricia Caroline Foster, Aug. 19, 1967 (div. Jan. 1986); children:James, Margaret. BA, Amherst Coll., 1967; MA, U. Pa., 1968, PhD, 1971. Asst. prof. econs. Cornell U., Ithaca, N.Y., 1972-79; vis. lectr. econs. U. Pa., Phila., 1979, research assoc. prof. Sch. Pub. and Urban Policy, 1979-80; assoc. prof. econs. Wayne State U., Detroit, 1980-86, prof., 1986—; cons. NIH, Bethesda, Md., 1980-84, The World Bank, Washington, 1983. Author: Economic-Demographic Interrelations in Developing Agricultural Regions, 1977; Fertility and Occupation, 1979. Contbr. articles to profl. jours. NIH grantee, 1974-77, 78-82. Mem. Internat. Union for Sci. Study Population, Econ. History Assn., Social Sci. History Assn. (bd. dirs. 1983-85, treas. 1985—), Am. Econ. Assn., Population Assn. Am., Am. Statis. Assn. Episcopalian. Avocations: numismatics, wine, book collecting. Office: Wayne State U Dept Econs Detroit MI 48202

HAINES, PERRY VANSANT, cattle company executive; b. Middletown, Ohio, Mar. 14, 1944; s. John Percy and Pendery (Spear) H.; m. Sidonie M. Sexton, 1982; 1 child, Pendery. A.B., Princeton U., 1967; M.B.A., Harvard U., 1970. Research asst. Harvard U., 1970-71; cons. Boston Cons. Group, 1971-74; exec. v.p. IBP, Inc. (formerly Iowa Beef Processors), Dakota City, Nebr., 1974—; dir. IBP, Inc., 1980—; v.p. Occidental Petroleum, Los Angeles, 1981—. Served with USMCR, 1967-68. Office: PO Box 515 Dakota City NE 68731

HAINES, STEPHEN JOHN, neurological surgeon; b. Burlington, Vt., Sept. 4, 1949; s. Gerald Leon and Frances Mary (Whitcomb) H.; m. Heather Lynn Halsted, Mar. 22, 1969; children: Christopher, Jeremy. AB, Dartmouth Coll., 1971; MD, U. Vermont, 1975. Diplomate Am. Bd. Neurological Surgery; diplomate Nat. Bd. Med. Examiners. Intern U. Minn., Mpls., 1975-76; neurol. surgery resident U. Pitts., 1976-81; asst. prof. neurosurgery U. Minn., Mpls., 1982-87, assoc. prof., 1987—, head. div. pediatric neurosurgery, 1985—; resident in neurol. surgery U. Pitts., 1976-81. Contbr. articles to profl. jour. Fellow ACS; mem. Am. Assn. Neurol. Surgeons (Van Wagenen fellow 1981), Congress Neurol. Surgeons, Soc. Clin. Trials. Office: U Minn Dept Neurosurgery 420 Delaware St SE Minneapolis MN 55455

HAINSFURTHER, WALTER JACOB, III, architect; b. Chgo., Oct. 17, 1954; s. Walter Jacob and Martha Ann (Felsenthal) H.; m. Betty Sue Golden, Oct. 9, 1983; 1 child, Sara Allison. BS Archtl. Studies, U. Ill., 1976; BArch, U. Ill., Chgo., 1978. Registered architect, Ill. Archtl. intern EnviroTechnics, Skokie, Ill., 1976-78, James March Goldberg, Lake Forest, Ill., 1978-79; architect Orville I. Kurtz & Assocs. Ltd., Des Plaines, Ill., 1979—. Bd. dirs. Jewish United Fund-Young Leadership Div., Chgo., 1985—, Jewish Children's Bur. Chgo., 1985—. Mem. AIA. Avocations: raquetball, softball, bicycling, reading, travel. Office: Orville I Kurtz & Assocs 2350 Devon Suite 111 Des Plaines IL 60018

HAISER, KARL FRANCIS, JR., accountant; b. Detroit, Dec. 5, 1942; s. Karl Francis Jahutskey and Mae Martha (Schram) H.; m. Linda Kay Clements, Nov. 18, 1967; children—Eric, Bryan, Justin. B.S., Ferris State Coll., 1965; M.B.A., Central Mich. U., 1967; diploma advanced acctg. Internat. Accts. Soc., 1973. C.P.A., Mich. Staff acct. Price Waterhouse & Co., C.P.A.s, 1966-71; asst. to controller Hygrade Food Products, Inc., Southfield, Mich., 1971-73; self-employed C.P.A., Grand Blanc, Mich., 1973—, mng. ptnr., 1987—; instr. Detroit Coll. Bus., 1983—; instr., advisor acctg. Mott Community Coll., 1983—. Twp. chmn. Planning Commn. and Bd. Appeals, 1974-76; cubmaster Boy Scouts Am.; founder Grand Blanc Jr. League Football. Served with USMC, 1967-69. Mem. Am. Inst. C.P.A.s, Mich. Assn. C.P.A.s., Pi Kappa Alpha. Republican. Lutheran. Home: 5186 Greenmeadows St Grand Blanc MI 48439 Office: 610 E Grand Blanc Rd Grand Blanc MI 48439

HAIST, KEITH LEROY, store owner; b. Pleasant Dale, Nebr., Feb. 6, 1923; s. Earnest Morton and Myrtle Bell (Dunten) H.; m. Norma Lee Woodward, July 25, 1948; children: Dean Woodward, Tim Arlin, Joy Louise. Student, U. Nebr.; cert. master watchmaker engr., Am. Acad. Sch. Horology, Denver, 1950. Watchmaker, jeweler Hilder Jewelers, York, Nebr., 1950, Sartor Jewelers, Lincoln, Nebr., 1951-53; owner Haist Jewelers, Mullen, Nebr., 1953-58, Arapahoe, Nebr., 1958-60, Hastings, Nebr., 1960—. Active in various Meth. Chs., Colo. and Nebr., Sunday sch. tchr., Meth. Youth Fellowship sponsor; 'foster father' to Am. Field Service Students; local fund raising chmn. Boys Scouts Am., 1954, com. mem. 1963. Served with U.S. Navy, 1943-46. Recipient Admiral in Nebr. Navy award Gov. Nebr., 1953. Mem. Nebr. Jewelers Assn., YMCA (local bd. dirs., Indian Guide leader, 1960-65), VFW, Am. Legion. Republican. Methodist. Club: Toastmasters (pres. 1964, 65). Lodges: Sertoma (pres. 1970, various awards), Masons. Avocation: rose gardening. Home: 2315 W 9th St Hastings NE 68901 Office: Haist Jewelers 219 N Lincoln Hastings NE 68901

HAJEK, ROBERT J., lawyer, real estate broker, commodity broker, nursing home owner; b. Berwyn, Ill., May 17, 1943; s. James J., Sr., and Rita C. (Kalka) H.; m. Maris Ann Enright, June 19, 1965; children—Maris Ann, Robert J., David, Mandie. B.A., Loras Coll., 1965; J.D., U. Ill., 1968. Bar: Ill. 1968, U.S. Tax Ct. 1970, U.S. dist. ct. (no. dist.) Ill. 1971, U.S. Ct. Appeals (7th cir.) 1972, U.S. Supreme Ct. 1972. Lic. real estate broker, Ill., Nat. Assn. Securities Dealers; registered U.S. Commodities Futures Trading Commn. ptnr. Hajek & Hajek, Berwyn, Ill., 1968-76; pres., bd. chmn. Hajek, Hajek, Koykar & Heytag, Ltd., Westchester, Ill., 1976-85; pres., chief exec. officer Land of Lincoln Ptnrs. Real Estate, Inc., Glendale Heights, Ill., 1985—; ptnr., owner Camelot Manor Nursing Home, Streator, Ill., 1978—, Ottawa Care Ctr., Ill., 1981—, Law Centre Bldg., Westchester, 1976—; owner Garfield Ridge Real Estate, Chgo., 1973-78, Centre Realty, Westchester, 1976-85; ptnr. Westbrook Commodities, Chgo., 1983; v.p., bd. mem., gen. counsel DeHart Gas and Oil Devel., Ltd., 1970-73; prin. Northeastern Okla. Oil and Gas Prodn. Venture, Tulsa, 1982—; exec. v.p., gen. counsel Garrett Plante Corp., 1978—, Ottawa Long Term Care, Inc., 1982—; bd. dirs. Land of Lincoln Savs. and Loan, 1981—, Home Title Services of Am., Inc., 1981—, Land of Lincoln Ins. Agy., Inc., 1982—, Medema Builders, Inc., 1983—, Land of Lincoln Ptnrs. Real Estate of Ill., Inc., 1984—, Land of Lincoln Ptnrs. Real Estate, Inc., 1984—, The Ill. Co., 1984—, Ill. Co. Properties, Inc., subs. of Ill. Co., 1984—, Ottawa Long Term Care, Inc., 1982—, Garrett Plante Corp., 1978—. Sr. boys' basketball coach Roselle Recreation Assn., Ill., 1981-83. Mem. ABA, Ill. Bar Assn., Nat. Assn. Realtors, Ill. Assn. Realtors, Northwest Suburban Bd. Realtors, Ill. Health Care Assn., Phi Alpha Delta. Republican. Roman Catholic. Clubs: Amateur Radio, No. Ill. DX Assn. Office: Land of Lincoln Ptnrs Inc 2081 Bloomingdale Rd Glendale Heights IL 60139

HAKES, WANDA FAYE, nursing educator; b. Narka, Kans., Apr. 14, 1930; d. John and Margaret Elizabeth (Holan) Chaloupka; m. Lester B. Hakes, Sept. 16, 1951; children—Anita Lytle, Frederick, Daniel, Carol Rohlfing. R.N., St. Elizabeth Hosp. Sch. Nursing, 1950. R.N., Nebr., Kans. Charge nurse St. Elizabeth Hosp., Lincoln, Nebr., 1950; staff nurse St. Joseph Hosp., Concordia, Kans., 1952-58, Gelvin-Haughey Clinic, Concordia, 1958-65; supr. Mennonite Hosp., Beatrice, Nebr., 1966-72; nursing instr. S.E. Community Coll., Beatrice, 1972—. Mem. Beatrice Community Hosp. Devel. Council, 1981—. Mem. Nat. Vocat. Assn., Nebr. Vocat. Assn., S.E. Nebr. League Nursing (sec.), Nat. League Nursing, S.E. Community Coll. Beatrice Campus Faculty Assn., League Nursing and Vocat. Assn. Clubs: Beatrice Bus. and Profl. Women's, Order Eastern Star.

HAKIM, ALI HUSSEIN, export company executive, consultant; b. Mushref, Lebanon, Aug. 13, 1943; came to U.S., 1973; s. Hussein A. and Sabah (Wazni) H.; m. Raafat M. Siklawi, July 2, 1972; children—Hussein, Ronny, Sameer, Mazen. B.S.B.A., Beirut U., 1970; postgrad. in acctg. Wayne State U., 1975; M.A. in Econs. and Politics, U. Detroit, 1980. Supr. Al-Mouharer Newspaper, Beirut, 1964-67; prin. Lebanese Soc. for Edn., Beirut, 1967-72; field services adviser Chrysler Corp., Detroit, 1973-75; owner, operator H & R Parking Co., Detroit, 1975-81; comptroller Met. Detroit Youth, 1979-82; pres. Hakim Export Import, Detroit, 1979-82, Hakim Export, Detroit, 1983—; pres. Gen. Bus. for Internat. Trade Corp., N.Y.C.; cons. to trading and investment agys., Africa, Middle East; budget cons. Met. Detroit Youth Found., 1983—. Research on U.S./China trade relations, 1980, U.S. monetary policy, 1981, internat. mktg., 1983. Mem. Republican Presdl. Task Force, 1982—. Mem. Am. Mgmt. Assn., Acctg. Aid Soc. Club: Senatorial (Washington).

HAKKINEN, RAIMO JAAKKO, aeronautical scientist; b. Helsinki, Feb. 26, 1926; came to U.S., 1949, naturalized, 1960; s. Jalmari and Lyyli (Mattila) H.; m. Pirkko Loyttyniemi, July 16, 1949; children—Bert, Mark. Diploma in aero. engring., Helsinki U. Tech., 1948; M.S., Calif. Inst. Tech., 1950, Ph.D. cum laude, 1954. Head tech. office Finnish Aero. Assn., Helsinki, 1948; instr. engring. Tampere Tech. Coll., Finland, 1949; design engr., aircraft div. Valmet Corp., Tampere, 1949; research asst. Calif. Inst. Tech., 1950-53; mem. research staff MIT, 1953-56; with Western div. McDonnell Douglas Astronautics Co., Santa Monica, Calif., 1956—, chief scientist phys. scis. dept., 1964-70; chief scientist flight scis. McDonnell Douglas Research Labs., St. Louis, 1970-82, dir. research, flight scis., 1982—; lectr. engring. UCLA, 1957-59; vis. assoc. prof. aeros. and astronautics MIT, 1963-64. Contbr. articles to profl. jours. Served with Finnish Air Force, 1944. Fellow AIAA (mem. fluid dynamics com. 1969-71, honors and awards com. 1975-83, tech. activities com. 1975-78, dir. at large 1977-79); mem. Am. Phys. Soc., Engring. Soc. in Finland, Cal. Inst. Tech. Alumni Assn., Am. Helicopter Soc. Inc., Sigma Xi. Home: 5 Old Colony Ln Saint Louis MO 63131 Office: PO Box 516 Saint Louis MO 63166

HALBEISEN, JOHN FRANCIS (JACK), industrial design consultant; b. Fremont, Ohio, Aug. 30, 1914; s. John Henry and Blanche Emma (Maillard) H.; m. Mary Louise Warnke, Jan. 14, 1939; children—John Francis Arthur, Eugene John, Mary Kay. Student, Toledo U., 1938-39, Cleve. Sch. Art, 1940-41, Wayne State U., 1943-45. Designer, Libbey Glass Co., Toledo, 1938-40, Gen. Motors, Detroit, 1940-45, Chrysler Corp., Highland Park, Mich., 1945-60; dir., design cons. Halbeisen Assocs., Dayton, 1960—. Patentee more than 90 devices in automotive technology. Holder 20 world records, Fedn. Aeronautique Internationale, Nat. Aeronautic Assn. as first man to fly east to west and west to east in an ultra-light aircraft. Mem. Am. Soc. Interior Designers (cons. designer, Design awards 1956, 58), Indsl. Designers Soc. Am. (cons.). Republican. Roman Catholic. Avocations: Flying; music; travel.

HALBERSTADT, KENNETH KEITH, ground support systems company executive; b. Champaign, Ill., Sept. 5, 1920; s. Harry B. and LaVerne Augusta (Moffett) H.; m. Hildred Marie Murphy, Aug. 27, 1966. Student U. Ill. Extension, 1939-41, Rock Island Arsenal, 1943, Ill. Inst. Tech., 1943. Engring. inspector U.S. Dept. War, Rockford, Ill., 1942-45; project engr. Barber Coleman Co., Rockford, 1945-64; with Modern Suspension Systems, Rockford, 1964-86, ret. 1986; pres., chief exec. officer Halberstadt & Assocs., 1987—. Sales and mktg. mgr. Assoc. elder First Presbyterian Ch., Rockford, 1975-79. Mem. Am. Inst. Indsl. Engrs. (sec. and 2d v.p. Winnebago chpt. 1981-83). Republican. Lodges: Shriners; Masons, Moose, K.T. (crusader comdr. 1986). Avocations: golf; hunting; fishing; bird watching. Home: 4932 Fenwick Close Rockford IL 61111 Office: Modern Suspension Systems Inc 333 18th Ave Rockford IL 61108

HALCOMB, F. JOSEPH, III, physician executive; b. Scottsville, Ky., Mar. 27, 1951; s. F. Joseph Jr. and Mariola (Shrewsbury) H.; m. Joan Marie Spears, June 1, 1974; children—Allison Archer, Alyssa Craig. B.S., U. Ky., 1974, M.D., 1978; M.S., MIT, 1980. Registered profl. engr., Ind.; diplomate Nat. Bd. Med. Examiners. Intern in internal medicine Albert B. Chandler Med. Ctr., Lexington, Ky., 1978-79; gen. practice medicine Halcomb and Oliver Clinic, Scottsville, 1979; postdoctoral research assoc. Mass. Gen. Hosp., Boston, 1979-80; assoc. med. dir. Zimmer, Inc. div. Bristol-Myers Corp., Warsaw, Ind., 1980-81, dir. new ventures, 1981-83, dir. new product devel., 1983-85, v.p. product devel., 1985—; adv. panel on orthopaedic and rehab. services FDA, 1985—; mem. Ky. Commn. on Alcohol and Drug Problems, 1974-75; mem. Contemporary Orthopaedics Surgeons Adv. Panel, 1983—. Contbr. sci. papers, articles to profl. publs. Patentee in field. Bd. dirs. Kosciusko Community YMCA, Warsaw, 1982—, Employee Fed. Credit Union, Warsaw, 1982-83. Mem. AMA (Physician Recognition award 1982, 85), Med. Alumni Assn., Am. Acad. Med. Dirs., Am. Acad. Family Physicians, Nat. Soc. Profl. Engrs., Ind. State Med. Assn., Ind. Acad. Family Physicians, Ind. Soc. Profl. Engrs., Kosciusko County Med. Soc., Bioelec. Repair and Growth Soc., Warsaw Area C. of C. (bd. dirs. 1986—), Sigma Alpha Epsilon (McChesney-Woodward Zeal award 1974), Mercedes-Benz Club Am. Presbyterian. Avocations: tennis; bicycling; photography; classic car restoration. Home: Route 7 Box 371-A Warsaw IN 46580 Office: Zimmer Inc PO Box 708 Warsaw IN 46580

HALDERMAN, GAIL LLEWELLYN, automotive executive; b. Tipp City, Ohio, June 14, 1932; d. Clyde Emerson and Ruth Emma (Eidemiller) H.; m. Barbara Jean Senter, Aug. 22, 1953; children: Kim, Karen, Kay, Carol. BA in Indsl. Design, Dayton (Ohio) Art Inst., 1954. Stylist various studios Ford Motor Co., Dearborn, Mich., 1954-55, design mgr. various studios, 1955-65, design exec., 1965-68, exec. dir., 1968-82, dir. car exterior design, 1982—; mem. nat. com. Corp. Designers Role in Industry, 1972, 73. Mem. Indsl. Design Soc. Am. (bd. dirs. 1956—, treas. 1969-70, chmn. 1971, 72), Dearborn Valley Home Owners Assn. (pres. 1974-76). Club: Dearborn Country. Avocations: golf, sailing, table tennis, pool. Home: 5795 Linden Dr Dearborn Heights MI 48127 Office: Ford Motor Co 21175 Oakwood Blvd Dearborn MI 48123

HALDERMAN, ROBERT RICHARD, farm management company executive, realtor; b. Wabash, Ind., Jan. 28, 1936; s. Howard H. and Marie E. (Zahm) H.; m. Janet Elizabeth Squires, June 26, 1960; children—F. Howard, Richard. B.S. in Agr., Purdue U., 1958. Cert. real estate broker, Ind., Mich., Ohio, Ill., Ky. Farmer, Wabash, Ind., 1952-58; area mgr. Halderman Farm Mgmt. Service, Inc., Wabash, 1958-60, area mgr., v.p., 1960-64, pres., 1964—; incorporator, dir. Frances Slocum Bank, Wabash, 1963—. Bd. dirs. United Fund of Wabash County, 1970; elder, trustee, deacon Presbyterian Ch., Wabash, 1958—. Served to capt. U.S. Army, 1959. Recipient Disting. Service award Wabash Jaycees, 1970. Mem. Ind. Soc. Farm Mgrs. and Rural Appraisers (v.p. 1966, pres. 1967), Big Bros., Northfield Athletic Booster Club (pres. 1983, 84, 85). Republican. Club: Wabash Country (bd. dirs. 1970). Lodge: Kiwanis (pres. 1965), Masons, Shriners. Avocations: golf; skiing; boating. Home: PO Box 297 Wabash IN 46992 Office: Halderman Farm Mgmt Service Inc PO Box 297 Wabash IN 46992

HALE, CAROL JEAN, civic association executive, city commissioner; b. Ann Arbor, Mich., July 2, 1942; d. Ward Karcher and Evelyn May (Gillson) Parr; m. Jan Raymond Hale, Aug. 21, 1964; children: David Dart, Matthew Joseph. BA in English and History, U. Mich., 1964, MA in Russian History, 1970. Cert. tchr., Mich. Tchr. Livonia (Mich.) Pub. Schs., 1965-69; civic worker Traverse City, Mich., 1970-85; exec. dir. Downtown Traverse City Assn., 1984-86; tchr.elem. schs. Traverse City, 1986—. Pres. Cen. Neighborhood Assn., Traverse City, 1976; sec. Grand Traverse Dept. Pub. Works, Traverse City, 1977—; mayor City of Traverse City, 1983-84; commr. City of Traverse City, 1977-85; mem. Downtown Devel. Authority, Traverse City, 1985—, Traverse City Planning Commn., 1986—. Recipient Dist. Service award Traverse City C. of C. Mem. Mich. Mcpl. League, LWV (local pres. 1975). Methodist. Lodges: Zonta (Woman of Yr. 1984), Eagles (Most Influential Community mem. 1984). Home: 439 6th Traverse City MI 49684 Office: PO Box 42 232 E Front Traverse City MI 49684

HALE, ROBERT MANSFORD, dentist; b. Bamberg, Fed. Republic Germany, Sept. 6, 1952; came to U.S., 1955; s. Sidney Isom Hale and Maria Kunigunda (Grieble) Zawicky; m. Linda Lou Walker, June 21, 1974; children: Tangie Marie, Kristie Lynn. BA, U. Mich., Flint, 1974; DDS, U. Mich., Ann Arbor, 1980. Gen. practice dentistry Davison, Mich., 1980—. Mem. ADA, Mich. Dental Assn., Genesee Dist. Dental Assn. Republican. Pentecostal. Lodge: Optimists. Avocations: sports, softball, bowling. Home: 9034 Creekview Grand Blanc MI 48439 Office: 7007 Davison Davison MI 48439

HALE, S. EUGENE, manufacturing company executive; b. St. Louis, Aug. 7, 1946; s. Everett Monroe and Thelma Louise (Smith) H.; m. Donna L. Abeln, May 26, 1973; children—Darren Eugene, Matthew Bernard. B.A. in Math., U. Mo., 1969. Programmer, Banquet Foods, St. Louis, 1969-72; sr. programmer Blackburn Co., St. Louis, 1972-74, supr. data processing, 1974-79, application systems mgr., 1979—. Mem. Assn. Systems Mgmt. Roman Catholic. Avocations: golf; reading.

HALE, SAMUEL WESLEY, JR., pastor; b. Chgo., Nov. 17, 1942; s. Samuel Wesley Sr. and Toledo Elizabeth (Dozier) H.; m. Gloria Marie Harris, Aug. 17, 1968; children: Samuel Wesley III, Lori Toledo, Jonathan Justin, Benjamin Prentiss. Student, U. Ill., 1960-61, Millikin U., 1961-62; BA, Am. Bapt. Theol. Sem., 1966; M of Div., So. Bapt. Theol. Sem., 1969. Ordained to ministry Bapt. Ch., 1965. Pastor Johenning Bapt. Ch., Washington, 1969-72; dir. religious activities Talladega (Ala.) Coll., 1972-73; dir. extension dept. Am. Bapt. Coll., Nashville, 1973-84; pastor Zion Missionary Bapt. Ch., Springfield, Ill., 1984—; bd. dirs. Christian Friends Ministries, Inc., Nashville; mem. adv. bd. Young Parent Support Services, Springfield, 1985. Composer religious songs. Bd. dirs. Greater Springfield Interfaith Assn., 1985; active Springfield Vicinity Misterial Alliance, 1984. Mem. Nat. Bapt. Congress of Christian Edn. (bd. dirs. 1971—), Contemporary Ministries Workshop (bd. dirs.). Democrat. Avocations: fishing, chess, badminton, basketball, softball. Office: Zion Missionary Bapt Ch 1601 E Laurel Springfield IL 62703

HALEY, GARY EUGENE, bank officer; b. Salem, Ind., Oct. 24, 1952; s. Isom T. and Thelma (Morris) H.; m. Victoria Louise Ford, July 1, 1978; children: Timothy, Gwendolen, Trevor, Alexander. BS, Ball State U., 1974, MA, 1979. Programmer analyst Gen. Telephone Electronics Data Services, Ft. Wayne, Ind., 1975-77; systems analyst Mchts. Nat. Bank, Indpls., 1977-78, Detroit Diesel Allison div. Gen. Motors Corp., Indpls., 1978-82; asst. v.p., sr. planning officer Am. Fletcher Nat. Bank, Indpls., 1982-84, v.p., mgr. strategic systems planning, 1984-87; sr. account mgr. Banc One Info. Services, Corp., Columbus, Ohio, 1987—. Mem. computer sci. adv. panel Ball State U., 1983—; mem. artificial intelligence com. Corp. for Sci. and Tech., Indpls., 1984—; lectr. Ind. U., Purdue U., Indpls., 1985—.

HALEY, JOHN DANIEL, civil engineer; b. Auburn, N.Y., Apr. 20, 1948; s. Amos William and Fern Evelyn (Anderson) H.; m. Joann Sexton, June 28, 1969; 1 child, John Daniel Jr. BSCE, U. Cin., 1975. Registered profl. engr., Ohio, Ky., Tex., Ga.; registered profl. surveyor, Ohio, Ky. Project engr. Lockwood, Jones & Beals, Dayton, Ohio, 1973-77, br. mgr., 1977-83, prin., 1983—; bd. dirs. Miami Valley Regional Transit Authority. Mem. curriculum com. Patterson Coop. High Sch., Downtown Dayton Assn., Dayton Devel. Council. Mem. Am. Congress on Surveying and Mapping, Profl. Land Surveyors of Ohio, Soc. for Mktg. Profl. Services, Nat. Assn. Indsl. and Office Parks, Urban Land Inst., NSPE. Republican. Club: Dayton Engrs. Lodge: Optimist. Home: 4801 Rushwood Circle Englewood OH 45322

HALEY, JOHNETTA RANDOLPH, musician, educator, university administrator; b. Alton, Ill., Mar. 19; d. John A. and Willye E. (Smith) Randolph; Mus.B. in Edn., Lincoln U., 1945; Mus.M., So. Ill. U., 1972; children—Karen, Michael. Vocal and gen. music tchr. Lincoln High Sch., E. St. Louis, Ill., 1945-48; vocal music tchr., choral dir. Turner Sch., Kirkwood, Mo., 1950-55; vocal and gen. music tchr. Nipher Jr. High Sch., Kirkwood, 1955-71; prof. music Sch. Fine Arts, So. Ill. U., Edwardsville, 1972—, dir. East St. Louis Campus, 1982—; adjudicator music festivals; area music cons. Ill. Office Edn., 1977-78; program specialist St. Louis Human Devel. Corp., 1968; interim exec. dir. St. Louis Council Black People, summer 1970. Bd. dirs. YWCA, 1975-80, Artist Presentation Soc., St. Louis, 1975, United Negro Coll. Fund, 1976-78; bd. curators Lincoln U., Jefferson City, Mo., 1974—, pres., 1978—; mem. Nat. Ministry on Urban Edn., Luth. Ch.-Mo. Synod, 1975-80; bd. dirs. Council Luth. Chs., Assn. of Governing Bds. of Univs. and Colls.; mem. adv. council Danforth Found. St. Louis Leadership Program, nat. chmn. Cleve. Job Corps, 1974-78; trustee Stillman Coll. Recipient Disting. Citizen award St. Louis Argus Newspaper, 1970; Cotillion de Leon award for Outstanding Community Service, 1977; Disting. Alumnae award Lincoln U., 1977; Disting. Service award United Negro Coll. Fund, 1979, SCLC, 1981; Community Service award St. Louis Drifters, 1979; Disting. Service to Arts award Sigma Gamma Rho, Fred L. McDowell award, 1986, Nat. Negro Musicians award, 1981, Sci. Awareness award, 1984-85, Tri Del Federated award, 1985, Bus. and Profl. Women's Club award, 1985-86, vol. yr. Inroad's Inc., 1986; named Duchess of Paducah, 1973; received Key to City, Gary, Ind., 1973. Mem. Council Luth. Chs., AAUP, Coll. Music Soc., Music Educators Nat. Conf., Ill. Music Educators Assn., Nat. Choral Dirs. Assn., Assn. Tchr. Educators, Midwest Kodaly Music Educators, Nat. Assn. Negro Musicians, Jack and Jill Inc., Friends of St. Louis Art Mus., The Links, Inc., Alpha Kappa Alpha, Mu Phi Epsilon, Pi Kappa Lambda. Lutheran. Clubs: Las Amigas Social. Home: 30 Plaza Sq Saint Louis MO 63103 Office: Box 20 B So Ill U Edwardsville IL 62026

HALIKAS, JAMES ANASTASIO, medical educator, psychiatrist; b. Bklyn., Nov. 26, 1941; s. Peter Simon and Olga Peter (Vavayanni) H.; B.S. (N.Y. State Regents scholar), Bklyn. Coll., 1962; M.D., Duke U., 1966; m. Anna May Van Der Meulen, Aug. 20, 1967; children—Peter Christopher, Anna Catherine. Intern, Barnes Hosp., St. Louis, 1966-67; resident psychiatry Barnes/Renard hosps., Washington U. Sch. Medicine, St. Louis, 1967-70; research fellow alcoholism and drug abuse Sch. Medicine, Washington U., St. Louis, 1969-70, instr. psychiatry, 1970-72, asst. prof., 1972-77, mem. com. on admissions, 1975-77; asso. prof. psychiatry U. Louisville Sch. Medicine, 1978, dir. div. social and community psychiatry, 1978; assoc. prof. psychiatry Med. Coll. Wis., Milw., 1978-84, dir. div. alcoholism and chem. dependency, 1978-84, mem. human research rev. com., 1981-84; prof. psychiatry, dir. residency tng. in psychiatry U. Minn. Med. Sch., Mpls., 1984—, mem. com. on the use of human subjects in research, 1985—, co-dir. chem. dependency treatment program U. Minn. Hosps. and Clinics, 1984—; asst. psychiatrist Barnes, Renard and Affiliated hosps., 1970-77; cons. Malcolm Bliss Mental Health Crt., St. Louis, 1970-77; dir. psychiat. div. Webster Coll. Student Health Service, Webster Groves, Mo., 1973-75; dir. Grace Hill Settlement House Psychiatry Clinic, St. Louis, 1973-77; clin. instr. dept. psychiatry Mo. Inst. Psychiatry, U. Mo., St. Louis, 1972-74; mem. profl. adv. com. Judevine Ctr. for Autistic Children, St. Louis, 1975-77; psychiat. research cons. Reproductive Biology Research Found., Masters and Johnson Inst., St. Louis, 1975-77. Mem. Mo. Gov.'s Adv. Council on Alcoholism and Drug Abuse, 1974-75; exec. com. Drug and Substance Abuse Council Met. St. Louis, 1973-77, pres., 1971-72; chmn. Children's Mental Health Services Council Met. St. Louis, 1973-74; host Sta. KMOX-TV weekly TV series Trips - the Teenage Point of View about Drugs, spring-summer 1971; adviser on drug abuse St. Louis County Juvenile Ct., 1970-72; mem. adv. bd. Drug Crisis Intervention Unit, St. Louis, 1971-77; mem. St. Louis Youth Ctr. profl. adv. com. Mo. Dept. Mental Health, 1977; adv. on drug abuse Drug Info. Ctr., St. Louis, 1970-74, Human Devel. Corp., St. Louis, 1970-73, Alliance for Regional Community Health, 1972-74; asso. psychiatrist, med. dir. for alcoholism services Jefferson County Alcoholism and Drug Abuse Center for Treatment and Research, Louisville, 1978; exec. and med. dir. River Region Mental Health-Mental Retardation Bd., Ky. Region VI Community Mental Health System, Louisville, 1978; dir. Wis. Alcoholism and Drug Abuse Research Inst., Milw., 1978-84; Sr. Scientist U. Wis., Milw., 1978-84; attending psychiatrist, dir. med. edn. DePaul Rehab. Hosp., Milw., 1978-84; dir. research and edn. in chem. dependency, sr. attending psychiatrist Milwaukee County Mental Health Complex, Milw., 1978-84, dir. psychiat. supervision div. long term care, 1983-84, dir. outpatient clinic, 1984, also chmn. or co-chmn. various coms.; sci. dir. DePaul Hosp. Found., Milw., 1978-84; assoc. psychiatrist U. Louisville Affiliated Hosps., 1978; attending psychiatrist Milw. Psychiat. Hosp., 1978-84, Columbia Hosp., Milw., 1980-84; attending psychiatrist U. Minn. Hosps. and Clinics, 1984—, Met. Med. Ctr., Mpls., 1985—; mem. planning com. Am. Med. Soc. on Alcoholism, 1977-78, mem. program com., 1983—, chmn. com. on med. edn., 1981—, mem. cert. com., 1985—, chmn. fellowship com., 1985—, Wis. state chmn., 1979-84; psychiat. cons. Social Security Disability Determination Service, 1984-87, Minn. Security Hosp., 1985—; mem. Wis. Alcohol and Drug Abuse Adv. Com., HHS, 1981-84; mem. Nat. Alcoholism Forum, 1978; co-chmn. clin. research task force Nat. Drug Abuse Conf., Seattle, 1978; mem. Mental Health Assn. Louisville, 1978, Louisville Council on Alcoholism, 1978; cons. Midwestern Area Alcohol Edn. and Tng. Program, 1976-77. Bd. dirs. Mental Health Assn. Met. St. Louis, 1973-77, chmn. St. Louis State Hosp. human research com., 1976-77; bd. dirs. Tellurian South Community, Inc., Madison, 1980—; mem. exec. council DePaul Rehab. Hosp., 1979-84; mem. med. appeals bd. Div. Motor Vehicles, State of Wis., 1980-84; mem. City of Mequon Bd. Appeals, 1980-84; mem. profl. adv. bd. Lactation Inst., Los Angeles, 1981—; mem. dist. study and adv. council Moundsview Sch. Dist., 1987—; also cons. Recipient NIMH Psychiatry Career Tchr. award in narcotics, drug abuse and alcoholism, 1972-75; diplomate Am. Bd. Psychiatry and Neurology, Nat. Bd. Med. Examiners. Mem. Am. Psychiat. Assn. (mem. Task Force on Substance Abuse Edn. in Psychiatry, 1985-87), Eastern Mo. Psychiat. Soc., Ky. Psychiat. Assn., Wis. Psychiat. Assn., Minn. Psychiat. Soc. (mem. com. on quality assurance and standards, 1987—), Am. Psycho-Pathol. Assn., Assn. for Med. Edn. and Research in Substance Abuse, N.Y. Acad. Scis., AAAS, Ky. Med. Assn., Research Soc. on Alcoholism, Assn. for Acad. Psychiatry, Am. Acad. Clin. Psychiatrists (bd. dirs. 1984—, chmn. med. edn. com. 1984—), Kappa Nu. Greek Orthodox. Contbr. numerous articles to profl. jours. Home: 22 Hill Farm Circle North Oaks MN 55110-8006 Office: U Minn Dept Psychiatry Box 393 Minneapolis MN 55455

HALING, THOMAS PARSONS, information systems strategy consultant; b. Detroit, June 25, 1953; s. Frank William Jr. and Jane Ellen (Parsons) H.; m. Nancy Irene Wright, Dec. 16, 1978. BBA, U. Mich., 1975; MBA, U. Va., 1977. Foundry analyst Power Generation div. Babcock & Wilcox, Barberton, Ohio, 1979-80; mgr. foundry prodn. control Nuclear Equipment div. Babcock & Wilcox, Barberton, Ohio, 1980-81, mgr. capacity mgmt., 1981-83, mgr. prodn. planning and control, 1983-84, mgr. info. systems, 1984-86; assoc. Booz Allen & Hamilton, Inc., Chgo., 1986—. Home: 245 N Dee Rd Park Ridge IL 60068 Office: Booz Allen Hamilton Inc 3 1st National Plaza Chicago IL 60602

HALKOWITZ, THERESA KNOP, interior designer; b. Racine, Wis., Nov. 14, 1955; d. Gerhardt Ernst and Bonne (Lettsome) Knop; m. James Joseph Halkowitz, Sept. 6, 1980; 1 child, Matthew James. BS, U. Wis., 1978. Designer Haworth, Holland, Mich., 1978-79, Interplan, Milw., 1979—. Mem. Am. Soc. Interior Designers (cert.). Lutheran. Avocations: sailing, downhill skiing, biking. Home: 2404 Dwight St Racine WI 53403 Office: Interplan PO Box 17356 Milwaukee WI 53217

HALL, BOBBY JIM, social service administrator, consultant; b. Andalusia, Ala., Feb. 27, 1943; s. Hurgon H. and Pearlie Mae (Bradshaw) H. BA, Stillman Coll., 1968; postgrad., Sangamon State U., Springfield, Ill., 1982—. Registered social worker, Ill. Mental health specialist Dixon (Ill.) State Sch., 1968-72; tech. asst. Dept. Children and Family Services, Springfield, 1972-75, tech. asst. coordinator, 1975-79, day care program planner, 1979-82, day care specialist, 1982-83, program devel. specialist, 1983—; sr. couns. Exec. Suite, Springfield, 1980-85; bd. dirs., cons. B.J. Hall and Assocs., Springfield, 1984—. Bd. dirs. Big Bros./Big Sisters, Springfield, 1984—; mem. exec. bd. Jerome Irvin Rep. Club, Springfield, 1985—; community rep. Headstart Policy Council, Springfield, 1982-86. Mem. Nat. Assn. Black Social Workers (founding bd. mem. Springfield 1975-80, treas. Springfield 1977-80, S award 1979), Attention Homes for Youth Inc. (program specialist 1979-86, Mentor 1984), West Cen. Ill. Health Care Assn. (program rep. 1986—), Republican. Baptist. Avocations: racquetball, golf, tennis. Home: 2929 Flowerbrook Ct Springfield IL 62702 Office: Dept Children and Family Services 406 E Monroe St Springfield IL 62701

HALL, CHARLES RUDOLPH, financial services executive; b. Marysville, Kans., Nov. 7, 1929; s. Percy Allen and Zella (Yaussi) H.; B.S., U. Kans., 1951; postgrad. Northwestern U., 1955-57, U. Wis., 1961; m. Helen Persson, July 19, 1952; children—Charles Rudolph, Timothy P., Jeffrey P. With Continental Ill. Nat. Bank & Trust Co., Chgo., 1955-81, asst. cashier, 1957-61, 2d v.p. nat. div., 1961-64, v.p. nat. div. group G, 1964-68, v.p. personnel div., 1968-70, sr. v.p. adminstrv. services, 1970-71, exec. v.p., 1971-75, exec. v.p. trust and investment services, 1975-81; chmn. bd., chief exec. officer Rollins Burdick Hunter Co., 1981-83; mng. dir. Merrill Lynch Capital Markets, Chgo., 1984—. Asso. St. Luke's Presbyn. Hosp., Chgo., 1965-76; bd. dirs. United Way Met. Chgo., 1970-83; bd. dirs., chmn. fin. devel. Am. Diabetes Assn. Greater Chgo., 1976-80; mem. adv. bd. Citizenship Council Met. Chgo., 1973-80; mem. bus. adv. bd. Nat. Alliance Businessmen, 1973-78; bd. dirs., mem. audit com. Ravinia Festival Assn., 1976-78, mem. investment com., 1982—; chief crusader Crusade of Mercy, 1975-76; mem. program task force United Way Met. Chgo., 1976-82, mem. exec. com., 1977, chmn. personnel com., 1977; bd. dirs., v.p. John Crerar Library, 1977—; chmn. New Trier Twp. High Sch. Bd. Caucus, 1971-72. Served with USNR, 1951-54. Mem. Chgo. Council Fgn. Relations (com. (1974—), Ill. C. of C. and Industry (labor relations com. 1969-71), Phi Delta Theta, Alpha Kappa Psi, Omicron Delta Kappa. Mem. Glencoe Union Ch. (trustee). Clubs: Chicago, Mid Am., Economic of Chicago; Skokie (Ill.) Country; Comml., Commonwealth, Lost Tree. Home: 800 Grove St Glencoe IL 60022 Office: 5500 Sears Tower Chicago IL 60606

HALL, DAVID MELVIN, osteopathic cardiologist; b. Cincinnati, Iowa, Dec. 25, 1941; s. Melvin Eugene and Hazel Naomi (Inns) H.; m. Nancy Jo Kissinger, Aug. 21, 1965; children—David Anton, Damon Melvin, Diana Nicole. B.S. in Zoology Edn., Northeast Mo. State U., 1964; D.O., Kirksville Coll. Osteo. Medicine, 1968. Intern, Flint (Mich.) Osteo. Hosp., 1969-70; resident in internal medicine Kirksville (Mo.) Osteo. Hosp., 1969-72; cardiology fellow Chgo. Coll. Osteo. Medicine, 1978-80; gen. internist internal medicine dept. Kirksville Coll. Osteo. Medicine, 1972-73, asst. prof. medicine, 1972-73; practice osteo. internal medicine, Oklahoma City, 1973-78; chmn. dept. internal medicine Hillcrest Osteo. Hosp., Oklahoma City, 1977-78; attending cardiologist Coll. Osteo. Medicine and Surgery, Des Moines, 1980-82, assoc. prof. medicine, 1980-82; practice osteo. medicine specializing in cardiology, Des Moines, 1982—; pres., chmn. dept. internal medicine Des Moines Gen. Hosp., 1987—; mem. adj. faculty U. Osteo. Medicine and Health Scis., Des Moines, 1983; editor Hawkeye Osteo. Jour., 1984-86; researcher pacemakers, anti-arrhythmic therapy. Mem. Am. Osteo. Assn., Am. Coll. Osteo. Internists, Iowa Heart Assn., Iowa Osteo. Med. Assn., Polk County Osteo. Med. Assn. Republican. Presbyterian. Contbr. articles to profl. jours. Home: 4209 Mary Lynn Dr Des Moines IA 50322 Office: 1440 E Grand St Des Moines IA 50316

HALL, DENNIS WILLIAM, printing company executive; b. Akron, Ohio, July 17, 1956; s. George Ernest Jr. and Leokadia Teresa (Popoff) H.; m. Mary Petrushkin, Aug. 30, 1980 (div. April 1986); 1 child, Jennifer Nicole. BSBA, U. Akron, 1979. Delivery driver Franklin Printing Co. Inc., Akron, 1972-80, v.p., 1980—. Democrat. Avocations: mechanics, reading, skiing, music, traveling. Home: 1623 Goodyear Blvd Akron OH 44305 Office: Franklin Printing Co Inc 923 Bank St Akron OH 44305

HALL, DONALD JOYCE, greeting card company executive; b. Kansas City, Mo., July 9, 1928; s. Joyce Clyde and Elizabeth Ann (Dilday) H.; m. Adele Coryell, Nov. 28, 1953; children: Donald Joyce, Margaret Elizabeth, David Earl. A.B., Dartmouth, 1950; LL.D., William Jewell Coll., Denver U., 1977. With Hallmark Cards, Inc., Kansas City, Mo., 1953—; adminstrv. v.p. Hallmark Cards, Inc., 1958-66, pres., chief exec. officer, 1966-83, chmn. bd., 1983—, chief exec. officer, 1983-85, also dir.; dir. United Telecommunications, Inc., Dayton-Hudson Corp., William E. Coutts Co., Ltd.; past dir. Fed. Res. Bank Kansas City, Mut. Benefit Life Ins. Co., Business Men's Assurance Co., Commerce Bank Kansas City, 1st Nat. Bank Lawrence. Pres. Civic Council Greater Kansas City; past chmn. bd. Kansas City Assn. Trusts and Founds.; Bd. dirs. Am. Royal Assn., Friends of Art, Eisenhower Found.; bd. dirs. Kansas City Minority Suppliers Devel. Council, Kans. City Minority Suppliers Devel. Council, Harry S. Truman Library Inst., Kansas City Symphony; past pres. Pembroke Country Day Sch., Civic Council of Greater Kansas City; trustee, past chmn. exec. com. Midwest Research Inst.; trustee Nelson-Atkins Museum of Art. Served to 1st lt. AUS, 1950-53. Recipient Eisenhower Medallion award, 1973; Parsons Sch. Design award, 1977; 3d Ann. Civic Service award Hebrew Acad. Kansas City, 1976; Chancellor's medal U. Mo., Kansas City, 1977; Disting. Service citation U. Kans., 1980. Mem. Kansas City C. of C. (named Mr. Kansas City 1972, dir.), AIA (hon.). Home: 6320 Aberdeen Rd Shawnee Mission KS 66208 Office: Hallmark Cards Inc 2501 McGee Trafficway Box 580 Kansas City MO 64141

HALL, DOROTHY MARIE REYNOLDS, educator; b. Columbus, Ohio, Dec. 22, 1925; d. Thomas Franklin and Nellie May (Nail) R.; student Ohio State U., 1973-79, Sinclair Community Coll., 1976; m. Grant Forest Hall; children—Stacy L., Cynthia Kay Hall Henderson, Mark Kevin. Dental asst. and office mgr., dental offices in Westerville, Ohio, 1954-68, Columbus, Ohio, 1968-70; dental asst., staff supr., clinic instr. Good Samaritan Dental Clinic, Columbus, 1970; instr., staff supr. Ohio State U. Coll. Dentistry, 1970-71; instr. adult edn. Eastland Vocat. Center, Groveport, Ohio, 1969; instr. dental assisting Eastland Career Ctr., 1972—; examiner Ohio Commn. on Dental Testing, Inc., 1977-78, 81—; chief examiner Ohio Dental Assts. Commn. on Testing, Inc., 1978-81, trustee-dir. 1977-80, examiner, 1978-81, chief examiner, 1984—. Mem. Columbus Dental Assts. Soc. (pres. 1968-69, Dental Asst. of Yr. 1980), Ohio Dental Assts. Assn. (pres. 1978-79, 80-81), Am. Dental Assts. Assn. (cert., registered dental asst.), Eastland Edn. Assn., Ohio Edn. Assn., NEA, Eastland Vocat. Assn. (pres. 1981-82), Ohio Vocat. Assn., Am. Vocat. Assn., Nat. Ret. Tchrs. Assn. (life mem.), Ohio Vocat. Tchrs. Assn. (chairperson S.E. sect. 1986—), Ohio Vocat. Asst. Tchrs. SE Region. Mem. Reformed Ch. Am. Club: Order Eastern Star. Author profl. publs.; developer, artist: A Manual of Lesson Plans for the Ohio Adult Dental Assistant Programs, 1981. Home: 4676 Big Walnut Rd Galena OH 43021 Office: 4465 S Hamilton Rd Groveport OH 43125

HALL, FRANK BRADEN, lawyer, speaker; b. Chgo., Jan. 24, 1917; s. Thrasher and Amalia (Linda) H.; m. Joan Brockhoff, May 11, 1957; children: Braden Brock, Scott Frank. BSEE, Ill. Inst. Tech., 1947; JD, DePaul U., 1956. Bar: Ill. 1956, U.S. Patent Office 1972; registered profl. engr., Ill. Instr., tech. cons. Indsl. Tng. Inst., 1948-49; engr. Beardsley & Piper div. Pettibone Corp., 1950-52, chief engr. elec. engring., 1952-59; sr. engr. Three E Co., 1959-60; assoc. elec. engr. Argonne Nat. Lab., 1960-64; chief control engr. Beardsley & Piper, 1965-72, patent atty., 1972-79; asst. corp. counsel Pettibone Corp., 1979-82, cons., speaker on product liability, 1982—. Author: Dictionary for Dismayed Defendants; contbr. articles to profl. jours. Served with USAAF, 1942-44. Mem. IEEE (sr. life), Chgo. Bar Assn., Am. Foundrymen's Soc. (award for sci. merit 1979), Patent Law Assn. Chgo., Nat. Soc. Profl. Engrs., SAR, Soc. Am. Magicians. Home: 855 N Northwest Hwy Park Ridge IL 60068

HALL, GORDON CLARKE, provincial judge; b. Cranbrook, B.C., Can., Oct. 3, 1921; s. Watson Smythe and Ellen (Leitch) H.; m. Agnet Margaret Rife, June 26, 1944; children: Nancy Margaret, David Malcolm, Douglas Rife. Student, U. Man., 1941, LLB, 1948. Assoc. Guy, Chappel and Co., Winnipeg, Man., 1948-56; ptnr. Thompson, Dilts, Jones, Hall and Dewar, 1956-65; judge Ct. of Queen's Bench, Man., from 1965; lectr. U. Man. Sch. Medicine, Winnipeg, 1954-65; judge Ct. Appeals for Man., Winnipeg, 1971—. Office: Ct of Appeals, Law Cts Bldg, Winnipeg, MB Canada R3C 0V8 *

HALL, HANSEL CRIMIEL, government official; b. Gary, Ind., Mar. 12, 1929; s. Alfred McKenzie and Grace Elizabeth (Crimiel) H. B.S., Ind. U., 1953; LL.B., Blackstone Sch. Law, 1982. Officer, IRS, 1959-64; gasoline service sta. operator, then realtor, Chgo., 1964-69; program specialist HUD, Chgo., 1969-73, dir. equal opportunity, St. Paul, 1973-75, dir. fair housing and equal opportunity, Indpls., from 1975; human resource officer U.S. Fish and Wildlife Serivce, Twin Cities, Minn.; cons. in civil rights; pres. bd. dirs. Riverview Towers Cooperative Assn., Inc.; 1984-87. Served with USAF, 1951-53; Korea. Mem. NAACP (Golden Heritage life mem.), Res. Officers Assn., Am. Inst. Parliamentarians, Ind. U. Alumni Assn.; Omega Psi Phi. Club: Toastmasters (past pres. Minnehaha chpt. 2563, past area gov.). Office: Fed Bldg Ft Snelling Saint Paul MN 55111

HALL, HELENE W., educator; b. Centralia, Ill., Sept. 17, 1926; d. James O. and Gladys (Hosman) Lawrence; B.S., Emporia State U., 1966, M.S., 1969, E.D.S., 1974; m. William E. Hall, June 27, 1948; children—Ronald William, Steven Charles, Jerry Victor. Sec., asst. to Med. Physicians & Dentists, Kansas City, Mo., 1966-69; tchr. Roosevelt Lab. High Sch., Emporia, Kans.; coordinator secondary sch. tchrs. Emporia State U., 1969-71, team leader Teacher Corps, 1971-73; instr., coordinator secretarial scis., word processing Kansas City Community Coll., 1973—. Mem. Nat. Bus. Edn. Assn., Am. Vocat. Assn., Kans. Vocat. Assn., Classroom Educators Adv. Com., Kans. Bus. Edn. Assn., Nat. Secretaries Assn., Office Edn. Assn., Assn. of Info. Systems Profls., Delta Pi Epsilon. Methodist. Home: 403 S 6th St Osage City KS 66523 Office: Kansas City Kans Community Coll 7250 State Ave Kansas City KS 66112

HALL, HOMER L., journalism teacher; b. Reeds, Mo., June 11, 1939; s. Columbus Terry and MArgie (Fain) H.; m. Lea Ann (Watson), Sept. 4, 1960; children: Lynlea, Ashley. BS in Edn., U. Mo., 1960; MS in Edn., U. Kans., 1965; postgrad, various insts. Tchr. North Kirkwood (Mo.) Jr. High, 1963-68, 70-73, Shawnee Mission, Kans., 1968-69; reporter Sedalia (Mo.) Democrat, 1969; tchr. Sedalia High Sch., 1969-70, Kirkwood High Sch., 1973—; dir. Ball State Journalism Workshops, Muncie, Ind., 1983-85, 87; tchr. summer journalism workshops, Mo., Ill., Tex., Ind., Calif., Wash., R.I., Iowa, Ariz. Author: (textbooks) Junior High Journalism, 1969 rev. 5 times, Senior High Journalism, 1985, Yearbook Guidebook, 1981 rev. 3 times; contbr. numerous articles to journalism publs. Tchr. Sunday sch. Kirkwood Baptist Ch., 1982—, deacon, 1985—. Served to 1st lt. U.S. Army, 1961-63. Named Mo. Journalism Tchr. of Yr., Mo. Interscholastic Press Assn., 1973, Mo. Tchr. of Yr., Mo. Dept. Edn., 1979, Nat. Journalism Tchr. of Yr., Dow Jones Newspaper Fund, 1982; recipient Gold Key award Columbia Scholastic Press Assn., Pioneer award Nat. Scholastic Press Assn., Merit medal Journalism Edn. Assn., Horace Mann award Mo. Nat. Edn. Assn. Mem. Mo. Journalism Edn. Assn. (past pres.), Kirkwood Community Tchrs. Assn., (past pres.), Sponsors of Sch. Publs. Greater St. Louis (sec., past pres.), Nat. Journalism Edn. Assn. (sec.), Phi Delta Kappa. Avocations: tennis, reading, writing, bridge, square dancing. Home: 698 Trailcrest Ct #5 Kirkwood MO 63122 Office: Kirkwood High Sch 801 W Essex Kirkwood MO 63122

HALL, JAMES ALAN, obstetrician-gynecologist; b. Indpls., Nov. 3, 1949; m. Kyle A. Carner, May 18, 1974; children: Audrey, Courtney, Lynly. AB, Ind. U., 1972, MD, 1975. Cert. Am. Bd. Ob-Gyn. Staff Logansport (Ind.) Clinic for Women, 1978—; asst. clin. prof. Ind U., Indpls., 1978—. Fellow Am. Coll. Ob-Gyn., ACS; mem. Cen. Assn. Ob-Gyn., Wabash Valley Ob-Gyn (pres.). Office: Logansport Clinic for Women Inc #6 Chase Park Logansport IN 46947

HALL, JAMES ROBERT, educator; b. Salem, Ill., Dec. 24, 1947; s. James Wesley and Patricia Joyce (Ellis) H. B.S., U. Ill., 1970. Cert. secondary tchr., Ill. Tchr. Murphysboro High Sch., Ill., 1970—. Author, compiler: (tng. man.) Key Club Faculty Advisors, 1975. Sunday sch. tchr. United Methodist Ch., Murphysboro, 1973-76, youth dir., 1973-76, mem. council on ministries, 1984—, trustee, 1984—; founder, dir. Christian Lay Council Youth Coffeehouse, 1973-75; mem. Murphysboro Recreation Bd., 1974-76, pres. 1975-76; community ambassador So. Ill. U. Area Services, 1975—; bd. dirs. Murphysboro Heart Fund, 1973-76, co-chmn., 1975-76; chmn. Murphysboro Muscular Dystrophy Assn., 1971-74; counsellor Little Grassy Youth Ch. Camp, 1973; steering com. Murphysboro Apple Festival, 1975—, exec. com., 1983—; bd. dirs. Murphysboro United Way, 1978—, Murphysboro Sr. Citizens Council, 1980-83, Resource Reclamation, Inc., 1979-85; vice chmn. Murphysboro Swimming Pool Project Commn., 1983-84, chmn., 1984—. Recipient Citizenship award Sta. WTAO Radio, 1983, 84, Ann. Community Service award Modern Woodmen Am., 1982, Citizen of Yr. award Murphysboro C. of C., 1984. Mem. NEA, Ill. Edn. Assn., Murphysboro Edn. Assn. Clubs: Key (advisor 1972—, adminstr. Ill.-Eastern Iowa dist. 1985—), Kiwanis (pres. 1977-78, lt. gov. dist. div. 1984-85, chmn. spl. club services Ill.-Eastern Iowa dist. 1984-85). Avocations: collecting books and plates; bowling; tennis. Home: 28 Candy Ln Murphysboro IL 62966 Office: Murphysboro High Sch 16th and Blackwood Dr Murphysboro IL 62966

HALL, JEFFREY LYNN, government official; b. Independence, Mo., Sept. 25, 1947; s. William H. and Margaret E. (Bales) H.; m. Brenda Marguerite Hall, July 30, 1978; children—Tracy Michelle, Jami Lynne, Bryan William, Todd Christopher. A.A.S., Longview Coll., 1978; B.S. in Data Processing, Avila Coll., 1980; M.A. in Bus. Adminstrn., Webster U., 1982. Cert. systems profl., 1985. Sr. programmer/analyst Ralston Purina Co., St. Louis, 1969-76; programmer/analyst Syscon, Inc., Edwardsville, Kans., 1977, Black & Veatch, Kansas City, Mo., 1977-80; systems analyst Iowa Beef Processors, Kansas City, 1980-81; project leader Adventist Health System, Overland Park, Kans., 1981-83; supr. systems and programming Water Dist. #1 Johnson County, Mission, Kans., 1983—; data processing instr. Nat. Coll., 1983—. Served with U.S. Army, 1966-68; Vietnam. Mem. Assn. Systems Mgmt. Seventh-day Adventist. Avocation: racquetball. Home: 8200 Evanston Raytown MO 64138 Office: Water Dist No 1 of Johnson County 5930 Beverly Mission KS 66202

HALL, JEFFREY STUART, newspaper executive; b. Boston, Nov. 13, 1951; s. Frederick Folsom Hall and Norma Bennett (Driscoll) Fox; m. Sue Lyddon, May 30, 1975; 1 child, Katherine McGregor. A.B., Stanford U., 1974; M.B.A., Harvard Bus. Sch., 1978. Pres. Seat-of-the-Pants Mgmt., Inc., Kansas City, Mo., 1978-79; various positions circulation and advt. Kansas City Star, Mo., 1979-82, v.p. mktg., 1982—. Developer trademark consumer product 1978; mem. editorial bd. Internat. Circulation Mgrs. Assoc. Update, 1980—. Co-chmn. Kansas City Spirit Festival, 1986; bd. dirs. Internat. Relations Council, 1985; chmn. Project Literacy, Kansas City, 1984-85. Mem. Kansas City Centurions C. of C. (award 1984). Roman Catholic. Club: Advt. (bd. dirs) 1983-84 (Kansas City). Avocations: skiing; tennis; soccer; personal computing. Office: Kansas City Star Co 1729 Grand Ave Kansas City MO 64108

HALL, JOHN HENRY, lawyer, historian, educator, adminstrator; b. Mound Bayou, Miss., Nov. 7, 1932; s. John H. and Icey M. (Roundtree) H.; m. Katie B. Green, Aug. 15, 1957; children—Jacqueline D., Jenifer D. Hall. B.S., Ind. U., 1970, M.S. in Edn., 1971, M.S. in Secondary Sch. Adminstrn., 1972; J.D., Southland U., 1981; Ed.D., Loyola U., Chgo., 1986. Bar: Ind. 1983, U.S. Supreme Ct. 1987. Foreman U.S. Reduction Co., East Chgo. Ind., 1957-62, shift supt., 1962-68; tchr. Gary Community Schs., Ind., 1962-74, asst. prin., 1975-84; sole practice law, Gary, 1983—; prof. law, racism and social change Ind. U., Gary, 1984; legal resource Gary Community Sch. Corp., 1983-84. Article writer Blacks in World History Information Newspaper (edn. and Community Service award 1983), 1979—. Supporter Mayor Richard Gordon Hatcher, Gary, 1976-83; campaign mgr. Katie Hall State Rep., Indpls., 1976, Katie Hall Congress, Gary, 1984; Sunday sch., BTU tchr., chmn. deacons Van Buren (Miss.) Bapt. Ch. Served with USAF, 1952-57. Mem. Gary Secondary Prins. Assn. (sec./treas. v.p., pres., Outstanding Leadership award 1982), ABA, Internat. Bar Assn., Nat. Bar Assn., Fed. Bar Assn., Ind. Bar Assn., Gary Bar Assn., Hammond Bar Assn., Lake County Bar Assn., Assn. Trial Lawyers Am., Phi Delta Kappa, Phi Alpha Delta. Democrat. Lodge: Masons.

HALL, JON EM, oil company executive; b. Columbus, Ohio, July 6, 1956; s. John Milton and Ordena Hill (High) H.; m. Merri Lynn Pugh, May 20, 1978; children—Jessie, Jennifer, Ross, Ashley. B.S. in Petroleum Engring., Marietta Coll., 1978. Registered profl. engr., Ohio. Petroleum engr. Amoco Prodn. Co., Brownfield, Tex., 1979-80, Houston, 1980-81, Atlas Energy Co., Warren, Ohio, 1981-83; asst. v.p., petroleum engr. Huntington Bank, Cleve., 1983-84; v.p. oil and gas ops. Royal Petroleum Properties, Inc., Cleve., 1984-86; chief tech. adv. Hall Energy, Inc., Powell, Ohio, 1982-86, pres., 1986—. Mem. Soc. Petroleum Engr. (bd. dirs. 1984-85), Soc. Profl. Well Log Analysts (v.p. 1984-85), Am. Assn. Petroleum Geologists, Ohio Oil and Gas Assn., Nat. Ohio Soc. Profl. Engrs. (cert. merit 1983). Republican. Methodist. Avocations: bowling; electric organ; sports. Lodge: Kiwanis. Home: 35454 Chesterfield Dr North Ridgeville OH 44039 Office: Hall Energy Inc PO Drawer G Powell OH 43065

HALL, KAY MARGARET, nurse; b. Lima, Ohio, July 24, 1943; d. Harold Ray and Ruth (Gordon) H.; m. Robert G. Jarvis, Oct. 23, 1976 (div. 1983). Diploma Miami Valley Hosp. Sch. Nursing, Dayton, Ohio, 1965; student Wright State U., 1974-77, U. Dayton, 1971, Universidad Technologica De Santiago, Santo Domingo, Dominican Republic, 1984—. R.N., Ohio. Charge nurse recovery room Miami Valley Hosp., Dayton, 1965-66; indsl. nurse Harris Seybold Co., Dayton, 1966-68; office nurse to physician, Dayton, 1968-69, 80-82; coordinator nurse Mobile Unit Clinics, OEO, 1969-72; emergency nurse Kettering Med. Ctr., Ohio, 1972-80, radiology nurse, 1979-80; chair N.A. delegation to world health council World's Children's Health, Geneva; nominated internat. chair over Americas by Mex., 1987—. Author: (manual) Procedures for Nursing Care in Radiology, 1977. Big sister Big Bros.-Big Sisters, Dayton, 1979-83. Recipient Citation Dominican Govt. Mem. Miami Valley Hosp. Sch. Nursing Alumni, Critical Care Nurses Dayton. Home: PO Box 1961 Kettering OH 45429

HALL, LARRY JOE, accountant; b. Ironton, Ohio, Jan. 4, 1944; s. Arthur Ralph and Opal Virginia (Tabor) H.; m. Gloria Ann Witten, May 25, 1972; 1 child, Thomas Brant. BS in Bus. Administrn., Morehead (Ky.) State U., 1967; MS in Acctg., U. Ky., 1973. CPA, W.Va. Acct. Ashland (Ky.) Oil, Inc., 1969-72, Somerville & Co., CPA's, Huntington, W.Va., 1973-74; supr. acctg. Armco, Inc., Middletown, Ohio, 1975—. Served as sgt. U.S. Army, 1968-69, Vietman. Mem. Am. Inst. CPA's. Republican. Mem. Christian Ch. Avocations: tennis, racquetball, jogging. Home: 9397 S Union Rd Miamisburg OH 45342 Office: Armco Inc 1801 Crawford St Middletown OH 45043

HALL, PAUL ANTHONY, microbiologist; b. St. Louis, Dec. 15, 1953; s. James Benjamin and Edna Lois (Hughes) H.; m. Deborah Lynn Tilton, May 31, 1975; 1 child, Erin Christine. BA in Biology, U. Mo., 1978. Registered microbiologist, Am. Acad. Microbiol. Microbiologist Ralston Purina Co., St. Louis, 1974-77, mgr. microbiology labs., 1977-80, mgr. microbiol. tech. services, 1980-83; mgr. microbiology research Anheuser Busch Co., St. Louis, 1983—. Contbr. articles to profl. jours. Mem. Nat. Am. Soc. Microbiology (local program chmn. 1984), Am. Soc. Microbiology (pres. Mo. br. 1983-85, nat. councilor 1985—), Regulatory Affairs Profl. Soc., Inst. Food Technologists. Home: 14 Arnold Dr Dupo IL 62239 Office: Anheuser Busch Corp R&D 1101 Wyoming St Saint Louis MO 63118

HALL, PHYLLIS A. HENRI, developer/fundraiser, consultant; b. Boston, Nov. 8, 1940; d. Samuel Henry and Edith)Salvin) Bloom; divorced; 1 child, Hilary Cynthia. BA, U. Calif., Berkeley, 1962; postgrad., MIT, 1973-74, Rockhurst Coll., 1980-83. Dir. research Harbridge House, Boston, 1964-70; research assoc. MIT, Cambridge, Mass., 1970-73; program adminstr. U. Hawaii, Honolulu, 1974-79, Mo. div. Community Devel., Kansas City, 1980-82; pres. Corp. Resource Cons., Kansas City, Mo., 1982—. Mem. Nat. Assn. Neighborhood Councils, 49/63 Neighborhood Coalition, South Town Council, Kansas City, 1986—, Friends of Art, Kansas City, 1986—; staff coordinator Mayor Charles B. Wheeler campaign, Kansas City, 1979. Mem. Nat. Soc. Fund Raising Execs. (bd. dirs.), Nat. Assn. Neighborhood Councils, Brush Creek Trolley Barn Assn., Greater Kansas City C. of C., Greater Kansas City Council Philanthropy, Nat. Assn. Female Execs., Brookside Neighborhood Assn. Democrat. Jewish. Avocations: fine arts, music. Home and Office: Corporate Resource Consultants 5800 Grand Ave Kansas City MO 64113

HALL, REBECCA ANN, educator; b. Dayton, Ohio, July 27, 1940; s. Noel Gould and Anna Frances (Pyle) Easton; m. Ted D. Hall, Dec. 21, 1963; 1 child, Robin Leigh. BS, Wittenberg U., 1961; MEd, Miami U., Oxford, Ohio, 1964, PhD, 1982. Tchr., counselor, public schs. curriculum coordinator, Brookville, Ohio, 1961-63, Carlisle, Ohio, 1963-65, Centerville City Schs., 1965—. Author: A history of Springboro, Ohio, 1815-1965, 1965, Personal Typing, 1979, Gregg Typing Series 7, 1982, Series 8, 1986. Mem., v.p. Clearcreek Bd. Edn., 1981-85. Mem. NEA, Ohio Edn. Assn., Nat. Bus. Edn. Assn., Ohio Bus. Tchrs. Assn., Am. Vocat. Assn., Ohio Vocat. Assn., Assn. Supervision and Curriculum Devel., Delta Pi Epsilon. Methodist. Home: 9668 Quailwood Trail Spring Valley OH 45370 Office: Centerville City Schools 500 E Franklin St Centerville OH 45459

HALL, RICHARD DAVID, chemical engineer, environmental consultant; b. Newark, Ohio, Mar. 30, 1932; s. David William Martin and Freda Jane (Zinn) H.; m. Marjorie Elma Schultz, Sept. 16, 1956; children—Jeffrey William, Colleen Dawn. B.S. in Chem. Engring., Ohio State U., 1960. Registered profl. engr., Ohio, Ark., Del., Calif., Tex. Chem. engr. Hercules Powder Co., Parlin, N.J., 1960-61; research engr. Barnebey-Chaney Co., Columbus, Ohio, 1961-62; asst. engr. Ohio Dept. Health, Columbus, 1962-65; regional environ. control mgr., spl. projects mgr. Diamond Shamrock Corp., Cleve., 1965-80; mgr. environ. affairs B.F. Goodrich Chem. Co., Independence, Ohio, 1980-82; pres., chem. engr. Hall's Environ. Assistance Co., Inc., Parma Heights, Ohio, 1982—; mgr. environ. affairs Nat. Distillers & Chem. Co., 1985-86; mem. air resources com. and water resources com. Chem. Mfrs. Assn., Washington, 1966-70; mem. chem. industry adv. com. Ohio River Valley Sanitation Compact, Cin., 1966-70. Author environ. statements for fed. and state legis. bodies. Water pollution analyst, author Cleve. Little Hoover Com., 1967. Served to sgt. U.S. Army, 1951-54, Korea. Mem. Am. Inst. Chem. Engrs., Water Pollution Control Fedn., Air Pollution Control Assn., Clermont County C. of C. Lutheran. Lodge: Masons. Avocations: gardening, singing. Home and Office: 6604 Loveland Miamiville Rd Loveland OH 45140

HALL, ROBBIE KEITH, manufacturing executive; b. Rensselaer, Ind., Aug. 14, 1951; s. Clifford and Alta Pauline (Spurgeon) H.; divorced; children: Tracy Ann, Dana Eileen; m. Denise Leanne Noel, Nov. 30, 1985. Student, Purdue U., Lafayette, Ind., 1979-82, Purdue U., Versaille, Ind., 1982—. Quality control mgr. Monon (Ind.) Trailer Inc., 1976-78; prodn. supt. Polymer Engring., Reynolds, Ind., 1980-81, quality control mgr., 1981-83; quality control mgr. Plastic Moldings, Osgood, Ind., 1983-86, process quality mgr. compression molding div., 1986—. Author: (manual) Product Quality at Polymer Engring., 1982, Certification of Plastic Molded Parts, 1985. Served with U.S. Army, 1973-76. Mem. Am. Soc. for Quality Control. Republican. Avocations: running, basketball, golf, geology, history. Home: PO Box 44 Osgood IN 47037 Office: Plastic Moldings Corp Rd 300 N PO Box 79 Osgood IN 47037

HALL, ROBIN RIDGELY, municipal administrator; b. Peoria, Ill., Apr. 12, 1942; s. Robert Ingersoll and Rutilia (Ridgely) H.; divorced; children: Jennifer, Charles. B, U. Ill., 1966, MS, 1974. Supt. recreation Urbana (Ill.) Park Dist., 1968-71, dir. parks and recreation, 1971—; cons. Mgmt. Learning Labs., Champaign, Ill., 1979—; lectr. U. Ill., Urbana, 1980-82, Ea. Ill. U., Charleston, 1986. Mem. Nat. Recreation and Park Assn. (Great Lakes Region Coordinating Council 1980-82), Ill. Park and Recreation Assn. (bd. dirs. 1979-83, pres. 1982, Robert Artz award 1984), U. Ill. Coll. Applied Life Studies Alumni Bd. (bd. dirs. 1979-82), Izaak Walton League Am. (bd. dirs. 1971-72), Urbana C. of C. (bd. dirs. 1986—). Presbyterian. Club: Illini Quarterback (bd. dirs. 1972-74). Lodge: Rotary (bd. dirs. Urbana chpt. 1986—). Avocations: reading, walking, genealogy, gardening. Office: Urbana Park Dist 901 N Broadway Urbana IL 61801

HALL, STEPHAN EUGENE, management consultant; b. Indpls., Apr. 28, 1942; s. Harold K. and Cora E. (Brown) H.; B.S. in Bus. Adminstrn., Northwestern U., 1964; m. Susan K. Bartholomew, Mar. 24, 1979. Vice pres., chief operating officer Cash, Inc., Indpls., 1961-68; mgmt. cons. Touche Ross & Co., Detroit, 1968-76; pres. S.E. Hall & Co., Birmingham, Mich., 1976—; treas. Airnet Inc.; dir. Birmingham Fin. Planning Corp.; chmn. Birmingham Advt. Assocs.; chmn. bd. Electronic Software, Inc. Mem. Birmingham Cablecasting Bd., 1980—; mem. Dean's Council, Northwestern U., 1975-80. C.P.A., Ind., Mich.; cert. mgmt. cons. Mem. Am. Inst. C.P.A.s, Inst. Mgmt. Cons., Mich. Assn. C.P.A.s, Ind. Soc. C.P.A.s, Beta Alpha Psi (hon.), Mu Alpha Theta (hon.). Clubs: Birmingham Athletic, Econ. of Detroit; Mill Reef (Antigua); Columbia (Indpls.). Home: 1120 Lyonhurst St Birmingham MI 48009

HALL, TONY P., congressman. m. Janet Dick, 1973; children—Jyl, Matthew. A.B., Denison U., 1964. Vol. Peace Corps, Thailand, 1966-67; mem. Ohio Ho. of Reps., 1969-72, Ohio Senate, 1973-78, 96th-100th Congresses from 3d Ohio Dist.; mem. house rules com., ranking majority mem., house select com. on hunger, chmn. internat. hunger task force.; mem. House Rules Com.; ranking majority mem. House Select Com. on Hunger; chmn. Internat. Hunger Task Force. Founder, mem. steering com. Congl. Friends of Human Rights Monitors; mem. bd. mgrs. Air Force Mus. Found.; trustee Holiday Aid; mem. adv. com. Emergency Resource Bank. Recipient Disting. Service Against Hunger award Bread for the World, 1984, 87, Tree of Life award Jewish Nat. Fund, 1986, Golden Apple award Nat. Assn. Nutrition and Aging Services Programs, 1986, Freedom award Asian Pacific Am. C. of C., 1986. Democrat. Clubs: Agonis, Trail's End. Office: 2448 Rayburn House Office Bldg Washington DC 20515

HALLENE, ALAN MONTGOMERY, elevator and escalator company executive; b. Moline, Ill., Mar. 12, 1929; s. Maurice Mitchell and Ruth (Montgomery) H.; m. Phyllis Dorene Welsh, June 16, 1951; children: Alan, Carol Louise, Janet Lee, James Norman. BS, U. Ill., 1951; postgrad., Oak Ridge Sch. Reactor Tech., 1951-52. Reactor engr. U.S. AEC, Oak Ridge and Chgo., 1951-53; sales engr. Montgomery Elevator Co., Moline, 1953-54, mgr. accessories div., 1954-57; br. mgr. Montgomery Elevator Co., Jacksonville, Fla., 1957-58, chief engr., 1958-60, v.p., 1960-64, exec. v.p., 1964-68, pres., 1968—, also bd. dirs.; mem. bus. adv. council U. Ill.; bd. dirs. 1st Midwest Bank of Moline, Butler Mfg. Co., Ill. Bell Telephone., Rolscreen Co., 1st Midwest Bancorp., Inc., The Inst. for Ill. Mem. Moline Dist. 40 Bd. Edn., 1966-70, Ill. Commn. on Atomic Energy, 1968-73, Ill. Gov.'s Adv. Council; mem. adv. com. tchr. corps HEW, 1970-73; bd. dirs. Moline Luth. Hosp., 1967-80, Western Golf Assn., 1972-77, Am. Coll. Testing Program, 1975-81, Augustana Coll., 1977-81; dir. The Inst. for Ill.; pres. U. Ill. Found.; trustee Butterworth Meml. Trust., Lincoln Acad. of Ill. Mem. U. Ill. Alumni Assn. (pres. 1973-75). Lodge: Rotary (pres. Moline chpt. 1961). Home: 1885 24th Ave A Moline IL 61265 Office: Montgomery Elevator Co 1 Montgomery Ct Moline IL 61265

HALLER, FRED JOSEPH, service company executive; b. Cleve., June 26, 1954; s. Fred Joseph and Jean May (Lemel) H.; m. Sarah Ross Luterick, June 18, 1977; children: Michael, Kelli. BS in Acctg., U. Akron, 1976, MS in Acctg., 1983. CPA, Ohio. Staff acct. Revco D.S., Inc., Twinsburg, Ohio, 1977-78; sr. auditor Coopers & Lybrand, Akron, Ohio, 1978-80; asst. controller Pentron Industries, Beachwood, Ohio, 1980-81; corp. controller Sancap Abrasives, Inc., Alliance, Ohio, 1981-86; pres., chief exec. officer Diet-Tek, Inc. (Nutra-Bolic Weight Reduction Systems), Dayton and Springfield, Ohio, 1986—. Mem. Am. Inst. CPA's, Ohio Soc. CPA's. Lutheran. Avocation: microcomputers. Home and Office: 10997 Jan Circle Uniontown OH 44685

HALLEWELL, LAURENCE, librarian, Portuguese literature educator; b. West Ham, Eng., Apr. 3, 1929; came to U.S., 1982; s. Herbert Joseph and Edith Ann (Moot) H.; m. Celestine Jane Hughes, Feb. 14, 1958; children: Mark Edmund, Rachel, Rebecca. BA, U. London, 1965; PhD, U. Essex, Colchester, Eng., 1975; MLS, Kent (Ohio) State U., 1985. Regional librarian Trinidad Cen. Library, San Fernando, Trinidad and Tobago, 1958-61; catalogue British Nat. Bibliography, London, 1961-64; asst. librarian U. Essex, 1965-77; dep. librarian Sch. Oriental and African Studies, London, 1977-78; prof. library sci. Universidade Fed. da Paraiba, João Pessoa, Brazil, 1979-82; Latin Am. bibliographer Ohio State U., Columbus, 1982-87; Ibero-Am. bibliographer U. Minn., Mpls., 1987—; Latin Am. editor Scarecrow Press, Metuchen, N.J., 1982—. Author: Books in Brazil, 1982, O Livro No Brazil, 1985; editor: Latin American Bibliography, 1978; contbr. articles to profl. jours. Served with British Army, 1947-49. Brazilian Fgn. Ministry scholar, 1970; OAS fellow, 1984. Fellow Library Assn. of United Kingdom; mem. Am. Library Assn., Latin Am.studies Assn., Soc. Latin Am. Studies, Seminar Acquistion Latin Am. Library Materials. Anglican. Home: 3226 Minnehaha Ave S Apt 304 Minneapolis MN 33406-2442 Office: U Minn 220 Wilson Library 309 19th Ave S Minneapolis MN 55455-0414

HALLIGAN, ROGER JOHN, JR., marketing communications consultant; b. Streator, Ill., Nov. 9, 1948; s. Roger John Sr. and Ruth Lorena (Brewer) H.; m. Beate Angelica Shubert, Apr. 21, 1973; 1 child, Alexis Morgan. BS, No. Ill. U., 1970. With Montgomery Ward & Co., Chgo., 1973; account supr. N.W. Ayer-ABH Internat., Chgo., 1973-76; group supr. Ruder, Finn & Rotman, Chgo., 1976-80; dir. advt. and pub. relations A.B. Dick Co., Niles, Ill., 1980-84; pres. mktg. communications cons. Halligan & Assocs., Chgo., 1984—. Served with U.S. Army, 1970-72. Mem. Nat. Computer Conf. (promotion chmn. 1986—), Publicity Club Chgo. (com. chmn. 1986). Roman Catholic. Avocations: golf, fishing, photography. Home: 3230 Park Pl Evanston IL 60201 Office: Halligan & Assocs Inc 444 N Michigan Ave Chicago IL 60611

HALLING, LEONARD WILLIAM, pathologist, laboratory administrator; b. Aurora, Ill., Apr. 1, 1927; s. Leonard Carl Gustave and Mildred Margaret (May) H.; m. Esther Suzanne Garon, June 18, 1957; children—Kevin Carl, Dale Brian, Julie Lynn. M.D., U. Vt., 1957. Diplomate Am. Bd. Pathology. Rotating intern Rose Hosp., Denver, 1957-58; resident in pathology Tripler Army Hosp., Honolulu, 1958-62; chief lab. Womack Army Hosp., Fayetteville, N.C., 1962-64; staff pathologist Armed Forces Inst. Pathology, Washington, 1965-67; dir. Hays Pathology Lab., Kans., 1967—; chief med. staff Hadley Regional Med. Ctr., Hays, 1972-73; pres. Kans. Found. Med. Care, Topeka, 1976. Bd. dirs. High Plains Edn. Consortium, Hays, 1975—; pres. Hays United Fund, 1976, Hays Arts Council, 1971. Fellow Coll. Am. Pathologists, Am. Soc. Clin. Pathologists; mem. Kans. Soc. Pathologists (past pres.). Republican. Presbyterian. Lodge: Rotary. Home: 3000 Tam O Shanter St Hays KS 67601 Office: Hays Pathology Labs PA 1300 E 13th St Hays KS 67601

HALLING, WILLIAM RUSSELL, accountant; b. Albert Lea, Minn., Jan. 3, 1939; s. Lawrence Russell and Romona Ione (Deeg) H.; m. Dianne Mary Spitzer, Jan. 28, 1961; children: Constance Jean, Barton Russell, Julie Ann. BA, Luther Coll., 1961. CPA, Mich., Minn., Ohio, Ill. Asst. acct. Peat Marwick Co., Mpls., 1961-78; local mng. ptnr. Peat Marwick Co., Toledo, 1978-81; ptnr. in charge audit dept. Peat Marwick Co., Chgo., 1981-86; local mng. ptnr. Peat Marwick Co., Detroit, 1986—; bd. dirs. Hist. Trinity, Detroit, Children's Hosp., Met. Affairs Corp., Cen. Bus. Dist. Assn., Luth. Brotherhood. bd. dirs. Luth. Social Services Ill., Chgo., 1985-86, Salvation Army, 1984-86; local fund raiser Luther Coll., Chgo., 1984-86. Mem. Am. Inst. CPAs, Nat. Assn. Accts., Mich. Assn. CPAs. Republican. Lutheran. Clubs: Detroit Athletic; Glenview (Chgo.). Avocations: skiing, tennis, golf, windsurfing. Home: 269 Chestnut Circle Bloomfield Hills MI 48013 Office: Peat Marwick Co 200 Renaissance Ctr Detroit MI 48243

HALLION, RICHARD PAUL, aerospace historian, museum consultant; b. Washington, May 17, 1948; s. Richard Paul and Marie Elizabeth (Flynn). B.A. with high honors in History, U. Md., 1970, Ph.D., 1975. Curator sci. and tech., curator space sci. and exploration Nat. Air and Space Mus., Smithsonian Instn., 1974-80; prof. history, instr. aerospace engring., U. Md., College Park, 1980-81, assoc. prof. gen. adminstrn., Univ. Coll., 1980-81; center historian Air Force Flight Test Ctr., Edwards AFB, Calif., 1982-86; dir. spl. staff office Aeronautical Systems Div., Wright-Patterson AFB, Ohio, 1986—; museum cons. Recipient Dr. Robert H. Goddard Hist. Essay award Nat. Space Club, 1980; Daniel and Florence Guggenheim fellow, 1974-75. Mem. AIAA (history manuscript award 1976, Young Engr./Scientist award Nat. Capitol sect. 1979), Aviation/Space Writers Assn. (writing citation 1977, 78, Space Lit. award 1979), Am. Astron. Soc., U.S. Naval Inst., Soc. History of Tech., Air Force Hist. Found. (mem. editorial adv. bd.), Air Force Assn. (life), U. Md. Alumni Assn. (life). Roman Catholic. Clubs: Wings (N.Y.C.); Read Room (Washington). Author: Supersonic Flight, 1972; Legacy of Flight: The Guggenheim Contribution to American Aviation, 1977; The Wright Brothers: Heirs of Prometheus, 1978; (with Tom D. Crouch) Apollo: Ten Years Since Tranquillity Base, 1979; Text Pilots: The Frontiersmen of Flight, 1981; Designers and Test Pilots, 1982; Rise of the Fighter, 1984; Naval Air War in Korea, 1986; contbr. articles to profl. jours. Office: Aeronautical Systems Div Spl Staff Office Wright-Patterson AFB OH 45433

HALLORAN, VICTOR DAVID, architect; b. Appleton, Wis., Jan. 19, 1927; s. David J. and Marie M. (Hoffman) H.; m. Ruth V. Krueger, May 24, 1950 (dec. Mar. 1983); children: Lili M., David E., James R., Thomas J., Corri J.; m. Jean E. Rhode, Oct. 19, 1984; stepchildren: Linda, Steven, Lori. Student, N.E. Wis. Tech. Inst., 1962-72. Registered architect, Wis. Archtl. draftsman R.N. LeVee, Appleton, 1949-51, Robert M. Connely, Appleton, 1951-52, Robert W. Surplice, Green Bay, Wis., 1952-72; owner, architect Surplice Assocs., Inc., Green Bay, 1973-85; architect Foth & Van Dyke, Green Bay, 1985—; instr. trades teaching N.E. Wis. Tech. Inst., Green Bay, 1964-72, judge, 1973-86. Contbr. articles to profl. jours. Bd. advisors Wis. State Code Rev. Bd., Madison, 1980-85. Served with U.S. Army, 1945-46. Mem. AIA, Wis. Soc. Architects (v.p., pres. 1976-78), Constrn. Specifiers Inst., Am. Correctional Assn., Nat. Jail Assn., Ashwaubenon Bus. and Profl. Assn. (bd. dirs. 1977-79). Presbyterian. Lodge: Rotary (v.p. Green Bay West club 1976, pres. 1977-78). Avocations: golf, bowling, cross country skiing, wood working, cabinetry. Home: 1283 Hickory Hill Dr Green Bay WI 54304 Office: Foth & Van Dyke Engrs Architects PO Box 19012 Green Bay WI 54307-9012

HALM, PETER ALFRED, financial planning executive; b. Ottawa, Ill., Nov. 2, 1943; s. Walter James and Dorothy Catherine (Zeller) H.; m. Mary Ann Fanti, Sept. 5, 1964; children: Ken, Lisa, Susan. BS, No. Ill. U., 1965. Tchr. Earlville Sch. Dist., Ill., 1965-68; ins. mgr. Equitable Ins. Co., Cedar Rapids, Iowa, 1968-82; pension cons. SCI Fin., Cedar Rapids, 1982-86; v.p. fin. planning exec. Berthel, Fisher & Fleischman, Inc., Cedar Rapids, 1986—; author, presenter continuing edn. life ins. Iowa jr. colls., 1982—. Bd. dirs. St. Jude Bd. Edn., Cedar Rapids, 1979-82; active March of Dimes, PTA seminars, Cedar Rapids, 1981—. Mem. CLU Assn. (program facilitator), Nat. Assn. Life Underwriters, Life Underwriters Tng. Council, Cedar Rapids Assn. Life Underwriters (bd. dirs. 1976-79). Lodge: KC. Avocations: golf, fishing. Home: 115 Rollingwood Dr NW Cedar Rapids IA 52405 Office: Berthel Fisher & Fleischman Inc 100 2d St NE Cedar Rapids IA 52407-4611

HALMAN, MARC ALLYSON, health care administrator; b. Ann Arbor, Mich., Aug. 5, 1951; s. Irving Elliott and Rose Anna (Schmerling) H.; m. Leslie Jill Martin, June 24, 1973; children: Joshua Michael, Seth Daniel. BSW, Eastern Mich. U., 1975; M in Soc. Adminstrn., U. Mich., 1981. Social worker U. Mich. Hosp., Ann Arbor, 1975-80, coordinator Cystic Firbrosis Ctr., 1980-82; administrv. mgr. pulmonary and critical care medicine U. Mich. Med. Sch., Ann Arbor, 1982-86, clin. adminstr. dept. radiation oncology, 1986—. Contbr. articles to health care jours. Exec. bd. dirs. Pastolal Care Services SE Mich., 1980-82; patient service commn. Metro Detroit Cystic Fibrosis Found., 1982-83; v.p. community relations Friends of Univ. Hosp., Ann Arbor, 1985—, pres.-elect, 1987—. Named one of Outstanding Young Men in Am. Jaycees, 1986. Mem. Med. Group Mgrs. Assn., Acad. Practice Assembly, Adminstrs. Internal Medicine, Nat. Council Univ. Adminstrs., Nat. Assn. Social Workers (v.p. Huron Valley chpt. 1979-80). Democrat. Jewish. Home: 3570 Frederick Dr Ann Arbor MI 48105 Office: U Mich Med Sch 3916 Taubman Ctr Ann Arbor MI 48109

HALMRAST, LYNN JAMES, psychologist; b. Wahpeton, N.D., Oct. 27, 1949; d. Gerhard Elmer and Lilly Halmrast; m. Dana Smith, Aug. 7, 1971 (div. Mar. 1980); 1 child, Nathan; m. Rae Mathews, Oct. 12, 1984; children: Meghan, Timothy. MS, Moorhead (Minn.) State U., 1974, specialty degree psychology, 1986, PhD, 1987. Lic. clin. psychologist, sch. psychologist. Psychologist Crookston (Minn.) Regional Interdist. Council for Exceptional Children, 1974-76, Independent Sch. Dist. #152, Moorhead, 1976—; coordinator psychol. services Edn. Cooperative, St. Cloud, Minn., 1980-81; pvt. practice psychology Moorhead, 1986—. Mem. Minn. Council for Exceptional Children (pres. 1987—). Lutheran. Avocation: crew member Hjemkomst Viking Ship Hjemkomst Heritage Ctr., Moorhead, 1980-82. Office: ISD #152 Townsite Ctr 810 4th Ave S Moorhead MN 56560

HALVERSON, PAUL KEITH, financial and accounting executive; b. Evanston, Ill., May 18, 1949; s. Roger Oscar and Helen Ann H. BA, Elmhurst Coll., 1972. V.p., Jr. and sr. class audit staff mgmt. trainee No. Ill. Gas Co., Aurora, Ill., 1969-71; auditor midwest regional audit office consol ops. GTE Service Corp., Des Plaines, Ill., 1971-74; sr. auditor GTE Service Corp., Des Plaines, 1974-75; gen. acctg. supr. GTE Directory Co., Des Plaines, 1975-78, asst. treas., officer, 1978-79, customer credit mgr., 1979; v.p. fin. Fox Ridge (Ill.) Press, 1979-80; head dept. acctg. data processing U.S. Envelope div. Westvaco, North Chicago, Ill., 1980-81; pres. Halverson Assoc., Des Plaines, 1981—; dir. fin., chief fiscal officer Cook County Sheriff, 1987. co-founder Maine Twp. (Ill.) Council on Alcoholism, 1974, v.p., 1974-77, pres. 1977-82; trustee Maine Twp., 1973-79, town clk., 1979-81, twp. supr. 1981—; sec.-treas. Town Trustees Assn., Cook County (Ill.), 1973, v.p., 1974-76, bd. dirs., 1974-77; mem. bd. liaison Maine Twp. com. on Youth, 1978-81; adv. bd. n.w. suburban counseling Salvation Army, 1982-87; mem. Chgo. Council on Fgn. Relations. Mem. Town Clks. Assn. Cook County (legis. com. 1980), Twp. Supr. Assn. (sec. treas. 1981-83, pres. 1983-86), Top. Ofcls. Cook County (pres. 1986—), Twp. Ofcls. of Ill., Govt. Fin. Officers Assn. (paratransit services chmn. 1985—). Republican. Office: 1700 Ballard Rd Park Ridge IL 60068

HAM, DONALD ALEXANDER, accountant; b. Winnipeg, Man., Can., Aug. 29, 1939; s. Ralph Carl Ham and Mary Kathleen (McMillan) Hitchcock; m. Carole Irene Rinkel, Oct. 27, 1967; children: Tina Marie, Robert Hugh. BS of Bus. in Acctg., U. Minn., 1967. CPA, Minn. Staff acct. Larson, Allen, Weishair & Co., Mpls., 1967-73, ptnr., 1973-86; Bd. dirs. First Nat. Bank International Falls, Minn., 1987—. Pres. endowment bd. Rainy River Community Coll., International Falls, 1987—, St. Thomas Sch., International Falls, 1987—. Served with U.S. Army, 1959-62. Roman Catholic. Lodge: Lions (pres. local chpt. 1975-76, sec. local chpt. 1979-80, Disting. Service award 1979-80). Avocation: golf. Home: Rt 8 PO Box 507 International Falls MN 56649

HAM, DONALD J., investment executive, veterinarian, legislator; b. Rapid City, S.D., May 30, 1934; s. Ernest B. and Nancy Jane (Hannum) H.; m. Arlene H. Hansen, Dec. 27, 1956; children—Jennifer L., Grady D. B.S., Colo. State U., 1956, D.V.M., 1958. Veterinarian Custer Vet. Clinic, Miles City, Mont., 1960-69; investment officer Dain Bosworth, Inc., Rapid City, 1969—, v.p., 1975—. Nat. committeeman Mont. Young Reps., 1966-69; county chmn. Pennington County Rep. Central Com., Rapid City, 1973-76; mem. S.D. Ho. of Reps., 1976—, majority whip, 1978-82, 87—, speaker of house, 1984-86. Served to lt. U.S. Army, 1958-60. Mem. Mont. Vet. Assn. (pres. 1968-69). Lutheran. Lodges: Lions, Elks. Avocations: skiing; tennis; golf. Home: 1116 Crestridge Ct Rapid City SD 57701 Office: Dain Bosworth Inc 722 St Joseph St Rapid City SD 57701

HAM, GEORGE ELDON, soil microbiologist, educator; b. Ft. Dodge, Iowa, May 22, 1939; s. Eldon Henry and Thelma (Cran) H.; m. Alice Susan Bormann, Jan. 11, 1964; children—Philip, David, Steven. B.S., Iowa State U., 1961, M.S., 1963, Ph.D., 1967. Asst. prof. dept soil sci. U. Minn., St. Paul, 1967-71, assoc. prof., 1971-77, prof., 1977-80; prof., head dept. agronomy Kans. State U., Manhattan, 1980—; dir. Kans. Crop Improvement Assn., Manhattan, 1980—, Kans. Fertilizer and Chem. Inst., Hutchinson, 1980—, Kans. Crops and Soils Industry Council, Manhattan, 1982—; cons. Internat. Atomic Energy Agy., Vienna, Austria, 1973-79. Assoc. editor Agronomy Jour., 1979-84. Contbr. articles to profl. jours. Asst. scoutmaster Indianhead council Boy Scouts Am., St. Paul, 1977-80; pres. North Star Little League, St. Paul, 1979-80. Served to sgt. U.S. Army, 1963-69. Fellow AAAS, Am. Soc. Agronomy (bd. dirs. council agrl. sci. and tech. 1985—), Soil Sci. Soc. Am.; mem. Crop Sci. Soc. Home: 2957 Nevada St Manhattan KS 66502

HAM, TAEWOO, elec. equipment mfg. corp. exec.; b. Korea, Mar. 13, 1953; came to U.S., 1963, naturalized, 1972; s. Inyong and Hynduck (Kim) H.; B.S., Pa. State U., 1975; postgrad. U. Pitts., 1976-78; MBA, Xavier U., 1986; m. Heiyoung Kim, Nov. 20, 1976; children—Anthony, Alexander. Jr. methods engr. Elliott Co., Jeannette, Pa., 1975-76, methods engr., 1976-77, supr. bills of material, 1977-79, mfg. engr., 1979-80; mfg. systems engr. Gen. Electric Co., Bridgeport, Conn., 1980-84, mgr. mfg. systems applications, program mgr. Automated Engine Assembly Ctr., Cin., 1984-85; mgr. technology modernization programs-engine assembly, 1985—. Mem. ASME (chmn. Pitts. chpt. 1980), Numerical Control Soc. (vice chmn. Pitts. chpt. 1980), Am. Inst. Indsl. Engrs., Soc. Mfg. Engrs. (Outstanding Young Mfg. Engr. award 1987). Home: 5508 Eagle Ln West Chester OH 45069 Office: Gen Electric Co 1 Neumann Way Cincinnati OH 45215

HAMACHEK, DON E., psychology educator; b. Milw., May 6, 1933; s. Evans O. and Marvis (Borgeson) H.; children: Daniel, Deborah. BA, U. Mich., 1955, MSW, 1957, PhD, 1960. Lic. psychologist, Mich. Teaching fellow U. Mich., Ann Arbor, 1958-60; prof. Mich. State U., East Lansing, 1960—. Author: Encounters with the Self, 1971, 2d rev. edit., 1978, 3d rev. edit., 1987, Encounters with Others, 1982, Psychology in Growth, Teaching and Learning, 1975, 3d rev. edit. 1985. Named Outstanding Alumnus, Lake Superior Coll., Sault Ste. Marie, Mich., 1974. Fellow Am. Psychol. Assn.; mem. Am. Assn. Counseling and Devel., Am. Group Psychotherapy Assn, Phi Kappa Kappa. Unitarian. Avocations: reading, running, windsurfing, fishing. Office: Mich State U 438 Erickson Hall East Lansing MI 48824

HAMAN, JERRY LEE, osteopathy educator; b. Williamsburg, Iowa, Mar. 8, 1947; s. Lawrence John and Mildred Maxine (Weaver) H.; m. Teresa Diane King; 1 child, Valerie. AS, Kirkwood Community Coll., Cedar Rapids, Iowa, 1971; BS, N.E. Mo. State U., 1973; MA in Sci. Edn., Northeastern Mo. U., Kirksville, 1974; DO, Kirksville Coll. Osteo. Medicine, 1978. Intern Parkview Hosp., Toledo, 1978-79; med. dir. New Madrid County Group, New Madrid, Mo., 1979-84; emergency room dir. Perry County Hosp., Perryville, Mo., 1984-85; instr. in gen. practice U. Health Scis., Kansas City, Mo., 1985—. Mem. Kansas City YMCA. Served as capt. USAR, 1980—. U.S. Pub. Health scholar, 1975-78. Mem. Am. Osteo. Assn., Am. Acad. Osteopaths, Am. Motorcycles Assn., Freedom of Road Riders. Republican. Home: Box 516 Kearney MO 64060

HAMANN, NORMAN LEE, SR., architect; b. Gypsum, Ohio, Jan. 27, 1936; s. Leonard Rolland and Agatha Gertrude (Bowen) H.; m. Berta Steigenberger, July 25, 1959; children: Norman L. Jr., Yvonne Marie, Richard John, Robert James, Thomas M.A. BArch, U. Mich., 1959. Registered architect Mich., Ind., Mass., Ill., Fla., Tex. Designer, draftsman Louis C. Kingscott & Assocs., Inc., Kalamazoo, Mich., 1960-63; project architect Richard Prince Architect, Kalamazoo, 1963-66; assoc., project architect Noordhoek & Scurlock, Architects, Kalamazoo, 1966-68; assoc. G.E. Diekma & Assocs., Kalamazoo, 1968-77; v.p., sec. Diekema/Hamann/Architects, Inc., Kalamazoo, 1977—. Prin. works include Heritage Housing for Elderly, Davenport, Iowa, Grand Ravine Sr. Housing, Allegan, Mich., Sheraton Hotel, Kalamazoo, Emergency Services Facility, City of Galesburg, Mich., City Hall/Police Dept./Fire Station, City of Three Rivers Mich., Library and Info. Ctr., Comstock Twp., Mich. Mem. Interfaith Forum on Religion, Art and Architecture, Am. Inst. Conservation Hist. and Artistic Works, Comstock Twp. Zoning Bd., 1963-71, Comstock Twp.Bldg. Bd. Appeals, 1967-69, Comstock Twp. Planning Commn., 1971-85, Comstock Zoning Bd. Appeals, 1975-81, 82-85; bd. dirs. Cath. Family Services, Kalamazoo, 1983-87, Mich. Archtl. Found., Detroit; v.p., bd. dirs. Comstock Community Ctr. Mem. AIA (sec. western Mich. chpt. 1979-80, v.p. western Mich. chpt. 1981, pres. western Mich. chpt. 1983, bd. dirs. 1984-85, Mem. of Yr. 1985), Mich. Soc. Architects (bd. dirs. 1984, sec. 1985, v.p. 1986). Avocations: carpentry, stamp collecting, travel. Office: Diekema/Hamann Architects Inc 6011 W Michigan Ave Kalamazoo MI 49009

HAMBERGER, LARRY KEVIN, clinical psychologist, educator; b. Fond du Lac, Wis., June 4, 1953; s. Lawrence Edward and Hilda Ella (Kleberg) H.; m. Nancy Jean Albee, June 30, 1979; 1 child, Heidi Jean. BS, U. Wis., Oshkosh, 1975; MA, U. Ark., 1979, PhD, 1982. Lic. psychologist, Wis. Internship Wood VA Med. Ctr., Milw., 1981-82; clin. instr. Med. Coll. Wis., Milw., 1982-83, asst. prof., 1983—; staff psychologist Mt. Sinai Med. Ctr., Milw., 1983; coordinator, dir. Men's Group Program SE Family Practice Ctr., Kenosha, Wis., 1983—; curriculum cons. Med. Coll. Wis., Milw., 1985—, stress mgmt. cons., 1982—; speaker various scientific meetings, 1979—. Author: Stress and Stress Management, 1984 (writer of yr. award 1984); contbr. articles and chpts. to profl. jours. Mem. Am. Psychological Assn., Wis. Psychological Assn., Soc. Tchrs. Family Medicine, Jaycees (v.p. Franklin, Wis. club 1984-85). Lutheran. Avocations: gardening, exercise, rock and mineral collecting, woodworking. Office: SE Family Practice Ctr PO Box 598 Tallent Hall Kenosha WI 53141

HAMBLIN, RODNEY DELANO, optometrist; b. Hayward, Okla., Mar. 24, 1933; s. Harve Arthur and Frances E. (Craig) H.; m. Lexie Ann Clester; Aug. 14, 1973; children: Terry, Kelly, Kimberly, Timothy. Student, Southwestern Coll., Winfield, Kans., 1951-52; OD, So. Coll. Optometry, 1957. Pvt. practice optometry Derby, Kans., 1957—. Mem. sch. bd. Unified Pub. Sch. Dist. 260, Derby, 1978-79. Served with U.S. Army, 1950-52, Korea. Mem. Am. Optometric Assn., Am. Optometric Found., Kans. Optometric Assn. (pres. 1970-71, Optometrist of Yr. 1977), Kans. Optometric Found., Derby C. of C. (sec. 1962), Beta Sigma Kappa. Republican. Presbyterian. Lodge: Kiwanis (pres. Derby 1961-62, Legion of Honor 1985). Avocation: fishing. Home: 8559 Hila Rd Derby KS 67037 Office: 437 E Madison Derby KS 67037

HAMBY, WARREN PATRICK, manufacturing company executive; b. Mobile, Ala., Apr. 16, 1935; s. Robert Scott and Anne Bridget (Fabre) H.; m. Lucille Isobel Prokop, May 25, 1959; children: Leslie, Tracy, Jeffrey, Matthew. BS in Indsl. Engring., U. Ala., 1960. Various mfg. positions Gen. Electric, various locations, 1960-78; plant mgr. Cooper Industries, Quincy, Ill., 1978-81, v.p., gen. mgr., 1981-84; pres. M-D Pneumatics, Inc., Springfield, Mo., 1984—, also bd. dirs.; bd. dirs. Bevis Industries, Providence. Served to cpl. USMC, 1953-55. Recipient Achievement award for Vocat. Edn., Dothan (Ala.) Bd. Edn., 1977. Mem. Indsl. Assn. Quincy, Houston County C. of C. (bd. dirs. 1975-77), Quincy C. of C. (bd. dirs. 1982-84), Quincy Coll. Pres. Assn. Lodge: Rotary. Avocations: golf, fishing. Home: 1527 S Bedford Rd Springfield MO 65804 Office: M-D Pneumatics Inc 4840 W Kearney Springfield MO 65803

HAMEISTER, LAVON LOUETTA, social worker; b. Blairstown, Iowa, Nov. 27, 1922; d. George Frederick and Bertha (Anderson) Hameister; B.A., U. Iowa, 1944; postgrad. N.Y. Sch. Social Work, Columbia, 1945-46, U. Minn. Sch. Social Work, summer 1952; M.A., U. Chgo., 1959. Child welfare practitioner Fayette County Dept. Social Welfare, West Union, Iowa, 1946-56; dist. cons. services in child welfare and pub. assistance Iowa Dept. Social Welfare, Des Moines, 1956-58, dist. field rep., 1959-64, regional supr., 1964-65, supr., specialist supervision, adminstrn. Bur. Staff Devel., 1965-66, chief Bur. Staff Devel., 1966-68; chief div. staff devel. and tng. Office Dep. Commr., Iowa Dept. Social Services, 1968-72, asst. dir. Office Staff Devel., 1972-79, coordinator continuing edn., 1979-86; farmer. Active in drive to remodel, enlarge Oelwein (Iowa) Mercy Hosp., 1952. Mem. Bus. and Profl. Women's Club (chpt. sec. 1950-52), Am. Assn. U. Women, Nat. Assn. Social Workers (chpt. sec.-elect 1958-59), Am. Pub. Welfare Assn., Iowa Welfare Assn., Acad. Cert. Social Workers. Lutheran. Home: 1800 Grand Ave West Des Moines IA 50265

HAMEL, LOUIS REGINALD, systems analysis cons.; b. Lowell, Mass., July 23, 1945; s. Wilfred John and Angelina Lucienne (Paradis) H.; A.A., Kellogg Community Coll., 1978; m. Roi Anne Roberts, Mar. 24, 1967 (dec.); 1 dau., Felicia Antoinette; m. Anne Louise Staup, July 2, 1972; children—Shawna Michelle, Louis Reginald III. Retail mgr. Marshalls Dept. Stores, Beverly, Mass., 1972-73; tech. service rep. Monarch Marking Systems, Framingham, Mass., 1973-74; employment specialist Dept. Labor, Battle Creek, Mich., 1977-78; v.p. corp. Keith Polygraph Cons. and Investigative Service, Inc., Battle Creek, Mich., 1978-79; indsl. engr., engine components div. Eaton Corp., Battle Creek, Mich., 1979-82; tooling and process engr. Kelley Tech. Services, Battle Creek, Mich., Clark Equipment Inc., 1983-84; tooling and mfg. engr., mfg. mgr. Trans Guard Industries Inc., Angola, Ind., 1983-85; facilitator employee involvement program Wohlert Corp., Lansing, Mich., 1985—; systems analysis cons., 1975—. Mem. Calhoun County Com. on Employment of Handicapped, Battle Creek, Mich., 1977-78; mem. U.S. Congl. Adv. Bd. Served with USN, 1963-71; Vietnam. Recipient Services to Handicapped award Internat. Assn. Personnel in Employment Security, Mich. chpt., 1978. Mem. Nat. Geog. Soc., Mich. Assn. Concerned Vets. (dir.), Nat. Assn. Concerned Vets., VFW. Democrat. Roman Catholic. Home and Office: 12240 Assyria Rd Bellevue MI 49021

HAMILL, CHRISTINA RAE, accountant; b. Detroit, Sept. 15, 1953; d. Carl R. and Shirley Danielson; m. Rick A. Hamill, July 10, 1976. B in Acctg., Mich. State U., 1975; MS in Taxation, Walsh Coll., 1983. CPA, Mich. Mgr. Ernst & Whinney, Detroit, 1975-84; prin. Arthur Young & Co., Detroit, 1984—. Mem. Am. Inst. CPA's, Mich. Assn. CPA's, Health Fin.

Mgrs. Assn., Mich. Women's Profl. Network (treas. Detroit chpt. 1985-86). Republican. Methodist. Club: Renaissance (Detroit). Office: Arthur Young & Co 100 Renaissance Ctr Detroit MI 48243

HAMILL, ROBERT L., biochemical research advisor; b. Youngstown, Ohio, Mar. 13, 1927; s. James Edwin and Jane Marie (Hope) H.; m. Meritta Ann Floyd, June 27, 1953 (div. 1975); children: Sebette Ann, Sheree Hope Hamill Zachary; m. Beverly Ann Pruett, Sept. 25, 1976. Student, Youngstown (Ohio) State U., 1947-48; BS in Chemistry, Ohio U., 1950; MS in Biochemistry, Mich. State U., 1953, PhD, 1955. Research asst. Mich. State U., E. Lansing, 1950-55; sr. biochemist Lilly Research Labs., Indpls., 1955-64, research scientist, 1964-69, research assoc., 1969-83, research advisor, 1983—; vice chmn. Intersci. Conf. on Antimicrobial Agts. and Chemotherapy. Contbr. numerous articles to profl. jours.; editor: Jour. Antibiotics, 1975—, Antimicrobial Agents and Chemotherapy, 1975-85; holder of over 70 patents in field. Served with USN, 1945-47, 51-53. Mem. AAAS, Am. Chem. Soc., Am. Soc. Microbiology, N.Y. Acad. Scis. Republican. Presbyterian. Club: Sertoma (Greenwood, Ind.). Home: 617 Brookview Dr Greenwood IN 46142 Office: Lilly Research Labs Eli Lilly and Co Lilly Corp Ctr Indianapolis IN 46285

HAMILTON, BETH ALLEMAN, information scientist, editor; b. Stewartstown, W.Va., Apr. 3, 1927; d. Hubert Charles and Gay Elizabeth (Zearley) Alleman; m. Rex Hamilton, Apr. 17, 1949; children: Shelley Hamilton Hutter, Meredith L., Eric R., Elizabeth Hamilton Gruhn, John Z. BS, W.Va. U., 1948; MA, Rosary Coll., 1969; CAS, U. Chgo., 1977. Chemist Standard Pharmacal, Chgo., 1948-49; tech. librarian Am. Meat Inst. Found., Chgo., 1949-51; research librarian Glidden Co., Chgo., 1952-53; owner, ptnr. Hamilton Truck Leasing, Elk Grove Village, Ill., 1957-63; editor, bus. analyst Internat. Minerals & Chem. Corp., Skokie, Ill., 1964-69; sci. librarian, assoc. prof. U. Ill., Chgo., 1969-72, adj. assoc. prof., 1972-79; exec. dir. Ill. Regional Library Council, Chgo., 1972-79; vis. lectr. Rosary Coll., 1970-71; vis. asst. prof. U. Ill. Grad Sch. Library Sci., Urbana, 1977-79. Editor: Libraries and Infomation Centers in the Chicago Metropolitan Area, 1973; Union List of Serial Holdings in Illinois Special Libraries, 1976, 77, Multitype Library Cooperation, 1977; (with others) As Much to Learn as to Teach: Essays in Honor of Lester Asheim, 1979, Chemical Engineering Data Sources: AIChE Symposium Series, 1986; contbr. articles to profl. jours. Mem. Arlington Heights (Ill.) Bd. Edn., 1966-70, Burr Ridge (Ill.) Bicentennial Commn., 1975-76; exec. v.p. Rep. Women's Club of Lyons Twp., Ill., 1975-76; librarian, tchr. First Presby. Ch. of Arlington Heights, 1960-69. Mem. ALA, Am. Chem. Soc., Spl. Libraries Assn. (joint task force with Nat. Commn. on Libraries and Info. Sci. on role of the spl. library), Beta Phi Mu. Home: 2420 Fir St Glenview IL 60025 Office: 5950 W Touhy Ave Niles IL 60648

HAMILTON, DAVID R., food service company executive. Pres. Szabo Food Serivce Inc., Oakbrook, Ill. Office: Szabo Food Service Inc 2000 Spring Rd Oakbrook IL 60521 *

HAMILTON, DAVID WENDELL, pathology assistant; b. Gregory, S.D., Feb. 20, 1953; s. Wendell Ralph and Doris Marie (Jacobsen) H.; m. Priscilla Ann Boyer, Mar. 12, 1983. B.S. in Math., U. Nebr., 1979, M.B.A., 1984. Pathologist's asst. Pathology Med. Services, Lincoln, 1976—. Bd. dirs. Friendship Force, Lincoln; programmer Mayor's Com. of Internat. Visitors, Lincoln. Fellow Am. Assn. Pathologist Assts.; mem. Nat. Assn. Med. Examiners, Biol. Photographers Assn., Nat. Histology Assn. Democrat. Lutheran. Avocations: reading; antique clock repair; hunting; fishing. Home: 5950 Bartholomew Circle Lincoln NE 68512 Office: Pathology Med Services 1919 S 40th St Lincoln NE 68506

HAMILTON, EDGAR JAMES, SR., municipal official; b. Baton Rouge, Aug. 10, 1944; s. Thomas James Hamilton and Edna Charlotte (Barnes) Woods; divorced; children: Edgar James, Reginald Felix; m. Sheila Renee Jefferson, June 23, 1979. BS, So. U., 1965; postgrad., Chgo. State U., 1967-69, Northeastern U., 1970-72; MA, Roosevelt U., 1975. Tchr. Chgo. Bd. Edn., 1965-81; dep. asst. supr. Cook County Ednl. Service Region, Chgo., 1981—; career counselor Chgo. Com. Urban Opportunity, 1968, 70, activity coordinator, 1969; cons. U. Ill., Sickle Cell Edn. program, Chgo., 1978. Pres. Judge Russell R. DeBow Scholarship Found., Chgo., 1985-86; mgr. campaigns 8th ward Dem. Orgn., Chgo., 1986; mem. Urban Youth Project, Chgo., 1986. Named one of Outstanding Young Men Am. U.S. Jaycees, 1979, Educator of Yr. Cook County Commr. Samuel Vaughan, 1983. Mem. Nat. Assn. Sch. Execs. (Cert. Achievement, 1982-87), Phi Delta Kappa, Alpha Phi Alpha. Lodge: Masons. Avocations: music, reading, cards, backgammon, outdoor activities. Home: 7430 S Bennett Ave Chicago IL 60649

HAMILTON, JAMES DARRELL, engineering executive; b. Buchanan, Tenn., Aug. 9, 1941; s. William Julius and Mary Ethel (Wimberley) H.; m. Pamela Zandra Diggs, Jan. 13, 1962; children: Christina Faye, William Alexander, James Matthew. Grad high sch., Buchanan. Mechanic McNutt Tractor & Implement Co., Paris, Tenn., 1959-64; set-up man machining dept. spl. products div. Emerson Electric Co., Paris, 1974-65, foreman machining dept., 1965-68, mfg. engr. machining dept., 1968-80, sr. divisional mfg. engr., 1980-86; mgr. mfg. engr., liaison fgn. ops. spl. products div. Emerson Electric Co., Hazelwood, Mo., 1986—. Republican. Mem. Ch. of Christ. Avocations: hunting, fishing, riding. Home: Rt 1 Box 14 Buchanan TN 38222 Office: Emerson Electric Co Spl Products Div 8400 Pershall Rd Hazelwood MO 63042

HAMILTON, LEE HERBERT, congressman; b. Daytona Beach, Fla., Apr. 20, 1931; m. Nancy Ann Nelson, Aug. 21, 1954; children: Tracy Lynn, Deborah Lee, Douglas Nelson. A.B., DePauw U., 1952, hon. degree; scholar, Goethe U., Frankfurt au Main, Germany, 1952-53; J.D., Ind. U., 1956; hon. degree, Hanover Coll. Mem. 89th— Congresses from 9th Dist. Ind., 1965—; chmn. select. com. to investigate covert arms transactions with Iran U.S. Congress, vice chmn. joint econ. com., chmn. subcom. econ. goals and intergovtl. policy; mem. subcom. internat. econ. policy, subcom. sci., research and tech., mem. foreign affairs com., subcom. Arms Control, Internat. Security and Sci.; chmn. subcom. Europe and Middle East; v.p. congrl. del. to U.S. Group Interparliamentary Union. Democrat. Office: US House of Reps 2187 Rayburn House Office Bldg Washington DC 20515

HAMILTON, PETE, chemical company purchasing executive; b. Shenandoah, Iowa, Feb. 19, 1931; s. Edwin Ross and Mary Celestia (Field) H.; m. Joan Revé Reese, Apr. 2, 1953; children: Sonia, Steve, Sandra, Shelly. Grad. high sch, Shenandoah. Editor Daily Sentinal, Shenandoah, 1955-73; purchasing mgr. Imperial Inc., Shenandoah, 1973—. Mem. council City of Shenandoah, 1976-80. Served as sgt. USAF, 1953-55. Mem. Shenandoah C. of C. (bd. dirs., pres. ambassadors for action). Democrat. Methodist. Lodge: Elks. Avocations: golfing, writing. Home: 301 W Summit Shenandoah IA 51601 Office: Imperial Inc W Sixth Shenandoah IA 51601

HAMILTON, RICHARD ALFRED, university administrator, educator; b. Pitts., Dec. 22, 1941; s. Robert Curtis and Dorothy Katherine (Sexauer) H.; BA, Otterbein Coll., 1965; MBA, Bowling Green State U., 1968; D in Bus. Adminstrn. (Univ. fellow 1968-71, Marathon Oil Co. dissertation fellow 1972), Kent State U., 1973. Production rate analyst dept. indsl. engring. RCA, Findlay, Ohio, 1966-67; computer systems analyst dept. market research Marathon Oil Co., Findlay, 1967-68; teaching fellow Coll. Bus. Adminstrn. Kent State U., 1968-71; assoc. prof. direct mktg. U. Mo., Kansas City, 1971—; pres. Mission Woods Cons., Inc.; cons. U.S. Senate Permanent Subcom. on Investigation, 1973-74, Midwest Research Inst. and Office of Tech. Assessment of U.S. Congress, 1974-75; speaker to profl. orgns. Recipient Cray Faculty award U. Mo., 1987. Mem. Am. Acad. Advt., Am. Inst. Decision Scis., Am. Mktg. Assn., Direct Mktg. Assn., Assn. MBA Execs., Sales, Mktg. Execs., Beta Gamma Sigma. Methodist. Author: (with David R. Bywaters) How to Conduct Association Surveys, 1976, Tourism U.S.A.-Marketing Tourism, Vol. 3, 1978; rev. editor Akron Bus. and Econ. Rev., 1977—. Home: 5306 Mission Woods Rd Mission Woods KS 66205 Office: Univ Mo Sch Adminstrn Kansas City MO 64110

HAMILTON, RICHARD PARKER, corporate executive; b. Worcester, Mass., Sept. 13, 1931; s. Ralph Ramsey and Doris Isabel (Waterhouse) H.; m. Nancy Marguerite Daniels, June 6, 1959; children: Jeffrey Richard, Jennifer Lynn, Kimberly Ann. B.B.A., U. Toledo, 1953; M.B.A., Ohio State U., 1954. Various positions Florsheim Shoe Co., Chgo., 1957-69, v.p., gen. mgr., 1969, pres., chief exec. officer, 1970-78; chmn., chief exec. officer retail stores div. Hart Schaffner & Marx, Chgo., 1978-80; pres., chief operating officer Hartmarx Corp., Chgo., 1981-84, chmn., chief exec. officer, 1985-86, now ret. Served with U.S. Army, 1955-56. Congregationalist. Club: Country (Northbrook, Ill.). Office: Hartmarx Corp 101 N Wacker Dr Chicago IL 60606 *

HAMILTON, ROBERT APPLEBY, JR., insurance company executive; b. Boston, Feb. 20, 1940; s. Robert A. and Alice Margaret (Dowdall) H.; student Miami U. (Ohio), 1958-62; m. Ellen Kuhlen, Aug. 13, 1966; children—Jennifer, Robert Appleby, III, Elizabeth. With Travelers Ins. Co., Hartford, Conn., Portland, Maine and Phila., 1962-65; with New Eng. Mut. Life Ins. Co., various locations, 1965—, regional pension rep., Boston, 1968-71, regional mgr., Chgo., 1972-83, sr. pension cons., 1983—. Mem. Republican Town Com., Wenham, Mass., 1970-72, Milton Twp., Ill., 1973-75; mem. Wenham Water Commn., 1970-72. C.L.U.; chartered fin. cons. Mem. Midwest Pension Conf., Am. Soc. Pension Actuaries (assoc.), Am. Soc. C.L.U.s, Am. Assn. Fin. Planners, Profit Sharing Council Am., Chgo. Council Fgn. Relations, Alpha Epsilon Rho. Republican. Home: 2 S 110 Hamilton Ct Wheaton IL 60187 Office: 10 S Riverside Plaza Suite 1710 Chicago IL 60606

HAMILTON, ROBERT MICHAEL, school system administrator; b. Washington, Iowa, June 12, 1945; s. Robert Martin and Francis Louise (Hoover) N.; m. Barbara Ann Hamilton, June 8, 1969; children: Lesley, Allison, Elizabeth, Anne. Student, St. Ambrose Coll., Davenport, Iowa, 1964-65; BBA, U. Iowa, 1968. Mgr. ops. Long Mfg., Davenport, 1972; dir. bus. affairs North Scott Community Sch. Dist., Eldridge, Iowa, 1972—; mem. Iowa State Bd. Pub. Instrn. Task Force on Sch. Fin., 1985. Mayor Town of Long Grove, Iowa, 1986—. Served to capt. U.S. Army, 1968-72, maj. Res. Mem. Assn. Sch. Bus. Ofcls. U.S and Can. (cert., reviewer 1986, cert. excellence 1983-86), Govtl. Fin. Officers Assn. of U.S. and Can. (cert. excellence 1985-86), Iowa Assn. Sch. Bus. Ofcls. (chmn. rules and by-laws com. 1985, chmn. legis. com. 1987), Ea. Iowa Govtl. Purchasing Assn. (pres. 1976-80, 81-82), Area Edn. Agy. Purchasing Assn. (pres. 1979, mem. economy task force 1986). Republican. Lutheran. Avocations: running, swimming, fishing, camping, golf. Office: N Scott Community Sch Dist 251 E Iowa St Eldridge IA 52748

HAMILTON, TED ALLEN, biostatistician; researcher; b. Niles, Mich., May 13, 1955; s. Harold Keith and Betty Lou (Knapp) H.; m. Jane Ann Long, Aug. 28, 1981. B.S. in Fisheries and Wildlife, Mich. State U., 1977; M.S. in Natural Resources, U. Mich., 1980, M.S. in Biostats., 1982. Fisheries biologist, statistician Ecol. Analysts, Inc., Northbrook, Ill., 1980-81; biostatistician, epidemiologist Ford Motor Co., Dearborn, Mich., 1982-83; coordinator, biostatistician dept. dermatology U. Mich. Hosp., Ann Arbor, 1983—. Mem. Am. Statis. Assn. Avocations: hiking, bird-watching, cooking, horticulture. Home: 3583 Pheasant Run Circle Apt 2 Ann Arbor MI 48104 Office: Univ Mich Hosp Dermatology Clin Research 1713 Taubman Ctr Ann Arbor MI 48109

HAMILTON, THOMAS MICHAEL, personnel consultant; b. Davenport, Iowa, Mar. 3, 1938; s. Burley Wilson and Aderienne Vera (Hartley) H.; m. Gayle Caroline Graff, Oct. 22, 1960; children: Sheila, Thomas. BS in Bus., Drake U., 1960, MS in Pyschology and Testing, 1971. Mgr. mktg., personnel N.W. Bell Telephone, Ottumwa, Des Moines, Clinton, Iowa, 1960-66; v.p. Personnel Incorp., Des Moines, 1966-71; pres. Thomas Hamilton & Assocs., Des Moines, 1971—. Bd. dirs. Fellowship of Christian Athletes, Des Moines, 1978—; bd. dirs, sec. YMCA, Des Moines, 1980—; vice chmn. Youth Homes of Iowa, Des Moines, 1971—. Served with USAF, 1960-64. Mem. Am. Soc. Personnel Adminstrn. (accredited), Des Moines C. of C. (chmn. econ. devel. speakers bur.). Republican. Methodist. Club: Des Moines Golf and Country (bd. dirs. 1980-84). Lodges: Rotary. Avocations: handball, fishing, golf. Home: 4706 Aspen Dr West Des Moines IA 50265 Office: Thomas Hamilton & Assocs Inc 100 Court Ave Suite 306 Des Moines IA 50309

HAMILTON, VERA ELLEN, educator, researcher; b. Clark County, Ohio, Dec. 14, 1934; d. Elmer and Clarice Mildred (Schindler) Overholser; m. Carl R. Welty, Mar. 13, 1954 (div. June 1967); children—Garry Lynn, Keith Alan; m. 2d, Nelson C. Hamilton, Mar. 6, 1971 (dec. Oct. 1985). A.A. in Bus. Adminstrn., Bliss Coll., Columbus, Ohio, 1982; B.B.A. in Comml. Credit and Fin., Urbana (Ohio) Coll., 1984. Keypunch operator Hobart Mfg. Co., Troy, Ohio, 1959-61, Kissell Co., Springfield, Ohio, 1961-63, Ohio Steel Foundry, Springfield, 1963-64; keypunch operator, clk.-typist, accounts payable clk., export clk., cost clk., timekeeper, purchasing expeditor Internat. Harvester Co., Springfield, 1964-71; asst. to husband in body shop bus., Springfield, 1971-73; keypunch operator, census preparer Community Hosp., Springfield, Ohio, 1973-76; data entry operator State Automobile Ins. Co., Columbus, Ohio, 1976-79; payroll clk., sec., credit adminstr., credit supr. Air Conditioning div. Magic Chef, Columbus, 1979-84; instr. pt. time Bliss Coll., 1984—; researcher, State Employment Relations Bd., 1986—. Mem. Nat. Assn. Credit Mgrs., Air Conditioning and Refrigeration Inst., Houston Assn. Credit Mgmt., Nat. Assn. Female Execs. Republican. Baptist. Home: 12 Hanford St Columbus OH 43206 Office: Bliss College 3770 N High St Columbus OH 43214

HAMLER, BRUCE WAYNE, retail executive; b. Columbus, Aug. 11, 1949; s. Herman Lester and Jayne (Thompson) H.; m. Connie Kae Corbett, Oct. 10, 1970; children: Heather Lynn, Wayne Thomas. Grad., U.S. Army Sch. Engrs., 1969; student, Columbus Tech. Inst., 1977-79, Columbus Police Acad., 1976, Columbus Police Acad., 1981. Sr. draftsman United Sheet Metal, Westerville, Ohio, 1972-76; archtl. interior designer Functional Planning Inc, Columbus, 1976-80; store designer Gold Circle Stores, Columbus, 1980-84, mgr. store planning, 1984—; archtl. interior designer Shremshock, Yoder Architects, Columbus, 1980-83. Inventor in field. Served with U.S. Army, 1968-70. Mem. Nat. Trust for Hist. Preservation, Am. Fedn. Police, Ohio Vol. Peace Officers Assn. Inc., Columbus Police Auxiliary Honor Guard. Office: Gold Circle Stores PO Box 63 6121 Huntley Rd Worthington OH 43085

HAMLIN, ALLENE GAY, civic worker; b. Highland, Ill., May 11, 1946; d. Israel Benjamin and Margaret Virginia (Eckmann) Hiken; ed. schs. for visually handicapped, secretarial tng.; m. Leonard Albert Hamlin, Oct. 12, 1968; children—Eric Garrett, Stephen Wayne. Mem. adv. sch. bd. Sunnyside Sch., 1979-80; comdr. Red Wing chpt. DAV Aux., 1978-82, chaplain state dept., 1979-80, sr. vice comdr., 1977-78, publicity chmn. Minn. dept., 1978-79, patriotic instr. Minn. dept., 1980-81, patriotic instr. dept. Minn., 1981-82, adj. Red Wing chpt., 1982-84, recipient past comdrs. pin, 1979; transcriber Braille books. Republican. Home: 1527 Central Ave Red Wing MN 55066

HAMLIN, JANE GREENE, curriculum specialist; b. Washington, Nov. 26, 1934; d. Roosevelt Brown and Mildred Lola (Hendrix) Greene; B.S., Purdue U., 1956; M.Ed., Nat. Coll. Ed., 1975; m. Richard Peter Hamlin, Aug. 11, 1956; children—Diane, Peter, David, Andrea. Tchr., N.W. Suburban Spl. Edn. Orgn., Palatine, Ill., 1974-80; curriculum specialist Behavior Edn. Center, Wheeling, Ill., 1980—. Mem. Northfield Village Caucus, 1981-85. Office Supt. Public Instrn. fellow, 1974. Mem. Ill. Council Exceptional Children (govt. relations regional coordinator), Assn. Supervision and Curriculum Devel., NEA, Phi Delta Kappa, Phi Mu (nat. career devel. dir.). Republican. Mem. United Ch. of Christ. Office: 1001 W Dundee St Wheeling IL 60090

HAMLIN, RICHARD EUGENE, former college president, banker; b. Royal, Iowa, June 2, 1925; s. Fred E. and Nancy Jane (Schuetz) H.; m. C. Joan Dahl, Aug. 14, 1949; children: Robert E., Elizabeth Ann. Student, Drury Coll., 1943; B.S., George Williams Coll., 1949; M.A., U. Omaha, 1952; Ph.D., U. Nebr., 1956. Exec. sec. South Omaha (Nebr.) YMCA, 1949-51; adult edn. dir. South Omaha (Nebr.) YMCA, Omaha, 1951-53; asso. dir. research nat. bd. South Omaha (Nebr.) YMCA, 1953-61; pres. George Williams Coll., 1961-83; chmn. bd., chief exec. officer Bank of Yorktown, Lombard, Ill., 1983-86; sr. v.p. Cole-Taylor Fin. Group, Northbrook, Ill., 1986—; chmn. bd. dirs. Cole Taylor Banks, Lombard and Skokie, Ill., 1986—; tchr. summer conf. Am. Youth Found., summer sch. U. Omaha.; Chmn. bd. Asso. Colls. Ill., 1977-78; vice chmn. Fedn. Ind. Ill. Colls. and Univs., 1977-78, chmn., 1978-81. Author: Hi-Y Today, 1955, A New Look at YMCA Physical Education, 1957; Co-editor: YMCA Yearbook, 1958-61. Mem. Am., Ill. psychol. assns., Downers Grove (Ill.) C. of C. (past chmn. bd.). Congregationalist. Clubs: University, Economic (Chgo.); Butterfield Country, DuPage. Home: 3908 Forest Dr Downers Grove IL 60515 Office: One Yorktown Ctr Lombard IL 60148

HAMM, JAMES MALCOLM, secondary educator; b. Parkersburg, W.Va., Feb. 20, 1947; s. Delmar Russell and Emma Jean (Carmichael) H.; divorced; children: Kimberly, Erin, Stephanie, Andrew. Student, U. Cin., 1965-67; BS in Secondary Edn., Ohio U., 1969; MEd, Xavier U., 1979. Cert. tchr. chemistry, data processing, computer sci., physical sci. High sch. tchr. Fed.-Hocking Sch., Stewart, Ohio, 1969-74, Southern Local Sch., Racine, Ohio, 1974-76, Blanchester (Ohio) Local Sch., 1976—; cons. Scholarship Testing Program, State of Ohio, 1979-83. Contbr. articles on sports to local newspaper, 1974-78; editor monthly newsletter automotive orgn., 1984-86. Mem. Ohio Edn. Assn., Nat. Edn. Assn. Lutheran. Lodge: Rotary (treas. 1985). Avocation: Chrysler car enthusiast.

HAMM, JOHN PETER, accountant, school system financial administrator; b. Iron Mountain, Mich., Mar. 11, 1934; s. Grant Charles and Gertrude Josephine (Genisee) H.; m. Dorisa Joy Beyer, Aug. 3, 1957; children: Jacqueline R., Stephanie A., Valerie J., Christopher G., John G., William P. BBA, Mich. State U., East Lansing, 1956. CPA, Wis., Mich. Sr. auditor Arthur Young & Co., Milw., 1957-62; sr. internal auditor Hwy. Trailer, Edgerton, Wis., 1962-65; chief acct. hosp., mgr. dept. internal audit U. Mich., Ann Arbor, 1965-70; treas. Property Devel. Group, Ann Arbor, 1970-72; assoc. supt. bus. and fin. Warren (Mich.) Consol. Schs., 1972—. Editor: (newsletter) Mich. Sch. Bus. Ofcls., 1981-83; contbr. articles to profl. jours. Served as capt. U.S. Army, 1957-59. Mem. Mich. Sch. Bus. Ofcls. (bd. dirs. 1983—, pres.-elect 1987-88), Am. Inst. CPA's, Assn. Sch. Bus. Ofcls., Macomb/St. Clare City Sch. Bus. Ofcls. (past pres, v.p., sec./treas). Republican. Roman Catholic. Clubs: Forest Brook Athletic (Ann Arbor), Travis Pointe Country. Lodge: Kiwanis (v.p. Ann Arbor club 1970). Avocations: jogging, antiques, sports. Home: 2817 Lillian Rd Ann Arbor MI 48104 Office: Warren Consol Schs 31300 Anita Warren MI 48093

HAMM, VERNON LOUIS, JR., management and financial consultant; b. East St. Louis, Ill., Mar. 14, 1951; s. Vernon Louis and Colleen Ann Hamm; B.S., Murray (Ky.) State U., 1973; M.B.A., St. Louis U., 1975; postgrad. Stanford U., 1975. Jr. exec. corp. accounts Brown Group, Inc., St. Louis, 1973-75; group supr. APC Skills Co., Palm Beach, Fla., 1975-77; account mgr. Inst. Mgmt. Resources, Los Angeles, 1977-78; dir. mgmt. devel. Naus & Newlyn, Inc., Paoli, Pa., 1978-82; pres. Mgmt. Alternatives Ltd., 1982—; mgmt., fin. and energy cons., 1975—; bd. dirs. Ryan's Family Steakhouses, Inc.; dir. Psychosystems Mgmt. Corp., N.Y.C. Mem. Am. Soc. for Tng. and Devel., Am. Prodn. and Inventory Control Soc., Murray State U. Alumni Assn. Contbr. articles to profl. publs.

HAMMAR, LESTER EVERETT, health care manufacturing company executive; b. Tillamook, Oreg., Dec. 15, 1927; s. Leo E. and Harriet L. (Parsons) H.; m. Margrit Steigl, May 9, 1964; children: Lawrence, Thomas, Stephanie. B.S., Oreg. State U., 1950; M.B.A., Washington U., 1964. With Montsanto Co., 1952-69; controller Monsanto-Europe, 1966-69; v.p., controller Smith Kline & French Labs., Phila., 1969-72, Abbott Labs., North Chgo., Ill., 1972—; dir. Hammar's Uniforms, Inc., Haven Fin. Corp. Ruling elder, clk. of session 1st Presbyterian Ch. of Lake Forest; mem. Interfaith Community Services. Served to 1st lt. F.A., AUS, 1951-52. Mem. Fin. Execs. Inst. (com. mem.), Am. Mgmt. Assn. (finance council). Club: 100 of Lake County (treas.). Home: 809 Timber Ln Lake Forest IL 60045 Office: Abbott Labs Abbott Park North Chicago IL 60064

HAMMARSTEN, JAMES FRANCIS, physician, educator; b. Grey Eagle, Minn., Mar. 25, 1920; s. Francis Ragnar and Julia Linnea (Hammargren) H.; m. Dorothea Marie Jung, Apr. 15, 1944; children: Linnea, James Eric, Richard. BS, U. Minn., 1943, MB, 1944, MD, 1945. Diplomate Am. Bd. Internal Medicine (bd. dirs. 1967-73, various other offices). Intern U. Okla. Hosps., Oklahoma City, 1944-45; resident in internal medicine U. Minn. Hosps., VA Hosp., Mpls., 1947-49; asst. prof. medicine U. Minn., Mpls., 1949-53, prof., 1962-66; from asst. prof. to prof. U. Okla., Oklahoma City, 1953-62, prof., head dept. medicine, 1966-78, Carl Puckett prof. pulmonary diseases, vice-chmn. dept. medicine, 1967-77; prof. medicine U. Okla. Health Scis. Ctr., Oklahoma City, 1977-78; prof. U. Wash., Seattle, 1978-87; disting. vis. prof. health scis. Boise State U., 1978-87; asst. chief med. services VA Hosp., Mpls., 1949-53; chief med. service VA Hosp., Oklahoma City, 1953-62, Boise VA Med. Ctr., 1978-81; chief of medicine St. Paul-Ramsey Hosp., 1962-66; cons. Internat. Union Against Tb; vis. prof. Laennec Hosp., Paris, 1977-78. Contbr. numerous articles to profl. jours. Served with U.S. Army, 1945-47, with USAF, 1953, col. USAR. Mem. AMA (alt. house dels. 1974-77, sec. council on diseases of chest 1974-77, counterpart dept. head Vietnam project 1967-75), ACP (master, re-certification com. 1971-73, Okla. Gov.'s council 1972-78), AAAS, Am. Lung Assn. (bd. dirs. 1968-80, 82—, various offices, Hall of Fame 1979), Am. Thoracic Soc. (pres. 1969-70, councilor-at-large 1962-64, 66-71, gen. med. sessions program com. 1963-65, chmn. med. sessions. program com. 1963, subcom. on fellowship 1966-67, others), Am. Heart Assn. (profl. edn. com. 1961-67, subcom. on pilot projects 1961-65, chmn. subcom. on pilot projects 1965-67, vice-chmn. profl. edn. com. 1963, others), Am.-Israel Med. Found. (trustee), Cen. Soc. Clin. Research (pres. 1968-69), Assn. Am. Physicians, Am. Geriatric Soc., Am. Clin. and Climatological Assn., Am. Coll. Chest Physicians (hon. fellow), Am. Fedn. Clin. Research, Assn. Am. Physicians, Am. Soc. Internal Medicine, Idaho County Med. Soc., Idaho State Med. Assn., Minn. Soc. Internatl Medicine, N.Y. Acad. Scis., Oklahoma County Med. Assn., Okla. Heart Assn., Okla. Soc. Internal Medicine, Okla. State Med. Assn., Okla. Thoracic Soc., Minn. Thoracic Soc., Soc. Exptl. Biology and Medicine, So. Soc. Clin. Investigation, Alpha Omega Alpha, Sigma Xi. Democrat. Lutheran. Lodge: Lions. Home: Rt 2 PO Box 192 Melrose MN 56352

HAMMEL, ERNEST MARTIN, health education administrator, educator; b. Ashtabula, Ohio, May 2, 1939; s. Eugene Christian and Etna Maria (Costas) H.; m. Martha Lorene Hertzer, Dec. 16, 1961; children—Eric John, James Martin. Student Hiram Coll., 1957-58; B.S., Heidelberg Coll., 1962; M.P.H., U. Mich., 1966, Ph.D., 1976. Sch. environ. health sanitarian Union County Health Dept., Marysville, Ohio, 1962-65; program planning specialist Mich. Commn. on Aging, Lansing, 1966-69; adminstr. local health dept. planning Mich. Dept. Pub. Health, Lansing, 1969-70; planning cons. Wayne County Health Dept., Eloise, Mich., 1970; program developer Mich. Assn. Regional Med. Programs, East Lansing, 1973-74, asst. dir. ops., 1975-76; exec. dir. Oakland Health Edn. Program, Rochester, Mich., 1976—; adj. prof., health services adminstrn. adviser Central Mich. U. Inst. for Personal and Career Devel., Mt. Pleasant, 1980—. Chmn. Oakland County Health Cable Communications Council, 1982-83; trustee Kenny Mich. Rehab. Found., Southfield, 1983—; mem. Republican City Com., Ann Arbor, Mich., 1972; troop com. chmn. Clinton Valley council Boy Scouts Am., 1981—. Behavioral Sci. fellow U. Mich., 1969-70, Behavioral Sci. Research fellow, 1971-72; grad. student Research grantee Rackham Sch. Grad. Studies, U. Mich., 1972; Pub. Health Service trainee U. Mich., 1965-66, 70-71, 72-73; contract Nat. Ctr. for Health Services Research and Devel., 1973. Mem. Assn. Am. Med. Colls., Am. Heart Assn., Am. Pub. Health Assn., Assn. Health Services Research, Assn. for Hosp. Med. Edn., Mich. Assn. for Med. Edn., Mich. Pub. Health Assn. U. Mich. Alumni Assn. Lutheran. Lodges: Masons, Shriners, Order of Eastern Star. Contbr. articles to profl. publs. Editor several med. care orgn. publs. Office: Oakland Health Edn Program Varner House Adams at Butler Rochester MI 48309-4401

HAMMER, CHERYL LYNN, engineer; b. New Kensington, Penn., Dec. 14, 1960; d. Clair Edward and Charlotte Ryan (Kerr) Eckels; m. Edgar Thomas Hammer III, May 28, 1982. BS in Mgmt. Engring. with honors, Grove City (Pa.) Coll., 1982. Cert. quality engr. Engr. Westinghouse Corp., Pitts., 1982-83, Consumers Power Co., Jackson, Mich., 1983-84; mfg. engr. Gen. Motors, Lansing, Mich., 1984—. Head organist Plum Creek Presbyn. Ch., Pitts., 1976-78; mem. Coll. Reps., Grove City, 1980-81; treas. Tammany Hills Condominium Assn., Lansing, 1986—; cons. project bus. Jr. Achievement. Nat. Presbyn. Agy. scholar, 1978. Mem. Am. Soc. for Quality

Control (cert.), Gamma Chi (fundraiser, gift chmn. 1980-82), Magna Cum Laude Soc. (pres. 1977-78). Republican. Lodge: Internat. Order Rainbow Girls (worthy advisor 1977-78). Avocations: physical fitness, reading, music. Home: 2925 Staten Ave #6 Lansing MI 48910 Office: Gen Motors B-O-C Lansing Div 920 Townsend St MC 4001 Lansing MI 48921

HAMMER, JOHN HENRY, II, hospital administrator; b. Bartlesville, Okla., Dec. 27, 1943; s. John Henry and Lucy (Macias) H.; B.B.A., St. Joseph's Coll., 1966; student U. Md. (Europe), 1968-69; M.B.A., U. Ill., 1984; m. Michele Evano, June 27, 1970; children—John Henry, Erica. Project mgr. Econ. & Manpower Corp., N.Y.C., 1971-73; asst. dir. human resources St. Catherine Hosp., East Chicago, Ind., 1974-80, pres. Employees Credit Union, 1974-80; dir. personnel Lakeview Med. Center, Danville, Ill., 1980-84, v.p., 1984—; bd. dirs. East Cen. Ill. Health Systems Agy., East Cen. Ill. Health Planning Orgn. Chmn., De La Garza Career Center Program Com., 1974-80. Served to capt. USAF, 1967-71, to maj. USAFR. Mem. Ind. Soc. Hosp. Personnel Adminstrn. (chmn. 1976-77, dir. 1977-79, pres. 1979-80), Am. Coll. Healthcare Execs. (bd. dirs. pvt. industry council 1983—), Am. Soc. Hosp. Personnel Adminstrn., Central Ill. Soc. Hosp. Personnel Adminstrs. (pres. 1984), Am. Soc. Personnel Adminstrn. Roman Catholic. Home: 1324 N Walnut Ave Danville IL 61832 Office: 812 N Logan Ave Danville IL 61832

HAMMER, OTTO ROBERT, manufacturing company executive, consultant; b. Arad, Romania, Aug. 25, 1946; came to U.S., 1952; s. Louis Hammer and Anna Peck; m. Patricia Ann Paulin, July 4, 1981. B MechE, CCNY, 1969. Cert. data processor. Staff scientist Sage Action, Inc., Ithaca, N.Y., 1970-72; area tech. specialist Tymshare, Inc., Syracuse, N.Y., 1972-76; group dir. Ernst & Whinney, Cleve., 1976-82; mgr. tech. services Rubbermaid, Inc., Wooster, Ohio, 1982—. Mem. Data Processing Mgmt. Assn., The Operation Research Soc. (membership chmn. 1979-80). Avocations: tennis, gardening. Home: 1345 Sugar Knoll Dr Akron OH 44313 Office: Rubbermaid Inc 1147 Akron Rd Wooster OH 44691

HAMMER, ROBERT WAYNE, television producer and director; b. Springfield, Mo., Oct. 12, 1947; s. Garold Cleo and Anne Louise (Bomhoff) H.; m. Sandra Sue Connelly, Aug. 15, 1970; children: Amy Louise, Abby Dean, Aaron Preston. Student, Friends U., Wichita, Kans., 1965-67, Wichita State U., 1967-70. Producer, dir. Sta. KAKE-TV, Wichita, 1966-71, Sta. WTOL-TV, Toledo, 1971-75; dir. creative services Sta. WBBH-TV, Ft. Myers, Fla., 1975-76; producer, dir. UAB Prodns., Cleve., 1976—; freelance talent coach, Cleve., 1982—. Longhouse chief Indian Guides, Strongville, Ohio, 1984—; bd. dirs. S.W. Cleve. br. YMCA, 1987—. Recipient Gold medal Internat. Film and TV Festival N.Y., 1984, Bronze Telly award TV Comml. Festival, 1985, Gold Telly award TV Comm., Festival, 1987. Mem. Nat. Acad. TV Arts and Scis. (Emmy award 1980, 84), Jaycees (bd. dirs. Berea, Ohio chpt. 1980-82). Republican. Methodist. Avocations: skiing, flying. Home: 774 Trotter Ln Berea OH 44017 Office: UAB Prodns 8443 Day Dr Parma OH 44129

HAMMER, ROGER ALLEN, publishing executive; b. San Francisco, Nov. 11, 1934; s. Paul A. and Margaret J. (Lilly) H.; children—Calli, Stephen. A.A., U. Calif.-Berkeley, 1954; B.A., U. Minn., 1973. News editor Mobile (Ala.) Daily Press Register, 1959-66; bur. chief UPI, Montgomery, Ala., 1966-69; account exec. Carl Byoir & Assocs., N.Y.C., 1969-77; group mgr. pub. relations Honeywell, Mpls., 1977-80; editor Hammer News Service, editor, pub. The Place in The Woods, pres. Hammer Enterprise, Golden Valley, Minn., 1980—; adult edn. tchr. Bd. dirs. Ala. Open and Sr. Bowl tennis tournaments, 1964-65; community liaison minority projects, Honeywell, Mpls., 1975-77. Served with AUS, 1957-59. Mem. Pub. Relations Soc. Am. (accredited), U.S. Tennis Assn., Native Sons of Golden West, Soc. Profl. Journalists. Democrat. Roman Catholic. Club: Minn. Press. Author: Black America, American Woman, 1980; The People (Native Americans), 1981; Hispanic America, 1984; My Own Book, 1987; pub. newsletter Read, America!. Office: 3900 Glenwood Ave Golden Valley MN 55422

HAMMER, SIGMUND IMMANUEL, retired geology and geophysics educator, consultant; b. Webster, S.D., Aug. 13, 1901; s. Ludvig Erikson and Laura Louise (Anderson) H.; m. Norma Lucille Johnson (dec. 1980); children—Sigmund Lewis, Mary Alice (dec.), John Phillip, Kirsten Norma Hammer Gardner, Paul Ludvig Norman, Laura Blanche Hammer Inglis (dec.), Douglas James, Ludvig Erikson; m. Doris E. Pullman Lomberg, 1985. Student Concordia Coll., 1919-21; B.A., St. Olaf Coll., 1924; Ph.D., U. Minn., 1929. Geophysicist, Gulf Oil Corp., Pitts., 1929-46, sect. head, 1946-67; lectr. U. Pitts., 1946-67, adj. mem. grad. faculty, 1963-67; prof. geology and geophysics, U. Wis., Madison, 1967-72, prof. emeritus, 1972—; cons. in exploration geophysics; exploration advisor United Nations Devel. Projects, Bolivia, 1972-75, Turkey, 1976-78; visiting prof. U. Mex., Mexico City, 1980, U. Minn., Duluth, 1981; mem. Appalachian Ultradeep Corehole Steering Com., 1987—. Contbr. articles to profl. jours. Organizing chmn. French Cultural Ctr. Western Pa., (1965-67; chmn. Norwegian classroom com. U. Pitts., 1962-66; pres. Nationality Council, U. Pitts., 1966-67; organizing pres. Am. Scandinavian Found., Pitts. chpt. 1964-66, Madison chpt. 1970-71. Mem. Am. Physical Soc., Soc. Exploration Geophysicists (hon.), (v.p. 1950-51, pres. 1951-52), Am. Geophysical Union (fellow), Am. Assn. Petroleum Geologists. Republican. Club: Cosmos (Washington). Avocations: Norwegian and American heritage and culture. Home: 110 S Henry St Apt 406 Madison WI 53703 Office: 1215 W Dayton St U Wis Weeks Hall Geol Scis Madison WI 53706

HAMMER, WILLIAM EARL, JR., information systems executive; b. Dayton, Ohio, Oct. 25, 1939; s. William Earl and Della (Nickel) H.; m. Beverly Gail Houston, June 15, 1963; children: Heidi Jo, Mark Jeffrey. B in Indsl. Engring., U. Dayton, 1962; MS in Indsl. Engring., Ohio State U., 1968. Cert. computer profl., Ill. Engr. Western Electric Co., Inc., Columbus, Ohio, 1962-64; planning engr. Western Electric Co., Inc., Columbus, 1964-67; sr. indsl. engr. The Duriron Co., Inc., Dayton, 1967-69, systems mgr., 1969-73, dir. info. systems, 1973—; mem. adv. bd. The Engring. Software Report, Clarkston, Ga., 1986—. Co-editor: Computer Integrated Manufacturing Systems, 1985; co-author: An Engineer's Guide to Spreadsheets, Word Processors & Data Base Managers, 1986. Fellow Inst. Indsl. Engrs. (pres. Dayton chpt. 1982-83, dir computer and info. systems div. 1983-84, v.p. area II, trustee 1987—); mem. Assoc. Info. Mgrs. Republican. Presbyterian. Club: Engrs. of Dayton (pres. 1986-87). Avocation: tennis. Office: The Duriron Co Inc 425 N Findlay St PO Box 1145 Dayton OH 45440

HAMMERSLEY, HOWARD ALAN, food products company account representative; b. Chgo., Jan. 29, 1962; s. Marshall Lester and Shirley Sylvia (Rosthantal) H. BS in Fin. Mktg., Ind. U., 1984. End-user rep. Land O'Lakes, Inc., Washington, 1984; sales rep. Land O'Lakes, Inc., Pitts., 1984-85; key acct. specialist Land O'Lakes, Inc., Altoona, Pa., 1985; acct. rep. Land O'Lakes, Inc., Columbus, Ohio, 1985-86, nat. accounts mgr., 1986—. Clubs: Ind. U. Alumni (Columbus) (treas.), Updowntowners (Columbus). Avocations: running, weightlifting, volleyball, basketball, sailing. Home: 5730 Shannon Heights Blvd Columbus OH 43220

HAMMON, ROBERT LEE, school administrator, educator; b. Macomb, Ill., Nov. 25, 1946; s. Victor Lee and Verna Elizabeth (Kerr) H.; m. Diane Kay Miner, Aug. 3, 1968; children: Robert James, Amanda Diane. BA in History, Western Ill. U., 1968, MS in Edn., 1970, D in Spl. Edn., 1971; PhD, U. Iowa, 1983. Cert. tchr., ednl. adminstr., adminstrv. supt. Tchr. Triopia Community Unit Sch. Dist., Concord, Ill., 1968-70; asst. high sch. prin. Maquoketa (Iowa) Community Unit Sch. Dist., 1971-73, high sch. prin., 1973-84; asst. supt. Sycamore (Ill.) Community Unit Sch. Dist., 1984—; grad. asst. Western Ill. U., 1970-71, U. Iowa 1982-83; asst. to dir. Inst. for Sch. Excecs., Iowa City, 1982-83; instr. Northern Ill. U., DeKalb, 1986—; del. 45th Supt. Work Conf., Tchrs. Coll. Columbia U., N.Y.C., 1986. Author monographs on collective bargaining, tchr. dismissal. Chmn. Pumpkin Festival Com., Sycamore, 1985-86. Ind. Dist. Ednl. Assn. fellow Kettering Found., 1974, 75, 76, 81; Disting. Educator award, Kettering Found.; Ill. State Tchrs. scholar, State of Ill. Mem. Am. Assn. Sch. Adminstrs., Ill. Assn. Sch. Adminstrs., Assn. Supervision and Curriculum Devel., Nat. Assn.. Pub. Employer Negotiators and Adminstrs., Sycamore C. of C. (v.p. 1984, pres. 1987-88). Methodist. Lodges: Rotary (Sycamore com. chmn.), Masons, Shriners, Optimists (v.p. Maquoketa). Home: 339 Parkside Dr Sycamore IL 60178 Office: Sycamore Community Unit Sch Dist 427 245 W Exchange St Sycamore IL 60178

HAMMOND, HAROLD LOGAN, pathology educator, oral pathologist; b. Hillsboro, Ill., Mar. 18, 1934; s. Harold Thomas and Lillian (Carlson) H.; m. Sharon Bunton, Aug. 1, 1954 (dec. 1974); 1 child, Connie; m. Pat J. Palmer, Aug. 1, 1985. Student Millikin U., 1953-57, Roosevelt U., Chgo., 1957-58; D.D.S., Loyola U., Chgo., 1962; M.S., U. Chgo., 1967. Diplomate Am. Bd. Oral Pathology. Intern, U. Chgo. Hosps., Chgo., 1962-63, resident, 1963-66, chief resident in oral pathology, 1966-67; asst. prof. oral pathology U. Iowa, Iowa City, 1967-72, assoc. prof., 1972-80, assoc. prof., dir. surg. oral pathology, 1980-83, prof., dir., 1983—; cons. pathologist Hosp. Gen. de Managua, Nicaragua, 1970—, VA Hosp., Iowa City, 1977—. Cons. editor: Revista de la Asociation de Nicaragua, 1970-71, Revista de la Federacion Odontologica de Centroamerica y Panama, 1971-77. Contbr. articles to sci. jours. Recipient Mosby Pub. Co. Scholarship award, 1962. Fellow AAAS, Am. Acad. Oral Pathology; mem. Am. Men and Women of Sci., N.Y. Acad. Scis., AAUP, Internat. Assn. Oral Pathologists, Internat. Assn. Dental Research. Avocations: collecting antique clocks, collecting gambling paraphernalia, collecting toys. Home: 1108 Weeber Circle Iowa City IA 52240-3359 Office: Univ Iowa Dental Sci Bldg Iowa City IA 52242-0101

HAMPL, JULIE LYNN, accountant; b. Russell, Kans., Aug. 22, 1956; d. Delmar L. and Mary Lou (Harper) H. BS in Bus. Adminstrn., Kans. State U., 1978. CPA, Kans., Mo. Staff acct. Touche Ross & Co., Kansas City, Mo., 1978-80; sr. acct. Touche Ross & Co., Kansas City, 1980-83, audit supr., 1983-86, recruiting dir., 1984-86, audit mgr., 1986—; instr. CPA rev. course U. Kans., Lawrence, 1985-87. v.p. Dimensions Unlimited, Kansas City, 1983; mem. fin. com. YWCA, Kansas City, 1984-85; trustee Village Ch., Prairie Village, Kans., 1986—; bd. dirs. Kansas City Consensus, 1987. Recipient Gold Key award State of Kans., 1978. Mem. Am. Inst. CPA's, Mo. Soc. CPA's (mem. state com. 1985-86), Eggs and Issues. Republican. Presbyterian. Club: Cen. Exchange (chmn. fin. com. 1984-86). Home: 3136 S 47th Terr Kansas City KS 66106 Office: Touche Ross & Co 1010 Grand Ave Suite 400 Kansas City MO 64106

HAMPTON, GLEN RICHARD, environmental engineer; b. Detroit, June 11, 1948; s. LaVerne P. and Virginia M. (Hubbard) H.; B.S. in Engring., Mich. Tech. U., 1973; m. Jane E. Fenlon, Jan. 30, 1981; children—Sarah Lynn, Melanie Anne. Project engr. Granger Engring., Inc., Cadillac, Mich., 1973-79; exec. v.p., dir. Chippewa Architects & Engrs., Inc., Kincheloe and St. Ignace, Mich., 1979-82; constrn. mgr. J.H. Granger and Assocs., Sault Ste. Marie, Mich., 1983—; cons. constrn. engring., environ. engring., civil engring., pollution control and solar energy. Registered profl. engr., Mich., Ky., Minn., Wis. Mem. Nat. Soc. Profl. Engrs., Mich. Soc. Profl. Engrs., ASCE (pres. N.W. Mich. chpt. 1980-82), Mich. Water Pollution Control Fedn., Mich. Soc. Civil Engrs., Nature Conservancy (dir. Mich. chpt.), Nat. Audubon Soc. Club: Kiwanis. Home: Route 2 Box 130 A Saint Ignace MI 49781 Office: Court St Sault Saint Marie MI 49783

HAMPTON, MARGARET JOSEPHINE, educator, decorating consultant; b. Princeton, Mo., Nov. 25, 1935; d. Leland Isaac and Margaret Ellen (Wendt) Heriford; m. Ronald Keith Hampton, July 20, 1957; children: Kevin Keith, Ronda René. BS, Samford U., 1957; MEd in Home Econs., U. Mo., 1974. Cert. vocat. home econs. tchr., Mo., Ala. Elem. tchr. Birmingham (Ala.) Pub. Schs., 1957; vocat. and home econs. tchr. Licking (Mo.) High Sch., 1957-68; tchr. Pattonville High Sch., Maryland Heights, Mo., 1968—; cons. North Cen. Schs. Accreditation Team, Columbia, Mo., 1970—, interior decorating Home Interiors, Dallas, 1981—; cons. lighting, home economist Intercounty Electric, Licking, 1963-67; supervising tchr. U. Mo., Columbia, 1972—; ednl. adv. council J.C. Penny Stores, St. Louis, 1978-80; cons. to food editor St. Louis County Star News, 1982-86. Author (with others) Mo. Family Relations Curriculum Guide, 1961-63. Mem. adv. council Parkway Sch. Dist., St. Louis, 1979-80, Mo. Gov.'s Conf. on Health and Drug Abuse, Jefferson City, 1986—. Mem. Nat. Assn. Vocat. Home Econs. Tchrs. (sec. 1983-85, pres. 1986—, editor and pub. jour. 1983-85), Am. Home Econs. Assn. (Mo. conf. chmn. 1979-80), Am. Vocat. Assn. (exec. bd. 1986—), Mo. Home Econs. Tchrs. Assn. (pres. 1979-81, Tchr. of Yr. award 1985 -86), St. Louis Suburban Home Econs. Tchrs. Assn. (pres. 1978-79), Future Homemakers Am. (advisor St. Louis chpt. 1957-86). Baptist. Home: 1514 Sugargrove Ct Creve Coeur MO 63146 Office: Pattonville High Sch 2497 Creve Coeur Mill Rd Maryland Heights MO 63043

HAMPTON, RONALD KEITH, educator, science curriculum consultant; b. Houston, Mo., May 16, 1934; s. William Arthur and Mary Elizabeth (Houser) H.; m. Margaret Josephine Heriford, July 20, 1957; children—Kevin Keith, Ronda Rene. B.S., Samford U., 1956; M.A.T., Duke U., 1964. Cert. tchr., Mo. Tchr. sci. Licking Sch. Dist., Mo., 1956-68; tchr. sci., sci. coordinator Jennings Schs., Mo., 1968—; evaluation team mem. No. Central Coll. & U., 1974-85. Author: (with R. Crooks) Life Science Mastery Learning Curriculum, 1982. NSF fellow, 1959-70. Baptist. Avocations: outdoor recreation, fishing, hunting, camping, travel. Home: 1514 Sugargrove Ct Creve Coeur MO 63146

HAMRA, SAM FARRIS, JR., lawyer, restaurateur; b. Steele, Mo., Jan. 21, 1932; s. Sam Farris and Victoria (Homra) H.; m. June Samaha, Apr. 1, 1956; children: Sam Farris III, Karen E., Michael K., Jacqueline K. BS in Bus., U. Mo., 1954, LLB, 1959. Bar: Mo. 1959. Assoc. Miller, Fairman, Sanford, Carr & Lowther, Springfield, Mo., 1959-65; sole practice Springfield, 1965—; pres., chmn. bd. Wendy's of SW Mo., Inc., Springfield, 1977—, Wendy's of Mo., Springfield, 1977—; vice chmn. Landmark Bank, Springfield; bd. dirs. Landmark Bancshares Corp., St. Louis; chmn. Law Day USA, 1960. Mem. vestry St. James Episcopal Ch., 1962-64, 69-71, lay reader, 1959-84; trustee Episcopal Diocese West Mo.'s Charitable Trust, 1984—; chmn. United Fund Kickoff Campaign, 1966; bd. dirs. devel. fund. U. Mo., 1981—; mem. boosters Southwest Mo. State U., Springfield; bd. dirs. Jr. Achievement of Middle Am., Inc., 1978-81; corp. chmn. Cerebral Palsy Telethon, 1981; bd. dirs. Lester E. Cox Med. Ctrs., Springfield, 1985—; bd. dirs., bd. govs. St. Jude Children's Research Hosp./ALSAC, Memphis, 1985—; Mo. fin. chmn. Gephardt for Pres. Com., 1985—; chmn. elect Springfield area Sports Hall of Fame com., 1986—; active Dem. Nat. Com., various state and nat. polit. campaigns. Named Springfield's Outstanding Young Man of Yr., 1966, Mo.'s Outstanding Young Man of Yr., 1967. Mem. ABA, Mo. Bar Assn., Greene County Bar Assn. (treas. 1966-67, bd. dirs. 1974-77), Legal Aid Assn. Greene County (bd. dirs. 1976-78), Mo. Inst. for Justice, Inc. (bd. dirs. 1980), Springfield C. of C. (bd. dirs. 1971-77, chmn. city council liaison com. 1974-75), Springfield Jaycees (pres. 1963-64), U. Mo. Alumni Assn. (athletic com. 1981-87), So. Fedn. Syrian and Lebanese Am. Clubs (chmn. bd. 1981-82, v.p. 1983-84, pres. 1984-85). Club: Tiger (U. Mo.), Hickory Hills Country (chmn. bldg. com. 1979-80), Cedars of the Ozarks (v.p. 1981). Lodge: Rotary (chpt. pres. Springfield Southeast 1967-68), Masons, Shriners. Home: 3937 Saint Andrews Dr Springfield MO 65804 Office: Two Corp Ctr Suite 2-200 1949 E Sunshine Springfield MO 65804

HAMRICK, FLORENCE AILEEN, director placement services; b. Chapel Hill, N.C., Mar. 10, 1959; d. Timmons Hicks Jr. and Aileen (Ailstock) H.; m. Kevin P. Condit. BA in English, U. N.C., 1981; MA in Coll. Student Personnel, Ohio State U., 1983. Asst. dir. student services Sheldon Jackson Coll., Sitka, Alaska, 1983-84; asst. dir. placement and career services Wichita State U., Kans., 1984—; activities asst. Ohio State U., Newark, Ohio, 1981-82; career counselor Ohio State U., Columbus, 1982-83. Mem. Am. Assn. Counseling and Devel., Am. Coll. Personnel Assn. Office: Wichita State U Campus Box 42 Wichita KS 67208

HANAWAY, DONALD JOHN, state attorney general; b. Stevens Point, Wis., Dec. 25, 1933; s. John Leo and Agnes Marie (Flatley) H.; B.B.A., U. Wis., 1958, LL.B., 1961; m. JoAnn R. Gaskell, June 21, 1958; children—Patrick James, Mary Kathleen, Michael John, Maureen Megan. Bar: Wis. 1961. Asst. dist. atty. Brown County, Green Bay, Wis., 1963-64, spl. prosecutor, 1967-78; city atty. City of De Pere (Wis.), 1964-72, 76-79, mayor, 1972-74; mem. firm Condon, Hanaway & Wickert, Ltd., Green Bay, 1969-84; mem. firm Hanaway, Kuehne & Dietz, Green Bay, 1984-86; mem. Wis. Senate, 1979-87, asst. minority leader, 1981-83; atty. gen. State of Wis., Madison, 1987—. Active various local govtl., civic and parish coms. Served with U.S. Army, 1954-56. Mem. ABA, Wis. Bar Assn., Brown County Bar Assn., Wis. Acad. Trial Lawyers, Wis. Sch. Attys. Assn. (charter), De Pere C. of C. (exec. sec. 1964-69). Republican. Club: Optimist (charter) (De Pere). Office: Office of Attorney Gen State Capitol Madison WI 53701

HANCOCK, ALAN CLELL, physician; b. Burr Oak, Kans., Sept. 24, 1935; s. Albert Clell and Gertrude Aline (Miller) H.; m. Phylis Ann Anderson, Dec. 28, 1956; children: Margaret Ann, Susan Christine. BS, Friends Univ., 1960; MD, U. Kans., Kansas City, 1964. Intern Bethany Med. Ctr., Kansas City, Kans., 1964-65; resident in radiology U. Kans. Med. Ctr., Kansas City, 1965-66; family practitioner Kansas City, 1966—; asst. dist. coroner Wyandotte County, Kansas City, 1968-80, dist. coroner, 1980—; adj. assoc. prof. Wichita (Kans.) State U., 1979-83. Med. dir. Kansas City Fire Dept. Paramedics, 1983-84. Mem. AMA, Kans. Med. Assn., Wyandotte County Med. Soc., Am. Acad. Family Practice. Republican. Avocations: flying, computer programming, photography, amateur radio. Office: 9201 Parallel Kansas City KS 66112

HANCOCK, JAMES BEATY, interior designer; b. Hartford, Ky.; s. James Winfield Scott and Hettie Frances (Meadows) H.; B.A., Hardin-Simmons U., 1948, M.A., 1952. Head interior design dept. Thornton's, Abilene, Tex., 1945-54; interior designer The Halle Bros. Co., Cleve., 1954-55; v.p. Olympic Products, Cleve., 1955-56; mgr. interior designer Bell Drapery Shops of Ohio, Inc., Shaker Heights, 1957-78, v.p., 1979—; lectr. interior design, Abilene and Cleve.; works include 6 original murals Broadway Theater, Abilene, 1940, mural Skyline Outdoor Theatre, Abilene, 1950, cover designs for Isotopics mag., 1958-60. Mem. Western Reserve Hist. Soc., Cleve. Mus. Art. Served with AUS, 1942-46. Recipient 2d place award for oil painting West Tex. Expn., 1940, hon. mention, 1940. Mem. Abilene Mus. Fine Arts (charter). Home: 530 Sycamore Dr Cleveland OH 44132

HANCOCK, JOAN HERRIN, executive search company executive; b. Indpls., Apr. 16, 1930; d. Roy Silvey and Glenna Olive (Metsker) Herrin; m. John Newton Hancock, May 12, 1951 (div. Feb. 1976); children—Glenna Jill Hancock Smith, Jeri Lee Hancock Moore, John Norman. B.A., Butler U., 1953. Career counselor Career Cons. Inc., Indpls., 1974-82; counselor, corp. officer Unique Alternatives Inc., Indpls., 1982-84, Alternatives Plus Inc., Indpls., 1984—; pres. Herrin & Assocs., 1986—. Precinct Committeeperson Democratic Party, Indpls; pres. Sch. #59 PTA, 1964, C.W.F. Allisonville Christian Ch., also mem. ch. bd., 1987—; active Camp Fire Girls. Mem. Central Ind. Assn. Profl. Cons. (sec. 1984-85, ethics com. 1980-81), Nat. Assn. Personnel Cons., State Assn. Personnel Cons., Am. Mgmt. Assn. (dir. membership 1986), Indpls. C. of C. (mem. community affairs council, pres. 1986—), Kappa Kappa Gamma (pres. Indpls. Assn. 1967-69; province dir. chpts. 1970-74, Mu club 1958-59, Betty Miller Brown award 1982). Mem. Christian Ch. (Disciples of Christ). Club: Hoosier 500 Toastmistress (pres. 1963) (Indpls.). Home: 4127 Timber Ct Indianapolis IN 46250 Office: Alternatives Plus Inc 9135 N Meridian Suite A8 Indianapolis IN 46260

HANCOCK, JOHN WALTER, accountant; b. Louisville, Oct. 8, 1947; s. John Wertz and Doris (Rowlett) H.; m. Elizabeth Ilsley Black, Apr. 16, 1971; children: Catherine Ilsley, Drew Birgham. BS, U. Nebr., Lincoln, 1969, MS, 1971; MBA, U. Nebr., Omaha, 1977. CPA, Nebr. Commd. 2d lt. USAF, 1971, advanced through grades to capt., 1974, resigned, 1976; sr. tax mgr. Peat, Marwick, Mitchell, Omaha, 1977-86; pvt. practice acctg. Omaha, 1986—; bd. dirs. Weitz Value Fund, Omaha. Treas., trustee, exec. com. Omaha Community Playhouse, 1979—, pres. bd. trustees, 1987—. Mem. Am. Inst. CPA's, Nebr. Soc. CPA's (sec. 1985—, pres.-elect 1987—, various coms.; Gold Cert. award 1978, Leadership award 1982, 84-85). Republican. Episcopalian. Office: 10330 Regency Pkwy Omaha NE 68114

HANCOCK, PATRICIA JEAN, body shop owner; b. Norfolk, Nebr., Oct. 18, 1945; d. John Joseph Fagan Jr. and Virginia Ruth (Simpson) Rauert; m. Robert Dale Hancock, Mar. 1, 1965; 1 child, Jennifer Lynn. BS in Math., U. Nebr., 1967, tchrs. cert., 1967, MAT in Math., 1971. Tchr. math., Palmyra, Nebr., 1967-68; grad. asst. U. Nebr., Lincoln, 1968-69; tchr. math. Pound Jr. High, Lincoln, 1969-74; sec.-treas. Bob's Body Shop, Grand Island, Nebr. Contbr. articles to profl. jours. Coordinator Bible sch. Trinity United Meth. Ch., 1983, 84, 85, leader 4-H Club, 1985—; mem. adminstrv. council ministries, 1984-86; tchr. Soc. Collision Repair Specialists. Mem. Nebr. Auto Body Assn. (sec., newsletter editor, convention organizer 1981-83). Clubs: Riverside Golf (Grand Island) (treas., v.p., pres. Ladies Golf Assn.). Avocations: golf, tennis, swimming, sewing, organ. Home: Route 1 Box 185 Cairo NE 68824 Office: Bob's Body Shop Inc 1800 W Lincoln Hwy Grand Island NE 68803

HAND, DIANE TELESCO, public relations executive; b. San Francisco, Oct. 4, 1946; d. Lee A. and Charlotte Umbreit Telesco; m. William Allen Hand, Jan. 19, 1968 (div. Aug. 1983). B.A., San Jose State U., 1967. Reporter, Santa Clara (Calif.) Jour., 1967-68, Seneca (S.C.) Jour., 1968-70; info. officer Va. Inst. Tech., Blacksburg, 1970-72, U.S. Dept. Agr., Washington, 1972-73; food editor The Times Mag., Army Times Pub. Co., Washington, 1973-76; communications specialist Dorn Communications, Mpls., 1976-82, account exec., 1982-83, account dir., 1983-84, v.p., 1984-85; account mgr. Fleishman-Hillard Inc., Kansas City, Mo., 1985-86, v.p., 1986—; cons. Va. Tech. Inst. Food Technologists Food Editors Conf., 1973-77. Mem. Nat. Fedn. Press Women (first place awards communications contest 1974, 75, 83), Pub. Relations Soc. Am., Press Women Minn. (founder, pres. 1977-79, Woman of Achievement 1982). Office: Fleishman Hillard Inc One Crown Ctr Kansas City MO 64108

HAND, ELBERT O., clothing manufacturing and retailing company executive. Pres. Hartmarx Corp., Chgo. Office: Hartmarx Corp 101 N Wacker Dr Chicago IL 60606 *

HANDLEMAN, DAVID, audio products company executive; b. 1914; married. With Handleman Co., Inc., Troy, Mich., 1937—, sec.-treas., 1946-66, chmn. dir., 1966—, also dir. Office: Handleman Co Inc 500 Kirts Blvd Troy MI 48084

HANDLER, ARLENE FRANCES, nurse; b. Chgo., Mar. 25, 1943; d. Hyman and Sophie (Twersky) Fridkin; m. Raymond Morton Handler, Dec. 7, 1962; children—Jonathan Alan, David Aaron, Deborah Lynn. Grad. Michael Reese Hosp. Sch. Nursing, Chgo., 1963; B.A. in Applied Behavioral Sci., Nat. Coll. Edn., 1981; B.S.N., U. Without Walls, Cin. R.N., Ill.; cert. sch. nurse, Ill. Staff nurse Michael Reese Psychiat. Hosp., Chgo., 1963-65; vol. nurse U.S. Air Force Hosp., Rantoul, Ill., 1965-67; staff nurse Lakeshore Psychiat. Hosp., Chgo., 1971; substitute sch. nurse Sch. Dist. 27, Northbrook, Ill., 1978-87, Stevenson High Sch., Prairie View, Ill., 1982-87, Hawthorne Sch., Vernon Hills, Ill., 1981-87; sch. nurse, Early Childhood Devel. Enrichment Ctr., Hoffman Estates, Ill, 1985—. Chmn. health and safety Sch. Dist. 27 PTA, Northbrook, 1974-78; co-chairperson screening com. Northbrook Caucus, 1976-78; mem., chairperson operation smoke detector Northbrook Safety Commn., 1977—; pres. Sch. Dist. 27 Council PTAs, Northbrook, 1978-80; v.p.-sch. Congregation Beth Shalom, Northbrook, 1981-83; vice chmn., chmn. by-laws Northbrook Plan Commn., 1982—. Co-honoree State of Israel Bonds, 1983. Mem. Michael Reese Nurses' Alumnae Assn., LWV, Ill. Assn. Sch. Nurses. Home: 4022 Rutgers Ln Northbrook IL 60062

HANDLER, RAYMOND MORTON, dermatologist, educator; b. Chgo., Oct. 23, 1937; s. William and Pearl (Greenband) H.; m. Arlene Frances Fridkin, Dec. 8, 1962; children—Jonathan, David, Deborah. B.S. in Medicine, U. Ill.-Chgo., 1959, M.D., 1961. Diplomate Am. Bd. Dermatology. Intern Michael Reese Hosp., Chgo., 1961-62; resident in dermatology U. Ill. Hosp., Chgo., 1962-65; pvt. practice medicine specializing in dermatology, Des Plaines, Ill., 1967—; clin. instr. dermatology U. Ill., Chgo., 1967-72, clin. asst. prof., 1972-77, clin. assoc. prof. dermatology, 1977—; chmn. sect. dermatology Luth. Gen. Hosp., Park Ridge, Ill., 1981—. Contbr. articles to profl. jours. Mem. Bd. Edn., Sch. Dist. 27, Northbrook, Ill., 1977—, pres. 1983-85, chmn. citizen's adv. council, 1974-77. Served to capt. USAF, 1965-67. Recipient State of Israel Bonds honor award Congregation Beth Shalom, 1982. Fellow Am. Acad. Dermatology, Acad. Psychosomatic Medicine; mem. Chgo. Dermatology Soc., Dermatology Found., others. Home: 4022 Rutgers Ln Northbrook IL 60062 Office: 8780 Golf Rd Des Plaines IL 60016

HANDLER, THOMAS JOHN, lawyer; b. Chgo., Mar. 8, 1956; s. Elmer J. and Jean M. (Neitzel) H.; m. Kimberly A. Cawley, July 3, 1982; 1 child, Ross B. BS in Accountancy, U. Ill., 1979; JD, DePaul U., Chgo., 1983. Bar: Ill. 1983, U.S. Dist. Ct. (no. dist.) Ill. 1983, U.S. Tax Ct. 1985. Dir. tax services CSO, Inc., Chgo., 1979-82; acct. Folisi Samz and Co., Schaumburg, Ill., 1981-82; acct., ptnr. Handler & Porter, Chgo., 1982-84; mng. ptnr. Handler and Assocs., Ltd., Chgo., 1983—; mng. ptnr. Shield Equities, Chgo., 1983—, Dayton Assocs., Chgo., 1984—; bd. dirs. Combined Marine Corp., Naperville, Ill. Contbr. articles to profl. jours. Mem. South Lakeview Neighbors Assn., Chgo., 1984-86. Named one of Outstanding Young Men Am., 1985, 86. Mem. ABA, Ill. State Bar Assn., Chgo. Bar Assn., Internat. Assn. Fin. Planners, Pi Kappa Alpha (bd. dirs. 1978-79, nat. rush dir. 1982—). Republican. Clubs: Mid-Day, Lakeshore Athletic (Chgo.). Avocations: tennis, travel, stamp collecting. Home: 1188 Asbury Winnetka IL 60093 Office: Handler and Assocs Ltd 123 N Wacker Dr Suite 1100 Chicago IL 60606-1769

HANDLEY, GEORGE WILLIAM, psychology educator; b. N.Y.C., Apr. 28, 1944; s. Albert Marvin and Gladys Martha (Campbell) H.; m. Anne Deborah Smith, Sept. 3, 1973; children: Ian Michael, Heather Gayle. BA cum laude, C.W. Post Coll., 1968; MS, U. Bridgeport, 1970; PhD, U. Tenn., 1972. Research asst. U. Bridgeport, Conn., 1968-70; assoc. prof. psychology Ohio State U., Lima, 1972—. Bd. dirs. Ottawa Valley Ctr. for Devel. Disadvantaged, Lima, 1980—. Mem. Nat. Inst. Mental Health (trainee 1971), Psi Chi. Office: Ohio State U 4240 Campus Dr Lima OH 45804

HANDS, STEVEN MICHAEL, marketing professional; b. Berea, Ohio, Nov. 16, 1959; s. Richard Stephen and Shirley Ann (Devine) H. BS in Gen. Engring., U. Ill., 1982; M Mgmt., Northwestern U., 1986. Registered engr. in tng., Ill. Sales engr. Barber-Colman Co., Lincolnwood, Ill., 1982-85; mktg. assoc. MCC Powers Process Controls, Skokie, Ill., 1985-86; market analyst MCC Powers Process Controls, Skokie, 1986—; ptnr. Micro Dynamics Computer Co., Des Plaines, Ill., 1986—. Mem. Am. Mktg. Assn., Instrument Soc. of Am. Republican. Roman Catholic. Home: 2326 Cannon Dr Mount Prospect IL 60056 Office: MCC Powers Process Controls 3400 Oakton St Skokie IL 60076

HANDSHY, ARTHUR W., department store executive. Pres. Lazarus Div., Columbus, Ohio. Office: Lazarus Div Town & High St Columbus OH 43215 *

HANDY, WILLIAM RUSSELL, newspaper editor; b. Trenton, N.J., June 14, 1950; s. Russell Phipps and Virginia (Parleir) H.; m. Barbara Houghton, Aug. 24, 1974; 1 child, Nicholas Russell. AB in Journalism, U. N.C., 1972; postgrad., Duke U., 1972-73. News editor Haines City (Fla.) Herald, 1973-74; reporter Lakeland (Fla.) Ledger, 1974-76; from reporter to asst. city editor to state editor Tampa (Fla.) Tribune, 1976-84; asst. mng. editor Wichita (Kans.) Eagle-Beacon, 1984-85, mng. editor, 1985—. Mem. Am. Soc. Newspaper Editors, AP Mng. Editors, Soc. Newspaper Design. Clubs: Wichita, Tallgrass (Wichita). Home: 310 N Pershing Wichita KS 67208 Office: The Wichita Eagle-Beacon Wichita Eagle & Beacon Pub Co Inc 825 E Douglas Ave Wichita KS 67201

HANDY, WILLIAM TALBOT, JR., bishop; b. New Orleans, Mar. 26, 1924; s. William Talbot Sr. and Dorothy Pauline (Pleasant) H.; m. Ruth Odessa Robinson, Aug. 11, 1948; children—William Talbot III (dec.), Dorothy D. Handy Davis, Stephen Emanuel, Mercedes Handy Cowley. Student, Tuskegee Inst., 1940-43; B.A., Dillard U., 1948, LL.D. (hon.), 1981; M.Div., Gammon Theol. Sem., 1951; S.T.M., Boston U., 1952. Ordained to ministry United Meth. Ch.; consecrated bishop. Pastor Newman Meth. Ch., Alexandria, La., 1952-59; pastor St. Mark Meth. Ch., Baton Rouge, 1959-68; v.p. United Meth. Pub. House, Nashville, 1968-78; dist. supt. Baton Rouge-Lafayette dist. United Meth. Ch., 1978-80; bishop Mo. area United Meth. Ch., St. Louis, 1980—; mem. exec. com. Bd. Higher Edn. and Ministry, Nashville, 1980—. Chmn. subcom. on voting rights U.S. Commn. on Civil Rights, 1959-68; mem. mayor's bi-racial adv. com. La. Adv. Com., Baton Rouge, 1965-66; life mem. NAACP, 1971—; vice chmn. bd. trustees Gammon Theol. Sem., Atlanta, 1970—; chmn. bd. trustees St. Paul Sch. Theology, Kansas City, Mo., 1980—. Served to staff sgt. AUS, 1943-46, ETO, PTO. Mem. Mo. Christian Leadership Forum. Lodge: Masons (33 degree). Avocation: collecting jazz and big band records. Office: United Meth Ch Mo Area 4625 Lindell Blvd Suite 424 St Louis MO 63108

HANEBORG, LARRY ROGER, beer distribution company executive, mechanical engineer; b. Denver, Sept. 16, 1944; s. Harold L. and Doris (Davidson) H.; m. Janice Higley, Aug. 28, 1965; children—Mark, Scott, Tad. B.S.M.E., Colo. State U., 1966. Indsl. engr., CF & I Steel Corp., Pueblo, Colo., 1966-69, asst. supt. mech. shops, 1969-77; pres. Coors Distbg., North Platte, Nebr., 1977-86; Founder Youth basketball program, 1977, youth football program, 1980; pres. North Platte Little League, 1983-84, North Platte Indsl. Corp., 1986-87; bd. dirs. Rough Riders Rodeo Assn., North Platte, 1982—, pres., 1985—. Recipient Life Mem. award Nebr. PTA, 1983, Lady Scout award, 1986; named Outstanding mem. Assn. Iron and Steel Engrs., 1975, Outstanding Coll. Supporter, Mid-Plains Coll., 1983. Mem. Nebr. Beer Wholesalers Assn., Nat. Beer Wholesalers Assn., Ducks Unltd. (chpt. pres. 1979-86), Nebr. Wildlife Protectors Assn. (bd. dirs. 1982-86). Republican. Methodist. Lodges: Rotary (bd. dirs. 1983-86), Elks. Avocations: hunting, snow skiing, fishing, golf, basketball. Office: Coors Distbg North Platte 642 N Willow St North Platte NE 69101

HANEBUTH, EDWARD ANDREW, sales executive; b. Rockford, Ill., Jan. 3, 1960; s. Harvey Wesley and Portia Marion (Andrew) H. AA, Rock Valley Coll., 1980; BA in Mktg., No. Ill. U., 1982. Statistician No. Ill. U., DeKalb, 1981-82; underwriter Northwestern Mut. Life Ins. Co., DeKalb, 1981-82; stereo cons. Columbia Audio Video, Rockford, Ill., 1982-83; tng. cons. V-Tip Inc., Rockford, 1983-85, regional v.p., 1985-87; ind. sales rep. Hydun Lab. Assocs., Reynoldsburg, Ohio, 1987—. Player Prairie State Games, Peoria, Ill, 1984, player/coach, 1985, head coach, 1986, volleyball chmn., 1987. Republican. Methodist. Avocations: golf, volleyball, handball. Home: 16540 Grove Creek Circle Pecatonica IL 61063 Office: Hydun Lab Assocs PO Box 111 Reynoldsburg OH 43068

HANELINE, KENNETH MICHAEL, comptroller; b. Cleve., June 22, 1958; s. Michael Vincent and Kathleen (Donelan) H.; m. Mary Catherine Ryan, Aug. 22, 1981; 1 child, Ryan Michael. BS in Acctg., Case Western Res. U., 1980; JD, John Marshall at Cleve. State U., 1986. CPA, Ohio. Data processing mgr. Rego Supermarkets Inc., Cleve., 1979-82, comptroller, 1982—; pvt. practice tax preparation, Westlake, Ohio, 1980—. Mem. Am. Inst. CPA's, Ohio Soc. CPA's, Beta Alpha Psi. Republican. Roman Catholic. Avocations: sailing, skiing. Home: 1931 King James Pkwy Suite #328 Westlake OH 44145 Office: Rego Supermarkets 4529 Industrial Pkwy Cleveland OH 44135

HANEY, DEBORAH ONSTAD, gynecologic nurse; b. Minot, N.D., Jan. 29, 1948; d. Vance Curtis and Eva Dorthea (Hoff) Onstad; m. Thomas Marlin Haney, July 25, 1971; children: Marlin Curtis Lee, Phillip Arthur Johan. BS in Nursing, U. N.D., 1971; grad. nurse practitioner tng. program, UCLA Med. Sch., 1976. Cert. Ob-Gyn nurse practitioner. Staff nurse United Hosp., Grand Forks, N.D., 1971-72; pub. health nurse 1st Dist. Health Unit, Minot, 1972-74, family planning nurse, 1974-76, staff nurse practitioner, 1976-77; clin. dir. Dakota Family Planning Ctr., Bismarck, N.D., 1979—; cons., nurse practitioner N.D. State Health Dept., Bismarck, 1978-79, educator family planning program, 1978-79; instr. U. N.D. Sch. Medicine, Bismarck, 1983—. Named one of Outstanding Young Women Of Am., 1979. Mem. Am. Nurses Assn., Council of Primary Health Care Nurse Practitioners, Nurse's Assn. of Am. Coll. Ob-Gyn (legis. com. 1980—), N.D. Pub. Health Assn., Sageway Honor Soc. Home: 908 Midway Dr Bismarck ND 58501 Office: Dakota Family Planning Ctr 203 E Front Ave Bismarck ND 58501

HANEY, J. TERRENCE, insurance consultant; b. Omaha, Nov. 26, 1933; s. James Cletus and Claire (Wilson) H.; m. Joanne M. Beach, Feb. 12, 1966 (div. Nov. 1971); children: Terrence L., Kim Marie, Robert R., J. Stephen, Patrick M. Student, Creighton U., 1952, U. Nebr., Omaha, 1981—. CLU. Salesman, unit mgr., div. mgr., dir. mass mktg. R.D. Marcotte & Assocs., Omaha, 1958-64; exec. v.p., gen. mgr. Ins. Cons., Inc., Omaha, 1964-85, pres., chief exec. officer, 1985—. Former pres. St. Margaret Mary Bd. Edn.; bd. dirs. Girls Club of Omaha; bd. dirs. Met. Tech. Community Coll. Found., 1987—. Mem. Nebr. Assn. Health Underwriters (past pres.), Internat. Assn. Health Underwriters (former bd. dirs.), Omaha Assn. Life Underwriters, Creighton U. Jaybacker Club (pres.). Republican. Roman Catholic. Clubs: Plaza, Plains Track, Happy Hollow Country, Toastmasters (past pres.). Lodges: Ak-Sar-Ben, Internat. Order of Rocky Mountain Goats. Avocations: jogging, physical fitness. Home: 407 N Elmwood Rd Omaha NE 68132 Office: Ins Cons Inc 200 Blackstone Centre Omaha NE 68131-3801

HANEY, JERRY LYNN, dentist; b. Independence, Mo., Sept. 5, 1955; s. Carl Ray and Elizabeth Anne (Hifner) H.; m. Sharon Kay Runyon, Oct. 6, 1984; 1 child, Joshua Lynn; stepchildren: Chrystal Jane Warren, Andrew George Warren. BS in Biology, Cen. Mo. State U., 1977; DDS, U. Mo., 1982. Gen. practice dentistry Odessa, Mo., 1982—. Treas. Calvary Bapt. Ch., 1983—, deacon, 1983—, mem. long range planning com., 1983. Mem. Delta Chi (pres. 1974-75). Republican. Lodge: Optimist (bd. dirs. 1984—). Avocations: racketball, chess. Home: 613 W McDowell Odessa MO 64076 Office: 404 N 4th Odessa MO 64076

HANEY, THOMAS MICHAEL, lawyer, educator; b. Evergreen Park, Ill., Oct. 1, 1938; s. Thomas Albert and Mary Etta (O'Toole) H.; m. Marian Conroy, May 28, 1966 (div. 1976). BA cum laude, Loyola U., Chgo., 1960; JD, U. Chgo., 1963, LLM, 1967; MBA, Loyola U., Chgo., 1971. Bar: Ill. 1963, U.S. Dist. Ct. (no. dist.) Ill. 1964. Assoc. McDermott, Will & Emery, Chgo., 1964-67, Internat. div. McDonald's Corp., Chgo., 1967-71; ptnr. Edwards, Haney et al, Chgo., 1971-75; instr., assoc. dean sch. law Loyola U., Chgo., 1975—. Contbr. articles to profl. jours. Mem. ABA (chmn. subcom. internat. law), Chgo. Bar Assn. (chmn. internat. law com.), Ill. State Bar Assn. (editor newsletter internat., chmn. internat. law sect.). Home: 1221 W Arthur Ave Chicago IL 60626 Office: Loyola U Sch Law 1 E Pearson St Chicago IL 60611

HANGEN, BRUCE BOYER, conductor, music director; b. Pottstown, Pa., Feb. 2, 1947; s. Paul Schaaber Jr. and Lillian Wintle (Mason) H. MusB, Eastman Sch. Music, Rochester, N.Y., 1970; postgrad., Berkshire Music Ctr., Tanglewood, Mass., 1972-73; D of Fine Arts (hon.), U. New Eng., Biddeford, Maine, 1982. Conducting asst. Buffalo Philharm., 1972-73; asst. condr. Syracuse (N.Y.) Symphony, 1972-73; asst. condr. Denver Symphony, 1973-76, assoc. condr., 1976-79; music dir., condr. Portland (Maine) Symphony, 1976-86, Omaha Symphony, 1984—; music panel Nat. Endowment for Arts, Washington, 1985-86. Recipient Eleanor Crane prize Berkshire Music Ctr., 1972; Bruce Hangen Day proclaimed by City of Portland, 1986. Avocation: bicycling. Office: Omaha Symphony Orch 310 Aquila Ct Omaha NE 68102-9998

HANIN, LEDA TONI, university administrator; b. Bronx, N.Y., Mar. 11, 1940; d. Paul Leopold and Milah (Russin) Wermer; m. Israel Hanin, June 12, 1960; children: Adam Jeffrey, Dahlia Beth. BA in Sociology, UCLA, 1962; cert. mktg., U. Pitts., 1978, MEd, 1984. Dir. confs. Western Psychiat. Inst., Pitts., 1974-77; dir. publicity Carnegie Inst., Pitts., 1977-81; dir. pub. and alumni relations grad. sch. indsl. adminstrn. Carnegie-Mellon U., Pa., 1981-86; dir. pub. relations grad. sch. bus. U. Chgo., 1986—. Winner CASE silver medal, 1987; 2-time winner Matrix prize for Pub. Communications, Women in Communications. Mem. Am. Assembly Collegiate Schs. Bus. (cons.), Pub. Relations Soc. Am. (pres. 1984-86, recipient prize 1986), Publicity Club Chgo. (recipient Silver Trumpet award 1987), United Mental Health Assn. (pres. 1984-86). Jewish. Club: Quadrangle (Chgo.). Avocations: theater, opera, travel, movies. Home: 1132 N Kenilworth Ave Oak Park IL 60302

HANIS, GREGORY RICHARD, hotel consultant; b. Milw., Sept. 21, 1950; s. Frank Richard and Beatrice Henrietta (Roos) H.; m. Ginger Ellen Sass, Oct. 19, 1974; 1 child, Lindsey Ellen. Account exec. Consol. Broadcasting, Milw., 1972-74; merchandise supr. Marshall Field and Co., Chgo., 1974-75; dir. mktg. Hotel Mgrs. and Hosts, Milw., 1975-80, Hotel Investors, Chevy Chase, Md., 1980-82; pres. Hospitality Marketers, Milw., 1982—; Pres. Waukesha (Wis.) Conv. Bur., 1982-84, bd. dirs. Mem. Meeting Planners Internat., Wis. Inn Keepers Assn. Avocations: downhill skiing, sailing, running, music. Office: Hospitality Marketers Inc 120 Bishops Way Suite 130 Brookfield WI 53005

HANK, BERNARD J., JR., elevator manufacturing company executive; b. 1929. BS, U. Notre Dame, 1951. Pres. Montgomery Elevator Co., Moline, Ill., 1964-68, chief exec. officer, chmn. bd. dirs., 1968—. Served to lt. (j.g.) USN, 1951-54. Office: Montgomery Elevator Co 30 20th St Moline IL 61265 *

HANKES, ELMER JOSEPH, residential building manager; b. Chgo., May 30, 1913; s. Nicholas and Camille (Mahler) H.; m. Barbara Ellen Sardeson, Mar 17, 1962; 1 child, Camilla Rose. BSME, Ill. Inst. Tech., 1941; postgrad., U. Minn., 1942-44. Registered profl. engr. Minn. Mech. engr. Gen. Electric Co., 1929-39; indsl. engr. U.S. Steel Co., 1941; project engr. Mpls. Honeywell,, 1942-45; founder, pres. Testscor, Inc., Mpls., 1945-75, Numeric Machining, Inc., Mpls., 1960-75; ret. 1976; founder, pres. Camilla Realty Corp., Mpls., 1961-82; mgr. student housing facility Willmar, Minn., 1982—; pres., bd. dirs. Hankes Found., Mpls. and Calcutta, India, 1986—; mem. U.S. Dept. Commerce trade missions to Norway-Denmark, 1963, Australia-New Zealand, 1964. Author Enterprises of Great Pith and Moment, 1982; patentee computers, instruments. Home and Office: 1768 Colfax Ave S Minneapolis MN 55403

HANKET, MARK JOHN, lawyer; b. Cleve., Jan. 28, 1943; s. Laddie W. and Florence J. (Kubat) H.; m. Carole A. Dalpiaz, Sept. 14, 1968; children—Gregory, Jennifer, Sarah. A.B. magna cum laude, John Carroll U., 1965; J.D. cum laude, Ohio State U., 1968; M.B.A., Xavier U., 1977. Bar: Ohio 1968. Atty. Chemed Corp., Cin., 1973-77, asst. sec., 1977-82, sec., 1982-84, v.p., sec., 1984-86, v.p., gen. counsel DuBois Chems. Div., 1986—. Com. chmn. Troop 850, Boy Scouts Am., 1984—;vice chmn. Cath. com. on scouting Archdiocese of Cin., 1986—. Served to capt. U.S. Army, 1968-73. Decorated Meritorious Service medal, Army Commendation medal with oak leaf cluster. Mem. ABA, Ohio Bar Assn. Office: DuBois Chems 1100 DuBois Tower Cincinnati OH 45202

HANKINS, DAVID LYNN, teacher; b. Waukegan, Ill., Sept. 6, 1945; s. Alex D. Sr. and Nellie (Holston) H. AS in Bus., So. Ill. U., 1965; BS in Elem. Edn., Ea. Ill. U., 1973, MA in Early Childhood Edn., 1974. Tchr. Spl. Edn. Dist. Lake County, Gurnee, Ill., 1973-77; tchr. Waukegan (Ill.) Pub. Schs., 1977-86, pre-vocat. coordinator, 1986—. Counselor, bd. dirs. Connection Crisis Line, Waukegan, 1974-75, Citizen Assistance Program, Waukegan, 1974-80. Served with USN, 1965-70, Vietnam. Democatr. Pentecostal. Avocations: genetics, horticulture, ornithology. Home: 12809 W Hart Waukegan IL 60087 Office: Spl Edn Dist Lake County 4440 W Grand Gurnee IL 60031

HANKINS, EDWARD RAY, educational administrator; b. Burden, Kans., Mar. 19, 1933; s. Daniel Ray and Ruth Ellen (Woodruf) H.; m. Rose Marie Nichols, June 26, 1955; children—Kammi Marie, Ken Alan. B.S., Pitts. State U., 1958, M.S., 1974. Asst. prin. Abilene High Sch. (Kans.), 1974-77; spl. needs specialist State Dept. Edn., Topeka, Kans., 1977-79, accreditation specialist, 1979-81, research coordinating Unit, 1981-82, vocational edn. coordinator, 1982-84, edn. program specialist, 1984—. Served to cpl. U.S. Army, 1953-55. Named Outstanding Young Educator Jr. C. of C., 1967. Mem. Am. Vocat. Assn., Kans. Vocational Assn., Kans Council Vocational Adminstrn., Phi Delta Kappa. Methodist. Avocations: Tennis, Tennis instructing.

HANKINS, RUTH ANNE, artist, graphic designer; b. Garden City, Mich., June 9, 1949; d. Theodore Roosevelt Jr. and Florence May (Stephenson) Jamieson; m. Michael William Hankins, May 9, 1969; children: Jennifer Anne, Micah Daniel. A in Comml. Art, Lansing Community Coll., 1983, A in Illustration, 1984. Graphic artist Delphi Stained Glass, Lansing, Mich., 1983-85; graphic designer Mich. Dept. Commerce, Lansing, 1985—. Author: (poetry) A Collection; designer (instant lottery game) Loose Change, 1979 (Monetary award), (catalog) Michigan Gift Guide, 1985 (Craftsman award). Avocations: writing, photography. Home: 818 N Cochran Charlotte MI 48813 Office: Mich Dept Commerce 565 Hollister Bldg 106 W Allegan Lansing MI 48913

HANKIS, ROY ALLEN, interior designer; b. Greenville, Mich., May 24, 1943; s. John LeRoy and Nila A. (Taylor) H.; interior design diploma Kendall Sch. Design, 1964; student Cranbrook Acad. Art, 1971. Dir. design, contract design firms, Grand Rapids and Detroit, Mich., 1964-73; owner, designer Roy Allen Hankis Interiors, Troy, Mich., 1974—; instr. interior design Henry Ford Community Coll., Dearborn, Mich., 1981—; trustee JONIRO Investment Co., Southfield, Mich., 1981—. Participating designer Detroit Symphony ASID Showhouse, Bloomfield Hills, Mich., 1985; designer Birmingham Jr. League-Mich. Design Ctr. Celebrity Room for Mich.'s first lady, 1985. Am. Soc. Interior Designers (dir. Mich. chpt. 1974), Christian Bus. Men's Com. Detroit. Baptist. Club: Rotary. Patentee. Home and Office: 5365 Breeze Hill Pl Troy MI 48098

HANKISON, JOHN ELLSWORTH, former transportation executive; b. Toledo, Ohio, Sept. 1, 1916; s. Otto Leroy and Lucy Sophia (Gabel) H.; m. Virginia Ann Werner, Apr. 11, 1942. Student, Ohio State U.; J.D., U. Toledo. Pres., chmn. bd. Midwest Haulers, Toledo, 1955-81; retired; dir. Ohio Citizens Bank, 1954, hon. dir., 1987; gen. counsel, pres., chmn. bd. dirs. Va. Surety Co., 1938-65. Bd. dirs. Toledo Humane Soc., 1965—, emeritus dir., 1987. Republican. Roman Catholic. Mem. Game Conservation Internat. (former dir.), Wildlife Conservation Fund Am., Toledo Mus. Art. Mem. East African Profl. Hunters Assn. (hon.), Nat. Rifle Assn., Ducks Unltd. (sponsor), Delta Theta Pi, Sigma Chi. Clubs: Heather Downs Country (Toledo) (dir., sec., chmn. bd. 1955-85), Shikar Safari Internat., Castalia Trout, Catawba Island and Yachtsman's Assn., Explorers, Mich. Polar Equator, Toledo, Rockwell Springs Trout, Belmont Country. Avocations: boating, fly fishing, photography.

HANKS, KATHRYN ANN, advertising executive; b. San Diego, Calif., July 25, 1947; s. Jacob Philip Adam and Bertha Margarite (Yacubik) Entler; m. Russell G. Fast, Feb. 16, 1968 (div. Aug. 1974); 1 child, Evyn Christina; m. William L. Hanks, Dec. 21, 1973 (div. Oct. 1983). Visual mdse. dir. Nordstrom, Inc., Portland, Oreg., 1970-73; advt. & dislplay dir. Einbender's, Inc., St. Joseph, Mo., 1974-76; visual merchandise dir. Townsend & Wall, St. Joseph, Mo., 1976-78; advt. mgr. Kirwan's Furniture, St. Joseph, Mo., 1978-80; proprietor Kathryn Hanks Agy., St. Joseph, Mo., 1980-84; pres., creative dir. Lionshare Mktg., St. Joseph, Mo., 1984—; Sec. Downtown, Inc., St. Joseph, 1981. Dancer Mo. Western State Coll. Dance Co., 1981-86, Mo. Theatre Resident Dance Co., 1985—. Bd. dirs. St. Joseph's YWCA, 1986—, Performing Arts Assn., St. Joseph, 1984-86. Recipient Visual Merchandising awards Display World Mag., Portland, 1972. Mem. St. Joseph C. of C., St. Joseph Area Women's Career Network (v.p. 1983), St. Joseph Ad Club (pres. 1984-86, recipient over 100 Addy awards 1978—), Nat. Agri-Mktg. Assn. (Best of NAMA Advt. award, 1985), Kansas City Art Dirs. Club, Kansas City Print Prodn. Club. Republican. Avocations: dancing, crafts, sewing, graphic design, music. Home and Office: Lionshare Mktg Inc 722 Francis Saint Joseph MO 64501

HANLEY, JAMES EUGENE, psychologist; b. Chgo., Mar. 14, 1946; s. Edward John and Elizabeth Mary (Marcott) H.; m. Joanne Catherine Doheny, Sept. 6, 1969; children: Edward, Robert, William. BA in Psychology, DePaul U., 1970, MA in Clin. Psychology, 1972; EdD in Beahvioral Sci., Nova U., 1978; cert. in Ednl. Adminstrn., No. Ill. U., 1985. Registered psychologist; cert. sch. psychologist. Coordinator psychol. services Aurora (Ill.) East Pub. Schs., 1973—; pvt. practice psychology Aurora, Ill., 1979—; lectr. Harper Community Coll., Palatine, Ill., 1973-75, Waubonsee Community Coll., Sugar Grove, Ill., 1979-84; cons. crisis intervention Assn. for Individual Devel., Aurora, 1983-85. Served to capt. U.S. Army Res., 1971-77. Mem. Ill. Sch. Psychologists Assn. Roman Catholic. Office: Aurora East Pub Schs Dist 131 417 S 5th St Aurora IL 60505

HANLEY, THOMAS PATRICK, obstetrician and gynecologist; b. St. Louis, Apr. 16, 1951; s. Thomas P. and Virginia Barbara (Lydon) H.; m. Patricia Ann McHargue, Dec. 27, 1975; children: Colleen, Thomas III, Timothy. BA, St. Louis U., 1973, MD, 1977. Diplomate Am. Bd. Ob-gyn. Intern St. Louis U., 1977-78, resident, 1978-81; practice medicine speciailizing in ob-gyn St. Louis, 1981-86; mem. staff St. Mary's Health Ctr., St. Louis U. Hosps., Deaconess Hosp., St. Louis Meml. Hosp.; asst. clin. prof. St. Louis U. Med. Sch., 1983—. Mem. AMA (physicians recognition award 1977-87), Am. Coll. Ob-gyn (physicians excellence award, 1986), Gynecol. Laser Soc., St. Louis Gynecol. Soc., St. Louis Metro Med. Soc. Republican. Roman Catholic. Avocation: golf. Office: 1035 Bellevue Suite 208 Saint Louis MO 63117

HANLEY, WILLIAM JOSEPH, marketing executive; b. N.Y.C., June 4, 1942; s. William Joseph and Margaret F. (O'Neil) H.; m. Jane Anne Atkinson, Jan. 29, 1972; children: Elizabeth A., Sarah O., Erin M., Liam J. BS in Acctg., Stonehill Coll., 1966. Various positions Sheraton Corp., Boston, 1971-78; v.p. mktg. services Americana Hotel Corp., N.Y.C., 1978-79; v.p. mktg. Pratt Hotel Corp., Dallas, 1979-82; sr. v.p. mktg. Radisson Hotel Corp., Mpls., 1982—. Mem. PTA, Bloomington, 1984—. Served to capt. U.S. Army, 1966-70, Vietnam. Decorated Bronze Star. Mem. Am. Soc. Travel Agts., Am. Soc. Assn. Execs., Hotel Sales Mgmt. Assn. Republican. Roman Catholic. Office: Radisson Hotel Corp 12805 Hwy 55 Minneapolis MN 55441

HANLON, EDWARD JAMES, restaurant owner; b. Melrose, Mass., May 8, 1950; s. Edward Francis and Mildred (Hardy) H.; m. Maureen Elizabeth O'Toole, June 27, 1971; children: Joyce Marie, Michelle Liegh, Patrick William. AA, Andover Inst., 1970. Mgr. Friendly Ice Cream, Springfield, Mass., 1976-78; dir. research and devel. Poppin Fresh Pies, Mpls., 1979-83; owner, operator Boston Subway, Hopkins, Minn., 1983—. Pres. City Ctr. Devel., Hopkins, 1984-86. Mem. Twin City West C. of C. (named entreprenuer of yr. 1986), Jaycees (named boss of yr. 1985, named one of 10 outstanding Minnesotans 1986). Club: Toastmasters (pres. 1980-81). Avocations: hockey, sailing. Office: Boston Subway 1019 Main St Hopkins MN 55343

HANLON, JAMES PAUL, management consultant; b. Bethlehem, Pa., Mar. 19, 1941; s. James Paul and Mary Louise (Rodfong) H.; m. Madelyn V. Vacca, Nov. 30, 1963; children: Eileen Louise, James Paul III. BS, Lehigh U., 1963. CPA, N.Y., Ill. Mng. ptnr. cons. services Midwest region Deloitte, Haskins & Sells, N.Y.C., 1963-69; ptnr. Deloitte, Haskins & Sells, Brussels, 1969-76, Tehran, Iran, 1976-79, Athens, Greece, 1979-80, Chgo., 1980—. Bd. dirs., mem. exec. com. Chgo. Youth Ctrs., 1985—. Mem. Am. Inst. CPA's, Ill. State Soc. CPA's. Avocation: vintage automobiles. Home: 639 Lincoln Ave Winnetka IL 60093 Office: Deloitte Haskins & Sells 200 E Randolph Dr Chicago IL 60601-6401

HANNA, DENNIS DONALD, dentist; b. Milw., Nov. 29, 1955; s. Donald Charles and Nancy Helen (Haberman) H.; m. Debora Howard, June 10, 1978 (div. Oct. 1984); children: Abigail Marie, Natalie Lynn; m. Janice Marie La Rosa, Sept. 6, 1986. BS, Marquette U., 1977, DDS, 1982; postgrad., U. Wis., Milw., 1978. Gen. practice dentistry West Allis, Wis., 1982—. Mem. ADA, Wis. Dental Assn., Greater Milw. Dental Assn., Am. Polit. Items Collectors, Milw. County Geneological Soc., Milw. County Hist. Soc. Roman Catholic. Avocation: collecting political items from 1840—. Office: 8411 W Cleveland Ave West Allis WI 53227

HANNA, GARY EUGENE, financial planner, retired federal agency adminsitrator; b. WaKeeney, Kans., June 23, 1936; s. Clarence Eugene and Clara (Henderson) H.; m. Joan Spicer, Aug. 13, 1961; children: Mark, Julie. BBA, Fort Hays State U., 1959. Cert. fin. planner, Kans. Field rep. Social Security Adminstrn., Hays, Kans., 1959-73; mgr. Social Security Adminstrn., Winfield, Kans., 1973-87, ret., 1987; with Profl. Investment Services, Inc., Winfield, Kans., 1987—; fin. planner Profl. Investment Service, Winfield, 1984—. Pres. Arts Council, Hays, 1973; chmn. bd. Cowley

County Mental Health, Winfield, 1985, Winfield Housing Authority, 1985. Mem. Internat. Assn. Fin. Planning, Social Security Mgrs. Assn., Inst. Cert. Fin. Planners. Presbyterian. Lodge: Rotary (pres. Winfield 1981, Paul Harris fellow 1985). Avocations: boating, art. Home: 2921 Lake Shore Dr Winfield KS 67156 Office: Profl Investment Services Inc 112 W 9th Winfield KS 67156

HANNA, GEORGE EDWARD, dentist, educator; b. Cedar Rapids, Iowa, June 16, 1957; s. Edward Joseph and Geraldine Kay (Haddy) H.; m. Beth Ann Thompson, Apr. 27, 1985. BS, U. Iowa, 1980, DDS, 1982. Percussion instr. Boddicker Sch. Music, Cedar Rapids, 1973-75; pvt. practive dentistry Cedar Rapids, 1982—; adj. faculty U. Iowa Coll. Dentistry, Iowa City, 1986—. Football, basketball coach kids leagues YMCA, Cedar Rapids, 1982-84. Mem. Acad. Gen. Dentists, Linn County Dist. Dental Soc. (chmn. children's dental health 1984-85), U. Iowa Dist. Dental Soc., Phi Eta Sigma, Omicron Kappa Upsilon. Greek Orthodox. Avocations: music, sports, water and snow skiing. Home: 2076 S Ridge Dr Coralville IA 52241 Office: 1953 1st Ave SE Cedar Rapids IA 52402

HANNA, JAMES A., advertising executive; b. Chgo., Aug. 29, 1950; s. Richard Francis and Mary Barbara (Piesciuk) H.; m. Cheryl Lynn Mannino, Apr. 8, 1972; children: Stacy Leigh, Kristen Ann. BA in Design, U. Ill., Chgo., 1972. Designer R. Head Design, Villa Park, Ill., 1972-74; pres. Hanna, Zappa & Polz, Oak Brook, Ill., 1974-84; account exec. Nalco Chem. Co., Naperville, Ill., 1984—. Pres. Coalition for Quality Edn., Villa Park and Lombard, Ill., 1983; bd. dirs. Elementary Sch. Dist. 45, Villa Park and Lombard, 1983—, sec., 1985—; del. Ill. Assn. Sch. Bds. Conv., 1986—. Roman Catholic. Avocations: travel, reading, art. Home: 1033 S Rand Rd Villa Park IL 60181 Office: Nalco Chem Co 1 Nalco Ctr Naperville IL 60566-1024

HANNA, MAGDY T., engineering educator; b. Alexandria, Egypt, June 2, 1953. BS with honors, Alexandria U., 1975; MS, Cairo U., 1980, U. Pitts., 1983; PhD, U. Pitts., 1985. Reseach asst. Inst. Nat. Planning, Cairo, 1976-80; teaching fellow dept. electrical engring. U. Pitts., 1981-85; vis. asst. prof. electrical and computer engring. dept. U. Iowa, Iowa City, 1985—; research asst. Nat. Radio Astronomy Observatory, Socorro, N. Mex., 1983; mem. com. Pitts. Conf. on Modeling and Simulation, 1981-85. Contbr. articles to profl. jours. Recipient Distinction award Inst. Nat. Planning, Cairo, 1977. Mem. IEEE (student), Soc. Exploration Geophysicists (student), Sigma Xi. Office: U Iowa Electrical and Computer Engring Iowa City IA 52242

HANNAH, JAMES BLAIN, lawyer; b. Mpls., Oct. 26, 1921; s. Hewitt Blain and Edna (Matre) H.; m. Rosemary Ethelyn Rathbun, Dec. 24, 1942; children—Holly Hannah Lewis, Duncan Rathbun. B.S. cum laude, Harvard U., 1942, J.D., 1948. Bar: Minn. 1948, U.S. Dist. Ct. Minn. 1948. Assoc. Synder, Gale, Hoke, Richards & Janes, Mpls., 1948-50; assoc. Mackall, Crounse & Moore, Mpls., 1950-59, ptnr., 1959-85, of counsel, 1985—. Chmn., campaign dir. March of Dimes, Nat. Found. Infantile Paralysis, Mpls., 1953-54; legal advisor, bd. dirs. Planned Parenthood of Minn., 1964-71; bd. dirs. Legal Aid Soc., Mpls., 1970-74, Citizens Com. on Pub. Edn., Mpls. Served to lt. USNR, 1942-46, PTO. Mem. ABA, Mpls. C. of C. (chmn. aviation com. 1957, Hundred Leaders of Tomorrow award 1953), Am. Legion. Unitarian. Clubs: Minikahda, 5:55, Harvard (Minn.) (pres. 1953). Avocations: skiing, sailing, tennis. Home: 7 E St Albans Rd Hopkins MN 55343 Office: Mackall Crounse & Moore 1600 TCF Tower Minneapolis MN 55402

HANNEMAN, JOSEPH EDWARD, financial controller; b. Lincoln, Nebr., May 29, 1960; s. Larry Edward and Joan L. (Traudt) H.; m. Patricia Marie Jenkins, June 12, 1982. BBA in Acctg., U. Iowa, 1982. CPA, Minn. Sr. auditor Touche Ross & Co., Mpls., 1982-85; fin. controller John H. Crowther Inc., Mpls., 1985—; alumni mem. Touche Ross & Co., Mpls., 1985—. Active Christ Presbyn. Ch., Mpls. Recipient 7th place award Nat. Weight Lifting Amateur Athletic Assn., Kansas City, 1976. Mem Minn. Soc. Pub. Accts., Am. Inst. CPA's, Hanneman Weightlifting Club (pres. Des Moines chpt. 1973-77), Delta Tau Delta (alumni). Republican. Home: 10213 Blaisdell Ave S Bloomington MN 55420 Office: John H Crowther Inc 3600 Multifoods Tower 33 S 6th St Minneapolis MN 55402

HANNEN, THOMAS JOHN, public housing administrator; b. Steubenville, Ohio, Nov. 15, 1934; s. Thomas Clellan and Lillian Eleanor (Robson) H.; m. Patricia Sue Welsh, Oct. 10, 1959 (div. 1964); 1 child, Kimberly Ann; m. B. Kathryn Cozzone, May 7, 1966; 1 child, Kathryn Marie. BBA, U. Steubenville, 1960. Cert. property mgr.; cert. pub. housing mgr. Various mgmt. positions Cuyahoga Met. Housing Authority, Cleve., 1961-83; asst. exec. dir. Rockford (Ill.) Housing Authority, 1983—. Mem. Nat. Assn. Housing and Redevel. Officials (nat. housing com. 1981—, bd. dirs. Ill. chpt. 1983—, bd. dirs. and v.p. for housing N. Cen. region 1985—), Ill. Assn. Housing Authorities, Assisted Housing Risk Mgmt. Assn. (bd. dirs. Ill. chpt. 1986—), Northern Ill. Council Housing Authorities, Inst. Real Estate Mgmt., Ohio Arts and Crafts Guild (past. mem. bd. dirs.). Avocation: stained glass. Home: 1123 North Ave Rockford IL 61103 Office: Rockford Housing Authority 330 15th Ave Rockford IL 61108

HANNERS, WILLIAM CHRIS, dentist; b. Columbus, Ohio, Nov. 25, 1951; s. Roger W. and Ruth (Black) H.; m. Kathleen Moore, July 3, 1976; children: Noah, Logan, Issac. BS, Capital U., 1975; DDS, Ohio State U., 1978. Gen. practice dentistry W. Chris Hanners, DDS & Assoc. Inc., Piketon, Ohio, 1978—; real estate developer Hanners Property Devel. and Mgmt. Co., Piketon, 1984—; cons. Hanners Consultings, Piketon, 1985—. Pres. Hanners Fund, Pike County, 1983—; bd. dirs. United Way, Waverly, Ohio, 1980-83, Cancer Soc., Pike County, 1982-85, Jr. Achievement, 1987. Mem. Pike County C. of C. (bd. dirs. 1984—, v.p. 1986-87). Democrat. Methodist. Avocations: reading, golf, playing the stock market. Office: PO Box 519 Piketon Profl Bldg Piketon OH 45661

HANNIG, VIRGIL LEROY, healthcare executive; b Breese, Ill., Dec. 22, 1943; s. Paulie Frank and Gladys Marie (Kapp) H.; m. Virginia Frances Born, May 29, 1965; children—Laura, Tim. B.S., So. Ill. U. C.P.A., Ill. Controller, asst. treas. So. Ill. Health Services, Carbondale, 1972-75; controller Providence Hosp., Cin., 1975, Springfield Community Hosp., Ill., 1975-77; v.p. fin. St. Mary's Hosp., Kankakee, Ill., 1977-83; v.p. fin. HealthCor, Kankakee, 1983-84, sr. v.p., 1985; pres. VentureCor, Inc., Kankakee, 1985; sr. v.p. ServantCor, Kankakee, 1985-86; dir. Kankakee County Catholic Credit Union. Bd. dirs. Kankakee chpt. ARC. Served with USAR, 1962-65. Fellow Healthcare Fin. Mgmt. Assn. (Robert J. McMahon award 1981, Robert H. Reeves award 1981, William G. Follmer award 1977; mem. Am. Coll. Hosp. Adminstrs., Am. Inst. C.P.A.s, Ill. Soc. C.P.A.s, Nat. Assn. Accts. Lodges: Rotary, Elks. Avocations: hunting, fishing, photography. Home: 1068 S Wildwood St Kankakee IL 60901

HANNON, NORMAN LESLIE, industrial management consultant; b. Ballymoney, No. Ireland, Dec. 31, 1923; came to U.S., 1963, naturalized, 1972; s. Arthur Gordon and Hilda Catherine Stewart-Moore (Denny) H.; B.S. in M.E., Queen's U., Belfast, No. Ireland, 1950; m. Patricia Ann Smale, June 2, 1951; children—Philip Leslie, Sarah-Louise, Michael John (dec.). Chief estimator British Tabulating Machines, No. Ireland, 1950-51; planning officer Hollerith Machines, South Africa, 1951-52; tech. sales engr. Babcock & Wilcox, South Africa, 1952-54; mgmt. cons. P.E. Cons. Group, London, 1954-63; supt. indsl. engring., adminstrn. mgr. Plastics and Fibers divs. Celanese Corp. U.S., Can., 1963-68; mgr. corp. devel. Forward Industries div. Will Ross, Inc., Kansas City, 1968-69; mgmt. cons. Richard Muther & Assos., Kansas City, Mo., 1969-72; dir. mgmt. services MAC Tools, Washington Ct. House, Ohio, 1972-73; dir. ops., mgr. adminstrn. and planning Gustin-Bacon div. Aeroquip Corp., Lawrence, Kans., 1973-77; v.p. Richard Muther & Assocs. Inc., Kansas City, Mo., 1977-83; sr. v.p., vice chmn. bd. Richard Muther & Assocs., Inc., 1983-85, The Leawood Group, Ltd., 1985—. Served with RAF, 1942-46. Chartered Engr., U.K., Australia, South Africa, Can.; cert. mgmt. cons. Mem. Instn. Mech. Engrs. (U.K.), Inst. Prodn. Engrs. (U.K.), Inst. Mgmt. Cons., Internat. Facility Mgmt. Assn. Address: c/o The Boreen RR 1 129 AZ Lawrence KS 66044 Office: The Leawood Group Ltd 4901 College Blvd Leawood KS 66211

HANRAHAN, ROBERT PHILIP, township official; b. Chgo., Nov. 9, 1932; s. Robert Michael and Margaret Estelle (Connolly) H.; m. Theresa A. Ieraci, Nov. 25, 1954; 6 children. B.S., U. Notre Dame, 1955, M.A., 1957. Cert. Ill. Assessing Ofcl. Faculty U. Notre Dame, South Bend, Ind., 1955-57; tchr. Niles West High Sch., Skokie, Ill., 1962-83; Realtor Kruger Realtors, Skokie, 1962-77; assessor Niles Twp. (Ill.), 1977—. Chairperson Human Relations Commn. of Morton Grove (Ill.); mem. Morton Grove Traffic and Safety Commn. Named Outstanding Citizen of Yr., Morton Grove Youth Commn., 1979. Mem. Cook County Twp. Assessor's Assn. (bd. dirs.), Twp. Ofcls. Ill., Internat. Assn. Assessing Officers (presenter paper nat. conv. 1985), Nat. Monogram Club. Home: 8233 N Austin Ave Morton Grove IL 60053 Office: Niles Twp Assessor's Office 5255 W Main St Skokie IL 60076

HANRATH, LINDA CAROL, librarian, archivist; b. Chgo., Aug. 22, 1949; d. John Stanley and Victoria (Fraint) Grzesiakowski; m. Richard Alan Hanrath, Nov. 1, 1980. BA in History, Rosary Coll., 1971, MA in Library Sci., 1974. Tchr. social studies Notre Dame High Sch., Chgo., 1971-75; outreach librarian Indian Trails Pub. Library, Wheeling, Ill., 1975-76, Arlington Heights (Ill.) Meml. Library, 1976-78; corp. librarian William Wrigley Jr. Co., Chgo., 1978—. Mem. Spl. Libraries Assn. (sec. Ill. chpt. 1984-86, chairperson library jobline com. 1981-83, 86-87, chairperson-elect food, agriculture and nutrition div. 1987—), Assn. Records Mgrs. and Adminstrs., Soc. Am. Archivists, Midwest Archives Conf., Beta Phi Mu. Republican. Roman Catholic. Avocations: needlework, skiing, reading, gourmet cooking. Home: 715 E Devon Ave Roselle IL 60172 Office: William Wrigley Jr Co 410 N Michigan Ave Chicago IL 60611

HANSELL, EDGAR FRANK, lawyer; b. Leon, Iowa, Oct. 12, 1937; s. Edgar Noble and Celestia Delphine (Skinner) H.; m. Phyllis Wray Silvey, June 24, 1961; children—John Joseph, Jordan Burke. A.A., Graceland Coll., 1957; B.B.A., U. Iowa, 1959, J.D., 1961. Bar: Iowa 1961. Mem. Nyemaster, Goode, McLaughlin, Emery & O'Brien, P.C., Des Moines, 1964—; ptnr. Nyemaster, Goode, McLaughlin, Emery & O'Brien, P.C., 1968—; bd. dirs. Britt Tech. Corp., The Vernon Co. Mem. editorial adv. bd. Jour. Corp. Law, 1985—. Bd. dirs. Des Moines Child Guidance Ctr., 1972-78, 81-87, pres., 1977-78; bd. dirs. Child Guidance Found., 1983—; trustee Iowa Law Sch. Found., 1975—, pres., 1983—; bd. dirs. Des Moines Community Playhouse, Inc., 1982-87, Iowa Sports Found., 1986—. Served with USAF, 1961-64. Mem. ABA, Iowa Bar Assn. (pres. young lawyers sect. 1971-72, gov. 1971-72, 85-87, mem. grievance commn. 1973-78, Merit award young lawyers sect. 1977, chmn. corp. and bus. law com. 1979-85, v.p. 1987—), Polk County Bar Assn. Home: 4001 John Lynde Rd Des Moines IA 50312 Office: Nyemaster Goode McLaughlin et al Hubbell Bldg Des Moines IA 50309

HANSELL, PHYLLIS SILVEY, psychologist; b. Versailles, Mo., Apr. 14, 1940; d. Wray D. and Ina (Brown) Silvey; m. Edgar Frank Hansell, June 24, 1961; children: John Joseph, Jordan Burke. A, U. Okla., 1963; MA, Drake U., 1970, EdD, 1984. Lic. psychologist, Iowa. Psychologist Des Moines Pub. Schs., 1975-80; counseling psychologist Drake U., Des Moines, 1980-83; pvt. practice psychology Des Moines, 1982—. Bd. dirs. Orchard Place, Des Moines, 1977—, Pub. Health Nurses Bd., Des Moines, 1964-69; commr. Des Moines Civil Rights Commn., 1970-73; v.p. bd. dirs. Orchard Place Found., Des Moines, 1983—. Mem. Am. Psychol. Assn., Am. Assn. Advancement of Behavior Therapy, Iowa Bd. Psychology Examiners, Iowa Psychol. Assn., Assn. Behavior Analysis, Midwestern Assn. Behavioral Medicine, Psi Chi. Club: Women's Exec. (Des Moines). Avocations: boating, tennis. Home: 4001 John Lynde Rd Des Moines IA 50312 Office: 1414 Woodland Des Moines IA 50309

HANSELL, RICHARD STANLEY, obstetrician, gynecologist, educator; b. Indpls., Nov. 18, 1950; s. Robert Mathy and Jewel (Martin) H.; m. Marni Jane Kent, May 26, 1973; children: Elizabeth, Victoria. BA, DePauw U., 1972; MD, Ind. U., 1976. Cert. Am. Bd. Obstetrics and Gynecology. Practice medicine specializing in ob-gyn Cedarwood Med. Ctr., St. Joseph, Mich., 1980-86; asst. prof. ob-gyn Ind. U., Indpls., 1986—; instr. Western Mich. U., Kalamazoo, 1980-86; med. bd. Planned Parenthood, Benton Harbor, Mich., 1980-86. Mem. AMA, Am. Coll. Ob-Gyn, Berrien County Med. Soc., Mich. State Med. Soc., Ind. State Med. Soc., Marion County Med. Soc. Presbyterian. Lodge: Kiwanis. Avocations: golf, fishing. Office: Ind U Med Sch Dept Ob-Gyn 926 W Michigan St Indianapolis IN 46223

HANSEN, ANDREW MARIUS, library association executive; b. Storm Lake, Iowa, Mar. 25, 1929; s. Andrew Marius and Margaret Mary (Van Wagenen) H.; m. Rina M. Smith, Feb. 24, 1967; 1 child, Neil S. B.A., U. Omaha, 1951; postgrad., U. Md., 1955; M.A., U. Minn., 1962; postgrad, U. Iowa, 1968-71. Librarian Bismarck (N.D.) Public Library, 1957-63, Sioux City (Iowa) Public Library, 1963-67; instr. Sch. of Library Sci., U. Iowa, Iowa City, 1967-71; exec. sec. ALA, Chgo., 1971-80; exec. dir. reference and adult services div. ALA, 1980—; vis. asst. prof. Ind. State U., Terre Haute, 1966. Pres. Friends of Wilmette Pub. Library, 1984-85. Served with USAF, 1951-55. Mem. N.D. Library Assn. (pres. 1958-59, sec., treas. 1962-63), Iowa Library Assn. (pres. 1967-68), Coalition Adult Edn. Orgns. (dir. 1972—), Ch. and Synagogue Library Assn. (treas. Northeastern Ill. chpt. 1985—), Chgo. Library Club (sec. 1983-84). Presbyterian. Home: 314 Skokie Ct Wilmette IL 60091 Office: American Library Assn 50 E Huron St Chicago IL 60611

HANSEN, CARL R., management consultant, b. Chgo., May 2, 1926; s. Carl M. and Anna C. (Roge) H.; m. Christia Marie Loeser, Dec. 31, 1952; 1 son, Lothar. M.B.A., U. Chgo., 1954. Dir. market research Kitchens of Sara Lee, Deerfield, Ill.; dir. market research Earle Ludgin & Co., Chgo.; service v.p. Market Research Corp. Am., 1956-67; pres. Chgo. Assoc. Inc., 1967—. Chmn. Ill. adv. council SBA, 1973-74; mem. exec. com. Ill. Gov.'s Adv. Council, 1969-72; resident officer U.S. High Commn. Germany, 1949-52; vice chmn. Rep. Cen. Com. Cook County; chmn. Young Rep. Orgn. Cook County, 1957-58, 12th Congl. Dist. Rep. Orgn., 1971-74, 78-82, Suburban Rep. Orgn., 1974-78, 82-86; del. Rep. Nat. Conv., 1968, 84; chmn. Legis. Dist. Ill., 1964—; del. Rep. State Conv., 1962-86; Elk Grove Twp. Rep. committeeman, 1962—; pres. John Ericsson Rep. League Ill., 1975-76; Rep. presdl. elector Ill., 1972; mem. Cook County Bd. Commrs., 1970, 74—; mem. Am. Scandinavian Found. Served to 1st lt. AUS, 1944-48, maj. Res. Mem. Am. Mktg. Assn., Am. Statis. Assn., Res. Officers Assn., Chgo. Hist. Soc., Planning Forum, Am. Legion. Clubs: Danish, Norwegian, Swedish (Chgo.). Lodges: Lions, Masons, Shriners. Home: 110 S Edward St Mount Prospect IL 60056 Office: 109 N Dearborn Chicago IL 60602

HANSEN, CARL RICHARD, JR., psychologist, researcher; b. Mankato, Minn., July 21, 1954; s. Carl Richard Sr. and Martha Elisabeth (Sorensen) H.; m. Constance Joann McLeod, June 27, 1981; 1 child, Carl Richard III. BA, BS, Viterbo Coll., 1976; MD, U. Minn., 1979, postgrad., 1979-82. Fellow in psychiatry U. Minn., Mpls., 1979-82; fellow in child psychiatry Yale U. Child Study Fellow, New Haven, 1982-84; pvt. practice child psychiatry North Haven, Conn., 1984-85, Golden Valley, Minn., 1985—; med. dir. child psychiatry service Golden Valley Health Ctr., 1987—; clin. dir. Greenshire Sch., Cheshire, Conn., 1984-85; cons. Golden Valley Health Ctr., 1985. Mem. U.S. Congl. Adv. Bd., 1985. Named one of Outstanding Young Men Am., 1981; recipient Eagle award Boy Scouts Am., 1969; fellow John A. Merck Found., Yale U., 1983-84, Leonard Berger, Yale U., 1983-84. Mem. AMA, AAAS, Am. Psychiat. Assn., Hastings Ctr., Sigma Xi. Republican. Lutheran. Office: 4101 Golden Valley Rd Ridgewood Bldg Golden Valley MN 55422

HANSEN, CRAIG EUGENE, insurance company executive; b. Algona, Iowa, Mar. 28, 1958; s. Dale Eugene and Jane Diane (Linquist) H. BS in Indsl. Adminstrn., Iowa State U., 1980; postgrad., Drake U., 1984—. Sr. bond underwriter USF&G Ins., Des Moines, 1980-86; bond. mgr. St. Paul Fire & Marine Ins. Co., Des Moines, 1986—. Mem. Surety Underwriters Assn. Lutheran. Avocations: golf, running. Home: 9073 Franklin Ave Des Moines IA 50322 Office: St Paul Fire & Marine Ins Co 1025 Ashworth Rd West Des Moines IA 50265

HANSEN, DAVID R., federal judge. Judge U.S. District Court of Northern Iowa, Cedar Rapids, 1986—. *

HANSEN, DAVID WEARE, optometrist; b. Maryville, Mo., Apr. 11, 1945; s. Lester Weare and Gretchen (Hosman) H.; m. Linda Jean Kubina, July 24, 1971; children—John David, Stephanie Jean. B.S., U. Iowa, 1967; B.S. in Visual Sci., Ill. Coll. Optometry, 1969, O.D., 1971. Lic. optometrist, Iowa. Gen. practice optometry, Des Moines, 1971—; contact lens cons. CIBA Vision Care, Atlanta, 1984—; clin. contact lens researcher Bausch & Lomb, Wesley Jessen, Alcon, Syntex, Precision Cosmet, Vision Ease; also others, Contbr. articles to medical jours. Active Grace Lutheran Ch., Iowa Assn. of Children with Learning Disabilities, Des Moines Civic Ctr.; bd. dirs. The Sci. Ctr. Iowa, 1981—, pres., 1984—; chmn. exhibits com. Sci. Ctr. 1982—, mem. action council 1974—. Fellow Am. Acad. Optometry (pres. Edn. Commn. 1984—), Coll. Optometrists in Vision Devel.; mem. Am. Optometric Assn., Iowa Optometric Assn., Mid-Iowa Optometric Soc., Central Iowa Devel. Vision Group. Republican. Avocations: photography; swimming. Home: 3001 Sylvania Dr West Des Moines IA 50265 Office: Optometric Assocs of Des Moines 2182 82nd St Des Moines IA 50322

HANSEN, DONALD, optometrist; b. Davenport, Iowa, May 11, 1926; s. Henry O. and Stella M. Hansen; m. Constance Lorraine Wolf, Oct. 19, 1934; children—Leslie Christine Hansen-Newman, Todd Whitney. B.A. Coe Coll., Cedar Rapids, Iowa, 1948; B.S. and O.D., Chgo. Coll. Optometry, 1951. Practice optometry The Main Vision Clinic, Davenport, 1951—; founder U.S. Farmers Food Bank. Charter mem. fin. accountability com. Am. div. Christian Blind Mission; advisor, cons. Heritage Found., Washington. charter mem. bd. dirs. Olypiads of Knowledge. Fellow Am. Acad. Corrective Optometry; mem. Am. Optometric Assn., Iowa Optometric Assn., Am. Coll. Syntonic Optometry. Club: Rock Island Arsenal Golf. Lodges: Rotary, Lions. Author: Winding America's Mainspring with Prepaid Social Security; Free World Social Security Using Free Enterprise Educational Trust. Home: 1117 Eastmere Dr Bettendorf IA 52722 Office: 1923 Main St Davenport IA 52803

HANSEN, ERIC PETER, lawyer; b. Mpls., June 12, 1951; s. Donald Arthur and Florence (Paulsen) H.; m. Janet G. Bostrom, Mar. 21, 1981; 1 child, Lindsey Elizabeth. B.A., St. Olaf Coll., 1973; J.D., Duke U., 1976. Bar: Minn. 1976, U.S. Dist. Ct. Minn. 1979, U.S. Ct. Appeals (8th cir.) 1979. Atty., 3M Co., St. Paul, 1976-80, div. atty., 1980-83, sr. atty., 1983—. Chmn. bill summary com. Berean League, Roseville, Minn., 1986—. Mem. Minn. Bar Assn. Republican. Mem. Christian Ch. Avocations: reading, skiing, tennis, golf. Office: 3M Co PO Box 33428 3M Ctr Saint Paul MN 55133

HANSEN, JAMES DAVID, accounting educator; b. Wilmar, Minn., June 5, 1947; s. Victor and Grayce H.; m. Margie J. Cramer, Sept. 7, 1969; children: John, Jennifer. BA, U. N.D., 1970; MBA, N.D. State U., 1982. CPA, N.D. Tchr. Sacramento, 1970-74; acct. Arthur Andersen & Co., St. Paul, 1977-79; tchr. acctg. N.D. State U., Fargo, 1979—, dir. Small Bus. Inst., 1984—; treas. Dakota Montessori, Fargo, 1981-86. Author: Computerized Accounting Instruction, 1985. Recipient George Washington Honor medal Freedoms Found., 1969. Mem. Am. Inst. CPA's, N.D. Soc. CPA's. Home: 9 Birch Ln Fargo ND 58103

HANSEN, JAMES OTTO, state educational administrator; b. Lead, S.D., Sept. 21, 1928; s. Harold J. and Lillian (Mattson) H.; B.S., Black Hills State Coll., 1952; M.A., U. No. Colo., 1956; Ed.D., U. S.D., 1968; m. Dora Laura Helmer, May 28, 1950; children—Linda Kay Hansen Whitney, Diana May Hansen Buseman, June Doreen. Tchr., prin. public schs., Philip, S.D., 1952-55; supt. schs., Wessington, S.D., 1956-60; supt. schs., Gregory, S.D., 1961-67; supt. schs., Madison, S.D., 1968-76; asst. supt. instrn. State of S.D., Pierre, 1976-77, dept. state supt., 1978-79, state supt. of elem. and secondary edn., 1979—; sec. S.D. Dept. Edn. and Cultural Affairs, 1985—. Served with USAF, 1946-49. Mem. NEA, Council Chief State Sch. Officers, Sch. Adminstrs. S.D. (Adminstr. of Yr., 1979), Phi Delta Kappa. Republican. Congregationalist. Clubs: Kiwanis, Rotary, Masons, Elks. Office: Kneip Bldg Pierre SD 57501

HANSEN, JOHN HERBERT, university administrator, accountant; b. Milw., Mar. 20, 1945; s. John Herbert and Elsie F. (Patri) H.; m. Christina Ann Lainey, Sept. 5, 1970. BBA, U. Wis., 1969; M in Acctg., U. Ill., 1973. CPA, Wis. Dir. fin. Marquette U., Milw., 1973—. corp. treas. Cath. League, Milw., 1982—. Served with USAF, 1970-73. Mem. Am. Inst. CPA's, Milw. Bond Club. Republican. Club: Rainbow Springs Country. Avocations: golf, gardening. Office: Marquette U 615 N 11th St Milwaukee WI 53233

HANSEN, JOHN WALKER, technical publications consultant; b. Edgar, Nebr., Aug. 28, 1934; s. Harry Hans and Elva Lorena (Short) H.; m. Eileen Ruth Nentwig, Aug. 2, 1958, children: Karen, Jill, David, Kristin. BA, Hastings Coll., 1954; postgrad., U. Minn., 1954-57. Tech. writer Pako Corp., Mpls., 1959-65, mgr. tech. pubs., 1965-86; pres. Hansen-Reshanov Cons. Inc., Mpls., 1986—. Author/pub.: Workday Breakfasts, 1979; co-author/pub.: 1986 Purchasing Directory for Technical Communicators, 1986. Served with U.S. Army, 1957-59. Mem. Soc. Tech. Communicators (sr., pres. Twin Cities chpt.). Avocation: gardening. Home: 8009 40th Ave N New Hope MN 55427 Office: Hansen-Reshanov Cons Inc 3140 Harbor Ln Suite 236 Plymouth MN 55441

HANSEN, KATHRYN GERTRUDE, former state official, association editor; b. Gardner, Ill., May 24, 1912; d. Harry J. and Marguerite (Gaston) Hansen; B.S. with honors, U. Ill., 1934, M.S., 1936. Personnel asst. U. Ill., Urbana, 1945-46, supr. tng. and activities, 1946-47, personnel officer, instr. psychology, 1947-52, exec. sec. U. Civil Service System Ill., also sec. for merit bd., 1952-61, adminstrv. officer, sec. merit bd., 1961-68, dir. system, 1968-72; lay asst. firm Webber, Balbach, Theis and Follmer, P.C., Urbana, Ill., 1972-74. Bd. dirs. U. YWCA, 1952-55, chmn., 1954-55; bd. dirs. Champaign-Urbana Symphony, 1978-81. Mem. Coll. and Univ. Personnel Assn. (hon., life mem., editor Jour. 1955-73, Newsletter, Internat. pres. 1967-68, nat. publs. award named in her honor 1987), Annuitants Assn. State Univs. Retirement System Ill. (state sec.-treas. 1974-75), Pres.'s Council U. Ill. (life), U. Ill. Alumni Assn. (life), U. Ill. Found., Campus Round Table U. Ill., Nat. League Am. Pen Women, AAUW (state 1st v.p. 1958-60), Champaign-Urbana Symphony Guild, Secretariat U. Ill. (life), Grundy County Hist. Soc., Delta Kappa Gamma (state pres. 1961-63), Phi Mu (life), Kappa Delta Pi, Kappa Tau Alpha. Presbyterian. Clubs: Monday Writers, Fortnightly (Champaign-Urbana). Lodge: Order Eastern Star. Author: (with others) A Plan of Position Classification for Colleges and Universities; A Classification Plan for Staff Positions at Colleges and Universities, 1968; Grundy-Corners, 1982; Sarah, A Documentary of Her Life and Times, 1984, Ninety Years with Fortnightly, Vols. I and II, an historical compilation, 1986; editor: The Illini Worker, 1946-52; Campus Pathways, 1952-61; This is Your Civil Service Handbook, 1960-67; author, cons., editor pubs. on personnel practices. Home: 1004 E Harding Dr Apt 307 Urbana IL 61801

HANSEN, LAURA ANN, sales executive; b. Elmhurst, Ill, July 26, 1959; d. Donald Charles and Patricia Ann (Dorian) H. BS, So. Ill. U., 1981. Pub. relations asst. MacArthur Found., Chgo., 1981-83; direct mktg. coordinator GTE Directories Corp., Des Plaines, Ill., 1983; telemkgt. supr. ABC/Tele1st, Bensenville, Ill., 1984-85; sales specialist Group W Cable, Chgo., 1985; telemkgt. mgr. Metrovision Cable, Blue Island, Ill., 1985—; cons. Chgo. Cable Cooperative, 1986—. Mem. Am. Soc. Tng. and Devel. Home: 2752 N Mildred #3 Chicago IL 60614 Office: Metrovision Inc 3026 W 127th St Blue Island IL 60406

HANSEN, LORRAINE (SUNNY) SUNDAL, counselor, educator; b. Albert Lea, Minn., Oct. 11, 1929; d. Rasmus O. and Cora B. Sundal; m. Tor Kjaerstad Hansen, Dec. 15, 1962; children—Sonja, Tor S. B.S., U. Minn., 1951, M.A., 1957, Ph.D., 1962; postgrad. U. Oslo, 1959-60. English tchr., St. Louis Park, Minn., 1951-53, Lab. Sch., U. Chgo., 1953-54; tchr. English and journalism Univ. High Sch., U. Minn., Mpls., 1954-57, counselor, dir. counseling, 1957-70; asst. prof., assoc. prof., prof. edn. psychology, 1962—, dir. project BORN FREE; cons. schs. and colls.; worldwide lectr., dir. workshops on career devel. and career edn. Author: Career Guidance Practices in School and Community, 1970; An Examination of Concepts and Definitions of Career Education, 1976; (with others) Educating for Career Development, 1975, 80; Career Development and Planning, 1982; Eliminating Sex Stereotyping in Schools, 1984. Editor: Career Development and Counseling of

Women, 1978; numerous BORN FREE publs., videotapes and TV courses. Contbr. articles to profl. publs., chpts. to books. Fulbright scholar, 1959-60; named Outstanding Leader in Edn. Mpls. YMCA, 1983; recipient Career Devel. Profl. Award Am. Soc. for Tng. and Devel., 1986. Fellow Am. Psychol. Assn.; mem. Am. Assn. for Counseling and Devel., Minn. Assn. for Counseling and Devel. (cert. recognition 1976, research award 1980, Outstanding Achievement award 1986), Nat. Career Devel. Assn. (pres. 1985-86), Internat. Assn. Ednl.-Vocat. Guidance, Internat. Round Table for Advancement of Counseling (exec. council, v.p. 1986—), Am. Sch. Counselors Assn., Am. Coll. Personnel Assn., Assn. for Counselor Edn. and Supervision (Nat. Disting. Mentor award 1985). Democrat. Congregationalist. Club: Minn. Women's Consortium. Office: U Minn Dept Edn 139 Burton Hall Minneapolis MN 55455

HANSEN, MICHAEL JUDE, dentist; b. Chicago Heights, Ill., Dec. 11, 1948; s. Holger Merlin and Cleopha Margaret (Donavan) H.; m. Katherine Ann Katz, Aug. 28, 1971; children: Kate, Joseph, Michael, Susan. BS, St. Norbert Coll., 1970; DDS, Loyola U., Chgo., 1974. Pvt. practice dentistry Cedarburg, Wis., 1974—; Sec.-treas. Ozaukee-Washington County Dental Soc., Cedarburg, 1975-76, v.p., 1976-77, pres., 1977-78. V.p. Cedarburg Jaycees, 1981, pres., 1982. Avocations: children, camping, fishing, hunting, riflery. Home: 4672 River Vista Dr Cedarburg WI 53012 Office: N57 W6296 Center St Cedarburg WI 53012

HANSEN, OLE VIGGO, chemical engineer; b. Detroit, May 6, 1934; s. Oluf Viggo and Carrie Alma (Wary) H.; m. Shirley Elizabeth Ford, Dec. 29, 1966; children: Victoria, Louisa. BSChemE, Wayne State U., 1956; equivalent of BS in Meteorology, Tex. A & M Univ., 1958. Registered profl. engr., Mich. Engr. tech. services 3M Co., Detroit, 1956-57; chem. engr. Fisher Body div. Gen. Motors, Detroit, 1960-64; mgr. mktg. Monsanto Co., St. Louis and Australia, 1964-76; dir. tech. mktg. Beltran Assocs., Inc., N.Y.C., 1976-78; mgr. mist eliminators Koch Engring. Co., Inc., Wichita, Kans., 1978—; bd. dirs. Divmesh of Canada, Ltd., Calgary, Alta., 1984-85. Contbr. articles to profl. jours. Served to capt. USAF, 1956-60. Mem. Am. Inst. Chem. Engrs. (session chmn. nat. meeting 1980). Avocations: 19th century history, classical music, travel. Home: 725 Fairland Wichita KS 67230 Office: Koch Engring Co Inc 4111 E 37th St N Wichita KS 67220

HANSEN, PATRICK WILLIAM, nurse; b. Milw., June 22, 1954; s. Donald Henry and Patricia Marian (Glisch) H.; m. Patricia Ann Cleary, May 27, 1978; children: Sean Patrick, Elizabeth Mary. AS in Nursing, Milw. Area Tech. Coll., 1978. Staff nurse Milw. County Med. Complex, Wauwatosa, Wis., 1978—. Mormon. Avocations: photography, sport fishing, target shooting. Home: 6890 Hwy Q Hartford WI 53027-9743 Office: Milw County Med Complex 8700 W Wisconsin Ave Wauwatosa WI 53226

HANSEN, RICHARD LOUIS, pharmaceutical company executive; b. Stillwater, Minn., Jan. 20, 1930; m. Linda Pugh, Mar. 16, 1957; children: Gregory, Susan, Beryl. BS, U. Minn., 1951; MS ChemE, Northwestern U., 1952. Devel. engr. fluorochems. 3M Co., St. Paul, 1952-54, market devel., new products, 1956-64, mgr. med. products, 1964-74, dept. mgr. diagnostics, 1977-80; mktg. dir. Riker Lab. 3M Co., Northridge, Calif., 1980-84; mgr. strategic planning Riker Lab. 3M Co., St. Paul, 1984—; mng. dir. 3M Singapore, 1974-77; bd. dirs. Littmann Meml. Found., Boston. Mem. Am. Inst. Chem. Engrs. (sect. chmn. 1958), Internat. Soc. Planning and Strategic Mgmt. Republican. Office: 3M Co Riker Labs Inc 225-1S-07 Saint Paul MN 55144

HANSEN, ROBERT ARNOLD, utilities company manager; b. La Crosse, Wis., Mar. 29, 1950; s. Arnold Marinus and Delores (Niedbalski) H.; m. Laurie Jo Lee, June 17, 1972; children: Heather, Hilary. BA in Acctg. and Bus. Adminstrn., Moorhead (Minn.) State U., 1971, MBA, 1983. CPA, Cert. Mgmt. Acct., Minn. Tax examiner II Minn. Dept. Revenue, Crookston, 1971-73; cost acct. FMC-Crane & Excavator, Cedar Rapids, Iowa, 1973-76; from acct. to mgr. tax dept. Otter Tail Power Co., Fergus Falls, Minn., 1976—. Bd. mgrs. Federated Ch., Fergus Falls, 1979-81; fund-raiser Minn. Ind. Reps., Fergus Falls, 1985-86. Named one of Outstanding Young Men Am., 1985. Mem. Am. Inst. CPA's (tax div.), Minn. Soc. CPA's, Edison Elec. Inst. (depreciation acctg. div.), Inst. Mgmt. Acctg., Fergus Falls Jaycees, (pres. 1977-83, 3d high state del., 1979, Outstanding Bd. Mem., 1979-81). Congregational. Club: Toastmasters (Fergus Falls) (sec. 1978). Lodge: Elks. Avocations: private pilot, swimming, bridge, bowling, skiing. Home: 1336 Hillcrest Ct Fergus Falls MN 56537 Office: Otter Trail Power Co 215 S Cascade Fergus Falls MN 56537

HANSEN, ROBERT EUGENE, accountant, educator; b. Decatur, Ill., Oct. 22, 1931; s. George Jesper and Arlowyne (Eckert) H.; m. Nancy May Wyant, Aug. 22, 1959; children: Julia, Eric, Joyce, Linda. CPA, Ohio, Ky. Asst. prof. acctg. U. Toledo, 1963-68, assoc. prof. acctg., 1968-74, prof., chair acctg. dept., 1978-86, prof. emeritus, 1986—; prof., chair acctg. dept. Morehead (Ky.) State U., 1974-78; prof. acctg. U. Detroit, 1986—; pres. Morehead State U. Fed. Credit Union, 1977-78; manuscript reviewer various pubs., 1980-86. Co-author: Development of Master of Taxation Graduate Program, 1986. Researcher, creator city charter Lakeview Heights, Ky., 1977-78. Mem. Am. Inst. CPA's, Inst. Internal Auditors (various offices 1965-69, Outstanding Service award 1972), Am. Acctg. Assn. (various coms. 1965-86), Ohio Soc. CPA's (various coms. 1963-86), Nat. Assn. Accts., Annual IRS Tax Inst. (coordinator, dist. dir. 1979-85), Beta Alpha Psi (faculty v.p. 1965-67, 84-86), Beta Gamma Sigma, Phi Kappa Phi. Avocations: woodworking, oil painting, golf, fishing. Home: 896 Sandalwood Rd W Perrysburg OH 43551 Office: U Detroit Coll Bus Adminstrn 4001 W McNichols Detroit MI 48221

HANSEN, ROBERT SUTTLE, chemist, educator; b. Salt Lake City, June 17, 1918; s. Charles Andrew and Bessie (Suttle) H.; m. Gilda Cappannari, Apr. 8, 1939; 1 son, Edward Charles. B.S., U. Mich., 1940, M.S., 1941, Ph.D., 1948; D.Sc. (hon.), Lehigh U., 1978. Asst. prof. chemistry dept. Iowa State U., Ames, 1948-51; asso. prof. Iowa State U., 1951-55, prof., 1955—, chmn., 1965-68, distinguished prof., 1967—; asso. chemist Ames Lab., Dept. Energy, 1948-55, sr. chemist, 1955—, chief chemistry div., 1965-68, dir., 1968—; cons. Procter & Gamble Co.; Mem. chemistry adv. panel NSF, 1971-75, materials research adv. com., 1976-80; mem. Gov.'s Sci. Adv. Council, 1977—, Iowa Energy Policy Council, 1978-86. Fellow AAAS, Iowa Acad. Sci. (Centennial Citation 1975); mem. Am. Chem. Soc. (past sec.-treas., chmn. colloid div., Kendall Co. award colloid chemistry 1966, Midwest award 1980, Iowa award 1987), Am. Phys. Soc., AAUP, Phi Beta Kappa, Sigma Xi, Phi Kappa Phi. Home: 2030 McCarthy Rd Ames IA 50010

HANSEN, ROBERT WAYNE, judge, editor; b. Milw., Apr. 29, 1911; s. Edwin A. and Martha (Siggelkow) H.; m. Dorothea Belle Awaus, Feb. 14, 1941; children: Karen Hansen Schat, John, Susan, Jim. LLB, Marquette U., 1933. Bar: Wis. 1933. Judge Wis. Dist. Ct., Milw., 1954-60, Wis. Circuit Ct., Milw., 1960-67; chief judge Milw. County, 1965-67; justice Supreme Ct. of Wis., Madison, 1967-78; res. judge State of Wis., 1978—. Lodge: Fraternal Order of the Eagles (editor Eagle mag. 1943-50, 1978—). Home: N48 W 3414 Jaeckels Dr Nashotah WI 53058

HANSEN, RUSSELL A., discount retail company executive. Chmn., pres., chief exec. officer, dir. Cook United, Inc., Cleve. Office: Cook United Inc 16501 Rockside Rd Cleveland OH 44137 *

HANSEN, SOREN, civil engineer; b. Copenhagen, Mar. 12, 1939; came to U.S., 1948; s. Anker Karl Andreas and Ingeborg (Astrup) H.; m. Mary Jane Hekker, June 12, 1965; children: Maia Allis, Kai Erik. BSCE, Cornell U., 1964, MSCE, 1965. Registered profl. engr., Ohio. Dir. engring. Stebbins Engring. and Mfg. Co., Watertown, N.Y., 1972-74; sr. project engr., mgr. Republic Steel Corp., Youngstown, Ohio, 1975-77; sr. staff engr. Republic Steel Corp., Cleve., 1977-81, mgr. project planning and control, 1982-84; environ. mgmt. engr. LTV Steel, Cleve., 1984-86; pres. InterGraphic Engring. Services, Cleve., 1985—. Mem. editorial bd. Project Mgmt. Jour., 1982—. Mem. ASCE, NSPE, Nat. Computer Graphics Assn. (membership com. 1984-85), Project Mgmt. Inst., Assn. Iron and Steel Engrs. (chmn. working group #4 1984-86). Unitarian. Avocations: gardening, reading.

HANSEN, TIM R., advertising executive; b. Racine, Wis., May 16, 1946; s. Ferdinand and Sylvia (Johnson) H.; m. Darlene S. Caskey, June 7, 1969; children: Kimberly, Melanie, Erik. A in Mktg., Gateway Tech. Inst., 1968; BS in Bus., Carthage Coll., 1984. Customer service supr. J I Case Co., Racine, Wis., 1970-74, with parts merchandising dept., 1974-80, sales devel. mgr., 1980-82, advt. mgr., 1982-84, mgr. pub. relations, sales promotion, advt., 1984—. Mem. Associated Gen. Contractors, Associated Equipment Distbrs., Constrn. Industry Mfrs. Assn. (pub. relations adv. bd. 1985—), Salmon Unltd. Clubs: Racine Ad. Avocations: fishing, hunting. Home: 1502 Laura Ave Racine WI 53406 Office: J I Case Co 700 State St Racine WI 53404

HANSEN, TIMOTHY JAMES, manufacturing company executive; b. Granite Falls, Minn., May 10, 1954; s. James Albert and Kathryn Ardis (Johnson) H.; m. Cheri Lynn Marschner, June 11, 1977; 1 child, Heidi. BS in Acctg., Mankato (Minn.) State U., 1976. CPA, Wis. Staff acct. Klinner Co., Medford, Wis., 1977-79; pvt. practice acct. Medford, 1979-85; supr. acctg. Tombstone Pizza Co., Medford, 1985—. Treas. Taylor City Big Bros./Big Sisters, Medford, 1979-85. Mem. Am. Inst. CPA's, Nat. Mgmt. Assn., Wis. Inst. CPA's (com. profl. conduct 1983—). Democrat. Lutheran. Avocations: raising quarter horses, softball, waterskiing. Home: N 3406 Bizer Dr Medford WI 54451 Office: Tombstone Pizza Corp PO Box 7000 Medford WI 54451

HANSEN, WENDELL JAY, clergyman, gospel broadcaster; b. Waukegan, Ill., May 28, 1910; s. Christian Hans and Anna Sophia (Termansen) H.; m. Bertelle Kathryn Budman, Mar. 9, 1933 (dec. Jan. 6, 1956); 1 child, Sylvia Larson; m. 2d, Eunice Evaline Irvine, Nov. 2, 1957; 1 child, Dean. Grad. Cleve. Bible Coll., 1932; A.B., William Penn Coll., 1938; postgrad. Gletch Berg Skule, Switzerland, 1939; M.A., U. Iowa, 1940, Ph.D., 1947. Ordained to ministry Recorded Friends, 1936, Evang. Reformed Ch., 1944; pastor chs., Grinnell, Iowa, Mpls. and Iowa City, 1934-47; evangelist with talking and performing birds, 1946—, mgr. gospel radio stas. Two Rivers, Wis., Menomonie, Wis., Peru, Ind., Wabash, Ind., East St. Louis, Ill., Indpls., 1952—; pres., chmn. of bd. WESL Inc., East St. Louis, 1962—, cons. radio and TV, 1970—; appointed adv. com. to Indpls. Prosecutor, 1986. Dir. St. Paul Inter-racial Work Camp, 1939; chmn. Minn. Joint Refuge Com., 1940-41. Recipient honor citation Nat. Assn. Broadcasters, 1980; Boss of Yr. award Hamilton County Broadcasters, 1979, award Boys Town, 1983, award Women of Faith, St. Louis, 1984. Mem. Internat. Platform Assn., Internat. Assn. Christian Magicians, Ind. Bird Fanciers, East St. Louis C. of C. (bd. dirs. 1981—), Pi Kappa Delta. Republican. Quaker. Club: Ind. Pigeon (best exotic bird award 1969, 75, 80). Lodge: Kiwanis. Contbr. articles to popular mags.

HANSON, ALLEN D., grain marketing and processing cooperative executive; b. 1936; married. With Harvest States Coops., St. Paul, 1958—; Pres., chief exec. officer Harvest States Coop., St. Paul, from 1982, now pres., chief sexec. officer. Office: Harvest States Coop PO Box 64594 Saint Paul MN 55164

HANSON, BRUCE EUGENE, lawyer; b. Lincoln, Nebr., Aug. 25, 1942; s. Lester E. and Gladys (Diessner) H.; m. Peggy Pardun, Dec. 25, 1972. B.A., U. Minn., 1965, J.D., 1966. Bar: Minn. 1966, U.S. Dist. Ct. Minn. 1966, U.S. Tax Ct. 1973, U.S. Ct. Appeals (8th cir.) 1973, U.S. Ct. Appeals (fed. cir.) 1983, U.S. Supreme Ct. 1970. Ptnr., Doherty, Rumble & Butler, St. Paul, 1966—. Mem. Ramsey County Bar Assn., Minn. State Bar Assn., Am. Acad. Hosp. Attys., Minn. Soc. Hosp. Attys. (bd. dirs.), Assn. Trial Lawyers Am. Order of Coif, Phi Delta Phi. Clubs: St. Paul Athletic; North Oaks Golf (Minn.). Home: 23 Evergreen Rd North Oaks MN 55110 Office: Doherty Rumble & Butler 1500 1st Nat Bank Bldg Saint Paul MN 55101

HANSON, BRYANT R., health care administrator; b. Price, Utah, Apr. 13, 1946; s. Rex R. and Christine (Passarella) H.; m. Annette Wilson, June 15, 1968; children: Tonya, Stephen. AB cum laude, Regis Coll., 1968; MS in Hosp. Adminstrn., Ohio State U., 1973. Asst. exec. dir. St. Francis Hosp., Blue Island, Ill., 1973-75, assoc. exec. dir., 1975-80, exec. dir., 1980—; preceptor Govs. State U., Park Forest, Ill., 1980—, Ohio State U., Columbus, 1980—; bd. dirs. Family and Mental Health Cook County, Oak Lawn, 1976-85, Met. Chgo. Healthcare Council. Mem. Blue Island Mayor's Adv. Com., 1980-85; hon. chmn. Los Amigos, Blue Island, 1982; bd. dirs. Community Fund South Cook County, 1978-80. Served with U.S. Army, 1968-71, Vietnam. Regis Coll. scholar, 1964-68; decorated Bronze Star. Mem. Blue Island C. of C. (bd. dirs. 1979-83), Am. Coll. Hosp. Adminstrs., Am. Acad. Med. Adminstrs., Ill. Hosp. Assn. (region pres. 1982-84), Cath. Hosp. Assn., Chgo. Conf. Cath. Hosps. (v.p. 1984-87), Met. Chgo. Health Care Council (bd. dirs. 1987-90). Roman Catholic. Lodges: Rotary (v.p. 1978-80), Deacons, K.C. (Blue Island). Avocations: golf, rose gardening. Home: 15304 Walnut Rd Oak Forest IL 60452 Office: St Francis Hosp 12935 S Gregory St Blue Island IL 60406

HANSON, CHARLES DENNIS, director of libraries; b. Whitehall, Wis., Nov. 2, 1944; s. Iver and Goldie Alice (Moe) H. BA, Eau Claire (Wis.) State U., 1966; MLS, U. Wis., 1970; PhD, Bowling Green (Ohio) State U., 1978. Instructional services librarian Aquinas Coll., Grand Rapids, Mich., 1973-75; chmn. reference dept. Findlay (Ohio) Pub. Library, 1975-76; head librarian North Baltimore Pub. Library, 1977-82, Ohio State U., Lima, 1982-85; dir. libraries Grosse Pointe Pub. Libraries, Mich., 1985—. Bd. dirs. Community Edn. Adv. Bd., Grosse Pointe Schs., 1986—. Mem. ALA, Pub. Library Assn., Assn. Coll. and Research Libraries, Library Adminstr. and Mgmt. Assn., Mich. Library Assn., Mich. Assn. Media in Edn. Democrat. Home: 449 Moran Rd Grosse Pointe Farms MI 48236 Office: Grosse Pointe Pub Library 10 Kercheval Ave Grosse Pointe MI 48236

HANSON, CHARLES EASTON, JR., museum director, consultant; b. Holdrege, Nebr., Apr. 4, 1917; s. Charles Easton and Irene Hazel (Adkins) H.; m. Eva Marie Phillips, Apr. 18, 1936; children: Charles Easton III, William Raymond, James Austin. Student, Kearney (Nebr.) State Coll., 1934-35, U. Colo., 1949-50. Chief engr. U.S. Corps. Engrs., Sioux City, Iowa, Liberal, Kans., 1942-43; planning engr. Bur. Reclamation, McCook, Nebr., 1946-51; adminstr. engr. U.S. Dept. Agriculture, Casper, Wyo., Washington, 1954-69; dir. Mus. Fur Trade, Chadron, Nebr., 1969-72, 74—; cons., lectr. Pubs. Mus., Chadron, 1969—, lectr. elderhostel program Chadron State Coll., 1983—. Author: (book) The Northwest Gun, 1955, The Plains Rifle, 1960, The Hawken Rifle, Its Place in History, 1979; editor Mus. Fur Trade publ., 1965—. Hon. chmn. Alexander Culbertson Meml. Commn, Orleans, Nebr., 1951; mem. Dawes County Travel Bd., Chadron, 1980—. Served with USAF, 1952. Recipient Henry Fonda Nebraskan award Gov. Nebr., 1985. Fellow Co. Mil. Historians; mem. Am. Soc. Arms Collectors, Fur Trade Days Assn., Mus. Assn. Am. Frontier (bd. dirs. 1949—, past pres.), Md. Arms Collectors, Potomac Corral Westerners (sheriff 1965), Phi Tau Gamma. Republican. Methodist. Avocations: travel, hunting. Home and Office: HC 74 Box 18 Chadron NE 69337

HANSON, DAVID BINGHAM, utility company executive; b. Moline, Ill., Oct. 12, 1931; s. Melvin L. and Laurine M. (Bingham) H.; m. Edith A. Kite, Sept. 2, 1966 (widowed Dec. 1980). Student, Blackhawk Coll., 1950, 56-60. Clk. Iowa Ill. Gas & Electric, Davenport, 1956-62, engring. technician, 1962-68, systems ops. supr., 1968-75, systems ops. engr., 1975-82, supt. systems ops. div., 1982—; mem. Mapp Ops. Commn., Minn., 1982—, Enerex Ops. Commn., Des Moines, 1983—, Mapp Pool Performance Subcom., Mpls., 1982—, Edison Elective Inst. Engring. & Operating Computer Commn., various locations, 1983—. Served to sgt. USAF, 1951-55, Korea. Mem. Edison Electric Inst., Am. Legion. Lodges: Kiwanis, Elks. Avocations: home computer, chess, golf, tennis. Home: 2252 E 47th St Davenport IA 52807 Office: Iowa Ill Gas & Electric Co 201 E 2d St Davenport IA 52801

HANSON, DUANE THEODORE, dentist; b. Brainerd, Minn., May 7, 1936; s. Theodore C. and Alvina C. (Racine) H.; m. Marian A. Torgelson, June 27, 1959; children: Susan, Shelly, Eric, Thomas, Michael. Student, Brainerd Jr. Coll.; BS, U. Minn., 1958, DDS, 1960. Dentist USAF, 1960-62; gen. practice dentistry Willmar, Minn., 1962—. Chmn. Willmar Sch. Bd., 1970-83; mem. Willmar Pub. Schs. Found., 1985—. Mem. Minn. Am. Dental Assn. (del. 1985—), West Ctr. Dental Study Club (v.p. 1964-66), Willmar Jr. C. of C. (v.p. 1964), Willmar C. of C. (bd. dirs. 1976-79). Roman Catholic. Lodge: Lions (pres. Willmar 1972), Elks, KC. Avocations: hunting, fishing, sailing. Home: 1029 Hill Rd Willmar MN 55201 Office: 1101 S 1st St Willmar MN 59201

HANSON, FRED T., lawyer; b. Wakefield, Nebr., Feb. 25, 1902; s. Peter H. and Hannah Ulrika (Anderson) H.; LL.B., U. Nebr., 1925; m. Helen Elizabeth Haddock, Nov. 12, 1928; 1 son John Fredrik. Admitted to Nebr. bar, 1925, since in pvt. practice; probate judge, 1931-42, pros. atty., 1927-30, 51-54; spl. asst. to U.S. atty. gen., 1954-62; life mem. Nat. Conf. Commrs. Uniform State Laws from Nebr., com. on uniform probate code. Bd. dirs. Nebr. dist. Luth. Ch.-Mo. Synod, 1976-80. Served as capt. AUS, 1942-46. Mem. Am. Judicature Soc., Am. Coll. Probate Counsel (regent), Am., Nebr., local bar assns., Am. Legion. Office: 316 Norris Ave Mc Cook NE 69001

HANSON, GARY WAYNE, state senator, real estate broker; b. Sioux Falls, S.D., Apr. 20, 1950; s. Wendell Holmes and Helen Alberta (Brumbaugh) H.; m. Sandra Kay Fredricks, June 20, 1970; children: Alicia Jayne, Wayne Allan, Stacy Elizabeth. BS, No. State Coll., Aberdeen, S.D., 1972. Owner, broker Hanson Realty, Sioux Falls, 1973—; expert witness real estate Circuit Ct. S.D., 1980—; appraiser, 1974—; mem. S.D. Senate, 1983—. Coach boys basketball, soccer, Sioux Falls, 1971—, girls basketball, soccer, volleyball, Sioux Falls, 1982—; mem. Nat. Rep. Legislators Assn., Washington, Named Outstanding Young Citizen Sioux Falls, 1985, Outstanding Young Citizen S.D., 1986. Mem. Sioux Falls Bd. Realtors (bd. dirs. 1981-85, pres. 1985-86), S.D. Legis. Affairs Com. Realtors, No. State Coll. Alumni Com. Methodist. Clubs: Jaycees (bd. dirs. 1975-76); Capitol (Pierre, S.D.). Lodge: Elks. Office: Hanson Realty 514 S Minnesota Ave Sioux Falls SD 57105

HANSON, GEORGE GUDMUNDUR, learning resources administrator, librarian; b. Chgo., Apr. 19, 1934; s. George William and Vigdis (Gudmundsson) H. BA, Northwestern U., 1956; MLS, U. Chgo., 1963; EdD, Loyola U., 1979. Cert. librarian, tchr. Tchr. Chgo. Pub. Schs., 1957-60; tchr. U.S. dependents sch. Keflavik, Iceland, 1961-62; librarian Truman Coll. (formerly Mayfair Coll.), Chgo., 1964—. Loyola U. fellow, 1978-79. Lutheran. Avocation: sailing, skiing. Offic: Truman Coll 1145 Wilson Ave Chicago IL 60640

HANSON, JAMES AUSTIN, museum director, state agency administrator; b. Haigler, Nebr., July 5, 1947; s. Charles Easton and Eva Marie (Phillips) H.; m. Ann Brown Miller, July 12, 1981. BS in Edn., Chadron (Nebr.) State Coll., 1969, MEd, 1970; PhD, U. Wyo., 1973. Cons. Wyo. State Mus., Cheyenne, 1970-73; dir. Panhandle-Plains Mus., Canyon, Tex., 1974-76; program coordinator Smithsonian Inst., Washington, 1976-81; pres. Austinia, Ltd., Chadron, 1981-85; dir. Nebr. State Hist. Soc., Lincoln, 1985—. Contbr. articles to profl. jours. Recipient Disting. Service award Mus. of Fur Trade, 1974; Smithsonian Inst. grantee, 1971, Nat. Mus. Act grantee, 1973. Mem. Explorer's Club. Lodges: Rotary (Four Way Test award 1965), Masons. Home: 2427 Woodsdale Blvd Lincoln NE 68502 Office: Nebr State Hist Soc PO Box 82554 1500 R St Lincoln NE 68508

HANSON, JOHN K., automobile manufacturing company executive; b. 1913. AA, Waldorf Coll., 1932; BS, U. Minn., 1934. Owner Hanson Furniture Co., 1937-62, Hanson Funeral Home, 1937-62; with Winnebago Industries Inc., Forest City, Iowa, 1958—, pres., 1959-71, 79-81, chmn. bd. dirs., 1971-75, 79—, vice chmn. bd. dirs., 1975-79. Office: Winnebago Industries Inc Junction 9 & 69 Forest City IA 50436

HANSON, JON GREGORY, real estate broker, consultant; b. Champaign, Ill., Nov. 8, 1956; s. Eldon Edward and Beverly Sue (Lindamore) H.; m. Nita Lynn Wheeler, July 2, 1983. AA in bus. and Real Estate Fin., Ohio Career Sch. Tech., 1984. Real estate broker HER Inc., Columbus, Ohio, 1981-83, David Hatcher Co., Columbus, 1983-84; pres. Fed. Equity Corp., Columbus, 1984—; Cons. Hanson Co., Columbus, 1982—; bd. dirs. Nick Koon Seminars, Inc., Columbus, 1986—. Author: Selling Sellers, 1983, Buying Bankless, 1985, Negotiate for Profit, 1986; editor (newsletter) Investors Update, 1984—. Mem. Ohio Investors Assn. (bd. dirs. 1981—, pres. 1981-86, 5 Yr. Service award 1986). Republican. Baptist. Home: 2934 Arrowhead Ct Columbus OH 43232 Office: Fed Equity Corp 3066 Noe Bixby Rd Columbus OH 43232

HANSON, KENNETH HAMILTON, lawyer; b. Chgo., Sept. 10, 1919; s. Clinton H. and Della (Bonson) H.; student North Park Coll., 1939-40; B.S., Northwestern U., 1943, J.D., 1949; m. Elaine F. Bleck, May 19, 1951; children—Christine E., Karen D., Kenneth Hamilton. Admitted to Ill. bar, 1949; practiced law, Chgo., 1949-53; atty. bus. devel. dept. First Nat. Bank Chgo., 1953-61; trial atty. Antitrust div. U.S. Dept. Justice, Chgo., 1961-83; mem. firm Brace & O'Donnell, Chgo., 1983—. Mem. edit. bd. law review. Served to lt. (j.g.) USNR, 1943-46. Mem. ABA (antitrust, litigation and corp. sects.), Ill. State Bar Assn., 7th Cir. Bar Assn., Am., Fed., Chgo. bar assns. (former chmn. Fed. Civil Procedure com.), Beta Theta Pi, Phi Delta Phi. Republican. Presbyn. Home: 955 Melody Rd Lake Forest IL 60045 Office: 332 S Michigan Ave Suite 1858 Chicago IL 60604

HANSON, LEE EDWIN, university administrator; b. Lansing, Mich., Sept. 24, 1947; s. Leroy Edwin and Ida Mildred (Chandler) H.; m. Claire Lenore Huling, Jan. 11, 1973 (div. Sept. 1981). B.A., Northwestern U., 1968, M.A.T., 1970. Instr., Kendall Coll., Evanston, Ill., 1970; tchr. Dist. 111 Schs., Highland Park, Ill., 1970-71; dir. devel. services Northwestern U., Evanston, Ill., 1971-82; dir. devel. services Washington U., St. Louis, 1982—; computer system design cons. for non-profit orgns., 1982—. Mem. Council Advancement and Support Edn., Phi Delta Kappa. Republican. Home: 220 N Forsyth Blvd Clayton MO 63105 Office: Washington U 1 Brookings Dr Box 1082 Saint Louis MO 63130

HANSON, MARK DOUGLAS, bank executive; b. Fargo, N.D., Aug. 11, 1957; s. Howard Eugene and Ruth Sigrin (Nelson) H.; m. Melanie Joy Sweeney, Sept. 11, 1982. BS in Fin. and Econs., St. Cloud (Minn.) State U., 1979. Mgmt. trainee TCF Savs. and Loan, Mpls., 1979-80, mgr. of electronic banking, 1980-82, mgr. checking, 1982-83, mgr. automatic teller machine network, 1983-85, asst. v.p., 1985—; Steering coms. TCF Employees Political Action Com., Mpls., 1985-86. Republican. Lutheran. Avocations: tennis, golf, antique collecting. Home: 6812 Sally Ln Edina MN 55435 Office: TCF Banking and Savs 801 Marquette Minneapolis MN 55402

HANSON, MARK JEFFREY, marketing executive; b. Mpls., Oct. 15, 1950; s. Homer O. and Madonna E. (Hinschberger) H.; m. Victoria Anne Zahler, Oct. 4, 1976; children: Krista, Brooke, Erin. BS, St. John's U., Collegeville, Minn., 1972, U. Minn., 1975; MBA, U. Minn., 1986. Fin. broker Equitable Life Ins. Co., Edina, Mpls., 1977-79; mktg. mgr. Health Cnt., Mpls., 1979-81, Buck Corp., Mpls., 1981—. Avocations: running, reading, music, photography. Home: 5180 Hooper Lake Rd Deephaven MN 55331

HANSON, MICHAEL LAWRENCE, labor union leader, construction equipment manufacturing company executive; b. Terre Haute, Ind., Mar. 1, 1942; s. Arnold Gilbert and Dorthy H.; foster s. Raymond and Annise Hirt; m. Dolores Ann Lanham, Mar. 11, 1967; children—Melinda Sue, William Eric. Student Ind. U., 1977-78. Cert. UAW. Lathe operator Ertels, Indpls., 1963-64; cleaner, installer Gen. Electric, Indpls., 1964; press operator Dormeyers, Rockville, Ind., 1965; with acids dept. P.R. Mallory, Greencastle, Ind., 1965-68; laborer J.I. Case Co., Terre Haute, 1975—; unionism lectr. Ind. State U. Vice pres. J.I. Case Co., chpt. UAW, 1976-77, pres., 1977-79; Labor rep., bd. dirs. Hamilton Mental Health Ctr., 1976-83; trustee, pres. J.I. Fed. Credit Union, 1975-76; pres. local PTO, 1979-80; active Wesley Chapel Methodist Ch., Berea Christian Ch., United Way Campaign, 1977; com. chmn. Wabash Valley council Boy Scouts Am., 1981—. Recipient certs. achievement and recognition Hamilton Ctr., Boy Scouts Am. Lodge: Masons. Avocations: hunting; swimming; bicycling; guns. Home: Route 17 Box 411 Brazil IN 47834 Office: J I Case Co PO Box 5215 Terre Haute IN 47805

HANSON, MONTE KENT, retail and broadcasting executive; b. Mexico, Mo., Jan. 11, 1955; s. Wilmer D. and Velma B. (Montague) H.; m. Glee Anne Brummitt, June 19, 1977; children—Josiah Kent, Lydia Michelle, Micah Franklin. B.S., Northeastern Mo. State U., 1977. Salesman, OCCO Feed Co., Oelwein, Iowa, 1973, dist. mgr., 1974-77; asst. mgr. K-Mart Corp., Mo., 1977-80; pres., gen. mgr. Faith Ctr., Kirksville, Mo., 1981—; pres., gen.

mgr. No. Mo. Christian Broadcasting, Inc., 1987—. Bd. dirs. Christian Life, Nazarene Ch., Mo., 1981, 82, 83. Named State Farmer, Future Farmers Am., Mo., 1973. Mem. Christian Booksellers Assn., Kirksville C. of C. (chmn. retail com. 1982), Nat. Fedn. Ind. Bus. Republican. Avocations: reading; Bible collecting; softball. Office: Faith Center 110 W Harrison St Kirksville MO 63501

HANSON, RANDY GALE, marketing research executive; b. Fulton, Mo., Jan. 19, 1959; d. Leo Irvin and Frances Mae (Griffin) H. AB in Stats. magna cum laude, U. Mo., Columbia, 1981, MA in Stats., 1982; postgrad. in bus., U. Kans., U. Mo., St. Louis, 1983—. Staff asst. Hallmark Cards, Kansas City, Mo., 1982-83, mktg. research analyst, 1983-85, sr. mktg. research analyst, 1985-86; sr. mktg. research mgr. Maritz Mktg. Research, St. Louis, 1986—. Recipient Outstanding Teaching award U. Mo. at Columbia Dept. Stats., 1982. Mem. Am. Mktg. Assn., Phi Beta Kappa, Sigma Alpha Epsilon (named to Order of the Phoenix 1982). Republican. Avocations: reading, fitness, cooking, bicycling, hiking. Home: 14407-4 Willowbend Pk Chesterfield MO 63017 Office: Maritz Mktg Research Inc 1395 N Highway Dr Saint Louis County MO 63099

HANSON, RICHARD LEON, music publisher; b. Bloomington, Ind., Oct. 19, 1946; s. Richard Arnold and Mary Ann (Fleener) H.; m. Sue Ann Harland, Oct. 27, 1964 (div. Nov. 1985); 1 child, Christena L.; m. Tina E. Blake, May 30, 1987. Student, Ind. U., 1964, 67. Pres. Ric Rac, Inc., Nashville, chmn. bd., 1985—, also pres. divs. Ric Rac Music, Rick Hanson Music, 1986—, Ric Rac Records, Rick Hanson Prodns., 1986—; performer Rick Hanson Show, 1980—; mem. Bloomington Songwriters Workshop, 1980—; pub., composer numerous songs. Mem. United Brotherhood Carpenters and Joiners Am., Nashville Songwriters Assn., Country Music Assn. Am. Fedn. Musicians, ASCAP, Ind. State Festivals Assn., 1987—.

HANSON, ROBERT ARTHUR, agricultural equipment executive; b. Moline, Ill., Dec. 13, 1924; s. Nels A. and Margaret I. (Chapman) H.; m. Patricia Ann Klinger, June 25, 1955. B.A., Augustana Coll., Rock Island, Ill., 1948. Various positions Deere & Co., Moline, 1950-62; gen. mgr. Deere & Co., Mexico, 1962-64, Spain, 1964-66; dir. mktg. overseas Deere & Co., 1966-70, v.p. overseas ops., 1972, sr. v.p. overseas div., 1973, dir., 1974—, exec. v.p., 1975-78, pres., 1978-85, chief operating officer, 1979-82, chmn., chief exec. officer, 1982—; bd. dirs. Procter & Gamble Co., Merrill Lynch & Co., Dun & Bradstreet Corp.; mem. Morgan Guaranty Trust Co.'s Internat. Council, N.Y.C., Council on Fgn. Relations. Trustee Com. for Econ. Devel.; trustee Mayo Found.; bd. dirs. Farm and Indsl. Equipment Inst. Served with USMCR, 1943-46. Home: 2200 29th Avenue Ct Moline IL 61265 Office: Deere & Company John Deere Rd Moline IL 61265

HANSON, ROBERT EUGENE, state official; b. Jamestown, N.D., Aug. 26, 1947; s. Louis J. and Kathlene A. (Wilmart) H.; m. Melody R. McFall, May 11, 1974; children: Jason Paul, Jamie Beth, Kristen Anne. BSBA, N.D. State U., 1968. Campaign scheduler N.D. Dem.-Non-Partisan League Party, Bismarck, 1968-70, campaign mgr., 1970; legis. aide Dem.-Non-Partisan League Legislators, Bismarck, 1971; youth coordinator State of N.D., Bismarck, 1971, dep. state treas., 1973-79, state treas., 1979—; also manpower planner N.D. Employment Security Bur.; spl. asst. Office N.D. Gov., Bismarck, 1971-73; chmn. State Investment Bd., 1979—. Vice chmn. Cen. Regional Conf. Nat. Conf. State Liquor Adminstrs., 1975, exec. sec.-treas., 1976—; chmn. Vets. Day, 1977, U.S. Savs. Bond., N.D., 1978; mem. state bd. dirs. N.D. PTA; Dem. candidate for State Pub. Service Commr., 1978. Served with U.S. Army, 1968-70. Decorated Bronze Star with oak leaf cluster; recipient Pi Omega award, 1968. Mem. Am. Soc. Pub. Adminstrs., Am. Legion, VFW, Blue Key. Roman Catholic. Club: N.D. Century. Lodge: Elks. Home: 304 Teton Ave Bismarck ND 58501 Office: Office of the State Treasurer State Capitol Bismarck ND 58501 *

HANSON, ROBERT PAUL, newspaper representation company executive; b. Chgo., May 22, 1944; s. John Peter and Margaret (Russell) B.; m. Virginia Marie Scholl, Aug. 28, 1965; children: Margaret, Jennifer, Robert, Erica. Student, DePaul U., Chgo., 1965-74. Salesman Des Plaines (Ill.) Pub., 1964-68; regional accounts mgr. Field Enterprises, Elk Grove Village, Ill., 1968-70; sales mgr. Paddick Publs., Arlington Heights, Ill., 1970-72; sales mgr., v.p. U.S. Suburban Press, Schaumburg, Ill., 1972—. Mem. Young Pres. Orgn. Roman Catholic. Club: Biltmore Country. Avocations: golf, baseball, racquetball, bridge, travel. Home: 431 Brookmont Ln Barrington IL 60010 Office: U S Suburban Inc 929 N Plum Grove Rd Schaumburg IL 60173

HANSON, RUSSELL FREDRIC, photographer; b. Mandan, N.D., Oct. 23, 1947; s. James Robert and Inez (Ohm) H.; m. Nancy Edmonds, Apr. 19, 1975; 1 child, Patricia Ri. AA, Bismarck (N.D.) Jr. Coll., 1968; BS, So. Ill. U., 1970. Photographer N.D. Dept. Tourism, Bismarck, 1970-75; chmn. dept. graphic arts Bismarck Jr. Coll., 1975-84; prodn. mgr. Guide mag., Fargo, N.D., 1984-86; dir. photography Hetland Ltd., Fargo, 1986—. Recipient numerous awards Outdoor Photographers of Am. Mem. Profl. Photographers Am. Lodge: Elks. Home: 3616 Rivershore Dr Moorhead MN 56560 Office: Hetland Ltd 1714 Main Ave Fargo ND 58103

HANSOTIA, BEHRAM JEHANBUX, financial and consumer services executive, management scientist; b. Bombay, Feb. 19, 1948; came to U.S., 1970; s. Jehanbux C. and Yadgar (Tarapore) H.; m. Anne Marie Healy, Dec. 26, 1975; 1 child, Zareen Anne. B in Tech., Indian Inst. Tech., Bombay, 1970; MS, U. Ill., 1971, PhD, 1973. Asst. prof. Bradley U., Peoria, 1973-77, assoc. prof., 1977-79; mgmt. sci. research analyst Caterpillar, Inc., Peoria, 1979-84, mgmt. sci. cons., 1984-85; research mgr. The Signature Group, Schaumburg, Ill., 1985-86, asst. v.p., 1986—; visiting scholar Stanford (Calif.) U., 1977; instr. pt. time Bradley U., 1983. Contbr. articles to profl. jours. U. Ill. fellow, 1973. Mem. Inst. Mgmt. Sci., Am. Mktg. Assn. Avocations: internat. travel, reading. Home: 814 Partridge Dr Palatine IL 60067 Office: The Signature Group 200 N Martingale Rd Schaumburg IL 60194

HANSOTIA, PHIROZE LOVJI, physician; b. Deolali, India, Nov. 8, 1937; came to U.S., 1962; s. Lovji Cowasji and Banu Lovji (Bhathena) H.; m. Marilyn Carol Fahning, Jan. 21, 1967; children: Eric Phiroze, Shirene Carole. BS, St. Xavier's Coll., Bombay, 1956; MD, Med. Coll., Nagpur, India, 1961. Diplomate Am. Bd. Psychiatry and Neurology, Am. Bd. Electroencephalography; lic. physican, surgeon, Wis. Intern Med. Coll., Nagpur, 1961-62; rotating intern Hamot Hosp., Erie, Pa., 1962-63; resident in pathology Cin. Gen. Hosp., 1963-64; resident in neurology U. Wis. Gen. Hosp., Madison, 1964-67; registrar in clin. electrophysiology Nat. Hosp., London, 1968; cons. in neurology Grant Med. Coll., Bombay, 1969; clin. neurologist, electroencephalographer Marshfield (Wis.) Clinic, 1970—, chmn. dept. neurosciences, 1974-78, mem. edn. com., 1972-84, mem. internal medicine residency com., 1981-84; assoc. clin. prof. neurology, U. Wis., Madison, 1971; bd. dirs. Marshfield Med. Found. Research Edn., mem. research awards com., 1983-86; examiner Am. Bd. Registration Electroencephalograph Technologists, Denver, 1980; assoc. examiner Am. Bd. Qualifications in Electroencephalography, 1981-86; chmn. St. Joseph's Hosp., Marshfield, 1975-78, mem. 1979-85; vis. prof. Med. Coll., Nagpur, 1985, Indira Gandhi Med. Coll., Nagpur, 1985, Grant Med. Coll., Bombay, 1985. Contbr. numerous articles to profl. jours. Pres. Washington Elem. Sch. P.T.A., Marshfield, 1979-80; v.p. New Visions Art Gallery Bd., Marshfield, 1984-85, pres. 1986. Fellow in epilepsy U. Wis. Hosp., Madison, 1967. Mem. Wis. Heart Assoc. (state task force on stroke 1971-75), Cen. Assn. Electroencephalographers (chmn. technicians edn. com. 1973-74, co-chmn. lab. standards and peer rev. com. 1976-77, sec. treas. 1980-82, pres. 1983-84, counsellor 1978-80), Wis. Epilepsy Assn. (v.p. midstate chpt. 1976-84), Wis. Neurology Soc. (sec., treas. 1977-78, v.p. 1978-79, pres. 1980-81), Am. Acad. Neurology (mem. com. 1977-79, history com. 1977-83), Am. Electroencephalographers Soc. (joint lab. rev. com. 1978, chmn. lab. accreditation com. 1980-82, 82-84, pres. bd. lab. accreditation 1983-86, counsellor 1984-87), Wis. Neurol. Soc. (pres. 1980-81), AMA (physicians recognition award 1977-86, Soc. Clin. Neurology (program co-chmn. 1985), Cen. Assn. Electroencephalographers (program chmn. 1978-79), Wis. Med. Soc., Wood County Med. Soc., Am. Epilepsy Soc., Soc. Clin. Neurologists, Neurol. Soc. India, N.Y. Acad. Scis., Clin. Sleep Soc., U. Wis. Alumni Assn. (life), Med. Explorers (pres. Marshfield post 1977-80). Democrat. Avocations: tennis, chess, skiing, racquetball, painting. Office: Marshfield Clinic 1000 N Oak Ave Marshfield WI 54449

HANSSEN, KENNETH RALPH, judge, barrister; b. St. Boniface, Man., Can., Jan. 5, 1945; s. Henning Osvald and Lillian Elvera (Timrose) H.; m. Elizabeth Anne Larter, Apr. 26, 1969; children: Mark Gregory, Corey Andrew, Kendra Elizabeth. BA, U. Man., 1965, LLB, 1968. Assoc. Duncan & Co., Morden, Man., 1969-71, ptnr., 1971-84; judge Ct. of Queen's Bench Province of Man., Winnipeg, Can., 1984—; lectr. Man. Bar Admission Course, Winnipeg, 1983—. Bd. dirs. Winnipeg Football Club, 1975—. Mem. Can. Bar Assn., Man. Bar Assn. (v.p. 1983-84). Lutheran. Avocation: sports. Office: Ct of Queen's Bench, New Law Cts Bldg, 408 York Ave 5th Floor, Winnipeg, MB Canada R3C 0P9

HANSSON, KELD, electronics company executive; b. Esbjerg, Denmark, Nov. 10, 1950; came to U.S., 1978; s. Erik and Inger Hansson; m. Julie Ann Smith, May 27, 1978. Student Aarhus (Denmark) Tech. Coll., 1968-69; cert. in elec. tech. Sonderborg Tech. Coll., Sonderborg, Denmark, 1970-74; student English Lang., Cambridge (Eng.) U., 1975-76. Technician Bang & Olufsen, Gloucester, Eng., 1975-76, service mgr., Brisbane, Australia, 1976-78, tech. mgr., Elk Grove Village, Ill., 1978-85, product mgr., 1985—. Mem. Audio Engring. Soc. Home: 850 Dracut Ln Schaumburg IL 60195 Office: Bang & Olufsen 1150 Feehanville Dr Mount Prospect IL 60056

HANVEY, JAN EUGENE, psychologist; b. Gaylord, Minn., July 7, 1947; s. Fred Whitney and Hildur Anne (Nygren) H.; m. Jannette Linda Skrede, Apr. 29, 1972 (div. Jan. 1977); m. Susan Marie Wilson, July 5, 1987. BA, U. Minn., 1973; MS, Winona (Minn.) State U., 1979; cert. jr. bus. adminstrn., U. Minn., 1973. Lic. psychologist, Minn. Mental health worker FMW Human Services, Fairmont, Minn., 1980-81; chem. dependency counselor Golden Valley (Minn.) Health Ctr., 1981-82; employee assistance counselor Human Resource Assocs., Mpls., 1982-83; psychologist Met. Mental Health Clinic, Mpls., 1983-85; pvt. practice psychology Mpls., 1983—; chem. dependency counselor Abbott Northwestern Hosp., Mpls., 1985-87; chem. dependency supr. Abbott Northwestern Behavioral Health Ctr., Brooklyn Center, Minn., 1987—; Speaker sta. KANO, Anoka, Minn., 1986—. Mem. Minn. Lic. Psychologists Assn., Minn. Chem. Dependency Assn. (cert.), N.W. Hennepin Human Services Council, Brooklyn Ctr. C. of C. (pub. relations com. 1986). Avocations: canoeing, computers, astrology, horse racing, public speaking. Home: 4150 Xenwood Ave S Saint Louis Park MN 55416 Office: Abbott Northwestern Behavioral Health Ctr 3300 County Rd 10 #306 Brooklyn Center MN 55429

HAPP, RICHARD THOMAS, manufacturing executive; b. Evanston, Ill., Apr. 29, 1951; s. George Mathias and Elizabeth D. (Platz) H. BEE, Purdue U., West Lafayette, Ind., 1973. Pres. Happ Electronics, Inc., Oshkosh, Wis., 1981—; pres. Discount Software House, Winnebago, Wis., 1982—. Mem. Soc. Mfr. Engrs. (membership com. 1985-86). Clubs: Lake Geneva Yacht (Race Com. award 1973), Inland Lake Yachting Assn. (Lake Geneva); Pegasus Riding (Neenah, Wis.) (charter). Avocations: sailing, computers. Home: 4640 Island View Oshkosh WI 54901

HAQUE, MALIKA HAKIM, pediatrician; b. Madras, India; came to U.S., 1967; d. S. Abdul and Rahimunisa (Hussain) Hakim; M.B.B.S., Madras Med. Coll., 1967; m. C. Azeez ul Haque, Feb. 5, 1967; children—Kifizeba, Masarath Nashr, Asim Zayd. Rotating intern Miriam Hosp., Brown U., Providence, 1967-68; resident in pediatrics Children's Hosp., N.J. Coll. Medicine, 1968-70; fellow in devel. disabilities Ohio State U., 1970-71; acting chief pediatrics Nisonger Center, 1973-74; staff pediatrician Children and Youth Project, Children's Hosp., Columbus, Ohio, also clin. asst. prof. pediatrics Ohio State U., 1974-80; clin. asso. prof. pediatrics Ohio State U., 1981—; pediatrician in charge community pediatrics and adolescent services clinics Columbus Children's Hosp.; cons. Central Ohio Head Start Program, 1974-79. Mem. Republican Presdl. Task Force, 1982—, Nat. Rep. Senatorial Com., 1985—, U.S. Senatorial Club. Recipient Physician Recognition award AMA, 1971-86, Gold medals in surgery, radiology, pediatrics and ob/gyn; Presdl. medal of Merit, 1982; diplomate Am. Bd. Pediatrics. Fellow Am. Acad. Pediatrics (Prep Fellowship award 1986); mem. Ambulatory Pediatric Assn., Central Ohio Pediatric Soc. Islam. Research on enuresis. Home: 5995 Forestview Dr Columbus OH 43213 Office: 700 Children's Dr Columbus OH 43205

HARAPIAK, HARRY MYRISLAW, province agency administrator; b. Winnipeg, Man., Can., Sept. 17, 1938; s. William John and Mary (Philipchuk) H.; m. Carol Anne Eastwood, May 17, 1962; children: Marianne, Mark, Christine, Kelly, Chad. Minister of No. Affairs Province of Man., Winnipeg, 1987—. Trustee Kelsey Sch., Man., 1974-80. New Democrat. Ukranian Catholic. Lodges: Elks, KC. Avocations: cross-country skiing, canoeing. Home: 49 Britannica Rd, Winnipeg, MB Canada R2N 1J4 Office: Ministry of No Affairs, Legis Bldg, Winnipeg, MB Canada R3C0V8

HARAPIAK, LEONARD ERNEST, provincial minister, farmer; b. Swan River, Man., Can.; m. Judy Didyk; 3 children. BA in Edn., U. Saskatchewan, Can., 1968. Cert. tchr., Can. Farmer Cowan, Man., Can., 1981—; mem. and minister Dept. Natural Resourses Govt. Man., Winnipeg, 1986—. Past pres. Aveyron Services, Swan River. New Democrat. Roman Catholic. Office: Ministry of Natural Resources, Legis Bldg, Winnipeg, MB Canada R3C 0V8

HARBAUGH, THOMAS EDWARD, psychologist; b. Washington, Nov. 10, 1940; s. Thomas Edward Sr. and Virginia Elizabeth (Witt) H.; m. Mary Patricia Lason, June 12, 1971; children: Thomas Edward, John Michael. BA, Marquette U., 1962; PhD, U. md., 1972. Lic. psychologist, Wis. Clin. psychologist Prince George's County Health Dept., Cheverly, Md., 1972-74, Gogebic County Mental Health Ctr., Ironwood, Mich., 1974-76, Unified Health Services, Shawano, Wis., 1976—; instr. Montgomery Coll., Takoma Park, Md., 1971-74; part time faculty No. Mich. U., Marquette, 1976; cons. Oconto County Unified Health Services, Oconto Falls, Wis., 1979—Menominee County Human Services Dept., Keshena, Wis., 1983—. Contbr. articles on psychology to newspapers; contbg. artist N.E. Wis. Audubon Soc. Calendar, 1981—. Scoutmaster Boy Scouts Am., Shawano, 1985—; bd. dirs. N.E. Wis. Audubon Soc., Green Bay, Shawano Presch., 1977. Served to capt. USMC, 1962-67. Grantee Inst. Child Study U. Md., College Park, Md., 1970-71. Mem. Am. Psychol. Assn., Wis. Psychol. Assn., Am. Soc. Clin. Hypnosis, Internat. Soc. Clin. Hypnosis, Am. Registry Lic. Psychologists and Mental Health Providers. Avocations: painting, wood carving, photography, camping. Home: W2899 Homewood Ave Shawano WI 54166 Office: Unified Health Services 420 E Green Bay St Shawano WI 54166

HARBECK, WILLIAM JAMES, real estate executive, lawyer, international consultant; b. Glenview, Ill., Dec. 16, 1921; s. Christian Frederick and Anna (Gaeth) H.; m. Jean Marie Allsopp, Jan. 20, 1945; children: John, Stephen, Timothy, Mark, Christopher. B.A., Wabash (Ind.) Coll., 1947; J.D., Northwestern U., 1950. Bar: Ill. 1950. Land acquisition atty. Chgo. Land Clearance Commn., 1950-51; with Montgomery Ward & Co., Chgo., 1951-81; asst. to pres., dir. corp. facilities Montgomery Ward & Co., 1968-70, v.p., dir. facilities devel., 1970-81; v.p. Montgomery Ward Devel. Corp., 1972-81; pres., chief exec. officer Montgomery Ward Properties Corp., 1974-81; pres. William J. Harbeck Assocs., 1981—; dir. Randhurst Corp., 1972-81, exec. com., 1975-79; bd. dirs. Internat. Council Shopping Centers, 1972-78, exec. com., 1975-78, govt. affairs com., 1977—, awards com., 1980-83, urban com. 1980-83, lectr., 1969—. Author articles in field; mem. editorial bds. profl. jours. Bd. dirs. Chgo. Lawson YMCA, 1973—, chmn. devel. com., 1979—, mem. exec. com., 1985—; bd. dirs. Greater North Michigan Ave. Assn., Chgo., 1979-81; chmn. constrn. com. Chgo. United, 1979-81; co-chmn. Chgo. Bus. Opportunities Fair, 1980-81; mem. real estate com. Chgo. Met. YMCA, 1982—, chmn. Bldg. Task Force, 1985—; mem. pres.'s council Concordia Coll., River Forest, Ill., 1969—, planning com. Inst. for Philanthropic Mgmt., 1985—; youth Bible and Bethel instr. Redeemer Luth. Ch., Highland Park, Ill., 1965, congregation pres., 1968-70, 85—, chmn. ch. growth com., 1982—; trustee Lutheran Ch. Mo. Synod Found., 1975-76, 81—, mem. Synodical mission study commn., 1974-75, mem. dist. research and planning com., 1981—, mem. task force on synodical constn. by-laws and structure, 1975-79; mem. research and planning com. No. Ill. Dist. Luth. Ch. Mo. Synod, 1984—; sponsor Luth. Chs. for Career Devel., 1979—; corp. chmn. U.S. Bond drive, Chgo., 1976; chief crusader Chgo. Crusade Mercy, 1976-78; div. chmn. Chgo. Cerebral Palsy campaign, 1977-78. Served to lt. (j.g.) USNR, 1942-46. Mem. Ill. Bar Assn., Luth. Layman's League, Alpha Sigma Kappa, Phi Alpha Delta, Pi Alpha Chi. Home and Office: 470 E Linden Ave Lake Forest IL 60045

HARBERGER, ARNOLD CARL, economist, educator; b. Newark, July 27, 1924; s. Ferdinand C. and Martha (Bucher) H.; m. Ana Beatriz Valjalo, Mar. 15, 1958; children: Paul Vincent, Carl David. Student, Johns Hopkins U., 1941-43; M.A., U. Chgo., 1947, Ph.D., 1950; Dr.h.c., U. Tucuman, 1979. Asst. prof. polit. economy Johns Hopkins U., 1949-53; asso. prof. econs. U. Chgo., 1953-59, prof., 1959—, chmn. dept., 1964-71, 75-80, Gustavus F. and Ann M. Swift disting. service prof., 1977—, dir. Center Latin Am. Econ. Studies, 1965—; vis. prof. MIT (Center Internat. Studies), New Delhi, 1961-62, Econ. Devel. Inst., IBRD, 1965, Harvard U., 1971-72, Princeton U., 1973-74, UCLA, 1983, 84, U. Paris, 1986; prof. econs. UCLA, 1984—; cons. IMF, 1950, U.S Pres.'s Materials Policy Commn., 1951-52, U.S. Treasury Dept., 1961-75, Com. Econ. Devel., 1961-78, Planning Commn., India, 1961-62, 73, Pan Am. Union, 1962-76, Dept. State, 1962-76, Central Bank, Chile, 1965-70, Planning Dept., Panama, 1965-77, Colombia, 1969-71; cons. Ford Found., 1967-77, Planning Commn., El Salvador, 1973-75, Budget and Planning Office, Uruguay, 1974-75, Can. Dept. Regional Econ. Expansion, 1975-77, Finance Ministry, Bolivia, 1976, Mex., 1976—; cons. Can. Dept. Employment and Migration, 1980-82, Indonesian Ministry Fin., 1981-82, 86, Can. Dept. Fin., 1982—, Chinese Ministry Fin., 1983. Author: Project Evaluation, 1972, Taxation and Welfare, 1974; Editor: Demand for Durable Goods, 1960, The Taxation of Income from Capital, 1968, Key Problems of Economic Policy In Latin America, 1970, World Economic Growth, 1985; Contbr. sci. papers to profl. jours. and govt. publs. Served with AUS, 1943-46. Guggenheim fellow; Fulbright scholar; faculty research fellow Social Sci. Research Council; Ford Found. faculty research fellow, 1968-69. Fellow Econometric Soc., Am. Acad. Arts and Scis.; mem. Am. Econ. Assn. (mem. exec. com. 1970-72), Western Econ. Assn. (v.p. 1987—), Royal Econ. Soc., Nat. Tax Assn., Phi Beta Kappa. Home: 4840 S Greenwood Ave Chicago IL 60615 Office: 1126 E 59th St Chicago IL 60637

HARBERT, TERRY LEE, social services administrator; b. Great Bend, Kans., Apr. 5, 1947; s. Howard Jess and Frances Elaine (Fulcher) H.; m. Jane Ann Omlor, June 7, 1969; (div. June 1971); m. Paula Louise Richardson, Apr. 1, 1972; 1 child, David Matthew. BA in Psychology, Kans. State U., 1969; MSW, U. Okla., 1971. Cert. social worker; lic. master social worker, Kans. Social worker VA Med. Ctr., Jackson, Miss., 1971-76; chief social work service VA Med. Ctr., Sheridan, Wyo., 1976-78, Knoxville, Iowa, 1978-85; chief social work service Colmery-O'Neil VA Med. Ctr., Topeka, 1985—; field instr. U. So. Miss., Hattiesburg, 1974-76, U. Utah, Salt Lake City, 1976-78, U. Iowa, Iowa City, 1978-85; adj. assoc. prof. U. Kans., Lawrence, 1985—. Contbr. articles to profl. jours. Vol. firefighter Barnett Reservoir Fire Dept., Brandon, Miss., 1973-75, emer. med. technician Clive (Iowa) Vol. Fire and Rescue Dept., 1980, rescue coordinator, 1981-84, asst. chief of dept., 1984-85. Served to capt. U.S. Army, 1972. Mem. Soc. for Hosp. Social Work Dirs. (pres. 1980), Nat. Assn. of Social Workers (pres. 1975), Assn. of VA Social Work Chiefs. Democrat. Presbyterian. Home: 3400 SW Skyline Pkwy Topeka KS 66614 Office: Colmery-O'Neill VA Med Ctr 2200 Gage Blvd Topeka KS 66622

HARBIN, SHIRLEY MEVERNA, city arts official, educator; b. Santa Cruz, Calif., Dec. 26, 1931; d. Fordyce Owen and Lillian Honorah (Erickson) Pengilly; m. Joseph Medrano, Dec. 27, 1956 (div. 1962); 1 child, Joseph Brian; m. Dean T. Harbin, Mar. 1963; 1 child, Paul Dean. Student, Muskegon Jr. Coll., 1950-52; BA, U. Mich., 1954, MA, 1960; PhD, Wayne State U., 1977. Tchr. Pontiac (Mich.) High Sch., 1954-57, Ypsilanti (Mich.) Jr. and Sr. High Sch., 1957-60, Detroit Pub. Schs., 1963; arts dir. City of Detroit, 1963—; instr. Wayne County Community Coll., Detroit, 1972-74, Wayne State U., Detroit, 1975—; costumes asst. Assn. Performing Arts, U. Mich., Ann Arbor, 1961-63; tchr. creative drama Ann Arbor Bd. Edn., 1961-63; dir. summer performing arts Camp Homestead Acres, Chelsea, Mich., 1961-62; program asst. children's show Oopsie, WWJ TV, 1971-76; cons. Oakland U., Mott Found. Continuing Edn. Creative Drama, 1965. Editor Bravo mag., 1984-86. Pres. Detroit Theatre Council, 1970—; sec./treas. Detroit Met. Black Arts, Inc., 1970-72, bd. dirs.; active Olympiad Internat. Theater Festival, Mich. and Ont., 1975, 79, 83, 87—. Recipient Bus. Women in the Arts award, YWCA, 1985. Mem. Am. Community Theatre Assn. (pres., chmn. royalty research com.), Community Theatre Assn. Mich. (bd. dirs. 1965-70), Internat. Assn. Theatre for Children and Youth (coordinator Show and Tell The World for Internat. Festival 1972), Detroit Inst. Arts, Detroit Theatre Assn. (chmn. festival 1972), Am. Community Theatre Assn. (pres. 1982-83), Am. Children's Theatre Assn. (chmn. nat. publicity 1969-71), Mich. Children's Theatre Conf. (co-chmn. 1970), Mich. Parks and Recreation Assn. (conv. speaker 1972, chmn. cultural arts, 1973—, Outstanding Program award 1980), Mich. Theatre Assn. (pres. 1980-81), Internat. Amateur Theatre Assn. (exec. dir., sec. gen. 1975—, editor newsletters 1986), SE Mich. Arts Forum (exec. editor newsletters 1978, editor 1985). Home: 1008 Ferdinand Detroit MI 48209 Office: City of Detroit 2735 W Warren Detroit MI 48208

HARBISON, STANLEY LINCOLN, social worker, religious counselor; b. Detroit, Jan. 30, 1937; s. Winfred A. and Ocie (Kelly) H.; m. Susan Winters, 1981; children—David L., Heather E. B.A. magna cum laude, Bethany Coll. (W.Va.), 1959; M.Div., Yale U., 1962; Ph.D., Vanderbilt U., 1975. Instr. history Eastern Mich. U., Ypsilanti, 1965-73, lectr. 1975, 78; lectr. social sci. Henry Ford Community Coll., Dearborn, Mich., 1973-78; instr. extension services U. Mich., Ann Arbor, 1975-76, nursing sch. research ethics com., 1979-80, lectr. religious studies, 1981; assoc. dir. Wesley Found., 1974-77; edn. dir. Ann Arbor West Side Meth. Ch., 1976-80; vol. services coordinator, caseworker Washtenaw County Juvenile Ct., Ann Arbor, 1979—; pres. Harbison Farms, Inc., 1985—. Mem. Ypsilanti City Council, 1977-80; exec. com. Southeast Mich. Council Govts., 1978-84; legis. com. Mich. Mcpl. League, 1979-80; union mgmt. negotiating team Washtenaw County Govt.; chmn. Mental Health Edn. Task Force; bd. dirs. Ypsilanti Area Futures, Inc., sec. inter-govtl. relations task force, volunteerism task force; adv. bd. alcoholism therapy Beyer Hosp.; v.p. Friends in Deed Ministries; coordinator Peaceable Community Games; exec. com. Interfaith Council of Congregations; exec. bd. local NAACP; organizer, convener Ypsilanti Area Social Agys. Forum; founder, chmn. Ypsilanti Youth Supporters; trustee Ypsilanti Sch. Bd., 1984—; del. Democratic State Conv.; elder, lay minister Christian Ch. (Disciples). Recipient Citizen of Yr. award Huron Valley chpt. Nat. Assn. Social Workers, 1982; So. Regional award scholar, 1959. Mem. Am. Acad. Religion, Am. Hist. Assn., Am. Soc. Ch. Hist., Am. Soc. Pub. Adminstrn., Nat. Council Crime and Delinquency, Mich. Assn. Sch. Bds. (fed. relations rep.), Nat. Ct. Appointed Spl. Advocates Assn., Beta Theta Pi. Author: The Social Gospel Career of Alva Wilmot Taylor, 1975. Contbr. articles on religious subjects to publs.; speaker local radio stas. Home: 1434 Collegewood Ypsilanti MI 48197 Office: 2270 Platt Rd Ann Arbor MI 48104

HARBOUR, MARY JO, home economics educator; b. Neodesha, Kans., Mar. 24, 1937; d. Henry William and Marie Velma (Peden) Kidd; m. Donald Ray Harbour, Aug. 24, 1958 (dec. Aug. 1982); children: Sara Marie, Diana Kay. BS in Home Econs. Edn., Kans. State U., 1960, MS in Consumer Econs., 1970. Mgr. advt. and display J.C. Penney's, Manhattan, Kans., 1958-61, office mgr., 1961-63; research asst., mgr. Homemaker Tng. Project, Kans. State U., Manhattan, 1968-71; instr. home econs. Manhattan Sch. Dist., 1973—; pres. Home Economists in Homemaking, Manhattan, 1965; mem. curriculum devel. adv. bd. Kans. State Dept. Home Econs., Topeka, 1981. Author numerous booklets on crafts, sewing and foods, 1982—; contbr. biweekly column Manhattan Mercury, 1982—, also articles to profl. jours. Pres., v.p. Theodore Roosevelt Sch. PTA, Manhattan, 1972-73; supt., tchr. vacation ch. sch., Manhattan, 1965-70; mem. recreation commn. adv. council Spl. Needs Population, Manhattan, 1983-84; mem. adv. bd. Flint Hills Tchr. Ctr., Ogden, Kans., 1980-81; projects leader 4-H Club, Manhattan, 1970-82. Presenter workshop Internat. Reading Conf., 1983. Mem. NEA (bldg. rep. 1977-83, local pres. 1986-87, mem. adminstrv. bd. 1987, local Tchr. of Yr. 1982), Am. Home Econs. Assn. (state Tchr. of Yr. 1982), AAUW. Republican. Presbyterian. Avocations: needlework, woodworking, walking, swimming, sewing. Home: 4807 Lakewood Ridge Manhattan KS 66502 Office: Manhattan Middle Sch 901 Poyntz Manhattan KS 66502

HARBUR, NATHAN CLAYTON, lawyer; b. Kansas City, Mo., Oct. 27, 1951; s. Clayton Joseph and Mildred Louise (Neumeyer) H.; m. Kathleen Pearce, Sept. 5, 1981. AB, Lafayette Coll., 1974; JD, U. Kans., 1977. Bar: Kans. 1977, U.S. Ct. Appeals (10th cir.) 1983. Assoc. then ptnr. Gardner and Davis, Olathe, Kans., 1977-84; ptnr. Watson, Ess, Marshall and Enggas, Olathe, 1985, Miller and Bash, PC, Overland Park, Kans., 1985—; instr. real estate law Johnson County Community Coll., Overland Park, 1979. Mem. ABA (dist. rep. young lawyers div. 1982-84), Kans. Bar Assn. (pres. young lawyers sect. 1981-82, Service awards 1984, 85), Johnson County Bar Assn., Assn. Trial Lawyers Am. Baptist. Lodge: Rotary. Avocations: weight tng., golf, basketball. Home: 8680 W 102d Terr Overland Park KS 66212 Office: Miller and Bash PC 9225 Indian Creek Pkwy Suite 790 Overland Park KS 66225

HARCOURT, MARION GOLDTHWAITE, social worker; b. Indpls., Aug. 18, 1928; d. John Louis and Helen (Whitehead) Goldthwaite; m. Robert Shaw Harcourt, Apr. 1, 1955 (div. Nov. 1979); children: Katherine, Shirley, John, Beth, David. BA, DePauw U., Greencastle, Ind., 1950; MS, Purdue U., 1953; MSW, Ind. U., 1976. Cert. clin. social work. Med. soc. worker Family Planning and Pub. Health, Indpls., 1977-78, Pub. Health Marion County, Indpls., 1978-81; family therapist Family Growth Ctr., Indpls., 1983-86; psychiat. social worker, family therapist Midtown Community Mental Health Ctr., Indpls., 1986—. Author: (chpt.) Child Sexual Abuse, 1986; contbr. articles to profl. jours. Mem. Nat. Assn. Social Workers (chair com. on ethics Ind. chpt. 1985—), Internat. Transactional Analysis Assn. (cert.), Am. Assn. Marriage and Family Therapists (clin.), Acad. Cert. Social Workers, MENSA, Intertel. Avocations: travel, China, photography, dog shows, computers. Home: 7755-D Newport Way Indianapolis IN 46256 Office: Family Growth Ctr 447 E 38th St Indianapolis IN 46205

HARDAWAY, JAMES, JR., accountant, consultant; b. Chgo., Sept. 26, 1955; s. James Sr. and Katherine Marie (Hailey) H.; m. Margo Karen Wolfe, Aug. 13, 1983; 1 child, Christina. BS, No. Ill. U., 1977; postgrad., Loop City Coll., 1982-83. CPA, Ill. Auditor Ill. Dept. Revenue, Oak Park, 1977-79; acct. Internat. Harvester, Schaumburg, Ill., 1979-80, City of Chgo., 1981-85; supr. acctg. Michael Reese Hosp., Chgo., 1985—; lectr. DuSable High Sch., Chgo., 1985; cons. in field. Mem. Am. Inst. CPA's, Ill. CPA's Soc. (polit. action com. 1985—). Democrat. Baptist. Club: Toastmasters. Avocations: baseball, basketball, bowling. Home: 281 Hoxie Calumet City IL 60409

HARDEN, ANITA JOYCE, nurse; b. Jackson, Tenn., May 17, 1947; d. Percy Lawrence and Majorie (Robison) H.; B.S. in Nursing, Ind. U., 1968; M.S. in Nursing, Ind. U.-Purdue U., Indpls., 1973; 1 son, Brian Robison Weir. Staff nurse Indpls. hosps., 1968-71; instr. Ind. U. Sch. Nursing, 1973-75; dir. continuing care Gallahue Mental Health Center, Indpls., 1975-80; mgr. psychiatry Community Hosp., Indpls., 1980-87, product line mgr. for psychiat. and mental health services, 1986—; dir. Psychiat. Services Community Hosp. North, 1987—; clin. asst. prof. Ind. U., 1977-82, clin. asso. prof., 1982—; clin. asso., trainer Suicide Prevention Service, Indpls., 1974-77; chmn. adv. bd. de-institutionalization project Central State Hosp., Indpls., 1978-79; mem. Ind. Council Community Mental Health Center, 1979-80. Recipient Outstanding Achievement in Professions award Center Leadership Devel., 1981. Mem. Ind. U. Alumni Assn., Christian Women's Fellowship, 500 Festival Assos., Coalition 100 Black Women (bd dirs.), Neal-Marshall Alumni Club, Alpha Kappa Alpha, Sigma Theta Tau, Chi Eta Phi. Mem. Christian Ch. (Disciples of Christ). Author articles in field. Home: 4057 Clarendon Rd Indianapolis IN 46208 Office: 7150 Clearvista Dr Indianapolis IN 46256

HARDEN, NORMAN EUGENE, marketing research company executive; b. Fond du Lac, Wis., May 3, 1934; s. Russell J. and Norma M. (Mayer) H.; m. Sondra Willoughby, Dec. 23, 1976; children: Gary, Cheryl, Jeffrey. B.S. magna cum laude, Lawrence U., Appleton, Wis., 1958. With A.C. Nielsen Co., a Dun & Bradstreet Co., Northbrook, Ill., 1958—, exec. v.p., 1968-76, pres., 1976—, also dir.; exec. v.p. Dun & Bradstreet, 1985—. Served with USAF. Club: Biltmore Country (Barrington, Ill.). Office: AC Nielsen Co Nielsen Plaza Northbrook IL 60062 *

HARDER, SARAH SNELL, university administrator; b. Chgo., Sept. 9, 1937; d. Frank Wen and Margaret Louise (Bryne) Snell; student U. Iowa, 1955-58; B.A., B.S. cum laude, U. Wis., LaCrosse, 1963; M.A., Bowling Green State U., 1966; m. Harry R. Harder, Feb. 7, 1964; children—Richard, Bentley, Jennifer, Aaron. Mem. faculty in English, Bowling Green State U., 1967-68; mem. faculty English, U. Wis., Eau Claire, 1968, adv. to older students, 1975-77, asst. to chancellor for affirmative action, 1975-78, asst. to chancellor for affirmative action and ednl. opportunity, 1978—; mem. U. Wis. regents' task forces on basic skills, status of women, minority/dis-advantaged students; cons. women's employment and equity, non-traditional programs in higher edn. Co-chmn. Nat. Women's Conf. Com., 1979-85; trustee Eau Claire Public Library, 1980-85, pres., 1984-85; chmn. bd. dirs. AAUW Ednl. Found., 1985—; founding bd. dirs. Wis. Women's Network; exec. Leadership Eau Claire, C. of C. Named one of 80 Leaders for the Eighties, Milw. Jour., 1979; 1st Excellence in Service award U. Wis.-Eau Claire, 1984. Dept. Edn. grantee, 1978—. Mem. AAUW (nat. pres. 1985—, dir. women's com., dir. legis. program com. mem. 1975—), LWV, Nat. Women's Polit. Caucus (award Wis. br.), Wis. Women's Council (chairperson), Delta Kappa Gamma (chpt. pres.), Alpha Lambda Delta. Democrat. Co-designer Beyond ERA—an Action Plan, 1982; contbr. articles to Redbook, Grad. Woman, Stateswoman. Home: U Wis Eau Claire WI 54701 Office: U Wis Library 2058 Eau Claire WI 54701

HARDIN, CAROLYN MYRICK, physiology educator, researcher; b. New Albany, Ind., Dec. 31, 1929; d. James Madison and Olive Cleon (Venner) M. B.A., George Washington U., 1958, M.A., 1959, Ph.D., 1969. Trainee psychophysiol. lab. Perry Point (Md.) VA Hosp., 1959-61; psychology technician Salem (Va.) VA Hosp., 1962-64; fellow, trainee in physiology George Washington U. Med. Ctr., Washington, 1964-69; instr. Meharry Med. Coll., Nashville, 1969-70, asst. prof. psychiatry and pharmacology, 1970-75, assoc. prof., 1976; assoc. prof. physiology Palmer Coll. Chiropractic, Davenport, Iowa, 1977-81, prof, 1981—. Treas. Hawthorne Dr. Townhomes Assn., Bettendorf, Iowa, 1981-83; mem.-at-large adminstrv. bd. Broadview United Meth. Ch., Bettendorf, 1982-86. Mem. Am. Physiol. Soc., Biophys. Soc., AAAS, Assn. Women in Sci., Iowa Acad. Sci., AAUP, Internat. Platform Assn., Sigma Xi. Democrat. Contbr. articles to profl. pubs. Home: 2503 Hawthorne Dr Bettendorf IA 52722 Office: 1000 Brady St PO Box 2455 Davenport IA 52803

HARDIN, CLIFFORD MORRIS, economist; b. Knightstown, Ind., Oct. 9, 1915; s. James Alvin and Mabel (Macy) H.; m. Martha Love Wood, June 28, 1939; children: Susan Carol (Mrs. L.W. Wood), Clifford Wood, Cynthia (Mrs. Robert Milligan), Nancy Ann (Mrs. Douglas L. Rogers), James. B.S., Purdue U., 1937, M.S., 1939, Ph.D., 1941, D.Sc. (hon.), 1952; Farm Found. scholar, U. Chgo., 1939-40; LL.D., Creighton U., 1956, Ill. State U., 1973; Dr. honoris causa, Nat. U. Colombia, 1968; D.Sc., Mich. State U., 1969, N.D. State U., 1969, U. Nebr., 1978, Okla. Christian Coll., 1979. Grad. asst. Purdue U., Lafayette, Ind., 1937-39, 40-41; instr. U. Wis., 1941-42, asst. prof. agrl. econs., 1942-44; asso. prof. agrl. econs. Mich. State Coll., 1944-46, prof., chmn. agrl. econs. dept., 1946-48, asst. dir. agrl. expt. sta., 1948, dir., 1949-53, dean agr., 1953-54; chancellor U. Nebr., 1954-69; sec. U.S. Dept. Agr., Washington, 1969-71; vice chmn. bd., dir. Ralston Purina Co., St. Louis, 1971-80; dir. Center for Study of Am. Bus., Washington U., St. Louis, 1981-83, scholar-in-residence, 1983-85; cons., dir. Stifel, Nicolaus & Co., St. Louis, 1980—; dir. Nappe-Babcock, Richmond, Halifax Engring., Inc., Alexandria, Va., The Cypress Fund, N.Y.C., Omaha br. Fed. Res. Bank of Kansas City, 1961-67, chmn., 1962-67. Editor: Overcoming World Hunger, 1969. Trustee Rockefeller Found., 1961-69, 72-81, Freedoms Found. at Valley Forge, 1973—, Winrock, Internat., Morrilton, Ark., 1984— , Am. Assembly, 1975—, U. Nebr. Found., 1975—; mem. Pres.'s Com. to Strengthen Security Free World, 1963. Mem. Assn. State Univs. and Land-Grant Colls. (pres. 1960, chmn. exec. com. 1961), Sigma Xi, Alpha Zeta, Alpha Gamma Rho. Home: 10 Roan Ln Saint Louis MO 63124 Office: 500 N Broadway Saint Louis MO 63102

HARDIN, MARTHA LOVE WOOD, civic leader; b. Muncie, Ind., Aug. 13, 1918; d. Lawrence Anselm and Bonny Blossom (Williams) Wood; m. Clifford Morris Hardin, June 28, 1939; children: Susan Hardin Wood, Clifford Wood, Cynthia Hardin Milligan, Nancy Hardin Rogers, James Alvin. Librarian U. Chgo., 1939-40. Contbr. articles to profl. jours. Chmn. Nebr. Heart Fund, 1967; vol. worker Lincoln Gen. Hosp., 1965, Clarkson Hosp., 1966; hon. chmn. Symphony Ball, Washington, 1970; mem. met. bd. YWCA, Washington, 1969-71, St. Louis, 1973—; mem. Women's Com. of Pres.'s Com. on Employment of Handicapped, 1970—, permanent mem. bd., 1970—; bd. dirs. St. Louis Speech and Hearing Clinic, St. Louis Met. YWCA, Cen. Inst. Deaf, St. Louis, 1986—; co-chmn. nat. fund-raising campaign U. Nebr. Found., 1977-80. Mem. DAR, PEO, St. Louis Geneal. Soc., Mortar Bd., Phi Beta Kappa, Pi Beta Phi. Clubs: Congl. (Washington), Old Warson Country, St. Louis, Wednesday. Home: 10 Roan Ln Saint Louis MO 63124

HARDIN, TOMMY JOE, electronics professional, photographer; b. Tacoma, Wash., May 13, 1947; s. Zachary Thomas Hardin and Doris Marie (Bezinque) Franchione. BS in Physics, Pittsburg (Kans.) State U., 1970, BS in Edn. Physics, 1974; postgrad., George Washington U., 1983. Technician Gulf Oil Chem. Co., Pittsburg, 1976-79; technician Quality Assurance Material Test Lab. Boeing Mil. Airplane Co., Wichita, Kans., 1979-80, quality assurance coordinator mil. programs, 1980-82, quality assurance corrective action analyst elec., electronics area, 1982-83, quality research and devel. mfg. devel. engr., 1983-86, coordinator product integrity audit group, 1986—; owner, photographer Free Lance Photography, Wichita, 1986—. Vol. coach, umpire Frontenac (Kans.) Little League Program, 1965-78; rep. materials and mfg. technology Good Neighbor Fund Membership Dr., Wichita, 1985. Mem. Am. Soc. Quality Control, Photographic Soc. Am. (charter mem. Santa Fe Trail and Okla. chpt.), Wichita Internat. Photography Exhibitors Soc. Democrat. Methodist. Clubs: Stereo Camera, Wichita Amateur Camera. Avocations: photography, reading, electronics projects, bowling, sports. Home: 1157 S Webb Rd Apt 1811 Wichita KS 67207

HARDING, ANDREW DAVID, insurance broker; b. Hannibal, Mo., Dec. 7, 1939; s. Andrew Duncan and Helen C. (Carroll) H.; m. Allene Berger, Aug. 10, 1939; children: James, Jennifer, Amy. BS in Fire Protection Engring., Ill. Inst. Tech., 1961. Registered profl. engr., Mo., Ill., Wis., Calif.; CPCU. Engr. fire protection Mo. Insp. Bur., St. Louis, 1961-66; safety engr. McDonnell Corp., St. Louis, 1966-67; cons. fire protection Aetna Life and Casualty, Hartford, Conn., 1967-71; v.p. Marsh & McLennan, Chgo., 1971—; cons., mgr. fire protection Sierra Group, Oak Brook, Ill., 1973-74. Chmn. fin. com. Gary Meth. Ch., Wheaton, Ill., 1981-82; treas. Wheaton North Fan Club, 1985-87. Mem. Soc. Fire Protection Engring., Soc. of CPCU (Chgo chpt. treas. 1982-83, sec. 1983-84, v.p. 1984-85, pres. 1986-87). Office: Marsh & McLennan Inc 222 S Riverside Chicago IL 60606

HARDING, BRUCE LEE, architect; b. Marshalltown, Iowa, Feb. 10, 1950; s. Russell Israel and Alice Lucille (Jay) H.; m. Sheila Ann Creedon, Aug. 20, 1977; children: Morgan Rae, Abbey Lee. BArch, Iowa State U., 1973; MArch, U. Wis., Milw., 1979. Assoc. Appier Marlof & Assoc., Rock Island, Ill., 1974-77, 79—. Bd. dirs. Mississippi Valley Spl. Olympics, Rock Island, 1986—. Mem. AIA (v.p. west Ill. chpt. 1985-86, pres. 1986-87), Rock Island Jaycees (pres. 1982-83). Republican. Mem. Soc. of Friends. Lodge: Kiwanis (pres. Rock Island chpt. 1981-82).

HARDING, JAMES WARREN, finance company executive; b. Montoursville, Pa., Nov. 9, 1918; s. James John and Alda (Edkin) H.; m. Emily Sue Landes, Mar. 22, 1941; 1 dau., Connie Sue (Mrs. Richard E. Fisher). B.A., Lycoming Coll., 1938, LL.D. (hon.); M.A., U. Chgo., 1940. With Kemper Cos., Chgo., 1940-84; accountant Kemper Cos., 1940-50, comptroller, 1960-68, exec. v.p., 1969; chmn. bd. Bank of Chgo., from 1969; pres. Kemper Corp., 1969-84, ret.; pres. Am. Underwriting Corp., Central Mortgage Co.; pres. Nat. Agts. Service Co., 1969—, also bd. dirs.; bd. dirs. Kemper Fin. Services, New Zealand Ins. Co. Contbr. articles to ins. and trade mags. Finance chmn. Crusade of Mercy, Chgo., 1964-65; trustee James S. Kemper Found., Mundelein Coll.; adv. bd. U. Chgo., Brigham Young U. Served with USNR, 1943-44. Recipient Hardy award Ins. Inst., 1946. Mem. Am. Mgmt. Assn., Econ Club, Financial Execs. Inst., Ins. Statis. Assn., Nat. Indsl. Conf. Bd., Ill. C. of C. (dir.), Phi Kappa Sigma. Republican. Methodist. Clubs: Chicago, University (Chgo.). Home: 1230 Thornbury Libertyville IL 60048 Office: Kemper Investors Life Ins Co 120 S LaSalle St Chicago IL 60603

HARDIS, STEPHEN ROGER, mfg. co. exec.; b. N.Y.C., July 13, 1935; s. Abraham I. and Ethel (Krinsky) H.; m. Sondra Joyce Rolbin, Sept. 15, 1957; children—Julia Faye, Andrew Martin, Joanne Halley. B.A. with distinction, Cornell U., 1956; M.P.A. in Econs, Woodrow Wilson Sch. of Pub. and Internat. Affairs, Princeton, 1960. Asst. to controller Gen. Dynamics, 1960-61; financial analyst Pfaudler Permutit Inc., 1961-64; staff asst. to controller 1964; mgr. corp. long-range planning Ritter Pfaudler Corp., 1965-68, dir. corporate planning, 1968; treas. Sybron Corp., Rochester, N.Y., 1969—; v.p. fin. Sybron Corp., 1970-77, exec. v.p. fin. and planning, 1977-79; vice chmn., chief fin. and adminstrv. officer Eaton Corp., Cleve., 1979—; dir. Soc. Corp., Soc. Nat., Inc., Nordson Corp., Shlegal Corp., Univ. Circle Inc. Past mem. Gov.'s Spl. Task Force on High Tech. Industry; past bd. dirs. Rochester Area Hosp. Corp., Rochester Area Ednl. TV Sta., Genesee Hosp.; trustee Cleve. Clinic. Served with USNR, 1956-58. Mem. Fin. Execs. Inst., MAPI Fin. Council, Phi Beta Kappa. Office: Eaton Corporation 1111 Superior Ave NE Cleveland OH 44114

HARDWICK, LEO PLINY, business educator; b. Boston, Feb. 4, 1930; s. Pliny S. and Nora M. Hardwick, m. Elizabeth Wirth; children: Katherine, James. AB, Tufts U., 1952; MBA, Boston U., 1956. Asst. editor EBASCO Services, N.Y.C., 1961-65; sr. assoc. editor Burroughs Clearing House, Detroit, 1966-69; free-lance writer various, Detroit, 1969—; adj. faculty various instns., Mich., 1977—; adj. asst. prof. Madonna Coll. and others, Livonia, Mich., 1980—. Author: How To Write Winning Reports, 1981. Served with U.S. Army, 1952-54. Mem. Am. Soc. Personnel Adminstrn. (editorial review com. 1980—). Home: 902 University Pl Grosse Pointe MI 48230

HARDWICK, PHILLIP KEITH, foundation executive, consultant; b. Richmond, Ind., Oct. 31, 1935; s. Herman Pearl and Emily cora (Richardson) H.; m. Patricia Ann Placke, Sept. 1, 1958 (div. 1976); children—Lucinda Kaye Hardwick Masterson, Phillip James; m. Karen Lynn Hickman, Nov. 20, 1976. B.S., Ind. U., 1959, M.S., 1963. Recreation assoc. Milw. Schs., 1959-61; supt. recreation Bloomington Parks, Ind., 1961-63; Indpls. Parks, 1963-67; campaign dir. United Way, Indpls., 1967-84; spl. asst. to pres. Marian Coll., Indpls., 1984-85; pres. Methodist Health Found., Indpls., 1985—; cons. P.K. Assocs., Indpls., 1983—. Bd. dirs. Indpls. Humane Soc., 1982—, Catholic Social Services, Indpls., 1985—. Recipient State High Sch. Football Official of Yr. award Ind. High Sch. Athletic Assn., 1985. Mem. Ind. Council Fund Raisers (bd. dirs. 1981-83, Profl. of Yr. award 1984). Republican. Lutheran. Clubs: Crooked Stick Golf, Speedway Golf (pres. 1982-84). Avocations: college and high school football official; golf. Home: 10740 Crooked Stick Carmel IN 46032 Office: Meth Health Found 1812 N Meridian St Indianapolis IN 46202

HARDY, BRIAN ELDON, engineering manager; b. Canton, S.D., May 21, 1952; s. Herbert Scott and Miriam Alice (Loken) H.; m. Elizabeth Marie Molyneaux, June 21, 1980; children: Allison Marie, Megan Kathrin, Matthew Scott. BSME, S.D. State U., 1976; MME, S.D. Sch. Mines & Tech., 1978. Design engr. John Deere & Co., Waterloo, Iowa, 1978-79; design engr. Electro-Magic Inc., Vermillion, S.D., 1979, chief engr., 1980-84; mgr. engring. Dale Electronics Inc., York, Nebr., 1984-87; sr. product engr. Dale Electronics Inc., Columbus, Nebr., 1987—. Patentee in field. Served with U.S. Army, 1972-73. Republican. Methodist. Club: Toastmasters (York). Avocations: flying, hunting, fishing. Home: 623 E 7th St York NE 68467 Office: Dale Electronics Inc 1122 23d St Columbus NE 68601

HARDY, E. VERNEDA, nurse; b. Pinckneyville, Ill., Feb. 1, 1927; d. Roy Nesbitt and Etta Mae (McIlrath) Brown; 1 dau., Marvel Ann Hardy Donovan. Diploma, Christian Welfare Hosp. Sch. Nursing, 1948; B.S. in Occupational Edn., So. Ill. U. Carbondale, 1984. Nurse, Christian Welfare Hosp., East St. Louis, Ill., 1948-52, St. Mary's Hosp., East St. Louis, 1952-61; nurse Pinckneyville (Ill.) Community Hosp., 1961-66, operating room supr., 1966—. Served with U.S. Army, 1945-48. Mem. Assn. Operating Room Nurses, So. Ill. U. Alumni Assn. Republican. Baptist. Club: Pinckneyville Bus. Women's. Home: 605 Saint Louis St Pinckneyville IL 62274 Office: 101 N Walnut St Pinckneyville IL 62274

HARDY, JAMES ALLEN, production agriculturist; b. Keokuk, Iowa, Apr. 17, 1959; s. Leonard Yetter Hardy and Audrey Helene (Damelio) Hartweg; m. Jenifer Ann Kell, Aug. 11, 1978; 1 child, Nathaniel. Real estate broker cert., Carl Sandburg Coll., 1985. Owner, operator Prairieland, Carthage, Ill., 1978—; bd. dirs. Hancock Service Co., Carthage. V.P. Hancock County Farm Bur., Carthage, 1985-87; trustee Prairie Twp., 1984—; treas. Carthage-Prairie Tax Assessment Dist., 1987—; mem. polit. action com. Activator, 1985—, county chmn. Slater Campaign Com., Macomb, Ill., 1984—; active Rep. precinct cen. com., Hancock, 1981—. Recipient Am. Farmer Degree, Future Farmers Am., 1980; Agrl. Leaders of Tomorrow award, Ill. Farm Bur., 1983. Mem. Carthage C. of C. (agrl. rep. 1983—, pres. 1987—). Republican. Methodist. Avocation: photography. Home and Office: Prairieland Rural Rt #2 Carthage IL 62321

HARDY, NORMAN E. (PETER), food and beverage company executive; b. Toronto, Ont., Can., Jan. 4, 1917; s. George and Myrtle (Dunsmore) H.; m. Dorothy Walter, Apr. 6, 1939; children: Eleanor Gayle, Beverley Georgine. Student, Pickering Coll., Ont. With Hardy Cartage Co. Ltd., 1935, Brewers' Warehousing Co. Ltd., 1948-49; mgr. Toronto Brewery, John Labatt Ltd., 1949-56, gen. mgr., 1956-59, v.p. beverages div., 1959, chmn. bd., past., dir.; bd dirs. Brascan Ltd., Noma Ind. Ltd., Union Enterprise; vice chmn., chief exec. officer Toronto Blue Jays Baseball Club. Served to lt. RCNVR, World War II. Clubs: The London, Mississauga Gold and Country, London Hunt and Country, Granite, Primrose. Office: John Labatt Ltd, 451 Ridout St N, London, ON Canada N6A 5L3

HARDY, RICHARD JOHN, loss prevention specialist; b. Chgo., Apr. 18, 1955; s. Arthur John and Elaine Barbara (Piotrowski) H.; m. Rosemary Ann Przybylski, June 11, 1977; 1 child, David. AA in Transp. and Biology, Daley Community Coll., 1979. Dir. safety Fast Motor Service, Brookfield, Ill., 1977-79; div. safety mgr. Gateway Transp., LaCrosse, Wis., 1979-80; regional safety supr. Interstate Motor Freight, Grand Rapids, Mich., 1981; regional loss prevention mgr. ARA/Smith's Transfer, Staunton, Va., 1982—. Mem. Ill. Trucking Assn., Nat. Com. for Motor Fleet Supr. Tng., Ill. Council Safety Suprs. Avocations: scuba diving, fishing, water skiing, snow skiing. Office: ARA/Smith's Transfer 4159 W 58th Pl Chicago IL 60629

HARDY, WILLIAM ROBINSON, lawyer; b. Cin., June 14, 1934; s. William B. and Chastine M. (Sprague) H.; m. Barbro Anita Medin, Oct. 11, 1964; children: Anita Christina, William Robinson. AB magna cum laude, Princeton U., 1956; JD, Harvard U., 1963. Bar: Ohio 1963, U.S. Supreme Ct. 1975. Life underwriter New Eng. Mut. Life Ins. Co., 1956-63; assoc. Graydon, Head & Ritchey, Cin., 1963-68, ptnr., 1968—; mem. panel comml. and constrn. industry arbitrators Am. Arbitration Assn., 1972—; reporter joint com. for revision of rules of U.S. Dist. Ct. for So. Dist. Ohio, 1975, 80, 83. Bd. dirs. Cin. Union Bethel, 1968—, pres., 1977-82; bd. dirs. Ohio Valley Goodwill Industries Rehab. Ctr., Cin., 1970—, pres., 1981—; mem Cin. Bd. Bldg. Appeals, 1976—, vice chmn., 1983, chmn., 1983—. Served to capt. USAR, 1956-68. Recipient award of merit Ohio Legal Ctr. Inst., 1975, 76. Mem. ABA, Ohio Bar Assn., Cin. Bar Assn., Am. Judicature Soc., Assn. Trial Lawyers Am., Ohio Acad. Trial Lawyers, 6th Circuit Jud. Conf. (life), AAAS, Ohio Soc. Colonial Wars (gov. 1979), Phi Beta Kappa. Mem. Ch. of Redeemer. Clubs: Princeton (N.Y.C.); Racquet (Cin.). Home: 1339 Michigan Ave Cincinnati OH 45208 Office: Graydon Head & Ritchey 1900 Fifth Third Ctr 511 Walnut St Cincinnati OH 45202

HARE, TY CHRISTIAN, controller; b. Kittaning, Pa., July 26, 1960; s. Millard L. and Peggy J. (Wilson) H.; m. Susan Wyncoop, June 29, 1985. BBA, U. Notre Dame, 1982. CPA. Staff acct. Deloitte haskins & Sells, Pitts., 1982-85; sr. acct. Deloitte haskins & Sells, Cin., 1985-86; controller Carnegie Constrn., Inc., Cin., 1986—. Mem. Am. Inst. CPAs, Pa. Inst. CPAs. Avocations: reading, music, golf. Home: 8684 Zenith Ct Cincinnati OH 45231 Office: Carnegie Constrn Inc 5 Circle Freeway Dr Cincinnati OH 45246

HARENS, PAUL ARTHUR, communications educator; b. Devil's Lake, N.D., May 7, 1951; s. Arthur Paul and Ellen Jane (Larsen) H.; m. Kathleen Marie Weniger, July 7, 1973; children: Michael Andrew, Nathan Paul. BA, Huron Coll., 1973; MA, U. S.D., 1982. Communications and debate coach Pierre (S.D.) Pub. Schs., 1973-79, U. S.D., Vermillion, 1979-80, Yankton (S.D.) Pub. Schs., 1980—. County chairperson Kundert for Gov., Yankton, 1985-86. Named Diamond Key Coach, Nat. Forensic League, Ripon, Wis., 1983. Mem. S.D. Communications Assn., S.D. Forensic Coaches Assn. (pres. 1985-86). Lodge: KC (bursar 1982-84, grand knight 1984-86). Avocation: collecting books. Home: 204 E 6th Yankton SD 57078

HARGENS, ROGER ALFORD, industrial salesman; b. Denison, Iowa, Oct. 31, 1952; s. Louie August and Eva Pearl (Alcorn) H.; m. Jane Ellen Yetter, Nov. 1974; children: Carey Rose, Ryan August, Amanda Jane. Indsl. salesman L.H. Kurtz Co., Des Moines, 1975-76, Interstate Machinery, Omaha, 1976-77, Iowa Machinery and Supply Co., Des Moines, 1977—. Mem. Soc. Mfg. Engrs. (membership chmn. 1982—). Republican. Roman Catholic. Avocations: golf, offroad motorcycling. Home: 6013 N Winwood Dr Johnston IA 50131

HARGER, LUANN LAWRENCE, educator; b. St. Louis, June 12, 1958; d. Paul Joseph and Virginia Rose (Fasholt) Lawrence; m. Gregory Dean Harger, June 21, 1980; 1 child, Christopher Paul. BS in Edn., Ind. U., 1980; MS in Reading, Butler U., 1984. Tchr. kindergarten Kiddie Kollege, Indpls., 1980-81; tchr. first and second grade Nobelsville (Ind.) Schs., 1981-82, tchr. second grade, 1982—; media cons. workshop speaker Prime Time Workshop, Indpls., 1985. Producer video tape The King Who Was Too Short, 1982, (1st in nation 1982), Jo The Eskimo Boy, 1983, (1st in region 1983), The Lady in the Harbor, 1984 (2d in region). Campaign worker Noblesville Reps., 1983. Mem. Delta Sigma Kappa (chmn. dance 1986-87, treas. 1987—). Avocations: exercising, walking, boating, reading, being outdoors. Home: 206 Ironwood Circle Noblesville IN 46060 Office: Hinkle Creek Elem Sch 595 S Harbour Dr Noblesville IN 46060

HARGER, MARK ALAN, manufacturing executive; b. Logansport, Ind., Dec. 28, 1954; s. Robert Dean and Anne Louise (DeLong) H.; m. Mary Elane Downey, Nov., 1978; children: Carli, Adam, Matthew. BSEE, Purdue U., 1978. Engr. field systems Texas Instruments, Knoxville, Tenn., 1978-80; mem. engring. staff RCA, Indpls., 1980-84; mgr. computer peripherals Gen. Elec., Portsmouth, Va., 1984-85; mgr. research and devel. Landis and Gyr, Lafayette, Ind., 1985—; pres. Datasoft Corp., Lafayette, 1986—. Patentee in field. Mem. Lafayette C. of C., Pi Kappa Alpha. Republican. Avocations: tennis, boating, fishing, sports cars. Office: Landis and Gyr 3601 Sagamore Pkwy N Lafayette IN 47903

HARGRAVE, SARAH QUESENBERRY, corporate foundation executive; b. Mt. Airy, N.C., Dec. 11, 1944; d. Teddie W. and Lois Knight (Slusher) Quesenberry. Student, Radford Coll., 1963-64, Va. Poly. Inst. and State U., 1964-67. Mgmt. trainee Thalhimer Bros. Dept. Store, Richmond, Va., 1967-68; Central Va. fashion and publicity dir. Sears Roebuck & Co., Richmond, 1968-73; nat. decorating sch. coordinator Sears Roebuck & Co., Chgo., 1973-74, nat. dir. bus. and profl. women's programs, 1974-76; v.p., treas., program dir. Sears-Roebuck Found., Chgo., 1976-87, program mgr. corp. contbns. and memberships, 1981-83, dir. corp. mktg. and pub. affairs, 1983-87; v.p. Northern Trust Co., Chgo., 1987—. Bd. dirs. Am. Assembly Collegiate Schs. Bus., 1979-82, mem. vis. com., 1979-82, mem. fin. and audit com., 1980-82, mem. task force on doctoral supply and demand, 1980-82; mem. Com. for Equal Opportunity for Women, 1976; chmn., 1978-79, 80-81; mem. bus. adv. council Walter E. Heller Coll. Bus. Adminstrn., Roosevelt U., 1979—; co-dir. Ill. Internat. Women's Yr. Ctr., 1975; mem. Chgo. Artists Coalition. Named Outstanding Young Women of Yr. Ill., 1976; named Women of Achievement State Street Bus. and Profl. Woman's Club, 1978. Mem. Assn. Humanistic Psychology, Am. Home Econs. Assn., Nat. Fedn. Bus. and Profl. Women's Clubs, Eddystone Condominium Assn. (v.p. 1978-86). Home: 421 W Melrose St Chicago IL 60657 Office: Northern Trust Co 50 S LaSalle St Chicago IL 60675

HARGREAVES, GEORGE MACDONALD, advertising executive; b. Highland Park, Mich., Sept. 6, 1927; s. George Wellock and Florence (Macdonald) H.; m. Catherine Mae Armstrong, Sept. 1, 1951; children: Amy J., George A., Jane C. BS in Physics, Hillsdale Coll., 1951. Research engr. Chrysler Corp., Highland Park, 1951-54; editor Soc. Mfg. Engrs., Detroit, 1954-59; mktg. mgr. Detroit Stamping Co., 1959-60; advt. mgr. Bendix Indsl. Controls, Detroit, 1960-61; chmn., treas. Common Sense Communications, Inc., Saginaw, Mich., 1961—. Author: Bench Saw Techniques, 1967. Served with USN, 1945-46. Mem. Bus. Profl. Advt. Assn. (cert. bus. communicator). Presbyterian. Club: Germania (Saginaw) (golf pres. 1982, bd. dirs.). Lodge: Kiwanis (pres. Saginaw 1971). Avocations: golf, music. Home: 124 Larch St Saginaw MI 48602 Office: Common Sense Communications Inc 602 S Michigan Ave Saginaw MI 48602

HARIHARAN, BRINDHA, accounting educator; b. Vadakanchery, Kerala, India, Sept. 14, 1945; d. C.R. and Thankam Ganapathy; m. P.R. Hariharan, May 26, 1967; 1 child, Selena. MA in English Lit., Govt. Victoria Coll., 1967; MBA, Ind. U., 1978. CPA, Ind. Dir. Three Rivers Montessori Sch., Ft. Wayne, Ind., 1968-74; asst. prof. St. Francis Coll., Ft. Wayne, 1978—; adj. faculty Ind. U., Ft. Wayne, 1974-76; jr. acct. Kern and Co., Ft. Wayne, 1976-78. Mem. Am. Inst. CPA's, Ind. CPA Soc. Hindu. Avocations: racquetball, reading. Home: 6025 Bohde Trail Fort Wayne IN 46835

HARITATOS, JAMES STEPHEN, social worker, gerontologist, educator; b. Rome, N.Y., Aug. 3, 1948; s. Jerry Nicholas and Lola Mary (Potanos) H.; m. Ann Spencer Watson, Aug. 14, 1971; children: Jana, Jonathan. BA, Valparaiso U., 1970; postgrad., Concordia Sem., 1970-72; advanced cert., St. Louis U., 1975, MSW, 1975. Cert. social worker. Project adminstr. Inst. Applied Gerontology St. Louis U., 1974; social services planner St. Louis Area Agy. Aging, 1975-77; aging services coordinator Pawnee Mental Health Services, Concordia, Kans., 1978; instr. allied health Cloud County Community Coll., Concordia, 1979—; resident services dir. Sunset Home, Concordia, 1979—; cons. social services curriculum Barton County Community Coll., Great Bend, Kans., 1978-82; dir. bereavement services Hospice N. Cen. Kans., Concordia, 1982-84, bd. dirs., chmn. fundraising com., 1986—; cons. social services hosps. and nursing homes, north cen. Kans., 1979—; facilitator Alzheimers Disease and Related Disorders Support Group, Concordia, 1986—. Guest editor, contbr. Social Services: Caring and Sharing Newsletter, 1986—. Leader adult Bible class Concordia Luth. Ch., 1979-84; mem. Human Relations Commn., Concordia, 1979-80; assoc. mem. Cloud County Commn. Aging, Concordia, 1978—. Recipient Pres.'s scholarship ea. dist. Luth.-Mo. Synod, Buffalo, 1966, Regents scholarship N.Y. State U. Regents, Albany, 1966,. Mem. Nat. Assn. Social Workers (chmn. Kans. chpt. long term care task force 1982-83), Gerontol. Soc. Am., Am. Soc. Aging, Gray Panthers, Nat. Council on the Aging. Democrat. Lutheran. Avocations: camping, swimming, singing in choral groups, piano, collecting stamps. Home: 533 E 7th Concordia KS 66901 Office: Sunset Home 620 2d Ave Concordia KS 66901

HARKIN, THOMAS R., U.S. Senator; b. Cumming, Iowa, Nov. 19, 1939; s. Patrick and Frances H.; m. Ruth Raduenz, 1968; children: Amy, Jenny. B.S., Iowa State U., 1962; J.D., Cath. U. Am., 1972. Mem. staff Ho. of Reps. Select Com. U.S. Involvement in S.E. Asia, 1970; mem. 94th-98th Congresses from 5th Iowa Dist., Sci. and Tech. Com., Agr. Com., U.S. Senate, 1984—, agr., appropriations and small bus. coms., labor and human resources com. Served with USN, 1962-67. Named Outstanding Young Alumnus Iowa State U. Alumni Assn., 1974. Democrat. Office: 316 Hart Senate Bldg Washington DC 20510

HARKINS, SISTER KATHLEEN LOUISE, educator; b. Chgo., Apr. 13, 1936; d. John Francis and Virginia Mary (Nass) H. BA, Barry U., 1963; MFA in Theatre, Cath. U., 1970; MA in Theology, Loyola U., Chgo., 1985. Joined Adrian Dominican Congregation, Roman Cath. Ch., 1954. Tchr., sec. Cath. elem. schs. Detroit and West Palm Beach, Fla., 1955-68; founder children's theater Rosarian Acad., West Palm Beach, 1963-68; lectr. theater Siena Heights Coll., Adrian, Mich., 1968-70; vis. tchr. creative drama Archdiocese Chgo., 1970-78; lectr. research theater and theology Loyola U., Chgo., 1978-82; pastoral assoc. St. Catherine of Alexandria Parish, Oak Lawn, Ill., 1982—; vis. lectr. theater and theology in liturgy Archdiocese Chgo., 1970—. Dir. numerous plays, 1964-70. Recipient Impact Tchr. award Nat. Cath. Edn. Assn., 1967. Mem. Chgo. Pastoral Assn., 8th Day Ctr. for Peace and Justice (pres. 1980—), Call To Action (pres. Chgo. chpt. 1983—), Preachers of the Word, Nat. Cath. Evangelization Assn., Ill. Theatre Assn. (bd. dirs. religion and theater 1978-81). Office: St Catherine of Alexandria Rectory 4100 W 107th Oak Lawn IL 60453

HARKINS, RICHARD WESLEY, marine engineer, naval architect; b. Duluth, Minn., Oct. 11, 1946; s. Wesley Ray and Vivian G. (LaBrosse) H.; m. Deborah Ann deGonzaque, Aug. 17, 1974; children: Ryan Wesley, Blair Ashley, Danielle Ashley. BS, U.S. Mcht. Marine Acad., Kings Point, N.Y., 1971; MSE in Naval Architecture and Marine Engring., U. Mich., 1976. Registered profl. engr., Ohio. 3d asst. engr. Hanna Steamship Corp., Cleve., 1971; 1st asst. engr. Poling Transp. Corp., N.Y.C., 1971-72; engr. Ingalls Shipbuilding Co., Pascagoula, Miss., 1972-74; fleet engr. Interlake Steamship div. Pickands Mather & Co., Cleve., 1976—. Author: (tech. paper) Investigation of Fuel Injection Cavitation, 1985 (Best Paper of 1985 Soc. Naval Architects and Marine Engrs.). Mem. Soc. Naval Architects and Marine Engrs. (ship machinery com. 1985, chmn. diesel panel 1985—, chmn. papers com. 1985-87, local sect. rep. 1985-87), ASTM (shipbuilding com. 1981—). Roman Catholic. Avocations: cross-country skiing, running, antique autos. Home: 2771 Hampton Rd Rocky River OH 44116 Office: Interlake Steamship div 629 Euclid Ave Suite 400 Cleveland OH 44114-3003

HARLAN, NORMAN RALPH, builder; b. Dayton, Ohio, Dec. 21, 1914; s. Joseph and Anna (Kaplan) H.; Indsl. Engring. degree U. Cin., 1937; m. Thelma Katz, Sept. 4, 1955; children—Leslie, Todd. Pres. Am. Constrn. Corp., Dayton, 1949—, Mainline Investment Corp., 1951—, Harlan, Inc., realtors; treas. Norman Estates, Inc. Mem. Dayton Real Estate Bd., Ohio Real Estate Assn., Nat. Assn. Real Estate Bds., C. of C., Pi Lambda Phi. Home: 303 Glenridge Rd Kettering OH 45429 Office: 2451 S Dixie Hwy Dayton OH 45409

HARLAN, WILLIAM ROBERT, JR., physician, educator; b. Richmond, Va., Nov. 1, 1930; s. William Robert and Helen J. (Weaver) H.; m. Linda Carol Mavencamp, Aug. 23, 1980; children: Elizabeth, William, Christopher, Nicole. B.A., U. Va., 1951; M.D. magna cum laude, Med. Coll. Va., 1955. Diplomate: Am. Bd. Internal Medicine, Am. Bd. Family Practice. Intern U. Wis., Madison, 1955-56; resident in medicine Duke U. Hosp., Durham, N.C., 1958-62; dir. Clin. Research Center, Med. Coll. Va., 1963-70; asso. dean U. Ala. Med. Sch., 1970-72; prof. medicine and community health scis. Duke U., 1972-74; prof. medicine and postgrad. medicine U. Mich., Ann Arbor, 1974—; asst. dean Med. Sch. U. Mich.; cons. World Bank; mem. sci. adv. bd. U.S. Air Force; mem. Armed Forces Epidemiology Bd., NIH study sects. and adv. councils. Contbr. articles to med. jours. Served with M.C. USN, 1956-58. Mem. ACP, Am. Heart Assn., N.Y. Acad. Sci., Sigma Xi, Alpha Omega Alpha. Episcopalian. Club: Country (Va.). Office: Chief of Staff VAMC 2215 Fuller Rd Ann Arbor MI 48105

HARLEY, ROY ANDREW, social worker, social services administrator; b. Mpls., Mar. 19, 1935; s. Andrew and Ann (Stenberg) H.; m. Karol L. Koeneman, Mar. 4, 1961; children: David A., Kristin L. AA, U. Minn., 1955; BA, Gustavus Adolphus Coll., 1959; MSW, U. Denver, 1963. Cert. social worker. Caseworker Hennepin County Ct. Service, Mpls., 1959-61, social worker, 1963-66; residential dir. Vasa Luth. Home, Red Wing, Minn., 1966-75; area residential dir. Luth. Social Services of Minn., Mpls., 1975-84, regional dir., 1984—; cons. Hiawatha Children's Home, Rochester, Minn., 1976, Lake City (Minn.) Nursing Home, 1978-83, Riverview Group Home, Namming, Minn., 1980—. Mem. Red Wing Planning Com., 1967-69, Red Wing City Council, 1969-75; chmn. bd. dirs. Goodhia-Wabsha Community Health, Red Wing, 1977-83; bd. dirs. S.E. Minn. Health Council, Rochester, 1980-83. Mem. Acad. Cert. Social Workers, AAMD, Nat. Assn. Social Workers (cert.), Pvt. Industry Council. Lodge: Masons. Avocations: skiing, fishing, hiking, outdoors.

HARLEY, SHEILA DAWNE, accountant; b. Santa Rosa, Calif., Apr. 14, 1945; s. Walter L. and Virginia V. (Carlson) R.; m. Jerry L. Harley, Nov. 20, 1977. BS in Bus. Adminstrn., Cen. Mo. U., 1978. CPA, Mo. Mem. audit staff Baird, Kurtz & Dobson, Springfield, Mo., 1977-78; staff accts. Roger Taylor, CPA, Springfield, 1978-79; staff acct. Jackson & Decker CPA, Springfield, 1979; ptnr. Decker & Harley, CPA's, Springfield, 1980—; ptnr. Indsl. Properties Investments, Springfield, 1986—; fin. ptnr. R.B. Investemnts, Springfield, 1985—; bd. dirs. Polar Printing, Inc., Springfield, 1986—. Chmn. Greene County Domestic Violence Shelter Bd., Springfield, 1985-86; treas. Salvation Army adv. bd., Springfield, 1984-86, U. Co-op. Extension Bd., 1982-86; bd. dirs. Green County Planning and Zoning Commn., Springfield, 1984—, Christian Found., Springfield, 1984—. Gen. Hap Arnold scholar USAF, 1963. Mem. Am. Soc. CPA's, Mo. Soc. CPA's, Am. Soc. Women Accts. (treas. 1983-84), Network of Springfield (treas. 1982-83, pres. 1983-84). Republican. Methodist. Lodge: Zonta (pres. 1981-82). Avocations: river boating. Office: Decker & Harley CPA's 805 W Battlefield Springfield MO 65807

HARLING, GENE, bank executive; b. 1946. BSBA, U. Fla., 1968; MBA, Wayne State U., 1969. Acct. Peat, Marwick, Mitchell and Co., 1971-79; with First Fed. Mich., Detroit, 1979—, now pres., chief operating officer. Served with U.S. Army, 1970-71. Office: First Fed of Mich 1001 Woodward Detroit MI 48226 *

HARLOW, DAVID MICHAEL, data processing executive; b. Pekin, Ill., Feb. 14, 1956; s. Robert David and Delores Jean (Painter) H.; m. Jill Susan Steger, June 17, 1978. AA, Ill. Cen. Coll., East Peoria, 1976; BA, Sangamon State U., 1986. Computer programmer Caterpillar Inc., Mossville, Ill., 1976-79; computer analyst Caterpillar Inc., Mossville, 1980-85; data base adminstr. Caterpillar Inc., East Peoria, 1986—. Mem. PEKIN Musicians Local 301, Peoria User Group, Phi Theta Kappa. Avocations: tennis, softball, chess, baseball, personal computer. Home: 115 Terrace Ln East Peoria IL 61611 Office: Caterpillar Inc 600 W Washington East Peoria IL 61630

HARLOWE, DIANE MARIE, hospital administrator; b. Bklyn., May 18, 1947; d. Ted and Edith (Nunziato) Coniglio; m. Hal Harlowe, July 30, 1979; children: Michael Darren, Matthew Ryan. BA, Georgian Court Coll., Lakewood, N.J., 1969; MS, Columbia U., 1974. Registered occupational therapist. Occupational therapist Letchworth Village, Thiells, N.Y., 1969-74; coordinator edn. and rehab. Lakeshore Manor, Madison, Wis., 1974-76; pvt. practice cons. Madison, Wis., 1976; dir. occupational therapy and speech services St. Mary's Hosp., Madison, Wis., 1977—; v.p., bd. dirs. Create-Ability Workshop, Madison, 1975-76; clinical asst. prof. U. Wis., Milw., 1979—; preceptor U. Wis., Madison, 1984—. Co-author: The ROM Dance, 1984; producer video and audio tapes The ROM Dance, 1984; co-author and producer Splints for Rheumatoid Arthritis, 1984; contbr. articles to profl. jours. Mem. steering com. Hal Harlowe for Dist. Atty., Madison, 1975—. Recipient grant for Create-Ability Workshop, Comprehensive Employment and Tng. Act, Madison, 1975; grantee Arthritis Found., 1978, 80, Arthritis Health Professions Assn., 1983-86. Mem. Arthritis Found., Arthritis Health Professions Assn., Wis. Occupational Therapy Assn., Am. Occupational Therapy Assn., Rehab. Internat. USA. Democrat. Office: St Mary's Hosp Med Ctr 707 S Mills St Madison WI 53715

HARMAN, DENNIS EUGENE, chemical executive; b. Fullerton, Calif., Nov. 17, 1939; s. Virgil R. and Juanita (Bierbower) H.; m. Connie Elyce Chapman, June 10, 1967; children: Jennifer Lynn, Kelly Elyce. BS, U. Ariz., 1962; M in Internat. Bus., Grad. Sch. for Internat. Mgmt., 1967. Mgr. mktg. south Atlantic region Ecolab, Inc., Brazil, 1968-77; sr. v.p. Pacific far east internat. ops. Ecolab, Inc., St. Paul, 1977-83, area v.p. Klenzade div., 1983—, v.p., dir. sales Klenzade div., 1985—; bd. dirs. CFR Corp., Mpls. Served to capt. USMC, 1962-66, Vietnam. Republican. Avocations: skiing, jogging, woodworking. Home: 7701 Stonewood Ct Edina MN 55435

HARMAN, DONALD LEE, nurse, educator, consultant; b. Titusville, Pa., Mar. 22, 1948; s. William Ceska and Eva Louise (Matha) H. B.S. in Edn., Edinboro Coll., 1970, M.S., 1972; A.A.S. in Nursing, Ohio U.-Zanesville, 1977. R.N., Ohio, Ill., Wis. Dir. out-patient services, Spencer Hosp., Meadville, Pa., 1974; in-service instr., Guernsy Meml. Hosp., Cambridge, Ohio, 1974-77; instr. in med., surg. and pediatric nursing Blessing Hosp., Quincy, Ill., 1977-79; pediatric staff nurse, Rush Presbyn. St. Luke's Hosp., Chgo., 1979; camp nurse Young Men's Jewish Council, Chgo., 1979; emergency room nurse Henrotin Hosp., Chgo., 1979, intervenous therapist, 1980; head instr. med. surg. nursing Madison (Wis.) Gen. Hosp. Sch. of Nursing, 1980-81, dir. nursing, edn., 1981-86, pres. bd. dirs. CommonHealth Co. Author: Energy-For All Reasons Facilitator's Guide. Del. to China U.S. Healthcare Systems, 1987. Recipient Copper Cup award, Madison Gen. Hosp., 1983. Del. to China to discuss U.S. Healthcare Systems. Mem. Am. Soc. Health, Edn. and Tng., Wis. Soc. for Health, Edn. and Tng., Wis. Soc. for Nursing Service Adminstrs. and Am. Nurses Assn., ANA Council for Continuing Edn. Methodist.

HARMON, PHILLIP LOUIS, lawyer; b. Bourne, Mass., Sept. 8, 1954; s. Russell Sanborn and Patsy (Bilger) H. BS, Cornell U., 1976; JD, Capital Law Sch., 1980. Bar: Ohio 1980, U.S. Dist. Ct. (so. dist.) Ohio 1981, D.C. 1982, U.S. Ct. Appeals (6th cir.) 1986. Law clk. to presiding justice Franklin County Probate Ct., Columbus, Ohio, 1976-78; bank officer Huntington Bank, Columbus, 1978-81; mgr. loan rev. Nat. Bank of Washington, 1981-82; asst. v.p. Shawmut Bank, Boston, 1983-85; sole practice Columbus and Washington, 1985—. Fin. advisor Elliott Richardson for Senate, Boston, 1984; mem. Rep. Nat. Com., Washington, 1983—. Mem. ABA (banking law subcom. 1981—), D.C. Bar Assn., Columbus Bar Assn. Office: 6649 N High St Suite 105 Columbus OH 43085

HARMON, R. E., transportation company executive. Pres. R.W. Harmon and Sons, Inc., Belton, Mo. Office: R W Harmon & Ss Inc 17327 S 71 Hwy Belton MO 64012 *

HARMS, PHYLLIS RAE MAHNKE, social services administrator; b. Milw., May 26, 1925; d. Louis William and Clara C.S. (Albrecht) Mahnke; m. Paul W.F. Harms, June 24, 1950; children: Steven P., Rae Antoinette, Claudia N., Nathan S., Caleb D., Seth S. BA, Valparaiso (Ind.) U., 1947; postgrad., Washington U., St. Louis, 1949. Sec. Immanuel Luth. Ch., Valparaiso, 1946-49; recorder Concordia Sem., St. Louis, 1949-50; tchr. Ashland (Oreg.) Schs., 1950-51; exec. asst. Ohio Nurses Assn., Columbus, 1977-85; adminstrv. asst. Luth. Social Services, Columbus, 1985—. Pres. Trinity Luth. Ch., Columbus, 1982-86; v.p. So. Ohio Synod Evang. Luth. Ch.in Am., 1987—. Mem. AAUW. Democrat. Avocation: ch. choir. Office: Luth Social Services 57 E Main St Columbus OH 43215

HARMSEN, LARRY JAMES, manufacturing executive, chemical engineer; b. Rock Rapids, Iowa, Aug. 1, 1939; s. Walter George and Lenore (Nelson) H.; m. Sally Ann Ringler, June 5, 1982; children: Jeffrey Scott, Peter Fraser Richards, Todd Michael. BSChemE, U. Iowa, 1962; LLB, LaSalle Extention U., Chgo., 1972. Registered profl. chem. engr., Minn. Dir. mfg. Honeywell Inc., Denver, 1980-82; mgr. research and devel. engring. Honeywell Inc., Rockford, Ill., 1982-83, v.p. engring. quality, 1983-84; v.p. engring. quality Motor and Control div. Pacific Sci., Rockford, 1984-85, v.p., dir., 1985—. Patentee plastic blood slide. Republican. Lutheran. Club: 351 Soccer. Avocations: golfing, skiing, fishing. Home: 4961 Brookview Rd Rockford IL 61107 Office: Pacific Sci Motor & Control Div 4301 Kishwaukee St Rockford IL 61109

HARNAGEL, JOHN ANDREW, school social worker; b. Des Moines, Mar. 18, 1944; s. Willard Wiegner and Madeleine (Franks) H.; m. Ardis Kay Vermazen, July 20, 1968; 1 child, Rachel Annette. BA, U. Iowa, 1966; MSW, Loyola U., Chgo., 1970. Cert. social worker, Ill. Caseworker Cook County Pub. Aid, Chgo., Ill., 1966-68; therapist Cen. Bapt. Children's Home, Lake Villa, Ill., unit supr., 1970-75, program adminstr., 1975-81; social worker Lake Villa Pub. Schs., 1981—; part-time pvt. practice Grayslake, Ill., 1972—; cons. Cen. Bapt. Children's Home, 1981-83, Allendale Sch. Boys, Lake Villa, 1985—. Bd. Edn. Grayslake Sch. Dist., 1979-86, pres. 1981-86; trustee Village of Grayslake, 1983—; gov. bd. Special Edn. Dist. Lake County, Ill., 1979-83; bd. dirs. Lake County Crisis Ctr., 1979-81, Cen. Bapt. Family Services, Lake Villa, 1984-85. Mem. Nat. Assn. Social Workers. Republican. Lodge: Lions. Avocations: watersports, gardening, reading, family vacations, writing. Home: 332 Highland Rd Grayslake IL 60030

HARNED, ROGER KENT, radiology educator; b. Madison, Wis., June 19, 1934; s. Lewis Boyer and Ermil Amelia (Caldwell) H.; m. Jacquelyn Sue Heal, Aug. 29, 1959; children: Roger Kent II, Jennifer Marie. BS, U. Wis., 1956; MD, U. Va., 1961. Am. Bd. Radiology. Intern Milw. County Gen. Hosp., 1961-62; resident in radiology Deaconess Hosp., Milw. Children's Hosps., 1964-67; instr. dept. radiology U. Va. Sch. Medicine, Charlottesville, 1967-68; from asst. to assoc. prof. radiology U. Nebr. Sch. Medicine, Omaha, 1969-79, prof. radiology, 1974—; cons. physician Omaha Vets. Hosp., 1969—; grad. faculty U. Nebr., Omaha, 1972—; peer rev. various med. jours. Contbr. articles on gastrointestinal radiology to profl. jours. Mem. Am. Coll. Radiology (fellow 1980, Armed Forces Inst. of Pathology disting. scientist position 1987-88), Radiological Soc. N.Am., Nebr. Radiological Soc. (pres. 1982-83), Soc. Gastrointestinal Radiologists (pres. elect 1986-87, pres. 1987-88). Republican. Presbyterian. Avocations: western art and history, photography, fly fishing. Home: 12624 Martha St Omaha NE 68144 Office: U Nebr Med Ctr Dept Radiology 42d & Dewey Ave Omaha NE 68105

HARNER, STEPHEN GLEN, otolaryngologist; b. Winston-Salem, N.C., Aug. 21, 1940; s. Casper Glendon and Wanda Rae (Carmichael) H.; m. Carla June Kelly, Aug. 24, 1963; children: Kelly Ann, Jeffrey Glenn. AB, Washington U., St. Louis, 1962; MD, U. Mo., 1965. Cert. Bd. Otolaryngology, 1971. Commd. 2d lt. U.S. Army, 1964, advanced through grades to maj.; intern Brooke Army Hosp, San Antonio, 1965-66; resident in surgery Reynolds Army Hosp., Ft. Sill, Okla., 1966-67; resident in otolaryngology Fitzsimons Army Hosp., Denver, 1968-70; asst. chief otolaryngology Letterman Army Hosp., San Francisco, 1970-73; resigned U.S. Army, 1973; staff otolaryngologist Mayo Clinic, Rochester, Minn., 1973—; assoc. prof. otolaryngology Mayo Med. Sch., 1986—. Contbr. articles to profl. jours. Bd. dirs. Hiawatha Homes, Rochester, 1980—, sec., 1986—. Named Tchr. of Yr., Mayo Fellow's Assn., 1979, 84, 86. Fellow ACS, Am. Acad. Otolaryngology, Am. Otologic Rhinologic & Laryngologic Assn., Am. Otologic Soc.; mem. AMA, Minn. Med. Assn., Zumbro Valley Med. Assn., Soc. Univ. Otolaryngologists. Lutheran. Avocatins: photography, travelling, boating, running. Office: Mayo Clinic 200 1st St SW Rochester MN 55905

HARNISH, ALBERT GUILFORD, JR., investment company executive; b. Boston, Feb. 9, 1934; s. Albert Guilford and Alice Francis (Conniff) H.; m. Joan Carol Sudbey, July 17, 1933; children: Steven G., Eric A., Christopher G. BS in Mgmt., Boston U., 1955; MBA in Fin., Golden Gate U., 1980. Commd. capt. U.S. Army, 1960, advanced through grades to lt. col., 1970, ret., 1976; pres. ISF, Inc., Virginia Beach, Va., 1977-80; sr. v.p. Dunn & Hargitt, Inc., Lafayette, Ind., 1980—. Author: Winning With Options, 1977; editor newsletter Market Guide, 1977-81. Decorated Bronze Star, Air medal, Legion of Merit. Mem. Nat. Futures Assn., Nat. Assn. Futures Trading Advisors, Internat. Assn. Fin. Planners, Assn. U.S. Army. Republican. Roman Catholic. Avocations: writing, photography. Home: 2106 Birch Ln Lafayette IN 47905 Office: Dunn & Hargitt Inc PO Box 1100 22 #2d St Lafayette IN 47902

HARO, JOHN CALVIN, architect; b. East Chicago, Ind., June 18, 1928; s. John Henry and Lydia (Lind) H.; m. Elizabeth Alison Smith, Dec. 26, 1954; children: John Stephen, Alexander James, Alison Margaret. Student, Mich. Technol. U., 1945-47; B.Arch., U. Mich., 1950; M.Arch., Harvard U., 1955. With firm Sanders & Malsin (Architects), Ann Arbor, Mich., 1950-51; firm Minoru Yamasaki & Assos., Detroit, 1952-54; with Albert Kahn Assos., Inc. (Architects & Engrs.), Detroit, 1955-73; asso. Albert Kahn Assos., Inc. (Architects & Engrs.), 1959-63, v.p., chief archtl. designer, 1963-73; also dir.; v.p., corporate dir. design Smith Hinchman & Grylls Assos., Inc. (Architects, Engrs., Planners), Detroit, 1973-77; v.p., dir. planning and design Albert Kahn Assos., 1977—; Instr. Boston Archtl. Center, 1954; adj. prof. Coll. Architecture and Design, U. Mich., 1972, 76, 77, Coll. Architecture and Urban Planning, U. Mich., 1976-78, chmn. alumni adv. bd., 1984—. Projects include physics and astronomy bldg., 1963, office and classroom bldg., 1971, both, U. Mich., Air Terminal Bldg, City Detroit, 1966; die and engring. facility, Gen. Motors Corp., Flint, Mich., 1968, also adminstrv. office bldg., Saginaw, Mich., 1969, southeastern br. facilities, Avon Products, Inc., Atlanta, 1970, Children's Hosp. of Mich, Detroit, 1971, office and pub. facilities, Washington Post, 1971, distbg. and mfg. facility, Eli Lilly Co., Indpls., 1974, Am. Motors Corp. office bldg, Southfield Mich., 1975, Owens Corning Fiberglas Tech. Center, Granville, Ohio, 1976, John Deere Engring. Mfg. Bldg, Waterloo, Iowa, 1976, Detroit Free Press, 1977, Ford Motor Co. Mfg. Bldg, Batavia, Ohio, 1980, Univ. Hosp., U. Mich., 1985. Mem. Detroit Inst. Arts, 1965—, Art. Assn. Birmingham, Mich., 1965—; mem. planning bd., City of Birmingham, 1971-76; trustee Founders Soc. Detroit Inst. Arts, 1974-80; bd. dirs. Birmingham Community House, 1976-79, New Center Area Council, 1978—, New Center Found., 1980—. Served to lt. (j.g.) USNR, 1951-52. Wheelwright Traveling fellow Harvard, 1960. Fellow A.I.A. (Gold medal from Detroit chpt. 1984); mem. Engring. Soc. Detroit, U. Mich. Coll. Architecture and Urban Design Alumni Assn. (chmn. bd. govs. 1985). Office: Albert Kahn Assos New Center Bldg Detroit MI 48202

HARP, DANA L., sales and marketing executive; b. Dayton, Ohio, Mar. 11, 1950; s. Lorrie Albert and Ruth Agnes (Pohlkotte) H.; m. Barbara Eichner, Aug. 21, 1971; children: Darren Matthew, Christine Elizabeth. Student, Sinclair Community Coll., 1969-71. Printing asst. Reynolds & Reynolds, Dayton, 1969-71, printing estimator, 1971-76, purchasing agt., 1976-78, sales rep., 1978-80; sales rep. John K. Howe Co., Dayton, 1981-83, v.p. sales, 1983—. Dir. projects Midwest chpt. Immune Deficiency Found., 1984—; active Bellbrook Wee Eagles. Mem. Ky. Bus. Advt. Assn., Adminstrv. Mgmt. Soc. Republican. Lodges: Lions. Avocations: basketball, golf. Home: 4100 Locus Bend Dr Dayton OH 45440

HARP, MICHAEL THOMAS, insurance company executive; b. Chgo., Feb. 13, 1946; s. Hugh T. and Rita M. (Charbonneau) H.; m. Sharon R. Collett, Apr. 20, 1968; children: Michelle, Troy, Tammy. BA in Econs., U. Nebr., Omaha, 1969; MBA, Cen. Mo. State U., 1976, MS in Indsl. Mgmt., 1978. Sr. field rep. Aetna Life & Casualty, Kansas City, Mo., 1971-80; resident v.p. Allied Group, Des Moines, 1980-83; v.p. comml. lines Md. Casualty, Balt., 1983-85; pres. and chief exec. officer Federated Rural Electric Ins. Co., Lenexa, Kans., 1985—. Served with U.S. Army, 1969-71. Club: Brookridge Country (Overland Park, Kans.). Avocations: boating, skiing, hunting, flying. Office: Federated Rural Electric Ins Co 11875 W 85th Lenexa KS 66215

HARPER, CHARLES MICHEL, food company executive; b. Lansing, Mich., Sept. 26, 1927; s. Charles Frost and Alma (Michel) H.; m. Joan Frances Bruggema, June 24, 1950; children: Kathleen Harper Wenngatz, Carolyn Harper, Charles Michel, Elizabeth Harper Murphy. BS in Mech. Engring, Purdue U., 1949; MBA, U. Chgo., 1950. Supr. methods engring. Oldsmobile div. Gen. Motors Corp., Detroit, 1950-54; indsl. engr. Pillsbury Co., Mpls., 1954-55; dir. indsl. engring. Pillsbury Co., 1955-60, dir. engring., 1961-66, v.p. research, devel. and new products, 1965-70, group v.p.-poultry, food service and venture businesses, 1970-74; exec. v.p., chief operating officer, dir. Conagra Inc., Omaha, 1974-76; pres., chief exec. officer Conagra Inc., 1976-81, chmn. bd., chief exec. officer, 1981—; bd. dirs. Norwest Corp., Valmont Industries, Inc., Peter Kiewit Sons', Inc., Burlington No., Inc.; exec. com. Nat. Commn. on Agrl. Trade and Export Policy, 1984—. Mem. council Village of Excelsior (Minn.), 1965-70, mayor, 1974; trustee Bishop Clarkson Meml. Hosp.; hon. chmn. Urban League Nebr. Membership Campaign, 1987; bd. dirs. Creighton U.; trustee Com. for Econ. Devel., Washington; pres. Mid Am. Council Boy Scouts Am., 1983-84. Served with AUS, 1946-48. Mem. U.S. C. of C. (bd. dirs., chmn. Food and Agriculture com.), Omaha C. of C. (chmn. 1979), Grocery Mfrs. Am. (bd. dirs. 1985—), Bus. Roundtable, Ak-Sar-Ben (gov.), U. Nebr.-Lincoln Coll. Bus. Admin. Alumni Assn. (hon. life), Beta Theta Pi. Office: ConAgra Inc One Central Park Plaza Omaha NE 68102

HARPER, ERNEST BOULDIN, JR., industrial merger consultant; b. Kalamazoo, Aug. 7, 1924; s. Ernest Bouldin and Lyssa Desha (Chalkley) H.; m. Catherine Matthews Weld, Oct. 7, 1961; children: Ernest Bouldin III, Catherine Matthews. BSEE, U. Mich., 1948; MBA, Harvard U., 1950. Sales mgr. Westinghouse Electric, Pitts., 1950-60; v.p. H.K. Porter, Pitts.,

1960-65; asst. to pres. ITT, N.Y.C., 1965-71; pres. E.B. Harper & Co., Lake Forest, Ill., 1971—. Mem. Am. Mktg. Assn., Assn. Corp. Growth, Midwest Planning Assn. (bd. dirs.). Republican. Episcopalian. Home: 509 College Rd Lake Forest IL 60045 Office: EB Harper & Co Inc 222 Wisconsin Lake Forest IL 60045

HARPER, GARY LEE, small business owner; b. Oakland City, Ind., May 25, 1937; s. Hallie Hansel and Annabell (Dishon) H.; m. Margaret Earl McConnell, Dec. 29, 1964. BS, Oakland City Coll., 1964; MS, U. Evansville, 1974. Instr. Carnegie Coll., Cleve., 1959-60; chemist Whirlpool Corp., Evansville, Ind., 1966-68; tchr. North Gibson Schs., Princeton, Ind., 1970-75; owner Oaks Printing Co., Oakland City, 1976-86. Publisher, editor Pike-Gibson Shopper, 1978-81. Pres. United Way of Gibson County, 1985; bd. dirs. United Way of Ind., Indpls., 1986—, Oakland City Coll. Found., 1983; rep. Rep. State Convention, Indpls., 1984-86. Served with U.S. Army, 1964-66. Recipient Vol. award United Way, 1985; named Future Ind. Leader Pub. Service Ind., 1984. Mem. NEA, Ind. State Tchrs. Assn. Republican. Methodist. Lodge: Kiwanis (pres. Oakland CIty 1983-84, lt. gov. Ind. 1986—), Elks, Shriners. Home and Office: 831 W College St Oakland City IN 47660

HARPER, JAMES EARL, III, paper industry executive; b. Bethesda, Md., Dec. 17, 1948; s. James E. Jr. and Dorothy Anne (Clark) H.; m. Sonja Theodora Aleida Huisert, Sept. 7, 1971 (div. June 1987); children: Tamara, Stephen; m. Beverly Deniece Tinsley, Aug. 3, 1987. BS in Engring., Johns Hopkins U., 1970; MBA, U. Pa., 1973. Sr. systems analyst Mgmt. Decisions Devel. Corp. div. Measurex Corp., Fairfield, Ohio, 1970-71, pres., 1981-86; pres. CIMCON Assocs., Fairfield, 1986—; bus. analyst Xerox Corp., Rochester, N.Y. and Greenwich, Conn., 1973-77; planning mgr. Xerox Corp., Rochester, 1979-81. Mem. Paper Industry Mgmt. Assn., Tech. Assn. Pulp and Paper Industry (author, presentor papers at conf. 1985, 87). Lodge: Rotary. Avocation: sailing. Home: 14 Palmer Ct Fairfield OH 45014 Office: Cimcon Assocs PO Box 9008 Fairfield OH 45014

HARPER, OLIVER WILLIAM, III, corporate plan consultant; b. Chgo., Nov. 25, 1953; s. Oliver William and Pauline W. (Simpson) H.; m. Patricia Ruth Hayes, Mar. 9, 1979; 1 son, Oliver William. B.A., U. Ill.-Chgo., 1978. Agt., Occidental Life of Calif., 1979; registered rep. Lincoln Nat. Life Ins. Co., Ft. Wayne, Ind., 1979-80; agt., registered rep. Penn Mut. Life Ins. Co., Phila., 1980-85; dir. employee benefit div. Penn Fin. Group, Chgo., 1981-85; chief exec. officer, exec. v.p. Corp. Plan Cons., Inc., 1985—. Dir. St. Edmund's Credit Union; co-chair bd. dirs. St. Edmund's Ch. Mem. Nat. Assn. Securities Dealers, Cert. Employee Benefit Specialists, Profl. Assn. Diving Instr., Chgo. Assn. Life Underwriters, Nat. Assn. Life Underwriters, Notaries Assn. Ill., U. Ill. Alumni Assn., Underwater Explorers Soc. Episcopalian. Club: Masons.

HARPER, RICHARD L., sales executive; b. Belleville, Ill., Mar. 28, 1956; s. Horace Edwin Jr. and Evelyn Ruth (Wright) H.; m. Joy Adair Clayton, May 31, 1986. BA, Principia Coll., 1980; MBA, U. Miami, 1982. Owner Kopyrich Printing, St. Louis, 1973-76; dist. mgr. Browning Mfg. Co., Maysville, Ky., 1983-84; sales engr. State Electric Co., St. Louis, 1985—; tchr. Belleville Area Coll., Granite City, Ill., 1985—; cons. Scharf Tax Services, St. Louis, 1984—. Contbr. articles to newspapers; photographer (video) Mo. Concert Ballet, 1986. Mem. work coms. First Ch. of Christ, Scientist, Brentwood, Mo., 1986 . Republican. Home: 7454 Hazel Ave Maplewood MO 63143 Office: State Electric Co 1977 Congressional Dr Saint Louis MO 63146

HARPER, ROGER WESLEY, consumer products co. exec.; b. Youngstown, Ohio, July 11, 1933; s. Harry Edward and Helen Marjorie (Young) H.; B.A., Wittenberg U., 1956. Sales rep. Shell Oil Co., Cleve., 1958-62, Chicopee Mills, Inc., N.Y.C., 1962-64; sales rep. H.H. Cutler Co., Grand Rapids, Mich., 1964-68; exec. v.p. Scharp Contemporary, Inc., Columbus, Ohio, 1968-77, now dir.; chmn., pres. Am. Leather Village, Inc., Columbus, 1977—. Served with U.S. Army, 1956-58. Lutheran. Home and Office: 622 Indian Mound Rd Columbus OH 43213

HARPER, STEPHEN RAY, data processing executive; b. Cin., Sept. 28, 1949; s. Robert Herrold and Eva Jeane (Alexander) H.; m. Becky Lou Jones, Aug. 12, 1972; children: Stephen Robert, Martha Anne. AAS in Computer Sci., Prairie State Coll., 1973. Programmer Evans Furs, Chgo., 1975-76; computer operator Thrall Car Mfg. Co., Chicago Heights, Ill., 1973-75, sr. programmer analyst, 1976-78; data processing mgr. Greene Cos. Internat., Oakbrook, Ill., 1978-83, Royal Crown Bottling Co., Chgo., 1983-86. Mem. Common User Group, Ill. System 38 User Group. Republican. Baptist. Home: 4730 W 183d St Country Club Hills IL 60477 Office: Royal Crown Bottling Co 2801 W 47th St Chicago IL 60632

HARPER, WILLIAM VICTOR, statistician, administrator; b. Blue Island, Ill., July 17, 1949; s. Cecil Victor and Ila Lily (Adderson) H. B.S. summa cum laude, Ohio State U., 1973, M.S., 1976, Ph.D., 1984. Statistician Ross Labs., Columbus, Ohio, 1976-77, mgr., 1977-78; research scientist Battelle Meml. Inst., Columbus, 1978-81, statistician, project mgr., 1981-86, sect. mgr., 1986—. Contbr. articles to profl. jours. Served with USAF, 1967-71. Mem. Am Statis. Assn., Am. Soc. Quality Control, Assn. Computing Machinery, Materials Research Soc., Columbus Statis. Assn. (pres. 1982-85). Presbyterian. Clubs: Running, Ski. Avocations: running; white water rafting; camping. Office: Battelle Project Mgmt Div 505 King Ave Columbus OH 43201

HARPER-NEAL, DEBORAH LEE, nurse; b. Indpls., July 1, 1955; s. Harry Webster Harper and Frances Lucille (Taylor) Neal; divorced; children: Jonathan Randolph, Jennifer Reneé, Jeremy Robert. Surgical Technologist degree, Ind. Vocat. Coll., 1975; Nursing degree, Ind. U., 1985. Scrub nurse Dr. R.W. Jones-Ob-Gyn., Indpls., 1975-80, Meth. Hosp., Indpls., 1980-85; prin. Harpers' Prep Child Care Facility, Indpls., 1985-86. Contr. articles to newspaper, 1986. Writer fine arts com. New Bethel Baptist Ch., 1984-86. Mem. Black Arts Cognizance Assn. (founder 1986—). Avocations: swimming, reading. Home: 3741 Graceland Ave Indianapolis IN 46208

HARR, GALE ANN, school psychologist; b. Youngstown, Ohio, June 21, 1955; d. William Brown and Marilyn Jean (Pratt) Roberts; m. Richard Kenneth Harr, Oct. 8, 1977; 1 child, Brandon Scott. BA, Mount Union Coll., 1977; MEd, Kent State U., 1979, EdS, 1981, postgrad. Cert. sch. psychologist, Ohio; cert. secondary tchr., Ohio. Substitute tchr. Summit County (Ohio) Schs., 1978-80; intern in sch. psychology Stow (Ohio) City Schs., 1980-81; sch. psychologist Maple Heights (Ohio) Schs., 1981-85, coordinator spl. pupil services, 1985—. Columnist Maple Heights Press., 1982—. Organizer, leader Chem. Abuse Reduced by Edn., Maple Heights, 1981—. Mem. Nat. Assn. Sch. Psychologists, Ohio Sch. Psychologists Assn. (planning com. 1986-87), Cleve. Assn. Sch. Psychologists (program com. 1986-87), Alpha Chi Omega. Avocations: reading, cooking, gymnastics, outdoor sports, music. Home: 2918 Chautauqua Dr Silver Lake OH 44224 Office: Maple Heights City Schs 5965 Dunham Rd Maple Heights OH 44137

HARR, LUCY LORAINE, association executive; b. Sparta, Wis., Dec. 2, 1951; d. Ernest Donald Harr and Dorothy Catherine (Heinz) Harr Vetter. B.S., U. Wis.-Madison, 1976, M.S., 1978. Lectr. U. Wis., Madison, 1977-82; asst. editor Everybody's Money Credit Union Nat. Assn., Madison, 1979-80; assoc. editor Everybody's Money Credit Union Nat. Assn., 1980-82, editor Everybody's Money, 1982-84, v.p. pub. relations, 1984—; dir. Ford Motor Co. Consumer Appeals Bd., Milw. Mgr. ann. report Credit Union Nat. Assn., 1984. Bd. dirs. Madison Area Crimestoppers, 1982-84. Recipient Clarion award, 1982. Mem. Women in Communications (pres. Madison profl. chpt. 1982-83, nat. v.p. programs 1986—), Internat. Assn. Bus. Communicators (program chmn. dist. meeting 1981), Am. Soc. Assn. Execs. (Gold Circle award 1984). Avocations: biking; reading. Home: Box 55143 Madison WI 53705 Office: Credit Union Nat Assn Inc Box 431 5710 Mineral Point Rd Madison WI 53701

HARRAL, WILLIAM MICHAEL, manufacturing company executive; b. Chillicothe, Ohio, Apr. 22, 1942; s. Edgar Augustas and M. Kathryn (Courtright) H.; m. Sydney Sue Laver, May 21, 1966; children: Michael Guy, James Richard. BS in Indsl. Engring., Ohio State U., 1965; MBA, U. Mich., 1968. Registered profl. engr., Ohio; cert. quality engr.; cert. reliability engr. Grad. fellow U. Mich., Ann Arbor; with Ford Motor Co., Dearborn, Mich., 1963-83, supr., 1967-73, mgr., 1973-83; dir. Arch Assoc., Northville, Mich., 1984—; bd. dirs. Hi Line Products; affiliate Computrain Inc.; assoc. Mgmt. Devel. Services Inc. Inventor engring. design. Mem. Ohio State U. Alumni, U. Mich. Alumni, Livonia C. of C., So. Wayne County C. of C., Am. Soc. Quality Control (vice-chmn. programs greater Detroit sect., nat. tech. publ. com. automotive div., chmn. tech. publs. promotion and distbn., authoring com. 1987), Automotive Industry Action Group (continuing quality project team, supplier cert. subcom., stats. applications subcom., Growth Opportunity Alliance of Greater Lawrence (research), Inst. Indsl. Engrs. (sr.) Engring. Soc. Detroit, Am. Soc. Tng. and Devel. (local, nat.). Republican. Methodist. Lodge: Masons. Avocations: reading, golf, auto racing. Home: 15770 Robinwood Dr Northville MI 48167

HARRELL, JAMES THOMAS, business executive; b. Newport, Ky., Oct. 21, 1936; s. William Thomas and Stella May (Jones) H.; B.B.A., U. Cin., 1960; M.B.A., Xavier U., 1969; certificate in mgmt. acctg., 1977. With Miami Margarine Co., Cin., 1963—, asst. controller, 1977—. Served with U.S. Army, 1962-63. Mem. Nat. Assn. Accts., Delta Sigma Pi, Beta Alpha Psi. Episcopalian. Home: 9191 New Haven Rd Harrison OH 45030 Office: 5226 Vine St Cincinnati OH 45217

HARRELL, JOHN LIMPUS, fundraising consultant; b. Frankfort, Ind., May 9, 1918; s. Jesse Albert and Mildred Vale (Limpus) H.; A.B., Franklin Coll., 1940; M.A., Ohio State U., 1941; m. Helen Vernon Schumacher, Nov. 23, 1943; 1 dau., Helen F. Asst. dir. Duluth (Minn.) Community Fund, 1941-43; exec. sec. Community Chest and War Chest, Green Bay, Wis., 1943-46; exec. dir. Community Chest, Watertown, N.Y., 1946-50, Cedar Rapids, Iowa, 1950-54; exec. dir. United Way of Wyandotte County, Kans., 1954-79; ret., 1979; fundraising cons., 1980—. Med. field agt. SSS, 1943-46; treas. Kans. Conf. Social Welfare, 1964-66; mem. Human Relations Commn., Kansas City, 1966-75, vice chmn., 1970-71; mem. Manpower Planning Bd., City-County Consortia, 1975-79; mem. citizens adv. com. Kans. Dept. Social Rehab. Services, 1976-79; bd. dirs., cons. Econ. Opportunity Found., Inc., 1965-79. Recipient Silver Bow award, Boy Scouts Am., 1972, Com. award, YMCA, 1972, Service award United Way of Am., 1972; Service Appreciation award Econ. Opportunity Found., Inc., 1974, Founder's award, 1976; Community Services Adminstrn. Service award, 1980; Appreciation awards AFL-CIO Tri-County Labor Council Eastern Kans., 1979, Cath. Social Services, 1979; Charter Dir. Recognition award Kans. Citizens Council on Aging, 1980. Mem. Kappa Delta Rho. Republican. Baptist. Clubs: Rotary, Elks. Home: Rural Route 1 Box 194B Michigantown IN 46057

HARRELL, ROBERT LEWIS, fire chief; b. Sedalia, Mo., May 5, 1944; s. Clarence R. Ray and Ada M. (Carver) H.; m. Patricia Ann Carnes, June 5, 1965; 1 child, Amber Flame. Assoc. in Sci., Penn Valley Community Coll., 1977. With Platter Rivial Mfg. Co., Sedalia, Mo., 1962-70; firefighter City of Sedalia, 1970-76; fire chief, City of Clinton (Mo.), 1976—; vol. fireman Pettis County Vol. Fire Dept., Sedalia, 1967-76. Chmn. Henry County chpt. ARC, Clinton, 1980-85; bd. dirs. Pettis County Muscular Dystrophy Assn., Sedalia, 1967-72; fund drive chmn. Muscular Dystrophy Assn., Kansas City chpt., Clinton, 1978-84; chmn. Clinton Tourism Com., 1985-86. Served with U.S. Army, 1965-67. Mem. Internat. Assn. Fire Chiefs (mem. emergency med. services com.), Mo. Fire Chiefs, Mo. Firefighters Assn., Nat. Fire Protection Assn., Mo. Emergency Mgmt. Assn., Profl. Fire and Fraud Investigators Assn. (bd. dirs.). Avocations: boating, fishing. Home: 1101 S Water Clinton MO 64735 Office: City Clinton Fire Dept 301 S Washington Clinton MO 64735

HARRELL, SAMUEL MACY, grain company executive; b. Indpls., Jan. 4, 1931; s. Samuel Runnels and Mary (Evans) H.; m. Sally Bowers, Sept. 2, 1958; children: Samuel D., Holly Evans, Kevin Bowers, Karen Susan, Donald Runnels, Kenneth Macy. B.S. in Econs., Wharton Sch., U. Pa., 1953. Pres., chmn. bd., chief exec. officer, chmn., exec. com. Early & Daniel Industries, Cin., 1971—; chmn. bd., chmn. ecec. com. Early & Daniel Co., Cin., 1971—; chmn. bd., chief exec. officer, chmn. exec. com. Tidewater Grain Co., Phila., 1971—; dir. Wainwright Bank & Trust Co., Wainright Abstract Co., Nat. Grain Trade Council, U.S. Feed Grains Council; mem. Chgo. bd. Trade. Served with AUS, 1953-55. Mem. Young Pres.'s Orgn., U. Pa. Alumni Assn. (past pres.), Terminal Elevator Grain Mchts. Assn. (dir.), Millers Nat. Fedn. (dir.), Assn. Operative Millers, Am. Soc. Bakery Engrs., Am. Fin. Assn., Council on Fgn. Relations, Fin. Exec. Inst., N.Am. Grain Export Assn. (dir.), Mpls. Grain Exchange, St. Louis Mchts. Grain Exchange, Buffalo Corn Exchange, Delta Tau Delta (Past prs. Ind. alumni). Presbyterian. Clubs: Columbia, Indpls. Athletic, Woodstock, Traders Point Hunt, Dramatic, Players, Lambs (Indpls.); Racquet (Phila.); University (Washington); Univ. (N.Y.C.). Lodges: Masons; Rotary. Home: 5858 Sunset Ln Indianapolis IN 46208 Office: 525 Carr St Cincinnati OH 45203

HARRIGAN, JINNI ANNE, medical educator; b. Cin., Nov. 15, 1946; d. Robert James and Virginia Anne (Diskin) H.; m. Dennis M. O'Connell, Apr. 17, 1982; 1 child, Kelly Marie. Cert. RN summa cum laude, St. Elizabeth's Hosp., Covington, Ky., 1967; BA in Psychology summa cum laude, U. Cin., 1975, MA, 1977, PhD, 1979. Cert. clin. psychologist, Ohio. Operating room nurse dept. surgery U. Cin., 1967-72, teaching/research asst. grad. studies, 1975-79, instr. dept. edn., 1979-80, asst. prof. Med. Sch., 1980-86, postdoctoral fellow clin. psychology, 1984-87, research dir. Dept. Family Medicine, 1984—, assoc. prof. Med. Sch., 1986—. Contbr. articles to profl. jours. U. Cin. Research Council grantee, 1979. Mem. Internat. Communication Assn., Am. Anthrop. Assn., Am. Psychol. Assn., Soc. Tchrs. Family Medicine, Friends of Women's Studies, NOW, Nat. Arbor Assn. Avocations: photography, pottery, jewelry making. Home: 3493 Brookline Ave Cincinnati OH 45220 Office: U Cin Dept Family Medicine Mail Location #582 231 Bethesda Ave Cincinnati OH 45267

HARRIMAN, RICHARD LEE, educator; b. Independence, Mo., Sept. 10, 1932; s. Walter S. and M. Eloise (Faulkner) H.; A.B., William Jewell Coll., 1953, Litt.D. (hon.), 1983. M.A., Stanford U., 1959. Instr., asst. prof. English U. Dubuque, Iowa, 1960-62; asst. prof. English, William Jewell Coll., Liberty, Mo., 1962, acting head English dept., 1965-69, dir. fine arts program, 1965—, asso. prof., 1966—. Treas. Kansas City Arts Council, 1980, sec., 1981. Served from pvt. to cpl., AUS, 1953-55. Woodrow Wilson fellow, 1957. Mem. Shakespeare Assn. Am., MLA, Assn. Coll. Univ. and Community Arts Adminstrs. (nat. exec. bd. 1975-78), Nat. Council Tchrs. English, AAUP, Lambda Chi Alpha, Sigma Tau Delta, Alpha Psi Omega. Meth. Home: Route 5 Box 6 Liberty MO 64068

HARRINGTON, LELAND RAY, service company executive; b. St. Louis, Mar. 24, 1946; s. James Franklin and Edith Mae (Clapp) H.; m. Ruth Lillian Longwell, Sept. 26, 1978; children: Monica S., Lori A., Winston S. Sales, security cons. Honeywell Corp., Tulsa, 1973-79; regional acct. mgr. Honeywell Corp., Dallas, 1980, regional sales mgr., 1981-82; nat. mgr. of nat. accts. Honeywell Corp., Mpls., 1982-83, br. gen. mgr. Twin Cities area, 1984—. Mem. Franklin Ave Bus. Assn. (pres.). Methodist. Avocations: piano, stamp collecting, golf, fishing, reading. Home: 8073 Timberlake Dr Eden Prairie MN 55344 Office: Honeywell Corp 2020 Bloomington Ave Minneapolis MN 55404

HARRINGTON, SHERMAN B., accountant; b. Jackson, Mich., Nov. 28, 1948; s. Bryce Eddile and Luella Evelyn (Dresselhouse) H.; m. Susan Lynn Filut, May 9, 1970; 1 child, Steven. BS in Bus., U. Mich., 1970, MS in Bus., 1971. Tax specialist Peat, Marwick, Mitchell & Co., Ann Arbor, Mich., 1970-76; tax mgr. Curtis, Bailey, Exelby & Sposito, Ann Arbor, 1976-79; ptnr. tax dept. Wright, Griffin, Davis & Co., Ann Arbor, 1979—. Pres. Washtenaw Estate Planning Council, Ann Arbor, 1980; elder, trustee 1st Presbyn. Ch., Ypsilanti, Mich., 1984-86; campaign treas. Thomas Shea for Dist. Judge, Ypsilanti, 1984; mem. allocation com. Washtenaw United Way, Ann Arbor, 1985-86; bd. dirs. Children Are People, Inc., Ann Arbor, 1986-87. Mem. Am. Inst. CPA's, Mich. Assn. CPA's (co-chmn. chpt. sec. 1986). Club: Chippewa Hills (Ypsilanti). Avocation: golf. Home: 340 Carriage Way Ypsilanti MI 48197 Office: Wright Griffin Davis & Co 480 City Center Bldg Ann Arbor MI 48104

HARRIS, ALLAN CLARENCE, banker; b. Martins Ferry, Ohio, Nov. 16, 1937; s. Henry Chester and Mary (Nedved) H.; m. Reba Mae Scott, May 25, 1957; children: Greggory Allan, Timothy Scott. Student, Am. Banking Inst., 1955-62. Various positions Toledo Trust Co., 1955—, mgr. securitites movement, 1973—. Deacon Judson Bapt. Ch., Toledo, 1983—; auditor Western Lake Erie Hist. Orgn., Toledo, 1980-85. Mem. Internat. Naval Research Orgn. (v.p. 1968—). Avocations: warship history, building radio-controlled model ships. Home: 1729 Lois Ct Toledo OH 43613 Office: Toledo Trust Co Operations Ctr Monroe St Toledo OH 43604

HARRIS, BOB FRANK, printing company executive, educator; b. Evansville, Ind., Mar. 12, 1941; s. Thomas and Anna Martha (Schumacher) H.; m. Barbara Jean Harris, Aug. 14, 1965; children—Brian James, Brent Earl. B.S., Ind. State U., 1965, M.S., 1967. Tchr. Montgomery County schs., Rockville, Md., 1965-66, Evansville-Vanderburgh Schs., Evansville, Ind., 1967-80; pres. Graphic Supply of Evansville, Inc., 1980-85. Chmn. Big Bend dist. Troop 350, Boy Scouts Am., mem. Buffalo Trace council; pres., Scott Twp. Civic Club, Evansville, 1974-76; tax adv. bd. Scott Twp., 1978-82; trustee, assessor Scott Twp., Vanderburgh, 1983—; mem. blood council ARC, Evansville, 1983—; pres. Scott Sch. PTA, 1982-85, New Harmony (Ind.) Schs., 1986—. Served with U.S. Army, 1960-63. Mem. NEA, Am. Indsl. Arts Assn., Ind. Indsl. Arts Assn., Phi Delta Kappa, Epsilon Pi Tau. Lodges: Masons, Shriners. Home: 1730 Montview Dr Evansville IN 47711 Office: Graphic Supply of Evansville Inc Rural Route #8 Box 168G Evansville IN 47711

HARRIS, BRUCE ALAN, dentist; b. Des Moines, July 1, 1952; s. William R. and Shirley A. (Menough) H. BS, St. Ambrose Coll., 1973; DDS, U. Iowa, 1977. Pres. bd. dirs. Green Balley Area Edn. Assn., Creston, Iowa, 1982-85; mem. Osceola (Iowa) City Council, 1983-85; mem. park bd. City of Osceola, 1985-87. Recipient Osceola Community Improvement award, 1986. Mem. ADA, Osceola C. of C. (bd. dirs. 1987—). Democrat. Lodges: Rotary, Wasted Knights. Office: 148 W Jefferson Osceola IA 50213

HARRIS, CHARLES ALFRED, JR., professional placement firm executive; b. Towson, Md., June 8, 1932; s. Charles Alfred and Della (Deady) H.; m. Helen Ann Fenney, June 15, 1960 (div. 1979); children—Charles Alfred III, Debbie A., Cindy A.; m. Elizabeth Marie Brush, Feb. 21, 1980. B.B.A., John Hopkins U., 1954; M.B.A., U. Miami, 1957; Ph.D., Calif. U.-Santa Ana, 1982. Chief exec. officer Industries Internat., Inc., Thousands Oaks, Calif., 1960-65; v.p. divisional/corporate Litton Industries, Inc., Beverly Hills, Calif., 1965-70; pres., chief exec. officer Harris & Assocs., Hamilton, Ohio, 1970—. Author: Cost and Budget Manual, 1969; Emergency E.D.P. Preparedness Plan, 1979; Executive Data Processing Management Manual, 1978. Mem. Nat. Assn. Personnel Cons., Nat. Assn. Acctg., Am. Mgmt. Assn., Ohio Placement Service, Data Processing Mgmt. Assn., Hamilton C. of C., Alpha Delta Phi. Republican. Episcopalian. Lodges: Masons, Shriners, Elks, Kiwanis. Avocations: golf; tennis; boating; barbershop quartet singing. Home and Office: Harris & Assocs 229 Heaton St Hamilton OH 45011

HARRIS, CHARLIE, educational administrator; b. Hayneville, Ala., Aug. 26, 1940; s. Willie F. and Lucy B. (Campbell) H.; m. Eula S. Sims, June 12, 1971. B.S., Ala. State U., Montgomery, 1963; M.S., Va. State U., Petersburg, 1970; Ph.D., Mich. State U., 1976. Cert. supt., vocat. dir., tchr., Mo., Del., Ill., Mich. Mgmt. exec. Vault Service Co., Montgomery, Ala. 1965—; occupational tchr. Fredericksburg (Va.) Pub. Schs., 1966-71, Lansing (Mich.) Sch. Dist., 1971-77; vocat. adminstr. Newark (Del.) Sch. Dist., 1977-81, Spl. Sch. Dist. of St. Louis County, 1981—; cons. vocat. edn. and mgmt. Served with U.S. Army, 1963-65. Mem. Am. Mgmt. Assn., Am. Assn. Sch. Adminstrs., Am. Vocat. Assn., Nat. Council Local Adminstrs., Nat. Assn. Indsl. and Tech. Tchr. Educators, Assn. Supervision and Curriculum Devel., Council Basic Edn., Am. Council Indsl. Arts Tchr. Edn., Mo. Vocat. Spl. Need, Assn., NAACP. Democrat. Author: Competency-Based Education: What It Spells for Teachers and Students, 1980, and other. Home: 1504 Royal Crest Ct Chesterfield MO 63017 Office: 13480 S Outer Forty Chesterfield MO 63017

HARRIS, CHAUNCY DENNISON, geographer, educator; b. Logan, Utah, Jan. 31, 1914; s. Franklin Stewart and Estella (Spilsbury) H.; m. Edith Young, Sept. 5, 1940; 1 child, Margaret. A.B., Brigham Young U., 1933; B.A. (Rhodes scholar), Oxford U., 1936, M.A., 1943, D.Litt., 1973; student, London Sch. Econs., 1936-37; Ph.D., U. Chgo., 1940; D.Econ. (honoris causa), Catholic U., Chile, 1956; LL.D. (h.c.), Ind. U., 1979. Instr. in geography Ind. U., 1939-41; asst. prof. geography U. Nebr., 1941-43; asst. prof. geography U. Chgo., 1943-46, asso. prof., 1946-47, prof., 1947-84, prof. emeritus, 1984—, dean social scis., 1955-60, chmn. non western area programs and internat. studies, 1960-66; dir. U. Chgo. Center for Internat. Studies, 1966-84; chmn. dept. geography U. Chgo., 1967-69, Samuel N. Harper Disting. Service prof., 1969-84, spl. asst. to pres., 1973-75, v.p. acad. resources, 1975-78; del. Internat. Geog. Congress, Lisbon, 1949, Washington, 1952, Rio de Janeiro, 1956, Stockholm, 1960, London, 1964, New Delhi, 1968, Montreal, 1972, Moscow, 1976, Tokyo, 1980, Paris, 1984; v.p. Internat. Geog. Union, 1956-64, sec.-treas., 1968-76; mem. adv. com. for internat. orgns. and programs Nat. Acad. Scis., 1969-73, mem. bd. internat. orgns. and programs, 1973-76; U.S. del. 17th Gen. Conf. UNESCO, Paris, 1972; exec. com. div. behavioral scis. NRC, 1967-70; mem. council of scholars Library of Congress, 1980-83, Conseil de la Bibliographie Geógraphique Internationale, 1986—. Author: Cities of the Soviet Union, 1970; editor: Economic Geography of the U.S.S.R, 1949, Internat. List of Geog. Serials, 1960, 71, 80, Annotated World List of Selected Current Geographical Serials, 1960, 64, 71, 80, Soviet Geography: Accomplishments and Tasks, 1962, Guide to Geog. Bibliographies and Reference Works in Russian or on the Soviet Union, 1975, Bibliography of Geography, Part I, Introduction to General Aids, 1976, Part 2, Regional, vol. 1, U.S., 1984, A Geographical Bibliography for American Libraries, 1985; contbr. sources of info. in the social scis. Encyclopaedia Britannica; contbg. editor: The Geog. Rev., 1960-73; contbr. articles to profl. jours. Recipient Alexander Csoma de Körösi Meml. medal Hungarian Geog. Soc., 1971, Lauréat d'Honneur Internat. Geog. Union, 1976; Alexander von Humboldt Gold Medal Gesellschaft für Erkunde zu Berlin, 1978; spl. award Utah Geog. Soc., 1985. Fellow Japan Soc. Promotion of Sci.; mem. Assn. Am. Geographers (sec. 1946-48, v.p. 1956, pres. 1957, Honors award 1976), Am. Geog. Soc. (council 1962-74, v.p. 1969-74; Cullum Geog. medal 1985), Am. Assn. Advancement Slavic Studies (pres. 1962, award for disting. contbns. 1978), Social Sci. Research Council (dir. 1959-70, vice chmn. 1963-65, exec. com. 1967-70), Internat. Council Sci. Unions (exec. com. 1969-72), Internat. Research and Exchanges Bd. (exec. com. 1968-71), Nat. Council Soviet and East European Research (dir. 1977-83), Nat. Council for Geog. Edn. (Master Tchr. award 1986); hon. mem. Royal Geog. Soc. (Victoria medal 1987), geog. socs. Berlin, Frankfurt, Rome, Florence, Paris, Warsaw, Belgrade, Japan, Chgo. (Disting. Service award 1965; dir. 1954-69, 82—). Home: 5649 S Blackstone Ave Chicago IL 60637 Office: Dept Geography U Chgo 5828 University Ave Chicago IL 60637

HARRIS, DAVID, supreme court justice; b. Jefferson, Iowa, July 29, 1927; s. Orville William and Jessie Heloise (Smart) H.; m. Madonna Theresa Coyne, Sept. 4, 1948; children: Jane, Julia, Frederick. BA, U. Iowa, 1949, JD, 1951. Sole practice Harris & Harris, Jefferson, 1951-62; dist. judge 16th Judicial Dist., Iowa, 1962-72; justice Iowa Supreme Ct., Des Moines, 1972—. Served with U.S. Amry, 1944-46, PTO. Mem. VFW, Am. Legion, Rotary. Roman Catholic. Avocation: writing poetry. Office: Iowa Supreme Court State Capitol Bldg Des Moines IA 50319

HARRIS, DAVID ANDREW, research engineer; b. Madison, Wis., Dec. 31, 1934; s. George William and May (Newberg) H. ; m. Nancy E. Freriks, July 3, 1957; children: Kristin E. Harris Elwell, Katherine E. Harris Landman. BS in Bldg. Industries, U. Wis., 1959; cert. in bldg. codes, U. Nebr., 1964; cert. modern bus. adminstrn., Alexander Hamilton Inst., 1971. Research engr. Nat. Gypsum Co., Buffalo, 1959-64, Johns Manville and Pabco, Emeryville (Calif.) and Manville, 1964-71; supr. acoustics and bldg. tech. Owens Corning Fiberglas, Toledo, 1971-83, sr. prod. technologist, 1983-86; owner Bldg. and Acoustic Design Cons., Toledo, 1986—. Author, editor: Planning and Designing the Office Environment, 1981; contbr. tech. articles to profl. jours.; patentee in field. Bd. dirs. Greenridge Community Assn., Castro Valley, Calif. 1966-67. Served with U.S. Army, 1953-55. Mem. ASTM, Noise Control Products and Materials Assn. (pres. 1984-86, exec. dir. 1987—), Acoustical Soc. Am., Inst. Noise Control Engrs., Office Landscape Users Group (bd. dirs. 1975—), Assn. Wall and Ceiling Contractors (task group chmn. 1984—). Clubs: Jolly Roger Sailing (Toledo) (fleet capt. 1982-84); C-22 Nat. Assn. (Eugene, Oreg.) (regional commodore 1986-87). Avocations: design racing sail boat, golf, walking. Home and Office: 4213 Partridge Ln Toledo OH 43623

HARRIS, DEBRA LYNNE, jewelry sales company executive; b. Columbus, Ohio, Oct. 26, 1956; d. Conrad London and Ruth Evelyn (Bergglas) H. B.S. in Bus., Ind. U., 1978. Founder, owner Gold Connection, Inc., Chgo., 1978—. Mem. Jewelers Bd. of Trade, Jewelers of Am.

HARRIS, DEL, professional basketball coach. B, Milligan Coll., Tenn.; M, Ind. U. Basketball coach Earlham Coll., Richmond, Ind., 1965-74, Houston Rockets, Nat. Basketball Assn., 1979-83; scout Milw. Bucks, Nat. Basketball Assn., 1983-86, asst. coach, 1986-87, head coach, 1987—. Office: Milwaukee Bucks 901 N Fourth St Milwaukee WI 53203 *

HARRIS, GLEN ALAN, evangelist; b. Connersville, Ind., Feb. 28, 1960; s. Richard Lee and Margaret Kathleen (Brown) H.; m. Angela Dee Ferguson, Aug. 4, 1984. Student, Tarrant County Jr. Coll., 1982; BS, Arlington (Tex.) Bapt. Coll., 1982; BTh., DD, Great Commn. Theol. Sem., Bowling Green, Ky., 1987. Crusade evangelist Calvary Bapt. Ch., Connersville, 1972-78; with pub. relations Arlington Bapt. Coll., 1978-82; founder, evangelist Local Ch. Ministries, Connersville, 1982—; tchr. Youth Worker's Seminar, 1983; guest speaker Kansas City Youth for Christ, 1985-86, I.B.F.I., Ft. Worth, 1987; mem. World Bapt. Fellowship Internat., Bapt. Bible Fellowship Internat. Editor: (newsletter) Influence, 1983; gospel recording artist. Guest speaker Fellowship of Christian Athletes, Kearny, Nebr., 1984. Mem. Southwide Bapt. Fellowship, Ind. Bapt. Fellowship Internat. Avocations: writing, drama, singing, tennis, baseball. Home: 2719 Grand Ave Connersville IN 47331 Office: Local Ch Ministries Calvary Bapt Ch PO Box 306 Connersville IN 47331

HARRIS, HAROLD HART, chemistry educator; b. Council Bluffs, Iowa, Mar. 12, 1940; s. Arthur Ankeny and Opal Ernestine (Hart) H.; m. Mary Elizabeth Cline, June 25, 1967; children: Matthew Marlin, Jill Elizabeth. BS in Chemistry, Harvey Mudd Coll., Claremont, Calif., 1962; PhD in Physical Chemistry, Mich. State U., 1967. Postdoctoral fellow U. Calif., Irvine, 1966-67, instr. chemistry, 1967-70; from asst. to assoc. prof. chemistry U. Mo., St. Louis, 1970—; cons. Solar Energy Research Inst., Golden, Colo., 1986—. Mem. Am. Chem. Soc. (sect. bd. dirs. 1987—), Am. Physical Soc., AAAS, Materials Research Soc., Fedn. Am. Scientists, Am. Assn. Univ. Profs. (chpt. pres. 1977), Sigma Xi. Unitarian. Avocations: running, woodworking. Home: 16 Country Fair Ln Creve Coeur MO 63141

HARRIS, JAMES HERMAN, pathologist, neuropathologist, consultant, educator; b. Fayetteville, Ga., Oct. 19, 1942; s. Frank J. and Gladys N. (White) H.; m. Judy K. Hutchinson, Jan. 30, 1965; children—Jeffrey William, John Michael, James Herman. B.S., Carson-Newman Coll., 1964; Ph.D., U. Tenn.-Memphis, 1969, M.D., 1972. Diplomate Am. Bd. Pathology; sub.-cert. in anatomic pathology and neuropathology. Resident and fellow N.Y.U.-Bellevue Med. Ctr., N.Y.C., 1973-75; adj. asst. prof. pathology N.Y. U., N.Y.C., 1975—; asst. prof. pathology and neuroscis. Med. Coll. Ohio, Toledo, 1975-78, assoc. prof., 1978-82, dir. neuropathology and electron microscopy lab., 1975-82; cons. Toledo Hosp., 1979-82, assoc. pathologist/neuropathologist, dir. electron microscopy pathology lab., 1983—, mem. overview com., credentials com., appropriations subcom. medisgroup, interquality task force; cons. neuropathologist Mercy Hosp., 1976—, U. Mich. dept. pathology, 1984—; cons. med. malpractice in pathology and neuropathology; mem. AMA Physician Research and Evaluation Panel; mem. ednl. and profl. affairs commn., exec. council Acad. Medicine; mem. children's cancer study group Ohio State U. satellite; mem. adv. com. to Blue Cross, mem. task force on Cost Effectiveness N.E. Ohio, tech. and issues com.; dir. PIE Mut. Ins. Co. Chmn. steering com. Pack 198, Boy Scouts Am.; chmn. fin. com., dir. bldg. fund campaign First Baptist Ch., Perrysburg, Ohio; faculty chmn. Med. Coll. Ohio United Way Campaign. Recipient Outstanding Tchr. award Med. Coll. Ohio, 1980; named to Outstanding Young Men Am., U.S. Jaycees, 1973; USPHS trainee, 1964-69, postdoctoral trainee, 1973-75; grantee Am. Cancer Soc., 1977-78, Warner Lambert Pharm. Co., 1978-79, Miniger Found., 1980 Toledo Hosp. Found., 1985, 86, Promedica Health Care Found., 1986. Mem. Am. Profl. Practice Assn., Lucas County Acad. Medicine (exec. council 1985—), Ohio State Med. Assn., Am. Assn. Neuropathologists (profl. affairs com., awards com., program com.), Internat. Acad. Pathologists, Ohio Soc. Pathologists, EM Soc. Am., Sigma Xi. Author med., sci. papers; reviewer Jour. Neuropathology and Exptl. Neurology. Home: 550 Oak Knoll Perrysburg OH 43551 Office: Toledo Mcpl Hosp Dept Pathology 2120 N Cove Blvd Toledo OH 43606

HARRIS, JEAN LOUISE, physician; b. Richmond, Va., Nov. 24, 1931; d. Vernon Joseph and Jean Louise (Pace) H.; m. Leslie John Ellis Jr., Sept. 24, 1955; children: Karen Denise, Pamela Diane, Cynthia Suzanne. B.S., Va. Union U., 1951; M.D., Med. Coll. Va., 1955; Sc.D. (hon.), U. Richmond, 1981. Intern Med. Coll. Va., Richmond, 1955-56; resident internal medicine 1956-57, fellow, 1957-58; fellow, Strong Meml. Hosp.-U. Rochester (N.Y.) Sch. Medicine, 1958-60; research assoc. Walter Reed Army Inst. Research, Washington, 1960-63; practice medicine specializing in internal medicine allergy Washington, 1964-71; instr. medicine Howard U. Coll. Medicine, Washington, 1960-68; asst. prof. dept. community health practice Howard U. Coll. Medicine, 1969-72; prof. family practice Med. Coll. Va., Va. Commonwealth U.; also dir. Center Community Health, 1972-77; sec. Human Resources Commonwealth of Va., 1978-82; v.p. state mktg. programs Control Data Corp., 1982-84, v.p. bus. devel., 1986—; lectr. dept. med. care and hosps. Johns Hopkins, Balt., 1971-73; asst. clin. prof. dept. community medicine Charles R. Drew Postgrad. Med. Sch., Los Angeles, 1970-73; adj. asst. prof. dept. preventive and social medicine UCLA, 1970-72; chief bur. resources devel. D.C. Dept. Health, 1967-69; exec. dir. Nat. Med. Assn. Found., Washington, after 1970; Cons. div. health manpower intelligence HEW, 1969—; mem. recombinant DNA adv. com. HEW Public Health Service-NIH, 1979-82; vice chmn. Nat. Commn. on Alcoholism and Alcohol Related Diseases, 1980-82. Trustee U. Richmond, active city council, Eden Prairie, Minn., 1987—. Recipient East End Civic Assn. award, 1955. Fellow Royal Soc. (Eng.); mem. Am. Pub. Health Assn., Richmond Med. Soc., Nat. Med. Assn., Am. Soc. Pub. Adminstrs., So. Inst. Human Resources (pres. 1980-81), Inst. Medicine/Nat. Acad. Scis., Beta Kappa Chi, Alpha Kappa Mu, Sigma Xi. Home: 10860 Forestview Cir Eden Prairie MN 55344 Office: Control Data Corp 8100 34th Ave S Minneapolis MN 55440

HARRIS, JEAN NOTON, music educator; b. Monroe, Wis., Feb. 21, 1934; d. Albert Henry and Eunice Elizabeth (Edgerton) Noton; B.A., Monmouth (Ill.) Coll., 1955; M.S., U. Ill., 1975, adminstrv. cert., 1980, Ed.D., 1985; m. Laurence G. Landers, June 7, 1955; children—Theodore Scott, Thomas Warren, Philip John; m. Edward R. Harris, Nov. 27, 1981; stepchildren—Adrianne, Erica. Tchr. music schs. in Ill. and Fla., 1955-76; tchr. ch. music for children, 1957-72; tchr. music Dist. 54, Schaumburg, Ill., from 1976; teaching asst. U. Ill., 1979. Named Outstanding Young Woman of Yr., Jaycee Wives, St. Charles, Mo., 1968; charter mem. Nat. Mus. Women in Arts. Mem. Music Educators Nat. Conf. (life), Ill. Music Educators Assn., Soc. Gen. Music Educators, Alliance for Arts Edn., NEA (life), Am. Choral Dirs. Assn., U. Ill. Alumni Assn. (life), Mortar Bd., Mensa, Delta Kappa Pi. Mem. United Ch. of Christ. Home: 914 Roxbury Ln Schaumburg IL 60194

HARRIS, JERRY LEE, systems analyst; b. Jackson, Mich., Oct. 25, 1939; s. Allen Royce and Julia Jean (Nimmo) H.; m. Carol Jean Covey, Apr. 18, 1959; children: Kimberly Lynne, Kelly Linea. Computer operator Consumers Power Co., Jackson, 1958-70, supr. ops., 1970-75, programmer analyst, 1975-82, systems analyst, 1982—. chmn. bd. First Ch. Christ, Jackson, 1980—. Avocation: video taping. Home: 3349 Spring Arbor Rd Jackson MI 49203 Office: Consumers Power Co P23-319 1945 Parnall Rd Jackson MI 49202

HARRIS, JOSEPH BENJAMIN, dentist; b. Richmond, Va., June 8, 1920; s. Joseph Brown and Alice (Burrell) H.; BS. summa cum laude, Va. Union U., 1949; D.D.S., Howard U., 1953; m. Pauline Elizabeth McKinney, June 19, 1955; children—Paula Jo, Joseph Carter, Joya Renee. Pvt. practice dentistry, Detroit, 1953—; dir. C.A. Howell & Co., mfr. and distbr. beauty supplies, 1967—, pres., chmn. bd., 1972—. Served with AUS, 1943-46. Recipient award Am. Soc. Dentistry for Children, 1953. Mem. Am., Nat., Wolverine, Mich., Detroit dental socs., Mich. Assn. Professions, Omicron Kappa Upsilon, Alpha Kappa Mu, Sigma Pi Phi, Omega Psi Phi. Home: 1190 W Boston Blvd Detroit MI 48202 Office: 2431 W Grand Blvd Detroit MI 48208

HARRIS, K. DAVID, lawyer, state supreme court justice; b. Jefferson, Iowa, July 29, 1927; s. Orville William and Jessie Heloise (Smart) H.; m. Madonna Therese Coyne, Sept. 4, 1948; children: Jane, Julia, Frederick. BA, U. Iowa, 1947, JD, 1951. Bar: Iowa 1951, U.S. Dist. Ct. 1957. Sole practice Jefferson, 1951-59; atty. Greene County, Iowa, 1959-62; judge 16th Dist. Ct., Iowa, 1962-72; assoc. justice Iowa Supreme Ct, Des Moines, 1972—. Served with U.S. Army, 1944-46, ETO. Republican. Roman Catholic. Home: 507 W Harrison Jefferson IA 50129 Office: Iowa Supreme Ct Box 107 Des Moines IA 50319

HARRIS, KEVIN MICHAEL, tax consultant; b. Centralia, Ill., Feb. 20, 1961; s. Basil Dean and Rita Louise (Cerny) H.;. BS, Ill. State U., 1983; postgrad., DePaul U., 1983—. CPA, Ill. Tax analyst Arthur Andersen & Co., Chgo., 1983—. Mem. Chgo. Council Foreign Relations, 1986. Mem. Am. Inst. CPA's, Ill. CPA Soc., Chgo. Area Runners Assn. (fin. com. 1986). Roman Catholic. Avocations: running, photography, gardening. Office: Arthur Andersen & Co 33 W Monroe Chicago IL 60603

HARRIS, KING W., manufacturing company executive; b. 1943. BA, Harvard U., 1964, MBA, 1965. With Pittway Corp., Northbrook, Ill., 1971—, v.p. alarm div., 1971-75, exec. v.p. electronics div., 1975-80, chmn. bd. dirs., chief exec. officer electronics div., 1980-84, now pres., bd. dirs. Office: Pittway Corp 333 Skokie Blvd Northbrook IL 60065 *

HARRIS, LEONARD, physician; b. N.Y.C., Oct. 29, 1927; s. Benjamin and Anna (Fradin) H.; m. Barbara Ann Peterson, Feb. 5, 1956; children: Jay, Daniel, Matthew. MD, N.Y.U., 1949. Diplomate Am. Bd. Pediatrics, Am. Bd. Psychiatry and Neurology. Intern Morrisania city Hosp., N.Y.C., 1949-50; asst. and chief resident in pediatrics Bronx Hosp., N.Y.C., 1950-52; resident in psychiatry U. Cin., 1969-71; resident in neurology Mt. Sinai Hosp., N.Y.C., 1952-53; fellow in child psychiatry U. Cin., 1971-73; practice medicine specializing in pediatrics N.Y.C., 1955-59; dir. pediatrics Holzen Hosp. and Clinic, Gallipolis, Ohio, 1959-69; practice medicine specializing in child psychiatry Cin., 1972—; cons. liaison Children's Hosp. Med. Ctr., Cin., 1976—, dir. behavioral unit, 1978—, dir. inpatient psychiatry, 1983—. Served to capt. USAF, 1953-55. Mem. Am. Psychiat. Assn., Am. Acad. Child Psychiatry. Jewish. Office: Childrens Hosp Med Ctr Elland and Bethesda Aves Cincinnati OH 45229

HARRIS, MARCELLA H. EASON (MRS. HARLEY EUGENE HARRIS), social worker; b. Augusta, Ark., Apr. 19, 1925; d. William Harvey and Hazel Faye (Haraway) Eason; B.A., Wilberforce U., 1947; M.S.W., Loyola U., Chgo., 1961; M.Ed. in Health Occupations, U. Ill., 1979; m. Harley Eugene Harris, June 15, 1952. Child welfare worker Ill. Dept. Pub. Welfare, 1952-54, caseworker Family Consultation Service, 1954-64; clin. social worker Winnebago County Mental Health Clinic, Rockford, Ill., 1964—, now clin. mgr. sustaining care services Janet Wattles Mental Health Center. Mem. Rockford Bd. Edn., 1965—, sec., 1965-69; trustee Swedish Am. Hosp.; bd. dirs. Rockford Local Devel. Corp.; mem. Allen Chapel African Methodist Episcopal Ch. Recipient Francis Blair award Ill. Edn. Assn., 1970, Service above Self award Rockford Rotary Club, 1971. Mem. Nat. Assn. Social Workers (chpt. vice chmn. 1960-61), Ill. Welfare Assn., Acad. Certified Social Workers, Nat. Council Negro Women, Rockford Jr. League (hon.), AAUW, Nat. Registry Health Care Providers in Clin. Social Work, Delta Kappa Gamma (hon.), Alpha Kappa Alpha. Club: Taus Sevice. Home: Cloisters Apt 1665 2929 Sunnyside Dr Rockford IL 61111 Office: 1325 E State St Rockford IL 61108

HARRIS, MARK WAYNE, oral surgeon; b. Las Vegas, N.Mex., Mar. 5, 1950; s. Arthur Wayne and Helen (Johnson) H.; m. Leisa Rogers, Jan. 5, 1980 (div. May 1985); 1 child, Brandon Michael. BCE, N.Mex. State U., 1972; DMD, U. Mo., Kansas City, 1978. Diplomate Am. Bd. Oral and Maxillofacial Surgeons. Engr. City of Santa Fe, 1972-74; assoc. prof. U. Mo., Kansas City, 1978; intern, then resident in oral and maxillofacial surgery Mayo Clinic, Rochester, Minn., 1978-81; practice medicine specializing in oral and maxillofacial surgery Assoc. Oral and Maxillofacial Surgeons, Mpls., 1981—; assoc. prof. oral and maxillofacial surgery U. Minn., Mpls., 1984—. Fellow Am. Assn. Oral and Maxillofacial Surgeons, Am. Coll. Oral and Maxillofacial Surgeons; mem. ADA, Sigma Tau, Chi Epsilon. Avocations: skiing, long distance running, mountaineering. Home: 22 West Point Pl Tonka Bay MN 55331 Office: Assoc Oral and Maxillofacial Surgeons 5901 Brooklyn Blvd Minneapolis MN 55416

HARRIS, MARY ANN, researcher, consultant; b. Moultrie, Ga., June 10, 1946; d. James Bobby and Mary Ola (Rooney) Brooks; m. John W. Harris, July 29, 1972; children: Paul, Justin. BS, Knoxville Coll., 1969; MA, Wayne State U., 1971; EdD, Nova U., 1986. Gerontology field supr. Case Western Res. U., Cleve., 1972-73; program dir. Fairhill Mental Health Ctr., Cleve., 1973-74; adj. instr. Cuyahoga Community Coll., Cleve., 1975-80; dir. sr. citizen ctr. City of Cleve., 1980-81; devel. officer Cleve. Adult Tutorial, 1981-86; research project assoc. U. Mich., Ann Arbor, 1986—; gerontology cons. Council for Econ. Opportunities, Cleve., 1981-83, Project Rainbow, Cleve., 1980—. Author: Grandparent Stuff-Riddles About Growing Old, 1985. Vol. Arthritis Found., Cleve., 1985-86; mem. East Cleve. Bd. Edn., 1979—; precinct committeeman East Cleve. Dem. Party, 1984—. Grantee Adminstrn. on Aging, 1979, Cuyahoga County Commisioners Office, 1985; recipient Mother of Yr. award Cleve. Call and Post Newspaper, 1984. Mem. Nat. Alliance of Black Sch. Educators, NAACP (chmn. com. 1985-86), Ohio Sch. Bds. Assn., Alpha Kappa Alpha (2d v.p. Cleve. 1985-86). Democrat. Avocations: creative writing, bowling, sewing. Home: 1326 E 143 St East Cleveland OH 44112 Office: U Mich IDD-IST UAW-Ford LIEPP 2200 Bonisteel Blvd Ann Arbor MI 48109

HARRIS, MICHAEL VERNON, leasing broker; b. Chgo., Dec. 19, 1957; s. Charles Vernon and Mary Lucille (Moore) H. BS in Bus. Mgmt., So. U., Baton Rouge, 1979. Corrugated sales rep. Owens-Ill., Miami, Fla., 1979-81; field sales eng. Honeywell, Dallas, 1980-82; account mktg. rep. IBM, Chgo., 1982-87; comml. office leasing broker Royal Le Page, Chgo., 1987—. Vol., role model Jobs for Youth, Chgo., 1985—, Chgo. Urban Group/Urbanites, 1986; mktg. coordinator Broadcast Housing Apostolic Ch. God, Chgo., 1985—; bd. dirs. S. Suburban Housing Ctr., Park Forest, Ill., 1986. Named one of Outstanding Young Men Am., 1981, 86. Mem. Homewood (Ill.) Bd. Realtors (bd. dirs. 1985—). Democrat. Mem. Apostolic Ch. Avocations: swimming, bowling, baseball, jazz. Home: 802 Glenwood Dyer Rd Glenwood IL 60425

HARRIS, MORTON EDWARD, mathematics educator; b. Bklyn., Apr. 27, 1934; s. Frank and Belle (Rubin) H.; m. Ilene Barmash Harris, July 9, 1967. BS, Yale U., 1955; MA, Harvard U., 1956, PhD, 1960. Asst. prof. Clark U., Worcester, Mass., 1960-61, Tufts U., Medford, Mass., 1961-65; asst. prof. U. Ill., Chgo., 1965-71, assoc. prof., 1971-74; assoc. prof. U. Minn., Mpls., 1974-76, prof., 1976—; vis. scholar U. Kiel, 1985, U. Essen, 1985, U. Chgo., 1985, 86, technion Israel Inst. Tech., 1985; speaker in field. Contbr. articles to profl. jours. Fellow NSF, 1955-60, 1965-80. Mem. Am. Math. Soc., Math. Assn. Am., Phi Beta Kappa. Republican. Jewish. Home: 4375 Coolidge Ave Saint Louis Park MN 55424 Office: U Minn Math Dept Minneapolis MN 55455

HARRIS, NANCY S., architect; b. Buenos Aires, Dec. 7, 1937; came to U.S., 1938; d. Louis Elbroch and Sylvia (Brodsky) Schacht; m. David Louis Harris, Aug. 11, 1957; children: Anne, Nathan, Elizabeth. Student, Antioch Coll., 1955-57, U. Ariz., 1972-75; BArch, U. Ky., 1978. Drafter Staggs & Fischer, Lexington, Ky., 1979; job capt. Mark McKechnie, Architect, Red Wing, Minn., 1981-84; owner, prin. Designing Woman, Red Wing, Minn., 1985—; appointed mem. bldg. com. T.B. Sheldon Meml. Auditorium, Red Wing, 1986—. Designer various local bldg. projects, 1981—. Mem. Mayor's Preservation Task Force, Red Wing, 1981, Red Wing City Council, 1983-85, County Dem. Cen. Com., Goodhue County, Minn., 1986—, LWV, Red Wing; del. Minn. Dem. Convs., 1982, 84, 86; sec. Cancer Soc., Red Wing, 1986—; bd. dirs., treas. Friends of History, Red Wing, 1986—. Grantee Ky. Arts Commn., 1979. Mem. AIA (assoc., Minn. chpt.), AAUW. Avocations: classical piano, reading, political activism. Home and Office: 1204 S Park St Red Wing MN 55066

HARRIS, NEISON, corporate executive; b. St. Paul, Jan. 24, 1915; s. William and Mildred (Brooks) H.; m. Bette Deutsch, Jan. 25, 1939; children: Katherine, King, Toni. AB, Yale U., 1936. Founder Toni Co.; pres. Toni div. Gillette Co., pres. Paper Mate div.; pres., bd. dirs. Pittway Corp., Northbrook, Ill., 1959-84, chmn. bd., 1984—; chmn. bd., chmn. exec. com., dir. Standard Shares, Inc. Named One of Ten Outstanding Young Men U.S., Jr. C. of C., 1948. Clubs: Standard, Lake Shore Country (Chgo.); Boca Rio Country (Boca Raton, Fla.). Office: Pittway Corp 333 Skokie Blvd Northbrook IL 60065

HARRIS, PHYLLIS IRENE, educator; b. Poplar Bluff, Mo., Aug. 10, 1927; d. Golly and Beulah Ruth (Tompkins) Hunter; m. Paul William Harris, May 27, 1950 (div. 1962); 1 son, Kevin Paul. B.S., Loyola U., Chgo., 1958; M.S., Chgo. State U., 1971, M.S., 1980; Ph.D., U. So. Ill., 1983. Tchr. mentally handicapped children Chgo. Pub. Schs., 1960—; week/study coordinator for handicapped Robeson High Sch.; tchr., counselor mentally handicapped adults Kennedy King Coll. Mem. Am. Fedn. Tchrs., NAACP, Council for Exceptional Children, Chgo. Assn. Retarded. Bahai. Home: 7729 S Cregier Ave Chicago IL 60649 Office: Chgo Pub Schs 6835 S Normal St Chicago IL 60621

HARRIS, R(AYMOND) WESLEY, business executive; b. Vinita, Okla., Feb. 17, 1940; s. Raymond N. and Ravanell A. (Pitts) H.; m. Renee E. LaFortune, June 2, 1962; children—Brian M., Daron J. B.S., Okla. State U., 1964, M.S. in Indsl. Engring. and Mgmt., 1965. Indsl. engr. E.I. duPont, Old Hickory, Tenn., 1965-68; with Hooker Chem. & Plastics Corp., Niagara Falls, N.Y., 1968-78, supt. plant services, 1973-74, project mgr. productivity improvement task force, 1974-75, corp. mgr. indsl. engring., 1975-78; v.p. Union Frondenberg U.S.A., Olney, Ill., 1978-84, pres., 1984—; v.p. B.U.A., Inc., Olney, 1978-84, pres., 1984—; pres., chief exec. officer Global Group Ltd., 1985—; dir. Richland Capital Group Inc., 1985—; cons. Weinmann Sports, Inc. Mem. planning and resource com. Olney Central Coll. Found., 1982, vice chmn. fin. com. and exec. com., 1983. Served to maj. USAFR, 1965—. Recipient Key to City of Olney, 1981, Congressman's award of Merit, 1981, Commendation award City of Olney, 1981. Mem. Am. Inst. Indsl. Engrs. (sec. chpt. 1974-75, pres. 1975-76, dir. 1976-77), Olney C. of C. (chmn. bus. and econ. devel. com. 1982-83), Alpha Pi Mu, Sigma Alpha Epsilon. Republican. Roman Catholic. Clubs: Petroleum, Richland County Country (dir. 1981—) (Olney). Lodges: Rotary, Elks. Home: 30 Willow Dr Olney IL 62450 Office: 1 Union Dr Olney IL 62450

HARRIS, RICHARD CARL, pharmacist; b. St. Johns, Mich., Jan. 18, 1951; s. Robert Gerald and Mabel Louise (Waidelich) H.; m. Carolyn Kay Willowick, Aug. 4, 1973; children: Julie Lynn, Kelly Michelle. BS in Pharmacy, U. Wis., 1974. Pharmacist Kealey Pharmacy, Janesville, Wis., 1975, Sherry Pharmacy, Stoughton, Wis., 1975-79; owner, pharmacist Harris Pharmacy, Waunakee, Wis., 1979—; asst. lab. instr. U. Wis. Sch. Pharmacy, Madison, 1976-78; pharmacy cons. Waunakee Manor Nursing Home, 1979—. Pres. Waunakee Eucmenical Bd., 1985. Fellow Am. Soc. Cons. Pharmacists; mem. Nat. Assn. Retail Druggists, Am. Pharm. Assn., Dane County Pharmacists Soc. (pres. 1978). Republican. Presbyterian. Avocations: skiing, hunting, running, sports. Home: 805 John St Waunakee WI 53597 Office: Harris Pharmacy 265 Village Hall PO Box 97 Waunakee WI 53597

HARRIS, RICHARD LEE, research chemist; b. Chgo., Nov. 1, 1934; s. Lee Merle Harris and Mae G. (Wood) Johnson; m. Carol Sue Wahlstrom, June 11, 1957 (div. Nov. 1977); children: Jay Alan, Susan Lee. BA in Chemistry, North Cen. Coll., Naperville, Ill., 1956; PhD in Organic Chemistry, U. Ill., 1960. Research chemist Du Pont, Niagara Falls, N.Y., 1960-64; research mgr. Diamond Shamrock, Painesville, Ohio, 1964—. Patentee in field. Mem. Rep. precinct com., Painesville, 1970-75. Mem. Am. Chem. Soc., U.S. Jaycees (v.p. 1961-64). Republican. Methodist. Home: 5245 N Ridge Apt #31 Madison OH 44057 Office: BioSpecific Technologies Inc PO Box 191 Painesville OH 44077

HARRIS, RICHARD STEVEN, systems consultant, programmer/analyst, educator; b. Kansas City, Kans., Aug. 3, 1949; s. George Joseph and Bonnie Jean (Knecht) H.; m. Phyllis Lea Stopp, Aug. 29, 1970; children: April Lea, Steven Erhardt. BA magna cum laude, Knox Coll.; MS in Edn., Western Ill. U. Cert. data processor, systems profl., data educator, computer programmer; high sch. teaching, Ill. sch. service profl., Ill., prodn. and inventory mgmt., personnel-guidance. Sci. tchr., counselor Brimfield (Ill.) High Sch., 1972-74, grad. of five factories, Galesburg, Ill., 1971-72, 74-80; plant mgr. Jacobson Barrel Corp., Milw., 1980-82; ind. systems cons. Milw. area, 1982-84; programmer Effective Mgmt. Systems, Milw., 1984-85; systems and programming tchr. Milw. Bus. Tng. Inst., 1985-86; programmer, systems analyst Systems For Profit, Inc., Milw., 1986—; systems and programming tchr. Milw. Area Tech. Coll., 1987—. Mem. Am. Prodn. and Inventory Control Soc. (instr., Milw. 1985-87), Assn. for Computing Machinery, Creation Sci. Soc. Milw. (program chmn. 1985-86), Creation Research Soc., Creation Social Sci. and Humanities Soc. Mem. United Pentecostal Ch. Avocations: bicycling, reading, studying, research activities, teaching ministry. Home and Office: 10853 S Nicholson Rd Oak Creek WI 53154

HARRIS, ROBERT ALLISON, biochemistry educator; b. Boone, Iowa, Nov. 10, 1939; s. Arnold E. and Marie (Wilcox) H.; m. Karen Kaye Dutton, Dec. 27, 1960; children—Kelly, Chris, Heidi, Shawn. B.S., Iowa State U., 1962; Ph.D., Purdue U., 1965. Asst. research prof. U. Wis., 1968-69; assoc. prof. biochemistry Ind. U. Med. Sch., Indpls., 1970-75, prof., 1975—, assoc. chmn. dept., 1983—. Co-editor: Isolation, Characterization, and Use of Hepatocytes, 1983; contbr. articles to profl. jours. Recipient Disting. Teaching award AMOCO, 1981, Young investigator award Ind. Diabetes Assn., 1977; Edward C. Moore award, 1985; Nat. Multiple Sclerosis Soc. fellow, 1966-68; established investigator Am. Heart Assn., 1969-74. Mem. Am. Soc. Biol. Chemists, Am. Oil Chemists Soc., Biochem. Soc., Am. Heart Assn., Am. Diabetic Assn., Am. Inst. Nutrition. Office: Ind U Sch Medicine Dept Biochemistry Indianapolis IN 46223

HARRIS, ROBERT EDWARD, farmer; b. Leavenworth, Kans., May 21, 1947. Grad. high sch., Leavenworth, 1965. Judge All Breeds Dairy Day, 4-H Club, Horton, Kans., 1961. Mem. Leavenworth County Farm Bur., Assn. Self Employed. Democrat. Baptist. Avocations: movies, reading. Home: Rt 3 Box 521 Leavenworth KS 66048

HARRIS, RONALD LEE, technology company executive; b. Lincoln, Nebr., Aug. 1, 1942; s. Lewis Eldon and Antonia (Synovec) H.; m. Christine Marie Olson, June 19, 1965; children—Bretton, Jennifer. B.S., U. Nebr., 1965, M.B.A., 1968. Cert. adminstrv. mgr. Vice chmn. Harris Labs., Inc., Lincoln, 1969-74, pres., 1974-84; pres. Fin. Systems, Inc., Kearney, Nebr., 1982—; pres. Harris Tech. Group, Inc., Lincoln, 1984—; cons. R.B. Harris Co., Lincoln. Trustee, U. Nebr. Found., 1982-83; bd. dirs. Lincoln Found., 1984-87; chmn. bd. dirs. Madonna Found., 1984-87; mem. Greater Lincoln Pvt. Industry Council, 1983-86. Mem. Am. Council Ind. Labs. (past pres.), Young Pres. Orgn., Adminstrv. Mgmt. Soc. (past pres.), Assoc. Industries Lincoln (past pres.), Lincoln C. of C. Republican. Methodist. Clubs: Adman's Gridiron, University. Avocations: golf, boating, racquetball. Home: 2215 The Knolls Lincoln NE 68512 Office: Harris Technology Group Inc 624 Peach St Box 80837 Lincoln NE 68501

HARRIS, ROSALIE SHONFELD, independent writer, public relations and corporate communications executive; b. Chgo., Feb. 4, 1944; d. Paul A. and Esther M. (Schulman) Shonfeld. B.A., Antioch Coll., 1966. Acct. exec. Daniel J. Edelman, Chgo., 1966-67, Clinton E. Frank, Chgo., 1967-69, Genesis/BBDM, Chgo., 1969-75; acct. mgr. Container Corp., Chgo., 1975-79; mgr. pub. communications Motorola, Inc., Schaumburg, Ill., 1979-81; account supr. Golin/Harris, Chgo., 1981-82; owner Rosalie Harris: Creative Solutions, Chgo., 1982—. Contbr. articles to various publs. Co-chmn. Friends of Hubbard St. Dance Co.; Bd. dirs. Chgo. String Ensemble. Recipient Headliner award Women in Communications, 1983. Mem. Women in Communications, Ind. Writers Chgo., Nat. Assn. Women Bus. Owners. Home and Office: 666 N Lake Shore Dr Suite 325 Chicago IL 60611

HARRIS, STANLEY GEORGE, adult educator; b. Oak Park, Ill., Mar. 3, 1916; s. Wilbur J. and Helen A. (Andrus) H.; m. Dorothy Katherine Damis, Aug. 27, 1943. AA, Wright Jr. Coll., 1937; BA, U. Chgo., 1941; MA, U. Mich., 1947, postgrad., 1947-51. Tng. specialist, mgr. Teletype Corp., Skokie, Ill., 1952-76; asst. dir. Maine, Oakton, Niles, Northfield adult edn. program Oakton Community Coll., Des Plaines, Ill., 1976-86. Contbr. articles to profl. jours. Pres. Niles Twp. Welfare Council, Skokie, 1975, Orchard Mental Health Ctr. Niles Twp., Skokie, 1976-86; chmn. United Way Fund Raising Campaigns, Skokie, 1977-78. Served to 1st sgt. U.S. Army, 1942-45. Mem. Adult Edn. Assn., Ill. Tng. Dirs. Assn., No. Ill. Indsl. Assn. (sect. chmn. 1960-62), Phi Kappa Sigma. (rushing chmn. 1940-41, advisor Ann Arbor 1945-47). Club: Publicity (Chgo.). Lodge: Kiwanis (pres. Skokie 1974-86). Avocation: theater. Home: 6956 N Kolmar Ave Lincolnwood IL 60646 Office: Oakton Community Coll 7701 Lincoln Ave Skokie IL 60077

HARRIS, STEVEN DALE, lawyer; b. Findlay, Ohio, Oct. 13, 1949; s. Kenneth Dale and Charlotte Louise (Rosebrook) H.; m. Ann Geppert, July 20, 1974; children—Stefan Geppert, Eliot Kendall. Student Salzburg U. (Austria), 1970; B.A., Bowling Green State U., 1971; J.D., Capital U., 1975. Bar: Ohio 1975. Legis. dir. Ohio Republican Party, Columbus, 1972-75; adminstrv. asst. Ohio Dept. Devel., Columbus, 1975; gen. counsel Ohio Energy Agy., Columbus, 1975-77; dir. Kans. Energy Office, Topeka, 1977-79; mgr. govt. policy analysis Sun Gas Co., Dallas, 1979-81; exec. v.p., gen. counsel, dir. Eagle Mountain Energy Corp., Reynoldsburg, Ohio, 1981-86, atty. Hiawatha Resources, Inc., 1986—. Mem. Wichita Energy Commn., 1978, Interstate Oil Compact Commn., Oklahoma City, 1981; trustee Columbus E. Soccer Assn., 1984—, pres., 1985—, coach, 1983—. Mem. Ohio State Bar Assn., Columbus Bar Assn., Eastern Mineral Law Found. Republican. Lutheran. Avocations: travel; photography; soccer; fishing. Office: Hiawatha Resources Inc 1456 Lancaster Ave Reynoldsburg OH 43068

HARRIS, TIMOTHY FRANCIS, accountant; b. St. Louis, Dec. 30, 1950; s. Arlo O. Jr. and Betty Jane (Sondhaus) H.; m. Julia J. Graul, Jan. 10, 1981; children: Matthew, Christine, Timothy Jr. BS, St. Louis U., 1973. CPA, Mo., Wis. Staff acct. Corrigan Constrn. Co., St. Louis, 1973; tax auditor Kerber, Eck & Braeckel, St. Louis, 1974-80; tax mgr., dir. mktg. Kerber, Eck & Braeckel, Milw., 1981-85, ptnr., 1985—. Mem. Am. Inst. CPA's, Wis. Inst. CPA's, Hosp. Fin. Mgmt. Assn., Cath. Health Assn., Wis. HomeHealth Orgn. Republican. Roman Catholic. Clubs: Milw. Athletic, Harlequin Rugby; Mo. Athletic (St. Louis). Home: N 24 W 22323 Elmwood Waukesha WI 53186 Office: 735 N Water St Milwaukee WI 53202

HARRIS, WILLIAM ALBERT, television news producer, journalist, consultant; b. Holyoke, Mass., Aug. 26, 1949; s. William Christopher and Jane Barbara (Siepierski) H.; m. Jane Marie Cushman, Oct. 8, 1982; children: Nicole Marie, Christopher Robert. AA, Holyoke Community Coll., 1968; BS, Boston U., 1971. Staff announcer Sta. WREB, Holyoke, 1963-69, Sta. WCRX-FM, Springfield, Mass., 1967-69; producer, dir. Sta. WWLP-TV, Springfield, 1969-72, reporter, anchor, 1972-77; exec. producer, anchor Sta. WJRT-TV, Flint, Mich., 1977—; v.p. Emergency Media Mgmt., Flint, 1983—. Chmn. communications United Way, Flint, 1979-80, campaign Cystic Fibrosis Found., Flint, 1981, telethon March of Dimes, Flint, 1984-86; dir. race Run for the Dimes Inc., Flint, 1984-86. Named Outstanding Vol. of Yr. Cystic Fibrosis Found., 1980-81; Emmy nominee New Eng. chpt. Nat. Acad. Arts and Scis., 1977; recipient Best Local Newscast award Mich. Associated Press, 1980, Spot News '81 award, Mich. AP. Mem. Radio/TV News Dirs. Assn., Soc. Profl. Journalists. Roman Catholic. Club: Riverbend Striders (Flint). Lodge: Ancient Order Hiberians in Am. Avocations: running, photography, restoring antique cars. Office: Sta WJRT-TV 2302 Lapeer Rd Flint MI 48502

HARRISON, DANIEL J., neurological surgeon; b. Peoria, Ill., Mar. 14, 1949; s. Hyman S. and Patricia F. (Moran) H.; m. Janie Jo Daubs, July 10, 1971. BS in Biochemistry, U. Ill., 1971; MD, U. Ill., Chgo., 1975. Diplomate Am. Bd. Neurol. Surgery. Intern in surgery U. Ill. Hosp., Chgo., 1975, resident in neurol. surgery, 1981; attending neurol. surgeon Good Samaritan Hosp., Downers Grove, Ill., West Suburban Hosp., Oak Park, Ill., Gottleib Hosp., Melrose Park, Ill.; neurol. surgeon West Suburban Neurolsurgical Assocs., Hinsdale, Ill. Mem. AMA, Congress Neurol. Surgeons.

HARRISON, JOSEPH WILLIAM, state senator; b. Chgo., Sept. 10, 1931; s. Roy J. and Gladys V. (Greenman) H.; B.S., U.S. Naval Acad., 1956; postgrad. Ind. U. Law Sch., 1968-70; m. Ann Hovey Gillespie, June 9, 1956; children—Holly Ann, Tracy Jeanne, Thomas Joseph, Amy Beth, Kitty Lynne, Christy Jayne. Asst. to pres. Harrison Steel Castings Co., Attica, Ind., 1960-64, sales research engr., 1964-66, asst. sec., 1966-69, sec., 1969-71, v.p., 1971-84, dir., 1968-84, mem. Ind. Senate, 1966—, majority leader, 1980—. Mem. Attica Consol. Sch. Bd., 1964-66, pres., 1966-67. Served with USN, 1956-60. Mem. Wabash Valley Assn., Am. Legion, Sigma Chi. Republican. Methodist. Lodges: Elks, Eagles. Home: 504 E Pike St Attica IN 47918 Office: PO Box 409 Attica IN 47918

HARRISON, VICKIE ELAINE, real estate appraiser, consultant; b. Louisiana, Mo., Oct. 17, 1959; d. Robert William Turpin and Mary Karen (Keith) Mikelson; m. Ronald Gene Harrison, Mar. 30, 1985. BA in Agrl. Bus. and Econ., U. Mo., 1981. Rev. appraiser Mo. Mass Appraisal, Independence, 1982-84, Bisen Appraisal Co., Buffalo, 1984; dep. assessor Lincoln County, Troy, Mo., 1984-85; pres., owner, appraiser Kinker Appraisal Service, Moscow Mills, Mo., 1985—. Mem. Nat. Assn. Ind. Fee Appraisers (v.p. St. Charles chpt. 1986—, pres.), Profl. Womens Appraisal Assn. (cert.), Lake St. Louis C. of C. Democrat. Presbyterian. Avocations: golf, skiing, antiques, baseball, reading. Home: Rural Rt 4 Box 44 Bowling Green MO 63334 Office: Kinker Appraisal Service Inc PO Box 100 634 Main St Moscow Mills MO 63362

HARRISON, WILLIAM FREDERICK, optometrist; b. Dresden, Ont., Can., Jan. 30, 1926; came to U.S., 1952; s. Albert and Laura Belle (Power) H.; m. Jeanette Lois Rea, Nov. 29, 1957. Student, Bradley U., 1952-56; BS in Optometry, Ill. Coll., Chgo., 1962, OD, 1963. Jeweller, watchmaker, engraver Harrison Jewellers, Chatham, Ontario, Can., 1946-52; horological engr. Elgin (Ill.) Nat. Watch Co., 1956-58; pvt. practice optometry Elgin, 1963—; bd. dirs. Sherman Hosp. Interested Men, Elgin, 1978-80, chmn. bd. 1981-82. Bd. dirs. Elgin Hist. Soc., 1986—. Served with Can. Navy, 1944-46. Mem. Am. Optometric Assn., Ill. Optometric Assn., Fox Valley Optometric Soc. (pres. 1968). Republican. Lodge: Kiwanis (bd. dirs. Elgin club 1983-85). Master watchmaker Horological Inst. Am., 1955, craftmember Brit. Horological Inst., 1955. Avocations: firearm engraving, engrossing. Home: 704 Diane Ave Elgin IL 60123-2626 Office: 232 N McLean Blvd Elgin IL 60123-3284

HARSTAD, CARL LESLIE, information manager; b. Cass Lake, Minn., Mar. 11, 1942; s. Lester Marvin Harstad and Leola (Patnaude) Fischer; m. Pamela Rae Lary, May 9, 1981. BA, U. Minn., 1971, MA, 1976. Area editor Faribault (Minn.) Daily News, 1971-72; staff writer Sun Newspapers, Wayzata, Minn., 1973-75; freelance writer Mpls., 1975—; mgmt. info. systems supr. Hennepin County Govt., Mpls., 1977-83; cons. computer mgmt. info. systems Mpls., 1983—; info. services coordinator Angiomedics, Plymouth, Minn., 1985—. Served with USN, 1961-65, Vietnam. Decorated Gallantry Cross Color (South Vietnam). Recipient Fire Photography award Minn. Fire Chiefs Assn., 1972; NSF scholar, 1959, St. Cloud State U. Alumni scholar, 1960. Mem. Soc. Profl. Journalists (bd. dirs. 1974-75), Minn. Astron. Assn. (sec. 1979-80, pres. 1980-81, editor newsletter 1975-84, 87—), Am. Meteor Soc., Am. Legion. Lutheran. Home: 4008 25th Ave S Minneapolis MN 55406 Office: Angiomedics 2905 Northwest Blvd Plymouth MN 55441

HART, CECIL WILLIAM JOSEPH, otolaryngologist, head and neck surgeon; b. Bath, Avon, England, May 27, 1931; came to U.S., 1957.; s. William Theodore Hart and Paulina Olive (Adams) Gilmer; m. Brigid Frances Molloy, June 15, 1957 (dec. Nov. 1984); children: Geoffrey Arthur, Paula Mary, John Adams; m. Doris Crystel Katharina Alm, Mar. 14, 1987; children: Kristen-Linnea Alm, Erik Alm, Britt-Marie Alm. BA, Trinity Coll., Dublin, Ireland, 1952, MB, BCH, BAO, 1955, MA, 1958. Diplomate Am. Bd. Otolaryngology. Intern Dr. Steevens Hosp., Dublin, Ireland, 1956, Little Co. Mary Hosp., Evergreen Park, Ill., 1957; mem. staff Little Co. Mary Hosp., 1958-59; resident in otolaryngology U. Chgo. Hosp. and clinic, 1959-62; instr. U. Chgo. Med. Sch., 1962-64, asst. prof., 1964-65; practice medicine specializing in otolaryngology Chgo., 1958—; mem. staff Northwestern Meml. Hosp., 1972—, Rehab. Inst. Chgo., 1965—, Children's Meml. Hosp., 1972—, Little Co. of Mary Hosp., 1977—, Community Meml. Gen. Hosp., La Grange, 1977—; teaching assoc. Cleft Palate Inst., 1968, dir. otolaryngology, 1969—; asst. prof. dept. otolaryngology and maxillofacial surgery Northwestern U. Med. Sch., 1965-75, assoc. prof., 1975—; lectr. dept. otorhinolaryngology Loyola U., 1972. Producer videos, movie; contbr. numerous articles to profl. jours. and mags.; also guest appearances various radio and TV talk shows. NIH fellow U. Chgo., 1962-63; NIH grantee, 1985-88. Fellow Am. Neurotology Soc. (pres. 1974-75, chmn. editorial review & publ. com. 1978-79), Am. Acad. Otolaryngology-Head and Neck Surgery (chmn. subcom. on Equilibrium 1980-86, computer com. 1987—), Am. Acad. Ophtalmology and Otolaryngology, ACS, Inst. Medicine Chgo., Soc. for Ear, Nose and Throat Advances in Children; mem. AMA, Brit. Med. Assn., Ill. State Med. Soc., Chgo. Med. Soc., Nat. Hearing Assn. (sci. adv. com. 1982—, bd. dirs. 1983—), Am. Cleft Palate Assn., Am. Council Otolaryngology, Chgo. Laryngological and Otological Soc. (v.p. 1975-76), Sigma XI, Northwestern Clin. Faculty Med. Assn. (vice chmn. 1976-78, pres. 1979-81), Barany Soc., Royal Soc. Medicine, Irish Otolaryngological Soc. Roman Catholic. Clubs: Cliff Dwellers, Carlton. Avocations: travel, baroque music, symphony, opera, tennis. Office: 707 N Fairbanks Ct Chicago IL 60611

HART, DAVID FLOYD, teacher; b. Saginaw, Mich., Oct. 11, 1949; s. Floyd E. and Lorraine M. (Domino) H.; m. Tamara T. Tuttle, Aug. 8, 1975. AA, Delta Community Coll., 1971; BS, Cen. Mich. U., 1972, MA, 1975, Specialist in Edn., 1982. Jr. high sch. tchr. language arts and health Bridgeport (Mich.)-Spaulding Community Sch. Dist., 1972-79, tchr. fourth and fifth grade, 1979-85, elem. tchr. phys. edn., 1985—; jr. high sch. football coach, Bridgeport-Spaulding Community Sch Dist., 1972-86, baseball coach, 1972—, high sch. varsity football asst. coach, 1987—. Mem. NEA, Mich. Edn. Assn., Bridgeport Edn. Assn., Am. Alliance for Health, Phys. Edn., Recreation and Dance, Internat. Lighting Class Assn., U.S. Yacht Racing Union, Am. Running and Fitness Assn., Am. Sailing Assn., Mich. High Sch. Coaches Assn., Mich. High Sch. Football Coaches Assn. Roman Catholic. Lodge: KC. Avocations: computers, reading, sailing, sports. Home: 3390 Dale Rd Saginaw MI 48603 Office: Bridgeport-Spaulding Community Schs 3878 Sherman St Bridgeport MI 48722-0613

HART, JACK MILES, communications consultant; b. Cozad, Nebr., June 21, 1924; s. Miles Gilbert and Edith Bertha (Abercrombie) H.; m. Mary Ellen Stauffer, June 5, 1943; children: Linda Kay Hart Stroh, Susan Jane. BA, U. Nebr., 1952. Farm and polit. editor Lincoln (Nebr.) Jour., 1952-59, editorial page editor, 1959-73, mng. editor, 1973-81; asst. to gov. State of Nebr., Lincoln, 1981-83; communications cons. InCom, Lincoln, 1983—; cons. Tabitha, Inc., Lincoln, 1983—; pub. Nebr. Resources Report, Lincoln, 1983. Commentator Sta. KRVN-AM, Lexington, Nebr., 1983-84. Pres. Nebr. Agr.-Bus., Lincoln, 1961, Lincoln Library Bd., 1968-69, Mo. Basin States Assn., 1984-85, Friendship Force of Lincoln, 1984-85; sec. Lincoln Found., 1979-80; lobbyist City of Lincoln, 1983-86. Served with USN, 1943-45. Recipient Am. Polit. Sci. award Am. Polit. Sci. Assn., 1956, Disting. Service award Nebr. Assn. Conservation Dists., 1957, Disting. Service award N.G. Assn. Nebr., 1963, Disting. Service award Lincoln Indian Ctr., 1981. Republican. Presbyterian. Lodges: Elks, Sertoma (bd. dirs. 1976-77, trustee Found. 1979-86). Avocations: travel, photography, reading, bridge. Home: 440 Lyncrest Dr Lincoln NE 68510

HART, JAMES HARLAN, emergency medicine physician; b. Hamilton County, Ill., Dec. 16, 1934; s. Gleason and Elizabeth Jane (Smith) H.; m. Sharon Lenore Darr, Sept. 20, 1937; m. 2d, Lora Rae Barnett, May 9, 1955; children—Shane, Kyle, Raelene. B.S., Southwestern State U., Weatherford, Okla., 1963; M.D., Okla. U., 1968. Intern, Mercy Hosp., Oklahoma City, 1968-69; resident in ob-gyn St. Anthony Hosp., Oklahoma City, 1969-72; practice medicine specializing in ob-gyn, Woodriver, Ill., 1972-77; emergency medicine physician St. Elizabeth Hosp., Danville, Ill., 1977, med. dir. emergency med. service, 1980—; practice medicine specializing in emergency medicine, Lincoln, Ill., 1977-80; emergency medicine physician, Danville, Ill., 1980; med. dir. emergency med. technicians program; clin. assoc. prof. U. Ill. Med. Sch., Urbana. Served with U.S. Army, 1957-59. Mem. Am. Coll. Emergency Physicians, AMA, Ill. State Med. Soc., Vermillion County Med. Soc. Republican. Home: Rural Route 2 Williamsport IN 47993 Office: St Elizabeth Hosp 600 Sager Ave Danville IL 61832

HART, JAY ALBERT CHARLES, real estate broker; b. Rockford, Ill., Apr. 16, 1923; s. Jabez Waterman and Monty Evangeline (Burgin) H.; student U. Ill., 1941-42, U. Mo., 1942-43, U. Miami (Fla.), 1952-56, Rockford Coll., 1961-62; m. Marie D. Goetz, July 16, 1976; children—Dale M., Jay C.H. Exec. v.p. Hart Oil Co., Rockford, 1947—; pres. Internat. Service Co., Pompano Beach, Fla., 1952-58; v.p. Ipsen Industries, Inc., Rockford, 1958-61; owner Hart Realtors, Rockford, 1961-86; owner Hart & Assocs., Rockford, 1987—; pres. Rock Cut Corp., 1978—; sec. Intra World, Inc., 1981-83; lectr. in field; trustee, sr. analyst Anchor Real Estate Investment Trust, Chgo., 1971-80. Dir. Winnebago County (Ill.) CD, 1975; dep. coordinator Winnebago County (Ill.) ESDA, 1976-86. Chmn. Rock River chpt. ARC, 1973, nat. nominating com., 1971, disaster chmn. Illiana div., 1972-80; bd. counselors Rockford Coll., 1974-80; emergency coordinator 9th Naval dist. M.A.R.S., USN, 1960-68, civilian adv. council, 1968-78. Office mgr. Citizens for Eisenhower, Chgo., 1952. Served with USAAF, 1943-46. Mem. Rockford Air Guild (pres. 1974, 76-77), Tamaroa Watercolor Soc. (v.p. 1974-80), Rockford Art Guild (dir.), Exptl. Amateur Radio Soc. (pres. 1960-80), Nat. Assn. Real Estate Appraisers, Soc. Indsl. and Office Realtors, Nat. Assn. Rev. Appraisers and Mortgage Underwriters, Nat. Assn. Realtors, Phi Eta Sigma. Mason (Shriner). Clubs: Univ., City. Author: Real Estate Buyers and Sellers Guide, 1961. Paintings in pvt., pub. collections; illustrations in numerous publs. Home: 2406 E Lane Rockford IL 61107 Office: 3701 E State St Rockford IL 61108

HART, JOSEPH KIRWIN, advertising executive; b. N.Y.C., Oct. 13, 1934; s. Edward Remington and Katharine (Kirwin) H.; m. Rosalie Palazzolo, Apr. 30, 1966; children: Joseph Jr., Brian Francis. BS, Georgetown U., 1956. V.p. Ross Roy Advt., Detroit, 1968-79, Meldrum and Fewsmith, Detroit, 1979-83, McCann Erickson Advt., Troy, Mich., 1983-87, Cahners Pub. Co., West Bloomfield, Mich., 1987—. Served to lt. USN, 1957-60. Mem. Bus. Profl. Advt. Assn. (cert. bus. communicator, bd. dirs. 1981—, Advt. Man of Yr., 1983), Adcraft Club of Detroit (publicity com. 1965—). Roman Catholic. Avocation: tennis. Home: 5781 Plum Crest Dr West Bloomfield MI 48322 Office: Cahners Pub Co 7459 Middlebelt Rd West Bloomfield MI 48322

HART, ROBERT FRANKLIN, statistical process control consultant, educator; b. Hinsdale, Ill., Dec. 2, 1930; s. Morris Broadway and Laura Louise (Miller) Bradfute; m. Annamae Stack, May 19, 1953 (div. Dec. 20, 1981); m. Marilyn Klotnia, July 11, 1982; children—Robert, David, Laura, Linda. B.S. in Engring., U. Ill., 1949; M.S. in Engring. Ill. Inst. Tech., 1963, M.S. in Bus., 1982; Ph.D. in Engring., Northwestern U., 1966. Registered profl. engr., structural engr., Ill. Asst. chief engine design engr. electro-motive div. Gen. Motors, La Grange, Ill., 1961-80, mgr. statis. control, 1980-81; cons. Robert Hart & Assocs., Ltd., Oshkosh, Wis., 1981—; researcher Coll. Bus., U. Wis.-Oshkosh, 1985—. Author: (with Marilyn Hart) Statistical Process Control Training Workbook, 1982. Mem. Am. Statis. Assn., Operation Research Soc. Am., Am. Soc. Quality Control, Tau Beta Pi, Sigma Tau, Chi Epsilon, Sigma Iota Epsion. Home: 816 Anchorage Ct Oshkosh WI 54901 Office: Coll Bus U Wis Oshkosh WI 54901

HART, ROBERT THOMAS, lawyer; b. St. Louis, Feb. 15, 1939; s. Richard Cleveland and Alice Veronica (Butler) H.; m. Janet L. Cyrier, Aug. 11, 1962; children: Stephanie, Kristine, Kathleen, Jennifer, Robert, Patricia. BS, St. Louis U., 1961, JD, 1963. Bar: Mo. 1963, U.S. Dist. Ct. (ea. dist.) Mo. 1964. Claims atty. Employers Group, St. Louis, 1963-65; br. legal mgr. Employers of Wausau, St. Louis, 1965-72; chief adminstrv. law judge State of Mo. Office Workers Compensation, St. Louis, 1972-77; ptnr. Kortenhof & Ely, St. Louis, 1977—; mcpl. judge City of Greendale, Mo., 1986—. Co-author: Missouri Workers Compensation Law. Mem. Mo. Bar Assn., Bar Assn. Met. St. Louis, Mo. Orgn. Def. Lawyers, Internat. Assn. Def. Counsel, Phi Delta Phi. Republican. Roman Catholic. Lodge: KC (treas. local club 1970-72). Avocations: coin collecting, hunting, fishing. Home: 480 Oakwood Ave Webster Groves MO 63119 Office: Kortenhof & Ely 1015 Locust Suite 300 Saint Louis MO 63101

HART, WILLIAM LEVATA, police chief; b. Detroit, Jan. 17, 1924; s. Charles John and Gessener Mae (Brock) H.; m. Laura Elaine Johnson, Nov. 25, 1950; children: Cynthia Renee, Jennifer Lynn. B.S., Wayne State U., 1977, M.Ed., 1978, Ed.D. in Ednl. Sociology, 1981; grad., FBI Nat. Acad., 1972. Coal miner Leechburg, Pa., 1940-43, 46-49; tool and die maker Ford Motor Co., 1950-52; with Detroit Police Dept., 1952—, insp., 1971-73, div. comdr., 1973-74, dep. chief hdqrs. bur., 1974-76, chief police, 1976—; instr. criminal justice Wayne State U.; bd. dirs. Criminal Law Revision Com., 1976—; chmn. bd. Detroit Met. Acad., 1978—; mem. U.S. Atty. Gen.'s Task Force on Violent Crime; witness juvenile justice subcom. of Senate Judiciary Com. on Juvenile Justice and Delinquency Prevention Program; appointed chmn. U.S. Atty. Gen.'s Task Force on Family Violence, 1983. Chmn. United Fund Drive, Detroit, 1978; mem. Mayor's Bus. and Labor Ad-Hoc Com.; bd. dirs. Boy Scouts Am., Boys Club of Met. Detroit. Served with USNR, 1943-46. Mem. Internat. Police Assn., Internat. Assn. Chiefs of Police, Nat. Exec. Inst., Police Found., Am. Acad. Profl. Law Enforcement, Mich. Assn. Chiefs of Police (crime prevention com., subcom. on use of deadly force), Wayne County Assn. Chiefs of Police, Major City Chiefs of Police Assn., Mich. Commn. Criminal Justice, Police Exec. Research Forum, Nat. Orgn. Black Law Enforcement Execs. (exec. bd.), Detroit Police Benefit and Protective Assn. (pres. trustees). Baptist. Clubs: Detroit Yacht, Masons. Office: Office of Police Chief 1300 Beaubien Detroit MI 48226

HART, WILLIAM THOMAS, judge; b. Joliet, Ill., Feb. 4, 1929; s. William Michael and Geraldine (Archambeault) H.; m. Catherine Motta, Nov. 27, 1954; children: Catherine Hart Fornero, Susan Hart DeMario, Julie Hart Boesen, Sally, Nancy. J.D., Loyola U.-Chgo., 1951. Bar: Ill. 1951, U.S. Dist. Ct. 1957, U.S. Ct. Appeals 7th cir. 1954, U.S. Ct. Appeals D.C. 1977. Asst. U.S. atty. No. Dist. Ill., Chgo., 1954-56; spl. asst. atty. gen. State of Ill., 1957-58; spl. asst. state's Cook County, Ill., 1960; judge U.S. Dist. Ct., Chgo., 1982—; mem. firm Defrees & Fiske, 1956-59; ptnr. Schiff, Hardin & Waite, 1959-82. Pres. adv. bd. Mercy Med. Ctr., Aurora, Ill., 1980-81; v.p. Aurora Blood Bank, 1972-77; trustee Rosary High Sch., 1981-82; bd. dirs. Chgo. Legal Assistant Found., 1974-76. Served with U.S. Army, 1951-53. Decorated Bronze Star. Mem. 7th Cir. Bar Assn., Law Club, Legal Club, Soc. Trial Lawyers, Union League Club of Aurora, Calif. (hon.). Office: US Dist Ct 219 S Dearborn St Chicago IL 60604 *

HARTENBACH, STEPHEN CHARLES, small business owner; b. St. Louis, Oct. 9, 1943. Student, Rockhurst Coll., 1961-62, St. Louis U., 1964-67. Salesman Revere Copper and Brass, N.Y.C., 1969-72; pres. Hartenbach Interiors, St. Louis, 1972-75; pres. and chmn. bd. dirs. Hartenbach Carpet, St. Louis, 1975—. Alderman City of Sunset Hills, Mo., 1979-83. Served to 1st lt. U.S. Army, 1964-68. Mem. Am. Soc. Appraisers (assoc.), Regional Commerce and Growth Assn., Down St. Louis, Inc. Republican. Roman Catholic. Club: Cooperstown Country (N.Y.) (house chmn.). Lodge: Elks. Office: 11088 Millpark Dr Suite 136 Maryland Heights MO 63043

HARTER, DAVID JOHN, oncologist, radiation therapist; b. Milw., Apr. 12, 1942; s. Herbert George and Marion Bertha (Kahl) H.; m. Diane Leigh Kuebler; children: Renée, Andrew, Susannah Lee. BA, U. Wis., Milw., 1964; MD, U. Wis., Madison, 1968. Diplomate Am. Bd. Radiology. Dir. Immanuel Radiation Treatment Ctr., Omaha, 1979—; asst. clin. prof. radiology U. Nebr. Coll. Med., Omaha, 1978—; dir. Great Plains Inst. U. Nebr., Lincoln. Pres. Am. Cancer Soc. Nebr. div., Omaha, 1983-84, bd. dirs. 1980—; vice chmn. Omaha Parks and Recreation Commn., 1983—; mem. Omaha Pub. Art Commn., adv. bd. U. Nebr. Sheldon Meml. Art Gallery. Served to lt. comdr. USN, 1968-72. Mem. AMA, Am. Coll. Radiology, Am. Soc. Therapeutic Radiologists, Am. Radium Soc., Am. Soc. Clin. Oncology, Gilbert H. Fletcher Soc. Club: Omaha Country, Omaha; Doctors of Houston. Home: 9927 Essex Rd Omaha NE 68114 Office: Immanuel Med Ctr 6901 N 72d St Omaha NE 68122

HARTIG, KATHLEEN FRANCES, medical supply executive; b. St. Louis, June 16, 1942; s. Russell J. and Teresa (Filla) Horrell; m. Glen C. Hartig, Sept. 7, 1963; children: Mark R., Laura A. AS in Mgmt., St. Louis Community Coll., 1985. Credit corr. Storz Instrument Co., St. Louis, 1975-78, sec. to controller, 1981-83, sales adminstr., 1983-85, contract adminstr., 1985—; office mgr. Sangamo Weston, St. Louis, 1978-79; account rep. Biermann O'Brien, St. Louis, 1979-81. Pres. Concord Young Reps., St. Louis, 1961, Mesnier Mothers Club, St. Louis, 1973-74; activities chmn. Affton Elks Auxiliary, 1985. Recipient Curator's award Mo. U., 1960. Avocations: cake decorating, crafts, reading, swimming. Office: Storz Instrument Co 3365 Tree Ct Ind Saint Louis MO 63122

HARTIGAN, JAMES J., airline executive; b. 1924. With United Air Lines, Inc., Chgo., Ill., 1942—; asst. mgr. sales United Air Lines, Inc., Mt. Prospect, Ill., 1961-63, sales mgr., 1963-67, asst. v.p. sales, 1967, v.p. passenger sales and services planning, 1968-71, v.p. system mktg., 1971-73, sr. v.p., gen. mgr. Western div., 1973-75, group v.p. ops. services, exec. v.p., 1975-81, pres., 1981-87, chief exec. officer, 1985-87, chmn., 1987—, also dir. Served with USN, 1943-45. Office: United Air Lines Inc PO Box 66100 Chicago IL 60666 *

HARTIGAN, NEIL F., attorney general Illinois, lawyer. former lieutenant governor Illinois; b. Chgo., May 4, 1938; S. David and Colletta Hogan; m. Marge Hartigan, June 9, 1962; children: John, Elizabeth, Laura, Bridget. Grad. social scis., Georgetown U., 1958; J.D., Loyola U., Chgo., 1961; LL.D. (hon.), Lincoln Coll., 1975. Bar: Ill. bar 1962. Formerly dep. adminstrv. officer City of Chgo.; legis. counsel City of Chgo. in Ill. 75th Gen. Assembly; then chief legal counsel Chgo. Park Dist.; lt. gov. Ill., 1973-77; pres., chief exec. officer Real Estate Research Corp., Chgo., 1977-79; dir. Real Estate Research Corp., 1977; sr. v.p. 1st Nat. Bank Chgo., 1977-83; sr. v.p., area head Western Hemisphere, 1979-83; atty. gen. State of Ill., 1983—; lectr. former mem. faculty John Marshall Law Sch. Active Am. Cancer Soc. drives; chmn. Nat. Conf. Lt. Govs., 1976; former mem. exec. com. Council State Govts.; bd. dirs. Georgetown U.; mem. vis. com. on public policy U. Chgo.; bd. dirs. Chgo. Conv. and Tourism Bur., TRUST, Inc., Lincoln Park Zool. Soc.; mem. exec. com. March of Dimes; chmn. Super-walk, 1978. Named One of 200 Hundred Young Ams. Most Likely To Provide New Generation of Leadership Time mag.; among Ten Outstanding Young Men of Yr. Chgo. Jr. C. of C., 1967; Man of Year Loyola U. Alumni Assn. and Chgo. Bar Assn., 1982; hon. pres. Spanish-speaking div. Jr. C. of C., Chgo. Mem. Am. Bar Assn., Ill. Bar Assn., Chgo. Bar Assn., Chgo. Assn. Commerce and Industry (v.p. urban affairs), Chgo. Council on Fgn. Relations, Young Presidents Orgn., Nat. Council on Aging, Irish Fellowship Club. Clubs: Economic, Executive, Rotary, K.C, Hundred of Cook County. Office: Office of Atty General 500 S 2d Springfield IL 62706 *

HARTING, JAMES JOSEPH, health administrator, consultant; b. St. Louis, Dec. 17, 1942; s. Paul Henry and Dorothy Edith (Adelman) H.; divorced; children: Noel, Amy. BA in Philosophy, Cardinal Glennon Coll., 1965; MSW in Social Work, Washington U., St. Louis, 1969. Child care worker Jewish Hosp., St. Louis, 1965; social worker Alton (Ill.) State Hosp., 1965-69; exec. dir. Alcohol and Drug Dependence Council, East St. Louis, 1969-77; dir. hosp. services div. Personal Performance Cons., St. Louis, 1977-79; pres. Harting Assocs., Inc., Fairview Heights, Ill., 1979—, Healthrite Systems, Inc., Belleville, Ill., 1983—; sec., treas. Corp. Health Resources, Inc., Albuquerque, 1986—. Mem. Am. Hosp Assn., Assn. Labor Mgmt. Adminstrs. and Cons. on Alcoholism, Alcohol and Drug Problems Assn. Avocations: tennis, golf. Home: 115 Fox Creek Belleville IL 62223 Office: Harting Assocs Inc 333 Salem Pl Suite 145 Fairview Heights IL 62208

HARTITZ, JOACHIM ERNST, chemical engineer, scientist; b. Dessau, Germany, Aug. 11, 1929; came to U.S., 1965; s. Ernst Karl and Hedwig (Klockengiesser) H.; m. Armgard Erika Weigel, Oct. 28, 1958; children—Marcos Dominik, Raina Carlotta. Ing. Chem., Ohm-Poly., Nurenberg,

Germany. Research engr. Bad. Anilin & Soda Fabrik, Ludwigshafen, Fed. Republic Germany, 1955-57; dep. mgr. Focke-Wulf Aircraft Co., Bremen, Fed. Republic Germany, 1957-59; plant mgr. Tubenplast S.A., Caracas, Venezuela, 1959-65; plant mgr. B.F. Goodrich Co., Ardee, Ireland, 1977-82, research fellow, Avon Lake, Ohio, 1965-77, 82—. Author: Polymer Engineering and Science, 1974. Patentee in field. Mem. Soc. Plastics Engrs. (sr.). Lodge: Masons. Home: 32833 Tanglewood Ct Avon Lake OH 44012 Office: BF Goodrich Chem Group Walker Rd Avon Lake OH 44012

HARTLE, RICHARD HENRY, publishing executive; b. Pitts., Mar. 7, 1931; s. Rupert William and Clementine Caroline (Schaub) H.; m. Mary Joyce Ryan, July 14, 1962; children: Thomas Ryan, Molly Katherine. BA, Pa. State U., State College, 1952. Sales rep. Latrobe (Pa.) Steel Co., 1955-59; mgr. splty. steel Edgecomb Steel Co., Hillside, N.J., 1959-61; sales rep. Look Mag., Cleve., 1961-63; regional mgr. Look Mag., Detroit, 1963-71; pres. Richard Hartle Assoc., Detroit, 1971—. Active Big Bros. Oakland County, Mihc., 1964-69; Bd. dirs. The Community House, Birmingham, Mich., 1982-85, pres. 1983-84, Saint Dunstan's Guild of Cranbrook, Bloomfield Hills, Mich., 1981-82. Served to 1st lt. USAF, 1952-54. Mem. The Adcraft Club, Detroit Advt. Assn. (pres. 1980-81). Republican. Roman Catholic. Club: Orchard Lake Country. Avocations: photography, music, golf, tennis, fishing. Office: Richard Hartle Assocs Inc 1025 E Maple Birmingham MI 48011

HARTLEY, JAMES MICHAELIS, manufacturing and printing co. exec.; b. Indpls., Nov. 25, 1916; s. James Worth and Bertha S. (Beuke) H.; student Jordan Conservatory of Music, 1934-35, Ind. U., Purdue U., Franklin Coll.; m. E. Lea Cosby, July 30, 1944; children—Michael D., Brent S. With Arvin Industries, Inc., 1934-36; founder, pres. J. Hartley Co., Inc., Columbus, Ind., 1937—. Pres., Columbus Little Theatre, 1947-48; founding dir. Columbus Arts Guild, 1960-64, v.p., 1965-66, dir., 1971-74; musical dir., cellist Guild String Quartet, 1963-73; founding dir. Columbus Pro Musica, 1969-74; dir. Regional Arts Study Commn., 1971-74; v.p. Ind. Council Republican Workshops, 1965-69, pres., 1975-77; pres. Bartholomew County Republican Workshop, 1966-67. Served with USAAF, 1942-46. Mem. NAM, Nat. Fedn. Ind. Bus. Office: 101 N National Rd Columbus IN 47201

HARTMAN, DAVID ELLIOTT, psychologist; b. N.Y.C., Jan. 9, 1954; s. Harry Wilson and Marian Phyllis (Milchin) H. AB, Vassar Coll., 1975; MA, Princeton U., 1978; PhD, U. of Ill., Chgo., 1982. Lic. psychologist, Ill. Intern Michael Reese Hosp.; asst. coordinator in emergency psychiatry Northwestern U. Hosp., Chgo., 1982; dir. psychology tng. Lincoln Park Clinic at Columbus Hosp., Chgo., 1985-86; dir. neuropsychology Cook County Hosp., Chgo., 1982—; adj. asst. prof. psychology U. Ill. Med. Ctr., Chgo., 1984—. Author: Neuropsychological Toxicology, 1987; mem. editorial bd. Archives Clin. Neuropsychology; contbr. numerous articles to profl. jours. Fellow NIMH. Mem. Am. Psychol. Assn. (pres. Chgo. chpt., edit. bd.), Ill. Psychol. Assn. (clin. chmn.), Phi Beta Kappa. Office: Cook County Hosp Dept Psychiatry 1835 W Harrison Chgo IL 60612

HARTMAN, EDWIN ALAN, psychology and business educator, consultant; b. Wisconsin Rapids, Wis., Oct. 15, 1944; s. Edwin John and Dorothy Marion (Polansky) H.; m. Diana Lynn Lindgren, Mar. 2, 1968; children—Elizabeth Ann, Amy Catherine. B.A., U. Wis.-Madison, 1968; M.A., Mich. State U., 1970, Ph.D., 1972. Research scientist Inst. Behavioral Research, Tex. Christian U., 1972-76; asst. prof. psychology and bus. adminstrn. U. Wis.-Oshkosh, 1976-79, assoc. prof. psychology and bus. adminstrn., 1979-83, acting asst. vice chancellor, 1984, prof., assoc. dean Coll. Bus. Adminstrn., 1985—; cons. Air Can., Am. Airlines, Eastern Airlines, First Nat. Bank Ft. Worth, Ft. Worth Nat. Bank, Oshkosh Truck Corp., Thilmany Pulp and Paper, Rockwell Internat.-Oshkosh div., Winnebago County, Waushara County, Trinity Valley Mental Health Authority, Tarrant County (Tex.), Wis. Assn. Sch. Bds., AT&T, Braniff Airlines, Kaiser-Permanente Med. Care Program. NDEA grad. fellow, 1968-71; NIMH grantee, 1979-82; HEW grantee, 1974-75. Mem. Am. Psychol. Assn., Acad. Mgmt., Fox Valley Personnel Assn., Midwest Psychol. Assn., Midwest Acad. Mgmt., Sigma Xi, Psi Chi. Presenter numerous confs.; contbr. chpts. to books, articles to profl. jours. Home: 2745 Montclair Pl Oshkosh WI 54901 Office: Clow Faculty U Wis Oshkosh WI 54901

HARTMAN, GARY MICHAEL, mechanical engineer; b. Auburn, Ind., Aug. 28, 1959; s. Robert Sammy and Glora Annette (Warner) H.; m. Domenica Nicolette Samargin, July 19, 1986. BSME, Tri-State U., Angola, Ind., 1981; postgrad., U. Mich., 1986—. Devel. engr. Bendix, South Bend, Ind., 1981-83, prod. engr., 1983-85; devel. mgr. Lucas Girling, Troy, Mich., 1985—. Advisor Jr. Achievement, South Bend, 1983-84. Mem. Soc. Automotive Engrs. (assoc., mem. brake subcom.). Republican. Avocations: skiing, scuba, gardening. Office: Lucas Girling 5500 New King St Troy MI 48007

HARTMAN, HERBERT ARTHUR, JR., oncologist; b. Halstead, Kans., Aug. 8, 1947; s. Herbert Arthur and Margrete Laverne (Schroeder) H.; m. Cynthia Craig, Dec. 26, 1971; m. April Craig, Herbert Arthur III. BA in Chemistry, U. Kans., 1969, MD, 1973. Diplomate Am. Bd. Internal Medicine, Am. Bd. Med. Oncology. Resident internal medicine U. Nebr. Med. Ctr., Omaha, 1973-76, fellow in med. oncology, 1976-78; oncologist Radiologic Ctr., Inc., Omaha, 1978-79, Sole Proprietorship, Omaha, 1979-80, Oncology Assocs., Omaha, 1980—; clin. asst. prof. internal medicine U. Nebr. med. Sch., 1979—. Contbr. articles to med. jours. Chmn. profl. edn. div. Nebr. Cancer Soc., 1985. Served to capt. USAFR. Fellow Am. Coll. Physicians; mem. AMA, Am. Soc. Internal Medicine, Am. Soc. Clin. Oncology, Nebr. Med. Assn., Metro Omaha Med. Soc., N.Y. Acad. Scis. Democrat. Episcopalian. Avocations: tennis, personal finance, reading. Home: 6211 Chicago Omaha NE 68132 Office: Oncology Assocs Immanuel Profl Plaza #13 6801 N 72d St Omaha NE 68122

HARTMAN, LENORE ANNE, physical therapist; b. Cleve., May 27, 1938; d. Howard Andrew and Emma Elizabeth (Beck) H. BS in Agriculture, Ohio State U., 1960, MS in Agriculture, 1963; postgrad., Kans. State U., 1963-67; cert. in phys. therapy, U. Kans., Delano, 1968. Staff phys. therapist R.J. DeLand Sch. for the Handicapped, Kansas City, Mo., 1969-74; chief phys. therapist Children's Mercy Hosp., Kansas City, 1974-78; relief staff Mass Gen. Hosp., Boston, 1969-70, staff phys. therapist, 1979—; clin. instr. phys. therapy St. Louis U., 1974-78, U. Ky., 1974-78, U. Mo., Columbia, 1973-78, U. Kans. Med. Ctr., Kansas City, 1974—; mem. med. adv. com. Hospice Care of Mid Am., Kansas City, 1984—; chapel organist, St. Luke's Hosp., Kansas City, 1978—. Ohio del. Internat. Farm Youth Exchange, Brazil, 1962; mem. Friends of Art Nelson Art Gallery, Kansas City. Mem. Am. Physical Therapy Assn. (del. to nat. 1975-76), Mo. Physical Therapy Assn. (chmn. northwest dist. 1974-76), Am. Guild of Organists (chmn. profl. concerns com. Greater Kansas City chpt. 1983), Japan Am. Soc., Ohio State U. Alumni Assn., Omicron Delta Epsilon, Phi Delta Gamma (contbr. articles to jour.). Avocations: sketching, sewing, dog obedience training, choir singing, gardening. Home: 6101 Delmar Fairway KS 66205 Office: Menorah Med Ctr 49th & Rockhill Rd Kansas City MO 64110

HARTMAN, MARSHA ANN MCLOCHLIN, accountant; b. St. Joseph, Mich., July 25, 1957; d. Charles Richard and Shirley Rose (Vendl) McL.; m. Garry Lee Hartman, Aug. 27, 1983. BS, Ind. U., 1980. Audit mgr. Coopers & Lybrand, Indpls., 1980—. Treas. Girls Clubs of Greater Indpls., 1986—. Mem. Am. Inst. CPA's, Ind. CPA Soc. (utilities com. 1986). Avocations: golfing, reading. Address: Coopers & Lybrand 2900 One American Square Indianapolis IN 46282

HARTMAN, ROBERT RAY, retired physician, medical consultant; b. Jacksonville, Ill., Feb. 17, 1914; s. Ray Adam and Blanche Margaret (Perry) H.; m. Beatrice Hayes, Feb. 20, 1937; children: Linda Skop, Suzanne Verticchio. AB, Ill. Coll., 1935; BM, Northwestern U., Chgo., 1940, MD, 1941; LLD (hon.), Ill. Coll., 1986. Diplomate Am. Bd. Ob-Gyn. Intern St. Louis City Hosp., 1939-40, resident in ob-gyn, 1940-43; practice medicine specializing in ob-gyn Jacksonville, 1946-85; chief of staff Passavant Hosp., Jacksonville, Ill., 1955, 66; assoc. clin. prof. ob-gyn Southern Ill. U., Springfield, 1976—; cons. Ill. Dept. Pub. Aid, 1974—, Ill. Dept. Pub. Health, Springfield, 1972-74, Ill. Maternal Welfare Com., 1954—, chmn., 1964-74; chmn. Ill. Maternal Welfare Com., 1964-74; sec. bd. trustees Ill. Coll., Jacksonville, 1963-86. Contbr. articles to profl. jours. Mem. Jacksonville Planning Com., 1959-67, chmn. 1962-67; mem. Mayor's Flood Control Com., Jacksonville, 1978-82; mem. Morgan County Bd. Health, Jacksonville, 1960-61, pres. 1968-80; mem. Ill. Com. Rewrite and Revise Pub. Aid Code, Springfield, Ill. 1978-81; trustee emeritus Ill. Coll., Jacksonville, 1986. Served to capt. U.S. Army, 1943-46. Recipient Cert. Appreciation, Morgan-Scott Med. Soc., 1979. Mem. AMA (alt. del. 1976-82), Ill. Ob-Gyn Soc. (pres. 1965-66), Am. Coll. Ob-Gyn, Internat. Coll. Surgeons, Ill. State Med. Soc. (trustee 1975-84, v.p. 1977, chmn. bd. trustees 1978-80), Am. Assn. Med. Assistance (nat. physician adv. 1982-84). Republican. Mem. United Ch. Christ. Club: The Club (Jacksonville (pres.). Lodges: Elks, Masons, Rotary (pres. 1951, Paul Harris fellow 1982). Avocations: philately, writing, travel. Home: 5B Justin Dr Jacksonville IL 62650

HARTMAN, WILLIAM JOSEPH, clinical psychologist; b. Chgo., June 23, 1913; s. William Albert and Linda Marietta (Jensen) H.; m. Merry Joy Lamb (div.); children: Harvey Strother, Steven Lee, Judith Ann, Roger Adam, Nina Lynn; m. Frances Celeste Gromaire. BA, State U. Iowa, 1941; MA, U. Mich., 1944; postgrad., George Washington U., 1947, U. Md., 1948, Washington Sch. Psychiatry, 1949. Psychologist Child Study Inst., Toledo, 1944, Bur. Prisons, Washington, 1944-51, State Reformatory, Green Bay, Wis., 1951-78; pvt. practice psychology Green Bay, 1978—. Chmn. fine arts Friends of the Library, Green Bay, 1985—; pres. Unitarian Fellowship, Green Bay, 1963l vol. counselor for handicapped Curative Workshop, Green Bay, 1986—. Served to sgt. USAF, 1942-44. Recipient Gov.'s Spl. award State of Wis., 1978. Mem. Am. Psychol. Assn., Wis. Psychol. Assn. (life), Am. Cancer Soc. (editor newsletter 1982), ACLU (bd. dirs. 1986), Artists Unlimited (founder Green Bay 1954). Democrat. Unitarian. Club: Green Bay Area Writers (pres. 1984-85). Avocations: painting, sculpture, writing, acting, wine-making. Home and Office: 1120 S Quincy St Green Bay WI 54301

HARTMANN, DONALD OTTO, SR., beverage corporation executive; b. St. Louis, Jan. 24, 1934; s. Otto Frederic and Mabel Lena (Schuessler) H.; B.S., U. Mo., 1963, M.Ed., 1964, Assoc. EED, 1966; m. Linda Lou Sparks, Sept. 8, 1962; children—Kimberly Lynn, Donald Otto, Jacqueline Marie, Michele Lee. Profl. scout exec. Boy Scouts Am., 1959-60; asst. prof. U. Mo., 1960-63; coordinator co-op. edn. Mo., 1963-67; dir. personnel, rehab. Goodwill Industries of Am., 1967-69; dir. forms mgmt., graphics communications, supply services Anheuser-Busch Cos., Inc., St. Louis, 1969—; tchr., counselor, cons. in graphic arts, forms design and mgmt., 1969—. Chmn. bd. Christian edn. United Ch. of Christ, St. Louis, 1974-77; bd. dirs. local bd. edn., 1972—, pres., 1973-76; active Boy Scouts Am., 1942—, Eagle Scout reviewer/presenter, 1960—; mem. community wide youth services panel United Way of St. Louis, 1970—; mem. White House Panel on Childhood Edn., Mo. Gov.'s Panel on Edn., 1977; active Lindbergh PTA, 1968—. Served with USN, 1953-59. Recipient Eagle Scout award Boy Scouts Am., 1952, Silver Explorer award, 1956, Gt. Grant award, 1962, Regional Service award, 1973, Silver Beaver award; Outstanding Loaned Exec. award United Way, 1970, Community Service award Girl Scouts U.S.A. Mem. Am. Sch. Bds. Assn., Nat. Sch. Bds. Assn., Mo. Sch. Bds. Assn., St. Louis Suburban Sch. Bds. Assn., In-Plant Mgrs. Assn., Council of Reprographics Execs., Am. Mgmt. Assn., Nat. Eagle Scout Assn. (St. Louis area council 1982), Phi Delta Kappa, Sigma Phi Epsilon (alumni bd. pres. 1963-70). Home: 4824 Gatesbury Dr Saint Louis MO 63128 Office: Anheuser-Busch Companies Inc One Busch Pl Saint Louis MO 63118

HARTMANN, RICHARD PAUL, accountant; b. Terre Haute, Ind., Sept. 4, 1934; s. Albert and Therese (Diekhoff) H.; m. Marcia Jean Von Blon, June 16, 1956; children—Richard Paul Jr., Jeffrey Bryan, Roger Allan. B.A., Capital U., 1956; student Officers Candidate Sch., Newport, R.I., 1956, U.S. Naval War Coll., 1969; postgrad. Xavier U., 1964-65, U. Dayton, 1965-66. C.P.A., Ohio, 1969. Sr. staff acct. Battelle & Battelle, C.P.A.s, Dayton, Ohio, 1960-69; owner, mgr. Richard P. Hartmann, C.P.A., Kettering, Ohio, 1970—. bd. dirs. Care Ctrs., Inc., Dayton, Longwood Broadcasting, Washington. Mem. City Council Kettering, 1977—; vice mayor City of Kettering, 1985—; treas. Holiday at Home, Inc., 1974—; mem. pres.'s council Capital U.; treas. Capital U. Alumni Bd., 1967-68; mem. Congrl. screeing coms. USN Acad.; treas. Ohio dist. Evang. Luth. Ch. Am., Ohio, 1987; bd. dirs. Kettering Community Improvement Corp., 1972—. Served with USNR, 1956-87, capt. Res. ret., 1987. Recipient Community Service award, Kettering, 1978, 79. Mem. Am. Inst. CPA's, Ohio Soc. CPA's, Kettering C. of C. (past pres.), Naval Inst., Nat. League Cities, Naval War Coll., Naval Res. Assn., U.S. Navy League (v.p. 1986), Miami Valley (Ohio) Mil. Affairs Orgn. (charter). Republican. Lutheran. Club: Exchange (Kettering pres. 1978-79). Office: 3560 Marshall Rd Kettering OH 45429

HARTMANN, RONALD C., engineering designer; b. St. Louis, Dec. 5, 1936; s. William and Dora (Kleinsorge) H.; m. Kathleen M. Ewers, May 3, 1958; children: Linda, Karen, Barbara. Engring. designer Anheuser-Busch, St. Louis, 1957—. Editor newsletter of Japanese Sword Soc. of U.S. Inc. Served with USN, 1954-57. Avocations: collecting and studying Japanese art, swords and related artifacts. Home: PO Box 4387 Saint Louis MO 63123

HARTMANN, RONALD JOSEPH, pharmacist; b. Waconia, Minn., Jan. 10, 1946; s. Gilbert Joseph and Eva Verna (Gorski) H.; m. Mary Jean Moldestad, Feb. 12, 1947; children—Carey Ayn, Matthew Joseph. B.S., U. Minn., 1969. Registered pharmacist, Minn. Pharmacy intern Matson Drug Co., Waconia, 1966-69, Abbott Hosp., Mpls., 1968-69; hosp. pharmacist Rochester (Minn.) Methodist Hosp., 1969-81; dir. pharmacy Spring Valley (Minn.) Meml. Hosp., 1974-75; dir. pharmacy Olmsted Community Hosp., Rochester, 1975-78; cons. pharmacist Mayo Clinic, Rochester, 1979-81; dir. pharm. services St. Olaf Hosp., Austin, Minn., 1981-83; owner Mapleton Drug, Mapleton, Minn.; mem. adj. faculty U. Minn. Mem., officer Rochester Area Barbershop Chorus, 1970-81; active Boy Scouts Am.; mem. Mapleton Area Planning Team, 1985; bd. dirs. Mapleton Community Home, 1985. Recipient Outstanding Achievement award Rexall Co., 1969. Fellow Am. Soc. Cons. Pharmacists; mem. Am. Pharm. Assn., Minn. State Pharm. Assn. (bd. dirs. 1979-83), Am. Soc. Hosp. Pharmacists, Minn. Soc. Hosp. Pharmacists, So. Minn. Soc. Hosp. Pharmacists (pres. 1974), Mapleton Area C. of C. (pres. 1987—), Kappa Psi (Scholastic award 1968), Rho Chi. Roman Catholic. Club: Sertoma. Home: 503 1st Ave SE Mapleton MN 56065 Office: Mapleton Drug Box 414 Mapleton MN 56065

HARTSELL, ROBERT NEAL, fire department officer, safety instructor; b. Elmwood Park, Ill., Mar. 26, 1937; s. Ralph Miles and Mary Alice (Napier) H.; m. Joan Cunningham, Mar. 3, 1956; children—Terry Lynn Tammy Dawn, Toni Renee, Daniel Robert. A.S. in Fire Sci., Triton Coll., River Grove, Ill., 1980; B.S., So. Ill. U., 1982; MPA, Ill. Inst. Tech., 1986. Fire fighter Chgo. Fire Dept., 1962-72, fire lt. Fire Prevention Bur., 1972-73, co. officer, 1973—, fire capt., 1980—, asst. dir. fire safety, 1986, comdg. officer air mask service; safety coordinator St. Joseph Hosp., 1979-83; fire safety instr. Mem. Republican Nat. Com. Served with USMC, 1954-57. Recipient commendations Chgo. Fire Dept., Mayor of Chgo., 1975, 1980. Mem. Internat. Soc. Fire Service Instrs., Fire Officers Assn., Am. Soc. Safety Engrs., Nat. Fire Protection Assn. Lodge: Internat. Order of Foresters. Home: 5525 N Nashville Ave Chicago IL 60656 Office: 558 W DeKoven St Chicago IL 60607

HARTSMAN, ELAINE EVELYN, consulting psychologist, educator; b. Milw., July 29, 1942; d. Max and Eleanor Regina (Kraus) H. BS in Psychology, U. Wis., Milw., 1964; MS in Rehab. Counseling, U. Wis., Madison, 1966; PhD, U. Minn., 1976. Cert. psychologist, Minn. Counselor Cooperative Sch. Rehab. Ctr., Minnetonka, Minn., 1966-72; case mgr. 916 Area Vocat. Tech. Inst., White Bear Lake, Minn., 1972-76; psychologist, facilitator St. Paul Pub. Schs., 1976—; pvt. practice psychology St. Paul, 1976—; supr. Walk-In Counseling Ctr., Mpls., 1982—; bd. dirs. Gestalt Inst., Mpls., 1984—. Mem. Minn. Psychology Bd. Mem. Democratic Farm Labor Party. Jewish. Avocations: reading, computer play, fine wines. Home: 1301 W 82d St Bloomington MN 55420 Office: 1885 University Ave W #121 Saint Paul MN 55104

HARTSOOK, ROBERT FRANCIS, educational administrator; b. Eureka, Kans., July 12, 1948; s. Herbert Edwin and Beverly Mercia (James) H. B.A., Kans. State Tchrs. Coll., 1970, M.S., 1972; J.D., Washburn U., 1979. V.p. Colby Community Coll., Kans., 1972-76; exec. v.p., chief exec. officer Kans. Engring. Soc., Inc., Topeka, 1978-82; v.p. Washburn U., Topeka, 1982-85, Wichita State U., Kans. 1985—. Bd. editors Washburn Law Jour. 1977-79, exec. editor, 1977-78. Commn. Kansas State Educ. Commn., Topeka, 1975-78; mem. adv. panel Gov.'s Commn. Criminal Admin., Topeka, 1975-78. Danforth Found. fellow, summer 1973. Mem. Council for Advancement and Support of Educ. (most improved univ. 1984, 86, exceptional achievement in fin. support 1985). Club: Wichita. Home: 9433 Bent Tree Circle Wichita KS 67226 Office: Wichita State U Wichita KS 67208

HARTSTEIN, JOHN MARK, electronics company executive; b. Mishawaka, Ind., Aug. 6, 1958; s. Theodore John and Joan Arlene (Bentley) H.; m. Cheryl June Bowling, MAy 31, 1980; 1 child, Daniel John. AA in Acctg. and Bus. Adminstrn., Michiana Coll. of Commerce, 1979. Cost analyst Skyline Corp., Elkhart, Ind., 1979-81; cost acct. Schult Homes Corp., Elkhart, 1981-84; estimator product mktg. Wells Electronics, Inc., South Bend, Ind., 1984—, product mktg. specialist, 1985—, internat. product and market devel. specialist, sales mgr. Can. div., 1987—. Treas. campaign Tommy Melton for State Rep., South Bend, 1981-82; officer, trustee, deacon Twin City Bapt. Ch., Mishawaka, 1987; mem. Osceola Communtiy Players, 1985. Republican. Avocations: referee, golf, softball, spectator sports. Home: 55801 Nursery Ave Mishawaka IN 46545 Office: Wells Electronics Inc 1701 S Main St South Bend IN 46613

HARTWIG, DANIEL J., environmental consultant; b. Milw., Mar. 27, 1949; s. Herman N. and Julia (Plevak) H.; m. Diane E. Meier, June 16, 1973; children: Matthew, Andrew, Jennifer, Timothy. BA in Environ. Engring., U. Wis., Milw., 1975; postgrad., U. Wis., Whitewater, 1976-81. Cert. safety profl., hazard control mgr., Wis. Safety cons. Limnetics, Inc., Milw., 1971-73; pvt. practice safety cons. Milw., 1973-75; dir. programs Wis. Council of Safety, Madison, 1975-78; pres. Daniel J. Hartwig Assocs., Inc., Oregon, Wis., 1978—; instr. Waukesha County (Wis.) Tech. Inst., 1977-79; lectr. in field, 1979—. Contbr. articles to profl. jours. Mem. Am. Soc. Safety Engrs. (profl., treas. 1985-86), Am. Indsl. Hygiene Assn. (profl.), Cons. Engrs. Wis., Triangle Frat. (pres. 1979-81), Fedn. Environ. Technologists. Roman Catholic. Club: Bklyn. Flying (Wis. pres. 1986-87). Lodge: Jaycees, Rotary. Avocations: softball, racquetball, antique cars. Home: 1518 Blue Heron Way Oregon WI 53575 Office: Daniel J Hartwig Assocs Inc 742 Market St Oregon WI 53575

HARTWIG, JOAN ELAINE, educator; b. Detroit, Mar. 5, 1936; d. Theodore Herman and Elfrieda Gertrude (Riske) Hock; m. William Carl Hartwig, July 7, 1956; children: Susan Marie Hartwig Chitlik, Karen Jean Hartwig Goodrich. BS, Mich. State U., 1958, MA, 1963. Admissions asst. Mich. State U., East Lansing, 1958-63, admissions counselor, 1963-65; counselor Lansing (Mich.) Community Coll., 1965—, instr., 1965-67, coordinator of articulation transfer program, 1965—, asst. prof., 1967-73, assoc. prof., 1973-77, instr. assertiveness classes, 1976-81, prof., 1977—; bd. dirs. Lansing Community Coll. Found. Editor: Transfer Articulation List, 1974, 76, 79, 84, 86. Mem. Mich. Assn. Collegiate Registrars and Admissions Officers (sec. 1978-80, pres. 1983-84), Mich. Personnel and Guidance Assoc. (legis. com. chair 1984-85), Mich. Assn. Higher Edn. (treas. Lansing Commmunity Coll. chpt. 1981—). Lutheran. Lodge: Zonta (dir. E. Lansing 1984-86, pres. 1986—). Avocations: calligraphy, reading, choral singing. Home: 1219 Lilac Ave East Lansing MI 48823 Office: Admissions Office-25 Lansing Community Coll. 430 N Capitol PO Box 40010 Lansing MI 48901

HARTZELL, ROBERT LEROY, foods manufacturing executive; b. Barron, Wis., June 23, 1941; s. Raymond A. and Ruth (Schrader) H.; m. Mary C. Ladlie, Sept. 5, 1964; children—Christopher, Elizabeth. B.S., U. Wis., 1963. Mgr. sales and mdseing. Wilson and Co., 1963-70; pres. North Star Foods, Inc., St. Charles, Minn., 1971—, North Star Freight, St. Charles, 1975—; bd. dirs. Whitewater Marathon, St. Charles, 1984—. Office: North Star Foods Inc PO Box 587 St Charles MN 55972

HARVEY, IRWIN M., carpet mill executive; b. Chgo., Apr. 24, 1931; s. Herman and Clara (Pomerantz) Harvey Smith; m. Marilyn G. Greenspahn, June 7, 1952; children: Beth I. Dorfman, Jill F. Harvey Stein, Gail L. B.S., Roosevelt U., 1952. Sales rep. Pinksy Floor Covering Co., Chgo., 1954-58; sales agt. Hyams & Harvey, Chgo., 1958-63; v.p., regional mgr. Evans & Black Carpet Mills, Elk Grove Village, Ill., 1963-67; v.p., dir. mktg. Evans & Black Carpet Mills, Dallas, 1967-68; chmn.-pres. Galaxy Carpet Mills Inc., Elk Grove Village, Ill., and Chatsworth, Ga., 1968-83, chmn., chief exec. officer, 1984—; bd. dirs., exec. com. Floor Covering Industry Found., Chgo., 1980—; mem. adv. bd. Acad. Design Sch., Chgo., 1978-83, Dallas Trade Mart, 1983—. Served with U.S. Army, 1952-54. Named Man of Year Floor Covering Industry Found., 1983. Mem. Carpet and Rug Inst. (dir. 1971—, exec. com. 1973-82, 1978-80), Chgo. Floor Covering Assn. Jewish. Home: 868 Thackeray Dr Highland Park IL 60035 Office: Galaxy Carpet Mills Inc 850 Arthur Ave Elk Grove Village IL 60007

HARVEY, KATHERINE ABLER, civic worker; b. Chgo., May 17, 1946; d. Julius and Elizabeth (Engelman) Abler; student La Sorbonne, Paris, 1965-66; A.A.S., Bennett Coll., 1968; m. Julian Whitcomb Harvey, Sept. 7, 1974. Asst. librarian McDermott, Will & Emery, Chgo., 1969-70; librarian Chapman & Cutler, Chgo., 1970-73, Coudert Freres, Paris, 1973-74; adviser, organizer library Lincoln Park Zool. Soc. and Zoo, Chgo., 1977-79, mem. soc.'s women's bd., 1976—, chmn. library com., 1977-79, sec., 1979-81, mem. exec. com., 1977-81 ; mem. jr. bd. Alliance Francaise de Chgo., 1970-76, treas., mem. exec. com., 1971-73, 75-76, mem. women's bd., 1977-80; mem. Fred Harvey Fine Arts Found., 1976-78; hon. life mem. Chgo. Symphony Soc., 1975—; mem. Phillips Acad. Alumni Council, Andover, Mass., 1977-81, mem. acad.'s bicentennial celebration com. class celebration leader, 1978, co-chmn. for Chgo. acad.'s bicentennial campaign, 1977-79, mem. student affairs and admissions com., 1980-81; mem. aux. bd. Art Inst. Chgo., 1978—; mem. Know Your Chgo. com. U. Chgo. Extension, 1981-84; mem. guild Chgo. Hist. Soc., 1978—; mem. women's bd. Lyric Opera Chgo., 1979—, chmn. edn. com., 1980, mem. exec. com., 1980-84 , treas. women's bd., 1983-84; mem. women's bd. Northwestern Meml. Hosp., 1979—, treas., chmn. fin. com., 1981-84, mem. exec. com., 1981—; bd. dirs. Found. Art Scholarships, 1982-83; bd. dirs. Glen Ellyn (Ill.) Children's Chorus, 1983—, founding chmn. pres.'s com., 1983; mem. women's bd. Chgo. City Ballet, 1983-84; trustee Chgo. Acad. Scis., 1986—; bd. dirs. Grant Park Concertd Soc., 1986—; adv. council med. program for performing artists Northwestern Meml. Hosp., 1986—. Mem. Antiquarian Soc. of Art Inst. Chgo. (life); bd. dirs. Grant Park Concerts Soc., 1986—. Clubs: Arts of Chgo., Friday (corr. sec. 1981-83), Casino (gov. 1982—, sec. 1984-85, 1st v.p. 1985-86, 2d v.p. 1986—), Cliff Dwellers. Home: 1209 N Astor St Chicago IL 60610

HARVEY, LEONARD A., corporate executive; b. St. Catharines, Ont., Can., Aug. 20, 1925; came to U.S., 1952, naturalized, 1960; m. Shirley Williams, Oct. 7, 1950; children: Brian, Bruce, Christopher. BS with honors, Queens U., 1950. With Borg Warner Chems. Inc., Parkersburg, W.Va., 1952—, pres., 1976-86; exec. v.p. Borg Warner Corp., Chgo., 1986—; bd. dirs. McGean Chem. Co., Parkersburg Nat. Bank, United Bancshares. Served with RCAF, World War II. Mem. Soc. Plastics Industry, Chem. Mfrs. Assn., Parkersburg C. of C. (pres. 1981-82, Can.-U.S. liaison com.). Office: Borg-Warner Corp 200 S Michigan Ave Chicago IL 60604

HARVEY, VIRGINIA PEASELEY, organization consultant; b. Richmond, Va.; d. Gabriel B. and Florence V. (White) Peaseley; B.S., in Chemistry, U. Md., 1929; M.S. in Phy. Edn., U. Wis., 1932; Ed.D. in Ednl. Psychology, Western Res. U., 1963; postgrad. Temple U., 1966-67; m. E. W. Harvey, Apr. 8, 1939 (div. 1958); 1 dau., Virginia Lynn Harvey Schmitt. Instr. U. Mich., 1932-38; asst. prof. Kent (Ohio) State U., 1938-42, 44-46-54, assoc. prof., 1954-64, prof., 1964-76, prof. emeritus, 1976—, faculty senate vice chairperson, 1973-74. Vis. prof. group dynamics Temple U., summer 1967; mem. Nat. Tng. Lab. Inst. Applied Behavioral Sci.; pres. V. Harvey & Assocs. Recipient Disting. Tchr. award Kent State U., 1971, Service award Phi Delta Kappa, 1972. Amy Morris Homans fellow, 1962-63; licensed psychologist, Ohio. Past pres. Kent Dist. Sch. Bd. Mem. Orgn. Devel. Network, Kappa Kappa Gamma, Alpha Psi Omega, Delta Psi Kappa, Phi Delta Kappa, Omicron Delta Kappa. Home: 1315 Greenwood Ave Kent OH 44240

HARVITH, JOHN DANA, college administrator; b. Detroit, Nov. 18, 1946; s. Samuel Gabriel and Rosella (Lebowitz) H.; m. Susan Merryman Edwards, June 15, 1972; 1 child, Rachel Edwards. AB, U. Mich., 1969, JD, 1973. Free-lance music critic The Ann Arbor (Mich.) News, 1971-78; writer cultural affairs Info. Services U. Mich., Ann Arbor, 1976-78; co-project dir. Phonograph Centenary Exhibit and Symposium U. Mich., Ann Arbor, 1977; dir. pub. relations Interlochen (Mich.) Ctr. for Arts, 1978-80; dir. news services Oberlin (Ohio) Coll., 1980—. Co-author: Karl Struss: Man With a Camera, 1976, Edison, Musicians, and the Phonograph, 1987; free-lance music critic Musical Am., Ann Arbor, 1973-79; contbr. articles to profl. jours. Mem. Spectrum, Oberlin, 1986—. NEH fellow, 1974, 75, Music Critics Inst. fellow, 1972, 73. Mem. Council Advancement and Support Edn. (Exceptional Achievement award 1984), Music Critics Assn., Firelands Assn. for Visual Arts. Democrat. Jewish. Avocations: collecting art and photography. Home: 78 S Professor St Oberlin OH 44074 Office: Oberlin Coll Office Communications 153 W Lorain St Oberlin OH 44074

HASANOGLU, NEZIH Z., osteopath; b. Istanbul, Turkey, Mar. 18, 1957; came to U.S., 1973; s. Baran Hasan and Nur Hilal (Ertan) H.; m. Debra Jean Toonen, June 23, 1979; children: Nezih, Kaplan, Taner. BS, U. Wis., Green Bay; DO, Chgo. Coll. Osteopathic Med. Pvt. practice osteopathic medicine Milw., 1983—. Avocations: soccer, skiing, golf. Home: 21520 Ann Rita Rd Brookfield WI 53005

HASCHEK-HOCK, WANDA MARIA, veterinary pathologist, toxicologist, educator, researcher; b. London, Sept. 7, 1949; came to U.S., 1974; d. Karol A. and Maria U. Adamska Haschek; m. Vincent F. Hock, Jr., Aug. 7, 1976. BVSc, Sydney U., Australia, 1972; PhD, Cornell U., 1977. Diplomate Am. Coll. Vet. Pathologists, Am. Bd. Toxicology. Postdoctoral fellow Cornell U., Ithaca, N.Y., 1977; research assoc. Oak Ridge (Tenn.) Nat. Lab., 1981-82, research staff mem. I, 1981-82; assoc. prof. veterinary medicine U. Ill., Urbana, 1982—; affiliate Inst. Environ. Studies, U. Ill., Urbana, 1983—; cons. Toxigenics, Inc., Decatur, Ill., 1982-83, Los Alamos (N.Mex.) Nat. Lab., 1986-87. Contbr. chpts. to books, articles to profl. jours. Fellow Am. Acad. Vet. and Comparative Toxicologists; mem. Am. Coll. Vet. Pathologists (editorial bd. 1984-86), Soc. Toxicology (editorial bd. 1984—), Soc. Toxicologic Pathologists, Am. Vet. Med. Assn., Phi Kappa Phi, Phi Zeta. Office: U Ill Dept Vet Pathobiology 2001 S Lincoln Urbana IL 61801

HASEGAWA, LEE PATTON, actress; b. St. Louis, Nov. 20, 1951; d. David Ravenscraft and MaryLee (Blank) Chiles; m. Clifton Masayoshi Hasegawa, July 28, 1973; children: Lee Toshiko, David Masanao. BA, Washburn U., 1973; MA, U. Mo., 1977. instr. Webster U., St. Louis, 1984-86; creative drama tchr. Theatre Project Co., St. Louis, 1979-87. Appeared Theatre Project Co. in Cat on a Hot Tin Roof, Little Foxes, Sister Mary Ignatius Explains It All For You; Repertory Theatre of St. Louis in The Marriage of Bette & Boo, The Dining Room, Streetcar Named Desire; TV performances include Mississippi, Ten Plus Two Tasks of Terrible Tim; author Mystery and History, Ancient Honor, Am. Indian Tales, Tall Tales; assoc. dir. Muny/Student Theatre Project, 1979-81; appeared in numerous indsl. films, TV and radio commercials. Mem. Cen. States Audition Assn. (co-chmn., founder), Actors Equity Assn., Am.Fedn. TV and Radio Actors, Screen Actors Guild, Equity Liason Bd. Democrat. Avocation: walking. Home and Office: 972 Warder Saint Louis MO 63130

HASELBY, RAY CLOYNE, internist, educator; b. Detroit, May 4, 1939; s. Cloyne and Grace Haselby; m. Connie F. Halberg, June 24, 1982; children—Lisa, Sam, Jessica, Emily, Cyrus, Danielle. A.B., U. Mich., 1961; D.O., Chgo. Coll. Osteopathy, 1969. With Peace Corps, Colombia, 1961-63; intern Chgo. Coll. Osteopathy, 1969-70, Cleve. Clinic Found., 1970-71; resident in internal medicine Cleve. Clinic Found., 1971-72, resident in infectious disease, 1972-74; mem. staff infectious disease sect., dept. internal medicine Marshfield Clinic (Wis.), 1974—; clin. asst. prof. medicine U. Wis.-Marshfield, 1974—; La. State U. fellow in tropical medicine, 1969; chmn. infection control com. St. Josephs Hosp., Marshfield; former pres. Marshfield Med. Research Found. Recipient Disting. Teaching award U. Wis. Med. Sch., 1978. Mem. Am. Osteo. Assn., Wis. Assn. Osteo. Physicians and Surgeons, Am. Soc. Microbiology, Infectious Disease Soc. Am. Contbr. articles to med. jours. Home: 1112 W State St Marshfield WI 54449 Office: Marshfield Clinic 1000 N Oak St Marshfield WI 54449

HASHMI, SAJJAD AHMAD, business educator, university dean; b. India, Dec. 20, 1933; m. Monica Ruggiero; children: Serena, Jason, Shawn, Michelle. BA, U. Karachi, 1953, MA, 1956; PhD in Insurance, U. Pa., 1962. Lectr. Ohio State U., Columbus, 1962-64; asst. prof. Roosevelt U., Chgo., 1964-66; prof. Ball State U., Muncie, Ind., 1966-83, chmn. dept. fin., 1973-83; Jones disting. prof., dean Sch. Bus., Emporia State U., Kans., 1983—; cons. to profl. ins. agts., Indspl., Louisville, Springfield, Ill.; speaker to profl. groups, 1983-84; tech. advisor Ind. Arts Commn.; appeared on TV and radio programs, testified before N.Y., Kans. and Ind. legis. coms. Author: Insurance is a Funny Business, 1972; Automobile Insurance, 1973; Contemporary Personal Finance, 1985; contbr. articles, revs., monographs to profl. publs. Named Prof. Yr. Ball State U. Students, 1971, Outstanding Tchr. of Yr., Ball State U., 1970. Mem. Am. Risk and Ins. Assn., Western Risk and Ins. Assn., Midwest Fin. Assn., Fin. Mgt. Assn., Emporia C. of C., Beta Gamma Sigma, Sigma Iota Epsilon, Alpha Kappa Psi, Gamma Iota Epsilon, Phi Kappa Phi. Club: Emporia Country. Lodge: Rotary. Home: 1702 Coronado Ave Emporia KS 66801 Office: Emporia State U Sch of Bus 1200 Commercial St Emporia KS 66801

HASKIN, ROBERT DOLPH, vocational service company owner; b. Kansas City, Mo., Dec. 31, 1944; s. Evert John and Thera Darlene (Dolph) H.; m. Katherine Jane Boddy, Aug. 12, 1967; children: David Robert, Scott Andrew. BA, Concord Coll., 1969; MA, Marshall U., 1972; cert. in Rehab. Counselor Tng., Va. Commonwealth U., 1972. Rehab. counselor W. Va. Dept. Vocat. Rehab., Huntington, 1972-73; clin. chief vocat. and ednl. services Rockford (Ill.) Meml. Hosp., 1973-77; dir. vocat. and ednl. services U. Wis. Hosp., Madison, 1977-82; supr. IMARC, Mpls., 1982-83; pvt. practice career and rehab. counseling Assesment and Vocational Services, Inc., Mpls., 1983—; cons. FMC Corp., Fridley, Minn., 1984—, Social Security Adminstrn., 1987—. bd. dirs. Rockford chpt. Nat. Spinal Cord Injury Found., 1976-77, Lake Harriet Christian Ch., Mpls., 1983—. Mem. Nat. Rehab. Assn., Nat. Assn. Rehab. Profls. in Pvt. Sector, Am. Assn. for Counseling and Devel., Minn. Assn. Rehab. Providers (sec. 1986—, mem. neutrality task force 1985), Rockford Jaycees (bd. dirs. 1975). Mem. Christian Ch. Avocations: sailing, swimming, theater. Home: 3905 Vincent Ave S Minneapolis MN 55410 Office: Assessment and Vocat Services 6135 Kellogg Ave S Suite 224 Edina MN 55424

HASKVITZ, SYLVIA EDIS, dietitian, writer, photographer; b. Mpls., Apr. 17, 1957; d. Marvin Harold and Dorothy (Cohen) H. BS in Nutrition and Dietetics, U. Tex., Houston, 1983. Dietitian Northwest Raquet and Swim Club, Mpls., 1983-85; nutrition cons., lifestyle educator Mpls., 1983—; dietitian eating disorders program Fairview Hosp., Mpls., 1986—. Vol. Am. Cancer Soc., Mpls., 1985—. Served with Tex. State Guard, 1982-83. Mem. Am. Dietetic Assn., Minn. Dietetic Assn. (speaker 1986—), Twin Cities Dist. Dietetic Assn., Sports and Cardiovascular Nutritionists. Club: Shalom (co-chmn. 1985—). Avocations: volleyball, calligraphy, photography, traveling, cross country skiing. Home: 2631 Xylon Ave S Minneapolis MN 55426 Office: Fairview Hosp 2312 S 6th St Minneapolis MN 55454

HASLEY, JOHN HOEFFLER, urologist; b. Ft. Wayne, Ind., Apr. 28, 1938; s. Henry and Rosalie (Hoeffler) H.; m. Marilyn Rose Seyfert, June 15, 1963; children—Mary Suzanne, John Charles. B.S., U. Notre Dame, 1959; M.D., Georgetown U., 1963. Diplomate Am. Bd. Urology. Intern Henry Ford Hosp., Detroit, 1963-64, resident in surgery, 1966-70; practice medicine specializing in urol. surgery Northwest Ohio Urol. Scis., Inc., Toledo, 1971—, pres., 1987—; chief med. staff St. Lukes Hosp., Maumee, Ohio, 1986—; treas., bd. dirs. Northwest Physicians, Inc., Toledo, 1985—; dir. Health Benefits Mgmt. Ohio, Toledo. Bd. dirs. Physicians Med. Care Found. Toledo. Served to lt. M.C., USNR, 1964-66. Mem. AMA, Ohio State Med. Assn. (del. 1980—), Acad. Medicine Toledo (v.p. 1982), Am. Fertility Soc., Ohio Urol. Soc., Northwest Ohio Urol. Assn. Republican. Roman Catholic. Clubs: Toledo; University (Notre Dame, Ind.). Home: 5553 Sturbridge Rd Toledo OH 43623 Office: Northwest Ohio Urol Scis Inc 5930 Huntingfield Blvd Toledo OH 43615

HASLEY, MICHAEL JAMES, manufacturing company executive; b. Cedar Rapids, Iowa, Oct. 31, 1946; s. Earl Andrew and Leone Marie (Wall) H.; m. Janice Margaret Michalek, June 15, 1968; children—Lisa Marie, Kimberly Joy, Scott Michael, Lauren Margaret. B.S. in Econ., Regis Coll., 1968. Vice pres. Quality Control Corp., Chgo., 1975-80, exec. v.p., 1980-83, pres., dir., 1983—; dir., pres. Qualiseal Tech. Ltd., Chgo., 1984—. Mem. Olph Men's Ch. Club, Glenview, Ill., 1985; sec., treas. Harwood Heights Indsl. Assn., Ill., 1979, pres., 1980. Served to lt. USNR, 1968-71. Mem. Nat. Assn. Corp. Dirs., Pres.'s Forum, Pres.'s Council, Am. Mgmt. Assn., Midwest Indsl. Mgmt. Assn., Tooling Mfg. Assn.,Fluid Sealing Assn. Republican. Roman Catholic. Club: Executive. Home: 1318 Pine St Glenview IL 60025

HASS, HERBERT EDWARD, lawyer, automotive products consultant; b. Chgo., July 21, 1919; s. Herman Reynold and Jeanette (Butler) H.; m. Marian Frances Bagg, Apr. 2, 1942; children: David Herbert, Jody Lynn. BA with honors, Andrews U., 1948; BTh, Seventh Day Adventist Sem., 1953; MA in Speech, Temple U., 1961; JD, U. Notre Dame, 1973. Bar: Mich. 1973, Pa. 1974, U.S. Dist. Ct. (we. dist.) Mich. 1976; ordained to ministry Lake Union Conf. Seventh Day Adventist, 1953. Dir. pub. relations Seventh Day Adventist State Confs., Ind., Ill., Pa., 1948-59, Faith for Today Internat. TV, L.I., N.Y., 1959-63; assoc. dir. devel. Loma Linda (Calif.) U., 1963-67; dir. pub. relations N.Y. Ctr., N.Y.C., 1967-70; found. dir., pub. relations dir. Southwestern Mich. Collge, Dowagiac, 1070-73; sole practice Berrian Springs, Mich., 1973—; gen. counsel Gen. Motors Consumers, Chgo., 1982—, cons. in area of defective automotive products; pres., cons. A-1 Adminstrs., Berrien Springs, 1979—; cons. Concerned Car Owners, Lansing, Mich., 1984—, Gen. Motor Products Groups, Chgo., 1983—, Phillipine Med. Sch. for entry into U.S. med. internships; pres. Comp In, Berrien Springs, 1977—; bd. dirs. Adventist Radio and TV, Ltd., London, Ont., Can. and U.S., 1985—. Author: (manuscript) Life and Work of Stephen Tyng, 1962 (citation 1962); contbr. ency. Hist. of N.Y. Ctr., 1966; editor TV program Telenotes, 1959-63. Bd. dirs. Pioneer Meml. Univ. Ch., Berrien Springs, 1965—. Served to tech. sgt. U.S. Army, 1942-45. Mem. ABA (various coms. 1974—), Mich. Bar. Assn. (various coms. 1973—), Pa. Bar Assn. (various coms. 1974—), Nat. Assn. Coll. and Univs. Attys., Am. Inst. for Prevention of Addition, Inc. (sec.-treas. 1987), Audubon Soc. Republican (mem. Washington club). Lodge: Optimists (Berrien Springs). Avocations: tennis, jogging, stamp collecting, woodworking. Office: 9160 US 31-33 Berrien Springs MI 49103

HASS, KATHLEEN JEAN, social work administrator; b. Ladysmith, Wis., Nov. 29, 1950; d. Marshall H. and Vernice L. (Tucker) Wiley; m. Edward L. Hass, Aug. 23, 1985. BA, U. Wis., Eau Claire, 1972; MA in Pub. Adminstrn., U. Wis., Oshkosh, 1986. Office mgr. Winter (Wis.) Motors, 1972-76; social worker Marian Nursing Home, Radisson, Wis., 1975-76; dir. Pierce County Office on Aging, Ellsworth, Wis., 1976—; social work cons. Stroms Group Homes, Ellsworth, 1986—, TAD Nursing Home, Plum City, Wis., 1980—. Bd. dirs. Turningpoint, River Falls, Wis., 1986-87. Mem. Wis. Social Service Assn. Office: Office on Aging Courthouse Box 670 Ellsworth WI 54011

HASSELL, ROBERT JOHN, finishing company executive; b. Washington, N.C.; s. Sidney Dawson and Clara (Brooks) H.; m. Donna Boylan, June 17, 1978; children: Rob, Kathryn, Anne. BS, Va. Polytech. Inst., 1973; MBA, Harvard U., 1980. CPA, Mass. Supr. Coopers & Lybrand, Boston, 1973-78; dir. sales and mktg. Bendix Corp., Cleve., 1980-84; v.p. finishing systems Ransburg Corp., Indpls., 1984—. Mem. Soc. Mfg. Engrs., Omicron Delta Kappa. Episcopalian. Home: 4950 Riley Mews Carmel IN 46032 Office: Ransburg Corp Box 88220 Indianapolis IN 46208

HASSELL, WAYNE, editor; b. Iron Mountain, Mich., Dec. 5, 1931; s. Conrad and Ruth Elvira (Anderson) H.; m. Mary Hilton, June 27, 1962; children: Barbara, Craig. Student, Bethel Coll., 1955-56, U. Mpls., 1956-59. Reporter The News, Iron Mountain, 1949-51; wire copy editor Pioneer Pres, St. Paul, 1956-67, news editor, 1967-83; asst. to exec. editor St. Paul Pioneer Press Dispatch, 1983—. Stamp columnist Pioneer Press, 1957—. Vol. cons. ARC, 1985-86; mem. communications bd. Episcopal Diocese, Mpls., 1985-86; mem. exec. bd. Soundings, Mpls., 1979-83; bd. dirs. Putting it All Together, St. Paul, 1985-86; vestry mem. St. Paul's Episcopal Ch. on the Hill, 1987—. Served with USMC, 1952-54, Korea. Mem. Am. Philatelic Soc., Am. Topical Assn., Internat. Soc. Japanese Philatelists. Clubs: St. Paul Athletic; War Cover. Avocation: stamp collecting. Home: 1765 Juno Ave Saint Paul MN 55116 Office: Pioneer Press Dispatch 345 Cedar Saint Paul MN 55101

HASSELLE, JAMES EUGENE, III, psychiatrist; b. Memphis, Apr. 30, 1935; s. James Eugene Jr. and Mary Francis (Sledge) H.; m. Norita Ledbetter, July 14, 1956 (div. 1974); children: Dawn Adair, Deborah Annette, Michael Andrew; m. Susan Darnell Vukmonich, Aug. 30, 1975; 1 child, Suzanne. Student, U. Tenn., 1953-55, MD, 1959. Diplomate Am. Bd. psychiatry and Neurology. Intern City of Memphis Hosp., 1959-60; resident Karl Menniger Sch. Psychiatry, Topeka, 1960-63; staff psychiatrist Tenn. Psychology Inst., Memphis, 1965-68; staff psychiatrist CF Menniger Hosp., Topeka, 1968-78, chief clin. service, 1974-78; med. dir. Bert Nash Community Mental Health Clinic, Lawrence, Kans., 1978-80; practice medicine specializing in psychiatry Lawrence, 1980—; cons. Memphis VA Hosp., 1967-68, Topeka VA Hosp., 1978, Rehab. Services, State of Kansas, 1984—; clin. supr. Karl Menniger Sch. Psychiatry, Topeka, 1968-78. Served to lt. commdr. USNR, 1963-65. Mem. AMA, Am. Psychiat. Assn., Kans. Med. Assn., Kans. Psychiat. Assn., Douglas County Med. Soc. (v.p. 1986). Avocations: outdoors, theater, art, reading. Home: Rural Rt 2 Box 247-A Lawrence KS 66046 Office: 346 Maine Lawrence KS 66044

HASSELQUIST, MAYNARD BURTON, lawyer; b. Amador, Minn., July 1, 1919; s. Harry and Anna M. (Froberg) H.; m. Lorraine Swenson, Nov. 20, 1948; children—Mark D., Peter L. B.S.L., U. Minn., 1941; J.D.L., U. Minn., 1947. Bar: Minn. 1948. Asst. mgr. taxation Gen. Mills Inc., Mpls., 1947-53; chmn. internat. dept. Dorsey & Whitney, Mpls., 1953-81, sr. ptnr.; dir. Graco Inc., Mpls., McLaughlin Gormley King Co., Mpls., ADC Telecommunications, Inc., Mpls., Wesco Resources, Billings, Mont., Soprea S.A., Paris. Gen. counsel, bd. dirs. Swedish Council Am.; past chmn. Japan-Am. Soc. Minn.; bd. dirs., counsel James Ford Bell Library; chmn. Fairview Hosps. Internat., Ltd., Cayman Islands. Served with USN, 1941-46. Mem. ABA, Minn. Bar Assn., Internat. Bar Assn., Am. Soc. Internat. Law. Republican. Lutheran. Club: Mpls. Office: Dorsey & Whitney 2200 First Bank Place East Minneapolis MN 55402

HASSETT, JACQUELYN ANN, nurse; b. La Crosse, Wis., Sept. 13, 1930; d. Frank Alois and Anne Helena (Milos) Spika; m. James John Hassett, Aug. 22, 1953; children—Barbara, Linda, Jean, Jane, Nancy, James David. Diploma in Nursing, St. Anthony de Padua Sch. Nursing, Chgo., 1951; BS, Barat Coll., 1977; MS, George Williams Coll., 1983. RN, Ill., Wis. Operating room nurse VA Hosp., North Chicago, Ill., 1951-54; part-time nursing positions St. Therese Hosp., Waukegan, Ill., 1954-58, Johnson Motors, Waukegan, 1958-64, VA Hosp., North Chicago, Ill., 1964-71; dir. health services Coll. of Lake County, Grayslake, Ill., 1971—, co-chmn. Inst. Self-Study for Rehab. Act 1973, 1978. Mem. Project SUCCEED, No. Ill., 1980-81; com. mem. Health Systems Agy. Kane-Lake-McHenry Counties, 1978-80; vol. Lake County Cancer Soc., 1975—, Am. Heart Assn., 1975—; bd. dirs. Med. Service Adv. Com. Lake County Health Dept., 1980—. Recipient Appreciation cert. Lake County Bd. Commrs., 1978; Meritorious Service award Am. Heart Assn., 1979-82; Outstanding award No. Ill. Council on Alcoholism, 1982, Commendation for Service Lake County (Ill.) Health Dept., 1986. Mem. Am. Coll. Health Assn. (council of dels. 1978-80, 83—), Mid-Am. Coll. Health Assn. (v.p. 1981-82, pres. 1983-84), No. Ill. Coll. Health Nurses Assn., Am. Legion Aux. Roman Catholic. Club: Altrusa (Waukegan). Home: 42749 Washington St Winthrop Harbor IL 60096 Office: Coll of Lake County 19351 W Washington St Grayslake IL 60030

HASSIN, DONALD JAMES, JR., district attorney; b. Ft. Knox, Ky., Sept. 18, 1949; s. Donald James and Margaret (Culley) H. BS, U.S. Mil. Acad., 1971; JD, Marquette U., 1981. Bar: Wis. 1981. Commd. 2d lt. U.S. Army, 1971, adv. through grades to capt., 1975; with 25th Inf. Div. U.S. Army, Schofield Barracks, Hawaii, 1972-77; asst. prof. mil. sci. Marquette U., Milw., 1977-78; resigned U.S. Army, 1978; currently maj. with Res; assoc. Cramer, Multhauf & Curran, Waukesha, Wis., 1981-84; sr. asst. dist. atty. City of Waukesha, 1984-87; asst. dist. atty. Waukesha County, 1987—. Mem. ABA, Waukesha County Bar Assn., Assn. NG Officers. Avocations: golf, skiing, fishing. Home: N22 W28832 Oak Ln Pewaukee WI 53072 Office: Waukesha County Dist Attys Office 515 W Moreland Blvd Waukesha WI 53186

HASSINGER, MARK ALAN, optometrist; b. Cleve., Jan. 4, 1956; s. Elwood Charles and June Bernice (Swaffield) H.; m. Angela Marie Federico, Aug. 18, 1984; 1 child, Jennifer Lynn. BS, Ohio State U., 1978; BS in Visual Sci., OD, Ill. Coll. Optometry, 1982. Lic. optometrist, Ohio, Wis., Ill. Assoc. optometrist Dr. Daniel Geiger, Parma, Ohio, 1983—; staff optometrist Ohio Permanente Med. Group, Willoughby, 1983-86; assoc. optometrist Dr. Ronald Mesnick, Lyndhurst, Ohio, 1983. Named one of Outstanding Young Mem of Am., 1984; Recipient Faculty Meml. award Ill. Coll. Optometry, Chgo., 1982. Mem. Phi Theta Upsilon (v.p. 1981-82). Avocations: sports, coin collecting, skiing.

HASSLER, DONALD MACKEY, II, English language educator, writer; b. Akron, Ohio, Jan. 3, 1937; s. Donald Mackey and Frances Elizabeth (Parsons) H.; m. Diana Cain, Oct. 8, 1960 (dec. Sept. 1976); children: Donald, David; m. Sue Smith, Sept. 13, 1977; children: Shelly, Heather. B.A. (Sloan fellow), Williams Coll., 1959; M.A. (Woodrow Wilson fellow), Columbia U., 1960, Ph.D., 1967. Instr. U. Montreal, 1961-65; instr. English Kent (Ohio) State U., 1965-67, asst. prof., 1967-71, assoc. prof., 1971-76, prof., 1977—, acting dean honors and exptl. coll., 1979-81, dir., 1973-83, coordinator writing cert. program, 1987—. Author: Erasmus Darwin, 1974, The Comedian as the Letter D: Erasmus Darwin's Comic Materialism, 1973, Asimov's Golden Age: The Ordering of an Art, 1977, Hal Clement, 1982, Comic Tones in Science Fiction, 1982, Patterns of the Fantastic, 1983, Patterns of the Fantastic II, 1984, Death and the Serpent, 1985, Isaac Asimov, 1987; mng. editor jour. Extrapolation, 1986—, co-editor, 1987. Co-chmn. Kent Am. Revolution Bicentennial Commn., 1974-77; deacon Presbyterian Ch., 1971-74, elder, 1974-77. Mem. Sci. Fiction Research Assn. (treas. 1983-84, pres. 1985-86), Phi Beta Kappa (pres. 1983-84). Lodge: Kiwanis (dir. 1974-76). Home: 1226 Woodhill Dr Kent OH 44240

HASTERT, (J.) DENNIS, U.S. Congressman; b. Aurora, Ill., Jan. 2, 1942; m. Jean Kahl, 1973; children: Joshua, Ethan. BA, Wheaton Coll., 1964; MS, No. Ill. U., 1967. Tchr., coach Yorkville (Ill.) High Sch.; mem. Ill. House Reps., Springfield, 1980-86, 100th Congress from Ill., Washington, 1987—. Lodge: Lions (Yorkville). Office: US House of Reps Office of House Mems Washington DC 20515 *

HASTINGS, GLEN RICHARD, II, hospital administrator, educator; b. Clovis, N.Mex., May 22, 1945; s. Glen Richard and Mary Evelyn (Milam) H.; m. Judith Ann Mitze, Oct. 1, 1967; children—Jay Dolphy, Katherine Ruth. B.S., U. Okla., 1967; M.B.A., Chapman Coll., 1975; M.H.A., U. Minn., 1977. Sports and gen. reporter Chickasha Daily Express, Okla., 1963-66; exec. dir., hosp. adminstr. St. Luke's Hosp., Kansas City, Mo., 1977—; asst. prof. Webster U., St. Louis, 1978—; clin. preceptor U. Minn., Mpls., 1980—; vice chmn. SLH Inc., Kansas City, 1984—; trustee Mo. Health Data Corp., 1985—. Author: Zero Based Budgeting, 1980; Product Line Management, 1985. Contbr. articles to profl. jours. Trustee Arthritis Found., Kansas City, 1978, Family and Childrens' Services, 1987; mem. Mid Am. Com. Health Care Costs, Kansas City, 1980; bd. dirs. Kansas City Area Hosp. Assn., 1978; mem. Blue River Fin. Com., Lee Summit, Mo., 1984; chmn. bd. dirs. Health Industry Data Inst., 1985; chmn. personnel com., sec. fin. com. First Baptist Ch. Raytown, Mo. Served to capt. USAF, 1967-75. Decorated Bronze Star. Recipient Pub. Health award Dept. Health, 1975. Mem. Am. Coll. Hosp. Adminstrs., Healthcare Fin. Mgmt. Assn., Am. Hosp. Assn., Kansas City Adminstrs. Assn., U. Minn. Alumni Assn. (preceptor 1977—), Kappa Alpha (sec. 1966-67). Lodge: Rotary. Avocations: personal computers; racquetball; basketball; tennis; golf. Home: 8412 Hawthorne Pl Raytown MO 64138 Office: St Lukes Hosp Wornall & 44th Sts Kansas City MO 64133

HASTINGS, JAMES WILLIAM, dentist; b. Oak Park, Ill., Oct. 14, 1941; s. James Joseph and L. June (Atherton) H.; m. Geraldine Mary Fischer; children: James Michael, Patrick William. BS in Dentistry, Ind. U., Indpls., 1963, DDS, 1966. Gen. practice dentistry Indpls., 1966—. Mem. ADA, Ind. Dental Assn., Indpls. Dist. Dental Soc. Republican. Home: 118 Timber Ln Brownsburg IN 46112 Office: 3850 Shore Dr #107 Indianapolis IN 46254

HASTINGS, KATHLEEN AGNES, social worker, psychotherapist; b. Lowell, Mass., Dec. 4, 1947; d. Roland Andrew and Marion Louise (Gray) De Mers; m. Charles Eugene Hastings Jr., Dec. 20, 1972; children: Kimberly Gene, Angela Rene, Brian Daniel. BS, Kans. Newman Coll., 1970; MSW, U. Kans., 1984. Social worker aide Bd. Edn., Wichita, Kans., 1970-71; job developer Model Cities Program, Wichita, 1971; drug counselor Moving Effectively for Social and Econ. Change, Wichita, 1972; med. social worker Wesley Med. Ctr., Wichita, 1972—; psychotherapist Coll. Hill Psychiat. Clinic, Wichita, 1984—; cons. U. of Kans. Sch. Medicine, Wichita, 1986. Parish youth dir. Cath. Youth Orgn., Wichita, 1982—. Mem. Nat. Assn. Social Workers, Acad. Cert. Social Workers. Democrat. Home: 125 N Berniece Wichita KS 67206

HASTINGS, MARGARET MITCHELL, health service executive, educator; b. Delaware County, Pa., Feb. 26, 1937; d. William Fish and Margaret (Henderson) Mitchell; m. Robert Allen Hastings, June 14, 1958; children: William, Margo. BA, Wellesley Coll., 1958; cert. in edn., Harvard U., 1958; MA, Nat. Coll., 1970; PhD, Northwestern U., 1975. Registered spl. edn. psychologist. Dir. ctr. for learning, mem. grad. faculty Nat. Coll., Evanston, Ill., 1971-76; exec. dir. State of Ill. Commn. on Mental Health and Devel. Disabilities, Chgo. and Springfield, Ill., 1976-85; vis. scholar Northwestern U., Evanston, 1985-86; prof. health resources mgmt., dir. MPH/MBA program U. Ill., Chgo., 1986—; pres. Policy and Mgmt. Inst., Inc., Chgo., 1986—. Author: Mental Health '77: A System in Transition, 1977, Mandated Planning for Mental Health, Developmental Disabilities and Substance Abuse, 1978, Issues '79: Politics, Planning, Funding and Advocacy, 1979, Financing Mental Health Services, 1985; editorial bd. Chgo. Reporter, 1985—; contbr. articles to profl. jours. Chairperson Health/Human Services Adv. Bd., New Trier Twp., Ill., 1982-86; mem. Alcohol, Drug Abuse and Mental Health Nat. Adv. Bd., 1985—, State Ill. Metabolic/Genetic Diseases Adv. Bd., 1984—; bd. dirs. Northwestern U. Sch. Edn., 1977—, Goodwill Industries, Chgo., 1979—, Skokie Valley Hosp. and Health Services Corp., 1981—, McCormick Theol. Sem., Chgo., 1984—. Recipient Dir.'s award for state leadership in mental health, Gov. Ill., 1976, Trevethan award for excellence in rehab. adminstrn. De Paul U. and Ray Graham Assn., 1983, Nat. Alumni Achievement award Northwestern U., 1985. Fellow Inst. Medicine Chgo.; mem. Davis Soc. for Knowledge Utilization (v.p. 1985—), Soc. Psychologists in Mgmt. (sec.-treas. 1985—), Am. Psychol. Assn. (mem. nat. pub. info. com. 1986—, div. 38 exec. council 1981—), Am. Pub. Health Assn., Acad. Mgmt., Am. Coll. Healthcare Execs. (speaker for nat. women's leadership 1986), Assn. Mental Health Adminstrs., Ill. Council on Home Health Services (chmn. long term home care state task force 1986—), Women's Health Exec. Network, Assn. Univ. Programs in Health Adminstrn., Am. Orthopsychiat. Assn., Gerontological Soc. Am. Clubs: Indian Hill, Mich. Shores, Plaza. Avocations: music, piano and voice composing, performing. Office: Policy and Mgmt Inst Inc. PO Box 228 Kenilworth IL 60043

HASTINGS, ROBERT EUGENE, city-county official; b. Council Bluffs, Iowa, June 17, 1932; s. Elmer Wayne and Lillian Irene (Potts) H.; student appraisal courses Omaha U., Iowa State U., Iowa Western Community Coll., 1967-78; m. Marcia Ann Martin, Aug. 2, 1969. Meter reader Council Bluffs Gas Co., 1950; clk. Milw. R.R., Council Bluffs, 1951-52; with Harding Cream Co., Omaha, 1952-54; clk. Safeway Stores, Council Bluffs, 1954-56; circulation mgr. World Herald Newspaper, Eastern Nebr., 1956-58; agt. Met. Life Ins., Omaha, 1958-59; asst. county assessor Pottawattamie County, Iowa, Council Bluffs, 1959-72; city assessor Council Bluffs, 1972-74; city-county assessor Pottawattamie County, 1974—; instr. appraisal Iowa Community Coll. Taxation and fin. steering com. Nat. Assn. Counties, Washington, 1974-79; pres. C of C Cee Bees (Goodwill Ambassadors), 1978; county govt. lobbyist, 1974-75; mem. Iowa State Assessors Edn. Commn., 1983-85. Recipient ICA degree, Iowa Inst. Certified Assessors. Mem. Internat. Assn. Assessing Officers (CAE degree; contbr. report 1974; profl. admissions com. 1981-85, mem. exec. bd. 1985-87, instr.), Nat. Assn. Review Appraisers (C.R.A. degree), Am. Soc. Appraisers (charter pres. Nebr. chpt. 1985-86, state dir. 1986-87), Iowa State Assn. Assessors, C. of C. (dir. 1975-77). Lutheran. Clubs: Kiwanis (pres. Downtown Council Bluffs 1976-77, On-To dist. Nebr.-Iowa Dist. conv. chmn. 1979, internat. conv. dist. chmn. 1983, 1987, club sec. 1983, lt. gov. div. 13, trustee Nebr.-Iowa Dist. 1981-82, dist. youth chmn. 1983-84, dist. community services chmn. 1985-86). Home: 72 Bellevue Ave Council Bluffs IA 51501 Office: Court House PO Box 1076 Council Bluffs IA 51502

HASTINGS, WILLIAM CHARLES, state supreme ct. judge; b. Newman Grove, Nebr., Jan. 31, 1921; s. William C. and Margaret (Hansen) H.; m. Julie Ann Simonson, Dec. 29, 1946; children—Pamela, Charles, Steven. B.Sc., U. Nebr., 1942, J.D., 1948. Bar: Nebr. bar 1948. With FBI, 1942-43; mem. firm Chambers, Holland, Dudgeon & Hastings, Lincoln, 1948-65; judge 3d jud. dist. Nebr., Lincoln, 1965-79, Supreme Ct. Nebr., Lincoln, 1979—. Pres. Child Guidance Center, Lincoln, 1962, 63; v.p. Lincoln Community Council, 1968, 69; vice chmn. Antelope Valley council Boy Scouts Am., 1968, 69; pres. 1st Presbyn. Ch. Found., 1968—. Served with AUS, 1943-46. Mem. Am. Bar Assn., Nebr. Bar Assn., Lincoln Bar Assn., Nebr. Dist. Judges Assn., Phi Delta Phi. Republican. Presbyterian (deacon, elder, trustee). Club: East Hills Country (pres. 1959-60). Home: 1544 S 58th St Lincoln NE 68506 Office: Nebr Supreme Ct State House Lincoln NE 68509

HATCH, HAROLD EUGENE, mortgage banker; b. Kansas City, Mo., June 26, 1935; s. Edgar E. and Myrtle Y. (Dunlap) H.; m. Jo Ann Manderino; children: Leslie Ann, Sarah Jane. BS, U. Mo., 1957; cert. Sch. Mortgage Banking, Northwestern U., Chgo., 1965. Asst. sec. United Mo. Mortgage Co., Kansas City, 1961-64, asst. v.p., 1964-68, v.p., 1968-81, exec. v.p., 1981-85, pres., 1985—; sr. v.p. United Mo. Bank of Kansas City, N.A., 1983—; bd. dirs. Crown Tours & Conv. Services, Kansas City. Chmn. Raytown Hist. Soc., 1963. Served as sgt. U.S. Army, 1957-59. Mem. Kansas City Bd. Realtors (com. chmn. 1964-66, bd. dirs. 1976), Lee's Summit Bd. Realtors (bd. dirs. 1967), Mo. Real Estate Assn., Mortgage Bankers Assn. Am., Mortgage Bankers Assn. Kansas City. Avocation: golf. Home: 6107 Harvard Raytown MO 64133 Office: United Mo Morgage Co 906 Grand Ave Kansas City MO 64106

HATCH, M. J., food products company executive. Pres. Codville Distributors, Winnipeg, Man., Can. Office: Codville Distbrs, 1800 Inkster Blvd, Winnipeg, MB Canada R3C 3J6 *

HATCH, ROBERT WINSLOW, food corporation executive; b. Hanover, N.H., Sept. 8, 1938; s. Winslow Roper and Dita Meiggs (Keith) H.; m. Nancy Packard Murphy, June 30, 1962; children: Kristin, Robert Winslow. B.A., Dartmouth Coll., 1960, M.B.A., 1962. Sales rep. Libby Glass Co., N.Y.C., 1961-62; research asst. Amos Tuck Sch., Hanover, 1962-63; with Gen. Mills, Inc., Mpls., 1963-84; product mgr. Gen. Mills, Inc., 1965-68, mktg. dir., 1968-71; exec. v.p. Gorton Corp., 1971-73, gen. mgr. protein div., 1973-75; gen. mgr. Golden Valley div., 1976; gen. mgr. Big G div., 1976-78, group v.p. splty. retailing, 1978-80, exec. v.p. splty retailing, collectibles and furniture, 1980-83, asst. to vice chmn. consumer non-foods, 1984; pres., chief exec. officer Interstate Bakeries Corp., Kansas City, Mo., 1984—; bd. dirs. Leslie Paper Co., Mpls., Sealright Corp., Kansas City. Exec. com. Mpls. Boys Club, 1978-83; pres. bd. East Side Neighborhood Services (Settlement House), from 1980; bd. dirs. YMCA, C. of C., Kansas City. Recipient Mpls. City Council's Com. on Urban Environment award, 1980. Republican. Presbyterian. Clubs: Calhoun Beach (pres. bd. govs. 1981-83); Kansas City, Carriage. Office: Interstate Bakeries Corp PO Box 1627 Kansas City MO 64141

HATCHER, RICHARD GORDON, former mayor; b. Michigan City, Ind., July 10, 1933; s. Carlton and Catherine Hatcher; m. Ruthellyn Marie Rowles, Aug. 8, 1976; children: Ragen Heather, Rachelle Catherine, Renee Camille. B.A., Ind. U.; J.D., Valparaiso U. Bar: Ind. bar. Practiced in East Chicago; formerly dep. prosecutor Lake County, Ind.; councilman-at-large Gary City Council, 1963-66; mayor of Gary 1967-87; former co-chmn. legis. action com., trustee, mem. human resources com., mem. exec. bd., chmn. adv. bd. U.S. Conf. Mayors, pres., 1980-81. Co-author commn. report on del. selection. Mem. steering com. on human resources devel. Nat. League Cities, past chmn. human resources com., 1974, also bd. dirs.; a founder Muigwithania, social and civic club; mem. Nat. Com. of Inquiry; mem. task force on presdl. TV debates 20th Century Fund; chmn. edn. subcom. Ind. adv. com. to U.S. Commn. Civil Rights; nat. chmn. bd. dirs. Operation PUSH, 1979-82; mem. exec. com. Nat. Urban Coalition; founder Nat. Black Caucus of Locally Elected Ofcls.; convenor Nat. Black Polit. Conv., Nat. Conf. on a Black Agenda for the 80's, 1980; pres. Nat. Conf. Democratic Mayors, 1977-78, Nat. Conf. Black Mayors, 1979-82, U.S. Conf. Mayors, 1980-81; mem. steering com. Nat. Black Assembly; chmn. Ind. State Black Caucus; active Urban League of NW Ind.; mem. adv. bd. Ind. U. N.W., Robert Woods Johnson Meml. Found.; chmn. Gary City Dem. Com.; mem. Ind. Dem. State Central Com., Nat. Dem. Com. on Del. Selection; mem. Dem. Nat. Com., vice chmn., 1980-85; mem. U.S. intergovtl. adv. commn. on edn. to Sec. of Edn.; chmn. bd. Trans-Africa; nat. chmn. Jackson for Pres., 1984; pres. Nat. Civil Rights Mus. and Hall of Fame, 1986—; mem., bd. dirs. Marshall U. Soc. of Yeager Scholars. Naemd one of 100 Most Influential Black Americans, Ebony Mag., 1971—. Mem. ABA, Ind. Bar Assn., Gary Bar Assn., NAACP (mem. exec. bd. Ind.).

HATCHER, THOMAS FOUNTAIN, mgmt. cons. co. exec.; b. Monroe, Mich., Dec. 26, 1931; s. Fountain H. and Cecilia E. (Boylan) H.; B.S., N.Y. U., 1968; m. Rosemary K. Downs, June 23, 1956; children—Mary Kathleen, Roberta Joan, Margaret Ann. With Equitable Life Assurance Soc., N.Y.C., 1955-71, mgr. learning systems, 1968-71; owner Thomas Hatcher Assos., Mpls., 1971-79; pres., owner Futures Unlimited, Inc., Mpls., 1979—. Mem. Nat. Speakers Assn., Am. Soc. Profl. Consultants. Roman Catholic. Author: The Definitive Guide to Long Range Planning, 1981. Home: 18525 Texas Ave Prior Lake MN 55372 Office: Futures Unlimited Inc 5200 W 73d St Minneapolis MN 55435

HATFIELD, CHARLES LEE, government administrator; b. McLeansboro, Ill., Dec. 15, 1953; s. Horace Hardin Hatfield and Shirley Frances (James) Dutton; m. Dana Dawn Cowan, June 16, 1979. AA, Ill. Cen. Coll., Peoria, 1974; BS, Ill. State U., Normal, 1976; postgrad., Sangamon State U., Springfield, Ill., 1978-81. Aide to candidate Brad Glass for State Treas., Springfield, 1977-78; adminstrv. asst. to dep. dir. Ill. Dept. Conservation, Springfield, 1978-80; account exec. WFMD Radio, Springfield, 1981-82; disability claims adjudicator Ill. Dept. Rehab. Services, Springfield, 1982-84, mgr. gen. services sect., 1984—; hist. documents broker. Precinct committeeman Sangamon County Rep. Cen. Com., Springfield, 1982—, chmn. Highrise/Nursing Home Com., 1984—; sgt. at arms Ill. Rep. State Conv., Springfield, 1982, del., 1982, 1984, del., Chgo., 1986, alt. del., Peoria, 1978; treas. Sangamon County Young Reps., Springfield, 1978-80; bd. dirs. Evening Rep. Club, Springfield, 1980-81. Governor's fellow State of Ill., 1977; named one of Outstanding Young Men of Am., 1985. Mem. U.S. Presdl. Campaign Memorabilia Club (pres. 1984—), Heart of Ill. Polit. Memorabilia Club. Methodist. Lodge: Masons. Avocations: collecting Americana and historical documents. Home: 1411 S State St Springfield IL 62704 Office: Ill Dept Rehab Services 623 E Adams St Springfield IL 62705

HATHAWAY, JOHN, financial trading executive; b. Lincoln, Ill., Mar. 24, 1945; m. Judith Ann De Smet, June 22, 1968; children: James Charles, Jed Aaron. BA, U. Ill., 1967; MBA, Loyola U., 1973. Mgr. personnel Carson Pirie Scott, Urbana, Ill., 1968-69; mgr. sales service Baxter-Travenol, Deerfield, Ill., 1969-75; mgr. internat. mktg. Miller and Co., Chgo., 1975-83; pres., chief exec. officer Interam. Corp., Mt. Prospect, Ill., 1983—. Chmn. nominating com. Sch. Dist. 25, Arlington Heights, Ill., 1980; trustee Arlington Heights Meml. Library, 1981—; mem. Art Inst. Chgo., 1976-83. Mem. Chgo. Assn. Commerce and Industry. Home: 501 S Beverly Ln Arlington Heights IL 60005

HATHAWAY, JOHN MICHAEL, engineer, paper products company executive; b. Akron, Ohio, Mar. 27, 1952; s. Lowell Robert and Ann Marie (Marcinkoski) H.; m. Betty Jo Bolender, July 12, 1975; children: Nathaniel David, Krystina Kylene. BSME, U. Notre Dame, 1974; MS in Indsl. Engring., Stanford U., 1975. Shift supr. Procter & Gamble, Green Bay, Wis., 1975-77, indsl. engr., 1977-79, maintenance mgr., 1979-81; project engr. Kimberly Clark, Neenah, Wis., 1982-84, supt. engring., 1984-85, dir. bldg. and office mgmt., 1985-87; mgr. engring. Kimberly Clark, 1987—. Inventions in field. Methodist. Avocations: fencing, water skiing. Home: 2595 Lost Dauphin Rd De Pere WI 54115 Office: Kimberly Clark Corp 2001 Marathon Ave Neenah WI 54956

HATLELID, J(OHN) MICHAEL, neurologist; b. Williston, N.D., Sept. 14, 1948; Ralph Sylvester and Mary Theresa (DesChenes) H.; Patti Marie Nemeth, June 27, 1984; 1 child, Tessa Elisabeth. BA, St. John's U., Collegeville, Minn., 1970; BS in Medicine, U. N.D., 1975; MD, Washington U., St. Louis, 1977. Diplomate Am. Bd. Psychiatry and Neurology. Intern Jewish Hosp., St. Louis, 1977-78; resident in neurology Barnes Hosp., St. Louis, 1978-81; fellow in neuropharmacology Washington U., 1981-84; practice medicine specializing in neurology St. Louis, 1984—. Mem. AMA, Am. Acad. Neurology. Avocations: birdwatching, oenology. Home: 25 Ladue Terr Saint Louis MO 63124

HATTERSLEY, ROBERT SHERWOOD, engineering manager; b. Dover, N.J., Sept. 4, 1931; s. William Joseph and Mabel Angela (Hall) H.; m. Jane Claire Williams, Aug. 22, 1958; children—Linda Jane, Robert Brent, Laura Beth. Registered profl. engr., Ohio, S.C. Engr. Procter & Gamble Co., Cin., 1957-61, group leader, 1961-66; plant engr., Quincy, Mass., 1966-73, sect. head, Cin., 1976—; ops. mgr. P & G de Mex., Mexico City, 1973-76. Author articles, reports. Served to 1st lt. C.E. USMC, 1954-57, Okinawa. Recipient medal Pi Tau Sigma, 1953. Mem. ASME (chmn. tech. and soc. div. 1983-85, nat. nominating com. 1982-85, issues mgmt. bd. 1983—), Nat. Soc. Profl. Engrs. (chpt. pres. 1986-87). Avocation: amateur cabinetmaker. Home: 8722 Long Ln Cincinnati OH 45231 Office: Procter & Gamble Co 11520 Reed Hartman Hwy Cincinnati OH 45241

HATTERVIG, ROBIN LYNN, dentist; b. Desmet, S.D., Apr. 4, 1958; d. Gene Willis and Harriet Ione (Larson) H. BS, U. S.D., 1980; DDS, U. Nebr., 1984. Gen. practice dentistry Howard, S.D., 1984—. Mem. ADA, S.D. Dental Assn. (So. dist.), S.D. Dental Found., Acad. Gen. Dentistry, Am. Soc. Dentistry for Children, Phi Beta Kappa, Omicron Kappa Upsilon. Republican. Lutheran. Club: Howard Community. Avocations: coin collecting, golf, tennis, bowling. Home: 222 E Park Ave Howard SD 57349 Office: 112 N Main St Box W Howard SD 57349

HATTERY, JEFFREY LYNN, utility company executive; b. Dover, Ohio, Feb. 6, 1953; s. Jay Calvin and Ethel Marie (Lengler) H.; m. Luanne Elizabeth Merner, Oct. 9, 1982. B.A., Mt. Union Coll., 1975; postgrad. Cleve. State U., 1983—. C.P.A. Audit staff Meaden and Moore C.P.A., Cleve., 1975-78; sr. auditor Consol. Nat. Gas Co., Cleve., 1978-80; rate analyst East Ohio Gas Co., Cleve., 1980-84, mgr. reports and stats., 1984—. Mem. Am. Inst. C.P.A.s, Ohio Soc. C.P.A.s, Nat. Assn. Accts. Episcopalian. Avocations: bicycling; skiing. Office: East Ohio Gas Co 1717 E 9th St Cleveland OH 44114

HATTIS, ALBERT D., business executive, educator; b. Chgo., Oct. 12, 1929; s. Robert E. and Victoria C. (Kaufman) H.; m. Fern Hollobow; children: Kim Allyson Hattis Mercer, Kay Arlene Hattis Draper, John Elmore, Michael Allen, Sharon Beth. BS with highest distinction, Northwestern U., 1948, postgrad. in bus. adminstrn., 1950, DD (hon.), 1968. Vice-pres., sec.-treas. Robert E. Hattis Engrs., Inc., Hattis Service Co., Inc., Deerfield, Ill., 1950-73; v.p., sec.-treas. Servbest Foods, Inc., Highland Park, Ill., 1973-78, exec. v.p., bd. dirs., 1987—; A.C. Equipment Co., 1978-80; pres., chief exec. officer Frigidmeats, Inc., Chgo., 1978-80; pres. Gits Enterprises, Inc., 1978-80, Double K Bar J Ranch, Inc., 1968—; prof. bus., holder Schwan Endowed Chair for Free Enterprise, S.W. State U., Marshall, Minn., 1981-88; dir. S.W. Minn. Small Bus. Devel. Ctr., 1984-87, S.W. Minn. Homegrown Economy Local Cooperation Office, 1984-88; chmn. Minn. Small Bus. Procurement Adv. Council, 1986-87. Exec. dir. The Lambs, Inc., Libertyville, Ill., 1980-81; trustee Orphans of the Storm Found., 1972-74, Cobblers Found., 1972-74; mem. adv. bd. Northwestern Psychiat. Inst., 1972-74; bd. dirs. Marshall Industries Found.; chmn. Marshall Planning Commn., 1982-85. Served to capt. USAF, 1946-48, 50-52. Mem. Assn. Pvt. Enterprise Edn., Internat. Council Small Bus., U.S. Assn. Small Bus. and Entrepreneurship, Minn. C. of C. (small bus. council 1984-87), Marshall Area C. of C. (bd. dirs.), Beta Gamma Sigma. Lodges: Lions, Rotary. Syndicated columnist, broadcaster Straight Talk, 700 newspapers, 400 radio stas. Home: 100 E Marshall St Marshall MN 56258 Office: 1256 Old Skokie Rd Highland Park IL 60035

HAU, THOMAS CALLOPY, accounting firm executive; b. Chgo., Sept. 5, 1935; s. Lawrence John and Marie Estelle (Callopy) H.; m. Gloria Ann Dressler, June 18, 1960; children: Lawarence, Kathleen, James, Robert, Cynthia, Nancy. BS, Loyola U., 1960. CPA, Ill. Staff acct. Arthur Andersen & Co., Chgo., 1960-61, sr. acct., 1961-66, mgr., 1966-71, ptnr., 1971—, mng. ptnr. small bus. div., 1983—; bd. dirs. Mt. Carmel Edn. Found, Chgo. Treas. Village of Glenwood, Ill., 1969-71, trustee, 1971-76; treas. Village of Olympia Fields, Ill., 1978-82. Served to cpl. U.S. Army, 1958-60. Mem. Am. Inst. CPA's (Elijah Watts Sells award, 1970), Ill. Soc. CPA's. Clubs: Olympia Fields Country; Metropolitan, Athletic Assn. (Chgo.). Home: 636 Brookwood Dr Olympia Fields IL 60461 Office: Arthur Andersen & Co 33 W Monroe St Chicago IL 60603

HAUCK, DANA RAY, farmer; b. Concordia, Kans., Sept. 6, 1949; s. Ray Vincent and Margaret Jeannette (Casey) H.; m. Marcia Ann Righter, Aug. 16, 1969; children: Michelle Lynn, Angeline Kay. BS in Animal Sci., Kans. State U., 1961. Gen. ptnr. Hauck and Hauck Farm, Delphos, Kans., 1962-76; owner, mgr. Pike Trail Cattle co., Delphos, 1976—; bd. dirs. State Bank Delphos; mem. honor awards selection com. USDA, Washington, 1986; mem. Dole Farm Adv. Bd., Washington, 1986. Bd. dirs. Delphos Co-op Assn., 1982—; elder First Presby. Ch., Delphos. Served with USNG 1970-76. Mem. Kans. Livestock Assn. (bd. dirs., vice chmn. cow-calf stocker council 1986-87), Nat. Cattleman's Assn. (agrl. policy com.), Alpha Zeta. Republican. Lodge: Masons, Elks. Avocations: hunting, skiing.

HAUEISEN, DEBORAH LUCILLE, insurance company executive; b. Portsmouth, Va., Aug. 20, 1954; d. Robert Allen and Vera Lucille (West) Hopkins; m. Glenn Henry Haueisen, Apr. 12, 1980; 1 child, Paul Arthur. ABA, Franklin U., 1984. Supr. ins. processing Nationwide Ins., Columbus, Ohio, 1975-78, analyst, supr., mgr. methods engring., 1978-86, mgr. systems and data, 1986—; cons. Productivity Mgmt. Assocs., Columbus, 1983. Mem. Civic Action Program, Columubs, 1985-87. Mem. Am. Inst. Indsl. Engrs. (assoc.). Office: Nationwide Ins 1 Nationwide Plaza Columbus OH 43216

HAUER, ANN, educator; b. Braddock, N.D., Sept. 19, 1942; d. Ray Joseph and Mildred Elizabeth (Kippes) Splonskowski; m. Jim Hauer, June 26, 1965; children: Todd, Missy. BA, Mary Coll., 1969; MA in Ednl. Adminstrn., U. N.D., 1981. Cert. elem. prin. Elem. tchr. Richholt Sch., Bismarck, N.D., 1970-74, tchr., asst. prin., 1974-76; tchr. Roosevelt Sch., Bismarck, 1976—; elem. rep. Bismarck Pub. Schs. Curriculum Steering Com., developer curriculum metrics, nutrition, career edn. Tchr. rep. N.D. adv. bd. Project Wild. Recipient Tchr. Yr award C. of C., 1987. Mem. NEA, N.D. Edn. Assn., Bismarck Edn. Assn. (govt. relations com., elem. negotiator, profl. rights and responsibilities chmn., pres.), Bismarck C. of C. (edn. com.), Phi Delta Kappa (v.p. 1985-86), Delta Kappa Gamma. Roman Catholic. Clubs: Apple Creek Tennis League, Apple Creek Country. Lodge: Elks. Home: 2600 Mercury Ln Bismarck ND 58501 Office: 613 Ave B West Bismarck ND 58501

HAUG, JAMES ALBERT, personnel director; b. Butler, Pa., Jan. 27, 1946; s. Walter Albert and Catherine H. (Kenst) H.; m. Linda Lee Virgili, Aug. 12, 1967; children: Kelly Ann, Robert Walter. BBA, Westminster Coll., 1967. Mgr. indsl. relations Midland Ross Corp., Sharon, Pa., 1967-77; mgr. human resources Huffy Corp., Dayton, Ohio, 1977-86; dir. human resources Reynolds & Reynolds, Celina, Ohio, 1986—. Mem. Ohio State Gov.'s Commn. on Labor/Mgmt. Relationships. Mem. Am. Soc. Personnel Adminstrs., Western Ohio Personnel Assn. Republican. Lodge: Kiwanis. Avocations: running, triathlons, competitive water skiing. Home: 905 Royal Oak Saint Marys OH 45885 Office: Reynolds & Reynolds Celina OH 45822

HAUGAN, HAROLD WALTER, plastics engr.; b. Stoughton, Wis., June 17, 1902; s. Paul Julius and Emma (Kildahl) H.; B.S., U. N.D., 1925, M.S., 1927; Ph.D., St. Andrews U., 1959. Adminstr. chemistry physics dept. York (Nebr.) Coll., 1939-41; instr. Eau Claire (Wis.) State Tchrs. Coll., 1941-43; research supr. U.S. ammunition plant, 1943-45; mem. research devel. staff Curtiss-Wright Research Lab., Cheektowaga, N.Y., 1945-47, Cornell U. Aero. Lab., 1947-49; devel. engr. Bell Aircraft Corp., 1949-54; prin. Harold Haugan Assos., Devel. Engrs., 1954-56; supr. plastics Mich. ordnance missile plant missile div. Chrysler Corp., 1956-63; plastics engr. space div. Chrysler Corp., New Orleans, 1963-68; promoter plastics edn. in schs. and libraries throughout U.S., 1968—; pioneer developer plastics for missiles and Saturn space boosters, 1947-68. Mem. Soc. Plastics Industry, Am. Chem. Soc., Am. Def. Preparedness Assn., AIAA, Ancient Astronaut Soc., Nat. Space Inst. Author tech. publs. in plastics engring. Home: 1396 Smith St Birmingham MI 48009

HAUGE, TRYGVE ARDELL, electronics executive; b. Fertile, Minn., Oct. 22, 1925; s. Thomas and Alma Constance (Christianson) H.; m. Beatrice Jean Halstad, Apr. 15, 1951; children: Cheryl, Brian, David. BSEE, N.D. State U., 1951; MSEE, U. Pitts., 1954; cert. mgmt., St. Thomas Coll., St. Paul, 1964. From engr. to dir. ops. Control Data Corp., Mpls., 1958-70; dir. ops. Arvin Magnetics, Mpls., 1970-72; dir. engring. and mfg. Sick Optik Electronic, Stillwater, Minn., 1973-80; pres. Tech. 80, Inc., Mpls., 1980—; cons. in field, Mpls., 1972-73. Served with USN, 1944-46. Office: Tech 80 Inc 658 Mendelssohn Ave N Minneapolis MN 55427

HAUGEN, CLIFFORD OLGAR, physician; b. Honeyford, N.D., Dec. 16, 1904; s. Ole Sjur and Gunhild T. (Staveteig) H.; m. Fern Catherine H. Breitweser, Aug. 6, 1935; 1 child, Clifford William. BS, U. N.D., 1926, MS, 1927; MD, U. Chgo., 1930. Asst. prof. anatomy U. N.D. Med. Sch., Grand Forks, 1930-35; student health physician U. N.D., 1933-35; gen. practice medicine Larimore, N.D., 1933—; staff mem. Deaconess Hosp., Northwood, N.D., 1935-86; acting pathologist N.D. Pub. Health Lab., Grand Forks, 1931; health officer City of Larimore, 1936—; med. examiner SSS, 1937; county physician Grand Forks County, N.D., 1939-43; surgeon Great No. and Burlington No. R.R.s, Larimore, 1939—. Pres. Evang. Luth. Ch. Council, Larimore, 1952; mem. Larimore City Council; chmn. bd. Larimore council Boy Scouts Am. Recipient Sioux award U. N.D. Alumni Assn. Mem. AMA, N.D. State Med. Assn. (Cert. Distinction 1969, 79), Grand Forks Dist. Med. Soc., Am. Acad. Family Physicians (charter), Sigma Xi. Republican. Lodges: Elks, Masons (worshipful master 1946). Avocation: world travel. Home: 303 E 3d St Larimore ND 58251 Office: 115 Towner Ave Larimore ND 58251

HAUGEN, ORRIN MILLARD, lawyer; b. Mpls., Aug. 1, 1927; s. Oscar M. and Emma (Moe) H.; m. Marilyn Dixon, June 17, 1950; children—Melissa, Kristen, Eric, Kimberly. B.S. in Chem. Engring., U. Minn., 1948, LL.B., 1951. Bar: Minn. 1951. Patent lawyer Honeywell, Inc., Mpls., 1951-59; patent lawyer Univac div. Sperry Rand, 1959-63; pvt. practice patent law Haugen & Nikolai, P.A., Mpls., 1963—. Pres. Arrowhead Lake Improvement Assn., Inc., Mpls., 1958-79. Served with USN, 1945-46. Mem. ABA, Minn. Bar Assn., Am. Patent Law Assn., Minn. Patent Law Assn., Minn. Trial Lawyers Assn., Minn. Acacia Alumni Assn., Inc. (pres. 1961-63), Acacia. Methodist. Lodge: Kiwanis. Home: 6612 Indian Hills Rd Edina MN 55435 Office: Internat Ctr Bldg Minneapolis MN 55402

HAUGH, BARBARA ANN, poet; b. Findlay, Ohio, Sept. 4, 1950; d. Raymond Leroy and Martha Wilma (De la Hamaide) H. BA in English, Ohio State U., 1980. Enlisted USAF, 1972, advanced through ranks to airman 1st class, discharged, 1974; enlisted USNG, 1974, advanced through ranks to ssgt.; supply clk. Rickenbacker Air Nat. Guard Base, Columbus, Ohio, 1981-86, Newark Air Force Base, Heath, Ohio, 1986—; resigned from ANG 1986. Author: (poetry books) Prism Poems, 1985, Comic Curios, 1987. Mem. Bus. and Profl. Women, Sierra Club. Presbyterian. Avocations: stamp collecting, writing, reading. Home: PO Box 488 Hebron OH 43025-0488 Office: Newark Air Force Station Heath Rd Heath OH 43056

HAUGH, ROBERT JAMES, insurance company executive; b. Milw., Jan. 19, 1926; s. John J. and Adeline (Bolmes) H.; m. Mary Jane Botsch, Oct. 15, 1949; children: Jane, William, Nancy. Ph.B., Marquette U., 1946, J.D., 1948. With St. Paul Fire & Marine Ins. Co., 1948—, sr. v.p. ops., 1976-78, pres., chief exec. officer, 1978—; pres., chief operating officer St. Paul Cos., Inc., 1982—, chmn., chief exec. officer, 1985—; trustee Underwriters Labs. Bd. dirs. ARC, St. Paul. Republican. Roman Catholic. Clubs: Minnesota. Office: St Paul Fire & Marine Ins Co 385 Washington St Saint Paul MN 55102 *

HAUPT, PAUL ANDREW, physician; b. Columbus, Ohio, June 7, 1949; s. Waldemar Albert and Patricia (Collmer) H.; m. Cheryl Ann Lawton, June 16, 1979; children: Andrew Waldemar, Travis Edward. BA in Physics, Syracuse U., 1971; DO, Ohio U., 1980. Internship Doctor's Hosp., Columbus, 1980-81; residency Mayo Clinic, Rochester, Minn., 1981-83; gen. practice medicine Menominee, Mich., 1983—. Med. examiner Menominee County, 1984—. Mem. AMA, Am. Osteo. Assn., Mich. State Med. Soc. Methodist. Avocations: running, sailing. Office: 1100 10th St Menominee MI 49858

HAUSAFUS, JOHN EARL, architect; b. Marshalltown, Iowa, Dec. 8, 1946; s. William Wayne and Margaret A. (Hastie) H.; m. Cheryl Ann Olmstead, May 26, 1973; children: Michael Todd, Tara Ann. AS, Marshalltown Community Coll., 1970; BArch, Iowa State U., 1973. Archtl. draftsman Englebrecht/Rice Architects, Des Moines, 1973-75; asst. prof. architecture Smith-Voorhees-Jensen, Des Moines, Iowa, 1975-80; project architects J.E.H. Architects, Des Moines, 1980-84, FEH Assocs. Inc., Des Moines, 1985—. Chmn. archtl. adv. com. City of Des Moines, 1986—. Mem. Constrn. Specifications Inst. (reg. award chmn. 1983-85, regional editor chmn. 1986-87 editor cen. Iowa chpt. 1978-82, pres. 1984-86, regional award 1983, 84, 85, Nat. award 1984, 85). Clubs: Bohemian, Cosmopolitan Internat. Des Moines (pres. 1982-83). Home: 3700 Rollins Ave Des Moines IA 50312 Office: FEH Assocs Inc 1115 Midland Fin Bldg Des Moines IA 50309

HAUSCHILD, DAVID LEE, farmer, water development specialist; b. Pierre, S.D., May 28, 1948; s. Leslie Joseph and Donna Artetta (Gillen) H.; m. Cheri Renee Green, Feb. 12, 1971; children: Jennifer, Caleb. Student, No. State U., 1968-69, Capitol U., 1985—. Lineman Martin Beach, Huron, S.D., 1968-70; farmer Hauschild Farms, Pierre, 1971—; Chmn. bd. Cendak Water Supply, Miller, S.D. Bd. dirs. S.D. Water Congress, Pierre, 1981-86, v.p., 1982-85; chmn. bd. Gymnastics for Kids, Pierre, 1985-86. Served with U.S. Army, 1969-70, Vietnam. Mem. Am. Legion (comdr. Blunt, S.D. chpt. 1973-75), VFW (comdr. Pierre chpt. 1986). Democrat. Methodist. Home and Office: 212 N Fir Pierre SD 57501

HAUSER, DAVID RAY, podiatrist; b. Jersey Shore, Pa., Mar. 7, 1955; s. Alfred L. and Henrietta J. (Speary) H.; m. Patricia McGregor, Aug. 18, 1978 (Sept. 1983). BA, Lycoming Coll., 1977; D in Podiatric Medicine, Pa. Coll., 1982. Diplomate Am. Bd. Podiatric Surgery. Intern, then resident Toledo; staff podiatrist Ctr. for Health Promotion, Toledo, 1983—; practice medicine specializing in podiatrics Sylvania, Ohio, 1983-84, Toledo, 1984—; dir. podiatry dept. Toledo Health Ctr., 1984—; bd. dirs. A.D.A. Lucas County Chpt., Toledo. Mem. Am. Podiatric Med. Assn., Ohio Podiatric Med. Assn., NW Ohio Acad. Podiatry, Phi Kappa Phi. United Methodist. Avocations: skiing, flying, jet skiing. Office: 3100 W Central Suite III Toledo OH 43606

HAUSER, LES JOHN, health care public relations and marketing consultant; b. Peoria, Ill., May 3, 1946; s. Warren George and Ethel May (Widmer) H.; m. Sharon Ann Carius, June 28, 1969; children Joshua, Kimberly. B.A. in English, Eureka Coll., 1969; M.S. in Mass Communications, Shippensburg State Coll., 1974. Communications coordinator, news editor Pa. Blue Shield Ins. Co., Camp Hill, 1973-75; mgr. pub. relations and advt. Del. Blue Cross/Blue Shield, Wilmington, 1975-76; dir. pub. relations Lansing (Mich.) Gen. Hosp., 1976-81; dir. community relations and devel. Mich. Hosp. Assn. Service Corp., Lansing, 1981-84; v.p. corp. planning and mktg. DePaul Health Ctr., St. Louis, 1984—; instr. Mich. State U., 1979-81, Lansing Community Coll., 1979; mem. pub. relations and mktg. com. Am. Osteo. Hosp. Assn., Chgo., 1979-80. Bd. dirs. Tri-County Emergency Med. Services Council, Lansing, 1979-81; mem. pub. relations adv. com. to pres. Wayne State U., Detroit, 1980-81. Served with U.S. Army, 1969-73. Named Outstanding Young Alumnus Eureka Coll., 1982. Mem. Acad. Hosp. Pub. Relations and Mktg. (MacEachern award 1978), Mich. Hosp. Pub. Relations Assn. (2 awards of achievement 1978), Pub. Relations Soc. Am. (founder, accredited, 1st pres. 1983), Am. Soc. Hosp. Pub. Relations, Am. Mktg. Assn., Cath. Health Assn. (publications com.), Am. Hosp. Assn. (publications com.). Methodist. Contbr. articles on to profl. jours. Home: 27 Cambrian Way Saint Charles MO 63301

HAUSERMANN, DALE RUSSELL, JR., merchant marine engineer; b. Mariemont, Ohio, June 26, 1953; s. Dale Russell and Helen Louise (Wilder) H. BS in Marine Engrng., U.S. Mcht. Marine Acad., 1975. Asst. engr. Crowley Maritime, Seattle, 1975-76; chief engr. Midland Enterprises, Cin., 1976—. Mem. Performance Ford Club of Am. Democrat. Avocations: car racing, car restoring. Home: 2020 Woodville Pike Goshen OH 45122

HAUSIG, JOHN HERMAN, restaurant industry executive; b. Omaha, Nov. 10, 1943; s. Otto Erich and Paula (Beck) H.; m. Deanna Jennings (div.); children: Eric Christopher, Brian Jennings. BA in Sociology, Omaha U., 1967; MS in Counseling, U. Nebr., Omaha, 1971. Account rep. Thomas J. Lipton, Omaha, 1967-69; Master Card rep. Omaha Nat. Bank, 1969-70; vocat. counselor Omaha Opportunities Industrialization Ctr., Omaha, 1971-73; v.p. ops. Ely's Restaurant (Cape Horn Ltd.), Grand Rapids, Mich., 1973—; bd. dirs., v.p. Grand Valley Mfg., Ltd., Grand Rapids; bus. cons. Grand Rapids Area C. of C., 1987—. Bus. chmn. M-37 Citizen's Group, Grand Rapids, 1976-79; bus. advisor work experience program Grand Rapids Pub. Schs., 1975-76. Served to sgt. USNG, 1961-67. Avocations: reading, outdoor sports, gardening, meditation. Home: 1425 Preston Ridge NW Grand Rapids MI 49504 Office: Ely's Restaurant 2701 Alpine Ave NW Grand Rapids MI 49504

HAUSKINS, DAVID EUGENE, data processing executive; b. Cedar Rapids, Iowa, Sept. 27, 1934; s. Orville James and Dorothy Alice (Ward) H.; m. Nadine Ann Melendy, Oct. 3, 1954; children: Tamra Dee VanNorman, Michelle Lynn. AS in Data Processing, San Diego Jr. Coll., 1970. Supr. data processing Gen. Dynamics Corp., San Diego, 1967-69, programmer analyst, 1969-70; programmer analyst Religious Book Discount House, Grand Rapids, Mich., 1970-71, dir. info. systems, 1971-72; programmer Meijer, Inc., Grand Rapids, 1972-73; systems analyst Miejer, Inc., Grand Rapids, 1973-85, programmer analyst, 1985—. Contbr. numerous articles to Congl. Record, newspapers and popular mags. Vol. Mich. state coordinator The Conservative Caucus, vol. Ronald Reagan's gubernatorial and presdl. campaigns; invited speaker various religious, civic, polit., academic groups; former candidate Ho. of Reps., Mich.; past-pres. Grand Rapids Bapt. Acad. Parent-Tchr. Fellowship, deacon Calvary Bapt. Ch., Grand Rapids; mem. White House Speakers Bur. Recipient Fred Meijer Community Service award, 1976, 77, Congress of Freedon Liberty award, 1975, 76; recipient Spl. Tribute Mich. Senate, 1986. Republican. Avocations: reading, sports. Home: 1460 Van Auken SE Grand Rapids MI 49508

HAUSLER, RUDOLF HEINRICH, research chemist; b. Zurich, Switzerland, Apr. 9, 1934; came to U.S., 1963; s. Robert Ruppert and Elsa (Figi) H.; m. Barbara Louise Corsaw, Feb. 5, 1972; 1 child, Natasha Louise. diploma chem. engring., Swiss Fed. Inst. Tech., Zurich, 1958, D.Tech.Scis., 1961. Research chemist, project leader Battelle Meml. Inst., Geneva, 1961-63; research chemist, research assoc. Universal Oil Products Co., Des Plaines, Ill., 1963-76; tech. dir. Gordon Lab., Inc., Great Bend, Kans., 1976-79; sr. research chemist corp. research and devel. Petolite Corp., St. Louis, 1979-81, prin. investigator, 1981-86, research fellow, 1986—; lectr. in field. Registered profl. engr., Calif. Mem. Electrochem. Soc. (chmn. Chgo. sect. 1967-68, councilor 1972—), Nat. Assn. Corrosion Engrs. (chmn. Chgo. sect. 1974-75), Chgo. Tech. Socs. Council (chmn. 1974-75), Am. Chem. Soc., Am. Soc. Metals. Unitarian-Universalist. Author, patentee in field. Office: Petrolite Corp 369 Marshall Ave Saint Louis MO 63119

HAUSMAN, ROBERTA BERNSTEIN, psychologist; b. Cambridge, Mass., Dec. 9, 1932; d. Israel and Gertrude (David) Bernstein; m. Malcolm Gilbert Idelson, Jan 13, 1956 (div. Aug. 1964); children: Eric Benjamin, Jonathan Marlowe, Janine Heather. BA, Syracuse U., 1953; MA, Tufts U., 1958; PhD, U. So. Calif., 1978. Lic. Psychologist. Research assoc. Wellesly (Mass.) Human Relations Service, 1954-57; lectr. Vassar Coll., Poughkeepsie, N.Y., 1962-66; assoc. prof. Hillsborough Community Coll., Tampa, Fla., 1968-71; lectr. U. Md., Heidelberg, Fed. Republic Germany, 1972-75, U. Mo., Kansas City, Mo., 1980-82; practice psychology Kansas City, 1978—; dir. Genesis Counseling Ctr., Kansas City, 1986—; cons. U. Mo. Law Sch., Oxford U. Summer Sch., 1984—, Nova U. Law Sch., Oxford U. Seminars, 1982-83. Author: Love that Hurts, Love that Heals, 1986; contbr. articles to profl jours and books. Bd. dirs. Jewish Community Ctr., Kansas City, 1983; group leader fine arts singles Village Presby. Ch., Kansas City, 1977—. Mem.Am. Psychol. Assn., Mo. Psychol. Assn., Kans. Psychol. Assn., Greater Kansas City Psychol. Assn., Am. Soc. Clin. Hypnosis, Internat. Soc. Clin. Hypnosis, Nat. Assn. Woman Bus. Owners. Club: Sketch-Box (Kansas City). Avocations: artist, skiing, tennis, bridge, travel. Office: Genesis Counseling Ctr 413 W 62d St Kansas City MO 64113

HAUSMAN, WILLIAM, psychiatry educator; b. N.Y.C., July 25, 1925; s. Jacob Henry and Tillie (Hoffman) H.; m. Lillian Margaret Fuerst, June 12, 1947; children: Steven David, Peter Douglas, Linda Louise Hausman Johnson, Clifford Alan. MD, Washington U., St. Louis, 1947. Diplomate Am. Bd. Psychiatry and Neurology. Commd. capt. U.S. Army, 1949, advanced through grades to col., 1964, ret., 1966; intern Coney Island Hosp., Bklyn., 1947-48; resident Worcester (Mass.) State Hosp., 1948-49, Inst. Pa. Hosp., Phila., 1949-50, 51-52; assoc. prof. Johns Hopkins U., Balt., 1966-69; prof. psychiatry, head dept. U. Minn., Mpls., 1969-80, prof. psychiatry, 1980—; cons. Levinson Inst., Belmont, Mass., 1975—. Contbr. articles to profl. jours. Fellow Am. Coll. Psychiatrists, Am. Psychiat. Assn., Am. Assn. Social Psychiatry; mem. Minn. Psychiat. Soc. Avocations: sailing, color photography, skiing. Home: 212 Parkview Terr Minneapolis MN 55416 Office: U Minn Dept Psychiatry 420 Delaware St SE Box 393 Mayo Minneapolis MN 55455

HAUSMAN, WILLIAM RAY, fund raising and management consultant; b. Bradford, Pa., Apr. 22, 1941; s. Raymond Harvey and Eleanor Janet (Freeman) H.; m. Rosalyn Schmidt, Aug. 16, 1963; children: Valerie Noelle, Stephanie Carol. AB, Wheaton (Ill.) Coll., 1963; MA, Trinity Evang. Div. Sch., 1966, DD (hon), 1981; student, North Park Theol. Sem., 1968-69; EdM, Harvard U., 1977. Ordained to ministry Evang. Covenant Ch., 1971. Minister Christian edn. Glen Ellyn (Ill.) Covenant Ch., 1966-69; registrar, dir. admissions Trinity Evang. Div. Sch., Deerfield, Ill., 1969-72, dean admissions and records, 1972-75, v.p. student affairs, 1975-77, assoc. dean, 1977-80; pres. North Park Coll. and Theol. Sem., Chgo., 1980-86; sr. interim minister Winnetka Covenant Ch., Ill., 1986-87; cons. Donald A. Campbell & Co., Inc., Chgo., 1986-87, v.p., 1987—; free-lance voice-over artist, 1986—. Mem. Lehigh County Hist. Soc. Club: Economics (Chgo.). Avocations: geneal. research, reading, travel, antiques. Home: 108 17th St Wilmette IL 60091 Office: Campbell & Co Inc 1 E Wacker Dr Chicago IL 60601

HAUSMANN, JOHN EDMUND, real estate executive, mayor; b. N.Y.C., Dec. 12, 1944; s. Otto Joseph and Rita Marie (Hourigan) H.; m. Susan Ellen Dow, Jan. 30, 1971; children: Maia Elizabeth, Ketti Louise, John Edmund II. BA, Union Coll., 1966; MBA, U. Va., 1970. Pres. Hausmann Enterprises, Hinsdale, Ill., 1983—. Mayor Village of LaGrange, Ill., 1980—, trustee, 1978-80; bd. dirs. Pace Suburban Bus div. Regional Transportation Authority, 1984—, St. Coletta's of Ill. Exceptional Children, 1985—, Uptown Fed. Savs., 1987—. Roman Catholic. Home: 300 S 7th Ave LaGrange IL 60525 Office: Hausmann Enterprises 911 N Elm St Hinsdale IL 60521

HAUWILLER, ROBERT PAUL, university administrator; b. St. Paul, June 24, 1934; s. Paul Heliodore and Bertha Elizabeth (Sherman) H.; B.S., St. Mary's Coll., Minn., 1956; M.S., U. Notre Dame, 1962; D.P.A., Nova U., 1985; m. Mary Agnes Walsh, Aug. 15, 1970. High sch. tchr., Ill., 1956-63; asst. prof. math., registrar Lewis U., Romeoville, Ill., 1963-68; dir. admissions and records, prof. math. Gov.'s State U., University Park, Ill., 1968-76; asst. registrar Chgo. State U., 1968-70, dir. instl. research and univ. relations, 1976-86, acting v.p. adminstrv. affairs, 1979; dir. instl. research, planning and grants, Joliet Jr. Coll., 1986—, NSF grantee, 1960-61. Mem. Am. Math. Assn., Phi Delta Kappa. Roman Catholic. Lodge: KC. Home: 9749 Mill Dr E Palos Park IL 60464 Office: Joliet Jr Coll 1216 Houbolt Ave Joliet IL 60436

HAVELKA, THOMAS EDWARD, choral director; b. Wheeling, W.Va., July 10, 1947; s. Alfred and Marilyn Eleanor (Hays) H.; m. Susan Kay Wilson, May 16, 1973; children: Trevor Hays, Havaleh Ann. BFA, Ohio U., 1969, MusM, 1975. Cert. tchr., Ohio. Music instr., chmn. fine arts dept. Bellaire (Ohio) Bd. Edn., 1969-74; choir dir., chmn. music dept. Coshocton (Ohio) City Bd. Edn., 1975—; founder Coshocton City Schs. Arts Festival, 1985—; state rep. All Am. Youth Honor Musicians, Miami, Fla., 1970—; asst. conductor All Am. Youth Honor Choir, 1970, 77-78, conductor, 1980—; adjudicator Internat. Choir Fest., Mexico City, 1978, Dulcimer Festival, Roscoe Village, Ohio, 1986-87, Show Choir Competition, Lancaster, Ohio, 1986, Show Choir Festival, Portsmouth, Ohio, 1986. Mem. Big Bros./Big Sisters Assn., Columbus, 1970—; dist. exec., chmn. bd. Boy Scouts Am., Coshocton, 1979-80; sect. leader, asst. accompanist Coshocton Community Choir, 1984—; active various theater groups, Coshocton and Wheeling, 1974—; singer St. Matthew's Episcopal Ch., Wheeling, W. Va., 1973-75; asst. organist Grace United Meth. Ch., Coshocton, 1986—. Mem. Ohio Edn. Assn., Ohio Music Edn. Assn. (asst. contest chmn., chmn. county membership com. 1977-78), Eastern Ohio Tchrs. Assn., Internat. Soc. for Music Edn., Internat. Fedn. for Choral Music., Am. Guild Organists, Am. Choral Dirs. Assn., Ohio Choral Dirs. Assn. (chmn. county membership 1978-79), Coshocton City Edn. Assn. (sec. 1984-85), Am. Film Inst., Met. Opera Guild, Kappa Kappa Psi, Phi Mu Alpha, Pi Kappa Lambda. Republican. Methodist. Avocations: travel, camping, backpacking, coin collecting. Home: 1628 Woodland Dr Coshocton OH 43812 Office: Coshocton High Sch 1209 Cambridge Rd Coshocton OH 43812

HAVEN, CARL OLE, hospital administrator; b. Detroit, July 13, 1940; s. Thomas Kenneth and Marion Lucile (Reading) H.; student Albion Coll., 1958-62; A.B., Wayne State U., 1968, M.A., 1976; postgrad. U. Mich., 1977; m. Patty Ann Foor, Aug. 3, 1975; children—Leslie, Brianne, Kathryn. With St. Joseph Mercy Hosp., Pontiac, Mich., 1956-57; operating technician, Grace Hosp., Detroit, 1960-61, adminstrv. resident, 1969-70, adminstrv. asst., 1970; emergency room, River Dist. Hosp., St. Clair, Mich., 1967; asst. hosp. dir., Harper-Grace Hosp., Detroit, 1971-81; dir. mgmt. Samaritan Health Center, Sisters of Mercy Health Corp., 1981-84; dir. mktg. A. Kuhlman & Co., Detroit, 1984—; pres. Pre-Paid Med. Legal Services, Inc.; cons. systems analysis and design for med. care delivery, Dominican Republic, 1977; profl. cons.; chmn. affiliated med. residency program, Wayne State U., 1973; chmn. fin. com. Associated Hosps. Processing Facility Corp., 1972; med. edn. com., Met. NW Detroit Hosp. Corp., 1978; cons. Mosman Electronics Inc. Com. chmn. Explorers Council 262, Dist. 13, Boy Scouts Am. Served with M.C., U.S. Army, 1962-65. Fellow Am. Coll. Hosp. Adminstrs.; mem. Am., Mich. (shared services com. 1978) Hosp. Assns., Greater Detroit Area Hosp. Council, Hosp. Fin. Mgmt. Assn. (advanced mem.), Alpha Kappa Delta. Contbr. articles to profl. hosp., med. jours. Home: 9150 Warner Rd Saline MI 48176 Office: 3939 Woodward Ave Detroit MI 48201

HAVENS, JOHN FRANKLIN, retired banker; b. Marietta, Ohio, May 14, 1927; s. William F. and Nola F. (Dysle) H.; m. Sally Luethi, June 19, 1950; children: John C., Thomas F., Ellen Havens Hardymon, Suzanne. BS, Ohio State U., 1949. Owner, operator real estate, constrn. and brokerage co. Columbus, Ohio, 1950-54; pres. Equitable Investment, Columbus, 1954-63; chmn. bd. dirs. U.S. Land Inc., Columbus, 1964-67, Homewood Co., Columbus, 1966-70; chmn. Franklin Bank, Columbus, 1970-80; chmn. bd. dirs. Banc One Corp., 1980-86, bd. dirs. emeritus; bd. dirs. W.W. Williams Co., Columbus, T.R.I., San Francisco, Evans Adhesive, Sanderville, Ga., TransAmerica Corp. Trustee Ohio State U., 1977-86, chmn., 1986, mem. Hosp.'s Bd., 1986—. Served with USCG, 1945. Named Outstanding Citizen, Columbus Citizen Jour., 1964, Outstanding Exec. Fin. Analyst Columbus Citizen Jour., 1969, Nat. Developer, Am. Builders Council, 1970; recipient Outstanding Achievement award Nat. Assn. Real Estate, 1966. Mem. Phi Gamma Delta. Methodist. Clubs: Varsity O (Columbus); Firestone Country (Akron) (gov.); Muirfield Village Golf (Dublin) (gov.). Office: Havens Havens & Hardymon 760 Northlawn Dr Suite A-2 Columbus OH 43214

HAVENSTEIN, GERALD BRYCE, geneticist; b. Manhattan, Kans., Sept. 2, 1939; s. August H. and Helen E. (Snodgrass) H.; m. Joyce Kay Withbroe, Aug. 24, 1963; children—Susan, Greg. B.S. in Agriculture, Kans. State U., 1961; M.S. in Genetics, U. Wis.-Madison, 1965, Ph.D. in Genetics, 1966. Staff geneticist H&N Inc., Redmond, Wash., 1967-76, dir. genetic research, 1976-86; chmn. dept. poultry sci. Ohio State U., Columbia, 1986—. Mem. Citizens Adv. Council-Gifted Edn., Lake Washington Sch. Dist., 1976-79. Mem. Poultry Sci. Assn., World's Poultry Assn., Poultry Breeders Am. (v.p. 1984, pres. 1985), Sigma Xi. Lutheran. Office: Ohio State U Dept Poultry Sci 674 West Lane Ave Columbus OH 43210

HAVERLAND, ELOISE KEPPEL, airlines executive; b. Pittston, Pa., Apr. 22, 1942; d. Henry Robert and Edna Louise (Keppel) Carichner; B.A., U. R.I., 1964; M.A., U. Chgo., 1978; children—Lisa, Bradley. With Personnel Devel., Inc., Palatine, Ill., 1972-77, Spiegel, Inc., Oak Brook, Ill., 1978-79; mgr. tng. and devel. Sun Elec. Corp., Crystal Lake, Ill., 1979-82, United Airlines, 1982—; tchr. women's program Harper Coll., Palatine; founder, pres. Nat. Network of Women in Sales. Mem. Am. Soc. Tng. and Devel., Ill. Soc. Tng. and Devel., Chgo. Sales Trainers Assn. Home: 338 N Benton St Palatine IL 60067 Office: PO Box 66100 EXOTD Chicago IL 60666

HAVERS, ROBERT WILLIAM, auctioneer, consultant, appraiser; b. Onaway, Mich., May 3, 1953; s. William John and Eleanor (Booth) H.; m. Susan Kaye Simpson, Aug. 6, 1977; 1 son, Jason Robert. Student Mo. Auction Sch., Saginaw Bus. Inst., Am. Mgmt. Assn. Lic. auction cons., appraiser. Auctioneer Cummins Auction Co., Omaha, Nebr., 1981; franchisee United Auctioneers, Omaha, 1982-84; owner, pres. Bob Havers, Auctioneers, Midland, Mich., 1977—; lectr. Central Mich. U., Mt. Pleasant, 1982; cons. Randy Garner, Auctioneers, Fairfield, Ohio, 1982—; ran benefit auction Scottish Rite, Kansas City, Mo., 1979. Author Procalamtion Nat. Auctioneers Week, 1980, 84. recipient Cert. Appreciation Trout Unlimited, 1982-85. Mem. Nat. Auctioneers Assn., Am. Entrepreneurs Assn., Smithsonian Inst., Am. Auction Inst. Democrat. Baptist. Club: Eagles. Avocations: country and bluegrass music, leathercraft. Home and Office: 700 E Haley St Midland MI 48640

HAVERSTICK, NED J., building developer; b. Dayton, Ohio, Oct. 3, 1942; s. Joseph B. and Helen (Jeager) H.; m. Camilla Wahl, Dec. 18, 1982; children: Jennifer, Stephanie, Sam, Alecia, Ben, Camilla Jr. Student, U. Cin., 1961-62; B in Bus., Eastern Ky. U., 1964. Pres. Haverstick Homes, Cin., 1970—. Served with USAF, 1972-77. Mem. Home Builders Assn. (pres. 1978), Engrs. Club Dayton. Republican. Presbyterian. Lodge: Kiwanis. Avocations: skiing, gardening, art collecting. Office: Haverstick Homes 1995 Madison Rd Cincinnati OH 45208

HAVILL, DIANA, university cardiology program administrator; b. Chgo., Dec. 19, 1943; d. Russell and Clara (Zaloudek) H. Owner, mgr. Olympia Inc., Crete, Ill., 1961-66; clin. coordinator U. Chgo., 1965-68; cardiology adminstr. U. Chgo., 1969—; fiscal adminstrv. cons. NIH, Bethesda, Md., 1970-75; research adminstrv. cons. in pvt. practice, Chgo., 1970—. Mem. Adminstrs. Internal Medicine. Lodge: Zonta (sec. Chgo. 1982-85, pres. 1987—). Avocations: horseback riding, hiking, swimming. Home: 5712 S Kenwood Chicago IL 60637 Office: U Chgo 5841 S Maryland Ave Box 423 Chicago IL 60637

HAWK, CAROLINE WINN, manufacturing company executive; b. Columbus, Ohio, Oct. 2, 1933; d. Thomas Parsons Winn and Gussie (Bailey) Raymond; m. David Nelson Hawk, June 13, 1954; children: Kathleen Ivy Hawk Ayle, Cynthia Bernice. Student, Ohio State U., 1951-54. Owner, mgr. Hawk's Card & Hobby Shop, Canton, Ohio, 1967-75; asst. to v.p advt. Citizen's Savs. Assn., Canton, 1967-70; gift buyer Stern & Mann Co., Canton, 1970-72; sales rep. Mut. N.Y. Ins. Co., Akron, Ohio, 1972-75; pres., owner Timber Line Products, Inc., Sugarcreek, Ohio, 1975—; distbr. Lincoln Logs, Ltd. Log Homes, Sugarcreek, 1979—. Arbitrator Better Bus. Bur. Mem. Am. Bus. Women's Assn. (treas., Boss of Yr. award 1978), Tuscarawas County C. of C. Lutheran. Office: Timber Line Products Inc Box 774 Sugarcreek OH 44681

HAWK, ROBERT STEVEN, library administrator; b. Athens, Ohio, June 6, 1949; s. John Paul and Mary Lois (Briggs) H.; m. Constance Lynne Jodoin, June 16, 1979. B.S., Wright State U., 1971; M.S. in L.S., U. Ky., 1974. Library asst. Dayton and Montgomery County Pub. Library, Dayton, Ohio, 1972-73; project dir. Miami Valley Library Orgn., Dayton, 1974-76; library devel. cons. State Library of Ohio, Columbus, 1976-77; librarian, asst. dir. main library Akron Summit County Pub. Library, 1977-79, librarian, asst. dir. brs., 1979-80, librarian, dir., 1980—. Host, writer: cable TV program INFOCUS, 1982. Mem. Gov's Pub. Library Fin and Support Com., Columbus, Ohio, 1983-86; mem. Ohio Multiple Interlibrary Coop. Com., 1980-81, Library and Info. Services to Citizens of Ohio Implementation Adv. Com., Columbus, 1983—; mem. adv. com. Kent State U. Sch. Library Sci., 1980—, U. Akron Continuing Edn. and Pub. Services, 1981—. Mem. ALA, Ohio Library Assn. (bd. dirs. 1982-85, v.p. 1985-86, pres. 1986-87), Beta Phi Mu. Methodist. Lodge: Kiwanis. Home: 311 Merriman Rd Akron OH 44303 Office: 55 S Main St Akron OH 44326

HAWK, SHARON HELEN KULA, cartographer; b. Granite City, Ill., Aug. 13, 1947; d. Alfred Joseph and Salomea Catherine (Wyciskalla) Kula; m. William Howard Hawk, June 18, 1968; children: William Daryl, Wendy Ann. BS in Geography, So. Ill. U., Edwardsville, 1979. Cartographer Def. Mapping Agy. Aerospace Ctr., St. Louis, 1979—; quality circle leader Def. Mapping Agy., 1986—. Catechism tchr. St. Mary's Cath. Ch., Edwardsville. Mem. Federally Employed Women (dep. tng. confs., v.p., program chairperson), Am. Soc. Photogrammetry, So. Ill. U.-Edwardsville Alumni Assn., Montclaire Meadows Assn. (treas.), Montclaire Pool Assn. Avocations: photography, horticulture, fishing, camping. Office: Def Mapping Agy Aerospace Ctr 3200 S 2d St Saint Louis MO 63118-3399

HAWK, STEVEN LYLE, agricultural products company executive, accountant; b. Moline, Ill., July 8, 1952; s. A. Lyle and Joan R. (Holland) H.; m. Nancy Elizabeth Brummet, Oct. 18, 1981; children: Jason Lyle, Sarah Elizabeth. AA, Blackhawk Coll., Moline, Ill., 1974; student, Western Ill. U., Macomb, 1982. Asst. mgr., accountant Farmers Elevator Coop., Fenton, Ill., 1972-77; area accountant IMC Corp., Erie, Ill., 1978; bus. mgr. Lindsay Klein Chevrolet-Oldsmobile Inc., Morrison, Ill., 1979—. Mem. Blackhawk Coll. Alumni Assn. (bd. dirs. 1983, pres. 1987—). Republican. Lutheran. Avocation: musician. Home: 5635 JDK Rd Erie IL 61250 Office: Lindsay Klein Chevrolet 627 E Lincolnway St Morrison IL 61270

HAWKINS, ALLEN WEBSTER, newspaper publisher; b. Advance, Mo., Dec. 15, 1925; s. Arthur Clifford and Winness (McNeely) H.; m. Gladys Ann Schmidt, Nov. 25, 1956. B in Journalism, U. Mo., 1947. Printer St. Francois Sounty Jour., Flat River, Mo., 1940-44; tchr. DeSoto (Mo.) Pub. Schs., 1944-45; news editor Russell (Kans.) Daily News, 1947-59; publisher Osawatomie (Kans.) Graphic, 1959—. Served to cpl. U.S. Army, 1950-52. Mem. Nat. Newspaper Assn. (treas. 1986—, bd. dirs. 1981—), Kans. Press Assn. (pres. 1970). Republican. Methodist. Lodge: Kiwanis, Masons, Shriners, Elks. Office: 122 Rohrer Heights Dr Osawatomie KS 66064 Office: Osawatomie Pub Co 635 Main St Osawatomie KS 66064

HAWKINS, BRETT WILLIAM, political science educator; b. Buffalo, Sept. 15, 1937; s. Ralph C. and Irma A. (Rowley) H.; m. Linda L. Knuth, Oct. 31, 1974; 1 child, Brett William. A.B., U. Rochester, 1959; M.A., Vanderbilt U., 1962, Ph.D., 1964. Instr. polit. sci. Vanderbilt U., 1963; instr. in polit. sci. Washington and Lee U., 1963-64, asst. prof., 1964-65; asst. prof. U. Ga., Athens, 1965-68; asso. prof. U. Ga., 1968-70; asso. prof. U. Wis., Milw., 1970-71, prof., 1971—. Author: Nashville Metro, 1964, The Ethnic Factor in American Politics, 1970, Politics in the Metropolis, 2d edit, 1971, Politics and Urban Policies, 1971, The Politics of Raising State and Local Revenue, 1978, Professional Associations and Municipal Innovation, 1981; contbr. articles to profl. jours. Mem. Phi Beta Kappa, Iota of N.Y. Home: 5318 N Kent Ave Whitefish Bay WI 53217 Office: U Wis Dept Polit Sci Milwaukee WI 53201

HAWKINS, ELLIS DELANO, metal processing company executive; b. Princeton, Ark., Feb. 13, 1941; s. Eddie and Anne Beadie (Smith) H.; m. Vera Mae Smith, Aug. 19, 1969 (div. Sept. 1979); children: Angela, Stacey, Rhonald. AA, Shorter Jr. Coll., 1958; BBA, Calif. Coast U., 1981, MBA, 1983. Cert. in statistical process control; lic. ins. agt., Ill. Operator drill press Choctaw Inc., Poyen, Ark., 1962-65; supr. Chrysler Corp., Detroit, 1965-76, Alcan Aluminum, Terre Haute, Ind., 1976—; pres., chief exec. officer Jes-El-Ed Inc., Chgo., 1980—; also bd. dirs. Jes-El-Ed Inc. Scoutmaster troop 48 Boy Scouts Am., Malvern, Ark., 1962; solicitor United Found., Detroit, 1971. Served with USN, 1958-62. Recipient Commendation Letter Tribune Star, 1986, Appreciation Letter, M.L. King Convocation Com., 1986. Mem. NAACP (life), Am. Legion (chmn. Spl. Olympics 1982—, plaque 1985). Democrat. Club: Chgo. Idlewilders (parlimentarian 1982-85). Lodge: Masons (sr. warden So. Dist. 1984—). Avocations: golf, bowling, short verse writing; profl. freelance photographer. Home: 12139 S Lafayette St Chicago IL 60628 Office: Jes-El-Ed Inc 3216 W 166th St Markham IL 60426

HAWKINS, JOHN LORIMER, auditor, accountant; b. Kansas City, Mo., Mar. 23, 1954; s. George Nicholas and Margaret Juanita (Garrison) H. BA magna cum laude, Avila Coll., 1975. CPA, Mo. Acct. Salvation Army, Kansas City, Mo., 1976-77; sr. internal auditor IRS, Kansas City, 1977—. Mem. Am. Inst. CPA's. Baptist. Avocations: running, hunting, fishing, softball, basketball. Home: 128 Seneca Lake Winnebago MO 64034 Office: IRS Internal Audit 2306 E Bannister Rd Kansas City MO 64131

HAWKINS, JUDY SHEPHERD, pharmacist; b. Emporia, Kans., Apr. 9, 1959; d. Robert Hershel and Augusta Hanah (Dickson) Shepherd; m. David Price Hawkins, June 7, 1986. BS in Pharmacy, U. Kans., 1982. Registered pharmacist, Kans. Staff pharmacist Olathe (Kans.) Med. Ctr., 1982—. Mem. Kans. Pharmacists Assn., Jr. League Kansas City, Kans. U. Alumni Assn., Gamma Phi Beta. Republican. Club: P.E.O. Sisterhood (Olathe).

HAWKINS, LAWRENCE CHARLES, management consultant, educator; b. Greenville County, S.C., Mar. 20, 1919; s. Wayman and Etta (Brockman) H.; m. Earline Thompson, Apr. 29, 1943; children—Lawrence Charles, Wendell Earl. B.A., U. Cin., 1941, B.Ed., 1942, M.Ed., 1951, Ed.D., 1970; AA (hon.), Wilmington Coll., 1979. Cert. sch. supt., Ohio. Elem./secondary tchr. Cin. Pub. Schs., 1945-52, sch. prin./dir., 1952-67, asst. supt., 1967-69; dean U. Cin., 1969-75, v.p., 1975-77, sr. v.p., 1977-83; vis. asst. prof. Eastern Mich. U., Ypsilanti, summers 1955-60; mem. Cincinnatus Assn., 1971—; bd. dirs. Wilmington (Ohio) Coll., 1980—; trustee Children's Home of Cin., 1978—; pres., chief exec. officer Omni-Man, Inc., 1981—. Bd. dirs. Bethesda Hosp., Cin., 1980—; vice chmn. Greater Cin. TV Ednl. Found., WCET-TV, 1983; Co-chmn. Cin. area NCCJ 1980—. Served to lt. USAAF, 1943-45. Recipient award of Merit, Cin. Area United Appeal, 1955, 73, cert. Pres.'s Council on Youth Opportunity, 1968, City Cin., 1968. Mem. NEA (life), Nat. Congress Parents and Tchrs. (hon. life; chmn. com.), Phi Delta Kappa, Kappa Delta Pi, Kappa Alpha Psi, Sigma Pi Phi.

HAWKINS, MICHAEL MURPHY, obstetrician, gynecologist; b. Houston, Sept. 8, 1948; s. George Luvern and Nancy Madelaine (Murphy) H.; m. Claudette Marie Cardenas, DEc. 28, 1972; children: Carolyn Marie, Jonathan Michael, Allison Ann. BA in Biochemistry, Rice U., 1971; MD, U. Tex., Dallas, 1975. Diplomate Am. Bd. Ob-Gyn. Intern, then resident Magee Women's Hosp. U. Pitts., 1975-79; staff obstetrician, gynecologist Kaiser-Permanente Med. Group, Santa Clara, Calif., 1979-82; practice medicine specializing in ob-gyn Zanesville, Ohio, 1982—; chmn. ob-gyn com. Bethesda Hosp., Zanesville, 1986; chmn. ob-gyn dept. Good Samaritan Med. Ctr., Zanesville, 1985-86. Fellow Am. Coll. Ob-Gyn; mem. AMA, Ohio

Med. Assn., Am. Fertility Soc., Muskingum Acad. Medicine. Republican. Avocations: computers, jogging, bridge. Home: 928 Eastward Circle Zanesville OH 43701-1554 Office: 840 Bethesda Dr Zanesville OH 43701

HAWKINS, RALPH G(ERALD), university media administrator; b. Lilbourn, Mo., June 12, 1930; s. Ralph N. and Marguriete (Landreum) H.; m. Dorothy Case, Aug. 6, 1955; children—Randy, Kim, Michael, Christopher. B.S.M.A. Kans. State Coll., 1958, M.S. in Edn., 1967; Ed.D., U. Ark., 1979. Lab. asst. Kans. State Coll., 1955-58; photo and editor, newspaper, Portageville, Mo., 1959-61; editor, pub. weekly newspapers, Clarkton and Gideon, Mo., 1962-64; dir. photography Kans. State Coll., Pittsburg, 1965-67; dir. graphics No. Ill. U., DeKalb, 1967-69; dir. ednl. media S.W. Mo. State U., Springfield, 1969—, assoc. prof. secondary edn., 1969—, supr. Media Ctr., 1983—. Deacon Presbyterian Ch., Springfield; mem. adv. bd. Springfield Cable TV. Served with USAF, 1951-55; Korea. Mem. Assn. Ednl. Communications Tech., Mo. Assn. Ednl. Tech., Phi Delta Kappa, Tau Kappa Epsilon. Democrat. Club: Univ. (pres.) (Springfield). Lodges: Elks, Kiwanis. Author multi-media show: Ed Media 2001, 1978. Home: 2020 S Oak Grove Springfield MO 65804 Office: SW Mo State U 901 S National Springfield MO 65804

HAWKINS, ROBERT LEWIS, III, lawyer; b. Moberly, Mo., Apr. 7, 1951. Student, Westminster Coll., 1969-70; BS, Cen. Mo. State U., 1976; JD, U. Mo., 1979. Spl. asst. prosecuting atty. Cole County, Jefferson City, Mo., 1979—; sole practice Jefferson City, 1979—; gen. counsel Mo. Telephone Assn., 1983—, Mo. Local Govt. Employees Retirement System, 1982—, Mo. Protection and Adv. Systems, Inc., 1985—; mem. exec. council Cole County Youth Ct., 1986—. Editor: The Missouri Partisan, 1985—. Deacon Faith Luth. Ch. Mo. Synod, Jefferson City, 1984—; bd. dirs. Cole County Hist. Soc., 1986—, Hist. City of Jefferson, Inc., 1986—. Mem. ABA, Mo. Bar Assn., Cole County Bar Assn., Confederate States Bar Assn., Mo. Assn. Prosecuting Attys., Supreme Ct. Hist. Soc., Mid.-Mo. Civil War Roundtable (sec./treas. 1985—), Mil. Order of Stars and Bars (Brigadier Gen. Francis Marion Cockrell chpt.), Sons of Confederate Veterans (comdr. Col. Pembroke S. Senteny camp 1985—). Democrat. Avocations: music, history, architecture, art and antiques. Home: 1744 Engelwood Dr Jefferson City MO 65101 Office: 221 E Capitol Ave PO Box 1497 Jefferson City MO 65102

HAWKINS, WALTER LENELL, manufacturing engineer; b. Louisburg, N.C., May 2, 1948; s. Leonard Marion and Ruth (Yarborough) H.; m. Charlene Ashe, Aug. 26, 1978; children: Brandon Lenell Ashe, Justin Cameron Ashe. BSME, N.C. A&T State U., 1970; MBA, Xavier U., 1976; postgrad. U. Cin., 1979, 87. Engr. Gen. Motors Corp., Warren, Mich., 1969; field engr. Dow Chem. Co., Wayne, Mich., 1970; program engr. Gen. Electric, Cin., 1970-71; project mgr. Procter & Gamble, Cin., 1971—, computer integrated mfg. and robotics resource, 1983—. Mem. Big Bros./Sisters Greater Cin., 1974—, bd. dirs., 1973-86, Let Every Adult Read Now, 1986; chpt. leader Young Astronaut Program, 1986. Recipient Ten Yr. award Big Bros./Sisters of Cin., 1983. Fellow Computer Mus.; mem. Soc. Mfg. Engrs., Robotics Internat., ASME, Engring. Soc. Cin. Baptist. Avocations: reading, specialized current events collection, bowling, exercising, etymology. Home: 1880 Fullerton Dr Cincinnati OH 45240 Office: Procter & Gamble Co Soap Plant 5201 Ivorydale Cincinnati OH 45217

HAWKINSON, RENEÉ, nurse; b. Sioux City, Iowa, May 15, 1961; s. Ray John and Nancy May (Coates) Carstensen; m. Jeffrey Vernon Hawkinson, Aug. 16, 1980; 1 child, Todd Michael. RN, St. Luke's Sch. Nursing, 1982. RN St. Luke's Regional Med. Ctr., Sioux City, Iowa, 1982—. Pledge raiser United Way, Sioux City, 1985-86. Democrat. Lutheran. Avocations: reading, aerobics. Home: 3218 Nebraska Sioux City IA 51104 Office: St Lukes Regional Med Ctr 2700 Stone Park Blvd Sioux City IA 51104

HAWLEY, SANDRA SUE, electrical engineer; b. Spirit Lake, Iowa, May 7, 1948; d. Byrnard Leroy and Dorothy Virginia (Fischbeck) Smith; m. Michael John Hawley, June 7, 1970; 1 child, Alexander Tristin. B.S. in Elec. Engring., U. Dayton, 1981; B.S. in Math. and Statistics, Iowa State U., 1970; M.S. in Statistics, U. Del., 1975. Research analyst State of Wis., Madison, 1970-71; research asst. Del. State Coll., Dover, 1972-73; asst. prof. math. and statistics Wesley Coll., Dover, 1974-81, chmn. dept. math. and computer sci., 1978-80; elec. engr. Control Data Corp., Bloomington, Minn., 1982-85; sr. elec. engr. Custom Integrated Circuits, 1985—. Contbr. articles to profl. jours. Elder, Presbyterian Ch. U.S.A., 1975—, mem. session Oak Grove Presbyn. Ch., Bloomington, 1985—. NSF scholar U. Dayton, 1981. Mem. IEEE, Assn. Women in Sci., Soc. Women Engrs., Am. Statis Assn. Home: 7724 W 85th St Circle Bloomington MN 55438 Office: Custom Integrated Circuits 4100 N Hamline Ave Saint Paul MN 55164

HAWLEY, WAYNE CURTIS, blood bank specialist; b. Johnson City, N.Y., July 27, 1946; s. Robert Briggs and Alta Irene (Johnson) H.; m. Diane Sue Mossbarger, June 9, 1973; children: Matthew, Dana, Debra. AB, Union Coll., Barbourville, Ky., 1968; cert. med. tech., Ohio State U., 1973, cert. SBB, 1975. Cert. med. technologist Am. Soc. Clin. Pathologists. Staff technologist Consol. Biomed. Labs., Dublin, Ohio, 1971-74, Ohio State U. Hosp., Columbus, 1974-75; edn. coordinator Cen. Ohio Red Cross, Columbus, 1975-77, Ohio State U. Hosp. Blood Bank, Columbus, 1977-82; coordinator blood bank Doctor's Hosp., Columbus, 1982-86; sect. head blood bank Grant Med. Ctr., Columbus, 1986—; mem. adv. com. Ft. Hayes Career Ctr., Columbus, 1976-78. Mem. Rep. Nat. Com., Washington, 1985—. Served with U.S. Army, 1968-71, Korea. Mem. Am. Assn. Blood Banks (edn. com. 1981-83), Ohio Assn. Blood Banks (chmn. legis. com. 1978-82, 84-86, chmn. awards com. 1978—), Union Coll. Alumni Assn. (scholar 1967-68). Mem. Grace Brethren Ch. Avocations: golfing, stained glass work. Home: 259 Chatham Rd Columbus OH 43214 Office: Grant Med Ctr Transfusion Service 111 S Grant Ave Columbus OH 43215

HAWTHORNE, DOUGLAS LAWSON, bank executive; b. Chgo., Feb. 10, 1942; s. Francis R. and Dorothea (Lawson) H.; m. Sally Archibald, Apr. 15, 1967; 1 child, Bryan Douglas. B.A., Wabash Coll., Crawfordsville, Ind., 1963; student, Grad. Sch. Bus., NYU, 1963-69. Mgmt. trainee Irving Trust Co., 1963-67; corp. credit mgr. Columbia Broadcasting Systems, 1967-69; from v.p., treas. to pres. Careers, Inc., 1969-71; dir. research and planning Third Nat. Bank and Trust Co. subs. Soc. Corp., Dayton, Ohio, 1971-74, v.p. corp. devel., 1974-75, sr. v.p., 1975-78, exec. v.p., 1978-82, pres., chief operating officer, 1982-84, pres., chief exec. officer, 1984-85; chmn. bd., chief exec. officer So. region Soc. Corp., Dayton, Ohio, 1985-86, chmn. bd. dirs., pres., chief exec. officer, 1987—, also dir.; chmn., chief exec. officer Society Bank, Dayton, 1986—; dir. XYOvest Inc.; mem. advisors bd. Ohio Bankers Assn.; vice-chmn. bd. dirs. MedAmerica Health Systems Corp. Div. chmn. United Way; treas., former trustee, mem. fin., audit and endowment coms. Miami Valley Hosp.; past v.p. adminstrn., exec. com., trustee Miami Valley council Boy Scouts Am.; grad. Leadership Dayton Program, 1976; trustee, mem. exec. com. Dayton Area C. of C.; trustee Dayton Art Inst.; chmn. Dayton/Montgomery County Conv. and Visitors Bur.; chmn. Summer Employment Encourages Kids, 1984; chmn. '85 U.S. Women's Golf Tournament; mem. Dayton Area Progress Council. Mem. Leadership Dayton Alumni Assn. Home: 4325 Delco Dell Kettering OH 45429 Office: Society Bank NA 34 N Main St Dayton OH 45402 *

HAWTHORNE, ELIZABETH M., education educator; b. Hartford, Conn., June 28, 1943; d. Samuel H. and Ruth (Grossman) Mirkin; m. John W. Hawthorne (div.); children: Arryn Martha, Jessica J., William J. II; m. Lawrence B. Mohr, Aug. 14, 1983. BS in Edn., Tufts U., 1965; MEd, Temple U., 1971; AM, U. Mich., 1981, PhD, 1985. Ednl. cons. YWCA Head Start Program, Alexandria, Va., 1974-76; project mgr. Nat. Inst. Advanced Studies, Washington, 1976-78; research assoc. U. Mich., Ann Arbor, 1983-85; dir. research The Carroll Group, Inc., Ann Arbor, 1985-86; asst. prof. edn. U. Toledo, 1986—. Author: Evaluating Employee Training, 1987. V.p. Tufts Alumni Council, Medford, Mass., 1975—; chmn. Washtenaw-Hill Hist. Dist. Study Commn., Ann Arbor, 1985-86; mem. Citizens Millage Com. City of Ann Arbor, 1986—; 1st v.p. Ann Arbor Art Assn., 1986—; trustee Oakland Community Coll., Bloomfield Hills, Mich., 1982-83. Mem. Assn. Study Higher Edn., Am. Ednl. Research Assn. Democrat. Jewish. Avocations: handcrafts, reading. Home: 1310 Hill St Ann Arbor MI 48104 Office: U Toledo Coll Edn and Allied Professions Toledo OH 43606

HAWTHORNE, FRANK WALKER, JR., foundation researcher, librarian; b. Lansing, Mich., Jan. 30, 1954; s. Frank Walker and June Marie (Caldwell) H.; m. Dottie M. Dilts, May 15, 1982. B.A., Western Mich. U., 1979, MLS, 1981. Prospect researcher RMH Found., Rochester, Minn., 1982—; reference librarian Rochester Pub. Library, 1982—. Mem. Rochester Human Rights Commn., 1985—, Minn. Episcopal Peace Commn., 1983-85. Mem. Minn. Prospect Research Assn. (v.p. 1984-87). Mem. League of Minn. Human Rights Commns. (del. 1985—), Democratic Farmers Labor Party. Avocations: reading, watercolors, cross country skiing. Home: 427 6th St SW Rochester MN 55902 Office: RMH Found 200 1st St SW Rochester MN 55905

HAY, RAYMOND A., steel and diversified manufacturing company executive; b. L.I., N.Y., July 13, 1928; m. Grace Mattson; children: John Alexander, Susan Elizabeth. B.S. in Econs., L.I. U., 1949; M.B.A., St. John's U., 1960. Mgr. Northeastern div. Monroe Calculating Machine Co. (now Monroe-Swede), 1958-61; with Xerox Corp., Rochester, N.Y., 1961-75; br. mgr. Xerox Corp., N.Y.C., 1961-62, zone mgr. Western Region, also asst. dir. sales ops. and dir. mktg., 1962-68, group v.p. and gen. mgr. info. systems, 1968, exec. v.p., to 1975; pres., chief operating officer LTV Corp., Dallas, from 1975, chief exec. officer, 1982—, also chmn., dir.; dir. First City Bancorp., Tex., Diamond Shamrock Corp. Bd. govs. Kennedy Ctr. for Performing Arts; trustee Dallas Mus. Fine Arts, Dallas Symphony Orch.; bd. dirs. Dallas Civic Opera Assn. Mem. Am. Mgmt. Assn., Nat. Sales Execs. Club: Dallas C. of C. (council steering com.). Office: LTV Corp 2001 Ross Ave PO Box 225003 Dallas TX 75265 *

HAY, ROBERT PETTUS, history educator; b. Eagleville, Tenn., Oct. 23, 1941; s. Ira James and Alice Elizabeth (Pettus) H.; m. Carla Jean Humphrey, Dec. 31, 1966. B.S. with highest honors, Middle Tenn. State U., Murfreesboro, 1962; Ph.D., U. Ky., 1967. Instr. history Middle Tenn. State U., summer 1964; lectr. history U. Ky., 1966-67; instr. history sch. edn. NDEA Inst., U. Ky., summer 1967; asst. prof. history Marquette U., Milw., 1967-71, assoc. prof., 1971—, asst. chmn. dept., 1975, chmn. dept., dir. grad. study, 1975-79. Assoc. history editor USA Today, 1980—; contbr. numerous articles and commentaries to hist., popular and profl. jours., book reviewer numerous publs.; author poetry. Mem. Milw. County Zool. Soc., Milw. Art Mus., Friends of Milw. County Pub. Mus., Tenn. State Mus. Assn. Univ. research grantee Marquette U., 1968; summer faculty fellow Marquette U., 1969, 73, life mem. Pres.'s Council Marquette U., U. Ky. Fellows. Commd. Ky. col., 1980; Woodrow Wilson fellow, 1962-63, 65-66; NDEA fellow, 1962-65; Nat. Endowment Humanities fellow, 1969-70. Mem. Orgn. Am. Historians (life), So. Hist. Assn. (life), Soc. Historians Early Am. Rep. (life), Tenn. Hist. Soc. (life), Am. Cath. Hist. Assn. (life), Milw. County Hist. Soc. (life), Ky. Hist. Soc. (life), Filson Club (life), Am. Hist. Assn. (life), Milw. Met. Historians Assn., East. Tenn. Hist. Soc. (life), West Tenn. Hist. Soc. (life), Inst. Early Am. History and Culture, Ctr. for Study of Presidency, Wis. Assn. Promotion of History, AAUP, Phi Alpha Theta, Pi Gamma Mu. Democrat. Roman Catholic. Clubs: Wisconsin, Helfaer Recreation Center, Atlanta Track. Avocations: running, gardening, poetry, weight-lifting, basketball. Home: 2146 Laura Ln Waukesha WI 53186 Office: Marquette U Dept History Milwaukee WI 53233

HAY, WILLIAM HENRY, physician; b. Chgo., Aug. 9, 1958; s. Henry Black and Helen Porthy (Fischer) H. BS in Biology, U. Ill., Chgo., 1979; MD, U. Ill., Rockford, 1983. Diplomate Am. Bd. Family Practice. Intern Rush-Christ Family Practice, Chgo., 1983-84, resident, 1984-86; fellow Rush Presbyn. St. Lukes Med. Ctr., Chgo., 1986-87. Asst. editor: The World Book Illustrated Home Med. Ency., 1987; contbr. articles to profl. jours. Mem. Nat. Council Against Health Fraud, 1982—, Ill. Council Against Health Fraud, 1987—, officers nominating com., 1987. Mem. AMA, Ill. State Med. Assn., Chgo. Med. Soc., Am. Acad. Family Physicians, Soc. Tchrs. Family Medicine, Physicians for Social Responsibility (bd. dirs. Chgo. chpt. 1986—), Internat. Physicians for Prevention of Nuclear War. Avocation: folk singing, guitar.

HAYASHI, TETSUMARO, educator, author, editor; b. Sakaide City, Japan, Mar. 22, 1929; came to U.S., 1954, naturalized, 1969; s. Tetsuro and Shieko (Honjyo) H.; m. Akiko Sakuratani, Apr. 14, 1960; 1 son, Richard Hideki. B.A., Okayama (Japan) U., 1953; M.A. (Rotary Internat. Jr. fellow), U. Fla., 1957; M.A., Kent State U., 1959, Ph.D., 1968. Assoc. dir. Culver-Stockton Coll. Library, Canton, Mo., 1959-63; instr. English Kent State U., Ohio, 1965-68; prof. English Ball State U., Muncie, Ind., 1977—; dir. Steinbeck Research Inst., 1981—. Author: Sketches of American Culture, 1960, John Steinbeck: A Concise Bibliography, 1967, Arthur Miller Criticism, 1969, Robert Greene Criticism, 1971, Shakespeare's Sonnets: A Record of 20th Century Criticism, 1972, Index to Arthur Miller: Criticism, 1976; editor: A Looking Glass for London and England (Thomas Lodge, Robert Greene), An Elizabethan Text, 1970, (with Richard Astro) Steinbeck: The Man and His Work, 1971, John Steinbeck: A Dictionary of His Fictional Characters, 1976; Steinbeck's Literary Dimension, 1973, A Study Guide to Steinbeck: A Handbook of His Major Works, 1974; also 13 other books, 10 monographs; founder, editor-in-chief: Steinbeck Quar., 1968—; gen. editor: Steinbeck Monograph Series, 1970—. Folger fellow, 1972, Am. Philos. Soc. fellow, 1975, 81, Am. Council Learned Socs. fellow, 1976; grantee Calif. Council for Humanities, 1981, 82, 85, Bernard Boyd Meml. Found. grantee, 1986. Mem. MLA, Midwest Modern Lang. Assn., Am. Studies Assn., Shakespeare Assn. Am., Internat. John Steinbeck Soc. (founder, pres.). Home: 1405 N Kimberly Ln Muncie IN 47304

HAYCOX, PHILLIP N., manufacturing company executive; b. Ft. Wayne, Ind., Feb. 8, 1935; s. Arthur Lee and Mildred I. (Markley) H.; m. Beverly Ann Winans, Feb. 14, 1954; children: Gregory Kent, Jeffery Edwin. BSME, Purdue U., 1957; car. Sale engr. Locke Steel, Huntington, Ind., 1958-65; regional mgr. Hull Corp., Hatboro, Pa., 1965-71; sales mgr. machine div. Van Dorn Plastic, Cleve., 1971-75; market mgr. poly-hi div. Manasha Corp., Ft. Wayne, 1975-80; pres. Hayco Inc., Ft. Wayne, 1980—. Leader Boy Scouts Am., Ft. Wayne, 1968-72. Mem. IEEE, Soc. Plastics Engr. (program com. 1985-86), Sigma Alpha Epsilon, Sigma Nu Epsilon Tau Tau.

HAYDEN, CHARLES BARRY, real estate developer; b. St. Louis, Sept. 8, 1943; s. Charles Francis and Marie Emily (Naumann) H.; m. Judith Ann Fister, Apr. 16, 1966; children: C. Brian, Cara, Laura, Allison. BSCE, U. Mo., Rolla, 1965, MS Engring. Adminstrn., 1970. Registered profl. engr., Mo., Ill., Okla., Fla.; registered broker, Mo. V.p. McCarthy Bros. Co., St. Louis, 1965-77; pres. The Hayden Co., St. Louis, 1977—; Bd. dirs. Mark Twain Bank, St. Louis. Served to 1st lt., U.S. Army, 1966-69. Mem. Nat. Assn. Home Bldrs. (bd. dirs., nat. rep. 1980—), Home Bldrs. Assn. St. Louis (pres. 1977—), Home Bldrs. Industry Advancement Fund (chmn. 1983—). Roman Catholic. Club: Forest Hills (St. Louis). Avocations: golf, tennis, reading. Office: The Hayden Co 1 The Pines Ct Saint Louis MO 63141

HAYDEN, HARROLD HARRISON, information company executive; b. Cin., Jan. 16, 1942; s. Harold Richard and Blanche Marie (Sargent) H. BA, Millikin U., Decatur, Ill., 1964; MA, DePaul U., Chgo., 1970. Dir. mktg. tng. Automatic Electric, Northlake, Ill., 1968-70; dir. Universal Tng. Co., Wilmette, Ill., 1970-80; pres. Performance Achievement Group, Chgo., 1980-85; v.p. Lead mgmt. Service, Chgo., 1985—. Author: (multimedia package) Successful Telephone Selling, 1979, Santa Fe Railroad Data, 1975, Best Ill. award, 1975; editor Secrets of Successful Telemarketing, 1985. Mem. Ohlmstead Hist. Soc., Riverside, Ill., 1985; bd. dirs. 44th Ward Bus. Com., Chgo., 1985-86. Recipient award Best Condo Bldg., Northside Real Estate Bd., Chgo., 1985. Mem. Am. Mktg. Assn., Am. Soc. Tng. and Devel. (bd. dirs. 1971-81, Best Tng. program 1975), Am. Mgmt. Assn. (speaker 1979-85). Clubs: Pin Point Ski, Chgo. Yacht. Avocations: sailing, skiing. Office: Lead Mgmt Services 1000 W Diversey Pkwy Chicago IL 60614

HAYDEN, JOHN MICHAEL, governor, insurance agent; b. Colby, Kans., Mar. 16, 1944; s. Irven Wesley and Ruth (Kelly) H.; m. Patti Ann Rooney, Aug. 26, 1968; children: Chelsi, Anne. B.S., Kans. State U., 1966; M.S., Ft. Hays State U., 1974. Exec. mgr. Rawlins County Promotional Council, Atwood, Kans., 1973-77; agt. E.C. Mellick Agy., Atwood, 1977—; speaker Kansas Ho. of Reps., until 1987; governor Kansas, Topeka, 1987—. Pres. U.S. Hwy. 36 Assn. Served to 1st lt. AUS, 1967-70, Vietnam. Mem. Am. Legion, VFW. Republican. Methodist. Club: Ducks Unltd. (Atwood). Lodge: Rotary (Atwood). Home: Governors Mansion State Capitol Topeka KS 67730 Office: Office of Gov State Capitol 2d Floor Topeka KS 66612-1590 *

HAYDOCK, WALTER JAMES, banker; b. Chgo., Dec. 14, 1947; s. Joseph Albert and Lillian V. (Adeszko) H.; student Harvard Bus. Coll., 1969-71, Daily Coll., 1971-73; B.S. in Acctg., DePaul U., 1976; m. Bonnie Jean Thompson, Aug. 22, 1970; children—Nicole Lynn, Matthew Michael. Computer operator, jr. programmer Pepper Constrn. Co., Chgo., 1972-73; input analyst Continental Bank, Chgo., 1973-76, data control supr., 1976-79, corporate fixed asset adminstr., 1979-83, properties systems analyst, 1983—; partner Day's End Motel, Wisconsin Dells, Wis., 1977—. Mem. Wis. Innkeepers Assn., Wisconsin Dells C. of C. Home: 14129 Somerset Ct Orland Park IL 60462 Office: Continental Bank 231 S LaSalle St Chicago IL 60693

HAYES, ARTHUR CHESTER, safety cons., state legislator; b. Ft. Wayne, Ind., Aug. 24, 1918; s. Walter F. and Marie P. (Hardesty) H.; B.S., Ind. U., 1948; m. Miriam E. Peck, Feb. 1, 1946 (dec. Nov. 1968); children—Arthur C., Bethany M., Gayle W. Crosby. Sales corr. Magnavox Corporation, 1948-54; supr. Budget State Hwy. Dept., 1954-58; owner Vernors Bottling Co., Ft. Wayne, 1959-63; became dist. mgr. Colonial Life & Accident Ins. Co., 1963; mem. Ind. Ho. of Reps., 1963-72, 77—, ho. mem. Ind. Statutory com. on Commn. on Protection and Advocacy for Developmentally Disabled, 1977-78; safety cons. Chmn. Interstate Cooperation Com., Recodification of Cities and Towns Commn.; mem. Sesquicentennial Commn.; chmn. speakers bur. Ind. Am. Revolution Bicentennial Commn.; mem. Ind. Am. Negro Emancipation Centennial Commn. Served with AUS, 1941-45. Mem. Ft. Wayne C. of C., Am. Legion. Clubs: Ft. Wayne Civitan (pres. 1963-68; lt. gov. Midwest 1967). Home: 2001 Oakland St Fort Wayne IN 46808 Office: State House Bldg Indianapolis IN 46204

HAYES, CARSON LEN, housing owner and agent; b. Bloomington, Ind., Aug. 1, 1960; s. Lenzy Curtis and Wilma Jean (Wampler) H.; m. Rebecca Lynn Kay, Mar. 9, 1985. BS, Ind. U., 1982, cert. real estate broker, 1983, cert. property and casualty ins. agt., 1984. Cert. HUD property mgr., Ind. Pres. Lenzy Hayes, Inc., Bloomington, 1982—. Active Richland Sr. Citizens Housing, Ellettsville, Ind., 1986, Ellettsville Sr. Citizens Housing, 1986, Richland Bean-Blossom Health Care, Inc., Elletsville, 1986. Recipient Arion award in music Arion Assn. 1977, John Phillip Sousa award Edgewood High Sch., Ellettsville, 1978. Mem. Am. Legion, Delta Chi. Democrat. Mem. Pentecostal Ch. Avocations: bicycling, horseback riding. Home: 2725 N Smith Pike Bloomington IN 47401 Office: Lenzy Hayes Inc 5665 W State Rd 46 Bloomington IN 47401

HAYES, CHARLES, religious organization executive, clergyman; b. Chgo., Aug. 4, 1950; s. Charles and Doris Yvonne (Davis) H. Degree in Theology, Emmaus Bible Sch., 1977; AA in Data Processing, Kennedy King Coll., 1982, AS in Acctg., 1985; BA, Chgo. State U., 1986. Lic. minister. Assoc. pastor St. Mary's Ch., Chgo., 1978—; instr. Kennedy King Coll., Chgo., 1980-82; pres. Christians Taking Action, Inc., Chgo., 1983—; bd. dirs. Organized Urban Resource, Inc., Chgo. Contbr. articles to profl. jours. Recipient Recognition award Ch. Christ, 1977, Appreciation award U.S. Com. for UNICEF, 1985. Democrat. Baptist. Avocations: horticulture, aquariums. Home: 6619 S Maryland Chicago IL 60637

HAYES, CHARLES A., Congressman; b. Cairo, Ill., Feb. 17, 1918; m. Edna J. Hayes; children: Barbara Delaney, Charlene Smith; 2 stepsons. Internat. v.p., dir. Region #412 United Food & Comml. Workers Internat. Union, AFL-CIO & CLC, 1968-83; mem. 98th-99th Congresses form Ill., 1983—; dist. dir. Dist. #41 UPWA, 1954-68; field rep., exec. v.p. Coalition Black Trade Unionists; v.p. Ill. State AFL-CIO, Operation PUSH, Chgo.; exec. bd. Chgo. Urban League; mem. Ill. State Commn. Labor Laws. Office: Ill Congressman Longworth House Office Bldg. Room 102 Washington DC 20515 *

HAYES, DAVID JOHN, former electrical component manufacturing company marketing executive; b. Indpls., July 30, 1943; s. Alfred Henry and Jean Alexander (Morrison) H.; A.B., Boston U., 1965; M.B.A., Cornell U., 1967. Mgmt. trainee Westinghouse Broadcasting Co., Chgo., 1967-68, Norwalk, Conn., 1968, Boston, 1968-71; nat. sales rep. NBC, Chgo., 1971-72; pres. Dana Enterprises, Chgo., 1972-75; v.p. mktg. Micron Industries Corp., Stone Park, Ill., 1975-83; dir. Haybec Enterprises, Inc., New Orleans Hotel Corp. Mem. Assn. M.B.A. Execs. Club Chgo., Salesmen with A Purpose (internat. v.p. 1980-81, Ill. pres. 1981-82), Ill. State Hist. Soc. (chmn. com. hist. markers 1980). Mem. Christian Ch. Clubs: Boston U. Chgo., Cornell Bus. Sch. Contbr. articles to Adminstrv. Sci. Quar. Home: 156 N Brainard Ave La Grange IL 60525

HAYES, DAVID JOHN ARTHUR, JR., association executive; b. Chgo., July 30, 1929; s. David J.A. and Lucille (Johnson) H.; m. Anne Huston, Feb. 20, 1963; children—David J.A. III, Cary. A.B., Harvard U., 1952; J.D., Ill. Inst. Tech.-Kent Coll. Law, 1961. Bar: Ill. Trust officer, asst. sec. First Nat. Bank of Evanston, Ill., 1961-63; gen. counsel Ill. State Bar Assn., Chgo., 1963-66; asst. dir. ABA, Chgo., 1966-68, div. dir., 1968-69, asst. exec. dir., 1969-87, v.p., 1987—; exec. dir. Naval Res. Lawyers Assn., 1971-75; asst. sec. gen. Internat. Bar Assn., 1978-80, Inter-Am. Bar Assn., 1984—. Contbr. articles to profl. jours. Served to capt. JAGC, USNR. Fellow Am. Bar Found.; mem. ABA, Ill. State Bar Assn. (ho. of dels. 1972-76), Nat. Orgn. Bar Counsel (pres. 1967), Chgo. Bar Assn. Club: Michigan Shores. Home: 908 Pontiac Rd Wilmette IL 60091 Office: ABA 750 N Lake Shore Dr Chicago IL 60611

HAYES, DORIS JEAN, data processing executive; b. Louisville, Ky., June 7, 1946; d. James Benedict and Rose Bernice (Ruley) H.; m. Joseph Alex Ritok Jr., Aug. 30, 1975; children: Christine Michelle, Stephanie Anne. BS summa cum laude, DePaul U., 1973; MBA with distinction, U. Mich., 1984. Tchr, Math and Sci. Chgo. Archdiocesan Sch. System, 1967-71; systems analyst Sears Roebuck & Co., Chgo., 1971-74; systems programmer Blue Cross/Blue Shield, Detroit, 1974-78; mgr. data processing Electronic Data Systems, Detroit, 1978—. Recipient Outstanding Performance award Gen. Motors Corp., 1983, 84. Mem. Beta Gamma Sigma. Office: Electronic Data Systems 2050 N Woodward Bloomfield Hills MI 48013

HAYES, EDWARD JAMES, manufacturing executive; b. Bklyn., Apr. 8, 1924; s. Patrick J. and Mary Francis (Miller) H.; m. Mary Theresa, Feb. 5, 1950; children: Mary Ellen, Edward Jr., Brian. BSME, MIT, 1950; MSME, U. Md., 1955. Registered profl. engr., Mich. Dir. research and devel. Kelsey-Hayes, Romulus, Mich., 1958-64; v.p. research engring. and quality control Kelsey-Hayes, Romulus, 1964-65, v.p. corp. research and devel., 1966-67, pres. and gen. mgr. wheel, drum and brake div., 1968-76, corp. v.p. research and devel. and engring., 1976—; corp. v.p. research and devel. and engring. Fruehauf div., Detroit, 1980-87, exec. v.p. tech. ops., sr. advisor to the chmn., 1987—; bd. dirs. E&E Engring., Detroit, Brembo S.p.A., Italy, FPS, Italy. Holder of 26 patents in brake field; contbr. articles to profl. jours. Pres. Long Branch Civic Assn., Silver Springs, Md., Green Point Civic Assn., Livonia, Mich.; del. Montgomery County Civic Fedn., Md. Served to capt. USAF, 1945, ETO. Recipient award for design and installation of playground equipment Silver Spring Police Dept. Fellow Engring. Soc. Detroit; mem. Soc. Profl. Engrs., Am. Inst. for Physics, AAAS, Sigma Xi. Clubs: Detroit Athletic; Grosse Point (Mich.) Yacht. Office: Fruehauf Corp R&D Div 10825 Harper Detroit MI 48213

HAYES, FRANK N., salt products company financial executive; b. Detroit, Jan. 14, 1938; s. Frank N. and Blanche C. (McDermott) H.; m. Gilda McGill, Mar. 26, 1977; children by previous marriage: William, Michael, Christopher, Kathleen. B.S. in Accounting, U. Detroit, 1960; M.B.A., Wayne State U., 1970. C.P.A., Mich. Auditor, accountant Price Waterhouse & Co., Detroit, 1959-63; gen. accounting mgr. Diamond Crystal Salt Co., St. Clair, Mich., 1963-68; asst. treas. Diamond Crystal Salt Co., 1968-71, treas., 1971-81, treas., chief fin. officer, 1981-85, v.p. fin., chief fin. officer, 1985—. Mem. Am. Inst. C.P.A.s, Mich. Assn. C.P.A.s, Fin. Execs. Inst., Beta Alpha Psi, Sigma Phi Epsilon. Home: 2932 Woodstock Circle Port Huron MI 48060 Office: 916 S Riverside Ave Saint Clair MI 48079

HAYES, GEOFFREY LEIGH, clergyman; b. Traverse City, Mich., June 1, 1947; s. Carl William and Shirley Margaret (Sanborn) H.; m. Sandra Lee Stricker, Dec. 27, 1969; children: Allyson Leigh, Rachel Anne. BA, Mich. State U., 1969; D in Religion, So. Calif. Sch. Theology, 1973. Ordained to ministry Meth. Ch., as deacon, 1970, as elder, 1974. Assoc. pastor First United Meth. Ch., Grand Rapids, Mich., 1973-78; pastor Asbury United Meth. Ch., Lansing, Mich., 1978—; mem. bd. ordained ministry west Mich. conf. United Meth. Ch., 1978—; pres. Lansing Area Council Chs., 1983. Contbr. articles to profl. jours. Mem. Alban Inst., Fellowship United Meths. in Worship, Music and Other Arts. Democrat. Avocations: singing, playing guitar, racquetball. Home: 2412 Post Oak Ln Lansing MI 48912 Office: Asbury United Meth Ch 2200 Lake Lansing Rd Lansing MI 48912

HAYES, HAROLD O., JR, manufacturing company executive; b. Evanston, Ill., Dec. 29, 1929; s. Harold O. and Frances E. (Henderson) H.; m. JoAnn Elaine Funkhouser, Dec. 24, 1951; children: Kenneth, Christopher, Jeffrey, Julie. BBA, Miami U., Oxford, Ohio, 1951; MBA, Northwestern U., 1955. Plant controller Walker Mfg., Lake Mills, Iowa, 1960-62, plant mgr., 1963-66; production mgr. HON Industries, Muscatine, Iowa, 1966-69; dir. mfg. Faultless div. Axia, Evansville, Ind., 1969-77; pres. and gen. mgr. Nestaway div. Axia, Cleve., 1978—; bd. dirs. Andamios Atlas. Served to lt. (j.g.) USCGR, 1951-53. Methodist. Avocations: golf, reading, photography, woodworking. Home: 80 Old Plank Ln Chagrin Falls OH 44022 Office: Axia Nestaway Div 9501 Granger Rd Cleveland OH 44125

HAYES, KENDALL PRESTON, marketing professional; b. Cleve., Mar. 18, 1929; s. Preston P. and Doris (Kendall) H.; m. Joan Pringle, Nov. 3, 1952 (dec. Mar. 1965); children: Dale Allison Hayes Clarke, Carolyn Lee, Kimberly Ann; m. Lois Goodchild, Aug. 19, 1967. AB, Duke U., 1951. Mktg. mgr. Arrow Pneumatics, Inc., Lake Zurich, Ill., 1971—. Served to lt. (j.g.) USN, 1951-53, Korea. Republican. Club: Lake Bluff Town and Tennis (pres. 1970). Home: 244 E North Ave Lake Bluff IL 60044 Office: Arrow Pneumatics Inc 500 N Oakwood Rd Lake Zurich IL 60047

HAYES, MARCIE LYNN, music educator, pianist; b. Canton, Ill., May 6, 1951; d. Leo G. May and Betty J. (Fanning) Hayes. BS in Piano cum laude, Ill. State U., 1986, postgrad. in psychology and music, 1986—. Mgr. Lewistown (Ill.) Plumbing, 1974-80; dir. B/N Suzuki Acad., Bloomington, Ill., 1980—. Author Childsplay (pre-sch. piano course), 1985. Mem. Mensa, Golden Key, Phi Kappa Lambda. Home: 917 W Market Normal IL 61761

HAYES, MARIA FERRARO, reproductive endocrinologist, educator; b. Indpls., Sept. 2, 1951; d. Leonard Martin and Nina Lou (Dillion) Ferraro; m. Robert Carmody Hayes Jr., June 7, 1980; children: Margaret Rose, Robert Carmody III. AB, Ind. U., 1972, MD, 1977. Diplomate Am. Bd. Ob/gyn. Resident in ob/gyn Wayne State U., Detroit, 1977-81, fellow reproductive endocrinology and infertility, 1981-83, asst. prof. endocrinology and infertility, 1983—; Jr. attending staff Hutzel Hosp., 1982—; active staff Harper Hosp., 1984—. Mem. AMA, Am. Coll. Ob/Gyn, Am. Fertility Soc., Mich. State Med. Soc., Wayne County Med. Soc., Cen. Assn. OB/Gyn, Arthur Metz Scholars, Phi Beta Kappa, Phi Rho Sigma. Roman Catholic. Home: 1250 Navarre Pl Detroit MI 48207 Office: CS Mott Ctr Human Growth and Devel 275 E Hancock Detroit MI 48201

HAYES, MARY JANE, pediatric dentist; b. Rochester, N.Y., Mar. 31, 1948; d. John Edward and Helen E. (Hendrick) H. BA, Rosary Coll., 1970; AM, U. Chgo., 1974; DDS, U. Ill., 1976, MS, 1978. Asst. prof. pediatric dentistry Northwestern U., Chgo., 1980—; pvt. practice pediatric dentistry Chgo., 1980—; lectr. U. Ill. Coll. Dentistry, Chgo., 1980—, DePaul U., Chgo., 1983—; ins. cons. specialist Blue Cross/Blue Shield, Chgo., 1984—. Bd. dirs. Infant Welfare Soc., Chgo., 1983—. Mem. ADA, Am. Acad. Pediatric Dentists, Ill. Soc. Pediatric Dentists (bd. dirs. 1985—, sec. 1987), Am. Assn. Women Dentists (treas. 1987). Home: 2648 N Bosworth Chicago IL 60614 Office: 919 N Michigan Chicago IL 60611

HAYES, MARY PHYLLIS, savings and loan association executive; b. New Castle, Ind., Apr. 30, 1921; d. Clarence Edward and Edna Gertrude (Burgess) Scott; m. John Clifford Hayes, Jan. 1, 1942 (div. Oct. 1952); 1 child, R. Scott. Student, Ball State U., 1957-64, Ind. U. East, Richmond, 1963; diploma, Inst. Fin. Edn., 1956, 72, 76. Teller Henry County Savs. and Loan, New Castle, 1939-41, loan officer, teller, 1950-62, asst. sec., treas., 1962-69, sec., treas., 1969-73, corp. sec., 1973-84; v.p., sec. Ameriana Savs. Bank (formerly Henry County Savs. and Loan), New Castle, 1984—; exec. sec. Am. Nat. Bank, Nashville, 1943-44; corp. sec. HCSS Corp., New Castle, 1984—; bd. dirs. Ameriana Ins. Co. Treas. Henry County Chpt. Am. Heart Assn., New Castle, 1965-67, 74-79, vol. Indpls. chpt. 1980—; membership sec. Henry County Hist. Soc., New Castle, 1975—; sec. Henry County Chpt. ARC, New Castle, 1976—. Recipient Gold medallian Am. Heart Assn., 1973, 20-Yr. award, 1983. Mem. Inst. Fin. Edn. (sec., treas. E. Cen. Ind. chpt. 1973—), Ind. League Savs. Insts. (25-Yr. award 1975), Psi Iota Xi (past sec., treas.). Mem. Christian Ch. Lodges: Altrusa (past officer, bd. dirs. New Castle chpt.), PEO (past chaplain, sec.). Avocations: music, travel, history, swimming. Office: Ameriana Savs Bank 2118 Bundy Ave New Castle IN 47362

HAYES, MICHAEL CHARLES, photographer; b. Rochester, Minn., Sept. 23, 1946; s. Charles Clement and Alice Lucille (Lundquist) H.; m. Nancee Jayne (Ralston); children: Andrew Michael, Kristen Ann. BA, U. Minn., 1971. Sr. photographer Gen. Mills Inc., Mpls., 1973-79, coordinator of visual presentation, 1979-86, supr. slide prodn., 1986—. Served as cpl. USMC, 1965-69, Vietnam. Mem. Minn. Indsl. Comml. Photographers Assn. Office: Gen Mills Photography 9200 Wayzata Blvd Golden Valley MN 55426

HAYES, RICHARD JOHNSON, association executive, lawyer; b. Chgo., May 25, 1933; s. David John Arthur and Lucille Margaret (Johnson) H.; m. Mary R. Lynch, Dec. 2, 1961; children: Susan, Richard, John, Edward. B.A., Colo. Coll., 1955; J.D., Georgetown U., 1961. Bar: Ill. 1961. Assoc. firm Barnabas F. Sears, Chgo., 1961-63, Peterson, Lowry, Rall, Barber and Ross, Chgo., 1963-65; staff dir. Am. Bar Assn., Chgo., 1965-70; exec. dir. Internat. Assn. Ins. Counsel, Chgo., 1970—; instr. various legal programs 1966—, Ins. Counsel Trial Acad., 1973—. Editor: Antitrust Law Jour, 1969—. Served to 1st lt. AUS, 1955-57. Mem. Am., Chgo. socs. assn. execs., ABA (chmn. prepaid legal services 1977-78), Ill. Bar Assn., Chgo. Bar Assn., Jr. Bar (chmn. 1965), Nat. Conf. Lawyers and Ins. Cos. (bd. dirs. 1983—), Phi Alpha Delta, Beta Theta Pi. Clubs: Rotary/One (Chgo.), Tower (Chgo.); Mich. Shores (Wilmette, Ill.). Home: 1920 Thornwood St Wilmette IL 60091 Office: 20 N Wacker Dr Chicago IL 60606

HAYES, THOMAS PATRICK, therapeutic radiology physician; b. Howard City, Mich., Apr. 29, 1926; s. Laurence William and Freda Augusta (Schanz) H.; m. Frances M. Lane, Aug. 14, 1948 (dec. Jan. 1978); children: Frances C., Thomas P. Jr., Julia L.; m. Geneva T. Mominee, Mar. 10, 1980. BS, U. Mich., 1946, MD, 1949. Diplomate Am. Bd. Radiology; cert. therapeutic radiology. Intern Indpls. Gen. Hosp., 1949-50; staff U.S. Naval Hosp., Portsmouth, Va., 1950, U.S. Naval Air Sta., Norfolk, Va., 1951, U.S.S. Mo., 1951-52; gen. practice medicine St. Joseph, Mich., 1953-66; resident in radiology Grad. Hosp., Phila., 1966-68; resident, asst. instr. U. Pa. Hosp., Phila., 1968-70; practice medicine specializing in radiotherapy Evansville, 1970—; dir. therapeutic radiology Deaconess Hosp., Evansville, Ind., 1974—, med. dir. therapeutic radiology, 1986—; sr. clin. instr. Nat. Cancer Inst., 1970. Contbr. articles to profl. and scholarly jours. Served to lt. USNR, 1950-52, ATO. Am. Cancer Soc. fellow, 1969. Mem. Vanderburgh County Med. Soc. (chmn. bd. censors 1982—), Am. Rare Minerals (bd. dirs. 1982—), Petroleum Club. Republican. Club: Oak Meadow Country. Avocations: photography, gardening, golf. Office: 350 Columbia Suite 420 Evansville IN 47710

HAYES, WALTER JOHN, data processing executive; b. N.Y.C., July 18, 1938; s. John C. and Mary (Mazgulski) Hayes; m. Dorothy Louise Hayes, Aug. 16, 1964; children—Walter, Daniel, Susan, Sarah. B.S. in Math., St. John's Coll., 1960, postgrad. 1960-62, 65-66, Athens Coll., 1967-68. Programmer/systems analyst Sperry Gyroscope Co., Lake Success, N.Y., 1963-66; sr. systems analyst/supr. Sperry Rand Space Support, Huntsville, Ala., 1966-68, info. systems mgr., 1968-69; regional data center mgr. Figgie Systems Mgmt. Group, Willoughby, Ohio, 1969-74, mgr. adminstrn., 1974-79, pres., 1979—; participant CAD/CAM Adv. Com., 1980—, Info. Resources Steering Com., 1981—, others; cons. in field. Mem. Figgie Polit. Action Com., 1981—, St. Anselm's Parish Council, Chesterland, Ohio, 1982—; bd. dirs. Fairmount Ctr., Russell, Ohio, 1985—. Served with USNG, 1955-61. Mem. Am. Prodn. and Inventory Control Soc., Assn. Data Processing Service Orgns. Republican. Roman Catholic. Club: Chagrin Valley Country. Home: 8680 Camelot Dr Chesterland OH 44026 Office: Figgie Systems Mgmt Group 4420 Sherwin Rd Willoughby OH 44094

HAYFORD, JOHN SARGENT, retail executive; b. Balt., Mar. 23, 1940; s. John Enoch and Anne Margaret (Weniger) H.; m. Barbara Jean McGann, Oct. 10, 1964; children: Kathryn, John, Patrick. BBA, Notre Dame U., 1962. CPA, Ind. With Ernst & Whinney, Chgo., 1963-77, ptnr., 1977-84; v.p. fin., treas. Marsh Supermarkets, Inc., Yorktown, Ind., 1984—. Mem. Am. Inst. CPA's (Elijah Watt Sells gold medal, 1966), Ind. Soc. CPA's. Republican. Roman Catholic. Clubs: Indpls. Sailing; Chgo. Yacht. Avocation: sailing. Home: 7715 Candlewood Lane Indianapolis IN 46250 Office: Marsh Supermkts Inc 501 Depot St Yorktown IN 47396

HAYHURST, THOMAS EDWARD, manufacturing company executive; b. Chgo., Nov. 8, 1953; s. Edward and Martha Ann (Milanowski) H.; m. Peggy Leigh Fritz, Apr. 30, 1977; children: Micah Thomas, Jansen Fritz. BS, Morehead State U., 1976. Diagnostic sales rep. Abbott Labs., Dayton, Ohio, 1982-83, account exec., 1984-85; nat. sales trainer Abbott Labs., Chgo., 1986—. Served to capt. USMC, 1976-81, with Res., 1981—. Mem. Lambda Chi Alpha Alumni Assn. (pres. 1986—). Republican. Lodge: Optimist (v.p. 1984-85). Avocations: woodworking. Home: 620 Appletree Ct Deerfield IL 60015 Office: Abbott Labs Abbott Park AP6D LL North Chicago IL 60064

HAYMAN, SHARON JOY, controller; b. Chgo., Dec. 3, 1961; d. Leslie Burt and Barbara Ann (Getz) H. BBA, U. Mich., 1984. CPA, Ill. Staff acct. Checkers, Simon & Rosner, Chgo., 1984-86; controller 312 Futures Inc., Chgo., 1986—; individual tax cons., Chgo., 1984—. Mem. Am. Inst. CPA's, Ill. Soc. CPA's. Jewish. Avocations: reading, collecting rare books. Home: 530 W Arlington #513 Chicago IL 60614 Office: 312 Futures Inc 222 W Adams Suite 1156 Chicago IL 60606

HAYMON, MONTE ROY, packaging manufacturing company executive; b. Bklyn., Sept. 23, 1937; s. Jack and Ann H.; m. Jane Ellen Kraft, June 26, 1960; children: Karen, Debra, Jacqueline. B.S.Ch.E., Tufts U., 1959; postgrad., Am. Internat. Coll., 1960-61; grad. advanced mgmt. program, Harvard U., 1980. Process engr. Monsanto Co., Springfield, Mass., 1960-62; mktg. mgr., then dir. mktg. Tenneco Plastics, Piscataway, N.J., 1962-68; v.p. mktg. Rexene Polymers Co., Paramus, N.J., 1968-73, v.p. mfg., 1973-76; v.p., gen. mgr. Tenneco Chems., Inc., Piscataway, 1976-80, group v.p., 1980-81; pres., chief operating officer Packaging Corp. Am., Evanston, Ill., 1981-82, pres., chief exec. officer, 1982—; dir. Electric Audio Dynamics, Inc. Bd. dirs. Evanston Econ. Devel. Corp. Served with USAR, 1959-60. Mem. Soc. Chem. Engrs., Am. Chem. Soc., Am. Paper Inst. (bd. dirs.), Fourdrinier Kraft Bd. Group (bd. dirs.), Inst. Paper Chemistry (trustee). Club: Harvard. Office: Packaging Corp of Am 1603 Orrington Ave Evanston IL 60204 *

HAYMONS, DAN LESTER, JR., hospital administrator; b. Lumber City, Ga., Nov. 20, 1936; s. Dan Lester and Amanda (Grace) H.; m. Bettye Lynn Manner, Mar. 28, 1964; children—Lesley Lynn, Christopher Daniel. B.A., Valdosta State Coll., 1958; M.H.A., U. Minn., 1963. Adminstrv. resident Bapt. Meml. Hosp., Memphis, 1962-63, adminstrv. asst., 1963-65; asst. adminstr. Erlanger Med. Ctr., Chattanooga, 1965-69; assoc. adminstr. St. Dominic Hosp., Jackson, Miss., 1969-72; adminstr., chief exec. officer Union Med. Ctr., El Dorado, Ark., 1972-79; pres., chief exec. officer N. Kansas City Hosp., 1979—; dir. Boatman's North Hills Bank, 1981—. Contbr. articles to profl. jours. Bd. dirs. Am. Cancer Soc., Northland unit, Kansas City, 1981—, pres., 1981-83; bd. dirs. Vis. Nurse Assn. Kansas City, 1980-84; mem. J.C. Penney Golden Rule Award Com., 1983-84. Served to lt. USN, 1958-61. USPHS traineeship, 1962. Mem. Am. Coll. Hosp. Adminstrs. (fellow), Kansas City Area Hosp. Assn. (dir. 1980- 84). Episcopalian. Clubs: Kansas City, Old Pike. Home: 500 NW Briarcliff Extension Kansas City MO 64116 Office: North Kansas City Hosp 2800 Hospital Dr North Kansas City MO 64116

HAYNE, LONNIE R(AY), state official; b. Star, Nebr., Sept. 18, 1940; s. Ralph and Ethel (Herman) H.; m. Gloria Pedersen, June 22, 1963; children—Lisa, Vicki. B.S., Dana Coll., 1962; M.A., U. Nebr., 1964. Mgmt. intern AEC, Las Vegas, Nev., 1964-65, procurement specialist, 1965; budget analyst Wis. Dept. Adminstrn., Madison, 1965-68, fed. aid analyst, 1968-70, budget dir., 1970-79; fiscal supr., Wis. Dept. Pub. Instrn., 1979—. Treas. adult chpt. Am. Field Service, Stoughton, 1984—. Johnson fellow, 1962; recipient Wall Street Jour. award, 1962. Mem. Am. Soc. Pub. Adminstrn. (treas. 1976-80), Assn. Career Employees. Republican. Lutheran. Avocations: school government, lay church work. Home: 2536 Ridgetop Rd Stoughton WI 53589 Office: Wis Dept Pub Instrn PO Box 7841 Madison WI 53707

HAYNES, CHRISTY RAY, accountant; b. Peoria, Ill., Nov. 21, 1939; s. Harold L. and Bernice (Christy) H.; m. Paulette J. Anderson, Dec. 27, 1964; children: Karen, Christopher. BS in Accountancy, U. Ill., 1967. CPA, Ind. Audit supr. Ernst & Whinney, Chgo. and Ft. Wayne, Ind., 1965-70; controller Midwestern United Life, Ft. Wayne, 1970-75; mng. ptnr. Haynes, Fenimore & Hall Inc., Anderson and Indpls., Ind., 1975—. Bd. dirs. Anderson Corp. for Econ. Devel., 1983—; active Com. to Elect Hardacre Mayor of Anderson, 1987—. Served with USAF, 1957-61. Mem. Am. Inst. CPA's, Ind. Assn. CPA's (pres. Muncie chpt. 1984-85), Anderson C. of C. (bd. dirs. 1983—). Republican. Lutheran. Office: Haynes Fenimore & Hall Inc 629 Nichol Ave Anderson IN 46015

HAYNES, FRANK MAURICE, business executive; b. Kansas City, Mo., June 1, 1935; s. William John and Marguerite Ida (Brown) H.; B.B.A., U. Colo., 1958; M.B.A. with honors, Roosevelt U., 1974; postgrad. Sch. Mgmt. Northwestern U., 1974-75; m. Arlene Claire Kidd, June 25, 1966; children—Jonathan Frank and Elizabeth Arlene (twins). Owner, operator Frank M. Haynes Ins. Agy., Chgo., 1960-65; pres. Employees Union Health & Welfare Agy., Inc., Chgo., 1965-72; cons. pension, health and welfare plans, Chgo., 1972-75; exec. v.p. W.J. Haynes & Co., Inc., Chgo., 1975-80, pres., 1980—. Served with U.S. Army, 1958-59. Recipient Wall St. Jour. award, 1974; certificate of merit Prudential Ins. Co., 1964; C.L.U. Mem. Am. Risk and Ins. Assn., Am. Soc. C.L.U.s, Internat. Found. Employee Benefit Plans, Beta Gamma Sigma. Home: 427 Sheridan Rd Kenilworth IL 60043 Office: 7045 N Western Ave Chicago IL 60645

HAYNES, JEAN REED, lawyer; b. Miami, Fla., Apr. 6, 1949; d. Oswald Birnam and Arleen (Weidman) Dow; m. William Rutherford Reed, Apr. 15, 1974 (div. Sept. 1981); m. Thomas Beranek Haynes, Aug. 7, 1982. AB with honors, Pembroke Coll., 1971; MA, Brown U., 1971; JD, U. Chgo., 1981. Bar: Ill. 1981, U.S. Dist. Ct. (no. dist.) Ill. 1983, U.S. Ct. Appeals (7th cir.) 1982. Tchr. grades 1-4 Abbie Tuller Sch., Providence, 1971-72; tchr./facilitator St. Mary's Acad., Riverside, R.I., 1972-74; tchr./head lower sch. St. Francis Sch., Goshen, Ky., 1974-78; law clk. U.S. Ct. Appeals (7th cir.), Chgo., 1981-83; assoc. Kirkland & Ellis, Chgo., 1983—. Sustaining fellow Art Inst. Chgo., 1982—, mem. aux. bd. 1986—. Mem. ABA (litigation sect.), Chgo. Bar Assn., Ill. Bar Assn. (life), Am. Judicature Soc. (life). Home: 179 East Lake Shore Dr Chicago IL 60611 Office: Kirkland & Ellis 200 E Randolph Dr Chicago IL 60611

HAYNES, MARY KATHERINE, nurse; b. Butler County, Mo., Oct. 2, 1931; d. Hershel Evert and Eva Mae (Hester) Heifner; cert. with highest honors, L P N Sch. Nursing, Poplar Bluff, Mo., 1960; R.N. with highest honors, Three Rivers Community Coll., 1973; B.Health Sci., Stevens Coll., Columbia, Mo., 1978; m. Robert W. Haynes, Aug. 14, 1948; children—Janice Haynes Thurman, Robert Randall. Nurse, Poplar Bluff Hosp., 1957-79, dir. nursing, 1974-79, nurse epidemiologist, 1975-79; adminstr. nursing service Richland Meml. Hosp., Olney, Ill., 1979-80, asso. adminstr., 1980—. Active PTA, 1958-70; troop leader Cotton Boll council Girl Scouts U.S.A., 1960-66; parliamentarian Democratic Woman's Club, 1962-65; instr. CPR, Mo. Heart Assn.; bd. advisers Three Rivers Community Coll. Sch. Nursing; mem. area project rev. com., bd. selection Comprehensive Health Planning Council of So. Ill. Southeastern Lung Assn. grantee, 1977. Mem. Assn. Practitioners of Infection Control, Assn. Infection Control Nurses. Club: Altrusa (dir. 1978). Home: 81 S Rickland Olney IL 62450 Office: 800 N Locust St Olney IL 62450

HAYON, YEHIEL, educator, publisher; b. Tel Aviv, Feb. 26, 1939; came to U.S., 1966; s. Jacob and Yaffa (Cohen) H.; m. Linda Beth Kern, June 16, 1968; children: Oren Jacob, Ronni Lea. BA, Tel Aviv U., 1965; MA, U. Tex., 1968, PhD, 1969. Prof. Hebrew Ohio State U., Columbus, 1969—; pub. Alpha Pub. Co., Columbus, 1985—; editor-in-chief Spl. Edit. Inc., Columbus, 1980—. Author: Modern Hebrew 1-3, 1970, Relativization in Hebrew, 1972; editor, founder jour. Hebrew Ann. Rev., 1977-81; editor book series, 1985—. Served to lt. Israeli Army, 1956-60. Mem. Assn. Jewish Studies. Jewish. Avocation: creative writing. Home: 41 N Merkle Rd Columbus OH 43209 Office: Ohio State U 1841 Millikin Rd Columbus OH 43210

HAYS, ANTHONY LYNN, broadcasting executive; b. Washington Court House, Ohio; Jan. 28, 1954; s. Roger Lynn and Doris Lou (Brown) H.; m. Linda Susan Varney, Oct. 12, 1979; 1 child, Ashley Lynn. Grad. Internat. Broadcasting Sch., Dayton, Ohio, 1975. Announcer, Sta. WCHO, Washington Court House, 1975-76, salesman, 1978-80, gen. mgr., 1984—; announcer, salesman Stas. WVAK/WUME, Paoli, Ind., 1976-78; sales mgr. Sta. WBEX, Chillicothe, Ohio, 1980-84. Mem. Ross County Republican Promotion Com., Chillicothe, 1984. Mem. Washington Court House C. of C. Methodist. Lodge: Rotary, Elks, Masons, Shriners. Avocations: fishing; genealogy; gardening and landscaping. Home: 5402 Plantation Pl New Holland OH 43145 Office: Sta WCHO 1535 N North St Washington Court House OH 43160

HAYS, BRADLEY GENE, bakery supply company executive; b. DeKalb, Ill., Jan. 6, 1957; s. William Gene and Joan Ellen (Spitz) H.; m. Kristine Ellen Tellison, Dec. 17, 1976 (div. July 1986); children—Michelle Joan, Andrea Jane, Jennifer Jean. Student Kishwaukee Jr. Coll., 1974-76; grad. Am. Inst. Baking, Chgo., 1976. Blending delivery salesman Chgo. Hol'n One Donut Co., 1974-76, sales mgr., 1976-78, exec., 1978-80, ops. mgr., 1980-82, pres., 1982—. Chmn. bldg. and grounds com. First Ch. of Christ Scientist, DeKalb. Republican. Home: 1512 Stonehenge Dr Sycamore IL 60178

HAYS, DENNIS EDWARD, data processing executive; b. Cin., Aug. 20, 1951; s. Harold Fred and Betty Catherine (Siebert) H.; m. Susan Rose Gross, Sept. 13, 1975; children: Katherine Anne, Brian Fredrick, Elizabeth Marie. AS, So. Ohio Coll., 1972; BS, U. Cin., 1983. Programmer R.L. Polk, Cin., 1974-76; programmer, analyst Kroger Co., Cin., 1976-78, Welco Industries Inc., Cin., 1978-81; mgmt. info. systems mgr. Randall Textron, Cin., 1981—. Soccer coach Mt. Healthy Youth Athletic Assn., 1985, 86, basketball coach, 1985 , tee ball coach, 1985, baseball coach, 1985. Mem. Delta Tau Kappa. Roman Catholic. Avocations: boating, bowling, coaching. Home: 9152 Ranchill Dr Cincinnati OH 45231 Office: Randall Textron 10179 Commerce Park Dr Cincinnati OH 45246

HAYS, GEORGE WAIGHT SECREST, librarian; b. Warren, Ohio, Oct. 9, 1954; s. Robert Collins and Sarah Lewis (Secrest) H.; m. Susan Kaye Abbuhl, May 21, 1977; children: Sarah Kathryn, George Waight Secrest II. BA, Mt. Union Coll., 1976; MSLS, Case Western Res. U., 1980. Head adult dept. Rodman Pub. Library, Alliance, Ohio, 1976—; mem. selection com. No. Ohio Film Cir., Elyria, 1985—. Canvasser Alliance Area Rep. Club, 1979—. Mem. ALA, Pub. Library Assn., Ohio Library Assn., Stark County Librarians (pres. 1979-80, 83-84), Psi Kappa Omega. Methodist. Lodge: Moose. Office: Rodman Pub Library 215 E Broadway St Alliance OH 44601

HAYS, H. BRADFORD, financial company executive; b. Pauls Valley, Okla., Sept. 15, 1943; s. Herbert Bradford and Ruth (Rice) H.; m. Laura Dobbs, May 27, 1967; children: Gregory, Jennifer, Graham. BBA, U. Okla., 1965; MBA, Northwestern U., 1966; JD, U. Ind., 1974. CPA, Okla. Fin. dir. Europe Eli Lilly Internat., London, Eng., 1981-86; dir. corp. tax planning Eli Lilly Internat., Eli Lilly & Co., Indpls., 1986—. Served to capt. USAF, 1966-71. Mem. Am. Inst. CPA's. Office: Eli Lilly & Co Lilly Corporate Ctr Indianapolis IN 46285

HAYS, MARILYN PATRICIA, real estate company executive; b. Yarrow, Mo., Sept. 19, 1935; d. John Dewey and Ruth (McKim) H.; m. Harold Clifton Ledbetter, Dec. 13, 1953 (div. 1972); children—Latricia Lyn, Lisa Ledbetter Cerio, David Clifton, Laura Lizanne; Harold Clifton, Jr.; m. Dean Leon Fortney, July 21, 1978. B.S., Northeast Mo. State U., 1958; broker cert. U. Fla., 1976; M.A., U. Mo., 1983; J.D., Washburn U., 1987. Lic. real estate broker, Mo., Kans., Fla., Grad. Realtors Inst. Fashion coordinator Ashells, Regina's Co., Kirksville, Mo., 1951-54; instr. pub. schs., Crocker, Novinger, Kirksville and University City, Mo., 1954-61; real estate salesstaff Goldman's Assocs., Daytona Beach, Fla., 1975-76; real estate broker Kellogg Century 21, Daytona Beach, 1976-78; pres. M.P. Hays Co., Olathe, Kans., 1978-82, Bucyrus, Kans., 1982—; cons. Goldman, Kellogg, Daytona Beach, 1975-78. Contbr. articles on real estate edn. to profl. jours. Pres. Fla. Osteopathic Med. Assn. Aux., Dist. IV, 1964-65, 73-74, pres.-elect, 1967-68; major chmn. Assn. of Jr. League, Daytona Beach, 1968-69, 72-73; Pan Hellenic del., 1972-78; adviser Ormond Beach Hosp. Guild, Fla., 1972-74. Scholar, Mo. Council PTAs, 1953, K.C., 1954; recipient Outstanding Sales Achievement award Kellogg Century 21, 1977. Mem. Miami County Bd. Realtors, Johnson County Bd. Realtors, Nat. Assn. Realtors, Kans. Assn. Realtors, ABA, Kans. Farm Bur., Women's Legal Forum, AAUW, Am. Quarterhorse Assn., Alpha Sigma Alpha, Phi Delta Phi. Republican. Roman Catholic. Clubs: Ormond Beach Woman's, Oceanside Country. Avocations: photography; cooking; horseback riding. Home: Route 1 Box 161 Bucyrus KS 66013 Office: M P Hays Co 223d St and State Line Rd Bucyrus KS 66013

HAYS, RICHARD JOSEPH, treasurer; b. Phila., Apr. 15, 1947; s. Richard Joseph and Helen May (Williams) H.; m. Sally Ann Gladney, July 25, 1969; children: Jennifer, Richard, Peter. BS in Bus. Adminstrn., Christian Bros. Coll., 1970. With various firms St. Louis, 1970-73; sr. internal auditor Chromalloy Am. Corp., St. Louis, 1973-75; controller Apted-Hulling, Inc., St. Louis, 1975-82, treas., 1982—. Bd. dirs., treas. Magdala Found., St. Louis, 1970—; bd. dirs. United Cerebral Palsey, St. Louis, 1987—. Mem. Am. Inst. CPA's, Nat. Assn. Accts., Mo. Soc. CPA's. Roman Catholic. Avocations: hunting, fishing, riding. Home: 1230 Carol Ann Pl Saint Louis MO 63122 Office: Apted-Hulling Inc 1103 Locust Saint Louis MO 63101

HAYS, ROBERT DAVIES, lawyer; b. Pitts., Apr. 12, 1927; s. Robert R. and Almeda (Davies) H.; m. Eloise Ruth Edwards, July 1, 1950; children: Janice L., Robert E. BBA, Ohio State U., 1950, JD, 1952. Bar: Ohio 1952, U.S. Dist. Ct. (so. dist.) Ohio 1952. Assoc. Alexander, Ebinger & Wenger, Columbus, Ohio, 1952-56; gen. counsel, sr. v.p. White Castle System, Inc., Columbus, 1956—. Bd. dirs. Better Bus. Bur. cen. Ohio, 1977—; sec., trustee Edgwar W. Ingram Found., Columbus, 1976—; bd. of trustees Julian Marcus Sr. Citizens Placement Bur., 1987—. Served with USNR, 1945-46. Mem. ABA, Ohio Bar Assn., Columbus Bar Assn., Am. Corp. Counsel Assn., Cen. Ohio Corp. Counsel Assn. (bd. dirs. 1983—), Foodservice and Lodging Inst. (bd. dirs. 1980—, pres. 1984-85), Ohio Council Retail Mchts. Chain Restaurants (chmn. 1984—, bd. dirs. 1984—), Columbus Jaycees (pres., bd. dirs. 1961, Outstanding Dir. 1959, Disting. Service award 1961). Republican. Clubs: Scioto Country (Columbus); Imperial Golf (Naples, Fla.). Avocations: golf, sports, reading. Office: White Castle System Inc 555 Goodale St Columbus OH 43215

HAYS, STEVEN WARREN, accountant, administrator; b. St. Louis, Sept. 13, 1958; s. Warren Eugene and Betty (Gustin) H. BSBA, U. Mo., 1980. CPA, Mo. Mgr. Rubin, Brown, Gornstein & Co., St. Louis, 1980—; instr. in field. Big bro. Big Bros. and Big Sisters, St. Louis, 1982-86. Mem. Am. Inst. CPA's, Mo. State Soc. CPA's, Home Builders Assn. St. Louis (edn. com.), Mortgage Bankers Assn. St. Louis. Avocations: softball, basketball, reading. Home: 201D Braeshire Manchester MO 63021 Office: Rubin Brown Gornstein & Co 3230 S Bemiston Saint Louis MO 63105

HAYS, THOMAS A., department store executive; b. Cleve., 1932; married. B.A., Wabash Coll., 1955. Pres. Venture Stores Inc. div. May Dept. Stores Co., St. Ann, Mo., 1972-82, chief exec. officer, 1980-82, chmn., 1982—; pres. The Hecht Co. div. May Stores Co., Washington, 1974—; with May Dept. Stores Co., St. Louis, 1969—, vice chmn., 1982-85, pres., 1985—, dir.; dir. Mercantile Trust Co., Mercantile Bancorp. Office: May Dept Stores Co 6th & Olive Sts St Louis MO 63101 *

HAYS, WILLIAM FRANCIS, physician; b. Herrin, Ill., May 28, 1947; s. Morris Henry and Lela Evelyn (Misker) H.; m. Sue Ellen Eichhorn, July 11, 1970 (div. 1983); children—Kelly, Karen, William B.; m. Pamala Kay Holder, Oct. 1, 1983. B.A., So. Ill. U., 1970; M.D., Northwestern U., 1977. Diplomate Am. Bd. Family Practice. Resident U. Ill.-Meth. Med. Ctr., Peoria, 1977-80; family practice, Herrin, Ill., 1980—; mem. staff Herrin Hosp., v.p., 1983—; clin. asst. prof. family practice So. Ill. U. Sch. Medicine, 1982—. Fellow Am. Acad. Family Practice; mem. Ill. State Med. Soc. (govt. affairs com. 1983-84, med. services com. 1986—, del. 1986-87), Ill. Assn. Family Practice (del. 1987). Methodist. Lodge: Elks. Office: 315 S 14th St Herrin IL 62948

HAYWARD, RICHARD ALDEN, city manager; b. Bakersfield, Calif., Nov. 4, 1952; s. Richard Bacom and Priscilla Elisabeth (Lane) H.; m. Rosalyn Kay Burkhart, May 21, 1977; 1 child, Richard David. B.A., Windham Coll., 1973; M.A., U. Toronto, 1975; M.P.A., U. Wyo., 1978. Adminstrv. asst. City of Gillette, Wyo., 1978-80, asst. to city adminstr., 1980-81, asst. city adminstr., 1981-82; city mgr. City of Napoleon, Ohio, 1982—. Bd. dirs. Henry County Sr. Ctr., 1982; mem. Pvt. Industry Council, 1983; trustee Napoleon Downtown Revitalization Corp., 1984. Recipient Small Employer of Yr. award, Govs. Commn. Handicapped, 1980. Mem. U.S. Fencing Assn. (exec. com. Wyo. div.), Internat. City Mgr. Assn., Ohio City Mgmt. Assn., Am. Soc. Pub. Adminstrs., Am. Pub. Works Assn., Napoleon Area C. of C. (bd. dirs. 1986). Presbyterian. Club: Optimists Internat. Avocations: geology; gardening; fencing; cross-country skiing. Office: City of Napoleon 255 W Riverview St Napoleon OH 43545

HAYZLETT, JEFFREY WAYNE, public relations executive; b. Charleston, W.Va., Nov. 11, 1960; s. William Frank Hayzlett and Henrietta Mae (Mangus) Brumbaugh; m. Tamara Lynn Anderson, July 2, 1982; 1 child, Lindsey Marie. BS in Govt. and Internat. Affairs, Augustana Coll., Sioux Falls, S.D., 1983. Dep. chmn. Senator George McGovern, Sioux Falls, 1980; field rep. Dem. Party of S.D., Sioux Falls, 1981-82; campaign mgr. Gov. O'Connor, Sioux Falls, 1982; staff asst. Congressman Tom Daschle, Sioux Falls, 1983-84; exec. dir. Am. Diabetes Assn., Sioux Falls, 1984-85; pres. Hayzlett & Assocs., Sioux Falls, 1984—; prof. pub. relations U. S.D., Vermillion, 1986—. Capt. Sioux Falls Plainsmen Rugby Team, 1982—; state dir. Sioux Falls Jaycees, 1985, bd. dirs. Camp for the Handicapped, 1985-86, Food Service Ctr.-Pantry, 1984, v.p., 1985, pres., 1986; sec. Sioux Falls Community Playhouse, 1985—. Recipient William C. Brownfield award S.D. Jaycees, 1984-85; named Officer of Quarter, Sioux Falls Jaycees, 1984-85, one of Outstanding Young Men of Am., 1982, 85. Mem. AM. Mgmt. Assn., Pub. Relations Soc. Am., Internat. Assn. Bus. Cons., Nat. Vol. Health Agys. S.D., S.D. Ad Fedn., S.D. Industry and Commerce Assn., Am. Assn. Diabetes Educators, Sioux Falls Area C. of C. (ambassador, legis. affairs com.). Lutheran. Avocations: rugby, hunting, reading. Home: 1120 W 22d St Sioux Falls SD 57105 Office: Hayzlett & Assocs Inc 330 N Main Ave Suite 301 Sioux Falls SD 57101

HAZEL, WILLARD RAYMOND, management information systems executive; b. Evansville, Ind., Jan. 10, 1946; s. James Euriah and Betty Doris (Moog) H.; m. Shirley Ann Melton, Aug. 31, 1964 (div. Aug. 1968); children: Douglas Michael, Kevin Lee; m. Janice Jean Hurt, Jan. 17, 1969. AS in Computer Sci., U. Evansville, 1974, BS in Bus. cum laude, 1977. Computer operator Old Nat. Bank, Evansville, 1964-65, computer programmer, 1965-66; programmer Potter & Brumfield, Inc., Princeton, Ind., 1967-68, chief programmer, 1968-69, systems analyst, 1970-71, sr. systems analyst, 1971-72, systems mgr., 1973-80, systems and program mgr., 1981—. Contbg. author: Production and Inventory Control Handbook, 1986, 2d edit. 1987. Bd. dirs. Gibson County United Way, 1981-84. Served with U.S. Army N.G., 1969-75. Mem. Am. Prodn. and Inventory Control Soc. (various offices Ohio Valley chpt.), Alpha Sigma Lambda. Lutheran. Lodge: Elks. Home: Rural Rt 2 Box 379 Princeton IN 47670 Office: Potter & Brumfield Inc 200 Richland Creek Dr Princeton IN 47671-0001

HAZELTINE, JAMES E, marketing educator; b. Lancaster, Pa., Oct. 16, 1941; s. James Ezra and Glenna Jane (May) H.; m. Charlotte Ann Hardin, Dec. 19, 1970 (div. July, 1986). BA, Franklin and Marshall Coll., 1963; student, U. Pa., 1968-69; MBA, U. Ky., 1979, Dr. Bus. Admin., 1986. Broadcaster various orgns. and locations, 1961-83; instr. U. Ky., Lexington, 1984-85; asst. prof. Ill. State U., Normal, 1985—; cons. Country Cos. Ins., Bloomington, Ill., 1986—. Served with U.S. Army, 1963-64, 68-69. Mem. Am. Mktg. Assn., Beta Gamma Sigma. Republican. Presbyterian. Avocations: boating, reading, computing. Office: Coll Bus Ill State U Normal IL 61761

HAZELTINE, JOYCE, state official. Sec. of state State of S.D. Office: Sec of State's Office 500 E Capitol Pierre SD 57501 *

HAZELTINE, MARK STEVEN, account executive; b. Beloit, Wis., Oct. 22, 1952; s. Donald Roger and Gladys Allene (Hanna) H.; m. Elizabeth Greene, Sept. 27, 1980; children: Philip Donald, Ross Michael. BA in Journalism, Ind. U., 1974. Account exec. Hoffman-York, Inc., Milw., 1974-76, Biddle Co., Chgo., 1976-78, Leo Burnett Co., Chgo., 1978-85, ABC Television Network, Chgo., 1985—. Recipient Outstanding Mktg. award, Hamburger U., McDonalds Corp., 1976. Mem. Broadcast Advt. Club of Chgo. Roman Catholic. Home: 2231 Coldspring Dr Arlington Heights IL 60004 Office: ABC Television Network 190 N State St Chicago IL 60601

HAZELTON, THOMAS FRANK, district park ranger; b. Cedar Rapids, Iowa, Apr. 25, 1955; s. Frank Taber and Marion Ella (Bellville) H. BS in Biology, Coe Coll., 1977; cert. conservation officer, Iowa Law Enforcement Acad., 1979, cert. peace officer, 1983. Cert. emergency med. technician. Park attendant Linn County (Iowa) Conservation Office, Marion, 1977-78, park ranger II, 1978-82, dist. supr., 1983—. Patentee recreation idea, 1986; contbr. articles to trade jours. Coordinator E. Cen. Iowa Spl. Olympics, Cedar Rapids, 1974—; bd. dirs. YMCA Camp Wapsie, Cedar Rapids, 1979—. Named Hon. Sports Marshall E. Cen. Iowa Spl. Olympics, 1977; recipient Cert. Appreciation LInn County Assn. Retarded Citizens, 1984. Mem. County Conservation Peace Officer's Assn. Iowa (pres. 1985—, resource person 1985—), Linn County Conservation Bd. Employees Assn. (sec./treas. 1979—), Phi Kappa Tau Alumni Assn., Phi Kappa Tau (chmn. bd. govs. 1981—, domain dir. 1984—, Outstanding Local Alumni 1984). Presbyterian. Office: Linn County Conservation 1890 County Home Rd Marion IA 52302

HAZELWOOD, WALTER CLAUDE, industrial engineer, manufacturing executive; b. Liberal, Kans., Jan. 17, 1947; s. Roy Elmo and Ruth Ella (Piety) H.; m. Marsha Lynn McCort, Jan. 5, 1968; children: Douglas A., John P., Sherri L. BS in Indsl. Engring., U. So. Fla., 1973. Cert. plant engr., Ohio. Indsl. engr. Whirlpool Corp., Findlay, Ohio, 1973-74, supr. maintenance scheduling, 1974-75, maintenance foreman, 1975, process engr., 1975-78; mgr. plant engring. Crown Controls Corp., New Bremen, Ohio, 1978-85, mgr. indsl. engring., 1985—. Elder Ch. of Christ, New Bremen, 1986—. Mem. Am. Inst. Indsl. Engrs. (sr., treas. Findlay chpt. 1973-75, sec. 1975-76, pres. 1976-78, bd. dirs. 1977-79), Am. Inst. Plant Engrs. (sr.). Republican. Lodge: Rotary (named Outstanding Young Profl. 1976). Home: 310 S Walnut New Bremen OH 45869 Office: Crown Controls Corp 40-44 S Washington New Bremen OH 45869

HAZEN, MARGARET JEAN, television personality, television and video producer; b. Salineville, Ohio, Jan. 6, 1944; d. Joseph Clarence and Margaret Viola (Wright) Myers; m. Andy D. Demyan; 1 child, Daniel A.; m. Raymond Dennis Hazen, Nov. 7, 1978; stepchildren: Lisa, Joan, Denny II, Marcella, Mary. Student, Kent (Ohio) State U., 1976-81. Various positions Gen. Electric Co., Cleve., 1969-83; producer, co-host Christian programs Sta. WDLI-TV, Louisville, 1983-86; co-host Denny and Marge Hazen Ministries program Sta. PTL TV and WTOF-AM-FM, Louisville, 1984—; co-founder The Christian Broadcast Ctr., Louisville, 1987—; indsl. video cons. Gen. Electric Co., Erie, Pa., 1981—; lectr. various civic groups. Producer (documentaries) for Cen. Bapt. Ch., Canton; videos including Korean Orphan Documentaries, 1983, industrial video tapes. Active Portage United Way. Democratic. Home: 8180 Ruble Ave NE Louisville OH 44641 Office: Station A PO Box 7317 Canton OH 44705

HAZLETT, PAUL EDWARD, data processing executive; b. Gallipolis, Ohio, Dec. 10, 1937; s. Vickers James and Wilma (Dickey) H.; m. Lynn Todd; 1 child, Esther. BBA, Cleve. State U., 1964. Freight sales N.Y. Cen., Cleve., 1964-66; with computer systems dept. Honeywell, Inc., Cleve., 1966-75; investment advisor Cleve., 1975-78; mgr. Fairview Gen. Hosp., Cleve., 1978—; adj. faculty Cuyahoga Community Coll., Cleve.; cons. in field. Candidate Cleve. City Council, 1975, 79. Served USAF, 1956-60. Avocations: jogging, racquetball. Home: 13317 Liberty Ave Cleveland OH 44135 Office: Fairview Gen Hosp 18101 Lorain Ave Cleveland OH 44111

H'DOUBLER, KURT EMERSON, dentist; b. Springfield, Mo., Jan. 29, 1956; s. Francis Todd Jr. and Joan Louise (Huber) H'D.; m. Mary Anne Onofrio, June 18, 1983. BA in Microbiology, U. Mo., 1978, DDS, 1983. Gen. practice dentistry Springfield, Mo., 1983—. Treas. Lakes County Rehab. Ctr., Springfield, 1985—. Mem. ADA, Mo. Dental Assn., Springfield Dental Soc. (chmn. profl. affairs 1986—), Jaycees Am. Republican. Presbyterian. Club: Hickory Hills Country (Springfield). Lodge: Masons, Shriners. Office: 948 S Jefferson Springfield MO 65806

HEACOX, JOHN LARRY, educator; b. Sikeston, Mo., Oct. 4, 1946; s. Eual W. and Lillas Geneva (Triplett) H.; m. Cathy Jean Rabaduex, Aug. 30, 1969; children—Kristopher, Bradley, Jeffrey. B.S. in Edn., Southeast Mo. U., 1968; M.Ed., Central Mo. U., 1982. Tchr., coordinator mktg. Sikeston (Mo.) Sr. High Sch., 1968—. First v.p. Three Rivers Muscular Dystrophy Assn., 1982-83; deacon, tchr. Sikeston 1st Baptist Ch.; recreation dir. for youth, Sikeston, Mo., summers, 1980—; pres. Dist. 12 Distributive Edn., 1985-86; bd. dirs. Little Piece of Heaven youth home. Recipient Outstanding Service awards Muscular Dystrophy Assn., 1980-83. Coach of Yr., 1976. Mem. Am. Vocat. Assn., Mo. Vocat. Assn., Mo. Tchrs. Assn., Nat. Assn. Ditributive Edn. Tchrs. Baptist. Club: Distributive Edn. of Am. Office: 200 S Pine St Sikeston MO 63801

HEAD, LINDA KUJAWA, radiologist; b. St. Paul, Mar. 1, 1952; d. Walter Andrew and Jerrie (Baloga) Kujawa; 1 child, Julie. BS in Medicine, Creighton U., 1972; MD, U. Nebr., 1975. Diplomate Am. Bd. Diagnostic Radiology. Resident in internal medicine U. Nebr. Med. Ctr., Omaha, 1975-77, resident in radiology, 1977-80, fellow in ultrasound, 1981-82, clin. instr. radiology, 1980-82, vol. radiologist, 1982—; radiologist Midlands Hosp., Papillion, Nebr., 1982—; sec. Midland Community Hosp. Found., Papillion, 1984—. Bd. dirs. Am. Cancer Soc., Bellevue, Nebr., 1984—. Mem. AMA, Am. Coll. Radiology, Nebr. Med. Assn., Radiology Soc. N.Am., Sarpy County Med. Soc., Am. Inst. Ultra Sonographers. Club: Altrusa. Home: 807 Ivy Ct Bellevue NE 68005 Office: 11111 Gold Coast Rd Papillion NE 68046

HEADINGS, RONALD LYNN, market research executive; b. Wichita, Kans., Jan. 15, 1960; s. Phillip L. and Estella Irene (Yutzy) H. BS in Econs., Bethel Coll., 1982, BA in Math., 1982; MBA Mktg., Ind. U., 1984. Brand supr. market research Procter and Gamble, Cin., 1984-86, field service coordinator market research, 1986—. Mennonite. Avocations: softball, volleyball, horticulture. Home: 6355 Corbly's Grant #15 Cincinnati OH 45230 Office: Procter and Gamble Box 599 Cincinnati OH 45201

HEADLEE, RAYMOND, psychoanalyst, educator; b. Shelby County, Ind., July 27, 1917; s. Ortis Verl and Mary Mae (Wright) H.; m. Eleanor Case Benton, Aug. 24, 1941; children—Sue, Mark, Ann. A.B. in Psychology, Ind. U., 1939, A.M. in Exptl. Psychology, 1941, M.D., 1944; grad., Chgo. Inst. Psychoanalysis, 1959. Diplomate: Am. Bd. Psychiatry and Neurology (examiner 1964—). Intern St. Elizabeth's Hosp., Washington, 1944-45; resident in psychiatry St. Elizabeth's Hosp., 1945-46; resident in psychiatry Milw. Psychiat. Hosp., 1947-48, pres. staff, 1965-70; practice medicine specializing in psychiatry and psychoanalysis Elm Grove, Wis., 1949—; clin. asst. prof. psychiatry Med. Coll. Wis., 1958-59, clin. asso. prof., 1959-62, clin. prof., 1962—, chmn. dept. psychiatry, 1963-70; prof. psychology Marquette U., 1966-76; Bd. dirs. Elm Brook (Wis.) Meml. Hosp., 1969-71. Author: (with Bonnie Corey) Psychiatry in Nursing, 1949; contbr. (with Bonnie Corey) numerous articles to profl. jours. Served to 1st lt. Ft. Knox Armored Med. Research Lab. AUS, 1945; to maj. at NIH, USPHS, 1953, Bethesda, Md. Fellow Am. Psychiat. Assn. (life), Am. Coll. Psychiatry; mem. State Med. Soc. Wis. (editorial dir. 1971-77), Wis. Psychiat. Assn. (pres. 1971-72). Clubs: Beefeater (London) (upper warder 1972—); Milw. Home: 12505 Gremoor St Elm Grove WI 53122 Office: 1055 Legion St Box 207 Elm Grove WI 53122

HEADLEE, WILLIAM HUGH, emeritus educator; b. Morristown, Ind., June 15, 1907; s. Walter C. and Nellie Ann (Adams) H.; A.B., Earlham Coll., 1929; M.S. (Rockefeller Found. fellow), U. Ill., 1933; Ph.D. (Rockefeller Found. fellow), Tulane U., 1935; cert. of proficiency in tropical and mil. medicine Army Med. Sch., 1943; m. Gabrielle Mills, Aug. 4, 1937; children—Joan Headlee Bowden, Anne. Instr. biology Am. U., Cairo, Egypt, 1929-31; research asst. internat. health div. Rockefeller Found., Cairo, 1930-32; asst. prin. Friendsville Acad., Tenn., 1933-34; instr. biology Purdue U., 1935-42, asst. prof. zoology, 1942-43; asst. prof. parasitic diseases Ind. U. Sch. Medicine, Indpls., 1943-46, asso. prof., 1946-53, prof., 1953-77, prof. emeritus, 1977—, parliamentarian of faculty, 1973-75, sec., 1973-74, exec. sec., 1974-75; dir. Parasitology Diagnostic Lab., Ind. U. Med. Ctr., 1943-57; cons. parasitologist dept. dermatology Indpls. Gen. Hosp., 1946-57; prof. parasitic diseases Ind. U. Sch. Med., 1953-77; prof. emeritus, 1977—; mem. faculty council Ind. U.-Purdue U.-Indpls., 1973-75, chmn. faculty bd. rev., 1974-75; chmn. dept. biology Nat. Pedagogic Inst., Caracas, Venezuela, 1937-38; sr. scientist USPHS Res., 1953-71; attache, med. parasitologist U.S. ops. mission Fgn. Ops. Adminstrn., Am. embassy, Bangkok, 1953-55; vis. prof. med. parasitology Sch. of Medicine, Chulalongkorn U. and Thailand Sch. Public Health, Bangkok, 1953-55; U.S. del. to 9th Pacific Sci. Congress, Bangkok, 1957; coordinator, dir. Ind. U.-AID, Pakistan Project to develop Jinnah Postgrad. Med. Center, 1957-66; asso. dir. Div. Allied Health Scis., Ind. U. Sch. Medicine, 1968; cons. epidemiologist Ind. Regional Med. Program, 1969-77. Bd. dirs. Central Ind. Council on Aging, 1979-82, mem. nominating com., 1979, long range planning com., 1979-82, program services com., 1978-81 ; del. Older Hoosiers Assembly of Commn. on Aging of State of Ind., 1977—, mem. at large, floor leader, 1982—, mem. aging network legis. com., steering com., 1978—; mem. Mayor's Adv. Com. on Aging and the Aged, Indpls., 1978-81; bd. dirs. Marion County Council on Aging, 1978-81; adv. council Ind. U. Center on Aging and Aged. Recipient Arts and Humanities award Shelbyville (Ind.) Rotary Club, 1980; John and Mary Markle Found. fellow, 1943, 44. Emeritus fellow AAAS (life, council 1957-62), Ind. Acad. Sci. (exec. com. 1944, chmn. zoology sect. 1944, mem. membership com. 1950-60, fellows com. 1972-77), Royal Soc. Tropical Medicine and Hygiene; emeritus mem. AAUP (sec.-treas. Ind. Conf. 1972-73, pres. 1974-75, Disting. Mem. award 1976), Am. Soc. Parasitologists (sr.; com. on hon. and emeritus mems. 1967), Am. Soc. Tropical Medicine and Hygiene (emeritus; program com. 1959, 60, nominating com. 1971), Sigma Xi (emeritus); mem. Soc. Internat. Devel., Internat. Coll. Tropical Medicine, Nat. Council on Aging, Nat. Ret. Tchrs. Assn., Ret. Profs. Ind., Soc. Ret. Execs., Am. Assn. Ret. Persons, Ind. Partners of Ams. (dir. 1978—, treas. 1986), Tulane U. Med. Alumni Assn. (life mem.), U. Ill. Alumni Assn. (life), Phi Sigma. Unitarian (bd. trustees 1953, 70-73, chmn. nominating com. 1970-71). Clubs: Ind. U. Emeritus, Earlham Coll. Emeritus. Contbr. numerous articles on epidemiology of parasite infections, med. edn., higher edn. to profl. jours., also poems and miscellaneous articles, manuals. Home: 762 N Riley Ave Indianapolis IN 46201

HEADLEY, KATHRYN WILMA, educator; b. Grand Rapids, Mich., Mar. 10, 1940; d. William L. and Kathryn (Mekkes) H. B.A., Hope Coll., 1967; M.Ed., Grand Valley Coll., 1981. Cert. tchr., Mich. Missionary, Reformed Ch. in Am., N.Y.C., summers, 1959-64; various ch. positions Ottawa Reformed Ch., West Olive, Mich., 1956—, Bible day camp dir., 1979-86; tchr. English and phys. edn. Jenison Pub. Schs. (Mich.), 1967—, head coach girls basketball, volleyball, 1967-78, head coach girls track, softball, 1967-73, head coach girls bowling, 1973-78, class advisor, 1983-87, numerous other sch. activities. coach girls soccer, basketball, Borculo Christian Sch., Mich., 1981—. Bd. dirs. Ottawa County Tchrs. Credit Union, Grand Haven, Mich., 1978—, v.p., 1984—. Mem. Mich. Edn. Assn. (rep.), NEA, Jenison Edn. Assn. (rep.), Mich. High Sch. Athletic Assn. (ofcl.), Hope Coll. Alumni Assn., Mich. Christian Endeavor Bd., Delta Kappa Gamma. Mem. Reformed Ch. in Am. Home: 9111 96th Ave Rural Rt 1 Zeeland MI 49464 Office: Jenison Pub Schs 2140 Bauer Rd Jenison MI 49428

HEADRICK, ROGER LEWIS, food company executive; b. West Orange, N.J., May 13, 1936; s. Lewis B. and Marian E. (Rogers) H.; m. C. Lynn Cowell, Sept. 29, 1962; children: Hilary R., Mark C., Christopher C., Heather R. A.B., William Coll., 1958; M.B.A., Columbia U., 1960. Fin. analyst Standard Oil (N.J.), Esso Eastern, Inc., N.Y.C., 1960-65; treas. Standard Oil (N.J.), Esso Eastern, Inc., Tokyo, 1965-70; v.p. Standard Oil (N.J.), Esso Eastern, Inc., Manila, 1970-73; treas., mgr. fin. and planning Standard Oil (N.J.), Esso Eastern, Inc., Houston, 1973-78; dep. controller Exxon Corp., N.Y.C., 1978-82; exec. v.p., chief fin. officer The Pillsbury Co., Mpls., 1982—; bd. dirs. Tonka Corp., Rahr Malting Co.; mem. adv. council, task force on income tax acctg. Fin. Acctg. Standards Bd. Trustee Dunwoody Indsl. Inst., Mpls., 1982—, The Blake Schs., 1983—, Fin. Execs. Research Found.; bd. dirs. The Guthrie Theater, 1985—. Served with Air Force Res. NG, 1960-66. Trustee Fin. Execs. Research Found.; mem. Fin. Execs. Inst. (com. corp. fin.), Council Fin. Execs.-The Conf. Bd. Office: Pillsbury Co 200 S 6th St Minneapolis MN 55402

HEAL, LAIRD WAYNE, social studies educator, consultant; b. Rhinelander, Wis., Apr. 7, 1933; s. Garold William and Albia (Miner) H.; widowed; children: Kim, Laird, Jodi, Gary, Andy, Loren, Dave. BA, Ripon (Wis.) Coll., 1955; MS, U. Wis., 1963, PhD, 1964. Prof. U. Ill., Champaign, 1975—. Contbr. articles to profl. jours. Mem. Am. Psychol. Assn., Am. Assn. Mental Deficiency. Home: 3202 Lakeshore Dr Champaign IL 61821 Office: U Ill 1310 S 6th St Champaign IL 61821

HEALEY, ROBERT WILLIAM, principal, computer consultant; b. Charleston, Ill., Sept. 29, 1947; s. William Albert and Ruth M. (Wiedenhoeft) H.; m. Sharon Barbara Grande, Aug. 7, 1982; children: William Robert, Steven Anthony. BS in Elem. Edn., Ea. Ill. U., 1970, MS in Ednl. Adminstrn., 1972; EdD in Curriculum and Supervision, No. Ill. U., 1977. Cert. elem. teaching K-9, gen. adminstrv. K-12, Ill. Prin. Glidden Elem. Sch., DeKalb, Ill., 1972-74, Lincoln Elem. Sch., DeKalb, 1974-83, Littlejohn Elem. Sch., DeKalb, 1983-84, Littlejohn and Cortland Elem. Schs., DeKalb, 1984-85, Jefferson Elem. Sch., DeKalb, 1986—; dir. Title I Elem. and Secondary Edn. Act., Pre-Sch. Base Line Program, 1972-74; dir. gifted edn. Bd. Edn. Negotiating Team, 1974-81, coordinator dist. testing and evaluation, 1981-84, coordinator spl. edn., 1984-86; mem. adv. bd. Evanston (Ill.) Educators Computer Software, 1983—; dir. testing DeKalb Sch. Dist. 428, 1986—; treas. No. Ill. Commn. for Gifted Edn., Oakbrook, 1980-82; mem. various elem. sch. planning and program councils, DeKalb, 1973—; coordinator numerous sch. programs, DeKalb, 1973—; leader numerous workshops DeKalb, 1976-85; sec. DeKalb Sch. Bd. Study com. on sch. lunch programs, 1976-77; cons. Scholastic Testing Service, 1980-83; chmn. dist. reading com., DeKalb, 1986—. Coordinator 10 yr. study of student achievement in DeKalb Schs., 1980-83; author numerous presentations, 1975-84; revisor DeKalb School District Parent Handbook, 1986; contbr. articles to profl. jours; inventor multi-purpose table and stage. Chmn. Task Force I DeKalb Sch. Dist., 1973-75; treas. No. Ill. Planning Commn., 1980-82; active Supts. Task Force on Spl. Edn., DeKalb, 1976-79, Mayor's Commn. DeKalb Planning Commn. for Yr. of Child, DeKalb, 1979, Dist. Computer Com., DeKalb, 1980-83, Dist. Revenue and Donations Com., 1980-83, Ill. PTA. Recipient Distinguished Program award Nat. Assn. for Tchr. Educators, Chgo., 1978; Named Citizen of the Day, WLBK Radio, DeKalb, 1983; Reading is Fundamental grantee Lincoln Sch., 1980-83, Ill. Ctr., 1980-83, Ill. Arts Council, Littlejohn Sch., 1984, Jefferson Sch., 1986. Mem. NEA (life), Nat. Assn. Elem. Prins., Ill. Prins. Assn., Assn. for Supervision and Curriculum Devel., Ill. Assn. for Supervision and Curriculum Devel., Soc. Am. Inventors, Ill. Council for Gifted Edn. Avocations: swimming, computer, home improvement. Home: 420 Sycamore Rd DeKalb IL 60115 Office: DeKalb Community Unit Sch Dist 145 Fisk Ave DeKalb IL 60115

HEALY, STEVEN MICHAEL, accountant; b. Chgo., July 20, 1949; s. Daniel Francis and Angelina (Massino) H. BA, U. Ill., Chgo., 1971; MBA, Rosary Coll., 1984. Br. mgr. Assocs. Capital Co., Chgo., 1971-74; credit analyst Motorola, Inc., Schaumberg, Ill., 1974-76; office mgr. Triple "S" Steel Corp., Franklin Pk., Ill., 1976-79; accounts payable supr. Zenith Electronics, Chgo., 1979-84; acctg. supr. Village of Oak Park, Ill., 1984-86; bus. analyst Cablevision of Chgo., Oak Park, 1986—. Mem. Oak Park Village Players Group; bd. dirs. Oak Park Employees Credit Union. Mem. Nat. Soc. Pub. Accts., Nat. Govt. Fin. Officers Assn., Ill. Govt. Fin. Officers Assn., U. Ill. Alumni Assn., Rosary Coll. MBA Alumni Assn. (founder, mem. soc. com. 1984—), Friends of the Oak Park Library, Friends of the Conservatory, Cath. Alumni Club. Club: Village Oak Park Chess (pres. 1984-86). Avocations: participation sports, reading, travel, writing, chess. Home: 728 S Ridgeland Ave Oak Park IL 60304 Office: Cablevision of Chgo 820 Madison Oak Park IL 60302

HEALY, THOMAS MARTIN, manufacturing company executive; b. Milw., May 9, 1921; s. Thomas and Helen (Galewski) H.; m. Ruth Marcella Johnson, Jan. 30, 1943; children: Kathleen Healy Brey, Maureen Ann Warzon, Timothy James, Eileen Marie, Daniel Michael. Student Milw. Area Tech. Sch., 1945-48; student U. Wisc., 1948-49. Engring. rep. Oilgear Co., Milw., 1952-59; mgr. Houston office, 1959-63, mgr. speciality sales, 1963-73, mgr. corp. devel., 1973-83, v.p. corp. devel., 1984-87; pres. Healy Assocs., Austin, Tex., 1987—. Campaigner Rep. Nat. Com. Served as non-commissioned officer USN, 1943-45, PTO. Mem. Am. Mgmt. Assn., World Future Soc., Am. Def. Preparedness Assn. Roman Catholic. Club: Onion Creek. Avocations: travel, philosophy, business and professional ethics.

HEANEY, GERALD WILLIAM, U.S. judge; b. Goodhue, Minn., Jan. 29, 1918; s. William J. and Johanna (Ryan) H.; m. Eleanor R. Schmitt, Dec. 1, 1945; children—William M., Carol J. Student, St. Thomas Coll., 1935-37; B.S.L., U. Minn., 1938, LL.B., 1941. Bar: Minn. bar 1941. Lawyer securities div. Dept. of Commerce Minn., 1941-42; mem. firm Lewis. Hammer, Heaney, Weyl & Halverson, Duluth, 1946-66; judge 8th Jud. Circuit, U.S. Court Appeals, 1966—. Mem. Dem. Nat. Com. from Minn., 1955; Bd. regents U. Minn., 1964-65. Served from pvt. to capt. AUS, 1942-46. Mem. Am., Minn. bar assns., Am. Judicature Soc. Roman Catholic. Office: US Court of Appeals Duluth MN 55802 *

HEAP, JAMES CLARENCE, retired mechanical engineer; b. Trinidad, Colo.; s. James and Elsie Mae (Brobst) H.; m. Alma Mae Swartzendruber. Registered profl. engr., Wis. Sr. mech. engr. Cook Electric Research Lab, Morton Grove, Ill., 1955-56; assoc. mech. engr. Argonne (Ill.) Nat. Lab., 1956-66; sr. project engr. Union Tank Car Co., East Chicago, Ind., 1966-71; sr. engr. Thrall Car Mfg. Co., Chicago Heights, 1971-77; research design engr. Graver Energy Systems, Inc., Chicago Heights, 1977-79; mech. cons. design engr. Pollak & Skan, Inc., Chgo., 1979-83, ret., 1983; cons. mech. design and stress analysis, 1965-83. Author: Formulas for Circular Plates Subjected to Symmetrical Loads and Temperatures, 1966; contbr. tech. papers to profl. jour.; patentee in field. Served with USAF, 1946-47. Mem. ASME. Lodge: Masons. Home: 1913 Lambert Ln Munster IN 46321

HEARD, WILLIAM ROBERT, insurance company executive; b. Indpls., Apr. 25, 1925; s. French and Estelle (Austin) H.; attended Ind. U.; m. Virginia Ann Patrick, Feb. 6, 1951; children—Cynthia Ann, William Robert, II. With Grain Dealers Mut. Ins. Co., 1948, exec. v.p., Indpls., 1978-79, pres., chief exec. officer, dir., 1979—; pres., chief exec. officer, dir. Companion Ins. Co., 1979—; chmn., dir., exec. com. Alliance Am. Insurers; chmn., exec. com. IRM; pres., dir. Grain Dealers Mut. Agy., Inc.; chmn. bd. 15 N. Broadway Corp. Served with USNR, 1942-46. Mem. Assn. Mill and Elevator Ins. Cos. (chmn., dir.), Ins. Inst. Ind. (dir., exec. com.), Mut. Reins. Bur. (dir., exec. com.), Indiana Better Bus. Bur. (dir., exec. com., vice chmn.), Excess of Loss Assn. (vice chmn., dir.), Sales and Mktg. Execs. Indpls. (past pres.), Sales and Mktg. Execs. Internat. (past dir.), Fla. 1752 Club (past pres.), Property and Casualty Ins. Council, Ind. Insurors Assn. (dir.), Hoosierland Rating Bur. (dir.), Ind. Mill and Elevator Rating Bur. (dir.), Ins. Claims Service (dir.), Property Loss Research Bur. (dir., chmn.), Mill and Elevator Rating Bur. (dir.), Mill and Elevator Fire Prevention Bur. (dir.), Econ. Club of Indpls., Am. Legion, Hon. Order Ky. Cols., Pi Sigma Epsilon. Club: Indpls. Skyline. Office: Grain Dealers Mut Ins 1752 N Meridian Indianapolis IN 46202

HEARN, J(AMES) WOODROW, bishop; b. MacIntyre, La., Mar. 7, 1931; s. John Elton and Alta (Fordham) H.; m. Anne Connaughton, Sept. 24, 1952; children: John Mark, Paul Woodrow, Diana Elizabeth Smith, Bruce Charles. AB, La. Tech. U., 1952; MST, Boston U. Sch. Theol., 1955, DST, 1965; postgrad., Harvard U., 1956; DDiv, Nebr. Wesleyan U., 1985. Ordained elder, United Meth. Ch., 1955. Exec. dir. Ft. Worth Council of Chs., 1966-69; program council dir. La. Conf. Chs., Shreveport, 1969-73; dist. supr. United Meth. Ch., Lake Charles, La., 1973-74; sr. pastor First United Meth. Ch., Baton Rouge, 1974-84; bishop United Meth. Ch., Lincoln, Nebr., 1984—. Trustee So. Meth. U., Dallas, Nebr. Wesleyan U., Lincoln, St. Paul Sch. Theology, Kansas City, Mo., Bryan Meml. Hosp., Lincoln; mem. bd. dirs. Global Ministries United Meth. Ch., Advance com. African Ch. Growth and Devel. Com. Mailing: PO Box 4553 Lincoln NE 68504 Office: NE Conf United Meth Ch 2641 N 49th St Lincoln NE 68504 *

HEARNE, EDWARD WARREN, III, writer, public relations executive; b. Jamestown, N.Y., Jan. 21, 1943; s. Edward Warren Jr. and Elizabeth (Brown) H.; m. Elizabeth Gould, Sept. 1, 1963 (div. Aug. 1977); 1 child, Joanna Megan; m. Clarice Strauch, Jan. 3, 1981;1 child, Edward Warren IV. BA, Coll. Wooster, 1965; MA, U. Chgo., 1966, postgrad., 1966-70. Dir. pub. rel. Inst. European Studies, Chgo., 1969-71; v.p. Independent Programming Assn., Chgo., 1980-81; pres. Healthcare Mktg. Assocs., Chgo., 1975-86, Here's Chgo., Inc., 1982-86, Ted Hearne Assocs., Chgo., 1971—. Producer, dir. (film) City of Dreams, 1983 (Houston Film Festival award 1983), (multi media) Heartbeat Chicago, 1983; contbr. articles to profl. jours. Office: Hearne Communications 20 N Michigan Ave Chicago IL 60602

HEARST, DAVID THURMAN, product development executive; b. St. Louis, May 2, 1947; s. Emmet and Donna Rose (Barnes) H.; m. Sharon Ann Becker, July 26, 1968; children: Racheal Christine, Jennifer Leigh. BS in Engring. Mgmt., U. Mo., Rolla, 1973, MS in Engring. Mgmt., 1974; postgrad., Case-Western Res. U., 1980—. Registered profl. engr., Mo. Program mgr. Air Products Inc., Allentown, Pa., 1975-77; asst. regional mgr. Liquid Air Corp., San Francisco, 1977-79; v.p. sales and mktg. AGA Gas Inc., Cleve., 1979-82; pres., chief exec. officer H&H Investment & Mgmt. Co., Chardon, Ohio, 1982—; pres., chief operating officer Area Tech. Inc., Hammond, Indiana, 1985—, also bd. dirs. Patentee cylinder identification device. Mem. Chardon Charter Review Com., 1985, Planning Com., 1986—. Served with USN, 1966-70, Vietnam. Grantee NSF, 1974. Mem. NSPE, Am. Soc. for Engring. Mgmt., Bar Coding Automotive Inst. Action Group (chmn. subcom.), Tau Beta Pi. Lodge: Rotary. Avocations: stock market, gardening. Home and Office: 465 South St Chardon OH 44024-9998

HEASEL, JOHN FREDERICK, office automations specialist; b. Cin., Mar. 30, 1934; s. Harry Frederick and Louise Alma (Peppers) Heasel; m. Linda Hartman, Aug. 6, 1960. Student, U. Cin., 1952-54, 58-59, Tulane U., 1963-67, La. State U., 1967-69; BBA, LaSalle U., 1974. Cert. office automation profl. Engr. AVCO Corp., Cin. and Richmond, Ind., 1959-63, Space div. Chrysler Corp., New Orleans, 1963-69; corp./dealer identity Chrysler Corp., Highland Park, Mich., 1969-78; fleet/facility engr. Chrysler Transport Inc., Detroit, 1978-80; logistics engr. Gen. Dynamics, Warren, Mich., 1980-83; mgr. office automation Gen. Dynamics, Troy, Mich., 1983—; instr. ethics tng. Gen. Dynamics, Troy, 1986; instr. microprocessors Apple Pub. Interest East, East Detroit, 1986. Contbr. articles to profl. jours. Active U.S Coast Guard Auxiliary, Mich., 1975—. Served with USN, 1954-58. Mem. Office Automation Soc. Internat., Nat. Mgmt. Assn., Auxop Assn. (founding, pres. 1984-85), Internat. Naval Research Orgn. (contrbg.). Clubs: Apple Core (Troy) (v.p. 1983—), Apple P.I.E. (East Detroit) (treas. 1986). Avocations: model bldg., personal computers, boating instr. Home: 22842 Avalon Saint Clair Shores MI 48080

HEATH, JON MICHAEL, mechanical designer; b. St. Paul, Sept. 9, 1938; s. Edward Gordon and Kathleen Evelyn (McFail) H.; m. Sharon Alice Bennett, June 18, 1960 (div. Nov. 1981); children: Julie, Paige, Paul, Colleen. Student, U. Minn., 1968-70. Draftsman Bros Incorp., Mpls., 1957-62, mech. designer, 1964-69; draftsman I Water Dept. City of Mpls., Mpls., 1962-64; project coordinator Raygo Corp., Mpls., 1969-72; staff designer Deltak Corp., Mpls., 1972—; cons. mech. design, Mpls., 1975-85. Copatentee heat recovery muffler for internal combustion engines, 1973, vertical firetube waste heat boiler, 1978. Coach Lake Region Hockey Assn., New Brighton, Minn., 1971-75. Mem. ASME. Presbyterian. Avocations: golf, bowling, guitar, reading. Home: 2740 Terraceview Ct Plymouth MN 55447 Office: Deltak Corp 13330 12th Ave N Minneapolis MN 55440

HEATH, MARIWYN DWYER, legislative issues cons.; b. Chgo., May 1, 1935; d. Thomas Leo and Winifred (Brennan) Dwyer; B.J., U. Mo., 1956; m. Eugene R. Heath, Sept. 3, 1956; children—Philip Clayton, Jeffrey Thomas. Mng. editor Chemung Valley Reporter, Horseheads, N.Y., 1956-57; self-employed freelance writer, platform speaker, editor Tech. Transls., Dayton, Ohio, 1966—; cons. Internat. Women's Commn., 1975-76; ERA coordinator Nat. Fedn. Bus. and Profl. Women's Clubs, 1974-82; mem. polit. and mgmt. coms. ERAmerica, 1976-82, exec. dir., 1982—; pres. Miami Valley Regioncal Transit Authority, 1986—. mem. Gov. Ohio Task Force Credit for Women, 1973; mem. Midwest regional adv. com. SBA, 1976-82; chmn. Ohio Coalition ERA Implementation, 1974-75. Bd. dirs. Dayton YWCA, 1968-74. Recipient various service awards; named One of 10 Outstanding Women of World, Soroptimist Internat., 1982. Mem. AAUW (dir. Dayton 1965-72; Woman of Year award Dayton 1974), Nat. Fedn. Bus. and Profl. Women's Clubs (pres. Dayton 1967-69, Ohio 1976-77; Woman of Year award Dayton 1974, Ohio 1974, 83), Ohio Women (v.p. 1983—, bd. dirs. 1977—), Assn. Women Execs., Women in Communications. Republican. Roman Catholic. Address: 10 Wisteria Dr Dayton OH 45419

HEATH, VERNON H., manufacturing company executive; b. 1929. Student, U. Minn., 1950. Cost acct. Malco Co., Mpls., 1950-51; with aero. lab. U. Minn.-Rosemount, 1951-56; with Rosemount, Inc., Eden Prairie, Minn., 1956—, pres., chief exec. officer, 1968—, also bd. dirs. Office: Rosemount Inc 12001 W 78th St Eden Prairie MN 55344 *

HEATHCOCK, JOHN EDWIN, clergyman; b. Detroit, Dec. 12, 1937; s. James Richard and Laurel Viola (Manwarren) H.; m. Kathryn Iva Trexler, Aug. 31, 1958 (div. 1978); children: Jean Marie, Jeffrey Daniel, Janet Iva; m. Elizabeth Ann Porter, Dec. 12, 1978. BS, Cen. Mich. U., 1966; M Div., Duke U., 1970, ThM, 1971; PhD, Internat. Coll., 1980. Ordained priest Episcopal Ch., 1984. Dir. pastoral care SW Texas Meth. Hosp., San Antonio, 1972-80, Amarillo (Tex.) Hosp. Dist., 1980-86, St. Luke's Hosp., Chesterfield, Mo., 1986—; cons. Perkins Sch. Theology So. Meth. U., Dallas, 1973-76, Oblate Coll., San Antonio, 1973-76; faculty Episc. Theol. Sem., Austin, Tex., 1973-78; exec. dir. Found. for Pastoral Care, Amarillo, 1980-86; faculty asst. Tex. Tech. Med. Sch., Amarillo, 1981-83. Profl. advisor Child Growth and Devel. Complex, Amarillo, 1985. Served to 1st lt. USAR, 1957-72. Fellow Coll. Chaplains, Am. Protestant Hosp. Assn.; mem. Assn. for Clin. Pastoral Edn. (supr. clin. pastoral edn., treas. 1975-78, chmn. cert. com. 1983-86), Am. Assn. for Marriage and Family Therapy, Tex. Psychotherapy Assn. (bd. dirs. 1978). Lodge: Masons (master 1969). Avocations: reading, woodworking, music, gardening, painting. Office: St Luke's Hosp 232 S Woods Mill Rd Chesterfield MO 63017

HEATHERSON, DAN MAURICE, mfg. co. exec.; b. La Porte, Ind., Feb. 4, 1947; s. Hugh Maurice and Florence Evelyn (Brady) H.; B.S. in Indsl. Mgmt., Purdue U., 1970; m. Patricia Louise Fogarty, Sept. 2, 1967; children—Jacqueline Anne, Danny Maurice, Michele Lee. Sect. indsl. engr. Colgate-Palmolive Co., Jeffersonville, Ind., 1970-71; sr. indsl. engr. AC Spark Plug div. Gen. Motors Corp., Flint, Mich., 1971-73; sr. indsl. engr. Joy Mfg. Co., Michigan City, Ind., 1974-76, mgr. mfg. engring., 1978-79, mgr. prodn. planning, 1979-82, mgr. prodn. planning and control, 1982-83, mgr. mfg. engring., 1983—; prodn. mgr. Penn Athletic Products Co., Phoenix, 1976-78. Founder, bd. dirs. Greater La Porte (Ind.) Pop Warner Football Assn., Inc., also head coach; past pres. Lake Porter Pop Warner Football Conf.; head coach La Porte Babe Ruth Baseball. Served with USMC, 1968. Mem. Am. Prodn. and Inventory Control Soc., Soc. Mfg. Engring., Computer and Automated Systems Assn. Roman Catholic. Club: Elks. Home: 403 Sunrise Blvd La Porte IN 46350 Office: 900 Woodland Ave Michigan City IN 46360

HEATON, CHARLES LLOYD, dermatologist, educator; b. Bryan, Tex., May 8, 1935; s. Homer Lloyd and Bessie Blanton (Sharp) H.; B.S., Tex. A&M U., 1957; M.D., Baylor U., 1961; M.A. (hon.), U. Pa., 1973. Intern, Jefferson Davis Hosp., Houston, 1961-62; resident Baylor U., 1962-65; sr. attending physician Phila. Gen. Hosp., 1965-69, chief of service, 1970-77; mem. dept. dermatology U. Pa. Sch. Medicine 66-78; asso. prof. dermatology U. Pa., 1973-78; assoc. prof. dermatology U. Cin., 1978-85, prof., 1985—. Served to lt. comdr. USPHS, 1965-67. Diplomate Am. Bd. Dermatology. Fellow Coll. Physicians of Phila., ACP; mem. AMA, Soc. Investigative Dermatology, Am. Venereal Disease Assn., Am. Dermatol. Assn., Cin. Dermatol. Soc. Author: Audiovisual Course in Venereal Disease, 1972; Chancroid: Current Therapy, 1975; (with D.M. Pillsbury) Manual of Dermatology, 1980; contbr. papers to profl. jours. Home: 5534 E Galbraith Rd Apt 25 Cincinnati OH 45236 Office: U Cin Coll Medicine Dept Dermatology 231 Bethesda Ave Cincinnati OH 45267

HEATON, JAMES WARDEN, management company executive; b. Clarksburg, W.Va., Jan. 21, 1952; s. Hiram Hayward and Rose Marie (Bramer) H.; m. Linda Marie Kline, Apr. 11, 1973; children—Robert D., Mary R., Joseph D. Officer Massillon Police Dept., Ohio, 1980-83, chief exec. officer, pres. Harrington & Rhodes, Massillon, 1983—; chmn. bd. Becker Mgmt. Inc., Massillon. Founder internat. police liaison team in Europe, 1977-79, Bowerston Police Dept., Ohio, 1980; regional coordinator domestic relations Cen. Intelligence Agy., 1985-86; co-founder United Vietnam Vets. Inc., Stark County, Ohio, 1982, exec. dir. Ohio Mil. Mus., 1984-85; mem. steering com. Ohio N.G. Territorial Militia Mus., 1984-85; founder Stark County Polit. Action Com., Massillon, 1984. Served as sgt. U.S. Army, 1972-80. Mem. Fraternal Order Police, Am. Fedn. Police, Am. Assn. Fin. Profls., Police Patrol Officers Assn. (pres.), Ohio Soc. Mil. History (co-founder), VFW, Am. Vets.(steering com.), U.S. Spl. Forces Assn., Mensa. Republican. Baptist. Home: 601 Amherst St SW Navarre OH 44662 Office: Becker Mgmt Assocs Inc 316 Lincoln Way E Massillon OH 44646

HEATON, PAMELA KIM, accountant; b. Kansas City, Kans., Nov. 14, 1956; d. Ronald Stuart and Kathleen E. (Wilson) Lamphear; m. James Vernon Heaton Jr., June 1, 1975; children: Alissa Ann, James Vernon III, Kyle David. BS, Kans. State U., 1982. CPA, Kans. Staff acct. Mize, Houser & Co., Topeka, 1982-85; sr. acct. CGF Industries, Inc., Topeka, 1985-87; instr. acctg. Kansas City Bus. Coll., 1987—; treas. Heidi and Peter Daycare Acad., Topeka, 1983-87. Asst. treas. Fairlawn Heights Wesleyan Ch., Topeka, 1985-87. Mem. Am. Inst. CPA's, Kans. Soc. CPA's (Gold Key award 1983). Republican. Home: 6922 Woodson Overland Park KS 66204 Office: Kansas City Bus Coll 1415 McGee Kansas City MO 64104

HEAVENRICH, HERBERT SAMUEL, management consultant; b. Omaha, Nebr., Oct. 13, 1922; s. Herbert Samuel and Sadie (Kirschbraun) H.; B.S.E., U. Mich., 1943; M.B.A., U. Chgo., 1953; postgrad. U. Wis., 1967-69; m. Jill Sherry, Apr. 26, 1954; children—Hope, Amy, Hollis, Avery, Adam. Research asst. Bemis Found., M.I.T., Cambridge, 1946-48; with HUD, Washington, 1950-52; builder, Milw., 1952-54; asst. to pres. Am. Houses Inc., N.Y.C., 1954-56; v.p., dir. Mortgage Assos., Inc., Milw., 1957-66; program dir. Big 10 Univ. Consortium on Pub. Policy, Econ. Growth & Tech., Madison, Wis., 1966-68; dir. city planning City of Milw., 1968-75; v.p. Anderson/Roethle Inc., Milw., 1975—; dir., owner Heavenrich & Co., Inc., 1980—. Bd. dirs. Milw. Mental Health Cons., Inc., 1980—; bd. dirs., treas. Milw. Urban League, 1960-66; pres. Republican Workshop of Wis., 1960-64. Served as lt. (j.g.) USNR, 1944-46. Bemis Found. grantee, 1949. Mem. Inst. Mgmt. Cons. Jewish. Club: Univ. (Milw.). Contbr. articles to profl. jours. Home: 2443 N Wahl Ave Milwaukee WI 53211 Office: 811 E Wisconsin Ave Milwaukee WI 53202

HEBDA, LAWRENCE JOHN, data processing executive; b. East Chicago, Ind., Apr. 9, 1954; s. Walter Martin and Barbara (Matzcynski) H.; m. Cynthia Ruth Aizkalns, June 17, 1978. BS, Purdue U., 1976; MBA, U. Iowa, 1983. Cert. data processor. Programmer Inland Steel Co., East Chicago, 1976-77; data analyst Deere & Co., Moline, Ill., 1977-82, systems analyst, 1982-83, project mgr., 1983-84, dealer systems cons., 1984-85, corp. planning analyst, 1985-87, systems edn. adminstr., 1987—. Mem. Nat. Rep. Congl. Com., 1982, 83, 84, 85; charter mem. Rep. Presdl. Task Force, 1980. Served with USN, 1972-75. Recipient Cert. Recognition, Nat. Rep. Congl. Com., 1982-85, Presdl. Achievement award Rep. Nat. Com., 1984. Mem. Data Processing Mgmt. Assn., Disabled Am. Vets. Comdr.'s Club, Am. Legion. Roman Catholic. Club: Toastmasters Internat. (assoc. area gov. 1983-84). Home: 2129 Lincolnwood Dr East Moline IL 61244 Office: Deere & Co John Deere Rd Moline IL 61265

HEBER, ALBERT JAMES, agricultural engineer; b. Parkston, S.D., Mar. 11, 1956; s. Alvin Eric and Leonida Louisa (Drefs) H.; m. Gloria Marie Folkers, June 5, 1977; children: Andrew, Noelle, Nathaniel, Joy. BS in Agrl. Engr., S.D. State U., 1978, MS in Agrl. Engring., 1979; PhD Engring., U. Nebr., 1984. Profl. engr., Kans. Research engr. II U. Nebr., Lincoln, 1981-84; asst. prof. Kans. State U., Manhatten, 1984—. Pres. Manhattan Parent Educators, 1985, 87; campaign chmn. Brookings County Election Com. for Dale Bell., Brookings, S.D., 1981. Nat. Pork Producers Council grantee, 1985; Kans. Dept. Econ. Devel. grantee, 1986. Mem. Am. Soc. Agrl. Engring., Am. Soc. Engring. Edn. Avocation: reading, sports, bible study, chess, piano. Office: Agrl Engring Dept Seaton Hall Manhattan KS 66506

HEBERT, MARY OLIVIA, librarian; b. St. Louis, Nov. 11, 1921; d. Arthur Frederick and Clara Marie (Golden) Meyer; certificate librarianship, Washington U., St. Louis, 1972; m. N. Hal Hebert, Sept. 9, 1943 (dec. Mar. 1969); children—Olivia, Stephen, Christina, Deborah, Beth, John, James. Secretarial positions in advt., 1942-43; v.p. Hebert Advt. Co., 1955-66; adminstrv. asst. communications Blue Cross, St. Louis, 1966-69, librarian, 1969—. Mem. Spl. Libraries Assn. (pres. St. Louis Metro chpt. 1984), St. Louis Med. Librarians, St. Louis Regional Library Network (council 1986-87). Roman Catholic. Office: 4444 Forest Park Blvd Saint Louis MO 63108

HECHT, HENRY WILLIAN, musician, educator; b. Montevideo, Minn., Nov. 27, 1932; s. Henry William Sr. and Lenora Harriet (Stebbins) H.; m. Deserré Ann Saltness, Sept. 5, 1954; children: Laura Marie Hecht Hoffman, Amy Louise Hecht Pennington. MusB, De Paul U., Chgo., 1959; MusM, Cath. U., Washington, 1978. Enlisted USN, 1951, advanced through ranks to sr. chief petty officer; instr. Sch. Music, USN, Washington, 1959-60; trombonist U.S. Navy Band, Washington, 1960-78; ret. USN, 1978; assoc. prof., band dir. Moody Bible Inst., Chgo., 1978—; tchr. artist Music and Drama Camp, Cedar Lake, Ind., 1982-86; clinician various music groups, USA, 1978—. Trombonist: recording) Ilse of Golden Dreams, 1957. Mem. Nat. Assn. Coll. Wind and Procussion Instruments, Bass Angler's Sportmans Soc., Christian Instrumental Dirs. Assn. Republican. Mem. Christian Repformed Ch. Avocations: fishing, golf. Home: 5124 S Wolf Rd Western Springs IL 60558 Office: Moody Bible Inst 820 N Lasalle Dr Chicago IL 60610

HECK, DAVID ALAN, orthopaedic surgery educator, mechanical engineering educator; b. Syracuse, N.Y., Nov. 20, 1952; s. William C. and Shirley W. (Wolthausen) H.; m. Kimberly Kay North, Sept. 27, 1980; children: William Donald, Andrew David. BS in Elect. and Computer Engring. cum laude, Clarkson Coll. Tech., 1973; MD, SUNY, Syracuse, 1977. Cert. AM. Bd. Orthopaedic Surgery. Intern in gen. surgery U. Minn., Mpls., 1977-78; resident in orthpaedic surgery SUNY, Syracuse, 1978-82; resident in orthopaedic biomechanics Mayo Clinic, Rochester, Minn., 1982-83; asst. prof. Ind. U. Sch. Medicine, Indpls., 1983-87, assoc. prof., 1987—; attending physician Ind. U. Med. Ctr., Indpls., 1983—, VA Med. Ctr., Indpls., 1983—, Riley Hosp., 1983—, Wishard Meml. Hosp., 1983—; adj. asst. prof. Sch. Mech. Engring. Purdue U., West Lafayette, Ind., 1984—; chief, orthopaedic surgery sect., VA Med. Ctr., 1983—, medipro advisor, 1986; bd. dirs. Indian Creek Hills, Inc., The Orthopaedic Rev. Course; lectr. various profl. orgns.; dir. Orthopaedic Biomechanics Lab. Ind. U. Med. Ctr., 1984—; mem. residency applicants rev. com., Ind. U., 1983—, orthopaedic chief's of services com., 1983—, search and screen com., 1984-86, adult ambulatory care com., 1986, orthopaedic basic sci. com., 1986. Contbr. numerous article to profl. jours. Sports medicine advisor White River Park, 1984—. Mem. AMA, Am. Coll. Sports Medicine, Am. Soc. Metals, Am. Soc. Biomechanics, Ind. Med. Assn., Marion County Med. Soc., Orthopaedic Research Soc., Knee Soc. (ex-officio, com. on evaluation), 7th Dist. Med. Soc., Eta Kappa Nu, Tau Beta Pi. Avocations: camping, canoeing, guns. Home: 11440 Valley Meadow Dr Zionsville IN 46077

HECK, GRACE FERN, lawyer; b. Tremont City, Ohio, Nov. 13, 1905; d. Thomas J. and Mary Etta (Maxson) H.; m. Leo H. Faust, May 25, 1977. B.A. cum laude, Ohio State U., 1928, J.D. summa cum laude, 1930. Bar: Ohio 1930, U.S. Dist. Ct. (so. dist.) Ohio 1932, U.S. Supreme Ct. 1960. Researcher, Nat. Commn. Law Observance and Enforcement, U.S. Dist. Ct. (so. dist.) Ohio, 1930-31, Ohio Judicial Council and Law Inst. Johns Hopkins U., 1931-32; prosecuting atty. Champaign County, Urbana, Ohio, 1933-37; sole practice, Urbana, 1937-43, 73-85, Springfield, 1947-73; assoc. Corry, Durfey & Martin, Springfield, 1943-47; mcpl. judge Champaign County, 1954-58. Exec. sec. War Price and Rationing Bd., Urbana, 1941-43; bd. trustees Spring Grove Cemetery Assn., 1954—; sec. bd. trustees Magnetic Springs Found., Ohio, 1957-62; pres. Ohio State U., Coll. Law Alumni Assn., Columbus, 1971-72; charter mem. Friends of Libraries Ohio State U., Friends of Hist. Costume and Textile Collection; mem. Nat. Council Coll. Law, Ohio State U. Columbus, 1971—; mem. Springfield Art Assn.; trustee Champaign County Arts Council, 1987—. Recipient Disting. Service award Ohio State U., 1971. Mem. Ohio State Bar Assn. (com. mem.), Champaign County Bar and Law Library Assn. (pres. 1965), Springfield Bar and Law library Assn. (sec. 1946-59, pres. 1963), ABA, Ohio State U. Alumni Assn. (2d v.p. 1956-58, adv. bd. 1962-73, Alumni Centennial award 1970), Order of Coif, Phi Beta Kappa, Zeta Tau Alpha, Kappa Beta Pi, Delta Theta Tau (nat. v.p. 1938-40, nat. pres. 1941-42, bd. trustees 1942-45). Democrat. Methodist. Clubs: Springfield Country (Ohio); Troy Country (Ohio); Altrusa. Lodge: Order of Eastern Star. Avocations: fishing, hunting, travel, photography, gravestone rubbings. Home: 134 W Church St Urbana OH 43078

HECK, RICHARD JOSEPH, biomedical engineer; b. Davenport, Iowa, Jan. 3, 1947; s. Laurence Stanley and Madonna Geneva (Kiefer) H.; m. Mary Anita Kelly, Nov. 24, 1973; children: Daniel Joseph, Kathryn Ann. BSEE, Iowa State U., 1970, MS in Biomed. Engring. and Elec. Engring., 1975. Engr. sales Trane Co., Des Moines, 1970-72; dir. biomed. services Iowa Meth. Med. Ctr., Des Moines, 1975-84; engr. biomed. Bio-Tech. Engring. Services, Des Moines, 1984—; cons. design engr. Audiology Assocs., Des Moines, 1979—; cons. engr. Des Moines Sci. Ctr., 1983—; instr., mem. adv. com. Community Coll. Des Moines, 1984—. Inventor narrow band noise generator. Mem. Cen. Iowa Biomed. Electronics Soc. (pres. 1982-84, v.p. 1985). Democrat. Roman Catholic. Avocations: electronics, carpentry, mechanics, computers, camping. Office: Iowa Meth Bio Tech Enging 1421 Walker St Des Moines IA 50316

HECK, VERNON EDWARD, accountant, lawyer, financial planner; b. Ste. Genevieve, Mo., Mar. 9, 1938; s. John Andrew and Anna Christine (Schmiederer) H.; m. Mary Jane Scherer, Sept. 14, 1963; children: Jeffrey Edward, Gregory Alan. AS in Commerce, St. Louis U., 1962, BS in Commerce, 1970; JD, Laclede Sch. Law, 1982. CPA, Mo. Jr. acct. James C. Thompson & Co., CPA's, St. Louis, 1956-58; sr. acct. L. Ray Schuessler & Co., CPA's, St. Louis, 1958-65, ptnr., 1965-68; ptnr. Elmer Fox & Co., CPA's, St. Louis, 1968-72; pvt. practice acctg. St. Louis, 1972—; bd. dirs. High Knoll Enterprises, Inc., Perryville, Mo., Let's Travel Inc., St. Louis, Home Trust Mercantile Bank, Perryville. V.p. fin. St. Louis Jaycees, 1966-67; treas. Amvets, 1981-83. Served with U.S. Army N.G., 1959-63. Mem. Aircraft Owners & Pilots Assn., Advt. Club Greater St. Louis. Club: Mo. Athletic. Lodges: Elks, Shriners (mem. Air Patrol), Knights of Haymakers of Greater St. Louis, Eagles. Avocation: flying. Office: 705 Olive Suite 724 Saint Louis MO 63101

HECKADON, ROBERT GORDON, plastic surgeon; b. Brantford, Ont., Can., Jan. 30, 1933; s. Frederick Gordon and Laura (Penrose) H.; B.A., U. Western Ont., 1954, M.D., 1960; postgrad. U. Toronto, 1960-66, U. Vienna, 1966; m. Camilla Joyce Russell, July 11, 1959; children—David, Louise, Peter, William, Barbara. Intern, Toronto Gen. Hosp., 1960-61; asst. resident Toronto Western Hosp., 1961, Toronto Wellesley Hosp., 1962, Toronto Gen. Hosp., 1962-63; resident in plastic surgery St. Michael's Hosp., Toronto, 1963, Toronto Western Hosp., 1964, Toronto Gen. Hosp., 1964, Toronto Hosp. for Sick Children, 1965; asst. resident orthopedics Toronto East Gen. Hosp., 1965-66; practice medicine specializing in plastic surgery, Windsor, Ont., Can., 1966—; chief med. staff Hotel Dieu; mem. staff Grace Hosp., Met. Hosp. (all Windsor). Served with RCAF, 1951-56. Fellow A.C.S.; mem. Canadian Med. Assn., Ont. Med. Assn., Essex County Med. Assn., Windsor Acad. Surgery, Royal Coll. Physicians and Surgeons, Can. Soc. Plastic Surgeons.

HECKERT, JOSIAH BROOKS, accountant, educator; b. Tescott, Kans., Jan. 22, 1893; s. Uriah E. and Nancy Jane (Roy) H.; m. Marie Hood, June 5, 1918. AB, Kans. Wesleyan U., 1916, DCS (hon.), 1941; postgrad., U. Kans., 1916-17; AM, U. Chgo., 1923; LLD (hon.), Simpson Coll., 1950. CPA, Ohio. Prof. econs. Simpson Coll., Indianola, Iowa, 1920-25; assoc. prof. acctg. Ohio State U., Columbus, 1925-45, prof. acctg., 1945—; pres. Columbus Blank Book Mfg. Co.; v.p. Dollar Fed. Savs. and Loan Assn., Avis Rent-A-Car System, Inc.; bd. dirs. indsl. and fin. corps. Author: Accounting Systems--Design and Installation, 1936, Distribution Costs--Analysis and Control, 1946; (with I.J. Stone) Wholesale Accounting and Control, 1935; (with W.E. Dickerson) Drugstore Accounting, 1943; (with J.D. Wilson) Controllership, 1952; contbg. editor to Accts. Handbook, 1943, Cost Acttg. Handbook, 1944. Mem. Am. Inst. Accts., Nat. Assn. Cost Accts. (past nat. dir., pres. 1952-53), Beta Gamma Sigma, Beta Alpha Psi, Lambda Chi alpha. Home: 2451 Brixton Rd Columbus OH 43221

HEDAHL, GORDEN ORLIN, drama educator, director, actor; b. Minot, N.D., Jan. 2, 1946; s. Chester Owen and Delores May (Johnson) H.; m. Kathleen Josephine Sawin, Sept. 2, 1967 (div.); children: Marc Oscar, Melissa Ann; m. Jean Louise Loudon, Dec. 31, 1983. BS, U. N.D., 1968, MA in Theater and Media, 1972; postgrad., Northwestern U., 1972; PhD, U. Minn., 1980. Postdoctoral fellow Purdue U., West Lafayette, Ind., 1981-82; grad. teaching asst. U. N.D., Grand Forks, 1968-70; instr. dept. theater and dance and communication U. Wis., Whitewater, 1970—; drama and film cons. Summer Migrant Program, Burlington, Wis., 1972-73; grad. teaching assoc. U. Minn., Mpls., 1974-75; actor Ind. Repertory Theatre, Indpls., 1981-82; freelance dir., actor, child drama and filmmaking cons. Author: (plays) Tall Tales and True, 1976, The Brothers Grimm, 1977, Land of the Rising Sun, 1979, Trolls and Other Fjord Folk, 1983, Andersen's Storybook, 1986, The Magic of Oz, 1987; editor: Technical Theatre Course Guide—K to 12, 1983, The Making of a Musical-Videotape, 1983, Wisconsin Theatre Course Guide, 1987. Gov. Gt. Lakes Region Children's Theatre Assn., 1977-78, 80-81, Community of Christ the Servant, 1980-81; bd. govs. Wis. Alliance for Arts Edn., 1985—. Recipient Outstanding New Dir. award Children's Theatre Assn. Am., 1977, Outstanding Educator award Whitewater Regional jaycees, 1980; U. Wis. Faculty Devel. grantee, 1981-82, Undergrad. Teaching Improvement grantee, 1982-83. Mem. Am. Assn. of Theatre for Youth, Assn. for Theatre in Higher Edn., Wis. Theatre Assn. (bd. govs. 1977-81, 82-86), Internat. Assn. Theatre for Children and Youth, Speech Communication Assn. Lutheran. Office: Univ Wisconsin Dept Theatre and Dance Whitewater WI 53190

HEDBERG, DALE TERRY, nurse anesthetist; b. Chgo., July 6, 1942; s. Arthur John and Gretchen (Gray) H.; m. Connie Duke, June 5, 1962 (div.); children: Dale C., Jeffrey D.; m. Patricia Ann James, Oct. 5, 1977; children: Dana A., Nathan C. BS in Nursing, No. Ill. U., 1970; Diploma in Anesthesia, Rush U., 1972; MA in Physiology, U. S.D., 1974. Registered nurse, Ill., Iowa; cert. registered nurse anesthetist, Ill., Iowa. Chief anesthetist, bus. mgr. Ottumwa (Iowa) Anesthesia Assocs., 1979-80; pvt. practice in anesthesia Hedberg Anesthesia Assocs., Ottumwa, 1980-83, Salem, Ill., 1983-84, Carlyle, Ill., 1984-85, Breese, Ill., 1985—; instr. various health related programs and assns. Com. mem. Boy Scouts Am., Trenton, Ill., 1986. Served with U.S. Army, 1961-69. Named Eagle Scout with palm Boy Scouts

Am., 1957. Mem. Am. Assn. Nurse Anesthetists (cert. Profl. Excellence 1978), Am. Psychotherapy Assn. (diplomate 1981—), Ill. Assn. Nurse Anesthetists, So. Ill. Anesthesia Assn. (sec. 1984—), Assn. to Advance Ethical Hypnosis. Republican. Clubs: Brown U. Exec., Nat. Assn. Unknown Players (Calif.). Avocations: tennis, bowling. Home and Office: Hedberg Anesthesia Assocs 195 N 7th Box 230 Breese IL 62230

HEDBERG, PAUL CLIFFORD, broadcasting executive; b. Cokato, Minn., May 28, 1939; s. Clifford L. and Florence (Erenberg) H.; m. Juliet Ann Schubert, Dec. 30, 1962; children: Mark, Ann. Student, Hamline U., 1959-60, U. Minn., 1960-62. Program dir. Sta. KRIB, Mason City, Iowa, 1957-58, Sta. WMIN, Mpls., 1959; staff announcer Time-Life broadcast Sta. WTCN-AM-TV, Mpls., 1959-61, Crowell Collier broadcast Sta. KDWB, St. Paul, 1961-62; founder, pres. Sta. KBEW Radio Blue Earth, Minn., 1963-81, Sta. KQAD and KLQL-FM, LuVerne, Minn., 1971; pres. stas. KMRS-AM and KKOK-FM, Morris, Minn., 1971—; founder, pres. Blue Earth Cablevision, Inc., 1973-82, Courtney Clifford Inc. (advt. rep.), Mpls., 1977-79; founder, owner Market Quoters Inc., Blue Earth, 1974—; founder, pres. Complete Commodity Options Inc., Blue Earth, 1977—; pres., owner Sta. KEEZ-FM, Mankato, Minn., 1977—; founder The Motion Graphics Group, 1983; founder, pres. Sta. KUOO-FM, Spirit Lake, Iowa, 1984—; owner Stas. KLSS and KLSS-FM, Mason City, Iowa, 1984—; mem. Minn. News Council, 1978-84. Bd. dirs. Minn. Good Roads, v.p., 1976-79, pres., 1979-81; bd. dirs. Blue Blue Earth Indsl. Service Corp., pres., 1970-76; dir. Spirit Lake Industries. Mem. Iowa Gt. Lakes Airport Commn., 1985—. Served with USCGR, 1962-70. Recipient Disting. Service award Blue Earth Jaycees, 1971. Mem. Minn. A.P. Broadcasters (pres. 1966, bd. dirs. 1976-78), Blue Earth C. of C. (Leadership Recognition award 1967, pres. 1967), Nat. Assn. Broadcasters (bd. dirs. 1985—) Minn. Assn. Broadcasters (radio bd. dirs. 1975-86 , v.p. 1980-81, pres. 1983-84), Iowa Gt. Lakes C. of C. (bd. dirs. 1985—). Lutheran. Clubs: Mason, Shriner, Kiwanis. Home: W Okoboji Rural Route Box 9379 Spirit Lake IA 51360 Office: KUOO Radio Bldg Hwy 9 W Spirit Lake IA 51360

HEDDEN, RUSSELL ALFRED, manufacturing company executive; b. Kearny, N.J., May 1, 1918; s. George Arthur and Anna (Meyer) H.; m. Dorothy Williams, June 15, 1939; children: Russell Alfred, Susanne, Linda Jean , Nancy Ellen, Richard Earl. B.S. in Mech. Engring., Newark Coll. Engring., 1941; postgrad., Gen. Motors Inst., 1939-40, NYU, 1944-45. Research asso. Nat. Indsl. Conf. Bd., N.Y.C., 1946-48; asst. to pres., budget dir. Carrier Corp., Syracuse, N.Y., 1948-51; controller, dir. mfg. S. Morgan Smith Corp., York, Pa., 1951-59; work mgr. Allis Chalmers Mfg. Co., West Allis, Wis., 1959-62; with Bendix Corp., 1962-72; pres. indsl. group Bendix Corp., Southfield, Mich., 1970-72; pres., chief operating officer Kearney & Trecker Corp., 1972-73, pres., chief exec. officer, from 1973, also dir.; pres., chief exec. officer Cross & Trecker Corp., from 1978, now chmn. bd.; dir. Marine Exchange Bank, Milw. Bd. regents Milw. Sch. Engring. Mem. Financial Execs. Inst., Nat. Machine Tool Builders Assn. (dir. 1970-72, chmn. 1978-79), Allied Products Inst. (trustee council technol. advancement). Republican. Episcopalian (vestryman, sr. warden). Clubs: Quayl Creek Country, Oakland Hills Country. Office: Cross & Trecker Corp 505 N Woodward Ave Bloomfield Hills MI 48013

HEDGCOCK, WILLIAM ROBERT, superintendent schools; b. Paris, Ill., Sept. 3, 1928; s. John Harrison and Virginia (McCaskill) H.; m. Naomi Ruth Harner, May 10, 1953; children—David, Ronald, Todd. B.S., U. Ill., 1951, M.Ed., 1952; postgrad. Ill. State U., 1967-70. Tchr. Rantoul High Sch., Ill., 1959-67; prin. Wapella High Sch., Ill., 1967-82; supt. Wapella Unit Dist., 1982—. Scoutmaster Arrowhead council Boy Scouts Am., 1951-52, 55-67; dir. Clinton Barbershop Chorus, Ill., 1969-78; choir dir. Clinton Presbyterian Ch., 1978—; bd. dirs. DeWitt County Red Cross Bd., Clinton, 1983—. Recipient 20 Yr. Scouter Key award Boy Scouts Am., 1966. Mem. Nat. Assn. Secondary Sch. Prins., Ill. Prins. Assn., Ill. Assn. Sch. Adminstrs. Republican. Presbyterian. Clubs: Soc. for Preservation and Encouragement of Barbershop Quartet Singing in Am. (Urbana, Clinton) (pres. 1962—), Gideons Internat. (Clinton) (sec. 1983—). Lodges: Masons (worshipful master 1956—). Served to cpl. U.S. Army, 1952-54. Avocations: barbershop quartet singing.

HEDGE, CYNTHIA ANN, lawyer; b. LaPorte, Ind., June 7, 1952; d. John S. and Edith Rae (Badkey) H. A.B., Ind. U., 1975; J.D., Valparaiso U., 1978. Bar: Ind. 1978, U.S. Dist Ct. (no. dist., so. dist.) Ind. 1978. Staff writer Ind. Dept. Commerce, Indpls., 1975; pub. relations asst. Ravinia Festival, Chgo., 1976; free-lance writer, LaPorte County, Ind., 1978—; dep. pros. atty. LaPorte County, 1978—; sole practice, Michigan City, Ind., 1978—; dir. Michiana Industries, LaPorte County. Chairperson, Child Abuse Adv. Team, LaPorte County, 1982—; bd. dirs., chairperson Parents and Friends of the Handicapped, Inc., 1986—; mem. bd. Bethany Lutheran Ch., LaPorte, 1982—, United Way, Michigan City, 1987—. Mem. ABA, Ind. Bar Assn., LaPorte County Bar Assn., Michigan City Bar Assn., Christian Legal Soc., Ind. U. Alumni Assn., AAUW, Michigan City C. of C. Home: 2912 N Regal Dr LaPorte IN 46350 Office: 601 Franklin Sq Michigan City IN 46360

HEDGES, MARK STEPHEN, clinical psychologist; b. Chgo., Feb. 15, 1950; s. Norman T. and Doris Mae (Walters) H.; B.S., Purdue U., 1972; M.A., U. S.D., 1974, Ph.D., 1977; m. Janice Finnie, Aug. 16, 1975; children—Anna, Miriam. Psychology intern Western Mo. Mental Health Center, Kansas City, 1975-76; dir. children and adolescent services, psychologist Northeastern Mental Health Center, Aberdeen, S.D., 1977—. Mem. exec. bd. New Beginning Center, 1978—. Mem. Am. Psychol. Assn., Phi Beta Kappa, Psi Chi, Phi Kappa Phi. Methodist. Club: Cosmopolitan. Office: Northeastern Mental Health Center 703 3d Ave SE Aberdeen SD 57401

HEDLAND, ROBERT WILFRED, marketing executive; b. Youngstown, Ohio, June 23, 1928; s. Rohdy Wilfred and Margaret (Hackett) H. BS in Edn., Youngstown State U., 1950; BS in Bus., Ohio State U., 1951; postgrad., Harvard U., 1971. Mgr. mktg. U.S. Steel, Cleve., 1953-58; v.p. mktg. The Wooster (Ohio) Brush Co., 1958—. Served to lt. (j.g.) USN, 1951-53. Home: 3165 Country Club Dr Medina OH 44691 Office: The Wooster Brush Co 604 Madison Ave Wooster OH 44691

HEDQUIST, JEFFREY PAUL, producer; b. Hartford, Conn., Apr. 25, 1945; s. Ernest Carl and Edna May (Stoeke) H.; m. Linda Anne Duris, June 12, 1976. BS in Psychology, Union Coll., 1967. Acct. exec. WNHC Radio-Triangle Publs., New Haven, 1968-70; exec. v.p., ptnr. Sound Concepts, Inc., Woodbridge, Conn., 1968-84; pres., owner Hedquist Prodns., Inc., Fairfield, Iowa, 1985—. Writer, producer radio commls. (Clio award 1974, 76-79, 87, Internat. Broadcasting award 1974, 77, 86-87, Retail Advt. Conf. award 1974, 78, 81, 83, 86-87, Addy award 1971-75, 78, 86). Devel. adv. council Maharishi Internat. U., Fairfield, 1987. Recipient Andy award Advt. Club of N.Y., 1974, 78, 80, 83, Francis W. Hatch award Advt. Club of Boston, 1972, 74. Mem. Assn. Multi-Image Internat. (Ami award 1982), Nat. Retail Mchts. Assn. (First award 1974, 77), AFTRA, Screen Actors Guild, Fairfield C. of C. Avocations: playing guitar and banjo, restoring 75 acre prairie, collecting sounds. Home: 1007 E Madison Fairfield IA 52556

HEDRICH, WILLIAM CLIFFORD, photographer; b. Chgo., June 21, 1912; s. Theodore Louis and Anna Sophia (Knudsen) H.; m. Te'a Dora Kre'mer, June 3, 1942; children—Ronald Ted, Paul Scott, Sandi Ann. Student, U. Ill., 1930-31, Inst. Design, Chgo., 1945-46, U.S. Army Motion Picture Sch., London, 1943. Partner Hedrich-Blessing Studio, Chgo., 1931-46; chmn. bd. Hedrich-Blessing Ltd., Chgo., 1946—; also dir. Hedrich-Blessing Ltd.; owner Hedrich Island Homes, St. Maarten, N.A., 1970—; dir. Oyster Pond Devel. Corp., St. Maarten, N.A. Photographer architecture and interiors, 1931—; one-man show The Gallery, Chgo., 1987; group shows with, Hedrich-Blessing, Mich. Sq. Rotunda, Chgo., 1935, Offices Perkins & Will, Chgo., 1967, Archtl. Photographers Am. exhibits, 1946-62, AIA Exhibit, 1978-79; also represented in permanent collections; photographs include Falling Water, a widely pub. archtl. photograph. Bd. dirs. Golden Sect. Soc., Boy Scouts Am., 1922-25. Served with U.S. Army, 1942-45. Decorated Bronze Star; recipient Gold medal award AIA, 1967, Archtl. Photographers Invitational award Pitts. Plate Glass, 1973, Spl. Disting. Profl. award Chgo. Design Market, also other awards; named to Photography Hall of Fame Santa Barbara, Calif., 1978. Mem. Profl. Photographers Am., Chgo. Photog. Guild. Lutheran. Club: South End Gun (Granville, Ill.). Office: 11 W Illinois St Chicago IL 60610

HEDRICK, FRANK EDGAR, aircraft company executive; b. Paola, Kans., June 20, 1910; s. Melvin Earl and Hulda Catherine (Mellor) H.; m. Harriet Elizabeth Miller, Sept. 17, 1949; D.B.A. (hons.), Southwestern Coll., 1975. Sales mgr. E.S. Cowie Electric Co., Wichita, Kans., 1935-40; sales mgr. Beech Aircraft Corp., Wichita, 1940-60, asst. to gen. mgr., 1940-45, v.p., coordinator, 1945-60, exec. v.p., 1960-68, pres., 1968-81, vice chmn. bd., chmn. exec. com., 1981-82, dir., chmn. fin. com. and bus. cons., 1982-83, dir. Beech Aircraft and chmn. fin. com., 1983—; dir., mem. fin. com. Raytheon Co.; pres. Hedrick Investments, Inc., 1982—. Mem. Gov.'s Task Force on Effective Mgmt., 1976; pres. Beech Aircraft Found. Named Gen. Aviation Man of Yr., 1976; recipient Golden Plate award Am. Acad. Achievement, 1976; Disting. Donor award Kans. Ind. Coll. Fund, 1982. Mem. Conquistadores del Cielo. Republican. Clubs: Crestview, Wichita Country; Burning Tree (Washington); Garden of Gods (Colorado Springs, Colo.); Cherry Hills Country (Denver).

HEDRICK, GEARY DEAN, small business owner; b. Wytheville, Va., Feb. 9, 1940; s. James Luther and Alma June (Webb) H.; m. Priscilla Ann Moore, Dec. 27, 1958; children: Geary Dean Jr., Darla Ann, Darren Keith. BA in Econs., Wofford Coll., 1975. Enlisted U.S. Army, 1960, advanced through ranks to sgt. major, 1978, ret., 1982; pres. Hedrick Gen. Maintenance/Contracting, Inc., Libertyville, Ill., 1982—. Del. Civic Ctr. Found. Libertyville, Inc., 1986—. Decorated Purple Heart, Bronze Star, DSM, Air medal; Cross of Gallantry with palm Rep. of Vietnam. Lodge: Lions (various offices 1984—). Avocations: hunting, fishing, swimming, weightlifting, football. Home and Office: 553A W Park Ave Libertyville IL 60048

HEDRICK, ROBERT ERNST, director human resources; b. Sherman, Tex., July 25, 1947; s. Ray Shields and Ernestine Bollinger H.; m. Caroline Lemley, Aug. 10, 1968; children: Sarah, Katherine. BA in Bus. and Econs., Wofford Coll., 1969; MBA, U. N.C., Greensboro, 1982. Personnel mgr. Beaunit Corp., S.C. and N.C., 1973-77; personnel mgr. Hanes Hosiery, Winston-Salem, N.C., 1977, mgr. compensation and benefits, 1978-80, dir. personnel services, 1980-82; dir. human resources Fuller Brush Co., Great Bend, Kans., 1983—. V.p. Kans. Employer Coalition on Health, Topeka, 1985, bd. dirs. 1985-86. Served to capt. U.S. Army, 1969-73, Vietnam. Mem. Am. Assn. Personnel Adminstrs., Community Hosp. Assn. Presbyterian. Club: Cen. Kans. Investment (Great Falls) (pres. 1986—). Home: 2924 Broadway Great Bend KS 67530 Office: Fuller Brush Co Westport Addition Great Bend KS 67530

HEEB, CAMILLE STOREY, physician, educator; b. Brookfield, Mo., May 26, 1944; d. Kenneth Paul and Virginia May (Bailey) Storey; children: Marsha, Sarah. BA with honors in Sociology, U. Kans., 1966, MS in Spl. Edn., 1967, MD, 1979. Corrective reading tchr., Chandler, Ariz., 1968-69; ednl. diagnostician Dept. Spl. Edn., Abilene, Tex., 1970-72; staff mem. dept. spl. edn. U. Kans., Lawrence, 1974-76, sponsor student chpt. Council for Exceptional Children; intern and pediatric resident U. Kans. Med. Ctr., 1979-81; pediatric resident Children's Mercy Hosp., Kansas City, Mo., 1981-82; staff physician Kans. Neurol. Inst., Topeka, 1982-84; pvt. practice, Topeka, Kans., 1984—; staff physician Stormont Vail Hosp., Topeka, St. Francis Hosp.; chmn. dept. pediatrics Meml. Hosp. Author: An Oral Language Development Program for the Educable Mentally Retarded, 1969. U.S. Office Edn./Bur. Handicapped fellow in spl. edn., 1966-67; U. Buffalo research grantee, 1968; recipient Daniel C. Darrow award, Paul Gyorgy award La Leche League. Mem. Council for Exceptional Children, Am. Assn. for Edn. Severely and Prodoundly Handicapped, PEO, AMA, Am. Acad. Pediatrics, Phi Beta Phi. Home: 3120 W 15th St Topeka KS 66604

HEEREMA, JAMES GARRIT, bank executive; b. Chgo., Aug. 12, 1955; s. John Jacob and Genevieve Laverne (VanSwol) H. BS in Bus. and Acctg., Eastern Ill. U., 1977. CPA, Ill. Acct. Peat, Marwick, Mitchell, Chgo., 1977-80; v.p., controller South Holland (Ill.) Trust & Savs. Bank, 1980-85, v.p., chief fin. officer, 1985—. Treas., bd. dirs. Am. Cancer Soc., South Holland, 1981-86. Mem. Ill. Soc. CPA's. Republican. Avocations: skiing, golf, tennis, softball. Office: South Holland Trust & Savs Bank 16178 South Park Ave South Holland IL 60473

HEERMANS, THOMAS WILLISON, industrial designer, design consultant; b. Milw., Apr. 24, 1926; s. Thomas Minton and Vera Rose (Baxter) H.; m. Elizabeth Hobson, June 24, 1950; children—Jill Marie, Thomas Minton, Jody Lynn, Janice Ann, Joy Elizabeth. B.S. in Design, U. Mich., 1961. Project engr. Argus Cameras, Inc., Ann Arbor, Mich., 1952-62; design engr. Hamilton Beach, Racine, Wis., 1962-64; mgr. product planning Ekco Housewares Co., Franklin Park, Ill., 1964-67; dir. indsl. design Regal Ware, Inc., Kewaskum, Wis., 1967—. Patentee in field. Served with USN, 1944-46. Mem. Color Mktg. Group (chairholder 1977—), Soc. Glass Decorators, Assn. Home Appliance Mfrs. (portable appliance engring. com. 1972—). Republican. Episcopalian. Avocations: fresh water aquarist, audiophile, photographer. Home: 258 Lincoln Dr S West Bend WI 53095 Office: Regal Ware Inc 1675 Reigle Dr Kewaskum WI 53040

HEEZEN, JAY ALLEN, veterinarian, farmer; b. Plankinton, S.D., May 23, 1944; s. Arie Merle and Jesse Evelyn (Harman) H.; m. Darlene E. Bloch, Aug. 29, 1970 (div. Dec. 1979); children—Jon, Jason; m. 2d, Phyllis Kay DeBoer, Jan. 13, 1981; children—Jay, Julie, Jennifer. B.S., U. Minn., 1966, D.V.M., 1968. Veterinarian, Vietnam, 1969-70; pvt. practice veterinary medicine, Plankinton, 1970—. Chmn. Plankinton Sch. Bd. Served to capt. U.S. Army, 1968-70. Bd. dirs. Plankinton Pub. Sch., 1982—. Mem. AVMA, S.D. Vet. Med. Assn., U.S. Assn. Sheep and Goat Practioners, VFW. Democrat. Methodist (tchr. Sunday sch.).

HEFFERN, GORDON EMORY, banker; b. Utica, Pa., Feb. 19, 1924; s. Claude E. and Lillian A (McKay) H.; m. Neva Lepley, Sept. 19, 1946; children: Mary Heffern Maddex, John, Robert, Richard. Student, Stevens Inst. Tech., 1944, U. Va., 1949. Asst. to pres., security analyst Peoples Nat. Bank of Charlottesville, Va., 1949-51; v.p. Nat. City Bank of Cleve., 1951-62, First Nat. City Bank of Alliance, Ohio, 1962-63; pres., chief exec. officer Goodyear Bank, Akron, 1963-74; pres., dir. Society Nat. Bank, Cleve., 1974-85, chmn., 1985—; pres., chief exec. officer, dir. Society Corp., Cleve., 1975—. Bd. dirs., chmn. fin. com. Mt. Union Coll.; mem. exec. bd., pres. Greater Cleve. council Boy Scouts Am.; bd. dirs. Univs. Hosps., Cleve., Bill Glass Evangelistic Assn.; mem. exec. com., treas. Downtown Cleve. Corp.; mem. session Fairmount Presbyterian Ch.; trustee John Carroll U. Served with USNR, 1942-46. Mem. Assn. Res. City Bankers, Bluecoats, Inc. (asst. treas.), Musical Arts Assn., Am. Def. Preparedness Assn., Univ. Circle. Republican. Clubs: Akron City, The Country, Pepper Pike, Portage Country, Union, Canterbury Golf; 50 (Cleve.). Home: 22450 Canterbury Ln Shaker Heights OH 44122 Office: Society Corp 127 Public Square Cleveland OH 44144 *

HEFFERNAN, JAMES HOWARD, pharmaceutical company executive; b. New Brunswick, N.J., Jan. 14, 1935; s. James Howard and Anne (Dougherty) H.; m. Margaret Theresa Stobitizer, Jan. 17, 1959; children: Margaret Anne Richards, James H. III, Michael, Daniel, Catherine. BS in Econs., Villanova U., 1956; MBA in Mgmt., Seton Hall U., 1966. Cert. purchasing mgr. Supr. N.J. Aluminum Extrusion Co., New Brunswick, 1958-59; buyer Western Electric Co., N.Y.C., 1959-67; sr. purchasing agt. Merck and Co., Inc., Rahway, N.J., 1967-74; mgr. field procurement Air Products and Chems. Inc., Allentown, Pa., 1974-83; dir. purchasing Marion Labs. Inc., Kansas City, Mo., 1983—. Candidate North Brunswick (N.J.) Mcpl. Com., 1972. Mem. Nat. Assn. Purchasing Mgrs. (chmn. chem. group 1982-84, Recognition award 1984), Pharm. Mfrs. Assn., Drug, Chem. and Allied Trades, Kansas City Purchasing Mgmt. Assn., Villanova U. Alumni Assn. (pres. New Brunswick chpt. 1959-74, pres. Allentown chpt. 1983). Lodge: Elks. Avocations: golf, skiing. Home: 11700 W 108B St Overland Park KS 66210 Office: Marion Labs Inc PO Box 9627 Kansas City MO 64134

HEFFERNAN, NATHAN STEWART, chief justice Wisconsin Supreme Court; b. Frederic, Wis., Aug. 6, 1920; s. Jesse Eugene and Pearl Eva (Kaump) H.; m. Dorothy Hillemann, Apr. 27, 1946; children: Katie (Mrs. Howard Thoms), Michael, Thomas. B.A., U. Wis., 1942, LL.B., 1948; student, Harvard U., 1943-44. Bar: Wis. 1948. Assoc. firm Schubring, Ryan, Peterson & Sutherland, Madison, Wis., 1948-49; practice in Sheboygan, Wis., 1949-59; partner firm Buchen & Heffernan, 1951-59; counsel Wis. League Municipalities, 1949; research asst. to gov. Wis., 1949; asst. dist. atty. Sheboygan County, 1951-53; city atty. City of Sheboygan, 1953-59; dep. atty. gen. State of Wis., 1959-62; U.S. atty. Western Dist. Wis., 1962-64; justice Wis. Supreme Ct., 1964—, chief justice, 1983—; lectr. mepl. corps., 1961-64; lectr. appellate procedure and practice U. Wis. Law Sch., 1971—; faculty Appellate Judges Seminar, NYU, 1972—; former mem. Nat. Council State Ct. Reps., chmn., 1976-77; office dir. Nat. Center State Cts., 1976-77, mem. adv. bd. appellate justice project; former mem. Wis. Jud. Planning Com.; chmn. Wis. Appellate Practice and Procedure Com., 1975-76; mem. exec. com. Wis. Jud. Conf., 1978—, chmn., 1983; pres. City Attys. Assn., 1958-59. Wis. chmn. NCCJ, 1966-67; past exec. bd. Four Lakes Council Boy Scouts Am.; gen. chmn. Wis. Democratic Conv., 1960, 61; mem. Wis. Found.; bd. visitors U. Wis. Law Sch., 1970-83, chmn., 1973-76; past mem. corp. bd. Meth. Hosp.; curator Wis. Hist. Soc.; trustee Wis. Meml. Union, Wis. State Library; trustee William Freeman Vilas Trust Estate. Served to lt. (s.g.) USNR, 1942-46; ETO, PTO. Recipient distinguished service award NCCJ, 1968. Fellow Am. Bar Found. ; mem. Am. Law Inst., Inst. Jud. Adminstrn. (mem. faculty seminar), ABA (past mem. spl. com. on adminstrn. criminal justice, mem. com. fed.-state delineation of jurisdiction, jud. adminstrn. com. on appellate ct., com. appellate time standards), Wis. Bar Assn., Dane County Bar Assn., Sheboygan County Bar Assn., Am. Judicature Soc. (dir. 1977-80, chmn. program com. 1979-81), Wis. Law Alumni Assn. (bd. dirs.), Nat. Conf. Chief Justices (bd. dirs.), Order of Coif, Iron Cross, Phi Kappa Phi, Phi Delta Phi. Congregationalist (former deacon). Clubs: Madison Lit. (pres. 1979-80); Harvard (Milw.), Harvard Bus. Sch. Home: 17 Thorstein Veblen Pl Madison WI 53705 Office: State Capitol Madison WI 53702

HEFFNER, SUZANNE ELIZABETH, public relations executive; b. Chgo., Nov. 17, 1941; d. Henry Edward and Lillian Elizabeth (Ferguson) H.; children—Robin E. Hackenbruch, Michelle D. Hackenbruch. Student Upsala Coll., 1959-63. Editorial assoc. Griswold-Eshleman, Cleve., 1963-65; v.p. Press Relations, Glen Ellyn, Ill., 1974-80; mktg. dir. Crawford Savs., Chgo., 1980-82; pub. relations dir. Pathway Fin., Chgo., 1982-85, corp. communications mgr., Fed. Res. Bank Chgo., 1985—; Mem. Wheaton-Warrenville High Sch. Parent Adv. Com., 1980-83; chmn. nominating com. Dist. 200 Sch. Bd., 1987—. Recipient Eagle award and certs. of excellence Chgo. Fin. Advertisers, 1979, cert. of excellence, 1982; Advt. award Savs. Instns. of Am., 1982. Home: 2S723 Winchester Circle Warrenville IL 60555 Office: 100 N State St Chicago IL 60602

HEFLER, WILLIAM LOUIS, elementary educator; b. New Albany, Ind.; s. Louis C. and Elizabeth (Grimes) H.; children: Sarah Elizabeth, Matthew Joseph. BS in Elem. Edn., Ind. U., 1980, MS in Elem. Edn., 1983. Tchr. 5th grade Washington Elem. Sch., Pekin, Ind., 1980—, chmn. various coms. Deacon Cen. Christian Ch., 1984-86; coach 5th grade soccer, softball, track, E. Washington Elem. Sch., 1981-84, coach 7th grade basketball 1981-85; state reviewer textbooks in math., sci., health, 1984-86. Named one of Outstanding Men Am., 1983, 85, Outstanding History Tchr. in Washington County, DAR, 1984. Mem. NEA, Nat. Sci. Tchrs. Assn., Nat. Council Tchrs. English, Nat. Council Social Studies, Ind. State Tchrs. Assn. (local pres. 1981-85, ins. trustee 1982-85, bd. dirs. 1986, chmn. various coms., del. various confs.), Ind. Council Tchrs. Math., Ind. Council Social Studies, Ind. Basketball Coaches Assn., Hoosier Assn. Sci. Tchrs., E. Washington Tchrs. Assn., Tau Kappa Epsilon, Phi Delta Kappa, Pi Lambda Theta, Kappa Delta Pi. Democrat. Home: 6673 Eagle Point Dr N Indianapolis IN 46254 Office: E Washington Elem Sch Rural Rt #2 Box E4 Perkin IN 47165

HEFLIN, LELAND EARL, bearing mfr.; b. Bolckow, Mo., Jan. 4, 1946; s. William Earl and Cleta Marie (Stuart) H.; student N.W. Mo. State U., 1963-65; B.S. in Bus. Adminstrn., U. Mo., Columbia, 1968, M.A. in Acctg., 1971; m. Barbara Sue Gilbert, May 19, 1968; children—Mark Alan, Matthew Lee. Supervisory acct. Peat, Marwick, Mitchell & Co., Richmond, Va., and Indpls., 1971-76; controller Park 100 Devel. Co., Indpls., 1976-77; v.p., treas. Waldemar Industries, Inc., Indpls., 1977—, also pres., dir. Terrecorp, Indpls., 1980—; former mem. faculty U. Richmond, Va. Commonwealth U., Butler U. Served with USMC, 1968-69. Mem. Am. Inst. C.P.A.s, Am. Mgmt. Assn., Soc. Mfg. Engrs. Club: Indpls. Sailing. Republican. Methodist. Home: 6265 N Chester Ave Indianapolis IN 46220 Office: 5455 W 86th St Indianapolis IN 46268

HEFNER, CHRISTIE A., publishing/entertainment company executive; b. Chgo., Nov. 8, 1952; d. Hugh Marston and Mildred Marie (Williams) H.; B.A. summa cum laude in English and Am. Lit., Brandeis U., 1974. Free lance journalist, Boston, 1974-75; spl. asst. to pres. Playboy Enterprises, Inc., Chgo., 1975-78, v.p., 1978-82, bd. dirs., 1979—, voce chmn., 1986—, pres., 1982—, chief operating officer, 1984 ; bd. dirs. Playboy Found.-Playboy Enterprises, Inc., Ill. chpt. ACLU. Recipient Agnes Underwood award Los Angeles chapter Women in Communications, 1984, Founders award Midwest Women's Ctr., 1986, Hunan Rights award Am. Jewish Com., 1987. Mem. Brandeis Nat. Women's Com. (life); mem. Com. of 200, Young. Pres. Orgn., Chgo. Network (bd. dirs), Mag. Pubs. Assn., Voters for Choice (editorial bd.), Am. Politics, Direct Mktg. Assn., Nat. Women's Polit. Caucus, Goodman Theatre, Phi Beta Kappa. Democrat. Office: Playboy Enterprises Inc 919 N Michigan Ave Chicago IL 60611

HEFNER, ELROY M., state legislator; b. Coleridge, Nebr., Dec. 12, 1923; grad. high sch.; m. Carol Rae Wilms, June 12, 1949; children—William, Douglas, Cynthia. Pres., part owner Hefner Oil & Feed Co.; mem. Nebr. Legislature, 1976, 80—. Former Mem. Coleridge Sch. Bd.; former mayor, Coleridge; former mem. Coleridge Fire Dept. Mem. Am. Legion, Nebr. Petroleum Marketers, VFW. Club: Coleridge Comml. (past pres.). Home: Box 36 Coleridge NE 68727

HEFNER, PHILIP JAMES, theologian; b. Denver, Dec. 10, 1932; s. Theodore Godfred and Elizabeth Helen (Mittelstadt) H.; m. Neva Lamae White, May 25, 1956; children: Sarah Elizabeth, Martha White, Julia Margaret, Rebecca Mittelstadt. BA, Midland Luth. Coll., 1954, LHD, 1982; BD, Chgo. Luth. Theol. Sem., 1959; MA, U. Chgo., 1961, PhD, 1962. Assoc. prof. systematic theology Hamma Div. Sch., Springfield, Ohio, 1962-64; prof. systematic theology Luth. Theol. Sem., Gettysburg, Pa., 1964-67; prof. systematic theology Luth. Sch. Theology, Chgo., 1967—, dir. grad. studies, 1979—; vis. prof. Japan Luth. Theol. Coll. and Sem., Tokyo, 1982. Author: Faith and the Vitalities of History, 1966, Promise of Teilhard, 1970; coauthor Defining America, Christian Dogmatics; assoc.-editor: Zygon: Jour. of Religion and Sci., 1980—, Dialog: A Theol. Jour., 1982—; contbr. numerous articles to profl. jours. Fulbright scholar U. Tuebingen, 1954-55; Rockefeller Found. Doctoral fellow, 1960-62, fellow Ctr. for Theol. and Natural Scis., 1985; recipient Franklin Fry award for Scholarship Luth. Brotherhood, 1977-78, Susan Colver Rosenberg award U. Chgo., 1963. Fellow Inst. on Religion in an Age of Sci. (pres. 1979-81, 84-87), Ctr. for Advanced Study in Religion and Sci. (grantee 1985), Soc. for Values in Higher Edn.; mem. Am. Acad. Religion (chmn. cons. on theology and sci. 1986-88), Internat. Luth./Reformed Dialogue, Luth. World Fedn., Geneva. Office: Luth Sch Theology at Chgo 1100 E 55th St Chicago IL 60615-5199

HEFTER, FREDRIC MYERS, social worker; b. Kankakee, Ill., May 1, 1928; s. Fred Charles and Daisy S. (Myers) H.; m. Martha K. McCorkle, June 13, 1966 (div. Feb. 1976); children: Fredric Morgan, Megan Alicia. BA, U. Ill., 1950, MSW, 1952. Cert. social worker. Community residence social worker VA Med. Ctr., Marion, Ind., 1961-69; asst. dir. Oscar Feigert Mental Health Ctr., Van Wert, Ohio, 1969-73; exec. dir. counseling service Family Counselors Services, Muncie, Ind., 1973-80; community care social worker VA Med. Ctr., Ft. Wayne, Ind., 1980-84, in-patient social worker, 1984-85; nursing home social worker VA Med. Ctr., Ft. Wayne, INd., 1985—. Coordinator G/L Help Line, Ft. Wayne, 1983—; treas. Up the Stairs Community Ctr., Ft. Wayne, 1985—, also bd. dirs. Mem. Nat. Assn. Social Workers, Nat. Conf. of Social Welfare. Jewish. Lodge: B'nai Brith. Home: 2730 Glenwood Ave Fort Wayne IN 40805 Office: VA Med Ctr 1600 Randall A Dr Fort Wayne IN 46805

HEGARTY, MARY FRANCES, lawyer; b. Chgo., Dec. 19, 1950; d. James E. and Frances M. (King) H. B.A., DePaul U., 1972, J.D., 1975. Bar: Ill. 1975, U.S. Dist. Ct. (no. dist.) Ill. 1976, U.S. Supreme Ct. 1980. Ptnr. Lannon & Hegarty, Park Ridge, Ill., 1975-80; sole practice, Park Ridge, 1980—; dir. Legal Assistance Found. Chgo., 1983—. Mem. revenue study com. Chgo. City Council Fin. Com., 1983; mem. Sole Source Rev. Panel, City of Chgo., 1984; pres. Hist. Pullman Found., Inc., 1984-85. Mem. Ill. State Bar Assn. (real estate council 1980-84), Chgo. Bar Assn., Women's Bar Assn. Ill. (pres. 1983-84), NW Suburban Bar Assn., Park Ridge Women Entrepreneurs. Democrat. Roman Catholic. Club: Chgo. Athletic Assn. Office: 301 W Touhy Park Ridge IL 60068

HEGEDUSICH, WILLIAM, military officer; b. Youngstown, Ohio, June 12, 1960; s. William Vincent and Cecilia Elizabeth (Blazo) H.; m. Susan Marie Zeh, May 26, 1984. AA, U. Md., 1983, BS, 1984. Commd. USAF, 1984, advanced through grades to 1st lt., 1986, computer operator, 1978-82; electronic warfare officer USAF, Minot AFB, N.D., 1984—; computer operator Capital Systems, Washington, 1984. Asst. scoutmaster Boy Scouts Am., Camp Springs, Md., 1978-82. Named Eagle Scout Boy Scouts Am., 1978; recipient Vigil Honor Boy Scouts Am., 1978. Mem. Armed Forces Communication and Electronic Assn. (award 1983, 84), Assn. Old Crows (Super Crow award 1986). Republican. Roman Catholic. Avocations: stamp collecting, computers, hiking, camping. Home: 101-2 Avion Way Minot AFB ND 58704 Office: 23 BMS Minot AFB ND 58705

HEGEMAN, GEORGE DOWNING, microbiology educator; b. Glen Cove, N.Y., Aug. 31, 1938; s. George Downing and Bonnie (Blair) H.; m. Sally Lorraine Lofgren, Aug. 26, 1961; children: Susan Elizabeth, Adrian Daniel. AB, Harvard U., 1960; PhD, U. Calif., Berkeley, 1965. Instr. bacteriology and immunology U. Calif., Berkeley, 1965, asst. prof. bacteriology, 1966-72; assoc. prof. microbiology Ind. U., Bloomington, 1972-79, prof. microbiology, 1979—; mem. sci. adv. bd. BioTrol, Inc., Mpls., 1985—. Patentee in field; contbr. articles to profl. jours.; mem. editorial review bd. Applied & Enivronmental Microbiology, 1984—. Mem. Community Market bd., Bloomington County, Ind., 1985—. USPHS fellow, 1962-66; grantee USPHS, NSF. Fellow Am. Acad. Microbilogy; mem. AAAS, Am. Soc. Microbiology, Am. Soc. Biol. Chemists, Forest Resources Assn. (past pres., v.p.). Avocations: beekeeping, forest resource activities. Office: Ind U Biology Dept Bloomington IN 47405

HEGEMIER, JUNE FRIEDA, special education director, school psychologist; b. New Bremen, Ohio, Oct. 3, 1934; d. Leroy Edward and Goldie Hirschfeld; m. Eugene E. Hegemier, July 16, 1955; children: David, Jonathan, Elizabeth. BA, WAshington U., 1956; MEd, U. Toledo, 1973. Lic. sch. psychologist, Ohio. Sch. psychologist Ottawa County Bd. Edn., Oak Harbor, Ohio, 1973-80; dir. spl. edn. Benton Carroll Salem Schs., Oak Harbor, 1980—; lic. sch. psychologist Giving Tree, Oak Harbor, 1982—; counselor, cons. Giving Tree, Oak Harbor, 1982—; trainer Hospice, Ottawa County, 1985—. Tchr. Sunday sch. United Ch. of Christ, Oak Harbor, 1955—; YWCA (bd. dirs. 1970-73). Mem. Nat. Assn. Sch. Psychologists, Ohio Sch. Psychologists Assn., Maumeem Valley Sch. Psychologists Assn., Ohi Assn. Pupil Personnel Adminstrs., Delta Kappa Gamma. Avocations: traveling, bicycling, boating, swimming.

HEGSTROM, GARY CLIFFORD, music educator; b. New Ulm, Minn., July 23, 1946; s. Clifford Waldemar and Velma Lucille (Emswiler) H.; m. Debra S. Schmidt, Aug. 7, 1983; 1 child, Jeffrey. BA in Music Edn. and Psychology, Luther Coll., Decorah, Iowa, 1968. Music educator Newark (Ill.) Schs., 1968-69, 71-74, Lake Mills (Wis.) Schs., 1974—; instr. brass instruments Conservatory of Music, San Antonio, 1970; prin. French hornist San Antonio Civic Orch., 1970; clinician French horn High Sch. Music Festivals, Chgo. area, 1971-74; adjudicator music festivals, Lake Mills, 1977—; French hornist Brass Ensemble, San Antonio, 1969-71. Specialist French horn U.S. Army Band, San Antonio, 1969-71. Served with U.S. Army, 1969-71. Home: W 8228 Sunset Ct Lake Mills WI 53551

HEGY, JEROME LEONARD, financial manufacturing executive; b. Hartford, Wis., Nov. 8, 1945; s. Philip Matthew and Irene Barbara (Kapler) H.; m. Janice Kathleen Moran, June 19, 1971; children: Brett, Chad, Nicole. BBA, St. Norbert Coll., 1967; postgrad., Marquette U., 1969-70; MBA, U. Wis., 1976. CPA, Wis. Staff acct. Am. Can Co., Milw., 1967-68; audit supr. Alexander Grant & Co., Milw., 1968-72; acctg. supr. Borg Textiles div. Bunker Ramo Corp., Milw., 1972-73; dir. fin. Cummins Wis. Inc., Milw., 1973-83; v.p. fin. DMT Corp., Waukesha, Wis., 1983-86; treas. Bostrom Seating Corp., Milw., 1986—. Mem. Wis. Inst. CPA's, Nat. Assn. Accts. (bd. dirs. 1985-86), Am. Inst. CPA's. Roman Catholic. Home: 21025 Heatherview Dr Waukesha WI 53186 Office: Bostrom Seating Corp 3326 E Layton Ave PO Box 600 Cudahy WI 53110

HEGYES, KENNETH FRANCIS, chemical company executive; b. Columbus, Ohio, Nov. 8, 1942; s. Frank Andrew and Elsie Adelaide (Saunders) H.; m. Betsy Ann Bryan, May 28, 1966; children: Laura, Bryan. BA, Rutgers U., 1965; MBA, Case Western Res. U., 1974. Mktg. mgr. health care div. Avery Internat., Painesville, Ohio, 1976-80, bus. mgr. diaper tape, 1978-80, bus. mgr. fabricator, 1980-86, bus. mgr. automotive, 1984-86; new bus. mgr. automotive Avery Internat., Detroit, 1986—; bd. dirs. Capital Tool Co., Cleve., H&M Realty, Cleve. Clubs: Rockwell Springs (Castalia, Ohio); Playhouse, Print (trustee 1984—) (Cleve.). Avocations: fishing, children's sports. Home: 22599 Byron Shaker Heights OH 44122

HEGYI, DOUGLAS FRANK, otorhinolaryngologist, plastic surgeon; b. Aurora, Ill., Mar. 13, 1945; s. Frank Julius and Grace Irene (Dziewior) H.; children: Justin Douglas, Jeffrey Douglas. Diploma Chgo. City Coll., 1968; BS in Psychology, Ill. Inst. Tech., 1971; DO, Chgo. Coll. Osteo. Medicine, 1976. Diplomate Nat. Bd. Examiners. Intern, Mt. Clemens Gen. Hosp., Mich., 1976-77; resident in otorhinolaryngology and oro-facial plastic surgery, Pontiac Osteo. Hosp., Mich., 1977-80; staff physician, treas. dept. opthalmology and otorhinolaryngology, 1980—, mem. teaching staff, 1980—; staff physician, sect. chief otorhinolaryngology Lapeer Gen. Hosp., Mich., 1980—, Caro Community Hosp., Mich., 1986—, Crittenton Hosp., Mich., 1986—; cons. staff Almont Community Hosp., Mich., asst. clin. prof. otorhinolaryngology Mich. State U., Coll. Osteo. Medicine, 1980—. Recipient Appreciation cert. Am. Cancer Soc., 1976; Named one of Hon. Order Ky. Col., 1987. Fellow Am. Acad. Otolaryngology, Skin Cancer Found. (hon.), Mich. Assn. Osteo. Physicians and Surgeons, Am. Acad. Cosmetic Surgery (assoc.), Osteo. Coll. Opthalmology and Otorhinolaryngology; mem. Atlas Club (life, cert. for Outstanding Service and Dedication 1976), Chgo. Coll. Osteo. Medicine Alumni Assn., Am. Osteo. Assn., Osteo. Coll. Ophthalmology and Otorhinolaryngology, Oakland County Osteo. Assn., Lapeer County Osteo. Assn., Am. Acad. Facial Plastic and Reconstructive Surgery. Roman Catholic. Lodges: Masons, Order of DeMolay. Office: 210 W Tienken Rochester MI 48064

HEH, GEORGE J., machine manufacturing executive; b. N.Y.C., Sept. 30, 1937; s. George C. and Georgia L. (Underreiner) H.; m. Carolyn Paige DeWitt, June 13, 1959; children: Rebecca Ann Heh Lindsay, George T. BA in Chemistry, U. Louisville, 1958, MBA, 1966. Mgr. materials Brunswick Corp., Lincoln, Nebr., 1968-73; plant mgr. Nordson Corp., Anderson, S.C., 1973-82; v.p. O&M Mfg. Corp., Houston, 1982-84; gen. mgr. Murray Turbomachinery Corp., Burlington, Iowa, 1984—; mem. adv. bd. Anderson Coll., 1981-82. Contbr. article to tech. jours.; patentee in field. Mem. Am. Chem. Soc., Am. Mgmt. Assn., Burlington C. of C. (chmn.). Republican. Roman Catholic. Lodge: Rotary. Home: 2609 Sunrise Ln Burlington IA 52601 Office: Murray Turbomachinery Corp 1101 Washington Ave Burlington IA 52601

HEIBERG, ELISABETH, radiology educator; b. Oslo, May 12, 1945; came to U.S., 1973; d. Erik Lyng and Gerd Augusta (Ursin-Holm) H.; m. J. David Malone, Mar. 25, 1970 (div.); children: Janina, Jonathan. Baccalaureat, Hartvig-Nissen, Oslo, 1964; MD, Royal Coll. Surgeons and Physicians, Dublin, Ireland, 1970. Diplomate Am. Bd. Radiology. Intern in surgery Jervis St. Hosp., Dublin, 1970-71; resident in medicine Nottingham (Eng.) City Hosp., 1971; resident in radiology Washington U., St. Louis, 1975-79; asst. prof. radiology St. Louis U. Hosp., 1979-85, assoc. prof., 1985—. Contbr. articles to profl. jours. Mem. Univ. City Symphony Orch., St. Louis, 1986—. Mem. AAUP, Am. Assn. Women Radiologists, Greater St. Louis Radiol. Soc., Am. Univ. Radiologists, Radiol. Soc. N.Am., Norwegian Soc. (sec. 1983-86, organizer singin group 1983-86). Avocations: violin, skiing, wind surfing, sci. fiction, volleyball. Home: 6959 Waterman Ave University City Saint Louis MO 63130 Office: St Louis U Hosp 1325 S Grand Saint Louis MO 63104

HEIDE, RICHARD THOMAS, lawyer; b. Lafayette, Ind., Feb. 2, 1931; s. Richard Jacob and Virginia Louise (Wells) H.; m. Evelyn Mae Thomas, Jan. 25, 1958; 1 son, Richard Wayne. B.S., Purdue U., 1957; L.L.B., Ind. U., 1960. Bar: Ind. 1961. Sole practice, Lafayette, Ind., 1962-72; ptnr. Heide & Gambs, Lafayette, 1972-74, Heide Gambs & Mucker, Lafayette, 1974-85, Heide Sandy Deets & Kennedy, Lafayette, 1985—. Chmn. Tippecanoe Democratic Central Com. Served with USN, 1951-55. Mem. ABA, Tippecanoe Bar Assn. (pres. 1986-87), 7th Circuit Bar Assn., Ind. Bar Assn. Mem. United Ch. of Christ. Clubs: Country (Lafayette), Grotto, Uptowners, Old Hickory. Lodges: Masons, Elks, Eagles, Moose.

HEIDEL, CHARLES MACLEISH, electric company executive; b. Detroit, July 19, 1925; s. Charles Richard and Anna Laura (MacLeish) H.; m. Barbara Cele, Aug. 7, 1948; children: Kerry, Kathy Heidel Okla, Kenneth, Keith, Karol. B.S. in Mech. Engring, Iowa State U., 1947. Registered profl. engr., Mich. With Detroit Edison Co., 1947—, mgr. engring., 1970-71, mgr. ops., 1971-73, v.p. engring. and constrn., 1973-75, exec. v.p. divs., 1975-77, exec. v.p. ops., 1977-81, pres., chief operating officer, 1981—; dir. 1st Fed. Savs. & Loan. Bd. dirs. Children's Hosp. Served in USNR, 1943-46. Mem. ASME, Engring. Soc. Detroit, Soc. Am. Mil. Engrs., Edison Electric Inst. Clubs: Detroit Athletic (Detroit), Econ. (Detroit). Office: Detroit Edison Co 2000 2nd Ave Detroit MI 48226 *

HEIDELBERG, HELEN SUSAN HATVANI, dentist; b. Greenville, Pa., July 30, 1957; d. Balazs Robert and Ilona Borbala (Nemeth) Hatvani; m. David Raymond Heidelberg, June 4, 1983; 1 child, David William. AA, Cuyahoga Community Coll., Parma, Ohio, 1977; BS in Biology magna cum laude, Cleve. State U., 1979; DDS, Case Western Reserve U., 1983. Resident in dentistry North Chicago (Ill.) VA Med. Hosp., 1983-84; assoc. dentist Steven D. Miller, DDS, Vernon Hills, Ill., 1984-85; gen. practice dentistry Norwalk, Ohio, 1986—. Mem. ADA, Ohio Dental Assn., N. Cen. Ohio Dental Soc., Great Lakes Dental Soc. (v.p. 1984), Norwalk C. of C. Avocations: jogging, canoeing, ceramics, gardening, needlecrafts. Home: 1945 Sleepy Hollow Rd Milan OH 44846 Office: Fisher-Titus Med Pk 266 Benedict Ave Norwalk OH 44857

HEIDENRICH, JOHN LOUIS, consulting firm executive; b. Freeport, Ill., Aug. 14, 1945. BS in Physics and Math, Western Ill. U., 1967. Evaluation lab. engr. micro-switch div. Honeywell, Freeport, 1968-69; sr. technician Hills McCanna Co., Carpentersville, Ill., 1970-72; asst. supr. engring. lab. Hills McCanna Co., Carpentersville, 1972-74, quality control engr., 1974-75, mgr. quality assurance/quality control, 1975-80, dir. quality assurance, 1980; v.p. N.C. Kist & Assocs., Inc., Naperville, Ill., 1980—. Home: 1136 Indian Dr Elgin IL 60120 Office: NC Kist & Assocs Inc 127-A S Washington St Naperville IL 60540

HEIDERSBACH, JOHN AUSTIN, marketing executive; b. Elmhurst, Ill., Nov. 6, 1942; s. Robert Henry and Dorothy (Duntemann) H.; m. Patricia Louise Yax, July 26, 1967 (div. Aug. 1974); children: Amy L., Ann M.; m. Ellen Kay Bakken, June 10, 1983; stepchildren: Kristofer K. Moffit, Matthew R. Moffit. BBA, U. Denver, 1970. Copywriter Valentine-Radford, Inc., Kansas City, Mo., 1972-73; account exec. Christenson, Barclay, Shaw, Kansas City, 1973-75; ptnr. Hedlund & Assocs., Mission, Kans., 1975-80; copy chief Gloria Aleff & Assocs., Waverly, Iowa, 1980-83; creative dir. Warren Anderson Advt., Davenport, Iowa, 1983-84; mktg. dir. Oster Communications, Cedar Falls, Iowa, 1984—. Stamp illustrator, Iowa Duck Stamp Design, Iowa Habitat Stamp Design, 1987. Vol. dir. Greater Kansas City March of Dimes, 1979-80, Cedar Valley chpt. March of Dimes, Waterloo, Iowa, 1981-83; bd. dirs. Cedar Valley Wetlands Found., Cedar Falls, Iowa, 1987. Served as sgt. U.S. Army, 1962-65. Mem. N.E. Iowa Mktg./Advt. Club. Avocations: wildlife and Western art, writing. Home: 319 Balboa Ave Cedar Falls IA 50613

HEIDRICK, GARDNER WILSON, management consultant; b. Clarion, Pa., Oct. 7, 1911; s. R. Emmet and Helen (Wilson) H.; m. Marian Eileen Lindsay, Feb. 19, 1937; children: Gardner Wilson, Robert L. B.S. in Banking and Fin, U. Ill., 1935. Indsl. dist. sales mgr. Scott Paper Co., Phila., 1935-42; dir. personnel Farmland Industries, Kansas City, Mo., 1942-51; assoc. Booz, Allen & Hamilton, Chgo., 1951-53; co-founder partner, chmn. Heidrick & Struggles, Inc., Chgo., 1953-82; co-founder, chmn. Heidrick Ptnrs., Inc., Chgo., 1982—; dir. Internat. Exec. Service Corp., Keller-Taylor Corp. Bd. dirs. U. Ill. Found.; bd. dirs. Keller Grad. Sch. Mgmt. Served with USNR, 1945-46. Recipient Pres.'s award U. Ill. Found., 1979. Mem. U. Ill. Alumni Assn. (past pres., Achievement award 1980), Phi Kappa Sigma. Clubs: Chicago (Chgo.), Tower (Chgo.); Hinsdale (Ill.) Golf (past pres.); University (N.Y.); Little Club (Gulfstream, Fla.); Country of Fla. (Delray Beach), Ocean (Delray Beach). Office: Heidrick Ptnrs Inc 20 N Wacker Dr Chicago IL 60606

HEIDT, JAMES ROBERT, retail company executive; b. Detroit, Feb. 20, 1951; s. George Leonard Heidt and Eleanore Jane (Madison) Sharpe; m. Christine Ann Smith, Sept. 11, 1976; children: Joshua James, Cody Rachel. Asst. mgr. nursery Youngs Nursery, Oak Park, Mich., 1965-67; mgr. warehouse Nat. Pet Supply, Ferndale, Mich., 1967-69; v.p., gen. mgr. Able Office Products, Ferndale, 1972—. Served with USAF, 1969-72, PTO. Lutheran. Avocations: running, woodworking, computers. Office: Able Office Products 1100 Woodward Heights Ferndale MI 48220

HEIGAARD, WILLIAM STEVEN, state senator, lawyer; b. Gardar, N.D. May 18, 1938; s. Oliver and Laufey (Erickson) H.; m. Paula Geston, 1960; children—Jody, Rebecca, Sara. B.A., U. N.D., 1961, J.D., 1967. Bar: N.D. 1967. Asst. atty. gen., Bismarck, N.D., 1967-68; state's atty., Cavalier County, N.D., 1970-75; mem. N.D. Ho. of Reps., 1980-81, N.D. State Senate, 1981—, majority leader. Served to 1st lt. U.S. Army, 1962-64. Mem. Am. Legion, Phi Delta Phi. Democrat. Lutheran. Lodges: Eagles, Elks. Office: PO Box 151 Langdon ND 58249

HEIGHWAY, JAMES EDWARD, electronics manufacturing executive; b. Chgo., Jan. 21, 1946; m. Oliver H. and Vivian M. (Wise) H.; m. Ellen Ann Komada, June 1, 1967; children: Jennifer Ann, Vivian Jean. BS, Elmhurst Coll., 1968; postgrad. bus. adminstrn., Case Western Res. U., 1985—. Sales mgr. Speedex Electronics, Rockford, Ill., 1967-69; dir. mktg. G.C. Electronics Co., Rockford, 1969-81; pres., chief exec. officer Mueller Electric Co., Cleve., 1981—; bd. dirs. Horizon Industries, Rockton, Ill., Mueller Electric, Cleve., Lawrence Corp., Chardon. Mem. Am. Mgmt. Assn., Am. Mktg. Assn., Pres. Assn., Electronic Industry Assn. (bd. dirs. 1984—). Republican. Roman Catholic. Avocation: horse breeding. Office: Mueller Electric Co 1583 E 31st St Cleveland OH 44114

HEILBRUNN, ROBERT E., steel company executive; b. Rochester, N.Y., Nov. 26, 1926; s. Robert J. and Madeleine (Stiefel) H.; m. Eleanor Beecher Wendt, Aug. 8, 1952; children: Susan, John, Ann. BA, U. Rochester, 1947. Asst. v.p. Buffalo Steel Corp., Tonawanda, N.Y., 1958-68; v.p. Copco Steel and Engring., Detroit, 1968-72, Allied Rochester Corp., 1972-77; gen. mgr. Dayton (Ohio) Fabricated Steel Co., 1977-83; pres. Abington Steel Corp., Dayton, 1983—, also bd. dirs.; bd. dirs. Miamisburg Machine Co. Pres. City Beautiful Commn., Dayton, 1983—, Easter Seal Soc., Dayton, 1984-85; chmn. River Festival, Dayton, 1981, Opera Gala, Dayton, 1983. Recipient Community Service award City of Dayton, 1984-85, Mayor's Econ. Devel. award City of Dayton, 1982. Republican. Unitarian. Clubs: Engrs., Miami Valley (Dayton). Home: 141 Squirrel Rd Dayton OH 45405 Office: Abington Steel Corp 6971 Brookville Salem Rd Brookville OH 45309

HEILER, JAMES LEE, dentist, horse breeder; b. Milan, Ohio, July 16, 1926; s. Leo Conrad and Madeline Marie (White) H.; m. Sharlene Linda Field, Apr. 18, 1953; children: Linda, Sherry, Marla, Jay, Robert. BA, Ohio State U., 1950, DDS, 1953. Gen. practice dentistry Cheviot, Ohio, 1953-55, Kenwood, Ohio, 1956-79, Milan, 1981—. Editor thoroughbred newsletter, 1982-84. Served with USN, 1945-46. Named to Ky. Colonel State of Ky., 1966. Mem. ADA, Ohio State Dental Assn., Internat. Assn. Anesthesiologists (charter). Avocation: flying. Home: 2918 Valley Ln Sandusky OH 44870 Office: 45 E Front Milan OH 44846

HEIMAN, MARVIN STEWART, financial services company executive; b. Chgo., Sept. 16, 1945; s. Samuel J. and Mildred (Miller) H.; m. Adrienne Joy Nathan, Aug. 7, 1966; children: Scott, Michelle, Adam. Student, Roosevelt U., 1963-67. Pres. Curtom Record Co., Chgo., 1969-80, Gold Coast Entertainment, Chgo., 1980-82; ptnr. Profl. Real Estate Securities Co., Lincolnwood, Ill., 1982-86; pres., chmn. bd. Sussex Fin. Group, Inc., Skokie, Ill., 1986; bd. dirs. Drovers Bank, Chgo.; ptnr. Cole Taylor Banks, Chgo., 1984—, bank examining com., 1986—; ptnr. Chgo. White Sox Am. League Baseball Club, 1981—. Mem. Rep. Nat. Com., 1980—. Mem. Internat. Assn. Fin. Planners, Real Estate Securities Syndication Assn. Am., Nat. Assn. Securities Dealers (registered rep.), Am. Jewish Com. (Humanitarian award 1978). Avocations: baseball, tennis, music. Office: Sussex Fin Group Inc 5215 Old Orchard Rd Skokie IL 60077

HEIMBURGER, RICHARD AMES, plastic and reconstructive surgeon; b. St. Louis, Jan. 17, 1936; s. Leroy Frances and Margaret Coleman (Smith) H.; m. Elizabeth Morgan, Dec. 23, 1964 (div. June 1979); children: Margaret, Richard Jr., Katherine; m. Mary Catherin Immegart, June 11, 1983. AB, Drury Coll., 1958; MD, Vanderbilt U., 1961. Diplomate Am. Bd. Plastic Surgery. Resident in plastic surgery U. Tex. Med. Br., Galveston, 1969-72; assoc. prof., chief plastic surgery U. Mo., Columbia, 1973-77; chief plastic surgery VA Hosp., Columbia, 1973-77; practice medicine specializing in plastic and reconstructive surgery Columbia, 1977—; assoc. clin. prof. dept. surgery St. Louis U. Med. Ctr., 1986—; staff Boone Hosp., Columbia, 1977—, St. Mary's Hosp., Jefferson City, 1977—; cons. Mo. Dept. Corrections, Jefferson City, 1977-84. Producer, dir. (movie) Burn Care of Hand, 1973, Hand Injury and Rehab., 1977. Dist. med. dir. Mo. div. Am. Cancer Soc., 1983—, bd. dirs. 1983—; mem. Mo. Govs. Com. Employing Handicapped, Jefferson City, 1977-82. Served to capt. USAF, 1964-66. Decorated Bronze Star. Fellow ACS; mem. Am. Assn. Hand Surgery (com. chmn. 1976-87), Am. Soc. Plastic and Reconstructive Surgery (edn. found. com. chmn.), So. Med. Assn. (chmn. plastic surgery 1981-82), Mo. State Med. Assn. (del. 1981-87). Lodge: Rotary (com. chmn.). Avocations: tennis, swimming, travel. Office: 1504 E Broadway Columbia MO 31444-9050

HEIMERICKS, GARY W., state official; b. Jefferson City, Mo., Feb. 17, 1951; d. Robert E. and Frances Ann (Rackers) H.; m. Belinda Kay Heimericks, May 26, 1973; children—Gary Christopher, Kimberly Kay. B.S., Lincoln U., 1973; M.S., U. Mo.-Columbia, 1977. Fiscal grants specialist Div. Planning and Budget, Mo. Dept. Social Services, Jefferson City, 1975-78, adminstrv. officer, 1978-81, dir. fin., 1981-85; dep. dir. Mo. Div. Med. Services, 1985-86; dir. mgmt. services Mo. Dept. Nat. Resources, 1986—; mgmt. cons. U. Mo., 1981. Coordinator blood drive ARC, Holts Summit, 1979-84; pres. North Sch. PTO, 1986. Mem. Am. Soc. Public Adminstrn. Roman Catholic. Lodge: Lions (sec. 1980-81). Home: RR 2 Box 27 Holts Summit MO 65043 Office: Dept Natural Resources PO Box 176 Jefferson City MO 65102

HEINE, CAROL JANE, optometrist; b. Terre Haute, Ind., July 11, 1953; d. Joseph Anthony and Betty Lee (Broussard) H. BS in Optometry, Ind. U., 1974, OD, 1978. Practice optometry specializing in contact lenses Terre Haute, 1978—; cons. Ind. U., Bloomington, 1979-80. Bd. dirs. Assn. Retarded Citizens, Terre Haute, 1982-83. Named one of the Outstanding Young Women of Am., 1978. Mem. Am. Optometric Assn. (Optometric Recognition award 1983-85), Ind. Optometric Assn. (dir. pub. info. 1986—, dir. dept. edn. 1981—), Western Ind. Optometric Soc. (sec. 1980-82, pres. 1982-84), Altrusa (bd. dirs. 1981-83, internat. relations chmn. 1985-86), Bus. and Profl. Women (Young Careerist award 1982), Terre Haute C. of C. (bd. dirs.), Ind. U. Optometry Alumni Assn. (pres. 1983), Gamma Phi Beta Alumni Assn. (rush advisor 1983—). Home: 2740 Thomas Ave Terre Haute IN 47805 Office: 2740 S 7th St Terre Haute IN 47802

HEINE, JAMES B., financial executive; b. Yankton, S.D., Apr. 8, 1956; s. Henry F. and Mary L. (Burbach) H.; m. Debra J. Burdick, Apr. 26, 1986. BA, Mt. Marty Coll., 1978; M in Bus. Tax, U. Minn., 1982; MBA, U. S.D., 1987. CPA, S.D. Staff auditor McGladrey Hendrickson & Pullen, Sioux Falls, S.D., 1978-80; sr. tax cons. Mpls., 1981-84; chief fin. officer Billion Cos., Sioux Falls, 1984—; sec. loan com. Farmers State Bank, Viborg, S.D., 1985—. Mem. Am. Inst. CPA's. Roman Catholic. Office: Billion Cos 3015 S Minnesota Ave Sioux Falls SD 57105

HEINE, RAYMOND ARNOLD CARL, bishop; b. Fort Wayne, Ind., May 28, 1922; s. William Frederick and Clara Margaretta (Gerberding) H.; m. Flora Margaretta Miller, Aug. 25, 1945; children—Ward William, Marian Ruth. A.B., Wittenberg U., 1943, D.D. (hon.), 1969; M.Div., Hamma Div. Sch., Springfield, Ohio, 1945. Pastor Whitestown-New Augusta Parish, Ind., 1945-47; asst. pastor Trinity Lutheran Ch., Fort Wayne, 1947-51; pastor Trinity Lutheran Ch., Grand Rapids, Mich., 1963-80, Christ Luth. Ch., Monroe, Mich., 1951-63; bishop Mich. Synod, Luth. Ch. in Am., Detroit, 1980—, mem. exec.bd., 1968-78, sec., 1974-78, dean dist. 2, 1970-80, mem. cons. com. on stewardship, 1982—. Trustee Carthage Coll., Kenosha, Wis., Luth. Sch. Theology, Chgo., bd. dirs. Luth. Social Services Mich., Detroit. Recipient merit award Suomi Coll., Hancock, Mich., 1982. Avocations: sailing; golf; reading. Home: 16030 Riverside Livonia MI 48154 Office: Luth Ch in Am Mich Synod 19711 Greenfield Rd Detroit MI 48235

HEINEMAN, BEN WALTER, corporation executive; b. Wausau, Wis., Feb. 10, 1914; s. Walter Ben and Elsie Brunswick (Deutsch) H.; m. Natalie Goldstein, Apr. 17, 1935; children: Martha Heineman Pieper, Ben Walter. Student, U. Mich., 1930-33; LL.B., Northwestern U., 1936; LL.D. (hon.), Lawrence Coll., 1959, Lake Forest Coll., 1966, Northwestern U., 1967; LHD, DePaul U., 1986. Bar: Ill. 1936. Pvt. practice law and govt. service Chgo., Washington, Algiers, 1936-56; chmn. bd. dirs. Four Wheel Drive Auto Co., 1954-57; founder, chmn. Farley/Northwest Industries, Inc., (formerly Northwest Industries), 1968-85; chmn. C. & N.W. Ry. Co., 1956-72; dir., chmn. exec. com., bd. dirs. 1st Nat. Bank, Chgo.; chmn. orgn. com. First Chgo. Corp., 1965-86; Chmn. White House Conf. to Fulfill These Rights, 1966, Pres.'s Task Force on Govt. Orgn., 1966-67, Pres.'s Commn. Income Maintenance Programs, 1967-69. Life trustee U. Chgo.; chmn. Ill. Bd. Higher Edn., 1962-69; trustee, mem. investment com. Savs. and Profit Sharing Fund of Sears Roebuck Employees, 1966-71; vis. com. dept. econs. Harvard, 1965-71; trustee, mem. exec. com., chmn. audit com. Rockefeller Found., 1972-78; bd. dirs. Lyric Opera, Chgo.; life trustee Orchestral Assn.; sustaining fellow Art Inst. Chgo. Fellow Am. Bar Found. (life), Am. Bar Assn., Am. Acad. Arts and Scis.; mem. Am. Law Inst. (life), Ill., Chgo. bar assns., Order of Coif, Phi Delta Phi (hon.). Clubs: Ephraim (Wis.) Yacht; Mid-America (Chgo.), Chicago (Chgo.), Casino (Chgo.), Commonwealth (Chgo.), Wayfarers (Chgo.), Economic (Chgo.), Standard (Chgo.), Quadrangle (Chgo.), Executives (Chgo.), Commercial (Chgo.), Chicago Yacht (Chgo.); Metropolitan, Carlton. Office: 9400 Sears Tower Chicago IL 60606

HEINEMANN, CHARLES ALAN, health care consultant, educator; b. Mpls., June 8, 1941; s. Elvin Frederick and Marguerite Florence (Witte) H.; m. Barbara Joann Perso, Nov. 6, 1965; 1 child, Andrew Charles. B.A., U. Minn., 1964, M. Hosp. Adminstrn., 1966. Adminstrv. resident St. Luke's Hosp., Milw., 1965-66; asst. adminstr., Union Hosp., Lynn, Mass., 1966-69; cons. Hamilton/KSA (formerly Hamilton Assocs.), Mpls., 1969-71, dir. systems and equipment planning, 1971—, prin., 1980—; mem. adv. group U.S. Dept. Health & Human Services, Washington, 1983; adj. instr. U. Minn., Mpls., 1969—; lectr. U. Wis., Eau Claire, 1979—. Author (unit lesson) Facility Development for Independent Study Program Hosp. Adminstrs., U. Minn., 1971—. Co-chmn. Greater Lynn Mental Health Assn., Mass., 1967-69; cubmaster Viking Council Boy Scouts Am., Mpls., 1982-83. Mem. Am. Hosp. Assn., Am. Coll. Hosp. Adminstrs.; fellow Am. Assn. Healthcare Cons. (cert., bd. dirs. 1983—, chmn. bd. dirs. 1986—). Republican. Mem. Christian Ch. Avocations: travel; photography; boating; fishing. Office: Hamilton/KSA 2021 E Hennepin Suite 450 Minneapolis MN 55413

HEINEMANN, LESLIE JAMES, dentist; b. Brookins, S.D., Jan. 5, 1955; s. Ralph Peter and Mabel Ann (Dubbelde) H.; m. Lisbeth Ann Fromelt, June 5, 1976; children: Jason, Mark, Kimberly, Melissa. Student, S.D. State U., 1973-76; BA, Augustana Coll., 1976-77; DDS, Loyola U., 1981. Gen. practice dentistry Fla., 1981—; adj. prof. S.D. State U., Brookings, 1981—; dental cons. Am. Health Edn. Council, Sioux Falls, 1983-86, Riverview Manor, Flandreau, S.D., 1981—. Mem. ADA, So. Dist. S.D. Dental Assn., Flandreau Jaycees (v.p. 1982-83), Omicron Kappa Upsilon, Alpha Sigma Pi. Republican. Roman Catholic. Lodge: Kiwanis. Avocations: hunting, trapping, golfing, tennis, farming. Home: Rural Rt 1 Box 25 Flandreau SD 57028 Office: 406 W Pipestone Flandreau SD 57028

HEINEMANN, WILLIAM, architect; b. Milw., Mar. 13, 1946; s. Henry Jr. and Alice Helen (Pinkalski) H.; m. Patricia Ann Doyne, Mar. 19, 1946; children: Megan Kate, Ryan William. AS in Archtl. Tech., MATC, 1978. Registered architect, Wis.; registered profl. engr., Wis. Substation draftsman Wis. Electric, Milw., 1964-65, archtl. designer, 1968-75; constrn. supt. Milw. County, 1975-81, dir. facilities, 1981-83, dir. architecture, 1983—. Tech. advisor Milw. County Commn. on Handicapped and Disabled, 1978—; chmn. St. Seton Bldg. Com., New Berlin, Wis., 1980-84. Served with U.S. Army, 1965-67, Vietnam. Mem. AIA, Wis. Soc. Architects, Constrn. Specifications Inst., Am. Pub. Works Assn., Milw. Zool. Soc. Roman Catholic. Lodge: Eagles. Avocations: fishing, skiing, swimming. Home: 11323 W Holly Ln Greenfield WI 53228 Office: Dept Pub Works 907 N 10th St Milwaukee WI 53233

HEINICKE, JANET LOUISE, educator, artist; b. Richmond, Ind., June 11, 1930; d. Homer Stroud and Mary DeMaris (Way) Hart; m. Herbert Raymond Heinicke, June 15, 1955; children: Peter, John, Mary Elizabeth, Mark, Sarah. BS, Wittenberg U., 1952; MS, U. Wis., 1955; MFA, EdD in Edn. Adminstrn., No. Ill. U., 1977, No. Ill. U., 1977. Supr. elem. art Goshen (Ind.) Pub. Sch., 1952-54; tchr. art Shaker Heights (Ohio) Pub. Sch., 1954-55; asst. prof. art Judson Coll., Elgin, Ill., 1960-62, 69-74; program coordinator Kankakee (Ill.) Community Coll., 1977-82; chmn. fine arts div. Simpson Coll., Indianola, Iowa, 1982—; guest artist, lectr. SW Community Coll., Creston, Iowa, 1985; guest artist, critic Iowa Amateur Artists Assn., Chariton, Iowa, 1985. Dir. Judson Coll. Art Gallery, 1969-74, chmn. profl. affairs com., 1969-74; chmn. faculty growth and devel. com. Kankakee (Ill.) Community Coll., 1977-82, chmn. campus beutification com., 1977-79; chmn. womens network group, Simpson Coll., 1983—; chmn. bldg. and planning com. Redeemer Luth. Ch., Indianola, 1984-85, Indianola Fine Arts Commn., 1984-85; mem. adv. panel community devel. Iowa Arts Council, 1986-87. Named one of Outstanding Young Women in Am., 1965. Mem. AAUW (regional v.p. northeast cen. region 1977-79, chmn. nat. com. structural change, 1979-81, pres. Indianola br. 1984—, bd. dirs. Iowa div. 1986—), Art Edn. Assn., Chgo. Artists Coalition, Assn. for Curriculum and Supervision Coll. Art Assn., Delta Kappa Gamma, Pi Lambda Theta, Alpha Lambda Delta. Home: 1302 W Boston Ave Indianola IA 50125 Office: Simpson Coll 701 N C St Indianola IA 50125

HEINIG, RUTH MIRIAM, drama professor; b. Benton Harbor, Mich., May 8, 1936; d. Ancil Roy and Olga Ida (Reschke) Beall; m. Edward Jeramiah Heinig, Dec. 18, 1965. BA, Valparaiso U., 1959; MA, U. Pitts., 1962, prof., 1975. Instr. Mt. Mercy Coll., Pitts., 1961-64; from asst. prof. to prof. Western Mich. U., Kalamazoo, 1964—. Author: Creative Drama for the Classroom Teacher, 1974, 2d edit., 1981, Creative Drama Resource Books, 1987; editor Children's Theatre Rev., 1975-78. Mem. Children's Theatre Assn. Am. (past pres.), Am. Theatre Assn. (bd. dirs. 1983-85), Children's Theatre Found. (bd. dirs. 1978—). Democrat. Home: 1805 Chevy Chase Kalamazoo MI 49008 Office: Western Mich U Communication Dept Kalamazoo MI 49008

HEININGER, STEVEN THOMAS, systems analyst; b. Indpls., Aug. 2, 1951; s. Thomas Ardry and Martha Elizabeth (Price) H.; m. Carlotta Jean Hartman, Aug. 7, 1976. AAS in Computer Technology, Purdue U., 1972, BS in Computer Technology, 1977. Production control supr. Ind. U., Indpls., 1974-76; sr. programmer Amax Coal Co., Indpls., 1976-79; systems analyst Norris Food Service, Indpls., 1979-82, Wabash Valley Power, Indpls., 1982-84, Dataflow Systems Inc., Indpls., 1984—; cons. in field, Indpls., 1982; owner SC Online Systems, Indpls., 1984-85. Active in ch. youth work. Republican. Lutheran. Home: 5502 Wagon Wheel Trail Indianapolis IN 46237-2073

HEINO, GREGORY LEE, accountant; b. Superior, Wis., Sept. 16, 1957; s. Leon Richard and Ruth Beverly (Karna) H.; m. Linda Rosemarie Paschkowski, Oct. 6, 1984. BA in Acctg., U. Wis., Superior, 1977. CPA, Wis. Jr. auditor Cooperative Auditing Services, Inc., Mpls., 1979-80, sr. auditor, 1980-86; ptnr. Paul Julin & Co., Mpls., 1986—. Mem. Nat. Soc. Accts. for Cooperatives (also Gt. Lakes chpt.). Lutheran. Home: 2315 E College Ave Appleton WI 54915 Office: Paul Julin & Co 7301 Zane Ave N Minneapolis MN 55443

HEINTZELMAN, ROSS GARFIELD, state ofcl.; b. Greensburg, Pa., Jan. 2, 1917; s. Ross Garfield and Bertha Lee (Acklin) H.; B.S., Ohio State U., 1948, M.A., 1950; m. Margery Isabel Major, Mar. 17, 1945; children—Christian Lee, Diane Kay. Engr. Timken Co., Canton, Ohio, 1936-60, supr. evaluation systems, 1960-73; chief labor relations State Inter-govtl. Personnel Adminstrn., Columbus, 1973-74; adminstrv. staff asst. Indsl. Commn. Ohio, Columbus, 1974—; cons. personnel relations. Councilman, Canton, Ohio, 1957-69; mem. Ohio Ho. of Reps., 1969-72. Served with USAAF, 1943-46. Recipient awards Am. Econ. Found., Polit. Sci. Acad., Police Boys Club, YMCA, Ohio Ednl. Assn.; Canton Tchrs. Man of Year award 1972; Appreciation award Ednl. Community Northeastern Ohio; Canton City Schs. award; Ohio Dental Assn. award; Mayor's citation. Home: 206 Grandview Ave NW Canton OH 44708

HEINTZMAN, DAVID ROGER, social services administrator; b. Bismarck, N.D., Apr. 15, 1951; s. Dan J. and Clara M. (Yetter) H.; m. Mimi Kim, May 31, 1979; 1 child, Kathryn Jane. BS in Bacteriology and Chemistry, N.D. State U., 1973; BS in Med. Tech., George Washington U., 1977. Supr. lab. Community Hosp., Warren, Minn., 1974-75; supr. ARC, Omaha, 1981-86, asst. adminstrv. dir., 1986—. Loaned exec. United Way of the Midlands, Omaha, 1985-86. Served with USN, 1975-81. Mem. Am. Soc. Tng. and Devel., Am. Assn. Blood Banks, Iowa Assn. Blood Banks, Omaha Safety Council. Democrat. Office: ARC Blood Services 3838 Dewey Ave Omaha NE 68105

HEINZ, EDWARD N., JR., mfg. co. exec.; b. Chgo., Nov. 27, 1914; s. Edward N. and Adeline (Kelly) H.; B.S. in Chem. Engring., Ill. Inst. Tech., 1937; m. Laurette F. Higgins, Oct. 22, 1943; children—Edward, Raymond, James, Pamela, Laurette, Joan, Mary Jayne. Vice pres., dir. Food Materials Corp., Chgo., 1937-67; pres., dir. Bell Flavors and Fragrances, Inc., Northbrook, Ill., 1967—. Served with U.S. Army, 1943-46. Mem. Flavor and Extract Mfrs. Assn. U.S. (past pres.), Am. Assn. Candy Technologists (past pres.), Serra Club Chgo. (past pres.), Am. Chem. Soc., Inst. Food Technologists, Am. Assn. Cereal Chemists. Clubs: N. Shore Country (Glenview, Ill.); JDM Country (Palm Beach, Fla.). Home: 22 Meadowview Dr Winnetka IL 60093 Office: 500 Academy Dr Northbrook IL 60062

HEINZ, JOHN PETER, lawyer, educator; b. Carlinville, Ill., Aug. 6, 1936; s. William Henry and Margaret Louise (Denby) H.; m. Anne Murray, Jan. 14, 1967; children: Katherine Reynolds, Peter Lindley Murray. A.B., Washington U., St. Louis, 1958; LL.B., Yale U., 1962. Bar: D.C. 1962, Ill. 1966, U.S. Supreme Ct. 1967. Teaching asst. polit. sci. Washington U., St. Louis, 1958-59, instr., 1960; asst. prof. law Northwestern U. Sch. Law, Chgo., 1965-68, assoc. prof., 1968-71, prof., 1971—, prof. law and urban affairs, 1972—, dir. program law and social scis., 1968-70, dir. research, 1973-74; affiliated scholar Am. Bar Found., Chgo., 1974—, vis. scholar, 1975-76, exec. dir., 1982-86. Author: (with A. Gordon) Public Access to Information, (with E. Laumann) Chicago Lawyers; contbr. articles to profl. jours. Served to capt. USAF, 1962-65. Grantee NIMH, 1970-72, NSF, 1970, 78-81, 84-86, CNA Found., 1972, Am. Bar Found., 1974—, Russell Sage Found., 1978-80. Fellow Am. Bar Found.; mem. Law and Soc. Assn., Am. Polit. Sci. Assn., ABA. Home: 525 Judson Ave Evanston IL 60202 Office: Northwestern U Sch Law 357 E Chicago Ave Chicago IL 60611

HEIPLE, JAMES DEE, judge; b. Peoria, Ill., Sept. 13, 1933; s. Rae Crane and Harriet (Birkett) H.; B.S., Bradley U., 1955; J.D., U. Louisville, 1957; Certificate in Internat. Law, City of London Coll., 1967; grad. Nat. Coll. State Judiciary, 1971; m. Virginia Kerswill, July 28, 1956; children—Jeremy Hans, Jonathan James, Rachel Duffield. Bar: Ill. 1957, Ky. 1958, U.S. Supreme Ct. 1962; partner Heiple and Heiple, Pekin, Ill., 1957-70; circuit judge Ill., 10th Circuit 1970-80; justice Ill. Appellate Ct., 1980—, presiding justice, 1985—. Vice pres., dir. Washington State Bank (Ill.), 1959-66; dir. Gridley State Bank (Ill.), 1958-59; village atty., Tremont, Ill., 1961-66, Mackinaw, Ill., 1961-66; asst. pub. defender Tazewell County, 1967-70., legal clerk Ill. Appellate Ct., 1968-70. Chmn. Tazewell County Heart Fund, 1960. Pub. Adminstr. Tazewell County, Ill., 1959-61; sec. Tazewell County Republican Central Com. 1966-70; mem. Pekin Sch. Bd., 1970; mem. Ill. Supreme Ct. Com. on Profl. Responsibility, 1978—. Recipient certificate Freedoms Found., 1975, George Washington honor medal, 1976. Mem. Ky., Ill. (chmn. legal edn. com. 1972-74, chmn. jud. sect. 1976-77, chmn. Bench and Bar Council 1984-85), Tazewell County (pres. 1967-68) bar assns., Ill. Judges Assn. (pres. 1978-79), Ky., Ill., Pa. hist. socs., Nat. Rifle Assn., S.A.R., Delta Theta Phi, Sigma Nu, Pi Kappa Delta. Methodist. Clubs: Filson; Union League (Chgo.). Lodge: Masons. Office: 524 Court St Pekin IL 61554

HEISE, VIRGIL E., accountant; b. Mpls., 1923; s. Theodore and Emma Marie (Benz) H.; m. Mavis M. Tychsen, May 5, 1949; children: Sandra, Jolynn, Natalie, Rhonda. Student, Macalester Coll., 1941-42, U. Minn., 1944-45. CPA, Minn. Staff acct. Holloway Knutson & Bowers, Mpls., 1945-53, Fiegen & Fiegen, Mpls., 1953-55; pvt. practice acctg. Mpls., 1955-87; cons. Arnott, Nilsestuen and Assocs., Mpls., 1987—. Dean counselors Viking council Boy Scouts Am., 1965-66. Served with USN, 1944. Mem. Min. Soc. CPA's. Lutheran. Lodges: Kiwanis (sec. 1965), Elks. Home: 7007 Jersey Circle Minneapolis MN 55427

HEISELMAN, DARELL ETHAN, physician, cardiologist, internist; b. Holton, Kans., Apr. 5, 1953; s. Therll and Neva Joyce (Robinson) H.; m. Sandra Louise Schwemmer, May 25, 1974 (div. Aug. 1977); m. Arlene C. Corpuz, Oct. 12, 1978; 1 child, Cassandra Jaye. BS, Kans. State U., 1975; DO, Kans. City (Mo.) Coll. Osteo. Medicine, 1979. Diplomate Am. Bd. Internal Medicine, Am. Bd. Cardiology. Intern in internal medicine Akron (Ohio) Gen. Med. Ctr., 1979-80, resident in internal medicine, 1980-82, fellow in cardiology, 1982-84, chief of critical care medicine, 1984—; fellow in critical care medicine Univ. Health Ctr., Pitts., 1983; asst. prof. Northeastern Okla. U. Coll. Medicine, 1987—; adv. health exec. bd. Ohio Edison Co., Akron, 1982—; investigator U. Pitts., 1985—; cardiology staff Akron Gen. Med. Ctr., 1986—. Fellow Am. Coll. Angiology, Am. Coll. Chest Physicians (council critical care 1986—), Am. Coll. Cardiology; mem. AMA, Ohio State Med. Assn., Summit County Med. Soc., ACP, Am. Soc. Internal Medicine, Ohio Soc. Internal Medicine, Soc. Critical Care Medicine, Ohio Soc. Critical Care Medicine, Coll. Osteo. Medicine (life), Am. Assn. Med. Systems and Informatics, Found. Critical Care Medicine (founding), Am. Fedn. Clin. Research, Am. Heart Assn. (trustee Akron dist. chpt. 1986—). Democrat. Roman Catholic. Club: Northeastern Ohio Apple. Avocations: ham radio, cuisine cooking. Home: 2435 Sourek Rd Akron OH 44313 Office: Akron Gen Med Ctr 400 Wabash Ave Akron OH 44307

HEISER, WILLIAM JOSEPH, radiologist; b. Bismarck, N.D., May 25, 1937; s. Joseph Theodore and Leone Elizabeth (Hildenbrand) H.; m. Nina Remdenok, Apr. 25, 1964; children: Monica Anne, Joseph Brian. BA in Math. magna cum laude, U. N.D., 1959; MD, Northwestern U., 1963. Diplomate Am. Coll. Radiology, Am. Coll. Quality Assurance and Utilization Rev. Physicians. Intern Mpls. Gen. Hosp., 1964; resident in radiology Northwestern U., Evanston, Ill., 1967; radiologist Henrotin Hosp., Chgo., 1970-86, chmn. dept. radiology, 1985-86; mem. staff Humana Hosp. Springfield (Ill.), 1987—, Carlinville (Ill.) Area Hosp., 1987—, Magnetic Resonance Ctr. Springfield, 1987—; physician cons. Rep. Health Care Rev. Services, Inc., Naperville, Ill., 1974—. Contbr. articles to profl. jours. Served to maj. USAR, 1967-70. Mem. AMA, Chgo. Med. Soc., Radiol. Soc. N.Am., VFW, Phi Beta Kappa, Sigma Xi, Phi Eta Sigma. Roman Catholic. Lodge: KC. Home: 3604 Spanish Trace Springfield IL 62702

HEISERMAN, OWEN RAND, association administrator; b. Mpls., June 25, 1945; s. Francis Henry and Charlotte Juneva (Rand) H.; m. Gail Jean Bonath, Apr. 7, 1973 (div. Nov. 1980); 1 child, Blair; m. Joyce Kay Best, July 3, 1981; 1 child, Lindsey. AA, Fergus Falls (Minn.) State Jr. Coll., 1965; BA magna cum laude, St. Olaf Coll., 1967; MA, U. Iowa, 1973. Vol. Peace Corps, Para, Brazil, 1967-70; campaign organizer Iowa Dem. Party, Monticello, 1976; housing dir. Mid-Iowa Community Action, Inc., Marshalltown, Iowa, 1977-84; resource development coordinator Iowa Assn. Community Action Dirs., Des Moines, 1985—. NDEA fellow U. Iowa, 1970-73; U.S. Fulbright Commn. lectureship, 1976-77. Mem. Iowa Community Action Assn., ACLU, Union of Concerned Scientists, Club Mac Midwest. Avocations: reading, woodworking, film, computing. Office: Iowa Assn Community Action Dirs Armory Bldg E First and Des Moines St Des Moines IA 50307

HEISLER, HAROLD REINHART, mgmt. cons.; b. Chgo.; s. Harold Reinhart and Beulah Mary (Schade) H.; B.M.E., U. Ill., 1954. Mgmt. cons. Ill. Power Co., Decatur, 1954—, mem. Nuclear Power Group, Inc., Argonne (Ill.) Nat. Lab., 1955-57; chmn. fossil fuel com., West Central region FPC, Chgo., 1966-68; chmn. evaluation com. Coal Gasification Group, Inc., 1971-75; chmn. Decatur Marine Inc., 1964-66; dir. Indsl. Water Supply Co., Robinson, Ill., 1975-77; pub. speaker in field; mem. Ill. Gov.'s Fuel and Energy Bd., 1970, Ill. Commerce Commn. Fuel and Energy Bd., 1971-75, Ill. Energy Resources Commn. Coal Study Panel, 1976-79, evaluation com. of kilngas process, 1976-80; mem. power plant productivity com. Ill. Commerce Commn., 1977-79; mem. com. on nuclear power plant constrn. Inst. Nuclear Power Ops. Mem. ASME, Nat., Ill. socs. profl. engrs., U. Ill. Alumni Assn., Sigma Phi Delta. Conceptual designer power plant sites and recreational lakes, Baldwin and Clinton, Ill. Home: 154 W Court Manor Pl Decatur IL 62522 Office: 500 S 27th St Decatur IL 62525

HEISLER, JEROLD LEE, marketing executive; b. Chgo., Sept. 25, 1938; s. Harold H. and Anne C. (Holland) H.; m. Lois R. Goldberg, Aug. 16, 1962; children: Eileen, Marcy. Student, Northwestern U., 1956-57; BA, U. Minn., 1960. Exec. v.p. Market Devel. Corp., St. Louis, 1979-85; sr. v.p. mktg. Metromail Corp., Lombard, Ill., 1985—. Trustee Village of Deerfield, Ill., 1977-83. Mem. Chgo. Assn. Direct Mktg. (pres. 1974-75). Home: 36 Oxford Dr Lincolnshire IL 60015 Office: Metromail Corp 360 E 22d St Lombard IL 60148

HEISLER, SHIRLEY CAROL, food service executive; b. Oshkosh, Wis., Sept. 9, 1936; d. Lowell Kenneth and Regina Katherine (Hubertus) Grasee; m. Thomas Frank Heisler, July 17, 1954; children: Robert Thomas, Dawn Marie. Grad. high sch., Oshkosh, 1954. Asst. product devel. Lenox Candles Inc., Oshkosh, 1972-75; prin. La Sure's Cake Cuisine and Cafe, Oshkosh, 1975—; cake decroator JC Penny's, Foun du Lac, Wis., 1973-74. Avocations: reading, crocheting. Home: 1570 Ripon Ln Oshkosh WI 54901

HEITKOTTER, LYNN ANN, sales executive; b. Chgo., Jan. 26, 1957; d. Frank Michael and Joan Mary (Lawson) Miller; m. Kurt Heitkotter, Oct. 7, 1978. Student, U. Ill., 1976-77, Chgo. Sch. Medicine, Palatine, 1977-78. With Lift Parts Mfg., Des Plaines, Ill., 1979-86, advt. asst., 1979, advt. mgr., sales mgr., 1979—. Mem. Material Handling Equipment Distbrs. Assn. Office: Lift Parts Mfg 333 E Touhy Ave Des Plaines IL 60018

HEITZMAN, FRANK EDWARD, architect; b. Litchfield, Ill., Aug. 24, 1946; s. Carroll Kramer and Mary Patricia (Hanafin) H.; m. Sandra Frensko, June 14, 1969; children: Christopher, Nicholas, Alexandra. BArch, U. Ill., 1970, MArch, 1975. Assoc. Skidmore, Owings & Merrill, Chgo., 1971-83; owner Heitzman Architects, Oak Park, Ill., 1983-85, 87—; ptnr. Heitzman & Thorpe Architects, Oak Park, 1986-87; instr. Triton Coll., River Grove, Ill., 1983—; adj. faculty interior design So. Ill. U., 1987—, mem. interior design program adv. com., 1987—. Chmn. accessibility code task force State Ill., Chgo., 1986; commr. Oak Park Landmarks Commn., 1979-86; mem. Mayor's Adv. Commn. Bldg. Code Amendments, Chgo., 1983-86. Triton Coll. grantee 1985; recipient Disting. Service award Landmarks Preservation Council, 1986. Mem. AIA (bd. dirs. Chgo. chpt. 1984—, bd. dirs. Ill. Council 1984—, first v.p., pres.-elect. Chgo. chpt. 1987—), Nat. Council Archtl. Registration Bds. (juror 1979, 86), Am. Soc. Interior Designers, Met. Planning Council, Landmarks Preservation Council Ill. (easement monitor 1983—). Democrat. Roman Catholic. Home: 1128 S Scoville Oak Park IL 60304 Office: Heitzman & Thorpe Architects 1033 South Blvd Oak Park IL 60302

HEKMATPANAH, JAVAD, neurosurgery educator; b. Isfahan, Iran, Mar. 25, 1934; came to U.S., 1957; m. Lyra Van Wein, Aug. 15, 1959; children: Daria, Kevin, Cameron. MD, U. Tehran, Iran, 1956. Diplomate Am. Bd. Neurol. Surgery, Am. Bd. Psychiatry and Neurology. Intern in psychiatry Chehrazi Hosp., Tehran, 1955-57; intern Mt. Sinai Hosp., Chgo., 1957-58; resident in neurosurgery U. Chgo. Hosp., 1961-64, instr., chief resident, 1963-64, asst. to assoc. prof. neurosurgery, 1964-75, prof. neurosurgery, 1975—; hon. prof. Sch. Medicine Pahlavi U., Iran, 1976; mem. Dorfman com. U. Chgo., curriculum com. dept. surgery, 1970-73, operating room com., 1976-78, dean adv. com., 1979-82, med. sch. admissions com., 1980-82; mem. council of the Univ. Senate, 1983-86. Mem. AMA, ACS, Am. Acad. Neurology, Cen. Neurosurg. Soc. (pres. 1974-75), Chgo. Med. Soc., Chgo. Neurol. Soc. (pres. 1979-80), Research Soc. Neurol. Surgeons, Sigma Xi. Office: U Chgo Sch Medicine Div Neurol Surgery 5841 S Maryland Ave Chicago IL 60637

HELBERT, JAMES RAYMOND, biochemist; b. Miles City, Mont., Aug. 4, 1918; s. Lu Roy and Maude Mae (Stevenson) H.; B.A. cum laude, St. John's U., Collegeville, Minn., 1947; M.S., Marquette U., 1958; Ph.D., Northwestern U., 1963; m. Bernice Cyganiak, July 9, 1949; children—Gregory, Helen, John, Monica. Chemist. Orthmann Labs., Inc., Milw., 1947-51; research chemist Red Star Yeast and Products Co., Milw., 1951-58; research biochemist, geriatrics research project VA Hosp., Downey, Ill., 1958-62, acting chief, 1962-63; research asso. div. clin. hematology dept. medicine Michael Reese Hosp. & Med. Center, Chgo., 1963-67; supr. biochem. and microbiol. research Miller Brewing Co., Milw., 1967-76; mgr. microbiol. research and adminstrv. affairs, 1976-85, ret., 1985; research asso. Marquette U., 1954-58; lectr. dept. biology Ill. Inst. Tech., Chgo., 1966; asst. prof. biochemistry Northwestern U., 1967-73; guest lectr. microbial biochemistry U. Wis., Milw., 1970. NIH fellow, 1960-63. Fellow Am. Inst. Chemists; mem. Am. Statis. Assn., Am. Chem. Soc., Inst. Food Technologists, Am. Soc. Brewing Chemists. Roman Catholic. Lodge: Eagles. Contbr. in field. Office: PO Box 330 Milwaukee WI 53201

HELBING, MICHAEL GERALD, artist; b. Elmhurst, Ill., Oct. 25, 1946; s. Clarance Henry and Patricia Marie (Waltz) B.; m. Wendy Ritchey, Oct. 11, 1986. Student, Purdue U., 1968; BFA, Ball State U., Muncie, Ind., 1973. Co-owner Clay Works Pottery, Noblesville, Ind., 1976-78; inspector Reid, Quibe, Allison, Wilcox, Indpls., 1978-79; prin. Helbing Studios, Indpls., 1981—; vis. artist Indpls. Mus. of Art, 1980, 84, St. Mary of the Woods, Terre Haute, Ind., 1985. One-man show Anderson (Ind.) Art Ctr., 1983; exhibited in group shows Contemporary Art Ctr., Cin., 1984, Indpls. Art. League, 1984, J.B. Speed Mus., Louisville; excuted murals Met. Arts Council of Indpls., 1979-81, Larkin Cons. Co., 1983, Acquisition and Restoration Corp., 1984-87, Fountain Commn., Dr. Karl Glander 1985-86. Served with U.S. Army, 1968-70. Avocations: cooking, observing life.

HELD, HOWARD GEORGE, accountant; b. Litchfield, Ill., Mar. 19, 1956; s. Lawrence J. and Dorothy R. (Grundy) H.; m. Linda Marie Coleman, July 28, 1979; children: Joseph, Bradley. BS, Bradley U., 1978. Staff acct. Murphey, Jenne, & Jones, Effingham, Ill., 1978-80; acct. Kentre, CPA, Altamont, Ill., 1980-83; acct., mgr. Scheffel & Co., Highland, Ill., 1983—. Youth sports mgr. Morrisonville (Ill.) Little League, 1971-75, Effingham Khoury League; umpire local high schs., Edwardsville, Ill., 1983—. Mem. Am. Inst. CPA's, So. Ill. chpt. of Ill. CPA Soc., Am. Legion (S-ship award 1974), Effingham Jaycees (pres. 1982-83). Roman Catholic. Lodge: KC. Home: 688 S Station Rd Edwardsville IL 62025 Office: Scheffel & Co 2 Woodcrest Profl Park Highland IL 62249

HELDER, BRUCE ALAN, metal products executive; b. Grand Rapids, Mich., July 1, 1953; s. Harry Martin and Margaret (Ditmar) H.; m. Arlene Faye Docter, May 29, 1975; children: Amanda Joy, David Ryan, Joel Brent, Jonathan Bruce, Brandon Michael. Student, Calvin Coll., 1972-73, Grand Valley State Coll., Allendale, Mich., 1974. Lic. realtor assoc.; cert. media specialist. Indsl. sales rep. Newman Communications, Inc., Grand Rapids, 1971-81; nat. sales mgr. Best Metal Products Co., Grand Rapids, 1981—; v.p. Venture Property Mgmt. Co. Mem. Real Estate Bd. Grand Rapids. Republican. Mem. Christian Reformed Ch. Home: 1336 Richwood Dr SE Grand Rapids MI 49508 Office: Best Metal Products Co 3570 Raleigh Dr Grand Rapids MI 49508

HELFER, HERMAN HYMAN, glass co. exec.; b. Chgo., Dec. 6, 1919; s. Harry and Sarah (Kurlansky) H.; student Herzl Jr. Coll., 1941; cert. U. Ill. Coll. Pharmacy, 1946; B.S. in Mktg., Roosevelt U., 1973, M.B.A., 1977; m. Frieda Hershkopf, Nov. 16, 1947; children—Joel, Harvey, Gail. With Novelty Glass & Mirror Co., Chgo., 1946—, gen. mgr., sec.-treas., 1960—; pres. Columbia Glass Co., Chgo., 1969—; pres. Columbia Automotive Galss Products, Inc. 1986; pres. Energipane Insulating Glass Corp.; sec.-treas. Temper-Pane Inc.; pres. Insulating Glass Ednl. Inst., 1980-81, seminar chmn., Chgo., 1981. Instr., Boys State, Springfield, Ill., 1966; chmn. Glazier's Pension and Welfare Funds, Chgo., 1969-73; div. exec. com. Jewish United Fund, 1981. Served with USAAF, 1943-46. Recipient Dealer of Yr. award Glass Digest, 1979. Mem. Am. Legion (post comdr. 1967-68), Assn. Glazing Contractors (pres. 1957-73), Nat. Glass Dealers Assn. (exec. com., pres. 1979-80, rep. to Consumer Safety Products Commn.), Flat Glass Mktg. Assn. (dir.), Nat. Assn. Store Fixture Mfrs. (asso.), Sealed Insulating Glass Mfrs. Assn. Jewish (sec., treas. synagogue). Lodges: B'nai B'rith (dir. sports lodge), Masons, Shriners. Contbr. articles to trade publs. Home: 8937 Forest View Rd Evanston IL 60203 Office: 4716 W Lake St Chicago IL 60644

HELFRICH, JOHN SAVAGE, neurologist; b. San Antonio, May 31, 1943; s. William R. and Alice (Savage) H.; widowed; children: John, James, Joseph, Jeffrey. AB cum laude, St. Michaels Coll., 1965; MD, Loyola U., Chgo., 1969. Diplomate Am. Bd. Psychiatry and Neurology. Intern Mary Hitchcock Hosp., Dartmouth Coll., Hanover, N.H., 1969-70; resident and fellow in neurology New Eng. Med. Ctr., Tufts U., Boston, 1970-73; neurologist Christie Clinic, Champaign, Ill., 1974—, dir. CT dept., head. neurology dept., 1976—; co-dir. EEG dept. Mercy Hosp., Urbana, Ill., 1974—; co-dir. EEG dept. Burnham Hosp., Champaign, 1976—, co-dir. CT scan, 1978. Recipient Preclin. Honor award Loyola U. Stritch Sch. Medicine, 1965-69. Mem. Am. Soc. NeuroImaging (cert. in neuroimaging), AMA, Am. Acad. Neurology, Ill. State Med. Soc., Champaign County Med. Soc., Alpha Epsilon Delta, Delta Epsilon Sigma, Phi Beta Pi. Republican. Roman Catholic. Home: 5 Lakepark Rd Champaign IL 61821 Office: Christie Clinic 101 W University Champaign IL 61820

HELGEMO, RISE COREY, advertising executive; b. Indpls., Sept. 11, 1949; d. Thomas J. and Louise Elizabeth (Audi) Corey; m. Gary N. Helgemo, July 2, 1983; children: Scott, Jon. BA, Rosary Coll., River Forest, Ill., 1971. Various managerial positions Ind. Bell Telephone Co., Indpls., 1971-80; direct mktg. mgr. GTE-Midwestern Telephone Ops., Westfield, Ind., 1980-82; dir. advt. Indpls. Bus. Jour., 1982—; mem. adv. bd. bus. Ivy Tech. Sch., Indpls., 1983—. Republican. Lutheran. Avocations: waterskiing, snow skiing. Home: 207 Sedwick Ct Noblesville IN 46060 Office: Indpls Bus Jour 3500 DePauw Blvd Suite 2070 Indianapolis IN 46260

HELLAND, ROBERT V., optical laboratory executive; b. Grand Forks, N.D., Jan. 31, 1939; s. Russell D. and Romaine (Cariveau) Guntzburger; m. Lois Anne Adam, June 6, 1959; children: Steven, Jennifer. BSBA, U. N.D., 1962. Supr. mfg. engring. Univac, St. Paul, 1964-71; mgr. prodn. MDS Atron, St. Paul, 1971-75, Delkor Industries, Mpls., 1975-79; pres. DBL Labs., Inc., St. Joseph, Minn., 1979—. Supr. Clear Lake (Minn.) Twp. Bd., 1986, 87; chmn. property and fin. com. St. Marcus Parish, Clear Lake, 1987. Republican. Roman Catholic. Office: DBL Labs Inc 280 Joseph St Saint Joseph MN 56374

HELLER, ABRAHAM, psychiatrist, educator; b. Claremont, N.H., Mar. 17, 1917; s. David and Rose Heller; m. Lora S. Levy, June 16, 1957; 1 child, Judith Rose. BA, Brandeis U., 1953; MD, Boston U., 1957. Diplomate Am. Bd. Med. Examiners, Am. Bd. Psychiatry and Neurology. Resident in psychiatry U. Colo., Denver, 1958-61; chief in-patient psychiatry Denver Gen. Hosp., 1961-65, asst. dir. psychiat. services, 1965-70, assoc. dir. psychiat. services, 1970-73, dir., community mental health services, 1970-72; chief psychiatry, dir. community mental health ctr. Newport (R.I.) Hosp., 1973-77; clin. assoc. prof. psychiatry Brown U., Providence, 1973-77; prof. psychiatry, community medicine Wright State U., Dayton, Ohio, 1977—, vice chmn. dept., 1980—. Fellow Am. Psychiat. Assn., Am. Orthopsychiat. Assn., Am. Assn. for Social Psychiatry; mem. Am. Pub. Health Assn., AAAS. Jewish. Home: 1400 Runnymede Rd Dayton OH 45419 Office: Wright State U Sch Medicine Dept Psychiatry Box 927 Dayton OH 45401

HELLER, CHARLES ANDREW, JR., electric utilities co. exec.; b. Teaneck, N.J., Mar. 18, 1929; s. Charles Andrew and Lillian Laura (Reuter) H.; m. Helen Johansen, July 19, 1952; children: Charles Andrew, Janice Maria, Richard Craig. B.A., Rutgers U., 1951; M.B.A., U. Pa., 1956; M.S. (Alfred P. Sloan fellow), M.I.T., 1966. With Am. Electric Power Service Corp., N.Y.C., 1956-63; with Ohio Power Co., Canton, 1963-68, 70—, v.p., 1974-76, exec. v.p., 1976-81, chief operating officer, 1976—, pres., 1981—; exec. asst. Wheeling Electric Co., W.Va., 1968-70; exec. v.p., dir. Ohio Electric Co.; v.p., dir. Cardinal Operating Co., Central Coal Co., Central Ohio Coal Co., Central Operating Co., So. Ohio Coal Co., Windsor Power House Coal Co., from 1976; v.p. Beech Bottom Power Co., Inc., Franklin Real Estate Co., from 1976, Ind. Franklin Realty, Inc., from 1976; dir. Ohio Electric Utility Inst., from 1976, pres., from 1978; dir. Central Trust Co. Northeastern Ohio, from 1975. Mem. Council for Reorganization of Ohio State Govt., 1967; dir. Canton Welfare Found., 1975-78; mem. Malone Coll. Adv. Bd., from 1976. Served to capt. USAF, 1951-53. Republican. Lutheran. Clubs: Canton, Brookside Country, Columbus Athletic. Lodges: Elks, Rotary. Office: Ohio Power Co 301 Cleveland Ave SW Canton OH 44702 *

HELLER, DICK DANIEL, JR., newspaper publisher; b. Decatur, Ind., May 22, 1929; s. Dick Daniel and Martha Delilah (Grant) H.; m. E. Jane Drew, Mar. 23, 1957; 1 child, Thomas Calvin. Student Ind. U., 1947-50, 54, U. Md., Augsburg, Germany, 1952-53; A.B., Syracuse U., 1956; postgrad. Ball State U., 1958-59, St. Francis Coll., 1964. Pres. Decatur Pub. Co., Ind., 1958—. Author: History of the Indiana Democratic Editorial Association, 1962. Editor: History of Adams County, Indiana, 1980. Editor newsletters: The Cardinal, 1979-84; The Craigellachie, 1980—. Historian, Adams County, 1980—; dir. Ind. Hist. Soc., 1982—, bd. dirs. genealogy sect. 1975—; chmn. Adams County-Decatur Sesquicentennial Com., 1984-86. Served as cpl. U.S. Army, 1951-54. Named Sagamore of Wabash, gov. of Ind., 1963, Ky. Col., gov. Ky., 1969; recipient End-to-End award Appalachian Trail Assn., 1973, Disting. Citizenship award Decatur Elks, 1975-76. Mem. Ind. Dem. Edn. Assn. (pres. 1965), Inland Daily Press Assn., Hoosier State Press Assn., UPI, Mid-Am. Press Inst., Decatur Trail Club (pres. 1984—). German Heritage Soc. (bd. dirs. Ind. chpt. 1984—). Avocations: bird watching; stamp collecting; genealogy; hiking. Home: Rural Route 3 Box 3 Decatur IN 46733 Office: Decatur Pub Co Inc 141 S 2d St Decatur IN 46733

HELLER, GRANT L., neurologist; b. Racine, Wis., Dec. 24, 1930; s. A. Grant and Edythe (Cohen) H.; m. Audrey P. Lecht, Aug. 14, 1954; children: Ronald, Lawrence, Michael, Steven, Brian. BS, Western Res. U., 1952, MD, 1956. Diplomate Am. Bd. Psychiatry and Neurology. Pvt. practice neurology Cleve., 1961—; clinical asst. prof. neurology Case Western Res. U., Cleve., 1981—. Contbr. articles to med. jours. Mem. bd. govs. U. Mich. Med. Ctr. Alumni Soc., 1976-82. Served as capt. U.S. Army, 1961-62. Fellow Am. Coll. Physicians, Am. Acad. Neurology; mem. Zeta Beta Tau (various offices), Phi Delta Epsilon (nat. pres. 1986-87). Office: 3619 Park East Beachwood OH 44122

HELLER, JAMES BRADLEY, architect; b. Cleve., Nov. 7, 1946; s. Milton Stanford and Rita (Albert) H.; m. Barbara Lynn Weiner, Aug. 9, 1969; children: Ryan, Kari, Darcy. BArch, Ohio State U., 1971. Registered architect, Ohio, NCARB, others. Architect Kekst Architects, Cleve., 1971-77, assoc., 1977-82, sr. v.p., 1982—. Assoc. chmn. Israel Bond Drive, Cleve., 1974, Jewish Welfare Fund, Cleve., 1984; vol. fireman City of Beachwood, Ohio, 1986—. Recipient Isreal Solidarity award State of Israel, 1976. Democrat. Avocations: softball, tennis, water skiing. Home: 24407 Tunbridge Ln Beachwood OH 44122 Office: Keeva J Kekst Assoc 1468 W 9th St #600 Western Reserve Bldg Cleveland OH 44113

HELLER, JOACHIM, health service manager, nurse, educator; b. Berlin, Oct. 11, 1938; came to U.S., 1951; s. Guenter and Hedwig (Ritter) H.; children: David, Brian. Cert. in Practicle nursing, Milw. Area Tech. Coll., 1964, Cert. in nursing, 1977; postgrad. U. Wis., Milw., 1977-79; BS in Nursing, Milton Coll., Wis., 1979; MS in Adminstrn. Leadership, U. Wis., Milw., 1981, PhD in Health Service Mgmt., 1982. Lic. practicle nurse, Wis.; RN, Wis.; registered emergency med. technician, Wis.; cert. edn. specialist, Wis. Surg. technician Misericordia Hosp., Milw., 1960-64; pub. health nurse Vis. Nurse Assn., Milw., 1964-66; staff nurse various hosps. and nursing homes, Milw., 1966-79; faculty, mgr. psychiat. unit Milw. County Mental Health Complex, 1979-83; health service and tng. mgr. House of Correction, Milwaukee County, 1983—; program evaluator, 1979—; cons. legal nursing intervention, 1981—. CPR affiliate faculty Wis. Heart Assn., 1980—; CPR instr. trainer Wis. Red Cross, 1984—; mem. Wis. Law Enforcement Standards Bd. Served with USMC, 1957-59. Mem. Nat. League of Nursing, Wis. League of Nursing, Am. Heart Assn., Wis. Heart Assn. (co-editor Heartbeat), Wis. Correctional Health Assn. (v.p. 1984—), Am. Correctional Assn., Wis. Correctional Assn., Milwaukee County Mental Health Task Force. Author: Program Evaluation, 1982; Disturbed Behavior Intervention, 1982. Contbr. articles in field to local profl. jours.

HELLER, MARK BRIAN, accounting firm executive; b. St. Louis, July 9, 1956; s. Ronald Lee and Geraldine (Tabachnic) H. BA in Speech and Communications, U. Mo., 1978, MBA in Mktg., 1980. Staff cons. Arthur Andersen & Co., St. Louis, 1980-83, sr. cons., 1983-84; mgr. Ernst & Whinney, St. Louis, 1984-86, sr. mgr. mgmt. cons. div., 1986—; speaker in field. Contbr. articles to profl. jours. Mem. Assn. for Prodn. Inventory Control Soc., Assn. for Retail Info. Systems, Purchasing Mgmt. Assn. (communication officer 1985—, pur-tech. com.1985—), St. Louis Retail Controllers Group (sec. 1986—), St. Louis Fedn., St. Louis Ambassador. Jewish. Club: Media (St. Louis). Avocations: piano, guitar, golf, writing music, sports.

HELLER, NANCY B., paralegal; b. Peoria, Ill., Mar. 22, 1956; d. Michael William and Joyce (Mendeloff) H. BA in Criminal Justice, Ind. U., 1978. Litigation paralegal Chester, Hoffman & Willcox, Columbus, 1978-84; labor paralegal Porter, Wright, Morris & Arthur, Columbus, 1984-85; litigation paralegal Vorys, Sater, Seymour & Pease, Columbus, 1985—. Vol. Indpls. Women's Prison, 1975-76, Bloomington Work Release Ctr., 1975-77, Franklin County Children's Services, 1979-80, Greater Columbus Arts Council, 1984—; mem. young leadership div. Columbus Jewish Fedn., 1982-84; v.p. fundraising, sec. B'nai Brith Women, 1980—. Named Outstanding Young Women in Am., 1983. Mem. Ohio Bar Assn. (legal assts. com.), Columbus Bar Assn. (lawyer/legal asst. com. 1983—, profl. ethics and grievance com. 1985—), Nat. Fedn. Paralegal Assocs. (profl. devel. com. 1985—, secondary rep. 1985—), Legal Assts. of Cen. Ohio (pres., v.p. membership com., chmn. continuing legal edn. com., sec., bd. dirs.), Alpha Epsilon Phi. Avocations: outdoor activities, reading, dancing, theatre. Home: 5861-B Hallworth Ave Columbus OH 43232 Office: Vorys Sater Seymour & Pease 52 E Gay St Columbus OH 43215

HELLER, PHILIP HENRI, physician; b. Des Plaines, Ill., Feb. 6, 1919; s. William Frederick and Magdalene (Henschel) H.; m. Ruth Wark, Apr. 28, 1945; children: Jeanne, Philip Henri, Nancy, Patricia, Mary. AB, U. Nebr., 1941; MD, Northwestern U., 1945. Diplomate Am. Bd. Family Practice. Intern St. Luke's Hosp., Chgo., 1944-45; assoc. staff St. Francis Hosp., Evanston, Ill., 1946-53; attending staff, staff officer Resurrection Hosp., Chgo., 1952-64, assoc. dir. family practice residency program, 1978-85; emeritus staff Resurrection Hosp., 1985—; attending staff Luth. Gen. Hosp., Park Ridge, Ill., 1959-78, hon. staff, 1978—, v.p., 1970-71, chmn. div. family practice and dir. Family Practice Ctr. and residency program, 1972-77; attending staff Holy Family Hosp., Des Plaines, 1960-74; asst. prof. U. Ill. Sch. Medicine, 1972-78. Pres. Des Plaines Bd. Health, 1949-63. Served to lt. comdr. USNR, 1945-46, 54-56. Fellow Am. Acad. Family Physicians; mem. Chgo. Med. Soc. (council mem. 1963-71, pres. Irving Park br. 1969-70), Ill. Acad. Family Physicians (pres. North Suburban br. 1959-60), Ill. Med. Soc., AMA, Soc. Tchrs. Family Medicine, Phi Rho Sigma. Mem. United Ch. Christ. Lodge: Masons.

HELLER, RANDALL LANE, JR., surgeon; b. St. Louis, Dec. 16, 1942; s. Randall Lane and Norma Alma (Knoll) H.; m. Suzanne Ruth Smith, Oct. 19, 1963 (div. Aug. 1973); m. Dorothy Louise Eckenfels, June 29, 1983; 1 child, Randall Lane III. BS, U. Mo., 1964, PhD, 1969; MD, U. Tex., 1976. Diplomate Am. Bd. Ob-Gyn. Intern Barnes Hosp., St. Louis, 1976-77, resident, 1977-80; practice medicine specializing in ob-gyn St. Louis, 1980—; mem. staff Barnes Hosp., St. Louis, Allied Hosp., St. Louis, St. Luke's Hosp., St. Louis; instr. chemistry U. Mo., 1968-69; asst. clin. prof. Wash. U., St. Louis, 1986—. Carl Bauer Research fellow U. Mo., 1967-68; Med. Student Research grantee 1973. Mem. AMA, Mo. Med. Assn., St. Louis Met. Med. Soc., Am. Coll. Ob-Gyn, St. Louis Maternity Hosp. Soc. (pres. 1983-85), Cen. Assn. Obstericians and Gynecologists. Avocations: hunting, fishing, flying. Home: 12823 Greenville Ln Saint Louis MO 63141 Office: Ob-Gyn Assocs Inc 1034 S Brentwood Blvd Suite 946 Saint Louis MO 63117

HELLER, ROBERT LEO, university chancellor, geology educator; b. Dubuque, Iowa, Apr. 10, 1919; s. Edward W. and May Olive (Bauck) H.; m. Geraldine Hanson, Sept. 26, 1946; children: Roberta, Katherine, Nancy. B.S., Iowa State U., 1942; M.S., U. Mo., 1943, Ph.D., 1950. Geologist U.S. Geol. Survey, 1943-44; mem. faculty U. Minn., Duluth, 1950—; prof. geology, chmn. dept. U. Minn., 1960-67, from asst. to provost to assoc. provost, 1965-76, provost, 1977-85, chancellor, 1985-87, chancellor emeritus, 1987—; dir. NSF earth sci. curriculum project U. Colo., 1963-65; mem. U.S. Nat. Com. Geology, 1977-81; editor Environment Times, 1976-80. Contbr. numerous articles to profl. publs. Vice pres. St. Louis County Heritage and Arts Ctr., 1974-77. Served to 2d lt. C.E., AUS, 1944-47. Recipient Neil Miner award Nat. Assn. Geology Tchrs., 1965, citation of merit Coll. Scis. and Humanities, Iowa State U., 1976, Comdrs. medal Order of Lion (Finland), 1981. Mem. Nat. Assn. Geology Tchrs. (pres. 1976-77), Am. Geol. Inst. (v.p. 1977-78, pres. 1978-79, Ian Campbell medal 1985), Council Sci. Soc. Presidents (vice chmn. 1980-81, chmn. 1981-82), Geol. Soc. Am., Paleontol. Soc., AAAS, Am. Assn. Petroleum Geologists, U. Minn. Alumni Assn. (Disting. Service award 1972). Office: Univ of Minn Duluth Office of the Chancellor Duluth MN 55812-2496

HELLSTRÖM, ÅKE ARVID, engineer; b. Norrkoping, Sweden, Aug. 30, 1943; came to U.S., 1975; s. Arvid and Lucia (Olsson) H.; m. Ingrid Stedt, May 20, 1967; children: Robert, Anders. BS in Mech. Engring., Polhemsskolan, Norrkoping, 1963; MS in Applied Physics, Chalmers U., Gothenberg, Sweden, 1969. System engr. Accuray, Sundsvall, Sweden, 1969-72; staff engr. Accuray, Sundsvall, 1972-75; sr. staff engr. Accuray, Columbus, Ohio, 1975-84; supr. design and devel. Accuray (merged with Combustion Engring.), Columbus, 1984—. Served with Swedish Army, 1966-69. Mem. Chalmers Engr. Assn. Home: 5714 Brinkley Ct Columbus OH 43220 Office: Combustion Engring PO Box 02650 Columbus OH 43202

HELLYER, CLEMENT DAVID, writer; b. Glendale, Calif., Aug. 15, 1914; s. Clement David and Frances Edna (Dodge) H.; m. Gertrude Gloria Phillips, Sept. 8, 1939; children: Gloria Penrose, David Phillips, John Christian. A.B., Principia Coll., 1936; M.S., Columbia, 1938; Beaumont fellow, U. Fla., 1950-52. Newspaper reporter San Diego Union-Tribune, 1939-41; pub. relations dir. San Diego C. of C., 1941-43; civilian aerial navigator USN, 1943-45; prof.journalism San Diego State Coll., 1947-49; dir. Centro Cultural Costarricense-Norteamericano, San Jose, Costa Rica, 1949-50; asst. dir. Sch. Inter-Am. Studies, U. Fla., 1950-52; vis. lectr. U.S. journalism Dept. State program leaders and specialists exchange, Latin Am. countries, 1952; Latin-Am. editor San Diego Union, 1953-60; freelance writer Sao Paulo and Rio de Janeiro, Brazil, 1960-64; writer, lectr. Latin Am. affairs 1950—; U.S. del. Jose Toribio Medina Centenary, Santiago, Chile, 1952; editor, pub. South Pacific Mail, Santiago, 1964-66; editorial dir. radio-TV sta. KOGO, San Diego, 1966-69; univ. editor, pub. affairs officer U. Calif., San Diego, 1969-74; owner Five Quail Books, 1978—. Author: (with Charles Mattingly) American Air Navigator, 1946, Story of the U.S. Border Patrol, 1963, Making Money with Words, 1981; Contbr. articles to prin. newspapers, periodicals U.S. Recipient Maria Moors Cabot award Columbia, 1959; 1st prize editorial competition Radio and TV News Dirs. Assn., 1968. Home: PO Box 278 Spring Grove MN 55974

HELMS, RONALD EUGENE, education educator; b. Grafton, W.Va., Aug. 3, 1945; s. Stanley Eugene and Rosemary (Cockrell) H.; m. Sharon Ann Verdigone, June 4, 1966; 1 child, Scott Michael. BA in Edn., Fairmont State Coll., 1966; MA in Polit. Sci., U. Dayton, 1968; PhD in Edn., Ohio State U., 1972. Tchr. Carlisle (Ohio) High Sch., 1966-69, Kettering (Ohio) City Schs., 1979—; adj. assoc. prof. edn. Wright State U., Dayton, Ohio, 1972—; assoc. prof. edn. U. Dayton, 1972—. Author: Cognitive Moral Development and Values Analysis, 1974; editor: Political Involvement, 1979, Social Studies: Theory into Practice, 1982; contbr. over 100 articles to profl. jours. Coach, referee Centerville (Ohio) Soccer, 1971-78; chmn. Centerville Sister Cities Com., 1979-83; mem. Centerville-Township Unification Com., 1978-80; expedition leader Boy Scouts of Am., Philmont, N. Mex., 1980. Recipient Teaching Excellance award Kettering Schs., 1980, named Outstanding Tchr., 1981; named Tchr. of Yr. Dayton Council for Social Studies, 1981. Mem. Assn. Govt. History (exec. dir. 1985—), Ohio Council Social Studies (pres. 1976-79, exec. dir. 1982-85), Nat. Council for Social Studies (bd. dirs. 1974-82), Ohio Assn. for Gifted Edn., Phi Delta Kappa. Club: Liederkrantz. Avocations: computer, soccer, tennis, camping, travel. Home: 7123 W Von Dette Centerville OH 45459 Office: Kettering City Schs 3775 Shroyer Rd Kettering OH 45429

HELMSTETTER, RICHARD JAMES, dentist; b. Madison, Minn., July 6, 1952; s. Clarence Warren and Edna Marie (Paul) H.; m. Debra Georgene Beck, Aug. 30, 1975; 1 child, Stacy Colette. BA, Concordia Coll., 1974; DDS, U. Minn., 1979. Gen. practice dentistry New Ulm, Minn., 1979—; instr. Canby (Minn.) Vocat. Tech., 1981—. Mem. Am. Dental Assn., Minn. Dental Assn., So. Dist. Dental Assn., Am. Heart Assn. (pres.-elect 1986). Republican. Lutheran. Club: New Ulm Country (bd. dirs. 1982-85, sec. 1982-83). Lodge: Sertoma (bd. dirs. 1980-83). Avocations: golf, racquetball. Home: 1017 17th St N PO Box 414 New Ulm MN 56073 Office: 2 N Minnesota St New Ulm MN 56073

HELSDINGEN, DANIEL JOHN, advertising executive; b. Chgo., Aug. 31, 1935; s. Henry Francis and Agnes Catherine (McHugh) H.; m. Mary Frances Nicholas, Jan. 25, 1958; children: Patricia Helsdingen Reed, Daniel, Joan, Mary, Thomas. BS in Commerce, DePaul U., 1957. Asst. advt. mgr. Inland Steel Co., Chgo., 1960-66; nat. advt. mgr. Blue Cross Assn., Chgo., 1966-67; v.p., account supr. Edward H. Weiss & Co., Chgo., 1967-71; exec. dir. Met. Chgo. Blood Council, 1971-74; sr. v.p. Lee King & ptnrs., Chgo., 1974-79; v.p., mgmt. supr. Campbell-Mithun, Inc., Chgo., 1979-86; assoc. Bools & Assocs., Chgo., 1986—. Mem. Gov's. blood bank task force Ill. Dept. Pub. Health, 1972-74, businessmen's task force Ill. Dept. Child and Family Services, 1970; bd. dirs. Mid-Am. Red Cross, 1978-86, Met. Chgo. Blood Council, 1974-77. Served with U.S. Army, 1957-62. Mem. Bus Profl. Advt. Assn. (cert. bus. communicator). Democrat. Roman Catholic. Home: 9021 S Francisco Ave Evergreen Park IL 60642 Office: Bools & Assocs 35 E Wacker Dr Chicago IL 60601

HELSEL, JESS F., metallurgical company executive; b. Deerfield, Ohio, Dec. 22, 1924; s. Jesse A. and Alice Agnes (Bruey) H.; student Kent State U., Akron U., Earlham Coll.; m. Barbara Jane Ebert, Mar. 1, 1947; children—Peter Fredrich, Jessica Jane, Leslie Alison. Supts., Wel-Met Co., Kent, Ohio, 1946-51, plant mgr., Salem, Ind., 1951-55; sales mgr. Ferraloy Co., Salem, 1955-57, pres., 1957-70; gen. mgr. powder metal products div. Gould, Inc., Salem, 1970-73, dir. bus. devel., 1973; pres. Helsel Metall. Co., Campbellsburg, Ind., 1974—, also dir.; pres., dir. Hel-Met, Inc., Helsel Metall. Internat. Corp. Chmn. bd. trustees Ind. Vocat. and Tech. Coll.; bd. dirs., exec. com. Found. Ivy Tech., also trustee state bd.; dir. Ind. Cert. Devel. Corp., Ind. Fiscal Policy; chmn. Ind. Small Bus. Council; dir. Ind. Fiscal Policy Inst. Served with USMRC, 1942-45. Decorated Purple Heart; named Hoosier Assoc. Mem. Soc. Automotive Engrs., Soc. Mfg. Engrs., Am. Soc. Metals, Am. Powder Metal Inst., Am. Ordnance Assn., Powder Metallurgy Parts Assn. (pres. 1965-67), Metal Powder Industries Fedn. (pres. 1967-69), Ind. State C. of C. (dir., chmn. exec. com., current chmn. bd.), Ind. Appaloosa Assn., Appaloosa Horse Club, Hoosier Horse Council. Republican. Home: RFD 3 Salem IN 47167 Office: Box 68 State Rd 60W Campbellsburg IN 47108

HELSTERN, RICHARD ANDREW, architect; b. Chgo., Jan. 4, 1931; s. Andrew Joseph and Grace Eleanor (Wolf) H.; m. Linda Lucile Lizut, Aug. 21, 1977; 1 child, Amina Katherine. Student, Inst. Design, Chgo., 1950-53; BA, So. Ill. U., Carbondale, 1959. Registered profl. architect, Ill. Project designer Skidmore, Owings & Merrill, Chgo., 1955-57, Perkins & Will, Architects, Chgo., 1960-65; lectr. So. Ill. U., 1965-69; prin. Shawnee Design Studio, Carbondale, 1972—, Richard Helstern, Architect, Carbondale, 1972—; design cons. Greater Egypt Regional Planning and Devel. Commn., Carbondale, 1970-72. Producer: (ednl. films) Five New Landscapes, 1973, Illinois: The State of the Future, 1979, Working for Better Health, 1985. Mem. Chgo. Heritage Com., 1959-61; founding mem. Save Hull House Com., Chgo., 1961-62. Served to sgt. U.S. Army, 1953-55, Korea. Recipient Annual Design award Nat. Service to Regional Councils, 1971, 74, Annual Design award Ednl. Exhibit Am. Assn. Sch. Adminstrs., 1964. Mem. AIA, Constrn. Specifications Inst. Avocation: photography. Home and Office: Rt 4 Union Hill Carbondale IL 62901

HELTON, KAREN ELIZABETH JOHNSON, industrial engineer; b. Dayton, Ohio, Oct. 13, 1962; d. Donn A. and Caroline Ruth (Liggett) Johnson; m. Richard Edwin Helton, Oct. 25, 1986. BSIE, U. Cin., 1986. Engring. mgmt. trainee Batesville (Ind.) Casket Co. (Hillenbrand Industries), 1986-87; project mgr., indsl. engr. Am. Power Equipment Co., Harrison, Ohio, 1987—. Mem. Inst. Indsl. Engrs. (assoc.). Baptist. Lodge: Order Eastern Star.

HELVEY, WILLIAM CLYDE, emergency medicine physician; b. West Palm Beach, Fla., Dec. 21, 1953; s. Wilfred D. and Alice G. (Campbell) H. BA, Miami U., Oxford, Ohio, 1975; MD, Ohio State U., 1978. Diplomate Am. Bd. Med. Examiners. Intern and res. Naval Regional Med. Ctr., Oakland, Calif., 1978-81; physician, pres. Waukegan (Ill.) Assocs., Ltd., 1983—. Served to lt. comdr. USN, 1978-83. Mem. Am. Coll. Emergency Physicians, AMA, Ill. State Med. Soc., Lake County Med. Soc. Methodist. Avocations: flying. Home: 11933 45th Ave Kenosha WI 53142 Office: Waukegan Assocs Ltd 1324 N Sheridan Rd Waukegan IL 60085

HEMBEL, ALAN GEORGE, development company executive; b. West Bend, Wis., Sept. 6, 1946; s. George Benjamin and Fern Louise (Resch) H.; m. Carmen Gran Kelsey, Jan. 22, 1972 (dec. 1985); children: Benjamin Alan, Sara Ann Louise. BBA with honors, U. Wis., 1971, MS in Real Estate, 1974. With CUNA Mut. Ins. Group, Madison, Wis., 1974-85, real estate adminstr., 1974-78, asst. v.p. real estate mgmt., 1978-85; with Marshall Erdman & Assocs., Inc., Madison, 1986—; instr. U. Wis. Extension, 1976-85; cons. in field. Served to maj., field arty. USAR, 1973—. Fellow Life Office Mgmt. Inst.; CLU. Republican. Lutheran. Home: 5308 Scenic Ridge Trail Middleton WI 53562 Office: Marshall Erdman & Assocs Inc 5117 University Ave Madison WI 53705

HEMINGER, EDWIN LLOYD, newspaper publisher; b. Findlay, Ohio, July 30, 1926; s. Russell Lowell and Golda (McClelland) H.; m. Barbara Jo Rieck, Sept. 20, 1952; children—Karl Lloyd, Margaret Ann Heminger Gordon, Kurt Frederick. B.A., Ohio Wesleyan U., 1948; M.S., Northwestern U., 1952; D. Jour. (hon.), Bethany Coll., 1980. Field sec. Delta Tau Delta, Indpls., 1948-49; asst. bus. mgr. Courier, Findlay, Ohio, 1952-59, pub., 1965—; v.p. Findlay Pub. Co., 1959-83, pres., 1983—, also dir.; pres. White River Broadcasting Co. Inc., 1983—; dir. AP, 1985—; dir. 5th 3d Bank of Northwestern Ohio, Celina Fin. Corp., Celina Mut. Ins. Co., Nat. Mut. Ins. Co., Nat. Gas & Oil Co., AP, 1985—. Pres. Findlay YMCA, 1965-67, United Way of Hancock County, 1969-70, Hancock Community Found., 1970-72, Hancock Hist. Mus. Assn., 1970-86; mem. Constl. Revision Commn., State of Ohio, 1970-77. Served with USNR, 1944-45, 50-51. Mem. Am. Newspaper Pubs. Assn. (dir. 1980—), Am. Newspaper Pubs. Assn. Found. (chmn. 1986-87), Ohio Newspaper Assn. (dir. 1979—), Newspaper Advt. Bur. (dir. 1980-86), State of Ohio Newspapers Found. (pres. 1979-80), Soc. Profl. Journalists, Nat. Press Club, Toledo Press Club, Inland Daily Press Assn. (pres. 1981), Ohio C. of C. (chmn. bd. 1977-79), Nat. Interfraternity Conf. (dir. 1979-87 , pres. 1986-87), Delta Tau Delta (nat. pres. 1972-74). Trustee, Findlay Coll., 1976—, Ohio Wesleyan U., 1977-85. Republican. Methodist. Clubs: Rotary, Findlay Country; Mid-Ocean (Bermuda); Belmont Country (Perrysburg, Ohio). Lodge: Elks.

HEMKER, PAUL WILLIAM, reinforced plastics company executive; b. Dayton, Ohio, Feb. 19, 1941; s. William Henry and Hildegard M. (Hartel) H.; m. Heide Cristel Hegele, Sept. 25, 1940; children: Eric William, Mark David. BSChemE, U. Cin., 1964; MBA, Cen. Mich. U., 1968. Plastics engr. Dow Chem. Corp., Midland, Mich., 1964-69; pres. Dynamic Plastics, New Paris, Ohio, 1969—. Council mem. St. Paul Luth. Ch., Richmond, Ind., 1974-80. Mem. Soc. Plastics Engrs. Republican. Clubs: Richmond Sail, Brookville (Ind.) Sail. Home: 4733 Meadowcrest Ln New Paris OH 45347 Office: Dynamic Plastics Inc 8207 St Rt 121 New Paris OH 45347

HEMMENS, THOMAS RAE, newspaper executive, marketing professional; b. Ottawa, Ill., July 29, 1937; s. Marcus Thomas and Lillian Mae (Griffin) H.; m. Doris Jean Lamb, June 22, 1957 (div. Feb. 1980); children: Thomas Rae Jr., Deborah Jean. Assembler Bentson Mfg., Aurora, Ill., 1955-57; sales, asst. dept. mgr. Sears Robeuck & Co., Aurora, 1957-59; with classified advt. sales Aurora Beacon News, 1959-68, retail advt. sales, 1968-81; advt. sales insert coordinator Naperville (Ill.) Sun, 1982-84, mktg. dir., 1984—. Bd. dirs. DuPage Bd. Jr. Achievement, 1984—; sect. leader Naperville YMCA Fund Drive, 1987. Mem. Naperville C. of C. (Ambassador of Yr. 1985, mem. Trade Fair Com. 1984—,chmn. ambassador com. 1986—, bd. dirs. 1987—), Lisle C. of C., Bolingbrook C. of C., Aurora C. of C. Republican. Lodges: Lions (chmn. publicity com. Naperville club 1986—), Moose. Avocations: photography, magic. Home: 18 Afton Dr Montgomery IL 60538 Office: Naperville Sun 9 W Jackson Naperville IL 60566

HEMPEL, LARRY C., marketing company executive, consultant; b. San Antonio, Dec. 8, 1944; m. Margaret M. Hempel, Aug. 13, 1966; children: Laura, Matt, Julia. BS, U. Mo., 1966; MA, Washington U., St. Louis, 1970. Spl. asst. fed. Reserve St. Louis, 1967-73; creative dir., cons. Maritz Mktg. Co., St. Louis, 1973-75; head coor. div. Tower Grove Bank, St. Louis, 1975-77; mgr. mktg. Centerre Bank, St. Louis, 1977-78; owner, operator, cons. Bank Aide Inc., St. Louis, 1978—; assoc. prof. St. Louis U. and Meramec Coll., 1971-77. Author copyright Profitability Focus Study, 1978. Served to sgt. N.G., USAF, 1966-72. Curator's scholar U. Mo., 1962. Mem. Ind. Community Banks Ill. Avocations: swimming, skiing, hiking, wilderness. canoeing. Home: 14445 Corallin Saint Louis MO 63017 Office: Bank Aide Inc 734 E Port Plaza Saint Louis MO 63146

HEMPHILL, BARRY ROMMEL, data processing executive; b. Phila., Apr. 9, 1936; s. Charles Wallen and Ruth (Rommel) Hemphill; m. Joyce Elaine Micheau, Apr. 20, 1957; children: Mark, Kirk, Tod. BS, Pa. State U., 1958. Various positions IBM Corp., Tampa and Miami, Fla., 1965-71; dir. computer services Cleve. State U., 1972-77; v.p. Blue Cross Northeast Ohio, Cleve., 1977-79; exec. dir. Coop Computer Ctr., Elmhurst, Ill., 1979-83; assoc. exec. dir. U S R.R. Retirement Bd., Chgo., 1983—. Mem., pres. Bay Village (Ohio) City Sch. Dist., 1976-79; trustee Glen Ellyn (Ill.) Library Bd., 1981-85. Mem. Assn. Computing Mgmt. Home: 649 A Shoreline Rd Lake Barrington IL 60010 Office: U S RR Retirement Bd 844 Rush St Chicago IL 60611

HEMPHILL, ROBERT JULES, mechanical engineer; b. Oak Park, Ill., Nov. 1, 1941; s. William Taylor and Luella Eileen (Evans) H.; m. Lora Lee

Wagner, Aug. 25, 1962; children: Todd, Mark, Scott. BS, Purdue U., 1963. Product engr. Sears Roebuck & Co., Chgo., 1964-73, sales engr., 1973-78, buyer, 1978-80; mgr. appliances and space conditioning Gas Research Inst., Chgo., 1980—; chmn. steering com. Gas Appliance Tech. Ctr., Cleve., 1983—. Contbr. articles to profl. jours. Mem. Am. Soc. Heating, Refrigeration & Air Conditioning, Gas Engrs. Soc., Phi Kappa Tau. Methodist. Avocations: boating, water sports. Office: Gas Research Inst 8600 W Bryn Mawr Ave Chicago IL 60631

HEMRY, TIMOTHY WAYNE, small business owner; b. Cleve., May 30, 1951; s. Francis Wayne and Ruth Evelyn (Bornemann) H.; m. Cathy Lynn Shoemaker, July 8, 1973; children: Aaron Daniel, Felicia Renea. BS in Edn., Kent (Ohio) State U., 1973. Cert. secondary tchr., Ohio. Organ builder Holtkamp Organ Co., Cleve., 1969-71; tchr. indsl. arts South Euclid and Lyndhurst City Schs., Ohio, 1973-78; pvt. practice organ builder Cleveland Heights, Ohio, 1976—. Mem. Am. Inst. Organ Builders (bd. dirs. 1983-85 edn. com. 1986—), Am. Guild Organists. Avocations: music, cabinet making, cycling. Home: 1052 Roanoke Rd Cleveland Heights OH 44121

HENDEE, JOHN H., JR., banker; b. 1926; married. B.A., Williams Coll., 1949; M.B.A., U. Wis., 1956. With 1st Wis. Nat. Bank of Milw., 1949—, sr. v.p., 1970-72, exec. v.p., 1972-76, pres., 1976—, dir. Office: First Wis Nat Bank of Milw First Wis Corp 777 E Wisconsin Ave Milwaukee WI 53202 *

HENDERSHOT, LYNDA RAE, physicians assistant; b. Bellaire, Ohio, May 24, 1952; d. Ray and Ida (Togliatti) Brubaker; m. William A. Baranich (dec.); m. David Michael Hendershot, Aug. 30, 1985. Registered nurse degree, Ohio Valley Sch. Nursing, 1973; student, Ohio State U., 1975-76, St. Joseph Coll., 1985—. Cert. CPR instr.; registered physician asst. Ohio Med. Bd.; cert. family nurse practitioner, Ohio; RN Ohio, W. Va., Pa. Staff nurse Bellaire (Ohio) City Hosp., 1973-74, Bellaire Clinic, 1974-76; physicians asst. Powhatan Health Ctr., Powhatan Point, Ohio, 1976—. Mem. Am. Acad. Physician Assts., Ohio Assn. Physician Assts., Am. Nurse Assn., Ohio Nurse Assn. Lodge: Order of the Eastern Star. Avocation: snow skiing. Home: 55139 Clover Rd Jacobsberg OH 43933 Office: Powhatan Health Ctr 63 Hwy South Powhatan Point OH 43942

HENDERSHOT, RICHARD JAMES, anesthesiologist; b. Columbus, Ohio, Nov. 7, 1946; s. Jack George Gilbert and Marjorie Marie (Fowler) H.; m. Saundra Lee Trotter, Dec. 27, 1969; children: Alison Rebecca, Benjamin Jennings. BS magna cum laude, Capital U., 1967; MD, Ohio State U., 1971. Diplomate Am. Bd. Anesthesiology. Asst. prof. U. Pitts., 1977-79; staff anesthesiologist St. Vincent/Deaconess Hosp., Billings, Mont., 1979-81, Research/Children's Mercy Hosp., Kansas City, Mo., 1981-83; anesthesiologist, dir. anesthesia services Meml. Hosp., Fremont, Ohio, 1983—; trustee Meml. Hosp., Fremont, 1987—. Fellow Am. Acad. Pediatrics; mem. AMA, Ohio State Med. Assn., Am. Soc. Anesthesiologists, Ohio Soc. Anesthesiologists, Internat. Anesthesia Research Soc., Soc. Cardiovascular Anesthesiologists, Soc. for Ambulatory Anesthesia, Soc. for Pediatric Anesthesia. Office: 125 N Arch St Suite C Fremont OH 43420

HENDERSON, EUGENE LEROY, lawyer; b. Columbus, Ind., July 21, 1925; s. Harry E. and Verna (Guffey) H.; m. Mary Louise Beatty, Sept. 6, 1948; children—Andrew, Joseph, Carrie Henderson Walkup. B.A., Franklin Coll., 1950; J.D., Harvard U., 1953. Bar: Ind. 1953. Assoc. Baker & Daniels, Indpls., 1953-59, ptnr., 1959-65; sr. ptnr. Henderson, Daily, Withrow & DeVoe and predecessor firms, Indpls., 1965—; bd. dirs. Maplehurst Group, Inc., Maplehurst Farms, Maplehurst Deli-Bake, Inc., PHD Venture Capital Corp.; sec. Ind. Fin. Investors, Inc. Mem. Ind. State Bd. Edn., 1984—; pres. Hoosier Art Salon; trustee Franklin Coll., Lacy Found.; bd. dirs. Indpls. Boys' Club. Served with U.S. Maritime Service, 1943-44, AUS, 1944-46. Mem. Indpls. Bar Assn., Ind. Bar Assn., ABA, Internat. Law Assn., Indpls. Mus. Art. Democrat. Clubs: Indpls. Athletic, Meridian Hills Country, Skyline, Venture, Lawyers, Econ. Lodge: Rotary. Home: 6225 Sunset Ln Indianapolis IN 46260 Office: Henderson Daily Withrow & DeVoe 2450 One Indiana Sq Indianapolis IN 46204

HENDERSON, FRANK ELLIS, state supreme court justice; b. Miller, S.D., Apr. 2, 1928; s. Frank Ellis and Hilda (Bogstad) H.; m. Norma Jean Johnson, Dec. 27, 1956; children: Frank Ellis, III, Kimberly, Patrick, Andrea, Eric, John, Anastasia, Matthew. LL.B., U. S.D., 1951. Bar: Fed. Dist. Ct. bar for Dist. S.D 1954. Practiced law Pennington County, S.D., 1953-74; judge 7th Jud. Circuit, State of S.D., 1975-78; justice S.D. Supreme Ct., Pierre, 1979—; mem. S.D. Senate, 1965-66, 69-70. Served to 1st lt. inf. U.S. Army, 1951-53, Korea. Decorated Bronze Star; Korean Service Medal, United Nations Medal. Mem. Pennington County Bar Assn., S.D. State Bar Assn., Am. Legion, VFW (nat. legal staff 1960-61), DAV (state staff judge adv. 1963-64, post comdr. 1962), Phi Delta Theta. Republican. Roman Catholic. Office: Supreme Ct State Capitol Bldg Pierre SD 57501 *

HENDERSON, GERALDINE JONES, school district library administrator; b. Chgo., Nov. 3, 1931; d. Robert David and Marie (Palasz) Jones; m. Clyde Dwight Henderson, Aug. 17, 1955; children—Jill Marie, Mark David. B.S. in Edn., So. Ill. U., 1949-52, M.S., 1955; M.A., Rosary Coll., 1964. Tchr. social studies Park Forest Schs. (Ill.), 1952-53; tchr. history Carbondale High Sch. (Ill.), 1953-55; speech therapist Hillside Elem. Sch. (Ill.), 1955-57; tchr. history, speech coordinator Downers Grove High Sch. (Ill.), 1957-60; tchr. history Naperville High Sch. (Ill.), 1960-61; head librarian Northwest High Sch., House Springs, Mo., 1972-76, Kirkwood High Sch. (Mo.), 1976-77; media specialist Title IVB program for non-pub. schs. Central Midwest Regional Ednl. Lab., St. Louis, 1978; dir. libraries Waterloo Community Unit Sch. Dist. 5 (Ill.), 1979—. Author, narrator video prodn. for Midwest Bapt. Gen. Conf., Christian Education: Lesson Preparation Goals, 1981. Tchr., coordinator ch. sch. Emmaus Bapt. Ch., Ballwin, Mo., 1981-83. Mem. ALA. Republican. Home: 408 Brass Lamp Dr Ballwin MO 63011 Office: Library Services Waterloo Community Unit Sch Dist 5 Bellefontaine Waterloo IL 62298

HENDERSON, HAROLD RICHARD, mechanical engineer; b. Winchester, Ind., June 9, 1927; s. Harold Kenneth and Helen Marie (Shaw) H.; m. Carole Beth Bender, Nov. 17, 1969; children—John Richard, Marilyn Ann Henderson Alexander, Scott Kenneth. B.S. in Mech. Engring., Tri-State Coll., Angola, Ind., 1949. Registered profl. engr., Ohio. Vice pres. engring. Lancaster Engring. (Ohio), 1953-59; v.p. engring. Arcair Co., Lancaster, 1959-78, v.p. ops., 1978—; dir. Gorsuch Enterprises, Lancaster, 1980—. Patentee in field. Ch. bd. dirs. Jr. Achievement Fairfield County, Lancaster, 1962; leader Central Ohio council Boy Scouts Am., 1963. Served with USNR, 1944-46. Mem. Nat. Welding Soc., Nat. Mgmt. Assn. (Silver Knight Mgmt. award 1982), Am. Soc. Testing Materials. Republican. Presbyterian. Lodge: Rotary. Avocations: Private pilot, stained glass. Home: 152 Lenwood Dr Lancaster OH 43130 Office: Arcair Co 3010 N Memorial Dr Lancaster OH 42130

HENDERSON, JAMES ALAN, engine company executive; b. South Bend, Ind., July 26, 1934; s. John William and Norma (Wilson) H.; m. Mary Evelyn Kriner, June 20, 1959; children: James Alan, John Stuart, Jeffrey Todd, Amy Brenton. A.B., Princeton U., 1956; Baker scholar, Harvard U., 1961-63. With Scott Foresman & Co., Chgo., 1962; staff mem. Am. Research & Devel. Corp., Boston, 1963; faculty Harvard Bus. Sch., 1963; asst. to chmn. Cummins Engine Co., Inc., Columbus, Ind., 1964-65; v.p. mgmt. devel. Cummins Engine Co., Inc., 1965-69, v.p. personnel, 1969-70, v.p. ops., 1970-71, exec. v.p., 1971-75, exec. v.p., chief operating officer, 1975-77, pres., 1977—, also dir.; dir. Cummins Engine Found., Inland Steel Co., Chgo., Ameritech, Chgo. Author: Creative Collective Bargaining, 1965. chmn. exec. com. Princeton U.; pres. bd. trustees Culver Ednl. Found. Served to lt. USNR, 1956-61. Presbyn. (elder). Home: 4228 Riverside Dr Columbus IN 47203 Office: Cummins Engine Co Inc Box 3005 Columbus IN 47202-3005

HENDERSON, JAMES ALLEN, engineering executive; b. San Francisco, Sept. 12, 1948; s. Robert M. and Joan Ardus (Nagel) H.; m. Jane Lesure, May 24, 1969 (div. July 1983). BSME, Iowa State U., 1970. Registered profl. engr., Wis., Tex. Staff engr. Allen-Bradley, Milw., 1970-79, El Paso, Tex., 1979-85; dir. engring. Milw. Brush Mfg., Menomonee Falls, 1985—. Mem. ASME (chmn. 1977-79, 84-85, bd. dirs. 1986), Soc. Mfg. Engrs. Home: 5324 W Bottsford Greenfield WI 53220 Office: Milw Brush Mfg PO Box 830 Menomonee Falls WI 53051

HENDERSON, JOE CHARLES, air force officer; b. Whitewright, Tex., July 31, 1941; s. Dove and Mildred Almeda (Powell) H.; m. Patricia Willis, Feb. 8, 1964; 1 child, Andrea. BS in Indsl. Art, North Tex. State U., 1965; MS in Systems Mgmt., U. So. Calif., 1976; postgrad., Air War Coll., 1986. Commd. 2d lt. USAF, 1965, aircraft maintenance officer, 1965-73; chief Pacific Asia force planning Hdqrs. USAF, Washington, 1973-77; dir. logistics Ministry Def., Rep. of Singapore, 1977-79; assoc. prof. aerospace studies Tex. A&M U., College Station, 1979-82; internat. logistics air force logistics command USAF, Kelly AFB, Tex., 1982-85; advanced through grades to col. USAF, 1985; dir. plans Hdqrs. Air Force Logistics Command, Wright-Patterson AFB, Ohio, 1986-87; vice comdr. air force Acquisition Logistics Ctr., Wright-Patterson AFB, 1987—; cons. ministry def. Rep. Singapore, 1977-79, forces armee Royal Vientianne, Laos, 1972, internat. logistics Govt.'s of Bahrain, Mex., Dominican Republican, Colombia, Peoples Rep. Vietnam, Uruguay, Switzerland, El Salvador, Rep. of Korea, Taiwan. Mem. Soc. Logistics Engrs., Air Force Assn., Air War Coll. Alumni Assn. Republican. Episcopalian. Avocations: racquetball, reading, mil. history. Home: 460 Chandler Dr Wright-Patterson AFB OH 45433 Office: AFALC/CV Wright Patterson AFB OH 45433

HENDERSON, LEWIS SEWAL, JR., dentist; b. Parsons, Kans., Oct. 19, 1926; s. Lewis Sewal and Elsie Mae (Bierschbach) H.; m. Betty Louise Young, June 6, 1949 (div.); children: Lewis S. III, Janelle Louise; m. Francis Anita Fisher, Jan. 11, 1985. AA, Parsons Jr. Coll., 1945; DDS, U. Kansas City, 1949. Pvt. practice dentistry Parsons, 1952—; pres. BHR Profl. Corp., 1972—; mem. dental staff Labette County Med. Ctr. Served with AUS, 1945, USN, 1949. Mem. ADA, Southeastern Kans. Dist. Dental Soc. (pres. 1960-61), Delta Signa Delta. Club: Parsons Country (pres. 1960-61). Lodges: Masons, Shriners. Home: 1401 Appleton Parsons KS 67357 Office: 1724 Broadway Parsons KS 67357

HENDERSON, MARK WILLIAM, librarian; b. Laurens, Iowa, Mar. 28, 1951; s. Loyd Earl and Margaret Irene (Devereaux) H.; m. Heather Eileen Jackson, Dec. 4, 1971 (div. Aug. 1986); children: Matthew, Sarah. BA, Wayne State Coll., 1973; MA, Iowa State U., 1979, U. Iowa, 1981. English tchr. South Hamilton Community Sch., Jewell, Iowa, 1974-79; librarian South Hamilton Community Sch., Jewell, 1979-81; librarian, media specialist Oskaloosa (Iowa) High Sch., 1981-85; print media specialist Dowling High Sch., West Des Moines, Iowa, 1985—. Mem. Western Iowa chpt. Muscular Dystrophy Assn., Des Moines, treas., 1983, v.p., 1985. Mem. Nat. Cath. Ednl. Assn., Iowa Ednl. Media Assn. (coordinator Intellectual Freedon award 1981—, bd. dirs. 1986—). Democrat. Roman Catholic. Home: 1800 Grand Ave #163 West Des Moines IA 50265 Office: Dowling High School St Joseph Ednl Ctr 1400 Buffalo Rd West Des Moines IA 50265

HENDERSON, MURRELL ELLIOTT, osteopathic physician; b. Wheatland, Wyo., Mar. 19, 1949; s. Ralph E. and Mansella D. (Davis) H.; m. Karen Koval, Sept. 13, 1974; children: Thomas, Rebekah, Benjamin. BS, U. Wyo., 1971; DO, Kans. City Coll. Osteo. Medicine, 1974. Gen. practice osteo. medicine Wadsworth, Ohio, 1976—; med. dir. PreventaMetrics, Akron, Ohio, 1985—. Vestry man Ch. of Resurrection, Sharon Ctr., Ohio. Mem. Am. Osteo. Assn., Coll. Osteo. Gen. Practitioners (cert.), Am. Osteo. Assn. Sports Medicine, Am. Coll. Sports Medicine, Am. Heart Assn., Am. Running and Fitness Assn., Assn. Fitness in Bus. Republican. Episcopalian. Avocation: gardening. Office: 2858 Market St Akron OH 44313

HENDERSON, RITA EVELYN, county official; b. Belcourt, N.D., Aug. 11, 1929; d. Joseph David and Mary Angeline (Herman) LaVerdure; m. George L. Lizotte, Jan. 21, 1946 (div.); children—George S., Lyman David; m. 2d, Alvy R. Henderson, Sept. 27, 1951. Student Belcourt Community Coll. (N.D.), 1978-79. Bookkeeper, sec. J.C. Penney, Wahpeton, N.D., 1948-50, Canfields, 1950-51; mgr. family farm, 1951-80; bookkeeper Rolette County Sr. Meals and Services, Rolla, N.D., 1980-82, project dir., 1982—. Mem. Rolette County Community Task Force; mem. Rolette County Bldg. Com.; v.p. Rolette County Council on Aging; bd. dirs. Region III Council on Aging, N.E. Health and Wellness; mem. N.D. Funding Task Force, 1985. Grantee Burlington No. Found., 1983; N.D. Community Found., 1983, World Relief Fund, 1984, Nat. Luth. Indian Bd., 1984, 85, William Randolph Hearst Found., 1985, N.D. Hwy. Dept., 1985. Mem. N.D. Project Dirs. Assn., Rolla Hosp. Aux. Democrat. Presbyterian. Lodges: Rebekah, Odd Fellows.

HENDERSON, ROGER EARL, manufacturing executive; b. Akron, Ohio, Mar. 11, 1947; s. Earl McKinley and Janice Irene (Bailey) H.; m. Mary Lou Henderson, Jan. 27, 1968 (div. June 1974); 1 child, Mark Anthony. Buyer Goodyear Aerospace, Akron, Ohio, 1965-68, B.F. Goodrich, Akron, 1968-70; v.p. Jay-Em Corp., Cuyahoga Falls, Ohio, 1970—; cons. Akron Regional Devel. Bd., Nat. Tool & Die Assn., Akron, 1984—. Served to sgt. U.S. Army Res., 1965-71. Home: 2087 Carlile Dr Uniontown OH 44685 Office: Jay-Em Corp 75 Marc Ave Cuyhoga Falls OH 44223

HENDERSON, ROSEMARY, librarian; b. Coffyville, Kans., July 15, 1936; d. Ray Aubrey and Irene Ora (Maxwell) Neale; m. Vance John Henderson, Mar. 9, 1957 (div.); 1 child, Jennifer Ann. AA, Stephens Coll., 1956; BS, Tex. Wesleyan Coll., 1959; M Library, Kans. State Tchrs. Coll., 1967; EdD, U. Kans., 1976. Asst. prof. librarianship U. N.D., Grand Forks, 1967-68; dir. learning resources Coffeyville Community Jr. Coll., 1968—; cons.-evaluator North Cen. Assn. Schs. and Colls., Kans. Library Network Bd., 1984—, vice-chairperson, 1985-87, chairperson, 1987—; mem. adv. council Emporia State U., 1986—. Reviewer Library Jour., 1970-74, Am. Reference Books Ann.-Libraries Unltd., 1974-80. Mem. Assn. Coll. and Research Libraries (chmn. community jr. coll. sect. 1975-76, sect. archivist, historian 1978—, editorial bd. 1986—), ALA (membership promotion task force 1978-81, nominating com. 1979, membership com. 1981-83), Kans. Library Assn. (sec. 1972-74, mem. council 1970-74, 78-83, 86-87, pres.-elect coll. and univ. libraries sect. 1981-83), Mountain Plains Library Asssn. (chmn. coll. and univ. sect. 1973-74). Home: 1206 West 5th St Coffeyville KS 67337 Office: Coffeyville Community Jr Coll Coffeyville KS 67337

HENDERSON, ROSS, business administration educator; b. Winnipeg, Man., Can., Aug. 5, 1928; s. Douglas Dudgeon and Annie Colville (Douglas) H.; m. Jeanette Kirk, Oct. 10, 1953; children—Scott Douglas, Craig Alexander, Eric Grant. B.Sc.M.E., U. Manitoba, 1955; M.B.A., Harvard U., 1957; Ph.D. in Bus., U. Western Ont., Can., 1975. Registered profl. engr., Man. Prin. Ross Henderson Ins. Co., Winnipeg, 1950-66; analyst U.S. Steel Co., Cleve., 1958-60; pres. Damascus Steel Products Ltd., Winnipeg, 1960-65; asst. gen. mgr. Dosco Steel Ltd., Montreal Works, Montreal, Que., Can., 1965-68; prof. bus. adminstrn. U. Man., Winnipeg, 1968—. Author: Plant Startup Productivity, 1975. Contbr. articles to profl. jours. Recipient Gov. Gen.'s medal, 1945; George F. Baker scholar, 1956; recipient Stanton award for Teaching Excellence, U. Man., 1977, Grad. Students' award for Teaching Excellence, U. Man., 1986. Fellow Fin. Analysts Fedn.; mem. Assn. Profl. Engrs. Man., Am. Soc. Quality Control. Avocations: running, swimming. Office: U Man, Dept Bus Adminstrn, Winnipeg, MB Canada R3T 2N2

HENDERSON, STEPHEN DOUGLAS, marketing executive, consultant; b. Bedford, Ind., Apr. 9, 1942; s. Leo Alton and Leah Lucille Henderson; m. Carol Sue Edmonds, Aug. 22, 1964; children: Stephen A., Kendrick K., Craig R. BS, Ind. U., 1964. Prodn. supr. Ford Motor Co., Warren, Mich., 1964-68; project mgr. Controlled Interval Sch., Rolling Hills Estates, Ohio, 1968-76; pres. Productivity Research, Indpls., 1976-77; unit v.p. Integrated Control Systems, Litchfield, Conn., 1977-78; prodn. engr. Stancor-Hamilton Standard Controls, Logansport, Ind., 1978-81, product marketing mgr., 1981-86; sales mgr. Thordarson Meissner, Mt. Carmel, Ill., 1986-87; regional sales mgr. Tamura Corp., Carson, Calif., 1987—; unit v.p. Integrated COntrol Systems, Litchfield, Conn., 1976-78. Mem. Electronic Industries Assn. Republican. Episcopalian. Lodge: Elks. Avocations: golf, swimming, hunting, fishing, reading.

HENDERSON, THOMAS CHARLES, pharmacist; b. Port Huron, Mich., Jan. 3, 1946; s. Kenneth James and Helen Elizabeth (Pressprich). AS, Port Huron Jr. Coll., 1968; BS in Pharmacy, Ferris State Coll., 1971; D of Pharmacy, Wayne State U., 1978. Staff pharmacist Port Huron Hosp., 1972-75, clin. pharmacist, 1977-86; pharmacist, owner The Medicine Shoppe, Kalamazoo, Mich., 1986—. Precinct del. St. Clair County Reps., 1983-84. Mem. Mich. Pharmacists' Assn., Southwest Mich. Pharmacists' Assn., St. Clair County Pharmacists' Assn. (pres. 1973-74, 78-79), Southeastern Mich. Soc. Hosp. Pharmacists. Home: 4329 Duke St C-4 Kalamazoo MI 49008 Office: The Medicine Shoppe 3721 S Westnedge Ave Kalamazoo MI 49008

HENDREN, GARY GENE, mathematics educator; b. Bethany, Mo., Feb. 15, 1939; s. Dwight Lyle and Helen Irene (Beeks) H.; m. Lonna Sharon McComas, Aug. 30, 1959 (div. Feb. 17, 1977); children: Sheri Ann, Jana Beth; m. Lynda Rose Lederman, Dec. 4, 1981. BS in Edn., N.E. Mo. State U., 1962, MA in Edn., 1966. Math. tchr. Riverview Gardens Sch. Dist., St. Louis, 1962-68; math. tchr. Parkway Sch. Dist., Chesterfield, Mo., 1968—, athletic coordinator, 1977—; off-campus instr. N.E. Mo. State U., St. Charles, 1968—; speaker math. and athletic confs. Named Outstanding Young Educator, Mo. Jaycees, 1972; recipient Pillar of Parkway award Parkway Sch. Dist., 1978, Faculty Dedication award Parkway Cen. High Sch., 1982. Mem. NEA (del. convs. 1978-80), Mo. Edn. Assn. (del. convs. 1978-79, mem. numerous North Cen. Assn. evaluation teams), Parkway Edn. Assn. (treas. 1976-77), Nat. Council Tchrs. Math. (local com. chmn. for confs. in St. Louis), Mo. Council Tchrs. Math. (pres. 1980-81, editor Math. Problems 1981—), Ill. Council Tchrs. Math., Math. Club Greater St. Louis (pres. 1975-76), Mo. Interscholastic Athletic Adminstrs. Assn., Nat. Interscholastic Athletic Adminstrs. Assn., Pi Mu Epsilon. Methodist. Club: Greater St. Louis Stamp (jr. advisor 1979—). Avocation: philately. Office: Parkway Central High Sch 369 N Woods Mill Rd Chesterfield MO 63017

HENDRICKS, LARRY DEE, internist, oncologist; b. Urbana, Ill., Mar. 14, 1942; s. Homer Dee and Forrest Erlene (Webber) H.; m. Mary Ann McFadden, July 9, 1965 (div. Oct. 1978); m. Teresita Fernandez, Sept. 8, 1979; Mark, Steve, Derrick, Jennifer, Lisa. BS, Alma Coll., 1964; DO, Chgo. Coll. Osteo. Medicine and Surgery, 1968. Diplomate Osteopath. Bd. Examiners, 1969. Intern Saginaw (Mich.) Osteo. Hosp., 1968-69, resident in internal medicine, 1969-72; practice osteopathic medicine Saginaw, 1972—. Mem. Am. Osteo. Assn., Am. Coll. Osteo. Internists, Mich. Assn. Osteo Physicians and Surgeons, Saginaw County Osteo. Soc. Republican. Roman Catholic. Avocations: golf, swimming, scuba diving. Office: 3400 Shattuck St Saginaw MI 48603

HENDRICKS, LEWIS TALBOT, forest products educator, consultant; b. Rome, N.Y., July 3, 1940; s. Clarence Murray and Thola P. (Brinkman) H.; m. Suzanne Haskins Rose, Aug. 25, 1962; children—Wendy, Heather. B.S., SUNY-Syracuse, 1961, M.S. in Wood Products Engring., 1962; Ph.D. in Forest Products, Mich. State U., 1967. Wood products technologist U.S. Dept. Agr. Forest Service, Duluth, Minn., 1964-67; asst. prof. forest products U. Minn.-St. Paul, 1967-71, assoc. prof., 1971-76, prof., 1976—, extension specialist; vis. prof. forest products lab. U. Wis., Madison, 1985-86; dir. Woodcraft Industries, St. Cloud, Minn.; forest products cons. Mem. Gov.'s Task Force value added wood products, 1981—. SBA grantee, 1982, 83. Mem. Forest Products Research Soc., Sigma Xi, Epsilon Sigma Phi, Gamma Sigma Delta. Methodist. Contbr. articles to profl. jours. Office: 220 Kaufert Lab 2004 Folwell Univ Minn Saint Paul MN 55108

HENDRICKS, TERENCE EUGENE, minister, urban planner; b. St. Louis, Sept. 14, 1952; s. Oliver Carl and Elee (Allen) H.; m. Janice Franklin, Mar. 25, 1972 (div. Oct. 1978); 1 child, Terence Eugene Jr.; m. Wendy Freenan, Dec. 6, 1980; children: Keria Deanne, Leah JoElle. BS in Geography, So. Ill. U., Edwardsville, 1974; BTh, Clarksville Sch. Theology, 1983. Ordained to ministry Bapt. Ch., 1984; cert. geography tchr., 1987. Dispatcher City of East St. Louis, Ill., 1971-75; motivational therapist Child Ctr., Centreville, Ill., 1975-76; youth counselor Youth Service Bur., East St. Louis, 1976-78; urban planner City of East St. Louis, 1978—. Columnist Beacon Newspaper, 1984; editor Community Devel. Newsletter, 1983-85. Asst. pastor Straightway Bapt. Ch., East St. Louis, 1974-82; adminstrv. asst. pastor Macedonia Bapt. Ch., East St. Louis, 1982—; bd. dirs. Foster Grandparents Program, East St. Louis, 1982—, Christian Rehab. Ctr., East St. Louis, 1978-82. Recipient I Dare You Leadership award Ralston Purina Co., St. Louis, 1970; named one of Outstanding Young Men of Am., 1985; scholar Ill. State Tchrs. Assn., 1970-74, Ill. State Gen. Assembly, 1981-84. Mem. Ministerial Alliance, NAACP. Democrat. Lodge: Masons (sr. deacon). Avocations: reading, speaking, bowling, fishing, tennis. Home: 6809 Russell Ave Centreville IL 62203 Office: City of East St Louis 1 Municipal Plaza East Saint Louis IL 62201

HENDRICKSON, JAMES NORMAN, controller, food products executive; b. Sioux City, Iowa, Nov. 14, 1945; s. Norman James and Elsie G. (Pierson) H.; m. Cynthia Lea Roy, Aug. 28, 1968 (div. Aug. 1978); m. Jacelyn Kay Yates, Dec. 29, 1979; children: Jolynn, Angelia, Jeremy. Student, Morningside Coll., 1964-67. Acctg. clerk Metz Baking Co., Sioux City, 1967-69; office mgr. Metz Baking Co., Omaha, 1969-73; office mgr. Metz Baking Co., Sioux City, 1973-78, dir. plant acctg., 1978-82, asst. v.p., controller, 1982-85, v.p., controller, 1985—. Served with USAR, 1966-72. Republican. Lutheran. Club: River City Anglers (Sioux City) (bd. dirs. 1986—). Avocations: fishing, boating, swimming. Office: Metz Baking Co 1014 Nebraska St Sioux City IA 51102

HENDRICKSON, JOHN CLARK, lawyer; b. Dayton, Ohio, Apr. 9, 1943; s. James Clark and June (Waddell) H.; separated; children: Katherine Ayres, Rebecca Clark. BA, U. Chgo., 1965; LLB, Columbia U., 1968; diploma, Nat. Inst. for Trial Adv., 1984. Bar: Ill. 1968, U.S. Supreme Ct. 1979. Assoc. Schiff, Hardin & Waite, Chgo., 1969-73; sole practice Chgo., 1973-79; assoc. Robert Plotkin & Assocs., Chgo., 1979-81; sr. trial atty. EEOC, Chgo., 1981—. Recipient Sustained Superior Performance awards EEOC, 1984, 86. Home: 1845 N Paulina St Chicago IL 60622 Office: Equal Employment Opportunity Commn 536 S Clark Chicago IL 60605

HENDRICKSON, LAWRENCE HILL, insurance company executive; b. Mpls., May 3, 1939; s. Laurence Jacob and Alocoque Loretta (Tierney) H.; m. Yvonne Janice Gulbro, (div. 1978); children—Laurie A., L. Gordon, Lisa K.; m. 2d Karen Lynne Sparks, May 14, 1983. B.A., U. Minn., 1961. Ins. salesman Sunlife Can. Ins. Co., Mpls., 1960-63; sales mgr. Am. Plan Life Ins. Co., Mpls., 1963-65; ptnr. Hendrickson-Karvonen & Assoc., Mpls., 1965-68; life ins. cons. Nordstrom-Larpenteur Agy., Inc., Mpls., 1968-71; exec. v.p., v.p. Minn.-Tex. Land and Cattle Balanced Fin. Planning, Inc., Mpls., 1971-81; mem. Pres.'s council Alexander Hamilton Life Ins. Co., 1982-87; pres. Lar-Mel Cons. Group, Inc., 1984—; chmn., chief exec. officer L.H. Hendrickson & Co., Mpls., 1981—; dir. Investment Corp. Am., Phila., 1974-78. Author: The Salary Continuation Plan, 1983; The Key Executive Plan, 1984. Named to All Stars, Western State Life Ins. Co., 1968-87, Man of Yr., Western States Life Ins. Co., 1968, 71, 73, 75, 79, 84-87; recipient Nat. Quality award Nat. Assn. Life Underwriters, 1972-87. Mem. Million Dollar Round Table, Top of the Table, Nat. Assn. Life Underwriters (nat. sales achievement award 1976-87). Republican. Roman Catholic. Clubs: Flagship Athletic (Eden Prairie, Minn.); Hazeltine Golf (Chaska, Minn.); Missions Hills Golf (Palm Springs, Calif.). Avocations: squash, golf. Home: 4790 Baycliffe Rd S Excelsior MN 55331 Office: LH Hendrickson & Co Inc 3600 W 80th St #140 Bloomington MN 55431

HENDRICKSON, LORRAINE UHLANER, business management educator, consultant; b. Washington, July 28, 1953; d. Julius Earl and Vera (Kolar) Uhlaner; m. Jack Reynold Hendrickson, Jr., Dec. 29, 1978; children: Eric Benjamin, Susan Abigail. A.B., Radcliffe Coll., 1973; Doctorandus, U. Leiden (Netherlands), 1976; M.A., U. Mich., 1976, Ph.D., 1980. Research asst. U. Leiden, 1973-74; asst. study dir. Inst. for Social Research, Ann Arbor, Mich., 1974-78; instr., asst. prof. Mich. State U., East Lansing, 1979-81; asst. prof. dept. mgmt. Coll. Bus., Eastern Mich. U., Ypsilanti, 1981-86, assoc. prof., 1986-84, dir. program devel. and research Ctr. for Entrepreneurship/ Coll. Bus. Service Ctr., 1986—; cons. StarPak Solar Systems Corp., Novi, Mich., 1981-85, dir., treas., 1976-85; cons. Livingston County Sheriff's Dept., Howell, Mich., 1981; cons. personnel mgmt. and orgnl. devel., Domino's Pizza Distbn., Inc., Ann Arbor, Mich., 1986—; del. White House Conf. on Small Bus., 1986; mem. adv. bd. Ann Arbor Innovation Ctr., 1986—; mem. bd. dirs. New Enterprise Forum, Ann Arbor, 1986—. Contbr. book revs. to Personnel Psychology, 1983, 84, papers to profl. confs. Sec., co-chmn. Mich. Alliance Small Bus., Lansing, 1981-83; mem. innovation and tech. task force Gov.'s Conf. on Small Bus., 1981; candidate state Democratic primary, 1982. Council for European Studies pre-dissertation fellow, U. Pitts., 1975. Mem. Acad. Mgmt., Am. Mgmt. Assn., Mich. Assn. Indsl. and Organizational Psychologists, Ypsilanti C. of C. (small bus. council 1986—), Home: 5757 Pontiac Trail Ann Arbor MI 48105 Office: Dept Mgmt Coll Bus Eastern Mich Univ Ypsilanti MI 48197

HENDRICKSON, MELISSA BATKA, protective services executive; b. Chgo., Aug. 13, 1955; d. Milan Edward and Mildred Emily (Chodora) Batka; m. William R. Hendrickson, June 6, 1981. BS, Western Ill. U., 1977; postgrad., DePaul U., 1979. Store detective Bonwit Teller, Chgo., 1977; insp. U.S. Treas. Bur. of Alcohol, Tobacco and Firearms, Chgo., 1978-81; special agent Def. Investigative Services div. U.S. Dept. Def., Chgo., 1981-84, sr. resident agt., team chief, 1984-86; sr. resident agt., team chief Def. Investigative Services div. U.S. Dept. Def., Chgo., Great Lakes, Ill., 1987—. Mem. Fed. Criminal Investigators Assn., Alpha Omicron Pi. Avocations: reading, physical fitness, jogging, gardening. Office: Def Investigative Service Resident Agy Great Lakes Bldg 3 Room 2 Great Lakes IL 60088

HENDRICKS-STERLING, DOROTHY, social services administrator; b. Superior, W.Va., Apr. 13, 1940; d. Joseph and Susie Elizabeth (Hunt) H.; m. Howard Thomas Sterling, Aug. 25, 1973; 1 child, Malik Thomas. BS in Home Econs., Cheyney State Coll., 1965; MS in Counseling, U. Pitts., 1971, cert. group specialist, 1971, PhD in Counseling Edn., Adolescent Psychology, 1974. Tchr. Pitts. Bd. Edn., 1965-69; counselor U. Pitts., 1969-71; counselor, asst. prof. Clarion (Pa.) State Coll., 1971-73; youth specialist Met. YWCA, Cleve., 1973-82, assoc. exec. dir., 1982-84; chief exec. office, pres. Ctr. Human Relations, Cleve., 1984—; cons., trainer Urban League, Cleve., 1973-75, Spanish Am. Commn., Cleve., 1975-80, Nat. Bd. YWCA, N.Y.C., 1982—. trainer Girl Scouts U.S.; pres. bd. dirs. Teen Fathers Program, Cleve., 1983—; bd. dirs. Frances Hollingsworth Calgie Found., Cleve., 1983—, Cleve. Area Bd. Realtors, 1984—, WomenSpace, Cleve., 1985—. Recipient Service award Teen Father Program, 1985-86. Mem. YWCA of U.S. (Service award 1981,83). Democrat. Methodist. Club: Toastmistress (charter mem., pres. Cleve. chpt. 1980-82). Home: 3810 Washington Blvd University Heights OH 44118 Office: Ctr Human Relations PO Box 9194 Cleveland OH 44101-3911

HENDRIKSE, RANDALL DON, computer company executive, consultant; b. Sheboygan, Wis., Oct. 12, 1949; s. John D. and Jeanette (Van Houten) H.; m. Kathleen Joyce Fieldhouse, Aug. 22, 1970; children—Christopher Michael, Timothy John. Student Calvin Coll., 1967-70; Assoc., Davenport Coll., 1970. Rate clk. Chair City Motor Express, Sheboygan, 1971-72, mgr. claims, 1972-76, mgr. data processing, 1976-82, Transpo Services, Sheboygan, 1982-84; pres., owner Accutech Computer Systems Ltd. U.S.A., Sheboygan, 1985—; cons. Software PM, Sheboygan, 1984-85; mem. adv. com. data processing Lakeshore Tech. Inst., Cleveland, Wis., 1984—. Elder, Christian Ref. Ch., Sheboygan, 1983—; announcer religious broadcasting, Sheboygan, 1973—; youth leader Cadets, Sheboygan, 1982—. Republican.

HENDRIX, STEPHEN JOSEPH, sales executive, freelance film and video producer; b. Lawrence, Kans., Aug. 13, 1956; s. Joseph William and Mildred Ailene (Wales) H.; m. Carol Kay Conley, June 7, 1980; children: Christopher Joseph, Holly Michelle. AS, B in Electronic Enging. Tech., Mo. Inst. Tech., 1979. Announcer Sta. KRMN, Cameron, Mo., 1976-78; announcer, egr. Sta. KEXS, Excelsior Springs, Mo., 1978-79; sales rep. Communication Systems Assocs., Cameron, 1979—. Built TV ministry First Assembly of God, St. Joseph, Mo., 1982-86. Singer Kansas City (Mo.) Youth for Christ, 1973-74; communications officer CAP, Cameron, 1984-85. Recipient guardian membership Nat. Fed. Ind. Bus., 1985. Mem. Am. Radio Relay League (life). Republican. Pentecostal. Lodge: Masons. Avocations: flying, amateur radio. Home: 303 N Prairie Hamilton MO 64644 Office: Communications Systems Assocs Inc 920 Ashland Dr Cameron MO 64429

HENDRIX, THOMAS CLAGETT, government official; b. Miraj, India, Sept. 3, 1920; s. Everett Jehu and Minnie Kate (Clagett) H.; came to U.S., 1924; B.A., Hastings Coll., 1942; J.D., Northwestern U., 1947; m. Carol Arden Crumpacker, Sept. 3, 1946 (div. Aug. 1966); children—Walker, Sarah, Anne, Kari; m. Dona Mae Farber, Oct. 2, 1981 (div. July 1982). Admitted to Mo. bar, 1948, Ill. bar, 1947; sole law, Kansas City, Mo., 1948-53; exec. sec. J.P. Hillelson, U.S. Congressman, Washington, 1953; legal asst., to chmn. NLRB, 1954-55, field atty., St. Louis, 1955-57, regional atty., Kansas City, Mo., 1957-69, regional dir., 1969-85, sole practice, Overland Park, Kans., 1985—. Served with USAAF, 1942-45. Home: 10439 Ash St Overland Park KS 66207 Office: PO Box 7442 Overland Park KS 66207

HENGESH, DONALD J., state corrections executive, military officer; b. Escanaba, Mich., June 4, 1944; s. Hazen Henry and Ruth Elizabeth (Boehnkamp) H.; m. Barbara Jean Hayes, Aug. 21, 1965 (div. Feb. 1983); children: Deborah Lynn, David Scott; m. Mary Bailey-Hengesh, June 25, 1983. BS, Cen. Mich. U., 1966; MS, Mich. State U., 1973; diploma, Air Command and Staff Coll., Maxwell AFB, Ala., 1977, Indsl. War Coll., Washington, 1980. Probation officer Mich. Dept. Corrections, Lansing, 1972-75, program mgr., 1975-77, program planner, 1977-78, adminstrv. asst., dep. dir., 1979-81, dir. community alternatives, 1981—. Coach and referee DeWitt (Mich.) team Am. Youth Soccer Orgn., 1979-85; scout leader Lansing council Boy Scouts Am., 1979-83; pres. St. Jude's Cath. Community, DeWitt, 1978-80. Served to maj. Mich. Air N.G., 1967—. Mem. Am. Corrections Assn., Nat. Guard Assn. U.S., Mich. Assn. Chiefs of Police, Mich. Corrections Assn., Nat. Guard Assn. Mich. Roman Catholic. Lodge: Lions (3d v.p. DeWitt chpt. 1987—). Avocations: design and building furniture. Home: 801 Andover DeWitt MI 48820 Office: Mich Dept Corrections 300 E Michigan Ave Lansing MI 48913

HENIKOFF, LEO M., JR., medical educator, university president; b. Chgo., May 9, 1939; m. Arlene Joan, Dec. 20, 1959; children—Leo M. III, Jamie Sue. M.D. with highest honors, U. Ill.-Chgo., 1963. Diplomate Am. Bd. Pediatrics, Am. Bd. Pediatric Cardiology. Intern Presbyn.-St. Luke's Hosp., Chgo., 1963-64; resident Presbyn.-St. Luke's Hosp., 1964-66, fellow in pediatric cardiology, 1968-69; clin. instr. U. Ill. Coll. Medicine, Chgo., 1964-66; clin. instr. pediatrics Georgetown U. Med. Sch., Washington, 1966-68; clin. asst. prof. Georgetown U. Med. Sch., 1968; asst. prof. U. Ill. Coll. Medicine, 1968-71; asst. prof. pediatrics Rush Med. Coll., Chgo., 1971-74; assoc. prof. Rush Med. Coll., 1974-79, asst. dean admissions, 1971-74, assoc. dean student affairs, 1974-76, assoc. dean med. scis. and services, 1976-79, acting dean v.p. med. affairs, 1976-78, prof. pediatrics, prof. medicine, 1984—; v.p. inter-instl. affairs Rush-Presbyn.-St. Luke's Med. Ctr., Chgo., 1978-79, pres., 1984—, trustee, 1984—; dean and v.p. med. affairs Temple U. Sch. Medicine, Phila., 1979-84; prof. pediatrics and medicine Temple U. Sch. Medicine, 1979-84; pres. Rush U., Chgo., 1984—; adj. attending Presbyn.-St. Luke's Hosp., 1969, asst., 1970-72, assoc., 1973-76, sr. attending, 1977-79, 84—; staff Temple U. Hosp., 1979-84; assoc. staff St. Christopher's Hosp. for Children, 1979-84; mem. Ill. Council of Deans, 1977-79; vice chmn. Chgo. Tech. Park, 1984-85, chmn., 1985-86; chmn. bd. Mid-Am. Health Programs, Inc., 1985—. Contbr. chpts. to books, articles to profl. jours. Bd. dirs. Fishbein Found., 1975-79, Chgo. Regional Blood Program, 1977-79, Sch. Dist. 69, 1974-75, Johnston R. Bowman Health Ctr. for Elderly, 1984—; bd. mgrs. St. Christopher's Hosp. for Children, 1979-84; bd. govs. Temple U. Hosp., 1979-84, Heart Assn. S.E. Pa., 1979-84; trustee Episcopal Hosp., 1983-84, Otho S.A. Sprague Meml. Inst., 1984—; mem. adv. bd. Univ. Village Assn., 1984—; mem. exec. com. Gov.'s Build Ill. Com.), 1985—. Served to lt. comdr. USPHS, 1964-68, Res. 1968—. Recipient Roche Med. award, 1962; Mosby award, 1963; Raymond B. Allen Instructorship award U. Ill. Coll. Medicine, 1966; Phoenix award Rush Med. Coll., 1977. Fellow Am. Acad. Pediatrics, Inst. Medicine Chgo., Coll. Physicians Phila.; mem. Assn. Am. Med. Colls. (chmn. nominating com. 1980, council of deans 1977-84, mem. audit com. 1984—), Pa. Med. Sch. Deans Com., AMA (council on ethical and jud. affairs 1984—), Pa. Med. Soc., Philadelphia County Med. Soc., Alpha Omega Alpha (chmn. nat. nominating com. 1981—, nat. dir. 1979—), Omega Beta Pi, Phi Eta Sigma, Phi Kappa Phi. Office: Rush-Presbyn St Luke's Med Ctr 1653 W Congress Pkwy Chicago IL 60612

HENK, EDWARD WILLIAM, dentist; b. Mpls., May 3, 1943; s. William Christopher and Genevieve Ann (Stotko) H.; m. Suzanne Louise Riendl, Dec. 26, 1972; children: Julia, William, Hillary. Student, St. Cloud (Minn.) State U., 1961-63; BS with distinction, U. Minn., 1965, DDS, 1967. Gen. practice dentistry Buffalo, Minn., 1969—; cons. Ebenezer Home, Buffalo, 1986—; bd. dirs. Retirement Ctr. Wright County. 1981—. Served to capt. USAF, 1967-69. Fellow Acad. Gen. Dentistry; mem. ADA, Minn. Dental Assn., Mpls. Dist. Dental Assn., Minn. Prosthodontic Soc., Am. Legion, Minn. Acad. Restorative Dentistry. Roman Catholic. Lodges: Rotary, KC. Home: 405 4th Ave NW Buffalo MN 55313 Office: 20 S 1st St Buffalo MN 55313

HENKE, ROBERT JOHN, lawyer, engineer; b. Chgo., Oct. 13, 1934; s. Raymond Anthony and May Dorothy (Driscoll) H.; m. Mary Gabrielle Handrigan, June 18, 1960; children—Robert Joseph, Ann Marie. B.S.E.E., U. Ill., 1956; M.B.A., U. Chgo., 1964; J.D., No. Ill. U., 1979, postgrad. John Marshall Law Sch. Bar: Ill. 1980, Wis. 1980, U.S. Dist. Ct. (no. dist.) Ill. 1980, U.S. Dist. Ct. (we. and ea. dists.) Wis. 1980, U.S. Supreme Ct. 1984; registered profl. engr., Ill., Wis. sr. elec. engr. Commonwealth Edison Co., Chgo., 1956-80; elec. engr. Peterson Builders, Sturgeon Bay, Wis., 1982-83; sr. elec., cost estimating engr. Sargent & Lundy Engrs., Chgo., 1985—; instr. econs. and criminal law NE Wis. Tech. Inst., 1981-82; asst. dist. atty. Door County, Wis., 1981, ct. commr., 1981-82; sole practice, Door County, 1981-84, Lake County, Ill., 1984—; dir. Scand, Door County. Vice chmn. Door County Bd. Adjustment, 1983-84; atty. coach Wis. Bar Found. High Sch. Moot Ct. Competition, Door County, 1984; vol. lawyers program, Lake County, Ill., 1985—. Served with USAR, 1958-63. Mem. ABA, Wis. Bar Assn., Door Kewaunee Bar Assn. (pres. 1983-84), Ill. Bar Assn. (vol. lawyers program Lake County chpt.), Chgo. Bar Assn., Lake County Bar Assn., Am. Judicature Soc., Ill. Soc. Profl. Engrs., Assn. Trial Lawyers Am., IEEE, NSPE, Am. Assn. Cost Engrs. Roman Catholic. Home: 835 D Country Club Dr Libertyville IL 60048 Office: Sargent & Lundy Engrs 55 E Monroe St Chicago IL 60603

HENKE, STEVEN JOHN, chemical company executive; b. Beatrice, Nebr., July 11, 1948; s. Gaylord George and Hilda Marie H. B.S., U. Nebr., 1970; M.B.A., Loyola U., Chgo., 1976; m. Janice Jo Barringer, Oct. 12, 1973. Research engr. Amoco Chems., Naperville, Ill., 1970-76, research supr., 1977—; tchr. plastics program Coll. DuPage, 1978-83, mem. plastics adv. bd., 1978-83. Recipient William Heusel award U. Nebr., 1966. Mem. Am. Ofcls. Assn., Soc. Advancement Materials Process Engring., Ill. High Sch. Assn. Recognized Football Ofcls., Phi Eta Sigma. Lutheran. Home: 6713 Cherry Tree Woodridge IL 60517

HENKEL, OTTO FREDERICK, JR., telephone company executive; b. Phila., May 25, 1955; s. Otto Frederick and Jean C. (Wadley) H.; m. Cynthia Ann Krieg, June 17, 1978. B.S. in Agr., Ohio State U., 1976, B.S. in Bus. Adminstrn., 1977. C.P.A., Ohio, Fla.; cert. internal auditor; cert. quality analyst; cert. mgmt. acct. Staff auditor Alexander Grant & Co., Dayton, Ohio, 1977-78, staff auditor, Cin., 1978-79; internal auditor Cin. Bell, Inc., Cin., 1980-83, corp. tax and acctg. researcher and planner, 1983—. Pres. Ross Citizens for a Better Community (Ohio), 1980-81; bd. dirs. Future Pioneers, Cin., 1983-84, treas. 1984-85. Mem. Inst. Internal Auditors (pres. 1984-85, v.p. 1983-84, treas. 1982-83, mem. internat. com. on membership, 1984-85, bd. govs. 1985-87), Inst. Mgmt. Acctg., Nat. Assn. Accts. (dir. 1981-83, sec. 1983-84, v.p. 1984-85, del. Ohio Council 1983-84, dir. Ohio Council 1984-86, pres. 1986-87, nat. com. on research 1987—), Ohio Soc. C.P.A.s, Fla. Soc. C.P.A.'s, Am. Inst. C.P.A.s, Ky. Soc. C.P.A.s, Assn. MBA Execs. Republican. Methodist. Home: PO Box 2847 Cincinnati OH 45201 Office: Cin Bell Inc 102-742 PO Box 2301 Cincinnati OH 45201

HENKEL, ZANE GREY, rehabilitation administrator; b. Denison, Iowa, Jan. 19, 1937; s. Franz Henry and Ennice Pearl (Hoskinson) H.; m. Beverly Grace Joy, June 18, 1960; children: Daniel Greyson, Stephen Christopher, Nathan Zachary, Philip Alexander. BA, Drake U., 1970; MEd, Auburn U., 1973. Cert. secondary tchr., Wis., Iowa. Free lance musician Des Moines, 1954-62; instr. music Elmer Conservatory, Milw., 1962-65; rehab. supr. State of Iowa, Des Moines, 1974-81; disabilty investigator and vocat. specialist Social Security Adminstrn., Des Moines, 1981—. Mem. Cen. Iowa United Profls. (pres. 1984-85), Phi Beta Kappa, Phi Kappa Phi. Avocations: foreign and domestic travel. Home: 8502 NW Jester Park Dr Polk City IA 50226 Office: Disability Br State of Iowa 510 E 12th St Des Moines IA 50319

HENLEY, JOEL DENNIS, accountant, tax consultant; b. Aberdeen, S.D., Sept. 3, 1956; s. Gerald Dennis and Nadene A. (Bierman) H.; m. Elizabeth Ann Hyde, Oct. 2, 1982. BS in Acctg. with honor, U. S.D., 1978. CPA, Minn. Staff acct. Dunmire, Short & Co., Gillette, Wyo., 1978-79; tax cons. Touche Ross & Co., Mpls., 1979-85, Coopers & Lybrand, Mpls., 1985—; speaker in field. Contbr. articles to profl. jours. Mem. Minn. Multi-Housing Assn.; bd. dirs. Concepts Family Living Inc., Mpls., 1984-86. Mem. Am. Inst. CPA's, Minn. Soc. CPA's. Lutheran. Club: Toastmasters (officer 1985-86). Home: 1520 Natchez Ave S Golden Valley MN 55416 Office: Coopers & Lybrand 1000 TCF Tower Minneapolis MN 55402

HENLEY, TERRY LEW, computer company executive; b. Seymour, Ind., Nov. 10, 1940; s. Ray C. and Barbara Marie (Cockerham) H.; m. Martha L. Gill, Mar. 26, 1961; children: Barron Keith, Troy Grayson. BS, Tri-State U., 1961; MBA, Loyola U., 1980, D in Psychology, 1982. Research and devel. engr. Halogens Research Lab., Dow Chem. Co., Midland, Mich., 1961-63, lead process engr., polymer plant, Bay City, Mich., 1964, supt. bromide-bromate plants, Midland, 1964-68; nat. sales mgr. Ryan Industries, Louisville, 1968-70; internat. sales mgr. Chemineer, Inc., Dayton, Ohio, 1970-77; cons. mktg., Xenia, Ohio, 1977-78; pres. Med-Systems Mgmt., Inc., Dayton, Ohio, 1978—. Author: Chemical Engineering, 1976; contbr. articles in field to profl. jours. Mem. Internat. Graphoanalysis Soc., Am. Inst. Chem. Engrs., Am. Mgmt. Assn., Med. Group Mgmt. Assn., Ohio Handwriting Analysts Assn., Soc. Integration Graphology. Home: 1167 Highview Dr Beavercreek OH 45385 Office: Med-Systems Mgmt Inc 8290 N Dixie Dr Dayton OH 45414

HENNEKES, DANIEL MARTINUS, mechanical engineer; b. Evansville, Ind., Feb. 7, 1946; s. Martinus E. and Louise (Schmidt) H.; m. Ruth Ann Fries, Jan. 6, 1968 (div. 1975); m. Sharon Alberta Snell, Apr. 5, 1975; children: Zachary, Chris. BSME, U. Ky., Lexington, 1968. Registered profl. engr., Ohio. With maintenance dept. Middletown (Ohio) Hosp., 1971-73; design engr. Cin. Milacron, 1969-71, 73-81, engring. supr., 1981-84, project mgr., 1984—. Patentee tool mount, robot tool system. Republican. Avocations: sailing, motor boating. Home: 302 Miami St Morrow OH 45152 Office: Cin Milacron 4701 Marburg Ave Cincinnati OH 45209

HENNENBERG, MICHAEL CHAIM, lawyer; b. Weiden, Fed. Republic Germany, Sept. 23, 1948; came to U.S., 1949; s. Jacob and Hildegard (Hohenleitner) H.; m. Susan Spitz, Mar. 7, 1982; children: Julia Esther, Deborah Pearl. B.S. in Bus. Adminstrn., Ohio State U., 1970; J.D., Cleve. State U., 1974. Bar: Ohio 1974, U.S. Dist. Ct. (no. dist.) Ohio 1974, U.S. Ct. Appeals (6th cir.) 1977, U.S. Supreme Ct. 1978. Dep. clk. Cuyahoga County Juvenile Ct., Cleve., 1972; law clk. Law Students Civil Rights Research Council, Cleve. Marshall Coll. Law, Cleve. State U., 1972-73; legal intern Pub. Defender's Office, Cuyahoga County, Cleve., 1973-74; ptnr., trial lawyer Greene & Hennenberg Co., L.P.A., Cleve., 1974—; panel chmn. Cuyahoga County Common Pleas Ct. Arbitration Commn., 1974—; guest lectr. profl. meetings; panelist legal topics, radio and TV shows. Contbr. articles to legal publs. Mem. Simon Wiesenthal Ctr. for Holocaust Studies; bd. dirs. Hebrew Free Loan Assn., 1979-83; Citizens League Greater Cleve.; vice chmn. ann. fund raising drive Jewish Community Fedn. Mem. Ohio Acad. Trial Lawyers (criminal law standing com.), Cleve. Bar Assn. (mem. criminal law sect. 1974—, chmn.; 1981-82, legis. liaison 1983-85 , mem. steering com. task force on violent crime 1982—, mem. jud. selection com. 1982-85, trustee 1985—), Cuyahoga Criminal Def. Lawyers Assn. (founder, editor quar. newsletter, pres. 1986-87), Ohio State Bar Assn., Assn. Trial Lawyers Am., Nat. Assn. Criminal Def. Lawyers, ABA, U.S. Supreme Ct. Hist. Soc., Cleve. State U. Law Alumni Assn. Home: 29200 Shaker Blvd Pepper Pike OH 44124 Office: Greene & Hennenberg Co LPA 801 Bond Court Bldg Cleveland OH 44114

HENNESSEY, DAVID CHARLES, public relations professional; b. Elgin, Ill., Mar. 6, 1949; s. John Quinn and Virginia Mary (Schultz) H.; m. Linda Huschle, Dec. 15, 1973. BA in English, St. John's U., Collegeville, Minn., 1971; Assoc. MLS, U. Mich., 1976. Asst. dir. Le Sueur-Waseca Regional Library, Waseca, Minn., 1976-77; acting dir. Le Sueur-Waseca Regional Library, Waseca, 1977, dir., 1978-79; pub. info. specialist St. Paul div. Pub. Health, 1980-84, St. Paul Dept. Planning and Econ. Devel., 1984—. Scriptwriter (videotape) On Your Behalf, 1987. Bd. dirs. Ramsey County unit Am. Cancer Soc., St. Paul, 1982; mem. pub. info. com. Minn. div. Am. Cancer Soc., Mpls., 1982—; bd. dirs., mem. exec. bd. The Eclectic Co., St. Paul, 1986—. Served with USCG, 1971-75. Recipient Award of Merit Minn. div. Am. Cancer Soc., 1982. Mem. Nat. Assn. Govt. Communicators, Minn. Assn. Govt. Communicators (v.p. adminstrn., No. Lights Excellence award, 1985, 86, 87). Democratic-Farmer-Labor. Roman Catholic. Avocations: reading, cross-country skiing, acting. Home: 1987 Sargent Ave Saint Paul MN 55105 Office: St Paul Dept Planning and Econ Development 25 W 4th St 13th Floor Saint Paul MN 55102

HENNESSEY, FRANK M., music, video, book computer software products and accessories distributor; b. 1938; married. Ptnr. Coopers & Lybrand, 1964-81; pres. Handleman Co., Troy, Mich., 1981—, also dir. Office: Handleman Co 500 Kirts Blvd Troy MI 48084

HENNESSEY, RICHARD EDWARD, accountant; b. Ft. Wayne, Ind., Sept. 14, 1951; s. Richard Kelly and Rose Mary (Ernst) H.; m. Martha Jane Duran, Dec. 22, 1973; children: Roseanne, Richard J. BS in Acctg., Ind. U., 1973. CPA, Ind. Staff acct. Price Waterhouse, Indpls., 1973-76, sr. tax acct., 1976-78, tax mgr., 1978-81, sr. tax mgr., 1981-84, ptnr., 1984, tax ptnr. in-charge, 1987—. V.p. Ind. Found. Bd. of Assocs., Bloomington, 1985—, Forum for Internat. Profl. Services, Indpls., 1986—; mem. Penrod Soc., Indpls., 1986—; pres. Indpls./World Skating Acad., 1986—. Mem. Am. Inst. CPA's, Ind. CPA Soc. Republican. Roman Catholic. Clubs: Woodstock (Indpls.), Indpls. Athletic. Avocations: squash, tennis, reading. Office: Price Waterhouse 2900 One Indiana Sq Indianapolis IN 46204

HENNESSY, DARLENE LENORE, human resource consultant; b. Macomb, Ill., Nov. 2, 1927; d. Colonel Kinsman and Maude Belle (Martin) Dean; divorced; children: Michael, Colleen, Robin. AA in Sociology, Coll. DuPage, 1972; BA in Sociology, Northeastern Ill., Chgo., 1977; MA in Social Sci., Northeastern Ill., 1978; MS in Counseling Psychology, George Williams Coll., Downers Grove, Ill., 1984. Cert. social and family therapist. Casework supr. State of Ill., Woodstock, Ill., 1972-77; counselor alcoholism Resurrection Hosp., Chgo., 1977-79; pvt. practice family therapy Glen Ellyn and Hoffman Estate, Ill., 1984—; coordinator family recovery programs Alcoholism Treatment Ctr. Alexian Bros. Med. Ctr., Elk Grove, Ill., 1979—. Mem. Am. Assn. Counseling Devel., Nat. Employment Counselors Assn., Internat. Graphoanalysis Soc., World Assn. Document Examiners, Women In Mgmt., Nat. Assn. Future Women, Ill. Assn. Addictions Counselors, Glen Ellyn C. of C. Avocations: stained glass, gardening. Home: 214 W Des Plaines Ln Hoffman Estates IL 60194 Office: H&K Assocs 799 Roosevelt Rd Bldg 6 Suite 303 Glen Ellyn IL 60137

HENNESSY, HAROLD RICHARD, physician; b. Two Harbors, Minn., Aug. 12, 1903; s. Maurice Alexander and Sarah Maude (Ousman) H.; B.A., Carleton Coll., 1926; B.S., U. Minn., 1930, M.B., 1930, M.D., 1931; cert. in public health U. Calif.-Berkeley, 1939; grad. U.S. Army Sch. of Mil. Govt., 1943; postgrad. U. Va., 1943; m. Helen Adele Lounsberry, July 24, 1930; children—Helen V., Irene E., Harold Richard, Marjorie J. Lic. physician, Minn., Calif., Ill. Intern, Calif. Lutheran Hosp., Los Angeles, 1930-31; resident Los Angeles City Health Dept., 1931-32; practice gen. medicine, Los Angeles, 1932-33; organizer, dir. Sutter-Yuba Bi-County Health Unit, Yuba City and Marysville, Calif., 1939; commd. 1st lt., M.C., U.S. Army, 1930, advanced through grades to col., 1946; chief med. unit instrs. sect. 9th Corps Area Presidio of San Francisco, 1940-41; chief indsl. med. officer Hdqrs. 9th Service Command, Salt Lake City, 1942-43; chief public health officer Hdqrs. Communications Zone G-5, ETOUSA, Hdqrs. SHAEF, 1944; chief public health officer Office of Surgeon, 15th U.S. Army, Belgium and Germany, 1945; cons. to surgeon gen. U.S. Army, 1947-52; cons. Office of Surgeon, 5th U.S. Army, 1962, ret., 1963; pvt. practice public health cons., Park Ridge and Winnetka, Ill., now Highwood, Ill.; mem. staff AMA, 1946-48; asst. sec. Council Indsl. Health, exec. officer com. profl. relations ACS, 1949-66. Decorated Bronze Star (U.S.); knight Order of Public Health (France); officer Order of Orange-Nassau with swords (Netherlands); Commemorative War Cross (Yugoslavia); recipient certs. of appreciation U.S. Army; hon. Ky. col., 1960; hon. mem. Indian Council, Clinton, Okla., named Chief White Arrow, 1960; named Hon. Citizen State of Tex., 1961, Hon. Col., Ala. State Militia, 1965, Hon. Adm. Tex. Navy, 1966; recipient Letter of Commendation, Pres. Harry S. Truman, 1971; Physician Recognition award AMA, 1980, 83; others. Fellow Am. Public Health Assn., Am. Assn. Indsl. Physicians and Surgeons; mem. Am. Assn. Sr. Physicians, Internat. Health Soc. (founder, 1st pres. 1949), Ret. Officers Assn. (Long Timers award 1983), Res. Officers Assn., Assn. Mil. Surgeons U.S., Fifty Yr. Club Am. Medicine, Mil. Order World Wars (mem. Silver Star roll Chgo. chpt.), Order of Lafayette (charter), Phi Beta Pi. Republican. Clubs: Officers (Ft. Sheridan, Ill.); Masons (Two Harbors, Minn.). Author geneal. books; contbr. articles to profl. jours. Home and Office: 10 E Hawthorn Pkwy Apt 422 Vernon Hills IL 60061

HENNEY, MAC LEE, lawyer; b. Columbus, Ohio, May 25, 1915; s. John Langford Wolbach and Ruth Oleta (Wilson) H.; m. Judith Ann Kauffman, May 29, 1947; children—Scott K., Cynthia Lee Henney Ayers, Deborah Lou Henney Krall, Christina Ann. J.D., Ohio State U., 1937. Bar: Ohio 1937. Sole practice, Columbus, Ohio, 1937-42; 1st officer Pan Am. Airways, Miami, Fla., 1942-46; mem. firm Henney & Walcutt, Columbus, 1946-60, Henney & Shaefer, 1960-70, White, Rankin, Henry, Morse & Mann, Columbus, 1970-85, White & Rankin, L.P.A., Columbus, 1985-87; counsel to Robins Preston & Beckett Co., Columbus, 1987—; corp. sec. Ohio Bar Title Ins. Co., 1955-87. Contbr. articles to profl. jours. Fellow Ohio State Bar Found.; mem. ABA, Ohio Bar Assn., Columbus Bar Assn. Republican. Episcopalian. Avocations: sailing; flying. Home: 2840 Canterbury Rd Columbus OH 43221 Office: Robins Preston & Beckett Co LPA 1328 Dublin Rd Columbus OH 43215

HENNING, WILLIAM CLIFFORD, cemetery consulting company executive; b. Kalamazoo, Oct. 21, 1918; s. Russell and Dott Lois (Stauffer) H.; B.A., Albion Coll. (Mich.), 1940; postgrad. Northwestern U. Law Sch., 1940-42, U. Mich. Law Sch., summer 1941; m. Charlotte Conrad, Sept. 14, 1946; children—Peggy J. Henning Berlin, Helen L. Henning Boddy. Sec., Sycamore (Ill.) C. of C., 1945-46; exec. sec. Allegheny County Funeral Dirs. Assn., Pitts., 1946-48, Am. Cemetery Assn., Columbus, Ohio, 1948-56; owner, pres. Am. Cemetery Cons., Inc., Springfield, Ohio, 1961—; sec., treas., gen. mgr. Rose Hill Burial Park, Springfield, Ohio, 1956-76. County chmn. United Appeals Fund, 1962; bd. dirs., 1964-67; moderator Snowhill United Ch. Christ, Springfield, 1958-60. Served to 1st lt. USAAF, 1943-45; PTO. Decorated Air medal with 2 oak leaf clusters. Mem. Am., Central Ohio (pres. 1958), cemetery assns., Ohio Assn. Cemetery Supts. and Ofcls. (pres. 1960), Am. Soc. Profl. Cons. Republican. Club: Springfield Lit. (pres. 1984). Lodges: Eagles, Kiwanis (pres. Springfield 1963), Masons. Contbr. articles to profl. jours. Home and Office: 6319 Plateau Dr Springfield OH 45502

HENRETTA, J(OSEPH) THOMAS, lawyer; b. Barberton, Ohio, Apr. 25, 1945; s. John Thomas and Edna (Kurchev) H.; m. Cathy Ann Litt, Dec. 27, 1968; children: David, Kevin, Megan. BA, U. Akron, 1968, JD, 1975. Asst. prosecuting atty. Summit County, Akron, Ohio, 1976-78; asst. atty. gen. State of Ohio, Columbus, 1978-84; ptnr. Scanlon & Henretta Co., LPA, Akron, 1984—. Bd. dirs. Akron Jewish Community Fedn., 1983; trustee Akron Jewish Ctr., 1983—; mem. adv. bd. Morley Health Ctr., Akron, 1985—; mem. cen. and exec. com. Summit County Dem. Party, Akron, 1976—. Served with U.S. Army, 1968-70. Mem. Assn. Trial Lawyers Am. (steering com. key person 1986—), Ohio Bar Assn. (Akron Bar Assn. (chmn. lawyer's assistance 1986—). Roman Catholic. Avocations: exercise, gardening, music. Home: 601 Haskell Dr Akron OH 44313 Office: Scanlon & Henretta 76 S Main St Akron OH 44308

HENRICH, ROBERT RICHARD, dentist; b. Queens, N.Y., Dec. 20, 1933; s. Milton Marvin and Matilda Elizabeth (Blecha) H.; m. Marie Agnes Delle Fave, Feb. 11, 1956; children: Robert P., Frank K., Elizabeth M., Christopher M. BS, U. Rochester, N.Y., 1955; DDS, Washington U., St. Louis, 1973. Registered profl. engr. Aircraft design engr. N.Am. Aviation, Columbus, Ohio, 1958-60; devel. engr. AFC Industries, St. Charles, Mo., 1960-68; cons. engring. sci. various orgns., 1968-74; instr. Washington U., 1972-75; gen. practice dentistry St. Charles, 1974—. Served to 1st lt. USMC,

1955-58. Recipient Scholastic Achievement award Internat. Coll. Dentists, 1973. Mem. ASME, ADA, Mo. Dental Assn. (various coms.). Avocations: bowling, amateur radio, duplicate bridge (national master), golf. Home: 3405 Wilshire Saint Charles MO 63301 Office: 2860 W Clay Saint Charles MO 63301

HENRIKSEN, NIEL CHRISTIAN, sales manager; b. Champaign, Ill., Sept. 2, 1960. Sales trainee Nabisco Brands, Inc., Champaign, 1982-83, sales rep., 1983-86; sales manager Nabisco Brands, Inc., Broadview, Ill., 1987—. Mem. Assn. MBA Execs., MBA Assn. (scholar 1986), Delta Mu Delta, Lambdi Chi Alpha (alumni of yr. 1984). Republican. Lutheran. Avocations: running, golfing, speed skating. Home: 5740 N Sheridan Rd Apt 7D Chicago IL 60660

HENRIKSON, VIRGINIA MARIE, accountant, financial planner. BA, St. Cloud (Minn.) State U., 1965. CPA, Minn; cert. fin. planner, Minn. Acct. Arthur Andersen & Co., Mpls., 1965-66, U. Minn., Mpls., 1966-74; tax acct. Olsen, Thielen & Co., St. Paul, 1980—, fin. planner, 1986. Mem. Am. Inst. CPA's, Inst. Cert. Fin. Planners, Internat. Assn. Fin. Planners Twin cities Assn. Fin. Planners, Minn. Soc. CPA's, Colo. Soc. CPA's, Am. Woman's Soc. CPA's, Minn. Woman's Soc. CPA's (pub. relations chair 1984-85, newsletter editor 1983-85). Office: Olsen Thielen & Co Ltd 223 Little Canada Rd Saint Paul MN 55117

HENRY, BRUCE EDWARD, city official, educator, management consultant; b. Cin., Apr. 26, 1952; s. Talmage Reed and Evelyn Louise (Hines) H.; m. Arlene Karen Schwiermann, Aug. 25, 1973; children—Jill Michelle, Brett Edward. B.A., U. Cin., 1974, M.P.A., 1975. Cert. peace officer, Ohio. Planning intern Ohio-Ky.-Ind. Regional Council Govts., Cin., 1974-75; asst. county adminstr. Clermont County, Batavia, Ohio, 1975-76, county adminstr., 1976-79; dir. mgmt. services Santoro Engring. Co., Batavia, 1979-81; instr. Am. govt. U. Cin., Batavia, 1979—; dir. pub. safety City of Blue Ash, Ohio, 1981-86, exec. pub. safety and pub. services, 1986—; chmn. bd. Clermont Met. Housing Authority, Batavia; dir. Clerrenton Corp., Maineville, Ohio. Various polit. positions, Clermont County, 1970-75; mem. exec. bd. Clermont County Youth Services Bur., 1973-75; mem. Clermont County Youth Devel. Council, 1975-77, Clermont County League Women Voters, 1975-79, Fed. exec. Bd.: Intergovtl. Affairs, 1978-79, Clermont Met. Housing Authority, 1979—, Gov.'s Law Enforcement Liaison Com., 1984—, Ohio Mcpl. League Legis. Policy Com., 1986, E911 Tech. Adv. Com. for Hamilton County, Ohio, 1986—, Hamilton County E 911 Rev. Bd., 1987—, State of Ohio Anti-Drug Allocation Adv. Com., 1987—; Clermont County rep., mem. various coms. Cin. Community Action Commn. Bd., 1976-77; mem. ednl. goal com. West Clermont Sch. Dist., 1975-77; mem. adv. com. Clermont County Family Services, 1976-79; vol. trustee, exec. com. alternate Ohio-Ky.-Ind. Regional Council Govts., 1976-78; trustee, Greater Community Chest and Council, 1983-85; chmn. Clermont County Community Chest, 1983-84; instr. Great Oaks Police Acad., 1983—; mem. search com. for health commr. Hamilton County Bd. Health, 1984. Recipient Am. Legion medal for Americanism, 1970, leadership awards Greater Cin. Community Chest and Council, 1980, 84, Campaign Vol. award Greater Cin. Community Chest and Council, 1981, planning award Greater Cin. Community Chest and Council, 1981-82; named Hon. Order of Ky. Cols., Commonwealth of Ky., 1977, Hon. Admiral, Commonwealth of Ky., 1986; scholarship U. Cin., 1970-74, grad. scholar, teaching asst. U. Cin., 1974-75. Mem. Ohio Assn. Pub. Safety Dirs. (pres. 1985-86), Ohio Assn. Chiefs Police, Internat. City Mgmt. Assn., Am. Soc. Pub. Adminstrn. (Greater Cin. Area chpt. Pub. Adminstr. of Yr. Program Specialist award 1987), Internat. Personnel Mgmt. Assn., Greater Cin. City Mgmt. Assn., Fraternal Order Police Assocs., Omicron Delta Kappa. Methodist. Lodge: Kiwanis (sec. 1984). Avocations: hunting; fishing; camping. Office: City of Blue Ash 4343 Cooper Rd Blue Ash OH 45242

HENRY, CRAIG ALLAN, quality assurance engineer, industrial engineering manager; b. Decatur, Ill., Aug. 26, 1944; s. Arthur Kendall and Shirley Mangan (Cornick) H.; Judith Ann Evans, June 17, 1962; children: Craig A., Melissa M., Heather C., Sarah K. Student, Millikin U., 1962-67, U. Wis., Whitewater, 1978-79; BSBA, Calif. Coast U., 1986, MBA, 1987. Indsl. engr. Cen. Foundry, Danville, Ill., 1968-72; indsl. engring. mgr. Hayes-Albion, Jackson, Mich., 1972-77, Gen. Castings, Waukesha, Wis., 1977-80; engring. mgr. Pressed Steel Tank, West Allis, Wis., 1979-80; cons. Milw., 1980-85; quality control mgr. Milw. Malleable Grey Iron, 1985-86. Capt. United Funds, 1968-72; advisor Jr. Achievement. Named one of Outstanding Young Men of Yr., U.S. Jaycees, 1976. Mem. Am. Foundry Soc. (indsl. engring. tech. com. 1976-86), Am. Soc. Quality Control, Inst. Indsl. Engring., Jaycees (various offices, J.C.I. membership). Club: Toastmasters. Lodge: Elks. Avocations: softball, basketball, hunting, woodworking, reading. Home: 907 Robins Ln Mukwonago WI 53149 Office: Milw Malleable Grey Iron Box 2039 Milwaukee WI 53201

HENRY, EDWARD FRANK, computer accounting service company executive; b. East Cleveland, Ohio, Mar. 18, 1923; s. Edward Emerson and Mildred Adella (Kulow) H.; B.B.A., Dyke Coll., 1948; student Cleve. Inst. Music, 1972; m. Nicole Annette Peth, June 18, 1977. Internal auditor E.F. Hauserman Co., 1950-52; office mgr. Frank C. Grismer Co., 1951-52; Broadway Buick Co., 1952-55; treas. Commerce Ford Sales Co., 1955-65; nat. mgr. Auto Acctg. div. United Data Processing Co., Cin., 1966-68; v.p. Auto Data Systems Co., Cleve., 1968-70; pres. Profl. Mgmt. Computer Systems, Inc., Cleve., 1970—, ComputerEase, Small Bus. Computer Ctrs. div. Profl. Mgmt. Computer Systems, Inc., 1985—, VideoEase Computerized Video Rental Systems div. Profl. Mgmt. Computer Systems, Inc., 1987—. Charter pres. No. Ohio Council Little Theatres, 1954-56; founder, artistic and mng. dir. Exptl. Theatre, Cleve., 1959-63; dramatic dir., actor various community theatres, 1955-65; actor Cleve. Playhouse, 1961-63; bd. dirs. Cleve. Philharmonic Orch., 1972-73. Served with USAAF, 1943-46; CBI. Notary public. Mem. Am. Mgmt. Assn., Nat. Assn. Accountants, Mil. Order World Wars, Air Force Assn. (life), Ky. Cols., Phi Kappa Gamma. Republican. Presbyterian. Clubs: Rotary, Acacia Country, Hermit, Univ., Cleve. Grays, Deep Springs Trout, Nat. Sojourners (Nat. Pres.'s cert. 1977-78, pres. Cleve. chpt. #23 1978), Heroes of '76 (comdr. Cleve. 1977). Lodges: Masons (33d degree), DeMolay (past master Cleve. chpt., Legion of Honor 1970), Ancient Accepted Scottish Rite (dramatic dir. 1967—), K.T., Grotto, Shriners (dramatic dir. 1968—, T.P.M. 1982-84), Cleve. Ct. #14, Jesters (dir. 1981, impresario 1984—, dramatic dir./producer 1971—), Kachina, SOBIB. Home: 666 Echo Dr Gates Mills OH 44040 Office: Profl Mgmt Computer Systems Inc 19701 S Miles Ave Cleveland OH 44128 also: 5840-A Mayfield Rd Mayfield Heights OH 44124

HENRY, HUNTER WOODS, chemical company executive; b. McComb, Miss., 1928. B.S., Miss. State U., 1950. With Dow Chem. Co., Midland, Mich., 1951—; dir. mfg. Dow Internat., 1964-66; dir. ops. Dow Chem. Latin Am., 1966-73, bus. devel. mgr., 1966-73; v.p. Dow Badische, 1973-76; mgr. organic chemicals dept. Dow Chem. U.S.A., 1976-77; mgr. Dow Mich. div., Midland, 1976-77; pres. Dow Quimica S.A., Brazil, 1977-82; corp. v.p. Dow Chem. U.S.A., Midland, 1982-83, pres., 1982—, corp. exec. v.p., 1983—, dir.; dir. Dow Corning Corp., Comerica Bank-Midland, Am. Indsl. Health Council. Office: Dow Chem USA 2020 Willard H Dow Ctr Midland MI 48640

HENRY, JAMES E., industrial engineer; b. Irvine, Ky., Mar. 14, 1942; s. Beverly B. and Hoyte Mae (Tipton) H.; m. Lucille Mullins, Aug. 12, 1978; children—Gregory, Teresa, Michael, Matthew. Indsl. engr. NCR Co., Dayton, Ohio, 1967-72, Springfield, Ohio, 1972-77; mgr. indsl. engring. Internt. Harvester Co., Fort Wayne, Ind., 1977-78, div. indsl. engr., 1978-79, mgr. indsl. engring., Chgo., 1979-82, corp. sr. indsl. engr., 1982-84; productivity mgr. Navistar Internat. Corp., 1984—. Home: 215 Winston Dr Bolingbrook IL 60439 Office: 401 N Michigan Ave Chicago IL 60611

HENRY, JOHN THOMAS, newspaper executive; b. St. Paul, May 30, 1933; s. Harlan A. and Roxane (Thomas) H.; m. Carla Joyce Lechthaler, Jan. 2, 1982; children: Alexandra, Elizabeth, J. Thomas, Catherine. B.B.A., U. Minn., 1955. With St. Paul Pioneer Press Dispatch, 1955—, asst. to publisher, then bus. mgr., 1971-76, gen. mgr., 1976—, pres., pub., 1985—. Vice pres. St. Paul Jr. C. of C., 1965-66; bd. dirs. St. Paul Jr. Achievement, Better Bus. Bur. of Minn., Boy Scouts Am., Minn. Coop. Office, Minn. Mus. Art, St. Paul Chamber Orch., St. Paul Downtown Council, United Hosps., Minn. Sci. Mus. Served with USAF, 1956-59. Recipient Disting. Service award Classified Advt. Mgrs. Assn., 1971. Mem. St. Paul C. of C. (chmn. bd. dirs. 1987). Home: 4436 Oakmede Ln White Bear MN 55110 Office: St Paul Pioneer Press Dispatch NW Publ Inc 345 Cedar St Saint Paul MN 55101

HENRY, LOREN FRED, shopping center management company executive; b. Mpls., Nov. 18, 1947; s. Fred and Elvira (Schmakel) H.; m. Donalee Jean Shemanek, Aug. 9, 1969; one child, Kelly Ann. BSBA, Winona (Minn.) State U., 1969. Property mgr. Klodt Constrn. Corp., Mpls., 1965-77; leasing rep. Developers Diversification, Moreland Hills, Ohio, 1977-82, dir. leasing, 1982-84; pres. Developers Diversified Mgmt. Inc., Moreland Hills, Ohio, 1984—; judge state career devel. Minn. Vocat. Tech. Schs., Mpls., 1974, 75. Served with U.S. Army, 1970-72. Mem. Internat. Council Shopping Ctrs., Minn. Apt. Assn., Golden Valley (Minn.) C. of C. (bd. dirs. 1975-76), Burnsville (Minn.) C. of C. Clubs: Braemar Mens (Edina, Minn.), Minn. Ad (Mpls.). Home: 20 Creekview Circle Moreland Hills OH 44022

HENRY, MICHAEL DANIEL, chiropractor; b. Chgo., Apr. 28, 1958. Student, U. Ill., 1976-79; BS, Nat. Coll. Chiropractic, Lombard, Ill., 1982, D of Chiropractic, 1983. Chiropractor, ptnr. Capitol Chiropractic Health Ctr., Springfield, Ill., 1983—. Bd. dirs. Land of Lincoln chpt. United Cerebral Palsy. Mem. Internat. Thermographic Soc., Am. Chiropractic Assn., Ill. Chiropractic Soc., Sangamon County Chiropractic Soc. (past pres.). Club: Am. Businessmen's. Lodge: Sertoma, B'nai Brith. Avocations: golf, scuba diving, weight tng., racquetball, triathlons. Home: 2626 S 5th St Springfield IL 62703

HENRY, ORMOND LEE, mechanical engineer, manufacturing executive; b. Youngstown, Ohio, July 28, 1937; s. Ormond Lee and Janet (Marshall) H.; m. Margaret M. Mixer, July 1, 1961; children: Betsy, Bruce, Matthew. BSME, Lehigh U., 1959; MBA, U. Mich., 1961; MS in Mech. Engring., Bradley U., 1966. V.p., gen. mgr. Neway Equipment Corp., Muskegon, Mich., 1965-74; group v.p. Bendix Automotive, Detroit, 1974-79; pres. Bendix Automotive, London, 1979-82; pres., chief exec. officer Castolin & Eutectic, Geneva, 1982-83; pres., chief operating officer RTE Corp., Brookfield, Wis., 1983-86; pres., chief exec. officer Champion Spark Plug Co., Toledo, 1986—. Mem. Phi Kappa Phi. Avocations: tennis; art collecting.

HENRY, PAUL BRENTWOOD, congressman; b. Chgo., July 9, 1942; s. Carl F. and H. I. (Bender) H.; m. Karen Anne Borthistle, Aug. 28, 1965; children: Kara Elizabeth, Jordan Mark, Megan Anne. B.A., Wheaton Coll., 1963; M.A., Duke U., 1968, Ph.D., 1970. Vol. Peace Corps, Liberia, 1963-64; vol. Peace Corps, Ethiopia, 1964-65; instr. polit. sci. Duke U., Durham, N.C., 1969-70; assoc. prof. Calvin Coll., Grand Rapids, Mich., 1970-78; mem. Mich. Ho. of Reps., Lansing, 1979-82, asst. minority floor leader, 1979-82; mem. Mich. Senate, Lansing, 1983-85, 99th-100th Congresses from 5th Mich. dist., Washington, 1985—. Author: Politics for Evangelicals, 1974, (with Stephen V. Monsma) The Dynamics of the American Political System, 1970. Mem. Mich. Bd. Edn., 1975-78; Kent County Republican chmn., Mich., 1975-76. Fellow Duke U., Durham, N.C. Mem. Am. Polit. Sci. Assn. Mem. Christian Reformed Ch. Office: Ho of Reps Office House Mems Washington DC 20515 *

HENRY, RICHARD ALAN, advertising executive, consultant; b. N.Y.C., June 23, 1954; s. Alan and Miriam Francis (Glicksman) H.; m. Suzanne Elizabeth Conlon, Nov. 26, 1980; children: Timothy, Claire. Student, U. Colo., 1972-74, Colo. State U., 1974-76. Prodn. adminstr. MGM Studios, Culver City, Calif., 1977-79; asst. dir. Donner & Goodmark, Los Angeles, 1978-80; assoc. producer Polygram Pictures, Los Angeles, 1980-81; prodn. supr. Gaylord Broadcasting, Los Angeles, 1981-82; exec. producer Sight & Sound Prodns., Mpls., 1982-83; sr. v.p. Bozell, Jacobs, Kenyon & Eckhardt, Mpls., 1983—; cons. in field. Active com. for a Drug Free Am. Mem. Dirs. Guild Am., Advt. Fedn. Minn., assoc. Art Dirs. and Copywriters Minn.(assoc.). Roman Catholic.

HENRY, RICHARD ALLEN, athletic director; b. Marion, Ohio, Dec. 2, 1946; s. Harold Franklin and Mildred Violet (Thomas) H.; m. Cathy Sue Lightner, Dec. 27, 1969; children: Christin Sue, Robyn Anne. BE, Ashland (Ohio) Coll., 1969; MEd, Kent (Ohio) State U., 1975. Cert. English and social psychology tchr., cert. secondary sch. adminstr. English tchr. John Sherman Jr. High Sch., Mansfield, Ohio, 1969-74, English tchr., dept. chmn., 1974-77; instr. communications skills N. Cen. Tech. Coll., Mansfield, 1973-77; English tchr. Mansfield Sr. High Sch., 1977—, athletic dir., attendance coordinator, 1981—; golf coach Mansfield Sr. High Sch., 1977—; cons., evaluator div. tchr. cert. Ohio Dept. Edn., Columbus, Ohio, 1972-74; evaluator N. Cen. Assn. of Colls. and Schs., 1985. Martha Holden Jennings Found. scholar Cleve., 1970-71. Mem. Nat. Interscholastic Athletic Adminstrn. Assn., Ohio High Sch. Athletic Dirs. Assn., Ohio Assn. Secondary Sch. Adminstrs., Acad. Golf Instrs., Nat. Golf Found., Phi Delta Kappa. Republican. Methodist. Club: Univ. (Mansfield). Lodge: Elks. Avocations: golf, racquetball, reading, travel. Home: 685 N Satinwood Circle Mansfield OH 44903 Office: Mansfield Sr High Sch 145 West Park Blvd Mansfield OH 44906

HENRY, RONALD WILLIAM, computer consultant, accountant; b. Chgo., Nov. 26, 1939; s. William F. and Catherine May (Hall) H.; m. Barbara Ann Henry, June 17, 1961 (div. Sept. 1976); children: Grant, Gayle. BA in Math., U. Minn., 1968; PhD (hon. degree), Sczamoc Tech. Inst., Budapest, Hungary, 1968, U. London, 1970; MA in Comparative Theology, U. London, 1971. Cert. in data processing; lic. pub. acct. Pres. Ednl. Systems, Inc., Mpls., 1962—; various managerial and exec. positions Control Data Corp., Mpls., 1965-70; ind. cons. Control Data Corp., London, 1970-82; testing mgr. Cray Research, Inc., Mpls., 1982-85; pres. Creative Bus. Enterprises, Inc., Mpls., 1984—; guest lectr. U. Minn., 1963-70, British Computing Soc., London, 1972-76; sr. instr. Inst. for Advanced Tech., Bethesda, Md., 1965-72, Inver Grove Community Coll., Inver Grove Heights, Minn., 1972-78; instr. Cen. Intelligence Agy., Arlington, Va., 1968-71; dir. computer devel. Vital Energy Corp., Edina, Minn., 1985-86. Author: Advanced Programming Techniques, 1972, Structured Analysis Design, 1973, Structured Data Base Development, 1978; co-designer software systems Allegro Linear Programming Systems, 1966. Bd. dirs. Minn. Assn. Mental Health, Mpls., 1968-72; precinct chmn. Rep. Party, Mpls., 1964-68; com. chmn. Hennepin County Citizen's League, Mpls., 1964-70. Mem. Nat. Soc. Pub. Accts., Entrepreneurs Internat., Mensa Internat. Avocations: gourmet cooking, jazz piano playing, racquetball. Home: 1900 E 86th St #318 Bloomington MN 55420 Office: Creative Bus Enterprises Inc 5753 2nd Ave S Minneapolis MN 55420

HENRY, THOMAS MITCHELL, lawyer, educator; b. Peoria, Ill., May 24, 1953; s. Warren Eugene and Alice Virginia (Tuttle) H.; m. Sandra Jane Perry, Oct. 6, 1979; 1 child, Jonathan Thompson. B.S., Ill. State U., 1975; J.D., So. Ill. U., 1978. Bar: Ill. 1978, U.S. Dist. Ct. (cen. dist.) Ill. 1978, U.S. Ct. Appeals (7th cir.) 1978. Assoc. W. D. Dersch, Peoria, 1978-81; ptnr. Henry & Henry Attys. at Law, Peoria, 1981-85; sole practice, Peoria, 1985—; adj. instr. bus. law Ill. Central Coll., 1981-87. Moderator Plymouth Congl. Ch., Chillicothe, Ill., 1981-83, chmn. refugee com., mem. mission com., 1981-84; pres. bd. dirs. Peoria Friendship House Christian Service, 1982-85. Mem. ABA, Ill. State Bar Assn., Peoria County Bar Assn. (civil practice coms., legal med. relations com.), Northside Businessmens Assn. (v.p. 1982-83, pres. 1985-87). Mem. United Ch. of Christ. Office: 1st National Bank Bldg Peoria IL 61602

HENSEL, HUBERT ADAM, obstetrician-gynecologist; b. Massillon, Ohio, Feb. 2, 1911; s. Raymond and Matilda Ann (Rohr) H.; m. Lucille Katrine Rogers, May 15, 1942 (dec. Nov. 1977); children: Sandra Jean, Raymond Lee, Carol Ann. BS in edn., Kent State U., 1938; MD, U. Louisville, 1943. Resident in ob-gyn Mt. Carmel Mercy Hosp., Detroit, 1944, Nashville Gen. Hosp., 1945; tchr. Stark County, North Lawrence, Ohio, 1934-39; intern Akron (Ohio) City Hosp., 1943; asst. resident ob-gyn. Mt. Carmel Mercy Hosp., Detroit, 1944; chief resident Nashville Gen. Hosp., 1945; practice medicine specializing in ob-gyn. Massillon, 1943—; pres. Massillon Bd. Health, 1982—. Pres. Acad. Medicine, Massillon, 1969, 77. Served to lt. (j.g.) USN, 1945-46, ETO, PTO. Mem. AMA, Am. Coll. Obstetrics and Gynecology, Ohio State Med. Assn. Republican. Roman Catholic. Avocations: writing, music, sculpting, oil painting. Home: 1135 Burd Ave Massillon OH 44646 Office: 845 8th St NE Massillon OH 44646

HENSELMEIER, SANDRA NADINE, training and development consulting firm executive; b. Indpls., Nov. 20, 1937; d. Frederick Rost Henselmeier and Beatrice Nadine (Barnes) Henselmeier Enright; m. David Albert Funk, Oct. 2, 1976; children: William H. Stolz, Jr., Harry Phillip Stolz II, Sandra Ann Stolz. AB, Purdue U., 1971; MAT, Ind. U., 1975. Exec. sec. to dean Ind. U. Sch. Law, Indpls., 1977-78; adminstrv. asst. Ind. U.-Purdue U., Indpls., 1978-80, assoc. archivist, 1980-81; program and communication coordinator Midwest Alliance in Nursing, Indpls., 1981-82; tng. coordinator Coll./Univ. Cos., Indpls., 1982-83; pres. Better Bus. Communications, Indpls., 1983—; adj. lectr. Ind. U.-Purdue U. at Indpls., 1971—, U. Indpls. Center Continuing Mgmt. Devel. and Edn., Indpls., 1984—. Author: Successful Customer Service Writing, Winning with Effective Business Grammar, Successful Telephone Communication and Etiquette; contbr. articles to profl. jours. Mem. ASTD, Assn. Bus. Communication, Assn. Profl. Writing Cons., Nat. Assn. Profl. Saleswomen, Indpls. C. of C., Ind. C. of C. Republican. Presbyterian. Avocations: traveling, walking, reading, learning new ideas. Office: Better Bus Communications 6208 N Delaware St Indianapolis IN 46220

HENSLEE, LAURA JANE, state agency administrator; b. Cin., Apr. 11, 1933; d. Forrest A. I and Carrie L. (Susselin) H.; 1 child, Angelita Stasiak. Student, Ohio State U., 1948. RN, N.J. Adminstr. Glendale Hosp., Grove City, Ohio, 1948-56; hosp. cons. Hill Burton Program Ohio Dept. Health, 1956-64; mem. personnel staff Gov. Jas. A. Rhodes, Ohio, 1964-72; asst. adminstr. State of Ohio Record Ctr., Columbus, 1972-80, adminstr., 1980-86; dir. Mt. Carmel Shaver Med. Ctr., 1987—. Republican. Avocations: tennis, golf. Home: 6404 Livingston Ave Reynoldsburg OH 43068

HENSLER, VICKI SANDRA, personnel management consultant, career consultant; b. Cleve., March 7, 1946; d. Arthur Bennett and Marilyn Vivian (Brauer) Fine; m. Paul Michael Dorner, June 11, 1966 (div. 1975); children—James Hugh, David Paul; m. Guy Jack Hensler, July 16, 1976. B.S., U. Ill., 1968, M.A., 1977, Ph.D., 1987. Pres. Career Ctr., Inc., Champaign, Ill., 1974-84; instr. Parkland Coll., Champaign, 1984—, dir. placement, 1987—; prin., cons. Profl. Personnel Mgmt., Champaign, 1984—; v.p. Downtown Electric, Inc., Urbana, Ill., 1984—; cons. Marine Am. Nat. Bank, Champaign, Franchise Mgmt. Systems, Inc., Champaign. Author: Journal of Parks and Recreation, 1966. Mem. Better Housing Com., Champaign, 1975; sec., bd. dirs. Ill. Adult and Continuing Edn. Assn., 1975-77; Mem. Am. Assn. Counseling and Devel., Am. Vocat. Assn., Am. Vocat. Rehab. Assn., Assn. Measurement and Evaluation, Nat. Employment Counselors Assn., Vocat. Guidance Assn., Champaign C. of C. (spl. projects com. mem. 1982—), Phi Delta Kappa. Republican. Jewish. Club: Executive (Champaign). Avocations: writing; teaching. Home: 3306 Stoneybrook Champaign IL 61821 Office: Round Barn Sta PO Box 6105 Champaign IL 61821

HENSLEY, CHAD, insurance company executive; b. 1924. Claims adjuster Mut. Casualty Co., Des Moines, 1949-52; with Preferred Risk Mut. Ins., Des Moines, 1952—, now pres., chief exec. officer. Served with AUS, 1943-46. Office: Preferred Risk Mutual Ins Co 1111 Ashworth Rd West Des Moines IA 50265 *

HENSLEY, GARY ALLEN, financial management consultant; b. Dearborn, Mich., Dec. 28, 1950; s. Leborn Edward and Juanita L. (Bivens) H.; m. Donna Jean Sumner, May 13, 1972. BBA, Saginaw Valley State Coll., 1973, MBA, 1986. Jr. acct., auditor Laine, Appold & Co., CPA's, Bay City, Mich., 1973-74; auditor, cons. Alexander Grant & Co., CPA's, Memphis, New Orleans, 1974-78, WFB & S, CPA's, Bay City, 1978-80; owner Acctg. & Mgmt. Services, Bay City, 1980-83; pres. Hensley Fin. Services, Inc., Bay City, 1983-84; treas. W.W. Hall & Assoc., Inc., Bay City, 1984—, also bd. dirs.; bd. dirs. Hensley-Tackman Optical Co., Bay City, 1976—. Contbr. articles to profl. jour. Trustee Bay City Schs. Bd. Edn., 1983-85, trustee, bd. treas., 1985-86, trustee, bd. sec., 1986-87, re-elected mem. 1987-91. Recipient Award of Merit Mich. Assn. Sch. Bds., 1985. Mem. Assn. Govt. Accts., Nat. Soc. Pub. Accts., Inst. Cert. Fin. Planners. Democrat. Baptist. Avocations: music, travel. Office: Wilson W Hall & Assocs Inc 708 S Euclid Ave Bay City MI 48706

HENSLEY, MARY LYNNE FLOYD, health care administrator; b. Covington, Ky., June 6, 1952; d. Robert Forsythe and Maysie McDowell (Williams) Floyd; m. Carl Evans Hensley II, Apr. 15, 1972; children: Carl Evans III, John Thomas, James Michael. Student, Am. U., Washington, D.C., 1970-71; AS, N.Y. State U., Albany, 1983; BBA with high distinction, U. Iowa, 1985. Acctg. technician VA Med. Ctr., Iowa City, 1982-86; adminstr. Dept. Neurology, U. Iowa, Iowa City, 1986—; mem. adv. com. Kirkwood Community Coll., Cedar Rapids, Iowa, 1986—. Mem. PTO, Iowa City, 1982—. Am. U. scholar, 1970-71, E. Lester Williams scholar, U. Iowa, 1984-85, Ponder Fund scholar U. Iowa, 1985. Mem. Nat. Assn. Accts., Med. Group Mgmt. Assn., Assn. Profl. and Faculty Women, Mortar Board, Omicron Delta Kappa, Beta Alpha Psi, Alpha Sigma Lambda, Beta Gamma Sigma, Phi Eta Sigma. Democrat. Presbyterian. Avocations: hiking, bicycling, reading. Office: U Iowa Dept Neurology 2153 RCP Iowa City IA 52242

HENSLEY, ROBERT PAUL, manufacturing company executive; b. Dayton, Ohio, Jan. 10, 1931; s. Cecil Paul and Edna Elizabeth (Muddell) H.; m. Carol Jean Kadel, Sept. 13, 1952; children: Diana Lynn, Kimberly Sue, Linda Carol. Degree in Acctg., Miami Jacobs Bus. Coll., 1951. Acct. Dayton Malleable Inc., Kettering, Ohio, 1951-63, supr. acctg., 1963-80, asst. treas., 1980-82; asst. sec., treas. Amcast Indsl. Corp. (formerly Dayton Malleable, Inc.), Kettering, 1982—. Mem. YMCA, Dayton, 1962—, Centerville (Ohio) Tax Appeal Bd., 1976—. Mem. Nat. Assn. Accts., Data Processing Mgmt. Assn., Risk Ins. Mgmt. Soc. (pres. 1986—). Republican. Avocations: golf, tennis, fishing. Office: Amcast Indsl Corp 3931 S Dixie Ave Kettering OH 45439

HENSON, PAUL HARRY, communications company executive; b. Bennet, Nebr., July 22, 1925; s. Harry H. and Mae (Schoenthal) H.; m. Betty L. Roeder, Aug. 2, 1946; children: Susan Irene Flury, Lizbeth Henson Barelli. B.S. in Elec. Engring, U. Nebr., 1948, M.S., 1950; hon. doctorates, U. Nebr., Ottawa U., Bethany Coll. Registered profl. engr., Nebr. Engr. Lincoln (Nebr.) Tel. & Tel. Co., 1941-42, 45-48, div. mgr., 1948-54, chief engr., 1954-59; v.p. United Telecommunications, Inc., Kansas City, Mo., 1959-60; exec. v.p. United Telecommunications, Inc., 1960-64, pres., 1964-73, chmn., 1966—, also dir.; dir. Armco, Duke Power; vice chmn. Pres.'s Nat. Security Telecommunications Adv. Com.. Trustee Midwest Research Inst., Tax Found., U. Nebr. Found., U. Mo. at Kansas City. Served with USAAF, 1942-45. Mem. Nat. Soc. Profl. Engrs., IEEE, Armed Forces Communications Electronics Assn., U.S. Telephone Assn. (dir. 1960-76, pres. 1964-65), Sigma Xi, Eta Kappa Nu, Sigma Tau, Kappa Sigma. Clubs: Mason (Shriner), Kansas City, Kansas City Country, Mission Hills Country, Castle Pines, El Dorado Country. Office: United Telecommunications Inc Box 11315 Kansas City MO 64112

HENSON, WILLIAM MICHAEL, real estate executive; b. Madisonville, Ky., Dec. 17, 1939; s. James William and Nell Kathryn (Offutt) H.; m. Deloris Ann Crane, Aug. 13, 1960; children: Michael, Dwane. Student, U. Evansville, 1968-69, 73. Lic. realtor, Ind.; lic. property mgmt. broker. Pres., chief exec. officer Henson Enterprises, Newburgh, Ind., 1960—; mgmt. broker property mgmt. sect. VA, Evansville, 1978—. Mem. Rep. Presdl. Task Force, Washington, 1986, Rep. Nat. Com. Mem. Nat. Assn. Realtors, Evansville Bd. Realtors. Club: U.S. Senatorial. Avocations: antique automobiles, boating. Home and Office: Henson Enterprises 10866 Spry Rd Newburgh IN 47630

HENTGES, JOSEPH THOMAS, academic administrator, consultant; b. St. Paul, July 17, 1941; s. Alvin Henry and Lorinda Edna (Frandrup) H.; m. Brigitte Leonore Mryczko (Aug. 13, 1966); children: John Joseph, Gary Michael. BS, Coll. St. Thomas, St. Paul, 1963, MA, 1970; edn. specialist degree, Mankato (Mich.) State U., 1976; PhD, Ohio State U., 1984. Tchr. Foley (Minn.) Pub. Sch., 1963-67, Park Sr. High, Cottage Grove, Minn.,

1967-75; asst. prin. Cannon Falls (Minn.) High, 1975-77; prin. Cannon Falls (Minn.) High Sch., 1977-80; research assoc. Ohio State U., 1980-82; supt. schs. Ind. Sch. Dist. 252, Cannon Falls, 1982-87, Woodstock (Ill.) Unit Sch. Dist. No. 200, 1987—; adv. bd. Mineral Springs Treatment Ctr., Cannon Falls, 1977-80; cons. and speaker on supt.-sch. bd. relationships. Author, co-editor: The American Sch. Superintendency, 1982. Chmn. Goodhue County Sch. Task Force on Chemical Health and Dependency, Red Wing, Minn., 1977-80; sr. coordinator Adventures in Attitudes, 1979-82. Named one of 100 top N.Am. sch. execs. in dists. of 2,500 or less students, Exec. Educator 100; Eikenberry fellow Ohio State U., 1982. Mem. Assn. Supervision and Curriculum Devel., Am. Assn. Sch. Adminstrs., Minn. Assn. Sch. Adminstrs., Woodstock C. of C. (bd. dirs.). Roman Catholic. Lodges: Rotary (membership chmn. Cannon Falls 1986), Lions (v.p. Cannon Falls 1985), K.C. Avocations: fishing, retriever dog tng., hunting, woodworking. Home: 720 Margaret Dr Woodstock IL 60098 Office: Woodstock Unit Sch Dist #200 501 W South St Woodstock IL 60098-3799

HENTHORNE, MARJORIE LUCILLE, designer, children's games manufacturing executive; b. Osawatomie, Kans., May 16, 1921; d. Benjamin F. and Mabel L. Emerson (Sturges) Henthorne; grad. Kansas City (Mo.) Jr. Coll., 1939; student Kansas City (Mo.) Art Inst., 1940-41, William and Mary Profl. Inst., Richmond, Va., 1942-43, King-Smith Sch., Washington, 1944-46; m. Huston Burns McClure, June 28, 1947; 1 dau., Jeanne Emerson. Freelance fashion designer, 1939—; Washington corr. Kansas City Star; chief French Lend Lease Control Office, Washington, 1943-45; aide to U.S. senator William F. Knowland of Calif., 1945-47; with Times-Harold News, Washington, 1947; propr., designer J.M.H. Products, Kansas City, Mo., 1975—. Mem. Nelson Atkins Mus. Art, Kansas City, Miami County, Kans. Geneology Soc., Mus. of Women and the Arts. Fin. and publicity chmn We the Women of Hawaii, 1953-54. Mem. Kansas City Women's C. of C., Columbia Arts Club Washington, Hist. Soc. State of Mo., Internat. Platform Assn., Universal Intelligence Data Bank of Am., Am. Women's Bus. Assn., Kansas City Internat. Relations Council, Westport Hist. Soc., Polit. Study Club Alumni Assn., Federated Women's Club. Mem. Christian Ch. Patentee games for children, designs. Club: Internat. Trade of Greater Kansas City, Inc. Address: 133 N Lawn St Kansas City MO 64123

HEPNER, MICHAEL JULES, allergist; b. Pitts., Oct. 1, 1952. BS, U. Mich., 1974; MD, U. Pitts., 1978. Diplomate Am. Bd. Internal Medicine, Am. Bd. Allergy and Immunology. Intern Washington (D.C.) Hosp. Ctr., 1978-79, resident, 1979-81; fellow in allergy Henry Ford Hosp., Detroit, 1981-83, mem. staff allergy div., 1983—. Fellow Am. Coll. Allergy; mem. AMA, ACP, Am. Acad. Allergy and Immunology. Office: Henry Ford Hosp Allergy div 2799 W Grand Blvd Detroit MI 48202

HEPNER, SONDRA LOUREEN, health care agency administrator; b. Chgo., Feb. 27, 1934; d. Phillip Charles and Florence Ida (Massell) Bell; m. Burt Upton, Jan. 15, 1952 (div. June 1974); children: Barbara, Susan Upton Douglass, Jody Jones; m. Ronald Allen Hepner, Aug. 20, 1974. BA, Northeastern Ill. U., 1973; MSW, Loyola U., Chgo., 1975. Cert. social worker, Ill. Treatment coordinator Riveredge Hosp., Forest Park, Ill., 1975-79; prin. Ctr. for Effective Living, Inc., Oak Park, Ill., 1978-80, pres., 1980-84; pres., chief exec. officer At Home Health, Inc., Oak Park, Ill., 1984-86. Newspaper columnist. Mem. Loyola Sch. Social Work Alumni Bd., Chgo., 1985-86; mem. women's aux. Gottleib Hosp. Mem. Nat. Assn. Social Workers (cert.), Assn. Mental Health Pvt. Practitioners Oak Park, Women's Adv. Council. Avocations: reading, sailing, camping, gardening, racquetball. Office: At Home Health Inc 715 W Lake St Oak Park IL 60301

HEPPERMANN, BERDELL JOHN, JR., printing company executive; b. St. Peters, Mo., Mar. 11, 1934; s. Berdell John and Loyola Ann (Doll) H.; m. Margie Ann Kohnen, June 16, 1956; children—John, Jeffrey, Jeannie, Timothy, Marla. Student U. Mo.-Rolla, 1955, Washington U., St. Louis, 1956-58. Design draftsman McDonnell Aircraft, St. Louis, 1956-58; mgr. Crest Bowl, Florissant, Mo., 1958-66; pres. Kimbell Printing & Stationary Co., Florissant, 1967—; ptnr. Kim-Hep, Florissant, 1979—, Old Mische Ranch, Warrenton, Mo., 1970—. Bd. dirs. Florissant Valley Sheltered Workshop, 1960—, North County YMCA, Florissant, 1978—. Served with USN, 1952-54. Mem. Nat. Office Products Assn. (lt. gov. dist. 12 1983-84), Am. Legion, Ducks Unltd., Florissant C. of C. (bd. dirs., officer, Outstanding Bus. Person award 1983). Roman Catholic. Lodges: Optimists (Florissant) (pres., lt. gov.), Rotary (pres.), K.C. Avocations: hunting; gardening. Home: 14707 Sinks Rd Florissant MO 63034 Office: Kimbell Printing & Stationery 865 Rue St Francois Florissant MO 63031

HERBATY, FRANK, federal agency executive; b. N.Y.C., July 5, 1923; s. Anthony and Mary (Garay) H.; m. Marilyn Miller, Feb. 11, 1950 (div. Mar. 1971); children: Laura, Denise, John, Lisa; m. Linda Ann Liverman, Nov. 24, 1971. B Mech. Engring., Coll. City of N.Y., 1944. Profl. engr. N.Y., Fla., Ariz.; Plant engring. mgr. Merganthaler Linotype, N.Y.C., 1955-58, Rohr Corp., Calif., 1958-60; v.p. Pope, Evans & Robbins, N.Y.C., 1960-64; dir. TWA, Kennedy Space Ctr., Fla., 1964-71; mgmt. cons. Middle West Service Co., Chgo., 1971-74; sr. program mgr. U.S. Dept. Energy, Argonne, Ill., 1974—; dir. research Pres. Carters Reorganization Project, Washington, 1977-78; pres. F. Herbaty & Assocs., Bolingbrook, Ill., 1983—. Author Cost Effective Maintenance Management, 1983, Teach Yourself to Sing, 1983. Recipient Commendation Pres. Carter, 1978. Mem. Am. Inst. Plant Engrs. (pres. 1964-71, Best Chapter of Yr., 1967). Avocations: music, golf, computers. Home: 253 Plainview Dr Bolingbrook IL 60439 Office: US Dept Energy 9800 S Cass Argonne IL 60439

HERBERT, DAVID LEE, lawyer, author; b. Cleve., Oct. 1, 1948; s. William Clayton and Virginia Margaret (Battersby) H.; m. Lynda Jane Rosenkranz, Aug. 23, 1970; children—Laurance, Jason, Meredith. B.B.A., Kent State U., 1971; J.D., U. Akron, 1974. Bar: 1974, U.S. Dist. Ct. (no. dist.) Ohio 1974, U.S. Ct. Appeals (6th cir.) 1984. Asst. prosecutor Stark County Prosecutor's Office, Canton, Ohio, 1974-80; ptnr. Herbert, Treadon, Benson & Frieg, Canton, 1975—; pres. Profl. Reports Corp., 1986—; assoc. prof. Kent State U. (Ohio), 1980—; pres., turstee Lake Twp. Trustees, Hartville, Ohio, 1983—; mem., sec., asst. chmn. Ohio Gov.'s Organized Crime Law Enforcement Cons. Com., Columbus, 1976-78; comml. arbitrator Am. Arbitration Assn., 1983—; mem., sec. Stark County Pub. Defender Com., Canton, Ohio, 1982—. Author: Attorneys' Master Guide to Psychology, 1980; Legal Aspects of Preventive and Rehabilitative Exercise Programs, 1984; Corporations of Corruption: The Systematic Study of Organized Crime, 1984; others; editor: The Exercise Standards and Malpractice Reporter, 1986—; contbr. articles to profl. jours. Bd. dirs. Stark County Jr. Achievement, Canton, Ohio, 1983; mentor, pupil enrichment program Lake Local Sch. Bd., Hartville, Ohio, 1981-83. Recipient Continuing Legal Edn. award ABA/Am. Law Inst., 1975. Mem. ABA (liaison to jud. adminstrn. div. 1972-73), Def. Research Inst., Am. Coll. Sports Medicine, Stark County Trustees and Clks. Assn., Stark County Bar Assn. (exec. com. 1984, grievance com. 1979-82), Akron/Canton Def. Lawyers Assn., Ducks Unltd., North Canton Jaycees (com. chmn. 1975-76). Republican. Home: 1055 Clearvale St NE Hartville OH 44632 Office: Herbert Treadon Benson & Frieg 4571 Stephen Cir NW Canton OH 44718-3629

HERBERT, EDWARD FRANKLIN, public relations executive; b. N.Y.C., Jan. 30, 1946; s. H. Robert and Florence (Bender) H.; m. Rhonda J. Scharf, Aug. 20, 1967; children—Jason Dean and Heather Ann (twins). B.S. in Communications, Syracuse U., 1967, M.S., 1969. Assoc. dir. pub. relations Am. Optometric Assn., Washington, 1971; community relations specialist Gen. Electric Co., Columbia, Md., 1971-73, pub. relations account supr., 1973-75; dir. pub. affairs Nat. Consumer Fin. Assn., Washington, 1975-78; regional dir. pub. relations Montgomery Ward Co., Balt., 1978-80, fin. info. services dir., Chgo., 1980-81, internal communications dir., 1981-82, corp. communications dir., 1982-83; regional dir. pub. relations MCI Communications Corp., Chgo., 1983-84; dir. communications MCI Midwest, MCI Telecommunications Corp., 1985—; adj. instr. Onondaga Community Coll. Served with U.S. Army, 1969-71. Mem. Pub. Relations Soc. Am., Chgo. Press Club, Sigma Tau Rho. Home: 830 Timber Hill Rd Highland Park IL 60035 Office: 205 N Michigan Ave Suite 3200 Chicago IL 60601

HERBIG, GUNTHER, conductor; b. Aussig, Germany, Nov. 30, 1931; s. Emil and Gisela (Hieke) H.; diploma Franz-Liszt-Hochschule, Weimar, Germany, 1956; m. Jutta Czapski, Oct. 30, 1958; children—Beate, Thomas. Mus. asst. Erfurt Theatre, 1956-57; condr. Deutsches Nat. Theatre, Weimar, 1957-62; prin. condr. Potsdam (Ger.) Theatre, 1962-66; condr. Berliner Sinfonie-Orchester, Berlin, 1966-72, chief condr., artistic dir., 1977-83; music dir. Detroit Symphony Orch., 1984—; chief condr., artistic dir. Dresden (Ger.) Philharmonic Orchester, 1972-77. Recipient Theodor Fontane Arts prize, 1964; German Democratic Republic Arts prize, 1970; Nat. prize German Democratic Republic, 1977. Mem. Composers League German Democratic Republic. Roman Catholic. Office: Detroit Symphony Orch Ford Auditorium Detroit MI 48226

HERBISON, PRISCILLA JOAN, social work educator, consultant; b. Mpls., Sept. 13, 1943; d. Charles W. and Vonda C. (Rogers) H. B.A., Coll. St. Catherine, St. Paul, 1965; M.S.W., U. Ill.-Urbana, 1969; J.D., U. Minn., 1982. Bar: Minn. 1983; cert. Acad. Cert. Social Workers. Social worker Catholic Social Service, St. Paul, 1965-67, Cath. Welfare Service, Mpls., 1969-71; prof. social work U. W.Va., 1971-74; prof., dir. social work program St. Cloud (Minn.) State U., 1974—, chmn. dept. sociology, anthropology and social work, 1985—; cons., researcher in law; staff aide to speaker of Ill. Ho. of Reps., 1968-69; founder, dir. early childhood ctrs. in rural Appalachia, 1971-72. Fairchild fellow, 1980. Mem. Acad. Cert. Social Workers, Nat. Assn. Social Workers, ABA, Christian Legal Soc., Lawyers Guild of St. Thomas More, Conf. Social Work Edn., Delta Theta Phi. Roman Catholic. Home: 1077 Sibley Memorial Hwy #500 Saint Paul MN 55118 Office: Saint Cloud State U 334-D Steward Hall Saint Cloud MN 56301

HERD, HAROLD SHIELDS, state supreme ct. justice; b. Coldwater, Kans., June 3, 1918. B.A., Washburn U., 1941, J.D., 1942. Bar: Kans. bar 1943. Partner firm Rich and Herd, Coldwater, 1946-53; individual practice law Coldwater, 1953-79; justice Kans. Supreme Ct., 1979—; mayor, Coldwater, 1949-53, county atty., Comanche County, Kans., 1954-58; mem. Kans. Senate, 1965-73, minority floor leader, 1969-73. Bd. govs. Washburn Law Sch., 1974-78; mem. Kans. Com. for Humanities, 1975-80, chmn. 1980. Mem. S.W. Bar Assn. (pres. 1977), Kans. Bar Assn. (exec. council 1973-80). Office: Kans Jud Center 301 W 10th St Topeka KS 66612 *

HERD, RICHARD MURLEN, maxillofacial surgeon; b. Indpls., Sept. 16, 1918; s. Murlen Burtis and Mary (Wolford) H.; m. Harriet Jean Erickson, June 27, 1949; children: Richard M. Jr., Eric Allen, Dorothy Jean. AB in Chemistry, Ind. U., 1941; DDS, St. Louis U., 1945. Intern U. Oreg., Portland, 1947-48; chief resident Wishard Hosp., Indpls., 1948-49, chief resident oral maxillofacial surgery, 1948-49; assoc. prof. oral maxillofacial surgery U. Louisville, 1949-58; practice dentistry specializing in oral maxillofacial surgery Indpls., 1959—; cons. Ind. U., 1962—; chmn. oral maxillofacial dept. Community Hosp., 1973-75, 85-87 Meth. Hosp., 1970-72, Winona Hosp., 1967-69, 84-86, St. Francis Hosp., 1964-67. Contbr. articles to profl. jours. Sponsor Indpls. council Boy Scouts Am., 1986—. Served to lt. (j.g.) USN, 1945-47. Recipient profl. award Am. Coll., 1960. Mem. Am. Coll. Oral Maxillofacial Surgeons, Am. Legion (chpt. comdr. 1986—), Am. Soc. (pres. Louisville chpt. 1955-57), Omicron Kappa Upsilon (scholastic award 1952). Republican. Lutheran. Lodges: Rotary, Moose, Masons, Shriners. Avocations: fishing, flying. Home: 6825 Creekside Ln Indianapolis IN 46220 Office: 5987 E 71st St Indianapolis IN 46220

HERINGTON, THOMAS MICHAEL, real estate corporation officer; b. Grand Rapids, Mich., Oct. 19, 1954; s. Thomas Arthur and Evelyn Margeret (Swiss) H.; m. Mary Ellen Vandenberg, Sept. 25, 1982; 1 child, Sarah VandenBerg. BA in History and Polit. Sci., Grand Valley State U., 1975. Lic. real estate broker, builder, gen. contractor. Salesperson Richardson Bus. Machines, Grand Rapids, 1978; dist. mgr. Murphy Oil Corp., El Dorado, Ark., 1979-82; owner Herington Real Estate, Grand Rapids, 1982—; pres. Herington Constrn. Inc., Grand Rapids, 1982—; v.p., dir. acquisitions Morgan Cos., Flint, Mich., 1985-86; gen. ptnr. Baum and Herington, Southfield, Mich., 1986—; gen. mgr., cons.Vandebunte Egg Co., Grand Rapids, 1983; lectr. real estate investment, 1985—. Vol. various Dem. and Rep. polit. candidates, Mich., 1973—; leader couple, lectr. Precana Conf. Cath. Ch., Grand Haven, Mich., 1983—. Office: Herington Real Estate and Constrn 345 State St SE Grand Rapids MI 49503

HERIP, WALTER MICHAEL, designer, educator; b. Cleve., Nov. 5, 1947; s. Walter and Stella (Burakoski) H. BFA in Indsl. Design, Cleve. Inst. Art, 1971; MA in Graphic Design, Kent State U., 1981. Ind. designer Herip Design, Peninsula, Ohio, 1971-80; pres. Herip Design Assocs., Inc., Hudson, Ohio, 1980—; asst. prof. art U. Akron, Ohio, 1976—; cons. design arts program Rubbermaid, Wooster, Ohio, 1984—, Ohio Dance, 1986—, Ohio Arts Council, Columbus, 1986—, Cleve. Mus. Natural History, 1987—. Patentee Child Resistant Closure, 1975; designer brochure for Akron Art Mus., 1986. Mem. Am. Inst. Graphic Arts. Soc. Typographic Art, Cleve. Soc. Communication Arts (recipient excellence award 1983), Peninsula Library and Hist. Soc. (pres. 1982-83, trustee 1977-83, 86—), Akron Art Mus. (chmn. visual arts com. 1979-80, chmn. comtemporaries group 1983), Nation Mus. Assn. (recipient excellence award 1986), Ohio Mus. Assn. (recipient excellence award 1986), Univ. and Coll. Design Assn. (recipient merit award 1978). Home: 1726 Main St Box 113 Peninsula OH 44264 Office: Herip Design Assocs Inc 36 E Streetsboro Hudson OH 44236

HERMAN, LAWRENCE FRANCIS, marketing executive, musician; b. Cleve., Oct. 7, 1952; s. Ralph John and Yolanda Benita (Cerio) H. B in Music Edn., Ind. U., 1976, MusM, 1977; MBA, Bowling Green State U., 1983. Trumpet instr. Interlochen (Mich.) Arts Acad., 1978-79; artist, lectr. Western Carolina U., Cullowhee, N.C., 1979-80; asst. dir. fundraising Northwood Inst., Midland, Mich., 1983-84; mktg. mgr. N.Am. Van Lines, Ft. Wayne, Ind., 1984-85; dir. mktg. Ft. Wayne Philharmonic, 1985—; prin. trumpet Asheville (N.C.) Symphony Orchestra, 1979-80; mktg. chmn. Forte Arts Found., Ft. Wayne, 1986. mem. mktg. com. Fine Arts Festival, Ft. Wayne, 1986. Named Outstanding Young Man of Am., 1984. Mem. Internat. Trumpet Guild, Am. Fedn. of Musicians, Assn. MBA Execs., Advt. Club Ft. Wayne. Roman Catholic. Home: 2219 Opechee Way Fort Wayne IN 46809 Office: Ft Wayne Philharmonic 222 W Berry Fort Wayne IN 46802

HERMAN, ROBERT DEAN, public administration educator, researcher; b. Harper, Kans., Jan. 6, 1946; s. Floyd Everett and Lois Virginia (Drake) H.; m. Charlotte Marion Davis, Aug. 22, 1971. B.A., Kans. State U., 1968; M.S., Cornell U., 1971, Ph.D., 1976. Asst. prof. U. Mo., Kansas City, 1972-77, assoc. prof. orgnl. behavior and community psychology 1977—. Contbr. chpts. to books, articles to profl. jours. Active Kansas City Consensus, 1984—; pres. Ctr. Developmentally Disabled, Kansas City, 1985-86. Mem. Am. Soc. Pub. Adminstrn., Assn. Voluntary Action Scholars, Am. Sociol. Assn. Avocations: racquetball; music; travel.

HERMAN, ROGER ELIOT, professional speaker, trainer, writer; b. San Francisco, Dec. 11, 1943; s. Carlton Martin and Estelle (Nadler) H.; m. Janet I. Meyer, June 22, 1969 (div. Feb. 1974); 1 child, Scott Philip; m. Sandra Jean Steckel, May 2, 1974; children: Bruce, Jeffrey, Jennifer. BA in Sociology, Hiram Coll., 1969; MA in Pub. Adminstrn., Ohio State U., 1977. Mgr. Rayco, Inc., Kent, Ohio, 1970-72; pvt. practice sales Stow, Ohio, 1972-76; pub. service dir. City Hilliard, Ohio, 1976-78; city mgr. City Rittman, Ohio, 1978-80; pres. Herman Assocs., Inc., Rittman, 1980—. Author: Disaster Planning for Local Government, 1982, Emergency Operations Plan, 1983; contbr. magazine columns, articles to profl. pubs. Commr. Ohio Boy Scouts Am., 1970, scoutmaster Tex. Boy Scouts Am., 1966-70. Served with U.S. Army, 1965-68. Named Most Interesting Person In Northeast Ohio, Cleve. mag., 1981, named one of Outstanding Young Men Am., 1976, 77, 78, 79; recipient Arrowhead award Boy Scouts Am., Ohio, 1969. Mem. Nat. Speakers Assn. (Ohio Speakers Forum ethics chmn. 1985-86), Am. Soc. Tng. and Devel. (program chmn. 1985-86, newsletter editor Northeast Ohio chpt. 1985-86), Ohio Jaycees (Hilliard pres. 1976-77, Blue Chip Disting. Service award 1977). Republican. Jewish. Club: Toastmasters (dist. lt. gov. Tex., Ohio 1965-80, Able Toastmaster award 1969). Avocation: writing. Office: Herman Assocs Inc 19 N Main St Rittman OH 44270

HERMAN, ROY ALAN, manufacturing company executive; b. Bronx, N.Y., July 9, 1943; s. Lee Herman and Jeanette (Rosenberg) H.; m. Sherry Lee Greenberg, June 7, 1964; children: Jennifer Leigh, Mark David. BS in Chemistry and Bus., MBA, Washington U., St. Louis, 1967. Tech. sales rep. Enjay Chem. Co., N.Y.C., 1967-71; product supr. Monsanto Co., St. Louis, 1971-72, product mgr., 1972-74; product mgr. Tubular Steel Inc., St. Louis, 1974-77; mktg. mgr. UNR Leavitt div. UNR, Inc., Chgo., 1977-84, v.p. mktg. and planning, 1984-86, pres., 1986—; mem. Com. on Pipe and Tube Imports, Washington, 1984—; assoc. dir. Nat. Assn. Steel Pipe Distbrs., Houston, 1986—. Contbr. articles to profl. jours. Avocations: bridge, tennis. Office: UNR Leavitt div UNR Inc 1717 W 115th St Chicago IL 60643

HERMANIES, JOHN HANS, lawyer; b. Aug. 19, 1922; s. John and Lucia (Eckstein) H.; m. Dorothy Jean Steinbrecher, Jan. 3, 1953. A.B., Pa. State U., 1944; J.D., U. Cin., 1948. Bar: Ohio 1948. Atty. Indsl. Commn. Ohio, 1948-50; asst. atty. gen. State of Ohio, 1951-57, asst. to gov., 1957-59; ptnr. Hermanies & Major (formerly Beall, Hermanies, Bortz & Major), Cin., 1976-82; mem. Ohio Supreme Ct., 1976-82; mem. Ohio Bd. Bar Examiners, 1963-68. Mem. Southwest Ohio Regional Transit Authority, 1973-76, trustee U. Cin., 1977—; bd. election Hamilton County, Ohio, 1984—; chmn. exec. com. Hamilton County Rep. Party, 1974—. Served with USMC, World War II. Mem. ABA, Ohio Acad. Trial Lawyers Assn., Am. Judicature Soc. Clubs: Bankers, Queen City, Highland Country. Home: 2110 Columbia Pkwy Cincinnati OH 45202 Office: Hermanies & Major 30 Garfield Pl Suite 740 Cincinnati OH 45202

HERMANN, DONALD HAROLD JAMES, lawyer, educator; b. Southgate, Ky., Apr. 6, 1943; s. Albert Joseph and Helen Marie (Snow) H. A.B. (George E. Gamble Honors scholar), Stanford U., 1965; J.D., Columbia U., 1968; LL.M., Harvard U., 1974; M.A. (Univ. scholar), Northwestern U., 1979, Ph.D., 1981. Bar: Ariz. 1968, Wash. 1969, Ky. 1971, Ill. 1972, U.S. Supreme Ct. 1974. Mem. staff, directorate devel. plans Dept. Def., 1964-65; With Legis. Drafting Research Fund, Columbia U., 1966-68; asst. dean Columbia Coll., 1967-68; mem. faculty U. Wash., Seattle, 1968-71, U. Ky., Lexington, 1971-72; mem. faculty DePaul U., 1972—, prof. law and philosophy, 1978—, dir. acad. programs and interdisciplinary study, 1975-76, assoc. dean, 1975-78, dir. Health Law Inst., 1985—; lectr. dept. philosophy Northwestern U., 1979-81; counsel DeWolfe, Poynton & Stevens, 1984—; vis. prof. Washington U., St. Louis, 1974, U. Brazilia, 1976; lectr. law Am. Soc. Found., 1975-78, Sch. Edn. Northwestern U., 1974-76, Christ Coll. Cambridge (Eng.) U., 1977, U. Athens, 1980; vis. scholar U. N.D., 1983; mem. NEH seminar on property and rights Stanford U., 1981; participant law and econs. program U. Rochester, 1974; mem. faculty summer seminar in law and humanities UCLA, 1978; Bicentennial Fellow of U.S. Constitution Claremont Coll., 1986; bd. dirs. Council Legal Edn. Opportunity, Ohio Valley Consortium, 1972, Ill. Bar Automated Research Corp., 1975-81, Criminal Law Consortium Cook County, Ill., 1977-80; cons. Adminstrv. Office Ill. Cts., 1975—; reporter cons. Ill. Jud. Conf., 1972—; mem. Center for Law Focused Edn., Chgo., 1977—; faculty Instituto Superiore Internazionale Di Science Criminali, Siracusa, Italy, 1978—; bd. dirs. Horizons Community Services, 1985—; cons. Commerce Fedn., State of São Paulo, Brazil, 1975; bd. dirs. Chgo. area AIDS Task Force Inc. Editor: Hosp. Law, 1986—, AIDS Monograph Series, 1987—. Bd. dirs. Ctr. for Ch.-State Studies, 1982—, Horizons Community Services, 1985—, Chgo. Area AIDS Task Force, 1987—. John Noble fellow Columbia U., 1968, Internat. fellow, NEH fellow, Law and Humanities fellow U. Chgo, 1975-76, Law and Humanities fellow Harvard U., 1973-74, Northwestern U., 1978-82, Criticism and Theory fellow Stanford U. 1981; NEH fellow Cornell U., 1982, Judicial fellow U.S. Supreme Ct., 1983-84, Bicentennial fellow of the U.S. Constitution, Claremont Coll., 1986. Mem. ABA, Ill. Bar Assn., Chgo. Bar Assn., Am. Acad. Polit. and Social Sci., Am. Law Inst., Nat. Health Lawyers Assn., Am. Soc. Law and Medicine, Am. Soc. Polit. and Legal Philosophy, Nat. Health Lawyers Assn., Am. Judicature Soc., Am. Philos. Assn., Soc. for Bus. Ethics, Soc. for Phenomenology and Existential Philosophy, Internat. Assn. Philosophy of Law and Soc., Soc. Writers on Legal Subjects, Internat. Penal Law Soc., Soc. Am. Law Tchrs., Am. Assn. Law Schs. (del., sect. chmn., chmn. sect. on jurisprudence), Am. Acad. Hosp. Attys., Ill. Assn. Hosp. Attys., Chgo. Hist. Preservation Soc., Evanston Hist. Soc., Northwestern U. Alumni Assn., Signet Soc. of Harvard. Episcopalian. Clubs: Hasty Pudding (Harvard); University, Quadrangle (Chgo.); Univ. (Evanston). Home: 1243 Forest Ave Evanston IL 60202 also: 880 Lake Shore Dr Chicago IL 60611 Office: De Paul Univ Coll Law 25 E Jackson St Chicago IL 60604

HERMANN, MARY KEVIN HOWARD, nurse, educator; b. St. Lawrence, Ky., Oct. 26, 1934; d. Charles Kevin and Mary M. Howard; R.N., St. Mary's Sch. of Nursing, Evansville, Ind., 1955; B.S. cum laude in Nursing, U. Evansville, 1970, M.A., 1972, M.S. in Nursing, 1974; Ed.D., Ind. U., 1984; m. Robert R. Hermann, Feb. 2, 1957; children—Michael R. (dec.), Barbara K., Leah M., Daniel J. Staff nurse St. Mary's Med. Center, Evansville, Ind., 1955-56, head nurse, 1956-58, asst. dir. nursing service, 1965-68; instr. nursing U. Evansville, 1970-73, asst. prof., 1973-76, assoc. prof., 1976-84, prof., 1984—, asst. dean baccalaureate program, 1974-80. Mem. adv. com. Am. Heart Assn. Program, Evansville, 1981. Mem. Am. Nurses Assn., Ind. Nurses Assn. (co-chmn. commn. on edn., chmn. task force on competencies, dir., dir. dist. 4 1982-84), Am. Assn. Critical Care Nurses. Home: 8011 Maple Ln Newburgh IN 47630 Office: 1800 Lincoln Ave Evansville IN 47702

HERMANN, ROBERT ANTHONY, accountant; b. Belleville, Ill., June 4, 1947; s. Anthony and Helen K. (Schneidewind) H.; m. Carole D. Zimmerman, oct. 8, 1983. BS, So. Ill. U., 1974. CPA, Mo., Ill. Staff acct. Rexall Drug Co., St. Louis, 1978-79, Stan Myrda, CPA, Fairview Heights, Ill., 1979-84; chief acct. Slay Industries, St. Louis, 1984-86; sr. auditor Harold Bohlmann & Co., CPA's, St. Louis, 1986—. Served to sgt. USAF, 1968-72, Vietnam. Am. Inst. CPA's, Mo. Soc. CPA's. Mem. United Ch. Christ. Avocation: model railroading. Home: 415 S Virginia Ave Belleville IL 62220

HERMSEN, LOUISE DORIS, marketing executive; b. Kenosha, Wis., June 13, 1952; d. Leon Paul and Jean Jesse (Telford) H. BA in Edn. magna cum laude, St. Norbert Coll., 1973; MBA in Mktg., U. Wis., Whitewater, 1975. Project specialist, mktg. JI Case subs. Tenneco Inc., Racine, Wis., 1976-78; mgr. sales devel. JI Case subs. Tenneco Inc., Racine, 1978-80, mgr. market devel. and services, 1980-84, mgr. market planning and pricing, 1984-85; dir. mktg. communications Harnischfeger corp., Milw., 1985—; guest lectr. Milw. area univs., 1979—. Vol. Milw. Area Girl Scouts U.S. Named one of Outstanding Young Alumni U. Wis., Whitewater, 1979, one of 13 Midwest Ad Women on the Rise, Ad Week mag., 1984. Mem. TEMPO-Profl. Women's Orgn. (com. mem.). Club: Sitmark Ski. Avocations: skiing, travel, theater, sailing. Office: Harnischfeger Corp PO Box 554 Milwaukee WI 53221

HERNANDEZ, RAMON ROBERT, public library director; b. Chgo., Feb. 23, 1936; s. Eleazar Dario and Marie Helen (Stange) H.; m. Fern Ellen Muschinske, Aug. 11, 1962; children: Robert Frank, Mary Martha. BA, Elmhurst (Ill.) Coll., 1957; BD, Eden Theol. Sem., St. Louis, 1962; MA, U. Wis., 1970. Co-pastor St. Stephen United Ch. Christ, Merrill, Wis., 1960-64; dir. youth work Wis. Conf. United Ch. Christ, Madison, 1964-70; dir. T.B. Scott Free Library, Merrill, 1970-75, McMillan Meml. Library, Wisconsin Rapids, Wis., 1975-83, Ann Arbor (Mich.) Pub. Library, 1983—. Editorial com. Songs of Many Nations Songbook, 1980; contbr. articles to profl. jours. Treas. Ann Arbor Homeless Coalition, 1985—; bd.dirs., sec., v.p. Riverview Hosp. Assn., Wisconsin Rapids, 1979-83. Mem. ALA, Wis. Library Assn. (Leadership award 1980, pres. 1980), Mich. Library Assn. Lodge: Rotary (pres. Merrill chpt. 1975, Community Service award 1975). Home: 1832 Covington Dr Ann Arbor MI 48103 Office: Ann Arbor Pub Library 343 S 5th Ave Ann Arbor MI 48104-2293

HERNANDEZ NIETO, HECTOR, philosophy and Spanish literature educator, researcher; b. Irapuato, Mex., Apr. 19, 1929; came to U.S. 1968, naturalized 1982; s. Santiago Hernandez and Felicitas Nieto; 1 child, Angelica Rocio. Baccalaureate, U. St. Thomas, Rome, 1959, Licenciate, 1960, Doctorate in Philosophy, 1964; M.A. in Classics, U. Ill., 1971, Ph.D. in Spanish, 1975. Dean students, prof. Colegio del Esp.S., Calahorra, Spain, 1960-62; prof. philosophy Instituto Superior de Estudios Eclesiasticos, Tlalpam, Mex., 1965-68; asst. prof. U. Ill., Chgo., 1972-77; chairperson Chgo. State U., 1977-83, prof., 1982—; founder Confedn. Latin Am. Students, Chgo., 1972, Spanish Club, Chgo., 1982. Author: Las raices metafisicas de la logica, 1971. Contbr. articles to profl. jours. Recipient Tchr. of Yr. award Chgo. State U., 1978, Outstanding Faculty award Chgo. State U., 1981. Roman Catholic. Avocations: computers, photography, short stories. Office: Chgo State U C-301 95th at King Dr Chicago IL 60628

HERNDON, BRADLEY J., bank executive; b. Terre Haute, Ind., May 22, 1957; s. Bill and Margaret (Church) H.; m. Nancy J. Bibb, July 20, 1979; 1 child, Lindsey Erin. BS with honors, Ind. State U., 1979; MBA with honors, U. Ind., Indpls., 1983. Chartered fin. analyst, 1986. Jr. portfolio mgr. Ind. Nat. Bank, Indpls., 1979-81, trust officer, 1981-83, asst. v.p., 1983-86, v.p., trust officer, 1986—. Bd. dirs., treas. Bright Way, Inc., Greenfield, Ind., 1986—, Multiple Sclerosis Soc. Indpls. Named one of Outstanding Young Men of Am., 1985. Fellow Indpls. Soc. Fin. Analyst Fedn. Republican. Lodge: Sertoma. Avocations: piano, reading, tennis. Home: 614 Hillcrest Ln Greenfield IN 46140 Office: Ind Nat Bank 1 Indiana Sq #622 Indianapolis IN 46266

HEROLD, KARL GUENTER, lawyer; b. Munich, Fed. Republic Germany, Feb. 3, 1947; s. Guenter K.B. and Eleonore E.E. (Arndt) H.; m. Helen Robinson, Sept. 14, 1968; children: Deanna, Donna, Nicole, Jessica, Christine. BS, Bowling Green State U., 1969; JD, Case Western Res. U., 1972. Bar: Ohio 1872, N.Y. 1985. Ptnr. Jones, Day, Reavis & Pogue, Cleve., 1972—; trustee Internat. and Comparative Law Ctr. Southwest Legal Found., Dallas, 1983; bd. dirs. Didier Taylor Refractories Corp., Cin., Redland Corp., San Antonio, v.p., Redland Credit Corp., San Antonio, v.p., Redland Fin. Inc., San Antonio, v.p., 1979-86. Trustee Cleve. Internat. Program, 1982—. Mem. ABA, Internat. Bar Assn., Order of Coif, Omicron Delta Kappa. Home: 2212 Edgeview Dr Hudson OH 44236 Office: Jones Day Reavis & Pogue North Point 901 Lakeside Ave Cleveland OH 44114

HEROLD, ROBERT DANIEL, organic chemist; b. Wabasha, Minn., Jan. 13, 1953; s. Allen Eldon and Beatrice May (Oestreich) H.; Lourdes Lucas, June 13, 1981; children: Wendy, Bettina. BS summa cum laude, U. Wis., Eau Claire, 1975; MS, MIT, 1977; PhD, Iowa State U., 1984. Sr. engr. Bendix Kansas City (Mo.) div. Allied-Signal Inc., 1984—; instr. chemistry Longview Community Coll., Lee's Summit, Mo., 1985. Mem. Am. Chem. Soc. (organic chemistry and polymer chemistry divs.), Am. Inst. Chemists, Sigma Xi, Phi Kappa Phi. Roman Catholic. Home: 11716 Fuller Ave Kansas City MO 64134 Office: Allied-Signal Inc Bendix Kansas City Div 2000 E 95th St Kansas City MO 64141

HERR, DEAN MARTIN, technical writer; b. Battle Creek, Mich., Aug. 17, 1955; s. Martin Lee and Carol Ellen (Horton) H. B.S. in Math., Mich. Tech. U., 1978, B.S. in Physics, 1981. Tech. writer Control Data Corp., Arden Hills, Minn., 1978-80, 81-83, Zycad Corp., Arden Hills, 1983-85. ETA Systems Inc., 1985—. Author, editor: Zycad Intermediate Form Tool Kit, 1984; ZIF Reference Manual, 1985. Mem. Mpls. Writers' Workshop, 1982. Mem. Am. Phys. Soc., Soc. of Mayflower Descs. in Minn. Republican. Baptist. Club: Mini-Unit (Mpls.). Home: 1360 Terrace Dr Apt 103 Roseville MN 55113 Office: ETA Systems Inc 1450 Energy Park Dr Saint Paul MN 55108

HERR, MARK CHARLES, architect; b. Milw., Dec. 15, 1952; s. Raymond Francis and Arline L. (Sternberg) H.; m. Kim Marie Huebner, Aug. 29, 1981; children: Diana, Andrew. BArch, U. Notre Dame, 1976. Registered architect, Wis., Minn., Iowa. Architect Zimmerman Design, Milw., 1976-78; architect Heike/Design Assoc., Milw., 1978-82, v.p., 1982-84, exec. v.p., 1984—. Major works include Tivoli Palm Garden, 1982 (Wis. Soc. Architects award), Kohler Design Ctr., 1986 (Wis. Soc. Architects award). Mem. AIA, Wis. Soc. Architects (2 awards 1982, 86), Nat. Council Architect Registration Bd., Nat. Trust Hist. Preservation, Elm Brook Hist. Soc. Club: Notre Dame of Milw. (bd. dirs. and com. chmn. 1980—). Avocations: cross country skiing, fishing, swimming. Home: 1417 American Ave Waukesha WI 53186 Office: Heike/Design Assocs Inc 13255 W Bluemound Rd Brookfield WI 53005

HERRERA, PAUL M., health science facility administrator; b. Toledo, Aug. 13, 1950; s. Paul Apolonio and Mary (Navarro) H.; m. Hilda Cantu, Dec. 15, 1973; children: David, Peter, Nina. BA, Bowling Green State U., 1972, MA in Rehab. Counseling, 1975; cert. rehab. counseling, cert. completion rehab. adminstrn., DePaul U. Probation officer Lucas County Adult Probation Dept., Toledo, 1972-74; community coordinator North Toledo Community House, 1974-76; rehab. counselor Stark County Bd. Mental Retardation/Devel. Disabilities, Canton, Ohio, 1976-78, dir. tng., 1978—; mem. com. on aging and devel. disabilities Northeastern Ohio U. Coll. Medicine Office Geriatric Medicine/Gerontology, Akron, 1983—, steering com. Joseph P. Kennedy Jr. Found. Grant. Author: Occupational Exploration for the Mentally Handicapped, 1982, Innovative Programming for the Aging and Aged Mentally Retarded/Developmentally Disabled Adult, 1983; editor (newsletter) ACCESS, 1986. Home: 2350 Nottingham NW Massillon OH 44646 Office: West Stark Ctr 7891 Hills and Dales Rd NW Massillon OH 44646

HERRES, ROBERT WENZEL, electrical inspector; b. Dayton, Ohio, Feb. 6, 1936; s. Wenzel George Jr. and Evelyn Mae (Snider) H.; m. Elfriede Anna Mühlen, Apr. 27, 1959 (div. Nov. 1968); children: David L., Roger A.; m. Judy Ruth Wilson, Mar. 13, 1972. Grad. high sch., Dayton, 1954. cert. electrical safety inspector, Ohio. Electrical inspector City of Dayton, 1980—; instr. Montgomery County Joint Vocat. Sch., 1984—; elec. contractor R.W. Herres Elect. Service, Dayton, 1960—. Mem. Internat. Assn. Elec. Inspectors. Democrat. Avocations: water sports, martial arts. Home: 1128 Burleigh Ave Dayton OH 45407 Office: City of Dayton Inspectional Services 101 W 3d St Dayton OH 45402

HERRICK, CLAY, JR., civic worker, retired advertising executive; b. Cleveland Heights, Ohio, Dec. 15, 1911; s. C. Clay and Alice Mabel (Merriam) H.; m. Ruth Eleanor Penty, Apr. 27, 1935; children: Clay Herrick III, Jill. BA, Adelbert Coll. of Western Res. U., 1934; diploma John Huntington Poly. Inst. Pub. relations dir. Gen. Tire & Rubber Co., Akron, 1940-45; creative dir. JP Smith creative printers for Eastman Kodak, Rochester, 1945-48; account exec. Fuller, Smith & Ross, Inc., 1948-58; v.p. Carpenter, Lamb & Herrick, Inc., 1958-64, pres., 1964-73; sr. v.p. Watts, Lamp, Kenyon & Herrick Inc., 1973-74, ret., 1974; pres. Western Res. Press, Inc., 1973-78, Landmarks Pub. Co., 1986—; instr. graphics Cleve. State U., 1968—, Cleve history Cuyahoga Community Coll., 1984—; originator, 1st chmn. Cleve. Printing Week celebrations, 1953 seminar leader In-Plant Printing Mgmt. Assn., 1978. Author: But It's So, 1934, Cleveland's Rich Heritage, 1975, Gags in Rhyme, 1983, Cleveland Landmarks, 1986; author monthly feature Cleveland Landmarks in Properties Mag., 1977-87; editor, pub. Graphic Artisan; editor Pioneer, Generally Speaking, Ad-Lib, Jaycee Current, Arco News, Harris Impressions, Candy Counter and Merchandiser, others. Pres. Early Settlers Assn.; chmn. Cleve. Landmark Commn.; v.p. Shaker Landmarks Commn.; chmn. Cleve. Hall Fame Commn.; v.p. Cleve. Bicentennial Commn.; pres. univ. alumni council Western Res. U.; fund chmn. Cleve. Ch. Fedn.; scoutmaster, cubmaster Boy Scouts Am.; pres. PTA; trustee YMCA, Shauffler div. Defiance Coll.; pub. relations bd. United Appeal; chmn. task force Cleve. Ambassadors, 1978; mem. pub. relations com. ARC Centennial, 1981; v.p. Cleve. Sr. Council, 1981-85, pres., 1985-86; deacon Fairmount Presbyn. Ch., Shaker Heights, Ohio, 1950-53, trustee, 1984-87; trustee Cleanland Rapid Recovery, 1983—; mem. Univ. Circle Council, 1982—; mem. Warehouse Dist., Rivers Bend Parks Corp., P.R. Community Midtown Corridor. Named Cleve. Graphic Arts Man of Year, 1965, Disting. Alumnus of Yr., Case Western Res. U., 1987; elected to Graphic Arts Hall of Distinction, 1977; recipient Heritage award New Eng. Soc., 1978, Americanism award Am. Legion, 1987; elected to Disting. Alumni Hall of Fame, Cleveland Heights High Sch., 1981, Cleve. Advt. Club Hall of Fame, 1981. Mem. Nat. Cartoonists Soc., Am. Assn. Advt. Agys. (chmn.), New Eng. Soc. (pres.; Man of Yr. 1977), Cleve. Cultural Gardens Fedn. (v.p., exec. sec.), Shaker Hist. Soc. (pres.), Cleve. Ad Club (v.p.), Founders and Patriots Am. (Ohio gov., lt. gov. nat. soc.), Fine Arts Assn. (trustee), Am. Advt. Fedn. (dist gov.; Advt. Man of Yr. 1974), Intercomm Communications Group (1st pres.), Cleve. Growth Assn. (speakers bur. 1980—), Cleve. Graphic Arts Council (organizer, pres., exec. sec. 1981-87), Adelbert Alumni Assn. Western Res. U. (pres.), SAR (past pres., sec.-treas. 1974-84, chaplain 1985—), Soc. Boonesboro, Order Ky. Cols., Sons and Daus. Pilgrims, Jamestowne Soc. (life), Cleve. Sr. Council pres. 1985-86, Cleve. Restoration Soc. (sec. 1981-85, pres. 1985-86), Delta Upsilon (alumni advisor 1981—), Sigma Delta Chi, Delta Sigma Rho, Pi Epsilon Delta. Clubs: Toastmasters Internat. (hon. life mem; co-founder 1st N.Y. club 1947), Cheshire Cheese (past pres. 4 times). Lodge: Rotary (trustee). Home: 16315 Fernway Rd Shaker Heights OH 44120

HERRICK, DAVID FRASER, banking executive; b. Ludlow, Mass., Oct. 8, 1947; s. William G. and Annie (Janes) H.; m. Carianne Muccino, May 12, 1973; children: Cara Lynn, Douglas. AB in Econs., Lafayette Coll., 1969; MBA, Am. Internat. U., 1973. Mktg. dir. Smith & Wesson, Springfield, Mass., 1969-71; advt. mgr. North & Judd, Middletown, Conn., 1971-73; v.p. Aetna Bus. Credit, East Hartford, Conn., 1973-81; sr. v.p. Assocs. Comml. Corp., Chgo., 1981-86, AT Comml. Corp., Rosemont, Ill., 1986—; dir. Nat. Comml. Fin. Assn., N.Y.C., 1986—. Contbr. articles to profl. banking jours. Bd. dirs. Midstate Transit Authority, Middletown, Conn., 1979-81; vice-chmn. Middletown Rep. Com., 1980-81. Republican. Clubs: Anvil (Dundee, Ill.), Monroe (Chgo.). Avocations: sports cars, photography, outdoors. Office: AT Comml Corp 5600 N River Rd Rosemont IL 60018

HERRICK, JEFFREY GLEN, dentist; b. Ames, Iowa, Apr. 1, 1953; s. John Berne and Gwen Jean (Netcott) H.; m. Wendy Beth Enders, July 10, 1976. BS in Zoology, Iowa State U., 1975; DDS, U. Iowa Coll. Dentistry, 1979. Gen. dentistry resident U. Iowa Hosp., Iowa City, 1979-80, gen. practice resident, 1980—. Mem. ADA, Iowa Dental Assn., Des Moines Dental Dist., Ames Area Dental Study Club. Avocations: running, golf, biking, reading, cross-country skiing. Office: 620 5th St Ames IA 50010

HERRICK, KENNETH GILBERT, air conditioning and refrigeration equipment manufacturing company executive; b. Jackson, Mich., Apr. 2, 1921; s. Ray Wesley and Hazel Marie (Forney) H.; m. Shirley J. Todd, Mar. 2, 1942; children: Todd Wesley, Toni Lynn. Student public and pvt. schs., Howe, Ind.; L.H.D. (hon.), Siena Heights Coll., 1974; H.H.D. (hon.), Adrian Coll., 1975, Detroit Inst. Tech., 1980; LL.D., Judson Coll., 1975; D. Engring. (hon.), Albion Coll., 1981. With Tecumseh Products Co., Mich., 1940-42, 45—; v.p. Tecumseh Products Co., 1961-66, vice chmn. bd., 1964-70, pres., 1966-70, chmn. bd., chief exec. officer, 1970—; dir. United Savs. Bank, Tecumseh, Mfrs. Nat. Bank Detroit, Gen. Telephone Co., Muskegon, Mich. Bd. dirs. Howe Mil. Sch.; pres. Herrick Meml. Hosp. Bd., 1970-81, from Herrick Found., 1970; mem. exec. adv. bd. St. Jude Children's Hosp., from 1978. Served with USAAC, 1942-45. Recipient Hon. Alumni award Mich. State U., 1975; Disting. Service award Albion Coll., 1975. Presbyterian. Clubs: Lenawee Country (Adrian, Mich.), Elks (Adrian, Mich.); Tecumseh Country (Tecumseh), Masons (Tecumseh). Office: Tecumseh Products Co 100 E Patterson Tecumseh MI 49286 *

HERRICK, TODD W., manufacturing company executive. Pres., chief operating officer Tecumseh (Mich.) Products Co. Address: Tecumseh Products Co 100 E Patterson St Tecumseh MI 49286 *

HERRIMAN, ALAN GEORGE, energy management engineer; b. Bowling Green, Ohio, Dec. 9, 1937; s. Loyd Raymond and Lelah Vee (Haines) H.; m. Norma Ann Sautter, Aug. 30, 1958; children: Philip Alan, Laura Jean (dec.). BSEE, Ohio No. U., 1959; MSc, Ohio State U., 1961. Sr. scientist Jet Propulsion Lab., Pasadena, Calif., 1962-70; energy mgmt. engr. Gen. Motors Corp., Defiance, Ohio, 1973—. Mem. Tau Beta Pi. Republican. Scientologist. Avocations: homebuilt aircraft construction, flying. Office: Gen Motors Cen Foundry PO Box 70 Defiance OH 43512

HERRIN, ROGER DEAN, podiatrist; b. Cave-in-Rock, Ill., Jan. 30, 1937; s. W.C. and Nigel (Blaine) H.; m. Mary Ann Potts (div.); children: Lysa Jo Herrin Saran, Steven Brent; m. Michelle Pett, Oct. 1983; 1 child, Michael Blaine. BS, Bethel Coll., 1960; postgrad., Ill. Coll. of Medicine, Chgo., 1963-65; D of Podiatric Medicine, Ill. Coll. Podiatric Medicine, 1969. Surgical diplomate; L.R. McCain cert. surgery. Mem. staff Harrisburg (Ill.) Med. Ctr. Inc., 1970—, Hardin County Gen. Hosp., Rosiclare, Ill., 1970—; v.p. Harrisburg Med. Ctr. Inc., 1973-76; cons. Vienna (Ill.) Correctional Ctr., Marion (Ill.) Prison, Ill. Youth Ctr., Harrisburg; cons. sports medicine various Ill. univs.; pres., owner RDK Mgmt. Service, Harrisburg, Bank of Galatia (Ill.); owner Hardin County Golf Club, Cave-in-Rock, Town & Country Shopping Ctr., Marion; concessionaire State Park Lodge, Cave-in-Rock, Ill. Author: (with Glen Seaborg) Problem Solving Approach in Teaching, 1961-62. vice chmn. Ill. Health Facilities Authority, Chgo., 1973-79. Mem. Am. Podiatric Med. Assn., Ill. Podiatric Med. Assn. Methodist. Clubs: Shawnee Hills Country (Harrisburg); Franklin County Country (Westfrankfort, Ill.). Avocations: golf, travel. Home: 20 Dogwood Pl Harrisburg IL 62946 Office: 203 N Vine St Harrisburg IL 62946

HERRING, DORIS LEE, business educator, consultant; b. Valdosta, Ga., June 28, 1933; d. Bartow Powell and Melanie (Small) H. BFA, Wayne State U., 1957, MAT, 1982. Adminstrv. asst. Wayne State U., Detroit, 1957-66, teaching asst., 1978-79; tchr., intern Detroit Pub. Schs., 1966-68; assoc. prof. Lewis Coll. of Bus., Detroit, 1979-80, asst. prof., 1981-83, prof., chairperson, 1983—; bd. dirs. D.L. Herring Enterprises, Detroit. Active Detroit Urban League, 1985—, Detroit Founders Soc., 1985—. Teaching intern. Nat. Tchrs. Corps. Dept. Edn. and Wayne State U., 1966-68. Mem. MLA, Nat. Council Tchrs. English, Nat. Assn. Study of Negro Life/History, Nat. Assn. Female Execs., Mich. Bus. Educators Assn., League of Women Voters, NAACP. Mem. Ch. of Christ. Club: Detroit Poetry Research Ctr. Avocations: chess, computer programming. Home: 759 Lawrence Ave Detroit MI 48202 Office: Lewis Coll Bus 17370 Meyers Rd Detroit MI 48235

HERRING, RAYMOND MARK, marketing executive, consultant; b. Nashville, Sept. 23, 1952; s. Raymond Benjamin and Alma Ruth (Murrell) H. BA, Baylor U., 1974, MA, 1976, EdD, 1983. Research and evaluation specialist McLennan County Med. Edn. and Research Found., Waco, Tex., 1979-82; dir. edn., pub. relations Providence Hosp., Waco, 1982-85, dir. ctr. for health promotion, 1983-85; v.p. John Leifer, Ltd., Shawnee Mission, Kans., 1985-86; pres. MHA Mktg. Services, Inc., Overland Park, Kans., 1986—; adv. bd. Upjohn Healthcare Services, Waco, 1984-85; editorial bd. Healthcare Mgmt. Rev., Overland Park, 1986—; bd. dirs. Tex. Soc. Hosp. Educators, 1983-85. Contbr. articles to profl. jours. Mem. HealthPlus, Overland Park; bd. dirs. Am. Diabetes Assn., Waco, 1984-85. Mem. Am. Mktg. Assn., Am. Soc. Healthcare Mktg. and Pub. Relations, Am. Soc. Healthcare Edn. and Tng. (com. chmn. 1985). Home: 11564 Caenen Overland Park KS 66210 Office: MHA Mktg Services Inc 6405 Metcalf Suite 421 Overland Park KS 66202

HERRMANN, ARTHUR DOMINEY, banker; b. Louisville, Sept. 29, 1926; s. Arthur Chester and Mattie Belle (Dominey) H.; m. Lucy Kindred, Apr. 7, 1951; children: Lucy W. Herrman Porter, Anne D. Herrman Phillips, Martha Kindred. BA, Ohio State U., 1947, JD, 1949; postgrad., Rutgers U., 1956. Bar: Ohio 1950. Asst. trust officer Huntington Nat. Bank, Columbus, 1951-56, pres., chief executive officer, 1972-75, also bd. dirs, chmn., 1980-81; pres., chief exec. officer Huntington Bancshares, Inc., 1975-81, also bd. dirs.; chmn., pres., chief exec. officer, dir. BancOhio Corp., 1981-84; chmn., dir. BancOhio Nat. Bank (mem. Nat. City Corp.), 1984—; bd. dirs. Nat. City Corp, N.Am. Broadcasting Co. Trustee Columbus Mus. Fine Art, from 1974, v.p. 1979-82, pres. 1982-84; trustee Ohio Dominion Coll. 1978—, chmn. 1984—; trustee Children's Hosp. of Columbus, 1985—, Ohio Cancer Found. 1977—; chmn. United Negro Coll. Fund Dr., 1984-85; trustee Capitol South Com. Urban Redevel. Corp., 1982—. Mem. Ohio Bankers Assn., Columbus Bar Assn., Ohio C. of C. (exec. com., trreas. 1979—), Columbus Area C. of C. (bd. dirs., vice chmn. exec. com. from 1983), Assn. Bank Holding Cos., Assn. Reserve City Bankers, Newcomen Soc., Sigma Chi, Phi Delta Phi. Clubs: Pres.' of Ohio State U.; Phi Delta Phi Legal Frat.; Cols.; Rocky Fork Hunt and Country; Castalia, Review. Office: BancOhio Nat Bank Office of Chmn 155 E Broad St Columbus OH 43251

HERRMANN, EUGENE DAVID, surgeon; b. Cin., Jan. 4, 1947; s. Eugene Raymond and Marjorie (Aull) H.; m. Mary Paula Schutte, Sept. 28, 1973; children: Eugene David Jr., Kelly Christine. BS, Georgetown U., Washington, 1969; MS, U. Mich., Ann Arbor, 1971; MD, Ohio State U., Columbus, 1974. Diplomate Am. Bd. Otolaryngology and Head-neck Surgery. Intern surgery U. Cin., 1974-75, resident surgery, 1975-76, resident otolaryngology and head-neck surgery, 1976-79; surgeon Raleigh (N.C.) Ear, Neck and Throat Assocs., 1979-81; pvt. practice Middletown, Ohio, 1981—; chmn. otolaryncology and ophthalmology Middletown Regional Hosp., 1984-86. Fellow Am. Acad. Otoloaryngology; mem. AMA, Ohio State Med. Assn., Butler County Med. Soc. Office: 500 S Breiel Blvd Middletown OH 45044

HERRMANN, THOMAS ANTHONY, civil engineer, consultant; b. St. Louis, Oct. 30, 1928; s. Anthony E. and Susan K. (Shinker) H.; B.S.C.E., Mo. Sch. Mines, Rolla, 1950; cert. USPHS, Cin., 1966; diploma U.S. Army Command and Gen. Staff Coll., 1978; m. Mary M. Finan, Apr. 7, 1951; children—John T., Marguerite A. Field engr. Sverdrup & Parcel, Inc., St. Louis, 1950-52; design engr. Russell & Axon, Inc., St. Louis, 1952-56; profl. engr. Williamson & Assos., St. Louis, 1956-66; v.p./mgr. civil, environ. div. Zurheide-Herrmann, Inc., St. Louis, 1966—. Served to col. C.E. USAR, 1950-86. Registered profl. engr., 10 states; registered land surveyor, Mo. Mem. Nat. Soc. Profl. Engrs. (past nat. dir.), Mo. Soc. Profl. Engrs. (pres. 1979-80, pres. St. Louis chpt. 1969-70, St. Louis Young Engr. of Yr. 1963, St. Louis Outstanding Engr. in Pvt. Practice 1980, St. Louis Engr. of Yr. 1981), Cons. Engrs. Council, ASCE, Am. Pub. Works Assn., Am. Water Works Assn. (Disting. Service ciation 1977), U. Mo. at Rolla Acad. Civil Engrs. (pres. 1987), Water Pollution Control Fedn., Mo. Water and Sewerage Conf., Soc. Am. Mil. Engrs., Res. Officers Assn., Chi Epsilon. Office: 4333 W Clayton Ave Saint Louis MO 63110

HERRMANN, THOMAS FRANCIS, database administrator; b. Kenosha, Wis., Sept. 28, 1951; s. Matthias Bernard and Sebastiana J. (Placente) H.; m. Gail Ann Sipsma, Oct. 25, 1975; children: Aaron Matthew, Joel Michael, Andrew Jacob, Justin Thomas. Student, Gateway Tech. Inst., Kenosha, 1969, U. Wis., Kenosha, 1973. Programmer Snap-On Tools Corp., Kenosha, 1975-79; project leader Jacobsen Mfg. Co., Racine, Wis., 1979-80; database analyst Jupiter Transp. Co., Kenosha, 1980-82; systems programmer Citibank S.D., Sioux Falls, 1982-85; database adminstr. Sandoz Crop Protection, Chgo., 1985-86; data processing cons. Applied Info. Devel., Inc., Oak Brook, Ill., 1986—. Editor newsletter Open Channel, 1985—. Candidate Common Council, Kenosha. Mem. Data Processing Mgmt. Assn. (reporter newsletter 1981-82). Roman Catholic. Clubs: USS Halsey (Sioux Falls), USS Voyager (Vernon Hills, Ill.). Avocations: sports, music, books. Office: 262 Hawthorn Village Commons Suite 114 Vernon Hills IL 60061

HERROLD, ANNE MARIE, pharmacist, research chemist; b. Anderson, Ind., Feb. 21, 1950; d. Walter Joseph and Esther Lillian (Seipel) Brewster; m. Robert Earl Herrold, Aug. 7, 1971; children—Amy Anne, Joseph Alden. B.S. in Pharmacy, Purdue U., 1973; M.B.A., Ind. U., Indpls., 1981. Registered pharmacist, Ind. Research chemist Eli Lilly & Co., Indpls., 1973-80. Patentee Sunscreen composition, 1981, cosmetic cream formulation, 1981, cosmetic lotion formulation, 1981, skin cell renewal regime, 1981, sensitive skin care regime, 1983, cosmetic cream formulation, 1983. Mem. Am. Pharm. Assn., Kappa Epsilon (sec. 1972-73; named Outstanding Woman Pharmacy Graduate 1973), Tri Kappa. Republican. Lutheran. Avocations: reading; playing organ; cooking. Home: 121 Westbourne Dr Brownsburg IN 46112

HERRON, DONALD PATRICK, lawyer, psychologist; b. Springfield, Ill. Feb. 6, 1954; s. Donald Franklin and Patricia Ann (Flynn) H.; m. Kristine Lydia Gish, Aug. 7, 1976. B.A. in Psychology and Sociology, U. Mo.-Kansas City, 1976, M.S. in Psychology, 1978, J.D., 1981. Bar: Mo. 1981, U.S. Dist. Ct. (we. dist.) Mo. 1981. Counselor, Johnson County Mental Retardation Ctr., Kans., 1976-77; lectr. in psychology, acad. adviser U. Mo.-Kansas City, 1977-80; assoc. Morris and Foust, Kansas City, 1981-85; ptnr. Herron and Lewis, Kansas City, 1985—; cons. psychology, Kansas City, 1978—. Author profl. papers in psychology. Named one of Outstanding Young Men in Am. Mem. ABA (litigation sect.), Mo. Bar Assn., Kansas City Bar Assn., Assn. Trial Lawyers Am., Mo. Trial Lawyers Assn., Nat. Assn. For Behavior Analysis, AAAS, Phi Delta Phi, Phi Kappa Phi, Psi Chi. Roman Catholic. Home: 8549 Wedd Overland Park KS 66212 Office: Herron and Lewis PO Box 2326 Rivergate Business Ctr Kansas City MO 64142

HERRON, ROLLAND EDWARD, osteopath; b. Salem, Ohio, Feb. 27, 1934; s. James William and Nora Evelyn (Dunn) H.; m. Joanne Hicks, Aug. 7, 1965; 1 child, Pamela Kay Binns. BS, Ohio State U., 1955; DO, Kirksville Coll. Osteo. Medicine, 1962. Pvt. practice osteopathic internal medicine Salem, Ohio, 1967—. Developer MediScript computer systems. Med. dir. Columbiana County Bd. of Health, 1985-86. Served with U.S. Army, 1955-56. Mem. Am. Osteo. Assn., Ohio State Med. Soc., Columbiana County Med. Soc. (past pres.). Republican. Lutheran. Avocations: computers; pvt. pilot, instrument rated. Home and Office: 816 N Lincoln Ave Salem OH 44460

HERSCHER, WALTER RAY, educator; b. Niles, Mich., Apr. 5, 1946; s. Frederick Leonard and Cecile Lillian (Burkybile) H.; m. Susan Kay Arnold, June 12, 1976; children—Anne Marie, Brian Craig. B.A., Kalamazoo Coll., 1966; M.A., U. Notre Dame, 1968; postgrad. U. Okla., 1968-70; M.S., U. Wis.-Oshkosh, 1986. Asst. mgr. SAGA Food Service, Kalamazoo Coll. and Nazareth Coll., Kalamazoo, Mich., 1971-73; social studies tchr. Appleton (Wis.) Pub. Schs., 1973—, head social studies dept., 1980-84, cross country coach Appleton West High Sch., 1973-84; instr. U. Wis.-Fox Valley Ctr., Appleton, 1979-81, Lakeland Coll., 1985—. Treas., Methodist Ch. Kum Dubls, 1982-83. Stone scholar Kalamazoo Coll., 1963-66; Hearst fellow U. Notre Dame, 1966-67. Mem. Nat. Council Social Studies, Wis. Council Social Studies, Kappa Delta Pi. Methodist. Club: Pace Setters. Home: 1341 W Cloverdale Dr Appleton WI 54914 Office: 610 N Badger St Appleton WI 54914

HERSEY, MARK, computer, infosystems engineer; b. N.Y.C., June 17, 1954; s. Fredrick Bromell and Ethel (Dougherty) H.; m. Marilyn Jean Rollo, Dec. 27, 1975. BS in Computer Sci., Mich. State U., 1975; postgrad., Calif. Tech. U., 1975; MS in Computer Sci., U. Mich., 1978. Programmer, analyst Mich. State U., East Lansing, 1974-77; systems programmer U. Mich., Ann Arbor, 1982-84; pres., cons. Hersey Micro Cons., Inc., Ann Arbor, 1984—. Avocations: bowling, chess. Office: Hersey Micro Cons Inc PO Box 8276 Ann Arbor MI 48107

HERSHEWAY, CHARLES EUGENE, marketing executive; b. Chgo., Apr. 23, 1933; s. Louis and Jean (Manfre) H.; student U. Ill., 1951-53; B.S., Northwestern U., 1959; m. Shirley Leyendecker, Jan. 19, 1957; children—Deborah Lynn, Louise Jeffrey; m. 2d, Priscilla Karas, Dec. 1, 1974. Editorial dir. Nat. Research Bur., Chgo., 1958-62; promotion mgr. Advt. Publs., Inc., Chgo., 1962-64; advt. mgr. Pfaelzer Bros. div. Armour Co., Chgo., 1964-67, mktg. mgr., 1967-70, sales mgr., 1970, v.p. mktg., 1970-74; pres. United Am. Food Processors Gourmet Fare, 1974-76, Mail Market Makers, Inc., Clarendon Hills, Ill., 1976-79; v.p. Lerner Scott Corp., 1979-84; v.p. mktg. Allen Bros., 1984-86; mktg. cons., 1986; pres. Gourmet Gift House, Broadview, Ill., 1986—. Served with USMCR, 1952-54, USN, 1954-58. Mem. Mail Advt. Club Chgo., Chgo. Federated Advt., Premium Industry Club, Sales Promotion Execs., Mail Advt. Author: NRB Retail Advt. and Sales Promotion Manual, vol. I, 1960, vol. II, 1961, vol. III, 1962; M.P. Brown Collection Letter Manual, 1961; Nat. Research Bur. Discount Store Manual, 1961. Contbr. articles to profl. jours. Home: 1450 Golden Bell Ct Downers Grove IL 60515 Office: Gourmet Gift House 1901-03 Cermak Rd Broadview IL 60153

HERSON, JULIAN, otolaryngologist; b. Lodz, Poland, June 1, 1910; came to U.S., 1942; s. Harry and Helen (Lickerman) Hirszzson; m. Helene Friedman; children: Eleanor, Albert. Docteur en Médecine, U. Paris, 1934, U. Bordeaux, France, 1936. Diplomate Am. Bd. Otolaryngology. Asst. dept. otolaryngology U. Bordeaux Clinics, 1935-36; intern Alexian Bros. Hosp., Chgo., 1943; practice medicine specializing in otorhinolaryngology Chgo., 1943—; staff Holy Cross Hosp., Chgo., 1944-53; staff Woodlawn Hosp., Chgo., 1950-51. Translator articles from French Jours. Served with French Army, 1938-40. Recipient Croix de Combattant, French Army, 1941; fellow Internat. Coll. Surgeons, 1960-62. Mem. AMA, Chgo. Med. Soc., Ill. State Med. Soc., Chgo. Laryngol. Soc. Avocations: music, philately. Office: 5430 S Kedzie Ave Chicago IL 60632

HERSZDORFER, PIERRE JACQUES, banker; b. Marseille, France, Apr. 20, 1939; came to U.S., 1955, naturalized, 1960; s. Julius and Paula (Roniger) H.; m. Doris Buntin, Dec. 24, 1968 (div. 1979). BS, NYU, 1968; student

Am. Inst. Banking. Mem. staff auditing dept. Irving Trust Co., N.Y.C., 1960-68; mem. staff comptroller's div. Citibank, N.Y.C., 1968-71; v.p. internat. div. Hartford Nat. Bank & Trust Co. (Conn.), 1971-79; v.p. Credit Agricole br. Caisse Nationale de Credit Agricole Paris, 1979-81; v.p. Union Commerce Bank Cleve., 1981; v.p., mgr. internat. banking dept. Norwest Bank Des Moines, N.A., 1981-84; v.p., mgr. internat. banking div. Mchts. Nat. Bank, Cedar Rapids, Iowa, 1984—; bd. dirs. Des Moines Fgn. Trade Zone Corp.; past lectr. Des Moines Area Community Coll., lectr. Kirkwood Community Coll.; past mem. faculty dept. bus. careers Manchester (Conn.) Community Coll. Mem. adv. bd. Des Moines Area Community Coll. Internat. Trade Studies, Kirkwood Community Coll., Internat. Trade Program, Ctr. Indsl. Research and Service, Iowa State U., Ames; mem. Iowa Dist. Export Council; past chmn. fraud detection and safeguard com. Council Internat. Banking. Served with U.S. Army Res., 1959-65. Mem. Des Moines World Trade Council, Des Moines Com. Fgn. Relations, Internat. Trade Bur., Cedar Falls-NE Iowa Internat. Trade Council, Davenport (Iowa)-Ill. Internat. Trade Assn., Sioux City-Siouxland Internat. Trade Assn., Robert Morris Assocs., Des Moines Art Ctr., Cedar Rapids Mus. Art, NYU Alumni Assn. Club: Embassy (Des Moines). Home: Cedar River Tower Cedar Rapids IA 52401 Office: 222 Second Ave NE Cedar Rapids IA 52401

HERTEL, DENNIS MARK, congressman, lawyer; b. Detroit, Dec. 7, 1948; s. John and Marie (Kaufmann) H.; m. Cynthia S. Grosscup, Sept. 2, 1971; children: Heather, Heidi, Katie, Mark. H.S. cum laude, Eastern Mich. U., 1971; J.D., Wayne State U., 1974. Bar: Mich. 1975. Tchr. public schs. Detroit, 1972-74; mem. Mich. Ho. of Reps., 1974-80, 97th-100th congresses from 14th Dist. Mich., 1981—. Mem. ABA, State Bar Mich., Wayne State U. Alumni Assn., East Warren Businessmen's Assn., Eastern Mich. U. Alumni, Grosse Pointe Jaycees, Steuben Soc. Am. Democrat. Clubs: St. Matthew's Mens, Lions. Office: US House of Representatives 218 Cannon House Office Bldg Washington DC 20515 *

HERTEL, JAMES ROBERT, insurance agency executive; b. Grand Rapids, Mich., June 7, 1929; s. George William and Kathryn Iris (Beukema) H.; m. Wilma Lucille Bylsma, Nov. 21, 1952; children—Jack Robert, Jane Ellen, Carol Ann. A.B., Calvin Coll., 1951. Salesman, Wurzburg Co., Grand Rapids, Mich., 1954-55; account exec. A. W. Hertel Agy., Holland, Mich., 1955-59; pres. James Hertel Agy., Fremont, Mich., 1959—; dir., sec. Old State Bank of Fremont (Mich.), 1971-86, pres., chief exec. officer, 1986—. Pres., Fremont Indsl. Devel. Corp., 1976—; pres. Fremont Econ. Devel. Corp., 1983. Served with AUS, 1951-54. Mem. Profl. Agts. Assn., Ins. Agts. Assn. Republican. Christian Reformed. Club: Rotary. Home: 3522 Ramshorn Dr Fremont MI 49412 Office: James Hertel Agy Inc 6 E Main St Box A Fremont MI 49412

HERTZ, KARL VICTOR, educational administrator; b. Indpls., Oct. 19, 1936; s. Victor Peter and Mary Martha (Hockensmith) H.; m. Carol Sue Gruber, Dec. 28, 1957; children—Karen Ann, Michael Karl, Sarah Jane. B.A., Marian Coll., 1961; M.S., Butler U., 1964; Ed.D., Ind. U., 1973. Cert. tchr., sch. adminstr., Ind., Ill., Wis. Tchr. English pub. schs., Indpls., 1960-63, chmn. English dept. Brebeuf High Sch., 1963-68, asst. prin., 1968-70, prin. 1970-73; prin., lectr. Lab. Sch., U. Chgo., 1973-75; prin. pub. sch., Munster, Ind., 1975-79; dir. secondary edn. Neenah Joint Sch. Dist., Wis., 1979-81, asst. supt., 1981-85; supt. Mequon-Thiensville Sch. Dist., Wis., 1984—; cons. to sch. dists. Bd. dirs. Jr. Achievement, Big Sisters. Recipient citation City of Indpls., 1973; citation Jesuit Secondary Edn. Assn., 1973; citation Bd. Dirs. Marian Coll.; Inst. Devel. Ednl. Activities fellow. Mem. Am. Assn. Sch. Adminstrs., Assn. Supervision and Curriculum Devel., Nat. Assn. Secondary Sch. Prins. Lodge: Rotary. Contbr. articles to profl. jours. Office: 5000 Mequon Rd Mequon WI 53092

HERTZ, RICHARD CORNELL, rabbi; b. St. Paul, Oct. 7, 1916; s. Abram J. and Nadine (Rosenberg) H.; m. Mary Louise Mann, Nov. 25, 1943 (div. July 1971); children: Nadine (Mrs. Michael Wertheimer), Ruth Mann (Mrs. Alain Joyaux); m. Renda Gottfürcht Ebner, Dec. 3, 1972. A.B., U. Cin., 1938; M.H.L., Hebrew Union Coll., 1942, D.D. (hon.), 1967; Ph.D., Northwestern U., 1948. Ordained rabbi 1942; asst. rabbi N. Shore Congregation Israel, Glencoe, Ill., 1942-47; asso. rabbi Chgo. Sinai Congregation, 1947-53; sr. rabbi Temple Beth El, Detroit, 1953-82, rabbi emeritus, 1982—; adj. prof. Jewish thought U. Detroit, 1970—, disting. prof. Jewish studies, 1980—; spl. cons. to pres. Cranbrook Ednl. Community, 1983-84; del. to internat. conf. World Union for Progressive Judaism, London, 1959, 61, Amsterdam, 1978, bd. dirs. union, 1973—; Lectr. Jewish Chautauqua Soc., 1942—; former mem. plan bd. Synagogue Council Am.; past mem. chaplaincy commn., former bd. dirs. Nat. Jewish Welfare Bd.; former mem. exec. com., vice chmn. Citizen's Com. for Equal Opportunity; mem. Mich. Gov.'s Com. on Ethics and Morals, 1963-69; mem. Mich. adv. council U.S. Commn. on Civil Rights, 1979-85; past mem. nat. bd. dirs. Religious Edn. Assn.; past adv. bd. Joint Distbn. Com.; former mem. nat. rabbinical council United Jewish Appeal; mem. rabbinic cabinet Israel Bonds, 1972—; pres. Hyde Park and Kenwood Council Chs. and Synagogues, Chgo., 1952. Author: Rabbi Yesterday and Today, 1943, This I Believe, 1952, Education of the Jewish Child, 1953, Our Religion Above All, 1953, Inner Peace for You, 1954, Positive Judaism, 1955, Wings of the Morning, 1956, Impressions of Israel, 1956, Prescription for Heartache, 1958, Faith in Jewish Survival, 1961, The American Jew in Search of Himself, 1962, What Counts Most in Life, 1963, What Can A Man Believe, 1967, Reflections for the Modern Jew, 1974, Israel and the Palestinians, 1974, Roots of My Faith, 1980, also articles in sci., popular publs. Dir. Am. Jewish Com., mem. nat. exec. bd., former hon. vice-chmn. Detroit chpt.; past dir. Mich. Soc. Mental Health, Jewish Family and Children's Services, United Community Services, Jewish Welfare Fedn. Detroit; v.p. Jewish Community Council Detroit; dir. United Found., Boys Clubs, Mich. region Anti-Defamation League; chmn. bd. overseers Hebrew Union Coll.-Jewish Inst. Religion, 1968-72; bd. govs. Detroit Inst. Tech., 1955-70; trustee Marygrove Coll., Detroit, 1986—. Served as chaplain AUS, 1943-46. Fellow Am. Sociol. Soc.; mem. Detroit Hist. Soc., Central Conf. Am. Rabbis (former nat. chmn. com. on Jews in Soviet orbit), Am. Jewish Hist. Soc., Am. Legion (dept. chaplain 1956-57), Jewish War Vets. (dept. chaplain 1958-59, 72—), Alumni Assn. Hebrew Union Coll.-Jewish Inst. Religion (past dir.). Clubs: Rotary (Detroit), Economic (Detroit) (dir.); Wranglers (past pres.), Great Lakes, Standard, Franklin Hills, Knollwood, Tam O'Shanter. Went on spl. mission for White House to investigate status Jews and Judaism in USSR 1959, mission for chief chaplains Def. Dept. to conduct retreats for Jewish chaplains and laymen, Berchtesgaden, Germany, 1973; mem. mission to Arab countries and Israel, Nat. Council Chs.-Am. Jewish Com., 1974; 1st Am. rabbi received in pvt. audience at Papal Palace by Pope Paul VI, 1963. Home: 4324 Knightsbridge Ln West Bloomfield MI 48033 Office: Temple Beth El 7400 Telegraph Rd at 14 Mile Birmingham MI 48010

HERTZBERG, EDWINA LEAYCRAFT, social work educator; b. Spring Lake, N.J., Nov. 21, 1930; d. Edwin Illensworth and Helen Winifred (Frey) Leaycraft; m. Robert Hastings Hertzberg, June 21, 1952; children: Catherine, Pamela, Amy, Gregory, Nicole, Mimi. AB, Cedar Crest Coll., 1953; MSW, U. Minn., 1972, postgrad., 1983—. Interviewer, researcher Minn. Ctr. for Social Work Edn., Mpls., 1972; community organizer Greater Mpls. Day Car Assn., 1972-73, exec. dir., 1973-77; asst. prof., chairperson dept. social work Augsburg Coll., Mpls., 1977-83, assoc. prof., 1983—; bd. dirs., past pres., sec. Minn. Conf. on Social Work Edn., Mpls.; mem. exec. com., bd. dirs. Ebenezer Soc., Mpls.; research asst. Ctr. for Urban and Regional, 1985-86; sec. Ebenezer Ctr. for Aging; mem. Ebenezer Found., Hennepin County Strategic Task Force on Socially Dysfunctional, 1986—. Contbr. articles to profl. jours. Vice chairperson 7th ward Dem. Farmer Labor Club, Mpls., 1966-68; chairperson State Dem. Farmer Labor Women's Workshop, Mpls., 1968; active Dem. Farmer Labor Feminist Caucus; social chair ctr. arts council Walker Art Ctr., Mpls., 1964-66. Recipient Faculty Growth award Am. Luth. Ch., Mpls., 1983; HUD fellow 1970-72. Mem. Nat. Assn. Social Workers (cert., bd. dirs. Minn. chpt. 1974-82, Disting. Service award 1985). Episcopal. Avocations: cross country skiing, camping, travel.

HERZ, DAVID A., neurosurgeon; b. Feb. 22, 1944; m. Myrna Blank, June 8, 1969; children: Adam, Scott. BS in Biology, Marietta Coll., 1965; MD, N.Y. Med. Coll., 1969. Diplomate Am. Bd. Neurol. Surgery. Intern in surgery Albert Einstein Coll. Medicine, Bronx, N.Y., 1969-70; resident in neurol. surgery Mcpl. Hosp. Ctr., Bronx, N.Y., 1970-75; instr. in neurol. surgery Eastern Va. Med. Sch., Norfolk, 1975-77; assoc. clin. prof. Mich. State U., East Lansing; neurosurgeon Neurosurgical Assocs. of Western Mich., Grand Rapids; mem. staff Blodgett Meml. Med. Ctr., Grand Rapids, Mich., Butterworth Hosp., Grand Rapids, Mary Free Bed Hosp. and Rehab. Ctr.; chief Neurotrauma and Neurosurgery St. Mary's Hosp. Contbr. numerous articles to profl. jours. Served to lt. commdr. USNR, 1975-77. Mem. AMA, Am. Coll. Surgeons, Congress Neurol. Surgeons (pub. relations com., sergent at arms com.), Am. Assn. Neurol. Surgeons (council state neurosurgical socs.), Cen. Neurosurgical Soc., Kent County Medical Soc. (chmn. med. liability com. 1985), Mich. Med. Soc., Mich. Assn. Neurol. Surgeons (past pres., past v.p., past bd. dirs., med. liability com.), Western Mich. Neurol. Soc. Home: 2860 Bonnell SE Grand Rapids MI 49506 Office: Neurosurgical Assocs of Western Mich 833 Lake Dr SE Suite 208 Grand Rapids MI 49506-1449

HERZ, DONALD RAYMOND, government financial executive, accountant; b. Hastings, Nebr., Apr. 18, 1949; s. Raymond George and Gladys Margaret (Hoelting) H.; m. Joyce Earlene Gaston, Aug. 26, 1972; children: Jeffrey, Jason, Jennifer, Jessica. BBA, U. Nebr., 1978. CPA, Nebr. Budget and fiscal officer Nebr. Crime Commn., Lincoln, 1972-78; acctg. supr. Johnson, Grant & Co., CPA's, Lincoln, 1979-84; mgr. acctg. systems State of Nebr., Lincoln, 1985—; pvt. practice acctg., Lincoln, 1985—. Recipient Regents Scholar award U. Nebr., 1974. Mem. Am. Inst. CPA's, Assn. Govt. Accts. (pres. 1985-86, nat. bd. dirs. 1987—), Nebr. Soc. CPA's (com. vice-chmn. 1986-87), Am. Mensa, Updowntowners. Democrat. Roman Catholic. Lodges: KC, Optimists (local treas. 1980-81). Avocations: reading, bridge, golf. Home: 1817 St Andrews Pl Lincoln NE 68512 Office: Dept of Adminstrv Services State Capitol Bldg Room 1206 Lincoln NE 68509

HERZBERG, DALE WAYNE, data processing executive; b. Troy, Mo., Nov. 30, 1955; s. Richard Nevin and Elizabeth Cathrine (Kammeier) H.; m. Linda Kathryn Wright, July 4, 1975; children: Janet Lynn, John Leo. BS, S.W. Mo. State U., 1977; postgrad., Fontbonne U., 1986—. Programmer analyst State of Mo., Jefferson City, 1977-79; sr. programmer analyst McDonnell Douglas, St. Louis, 1979—. Mem. Wentville Jaycees (pres. 1982-83), Nat. Rifle Assn. Lutheran. Avocations: hunting, trap shooting, fishing, antiques. Home: 20 Kingsway Wentzville MO 63385 Office: McDonnell Douglas 325 S McDonnell Blvd Hazelwood MO 63385

HERZING, THOMAS WAYNE, university administrator, communications consultant; b. St. Cloud, Minn., June 30, 1939; s. Albert Joseph and Lorraine Elizabeth (Lardy) H.; m. Marlene Marie Zwilling, June 10, 1961; children: Mark Vincent, Lisa Marie, Paul Thomas, Rachel Mary. BA, St. Johns U., 1961; MA, Marquette U., 1963; PhD, U. Wis., 1972. Asst. prof. St. Joseph's Coll., Rensselaer, Ind., 1962-67; prof. English U. Wis., Oshkosh, 1967—, asst. to dean, 1976-77, asst. dean, 1977-78, assoc. dean, 1978-80, asst. to chancellor, 1980-86, asst. chancellor, 1986—; pres. Tomar Cons., Oshkosh, 1986—. Author: Reasoning for Writing, 1971, Language in the Public Eye, 1974, Corporate History, 1986. Chmn. Cable TV Franchise Com., Oshkosh, 1986-87; trustee Oshkosh Libraries, Winnefox Consortium. Me. Nat. Council Tchrs. English, Am. Internat. and Midwest Socs. for Study Eighteenth-Century Literature, Nat. Assn. Coll. Univ. Bus. Officers. Roman Catholic. Avocations: writing, salmon fishing, sports cars. Home: 937 Vine St Oshkosh WI 54901 Office: U Wis 800 Algoma Blvd Oshkosh WI 54901

HERZOG, DORREL NORMAN ELVERT (WHITEY HERZOG), baseball manager; b. New Athens, Ill., Nov. 9, 1931. Infielder, outfielder Washington Senators, 1956-58, Kansas City Athletics, 1958-60, Balt. Orioles, 1961-62, Detroit Tigers, 1963; scout Kansas City Athletics, 1964, coach, 1965; coach N.Y. Mets, 1966, dir. player devel., 1967-72; mgr. Tex. Rangers, 1973; coach Calif. Angels, 1974-75, interim mgr., 1974; mgr. Kansas City Royals, 1975-79, St. Louis Cardinals, 1980—. Named Sporting News Man of Year, 1982, Nat. League Mgr. of Year, 1985. Office: care St Louis Cardinals Busch Meml Stadium 250 Stadium Plaza Saint Louis MO 63102

HERZOG, GODOFREDO MAX, physician; b. Chemnitz, Germany, Jan. 12, 1931; s. Heinrich and Louise (Gittler) H.; came to U.S., 1950, naturalized, 1960; B.S., La. State U., 1953; M.D., Washington U., St. Louis, 1957; m. Eva R. Muller, Sept. 2, 1956; children—Jacques A., Patricia M., Elsa M. Intern, Jewish Hosp., St. Louis, 1957-58, Sch. Aerospace Medicine, San Antonio, Tex., 1960; resident in surgery Jewish Hosp., Cin., 1958-59; resident in ob-gyn Jewish Hosp., St. Louis, 1964-67; instr. ob-gyn Washington U., St. Louis, 1967—; practice medicine, specializing in ob-gyn, St. Louis, 1967—; chmn. dept. ob-gyn Christian Hosps. NE/NW, St. Louis; sr. med. cons. Premenstrual Program Ctr., St. Louis; gynecol. cons. med. laser program DePaul Hosp., St. Louis; cons. in field. Med. adviser, bd. dirs. Life Seekers, Planned Parenthood, Abortion Rights Alliance; mem. Hispanic Leadership Conf., St. Louis. Served to capt. M.C., USAF, 1959-64. Diplomate Nat. Bd. Med. Examiners, Am. Bd. Ob-Gyn. Fellow Am. Coll. Ob-Gyn; mem. AMA, St. Louis Met. Med. Soc., Pan Am., Israel, Mo. med. assns., Mo., St. Louis gynecol. socs., Am. Soc. Gynecol. Laparoscopists, Am. Fertility Soc., Gynecologic Laser Soc. Jewish. Contbr. articles to profl. publs. Home: 9 Wendover St Saint Louis MO 63124 Office: 77 Westport Plaza Dr Suite 265 Saint Louis MO 63141

HESBURGH, THEODORE MARTIN, clergyman, former university president; b. Syracuse, N.Y., May 25, 1917; s. Theodore Bernard and Anne Marie (Murphy) H. Student, U. Notre Dame, 1934-37; Ph.B., Gregorian U., 1939; postgrad., Holy Cross Coll., Washington, 1940-43; S.T.D., Cath. U. Am., 1945; S.T.D. hon. degrees, Bradley U., LeMoyne Coll., U. R.I., Cath. U. of Santiago, Chile, Dartmouth, Villanova U., St. Benedict's Coll., Columbia, Princeton, Ind. U., Brandeis U., Gonzaga U., U. Calif. at Los Angeles, Temple U., Northwestern U., U. Ill., Fordham U., Manchester Coll., Atlanta U., Wabash Coll., Valparaiso U., Providence Coll., U. So. Calif., Mich. State U., St. Louis U., Cath. U. Am., Loyola U. at Chgo., Anderson Coll., State U. N.Y. at Albany, Utah State U., Lehigh U., Yale, Lafayette Coll., King's Coll., Stonehill Coll., Alma Coll., Syracuse U., Marymount Coll., Hobart and William Smith Coll., Hebrew Union Coll., Cin., Harvard. Entered Order of Congregation of Holy Cross, 1934; ordained priest Roman Catholic Ch., U. Notre Dame, 1943; chaplain Nat. Tng. Sch. for Boys, Washington, 1943-44; vets. chaplain U. Notre Dame, 1945-47, asst. prof. religion, head dept., 1948-49, exec. v.p., 1949-52, pres., 1952-87; trustee Chase Manhattan Bank. Author: Theology of Catholic Action, 1945, God and the World of Man, 1950, Patterns for Educational Growth, 1958, Thoughts for Our Times, 1962, More Thoughts for Our Times, 1965, Still More Thoughts for Our Times, 1966, Thoughts IV, 1968, Thoughts V, 1969, The Humane Imperative: A Challenge for the Year 2000, 1974, The Hesburgh Papers: Higher Values in Higher Education, 1979. Former dir. Woodrow Wilson Nat. Fellowship Corp.; mem. Civil Rights Commn., 1957-72; mem. of Carnegie Commn. on Future of Higher Edn.; chmn. U.S. Commn. on Civil Rights, 1969-72; mem. Commn. on an All-Volunteer Armed Force, 1970; chmn. with rank of ambassador U.S. delegation UN Conf. Sci. and Tech. for Devel., 1977—; Bd. dirs. Am. Council Edn., Freedoms Found. Valley Forge, Adlai Stevenson Inst. Internat. Affairs; past trustee, chmn. Rockefeller Found.; trustee Carnegie Found. for Advancement Teaching, Woodrow Wilson Nat. Fellowship Found., Inst. Internat. Edn., Nutrition Found., United Negro Coll. Fund, others; chmn. Overseas Devel. Council; chmn. acad. council Ecumenical Inst. for Advanced Theol. Studies, Jerusalem. Recipient U.S. Navy's Disting. Pub. Service award, 1959; Presdl. Medal of Freedom, 1964; Gold medal Nat. Inst. Social Scis., 1969; Cardinal Gibbons medal Cath. U. Am., 1969; Bellarmine medal Bellarmine-Ursuline Coll., 1970; Meiklejohn award A.A.U.P., 1970; Charles Evans Hughes award Nat. Conf. Christians and Jews, 1970; Merit award Nat. Cath. Ednl. Assn., 1971; Pres.' Cabinet award U. Detroit, 1971; Am. Liberties medallion Am. Jewish Com., 1971; Liberty Bell award Ind. State Bar Assn., 1971, Laetare medal Univ. Notre Dame, 1987; others. Fellow Am. Acad. Arts and Scis.; mem. Internat. Fedn. Cath. Univs., Freedoms Found. (dir., mem. exec. com.), Nutrition Found., Commn. on Humanities, Inst. Internat. Edn. (pres., dir.), Cath. Theol. Soc., Chief Execs. Forum, Am. Philos. Soc., Nat. Acad. Edn., Council on Fgn. Relations (trustee). Office: Univ Notre Dame Pres Emeritus Notre Dame IN 46556 *

HESEMAN, CALVIN RICHARD, civil engineer, utilities engineer; b. Centralia, Ill., June 23, 1950; s. Orville Henry and Vera M.A. (Rommelmann) H.; m. Monica Schmitt, Aug. 14, 1971; children: Eric, Dirk, Natalie. BSCE with honors, U. Mo., Rolla, 1972. Registered profl. engr., Ill. Gas engr. Ill. Power Co., Decatur, 1972-74, asst. gas supt., 1974-77, compliance engr., 1977-79, indsl. sales engr., 1979-83, supr. gas planning, 1983-84, dir. gas and structural design, 1984—. Advisor Jr. Achievement, Decatur, 1979-80; v.p. Mount Zion chpt. Ill. Counicl for Gifted Edn., 1986—. Mem. ASME (gas piping tech. com. 1985-86), Am. Gas Assn., Mount Zion Jaycees (mgmt. v.p. 1986—), Jr. Engring. Tech. Soc. (adv. bd. 1985-86). Republican. Presbyterian. Home: 600 Fawn Ct Mount Zion IL 62549 Office: Ill Power Co 500 S 27th St Decatur IL 62525

HESS, BARTLETT LEONARD, clergyman; b. Spokane, Wash., Dec. 27, 1910; s. John Leonard and Jessie (Bartlett) H.; B.A., Park Coll., 1931, M.A. (fellow in history 1931-34), U. Kan., 1932, Ph.D., 1934; B.D., McCormick Theol. Sem., 1936; m. Margaret Young Johnston, July 31, 1937; children—Daniel Bartlett, Deborah Margaret, John Howard and Janet Elizabeth (twins). Ordained to ministry Presbyn. Ch., 1936; pastor Effingham, Kan., 1932-34, Chgo., 1935-42, Cicero, Ill., 1942-56, Ward Meml. Presbyn. Ch., Detroit, 1956-68, Ward, Presbyn. Ch., Livonia, Mich., 1968-80, Presbyn. Ch., 1980—. Tchr. ch. history, bible Detroit Bible Coll., 1956—, bd. dirs., 1956—; minister radio sta. WHFC, Chgo., 1942-50, WMUZ-FM, Detroit, 1958-68, 78—, WOMC-FM, 1971-72, WBFG-FM, 1972—; missioner to Philippines, United Presbyn. Ch. U.S.A., 1961; mem. Joint Com. on Presbyn. Union, 1980; adviser Mich. Synod council United Presbyn. Ch.; mem. com. Billy Graham Crusade for S.E. Mich., 1976; mem. adminstrv. com. Evang. Presbyn. Ch., 1980—. Mem. Organizer Friendship and Service Com. for Refugees, Chgo., 1940. Bd. dirs. Beacon Neighborhood House, Chgo., 1945-52, Presbyns. United for Bibl. Concerns, 1975-80; pres. bd. dirs. Peniel Community Center, Chicago, 1945-52. Named Pastor of Year, Mid-Am. Sunday Sch. Assn., 1974; recipient Service to Youth award Detroit Met. Youth for Christ, 1979. Mem. Cicero Ministers Council (pres. 1951), Phi Beta Kappa, Phi Delta Kappa. Author: (with Margaret Johnston Hess) How To Have a Giving Church, 1974; (with M.J. Hess) The Power of a Loving Church, 1977, How Does Your Marriage Grow, 1982, Never Say Old, 1984; contbr. articles in field to profl. jours. Traveled in Europe, 1939, 52, 55, 68; also in Greece, Turkey, Lebanon, Syria, Egypt, Israel, Iraq; condr. tour of Middle East and Mediterranean countries, 1965, 67, 73, 74, 76, 78, 80, China and Far East, 1982; missioner, India, 1981, Brazil, 85, 86. Home: 16845 Riverside Dr Livonia MI 48154 Office: 17000 Farmington Rd Livonia MI 48154

HESS, JONATHAN LOUIS, psychology educator, clinical neuropsychologist; b. South Milwaukee, Wis., Aug. 8, 1940; s. A. Raymond and Ruth Ellen (Pakiser) H.; m. Loretta Bridget Keighron, Aug. 23, 1970; 1 child, Deidre Marie. BA, Wheaton Coll., 1962; MA, No. Ill. U., 1964; PhD, Purdue U., 1969. Registered psychologist, Ill. Vis. asst. prof. psychology Wesleyan U., Middletown, Conn., 1969-70; asst. prof. biobehavioral sci. U. Conn., Storrs, 1970-73; prof. psychology Sangamon State U., Springfield, Ill., 1973—; clin. neuropsychologist Meml. Med. Ctr., Springfield, 1980—; adj. faculty depts. psychiatry and pharmacology So. Ill. U., Springfield, 1974—; dir. cognitive rehab. program Meml. Med. Ctr., Springfield, 1986—; med. cons., task force mem. Ill. Dept. Rehab. Services, Springfield, 1986—. Mem. N.Y. Acad. Scis., Nat. Head Injury Found., Ill. Head Injury Assn. (bd. advisors), Internat. Neuropsychol. Soc., Cen. Ill. Psychologists Soc., Sigma Xi. Avocations: piano, guitar, opera, theatre, sports. Office: Sangamon State U Psychology Program Shepard Rd Springfield IL 62708 also: Meml Med Ctr 800 N Rutledge Springfield IL 62703

HESS, LEE HOWARD, restaurant chain executive; b. Chgo., Mar. 1, 1947; s. Segel Henry and Jane (Kornblith) H.; m. Irene Levine, Nov. 12, 1978; 1 child, Michael. BA, U. Mich., 1968; MA, Stanford U., 1969; MBA, Harvard U., 1972. V.p., chief fin. officer Twenty First Century Corp., N.Y.C., 1972-80; pres. TGI Splty. Restaurants, N.Y.C., 1981; sr. v.p. Wendy's Internat., Dublin, Ohio, 1981—. Home: 405 W 6th Ave Columbus OH 43201 Office: Wendy's Internat Inc 4288 W Dublin Granville Rd Dublin OH 43017

HESS, MARGARET JOHNSTON, religious writer, educator; b. Ames, Iowa, Feb. 22, 1915; d. Howard Wright and Jane Edith (Stevenson) Johnston; B.A., Coe Coll., 1937; m. Bartlett Leonard Hess, July 31, 1937; children—Daniel, Deborah, John, Janet. Bible tchr. Community Bible Classes Ward Presbyn. Ch., Livonia, Mich., 1959—, Christ Ch. Cranbrook (Episcopalian), Bloomfield Hills, Mich., 1980—. Co-author: (with B.L. Hess) How to Have a Giving Church, 1974, The Power of a Loving Church, 1977, How Does Your Marriage Grow?, 1983, Never Say Old, 1984; author: Love Knows No Barriers, 1979; Esther: Courage in Crisis, 1980; Unconventional Women, 1981, The Triumph of Love, 1987; contbr. articles to religious jours. Home: 16845 Riverside Dr Livonia MI 48154

HESS, ROBERT JOHN, manufacturing company executive; b. Aurora, Ill., Sept. 13, 1937; s. Christopher and Marian (Wagner) H.; m. Judith A. Ernst, Aug. 13, 1960 (div.); children: Robert M., Richard C., Patricia K., Margaret M., Marilyn A.; m. Barbara Jean Gentry, Sept. 10, 1983; children: Brittany, Kristine. BS, Loyola U., 1960; MBA, U. Chgo., 1978. CPA, Ill. Cost acct. Automatic Electric, Northlake, Ill., 1960-62; supr. gen. acctg. Pipeline Service Corp., Franklin Park, Ill., 1962-68; corp. controller Masonite Corp., Chgo., 1968-84; exec. v.p. Superior Toy and Mfg. Co., Inc., Chgo., 1984—. Served to capt. USAR, 1960-68. Home: 1605 Royal Oak Rd Darien IL 60559 Office: Superior Toy and Mfg Co Inc 3417 N Halsted St Chicago IL 60657

HESSE, ELMER FRANK, academic administrator; b. St. Louis, Mar. 4, 1950; s. Elmer Frank and Leta Marie (Sanders) H.; m. Charlotte Coburn, July 8, 1972; children: Shannon Elise, Sarah Frances. BS, Ball State U., 1972, MS, 1976. Systems analyst Blue Cross/Blue Shield, Jacksonville, Fla., 1977-78; programmer Ball State U., Muncie, Ind., 1972-74, programmer, analyst, 1974-77, assoc. dir., 1978-83; dir. computing Wright State U., Dayton, Ohio, 1983—; cons. Muncie Pub. Schs., 1977-82, various orgns., Muncie and Dayton, 1977—. Orgn. rep. CAUSE, EDUCOM, GUIDE, SHARE. Recipient Faith in God award and Leadership cert. Muncie C. of C., 1983. Mem. Assn. Computing Machinery, Dayton Art Inst. Presbyterian. Lodge: Kiwanis. Avocations: jogging, walking, bird watching, coin collecting. Home: 215 Maysfield Rd Dayton OH 45419 Office: Wright State U 3640 Colonel Glenn Dayton OH 45435

HESSEL, JOSEPH CHARLES, accountant; b. St. Louis, Aug. 31, 1956; s. Joseph Michael and Rosemary (Peterman) H.; m. Marie Elizabeth Watkins, June 18, 1983; 1 child, Stephanie. BSBA, Southeast Mo. State U., 1978. CPA, Mo.; cert. bank EDP auditor. Standard cost acct. Wagner div. McGraw Edison Co., St. Louis, 1979-81; internal auditor Lukens Gen. Industries, Inc., St. Louis, 1981-82; asst. controller Ludlow Saylor div. and Gruendler Crusher div. Lukens Gen. Industries, Inc., St. Louis, 1982-84, Cass Bank and Trust Co., St. Louis, 1984—. Mem. Am. Inst. CPA's, Nat. Assn. Accountancy, Acctg. Research Assn., Mo. Soc. CPA's, Sigma Phi Epsilon. Roman Catholic. Avocations: men's softball, fishing. Office: Cass Bank & Trust Co 10th & Olive St Saint Louis MO 63101

HESSLER, WILLIAM GERHARD, data processing executive; b. Chgo., May 20, 1926; s. William Gerhard and Rosemary (Kalb) H.; m. Kazuko Yonetsu, June 2, 1956; children: Martha, George, Kay, Emmy. BSEE, Purdue U., 1946; MBA, Northwestern U., 1956. Cert. data processor. Tech. intelligence investigator U.S. Army, Tokyo, 1947-50; electronics engr. signal corps. U.S. Army, Yokohama, Japan, 1952-54; mfg., devel. engr. Western Electric, Chgo., 1955-61; engring. specialist Goodyear Aerospace Corp., Akron, Ohio, 1961-65; computer applications programmer analyst Goodyear Tire & Rubber Co., Akron, 1965-83, computer operating systems programmer, 1983-87; cons. Cutler-Williams, Middleburg Heights, Ohio, 1987—; tax cons. and return preparer H & R Block, Greater Akron, 1969-80, Akron Nat. Tax & Notary, 1981, Hammer Tax Service, Akron, 1982—; cons. in field, 1982—; agt. enrolled to practice before the U.S. Dept. Treasury IRS, 1984—. Scoutmaster Boy Scouts Am., Silver Lake, Ohio, 1972-77. Served with U.S. Army, 1950-52, Korea. Mem. Ohio Soc. Enrolled Agts. Roman Catholic. Avocation: amateur radio. Home: 3046 Lake Rd Silver Lake OH 44224 Office: Cutler-Williams 7261 Engle Rd Suite 409 Middleburg Heights OH 44130

HESSLUND, BRADLEY HARRY, manufacturing engineer; b. Mpls., June 27, 1958; s. Harry A. and Dorothy (Tishi) H. AA, Normandale Community Coll., 1978; BS, U. Wis., Menomonie, 1981; MBA, U. Pitts., 1984. Indsl.

engr. Thermo King Corp. sub. Westinghouse Electric Corp., Bloomington, Minn., 1981-82; quality engr. Westinghouse Electric Corp., Beaver, Pa., 1983; cost engr. IBM Corp., East Fishkill, N.Y., 1984-85; mfg. engring. supr. Fed.-Hoffman Inc., Anoka, Minn., 1985—. Republican. Lutheran. Office: Hoffman Engring Co 900 Ehlen Dr Anoka MN 55303

HESTAD, BJORN MARK, metal distributing company executive; b. Evanston, Ill., May 31, 1926; s. Hilmar and Anna (Aagaard) H.; student Ill. Inst. Tech., 1947; m. Florence Anne Ragusi, May 1, 1948; children—Marsha Anne Hestad Chastain, Patricia Lynn Krueger, Peter Mark. Sales corr., Shakeproof, Inc., Chgo., 1947-50; indsl. buyer Crescent Industries, Inc., Chgo., 1950-51; purchasing agt. Switchcraft, Inc., Chgo., 1951-73, materials mgr., 1973-74, dir. purchasing, 1974-77; pres. Tool King, Inc., Wheeling, Ill., 1977—; pres. H & H Enterprises of Northfield. Mgr. youth orgns. Northfield Jr. Hockey Club, 1968-71, Winnfield Hockey Club, 1972-73; bus. mgr. West Hockey Club, 1973-74. Served as cpl. USAAF, 1944-46. Mem. Tooling and Mfg. Assn., Sons of Norway. Republican. Mem. United Ch. Christ. Clubs: Waukegan Yacht, Lions. Home: 850 Happ Rd Northfield IL 60093 Office: Tool King Inc 275 Larkin Dr Wheeling IL 60090

HESTER, JAMES FRANCIS, JR., fastener mfg. co. exec.; b. Chgo., May 6, 1928; s. James Francis and Marion A. (Meservey) H.; student Marquette U., 1948; B.S. in Commerce, De Paul U., 1951; m. Doris Bauer, Nov. 17, 1951; children—James III, Timothy, Maureen, Stacie, Deidre. Credit mgr. St. Joseph Hosp., Chgo., 1950-53; with Am. Rivet Co., Inc., Franklin Park, Ill., 1953—, v.p., dir., 1960—, sec., 1981—. Served with U.S. Army, 1946-47. Mem. Franklin Park C. of C. (dir. 1967-70), Ill. Mfg. Assn., Chgo. Assn. Commerce and Industry, Purchasing Mgmt. Assn. Chgo., Nat. Assn. Purchasing Mgmt., Chgo. Midwest Credit Mgmtm. Assn., NAM, N.W. Suburban Mfrs. Assn. (dir. 1967-70, pres. 1976-77). Roman Catholic. Club: River Forest Golf (Elmhurst, Ill.) (dir. 1984-86, sec. 1985, 86). Office: 11330 W Melrose St Franklin Park IL 60131

HESTER, J(AMES) SCOTT, architect; b. High Point, N.C., Oct. 23, 1945; s. Walter Filmore and Rebecca Pitts (Crowder) H.; m. Mary Katherine Viger, Aug. 23, 1969; children: Kathryn Kern, Holly Hughes, Susan Scott, James Scott. Student, Duke U., 1963-64; BArch, U. Mich., 1969; MArch, U. Pa., 1970. Registered architect, N.Y., D.C. Architect SH&G, Inc., Detroit, 1970-78, Ford & Earl Design, Warren, Mich., 1978-80; v.p., dir. EPR, Inc., Washington, 1980-82; Dir. Space Design Internat., Cin., 1983-86. Mem. Eagle Scouts of Am. Assn., 1958. Mem. Am. Inst. Architects, SAR. Republican. Episcopalian. Clubs: Chevy Chase (Md.); Detroit Country. Home: 214 Rugby Ave Terrace Park OH 45174 Office: 309 Vine St Suite 445 Cincinnati OH 45202

HETH, DIANA SUE, social services director; b. Robinson, Ill., Sept. 25, 1948; d. Quentin Wilson and Marguerite (Byrd) Abraham; m. Kenneth Lewis Greider, Aug. 16, 1970 (div. Mar. 1985); children: Kathryn Elizabeth, Susan Nicole, Jonathan Abraham; m. Harold Eugene Heth; 1 child, Joseph Brockwell. BSE, Eastern Ill. U., 1970; postgrad. in Social Work, U. Ill. Exec. instr. Nat. Assn. Downs Syndrome, Chgo., 1976-77, Heartland Hospice, Effingham, Ill., 1983—. Vol. Belleville (Ill.) Hospice, 1981-83. Mem. Ill. State Hospice Orgn. (bd. dirs. 1985-86), Ill. Pub. Health Assn., County Orgn. Service Providers. Republican. Methodist. Clubs: Newcomers (Effingham) (pres. 1984-85), Compassionate Friends (Effingham) (bd. dirs. 1985—). Avocations: bridge, bowling, needlework, gardening, cooking club. Home: Rt 1 Box 63 Shumway IL 62461 Office: Heartland Hospice PO Box 1077 Effingham IL 62401

HETH, MICHAEL LEWIS, safety manager; b. Waterloo, Iowa, May 27, 1951; s. Herbert Lewis and Beverly Joyce (Smith) H.; m. Jolene F. Lyons, Aug. 23, 1971; children: Kasey, Tim. BA in Safety, U. No. Iowa, 1975. Cert. safety mgr., hazard control mgr. Compliance safety and health officer Iowa Dept. Labor, Des Moines, 1976-83; mgr. safety and health Chamberlain Nat., Waterloo, Iowa, 1983-86; mgr. environ. scis. Frye Copysystems, Des Moines, 1986—; pres. Loss Control Mgmt., Ankeny, Iowa, 1981—. Bd. dirs. Iowa Safety Council, Des Moines, 1983—. Served with U.S. Army, 1970-71, Vietnam. Mem. Am. Soc. Safety Engrs., Nat. Fire Protection Assn., Am. Assn. Indsl. Hygienists. Presbyterian. Lodge: Elks. Avocation: computers. Home: 3026 NW 83d Ankeny IA 50021 Office: Frye Copysystems 2209 Bell Ave Des Moines IA 50321

HETRICK, MICHELLE, truck parts company executive; b. Columbus, Ohio, Sept. 25, 1958; d. Saverio and Domenica Margaret (Zappia) Caruso; m. Lynn Paul Hetrick, Apr. 12, 1980; 1 dau., Vanessa Lynn. A.A., Stark Tech. Coll., Canton, Ohio, 1978. Vice-pres. Lynn Truck Parts Corp., Massillon, Ohio, 1979—. Mem. Massillon C. of C., Nat. Assn. Female Execs., Stark Tech. Alumni Assn., Internat. Truck Parts Assn. Republican. Roman Catholic. Clubs: Canton Jr. Woman's, Arboretum Garden, Timken Mercy Service League (Canton). Avocations: skiing; tennis; snowmobiling. Office: Lynn Truck Parts Corp 739 3d St SE Massillon OH 44646

HETTINGA, DONALD ROY, English educator; b. Grand Rapids, Mich., Nov. 7, 1953; s. Roy and Marjorie (Battjes) H.; m. Kimberly Ann Gilmore, Aug. 27, 1977; children: Caitlin, Zane. BA, Calvin Coll., 1976; MA, U. Chgo., 1977, PhD, 1983. Instr. Grand Valley State Coll., Allendale, Mich., 1981-83; asst. prof. Calvin Coll., Grand Rapids, Mich., 1983—. Contbr. articles and revs. to mags., profl. jours. and newspapers. Cons. Grand Rapids Area Council for the Humanities, 1984-85. Writing fellow Mrs. Giles Whiting Found., 1982-83. Mem. Modern Language Assn., Nat. Council Tchrs. English, Conf. on Coll. Composition and Communication, Conf. on Christianity and Lit. Mem. Christian Reformed Ch. Office: Calvin Coll Dept English Grand Rapids MI 49507

HEUBECK, ROBERT LESLIE, insurance company executive; b. Balt., Apr. 2, 1946; s. Leonard Henery and Hazel Madelyn (Howard) H.; m. Deborah Jane Oplinger, Nov. 7, 1970; children: Kurt David, Kate Dyanna. BS in Mktg., U. Balt., 1968. Salesman Noxell Corp., Balt., 1971-74; gen. mgr. Paul Revere Life Ins. Co., Mass., 1974-80; gen. agent Am. United Life, Indpls., 1981—. Served with Pa. NG, 1968-74. Recipient Commendation Medal State of Pa., 1973. MeMem. Akron Life Underwriters Assn. (trustee), Nat. Life Underwriters Assn., NE Ohio Assn. Health Underwriters, Nat. Assn. Health Underwriters. Republican. Mem. Ch. Christ. Club: Revere Soccer (Bath, Ohio)(bd. dirs. 1980-85, charter). Lodge: Masons. Home: 2126 Kemery Rd Akron OH 44313 Office: PO Box 2709 843 W Cleve-Mass Rd Bath OH 44210

HEUER, ARTHUR BARNES, manufacturing company executive; b. St. Louis, July 6, 1931; s. Scott and Maurine (Barnes) H.; m. Norma Ball, Apr. 10, 1954; children: Linda B., Mary Lisa Heuer Stoll, Arthur B. Jr. BS, U. Va., 1954, MA, 1958. Sales rep. Cities Service Oil Co., N.Y.C., 1957-59, St. Louis, 1959-61; asst. sales mgr. Engel Industries, Inc., St. Louis, 1961-64, sales mgr., 1965-76, v.p. sales and mktg., 1976—; cons. parent relations and travel Camping and Edn. Found., Columbus, Ohio, 1959-86. Served with U.S. Army, 1954-56. Mem. U. Va. Alumni Assn. (pres. St. Louis chpt. 1960-61). Presbyterian. Club: Creve Coeur (Mo.) Racquet. Avocations: canoeing, woodworking. Home: 11322 Clayton Rd Frontenac MO 63131 Office: Engel Industries Inc 8122 Reilly Ave Saint Louis MO 63111

HEUER, RONALD EUGENE, tunneling geotechnical consultant, civil engineer, engineering geologist; b. Pontiac, Ill., Apr. 7, 1940; s. George Ernest and Rosemary (Quinn) H.; m. Debra Lynn Virgens, May 8, 1981; children by previous marriage: Janna Leigh, Garrick Todd. BSCE, U. Ill., 1963, MS in Geology, 1965, PhDCE, 1971. Registered engr., Calif., Ill., Va., N.Y. Sr. engr., geologist, A.A. Mathews Inc., Arcadia, Calif., 1969-73, Rockville, Md., 1973-74; sr. engr., geologist, Foster Miller Assocs., Alexandria, Va., 1974-75; geotech. cons., Champaign and McHenry, Ill., 1975—; assoc. prof. civil engring. U. Ill., Urbana, 1975-78; mem. Nat. Com. Tunneling Tech., NSF, 1973-78, Nat. Com. Rock Mechanics, 1975-78. Contbr. papers to profl. publs. and confs. Recipient Bronze Tablet, U. Ill., 1963; NSF fellow, 1963-64. Mem. ASCE, Assn. Engring. Geologists, Am. Arbitration Assn. Clubs: Nat. Rifle Assn., League Am. Wheelmen. Avocations: Bicycle touring, photography, firearms.

HEUKE, THOMAS EUGENE, general dentistry; b. Lincoln, Nebr., May 25, 1952; s. Willard G. and Carolyn (Schmidt) H.; m. Joan Marie Cherek, May 20, 1978; children: Heather Anna, Thomas Eugene Jr. Student, U. Nebr., 1972, DDS, 1976. Lic. dentist, Nebr. Gen. practice dentistry Lincoln, 1976—; lab. and clin. instr. U. Nebr., Lincoln, 1985—. Bd. dirs. Lincoln Westside Orgn., 1983. Recipient Nebr. Master Angler award, 1984. Mem. ADA, Nebr. Dental Assn., Lincoln Dist. Dental Assn. Democrat. Lutheran. Avocations: genealogy, photography, sculpting, fishing. Home: 619 Garfield Lincoln NE 68502 Office: 201 Capitol Beach Blvd Suite 14 Lincoln NE 68528

HEULE, MICHAEL JOHN, architect; b. Winona, Minn., Oct. 5, 1955; s. Richard Irving and Rose Mary (Sahr) H.; m. Elizabeth Ann Vance, May 24, 1986. BArch cum laude, Kans. State U., 1984. Intern architect Bucher, Willis & Ratliff, Salina, Kans., 1983-85; staff architect Bucher, Willis & Ratliff, Kansas City, Mo., 1984, Howard, Needles, Tammen & Bergendoff, Kansas City, 1984-86; project architect Hedeen Architects, Lenexa, Kans., 1986—. Served with U.S. Army, 1976-79, Republic of Germany. Mem. AIA (assoc., membership com. 1985, programs com. 1986), Tau Sigma Delta, Phi Kappa Phi. Roman Catholic. Home: 316 W 46th St 1W Kansas City MO 64112 Office: Hedeen Architects 7914 Quivira Rd Suite D Lenexa KS 66215

HEULER, LEROY AUGUST, construction company executive; b. Milw., Apr. 28, 1931; s. Lester Arthur and Florence Ella (Spalzbury) H.; m. Patricia Ann Grayson, Sept. 13, 1952; children: Cheryl, James, John, Lisa. BSBA, Marquette U., 1953. Treas. Glendale Tiles, Inc., Milw., 1953-58; pres. Heuler Tile Co., Wauwatosa, Wis., 1958—. Pres. Hapatha Luth. Ch., Milw., 1958-60; bd. dirs. Elm Grove (Wis.) Luth. Ch., 1968-74. Mem. Assn. Tile Contractors Milw., Milw. Assn. Commerce, Luth. Layman's League, Delta Sigma Pi. Republican. Clubs: Westmoor Country (bd. dirs., v.p.), Concordia Century. Home: 1700 Legion Dr Elm Grove WI 53122 Office: 730 N 109th St Wauwatosa WI 53226

HEUPEL, DONALD DEAN, manufacturing executive; b. Elgin, N.D., Feb. 14, 1947; s. Arthur and Martha Magdalene (Kirsh) H.; m. Janet Carol Steckler, Oct. 19, 1968; children: David, Julie. BSME, N.D. State U., 1968; MBA, U. S.D., 1972. Prodn. coordinator Universal Mfg. Co., Algona, Iowa, 1972-77, v.p., 1977-85, pres., 1985—; also bd. dirs. Universal Mfg. Co., Algona. Chmn. Algona Mcpl. Airport Commn., 1985—. Served to 1st lt. U.S. Army, 1968-70, Vietnam. Republican. Roman Catholic. Lodge: Kiwanis (pres. Algona chpt. 1981-82). Avocations: sports, aviation. Home: 219 South Ave Algona IA 50511 Office: Universal Mfg Co 405 Diagonal St Algona IA 50511

HEURING, RICKEY LYNN, accountant; b. Cape Girardeau, Mo., June 10, 1951; s. Albert Louis and Carma Nell (Wills) H.; m. Debra Ann Wist, July 29, 1972; children: Karl Lewis, Darren Andrew, Blake Allen. AA in Computer Sci., BS in Acctg., S.E. Mo. State U., 1973. Retail acct. Wetterau Inc., Scott City, Mo., 1974-75, asst. retail acctg. mgr., 1975-77, retail acctg. mgr., 1979-83; owner Heuring Acctg., Scott City, 1983—. Sec. KC, Scott City, 1976. Served with USNG, 1972-78. Mem. Nat. Soc. Pub. Accts. Roman Catholic. Lodge: Optimists (bd. dirs. Scott City club 1985). Home: Rt 1 PO Box 1103 Scott City MO 63780 Office: Heuring Acctg Services PO Box 1007 Scott City MO 63780

HEUSCHELE, SHARON JO, college dean; b. Toledo, Ohio, July 12, 1936; 1 child, Brent Philip. BE, U. Toledo, 1965, MEd, 1969, PhD, 1973. Cert. elem., secondary tchr., Ohio. Asst. prof. Ohio Dominican Coll., Columbus, 1970-73, St. Cloud U., Minn., 1973-74; assoc. prof. Ohio State U., Columbus, 1974-79; dean instl. planning Lourdes Coll., Sylvania, Ohio, 1980—; cons. U. Hawaii, 1979, others. Bd. dirs. Trinity-St. Paul Inner City Program, Toledo, 1968; cons. Ohio Civil Rights Commn., 1972. Recipient citation U. Toledo, 1979, Journalistic Excellence award Columbia Press Assn., 1954; U. Toledo fellow, 1967-69. Mem. Am. Council Edn., Ohio Conf. Coll. and Univ. Planning, Soc. Coll. and Univ. Planning (com. 1984-85), Phi Theta Kappa, Phi Kappa Phi (citation 1973), U. Toledo Alumni Assn., U.S. Coast Guard Aux. Lutheran. Avocations: fossil and mineral collecting, poetry, horseback riding. Office: Lourdes College 6832 Convent Blvd Sylvania OH 43560

HEVIER, RICHARD SCOTT, real estate executive; b. Waukesha, Wis., July 29, 1957; s. Ronald John and Anne Lee (Adams) H.; m. Cheryl Lynn Beebe, May 9, 1981. Student, U. Wis., LaCrosse, 1974-77, 78, U. Wis., Oshkosh, 1977-78. Lic. real estate broker, Wis. Sales rep. Bob Deal Realty Corp., LaCrosse, 1974-79; dir. HUD developments Hoeschler Realty Corp., LaCrosse, 1980-81; dir. financing, NRG Homes, Inc., LaCrosse, 1981-86, also chmn., 1985-86; pres. TecStar Corp., LaCrosse, 1984—. Candidate 32d dist. Wis. Senate, 1976, 34th dist. Wis. Assembly, 1982; delegate 3d dist. Wis. GOP convention, 1976-84; advocate LaCrosse Citizen Advocacy, 1984-87; mem. Apostolate for Family Consecration, 1986—. Mem. Onalaska (Wis.) Jaycees (Brownstone award 1979), Phi Kappa Delta. Roman Catholic.

HEWAK, BENJAMIN, chief justice; b. Winnipeg, Man., Can., Nov. 12, 1935; s. Michael and Stephania (Kokowska) H.; children: Deborah, Donna, Darcia. BA, U. Man., 1956, LLB, 1960. Crown atty. Govt. of Man., Winnipeg, 1960-65; ptnr. Pollock, Nurgitz, Bromley, Myers and Hewak, Winnipeg, 1965-71; judge County Ct. Winnipeg, 1971-77; judge Ct. of Queen's Bench of Man., Winnipeg, 1977-85, chief justice, 1985—. Mem. Can. Bar Assn., Can. Judges Conf., Can. Jud. Council, Can. Inst. Adminstrn. Justice. Ukrainian Catholic. Home: 2006 7 Evergreen Pl, Winnipeg, MB Canada R3C 0P9 Office: Ct of Queen's Bench, Law Cts Bldg, 408 York Ave, Winnipeg, MB Canada R3C 0P9

HEWES, ROBERT CHARLES, radiologist; b. Balt., Feb. 14, 1953; s. Gordon Cecil and Gladys Dorothy (Barringham) H.; m. Judith Renee Lacy, Mar. 23, 1975; children: Christy, Amy, Jeremy. Student, Columbia Union Coll., 1973; BS, Loma Linda U., 1976, MD. Diplomate Am. Bd. Med. Examiners. Resident in radiology Loma Linda (Calif.) U., 1978-81, asst. prof. radiology, 1983-84; fellow in orthopedic radiology Hosp. for Spl. Surgery Cornell U. Med. Ctr., N.Y.C., 1981-82; fellow in interventional radiology Johns Hopkins U. Hosp., Balt., 1982-83; asst. prof. Wright State U.; mem. staff Kettering (Ohio) Med. Ctr., vice chmn. dept. radiology, 1985—. Contbr. articles on radiology to profl. jours. Recipient cert. merit Am. Roentgen Ray Soc., 1983. Mem. AMA, Radiol. Soc. North Am., Soc. Cardiovascular and Interventional Radiology. Republican. Adventist. Avocations: radio-controlled airplanes, ham radio, woodworking, sports. Office: Kettering Med Ctr Dept Radiology 3535 Southern Blvd Kettering OH 45429

HEWETT, KATHLEEN ANN, information management executive, educator; b. St. Paul, Aug. 20, 1954; d. Robert Albert and Bernice Ann (Peschel) McGown; m. Charles Wadsworth Hewett, Nov. 26, 1983. BA, Coll. St. Catherine, 1981; M in Scientia Bibliothecaria, U. Wales, Aberystwyth, 1983. Asst. reference librarian Hamline U., St. Paul, 1979-80; tech. services asst. Legisl. Reference Library, St. Paul, 1981; mgr. library Rider, Bennett, Egan & Arundel Law Firm, Mpls., 1982; mgr. records and info. systems Dorsey and Whitney Law Firm, Mpls., 1982—; mem. adj. faculty Coll. St. Catherine, St. Paul, 1986—. Mem. Am. Mgmt. Assn., Assn. Record Mgrs. and Adminstrs. (editor Twin Cities chpt. annual report 1985), Soc. Indexers, Minn. Assn. Law Librarians, Minn. Online Users Group. Avocations: birding, hiking, fishing, ice skating. Home: 780 W Wentworth Ave Mendota Heights MN 55118 Office: Dorsey & Whitney Law Firm 2200 First Bank Place Minneapolis MN 55402

HEWITT, JAMES WATT, lawyer; b. Hastings, Nebr., Dec. 25, 1932; s. Roscoe Stanley and Willa Manners (Watt) H.; student Hastings Coll., 1950-52; B.S., U. Nebr., 1954, J.D., 1956; m. Marjorie Ruth Barrett, Aug. 8, 1954; children—Mary Janet, William Edward, John Charles, Martha Ann. Bar: Nebr. 1956. Practice, Hastings, 1956-57, Lincoln, Nebr., 1960—; v.p., gen. counsel Nebco, Inc., Lincoln, 1961—; vis. lectr. U. Nebr. Coll. Law, 1970-71; adj. fellow univ. studies U. Nebr., 1978—; dir. Vistar Bank (formerly Gateway Bank), Lincoln. Mem. state exec. com. Rep. Party, 1967-70, mem. state central com., 1967-70, legis. chmn., 1968-70. Bd. dirs. Lincoln Child Guidance Center, 1969-72, pres., 1972; bd. dirs. Lincoln Community Playhouse, 1967-73, pres., 1972-73; trustee Bryan Meml. Hosp., Lincoln, 1968-74, 76-82, chmn., 1972-74; trustee U. Nebr. Found., 1979—. Served to capt. USAF, 1957-60. Mem. Am. (Nebr. state del. 1972-80, bd. govs. 1981-83), Nebr. State (chmn. ins. com. 1972-76, chmn. pub. relations com. 1982-84, pres. 1985-86), Fed., Lincoln bar assns., Newcomen Soc., Am., Nebr., Lincoln rose socs., Round Table, Beta Theta Pi, Phi Delta Phi. Congregationalist. Clubs: University, Country of Lincoln (Lincoln). Home: 2990 Sheridan Blvd Lincoln NE 68502 Office: 1815 Y St PO Box 80268 Lincoln NE 68501

HEWITT, RANDALL HOWARD, accountant; b. Butler, Pa., June 30, 1954; s. Loren Howard and Betty Ruth (Shaeffer) H.; m. Susan Ray Yocum, Nov. 17, 1979; children: Emily Ann, Ross Howard. BS in Acctg., Ind. U.-Purdue U., Indpls., 1976. CPA, Ind. Sr. acct. George S. Olive & Co., CPA's, Indpls., 1978-83; sr. auditor Nat. Bank Greenwood, Ind., 1983-86; audit adminstr. Mchts. Nat. Corp., Indpls., 1986—. Mem. Am. Inst. CPA's, Ind. CPA Soc., Inst. Internal Auditors, Johnson County (Ind.) Investors Unlimited (ptnr., treas. 1983—). Avocations: investing, golf, water sports, softball, basketball. Office: Mchts Nat Corp One Merchants Plaza Indianapolis IN 46255

HEWITT, THOMAS EDWARD, financial executive; b. West Lafayette, Ind., Sept. 7, 1939; s. Ernest Edward and Katherine (Thelen) H.; B.A., Dartmouth Coll., 1961, M.B.A., 1962; m. Jeraldine Lee Spurgeon, June 16, 1962; children—Debora Lynn, Laura Jean, Gregory Spurgeon. Staff acct. Ernst & Whinney, Chgo., 1966-67, acct. in charge, 1967, sr. acct., 1967-69; controller Thorne United Inc., Addison, Ill., 1969-70, sec.-treas., 1970; supr. Ernst & Whinney, Chgo., 1971-76; controller Waterloo (Iowa) Industries, Inc., 1976-79, v.p. fin., 1979—, also bd. dirs. 1986—. Treas., Salvation Army, Waterloo, 1977-78, 80-82, Cedar Valley United Way, 1983-87, Covenant Med. Ctr., 1986-87, St. Francis Hosp., 1986-87; assoc. campaign chmn. United Way of Black Hawk County, 1981, 82; spl. project chmn. Chgo. Jaycees, 1969; trustee Westminster United Presbyterian Ch., 1984-86, vice-chmn., 1985. Served to capt. USMC, 1962-66. Named to Pres.'s Honor Club, Beatrice Foods Co., 1980; NROTC regular scholar, 1957-62; C.P.A., Ill. Mem. Am. Inst. C.P.A.s, Nat. Assn. Accts., Am. Mgmt. Assn. Club: Sunnyside Country (treas. 1984, pres. 1985; trustee, 1986—). Lodge: Elks. Home: 1105 Prospect Blvd Waterloo IA 50701 Office: Waterloo Industries Inc 999 Home Plaza Waterloo IA 50701

HEWITT, WILLIAM RALPH, industrial engineer; b. Dayton, Ohio; s. William Robert Hewitt and Irene Leah (Seibel) Johannsen, July 6, 1968; children: William Arthur, Cynthia Lee, Anita Jane. BS Indsl. Supervision, Wilmington Coll., 1968. Indsl. engr. Frigidare div. Gen. Motors Corp., Dayton, 1968-78; sr. indsl. engr. Micro Devices div. Emerson Electric, Dayton, 1978-80; div. indsl. engr. Mead Products div. Mead Corp., Dayton, 1980-81; corp. indsl. engr. Copeland Corp., Sidney, Ohio, 1981-82; chief indsl. engr. James David Inc., Hamilton, Ohio, 1982-84; methods engr. Supermet div. Stanadyne Inc., Trotwood, Ohio, 1984-87; sr. indsl. engr. Standard Register Co., Dayton, 1987—. Mem. planning commn. City of Moraine, Ohio, 1973; fire fighter Moraine Fire Dept. Mem. Internat. Assn. Quality Circles (bd. dirs. 1986—), Inst. Indsl. Engrs. (sr.). Republican. Mem. Christian Ch. Avocations: photography, softball, hunting, fishing, Red Cross first aid and CPR instr. Home: 3164 Dorf Dr Moraine OH 45418

HEYING, JOSEPHINE MARIE, diversified companies executive; b. West Union, Iowa, May 22, 1916; d. John Herman and Katherine (Schmitt) Langreck; m. H.L. Heying, 1937; children: Terrance Jon, Sondra Kay, Charles Hilary, Therese Jo. With Heying Chick and Supply, West Union, Iowa, 1945-70; sec. to state sen. Des Moines, 1964-68, 72-76; owner Heying Enterprises, West Union, 1970—; pres. Heying Firms, Inc., West Union, 1980—. Pres. Fayette Co. (Iowa) Tourism, chmn. Regional Tourism; past pres. Holy Name Rosary Soc.; tchr. Holy Name, 1980-87; appointee Gov.'s Task Force on Efficiency in Govt., 1983; hon. bd. mem. State Iowans for Tax Relief. Avocations: bridge, bowling, golfing, writing. Home: 115 Jefferson St West Union IA 52175 Office: 700 W Bradford St West Union IA 52175

HEYMAN, FLAVEL JOSEF, optometrist; b. Upper Sandusky, Ohio, Jan. 11, 1957; s. Flavel Joseph and Clara Marie (Thiel) H.; m. Diane Beth Loseke, Dec. 12, 1981; 1 child, Flavel Jay. BS, Ohio State U., 1979, OD, 1983. Practice medicine specializing in optometry Paxton, Ill., 1983—. Mem. Am. Optometric Assn., Ill. Optometric Assn. Club: Service. Lodge: Rotary (pres. Paxton club 1985-86). Home: 11 Allison Dr Paxton IL 60957 Office: 145 W Center St Paxton IL 60957

HEYSE, WARREN JOHN, publishing company executive; b. Milw., Oct. 13, 1923; s. Raymond Henry and Harriet Margaret (Regner) H.; m. Roxybelle Brown, July 9, 1949; children: Roxanne, Jennifer, Nanette. B.S., U. Wis., 1948; postgrad., Marquette U. Law Sch., 1949; M.S., UCLA, 1950; postgrad., U. Minn., 1952. Classified advt. salesman Milw. Jour., 1952-55, retail advt. supr., 1955-59, classified advt. mgr., 1959-66, asst. advt. dir., 1966-68, v.p., dir. mktg., devel., 1968-73; sr. v.p. Jour. Communications Inc., 1973-77, exec. v.p., 1977-83, pres., 1983—; pres. Jour./Sentinel Inc. (pub. Milw. Jour.), 1977-84, vice chmn. bd., 1984—; bd. dirs. MJE, Perry Printing, Midwestern Relay Inc. (all Jour. Co. subs.), 1973—; vice chmn. WTMJ, Inc.; trustee Jour. Stock Trust, 1976—. Gen. chmn. United Way, 1969, bd. dirs., 1970-76; bd. dirs. Vis. Nurses Assn., 1971-76, ARC, 1972-74; bd. dirs. Milwaukee County council Boy Scouts Am., 1975—, pres., 1984-85; bd. dirs. St. Joseph Hosp., 1970-78, Greater Milw. Com., 1977—, U. Wis. Found., 1980—; bd. dirs. United Performing Arts Fund, 1978-86, co-chmn., 1979. Served with inf. U.S. Army, 1943-46, ETO. Recipient McGovern award for classified advt., 1979, Wis. Newspaper Pub. of Yr. award, 1983, 84. Mem. Sigma Alpha Epsilon, Sigma Delta Chi, Kappa Tau Alpha. Methodist. Clubs: University, Bascom Hill Soc. (U. Wis., Madison), Circumnavigator. Lodge: Rotary. Office: Journal Communications Inc 333 W State St Milwaukee WI 53201

HEYWOOD, ROBERT MONROE, allergist; b. Washington, Aug. 11, 1927; s. Arthur Adelbert and Irene Clara (Nielsen) H.; m. Meda Louise Brown, Aug. 14, 1953; children: Christopher, Craig, Brian, Anne. BS, U. Wis., 1950; MD, George Washington U., 1954. Intern USN Hosp., Bethesda, Md., 1954-55; resident in internal medicine U. Mich., Ann Arbor, 1956-59, resident in allergy, 1959-60; practice medicine specializing in allergy and immunology Marshfield (Wis.) Clinic, 1960—; med. dir. asbestos control program Weyerhaeusen Co., Tacoma, Washington, 1974-78, 85—; assoc. clinical prof. internal medicine U. Wis. Med. Sch., Madison, 1961—. Police and fire commr., Marshfield, 1983—. Served to lt. USNR, 1954-56. Fellow Am. Acad. Allergy and Immunology. Presbyterian. Avocation: collecting guns. Home: 1204 W Fifth Marshfield WI 54449 Office: Marshfield Clinic 1000 N Oak St Marshfield WI 54449

HEZLEP, WILLIAM EARL, theater educator, playwright; b. Turtle Creek, Pa., Sept. 14, 1936; s. Harry Morsan and Anne May (Simpson) H.; m. Norma Simpson, Apr. 1965 (dec. Nov. 1976); m. Diane DeSutter, Aug. 1977 (dec. May 1982); m. Ruth Eloise Jacobson, June 3, 1983; children: Dirk Morgan, Erin Casey. BA, Westminster Coll., 1961; MA, Wayne State U., 1965, PhD, 1973. Asst. prof. theatre Southwest Minn. State U., Marshall, 1968-72, assoc. prof. theatre, dept. chmn., 1973-76, prof. theatre, 1976—; free lance actor, Pitts., 1961-63, Detroit, 1966-68. Author: (plays) Pipestone Cafe, 1977, It's A Living, 1978, Time Pockets, 1979, Nessie, 1980, Ghost Town, 1981, Pharaoh's Dagger, 1982, Cayman Duppy, 1984, Obit For A Polar Bear, 1985; dir. Southwest Summer Theater, Marshall, 1968-77. Served to petty officer 2d class, USN, 1954-57. Wayne State U. fellow, 1963-68. Mem. Screen Actors Guild, Dramatists Guild, Minn. Edn. Assn. of NEA. Lodge: Order of DeMolay. Avocations: fishing, sailing, archaeology. Home: 100 W Lyon Marshall MN 56258 Office: Southwest Minn State U Dept Speech Communication & Theater Marshall MN 56258

HIARING, VAUGHN LYNN, restaurant owner, bookstore owner; b. Madison, S.D., July 22, 1949; s. Merlin Elbridge and Allia Juanita (Alfson) H.; m. Virginia Sue Sifert, Oct. 13, 1973; children: Ian Eric, Courtney Anne. Grad., Madison High Sch., 1967. Mgr., co-owner Truck Haven Cafe, Clarinda, Iowa, 1976-81; owner Vaughn's Books, Clarinda, 1981—; owner, mgr. Clarinda Cafe, 1984—. Pres. PTL, Immanuel Luth. Sch., 1986-87. Served with U.S. Army, 1970-72. Mem. C. of C., Glenn Miller Birthplace

Soc. Lutheran. Avocations: running, baseball card collector, reading. Home: 900 S 20th St Clarinda IA 51632 Office: Clarinda Cafe 1106 S 16th St Clarinda IA 51632

HIATT, HAROLD, psychiatry educator; b. Wilmington, Ohio, Oct. 15, 1921; s. Burritt Mills and Pearl (Peele) H.; m. Jennie Fennell, Feb. 14, 1961 (dec. June 1976); 1 child, Harold D.; m. Marjorie McCullough, Apr. 14, 1984; children: Christine, Cynthia. BS, Wilmington Coll., 1943; MD, U. Cin., 1946. Diplomate Am. Bd. Psychiatry. Chief resident dept. psychiatry U. Cin., 1951-52; instr. psychiatry U. Cin. Med. Ctr., 1952-64, assoc. prof., 1964-74, prof., 1974—; chief psychiat. service Cin. VA Hosp., 1954-79. Contbr. articles to profl. jours., chpts. to books. Bd. dirs. Jr. League of Cin., 1962-75. Served to capt. Med. Corps, 1947-49. Fellow Am. Coll. Psychiatrists (mem. coms.), Am. Psychiat. Assn. (life., Ohio rep. 1969-80); mem. Ohio Psychiat. Assn. (pres. 1968-69, 25 Yr. Leadership cert. 1976, Disting. Service award, 1980), Cin. Coll. Med. Alumnal Assn. (pres. 1981). Mem. Soc. Friends. Club: Faculty. Avocations: golfing, life drawing, tree farming, writing. Home: 7448 Indian Creek Rd Cincinnati OH 45230 Office: U Cin Med Ctr 231 Bethesda Ave Mail LOC 559 Cincinnati OH 45267

HIATT, JOHN ERIC, accountant; b. Marion, Ind., Sept. 29, 1957; s. Fred M. and Jane Ann (Matchette) H.; m. Mary Lee Gartland, Oct. 25, 1980; children: Matthew E., Melissa E. BS, Ind. U., 1980. CPA, Ind., Nebr. Supr. payroll, accounts receivable, EDP UARCO, Inc., Watseka, Ill., 1980-82; mgr.-in-charge Hall & Thomas, CPA's, Elwood, Ind., 1982-84; audit mgr. Touche Ross & Co., Lincoln, Nebr., 1984—; asst. prof. Taylor U., Upland, Ind., 1983. Treas. Assn. for Retarded Citizens, Lincoln, 1985—. Mem. Am. Inst. CPA's, Nebr. Soc. CPA's. Republican. Avocations: golf, tennis, scuba diving. Home: 5421 S Dove Ln Lincoln NE 68516 Office: Touche Ross & Co 1040 NBC Ctr Lincoln NE 68508

HIBBARD, DWIGHT H., telecommunications company executive; b. 1923, Hadley, Mass.; married. BA, Amherst Coll., 1947; BSEE, MIT, 1949. With So. Bell Telephone Co., 1949-61; with AT&T Co., 1962-64; with Cin. Bell, Inc., 1964—, chief engr., then gen. plant mgr., 1966-68, v.p. personnel relations info., 1968-72, v.p. revenue requirements, 1972-74, v.p. ops, 1974-78, exec. v.p. purchasing, 1978-83, pres., 1983—, chief exec. officer, 1984—, chmn., 1985—, also bd. dirs.; also chmn., chief exec. officer, former pres., bd. dirs. Cin. Bell Telephone Co. (subs. Cin. Bell, Inc.); bd. dirs. Ohio Nat. Life Ins. Co., Cen. Bankcorp., Inc., Teradyne Inc. Served to lt. (j.g.) USN, 1943-45. Office: Cin Bell Inc 201 E 4th St Cincinnati OH 45202 *

HIBBE, DOUGLAS WARREN, association executive; b. Jersey City, Apr. 11, 1921; s. Elmer Herman and Bertha Catherine (Rogers) H.; m. Eleanor Alicia Bory, Feb. 20, 1943; children—Sharyn, Craig, Jill. B.S., NYU, 1948, J.D., 1951; postgrad. Army Lang. Sch., Monterey, Calif., 1962. Clk., Dun & Bradstreet, Inc., N.Y.C., 1945-46; ins. clk. Royal Liverpool Group, N.Y.C., 1946-48; ins. underwriter Phoenix London Group, N.Y.C., 1949-51; spl. agt. FBI, Washington, and various locations, 1951-77; legis. counsel Nat. Fraternal Congress Am., Chgo., 1979—. Served with USMC, 1941-45; ETO, PTO. Recipient Meritorious awards FBI, 1955, 61, 62. Mem. Assn. Fraternal Benefit Counsel, Soc. Former Spl. Agts. FBI, Phi Delta Phi. Republican. Home: 130 S Ellsworth St Naperville IL 60540 Office: Nat Fraternal Congress Am Hdqrs Office 1300 Iroquois Dr Suite 260 Naperville IL 60540

HICKEY, JOHN THOMAS, electronics company executive; b. Chgo., Oct. 28, 1925; s. Matthew J., Jr. and Naomi (Pope) H.; m. Joanne R. Keating, Sept. 17, 1949; children: Kathleen Hickey Coakley, John, Michael, James, Roger. B.S. in Commerce, Loyola U., Chgo., 1948; M.B.A., U. Chgo., 1952. With Motorola Inc. (and subs.), 1948—, gen. mgr. semicondr. div., 1955-58, asst. to pres., 1958-62, dir. long range planning, 1962-65, v.p. planning, 1965-70, v.p. finance, sec., 1970-74, sr. v.p., chief fin. officer, dir., 1974-84, exec. v.p., chief fin. officer, dir., 1984-86, chmn. fin. com., dir., 1986—; dir. Benefit Trust Life Ins. Co. Served with AUS, 1944-46. Club: Skokie Country (Glencoe). Home: 614 South Ave Glencoe IL 60022 also: PO Box 1065 Sea Island GA 31561 Office: Motorola Inc 1303 E Algonquin Rd Schaumburg IL 60196

HICKEY, M. JOE, college dean, retired naval officer; b. Armington, Ill., Sept. 15, 1933; s. Karle Merton and Edna Elizabeth (Kistler) H.; m. Norma Deane Neth, Oct. 31, 1959 (div. 1964). B.S., George Washington U., 1975; M.S., Western Ill. U., 1978. Enlisted U.S. Navy, 1956, commd. ensign, 1966, advanced through grades to lt. comdr., 1974, ret., 1977; div. chmn. allied health Nat. Coll., Rapid City, S.D., 1979-80; sr. program dir. Robert Morris Coll., Carthage, Ill., 1980-83, dean of students, 1983—. Mem. Carthage C. of C., Am. Assn. Med. Assts. (on-site visitor 1980—), Ret. Officers Assn. Republican. Avocations: Civil war history; antiques; general and herb gardening; pioneer skills. Home: 410 N Madison Carthage IL 62321 Office: Robert Morris Coll College Ave Carthage IL 62321

HICKMAN, DAVID MICHAEL, paper tableware manufacturing company executive; b. Salem, Oreg., Dec. 11, 1942; s. Vernon Combs and Margaret Irene (Copley) H.; student public schs.; m. Karen Joyce Cox, Aug. 24, 1968; children—Sean Michael, Shannon Lee. Terr. mgr. Brown & Williamson Tobacco Co., 1964-66, Gibson Greeting Cards, Inc., 1966-69; chain drug specialist Coty, Inc., 1970-73; pres., owner Expressions, Seattle, 1973-75; v.p. sales Paper Art Co., Inc., Indpls., 1975-78, exec. v.p., 1978—; pres., owner Paper Artery Co., Inc., 1979—, Shaniko Mktg. Co., 1978—, Paper Art Co., Inc., 1983—; pres. Dave Hickman & Assocs., 1986—. Served with U.S. Army, 1960-63. Republican. Presbyterian. Home: PO Box 389 DePoe Bay Dr Indianapolis IN 46250 Office: 3500 N Arlington Ave Indianapolis IN 46218

HICKMAN, LESTER ANSLEY, educator, administrator; b. St. Clair Twp., Ohio, Apr. 5, 1927; s. James Harvey and Nannie Ola (Robinson) H.; m. Elaine Taylor, Aug. 19, 1950; children—Philip Jeffrey, David Kim, Timothy Craig, Elizabeth Ann. B.S. in Edn., Geneva Coll., 1954; M.S., U. Pitts., 1956; postgrad. U. Toledo, 1972, Ed.D., 1978. Tchr., Highlandtown (Ohio), 1951-54; prin. Beaver (Ohio) Local Schs., 1954-56; supt. Hopedale (Ohio) Local Schs., 1956-60; dir. Colegio Americano para Varones, Barranquilla, Colombia, 1960-65; prin. East Liverpool (Ohio) Sch., 1965-67, tchr., 1976—; prin. Greenford (Ohio) High Sch., 1967-69; supr. Millcreek-West Unity Sch. Dist., Ohio, 1969-73; chmn. edn. dept. Roberts Wesleyan Coll., 1973-76. Pastor Mt. Zion United Meth. Ch., 1985—. Served with U.S. Army, 1945-47. Mem. NEA (life), Phi Delta Kappa. Presbyterian (elder). Author: A Study of the Effect of the Exemplary Center for Reading Instruction Program on Reading Scores, 1978. Home: 47458 Bell School Rd East Liverpool OH 43920 Office: W 8th St East Liverpool OH 43920

HICKOK, DAVID KEITH, pediatrician, educator; b. Kalamazoo, Mich., Aug. 4, 1936; s. Keith and Laura L (Lane) H.; m. Rhea Marie Crandall, Nov. 30, 1957 (div. June 1982); children—Michael David, Mark Allen, Steven Edward, Robert Blair; m. Marlene Diane Myers, Dec. 18, 1982; children: Kathryn Lynne, Andrew Myers. B.S., Mich. State U., 1958; M.D., U. Mich., 1962. Diplomate Am. Bd. Pediatrics. Intern Bronson Methodist Hosp., Kalamazoo, 1962-63, resident in pediatrics, 1963-64; resident Univ. Hosp., Ann Arbor, Mich., 1964-66; practice medicine specializing in pediatrics, Kalamazoo, 1968-82; clin. instr. Pediatrics and Communicable Diseases, U. Mich Med. Sch., Ann Arbor, 1980—; asst. dir. Southwestern Mich. Area Health Edn. Ctr., Kalamazoo, 1982—; asst. prof. pediatrics and human devel. Coll. of Human Medicine, Mich. State U., 1982—. Dist. chmn. Southwest Mich. council Boy Scouts Am., 1968—; bd. dirs. Family Health Ctr., Kalamazoo, 1970-74, Child Abuse Evaluation and Treatment Ctr., 1985—; active Boy Scouts Am. Served to capt. U.S. Army, 1966-68. Recipient Dist. Award of Merit, Boy Scouts Am., 1980, Silver Beaver award, 1982. Fellow Am. Acad. Pediatrics; mem. Western Mich. Pediatric Soc., Mich. State Med. Soc., Kalamazoo Acad. Medicine. Mem. Ch. Reformed. Lodge: Rotary. Avocation: scouting. Office: Southwestern Mich Area Health Edn Ctr 64 E Bronson Med Ctr 252 E Lovell St Kalamazoo MI 49007

HICKROD, GEORGE ALAN, educational administration educator; b. Fort Branch, Ind., May 16, 1930; s. Hershell Roy and Bernice Ethel (Karnes) H.; m. Ramona Dell Poole, 1952 (div.); m. Lucy Jen Huang, June 17, 1964; 1 stepson, Goren Wallis Liu. A.B., Wabash Coll., 1954; M.A., Harvard U., 1955; Ph.D., Harvard U., 1966. Asst. prof. ednl. and social scis. Muskingum Coll., 1962-67; assoc. prof. ednl. adminstrn. Ill. State U., Normal, 1967-71, prof., 1971-83, disting. prof., 1983—, dir. Ctr. for Study Ednl. Fin., 1974—. Contbr. articles on ednl. fin. to profl. jours., chpts. to books. Served with USMC, 1950-52, Korea. State of Ill. and U.S. Govt. grantee. Mem. Am. Edn. Fin. Assn. (v.p. 1983-84, pres. 1984-85). Democrat. Unitarian. Clubs: Scottish-Am. Soc. Central Ill. (past chief), Clan Wallace Internat. Lodges: Masons, Elks. Avocations: history; genealogy; travel; cooking. Home: 2 Turner Rd Normal IL 61761

HICKS, CLAYTON N., optometrist; b. Columbus, Ohio, May 2, 1943; s. Amos Nathaniel and Augusta (Asby) H. BS in Microbiology, Ohio State U., 1964, OD, 1970. Microbiologist Ohio Dept. Health, 1964-70; clin. instr. Ohio State U. Coll. Optometry, Columbus, 1970—; practice medicine specializing in optometry Columbus, 1970—; vision cons. Ohio Dept. HHS, 1976—; conv. planner, Columbus, 1982—. Mem. Martin Luther King Jr. Holiday Commn., 1986—, Driving Park Mental Health Comm., 1985—, Nat. Black Leadership Roundtable, 1984—; mem. nat. adv. council United Negro Coll. Fund. Recipient Polit. Leadership award 29th Dist. Citizen's Caucus, 1986. Mem. Nat. Optometric Assn. (pres. 1983-85, Optometrist of Yr. 1982), Neighbor House House Inc. (pres. 1978-81), Alpha Phi Alpha (pres. Columbus chpt. 1981-83, Outstanding Service award 1981). Lodge: Lions (pres. Columbus inner city club 1977-80). Home: 4961 Wintersong Ln Westerville OH 43081 Office: Driving Park Vision Ctr 1489 Livingston Ave Columbus OH 43205

HICKS, DWIGHT LEE, accountant; b. Clarinda, Iowa, Oct. 1, 1948; s. Talton G. and Dorothy (Cerven) H.; m. Patricia Kay Combs, Aug. 31, 1969; children: Jill, Megan, Lucas. BBA, U. Iowa, 1971; postgrad., Simpson Coll., 1981-84. CPA, Iowa. Office mgr. FS Services, Allison, Iowa, 1971-74; supr. A.C. Nielsen Co., Mason City, Iowa, 1974-78; bus. mgr. Wakonda Club, Des Moines, 1978—; controller South Iowa Meth. Homes, Inc., Des Moines, 1987—. Mem. Am. Inst. CPA's. Democrat. Methodist. Avocations: sports, camping. Home: 711 W Clinton Indianola IA 50125 Office: South Iowa Meth Homes Inc 3520 Grand Ave Des Moines IA 50312

HICKS, GERALD W., II, accounting firm executive; b. Mankato, Minn., July 12, 1954; s. Gerald W. Sr. and Evelyn M. (Anderson) H.; m. Mary J. Hicks, July 3, 1976; children: Jesse, Sara, Stephanie, Lauren. BS cum laude, Mankato State U., 1976. Supr. acctg. Touche Ross and Co., St. Paul, 1976-80; mgr. acctg. Gazzola, Wolf, Etter and Co., North Mankato, Minn., 1980-83, ptnr., 1984—; speaker tax related topics, 1986. Mem. fin. com. Holy Rosary Ch., North Mankato, 1983—, mem. ch. stewardship com., 1987—; advisor to bd. dirs. Children's Adv. Programs of Mankato, 1985—; budget panel coordinator United Way, Mankato, 1985—, bd. dirs., 1986—. Mem. Am. Inst. CPA's, Minn. Soc. CPA's. Roman Catholic. Lodge: Sertoma. Avocations: coaching childrens baseball, golf. Office: Gazzola Wolf Etter and Co 1120 South Ave North Mankato MN 56001

HICKS, HELEN ANNE, financial analyst; b. Chgo., Jan. 18, 1962; d. Harold Francis and Norine Frances (McNamara) H.; m. Terence W. Dempsey, June 6, 1987. BS, U. Ill., Chgo., 1984; MBA, U. Ill., 1986. Asst. mgr. Dunkin Donuts, Chgo., 1977-80; finance teaching asst., then instr. Univ. Ill at Chgo., 1984-86, database teaching asst., cons., 1985; research assoc. Drexel Burnham Lambert, Chgo., 1987—. Mem. Anti-Cruelty Soc. Chgo. Recipient 7 undergrad. scholarships, 3 grad. fellowships. Mem. Nat. Wildlife Fedn., U. Ill. Alumni Assn. (life), Alpha Lambda Delta, Beta Gamma Sigma, Phi Eta Sigma, Phi Kappa Phi. Democrat. Roman Catholic. Avocations: wildlife and nature conservation, photography, bird watching, drawing.

HICKS, HERBERT RAY, minister; b. Sardimia, Ohio, Oct. 21, 1939; s. James Blackburn and Lavina Marie (Donohoo) H.; m. Shirley McCleese, Mar. 25, 1960; 1 child, John Mark Hicks. AB, Cin. Christian Coll., 1962; BTh, Cin. Christian Sem., 1963; M in Div. with honors, Lexington Theol. Sem., 1968, D in Min., 1972. Ordained to ministry Christian Ch., 1968. Pastor 1st Chirstian Ch., Clifton Forge, Va., 1972-76; pastor Graham Christian Ch., Bluefield, Va., 1976-83, Zanesville, Ohio, 1983—. Author: An Historical Study of The Society of Friends, 1968. Lodge: Rotary, Masons, Shriners. Avocation: computer programming. Office: 1st Christian Ch 3000 Dresden Rd Zanesville OH 43701

HICKS, JAMES EARL, artist; b. Joliet, Ill., June 17, 1951; s. Basil Clark and Marie (Ballun) H.; m. Christine Elizabeth Marsh, Jan. 10, 1976; 1 child, Patricia Lyn. Student design, Joliet Jr. Coll., 1969-70; diploma illustration, Kendall Sch. Design, Grand Rapids, Mich., 1972; pvt. studies in marbelization with, Don Guyot, Seattle, 1986. Artist Rospatch Label Co., Grand Rapids, 1970-71; master desinger Am. Greetings Corp., Cleve., 1972—; sec. Artists' Concerns Com., Cleve., 1985—. Creator Feature Artists' Wall, Cleve., 1986-87; illustrator: (book) Porfl. Floral Arrangements, 1979; illustrator 1985 Christmas Seal. Republican. Presbyterian. Club: NE Yacht (Cleve.) (cruise chmn. 1987—). Avocations: coins, shells, sailing, golf, cross country skiing. Home: 1438 Rycroft Ave Lakewood OH 44107 Office: Am Greetings Corp American Rd Cleveland OH 44111

HICKS, JAMES THOMAS, physician, lawyer; b. Brownsville, Pa., June 5, 1924; s. Thomas and Florence Julia (O'Donnell) H.; B.S., U. Pitts., 1945, A.B., 1946, M.S., 1946; Ph.D., George Washington U., 1950; M.D., U. Ark., 1956; J.D., DePaul U., 1975; m. Ellen Elliott, Aug. 25, 1950; children—Ellen, Mary Jo. Intern USPHS, Balt., 1956-60; resident VA Hosp., Pitts., 1958-60; admitted to Ill. bar, 1977, U.S. Ct. of Appeals, 1977, Pa. bar, 1977 U.S. Supreme Ct. Bar, 1980; practice medicine specializing in forensic and legal medicine, River Forest, Ill., 1964—; dir. labs. Oak Park (Ill.) Hosp., 1964—; pres. Oakton Service Corp., 1968—; Oakton Service Corp. of Pa. Served with USPHS, 1956-57. Fellow Nat. Cancer Inst., 1949-50. Fellow ACP, Internat. Coll. Surgeons; mem. AMA, ABA, Ill. Bar Assn., Pa. Bar Assn., Assn. Am. Trial Lawyers, Am. Assn. Hosp. Lawyers, Sigma Xi. Clubs: Univ., Whitehall, Oak Park Country, Carlton. Contbg. editor Hosp. Formulary Mgmt., 1966-70. Home: 7980 W Chicago Ave River Forest IL 60305 Office: 520 Maple Ave Oak Park IL 60304

HICKS, JUDITH EILEEN, nursing administrator; b. Chgo., Jan. 1, 1947; d. John Patrick and Mary Ann (Clifford) Rohan; m. Laurence Joseph Hicks, Nov. 22, 1969; children—Colleen Driscoll, Patrick Kevin. B.S. in Nursing, St. Xavier Coll., Chgo., 1969; M.S. in Nursing, U. Ill.-Chgo., 1975. Staff nurse Mercy Hosp., Chgo., 1969-70, nursing supr., 1970-73; cons. continuing edn. Ill. Nurses Assn., Chgo., 1974-75; dir. obstetrics and gynecology nursing Northwestern Meml. Hosp., Chgo., 1975-81; v.p. nursing Children's Meml. Hosp., Chgo., 1981-86; pres. Children's Meml. Home Health, Inc., 1986—, Children's Meml. Nursing Services, 1986—; dir. Near North Health Corp., Chgo., 1982—. Mem. Ill. Hosp. Assn. (chmn. Council on Nursing 1982-83), Inst. Medicine, Am. Soc. Nursing Adminstrs., Women's Health Exec. Network (pres. 1984-85). Roman Catholic. Home: 2206 Beechwood St Wilmette IL 60091 Office: Children's Meml Hosp 2300 Childrens Plaza Chicago IL 60614

HICKS, JUDITH KAE, educator; b. Grundy Center, Iowa, Feb. 2, 1940; d. Bertram Lyle and Victoria Marie (Smith) Robinson; m. John Richard Hicks, June 15, 1969; children—Jeremy Robinson, Sarah Elizabeth. B.A. in History, Wartburg Coll., 1963; student Colo. State Coll., 1960-61. History tchr. Nokomis Community Dist. 22 (Ill.), 1963-67, 68-69; social studies tchr. Greenview Sch. System (Ill.), 1967-68; tchr. history Webber Twp. High Sch., Bluford, Ill., 1978—; trustee Egyptian Area Schs. Employees Benefit Trust, 1983-85. Mem. AAUW, NEA, Ill. Edn. Assn., Webber Secondary Edn. Assn. (pres. 1983-84), Webber Twp. Edn. Assn. (pres. 1984-85). Methodist. Club: PEO. Home: 1806 Pace Ave Mount Vernon IL 62864 Office: Webber Twp High Sch S Main St Bluford IL 62814

HICKS, KENNETH WILLIAM, bishop; b. LaHarpe, Kans., June 18, 1923; s. Earl Franklin and Ertie Leona (Williams) H.; m. Lila Elaine Goodwin, Aug. 11, 1946; children: Linda Diane, Debra Dawn. B.A., York (Nebr.) Coll., 1947; M.Th., Iliff Sch. Theology, Denver, 1953; D.D. (hon.), Nebr. Wesleyan U., 1970, Westmar Coll., LeMars, Iowa, 1977; LL.D. (hon.), Philander Smith Coll., 1978. Ordained to ministry United Methodist Ch., 1952; pastor chs. in Nebr. and Colo., 1945-68; dist. supt. Central dist. United Meth. Ch., Kearney, Nebr., 1968-73; sr. pastor Trinity United Meth. Ch., Grand Island, Nebr., 1973-76; bishop Ark. area United Meth. Ch., Little Rock, 1976-84, Kans. area East, Topeka, 1984—. Trustee So. Meth. U., St. Paul Sch. Theology, Kansas City, Mo., Hendrix Coll., Conway, Ark., Meth. Hosp., Memphis, Philander Smith Coll., Little Rock; Trustee Lydia Patterson Inst., El Paso, Tex.; Trustee Meth. Children's Home, Little Rock; chmn. United, Negro Coll. Fund Ark., 1977. Named Alumus of Year Iliff Sch. Theology, 1977. Democrat. Clubs: Lions, Rotary, Shriners. Office: United Meth Ch Kans Dist E PO Box 4187 Topeka KS 66604 *

HICKS, PATRICIA LYNN, probation officer; b. Pontiac, Mich., June 17, 1953; d. William E. Bevan and Priscilla Alien (Duncan) Bort; m. Randall William Hicks, Oct. 14, 1978 (div. Mar. 1985); children: Melissa B., Ashley William, Efrim Bradley. BSW, Western Mich. U., 1975. Lic. social worker, Mich. Crisis intervention worker Bronson Hosp., Kalamazoo, 1974-77; counselor Youth Service Bur., Centreville, Mich., 1977-80; probation officer Probate Court, Centreville, 1980-86. Tchr. Sunday sch. Jone Bible Ch., 1986; dir. Meth. Youth Fellowship, 1977-81. Avocations: sports, crafts. Office: Probate Ct Centreville MI 49032

HICKS, SAMUEL IRVING, teacher educator; b. Stormville, N.Y., Apr. 4, 1902; s. Irving J. and Elizabeth (Tripp) H.; A.B., U. Mich., 1924; M.A., Columbia, 1927; Ed.D., Columbia U., 1947; postgrad. N.Y. U., 1931-33; m. Margaret Anderson, Jan. 7, 1924; children—Eleanor (Mrs. Peter Werenfels), Virginia (Mrs. John Karl). Tchr., Boyne City (Mich.) High Sch., 1924-26; prin. jr. and sr. high sch., Dobbs Ferry, N.Y., 1926-29; supt. schs., Central Park, N.Y., 1929-32, Pearl River, N.Y., 1932-58; coordinator services to adminstrs. citizenship edn. project Columbia U., 1954-56; prof. edn. Ohio U., Athens, 1958—, dir. Center for Ednl. Research and Service, 1960-66, coordinator ednl. placement, 1972-87; dir. Inst. Edn., Ahmadu Bello U., Nigeria, 1966-70; exec. sec. SEOKWA Council Adminstrv. Leadership, 1972—. Mem. Am. Ednl. Research Assn., N.Y. State Ednl. Research Assn. (past pres.), Am. Assn. Sch. Adminstrs., Nat. Conf. Profs. Ednl. Adminstrn., Comparative and Internat. Edn. Soc., Assn. Sch. Bus. Ofcls., Am. Ednl. Fin. Assn., AAUP, Kappa Delta Pi, Phi Kappa Phi Phi Delta Kappa. Clubs: Athens Rotary, Rotary (Zaria, Nigeria), Pearl River (past pres.). Home: 48 Briarwood Dr Athens OH 45701 Office: 48 Briarwood Dr Athens OH 45701

HICKS, TIMOTHY GERALD, lawyer; b. Pontiac, Mich., Aug. 4, 1952. BA, Cen. Mich. U., 1974, MA, 1977; JD, T.M. Cooley Law Sch., Lansing, Mich., 1983. Bar: Mich. 1983, U.S. Dist. Ct. (ea. dist.) Mich. 1983. High sch. tchr. Deckerville (Mich.) Schs., 1974-76; high sch. counselor Stock Bridge (Mich.) Schs., 1977-82; research atty. Ingram County Ct., Mason, Mich., 1983; assoc. Lyon & Hackett, Cheboygan, Mich., 1983-85, Parmenter, Forsythe, Rude, VanEpps, Briggs & Fauri, Muskegon, Mich., 1985—. Chmn. Cheboygan County Reps., 1985; county coordinator Bill Lucas for Gov., Muskegon, 1986. Mem. ABA, Mich. Bar Assn., Cheboygan County Bar Assn. (sec. 1984-85), Muskegon County Bar Assn., Am. Trial Lawyers Assn. Lodge: Kiwanis (bd. dirs. Cheboygan 1985, bd. dirs. Muskegon 1986). Avocations: sports, photography. Home: 1571 Geenwich Muskegon MI 49441 Office: 500 Lumberman's Bank Bldg Muskegon MI 49443

HIEBEL, JOANN HELEN, advertising agency executive; b. Hinckley, Minn., Dec. 7, 1936; d. Joseph Nicholas and Lillian Anna (Korbel) Williams; m. Kenneth John Hiebel, Sept. 5, 1959 (div. Apr. 1981); children—Caroline Kathleen, Michael John. Student Coll. of St. Benedict; B.A., U. Minn., 1958. Adminstrv. asst. Admiral-Merchants, St. Paul, 1958-63; tchr. piano, Mpls., 1964-74; adminstrv. asst. Minn. Opera Co., St. Paul, 1974-77; advt. assoc. Coulter & Assocs., Mpls., 1977-79; mgr. pub. relations Profl. Instruments, Mpls., 1979-81; owner, pres. chief exec. officer Jo Ann Hiebel & Assocs., Mpls., 1981—; exec. dir. Minn. Tooling and Machining Assn., 1981—; advt. rep. and pub. assoc. Bolger Publs., Mpls., 1982-85. Bd. dirs. Exec. Manor Condominium Assn., Mpls., 1980-81, Kidney Found. of Upper Midwest, St. Paul, 1983—; del. Minn. Conf. on Small Bus., Mpls., 1981, 87; mem. Mrs. Jaycees, St. Anthony, Minn., 1963-70. Mem. Nat. Assn. Women Bus. Owners, Advt. Fedn. Minn., Sales and Mktg. Execs.-Mpls., Minn. Soc. Assn. Execs., Minn. Assn. Commerce and Industry, Gamma Phi Beta. Republican. Home: 1235 Yale Pl Minneapolis MN 55403 Office: Hiebel & Assocs Inc 6700 Excelsior Blvd Minneapolis MN 55426

HIEBER, BARBARA E., railroad executive; b. East Chicago, Ind., Jan. 30, 1939; d. Fred H. Hieber and Barbara V. Jankauskas; children: Susan Poloncak Wilk, Steven M. Poloncak Thomas Gregory Wilk. Cert. in transp. mgmt. Calumet Coll., 1974; cert. in advt. studies Inst. Advanced Advt., Medill Sch. Journalism, Northwestern U., 1983; BBA, DePaul U., 1987. Mech. draftsman Combustion Engring. Inc., East Chicago, 1957-60; engring. technician Gen. Am. Transp. Corp., 1961-63, Pullman Standard Co., 1970-71, McKee-Berger-Mansueto Co., 1971-72; traffic and transp. generalist Am. Maize, Hammond, 1973-74, Ind. Harbor Belt R.R., Hammond, 1974-78; traffic and transp. generalist Santa Fe Ry., Chgo., 1978-79, acct., 1979, splty. advt. coordinator Advt. Direction Inc., Chgo., 1979-83; cost and research analyst Santa Fe So. Pacific Corp., Chgo., 1983—, Am. Assn. Advt. Agys. fellow, 1983. Mem. Womens Advt. Club Chgo. (chmn. ethics legis. com. 1982-85), Am. Advt. Fedn., Cost Analysis Orgn. Assn. of Am. R.R.s, Am. Council R.R. Women. Home: 277 Stony Island Calumet City IL 60409 also: Rt 1 Box 267 Lake Bruce Kewanna IN 46939 Office: Santa Fe Railway 224 S Michigan Ave Chicago IL 60604

HIEBER, RANDALL ROBERT, optometrist, consultant; b. Bucyrus, Ohio, Dec. 1, 1954; s. E. Richard and Irene (Brause) H.; m. Rebecca Ann Heinlen, June 13, 1976; children: Ryan Randall, Richard Robert. BS in Biochemistry, Bluffton Coll., 1976; D in Optometry, Ohio State U., 1979. Clin. investigator Ohio State U., Columbus, 1979-80; pvt. practice optometry Galion, Ohio, 1979—; clin. investigator Ohio State U., Columbus, 1979-80, Polymer Technology, 1986; clin. instr. Ohio State U., 1979-81; lectr. Am. Hydron, N.Y.C., 1986. Eyecare profl. Men for Missions, Haiti, 1983; deacon Missionary Alliance Ch., Galion, 1985-86; bd. dirs. adv. council Galion Sch. Bd., 1985-86; bd. dirs. Galion YMCA, 1985-86. Recipient Outstanding Recognition award Am. Optometry Assn., 1985; named one of Outstanding Young Men Am., 1985. Mem. Ohio Optometric Assn., Am. Optometric Assn., Contact Lens sect. of Am. Optometric Assn. (charter), Better Vision Inst., Galion C. of C. Republican. Mem. Christian Missionary Alliance Ch. Lodges: Lions (bd. dirs. Galion club), Elks. Avocations: antiques, woodworking, wood carving, golf, racquetball. Office: 337 Hwy W Galion OH 44833

HIEBERT, ELIZABETH BLAKE, civic worker; b. Mpls., July 18, 1910; d. Henry Seavey and Grace (Riebeth) Blake; student Washburn U., 1926-30; B.S., U. Tex. 1933; m. Homer L. Hiebert, Aug. 29, 1935; children—Grace Elizabeth (Mrs. John E. Beam), Mary Sue (Mrs. Donald Wester), John Blake, Henry Leonard, David Mark. Sec. Topeka Regional Sci. Fair, 1958-60, bd. dirs., 1964—; bd. dirs. YMCA 1968-74, Topeka (Kans.) Friends of the 300; water safety instr. and swimming tchr. of handicapped; freelance writer; former mem. Shawnee County Advocacy Council on Aging; Shawnee County chmn. Arthritis Found. Hon. fellow Harry S. Truman Library; recipient Paul Harris award Rotary, 1985. Mem. D.A.R., Daus. Am. Colonists, AAUW (dir. 1944-62, 65—), N.E. Hist. and Geneal. Soc., Tex. U. Alumni, Am. Home Econs. Assn., Shawnee County Med. Aux. (past pres.), Nat. Audubon, Met. Mus. Art, P.E.O. (past local pres. coop. bd.), Topeka Art Guild, Nat. Soc. Ancient and Hon. Arty., Nat. Trust Historic Preservation, Internat. Oceanographic Found., Nat. League Am. Pen Women (pres. Topeka 1970-72), Washburn Alumnae Assn., Am. Assn. State and Local History, Colo. Hist. Assn., Shawnee County Hist. Soc., Mont., Minn., Kans. hist. socs., Smithsonian Assos., Oceanic Soc., Internat. Platform Assn., Topeka Friends of the Library, Cousteau Soc., Am. Assn. Zookeepers, Nat. Assn. for Mature People, Am. Assn. Ret. Persons, K.U. Spencer Mus. Art, Conn. Soc. Genealogists, Nat., New Eng. geneal. socs., Topeka Beautification Assn. (sec.), People to People, Archives Assos., Am. Space Found., Mus. Fine Arts Boston, Kans. Reading Assn., Am. Assn. Museums, San Diego Zool. Soc., Nat. Space Inst., Oriental Inst., Delta Kappa Gamma (hon.), Delta Gamma, others. Club: Topeka Knife and Fork. Editor children's page Household mag., 1934-39. Home: 1517 Randolph Topeka KS 66604

HIEBERT, WILLIAM JOHN, family therapist; b. Mt. Lake, Minn., Sept. 20, 1938; s. Nicolei J. and Evelyn Sarah (Falk) H. Student, Antioch Coll., 1958; BA, U. Minn., 1961; MDiv., Northwestern Luth. Theol. Sem., 1964;

MST, Andover Newton Theol. Sch., 1967. Dir. edn. services Marriage and Family Counseling Service, Rock Island, Ill., 1968—; gen. chmn. Perspectives in Family Therapy Internat. Seminars, Essex, Conn., 1983—. Editor: Counseling in Marital and Sexual Problems, 1985; founding editor Family Therapy News, 1979-85; editor Ill. Family Therapist, 1986—. Fellow Am. Assn. Marital and Family Therapy (approved supr., editor 1979-85, Disting. Service award 1985, Disting. Pres. award 1986); mem. Am. Family Therapy Assn., Am. Assn. Pastoral Counselors. Democrat. Methodist. Home: 1450 18th Ave C4 Rock Island IL 61201 Office: Marriage & Family Counseling Service 1800 3d Ave #512 Rock Island IL 61201

HIER, DANIEL BARNET, neurologist; b. Chgo., Mar. 23, 1947; s. Stanley W. and Jean (Schrager) H.; m. Myra Goldberg, Aug. 30, 1981; 1 child, Benjamin Philip. BA, Harvard U., 1969, MD, 1973. Medical intern Bronx Mcpl. Hosp., N.Y.C., 1973-74; neurology resident Mass. Gen. Hosp., Boston, 1974-77, neurology fellow, 1977-79; neurologist Michael Reese Hosp., Chgo., 1979—, chmn. neurology, 1986—. Fellow Am. Acad. Neurology, Am. Heart Assn. (stroke council). Home: 641 W Willow Chicago IL 60616 Office: Michael Reese Hosp 2900 S Ellis Ave Chicago IL 60616

HIETPAS, JEAN LUCILLE, social program director, educator; b. Appleton, Wis., Jan. 29, 1955; d. Arthur Peter and Irene Marie (Timmers) H. BS, U. Wis., Milw., 1980, MS, 1985. Cert. alcohol and drug abuse therapist; registered occupational therapist. Psychotherapist DePaul Hosp., Milw., 1980-86, program dir., 1986-87; lectr. in occupational therapy U. Wis., Milw., 1984-86; program dir. Elmbrook Meml. Hosp., Brookfield, Wis., 1987—. Coordinator Wis. Occupational Mental Health Assn., Milw., 1984, 85. Recipient Wis. Occupational Therapy Recognition award Wis. Occupational Therapy Assn., Milw., 1985. Mem. Wis. Assn. Alcohol and other Drug Abuse, Am. Occupational Therapy Assn. Avocations: aikido, internat. travel. Office: Elmbrook Meml Hosp 19333 W North Ave Brookfield WI 53005

HIEU, NGUYEN-TRUNG, social science educator, voluntary agency executive; b. Nghe-An, Viet Nam, Dec. 15, 1946; came to U.S., 1974, naturalized, 1980; s. Ngoc-Duc and Thu-Ba (Nguyen) N.; B.A., U. Saigon, 1970; M.A., Govs. State U., 1975, 76, 77, 78; M.Ed., Loyola U., Chgo., 1979, Ed.D., 1985; C.A.S., U. Chgo., 1980; Ph.D., Heed U., 1981. Tchr., Viet Nam Ministry Edn., Saigon, 1966-67; tng. officer U.S. AID, Viet Nam, 1968-69; instr. Nat. Sch. Social Work, Viet Nam, 1970-74; tchr. counselor Jones Community Ctr., Inc., Ill., 1974-75; counselor Catholic Charities, Lombard, Ill., 1975-76; tchr. Chgo. Bd. Edn., 1977—; instr. Nat. Coll. Edn., Chgo., 1979—; founder, pres. NghiaSinh Internat., Saigon, Chgo., 1963—; exec. dir. Social Service Ctr., Saigon, 1968-70; prin. NghiaViet High Sch., Saigon, 1971-74; exec. dir. Vietnamese Community for Human Devel. Inc., Chgo., 1976-80. Author: English-Vietnamese Idioms, 1977, 2d edit., 1981; Nineteen Songs for Love and Peace, 1974; English-Vietnamese Social Science Concepts, 1972. Editor: Lien-Nghia News, 1963—. Mem. Ill. Bilingual Adv. Council, Chgo., 1978-82, Asian Am. Adv. Council to Gov. Ill., 1983—; dir. Access, Inc., Chgo., 1979-84; sponsor more than 1,000 refugees, Chgo., 1975-84. Recipient Nat. Medal of Youth, 1969, Nat. Medal of Edn., 1970, Nat. Medal of Social Service, 1971, Nat. Medal of Labor, 1972; Edn. award Ill. Bd. Edn., 1979; Citizen of Yr. award Chgo. Citizenship Council, 1981; Pres.'s Vol. award White House, 1983-84. Mem. Nat. Assn. Vietnam-Am. Edn., Asian Am. Educators, Ill. Bilingual Edn. Assn., Chgo. Bilingual Educators Assn., Chgo. Citizenship Council. Office: Nat Coll Edn 18 S Michigan Ave Chicago IL 60603

HIGBIE, J(OHN) RICHARD, hospital adminstrator; b. Wooster, Ohio, Dec. 2, 1935; s. John Richard and Truth (Hewitt) H.; married June 15, 1957; children: John Richard III, Jill Anne, Peter Scott. BSBA, U. Akron, 1961. Employment supr. Akron Gen. Hosp., Akron, Ohio, 1957-59; employment interviewer B.F. Goodrich Co., Akron, 1960; personnel dir. Akron City Hosp., 1961-66; profl. employment mgr. PPG Industries, Barberton, Ohio, 1967; exec. v.p. Children's Hosp. Med. Ctr., Akron, 1968—; chmn. Advance Inc., Akron, 1971-76; mem. exec. com. Children's Hosps. Automated Med. Programs, Columbus, Ohio, 1978-82. pres. United Services for Handicapped, Akron, 1981-83; trustee Cancer Soc. Summit County, Akron, 1975-80, Portage Path Community Mental Health Ctr., Akron, 1972—, treas. 1977-81. Mem. Am. Coll. Healthcare Execs., Am. Hosp. Assn., Ohio Hosp. Assn., Med. Educators Assn., Am. Soc. for Personnel Adminstrs. (pres. Akron 1966-67), Nat. Assn. Children's Hosps. and Related Insts. (chmn. nat. monitrend com., 1980—). Clubs: Cascade (Akron); Prestwick Country (Uniontown, Ohio). Home: 3800 Glen Eagles Blvd Uniontown OH 44685-8824 Office: Childrens Hosp Med Ctr 281 Locust St Akron OH 44308

HIGGINBOTHAM, SUZANNE GUGE, financial company executive; b. St. Louis, Oct. 16, 1926; d. Lee Brown and Louise Suzanne (Reitz) Guge; m. William H. Higginbotham, Oct. 4, 1970; m. Carl H. Koch, Jan. 18, 1951 (div. June 1969); 1 stepchild, Patricia Koch. Student Washington U., 1955-59. Personnel mgr. Safeco Ins. Co., St. Louis, 1954-69; dir. personnel Volkswagen Ins. Co., St. Louis, 1969-76, Swank Motion Pictures, St. Louis, 1976-77; exec. dir. YWCA Met. St. Louis, 1977-85; human resource cons., 1985-86; account executive Charlotte S. Cohen & Co., Inc., Investments, 1986—; mem. faculty Creative Problem Solving Inst., State Coll., Buffalo, 1971—. Contbr. articles to ins. and personnel jours. Bd. dirs. Confluence, Citizens Action Group, St. Louis, 1983—. Mem. Indsl. Relations Assn., Ins. Women St. Louis (pres. 1964-65), Personnel Assn. Greater St. Louis (pres. 1979-80), Personnel Assn. Greater St. Louis (bd. dirs. 1969-84), Group Action Council Greater St. Louis (chmn. 1968), Women's Info. Network, St. Louis Forum Exec. Women's Network. Republican. Home: 890 Judson Manor Dr Saint Louis MO 63141

HIGGINS, ANDREW JACKSON, state supreme ct. justice; b. Platte City, Mo., June 21, 1921; s. Andrew Jervy and Frances Beverly H.; m. Laura Joan Brown, Oct. 30, 1948; children: Susan Louise, Laura Frances. A.B., Central Coll., 1943; LL.B., Washington U., St. Louis, 1948. Bar: Mo. bar 1948. Practice law Platte City, 1948-60; former pros. atty. Platte County; former mayor Platte City; judge Jud. Circuit 6, 1960-64; commr. Mo. Supreme Ct., Jefferson City, 1964-81; assoc. justice Mo. Supreme Ct., 1981—. Past chmn. Platte County Democratic Central Com. Served with USN, 1943-46. Mem. Sigma Alpha Epsilon, Delta Theta Phi. Address: Mo Supreme Ct PO Box 150 Jefferson City MO 65102 *

HIGGINS, FRANCIS EDWARD, educator; b. Chgo., Nov. 29, 1935; s. Frank Edward and Mary Alyce (Fahey) H.; B.S., Loyola U., Chgo., 1959, M.A., 1964; postgrad. Exeter Coll., Oxford (Eng.) U., 1962, Am. U. Beirut, 1966, McGill U., Montreal, Que., Can., 1967; adminstrn. cert. St. Xavier Coll., 1971; Ed.D., U. Sarasota, 1977. Tchr., Washington Jr. High Sch., Chicago Heights, Ill., 1959; tchr. Chgo. Vocat. High Sch., 1960-68, dept. chmn., 1964; asst. prof. social sci. Moraine Valley Community Coll., 1968-69; tchr. history Hillcrest High Sch., Country Club Hills, Ill., 1969—; instr. nursing continuing edn. St. Francis Coll., 1978—. Mem. pres.'s council St. Xavier Coll., 1978—; mem. St. Germaine Sch. Bd., 1972-73, St. Alexander Sch. Bd., 1978-84; active Chgo. council Boy Scouts Am., 1969-77, asst. dist. commr., 1971-75, mem. dist. scout com., 1976-77; co-historian Palos Heights Silver Jubilee Com., 1984. Recipient Disting. Service award Chgo. council Boy Scouts Am., 1974; Brit. Univ. scholar, 1962; Fulbright fellow, summer 1966; English Speaking Union fellow, 1967. Mem. Ill. Hist. Soc., Del. Hist. Soc., Am. Cath. Hist. Soc., Nat. Council Social Studies, Ill. Council Social Studies, Nat. Curriculum and Supervisory Assn., Ill. Supervisory Assn., Ill. Assn. Supervision and Curriculum Devel. (editorial rev. bd. Jour. 1984-86), Chgo. Hist. Soc., Nat. Hist. Soc., Brit. Hist. Assn., Brit. Hist. Assn., Nat. Soc. Study Edn., Phi Delta Kappa, Phi Gamma Mu. Republican. Roman Catholic. Contbr. revs. to Am. Cath. Hist. Jour., History Tchr. Jour. Home: 7660 W 131st St Palos Heights IL 60463 Office: Hillcrest High Sch 175th and Pulaski Rd Country Club Hills IL 60477

HIGGINS, JAMES JOSEPH, environmental consultant; b. Massillon, Ohio, May 15, 1920; s. John P. and Stella M. (Warth) H.; m. Gloria L. Pepoon, Aug. 20, 1949; children: Bruce J., Keith W., Anita L., Suzanne M. B in Chem. Engring., Ohio State U., 1942; MS, Lawrence Coll., 1948, PhD, 1951. Chem. engr. Fox River Paper Co., Appleton, Wis., 1946, Union Bag & Paper Co., Savannah, Ga., 1947; chemist Morris Paper Mills, 1948; devel. chemist Ohio Boxboard Co., Rittman, 1950-54; paper mill supt. Packaging Corp. Am., Rittman, 1954-57, research group leader, research and devel. mgr., 1958-61, dir. tech. services and environ. control, Grand Rapids, Mich., 1961-85; pvt. practice environ. cons., Grand Rapids, 1985—. Contbr. articles to profl. jours.; patentee in field. Served to capt. C.E., U.S. Army, 1942-46. Fellow Am. Inst. Chemists; mem. Am. Inst. Chem. Engrs., Sigma Xi. Home and Office: 2035 Wilshire Dr SE Grand Rapids MI 49506

HIGGINS, MARLA ANN, speech and language pathologist; b. Sandusky, Ohio, Aug. 17, 1951; d. Ralph John and Grace Lucile (Karbler) Keller; m. John Robert Higgins, Sept. 21, 1974; children: Jane Ann Higgins, Katherine Ann. BS in Edn., Bowling Green State U., 1973. Lic. speech pathologist. Speech pathologist Perkins Schs., Sandusky, 1973-75, Erie County Bd. Edn., Sandusky, 1976—; part-time U.S. customs insp., Sandusky, 1974—; treas. South Shore Machine, Sandusky, 1981—. V.p. Sts. Peter and Paul Bd. Edn., Sandusky, 1985-86. Mem. Ohio Speech and Hearing Assn., Kappa Delta Pi, Sigma Alpha Eta. Democrat. Roman Catholic. Avocations: antiques, fitness programs. Home: 1118 Buckingham St Sandusky OH 44870

HIGGINS, ROBERT ARTHUR, electrical engineer, educator, consultant; b. Watertown, S.D., Sept. 5, 1924; s. Arthur C. and Nicoline (Huseth) H.; m. Barbara Jeanne Fagerlie, 1958; children—Patricia Suzanne, Daniel Alfred, Steven Robert. B.E.E. with honors, U. Minn., 1948; M.S.E.E., U. Wis., 1964; Ph.D. in Elec. Engring., U. Mo., 1969. Registered profl. engr. Engr. Schlumberger Well Survey Corp., Tex., 1948-57; research technologist Mobil Research and Devel. Corp., Tex., 1958-61; research engr. United Aircraft Research Labs., Conn., 1965; staff specialist Remote Sensing Inst., S.D., 1969-71; asst. prof. elec. engring. S.D. State U., 1969-74, assoc. dir. Engring. Expt. Sta., 1973-77, prof. elec. engring., 1974-79; prof. elec. engring. Mankato State U., 1980; prin. engr. Sperry Univac, 1981-85; prof. elec. engring. St. Cloud State U., Minn., 1985—; cons. Control Data Corp., 1977-80, Lawrence Livermore Lab., 1971-73, U.S. Air Force Office Sci. Research, Fla., 1976; project dir., cons. NSF, 1973-80. Contbr. articles to profl. jours. Bd. dirs. Eden Prairie Bd. Edn., Minn., 1982-85. Served with AUS, 1943-46. NASA fellow, 1966-68; grantee NSF, 1966, 72, 74, 86, AEC, 1971-73, Office Water Resources Research, 1971-74. Mem. NSPE, IEEE (sr.), Sigma Xi. Lutheran. Club: Flagship Athletic. Home: 11260 Windrow Dr Eden Prairie MN 55344 Office: St Cloud State U Elec Engring Dept Saint Cloud MN 56301

HIGGINSON, JERRY ALDEN, JR., bank executive; b. Mt. Vernon, Ill., July 21, 1957; s. Jerry Alden Sr. and Beverly Joyce (York) H.; m. Leah Jane Murray, June 11, 1983; 1 child, Sara Elisabeth. BA, Graceland Coll., Lamoni, Iowa, 1979; postgrad., So. Ill. U., 1979; postgrad. sch. banking, So. Meth. U., 1987—. Trust officer, asst. cashier Salem (Ill.) Nat. Bank, 1979-80; trust officer MidAm. Bank and Trust, Carbondale, Ill., 1980-82; asst. v.p., trust officer NBC Bank-San Antonio, 1982—; instr. Am. Inst. Banking, San Antonio, 1984—. Pres. San Antonio Symphony Soc., 1985-86; treas., pres. San Antonio Clean and Beautiful Com., 1986-87; pres. bd. trustees San Antonio Area Found., 1986-87; bd. dirs. Beautify San Antonio, 1987—. Mem. Symphony Soc. San Antonio, San Antonio Baroque Music Soc., San Antonio Conservation Soc. Republican. Mem. Reorganized Ch. Jesus Crist of Latter-day Saints. Club: Knife & Fork of San Antonio. Lodge: Rotary.

HIGGS, CATHLEEN ANNE, vocational rehabilitation counselor; b. Garden City, Mich., Nov. 20, 1951; d. David Griffin Higgs and Charlotte (Hathorne) Riddle; Charles William Riddle (stepfather); m. Scott Allen Grigg, Mar. 15, 1986. BS, Mich. State U., 1972, MA, 1979. Rehab. counselor Mich. Rehab. Services, Lansing, 1979-83; vocat. counselor Mich. State U., East Lansing, 1983—; liaison rehab. engring. project Mich. State U., 1979-82, adj. faculty rehab. masters program, 1983—; cons. and presentor rehab. masters program Drake U., Des Moines, 1986. Recipient Ruby Neely Hon. award Mid-Mich. Multiple Sclerosis Soc., 1983-84. Mem. Mich. Rehab. Assn. (bd. dirs. 1982-83), Mich. Rehab. Counseling Assn. Avocations: traveling, camping, bicycling. Home: 503 Manchester DeWitt MI 48820

HIGH, DOROTHY HELEN FRANK, city recreation administrator; b. Lincoln, Nebr., Feb 3, 1935; d. Theodore Ludwig and Lillian Winifred (Schellberg) F.; m. Duane High, Nov. 18, 1955; children—Ted Frank, Catherine Nadine. B.S. in Edn., U. Nebr., 1956; M.S. in Edn., Chadron State Coll., 1967. Instr. phys. edn. Lincoln Pub. Schs., Nebr., 1956-58, Alliance City Schs., Nebr., 1964-67, Scottsbluff Pub. Schs., Nebr., 1967-69, Hiram Scott Coll., Scottsbluff, 1969-71; asst. prof. edn., Tarkio Coll., Mo., 1971; recreation supr. City of Scottsbluff, 1973—. Mem. adv. bd. Nebr. Council Ednl. TV, Lincoln, 1968-70, Nebr. Dept. Edn., 1970; bd. dirs. Southeast Recreation Ctr., Scottsbluff, 1975-80, Jaycee Sr. Ctr., Scottsbluff, 1978-82; mem. adv. bd. Foster Grandparent Program, Scottsbluff, 1983—. Mem. Am. Assn. Leisure and Recreation (pres.-elect 1985-86, pres. 1986-87), Am. Alliance Health, Phys. Edn., Recreation and Dance (bd. govs. 1986-87, pres. central dist. 1982-84, Honor award 1975), Nebr. Assn. Health, Phys. Edn., Recreation and Dance (pres. 1972-73, Honor award 1970), Am. Soc. Aging. Republican. Lutheran. Club: Soroptimist Internat. of Scotts Bluff County (pres. 1978-79). Avocations: tennis; swimming. Home: 2210 7th Ave Scottsbluff NE 69361 Office: City of Scottsbluff 1818 Ave A Scottsbluff NE 69361

HIGHT HELLENS, LAWRENCE OTHELLO, scriptwriter, illustrator; b. Chgo., Sept. 28, 1922; s. Frank James Hellens and Barbara Ann (Johnson) Hight; m. Gloria R. Winters, (div. 1951); children: Larnel Jerry, Anita Catherine (dec.); m. Marletta Martenia, Sept. 23, 1963; m. Helen Libbie Colburn, May 23, 1970; children: Ruth Naomi, Claire Samantha, Paul Lawrence, Jasamine Maude, Harriet Ann. Student, Atlanta U., 1943, Art Inst. Chgo., 1947-51, Radio Inst. Chgo., 1951-52, Commercial Art Inst. Chgo., 1950-52; DD (hon.), Ch. Gospel Ministry, Chula Vista, Calif., 1986. Co-founder, producer, playwright Harlem Co-op Theatrical, Chgo., 1947-51; founder in chief, writer Artesia Pub. Co., Chgo., 1952-54; co-founder, commercial artist Tri-Art Studios., Chgo., 1955-58; founder, pres. Sound Track Prodns., Chgo., 1959-67; founder, dir., TV producer, scriptwriter LOHAE Studio Creative, Chgo., 1967—. Creator meml. posters Kennedy-King, 1963-69; polit. posters for Harold Washington, 1983. Founder, bd. dirs. Nat. Alliance Artists for Polit. Action, Chgo., 1984—; founder, minister Temple Kethra E' DA, 1986—. Served with USAAF, 1943-46. Recipient 1st prize Chgo. Park Dist. Art Contest, 1947, Chgo. Poets award Friends of Chgo. Poets, Chgo. Cultural Ctr., 1965. Mem. Internat. Black Writers, Soc. Black Poets. Democrat. Mem. Ch. Universal Life Sci. Found. Lodges: Roscrucians, Mayans. Avocations: hist. research, bibl. research, lectures. Home and Office: 9633 S Prospect Chicago IL 60643

HIGI, WILLIAM L., bishop; b. Anderson, Ind., Aug. 29, 1933. Student, Mt. St. Mary of the West Sem., Xavier U. Ordained priest Roman Cath. Ch., 1959. Bishop Lafayette, Ind., 1984—. Address: Office of Archdiocese 610 Lingle Ave PO Box 260 Lafayette IN 47902 *

HIGLEY, DAVID GRADY, optometrist; b. Ypsilanti, Mich., June 18, 1949; s. Harold George and Margaret Anne (Corbitt) H. BS, Pacific U., 1971, OD, 1973. Cert. vision therapist, orthokeratologist. Pvt. practice optometry Rockford, Mich., 1973—; dir. optometry Thomas Optical, Muskegon, Mich., 1986; cons. Sterling Vision, Sterling Heights, Mich., 1984-86. Pres. Rockford Community Theatre, 1981-86; commr. Rockford Arts Council, 1982-84; active Grand Rapids (Mich.) Civic Theatre, 1974-86. Named Best Actor, Cedar Springs Players, 1977, Best Supporting Actor, Cedar Springs Players, 1978. Mem. W. Mich. Optometric Assn., Mich. Optometric Assn., Am. Optometric Assn., Optometric Extension Program, Contact Lens Sect., Rockford Jaycees (Jaycee of the Mo. 1974), Rockford Hist. Soc. Republican. Lodge: Lions (chmn. sight conservation com.). Avocation: sports. Home: 1157 Iroquois Dr SE Grand Rapids MI 49506 Office: 5202 Northland Dr NE Grand Rapids MI 49505

HILBY, WALTER JOSEPH, engineer; b. Coon Valley, Wis., Sept. 15, 1932; s. Valentine L. and Anna M. Hilby; m. Mary D. Grundy, Sept. 5, 1959; children: Howard L., Kim M. Rowland. BS in Structural Engring., Finlay Engring. Coll., 1958; MA in Pub. Adminstrn., Sangamon State U., 1980. Registered profl. and structural engr., Ill. Civil engr. Ill. Dept. Transp., Springfield, Ill., 1958—. Served with U.S. Army, 1953-55, Germany. Roman Catholic. Lodge: KC. Office: Ill Dept of Transp 2300 So Dirksen Pkwy Springfield IL 62764

HILDEBRAND, MICHAEL JOSEPH, banker; b. Sheboygan, Wis., Oct. 1, 1945; s. Joseph Leonard and Laverne (Lamb) H.; m. Wilma Maria Gietman, July 11, 1970; children: Kristin Ann, Joseph Michael. BS in Econs., U. Wis., Oshkosh, 1968. Nat. bank examiner Comptroller of the Currency, Appleton, Wis., 1968-72; v.p. 1st Nat. Bank, Menasha, Wis., 1972-75; v.p. Nat. Exchange bank, Fond du Lac, Wis., 1975-80, 1st v.p., 1980—. Past pres. United Way Fond du Lac; past chmn. bd. rev. for taxes, Fond du Lac, 1981-86; mem. Area Econ. Authority, 1980—, chmn., 1981; mem. Chancellors Council of Advisors U. Wis., Oshkosh, 1982—. Mem. Fond du Lac County Bankers Assn. Roman Catholic. Lodges: Rotary, Kiwanis (Kiwanian of Yr. 1978-79, past pres.). Avocations: golf, skiing. Home: 751 Sterling Dr Fond du Lac WI 54935 Office: Nat Exchange Bank and Trust 130 S Main St Fond du Lac WI 54935

HILDEBRANDT, RICHARD JOHN, obstetrician/gynecologist, educator, academic director; b. Harrisburg, Pa., Dec. 21, 1932; s. Carl Emil and Ruth Mable (Meharry) H.; m. Frances Olsen, Sept. 16, 1937; children: Kristen, Allison, David Carl. BS with honors, The Citadel, 1955; MD, Duke U., 1959. Diplomate Am. Bd. Ob-Gyn., Am. Bd. Maternal Fetal Medicine. Intern in medicine Duke U. Sch. Medicine, 1959-60; asst. resident Ob-gyn Sch. Medicine U. Fla., Gainesville, 1960-63, chief resident, instr. Ob-gyn, 1963-64, postdoctoral fellow in Microbiology, 1962-63, asst. prof., 1966-71; research fellow NIH, Bethesda, Md., 1964-66; from assoc. prof. to clin. prof. Pa. State U., Hershey, 1971-84; dir. ob-gyn dept. PolyClinic Med. Ctr., Harrisburg, 1976-84; dir. ob-gyn dept., prof. Wright State U., Dayton, Ohio, 1984-87; with Miami Valley Hosp. Perinatal & Gynecol. Ultrasound Imaging Ctr., Dayton, 1987—; bd. dirs. Social Health Services, Dayton; med. dir. Perinatal Health Ctr., Dayton, 1984-87, co-chmn. perinatal adv. council region II, 1986. Mem. St. Paul's Hunger Task Force, Dayton, 1985-86, chmn., 1987. Served to lt. comdr. USPHS, 1964-66. Macy Faculty fellow Josiah Macy Found., 1966-69. Fellow Am. Coll. Ob-Gyn; mem. Social Health Assn. (bd. dirs. 1986—), Soc. Gynecologic Investigation, Soc. Perinatal Obstetricians. Republican. Episcopalian. Home: 3449 Indian Hill Dr Dayton OH 45429 Office: Miami Valley Hosp Perinatal & Gynecol Ultrasound Imaging Ctr 1 Wyoming St Dayton OH 45409

HILDRETH, PATRICIA YVONNE, accounting executive; b. Clinton, Ind., Mar. 15, 1934; d. Leonard Adam and Wilma Vivian (Scifres) Prulhiere; m. James A. Hildreth, Jan. 20, 1954; children: John Alan, Patti Virginia, David Michael, Brian Spencer. Student Jackson Community Coll., 1974-80, Eastern Mich. U., 1980-81. Sales clk. Yeager Co., Akron, Ohio, 1951-52; acctg. clk. B.F. Goodrich Co., Akron, 1952-54; owner bookkeeping firm P.Y. Hildreth, Akron, 1965-72; owner Jackson Small Bus. Service (Mich.), 1972—; cons. in field. Millage campaign chmn. Jackson Pub. Sch., 1977, mem. various coms., 1972-81; active Girl Scouts U.S.A., Akron and Jackson; pres. PTA, Akron, 1968-70; treas. Jackson Med. Ctr. Inc., 1980-82. Mem. Ind. Accts. Assn. of Mich. (edn. com. 1983-84). Republican. Mem. Ch. of Christ. Lodge: Civitan (treas. Jackson club 1981-85, mem. various coms.). Office: Jackson Small Bus Service 2300 W Michigan Ave Jackson MI 49203

HILDRETH, R(OLAND) JAMES, foundation executive, economist; b. Des Moines, Nov. 26, 1926; s. Roland James and Emma (Lehman) H.; m. May Helen Carlson, June 8, 1947; children: Christine, Jeffrey, Paul. B.S., Iowa State U., 1949; M.S. in Indsl. Econs., 1950; Ph.D. in Econs., 1954; postgrad. in econs., U. Minn., 1950-52. Instr. Augsburg Coll., Mpls., 1950-52; asst. prof. agrl. econs. and sociology Tex. A&M U., 1954-58; with Tex. Agr. Experiment Sta., 1954-62, research coordinator W. Tex., 1958-59, asst. dir., 1959-62; asso. mgr., dir. Farm Found., Chgo., 1962-70; mgr., dir. Farm Found., 1970—; joint council Food and Agrl. Scis., USDA, 1978-85; cons. council edn. Am. Veterinary Med. Assn., 1977-87. Contbg. author: Changing Patterns in Fertilizer Use, 1968; Editor: Readings in Agricultural Policy, 1967; Co-editor, contbg. author: Methods for Land Economics Research, 1966. Mem. nat. council Boy Scouts Am., 1973-75; mem. advisory com. Council on Rural Health, AMA, 1970-77; mem. advisory council on consumer affairs Am. Bankers Assn., 1971-73; mem. citizens advisory com. Coll. Phys. Edn., U. Ill., 1966-69; bd. dirs. Lutheran Gen. Hosp., Park Ridge, Ill., 1970-82, Nat. Center for Vol. Action, 1970-72. Served with U.S. Army, 1945-47. Recipient Henry A. Wallace award Iowa State U., 1981. Fellow Am. Agrl. Econs. Assn. (pres. 1977-78); Mem. Internat. Assn. Agrl. Economists (sec.-treas. 1973—), Am. Country Life Assn. (past pres.). Home: 381 Poplar Ave Elmhurst IL 60126 Office: 1211 W 22d St Oak Brook IL 60521

HILDT, JOANNE EILERS, marketing consultant; b. St. Cloud, Minn., Dec. 10, 1946; d. Gerald Herman and S. Blanche (Lawton) Eilers; m. Peter Bogert Hildt, Dec. 31, 1975. BS, St. Cloud State U., 1968; postgrad., U. Minn., Mich. State U. Cert. Mktg. Dir. Nat. promotion coordinator Vasarette, Mpls., 1973-75; promotion dir. Har Mar Mall, St. Paul, 1975-78; mktg. dir. Yorktown Shopping Ctr., Lombard, Ill., 1978-82; owner Hildt & Assocs., Bloomingdale, Ill., 1982—; bd. dirs. Greater Woodfield Conv. and Visitors Bur., Schaumburg, Ill. Contbg. columnist Jones Report Newsletter, 1981—, Shopping Ctr. World mag., 1981—. Mem. Old Town Commn., Bloomingdale, 1979-82, chmn. 1980-82; plan commr. Planning and Zone Bd., Bloomingdale, 1982-83; trustee Village of Bloomingdale, 1983—. Named Vol. of Yr., Mpls. Aquatennial, 1974, 75; recipient Liberty Bell award DuPage Law Assn., DuPage County, Ill., 1981. Mem. Internat. Council Shopping Ctrs. (state com. 1986—, Maxi award 1980), Chgo. Area Mktg. Dirs. Assn. (newsletter editor 1981—), Bloomindale C. of C., DuPage County Devel. Commn. Avocation: travel. Office: Hildt & Assocs 110 S 3d St Bloomingdale IL 60108

HILER, JOHN PATRICK, congressman, former foundry executive; b. Chgo., Apr. 24, 1953; s. Robert J. and Margaret F. H.; m. Catherine Sands. B.A., Williams Coll., 1975; M.B.A., U. Chgo., 1977. Mktg. dir. Charles O. Hiler and Son, Inc., Walkerton, Ind., 1977-80, Accurate Castings Co., La Porte, 1977-80; Mem. 97th-100th congresses from 3d Ind. Dist. Del. Ind. Rep. Conv., 1978, 80; trustee LaLumiere Sch., LaPorte; del. White House Conf. Small Bus., 1980; del. Rep. Nat. Conv., 1984. Mem. LaPorte C. of C. Roman Catholic. Office: River Glen Office Plaza 501 E Monroe Room 120 South Bend IN 46601 also: 407 Cannon House Office Bldg Washington DC 20515

HILFINGER, DEAN FARRAR, architect; b. Winfield, Kans., Aug. 10, 1912; s. Roy Morton and Faye (Farrar) H.; m. Avis E. Elmendorf, May 27, 1943; children—DeAnne, Sharmon. BA, S.W. Coll., 1932; BS Archtl. Engring. with honors, U. Ill., 1935; DSc (hon.), Southwestern Coll., 1985. Registered architect, Ill. and 34 other states; registered profl. engr., Ill. Archtl. draftsman George E. Ramey and Co., Champaign, Ill., 1935-57; archtl. draftsman Lundeen and Roozen, Bloomington, Ill., 1937-38; prin. Lundeen and Hilfinger, Bloomington, Ill., 1938-64, Lundeen, Hilfinger and Asbury, Bloomington, Ill., 1965-73, Hilfinger, Asbury, Cufaude and Abels, Bloomington, Ill., 1973—; vis. lctr. U. Ill., 1973. Author: Reducing Liability in your Architectural Practice, 1987, Reducing Liability in your Engineering Practice, 1987; contbr. chpts. to handbooks in field. Pres., bus. mgr., exec. com. Bloomington Normal Symphony Soc., 1951-85; pres., bd. dirs. Bloomington Library Bd., 1952-74. Ill. Sr. Olympic tennis winner, 1982-84. Fellow AIA (treas. 1967-69, Edward C. Kemper award 1984, Cert. Exceptional Service award 1981); mem. Constrn. Specifications Inst. (cert. constrn. specifier), Am. Concrete Inst., ASTM, Internat. Union Architects (dep. v.p. 1970-72, AIA del. 1965, 69, 72, 75). Republican. Club: Young Men's (Bloomington) (pres. 1971-72). Lodge: Rotary (bd. dirs. 1977-80). Avocations: chamber music; tennis. Home: 44 Country Club Pl Bloomington IL 61701 Office: Hilfinger Asbury Cufaude & Abels 318 W Washington St Box 3216 Bloomington IL 61701

HILGART, ARTHUR A., JR., pharmaceutical company executive; b. Chgo., Mar. 6, 1936; s. Arthur and Naomi (Nelson) H.; m. Carolyn Charleston, June 15, 1957; children—John Arthur, Joshua Carl. A.B., Shimer Coll., 1953; M.B.A., U. Chgo., 1955. With The Upjohn Co., Kalamazoo, Mich., 1957—, exec. dir. corp. planning and devel. 1982—; guest lectr. Kalamazoo Coll., Western Mich. U.; bd. dirs. Upjohn Healthcare Services, Cobb-Vantress Inc. Pres., Reproductive Health Care Ctr./Planned Parenthood; pres. Kalamazoo Civic Players; founding bd. dirs. ACLU of Western Mich.; past pres. Kalamazoo Council on Human Relations. Mem. Am. Econ. Assn., AAAS, Soc. Long-Range Planning (London). Home: 1801

Evanston Kalamazoo MI 49008 Office: The Upjohn Co 7000 Portage Rd Kalamazoo MI 49001

HILGENDORF, ROBERT LEE, automotive and aerospace company executive; b. San Jose, Ill., Dec. 9, 1936; s. Clarence Herman and Elsie Florence (Rademaker) H.; m. Barbara Ann Koschnick, June 4, 1975. BA, So. Ill. U., 1958, MA, 1959; MS, Purdue U., 1963. Lic. psychologist, Ohio. Commd. 2d lt. USAF, 1959, advanced through ranks to lt. col., 1976, ret., 1979; dir. engring. Midland Ross Corp., Urbana, Ohio, 1979-85; exec. v.p. Johnson Industries Corp., Urbana, 1985—; aerospace cons. Northrop Electro-Mech. Corp., Anaheim, Calif., 1979-82. Contbr. articles to profl. jours. Tufts U. Bd. Trustees scholar, State of Ill. scholar; recipient grad. research asistantship U.S. Office Edn. Mem. AIAA, Human Factors Soc., Soc. Automotive Engrs. Club: Dayton (Ohio) Racquet. Avocations: agriculture. Home: 8168 Detrick-Jordan Pike New Carlisle OH 45344 Office: Johnson Industries Corp 605 Miami St Urbana OH 43078

HILGER, DAVID JOHN, marketing executive; b. Wauseon, Ohio, Feb. 4, 1954; s. John David and Joan Ester (Smith) H. BS, U. Toledo, 1977, MBA, 1983. Fin. cons. Conway, Stevenson & Assocs., Toledo, 1980-83; mktg. specialist AT&T, Toledo, 1983-85; fin. and planning specialist E.D.S., Southfield, Mich., 1985-86; mktg. exec. Burroughs Corp., Holland, Ohio, 1986—; instr. U. Toledo, 1983-84, Owen Tech. Coll., Toledo, 1984-86. Recipient Community Service award Grad. Council U. Toledo, 1983. Office: Burroughs Corp 6733 Airport Hwy Holland OH 43528

HILGERS, THOMAS WILLIAM, obstetrician-gynecologist; b. Mpls., Aug. 9, 1943; s. Robert and Ann Hilgers; m. Susan K. Bastyr; children: Paul, Stephen, Michael, Teresa. BS in Natural Sci., St. John's U., 1964; MD, U. Minn., 1969. Diplomate Am. Bd. Ob-Gyn. Intern Rochester (Minn.) Gen. Hosp., 1969-70; fellow in ob-gyn Mayo Grad. Sch., Rochester, 1970-73; chief resident ob-gyn Ohio Med. Coll., Toledo, 1973-74; asst. prof. ob-gyn St. Louis U., 1974-77; asst. prof. ob-gyn Creighton U., Omaha, 1977-80, assoc. prof. ob-gyn, 1980-85; dir. Pope Paul VI Inst., Omaha, 1985—; bd. dirs. Creighton U. Natural Family Planning Ctr., 1977-85, St. Louis U. Natural Family Planning Ctr., 1974-77; tchr. edn. program Pope Paul VI Natural Family Planning Creighton U., 1979—. Contbr. articles on human reproduction to profl. jours. Mem. Am. Acad. Natural Family Planning (ad hoc sci. adv. com. 1984—, ad hoc com. study commns. 1983—), Am. Coll. Obstetricians and Gynecologists, Omaha Ob-Gyn Soc., Omaha Midwest Clin. Soc. Roman Catholic. Avocation: U. Nebr. football. Office: Pope Paul VI Inst 6901 Mercy Rd Omaha NE 68106

HILKE, EILEEN VERONICA, educator; b. Milw., Sept. 23, 1950; d. Arthur and Dorothy (Ingich) Gehlen; m. Thomas Hilke, July 13, 1974. B.S., U. Wis.-Eau Claire, 1972; M.Ed., Marquette U., 1977; Ph.D., U. Wis.-Milw., 1983. Tchr. elem. sch., Sheboygan Falls, Wis., 1972-77; assoc. prof. Lakeland Coll., Sheboygan, 1977—, chmn. dept. edn. and psychology, 1978—, chmn. div. social sci., 1981—. Bd. dirs. Mental Health Assn.; clerk Bd. of Edn., 1986. Recipient Citizenship award DAR, George Washington Honor medal, 1987; named One of Outstanding Young Women Am., 1981; Delta Kappa Gamma scholar. Mem. Interlake Reading Assn. (pres., program chmn.), Wis. Reading Assn. (dir.), Internat. Reading Assn. (sect. leader Great Lakes region), Nat. Council Social Studies (tchr. edn. com. 1986), Wis. Ednl. Research Assn., Assn. for Supervision and Curriculum Devel., Wis. Math. Council, NEA, Northeastern Wis. Edn. Assn. (v.p.), Wis. Council for Social Studies (dir.), Wis. Assn. Colls. Tchr. Edn. (pres., exec. bd.), AAUW, Am. Personnel and Guidance Assn., Phi Delta Kappa (pres., dir., historian), Delta Kappa Gamma (rec. sec., exec. bd.). Author: Elementary Education as a Profession, 1981; contbr. articles to profl. jours. Office: Lakeland Coll Sheboygan WI 53081

HILL, BEVERLY ELLEN, health sciences educator; b. Albany, Calif., May 20, 1937; s. Bert E. and Catherine (Doyle) H. BA, Coll. Holy Names, 1960; MS in Edn., Dominican Coll., 1969; EdD, U. So. Calif., 1978. Producer, dir. Health Scis TV U. Calif., Davis, 1966-69, coordinator Health Scis. TV, 1969-73; asst. dir. IMS U. So. Calif., Los Angeles, 1973-76, asst. dir. continuing edn., 1976-80, dir. biocommunications, 1976-80; dir. Med. Ednl. Resources Program Ind. U. Sch. Medicine, Indpls., 1980—; Presenter Cath. U. Nijmegen, Netherlands, 1980, 81, European Symposium on Clin. Pharmacy, Brussels, 1982, Barcelona, Spain, 1983. Contbr. articles to profl. jours. Pres. Indpls. Shakespeare Festival, 1982-83; mem. subcom. Ind. Film Commn., Indpls., 1984—. Recipient first place in rehab. category 4th Biannual J. Muir Med. Film Fest., 1980. Mem. Assn. Biomed. Communications (bd. dirs. 1985—), Health Scis. Com. Assn. (bd. dirs. 1976-79, First Place Video Festival, 1979), Assn. for Edn. Communications and Tech. Avocations: painting, travel, archeology, music, tennis, swimming. Home: 5259 W 59th St Indianapolis IN 46254 Office: Med Ednl Resources Program 1226 W Michigan St BR 156 Indianapolis IN 46223

HILL, CHRISTOPHER DAVID, auditor; b. Clarinda, Iowa, July 11, 1961; s. Donald David and Janet Elaine (Eilers) H.; m. Angela Crouse, Dec. 31, 1983. BS, NW Mo. State U., Maryville, 1983. CPA, Mo. Staff acct. Ernst & Whinney, Kansas City, Mo., 1983-85, sr. acct., 1985—. Fellow Life Mgmt. Inst., Life Office Mgmt. Assn., Inc., mem. Am. Inst. CPA's, Mo. Soc. CPA's. Republican. Lutheran. Avocations: golf, tennis, weight lifting. Office: Ernst & Whinney 1100 Main 2000 City Ctr Sq Kansas City MO 64105

HILL, CHRISTOPHER JOHN, data processing executive; b. Watervliet, Mich., Aug. 14, 1949; s. Leonard and Jeanne (Manby) H.; m. Sally Pugsley, Oct. 20, 1978; children: Matthew, Michael. Student, Western Mich. U., 1967; BS in Med. Tech., Mich. State U., 1971; student, U. Ariz., 1977. Mgr. Advanced Med. Research, Pontiac, Mich., 1971-72, 73; research scientist Ames Research div. Miles Labs., Elkhart, Mich., 1974-76, U. Ariz. Med. Coll., Tucson, 1977; instructional mgr. Van Buren Sch. Dist., Lawrence, Mich., 1978-81, dir. computer ops., 1978—; mem. data processing faculty Southwestern Mich. Coll., Dowagiac, Mich. Mem. Data Processing Mgmt. Assn., Lake Mich. User Group Hewlett Packard. Home: 720 Delaware Ct Lawton MI 49065 Office: Van Buren Intermediate Sch Dist 700 S Paw Paw St Lawrence MI 49064

HILL, DARYL KENT, orthodontist; b. Gary, Ind., Aug. 13, 1954; s. Raymond Guy and Evelyn Ester (Anderson) H. BA in Chemistry and Biology, Ind. U., 1976; DMD, Tufts U., 1979; MS in Orthodontics, U. Ill., Chgo., 1981. Practice dentistry specializing in orthodontics Munster, Ind., 1981—. Mem. ADA, Northwest Ind. Dental Assn. (bd. dirs. 1984—), Am. Assn. Orthodontists, Munster C. of C., Ind. U. Alumni Assn. (bd. dirs. 1984-85). Avocations: flying, scuba diving, sky diving, skiing, water skiing. Home: 145 Shorewood Dr Valparaiso IN 46383 Office: 8231 Calumet Ave Munster IN 46321

HILL, DAVID WILLIAM, design company executive; b. Youngstown, Ohio, Mar. 1, 1949; s. Eugene David and Eleanore Ruth (Welsh) H.; m. Penny M. Simon, Dec. 31, 1983 (div. Sept. 1986). Cert., USAF Sch. Acctg. and Fin., 1969. Cert. credit and fin. analyst Dun and Bradstreet. Office mgr. Oxford (Ohio) Auto Parts, 1971-72; sec. Mobile Enterprises, Inc., Ft. Wayne, Ind., 1973-78; owner, pres. Hill Ins. Agy., Ft. Wayne, 1978-82; v.p. Royal Oak Fin. Services, Inc., Ft. Wayne, 1983-84; exec. v.p. MidAm. Design Services, Inc., Ft. Wayne, 1984—, also bd. dirs.; bd. dirs. Miltec Engring. and Mfg. Co., Inc., Ft. Wayne, Blankenship Acquisition, Inc., Ft. Wayne; v.p., bd. dirs. Typhoid Larry O'Leary's, Ft. Wayne, 1985—. Dep. registrar Bd. Election, Ft. Wayne, 1973-76; Dem. precinct committeeman, Ft. Wayne, 1973-76, asst. precinct committeeman, Youngstown, 1963-70. Served with USAF, 1969-70. Mem. Ind. Assn. Convenience Stores, Ft. Wayne C. of C., Am. Legion, Ft. Wayne Women's Golf Assn. (main speaker 1984, Golf Digest Field Adv. Network 1987—). Lutheran. Club: Minot (N.D.) Mut. Investment (pres. 1969-70), Wayne Elks Country (bd. govs. 1981-85). Lodge: Elks (exalted ruler 1984-85). Home: 4931 Pinebrook Dr Fort Wayne IN 46804 Office: MidAm Design Service Inc 10206 Lima Rd Fort Wayne IN 46818

HILL, DELMAS CARL, retired sr. judge; b. Wamego, Kans., Oct. 9, 1906; s. Ray G. and Elfie E. (Smith) H.; m. Katherine V. Hooven, July 29, 1933 (dec. Jan. 1978); m. Wilma B. Jennings, Mar. 4, 1981. LL.B., Washburn Coll., 1929; LL.D., 1958. Bar: Kan. bar 1929. Practiced in Wamego, 1929-43, 46-49; county atty. Pottawatomie County, Kans., 1931-34; asst. U.S. atty., Dist. Kans., 1934-36; gen. counsel Kans. State Tax Commn., 1937-39; chmn. Democratic State Com., 1946-48; U.S. dist. judge 1949-61, U.S. circuit judge, 10th circuit, 1961-77, sr. judge, 1977—. Served with AUS, 1943-46; prosecution staff in trial of Gen. Yamashita 1945, Manila, P.I. Episcopalian. Home: 5051 E Lincoln Wichita KS 67218

HILL, DONAL DEAN, osteopathic physician; b. Fairfield, Iowa, Aug. 16, 1953; s. Gerald R. and Nada Lavelle (Hanna) H.; m. Mary Mieko Williams, Apr. 9, 1977; children: Heather Ellen, Holly Marie, B.S. cum laude, Iowa Wesleyan Coll., 1976; D.O. with honors, U. Osteo. Medicine and Health Scis., Des Moines, 1979. Intern, Des Moines Gen. Hosp., 1979-80; ptnr. Med. Arts Clinic, Fairfield, Iowa, 1980—; mem. staff U. Osteo. Medicine and Health Scis., Des Moines, 1981-82; vice chmn. staff Jefferson County Hosp., 1983, chief of med. staff, 1984; mem. Pub. Health Adv. Bd. Mem. fin. comm., deacon 1st Bapt. Ch. Recipient Outstanding Freshman award Iowa Wesleyan Coll., 1977; Charles Reed award U. Osteo. Medicine and Health Scis., 1979. Mem. Iowa Med. Soc., Iowa Osteo. Med. Soc., Am. Osteo. Assn., Osteo. Nat. Alumni Assn., Iowa Acad. Osteopathy, Jefferson County Med. Soc. (chmn. 1984), S.E. Iowa Osteo. Med. Soc. (pres. 1982-84), Iota Phi (hon.), Beta Beta Beta Soc. Republican. Clubs: Rotary Golf, Country (Fairfield). Home: 401 Heatherwood Circle Fairfield IA 52556 Office: Medical Arts Clinic 408 S Maple Fairfield IA 52556

HILL, FAY GISH, librarian; b. Resnnelaer, Ind., Sept. 19, 1944; d. Roy Charles and Vergie (Powell) Gish; m. John Christian Hill, May 20, 1967; 1 child, Christina Gish. BA, Purdue U., 1967; MLS, U. Tex., 1971. Asst. librarian basic reference dept. Tex. A&M U., Coll. Station, 1972, assoc. librarian sci. ref. dept., 1972-74, acting head librarian sci. reference dept., 1975; reference librarian Cen. Iowa Regional Library, Des Moines, 1984—. Troop leader Girl Scouts U.S., Ames, Iowa, 1983—; bd. dirs. Friends of Foreign Wives, Ames, 1982-86. Mem. Am. Library Assn. Presbyterian. Avocation: collecting antiques. Home: Rural Rt 4 Squaw Valley Ames IA 50010 Office: Cen Iowa Regional Library Reference 515 Douglas Ave Ames IA 50010

HILL, GARY, social services company executive. s. Leo and Betty H.; m. Cece Hill. BS, U. Nebr. Pres. Contact Ctr., Inc.; chmn. bd. dirs. Northwest Metal Co.; speaker major univs., the FBI Acad., the Nat. Tng., Nat. Inst. Corrections, bus. mgmt. seminars, library assns.; cons. Pres. Task Force, UN, various fed., state and local agencies. Bd. dirs. more than 50 civic orgns.; chmn. UN Nongovt. Orgns. Alliance on Crime Prevention and Criminal Justice; mem. nat. campaign cabinet United Jewish Appeal Served with U.S. Army, 1961-63. Recipient over 200 local, state, nat. and internat. awards; named One of Am.'s 10 Most Outstanding Young Men. Lodge: Elks. Subject of Dec. 1986 Reader's Digest story. Avocations: cross-country motorcycle riding, ultramarathons, triathalons. Office: Contact Ctr Inc PO Box 81826 Lincoln NE 68501

HILL, GARY RAY, savings and loan executive; b. Ames, Iowa, Apr. 5, 1947; s. Arthur B. Hill and Ethel (Lemens) Harris; m. Phyllis Lohr, May 29, 1970; children: Deborah, Rebecca. BS in Acctg. magna cum laude, Mankato State U., 1975, MBA, 1978. CPA, Iowa. Customer service rep. 3M Co., Mpls., 1969-73; staff acct. Peterson & Co., Mankato, Minn., 1975-79; sr. internal auditor Gen. Telephone of Midwest, Grinnell, Iowa, 1979-81; v.p., treas. Mid-Iowa Savs. and Loan, Newton, Iowa, 1981—, also bd. dirs. Com. chmn. United Way, Newton, 1986; adv. dir. Salvation Army, Newton, 1982—; council mem., treas. 1st Luth. Ch., Newton, 1983—. Served with USAF, 1965-69. Mem. Am. Inst. CPA's, Iowa Soc. CPA's, Iowa Fin. Mgrs. Soc. (exec. com. 1983—, pres. 1986-87, bd. dirs. 9th dist. 1987—). Lodge: Kiwanis (bd. dirs. Newton club 1983-85). Avocations: gardening, fishing, basketball. Home: 1526 S 15th Ave W Newton IA 50208 Office: Mid Iowa Savs & Loan PO Box 687 Newton IA 50208

HILL, HOWARD EUGENE, accountant; b. Chgo., July 4, 1958; s. Thelma (Hill) King. BS in Accountancy and Fin., No. Ill. U., 1980. CPA, Ill.; lic. ins. agt., Ill. Staff acct. U.S. Gypsum Co., Chgo., 1980-82; auditor McDonald's Corp., Oak Brook, Ill., 1982-84, acctg. supr., 1984-85; ptnr. Bolling & Hill CPA's, Chgo., 1985—. Author Bolling & Hill Quarterly Report, 1986-87. Mem. Am. Inst. CPA's, Ill. CPA Soc., Nat. Assn. Black Accts. (v.p. 1985-86), New Chgo. Com., No. Ill. U. Black Alumnus Assn. (chmn. 1987), Nat. Assn. Securities Dealers. Avocations: reading, politics, tennis, softball, travel. Home: 11014 S Edbrooke Chicago IL 60628 Office: 8527 S Stony Island Chicago IL 60617

HILL, JAMES, JR., accountant; b. Balt., Aug. 20, 1941; s. James Hill; m. Carole Jones, Feb. 19, 1972; children: James III, Brian. BS, Cen. State U., Wilberforce, Ohio, 1964; MBA, U. Chgo., 1967. CPA, Ill. Cost acct. Union Carbide, Niagara Falls, N.Y., 1964-65; staff auditor Alexander Grant, Chgo., 1967-69; dep. dir. Chgo. Econ. Devel. Corp., Chgo., 1969-70; mng. ptnr. Hill, Taylor & Co., Chgo., 1972—. Named one of Chgo.'s Ten Outstanding Young People, 1976; recipient Bus. Adminstrn. Alumni award Cen. State U., 1978, Little Gold Oilcan award Chgo. Bus. Opportunities Fair, 1969. Mem. Ill. CPA Soc. (bd. dirs. 1983-86), Am. Inst. CPA's (com. 1976—), State Accountancy of Ill. (bd. dirs. 1980—), Chgo. Commons Assn. (bd. dirs.). Club: Economic (Chgo.). Lodge: Rotary. Office: Hill Taylor & Co 116 S Michigan Ave Chicago IL 60603

HILL, JAMES ALLEN, orthopaedic surgeon; b. Chgo., Sept. 14, 1949; s. James Allen and Doretha (Lowe) H.; m. Sandra Denise Small, Oct. 18, 1969; children: Janine, Melanie, Ryan. BA, Northwestern U., 1967-71, MD, 1974. Diplomate Am. Bd. Orthopaedic Surgery. Intern Evanston (Ill.) Hosp., 1974; resident in orthopaedic surgery Northwestern U., Chgo., 1975-79; fellow in sports medicine Nat. Athletic Inst. Health, Inglewood, Calif., 1979-80; from instr. to assoc. prof. orthopaedic surgery Northwestern U., Chgo., 1980-84, asst. prof., co-dir. sports medicine, 1980—, admissions com., 1982—, chmn. implemetation com. Motion Analysis Lab., 1982—; team physician Chgo. Hustle, 1980-81, Nat. Sports Festival IV, Baton Rouge, La., 1985; cons. Chgo. Cubs, 1981-83, NFL, 1982—; vol. physician U.S. Olympic Team, 1984; crew chief drug control program, U.S. Olympic Festival, Houston, Tex., 1986; mem. staff Northwestern Meml. Hosp., Cook County (Ill.) Hosp., VA Lakeside Med. Ctr., Children's Meml. Hosp., Rehab. Inst. Chgo. Mem. publs.-editorial bd., Sports Medicine Digest, 1984—; contbr. articles to profl. jours. Mem. pres. adv. council Kennedy-King Coll., 1981; bd. dirs. Martin Luther King Boys Club, 1980—, Comprehensive Research and Devel., 1978—, Health-er-cize, 1984—. Served to maj. USAR. Recipient Zimmer Research award Orthopaedic Research and Edn. Found., 1983; Berg-Sloat Traveling fellow Orthopaedic Research and Edn. Found., 1980; A.B.C. Traveling fellow Am. Orthopaedic Assn., 1985; grantee NIH, 1983, Orthopaedic Research and End. Found., 1984. Fellow Am. Coll. Sports Medincine; Am. Acad. Orthopaedic Surgeons (com. sports medicine), ACS, AMA, Am. Med. Joggers Assn., Am. Med. Soccer Assn., Am. Orthopaedic Soc. Sports Medicine, Am. Shoulder and Elbow Surgeons, Arthroscopy Assn. N.Am., Chgo. Med. Soc., Chgo. Com. on Trauma, Chgo. Orthopaedic Soc., Chgo. Area Runners Assn. (med. com.), Cook County Physician's Assn., Ill. Orthopaedic Soc. (membership com. 1985—), Ill. Med. Soc. (sports medicine com. 1983—), Chgo. Inst. Medicine, Internat. Arthroscopy Assn., Internat. Soc. Biomechanics in Sports, J. Robert Gladden Orthopaedic Soc., Nat. Med. Assn., Orthopaedic Research Soc., Orthopaedics Overseas, Inc., Robert K. Kerlan Fellowship Soc., Herodicus Soc., Midwest Bio-Laser Inst. Baptist. Avocations: running, reading. Office: Northwestern U Dept Orthopaedics 845 N Michigan Ave Suite 922E Chicago IL 60611

HILL, JAMES CARTER, steel company executive; b. East Orange, N.J., Nov. 4, 1947; s. Otto Herman Jr. and Ruth Elizabeth (Stark) H.; m. Ann Beal Johnson, June 21, 1969; children: Heather Elizabeth, Ryan James. BS, Lehigh U., 1969; MS, Northwestern U., 1973. Metallurgist Inland Steel Co., East Chgo., 1969-75; quality control mgr. MST div. Quanex, St. Lyon, Mich., 1975-80, ops. supt. MST div., 1980; plant mgr. ATD div. Quanex, South Plainfield, N.J., 1980-82, gen. mgr. ATD div., 1982-83; group pres. Quanex Tube Group, Livonia, Mich., 1983—. Republican. Methodist. Avocations: tennis, travel, bridge, family, reading. Office: Quanex Tube Group 17177 N Laurel Park Dr Livonia MI 48152

HILL, JAMES HOWARD, physician; b. Howell, Mich., June 10, 1947; s. Harold Charles and Lavina Blanche (Sears) H.; m. Cynthia Jane Nelson, June 25, 1971; children: Lander Roan, Peter Anders, Anne Elizabeth, Brigitta Christiane, Andrew Nicholas. BS, U. Mich., 1969, MD, 1974, MS, 1979. Diplomate Am. Bd. Otolaryngology. Resident in surgery The Meml. Hosp., Worcester, Mass., 1974-75; resident in otorhinolaryngology U. Mich. Med. Ctr., Ann Arbor, 1975-79; dir. sect. head and neck cancer, dept. Otolaryngology, Eye and Ear Infirmary U. Ill. Coll. Medicine, Chgo., 1982—; Bd. dirs Midwest Bio-Laser Inst., Chgo., 1985—. Contbr. articles to profl. jours., chpts. to books. Served to maj. U.S. Army, 1979-82. Fellow ACS, Am. Acad. Otolaryngology; mem. Soc. Univ. Otolaryngologists, Am. Acad. Facial Plastic and Reconstructive Surgery. Home: 120 E George St #500 Bensenville IL 60106 Office: U Ill Dept Otolaryngology Head and Neck Surgery 1855 W Taylor St Suite 242 Chicago IL 60612

HILL, JOHN HEMMINGSON, virologist, plant pathologist; b. Evanston, Ill., Feb. 19, 1941; S. Robert Kermit and Adelaide (Nyden) H.; m. Laani May Fong, Aug. 5, 1967; children: Brent, Bryce, Bjork. BA, Carleton Coll., 1963; MS, U. Minn., St. Paul, 1966; PhD, U. Calif., Davis, 1971. Asst. prof. Iowa State U., Ames, 1972-78, assoc. prof., 1978-82, prof., 1982—. Asst. scoutmaster Boy Scouts Am., Ames, 1982—; session mem. Collegiate Presbyn. Ch., Ames, 1987. Mem. Am. Soc. Virology (Am. type culture collection exec. com. 1986—), Am. Phytopathological Soc., Sigma Xi, Gamma Sigma Delta. Avocations: railroading, skiing. Home: 2800 Duff Ames IA 50010 Office: Iowa State U Dept Plant Pathology 403 Bessey Hall Ames IA 50011

HILL, JOHN NAPIER, graphic designer, advertising executive; b. Lanark, Scotland, Jan. 25, 1933; came to U.S., 1950; s. Robert Hill and Margaret (McIlroy) Teeling; m. Monica Misset, Apr. 3, 1965; children: John N., Stephen M., Alison M. BA, Art Inst. Chgo., 1962. Art dir. Burton Browne Advt., Chgo., 1964-66, Elias Schaeffer, Chgo., 1966-68; owner, mgr. John Hill Design, Chgo., 1968-70; v.p. Seery Hill Assocs., Oak Brook, Ill., 1970-75; pres. John Hill Assocs., Oak Brook, 1975—. Served to cpl. U.S. Army, 1953-55, Korea. Mem. Road Am. (bd. dirs. 1980—). Roman Catholic. Avocations: road racing, photography, traveling. Office: John Hill Assocs 210 W 22d St Suite 112 Oak Brook IL 60521

HILL, JOHN STEVEN, accountant; b. Clarion, Iowa, Jan. 20, 1957; s. Alva Dale and Anne (Cerny) H.; m. Kristin Lisa Reis, Nov. 18, 1978; children: J. Stanton, Jacob Reis. BS in Indsl. Adminstrn. and Econs., Iowa State U., 1979. CPA, Iowa. Sr. audit mgr. Peat Marwick Main and Co., Des Moines, 1979—. Chmn. panel United Way Cen. Iowa, Des Moines, 1986—, bd. dirs., 1987—. Mem. Am. Inst. CPA's, Ind. Soc. CPA's, Nat. Assn. Accts. (dir. spl. activities 1985, dir. mem. acquisition 1986, bd. dirs. 1987—). Republican. Methodist. Avocations: golf, running. Home: 8903 Urbandale Ave Urbandale IA 50322 Office: Peat Marwick Main Co 2500 Ruan Center Des Moines IA 50309

HILL, JONAS LEE, SR., social services administrator, educator; b. Highland Park, Mich., Dec. 7, 1947; s. Willie James Hill and Mary Ann (Morris) Hill-Long; m. Sandra Jean Huff-Hill, Jan. 29, 1968; children: Shirelle L., Asanti T., Jonas L. Jr. BS, Mercy Coll., Detroit, 1982; MA, Wayne (Mich.) State U., 1985. Clk. Mich. Dept. Correction, Detroit, 1979-82; employment coordinator Wayne County Probation Dept., Detroit, 1979-83; juvenile counselor Wayne County Youth Home, 1982—; social worker St. Francis Homefor Boys, Detroit, 1983—, dir. social services, 1985—; therapist, clinician U.S. Dept. Mental Health, Allen Park, Mich., 1985. Served with U.S. Army, 1968-69, Vietnam. Fellow Mich. Correction Assn.; mem. Am Assn. Counseling Devel., Child Welfare League Am., Nat. Assn. Social Workers. Democrat. Baptist. Club: Profl. Men's. Lodge: Optimists. Avocations: bowling, photography, racquetball, tennis, record collecting. Office: St Francis Home for Boys 2701 Fenkell Ave Detroit MI 48238

HILL, KENNETH DOUGLAS, food service executive; b. Owosso, Mich., Feb. 8, 1934; s. Douglas and Margaret Elizabeth H.; m. Elizabeth Jane Kunderer, Nov. 26, 1960; 1 son, Michael Scott. BA, Mich. State U., 1952-56. Asst. mgr. Golden Ox Restaurant, Kansas City, Mo., 1956-58; mgmt. trainee John R. Thompson Co., Skokie, Ill., 1958-59; asst. mgr. Holiday Inn Chain, Wichita Falls, Tex., 1959-60; gen. mgr. Cheshire Inn & Lodge, St. Louis, 1960-66; pres. Gilbert-Robinson Inc., Kansas City, Mo., 1967-85; pres., chief exec. officer Signature Foods Inc., Kansas City, 1985—. Recipient Nat. Spirit of Life award City of Hope, 1982. Mem. Nat. Restaurant Assn. (bd. dirs.), Mo. Restaurant Assn. (bd. dirs., past pres. Kansas City chpt.), Young Pres. Orgn. Republican. Congregationalist. Avocations: boating, water sports, snow skiing. Home: 1232 W 63d St Kansas City MO 64113 Office: Signature Foods Inc 800 W 47th St Suite 555 Kansas City MO 64113

HILL, LLOYD LESTER, JR., health care executive; b. Nacagdoches, Tex., Jan. 8, 1944; s. Lloyd Lester and Ruby (Murchison) H.; m. Carol Ann London, Dec. 20, 1964; children—Ronald Lloyd, Brandt Lloyd; m. Sueann Staggs, June 25, 1978; 1 son, Joshua Lloyd. Student psychology N. Tex. State U., 1962-65; student U. Tex., 1965-67, Columbia U., 1980—; M.B.A., Rockhurst Coll., 1985. Dist. sales mgr. Marion Health and Safety div. Marion Labs., Dallas and Los Angeles, 1969-74, regional sales mgr., Chgo., 1974-76, mgr. new bus. devel., Kansas City, 1976-77, dir. sales, 1977-79; regional mgr. Norton SPD, Cranston, R.I., 1979-80; sr. v.p. Kimberly Services Inc., Kansas City, Kans., 1980—, dir., 1982—; cons. Carlton Mgmt. Inc., Kansas City, Mo., 1981—. Vice pres. adminstrn., organizer Santa Fe Blazers Swim Team, Overland Park, Kans., 1976-78. Mem. Home Health Supplemental Staffing Assn. Republican. Methodist. Office: Kimberly Services Inc 2500 W 110th Overland Park KS 66210

HILL, MARK RICHARD, controller; b. Streator, Ill., Apr. 29, 1952; s. Richard Earl and Marilyn Jean (Thompson) H.; m. Patricia Jeanne Eisenach, May 25, 1974; children: Mark Richard Jr., Elizabeth Anne. BS, Fla. State U., 1976; MBA, Winthrop Coll., 1983. CPA, Fla. Sr. auditor Peat, Marwick, Mitchell and Co., Jacksonville, Fla., 1976-78; internal audit mgr. Dominion Bankshares Corp., Roanoke, Va., 1978-81; v.p. First Union Comml. Corp., Charlotte, N.C., 1981-84; comptroller First Nat. Bank Cin., 1984-85; controller Household Internat. Bank, Prospect Heights, Ill., 1985—. Served with USN, 1971-74. Mem. Am. Inst. CPA's, Fin. Mgrs. Soc. Republican. Avocations: sailing, scuba diving. Home: 622 Valley Ln Palatine IL 60067 Office: Household Internat 2700 Sanders Rd Prospect Heights IL 60070

HILL, NED CROMAR, finance educator, consultant; b. Salt Lake City, Dec. 18, 1945; s. Richard G. Sharp and Bettie (Cromar) Hill; m. Claralyn Martin, Nov. 26, 1968; children: Evan M., Jonathan C., Aaron R., Joseph B., Alison. Student, Brigham Young U., 1967; BS, U. Utah, 1969; MS, Cornell U., Ithaca, N.Y., 1971; PhD, Cornell U., 1976. Cert. cash mgr. Asst. prof. fin. Cornell U., 1976-77; asst. prof. fin. Ind. U., Bloomington, 1977-81, assoc. prof. fin., 1981—; cons. Hill Fin. Assocs., Bloomington, 1978—. Author: Essentials in Cash Management, 1984, Short-Term Financial Management, 1987; co-founder Jour. Cash Mgmt., 1981. Stake pres. Ch. Jesus Christ of the Latter Day Saints, 1982—; fin. v.p. Boy Scouts Hoosier Trails Council, Bloomington, 1980-86. Served with U.S. Army, 1971-72. Mem. Nat. Corp. Cash Mgmt., Fin. Mgmt. Assn. (bd. dirs. 1986—), Phi Beta Kappa, Phi Kappa Phi. Republican. Avocations: vocal music, canoeing, camping, photography. Office: Ind U Sch Bus Dept Fin Bloomington IN 47405

HILL, NELSON DAVID, publishing executive, lay minister; b. Steamboat Springs, Colo., Sept. 23, 1949; s. Nelson Hawkins and Virginia Bertha (Tillett) H.; m. Pamela Marie Paul, June 13, 1970; children: Jaclyn Nicole, Ryan Garth. BA, Grand Valley State Coll., 1973. Advt. asst. Moody Press, Chgo., 1968-70; advt. asst. Zondervan Corp., Grand Rapids, Mich., 1970-73, prodn. mgr., 1973-76, dept. mgr., 1977-84, gen. mgr. direct mktg., 1985—. Contbr. articles to mags. Treas. Kent County Rep. Com., Grand Rapids, 1973-75; chmn. gubernatorial campaign, Grand Rapids, 1974. Mem. Direct Mktg. Assn., Christian Booksellers Assn. Mem. Evang. Covenant Ch. Home: 4580 Restmor Grandville MI 49418 Office: Zondervan Corp 1415 Lake Dr SE Grand Rapids MI 49506

HILL, PAMELA JEAN, pharmacist; b. Indpls., Nov. 4, 1958; d. Cecil Johnnie and Marguerite Alice (Budrech) H. BS, Butler U., 1982; postgrad in Pub. Health, 1983—. Lic. pharmacist, Ind. Staff pharmacist Ind. U. Hosps., Indpls., 1983-85; resident, 1983; dir. pharmacy services Care Mark Home Health Care of Am., Indpls., 1985-86; pharmacist, cons. PH Cons. 1986—; nutrition cons. Care Mark Home Health Care of Am., 1985-86. Author: Nutritional Handbook Indiana University Hospitals, 1985; (with others) Help! I'm Parenting My Parent, 1987; producer videotape series, Corinthian Pharmacy; contbr. articles to profl. jours. Sec. music com. Southport Presbyn. Ch., Ind., 1985—. Mem. Am. Soc. Parenteral/Enteral Nutrition, Am. Soc. Hosp. Pharmacists, Ind. Pharmacists Assn., Ind. Soc. Hosp. Pharmacists, Ind. Soc. Parenteral/Enteral Nutrition, Nat. Assn. Female Execs. Butler U. Band Alumni Assn. (pres. 1985—). Republican. Presbyterian. Avocations: flute playing, theater, needlework, art. Office: PH Cons 7547 Cynthia Dr Indianapolis IN 46227

HILL, PATRICIA JO, media specialist, educator; b. Muncie, Ind., Oct. 28, 1944; d. Frederic Burnside and Elizabeth Becom (Zaring) Harbottle; m. Charles Francis Hill; 1 son, Thomas Frederic. B.S., Ball State U., 1964, M.A., 1978, Ed.S., 1981. Instr., head immunology dept. Ball Meml. Hosp., Muncie, Ind., 1963-74; tchr. emotionally disturbed Indpls. Pub. Schs., 1974-75, lead tchr. severe/profound mentally retarded, 1979-84, tchr. moderately mentally handicapped, 1986—; media specialist in spl. edn., 1984-86; cons. Prescription Learning Corp., 1975-76. Dir. pub. edn. Am. Cancer Soc., Lawrence Twp., Indpls.; Ind. vol. rep. Fed. Transp. and Archtl. Barriers Bd.; participant 21st Leadership Series between C. of C. and Inpls. Pub. Schs. NSF grantee, 1961; Shroyer scholar Mchts. Nat. Bank Muncie, 1972; Indpls. Pub. Schs. scholar, 1981. Mem. Council Vols. and Orgns. for Handicapped, Assn. Behavioral Analysts, Council Exceptional Children (tech. and media div.), Assn. Supervision and Curriculum Devel., Indpls. Edn. Assn. (bargaining team). Methodist. Home: 7330 Scarborough Blvd E Indianapolis IN 46256 Office: 3650 Cold Spring Rd Indianapolis IN 46222

HILL, PENNY GARRISON, computer analyst, systems programmer; b. Phila., Sept. 2, 1944; d. Edward William and Anne Tanguay (Flick) Garrison; m. Ralph Julian Hill Jr., Aug. 31, 1968 (div. Jan. 1974); 1 child, Christopher Townsend. BA in Math., Psychology, U. Del., 1966. Computer programmer, analyst N.C. State U., Raleigh, 1966-68, Vitro Labs., Wheaton, Md., 1968-69; instr. programming tech. Control Data Inst., Arlington, Va., 1969-70; sr. programmer-analyst Fairfax (Va.) Hosp., 1970-74; sr. application analyst, systems engr. Dimension Inc., Reston, Va., 1974-75; sr. cons. Cincom Systems, Cin., 1975-76, 77-80; sr. systems cons. Genasys Systems Inc., Rockville, Md., 1976-77; sr. software engr. MicroPro Internat., San Rafael, Calif., 1980-81; pvt. practice computer cons. Bonner Springs, Kans., 1981-83; mgmt. info. systems tech. services analyst Hallmark Cards Inc., Kansas City, Mo., 1984—. Vol. Mid Am. Hospice, Kansas City, 1984—. Mem. Am. Assn. Artificial Intelligence. Office: Hallmark Cards Inc 2501 McGee MD 352 Kansas City MO 64141-6580

HILL, ROBERT ARLEN, architect; b. Denver, Apr. 29, 1937; s. Wilfred Garland and Blanche Ann (Barada) H.; m. Gigi Lauridson, Dec. 21, 1968; children—Karen, Jeffrey. B.Arch., Iowa State U., 1961. Cert. architect, Nebr. Project architect Leo A. Daly Co., Omaha, 1961-68; v.p. Hellmuth Obata & Kassabaum, St. Louis, 1968—. Vice chmn., sec. Brentwood Planning and Zoning Bd., 1978—. Served to cpl. Army N.G., 1961-65. Mem. AIA, Phi Kappa Psi. Republican. Mem. United Ch. of Christ. Lodge: Lions. Home: 1931 Parkridge St Brentwood MO 63144 Office: 100 N Broadway St Saint Louis MO 63102

HILL, ROBERT CRAIG, dentist; b. Oklahoma City, Okla., Feb. 12, 1940; s. Earl Chester and Frieda Lucile (Craig) H.; m. Karen Kay Brunner, June 12, 1965; children: Craig Mitchell, Jason Ronald. BS, Okla. State U., 1962; DDS, U. Mo., Kansas City, 1966. General practice dentistry North Kansas City, Mo., 1966—. Mem. Northland Community Choir, Kansas City, Mo., 1980—. Mem. Mo. Dental Assn., ADA, Greater Kansas City Dental Soc., Clay-Platte Study Club, Northland Men's Garden Club (charter). Avocations: gardening, philately, fishing, reading. Home: 20 NW 43 Terr Kansas City MO 64116 Office: 2180 Swift Ave North Kansas City MO 64116

HILL, ROBERT JOHN, corporate and charter services chief pilot; b. Unity, Ohio, June 29, 1932; s. Harry H. and Alice Jo (Blair) H.; m. Eve Marie Duke, Feb. 16, 1957; children: Kathleen, Randall, Scott. BBA, Youngstown State U., 1960; postgrad. in aviation tech., U. Miami, 1963; postgrad. in aviation, Flight Safety Inst., 1973-86. Cert. various instr. and transp. ratings, FAA. Pilot Beckett Aviation, Youngstown and Cleve., Ohio, 1967-77; ops. inspector FAA, Indpls., 1977-78; pilot Republic Steel, Cleve., 1979-82; pres. R.J. Hill, Inc., Strongsville, Ohio, 1983—; chief pilot Flight Ops., Inc., Cleve., 1984—; cons. Savors Aviation, Negley, Ohio, 1968-71, Brunswick (Ohio) Aviation, 1985-86. Asst. leader Boy Scouts Am., North Lima, Ohio, 1968-71; advisor Youth Riding Club, Strongsville, 1974-76; coleader Teen Aviation Group, Columbiana, Ohio, 1984. Served with USN, 1950-54, Korea. Mem. Nat. Bus. Aircraft Assn. (assoc.), Exptl. Aircraft Assn. (v.p. 1983—), Quiet Birdmen, DAV. Methodist. Avocations: aircraft restoration, golf. Home: 16554 Whitney Rd Strongsville OH 44136 Office: Flight Ops Inc 6200 Riverside Dr Cleveland OH 44135

HILL, ROBERT WAYNE, utility executive; b. Richmond, Ind., July 10, 1927; s. H. Wayne and Kathryn G. (Weimer) H.; m. Bonnie J. Dishman, June 22, 1948; children: Robert W., Susan Jane Hill deArmendi. B.S.E.E., Purdue U., 1951. Registered profl. engr., Ind. Engr. in charge elec. distn. Indpls. Power & Light Co., 1970-73, asst. v.p. engring. and constrn., 1973-77, v.p. transp. and distbn., 1977-79, sr. v.p. ops., 1979-80, exec. v.p., 1980-81, pres., chief operating officer dir., 1981—; bd. dirs. Indpls. Econ. Devel. Corp.; bd. trustees N.Am. Electric Reliability Council.; adv. council Rogers Group, Inc. Mem. exec. bd. East Central Area Reliability Agreement, Canton, Ohio; dir. Ind. Electric Assn.; bd. dirs. Greater Indpls. Progress Com., United Way Cen. Ind. . Served with USN, 1945-46. Mem. IEEE, Indpls. C. of C., Am. Mgmt. Assn. (pres.'s assn.), Eta Kappa Nu. Clubs: Crooked Stick Golf, Columbia, Indpls. Athletic, Skyline, Greenfield Elks. Office: Indpls Power & Light Co 25 Monument Circle Indianapolis IN 46206 *

HILL, ROBYN LESLEY, artist, designer; b. Sydney, Australia, Apr. 28, 1942; d. Frank Bragg and Florence Margorie (Turnham) H. Grad., Nat. Art Sch., Sydney, 1962; studies with Edward Betts, Claude Croney, Fred Leach, Maxine Masterfield, 1969-85. Art mistress S.C.E.G.G.S., Sydney, 1963-66; art dir. Am. Greetings, Cleve., 1967-78; sr. program dir. Those Characters From Cleve., 1978-87. Creative, designer (TV program) The Special Magic of Herself the Elf (Can. Emmy award 1982). Mem. Nat. Watercolor Soc. (signature), Nat. Watercolor USA Hon. Soc. (award Springfield Art Mus. 1984), Ohio Watercolor Soc. (So. Ohio Bank award 1983), North Coast Collage Soc., Ky. Watercolor Soc. Episcopalian. Home: 27000 Lakeshore Blvd Euclid OH 44132 Office: Those Characters from Cleve 8800 E Pleasant Valley Rd Cleveland OH 44131

HILL, W. CLAYTON, management consultant; b. New Hampton, Mo., Sept. 24, 1916; s. Charles A. and Elva E. (Riggins) H.; B.S. in Bus. Adminstrn., U. Mo., 1937; m. Dorothy L. Crosby, Aug. 24, 1938; children—Charles W., Douglas L. Acct., Gen. Elec. Co., Bridgeport, Conn., 1937-41; sales mgmt. IBM Corp., 1941-50; asst. to pres. Gen. Elec. X-Ray Corp., Milw., 1950-53; v.p. Hotpoint Co. div. Gen. Elec. Co., Chgo., 1953-57; cons., mgr. planning Gen. Elec. Co., N.Y.C., 1957-62; dir. planning Am. Can Co., 1962-64; mgmt. cons. C. Hill Assocs., Greenwich, Conn., 1964-80, Prairie Village, Kans., 1980—; instr. Marquette U., 1950-53; cons. RCA Corp., Sperry Co., Ford Motor Co., Pet, Inc., Gen. Elec. Co., Monsanto Co., H&R Block, Inc., Farmland Industries, Inc., United Telecommunications, Inc., others. V.p. Somerset Manor; mem. adv. council Bus. Sch., U.Mo., City of Prairie Village. Served with Signal Corps, AUS, 1943-46. Decorated Army Commendation Medal. Mem. Am. Mktg. Assn., Nat. Assn. Accts., Sales Exec. Club N.Y.C., U. Mo.-Kansas City Bus. Sch. Alumni Assn. (pres.), U. Mo. Columbia Alumni Assn. Office: 8713 Catalina Dr Prairie Village KS 66207

HILL, WINFRED FARRINGTON, psychology educator; b. Chelsea, Mass., May 23, 1929; s. Roy Wesley and Lura Lois (Cole) H.; m. Libby May Kaplan, June 14, 1957; children—Alison Renee, Linda Suzanne. A.B., Yale U., 1950; M.A., Northwestern U., 1951; Ph.D., Stanford U., 1954. Instr. psychology Harvard U., 1956-57; from asst. prof. to prof. Northwestern U., Evanston, Ill., 1957—; research cons. Downey (Ill.) VA Hosp., 1963-70. Author: Learning: A Survey of Psychological Interpretations, 1963, 4th edit., 1985, Psychology, Principles and Problems, 1970, Principles of Learning: A Handbook of Applications, 1981. Served with AUS, 1954-56. Research grantee NSF, 1958-64; research grantee Nat. Inst. Mental Health, 1965-68; Center Advanced Studies Behavioral Scis. fellow, 1966-67. Fellow Am. Psychol. Assn., AAAS; mem. Midwestern Psychol. Assn. (sec.-treas. 1970-73, pres. 1974-75, conv. mgr. 1986—), AAUP, Psychonomic Soc., Sigma Xi. Home: 2715 Woodland Rd Evanston IL 60201

HILLE, MICHAEL JOHN, library director; b. Shawano, Wis., Dec. 23, 1943; s. Arthur Fred and Ruth Roselyn (Redmann) H.; m. Marilyn Lou Mueller, Sept. 18, 1976; children—Jason, Lisamarie. B.S., U. Wis.-Oshkosh, 1965; M.S., U. Milw., 1971. Head librarian West Milw. High Sch., 1965-73, Nathan Hale High Sch., West Allis, Wis., 1973-74; dir. Shawano City-County Library, Wis., 1974—; adv. com. Nicolet Library System. Bd. dirs. Shawano County Hist. Soc., 1975—. Mem. Wis. Library Assn., Wis. Audio-Visual Circuit (bd. dirs. 1983—). Republican. Lutheran. Lodge: Rotary. Avocations: tennis, reading, painting, basketball, gardening. Home: Route 1 Pine Rd Cecil WI 54111 Office: Shawano City-County Library 128 S Sawyer St Shawano WI 54166

HILLENBRAND, CHARLES REYNOLD, psychiatrist, educator; b. Chgo., Nov. 11, 1943; s. Charles John and Wilma Grace (Dowthitt) H.; m. Stephanie Jean Zayachek, June 27, 1970; children: Stephanie Anne, Sarah Heather, Jonathan Frederick. BS in Biology, Loyola U., Chgo., 1965; MD, Loyola U., Maywood, Ill., 1969. Diplomate Nat. Bd. Med. Examiners, Am. Bd. Psychology and Neurology. Intern Milw. County Gen. Hosp., 1970; resident in psychiatry Loyola U. Hosp., Maywood, 1973; dir. cons. psychiatry Loyola U., Maywood, 1975-76; pvt. practice psychiatry Elk Grove, Ill., 1975—; clin. assoc. prof. psychiatry Loyola U., Maywood, 1982—; Cons. psychiatrist Presdl. Amnesty, Ft. Harrison, Ind., 1974-75, Elk Grove Police Dept., 1976—, Mercy Med. Ctr., Aurora, Ill., 1978—; attending psychiatrist Loyola U., Maywood, 1975—, Alexian Bros. Med. Ctr., Elk Grove, 1976—; instr. Cook County Grad. Sch. Medicine, Chgo., 1973—; vis. lectr. various med. schs., 1973—. Served to maj. U.S. Army, 1973-75. Mem. Am. Psychiat. Assn., Ill. Psychiat. Soc., Ill. Assn. Gen Hosp. Psychiatrists, Chgo. Found. for Med. Care. Roman Catholic. Avocations: reading, stained glass constrn., piano, organ, guitar. Home: 234 S Illinois Villa Park IL 60181 Office: Alexian Bros Med Plaza 850 Biesterfield Suite 3005 Elk Grove Village IL 60007

HILLENBRAND, DANIEL A., manufacturing company executive; b. 1923; married. Student, Purdue U. With Hillenbrand Industries, Inc., Batesville, Ind., 1946—, dir. purchasing, 1946-64, v.p., dir. mktg., 1964-69, pres. subs. Batesville Casket Co., 1969-72, chmn. bd., pres., chief exec. officer parent co., 1972-81, chmn. bd., chief exec. officer, 1981—, also dir. Office: Hillenbrand Industries Inc Hwy 46 East Batesville IN 47006 *

HILLENBRAND, W. AUGUST, manufacturing company executive; b. 1940; married. B.S. in Mgmt., St. Joseph's Coll., 1965. With Hillenbrand Industries, Batesville, Ind., 1958—, asst. to pres., 1965-70, v.p. ops., 1970-79, exec. v.p., 1979-81, pres., chief operating officer, 1981—, also dir. Office: Hillenbrand Industries Inc Hwy 46 East Batesville IN 47006 *

HILLER, JOHN RICHARD, physicist, educator; b. Scranton, Pa., July 3, 1953; s. John Robert and Lillian Mae (Hummer) H.; m. Sharon Gay Pollock, June 27, 1981. BS, Drexel U., Phila., 1976; MS, U. Md., 1978, PhD, 1980. Physicist Harry Diamond Labs., Woodbridge, Va., 1975-76; with Inst. Advanced Study, Princeton, N.J., 1980-82; research assoc. Purdue U., West Lafayette, Ind., 1982-84; asst. prof. physics U. Minn., Duluth, 1984—. Contbr. articles to profl. jours. NSF grad. fellow, 1976, Albert Einstein fellow, 1981; faculty research grantee, U. Minn., 1985, 86. Mem. Am. Phys. Soc. Home: 2520 N Tischer Rd Duluth MN 55804 Office: U Minn Dept Physics 10 University Dr Duluth MN 55812

HILLESHEIM, STEVEN JOHN, dentist; b. Chgo., Apr. 18, 1958; s. John Joseph and Evelyn Christina (Bonvino) H.; m. Barbara Ann Fitzsimmons, Oct. 4, 1985 (divorced). BS, Loyola U., Chgo., 1980; DDS, Loyola U., Maywood, Ill., 1984. Practice gen. dentistry Paul A. Difranco DDS, Des Plaines, Ill., 1984—, River Forest, Ill., 1985—; cons. KC Ednl. Media, Des Plaines, Ill., 1986—. Mem. ADA, Chgo. Dental Soc., Ill. State Dental Soc., Delta Sigma Delta. Republican. Roman Catholic. Home: 508 Bonnie Brae River Forest IL 60305 Office: 7321 W Lake St River Forest IL 60305

HILLMAN, DOUGLAS WOODRUFF, federal judge; b. Grand Rapids, Mich., Feb. 15, 1922; s. Lemuel Serrell and Dorothy (Woodruff) H.; m. Sally Jones, Sept. 13, 1944; children: Drusilla W., Clayton D. Student, Phillips Exeter Acad., 1941; A.B., U. Mich., 1946, LL.B., 1948. Bar: Mich. 1948, U.S. Supreme Ct. 1967. Assoc. Lilly, Luyendyk & Snyder, Grand Rapids, 1948-53; partner Luyendyk, Hainer, Hillman, Karr & Dutcher, Grand Rapids, 1953-65, Hillman, Baxter & Hammond, 1965-79; U.S. dist. judge Western Dist. Mich., Grand Rapids, 1979—; chief judge Western Dist. Mich., 1986—; instr. Nat. Inst. Trial Advocacy, Boulder, Colo. Chmn. Grand Rapids Human Relations Commn., 1963-66; chmn. bd. trustees Fountain St. Ch., 1970-72; pres. Family Service Assn., 1967. Served as pilot USAAF, 1943-45. Decorated D.F.C., Air medal.; Recipient Annual Civil Liberties award ACLU, 1970. Fellow Am. Bar Found.; Mem. Am. Bar Assn., Mich. Bar Assn. (chmn. client security fund), Grand Rapids Bar Assn. (pres. 1963), Am. Coll. Trial Lawyers (Mich. chmn. 1979), 6th Circuit Jud. Conf. (life), Internat. Acad. Trial Lawyers, Fedn. Ins. Counsel, Internat. Assn. Ins. Counsel, Internat. Soc. Barristers (pres. 1977-78), Nat. Bd. Trial Advocacy. Clubs: M (U. Mich.); University (Grand Rapids); Rotary, Torch. Office: 110 Michigan St NW 682 Grand Rapids MI 49503

HILLMAN, STANLEY ERIC GORDON, former corporate executive; b. London, Eng., Oct. 13, 1911; came to U.S., 1951, naturalized, 1957; s. Percy Thomas and Margaret Eleanor Fanny (Lee) H.; m. May Irene Noon, May 2, 1947; children: Susan, Deborah, Katherine. Ed., Holyrood, Tonbridge schs., Eng. With Brit.-Am. Tobacco Co., Ltd., London, Shanghai, 1933-47; dir. Hillman & Co., Ltd., Cosmos Trading Co., FED Inc., U.S.A., Airmotive Supplies Co. Ltd., Hong Kong, 1947-52; v.p. Gen. Dynamics Corp., 1953-61; v.p., group exec. Am. Machine & Foundry Co., N.Y.C., 1962-65; v.p., dir. Gen. Am. Transp. Corp., 1965-67; pres., vice chmn., dir. IC Industries, 1968-78; bankruptcy trustee Chgo., Milw., St. Paul & Pacific R.R., 1978-79; dir. Bandag Corp., Conrail Corp., Axla Corp. Trustee Gen. Growth Properties. Clubs: Chgo., Mid Am. (Chgo.); Onwentsia, Royal Poinciana. Home: 414 Thorne Ln Lake Forest IL 60045

HILLSTORM, CARLYLE ROBERT, farmer; b. Phila., Aug. 30, 1939; s. Philip W. Hillstorm and Olga C. (Siegel) H.; m. Sally Ann Stevens, June 3, 1967; children: Michael, Mary Ann, Melinda, Michele. BS, N.D. State U., 1961, MS, 1971. Asst. county agt. N.D. Extension Service, Langdon, 1964-66; county agt. N.D. Extension Service, Cando, N.D., 1966-73; farm owner and operator Hensler, N.D., 1973—. Chmn. Selective Services Bd., Hensler, 1985-86; vice chmn. Oliver County Farm Bur.,Hensler, 1985-86; treas. Oliver County Crop and Livestock Assn., 1976-82. Served with U.S. Army, 1962-63. Roman Catholic. Lodge: KC. Home: Box 116 Hensler ND 58547

HILLYER, BERNARD CHARLES, physician; b. Washington, May 10, 1944; s. Bernard H. and Renee Agness (Enders) H.; m. Linda Jean Speece, May 2, 1970; children: Chad, Jill, Amanda. BS, U. N.D., 1966; MD, U. Nebr., Omaha, 1970. Intern Sacred Heart Hosp., Spokane, Wash., 1971; resident St. Francis Hosp., Wichita, Kans., 1975; mem. staff Cass County Meml. Hosp., Atlantic, Iowa, 1973-81; gen. practice medicine Knoxville, Iowa, 1981—; mem. staff Knoxville Area Community Hosp., 1981—. Served to capt. U.S. Army, 1971-73. Mem. Marion County Med. Soc. (pres. 1986). Knoxville C. of C. (v.p. 1985-86). Republican. Roman Catholic. Avocations: racquetball, hunting, boating, golf, photography. Home: 1205 Levin Dr Knoxville IA 50138 Office: 1202 W Howard St Knoxville IA 50138

HILL-YOUNG, JENNIFER NELL, health agency adminstrator; b. Kansas City, Mo., Aug. 11, 1949; d. James and Mildred (Fowler) Hill; m. Youdoran Young, May 13, 1977. BA in English, U. Mo., 1971, MPH, 1973; Assoc. in Nursing, Penn Valley State U., 1985. Program coordinator U. Mo., Columbia, 1974-79; health educator Wayne Miner, Kansas City, 1979-81; health planner MAHSA, Kansas City, 1981-82; assoc. dir. Adolescent Resources Corp., Kansas City, 1982—; cons. Support Ctr., Houston, 1986—. Mem. Am. Pub. Health Assn., Black Caucus of Health Workers, Phi Delta Kappa, Alpha Kappa Alpha. Roman Catholic. Avocations: computers, needlepoint, reading, aerobics. Office: Adolescent Resources Corp 4011 Washington Kansas City MO 64111

HILPERT, BRUNETTE KATHLEEN POWERS (MRS. ELMER ERNEST HILPERT), civic worker; b. Baton Rouge; d. Edward Oliver and Orvilla (Nettles) Powers; A.B., La. State U., 1930, B.S. in L.S., 1933; postgrad. Columbia U., 1937; m. Elmer Ernest Hilpert, Aug. 1, 1938; children—Margaret Ray, Elmer Ernest II. Catalogue, La. State U. Library, Baton Rouge, 1930-36, La. State U. Law Sch. Library, 1936-38; librarian Washington U. Law Sch. Library, St. Louis, 1940-42; reference librarian Washington U. Library, St. Louis, 1952-54. Drive capt. United Fund, St. Louis, 1956; del. White House Conf. on Edn., St. Louis, 1962; trustee John Burroughs Sch., 1959-63; bd. dirs. Grace Hill Settlement House, 1957-63, v.p., 1960-62; bd. dirs. Internat. Inst., 1964-68; bd. dirs. Neighborhood Health Center, 1964-67, sec., 1964—; dir. Arts and Edn. Council, 1967-87; pres., dir. Women's Assn. St. Louis Symphony Soc., 1969-71; exec. com., dir. St. Louis Symphony Soc., 1969—; bd. dirs. Miss. River Festival, 1969-74; dir. women's adv. bd. Continental Bank & Trust Co., 1970-77, 79—; bd. dirs. St. Louis Inst. Music, 1971-75; bd. dirs. St. Louis String Quartet, 1971-77, pres., 1975-77; bd. dirs. Community Music Sch., 1973-75, Little Symphony Concerts Assn., 1975-78, St. Louis Conservatory and Schs. for Arts, 1975-84, Dance Concert Soc., 1977-81, Women's Aux. Bd. Bethesda Gen. Hosp., 1981—. Recipient Woman of Achievement award St. Louis Globe Democrat, 1967. Mem. Nat. Soc. Arts and Letters (dir. 1964-65, 80-82), Delta Zeta. Republican. Presbyterian. Clubs: Wednesday (rec. sec. 1963-64), University. Home: 630 Francis Pl Apt 1-N Saint Louis MO 63105

HILPERT, DALE W., retail shoe company executive. BS, U. Wyo., 1966; MBA, U. Denver, 1970. With Dayton Hudson Corp., Mpls., 1970-76, Cook United, Inc., Cleve., 1976-78, May Dept. Stores, St. Louis, 1978-80; with Volume Shoe Corp., Topeka, Kans., 1980—, chief fin. officer, sr. v.p., 1980-81, exec. v.p., 1981-82, now chmn., chief exec. officer, dir., 1982—. Office: Volume Shoe Corp 3231 E 6th St Topeka KS 66607 *

HILTON, FRANK LINDEN, physician; b. Terre Haute, Ind., Nov. 12, 1944; s. Frank Farnsworth and Clara Della (Sankey) H.; children: Jennifer, Ryan. BS, Ind. State U., 1966; MD, Ind. U. Sch. Medicine, 1970. Diplomate Am. Bd. Gynecology. Dir. ob-gyn edn. St. Mary's Med. Ctr., Evansville, 1979—; pres. Evansville (Ind.) Obtet. and Gynecol. Assocs., Inc., 1986—; asst. clinical prof. ob-gyn Ind. U. Sch. Medicine, 1982—. Served as capt. U.S. Army, 1971-72. Recipient Arthur Griep award House Staff St. Mary's Med. Ctr., 1979, 86. Mem. AMA, Gyneecologic Laser Soc., Vanderburgh County Med. Soc. (pres. 1985-86), Ind. State Med. Assn., Am. Soc. for Colposcopy and Cervical Pathology, Am. Fertility Soc. Roman Catholic. Avocation: flying. Home: 7821 Peach Blossom Ln Evansville IN 47715 Office: Evansville Ob-Gyn Assocs 326 S E 7th Evansville IN 47713

HILTON, STANLEY WILLIAM, JR., theatrical manager, director; b. Phila., Mar. 24; s. Stanley William and Jennie (Parsons) H.; B.A., Fisk U., 1959; postgrad. Temple U.; m. Inge Himmersbach, Dec. 1962; 1 child, Richard H. Office mgr., resource cons., social worker Cook County Dept. Pub. Aid, Chgo., 1961-70; coordinator, ednl. and vocat. counselor Community Coll. Dist., San Francisco, 1971-74; co. mgr. prodn. Hair, Chgo., 1968, San Francisco, 1969; mgr. Orpheum Theatre, San Francisco, 1970; co. mgr. prodns. No Place To Be Somebody, 1971, My Fair Lady, 1973, San Francisco, Jesus Christ Superstar, 1973, Winner Take All, Los Angeles, 1976, Eleanor, Chgo., 1976; gen. mgr. Street Dreams, Chgo., 1982; dir. park and theatre ops. Art Park, Lewiston, N.Y., 1974; exec. dir. Blackstone Theatre, Chgo., 1974-86; bd. dirs. The Ctrs. for New Horizons, Chgo., 1976-79, The Acad., Art, Music, Dance, Theatre, Chgo., 1980-84. Mem. Assn. Theatrical Press Agts. and Mgrs. Home: 1540 N State Pkwy Chicago IL 60610 Office: 60 E Balbo St Chicago IL 60605

HILTY, WILLIAM JACOB, retired association executive; b. Bucyrus, Ohio, Dec. 1, 1921; s. Harold Eugene and Gladys Marie (Heinlen) H.; m. Davelyn Lawrence, July 15, 1942; children: Harold Lawrence, Amanda Sue, Melissa Kay, Laura Ann. Advt. mgr. Flexible Bus. Co., Loudonville, Ohio, 1948-51; account exec. Fuller, Smith & Ross, Cleve., 1951-59; dir. communications Am. Soc. Metals, Metals Park, Ohio, 1969-71, IEEE, N.Y.C., 1971; mng. dir. expositions and publs. Soc. Mfg. Engrs., Dearborn, Mich., 1971-81, exec. v.p., gen. mgr., 1981-86. Served to maj. USAF, 1941-45, ETO. Mem. Nat. Assn. Exposition Mgrs. (pres. 1970).

HINCKLEY, BARBARA PRENTISS, political scientist, educator; b. Boston, Aug. 12, 1937; children—Sandra, Karen. A.B., Mt. Holyoke Coll., 1959, LL.D. (hon.), 1984, Ph.D., Cornell U., 1968. Asst. prof. U. Mass., Amherst, 1968-70, Cornell U., Ithaca, N.Y., 1970-72; assoc. prof. poli-sci. U. Wis.-Madison, 1972-74, prof., 1974—; cons. house elections ABC News, N.Y.C., 1982, 84. Author: The Seniority System in Congress, 1971; Congressional Elections, 1981; Stability and Change in Congress, 3rd edition, 1983; contbr. articles to profl. jours. Guggenheim fellow, 1975; recipient Hawkins Prof. award U. Wis., 1983. Mem. Am. Polit. Sci. Assn. (v.p. 1975), Legis. Studies Group (pres. 1979-80). Office: U Wis Dept Polit Sci 1050 Bascom Mall Madison WI 53706

HINCKLEY, CHARLES CLARENCE, insurance company executive; b. Wausau, Wis., Feb. 11, 1933; s. Clarence Charles and Ada Marie (Kronenwetter) H.; m. Ellen Ann Conaghan, July 29, 1961; children: Charles III, Molly, Andrew, Alison. B.S., Marquette U., 1955, J.D., 1958; LL.M., Wayne State U., 1973; MBA, Xavier U., 1986. Bar: Wis. 1958, Ohio 1974. With Northwestern Mut. Life Ins. Co., Milw., 1958-61, Home Life Ins. Co., N.Y., 1964-73; with Union Central Life Ins. Co., Cin., 1961-64, 73—, assoc. gen. counsel, v.p., gen. counsel, sr. v.p., exec. v.p., 1973-83, pres., 1983-85; pres., chief operating officer 1983-85, pres., chief exec. officer, 1986—, also bd. dirs., 1977—; Bd. dirs. Cen. Trust Co., N.A., Manhattan Nat. Corp., 1986—, pres., chmn., chief exec. officer, 1987—; chmn. bd. dirs. Manhattan Life Ins. Co., Manhattan Nat. Life Ins. Co. Contbr. articles to profl. jours. Gen. chmn. YMCA Capital Campaign, Cin., 1986; past pres. bd. Cath. Social Services, S.W. Ohio; chmn. bd. trustees Summit Country Day Sch., 1981—; trustee Community Chest and United Appeal, Cin., 1983—; bd. dirs. Cin. Bus. Com. Mem. Assn. Life Ins. Counsel, ABA, Assn. Life Underwriters, Nat. Assn. Life Underwriters, Ohio Assn. Life Underwriters., Million Dollar Round Table (life), Greater Cin. C. of C., 1986—. Clubs: Cin. Country; Queen City: Commonwealth: Bankers (Cin.). Home: 3160 Victoria Ave Cincinnati OH 45208 Office: Union Cen Life Ins Co PO Box 179 Cincinnati OH 45201

HINCKLEY, WILLIAM LAWRENCE, education educator; b. Oxnard, Calif., June 9, 1938; s. Lawrence Bradford and Mildred (Coombs) H.; m. Sara Lee Townley, Oct. 14, 1961; children: James Bradford, Susan Lee. BA, Stanford U., 1960, MA, 1965, EdD, 1969. Tchr. Los Altos (Calif.) High Sch., 1963-65; tchr., research asst. Stanford U., 1965-67; project adminstr. ESEA, Maryville, Mo., 1967-68; prof. N.W. Mo. State U., Maryville, 1968—. Contbr. articles to profl. jour. Served to lt. (j.g.) USN, 1960-63. Research grantee Dept. HEW, 1971-73. Mem. Network Profs. Secondary

Edn., Phi Delta Kappa (chapters pres. 1974-75). Republican. Episcopalian. Club: Maryville Country. Lodge: Rotary (pres. 1976-77). Avocations: boating, golf. Office: Northwest Mo State U Maryville MO 64468

HINDERBERGER, STEPHEN JOHN, financial executive; b. St. Louis, May 18, 1954; s. Joseph Eugene and Audrey Lucille (Kreiger) H.; m. Ann Marion Puglisi, July 30, 1976; children: Kate, Laura, Bryan. BS in Acctg. magna cum laude, St. Louis U., 1975. CPA, Mo. With audit staff Touche Ross and Co., St. Louis, 1975-78; asst. mgr. external reporting The May Dept. Stores Co., St. Louis, 1978-79, mgr. external reporting, 1979-82, dir. seasonal planning, 1982-84; div. v.p., asst. to pres. Famous-Barr, St. Louis, 1984-87; dir. capital planning and control The May Dept. Stores Co., St. Louis, 1987—. Mem. Am. Inst. CPA's., Mo. Soc. CPA's. Avocation: golf. Home: 4621 Grandcastle Dr Saint Louis MO 63128 Office: The May Dept Stores Co 611 Olive St Saint Louis MO 63101

HINDO, WALID AFRAM, radiology educator, oncologist; b. Baghdad, Iraq, Oct. 4, 1940; came to U.S. 1966, naturalized 1976; s. Afram Paul and Laila Farid (Meshaka) H.; m. Fawzia Hanna Batti, Apr. 20, 1965; children—Happy, Rana, Patricia, Heather, Brian. M.B., Baghdad U., 1964, Ch.B., 1964. Diplomate Am. Bd. Radiology. Instr. radiology Rush Med. Coll, Chgo., 1971-72; asst. prof. Northwestern U., Chgo., 1972-75; assoc. prof. medicine and radiology Chgo. Med. Sch., 1975-80, prof., chmn. dept. radiology, 1980—; cons. Ill. Cancer Council. Contbr. articles on cancer treatment to profl. jours. Bd. dirs. Lake County div. Am. Cancer Soc., Ill., 1975-80. Served to lt. M.C., Iraq; Army, 1965-66. Named Prof. of Yr., Chgo. Med. Sch., 1981, 82, 83, 85. Mem. Am. Coll. Radiology, Am. Soc. Acad. Radiologists, Am. Soc. Therapeutic Radiologists. Republican. Roman Catholic. Home: 2789 Greenwood Rd Northbrook IL 60062 Office: Univ of Health Scis Chgo Med Sch 3333 Greenbay Rd North Chicago IL 60064

HINER, HENRY NORTON, pharmacist; b. Ashland, Ohio, July 29, 1938; s. John P. and Edith (Norton) H.; m. Norma Jean Shumaker, June 16, 1963; children: Mark Andrew, David Michael. BS in Pharmacy, Ohio No. U., 1961. Pharmacist, mgr. Hurst's Pharmacy, Ashland, 1961-66; owner, pres. Hiner's Pharmacy, Inc., Ashland, 1966—. Pres. United Appeal of Ashland County, 1974; bd. dirs. Ashland County Health, 1984. Mem. Ohio State Pharm. Assn., Ashland Downtown Merchants Assn., Ashland Area C. of C. (bd. dirs. 1980-83). Republican. Lutheran. Clubs: Young Men's Bus. (treas. Ashland chpt. 1975-76, pres. 1986-87). Lodges: Masons, Shriners (pres. Ashland County chpt. 1983). Avocations: downhill and cross country skiing, golf, needlepoint. Home: 607 Country Club Ln Ashland OH 44805 Office: Hiners Pharmacy Inc 34 W Main St Ashland OH 44805

HINER, MARJORIE LOU, trucking company executive; b. Crawfordsville, Ind., June 5, 1944; d. Isaac Edwin and Dortha Eileen (Odell) Hoss; BS, Ball State U., 1966, MA, 1970; m. Homer F. Hiner, July 14, 1972; children: Richard, David, Marcy. Tchr., Maconaquah High Sch., Bunker Hill, Ind., 1966-67; substitute tchr. various schs., 1970-73; with Hiner Transport, Inc., Huntington, Ind., 1973—, owner, sec.-treas. bd. dirs., 1973—; bookkeeper, dir. Hiner Mgmt. Services, Inc. Bd. dirs. Huntington County United Way, Huntington Meml. Hosp. Found., mem. adv. bd. Salvation Army; chmn. bd. dirs. Huntington County Crime Stoppers, Inc. Mem. Nat. Assn. Female Execs., Am. Bus. Women's Assn. Mem. Ind. Motor Truck Assn., Huntington C. of C. (bd. dirs.), South Side Bus. Assn., Ball State U. Alumni Assn., Psi Iota Xi, Alpha Phi. Republican. Home: 1979N-600W Andrews IN 46702 Office: PO Box 621 Huntington IN 46750

HINES, CURTIS LEE, educational administrator; b. Decatur, Ill., Apr. 3, 1945; s. Sylvester and Nobie (Hempstead) H.; m. Lexanna Marie Johnson, Aug. 18, 1968 (div. 1974); m. Elinor Diane Ellis, July 25, 1978; children: Rayna Lynn, Shayla Ann, Kayla Karin. BS in Edn., N.E. Mo. State U., 1969, MS in Edn. Counseling, 1970. Cert. ednl. counselor, sch. adminstr., Ill. Tchr. driver edn. Eastridge High Sch., Kankakee, Ill., 1969-70, counselor, 1970-74, head wrestling coach, 1969-74; counselor Dept. Pub. Aid, Kankakee, 1972; part-time instr. psychology, sociology, polit. sci., health Kankakee Community Coll., 1972-74; dean of students Evanston (Ill.) Twp. High Sch., 1974-80, dean bldg. services, 1980—, Atlanta, Ga., 1981-86, regional mgr., 1986—. Founder, past pres., mem. exec. bd. Concerned Blacks for Sch. and Community Improvement, Evanston; life mem. NAACP, mem. exec. bd. North Shore br., 1977-81, chmn. edn. com., 1977-79; mem. Chgo. chpt. People United to Save Humanity, 1980—. Mem. Ill. Edn. Assn., NEA, Am. Personnel and Guidance Assn., Ill. Personnel and Guidance Assn., Nat. Alliance Black Sch. Educators (local sch. commn. task force), Lake County Alliance Black Sch. Educators (chairperson budget), Phi Delta Kappa, Kappa Delta Pi., Omega Psi Phi. Baptist. Home: 2305 N Sheridan Rd Waukegan IL 60087 Office: Evanston Twp High Sch 1600 Dodge St Evanston IL 60201 Office: A L Williams Co 750 Arthur St Elk Grove Village IL 60007

HINES, JAMES WILLIAM, bank executive; b. Connellsville, Pa., July 8, 1950; s. James W. Sr. and Bernadine (Moore) H.; m. Marilyn Sallach, Sept. 30, 1972; children: Kevin, Scott. BA in Econs., Allegheny Coll., 1972; MBA in Mgmt., Baldwin-Wallace Coll., 1986. Mgr. SAGA Foodservice, Menlo Park, Calif., 1970-73; mgmt. intern Cardinal Fed. Savs. Bank, Cleve., 1973-75, br. mgr., 1975-79, mgr. tng. and devel., 1979-81, v.p., mgr. facilities and adminstrn., 1981—; instr. Lorain County Community Coll., Elyria, Ohio, 1978-82, Inst. Fin. Edn., Cleve., 1982-84; bus. cons. Jr. Achievement Project Bus., 1985—. Mem. North Olmsted (Ohio) Transp. Study Team, 1984—, North Olmsted Community Council, 1985-86, North Olmsted Bd. Edn., 1987—; pres. Deerfield N. Homeowners Assn., 1983-85. Served with USN, 1971-73. Mem. Purchasing Mgmt. Assn. Cleve., Nat. Purchasing Mgmt. Assn., Soc. Telecommunication Profls., Administrv. Mgmt. Soc., Mich. Ohio Telecommunication Assn., Bldg. and Mgrs. Assn., North Olmsted Jaycees (pres. 1985-86). Republican. Presybterian. Home: 24317 Woodmere Dr North Olmsted OH 44070 Office: Cardinal Fed Savs Bank 150 Euclid Ave Cleveland OH 44114

HINES, SUSAN ANN, nurse, educator; b. Detroit, Dec. 13, 1949; d. George C. and Linda (Shadid) Naufel; m. George G. Jr., Nov. 13, 1971; children: George Naufel, Kimberly Suzanne. Cert., Springfield Sch. Practical Nursing, 1969; student, Lincolnland Community Coll., 1986—. Lic. practical nurse, Ill. Rehab. nurse Dirksen House Healthcare, Springfield, Ill., 1969-72; nurse supr. UpJohn Services, Springfield, Ill., 1976=80; nurse mgr. Equifax-Physical Measurements, Springfield, 1980—. Mem. Springfield Life Underwriters Assn., Gen. Agy. Mgmt. Assn. (bd. dirs. 1985—). Avocations: reading, gourmet cooking, antiques, travel. Home: 59 Woods Mill Rd Sherman IL 62684 Office: Physical Measurements Info 801 S Durkin Dr Springfield IL 62704

HINKE, MARVIN L., radiologist, educator; b. Stanley, Wis., Jan. 21, 1930; s. Henry Benjamin and Nellie Grace (Dresel) H.; children: Ann, David, Peter, Richard. BS, MD, U. Wis., Madison, 1952; MD, U. Wis., 1955. Diplomate Am. Bd. Radiology. Intern Med. Coll. Va., Richmond, 1955-56; surgery resident Marshfield Clinic, 1958-59, staff radiologist, 1963-86; resident in radiology U. Wis., 1959-62, instr. radiology, 1962-63; assoc. prof. Med. Sch. U. Wis., Madison, 1985—; mem. clin. teaching staff U. Wis.; chmn. dept. radiology, Marshfield Clinic, 1977-79. Served to capt. U.S. Army, 1956-58. Fellow Am. Coll. Radiology; mem. AMA, Radiologic Soc. N.Am., Wis. Radiol. Soc., Assn. U. Radiologists, Wis. State Med. Soc.. Avocations: sailing, skiing, gardening, history, travel, music. Home: 3100 Lake Mendota Dr Apt 406 Madison WI 53705 Office: U Wis Hosp and Clinics 600 Highland Ave Madison WI 53792

HINKEL, JAY CRAIG, lawyer; b. Larned, Kans., Jan. 22, 1954; s. Leonard Elmer Adam and Shirley Ann (Sloan) H.; m. Deborah Ann Beal, Sept. 1, 1979; 1 child, Nathaniel. Diplomate, U. Siena, Italy, 1973; BA, U. Kans., 1976, BS, 1978, JD, 1981. Bar: Kans. Assoc. Smith Law Office, Garden City, Kans., 1981-82; sole practice Garden City, Kans., 1982-84; county prosecuting atty. Finney County, Garden City, Kans., 1984—; bd. dirs. adv. bd. Garden City Community Coll. Criminal Justice program, 1985—, Status offenders programs, 1984—, instr. bus. law, 1984-85; instr. Finney County Sheriff's Dept., 1985—. Bd. dirs. Family Crisis Services, Garden City, 1986—, Community Concerts Assn. S.W., Kans., 1984—; precinct committeeman Finney County Republicans, Garden City, 1984—; elder First Christian Ch. Named Outstanding Young Man Am. Internat. Jaycees, 1982. Mem. Finney County Bar Assn., Kans. County & Dist. Attys. Assn., Kans. Bar Assn., Nat. Dist. Attys. Assn. Republican. Lodge: Lions. Avocations: downhill skiing, reading, golf. Home: 2706 Shamus Garden City KS 67846 Office: Finney County Courthouse 824 Saint John St Garden City KS 67846

HINKLE, BENNY STEWART, food company executive; b. Blackstar, Ky., May 5, 1942; s. Everett Disoel and Mabel Bell (Young) H.; m. Marlene Mary Reichert, July 12, 1966; 1 dau., Dawn Michelle. A.S., Sinclair Coll., 1967; Comml. Pilot, Burnside Ott Aviation Sch., Ft. Lauderdale, 1967. With Dayton Tire & Rubber (Ohio), 1964-67; pilot Burnside-Ott, Ft. Lauderdale, 1967-69; pilot, ins. sales CUNA Mut. Ins., Madison, Wis., 1969-81; pres. L. J. Products Co., Dayton, Ohio, 1981—; cons. L. J. Products, Dayton, 1981—. Served with USAF, 1960-64. Home: 1378 Wilhelmina Dr Vandalia OH 45377 Office: L J Products Co 921 Bridge St Dayton OH 45407

HINKLE, DONALD EARL, lawyer, tax executive; b. Linton, Ind., Feb. 13, 1952; s. A. Earl and Mary Ellen (Birt) H.; m. Mary Elizabeth Haag, Aug. 7, 1976; children: Lauren Rebecca, Gregory Earl. BS in Bus., Ind. U., 1974, JD, 1976. Bar: Ind. 1976, U.S. Dist. Ct. (so. dist.) Ind. 1976. Tax mgr. Arthur Andersen and Co., Indpls., 1976-83; dir. taxes Banc One Ind. Corp., Indpls., 1983—. Mem. ABA, Ind. State Bar Assn., Am. Inst. CPA's, Ind. CPA Soc., Tax Execs. Inst. Avocations: auto racing, photography. Home: 8914 Kirkham Rd Indianapolis IN 46260-1641 Office: Banc One Ind Corp 111 Monument Circle Indianapolis IN 46277-3066

HINKLE, ROBERT DOUGLAS, naturalist, educator; b. Hillsdale, Mich., June 23, 1946; s. Kennedy J. and Marcele Erma (Summers) H.; m. Paula Kramer, Nov. 25, 1985. BS, Mich. State U., 1969, MS, 1971, PhD, 1976. Staff naturalist Woldumar Nature Ctr., Lansing, Mich., 1969-75; instr. environ. studies Mich. State U., East Lansing, 1974-76, asst. prof., 1976-78; asst. prof. Johnson (Vt.) State Coll., 1978-82, chmn. dept. environ. studies, 1980-82; chief naturalist Cleve. Metroparks, 1982—; cons. East Lansing Pub. Schs., 1973, Johnson Pub. Schs., 1981-82. Author, editor: (labratory manual) Supplementary Materials for Environmental Education, 1975; author monthly column on environment, 1982—. Recipient Excellence in Undergrad. Teaching award Mich. State U., 1975. Mem. Assn. Interpretive Naturalists (dep. dir. region 8, regional vice-dir. 1985—), Mich. Environ. Edn. Assn. (bd. dirs. 1976-82), The Wildlife Soc., AAAS, Am. Soc. Mammalogists, Beta Beta Beta, Alpha Zeta. Home: 9756 Eastland Rd Strongsville OH 44136 Office: Cleveland Metroparks 4101 Fulton Pkwy Cleveland OH 44144

HINKLIN, ALAN DEE, architect; b. Marion, Ohio, Feb. 19, 1937; s. Irvin Melvin and Veryl (Sanders) H.; m. Florence Abigail Campton, June 8, 1963; children: Matthew Alan, Erin Christopher. BArch, U. Cin., 1962. Student architect Charles Oborn Architect, Marion, 1956-58, Edwards and Burris, Marion, 1958-63; with Skidmore, Owings & Merrill, Chgo., 1963—, ptnr., 1984—; lectr. Continental Bank, Chgo., 1979-84; speaker A/E/C Systems '86, Chgo., 1986. Chief crusader United Fund Crusade of Mercy, Chgo., 1984. Mem. AIA, Profl. Services Mgmt. Assn., Chgo. Bldg. Congress. Club: Metropolitan, Univ., Monroe (Chgo.). Office: Skidmore Owings & Merrill 33 W Monroe Chicago IL 60603

HINMAN, MYRA MAHLOW, educator; b. Saginaw County, Mich., Jan. 11, 1926; d. Henry and Cynthia (Mims) Mahlow; B.S., Columbia U., 1946; M.A., U. Fla., 1954, Ph.D., 1959; m. George E. Olstead, 1948 (div. 1967); 1 son, Christopher Eric; m. 2d, Charlton, Hinman, 1968 (dec. 1977); 1 stepdau., Barbara. Asst. prof. Memphis State U., 1959-61; instr. U. Kans., Lawrence, 1961-63, asst. prof., 1963-68, asso. prof. English lit., 1968—. Travel grantee Am. Council Learned Socs., 1966. Mem. MLA, Internat. Arthurian Soc., Shakespeare Assn. Am., U. Va. Bibliog. Soc., AAUP, Kans. Folklore Soc., Midwest Modern Lang. Assn., S. Atlantic Modern Lang. Assn., United Burmese Cat Fanciers, Am. Shorthair Cat Assn., Phi Kappa Phi. Asst. editor: Hinman Text, Complete Works of Shakespeare. Contbr. articles to profl. jours. Home: 1932 Maine St Lawrence KS 66046 Office: Wescoe Hall Univ Kans Lawrence KS 66045

HINNENKAMP, DAVID HENRY, accountant; b. Melrose, Minn., May 23, 1962; s. Herbert Paul and Marie Rose (Dickhaus) H.; m. Carla Catherine Pohlmann, May 23, 1987. BS in Acctg., St. Cloud (Minn.) State U., 1984. CPA, Minn. Acct. Kern, Poganski & Hirschfeld, Ltd., St. Cloud, 1983-86, Princeton, Minn., 1986—; guest speaker various colls. and univs; instr. Community Edn., Princeton, 1986—. Mem. Am. Inst. CPA's, Minn. Soc. CPA's, Mcpl. Fin. Officers' Assn. Republican. Roman Catholic. Lodge: Rotary. Avocations: baseball, basketball, softball, skiing, golf. Home: 923 W Branch St #4 Princeton MN 55371 Office: Kern Poganski & Hirschfeld Ltd 501 S 4th St Suite 202 Princeton MN 55371

HINNRICHS-DAHMS, HOLLY BETH, educator; b. Milw., Oct. 31, 1945; d. Helmut Ferdinand and Rae W. (Beebe) H.; m. Raymond H. Dahms, June 11, 1983 (dec. Oct. 2, 1983). Student U. Wis.-Milw., 1963-64, 66, 79—, Chapman Coll., 1965, 67, Internat. Coll. Copenhagen, summer 1968, Temple U., summer 1970, B.A., Alverno Coll., 1971; postgrad. Marylhurst Coll., 1972, Chapman Coll. World Campus Afloat, summers 1973, 74, Inst. Shipboard Edn., 1978, 79. Vice pres. Hinnrichs Inc., Germantown, Wis., 1964-72; tchr. Germantown Recreation Dept., 1965; coach Milw. Recreation Dept., 1966-67; rep. for Wis., Chapman Coll., Orange, Calif., 1967; clk. Stein Drug Co., Menomonee Falls, Wis., 1967-72; tchr. Milw. area Catholic Schs., 1967-72, 83—; asst. mgr. Original Cookie Co. (Mother Hubbard's) Cookie Store, Northridge Mall, Milw., 1977-84, SAU-U Warehouse Deli, 1984-85, mgr. office, 1985—; substitute tchr. pub. schs. Milw. area, 1975-80, 83—; tchr. Indian Community Sch., Milw., 1971-72, Martin Luther King Sch., 1973-74, Crossroads Acad., Milw., 1974-75, Harambee Community Sch., 1980-83; tutor Brookfield (Wis.) Learning Ctr., 1986—; Midwest rep. World Explorer Cruises, 1978—. Mem. Wis. math. Council, Nat. Council Tchrs. Math., Internat. Inst. Milw. Friends of Museum, Alpha Theta Epsilon. Christian Scientist. Traveled 63 countries; contbr. articles on travel to various publs. Home: W140 N9766 Hwy 145 Germantown WI 53022

HINRICHSEN, THOMAS PETER, importing executive; b. Muscatine, Iowa, Jan. 16, 1956; s. Thomas P. and Bernice M. (Mittman) H. AS, Eastern Iowa Community Coll., 1976; BS, Iowa State U., 1981. CPA, Iowa. Sr. acct. Cain, Ellsworth & Co., CPA's, Sheldon, Iowa, 1981-86; gen mgr. K-T Industries, Sheldon. Mem. Am. Inst. CPA's, Iowa Soc. CPA's. Republican. Club: Sheldon Country (treas., bd. dirs. 1985—). Lodge: Jaycees (treas. Sheldon chpt. 1985). Avocations: golf, travel. Home: 201 N 17th Ave #3 Sheldon IA 51201 Office: K-T Industries Box 123 Sheldon IA 51201

HINSHAW, CHARLES THERON, physician; b. Wichita, Kans., Jan. 31, 1932; s. Charles Theron and Mary Gwyn (Whiteman) H.; m. Karol King, June 20, 1957 (div. May, 1979); children: Charles Theron III, Mary Karolyn. BA, U. Kans., 1954, MD, 1958. Cert. Am. Bd. Pathology-Anat. and Clin, Am. Bd. Nuclear Medicine. Pathologist Hutchinson (Kans.) Hosp., 1965-79; dir. Bioctr. Lab., Wichita, 1979-83; physician, ecologist Garvey Ctr., Wichita, 1983-84; practice specializing in ecological medicine Wichita, 1984—; med. dir. Sci. Lab., Wichita, 1979-83, Ice Dream Internat., Sarasota, Fla., 1984—; lab. dir. Urban Ministries, Wichita, 1985—. Coauthor 7 articles in med. jours. Chmn. Sen. Bob Dole Com., Reno County, Kans., 1968, 74; bd. dirs. YMCA, Hutchinson, Kans., 1969-70, Kans. chpt. Am. Cancer Soc., 1972. Served to capt. USAF, 1959-61. Fellow Am. Soc. Clin. Pathologists (sec. adv. council 1974), Coll. Am. Pathologists; mem. AMA, Am. Acad. Environ. Medicine, Kans. Soc. Pathologists. Republican. Presbyterian. Avocations: golf, tennis, skiing, racquetball. Home: 5101 Kings Row Wichita KS 67208 Office: 1133 E 2d St Wichita KS 67214

HINSHAW, GAIL LAVERNE, management information systems specialist; b. Greensburg, Kans., Jan. 11, 1951; s. Laverne Craft and Ruby (Ellis) H.; m. Sheila Ruth Ratcliff, Dec. 20, 1970; children: Darren, Lisa. BS, Fort Hays State U., 1972, MS, 1974. Tchr., prin. Unified Sch. Dist. 474, Haviland, Kans., 1973-77; dist. exec. Boy Scouts Am., Springfield, Mo., 1977-80; mgr. Paul Mueller Co., Springfield, 1980—, mgr. mgmt. info. systems, 1985—. Bd. dirs., pres. Springfield Speech and Hearing Ctr., Springfield, 1980-84; chmn. adv. com. Ctr. for Bus. Research, Springfield, 1985—; mem. adv. com. Graff Vocat. Tech. Ctr., Springfield, 1983-84. Named Eagle Scout Boy Scouts Am., 1966. Mem. Data Processing Mgmt. Assn. Republican. Mem. Nazarene Ch. Avocation: aviation. Home: Rt 3 Box 207-20 Strafford MO 65757 Office: Paul Mueller Co Box 828 Springfield MO 65801

HINTON, DAVID BRUCE, investment broker; b. Marshalltown, Iowa, Apr. 21, 1950; s. Cecil Marion and Dorothy Elizabeth (Kanzok) H.; m. Mary Claire Pleiss, Aug. 21, 1971; 1 child, Alexandra Friederike. Student, Heidelberg, W.Ger., 1970-71; BA, Drake U., 1972; MA, U. Iowa, 1974. Registered rep. R.G. Dickinson & Co., Des Moines, 1976-77; asst. v.p. Piper Jaffray & Hopwood, Des Moines, 1977-83; v.p. mktg. R.G. Dickinson & Co., Des Moines, 1983—; lectr. univs. in Germany, 1974-76. Author: The Films of Leni Riefenstahl, 1978, A Place to Grow: Revitalizing Iowa's Economy, 1983. Mem. Iowa Devel. Commn., 1982—; chmn. Des Moines Com. Fgn. Relations, 1978—; exec. com. Des Moines Bur. Econ. Devel., 1982—. Mem. Iowa Investment Bankers Assn., Securities Industry Assn. (govt. relations com.), Soc. for Iowa's Future (founding chair), World Future Soc. Republican. Unitarian. Club: Des Moines. Home: 1617 Buffalo Rd West Des Moines IA 50265 Office: care of RG Dickinson & Co PO Box 9111 Des Moines IA 50306

HINZMAN, GERALD RICHARD, chief of police; b. Amana, Iowa, Oct. 4, 1947; s. Earl John and Fern Vernice (Douglass) H.; m. Linda Louise Gardner, Mar. 8, 1980; children: Paula, Lisa, Sarah. AA in Law Enforcement, Kirkwood Coll., Cedar Rapids, Iowa, 1974; BBA and BA in Criminal Justice, Mt. Mercy Coll., Cedar Rapids, 1976; M of Pub. Adminstrn., Iowa State U., 1977. Patrol officer Cedar Rapids Police Dept., 1970-72, helicopter pilot, 1972-74, detective, 1974-77, lt., 1977-78, capt., 1978-85, chief, 1985—. Altar asst. Peace Luth. Ch., Cedar Rapids, 1981—; bd. dirs. Community Dispute Ctr., Cedar Rapids, 1983—, Found. II Youth Shelter, Cedar Rapids, 1984—, Child Protection Ctr., Cedar Rapids, 1985—, Crime Stoppers, Cedar Rapids, 1985—, YMCA, Cedar Rapids, 1985—. Served to sgt. U.S. Army, 1966-68. Recipient Disting. Alumni award Mt. Mercy Coll., 1985. Mem. Internat. Assn. Chiefs of Police, Iowa Police Execs. Forum, Soc. Mayflower Descendants. Lodges: Masons, Rotary. Avocation: genealogy. Home: 2834 33d Ave SW Cedar Rapids IA 52404 Office: Cedar Rapids Police Dept 310 2d Ave SW Cedar Rapids IA 52404

HIPPS, DONNA MARIE (MRS. ROBERT O. HIPPS), librarian; b. Waterloo, Iowa, May 18, 1925; d. George Fred and Mamie Jean (Livingston) Westlic; B.S., Iowa State U., 1946; M.A., U. Minn., 1963; m. Robert O. Hipps, Aug. 9, 1946; Children—Alan, Margaret (Mrs. Douglas A. Peters), James. Tchr. pub. schs., Iowa, 1946-48; teaching asst. Univ. High Sch., U. Minn., Mpls., 1960-63; librarian Lincoln High Sch., Bloomington, Minn., 1963-70; library specialist Jefferson High Sch., Bloomington, 1970-74, dir. resource center, 1974-75, media dir., 1975—. Mem. Am. Fedn. Tchrs., NEA, LWV (state treas. 1958-59, dir. Edina 1955-58), Am. Field Service, AAUW, Sigma Kappa, Beta Phi Mu. Methodist. Home: 6604 Dakota Trail Edina MN 55435 Office: 4001 W 102d St Bloomington MN 55431

HIRSCH, ARLENE SHARON, career counselor; b. Chgo., Mar. 18, 1951; d. Kurt S. and Irma Hirsch. BA, U. Iowa, 1973; MA, Northwestern U., 1983. Supr. Horwitz, Anesi, Chgo., 1974-76; adminstr. Panter, Nelsm & Bernfield, Chgo., 1976-81; pvt. practice career counseling Chgo., 1983—; cons. Robert Morris Coll., Chgo., 1984—; adult edn. instr. Discovery Ctr., Chgo., 1984—, Latin Sch., Chgo., 1985—; instr. DePaul U., Chgo., 1985—. Editor jour. Contemporary Issues in Career Development, 1986—; career advice columnist, Chicagoland Job Source, 1985—, Shop Talk, 1985—, Career Moves, 1985—. Cons. Women Employed, Chgo., Midwest Women's Ctr., Chgo., YWCA-Career Services, Chgo. Mem. Am. Assn. Counseling and Devel., Nat. Assn. Women Bus. Owners, Profl. Career Counselors Network. Avocations: aerobics, softball. Home and Office: 850 N State St Chicago IL 60610

HIRSCH, BRUCE WANGMAN, nursing home administrator; b. Chgo., Jan. 5, 1946; s. S. Carl and Stina Elvira (Leander) H. BA, No. Ill. U., 1971, MA, 1975; postgrad., Nova U. Lic. nursing home adminstr., Ill.; cert. mental health adminstr., Ill. Mental health adminstr. Tinley Park (Ill.) Mental Health Ctr., 1973-76; unit dir. W.A. Howe Ctr., Tinley Park, 1976-84; mgmt. cons. Data Mgmt. Assoc., Springfield, Ill., 1984; prin., cons. Humble King & Assocs., Springfield, 1985-86; facility dir. Herrick House, Bartlett, Ill., 1986—. Organizer St. Nicholas Tenants Orgn., Springfield, 1985. Mem. Am. Assn. Mental Deficiency (treas. 1984-86), Assn. Mental Health Adminstrs. (cert.), Assn. Retarded Citizens, Child Care Assn., Pi Alpha Alpha. Unitarian. Avocations: folk singer, guitarist. Office: Herrick House Children's Ctr 1 W Bartlett Rd Bartlett IL 60103

HIRSCH, CHRISTIAN RICHARD, mathematics educator; b. Le Mars, Iowa, Mar. 6, 1944; s. Chris Richard and Margaret Katherine (Wiltgen) H.; children: Emily, Anne, Jennifer. BA, U. Iowa, 1966; MA, Creighton U., 1969; MS, U. Ill., 1970; PhD, U. Iowa, 1972. Math. tchr. South High Sch., Omaha, 1966-67; chmn. math. dept. Notre Dame Acad., Omaha, 1967-69; spl. research asst. Iowa Testing Programs, Iowa City, 1971-72; vis. prof. U. Manitoba, Winnipeg, Can., 1972-73; prof. Western Mich. U., Kalamazoo, 1973—; mem. adv. bd. Kalamazoo Area Math. and Sci. Ctr., 1985—. Author: Geometry 2d edit., 1984, Trigonometry and Its Applications, 1985; editor: The Secondary School Math. Curriculum, 1985, also jours.; contbr. articles to profl. yearbooks and jours. Fellow NSF, 1969-70; NSF grantee, 1980, 81, 82. Mem. Am. Assn. Univ. Profs., Math. Assn. Am., Mich. Council Tchrs. Math. (v.p. 1981-85, pres. elect), Nat. Council Tchrs. Math. (mem. Commn. Standards for Sch. Math. 1986—), Sch. Sci. and Math. Assn. (bd. dirs. 1986—), Phi Delta Kappa. Democrat. Roman Catholic. Avocations: tennis, biking, swimming. Home: 6121 Torrington Rd Kalamazoo MI 49009 Office: Western Mich U Dept Math Kalamazoo MI 49008

HIRSCH, EDWARD, advertising executive; b. St. Louis, Dec. 3, 1924; s. Louis and Rose (Goldman) H.; m. Gloria Simon, Feb. 3, 1957; children: Irl B., Lynn, James S. BS, Washington U., St. Louis, 1949. Salesman Retailers Mkt. News, St. Louis, 1949-50; advt. mgr. Accounts Supervision Co., St. Louis, 1950-52; creative supr. Winius-Brandon Co., St. Louis, 1952-72; creative v.p. Sayers Communications, St. Louis, 1972-86. Editor: The Baby Team, 1979. Mem. Advt. Club St. Louis (Outstanding mem. 1949), Bus. and Profl. Advt. Assn. Democrat. Jewish. Lodge: B'nai Brith. Avocations: tennis, reading. Home and Office: Hirsch Communciations 7441 Byron Pl Clayton MO 63105

HIRSCH, JOHN STEPHEN, artistic director; b. Siofok, Hungary, May 1, 1930; emigrated to Can., 1947; s. Joseph and Ilona (Horvath) H. Student, Israel Gymnasium in, Budapest; D.Litt. (hon.), U. Man., 1966; also hon. fellow, Univ. Coll.; LL.D. (hon.), U. Toronto, 1967. lectr. Columbia, N.Y. U.; theatre cons. Can. Council, Ont. Arts Council; cons. BBC/PBS Shakespeare Project for Children's TV, 1978; cons. artistic dir. Seattle Repertory Theatre, 1979—. Dir. first play: The Time of Your Life at Little Theatre, Winnipeg, Man., Can., 1951; dir., Stratford Shakespearean Festival, Ont., 1965, The Cherry Orchard, Henry VI, 1966, Richard III, The Tempest, 1982, A Midsummer Night's Dream, The Three Musketeers, 1968, Satyricon, 1969; dir. first play in New York: Lorca's Yerma, Vivian Beaumont, for Repertory Theater of Lincoln Center, 1966; Galileo, 1967, St. Joan, 1968, The Time of Your Life, 1969, Beggar on Horseback, 1970, Playboy of the Western World, Antigone, 1971; dir.: Broadway prodn. of We Bombed in New Haven, 1968, AC/DC, for Chelsea Theater Center, 1970; for Theatre du Nouveau Monde, Mere Courage, 1964, for the Habimah, Tel Aviv, The Seagull, 1970; asso. artistic dir., Stratford (Ont.) Shakespearean Festival, 1967-69, artistic dir., Stratford (Ont.) Shakespearean Festival, 1981—, founder, Rainbow Stage, Theatre 77, Man. Theatre Centre; entered film prodn. in Can. with: In The Shadow of the City, 1955; first directed on TV, in 1954; and has since directed: The Three Musketeers; co-artistic dir., Stratford Festival Theatre, 1968-69; dir.: Midsummer Nights Dream, Mpls. Theatre, 1972, The Dybbuk, Los Angeles prodn. Mark Taper Forum, 1975, Maggie Smith in The Three Sisters, Stratford Festival, 1976, The Tempest, Mark Taper Forum, 1979, Number Our Days, Mark Taper Forum, 1979; exec. producer: Sarah, 1976; head TV drama, English service div. CBC, 1976-78; History of the American Film, Nat. Arts Centre, Ottawa, 1979; Author: children's plays Rupert the Great; New Translation and Adaptation of Ansky's The Dybbuk.; Contbr. articles to profl. jours. Bd. dirs. Theatre Communications Group, Royal Winnipeg Ballet. Recipient Order of Can. medal, Outer Circle Critics award for St. Joan, Obie award for AC/DC, Canadian Authors Assn. award for transl. and adaptation The Dybbuk.

HIRSCH, LORE, psychiatrist; b. Mannheim, Fed. Republic of Germany, July 8, 1908; came to U.S., 1940; d. Erwin Hirsch and Marie Kiefe; m. Eugene Hesz, Jan. 25, 1958 (div. Oct. 1968). MD, Karl Ruprecht U., Heidelberg, Fed. Republic Germany, 1937. Diplomate Am. Bd. Neurology and Psychiatry. Intern Greenpoint Hosp., Bklyn., 1942-43; resident Bellvue Hosp., N.Y.C., 1943-48; sect. chief VA Hosp., Bronx, N.Y., 1949-54; dir. psychiatry Wayne County Gen. Hosp., Mich., 1954-55; dir. outpatient services Northville (Mich.) Regional Hosp., 1955-58; practice medicine specializing in psychiatry Dearborn, 1958—. Contbr. numerous articles to profl. jours. Fellow Am. Psychiat. Assn. (life); mem. AMA (life), Mich. Med. Soc., Wayne County Med. Soc., Mich. Psychiat. Soc. Unitarian-Universalist. Avocations: books, theatre, travel. Home: 212 S Melborn St Dearborn MI 48124 Office: 2021 Monroe St Dearborn MI 48124

HIRSCH, MARY MARGARET, dentist; b. Milw., Oct. 22, 1956; d. Clifford William and Irene Mary (Jones) H.; m. Craig Jeffrey Madsen, July 25, 1981. BS in Natural Sci., U. Wis., 1978; DDS, Marquette U., 1982; student, U.S. Dental Inst., Skokie, Ill., 1986—. Dentist Madison Family Dental Clinic, 1982-85, Madsen & Hirsch, Madison, 1985—. Mem. ADA, Dane County Dental Soc., Wis. Dental Assn., Am. Acad. Gen. Dentistry, Am. Assn. Functional Orthodontics, Am. Assn. Women Dentists. Roman Catholic. Club: Toastmasters. Office: Madsen & Hirsch 6313 Odana Rd Madison WI 53719

HIRSCH, NORMA JEAN, neonatologist; b. Charles City, Iowa, Aug. 2, 1944; d. Milton Charles and Dorothy Leona (Lacour) H. B.S., Iowa State U., 1966; M.D., U. Iowa, 1970. Diplomate Am. Bd. Pediatrics. Intern pediatrics Children Med. Ctr., Dallas, 1970-71, resident, 1971-73; fellow in pediatric nephrology Ind. U., Indpls., 1973-74; asst. prof. pediatrics U. Tex., Dallas, 1974-75; fellow in neonatology Baylor Coll. Medicine, Houston, 1975-77; neonatologist, clin. asst. prof. Baylor U. Med. Ctr., 1977-79; clin. asst. prof. pediatrics U. Iowa, Iowa City, also staff Newborn Care Cons., P.C., Des Moines, 1979—; clin. asst. prof. pediatrics U. Iowa, Iowa City, 1979—; med. dir. Variety Club Newborn Intensive Care Nursery, 1981—. Author, editor numerous med. publs. Bd. dirs. Sherman Hill Assn., 1983—. Named Woman of Achievement, YWCA, 1983. Fellow Am. Acad. Pediatrics (Iowa chpt. liason to state legis., liason to healthy mothers, healthy babies coalition); mem. AMA, Am. Med. Womens Assn., Iowa Med. Soc., Polk County Med. Soc. Democrat. Lutheran. Club: Embassy. Office: Newborn Care Cons PC PO Box 4566 Des Moines IA 50306

HIRSCH, SAMUEL ROGER, allergist; b. Chgo., Dec. 19, 1930; s. Bernard Bruno and Lucille (Hoffman) H.; m. Adrienne Cogan, Aug. 22, 1954; children: Daniel, Michael, Sharon, Brian. BA, U. Wis., 1953, MD, 1956. Intern Ill. Research and Edn. Hosp., Chgo., 1956-57, resident, 1957-58; resident VA Med. Ctr., Milw., 1960-63, chief allergy and pulmonary research lab., 1975-85; practice medicine specializing in allergy Milw., 1963—; Assoc. clin prof. Med. Coll. Wis., Milw., 1975—, U. Wis., Milw., 1980—. Author Allergy Cookbook and Food Buying Guide, 1982; contbr. articles to profl. jours. Served to capt. USAF, 1958-60. Fellow ACP, Am. Coll. Chest Physicians, Am. Acad. Allergy and Immunology (chmn. audio visual com. 1982), Am. Coll. Allergists; mem. AMA (Physicians Recognition award 1971, 80, 82, 85), Wis. Allergy Soc. (pres. 1975-77). Avocation: banjo strumming. Office: Allergic Diseases SC 5020 W Oklahoma Ave Milwaukee WI 53219

HIRSCHENBERGER, RICHARD HENRY, psychologist; b. Grosse Point, Mich., Jan. 29, 1950; s. Henry Anthony and Kathleen Patricia (Byrne) H.; 1 child, Kristie. Student, St. Thomas Coll., St. Paul, Minn., 1968-71; BS in Psychology, DePaul U., 1972; MS in Behavior Modification, So. Ill. U., 1975. Lic. psychologist, Minn. Behavior specialist Carbondale, Ill., 1974-75; behavior modification coordinator Dubuque, Iowa, 1975-80; psychologist Brainerd (Minn.) Regional Human Services, 1980—. Exec. com. mem. Minn. State Council for the Handicapped. Mem. Assn. Behavior Analysis, Minn. Assn. Behavior Analysis (exec. com.), Minn. Licensed Psychologists, Handicapped Action Assn. (pres.). Home: 4321 Cedardale Ln Baxter MN 56401 Office: Brainerd Regional Human Services Ctr 1777 E Oak St Brainerd MN 56401

HIRSCHFIELD, A. A., provincial judge. Judge Ct. of Queen's Bench, Winnipeg, Man., Can. Office: Ct of Queen's Bench, Law Cts Bldg, Winnipeg, MB Canada R3C 0V8 *

HIRSCHMAN, SHERMAN JOSEPH, lawyer, accountant, educator; b. Detroit, May 11, 1935; s. Samuel and Anna (Maxmen) H.; m. Audrey Hecker, 1959; children—Samuel, Shari. B.S., Wayne State U., 1956, J.D., 1959, LL.M., 1968. Bar: Mich. 1959, Fla. 1983, Wis. 1984; C.P.A., Mich., Fla.; cert. tax lawyer, Fla. Practice, Mich., 1959—; instr. comml. law Detroit Coll. Bus., 1971—. Served with U.S. Army Res., 1959-62. Mem. Mich. Bar Assn., Fla. Bar Assn., Wis. Bar Assn. Office: 29870 Middlebelt St Farmington Hills MI 48018 also: 3101 W Buffalo Tampa FL 33557

HIRSH, WILLIAM CLIFFORD, manufacturing engineer; b. Syracuse, N.Y., Dec. 7, 1959; s. William Thomas Hirsh and Leona Margaret (Peterson) Carbonaro; m. Sally Ann Metzler, June 2, 1984. AS, AS in Engring. Sci., Mohawk Valley Community Coll, 1981; BSME, Syracuse U., 1983. Supr. maintenance Miller Brewing Co. Cen. N.Y. Bottle Co., Auburn, 1983; mfg. engr. Gen. Motors Truck and Bus. Flint (Mich.) Metal Fabricating, 1984—. Named Eagle Scout, Boy Scouts Am., 1974; recipient James Brink Sportsmanship award Baldwinsville and Acad. Cen. Schs., 1978; scholar N.Y. State Regents Found., 1978, Baldwinsville Community, 1978, James Walter Carrier, 1982. Mem. ASME (assoc.). Avocations: stamp collecting, hunting, fishing, trapping, gardening. Home: 401 Lincoln St Fenton MI 48430 Office: Gen Motors Truck/Bus Flint Metal Fabricating G2238 W Bristol Rd Flint MI 48553

HIRST, ROBERT LYNN, senior internal auditor; b. Boulder, Colo., May 9, 1947; s. LeRoy John and Betty jo (Curtis) H.; m. Mary M. Schlicher, Aug. 25, 1968 (div. June 1983); m. Kelly D. Holzman, Jan. 14, 1984. BA, Southwestern Coll., 1969. Cert. internal auditor. Social worker Kans. Social and Rehab. Services, Wichita, 1969-73, unit supr. welfare, 1973-81; internal auditor The Coleman Co., Inc., Wichita, 1981-87, sr. internal auditor, 1987—. Treas. Coventry Homeowners Assn., Wichita, 1986. Mem. Soc. Bib. Lit., Inst. Internal Auditors, Alban Inst. Associated Parishes. Avocations: music, reading, photography. Home: 1450 S Webb Rd #423 Wichita KS 67207 Office: The Coleman Co Inc 250 N St Francis Wichita KS 67201

HISCHKE, PAUL HAROLD, info systems executive; b. Oconto Falls, Wis., June 15, 1945; s. Frederick Carl and Martha Marie (Struck) H.; m. Lynne Baker, 1965 (div. 1971); m. Lynn Karen Buchman, Nov. 12, 1973; children: Julie, James. Student, U. Wis., 1971. Acct. Mueller Climatrol, Milw., 1969-73; engring. analyst Accurate Indsl. Devel., Milw., 1973-76, Jos. Schlitz Brewing Co., Milw., 1976-80; mgmt. info. systems and data processing mgr. CH2M Hill, Milw., 1980-85; systems project mgr. Milw. Met. Sewerage Dist., 1985—. Served with USN, 1966-68. Democrat. Roman Catholic. Home: 2944 S 12th St Milwaukee WI 53215 Office: Milw Met Sewerage Dist 735 N Water St Milwaukee WI 53202

HITCHCOCK, DONALD SIMON, architectural engineering company executive; b. Putnam County, Ohio, May 12, 1929; s. George Clinton and Teresa Fern (Ridenour) H.; m. Gwenna F. Hicks, July 4, 1955; children: Thomas, Michael, James. B.S. in Engring., U.S. Mcht. Marine Acad., 1951; M.M. in Fin., Northwestern U., 1980. Registered profl. engr., Ill., Ohio, Ind., W.Va. Sr. engr. Central Foundry div. Gen. Motors Corp., Defiance, Ohio, 1955-69; exec. v.p. Lester B. Knight & Assocs., Inc. (architects/engrs.), Chgo., 1970—. Past pres. Anthony Wayne Sch. PTA, Defiance; past mem. Traffic Safety Commn., Western Springs, Ill.; trustee Foundry Edn. Found.; mem. indsl. adv. bd. So. Ill. U. at Carbondale. Served to lt. USNR, 1951-54. Mem. Foundry Equipment Mfrs. Assn. (past pres.), Nat. Soc. Profl. Engrs., Am. Foundrymen's Soc., Western Soc. Engrs., Ill. Soc. Profl. Engrs., Chgo. Bldg. Congress (dir.), Chgo. Acad. Scis. (v.p.), Soc. Am. Mil. Engrs., Nat. Council Engring. Examiners (registered). Presbyterian. Clubs: Chgo. Athletic Assn., Tavern, Economic (Chgo.); La Grange Country. Home: 3801 Central Ave Western Springs IL 60558 Office: Lester B Knight & Assocs Inc 549 W Randolph St Chicago IL 60606

HITCHCOCK, ROBERT FRANK, mechanical engineer; b. Chgo.; s. Robert Oan and Helen Anntenet (Riha) H.; m. Mary Dawn O'Hara, June 23, 1973; children: Robert A., Kelly M. AS in Mech. Tech., Coll. DuPage, 1970; BS in I&T, No. Ill. U., 1972. Design engr. Wire Cloth Products, Bellwood, Ill., 1973-75; design engr. Nat. Metal Products, Bensonville, Ill., 1975-76, plant engr., 1976-78; project engr. Advt. Metal DisPlay, Chgo., 1976; chief engr. Sealed Power Corp., Des Plaines, Ill., 1978-84; mgr. tool and product engring. Ekco Products Inc., Wheeling, Ill., 1984—. Inventor method of assembling metal and plastic, method and design for auto air conditioner dehydrator dryer. Mem. Vill. Planning Commn., Glendale Heights, Ill., 1983. Mem. Soc. Mfg. Engrs. Roman Catholic. Office: Ekco Products Inc 777 Wheeling Rd Wheeling IL 60090

HITCHCOCK, ROGER ELROY, accountant; b. Midland, Mich., Mar. 4, 1955; s. Carl Elroy and Glenna May (Brubaker) H.; m. Gail Ann Szczepanski, Sept. 30, 1977; children: Troy, Paige, Andrea. Assocs. in Bus., Mid-Mich. Community Coll., 1979; BBA, Cen. Mich. U., 1981. CPA, Mich. Staff acct. Price Waterhouse, Battle Creek, Mich., 1981-83; sr. acct. Laine, Appold & Co., Bay City, Mich., 1983—. Served as sgt. USAF, 1973-77. Mem. Am. Inst. CPA's, Mich. Assn. CPA's. Roman Catholic. Home: 4547 SE Lewis Dr Bay City MI 48706 Office: Laine Appold & Co 720 Livingston Bay City MI 48708

HITE, LINDA MCNEIL, assistant university dean; b. Steubenville, Ohio, Sept. 23, 1952; d. Charles E. and Ruth Ann (George) McNeil; m. Richard L. Hite, May 22, 1982. BA, Mt. Union Coll., 1974; MEd, Edn. Specialist, Kent State U., 1976; PhD, Purdue U., 1983. Cert. counselor. Counselor Cuyahoga Community Coll., Warrensville Hts., Ohio, 1976-77; adminstrv. asst. Kent State U., 1976-77; counselor Purdue U., West Lafayette, Ind., 1977-84, asst. dean students, 1984—. Mem. Nat. Assn. Women Deans Adminstrs. and Counselors (directorate 1983-85, div. chmn. 1986—), Am. Assn. Counseling and Devel. Home: 2308 Butler St Lafayette IN 47905 Office: Purdue U Dean of Students Office Hovde Hall West Lafayette IN 47907

HITT, WILLIAM DEE, organizational psychologist; b. Lexington, Ky., Feb. 18, 1929; s. Sellers William and Clyde (Barnes) H.; m. Diane Frances Umbaugh, Jan. 26, 1957; children: Jennifer, Jodi, Julie, Jill. BA, U. Ky., 1951; MA, Ohio State U., 1954, PhD, 1956. Research psychologist Battelle Meml. Inst., Columbus, Ohio, 1957-59, chief behavioral scis. div., 1960-70, dir. ctr. for improved edn., 1971-76, dir. mgr. devel., 1977—. Author: Education as a Human Enterprise, 1973, Managment in Action, 1985. Served to 1st lt. USAF, 1951-53. Mem. Am. Psychol. Assn., Am. Mgmt. Assn., Sigma Xi. Avocation: studying philosophy. Home: 223 W Southington Worthington OH 43085 Office: Battelle Meml Inst 505 King Ave Columbus OH 43201

HIXENBAUGH, MELISSA JEANNÉ, Arabian horse breeder; b. St. Louis, June 7, 1950; d. Evert O. and Alta (Fally) Scoles; m. Larry Gene Hixenbaugh, Aug. 28, 1971. AA, Kaskaskia Coll., 1970. Several clerical positions various, Centralia, Ill., 1968-86; owner, mgr. Lar-Mel Ranch, Centralia, 1977—; coordinator hourse units Centralia Halloween Parade, 1980-83. Mem. Am. Horse Shows Assn., Internat. Arabian Horse Assn., Arabian Horse Registry, Internat. Side Saddle Orgn., Pyramid Soc. Baptist. Clubs: Walnut Hill Saddle (bd. dirs. 1984-86, v.p. 1987—), Ill. Arabian Horse Assn., Abu Horse Club, Arab, Inc., Mo. Arabian Horse Assn. Avocations: collecting dolls, horse models, and postcards, dancing, riding. Home and Office: Rt 4 Box 146A Centralia IL 62801

HLADKY, JOSEPH F., III, publishing executive; b. Cedar Rapids, Iowa, Mar. 20, 1940; s. Joseph F. Jr. and Jane (Miller) H.; m. Katherine S. Kanealy; children: Elizabeth, Katherine. BA, U. Iowa, 1962. Trainee Bank Calif., Berkeley, 1962-63; dist. circulation supr. The Gazette Co., Cedar Rapids, 1963-65, display advt. salesman, 1965-70, prodn. mgr., 1970-77, v.p., 1972-80, pres., 1980—; bd. dirs. Banks of Iowa, Merchants Nat. Bank. Bd. dirs Coe Coll., Cedar Rapids, 1981—. Mem. Am. Soc. Newspaper Editors, Am. Newspaper Pubs. Assn. (tech. com. 1984—, bd. dirs., vice chmn. tech. com. 1986—), Iowa Newspaper Assn., Inland Daily Press Assn., Nat. Assn. Broadcasters, Cedar Rapids C. of C. (bd. dirs. 1984—). Club: Cedar Rapids Country. Lodges: Masons, Shriners. Home: 345 34th St SE Cedar Rapids IA 52403 Office: The Gazette Co 500 3d Ave SE Cedar Rapids IA 52401

HLAVAY, JAY ALAN, geologist; b. Pitts., Sept. 30, 1956; s. Joseph and Margaret Marie (Danjou) H.; m. Sandra Kay Yoho, July 15, 1978 (div. Apr. 1985). Student, Rutgers U., 1979; BS in Geology magna cum laude, U. Pitts., 1983. Geologist RSC Energy Corp., New Philadelphia, Ohio, 1983-85; dist. geologist Carless Resources Inc., New Philadelphia, 1985—. Navy ROTC scholar, 1974; recipient Appreciation award Tuscarawas Valley Desk and Derrick Club, 1985, 86. Mem. An. Assn. Petroleum Geologists, Ohio Geol. Soc., Soc. Profl. Well Log Analysts, Pitts. Geol. Soc., Ohio Oil and Gas Assn., Computer Oriented Geol. Soc., Pitts. Assn. Petroleum Geologists, Sigma Gamma Epsilon. Home: Rt 4 Box 503BB Dover OH 44622 Office: Carless Resources Inc Rt 2 Box 2174 New Philadelphia OH 44663

HLAVIN, PETER JOSEPH, investment banker; b. Evergreen Park, Ill., Jan. 7, 1958; s. Joseph Raymond and Genrose (Smith) H. BBA, U. Iowa, 1980; MBA, Ind. U., 1982. Banking officer RepublicBank, Dallas, 1982-84; assoc. Rauscher Pierce Refsnes, Inc., Dallas, 1984-86; v.p. Mesirow Fin. Corp., Chgo., 1986—. Author: (book) Instructional Business Case, Energy Lending: Penn Circle National Bank, 1984. Advisor Jr. Achievement, Dallas, 1984. Office: Mesirow Fin Corp 350 N Clark St Chicago IL 60610

HO, ALFRED RONALD, accountant; b. Kowloon, Hong Kong; came to U.S., 1953; s. Ronald and Lucy (Young) H.; m. Sherry Fong Moy, Feb. 20, 1970; children: Jennifer, Tamera, Katherine, Jeremy. BSBA, U. Mo., St. Louis, 1973. CPA, Mo. Agt. IRS, 1973-77; tax acct. Rubin, Brown, Gornstein & Co., CPA's, 1977-78; pvt. practice acctg. St. Louis, 1978—. Served with USAR, 1971-77. Mem. Am. Inst. CPA's, Mo. Soc. CPA's. Home: 2195 Parasol Chesterfield MO 63017 Office: 11431 Gravois Saint Louis MO 63126

HO, DAVID K., manufacturing company executive; b. Honolulu, Mar. 5, 1948; s. Raymond T.Y. and Ellen T.Y. (Fong) H.; m. Joan Yee, July 6, 1968 (div. Apr. 1982); 1 child, Michael J.; m. Patricia Ann McAndrews, June 25, 1983. BS in Indsl. Engring., U. So. Calif., 1970; MBA, Butler U., 1976; MS in Acctg., U. Wis., Whitewater, 1981. Indsl. engr. FMC Corp., Los Angeles, 1970-73; mgr. production planning and inventory control FMC Corp., Indpls., 1973-77; materials mgr. Butler Mfg. Co., Ft. Atkinson, Wis., 1977-81; systems mgr. Butler Mfg. Co., Kansas City, Mo., 1981-82; dir. materials and systems Behlen Mfg. Co., Columbus, Nebr., 1982-84, v.p. operations, 1984—; also bd. dirs. Behlen Mfg. Co., Columbus. Mem. acctg. adv. bd. City of Columbus, 1986—. Mem. Inst. Indsl. Engrs. (sr.), Am. Production and Inventory Control Soc. Republican. Baptist. Home: 8907 N 52d Ave Omaha NE 68152

HO, JAMES CHIEN-MING, science educator; b. Kiengsu, China, July 31, 1937; came to U.S., 1961; s. Jungsiao and Jing Po (Huang) H.; m. Lydia S. Hsu, Aug. 8, 1964; children: Claudia, Marilyn. BSCE, Nat. Taiwan U., Taipei, 1959; MS in Chemistry, Univ. Calif., Berkeley, 1963, PhD in Chemistry, 1966. Research fellow Lawrence Radiation Lab., Berkeley, Calif., 1966-67; sr. scientist Battelle Meml. Inst., Columbus, Ohio, 1967-71; assoc. prof. physics Wichita State U., Kans., 1971-76, prof., 1976—, prof. physics and chemistry, 1985—; sr. resident research assoc. Nat. Research Council, Dayton, Ohio, 1972, 1973, 1975; vis. prof. Chemistry Univ. Calif.-Berkeley, 1977-78. Contbr. articles to profl. jours. Pres. Wichita Asian Assn., 1981-82; chmn. bd. dirs. Wichita Indo-Chinese Center, 1983-84; mem. Sister City Adv. Bd., Wichita, 1985—; bd. dirs. S. Cen. Kans. Econ. Devel. Dist., 1985—, Wichita area council Girl Scouts U.S., 1985—. Recipient 10 Who Care award Sta. KAKE-TV, 1984. Mem. ASTM, AAAS, Am. Phys. Soc., Am. Chem. Soc., Sigma Xi. Office: Wichita State U Physics Dept Wichita KS 67208

HO, LEO CHI CHIEN, education administrator; b. Tai Hu, An-Wei, Republic of China, Sept. 2, 1940; came to U.S., 1964, naturalized, 1971; s. Yu Yuan and Hung (King) H.; m. Julie Yu-Ling Hou, May 11, 1967; children: Albert, Alexander. BA, Nat. Cheng Chi U., Taipei, Republic of China, 1964; MLS, Atlanta U., 1967; PhD, Wayne State U., 1975. Librarian Tex. Tech U., Lubbock, 1966-69; dir. China Sci. Pub., Taylor, Mich., 1969-77; bus. librarian Detroit Pub. Library, 1970-75; librarian Washtenaw Community Coll., Ann Arbor, Mich., 1977—; pres. Fin. Brokers' Exchange, Farmington Hills, Mich., 1978-87; edn. adminstr. Sylvan Learning Ctr.Mich., West Bloomfield, 1987—; bd. dirs. Sylvan Learning Ctr. of Mich. Mem. adv. council Guide to Ethnic Museums, Libraries, and Archives in the U.S., 1984. Bd. govs. Internat. Inst. of Greater Met. Detroit, 1985—; commr. Mich. Gov.'s Adv. Com. on Asian Affairs, Lansing, 1986—. Mem. Detroit Chinese Cultural Ctr. (pres. 1984-86, Outstanding Service award 1984), Assn. Chinese-Ams. (v.p. 1985—). Lodge: Rotary. Home: 35126 Glengary Circle Farmington Hills MI 48018 Office: Sylvan Learning Ctr 5755 W Maple Suite 115 West Bloomfield MI 48033

HO, ROBERT EN MING, physician; b. Honolulu, Nov. 13, 1942; s. Donald Tet En Ho and Violette (Weeks) Gould; m. Edie Olsen, June 27, 1964; children: Lisa, Amy. BS cum laude, Mich. State U., 1964; MD, Wayne State U., 1968. Diplomate Am. Bd. Neurol. Surgery. Surg. intern Detroit Gen. Hosp., 1968-69, surg. resident, 1969-70, neurosurg. resident, 1972-76; microsurg. fellow Neurochirurgische Universtatskilinik, Zurich, Switzerland, 1976; instr. dept. neurosurgery Wayne State U., Detroit, 1977-79, dir. dept. neurosurgery Gertrude Levin Pain Clinic, 1977-80, asst. prof., 1979-84, chief neurosurg. services Health Care Inst., 1979-84, founder, dir. Microneurosurg. Lab., 1977—, clin. asst. prof., 1984—; dir. neuroscis. intensive care unit Harper Hosp., Detroit, 1980-84; mem. audit com. Detroit Gen. Hosp., 1977-80, mem. med. device com., 1977-80, mem. credentials com., 1978-84; sec., treas. Detroit Neurosurg. Acad. Program Com., 1978-84; mem. emergency room com. Harper Hosp., 1980-84, neuroscis. intensive care unit com., 1980-84; dir. Oakland-Macomb PPO; chief neurol. sect. William Beaumont Hosp., Troy, Mich., trustee, 1986—; presenter of numerous exhibits, profl. papers; organizer numerous med. meetings.; lectr. in field. Contbr. articles to profl. jours. Served with U.S. Army, 1970-72, Vietnam. Recipient Intern of Yr. award Detroit Gen. Hosp., 1969. Mem. AMA, ACS, Congress Neurol. Surgeons, Detroit Neurosurg. Acad., Mich. Assn. Neurol. Surgeons (sec.-treas. 1979-82, v.p. 1982-84, pres. 1984-86, bd. dirs. 1986—), Mich. State Med. Soc., Oakland County Med. Soc., Wayne County Med. Soc., Internat. Coll. Surgeons (U.S. sect.), Am. Assn. Neurol. Surgeons (spinal disorders sect. 1981, cerebrovascular surgery sect.). Office: 44199 Dequindre Rd Suite 402 Troy MI 48098

HO, TERRY JAUSHONG, physician; researcher; b. Shin-chu, Taiwan, Feb. 16, 1939; came to U.S., 1970, naturalized, 1975; s. Tein-chen and Fong (Chen) H.; m. Gloria Lomero Reyes, May 17, 1973; 5 children. B. Eng., Cheng-Kung U., Tainan, Taiwan, 1962, M.D., 1969. Diplomate Am. Bd. Ob-Gyn. Intern, Elizabeth Gen. Hosp., N.J., 1970-71; resident in ob-gyn N.J. Med. Sch., Newark, 1971-75; practice medicine specializing in ob-gyn Greene County Hosp., Linton, Ind., 1975-77, Union Hosp., Regional Hosp., Terre Haute, Ind., 1977—; instr. N.J. Med. Sch., 1974-75; chmn. dept. ob-gyn Greene County Hosp., 1975-77, dept. ob-gyn, Regional Hosp., 1982-83; assoc. faculty Ind. U. Sch. Medicine, Indpls., 1979. Fellow A.C.S., Am. Coll. Obstetricians, Gynecologists; mem. Am. Fertility Soc., Vigo County Med. Soc., AMA. Avocations: oil painting. Home: PO Box 508 Riley IN 47871 Office: 1724 W 7th St Terre Haute IN 47804

HOAG, DAVID H., steel company executive; b. 1939; married. BA, Allegheny Coll., 1960. With LTV Steel Co., Cleve., 1960—, sales trainee, 1960-61, salesman Cin. and Chgo. dist. sales offices, 1961-68, asst. prodn. mgr. standard pipe, 1968-69, prodn. mgr. standard pipe, then asst. dist. sales mgr. Pitts. dist. sales offices, 1968-75, then prodn. mgr. hot rolled sheet, then mgr. tubular prodn. sales, then gen. sales specialty steels, 1968-75, gen. mgr. mktg., 1975-77, v.p. mktg. services, 1977-79, pres. basic steel Eastern div., 1979-82, exec. v.p., from 1982, now pres., chief operating officer, also bd. dirs.; former group v.p. parent co. LTV Corp., Dallas, now exec. v.p., bd. dirs. Office: LTV Steel Co Inc 25 W Prospect Ave Cleveland OH 44115 Other Office Address: LTV Steel Company 25 W Prospect Ave Cleveland OH 44115 *

HOAG, JOHN ELLIS, farmer; b. Elyria, Ohio, Feb. 23, 1939; s. Ellis DeForest and Erna I. (Dewald) H.; m. Patricia Jane Gregg, Sept. 2, 1961; children: David, Heather, Gary. BS, Miami U., Oxford, Ohio, 1961. Staff acct. Peat Marwick Mitchell, Cleve., 1962-66; apprentice grower Hoags Greenhouse, Elyria, 1966-69, mgr., grower, 1969-84, pres., gen. mgr., 1984—; sec., treas. Cleve. Growers Mktg. Co., 1980—, also bd. dirs.; bd. dirs. Greenhouse Vegetation Packing Co., Berea, 1981—; trustee Lakewood Park Cemetery, Rocky River, Ohio, 1984—. Pres. local parent-tchr. fellowship, Sheffield, 1970-72; bd. dirs. Sheffield (Ohio) Lake Schs., 1972-76. Named Outstanding Citizen, Jaycees, 1974. Mem. Ohio Greenhouse Assn., Cleve. Greenhouse Vegetation Growers Assn. (bd. dirs. 1984-87). Home: 5336 Abbe Rd Elyria OH 44035 Office: Hoags Greenhouse Inc 5319 Abbe Rd Elyria OH 44035

HOAGENSON, CONNIE LOU, practical nurse educator; b. Independence, Mo., Dec. 14, 1937; d. Kenneth John and Annabell (Bly) Smith Mosley; m. Evan Walter Seedorf, July 20, 1958 (div. Apr. 1970); m. Richard Eugene Hoagenson, Dec. 28, 1970; 1 son, Lloyd Walter. B.S., Coll. St. Francis, Joliet, Ill., 1982; R.N., Research Hosp., Kansas City, Mo., 1958. Cert. tchr., Mo. Inservice coordinator Jackson County Hosp., Kansas City, 1966-68; inservice instr. St. Joseph Hosp., Kansas City, 1968-70; surg. nurse Independence Sanitarium, 1970-71; instr. surg. technologists Health Occupations, Independence, 1971-81, instr. practical nurses, 1981—, coordinator daily activities, 1981—; author poetry. Mem. nurture com. Lutheran Ch. Mo. Synod, St. Louis, 1982—; tchr. midweek sch. St. Paul's Luth. Ch., Independence, 1981—; mem. Kansas City ARC, 1958—; bd. dirs. Beautiful Savior Home, Belton, Mo., 1980-82. Mem. Mo. State Assn. Health Occupation Educators (pres. 1985-86), Mo. Vocat. Assn. Democrat. Home: 1417 Millburn St Independence MO 64056 Office: Health Occupations 1509 W Truman St Independence MO 64050

HOAGLAND, JAMES LEE, electrical distribution executive; b. Oak Park, Ill., Nov. 2, 1922; s. Walter P. and Lola L. (Lee) H.; m. Florence E., Jan. 15, 1947; children: James, Edward, John, Peter. B.A., Colgate U., 1944. With Graybar Electric Co., 1946—; regional mgr. Graybar Electric Co., Chgo., 1972-75; v.p. Graybar Electric Co., 1975-78; exec. v.p. Graybar Electric Co., N.Y.C., 1979-80; pres., chief exec. officer Graybar Electric Co., 1980—, also dir.; dir. Centerre Bank N.A. Bd. dirs. St. Louis Symphony, Met. St. Louis YMCA, Arts and Edn. Council. Served with USNR, 1942-46. Clubs: St. Louis, Log Cabin, Old Warson Country; Union League (N.Y.C.). Office: Graybar Electric Co Inc 34 N Meramec Ave Saint Louis MO 63105 *

HOAGLUND, JAMES B., manufacturing company executive. Chmn., chief exec. officer McQuay Inc., Mpls. Office: McQuay Inc 13600 Industrial Park Blvd Minneapolis MN 55441 *

HOARD, CHARLES MASON, JR., communications company executive; b. Jefferson City, Mo., Oct. 1, 1955; s. Charles Mason Sr. and Yvonne (Walker) H.; m. Marcia Veronica, Oct. 5, 1982 (div. Dec. 1984). B in Gen. Studies, U. Kans., 1977; MA, Ohio U., 1979. Dir. ops. Sta. WAWA/WLUM-FM, Milw., 1979-80; gen. mgr. Cox Cable Communications, Maywood, Ill., 1980-82; dist. bus. mgr. Continental Cablevision, Dolton, Ill., 1982-85; area gen. mgr. Ameritech Mobile Communications, Schaumburg, Ill., 1985—; pres. The Comuplink Corp., Arlington Heights, Ill., 1985—. Mem. Minorities in Cable and New Technology (exec. bd. dirs. 1982—). Baptist. Home: 4130 Mallard Dr #6 Arlington Heights IL 60004 Office: Ameritech Mobile Communications 1515 Woodfield Rd #1400 Schaumburg IL 60173

HOARD, DOUGLAS LEE, accountant; b. Carson City, Mich., Dec. 9, 1958; s. Russell Lee and Carol (Lytle) H.; m. Ellen Renee Marco, Aug. 13, 1983. BBA, Cen. Mich U., 1982. CPA, Mich. Prin. Roslund Prestage CPA's, Alma, Mich., 1982—; bd. dirs. Gratiot Community Credit Union, Alma, Mich. 1985—. Mem. Am. Inst. CPA's, Mich. Soc. CPA's. Republican. Lodges: Rotary, Elks. Avocations: golf, computers. Home: 1203 S Swegles Saint Johns MI 48879 Office: Roslund Prestage CPA's 308 Gratiot Ave Alma MI 48801

HOARE, JAMES PATRICK, research chemist; b. Denver, Jan. 9, 1921; s. Patrick Joseph and Mary Josephine (Breen) H.; m. Therese Clare Tressel, Aug. 29, 1953; children: Karen Marie, Patrick James, John Paul. BS, Regis Coll., 1943; MS, The Cath. U. of Am., 1948, PhD, 1949. Instr. physics and chemistry Trinity Coll., Washington, 1949-52, asst. prof. physics and chemistry, 1952-54; phys. chemist. U.S. Naval Research Labs, Washington, 1954-57; prin. research engr. Ford Motor Co., Dearborn, Mich., 1957-60; sr. research chemist Gen. Motors Corp., Warren, Mich., 1960-79; research fellow Gen. Motors Corp. Research Labs., Warren, 1979—. Author: The Electrochemistry of Oxygen, 1968; contbr. chpts. to books. Judge Nat. and Internat. Sci. Fairs, Detroit; active Rep. Presdl. Task Force and U.S. Senatorial Club; tenor St. Agatha Chorale. Served with USN, 1944-46, PTO. Fellow Mullen, Cath. U. Am.; recipient John Campbell medal for Outstanding Basic Research on Oxygen, Gen. Motors Research Labs., 1982, John Campbell medal for Outstanding Basic Research on Chromium, Gen. Motors Research Labs., 1985, Alumni Sci. Achievement award, Cath. U. Am., 1984. Mem. Electrochem. Soc. (bd. dirs. 1971-73), Am. Chem. Soc., Internat. Soc. Electrochemistry, N.Y. Acad. Sci., Am. Electroplates Soc. (Gold Medal 1985, Silver Medal 1981, 83), Sigma Xi. Republican. Roman Catholic. Avocations: bowling, tennis, swimming, music composition, singing. Home: 26065 Dover Redford MI 48239 Office: Gen Motors Research Labs Dept 37 12 Mile and Mount Rds Warren MI 48090

HOBBS, DEAN GLENN, marine transportation manager, marine master pilot; b. Ann Arbor, Mich., Mar. 11, 1954; s. Charles R. and Zelma D. Spaulding; m. Brenda Jo Goldammer, Apr. 2, 1977; children—Annette Camelia, Cortney Jo. AAS, Gt. Lakes Maritime Acad., 1976; student Thornton Community Coll., 1980; BS in Bus. Mgmt., Regents Coll., 1987. Cadet, U.S. Steel Corp. Gt. Lakes Fleet, 1974, Amoco Oil Co., Gt. Lakes, 1975; 1st class tanker pilot Amoco Oil Co., Gt. Lakes Ops., 1976-79, master tanker pilot, 1979, coordinator marine services, Whiting, Ind., 1980-81, supr. ops. marine, 1981-84, supt. marine ops., 1985-86; fleet analyst Mich. Dept. Commerce, Traverse, 1986—; instr. Gt. Lakes Maritime Acad., 1979. Bd. visitors Gt. Lakes Maritime Acad., also bd. dirs. Alumni Assn. Mem. Internat. Ship Master's Assn., Soc. Naval Architects and Marine Engrs., Profl. Mariners Assn., U.S. Naval Inst. Clubs: Propellor (Chgo.), Toastmasters.

HOBBS, JAMES ALLEN, insurance executive; b. Richmond, Ind., July 28, 1930; s. Vernon D. and Benona H. (Heath) H.; m. Ann House, Dec. 27, 1952; children: Alan, Larry. B.S. in Bus, Ind. U., Bloomington, 1952. With Lafayette Life Ins. Co., Ind., 1954—; exec. v.p., sec., dir. Lafayette Life Ins. Co., 1968—. Bd. dirs. Lafayette Parks and Recreation Dept.; mem. lay adv. bd. St. Elizabeth Hosp.; bd. dirs. Mus. Art; mem. bd. pensions and ins. N. Ind. Meth. Ch.; trustee Trinity Meth. Ch. Served with USAF, 1952-54. Fellow Life Mgmt. Inst.; mem. Lafayette C. of C. (dir.), Life Office Mgmt. Assn. Republican. Methodist. Home: 907 Lazy Ln Lafayette IN 47904 Office: 2203 S 18th St Box 7007 Lafayette IN 47903

HOBBS, JAMES CALVIN, communications exec.; b. Harlingen, Tex., May 1, 1938; s. Edward and Bessie Mae (Jackson) H.; student N.Mex. State U., 1955-57; B.J., U. Mo., 1959, B.A. in Math, 1961, M.A. in Journalism, 1961; m. Marijo Caposell, July 11, 1970; children—Rachel Elizabeth, Jared Charles. Publs. editor Trane Co., La Crosse, Wis., 1962-65; publicist Dow Corning Corp., Midland, Mich., 1965-68; account exec., account supr. Ketchum, McLeod & Grove, Pitts., 1968-72; exec. v.p. Dave Brown & Assos., Inc., Oakbrook, Ill., 1972-85; creative dir. Loran Nordgren & Co., Inc., Frankfort, Ill., 1985-87; account exec. D.L. Arends Advt., Inc., Oakbrook, 1987—. Served with M.P., U.S. Army, 1962. Recipient Golden Quill award Pitts. Communications Assn., 1971. Mem. Soc. Tech. Communicators (chmn. Pitts. 1971-72), Public Relations Soc. Am., Am. Med. Writers Assn., Chgo. Headline Club, Profl. Photographers Am., Kappa Tau, Phi Alpha Mu, Sigma Alpha Epsilon, Sigma Delta Chi. Presbyterian. Club: Elks. Contbr. articles to profl. jours. Home: 3026 W 76th St Woodridge IL 60517 Office: 900 Jorie St Suite 70 Oakbrook IL 60521

HOBERG, GLENN, osteopathic physician; b. Burnstad, N.D., Oct. 12, 1927; s. Ole and Nora Christian (Land) H.; m. Georgia Mae Prouty; children: Mark, Glynn Laurel, Nora, Gordon. DO, Kirksville Coll., 1958. Cert. Am. Coll. Gen. Practice. Intern Saginaw (Mich.) Osteo. Hosp., 1958-59; pvt. practice osteo. medicine Med. Block Ltd., River Falls, Wis., 1959—; chief of staff River Falls City Hosp., 1966-76; chief of staff Hudson (Wis.) Hosp., 1981-82, also bd. dirs. Served to USN, 1945-52; col. M.C. Wis. N.G. Republican. Lutheran. Avocation: farming. Office: Med Block Ltd 504 S Main St River Falls WI 54022

HOCEVAR, GREGORY PAUL, metal processing specialist; b. Cleve., May 30, 1948; s. Charles F. and Elizabeth (Bezdek) H.; m. Elaine F. Mismas, Oct. 24, 1970; children: Gregory P. Jr., Matthew J., Ryan J., Sarah A. BS, Dyke Coll., 1970; MBA, Lake Erie Coll., 1983. Cert. purchasing mgr., Ohio. Staff acct., then asst. supr. acctg., then controller staff Pickands Mather & Co., Cleve., 1970-81, purchasing agt., 1981—; part-time evening prof. mgmt. and mktg. courses Dyke Coll. Mem. Nat. Assn. Purchasing Mgmt., Cleve. Purchasing Mgmt. Assn. (chmn. membership com., bd. dirs. 1986—), Lake County Golf Assn. Roman Catholic. Avocations: racquet sports, golf. Home: 14780 Russell Ln Novelty OH 44072 Office: Pickands Mather & Co 1100 Superior Ave Cleveland OH 44114

HOCH, LINDA LOU, educator, computer specialist; b. Quincy, Ill., Jan. 12, 1952; d. Edward George and Selma Elizabeth (Flick) Windoffer; m. Arnold Joseph Hoch, Aug. 18, 1973; children: Angela, Randall, Renee. BS in Edn., NE Mo. State U., 1973, M in Bus. Edn., 1975, computer cert., 1980. Computer bus. edn. instr. Westran, Huntsville, Mo., 1973—. Contbr. articles to newspapers and mags. Mem. Bus. and Profl. Standards, 1973—; dist. chmn. Cystic Fibrosis Found., Randolph County, Mo., 1975-77. Mem. Nat. Bus. Edn. Assn., North Cen. Bus. Edn. Assn., Mo. State Tchrs. Assn., Westran Community Tchrs. Assn. (pres. 1978-79), Future Tchrs. Am. (Mo. state advisor 1985-86, NE dist. advisor 1985—), Internat. Women in Leadership, Pi Omega Pi, Phi Delta Kappa, Alpha Phi Sigma. Roman Catholic. Club: Moberly's Women Aglow (Moberly, Mo.). Avocations: reading, sewing, cooking, computer programming.

HOCHSTEDLER, RITA TAYLOR, controller; b. Greencastle, Ind., July 5, 1960; d. Robert E. and Joan Marie (Staub) Taylor; m. Kevin Ray Hochstedler, Sept. 26, 1986. BS, Ind. State U., 1982. CPA, Ind. Staff acct. McGladrey, Hendrickson & Pullen, Indpls., 1983-85, South Bend, Ind., 1985-87; controller E.H. Tepe Co., Inc., South Bend, 1987—. Fellow Am. Soc. CPA's, Ind. CPA Soc., Am. Soc. Women Accts.

HOCHSTETLER, LEROY, small business owner; b. Nappanee, Ind., Jan. 1, 1939; s. Daniel H. and Lovina Hochstetler; m. Malinda Schmucker, June 18, 1957; children: Rebbeca, Linda, Nathan. Owner Hochstetler Well Drilling, Bremen, Ind., 1968—, Wellco Tool Pro., Bremen, 1970—, Rentown Shoppe, Bremen, 1972—, Burlington Wholesale, Bremen, 1980—. Home: 1533 3d Rd Bremen IN 46506

HOCHWALD, WERNER, educator, economist; b. Berlin, Germany, Jan. 21, 1910; s. Moritz and Elsa (Stahl) H.; m. Hilde Landenberger, Jan. 28, 1938 (dec. June 1958); children: Miriam Ruth, Eve Fay. Student, U. Freiburg, 1928-29; LL.B., U. Berlin, 1933; B.S., Washington U., St. Louis, 1940, A.M., 1942, Ph.D., 1944. Counsel Com. on Aid and Reconstrn., 1933-38; instr. ASTP, 1942-44; instr. to asso. prof. Washington U., St. Louis, 1944-49; prof. Washington U., 1950—, chmn. dept. econs., 1955-63, Tileston prof. polit. economy, 1958—; Kennedy Disting. prof. econs. U. of the South, 1981; cons. Fed. Res Bank of St. Louis, 1947-58; mem. citizens budget com., St. Louis. Author: Local Impact of Foreign Trade, 1960, An Economist's Image of History, 1968, The Rationality Concept in Economic Analysis, 1971; Contbg. author: Twentieth Century Economic Thought, 1950, Studies in Income and Wealth, 1957, Local Economic Activity and Foreign Trade, 1958, Design of Regional Accounts, 1962, Southern Economic Development, 1964, The Idea of Progress, 1973, Encyclopedia of Economics, 1981. Mem. Am. Econ. Assn., So. Econ. Assn. (pres. 1966-67), Midwest Econ. Assn., Nat. Bur. Econ. Research, Am. Statis. Assn. (nat. council 1950-52), Econometric Soc., Econ. History Assn., Internat. Assn. for Research in Income and Wealth, Phi Beta Kappa (chpt. pres.). Home: 6910 Cornell Ave University City MO 63130 Office: Dept Econs Washington U Saint Louis MO 63130

HOCK, PHILLIP HERSCHEL, pharmacist; b. Bowling Green, Ohio, Nov. 17, 1935; s. Clarence Herschel and Kathryn Eudora (Mansfield) H.; m. Jeannine North, Dec. 7, 1956 (div. Dec. 1975); children: Lori Ann Hock Shue, Molly, Elissa, James, Kathryn; m. Ramona LaVerne English, Jan. 5, 1976; 1 child, Phillip Adam. BS in Pharmacy, Ohio No. U., 1957. Registered pharmacist, Ohio, Mich., S.C. Owner Hock Pharmacy, Grand Rapids, Ohio, 1960-77, Hock Saxon Pharmacy, Sylvania, Ohio, 1976-79, Hock Pharmacy, Inc., Delta, Ohio, 1972-86; pharmacist Rite Aid Drug Co., Inc., Toledo, Ohio, 1986—. Mem. Grand Rapids City Council, 1964-71. Republican. Lutheran. Lodge: Masons. Avocations: gardening, golfing. Home: 18670 Main St Tontogany OH 43565

HOCKEIMER, HENRY ERIC, government official; b. Winzig, Germany, Apr. 3, 1920; came to U.S., 1946, naturalized, 1951; s. Erich and Gertrude (Masur) H.; m. Margaret Feeny, May 26, 1956; children: Ellen Patricia, Henry Eric. Student, RCA Insts., 1946-47; electronics and bus. mgmt., N.Y.U., 1948-51. With Philco-Ford Corp., Phila., 1947—; gen. mgr. communications and tech. services div. Philco-Ford Corp., 1962-63, corp. v.p., 1963-72; v.p., gen. mgr. refrigeration products div. Philco-Ford Corp., Connorsville, Ind., 1972-75; pres. Ford Aerospace & Communications Corp., Dearborn, Mich., 1975-85; v.p. Ford Motor Co., 1981-85; cons. USIA, Washington, 1985-86; dep. dir. TV and film service USIA, 1985—. Bd. dirs. Detroit Symphony, Hampton Inst.; bd. regents Cath. U. Am., Hampton U. Mem. Franklin Inst., Engring. Soc. Detroit, Electronic Industries Assn. Clubs: Capitol Hill (Washington); Renaissance, Detroit Econ., Nat. Space. Office: USIA 601 'D' NW Washington DC 20547

HOCKENBERG, HARLAN DAVID, lawyer; b. Des Moines, July 1, 1927; s. Leonard C. and Estyre M. (Zalk) H.; m. Dorothy A. Arkin, June 3, 1953; children—Marni Lynn Vrona, Thomas Leonard, Edward Arkin. B.A., U. Iowa, 1949, J.D., 1952. Bar: Iowa 1952. Assoc. Abramson & Myers, Des Moines, 1952-58; mem. firm Abramson, Myers & Hockenberg, Des Moines, 1958-64; sr. ptnr. firm Davis, Hockenberg, Wine, Brown , Koehn & Shors, predecessor, Des Moines, 1964—; dir. West Des Moines State Bank; trustee CPL Real Estate Investment Trust. Pres. Des Moines Jewish Social Service Agy., 1958-60; mem. Internat. Relations and Nat. Security Adv. Council, Republican Nat. Com., 1978; chmn. Council Jewish Fedns., Small Cities Com., 1970-71; mem. exec. com. Am. Israel Pub. Affairs Com.; pres. Wilkie House, Inc., Des Moines, 1965-66, Des Moines Jewish Welfare Fedn., 1973-74. Served with USNR, 1945-46. Mem. Des Moines C. of C. (chmn. 1986, chmn. bur. econ. devel. 1979, 80, bd. dirs. 1986), Greater Des Moines C. of C. (chmn. 1986), Delta Sigma Rho, Omicron Delta Kappa, Phi Epsilon Pi. Republican. Clubs: Des Moines, Pioneer, Wakonda. Home: 2880 Grand Ave Des Moines IA 50312 Office: Davis Hockenberg Wine Brown Koehn & Shors 2300 Financial Center Des Moines IA 50309

HOCKENBROCHT, DAVID WILLIAM, mfg. and oil co. exec.; b. Williamsport, Pa., Mar. 17, 1935; s. William Robert and May Elizabeth (Dietrick) H.; m. Joan Carol Ferguson, Aug. 4, 1956; children: Robin Gaye, Douglas David. B.S., Allegheny Coll., 1957; M.B.A., Western Res. U., 1965. Gen. mgr. subs. Standard Oil Co. of Ohio, Cleve., 1957-68; v.p. mktg. Curtis-Noll Corp., Cleve., 1968-71; pres. Auto & Acro Inc., Cin., 1971-73; dir. corp. acquisitions Firestone Tire & Rubber Co., Akron, Ohio, 1973-78; pres., chief operating officer, dir. Sparton Corp., Jackson, Mich., 1978—; also dir. Sparton Corp. Served to capt. USAF, 1958-60. Republican. Mem. Free Methodist Ch. Office: Sparton Corp 2400 E Ganson St Jackson MI 49202 *

HOCKENBURY, ROBERT WALTER, purchasing executive; b. Somerville, N.J., Feb. 14, 1949; s. Walter and Marjorie (Brittner) H.; m. Janet Claire Feilen, Aug. 14, 1971; children: Melanie Ann, Alison Blair. A in Applied Sci., Milw. Sch. Engring., 1970, BS, 1972. Design engr. CTC Marlin, Milw., 1972-77; mfg. supr. Graham Co., Milw., 1977-78, Delco Electronics, Oak Creek, Wis., 1978-79; sr. buyer Johnson Controls Inc., Milw., 1979—; instr. Waukesha County Tech. Inst., Pewaukee, Wis., 1977-79. Patentee digital trans. controller. Asst. coach Town Mukwonago (Wis.) Athletic Assn. Served with USAR, 1972—. Avocations: baseball, gardening. Office: Johnson Controls Inc 507 E Michigan St Milwaukee WI 53201

HOCKETT, MARCIA EILEEN, nurse, cardiovascular clinical nurse specialist; b. Dayton, Ohio, Jan. 10, 1948; d. Howard Sr. and Mary Louise (Jennings) Dozier; m. Clarence Hockett, Jr., Sept., 16, 1967. AS, Sinclair Community Coll., 1975; BS in Nursing, Miami U., Oxford, Ohio, 1981; MA, Ohio State U., 1986, postgrad. 1986—. Staff nurse intensive care, 1975-83, cardiovascular clin. nurse specialist, 1983—; adj. faculty clin. nursing Wright State U., 1984—. Vol., ARC, Dayton, 1983; mem. Cardiac Rehab. Task Force, Dayton, 1983. Grad. Traineeship grantee, Ohio State U., 1982. Mem. Am. Assn. Critical Care Nurses (pub. affairs com. 1983-85), Ohio Nurses Assn. (2d v.p. 1985—), Dist. Ten Nurses Assn. (bd. dirs. 1986—), Am. Heart Assn., Cardiovascular Council on Nursing, Sigma Theta Tau. Democrat. Baptist. Home: 5268 Torch Ln Dayton OH 45427 Office: VA Med Center 4100 W 3d St Dayton OH 45428

HOCKETT, TERRY GEORGE, investment company executive; b. Chgo., Mar. 3, 1949; s. George Curtis and Mary (Smith) H. BS in Bus., No. Ill. U., 1976, MS in Fin., 1982. Fin. analyst Bank of Am., San Francisco, 1976-78; v.p. Dowse Securities, San Francisco, 1978-80; cons. San Francisco, 1980-82; v.p. Lotsoff Capital, Chgo., 1982-86; sr. v.p. Lotsoff Systems, Chgo., 1982-86; cons. Equity Preservation Inc., Northfield, Ill., 1986—. Co-author: Gold Trading: A Computerized Evaluation of Trading Systems, 1981. Served with USN, 1968-71, Vietnam. Named one of Outstanding Young Men in Am., 1981. Mem. Tech. Securities Analysts Assn. San Francisco, DAV, Chgo. Hearing Soc., Chgo. Art Inst., Beta Gamma Sigma. Avocations: guitar, sailing, golf, fishing, reading. Home: 915 W Montana #26 Chicago IL 60614 Office: Equity Preservation Inc 790 Frontage Rd Northfield IL 60093

HODA, QAMRUL, physician; b. Jamshedpur, India, Feb. 2, 1942; came to U.S., 1969; s. Syed Anwarul and Ummatuz (Zohra) H.; I. Sci., St. Xavier's Coll., Ranchi, India, 1960; M.B.B.S., P.W. Med. Coll., Patna, India, 1965; M.D. in Pediatrics, Patna U., 1968; m. Nikhat Bano, June 14, 1972; children—Syed Tanveer, Tasnim. Intern, St. Joseph Mercy Hosp., Pontiac, Mich., 1969-70, now staff mem.; resident in pediatrics, Pontiac Gen. Hosp., 1970-72, now staff mem., cons. in pediatric nephrology, 1975—; resident Hosp. for Sick Children, Toronto, Ont., Can., 1972-73; teaching fellow in nephrology and ambulatory pediatrics Wayne County Gen. Hosp., Pontiac, 1974-75; pvt. practice medicine specializing in pediatrics and pediatric nephrology, Pontiac, 1975—. Fellow Am. Acad. Pediatrics; mem. Mich. Med. Soc., Oakland County Med. Soc., Detroit Pediatric Soc. Office: 185 Elizabeth Lake Rd Pontiac MI 48053

HODAPP, LARRY FRANK, accountant; b. Dayton, Ohio, Feb. 13, 1956; s. Ruey Frank Jr. and Carol Rose (Coons) H.; m. Susan Ann Harris, July 1, 1978; 1 child, Ryan Frank Harris. BS in Acctg. with honors, Ind. U., 1978. CPA, Ohio. Staff acct. Deloitte Haskins & Sells, Dayton, Ohio, 1978-79, sr. asst. acct., 1979-81, sr. acct., 1981-84, mgr., 1984—. Chmn. Miami Valley Regional Bicycle Com., Dayton, 1980—; fin. and site dir. Thunder Rd. Bike-A-Thon, Dayton, 1982—. Mem. League Am. Wheelmen/Bicycle USA (nat. dir., treas. Balt. 1982—), Inst. Fin. Mgrs., Am. Inst. CPA's, Ohio Soc. CPA's. Club: Toastmasters (pres. 1985-86). Lodge: Rotary (bd. dirs. Kettering club 1986-87, sec. 1987—). Avocations: bicycling, golf, stocks. Home: 4724 Bokay Dr Dayton OH 45440 Office: Deloitte Haskins & Sells 2200 Kettering Tower Dayton OH 45423

HODAPP, LEROY CHARLES, bishop; b. Seymour, Ind., Nov. 11, 1923; s. Linden Charles and Mary Marguerite (Miller) H.; m. Polly Anne Martin, June 12, 1947; children: Anne Lynn Hodapp Gates, Nancy Ellen Hodapp Wichman. A.B., U. Evansville, Ind., 1944, D.D., 1961; B.D., Drew Theol. Sem., Madison, N.J., 1947; L.H.D., Ill. Wesleyan U., 1977; D.D., McKendree Coll., 1978, Wiley Coll., 1980. Ordained to ministry Methodist Ch., 1947; pastor chs. in Ind. 1947-65; supt. Bloomington (Ind.) Dist. Meth. Ch., 1965-67, supt. Indpls. West Dist., 1967-68, supt. Indpls. N.E. Dist., 1968-70; dir. S. Ind. Conf. Council, 1970-76; bishop Ill. area United Meth. Ch., Springfield, 1976—; pres. United Meth. Gen. Bd. Ch. and Soc., 1980—. Coeditor: Change in the Small Community, 1967. Democrat. Office: 2427 E 2d St Bloomington IN 47401 *

HODDER, KENT HOLMES, film and video producer, director; b. Lincoln, Nebr., Nov. 5, 1956; s. William and Sue (Holmes) H. Assoc. producer documentary unit Moore on Sunday Sta. WCCO TV, Mpls., 1978-79, assoc. program producer PM Mag., 1979-81, asst. dir. programming and devel., 1981-83; creative dir. Prodn. 4 Studios, Mpls., 1983-86; pres. Met. Prodns. Inc., Mpls., 1985—; tchr. film U. Minn., Mpls., 1977-78; cons. in field, 1979-83. Author/producer: (TV drama) One Who Stole at Christmas, 1984 (Iris award 1984); producer (TV drama) Gift of the Magi, 1983. Recipient Tellies award U.S. Regional Comml. Awards, 1979, 80, 81, 82, 83, 84, 85, 86, Gold Achievement award Chgo. Film Festival, 1985, Service to Children award Nat. Assn. Broadcasters, 1986; Winner of Show, I.T.V.A., 1985. Mem. Nat. Assn. TV Arts and Scis. (Mpls./St. Paul chpt., chmn. membership com. 1986—), Am. Film Inst., Advt. Fedn. Minn. Home: 2288 Loop Station Minneapolis MN 55402 Office: Met Prodns Inc 2800 Foshay Tower Minneapolis MN 55402-2907

HODDER, WILLIAM ALAN, fabricated metal products company executive; b. Lincoln, Nebr., May 6, 1931; s. Ernest Chesley and Velma Catherine (Warren) H.; m. Suzanne Holmes, Apr. 3, 1954; children: Kent, Laurie, Susan, Mark, Beth. B.A., U. Nebr., 1954; grad., Programs and Mgmt. Devel. Program, Harvard, 1961. Mktg. positions IBM Corp., 1954-66; v.p. orgn. planning and devel. Dayton Co., Mpls., 1966-68; sr. v.p. Dayton Hudson Corp., 1970-73, dir., 1971-73; pres. Target Stores, 1968-73; pres., dir. Donaldson Co., Inc., Mpls., 1973—, chief exec. officer, 1982—, chmn. bd., 1984—; dir. Norwest Corp., Tennant Co., Network Systems Corp., Cowles Media Co., Northwestern Nat. Life Ins. Co., Moniterm Corp. mem. Minn. Bus. Partnership. Trustee Macalester Coll.; bd. overseers Coll. Bus. Adminstrn., U. Minn. Served with AUS, 1954-56. Mem. Chief Execs. Orgn., Inc., Soc. Automotive Engrs., Harvard Bus. Sch., Club Minn. (dir., past pres.). Clubs: Minneapolis, Minikahda. Home: 11 Circle West Edina MN 55436 Office: Donaldson Company Inc 1400 W 94th St Minneapolis MN 55431

HODEL, MERLE ALVIN, airline executive, flight educator, captain; b. Roanoke, Ill., Mar. 25, 1941; s. Alvin Amos and Emma (Fanny), H.; m. Gayle Ann Tanner, June 10, 1967; children—Martin Merle, Michelle D. B.S., So. Ill. U., 1967, M.S. in Edn., 1972. Chief pilot, chief flight instr. Airgo, Inc., Carbondale, Ill. 1968-70, asst. mgr. flying, capt., dispatcher, Air Ill., Inc., Carbondale, 1970-77; pilot Mobil Corp., Chgo., 1977-79; flight mgr., check airman, ground sch. instr., capt., Midway Airlines, Chgo., 1979—; bd. dir. Coll. DuPage Travel & Tourism Dept., Glen Ellyn, Ill., 1984—. Mem. Am. Biog. Inst. Research Assn., Aerospace Edn. Assn., Am. Soc. Aerospace Edn., Am. Assn. Flight Instrs., Ill. Pilots Assn., Pilots Internat. Assn., Nat. Aeronautics Assn., Aircraft Owners and Pilots Assn., Seaplane Pilots Assn., Phi Delta Kappa, Kappa Delta Pi. Republican. Avocation: computing. Home: 6028 Ridgeway Drive Woodridge IL 60517 Office: Midway Airlines 5700 S Cicero Ave Chicago IL 60638

HODEN, GARRY PHILLIP, manufacturing company executive; b. Duluth, Minn., July 12, 1948; s. Vernon Gustav and Patricia Ann (Garrison) H.; m. Mary Margaret Brinkmeier, July 10, 1970; children: Deirdre Mary, Derek Garrison. BA in Acctg., U. Minn., Duluth, 1970; MBA, St. Thomas Coll., 1981. CPA. Staff acct. Laventhol & Horwath, Mpls., 1970-75; audit supr. Grant Thorton, Mpls., 1975-78; corp. cost acct. mgr. Graco Inc., Mpls., 1978-86; v.p. fin. and administrn. Medallion Kitchens, Inc., Waconia, Minn., 1986—. Served with U.S. Army, 1970-72. Mem. Am. Inst. CPA's (hon. mention Elijah Watt Sells award 1974), Minn. Soc. CPA's, Crystal (Minn.) Jaycees (pres. 1976). Republican. Roman Catholic. Avocations: golf, hockey. Home: 8400 46th Ave N New Hope MN 55428 Office: Medallion Kitchens Inc 180 Industrial Blvd Waconia MN 55387

HODES, BARBARA, organizational consultant; b. Chgo., Nov. 30, 1941; d. David and Tybe Zisook; m. Scott Hodes, Dec. 19, 1961 (div. 1977); children: Brian, Valery; m. A. Bruce Schimberg, Dec. 29, 1984. BS, Northwestern U., 1962. Ptnr. Just Causes, cons. not-for-profit orgns., Chgo., 1978-86 ; cons. in philanthropy and organizational devel., 1987—; Chgo. cons. Population Resource Ctr., 1978-82. Woman's bd. dirs. Mus. Contemporary Art; bd. dirs., vice chmn. Med. Research Inst. Council, Michael Reese Med. Center; bd. dirs., chmn. Midwest Women's Ctr.; trustee Francis W. Parker Sch. Office: 209 E Lake Shore Dr Chicago IL 60611

HODES, HERBERT CHARLES, obstetrician gynecologist; b. Kansas City, Mo., Aug. 6, 1943; s. Michael and Dorothy (Kalis) H.; m. Andrea Faye Bornstein, Dec. 24, 1967; children: Traci, Carrie, Gregory, Garrett. BS, U. Mo., 1965; MD, Kans. U., 1969. Diplomate Am. Bd. Ob-Gyn. Intern St. Francis Hosp., Wichita, Kans., 1969-70; resident in ob-gyn. Kans. U. Med. Ctr., Kansas City, 1971-74; assoc. ob-gyn. Med. Ctr., PA, Hutchinson, Kans., 1974-77; practice medicine specializing in ob-gyn. Overland Park, Kans., 1977—; staff physician Shawnee Mission (Kans.) Med. Ctr., 1977—, Humana Hosp., Overland Park, 1980—. Served to lt. USNR, 1971-73. Fellow Am. Coll. Ob-Gyns., Am. Fertility Soc.; mem. AMA, Kans. Med. Soc., Kans. City Gyn. Soc., Gynecol. Laser Soc., Am. Assn. Gyn. Laparoscopists, Alpha Epsilon Pi. Avocations: jogging, scuba diving. Office: 4840 College Blvd Suite 100 Overland Park KS 66211

HODGE, ERNEST VANCE, banker; b. San Francisco, July 10, 1945; s. Meredith Vance and Julia Charlene (Robinson) H.; m. Claire Anne Burghardt, Dec. 18, 1968; children: Deborah, Susan. BA, Westminster Coll., 1967; MBA, U. Kans., 1971; grad., U. Wis., 1979. 2d v.p. Continental Ill., Chgo., 1971-82; v.p. Nat. Westminster Bank, Chgo., 1982-86. Treas. Walker Sch. PTA, Clarendon Hills, 1982-84. Served to sgt. USAF Res. Mem. Am. Bankers Assn. Republican. Presbyterian. Club: Oak Brook Polo. Home: 300 Harris Clarendon Hills IL 60514

HODGE, JAMES ROBERT, psychiatrist; b. Martins Ferry, Ohio, Jan. 28, 1927; s. Robert Gabriel and Ethel Melissa (Ashton) H.; m. Marilyn Jane Dinklocker, June 10, 1950; children: Sharon, Scott. B.S., Franklin and Marshall Coll., 1946; M.D., Jefferson Med. Coll., 1950; M.A., U. Akron, 1981. Intern U.S. Naval Hosp., St. Albans, N.Y., 1950-51; resident Menninger Sch. Psychiatry, Topeka, 1951-52, U.S. Naval Hosp., Oceanside, Calif., 1952-53, Univ. Hosps., Cleve., 1954-55; USPHS fellow in adult psychiatry Sch. Medicine Case-Western Res. U., 1955-56; practice medicine specializing in psychiatry Akron, Ohio, 1956—; head psychiatry Akron City Hosp., 1962-75, cons. staff, 1975-79, chmn. dept. psychiatry, 1979-85; assoc. program dir., clinic dir. St. Thomas Med. Ctr., 1986—; adj. prof. psychology U. Akron, 1963-85; prof. psychiatry Northeastern Ohio Univs. Coll. Medicine, 1980—; mem. council chiefs psychiatry Northeastern Ohio U. Coll. Medicine, Akron, 1974-76, 79—, dir. psychiat. residency tng. program, 1981-83, chmn. dept. of psychiatry, 1982—; grad. faculty in psychology Fla. Inst. Tech., 1976-83. Author: Practical Psychiatry for the Primary Physician, 1975, also articles in med. and psychiat. jours.; feature writer: Med. Times mag; producer: movie The Use of Hypnosis in Psychotherapy, 1975. Served to lt. USNR, 1944-45, 50-51, 52-54. Recipient spl. recognition award Ohio Psychiat. Assn., 1976, Meritorious Service award Ohio Psychiat. Assn., 1981. Fellow Am. Psychiat. Assn., Am. Soc. Clin. Hypnosis, Internat. Soc. Clin. and Exptl. Hypnosis, Acad. Psychosomatic Medicine, Am. Coll. Psychiatrists; mem. Am. Psychol. Assn., Ohio Psychiat. Assn. (pres. 1980-81), Central Neuropsychiat. Assn. (v.p. 1986-87). Home: 295 Pembroke Rd Akron OH 44313 Office: Dept Psychiatry St Thomas Med Ctr 444 N Main St Akron OH 44310

HODGES, ALBERT WILLFRED, retired music educator; b. Greensburg, Kans., Aug. 1, 1914; s. Albert Alton and Allatha Rebecca (Baer) H.; m. Ruby Winifred Dunlap, June 10, 1942; children—Woodrow Joe, Donald Albert. Mus.B., Southwestern Coll., 1936; Grad. Army Music Sch., Washington, 1943; M.Music Edn., U. No. Colo., 1957; postgrad. U. Ky., 1967-68. Music tchr., band dir. Kans. pub. schs., 1936-41; dir. Air Force Band, 1943-46; band dir. pvt. lesson instr. Kearney, Nebr. pub. schs., 1946-54; dir. bands, music edn. Southwestern Coll., Winfield, Kans., 1955-73; dir. music therapy State Hosp. Tng. Ctr., Winfield, 1973-78; pvt. tchr. instrumental lessons, 1978—; ret., 1978; adjudicator music contests Kans., Okla., Mo. and Nebr. pub. schs., 1946—; clinician music, bands, Kans., Okla. and Nebr. pub. schs., 1946—. Mem. Winfield Oratoria Soc., 1955-84 , pres., 1978-84 .

Mem. Music Educators Nat. Conf., Kans. Music Educators Assn. (Hall of Fame 1976), Coll. Band Dirs. Nat. Assn. (chmn. Kans. State sect. 1957-73), Am. Legion, Phi Mu Alpha Sinfonia, Phi Beta Mu (nat. com rules and bylaws). Republican. Methodist. Avocations: handicrafts; sports. Home: 1513 Olive Winfield KS 67156

HODGES, JAMES ALFRED, JR., financial executive; b. N.Y.C., May 30, 1938; s. James Alfred and Virginia Rose (Howard) H.; m. Gail Barbara Taylor, June 17, 1961. A.B., Cornell U., 1960; M.B.A., U. Chgo., 1962. C.P.A., Ill. With Amax, Inc., Greenwich, Conn., 1966-71; asst. treas. PPG Industries, Inc., Pitts., 1971-76; corp. treas. Baxter Travenol Labs., Inc., Deerfield, Ill., 1976-80; v.p. fin. and treas. Sargent-Welch Sci. Co., Skokie, Ill., 1981-85; v.p. fin. and adminstrn., chief fin. officer Pansophic Systems Inc., Oak Brook, Ill., 1985-86, sr. v.p. fin. and adminstrn, chief fin. officer, 1987—. Mem. Fin. Execs. Inst., Am. Inst. C.P.A.s, Ill. Soc. C.P.A.s. Club: Cornell U. of Chgo. Home: 1257 Deerpath Lake Forest IL 60045 Office: Pansophic Systems Inc 709 Entriprise Dr Oak Brook IL 60521

HODGES, LAURENT, physics educator; b. Houston, Jan. 16, 1940; s. Lee and Léone (Camus) H.; m. Linda Feitl, Sept. 10, 1966; children: Andrew Carlos, Katherine Anne. AB summa cum laude, Harvard U., 1960, PhD, 1966. Physics prof. Iowa State U., Ames, 1968—. Author: Environmental Pollution, 1973, 2d edit., 1977. Mem. Am. Physical Soc., Am. Assn. Physics Tchrs. Am. Solar Energy Assn. Democrat. Roman Catholic. Avocations: gardening, beekeeping, photography, astronomy. Home: 2115 Coneflower Ct Ames IA 50010 Office: Iowa State U Physics Dept Ames IA 50011

HODGES, RALPH LEE, pharmacist; b. Liberal, Kans., June 14, 1948; s. Basil Lee and Winifred Barbara (Ragsdale) H.; m. Terri Ann Ricketts, Apr. 22, 1973; children: Ryan Lee, Jaime Renae. BS in Pharmacy, Southwestern State Coll., Weatherford, Okla., 1971. Registered pharmacist, Kans., Colo., Okla.; emergency med. technician, Kans., 1973-80. Pharmacist Sublette (Kans.) Drug Store, 1971-76; staff pharmacist Humana Hosp., Dodge City, Kans., 1977-81, 83—; chief pharmacist Med. Ctr. Pharmacy, Dodge City, 1981-83; cons. pharmacist Minneola (Kans.) Dist. Hosp., 1986—; CPR instr. Am. Heart Assn., 1973-80. Master instr. hunter safety Kans. Fish and Game Commn. Mem. Kans. Pharm. Assn., Kans. Soc. Hosp. Pharmacists, Nat. Rifle Assn. (life). Democrat. Avocations: hunting, fishing, water skiing, downhill skiing, archery. Home: 104 Crestview Dr Dodge City KS 67801 Office: Humana Hosp 3001 Ave A Dodge City KS 67801

HODGMAN, VICKI JEAN, school system administrator; b. Joliet, Ill., May 22, 1933; d. Joseph and Mary (Desman) Mikolic; divorced; children: Michael James, Tudy Magnuson, Kathy Lynn. BEd, Ill. State U., 1954, MEd, 1970; postgrad., U. Bridgeport, 1972, U. Hawaii, 1982, No. Ill. U., 1978, 79, 80, Nat. Coll., 1983, 86, U. Utah, 1984. Cert. tchr., Ill., Md. Tchr. Will County (Ill.) Pub. Schs., Joliet, Rockdale and Lockport, 1954-55, 58-68, Balt. County (Md.) Pub. Schs., Sparrow's Point, 1955-56, McLean County (Ill.) Pub. Schs., Heyworth, 1957; tchr. spl. edn. So. Will County Coop. for Spl. Edn., 1969-79, supr., coordinator, 1979—; sec. Pulse-Chicagoland Spl. Edn. Suprs., 1983-85. Vol. Youth with a Mission, Gospel Outreach, 1985; treas. Women's Ch. Council, Rockdale, Ill., 1966-67, Band Parents Assn., Rockdale, 1966-67. Mem. Council Exceptional Children, Ill. Council Exceptional Children, Ill. Council Children with Behavior Disorders (bd. dirs. 1986-87), Will County Reading Assn., Ill. Alliance for Exceptional Children and Adults, Assn. for Children with Learning Disabilities, Assn. for Supervision and Curriculum Devel., Secondary Reading League, Heritage Quilters Guild. Republican. Mem. Assembly of God Ch. Avocations: sewing, quilting, world travelling. Home: 310 Reedwood Dr Joliet IL 60436 Office: So Will County Co-op Spl Edn 106 Tryon Channahon IL 60436

HODGSON, ARTHUR CLAY, lawyer; b. Little River, Kans., Aug. 22, 1907; s. Edward Howard and Flora Cleveland (Perry) H.; m. Annie Letitia Green, Jan. 5, 1939; children—Richard, David, Edward, Alice Anne, James. A.B., U. Kans., 1929; J.D., George Washington U., 1937. Bar: Kans. 1936, D.C. 1936, U.S. Supreme Ct. 1950. Sole practice, Washington, 1936-38; practice, Lyons, Kans., 1938—, ptnr. Hodgson & Kahler, 1969—. Pres. Lyons Jaycees; bd. dirs. Lyons C. of C. Served with USN, 1943-45. Mem. Kans. Trial Lawyers Assn., Assn. Trial Lawyers Am. (bd. govs. 1973-76), Rice County Bar, S.W. Kans. Bar, Kans. Bar Assn. (del., disting. service award 1985), ABA (ho. of dels. 1976-82). Democrat. Congregationalist. Clubs: Rotary (Lyons); Masons (Little River). Home: Rural Route Little River KS 67457 Office: 119 1/2 W Main Lyons KS 67554

HODGSON, GARY FRANCIS, educational administrator; b. Cadillac, Mich., July 24, 1941; s. Myles Wesley Hodgson and Beatrice Otilia (Denzel) Budnick; m. Johanna Wilhelmina Keur, Aug. 27, 1966; children—Jennifer, Elizabeth. B.S., Western Mich. U., 1964, postgrad., 1977-78; M.Ed., Kent State U., 1972; postgrad., Mich. State U., 1983—. Cert. secondary prin., Mich. Dir., tchr. Dawntreader Alternative High Sch., Kalamazoo, 1972-74; career edn. cons. Kent Intermediate Sch. Dist., Grand Rapids, Mich., 1974-75; alternative edn. tchr. East Kentwood High Sch., Mich., 1975-78; asst. prin. West Ottawa High Sch., Holland, Mich., 1978-80; prin. West Ottawa Middle Sch., Holland, 1980—; career edn. cons., Hastings, Mich., 1975-79; middle schs. cons., Holland, 1981—; career edn. instr. Western Mich. U., Kalamazoo, 1976. Contbg. editor: Career Education Resource Guide, 1975. Designer mentorship program, 1983. Mem. exec. council Hope Ch., Holland, 1981—; mem. Holland Area Arts Council, 1981—. Recipient Cert. of Appreciation, Mich. State Bd. Edn., 1984, Excellence in Edn. award U.S. Dept. Edn., 1983; Profl. Devel. Consortium grantee, 1981, 82, 85. Mem. Mich. Assn. of Academically Talented, Ottawa County Middle Level Educators (chmn. 1983), Nat. Assn. Secondary Prins., Mich. Assn. Secondary Prins., Assn. for Supervision of Curriculum Devel., Nat. Middle Sch. Assn., Ottawa Area Sch. Adminstrs., Common Cause, Amnesty Internat., Bread for the World, Jacques Cousteau Soc. Mem. Reformed Ch. Am. Avocations: travel, reading, racquetball. Office: West Ottawa Middle Sch 3700 140th Ave Holland MI 49424

HODGSON, THOMAS RICHARD, health care executive; b. Lakewood, Ohio, Dec. 17, 1941; s. Thomas Julian and Dallas Louise (Livesay) H.; m. Susan Jane Cawrse, Aug. 10, 1963; children—Michael, Laura, Anne. B.S. in Chem. Engring, Purdue U., 1963; M.S.E., U. Mich., 1964; M.B.A., Harvard U., 1969. Devel. engr. E.I. Dupont, 1964; assoc. Booz-Allen & Hamilton, 1969-72; with Abbott Labs., North Chicago, Ill., 1972—; gen. mgr. Faultless div. Abbott Labs., 1976-78, v.p. gen. mgr. Hosp. div., 1978-80, pres. Hosp. div., 1980-83, group v.p., pres. Abbott Internat. Ltd., 1983-84, exec. v.p. parent com., 1985—, also dir.; dir. View Engring., Simi Valley, Calif. Mem. Lake Forest (Ill.) Bd. Edn. Served with Chem. Corps U.S. Army, 1965-67. Baker scholar; NSF fellow; recipient Disting. Engring. Alumni award Purdue U., 1985. Mem. Chgo. Council Fgn. Relations, Phi Eta Sigma, Tau Beta Pi. Clubs: Economic of Chgo., Knollwood. Home: 1015 Ashley Rd Lake Forest IL 60045 Office: Abbott Internat Ltd Bannockburn Lakes Office Plaza 2355 Waukegan Rd Deerfield IL 60015

HODJAT, YAHYA, metallurgist; b. Tehran, Iran, Aug. 8, 1950; came to U.S., 1977; s. Javad and Robabeh (Fayaz) H.; m. Patricia Anne Gray, Dec. 17, 1980. BS, Arya-Mehr U., Tehran, Iran, 1972; MS, Ohio State U., 1978, PhD, 1981. Engr. trainee August Thyssen Corp., Oberhausen, W. Ger., 1974-75; project mgr. Pahlavi Steel Corp., Ahwaz, Iran, 1975-77; grad. research assoc. Ohio State U., Columbus, 1977-81; dir. ops. Intercontinental Metals, Miami, 1981-82; research scientist The Standard Oil Co., Cleve., 1982-83; mgr. pulley devel. Dyneer Corp., Bloomfield Hills, Mich., 1983—; cons. Intercontinental Metals Corp., Miami, 1978-80. Asst. inventor Pyro-Technique Silver Refining, 1980. Served to lt. Iranian Imperial Army, 1972-74. Mem. AIME, Am. Soc. Metals, Am. Foundrymen's Soc., Alpha Sigma Mu. Home: 45200 Keding St Apt 304 Utica MI 48087 Office: Dyneer Corp 1133 W Long Lake Rd Bloomfield Hills MI 48013

HODSON, THOMAS WILLIAM, health care company executive; b. Phila., Nov. 25, 1946; s. William K. and Marguerite M. (Hendrick) H.; m. Constance Gail Stirling, July 5, 1969; children: Hollistir S., Andrew S. B.S. in Bus. Adminstrn. and Econs, Lehigh U., Bethlehem, Pa., 1968; M.B.A., Harvard U., 1974. With Baxter Travenol Labs., Inc., 1974—; treas. Baxter Travenol Labs., Inc., Deerfield, Ill., 1980-84, v.p., 1984—. Bd. dirs. Better Govt. Assn., 1986—. Served to lt. USNR, 1969-72. Roman Catholic. Home: 911 Forest Glen W Winnetka IL 60093 Office: 1 Baxter Pkwy Deerfield IL 60015

HOECKER, ALBERT ROBERT, pipe and piling supply company executive; b. Chicago Heights, Ill., Sept. 26, 1940; s. Albert W. and Margret (Grimm) H.; m. Sandra J. Roemer, Mar. 20, 1965 (div. Apr. 1973); children: Scott A., Bonnie Lyn; m. Judith A. Mussen, Jan. 3, 1976; children: Julie P., Cindy M. Assoc. in Bus., Bloom Community Coll., 1960. Salesman Thorn Creek Realty, Chicago Heights, 1963-65, Nero Co., Chgo., 1965-67; pres., chief exec. officer The ALA Co. Ltd., South Chicago Heights, Ill., 1967-76, Albie Co., Chicago Heights, 1976-81, Prairie Pipe and Piling Supply, Inc., Steger, Ill., 1981—. Served as pfc. USMC, 1960-63. Mem. Nat. Assn. Steel Pipe Distbrs., So. Suburban Builders Assn., Am. Legion, AMVETS. Lodges: Kiwanis, Moose. Home: 3495 Chalet Ln Crete IL 60417 Office: Prairie Pipe & Piling Supply Inc 24 E 36th Pl PO Box 2 Steger IL 60475

HOEFS, PAUL THEODORE, II, rancher; b. Wood Lake, Nebr., Nov. 30, 1926; s. Paul A. and Margaret (Roberts) H.; m. Patricia Anderson; children—Paul, Sheri, Mary, Jan, Bonnie, John, Patricia, Jim, Mark. Grad. Campion Jesuit Mil. Acad. Aerobatic and spray pilot; farmer, Wood Lake, Nebr. Mem. Wood Lake Vol. Fire Dept., 1972-76; mem. Class 6 Sch. Bd., Wood Lake; pres. Wood Lake Sch. Dist. 7; dir. Sch. Dist. 195; pres. Cherry County (Nebr.) Hosp. Bd., also pres. Found.; bd. dirs. Greater Nebr. Health System Agy.; trustee Sacred Heart Ch. Mem. Nebr. Stock Growers Assn. (vice chmn. brand and theft com. 1972, chmn. pub. lands 1978, v.p. 1980, pres. elect 1981, pres. 1982), Nat. Cattle Assn. (bd. dirs.), Aircraft Owners and Pilots Assn., S.D. Stock Growers Assn., Farm Bur., Sandhills Cattle Assn. (bd. dirs.), Livestock Merchandising Inst. (trustee), Fed. Land Bank Assn. Valentine (Nebr.) (pres. 1974, bd. dirs.). Roman Catholic. Lodge: KC. Address: Skull Lake Ranch PO Box 727 Wood Lake NE 69221

HOEKSTRA, ANDREW LOUIS, psychiatrist; b. Grand Rapids, Nov. 26, 1919; s. Peter A. and Alice Jacoba (Clausing) H.; m. Portia Kellog Rich, Nov. 26, 1940; children: Peter (dec.), Anna, Margaret, Elizabeth, Andrea, Mary, Catherine, John. SB, U. Chgo., 1941; MD, U. Colo., Denver, 1945. Diplomate Am. Bd. psychiatry and Neurology. Psychiatrist Pine Rest Christian Hosp., Grand Rapids, 1951-52; gen. practice psychiatry Grand Rapids, 1952-68; med. dir. Ionia County Mental Health Clinic, Ionia, Mich., 1966-72; supt. Jacksonville (Ill.) State Hosp., 1972-76; psychiatrist McFarland Mental Health Clinic, Springfield, Ill., 1976—; cons. Grand Rapids Ghild Guidance Clinic, 1952-57, Montcalm Mental Health Clinic, Stanton, Mich., 1968-70. Served to capt. U.S. Army, 1946-49. Fellow Am. Psychiat. Assn. (life). Roman Catholic. Avocations: music, poetry. Home: 717 S Park Ave Springfield IL 62704 Office: McFarland Mental Health Ctr 901 Southwind Springfield IL 62704

HOEL, ROGER SATRANG, conductor; b. Chgo., Oct. 30, 1938; s. Bjarna and Ninnia Olga (Huggenvik) H.; m. Donna Ruth Harms, May 20, 1961; children—Elizabeth Ann, Gregory Roger. B.S., St. Olaf Coll., 1960; M.S., U. Minn., 1963; M.A., Cornell U., 1966; B.A., Augsburg Coll., 1973. Asst. Conductor St. Paul Civic Orch., 1964-68, St. Paul Chamber Orch., 1968-69; assoc. conductor Bloomington Symphony Orch., Minn., 1966-70; music dir., conductor Apollo Male Chorus, Mpls., 1977—; music dir., prin. conductor, founder Minnetonka Orchestral Assn., Minn., 1974—; minister music Edgewater Emmanuel Ch., 1966—; founder Minnetonka Symphony Orch., 1974, Minnetonka Children's Choir, 1976, Minnetonka Chorale, 1976, Minnetonka Chamber Orch., 1976, Minnetonka Civic Orch., 1976, Minnetonka Sr. Chorale, 1980, Minnetonka Youth Orch., 1980. Mem. fine arts com. Hopkins Sch. Dist., 1982-84, curriculum council, 1984; bd. dirs. Hopkins Assn. Children with Learning Disabilities, 1977. Recipient Citizen of Yr. award Minnetonka C. of C., 1977, Master Tchr. award Hopkins Sch. Dist., 1979, 2d place award Am. Choral Festival, Mpls., 1981, 2d prize Internat. Music Eisteddfod, Llangollen, Wales, 1982. Mem. Nat. Com. on Male Choruses, Nat. Com. on Children's Choirs, Internat. Children's Choir Assn., Conductor's Guild, Nat. Assn. Tchrs. of Singing, Bach Soc. (bd. dirs. 1984). Lutheran. Club: Evergreen (Mpls.). Avocations: Lincoln history; skiing; running. Home: 5216 Mayview Rd Minnetonka MN 55345 Office: Minnetonka Orchestral Assn 1001 Hwy 7 Hopkins MN 55343

HOELTKE, GARY MARTIN, research executive; b. Grand Island, Nebr., Dec. 2, 1936; s. Walter and Nelda (Roby) H.; m. Linda Rose Fahrlander, Sept. 6, 1959; children: Carol, Alice. BEd, U. Nebr., 1958, MEd, 1959, EdD, 1966. Lic. psychologist, Nebr. Tchr. Hastings (Nebr.) Pub. Sch., 1958-59; instr. Ohio State U., Columbus, 1959-60; guidance dir. Clay County Schs., Spencer, Iowa, 1960-62; sch. psychologist Pottawattamie County Schs., Council Bluffs, Iowa, 1962-64; assoc. prof. U. Kans., Lawrence, 1964-70; from v.p. to sr. v.p. Selection Research Inc., Lincoln, Nebr., 1983. Co-Author: Learning Style Identification, 1981; contbr. articles to profl. jours. Mem. Am. Psychol. Assn., Am. Ednl. Research Assn. Home: 7320 Briarhurst Lincoln NE 68506 Office: Selection Research Inc 301 S 68th Lincoln NE 68505

HOENE, ROBERT EDWARD, S.J., pastoral care director; b. Duluth, Minn., Mar. 21, 1920; s. Arthur C. and Vera Katherine (Vollmer) H. AB, St. Louis U., 1944, MA in Classics, Licentiate in Philosophy, 1947; MS in Biology, Marquette U., 1958; MS in Psychology, Loyola U., 1962, PhD in Psychology, 1963. Ordained priest Roman Catholic Ch., 1953; lic. psychologist, Wis. Instr. St. John's Coll., Belize, 1947-50; asst. prin. Campion High Sch., Prairie du Chien, Wis., 1955-56; asst. prof. Marquette U., Milw., 1963-80; dir. pastoral care St. Joseph Ctr. Mental Health, Omaha, 1986—; research assoc. (base-line study in human genetics for U.S. genepool) Argonne Nat. Lab., 1956-60; cons. Good Shepherd Sisters, St. Paul, 1961-86, Misericorde Sisters, Milw., 1964-80; research assoc. Child Welfare League Am., N.Y.C., 1966-68. Author: (book) The Unadjusted Delinquent Girl, 1986; contbr. articles to profl. jours. Mem. Am. Psychol. Assn., Nat. Assn. Cath. Chaplains (dir. region IX 1984-86), Nebr. Psychol. Assn., Wis. Acad. Arts, Scis., Letters. Avocations: oil painting, tennis, skiing. Home: Creighton U Jesuit Community Omaha NE 68178 Office: St Joseph Ctr Mental Health 819 Dorcas Omaha NE 68108

HOENECKE, KARL F., signal company executive; b. Ann Arbor, Mich., Apr. 1, 1930; s. Edgar Herman and Meta Amelia (Bunge) H.; m. Gretchen Riggs, Aug. 16, 1952; children: Meta, Sarah, Gretchen. B.A., U. Mich., 1954, M.B.A., 1955; A.M.P., Harvard U., 1968. Sales mgr. Univ. Microfilms Inc., Ann Arbor, 1955-57; pres. Graphic Systems Rockwell Internat., Chgo., 1957-75; chmn., pres. Fed. Signal Corp., Oak Brook, Ill., 1975—; mem. N.Y. Stock Exchange Adv. Com.; dir. Am. Nat. Bank and Trust, Chgo., Puritan-Bennett Corp., Kansas City. Mem. com. Chgo. Symphony Orch., 1985; trustee Glenwood Sch. for Boys, Ill., 1974; bd. dirs. Community House Hinsdale, Ill., 1984-85. Mem. Chgo. Assn. Commerce and Industry (bd. dirs. 1984—), Ill. Mfrs. Assn. (bd. dirs. 1974),. Clubs: Chicago, Mid Am. (bd. dirs., sec. 1981-84). (Chgo.); Hinsdale Golf. Office: Fed Signal Corp 1415 W 22nd St Oak Brook IL 60514 *

HOERLE, ARNO JOSEPH, logistics manager; b. Columbus, Nebr., Dec. 22, 1938; s. Elmer Edmond and Leona Willimena (Hollmann) H.; m. Renate Mueller, July 7, 1944; children: Michael Carl, Mark Alan. BS in Acctg., Hampton Inst., 1974; MA, Webster U., 1985. Cert. comml. pilot. Commd. 2d lt. U.S. Army, 1958, advanced through grades to lt. col., 1981; various aviation and logistics assignments Cobra AH-1 Program Office, 1958-83; ret. U.S. Army, 1983; logistics mgr. Boeing Mil. Airplane Co., Wichita, Kans., 1983—. Mem. Soc. Logistics Engrs. Republican. Lutheran. Office: Boeing Military Airplane Co Oliver Wichita KS 67277

HOERNEMAN, CALVIN A., JR., educator; b. Youngstown, Ohio, Sept. 30, 1940; s. Calvin A. and Lucille A. (Leiss) H.; m. Cheryl L. Morand, Aug. 10, 1973; children: David, Jennifer, Christina. BA, Bethany Coll., 1962; MA, Mich. State U., 1964. Mem. faculty Delta Coll., University Center, Mich., 1966—, prof. econs., 1976—; pres. Bus. Software Solutions, 1986—; cons. Prentice-Hall, Acad. Press, Goodyear Pub., Random House Pub. Author: Poverty, Wealth and Income Distribution, 1969; co-author: "Caper" Principles of Economics Software Study Guide; contbr. articles to various publs. Recipient Recognition award AAUP, 1972, Bergstein award Delta Coll. Grad. Class, 1972. Mem. Am. Econ. Assn., Midwest Econ. Assn., AAUP, Wine Educators Soc. Home: 5712 Lamplighter Ln Midland MI 48640 Office: Delta Coll University Center MI 48710

HOERNER, JOHN LEE, department store executive; b. Lincoln, Nebr., Sept. 23, 1939; s. Robert L. and Lulu (Stone) H.; m. Susan Kay Morgan, Nov. 12, 1959 (div. Nov. 1971); m. Anna Lea Thomas, Feb. 16, 1973; children: John Scott, Joanne Lynne. B.S., B.A., U. Nebr., 1961. Vice pres. Hovland-Swanson Co., Lincoln, Nebr., 1959-68; gen. mdse. mgr. Woolf Bros., Kansas City, Mo., 1968-71; sr. v.p. Hahne's, Newark, 1971-80; pres., chief exec. officer H & S Pogve Co., Cin., 1981, L.S. Ayres & Co., Indpls., 1982-87; chmn., pres., chief exec. officer Debenhams div. Burton Group plc, Indpls., 1986—; v.p. Associated Dry Goods Corp., N.Y.C., 1981-86; dir. Mchts. Nat. Corp., Indpls. Author: Ayres Adages, 1983. Campaign mgr. Denny for Congress Com., Lincoln, Nebr., 1966. Republican. Clubs: Spring Valley Hounds (New Vernon, N.J.); Watching Riding and Driving (Summit, N.J.) (former pres.); Camargo Hunt, Queen City (Cin.); Traders Point Hunt (treas.), University, Woodstock (Indpls.). Home: 5635 Sunset Ln Indianapolis IN 46208 Office: Debenhams div Burton Group 3055 N Meridian St 3B Indianapolis IN 46208 *

HOESL, DONALD LEONARD, optometrist; b. Grand Forks, N.D., Aug. 10, 1925; s. George Joseph and Rosella Marie (Beauchamp) H.; m. Anne Blanche Henrikson, June 14, 1958; children: John, Pamela, Carla, Linda. OD, No. Ill. Coll. Optometry, Chgo., 1951. Pvt. practice optometry Rolla, N.D., 1952—. Pres. Rolla Comml. Club, 1957; chmn. bd. dirs. Rolla Community Hosp., 1973-77; religious instr. St. Joachim Cath. Ch., Rolla, 1970-73, trustee, 1975-78. Served with USN, 1943-46, PTO. Mem. Am. Optometric Assn., N.D. Optometric Assn. (pres. 1957-58), N.D. Vision Services Inc. (pres. 1975-76), Am. Legion (fin. officer Rolla 1954-76). Lodge: KC (fin. sec. 1968-83). Avocations: hunting, fishing, gardening, reading. Home and Office: Vision Ctr PO Box 669 Rolla ND 58367

HOEWISCH, WALMER HOEWISCH, quality engineer; b. Weyauwega, Wis., Mar. 10, 1938; s. Willhelm A. and Norma B. (Bauer) H.; m. Maxine R. Schwebs, Feb. 10, 1962; children: Kirk, Stacy, Allison, Andrea, Brooke, Elise. BEE, U. Wis., 1961, BBA in Prodn. Mgmt., 1962. Cert. quality engr. Quality engr. Square D Co., Milw., 1962-65, test. supr., 1965-68, gen. foreman inspections, 1968-71; asst. quality mgr. Chrysler Outbd., Hartford, Wis., 1971-72; quality mgr. Ray-O-Vac, Appleton, Wis., 1972-79; quality mgr. Speed Queen Co., Ripon, Wis., 1979-84, corp. mgr. quality engring., 1984—. Mem. bd. Hortonville (Wis.) Schs.; pres., treas., sec. Beautiful Savior Luth. Ch., Mequon, Wis., 1965-73; pres., treas. Bethlehem Luth. Ch., Hortonville, 1975-78, 80. Mem. Am. Soc. Quality Control (sr.). Republican. Club: Investment (Milw.) (pres. 1973). Home: Rt 3 Box 146 Hortonville WI 54944 Office: Speed Queen Co Shepard St Ripon WI 54971

HOEY, RITA MARIE, public relations executive; b. Chgo., Nov. 4, 1950; d. Louis D. and Edith M. (Finnemann) Hoey; m. Joseph John Dragonette, Sept. 4, 1982. BA in English and History, No. Ill. U., 1972. Asst. dir. Nat. Assn. Housing and Human Devel., Chgo., 1975; public relations account exec. Weber Cohn & Riley, Chgo., 1975-76; publicity coordinator U.S. Gypsum Co., Chgo., 1976-77; with Daniel J. Edelman, Inc., Chgo., 1977-84, sr. v.p., 1981-84; exec. v.p. Dragonette, Inc., Chgo., 1984—. Mem. Pub. Relations Soc. Am., Women in Communications. Home: 3416 S Cherry Valley Woodstock IL 60098 Office: 303 E Wacker Dr Suite 218 Chicago IL 60601

HOFF, LAWRENCE CONRAD, pharmaceutical company executive; b. Fresno, Calif., Jan. 19, 1929; s. Conrad and Katherine H.; m. Jacqueline Goodyear, Jan. 27, 1950; children—M. Catherine, Frederick L., Lisa J. A.B. in Econs., Stanford U., 1950; SC.D. in Pharm. (hon.), Mass. Coll. Pharm. & Allied Health Sci., 1981. With sales The Upjohn Co., Kalamazoo, 1950-66, dir. domestic pharm. ops., 1966-69, v.p. domestic pharm. mktg., 1969-74, v.p., gen. mgr. domestic pharm. ops., 1974-77, exec. v.p., 1977-84, pres., 1984—; bd. dirs., exec. com. Council on Family Health, N.Y.C., 1976—; bd. trustees, chmn. Nat. Found. Infectious Diseases, Washington, 1976-81; bd. dirs., exec. com., v.p. Proprietary Assn., Washington, 1979-85; nat. adv. com. Kellogg Pharm. Clin. Scientist Program, Mpls., 1980; bd. dirs. First Am. Bank Corp. Bd. trustees Borgess Med. Ctr., Kalamazoo, 1982. Mem. Pharm. Mfr.'s Assn. (chmn. 1987—, bd. dirs. 1984), Am. Fedn. Pharm. Edn. (bd. dirs. 1980). Republican. Episcopalian. Club: Kalamazoo Country. Office: Upjohn Co 7000 Portage Rd Kalamazoo MI 49001

HOFFARD, GARY MARK, optometrist; b. Foston, Minn., May 5, 1948; s. Mark Clinton and Regina (Striefel) H.; m. Sheila Cray, Apr. 8, 1978; children: Justin, Davin, Cyndi, Brian, Angela. Student, Bemidji State U., 1966-68; OD, South Coll. Optometry, 1972; postgrad., U. Minn., 1975-76. Optometrist U.S. Army, Korea, 1972-73; chief optometry clinic U.S. Army, Indpls., 1973-74; pvt. practice optometry Elk River, Minn., 1974—; chief optometry clinic, USAR, Ft. Snelling, Minn., 1975-77; cons. Shire Home for Mentally Retarded, Elk River, 1978—. Den leader Boy Scouts Am., Elk River, 1984-86, com. chmn., 1986—. Served to capt. U.S. Army, 1972-74. Named one of Outstanding Young Men of Am., 1985. Fellow Am. Acad. Optometry; mem. Am. Optometric Assn., Minn. Optometric Assn., Met. Dist. Optometric Soc., Elk River C. of C., Minn. Jaycees (v.p. Ramsey club 1982-85, named v.p. of quarter 1985). Roman Catholic. Lodges: K.C., Eagles. Office: 661 Main PO Box 44 Elk River MN 55330

HOFFEN, JEFFREY AARON, dentist; b. Chgo., Apr. 16, 1959; s. Marvin Jerome and Rosalie (Platt) H. BS, U. Ill., Chgo., 1980, DDS, 1983; postgrad. in bus., U. Chgo., 1986—. Lic. dentist, Ill. Dentist Harvey (Ill.) Dental Assn., 1983—; dental cons. Lincoln Park Terrace, Chgo., 1984-85. Mem. Ill. Found. Dentistry for Handicapped, Am. Dental Vols. for Israel (Vol. award 1984), Chgo. Area Runners Assn., Phi Eta Sigma. Avocations: herpetology, running. Home: 6611 Navajo Lincolnwood IL 60646 Office: Harvey Dental Assn 163 E 154th Harvey IL 60612

HOFFERT, KENNETH EDWARD, dentist; b. Detroit, Mar. 12, 1942; s. Edward Christian and Mildred Genevieve (Townshend) H.; m. Janice Marie Masterson, Oct. 26, 1968; children: Kelley Ann, Llanda Marie, Gregory Kenneth. DDS, U. Detroit, 1967. Gen. practice dentistry Trenton, Mich., 1967—. Bd. dirs. Seaway Chorale & Orch. Inc., Trenton; mem. Grosse Ile (Mich.) Hist. Soc. Mem. ADA, Mich. Dental Assn., Detroit Dist. Dental Soc. Roman Catholic. Lodge: Kiwanis (pres. Trenton club 1985-87). Avocation: model railroading. Office: 1680 Kingsway Ct Trenton MI 48183

HOFFERT, PHILLIP, architect; b. Tiffin, Ohio, May 1, 1943; s. Morris and Miriam (Konkle) H.; m. Roberta Lee Fieldhouse, Jan. 19, 1966; children: Garrett, Ethan. BArch, Ohio U., 1966. Registered architect, Ohio, N.J. Assoc. Saseen & Booyls, Atlantic City, 1966-70; job capt. Deer & Cornachione, Copley, Ohio, 1970-75; prin. Kreeger & Assocs., Copley, 1975-85; project architect Voinovich Cos., Cleve., 1985—. Mem. AIA, Architects Soc. Ohio, Nat. Council Archtl. Registration Bds. Clubs: Mens Garden, Torch (Akron) (treas. 1984-85). Lodge: Masons (pres. fellowship club). Avocations: sailing, computers. Office: Voinovich Cos 2060 E 9th St 1st Floor Cleveland OH 44115

HOFFMAN, CELESTE MARIE, customer training specialist; b. Fairbury, Ill., Aug. 27, 1962; d. William Henry and Helen Louise (Kreeb) H. AS, Parkland Coll., 1982; BS in Bus., Western Ill. U., 1984. Customer tng. specialist TRT Telecommunications, Oakbrook Terr., Ill., 1984—. Office: TRT Telecommunications 1 S 450 Summit Ave Suite 260 Oakbrook Terrace IL 60181

HOFFMAN, CLYDE HARRIS, dean emeritus technical institute; b. Jamestown, N.D., Mar. 24, 1925; s. Clarence William and Ada Catherine (Gensrich) H.; B.S.E.E., U. N.D., 1950; M.S.E.E., U. Notre Dame, 1952, Ph.D. in Applied Mechanics, 1962; m. Betty Myra Ledingham, May 29, 1950. Instr. elec. engring. U. Notre Dame, 1951-52, asst. prof., 1953-62; project engr. Jack & Heintz, Inc., Cleve., 1952-53; asso. prof. elec. engring. Ill. Inst. Tech., Chgo., 1962-70, also head elec. engring. dept. Kabul (Afghanistan) U., 1966-68; mgr. IIT/TV Instructional Television Network, 1968-70; tng. mgr. Page Communications Engrs. INTS Program, Tehran, 1970-72; dir. tech. and vocat. tng. Harza Engring. Co., Chgo., 1972-73; 1st officer, program specialist UNESCO, Paris, 1973-78; mgr. transit communications systems IIT Research Inst., Chgo., 1978-80; dean acad. affairs DeVry Inst. Tech., Chgo., 1980-85; prin. Edutech Assocs. Cons., 1986—; evaluation panels undergrad. sci. instructional equipment program NSF, 1963-65; mem.

Nat. Acad. Scis. adv. com. to electronics instrumentation div. Nat. Bur. Standards, 1965-68; mem. Nat. Def. Exec. Res., U.S. Dept. Transp. trustee Nat. Electronics Conf., Inc. Sustaining mem. Republican Nat. Com.; mem. nat. adv. bd. Am. Security Council. Served with inf. AUS, 1943-46; ETO, PTO. Decorated Bronze Star; registered profl. engr., Ill., Ind., Calif. Mem. Instrument Soc. Am. (sr. mem., governing bd. 1964-65, v.p. Chgo. sect. 1980-81, v.p. dist. 6 1986—), IEEE (sr.), Am. Def. Preparedness Assn. (life), DAV, (life), Nat. Rifle Assn. (life), Nat. Assn. Watch and Clock Collectors, Am. Soc. Tng. and Devel., Am. Legion, Inst. Radio Engrs. (chmn. South Bend sect. 1960-61), IEEE (exec. com. Chgo. 1964-65), Am. Ordnance Assn., AAAS, ASME, Assn. Computing Machinery, Am. Soc. Engring. Edn., Nat. Electronics Conf. (dir. 1957-64), Art Inst. Chgo. Republican. Club: Elks. Contbr. numerous articles to profl. jours. Home: 184 Cascade Dr Indian Head Park IL 60525 Office: PO Box 275 Western Springs IL 60558

HOFFMAN, HILDRED COHEN, psychiatric social worker; b. Kansas City, Kans., Jan. 22, 1935; d. Joseph and Margaret (Pollock) C.; m. Edward Lewis Hoffman, Apr. 5, 1955 (div. May 1974); children: Michael, Martha, Susan, Andy. Student, Smith Coll., 1953-55; BA, U. Mo., Kansas City, 1955-57; MSW, Kansas U., 1966, postgrad., 1983—. Mem. staff Family & Children's Services, Kansas City, Mo., 1966-70, Ozanam Home for Boys, Kansas City, Mo., 1970-72; pvt. practice psychiat. social work Prairie Village, Kans., 1973—; bd. dirs. Rosedale State Bank, Kansas City, Kans., pres., 1980, cons. 1981-85. Mem. Internat. Transactional Analysis Assn. (clin.), Nat. Assn. Social Workers (clin.), Am. Assn. Marriage & Family Therapy (clin.), Am. Group Psychol. Assn., Nat. Council Jewish Women (pres. Kansas City, Mo. chpt. 1973-74). Republican. Jewish. Club: Oakwood Country (Kansas City, Mo.). Avocations: golf, aerobics, flying, reading, skiing. Home: 2101 Brookwood Shawnee Mission KS 66208 Office: 3700 W83 Prairie Village KS 66208

HOFFMAN, JAMES PAUL, lawyer, hypnotist; b. Waterloo, Iowa, Sept. 7, 1943; s. James A. and Luella M. (Prokosch) H.; m. Debra L. Malone, May 29, 1982; 1 dau., Tiffany K. B.A., U. No. Iowa, 1965, J.D. U. Iowa, 1967. Bar: Iowa 1967, U.S. Dist. Ct. (no. dist.) Iowa 1981, U.S. Dist. Ct. (so. dist.) Iowa 1968, U.S. Dist. Ct. (so. dist.) Ill, U.S. Tax Ct. 1971, U.S. Ct. Appeals (8th cir.) 1970, U.S. Supreme Ct. 1974. Sr. mem. James P. Hoffman, Law Offices, Keokuk, Iowa, 1967—; chmn. bd. Iowa Inst. Hypnosis. Fellow Am. Inst. Hypnosis; mem. ABA, Iowa Bar Assn., Lee County Bar Assn., Assn. Trial Lawyers Am., Ill. Trial Lawyers Assn., Iowa Trial Lawyers Assn. Democrat. Roman Catholic. Author: The Iowa Trial Lawyers and the Use of Hypnosis, 1980. Home and Office: Middle Rd PO Box 1066 Keokuk IA 52632

HOFFMAN, JAMES R., bishop; b. Fremont, Ohio, June 12, 1932. Ed., Our Lady of Lake Minor Sem., Wawasee, Ind., St. Meinrad Coll., Mt. St. Mary Sem., Norwood, Ohio, Cath. U. Am. Ordained priest Roman Cath. Ch., 1957; ordained titular bishop of Italica and aux. bishop of Toledo 1978, apptd. bishop of Toledo, 1980. Office: Bishop's Residence 2544 Parkwood Ave Toledo OH 43610

HOFFMAN, JOAN BENTLEY, public relations consultant; b. Trenton, N.J., Dec. 7, 1946; d. Harold William and Harriet Maude (Stallings) Bentley; m. Michael Charles Hoffman, July 31, 1971; children: Amy, Cara, Jennifer. AB, Goucher Coll., 1969; M, Yale U., 1971. Traffic coordinator Sta. WBAL (NBC) Radio, Balt., 1970-71; music tchr. Pleasant Plains Elem. Sch., Balt., 1972-75; accompanist, coach Wheaton (Ill.) Coll. Suzuki Program, 1980-85, music theory instr., 1985—; cons. pub. relations, Wheaton, 1979—. Music dir. (plays) St. Matthews Dramatic Soc., Balt., 1973, 74, Wheaton Drama, 1985. Dem. precinct capt., Wheaton, 1984—; treas. Glen Ellyn (Ill.) Jr. Woman's Club, 1984-85, v.p., 1985; sec. 5th Dist. Ill. Jr. Woman's Clubs, 1986—. Club: Goucher Coll. (Chgo.) (pres. 1982—). Home: 25W 624 Summerfield Ct Wheaton IL 60187

HOFFMAN, JOHN HARRY, lawyer, accountant; b. Chgo., June 18, 1913; s. Dave and Rose (Gewirtzman) H.; J.D., John Marshall Law Sch., 1938; m. Gwen Zollo, Dec. 30, 1949; children—Alana Sue Glickson, Edward Jay, Gayle Beth Hoffman Olsen. Bar: Ill. 1938, U.S. Supreme Ct. 1956. Practice law, Chgo., 1938—; propr. John H. Hoffman & Co., 1952—, ptnr., 1966—; pres. John H. Hoffman, P.C., 1972. C.P.A., Ill. Mem. ABA, Ill. Bar Assn., Chgo. Bar Assn., Decalogue Soc., Am. Inst. C.P.A.s, Ill. Soc. C.P.A.s. Club: Twin Orchard Country (Long Grove, Ill.). Lodges: Masons (32d degree), Shriners, B'nai B'rith. Office: 221 N LaSalle St Chicago IL 60601

HOFFMAN, JOSEPH JAMES, JR., clinical psychologist; b. Killeen, Tex., Sept. 10, 1954; s. Joseph James Sr. and Jacquiline Mary (Sweeney) H.; m. Roseann Marie Bobnar, Dec. 30, 1979; children: Joseph James III, Paul Michael, Matthew William. BA magna cum laude, U. Mo., 1976; MA, So. Ill. U., 1979; PhD, Utah State U., Logan, 1982. Lic. psychologist, Iowa. Mental health counselor Tri County Mental Health Ctr., Carrollton, Ill., 1977-79; cons. Mater Clinic, Knoxville, Iowa, 1984-86; clin. psychologist VA Med. Ctr., Knoxville, 1982-87, dir. tng., 1985-86; psychologist Colarelli, Meyer and Assocs., Clayton, Mo., 1987—. Contbr. articles to profl. jours. Mem. Am. Psychol. Assn., Iowa Psychol. Assn., Novi Psi. Roman Catholic. Avocations: sports, travel, poker. Home: 12160 Plainsman Dr Creve Coeur MO 63146 Office: Colarelli Meyer and Assocs 7751 Carondelet Ave Clayton MO 63105

HOFFMAN, LAWRENCE MICHAEL, dentist; b. St. Louis, July 9, 1951; s. Stanley and Estelle (Katz) H.; m. Phyllis Lee Paul, July 20, 1975; children: Lesley Ann, Molly Suzanne, William Paul. BA, Ind. U., 1972; DMD, Washington U., 1976. Instr. clin. dentistry Washington U., St. Louis, 1977; resident Jewish Hosp., St. Louis, 1977-78, chief dental clinic, 1979-86; gen. practice dentistry St. Louis County, 1978—; dental cons. Health Care Network, 1984—; nat. dental dir. Metlife Health Care Mgmt., 1985—. Author: Dick Clark's 25 Years of Rock and Roll, 1981; corr. St. Louis Jouralism Rev., 1980—, Billboard mag., 1982-85. Recipient Sr. Citizen's Service award City of St. Louis, 1978. Mem. ADA, Mo. Dental Assn., St. Louis Dental Soc. Club: Current Topics (pres. 1983-85). Office: 10287 Clayton Rd Suite 350 Saint Louis MO 63017-1115

HOFFMAN, LOUIS, psychiatrist; b. Detroit, Nov. 5, 1922; s. Nathan and Yetta (Schectman) H.; m. Florence Rubinstein, June 15, 1947; children: Andrew R., Karen Hoffman, Judith Baumgarten Hoffman, Anne Cohen. MD, Wayne State U., 1950. Diplomate Am. Bd. Psychiatry and Neurology. Rotating internship Grace Hosp., Detroit, 1950-51; resident Pontiac (Mich.) State Hosp., 1951-54, dir. Out-patient Psychiat. Clini, 1954-55; practice psychiat. Detroit and Southfield, Mich., 1969—; mem. staff William Beaumont Hosp., Royal Oak, Mich.; clin. asst. prof. dept. psychiatry Wayne State U., 1957—; assoc. in ob-gyn Wayne STate U., 1973—. Served with inf. U.S. Army, 1943-45. Mem. AMA, Am. Psychiatric Assn., Mich. Psychiatric Assn., Mich State Med. Assn., Oakland County Med. Soc., Wayne County Med. Soc. Avocations: horseback riding, jumping, swimming, archaeology. Home: 26376 Huntington Rd Huntington Woods MI 48070 Office: 21701 W Eleven Mile Rd Suite 9W Southfield MI 48076

HOFFMAN, MICHAEL CHARLES, otolaryngology; b. N.Y.C., Mar. 9, 1947; s. Arthur and Julia (Cherepanya) H.; m. Joan Bentley, July 31, 1971; children: Amy Elizabeth, Cara Christine, Jennifer Michelle. BA, Johns Hopkins U., 1969, postgrad., 1969-71; MD, U. Md., Balt., 1976. Resident in gen. surgery U. Md. Hosp., Balt., 1976-77, resident in otolaryngology, 1977-80; dir. hearing and speech ctr. Greater Balt. Med. Clinic, 1971-72; practice medicine specializing in otolaryngology Glen Ellyn Clinic, Ill., 1980—. Fellow Am. Acad. Otolaryngology; mem. AMA, Ill. State Med. Soc., Dupage County Med. Soc., Md. Surg. Soc. Avocations: fishing, boating, skiing. Office: Glen Ellyn Clinic SC 454 Pennsylvania Ave Glen Ellyn IL 60137

HOFFMAN, PATRICIA PATRICK, psychologist; b. Paragon, Ind., Jan. 1, 1925; d. Bruce Tadd and Kathryn Jane (Moyer) Patrick; m. Paul G. Hoffman, Jan. 27, 1945; children: Jane, Mary Ann, Nancy, John, Peter. BA, Carleton Coll., 1945; MS, St. Cloud (Minn.) State U., 1964; PhD, Union Grad. Sch., Cin., 1982. Lic. cons. psychologist, Minn. Social worker Stearns Social Services, St. Cloud, Minn., 1964-66; instr. St. Cloud State U., 1966-76, from asst. to assoc. prof., 1976-86, prof. psychology, 1986—, also mem. faculty assoc. exec. council, research grant com., speakers bur.; cons. in field. Bd. dirs., mem. speakers bur. St. Cloud Area Women's Shelter, 1984—. Mem. Am. Psychol. Assn. (various divs.), Minn. Psychol. Assn., Cen. Minn. Psychol. Assn., DAR (past pres.). Mem. Democratic Farm Labor Party. Presbyterian. Avocations: antiques, sports, bridge. Home: 33 Highbanks Pl Saint Cloud MN 56301 Office: St Cloud State U Counseling Ctr Saint Cloud MN 56301

HOFFMAN, RICHARD GEORGE, psychologist; b. Benton Harbor, Mich., Oct. 6, 1949; s. Robert Fredrick and Kathleen Elyce (Watts) H.; m. Julia Ann May, Dec. 18, 1970; children: Leslie Margaret, Michael Charles, Angela Lynn, Jennifer Elizabeth. BS with honors, Mich. State U., 1971; MA in Psychology, Long Island U., 1974, PhD in Clin. Psychology, 1980. Lic. con. psychologst. Instr. pediatrics U. Va., Charlottesville, 1977-80; asst. prof. pediatrics and family med. U. Kans., Wichita, 1980-84; asst. prof. behavioral sci. U. Minn., Duluth, 1984—, dir. neuropsychology lab., 1986—, dir. Edwin Eddy Neurocommunication lab., 1987—; assoc. dir. Child Evaluation Ctr., Wichita, 1981-82; dir. adminstrn. Comprehensive Epilepsy Clinic, Wichita, 1983-84; cons. psychologist U. Assocs., P.A., Duluth, 1984—. contbr. articles to profl. jour. Pres. Home and Sch. Assn., St. Michael's Sch., Duluth, 1986. NIH Research grantee, 1985; USCG Research grantee, 1986; Research grantee Sch. Medicine U. Kans., 1984, U. Minn., 1986. Mem. Am. Psychol. Assn., Nat. Acad. Neuropsychologists, Soc. Behavioral Medicine, Soc. Tchrs. Family Medicine, Cen. Va. Behavioral Assn. (pres. 1979-80). Democrat. Roman Catholic. Lodg: KC. Avocations: bicycling, hiking, tennis. Home: 219 Occidental Blvd Duluth MN 55804 Office: U Minn Dept Behavioral Scis Duluth MN 55812

HOFFMAN, WILLIAM KENNETH, obstetrician, gynecologist; b. Milw., Jan. 18, 1924; s. William Richard and Marian (Riegler) H.; student U. Wis., 1942-43; student U. Pa., 1943-44, postgrad, 1954-55; M.D., Marquette U., 1947; m. Peggy Folsom, July 28, 1952; children—Janet Susan, Ann Elizabeth. Intern, Columbia Hosp., 1947-48, resident in obstetrics and gynecology, 1948-49, mem. staff, 1949—; preceptor R.E. McDonald, M.D., Milw., 1949-50; resident in ob-gyn U. Chgo., 1950-51; practice medicine specializing in ob-gyn, Milw., 1955-74; mem. staff, Columbia Hosp.; dir. health service U. Wis.-Milw., 1974—, cons. Sch. Nursing, 1976-77, clin. assoc. prof., 1979—, vice chmn., mem. instl. rev. bd., 1976—, mem. instl. safety and health com., 1981—, chmn., 1984—. Mem. Am. Coll. Ob-Gyn, Am. Coll. Health Assn., Am. Coll. Sports Medicine, Milw. Acad. Medicine, N.Y. Acad. Scis., Royal Soc. Medicine, Am. Cancer Soc. (public edn. com. Milw. div., bd. dirs. 1983—). Home: 4629 N Murray Ave Milwaukee WI 53211

HOFFMANN, GEORGIANNA GRACE STRACKE, psychotherapist; b. Flint, Mich., Dec. 8, 1933; d. George Adam and Mary Elizabeth (Saunders) Stracke; m. Louis Gerhard Hoffmann, Nov. 4, 1955; children: Julianna Tobi Hoffmann Passalacqua, Eugenie Claire. Diploma in nursing, The Ch. Home and Hosp. Nursing, 1955; BS in Nursing, Johns Hopkins U., 1959; MA in Psychiatric Nursing, U. Iowa, 1970. Registered nurse, Md., Iowa. Faculty The Ch. Home and Hosp., Balt., 1956-59; psychotherapist Mid-Eastern Iowa Community Mental Health Ctr., Iowa City, 1970-82; pvt. practice psychotherapy, cons. Ctr. for Marital and Sexual Counseling, Iowa City, 1973—; coordinator family stress clinic, family practice dept. U. Iowa Coll. Medicine, Iowa City, 1982—. Mem. Am. Nurses Assn., Am. Assn. Sex Educators, Counselors and Therapists (cert. sex therapist), Am. Assn. for Marriage and Family Therapy (clin., bd. dirs. Iowa chpt. 1983-85), Soc. Tchrs. of Family Medicine, Sigma Theta Tau, Internat. Wives Club (Am. chmn. 1967). Democrat. Episcopalian. Avocations: knitting, biking, skiing, dancing, poetry writing. Home: 1016 E College St Iowa City IA 52240 Office: Family Stress Clinic U Iowa Dept Family Practice Steindler Bldg Room 2018 Iowa City IA 52240

HOFFMANN, SISTER JOAN MARIE, nursing administrator; b. Milw., Sept. 6, 1923; d. Peter Nicholas and Anna Marie (Shummacher) H. BS in Nursing, St. Ambrose Coll., Davenport, Iowa, 1952; MS in Nursing Edn., Marquette U., 1959; M in Nursing Adminstrn., U. Minn., 1962. Joined Sisters of Mercy, Roman Cath. Ch., 1945; RN, Ill., Iowa, Wis. Asst. dir. nursing Mercy Hosp., Chgo., 1962-63; dir. nursing Mercy Hosp., Davenport, 1963-65, dir. edn., 1971—; dir. nursing Mercy Hosp., Janesville, Wis., 1965-66; hosp. adminstr. Mercy Hosp., Marshalltown, Iowa, 1967-69; also bd. dirs. Mercy Hosp., Iowa City and Clinton, Iowa; exec. dir. Iowa Bd. Nursing, 1970. Mem. Am. Soc. Healthcare, Am. Coll. Healthcare Execs., Am. Cancer Soc. (hon. life Iowa div.), Am. Hosp. Assn., Iowa Hosp. Assn. (pres. 1980, 85), Iowa Soc. Healthcare Edn. and Tng. (Lou Holloway Mentorship award, 1986). Avocation: stamps. Home: 1638 W 29th St Apt 9 Davenport IA 52804 Office: Mercy Hosp W Central Pkwy at Marquette Davenport IA 52804

HOFFMANN, MAURINE WATSON, library adminstrator; b. Evanston, Ill., June 28, 1933; d. Maurice Stephen and Louise (Stephenson) Watson; m. Robert Ernst Hoffmann, July 18, 1953 (div. June 1969); children: Barbara Gale, Janet Irene, Burton Ernst; m. Robert Walter Bilhorn, Apr. 21, 1984. Student, U. Wis., Madison, 1951-53, 70-73, BS in Polit. Sci., 1971, MLS, 1973; student, U. Wis., Oshkosh, 1967-70. Librarian WARF Inst., Madison, 1973-75; coordinator Madison Area Library Council, 1975-76; asst. adult services librarian Lake County Pub. Library, Merrillville, Ind., 1976-78; library adminstr. Matteson (Ill.) Pub. Library, 1978-86, Elmwood Park (Ill.) Pub. Library, 1986—. Book reviewer Booklist mag., 1979—. Past team capt., various other offices United Fund, Oshkosh; past bd. dirs. Community Concerts Assn., Oshkosh; past leader Camp Fire Girls, Oshkosh. Ziegler Found. scholar, 1971. Mem. ALA, Ill. Library Assn., Chgo. Library Club. Club: Lake Shore Ski (Chgo.) (summer events dir. 1983-84). Lodge: PEO (corr. sec. Chgo. 1985-87, v.p. 1987—). Avocations: skiing, sailing, bridge, sewing, reading. Home: 405A Eugenie St Chicago IL 60614 Office: Elmwood Park Pub Library 4 Conti Pkwy Elmwood Park IL 60443

HOFFNER, VERNON RUSSELL, JR., data processing executive; b. Flint, Mich., Aug. 22, 1942; s. Vernon Russell Sr. and Doris Louise (Wilson) H.; m. Nancy Rae Wilson, June 11, 1966; children: Carrie Elizabeth, Stephen Christopher. AS, Flint Jr. Coll., 1962; BS, U. Mich., 1964; MBA, Cen. Mich. U., Mt. Pleasant, 1970; PhD, Mich. State U., East Lansing, 1975. Programmer IBM Corp., Rockville, Md., 1964-67; systems analyst Dow Corning, Midland, Mich., 1967-70; prof. Eastern Mich. U., Ypsilanti, 1973-77; cons. Gen. Motors Corp., Detroit, 1977-83; mgr. Spring Arbor Distbrs., Belleville, Mich., 1983—; ptnr. Tarabusi Assocs., Inc., 1985—, pres., Farmington, Mich., 1986. Contbr. articles to profl. jour. Clk., pres., Ward Presby. Ch., Livonia, Mich., 1986. Mem. Assn. Systems Mgmt. (sec. 1983-84). Avocations: sailing, skiing, swimming, reading, computers. Home: 21832 Parklane Ct Farmington Hills MI 48024 Office: Spring Arbor Distbrs 10885 Textile Rd Belleville MI 48111

HOFMAN, JOHN ERWIN, accountant; b. St. Louis, Mar. 6, 1960; s. James A. and Marian G. (Stevens) H.; m. Mary Shea, June 3, 1983. BBA, U. Mo., 1982. CPA, Mo. Staff acct. Price Waterhouse, St. Louis, 1984—. Treas. Citizens Against Annexations and Incorporating, St. Louis County, 1986. Named one of Outstanding Young Men of Am., U.S. Jaycees. Mem. Am. Inst. CPA's, Mo. Soc. CPA's. Roman Catholic. Office: PO Box 1432 Maryland Heights MO 63043

HOFMAN, LEONARD J., clergyman. Stated clk. Christian Reformed Ch. N.Am., Grand Rapids, Mich. Office: Christian Ref Ch of N Am 2850 Kalamazoo Ave SE Grand Rapids MI 49560

HOFMAN, WILLIAM BRADLEY, otolaryngologist; b. Birmingham, Mich., July 5, 1932; s. Louis Charles and Martha Loyola (Rosso) H.; m. Sherry Ann Burns, July 1, 1961; children: William Christopher, Jennifer Lynn, Melissa Ann. BA, Miami U., Oxford, Ohio, 1953; MD, U. Cin., 1958. Diplomate Am. Bd. Otolaryngology. Attending staff The Christ Hosp., Cin., 1973—, Children's Hosp., Cin., 1977—; pvt. practice specializing in otolaryngology Cin.; mem. courtesy staff Mercy Hosp., Cin., 1969—, Deaconess Hosp., Cin., 1975—, adminstrv. and teaching staff Bethesda Hosps., Cin., 1975—; asst. clin. prof. U. Cin. Hosp., 1970—; cons. staff Clinton Meml. Hosp., Wilmington, Ohio, 1973—. Served with USPHS, 1959-61. Spl. fellow in head and neck surgery, NIH, 1966-67; Am. Cancer Soc. fellow, 1967-70. Mem. AMA, ACS, Am. Acad. Otolaryngology, Am. Acad. Facial Plastic and Resoncstructive Surgery, Ohio Soc. Otolaryngology, Ohio State Med. Assn., Acad. Medicine of Cin., Cin. Otolaryngologic Soc. Republican. Club: Kenwood Country (Cin.). Avocations: golf, travel, reading, furniture refinishing. Office: 7777 Montgomery Rd Cincinnati OH 45236

HOFRICHTER, DAVID ALAN, international management consulting firm executive; b. Lakewood, Ohio, July 10, 1948; s. David Christian and Virginia Amelia (Rickley) H.; m. Carol Ann Rybak, May 15, 1971; children—Kristin Ann, Matthew David. B.A., Baldwin-Wallace Coll., 1970; M.A., Duquesne U., 1972, Ph.D., 1976. Assoc., Hay Assocs., Pitts., 1977-78, prin., 1978-80, dir. orgn. and manpower services, 1980-81, gen. mgr., Cin., 1981—, ptnr., gen. mgr., 1983-85, v.p., gen. mgr., Cin., 1985-86, sr. v.p., gen. mgr., Chgo., 1986—, bd. dirs. Nat. Health Care Practice, Chgo., 1985—. Author: Executive Compensation in Health Care, 1986. Mem. Am. Psychol. Assn., Am. Soc. Cons. Mgmt. Engrs., Fin. Planning Assn. for City Chgo., Pa. Psychol. Assn. Republican. Roman Catholic. Clubs: Ruth Lake Country (Hindsdale, Ill.); Beckett Ridge Country (Cin.); Oak Brook (Ill.) Polo. Avocations: golf, swimming, polo. Home: 60 Derby Ct Oak Brook IL 60521 Office: Hay Group 1 E Wacker Dr Chicago IL 60601

HOFSTAD, RALPH PARKER, agricultural cooperative executive; b. Phila., Nov. 14, 1923; s. Ottar and Amelia (Davis) H.; m. Adeline Smedstad, June 14, 1947; children: Diane (Mrs. Roger Dunker), Barbara (Mrs. Dan McClanahan), James, Ron, Tom, Susan. Student, Hamline U., 1942-43, Gustavus Adolphus Coll., 1943-44, Northwestern U., 1944, U. Minn., 1946-47; B.B.A., Northwestern U., 1948. Accountant F S Services, Bloomington, Ill., 1948-51; mgmt. ops. F S Services, 1953-65; pres. Farmers Regional Coop (Felco), Ft. Dodge, Iowa, 1965-70; sr. v.p. agrl. services Land O' Lakes Inc., Ft. Dodge, 1970—; pres. Land O' Lakes Inc., Mpls., 1974—; bd. dirs. Hon Industries, Muscatine, Iowa, Control Data Corp., Mpls. Trustee Hamline U., St. Paul, U. Minn. Found., St. Paul, Better Bus. Bur., Minn.; bd. dirs. Goodwill Industries Am., 1977—. Served with USNR, 1943-46. Mem. Grocery Mfrs. Am. (bd. dirs. 1983), Nat. Council Farmer Coops. (bd. dirs. 1973—), Mpls. C. of C. Methodist. Home: 8621 Basswood Rd Eden Prairie MN 55344 Office: Land O'Lakes Inc 4001 Lexington Ave Arden Hills MN 55112

HOGAN, HARLAN ROBERT, voice-over actor; b. Chgo., Sept. 30, 1946; s. Harlan Vincent and Marjorie Catherine (Thurber) H.; m. Jayne Francis Milazzo, Apr. 12, 1969 (divorced); children: Jameson, Graham. BFA, Ill. Wesleyan U., 1968. Announcer Sta. WHUT-radio, Anderson, Ind., 1968-69, Sta. WCLR-radio, Skokie, Ill., 1969-71; advt. mgr. Advanced Systems, Elk Grove, Ill., 1971-74; pres., voice over actor Wordsworth, Inc., Chgo., 1974—. Recipient Golden Trumpet award Chgo. Pub. Relations Club, 1976, Best Commls. award Worlds Best Commls., 1985. Mem. Screen Actors Guild (v.p. Chgo. 1983-84), Internat. Brotherhood of Magicians. Club: Waukegan Yacht. Avocations: sailing, magic, bicycling. Home: 1030 N State Apt 11C Chicago IL 60610

HOGAN, MICHAEL RAY, insurance company executive; b. Newark, Ohio, Apr. 21, 1953; s. Raymond Carl and Mary Adele (Whalen) H.; m. Martha Ann Gorman, July 24, 1976; children: Colleen Michael, Patrick Gorman. BA, Loyola U., Chgo., 1978; M in Mgmt. with distinction, Northwestern U., 1980. Assoc. McKinsey & Co., Inc., Chgo., 1980-81, engagement mgr., 1982-83; sr. v.p., treas. FBS Ins. Co., Mpls., 1984-85; group v.p., gen. mgr. Gen. Am. Life Ins. Co., St. Louis, 1986, v.p., 1987—; cons. Swedish Trade Commn., Chgo., 1978, Lee Wards Creative Crafts Co., Elgin, Ill., 1979. Contb. articles to profl. jours. Active Experience St. Louis, 1986, Leadership St. Louis, 1987—. F.C. Austin Found. scholar, 1978-80, Phi Gamma Nu scholar, 1980; recipient Richard M. Clewett award Northwestern U., 1980. Mem. Am. Mktg. Assn., Beta Gamma Sigma. Democrat. Roman Catholic. Club: Stadium (St. Louis). Avocations: reading, family, golf, travel. Home: 12870 Nanell Ln Saint Louis MO 63127 Office: Gen Am Life Ins Co 13045 Tesson Ferry Rd Saint Louis MO 63128

HOGAN, TIMOTHY S., judge; b. Wellston, Ohio, Sept. 23, 1909; s. Timothy S. and Mary Adele (Deasey) H.; m. Evalon Roberts, Dec. 27, 1934; children—Nancy Ann (Mrs. Fred Dutton), Margaret M. (Mrs. John H. Wyant), Timothy S. III. A.B., Xavier U., 1930, LL.D., 1976; J.D., U. Cin., 1931. Bar: Ohio bar 1931. Pvt. practice with firm Cohen, Baron, Todd & Hogan, Cin., 1931-66; spl. counsel, atty. gen. Ohio, 1937-41, 48-50; U.S. dist. judge So. Dist. Ohio Cin., 1966—; chief judge 1976-78; lectr. trial practice U. Cin. Law Sch., 1950-62. Mem. Clermont (Ohio) County Planning Commn., 1958-62; Del.-at-large Ohio Democratic Nat. Conv., 1952. Served to lt. col. USAAF, 1942-46. Mem. Fed., Ohio, Cin., Clermont County bar assns., Order of Coif. Roman Catholic. Home: 3810 Eileen Dr Cincinnati OH 45209 Office: U S Dist Ct 829 U S Courthouse & P O Bldg 5th & Walnut Sts Cincinnati OH 45202

HOGER, DAVID EDWIN, manufacturing company executive; b. Paw Paw, Mich., Oct. 31, 1936; s. Wayne Edwin and Harriet Jane (Wiersba) H.; m. Phyllis Joan Johnson, Aug., 1956 (div. Feb. 1972); children—Bradley Jon, Wendy Sue; m. Sandra Jayne Ignatz, Mar. 23, 1972; children—Jill Marie, Heather Leigh. Student Western Mich. U., Kalamazoo Coll. Prodn. mgr. A. F. Murch Corp., Paw Paw, Mich., 1965-70; gen. mgr. Jessco Inc., Dowagiac, Mich., 1970-72; plant mgr. Richardson Homes, Waco, Tex., 1972-75; gen. mgr., v.p. Jessco, Inc., Dowagiac, 1975—; group v.p., chief exec. officer Jessco div. Rospatch Corp., 1980—; v.p. Tiffin Enterprise subs. Rospatch Corp., Tiffin, Ohio, 1984—. Trustee Village of Paw Paw, Mich., 1964-69, pres., 1969-71; supr. Silver Creek Twp., Dowagiac, 1978-81; trustee, pres., sec. Dowagiac Union Sch. Dist., 1981—; bd. dirs. Cass County United Way, 1981—. Republican. Methodist. Lodges: Lions (treas. Paw Paw 1965), Rotary (bd. dirs. local). Avocations: fishing; wood working. Home: 514 Green St Dowagiac MI 49047 Office: Jessco Div Rospatch Corp 202 Spaulding St Dowagiac MI 49047

HOGINS, MILDRED HOLDAR, medical technologist; b. Russelville, Ark., Jan. 18, 1939; d. Luther and Francess Eythl (Briscoe) Holdar; cert. in med. tech. Hillcrest Med. Center, Tulsa, 1963; B.S. in Biology, U. Mo., Kansas City, 1969; M.A. in Mgmt. and Supervision, Central Mich. U., 1976; m. Albert Gumbs; 1 son, Mark H. Hogins. Med. technologist St. Joseph Hosp., Tucson, 1964-66; bacteriologist Providence Hosp., Anchorage, Alaska, 1966-67; med. technologist St. Margaret Hosp., Kansas City, Kans., 1967-68, Providence Hosp., Kansas City, Kans., 1969-71; edn. coordinator Sch. Med. Tech., also asst. chief med. technologist Providence-St. Margaret Health Center, Kansas City, Kans., 1971-76, chief med. technologist, 1976—. Bd. dirs. Mill Creek Run Home Owners Assn., 1979-82, 85—, Plaza Acad., Kansas City, Mo., 1982-84. Mem. Clin. Lab. Mgrs. Assn. (bd. dirs. Kansas City chpt. 1985—), Nat. Assn. Female Execs., Am. Soc. Clin. Pathologists, Kans. Soc. Med. Tech. (conv. chmn. 1975), Greater Kansas City Soc. Med. Tech. (treas. 1980), U. Mo. Kansas City Alumni Assn., Central Mich. U. Alumni Assn., Mensa (bd. dirs. Mid-Am. chpt. 1983-87). Home: 14076 W 88th Terr Lenexa KS 66215 Office: 8929 Parallel Pkwy Kansas City KS 66112

HOGLUND, STEPHEN, jewelry designer, goldsmith, blacksmith; b. Virginia, Minn., Mar. 3, 1955; s. Carl O. and Lorraine Marie (Fahlstedt) H. Student in Art Metals, St. Cloud State Coll., 1973-75, U. Wis., LaCrosse, 1975-76; student, Stewarts Internat. Sch. for Jewelers, 1985. Designer, goldsmith J. Buzoguny Designs/Goldsmith Shop, Key West, Fla., 1978-80; owner, designer Superior Designs, Grand Marais, Minn., 1980—. Designer mus. quality jewelery peices featureing N.Am. gemstones and artifacts in gold on exhibit at C.G. Rein Gallery, Santa Fe, Mpls. and Scottsdale, Ariz. Recipient 1st place Metals award Lutsen (Minn.) Art Show, 1978, 79, Lake Superior '77 award Tweed Mus., Duluth, 1977. Mem. Jewelers of Am. (2d place award Minn. br. Jewelry Design Contest). Avocations: sailing, sailboarding. Home and Office: Superior Designs PO Box 882 410 W Hwy 61 Grand Marais MN 55904

HOGUE, RICHARD EUGENE, technical writer; b. Laramie, Wyo., Oct. 3, 1932; s. Harry Samuel and Billie Francis (Hinds) Shacklett; m. Margaret Ann Hogue, Jan. 20, 1957; children: Richard William, Michael Gene. Student, Augusta (Ga.) Coll., 1975, BA in Psychology, 1983. Enlisted U.S. Army, 1951, advanced through ranks to warrant officer, 1966, retired, 1983; writer ITT, Ft. Wayne, Ind., 1983—. Contbr. articles to mags. Decorated Legion of Merit. Mem. Soc. Logistical Engrs. Lodge: Masons. Avocation: chess. Home: 3338 Marias Dr Fort Wayne IN 46815 Office: ITT A/OD PO Box 3700 Fort Wayne IN 46801

HOGUET, DAVID DILWORTH, rental furniture executive; b. Sharon, Conn., Aug. 16, 1951; s. Joseph Lynch Hoguet and Diana Wood (Dilworth) Wantz; m. Karen Meisel, Oct. 9, 1983; 1 child, Jennifer Leigh. BA in History, U. Pa., 1973; MBA in Fin., NYU, 1975. With W.R. Grace, N.Y.C., 1975-1980; treas. Chemed Corp., Cin., 1981-1983, v.p. fin., treas., 1984-86; pres. Globe Furniture Rentals, Cin., 1986—; bd. dirs. Roto Rooter, Inc. Fundraiser Brooks Sch., North Andover, Mass., 1978—. Mem. Fin. Exec. Inst., Am. Mgmt. Assn., Nat. Investors Relations Inst. Clubs: Losantiville, Bankers, Racquet. Avocation: squash. Home: 2658 Grandin Rd Cincinnati OH 45208 Office: Globe Furniture Rentals 1925 Greenwood Ave Cincinnati OH 45246

HOHENSTEIN, ALAN RAYMOND, appraisal and valuation consultant; b. Mpls., Nov. 11, 1936; s. Gilbert Wyle and Alice Ann (Delaney) H.; m. Shirley Dianne Culton, Apr. 4, 1970 (div. 1980); children—Jeffrey Owen, Steven Francis. Student St. Cloud State U., 1955-59. Exec. v.p. Premium Corp., Mpls., 1965; v.p. fin. D.I. Leasing Corp., Mpls., 1968-70; asst. investment mgr. Prudential Ins. Co., 1971-73; v.p. Affiliated Leasing Corp., Madison, Wis., 1973-74; regional v.p. Marshall and Stevens, Inc., Mpls., 1975—; v.p. Affiliated Leasing Corp., Madison, Wis., 1973-74. Spl. advisor U.S. Congl. Adv. Bd. Served with U.S. Army, 1959-61. Mem. Nat. Assn. Accts. Episcopalian. Club: Wayzata Yacht. Home: 5104 W 70th St Edina MN 55435 Office: 12 S 6th St Suite 930 Minneapolis MN 55402

HOHENSTEIN, JAMES BRYAN, architect, graphic designer; b. Lincoln, Nebr., Aug. 7, 1948; s. William Nels and Lillian Sarah (Hunt) H.; B.Arch., U. Nebr. at Lincoln, 1972; m. Donna Rae Gruenemeier, Dec. 27, 1969; children—Heather Suzanne, James Bryan, Tara Fae. Design architect Reynolds, Smith & Hills, Tampa, Fla., 1972-73, Bahr, Hanna, Vermeer & Haecker, Omaha, 1973-75, Henningson, Durham & Richardson, Omaha, 1975-81; head designer med. architecture Kirkham & Michael Assos., 1981-84; design mgr. Henningson Durham & Richardson, Omaha, 1984—; contbg. illustrator The Landmark mag.; partner Hohenstein-Dance Studio, graphic and photographic design. Recipient Asso. Arts award AIA, 1976. Mem. Nebr. Soc., AIA. Club: Ak-Sar-Ben.

HOHNSTEIN, MIKE ROBERT, salesperson, entrepreneur; b. Kansas City, Mo., June 21, 1959; s. Robert P. and Clair (Bade) H.; m. Renae S. Hoggatt, June 13, 1981; children: Benjamin, Katie. Grad., Kearney (Nebr.) State, 1982. Sales rep. Dutton-Lainson Co., Hastings, Nebr., 1982-84, Yellow Freight System, Inc., Kearney, 1984—; owner, pres. Scholarship Matching Service, Minden, Nebr., 1986—. Mem. Cen. Nebr. Traffic Club (2d v.p. 1987—), Jaycees, Sigma Phi Epsilon. Home: 643 E Holland Minden NE 68959

HOISINGTON, CHARLES WILLIAM, commodity trading advisor; b. Columbus, Ohio, Feb. 4, 1939; s. Charles William and Helen Marie (Warner) H.; m. Patricia Ann Smith, June 3, 1963 (div. Aug. 1981); children: Amy B., Charles W. Jr. BEd, Ohio State U., 1967. Registered commodity trading advisor. Pvt. practice commodity trading advisor Columbus, 1975—; cons. in field. Officer Columbus Fathers; participant Big Bros. Assn. Avocation: outdoors activities. Home and Office: 188 Fairway Dr Columbus OH 43214-1750

HOISINGTON, DOUGLAS GEORGE, oil company executive; b. Fairfield, Ill., Sept. 28, 1951; s. George Howard and Iloe Charlene (Lund) H.; m. Paula Kristin Allen, Jan. 7, 1972; children: Chelsea, Chandler. BS in Petroleum Engring., U. Kans., 1979. Prodn. engr. Conoco, Inc., Oklahoma City, 1979-81; dist. engr. Coquina, Inc., Oklahoma City, 1981-82; div. engr. Star Resources, Oklahoma City, 1982; v.p. prodn. Allen Drilling Co., Great Bend, Kans., 1982—; bd. dirs Peoples State Bank, Ellinwood, Kans. Mem. Am. Petroleum Inst., Ind. Petroleum Assn. of Am., Kans. Ind. Oil and Gas Assn., Soc. of Petroleum Engrs. (jr.), Phi Mu Alpha Sinfonia. Avocations: golf, reading, racquetball.

HOISLBAUER, WILLIAM IGNATIUS, real estate developer; b. Cleve., July 16, 1937; s. William and Mary (Jankowicz) H.; m. Virginia Ruth Koskey, Aug. 16, 1958 (div. Nov. 1965); children: Holly Suzanne, William Stephen; m. Judith Kay Naklizki, June 27, 1970. Student, Wayne State U., 1955-57; AA in Bus. Adminstrn., Fenn Coll., 1960. Pres. Hoislbauer Builders, Cleve., 1959—, Hoislbauer Realty, Cleve., 1966—; bd. dirs. Three Bills Inc., Cleve., H & F Bldg. Co., Cleve. Chief exec. officer Seven Hills (Ohio) Aux. Police, 1964-73. Served to commodore USCG, 1986-87. Mem. Seven Hills C. of C. (trustee 1960-69). Republican. Roman Catholic. Avocations: boating, bowling, traveling.

HOKE, ROBERT ALAN, aquatic ecologist; b. Tiffin, Ohio, Oct. 4, 1954; s. Robert Ray and Joy Ann (Bollinger) H.; m. Lori Jean Laskowski, July 12, 1980 (div. Apr. 1986); 1 child, Ian Ray. Bs, Bowling Green State U., 1976, MS, 1981. Cert. environ. profl., assoc. fisheries scientist. Biochem. tech. U. S. Environ. Protection Agy., Chgo., 1976; research assoc. Heidelberg Coll., Tiffin, 1976-79; sr. biologist Aqua Tech. Environ. Cons., Inc., Melmore, Ohio, 1980-82; vol. U.S. Peace Corps, Cebu, Philippines, 1982-84; prin. biologist Aqua Tech. Environ. Cons. Inc., Melmore, 1984-87. Contbr. articles to profl. jour. U.S. Environ. Protection Agy. grantee, 1977, 81. Mem. Nat. Assn. Environ. Profls., Ohio Acad. Sci., N.Am. Benthological Soc., Soc. Environ. Toxicol. and Chem., Am. Fisheries Soc., Sigma Xi. Avocations: camping, fishing, woodworking. Home: 1920 Alpha St Lansing MI 48910 Office: Mich State U Pesticide Research Ctr Room 201 East Lansing MI 48824

HOKIN, EDWIN E., steel manufacturing company executive. Chmn. exec. com. UNR Industries, Inc., Chgo. Office: U N R Industries Inc 332 S Michigan Ave Chicago IL 60604 *

HOLBEIN, GARY L., dentist; b. Findlay, Ohio, Feb. 3, 1949; s. George Louis and Erma Dorothea (Garno) H.; m. Deborah Kay, Dec. 22, 1975; children: Amanda Leigh, Maggie Leigh. BS in Pharmacy, U. Cin., 1972; DDS, Ohio State U., 1975. Practice dentistry Bay City, Mich., 1975—; lectr. in pharmacology Delta Coll., University Ctr., Mich., 1985—. Mem. ADA, Ohio State Pharm. Assn., N. Cen. Ohio Dental Assn. (treas. 1978), Chgo. Dental Soc., Saginaw Valley Dental Soc. Home: 2047 Reppuhn Bay City MI 48706 Office: 1112 S Euclid Bay City MI 48706

HOLBROOK, AMY LEE, marketing manager; b. Columbus, Ohio, July 1, 1958; d. Joseph R. and Wilma E. (Semones) H. Student, Ohio State U., 1976-77; BBA, Franklin U., 1981. Sales adminstr. Adria Labs, Inc., Dublin, Ohio, 1979-82; tech. sales rep. Transmet Corp., Columbus, 1982-85, mktg. mgr., 1986—. Mem. Cen. Ohio Indsl. Marketers (bd. dirs., treas. 1986), Am. Soc. Metals, Soc. Plastics Engrs., Soc. Tech. Communication. Democrat. Methodist. Avocations: travel, reading, camping. Home: 3779 Habitat Dr Columbus OH 43228 Office: Transmet Corp 4290 Perimeter Dr Columbus OH 43228

HOLDEMAN, RICHARD JOHN, JR., financial executive; b. Goshen, Ind., Jan. 13, 1943; s. Richard John and Hilda Jean (Wintermute) H.; m. Carol Ann Hyatte, June 5, 1965; children: Tracy, Jeffrey, Jennifer, William. BS, Tri State Coll., 1965. Acct. CTS Corp., Elkhart, Ind., 1965-70; controller LaPorte (Ind.) Plastics, 1970-72; asst. controller Swinger, Elkhart, 1972-74; v.p. fin. Jayco, Ind., Middlebury, 1974—. Treas., dir. HOME, Elkhart, 1975-77; v.p., treas. Middlebury Little League, 1980-86; fund raising chmn. ARC, Elkhart, 1980. Republican. Methodist. Avocations: swimming, skiing, bowling. Home: 57531 CR 18 Goshen IN 46526 Office: Jayco Inc 58075 SR 13 S Middlebury IN 46540

HOLDEMAN, ROBERT LEWIS, II, architect, artist; b. Elkhart, Ind., June 11, 1941; s. Robert Lewis and Saritea (Lorenz) H.; m. Jane Day, Aug. 22, 1964; children—Robert Scott, John Edward. B.S. in Architecture, U. Cin., 1965. Assoc., Field, Graheck, Bell & Kline, Traverse City, Mich., 1965-70, David L. Stiffler, Traverse City, 1970-75; prin. Architecture/Artistry/Interiors Inc., Traverse City, 1975—; ptnr. Welch, Holdeman Studio (stained glass). bd. dirs. Traverse City Arts Council; trustee Traverse City Osteopathic Hosp. Mem. AIA, Mich. Soc. Architects, Mich. Soc. Artists and Craftsmen, Internat. Soc. Artists. Methodist. Creator stained glass windows: St. Francis Church, TBA Credit Unions, Hagerty Ins. Agy. (all Traverse City), many residences; bronze sculpture, Munson Med. Center. Home: 2629 Nelson Rd Traverse City MI 49684 Office: 1004 E 8th St Traverse City MI 49684

HOLDEN, EDGAR HOWARD, state legislator; b. Tama, Iowa, Mar. 24, 1914; s. Glen and Laura (Warner) H.; m. Rachel O. Brown, 1937. Mem. Iowa Ho. Reps., 1967-75, Iowa Senate, 1978—. Adv. bd. Salvation Army. Served with AUS, 1943-45. Mem. Gideons, C. of C., Am. Legion. Presbyterian. Lodge: Rotary. Home: 2246 E 46th Davenport IA 52807

HOLDEN, GEORGE T., business forms executive; b. Mpls., July 31, 1945; s. Harold L. and Harriet (Thwing) H.; m. Cristy Jane Muller, Aug. 22, 1982; children: Elizabeth, Tricia. BBA, Northwestern U., 1967; MBA, Harvard U., 1970. With brand mgmt. Proctor & Gamble, Cin., 1970-72; pres. Holden Bus. Forms Co., Mpls., 1972—. Served to 2d lt. USNG, 1967-74. Mem. Black Leaf Soc. of Internat. Bus. Forms Industry (past chmn.), Ash Khan Soc. of Printing Industry Am. Clubs: Harvard (past pres. Lodge: Masons. Avocation: sports. Office: 607 Washington Ave N Minneapolis MN 55401

HOLDERMAN, JAMES F., JR., federal judge; b. 1946. BS, U. Ill., 1968, JD, 1971. Judge U.S. Dist. Ct. (no. dist.) Ill., Chgo., 1985—; asst. U.S. atty. City of Chgo., 1972-78; ptnr. Sonnenschein, Carlin et al, Chgo., 1978-85; judge U.S. Dist. Ct. (no. dist.) Ill., Chgo., 1985—; lectr. law U. Chgo., 1983—. Office: U S Dist Ct 219 S Dearborn St Room 2146 Chicago IL 60604

HOLGAARD, CONRAD J., manufacturing company executive. Chmn. Raven Industries, Inc., Sioux Falls, S.D. Office: Raven Industries Ins PO Box 1007 Sioux Falls SD 57101 *

HOLIDAY, GREGORY, administrative law judge; b. Detroit, Nov. 27, 1951; s. Christor and Merdis (Jackson) H.; m. Zenobia Ann Watts, Mar. 24, 1985; 1 child, Kai Alano. Student, Ferris State Coll., 1970; BS, Eastern Mich. U., 1974; JD, U. Detroit, 1977; postgrad., Inst. of Continuing Legal Edn., 1977-87. Bar: Mich. 1977, U.S. Dist. Ct. (ea. dist.) Mich. 1978, U.S. Supreme Ct. 1983. Staff atty. Oakland County Legal Aid, Royal Oak Twp., Mich., 1977-80; supervising atty. Oakland Livingston Legal Aid, Ferndale, Mich., 1980-81; adminstrv. law judge Mich. Dept. Licensing and Regulation, Lansing, 1981-83, adminstrv. law judge, acting dir., 1983-85; faculty advisor Nat. Jud. Coll., Reno, 1982-85, 87; chmn. state coordinating planning commn. Nat. Conf. Adminstrv. Law Judges, Washington, 1985—; coordinator, host 1986 Adminstrv. Law Program, Ann Arbor, Mich., 1986. Contbr. articles to profl. jours. Arbitrator Better Bus. Bur. Met. Detroit, 1981—; trustee Otis Bryant Jr. Scholarship Fund, Oak Park, Mich., 1981—; chmn. Citizens Task Force for Royal Oak Twp., Oakland County, Mich., 1984—; pres. Huntington Estates Homeowner Assn., Oak Park, 1986—; dir. S.E. Mich. State Employees Fed. Credit Union, Southfield, Mich., 1987—. Reginald H. Smith fellow, 1977-79; recipient Spirit of Black Enterprise award Sanders and Assocs., 1985. Mem. ABA (chmn. com. 1985—), Nat. Bar Assn., Assn. Black Judges of Mich., Nat. Conf. Adminstrv. Law Judges (exec. com. 1986—), Mich. Bar Assn. (exec. council adminstrv. law sect. 1986—). Baptist. Clubs: Park Pl. Investment (Oak Park) (pres. 1982-84); Econ. of Detroit (jr. exec. 1981-86). Avocations: golf, tennis, racquetball, whist, bicycling. Home: 8757 Kenberton Dr Oak Park MI 48237 Office: Mich Dept Licensing and Regulation 611 W Ottawa 2d Floor Lansing MI 48909

HOLIDAY, LOIS ANN, lawyer; b. Franklin, Ind., June 6, 1954; d. Dale Wesley and Helen Rosemary (Blaich) Jones; m. James Ernest Holiday, Aug. 5, 1978; children: Wesley Ernest, Walter Ernest. BS, Ind. State U., 1975; postgrad. Pepperdine U., 1977-78; JD, Western State U., Fullerton, Calif., 1981. Bar: Ind. Staff atty. Ind. State Dept. Pub. Welfare, Indpls., 1981-83; dep. prosecutor Johnson County, Franklin, Ind., 1983—; mem. bar com. profl. fitness Ind. State Supreme Ct. Precinct committeeman Sugar Creek Twp., New Palestine, Ind., 1984—; bd. dirs., past chmn. Interlocal Community Action Program, New Castle, 1982-86. Mem. Hancock County Bar Assn., Ind. State Bar Assn. (legis. com. juvenile and domestic sect.), Indpls. Bar Assn., Ind. Rural Lawyers Assn., Johnson County Bar Assn. Congregationalist. Republican. Avocations: bowling, camping, antique collecting. Home: Rural Route 4 Box 270 New Palestine IN 46163 Office: Johnson County Prosecutor's Office Courthouse Annex Franklin IN 46131

HOLIGA, LUDOMIL ANDREW, metallurgical engineer; b. Dayton, Ohio, Dec. 7, 1920; s. Andrew and Antonia Margaret (Sefcek) H.; m. Aryetta Lillian Mernedakis, Feb. 6, 1960; children—David, Carol, Millard, Timothy, Michael. Engr. assoc., Sinclair Coll., 1948; B.Sc., Calgary Coll. Tech., 1974, M.M.E., 1975. Cert. mfg. engr. Engr. designer Wright Patterson AFB, Ohio, 1941-54; contract designer Product Design Services, Inc., Dayton, Ohio, 1955-60; with Dayton Progress Corp., 1961—, dir. corp. devel., 1972-73, dir. research and tech. edn., 1974—. Research on cutting clearances for perforating metals in stamping dies. Served with USAAF, 1942-45, AUS, 1951-52. Mem. Soc. Mfg. Engrs. (chmn. standards com. 1963-72), Ohio Research and Devel. Found., Foremans Club, Am. Metal Stamping Assn. Lutheran. Home: 2025 Oak Tree Dr E Kettering OH 45440 Office: Dayton Progress Corp 500 Progress Rd Dayton OH 45449

HOLL, CARL W., JR., radiologist; b. Wabash, Ind., Oct. 14, 1933; s. Carl W. and Ruth Eve (Hornish) H.; m. Donna Jean Bartels, Apr. 15, 1961; children: Cheryl, Mark, Michael. AB, Manchester Coll., 1954; MD, Ind. U., 1958. Diplomate Am. Bd. Radiology. Commd. USAF, 1956, advanced through grades to col., 1973, retired, 1976; intern UCLA, 1958-59, radiology resident, 1963-67; chief diagnostic radiology Wilford Hall Hosp., San Antonio, 1967-69; chmn. dept. radiology USAF Hosp., Wiesbaden, Fed. Republic Germany, 1969-73, Keesler AFB, Miss., 1973-76; radiologist Community Hosp., Indpls., 1977—. Republican. Lutheran. Office: Community Hosp 1500 N Ritter Indianapolis IN 46219

HOLLADAY, ROBERT LAWRENCE, physician; b. Hillsboro, Ohio, Apr. 9, 1932; s. Clarence Carson and Helen (Brown) H.; m. Lavonne Lynd Beard; children: Scott Raymond, Lawrence Alan, Bruce Robert. BA, Ohio State U., 1954, MD, 1958. Intern St. Rita's Hosp., Lima, Ohio, 1958-59; gen. practice medicine Lima, 1959—. Fellow Am. Acad. Family Practice, Ohio Acad. Family Practice, Lima Acad. Family Practice (pres. 1985-86); mem. AMA, Ohio State Med. Assn. Republican. Methodist. Club: U.S. Power Squad. Lodge: Elks. Avocations: boating, photography. Home: 2874 Sands Rd Lima OH 45805 Office: 2609 Breese Rd Lima OH 45806

HOLLAND, HAROLD HERBERT, banker; b. Clifton Forge, Va., Feb. 11, 1932; s. Tristum Shandy and Ida Blanche (Paxton) H.; m. Nellie Mae Thomas, Jan. 15, 1955; children—Richard Long, Michael Wayne. Student, Coll. of William and Mary, 1953-54; BA, George Washington U., 1957, MBA, 1958. Tech. asst. Fed. Res. Bd., Washington, 1959-61; v.p. Falls Church Bank, Va., 1961-67; exec. v.p. Bank of New River, Radford, Va., 1967-70; pres., chief exec. officer Farmers Nat. Bank, Salem, Va., 1970-75; chmn., pres., chief exec. officer, dir. Am. Nat. Holding Co., Kalamazoo, 1975-86, Am. Nat. Bank & Trust, Kalamazoo, 1975-86; chmn. bd., dir. Kalamazoo Econ. Devel. Corp., 1977-84; dir. Wynfield Prodns.; chmn. Old Kent Bank of Kalamazoo, 1986-Apr., 1987. Exec. council, v.p. S.W. Mich. council Boy Scouts Am., Kalamazoo, 1976-86; county co-chmn. Gilmore for Congress, 1981; trustee I.S. Gilmore Found.; bd. dirs. Kalamazoo Conv. and Visitors Bur., 1981-82, Jobs for Mich. Grads., 1985—, Downtown Tomorrow, Inc., 1985—, West Mich. Telecommunications Found.; chmn. Kalamazoo 2000 Econ. Devel. Com., 1982; pres. Va. Mental Health Found., 1974-75; chmn., bd. dirs. Western Mich. U. Found., 1985—; trustee Borgess Hosp., 1986—, I.S. Gilmore Found., 1976—; chmn. Borgess Captial Campaign, 1986; mem. City of Kalamazoo Pension Divestiture Study Com. Recipient Disting. Service award U.S. Jaycees, 1965, Silver Beaver award Boy Scouts Am., 1986. Mem. Mich. Bankers Assn. (mem. strategic planning com.), Assn. of Bank Holding Cos. (dir. 1978-81), Kalamazoo County C. of C. (pres. 1981, chmn. strategic planning com. 1984). Republican. Methodist. Clubs: Park, Kalamazoo Country, Beacon. Lodge; Rotary (pres. 1974). Home: 1786 Greenbriar Kalamazoo MI 49008

HOLLAND, PATRICIA ANN, physical therapist, restaurant owner; b. Indpls., Mar. 25, 1933; d. William Martin and Kathryn (Kavanagh) H.; m. Oliver L. Pipkin, Sept. 8, 1986. BS in Physical Therapy, St. Louis U., 1955; MS in Edn. and Psychology, Butler U., 1968. Registered physical therapist. Physical therapist Ind. U. Med. Ctr., Indpls., 1955-64; physical therapist, pre sch. tchr. St. Mary's Child Ctr., Indpls., 1964-68; physical therapist supr. Wishard Meml. Hosp., Indpls., 1972-74; physical therapist Hosp. Based Home Care, VA Hosp., Indpls., 1979-86. Chairperson Ind. black Expo Jazz Concert, Indpls., 1982-86; sec. West Montgomery Jazz Fest, Indpls., 1983-86. Mem. Am. Physical Therapy Assn. (sec. 1955-58), 54th and College St. Mcht. Assn. (sec. 1985-86). Avocatios: cooking and baking, yoga, swimming. Home: 4605 Washington Blvd Indianapolis IN 46205 Office: The Place to Start Restaurant 5377 N College Ave Indianapolis IN 46220

HOLLAND, ROBERT WARREN, small business owner, entrepreneur; b. Toledo, June 19, 1954; s. Richard Ivan and Pearl Louise (Hiatt) H.; m. Corrine Marie Bondy, Dec. 31, 1984; 1 child, Justin Robert. Grad. high sch., Toledo, 1972; student, U. Toledo, 1972-75. Regional mgr. Sportfame Inc., Toledo, 1974-82; sole proprietor Team Mates, Toledo, 1982—; baseball coach DeVilbiss High Sch., Toledo, 1973-77, 80—. active Old Newsboy Charity paper Drive, Toledo; baseball coach Raymer Elem. Sch., Toledo, 1970-80, St. Thomas Cath. Youth Orgn., Toledo, 1981, 82, basketball coach, 1978-82. Republican. Lutheran. Avocations: softball, basketball, golf, reading, music. Home: 5547 Gay St Toledo OH 43613 Office: Team Mates 840 E Broadway Toledo OH 43605

HOLLAND, RUTH ELIZABETH, limnology research scientist; b. Weatherly, Pa., Apr. 17, 1936; d. Charles Frederick and Ruth Mae (Krick) H.; m. Alfred Merle Beeton, June 4, 1966; children: Jonathan Eugene, Daniel Paul. BA, St. Olaf Coll., 1958; MS, U. Mich., 1962. Fisheries research biologist U.S. Bur. Comml. Fisheries, Ann Arbor, Mich., 1963-66; research specialist U. Wis. Ctr. Great Lakes Studies, Milw., 1966-76; research investigator U. Mich. Atmospheric and Oceanic Scis., Ann Arbor, 1976—; research assoc. dept oceanography Oreg. State U., Corvallis, 1982; cons. Indsl. Biotest, Northbrook, Ill., 1970, Atty. Gen. State Wis., Madison, 1972, 73. Contbr. articles to profl. jours. Treas. Newport Elem. PTSO, Ann Arbor, 1980-81, v.p. Forsythe Jr. High PTSO, 1983-84, curriculum chmn., 1984-86; den mother, com. chairwoman Cub Scouts Am., Ann Arbor, 1979-82. Fellow AAAS; mem. Internat. Soc. Diatom Research, Am. Soc. Limnology and Oceanography, Societas Internat. Limnologiae, Freshwater Biol. Assn. Great Britain. Lutheran. Avocations: travel, theater, music, reading, photography. Home: 2761 Oakcleft Ct Ann Arbor MI 48103 Office: Atmospheric & Oceanic Scis Hayward Blvd Ann Arbor MI 48103

HOLLANDER, ADRIAN WILLOUGHBY, computer software company executive; b. Sumter, S.C., Oct. 12, 1941; s. Willard Fisher and Mildred Hanna (Willoughby) H.; m. Eleanor Busby Smith, May 26, 1963; children: Richard, David, Robert. BS, Iowa State U., 1963. CPA; cert. info. system auditor, internal auditor. Mem. audit and cons. staff Arthur Andersen and Co., Chgo., 1965-71; auditor Beverly Bancorporation, Chgo., 1971-73; v.p. Cullinane Corp., Chgo., 1973-78; auditor Cen. Nat. Bank in Chgo., 1978-79; pres. EDP Audit Assocs., Inc., Summit, Ill., 1980; pres. Complus, Inc., Hickory Hills, Ill., 1982-87, Chgo., 1987—; cons., owner EDP Audit Service, Chgo., 1979—. Contbr. articles to profl. jours. Trustee St. Paul's Union Ch., Chgo., 1973-75; bd. dirs. Beverly Improvement Assn., Chgo., 1972—; council of dels. Beverly Area Planning Assn., Chgo., 1980-85; del. Chgo. Agenda for Pub. Edn., 1983—. Served to 1st lt. U.S. Army, 1963-65. Mem. Am. Inst. CPA's, Ill. CPA Soc., EDP Auditors Assn., Inst. Internal Auditors, Nat. Soc. Chartered Bank Auditors (cert.). Republican. Avocations: fishing, camping, scouting. Home: 9360 S Pleasant Ave Chicago IL 60620 Office: Complus Inc 9500 S Vanderpoel Chicago IL 60643

HOLLANDER, DORIS ANN, psychologist, consultant, businesswoman; b. St. Louis, Oct. 13, 1941; d. Samuel and Rose (Heller) H.; m. Jerrold Blumoff, June 9, 1963; children: Sam, Rebecca. BA, Washington U., St. Louis, 1964; MA with distinction, DePaul U., 1972; PhD, Loyola U., Chgo., 1979. Caseworker Mo. Div. Welfare, St. Louis, 1964-65; research assoc. Inst. Juvenile Research, Chgo., 1967-68; instr. ednl. psychology Loyola U., Chgo., 1972-73; psychologist, program developer Women's Achievement Program, Hammond, Ind., 1976-78; pres. Whole Food & Grain Depot, Oak Park, Ill., 1972-78; asst. prof. psychology Webster U., St. Louis, 1979-83, co-chmn. psychology dept., 1982-83; pres. New Options, Inc., 1983—; co-chmn. psychology, sociology and anthropology, dir. adult learner project, Webster U.; lectr. Washington U. Sch. Bus. Exec. v.p., program chmn. Oak Park Mental Health Bd., 1976-79. Editor Mo. Psychologist. Mem. Assn. Community Mental Health Authorities Ill. (del.), Am. Psychol. Assn., Southeastern Psychol. Assn., Mo. Psychol. Assn. (sec. 1985-86, pres. 1987—, chmn. women's issues com. 1983-84), St. Louis Network Women Psychologists (coordinator 1981-84, pres. 1982-84, bd. dirs. 1984-87, historian 1985-87), Soc. Psychologists Mgmt. (bd. dirs.), St. Louis Psychol. Assn. (program chmn. 1984-85, pres. 1985-86). Home: 6330 Alexander Dr Saint Louis MO 63105 Office: 235 S Meremac Blvd Suite 1032 Saint Louis MO 63105

HOLLANDER, STANLEY CHARLES, marketing educator; b. Balt., Aug. 2, 1919; s. Abraham A. and Selma (Langfeld) H.; m. Selma Dorothy Jacobs, Dec. 16, 1956. BS, NYU, 1941; MA, Am. U., 1946; PhD, U. Pa., 1954. Trainee, asst. mgr. Neisner Bros., various locations, 1941-43; analyst Neisner Bros., 1943-45, Charles Stoen Co., N.Y.C., 1946; cons. Office Price Adminstrn., Washington, 1945-47; instr. dept. mktg. U. Buffalo, 1947-49; instr. dept. mktg. U. Pa., Phila., 1949-54, assoc. prof., 1956-58; asst. prof. Sch. Bus. U. Minn., Mpls., 1954-56; assoc. prof. mktg. Mich. State U., East Lansing, 1958-59, prof., 1959—. Author: Retail Price Policies, 1958; Multinational Retailing, 1958; Restraints on Retail Competition, 1965; author (with D.J. Duncan) Modern Retailing Management, 1972, 77, (with R. Savitt), 83; editor: Exploration in Retailing, 1959; (with R. Moyer) Markets and Marketing in Developing Countries, 1968; (with J. Boddewyn) Public Policy Toward Retailing, 1972; Passenger Transportation, 1968; Business Consultants and Clients, 1963; Management Consultants and Clients, 1972; also articles. Recipient NYU Inst. Retail Mgmt. award, 1964; named disting. scholar Mich. State U., 1982. Mem. Am. Mktg. Assn., Am. Coll. Retailing Assn. (pres. 1986—), Am. Econ. Assn., Acad. Mktg. Sci. (bd. govs. 1986—), Bus. History Conf., AAUP, Phi Kappa Phi, Beta Gamma Sigma, Eta Mu Pi. Jewish. Club: University (Lansing). Office: Mich State U 321 Eppley Ctr East Lansing MI 48824

HOLLENBAUGH, FLORENCE ALMA, nurse, consultant; b. Lakewood, Ohio, Mar. 1, 1929; d. Melvin A. and Dorothy F. (Geiger) Heidloff; m. William J. Hollenbaugh, Feb. 11, 1955 (dec. Apr. 1981); 1 son, William. Student Western Res. U. Sch. Nursing, Cleve., 1946-50; cert. U. So. Calif. Sch. Pub. Adminstrn., 1956; student Harvard Med. Sch., 1977, 79, 81, 83, 84. R.N., Ohio. Head nurse Univ. Hosps., Cleve., 1950; clin. instr. Vis. Nurse Assn., Cleve., 1951-52; police officer, Lakewood, 1954-58; pub. health nurse Medina County (Ohio), 1958-61; inservice educator Lodi (Ohio) Community Hosp., 1961-76; nurse epidemiologist S.W. Gen. Hosp., Middleburg Heights, Ohio, 1976—; guest lectr. Cleve. State U., Kent State U., Baldwin-Wallace Coll. Mem. Army emergency relief com. ARC. Midpark Homeowners Assn. Served to 1st lt. Nurse Corps, U.S. Army, 1952-54. Stuart Pharms. grantee, 1981. Mem. Assn. for Practitioners Infection Control (pres. chpt. 1980, chmn. bd. 1981, 82, nat. adv. com.), Assn. Hosp. Risk Mgrs., Assn. Advancement Med. Instrumentation, Medina County Nurses Assn. (pres.), Pentagon Council Hosp. Inservice Edn. (chmn.), Akron Hosp. Assn. (edn. com.), Am. Soc. Hosp. Engrs., Res. Officers Assn., Am. Legion. Republican. Mem. United Ch. of Christ. Clubs: Women's Fellowship (Middleburg Heights); Lake Erie Sci. Ctr. (Bay Village, Ohio). Contbr. articles to profl. jours. Home: 15264 Hemlock Ln Middleburg Heights OH 44130 Office: Southwest Gen Hosp 18697 E Bagley Rd Middleburg Heights OH 44130

HOLLENBERG, PAUL FREDERICK, pharmacology educator; b. Phila., Sept. 18, 1942; s. Frederick Henry and Catherine (Dentzer) H.; m. Emily Elizabeth Vanootighem, May 6, 1967; children: Kathryn Mary, David Paul. BS in Chemistry, Wittenberg U., 1964; MS in Biochemistry, U. Mich., 1966, PhD in Biochemistry, 1969. Postdoctoral fellow U. Mich., Ann Arbor,

1969, U. Ill., Urbana, 1969-72; asst. prof. Northwestern U., Chgo., 1972-81, assoc. prof., 1981-84, prof. pathology and molecular biology, 1984-87; prof. pharmacology, chmn. dept. Wayne State U. Sch. Medicine, Detroit, 1987—. Schweppe Found. research fellow, 1974-77; NIH research grantee, 1974—. Mem. Am. Chem. Soc., Am. Soc. Biol. Chemists, Am. Soc. Pharmacological and Experimental Therapy, Am. Assn. for Cancer Research, Society of Toxicology. Avocations: reading, running, golf. Home: 5283 Provincial Bloomfield Hills MI 48013 Office: Dept Pharmacology Sch Medicine Wayne State U 540E Canfield Detroit MI 48201

HOLLENKAMP, PATRICIAN KAYLOR, psychotherapist; b. Kingsport, Tenn., Jan. 21, 1944; d. Cecil Franklin and Nola Berniece (Pridemore) Burchette; m. Robert Wayne Kaylor, June 5, 1965 (div, 1972); 1 child, Dawn Burchette Kaylor; m. Theodore Joseph Hollenkamp IV, Aug. 27, 1984. BA, Wake Forest U., 1965; MSW, U. Tenn., 1968; cert. clin. specialist, Ctr. Humanistic Studies, Detroit, 1982; PhD in Clin. Psychology, Union of Experimenting Colls. and Univs., Cin., 1985. Lic. psychologist, marriage counselor; cert. social worker. Child welfare worker State of Tenn., Hawkins County, 1965-66; dir. child welfare State of Tenn., Sullivan County, 1966-68; clin. social worker, supr. Oakland County, Southfield, Mich., 1968-71; program dir. Providence Hosp., Southfield, 1971-73; pvt. practice social work, specialist in psychology of work Birmingham, Mich., 1973—; field instr. U. Mich., Ann Arbor, Wayne State U., Detroit, 1969-73; instr. dept. social work U. Detroit, 1975; lectr. on stress mgmt.; cons. mgmt. tng. Wayne County Assn. for Retarded, 1986; cons. SSI, Chgo., 1986. Active Birmingham Unitarian Ch., 1979—; tchr. community edn. courses, 1979—. Mem. Am. Assn. Marriage and Family Therapists (clin.), Am. Group Psychotherapy Assn. (chair membership com. 1976-78, nat. membership com. 1978-81), Mich. Soc. Clin. Social Work (tras., liaison to Gov.'s Task Force Com.). Democrat. Club: Forest Lake Country. Lodge: Zonta Internat. (bd. dirs. Southfield area 1986—). Avocations: cross country skiing, hiking, canoeing, writing, bridge. Office: Adams Psychol Assn 801 S Adams Suite 200 Birmingham MI 48011

HOLLER, JOSEPH, psychologist, consultant; b. Witt, Ill., Dec. 15, 1932; s. Joseph Henry and Jane (Summers) H.; m. Martha Carolyn Delashmit, Apr. 17, 1954 (div. Feb. 1971); 1 child, Joseph. BS magna cum laude, Ball State U., 1972, MA in Clin. Psychology, 1973, MA in Counseling Psychology, 1974; PhD in Counseling Psychology, Purdue U., 1977. Lic. psychologist, clin. marriage and family therapist; lic. arborist. Landscape designer Gaar's, Inc., Chesterfield, Ind., 1960-65; pres. Landscape Assocs., Paris, 1965—; sr. ptnr., cons. psychologist Joseph Holler & Assocs., Paris, 1972—; artist-in-residence Purdue U., 1984-85, vis. scholar, 1979—; cons. psychologist Indian Affairs, Pine Ridge, S.D., 1980, Eastern Mont., Glendive, 1982-83. Contbr. numerous articles in field aired on nat. pub. radio. Mem. Chesterfield Boosters Club, 1961-65, City Beautification Com., Anderson, Ind., 1965-69. Served with USAF, 1952-56. Mem. Am. Psychol. Assn., Am. Assn. Marriage and Family Therapy, Am. Orthopsychiat. Assn., Am. Personnel Assn. Methodist. Lodges: Kiwanis (pres. Chesterfield chpt. 1961-66), Masons. Avocations: hiking, gardening, crossword puzzles, writing, lang. study. Home and Office: 207 Ann St Paris IL 61944-1218

HOLLEY, H. STEELE, physician, anesthesiologist, educator; b. Cape Girardeau, Mo., June 15, 1935; s. Herbert Steele and Charlotte (Maybury) H.; m. Judith Karen Miller, Sept. 24, 1962; children: Christine, Karen, Kimberly. AB, Cen. Coll., Fayette, Mo., 1957; MD, Washington U., St. Louis, 1961; MSc, McGill U., Quebec, Can., 1965. Diplomate Am. Bd. Anesthesiology. Vice chmn. dept. anesthesiology Northwestern U., Chgo., 1976-85; med. dir. operating rooms Northwestern Meml Hosp., Chgo., 1978-85; assoc. prof. anesthesiology Northwestern U., 1979—. Contbr. articles to profl. jours. Served with USNR, 1965-67. Mem. AMA, Am. Soc. Anesthesiology, Ill. Med. Soc., Ill. Anesthesiology Soc. Republican. Office: Northwestern Meml Hosp 710 Fairbanks Ct Chicago IL 60611

HOLLEY, LARRY JAMES, entrepreneur; b. Eaton Rapids, Mich., July 28, 1941; s. Chester James and Marion Alma (Peckham) H.; m. Judith Marie Gardner, July 7, 1962; children: David Wayne, Déborah Marie, Dawn Marie. Student, Marion (Ind.) Coll., 1960; cert. in real estate, Holloway Inst., 1986. Owner HoBo Fireworks, Eaton Rapids, 1976-86, Holley's Bear Den Inc., Eaton Rapids, 1978-86, Calico Kitchen Millers, Eaton Rapids, 1980-86. Mayor Eaton Rapids, 1981-85; Rep. precinct, state del., 1986; leader Downtown Devel. Authority, 1982. Recipient Outstanding Achievement award City of Eaton, 1985. Mem. Mich. Fast Food and Soft Swirl Assn., Mich. Sheriffs Assn., Mich. Jaycees (pres. 1977-79, 1st Place Award 1978). Methodist. Lodge: Kiwanis (2d v.p. 1986). Avocation: fireworks, pyrotechnics. Home: 1431 Water St Eaton Rapids MI 48827 Office: Holleys Bear Den Inc 829 S Main St Eaton Rapids MI 48827

HOLLEY, LAWRENCE ALVIN, retired labor union official; b. Elkhart, Ind., Nov. 7, 1924; s. Olin Coet and Carrie (Erwin) H.; m. Joyce Reed, Mar. 5, 1946; 1 child, Claudia Joyce. Student pub. schs., Elkhart. Bus. rep. Vancouver (Wash.) Aluminum Trades Council, 1951-57; pres. Wash. State Card and Label Council, 1952-57; internat. rep. Aluminum Workers Internat. Union, St. Louis, 1957-65, wage engr., 1965, research and ednl. dir., 1967-75; dir. Region 5 Aluminum Workers Internat. Union, Vancouver, Wash., 1975-77; pres. Aluminum Workers Internat. Union now Aluminum, Brick and Glass Workers Internat. Union, St. Louis, 1977-85; farmer La Center, Washington, 1985—; v.p. Union Label and Service Trades Dept., AFL-CIO, 1980-85, exec. bd. Maritime Trades Dept., 1981-85. Served with U.S. Army, 1943-46, PTO. Decorated Bronze Star with oak leaf cluster. Mem. Am. Legion. Democrat. Club: Voyageur 40/8. Lodge: Eagles. Office: Aluminum Brick & Glass Workers Internat Union 3362 Hollenberg Dr Bridgeton MO 63044

HOLLIS, HAROLD BINKLEY, insurance company executive; b. Princeton, Ind., July 18, 1906; s. John S. and Jessie B. (Binkley) H.; B.S., Purdue U., 1928; m. Martha Jane Gehlman, Oct. 15, 1937; children—Richard, John, Barbara Hollis McWalter, Kenneth L. and Nancy J. Hollis Huston (twins). Engr., Ill. Hwy. Dept., Paris, 1928, bridge engr., Springfield, 1931-42; civil engr. Mo. Pacific R.R., Nevada, Mo., 1929; purchasing agt. Remington Rand Co., Springfield, Ill., 1942-45; ptnr. Koke Mill Subdiv. Mgr. baseball team Little League, 1952-54, Pony League, Colt League, 1954-56. Clubs: Masons, Shriners, Springfield Purdue Alumni (pres. 1937-38, 41-42, 49-50, 83-84). Home: 1305 Wood Mill Dr Springfield IL 62707 Office: 405 S Grand Ave W Springfield IL 62704

HOLLIS-ALLBRITTON, CHERYL DAWN, retail paper supply store executive; b. Elgin, Ill., Feb. 15, 1959; d. L.T. and Florence (Elder) Saylors; m. Thomas Allbritton, Aug. 10, 1985. BS in Phys. Edn., Brigham Young U., 1981; cosmetologist Sch. Beauty Culture, Berwyn, Ill., 1981. Retail sales clk. Bee Discount, North Riverside, Ill., 1981-82, retail store mgr., Downers Grove, Ill., 1982, Oaklawn, Ill., 1982-83, St. Louis, 1983; retail tng. mgr. Arvey Paper & Supplies, Chgo., 1984, retail store mgr., Columbus, Ohio, 1985—. Mem. Nat. Assn. Female Execs. Republican. Mormon. Avocations: cosmetology, reading, travel. Office: Arvey Paper & Supplies 431 E Livingston Columbus OH 43215

HOLLOWAY, DONALD PHILLIP, librarian; b. Akron, Ohio, Feb. 18, 1928; s. Harold Shane and Dorothy Gayle (Ryder) H.; B.S. in Commerce, Ohio U., Athens, 1950; J.D., U. Akron, 1955; M.A., Kent State U., 1962. Title examiner Bankers Guarantee Title & Trust Co., Akron, 1950-54; acct. Robinson Clay Product Co., Akron, 1955-60; librarian Akron-Summit Pub. Library, 1962-69, head fine arts and music div., 1969-71, sr. librarian, 1972-82. Payroll treas. Akron Symphony Orch., 1957-61; treas. Friends Library Akron and Summit County, 1970-72. Mem. Music Library Assn., Am., Ohio, Akron bar assns., Ohio Library Assn., ALA, Nat. Trust for Hist. Preservation, Internat. Platform Assn., Soc. Archtl. Historians, Coll. Art Assn., Art Libraries North Am. Republican. Episcopalian. Club: Nat. Lawyers (Washington). Home: 601 Nome Ave Akron OH 44320

HOLLOWAY, JAMES BRIAN, accountant; b. Bowling Green, Ohio, Apr. 22, 1957; s. Frederich Henry and Joyce Lee (Schwecheimer) H. BS in Bus. Adminstrn., Bowling Green State U., 1979. CPA, Ill. Sr. mgr. Peat, Marwick, Mitchell & Co., Chgo., 1979-86; mgr. fin. reporting Victoria's Secret Mail Order, Columbus, Ohio, 1986—. Mem. Am. Inst. CPA's, Ill. CPA Soc. Methodist. Club: Sierra (Des Plaines Valley chpt.) (treas. 1981-82). Home: 2090 Brookhurst Ave Columbus OH 43229 Office: Victoria's Secret Mail Order 2 Limited Pkwy Columbus OH 43216

HOLLRAH, JOHN ROBERT, architect; b. St. Charles, Mo., Sept. 17, 1952; s. Vernon Henry and Hildegard Ann (Richterkessing) H.; m. Minnie Sarah Clyde, Aug. 14, 1982; children: John Dietrich, Michael Benjamin. BArch, Kans. State U., 1978. Registered architect, Kans. Job capt. Law, Kingdon P.A., Wichita, Kans., 1978-81; architect Wilson Darnell and Assocs., Wichita, 1981-83; project architect Gossen, Livingston and Assocs., Wichita, 1983-85, Black and Veatch, Kansas City, Mo., 1985—. Served as sgt. USMC, 1970-73. Mem. AIA, Kans. Soc. Architects, Nat. Audubon Soc., Sierra Club. Lutheran. Avocations: hiking, rowing, golf. Office: Black and Veatch Engrs Architects 1500 Meadowlake Pkwy Kansas City MO 64114

HOLLY, JOHN, producing director, stage manager, actor; b. St. Louis, May 6, 1944; s. Jack Edwin and Harriet (Shellenberger) Williamson; children—Holly, Robin, Jacki. B.A. in Drama, Ariz. State U., 1966. Actor, stage mgr., dir., various theatre and TV prodns., 1963-72; prodn. stage mgr. Theatre Now, Inc., N.Y.C., 1972-74; gen. mgr. Music Theatre of Wichita, Kans., 1974-79, producing dir., 1979—; artistic dir. Wichita Children's Theatre, 1977-84; v.p., dir. Marketing Concepts, Inc., N.Y.C.; prodn. mgr. Wichita Symphony Soc.; guest prof., dir. Wichita State U., 1975-82; TV prodn. specialist U.S. Army, 1969-71. Vice pres. Conv. and Visitors Bur. Wichita, 1983-84; profl. chmn. Assn. Kans. Theatre, 1976-79; dir. Wichita Arts Council, 1979-84. Named to Outstanding Young Men Am. Nat. Jaycees, 1977; recipient Am. Spirit Honor medal Arms Service, 1970. Mem. Actors Equity Assn., Internat. Alliance Theatrical Stage Employees, Nat. Alliance Musical Theatre Producers (v.p.), Bobkats Internat. (pres. 1976—), Theatre Communications Group (assoc.), Wichita C. of C. Republican. Office: Music Theatre of Wichita 225 W Douglas St Wichita KS 67202

HOLM, RICHARD EUGENE, quality and industrial engineer; b. Portland, Oreg., Mar. 29, 1946; s. Harold Joseph and Gladys Alberta (Kempf) H.; m. Patricia Alice Welch, Oct. 4, 1969; children: Jennifer Lynn, Tricia Leigh. BA, Washington State U., 1968; MBA, Ind. U., 1975. Cert. quality engr., reliability engr.; registered profl. engr. Materials handling engr. Ford Motor Co., Dearborn, Mich., 1968-74; reliability engr. Am. Motors Co., Detroit, 1974-77; supr. quality engring. John Deere & Co., Waterloo, Iowa, 1977—; quality and mfg. cons. Arthur Young, Detroit, 1987—; cons. Iowa Devel. Com., Des Moines, 1984, Iowa State U., Amie, 1986; instr. quality engring. courses; lectr. various profl. groups. Leader bldg. fund program YMCA, Waterloo, 1981, leader fund dr. Columbus High Sch., Waterloo, 1985, 86; pres. St. Edwards Booster Club, 1987. Served with U.S. Army, 1968. Mem. Am. Soc. Quality Control (pres. 1982, 83, bd. dirs. 1984—). Republican. Lodges: Masons (sr. warden Detroit 1977), Elks. Avocations: racquetball, golf, fishing, softball. Home: 1333 Olympic Dr Waterloo IA 50701 Office: John Deere Tractor Works PO Box 3500 Dept 422 Waterloo IA 50704

HOLM, ROGER HERBERT, purchasing executive; b. New London, Minn., Aug. 6, 1930; s. Herbert A. and Ruth O. (Olson) H.; m. Eleanor E. Stuneck, Aug. 12, 1961; children—Michael Stephanie, Mary. Student pub. schs., New London. With Assoc. Loan Co., Mpls., 1960-63; asst. mgr. Northtown Fin. Co., Mpls., 1963-66; bus. mgr. Unity Med. Ctr., Fridley, Minn., 1966-73, dir. materials mgmt., 1973—. Mem. Healthcare Materials Mgmt. Soc., Upper Midwest Hosp. Purchasing Assn. (pres. 1983), Twin City Purchasing Mgmt. Assn., Minn. Assn. for Hosp. Safety and Security, Hosp. Fin. Mgmt. Assn. (pres. 1972-73). Roman Catholic. Home: 502 5 1/2 St Elk River MN 55330 Office: Unity Med Ctr 550 Osborne Rd Fridley MN 55432

HOLMAN, JAMES LEWIS, financial and management consultant; b. Chgo., Oct. 27, 1926; s. James Louis and Lillian Marie (Walton) H.; m. Elizabeth Ann Owens, June 18, 1948 (div. 1982); children: Craig Stewart, Tracy Lynn, Mark Andrew; m. Geraldine Ann Wilson, Dec. 26, 1982. BS in Econs. and Mgmt., U. Ill., Urbana, 1950, postgrad., 1950; postgrad. Northwestern U., 1954-55. Traveling auditor, then statistician, asst. controller parent buying dept. Sears, Roebuck & Co., Chgo., 1951-54; asst. to sec.-treas. Hanover Securities Co., Chgo., 1954-65; asst. to controller chem. ops. div. Montgomery Ward & Co. Inc., Chgo., 1966-68; controller Henrotin Hosp., Chgo., 1968; bus. mgr. Julian, Dye, Javid, Hunter & Najafi, Associated, Chgo., 1969-81, cons. 1981-84; vol. cons., adminstrv. asst. Fiji Sch. Medicine, Suva, U.S. Peace Corps, 1984-86, cons., 1987—; cons., dir., sec.-treas. Comprehensive Resources Ltd., Glenview (Ill.), Wheaton (Ill.) and Walnut Creek, Calif., 1982; bd. dirs., sec.-treas. Medtran, Inc., 1980-83; sec. James C. Valenta, P.C., 1979-82; sponsored project adminstr. Northwestern U., Evanston, Ill., 1984—. Sec., B.R. Ryall YMCA, Glen Ellyn, Ill., 1974-76, bd. dirs., 1968-78; trustee Gary Meml. United Meth. Ch., Wheaton, 1961-69, 74-77; bd. dirs. Goodwill Industries Chgo., 1978-79, DuPage (Ill.) Symphony, 1954-58, treas., 1955-58. Served with USN, 1944-46. Baha'i. Lodge: Kiwanis (bd. dirs. Chgo. 1956-60, bd. dirs. youth found. 1957-60, pres. 1958-60). Office: 3 Wheaton Ctr Suite 302 Wheaton IL 60187

HOLMAN, JOHN FREDRICK, manufacturing executive, mechanical engineer; b. Stevens Point, Wis., Nov. 19, 1945; s. John S. and Winifred I. (Plank) H.; m. Cheryl E. Gyrion, Feb. 5, 1966; children: Lisa Catherine, Megan Leigh. BSME, U. Wis., 1970. Engr. IPM Corp., Columbus, Ohio, 1970-77; engring. mgr. Pure Carbon Co., Coudersport, Pa., 1977-81; plant mgr. Advance Products Corp., Beaver Dam, Wis., 1981-84; pres. Dymet Corp., Muskegon, Mich., 1984—; Patentee chem. process for impregnation of powder metallurgy parts, 1973. Mem. Coudersport Borough Council, 1980; bd. dirs. Cogeneration Plant Bd., Coudersport, 1980. Mem. Am. Powder Metallurgy Inst. Republican. Lodge: Rotary (Beaver Dam internat. student exchange com. 1983) , Masons. Avocations: old cars, woodworking, skiing. Home: 1188 Yorkshire Dr Muskegon MI 49441 Office: Dymet Corp 1901 Peck St Muskegon MI 49443

HOLMAN, W. H., JR., food products company executive. Chmn. Topco Assocs., Inc., Skokie, Ill. Address: Topco Assns Inc 7711 Grosse Pointe Rd Skokie IL 60076 *

HOLMAN, WILLIAM BAKER, surgeon, coroner; b. Norwalk, Ohio, Mar. 22, 1925; s. Merlin Earl and Rowena (Baker) H.; m. Jane Elizabeth Henderson, June 24, 1951; children—Craig W., Mark E., John S. B.S., Capital U., 1946; M.D., Jefferson Med. Coll., 1950. Intern, St. Luke's Hosp., Cleve., 1950-51, resident in gen. surgery, 1951-52, 55-57; practice medicine specializing in surgery, Norwalk, 1957—; coroner Huron County, Norwalk, 1962—, health commr., 1985—; asst. clin. prof. surgery Med. Coll. Ohio at Toledo, 1984—; Bd. dirs. REMSNO, Toledo, 1974—, Norwalk Profl. Colony, 1983—; mem. exec. com. Huron County Republican Com., Norwalk, 1980. Served to 1st lt. U.S. Army, 1952-54; Korea. Fellow ACS; mem. AMA, Ohio State Med. Assn., Huron County Med. Soc. (pres. 1978), Ohio State Coroners Assn., Nat. Assn. Med. Examiners. Lutheran. Avocations: boating; photography; stamp collecting; gun collecting. Home: 39 Warren Dr Norwalk OH 44857 Office: 257 Benedict Ave Norwalk OH 44857

HOLMAY, PATRICK JAMES, computer consultant; b. Saipan, Mariana Islands, June 11, 1957; s. Richard Edward and Mary Margaret (Schultz) H.; m. Mary Jane Roske, Aug. 25, 1979; children: Daniel, Nicholas. BS, St. John's U., Collegeville, minn., 1980. Computer programmer/analyst St. John's U., Collegeville, 1980-81, instr. computer sci., 1981-83, mgr. academic computer ctr., 1981-87; cons. Analysts Internat. Corp., Mpls., 1987—; cons. in field, St. Cloud, Minn., 1985—. Contbg. author: Business Consulting, 1985; contbr. articles to profl. jours. Computer instr. Land of Lakes Girl Scout Council, St. Cloud, 1983-87. Mem. Assn. Computing Machinery, Data Processing Mgmt. Assn., Soc. Data Educators. Office: Analysts Internat Corp 7615 Metro Blvd Minneapolis MN 55435

HOLMBERG, JOYCE, state legislator; b. Rockford, Ill., July 19, 1930; m. Eugene Holmberg; 2 daus. B.A., No. Ill. U.; M.A., Alfred Adler Inst., Chgo. Mem. Ill. State Senate from 34th Dist., 1983—. Democrat. Office: Ill State Capitol Bldg Springfield IL 62706

HOLMES, CARL DEAN, farmer, state legislator; b. Dodge City, Kans., Oct. 19, 1940; s. Haskell Amos and Gertrude May (Swander) H.; m. Willynda Coley, Nov. 29, 1986. Student, Kans. U., 1958-60; BBA, Colo. State U., Ft. Collins, 1962. Mgr. Holmes Motor Co., Plains, Kans., 1962-65; v.p. Holmes Chevrolet, Inc., Meade, Kans., 1962-78; owner Holmes Sales Co., Plains, 1965-80; land mgr. Holmes Farm, Plains, 1962—. Chmn. Greater Southwest Regional Planning Commn., Garden City, Kans., 1980-82; del. Rep. Dist. Conv., Great Bend, Kans., 1984, Rep. State Conv., Topeka, 1984; mayor City of Plains, 1982—; mem. 125 dist. Kans. Ho. Reps., Topeka, Kans., 1985—; precinct committeeman, Meade County Reps., 1986—, pres. Kans. Mayors Assn., 1984-85; v.p. League Kans. Municipalities, 1986-87. Mem. Liberal C. of C. Methodist. Lodge: Masons. Avocations: flying, photography. Home and Office: Box 578 Plains KS 67869

HOLMES, EDWARD THORROLD, computer information systems specialist; b. Herrin, Ill., June 6, 1940; s. Edward C. and Alice L. (Manning) H.; m. Ruby J. Yates, Nov. 16, 1962; children: Stephanie Ann, Edward M. BA, So. Ill. U., Carbondale, 1962. Systems analyst Alcoa, Newburgh, Ind., 1965-68; systems analyst Whirlpool Corp., Evansville, Ind., 1968-75, sr. systems analyst, 1975-81, systems supr., 1981—. Served with USAF, 1962-65, lt. col. Ind. Air NG, 1965-71. Mem. NG Assn., Ind. NG Assn., Whirlpool Mgmt. Club. Office: Whirlpool Corp Hwy 41 Evansville IN 47727

HOLMES, HOWARD SUMNER, executive; b. Chelsea, Mich., July 24, 1913; s. Howard Samuel and Mabel Irene (White) H.; m. Mary Ernestine Blodgett, June 12, 1943; children: Howard, Christine, Kathryn, William, Andrea. Student Princeton U., 1932; B.S. in Mech. Engring., U. Mich., 1937; D.Sci. in Bus. Adminstrn. (hon.), Cleary Coll., 1983. Pres., dir. Chelsea Milling Co. (Mich.), from 1946; v.p., dir. C&C Carton Co., Marshall, Mich., from 1972; dir. Domino's Pizza Co., Ann Arbor, Mich., Mennel Milling Co., Fostoria, Ohio; dir., exec. com. Millers Nat. Ins. Co., Chgo.; exec. bd., treas. Wheat Industry Council, Washington, 1980—. Mem. div. bd. Catherine McAuley Health Ctr., Ann Arbor; chmn. devel. council St. Joseph Mercy Hosp.; bd. dirs. devel. council U. Mich.; trustee Portage council Boy Scouts Am. Mem. Millers Nat. Fedn. (exec. com., former bd. chmn.), Mich. Millers Assn. (pres.), Tau Beta Pi, Alpha Delta Phi. Republican. Congregationalist. Clubs: Princeton (N.Y.), Athletic (Detroit), Univ. (Chgo.), Barton Hills Country (Ann Arbor), Masons. Home: 175 Underdown Rd Ann Arbor MI 48105

HOLMES, JOHN ROBERT, communications teacher; b. Milw., Feb. 20, 1952; s. Robert J. and Hildegarde M. (Huber) H.; m. Patricia Mary (Annesley), May 22, 1976. BA, U. Wis., Milw., 1977; MA, Marquette U., 1984. Cert. tchr., Wis. Tchr. communications media Milw. Pub. Schs., 1978—, Marquette U. div. continuing edn., Milw., 1986—. Mem. Wis. Communication Assn., SPEECH Communication Assn., Internat. TV Assn., Am. Fedn. Musicians, Sherlock Holmes Soc. of London, Phi Delta Kappa. Avocation: travel. Home: 9405 W Hadley St Milwaukee WI 53222 Office: Milw Pub Schs PO Drawer 10K Milwaukee WI 53201-8210

HOLMES, MARY PATRICIA, academic administrator; b. Cleve., Jan. 20, 1952; d. Frank Joseph and Margaret Mary (Lavelle) Geib; m. Thomas William Holmes, Aug. 23, 1974; children: Erin, Ryan, Matthew. BS, U. Dayton, 1974, MS, 1975. Asst. dir. recreational sports U. Dayton, Ohio, 1974-78; physical edn. instr., dir. intramural sports North Harris Coll., Houston, Tex., 1978-79; assoc. dir. recreational sports Miami U., Oxford, Ohio, 1979—; cons. Square D Corp., Avon Products, Oxford, 1984-86; workshop clinician Pres. Council on Physical Fitness and Sports, 1982—. Editor (Book) Process and Concepts in Recreational Sports, 1983; contbr. 25 articles to recreation jours. Served with U.S. Army, 1979—. Named one of Outstanding Women of Am., 1980. Mem. Nat. Intramural Recreational Sports Assn. (v.p. 1980-82, Leadership award 1982, jour. editorial bd. 1977-81), Ohio Recreational Sports Assn. (state dir. 1974-78), Omicron Delta Kappa. Roman catholic. Avocations: tennis, squash, antique hunting, reading. Home: 210 Ridge Ave Oxford OH 45056 Office: Miami U Withrow Ct Oxford OH 45056

HOLMES, MICHAEL PATRIC, investment company executive; b. San Diego, Oct. 28, 1952; s. Melvin Lawrence and Virginia Edith (Loethen) H.; m. Elizabeth Ellen Maddox, Sept. 8, 1979; 1 child, Daniel Padric. BS in Phys. Edn. and Eng. Lit., William Jewell Coll., 1975; diploma in Iraqi Arabic, Def. Lang. Inst., 1971. Investment exec. Stifel Nicolaus Inc., Leawood, Kans., 1976-81; investment officer Dain Bosworth Inc., Overland Park, Kans., 1981-83; v.p., resident mgr. WZW Fin. Services, Westwood, Kans., 1983-85; exec. v.p., co-founder VSR Fin. Services, Leawood, 1985—, also bd. dirs.; lectr. various orgns.; bd. dirs. ShowMe Enterprises, Kansas City, Mo., Heartland Mgmt., Leawood, ptnr. 1986—. Contbr. articles to $100,000 Portfolio newsletter. Vol. Angel's Haven, Md., 1972-74; bd. dirs. Rose Brooks Home for Battered Women, Kansas City, 1984, Kansas City Wheelchair Athletics, 1984—, Spaniacs, Kansas City, 1985—. Served with USAF, 1971-74. Mem. Internat. Assn. Fin. Planners, Planners Am. (various awards), VFW. Republican. Roman Catholic. Office: VSR Fin Services Inc 8012 State Line Rd #104 Leawood KS 66208

HOLMES, RICHARD WINN, state supreme ct. justice; b. Wichita, Kans., Feb. 23, 1923; s. Winn Earl and Sidney (Clapp) H.; m. Gwen Sand, Aug. 19, 1950; children—Robert W., David K. B.S., Kans. State U., 1950; J.D., Washburn U., 1953. Bar: Kans. bar 1953, U.S. Dist. Ct. bar 1953. Practice law Wichita, Kans., 1953-77; judge Wichita Mcpl. Ct., 1959-61; instr. bus. law Wichita State U., 1959-60; justice Kans. Supreme Ct., 1977—. Served with USNR, 1943-46. Mem. Kans., Topeka, Wichita bar assns., Am. Judges Assn. (founder, bd. govs. 1980—). Home: 2535 Granthurst Ave Topeka KS 66611 Office: Kansas Judicial Center Topeka KS 66612

HOLMES, ROBERT ALLEN, lawyer, educator, consultant, lecturer; b. Sewickley, Pa., Dec. 12, 1947; s. Lee Roy John and Nellie Ann (Kupits) H.; m. Linda Lee Freeman Aug. 16, 1969; children—Wesley Paige, Ashley Reagan. B.A. in Bus. Adminstrn., Coll. William and Mary, 1969, J.D., 1972. Bar: Md. 1972, U.S. Dist. Ct. Md. 1972, Va. 1973, U.S. Dist. Ct. (ea. dist.) Va. 1973. Assoc. Ober, Grimes & Shriver, Balt., 1972-73, Kellam, Pickrell & Lawler, Norfolk, Va., 1973-75; ptnr. Holliday, Holmes & Inman, Norfolk, 1975-77; asst. prof. law Bowling Green State U., Ohio, 1977-82, assoc. prof., 1982—; dir. Purchasing Law Inst., 1979—, EEO-Affirmative Action Research Group, 1978—; lectr. profl. seminars and workshops throughout country on discrimination and affirmative action law. Author: (books) (with others) Computers, Data Processing and the Law, 1984; numerous manuals on discrimination and affirmative action law. Contbg. editor, monthly columnist Midwest Purchasing, 1983-84. Recipient Outstanding Young Man award William and Mary Soc. Alumni, 1973. Mem. Md. Bar Assn., Va. Bar Assn., Am. Bus. Law Assn., Am. Soc. Personnel Adminstrs., Nat. Assn. Purchasing Mgmt., Mensa. Republican. Home: 1034 Conneaut Ave Bowling Green OH 43402 Office: Bowling Green State U Legal Studies Dept Bowling Green OH 43403

HOLMES, ROBERT EDWARD, justice Ohio Supreme Ct.; b. Columbus, Ohio, Nov. 14, 1922; s. Harry Barclay and Nora Jane (Birney) H.; m. Jean Wren; children—Robert Edward, Hamilton Barclay. A.B., Ohio U., 1943, LL.B., 1949. Bar: Ohio bar. Practiced law 1949-69; mem. Ohio Ho. of Reps., 1960-69; judge 10th Dist. Ct. Appeals, Columbus, 1969-78; justice Ohio Supreme Ct., Columbus, 1979—. Pres. Columbus Area Internat. Program, Council Internat. Programs; founder Columbus Community Camp; bd. dirs. Boy Scouts Am., Salvation Army, Pilot Dogs, Inc. Served with USN, 1944-46. Mem. Columbus Bar Assn., Ohio Bar Assn., Am. Bar Assn. Republican. Office: Supreme Ct Ohio 30 E Broad St Columbus OH 43215 *

HOLMES, SUE BAIRD, clinical nurse specialist; b. Dixon, Ill., June 9, 1955; d. Dale Edman and Mary Louise (Dysart) Baird; m. Dennis Franklin Holmes, Apr. 27, 1985. BS in Nursing, No. Ill. U., 1977; MS in Nursing, U. Ill., 1983. Asst. head nurse Community Gen. Hosp., Sterling, Ill., 1979-82; clin. nurse specialist St. Joseph's Hosp., Milw., 1984—; pres. Wis. Orthopedic Nurses, Inc., 1985—; mem. faculty Marquette U., Milw., 1985—. Contbr. articles to profl. jours. Mem. Am. Nurses Assn., Wis. Nurses Assn. (sec. clin. nurse specialists council 1985—), Milw. Dist. Nurses Assn. (membership chmn. 1984—), Nat. Assn. Orthopedic Nurses, Nursing Diagnosis Assn., Sigma Theta Tau. Avocation: horseback riding. Home: 7681-

A N 99th St Milwaukee WI 53224 Office: St Joseph Hosp 5000 W Chambers Milwaukee WI 53210

HOLMES, WILLIAM RICHARDSON, vocational counselor; b. Payne, Ohio, Apr. 13, 1933; s. Phillip Richardson and Alta Marie (Enz) H.; divorced; children: Richard Paul, Laura Kathleen. BS, Bowling Green State U., 1959. Lic. real estate broker, N.Mex. Social worker Crawford County Welfare Dept., Bucyrus, Ohio, 1963-65; adminstr. Defiance (Ohio) County Welfare Dept., 1965-68; social worker Allen County Welfare Dept., Ft. Wayne, Ind., 1968-76; assoc. broker Reliable Realtors, Roswell, N.Mex., 1976-78; asst. dir. Social Security div. Pub. Employees Retirement Bd. State of N.Mex., Santa Fe, 1978-79; job placement dir. Goodwill Industries, Lima, Ohio, 1979; sr. counselor III Bur. Vocat. Rehab., Marion, Ohio, 1980—. Mem. Gov.'s Com. on Hiring the Handicapped, 1981-82 mem. State Council of Counselors, 1982—. Mem. Profl. Social Workers. Methodist. Lodge: Moose. Avocations: photography, travelling. Home: 963 Chateau Dr Marion OH 43302 Office: Bur Vocat Rehab 749 E Center St Marion OH 43302

HOLOHAN, O. J., industrial and interior designer; b. Detroit, Sept. 18, 1936; s. James Frances and Ernestine Flora (Neumann) H.; degree in Indsl. Designs and Interiors, Cleve. Inst. Art, 1961; m. Laurinda Anne Loewe, Oct. 25, 1969; children—Eric James, Shauna Lynn, Brian James. Illustrator to Pres. D. Eisenhower, 1957-58; art dir. TV sta., Washington, 1958-59; dir. design O.J.K. Designers div. F.W. Roberts, Cleve., 1962-67; pres. O.J. Holohan Assocs., Inc., Burton, Ohio, 1967—, Inarco, Twinsburg, Ohio, 1984—; judge design juries. Served with U.S. Army, 1957-59. Recipient Merit award Nat. Stationary and Office Equipment Assn., 1962; Design award 2d place Nat. Office Furniture Assn., 1963; Design award, 1965; 1st and 2nd place awards Office Interior Design Mag., 1965; hon. mention award S.M. Hexter Co., 1975. Mem. Inst. Bus. Designers (founding, award for lounge group 1982-83), Zool. Assn. Am., Nat. Office Furniture Assn. Home: 2 Serenity Pk 12175 Snow Rd Burton OH 44021 Office: 1 Serenity Pk 12175 Snow Rd Burton OH 44021

HOLOYDA, BASIL B., physician; b. Chgo., Nov. 12, 1953; s. Walter and Margaret (Nigiwski) H.; m. Patricia Ann Doyle, Oct. 20, 1979; children: Christopher Michael, Kathleen Ann, Brian James. B in Med. Sci., Northwestern U., 1973, MD, 1977. Diplomate Am. Bd. Psychiatry and Neurology; cert. EEG. Intern Northwestern U., Chgo., 1977-78, resident in neurology, 1978-81; fellow clin. neurology Mayo Clinic, Rochester, Minn., 1981-82; dir. clin. neurophysiology lab. St. Mary's Hosp., Madison, Wis., 1982—, Dean Med. Ctr., Madison, Wis., 1982—; mem. psychiatry patient review commn. St. Mary's Hosp., 1983—, clin. neurophysiology commn., 1984—. Fellow Am. EEG Soc.; mem. Am. Acad. Neurology, Cen. Assn. EEG, Wis. Neurol. Soc., AMA, Alpha Omega. Roman Catholic. Avocations: music, literature, travel. Home: 5 Canvasback Circle Madison WI 53717 Office: Dean Med Ctr 1313 Fish Hatchery Madison WI 53715

HOLSCHER, DAVID COLLINS, corporate communications executive; b. Ashtabula, Ohio, Nov. 27, 1950; s. John Noble and Vera Francis (Collins) H.; m. Vicky Lynn Campbell, June 30, 1974; children: TOdd David, Mary Katherine. BA in English, Yale U., 1974. Pubs. specialist office of personnel services Ohio State U., Columbus, 1974-76, promotion mgr. telecommunications ctr., 1976-80; mktg. communications mgr. Informatics Gen. Corp., Columbus, 1980-82; communications coordinator Liebert Corp., Columbus, 1982-86; mktg. and fin. communications mgr. Accuray Corp., Columbus, 1986—. Contbr. articles to profl. jours. Trustee Actions for Children Council, Columbus, 1976-79. Mem. Pu. Relations Soc. Am., Cen. Ohio Indsl. Marketers Assn. (pres. 1983). Democrat. Episcopalian. Avocations: photography, soccer, golf, hiking, camping. Home: 301 Park Blvd Worthington OH 43085 Office: Accuray Corp 650 Ackerman Rd Columbus OH 43202

HOLSCHER, RICHARD HARRY, bank executive; b. Columbus, Ohio, Dec. 18, 1928; s. Harry Heltman and Helen (Harding) H.; m. Donna Elizabeth Lyons, Feb. 3, 1951; children: Deborah Holscher Borkin, David. BS in Commerce and Law, U. Ill., 1951, JD, 1955. Bar: Ill. 1955. With First Wis. Nat. Bank of Milw., 1964—, exec. v.p., sr. v.p. comml. group, 1987—; exec. v.p. First Wis. Mortgage Co., Milw., 1973—. Trustee, treas. Family Hosp., Milw., 1984-85; pres., bd. dirs. Milw. County Hist. Soc., 1965-83, Wis. Humane Soc., 1975-83; bd. dirs. Milw. Repertory Theater. Served with USN, 1946-48; served to 1st lt. U.S. Army, 1951-53. Mem. Wis. Mortgage Bankers Assn., Robert Morris Assocs. Club: Ozaukee Country. Avocations: sailing, hiking. Home: 2220 W Applewood Ln Glendale WI 53209 Office: First Wis Nat Bank Milw 777 E Wisconsin Ave Milwaukee WI 53202

HOLSCHUH, JOHN DAVID, judge; b. Ironton, Ohio, Oct. 12, 1926; s. Edward A. and Helen (Ebert) H.; m. Carol Stouder, Aug. 13, 1927; 1 son, John David. B.A., Miami U., 1948; J.D., U. Cin., 1951. Bar: Ohio bar 1951. Law clk. U.S. Dist. Ct. judge, 1952-54; mem. firm Alexander, Ebinger, Holschuh, Fisher & McAlister, Columbus, Ohio, 1954-80; judge U.S. Dist. Ct. for so. dist. Ohio, 1980—; mem. com. on codes of conduct Jud. Conf. U.S., 1985—; adj. prof. law Coll. Law, Ohio State U., 1970. Pres. bd. dirs. Neighborhood House, 1969-70. Fellow Am. Coll. Trial Lawyers; mem. Order of Coif, Phi Beta Kappa, Omicron Delta Kappa. Home: 2630 Charing Rd Columbus OH 43221 Office: 85 Marconi Blvd Columbus OH 43215

HOLSHOUSER, THOMAS CHARLES, architect; b. Cape Girardeau, Mo., May 1, 1939; s. Charles Mason and Velma Drewseal (Allen) H.; m. Judith Sue Gleason, July 15, 1966; 1 child, Kimberly Kay. Diploma in architecture, Ranken Trade Sch., 1961. Registered architect, Mo., Ill. Draftsman Boardman, Cape Girardeau, Mo., 1961-67, Phillips Assocs., Cape Girardeau, 1967-71; prin. Holshouser & Assoc., Cape Girardeau, 1971—. Mem. AIA, Mo. Assn. Bldg. Officials and Inspectors, Architects of So. Mo., Mo. Council Architects, St. Louis chpt. AIA, Cape Girardeau C. of C. Lodges: Rotary, Elks, Masons. Avocations: power boating, woodworking. Home: 2401 Erna St Cape Girardeau MO 63701 Office: Holshouser & Assocs 219 N Clark Ave Cape Girardeau MO 63701

HOLST, MARTIN THORVALD, small business owner; b. Cedar Falls, Iowa, Oct. 21, 1922; s. Thorvald Bodholdt and Mary (Rasmussen) H.; m. Evelyn Ruby Prostine, June 16, 1957; children: Martin Paul, John Christian, Paul David, David Thor. BA, Iowa State Tchrs. Coll., 1944; MBA, Stanford U., 1947. Salesman Holst Bus. Products, Cedar Falls, Iowa, 1947-62, ptnr., 1962-67, owner, 1967—. sec., treas., pres. Cedar Falls Band Inc., Cedar Falls, 1938-85; pres. bd. dirs. Cedar Falls Pub. Library, 1948-85. Republican. Lutheran. Lodge: Lions (bd. dirs. Cedar Falls 1962-65). Avocations: tennis, photography, collecting and restoring sports cars, camping. Home: 2620 Ashland Ave Cedar Falls IA 50613 Office: Holst Bus Products 211 Washington Cedar Falls IA 50613

HOLSTON, JAMES LLOYD, manufacturing company executive; b. Jackson, Miss., Apr. 27, 1951; s. James William and Bennie Lou (Hunnicutt) H.; m. Janet Karen Satterthwaite, Apr. 3, 1982; children: Rachel Elise, Sarah Elizabeth. BA, U. Okla., Norman, 1978; MBA, Ind. U., South Bend, 1985. Cert. data processor; cert. systems profl. Programmer St. Anthony Hosp., Oklahoma City, 1971-78; programmer, analyst First Nat. Bank, Oklahoma City, 1979-80, Clark Equipment Co., Buchanan, Mich., 1980-81; info. resource mgmt. cons. Price Waterhouse, South Bend, 1981-87; project mgr. Bendix Energy Controls div. Allied Signal, Inc., South Bend, 1987—. Mem. Assn. for Systems Mgmt. (sec. 1983-84, bd. dirs. 1984-85), Ind. U. Alumni Assn. (mem. adv. com. 1985—). Methodist. Avocations: microcomputers, photography, gardening, vocal music. Home: 1428 Sunnymede Ave South Bend IN 46615 Office: Bendix Energy Controls 717 N Bendix Dr South Bend IN 46620

HOLT, GILBERT ANTHONY, allergist/immunologist, educator; b. Bridgeport, Conn., July 20, 1942; s. Gilbert Anthony and Catherine (Henry) H.; m. Aurea Lugod, Nov. 9, 1964; children: Catherine Mary, Deborah Aimee, James Anthony. BA, Fairfield U., 1964; MD, M of Surgery, McGill U., Montreal, Can., 1969. Diplomate Am. Bd. Internal Medicine, Am. Bd. Allergy and Immunology. Commd. 2d lt. USAF, 1971, advanced through grades to lt. col., serving as med. officer, 1971—; intern E.J. Meyer Meml., Buffalo Gen. Hosps., Buffalo, 1969-71; resident allergist Walter Reed Army Med. Ctr., Washington, 1975-76; fellow allergy Georgetown U., Washington, 1976-78; assoc. clin. prof. medicine Wright State U., Fairborn, Ohio, 1979—; resigned USAF, 1984; practice medicine specializing in allergy and immunology Dayton and Springfield, Ohio, 1984—. Mem. ACP, Ohio Soc. Allergy and Immunology. Republican. Roman Catholic. Home: 3773 S Greenbrier Dr Fairborn OH 45324-9722 Office: 2624 Lexington Ave Springfield OH 45505

HOLT, GLEN EDWARD, library adminstrator; b. Abilene, Kans., Sept. 14, 1939; s. John Wesley and Helen Laverne (Schrader) H.; m. Janice Elaine Ming, May 30, 1958; children: Kris, Karen, Gordon. BA, Baker U., 1960; MA, U. Chgo., 1965, PhD, 1975. From instr to asst. prof. Wash. U., St. Louis, 1968-82; dir. honors div. Coll. Liberal Arts, U. Minn., 1982-87; exec. dir. St. Louis Pub. Library, 1987—; cons. NEH, Washington, 1980-82, Chgo. Hist. Soc., 1976-79, Mo. Hist. Soc., St. Louis, 1979—; cons. City of Chgo., 1983. Co-editor: St. Louis, 1975; co-author: Chicago, A Guide to the Neighborhoods, 1979; author: St. Louis Historical Moments, 1986. State adv., bd. dirs. Minn. Gifted and Talented Adv. Bd., 1986-87; bd. dirs. Nat. Mus. Transport., St. Louis, 1980-85, U. Minn. Campus YMCA, Mpls., 1985-87. Woodrow Wilson Found. fellow, 1963-64, Danforth Fellow, 1963-68; NEH grantee 1976-78. Mem. Orgn. Am. History, Am. Assn. State and Local History, Am. Assn. Mus., Am. Library Assn. Club: Press, Media (St. Louis). Avocations: photography, collecting paperweights and books. Home: 4954 Lindell Blvd Apt 4-W Saint Louis MO 63108 Office: St Louis Pub Library 1301 Olive St Saint Louis MO 63103

HOLT, JANA DEANNE, elementary school teacher; b. Joplin, Mo., July 31, 1957; d. Homer V. and Donna Gwendolyn (Patton) Wallace; m. Matthew Kemp Holt, May 24, 1980; 1 child, Melanie Janelle. BS in Edn., Southwest Bapt. U., 1979. Tchr. Avilla (Mo.) Elem. Sch., 1979; tchr. Webb City (Mo.) Dist. R-7, 1979-84, ESL program tutor, 1985—; pvt. tutor, Carterville, Mo., 1985—. Sponsor United Meth. Youth Fellowship, 1984—; mem. United Meth. Women (pres. 1984). Mem. Webb City Community Tchrs. Assn. (exec. com. 1983-84). Democrat. Methodist. Avocation: writing children's lit. Home: 1909 Aylor Webb City MO 64870 Office: Webb City Sch Dist R 7 411 N Madison Webb City MO 64870

HOLT, KEITH FONNER, architect; b. Flint, Mich., Aug. 30, 1951; s. Ross Eugene and Wanda Bessie (Pocza) H.; m. Sandra Sue Florida, June 15, 1985. Student, Mott Community Coll., 1969-71; BArch, Ariz. State U., 1975. Registered architect, Mich. Designer Gene Terrill Assoc., Flint, 1971, Ellis, Arndt & Truesdel, Flint, 1972, Sedgewick-Sellers, Inc., Flint, 1973-74, Conde, Inc., El Paso, Tex., 1976-77; project architect SSOE, Inc., Flint, 1977—. Mem. AIA (treas. Flint chpt. 1983-84, v.p. Flint chpt. 1985, pres. Flint chpt. 1986), Mich. Soc. Architects, Nat. Council Archtl. Registration (cert. 1982). Avocations: reading, painting, drawing. Home: 1910 Montclair Flint MI 48503 Office: SSOE Inc 200 Mott Found Bldg Flint MI 48502

HOLT, NOEL CLARK, minister; b. Cape Girardeau, Mo., Dec. 8, 1935; s. Archie N. and Dorothy G. (Shaw) H.; m. Rosalee Powell, Feb. 27, 1955; children: Sidney Clark, Jennifer Lee, Julie Powell. BA, Cen. Coll., Fayette, Mo., 1959; MDiv, Garrett Theol. Sem., 1963; DMin, Princeton Sem., 1983. Founding minister Kingswood Ch., Buffalo Grove, Ill., 1963-71; sr. minister Faith Ch., Dolton, Ill., 1971-77, First Ch., Park Ridge, Ill., 1977-80, Trinity Ch., Wilmette, Ill., 1980-85, Baker Meml. Ch., St. Charles, Ill., 1985—; dir. recruitment Bd. Ordained Ministry, Chgo., 1985—. Mem. ACLU. Club: Union League. Avocations: sailing, travel, photography. Home: 307 Iroquois Ave Saint Charles IL 60174 Office: Baker Meml United Meth Ch 307 Cedar Ave Saint Charles IL 60174

HOLTAM, LORRAINE SANDRA, pharmacist, clinical researcher; b. Edinburgh, Scotland, June 22, 1958; d. Roland Howard Weir and Sheena Elizabeth (Charters) Watkins; m. John Benjamin Holtam Jr., Oct. 4, 1980. BS in Pharmacy, Drake U., 1979. Registered pharmacist, Iowa, Ill. Research pharmacist Abbott Labs., North Chgo., 1979-83, clin. research assoc., 1983-87; sr. clin. research assoc. Abbott Labs., Abbott Park, Ill., 1987; regional clin. research assoc. Adria Labs., Atlanta, 1987—. Mem. Am. Pharm. Assn., Assn. Clin. Pharmacology, Ill. Pharmacist Assn., Iowa Pharmacist Assn., Chicagoland Pharm. Discussion Group (sec., treas. 1985-86, com. chmn. 1986-87)., Drake U. Chgo. Area Alumni Assn. (Chgo. area chmn. 1984—). Avocations: alumni activities, knitting, geneology research.

HOLTEN, JAMES J., meat processing company executive; b. Granite City, Ill., Apr. 9, 1940; s. Elwyn H. and Ilene P. (Hoopengarner) H.; m. Shirley Ann Taylor, Dec. 18, 1976; children: Tyanna Bechtoldt, Gregory. BS, So. Ill. U., Edwardsville, 1965. With Holten Meat Inc., East St. Louis, Ill., 1961-65, sec., 1965-75, pres., 1975-85, chief exec. officer, chmn. bd. dirs., 1985—. Served with USAF, 1963-69. Mem. Young Pres's. Orgn. Republican. Roman Catholic. Avocation: boating. Home: 4 E Beacon Hill Rd Fairview Heights IL 62208 Office: Holten Meat Inc 919 Lynch PO Box 129 East Saint Louis IL 62201

HOLTER, ARLEN ROLF, cardiothoracic surgeon; b. Sullivan's Island, S.C., Feb. 1, 1946; s. Arne and Helen (Soderberg) H.; m. Elizabeth Anne Reid, Nov. 9, 1974; children—Matthew Arlen, Peter Reid, Andrew Douglas. B.S., Stanford U., 1968; M.S., U. Chgo., 1971, M.D., 1973. Diplomate Am. Bd. Thoracic Surgery; Am. Bd. Surgery. Intern in surgery Mass. Gen. Hosp., Boston, 1973-74, resident in surgery, 1974-78; sr. registrar in cardiac surgery Southampton Chest Hosp., Eng., 1978; resident in cardiac surgery Yale U., New Haven, 1978-80; practice medicine specializing in cardiothoracic surgery, Mpls., 1980—; instr. surgery Yale U., 1979-80. Contbr. articles to profl. jours. Recipient Franklin McLean research award U. Chgo., 1973. Fellow ACS, Am. Coll. Cardiology, Am. Coll. Chest Physicians; mem. Soc. Thoracic Surgeons, Pan Pacific Sur. Soc. Lutheran. Avocations: marathon running; skiing; photography. Office: Cardiothoracic Cons PA 6545 France Ave S Minneapolis MN 55435

HOLTGREVEN, DOUGLAS ALLEN, electronics sales and marketing executive; b. Lima, Ohio, Sept. 25, 1957; s. Charles Thomas and Evelyn Kathryn (Gores) H. A in Elec. Mech. Engring., Alfred (N.Y.) State U., 1977. Br. mgr. Holtgreven Scale & Electronics, Middletown, 1980-82; nat. sales mgr. Holtgreven Scale & Electronics, Findlay, Ohio, 1982-85; v.p. mktg. Holtgreven Scale & Electronics, Findlay, 1985—. Mem. Internat. Soc. Weighing and Measurement, Am. R.R. Engring. Assn., Ohio Feed and Grain Assn., Ind. Feed and Grain. Republican. Roman Catholic. Club: Findlay Country. Lodge: Elks, KC. Avocations: softball, bowling, skiing. Home: 930 McManness Ave Findlay OH 45840 Office: Holtgreven Scale & Electronics 420 E Lincoln St Findlay OH 45840

HOLTKAMP, DORSEY EMIL, medical research scientist; b. New Knoxville, Ohio, May 28, 1919; s. Emil H. and Caroline E. (Meckstroth) H.; m. Marianne Church Johnson, Mar. 20, 1942 (dec. 1956); 1 son, Kurt Lee; m. Marie P. Bahm Roberts, Dec. 20, 1957 (dec. 1982); stepchildren: Charles Timothy Roberts, Michael John Roberts; m. Phyllis Laurence Bradfield, Sept. 1, 1984. Student, Ohio State U., 1937-39; AB, U. Colo., 1945, MS, 1949, PhD, 1951. Sr. research scientist biochemistry sect. Smith, Kline & French Labs., Phila., 1951-57, endocrine-metabolic group leader, 1957-58; head endocrinology dept. Merrell-Nat. Labs. div. Richardson-Merrell, Inc., Cin., 1958-70, group dir. endocrine clin. research, med. research dept., 1970-81; group dir. med. research dept. Merrell Dow Pharms. subs. Dow Chem. Co., Cin., 1981—. Research and publs. on various phases endocrinology, pharmacology, tumor metabolism, fertility-sterility control, biochemistry, teratology, inflammation, nutrition; research and devel. on new drugs. U. Colo. Med. Sch. fellow, 1946, biochemistry research fellow, 1948-51. Fellow AAAS; mem. AMA (affiliate), Am. Soc. Clin. Pharm. and Therapeutics, Endocrine Soc., Am. Fertility Soc., Am. Chem. Soc., Am. Soc. Pharmacology and Exptl. Therapeutics, N.Y. Acad. Sci., Ohio Acad Sci., Soc. Exptl. Biology and Medicine, Sigma Xi, Nu Sigma Nu. Republican. Presbyterian. Home: 130 S Liberty-Keuter Rd Lebanon Oh 45036 Office: Merrell Dow Pharms 2110 E Galbraith Rd Cincinnati OH 45215

HOLTON, EARL D., retail company executive; b. 1934. With Meijer, Inc., Grand Rapids, Mich., 1952—, v.p., 1967-76, then exec. v.p., now pres., dir. Office: Meijer Inc 2727 Walker Ave NW Grand Rapids MI 49501 *

HOLTZ, GLENN EDWARD, band instrument manufacturing executive; b. Detroit, Jan. 15, 1938; s. Edward Christian and Evelyn Adele (Priehs) Foutz H.; m. Mary Eleanor Russell, Nov. 25, 1981; children by previous marriage—Robert, Kimberly, Rene, Letitia, Kimberly, Pamela. B. Mus. Edn., U. Mich., 1960, M. Mus. Edn., 1964; cons. motivation student Personnel Dynamics, Mpls., 1980. Mus. tchr. Middleville High Sch. (Mich.), 1960-62; dist. mgr. Selmer Co., Elkhart, Ind., 1965-74, sales mgr., 1974-76; pres. Knapp Mus. Co., Grand Rapids, Mich., 1976-80; v.p. mktg. sales Gemeinhardt/CBS, Elkhart, 1981-83, gen. mgr., 1983—, also pres. CBS Columbia Music Div., 1984, v.p. CBS, 1985; pres. Steinway Music Properties (formerly CBS Columbia Music Div.), 1985; pres. Gemeinhardt Co., Inc. seminar leader Sch. Band Movement Phase II Gemeinhardt, Elkhart, 1982-83. Dist. gov. Lion's Internat., Jackson, Lansing, Battle Creek, Mich., 1970-71; pres. Middleville Bd. Edn., 1964-66. Recipient Disting. award Lion's Internat., Mich., 1971. Mem. Nat. Assn. Band Instrument Mfrs. (pres. 1986-88), Am. Music Conf. (bd. dirs. 1987—). Republican. Office: Gemeinhardt PO Box 788 Elkhart IN 46515

HOLTZ, KATHLEEN MARIE, small business owner; b. Tawas, Mich., May 17, 1960; d. Clarence Harold and Mary Katherine (Patterson) H. Student, Cen. Mich. U., 1978-82. Owner Pirate's Cove Pet Ctr., Mt. Pleasant, Mich., 1980—; lectr. Cen. Mich. U., various local profl. assns. Mem. Pet Industry Joint Adv. Council, Mich. Profl. Pet Groomers Assn. Lutheran. Lodge: Order Eastern Star. Avocations: skiing, swimming, tennis, racquetball, sewing. Home: 1612 Mary Ann St Mount Pleasant MI 48858 Office: Pirate's Cove Pet Ctr 2207 S Mission Suite B Mount Pleasant MI 48858

HOLZ, ANTHONY DAVID, rabbi; b. Cape Town, South Africa, May 1, 1942; came to U.S., 1964; s. Erich and Ursula (Kassel) H.; m. Judith Devine, Nov. 27, 1966; children: Meiera, Jessa, Dara. MA in Hebrew Lit., Hebrew Union Coll., 1970, postgrad., 1970-72, 77-81. Ordained rabbi, 1970. Hillel advisor Miami U., Oxford, Ohio, 1970-72; rabbi Progressive Jewish Congregation, Pretoria, South Africa, 1972-77, Temple Israel, Paducah, Ky., 1977-81, Cong Beth Tikivah, Columbus, Ohio, 1981-83, Temple Israel, Duluth, Minn., 1983—; v.p. Institute of Creative Judaism, Cin., 1971—; chaplain Fed. Prison Camp, Duluth, 1985—. Author: (with others) Funeral & Memorial Services, 1979. Bd. advisors Lake Superior Chamber Orch.; bd. dirs. NAACP, Duluth, 1984—. Mem. Cen. Conf. on Am. Rabbis, Mid-Western Assn. Reform Rabbis. Lodge: Rotary. Home: 2614 E Superior St Duluth MN 55812 Office: Temple Israel 1602 E 2d St Duluth MN 55812

HOLZ, HARRY GEORGE, lawyer; b. Milw., Sept. 13, 1934; s. Harry Carl and Emma Louise (Hinz) H.; m. Nancy L. Heiser, May 12, 1962; children: Pamela Gretchen, Bradley Eric, Erika Lynn. BS, Marquette U., 1956, LLB, 1958; LLM, Northwestern U., 1960. Bar: Wis. 1958, Ill. 1960. Teaching fellow Northwestern U. Sch. Law, 1958-59; assoc. Sidley & Austin, Chgo., 1960; ptnr. Quarles & Brady, Milw., 1968—; lectr. law securities regulation U. Wis. Law Sch., 1971-74; adj. prof. securities regulation law Marquette U. Sch. Law, 1976—; mem. faculty program on antitrust law Wis. State Bar Advanced Tng. Seminars, 1975-82, mem. faculty program on securities law, 1975—. Bd. visitors Marquette U. Sch. Law, 1986. Served to capt. C.E. U.S. Army, 1960-67. Mem. ABA (Robinson-Patman com., corp. counsel com.), Wis. Bar Assn. (chmn. dir. corps., banking and bus. law sect. 1978-79, bd. dirs. 1978-83, corp. and bus. laws com. 1985—), Milw. Bar Assn., Bar Assn. 7th Fed. Circuit, Marquette U. Sch. Law Woolsack Soc. (bd. dirs.), Beta Gamma Sigma. Lutheran. Clubs: Milw. Athletic, Western Racquet. Office: Quarles & Brady 411 E Wisconsin Ave Milwaukee WI 53202

HOLZER, RICHARD JEAN, lawyer; b. Easton, Pa., Jan. 31, 1940; s. J. A. and Ann C. (Carta) H.; B.A., Gettysburg Coll., 1961; M.B.A., U. Dayton, 1971; student N.Y. U., 1968-69; J.D., Salmon P. Chase Coll. Law, No. Ky. State U., 1975; m. Charlotte L. Branson, Aug. 15, 1964; children—Richard Jean, C. Christopher. Field rep. INA, Pitts., 1961-66; asso. R. D. Griewahn & Assos., Erie, Pa., 1966-68; mgr. compensation and benefits Curtis-Wright Corp., Woodridge, N.J., 1968-69; mgr. personnel services, McCall Printing Co., Dayton, 1969-70; labor relations adminstr. City of Dayton, 1970-75; admitted to Ohio bar, 1975; atty. pub. sector labor and corp. law, ptnr. Pickrel, Schaeffer and Ebeling, Dayton, 1975—; law dir. City of Englewood (Ohio); asst. prof. U. Dayton, 1976-77, Wright State U., 1979-80. Com. chmn. Montgomery County Personnel Task Force, 1979—; soccer coach Northmont Bd. Edn., 1983—. Served with U.S. Army, 1962-64. Recipient Book award for labor law No. Ky. State U. Mem. Am. Soc. Personnel Adminstrs., Nat. Pub. Employers Labor Relations Assn., Ohio Pub. Employers Labor Relations Assn., Ohio League Mcpl. Attys., Ohio Council Sch. Bd. Attys. (vice chmn.), Ohio State Bar Assn., Fed. Bar Assn., Dayton Bar Assn., Scabbard and Blade, Phi Alpha Delta, Lambda Chi Alpha. Lutheran (council 1976—, pres. council 1978-79). Home: 10887 Putnam Rd Englewood OH 45322 Office: 2700 Kettering Tower Dayton OH 45423

HOLZMAN, SHELDON PAUL, accountant; b. Chgo., Sept. 26, 1946; s. Al and Sally (Rutizer) H.; m. Elaine Beth Weiss, Apr. 7, 1968; children: Burton, Michael. BS in Acctg., DePaul U., 1972. CPA, Ill., Wis., Iowa. Acct., supr. Panel, Kerr, Forster & Co., Chgo., 1966-75; sr. mng. ptnr. Bernstein & Bank, Ltd., Chgo., 1975-82; ptnr. Laventhol & Horwath, Chgo., 1982—. Mem. Satellite Council Channel 11 WTTW, Chgo., 1986—; chmn. mcpl. audit adv. bd. State of Ill., 1985—. Served with U.S. Army, 1968-70. Mem. Am. Inst. CPA's (com. mem. 1975-76), Ill. CPA Soc. (chmn. ethics govtl. com. 1985—), Govt. Fin. Officers Assn., Ill. Assn. Sanitary Dists., Airport Ops. Council Internat., Newcomen Soc. Am. Democrat. Jewish. Club: River (Chgo.). Office: Laventhol & Horwath 300 S Riverside Plaza Chicago IL 60606

HOMAN, GERLOF, pharmaceutical company executive; b. Bandung, Indonesia, Feb. 10, 1930; came to U.S., 1973; s. Freerk Hinrik and Joan (Groosjohan) H.; Ph.D. in Organic Chemistry, U. Amsterdam, 1952, M.Clin. Pharmacy, 1961; m. Siekelina Rogaar, Oct. 10, 1955; children—Irma, Astrid, Floris, Paul. Plant mgr. Vitamin D Factories, Weesp, Netherlands, 1956-59; plant mgr. pharm. cos., Holland, India, 1960-63, 63-68, gen. pharm. mgr., 1968-72; gen. mgr. K-V Pharm. Co., St. Louis, 1973-75; dir. research and devel. Cartrix, Brentwood, Mo., 1975—, now v.p. research and devel. Survival Tech. Inc. Mem. Pharm. Mfrs. Assn., Assn. Clin. Pharms. Royal Dutch Soc. Chemistry, Parenteral Drug Assn. Author books in field. Patentee in field. Home: 748 Elkington St Louis MO 63132 Office: Survival Tech Inc 2615 S Hanley Saint Louis MO 63144

HOMANDBERG, GENE ALVIN, biochemist; b. Inwood, Iowa, June 7, 1950; s. Alvin Arne and Darleen Winnifred (Keith) H. BS, U. S.D., 1972, PhD, 1976. Undergrad. research asst. biochemistry dept. U. S.D., 1969-72, grad. research asst., 1972-76, teaching asst. biochemistry, 1973-74, postdoctoral research assoc., 1976; NIH trainee, 1972-73; postdoctoral research assoc. Purdue U., West Lafayette, Ind., 1976-78; postdoctoral fellow Lab. Chem. Biology, Nat. Inst. Arthritis, Metabolism and Digestive Diseases, NIH, Bethesda, Md., 1978-80; cancer research scientist II dept. molecular biology Roswell Park Meml. Inst., Buffalo, 1980-81; asst. scientist dept. medicine Mt. Sinai Med. Ctr., Milw., 1981—; asst. prof. U. Wis. Med. Sch., Milw., 1981-85, assoc. prof., 1985-86; sr. biochemist Abbott Labs., Abbott Park, Ill., 1986—. Grantee Nat. Heart and Lung Inst., 1983-85. Mem. Am. Chem. Soc., AAAS, Am. Soc. Biol. Chemists, Am. Heart Assn., Sigma Xi. Democrat. Lutheran. Contbr. articles to biochem. jours. Home: 840 Westmoreland Dr Apt 9 Vernon Hills IL 60061 Office: Abbott Labs Bldg 9A Dept 472 Abbott Park IL 60064

HOMMA, HITOSHI, physicist; b. Akita, Japan, Mar. 28, 1948; s. Fumio and Miyoko (Takeshima) H.; m. Mayumi Iwamoto, June 30, 1979; children: Shunsuke Sean, Emmi. B in English, Tohoku U., 1971, M in English, 1973; MS, U. Mich., 1982, PhD in Physics, 1984. Researcher Fujitsu Labs., Kowasaki, Japan, 1973-78; postdoctoral fellow Argonne (Ill.) Nat. Lab., 1984-87, asst. physicist, 1987—. Mem. Am. Physical Soc. Avocations: jogging, classical music, tennis. Home: 16 W 505 Mockingbird Ln #105 Hinsdale IL 60521 Office: Argonne Nat Lab 9700 S Cass Ave Argonne IL 60439

HOMSI, RATEB K., physician; b. Damascus, Syria, Mar. 1, 1929; came to U.S., 1955, naturalized, 1964; s. Khaled M. and Munira (Nahas) H.; m. Laura Jean Morgan, Sept. 3, 1958; children—Terence, Ray, Kenneth. B.S.,

Coll. Scis., Damascus, 1947; M.D., Coll. Medicine, Damascus, 1953. Diplomate Am. Bd. Surgery, Intern, Huron Road Hosp., Cleve., 1955-56; resident St. Vincent's Hosp., Jacksonville, Fla., 1957-60; gen. surgeon Community Meml. Hosp., Cheboygan, Mich., 1963-68, chmn. dept. surgery, 1968-84, med. dir., 1983—. Fellow Am. Soc. Abdominal Surgeons, Internat. Coll. Surgeons; mem. Mich. State Med. Soc., AMA, Assn. Arab-Am. Univ. Grads., Nat. Arab Am. Assn. Avocations: Golf, bridge. Home: 457 Foote Rd Cheboygan MI 49721 Office: Community Meml Hosp 802 S Main St PO Box 99 Cheboygan MI 49721

HONAKER, JANICE MARIE, medical association administrator; b. Peoria, Ill., Oct. 13, 1957; d. William Frederick and Mary Anne (Svymbersky) H. BS, U. Iowa, 1979; M Health Services, Coll. of St. Francis, Joliet, Ill., 1986. Unit mgr. St. Francis Med. Ctr., Peoria, 1980-82, asst. dir. planning, 1982-84, dir. planning, 1984—; moderator design class Bradley U., Peoria, 1983, Ill. Community Coll., East Peoria, Ill., 1984. Mem. Parish Life Team, Peoria, 1982-83. Mem. East Peoria C. of C. (ambassador 1985-86), U. Iowa Alumnae Assn., Alpha Xi Delta (pres. 1981, 83, 1979 pledge trainer). Roman Catholic. Home: 612 Westwood Peoria IL 61614 Office: St Francis Med Ctr 530 NE Glen Oak Ave Peoria IL 61637

HONG, JOHN JOONPYO, physician; b. Seoul, Republic of Korea, Aug. 27, 1938; Came to U.S., 1968; s. Myung Kil and Kil Sang (Song) H.; m. Judith Kyuwon Lee, May 12, 1965; children: Richard, Rosamond, Raymond. Grad. premedical sch., Seoul Nat. U., 1960, MD, 1964, M in Med. Sci., 1966, postgrad., 1967. Diplomate Am. Bd. Abdominal Surgery. Intern The Victoria Gen. Hosp., Halifax, N.S., Can., 1967-68; resident in surgery Aultman Hosp., Canton, Ohio, 1968-69, Fairview Gen. Hosp., Cleve., 1969-72; mem. med. staff Deaconess Hosp. of Cleve., 1974-86; owner, operator Brook Park (Ohio) Med. Clinic, 1980—; mem. med. staff S.W. Gen. Hosp., Middleburg Heights, Ohio, 1976-86. Fellow Am. Soc. Abdominal Surgeons, Internat. Coll. Surgeons; mem. Acad. Medicine of Cleve., Ohio State Med. Assn., Korean Assn. Greater Cleve. (pres. 1979), Brook Park C. of C. Avocations: violin, classical and latin music, golf, travel. Home: 2684 Goldwood Dr Rocky River OH 44116 Office: Brook Park Med Clinic 15400 Snow Rd Brook Park OH 44142

HONIG, LAWRENCE EDWARD, retail executive; b. Spartanburg, S.C., Jan. 19, 1948; s. O. Charles and Jean Gates (Davis) H.; m. Ellen Stokes, Aug. 7, 1971. B.A., Washington and Lee U., 1970, B.S., 1970; M.A., U. Tex.-Austin, 1972; M.B.A., Harvard U., 1975. Assoc. Loeb, Rhoades & Co., N.Y.C., 1972-73; prin. McKinsey & Co., Chgo., 1975-82; exec. v.p. May Dept. Stores Co., St. Louis, 1982-85, vice chmn., 1986—, also bd. dirs. Author: John Henry Brown, 1972. Served to capt. U.S. Army, 1971-72. Club: Capital City (Atlanta). Office: May Dept Stores Co 6th & Olive Sts Saint Louis MO 63101

HONKE, SUE ANN, financial executive; b. Flint, Mich., Feb. 4, 1948; d. Ivan L. and Frances E. Tuttle; grad. Victor Bus. Sch., 1969; student U. Mich., 1970-73; m. Alfred A. Honke, June 27, 1981; children—Victoria Sue, Byron D. Med. sec. Univ. Hosp., 1966-69; adminstrv. asst. Inland Scholtz Modular Housing, 1971-72; adminstr., acct. Washtenaw County Rd. Commn., 1972-76; office mgr. Moehrle, Inc., Ann Arbor, Mich., 1976-79; fin. mgr. Lovejoy Tiffany & Assocs., Inc., Ann Arbor, 1979-80, dir. fin. and adminstrn., 1980-83, v.p., gen. mgr., 1983—. Mem. Nat. Assn. Female Execs., Nat. Assn. Accts., Am. Mgmt. Assn., Credit Women Internat. Office: Lovejoy Tiffany & Assocs Box 8259 Ann Arbor MI 48107

HONNOLD, DENNIS DYER, agricultural business executive; b. Des Moines, June 18, 1942; s. Willard Lehman and Opal (Dyer) H.; m. Penny Ward, Sept. 4, 1965; children: Daniel, Jeff. BA in Chemistry, Millikin U., 1968; MS in Food Sci., U. Ill., 1972. Analytical chemist Staley Continental Inc., Decatur, Ill., 1963-67, prodn., process devel. chemist, 1968-73, tech. service salesman, 1973-74, product mgr., 1974-80, mktg. mgr., 1981-85, dir. acctg. and adminstrn., protein div., 1985—. Treas. Sinawik Park Bd., Decatur, 1980-83; pres. High Sch. Band Boosters, Decatur, 1985-87. Mem. Inst. Food Technologists (profl.), Am. Meat Inst. Presbyterian. Avocations: gardening, tennis, golf. Home: 236 Silver Dr Decatur IL 62521 Office: Staley Continental Inc PO Box 151 Decatur IL 62525

HOOD, LESLIE LYNN, publishing executive; b. Indpls., June 24, 1948; s. John Marquis and Gloria (Bennett) H.; m. Jean Marie Rawlings, Dec. 12, 1969; children—Derek, Heath, Brecka, Shamene. B.S., Mo. Valley Coll., 1970. Student personnel adminstr. Mo. Valley Coll., Marshall, 1969-71; ministerial degree Berear Coll., 1985. Ordained to ministry, 1985. Dist. dir. Crossroads of Am. council Boy Scouts Am., Indpls., 1971-74, fin. dir. Dan Beard council, Cin., 1974-83; v.p. Lay Leadership Internat., Christian lit. pub. co., Fairfield, Ohio, 1983—; pres. C.C.S. Consultants, Cin., 1980—; bd. dirs. Santa Marie Neighborhood, Cin., 1976-80, H.I.P. Inc., Cin., 1977-79. Author: Financing Local Institutions, 1981; Baptist Church in Scouting, 1983. Named Eagle Scout, 1965. Kansas City Council Higher Edn., 1969. Mem. Nat. Soc. Fund Raising Execs. (cert.; Honors scholar 1983; mem. exec. bd. 1980—), Cin. Soc. Fund Raisers, Advt. Council. Republican. Mem. Assemblies of God, Nat. Assn. Ch. Bus. Adminstn. (v.p. 1987). Clubs: Hamilton (Ohio); Kiwanis (Cin.). Lodge: Elks. Avocations: hiking; camping; canoeing. Home: 5841 Gilmore Dr Fairfield OH 45014 Office: Lay Leadership Internat 1267 Hicks Blvd Fairfield OH 45014

HOOGSTRA, FAY BEE, accountant; b. St. Paul, Oct. 5, 1961; d. Merlin Henry and Virginia Lylian (Schaffer) H. BS, U. Wis., Green Bay, 1983. CPA, Wis. Acct. Gen. Motors, Janesville, Wis., 1983; acct., auditor Van Der Jagt Buss & Assocs., Sheboygan, Wis., 1984-87; acct. Kohler (Wis.) Co., 1987—. Mem. Nat. Assn. Accts., U. Wis. Green Bay Alumni Assn. Republican. Presbyterian. Club: Toastmasters. Avocations: jogging, tennis, sports, dancing, reading. Home: 2113 Wiemann St Sheboygan WI 53081 Office: Kohler Co Kohler WI 53044

HOOK, JOHN BURNEY, investment company executive; b. Franklin, Ind., Sept. 6, 1928; s. Burney S. and Elsie C. (Hubbard) H.; m. Georgia Delis, Feb. 8, 1958; children—David, Deborah. BS, Ind. U., 1956, MBA, 1957. CPA, Ohio.; cert. fin. acct. Store mgr. Goodman-Jester, Inc., Franklin, Ind., 1949-50; auditor Ernst & Ernst, Indpls., 1953-56; financial analyst Eli Lilly & Co., Indpls., 1957-59; gen. ptnr. Ball, Burge & Kraus, Cleve., 1966-70; pres., dir. Cuyahoga Mgmt. Corp., 1966-81; mng. ptnr. Hook Ptnrs., Cleve., 1984—. Mem. Am. Inst. CPAs, Am. Inst. Chartered Financial Analysts. Republican. Methodist. Clubs: Cleve. Athletic, Union (Cleve.); Lakewood Country. Home: 435 Bates Dr Bay Village OH 44140 also: 1856 Beachside Tennis Villas Hilton Head Island SC 29928 Office: 815 National City Bank Bldg Cleveland OH 44114

HOOK, WILLIAM FRANKLIN, radiologist; b. Williston, N.D., May 26, 1935; s. Charles Ellis and Ann (Franklin) H.; m. Margo Joanne Booth, June 21, 1958 (div. Sept. 1968); children: William, Christopher, Paul; m. Merry Jean Schimke, Nov. 26, 1968 (div. 1987); 1 child, Kari Ann. AB, Stanford U., 1957; MD, Jefferson Med. Coll., 1961. Diplomate Am. Bd. Radiology, Am. Bd. Nuclear Medicine. Staff radiologist O&R Clinic, Bismarck, N.D., 1969-74; dir. nuclear radiology O&R Clinic, Bismarck, 1983—; chief dept. radiology Bismarck Hosp., 1970-74; dir. dept. radiology Mandan (N.D.) Hosp., 1974-81; staff radiologist Meth. Hosps., Dallas, 1981-83; asst. clinical prof. U. N.D., 1978—. Author: Common Sense and Modern First Aid, 1967; contbr. articles profl. jours. Served to lt. USNR, 1961-64, col. res. Mem. AMA (Physician's Recognition award 1983-86), Am. Coll. Radiology, Soc. Nuclear Medicine, N.D. State Radiol. Soc., 6th Dist. Med. Soc. Lutheran. Avocations: hunting, golf. Home: Rural Rt 5 Box 145A Bismarck ND 58501 Office: O&R Clinic 222 N 7th St Bismarck ND 58501

HOOKER, DAVID NEIL, financial executive, accountant; b. Anderson, Ind., Mar. 12, 1950; s. Robert Kieth and Evelyn Marie (McElhoe) H.; m. Mary Margret Wickert, Aug. 12, 1972; children: Andrew, Jessica. BS in Acctg., Ball State U., 1972. CPA, Ill. Audit asst. S.D. Liedesdorf & Co., Chgo., 1972-74, audit sr., 1974-77, audit mgr., 1977; asst. controller Telemed Corp., Hoffman Estates, Ill., 1977-79; controller Telemed Corp., Hoffman Estates, 1979-84; corp. mgr. Elmhurst (Ill.) Meml. Hosp., 1985-86; chief fin. officer Travelers/Diebold Tech. Co., Itasca, Ill., 1986—. Mem. Am. Inst. CPA's, Ill. CPA Soc. Republican. Methodist. Avocations: family, outdoor activities, sports. Home: 340 Southampton Dr Geneva IL 60134 Office: Travelers/Diebold Tech Co One Pierce Pl Suite 550 Itasca IL 60143

HOOKER, JAMES TODD, manufacturing executive; b. Ashland, Ohio, Dec. 21, 1946; s. Melvin Todd and Harriett (Lutz) H.; m. Sallie Foulkrod Utz, Feb. 22, 1975; 1 child, Stephanie Rae. BSBA magna cum laude, Ashland Coll., 1973. Advt. mgr. The Gorman-Rupp Co., Mansfield, Ohio, 1974-76; mfg. engr. The Gorman-Rupp Co., Mansfield, 1976-79, asst. service mgr., 1979-80, gen. service mgr., 1980-86, asst. sales mgr., 1986—. Solicitor United Way, Mansfield, 1982, 83, 87. Served with USN, 1966-69, Vietnam. Decorated Vietnamese Gallantry Cross. Republican. Presbyterian. Home: 1090 Trout Dr Mansfield OH 44903 Office: The Gorman-Rupp Co 305 Bowman St Mansfield OH 44903

HOOKER, JOHN HENRY, radiologist; b. Dixon, Mo., Sept. 30, 1924; s. Henry Greenleaf and Grace Frances (Wells) H.; m. Betty Lou Wells, Apr. 26, 1952; 1 child, Jennifer Lou. Student pre-medicine, U. Mo., 1942-45; MD, U. Tenn., 1949; cert. radiology, St. Louis City Hosp., 1961. Cert. Am. Bd. Radiology. Radiologist Alton (Ill.) Meml. Hosp., 1961-69, dir. dept. radiology, 1969—; past pres. med. staff Alton Meml. Hosp., Community Meml. Hosp., Madison County Med. Soc. Served to capt. U.S. Army, 1955-57. Mem. AMA, Am. Coll. Radiology, Radiol. Soc. N.Am., Am. Inst. Ultrasound in Medicine. Republican. Presbyterian. Avocations: travel, photography, geneology. Home: 19 Fairmont Alton IL 62002 Office: Alton Meml Hosp 1 Memorial Dr Alton IL 62002

HOOPER, GRACE ISABEL, library educator; b. Cleve., July 1, 1918; d. Cornelius Fitzgerald and Grace Evelyn (True) Maloney; m. John George Hooper, Apr. 18, 1953 (dec. July 1973); children: John David, Dale Thomas. AB, Ursuline Coll. for Women, Cleve., 1941; MLS, Case Western Res. U., 1945. Cert. secondary sch. tchr., Ohio. Media specialist Univ. Sch. for Boys, Hunting Valley, Ohio, 1965-69; library dir. Elyria (Ohio) High Sch., 1969-79; research librarian Magnificat High Sch., Rocky River, Ohio, 1979—. Pres. Great Lakes secondary curriculum Youth for Tomorrow's Lakes, Inc., Elyria, 1983—; trustee Cleve. Waterfront Coalition, 1986—. Recipient Martha Holden Jennings award, 1975, 84. Mem. Am. Assn. Univ. Women, Ohio Ret. Tchrs. Assn., Great Lakes Hist. Soc., Altrusa Internat. (pres. Elyria chpt. 1978-80, Rocky River, 1983—). Republican. Roman Catholic. Avocations: reading, music, travel, ice skating, sailing.

HOOPER, JAMES MURRAY, service association executive; b. Waco, Tex., Jan. 4, 1928; s. Murray Robertson and Ersey (Cawthon) H.; m. Lorraine Marian Voehl, Mar. 9, 1967; children—William David, John Charles, Walter Brooks, Paul Ryan. B.Arch., Tex. Tech U., 1953. Vol., staff positions Peace Corps, Bolivia, Guatemala, Colombia, 1962-69; dir. Brazil, Rio de Janeiro, 1969-71; owner N.Mex. Office Supply Co., Santa Fe, 1971-72; adminstrv. officer Ohio Dept. Fin., Columbus, 1972-76; exec. dir. Sertoma Internat., exec. v.p. Sertoma Found., Kansas City, Mo., 1976—. Served with USN, 1946-48. Mem. Am. Soc. Assn. Execs., Mid Am. Soc. Assn. Execs. Club: Sertoma (Kansas City, Mo.). Office: Sertoma Internat 1912 E Meyer Blvd Kansas City MO 64132

HOOPER, SUSAN JEANNE, nurse, military official; b. Rapid CIty, S.D., Aug. 4, 1950; d. Hugh McNiell and Bertha Regina (Mahlberg) Thomas; m. John D. Lanham, Oct. 6, 1976 (div. Aug. 1979); m. Robert Edward Hooper, Feb. 21, 1981; children: Cassandra, Robert Brian. RN Diploma, Presbyn. Sch. Nursing, 1971; BS in Psychology, U. Dubuque, 1973; cert. midwife, Frontier Nursing Service, 1975; MS in Nursing, Vanderbilt U., 1979. RN. Staff RN, asst. head nurse Presbyn. Med. Ctr., Denver, 1971-72; dir. student health U. Dubuque, Iowa, 1972-73; dist. RN, preceptor family nurse practitioner clin. inst. Frontier Nursing Service, Hyden, Ky., 1973-75; staff RN, home health nurse St. Joseph Hosp., Florence, Colo., 1975-76; commd. 1st lt. U.S. Army, 1976, advanced through grades to maj., 1986; nurse, midwife U.S. Army, Ft. Campbell, Ky., Ft. Hood, Tex., Frankfurt, Fed. Republic Germany, 1976-79, 79-83, 83-86; head nurse post partum U.S. Army, Ft. Riley, Kans., 1986—; pediatric nurse practitioner Custer County Health Dept., Westcliff, Colo., 1975-76. Mem. Colo. Nurse's Assn., Nurse's Assn. Am. Coll. OBGYN, Am. Nurse's Assn., Am. Coll. Nurse Midwives. Roman Catholic. Avocations: needlepoint, counted cross stitch, sewing, reading. Home: 142 N Dartmouth Manhattan KS 66502 Office: US Army Meddac IACH Fort Riley KS 66442

HOOPINGARNER, JOHN MARTIN, lawyer, educator; b. Dover, Ohio, May 8, 1954; s. Dallas Stanley and Josephine (Agosti) H.; m. Susan Scott Hanhart, July 17, 1976; Children: Scott David, Katherine Ann. BA, Muskingum Coll., 1976; JD, Ohio No. U., 1979. Bar: Ohio 1979, U.S. Dist. (no. dist.) Ohio 1979, U.S. Dist. Ct. Appeals (6th. cir.) 1983, U.S. Supreme Ct. 1984. Assoc. Smith Rnner Hanhart Miller & Kyler, New Philadelphia, Ohio, 1979-85; ptnr. Hanhart Miller & Kyler, New Philadelphia, 1985—; instr. real estate law Kent State U., New Philadelphia, 1986—. Bd. dirs. Tuscarawas County Bd. Mental Retardation and Devel. Disabilities, New Philadelphia, 1981—, chmn. 1983—, Tuscarawas County YMCA, 1982-85, Am. Cancer Soc., Tuscarawas County, 1985—, Tuscarawas County C. of C., 1981-85; bd. trustees, sec. Ohio Assn. County Bds. Mental Retardation & Devel. Disabilities, 1987—. Mem. ABA (real property, probate and trust law sect.), Ohio Bar Assn. (bd. govs. young lawyers sect.), Tuscarawas County Bar Assn. (pres. 1985-86), Dover Jaycees (bd. dirs. 1981-84). Democrat. Club: Union County (Dover). Lodge: Elks. Home: 320 East 14th St Dover OH 44622 Office: Hanhart Miller & Kyler 405 Chauncey Ave PO Box 668 New Philadelphia OH 44663

HOOPS, DONALD LEE, medical association administrator; b. Villa Grove, Ill., Oct. 16, 1934; s. Adolph L. and Effie O. (Ringo) H.; m. Geraldine M. Rotter, Aug. 26, 1962; children: Michael, Susan, Mary. BS, Eastern Ill. U., 1956, MS in Edn., 1960; PhD, So. Ill. U., 1970. Mgr. edn. Westinghouse Mgmt. Corp., Ind., 1962-65; asst. prof. Northeastern Ill. U., Chgo., 1965-70; ednl. dir. United Dairy Assn., Rosemont, Ill., 1970-79; exec. dir. Am. Occupational Medicine Assn., Arlington Heights, Ill., 1979—; cons. Litton Industries, Chgo., 1963-65. Author: Behavioral Objectives Review, 1970, Book of Christmas Letters, 1985. Bd. dirs. Northwest Suburban Towns Club, 1975-80. Served to 1st lt. U.S. Army, 1957-59. Home: 18 Wildwood N Prospect Heights IL 60070 Office: Am Occupational Medicine Assn 2340 S Arlington Heights Rd Arlington Heights IL 60005

HOORT, GLENN A., podiatric surgeon; b. Lansing, Mich., Mar. 3, 1951; s. John Calvin and Florence Alice (Nichols) H.; m. Marga Lizbeth Helder, Aug. 10, 1974; children: Deborah, Thomas, Cathrine, Laura. BS, Calvin Coll., 1973; D of Podiatric Medicine, Ill. Coll. Podiatric Medicine, 1978. Practice podiatric surgery Holland, Mich., 1980—. Mem. Am. Podiatric Med. Assn., Mich. State Podiatric Med. Assn., Holand C. of C. Republican. Mem. Christian Reformed Ch. Lodge: Rotary. Home: 382 Big Bay Dr Holland MI 49424 Office: 291 Lakewood Blvd Holland MI 49424

HOOTEN, WILLIAM FOSTER, JR., wholesale executive; b. St. Louis, Aug. 13, 1926; s. William Foster and Ida B. (Willis) m. Joanne Jeans, Aug. 1, 1949; children: William F. III, Marcia Ann Godfrey, Suzanne Brownlee. BJ, U. Mo., Columbia, 1950. Sales rep. London Guarantee and Accident Co., St. Louis, 1950; corp. v.p. and dir. Western Auto Stores, Inc., Kansas City, Mo., 1952-77; v.p. Leiter's Designer Fabrics, Inc., Kansas City, Mo., 1978-80; pres. Liberty Distbrs., Inc., Des Plaines, Ill., 1980—; also dir. Liberty Distbrs., Inc. (Trustworthy Hardware Stores), Des Plaines, Ill.; mem. adv. bd. Home Ctr. Show, Chgo., 1985—. Contbr. numerous travel articles to Kansas City Star, 1977-79. Elder Cardinal Drive Ch. of Christ, Rolling Meadows, Ill., 1982-85, Overland Park (Kans.) Ch. of Christ, 1975-80, San Jose Ch. of Christ, Jacksonville, Fla., 1965-70; trustee Abilene (Tex.) Christian U., 1980—, Mich. Christian Coll., Rochester (Detroit), 1981-86. Served with USN, 1944-46, PTO, to 1st lt. U.S. Army, 1950-52. Mem. Am. mgmt. Assn., Des Plaines C. of C., Sigma Nu. Republican. Lodges: Rotary, Civitan. Avocations: jogging, history studies, ednl. travel, public speaking. Home: 8710 Ensley Ln Leawood KS 66206 Office: Liberty Distbrs Inc 2570 Devon Ave Des Plaines IL 60018

HOOVER, CHARLES M., appliance corporation executive; b. Okla., 1920. Ed., Okla. State U., 1942. Gen. sales mgr. Marquette Corp., 1942-60; with Roper Corp., Kankakee, Ill., 1960—; chmn. bd., chief exec. officer Roper Corp., 1967—, also dir.; chmn. bd., pres., chief exec. officer Roper Sales Corp.; pres. Eastern Products Corp. Office: Roper Corp 1906 W Court St Kankakee IL 60901 *

HOOVER, EARL REESE, savings association executive, lawyer; b. Dayton, Ohio, Nov. 19, 1904; s. John Jacob and Flora Maude (Brosier) H.; m. Alice Lorene Propst, Dec. 18, 1931; 1 child, Richard Wilson. A.B., Otterbein Coll., 1926, LL.D., 1955; J.D., Harvard U., 1929; LL.D., Salem Coll., 1961. Asst. atty. gen. State of Ohio, Columbus, 1930-31, 32; assoc. Mooney, Hahn, Loeser, Keough & Beam, Cleve., 1933-46; sole practice, Cleve., 1946-50; instr. bus. Fenn Coll. (now Cleve. State U.), 1950-51; law dir. Town of Aurora, Ohio, 1949-50; judge Common Pleas Ct. of Cuyahoga County, Cleve., 1951-69; sr. v.p. Shaker Savs. Assn., Shaker Heights, Ohio, 1969-80, mem. adv. bd. dirs., 1977-80; sr. v.p. Ohio Savs. Assn., 1980—; guest speaker numerous clubs, assns. Author: Cradle of Greatness: National and World Achievements of Ohio's Western Reserve, 1977. Bd. dirs. Cleve. Law Library, 1942-54, Citizens Bur., 1945-53; bd. dirs. Cleve. Roundtable of NCCJ, 1946-52, mem. exec. com., 1950-52, treas., 1950-52, chmn. food industry com Cleve. Health Council, 1942-46; trustee, mem. exec. com. Nationalities Services Ctr., 1953-56; mem. Cleve. Landmarks Commn., 1974-82; exec. bd. dirs. Greater Cleve. Bicentennial Commn., 1975-76; trustee Cleve. Masonic Library Assn., 1973-83; chmn. pub. relations com. Anti-Tv League of Cleve. and Cuyahoga County, Cleve., 1963-65; trustee Otterbein Coll., 1935-60, chmn. alumni relations and publicity com. of bd. trustees, 1945-60; mem. men's com. Cleve. Playhouse, 1950-57; bd. dirs. Neighborhood Settlement Assn., 1951-58; exec. bd. dirs. Greater Cleve. council Boy Scouts Am., 1956-59, chmn. council's Ct. of Honor, 1949-55, chmn. Newton D. Baker Dist., 1956-59, rep. to Nat. Council, 1957; bd. dir. Cleve. Ch. Fedn., 1955-58, Western Res. Hist. Soc., 1968—, Shaker Hist. Soc., 1969-81, v.p., 1970-71; bd. dirs. Religious Heritage of Am., 1958-59; v.p. Ripon Club (Rep. Club), 1949; mem. exec. Cleve. Civil War Round Table, 1969-70. Named Father of Hall of Fame Otterbein Coll., 1968; recipient Disting. Alumnus award Alumni Assn. of Otterbein Coll., 1970, award for Outstanding Service to Scouting Boy Scouts Am., Southwest Dist., 1972. Mem. Bar Assn. Greater Cleve., Cleve. Bar Assn. (rep. to Council of Dels. of Ohio State Bar Assn. 1937-38, chmn. coms.), Ohio State Bar Assn. (chmn. coms.), Cuyahoga County Bar Assn., Early Settlers Assn. of Western Res. (pres. 1971-72, bd. dirs. 1967—, mem. com. establishing Hall of Fame 1971), Harvard Alumni Assn. of Cleve., Harvard Law Sch. Alumni Assn., Otterbein Coll. Alumni Assn. (nat. pres.). Mem. United Ch. of Christ. Clubs: City (v.p. 1948, bd. dirs. 1946-48), Cleve. Shrine Luncheon (pres. 1959, bd. dirs. 1957-59), Cleve. Advt., Hundred Club (pres. 1938), Republic (bd. dirs. 1940-41, 44-48, pres. 1947). Lodges: Rotary (chmn. projects, emcee civic luncheons), Kiwanis of Cleve. (bd. dirs. Found. 1963-66, v.p. 1965-66), Masons, Shriners, Jesters. Office: Ohio Savs Assn 13109 Shaker Sq Cleveland OH 44120

HOOVER, HERBERT ARNOLD, chemical manufacturing company executive; b. Chgo., Jan. 28, 1930; s. Arnold Elton and Inez Charlotte (Kriegsman) H.; m. Jeanette Mary Saule, Dec. 30, 1955; children: Jennifer Mary, Christopher Arnold. BS in Chem., U. Ill., 1952; MBA, Northwestern U., 1955. With Procter & Gamble, Cin., 1956-64; div. gen. mgr. E.R. Carpenter Co., Richmond, Va., 1965-69; v.p. then pres. Acheson Industries, Port Huron, Mich., 1970—; bd. dirs. eleven subs of Acheson Industries; Mich. Bank PH. Served to capt. USMCR, 1952-54, Korea. Nat. Assn. Mfrs. (bd. dirs.), Mich. Mfrs. Assn. (bd. dirs.), Delta Chi, Beta Gamma Sigma. Republican. Episcopalian. Clubs: De Noailles (Marseilles, France); Moor Park Golf (London); Port Huron Golf. Home: 4 Anweiler Ln Port Huron MI 48060 Office: Acheson Industries PO Box 8 511 Fort St Port Huron MI 48060

HOOVER, LAWRENCE RICHARD, utility executive; b. Canton, Ohio, Apr. 10, 1935; s. Richard Seiler and Helen Elizabeth (Marietta) H.; m. Nancy Louise Weaver, Sept. 9, 1938; children: Charles Howard, Stephen Lawrence, Timothy Richard, William Frank. BSEE, MIT, 1957. Profl. engr., Ohio. Engr. Am. Elec. Power Service Corp., N.Y.C., 1957-1958; power engr. Ohio Power Co., Canton, 1958-66, rates dir., 1966-79, v.p., 1979—; bd. dirs. Am. Elec. Power Service Corp., Columbus. Chmn. Aultman Hospital, Canton. Republican. Mem. United Ch. of Christ. Avocations: tennis, skiing, woodworking. Office: Ohio Power Co PO Box 400 301 Cleveland Ave S W Canton OH 44701

HOOVER, LOLA MAE, communications company manager; b. Monticello, Ark., Apr. 1, 1947; d. Victor Arthur and Essie (Humphries) Piper; divorced; 1 child, Larry Wayne. With prodn. dept. AT&T, West Chgo., 1965-78, 1st level shop mgr., 1978-83, warehouse mgr., 1983-84, office mgr., 1984-86; with Mfg. Resource Planning project, 1986-87, leader Mfg. Resource Planning project, 1987—; devel. quality excellence program, 1986. Baptist. Home: 207 Briar Ln North Aurora IL 60542 Office: AT&T Info Systems 1700 Hawthorne Ln West West Chicago IL 60185

HOOVER, THOMAS JOHN, dentist; b. Woodstock, Ill., May 31, 1949; s. Doyne and Olive Elizebeth (Martinson) H.; m. Roberta Jean Kalina, Aug. 28, 1971; children: Matthew Thomas, Alexis Ann, Sarah Elizabeth. AA, U. Md., 1975; BS, No. Ill. U., 1979; DDS, U. Ill., Chgo., 1983. Assoc. Robert T. Sven DDS, Antioch, Ill., 1983-86; ptnr. N. Suburban Dental Assocs., Hoffman Estates, Ill., 1986—; clin. instr. U. Ill., Chgo., 1983-86; speaker in field, 1980—. Spl. advisor Crystal Lake (Ill.) Manor Park Dist., 1985-86, mem. adv. bd., 1986. Served to staff sgt. USAF, 1969-75. Mem. ADA, Ill. Dental Soc., Chgo. Dental Soc., Delta Sigma Delta (treas. 1982-83, asst. dep. 1984-86, Outstanding Sr. 1983), Phi Sigma, Am. Legion. Lodge: Masons. Avocations: walking, racquetball, swimming. Home: 4902 Drive-In Ln Crystal Lake IL 60014 Office: N Suburban Dental Assocs 1786 Moon Lake Blvd Hofmann Estates IL 60194

HOOVER, THOMAS WAYNE, security equipment company executive; b. Chgo., Dec. 27, 1936; s. Joseph Wayne and Eileen Cecelia H.; A.B. in Econs., Loyola U., Chgo., 1969; children—Thomas Wayne, Caroline M., David M., Matthew R., Mark J. Sales and mktg. ofcl. Belden Corp., Chgo., 1963-69; sales and mgmt. ofcl. Diebold, Inc., Chgo., 1969-75; pres. Ill. Nat. Safe Corp., River Forest, 1975—. Served with USAF, 1956-59. Mem. Nat. Ind. Bank Equipment Suppliers Assn. Republican. Roman Catholic. Club: Union League (Chgo.). Office: 7308 Central St River Forest IL 60305

HOPE, JERRY LEE, engineering manager; b. Hillsboro, Ill., Feb. 27, 1936; s. Paul E. and Lena M. (Ricker) H.; m. Jeanne M. Rice, June 20, 1959; children: Kristine L., Paul E. II. BSEE, Washington U., 1959. Application engr. Elliott Equipment Co., Jeannette, Pa., 1959-60; supt., chief engr. Swift & Co., Chgo., 1960-73; cons. engr. Globe Engr. Co., Chgo., 1973-83; corp. engrng. mgr. OSI Industries, Inc., Aurora, Ill., 1983—; cons. food processing, 1980—. Contbr. articles to profl. jours. Asst. dir. Emergency Services, St. Charles, Ill., 1972-80; deacon, elder Fox Valley Presbyn. Ch., Geneva, Ill., 1976—; bd. dirs. Norris Recreation Ctr., St. Charles, Ill., 1986—; mem. St. Charles Downtown Redevel. Citizen's Adv. Bd., 1987—. Mem. Am. Soc. Heating, Refrigerating, and Air-Conditioning Engrs., Inc., Inst. Food Technologists; St. Charles C. of C. (bd. dirs. 1972-74, Disting. Service award 1973), Nat. Rifle Assn. Club: St. Charles Sportsmen (bd. dirs. 1978-84). Lodges: Masons, Elks. Avocaitons: hunting, fishing, taxidermy. Office: OSI Industries Inc 1225 Corporate Blvd Aurora IL 60507-2018

HOPEN, DIANNE BROWN, French educator, educational administrator; b. St. Paul, Dec. 30, 1947; d. Maurice Leander and Ann Edith (Kell) Brown; m. Allan Nels Hopen, Aug. 16, 1969. B.S. in Edn., U. Minn., 1969, M.A. in Edn., 1980; cert. of participation Université Catholique d'Angers (France), 1978; student Université de Nantes (France), 1985. Teaching cert., Minn. Tchr. French and Am. history St. Paul Pub. Schs., 1969—; dean French Lang. Village Programs, Concordia Coll., Moorhead, Minn., 1972-85, dir. French Mini Programs, 1973-80, dir. French Tchr. Immersion Experiences, 1973-85, tchr./counselor Mpls. Pub. Schs. Lang. Camp, summers 1970, 71; group leader student trips to France, Intercultural Student Experiences, 1973—; French tchr. Twin City Inst. for Talented Youth, summers 1970, 71; Fulbright exchange tchr., France, 1985; mem. Com. of 11, Minn. Dept. Edn., 1975-78, trainer, 1978; guest French govt. Franco-Am. Ednl. Colloquium, Paris, 1986. Recipient 5 mini grants, St. Paul Pub. Schs., 1972-75, 87, Julius Braufman award for excellence in edn. Minn. Bus. Found., 1984, Percy Fearing award for devel. creative lang. materials, 1986; named Honor Roll

Tchr. of Excellence, Minn. Tchr. of Yr. Com., 1976. Mem. Am. Assn. Tchrs. of French (regional rep. to nat. exec. council for Mid-Central U.S. 1982—), Minn. Council on Teaching Fgn. Langs., Am. Council on Teaching Fgn. Langs. Author: Un Nouveau Jour., 1973; Leader's Handbook for Mini Programs, 1976; co-author: French Language Village Instruction Program, 1982; editor: Les Chansons du Lac du Bois (French songbook), 1982, Activity and Sport Instruction Program: Guidebook for Counselors, 1982, Medical Care Manual, 1983, Counselor Handbook, 1983, Dean's Handbook, 1983. Home: 250 Edgewood Ln West Saint Paul MN 55118 Office: Humboldt Secondary Complex 30 E Baker St Saint Paul MN 55107

HOPEN, HERBERT JOHN, horticulture educator; b. Madison, Wis., Jan. 7, 1934; s. Alfred and Amelia (Sveum) H.; m. Joanne C. Emmel, Sept. 12, 1959; children: Timothy, Rachel. BS, U. Wis., 1956, MS, 1959; PhD, Mich. State U., 1962. Asst. prof. U. Minn., Duluth, 1962-64; prof. U. Ill., Urbana, 1965-85, prof., acting head, 1983-85; prof. horticulture, chmn. dept. U. Wis., Madison, 1985—. Mem. AAAS, Am. Soc. for Hort. Sci., Weed Sci. Soc. Am., North Cen. Weed Control Conf., Sigma Xi, CAST. Avocations: reading, gardening. Office: U Wis Dept of Horticulture 1575 Linden Dr Madison WI 53706

HOPKINS, EDWARD DONALD, manufacturing executive; b. Little Rock, Apr. 16, 1937; s. Edward J. and Mildred Irene (Thompson) H.; m. Dawn Dee Fritz, June 12, 1965; children—Mark Edward, Scott Edward, Paige Noel. B.S., U.S. Air Force Acad., 1960; M. Aerospace Mgmt., U. So. Calif., 1967. Unit mgr. Gen. Electric Co., Cin., 1967-69; v.p. mktg. Tri-City Bldg., Cin., 1969-70; group v.p. Rochester Inst. Systems, N.Y., 1970-74; div. pres. Gould Inc., Phila., 1974-80; group v.p. Sherwin Williams Co., Cleve., 1980-83; pres., chief operating officer Interlake, Inc., Oak Brook, Ill., 1983—; bd. dirs. Sealed Power Corp. Served with USAF, 1956-67. Office: Interlake Inc 2015 Spring Rd Oak Brook IL 60521

HOPKINS, HAROLD A., JR., clergyman. Bishop, Episcopal Ch., Fargo, N.D. *

HOPKINS, JAMES MICHAEL, business administration educator; b. Lynch, Nebr., Jan. 15, 1946; s. Hollie Russell and Mary Beatrice (Chavala) H.; m. Cheryl Lee Timmerman, Mar. 29, 1970; children: Heath, Troy, Justin. BS in Acctg. with high distinction, Ferris State Coll., 1971; MA, U. Nebr., 1973. CPA, Iowa, Nebr. Supr. Fox & Co., Omaha, 1973-78; tax mgr. Williams & Co., Sioux City, Iowa, 1978-80, Postal Fin. Co., Sioux City, 1980-82; dir. fin. Sioux Honey Assn., Sioux City, 1982-86; asst. prof. Morningside Coll., Sioux City, 1986—. acting pres. Sioux City Tax Group, 1982-84; dir. Tax Research Conf., Sioux City. Treas. St. Mark Luth. Ch., Sioux City, 1980-81. Served to staff sgt. USAF, 1966-70. Mem. Am. Inst. CPA's, Iowa Soc. CPA's, Northwest Iowa CPA's, Estate Planning Council of Greater Siouxland (exec. com.). Lodge: Optimists (pres. 1979-80, v.p. 1984-85). Home: 2825 S Maple St Sioux City IA 51106 Office: Morningside Coll 110 Lincoln Ctr Sioux City IA 51106

HOPKINS, MALCOLM T., insurance company executive. Chmn. Drum Fin. Corp., Omaha. Office: Drum Fin Corp 105 S 17th St Omaha NE 68102 *

HOPKINS, MARTHA JEAN, production company executive; b. Chgo., Dec. 17, 1940; s. John L. and Idamae (Humiston) H.; B.A., Denison U., 1962; M.Ed., Nat. Coll. Edn., 1966, M.M. (MBA) Northwestern U., 1986. Staff editor Laidlaw Bros., River Forest, Ill., 1969-74; project dir. Ency. Brit. Ednl. Corp., Chgo., 1974-77, sr. producer, 1977-79, dir. prodn. planning and research, 1979-83, dir. planning, 1983—; presenter Nat. Council Geographic Edn.; guest speaker Columbia Coll.; cons. Sadlier Pubs. Mem. Assn. Supervision and Curriculum Devel., Internat. Reading Assn., Nat. Council Tchrs. English Nat. Council Social Studies, Nat. Council Tchrs. Math., AAAS, Nat. Sci. Tchrs. Assn., Am. Soc. Tng. and Devel., Chgo. Council Fgn. Relations. Clubs: Sierra, Canyon. Author/producer: Open Box: Ideas for Creative Expression, 1977; That's Fantastic!, 1978; That's Incredible!, 1979; A Likely Story (Learning Filmstrip of Yr. award, 1979), PRS (Design '75 award). Home: 4300 N Marine Dr Chicago IL 60613 Office: 425 N Michigan Ave Chicago IL 60611

HOPKINS, SHEILA MARIE, pharmacist; b. Mpls., Sept. 24, 1954; m. Larry I. Hopkins, Oct. 2, 1982. BS in Pharmacy, Drake U., 1976; MBA, Ill. Benedictine Coll., 1985. Registered pharmacist, Ill. Pharmacist St. Mary's Hosp., Galesburg, Ill., 1976-78; pharmacist Good Samaritan Hosp., Downers Grove, Ill., 1978-81, pharmacy supr., 1981-85, pharmacist, 1985—; skin care cons. Mary Kay Cosmetics, 1985—. Mem. exec. bd. United Meth. Women at Community United Meth. Ch. Mem. Am. Pharm. Assn., Am. Soc. Hosp. Pharmacists, No. Ill. Council of Hosp. Pharmacists, Lambda Kappa Sigma. Avocations: sports, family, outdoor activities, cooking, crafts.

HOPKINS, WILLARD GEORGE, health care administrator; b. Balt., Mar. 30, 1940; s. George Conrad and Laura Elizabeth (Elwell) H.; m. Valerie Jewell Hopkins, June 22, 1963; children—Michelle Marie, Tiffany Lynn. B.S. in Civil Engring., U. Md., 1963; M.H.A., Cornell U., 1969, M.B.A., 1969. Cons. Arthur Young & Co. San Francisco, 1969-74, health cons., practice dir., 1974-76, dir. health care, cons. practice dir., Washington, 1976-78; health cons., practice dir. Booz Allen & Hamilton, Washington 1977-79; exec. v.p. Scottsdale Meml. Hosp., Ariz., Scottsdale Meml. Health Service Co., 1979-83; exec. dir. Mednet/Euclid Clinic Found., Ohio, 1983-87; pres. Health Futures, Ariz., 1987—. Served with USPHS, 1963-69. Fellow Am. Coll. Hosp. Execs., Soc. Advanced Med. Systems; mem. N.Am. Soc. Corp. Planning, Am. Health Planning Assn., NAM, Assn. Univ. Programs in Health Adminstrn., Comprehensive Health Planning Assn. Contra Costa County (bd. dirs. 1973-77). Mem. editorial adv. bd. Am. Jour. Health Planning, 1976-79; contbr. articles to profl. jours. Presbyterian. Lodge: Rotary.

HOPP, NANCY SMITH, fund-raising executive, free-lance writer; b. Aurora, Ill., Nov. 1, 1943; d. C. Dudley and Margaret (McWethy) Smith; m. Edward Thompson Reid, July 19, 1963 (div. Feb. 1966); 1 child, Edward Thompson Jr.; m. James C. Hopp, Feb. 4, 1978. Cert., Chgo. Sch. Interior Design, 1965; BA in Social Scis., Aurora U., 1968, MS in Bus. Mgmt., 1982. Dir. pub. relations WLXT-TV, Aurora, 1969-70; bookstore mgr. Waubonsee Coll., Sugar Grove, Ill., 1970-79, dir. purchasing, 1979-85, dir. pub. relations, 1984-85; dir. devel. Assn. for Individual Devel., Aurora, 1985—; pres. office staff group Waubonsee Community Coll., 1974-75, site devel. and nature trail coordinator, 1974-85. Editor: Volunteers Make the Difference, 1982; author Pigeon Woods Cookbook; producer (film) Caring Counts; contbr. articles to profl. jours. Bd. dirs. Family Support Ctr., Aurora, 1984—; mem. adv. council Mercy Ctr. Health Care, Aurora, 1985—; moderator New Eng. Congl. Ch., Aurora, 1983; counselor Boy Scouts Am.; charter mem. bd. dirs. Aurora Community Coordinating Council, 1985-86; mem. grad. adv. bd. Aurora U., 1982—; mem. mktg. com. YWCA, 1986—; mem. Block Grant Working Com., Aurora, 1987—. Named Woman of the Day WAIT-AM radio, Chgo., 1974; recipient citation U.S. Dept. Health , Edn. and Welfare, 1969. Mem. Women in Mgmt. (bd. dirs., sec., treas., Nat. Charlotte Danstrom Woman of Achievement award 1984), Nat. Soc. Fund-raising Execs. (ethics com. Chgo. chpt. 1987—), Aurora Area Fundraisers, Exchange Club. Republican. Lodge: Altrusa. Avocations: water sports, auto racing, billiards, art, lit. Home: 175 S Western Ave Aurora IL 60506 Office: Assn Individual Devel 309 W New Indian Trail Ct Aurora IL 60506

HOPPERT, EARL W(ILLIAM), clergyman, educator, pastoral counselor; b. Duluth, Minn., Nov. 14, 1939; s. Glenn A. and Margaret J. (Server) H.; m. Candice N. Leuthold, Dec. 26, 1974; children—Lesley, Kelly. A.A. with honors, N.D. State Sch. Sci., 1959; B.A. magna cum laude, Yankton Coll., 1961; M.Div., Andover Newton Theol. Sch., 1965; postgrad. Trinity Coll., Glasgow U., 1965-68; D.Min. in Pastoral Care and Counseling, Christian Theol. Sem., Indpls., 1982. Ordained to ministry United Ch. Christ, 1965. Asst. pastor The Tron Ch., Balornock, Glasgow, Scotland, 1967-68; pastor 1st Congl. Ch., Eastlake, Colo., 1968-72, United Ch. Christ Westminster (Colo.), 1968-72; chaplain resident Methodist Hosp., Rochester, Minn., 1972-73; chaplain intern/resident St. Luke's Hosp., Milw., 1973-75; chaplain educator Central State Hosp., Indpls., 1975—, head dept. pastoral care, 1975—, founder, chmn. patient advocacy com., 1979-84; clin. pastoral edn. supr., mem. faculty Christian Theol. Sem., Indpls., 1976—, counselor Pastoral Counseling Services, 1980—. Leader Kick the Habit Clinics, Wis. Lung Assn., 1974-75. Turner fellow, 1965; Ind. Dept. Mental Health grantee, 1976-82; recipient numerous scholarships; recipient Dist. Service award DeMolay. Mem. Assn. Clin. Pastoral Edn. (cert. chaplain supr.; life mem.), Am. Assn. Marriage and Family Therapy (clin.), Am. Assn. Pastoral Counselors (cert.), Council Health and Human Services Ministries (assoc.), Internat. Preview Soc. Lodge: Masons. Contbr. to profl. publs. Home: 9001 Caminito Ct Indianapolis IN 46234 Office: 3000 W Washington St Indianapolis IN 46222

HOPPES, GARY JON, vocational educator; b. Davenport, Iowa, Oct. 9, 1946; s. James William and Viola Pearl (Johnson) H.; B.A. in Indsl. Edn., U. No. Iowa, 1973; M.S. in Indsl. Vocat./Tech. Edn., Iowa State U., 1976. Instr., coordinator vocat. programs Lakenheath Am. High Sch., RAF Lakenheath, Eng., 1973-74; tech. writer, tng. dept. Cherry Burrell Co., Cedar Rapids, Iowa, 1974-75; grad. research asst., spl. needs Iowa State U., 1975; program coordinator Alternative Edn. Ctr., Marion (Iowa) Ind. Sch., 1976-78; instr., coordinator collision repair program Kirkwood Community Coll., 1978-86; assoc. dean., Dodge City (Kans.) Community Coll., 1986—; vocat. cons. to trade and indsl. programs. Served with USN, 1965-69; Vietnam. Decorated service medal with 5 Bronze Stars, Navy Achievement medal; recipient Order of Arrow award Boy Scouts Am., 1961, Life Scout award, 1963. Mem. Council Vocat. Edn., Am. Vocat. Assn., Iowa Vocat. Assn., Nat. Assn. Indsl. and Tech. Tchr. Educators, Epsilon Pi Tau. Lutheran. Club: Vocat. Indsl. Clubs Am. Author: Working Papers Special Needs Population, 1976; The Administrator's Role in Establishing and Maintaining A Vocational Cooperative Education Program, 1976; Photojournalism, A Guide, 1978. Home: Dodge City Community Coll 2501 N 14th Ave Dodge City KS 67801 Office: 6301 Kirkwood Blvd Linn Hall 113 Cedar Rapids IA 52406

HOPPIN, FREDERIC BARRY, realtor; b. Pawnee, Ill., Nov. 1, 1914; s. Frank Horace and Maude Elizabeth (Sloman) H.; m. Ruth Clara Hoffman, Aug. 14, 1943. BS, U. Ill., 1941. Assoc. supr. Farm Security Adminstrn., Watseka, Ill., 1941-42; supr. Farmer Home Adminstrn., Harrisburg, Ill., 1946-47; county farm advisor Fed. Extension, McLeansboro, Ill., 1947-49, Lincoln, Ill., 1949-56; real estate broker Lincoln, 1956—. Mem. U. Alumni Assn. (life, Loyalty award), Coll. Agriculture Alumni Assn. (past pres.), various other organizations affiliated with U. Ill., Ill. Shorthorn Breeders Assn., Logan County Bd. Realtors (charter pres.), Nat. Assn. Realtors, Ill. Nat. Inst. Farm and Land Brokers, Ill. Assn. Realtors (legis. com. mem.), Ill. Polled Shorthorn Assn. Republican. Methodist. Lodge: Rotary. Home: 1401 N Union Lincoln IL 62656 Office: 408 Pulaski Lincoln IL 62656

HOPPING, EARLE ALBERT, executive placement counselor; b. Glen Cove, N.Y., July 6, 1943; s. Earle Albert and Mary Rita (McLaughlin) H.; m. Judith Ann Streit, Nov. 15, 1964 (div. 1974); m. Doreen Joyce Moore, May 31, 1975; children—Michael, Billi, Lori, Lucy, Kathleen, Molly, Todd. B.S. in Elec. Engring., Milw. Sch. Engring., 1969; M.B.A., N.D. State U., 1983. fed. acct. rep. Control Data Corp., Washington, 1969-72; field rep. Neca, Chgo., 1972; asst. mgr., tng. dir. Dakotas chpt., Neca, Fargo, N.D., 1972-85; pres. Dunhill of Fargo, Inc., N.D., 1985—; cons. in field. Mem. State Bd. Adv. Com. for Vocat. Edn., N.D., 1975-78; mem. Job Service Adv. Com., N.D., 1980-83. Served with USN, 1960-64. Recipient Spl. Recognition award U.S. Dept. Labor, 1977. Mem. IEEE, Illuminating Engring. Soc. (pres. Red River chpt. 1975-76), N.D. Safety Council (pres. 1978-80, chmn. bd. dirs. 1980-81), Am. Legion. Republican. Lutheran. Lodges: Elks, Eagles, Optimist. Avocations: golf; bowling; computers. Home: 1215 S 15th St Moorhead MN 56560 Office: Dunhill of Fargo Inc 51 Broadway Suite 604 Fargo ND 58102

HOPSON, MICHAEL WILLIAM, bank examiner; b. Corydon, Iowa, Sept. 8, 1959; s. Kenneth James Hopson and Alberta Kathryn (Johnson) Oliver; m. Karen Marlene Knust, Aug. 22, 1981. BA, Simpson Coll., 1982. Bank examiner I to IV Iowa Div. Banking, Des Moines, 1982-86, bank exam. analyst, 1986—. Simpson Coll. scholar, Indianola, Iowa, 1978-82; recipient Bizad Club award, Soc. for Advancement of Mgmt., Simpson Coll., 1982. Mem. Lakewood Village Assn. (bd. dirs. 1987—), Lambda Chi Alpha Alumni Assn. (bd. dirs. 1986—, Housing Corp. 1986). Democrat. Baptist. Avocations: golf, history, reading. Home: 4818 Lakewood Dr Norwalk IA 50211 Office: IA Div Banking 530 Liberty Bldg 418 6th Ave Des Moines IA 50309

HORECKA, RICHARD ROBERT, physician; b. Owatonna, Minn., Dec. 30, 1952; s. Robert Gene and Donna Mae (Johnson) H.; m. Anita Lorraine Wellman, Aug. 4, 1984. BA, Concordia Coll., 1975; MD, U. Minn., 1980. Diplomate Am. Bd. Family Physicians. Resident in family practice U. Minn. Dept. Family Practice, Mpls., 1980-83; practice medicine specializing in family practice Affiliated Med. Ctrs., Benson, Minn., 1983—; clin. instr. Dept. Family Practice U. Minn., Mpls., 1986—; bd. rep. Affiliated Med. Ctrs., Willmar, Minn., 1986—. Pres. Benson area C. of C., 1986; adv. human services S.W. Minn. Initiative Fund, Granite Falls, 1986-87; mem. region 6W Benson Econ. Devel. Commn., 1985—. Recipient Teaching award Parke-Davis, Inc., 1983. Fellow Am. Acad. Family Physicians; mem. Minn. Acad. Family Physicians (resident dir.), Mid-Minn. Med. Soc. (pres. 1987—), Ramsey County Med. Soc. (bd. dirs. 1982-83), AMA, Minn. Med. Soc., Jaycees (v.p. Benson chpt. 1984-85). Lutheran. Lodge: Kiwanis (pres. Benson club 1986-87). Avocations: fishing, travel, reading, racquetball, gardening. Home: 320 11th St S Benson MN 56215 Office: Benson Med Ctr 1805 Wisconsin Ave Benson MN 56215

HOREVITZ, RICHARD PAUL, psychologist; b. Chgo., May 26, 1945; s. Irving Paul and Betty Joy (Kaplan) H.; m. Joan Peters, June 23, 1968 (div. Nov. 1974); m. Alice Victoria Blacksin, Sept. 10, 1980; children: Elizabeth, Alexandra; stepchildren: Emilie, Raphael. BA, U. Mich., 1967; MA, U. Chgo., 1970; PhD, Union Grad. Sch., 1976. Lic. psychologist, Ohio; Diplomate Am. Bd. Psychol. Hypnosis. Asst. prof. sociology Rosary Coll., River Forest, Ill., 1970-71; dir. edn., research Inst. Psychotherapy, Chgo., 1973-76; prof. Govs. State U., Park Forest, Ill., 1977-78; assoc. dir. Associated Mental Health Services, Chgo., 1980—; clin. assoc. dept. psychology U. Ill., Chgo., 1984—. Contbr. articles to profl. jours. Woodrow Wilson fellow, 1967-68, U. Chgo. fellow, 1968-69, Kent-Danforth Found. fellow. Fellow Am. Orthopsychiat. Assn.; mem. Am. Psychol. Assn. (exec. com. 1982-86), AAAS, Soc. Clin. and Exptl. Hypnosis (exec. com. Div. 30 1980—), Soc. Psychotherapy Research, Internat. Soc. Study Multiple Personalities. Home: 861 Prospect Ave Winnetka IL 60093 Office: Assn Mental Health Services 230 N Michigan Ave 3200 Chicago IL 60601

HORGAN, CORNELIUS OLIVER, applied mechanics and mathematics educator; b. Cork, Ireland, May 16, 1944; m. Myra O'Callaghan; children: Olivia, David. BS, Univ. Coll., Cork, 1964, MS, 1965; PhD, Calif. Inst. Tech., 1970; DSc, Nat. U. Ireland, Dublin, 1983. Lectr. U. Mich., Ann Arbor, 1970-72; sr. research assoc. U. East Anglia, Norwich, U.K., 1972-74; assoc. prof. U. Houston, 1974-78; prof. applied mechanics and math. Mich. State U., East Lansing, 1978—; vis. prof. Northwestern U., Evanston, 1977-78, Calif. Inst. Tech., Pasadena, 1984-85. Contbr. over 65 publis. in field of theoretical mechanics and applied math. Fellow Am. Acad. Mechanics; mem. ASME (chmn. tech. com. 1981—), Am. Math. Soc., Soc. Engring. Sci., Soc. for Indsl. and Applied Math. Home: 1646 Boulevard Dr Okemos MI 48864 Office: Mich State U East Lansing MI 48824

HORISBERGER, DON HANS, musician; b. Millersburg, Ohio, Mar. 2, 1951; s. Hans and Jeanette (Grossniklaus) H. MusB, Capital U., 1973; MusM, Northwestern U., 1974, MusD, 1985. Dir. music 1st Presbyn. Ch., Waukegan, Ill., 1976—; sect. leader Chgo. Symphony Chorus, 1977—; dir. Waukegan Symphony Chorus, 1979—; lectr. in music Capital U., Columbus, Ohio, 1974-75; asst. to lang. coach Chgo. Symphony Chorus, 1978—. Fulbright-Hayes grantee 1975. Mem. Am. Choral Dirs. Assn., Assn. Profl. Vocal Ensembles. Home and Office: 5455 N Sheridan Rd #3601 Chicago IL 60640

HORKY, REGINALD PATRICK, jewelery store owner; b. Flint, Mich., July 18, 1952; s. Stanley Joseph and Helen Mary (Gasparovic) H.; m. Melinda Ellen Mizikow, April 18, 1977; children: Reginald, Elisa. Cert. diamond grading. Goldsmith Diamond Exchange, Flint, 1975-77; owner R. Horky Co., Flint, 1977-80, Swartz Creek, Mich., 1980-83; owner Reginalds Fine Jewelry, Swartz Creek, 1983-85, Elegance in Diamonds, Grand Blanc, Mich., 1985—; apprenticed to Paul Marciszewski, M. Paul & Sons, Flint, 1971—, Jim Alphin, Jim Alphin Mfg. Jeweler, Inc., Dallas, 1975—. Patentee methods of mfg. Recipient cert. appreciation USMCR, 1985, plaque of appreciation Boy Scouts Am., 1986. Mem. Left Bank Art Gallery. Republican. Roman Catholic. Avocations: painting, sclupture, electronics, physics reading. Office: Elegance in Diamonds 12235 S Saginaw St Grand Blanc MI 48439

HORMAN, JAMES ARLAN, accountant; b. La Crosse, Wis., Mar. 22, 1942. BS, U. Wis., 1965, BBA, 1976. CPA, Wis. Chemist, mgr. Olin Corp., Baraboo, Wis., 1966-75; acct. Fishkin, Dippel and McNevin, Baraboo, 1976-81; officer Fishkin, Dippel and McNevin, S.C., Baraboo, 1982—. Mem. Am. Inst. CPA's, Wis. Inst. CPA's, Accts. Computer Users Tech. Exchange. Republican. Home: 1026 6th St Baraboo WI 53913 Office: Fishkin Dippel & McNevin SC PO Box 150 Baraboo WI 53913

HORMOZI, HORMOZ, chemical engineer; b. Kermanshah, Iran, July 19, 1936; came to U.S., 1959; s. Abbass and Moneer (Golestani) H.; m. Nahid Afshar, Dec. 23, 1976; 1 child, Shirin Moneer. B.S. in Chem. Engring., Ariz. State U., 1964; M.B.A., Mankato State U., 1979. Registered profl. engr., Tex. Plant Low density polyeth supr. Dow Chem. Co., Freeport, Tex., 1964-66, engr., 1966-70; low density polyeth supt. U.S.I. Chem. Co., Morris, Ill., 1970-75, plant mgr., Mankato, Minn., 1975-79, Streamwood, Ill., 1979—. bd. dirs. Suburban Bank, Bartlett, Ill. Active Heart Fund, 1968; bd. dirs. Streamwood chpt. Am. Cancer Soc., 1981—; active mem. People to People Internat., 1962—; Econ. Devel. Commn., Streamwood, 1986—. Recipient Mayor's award Lake Jackson, 1969. Mem. Soc. Plastics Engrs. (dir. 1980—), Streamwood C. of C. (dir. 1981—). Baha'i. Home: 1010 Douglas Rd Elgin IL 60120 Office: 601 E Lake St Streamwood IL 60107

HORN, GARY ALLEN, pharmacist; b. Hamilton, Ohio, July 29, 1949; s. Louise M. Horn; m. Jan Louise Thieman, May 19, 1973 (div. Sept. 1976); 1 child, Jason Roderick; m. Lucinda Anne McKamey, Apr. 29, 1978; children: Stephanie Leigh, Travis Jeremy. BS, Ind. U., 1973, Butler U., 1976. Pharmacist, mgr. C&E Drugs, Inc., Indpls., 1976-77; staff pharmacist Tipton County (Ind.) Meml. Hosp., 1977-78, dir. pharmacy, 1978—. Mem. Ind. Pharm. Assn., Ind. Soc Hosp. Parmacists, Am. Soc. Hosp. Pharmacists. Roman Catholic. Club: Runners Forum (Indpls.). Lodge: KC. Avocations: running, gardening, collecting baseball cards, bowling, snowmobiling. Home: PO Box 5003 Zionsville IN 46077 Office: Tipton County Meml Hosp 1000 S Main St Tipton IN 46072

HORN, JOHN BENTON, insurance executive; b. Columbus, Ohio, Oct. 24, 1927; s. John G. Horn and Lillian Louise (Roberts) Story; m. Marie Helen McDonough, Aug. 23, 1948; children: Christine D., Karen C., Myra J. Cert. in acctg., Bliss Coll., 1949. CPCU. V.p. underwriting Grange Mutual Cos., Columbus, 1972-74, v.p. ins. ops., 1974-79, v.p. corp. programs, 1979-84, sec., dir. corp. facilities, 1984—. Treas. Cen. Buying Ctr. and Franklinton Food Pantry, Columbus, 1984-85; pres. Cen. Ohio Camp Fire Council, Inc., 1986—. Served with U.S. Army, 1946-47, PTO. Mem. Soc. Charter Propery and Casualty Underwriters, Nat. Assn. Mut. Ins. Cos. (merit award 1986), Am. Inst. CPCU (Profl. Leadership Scroll 1983). Republican. Presbyterian. Lodges: Kiwanis (pres. 1980-81), Moose. Club: Oakhurst Country. Avocations: golf, bowling. Home: 12397 Center Dr Orient OH 43146 Office: Grange Mut Cos 650 S Front St Columbus OH 43206

HORN, WILLIAM KEELEY, accountant; b. Hibbing, Minn., Feb. 18, 1955; s. Walter Edwin Jr. and Lois Ann (Hanson) H.; m. Randi Marie Roisum, Sept. 20, 1980; children: Kirsten Leigh, David Kenneth. BA, Gustavus Adolphus Coll., 1977. CPA, Minn. Staff tax acct. McGladrey, Hendrickson & Pullen, Mpls., 1977-81; ptnr. McGladrey, Hendrickson & Pullen, Bloomington, Minn., 1984—; tax mgr. Arthur Young & Co., Mpls., 1981-84. Mem. Am. INst. CPA's, Minn. SOc. CPA's (chmn. tax conf. com. 1986—), Twin West C. of C., Bloomington C. of C. Republican. Lutheran. Club: Flagship Athletic (Eden Prairie, MInn.). Lodge: Masons. Avocations: golf, fishing, sailing. Office: McGladrey Hendrickson & Pullen 3600 W 80th St #500 Bloomington MN 55431

HORNBACK, DAVID IRA, data processing executive; b. Noblesville, Ind., Nov. 19, 1945; s. Arthur Raymond and Helen Edel (Wilson) H.; m. Charlotte Dale Kline, May 4, 1974; children: Michael David, Angela Michelle. BS in Indsl. Mgmt., Purdue U., 1969. Systems analyst Procter & Gamble, Cin., 1969, sr. systems analyst, 1971-73, 1981-85; mgr. data processing Hewitt Soap Co., Dayton, Ohio, 1973-81; dir. data processing Triad-Utrad div. Magnetek Corp., Huntington, Ind., 1985—, Jefferson Electric div. Magnetek Corp., Downers Grove, Ill., 1985—. Chmn. christian life bd. First Ch. of Nazarene, Loveland, Ohio, 1982-85. Servedwith U.S. Army, 1969-71. Decorated Bronze Star. Republican. Avocations: gardening, fishing. Home: 554 E 300 N Huntington IN 46750 Office: Triad-Utrad 1124 E Franklin St Huntington IN 46750

HORNBY, GREGORY PAUL, hazardous waste disposal and oil reclamation executive; b. Lincoln Park, Mich., Apr. 25, 1959; s. Carl William and Geraldine Francis (Williams) H.; m. Patricia Ann Tarwacki, Aug. 17, 1985; 1 child, Gregory Carl. BBA with distinction, U. Mich., 1981. Sr. fin. analyst Fisher Body div. Gen. Motors Corp., Detroit, 1981-83; gen. mgr., chief fin. officer Environ. Waste Control, Inc., Inkster, Mich., 1983—. Mem. Liquid Indsl. Control Assn. (officer, bd. dirs.), U. Mich. Alumni Assn. Republican. Roman Catholic. Club: Grosse Ile Golf and Country, Detroit Athletic. Avocations: golf, weightlifting, photography, boating. Home: 14344 Heritage Riverview MI 48192 Office: Environ Waste Control Inc 27140 Princeton Ave Inkster MI 48141

HORNE, PAUL DENNIS, protection services official; b. Toledo, Nov. 22, 1950; s. Elmer Chadbourne and Rita Cecelia (Mauter) H.; m. Jeanne Ann Junkins, Aug.8, 1975; 1 child, Matthew Joseph. AS, Owens Tech. COll., 1978; BS, U. Toledo, 1980; grad., Harvard Trade Union Program, 1987. Fire fighter Toledo Fire Div., 1973-80, lt., 1980—. Mem. steering com. City of Toledo Tax Levy, 1982—. Served to sgt. USAF, 1968-72, Vietnam. Mem. Internat. Assn. Firefighters, Ohio Assn. Profl. Fire Fighters (workers compensation and pension coordinator 1983-85), Toledo Fire Fighters Union (workers compensation rep. local 92 1974-80, sec. 1978-80, pres. 1982—), AFL-CIO, U. Toledo Alumni Assn., Cen. Cath. Alumni Assn., Vietnam Vets. of Am. Avocations: guitar, bicycling, cross country skiing, reading. Home: 1520 Creekwood Ln Toledo OH 43614 Office: Toledo Fire Fighters 714 Washington Toledo OH 43624

HORNE, TIMOTHY J., lawyer; b. Toledo, Sept. 23, 1949; s. Elmer Chadbourn and Rita Cecelia (Mauter) H.; m. Pamela Rae Runion, Nov. 16, 1973; children: Devon Rae, Erin Rebecca. BA, Coll. Wooster, 1971; MS in Edn., U. Toledo, 1975, JD, 1985. Bar: Ohio 1985, Mich. 1986. Tchr., coach Sylvania (Ohio) City Schs., 1976-85; assoc. Gallon, Kalniz & Iorio Co., L.P.A., Toledo, 1985—. Editor Toledo U. Law Rev., 1984-85. Mem. ABA, Am. Trial Lawyers Assn., Mich. Bar Assn., Order of Coif, Ohio Bar Assn., Phi Kappa Phi. Republican. Roman Catholic. Avocations: weight lifting, bicycling, reading. Home: 2251 Middlesex Dr Toledo OH 43606 Office: Gallon Kalniz & Iorio Co LPA 5550 W Central Toledo OH 43615

HORNER, CHARLES DALLAS, lawyer; b. Kansas City, Mo., Mar. 21, 1939; s. Bryan Ridgway and Alma Louise (Dallas) H.; m. Mary Katherine Hall, Aug. 18, 1962; children: Charles Walton, Katherine Hall, Stephen Bryan. BA, Princeton U., 1961; JD, U. Mich., 1964. Bar: Mo. 1964, Kans. 1985. Assoc. atty. Watson, Ess, Marshall & Engass, Kansas City, 1964-69; ptnr. Hillix, Brewer, Hoffhaus, Whittaker & Horner, Kansas City, 1969—, mng. ptnr., 1985—; bd. dirs., exec. com. St. Luke's Mo. Hosp., Kansas City, 1979—, chmn. Mid-Am. Heart Inst., 1985—; sec. Wyandotte Garage Corp., Kansas City, 1983—; bd. dirs. Mid-Am. Healthnet, Inc., Kansas City. Author: Real Estate Tax Shelters, 1982. Legal advisor Downtown Council, Kansas City, 1982—; treas. Audrey Langworthy Kans. Senate campaign, 1984; chmn. tax policy com. Johnson County (Kans.) Rep. Party, 1984—; vestry, chancellor St. Andrews Episcopal Ch., Kansas City, 1968-84. Mem. ABA (real property and trusts sect.), Mo. Bar Assn., Lawyers Assn. Kansas City, Kansas City Bar Assn. Club: Kansas City Country (Johnson County); Univ., Mercury (bd. dirs., v.p., pres.)(Kansas City). Lodge: Rotary (pres.

Kansas City chpt.). Avocations: tennis, sailing, amateur radio. Home: 6143 Reinhardt Dr Shawnee Mission KS 66205 Office: Hillix Brewer Hoffhaus Wittaker & Horner 911 Main Suite 2700 PO Box 13367 Kansas City MO 64199

HORNG, MENG YANG, obstetrician, gynecologist; b. Taiwan, Republic of China, Jan. 3, 1940; came to U.S., 1969; s. Kong T. and Ching S. (Kuo) H.; m. Linda Tung Horng, Oct. 6, 1966; children: Wendy, Aaron. MD, Kaohsiung Med. Coll., Taiwan, 1965. Intern Mt. Carmel Mercy Hosp., Detroit, 1969-70, resident, 1970-73; resident Providence Hosp., Southfield, Mich., 1972-73; practice medicine specializing in ob-gyn Bloomington, Ill., 1974—; chief ob-gyn St. Joseph Hosp. Med. Ctr., Bloomington, 1978-79, 82-83, 86—, chief med. staff, 1983-84. Fellow Am. Assn. Gynecol. Laparoscopists, Am. Coll. Ob-Gyn; mem. AMA, Ill. Med. Soc., McLean County Med. Soc. Republican. Presbyterian. Lodge: Rotary. Home: 5 Northcrest Ct Bloomington IL 61701 Office: 107 N Regency Dr Bloomington IL 61701

HORNICKEL, ROBIN RAE, accountant; b. Corydon, Ind., Oct. 21, 1958; d. Ronald Evans and Alice Mae (Winders) H. BS, Ball State U., 1981. CPA, Ind. Staff acct. Walker & Weber, Indpls., 1981-86; controller Eaton & Lauth Cos., Inc., Indpls., 1986—. Mem. Am. Inst. CPA's, Ind. Soc. CPA's. Club: YMCA. Avocations: running, racquetball, weightlifting, aerobics.

HORNING, WILLIAM LESLIE, school counselor; b. Crestline, Ohio, July 12, 1938; s. Paul A. and Magdalene A. (Schaub) H.; m. Marilyn Joan Armstrong, Aug. 9, 1958; children: Linda, Michael, Joseph, Anthony, Monica, Lisa. BS, Ohio State U., 1973; MEd, Bowling Green State U., 1977, diploma Ednl. Specialist, 1982. Ordained deacon Roman Cath. Ch., 1974. Various managerial positions Penn-Cen. R. R., Chgo., 1956-70; tchr. Sacred Heart Sch., Bethlehem, Ohio, 1970-72; principal, tchr. Crestline (Ohio) Schs., 1973-86, guidance counselor, 1986—; adjunct prof. Ashland (Ohio) Coll., 1986-87; instr. Diaconate Office, Toledo, 1986-87. Mem. Crawford County Needs Assessment Bd., 1985, Crestline Police Dept. Community Adv. Bd., 1986-87, Crawford County Youth Services Bd., 1987. Named Outstanding Tchr., 1974, 75; recipient Jennings scholarship Martha Jennings Found., 1976. Mem. Ohio Assn. Elem. Sch. Adminstrs. (zone 4 legis. rep. 1985-86), Crestline Edn. Assn. (Outstanding Adminstr. 1982), St. Vincent DePaull Soc., Crestline Ministerial Assn., Phi Delta Kappa. Democrat. Roman Catholic. Lodges: Knights of Columbus (Family of the Month 1983, local sec.), Lions (local v.p. 1985-87, dist. chaplain). Avocations: jogging, reading, travelling. Home: RD #2 Box 220 Crestline OH 44827 Office: Crestline Bd Edn 215 N Cocumbus St Crestline OH 44827

HORNSBY, ELIZABETH CAMILLE, insurance company executive; b. Detroit, July 26, 1954; d. J. Eugene and Irene (Sanford) Kangas; children: Caelan Mary, Christopher Johnson. BS, Old Dominion U., 1975. Agt. pres.'s council N.Y. Life Ins. Co., Skokie, Ill., 1984-86, mgr. sales, 1986—. Mem. Nat. Assn. Life Underwriters, Gen. Agy. Mgrs. Assn., N.Y. Life Women's Network. Roman Catholic. Office: NY Life Ins Co 8831 Gross Pointe Rd Skokie IL 60077

HOROWITZ, FRED L., dentist, educator, consultant; b. Chgo., June 10, 1954; s. Jacob and Celia (Morgenstern) H. BA, Washington U., St. Louis, 1976, DMD, 1979; cert. of residency, Sinai Hosp. Detroit, 1980. Practice dentistry Chgo., 1981—; cons. Sinai Hosp. Detroit, 1980—; chief dental cons. Charter Barclay Hosp., Chgo., 1985—; mem. med. teaching staff Michael Reese Hosp., Chgo., 1984—, Ravenswood Hosp., Chgo., 1983—; mem. instl. rev. bd. Ravenswood Health Care Corp., Chgo., 1985—; bd. dirs. Plan Adminstrs. Ill., Inc., corp. dental dir. First Commonwealth Dental Care, Inc. Contbr. articles to Ravenswood Hosp. publs. Mem. Am. Assn. Hosp. Dentists, Acad. Gen. Dentistry, Alpha Omega (leadership award 1979). Office: Ravenswood Health Care Ctr 4211 N Cicero Chicago IL 60641

HOROWITZ, STEVEN LESLIE, physician; b. Bklyn., June 10, 1950; s. Jack M. and Lois Jean (Luskin) H.; m. Sandra Willner, Aug. 25, 1974; children: Jeanne, David. BA, U. Pa., 1971; MD, Jefferson Med. Coll., 1975. Diplomate Am. Bd. Otolaryngology. Resident in gen. surgery Hahnemann Hosp., Phila., 1975-76; resident in otolaryngology U. Ill. Hosp., Chgo., 1976-79; practice medicine with multispecialty group Suburban Heights Med. Ctr., Chicago Heights, Ill., 1979—; staff St. James Hosp., Chicago Heights, 1979—. Contbr. articles to profl. jours. Bd. dirs. South Suburban Jewish Community Ctr., 1980-85, Congregation Am Echad, 1981—, South Suburban Community Day Sch., 1982—. Fellow ACS (admissions com. 1981), Am. Acad. Otolaryngology. Clubs: Rolls Royce Owners, Pierce-Arrow Soc., Classic Car Of Am., Lincoln Continental Owners. Lodge: B'nai B'rith. Avocations: radio control airplanes, oil painting, sculpting, antique automobiles, tennis. Office: Suburban Heights Med Ctr 333 Dixie Hwy Chicago Heights IL 60411

HORROCKS, LLOYD ALLEN, physiological chemistry educator, treasurer; b. Cin., July 13, 1932; s. Robert and Martha (Keeler) H.; m. Marjorie Lee Werstler, June 30, 1956; children: Richard A., Rebecca A. Horrocks Haxe. BA in Chemistry with honors, Ohio Wesleyan U., 1953; MS in Physiol. Chemistry, Ohio State U., 1955, PhD in Physiol. Chemistry, 1960. Research assoc. neurochemistry lab. Cleve. Psychiat. Inst., 1960-68; sr. clin. instr. neurosurgery Case Western Res. U., Cleve., 1965-66; from asst. prof to prof. physiol. chemistry Ohio State U., 1968—; mem. project rev. com. NIH Neurol. Disorders Program, 1981-85; vis. prof. NATO, Nat. Research Council of Italy, 1986; chmn. numerous coms. on profl., ednl., adminstrv., and acad. policies; lectr. on biochemistry Ohio State U. Editor: (with others) Phospholipids in the Nervous System, Volume I: Metabolism, 1982, Volume II: Physiological Roles, 1985, Phospholipid Research and the Nervous System: Biochemical and Molecular Pharmacology, 1986; (jour.) Neurochem. Pathology, 1982—; assoc. editor Lipids, 1985-87; mem. editorial bd. Jour. Lipid Research, 1976-83; mem. editorial bd. Jour. Neurochemistry, 1978-85, advisory bd., 1976-77. Served to lt. USAF, 1955-58. Grantee, NIH, 1961—, Spinal Cord Research Found., 1986-87; NIH spl. fellow, 1964; Macy Faculty scholar U. Louis Pasteur, 1974;. Mem. Internat. Soc. for Neurochemistry (mem. spl. coms. 1978-79, 79-81, 85-87, co-organizer Satellite Symposia, 1980-81, 82-83, 84-85, mem. Council 1981-85), Internat. Soc. for Devel. Neurosci., European Soc. for Neurochemistry, AAAS, AAUP, Am. Soc. Biol. Chemists, Am. Soc. for Neurochemistry (local chmn. 1973, program chmn. 1987—), Soc. for Neurosci. (cen. Ohio chpt. sec., treas. 1972-73, chmn. 1973-74, 76-78), Biochem. Soc., Omicron Delta Kappa, Phi Lambda Upsilon, Sigma Xi. Home: 328 W 6th Ave Columbus OH 43201 Office: Ohio State U 1645 Neil Ave Hamilton Hall #214 Columbus OH 43210

HORSEFIELD, DAVID REID, environmental engineer; b. Oak Park, Ill., Jan. 24, 1931; s. Raymond Ernest and Ellen (Crawford) H.; m. Rigmor Wienke, Feb. 16, 1957; children—Steven Reid, Robert David; m. 2 Joan Betty Weber, Nov. 11, 1972. B.S. in Civil Engring., U. Mass., 1952; M.S. in San. Engring., U. Mich., 1956. Registered profl. engr., N.Y., 18 other states. Engr., Camp Dresser & McKee, Boston, 1960-69, v.p., 1970-72, dir., sr. v.p., ptnr., Boston and Milw., 1972-82, sr. tech. cons., Milw., 1982—; cons. environ. engr., Mequon, Wis., 1982—; dir. Warzyn Engring., Inc., Madison, Wis. Vice pres.-ch. council, 1978-83; mem. Luther Manor Aux., 1983-86. Served to 1st lt. USAF, 1952-54; Korea. Recipient Service award Water Pollution Control Fedn., 1981; U. Mass. Engring. Alumni Assn. award, 1976; san. sect. award Boston Soc. Civil Engrs., 1969, Desmond Fitzgerald award, 1969. Fellow ASCE; mem. Am. Acad. Environ. Engrs. (trustee 1976-78), Water Pollution Control Fedn. (dir. 1981-83), Am. Water Works Assn., Am. Cons. Engrs. Council (peer reviewer). Republican. Lutheran. Contbr. articles to profl. jours.; developed total solids mgmt. plan for Milw. Met. Sewerage Dist., 1978.

HORSLEY, JACK EVERETT, lawyer, author; b. Sioux City, Iowa, Dec. 12, 1915; s. Charles E. and Edith V. (Timms) H.; m. Sallie Kelley, June 12, 1939 (dec.); children: Pamela, Charles Edward; m. Bertha J. Newland, Feb. 24, 1950 (dec.); m. Mary Jane Moran, Jan. 20, 1973; 1 child, Sharon. AB, U. Ill., 1937, JD, 1939. Bar: Ill. 1939. With Craig & Craig, Mattoon, Ill., 1939—, sr. counsel; vice chmn., bd. dirs. Cen. Nat. Bank, 1976—, Harlan Moore Heart Research Found., 1968—; mem. lawyers adv. council U. Ill. Law Forum, 1960-63; lectr. Practising Law Inst., N.Y.C., 1967-73, Ct. Practice Inst., Chgo., 1974—, U. Mich. Coll. Law Inst. Continuing Legal Edn., 1968; vis. lectr. Orange County (Fla.) Med. Soc., 1975, San Diego Med. Soc., 1970, U. S.C., 1976, Duquesne Coll., 1970; chmn. rev. com. Ill. Supreme Ct. Disciplinary Commn., 1973-76. Narrator: Poetry Interludes, Sta. WLBH-FM; author: Trial Lawyer's Manual, 1967, Voir Dire Examinations and Opening Statements, 1968, Current Development in Products Liability Law, 1969, Illinois Civil Practice and Procedure, 1970, The Medical Expert Witness, 1973, The Doctor and the Law, 1975, The Doctor and Family Law, 1975, The Doctor and Business Law, 1976, The Doctor and Medical Law, 1977, Testifying in Court, 1973, 2d edit., 1983, 3d edit., 1987, Anatomy of a Medical Malpractice Case, 1984; contbr. articles to profl. jours. including RN Mag. and Forensic Scis.; cons., contbr. Med. Econs., 1969—; legal cons. Mast-Head, 1972—. Pres. bd. edn. Sch. Dist. 100, 1946-48; bd. dirs. Harlan Moore Heart Research Found., 1968—; vol. reader in recording texts Am. Assn. for Blind, 1970-72. Served to lt. col. U.S. Army, 1942-46. Fellow Am. Coll. Trial Lawyers; mem. ABA, Ill. Bar Assn. (exec. council ins. law 1961-63, lectr. law course for attys. 1962, 64-65, Disting. Service award 1982-83), Coles-Cumberland Bar Assn. (v.p. 1968-69, pres. 1969-70, chmn. com. jud. inquiry 1976-80, chmn. meml. com. 1981—), Am. Arbitration Assn. (nat. panel arbitrators), U. Ill. Law Alumni Assn. (pres. 1966-67, Alumni of Month Sept. 1974), Ill. Def. Counsel Assn. (pres. 1967-68), Soc. Trial Lawyers (chmn. profl. activities 1960-61, bd. dirs. 1966-67), Adelphic Debating Soc., Assn. Ins. Attys., Internat. Assn. Ins. Counsel, Am. Judicature Soc., Appellate Lawyers Assn., Scribes, Delta Phi (exec. com. alumni assn. 1960-61, 67-68), Sigma Delta Kappa. Republican. Lodge: Masons (32 degree). Home: 50 Elm Ridge Mattoon IL 61938 Office: Craig & Craig 1807 Broadway PO Box 689 Mattoon IL 61938

HORST, BRUCE EVERETT, mfg. co. exec.; b. Three Rivers, Mich., Feb. 17, 1921; s. Walter and Genevieve (Turner) H.; m. Patricia Kranish, Oct. 4, 1969; children—Michael, Diane, Mark. B.S. in Bus. and Engring. Adminstrn, Mass. Inst. Tech., 1943. With Barber-Colman Co., Rockford, Ill., 1946—; pres. Barber-Colman Co., 1965-75, vice chmn. bd., 1975-76; pres. Mid-States Screw Corp., 1976—, Redin Corp., 1979—. Bd. dirs. Rockford YMCA, 1964—, pres., 1965-67. Served to 1st lt. USAAF, 1943-45. Decorated Air medal. Clubs: Rotary; Forest Hills Country (Rockford) (past sec.); Univ. (Rockford). Home: 2625 Harlem Blvd Rockford IL 61103 Office: 1817 18th Ave Rockford IL 61108

HORST, RICHARD HARLEY, accountant, auditor; b. St. Louis, Oct. 7, 1958; s. Richard Joseph and Lovena Ethel (Casady) H.; m. Mary Alice Stauder, June 25, 1983. BSBA in Acctg., St. Louis U., 1980. CPA, Mo.; cert. internal auditor. Sr. staff auditor Arthur Young & Co., St. Louis, 1980-84; corp. auditor Southwestern Bell Corp., St. Louis, 1984-86, mgr. audit adminstrn., 1986—; instr. St. Louis Community Coll., Meramec, Mo., 1986—. Mem. Am. Inst. CPA's, Nat. Assn. Accts., Mo. Soc. CPA's (relations with educators com.), Greater St. Louis Bowling Assn. (chmn. budget fin. com. 1985-86, chmn. audit com. 1986-87). Roman Catholic. Lodge: KC. Avocations: golf, antique car restoration, model railroading, bowling. Home: 1250 Pine Trails Fenton MO 63026 Office: Southwestern Bell Corp 1 Bell Ctr 39-A-7 Saint Louis MO 63101

HORSTICK, DONALD EUGENE, data processing executive; b. Harrisburg, Pa., Nov. 26, 1937; s. George E. and Mae C. (Dudley) H.; m. Miriam Louise Dayhoff, Feb. 19, 1961. BBA summa cum laude, Franklin U., 1976. Cert. info. systems auditor, systems profl., quality analyst. Systems and programming supr. Nationwide Ins., Columbus, Ohio, 1969-73, systems and programming mgr., 1973-78, EDP audit mgr., 1978—. Served to sgt. U.S. Army, 1961-63. Mem. EDP Auditors Assn. (bd. dirs. cen. Ohio chpt. 1980—, sec. 1982-83, 86-87, v.p. 1983-84, 87—, pres. 1984-85). Republican. Methodist. Avocation: gospel singing group. Home: 1910 Surrey Dr Blacklick OH 43004 Office: Nationwide Ins 1 Nationwide Plaza Columbus OH 43216

HORSTMAN, VERN DAVID, human resource director; b. La Crosse, Wis., Mar. 2, 1957; s. LaVern H. and Joyce A. (Thielker) H.; m. Jane T. Malin, June 10, 1978; 1 child, David. BS in Psychology, U. Wis., La Crosse, 1980; postgrad., U. Nebr., Omaha, 1981; M in Labor and Indls. Relations, Mich. State U., 1983. Indsl. relations analyst Ford Motor Co., Sandusky, Ohio, 1983-85; supr. salaried personnel Ford Electronics and Refrigeration Corp., Bedford, Ind., 1985-86, supr. labor relations, 1986—. Mem. Am. Soc. Personnel Adminstrs., S. Cen. Ind. Personnel Assn., Indsl. Relations Research Assn., Mich. State Alumni Assn., U. Wis.-La Crosse Alumni Assn. Avocations: reading, gardening, photography, tropical fresh-water aquariums, astronomy. Office: Ford Electronics and Refrigeration Corp 3120 W 16th Bedford IN 47421

HORTER, CHARLES MARK, personnel administrator; b. Grafton, N.D., July 7, 1950; s. Werner Henry and Donna Ann (Markholt) H.; m. Julie Ann Marynik, Oct. 25, 1975; children: Rachel, Stacey, Andrea. BS in Pub. Adminstrn., U. N.D., 1972, MS in Pub. Adminstrn., 1978. Coordinator personnel programs N.D. League of Cties, Bismarck, 1974-75; tng. officer N.D. State Hwy. Dept., Bismarck, 1975-77, asst. personnel dir., 1977-81; personnel dir. Super Valu Stores, Inc., Bismarck, 1981—; cons. U.S. Civil Service Commn., Denver, 1975. Chmn. evaluation com. N.D. Council Vocat. Edn., Bismarck, 1986; mem. com. Gov.'s Employment and Tng. Forum, Bismarck, 1986; chmn. Bismarck Folkfest Airshow, 1985-86; mem. com. Bismarck Jr. Coll. Bus. Adv. Com., 1986, U. N.D. Sioux Boosters Club, 1980-86. Mem. Am. Soc. Personnel Adminstrn. (pub. affairs officer 1986—), Cen. Dakota Personnel Assn. (chmn. tng. com. 1984-85, chmn. future planning com. 1986—). Roman Catholic. Coubs: Capitol Curling (Bismarck) (publicity com. 1985—). Avocations: curling, boating, fishing, golf. Home: 3200 Ave C East Bismarck ND 58501 Office: Super Valu Stores Inc 707 Airport Rd PO Box 5506 Bismarck ND 58502

HORTON, JOHN EDWARD, periodontist, educator; b. Brockton, Mass., Dec. 30, 1930; s. Harold Ellsworth and Anita Helen (Samuelson) H.; children—m. Jacqueline A. Hansen, June 10, 1951; John Edward, Janet Elaine, James Elliot, Jeffrey Eugene, Joseph Everett; m. Susan Drake, Aug. 4, 1984. B.S., Providence Coll., 1952; D.M.D., Tufts U., 1957; M.S.D., Baylor U., 1965; M.A., George Washington U., 1978. Commd. 1st lt. U.S. Army, 1957, advanced through grades to col., 1972; cons. to surgeon U.S. Army, Europe, 1967-70; guest scientist dept. immunology Nat. Inst. Dental Research, Bethesda, Md., 1970-73; chief depts. microbiology and immunology Inst. Dental Research U.S. Army, 1973-77, ret., 1977; lectr. Johns Hopkins U. Sch. Pub. Health, 1975-79; asst. professorial lectr. George Washington U., Washington, 1972-74, assoc. professorial lectr., 1974-76, professorial lectr., 1976-77; assoc. prof., chmn. program dir. dept. periodontology Harvard U. Sch. Dental Medicine, 1977-81; prof., chmn., program dir. dept. periodontology Ohio State U. Coll. Dentistry, Columbus, 1981—; cons. VA Med. Ctr., West Roxbury and Brockton, Mass., 1978-81; cons. div. research grants NIH, 1973-86, VA Out-Patient Ctr., Columbus, U.S. Air Force Med. Ctr., Wright Patterson AFB, U.S. Army Inst. Dental Research. Editor: Mechanisms of Localized Bone Loss, 1978. Contbr. numerous articles to profl. jours. Decorated Commendation medal, Meritorious Service medal, Legion of Merit. Fellow AAAS, Am. Pub. Health Assn., Internat. Coll. Dentists, Royal Health; mem. Omicron Kappa Upsilon, Phi Delta Kappa, Sigma Xi. Office: Ohio State Univ Coll Dentistry Dept Periodontology 305 W 12th Ave Columbus OH 43210

HORTON, KEITH ALLYN, psychiatrist; b. Sayre, Pa., July 15, 1933; s. Clayton Darwin and Marion Esther (Hicks) H.; m. Elizabeth Ann Winters, Mar. 1, 1969; children: Laura M., Amy D. AB, U. Pa., 1955; MD, Albany Med. Coll., 1960. Intern Lankenau Hosp., Phila., 1960-61; resident Inst. Phila. Pa. Hosp., 1961-64; practice medicine specializing in psychiatry and psychoanalysis Mpls., 1978—; cons. Phila. YMCA Group Ctr., Phila., 1964-78, Episcopal Acad., Phila., 1970-78, The Hill Sch., Pottstown, Pa., 1975-78, Children's Med. Ctr., Mpls., 1980-86. Served to capt. U.S. Army, 1966-68. Named Tchr. of Yr., U. Minn. Psychiat. Residents, 1982, 84, 86. Fellow Am. Psychiat. Assn., Am. Soc. Adolescent Psychiatry; mem. Am. Psychoanalytic Assn., Chgo. Psychoanalytic Soc. Republican. Episcopalian. Clubs: Merion Golf (Ardmore, Pa.); Minikahda (Mpls.). Avocations: golfing, skiing, bridge. Home and Office: 3141 Dean Ct #C1101 Minneapolis MN 55416

HORTON, RICHARD ADAM, nature center executive, environmental educator; b. Cleve., May 14, 1943; s. Adam Morrow and Florence Adelia (Gratz) H.; m. Ruth Ellen Lambert, Aug. 10, 1968 (div. Oct. 1979); children: Brian Richard, Chad Alan; m. Karen Kay Rosengarten, Aug. 22, 1980; 1 child, Megan Rose. BA, Hiram Coll., 1965; MEd, Kent State U., 1968; postgrad. Gestalt Inst. of Cleve., 1973-75, Inst. for Earth Edn., 1977-84. Cert. tchr. high sch., Ohio.; cert. trainer Inst. Earth Edn. Tchr. sci. Warrensville Jr. High Sch., Warrensville Heights, Ohio, 1965-68, chmn. dept. sci., 1966-68; tchr. sci. Univ. Sch. for Boys, Shaker Heights, Ohio, 1968-75, dir. lower sch. sci., 1970-75; summer naturalist Shaker Lakes Regional Nature Ctr., 1971, 74, 75, dir., 1975—; coordinator Ohio Valley Region/Inst. for Earth Edn., Warrenville, Ill., 1981—; chmn. natural sci. ctrs. conf. Nat. Sci. for Youth Found. and Nat. Audubon Soc., 1986. Author sci. programs, family camp programs. Mem. task force Presbytery of the Western Res., Cleve., 1983-84; dir., program designer/All-Church Camp, Forest Hill Ch., Cleveland Heights, Ohio, 1982, 83, 84; mem. citizens adv. com. City of Shaker Heights planning com., 1980; mem. Joint Com. on Doan Brook Watershed, Cleve., 1975—, chmn., 1978-79; mem. exhibit adv. com. Cleve. Children's Mus. Recipient Disting. Service award City of University Heights, 1986. Mem. Inst. for Earth Edn. (assoc., Chmn.'s award 1987), Nat. Sci. Tchrs. Assn., Natural Sci. for Youth Found., Northeast Ohio Inter-Mus. Council (vice chmn. 1979-83), Ohio Mus. Assn. (treas. 1980-83), Cleve. Regional Council of Sci. Tchrs., Phi Delta Kappa, Beta Beta Beta. Democrat. Presbyterian. Club: Group Couples (Cleveland Heights). Avocations: gardening; creating backyard wildlife habitats; cooking; cross-country skiing. Office: Shaker Lakes Regional Nature Ctr 2600 S Park Blvd Cleveland OH 44120

HORTON, ROBERT ANDREW, engineer executive; b. Oradell, N.J., Feb. 22, 1929; George Francis and May (Acker) H.; m. Lillian Marie Brandow, Sept. 23, 1950; children: Robert A., William T., Thomas J., Nancy K. BChemE, Cooper Union Sch. Engring., 1955. Chemist Austenal, Inc., Dover, N.J., 1955-59; pilot plant mgr. Precision Metal Smiths, Inc., Cleve., 1959-72, dir. research and devel., 1972-80; sect. mgr., project leader TRW, Inc., Cleve., 1980-86; mgr. casting tech. PCC Airfoils, Inc., Cleve., 1986—. Contbr. papers to tech. jour.; holder of 33 U.S. Patents. Fellow Am. Inst. Chemists; mem. AAAS, Am. Ceramic Soc., Am. Soc. for Metals, Ductile Iron Soc. (mem. research com. 1976-80), Investment Casting Inst. (pattern materials com. 1986). Avocations: jazz, sports. Home: 12781 Caves Rd Chesterland OH 44026 Office: PCC Airfoils Inc 23555 Euclid Ave Cleveland OH 44117

HORTON, ROBERT BAYNES, petroleum company executive; b. Bushey, Eng., Aug. 18, 1939; s. William H. Horton and Dorothy Joan (Baynes) Dunn; m. Sally Doreen Wells, July28, 1962; children: Simon, Ruth. BSME, U. St. Andrews, Scotland, 1960; MS, MIT, 1971. With Brit. Petroleum Ltd. (now BP PLC), London, 1957-86; gen. mgr. BP Tankers, London, 1975-76, gen. mgr. corp. planning, 1976-79; mng. dir. BP plc, 1983-86; chmn., chief exec. officer Standard Oil Co., Cleve., 1986—, also bd. dirs.; bd. dirs. API, Nat. City Corp. Trustee Case Western Res. U., Cleve.; mem. Com. for Econ. Devel., MIT Corp. Fellow Royal Soc. Arts; mem. Nat. Petroleum Council, Chem. Industries Assn. (pres. 1982-84), Bus. Roundtable, Bristish Inst. Mgmt. (companion, vice chmn. 1984—), Musical Arts Assn. (trustee), Univ. Circle Inc. (trustee). Anglican. Clubs: Carlton (London); Leander (Henley, Eng.); Union, Country (Cleve.). Avocations: music, hunting, political biography. Office: The Standard Oil Co 200 Public Sq Cleveland OH 44114-2375

HORTON, ROBERT PETER, materials executive; b. Wahpeton, N.D., Mar. 31, 1951; s. James Aaronand Marcelle Anna Marie (Reitan) H.; m. Greta Marie Björn, Feb. 14, 1976; children: Eric Andrew, Kari Elise. BS in Econs., USAF Acad., Colorado Springs, 1973; MBA, Northeastern U., Boston, 1981. Commd. 2d lt. USAF, 1973, advanced through grades to capt., 1976, resigned, 1979; mfg. Systems Analyst The Stanley Works, New Britain, Conn., 1981-82; prodn. control mgr. The Stanley Works, Sabina, Ohio, 1982-84; forecasting mgr. The Stanley Works, Washington Ct. House, Ohio, 1984-86, materials mgr., 1986—. Served to maj. USAFR. Mem. Am. Prodn. Inventory Control Soc., Beta Gamma Sigma. Presbyterian. Avocations: racquetball, photograph, skiing, camping. Home: 5995 Locust Grove Rd Washington Court House OH 43160 Office: The Stanley Works S Fayette St Washington Court House OH 43160

HORTON, YVONNE ROULHAC, home economist, training consultant; b. Phila., Mar. 23, 1949; d. Christopher Maxwell and Nellie (Gordon) Roulhac; m. James Horton, Apr. 21, 1973 (div. July 1980); 1 child, James Christopher. BS, Howard U., 1970, MS, 1973; postgrad., U. Ill., 1981—. Instr. retailing Opportunities Industrialization Ctr., Washington, 1970-73; lectr. Mundelein Coll., Chgo., 1973-74, Chgo. State U., 1974; advisor home econs. Coop. Extension Service U. Ill., Chgo., 1979—. Den mother University Park council boy Scouts of Am., 1984. Mem. Am. Home Econs. Assn. Clubs: Links (local 1st pres. 1976-78), Jack and Jill. Avocation: needlecraft. Home: 712-3 Marina Ct University Park IL 60466 Office: U Ill Coop Extension Service 6234 S Western Ave Chicago IL 60636

HORVATH, JAMES JULIUS, sugar company executive; b. Milw., July 19, 1945; s. Julius and Marilyn A. (Wilson) H.; m. Carol A. Warren, Jan. 6, 1968; children: Bradley J., Brian J. BBA, U. Wis., Milw., 1967, MBA, 1969. From fin. analyst to mgr. fin. Miller Brewing Co., Milw., 1969-76, mgr. treasury, 1976-78, dir. acctg., 1978-81, dir. mgmt. info. services, 1981-85; v.p. finance Am. Crystal Sugar Co., Moorhead, Minn., 1985—. Bd. dirs. Red River Human Services Found., Fargo, N.D., 1985—; fin. dir. Fargo Council Boy Scouts Am., 1987—. Office: Am Crystal Sugar Co 101 N 3rd St Moorhead MN 56560

HORWITZ, DONALD PAUL, restaurant chain executive; b. Chgo., Feb. 5, 1936; s. Theodore J. and Lillian H. (Shlensky) H.; m. Judith Robin, Aug. 23, 1964; children—Terry Robin, Linda Diane, Gail Elizabeth. BS, Northwestern U., 1957; JD, Yale U., 1960. Bar: Ill. bar 1961, D.C. bar 1961, U.S. Supreme Ct 1966; C.P.A., Ill. With atty.'s gen. honors program Dept. Justice, 1961-63; atty. firm Gottlieb & Schwartz, Chgo., 1963-66; with Arthur Young & Co. (C.P.A.'s), Chgo., 1966-72; ptnr. Arthur Young & Co. (C.P.A.'s), 1971-72; exec. v.p., sec., dir. McDonald's Corp., Oak Brook, Ill., 1972—; dir. CML Labs.; lectr. Grad. Sch. Commerce, DePaul U., Chgo. Contbr. articles to profl. jours. Mem. caucus nominating com. Village of Glencoe, Ill., 1975-78; bd. dirs. Chgo. Med. Sch./U. Health Scis., Recordings for Blind; vice chmn., bd. dirs., vice chmn. bd. Highland Park Hosp.; bd. dirs. Anti-Defamation League; hon. trustee St. Augustine's Coll., Chgo., St. Augustine Coll., Chgo. Mem. Am. Bar Assn., Ill. Bar Assn., Chgo. Bar Assn., Am. Inst. CPA's, Ill. Soc. CPA's. Club: Briarwood Country (pres., dir.). Office: McDonalds Corp 1 McDonald Plaza Oak Brook IL 60521

HORWITZ, HARRY, physician, educator; b. London, Mar. 20, 1927; came to U.S., 1960, naturalized, 1965; s. Benjamin and Doris Horwitz; m. Jeanna Doreen Segal, Mar. 18, 1958; children—Ruth, Caroline. M.D., U. London, 1950. Diplomate Am. Bd. Therapeutic Radiology. Intern Met. Hosp., London, 1950-51; intern St. Bartholomew's Hosp., London, 1951-52, resident, 1954-58; sr. resident Addenbrooke's Hosp., Cambridge, Eng., 1958-60; fellow Mt. Sinai Hosp., N.Y.C., 1959; prof. radiology U. Cin., 1960—; pres. Oncology Assocs., Inc., Cin., 1972—. Contbr. articles to med. jours. Bd. dirs. Am. Cancer Soc., 1967—. Served with RAF, 1952-54. Am. Cancer Soc. grantee, 1960-63, USPHS grantee, 1961, 62, 63. Fellow Royal Soc. Medicine, Am. Coll. Radiology; mem. AMA, Brit. Med. Assn., Am. Roentgen Ray Soc., Radiol. Soc. N.Am., Am. Soc. Clin. Oncology, Cancer Control Council, Radiol. Soc. Greater Cin. (past pres.). Clubs: Queen City (Cin.); Indian Hill; Camargo Hunt, Kenwood Country. Lodge: Lodge of Hospitality. Home: 9355 Holly Hill Cincinnati OH 45243 Office: 3120 Burnet Ave Suite 103 Cincinnati OH 45229

HORWITZ, IRWIN DANIEL, otolaryngologist, educator; b. Chgo., Mar. 31, 1920; s. Sol and Belle (Stern) H.; m. Isabel Morwitz, July 23, 1944; children—Steven, Judd, Clare. B.S., U. Ill., 1941, M.D., 1943. Intern Cook County Hosp., Chgo., 1944; resident Ill. Eye and Ear Infirmary, Chgo., 1946-48; practice otolaryngology Chgo., 1948—; clin. prof., head div. otolaryngology Chgo. Med. Sch., 1969; prof. Rush Med. Sch., 1976—; formerly chief div. otolaryngology Mt. Sinai Hosp., former pres. med. staff. Contbr. articles profl. jours. Served to capt., M.C. AUS, 1944-46. Fellow A.C.S.; mem. AMA, Chgo. Otol. and Laryngol. Assn., Am. Acad. Ophthalmology and Otolaryngology, Ill., Chgo. med. socs. Home: 6431 N Knox St Lincolnwood IL 60646 Office: 55 E Washington St Chicago IL 60602

HORWITZ, ROBERT HENRY, political science educator; b. El Paso, Tex., Sept. 3, 1923; s. David and Louise (Mendelsohn) H.; m. Noreen Margaret Surti, Jan. 1948; children: Susheila Louise, David D. BA, Amherst Coll., 1949; MA, U. Hawaii, 1950; PhD, U. Chgo., 1954; LHD (hon.), Kenyon Coll., 1987. Asst. prof., researcher U. Hawaii, 1948-51; research asst. com. for study citizenship edn. U. Chgo., 1953-55; from asst. prof. to prof. polit. sci. Mich. State U., East Lansing, 1956-66; prof. polit. sci., chmn. dept. Kenyon Coll., Gambier, Ohio, 1966—, dir. Pub. Affairs Conf. Ctr., 1976-78. Co-author: John Locke's Questions Concerning the Law of Nature, 1986; editor: The Moral Foundations of the American Republic, 1977; contbr. articles to profl. jours. Served with AUS, 1942-46, ETO, PTO. Decorated Bronze Star; decorated Combat Inf. badge; fellow Emil Schwartzhaupt Found., 1953-55, Rockefeller Found., 1959, Ford Found., 1956-58; Earhard Found. fellow, 1972, NEH fellow, 1973-76. Mem. AAUP, Am. Polit. Sci. Assn., Am. Soc. Polit. and Legal Philosophy. Jewish. Office: Kenyon Coll Dept Polit Sci Gambier OH 43022

HORWITZ, RONALD M., business administration educator; b. Detroit, June 25, 1938; s. Harry and Annette (Levine) H.; m. Carol Bransky, Mar. 30, 1961; children: Steven, Michael, David, Robert. BS, Wayne State U., 1959, MBA, 1961; PhD, Mich. State U., 1964. CPA, Mich. Prof. fin. U. Detroit, 1963-73, 75-79; healthcare cons., dir. personnel devel. Arthur Young & Co., Detroit, 1974-75; dean Sch. Bus. Adminstrn., prof. finance Oakland U., Rochester, Mich., 1979—. Contbr. articles to profl. jours. Mem. adv. bd. Providence Hosp., Southfield, Mich., 1979—; trustee adv. panel Greater Detroit Health Council, 1980—. Stonier fellow Am. Bankers Assn., 1963. Mem. Healthcare Fin. Mgmt. Assn. (bd. dirs. 1976-80), Mich. Assn. CPA's (grantee 1960), Am. Inst. CPA's, Fin. Mgmt. Assn., Am. Acctg. Assn., Acctg. Aid Soc. Detroit (founder), Mich. Bridge Assn. (pres. 1974-76). Avocation: bridge (life master, tourney chmn. Motor City regional). Office: Oakland U Sch of Bus Adminstrn Rochester MI 48309-4401

HOSCHETTE, JOHN ARNOLD, engineer; b. St. Paul, Oct. 10, 1952; s. Vernon Peter and Veronica (Schueller) H.; m. Linda Kathrine Mastel, Aug. 3, 1974; children: Tina, John G. BSEE, U. Minn., 1974, MSEE, 1975, cert. bus. adminstrn., 1983. E-O Engr. Northrop Corp., Hawthorne, Calif., 1975-77; sr. engr. Honeywell, Mpls., 1977-82, sr. scientist, 1982-85, sr. prin. engr., 1985—. Contbr. articles to profl. jours. Mem. Soc. Photographic and Indsl. Engrs. Roman Catholic. Office: Honeywell 10400 Yellow Circle Hopkins MN 55343

HOSEK, JOHN EDWIN, financial analyst; b. Balt., June 19, 1947; s. John Jerome and Lillian Anne (Caywood) H.; m. Rebecca Doris Hinton, Dec. 13, 1975; 1 child, Leigh Christine. BS, Abilene (Tex.) Christian Coll., 1969; MS, Abilene Christian U., 1979. With J.C. Penney Co., Arlington, Tex., 1970-74; cost and budget analyst Gen. Dynamics Corp., Ft. Worth, 1975-77, sr. fin. analyst, 1977-78; contract price analyst negotiator USAF, Wright-Patterson AFB, Ohio, 1978-86, sr. cost/price analyst negotiator, 1986—. Treas. and deacon Huber Heights (Ohio) Ch. of Christ, 1983-86. Served with USN, 1969. Recipient Small Bus. Inst. award SBA, 1975. Mem. Nat. Contract Mgmt. Assn., Nat. Mgmt. Assn. (treas. Ft. Worth chpt. 1975-76), Pi Beta Sigma (advisor Abilene chpt. 1974-75). Republican. Lodge: Lions (v.p. Abilene chpt. 1974-75). Avocation: golf. Home: 7639 Rustic Woods Dr Huber Heights OH 45424 Office: USAF ASD/PMFC Area B Bldg 16 Wright-Patterson AFB OH 45433

HOŚKINS, JAMES JAY, chemical engineer; b. Toledo, Nov. 27, 1950; s. James Jackson and Marcella Marion (Rawlins) H.; m. Denise Elaine Neumann, June 15, 1973; 1 child, Matthew James. BS in Chem. Engring., U. Toledo, 1972, MS Chem. Engr., 1974; MBA, Xavier U., 1982. Chem. engr. Procter & Gamble, Cin., 1973-77, project leader, 1977-79, brand asst., 1983, section head, 1979-82, 83—. Patentee liquid cleansing product with skin feel additives. Account mgr. United Appeal, Cin., 1986. Mem. Am. Inst. Chemical Engrs. (assoc.). Republican. Club: Toastmasters (past pres.) (Cin.). Avocations: jogging, hiking, reading. Home: 10096 Sonya Ln Cincinnati OH 45241 Office: Procter & Gamble Co 11511 Reed Hartman Hwy Cincinatti OH 45241

HOSMER, CHARLES BRIDGHAM, JR., historian, educator; b. Naples, Italy, Feb. 23, 1932; s. Charles Bridgham and Faye (Durham) H.; m. Jeralyn Prugh, Dec. 27, 1955; children: Kathryn, Jonathan Prescott. BA, Principia Coll., 1953; MA, Columbia U., 1956, PhD, 1961. Tchr. pub. schs., South Huntington, N.Y., 1956-59; from instr. to full prof. Principia Coll., Elsah, Ill., 1960—, Jay P. Walker prof. history, 1972—. Author: Presence of the Past, History of Preservation, 1965, Preservation Comes of Age, 1981; (with others) Elsah: A Historic Guidebook. Mem. Ill. Hist. Sites Adv. Council, Springfield, 1969-76; pres. Hist. Elsah Found., 1971—; chmn. Elsah Zoning Bd., 1973-79. Served as cpl. U.S. Army, 1953-55. Named Disting. Assoc., Eastern Nat. Park and Monument Assn., Phila., 1981. Mem. Am. Hist. Assn., Orgn. Am. Historians, Am. Assn. State and Local History, Soc. Archtl. Historians, Nat. Trust Hist. Preservation. Democrat. Christian Scientist. Avocation: collecting books on architecture. Home: PO Box 155 Elsah IL 62028 Office: Principia Coll Elsah IL 62028

HOST, DAN R., optometrist; b. Kokomo, Ind., May 26, 1953; s. Raymond A. and Martha A. (Addison) H.; m. Nancy K. Snyder, Aug. 9, 1975; children: Brian D., Amy M. BS, Ind. U., 1975, OD, 1977. Intern IU External Clinic, Ft. Campbell, Ky., 1975; gen. practice optometry Huntington, Ind., 1979—. Served to lt. USN, 1977-79. Mem. Am. Optometrist Assn., Ind. Optometrist Assn., Northeastern Ind. Optometric Soc. Republican. Lodge: Optimist Internat. (pres. local chpt. 1985-86). Avocations: basketball, raquetball, golf. Home: 6254 W 465 N Huntington IN 46750 Office: 518 N Jefferson St Huntington IN 46750

HOSTETLER, GORDON LEE, pharmaceutical company executive; b. Hastings, Nebr., June 20, 1934; s. Wilbur and Velma Emeline (Lapp) H.; m. Phyllis Fay Davenport, July 2, 1960; children: Michael Alan, Elaine Melissa. BA, Goshen Coll., 1959. Cert. quality engr. Chemist Miles Labs., Inc., Elkhart, Ind., 1959-63, supr. quality assurance, 1963-67; mgr. quality assurance Miles Labs., Inc., West Haven, Conn., 1967-72; mgr. quality assurance Miles Labs., Inc., Elkhart, 1972-76, dir. quality assurance, 1976—. Contbr. articles on stability to profl. jours. Mem. Am. Soc. for Quality Control (chmn. South Bend sect. 1986-87). Mem. Unitarian Ch. Avocations: photography, music collecting. Home: 58319 CR 7 Elkhart IN 46517 Office: Miles Labs Inc Box 340 Elkhart IN 46517

HOSTETLER, ROBERT D., electronics company executive; b. 1942. BS, Purdue U., 1964, MS, 1965. With CTS Corp., Elkhart, Ind., 1965—, dir. corp. planning, 1965-67, asst. treas., 1967-77, v.p., 1977-79, exec. v.p., treas., mem. exec. com., 1979-80, pres., mem. exec. com., 1980-81, now chmn., pres., chief exec. officer. Office: CTS 905 N West Blvd Elkhart IN 46514 *

HOSTETTER, EDWARD D., protective services official; b. Canton, Ohio, July 24, 1950; s. Walter Aaron and Mary Ellen (Sheaters) H.; m. Jeanne Ellen Tamper, Nov. 10, 1983; chldren: Traci Lynn, Victoria Lenore. Student, Kent State U., 1969-72, 68-69. Cert. Law Enforcement Instr. With M. O'Neil Co., Canton, 1968-76; security officer Buckeye Protective Service, Canton, 1976-78, tng. office, 1978-80, dir. tng., 1980-83; police officer Canton Police Dept., 1977—; pres. Hostetter & Assocs., Inc., Canton, 1985—; dir. Vanguard Security Tng., Canton, 1985—. Mus. dir., prin. conductor North Canton Community Band, 1976—. Mem. Am. Fedn. of Police (pres. Canton chpt. 1982-85, state pres. 1982—), Am. Soc. Indsl. Security, Acad. Security Educators and Trainers. Republican. Mem. Christian Ch. Avocations: music, target shooting, reading. Office: Vanguard Security Tng PO Box 80096 Sta C Canton OH 44708

HOSTETTER, HAROLD VICTOR, union official; b. Coshocton, Ohio, May 7, 1928; s. Wilbert B. and Minnie Ellen (Emler) H.; m. Lily Ruth Patterson, June 9, 1945 (div. 1981); m. 2d, Wilma Jean Sharrer, Nov. 16, 1981; children—Patricia Ellen, Derek William. Student pub. schs., West Lafayette, Ohio. Tool and diemaker Steel Ceilings, Inc., Coshocton, 1946-63; dist. dir. Internat. Assn. Machinists Dist. 28, Zanesville, Ohio, 1963—; v.p. Ohio State Machinists, Columbus, 1974—, Ohio AFL-CIO, Columbus, 1978—; nat. planner Machinists Non-Partisan Polit. League, Washington, 1980—; bd. dirs. Gradall Co., New Philadekphia. Bd. dirs. Goodwill Industries, Zanesville, 1976-80. Democrat. Methodist. Lodges: Elks, Masons (master 1961), Order Eastern Star, Moose. Home: 5445 Heritage Dr Nashport OH 43830 Office: Internat Assn Machinists Dist 28 1526 Bluff Zanesville OH 43701

HOTALING, ANDREW JAY, pediatric otolaryngologist; b. Glen Ridge, N.J., May 16, 1946; s. William Edgar and Jean (Perrino) H.; m. Sylvia Marie Morris, Apr. 29, 1978; children: James Morris, Jeffery Morris. AB, Dartmouth Coll., 1968; MD, Case Western Res. U., 1979. Intern in surgery Case Western Res. U., Cleve., 1979-81; resident in otolaryngology Northwestern U., Chgo., 1981-84; fellow in pediatrics and otolaryngology Children's Hosp. Pitts./ U. Pitts., 1984-85; assoc. attending physician Children's Hosp. of Mich., Detroit, 1985—. Served to lt. USN, 1968-73, PTO. Fellow Am. Acad. Otolaryngology Head and Neck Surgery; mem. AMA, Soc. Ear, Nose and Throat Advances for Children, Inc. Avocations: jogging, skiing, sailing. Home: 410 Lakeland Ave Grosse Pointe MI 48230 Office: 4400 Town Ctr Suite 250 Southfield MI 48075

HOTCHNER, BEVERLY JUNE, psychologist; b. East St. Louis, Ill., July 13, 1928; d. Benjamin E. and Jennie Louise (Komar) Novack; m. Selwyn Ross Hotchner, Nov. 22, 1951; children: Kirby Ross, Bradley Ross. BS, U. Ill., 1950; PhD, Washington U., 1972. Lic. psychologist, Mo.; cert. sex therapist, educator, Mo. Asst. prof. dept. behavioral sci. So. Ill. U. Sch. Dental Medicine, Edwardsville, 1973-75, acting chairperson dept. behavioral sci., 1974-75; founder, exec. dir. Ctr. Human Concern, St. Louis, 1975—; pvt. practice psychology St. Louis, 1979—; cons. St. Luke's Hosp., St. Louis, 1979—. Mem. Am. Psychol. Assn., Mo. Psychol. Assn., St. Louis Psychol. Assn., Am. Assn. Sex. Educators, Cons., Therapists (tng. dir. 1976-77, chairperson Plainstate region 1976-78, mem. nat. sex therapy cert. com. 1977-78), Soc. Sci. Study Sex (nat. bd. dirs. 1987), Am. Assn. Marriage and Family Therapy, Phi Beta Kappa, Alpha Lamba Delta, Kappa Delta Pi. Home and Office: 7206 Cornell Saint Louis MO 63130

HOTZLER, MARK ALLEN, commercial real estate broker; b. Okabena, Minn., Apr. 3, 1956; s. Warren Jacob and Elaine D. (Loeschen) H.; m. Jane Marie Amundgaard, June 28, 1980; children: Stephanie Marie, Jaclyn Jane. AA, Worthington (Minn.) Community Coll., 1976; BSBA, Southwest State U., Marshall, Minn., 1980. Real estate broker and developer Armstrong Real Estate, Lakefield, Minn., 1976-79; comml. property mgr. Towle Real Estate, Mpls., 1981-85; comml. real estate broker Towle Real Estae, Mpls., 1985—. Mem. Inst. Real Estate Mgmt. (cert. property mgr.), Internat. Council Shopping Ctrs., Nat. Bd. Realtors, Minn. Bd. Realtors (cert. comml. investment mgr.), Burnsville C. of C. Avocations: sports, cooking, photography. Home: 13012 Oliver Ave S Burnsville MN 55337 Office: Towle Real Estate 330 Second Ave S Minneapolis MN 55402

HOUCHINS, DANIEL THOMAS, bank executive; b. Bellefontaine, Ohio, Oct. 8, 1955; s. Grover Thomas and Ethel Marie (Steggeman) H. BS in Acctg., Ohio State U., 1978. CPA, Ohio. Audit staff Alexander Grant & Co., CPAs, Columbus, Ohio, 1978-81; internal audit staff Huntington Banks, Columbus, 1981-82, internal audit sr., 1982-84, asset based audit mgr., 1984—; pvt. practice acctg., Columbus, 1981—. Mem. Am. Inst. CPAs, Ohio Soc. CPAs, Beta Gamma Sigma. Republican. Roman Catholic. Avocations: golf, coin and paper money collecting. Home: 6000 Hildenboro Dr Dublin OH 43017 Office: Huntington Banks 41 S High St Dept HC0822 Columbus OH 43260

HOUCK, JOHN BUNN, psychologist, priest; b. Little Rock, Apr. 21, 1936; s. Jesse French and Jane (Cleaver) H.; m. Dawn Kyoko Aoto, June 30, 1964; children: Fawn Elizabeth, Florence Anne. BS, Miss. State U., 1958; MDiv, Seabury-Western Sem., 1964; MA, U. Chgo., 1968; PhD, Ill. Inst. Tech., 1974. Registered psychologist; ordained priest. Minister United Campus Ministry Ill. Inst. Tech., Chgo., 1968-76; pastor South Community Ch., Chgo., 1973-80; exec. dir. Pastoral Counseling Service, Chgo., 1976—; dir. Wholistic Health Ctr., Oak Park, Ill., 1979-81; pvt. practice psychologist Oak Park, 1983—; bd. dirs. Contact Chgo., 1982—. Mem. Am. Assn. Pastoral Counselors, Am. Psychol. Assn., Internat. Transactional Analysis Assn. Home and Office: 1453 E Park Pl Chicago IL 60637

HOUDE, LEE FRANCIS, engineer; b. Worcester, Mass., Oct. 3, 1946; s. Russell Henry and Jean Marie (Kirby) H.; m. Mary Margaret Kruger, Aug. 12, 1968 (div. Mar. 1985); children: Andrew, David. B in Indsl. Engring., Gen. Motors Inst., Flint, Mich., 1969. Registered profl. engr., Mich. Plant engr. Assembly div. Gen. Motors, Framingham, Mass., 1964-78; mfg. developer Gen. Motors, Warren, Mich., 1978-79, mfg. analysis specialist Assembly div., 1979-84; mfg. engr. Saturn Corp., Troy, Mich., 1984—. Bd. dirs. Charles River Watershed Assn., Cambridge, Mass., 1974-76. Mem. Engring. Soc. of Detroit, Mich. Ind. Hygiene Soc. Lodge: Elks (local sec. 1985—). Avocations: hunting, fishing, camping, scuba diving. Home: 8971 Pippen Dr Romeo MI 48065 Office: Saturn Corp PO Box 7025 Troy MI 48007

HOUGH, CHARLES NEFF, JR., manufacturing company executive; b. Chgo., July 10, 1934; s. Charles N. and Helen Evans (Hamilton) H.; m. Bonnie Jean Wallace, Aug. 27, 1955; children: Charles N. III, Steven W., Mark H., Douglas G., Heidi H. BS, Northwestern U., 1956. Mgr. Kengrip div. Kennametal Inc., Latrobe, Pa., 1960-70; v.p. sales and mktg. Hunter Engring., St. Louis, 1970-78; v.p. mktg. Sun Electric Corp., Crystal Lake, Ill., 1978-81; v.p. sales Alloy Automotive, Chgo., 1981-84; v.p., gen. mgr. OTC tool and equipment div. Sealed Power Corp., 1984—. Active ARC, United Fund, Crippled Children, Boy Scouts Am., various locations; active Episc. chs., various locations. Recipient 25 Yrs. Service to the Industry award Automotive Hall of Fame, 1986. Mem. Automotive Service Industry Assn. (bd. dirs. 1984—), Nat. Tire Dealers and Retreaders Assn. (Faith in Am. Bus. award 1978). Republican. Club: Owatonna Country. Lodges: Elks, Shriners. Avocations: tennis, golf, cooking, hunting, fishing. Home: 40 Kirk Pl Owatonna MN 55060 Office: OTC div Sealed Power Corp 655 Eisenhower Dr Owatonna MN 55060

HOUGH, DAVID BRUCE, internist; b. Enid, Okla., Mar. 31, 1946; s. Guthrie Wayne and Naomi Colene (Spaulding) H.; m. Merrilee Murphy, June 1, 1972 (div. Sept. 1978); children: James, Mary, David; m. Elizabeth Ann Sloat, Apr. 27, 1979. BA, Phillips U., 1968; DO, Chgo. Coll. Osteo. Medicine, 1974. Intern Mt. Clemens (Mich.) Gen. Hosp., 1974-75, resident in internal medicine, 1975-78; physician Mich. Internal Medicine Assocs., PC, South Bend, Ind., 1978—; chief of staff Mich. Community Hosp., 1981, 83-84, bd. dirs., 1983-84; v.chmn. Omni Health Care Systems, 1985-86; mem., bd. dirs. St. Joseph County Hospice, 1985-86. Mem. Am. Osteo. Assn., Am. Coll. Osteo. Internists, Am. Heart Assn. Avocations: hunting, golf. Home: 1734 Bond St Niles MI 49120 Office: Mich Internal Medicine Assoc PC 2505 E Jefferson South Bend IN 46615

HOUGH, FREDERICK JOHN, II, chiropractic coll. ofcl.; b. Chgo., Sept. 14, 1936; s. Frederick John and Eleanora Francis (Cyra) H.; A.A., Coll. of DuPage, 1975; B.A., Elmhurst Coll., 1976; divorced; children—Frederick, Michael, Neil, Linda, Laura. Cost acct. Wilson Sporting Goods Co., 1957-58; office mgr. Howell Tractor and Equipment Co., 1958-60; pres. Great Lakes Sci. Corp., Lombard, Ill., 1960-74; corp. v.p., chief fiscal officer, v.p. adminstrn., Nat. Coll. Chiropractic, Lombard, 1974—; instr. investing, fin., bus. and law, 1974—; lectr., bus. and investment adv., 1974—. Served with USMC, 1954-57. Lic. real estate broker, Ill., Wis. Mem. 1st Marine Brigade, Fleet Marine Force, VFW (chpt. treas.), Delta Mu Delta. Republican. Methodist. Home: 326 S Monterey St Villa Park IL 60181 Office: Nat Coll Chiropractic 200 E Roosevelt Rd Lombard IL 60148

HOUGH, JANE RUTH ELDER, soprano, educator; b. Tacoma, Wash., May 22, 1923; d. Roger Emerson and Mabel (Bradway) Elder; m. Eldred Wilson Hough, Dec. 28, 1948; children—Christine Elizabeth Hough Smith, Phyllis Jane Hough Wheeler, Roger Eldred, Carl Emerson. B.S. in Physics, U.Wash., 1945; B.A. in Music, Occidental Coll., 1946; M.L.S., U. Maine, 1975; M.M.Ed. in Music, Miss. State U., 1982. Mathematician, U.S. Govt. Army Ordnance, Los Angeles, 1946-49; soprano, symphony chorus, Los Angeles, 1946-48, Opera Theater, U. Maine, Orono, 1975, Bangor Community Theater (Maine), 1976; soloist Symphony Chorus, Starkville, Miss., 1976-82; operatic soprano Midland Repertory Players, Alton, Ill., 1983—; instr. singing, Carrollton, Ill., 1982—. Mem. Nat. Assn. Tchrs. of Singing, ALA, Sigma Alpha Iota Alumnae (treas. Tulsa 1951-52, organizer, 1st pres. Austin, Tex. 1959-61, Sword of Honor 1960), P.E.O. (1st pres. chpt. KZ Carbondale, Ill. 1967-69), AAUW, DAR, Alpha Omicron Pi. Methodist. Club: Nocturne Music (pres. 1979-81). Home: PO Box 90 Carrollton IL 62016

HOUGHTBY, CAROL MARY, accountant; b. Portland, Conn., Dec. 12, 1960; d. William Earl and Elizabeth Ann (Porter) H. BS, Lehigh U., 1982. CPA, Minn. Staff auditor Laventhol & Horwath, Mpls., 1982-84, sr. auditor, 1984-85; sr. internal auditor MSI Ins. Co., Arden Hills, Minn., 1985-86; acct. mktg. services, cons. Western Life Ins. Co., Woodbury, Minn., 1986—. Fin. adv. bd. Mpls. Theatre in the Round, 1984—; vol. Big Bros./Big Sisters, Mpls., 1984. Mem. Am. Inst. CPA's, Minn. Soc. CPA's (mem. industry sub-com.), Lehigh U. Alumni Club (founder, pres. 1984—). Avocation: gardening. Home: 1659 Juliet Ave Saint Paul MN 55105 Office: Western Life Ins Co PO Box 64271 Saint Paul MN 55164

HOUGHTON, PETER BRIAN, airline company executive; b. Taylor, Tex., Jan. 25, 1951; s. James F. and Jeanne (Bull) Houghton; m. Deborah Anne Collins, Oct. 18, 1970; children: Robert, William. BS, Moorhead State U., 1971; MBA, Mich. State U., 1973; JD, William Mitchell Coll. Law, 1980. Bar: Minn. 1980. Sales rep. Northwest Airlines, Mpls., 1973-75; cargo sales mgr. Northwest Airlines, St. Paul, 1975-80, pricing dir., 1980-85, airline planning div., 1985—, dir. adminstrn. data processing, 1986—. Mem. ABA, Minn. State Bar Assn. Lutheran. Avocations: golf, running. Office: Northwest Airlines Minneapolis-Saint Paul Airport Saint Paul MN 55111

HOUK, KATHLEEN ANN, dentist; b. Salem, Ohio, May 18, 1953; d. John Robert and Irene Anna (Fleischer) Shepherd; m. George Wayne Houk, June 15, 1974; children: Annie Michelle, Katie Marie. DDS, Ohio State U., 1977. Lic. dentist, Ohio. Gen. practice dentistry Poland, Ohio, 1977—. Advisor Greenford Happy Helpers 4-H Club, Mahoning County, Ohio, 1971-75; supt. vacation bible sch. Emmanuel Luth. Ch., New Springfield, Ill., 1977-78. Named Dairy Princess Buckeye Dairy Boosters, Mahoning County, Ohio, 1970. Mem. ADA, Ohio Dental Assn., Corydon Palmer Dental Soc. (adv. council), Mahoning County Young Farmers Assn. (v.p. 1979-86), Mahoning County Farm Bur. (sec. 1979-86). Avocation: collecting music boxes, primitive Am. antiques. Home: 2700 E Middletown Rd Poland OH 44514 Office: 2600 E Middletown Rd Poland OH 44514

HOUK, LISA ANN, advertising company account executive; b. Rolla, Mo., July 10, 1960; d. Gael Owen and Mary Jean (Mathers) Westerhoff; m. F. John Houk, Nov. 29, 1986. BA in Telecommunications, Ind. U., 1982. Sales coordinator Winston Network, Chgo., 1984, account exec., 1984—. Mem. Phi Mu Alumnae (v.p. Chgo. West Suburban chpt. 1983-85, chpt. pres. 1986—). Office: Winston Network 211 E Ontario St Chicago IL 60611

HOUK, ROBERT E., utility company executive. Pres. bd. dirs. Citizens Gas and Coke Utility, Indpls. Office: Citizens Gas & Coke Utility 2020 N Meridian St Indianapolis IN 46202 *

HOULE, DAVID ECKHARDT, restaurant executive; b. Chgo., July 3, 1948; s. Cyril Orvin and Bettie Eckhardt H. B.A. in Fine Arts, Syracuse U., 1969. With systems office U. Chgo. Library, 1969-72; with Ward-Griffith Newspapers, 1974-76; account exec. NBC-TV, 1976-78; sr. account exec. CBS-TV, Chgo., 1978-81; dir. sales Warner Amex Satellite Entertainment Co., Chgo., 1981-84; v.p. advt. sales MTV Networks Inc., 1984-85; chmn. bd., chief exec. officer Mama Mia! Pasta Restaurant Co., Chgo., 1984—. Mem. film ctr. com. Sch. of Art Inst., Chgo.; friend Hubbard St. Dance Co. Office: Mama Mia! Pasta Restaurant Co 116 S Michigan Ave Chicago IL 60603

HOULE, THOMAS JOSEPH, electronics company sales executive; b. St. Paul, Feb. 4, 1938; s. Wilfred Theodore and Gladys (Irene) H.; m. Georgia Anne Burlingame, Oct. 5, 1957; children: Mary, John, George, Benjamin. BA, U. Minn., 1965. Tech. writer Univac, St. Paul, 1965-67; advt. mgr. Medtronic, Mpls., 1967-72, Marquette Electronics, Milw., 1972-75; dist. sales mgr. Doerr Electric, Cedarburg, Wis., 1975—. Contbr. articles to hobby mags. Republican. Roman Catholic. Avocations: model aircraft and ship design and construction, photography, history, woodworking. Home: 11333 N Lake Shore Dr Mequon WI 53092 Office: Doerr Electric Corp Box 67 Cedarburg WI 53012

HOULTON, LOYCE J., artistic director, choreographer; b. Proctor, Minn., June 13, 1926; d. Andrew and Ragna M. Johnson; m. William H. Houlton, July 28, 1950; children: Laif, Joel, Lise, Andrew. B.A., Carleton Coll., 1946, Hum.D. (hon.), 1981; M.A., NYU, 1950. Mem. dance adv. panel Minn. State Arts Council, 1972-75. Artistic dir., Minn. Dance Theatre, Mpls., 1962—; artistic dir. emeritus Ballet Mich., Ballet Austin, Dance Theater of Harlem, A Dancer's Place, New Sch. of Dance; choreographer for, Berlin Deutsche Oper Ballet, Washington Ballet, Dayton (Ohio) Ballet, Louisville Ballet, Pacific N.W. Ballet, Pa. Ballet, Pauline Koner Dance Consert, N.Y.C., Tulsa Ballet Co., subject of film Loyce. Recipient Plaudit award Nat. Dance Assn., 1980; Minn. State Arts Bd. choreographic fellow, 1978-79; Nat. Endowment for Arts Class A choreographic grantee. Mem. Nat. Assn. Regional Ballet (pres. Mid-States region 1972-73, dir. 1975—).

HOUPIS, CONSTANTINE HARRY, electrical engineering educator; b. Lowell, Mass., June 16, 1922; s. Harry John and Metaxia (Gourokous) H.; student Wayne U., 1941-43; BS, U. Ill., 1947, MS, 1948; postgrad. Ohio State U., 1952-56; PhD, U. Wyo., 1971; m. Mary Stephens, Aug. 28, 1960; children: Harry C., Angella S. Spl. research asst. U. Ill., 1947-48; devel. elec. engr. Babcock & Wilcox Co., Alliance, Ohio, 1948-49; instr. elec. engring. Wayne State U., 1949-51; prin. elec. engr. Battelle Meml. Inst., Columbus, Ohio, 1951-52; prof. elec. engring. Air Force Inst. Tech., Wright-Patterson AFB, Ohio, 1952—; guest lectr. Nat. Tech. U. Athens, 1958, U. Patras, 1984, Weizmann Inst. Sci., 1984; cons. Air Force Flight Dynamics Lab. Served with AUS, 1943-46. Recipient Outstanding Engr. award Dayton area Nat. Engrs. Week, 1962. Fellow. IEEE; mem. Am. Soc. Engring. Edn., Am. Hellenic Edn. Progressive Assn., Tau Beta Pi, Eta Kappa Nu, Sigma Chi. Mem. Greek Orthodox Ch. Author: (with J.J. D'Azzo) Feedback Control System Analysis and Synthesis, 1960, 2d edit., 1966; Principles of Electrical Engineering: Electric Circuits, Electronics, Energy Conversion, Control Systems Computers, 1968; Linear Control Systems Analysis and Design: Conventional and Modern, 1975, 3d edit., 1988; (with J. Lubelfeld) Outline of Pulse Circuits; (with G.B. Lamont) Digital Control Systems: Theory Software, Hardware, 1985; also articles on automatic controls in profl. jours. U.S., Eng., Greece. Home: 1125 Brittany Hills Dr Centerville OH 45459 Office: Air Force Inst Tech Wright-Patterson AFB OH 45433

HOURIGAN, DIANE RENAE, dentist; b. Friend, Nebr., July 7, 1949; s. Arnold George and Lois Maxine (Stanley) Frankforter; m. Patrick Raymond Hourigan, Sept. 5, 1970 (div. 1975). BS, York Coll., 1968; DDS, U. Nebr., 1981. Gen. practice dentistry Shelton, Nebr., 1981-83, Kearney, Nebr., 1983—; clin. instr. dentistry U. Nebr., Lincoln, 1981; clin. inst. Cen. Community Coll., Hastings, Nebr., 1982-83, adv. com. dental hygiene, 1982—. Bd. dirs. Kearney Area Community Ctr., 1986. Mem. ADA, Nebr. Dental Assn. (legis. liason 1986), Buffalo County Dental Soc., Northwest Dist. Dental Soc. (pres. 1984-85), Am. Soc. Dentistry for Children. Democrat. Roman Catholic. Avocations: racquetball, travel. Office: 3720 Ave A Box 1240 Kearney NE 68848-1240

HOUSE, CARLEEN FAYE, medical researcher, systems analyst; b. Sparta, Wis., Dec. 14, 1950; d. Clarence Frederick and Ida Mae (Murdock) Anderson; m. Gregory Allen House, Aug. 25, 1984. BS, U. Wis., 1978, MS, 1982. Cert. engr., Wis. Prin. Customized Research and Design, 1979-81; sci. tchr. Wis. Ednl. System, 1981-82; systems engr. Hewlett Packard, 1982-83, systems analyst, 1983-86, MIS dir., 1986—; chief exec. officer House Research, 1986—; dir. devel. House Properties One, 1985—; pres. HPII Ltd. Partnership, 1986—. Mem. Women in Engring., Aircraft Owners and Pilots Assn., Omicron Nu, League of Women Voters. Republican. Lutheran. Avocations: flying, horticulture, skiing. Home and office: 10579 Point Pleasant Rd Chisago City MN 55013

HOUSE, CHARLES BREWER, JR., college president, educator; b. Galesburg, Ill., June 24, 1927; s. Charles Brewer and Sarah Margueritte (Ostrander) H.; m. M. June Hornby, Apr. 9, 1950; children: Charles, David, Stephen, James, Robert. BS, U. Nebr., 1949; MDiv, Princeton Theol. Sem., 1955; PhD, Mich. State U., 1975. Ordained to ministry Presbyterian Ch. Assoc. pastor Westminster Presbyn. Ch., Grand Rapids, Mich., 1955-58; asst. prof. religion and chaplain Alma Coll., Mich., 1958-64; vis. prof. humanities U. Nigeria, Nuskka, 1964-67; lectr. humanities Mich. State U., East Lansing, 1967-69; exec. asst. to pres. Central Mich. U., Mount Pleasant, 1969-82; pres. State U. N.D., Valley City, 1982—; mem. Synod Adv. Council on Presbyn. Colls., Bloomington, Mich., 1983—, Mich. Council for Humanities, East Lansing, 1973-78. Served to lt. USN, 1945-52, PTO. Mem. Valley City C. of C. (bd. dirs. 1982), Sigma Iota Epsilon, Phi Delta Kappa. Lodges: Rotary, Elks, Eagles. Avocations: sailing, cross country skiing, backpacking, wood carving, music. Home: 159 Viking Dr Valley City ND 58072

HOUSE, JERRY L., otolaryngologist; b. Elwood, Ind., Sept. 4, 1950; s. Joseph Lee and Mary Margaret (Faust) H.; m. Sharon R. Ross, June 8, 1974; children: Johnathan, Katherine, Brian. AB, Ind. U., 1972, MD, 1975. Diplomate Am. Bd. Otolaryngology. Intern Meth. Hosp., Indpls., 1975-76, resident surgery, 1976-77; resident in otolaryngology Ind. U. Med. Ctr., Indpls., 1977-80; vis. physician Kantonspital, Zürich, Switzerland, 1980; clin. fellow in otology and neurotology Otologic Med. Group and House Ear Inst., Los Angeles, 1981; practice medicine specializing in otolaryngology Indpls., 1981—; staff mem. Humana Hosp., Indpls., St. Vincent's Hosp., Indpls.; staff mem., med. dir. audiology and prin. investigator cochlear implant investigations Meth. Hosp., Indpls.; asst. clin. prof. Ind. U. Sch. Medicine; speaker in field. Contbr. articles to profl. jours. Mem. AMA, Am. Acad. Otolaryngology, Marion County Med. Soc., Ind. Med. Soc., Am. Auditory Soc., Ind. Assn. of the Deaf, Ind. Assn. Hearing Impaired Children (bd. dirs.), Soc. Neurovascular Surgery, Acoustic Neuroma Assn., Indpls. Speech and Hearing Ctr. (bd. dirs.), House Ear Inst., Alumni Fellowship Group. Home: 6856 Fox Lake North Dr Indianapolis IN 46278 Office: 9102 N Meridian St #525 Indianapolis IN 46260

HOUSEMAN, GERALD L., political science educator, writer; b. Marshalltown, Iowa, Apr. 12, 1935; s. Lawrence D. and Mary N. (Smith) H.; m. Penelope Lyon, Feb. 11, 1961; children: Christopher, Elisabeth, Victoria. BA, Calif. State U., Hayward, 1965, MA, 1967; PhD, U. Ill., 1971. Asst. prof. polit. sci. Ind. U., Ft. Wayne, 1971-76, assoc. prof., 1976-82, prof., 1982—; vis. prof. Brock U., St. Catharines, Can., summer 1970, New Coll., Durham, Eng., 1975-76, Calif. State Polytech. U., San Luis Obispo, 1983-84, U. Calif., Irvine, 1984-85, St. Mary's Coll. Calif., 1985-86. Mem. Transit Authority Bd., Ft. Wayne, 1973-75; city plan commr., 1982-83; active ACLU, Anti-Defamation League. Served with USMC, 1954-57. Grantee NSF, 1970, Ford Found., 1973, 74, NEH, 1977-78, 87; Ind. U. fellow, 1973, 74, 77. Mem. Am. Polit. Sci. Assn. (seminar grantee 1980, 81), Caucus for a New Polit. Sci. Jewish. Author: (with H. Mark Roelofs) The American Political System, 1983; G. D. H. Cole, 1979; The Right of Mobility, 1979; City of the Right: Urban Applications of American Political Thought, 1982, State and Local Government: The New Battleground, 1986.

HOUSER, H. DAVID, bank executive; b. Ft. Wayne, Ind., Aug. 24, 1944; s. Harold H. and Geraldine (Buhl) H.; m. Carol Sue Lotter, Nov. 22, 1967; children: Michael David, Nicole Suzanne. BS, Ball State U., 1967. Asst. cashier Anthony Wayne Bank, Ft. Wayne, 1967-70; asst. v.p. Ind. Bank, Ft. Wayne, 1970-78; v.p. Auburn (Ind.) State Bank, 1978-83; pres., chmn. Knisely Nat. Bank, Butler, Ind., 1983—. Treas. Auburn YMCA, 1980—; pres. Auburn Port Authority, 1985; bd. dirs. Howe Mil. Acad., Howe, Ind., 1978—; chmn. bd. dirs. DeKalb Meml. Hosp., Auburn, 1978—. Served with U.S. Army, 1967-72. Mem. Ind. Bankers Assn. (bd. dirs. 1986—), Robert Morris Assocs., Butler C. of C. (bd. dirs. 1983—). Republican. Lutheran. Club: Greenhurst Country (Auburn). Lodges: Masons, Shriners. Avocations: flying, golf. Home: 135 Zona Dr Auburn IN 46706

HOUSER, MARTHA JEAN, author, educator; b. Detroit, Apr. 20, 1928; d. Philip Leonard and Rose (Meszaros) Tucker; m. Mortimer Clarke Houser, Sept. 3, 1947; children—Leonard Paul, Rosemary Houser Taylor, Julia Houser Cassidy. B.S. cum laude, Kent State U., 1971, M.Ed., 1975. Pvt. piano and organ tchr., Oreg. and Ohio, 1950-65; tchr. La Brae Local Schs., Leavittsburg, Ohio, 1966-81, reading specialist Bascom Elem. Sch., 1974-81; Right to Read dir., La Brae Local Schs., Ohio Dept. Edn., 1979-81. Annie Webb Blanton grad. scholar Delta Kappa Gamma, 1973; Ohio Dept. Edn. Tchr. grantee, 1980. Mem. Trumbull Area Reading Assn. (past pres.), NEA, AAUW, Music Tchrs. Nat. Assn., Nat. Retired Tchrs. Assn., Ohio Retired Tchrs. Assn., Trumbull Retired Tchrs. Assn., Delta Kappa Gamma, Kappa Delta Pi. Clubs: Amateur Radio Relay League (Warren, Ohio), Holborn Herb Growers Guild. Home: 2700 Heather Ln NW Warren OH 44485

HOUSER, RICHARD LYNN, banker; b. Butler, Ind., June 9, 1947; s. Frank F. and Viola M. (Hose) H.; m. Patty Jo Hudson, Oct. 31, 1968; (div. Nov. 1978); children—Tammy V., Richard Dean; m. Joyce E. Dunlap, Nov. 18, 1978. Student St. Francis Coll., Ind., 1964-65, Ind. U., 1970-75. Mgr., Am. Credit Corp., Charlotte, N.C., 1970-74; sr. v.p. Citizens Nat. Bank, Columbia City, Ind., 1974—; owner, operator H & B Bookstore, Columbia City, 1982—. Contbr. poetry to anthologies. Mem. exec. com. Ft. Wayne Credit Bur., Ind., 1981—; bd. dirs. Ft. Wayne Better Bus. Bur., 1980—; pres. Columbia City .Civic Theatre, 1981-82; bd. dirs. Jr. Achievement, 1975-83. Served with USMC, 1965-69, Vietnam. Mem. Robert Morris Assocs., No. Ind. Bankers Assn., Ind. Bankers Assn., Am. Bankers Assn., Assn. Profl. Poets, Nat. Manufactured Housing Assn., Columbia City C. of C. (bd. dirs. 1976-82, pres. 1978-80). Clubs: Poetry (Columbia City); Elks Country (Fort Wayne); Orchard Ridge Country. Lodge: Elks. Avocations: reading; computers; golf; basketball. Office: PO Box 510 Columbia City IN 46725

HOUSTON, JEROME ALLEN, marketing executive; b. Racine, Wis., May 1, 1952; s. Ralph Robert and Grace Marie (Spaulding) H.; m. Vivian Renee Borst, Sept. 1, 1979; 1 child, Jonathan Edward. BA in History and S. Asian Studies, U. Wis., 1974. Vol. U.S. Peace Corps, Korat, Thailand, 1974-76; tech. writer Snap-on Tools Corp., Kenosha, Wis., 1977-79, Pako Corp., Mpls., 1979-82; mktg. mgr. DataMyte Corp., Minnetonka, Minn., 1982—; instr. in statistics Hennepin Tech. Inst., Mpls., 1985—. Author, editor: DataMyte Handbook, 1984; producer: (videotape) If You Are Really Serious About Quality, 1986. Mem. Soc. for Tech. Communication, Am. Soc. for Quality Control, Bus. and Profl. Advt. Assn. Avocations: sailing, running, swimming, blue grass and sitar music. Home: 12210 24th Ave N Plymouth MN 55441 Office: DataMyte 14960 Industrial Rd Minnetonka MN 55345

HOUSTON, WILLIAM ROBERT MONTGOMERY, ophthalmic surgeon; b. Mansfield, Ohio, Nov. 13, 1922; s. William T. and Frances (Hursh) H.; B.A., Oberlin Coll., 1944; M.D., Western Res. U., 1948; m. Marguerite LaBau Browne, Apr. 25, 1968; children—William Erling Tenney, Marguerite Elisabeth LaBau, Selby Cabot Truitt Vanderbilt. Intern, Meth. Hosp. Bklyn., 1948-49, Ill. Eye and Ear Infirmary, Chgo., 1949-50; resident N.Y. Eye and Ear Infirmary, 1950-52; practice medicine specializing in ophthalmic surgery, Mansfield, 1952—; mem. staffs Mansfield Gen. Hosp., Peoples Hosp., Mansfield, N.Y. U. Bellevue Med. Center, N.Y.C.; assoc. prof. clin. ophthalmology N.Y. U. Sch. Medicine. Pres. Mansfield Symphony Soc., 1965-68, Mansfield Civic Music Assn., 1965; mem. Mansfield City Sch. Bd., 1962-65, v.p., 1965. Served to capt. M.C. USAF, 1952-55. Diplomate Am. Bd. Ophthalmology. Recipient Honor award Acad. Ophthalmology. Fellow Internat. Coll. Surgeons; mem. SAR (color guard 1961-71), Ohio Hist. Soc. (life), Western Res. Hist. Soc. (life fellow), N.Y. Geneal. and Biog. Soc. (life), Ohio Geneal. Soc. (trustee 1955—). Editor, Ohio Records and Pioneers Families, 1970—. Address: 456 Park Ave W Mansfield OH 44906

HOUTS, W. WALLACE, educator, real estate consultant; b. Rockford, Iowa, Oct. 30, 1927; s. John Max and Caroline (Talbot) H.; m. Beverly Swahn, Aug. 2, 1953; children—Robert, Mary Jane, Richard, Charles, Chris. B.A., Iowa Wesleyan Coll., 1950; M.A., State U. Iowa, 1951. Cert. tchr., Minn. Art supr. Omaha Pub. Schs., 1951-53; art tchr. Richfield Pub. Schs., Minn., 1953-84; investment cons. Ebbco Co., Mpls., 1964—. Dist. commr. Viking council Boy Scouts Am., Mpls., 1977-79, dist. chmn., 1982-86, nat. jamboree leader, 1973, 77, 81. Served as cpl. U.S. Army, 1946-47. Recipient Award of Merit, Miniwicota Dist. Boy Scouts Am., 1973, Scouter of Yr. award 1984, Silver Beaver award Viking council Boy Scouts Am., 1975, God and Service award United Meth. Chs., 1987. Mem. Richfield Fedn. Tchrs., Minn. Fedn. Tchrs., Am. Fedn. Tchrs., Minn. Art Educators Assn., Kappa Pi, Sigma Phi Epsilon. Republican. Methodist. Lodge: Rotary. Avocations: photography; sports; calligraphy. Home: 10210 Parkview Circle Bloomington MN 55431 Office: Ebbco Co 4940 Viking Dr Suite 688 Edina MN 55435

HOVERSTEN, O. HENRY, accountant, minister, educator; b. Thompson, Iowa, Sept. 29, 1922; s. Albert and Astrid (Rosvold) H.; m. Janice Gail Glauner, Dec. 22, 1949; children: William, Daniel, Paul, Carol. BA, U. Minn., 1947; MBA, Harvard U., 1950; MDiv, Trinity Luth. Seminary, 1967. CPA, Ohio; cert. mgmt. acct., internal auditor; ordained to ministry Luth. Ch., 1967. Field auditor N.Y. Term. Wholesale Co., St. Paul, 1947-48; dir. oil and gas taxes Gulf Oil Corp., Pitts., 1950-64; prof., dept. chmn. Capital U., Columbus, Ohio, 1969-86; dean Grad. Sch. Adminstrn. Capital U., Columbus, 1986—. Served as lt. j.g. USN, 1943-46, PTO. Mem. Pitts. Harvard Bus. Sch. Club (pres. and chmn. bd. dirs. 1962-63), Pitts. U. Minn. Alumni Club (pres. and chmn. bd. dirs. 1961-62), Chi Psi. Republican. Home: 207 S Ardmore Columbus OH 43209

HOVIJITRA, SUTEERA TANTITEERACHARI, dentist, researcher; b. Bangkok, Aug. 3, 1944; came to U.S., 1972; s. Tienchai and Sae I. Tantiteerachart; m. Chamnan Hovijitra, Aug. 15, 1972; children: Ray S., Norman T. DDS cum laude, Mahidol U., 1968, postgrad. cert., 1970; MSD, Ind. U., 1976, DDS, 1981. Instr. Mahidol U., Bangkok, 1970-72; grad. asst. Ind. U., Indpls., 1972-74, asst. prof., 1974-76; asst. prof. U. Ky., Lexington, 1976-79; assoc. prof. Ind. U., Indpls., 1979—. Mem. ADA, Am. Acad. Crown and Bridge Prothodontics, Ind. Assn. Women Dentist, West Side Study Club, Ind. U. Alumni Assn. Home: 4504 Hidden Orchard Ln Indianapolis IN 46208 Office: 3750 Gulon Rd Indianapolis IN 46222 Office: Ind U Dental Sch 1121 W Michigan St Indianapolis IN 46202

HOWALD, ALAN BERT, management consultant; b. Brazil, Ind., Jan. 23, 1945; s. Vern Fredrick and Marie Martin H.; m. Judith Ann Riddell, June 19, 1963 (div. Jan. 1981); children: Troy, Deborah; m. Linda Sue Lanning, Feb. 16, 1985. BS, Ind. State U., 1968. Personnel adminstr. Bank One, Columbus, Ohio, 1968-73; personnel mgr. AccuRay Corp., Columbus, 1973-79; mgmt. cons. William Alan Assocs., Columbus, 1979-81; sr. mgmt. cons. J.W. Hickey Assoc., Columbus, 1981—; chmn. scholarship com. J.W. Hickey, Columbus, 1983—; speaker seminars. Loaned exec. United Way, Columbus, 1972, Nat. Alliance Businessmen, Columbus, 1972. Mem. Am. Compensation Assn., Employment Mgmt. Assn. (com. mem. 1975-77), Cen. Ohio Mgmt. Assn. (instr. 1976-84). Republican. Methodist. Avocations: flying, fishing, travel. Office: JW Hickey & Assocs 4391 E 17th Ave Columbus OH 43219

HOWARD, ALAN CHARLES, English educator; b. Manistee, Mich., Aug. 27, 1944; s. Edmund Witherell and Esther Marie (Watrous) H.; m. Lois Marie Zimmer, June 20, 1965; children: Jennifer, Rebecca. AB in English, Cen. Mich. U., 1967; MA in English, U. Mich., 1968. Lectr. English Southgate Tech. Coll., London, 1975-76; asst. prof. English Bay de Noc Community Coll., Escanaba, Mich., 1968-75, 76—. Pres. Bay Area Campus Ministry, Escanaba, 1985—; sec., v.p. PTO, Escanaba, 1983-85; mem. council on ministries First United Meth. Ch., Escanaba, 1980—; trustee Escanaba Pub. Library, 1980—,. Fulbright grantee, 1975-76; named one of Outstanding Young Men of Am. U.S. Jaycees, 1977. Mem. Nat. Council Tchrs. of English, Conf. Coll. Composition and Communication. Avocations: travel, photography, cooking, creative writing. Home: 301 S 13th St Escanaba MI 49829 Office: Bay de Noc Community Coll College Ave Escanaba MI 49829

HOWARD, ALICE LAVERNE, bank executive; b. Blythesville, Ark., Apr. 4, 1943; d. Luther M. and Alice R. (Kinnision) Ford. Student, U. St. Louis, 1970—. Ops. officer, administrv. asst. Centerre Bank, St. Louis, 1977-80, dir. ops. tng., 1979-80, asst. v.p. mgr. domestic wire ctr., 1980-81, asst. v.p., mgr., domestic ops., 1981-82, v.p., mgr. air transport assn. of Am. dept., 1981-82, v.p., mgr. administrv. services div., 1983-86, v.p., mgr. retail ops. div., 1986—. Officer Santa's Helpers, St. Louis, 1972—; dir. Women's Self Help Ctr., 1986—. Recipient Leadership award YWCA, Metro St. Louis, 1984. Mem. Am. Inst Banking (bd. dirs. St. Louis chpt. 1984—). Avocations: reading, walking, fishing. Home: 1612 Forestedge Dr Saint Louis MO 63138 Office: Centerre Bank N A 1 Centerre Plaza Saint Louis MO 63101

HOWARD, DAVID MORRIS, missionary; b. Phila., Jan. 28, 1928; s. Philip E. Jr. and Katharine (Gillingham) H.; m. Phyllis Gibson, July 1, 1950; children—David, Stephen, Karen Elisabeth, Michael. A.B., Wheaton Coll., 1949, M.A. in Theology, 1952; LL.D., Geneva Coll., 1974; L.H.D., Taylor U., 1978. Ordained to ministry, 1952; asst. gen. dir. Latin Am. Mission, Colombia S.Am., Costa Rica, C.Am., 1953-68; missions dir. Inter-Varsity Christian Fellowship, Madison, Wis., 1968-76, asst. to pres., 1976-77; dir. Urbana Student Missionary Convs., 1973, 76; dir. Consultation on World Evangelization, Pattaya, Thailand, 1977-80; gen. dir. World Evangel. Fellowship, Wheaton, Ill., 1982—. Author: Hammered as Gold, 1969, reprinted as The Costly Harvest, 1975; Student Power in World Missions, 1979; How Come, God?, 1972, By the Power of the Holy Spirit, 1973; Words of Fire, Rivers of Tears, 1976, The Great Commission for Today, 1976, The Dream That Would Not Die, 1986, What Makes a Missionary, 1987. Adv. life trustee Wheaton Coll. Office: World Evangel Fellowship PO Box WEF Wheaton IL 60189

HOWARD, GEORGE STEPHEN, psychology educator; b. Bayonne, N.J., June 8, 1948; s. John Marion and Margaret Marian (Jordan) H.; m. Nancy A. Gulanick, June 15, 1974; children: John, Greg. BA, Marist Coll., 1970; MA, So. Ill. U., 1972, PhD, 1975. Assoc. prof. clin. psychology Houston, 1975-81, faculty resources, 1977-79; asst. prof. psychology U. Notre Dame, Ind., 1981-87, chmn. dept. psychology, 1985—; Cons. to academic v.p., Wichita, 1974-75. Author: Basic Research Methods in the Social Sciences, 1985, Dare We Develop a Human Science?, 1986; mem. editorial bd. Jour. Counseling Psychology, 1981. Fellow Am. Psychol. Assn. Roman Catholic. Home: 17044 Hampton Dr Granger IN 46530 Office: U Notre Dame Dept Psychology Notre Dame IN 46556

HOWARD, JAMES JOSEPH, III, utility company executive; b. Pitts., July 1, 1935; s. James Joseph Jr. and Flossie (Wenzel) H.; m. Donna Joan Fowler, Aug. 31, 1955; children: James J. IV, Catherine A., Christine A., William F. BBA, U. Pitts., 1957; MS, MIT, 1970. With Bell Telephone of Pa., Pitts., 1957-78, v.p., gen. mgr., 1976-78; v.p. ops. Wis. Telephone Co., Milw., 1978-79, exec. v.p., chief operating officer, 1979-81, pres., 1981-83, chmn., chief exec. officer, 1983; pres., chief operating officer Ameritech, Chgo., 1983-87, dir.; pres., chief exec. officer No. States Power Co., Mpls., 1987—; bd. dirs. Square D Co., Palatine, Ill., Walgreen Co., Deerfield, Ill., No. States Power Co., Mpls. Bd. trustees Coll. of St. Thomas, St. Paul, Minn. Sloan fellow MIT, 1969. Mem. Conf. Bd. Clubs: Chgo., Comml., Econ.; Milw. Country; Duquesne, Oakmont Country (Pitts.), Minn., Mpls. Athletic. Office: No States Power Co 414 Nicollet Mall Minneapolis MN 55401

HOWARD, JAMES R., food packing company executive. Chmn. Black Hills Packing Co., Rapid City, S.D. Office: Black Hills Packing Co. Drawer 2130 Rapid City SD 57709 *

HOWARD, JERRY ARTHUR, children's home executive, consultant; b. Huntington, Ind., Oct. 13, 1940; s. Arthur W. and Esta G. (Herrmann) H.; m. Wanda Lee James, June 17, 1962; children—Jonathan A., James T. B.S., Greenville Coll., 1962; M.S., Purdue U., 1965, Ph.D., 1974. Tchr. jr. high sch. Carroll Consol. Sch., Flora, Ind., 1962-65; prin. Culver (Ind.) Schs., 1965-69; NDEA fellow Purdue U., West Lafayette, Ind., 1970-72; prin. North Miami Sch. Corp., Denver, Ind., 1972-73; asst. dir. stewardship dept. Free Meth. World Hdqrs., Winona Lake, Ind., 1974-79; dir. devel. Salem Children's Home, Flanagan, Ill., 1979—; guest instr. Greenville Coll., Ill., 1983, Huntington Coll., Ind., 1984; cons. Ont. Conf., Free Meth. Ch., Toronto, Ont., Can., 1974; chmn. audio/visual com. Free Meth. World Conv., 1978-79; ch. chmn. Hope Fellowship Evang. Mennonite, Wabash, Ind., 1983-86; cons. estate planning Evang. Mennonite Conf., Ft. Wayne, Ind., 1979—. Contbr. articles to profl. jours. Named Hon. Farmer North Miami chpt. Future Farmers Am., 1973; NDEA fellow Purdue U., 1970. Mem. Am. Mgmt. Assn., Christian Stewardship Council, Phi Delta Kappa, Phi Alpha Theta. Republican. Mennonite. Home: Box 252 Rural Route 1 Akron IN 46910

HOWARD, JOHN R., food packing company executive. Pres. Black Hills Packing Co., Rapid City, S.D. Office: Black Hills Packing Co Drawer 2130 Rapid City SD 57709 *

HOWARD, LEE CROWLEY, pharmaceutical executive; b. Columbus, Ga., May 7, 1958; s. John Edward and Marian Davis (Richardson) Crowley; m. Steven Ray Howard, July 18, 1981. BS in Pharmacy, U. Colo., 1981; MBA, Ind. U., 1987. Lic. pharmacist, Ky., Ind. Staff pharmacist N.K.C. Inc., Louisville, 1981-83, Jewish Hosp., Louisville, 1982-83; dir. pharmacy Jennings Community Hosp., North Vernon, Ind., 1983-85; staff pharmacist Jackson County Pharmacy, Seymour, Ind., 1985-86, Union Hosp., Terre Haute, Ind., 1986-87; mktg. assoc. Eli Lilly and Co., Indpls., 1987—; aerobics instr. Shapenastics, Louisville, 1983-84. Mem. Ind. Soc. Hosp. Pharmacists, Wabash Pharm. Soc., MBA Assn. Ind. U., Rho Chi, Beta Gamma Sigma. Clubs: Marketing, GWB (Bloomington, Ind.). Avocations: aerobics, walking, golf, skiing, bicycling.

HOWARD, PHILIP MARTIN, insurance agent; b. Chgo., Dec. 16, 1939; s. Anthony Gerald and Mary Elizabeth (Smith) H.; m. Diane R. Miller, Sept. 12, 1964; children: Anne Marie, Philip Martin II, Kevin Vincent. Student Chgo. parochial schs. Laborer, tree trimmer Chgo. Bur. Forestry, 1963-66; sales rep. O.H. div. Bell & Howell, Chgo., 1966; sr. account agt. Allstate Ins. Co., Chgo., 1967—; ins. officer Mt. Greenwood Youth Baseball, Chgo., 1981-86. Served with USMCR, 1962-67. Roman Catholic. Home: 11324 S Lawndale Ave Chicago IL 60655 Office: 7000 W 111th St Worth IL 60482

HOWARD, ROBERT FREDERICK, hotel company executive; b. Buffalo, June 24, 1947; s. William Robert and Alice Louise (Bangert) H.; m. Clare Ada Heaton, Oct. 7, 1969; 1 child; Christopher R. BS in Hotel Adminstrn., Cornell U., 1969; MBA, Syracuse U., 1971. Desk clk., bartender Winegardner & Hammons, Inc., Syracuse, N.Y., 1969-71; corp. planning analyst Flagship Internat. subs. Am. Airlines, Inc., N.Y.C., 1971-73; cons. David J. Burgos & Assoc., N.Y.C., 1973-74; comptroller Anchorage Hotel, Antigua, West Indies, 1974-77; fin. dir. Jumer's Castle Lodge, Inc., Peoria, Ill., 1977-79, v.p., 1979—, also bd. dirs. Chmn. Cornell Alumni Secondary Schs. Com., Down State, Ill., 1986; coordinator Workshop in Bus. Opprtunities, Harlem, N.Y., 1971-74. Regents scholar Cornell U., 1965-69; recipient Pub. Service award Workshop in Bus. Opportunities, 1973. Mem. Cornell Soc. Hotelmen, Nat. Restaurant Assn. Republican. Avocations: travel, tennis, restoring old homes. Home: 612 Fondulac Dr East Peoria IL 61611 Office: Jumer Hotels Ltd 3126 SW Adams St Peoria IL 61605

HOWARD, ROBERT M., food products manufacturing company executive; b. 1923; married. B.S. in Engring., U. Minn., 1947. With Internat. Multifoods Corp., Mpls., 1947—, dir. engring. and milling, 1957-63, regional prodn. mgr. U.S. flour milling div., 1963-69, v.p. and gen. mgr. indsl. foods div., 1969-83, exec. v.p., 1981-85; pres. Internat. Multifoods Corp., 1986—. Served with USNR, 1944-46. Office: Internat Multifoods Corp 733 Marquette Ave 1200 Multifoods Bldg Minneapolis MN 55402 *

HOWARD, THOMAS EDWARD, JR., tax consultant; b. St. Louis, July 31, 1956; s. Thomas Edward and Marie Anthony (Hory) H.; m. Barbara Ann Walczyk, Oct. 6, 1978; 1 child, Ryan Thomas. BSBA cum laude, St. Louis U., 1978. CPA, Mo. Sr. tax mgr. Peat, Marwick, Main & Co., St. Louis, 1978—; mem. faculty Ill. Bankers Sch., Carbondale, 1981-85; speaker Mo. Bankers Assn., St. Louis, 1986; bd. dirs. Mo. Pacific Credit Union, St. Louis. Contbr. articles to profl. jours. Fund raiser Multiple Sclerosis Soc., St. Louis, 1986; bd. dirs. MS150 Bike Ride, St. Louis, 1987. Mem. Am. Inst. CPA's, Mo. Soc. CPA's. Roman Catholic. Club: Media. Avocations: cycling, running, golf. Home: 6411 Woodbine Ct Saint Louis MO 63109 Office: Peat Marwick Main & Co 1010 Market St Saint Louis MO 63109

HOWARD, WILLIAM M., engineer executive; b. Chgo., Jan. 28, 1935; s. Cyril Marshall and Leeta Miriam (Darling) H.; m. Patricia Jean Howard, Aug. 31, 1957 (div. June 1984); children: Bonnie Jean, Craig Marshall; m. Mary Elizabeth Collins, Oct. 18, 1986. BS in Civil Engring., U. Wis., 1958, BBA in Indsl. Mgmt., 1960, MBA in Indsl. Mgmt., 1968. Registered profl. engr., Wis. Product engr. Eastman Kodak, Rochester, N.Y., 1960-66; v.p. Hooper Constrn. Corp., Madison, Wis., 1966-79; pres. Power Span, Inc., Hayfield, Minn., 1979-83, Power Line Systems, Inc., Madison, 1983—; instr. U. Wis. Madison, 1957-58, Rochester Inst. Tech., 1964-66; lectr. U. Wis. Madison, 1986—. Patentee R.R. loading system for concrete poles, 1985. Exec. dir. Madison Scouts Drum & Bugle Corps., 1968-80; founder, bd. dirs. Drum Corps. Internat., Lombard, Ill., 1971-80, Drum Corps. Midwest, Milw., 1974-80; dep. mgr. Jonathan Barry for gov., Madison, 1986. Served to capt. U.S. Army, 1958-60. Mem. ASCE, ASTM, IEEE, Am. Concrete Inst., Tau Beta Pi, Chi Epsilon. Republican. Avocations: skiing, tennis, sailing, canoeing, camping. Home: 5214 Hedden Circle Middleton WI 53562 Office: Power Line Systems Inc 6701 Seybold Rd Madison WI 53719

HOWARDS, ROBERT, marketing executive; b. Brussels, May 4, 1945. BBA, U. Miami, 1967; MBA, U. Houston, 1970. Sr. mktg. analyst Exxon USA, Houston, 1967-74; dir. children's mktg. Burger King Corp., Miami, Fla., 1974-80; mgr. promotional services Seven Up Co., St. Louis, 1980-83; v.p. advt. and promotion Playboy Enterprises, Chgo., 1983-84; sr. v.p. Rogers Merchandising, Lombard, Ill., 1984—. Avocations: tennis, photography. Office: Rogers Merchandising Inc 1 Imperial Pl Lombard IL 60148

HOWCOTT, J(AMES) FRED, human services consultant; b. White Plains, N.Y., Sept. 11, 1931; s. Thyrul C. and Gertie (Fitchett) H.; m. Jeffernell O. Green; children: Terry Lynn, Sonya Rene. AB, Cen. State U., 1956; MSW, Wayne State U., 1960; postgrad., U. Mich., 1978—. Cons. Wayne County Juvenile Ct., Detroit, 1960-64; adminstr. Mich. Dept. Health, Detroit, 1964-68; exec. dir. Neighborhood Services Orgn. Community Mental Health Program, Detroit, 1968-72; cons. Detroit, 1972-74; prof. social work Wayne State U., Detroit, 1974-81; exec. dir. Todd-Phillips Childrens Home, Detroit, 1981—. State dir. Com. to Reelect the Pres., Detroit, 1972; Rep. precinct del. Mich., 1980—; bd. dirs. Community Case Mgmt., Detroit, 1980—, Episc. Diocese Sch. Theology, Detroit, 1983-85; cons. Wolverine Bapt. Conv. 1981—. Served with U.S. Army, 1952-54, Korea. Mem. Nat. Assn. Social Workers (chmn. nomination and leadership devel. com. 1980-84), Council Social Work Edn., Nat. Assn. Black Social Workers (founding), Omega Psi Phi (vice basilus 1968-72). Episcopalian. Lodges: Masons, Optimists. Avocations: golf, travel, racquetball, music, antiques. Home: PO Box 21002 Detroit MI 48221 Office: Todd-Phillips Childrens Home 1561 Webb Detroit MI 48206

HOWDER, DELORIS JEAN, designer, manufacturer; b. Muscotah, Kans., Dec. 28, 1926; d. Ernest Oscer and Lona Ethel (Wiley) Hollenbeck; student Nat. Sch. Dress Design, 1953-54; m. Wilbern B. Obbards; 1 son, Glen Alan; m. 2d, Richard Joseph Howder, Jan. 29, 1968. With Horton Garment Co. (Kans.), 1948-54; with Paramount Studios, Hollywood, Calif., 1955; owner, designer Deloris Square Dance Dresses, Long Beach, Calif., Springfield, Mo., Seligman, Mo., and Horton, 1957—. Mem. Horton C. of C. (mem. arts and crafts show com. 1979, mem. arts, crafts and flea market 1983-84), Nat. Costume Assn., Parents Without Partners (editor newsletter 1979-82, N.E. Kans. chpt. 1071 membership dir. 1982-83). Office: 847 Central Horton KS 66439

HOWE, DONALD EDWARD, broadcast producer; b. Aurora, Colo., May 12, 1962; s. Donald Burton Howe and Madeline Ella Brown. BA in Telecommunications, Mich. State U., 1984. Broadcast producer, prodn. mgr. Mars Advt., Southfield, Mich., 1986—; ptnr., cons. Screenlogic, Walled Lake, Mich., 1986—. Photography instr. Boys' and Girls' Club Lansing, 1981-82. Recipient Jim Cash award Mich. State U., 1984; Art Stokus Meml. scholar, 1980. Mem. Detroit Producers Assn. Democrat. Home: 1839

Alton Circle Walled Lake MI 48088 Office: Mars Advt Co 24209 Northwestern Hwy Southfield MI 48075

HOWE, G(ARY) WOODSON, newspaper editor; b. Sioux City, Iowa, Feb. 15, 1936; s. Robert Blanchard and Marjorie Murray (Woodson) H.; m. Anda Grinbergs, Aug. 17, 1968; children—Marisa, Evan. B.A. in Am. Studies, Yale U., 1958. Reporter Lincoln Star, Nebr., 1961-62; reporter Omaha World Herald, 1962-67, city editor, 1967-71, adminstrv. asst. to pres., 1971-75; v.p. Omaha World Herald Co., 1975—; corp. sec. Omaha World Herald, 1974-80, v.p., exec. asst. to pres., 1975-79, v.p., exec. editor, 1979-85, editor, 1985—; dir. Omaha World Herald Co., 1974—. Mem. met. bd. Omaha YMCA, 1975-81; mem. exec. com. Health Planning Council Midlands, 1976-78; mem. Omaha Performing Arts Ctr. Corp. Bd., 1974—; co-chmn. United Way Midlands, 1978; trustee Joslyn Art Mus., 1980—. Served to lt. (j.g.) USN, 1958-61. Recipient Journalist of Yr. award Creighton U., 1967. Mem. Soc. Profl. Journalists, Am. Soc. Newspaper Editors, Sigma Delta Chi. Home: 2315 S 103rd St Omaha NE 68124 Office: Omaha Herald-World Co World-Herald Square Omaha NE 68102

HOWE, HILARY ELEANOR, publishing sales executive; b. London, Dec. 3, 1942; d. Thomas James Jackson and Mary Gladys Jackson (Lubbock) H.; divorced; 1 child, Dvid Thomas Yob. BA in Mktg. and Advt., Wayne State U., 1961-65. Adminstv. asst. pub. relations Leo Burnett Advt., Southfield, Mich., 1966-68; media dir. Planned Mktg. and Advt., Birm, Mich., 1968-78, The AD Works, Southfield, 1978-80, Sohigian & Ptnrs., Southfield, 1979-82; assoc. media dir. Ross Roy, Detroit, 1982-84; regional sales mgr. Am. Newspaper, Detroit, 1983—. Mem. Sales Assn., AD Craft Club. Republican. Episcopalian. Avocations: boating, swimming, skiing, fly fishing, snorkeling. Home: 27484 Evergreen Lathrup Village MI 48076

HOWE, JOHN KINGMAN, sales and marketing executive; b. Everett, Wash., Nov. 7, 1945; s. John Cutler and Nancy Carpenter (Kingman) H.; m. Loretta Kerr, Aug. 27, 1966; children—Steven Cutler, Nancy Kingman. Student Ohio State U., 1963-65. Field technician Data Corp., Dayton, Ohio, 1965-66; letter carrier U.S. Post Office, Dayton, 1966; sales rep. E.S. Klosterman Co., Dayton, 1966-71, v.p. 1971-72; v.p. sales, dir. Springfield Binder Corp., Ohio, 1981-84, pres., chief exec. officer, 1984—; pres. The John K. Howe Co., Dayton, Ohio, 1972-87, chmn., chief exec. officer, dir. 1987—; pres., dir. Cutler-Kingman, Inc., Dayton, 1979-86; gen. ptnr. H&B Enterprises, Dayton, 1977—, Design Investment Properties, Dayton, 1979-86, BMR Properties, Ltd., Dayton, 1979-82; adminstr. John K. Howe Co./Profit Sharing, Dayton, 1973—, John K. Howe Co./Pension Plan, 1976—; owner Androscoggin Designs, Dayton, 1979— . Pres. South Dixie Bus. Assn., Kettering, Ohio, 1978-82. Mem. Adminstrv. Mgmt. Soc. Internat., Dayton C. of C. Republican. Presbyterian. Home: 628 Cushing Ave Dayton OH 45429 Office: John K Howe Co Inc 2435 S Dixie Ave Dayton OH 45409

HOWE, RAYMOND BRADLEY, security systems consultant; b. N.Y.C., Aug. 25, 1920; s. Herbert R. and Ruth (Bradley) H.; m. Faye M., Aug. 6, 1950 (div. Sept. 1978); children: Anthony, Carolyn, Chris, Mary Ellen, Jennifer, John, Charles; m. Joy R. Throckmorton, Sept. 21, 1978; 1 child, Tracy. BS, U. Md., 1949. Research scientist USDA, Beltsville, Md., 1949-50; spl. agt. FBI, Washington, 1950-78; pres. Ray Howe & Assocs., Lees Summit, Mo., 1978—; Chmn. Lynwood Racing Stables, Lees Summit, 1985—. Author: (cartoon book) Fall Semester '84, 1984; contbr. articles in field to Ripples mag., 1983-84. Chmn. Security Com., Village of Lakewood, Mo., 1983. Served to capt. A.C., U.S. Army, 1942-46, ETO. Decorated Air medal with clusters. Mem. Soc. Former Spl. Agts. FBI (chmn. Kansas City chpt. 1986), Cartoonists Guild, Thunderbolt Assn., VFW (vice comdr. 1986). Republican. Club: Lakewood Country (Lees Summit). Avocation: owning and training thoroughbred race horses. Home: 238 Bayview Dr Lees Summit MO 64063

HOWE, RICHARD RAY, lawyer; b. Decatur, Ill., Aug. 23, 1932; s. Elbert Davis and Marie (Harris) H.; A.B., U. Mo., 1954, J.D., 1959; m. Elaine Bondurant, Apr. 17, 1954; children—Richard R., Scott W., Dale A., Tracy. Admitted to Mo. bar, 1959, since practiced in Canton. Mem. Canton Bd. Edn., 1962-68, sec., 1962-67, v.p., 1967-68. Pros. atty. Lewis County (Mo.), 1969-72; commr., also chmn. Commn. to Reapportion Mo. Legislature, 1971. Mem., vice chmn. Mo. Commn. on Human Rights, 1974-76. Chmn., Republican Central Com. Lewis County, 1971-76, 79—; chmn. 9th Congl. Dist. Rep. Com., 1974-76. Trustee Canton Pub. Library, 1961-70. Served with USAF, 1955-57. Mem. Am. Bar Assn., Assn. Trial Lawyers Am., Am. Judicature Soc., Alpha Tau Omega, Phi Alpha Delta. Mason, Kiwanian. Home: Rural Route 2 Canton MO 63435 Office: 436 Lewis St Canton MO 63435

HOWE, ROBERT BRUCE, hematologist, educator; b. Elgin, Ill., Feb. 13, 1936; s. Francis W. and Esther (Dorow) H.; m. Sondra Ann Wieland, Aug. 12, 1961; children: Deborah, Philip, Stephen. BS, Union Coll., Schenectady, N.Y., 1958; MD, Harvard U., 1962. Intern, then resident U. Minn., 1962-67; asst. clin. dir. Nat. Cancer Inst., Bethesda, Md., 1967-70; prof. med. U. Minn., Mpls., 1970—, chief Gen. Medicine div., 1985—; cons. VA Hosp., Mpls., 1970—. Contbr. numerous articles on bile pigment metabolism and hematology to profl. jours, chpts. to books. Served to lt. comdr. USPHS, 1967-69. Fellow ACP, Internat. Soc. Hematology; mem. AAAS, Am. Soc. Hematology, AM. Fedn. for Clin. Research, Soc. for Gen. Internal Medicine , Leukemia Soc. Am. (bd. councilmen), Sierra Club. Avocations: sailing, skiing. Home: 135 Chevy Chase Dr Wayzata MN 55391 Office: Univ Minn Med Sch 512 Delaware St Minneapolis MN 55455

HOWE, STANLEY MERRILL, manufacturing company executive; b. Muscatine, Iowa, Feb. 5, 1924; s. Merrill Y. and Thelma F. (Corriel) H.; m. Helen Jensen, Mar. 29, 1953; children: Thomas, Janet, Steven, James. B.S., Iowa State U., 1946; M.B.A., Harvard U., 1948. Prodn. engr. HON Industries, Muscatine, Iowa, 1948-54; v.p. prodn. HON Industries, 1954-61, exec. v.p., 1961-64, pres., 1964—, chmn., 1984—, also dir.; chmn. bd. Corry Heibert Corp., Heatilator Inc., Budget Panels, Inc., Murphy-Miller Co.; pres. Prime-Mover Co. Trustee Iowa Wesleyan Coll.; chmn. Muscatine Community Health Found. Gerard Swope fellow Harvard U., 1948. Mem. NAM, Iowa Mfrs. Assn., Am. Mgmt. Assn. Methodist. Clubs: Rotary, Elks, 33. Office: Hon Industries Inc 414 E 3d St Muscatine IA 52761

HOWELL, DAVID JOSEPH, oral surgeon, educator; b. Indpls., Feb. 22, 1952; s. Joseph Dumas and Virginia Ann (Roberts) H.; m. Cathy Diane Trittipo, July 31, 1976; 1 child, Pamela Diane. AB, Ind. U., 1975, DDS, 1981; cert., U. Tenn., 1984. Cert. Oral and Maxillofacial Surgery. Asst. prof. Ind. U., Indpls., 1984—; practice dentistry specializing in oral and maxillofacial surgery Ind. U., Bloomington, 1984—. Recipient Glen Pell Meml. Scholastic award Ind. Soc. Oral and Maxillofacial Surgeons. Mem. Am. Assn. Oral and Maxillofacial Surgeons, ADA, Ind. Dental Assn., Delta Sigma Delta (acad. alumni award 1981). Methodist. Avocation: skiing. Home: 4240 Penn Ct Bloomington IN 47401

HOWELL, HONOR SHARON, minister; b. Seguin, Tex, Oct. 12, 1947; d. Joe Milam and Mary Elizabeth (McKay) H. BA, Austin Coll., 1970; MDiv, St. Paul Sch. Theology, 1973. Youth minister Key Meml. United Meth. Ch., Sherman, Tex., 1969-71, Second Presbyn. Ch., Kansas City, Mo., 1971-72; pastor Edwardsville United Meth. Ch., Kans., 1972-75; assoc. program dir. Council on Ministries, Topeka, 1975-80; v.p. St. Paul Sch. Theology, Kansas City, Mo., 1980-85; sr. pastor St. Mark United Meth. Ch., Overland Park, Kans., 1985—; pres. Commn. on Status and Role of Women in United Meth. Ch., Evanston, Ill., 1984—; chmn. personnel com. Council on Ministries, Topeka, Kans., 1984—. V.p. ReStart Bd. Dirs. Mem. NOW, ACLU, Christian Educators Fellowship, Nat. Assn. Female Execs., Smithsonian Assocs., Internat. Assn. Women Ministers, Amnesty Internat., Nat. Mus. Women in Arts (charter). Democrat. Home: 6600 Reeds Dr Mission KS 66202 Office: St Mark United Meth Ch 6422 Santa Fe Dr Overland Park KS 66202

HOWELL, L(OUIS) MICHAEL, surgeon; b. Oakes, N.D., Sept. 3, 1941; s. Joe W. and Virginia C. (Mikkelson); m. M. Michela Cook, Feb. 4, 1967; children: Angela, Kristine, Michael, Melinda. Student, Gonzaga U., 1959-62; BS, U. N.D. Med. Sch., 1964; MD, Georgetown U., 1966. Intern U. Chgo. Med. Sch., 1966-67; resident U. Ind. Med. Sch., Indpls., 1967-68; resident in surgery Swedish Hosps., Seattle, 1968-71; chief of surgery U.S. Army Hosp., Ft. Meade, Md., 1971-73; surgeon Fargo (N.D.) Clinic, 1973—; clin. prof. surgery U. N.D. Med. Sch. Contbr. articles to profl. jours. Pres. 1st. Dist. Med. Soc., Fargo, 1981; mem. exec. bd. Fargo C. of C., 1980-83; chmn. N.D. Med. Polit. Action Com., 1978-80; mem. exec. bd. N.D. Golf Assn., 1983—. Served to maj. U.S. Army, 1971-73. Fellow ACS; mem. AMA, Am. Soc. Bariatric Surgery, N.D. Med. Soc. Republican. Roman Catholic. Lodge: Rotary. Avocations: golf, racquetball, reading. Home: 173 S Woodcrest Fargo ND 58102 Office: Fargo Clinic Fargo ND 58102

HOWELL, ORVIE LEON, geologist; b. Wichita, Kans., Sept. 4, 1931; s. Orville Clements and Hettie-Elizabeth (Brock) H.; divorced; children—Dale, Richard, Susan, Sally. B.S. in Geology, Wichita State U., 1954. Geologist, Lion Oil Co., Wichita, Kans., 1954-58; dist. geologist Lario Oil and Gas Co., Wichita, 1958-63, gen. mgr. Hinkle Oil Co., Wichita, 1973—. Fund raiser United Way, Wichita, 1970-83; sec. adv. com. dept. geology Wichita State U., 1983—. Mem. Am. Assn. Petroleum Geologists (speaker 1969-70, co-editor jour. 1969-70), Kans. Geol. Soc. (pres. 1968-69), N.Mex. Geol. Soc., Am. Inst. Profl. Geologists, Rocky Mountain Assn. Geologists, Kans. Ind. Oil and Gas Assn. Republican. Methodist. Clubs: Tallgrass Country, Crestview Country, Petroleum (Wichita). Avocations: Flying, travel. Home: 9031 Lakepoint Dr Wichita KS 67226 Office: Hinkle Oil Co 1016 Union Ctr Wichita KS 67202

HOWELL, STEPHEN HAVILAND, utility executive; b. Bethlehem, Pa., May 21, 1932; s. Richard and Marion (Mekeel) H.; m. Ann E. Adams, June 19, 1954; children—Cathy, Susan, David, Thomas. B.S.E., Princeton U., 1954; M.S. in Indsl. Mgmt. (Sloan fellow), M.I.T., 1966. Registered profl. engr., Mich. Exec. v.p. Consumers Power Co., Jackson, Mich., 1980—. Served with USNR, 1954-56. Mem. Soc. Petroleum Engrs., Am. Assn. Petroleum Geologists, Atomic Indsl. Forum. Republican. Presbyterian. Home: 3923 Harwich Ln Jackson MI 49201 Office: Consumers Petroleum Co 212 W Michigan Ave Jackson MI 49201

HOWERTON, JOHN DOUGLAS, systems analyst; b. Galesburg, Ill., Apr. 1, 1957; s. James Raymond and Bonny Jean (Beckner) H.; m. Melinda Marie Stevens, June 7, 1980; children: Amy, Steven. AS, Lincoln Land Community Coll., 1977; BS, Millikin U., 1979. Data processing mgr. Capitol Bank, Springfield, Ill., 1979-81; prodn. planning analyst Banks of Iowa Computer Services, Cedar Rapids, 1981-84; sr. hardware analyst Banks of Iowa Computer Services, Cedar Rapids, Iowa, 1984-86, product mgr. for delivery systems, 1986—. Republican. Methodist. Avocations: softball, reading, travel. Home: 1068 Rainbow Blvd Hiawatha IA 52233 Office: Banks of Iowa Computer Services PO Box 1847 Cedar Rapids IA 52406

HOWIE, MICHAEL GLEN, state agency administrator; b. Red Bud, Ill., June 22, 1949; s. Orville Glen and Clara Ione (Shemonic) H. BA in Psychology, McKendree Coll., Lebanon, Ill., 1971; MA in Psychology, U. Richmond, Va., 1973. Psychologist I Ill. Dept. Mental Health, CHester, 1973-74; psychologist II and Adminstrv. asst. Chester Mental Health Ctr., 1974-78, adminstrv. asst. to facility dir., 1978-83; dep. coordinator forensic psychiatry Ill. Dept. Mental Health and Developmental Disabilities, Chester, 1983-84; dep. assoc. dir. div. policy and spl. programs Ill. Dept. Mental Health and Developmental Disabilities, Springfield, 1984—. Mem. Am. Assn. Correctional Psychologists, BMW Motorcycle Owners Club, BMW Car Club Am. Lodge: Elks. Avocations: motorcycling, camping, hiking, boating. Home: 1121 Crescent Ln Springfield IL 62704 Office: Ill Dept Mental Health and Developmental Disabilities 401 S Spring St Springfield IL 62706

HOWLAND, JOHN GORDON BROWN, venture capitalist; b. Norfolk, Va., Nov. 26, 1942; s. John B. and Diana L. (Gray) H.; m. Karen H. Chastain, Feb. 17, 1968; children—John Paul, Nicholas Chastain. B.S., U.S. Naval Acad., 1964; M.B.A., NYU, 1972. Corp. banking officer Citibank, N.Y.C., 1969-72; asst. treas. Am. Hosp. Supply Corp., Evanston, Ill., 1972-74; treas. CF Industries, Chgo., 1974-75; fin. cons., Chgo., 1975-76; treas. Skil Corp., Chgo., 1977-79; founder, pub. Cashflow Mag., Glenview, Ill., 1979-86; pres., Coordinated Capital Resources, 1986—. Chmn. fin. com. Sch. Dist. 34, 1978; founder Glenview Soccer Program (AYSO), 1982; mem. Nat. bd. dirs. Am. Youth Soccer Orgn., 1985-87; bd. dirs. High Sch. Dist. 225, 1987—. Served to lt. USN, 1964-69; Vietnam. Mem. Nat. Corp. Cash Mgmt. Assn. (founder), Fin. Execs. Inst. Clubs: Econ. of Chgo.; Rotary (Glenview) (past pres.). Office: 1807 Glenview Rd Suite 205 Glenview IL 60025

HOWLETT, ROBERT GLASGOW, lawyer; b. Bay City, Mich., Nov. 10, 1906; s. Lewis Glasgow and Anne Lucile (Hurst) H.; m. Barbara Withey, Sept. 19, 1936; children: Eleanor Howlett Burton, Craig G., Douglas W. BS, Northwestern U., 1929, JD, 1932. Bar: Ill. 1932, N.Y. 1940, D.C. 1944, Mich. 1947, Tenn. 1947. Ptnr. Varnum Riddering Schmidt & Howlett, Grand Rapids, Mich., 1949-83; of counsel Varnum Riddering, Schmidt & Howlett, Grand Rapids, Mich., 1983—; mem. Mich. Employment Relations Commn., 1963-76, chmn., 1964-76; chmn. Fed. Service Impasses Panel, 1976-78, 82-84, mem., 1984—; sec., bd. dirs. Light Metals Corp., Elston Richards Inc.; mem. Fgn. Service Impasse Disputes Panel, 1976-78, 81—; industry mem. shipbldg. commn. Nat. War Labor Bd., 1943-45; spl. asst. atty. gen., dept. aero. State of Mich., 1957-61; vis. prof. Mich. State U., East Lansing, 1972, 75. Contbr. articles to profl. jours. Chmn. Kent County Republican Com., 1956-61; del. Rep. Nat. Conv., 1960. Mem. ABA, Grand Rapids Bar Assn. (pres. 1962-63), State Bar Mich., Nat. Acad. Arbitrators, Indsl. Relations Research Assn. (pres. Detroit chpt. 1978-79), Soc. Profls. in Dispute Resolution (pres. 1974-75), Assn. Labor Relations Agys. (pres. 1977-78), Am. Arbitration Assn. (bd. dirs. 1975—, Disting. Service award 1982). Clubs: Kent Country, Peninsular (Grand Rapids). Home: 2910 Oak Hollow Dr SE Grand Rapids MI 49506 Office: Varnum Riddering Schmidt & Howlett Suite 800 171 Monroe St NW Grand Rapids MI 49503

HOWLEY, C. JOE, healthcare sales educator; b. Mankato, Minn., Dec. 25, 1927; s. Charles Lester and Mary (Burns) H.; m. Virginia Rose Tritchler, Feb. 5, 1951; children: Mark, Kathleen, Nancy, Paul, Matthew, John, Joseph. BS, Mankato State U., 1950. Salesman Northwestern Welco, Pitts., 1950-55; sales mgr. Kendall Sales Edn. Ctr., Barrington, Ill., 1955-60, mgr. dist., regional sales, 1960-77, dir. profl. sales edn., 1977—. Contbr. articles to profl. jours. Served with USN, 1945-46. Nat. Soc. Sales Tng. Execs. (various offices, pres. 1988), Am. Soc. Tng. Dirs. Roman Catholic. Avocation: running. Home: 461 Meridian Crystal Lake IL 60014 Office: Kendall Sales Edn Ctr 600 Hart Rd Rm 230 Barrington IL 60010

HOWREN, PHILIP BRUCE, osteopath; b. Youngstown, Ohio, Nov. 17, 1950; s. Bruce Harold and Austa Marie (Hojer) H.; m. Phyllis Yvonne Duvall, Nov. 30, 1985; children: Trisha, Michael. BS, Youngstown State U., 1972; DO, U. for Health Scis., Kansas City, Mo., 1976. Cert. in emergency medicine, 1984. Intern Brentwood Hosp., Cleve., 1976-77, emergency physician, 1977—; emergency physician Cuyahoga Falls (Ohio) Gen. Hosp., 1977-80; critical care physician Lorain (Ohio) Community Hosp., 1978-83; dir. Brentwood Ambulatory Care Ctr., Sagamore Hills, Ohio, 1980—; advisor various mcpl. rescue squads, 1980—; rep. State of Ohio Emergency Med. Services Commn., 1986. Mem. Am. Coll. Osteo. Emergency Physicians, Am. Coll. Emergency Physicians, Am. Osteo. Assn., Ohio Osteo. Assn., Cleve. Acad. Osteo. Medicine (tng. com. 1984), Stow Jaycees (bd. dirs. 1980-84, Jaycee of Yr. 1982), Sigma Sigma Phi. Republican. Club: Silver Lake Country. Avocations: golf, skiing, carpentry, woodworking. Office: 7530 Carter Rd Sagamore Hills OH 44067

HOXTELL, EUGENE ORVILLE, dermatologist; b. Fargo, N.D., Aug. 21, 1944; s. Orville Theodore and Emma Emelia (Leininger) H.; m. Sharron Lee Johnson, Dec. 16, 1967; children—Jeffrey, Kirsten. B.S., U. Minn., 1967, M.D., 1969, M.S., 1976. Diplomate Am. Bd. Dermatology, Am. Bd. Dermatopathology. Staff dermatology Central Plains Clinic, Sioux Falls, S.D., 1976-82; practice medicine specializing in dermatology Dermatology Assocs., Sioux Falls, 1982—; cons. VA Hosp., Sioux Falls, 1976—. Contbr. articles to profl. jours. Pack leader Webelos, Boy Scouts Am., Sioux Falls, 1983. Served to maj. USAF, 1971-73. Fellow Am. Acad. Dermatology, Am. Soc. Dermatopathology, Am. Soc. Dermatologic Surgery; mem. AMA, Soc. Investigation Dermatology. Republican. Lutheran. Avocations: sailing, flying, photography. Home: 3812 Birchwood Ave Sioux Falls SD 57103 Office: Dermatology Assocs 1201 S Euclid St Sioux Falls SD 57105

HOXWORTH, DAN HARDY, economist; b. Cape Girardeau, Mo., June 10, 1960; s. Gerald Monroe and Frances Lee (Hardy) H.; m. Louise Anne Frezza, July 23, 1983; children: Ian William, Kellen Lewis. BA with honors in Econs., U. Mo., 1982. Asst. economist Fed. Res. Bank, Kansas City, Mo., 1982-86; cons. Tenenbaum-Hill Assocs., Kansas City, 1986—. Pres. West Plaza Neighborhood Assn., Kansas City, 1985, 86, 87; bd. dirs. Westport Citzens Action Coalition, 1987. Curator's scholar, U. Mo., 1978, Univ. scholar, U. Mo., 1982. Mem. Inst. Property Taxation, Phi Beta Kappa. Democrat. Unitarian Universalist. Club: Mid-Am. Masters (Kansas City). Avocations: running, neighborhood organizing, outdoor nature activities, politics. Home: 4322 Fairmount Ave Kansas City MO 64111 Office: Tenenbaum-Hill Assoc PO Box 30330 Kansas City MO 64112

HOYNE, THOMAS TEMPLE, dentist; b. Salina, Kans., May 13, 1935; s. John Thomas and Opal Louise (Fisher) H.; m. Naomi Jeanette Nelson, June 21, 1961. BS in Chemistry, U. Kans., 1957; DDS, U. Kansas City, Mo., 1963. Gen. practice dentistry Stover, Mo., 1963—; cons. Handicapped Dental Patients of Mo., 1980-83. Contbr. articles on archeology to profl. jours. Scoutmaster to council exec. bd. Boy Scouts Am., Stover, 1963—. Served to 1st lt. U.S Army, 1957-59. Recipient Silver Beaver award Boy Scouts Am., 1972, Silver Lamb award Boy Scouts Am. and Luth. Ch., 1976. Mem. ADA, Mo. dental Assn., Royal Soc. Health, U. Kans. Chemistry Dept. Alumni Assn., State Mo. Archeol. Soc. (trustee 1987—), W. Cen. Mo. Archeol. Soc. (pres. 1986, 87), Morgan county Archeol. Soc. (pres. 1963-68). Republican. Lutheran. Lodge: Lions. Avocations: Am. archaeology, mil. history, camping, fishing. Home: Woodland Dr and Hughes Ave Stover MO 65078 Office: Mimosa Dr and Hwy 52 Stover MO 65078

HOYT, DON, SR., association executive; b. North Adams, Mich., Mar. 28, 1930; s. George Washington and Frances (Monroe) H.; m. Dorothy Hess, Mar. 7, 1947 (div. Oct. 1952); m. Ella Mae Lake, Dec. 20, 1952; children—Peggy, Jerry, Linus, Don Jr., Becky, Barbara. Pres. Nat. Trappers Assn., Bloomington, Ill., 1977—. Home: 15412 Tau Rd Marshall MI 49068 Office: Box 3667 216 N Center St Bloomington IL 61701

HOYT, JOHN CLAXTON, automotive parts company executive; b. Boston, Oct. 29, 1930; s. William Fenn Hoyt and Harriet (Claxton) Jones; m. Mary Alice Louden, July 26, 1958; children: Judith Ann, Elizabeth Jean, Robert Fenn. AB, Hamilton Coll., 1952; MBA, U. Pa., 1954. Chief statistician Nat. Machine Tool Builders Assn., Cleve., 1955-57; market analyst Standard Oil Co., Cleve., 1957-62; supr., dir. mktg. research Champion Spark Plug Co., Toledo, 1962—; chmn., pres. Gt. Lakes Mktg. Assocs., Inc. Toledo, 1964-85; v.p., dir. Vellmar Foods, Inc., Toledo, 1976-80; gen. ptnr. Hodges Devel. Co., Toledo, 1979-85. Co-author: Leading Cases in Marketing Research, 1971. Pres. Lucas County Bd. Edn., Toledo, 1977, 81, 85—, Grace Community Ctr., toldo, 1983-86; chmn. Toledo Area Pvt. Industry Council, 1981—, Toledo Area Salvation Army Bd., 1983-86; bd. dirs. Penta County Joint Vocat. Sch., Perrysburg, Ohio, 1984—. Recipient Silver Beaver award Boy Scouts Am., Toledo, 1968, Vigil Honor award Boy Scouts Am., 1967. Mem. Am. Mktg. Assn. (v.p. Ohio chpt. 1965-66), Automotive Market Research Council (pres. 1967-68), Automotive Service Industry Assn., Automotive Parts and Accessories Assn. Republican. Mem. United Ch. Christ. Clubs: Toledo Tennis, Toledo Racquet. Lodge: Masons. Home: 4140 Northmoor Toledo OH 43606 Office: Champion Spark Plub Co PO Box 910 Toledo OH 43661

HOYT, RANDAL LEE, mechanical engineer; b. Laddonia, Mo., Dec. 22, 1958; s. Glenroy John and Anita Rose (Williams) H.; m. Maria Elena Caras, Mar. 2, 1985; 1 child, Megan Brooke. BSME, U. Mo., Rolla, 1981. Cert. mech. engr., Ill. Project engr. John Deere Harvester Works, East Moline, Ill., 1979—; regional mgr. A.L. Williams & Assocs., Inc., 1985—. Loaned exec. United Way Campaign, Quad-Cities, Ill., 1982, acct. exec., 1983; solicitor Christ the King Cath. Ch., Moline, Ill. 1986. Avocations: softball, volleyball.

HOYT, RICHARD COMSTOCK, econs. consulting co. exec.; b. St. Paul, Sept. 30, 1939; s. Charles Richardson and Minnie (Comstock) H.; B.S., Kans. State U., 1961; M.S., U. Minn., 1968, Ph.D., 1972; m. Ingrid Langensiepen, Oct. 24, 1964; children—Monika Anna, Derek Richard. Milling engr. Tennant & Hoyt Co., Lake City Minn., 1971-72, pres., 1972; research asst. U. Minn., 1968-71; pres. Analytics, Inc., Excelsior, Minn., 1973—; lectr. in field. Served with C.E., U.S. Army, 1962-65. Mem. Am. E.on. Assn., Am. Agrl. Econ. Assn., Mgmt. Sci. Assn. Republican. Contbr. articles in field to profl. jours. Home: 5975 Ridge Rd Excelsior MN 55331 Office: 464 2d St Excelsior MN 55331

HOZAK, NORMAN L., chemical engineer; b. Owosso, Mich., Aug. 20, 1936; s. Rudolph and Elinor I. (Barnefski) H.; m. Ruth Eileen Engwis, Sept. 28, 1957; children: Susan, Anne, Douglas, Kenneth, Gregory. BChemE, U. Mich., 1959, MChemE, 1960. Chem. engr. Dow Chem. Co., Midland, Mich., 1960-63, asst. supt., 1963-66, project engr., 1966-68, supt. engring., 1968-70, project supt. engring., 1970-86, assoc. engring. cons., 1986—. Pres. Midland Concert Band, 1977-86; mem. fin. bd. Mich. Area Polit. Action Com., Midland, 1984-87; precinct del. Midland County Rep. Conv., 1986-88. Mem. Am. Inst. Chem. Engrs., U. Mich. Alumni (pres.1968), Alphi Chi Sigma. Republican. Clubs: Apple Computer, 660 Investors (Midland) (pres. 1984). Lodge: Kiwanis (com. chmn., bd. dirs. Kiwassee 1980-84). Home: 3810 Boston Midland MI 48640

HRBEK, GEORGE WILLIAM, electrical engineer, electronics company executive; b. Oak Park, Ill., Dec. 27, 1927; s. George and Emily (Knourek) H.; m. Geraldine Barbara Shaw, June 27, 1953; children—George M., William D., Barbara K. B.S.E.E., Ill. Inst. Tech., 1953; M.S.E.E., Northwestern U., 1964. Engr., Sperry Gyroscope Co., Great Neck, N.Y., 1953-54; mgr. electron device research Zenith Radio Corp., Chgo., 1956-77, dir. video engring., Glenview, Ill., 1980—; mgr. mfg. research Motorola, Inc., Schaumburg, Ill., 1977-79; mgr. research Ardev Inc., Palo Alto, Calif., 1979-80; tech. speaker in field. Served with U.S. Army, 1954-56. Mem. IEEE (sr.), Sigma Xi, Eta Kappa Nu Assn. Republican. Roman Catholic. Club: Yacht (Milw.). Contbr. articles in field to tech. publs. Patentee in field. Office: Zenith Electronics Corp 1000 Milwaukee Ave Glenview IL 60025

HRINKO, DANIEL DEAN, clinical counselor; b. Springfield, Ohio, Dec. 14, 1955; s. Peter and Jean Ayr (Wallace) H.; m. Lisa Marie Rykowski, Oct. 23, 1976; children—Peter Daniel, Matthew David. B.A., Muskingum Coll., 1976; M.A., Ball State U., 1977. Cottage therapist Oesterlen Services for Youth Ctr., Springfield, Ohio, 1978-79; dir. day treatment Dayton (Ohio) Youth Drug Program, 1980-82; pvt. practice adolescent and family counseling, Springfield, Ohio, 1982-84; dir. assessment Alcohol and Drug Council Clark County, 1984-86; therapist adolescent psychiat. unit, Dettmer Hosp., Troy, Ohio, 1986-87, unit coordinator adolescent psychiatric unit, Dettmer Hosp. Troy, 1987—; cons. agys. Vol. German Twp. Fire Dept., 1978—. Mem. Am. Psychol. Assn. Lutheran. Lodge: Masons (past master). Address: 3643 Troy Rd Springfield OH 45504

HRIVNAK, JOHN ANDREW, architect; b. Elyria, Ohio, May 7, 1952; s. Andrew and Betty Jane (Schaeffer) H.; m. Jill Annette Franks, Dec. 14, 1974; children: David Jonathan, Daniel Joshua, Andrew James, Stephen Michael. BBA, Wittenberg U., 1974; MBA in Mgmt.and Fin., Xavier U., 1976; MArch, U. Cin., 1978. Registered architect, Ohio. Mktg. dir. BHDP Architects, Cin., 1977-81; asst. dir. archtl. programs HDR, Omaha, 1981-84, nat. dir. continuing care program, 1984-85; mktg. dir., project architect Roger L. Schutte & Assocs., Omaha, 1985—; prin. Renaissance Retirement Villages, Omaha, 1985—; lectr. retirement community design and devel. Laventhol & Horwath, 1985-86; cons. SBA, 1982-85. Mem. Nebr. Rep. Cen. Com., Douglas County Young Reps., Freedom Council; del. Rep. Conv. Mem. AIA, Nat. Assn. Sr. Living Industries, Am. Assn. Retirement Communities, Am. Assn. Housing for the Aged, Nat. Council Archtl. Rev. Bds., Nat. Fedn. Ind. Businessmen, Urban Land Inst. (guest speaker retirement community design and devel. 1985), Soc. for Mktg. Profl. Services. Club: 1000 (Virginia Beach, Va.). Avocations: tennis, soccer, vocal performance, parenting. Home: 11448 Queens Dr Omaha NE 68164 Office: Renaissance Retirement Villages 8801 W Center Rd Suite 304 Omaha NE 68124

HSIUNG, HANSEN MAXWELL, research scientist; b. Han Kow, Hu-Pei, Republic of China, May 12, 1947; came to U.S., 1970, permanent resident, 1982; s. Sow-Tsow and Wei-Mei Chia H.; m. Ling-Ann Wei, Jan. 29, 1972; children—Amy W., Wayne. B.S. in Chemistry, Nat. Taiwan U., Taipei, 1969; M.S. in Biochemistry, U. Ill.-Urbana, 1972, Ph.D. in Organic Chemistry, 1975. Research assoc. Nat. Research Council of Can., Ottawa, Ont., 1977-80; sr. biologist Eli Lilly & Co., Indpls., 1980—. Mem. AAAS. Home: 108 W 88th St Indianapolis IN 46260 Office: Lilly Corp Ctr 307 E McCarty St Indianapolis IN 46285

HSU, DER-ANN, statistician, financial researcher; b. Canton, Peoples Republic of China, Dec. 9, 1943; s. Jen-Lin and Su-Yun (Lee) Hsu; m. Jane C. Hsu, July 27, 1974; children—Patricia, Andrew. B.A. in Econs., Nat. Taiwan U., Tapei, 1965; Ph.D. in Bus. Statistics, U. Wis., Madison, 1973. Research asst. prof. Princeton U., N.J., 1974-77; asst. prof. U. Wis., Milw., 1977-79, assocs. prof., 1979-83, prof. statistics and finance, 1983-87, disting. research prof. fin., 1987—; cons. FAA, Atlantic City, 1977—, various investment cos., 1986—. Contbr. articles to profl. jours. Recipient Outstanding Research award Sch. Bus. Adminstrn., U. Wis., 1984; Research Com. award Grad. Sch., U. Wis., 1985. Fellow Royal Inst. Nav., Royal Statis. Soc.; mem. Am. Statis. Assn., Inst. Mgmt. Scis., Am. Finance Assn. Avocation: violin. Home: 9485 N Range Line Rd River Hills WI 53217 Office: Sch of Bus Adminstrn U Wis PO Box 742 Milwaukee WI 53201

HSU, JAMES, architect; b. Kowloon, Hong Kong, Dec. 31, 1951; came to U.S., 1971; s. Liang Shing and Bih (Yuen) H. Student engring., Pacific Luth. U., 1971-73; BArch with high honors, Ill. Inst. Tech., 1977, MArch, 1981. Jr. architect Skidmore Owings and Merrill, Chgo., 1976-77; sr. architect Minoru Yamasaki and Assocs., Troy, Mich., 1981—. Pacific Luth. U. scholar, 1972, Women's Archtl. League scholar, 1976, Ill. Inst. Tech. scholar, 1978-80, Graham Found. scholar, 1981. Mem. AIA (assoc.). Avocations: computers, electronics, swimming. Home: 597 Kirts Blvd Apt 101 Troy MI 48084 Office: Minoru Yamasaki and Assocs 350 W Big Beaver Rd Troy MI 48084-4100

HU, STEPHEN NAI-KAI, statistician, researcher; b. Nanking, China, Dec. 6, 1933; came to U.S., 1957; s. Mai and Su-lian (Wu) H.; m. Louisa Shu-fong Lee, Sept. 6, 1969; 1 child, Nancy. B.A., Nat. Taiwan U., 1955; M.S., U. Tenn., 1958; Ph.D., U. N.C., 1966. Instr. Western Carolina Coll., Cullowhee, N.C., 1964-67; asst. prof. U. Detroit, 1967-74; statistician Mich. Dept. Transp., Lansing, 1976—. Mem. Am. Statis. Assn. Home: 3854 New Salem Circle Okemos MI 48864

HUBAND, C., provincial judge. Judge Man. Ct. of Appeals, Winnipeg. Office: Ct of Appeals, Law Cts Bldg, Winnipeg, MB Canada R3C 0V8 *

HUBBARD, ARTHUR THORNTON, chemistry educator, electrochemist; b. Alameda, Calif., Sept. 17, 1941; s. John White and Ruth Frances (Gapen) H.; m. Pratinmas Bougssudhiraks, Mar. 25, 1976; children: David A., Lynne F. BA, Westmont Coll., 1963; PhD, Calif. Inst. Tech., 1967. Prof. chemistry U. Hawaii, Honolulu, 1967-76, U. Calif., Santa Barbara, 1976-86; prof. chemistry U. Cin., 1986—, dir. surface ctr., 1986—. Contbr. numerous articles to sci. jours. Grantee NSF, NIH, Air Force Office Sci. Research, U.S. Dept. Energy. Mem. Am. Chem. Soc. (assoc. editor 1984—), Electrochem. Soc. Office: U Cin Dept Chemistry Cincinnati OH 45221

HUBBARD, BURRITT SEYMOUR, JR., financial consultant; b. Ashtabula, Ohio, July 13, 1923; s. Burritt Seymour and Elizabeth (Harmon) H.; m. Joanne Janis White, Dec. 20, 1950; children: Burritt William, Richard Seymour, Gretchen Elizabeth. BS, Babson Coll., 1949. Adminstrv. asst. Ashtabula Corrugated Box, 1949-51; factory mgr. Ashtabula Box Socket Co., 1956-61, Inland Container, Indpls., 1952-56; treas., asst. to pres. Molded Fiber Glass Co., Ashtabula, 1961-68; fin. cons. Ashtabula, 1968—; bd. dirs., treas. Cleve. Armatur. Past pres., trustee Civic Devel. Corp., Ashtabula, 1959-86; trustee St. Peter's Found., Ashtabula, 1963—; trustee endowment fund Episcopal Diocese Ohio, Cleve., 1983—; chmn. Job Devel. Task Force, Ashtabula, 1984—, Episcopal Lake Region Council, Painesville, Ohio, 1984-86. Served with U.S. Army, 1943-45, ETO. Mem. Cleve. Soc. Security Analysts, Fin. Analyst Fedn., Internat. Assn. Fin. Planners. Republican. Club: Ashtabula Country (trustee). Avocations: tennis, golfing, skiing. Home: 4105 Edgewater Dr Ashtabula OH 44004 Office: PO Box 547 Ashtabula OH 44004

HUBBARD, DEAN LEON, university president; b. Nyssa, Oreg., June 17, 1939; s. Gaileon and Rhodene (Barton) H.; m. Aleta Ann Thornton, July 12, 1959; children—Melody Ann, Dean Paul John, Joy Marie. B.A., Andrews U., 1961, M.A., 1962; diploma in Korean Lang., Yunsei U., Seoul, Korea, 1968; Ph.D., Stanford U., 1979. Dir. Seventh-day Adventist English Lang. Schs., Seoul, 1966-71; asst. to pres. Loma Linda U., Calif., 1974-76; acad. dean Union Coll., Lincoln, Nebr., 1976-80, pres., 1980-84; pres. NW Mo. State U., Maryville, 1984—; pres. Dean L. Hubbard and Assocs., Inc., 1976—; dir. Adventist Health Systems-Eastern and Middle Am., 1984-87. Chmn. bd. United Way, Lincoln, 1980-84; bd. dirs. Mt. St. Clare Coll., Clinton, Iowa, 1985—. Lodge: Rotary. Avocation: classical music. Office: NW Mo State Univ Office of the Pres Maryville MO 64468-6001

HUBBARD, JOHN M., golf course administrator; b. Beech Creek, Pa., Feb. 13, 1916; s. Morris R. and Ina May (Putman) H.; m. Virginia A. Nelson, June 4, 1938; children: Robert, Nancy. Student, Gen. Motors Engring. and Mgmt. Inst., 1938, U. Detroit, 1939. Sr. engr. Fisher Body, Warren, Mich., 1935-74; pres. Oxford Hills Golf and Country Club, Pontiac, Mich., 1974—; advisor Ferris State Coll., Big Rapids, Mich., 1960-74. Mem. Soc. Engring. Illustrators (bd. dirs., Outstanding Achievement award 1981). Republican. Lodges: Rotary (bd. dirs. Oxford club 1981-82), Elks, Masons (master mason 1960-61). Designed Oxford Hills Golf Course, 1961. Home: 350 E Drahner Oxford MI 48051 Office: Oxford Hills Golf and Country Club 300 E Drahner Oxford MI 48051

HUBBARD, LINCOLN BEALS, medical physicist, consultant; b. Hawkesbury, Ont., Can., Sept. 8, 1940; s. Carroll Chauncey and Mary Lunn (Beals) H.; came to U.S., 1957; m. Nancy Ann Krieger, Apr. 3, 1961; children—Jill, Katrina. B.S. in Physics, U. N.H., 1961; Ph.D., MIT, 1967. Diplomate Am. Bd. Radiology; cert. health physicist Am. Bd. Health Physics. Postdoctoral appointee Argonne Nat. Lab., 1966-68; asst. prof. math. and physics Knoxville Coll. (Tenn.), 1968-70; asst. prof. physics Furman U., Greenville, S.C., 1970-74; chief physicist Mt. Sinai Hosp., Chgo., 1974-75, Cook County Hosp., Chgo., 1975—; ptnr. Fields, Griffith, Hubbard & Broadbent, Inc., 1978—; assoc. prof. med. physics, Rush U., 1986— . Mem. Am. Assn. Physicists in Medicine, Am. Coll. Radiology, Am. Phys. Soc. Author: (with S.S. Stefani) Mathematics for Technologists, 1979, (with G. B. Greenfield) Computers in Radiology, 1984. Home: 4113 West End Rd Downers Grove IL 60515 Office: PO Box 367 Hines IL 60141

HUBBARD, STANLEY STUB, broadcast executive; b. St. Paul, May 28, 1933; s. Stanley Eugene and Didrikke A. (Stub) H.; m. Karen Elizabeth Holmen, June 13, 1959; children: Kathryn Elizabeth, Stanley Eugene, Virginia Anne, Robert Winston, Julia Didrikke. BA, U. Minn., 1955. With Hubbard Broadcasting, St. Paul, 1950—, pres., 1967—; pres. U.S. Satellite Broadcasting Co., Inc. Chmn. St. Croix Valley Youth Ctr., 1968—; trustee Hubbard Found.; bd. dirs. St. Paul Ramsey United Arts Council, U. Minn. Friends of the Gen. Coll., Sci. Mus. of Minn., Psychoanalytic Found. Minn., U. Minn. Found., Guthrie Theatre. Mem. Minn. Broadcasters Assn., Internat. Radio and TV Soc., Broadcast Pioneers., St. Paul C. of C. (bd. dirs.), Minn. Execs. Orgn., World Bus. Council. Clubs: Minneapolis; Minnesota; St. Paul Athletic, Town and Country (St. Paul); St. Croix Yacht, St. Croix Sailing (Lakeland, Minn.); St. Petersburg (Fla.) Yacht; Bal Harbour, Indian Creek Country, Ocean Reef, Key Largo Anglers, Surf Curb. Home: 2289 River Rd S Lakeland MN 55043 Office: Hubbard Broadcasting Inc 3415 University Ave Saint Paul MN 55114

HUBBELL, FRED, department store company executive. Chmn., chief exec. officer Younkers, Inc., Des Moines. Office: Younkers Inc 7th & Walnut Sts Des Moines IA 50397 *

HUBBELL, JAMES WINDSOR, JR., insurance company executive; b. Des Moines, Iowa, May 17, 1922; s. James Windsor and Harriet Amanda (Cox) H.; m. Helen Houx, June 8, 1946; children: James, Harriet, Frederick, Michael. Student, Harvard U., 1941-46. Bd. dirs. Equitable of Iowa Cos., Des Moines, 1961—, pres., chmn. bd. dirs., chief exec. officer, 1976—; bd. dirs. F.M. Hubbell Son & Co. Trustee Simpson Coll., Indianola, Iowa, 1974—. Served with USN, 1943-45. Mem. Des Moines C. of C. (pres. 1972). Episcopalian. Clubs: Porcellian, Wakonda, Lost Tree. Office: Equitable of Iowa Cos 699 Walnut St PO Box 9107 Des Moines IA 50306

HUBBS, RONALD M., retired insurance company executive; b. Silverton, Oreg., Apr. 27, 1908; s. George W. and Ethel (Burch) H.; B.A., U. Oreg.; LL.D. (hon.), William Mitchell Coll. Law, Macalester Coll. H.L.D., (hon.), Carleton Coll., m. Margaret S. Jamie, Sept. 9, 1935; 1 son, George J. With St. Paul Fire & Marine Ins. Co., 1936-77, asst. to pres., 1948-52, v.p., 1952-59, exec. v.p., 1959-63; pres., chief exec., 1963-68, chmn., 1968-73; pres., chief exec. officer St. Paul Cos., Inc., 1968-73, chmn., 1973-77; past dir. Western Life Ins. Co., chmn. Toro Credit Co.; past chmn. AFIA Worldwide Ins. Past bd. dirs. Minn. Council on Econ. Edn.; bd. dirs., founding trustee Twin Cities Pub. TV Corp.; trustee James H. Hill Reference Library; adv. bd. U. Minn. Sch. Mgmt.; task force U. Minn. Writing Standards, Lt. Gov. Minn. on Womens' History Ctr.; Gov.'s Adv. Com. on Literacy; bd. dirs. emeritus William Mitchell Coll. Law; trustee Coll. St. Thomas, Carleton Coll.; chmn. bd. trustees F.R. Bigelow Found.; past trustee, past chmn. Ins. Inst. Am.; mem., past chmn. pres.'s council St. Catherine's Coll.; gov. Internat. Inst. Seminars, Inc.; bd. dirs. Charles Lindbergh Fund, Cath. Digest; bd. overseers emeritus U. Minn. Sch. Mgmt.; bd. dirs. Inst. Philos. Research; trustee St. Paul Found., North Star Found.; bd. overseers Hill Monastic Manuscript Library and Univ. Without Walls; trustee Sci. Mus. Minn. elector Ins. Hall Fame. Served from 1st lt. to col. AUS, World War II. Decorated Legion of Merit; recipient St. Thomas Aquinas medal Coll. St. Thomas; creative leadership in adult edn. award MACAE; Life-long learning award Met. State U.; Disting. Community Builder award Indianhead council Boy Scouts Am.; Great Living St. Paulite award St. Paul C. of C.; Pres. Council award Minn. Pvt. Colls.; King's medal Carl XVI Gustaf of Sweden; Disting. Service award Minn. Humanities Comm.; others. Mem. Am. Inst. Property and Liability Underwriters (past chmn., trustee), Orgn. Am. Historians, Minn. Hist. Soc. (past pres.), Co. Mil. Historians, Sherlock Holmes Soc. of London, Orchid Soc., Alpha Tau Omega, Phi Delta Phi, Scabbard and Blade, Friars, Beta Gamma Sigma. Episcopalian (past trustee diocese Minn.). Club: Minn. (past pres.). Home: 689 W Wentworth Ave #102 Saint Paul MN 55118 Office: 385 Washington St Saint Paul MN 55102

HUBER, J. PATRICK, warehousing executive; b. Fremont, Ohio, Sept. 24, 1940; s. Chauncey E. and Dorothy E. (Hetrick) H.; m. Sandra S. George, Aug. 27, 1961 (div. Sept. 1978); children: Ranelle, Jay, Mark; m. Bonnie L. Nilson, Feb. 17, 1981. BA, Ohio Wesleyan U., 1962. Terminal mgr. Mohawk Motor, Tiffin, Ohio, 1962-68, v.p. sales, 1968-70; pres. Warehouse Assocs., Lima, Ohio, 1970—; bd. dirs. Met. Bank, Lima; mng. ptnr. Lima Leasing, 1973—, Cemp Enterprise, Lima, 1972—, Dot Lines Cartage, Lima, 1974—. Bd. dirs. Lima YMCA, 1980—. Republican. Methodist. Club: Shawnee Country (Lima) (v.p. 1984—). Lodge: Elks. Home: 107 Hawthorne Lima OH 45805 Office: PO Box 1422 Lima OH 45802

HUBER, JOAN ALTHAUS, sociology educator; b. Bluffton, Ohio, Oct. 17, 1925; d. Lawrence Lester and Hallie Moser (Althaus) H.; m. William Form, Feb. 5, 1971; children: Nancy Rytina, Steven Rytina. B.A., Pa. State U., 1945; M.A., Western Mich. U., 1963; Ph.D., Mich. State U., 1967. Asst. prof. sociology U. Notre Dame, Ind., 1967-71; asst. prof. sociology U. Ill., Urbana-Champaign, 1971-73; assoc. prof. U. Ill., 1973-78, prof., 1978-83, head dept., 1979-83; dean Coll. Social and Behavioral Sci., Ohio State U., Columbus, 1984—, Coll. Arts and Sciences, Ohio State University, Columbus, 1987—. Author: (with William Form) Income and Ideology, 1973, (with Glenna Spitze) Sex Stratification, 1983. Editor: Changing Women in a Changing Society, 1973, (with Paul Chalfant) The Sociology of Poverty, 1974. NSF research awardee, 1978-81. Mem. Am. Sociol. Assn. (v.p. 1981-83), Sociologists for Women in Soc., Midwest Sociol. Soc. (pres. 1979-80). Home: 1439 London Dr Columbus OH 43221 Office: Ohio State U 166 Denney Hall 164 W 17th St Columbus OH 43210 *

HUBER, KATHERINE JEANNE, steel company executive; b. Wyandotte, Mich., Sept. 21, 1958; d. William Randolph and Sarah Louise (McCarron) Martin; m. Donald James Huber, Jan. 16, 1981. BS in Math., U. Mich., Dearborn, 1980; MS in Applied Math., Purdue U., Hammond, Ind., 1985. Mgmt. trainee Nat. Steel Corp., Ecourse, Mich. and Portage, Ind., 1980-82; div. analyst Nat. Steel Corp., Portage, 1982-84, supr. cost and methods, 1984-85, supr. forecasting and services, 1985-86; standards supr. Cold Roll Products, 1987—; tutor math. Nat. Steel Corp., 1985—. Mem. Inst. Indsl. Engrs. (membership dir. 1983-84, chpt. v.p. 1984-86, pres. 1987—), Midwest Steel Supr. Assn. (bd. dirs. 1983-84, treas. 1984-85, pres. 1985-86), Midwest Steel Employees Assn. (social com. 1985-86, treas. 1987—), Nat. Assn. Accts. Democrat. Roman Catholic. Home: 1650 Coleman Porter IN 46304 Office: Nat Steel Corp Hwy 12 Portage IN 46304

HUBERT, JEAN-LUC, chemical executive; b. Metz, Moselle, France, Mar. 13, 1960; s. Andre and Franziska (Schmidt) H. Diplome Ingenieur, Ecole Centrale Paris, 1982, advanced engring., 1982; MS in Mech. and Nuclear Engring., Northwestern U., 1985. Simulation engr. Didier Werke, Wiesbaden, Fed. Republic Germany, 1981; engr. Iron and Steel Research inst., Metz, France, 1983; applications engr. L'Air Liquide, Paris, 1985-86; mgr. cryogenic research Liquid Air Corp., Countryside, Ill., 1986—. Served to 2d lt. French Navy, 1982-83. Tuition fellow Georges Lurcy Found., 1984, Henri Blanchenay fellow French Inst., 1984, Bieneck/Didier fellow, Fed. Republic of Germany, 1984. Mem. Am. Soc. Mech. Engrs. (assoc.), Internat. Inst. Refrigeration (assoc.), Inst. Food Technologists. Home: 6103 Knollwood Rd Willowbrook IL 60514 Office: Liquid Air Corp Chgo Research Ctr 5230 S East Ave Countryside IL 60525

HUCKE, MICHAEL RAY, accountant; b. Dayton, Ohio, Apr. 29, 1942; s. Melvin Louis and Edythe Evangeline (Lisk) H.; children—John, Elizabeth, Timothy. B.S., Capital U., 1964; M.A., Wichita State U., 1966; postgrad. Okla. State U. Asst. prof. acctg. Carroll Coll., Waukesha, Wis.; fin. specialist Gen. Electric Co., Milw., 1975-77; mgr. fin. planning NCR, Dayton, Ohio, 1977-83; owner Hucke Acctg. Services, Dayton, 1983—. Chmn. bd. dirs. Wernle Children's Home, Richmond, Ind., 1985-86; pres. Epiphany Luth. Ch., Centerville, Ohio, 1984. Mem. Inst. Mgmt. Acctg., Nat. Assn. Tax Practitioners. Republican. Methodist. Home: 2-B Belle Meadows Dr Trotwood OH 45426 Office: Hucke Acctg Services 509 Windsor Park Dr Dayton OH 45459

HUCKER, DAVID RUSSELL, teacher; b. St. Louis, July 26, 1950; s. Russel Oscar and Arleen Anna (Hoffman) H.; m. Vera Madelyn Christopher, Nov. 3, 1972; children: Jaanna, Brian. BS in Edn., Cen. Mo. State U., 1972. Cert. automotive technician. Tchr., supr. St. Louis Pub. Schs., 1972-74, Dept. Def. Overseas Dependants Schs., Okinawa, Japan, 1974-77; machine designer, draftsman Ferguson Machine Co., St. Louis, 1977-78; tchr., supr. Ladue Pub. Schs., St. Louis, 1978—. Mem. Internat. Technology Educators Assn., Mo. State Tchrs. Assn., Profl. Assn. Diving Instrs. (divemaster). Mem. United Ch. of Christ. Avocations: scuba diving.

HUDDLESTON, DONALD DEON, food products executive; b. Ft. Dodge, Iowa, Mar. 18, 1940; s. Floyd Lionel and Dorothy Myrtle (Laughlin) H.; m. Betty JoAnn Bauman, July 15, 1967; children: Daniel Michelle, Tamara Ann, Jason Lincoln. AA, Ft. Dodge Community Coll., 1964; BS, Colo. State U., 1967. Mgr. quality assurance Birds Eye Gen. Foods, Waseca, Minn., 1967-70, Jell-O Gen. Foods, Chgo., 1970-72, Kitchens of Sara Lee, New Hampton, Iowa, 1972-85; tech. dir. Hollywood Brands, Centralia, Ill., 1983-84, dir. mfg., 1984—. Served as sgt. USMC, 1958-62. Mem. Am. Soc. Quality Control, Inst. Food Technologists, Nat. Confectioners Assn. (mem. tech. com. 1985—). Republican. Roman Catholic. Lodge: Elks, Masons. Avocations: hunting, fishing, reading, computers, canoeing. Home: Box 251C Meadow Ln Centralia IL 62801 Office: Hollywood Brands Inc 836 S Chestnut Centralia IL 62801

HUDDLESTON, SHARON, physical education educator, consultant; b. Texarkana, Tex., Aug. 28, 1945; d. Clovis and Bertha Faye (Shannon) H. B.S., Stephen F. Austin U., 1968, M.S., 1969; Ph.D., U. Iowa, 1981. Instr., coach Midwestern U., Wichita Falls, Tex., 1969-70, Stephen F. Austin U., Nacagdoches, Tex., 1970-72; coach U. Wis., Madison, 1972-73; grad. teaching and research asst. U. Iowa, Iowa City, 1978-80; asst. prof. phys. edn. U. No. Iowa, Cedar Falls, 1973—, sport psychology cons., 1981—; self def. cons. Sexual Assault Intervention Ctr., Waterloo, Iowa, 1983—. Recipient Laura Tuttle Meml. Grad. award U. Iowa, Iowa City, 1979, Sims Riddle award, 1980. Mem. AAHPER and Dance, NEA, N.Am. Soc. Psychology Sport and Phys. Activity, Iowa State Edn. Assn., Iowa Assn. Health, Phys. Edn., Recreation and Dance (research chmn. 1984-86). Democrat. Office: U No Iowa East Gymnasium Cedar Falls IA 50614

HUDIK, MARTIN FRANCIS, hospital administrator, educator, consultant; b. Chgo., Mar. 27, 1949; s. Joseph and Rose (Ricker) H. BS in Mech. and Aerospace Engring., Ill. Inst. Tech., 1971; BPA, Jackson State U., 1974; MBA, Loyola U., Chgo., 1975; postgrad. U. Sarasota, 1975-76. Cert. health care safety mgr., hazard control mgr., hazardous materials mgr.; cert. police and security firearms instr., Ill. and Nat. Rifle Assn. With Ill. Masonic Med. Ctr., Chgo., 1969—, dir. risk mgmt., 1974-79, asst. adminstr., 1979—; lt. tng. div. Cicero (Ill.) Police Dept., part-time 1971—; instr. Nat. Safety Council Safety Tng. Inst., Chgo., 1977-85; cons. mem. Council Tech. Users Consumer Products, Underwriters Labs., Chgo., 1977—; instr., lt. U.S. Def. Civil Preparedness Agy. Staff Coll., Battle Creek, Mich., 1977-85. Pres. sch. bd. Mary Queen of Heaven Sch., Cicero, 1977-79, 84-86; pres. Mary Queen of Heaven Ch. Council, 1979-81, 83-86; pres. I.M.M.C. Employee Club, 1983-86. Ill. State scholar, 1969-71. Mem. Am. Coll. Hosp. Adminstrs., Am. Soc. Hosp. Risk Mgmt., Nat. Fire Protection Assn., Am. Soc. Safety Engrs., Am. Soc. Law and Medicine, Ill. Hosp. Security and Safety Assn. (co-founder 1976, founding pres. 1976-77, hon. dir. 1977-82), Cath. Alumni Club Chgo. (bd. dirs. 1983-84, 86, exec. bd 1984, 86), Mensa, Pi Tau Sigma, Tau Beta Pi, Alpha Sigma Nu. Republican. Roman Catholic. Lodges: KC (Cardinal council), Masons. Office: 836 W Wellington Ave Chicago IL 60657

HUDNUT, WILLIAM HERBERT, III, mayor; b. Cin., Oct. 17, 1932; s. William Herbert, Jr. and Elizabeth (Kilborne) H.; m. Susan G. Rice, Dec. 14, 1974; children from previous marriage: Michael Conger, Laura Anne, Timothy Norton, William Herbert IV, Theodore Beecher. B.A. magna cum laude, Princeton, 1954; M.Div. summa cum laude, Union Theol. Sem., N.Y.C., 1957; D.D., Hanover Coll., 1967, Wabash Coll., 1969; LL.D., Butler U., 1980, Anderson Coll., 1982, Franklin Coll., 1983; Litt.D., Ind. Central U., 1981. Ordained to ministry Presbyn. Ch., 1957; asst. minister Westminster Ch., Buffalo, 1957-60; pastor 1st Presbyn. Ch., Annapolis, Md., 1960-63; dir. Westminster Found., Annapolis, 1960-63; sr. minister 2d Presbyn. Ch., Indpls., 1963-72; mem. 93d Congress from Ind., 1973-74; dir. dept. community affairs Ind. Central U., Indpls., 1975; mayor Indpls., 1976—; mem. Presdl. Adv. Com. on Federalism, 1981—; pres. Nat. Conf. Rep. Mayors, 1987. Author: Minister/Mayor, 1987; editor: Union Sem. Quar. Rev, 1956-57; Contbr. sermons, articles to profl. publs. Mem. Bd. Pub. Safety, Indpls., 1970-71; Pres. Anne Arundel County Mental Health Assn., 1961-63; pres., bd. dirs. Marion County Mental Health Assn., 1966-68, Westminster Found., Purdue U., 1969-73; bd. dirs. Community Service Council Met. Indpls., 1964-68, Weekday Religious Edn., Marion County, 1964-69, Family Service Assn., 1966-72, Ind. Mental Health Assn., 1968-69, Flanner House, 1968-72; pres. trustees Darrow Sch., New Lebanon, N.Y., 1968-75; bd. dirs. Nat. League Cities, 1977—, pres. bd. dirs., 1981; bd. dirs. Ind. Assn. Cities and Towns, 1976—, pres. bd. dirs., 1979; mem. Intergovtl. Sci., Engring. and Tech. White House Adv. Panel, 1976-77, U.S. Conf. Mayors; adv. bd. Am. Fedn. Small Bus.; mem. New Coalition Welfare Reform Task Force, 1976-77, Task Force on Fed. Deficit, 1981; mem. adv. Commn. on Intergovtl. Relations, 1984; bd. dirs. Indpl. Center Adv. Research, 1976—, Humane Soc., 1983—; trustee Roosevelt Ctr. Am. Policy Studies, Washington, 1984—. Recipient Russell G. Lloyd Disting. Service award Ind. Assn. of Cities and Towns, 1985; named All-Pro City Mgmt. Team City and State Mag., 1986. Mem. Ind. Rep. Mayor's Assn. (pres. 1980), Nat. Conf. of Rep. Mayors and Mcpl. Elected Officials (pres. 1987), Rep. Nat. Com., Phi Beta Kappa. Republican. Clubs: Indianapolis (Indpls.), Columbia (Indpls.), Sertoma (Indpls.), Kiwanis (Indpls.), Masons (Indpls.) (33 deg.), Moose (Indpls.). Office: 2501 City-County Bldg Indianapolis IN 46204

HUDSON, CELESTE NUTTING, educator, reading clinic administrator, consultant; b. Nashville, Sept. 18, 1927; d. John Winthrop Chandler and Hilda Bass (Alexander) Nutting; m. Frank Alden Hudson III, Dec. 30, 1948 (dec.); children—Frank Alden IV (dec.), Jo Ann Hudson Algermissen, Celeste Jane Hudson Hayes, John Winthrop Nutting. B.S., Oreg. Coll. Edn., 1952; M.S., So. Ill. U., 1963, Ph.D., 1973. Cert. tchr., Tenn., Oreg., Mo., Iowa. Tchr. pub. schs., Crossville, Tenn., 1949-51, Salem, Oreg., 1952-53, West Walnut Manor and Jennings, Mo., 1953-54, Normandy Sch. Dist., St. Louis County, Mo., 1954-66; reading coordinator Sikeston (Mo.) Pub. Schs., 1966-71; traveling cons. Ednl. Devel. Labs., Huntington, N.Y., 1970-71; mem. clin. staff So. Ill. U. Reading Ctr., 1972; asst. prof. edn. St. Ambrose Coll., 1972-75, U. Tenn.-Chattanooga, 1975-76; project dir. Learning Skills Ctr., St. Ambrose Coll., 1976-80, asst. prof. edn., 1976-78, assoc. prof., 1979-86 , dir. elem. edn., 1972-75, 76—, chmn. dept. edn., 1980-84, div. chmn., 1984—, prof. edn., 1986—, dir. Reading Clinic, 76—; cons. reading. Mem. Kimberly Village Bd., Davenport, Iowa, 1979-83. Mem. Assn. Tchrs. Educators, Assn. Supervision and Curriculum Devel., Internat. Reading Assn. (Scott County council), Am. Assn. Colls. Tchr. Edn., Assn. Tchr. Educators, New Eng. Women (past pres.), Women in Ednl. Adminstrn., DAR, United Daus. Confederacy, Alpha Delta Kappa (past pres.), Kappa Delta Pi, Phi Delta Kappa. Methodist. Author: Handbook for Remedial Reading, 1967; Cognitive Listening and the Reading of Second Grade Children, 1973. Office: Saint Ambrose Coll Davenport IA 52806

HUDSON, DENNIS LEE, lawyer, government official; b. St. Louis, Jan. 5, 1936; s. Lewis Jefferson and Helen Mabel (Buchanan) H.; m. Linda Kay Adamson; children—Karen Marie, Karla Sue. B.A., U. Ill., 1958; J.D., John Marshall Law Sch., 1972. Bar: Ill. 1972, U.S. Dist. Ct. (so. dist.) Ill. 1972, U.S. Dist. Ct. (no. dist.) Ill. 1972. Insp., IRS, Chgo., 1962-72; spl. agt. GSA, Chgo., 1972-78, spl. agt.-in-charge, 1978-83, regional insp. gen., 1983—; supervisory spl. agt., Dept Justice-GSA Task Force, Washington, 1978. Bd. govs. Theatre Western Springs, Ill., 1978-81; deacon Grace Lutheran Ch., LaGrange, Ill., 1977-81. Served with U.S. Army, 1959-61. John N. Jewett scholar, 1972. Mem. ABA, Ill. Bar Assn., Assn. Fed. Investigators. Home: PO Box 113 Western Springs IL 60558 Office: Office Insp Gen GSA Suite 408 230 S Dearborn St Chicago IL 60604

HUDSON, HAROLD DON, veterinarian; b. Audrain County, Mo., Nov. 22, 1943; s. Harold F. and Greta Arlene (Boyd) H.; A.A., Hannibal (Mo.) La Grange Coll., 1963; B.S., U. Mo., 1967, D.V.M., 1970; m. Carole Jacqueline Spence, Aug. 30, 1964; children—Dale Brent, Kim Marie. Assoc. Clarinda (Iowa) Vet. Clinic, 1970-71, Bethany (Mo.) Vet. Clinic, 1971-72, Vet. Clinic, Mexico, Mo., 1972—. Mem. AVMA, Mo. Vet. Med. Assn., Am. Assn. Bovine Practitioners, Am. Assn. Swine Practitioners. Baptist. Home: 933 Emmons St Mexico MO 65265 Office: 1624 Hwy 54 E Mexico MO 65265

HUDSON, JOHN EARL, social worker, psychology researcher; b. Detroit, Jan. 25, 1952; s. Ralph Joseph and Aurelia Emma (Walton) H.; m. Camille Diane Bailey, Jan. 12, 1974; children: Shannon, Courtney. BS, Eastern Mich. U., 1973, MA, 1975; PhD, U. Toledo, 1984. Cert. social worker, Mich. Instr. Schoolcraft Coll., Livonia, Mich., 1975; social worker State of Mich., Detroit, 1973-86; researcher Oak Manor Clinic, Detroit, 1986—. Author song lyrics. Coach Ypsilanti (Mich.) Twp. Recreation, 1986-87; mem. citizens adv. com. Willow Run Schs., 1986-87. Mem. Mich. Assn. Emotionally Disturbed Children, United Auto Workers, Superior Twp. Jaycees (v.p. 1986-87, William Browning award, 1985), Eastern Mich. U. Alumni Assn. Home: 8621 Heather Dr Ypsilanti MI 48198

HUDSON, MICHAEL WESLEY, banker; b. Lafayette, Ind., Sept. 23, 1945; s. Wesley Talmadge and Anna Ruth (Hurn) H.; m. Linda Louise Mathis, Sept. 25, 1965; children—Clinton Michael, Sherry Ann. Grad. Am.

Inst. Banking, 1971; student Purdue U., 1977-78. Br. mgr., officer Purdue Nat. Bank, Lafayette, 1967-78; v.p. State Bank Oxford (Ind.), 1978—, lic. real estate broker. Pres., Warren County Young Democrats, 1975—; del. Ind. Dem. Conv., 1976; trustee Adams Twp., 1975-82; sec. treas. Pine Village Fire Dept.; mem. Warren County Sheriff Merit Bd. Served with U.S. Army, 1965-67. Mem. Am. Inst. Banking. Roman Catholic. Lodge: Lions. Home: RR 1 Box 116 Pine Village IN 47975 Office: 100 S Justus St Oxford IN 47971

HUDSON, ROBERT PAUL, medical educator; b. Kansas City, Kans., Feb. 23, 1926; s. Chester Lloyd and Jean (Emerson) H.; m. Olive Jean Grimes, Aug. 1, 1948 (div. 1963); children—Robert E., Donald K., Timothy M.; m. Martha Isabelle Holter, July 10, 1965; children—Stephen, Laurel. B.A., U. Kans., 1949; M.D., 1952; M.A., Johns Hopkins U., 1966. Instr., U. Kans.-Kansas City, 1958-59, assoc. in medicine, 1959-63, asst. prof., 1964-68, assoc. prof., 1968—, prof., chmn. history of medicine, 1968—. Author: Disease and its Control, 1983. Contbr. articles to profl. jours. mem. editorial bd. Bull. History of Medicine, Balt., 1981—. Served to 1st lt. U.S. Army, 1953-55. Fellow ACP; mem. Am. Assn. for History of Medicine (pres. 1984—), Am. Osler Soc. (bd. govs., pres. 1987—). Home: 12925 Frontier Rd Olathe KS 66061 Office: Kans U Med Ctr 39th and Rainbow Kansas City KS 66103

HUDSON, TERRI ELIZABETH, physical therapist; b. Abilene, Kans., Dec. 15, 1953; d. Alvin Ward and Louise Rugo (Hampton) G.; m. Steven Lee, Aug. 11, 1973; children: Amanda Louise, Jeffrey Ward. BS in Gen. Sci., Ft. Hays State U., Kans., 1976; BS in Phys. Therapy, Kans. U., 1976. Staff phys. therapist St. Francis Hosp., Wichita, Kans., 1977—; cons. cardiac rehab. St. Francis Hosp., 1982—. Mem. Am. Phys. Therapy Assn., Kans. Phys. Therapy Assn. Avocations: reading, needlepoint, craft. Home: 275 S Gleneagles Ct Wichita KS 67209 Office: St Francis Hosp Phys Therapy 929 N St Francis Wichita KS 67207

HUDSPETH, DONNA GALASSI, psychologist, educator; b. Springfield, Ill.; d. Vincent and Mary Elizabeth (Foykier) Galassi; m. Lionel M. Hudspeth, July 23, 1970. AA, Springfield (Ill.) Coll., 1963; BA, Ill. Coll., 1965; MA, Bradley U., 1967; postgrad. in psychology U. Ill., 1972. Lic. psychologist, Ill.; cert. sch. psychologist, Ill. Instr. psychology Lincoln Land Coll., Springfield, Ill., 1969-76, Sangamon State U., Springfield, 1967-83; clin. psychologist Baumann Clinic, Springfield, 1976-80; psychologist Springfield pub. schs., 1967—; psychologist Psychol. Assocs., Springfield, 1980-85; pvt. practice Centrum Psychol., 1985—; cons. Hope Sch., 1982—; mem. Ill. Status Offenders Bd. Mem. Am. Psychol. Assn., Ill. Psychol. Assn., Nat. Health Service Providers, Springfield Edn. Assn. (officer), NEA, Ill. Edn. Assn., Women in Healthcare, Springfield Art Assn., Women in Mgmt., Women in Healthcare Women's Profl. Orgn. Springfield. Office: 319 E Madison Suite D Springfield IL 62703

HUEBSCHMAN, MARTIN JOHN, JR, manufacturing executive; b. Balt., Apr. 25, 1947; s. Martin John and Elizabeth (Rosenberger) H.; m. Carol Ann Hall, Jan. 15, 1967 (div. Aug. 1971); 1 child, Martin John 111; m. Barbara Kathleen Cummings, June 23, 1973; children: Eric Sean, Kevin James. BBA, Cleve. State U., 1972; JD, Cleve. Marshall Law Sch., 1976. Bar: Ohio, 1976. Asst. treas. Nordson Corp., Cleve., 1976-80, treas., 1980-84; sr. v.p. fin. and planning Met-Coil Systems Corp., Cedar Rapids, Iowa, 1984-86, pres., chief operating officer, 1986—; also bd. dirs. Met-Coil Systems Corp., Cedar Rapids. Pres., v.p., treas. Lake of the Falls Condominium, Olmsted Falls, 1973-76; trustee Lake Ridge Acad., Elyria, 1984; bd. dirs., pres., campaign chmn. United Way of Greater Lorain County, 1982-84. Mem. Nat. Machine Tool Builders' Assn., ABA, Nat. Investor Relations Inst. Risk & Ins. Mgmt. Soc., Young Pres. Orgn. Republican. Methodist. Clubs: Elmcrest Country, Investment. Avocations: computers, sports, reading, traveling. Home: 130 Tomahawk Trail SE Cedar Rapids IA 52403 Office: Met-Coil Systems Corp 425 2d St SE 11th Fl Cedar Rapids IA 52401

HUEHOLT, THOMAS WAYNE, accountant; b. Clinton, Iowa, Feb. 19, 1938; s. Frederick and Juliette Josephine (Ohrt) H.; m. Donna Lee Huenolt, June 8, 1963; children: Claire Marie, Melissa Lynn, Christiana. BA, St. Ambrose Coll., 1970. Asst. div. controller Dispenser div. Eaton Corp., Glen Ellyn, Ill., 1966-70; asst. treas. Store Kraft Mfg., Beatrice, Nebr., 1970-75; controller Hyland Mfg. Co., Osceola, Iowa, 1975-77, Compressor Controls Corp., Des Moines, 1977-82; treas. Lortex, Inc., Des Moines, Iowa, 1977—. Pres. Dowling Bank Boosters, Des Moines, 1982-83; bd. dirs. Osceola C. of C., 1977; mem. Polk County Rep. Cen. Com., 1985—; mem. parish council St. Bernard's Ch., Osceola, 1975-77, St. Joseph's Ch., Beatrice, 1971-75, Sacred Heart Ch., Clinton, Iowa, 1965-70. Mem. Nat. Assn. Accts. (bd. dirs. 1984—), Nat. Assn. Credit Mgrs. Republican. Roman Catholic. Club: Des Moines Cycle. Lodge: Optimists (local bd. dirs. 1971-75. Avocations: bicycling, politics. Home: 1406 60th Des Moines IA 50311 Office: Lortex Inc PO Box 1936 Des Moines IA 50306

HUENEFELD, WESLEY CARL, agricultural conservationist; b. Aurora, Nebr., Aug. 19, 1909; s. Carl Henry and Grace Leon (Davis) H.; m. Beth Iova Stilgebouer, Aug. 14, 1938 (dec. 1976); children—Ann, Arthur, Ethel, Lynn, Patricia; m. Emma Louise Yerkes, Aug. 25, 1978. B.A., U. Nebr., 1935. Farmer, Aurora, Nebr., 1938-85; conservationist, historian, mus. builder County Nebr. Centennial Com., Hamilton County, Nebr., 1965; pres. Hamilton County Hist. Soc., Aurora, Nebr., 1965-85; planner Plainsman Mus., Aurora, 1976—. Designer, planter Nebs. Tree Farm Conservation Tree Farm, 1959; designer, dir. Plainsman Mus., Plainsman Agr. Mus., 1972-85; landscape architect Aurora Pub. Schs., mus., pub. bldgs., 1959-85. Sec. Hamilton County Fair Bd., 1955-63; county chmn. Hamilton County Am. Bicentennial Com., Hamilton County, Nebr., 1976; dir., planner Prodn. Hist. Murals, Mosaics and Celestial Scene in Plainsman Mus., 1974-80. Recipient A. E. Sheldon award Nebr. State Hist. Soc., Lincoln, 1977; named Neb. Outstanding Tree Planter, Neb. Forestry Dept., Nebr. Dept. Forestry, Wildlife and Fisheries, 1979; recipient Silver Tree Farm cert. Nebr. Tree Farm Program and Am. Forestry Inst., 1985. Republican.

HUENEMANN, KURT EDWARD, data processing executive; b. Piqua, Ohio, Mar. 2, 1961; s. William Arthur and Jean Susan (Seward) H.; m. Lynn Marie Ridley, June 25, 1983; 1 child, Jeffrey. BS, Heidelberg Coll., 1983; postgrad., Bowling Green State U., 1983—. Computer ops. mgr. Heidelberg Coll., Tiffin, Ohio, 1983—; cons. various profl. orgns. Lodge: Kiwanis (bd. dirs. 1986). Avocations: model building, bowling, gardening. Home: 362 Walker St Tiffin OH 44883 Office: Heidelberg Coll 310 E Market St Tiffin OH 44883

HUENNEKENS, NANCY MAE, teacher; b. La Crosse, Wis., July 22, 1949; d. James Wilbert and Majorie Mae (Hale) Gums; m. Richard Arthur Huennekens, Oct. 16, 1976; 3 children. BS, U. Wis., Eau Claire, 1971; cert. in reading, Carthage Coll., Kenosha, 1982. cert. tchr., Wis. Tchr. Racine (Wis.) Unified Schs., 1971-82, reading resource tchr., 1982—. Roman Catholic. Avocations: running, cross country skiing, family, cooking. Home: 433 Mulberry Ln Racine WI 53402

HUERTER, JOSEPH PATRICK, lawyer; b. Wetmore, Kans., Mar. 17, 1960; s. Edwin H. and Bernadine R. (Driscoll) H.; m. Susan D. Anderson, July 11, 1981; 1 child, Andrew Joseph. BA in Polit. Sci., Communications, Benedictine Coll., 1981; JD, Washburn U., 1983. Bar: Kans. 1983, U.S. Dist. Ct. Kans. 1983, U.S. Ct. Appeals (10th cir.) 1985. Ptnr. Tenopir & Huerter, Topeka, Kans., 1983—. Pres. Kans. Young Dems., 1982-83; mem. council City of Topeka, 1985—. Mem. ABA, Kans. Bar Assn., Assn. Trial Lawyers Am., Kans. Trial Lawyers Assn. Democrat. Roman Catholic. Office: Tenopir & Huerter 420 SE 29th Topeka KS 66605

HUESER, ROBERTA JEAN, city official; b. Dallas, Iowa, Oct. 3, 1932; d. Carl Robert and Lucille Julia (Logue) Wheeler; student Wayne (Nebr.) State Coll., Colo. State Coll., Greeley, Northwestern Coll., Orange City, Iowa; m. William Joseph Hueser, June 1, 1956; children—Kyle Robert, Jon William. Sch. tchr. in Iowa, 1953-63; city clk. George (Iowa), 1977—. Chmn. bd. George Bicentennial Mus., 1976-86; adv. bd. George Good Samaritan Center, 1978-87; chmn. George Centennial Celebration; treas. bd. dirs. Evergreen Lawn Cemetery. Mem. Lyon County Mcpl. League (sec.-treas. 1977-78, 84-85). Democrat. Mem. Ch. of Christ. Club: Facts and Fun (pres. 1978-80). Co-author: In and Around George 1872-1912. Home: 209 W Ohio Ave George IA 51237 Office: City Hall 120 1/2 S Main Saint George IA 51237

HUESMANN, LOUIS CASS, II, physician; b. Indpls., Sept. 25, 1931; s. Louis M. and Virginia (Pearce) H.; m. Margaret Simpson Bateman, Sept. 4, 1953; children: Jessica, Louis, Natalie, Perry, Matthew. DVM, Ohio State U., 1955; MD, Ind. U., 1959. Intern Cin. Gen. Hosp., 1959-60; resident in gen. surgery Ind. U. Med. Ctr., 1960-61; resident in orthopedics Henry Ford Hosp., Detroit, 1963-64, Columbia Hosp., Columbia, S.C., 1964-66, Northwestern U., Chgo., 1966; orthopaedic surgeon Medical Office of Robert C. Grier, Greenville, S.C., 1966, F.C. Smith Clinic, Marion, Ohio, 1967-76; practice medicine specializing in orthorpaedic surgery Delaware, Ohio, 1976—; field med. cons. Ohio Bur. Vocat. Rehab., Marion, 1980-86; cons. bd. health City of Delaware, 1980-86. Served to capt. U.S. Army, 1961-63. Fellow ACS; mem. Am. Coll. Orthopaedic Surgeons, Ohio Med. Assn., Delaware County Med. Soc., Peer Review Assn. (v.p. 1983—). Republican. Mem. Brethern Ch. Office: 494 W Central Ave Delaware OH 43015

HUESTIS, WILLIAM (BILL) D'AUBIGNY, manufacturing company executive; b. Gloversville, N.Y., Oct. 15, 1923; s. John Lamb and Marion Helen (Sherburne) H.; m. Dorothy Minette Fuller, Sept. 8, 1943; children: David Lee, Susan Kay, Scott Eugene, Barbara Jean. Grad., High Sch., Stillwater, Minn., 1941. Salesman Montgomery Ward, St. Paul, 1946-48, Graybar Electric Co., St. Paul, 1948-50, Werners, Inc., South St. Paul, 1950-53, Admiral Corp., St. Paul, 1953-56; pres., owner, operator L.P. Gas Equipment Co., St. Paul, 1957-86, Road Rescue, Inc., St. Paul, 1976—; bd. dirs. DS & B Realty, St. Paul, DSB Corp., St. Paul. Bd. dirs. St. Paul Winter Carnival Assn., 1986—; chmn. bd. dirs. Dist. 12 Citizenss Council, St. Paul, 1979-83; dir. adv. council Energy Park, St. Paul, 1981—. Recipient Entrepreneurial award Minn. Bus. Hall Fame, 1982, 84, 85; named Minn. Small Bus. Man Yr., Nat. SBA, 1986. Mem. Midway Civic and Commerce Assn. (bd. dirs. 1973—), Minn. Assn. Commerce and Industry (bd. dirs. 1985—), Minn. Inventors Council (bd. dirs. 1985—), St. Paul Area C. of C. (v.p., bd. dirs. 1983—, named small bus. man of yr.1986). Republican. Mem. United Ch. Christ. Lodge: Rotary (Paul Harris fellow 1986). Avocations: gardening, woodworking, music, real estate. Office: Road Rescue Inc 1133 Rankin St Saint Paul MN 55116

HUEY, BRUCE EDWARD, accounting executive; b. Chgo., July 15, 1947; s. Floyd Edward and Mary Frances (Brusic) H.; m. Carol Joan Miller, May 31, 1975; children: Ross Floyd, Erica Marie. BS in Commerce with highest honors, De Paul U., 1974, MS in Taxation, 1978. CPA, Ill. Prin. Arthur Young & Co., Chgo., 1974-85; ptnr. Friedman & Huey Assocs., Chgo. and Homewood, Ill., 1985—; lectr. De Paul U., Chgo., 1978—. Author (tng. manual) Income Taxation of Estates, Trusts, and Decedents, 1986; contbr. articles to profl. jours. Trustee Erikson Inst., Chgo., 1984—, Wyler Children's Hosp., Chgo., 1984—. Mem. Am. Inst. CPA's, Ill. CPA Soc., Beta Alpha Psi, Beta Gamma Sigma. Roman Catholic. Avocations: horticulture, woodworking. Office: Friedman & Huey Assocs PO Box 1055 Homewood IL 60430

HUF, CAROL ELINOR, tax service company executive; b. Milw., Apr. 21, 1940; d. William Weiss and Florence H. (Melcher) Weiss Lange; m. Walter Franklin Huf, Sept. 9, 1961; children—Mardell Leslie, Walter Albert III. Student Valparaiso U., 1958-60, Waukesha County Tech. Inst., 1968-69. Tax preparer H & R Block, Milw., 1967-84, instr. tax sch., 1969-83; job service interviewer State of Wis., Waukesha, 1984; pres. Personalized Tax Service, Inc., West Allis, Wis., 1984—, div. mgr. A.L. Williams, 1986. Vol. worker Girl Scouts US, Waukesha, 1970-80, Boy Scouts Am., Waukesha, 1975—; swimming referee Wis. Interscholastic Athletic Assn., Milw., 1972-84. Recipient awards Boy Scouts Am. Mem. Wis. Womens Pub. Links Golf Assn. (sr. v.p. 1986—, state tournament chairperson 1987), Wis. Assn. Accts., Met. Swimming Ofcls. Lutheran. Clubs: Edgewood Golf (Big Bend, Wis.) (pres. 1984—). Home: 17825 Westward Dr New Berlin WI 53151 Office: Personalized Tax Service Inc 10533 W National Ave West Allis WI 53227

HUFF, C(LARENCE) RONALD, public administration and criminology educator; b. Covington, Ky., Nov. 10, 1945; s. Nathaniel Warren G. and Irene Opal (Mills) H.; m. Patricia Ann Plankenhorn, June 15, 1968; children—Tamara Lynn, Tiffany Dawn. B.A., Capital U., 1968; M.S.W., U. Mich., 1970; Ph.D., Ohio State U., 1974. Social worker Franklin County Children's Services, Columbus, Ohio, 1968; social work intern Pontiac (Mich.) State Hosp. and Family Service Met. Detroit, 1969-70; dir. psychiat. social work Lima (Ohio) State Hosp., 1970-71; psychiat. social worker Northwest Community Mental Health Ctr., Lima, 1971-72; grad. teaching assoc. Dept. Sociology, Ohio State U., 1972-74; asst. prof. social ecology U. Calif.-Irvine, 1974-76; asst. prof. sociology Purdue U., 1976-79; assoc. prof. pub. adminstrn., dir. program for study of crime and delinquency Ohio State U.-Columbus, 1979-87, prof., 1987—; cons. ABA, NSF, Bur. Justice Stats., Nat. Inst. Justice, Nat. Inst. Corrections, Nat. Inst. Juvenile Justice and Delinquency Prevention, others. Recipient Nat. Security award Mershon Found., 1980; prize New Eng. Sch. Law, 1981; Outstanding Teaching award, 1985; ABA grantee, 1974-77; Purdue U. grantee, 1978; Dept. Justice grantee, 1978-79; Ohio Dept. Mental Health grantee, 1982-83, 84-85, 85-87, Gov.'s Office Criminal Justice grantee, 1985—. Fellow Western Soc. Criminology; mem. Acad. Criminal Justice Scis., AAUP, ABA, Am. Correctional Assn., Am. Soc. Pub. Adminstrn., Am. Soc. Criminology (exec. bd.), Am. Sociol. Assn., Internat. Sociol. Assn., Nat. Council on Crime and Delinquency, Phi Kappa Phi. Author: The Mad, the Bad and the Different: Essays in Honor of Simon Dinitz, 1981; Attorneys as Activists: Evaluating the American Bar Association's BASICS Program, 1979; Contemporary Corrections: Social Control and Conflict, 1977; Planning Correctional Reform, 1975; others; contbr. articles to profl. jours., chpts. to books. Home: 1825 Snouffer Rd Worthington OH 43085 Office: Ohio State U 202C Hagerty Hall 1775 College Rd Columbus OH 43210

HUFF, DAVID RICHARD, funeral home executive; b. St. Joseph, Mo., Aug. 24, 1948; s. Harry Francis and Frances Emily (Knopinski) H.; m. Catherine Ann Chitwood, Aug. 7, 1976. BA, Rockhurst Coll., 1970; postgrad., Fla. State U., 1975-76; PA, U.S. Med. Ctr., 1975. Lic. funeral dir., Mo.; lic. educator, Mo. Tchr. St. Francis Sch., St. Joseph, 1970; med. records clk. Fed. Prison Health Systems, Leavenworth, Kans., 1971, hosp. adminstrv. asst., 1971-73, physician asst., 1974-84; asst. hosp. adminstr. Fed. Prison Health Systems, El Reno, Okla., 1977-79; health systems adminstr/ Fed. Prison Health Systems, Big Spring, Tex., 1979-84; fiscal affairs office mgr. Heaton-Bowman-Smith Funeral Home, Inc., St. Joseph, 1984—. Coordinator community health screenings City of Big Spring, 1980-84; bd. suprs. Citizens Fed. Credit Union, Big Spring, Tex., 1981-84, sec. 1983-84; bd. dirs. Am. Heart Assn., Big Spring, 1982-83; hon. bd. dirs. Rockhurst Coll., Kansas City, 1983—. Mem. Mo. Funeral Dirs. Assn., St. Joseph C. of C.. Democrat. Roman Catholic. Clubs: Century (Kansas City), Royal LeBlond, Diplomat's, Ambassador's (St. Joseph). Lodge: KC. Avocations: gardening, philatelic collection. Home: 4211 Buckingham Ct Saint Joseph MO 64506 Office: Heaton-Bowman-Smith Funeral Home Inc 3609 Frederick Blvd Saint Joseph MO 64506

HUFF, DENNIS LEE, banker; b. Elkhart, Ind., June 14, 1947; s. Bernard B. and Rachel E. (Fike) H. BMus cum laude, North Cen. Coll., 1969; MMus, DePauw U., 1971. From teller to asst. v.p. Midwest Commerce Banking Co., Elkhart, 1971-83; asst. v.p. Valley Am. Bank, South Bend, Ind., 1983-86, v.p. 1986—; fin. ind. cons. Automation Strategies, Inc., Elkhart, 1986-87. Organist/choirmaster Castle United Meth. Ch., Elkhart, 1971-83; organist Cen. Christian Ch., Elkhart, 1983—. Mem. Am. Guild Organists, Assn. Systems Mgmt., Michiana Fin. Microcomputers Users Group, Elkhart PC Users Group, Internat. Edsel Club, Edsel Owners Club, Elkhart Vintage Auto. Avocations: classic cars, philately, syngraphy, photography, personal computers. Home: 809 Hiawatha Dr Elkhart IN 46517 Office: Valley Am Bank PO Box 328 South Bend IN 46624

HUFF, JOHN DAVID, church administrator; b. Muskegon, Mich., Nov. 20, 1952; s. Lucius Barthol and Marian (Brainard) H.; m. Diane Lynn Church, May 17, 1975; children: Joshua, Jason, Jessica. B in Religious Edn., Reformed Bible Coll., 1977; MA in Sch. Adminstrn., Calvin Coll., 1983; postgrad., Western Mich. U. Cert. ch. educator. Dir. edn. 1st Christian Reformed Ch., Visalia, Calif., 1977-79, Bethany Reformed Ch., Grand Rapids, Mich., 1979-83, Haven Reformed Ch., Kalamazoo, 1983—; tchr. trainer, mem. tsak force on evangelism and renewal Synod of Mich. Reformed Ch. in Am., 1987—. Vice chmn. Youth Com. Bill Glass Crusade, Visalia, 1978, chmn. Cen. Valley Ch. Workers Conf., Visalia, 1978; mem. Youth Com. City-Wide Easter Services, Visalia, 1979; trustee Reformed Bible Coll., Grand Rapids, 1984—, mem. exec. com., 1985—, asst. sec. bd. dirs., 1986—); chmn. Southwest Mich. Christian Discipleship Com., 1984-85. Recipient DeVos award Reformed Bible Coll., 1977; Mich. State scholar, 1970. Mem. Biblical Archeol. Soc., Christian Educators-Reformed Ch. Am., Inst. for Am. Ch. Growth (cons. 1986—), Cen. Valley Youth Ministers (sec. 1978-79), Delta Epsilon Chi. Republican. Avocations: reading, racquetball, golf, civil war info. Home: 5150 Simmons Kalamazoo MI 49004 Office: Haven Reformed Ch 3210 Virginia Kalamazoo MI 49004

HUFF, WILLIAM E., refining company executive; b. 1928; married. B.B.A., Butler U., 1960. With Nat. Liquor Corp., 1952-56; pres. Hoosier Coal & Oil Co. Inc., 1956-73; with Rock Island Refining Corp., Indpls., 1973—, v.p., treas., 1973-79, sr. v.p. fin., 1979-83, pres., 1983—, dir. Served with U.S. Army, 1949-52. Office: Rock Island Refining Corp PO Box 68007 Indianapolis IN 46268 *

HUFFER, DAN L., banker; b. Lima, Ohio, July 7, 1937; s. Harold E. and Margaret (VanMeter) H.; m. Phyllis J. Reiff, Dec. 31, 1957; children: Mark E., Michelle E. Lencke. BS in Acctg., Ohio State U., 1961. CPA, Ohio. Audit mgr. Price Waterhouse, Cleve., Columbus, Ohio, 1961-72; auditor The Borden Co., Columbus, 1972-74; sr. v.p., chief fin. officer BancOhio Corp., Columbus, 1974-84; exec. v.p., chief fin. officer Centerre Bancorp., St. Louis, 1984—. Trustee Columbus Zool. Assn., 1975-80, Franklin U., Columbus, 1982-84; pres. Phi Kappa Tau Found., Columbus, 1981-84. Mem. Am. Inst. CPA's, Ohio Soc. CPA's, Assn. Bank Holding Cos., Fin. Execs. Inst. (bd. dirs. 1982-84), The Treas.'s Club. Republican. Presbyterian. Clubs: Bellerive Country, St. Louis; Brookside Country (Columbus). Avocations: golf, tennis, skiing, sailing. Home: 13332 Fairfield Sq Dr Chesterfield MO 63017 Office: Centerre Bancorporation One Centerre Plaza Saint Louis MO 63101

HUFFER, JAMES MORSE, orthopaedic surgeon, educator; b. Madison, Wis., Jan. 20, 1934; 3 children from 1st marriage; 4 stepchildren from current marriage. SB, U. Chgo., 1954, MD, 1958. Intern Strong Meml. Hosp., Rochester, N.Y., 1958-59, resident in orthopaedic surgery, 1959-60; practice medicine specializing in orthopaedic surgery Madison, 1962—; instr. dept. surgery U. Wis., Madison, 1965-66, asst. prof. dept. surgery, 1966-72, assoc. prof. dept. surgery, 1972—. Contbr. articles to profl jours. Served with USAF, 1960-62. Fellow ACS; mem. AMA, Wis. Med. Soc. (com. safe transp., com. peer review), Wis. Othopaedic Soc., Mid-Am. Orthopaedic Soc., Madison Orthopaedic Soc., Dane County Med. Soc., Clin. Orthopaedic Soc. Home: 3968 Plymouth Circle Madison WI 53705 Office: Bone & Joint Surgery Assoc 2704 Marshall Ct Madison WI 53705

HUFFMAN, CARL EDWARD, JR., professional speaker, management trainer; b. Indpls., July 29, 1937; s. Carl Edward and Marie G. (Bolinger) H.; m. Judith A. Koziol, Mar. 10, 1973; children—Carl Edward, Natalie Ann Marie. B.A. in Speech and Theatre, Ind. U., 1975. Dist. mgr. McLean Employees. Credit Union, Winston-Salem, N.C., 1964-67; medicare-medicaid coordinator Ind. Blue Cross, Indpls., 1967-75; dist. mgr. Wis. PSRO, Madison, 1975-77; exec. dir. Ind. PSRO, Indpls., 1977-78; chief exec. officer MESA, Buffalo Grove, Ill., 1978-81; pres. Huffman Enterprises, Elgin, Ill., 1981—; instr. Am. Mgmt. Assn., N.Y.C., 1980—; mem. faculty Aurora U. Mgmt. Ctr., Am. Coll. Health Care Adminstrs. Author: The Quick Fix, 1987, also article. Pres. St. Mary's Sch. Edn. Com., Elgin, 1984-85. Recipient Award for Excellence, Univ. Forum, Ind. U., Indpls., 1974; winner 1st pl. oratory Univ. Forum Ind. U.-Purdue U., Indpls., 1974. Mem. Nat. Speakers Assn. (pres. elect Ill. chpt. 1985, pres. 1986-87), Ill. Tng. and Devel. Assn. (chmn. 1983), Chgo. Sales and Tng. Assn. Republican. Roman Catholic. Clubs: Toastmasters (pres. Schaumburg, Ill. 1981-82, Communication and Leadership award 1987), Jaycees (v.p. Indpls. 1964-67). Avocations: Camping; travel. Home: 358 Shiloh Ct Elgin IL 60120 Office: Huffman Enterprises Inc PO Box 1311 Elgin IL 60121

HUFFMAN, DENNIS DON, metallurgy researcher; b. Lima, Ohio, May 21, 1942; s. Donald D. and Eleanor Louise (Foulkes) H.; m. Judith Ann McDonald, Apr. 7, 1962; children: Todd D., Craig D., Brad D. BS in Metallurgy, Case Inst. Tech., 1964; postgrad. in metallurgy, U. Pitts., 1965-69. Service metallurgist Latrobe (Pa.) Steel Co., 1964-70, supervising metall. engr., 1970-75; sales mgr. cast masters div. Latrobe (Pa.) Steel Co., Bowling Green, Ohio, 1975-82; sect. leader Timken Research, Canton, Ohio, 1982-86, mgr. primary steel processing, 1986. Contbr. articles profl. jours. Commr. Pennysburg (Ohio) Youth Athletic Assn., 1976-82; ruling elder Presbyn. Ch., Latrobe, 1972. Mem. Am. Soc. Metals (nat. chmn., various coms., chmn. handbook com.), Am. Iron and Steel Inst. (nat. chmn. sensor com., 1983—), Am. Die Casting Inst., Soc. Die Casting Engrs., ASTM, AIME, Latrobe Jaycees. Republican. Methodist. Club: Exchange (Canton pres. elect 1986—). Lodge: Rotary. Avocations: athletics, woodworking. Home: 2444 Foxway Circle NW North Canton OH 44720 Office: Timken Research 1835 Dueber Canton OH 44706

HUFFMAN, GARY CLAUDE, finance company executive; b. Springfield, Ill., Dec. 4, 1944; s. Claud A. and Eula L. (Fritsch) H.; m. Susan P. Beville, Sept. 27, 1969; children: Heather, Claudia. BS in Bus. Adminstrn., Olivet Nazarene U., 1966; MBA, Sangamon State U., 1981. Sales exec. Glidden-Durkee/SCM, Balt. and Chgo., 1969-71; branch mgr. Huffman Fin. Co., Springfield, 1971-73, pres., 1978—; nat. acct. mgr. Xerox Corp., Springfield, 1973-78; mem. adv. bd. Consumer Credit Counselling Service, Springfield, 1979—, ind. sect. Am. Fin. Services Assn., Washington, 1986—; bd. dirs. Ill. Fin. Services Assn., Chgo., pres. 1979—, chmn., 1986—. mem. com. Gov.'s Prayer Breakfast, Springfield, 1979—, Ill. Task Force Fin. Services, Springfield, 1985—; bd. dirs. Am. Cancer Soc., Springfield, 1986—. Served to 1st lt. U.S. Army, 1966-69. Mem. Am. Bus. Club (bd. dirs. 1978-80). Republican. Methodist. Lodge: Sertoma Internat. (treas. 1986—). Avocations: golf, tennis, jogging. Home: 107 Pinehurst Dr Springfield IL 62704 Office: Huffman Fin Co 424 E Monroe Springfield IL 62701

HUFFMAN, GORDON SETH (TIM), JR., clergyman, religion educator; b. Pitts., Mar. 26, 1943; s. Gordon Seth and Janet Kathryn (Koster) H.; children: Todd Andrew, Kevin Scott. BA, Capital U., 1964; BD, Luth. Theol. Sem., Columbus, Ohio, 1968; PhD, U. St. Andrews, Scotland, 1977. Ordained to ministry Am. Luth. Ch., 1972. Assoc. pastor Div. Luth. Ch., Parma Heights, Ohio, 1971-75; prof. systematic theology Luth. Theol. Sem., Hong Kong, 1976-79; chmn. christian mission Trinity Luth. Sem., Columbus, 1979—; mem. governing bd. Inst. Mission in U.S.A., Columbus, 1984—. Mem. Internat. Assn. Mission Studies, Am. Soc. Missiology, Assn. Profs. Mission. Democrat. Office: Trinity Luth Sem 2199 E Main St Columbus OH 43209

HUFFMAN, H. ARLENE, banker; b. Paxton, Ill., June 18, 1933; d. Edward V. and Mabel R. (Johnson) Bankson; m. Richard M. Huffman, Nov. 25, 1953; children—Melinda Huffman Etter, Mark, David. Student Ind. Bus. Coll. With Community State Bank, Royal Center, Ind., 1969—, asst. cashier, 1969-75, asst. trust officer, 1975-78, ins. dept. mgr., 1978—. Helper for elderly Helping Hands, Royal Center; past pres. Progressive Club, Royal Center. Mem. Ind. Agts. Assn. Office: Community State Bank 101 Chicago St Royal Center IN 46978

HUFFMAN, IRENE DOROTHY, wine marketing specialist; b. Joliet, Ill., Oct. 8, 1947; s. Bernard John McShane and Dorothy C. (Cheney) Boster; m. James Earl Huffman, Nov. 29, 1969. Student, No. Ill. U., 1964-66; AAS, Black Hawk Coll., 1979; BA, Western Ill. U., 1983. Computer operator Joliet Army Arsenal, 1966-72; computer programmer Bear Mfg., Rock Island, Ill., 1974-76; computer operator Deere Harvester Works, East Moline, Ill., 1976-80, computer programmer, 1980-83; computer standards coordinator Deere & Co. Harvester Works, East Moline, 1983-85; wine mktg. specialist Dimitri Wine & Spirits, Inc., Rock Island, Ill., 1986—; instr. wine Black Hawk Coll., Moline, Ill., 1984—; guest appearance Sta. WHBF-TV, Moline. Wine judge Miss. Valley Fair, Davenport, Iowa, 1981-82, Midwestern Wine Seminar, Lacrosse, Wis., 1985; mem. tech. team Nat. Restaurant

Assn. Wine Competition, Chgo., 1985; contbr. articles on wine to profl. jours.; filmed wine segments for Sta. WQPT-TV, Moline, 1986-87. Vol. Friends of Lane Evans, Rock Island. Recipient 3d place award profl. div. Gejas Wine Competition, Chgo., 1986. Mem. NOW, Career Women's Network (bd. dirs. 1984-86), Soc. Wine Educators, Les Amis du Vin, Am. Inst. Wine and Food. Methodist. Avocation: wine appreciation activities. Home: 1225 W 5th St Milan IL 61264

HUFFMAN, MICHAEL ROBERT, manufacturing executive; b. Ft. Madison, Iowa, July 19, 1955; s. Rupert Warren and Rose Mary (Hoenig) H.; m. Roxanna Jolene Huffman; children: Brooke Lindsey, Jason Michael. Student, Southeastern Coll., Burlington, Iowa, 1973-75. Machinist Huffman Welding and Machine, Inc., Ft. Madison, Iowa, 1973-80, with purchasing div., 1980-83, mgr., 1983-85, plant mgr., 1985—. Republican. Home: 1202 Ave B Fort Madison IA 52627 Office: Huffman Welding & Machine Inc Rural Rt #2 Box 36 Fort Madison IA 52627

HUFFMAN, WENDELL ALAN, real estate corporation officer; b. Wichita, Kans., Mar. 4, 1952; s. Eugene Wendell and Darlene Rosetta (Cowell) H.; m. Kathryn Ruth Felmer, May 19, 1984; children: James Robert, Whitney Kathryn. BBA, Wichita State U., 1975. Police officer City of Wichita, 1974-76; property mgr. Talley Investment, Wichita, 1976-78; v.p. Harter, Inc., Wichita, 1978-80; owner Key Mgmt. Co., Wichita, 1980—; instr. Registered Apt. mgr. Service, Wichita, 1977—. Mem. Inst. Real Estate Mgmt. (pres. Wichita chpt. 1983, governing council 1986-88), Wichita C. of C., Ducks Unlimited (com. mem.). Republican. Methodist. Avocations: hunting, skiing, softball. Office: Key Mgmt Co 919 West Second Wichita KS 67203

HUFFMAN-HINE, RUTH CARSON, adult education administrator, educator; b. Spencer, Ind., Sept. 13, 1925; d. Joseph Charles Carson and Bess Ann Taylor; m. Joe Buren Hine; children: Paulette Walker, Larry K., Annette M. AA in Fine Arts, Ind. Cen. Coll., 1967; BS in Edn., Butler U., 1971; MS in Adult Edn., Ind. U., 1976. Cert. elem. edn. Subs. tchr. Met. Sch. Dist. Wayne Twnshp., Indpls., 1956-60; tchr. of homebound Met. Sch. Dist. Decatur Twnshp., Indpls., 1964-66; adult edn. tchr. Met. Sch. Dist. Wayne Twnshp., Indpls., 1971-75, adminstr. adult edn., 1975—; cons. Ind. Adoption System, Indpls., 1985—; regional rep. Ind. Assn. Adult Adminstrs., 1984—; program rep. Ind. Literacy Coordinators, Indpls., 1985—; speaker, mem. literacy research and evaluation com. Ind. Adult Literacy Coalition, Indpls., 1980-86. Co-author Learning for Everyday Living, 1978, Table Approach to Education, 1984, Developing Educational Competencies for Individuals Determined to Excel, 6 vols., 1980 (ERIC System award 1980), (ERIC System award 1985), Collection, Evaluation, Dissemination of Special Research Projects, 1984. Vice com. person Rep. Orgn., Indpls., 1968-72. Mem. Internat. Reading Assn. (Celebrate Literacy award 1984), Ind. Assn. for Adult Edn. (treas. 1984—, Outstanding Adult Educator 1979), Beta Phi Delta (pres. 1986—), Delta Kappa Gamma (v.p. 1985-86, fellowship chmn. 1982-84), Phi Delta Kappa. Republican. Mem. Christian Ch. Avocations: reading, music, bicycling. Home: 50 Abner Creek Pkwy Danville IN 46122 Office: Met Sch Dist Wayne Twnshp 1200 N Girls School Rd Indianapolis IN 46214

HUFFNAGLE, NORMAN PARMLEY, physicist; b. Honolulu, Dec. 26, 1941; s. Norman Sylvester and Helen Louis (Parmley) H.; m. Cleda May Walker, June 7, 1980; children: Mitchell Walker, Norman Walker, Donley Walker Jr., Kent Norman, Craig Benjamin, Christian Thomas. BA, Drake U., 1963; MS in Sci. Edn., U. Nebr., 1969. Physicist Mine Def. Lab. USN, Panama City, Fla., 1963-66; mem. tech. staff Hughes Aircraft, Canoga Park, Calif., 1969-72; staff engr. Martin Marietta Corp., Orlando, Calif., 1972-78; mgr. Electro-Optics Systems div. Boeing Mil. Airplane Co., Huntsville, Ala., 1978-83, sr. staff engr. Honeywell Def. Systems div., 1983-87; mgr. advanced concepts Northrop Electro-Mech. Div., Anaheim, Calif., 1987—; dir. Village Green Lighting Dist. Patentee in sonar and signal processing, lasers and fiber/optics controls. Mem. Acoustical Soc. Am., Soc. Auto. Test Engring., Martin Marietta Mgmt. Club, Boeing Mil. Airplane Co. Mgmt. Club, Honeywell Mgmt. Club, Sigma Xi. Republican. Home: c/o Norman Walker 1601 W MacArthur Apt 32H Minnetonka MN 55343

HUFSCHMIDT, ALVIN JAMES, wire company executive; b. Pitts., Oct. 19, 1946; s. Alvin John and Ethel A. (Schenck) H.; m. Carol Batz, Aug. 24, 1968; 1 child, Amy. BS in Indsl. Engring., Cleve. State U., 1969. Materials mgr. Fincor div. Rockwell Internat., York, Pa., 1970-77; materials mgr. Morse Controls div. Incom Internat., Hudson, Ohio, 1977-83; corp. material mgr. Electronic Engring. Co., Brecksville, Ohio, 1983-86; corp. materials mgr. Am. Spring Wire Corp., Bedford Heights, Ohio, 1986—. Fellow Am. Prodn. and Inventory Control Soc. (cert. 1979). Avocations: sailing, tennis.

HUGGHINS, MILDRED KAUFMAN SHIELDS, musician; b. Joplin, Mo., Mar. 29, 1929; d. Arley Bryan and Mildred Johanna (Kaufman) Shields; m. Ernest Jay Hugghins, Aug. 12, 1952; children: Susan Jane, Arley Jay, Mildred Kay. MusB, BA, Hendrix Coll., 1950; MusM, U. Ill., 1952. Organist various chs., Conway, Ark., 1946-50; asst. organist Episc. Ch., Champaign, Ill., 1950-52; organist Pulaski Heights Meth. Ch., Little Rock, Ark., 1951, First Luth. Ch., Brookings, S.D., 1953-59; organist, worship planner 1st United Meth. Ch., Brookings, 1960—; pvt. tchr. organ, piano, Brookings, 1952—; accompanist, organist Prairie Chorale, Brookings, 1985—. Writer art column Brookings Register, 1979—. Trustee Brookings Pub. Library, 1968-77; pres. Brookings Area Art Council, 1975-77, exec. sec., 1979—; mem. auction com. Evening for the Arts benefit, 1976-80; mem., founder Community Cultural Ctr., Brookings, 1976—. Mem. Am. Guild Organists (dean 1982-84), Nat. Fedn. Music Clubs (Aeolian Music Club pres., 1964-65), Fellowship United Meths. in Worship, Music & Other Arts, Meml. Art Ctr. Guild, AAUW, LWV, DAR. Democrat. Club: PEO Faculty Women's. Lodges: Job's Daughters (dir. music 1969-79), KiWives Internat. (pres. 1984-85). Avocations: sewing, reading, hiking, travel. Home: 1034 6th Ave Brookings SD 57006

HUGGINS, CHARLES BRENTON, surgical educator; b. Halifax, N.S., Can., Sept. 22, 1901; s. Charles Edward and Bessie (Spencer) H.; m. Margaret Wellman, July 29, 1927; children: Charles Edward, Emily Wellman Huggins Fine. BA, Acadia U., 1920, DSc (hon.), 1946; MD, Harvard U., 1924; MSc, Yale, 1947; DSc (hon.), Washington U., St. Louis, 1950, Leeds U., 1953, Turin U., 1957, Trinity Coll., 1965, U. Wales, 1967, U. Mich., 1968, Med. Coll. Ohio, 1973, Gustavus Adolphus Coll., 1975, Wilmington (Ohio) Coll., 1980, U. Louisville, 1980; LLD (hon.), U. Aberdeen, 1966, York U., Toronto, 1968, U. Calif., Berkeley, 1968; D of Pub. Service (hon.), George Washington U., 1967; D of Pub. Service (hon.) sigillum magnum, Bologna U., 1964. Intern in surgery U. Mich., 1924-26, instr. surgery, 1926-27; with U. Chgo., 1927—, instr. surgery, 1927-29, asst. prof., 1929-33, assoc. prof., 1933-36, prof. surgery, 1936—, dir. Ben May Lab. for Cancer Research, 1951-69, William B. Ogden Disting. Service prof., 1962—; chancellor Acadia U., Wolfville, N.S., 1972-79; Macewen lectr. U. Glasgow, 1958, Ravdin lectr., 1974, Powell lectr., Lucy Wortham James lectr., 1975, Robert V. Day lectr., 1975, Cartwright lectr., 1975. Trustee Worcester Found. Exptl. Biology; bd. govs. Weizmann Inst. Sci., Rehovot, Israel, 1973—. Decorated Order Pour le Mérite Germany; Order of The Sun Peru; recipient Nobel prize for medicine, 1966, Am. Urol. Assn. award, 1948, Francis Amory award, 1948, AMA Gold medals, 1936, 40, Société Internationale d'Urologie award, 1948, Am. Cancer Soc. award, 1953, Bertner award M.D. Anderson Hosp., 1953, Am. Pharm. Mfrs. Assn. award, 1953, Gold medal Am. Assn. Genito-Urinary Surgeons, 1955, Borden award Assn. Am. Med. Colls., 1955, Comfort Crookshank award Middlesex Hosp., London, 1957, Cameron prize Edinburg U., 1958, Valentine prize N.Y. Acad. Medicine, 1962, Hunter award Am. Therapeutic Soc., 1962, Lasker award for med. research, 1963, Gold medal Virchow Soc., 1964, Laurea award Am. Urol. Assn., 1966, Gold medal Worshipful Soc. Apothecaries of London, 1966, Gairdner award Toronto, 1966, Chgo. Med. Soc. award, 1967, Centennial medal Acadia U., 1967, Hamilton award Ill. Med. Soc., 1967, Bigelow medal Boston Surg. Soc., 1967, Disting. Service award Am. Soc. Abdominal Surgeons, 1972, Sheen award AMA, 1970, Sesquicentennial Commemorative award Nat. Library of Medicine, 1986; Charles Mickle fellow, 1958. Fellow ACS (hon.), Royal Coll. Surgeons Can. (hon.), Royal Coll. Surgeons Scotland (hon.), Royal Coll. Surgeons England (hon.), Royal Soc. Edinburgh (hon.); mem. Am. Philos. Soc., Nat. Acad. Scis. (Charles L. Meyer award for cancer research 1943), Am. Assn. Cancer Research, Canadian Med. Assn. (hon.), Alpha Omega Alpha. Home: 5807 Dorchester Ave Chicago IL 60637 Office: Univ of Chgo Ben May Lab for Cancer Research 950 E 59th St Chicago IL 60637

HUGGINS, CHARLOTTE SUSAN HARRISON, author, educator, travel specialist; b. Rockford, Ill., May 13, 1933; d. Lyle Lux and Alta May (Bowers) H.; student Knox Coll., 1951-52; A.B. magna cum laude, Radcliffe Coll., 1958; M.A., Northwestern U., 1960, postgrad., 1971-73; m. Rollin Charles Huggins, Apr. 26, 1952; children—Cynthia Charlotte Peters, Shirley Ann Cooper, John Charles. Asst. editor Hollister Publs., Inc., Wilmette, Ill., 1959-65; tchr. advanced placement English New Trier High Sch. East, Winnetka, Ill., 1965—, asst. sponsor Echoes, 1981, Trevia, 1982, 83; pres. Harrison Farms, Inc., Lovington, Ill., 1976—; instr., travel expert New Trier Adult Edn. Keys to the World's Last Mysteries, 1986—, Cambodia: A Place in Time, 1987. Mem. women's bd. St. Leonard's House, Chgo., 1965-75; Central Sch. PTA Bd., Wilmette, 1960-64; mem. jr. bd. Northwestern U. Settlement, Chgo., 1965-75. Recipient DAR Citizenship award, 1953, Phi Beta Kappa award, 1957; Am. Legion award, 1959; named Master Tchr., New Trier High Sch., 1979. Mem. NEA, Ill. Edn. Assn., New Trier Edn. Assn., Nat. Council Tchrs. English, Ill. Assn. Tchrs. English, MLA, Northwestern U. Alumni Assn., Jr. Aux. U. Chgo. Cancer Research Bd., Mary Crane League, Pi Beta Phi. Clubs: Nat. Huguenot Soc., Ill. Huguenot Soc., Womans' of Wilmette, Mich. Shores, Knox Coll.; Univ. Club of Chgo., Radcliffe Coll. (Chgo.). Author: A Sequential Course in Composition Grades 9-12, 1979; A History of New Trier High School, 1982, Passage to Anaheim: An Historical Biography of Pioneer Families, 1984. Home: 700 Greenwood Ave Wilmette IL 60091 Home: Ptarmigan Meadows Creede CO 81130 Office: 385 Winnetka Ave Winnetka IL 60093

HUGGINS, HOSIAH, JR., management consultant; b. Cleve., Aug. 17, 1950. BA, U. Akron, Ohio, 1974. Mktg. rep. Amalgamated Stationers Co., Cleve., 1974-77, v.p. sales, 1977-80; mktg. rep. Xerox Corp., Cleve., 1980-82, sr. mktg. rep., 1982-83; pres. Insight & Attitudes, Inc., Cleve., 1983—. Named one of Outstanding Young Men of Am., 1981, Man of Yr., Bel-Air Civic Club, 1983, one of 83 Most Interesting People, Cleve. mag., 1983; recipient Disting. Leadership award United Negro Coll. Fund, 1982-84, Pres.' award Mid-Am. Assn. Ednl. Opportunity Personnel, 1983, Leadership award Alliance Black Telecommunicaions Employees of AT&T. Mem. Am. Mktg. Assn., Am. Soc. Tng. and Devel., Inst. Mgmt. Cons., Nat. Assn. Mgmt. Cons. (nat. pres. 1987), Nat. Assn. Mktg. Developers, Nat. Speakers' Assn., Sales and Mktg. Execs. Democrat. Roman Catholic. Home: 10930 Wade Park Cleveland OH 44106 Office: Insight & Attitudes Inc 3101 Euclid Office Plaza Suite 501 Cleveland OH 44115

HUGHES, BARBARA ANN LEROY, association executive; b. Mich. City, Ind., Feb. 22, 1932; d. Archibald Francis and Virgie Elizabeth (Matzke) LeRoy; m. Robert Jon Hughes, June 25, 1955; children—Elizabeth Ann Hitomi, Clare Frances, William LeRoy. B.S. in Chemistry, Purdue U., 1954; postgrad., 1954-55, 75-80. Chemist Pillsbury Co., Mpls., 1955-56; editor, reporter Sun Newspaper, Mpls., 1965-71; environ. program dir. Am. Lung Assn. Hennepin County, Mpls., 1973-82, exec. dir. St. Paul, 1983—. Editor Clean Air Newsletter, 1973—; contbr. to Congl. report, 1980. Chmn. trustees Anoka County Library, Blaine, Minn., 1962-65; chmn. Fridley Cable TV Adv. Bd., Minn., 1972-77, 81—; chmn. KUOM Radio Adv. Bd., 1980—; mem. Environ. Quality Bd., St. Paul, 1983—. Named Fridley Sun Woman of Yr. Fridley Sun Newspaper, 1972; recipient Outstanding Service award Minn. Library Assn., 1973; Pub. Citizen award Minn. Pub. Interest Research Group, 1982. Mem. Minn. Pub. Health Assn., Upper Midwest Air Pollution Control Assn. (pres. 1977), Congress Lung Assn. Staff (com. chmn. 1975-80), LWV (state bd. 1968-71). Democratic. Unitarian. Club: Sierra (Mpls.). Avocations: reading; skiing; theater; fishing. Home: 548 Rice Creek Terr Fridley MN 55432 Office: Am Lung Assn Ramsey County 614 Portland Ave Saint Paul MN 55102

HUGHES, BELDON EARL, coal company executive; b. Linton, Ind., May 6, 1947; s. Earl David and Juanita (Davis) H.; m. Kathryn Lorraine Jarman, Mar. 5, 1967 (div. May 1980); 1 child, Aimeé Lorraine; m. Kelly Denise McCarty, June 21, 1980; children: Kimberly Denise, Krista Diane. Student, Lamar U., 1965-66, Vincennes (Ind.) U., 1966-67. Maj. Knox County Police Dept., Vincennes, 1971-78; owner, mgr. The Plumbing Shop, Bicknell, Ind., 1978-80; dir. health safety tng. Green Constrn. Ind. Inc., Cannelburg, 1980—. Served to staff sgt. USAF, 1966-70. Named Law Officer of Yr. Am. Legion Ind., Hon. Order Ky. Coln., Gov. of Ky., 1985; recipient Acad. Police Sci. award Nat. Law Enforcement Acad., Washington, 1975. Mem. Ind. Coal Council (legis. com. 1983—, gov. affairs com. 1983—, bd. dirs. 1984—), Nat. Safety Council (indsl. div.), Ind. Coal Mining Inst., U.S. Jaycees (named Outstanding Young Man Yr. 1977). Lodges: Elks (Esquire 1984-85), Moose. Avocations: basketball, golf, fishing. Home: PO Box 3 Westphalia IN 47596 Office: Green Contrn Ind Inc PO Box 67 Cannelburg IN 47519

HUGHES, DAVID, architect; b. N.Y.C., Dec. 24, 1947; s. Willie Dixon and Lossie (Kittrell) Hughes; m. Geralynne Regina Ingram, July 21, 1969 (div. Jan. 1980); children: Latif, Ahmed, Titanya, Aisha, David II. BArch, Columbia U., 1974; M in Urban Planning, CCNY, 1975. Registered architect, Ohio; lic. landscape architect, Ohio; lic. planner, N.J. Prin. David Hughes, Cons., Cleve., 1977—; project architect Madison Internat., 1983-85; prof. architecture Kent (Ohio) State U., 1985—; master planner City of East Cleveland, Ohio, 1986—. Mem. AIA, Am. Planning Assn. Baptist. Avocations: photography, world travel. Home: 55 Barrett Rd #309 Berea OH 44017

HUGHES, DAVID H., manufacturing executive; b. Kansas City, Mo., Sept. 9, 1928; s. Hilliard W. and Mary (Histed) H.; m. Dorothy H. Halsey, Dec. 19, 1950; children: David, Avery, Steven, Betsey. B.S.E., Princeton U., 1949; M.B.A., Harvard U., 1952. Vice chmn. Hallmark Cards, Kansas City, Mo., also bd. dirs.; bd. dirs. Yellow Freight Systems, Overland Park, Kans. Trustee Hall Family Found., Kansas City, Mo.; chmn. Midwest Research Inst., Kansas City; past chmn. bd. Sunset Hill Sch., Kansas City; past pres. Jr. Achievement Greater Kansas City; past bd. dirs. Boys' Club Kansas City, INROADS, Kansas City; bd. dirs., trustee Children's Mercy Hosp., Kansas City; pres. St. Luke's Hosp. Found. Served to 2d lt. USAF, 1952-53. Mem. Greater Kansas City C. of C. (past v.p., past dir.). Republican. Presbyterian. Clubs: Kansas City Country (pres. 1982) (Mission Hills, Kans.); River (dir. 1981-83) (Kansas City, Mo.). Avocations: golf, sailing.

HUGHES, GARY JOSEPH, school administrator; b. Flint, Mich., Aug. 25, 1948; s. Christopher John and Mary Josephine (King) H.; m. Frances Eleanora Schauf, Aug. 18, 1972. BA, Marquette U., 1970; MA, Cen. Mich. U., 1971; MBA, Wayne State U., 1975; EdD, Internat. U., St. Louis, 1984. Cert. secondary tchr., Mich. Guidance counselor Lake Orion Schs., Mich., 1973-75, guidance dir., 1975-79, basketball coach, 1973-79; high sch. adminstr., Allegan Schs., Mich., 1979-80, Lawton Pub. Schs., Mich., 1980-81; prin., curriculum dir. Goodrich Area Schs., Mich., 1981-85; adminstrn. asst. Troy (Mich.) Sch. Dist., 1985-86; asst. supt. Durand (Mich.) Area Schs., 1986—; cons., Grand Blanc, Mich., 1984. Author: Impact of Role of Spouse, 1984; contbr. articles to profl. jours. Inst. Edn. Leadership fellow 1984-85. Mem. Jaycees, Genesee 8 Conf. (pres. 1984-85), Southwestern Athletic Conf. (pres. 1980-81), Adminstrv. Council Internat. U., Oakland Personnel and Guidance Assn. (Recognition award 1979), Phi Delta Kappa (Recognition award 1984). Roman Catholic. Avocations: sports; woodworking. Home: 5594 Old Franklin Grand Blanc MI 48439 Office: Durand Area Schs 310 N Saginaw Durand MI 48429

HUGHES, GENE WYATT, construction company executive; b. Dayton, Ohio, Feb. 20, 1926; s. John Clayborne and Catherine (Wyatt) H.; Julie Clare Loeffel, May 22, 1964; children: Robert, Meredith, John. BA, Williams Coll., 1950; MS, Stanford U., 1960; MBA, U. San Francisco, 1970. Registered profl. engr., Ohio. Project engr. Hughes Simonson, Dayton, 1954-59; dept. mgr. Scott Co. of Calif., Oakland, 1960-67; project mgr. Swinerton-Walberg, San Francisco, 1967-70; v.p. Hughes Bechtol, Dayton, 1970-82, pres., chief exec. officer, 1982-84; pres. Frebco, Inc., Dayton, 1984—. Adv. com. Sinclair Community Coll., 1980—. Served with USNR, 1944-46, PTO. Mem. ASHRAE (chpt. v.p. 1974-75), Internat. Exec. Service Corps, Mech Contractors Assn. (bd. dirs.), Am. Arbitration Assn. Republican. Presbyterian. Club: Dayton Country. Lodge: Rotary (pres. Oakwood chpt. 1983-84). Avocations: skiing, golf, running, exercise, music. Office: Frebco Inc PO Box 176 Wright Bros Sta Dayton OH 45409

HUGHES, HOWARD BOS, photographer; b. Chgo., Oct. 2, 1938; s. William B. and Wilhelmina (Bos) H.; m. Lynn Edith Bukoll, Aug. 10, 1963; children—Heather, Kelly. B.A., Hope Coll., 1961; B.F.A., Art Inst. Chgo., 1980. With Am. Oil Co., Chgo., 1961-65; registered rep. Wayne Hummer & Co., Chgo., 1965-70; asst. v.p. Palatine Nat. Bank, Ill., 1970-72; prin. Howard B. Hughes Photography, Palatine, 1972—. Bd. govs. Lutheran Social Services, Chgo., 1980—; Republican precinct capt., Palatine, 1975—; treas. United Luth. Ch., Oak Park, Ill., 1966-68. Recipient 1st pl. photo award 7th Internat. Human Unity Conf., 1980. Mem. Profl. Photographers Am., Beta Theta Pi. Republican. Club: Medinah Country (Ill.) (photographer 1980—). Avocations: golf; running. Home: 1791 Prestwick Dr Inverness IL 60067

HUGHES, JEROME MICHAEL, educator, state senator,; b. St. Paul, Oct. 1, 1929; s. Michael Joseph and Mary (Malloy) H.; m. Audrey M. Lackner, Aug. 11, 1951; children—Bernadine, Timothy, Kathleen, Rosemarie, Margaret, John. B.A., Coll. of St. Thomas, St. Paul, 1951; M.A., U. Minn., 1958; Ed.D., Wayne State U., Flint, Mich., 1970; postdoctoral fellow, U. Minn., 1985. Tchr. Shakopee Sch. Dist., Minn., 1951-53; tchr. St. Paul Sch. Dist., 1953-61, counselor, 1963-66, research asst., 1966-67, edn. cons., 1968—; mem. Minn. Senate, St. Paul, 1966—, chmn. edn. com., 1973-82, chmn. elections and ethics com., 1983—, pres., 1983—; mem. faculty U. Minn., 1986; mem. Edn. Commn. of States, Denver, 1973—; dir. State Legis. Leaders Found., Boston, 1983—; mem. Nat. Community Edn. Adv. Council, Washington, 1980-83; mem. Nat. Conf. State Legislature State/Fed. Assembly, 1983—. Mott fellow, 1967-68; Ford Found. fellow George Washington U., 1974-75; Bush Summer fellow, U. Calif., 1975; Disting. Policy fellow George Washington U., 1977-78; postdoctoral fellow U. Minn., 1980-81; recipient Pennell award Minn. Fedn. Tchrs., 1974; Disting. Service award Minn. Elem. Sch. Prins. Assn., 1982; named Community Educator of Yr. Minn. Community Edn. Assn., recipient other awards. Mem. Phi Delta Kappa. Mem. Democratic Farm Labor Party. Roman Catholic. Avocations: travel; reading; fishing; dancing. Home: 1978 Payne Ave Maplewood MN 55117 Office: Saint Paul Pub Schs 360 Colborne St Saint Paul MN 55102

HUGHES, LARRY CHARLES, osteopath; b. Princeton, Ind., May 8, 1953; s. Charles P. and Kathryn (Stewart) H.; m. Sarah Jane Kifer, Aug. 15, 1975; children: Brian Paul, Amy Ann, Michael Thomas. BS, U. Notre Dame, 1976; DO, Kirksville Coll. Osteo. Medicine, 1980. Diplomat Nat. Bd. Examiners Osteopathic Physicians and Surgeons. Intern Southbend (Ind.) Osteo. Hosp., 1980-81; pvt. practice osteopath Mooresville, Ind., 1981—; v.p. Profl. Asbestos Disposal Corp., 1986—; med. dir. Heritage Home Health Care, Martinsville, Ind., 1981—, Millers Merry Manor Nursing Home, Mooresville, 1984—; chmn. utilization rev. com., mem. exec. com. Morgan County (Ind.) Meml. Hosp. Pres. Mooresville Area Sr. Ctr., Inc., 1984—, Coordinated Aging Services for Morgan County, Martinsville, 1985—. Named Outstanding Citizen award City of Evansville, 1970; Cert. Merit Coordinated Aging Services of Morgan County, 1986. Mem. Ind. Assn. Osteo. Physicians and Surgeons (pres. 1984-85), Morgan County Med. Soc. Republican. Roman Catholic. Avocations: hunting, fishing, golf. Home: 110 Charmil Dr Mooresville IN 46158 Office: 430 E St Clair St PO Box 187 Mooresville IN 46158

HUGHES, LARRY NEAL, environmental engineer; b. West Plains, Mo., Aug. 19, 1941; s. Wilbur Emerson and Ruby Bernice (Johnson) H.; m. Carolyn Sue Mason, Mar. 22, 1968; children—John Thomas, Amanda Christine. B.S.C.E., Bradley U., 1964; M.S. in Pub. Health Engring., U. Hawaii, 1967. Registered profl. engr., Fla., Ill.; cert. sewage treatment works operator, class 1, Ill. E.P.A. Civil engr. Dept. Transportation, Peoria, Ill., 1964-65; asst. dist. chemist Greater Peoria San. Dist., 1967-70, dir. waste treatment facilities, 1970—. Contbr. articles to profl. jours. Roundtable commr. staff W.D. Boyce Council Boy Scouts Am., Peoria, 1981-83, cubmaster, 1981-83, scouting coordinator, 1983—, asst. cubmaster, 1980-81. Recipient Scouter's Tng. award, Woodbadge award, Eagle Scout award, all Boy Scouts Am. Fellow ASCE; mem. Am. Acad. Environ. Engrs. (diplomate), Nat. Soc. Profl. Engrs., Ill. Soc. Profl. Engrs., Water Pollution Control Fedn. (Hatfield award 1985), Ill. Assn. Water Pollution Control Operators (pres. 1986-87), Ill. Water Pollution Control Assn., Central States Water Pollution Control Assn. (Operating award 1974), Ducks Unltd., National Rifle Assn., Bass Anglers Sportsman Soc., Pi Kappa Alpha. Avocations: hunting, fishing, hiking, camping. Office: 2322 S Darst St Peoria IL 61607

HUGHES, RALPH CARMEN, diversified manufacturing company executive; b. Hagerstown, Ind., Oct. 19, 1927; s. Ralph Carlton and Euveda Bosman (Canaday) H.; m. Charlotte Ann Bronnenberg, Mar. 27, 1948; children: Jane Ann, Ralph Charles, Cynthia Jo, William Curtis. BSA, Purdue U., 1950. Asst. agrl. editor Purdue U., West Lafayette, Ind., 1950-54; copywriter John Deere & Co, Moline, Ill., 1954-60, advt. mgr., 1960-84, dir. advt., 1984—. Republican. Office: Deere & Co John Deere Rd Moline IL 61265

HUGHES, SUSAN LANE, social worker, health services researcher, gerontologist; b. Boston, Feb. 2, 1943; d. John Joseph and Agnes Thomasine (Lane) Mooney; m. Edward F.X. Hughes, Feb. 11, 1967; children—Edward Francis, John Patrick, Dempsey Lane. B.A., Manhattanville Coll., Purchase, N.Y., 1964; M.S.W., Simmons Coll., Boston, 1966; D.S.W., Columbia U., 1981. Social worker Mass. Gen. Hosp., Boston, 1966-67, Presbyn. Hosp., N.Y.C., 1967-69, 70-74; Project dir. Ctr. for Health Services Research, Northwestern U., Evanston, Ill., 1977-81, program dir., 1981—; research cons. Five Hosp. Homebound Program, Chgo., 1977—, Am. Found. for Blind, N.Y.C., 1976-77; mem. com. to plan maj. study of nat. long-term care policies Inst. Medicine, 1985. Author: Long Term Care: Options in an Expanding Market, 1986; contbr. articles to profl. publs., chpts. to books. Mem. nursing home adv. council Office of Ill. Atty. Gen., Chgo., 1984—, Adv. Com. for Maturing Adult, Chgo. Health Dept., 1984—. Kellogg Found. fellow, 1979. Mem. Am. Pub. Health Assn., Assn. Health Services Research, Gerontol. Soc. Am. Democrat. Roman Catholic. Avocations: swimming, sailing, gardening, mystery reading. Home: 810 Lincoln St Evanston IL 60201 Office: Northwestern U Ctr Health Services 629 Noyes St Evanston IL 60201

HUGHES, SYLVESTER (SLY), social services administrator; b. Peoria, Ill., May 8, 1948; s. Hattie Lee (Hughes) Stuckey. AA, Ellsworth Coll., 1972; BA, Simpson Coll., 1974; MA, Drake U., 1979. Community correctional service worker Iowa Dept. Social Services, Des Moines, 1974-79, program planner, 1978-80; corp. staff Des Moines Register, 1980-82, asst. dir. community affairs, 1980-82; asst. to dir. Park and Recreations, Des Moines, 1982—. Bd. dirs. Big Bros. and Sisters, 1970-80, Oak Ridge Bd., Des Moines; mem. Black Leadership Council, Des Moines, Gov's. Homecoming 1986, Des Moines, City Mgrs. Equal Employment Opportunity Adv. Com., Des Moines. Served with USN, 1967-70, Vietnam. Mem. Blacks in Mgmt., Iowa Parks and Recreation Assn., Omega Psi Phi. Democrat. Baptist. Home: 1164 Americana Ct #14 Des Moines IA 50314

HUGHES, WENDY LENORE, engineer; b. Stamford, Conn., Mar. 19, 1961; d. Joseph Lawrence II and Greta Alice (Feldtmose) Mitchell; m. Thomas Williams Hughes, May 25, 1985; children: Eric Lee, Jill Elane. BSCE, U. Dayton, 1983, postgrad. in engring. mgmt., 1983—. Technician Monsanto Research Corp., Miamisburg, Ohio, 1982-83, quality control engr., 1983-85, surveillance engr., 1985—. Mem. Am. Inst. Chem. Engrs. (chmn. 1986-87), Soc. for Creative Anachronism. Republican. Lutheran. Avocations: medieval history and customs research, reading, investing, hist. arts and scis. Home: 274 Cora Dr Carlisle OH 45005

HUGHES, WILLIAM OWEN, accountant; b. Garden City, Kans., Oct. 13, 1914; s. John Perry and Leona (Green) H.; m. Zola Andrews, July 4, 1937; children—Steven Perry, B. Acctg., Park Coll., Denver, 1936; cert. in acctg. Northwestern U., 1947. Acct., dist. mgr. Internat. Harvester, Chgo., 1940-72; acct., mgr. Andrews Bus. Services, Kansas City, Mo., 1972-79; acctg. exec. Internat. Exec. Service Corp., Stamford, Conn., 1980—. Recipient Service to Country award Internat. Exec. Service Corps, 1980-81. Mem. Nat.

Soc. Pub. Accts., Nat. Assn. Tax Cons. (dir. 1971-83), Overland Park C. of C., Nat. Model R.R. Assn. Methodist. Home: 9816 Horton Dr Overland Park KS 66207

HUGHEY, MICHAEL JOHN, obstetrician-gynecologist; b. Chgo., July 2, 1948; s. Merle Stanley and Elaine (Cartmel) H.; m. Kathleen Bailey, June 18, 1977; children Andrew Bailey, Scott Bailey. A.B., Princeton U., 1970; M.D., Loyola U., Chgo., 1974. Diplomate Am. Bd. Ob-Gyn. Intern, Evanston Hosp., Ill., 1974-75; resident in ob-gyn, Northwestern U., Chgo., 1974-78; instr. ob-gyn, 1978-80, asst. prof., 1980—; obstetrician North Care Med. Group, Evanston, Ill., 1978—, chmn. dept. ob-gyn, 1981—, v.p., 1981—, also dir. Author: The Complete Guide To Pregnancy, 1984. Contbr. articles to profl. jours. Ruling elder First Presbyterian Ch. Wilmette, Ill., 1983—. Fellow Am. Coll. Obstetricians and Gynecologists; mem. AMA, Chgo. Med. Soc., Ill. State Med. Soc., Am. Inst. Ultrasound in Medicine. Club: Mich. Shores (Wilmette). Office: NorthCare Med Group 500 Davis St Evanston IL 60201

HUGHS, HERB, computer parts manufacturing executive. Pres. UIS Co., Overland Park, Kans. Office: UIS Co 9300 Metcalf Overland Park KS 66212 *

HUHEEY, MARILYN JANE, ophthalmologist; b. Cin., Aug. 31, 1935; d. George Mercer and Mary Jane (Weaver) H.; B.S. in Math., Ohio U., Athens, 1958; M.S. in Physiology, U. Okla., 1966; M.D., U. Ky., 1970. Tchr. math. James Ford Rhodes High Sch., Cleve., 1956-58; biostatistician Nat. Jewish Hosp., Denver, 1958-60; life sci. engr. Stanley Aviation Corp., Denver, 1960-63, N.Am. Aviation Co., Los Angeles, 1963-67; intern U. Ky. Hosp., 1970-71; emergency room physician Jewish Hosp., Mercy Hosp., Bethesda Hosp. (all Cin.), 1971-72; ship's doctor, 1972; resident in ophthalmology Ohio State U. Hosp., Columbus, 1972-75; practice medicine specializing in ophthalmology, Columbus, 1975—; mem. staff Univ. Hosp., Grant Hosp., St. Anthony Hosp., 1975-79; clin. asst. prof. Ohio State U. Med. Sch., 1976-84, clin. assoc. prof., 1985—, dir. course ophthalmologic receptionist/aides, 1976; mem. Peer Rev. Orgn. Bd., 1986—, Ohio Optical Dispensers Bd, 1986—. Dem. candidate for Ohio Senate, 1982. Diplomate Am. Bd. Ophthalmology. Fellow Am. Acad. Ophthalmology; mem. AAUP, Am. Assn. Ophthalmologists, Ohio Ophthalmol. Soc. (bd. govs. 1984—, del. to Ohio State Med. Assn. 1984—), Franklin County Acad. Medicine (profl. relations com. 1979-82, legis. com. 1981—, edn. and program com. 1981—, chmn. 1982-85, chmn. community relations com. 1987—), Ohio Soc. Prevent Blindness (chmn. med. adv. bd. 1978-80), Ohio State Med. Assn. (dr.-nurse liaison com. 1983—), Columbus EENT Soc., Life Care Alliance (pres. sustaining bd. 1987—), LWV, Columbus Council World Affairs, Columbus Bus. and Profl. Women's Club, Columbus C. of C., Grandview Area Bus. Assn., Federated Dem. Women of Ohio, Columbus Area Women's Polit. Caucus, Phi Mu. Clubs: Columbus Met. (forum com. 1982—, fundraising com. 1983-84, chmn. 10th anniversary com. 1986), Mercedes Benz (dir. 1981-83), Zonta, (program com. 1984-86, chmn. internat. com. 1983), Herb Soc. Home: 2396 Northwest Blvd Columbus OH 43221 Office: 1275 Olentangy River Rd Columbus OH 43212

HUIATT, RONALD DEAN, college administrator, researcher; b. Kansas City, Mo., Dec. 25, 1950; s. Donald Eugene and Ethel Mae (Osborn) H.; m. Rhonda Helen Rodwell, June 9, 1974. BA, U. Mo., 1973; MA, Ohio State U., 1975. Researcher State of Ohio, Northfield, 1978-80, Pisces Project, Akron, Ohio, 1980-84; dir., donor research Oberlin (Ohio) Coll., 1984—; ptnr. research and program evaluation for the human services, Cleve., 1978-80. Co-editor: Multi-State Info. Systems Conference Proceedings, 1981. Mem. Council Advancement and Support Edn., Am. Saddlebred Horse Assn., Am. Horse Shows Assn. Democrat. Avocations: showing horses, sports. Home: 5471 Lance Rd Medina OH 44256 Office: Oberlin Coll Devel Office Bosworth Hall Oberlin OH 44074

HUITEMA, BRADLEY EUGENE, psychologist, design consultant, educator; b. Hammond, Ind., July 28, 1938; s. Roy and Doris (Yeater) H.; m. Kathryn Ann Brock, Sept. 2, 1961 (div.); children—Craig Bradley, Laura Lynn. B.A., So. Ill. U., 1961; M.A., Western Mich. U., 1962; Ph.D., Colo. State U., 1968. Research prof., Oreg. State System of Higher Edn., Monmouth, 1967-68; prof. psychology, Western Mich. U., Kalamazoo, 1968—; research design cons. Anova Research, Inc. Research psychologist U.S. Army, 1962-64. Mem. Am. Psychol. Assn., AAAS, Am. Statis. Assn., Soc. of Behavioral Medicine. Author: The Analysis of Covariance and Alternatives, 1980, Bonferonni Statistics: Tables and Pllications, 1987. Home: 113 Braemar Ln Kalamazoo MI 49007 Office: Western Mich U Psychology Dept Kalamazoo MI 49008

HUIZENGA, BERNARD ANDREW, orthopedic surgeon; b. Waupun, Wis., Mar. 23, 1939; s. William E. and Johanna (Tamminga) H.; m. Judith L. Wilson, June 9, 1962; children: Beth, Jill, Jane. BA, U. Wis., 1959, MD, 1962. Diplomate Am. Bd. Orthopedic Surgery. Intern with U.S. Army Wm. Beaumont Gen Hosp., El Paso, Tex., 1962-63; resident in gen. surgery Wood VA Hosp., Milw., 1965; resident in orthopedic surgery Columbia Hosp., Milw., 1966; mem. staff Orthopedic Assocs. Milw., S.C., 1969—, Milw. children's Hosp., 1966-67, Milw. County Hosp., 1967-68, VA Hosp., Milw., 1968-69; assoc. clin. prof. Med. Coll. Wis., Milw., 1965—. Served to capt. U.S. Army, 1962-65. Fellow Scoliosis Research Soc., Am. Acad. Orthopedic Surgery; mem. Midwest Orthopedic Assn., Wis. State Orthopedic Soc., Milw. Orthopedic Soc. Office: Orthopedic Assoc Milw SC 4036 N 51st Milwaukee WI 53216

HUIZENGA, DAVID LEE, accountant; b. Grand Rapids, Mich., July 19, 1958; s. Leo A. and Barbara J. (Skestone) H. BSBA, Aquinas Coll., 1980; M in Taxation, Grand Valley State Coll., 1984. CPA, Mich. Acct. State of Mich., Grand Rapids, 1980, Linden Manske CPA, Grand Rapids, 1980-82; tax mgr. Seidman & Seidman, Grand Rapids, 1982—. Contbr. articles to Detroit Free Press, profl. jour. Mem. Am. Inst. CPA's, Mich. Assn. CPA's (state tax com.), Grand Rapids Jaycees (bd. dirs. 1984—). Republican. Club: Athletic (Grand Rapids). Avocations: golf, racquetball, basketball, softball, family picnics. Office: Seidman & Seidman 99 Monroe NW Suite 800 Grand Rapids MI 49503

HUIZENGA, DONALD LEE, manufacturing company executive; b. Muskegon, Mich., Nov. 8, 1946; s. Donald Irving and Anita J. (Wraalstad) H.; m. Alice Jane Petersen, Aug. 23, 1968; children: Jason Donn, Jaime Lynn. BS, Drake U., 1968. With Old Kent Bank & Trust, Grand Rapids, Mich., 1968-77, v.p. trust ops., 1976-77; pres. Cedar Springs (Mich.) Castings, Inc., 1977—; mem. govt. adv. council Gulf Oil, 1982-86. Bd. dirs. Grand Rapids (Mich.) chpt. Am. Cancer Soc., 1975-77, Rockford Ambulance Co., 1985—; adv. bd. Sch. Engring., Western Mich. U., 1985—; trustee Cedar Springs Edn. Found. Served with U.S. Army, 1968-70, USAR, 1970-74. Mem. Cedar Springs C. of C. (bd. dirs. 1980-85, Citizen of Yr. 1982), Foundry Assn. Mich. (bd. dirs. 1979—, v.p. 1982-83, pres. 1984-86), Am. Inst. Banking (pres. 1976-77), Am. Foundrymens Soc. Republican. Lutheran. Club: Grand Rapids Econs. Lodges: Rotary (local bd. dirs. 1980-84, pres. 1982-83), Lions (local pres. 1972-73). Office: 69 W Maple St Cedar Springs MI 49319

HULESCH, WILLIAM STANLEY, physician; b. Cleve., Apr. 28, 1946; s. Stanley and Beatrice R. (Suchma) H.; B.S., U. Dayton, 1968; M.D., Loyola U., Chgo., 1972; m. Jane S. Liebel, Aug. 9, 1969. Resident in family practice MacNeal Hosp., Berwyn, Ill., 1972-75; practice medicine specializing in family practice, Downers Grove, Ill., 1975—; clin. assoc. prof. U. Ill.; past chmn. family practice dept. Good Samaritan Hosp.; past chmn. family practice dept. Hinsdale Hosp.; mem. faculty George Williams Coll., Hinsdale Hosp. Family Practice Residency; pres. D.G. Family Practice, H.S.M. Inc. Advisor, Downers Grove Sch. System, Hinsdale Sch. System. Diplomate Am. Bd. Family Practice, Nat. Bd. Med. Examiners. Fellow Am. Acad. Family Physicians (chmn. by-laws com. 1987—); mem. AMA (Physicians Recognition award), Ill. Acad. Family Physicians (dir., chpt. pres., chmn. bd., pres. 1986), Family Health Found., Ill., Alpha Epsilon Delta. Republican. Editorial research bd. Sports Medicine. Office: 6800 Main St Downers Grove IL 60515

HULETT, WILLIAM, hotel services company executive. Pres. hotel div. Stouffer Hotel Mgmt. Corp., Solon, Ohio. Office: Stouffer Hotel Mgmt Corp 29800 Bainbridge Solon OH 44139 *

HULL, GARY LEROY, education educator, dean; b. Berwick, Ill., Oct. 12, 1941; s. LeRoy M. and Gladys S. (Williams) H.; m. Janice Ann Reeves, Aug. 21, 1965; children: Matthew, Garth. BS, Western Ill. U., 1964; MS, Ind. U., 1967; PhD, Mich. State U., 1972. Cert. elem. and high sch. tchr., Ill., Mich., Ga. Tchr. Schaumburg (Ill.) Schs., 1964-67; adminstr. Thornton High Sch. Dist., Harvey, Ill., 1967-68; from instr. to asst. prof. edn. U. Ga., Athens, 1968-72; asst. prof., dir. Kent (Ohio) State U., 1972-73; prof., chmn. So. Ill. U., Edwardsville, 1973-84, prof., assoc. dean, 1984—; cons. Ill. State Bd. Edn., Springfield, 1975—, Battelle, Research Triangle, N.C., 1979-84, Diversified Tech. Service, El Paso, Tex., 1983—, Allen Corp. of Am., Dallas, 1985—. Contbr. articles to profl. jours., govt. publs., govt. studies. Pres. Homeowners Assn., Edwardsville, 1974-76; mem. Madison County (Ill.) Reps., 1975—. Mem. Assn. for Supervision and Curriculum Devel., Assn. for Ednl. Communications and Tech., Am. Ednl. Research Assn., Phi Delta Kappa. Methodist. Club: Sunset Hills Country. Lodge: Lions. Avocations: jogging, golf. Home: 823 Amherst Pl Edwardsville IL 62025 Office: So Ill U Sch Edn Edwardsville IL 62025

HULL, ROGER HAROLD, college president; b. N.Y.C., June 18, 1942; s. Max Harold and Magda Mary (Stern) H.; m. Anne Elizabeth Dyson, July 4, 1980; 1 child, Roberto Franklin. A.B. cum laude, Dartmouth Coll., 1964; LL.B., Yale U., 1967; LL.M., U. Va., 1972, S.J.D., 1974. Bar: N.Y. 1968. Assoc. firm White & Case, N.Y.C., 1967-71; spl. counsel to gov., Va., 1971-74; spl. asst. to chmn., dep. staff dir. Interagy. Task Force Law of Sea, NSC, 1974-76; v.p. devel. Syracuse (N.Y.) U., 1976-79, v.p. devel. and planning, 1979-81; pres. Beloit (Wis.) Coll., 1981—; dir. M&I Bank, Beloit; mem. U.S. del. Law of Sea Conf., 1974-76; adj. prof. Syracuse U. Law Sch., 1976-81; Bd. visitors Coll. William and Mary, Williamsburg, Va., 1970-74; mem. public instns. task force Assn. Gov. Bds., 1975. Author: The Irish Triangle, 1976; co-author: Law and Vietnam, 1968. Mem. Am. Bar Assn., Young Pres.' Orgn., Am. Soc. Internat. Law., Council on Fgn. Relations(Chgo.). Clubs: Beloit Country; Yale (N.Y.C.). Office: Beloit Coll Beloit WI 53511

HULLINGER, CRAIG HARLAN, city planning consultant; b. Brookings, S.D., Dec. 1, 1947; s. Clifford Harlan and Louise Edna (Liffengren) H.; m. Elizabeth S. Ruyle, Oct. 24, 1985; children: Clint, Bret, Leigh Ann. B.A., Govs. State U., 1975, M.A., 1976; postgrad. U. Ill., 1980. Exec. dir. Will County Planning Dept., Joliet, Ill., 1973-77; planner, acting mgr. City of Park Forest South, Ill., 1977-78; chief devel. Prairie Devel. Ltd., Crete, Ill., 1978-80; pres. Planning Devel. Services, Chgo., 1980—; cons. to cities in Ind., Ill. and Mich., 1978—. Candidate, Will County Bd., Frankfort, Ill., 1979, precinct committeeman, 1980. Served to lt. col. USMC, 1966-71, Vietnam. Recipient Navy Commendation medal. Mem. Am. Inst. Cert. Planners, Am. Planning Assn., Misericordia Parents Assn. (chmn. ways and means com. 1981-83), Marine Corps Res. Officers Assn. (sec. 1983-84), Plank Rd. Trail Assn. (bd. dirs. 1984—), Friends of Park. Lutheran.

HULLINGER, G. E., manufacturing company executive. Pres. Warner-Ishi Corp., Decatur, Ill. Office: Warner-Ishi Corp 707 Southside Dr Decatur IL 62525 *

HULLINGER, MICHAEL DUANE, construction executive; b. Osceola, Iowa, Oct. 17, 1950; s. Duane Winford and Caroline Louise (James) H.; m. Joan DeVee Mullenburg, Nov. 21, 1970; children: Michelle, Matthew. BSIndslE, Iowa State U., 1973. Field supt. Todd & Sargent, Ames, Iowa, 1973-76, project mgr., 1976-79; field project mgr. T.E. Ibberson, Mpls., 1979-81; asst. mgr. of projects Fling Constrn. Mgmt., Columbus, Ohio, 1981-82, mgr. of projects, 1981-85; v.p. F & P Mgrs., Inc. (formerly Fling Constrn. Mgmt.), Columbus, Ohio, 1985-86, also bd. dirs. Project mgr./team leader constrn. and design open structure to minimize grain dust explosions, 1981-83, for state of the art clay handling facility, 1983-84. Coach, asst. coach Dublin (Ohio) Youth Orgn., 1984—. Mem. Project Mgmt. Inst. Democrat. Methodist. Avocations: flying, hunting, skiing.

HULLVERSON, JAMES EVERETT, JR., lawyer, educator; b. St. Louis, Sept. 20, 1953; s. James Everett and Shirley (Shaughnessey) H.; m. Laure Albers Bauer, Oct. 7, 1977; children—Everett James, Leigh Bauer. B.A., Yale U., 1975; J.D. cum laude, St. Louis U., 1978. Bar: Mo. 1978, U.S. Dist. Ct. (ea. dist.) Mo. 1978, Ill. 1979, U.S. Supreme Ct. 1981, U.S. Ct. Appeals (8th cir.) 1983; diplomate Am. Bd. Profl. Liability Attys.; cert. civil trial adv. Nat. Bd. Trial Advocacy. Ptnr. Hullverson, Hullverson & Frank, Inc., St. Louis, 1978—; adj. assoc. prof. law St. Louis U., 1983—; faculty Nat. Coll. Advocacy, 1983, 85; lectr. in field. Contbr. chpts. to books; author seminar program. Active Attys. Motivated for Mo. Mem. Assn. Trial Lawyers Am., Ill. Trial Lawyers Assn., Mo. Assn. Trial Attys., Mo. Bar Assn., Am. Soc. Law and Medicine. Roman Catholic. Clubs: Mo. Athletic, St. Louis Masters Swim, Yale (St. Louis). Home: 7937 Teasdale Ct University City MO 63130 Office: Hullverson Hullverson & Frank Inc 1010 Market St Suite 1550 Saint Louis MO 63101

HULS, WAYNE ROBERT, accountant; b. Mitchell, S.D., Feb. 23, 1956; s. Robert William and Dolores (Weber) H. BSBA in Acctg., U. S.D., 1978. Supr. Touche Ross & Co., Mpls., 1978-84; asst. controller Pillsbury Co.—Feed div., Mpls., 1984-87; acctg. mgr. materials mgmt. Pillsbury Co., Mpls., 1987—. Treas. Senate dist. #45 Ind. Reps., Mpls., 1985-87, chmn., 1987—; treas. Hennepin County Ind. Reps., Mpls., 1986—. Mem. Am. Inst. CPA's. Roman Catholic. Avocations: backpacking, racquetball. Home: 2120 Windsor Way Golden Valley MN 55422-4147 Office: The Pillsbury Co Pillsbury Ctr MS 1934 Minneapolis MN 55402

HULSEBOSCH, CHARLES JOSEPH, truck manufacturing company executive; b. N.Y.C., Dec. 14, 1933; s. Albert J. and Marie (Gough) H.; m. Elizabeth Ferguson, July 6, 1957; children—Albert, Daniel, Joseph, Kristine, Thomas, Howard, John. A.B., Dartmouth, 1955; M.B.A., Amos Tuck Sch., 1956. Financial analyst Ford Motor Co., 1956-60; from budget mgr. to controller Renault, Inc., N.Y.C., 1960-63; with United Fruit Co., 1963-69, treas., 1967-69; v.p., treas. Libby, McNeill & Libby, 1969-74, v.p. fin., 1974-77; also dir.; v.p. fin., treas., dir. Oshkosh Truck Corp., Wis., 1978—; part owner Wis. Flyers, Continental Basketball Assn. Mem. Oshkosh City Council, 1981-85. Mem. Fin. Execs. Inst., Newcomen Soc., Zeta Psi. Republican. Roman Catholic. Club: Oshkosh Power Boat, Oshkosh Country. Home: 2015 Menominee Dr Oshkosh WI 54901 Office: 2307 Oregon St Oshkosh WI 54901

HULSMAN, CARL HENRY, manufacturing company executive; b. Medina, Ohio, Feb. 21, 1929; s. John Ernest and Louise (Kirstein) H.; m. Jane Gay Tripp, Sept. 4, 1954; children—John Charles, Ann Elizabeth, Jean Ellen. B.S. magna cum laude, Kent State U., 1955. Pub. accountant Walthall & Drake, Cleve., 1955-62; controller Work Wear Corp., Cleve., 1962-86, v.p., controller, 1986—. Served with inf. U.S. Army, 1946-52. Mem. Ohio Soc. C.P.A.'s, Beta Gamma Sigma. Home: 21173 Endsley Ave Rocky River OH 44116 Office: 1768 E 25th St Cleveland OH 44114

HULTGREN, DENNIS EUGENE, farmer; b. Union County, S.D., Mar. 19, 1929; s. John Alfred and Esther Marie (Johnson) H.; grad. high sch.; m. Nelda Ethelyn Olson, Aug. 3, 1957; children—Nancy Hultgren Klemme, Jean Hultgren Doty, Jahn Dennis, Ruth Dorothy Hultgren Henneman. Farmer, Union County, 1953—; commr., chmn. Union County Planning and Zoning Bd., 1972-83; mem. bd. bylaw revision Union County Electric Co., 1983-85. Pres. bd. Union Creek Cemetery, 1958—; pres. bd. mgrs. Union-Sayles Watershed Dist., 1965-70. Treas., Sioux Valley Twp., Union County, 1980—; treas., bd. dirs. W. Union Sch., 1957-67; chmn. Union County Sch. Bd., 1961-68; pres. Alcester (S.D.) Sch. Bd., 1970-77; chmn. Alcester PTA, 1967-68; mem. tech. bd. rev. Southeastern Council Govts., Sioux Falls, S.D., 1976-77; bd. dirs. Siouxland Interstate Met. Planning Council, Sioux City, Iowa, 1977-83, sec. council ofcls., 1978-83; bd. dirs. Old Opera House Community Theater, Akron, Iowa, Akron Area Action Assn., 1983-85, 1983-84, Akron Devel. Corp., 1985—; Rep. precinct committeeman, 1970—, Union County Rep. Cen. Com., 1970—; mem. S.D. State Bd. Equalization, 1987—. Served with AUS, 1951-53, Korea. Recipient outstanding dedication and service award Old Opera House Community Theatre, 1984, Sioux City Siouxland Disting. Citizen award Siouxland Interstate Met. Planning Council, 1983, Jefferson award Sta. KELO-TV, 1985, Outstanding Community Service award Lions Internat., 1985. Mem. Farm Bur., Farmers Union (exec. bd. Union County 1987—), S.D. Livestock Feeders Assn., Nat. Cattlemen's Assn., Associated Sch. Bds. S.D. (Merit award 1976), Am. Legion (exec. bd. Akron 1978—, comdr. Akron 1980-81, historian 1981—, trustee 1983—), VFW. Lutheran (mem. bd. 1967-70, 82-84, lay chmn. 1970, 82—chmn. centennial com. 1974). Address: Hulteboda Farm Box 147 Route 2 Akron IA 51001

HULTGREN, LENNART SVEN, engineer; b. Ludvika, Sweden, Mar. 18, 1950; came to U.S., 1974; s. Sven Olof and Beeri Lilian (Eriksson) H.; m. Azam Ahmadi-Moghadam, 1983. BS in Engring. Physics, Uppsala U., 1973; MS in Aero. and Astronautical Engring., MIT, 1975, PhD, 1978. Research engr. Aero. Research Inst. of Sweden, Stockholm, 1973-74; postdoctoral assoc. MIT, Cambridge, Mass., 1978-79; vis. asst. prof. Ill. Inst. Tech., Chgo., 1979-80, asst. prof., 1980-85, assoc. prof., 1985-87; aerospace engr. Lewis Research Ctr. NASA, Cleve., 1987—; cons. Aero. Research Inst. of Sweden, Stockholm. Mem. Am. Phys. Soc. (fluid dynamics div.), AIAA, Am. Acad. Mechanics, Sigma Xi. Office: NASA Lewis Research Ctr MS 5-9 21000 Brookpark Rd Cleveland OH 44135

HUMAY, PRISCILLA MARIE, artist, illustrator b. Chgo.; d. Francis Joseph and Helen Barbara (Balun) Humay; children: Michele Lepore Erickson, Anton Witek, Priscilla Louis, Demetrious Louis. B.F.A., Art Inst. Chgo., 1969; M.S. in Visual Design, Inst. Design, Ill. Inst. Tech., 1971; postgrad. Charles U., Prague, Czechoslovakia, 1972, 73. Tchr., Deerpath Art League, Lake Forest, Ill., 1983—, Jewish Cultural Ctrs., Chgo., 1971; lectr. Willowbrook High Sch., 1971, Oakton Community Coll., Morton Grove, Ill., 1974, Govs. State U., Park Forest, Ill., 1974; gallery co-dir. ARC Gallery and Ednl. Found., Chgo., 1978-79; gallery co-dir., art festival coordinator, bd. dirs. Alumni Assn. Sch. of Art Inst. Chgo., 1975, 76; med. illustrator, graphic designer, visual designer, illustrator, 1973—; solo exhibits include Oak Park, 1967, Gallery at Garrett at Northwestern U., 1975, ARC Gallery, 1974, 76, Illini Union Gallery, U. Ill., Champaign-Urbana, 1978; participant group exhibits, also juried exhibit Films by Women 1974, Mus. of Art Inst. Chgo.; works represented in collections of Main Bank of Chgo., Household Internat. Corp., Citizens Bank of Waukegan, pvt. collections, U.S., W.Ger., Holland, Czechoslovakia; juror for animated film Chgo. Internat. Film Festival, 1978. Pres. Lake Forest-Lake Bluff Jr. Women, 1981-82; founder, dir. Lake Forest-Lake Bluff Concerned Citizens for Peace, 1982, 83; chmn. of events Art for Nuclear Weapons Freeze at Richard Gray Gallery, Chgo., 1983; pres. Lake Bluff-Lake Forest Com. of Arden Shore Assn. Home for Boys, 1982; pres. Arden Shore Assn. Home for Boys, 1983, 84; treas. bd. Deerpath Art League, 1983, 84; chair Art for a Nuclear Weapons Freeze, Gray Gallery, Chgo., 1983. Recipient cert. of merit Chgo. Internat. Film Festival, 1971, jury award Evanston (Ill.) Art Festival, 1971, purchase awards Citizens Bank of Waukegan, 1982, Household Internat. Corp. Collection, 1982, 2d place graphics award Fall Festival Deerpath Art League, Lake Forest, 1982, 1st place graphics award, 1983. Mem. AAUW. Home and Office: 381 Pierce Ct Vernon Hills IL 60061

HUMBLE, JIMMY LOGAN, transportation company road engineer; b. Columbia, Ky., Dec. 6, 1944; s. William Rymon and Maxine (Brockman) H. B.S. in Elem. Edn., Western Ky. U., 1972. Field reporter Adair County, Columbia, 1963-66; surveyor Agr. Stabilization Com., Muskingum County Edn. Dept., Zanesville, Ohio, 1966-73; road engr. ARA/Smith's, Columbus, Ohio, 1974—; trustee Teamster's Local 413, Columbus, 1983-85. Mem. Fraternal Order Police, Smithsonian Instn., Regenerative Agr. Assn., Pub. Library Columbus and Franklin County (fellow). Democrat. Methodist. Clubs: Ohio Auto, Centurian (Columbus); 4-H (Columbia); Future Farmers Am. Sentinel. Avocations: reading; travel; writing. Home: 351 Garden Heights Ave PO Box 28098 Columbus OH 43228-0098

HUME, HORACE DELBERT, manufacturing company executive; b. Endeavor, Wis., Aug. 15, 1898; s. James Samuel and Lydia Alberta (Sawyer) H.; student pub. schs.; m. Minnie L. Harlan, June 2, 1926 (dec. May 1972); 1 son, James; m. 2d, Sarah D. Lyles Rood, Apr. 6, 1973. Stockman and farmer, 1917-19; with automobile retail business, Garfield, Wash., 1920-21, partner and asst. mgr., 1921-27; automobile and farm machine retailer, Garfield, partner, mgr., 1928-35, gen. mgr. Hume-Love Co., Garfield, 1931-35, pres., 1935-57; partner, gen. mgr. H.D. Hume Co., Mendota, Ill., 1944-52; pres. H.D. Hume Co., Inc., 1952—; partner Hume and Hume, 1952-72; pres. Hume Products Corp., 1953—; pres., dir. Hume-Fry Co., Garden City, Kans., 1955-73; dir. Granberry Products, Inc., Eagle River, Wis. Mayor, Garfield, Wash., 1938-40. Bd. dirs. Mendota Hosp. Found., 1949-73, pres., 1949-54; bd. dirs. Mendota Swimming Pool Assn.; mem. City Planning Commn., 1953-72, chmn., 1953-69; mem. Regional Planning Commn., LaSalle County, Ill., 1965-73, chmn., 1965-71; mem. Schs. Central Com., 1953—, LaSalle County Zoning Commn., 1966—, LaSalle County Care and Treatment Bd., 1970-73; chmn. Mendota Watershed Com., 1967-73. Mem. Am. Soc. Agrl. Engrs., Eagle River (Wis.) C. of C. (pres., dir. 1962-63), Mendota C. of C. (pres. 1948-49, dir. 1946-49, Community Service award 1972). Republican. Presbyterian (elder). Clubs: Kiwanis (pres. 1953, dir. 1954), Masons, Shriners, Order Eastern Star, Elks; Lakes (Sun City, Ariz.). Patentee in various fields. Home: 709 Carolyn St PO Box 279 Mendota IL 61342 Office: 1701 1st Ave Mendota IL 61342

HUMES, LAWRENCE THOMAS, chemical company executive; b. Camden, N.J., May 7, 1934; s. George and Virginia (Cook) H.; m. Ruth Ann Fleming, Oct. 21, 1961; children: Christopher Rol, Nathan Todd. BSBA, Drexel U., 1957. Staff acct. Nat. Tube div. US Steel, McKeesport, Pa., 1957-66; sr. analyst USS Chems., Pitts., 1966-74; mgr. acctg. Aristech Chem., Haverhill, Ohio, 1974—. Served with U.S. Army, 1961. Republican. Baptist. Avocations: golf, reading. Home: 2725 Brookhaven Dr Wheelersburg OH 45694 Office: Aristech Chem Corp PO Box 127 Ironton OH 45638

HUMITA, TIBERIUS TED, educator; b. Clui, Romania, Dec. 20, 1913; came to U.S., 1951, naturalized, 1956; s. Teodor and Teodosia (Abrudan) H.; m. Sophie Kisch, Sept. 20, 1954. Student U. Bucharest (Romania), 1937-39, U. Rome (Italy), 1946-50; BA, Wayne State U., 1958, MA in Polit. Sci., Tchrs. Coll., 1960, secondary teaching certificate, 1961. Sec., v.p. Romanian Polit. Refugee Welfare Com., Rome, Italy, 1948-50; worker, timekeeper, payroll clk. Chrysler Corp., Highland Park, Mich., 1951-60; tchr. fgn. langs. Detroit Pub. Schs., 1961-80. Corr., Romanian News America, Cleve., 1964—. Romanian cons. Greater Detroit Ethnic Group Project, 1968-75. Candidate, Mich. Constl. Conv., 1961; chmn. Romanian sect. nationalites div. Mich. Dem. Com., 1960—, v.p., 1965-66, treas., 1968-70. Contbg. mem. Iulia Maniu Found., N.Y., 1965—. Served to 1st lt. Romanian Army, 1939-40; polit. prisoner, Buchenwald, Germany, 1942-44. Recipient Service award Nationalites div. Mich. Dem. Com., 1967, M. Banciu award Romanian of Year, 1978, Aron Cotrus award, 1979; Fonds European Secour Etud. Etranger, Switzerland scholar, 1949-50; Nat. Def. Edn. Act grantee N.Y. State U., 1963; Fed. grantee, P.R., 1966. Mem. Internat., Am. polit. sci. assns., Am. Fedn. Tchrs., Am. Acad. Polit. and Social Sci., Mich. Fgn. Lang. Assn., Am. Council Fgn. Lang. Tchrs. Editor Bull. Romanian Am. Nat. Com., Detroit, 1958-63; dir. sci. book exhibit Internat. Congress Dialectology. Louvain, Belgium, 1960. Home: 16424 Lincoln St East Detroit MI 48021

HUMKE, RAMON L., telecommunications executive; b. Quincy, Ill., Nov. 19, 1932; s. E.G. and Florence K. (Koch) H.; m. Carolyn Jacobs, Nov. 20, 1955; 1 child, Steven K. Ed., Quincy Coll., Ill., 1952-53, Springfield Coll., Ill., 1956-58, Carleton Coll., 1968. Various mgmt. positions Ill. Bell Telephone Co., 1951-73; v.p. personnel Ill. Bell Telephone Co., Chgo., 1978-82; dir. forecasting and productivity AT&T, N.Y.C., 1973-76; v.p. corp. affairs Ameritech, Chgo., 1982-83; pres., chief exec. officer Ind. Bell Telephone Co. Inc., Indpls., 1983—; dir. Am. Fletcher Corp., Indpls., Am. Fletcher Nat. Bank, Indpls., Ameritech Services, Inc., Chgo., Meridian Ins. Group. Chmn. Indpls. U.S. Govt. Bond Drive, 1984-85; vice chmn. United Way Greater Indpls., 1985; gen. campaign chmn. United Way of Cen. Ind., 1986; chmn. Ind. Symphony, 1985—; mem. adv. com. Krannert Sch. Bus., Purdue U., 1984-85. Served to 1st lt. U.S. Army, 1953-56, Europe. Named to Order Ky. Cols., 1983, Ark. Travelers, 1985; recipient medal of Merit, U.S. Treasury Dept., 1984, 85. Mem. Telephone Pioneers Am. (pres. 1985-86), Ind. Telephone Assn. (bd. dirs. 1984—), Ind. State C. of C. (exec. com.

1984—). Clubs: Indpls. Athletic, Columbia, Crooked Stick Golf (Indpls.); Meridian Hills Country; Skyline (bd. govs.). Avocations: golf, wilderness hiking, U.S. history. Office: Ind Bell Telephone Co Inc 240 N Meridian St Indianapolis IN 46204

HUMMEL, DANIEL GEORGE, optometrist; b. Sharon, Pa., June 8, 1905; s. Peter Ferdinand and Rosene (Adeline) H.; m. Hildegarde Rose Schiff, Apr. 26, 1943; children: Kurz, Marian Ruth. BS, Ohio State U., 1928; OD, Phila. Optical, 1950; D Ocular Sci. (hon.), Chgo. Coll. Optometry, 1951. Pvt. practice optometry Cleve. Recipient Disting. Service award Disting. Service Found. of Optometry, 1949. Fellow AAAS; mem. Am. Acad. Optometry (life, various offices and coms. 1938-60, pres. 1949-50, Eminent Service award 1961), Am. Optometric Assn., Ohio Optometric Assn. Cleve. Optometric Assn., Cleve. Acad. Optometry. Republican. Presbyterian. Lodge: Kiwanis. Office: 7029 Royalton Rd North Royalton OH 44133

HUMPHREY, BLAKE B., electronics company executive. Pres. Mallory Timers Co., Indpls. Office: Mallory Timers Co 3029 E Washington St Indianapolis IN 46206 *

HUMPHREY, HUBERT HORATIO, III, Minnesota attorney general; b. Mpls., June 26, 1942; s. Hubert Horatio and Muriel (Buck) H.; m. Nancy Lee Humphrey, Aug. 14, 1963; children: Lorie, Pam, Hubert Horatio IV. B.A. in Polit. Sci., Am. U., Washington, 1965; J.D., U. Minn., 1969. Bar: Minn. Sole practice law 1970-82; mem. Minn. State Senate, 1972-82; atty. gen. State of Minn., St. Paul, 1983—. Bd. mgmt. Northwest br. YMCA. Mem. ABA, Minn. Bar Assn., Hennepin County Bar Assn. Mem. Democratic-Farmer-Labor Party. Home: 8116 40th Ave N New Hope MN 55427 Office: Office of Atty General 102 State Capitol Saint Paul MN 55155 *

HUMPHREY, MARIAN JEAN, systems engineer; b. Springfield, Ill., Aug. 27, 1953; d. Lowell Keith and Betty Jean (Rogers) H. Student, Springfield Coll. Ill., 1973-75; BA in Music Edn., MacMurray Coll., 1977; studying voice with Martha Sheil, U. Mich. Systems engr. IBM Corp., Ft. Wayne, Ind., 1977-80, Lima, Ohio, 1980-82, Toledo, 1982—. Mem. Ft. Wayne Philharmonic Chorale, 1978-81, Toledo Symphony Chorale, 1982—; Big Sister Big Bros.-Big Sisters N.W. Ohio, Toledo, 1986—. Republican. So. Baptist. Avocations: reading, gardening. Home: 1255 S Byrne Apt B213 Toledo OH 43614

HUMPHREY, NEIL DARWIN, university president; b. Idaho Falls, Idaho, May 20, 1928; s. Clair Pierce and Freda (Hatfield) H.; m. Mary Pat Smith, Aug. 21, 1950; childern: Ann, Therese. BA in Polit. Sci., Idaho State U., 1950; MS in Govt. Mgmt., U. Denver, 1951; EdD, Brigham Young U., 1974. Exec. sec. Nev. Taxpayers Assn., 1955-59; budget dir. Nev., 1959-61; bus. mgr. U. Nev., 1961-64, v.p. fin., 1964-67, acting pres., 1967-68; chancellor U. Nev. System, 1968-77; pres. U. Alaska, 1977-78; v.p. for fin. affairs Youngstown (Ohio) State U., 1978-79, exec. v.p., 1979-84, pres., 1984—; bd. dirs. Comml. Shearing, Inc., First Fed. Savs. and Loan Assn. Youngstown. Home: 41 Poland Manor Poland Village OH 44514 Office: Youngstown State U Youngstown OH 44555

HUMPHREYS, ALICE KAREN, social worker, educator; b. Kansas City, Mo., June 15, 1938; d. Henry Eugene and Meredith Kathryn (Geiger) Gould; m. Donald Haslam Humphreys, July 1, 1961; children: Douglas, Alyson, John E., Meredy, Hutch, Hank. BA, U. Kans., 1960, MSW, 1981; MA in Teaching, Harvard U., 1961; postgrad. study in family systems, Georgetown U., 1983-86. Cert. social worker, Kans. Tchr. Great Bend (Kans.) High Sch., 1964-79; dir., family therapist Cath. Social Services, Great Bend, 1981—; instr. Barton County Community Coll., Great Bend, 1984—; cons. Cath. Social Services, Great Bend., 1985—. Pres. Barton County Kans. U. Alumni, Great Bend, 1970-74. Mem. Nat. Assn. Social Workers, Acad. Cert. Social Workers, Phi Beta Kappa. Avocations: swimming, writing, reading. Home: 3105 Broadway Great Bend KS 67530 Office: Cath Social Services 2546 20th St Great Bend KS 67530

HUMPHREYS, HOLLY E., accountant, computer systems consultant; b. East Chicago, Ind., May 31, 1947; d. Wilson Lee and Esther (Egger) H.; m. John William Loeb, Sept. 14, 1979 (div. Jan. 1986). BS, Purdue U., 1969; cert. acctg., U. Pitts., 1972. CPA, Pa. Acct. Price Waterhouse Co., Pitts., Chgo., 1972-75; asst. controller Pullman, Inc., Chgo., 1975-77; controller Hillman's Inc., Chgo., 1977-79, Silvestri Corp., Chgo., 1979-80; v.p. GMP Services Inc., Chgo., 1982—. Treas. Better Boys Found., Chgo., 1979—, mem. exec. com., program com.; treas. Merit Music Program, Inc., Chgo., 1981—. Avocations: photography, travel. Home: 4300 N Marine Dr Chicago IL 60613

HUMPHREYS, JAMES BURNHAM, hospital administrator; b. Fulton, Mo., July 25, 1941; s. James Carroll and Mary Thelma (Burnham) H.; m. Emily Elaine Earl, Oct. 2, 1971; children—Erica, James Burnham II. B.A., Westminster Coll., 1963; M.S., Trinity U., San Antonio, 1969. Adminstrv. resident Meml. Hosp., Lufkin, Tex., 1967-68, asst. adminstr., 1968-69; with St. Lukes Hosps., St. Louis, 1969—, assoc. adminstr., 1974-78, v.p. ops., 1978-84, v.p. adminstrn., 1984—; mem. adj. faculty Washington U., 1976—. Served to 1st lt. AUS, 1964-66 Fellow Am. Coll. Hosp. Adminstrs.; mem. Am. Mgmt. Assn., Am. Hosp. Assn., Hosp. Assn. Met. St. Louis. Democrat. Presbyterian. Lodge: Rotary (bd. dirs. Kirkwood club). Home: 507 Bambury Way Kirkwood MO 63122 Office: 232 S Woods Mill Rd Saint Louis MO 63017

HUMPHRIES, BEVERLY NELL (MRS. DONALD R. HUMPHRIES), librarian; b. Gatesville, Tex., July 3, 1930; d. E.B. and Nora H. (Nelson) Harris; A.A., Clifton Jr. Coll., 1946-48; B.S., N. Tex. State U., 1950; M.S., So. Ill. U., 1971; m. Donald R. Humphries, May 27, 1951; children—Brett, Joel. Elem. tchr. Balmorhea (Tex.) Pub. Schs., 1948-49; res. librarian Tex. Technol. U., Lubbock, 1950-51; elem. tchr. Fairbanks (Alaska) Sch. Dist., 1952-54; serials and documents librarian Tex. A. and M. U., College Station, 1954-57; periodicals librarian Davenport (Iowa) Pub. Library, 1957-59; librarian Monticello Coll., Godfrey, Ill., 1965-71, Lewis and Clark Community Coll., Godfrey, 1971—. Bd. dirs. Greater Alton Concert Assn., 1968-80. Mem. Am., Ill. library assns. Club: Zonta. Office: Lewis and Clark Community Coll Godfrey IL 62035

HUND, ROBERT ARTHUR, corporate executive; b. Detroit, Apr. 12, 1927; s. Arthur Alexander and Ruth Rose (Thomas) H.; m. Carole Kathleen Olson, July 9, 1950; children—Kathie, June, Cynthia, Jonathan. B.S. in Music Edn., Wayne State U., 1951; student Cin. Conservatory of Music, 1952, NYU, 1953. Cert. tchr., Mich. Mgr., Henry I Cristal Co., Detroit, 1957-63; v.p. Roy Clark, Inc., 1963-67; pres., Robert Hund Inc., Farmington, 1967—; mng. dir. Marble Inst. of Am., Farmington, Mich., 1980—. Editor manual on marble design, mag. Through the Ages. Served to sgt. U.S. Army, 1945-47. Decorated Commendation Ribbon. Mem. Am. Nat. Standards Inst., Am. Soc. Interior Designers (pres., citation Mich. chpt. 1981), Am. Soc. Testing and Materials (com. C-18), AIA (profl. mem. Detroit chpt.). Office: Robert Hund Inc 33505 State St Farmington MI 48024

HUNDER, GENE GERALD, physician; b. Lake City, Minn., Feb. 7, 1932; s. Tilman James and Melita Henrietta (Bremer) H.; m. Janet Gretchen Hunt, July 26, 1956; children—Heidi, Jennifer, Gregory, Grant, Naomi, Stephanie. Student, St. Olaf Coll., 1950-52; B.A., U. Minn.-Mpls., 1954, M.D., 1958, M.S., 1963. Diplomate Am. Bd. Internal Medicine. Intern, Strong Meml. Hosp., Rochester, N.Y., 1958-59, resident, 1959-61; resident Mayo Clinic, Rochester, Minn., 1961-64; instr. internal medicine Mayo Grad. Sch., Rochester, Minn., 1966-67, asst. prof. internal medicine, 1968-73, assoc. prof., 1973-78, prof., 1978—, full mem. internal medicine, 1981—, cons. internal medicine and rheumatology, prof. internal medicine Mayo Clinic, Mayo Found., 1978—, head sect. rheumatology Mayo Clinic, 1976-81, chmn. rheumatology research com., 1976-81, 87, chmn. clin. investigator tng. program Mayo Grad. Sch., 1981-84. Co-author: Physical Examination of the Joints, 1978; Editor: Rheumatology, 1978; Assoc. editor: Jour. Lab. and Clin. Medicine, 1979-81. Mem. editorial bd. Jour. Arthritis and Rheumatism, 1973-83, Jour. Rheumatology, 1982—, Jour. Musculoskeletal Medicine, 1983—, Scandinavian Research Journal, 1986—. Contbr. numerous sci. articles to med. jours. Mem. ho. dels. Arthritis Found., Atlanta, 1980-83, trustee, 1985—; mem. exec. com. Minn. Arthritis Found., Mpls., 1984—. Philip Showalter Hench lectr. Ariz. Med. Soc., Phoenix, 1965; Charles W. Thomas lectr. Med. Coll. Va., Charlottesville, 1979; Carl Pearson lectr. Los Angeles County Med. Assn., 1983. Nu Sigma Nu scholar, 1955; Minn. Med. Found. acad. scholar, 1955; Fellow ACP (pres. Minn. chpt. 1985—); mem. AMA, Am. Assn. Immunologists, Am. Fedn. Clin. Research, AAAS, Cen. Clin. Research Club, Cen. Soc. Clin. Research (mem. program com.), Am. Soc. Clin. Rheumatology (pres.), Am. Rheumatism Assn. (mem. exec. com. 1976-77, v.p. cen. region 1987), Phi Beta Kappa, Alpha Omega Alpha. Republican. Lutheran. Home: 1305 Folwell Dr SW Rochester MN 55902 Office: Mayo Clinic 200 1st St SW Rochester MN 55905

HUNDHAUSEN, DAVID FRANK, theater educator; b. Milw., May 17, 1939; s. Harvey Raymond and June Marion (Putnam) H.; m. Patricia Moore Peters, Sept. 24, 1966; children: Ellen, Christopher, Anne. BS in Edn., U. Wis., 1961; MA in Dramatic Art, U. Iowa, 1965; postgrad., U. Wis., Madison, 1969-71, U. Wis., Milw., 1982. Tchr. West Allis (Wis.) Schs., 1961-63; prof. U. Wis., Manitowoc, 1965-66, Waukesha, 1966—; cons. Waukesha Block PArents, Waukesha, 1985-86. Author: (Play) Tune OUt, Tune In, 1979, The Dream Maker, 1982, The Waukesha Show, 1984; co-author: (play) Once Upon a Puppet, 1987. Chmn. event and planning Waukesha Sesquicentennial Celebration, 1983-84; mem. com. Waukesha YWCA Art Affair, 1987; bd. dirs. Waukesha Civic Theater, 1976-79, 82-85. Grantee U. Wis., 1982; recipient Community Service award Friends and Alumni of U. Wis. at Waukesha, 1985. Mem. Wis. Theatre Assn., Phi Beta Kappa. Avocation: travel, plays, concerts, ballet, cross country skiing. Home: 2942 Madison St Waukesha WI 53188

HUNGATE, WILLIAM LEONARD, judge, former congressman; b. Benton, Ill., Dec. 14, 1922; s. Leonard Wathen and Maude Irene (Williams) H.; m. Dorothy N. Wilson, Apr. 13, 1944; children: William David, Margie Kay (Mrs. Branson L. Wood III). A.B., U. Mo., 1943; LL.B., Harvard U., 1948; LL.D. (hon.), Culver-Stockton Coll., Canton, Mo., 1968; J.D. (hon.), Central Meth. Coll., Fayette, Mo., 1975. Bar: Mo. 1948, Ill. 1949, U.S. Supreme Ct 1960, D.C. 1967. Practiced law Troy, Mo., 1948-68, St. Louis, 1977-79; sr. partner firm Hungate and Grewach, 1956-68; partner firm Thompson and Mitchell, St. Louis, 1977-79; judge U.S. Dist. Ct. Eastern Dist. Mo., 1979—; pros. atty. Lincoln County, Mo., 1951-55; spl. asst. atty. gen. of Mo. 1958-64; research adminstrn. criminal justice in U.S. Am. Bar Found., 1956; mem. 88th-94th congresses, 9th Dist. Mo.; mem. judiciary com., chmn. subcom. criminal justice, select com. on small bus., chmn. subcom. on activities of regulatory agys.; vis. prof. polit. sci. U. Mo., St. Louis; also composer. Trustee William Woods Coll.; chmn. small bus. adv. com. Treasury Dept., 1977; chmn. Mo. Gov.'s Commn. on Campaign Reform and Ofcl. Conduct, 1978-79; mem. Adv. Com. on Criminal Rules, 1977—. Mem. Ill. Bar Assn., Fed. Bar Assn., ABA (nat. conf. of fed. trial judges exec. com. 1980—, chmn. 1985-86), Mo. Bar Assn., D.C. Bar Assn., Harvard Law Sch. Assn. Mo. (pres. 1962-64, 83-84, council mem.), ASCAP, Mo. Squires, Jud. Conf. U.S. (budget com.), 8th Cir. Dist. Judges Assn. (pres. 1984-86, mem. budget com. of Jud. Conf. U.S.). Mem. Christian Ch. (chmn. bd. 1964). Club: Kiwanian (Troy) (pres. 1951, lt. gov. 1959). Home: 26 Chapel Hill Estates Town and Country MO 63131 Office: U S Dist Ct 1114 Market St Saint Louis MO 63101

HUNGER, J. DAVID, business educator; b. New Kensington, Pa., May 17, 1941; s. Jackson Steele and Elizabeth (Carey) H.; m. Betty Johnson, Aug. 2, 1969; children: Karen, Susan, Laura, Merry. BA, Bowling Green (Ohio) State U., 1963; MBA, Ohio State U., 1966, PhD, 1973. Selling supr. Lazarus Dept. Store, Columbus, Ohio, 1965-66; brand asst. Procter and Gamble Co., Cin., 1968-69; asst. dir. grad. bus. programs Ohio State U., Columbus, 1970-72; instr. Baldwin-Wallace Coll., Berea, Ohio, 1972-73; prof. U. Va., Charlottesville, 1973-82; strategic mgmt. prof. Iowa State U. Coll. Bus., Ames, 1982—; prof. bus. George Mason U., Fairfax, Va., 1986-87; cons. to bus., fed. and state agys. Served to capt. Mil. Intelligence, U.S. Army, 1966-68. Decorated Bronze Star. Mem. Acad. Mgmt., N.Am. Case Research Assn., Midwest Case Research Soc., Strategic Mgmt. Soc. Author: (with T.L. Wheelen) Strategic Management and Business Policy, 1983, rev. edit., 1986, An Assessment of Undergraduate Business Education in the U.S., 1980, Strategic Management, rev. edit., 1987, Cases in Strategic Management and Business Policy, 1987; contbr. articles to publs. Office: Iowa State U Coll of Bus 300 Carver Hall Iowa State U Ames IA 50011

HUNGERFORD, BRIAN EDWARD, financial executive; b. Maiden Rock, Wis., Feb. 6, 1955; s. Edward Judson and Elizabeth Mary (Brookshaw) H.; m. Marie Welborn, Sept. 6, 1985. BA, U. Minn., 1981; MBA, U. Wis., 1983. Sr. fin. analyst Oscar Mayer Foods Corp., Madison, Wis., 1983-85; sr. supr. accounts payable Target Stores, Mpls., 1985—. Roman Catholic. Home: 5108 Penn Ave S Minneapolis MN 55419 Office: Target Stores 6499 University Ave NE Fridley MN 55432

HUNKEL, CARY CHRISTIANA, artist; b. Milw., June 18, 1945; d. Victor Henry and Pearl Bernice (Stoecklin) H.; m. James Atlee Bucklew, Mar. 9, 1985; 1 child Victor Gauss. BA, U. Wis., 1967, MS, 1969, MFA, 1981. Lectr. U. Wis., 1969-81; contract. artist Wis. State Hist. Soc., Madison, 1984-85; free-lance artist 1981—. Exhibited at Wausau Birds In Art Show, 1982, 84, 87, Watercolor Wis., 1985, Great Lakes Wildlife Art Show, 1986. Mem. Madison Audubon Soc. (sec. 1983—) Goose Pond Santuary (sec. 1983—). Avocations: sailing, ice hockey. Home: 1306 Eberhardt Ct Madison WI 53715

HUNSAKER, TRACY ANNE, lawyer; b. St. Louis, Aug. 13, 1959; d. Raymond Thomas Hunsaker and Dorothy Jayne (Hickman) Hunsaker Reilly. BA, U. Dayton, 1981; JD, St. Louis U., 1984. Bar: Mo. 1984, Ill. 1985. Atty. Mo. State Hwy. and Transp. Dept., St. Louis, 1984—. Mem. ABA, Mo. Bar Assn. (eminent domain com., legis. com.), St. Louis Metro. Bar Assn. (chmn. legis. com., golf com., sec. trial sect. 1985—, legis. com., continuing legal edn. com., media com., edn. com.), Woman Lawyers Assn. (chairperson legis. com., sec.), Lawyers Assn., Assn. Trial Lawyers Am. (assoc.). Avocations: golf, racquetball, biking, writing, painting. Office: Mo State Hwy & Transp Dept 329 S Kirkwood Saint Louis MO 63122

HUNSICKER, RONALD JAY, health care executive; b. Norristown, Pa., Aug. 8, 1945; s. Christian D. and Florence H. (Gottshall) H.; m. Joyce M. Brunner, June 20, 1968 (div. June 1985); children: Jonathan Jay, Angela Dawn; m. Kendall P. Keech, Dec. 14, 1985. BA, Bluffton Coll., 1967; M Div, Mennonite Bibl. Sem., 1971; D of Ministry, Princeton Theol. Sem., 1982. Pastor Charleswood Mennonite Ch., Winnipeg, Manitoba, Can., 1970-75; chaplain Oaklawn Psychiat. Ctr., South Bend, Ind., 1980-85; v.p. Meml. Hosp., South Bend, 1985—; cons. Coll. Chaplains, Chgo., 1984. Contbr. various articles on marriage and family issues to profl. jours. Fellow Coll. Chaplains; mem. Am. Assn. Marriage and Family Therapists (clin.), Assn. Clin. Pastoral Edn. (cert. supr. 1977—). Avocations: fishing, skiing, jogging. Home: 51444 Jodie Lynn Dr Granger IN 46530 Office: Meml Hosp 615 N Michigan St South Bend IN 46601

HUNT, DAVID ALLEN, organic chemist; b. Huntington, W.Va., Dec. 4, 1952; s. Bernard Ray and Nadine Dora (Meadows) H.; m. Susan Lynne Sullivan, Dec. 21, 1973; children: Jessica Ryan, Ashley Lauren. BS in Chemistry, Marshall U., 1973, MS in Organic Chemistry, 1975; PhD in Organic Chemistry, Duke U., 1979. Sr. chemist Union Carbide Tech. Ctr., South Charleston, W.Va., 1979-81, Molecular Structure/Composition Skills Ctr., Agrl. Products Co., 1980-81; sr. scientist organic chemistry Becton Dickinson Research Ctr., Research Triangle Pk., N.C., 1981-84; sr. research chemist PPG Industries Biochems., Barberton, Ohio, 1984—. Contbr. articles to profl. jours. Served with U.S. Army, 1971-77. Ashland Oil Co. fellow, 1973, FMC Corp. fellow, 1975. Mem. AAAS, N.Y. Acad. Sci., Am. Chem. Soc. (named Outstanding Sr. Chemist Ohio Valley sect. 1974), Sigma Xi, Phi Lambda Upsilon, Chi Beta Phi, Omicron Delta Kappa. Methodist. Home: 4680 Treetop Dr Copley OH 44321 Office: PPG Industries Biochemicals PO Box 31 Barberton OH 44203

HUNT, DOUGLAS EDWARD, social services adminstrator; b. Greenville, Ohio, July 2, 1948; s. Howard Edward and Ruth Annalee (Horine) H. BS in Biology and Gen Sci. Vocat., cert. tchr., Ohio State U., 1972; M in Edn. Adminstrn., Wright State U., 1975. Fin. and med. supr. Darke County Human Services, Greenville, Ohio, 1975-80, dir., 1980—. Mem. Community Action Com., Community Block Grant; bd. dirs. Salvation Army. Named one of Outstanding Young Men Am. Mem. Ohio Community Services Dirs. Assn., Crippled Children and Adult Soc. Republican. Methodist. Lodges: Kiwanis (pres. 1986—), Masons. Home: 367 SR 726 New Madison OH 45346 Office: Darke County Human Services 802 E 4th St Greenville OH 45331

HUNT, G(ERARD) PATRICK, account executive; b. Detroit, Nov. 6, 1959; s. Henry Stanley and Louise Gloria (Holtmeyer) H. BBA in Fin., U. Minn., 1981. Pres., pub. and art dir. Canyon Times Newspaper, Inc., Salt Lake City, 1981-84; dir. vertical market sales Century Software, Sandy, Utah, 1984-85; account exec. Fallon McElligott, Mpls., 1985—. Mem. Utah Nordic Skiers Assn. Avocations: yacht racing, skiing, mountaineering. Home: 5408 Sanibel Dr Minneapolis MN 55408 Office: Fallon McElligott 701 4th Ave S Minneapolis MN 55415

HUNT, GRACE MENDENHALL, artist; b. Cin., Oct. 21, 1915; d. Graham Putnam and Frances Carisle (Mendenhall) H. B.A., Vassar Coll., 1937; student Cin. Art Acad., 1938-40. Portrait painter; one-woman shows include: Woman's Exchange, 1954, Univ. Club, 1962; portraits exhibited in Mich., Ind., N.J., Conn., Okla., Ky. and Washington. Mem. Cin. Woman's Art Club (past treas.), Profl. Artists Cin. (past treas.), Woman's Art Club Cin. Coll. Art. Republican. Roman Catholic. Home and Office: 164 Glenmary Ave Cincinnati OH 45220

HUNT, JEFFREY BRIAN, lawyer; b. Huntington, W.Va., Sept. 23, 1958; s. Bernard Ray and Nadine Dora (Meadows) H.; m. Krista Moorman, May 14, 1983. BA magna cum laude, Marshall U., 1980; JD summa cum laude, U. Ky., 1983. Bar: Mo. 1983, Ill. 1984, U.S. Dist. Ct. (ea. dist.) Mo. 1984, U.S. Ct. Appeals (8th cir.) 1984. Assoc. Peper, Martin, St. Louis, 1983, Lewis and Rice, St. Louis, 1983—; adj. instr. Washington U., St. Louis, 1983—. Mem. ABA, Assn. Trial Lawyers Am., Bar Assn. of Met. St. Louis, Order of the Coif, Omicron Delta Kappa. Democrat. Methodist. Avocations: tennis, softball, baseball, basketball, golf. Home: 1240 Orchard Village Ln Manchester MO 63021 Office: Lewis and Rice 611 Olive Suite 1400 Saint Louis MO 63101

HUNT, LAMAR, profl. football team exec.; b. 1933; s. H. L. and Lyda (Baker) H.; m. Norma Hunt; children: Lamar, Sharon, Clark. Grad., So. Meth. U. Founder, owner Kansas City Chiefs, NFL, 1959—, pres., 1959-76, chmn., 1977-78; founder, pres. AFL, 1959; (became Am. Football Conf.-NFL 1970); pres. Am. Football Conf., 1970—; dir. Great Midwest Corp., Interstate Securities, Traders' Nat. Bank. Bd. dirs. Profl. Football Hall of Fame, Canton, Ohio. Named Salesman of Year Kansas City Advt. and Sales Execs. Club, 1963; Southwesterner of Year Tex. Sportswriters Assn., 1969. Office: Kansas City Chiefs One Arrowhead Dr Kansas City MO 64129 *

HUNT, ROBERT CHESTER, construction company executive; b. Dayton, Ohio, 1923. Grad., Case Inst. Tech., 1942. With Huber Hunt & Nichols Inc., Indpls., 1947—, sec., 1950-51, gen. mgr., 1951-52, v.p., 1952-56, chmn. bd., pres., 1956—, chmn. bd., dir.; dir. Am. Fletcher Nat. Bank. Office: Huber Hunt & Nichols Inc 2450 S Tibbs Ave Indianapolis IN 46206 *

HUNT, ROBERT WAYNE, manufacturing company executive; b. Tipton County, Ind., May 28, 1940; s. Wayne G. Hunt and Janet Marie (Harris) Messick; m. Sandra Jean Kuhlman, June 22, 1963; children—Rhonda Jean, Jeffrey Robert. B.S. in Bus. Adminstrn., U. Evansville, 1963. Sr. mktg. exec. Ford Motor Co., Phila., 1965-71; dir. adminstrn., personnel W.E. Walker Co., Jackson, Miss., 1971-73; plant mgr. Northwest Industries, Jackson, 1973-80; asst. v.p. mfg., UNR-Leavitt Co., Chgo., 1980-81, v.p. mfg., 1981-82, v.p. ops., 1982-84, sr. v.p. ops., 1984—; chmn. energy Miss. Mfrs. Assn., Jackson, 1979-80. Dist. commr., Boy Scouts Am., Canton, Ohio, 1969. Recipient Outstanding Leadership award Internat. Brotherhood Elec. Workers, Jackson, 1980. Mem. Am. Mgmt. Assn. Republican. Methodist. Home: 5900 Oakwood Dr #3L Lisle IL 60532 Office: UNR Leavitt 1717 W 115th St Chicago IL 60643

HUNT, ROGER SCHERMERHORN, hospital administrator; b. White Plains, N.Y., Mar. 7, 1943; s. Charles Howland and Mildred Russell (Schermerhorn) H.; m. Mary Adams Libby, June 19, 1965; children: Christina, David. B.A., DePauw U., 1965; M.B.A., George Washington U., 1968. Adminstrv. resident Lankenau Hosp., Phila., 1966-68; asst. adminstr. Hahnemann Med. Coll. and Hosp., Phila., 1968-71; hosp. dir. Hahnemann Med. Coll. and Hosp., 1971-74, assoc. v.p., hosp. adminstr., 1974-77; dir. Ind. U. Hosps., Indpls., 1977-84; chmn. Alliance of Indpls. Hosps., 1981; pres. Lutheran Gen. Hosp., Park Ridge, Ill., 1984—; sec.-treas. Delaware Valley Hosp. Laundry, 1969-77; trustee Nat. Benefit Fund of Nat. Union Hosp. and Health Care Employees, 1973-77; bd. dirs. Phila. Blood Center, 1972-74; pres. United Hosp. Services, 1979-81; assoc. prof. hosp. adminstrn. Ind. U. Sch. Medicine, 1977-84; vice chmn. Pa. Emergency Health Services Council, 1975-77; pres. Chester County Emergency Med. Service Council, 1971-77. Pres. Wayne Area Jr. C. of C., 1970-71, state dir., 1971-72. Fellow Am. Coll. Healthcare Execs. (regent for Ind. 1984, Postgrad. tng. award 1968); mem. Am. Hosp. Assn., Ill. Hosp. Assn., Ind. Hosp. Assn. (bd. dirs. 1982-84), Met. Chgo. Healthcare Council (dir. 1986). Lodge: Rotary. Office: Luth Gen Hosp 1775 Dempster St Park Ridge IL 60068

HUNT, SONDRA KAY GORDON, employment specialist, writer; b. Middletown, Ohio, June 2, 1937; d. John Charles and Ora Lillie (Stewart) Gordon; A.A. magna cum laude, U. Cin., 1975; m. Ralph J. Bays, Feb. 17, 1956 (dec. 1969); children—Sherry Kay, Cynthia Rae, Robert Jay; m. Harold Eugene Hunt, May 23, 1985. Reporter, ch. editor Middletown Jour., 1955-56; mng. editor Warren County Reporter, Lebanon, Ohio, 1966-72; corr. Franklin (Ohio) Chronicle, 1974-78; free lance journalist, 1973—, family therapist Mary Haven Youth Center, Lebanon, Ohio, 1980-83; spl. places ops. Supr. U.S. Bur. Census, 1980. Mem. Ohio Gov.'s Traffic Safety Com., 1972-76; mem. Warren County Bd. Mental Health and Retardation, 1972-80, chmn., 1974-80; chmn. dist. one planning council Ohio Dept. Mental Health 1977-80; mem. exec. bd. Ohio Community Mental Health Assn., 1979-80; mem. citizens adv. com. Lebanon Correctional Instn., Lebanon, 1971—; sec. Warren County Safety Council, 1972-76; mem. citizens com. Ohio Dept. Rehab. and Corrections 1976-82; bd. dirs. Warren County com. Ohio Easter Seal Soc. for Crippled Children and Adults, 1967—; mem. Warren County Bd. Elections, 1974-80, Warren Profl. Health Adv. Com.; bd. dirs. Warren United Appeal; asst. to organizer Warren County Disaster Services, 1975; former sec. Warren County Disaster Services Orgn.; sec., Warren County Democratic Women's Club, 1963-67, Warren County Dem. Central and Exec. Com., 1965-80; precinct committeeman Dem. party, 1964-80; mem. land use subcom. Ohio-Ky.-Ind. Council Govts., 1975—; sec. Warren County Interagy. Council, editor newsletter; Sunday sch. tchr. Methodist Ch., 1963-72; bd. mem. Big Bros./Sisters; pres. Warren County Alcoholism/Drug Abuse, Inc.; Ohio Assn. Bds. County Visitors (pres. 1981). Winner 1st pl. Beta Sigma Phi internat. short story contest, 1964, Ohio Dept. Hwy. Safety Media contest, 1970. Mem. Nat. Council Crime and Delinquency, Internat. Platform Assn., Phi Kappa Epsilon, Alpha Sigma Lambda. Address: 3730 Beatrice Dr Franklin OH 45005

HUNT, SUSAN MONICA, lawyer; b. Akron, Ohio, May 18, 1952; d. Russell Bliss and Martha (Pankau) H. BEd, U. Kans., 1975; M in Adminstrn. of Justice, Wichita State U., 1983; JD, U. Kans., 1986. Bar: U.S. Dist. Ct. (we. dist.) Mo. 1986, U.S. Ct. Appeals (7th and 8th cirs.) 1987. Tchr. Turner (Kans.) High Sch., 1975-80; forensic chemist Kansas City (Mo.) Police Dept. Crime Lab., 1980-84; assoc. Koenigsdorf, Wyrsch & Ramsey., Kansas City, 1986—. Author: (book) Investigation of Serological Evidence, 1984; (with others) Specific Requests for Exculpatory Evidence After U.S. v. Bagley, 1986. Recipient Am. Jurisprudence in Property award Lawyers Co-Operative Pub. Co.-Bancroft Whitney Co., 1984, Fisher award in Trial Advocacy, 1986. Mem. ABA, Mo. Bar Assn., Kansas City Met. Bar Assn., Nat. Assn. Criminal Defense Lawyers, Mo. Assn. Criminal Defense Lawyers. Presbyterian. Lodge: Soroptimist Internat. Avocations: antiques. Home: 5607 Roeland Dr Roeland Park KS 66205

HUNT, WILLIAM LUTHER, III, sales and marketing executive; b. Washington, Jan. 21, 1939; s. William L. and Lois (Trimmer) H.; m. Judith Fellows Ingraham, Sept. 3, 1960; children: Caroline, Jenifer, Alison. BA in

Econs. with honors, U. Va., 1962; postgrad., MIT, 1967; postgrad. in mktg. mgmt. program, Harvard U., 1977. Dist. sales mgr. Sunbeam Corp., Chgo., 1962-66; nat. field sales mgr. Cornwall Corp., Boston, 1966-75; v.p. sales and mktg. Patton Electric Co., Inc., New Haven, Ind., 1975—; lectr. Ind. Entrepreneurial Workshop, Ft. Wayne, 1985. Contbr. articles to trade mag. Served with USN, 1957-59. Recipient S.P.O.K.E. award, U.S. Jaycees, 1967. Mem. Nat. Housewares Mfrs. Assn., Assn. Home Appliance Mfrs. (heater exec. com. 1984-87, bd. dirs. portable appliance div. 1984-87; chmn. fan exec. com. 1985-87), Am. Fan Assn. (pres. 1984-87), Am. Mgmt. Assn., Home Ventilating Inst. (bd. dirs. 1983), U.S. C. of C., Arlington (Va.) Jaycees, U. Va. Alumni Assn. (life), Alpha Tau Omega (pledge chmn.). Methodist. Avocations: golf, tennis, fishing, gardening, reading. Home: 10808 Morning Mist Trail Fort Wayne IN 46804 Office: Patton Electric Co Inc 15012 Edgerton Rd New Haven IN 46774

HUNTER, BRIAN J., agricultural engineer; b. Creston, Iowa, July 11, 1947; s. Doyle J. and Dorothy Belle (Gray) H.; m. Diane Catherine Castle, Nov. 30, 1974; children: Jill Catherine, Breanne Lynn. BS in Agrl. Engring., Iowa State U., 1971, BSCE, 1972. Registered profl. civil engr., Iowa; lic. land surveyor, Iowa. Asst. county engr. Montgomery County, Red Oak, Iowa, 1972-77; county engr. Ringgold County, Mt. Ayr, Iowa, 1978; project engr. Associated Engrs., Ft. Dodge, Iowa, 1978-79; asst. county engr. Pottawattamie County, Council Bluffs, Iowa, 1979—; speaker career fairs, service clubs, continuing edn. workshops. Picnic chmn. St. Patrick's Parish, Council Bluffs, 1984-86; chmn. City Planning Commn., 1987, Council Bluffs, 1986—. Mem. ASCE, NSPE, Iowa Engring. Soc. (pres. Grenville Dodge chpt. 1984-85), Soc. Land Surveyors Iowa. Roman Catholic. Clubs: Toastmasters (local pres. 1987), St. Patrick's Men's (com. chmn.). Home: 274 Elmwood Dr Council Bluffs IA 51501

HUNTER, CHARLES DAVID, retail company executive; b. Alameda, Calif., Dec. 3, 1929; s. Adin Wesley and Bertha Anna (Mayer) H.; m. Alice Betty Trinski, Nov. 6, 1954 (dec. 1970); children: Jeffrey Paul, Karen Sue, Brian David, Robert Stephen; m. Joy Ann Morris, Jan. 12, 1973. A.A., Modesto Jr. Coll., 1949; B.S., U. Calif.-Berkeley, 1951. Staff auditor, mgr. Arthur Andersen & Co., Chgo., 1955-66; asst. controller Walgreen Co., Chgo., 1967-69; controller Walgreen Co., 1969-71, v.p. adminstrn., 1971-78, exec. v.p., 1978—. Served to lt. USNR, 1952-55. Mem. Financial Execs. Inst., Am. Inst. C.P.A.s, Ill. Soc. C.P.A.s, Chgo. Retail Financial Execs. Assn. (pres. 1971-72). Home: 1589 S Garden St Palatine IL 60067 Office: 200 Wilmot Rd Deerfield IL 60015

HUNTER, CHARLES ORVIS, psychologist; b. Warren, Ohio, Aug. 6, 1943; s. George H. and Gayle (Bandy) H.; m. Susan Wynn Clough, Aug. 1, 1972; children: Christopher B., Matteau Charles. BS in Edn. and Sociology, Findlay Coll., 1969; MS in Psychology, St. Francis Coll., 1971. Asst. dir. Irene Byron Drug Rehab. Ctr., Ft. Wayne, Ind., 1971-72; clin. psychologist Mental Health Ctr. of Western Stark County, Inc., Massillon, Ohio, 1972-77; dir. psychol. services Child and Adolescent Service Ctr., Canton, Ohio, 1977-79; exec. dir. Child and Adolescent Service Ctr., Canton, 1979-81; pvt. practice in psychology Canton, 1976—; guest lectr. Massillon City Hosp. Sch. Nursing, 1975-76; cons. in field. Contbr. articles to newspaper. Served to capt. Ohio Army N.G., 1966-72. Named one of Outstanding Young Men Am., 1974, Outstanding Alumnus Findlay Coll., 1978; recipient Cert. Commendation Mental Health Assn. of Stark County, 1975, Cert. Commendation North Lawrence Police Dept., 1976. Mem. Acad. for Edn. and Research in Profl. Psychology (trustee, treas.), Ohoi Psychol. Assn. (membership com.), State Assn. Psychology and Psychology Assts. (cert. commendation 1978), N.E. Ohio Psychol. Assn., Am. Psychotherapists Guild. Home: 228 21st NW Canton OH 44709 Office: 4450 Belden Village Ave Suite 205B Canton OH 44718

HUNTER, DENNIS LEON, optometrist; b. San Mateo, Calif., Feb. 7, 1948; s. Manuel Wayman and Marilyn Jean (Fassett) H.; m. Marilyn Jean Wanless, Aug. 23, 1969. BS, U. Calif., Berkeley, 1970, OD, 1972. Pvt. practice optometry Marshall, Mo., 1975—; optometry cons. USAF, Whiteman AFB, Mo., 1976. Mem. adv. bd. Mo. Medicare, Jefferson City, Mo., 1983—; mem. Econ. Devel. Bd., Marshall, 1985—. Served to capt. USAF, 1971-75. Fellow Am. Acad. Optometry; mem. Am. Optometric Assn. (charter contact lens sect.), Mo. Optometric Assn. (trustee 1983—), Mo. Optometric Found. (life). Republican. Presbyterian. Lodge: Lions (pres. Marshall 1981). Avocations: golf, softball, volleyball, little league coaching. Home: 550 S Lake Dr Marshall MO 65340 Office: Drs BuBois & Hunter 302 W Morgan Marshall MO 65340

HUNTER, DOUGLAS LEE, elevator company executive; b. Greeley, Colo., May 3, 1948; s. Delmer Eural and Helen Converse (Haines) H.; m. Janet Lee Snook, May 26, 1970; children—Darin Douglas, Joel Christopher, Eric Andrew, Jennifer Lee. Student Phillips U., Enid, Okla., 1966-70; B.A. cum laude, Sioux Falls Coll., 1979; postgrad. N.Am. Bapt. Sem., Sioux Falls, 1977-79. Elevator constructor Carter Elevator Co., Inc., Sioux Falls, S.D., 1971-72, rep., 1972-74, controller, 1974-78, sec.-treas., 1978-82, v.p., 1982-87, pres. 1987—; ptnr. Lifters Ltd., Sioux Falls, S.D., 1984—, chief exec. officer 1987— . Creator, editor: Body Building Manual for the Christian Church in the Upper Midwest, 1983. Mem. gen. bd. Christian Ch. (Disciples of Christ), Indpls., 1984-88; mem. regional bd. Christian Ch. in the Upper Midwest, Des Moines, 1985-87 ; bd. dirs. Glory House, Sioux Falls, 1983-86 ; teaching leader Bible Study Fellowship, Sioux Falls, 1981—; vice chmn. Greater Sioux Empire Billy Graham Crusade, 1986-87 . Named Outstanding Young Religious Leader, Jaycees, Sioux Falls, 1974. Mem. S.D. Family Bus. Council, Sen. Larry Pressler's Small Bus. Adv. Com., Nat. Assn. Elevator Contractors, Constrn. Specifications Inst., Christian Businessmen's Com. U.S.A. Republican. Club: Rotary. Avocations: golf; tennis; reading; music. Home: 1605 Shafer Dr Sioux Falls SD 57103 Office: Carter Elevator Co Inc 2504 S Duluth Ave Sioux Falls SD 57105

HUNTER, ELMO BOLTON, U.S. judge; b. St. Louis, Oct. 23, 1915; s. David Riley and Della (Bolton) H.; m. Shirley Arnold, Apr. 5, 1952; 1 child, Nancy Ann (Mrs. Ray Lee Hunt). A.B., U. Mo., 1936, LL.B., 1938; Cook Grad. fellow, U. Mich., 1941. Bar: Mo. bar 1938. Sole practice Kansas City, 1938-45; sr. asst. city counselor 1939-40; ptnr. Sebree, Shook, Hardy and Hunter, 1945-51; state circuit judge Mo., 1951-57; Mo. appellate judge 1957-65, U.S. dist. judge, 1965—, now sr. judge; instr. law U. Mo., 1952-62. Contbr. articles to profl. jours. Mem. Bd. Police Commrs., 1949-51; Trustee Kansas City U., Sch. of Ozarks; fellow William Rockhill Nelson Gallery Art. Served to 1st lt., M.I. AUS, 1943-46. Recipient First Annual Law Day award U. Mo., 1964. Fellow ABA; mem. Fed., Mo. bar assns., Jud. Conf. U.S. (chmn. ct. adminstrn. com.), Am. Judicature Soc. (bd. govs., mem. exec. com., pres.), Acad. Mo. Squires, Order of Coif, Phi Beta Kappa, Phi Delta Phi. Presbyterian (elder). Office: U S Dist Ct U S Courthouse 811 Grand Ave Room 659 Kansas City MO 64106

HUNTER, HARLEN CHARLES, orthopedic surgeon; b. Estherville, Iowa, Sept. 23, 1940; s. Roy Harold and Helen Iola (King) H.; m. JoAnn Wilson, June 30, 1962; children—Harlen Todd, Juliann Kristin. B.A., Drake U., 1962; D.O., Coll. Osteo. Medicine and Surgery, Des Moines, 1967. Diplomate Am. Osteo. Bd. Orthopedic Surgery. Intern Normandy Osteo. Hosp., St. Louis, 1967-68, resident in orthopedics, 1968-72, chmn. dept. orthopedics, 1976-77; founder, orthopedic surgeon Mid-States Orthopedic Sports Medicine Clinics of Am., Ltd. (St. Louis Orthopedic Sports Medicine Clinic , Urbandale, St. Peters, and Chesterfield), 1977—; mem. staff Normandy Osteo. Hosp., St. Louis, St. Peters Community Hosp. (Mo.); clin. instr. Kirksville Coll. Osteo. Medicne; orthopedic cons., team physician to high schs.; pres. Health Specialists, Inc. mem. med. adv. bd. Mo. Athletic Activities Assn.; cons. sports medicine Sports St. Louis newspaper; founder Ann. Sports Medicine Clinic for Trainers and Coaches; nat. lectr. various social, profl. orgns.; adj. clin. assoc. prof. Coll. Osteo. Surgery, Des Moines; orthopedic surgeon Iowa State Boys Basketball Tournament, 1966-85. Contbr. articles to profl. publs. Recipient Clinic Speaker award Iowa High Sch. Baseball Coaches Assn., 1982, 83. Fellow Am. Coll. Osteo. Surgeons, Am. Osteo. Acad. Orthopedics (past chmn. com. on athletic injuries); mem. Am. Osteo. Assn., Mo. Assn. Osteo. Physicians and Surgeons, Am. Coll. Sports Medicine, Am. Orthopedic Soc. Sports Medicine (del. sports medicine exchange program to China 1985), AMA, St. Louis Met. Med. Assn. Republican. Methodist. Lodges: Masons (Des Moines); Shriners. Home: 1230 Walnut Hill Farm Chesterfield MO 63017 Office: St Louis Orthopedic Sports Medicine Clinic 14377 Woodlake Chesterfield MO 63017

HUNTER, JAMES GALBRAITH, JR., lawyer; b. Phila., Jan. 6, 1942; s. James Galbraith and Emma Margaret (Jehl) H.; m. Pamela Ann Trott, July 18, 1969 (div.); children—James Nicholas, Catherine Selene. B.S. in Engring. Sci., Case Inst. Tech., 1965; J.D., U. Chgo., 1967. Bar: Ill. 1967, U.S. Dist. Ct. (no. dist.) Ill. 1967, U.S. Ct. Appeals (7th cir.) 1967, U.S. Ct. Claims, 1976, U.S. Ct. Appeals (4th and 9th cirs.) 1978, U.S. Supreme Ct. 1979, U.S. Dist. Ct. (cen. dist.) Ill. 1980, Calif. 1980, U.S. Dist. Ct. (cen. and so. dists.) Calif. 1980, U.S. Ct. Appeals (5th cir.) 1982, U.S. Ct. Appeals (fed. cir.) 1982. Assoc. Kirkland & Ellis, Chgo., 1967-68, 70-73, ptnr., 1973-76; ptnr. Hedlund, Hunter & Lynch, Chgo., 1976-82, Los Angeles, 1979-82; ptnr. Latham & Watkins, Hedlund, Hunter & Lynch, Chgo. and Los Angeles, 1982—. Served to lt. JAGC, USN, 1968-70. Mem. ABA, State Bar Calif., Los Angeles County Bar Assn., Chgo. Bar Assn. Clubs: Metropolitan (Chgo.), Chgo. Athletic Assn., Los Angeles Athletic. Exec. editor U. Chgo. Law Rev., 1966-67. Office: Sears Tower Suite 6900 Chicago IL 60606 also: 555 S Flower St Los Angeles CA 90071

HUNTER, JOHN SAMUEL, III, environmental engineer; b. Denver, Oct. 1, 1941; s. John Samuel II and Margaret A. (Oliver) H.; m. Coralie Overbeck, Dec. 27, 1963; children: John Samuel, Karlene Annette, Laura Mary-Alexia. BSCE, Colo. State U., 1964; MS Enviorn. Health Engring., U. Minn., 1965; PhD, Colo. State U., 1978. Diplomate Am. Acad. Environ. Engrs.; registered profl. engr., Colo. Environ. engr. USAF, 1964-70, 3M Co., St. Paul, 1973—. Contbr. environ. engring. articles to tech. jours.; patentee in field. Active sch. bd. Calvary Assembly Acad., White Bear Lake, Minn., 1981-85; scoutmaster troop White Bear Lake Council Boy Scouts Am., 1978-80. Served to capt. USAF, Vietnam. Recipient Radebaugh award Cen. States Water Pollution Control Assn., 1982, IR-100 award Indsl. Research mag., 1983. Fellow Am. Soc. Civil Engrs.; mem. The Filtration Soc., Cen. States Water Pollution Control Assn., Water Pollution Control Fedn. Avocations: photography, gardening, snow skiing. Home: 1867 3d St White Bear Lake MN 55110 Office: 3M Co EE & PC 21-2W PO Box 33331 Saint Paul MN 55133

HUNTER, JOSEPH EDWARD, musician, consultant; b. Jackson, Tenn., Nov. 19, 1927; s. John G. and Vada Idona (Dreke) H.; m. Mable Daisy Miller, June 15, 1957 (div.); children—Joseph Jr., Michelle Dana. Student Lane Coll., U. Detroit, Detroit Inst. Tech. Profl. pianist, 1956-59; pianist, arranger, band leader Motown Record Corp., Detroit, 1959-61; band leader with Jackie Wilson, 1961; musical dir. Pied Piper records, 1967-68; musical dir. cons. Brohun Pub., 1968—; cons. various chs., rec. artists and firms. Served with USAF, 1946-49. Recipient awards Black Music Found., Upper Room, Mother Waddles' Perpetual Mission. Mem. Nat. Com. for Rec. Arts, Detroit Fedn. Musicians. Lodge: Masons. Composer numerous published songs. Office: 19935 Orleans Detroit MI 48203

HUNTER, MATTIE, human services executive; b. Chgo., June 1, 1954; d. Lucious and Flabe (Davis) H. BA, Monmouth (Ill.) Coll., 1976; MA, Jackson (Miss.) State U., 1982. Summer counselor Chgo. Housing Authority, 1972-76; asst. mgr. Whitney's Fashions, Chgo., 1976; tng. specialist City Colls. of Chgo., 1977-81; youth service worker Dept. Human Services City of Chgo., 1977-81; program dir. Human Services Devel. Inst. Chgo., 1982-85, exec. asst. to pres., 1985—; conf. planner, community liaison, and mktg. Bakeman & Assocs., Chgo., 1986—. Author: (newsletter) Nat. Elk Alcoholism Commn., 1982. Mem. Community Devel. Adv. Council City of Chgo., 1986; mem. steering com. Cook County Democratic Women, Chgo., 1985—; staff asst. Polit. Action Conf. of Ill., Chgo., 1984—; vol. Warren county Rep. Orgn., Monmouth, 1975; fundraiser Nat. Polit. Congress of Black Women, Chgo., 1985—; vol. coordinator Hands Across Am., Chgo., 1986, March of Dimes Telethon, Chgo., 1979-81, Muscular Distrophy, Chgo., 1980, 81, 85, local adv. council Chgo. Housing Authority, 1968-76; precinct coordinator congl. dist. race, Chgo., 1980, 1976, 3rd Ward Regular Democratic Orgn., Chgo., 1970-72; asst. ward coordinator Washington for Mayor City of Chgo., 1983; surveyor Joint Ctr. for Polit. Studies, Washington, 1973; ambassador of mercy United Way, Chgo.; vice chmn. adv. council Chgo. Intervention Network Dept. of Human Services, 1985—, convocations com. Monmouth Coll., 1973-74, cultural affairs com., 1975-76; bd. dirs. Black Leadership Roundtable of Ill., Chgo., 1986—. Named one of Outstanding Young Women Am., 1985; recipient award of Appreciation, Dept. Human Services City of Chgo., 1981, award of Gratitude, Human Resources Devel. Inst. Chgo., 1984. Mem. Notaries Assn. of Ill., Inc., Nat. Black Alcoholism Council (chmn. Orgn. Devel. Com., award of Appreciation), Nat. Forum Black Pub. Adminstrs., Nat. Assn. for Female Execs. Democrat. Baptist. Avocations: volleyball, softball, bowling. Home: 8819 S Throop St Chicago IL 60620

HUNTER, NEVIN DORAN, political science educator; b. July 15, 1938; married; 5 children. BS in Polit. Sci., Brigham Young U., 1963, MS in Polit. Sci., 1965; PhD in Polit. Sci., U. Wash., 1971. Asst. prof. polit. sci. Simpson Coll., Indianola, Iowa, 1966-69; asst. prof. polit. sci. Mankato (Minn.) State U., 1969-71, assoc. prof. polit. sci., 1971-79, prof. polit. sci., 1979—; vis. prof. polit. sci. St. John's Univ., Collegeville, Minn., 1969; pub. info. specialist U.S. Army Corps Engrs., 1975, 76; assoc. dir. and faculty fellow Gen. Mgmt. Tng. Ctr., Washington, 1976-77; project dir. justice system improvement study State of Minn. Crime Control Plannig Bd., 1979-80; exec. dir. leadership VA, U.S. VA, Washington, 1983-84; Chief Justice appointee to Minn. Commn. on Bi-centennial of U.S. Constn.; lectr. U.S. Constn. for Minn. Humanities Commn. Contbr. articles to profl. jours. St. John's U. grantee, 1969, Probationed Offender and Rehab. Tng. Program grantee, 1973, Mankato State U. grantee, 1984, Fed. Law Enforcement Assistance Adminstrn. grantee. Home: 115 W 9th St Mankato MN 56001 Office: Mankato State U Polit Sci Dept Mankato MN 56001

HUNTER, ROBERT TYLER, investment management company executive; b. Peoria, Ill., Jan. 14, 1943; s. Thomas Oakford and Joan (Sargent) H.; m. Mary Michelle Tyrrell, June 12, 1965. A.B., Harvard U., 1965. Pres. First Union Trust Co., Kansas City, Mo., 1973-81; sr. v.p., trust div. mgr. Centerre Bank, Kansas City, 1981-84; v.p., mgr. client services and mktg. DST Systems, Inc., Kansas City, 1984-85; sr. v.p. mktg. Waddell & Read Asset Mgmt. Co., Kansas City, 1985—Treas. M.S. Soc., Mission, Kans.; bd. dirs. Boys and Girls Club, Kansas City; trustee Menorah Hosp. Found., Kansas City; bd. govs. Kansas City Philharmonic Assn.; bd. dirs., com. chmn. Kansas City Youth Symphony. Fellow Fin. Analyst Fedn.; mem. Fin. Analyst Soc. Kansas City, Corp. Fiduciaries Soc. of Kansas City (past pres.), Estate Planning Assn. Republican. Roman Catholic. Clubs: Harvard/Radcliffe (pres. 1983-85); Kansas City Rcquet (Merriam, Kans.). Avocations: tennis; swimming; reading; coaching. Home: 8215 Noland Rd Lenexa KS 66215 Office: Waddell & Reed Asset Mgmt Co 2400 Pershing Rd Kansas City MO 64108

HUNTER, VICTOR LEE, marketing executive, consultant; b. Garrett, Ind., Mar. 1, 1947; s. John Joseph and Martha May (Brown) H.; m. Linda Ann Loudermilk, Dec. 19, 1969; children: Jed, Andrew, Matthew, Holly. BS, Purdue U., 1969; MBA, Harvard U., 1971. Dir. mktg. Kreuger, Inc., Green Bay, Wis., 1971-75; pres. B&I Furniture, Milw., 1975-81, Hunter Bus. Direct, Milw., 1981—; bd. dirs. Bus. Marketers Group, Inc., Milw. Lay leader United Meth. Ch., Whitefish Bay, Wis., 1985. Mem. Direct Mktg. Assn., Wis. Direct Mktg. Club, Bus. to Bus. Direct Mktg. Council. Office: Hunter Bus Direct 8793 N Port Washington Milwaukee WI 53217

HUNTER, WILLARD BOWEN, chemical executive; b. Midland, Mich., Mar. 8, 1944; s. Melvin Jasper and Naomi Mary (Bowen) H.; m. Russelle Cordes, June 2, 1973 (div. Sept. 1986); 1 child, Bowen. BS, Tex. Wesleyan Coll., 1967; MA in Internat. Mgmt., Am. Grad. Sch. Internat. Mgmt., 1973. Engr. internat. sales Ritter div. Sybron Corp., Rochester, Mass., 1973-75; salesman Dow Chem., Boston, 1976-79, bus. analyst Dow Chem., Midland, Mich., 1980-82, mgr. mktg. research, 1982—. Bd. dirs. Midland Music Soc., 1982-86; chmn. arrangement com. CROP Walk, Midland, 1986—. Served with USN, 1968-72. Methodist. Club: Torch (bd. dirs. 1986—) (Saginaw, Mich.). Lodges: Rotary (program chmn. Midland club 1985-87, bd. dirs. 1987—), Masons (sr. warden Wellesley club 1979-80), Order of Eastern Star (worthy patron Wellesley club 1979-80). Avocations: hiking, bridge, golf, tennis, fgn. langs. Home: 5417 Wanetah Dr Midland MI 48640 Office: Dow Chem Plastics Dept 2040 WH Dow Ctr Midland MI 48640

HUNTRESS, BETTY ANN, former music store propr.; b. Poughkeepsie, N.Y., Apr. 29, 1932; d. Emmett Slater and Catherine V. (Kihlmire) Brundage; m. Arnold Ray Huntress, June 26, 1954; children: Catherine, Michael, Carol, Alan. BA, Cornell U., 1954. Tchr. high sch., Bordentown, N.J., 1954-55; part-time asst. to prof. Delta Coll., Northwood Inst., Midland, Mich., 1958-71; part-time tchr. Midland Pub. Schs., 1968-79, 83—; owner, mgr. The Music Stand, Midland, 1979-82. Bd. dirs. Midland Center for Arts, 1978-86 ; v.p. MCFTA (Arts Center), 1980-84 ; mem. charter bd. mgrs. Matrix Midland Ann. Arts and Sci. Festival, 1977-80; cons. Girl Scouts Am., 1964-76; mem. Mich. Internat. Council, 1975-76; bd. mem. Adult Literary Council Midland County, 1986—. Named Midland Musician of Yr., 1977. Mem. Music Soc. Midland Center for Arts (dir. 1971-86, chmn. 1976-79), AAUW (dir. 1962-73, pres. 1971-73, mem. Mich. state div. bd. 1973-75, 1st v.p. Mich. state div. 1983-85 , outstanding woman as agt. of change award 1977, fellowship grant named in her honor 1976), Midland Symphony League Soc. (2d v.p.), LWV (bd. dirs. 1986—), Community Concert Soc., Kappa Delta Epsilon, Pi Lambda Theta, Alpha Xi Delta. Republican. Presbyterian. Home: 5316 Sunset Dr Midland MI 48640

HUNTZINGER, ROGER JAY, newspaper executive; b. Pendleton, Ind., June 18, 1952; s. Delbert and Evelyn (Burdette) H.; m. Jill Ellen Jones, Nov. 21, 1982; children: Heather, Nathan. BS, Ball State U., 1974. Dist. mgr. The Republic, Columbus, Ind., 1976-77, motor route supr., 1977-78, asst. circulation mgr., 1978-80, circulation mgr., 1980-84; gen. mgr. Herald Jour., Monticello, Ind., 1984—. bd. dirs. Jr. Achievement, Columbus, Ind., 1980. Mem. Hoosier State Press Assn., Inland Daily Press Assn., Internat. Newspaper Promotion Assn., Ind. Rep. Editorial Assn., Monticello C. of C. (bd dirs. 1986). Lodge: Rotary. Home: PO Box 839 Monticello IN 47960 Office: PO Box 409 114 S Main Monticello IN 47960

HUPALO, KATHLEEN FIXSEN, lawyer; b. Sheridan Twp., Minn., Jan. 21, 1945; d. Orman Bernard and Margery Elizabeth (Swartz) Fixsen; m. Ivan Hupalo, May 24, 1964; 1 son, Peter. B.A. in Sociology, U. Minn., 1976, J.D., 1981. Bar: Minn. 1981, U.S. Dist. Ct. Minn. 1982, U.S. Ct. Appeals (8th cir.) 1982. Sole practice, St. Paul, 1981-84; atty. Am. Indian Health Agy., St. Paul, 1984; human rights law enforcement officer Minn. Dept. Human Rights, 1985—. Contbr. articles to legal jours. Atty. Nursing Home Rights, Mpls., 1982; den mother Boy Scouts Am., 1976; mem. West Side Neighborhood House, St. Paul, 1976—, West Side Citizens Edn., 1976. Mem. ABA, Minn. State Bar Assn., Ramsey County Bar Assn., Minn. Women Lawyers Inc., Minn. Alumni Assn., Lex Alumnae. Home: 684 Delaware Ave Saint Paul MN 55107

HURAND, GARY JAY, franchise executive; b. Flint, Mich., Oct. 26, 1946; s. Arthur and Bess H.; m. Carol Levine, May 17, 1970; children—Joshua, Sara. B.S., Mich. State U., 1969. Dir. ops. and mgmt. Diversified, Inc., Flint, 1969-70, v.p., 1971; v.p. Dawn Donut Systems, Inc., Flint, 1970-71, pres., 1971—; v.p. Flint Motor Inn, 1971—; Mem. Flint C. of C., Mich. State U. Alumnae (life), Sales and Mktg. Execs. Flint, Young Pres. Orgn. Jewish. Home: 2040 Walden Ct Flint MI 48504 Office: G-4300 W Pierson Rd Flint MI 48504

HURD, PAUL MICHAEL, hospital administrator; b. Sheldon, Iowa, Sept. 8, 1945; s. Paul Anthony and Elisabeth (Reim) H.; m. Linda Jane Darrah, July 13, 1968; 1 child, Darran Paul. BBA, U. Iowa, 1967; MBA, U. Toledo, 1983. Asst. mgr. KMart Corp., Iowa, Ill., 1967-70; asst. purchasing agt. U. Iowa, Iowa City, 1970-77; materials dir. St. Luke's Hosp., Maumee, Ohio, 1977-86; hosp. adminstr. Community Meml. Hosp., clarion, Iowa, 1986—. Mem. Am. Coll. Healthcare Execs., Am. Hosp. Assn., Iowa Hosp. Assn. Democrat. Roman Catholic. Lodge: Lions. Home: 419 11th St NE Clarion IA 50525

HURD, ROBERT JAMES, dentist; b. Pontiac, Mich.; s. Homer and Roberta Ann (Reynolds) H.; m. Kendra Kay Crowell; 1 child, Tracy Lynn. AS, Lincoln Land Coll., 1973; DDS, So. Ill. U., Edwardsville, 1976. Dental technician Long Dental Studio, Springfield, Ill., 1966-73; gen. practice dentistry Springfield, 1976—. Served with U.S. Army, 1963-66. Mem. ADA, Ill. State Dental Soc., G.V. Black Dental Soc. (exec. council 1976—). Republican. Presbyterian. Lodges: Lions, Elks. Home: N Walnut St Rd Rochester IL 62563 Office: 6 Drawbridge Springfield IL 62704

HURD, ROGER ALLAN, data processing company sales professional; b. Highland Park, Mich., Sept. 15, 1956; s. Byron Thomas and Barbara (Ekeroth) H.; m. Catherine Joan Evans, Dec. 29, 1978; children: Evan McKinley, Tyler Allan. BA, Cornell U., 1978, MBA, 1980. Sales rep., sales mgr. Southwestern Co., Nashville, 1977-80; mktg. rep. Sykes Datatronics, Rochester, N.Y., 1981-83; networking cons. Wang Labs., Oakbrook, Ill., 1983-85; account rep. Wang Labs., Chgo., 1985—. Deacon Summerville Presbyn. Ch., Rochester, 1982. Mem. Soc. for Preservation and Encouragement Barber Shop Quartet Singing in Am. (West Town's Chorus). Club: Cornell U. of Chgo. (membership chmn. 1986). Avocation: singing. Office: Wang Labs 444 N Michigan Chicago IL 60611

HURD, THOMAS ROBERT, architect, consultant; b. Payton, Iowa, Feb. 21, 1951; s. Joseph William and Lathelma Rozella (Griggs) H.; m. Nancy Ann Ziegler, May 31, 1975; children: Emily, Kyle, Alyse. BArch, Iowa State U., 1973, MArch, 1979. Registered architect, Iowa. Draftsman Waggoner Mahaffey & Bowman, Mason City, Iowa, 1973-74, designer, 1978-83; prin. Spatial Designs Architects, Mason City, 1983—. Democrat. Roman Catholic. Avocations: skiing, tennis, golf. Office: Spatial Designs 102 West Side Offices Mason City IA 50401

HURKMAN, DIANE LEE, cytopathology educator; b. Appleton, Wis., June 17, 1950; d. Arthur Joseph and Esther Lena (Prokash) DeDecker; m. Ronald James Hurkman, Mar. 24, 1973; children: Sonya, Reed, Natasha. Student in biology, U. Wis., Stevens Point, 1968-71; student in cytology, State Lab. of Hygiene, Madison, Wis., 1971-72. Registered med. technologist. Instr. cytopathology Mayo Clinic, Rochester, Minn., 1973-84; edn. coordinator U. Nebr. Med. Ctr., Omaha, 1984-87; free-lance med. research writer and copy editor Omaha, 1987—. Author: Cytologic Detection of Multiple Myeloma in Cervical Pap Smear, 1983, Cytopathology of Opportunistic Infection in Bronchoalveolan Lavage, 1986. Speaker Am. Cancer Soc., Rochester, 1983. Am. Cancer Soc. grantee, 1971. Mem. Am. Soc. Clin. Pathologists, Am. Soc. Cytology, Internat. Soc. Clin. Lab. Technologists, Heart of Am. Soc. Cytology. Republican. Roman Catholic. Avocations: sailing, writing novels. Home and Office: 1286 S 163d Ave Omaha NE 68130

HURL, RODNEY BECK, physician; b. Shelby, Ohio, Feb. 25, 1930; s. Robert Davis and Esther Helen (Beck) H.; B.S., Bethany (W.Va.) Coll., 1951; M.D., Temple U., 1955; m. Judith Rothrock, July 17, 1955; children—Megan, Marcy, Jeffrey. Rotating intern Mt. Carmel Hosp., Columbus, Ohio, 1955-56, resident in family practice, 1959; practice medicine specializing in family practice, Marysville, Ohio, 1959—; pres. R.B. Hurl M.D. Inc., 1970—; mem. staff Meml. Hosp., Marysville, Riverside Meth. Hosp., Columbus; pres., dir. Marysville Rest Homes, Mildon Park Assos. Inc.; dir. Marysville Newspapers Inc. Trustee Bethany (W.Va.) Coll., 1971—, chmn. devel. com., 1974—, also mem., sec. exec. com., mem. nominating com.; mem. Union County Mental Health Bd., 1970-80, pres., 1978-80; pres. Marysville City Parks and Recreation Commn., 1974-78. Served to capt. M.C., USAF, 1956-58. Recipient Outstanding Alumni Service award Bethany Coll., 1978; diplomate Am. Acad. Family Practice. Mem. AMA, Am. Acad. Family Practice, Ohio Med. Assn., Ohio Acad. Family Practice, Central Ohio Acad. Family Practice (dir. 1979-80), Union County Med. Assn. Republican. Lutheran. Club: Masons. Home: 381 Hickory Dr Marysville OH 43040 Office: 211 Stocksdale Dr Marysville OH 43040

HURLBUT, RICHARD WADE, psychologist; b. Stevens Point, Wis., Oct. 23, 1950; s. Kenneth Edward and Elizabeth (Swan) H.; m. Connie Haack-Hurlbut, Sept. 17, 1977. BS, U. Wis., 1972, MS, 1976, PhD, 1979. Lic. Psychologist. Intern in psychology Wis. Div. of Corrections, Madison, 1979-80, staff psychologist, 1980-82, sr. staff psychologist, 1982-83; gen. practice psychology Mid-Wis. Psychotherapy Assocs., Stevens Point, 1981—; adj. prof. U. Wis., Stevens Point, 1984-86; cons. Homme Home for boys, Wittenberg, Wis., 1984—, Luth. Social Service, Shawno, Wis., 1984—, Assoc. Cons. Services, Marshfield, Wis., 1984—; co-owner, v.p. Heath Maintanance Services, Stevens Point, Wis., 1983—. Mem. Soc. Clin. and Cons. Psychologist (pres. 1984-85), Am. Psychol. Assn., Wis. Psyhol. Assn. Democrat. Avocations: flying, scuba diving, skiing, travel. Office: Mid Wis Psychotherapy Assocs 100 Bremmer St Stevens Point WI 54481

HURLEY, MARJORIE BRYAN, bank executive; b. Ft. Worth, Feb. 13, 1941; d. Everett and Ollie Rhea (McKinney) Bryan; m. Doyle Andrew Hurley, Mar. 15, 1958; children: Gregory Dean, Jeffrey Alan. Cert. in bank mktg., U. Colo., 1978; cert. in bank mktg. mgmt., U. Ga., 1984. Asst. mktg. Bank of the S.W. (now MBank-Houston), Houston, 1965-75; asst. v.p., dir. mktg. (now First Am. Bank) Union First Nat. Bank, Washington, 1975; v.p., dir. mktg. United Mo. Bancshares, Inc., Kansas City, 1979—. Advisor: (textbook) Marketing for Bankers, 1982. Mem. Advt. Club of Kansas City (treas. 1985-86, sec. 1986-87, bd. dirs. 1984—, Ad Woman of Yr. award 1983), Bank Mktg. Assn. Republican. Baptist. Avocations: antiquing, gardening, refinishing furniture. Office: United Mo Bancshares Inc PO Box 419226 Kansas City MO 64141-6226

HURLEY, PATRICK JAMES, psychologist; b. Moorestown, N.J., Nov. 29, 1947; s. Robert Edward and Agnes (Workman) H.; m. Cheryl Lynn Ambrose, Aug. 23, 1969; 1 child, Shawn Patrick. BS, U. Dayton, 1969; MA, Wright State U., 1973. Lic. psychologist, Ohio. Intern Adams County Schs., West Union, Ohio, 1972-73; psychologist New Lexington (Ohio) Schs., 1973-85; clin. dir. Thompkins Ctr., Cambridge, Ohio, 1984-86; dir. behavioral sci. Health Sphere, Newark, Ohio, 1985—; pvt. practice psychology Somerset, Ohio; sec. bd. dirs. Family Tree, Zanesville, Ohio; bd. dirs. Nelsonville (Ohio) Children's Ctr.; pres. Friends Pregnancy Counseling, New Lexington, 1982—. Mem. Ohio Sch. Psychology Assn., Nat. Assn. Sch. Psychologists. Roman Catholic. Avocations: woodworking, antiques. Home: 3245 Dutch Ridge Rd SE Rt 1 New Straitsville OH 43766 Office: Health Sphere 1873 Tamarack Newark OH 43055 Office: 313 North Dr Somerset OH 43783

HURST, CHARLES BLAKE, farmer; b. Fla., Apr. 21, 1957; s. Charles Leroy and Mildred Mae (Nelson) H.; m. Julia Louise Renken, Aug. 27, 1977; children: Katherine Lee, Rebecca Ann, John Benton. BS in Agriculture, U. Mo., 1978. Farmer Hurst Farms, Tarkio, Mo., 1978—. Mem. Am. Farm Bur. (young farmer com. 1986), Mo. Farm Bur. (chmn. young farmer com. 1985, resolutions com. 1982, 85), N.W. Mo. Farmers Action (vice chmn. 1985-86), Atchison County Farm Bur. (pres. 1984-87). Republican. Baptist. Home and Office: Rural Rt 1 Box 24 Westboro MO 64498

HURST, DURWOOD QUENTIN, criminal investigator; b. East St. Louis, Ill., Nov. 21, 1942; s. Forrest Washington and Virginia Elanor (Davis) H.; m. Carolyn Jean Stafford, June 5, 1971; children: Christopher, Jeffery, Bradley, Jason. Student, Belleville (Ill.) Jr. Coll. Police officer Caseyville (Ill.) Police Dept., 1960-70; inspector Office of Sec. of Stateof Ill., Springfield, 1960-65; dep. sheriff St. Clari County, Ill., 1965-70; investigator Appellate Defender's Office, Mt. Vernon, Ill., 1970—; chief exec. officer D.Q. Hurst Corp., Coulterville, Ill., 1977—; dep. coroner Randolph County, Ill., 1978-82. Precint committeeman Randolph County Dems.; chmn. Coulterville Draft Bd., 1986—. Avocations: golf, fishing, hot ari ballooning, helicopters. Home and Office: Box 485 Coulterville IL 62237-0485

HURT, FLOYD ROBERT, corporation official, farmer; b. Belfield, N.D., Jan. 24, 1936; s. Louis James and Gladys Cecile (Owen) H.; m. Muriel Ethel Brown, Jan. 17, 1958; children—Floyd Robert, Linda Kay. Student schs. Belfield, N.D. Roughneck, Rutledge Drilling Co., 1959-62; driller, Noble Drilling Co., 1962-65; roustabout Amerada Corp., 1965-67; lease foreman Amerada-Hess Corp., Belfield, 1967-71, field maintenance supr., 1971-73, area supt., 1973-80, dist. supt., 1980—, asst. producer tng. films. City council mem. South Heart, N.D., police commr., 1978-82, civil def. commr. 1986—; elder United Presbyterian Ch., Belfield. Mem. adv. council Bur. Land Mgmt., Dickinson. Served with USAF, 1955-59. Recipient Safety award Noble Drilling Co., 1965. Lodges: Masons, Shriners, Order Eastern Star (past patron, Elks, Eagles, Royal Arch Masons. (temple comdr.).

HURTER, ARTHUR PATRICK, economist, educator; b. Chgo., Jan. 29; s. Arthur P. and Lillian T. (Thums) H.; m. Florence Evalyn Kays; children—Patricia Lyn, Arthur Earl. BSCE, Northwestern U., MSCE, MA in Econs., PhD in Econs. Chem. engr. Zonlite Research Lab., Evanston, Ill., 1957-58; assoc. dir. Research Transp. Ctr., Northwestern U., Evanston, Ill., 1963-65, asst. prof. dept. Indsl. Engring. and Mgmt. Scis. Tech. Inst., 1962-66, prof., 1970—, chmn. dept., 1969—, assoc. prof. fin. Grad. Sch. Mgmt., 1969-70, prof., 1970—; cons. U. Chgo., ESCOR, Sears Roebuck & Co., Standard Oil of Ind., Ill.; bd. dirs. Ill. Environ. Health Research Ctr., 1972-77; mem. com. Sci. Tech. Adv., Ill. Inst. Natural Resources, 1980-84. Author: The Economics of Private Truck Transportation, 1965, Facility Location and the Theory of Production, 1987; contbr. articles to profl. jours. Pres. Council St. Scholastical High Sch., 1972-80; elder Granville Ave. Presbyterian Ch., 1976—. Grantee Resources for the Future, 1964, Office of Naval Research, 1965, NSF, Social Sci. Research Council dissertation fellow. Mem. Am. Econ. Assn., Regional Sci. Assn., Ops. Research Soc. Am., Inst. Mgmt. Scis., Inst. Indsl. Engrs., Sigma Xi, Phi Lambda Upsilon, Tau Beta Pi. Home and Office: 1505 W Norwood Chicago IL 60660

HURTTE, JAMES EDWARD, mining and safety engineer; b. Taylorville, Ill., Dec. 14, 1951; s. Rayford C. and Dorothy L. (Chlebus) H.; m. Donna Lee Hoy, Jan. 8, 1972; children: Eric, Christopher, Travis. BS in Mining Engring., U. Mo., 1974. Cert. mine examiner, instr., mine mgr., shaft and slope supr., Ill. Mine engr. Peabody Coal Co., Pawnee, Ill., 1974-76, underground supr., 1976-82; safety mgr. Peabody Coal Co., Pawnee, 1982—; mapman Mine Rescue Team, Pawnee, 1977-84, tng. instr. 1984—. Mem. Taylorville Parent-Tchrs. Assn., 1981-86; mem. exec. bd. Red Bland Littl eLEague, Taylorville, 1985-86; pres. St. Mary's Parish Council, Taylorville, 1986. Mem. Ill. Mining Assn., Holmes Safety Assn. (exec. bd. 1985-86), Nat. Mine Rescue Assn. Roman Catholic. Avocations: hunting, fishing, baseball, carpentry. Home: 1108 W Poplar Taylorville IL 62568 Office: Peabody Coal Co Box 158 Pawnee IL 62558

HURWITZ, MARTIN GERALD, investment analyst, educator; b. Revere, Mass., July 24, 1940; s. Benjamin and Rose (Yaffee) H.; m. Anne Lewinnek, May 5, 1985; children: Gregg J., Richelle H. BS, MIT, 1962, MS, 1964, MBA, 1973; B in Pub. Acctg., Walton Sch., Chgo., 1977. Mgr. Boston ops. Logicon, Bedford, Mass., 1971-73; gen. mgr. Zenith Electronics, Glenview, Ill., 1973-83; investment analyst Prescott, Ball and Turben, Chgo., 1983—; asst. prof. Lowell (Mass.) Tech. Inst., 1965-66; adj. prof. Lake Forest (Ill.) Coll., 1979—, Ill. Inst. Tech., Chgo., 1986—. Contbr. articles to profl. jours. Alfred P. Sloan Found. fellow. Avocations: bridge, antiques, computers. Home: 1434 S Yale Arlington Heights IL 60005 Office: Prescott Ball & Turben 230 W Monroe Chicago IL 60606

HUSAR, JOHN PAUL, newspaper columnist; b. Chgo., Jan. 29, 1937; s. John Z. and Kathryn (Kanupke) H.; A.A., Dodge City Coll., 1958; B.S. in Journalism, U. Kans., 1962; m. Louise Kay Lewis, Dec. 28, 1963; children—Kathryn, Laura. Reporter, Clovis (N.Mex.) News-Jour., 1960; night wire editor Okinawa Morning Star, 1961; city editor Pasadena (Tex.) Daily Citizen, 1962; bus. editor Topeka Capital-Jour., 1963; regional news editor Wichita (Kans.) Beacon, 1963-65; sports columnist and writer Chgo. Tribune, 1966—. Chmn., Village of Willow Springs (Ill.) Zoning Commn., 1975-77; mem. Ill. Forestry Adv. Com., 1981-82; mem. adv. com. Ill.-Mich. Canal Nat. Heritage Corridor, 1982; profl.-in-residence U. Kans. Sch. Journalism, 1985. Served with U.S. Army, 1960-62. Recipient 1st pl. award in sportswriting Ill. UPI, 1977, Ill. AP, 1984, 1st pl. award in feature writing Bowling mag., 1979, environ. reporting award Chgo. Audubon Soc., 1979, Disting. Alumnus award Dodge City Coll., 1983, 2d pl. award for public service reporting Ill. AP, 1980, 2d pl. award for sports column writing, 1981, spl. writing award Chgo. Tribune, 1980, Jacob A. Riis award Friends of Parks, 1981, Peter Lisagor award Chgo. chpt. Sigma Delta Chi, 1985, Du-Pont Stren Edit. Excellence award, 1986. Mem. Golf Writers Assn. Am. (past dir.), Baseball Writers Assn. Am., Outdoor Writers Assn. Am., Phi Kappa Theta. Office: 435 N Michigan Ave Chicago IL 60611

HUSARIK, ERNEST A., ednl. adminstr.; b. Gary, Ind., July 2, 1941; married, 2 children. BA in History, Olivet Nazarene Coll., Kankakee, Ill., 1963; MS in Ednl. Adminstrn., No. Ill. U., DeKalb, 1966; PhD in Ednl. Adminstrn. and Curriculum Devel., Ohio State U., Columbus, 1973; m. Elizabeth Ann Bonnette; children: Jennifer, Amy. Supt., Ontario (Ohio) Pub. Schs., 1973-75; supt. Euclid (Ohio) Pub. Schs., 1975-86, Westerville (Ohio) Pub. Schs., 1986—. Mem. tchr. edn. and cert. adv. commn. Ohio Dept. Edn.; mem. Westerville City Shade Tree Commn.; mem. adv. and distbn. com. Martha Holden Jennings Found.; mem. alumni adv. council Ohio State U.; mem. Franklin County Ednl. Council. Mem. Am. Assn. Sch. Adminstrs., Buckeye Assn. Sch. Adminstrs. (dir.), Nat. Assn. Supervision and Curriculum Devel., Ohio Assn. Supervision and Curriculum Devel., Greater Cleve. Sch. Supts. Assn. (past pres.), Mid-Am. Assn. Sch. Supts., Euclid C. of C. (past pres.), Waterville C. of C. (bd. dirs.), Olivet Nazarene Coll. Alumni Assn. (past mem. alumni bd. dirs.), Phi Delta Kappa (past chpt. pres.), Sigma Tau Delta. Contbr. articles in field to profl. jours. Home: 1029 Wood Glen Rd Westerville OH 43081 Office: 336 S Otterbein Ave Westerville OH 43081

HUSAYNU, RYAN ANTHONY, lawyer; b. Detroit, June 14, 1959; s. Hakki Hermez and Suad Mary (Ankawi) H. BA, U. Detroit, 1980, MBA, JD, 1983. Bar: Mich. 1984, U.S. Dist. Ct. (ea. dist.) Mich. 1984. Assoc. Harvey, Kruse, Westen & Milan, P.C., Detroit, 1984—. Mem. ABA, Mich. Bar Assn., Detroit Bar Assn., Cath. Lawyers Detroit, Delta Theta Phi (bd. dirs. met. Detroit senate 1983—). Home: 7357 Cathedral Birmingham MI 48010 Office: Harvey Kruse Westen & Milan PC 1590 First Nat Bldg Detroit MI 48226

HUSBAND, RICHARD LORIN, SR., business executive; b. Spencer, Iowa, July 28, 1931; s. Ross Twetten and Frances Estelle (Hall) H.; A.A., Rochester State Community Coll., 1953; A.B., U. Minn., 1954; m. Darlene Joyce Granberg, 1954; children—Richard Lorin, Thomas Ross and Mark Thurston (twins), Julia Lynn, Susan Elizabeth. Pres., Orlen Ross Inc., Rochester, Minn., 1962—; partner The Gallery, European antiques, china, gifts, Rochester, 1968—, Millenium III, home furnishings, Rochester, 1975—. Nat. Editor: The Mayflower Quaterly. Active Episcopal Diocese of Minn., 1951-52, 58—, nat. dept., 1969-73, alt. dept., 1973-75; trustee Seabury Western Theol. Sem., 1975-87, exec. com., 1983-84, 2d v.p., 1976-87; founder Rochester Arts Council, Rochester PTA Community Coll. Scholarship Program, H.D. Mayo Meml. Lecture in Theology, others; pres. Olmsted County (Minn.) Hist. Soc., 1976-77; bd. dirs. Rochester Symphony Orch., Choral, Opera, 1970-78, pres., 1974-75; del. Olmsted County Republican Com., 1974-82; mem. exec. council Minn. Hist. Soc., 1984—. Recipient Disting. Service award Rochester Jaycees, 1965, Fifty Mem. award YMCA, 1968, award for Minn. Bicentennial, Gov. Minn., 1976; named 1 of Minn's, 10 Outstanding Young Men, Minn. Jaycees, 1966, Disting. Christian Service award Seabury Western Sem. Mem. Minn. Home Furnishings Assn. (pres. 1976-79, trustee 1968—), First Dist. Hist. Assembly Minn. (pres. 1969-71), Minn. Retail Fedn. (trustee 1972—), Olmsted County Archeology Soc. (founder), Rochester Civil War Roundtable (founder), Rochester Revolutionary War Roundtable (founder), Rochester Arts Council (founder), Am., Nat. (charter), Minn., Norwegian/Am. hist. socs., Minn. Archeology Soc., Am. Assn. State and Local History, U. Minn. Alumni Assn. (life), U. Minn. Alumni Club (charter) Rochester C. of C., Alpha Delta Phi Alumni Assn., Soc. Mayflower Descs. (trustee Minn., dep. gov. 1983—), SAR (Minn. pres. 1980-82), Descs. Colonial Clergy, Sons Union Vets of Civil War, Minn. Territorial Pioneers (trustee 1978—, pres. 1981-84), Soc. Archtl. Historians. Clubs: Rotary (historian 1980-82) (Rochester); Sertoma (Austin) (founder). Public speaker. Home: 1820 26th St NW Rochester MN 55901 Office: Orlen Ross Inc 105 N Broadway Rochester MN 55904

HUSBAND, WILLIAM SWIRE, computer industry executive; b. Hinsdale, Ill., Dec. 18, 1939; s. William Thompson and Arlene Martha (Frey) H.; m. Janet Goatley, Nov. 26, 1965; children—Scott, Andrea. B.S., Iowa State U., 1962. Mktg. rep. IBM, San Francisco, 1966-70; dist. mktg. mgr. DPF, Des Plaines, Ill., 1971-78; v.p. Celtic Computer Investment Co., Palatine, Ill., 1978; pres. 20th Century Systems, Inc., Palatine, 1978—. Presented symposium for U. Calif.- Berkeley at Systems Technology Inst., Milan,1987. Author, pub.: Computer Acquisition and Disposition Planning, 6th edit., 1986. IBM Technology and Product Strategies in the 80's, 1986; contbg. editor Computer Econs. mag., 1986—. Active Buehler YMCA, Palatine Boys' Baseball, 1978-85. Served to lt. (j.g.) USN, 1962-66. Republican. Presbyterian. Office: 20th Century Systems Inc 330 W Colfax Ave Palatine IL 60067

HUSBY, JOHN RICHARD, medical association administrator, health science educator; b. Traverse City, Mich., Apr. 2, 1950; s. Leon Wilford and Doris Ann (McKasson) H.; m. Lois Eileen Frederick, Apr. 9, 1983. BA, U. Mich., Flint, 1973; MA, Cen. Mich. U., Mt. Pleasant, 1981; postgrad., Mich. State U., 1985—. Cert. social worker, Mich. Counselor Nat. Council Alcoholism, Flint, 1979-80; sr. therapist Hurley Med. Ctr., Flint, 1981-83; psychotherapist Inst. Mental Health, Flint, 1982-83; outpatient therapist Tuscola County Community Mental Health, Caro, Mich., 1983-84; pres. J.R. Husby & Assocs., Lansing, Mich., 1982—; dir. mktg. The Meml. Hosp., Owosso, Mich., 1986-87; adj. faculty Baker Coll., Owosso, 1985—. vol. staff aide David Hollister, Mich. Ho. of Rep., 1986. Mem. Am. Alliance Health, Phys. Edn., Recreation and Dance. Democrat. Episcopalian. Avocation: cross-country skiing.

HUSER, LAWRENCE ROY, sales and marketing executive; b. Detroit, Apr. 24, 1945; s. Walter George and Mildred Elenor (Rhodel) H.; m. Mary Ellen Gammicchia, May 9, 1970; children: Jenna Lynn, Jessica Lee. BS in Engring., Western Mich. U., 1967; MBA, Wayne State U., Detroit, 1971. Sales egnr. Ingersoll-Rand Co., Kalamazoo, 1971-75; br. mgr. Ingersoll-Rand Co., Detorit, 1975-80; internat. mktg. mgr. Ingersoll-Rand Co., Charlotte, 1980-84; pres., dir. Program World Inc., Charlotte, 1984-85; v.p. sales and mkgt. Avondale Industries, Inc., Mayville, Wis., 1985—; cons. Air Systems, Charlotte, N.C., 1984;. Mem. Charlotte Ambassadors, 1984-85. Mem. Sales and Mktg. Execs. Milw. Republican. Lutheran. Avocations: tennis, boating, skiing. Home: 19165 Killarney Way Brookfield WI 53005 Office: Avondale Industeries Inc PO Box 28 Mayville WI 53050

HUSK, DONALD ESTEL, state official Indiana; b. Oakland City, Ind., Dec. 10, 1925; s. George Raymond and Hazel Rita (Ashley) H.; grad. high sch.; m. Velma Cunningham, June 7, 1946; children—Robert, Mark. With Hoosier Cardinal, Inc., Evansville, Ind., 1946; asst. cashier English State Bank (Ind.), 1949; with Ind. Dept. Financial Instns., 1953—, sr. examiner, 1958-70, supr. div. banks and trust cos., Indpls., 1970-86; dep. dir. depository instns., 1986—. Served with USNR, 1943-46. Certified fin. examiner. Mem. Hist. Record Assn., Soc. Fin. Examiners. Clubs: Masons, Plainfield Optimists. Home: 424 Wayside Dr Plainfield IN 46168 Office: 1024 State Office Bldg Indianapolis IN 46204

HUSK, GORDON J, bank president; b. Martinsville, Ind., Apr. 3, 1934; s. George Raymond and Hazel Retta (Ashley) H.; m. Marian Adeline May, May 26, 1956; children: Gordon Michael, Steven Jay. U. Ga., 1966, Ind. U., 1969. Asst. zone mgr. Internat. Harvester, Indpls., 1958-61; state examiner Indpls., 1961-62; examiner Fed. Home Loan Bank Bd., Indpls., 1962-64, sr. v.p., chief supervisory agt., 1964-84; pres. First Fed. Savs. Bank and Trust, Pontiac, Mich., 1984-86, also bd. dirs; chmn., bd. dirs., pres. Pioneer Fed. Savs., Mason City, Iowa, 1987—. Served with USNR. Methodist. Club: Euchre and Cycle (Mason City). Lodge: Masons. Avocation: boating. Home: 1 Country Club Pl Clear Lake IA 50428 Office: Pioneer Fed Savs 124 N Washington Mason City IA 50401

HUSMAN, LOIS ARLENE, psychotherapist; b. Chgo., July 24, 1937; s. Nathan H. and Harriet (Bernstein) Schwartz; m. David L. Husman, Jan. 23, 1957 (div. Mar. 1969); children—Melinda, Lori. Student Northwestern U., 1954-57; B.G.S., Roosevelt U., 1972; M.S.W., U. Ill., 1974. Social worker A.E.R.O. spl. edn. sch., 1974-79; psychotherapist in pvt. practice, Chgo., 1979—. Mem. Chgo. Symphony Orch. Assn., Art Inst. Chgo., Chgo. Council Fgn. Relations, Nat. Assn. Social Workers, Am. Orthopsychiat. Assn. Home: 1430 Astor St Apt 10-C Chicago IL 60610 Office: 111 N Wabash St #1202 Chicago IL 60602

HUSS, STEPHEN FORGEY, mental health care executive; b. Evansville, Ind., Sept. 17, 1945; s. Ernie Rupert and Frances Juanita (Forgey) H.; children: Michael Blair, Justin Todd. BE, U. Cen. Ark., 1967; MA, Southeast Mo. State U., 1972; postgrad., St. Louis U., 1985—. Cert. social studies tchr., Mo., Ark. (life), alcoholism and drug abuse counselor. Tchr. social studies Hillsboro (Mo.) Secondary Schs., 1967-74; chief exec. officer Community Treatment Inc., Festus, Mo., 1974—; part-time instr. Jefferson Coll., Hillsboro, 1967-74; adj. asst. prof. social work, St. Louis U.; vol. dir. Community Treatment Inc., 1973-74; mem. Eastern Mo. Regional Adv. Com. for Alcohol and Drug Abuse, clin. adv. bd. Mo. Dept. Mental Health, 1974-87; cert.instr., adminstr. Alcohol Related Traffic Offenders' Program, 1984; guest lectr. numerous local social and profl. groups; participant numerous workshops, insts. and confs. in health and edn. field. Contbr. articles to profl. jours. Dir. Hillsboro R-3 Bd. Edn., 1986—; mem. Citizen's Study Group on Youth in Jefferson County, advisor Explorer Scouts, Coach YMCA Basketball League, mem. Home Econs. Adv. Com., Crystal City (Mo.) and Hillsboro Sch. Dists; del. Midwest Model UN; lay and youth leader Meth. Ch., adminstrv. council Hillsboro Meth. Ch. Recipient Friend of Edn. awards, Hillsboro R-3 Dist., Jefferson County Tchrs., 1984. Mem. Nat. Assn. Alcoholism Counselors, Mo. Assn. Alcoholism Counselors, Jefferson County Guidance and Counselors Assn., Jefferson County Community Services Forum, Mo. Assn. Alcohol and Drug Abuse Programs, Mo. Coalition Community Health Ctrs., Phi Alpha Theta. Democrat. Home: PO Box 231 Hillsboro MO 63050 Office: PO Box 505 Festus MO 63028

HUSS, WILLIAM LEE, accountant; b. Kaukauna, Wis., May 18, 1956; s. Donald John and Elaine Mary (Vandenberg) H.; m. Beth Ellen Braun, Oct. 4, 1980 (div. Sept. 1984); m. Carol Ann Lindemann, Dec. 26, 1987. BBA, U. Wis., Oshkosh, 1978. CPA, Wis. Staff acct. Clifton, Gunderson & Co., Neenah, Wis., 1979-80; controller, sec.-treas. Chief Equiptment, Inc., Oshkosh, 1980-83; tax and systems mgr. Exptl. Aircraft Assn., Oshkosh, 1983—; acctg. prof. Marian Coll., Fond du Lac, Wis., 1986—; acctg. instr. Fox Valley Tech. Inst., Oshkosh, 1980—. Adv. editor book revs. McGraw Hill Book Co., 1983. Vol. Big Brother, 1976—; pres., bd. dirs. Big Brothers of Oshkosh, 1985—. Fellow Wis. Inst. CPA's; mem. Am. Inst. CPA's. Roman Catholic. Avocations: astronomy, reading, bicycling, racquetball, coin and book collecting. Home: 575 W Snell Rd Oshkosh WI 54901 Office: Exptl Aircraft Assn Wittman Airfield Oshkosh WI 54901-3086

HUSSEIN, RAFAAT MAHMOUD, engineering educator; b. Cairo, June 12, 1950; came to U.S., 1983; s. Mahmoud Morsi Hussein and Saadia (Wahba) Amin; m. Paige Carpenter, Aug. 15, 1983; 1 child, Mohamed Ben-Abdu Allah Rafaat. BCE, El-Azhar U., Cairo, 1974; M of Bldg. Engring., Concordia U., Montreal, Can., 1978, PhD in Mechanics of Solids and Structures, 1980. Lectr. El-Azhar U., 1974-76; research assoc. Concordia U., 1976-80; structural specialist Lavalin Cons., Inc., Montreal, 1980-83; asst. prof. engring. N.J. Inst. Tech., Newark, 1983-85, Evansville (Ind.) U., 1985—. Author: Composite Structures, 1986, (with others) Handbook of Civil Engring, 1986; contbr. articles to profl. jours. Mem. ASCE (assoc., com. on wood 1984—, com. cold-formed mems.), Am. Acad. Mechanics, Am. Concrete Inst. (com. on slabs). Home: PO Box 14004 Evansville IN 47714-6004 Office: U Evansville 1800 Lincoln Ave Evansville IN 47714

HUSSEY, LAWRENCE ELLIOTT, sales executive; b. Mich. City, July 16, 1956; s. Austin Elliott and Jennie Ann (Magro) H.; m. Celeste Marie Timm, Jan. 5, 1985; 1 child, Nicholas Lawrence. BS, Purdue U., 1980. Customer service rep. Jet Fabricators, Inc., Michigan City, 1974-78, mgr. product control, 1978-82, sales mgr., 1982-83, v.p. sales, 1983-87, exec. v.p., 1987—, also bd. dirs. Bd. dirs. United Way of Michigan City/Michiana, 1982-83, mem. budget and allocation com., 1980—; bd. dirs. YMCA Michigan City, 1983-86; pres. Sacred Heart Ch. Parish Council, Michigan City, 1985-86. Mem. Am. Soc. Quality Control, LaPorte County Personnel Assn. Roman Catholic. Lodge: Kiwanis. Avocations: reading, golf, gardening. Home: 914 Roeske Trail Michigan City IN 46360 Office: Jet Fabricators Inc Hwy 212 Michigan City IN 46360

HUSTAD, THOMAS PEGG, marketing educator; b. Mpls., June 15, 1945; s. Thomas Earl Pegg and John Charles and Dorothy Helen (Anderson) H.; B.S. in Elec. Engring., Purdue U., 1967, M.S. in Indsl. Mgmt., 1969, Ph.D. in Mktg., 1973; m. Sherry Ann Thomas, Jan. 30, 1971; children—Kathleen, John. Vis. asst. prof. Purdue U., West Lafayette, Ind., 1971-72; asst. prof. Faculty of Adminstrv. Studies, York U., Toronto, 1972-74, assoc. prof., 1974-76, asso. prof., mktg. area coordinator, 1976-77; asso. prof. mktg. Sch. Bus., Ind. U., Bloomington-Indpls., 1977-82, prof., 1982—, chmn. M.B.A. program, 1983-85 , program chmn. Ind. U. Ann. Bus. Conf., 1983, 84, cofounder Ind. U. Exec. Forum; exec. dir. Ind. U. Internat. Bus. Forum, 1981-85;cons. N. Am. corps., Can. Govt.; condr. seminars for U.S., Can. and Venezuelan industry. Mem. Am. Mktg. Assn. (award 1973), Product Devel. and Mgmt. Assn. (program chmn. 3d ann. conf., v.p. confs. 1979, pres. elect 1980, pres. 1981, dir. 1982-83, chmn. publ. com. 1982-84, sec./treas. 1984—), Ancient and Hon. Arty. Co. Mass., Internat. Assn. Jazz Record Collectors, Phi Eta Sigma, Tau Beta Pi, Beta Gamma Sigma. Author: Approaches to the Teaching of Product Development and Management, 1977; editor: International Competition: The American Challenge, 1986; founder, editor: Jour. Product Innovation Mgmt.; contbr. articles to books and profl. jours. Home: 8931 Butternut Ct Indianapolis IN 46260 Office: Sch Business Indiana U Bloomington IN 47405

HUSTEAD, RUSSELL MARTIN, gynecologist/obstetrician; b. New Haven, Conn., Mar. 9, 1953; s. Robert Frank and Betty Jo (Cope) H.; m. Susan Schmidt; children: Hunter, Taylor. Student, Yale U., 1971-73; BSEE with highest distinction, U. Kans., Lawrence, 1975; MD, U. Kans., Kansas City, 1978. Diplomate Am. Bd. Ob-Gyn. Intern, then resident in ob-gyn Mayo Clinic, Rochester, Minn., 1978-82; practice medicine specializing in ob-gyn Kansas City, Mo., 1982—. Fellow Am. Coll. Ob-Gyn (jr.), Mo. Pilot's Assn. Republican. Methodist. Avocations: piloting, hunting, amateur radio, building and flying radio-controlled aircraft. Home: 10809 Horton Overland Park KS 66211 Office: 1010 Carondelet #328 Kansas City MO 64114

HUSTED, STEWART WINTHROP, business educator; b. Roanoke, Va., Oct. 22, 1946; s. John Edwin and Katheryn Faye (Stewart) H.; m. Kathleen Lixey, June 22, 1974; children: Ryan Winthrop, Evan William. BS, Va. Poly. Inst. & State U., 1968; MEd, U. Ga., 1972; PhD, Mich. State U., 1977. Trainee Macy's Dept. Stores, Atlanta, 1967, Heironomus Dept. Stores, Roanoke, Va., 1967; mktg. edn. coordinator and tchr. Towers High Sch., Decatur, Ga., 1972-75; vocat. counselor Lansing (Mich.) Community Coll., 1975-76; prof. bus. Ind. State U., Terre Haute, 1976—; reviewer McGraw-Hill, N.Y.C., 1983—. Author: (with Sam Certo, Max Douglas) Business, 1st ed., 1984, 2d ed. 1987, (with Ralph Mason, Pat Rath) Marketing Practices and Principles, 4th ed., 1986, (with others) Cooperative Occupational Education, 5th ed., 1988; contbr. articles to profl. jours. Rep. to Interstate Distributive Edn. Curriculum Consortium, Ind. Dept. Pub. Instrn., 1978-85, also trustee. Bd. dirs., treas. Big Bros./Big Sisters, 1977-80. Served to lt. col. USAR, 1968—. Named to Mktg. Edn. Hall of Fame, 1974; U.S. Office Edn. EPDA Nat. fellow, 1975-76. Mem. Am. Vocat. Assn., Am. Soc. Tng. and Devel., Am. Mktg. Assn., Mktg. Edn. Assn., Delta Pi Epsilon, Beta Gamma Sigma, Epsilon Delta Epsilon (Research award 1978). Methodist.

HUSTON, JONATHAN BOYD, computer programmer, writer; b. Cleve., June 12, 1964; s. Dewey Orvin and Constance May (Shipp) H.; m. Karen Jean Purnhagen, Aug. 22, 1985; 1 child, Alicia May. BS in Systems Analysis, U. Dayton, 1986. Computer cons. engring. dept. U. Dayton, Ohio, 1983, TDM, Gen. Electric, Evendale, Ohio, 1984; computer cons. ASD/ENSSS, Wright Patterson AFB, Fairborn, Ohio, 1985-87; computer analyst Data Processing Dept. Profl. Mktg. Communications Inc., Dayton, 1987—. Sec.-treas. Sci. Fiction Fans Am., Dayton, 1983. Presdl. scholar U. Dayton, 1982. Mem. Datari Users Group (v.p. 1984-86), ST Users Group (v.p. 1986). Republican. Pentecostal Protestant. Home: 6320 Keeler St Huber Heights OH 45424-1714

HUTCH, THOMAS BRENT, SR., biologist, consultant; b. Jackson, Tenn., Feb. 10, 1953; s. A. James and Anna Mae (Peoples) H.; m. Debra Jo-Ed Maynard, Dec. 17, 1978; 1 child, Thomas Brent Jr. Student, Fisk U., 1971-72; BS in Biology, Morehouse Coll., 1977. Dir. tech. staff biology dept. Morehouse Coll., Atlanta, 1977-80; with biomed. research dept. Abbott

Labs., Abbott Park, Ill., 1981—. Treas., bd. dirs. Manchester Knoll Coop., North Chicago, Ill., 1984—; mem. Rep. Nat. Com., Washington, 1987—;. Mem. Am. Chem. Soc., Am. Soc. Microbiology, Am. Soc. Medicinal Chemistry, Midwest Assn. Housing Coops., Nat. Geog. Soc., Am. Film Inst., Chgo. Council Fgn. Relations, Smithsonian Inst., Art Inst. Chicago. Roman Catholic. Avocations: tennis, golf, horseback riding. Office: Abbott Labs D-47T AP9A Abbott Park IL 60064

HUTCHENS, GALE DEAN, excavating company owner, farm owner; b. Assumption, Ill., Oct. 30, 1933; d. Jacob Ellis and Beulah Mamie (Finks) H.; m. Nelda Lorene Epperson, June 17, 1951; children: Diane Elaine Hutchens Jenkins, Gary Lynn. Grad. high sch., Assumption, Ill. Pres. Freedom Ready Mix, Decatur, Ill., 1981-84, Cloud 9 Ultralights, Decatur, 1982-86; pres., owner Gale D. Hutchens Excavating, Decatur. Elder, Sunday Sch. supt. Elm Grove Ch. of God, Decatur. Mem. Nat. Fedn. Ind. Bus. Home and Office: 935 E Tohill Rd Decatur IL 62521

HUTCHENS, ROBERT DOUGLAS, physical chemist, consultant; b. Dayton, Ohio, Dec. 11, 1946; s. David Dale and Mary Frances H.; m. Joyce Elaine Herbst, Oct. 27, 1973; children—Kenneth James, Brian Douglas. Student, Washington & Lee U., 1964-66; B.S. in Chemistry, U. Mich., 1968; Ph.D., U. Pitts., 1972. Engr., Air Force Materials Lab., Wright-Patterson AFB, Ohio, 1972-79; mgr. materials devel. Raytheon Co., Waltham, Mass., 1979-82; prin. sr. engr. Universal Tech. Corp., Dayton, Ohio, 1982-84; with Gen. Research Corp., Dayton, 1984-85 ; mgr. cons. services, Solion Systems, Dayton, 1985—. cons. electronics. Served to 1st lt. USAF, 1972-75. Named Engr. of Year, Air Force Materials Lab., 1979; NASA fellow, 1969, Andrew Mellon fellow, 1971. Mem. Sigma Xi. Presbyterian. Contbr. articles to profl. jours. Home: 8844 Rooks Mill Ln Centerville OH 45459 Office: 1271 N Fairfield Rd Dayton OH 45432

HUTCHESON, SUSANNA KAYE, insurance executive, business writer; b. ElDorado, Kans., Jan. 8, 1944; d. Harold G. and E. Irene (Wedding) H.; student Butler County Community Coll., 1970-71, Kans. U., 1966-67. Soc. writer Joplin (Mo.) Globe, 1973; writer Antioch (Calif.) Daily Ledger, 1974; advt. mgr. Mulvane (Kans.) News, 1976—, columnist Points to Ponder, 1976—; freelance writer, Speciality Salesman Mag., Am. Salesman, Salesman's Opportunity, others, 1967—; pres. SKAY Features, 1977—, Skay Enterprises, Inc., 1977—; owner Hutcheson Ins. Agy., 1983—; gen. agt. Howard Life Ins. Co., Lakewood, Colo.; editor Altoona (Kans.) Tribune, 1977—; owner Park City (Kans.) Press, 1977—; ins. agt. Bankers Life & Casualty Co., Chgo., 1979—. Mem. Bus. and Profl. Women, Authors Guild, Author League Am., Assoc. Bus. Writers Am., Nat. Assn. Exec. Women, Women in Energy. Republican.

HUTCHINS, DONALD BYRON, tire company executive; b. Toledo, July 27, 1948; s. Donald Byron and Camilla Jane (Omey) H.; m. Jill Janice Rood, Aug. 23, 1969; children—Jennifer, Samantha. B.A., U. Mich., 1970, M.B.A., 1973. C.P.A., Mich., Ohio. Sr. auditor Coopers & Lybrand, Detroit, 1974-76, audit supr., 1976-78, audit mgr., 1978-81, lead mgr. Emerging Bus. Sect., 1978-81; mgr. fin. reporting Firestone Tire & Rubber Co., Akron, Ohio, 1981-83, asst. controller, 1983—. Membership recruiter Jr. Achievement, Detroit, 1979. Mem. Nat. Assn. Accts. (dir. community affairs 1983-84), Am. Inst. C.P.A.s, Mich. Assn. C.P.A.s, Ohio Soc. C.P.A.s (mem. industry liaison com. 1982). Episcopalian. Club: University (Detroit). Contbr. internal pubs. Office: Firestone Tire & Rubber Co 1200 Fireston Pkwy Akron OH 44317

HUTCHINSON, DUANE DOUGLAS, storyteller, writer, clergyman; b. Elgin, Nebr., June 16, 1929; s. William Clyde and Eva Susan (Martin) H.; m. Marilyn Ann Burton, Sept. 3, 1950; children—Stephen Kent, James Wesley. B.A. in Edn., Kearney State Coll., 1953; Th.M., Perkins Sch. Theology, So. Meth. U., 1956; postgrad. U. Chgo., 1956-57; M.A. in English, U. Nebr., 1979. Ordained to ministry United Methodist Ch., 1954; cert. pub. sch. tchr., Nebr. Pastor, Chester and Hubbell, Nebr., 1957-61; teaching fellow Centennial Coll., U. Nebr., 1979-81; campus minister U. Nebr., 1961-79; travelling storyteller Nebr. Arts Council and Iowa Arts Council, 1979—; condr. writing and storytelling workshops. Author: Doc Graham: Sandhills Doctor, 1970; Exon: Biography of a Governor, 1973; Images of Mary, 1971; Savidge Brothers: Sandhills Aviators, 1982; Storytelling Tips: How to Love, Learn and Relate a Story, 1983, A Storyteller's Ghost Stories, 1987. County del. Democratic party; past pres. local chpt. UN Assn. Mem. Nat. Assn. Preservation and Perpetuation of Storytelling, Nebr. Library Assn., Nat. Council Tchrs. English. Home: 3445 Touzalin Ave Lincoln NE 68507

HUTCHINSON, FREDERICK EDWARD, organization executive; b. Atkinson, Maine, June 1, 1930; s. Malcolm Eugene and Gertrude (Sargeant) H.; m. Dione Kendall Williams, Sept. 6, 1952; children: Juliana, Karen. B.S., U. Maine, 1953, M.S., 1958; Ph.D., Pa. State U., 1966. Mem. faculty dept. plant and soil scis. U. Maine at Orono, 1953-72, prof. soil sci., 1967-72, chmn. dept., 1971-72, dean Coll. Life Scis. and Agr., dir. expt. sta., 1972-75, v.p. for research and pub. service, 1975-80, 81-82, acting v.p. acad. affairs, 1980-81; exec. dir. Bd. for Internat. Food and Agr. Devel., 1982-85; dir. Ohio Agr. Research and Devel. Ctr., 1985-86; v.p. for agrl. adminstrn. Ohio State U., Columbus, 1986—; mem. bd. govs. ICRISAT, Hydrebad, India, 1978-82, CIAT, Cali, Columbia, 1985—. Chmn. bldg. fund dr. U. Maine, 1973-75; mem. adv. bd. Maine Rural Environ. Conservation Program, 1974-78, commn. on missions N.W. United Meth. Ch., Columbus, 1986—; chmn. joint research com. AID, 1977-80. Served with AUS, 1948-49. Fellow Am. Inst. Chemists, AAAS, Soil Conservation Soc. Am.; mem. Am. Soc. Agronomy (Outstanding Tchr. award N.E. chpt. 1971); fellow Soil Conservation Soc.; mem. Soil Sci. Soc., Audubon Soc., Sigma Xi, Phi Kappa Phi, Alpha Zeta. Republican. Methodist (chmn. ch. bldg. com. 1967-73). Home: 541 Teteridge Rd Columbus OH 43214 Office: Ohio State U 100 Agrl Adminstrn Bldg 2120 Fyffe Rd Columbus OH 43210

HUTCHINSON, GRACE ANN, physical education instructor; b. Sandusky, Ohio, May 13, 1949; d. John Oscar and Martha Louise (Olcott) H. Student Hope Coll., 1967-68; B.S.E., No. Ill. U., 1972; postgrad. So. Ill. U., 1972-73, postgrad. Bowling Green U., 1978-80. Cert. tchr., Ohio. Program dir. Plymouth Shore, Lakeside, Ohio, 1968-72; grad. asst. Southern Ill. U., Carbondale, 1972; phys. edn. instr. Joliet Twp. Schs. (Ill.), 1973-76; phys. edn. instr. Norwalk City Schs. (Ohio), 1977—; coach, counselor Ohio Northern U. Volleyball Camp, Ada, 1982—; speaker at confs., symposium speaker 1983, 86. AA State All-Star Coach; Named Coach of All-Star Match Crestview Booster Club, Ashland, Ohio, 1983; named Coach of All-Star Match Ont. Booster Club, Mansfield, Ohio, 1983, Dist. 6AA Coach of Year, 1984, 86, AA Coach of Yr.-All-State Hon. Mention, 1983, 84, AA Coach of Yr. Ohio, 1986. Mem. NEA, Ohio Assn. Health Phys. Edn. Dance, Nat. Volleyball Coaches Assn., Ohio High Sch Volleyball Coaches Assn. (Dist. 6 rep. 1983-85, Dist. 6 pres. 1984-85, pres. 1987-88), Ohio Edn. Assn. (state assn. v.p. 1985-86). Republican. Office: Norwalk High Sch 80 E Main St Norwalk OH 44857

HUTCHISON, JOHN ALLAN, pharmacist; b. Davenport, Iowa, Aug. 24, 1944; s. Robert P. and Doris R. (Ruble) H.; m. Patricia Ann Willging, Mar. 1, 1969 (div. Jan. 1973); m. Jean Marie Foster, June 7, 1975; children: Jeffrey, Mark. BS in Pharmacy, Drake U., Des Moines, 1967. Lic. pharmacist, Ill., Iowa. Pharmacist Schlegel Drug, Davenport, Iowa, 1967-70; pharmacist, ptnr. Pharmacy Ctr., Mt. Carroll, Ill., 1970—; pharmicist, ptnr. Lanark (Ill.) Pharmacy, 1980—. Mem. Am. Pharm. Assn., Ill Pharmacists Assn., Am. Soc. Cons. Pharmacists, Northwest Ill. Pharmacists Assn. Republican. Avocations: boating, water skiing, snow skiing. Home: 501 S West St Mount Carroll IL 61053 Office: Pharmacy Ctr 101 W Market St Mount Carroll IL 61053

HUTCHISON, PETER MURRAY, social worker; b. Detroit, Aug. 30, 1951; s. Thomas Murray and Louise Mary (Whytock) H.; m. Gail Diane Larson, Apr. 1, 1977; 1 child, Thomas Murray II. BS, Mich. State U., 1973. Lic. social worker, Mich. Campcraft specialist Detroit Bd. Edn., 1969-72; juvenile caseworker Genesee County Probate Ct., Flint, Mich., 1973—; cons. State of Mich., Lansing, 1985. Pres. Flint Planned Parenthood, 1979; music, nominating, stewardship coms. First Congl. Ch., Grand Blanc, Mich., 1986. Mem. Juvenile Justice Assn. Mich. (bd. dirs. 1977-78, vice-chmn. 1978-79), Pipers and Pipe Band Soc. Ont., Greater Flint Hockey Assn. (coach). Avocations: golf, playing bagpipes. Home: 1041 Davenport Burton MI 48529 Office: Genesee County Probate Ct 919 Beach St Flint MI 48502

HUTCHISON, STANLEY PHILIP, insurance company executive, lawyer; b. Joliet, Ill., Nov. 22, 1923; s. Stuart Philip and Verna (Kinzer) H.; m. Helen Jane Rush, July 25, 1945; children: Norman, Elizabeth. B.S., Northwestern U., 1947; LL.B., Kent Coll. Law, 1951. Bar: Ill. 1951. Legal asst. Washington Nat. Ins. Co., Evanston, 1947-51; asst. counsel Washington Nat. Ins. Co., 1951-55, asst. gen. counsel, 1955-58, asso. gen. counsel, 1958-60, gen. counsel, 1960-63, v.p., gen. counsel, dir., 1963-66, exec. v.p., gen. counsel, dir., 1966-67, exec. v.p., gen. counsel, sec., dir., 1967-70, chmn. exec. com., 1970-73, vice chmn. bd., 1974-75, chmn. bd., chief exec. officer, 1976—; pres. Wash. Nat. Corp., 1970—, chief exec. officer, 1978—, chmn. bd., 1983—; dir. Washington Nat. Life Ins. Co. N.Y, United Presdl. Life Ins. Co., Ind. Mem. pres.'s council Nat. Coll. Edn., 1977—, adv. council Kellogg Grad. Sch. Mgmt. Northwestern U., 1981—; bd. dirs. Evanston Hosp. Corp., 1983—. Served to lt. (j.g.) USNR, 1942-46. Mem. Ill. C. of C., Evanston C. of C. (pres. 1973-74), ABA, Ill. Bar Assn., Assn. Life Ins. Counsel, Am. Council Life Ins., dir. (1977-81), Ill. Life Ins. Council (dir. 1978—, pres. 1983-85), Ins. Econs. Soc. Am. (dir. 1977-85, chmn. 1981-82), Health Ins. Assn. Am. (bd. dirs. 1984—, chmn. 1987—). Home: 830 Heather Ln Winnetka IL 60093 Office: Washington Nat Corp 1630 Chicago Ave Evanston IL 60201

HUTSON, ALAN ROBERT, apparel company executive; b. Boston, Apr. 16, 1945; m. Jane Palmour, Dec. 16, 1967; 1 child, Alan Jr. BBA, U. Fla., 1968; MBA, Harvard U., 1973. Nat. sales mgr. Work Wear Corp., Cleve., 1977-80, v.p. mktg. div., 1980-86; exec. v.p. U.S. ops. Work Wear Corp., Chagrin Falls, Ohio, 1986—. Served to 1st lt. U.S. Army, 1968-71. Republican. Episcopalian.

HUTSON, JEFFREY WOODWARD, lawyer; b. New London, Conn., July 19, 1941; s. John Jenkins and Kathryn Barbara (Himberg) H.; m. Susan Office, Nov. 25, 1967; children—Elizabeth Kathryn, Anne Louise. A.B., U. Mich., 1963, LL.B., 1966. Bar: Ohio 1966, Hawaii 1970. Assoc. Lane, Alton & Horst, Columbus, Ohio, 1966-74, ptnr., 1974—. Served to lt. comdr. USN, 1967-71. Fellow Am. Coll. Trial Lawyers; mem. ABA, Ohio Bar Assn. (past chmn. litigation sect.), Ohio Assn. Civil Trial Attys. (past pres.), Columbus Bar Assn., Internat. Assn. Ins. Counsel. Republican. Episcopalian. Clubs: Scioto Country, Athletic. Avocations: cycling; cross country skiing; reading; music. Office: Lane Alton & Horst 155 E Broad St Columbus OH 43215

HUTSON, JERRY WAYNE, food products executive, consultant; b. Sachse, Tex., Dec. 1, 1935; s. Lee Bryant and Cleo Estelle (Lane) H.; m. Nancy Dee Norton, Nov. 8, 1969. BA Tex. Christian U., Ft. Worth, 1958; M in Mgmt. Northwestern U., 1982; regional phys. dist. mgr. Kraft, Inc., Decatur, Ga., 1975-77; mgr. materials planning Kraft, Inc., Glenview, Ill., 1977-82, mgr. logistics analysis, 1982-83, v.p. distbn. ops., 1985—; dir. logistics-Europe Kraft, Inc., Lausanne, Switzerland, 1983-85. Mem. Council Logistics Mgmt., Grocer Mfrs. Assn. Republican. Disciple of Christ. Avocations: tennis, skiing.

HUTTER, JACK WILLIAM, podiatrist; b. Milw., Oct. 30, 1950; s. Herman Joseph Hutter and Virginia Fae (Fiebrantz) Stanaway; m. Jane Ellen Grossman, Sept. 15, 1973; children: Jennifer Jane, Justin William. BS cum laude, U. Wis., Milw., 1977; D Podiatry cum laude, Ill. Coll. Podiatric Medicine, 1981. Diplomate Am. Bd. Podiatric Surgery. Resident in podiatric surgery Lakeview Hosp., Wauwatosa, Wis., 1981-82, mem. podiatry staff, 1982—; pvt. practice podiatry Oconomowoc, Wis., 1982—; med. audit com., infection control com. Lakeview Hosp., Wauwatosa, Wis., 1983—, exec. com. podiatry staff, 1985-86, 86-87, surg. residency com. podiatry staff, 1986—. Fellow Am. Coll. Foot Surgeons; mem. Acad. Ambulatory Foot Surgeons, Am. Podiatry Assn., Wis. Soc. Podiatric Medicine, Ill. Coll. Podiatric Medicine Alumni Assn. (Scholarship award 1979-80, 80-81), U. Wis.-Milw. Alumni Assn. (life). Roman Catholic. Avocations: art, music, golf, tennis. Home: 613 Washington St Oconomowoc WI 53066 Office: 422 Summit Ave Oconomowoc WI 53066

HUTTON, BEN OSCAR, university program director, educator; b. Cassville, Mo., Dec. 17, 1932; s. Oscar B. and Ruth C. (Dunn) H. m. Sue Easley, Feb. 20, 1955; children: Jeff, Steve. BS, SW Mo. State U., 1958; MEd, Drury Coll., 1961; EdD, U. Ark., 1968. Cert. therapist. Prof. psychology and edn. Southeast Mo. State U., Cape Girardeau, 1967-74; prof. counseling psychology U. So. Miss., Hattiesburg, 1974-80; prof., chmn. counseling and human devel. Walsh Coll., Canton, Ohio, 1982—; dir. grad. studies Walsh Coll., Canton, 1982—; VA counselor, SE Mo. State U., Cape Girardeau, 1968-74; vis. prof. Pittsburg (Kans.) State U., 1981; practicum supr. Inst. Reality Therapy, Los Angeles, 1983, faculty, 1985. Editor Readings and Case Studies in Reality Therapy, 1985; contbr. articles to profl. jours. Served with USN, 1951-55, Korea. Mem. Am. Psychol. Assn., Am. Assn. for Counseling and Devel., Am. Assn. for Marriage and Family (clin.), Ohio Assn. for Counseling and Devel. Avocations: reading, travel. Home: 861A 44th St NW Canton OH 44709 Office: Walsh Coll 2020 Easton St NW Canton OH 44720

HUTTON, EDWARD LUKE, chemical company executive; b. Bedford, Ind., May 5, 1919; s. Fred and Margaret (Drehobl) H.; m. Kathryn Jane Alexander; children—Edward Alexander, Thomas Charles, Jane Clarke. B.S. with distinction, Ind. U., 1940, M.S. with distinction, 1941. Dep. dir. Joint Export Import Agy. (USUK), Berlin, Fed. Republic Germany, 1946-48; v.p. World Commerce Corp., 1948-51; asst. v.p. W.R. Grace & Co., 1951-53, cons., 1960-65, exec. v.p., gen. mgr. Dubois Chems. div., 1965-66, group exec. Specialty Products Group and v.p., 1966-68, exec. v.p., 1968-71; cons. internat. trade and fin. 1953-58; fin. v.p., exec. v.p. Ward Industries, 1958-59; pres., chief exec. officer Chemed Corp., Cincinnati, 1971—, dir.; chmn. Omnicare, Inc., Cincinnati, 1981—; dir. Omnicare, Inc.; chmn., dir. Roto-Rooter, Inc., 1984—; dir. DuBois Germany, Am. States Ins. Co. Co-chmn. Pres.'s Pvt. Sector Survey on Cost Control, exec. com., subcom. Recipient Disting. Alumni Service award Ind. U., 1987. Mem. Internat. Platform Assn., Dirs.' Table, AAUP (governing bd. dirs. 1958—), Newcomen Soc. Clubs: Downtown Assn., Econs., Princeton, University (N.Y.C.), Queen City, Bankers (Cin.), Cincinnati. Home: 6680 Miralake Dr Cincinnati OH 45243 Office: Chemed Corp 1200 DuBois Tower Cincinnati OH 45202

HUTTON, JOHN JAMES, medical researcher, medical educator; b. Ashland, Ky., July 24, 1936; s. John James and Alice (Virgin) H.; m. Mary Labach, June 13, 1964; children: Becky, John, Elizabeth. AB, Harvard U., 1958, MD, 1964. Diplomate Am. Bd. Internal Medicine. Sect. chief Roche Inst., Nutley, N.J., 1968-71; prof. medicine U. Ky., Lexington, 1971-79, U. Tex., San Antonio, 1980-84; prof. pediatrics U. Cin., 1984-87, dean Coll. Medicine, 1987—. Editor Internal Medicine, 1983; contbr. articles to profl. jours. Mem. Am. Soc. Hematology, Assn. Am. Physicians, Am. Soc. Clin. Investigation, NIH (biochemistry study sect.). Office: U Cin ML #555 MSB E-251 Cincinnati OH 45267

HUTTON-SEREDA, SHERYL LOUISE, association official; b. Cleve., Dec. 3, 1946; d. Murray Eugene and Marion Louise Garnett. BS in Biochemistry and Nutrients, U. Nebr., 1970. Assoc. producer Sta. WKYC-TV, NBC, Cleve., 1971-78; sales rep. Chase Bag Co., Chagrin Falls, Ohio, 1978-79; pub. relations dir. City of Cleveland Heights (Ohio), 1979-83; dir. communications Greater Cleve. Hosp. Assn., 1983—. Mem. spl. edn. adv. council Shaker Heights (Ohio) Bd. Edn.; bd. dirs. Pre-Term Clinic, The Art Studio for Physically and mentally handicapped, Friends of Shaker Square. Recipient Gavel award ABA, 1976, CINE award Council Internat. Nontheatrical Events, 1976, award of appreciation Cleve. Home and Flower Show, 1981, 3M Corp. Innovators award, 1986, Award for Mgmt. Innovation, Found. of Am. Coll. Healthcare Execs. Mem. Pub. Relations Soc. Am., Am. Coll. Healthcare Mktg. Home: 2671 Haddam Rd Shaker Heights OH 44120

HUTZELL, ROBERT RAYMOND, clinical psychologist; b. Des Moines, Dec. 6, 1948; s. Robert Roy and Dorothy Mae (Oldham) H.; m. Vicki Lynn Shinn, Aug. 31, 1969; children: Daisy Lynn, Angela Kathreen. BS with honors and distinction, U. Iowa, 1971; MS, Fla. State U., 1973, PhD, 1975. Trainee, intern Southeastern U.S. VA, 1972-75; clin. psychologist VA, Biloxi, Miss., 1975-76, Knoxville, Iowa, 1976—, dir. Behavioral Health Clinic; dir. psychol. services Mater Clinic, Knoxville, 1983—; adj. faculty U. Iowa, Iowa City, 1978-83; conducts profl. tng. workshops. Mem. editorial adv. bd. The Hospice Jour.; author various books, newspaper column; contbr. articles to profl. jours. and chpts. to books. Recipient Performance award VA, 1978, 81-86. Mem. Am. Psychol. Assn. (Psychologists in Pub. Service cert. of recognition 1983), Midwestern Psychol. Assn., Southeastern Psychol. Assn., Iowa Psychol. Assn. (editor newsletter 1978-86, pres.-elect 1987, Merit award 1986), Nat. Orgn. VA Psychologists (newsletter editor 1984—, trustee 1987—, cert. of recognition 1985), Inst. Logotherapy (diplomate; regional dir. 1984—, Iowa chpt. pres. 1983-87), Iowa Nut Tree Growers Assn. Methodist. Home: Drawer 112 Knoxville IA 50138 Office: VA Med Center Knoxville IA 50138

HYATT, JOEL Z., lawyer, management services company executive; b. Cleve., May 6, 1950; s. David and Anna (B.) Zylberberg; m. Susan Metzenbaum, Aug. 24, 1975; children: Jared Z., Zachary Robert. B.A., Dartmouth Coll., 1972; J.D., Yale U., 1975. Founder, sr. ptnr. Hyatt Legal Services, Kansas City, Mo.; pres., chief exec. officer Block Mgmt. Co., Kansas City, Mo. Bd. fellows Brandeis U.; asst. treas. Democratic Nat. Com., 1981-83; bd. dirs. Ctr. for a New Democracy; founding mem. U.S. Senate Democratic Leadership Circle; mem. nat. young leadership cabinet United Jewish Appeal; mem. nat. exec. com. Am. Jewish Congress. Mem. Young Pres.'s Orgn. Office: Hyatt Legal Services 4410 Main St Kansas City MO 64111

HYDE, HENRY JOHN, congressman; b. Chgo., Apr. 18, 1924; s. Henry Clay and Monica (Kelly) H.; m. Jeanne Simpson, Nov. 8, 1947; children: Henry J., Robert, Laura, Anthony. Student, Duke U., 1943-44; B.S., Georgetown U., 1946; J.D., Loyola U., Chgo., 1949. Bar: Ill. Mem. Ill. Gen. Assembly, 1967-74, 97th-99th congresses from 6th Ill. Dist. Served with USN, 1944-46. Mem. Chgo. Bar Assn. Republican. Roman Catholic. Home: 120 E George St Bensenville IL 60106 Office: 2104 Rayburn House Office Bldg Washington DC 20515

HYDE, WILLIAM KENT, lawyer; b. Aberdeen, S.D., Feb. 5, 1955; s. Charles Williams and Jessie Ellen (Strader) H. BA, Northwestern U., 1977, MA, 1979; JD, U. S.D., 1983. Bar: S.D. 1983. Law clk. to presiding justice S.D. Supreme Ct., Pierre, 1983-84; sole practice Aberdeen, 1984—. Editor: (poetry) Eighty Times Around the Sun, 1986. Chmn. S.D. Capital of the Age of Enlightenment, Aberdeen, 1981—. Recipient First Place award S.D. State Poetry Soc. Contest, Sioux Falls, 1984, First Place award Christmas Story Contest, Aberdeen Am. News, 1985. Mem. S.D. Bar Assn. Club: Fireside Poetry (Aberdeen). Lodge: Kiwanis. Avocations: teacher transcendental meditation, writing, bicycling, lecturing. Home: 1523 Marsie Circle Aberdeen SD 57401 Office: Hyde Law Office 321 Citizens Bldg Aberdeen SD 57401

HYDEN, ELAINE, auditor; b. Herrin, Ill., Jan. 10, 1949; d. Luther H. and Dorothy (Roberts) H.; m. Thomas J. Ziglinski. BS in Journalism, So. Ill. U., Carbondale, 1971; BS in Acctg., So. Ill. U., 1980. CPA, Ill.; cert. internal auditor. Cost acct. So. Ill. U., 1972-78, internal auditor, 1980-84, internal audit mgr., 1984-85; exec. dir. audits So. Ill. U., Carbondale, Springfield and Edwardsville, 1985—; bd. dirs. SIU Credit Union, Carbondale, 1984—. Bd. dirs. Carbondale Women's Ctr., 1982-83. Named one of Outstanding Young Women of Am., 1984. Mem. Am. Inst. CPA's, Ill. CPA Soc., Inst. Internal Auditors (cert. of excellence 1983). Avocation: genealogy. Home: 415 Elles Ave Carterville IL 62918 Office: So Ill U Internal Audit Office 111 Greek Row Carbondale IL 62901

HYDEN, HOWARD EVERT, computer company marketing executive; b. Chgo., June 27, 1941; s. Hans Oscar and Edythe Dorothy (Kallberg) H.; m. Margaret Malloy, Feb. 17, 1972 (div. Feb. 1974); m. Dorothy Louise Hyden, July 17, 1976; children: Shannon Michele Daley, Kent Stewart, Tiffany Nichole. Student, U. Ill.; MBA, Pepperdine U., 1980. Region mgr. Control Data Corp., Irvine, Calif., 1979-81; nat. sales exec. Control Data Corp., Mpls., 1981-82, gen. mgr. div. govt. ednl. services, 1982-83, academic edn. mktg. exec., 1983-84, corp. mktg. exec., 1984—. Served with USN, 1962-66. Republican. Lutheran. Home: 7415 Hyde Park Dr Edina MN 55435 Office: Control Data Corp 8100 34th Ave S Minneapolis MN 55440

HYNDMAN, ROBERT C., chemical company executive. BSChe Washington U., 1950, MBA Northwestern U., 1956. Field salesman gen. chems. Dow Chem. Co., 1950-54; with Morton Chem. Co., 1954-79, field salesman, 1954-56, mgr. sales eastern dist., 1956-60, mgr. sales inorganic chems., 1960-64, mgr. packaging products, 1964-68, v.p. 1968-72, exec. v.p., gen. mgr., 1972-73, pres., 1973-79; with Morton Salt Co., 1979-81; pres. Morton Norwich, 1981-82; exec. v.p. Morton Thiokol, Inc., Chgo., 1982-84; pres., chief operating officer, 1984—, also dir. Office: Morton Thiokol Inc 110 N Wacker Dr Chicago IL 60606 *

HYRE, JAMES G., school superintendent; b. Burnsville, W.Va., Mar. 15, 1941; s. Dixie Andrew and Elizabeth M. (Marple) H.; m. Barbara Ann Zinszer, Sept. 19, 1964; children: Pamela, James Jr. BS, Ohio State U., 1963; MEd, Westminster Coll., New Wilmington, Pa., 1967; EdD, U. Akron, Ohio, 1975. From tchr. to asst. prin. Brookfield (Ohio) Local Sch., 1965-69; asst. prin. Stow (Ohio) City Schs., 1969-71; jr. high sch. prin. Ravenna (Ohio) City Schs., 1971-73; high sch. prin., personnel dir. Warren (Ohio) City Schs., 1975-77; supt. Howland Local Schs., Warren, 1977-79, Canton (Ohio) City Schs., 1979-82, Columbus (Ohio) City Schs., 1982—. Mem. adv. bd. United Negro Coll. Fund, Columbus, 1982—; trustee Columbus Conv. Bur., 1982—, Grant Med. Ctr., Columbus, 1986, Columbus Zoo, 1986, Ctr. of Si. and Industry, 1986; bd. dirs. Pvt. Industry Council, Columbus, 1986, Boy Scouts Am., Columbus, 1986. Named Supt. of Yr., Ohio Sch. Counselors Assn., 1986. Mem. Am. Assn. Sch. Adminstrs., Buckeye Assn. Sch. Adminstrs. (Leadership award 1986), Ohio Sch. Bds. Assn., Phi Delta Kappa. Presbyterian. Club: Capital (Columbus). Avocation: golf. Office: Columbus City Sch Dist Office of the Superintendent 270 E State St Columbus OH 43215

HYSELL, NILES ANDREW, JR., marketing executive; b. Mpls., Dec. 10, 1946; s. Niles Andrew Sr. and Naomi Victoria (Lee) H.; m. Jennifer Zehr, June 2, 1983; children: Andrew, Matthew. BA, St. Olaf Coll., 1968. Territory mgr. Cargill, Inc., Concord, N.H., 1972-73; product mgr. Cargill, Inc., Lansing, N.Y., 1973-75, sales mgr., 1975-79; regional mgr. Cargill, Inc., Cin., 1980-84; mktg. mgr. Cargill, Inc., Mpls., 1984—; instr. Jaycees Project Bus., Mpls., 1984-85; cons. Met. Econ. Devel. assn., Mpls., 1984—, Mgmt. Assistance Project, Mpls., 1984—, Govs. STEP Program, St. Paul, 1985. Active Campaign Pvt. Colls., St. Paul, 1985-86; chmn. Cargill div. United Way, Mpls., 1985; bd. dirs. Sylman Chamber Ensemble, 1985. Served to sgt. U.S. Army, 1969-72. Mem. Am. Mktg. Assn., Nat. Account Mktg. Assn., Ingredient Fodd Technologists Assn., Water Quality Assn., Salt Inst. Republican. Lutheran. Avocations: tennis, skiing, piloting, jogging. Home: 4811 Spring Circle Minnetonka MN 55345 Office: Cargill Co PO 5621 Minneapolis MN 55440

HYSLOP, DAVID JOHNSON, arts administrator; b. Schenectady, June 27, 1942; s. Moses McDickens and Annie (Johnson) H.; m. Sandra Wheeler, June 25, 1978; children—Kristopher Jae, Alexander; stepchildren—Marc Langhammer, Monica Langhammer. B.S. in Music Edn, Ithaca Coll., 1965. Elem. sch. vocal music supr. Elmira Heights, N.Y., 1965-66; mgr. Elmira Symphony Choral Soc., 1966; asst. mng. dir. Minn. Orch., Mpls., 1966-72; gen. mgr. Oreg. Symphony Orch., Portland, 1972-78; exec. dir. St. Louis Symphony Soc., 1978—. Trustee Nat. Com. on Symphony Orch. Support; bd. dirs. St. Louis Conservatory and Schs. for Arts, Portland State U., Chamber Music N.W.; lobbyist Com. for Arts in Mo. Martha Baird Rockefeller grantee, 1966. Mem. Am. Symphony Orch. League. Clubs: Mo. Athletic (St. Louis), Univ. (St. Louis). Home: 7131 Pershing Saint Louis MO 63130 Office: Saint Louis Symphony Orch 718 N Grand St Saint Louis MO 63103

HYZER, DAVID WILLIAM, architect, civil engineer; b. Janesville, Wis., Mar. 10, 1950; s. William Gordon and Mary Ann (Bandt) H.; m. Marcia Phillipps, Aug. 10, 1975; 1 child, Joel David. BCE, U. Wis., 1975. Registered profl. engr., Wis.; registered architect, Wis. Design engr. Gen. Engring., Portage, Wis., 1976-81; prin. engr. Strang Ptnrs., Madison, Wis., 1981—, also b. dirs. Commr. Middleton (Wis.) Pub. Works, 1985—, Water Utility Bd., Middleton, 1985—, Sewer Utility Bd., Middleton, 1985—, Wis. Structural Review Bd., Madison, 1985. Mem. AIA, Wis. Soc. Architects. Lodge: Rotary (bd. dirs. Middleton chpt. 1984-86). Home: 7103 Parkshore Ct Middleton WI 53562 Office: Strang Ptnrs Inc 3800 Regent St Madison WI 53705

IACCHEO, ARMAND RICHARD, meteorology executive, consultant; b. N.Y.C., Apr. 24, 1923; s. Armand and Anne Aurora (DiPietro) I.; m. Carole Armanda Soi, Mar. 30, 1946; children—Sandra Ann Iaccheo Lord, Karen E. Iaccheo Joest. Student, U. Calif.-Berkeley, 1941-42; degree in meteorology USAAF-TTC, 1943 B.S. in Natural Sci., Washington U., St. Louis, 1952. Cert. cons. meteorologist. Spl. Services meteorologist U.S. Weather Bur., 1949-52; research meteorologist, 1947-48; v.p. Weather Corp. Am., 1952-68, v.p., gen. mgr., St. Louis, 1970-84, pres. 1985—; dir. environ. info. services Travelers Research Ctr., Hartford, Conn., 1969; cons. Served to capt. USAAF, 1942-46; ETO. Mem. Am. Meteorol. Soc., Nat. Council Indsl. Meteorologists (pres.-elect), Mo. Council Meteorol. Edn. and Research, Am. Meteorol. Soc. (chmn. St. Louis chpt. 1954, 61, Seal of Approval for radio weather broadcasting), Washington U. Alumni Assn. Office: Weather Corp of America 5 American Industrial Dr Saint Louis MO 63043

IACOBELLI, JOHN LOUIS, economist; b. Cleve., Dec. 24, 1931; s. Joseph and Theresa (Caporaso) I.; m. Eleanor M. Mandala, Sept. 3, 1956; children: Joseph, Andrew, Christopher. BS, Kent State U., 1955, MA, 1965; PhD, U. Tex., 1969. Sr. sales rep., ter. mgr. NCR, Cleve., 1957-64; asst. prof. labor and indsl. relations Cleve. State U., 1968-71, assoc. prof. mgmt. and labor, 1971-76; prof. econs. Wright State U., 1976-78, chmn. dept., 1976-78; pres. Delphi Assocs., Inc., Cleve., 1972-75; economist, spl. rep. Columbus Mut. Life Ins. Co., 1980-86; v.p. Advance Planning Concepts, Inc., 1983-86; registered rep. Integrated Resources Equity Corp., 1983-85; registered rep., prin. Lowry Fin. Services Corp., 1985—; economist, pres. I.A. Bell Fin. and Econ. Planning, Inc., 1986—; registered investment advisor, 1986; gen. agt. various life ins. cos., 1986; cons. in field. Contbr. articles to profl. jours. Served with U.S. Army, 1955-57. U.S. Dept. Labor grantee, 1967-68, HUD and Nat. League of Cities grantee, 1973-74. Mem. Am. Econ. Assn., Indsl. Relations Research Assn., Acad. Mgmt., Internat. Assn. Fin. Planners, Nat. Assn Securities Dealers (mem., broker 1985—), Christian Family Movement, Delta Sigma Pi. Home: 19953 Idlewood Trail Strongsville OH 44136 Office: 11925 Pearl #103 Cleveland OH 44136-3343

IACOBELLI, MARK ANTHONY, dentist; b. Cleve., Aug. 27, 1957; s. Anthony Peter and Irene Margaret (Pordash) I.; m. Lauren Patricia Slapak, May 23, 1981. BS, Case Western Res., 1979, DDS, 1982. Dentist, co-owner Iacobelli & Iffland, Canton, Ohio, 1982-85; gen. practice dentistry Parma, Ohio, 1985—. Co-chmn. Padua Franciscan Devel. Drive, Parma, 1986. Named one of Outstanding Young Men Am., 1982. Mem. ADA, Ohio Dental Assn., Cleve. Dental Assn., Am. Assn. Functional Orthodontics. (Achievement award 1982), Acad. Gen. Dentistry. Republican. Roman Catholic. Avocations: boating, fishing, skiing, golf. Home: 6552 Queens Way Brecksville OH 44141 Office: 6681 Ridge Rd Suite 405 Parma OH 44129

IACOCCA, LIDO ANTHONY (LEE IACOCCA), automotive manufacturing executive; b. Allentown, Pa., Oct. 15, 1924; s. Nicola and Antoinette (Perrotto) I.; m. Mary McCleary, Sept. 29, 1956 (dec.); children—Kathryn Lisa, Lia Antoinette. BS, Lehigh U., 1945; ME, Princeton U., 1946. With Ford Motor Co., Dearborn, Mich., 1946-78; successively mem. field sales staff, various merchandising and tng. activities, asst. dirs. sales mgr. Ford Motor Co., Phila.; dist. sales mgr. Ford Motor Co., Washington, 1946-56; truck mktg. mgr. div. office Ford Motor Co., 1956-57, car mktg. mgr., 1957-60, vehicle market mgr., 1960, v.p.; gen. mgr. Ford Motor Co. (Ford div.), 1960-65, v.p. car and truck group, 1965-69, exec. v.p. of co., 1967-69, pres. of co., 1970-78; also pres. Ford Motor Co. (Ford N.Am. automobile ops.); pres., chief operating officer Chrysler Corp., Highland Park, Mich., 1978-79, chmn. bd., chief exec. officer, 1979—. Past chmn. Statue of Liberty-Ellis Island Centennial Commn. Wallace Meml. fellow Princeton U. Mem. Tau Beta Pi. Club: Detroit Athletic. Office: Chrysler Corp 12000 Chrysler Dr Highland Park MI 48288

IAGULLI, GERALD LEE, data porcessing manager; b. Toledo, Dec. 5, 1948; S. Donald Robert and Caroline Jean (Maedel) I.; m. Nancy Helen Nunemaker, Mar. 20, 1970; children: Carly Ann, Nicholas Dominic. AA, U. Toledo, 1969, BBA, 1976. Computer operator Owens-Ill., Inc., Toledo, 1969-72, programmer, analyst, 1972-79, fin. analyst, 1979-80; dir. ops. Royal Petroleum, Inc., Cleve., 1980-82; mgr. info. ctr. Toledo Edison Co., Toledo, 1982—; exec. v.p. Tri-Nalysis, Toledo, 1979—. Home: 6837 Shieldwood Toledo OH 43617 Office: Toledo Edison Co 300 Madison Ave Toledo OH 43652

IAKOVOS, ARCHBISHOP DEMETRIOS A. COUCOUZIS, clergyman; b. Imvros, Turkey, July 29, 1911; s. Athanasios and Maria Coucouzis. Grad., Theol. Sch. of Halki, Ecumenical Patriarchate, 1934; S.T.M., Harvard, 1945; D.D., Boston U., 1960, Bates Coll., 1970, Dubuque U., 1973, Assumption Coll., 1980; L.H.D., Franklin and Marshall Coll., 1961, Southeastern Mass. Tech. Inst., 1967, Am. Internat. Coll., 1972, Catholic U., 1974, Loyola Marymount U., 1979, Queen's Coll., 1982; LL.D., Brown U., 1964, Seton Hall U., 1968, Coll. of Holy Cross, 1966, Fordham U., 1966, Notre Dame U., 1979, N.Y. Law Sch., 1982, St. John's U., 1982; H.H.D., Suffolk U., 1967, Stonehill Coll., 1980; D.S.T., Berkeley Div. Sch., 1962, Gen. Theol. Sem., 1967, Thessalonica U., 1975; Lit.D., PMC Colls., 1971; others. Ordained deacon Greek Orthodox Ch., 1934; archdeacon Greek Orthodox Ch., Met. Derkon, 1934-39, Greek Archdiocese; prof. Archdiocese Theol. Sch., Pomfret, Conn., 1939; ordained priest 1940; parish priest Hartford, Conn., 1940-41; preacher Holy Trinity Cathedral, N.Y.C., 1941-42; parish priest St. Louis, 1942; dean Cathedral of Annunciation, Boston, 1942-54; dean Holy Cross Orthodox Theol. Sch., Brookline, Mass., 1954, now pres.; bishop of Holy Cross Orthodox Theol. Sch., Melita, Malta, 1954-56; rep. Ecumenical Patriarchate, World Council Chs., Geneva, 1955-59; then copres. council Ecumenical Patriarchate, World Council Chs., 1959-68; elevated to Metropolitan, 1956; archbishop, N. and S. Am., Holy Synod of Ecumenical Patriarchate, 1959—; Chmn. Standing Conf. Canonical Bishops in the Americas; mem. adv. bd., v.p. Religion in American Life. Author works in Greek, French, English, German. Pres. St. Basil's Acad., Garrison, N.Y.; chmn. trustees Hellenic Coll., Brookline; trustee Anatolia Coll., Salonika, Greece. Recipient Man of Yr. award B'nai B'rith, 1962; recipient Nat. award NCCJ, 1962, Clergyman of the Yr. award Religious Heritage Am., 1970, Presdl. Citation as Disting. Am. in Voluntary Service, 1970, Man of Conscience award Appeal of Conscience Found., 1971, Presdl. Medal of Freedom, 1980, Interreligious award Religion in Am. Life, 1980, Clergyman of Yr. award N.Y.C. Council Churches, 1981. Mem. Am. Bible Soc. (bd. mgrs.). Address: Greek Orthodox Church Forty East Burton Place Chicago IL 60610 *

IAMS, JACK LOUIS, architect; b. Marietta, Ohio, June 1, 1929; s. Hillis D. and Wilda (Lindamood) I. BS, Marietta Coll., 1951; BArch, U. Cin., 1956. Staff architect Scott & Eesley, Marietta, 1952-55, Frank, Lindberg & Mackey, Columbus, Ohio, 1961-65, Kayser & Mould, Columbus, 1966-74; pvt. practice architecture Columbus, 1975—. Served to capt. USAF, 1956-59. Mem. AIA. Lodge: Masons. Home: 332 6th St Marietta OH 45750

IANNANTUONO, CHRISTOPHER JAMES, manufacturing company executive; b. Tiffin, Ohio, Oct. 2, 1958; s. Tony and Verland Irene (Anderson) I.; m. Christine Marie Cook, June 25, 1982; children: Anthony Francis, Amy Christine. BBA, Heidelberg Coll., Tiffin, 1981; MBA, Ashland (Ohio) Coll., 1983. Assoc. indsl. engr. Timken Co., Bucyrus, Ohio, 1981-83, indsl. and systems engr., 1983-86, supr. tng. and personnel, 1986—. Indsl. chmn. Bucyrus Area United Way Fund Drive, 1986. Mem. Am. Prodn. and Inventory Control Soc., Jaycees. Roman Catholic. Lodge: KC. Office: The Timken Co Rt 30 Bucyrus OH 44820

IANNOLI, JOSEPH JOHN, JR., university development executive; b. Worcester, Mass., Oct. 28, 1939; s. Joseph John and Alice Bernadette (Moore) I.; A.B., Franklin and Marshall Coll., 1962; M.A., Syracuse U., 1967; m. Gail V. Cummings, Oct. 21, 1972; children—Juliet, Christopher. Devel. officer Franklin & Marshall Coll., Lancaster, Pa., 1965-68; asso. dir. med. devel. U. Miami, 1968-70; adminstr. Children's Hearing and Speech Ctr., 1970-73; asst. dir., cons. Am. Bankers Assn., Washington, 1973-74, Marts & Lundy, Inc., N.Y.C., 1974-78; dir. capital support U. Hartford, Conn., 1978-82; v.p. devel. Ripon (Wis.) Coll., 1982—; sr. cons. J.M. Lord & Assos.; lectr. in field. Bd. dirs. Wau-Bun council Girl Scouts U.S.A. Recipient Samuel McDonald Humanitarian award, 1958. Cert. fund raising exec. Mem. Nat. Soc. Fund Raising Execs., Council for Advancement and Support of Edn., Fund Raising Inst., Bushnell Meml. Steering Com., 1980-82; bd. dirs. Ripon area C. of C. Office: Box 248 Ripon Coll Ripon WI 54971

IAQUINTA, LEONARD PHILLIP, university development and alumni official; b. Kenosha, Wis., Aug. 1, 1944; s. Anthony Sam and Mary Natalie (Gallo) I. BJ, Northwestern U., 1966; M in Journalism, Columbia U., 1967. Dir. World Studies Data Bank Acad. for Ednl. Devel., N.Y.C., 1969-76; dir. field services Alumni Relations Northwestern U., Evanston, Ill., 1977-81; dir. Nat. Alumni Program Columbia U., N.Y.C., 1981-82; devel. and alumni officer CUNY, 1982-86; dir. devel. and alumni affairs Indiana-Purdue Univs. at Fort Wayne, 1986—. Asst. editor: Notes on Negotiating, 1974; contbr. articles to profl. jours.; author various devel. manuals. Exec. dir. Kenosha United Way, 1976-77; mem. Fort Wayne Area Fundraisers, 1987—, Council for Advancement and Support of Edn., 1977—. Mem. Soc. for Profl. Jours., NE Ind. Fundraisers, Ind. Council Fundraising Execs., Ind. Planned Giving Group, Sigma Delta Chi. Congregationalist. Lodge: Rotary. Avocations: gardening, reading, travel. Home: 2518 Eastbrook Dr Fort Wayne IN 46805 Office: Indiana/Purdue U 2101 Coliseum Blvd E Fort Wayne IN 46805

ICARD, LARRY DENNIS, social work educator, consultant; b. Lenoir, N.C., Aug. 4, 1949; s. Fred C. and Lorean M. (Thomas) I. B.A. in Sociology, Johnson C. Smith U., Charlotte, N.C., 1972; M.S.W., W.Va. U., 1975. Dir. minority recruitment Dis-Tran Personnel, Garland, Tex., 1972; pub. welfare worker Tex. Dept. Pub. Welfare, 1973; instr. dept. sociology and social work U. Wis.-Superior, 1976; asst. prof. social work Sch. Social Work, W.Va. U., Morgantown, 1976-80; asst. prof. Sch. Social Work, U. Cin., 1980-86, assoc. prof., 1986—; chmn. baccalaureate social work program, 1980—; cons. orgnl. devel. and undergrad. social work edn. Contbr. several chpts. to books on social work. Vice pres. Cin. Mental Health Assn., 1982-85; trustee Humans United for Better Services Inc., Cin.; human services adv. com. City of Cin. Mem. Nat. Assn. Black Social Workers, Council Social Work Edn., Nat. Assn. Baccalaureate Program Dirs. (v.p. 1984-86). Researcher in mental health. Office: Sch Social Work U Cin Cincinnati OH 45221

ICKOWICZ, GARY PEARCY, sales consultant, buyer, broker auto leasing; b. Toronto, Ont., Can., July 23, 1954; s. Joseph and Rose (Miller) I.; m. Gloria R. Levy. Student Ohio State U., 1972-75; A. Bus. Mgmt., Cuyahoga Community Coll., Cleve., 1983; BBA Ursuline Coll., Cleve., 1985—. Asst. mgr. Mogol's Mens Wear, Columbus, Ohio, 1975-76; mgmt. trainee Schottenstein's, Columbus, 1976-78; mgr. men's clothing Value City, Indpls., 1978-79; sales mgr., buyer J. Ickowicz Fur Salon, Inc., Cleve., 1979-84; sales cons. Allied Lighting Services Inc., Beachwood, Ohio, 1984-86 , sales mgr., Solon, Ohio, 1984—. Mem. Jewish Big Bro. Assn.; coach Tris Speaker Little League; active Ohio State Rep. campaign. Mem. Cleve. Fur Inst. Democrat. Jewish. Lodge: Masons. Home: 2049 S Green Rd South Euclid OH 44121 Office: 14427 Cedar Rd South Euclid OH 44121

IDE, DAVID ERWIN, marketing consultant; b. Tarentum, Pa., Nov. 11, 1942; s. Erwin H. and Flora (Grine) I.; married, Sept. 12, 1982; children: Laura, Eric. BA, Bowling Green Coll., 1964. Copywriter Fuller & Smith, Cleve., 1967-69, D'Arcy Corp., Cleve., 1969-71; research dir. Nationwide Advt. Service, Inc., Cleve., 1971-86; cons. mktg. research Lakewood, Ohio, 1986—. Home and Office: 1057 Sylvan Ave Lakewood OH 44107

IDE, KAMY LORRAINE, communications executive; b. Cadillac, Mich., Sept. 4, 1954; d. Roy William and Julia (Tisi) Hansen; m. Donald Eugene Ide, May 26, 1973; children: Rene N., Thomas D. AA, Lakewood Coll., 1977. Mng. editor Osceola Herald, Reed City, Mich., 1973; news editor Evart (Mich.) Rev., 1973-74; mng. editor Vadnais Heights Little Can. Press, White Bear, Mich., 1974-75; owner Pride Pub. Relations, St. Paul, 1976-77; v.p., dir. advt. Ide Inc., St. Paul, 1977—; cons. newspaper publicity Corpus Christi Sch., St. Paul, 1985-86. Contbr. articles to Minn., Mich. newspapers, 1970—. Mem. Home Sch. Assn. (v.p. Corpus Christi Schs. 1985-86). Republican. Roman Catholic. Avocaitons; fiction writing, photography.

IDERAN, CHARLES MICHAEL, therapist; b. Brownwood, Tex., Sept. 26, 1946; s. Noel Graves and Phyllis Irene (Bell) Olden; m. Mary Louise Rohr, June 14, 1969; children: David Charles, Trisha Michelle, Katherine Elizabeth. BA, Luther Coll., 1968; M Div, Wartburg Theol. Sem., 1974; D of Ministry, Luth. Sch. Theology, 1981. Tchr. Houston (Minn.) Pub. Schs., 1968-70; minister Otter Creek Luth. Parish, Highland, Wis., 1974-76, St. John's Luth. Ch., Johnson Creek, Wis., 1976-79; therapist Ctr. for Life Skills, Chgo., 1980-87, dir. tng., 1983-87; co-founder Genesis Therapy Ctr., Oak Forest, Ill., 1987; Adj. prof. Sem. Conservatory for Urban Pastor Edn., Chgo., 1980—, No. Bapt.Theol. Sem., Lombard, Ill., 1983—. Pres. R.C.A., Watertown, Wis., 1975-76; mcpl. judge Village of Johnson Creek, 1975-76; pres. Christian Care Ctr., Chgo., 1985—. Mem. Am. Assn. for Marriage and Family Therapy (approved supr.), Orthopsychiat. Assn., Christian Assn. for Psychol. Studies. Avocations: golf, handball. Home: 516 Buckley Ct University Park IL 60466 Office: Ctr for Life Skills 858 N Clark Chicago IL 60610

IDOL, LORNA JEANNE, researcher, teacher educator, author; b. Glenwood Springs, Colo., Mar. 7, 1947; d. Loren Ellis and Lana (Gregory) Idol; m. J. Frederick West, Oct. 18, 1986; 1 child, Paz Timoteo. Student U. Denver, 1965-67; BS in Edn., U. Nev., 1969, MEd, 1974; PhD in Edn., U. N.Mex., 1979. Cert. spl. edn. tchr., Nev. Counselor Wiltwyke Sch. for Boys, Ossining, N.Y., summer 1970; supr. tchr. Student Teaching Program, Dept. Spl. Edn., U. Nev., Reno, 1970-74; tchr. Washoe County Sch. Dist. Vets. Meml. Elem. Sch., Reno, 1970-74; grad. asst. spl. edn. U. N.Mex., Albuquerque, 1975, field supr. Spl. Edn., 1977-78, instr., 1976-78; tchr., lang. acquisition Albuquerque Pub. Schs., 1976; grad. intern Lovelace-Bataan Clinic Albuquerque, 1976; vis. lectr., coordinator Resource/Cons. Tchr. Program, Dept. Spl. Edn., U. Ill., Urbana, 1979-86, dir. Lab. for Reading Improvement, Ctr. for Study of Reading, 1985—, instr. grad. courses; vis. scholar U. Tex. Austin, 1986-87; cons. pub. sch. in-service tchr. edn.; statis. analysis cons. Author: Special Educators Consultation Handbook, 1983, Collaborative Consultation, 1986, Models of Curriculum-Based Assessment, 1986; editor: Grace Fernald's Remedial Technique in Basic Short Subjects, 1987; sr. editor: Remedial and Spl. Edn. Jour., 1987—; mem. editorial bd. Jour. Tech. Edn. and Spl. Edn., 1984-87; also articles. Recipient Scholars' Travel award U. Ill., 1981, 83, 84-86, Outstanding Presentation award Internat. Council for Exceptional Children, 1981; U. Nev. fellow, 1974. Mem. Council Exceptional Children (rep. to Bd. Govs. from Tchr. Edn. div. 1984-87), Council Children with Learning Disabilities, Nat. Reading Council, Internat. Reading Assn., Am. Ednl. Research Assn. Democrat. Methodist. Office: 1310 S 6th St Suite 288 Edn Bldg Champaign IL 61820

IDSTEIN, JAMES RICHARD, controller; b. Chgo., May 10, 1953; s. Richard Lawrence and Geraldine Mary (Driscoll) I.; m. Lynn Patecky, June 10, 1978; children: Brian James, Karen Lynn. AA, William Rainey Harper Coll., 1973; BS in Acctg., No. Ill. U., 1975; MBA, DePaul U., 1987. CPA, Ill. Staff acct. Edwin Olszanski, CPA, Park Ridge, Ill., 1976-79; controller VLS Protective Coatings, Des Plaines, Ill., 1979—, also bd. dirs.; controller Byron Ellis Assocs., Des Plaines, 1979—, also bd. dirs.; bd. dirs. Burrill Corp., Des Plaines, 1979—. Mem. Am.Inst. CPA's, Nat. Assn. Accts., Ill. CPA Soc., Delta Mu Delta, Beta Alpha Psi. Republican. Roman Catholic. Home: 731 Cutter Ln Elk Grove Village IL 60007 Office: Byron Ellis Assocs Inc 650 First Ave Des Plaines IL 60016

IEHL, BRUCE HERBERT, financial consultant; b. Chgo., May 5, 1949; s. Charles Herbert and Helen Marie (Leavitt) I.; m. Lynda Alice Reed, Aug. 20, 1971 (div. 1981); children: Wendy Robyn, Allison Peaches; m. Carmen Elizabeth Tobar, Aug. 24, 1986. BS in Physics, U. Ill., 1971. Pvt. cons. Bellflower, Ill., 1976-79; site dir. Truman Coll., Chgo., 1979-81; pres. First Personal Trust Co., Bellflower, 1981—; distributer Success Motivation Inst., Inc., 1978—. Served with USAF, 1971-76. Mem. Soc. Computer Simulation, Planetary Soc. Methodist. Home: Rural Rt 1 Bellflower IL 61724

IGIELSKI, KEVIN MARCHEL, accountant; b. Chgo., Oct. 3, 1962; s. Ronald Joseph and Roberta (Forst) I.; m. Diane M. Slouka, Sept. 13, 1986. BS in Acctg., Ea. Ill. U., 1984. Gen. acct. Do All No. Ill. Co., Des Plaines, Ill., 1984; field examiner state regulating agy. Ill. State Dept. Ins., Chgo., 1984-86; ins. controls analyst Bankers Life and Casualty, Chgo., 1986—. Republican. Roman Catholic. Avocations: photography, music, philosophy. Home: 207 Regency Dr #549 Bloomingdale IL 60108

IGLESKI, THOMAS ROBERT, lawyer, insurance company executive; b. Chgo., June 16, 1934; s. William E. and Wanda M. I.; m. Arline Skowronski, Nov. 10, 1962; children—Mark, Laura. B.B.A., U. Notre Dame, 1955; J.D., De Paul U., 1962. Bar: Ill. 1962, U.S. Supreme Ct. 1968. Atty. CNA Ins. Cos., Chgo., 1962-68; corp. sec., asst. gen. counsel CNA Ins. Cos., 1972—, v.p., 1977—; corp. counsel CNA Fin. Corp. subs. CNA Ins. Cos., Chgo., 1968-72. Served with U.S. Army, 1956-58. Mem. Am., Ill., Chgo. bar assns., Am. Soc. Corp. Secs. Clubs: Calumet Country, Union League. Home: 19110 Pierce Ave Homewood IL 60430 Office: CNA Insurance Cos CNA Plaza Chicago IL 60685

IGLEWSKI, RUDOLPH DANIEL, construction company executive, real estate broker; b. Dallas, Aug. 15, 1948; s. John Andrew Iglewski and Genieve Hills; m. Sandra Sue Seabright, Apr. 4, 1970; children: Rudolph Daniel, David Wayne. Student, U. Wis., Superior, 1967-70; cert. in real estate, Adams (Wis.) Tech. Coll., 1981. Carpenter Local 836, Janesville, Wis., 1970-73; asst. project mgr. TMW Joint Ventures, Colorado Springs, Colo., 1973-74; mng. supr. Adams & Leonard, Tulsa, 1977-79, J.D. Bergman Corp., Wisconsin Dells, Wis., 1978-87; ptnr. C & G Enterprises, Wisconsin Dells, 1985—; owner Cen. Wis. Builders, Wisconsin Dells, 1987—; insp. Dept. Indsl. Labor and Human Relations, Madison, Wis., 1985—; broker Cen. Wis. Realty, Wisconsin Dells, 1987—. Cubmaster Cub Scouts, Wisconsin Dells. Served with USNG, 1970-76. Democrat. Roman Catholic. Avocations: family, fishing, bowling. Home and Office: 839 Grouse Dr Wisconsin Dells WI 53965

IHBE, THOMAS SCOTT, infosystems specialist; b. Green Bay, Wis., Dec. 14, 1958; s. Gordon M. and Patricia (Herzer) I.; m. Stephanie M. Morris, Apr. 24, 1982. BS in Indsl. Engring., BBA in Acctg., U. Wis., 1981; MBA in Ops. Mgmt., U. Minn., 1986. Indsl. engr. 3M, St. Paul, 1982-83, systems analyst, 1983-84, systems devel. supr., 1984—. Advisor Jr. Achievement, St. Paul, 1982. Mem. Am. Prodn. and Inventory Control Soc. (cert.). Republican. Methodist. Avocation: sailing. Office: 3M 850 Bush Ave Saint Paul MN 55144

IHLANFELDT, WILLIAM, university administrator, consultant; b. Belleville, Ill., Dec. 12, 1936; s. Raymond William and Olivia Anna (Boycourt) I.; m. D. Jeannine Huguelet, May 7, 1978; children—Troy, Kimberly, Holly. B.S., Ill. Wesleyan U., 1959, LL.D., 1980; M.A., Northwestern U., 1963, Ph.D., 1970. Adminstr., Monticello Coll., Godfrey, Ill., 1959-60; tchr., coach Rich Twp. High Sch., Park Forest, Olympia Fields, Ill., 1960-64; dir. fin. aid Northwestern U., Evanston, Ill., 1964-67, dean admission and fin. aid, 1973-78, v.p. instnl. relations, dean admissions, 1978—; chmn. pub. policy Consortium Financing Higher Edn., Cambridge, Mass., 1979-83; chmn. Fedn. Ill. Ind. Colls. and Univs., Springfield, 1981-83; vice chmn. Econ. Devel. Corp., 1983—; mem. exec. com. Student Loan Mktg. Assn., Washington, 1975—; cons. in field. Author: Achieving Optimal Enrollments and Tuition Revenues, 1980; contbr. chpts. to books, articles to profl. publs. Founder, Northwestern U. Chgo. Action Project, Evanston, 1966; Evanston/Univ. Research Park, 1984, chmn., chief exec. officer, 1986—; co-author Ill. Ind. Higher Edn. Loan Authority, Northbrook, Ill., 1981. Wieboldt Found. grantee, 1966, 67, 68. Mem. Am. Assn. Higher Edn., Coll. Entrance Exam. Bd. (service award 1978), Phi Delta Kappa. Club: Indian Hill (Winnetka, Ill.). Avocations: tennis, skiing. Office: Northwestern Univ 633 Clark St Evanston IL 60201

IHLE, HERBERT DUANE, food company executive; b. Ames, Iowa, July 8, 1939; s. Joe and Martha Marie (Larson) I.; m. Catherine Eileen Klein, Dec. 27, 1959; children—Brenda Kirsten, Valerie Anne, Michael David. A.A., Waldorf Jr. Coll., Forest City, Iowa, 1959; B.A., Concordia Coll., Moorhead, Minn., 1961; M.S., U. Minn., 1963. Dir. fin. planning Pillsbury Co., Mpls., 1976-78, sr. v.p. fin. Burger King, 1979-80, v.p. fin. foods, 1980-81, v.p., controller, 1981-82, exec. v.p., chief fin. officer Burger King, 1982-83, sr. v.p., controller, 1983—, treas., 1987—; dir. Burger King Corp., Miami, Fla., Pillsbury Commodity Services, Chgo. Mem. Fin. Execs. Inst. (com. on corp. reporting, SEC subcom.). Bd. dirs. Luth. Brotherhood, Mpls. Republican. Clubs: Mpls., Mpls. Athletic. Avocation: tennis. Home: 6208 Fox Meadow Ln Edina MN 55436 Office: Pillsbury Co 200 S 6th St Minneapolis MN 55402

IHLE, ROGER L., electrical engineer; b. Cleghorn, Iowa, Oct. 10, 1918; s. Charles W. And Lenora I. (Ohler) I.; m. Marilyn Henderson; children: R. Charles, Christopher L. BSEE, Iowa State U., 1940. Registered profl. elec. engr., Nebr., Iowa, S.D. Commd. 2d lt. USAF, 1941, advanced through grades to lt. col., 1954, elec. counter measures officer, 1941-45, 51-52, ret., 1961; prin. Krueger Ihle Electric, Norfolk, Nebr., 1947-70; dir. engring. and maintenence Immanuel Med. Ctr., Omaha, 1970-73, Meth. Med. Ctr., Des Moines, 1973-78; dir. engring. services Good Samaritan Hosp., Kearney, Nebr., 1978—. Fellow Am. Soc. Hosp. Engrs.; mem. NSPE (sec.-treas., pres. elect, pres., state bd. dirs., 1983—), Nebr. Insts. of Health Care Engrs. (pres. 1983-85, vice chmn. 1987-88). Democrat. Presbyterian. Lodges: Kiwanis (bd. dirs. Kearney club 1986-87), Elks. Avocations: gardening, fishing, hunting. Home: 29 Lakeside Dr Kearney NE 68847 Office: Good Samaritan Hosp 31st and Central Kearney NE 68847

IKEN, JAMES LEO, architect; b. Fargo, N.D., Dec. 27, 1953; s. Lyle Roland and Elizabeth (Welsh) I.; m. Cynthia Marie Cardoso, June 25, 1982. BArch, N.D. State U., 1978; MBA, Boston U., 1983. Registered architect, Wis., Minn., Nebr. Intern architect Loewll Hanson Architect, Spring Valley, Wis., 1978-79; staff cons. Burndy Corp., Mpls., 1979-80; engring. contract specialist Hdqrs. Strategic Air Command, Omaha, 1983-84, chief logistics mgmt., 1984-85, chief housing programs, 1985—. Served to capt. USAF, 1980-83. Mem. AIA, Soc. Am. Mil. Engrs., Jaycees (bd. dirs. Plattsmouth, Nebr. chpt. 1985-86). Republican. Roman Catholic. Avocations: skiing, flying, golf. Home: 926 Scott St Plattsmouth NE 68048

IKENBERRY, STANLEY OLIVER, university president; b. Lamar, Colo., Mar. 3, 1935; s. Oliver Samuel and Margaret (Moulton) I.; m. Judith Ellen Life, Aug. 24, 1958; children: David Lawrence, Steven Oliver, John Paul. BA, Shepherd Coll., Shepherdstown, W.Va., 1956; MA, Mich. State U., 1957, PhD, 1960, LLD (hon.); LLD (hon.), Millikin U., Ill. Coll., Rush U. Instr. Office Evaluation Services, Mich. State U., 1958-60, instr. instl. research, 1960-62; asst. to provost for instl. research, asst. prof. edn. W.Va. U., 1962-65, dean Coll. Human Resources and Edn., assoc. prof. edn., 1965-69; prof., assoc. dir. Ctr. Study Higher Edn., Pa. State U., 1969-71, sr. v.p., 1971-79; pres. U. Ill., Urbana, 1979—; pres. bd. dirs. Appalachia Edn. Lab., 1965-69; bd. dirs. Am. Council on Edn., Harris Bankcorp, Chgo., Franklin Life Ins. Co., Springfield, Pfizer, Inc., N.Y.C. Contbr. articles to profl. jours. Co-chmn. Ill. Gov.'s Commn. on Sci. and Tech., 1982—; trustee, chmn. Carnegie Found. for Advancement Teaching; bd. dirs. Nat. Sci. Ctr. Named hon. alumnus Pa. State U. Mem. Am. Ednl. Research Assn. (bd. dirs.), Am. Assn. Higher Edn. (bd. dirs., Nat. Assn. State Univs. and Land-Grant Colls. (pres.-elect), Am. Assn. Instl. Research, Nat. Soc. Study Edn. Clubs: Chgo., Econ., Comml., Mid-Am., Tavern (Chgo.); Champaign Country. Office: Univ of Ill Cen Office Office of the Pres Urbana IL 61801

ILIADIS, NICK, mechanical engineer; b. Athens, Greece, Nov. 23, 1951; came to U.S., 1956; s. Nickolas Iliadis and Agatha Colesnicenco; m. Susan Linda Fidler, June 28, 1975; children: Michelle Brooke, Jamie Lynn. BME, U. Ill., Chgo., 1974; A in Physics, U. London, 1978. Registered profl. mfg. engr., Ill. Mfg. engr. Alphatype Corp., Niles, Ill., 1974-76, EMI MEd. Inc., Northbrook, Ill., 1976-81; mech. engr. Williams Electronics, Chgo., 1981-84; project engr. Safety-Kleen Corp., Elgin, Ill., 1984-85, mgr. quality assurance, 1985—. Mem. ASME, Soc. Mfg. Engrs. (sr., instr. engring. systems 1983—),

Soc. Bio-med. Engrs. Avocations: collecting movies, writing software, home electro-mechanics, golfing, bowling. Office: Safety-Kleen Corp 777 Big Timber Rd Elgin IL 60123

ILIC-SPONG, MARIJA, engineering educator; b. Zaječar, Yugoslavia, Feb. 11, 1951; came to U.S., 1977; d. Dragoljub N. and Vera (Djordjevic) Ilic; m. Mark William Spong, Feb. 10, 1980; children: Matthew, John. BS in Engring., U. Belgrade, Yugoslavia, 1974, MS in Engring., 1976; MS, Washington U., St. Louis, 1979, DSc, 1980. Asst. prof. engring. Drexel U., Phila., 1981-82, Cornell U., Ithaca, N.Y., 1982-84, U. Ill., Urbana, 1984—; cons. Gen. Electric, Schenectady, N.Y. Contbr. articles to profl. jours.; patentee in field. Recipient First Presdl. Young Investigators award NSF, 1984. Mem. IEEE. Home: 2203 Wyld Dr Urbana IL 61801 Office: U Ill 1406 W Green Urbana IL 61801

ILORETA, ALFREDO T., urologist; b. Sinait, Philippines, Dec. 9, 1947; s. Basilio and Hipolita (Tabutol) I.; m. Maria Delia Calo; children—Alfred Marc, Francis, Joseph. B.S., Far Eastern U., Manila, 1966; M.D. cum laude, U. Santo Tomas, Manila, 1971. Rotating intern St. Thomas Hosp., Akron, Ohio, 1972-73, resident in surgery, 1973-74; resident in surgery St. Luke's Hosp., Bethlehem, Pa., 1974-75; resident in urology Albert Einstein Coll. Medicine, Bronx, N.Y., 1975-79, Sloan-Kettering Meml. Cancer Ctr., N.Y.C., 1978; practice medicine specializing in urology, Topeka, Kans., 1979—; chief of urology VA Med. Ctr.; staff urologist Topeka Urology Clinic, 1982—. Contbr. articles to profl. jours. Mem. Am. Urological Assn., Am. Soc. Clin. Urologists. Home: 6950 SW 33d St Topeka KS 66614 Office: 1516 W 6th St Topeka KS 66606

ILTIS, JOHN FREDERIC, advertising and public relations company executive; b. Chgo., Dec. 14, 1940; s. Frederic and Alice Henrietta (Nachman) I.; m. Gillian Ann Cane, Nov. 20, 1976; children: Claire Alexandra, Annika Leigh. Student, Lincoln Coll., 1962; A.A., Bradley U., 1964. Advt. and pub. relations asst. Balaban & Katz Theatres, Chgo., 1965-68; midwest dir. advt and pub. relations Universal Pictures, Chgo., 1968-69; field ops. dir. Universal Pictures, N.Y.C., 1969-70; owner, operator film prodn. and mktg. co. London, 1971-73; pres. John Iltis Assocs., entertainment, advt. and pub. relations, Chgo., 1973—; instr. pub. relations Columbia Coll., Chgo. vice chmn. Community Film Workshop of Chgo.; mem. adv. bd. Film Ctr., Art Inst. Chgo.; bd. dirs. Lawyers for Creative Arts, Chgo., Variety Club Ill.; mem. adv. bd. DePaul U. Theatre Sch., Chgo. Served with U.S. Army, 1964. Mem. Acad. Motion Picture Arts and Scis., Publicity Club Chgo., Chgo. TV Acad., Publicists Guild, Broadcast Advt. Club. Home: 3844 Kenmore Ave Chicago IL 60613 Office: John Iltis Assocs 666 N Lake Shore Dr Chicago IL 60611

IMBLER, JOHN MARK, church executive, clergyman; b. Kokomo, Ind., Mar. 27, 1945; s. Chester and Jeanette (Ferguson) I.; m. Toni Wine, Sept. 3, 1967; children: Andrew, Bethany, Catherine. BA, Butler U., 1967; MDiv., Christian Theol. Sem., 1971, STM, 1981; DD, Columbia Coll., 1987. Ordained to ministry Christian Ch. (Disciples of Christ), 1974. Counselor Indpls. Skills Ctr., 1971-74, asst. dir., 1974-76; dir. vocat. services State of Ind., Indpls., 1976-79; dir. instl. services div. higher edn. The Christian Ch. (Disciples of Christ), 1979-81; v.p. div. higher edn. The Christian Ch. (Disciples of Christ), St. Louis, 1981—; Mem. Task force on Ministry, The Christian Ch. (Disciples of Christ), 1984—, study task group Assn. Theol. Sch., 1981; treas. ADTD, St. Louis, 1979—. Assoc. editor Disciples Theol. Digest, 1986—; contbr. articles to ch. jour. Active Lindbergh Sch. Dist. Citizen's Adv. Council, St. Louis, 1983-85, 87. Named one of Outstanding Young Men Am, 1980. Mem. Am. Acad. Religion, Soc. For Advancement Continuing Edn. for Ministry, Disciples Christ Hist. Soc. (life). Avocations: sports, reading. Office: Div Higher Edn Christian Church (Disciples of Christ) 11780 Borman Dr Suite 100 Saint Louis MO 63146

IMBURGIA, LOUIS ANTHONY, dentist; b. Chgo., Feb. 9, 1958; s. Anthony and Michaelina (Aiello) I.; m. Rosemary Imburgia. BS in Biology, Loyola U., Chgo., 1980; DDS, Loyola U., Maywood, Ill., 1984. Gen. practice dentistry Chgo., 1984—; lectr. City Coll. Chgo., 1985—; cons. Dobson Nursing Home, Evanston, Ill., 1985-87. Mem. ADA, Ill. Dental Soc., Chgo. Dental Soc. (mediation com. 1985—), Acad. Gen. Dentistry, Arcolian Dental Arts. Club: United Italian Am. (Chgo). Office: 5918 W Irving Park Rd Chicago IL 60634

IMERGOOT, LYNN CAROL, athletic director; b. Bronx, N.Y., Dec. 29, 1948; d. Bernard Jack and Selma (Goldberg) Stockman; m. Michael Harris Imergoot, Dec. 23, 1973 (div.); children: Douglas Elliot, Jennifer Hope. AB, Lehman Coll. CUNY, 1969; MS, U. Ill., 1970. Cert. phys. edn. tchr., Mo., N.Y. Phys. edn. tchr. White Plains (N.Y.) High Sch., 1970-72; phys. edn. instr. Washington U., St. Louis, 1972-77, coordinator women's sports, 1977-84, asst. athletic dir., 1984—; coach women's tennis Washington U., 1975—; v.p. Midwest Camp Cons., Maryland Heights, Mo., 1978—; mem. adv. com. St. Louis Post-Dispatch Scholar-Athlete Award, 1978-84. Contbr. articles to profl. jours. Vol. Channel 9 Auction, St. Louis, 1981-84; solicitor United Way Campaign, 1983-84. Recipient A.W. Neidhard award Lehman Coll., 1969; Thomas Hunter scholar, 1965. Mem. Council of Collegiate Women Athletic Adminstrs., Internat. Assn. Phys. Edn. and Sport for Girls and Women, Am. Alliance for Health, Phys. Edn., Recreation and Dance, Intercollegiate Tennis Coaches Assn., Mo. Assn. Health, Phys. Edn., Recreation and Dance (Helen Manley award 1984). Democrat. Jewish. Avocation: tennis. Home: 1785 Red Coat Dr Maryland Heights MO 63043 Office: Washington U Dept Athletics One Brookings Dr PO Box 1067 Saint Louis MO 63130

IMESCH, JOSEPH LEOPOLD, bishop; b. Grosse Pointe Farms, Mich., June 21, 1931; s. Dionys and Margaret (Margelisch) I. B.S., Sacred Heart Sem., 1953; student, N.Am. Coll., Rome, 1953-57; S.T.L., Gregorian U., Rome, 1957. Ordained priest Roman Catholic Ch., 1956; sec. to Cardinal Dearden, 1959-71; pastor Our Lady of Sorrows Ch., Farmington, Mich., 1971-77; titular bishop of Pomaria and aux. bishop of Detroit 1973-79; asst. bishop N.W. Region, 1977-79; bishop of Joliet Ill., 1979—. Office: Chancery Office 425 Summit St Joliet IL 60435 *

IMMER, BERYLE JEAN, nurse; b. Oklahoma City, Mar. 25, 1937; d. George Guy and Blanche Ermal (Garrett) Clesson; m. Robert Glenn Immer, June 23, 1962; children: Joy Lynn, Michael Guy, Steven Frederick. Diploma in Nursing, Independence Sanitarium and Hosp. Sch. Nursing, 1959; AA, Graceland Coll., 1959; BS in Nursing, U. Colo., 1961; MEd, U. Mo., 1981. Pub. health nurse Graham County Health Dept. Safford, Ariz., 1961-62; nursing instr. Independence Sanitarium Hosp. Sch. Nursing, Mo., 1965-67; pub. health nurse City Health Dept., Independence, 1967-68; instr., coordinator practical nursing programs Kansas City (Mo.) Sch. Dist., 1975-81; coordinator adult health occupations programs Independence Sch. Dist., 1981-87; dir. assoc. degree nursing program Park Coll., Parkview, Mo., 1987—; mem. program of practical nursing task force Mo. Council Practical Nursing Educators, 1984-86; expert witness on nursing edn.; nurse educator cons. Park Coll., 1986-87. Mem. Mo. House Com., 1983; bd. dirs., sec. Ctr. Pl. Credit Union, 1982-85; mem. bldg. com. Gudgell Park Congregation, Reorganized Ch. of Jesus Christ of Latter Day Saints, 1983-87, organ com., 1984-86; sec. Independence Mo. Sch. Dist. Vocat. Adv. Com., 1982—. Mem. Nat. League Nursing, Am. Vocat. Assn., Mo. Vocat. Assn. (policy com. 1986-87), Mo. Project Aware, Mo. Council Vocat. Adminstrs., Orgn. for Advancement Assoc. Degree Nursing. Avocations: piano, organ, painting. Office: Park Coll Dept Nursing 8700 River Park Dr Parkville MO 64152

IMMKE, KEITH HENRY, lawyer; b. Peoria, Ill., Jan. 18, 1953; s. Francis William and Pearl Lenora (Kime) I. BA, U. Ill., 1975; JD, So. Ill. U., 1978. Bar: Ill. 1978, U.S. Dist. Ct. (so. and ea. dists.) Ill. 1979. Assoc. Lawrence E. Johnson & Assocs., P.C., Champaign, Ill., 1979—. Mem. ABA, Ill. State Bar Assn., U. Ill. Alumni Assn., Phi Kappa Phi, Pi Sigma Alpha, Phi Alpha Delta. Office: Lawrence E Johnson & Assocs PC 202 W Hill St Champaign IL 61820

IMP, JOHN MICHAEL, clinical psychologist; b. Milw., Nov. 8, 1944; s. John Frank and Irene Leona (Gawin) I.; m. Donna Marie Bartolone, Nov. 23, 1975; children: Julie Marie, Michael Benjamin. BA in Psychology, Marquette U., 1968, MS in Clinical Psychology, 1972; postgrad., Cardinal Stritch Coll., Milw., 1972; PhD in Ednl. Psychology, Marquette U., 1976. Lic. psychologist, Wis. Psychometric asst. Milw. Pub. Schs., 1974-76; staff psychologist Bur. of Prisons, Alderson, W.Va., 1977-79, Oxford, Wis., 1979—. Author: FCI Alderson Relaxation Training Manual, 1978, (audio cassette) Relax on Cue, 1982. Pre-marital counselor St. Mary's Cath. Ch., Portage, Wis., 1986, mem. fundraising com. Served with U.S. Army, 1968-70. Recipient George Washington Honor medal Freedom Found., 1972. Mem. Psi Chi (pres. 1971-72), Phi Delta Kappa. Avocations: fishing, target shooting, do-it-yourself projects, inventing, book collecting. Home: W 8407 Foote Dr Portage WI 53901 Office: Fed Correctional Instn Box 500 Oxford WI 53952-0500

IMUS, JOHN FRANKLIN, real estate exec.; b. Takoma Park, Md., Feb. 26, 1958; s. Harold Raymond and Margaret Ester (Goodman) I. Student, U. Wash., 1976-77; BBA, U. Tex., 1982. V.p. Devel. Control Corp., Northfield, Ill., 1984—. Mem. Internat. Council Shopping Ctrs., Urban Land Inst. Republican. Methodist. Avocations: music, skiing, scuba diving, hunting, travel. Home: 2140 Ash Ln Northbrook IL 60062 Office: Devel Control Corp 550 Frontage Rd Suite 388 Northfield IL 60093

IMWALLE, MARK DAVID, diagnostic radiologist; b. Cin., Sept. 23, 1943; s. George and Helen Marie (O'Connell) I.; m. Linda E. Elliott, Mar. 9, 1968; children: Mark Andrew, David, Stephen, Karl, Daniel. BS in Philosophy, Xavier U., 1965; MD, U. Cin., 1969. Diplomate Am. Bd. Radiology, Am. Bd. Nuclear Medicine. Intern Good Samaritan Hosp., Cin., 1969-70; resident in radiology U. Cin., 1970-73; staff radiologist Toledo Hosp., 1973-74, Ft. Hamilton (Ohio) Hosp., 1974-76, Mercy Hamilton (Ohio) Hosp., 1977—, Mercy Fairfield (Ohio) Hosp., 1977—. Mem. Am. Coll. Radiology. Republican. Roman Catholic.

INDURANTE, PETER JOSEPH, property tax consultant and appraiser; b. Chgo., Aug. 4, 1950; s. Frank J. and Millicent Anna (Wurst) I. BBA in Finance, Loyola U., Chgo., 1972; MBA, DePaul U., 1978. Mgmt. trainee GATX Corp., Chgo., 1972-73, tax analyst, 1973-78, property tax mgr., 1978-79, asst. dir. tax, 1979-82; owner, chief cons. Peter J. Indurante Property Tax Cons. & Appraisal, Schaumburg, Ill., 1982—, coordinator and prin. speaker for ann. rail car tax seminars, 1985, 86; authorized tax agent various corps. Editor, publisher, author (monthly newsletter) State Tax Letter for Rail Car Owners and Mgrs., 1983—; (booklet) Rail Car Taxes: Theory, Valuation Compliance, Negotiation and Protest, 1985. Mem. Railway Progress Inst. (state tax com.). Avocations: golf, banjo, writing letters to newspaper editors. Office: 1622 E Algonquin Rd Suite K1 Schaumburg IL 60173

INFIELD, MARTHEA MAE, mental health service executive; b. Cleve., Dec. 31, 1929; d. Neil Edward and Freda Margaret (Schray) Bowler; m. Dwight Hosak Infield, Nov. 14, 1953; children—Susan, Dwight David, Donald, Elisabeth. B.B.A., Fenn Coll., 1952; M.S., Case Western Res. U., 1970. Asst. to overseas div. mgr. Goodyear Tire & Rubber, Akron, Ohio, 1953-54; social worker Lucas County Welfare Dept., Toledo, 1964-65; social worker protective services Cuyahoga County Welfare Dept., Cleve., 1967-68; crisis counselor Crisis Intervention Team, Cleve., 1970-72, coordinator, 1972-74, exec. dir. CIT Mental Health Services, 1974—. Republican. Presbyterian. Home: 8381 Celianna Strongsville OH 44136 Office: CIT Mental Health Services 2177 S Taylor Rd University Heights OH 44118

INGBER, ABIE I., rabbi; b. Montreal, Quebec, Can., Mar. 30, 1950; s. Wolfe and Fania (Paszht) I.; m. Shelley Sandra Nadler, Aug. 19, 1973; children: Avital Nadler, Dorit Peck. BS, McGill U., Montreal, 1971; MA in Hebrew Letters, Hebrew Union Coll.-Jewish Inst. Religion, 1976. Ordained rabbi, 1977. Exec. dir., rabbi Hillel Found., Cin., 1977—; homiletics instr. Hebrew Union Coll.-Jewish Inst. Religion, Cin., 1984—. Author: (books) Cook Unto Others, 1983, Assessing the Significance of the Holocaust, 1987. bd. dirs. Cin. Council for Soviet Jews, 1980—, Clifton Town Meeting, Cin., 1985—, Gov. Celeste's Holocaust Com., Columbus, Ohio, 1986; v.p. Interfaith Holocaust Found., Cin., 1983—. Recipient Haber award City of Washington; named hon. Ky. col., 1987. Mem. Cen. Conf. Am. Rabbis, Campus Ministries Assn. (chmn. 1984-85), Assn. Hillel Jewish Campus Profls. (pres. 1984-86), Am. Jewish Com. Avocation: cooking. Office: Hillel Found 2615 Clifton Ave Cincinnati OH 45220

INGERSOLL, JOHN THOMAS, manufacturing company executive; b. Huntington, W.Va., July 14, 1939; s. John Fredrick and Glenn Claire (Pirrung) I.; m. Martha Mae Miller, Jan. 23, 1960; children—Cynthia Claire, Catherine Elizabeth, Laura Ellen. B.B.A.; student Marshall U., 1957-62, Toledo U., 1965, UCLA, 1968, Purdue U., 1970, Northwestern U., 1985. With Owens-Ill., Inc., Toledo, Ohio, 1964—, dir. corp. staff adminstrn., 1975-78, v.p., dir. total compensation, 1978-85, v.p. exec. compensation and succession planning, 1985—; dir. planning and program control HUD, Washington, 1971-72. Chmn. Toledo Area Govtl. Research Assn. Studies, 1976-78; elder Glendale Presbyterian Ch., 1979—. Served to 1st lt. U.S. Army, 1962-64. Mem. Vanderbilt Group, Presdl. Interchange Exec. Assn. (Outstanding Achievement award 1972), Am. Compensation Assn., Sigma Alpha Epsilon. Presbyn. Home: 4838 Eastwick Dr Toledo OH 43614 Office: Owens-Ill Inc One Sea Gate Toledo OH 43666

INGLE, JAMES HOBART, engineering technician; b. Dayton, Ohio, Nov. 30, 1951; s. Hobart Baird and Helen Elizabeth (Miller) I.; m. Maryann Kiel, May 9, 1987. A.A.S., Mich. Technol. U., 1972; postgrad. Bay-de-Noc Community Coll., Escanaba, Mich., 1973. Cert. engring. technician Nat. Inst. Cert. in numerous Engring. Technologies. Mem. survey crew Davis Surveying, Escanaba, summers 1970-71, survey crew chief, 1972-73; survey crew chief, constrn. insp. Coleman Engring. Co., Escanaba, 1974-75; hwy. constrn. insp. Mich. Dept. Transp., Crystal Falls, 1975; constrn. insp. Soil Testing Services, Inc. (now STS Cons. Ltd.), Marquette, Mich., 1976—, also office mgr., area mgr., sr. engring. technician. Mem. Am. Soc. Cert. Engring. Technicians, Mich. Technol. U. Alumni Assn., Marquette Jaycees (dir. 1977-79, treas. 1978-79, community action v.p. 1979-80, pres. 1980-81, chmn. 1981-82), Mich. Jaycees (region instnl. coordinator 1983-84, region 1 dir. 1984-85 dist. B dir. 1982-83, senator), Escanaba Jaycees. Club: Mich. Technol. U. Huskies (Houghton). Lodge: Elks. Home: Star Route Box 447 Gwinn MI 49841 Office: 1909 Enterprise St Marquette MI 49855

INGLE, SUD RANGANATH, management consultant; b. Pune, India, Oct. 6, 1942; Came to U.S., 1965; s. Ranganath V. and Sita R. I.; m. Neelima Kulkarni Ingle, June 21, 1970; children: Geeta, Vinita. B in Engring., Coll. Engring., Pune, 1964; MS in Indsl. Engring., Purdue U., 1966; MBA, U. Wis., Oshkosh, 1972. Quality control engr. Giddings and Lewis, Fond du Lac, Wis., 1966-70; quality control engr. Mercury Marine, Fond du Lac, 1970-77, gen. mgr., 1977-82; pres. Quality Circles Services, Fond du Lac, 1982—; cons., trainer in field. Author: Quality Circles Master Guide, 1982, Quality Circles in Service Industries, 1983, In Search of Perfection, 1985. Mem. Fond du Lac Art Council, 1970; local rep. Fox Valley India Soc., Appleton, Wis. 1979. Mem. Internat. Assn. Quality Control (founding), Am. Soc. Quality Control. Home: 812 Forest Circle Fond du Lac WI 54935 Office: PO Box 812 Fond du Lac WI 54935

INGRAHAM, VIVIAN JUNE LOWELL, employment specialist; b. Omaha, June 1, 1922; d. John Calvert and Pearl Mabel (Whitscell) Lowell; m. Edwin L. Ingraham, 1948; children: Richard D., Leroy Lowell, John Edwin, Jeffrey Scott.; m. 2d, Clarence Parson, Sept. 7, 1969. Student U. Nebr., Omaha. Supr. customer service Met. Utilities Dist., 1940-46; news reporter sta. KBON, Omaha, 1962-67; med. transcriber VA Hosp., Omaha, 1971-73; exec. dir. Gt. Plains Council Girl Scouts U.S.A., Omaha, 1973-75; job developer City of Omaha, 1976-81; employment coordinator CETA, Iowa, 1981-83; employment specialist Crawford Rehab. Services, Omaha, 1983-85; owner, mgr. VIP Enterprises, Omaha, 1985—. Exec. com. Mid-Am. Council Boy Scouts Am., 1960—, Fontenelle Dist. Boy Scouts Am., 1958-76; youth coordinator Douglas County ARC, 1965-70; dist. II dir. Nebr. State PTA, 1964-68; v.p. Omaha PTA Council, 1966-68; pres. Walnut Hill Sch. PTA, 1958-60, Monroe Sch., 1965-67, Fontenelle Schs., 1962-64; dist. del. Rep. party; state PTA hon. life mem. Panelist: Discrimination and Its Effect on Children, 1970; author: (booklet) A Look at PTA, 1966; contbr. articles to religious mags. Recipient Hon. Nat. Life PTA award, 1972, Good Neighbor award Ak-Sar-Ben, 1970, Brotherhood Week-Good Neighbor award NCCJ, 1967, Service award ARC, 1968-71, Outstanding Citizen award Omaha Pub. Schs.; named Nat. Officer (Stewards) Nat. Presbyn. Mariners, 1960-66, Hon. Adm. Nebr. Navy. Mem. Profl. Assn. Girl Scout Execs. Presbyterian. Office: VIP Enterprises Benson Sta PO Box 4604 Omaha NE 68104

INGRAM, EDGAR W., JR., restaurant franchise company executive; b. 1910. Student, Cornell U. With White Castle System, Inc., Columbus, Ohio, 1931—, pres., chief exec. officer, 1966-79, chmn. bd. dirs., 1979—. Office: White Castle System Inc 555 W Goodale St Columbus OH 43215 *

INGRAM, EDGAR W., III, restaurant franchise company executive; b. 1951. BSBA, Bowling Green (Ohio) State U., 1972. With White Castle System, Inc., Columbus, 1972—, pres., chief exec. officer, 1979—. Office: White Castle System Inc 555 W Goodale St Columbus OH 43215 *

INGRAM, LOIS SWINTON, pharmacist; b. Galesburg, Ill., Oct. 13, 1934; d. Wayne and Hope Gurnee (Giddings) Swinton; B.S., St. Louis Coll. Pharmacy, 1963; M.A., Webster U., 1985; m. William Ingram, Mar. 21, 1954; children—Susan, William Scott. Pharmacist, Bakers Rexall Drug Store, Keokuk, Iowa, 1963-69; dir. pharacy Graham Hosp., Keokuk, 1969-74; pharmacist Osco Drug Store, Keokuk, 1974-75; dir. pharmacy St. Lukes Hosp. West, Chesterfield, Mo., 1975—. Mem. Am. Soc. Hosp. Pharmacists, Mo. Soc. Hosp. Pharmacists, St. Louis Soc. Hosp. Pharmacists. Republican. Episcopalian. Home: 710 Wild Walnut St Manchester MO 63011 Office: 232 Wood Mill Rd Chesterfield MO 63017

INGRAM, ROBERT PALMER, magazine publisher; b. Norfolk, Va., July 21, 1917; s. Robert Palmer and Margaret (Wible) I.; m. Mary Elizabeth Renfro, Sept. 30, 1949; children: Marsha Jill, Robert Palmer. Student, Washington and Lee U., 1935-36, U. Pitts., 1936-37. Salesman Anchor Hocking Glass Corp., Grand Rapids, Mich., 1942-45, Kansas City, Mo., 1945; pres. Robert P. Ingram & Co., Kansas City, 1946—, Tracy Devel. Co., Mo., 1963—, Ingram Investment Co., Mo., 1964—, LaSalle Leasing Co., Mo., 1971—, Stas. KXTR and KBEA, Lenexa, Kansas City Bus. Advt. Co.; pub. The Ind. mag., 1983—; bd. dirs. Rubbermaid Inc., Harzfelds, Inc., Am. Cablevision of Kansas City. Mem. capital requirements for pub. schs. com., Kansas City, 1969; chmn. fin. com. Jackson County Reps., 1966; trustee U. Mo., Kansas City, M.W. Research Inst.; pres. Downtown, Inc., 1970-72; bd. dirs. Civic Council Greater Kansas City. Mem. Nat. Alliance Businessmen (met. chmn. 1969), Kansas City C. of C. (past pres.), Am. Royal Assn. (bd. govs.), Downtown, Inc. (pres. 1970-72). Clubs: Kansas City, Carriage (Kansas City); Governor's (Palm Beach, Fla.). Office: 306 E 12 St Kansas City MO 64106

INGRAM, TERRENCE NEALE, insurance agent; b. Shullsburg, Wis., Nov. 21, 1939; s. Forrest R. and Ida D. (Fiedler) I.; m. Nancy June Fleming Laun, May 30, 1981. B.S., U. Wis.-Platteville, 1961. Instr. physics and math. U. Wis., Platteville, 1961-64; Bald Eagle researcher, 1964-65; bird instr. Wis. Audubon Camp, 1964-65; tchr. high sch., Mauston, Wis., 1965-66, Cuba City, Wis., 1966-67; instr. physics U. Wis., Platteville, 1967-68; tchr. high sch., Harvard, Ill., 1968-70; field underwriter N.Y. Life Ins. Co., 1970-84; ind. agent, 1984—; founder, pres., exec. dir. Eagle Valley Environmentalists, 1972-84, The Eagle Found., 1984—. Editor: Inland, 1961-65. Bd. dirs. North Central Audubon Council, 1966-70; bd. dirs. Ill. Audubon Soc., 1963-70, v.p., 1970. Recipient Honor Roll award Izaak Walton League Am., 1976; Sol Feinstone Environ. award SUNY-Syracuse, 1979; Protector of Environment award Chgo. Audubon Soc., 1981. Mem. Assn. Life Underwriters, Wis. Acad. Sci., Northwest Ill. Guernsey Assn. (pres. 1982—), Inland Bird Banding Assn. (pres. 1983-85). Republican. Editor: Bird Banding News, 1961-65. Coordinator: No. Am. Bird Bander, 1984—. Home: 8384 N Broadway Apple River IL 61001 Office: 300 Hickory St Apple River IL 61001

INKLEY, SCOTT RUSSELL, hospital administrator, physician, educator; b. Cleve., Mar. 8, 1921; s. Edwin A. and Isabella Bell (Russell) I.; m. Josephine Newcomer, Feb. 13, 1943; children: Josephine Christian, Leslie Logan, Scott Russell Jr., Sabrina Ann. Student, Harvard U., 1942; MD, Western Res. U., 1945. Intern Univ. Hosps. of Cleve., 1945-46, asst. resident, 1948-49, teaching fellow in medicine, 1949-50, chief med. resident, 1950-51, asst. physician in medicine out-patient dept., 1951-56, asst. physician dept. medicine, 1955-66, assoc. physician, 1966-68, physician, 1968—, physician-in-charge pulmonary function lab., 1962-77, dir. inhalation therapy dept., 1966-78, chief pulmonary diseases, 1968-78, chief of staff, 1978-82, pres., chief exec. officer, 1982-86, cons., 1986—; instr. dept. medicine Case Western Res. U., Cleve., 1951-54; sr. instr. Case Western Res. U., 1954-55, asst. prof., 1955-56, assoc. clin. prof., 1966-73, assoc. prof., 1973-76, prof., 1976—; bd. dirs. Huntington Nat. Bank. Contbr. articles to profl. jours. Past pres. Cleve. Med. Library Assn.; trustee Cleve. Mus. Natural History; trustee Judson Park Retirement Community, United Way, Univ. Circle Inc., U. Hosps. of Cleve. (hon.). Served to capt. M.C. U.S. Army. Fellow Am. Coll. Chest Physicians, ACP; mem. Am. Heart Assn., Am. Thoracic Soc., AMA, Central Soc. Clin. Research, Am. Acad. Med. Dirs., Ohio State Med. Assn., Cleve. Acad. Medicine, Sigma Xi. Republican. Episcopalian. Clubs: Union, Tavern, Chagrin Valley Hunt; Harvard (N.Y.C.). Home: 13500 County Line Rd Chagrin Falls OH 44022 Office: Univ Hosps of Cleve 2074 Abington Rd Cleveland OH 44106

INKS, ALLEN WALCOTT, engineer; b. Austin, Tex., Oct. 23, 1954; s. Allen Lee and Cordelia Catherine (Rugeley) I.; m. Kitty Kit Ching Chung, May 1979. AS in Electronics, Gavilan Coll., Gilroy, Calif., 1982; AAS in Nuclear Power Plant Ops. Tech. magna cum laude, Monroe (Mich.) Community Coll., 1984; BS in Mech. Engring. Tech., Wayne State U., 1986. Cert. sr. reactor operator, Mich. Enlisted USN, 1972, advanced through ranks to petty officer first class, 1978, engring. watch supr. USS Ethan Allen, elect. div. supr., resigned, 1980; nuclear supervising operator Detroit Edison Co., 1981—, shift tech. adviser, engr., 1987—. Arbitrator Better Bus. Bur., Detroit, 1987. Mem. Am. Nuclear Soc., Mich. Nuclear Soc. (exec. com. 1987—), Mensa. Republican. Episcopalian. Avocation: sailing. Home: 9854 Lorden Dr Erie MI 48133 Office: Detroit Edison Co 6400 N Dixie Hwy 135 TAC Fermi-2 Newport MI 48166

INKS, GERALD DUANE, television station engineer; b. Dayton, Ohio, Sept. 4, 1961; s. Duane G. Inks and Martha Lynn (Winfrey) Ridge. Assoc. Sci. in Elec. Engring. Tech., Purdue U., 1981; student Ind. U./Purdue U.-Indpls., 1982—. Studio engr. Neon Cornfield Rec. Studios, Indpls., 1978, Frontier Studios, Indpls., 1979; salesman Radio Shack, Indpls., summer 1981; TV engr. WISH-TV, Indpls., 1982—. Investigator, Castleton Fire Dept., Indpls., 1982—, capt. fire prevention, 1983—; spl. dep. Marion County Sheriff's Dept., Indpls., 1984—. Hoosier scholar State of Ind., 1979. Mem. Marion County Vol. Firemen's Assn., Marion County Dep. Sheriff's Lodge, Indpls. Repeater Assn., Internat. Thespian Soc. (pres. 1977). Methodist. Avocations: airplane pilot; computers; electronics; amateur radio. Home: 8512 Wakefield Ct Indianapolis IN 46256 Office: WISH-TV 1950 N Meridian Indianapolis IN 46220

INMAN, LYDIA LUCILLE, retired university dean; b. Collins, Iowa, June 28, 1918; d. Stephen Wall and Florence Iva (Dickson) I. B.S., Iowa State U., 1940, M.S., 1950; Ph.D., U. Minn., 1963. Tchr. home econs. secondary schs., Iowa, Ill., 1940-48; research fellow, instr. dept. household equipment Iowa State U., Ames. 1948-51, asst. prof., 1955-57, assoc. prof., 1957-65, prof., 1965-73, chmn., 1963-66, coordinator resident instrn., 1966-73; vis. instr. dept. home mgmt. Mich. State U., East Lansing, 1951; assoc. prof. dept. household sci. Okla. A&M U., Stillwater, 1951-55; head div. home econs. Northeast Mo. State U., Kirksville, 1973-83, acting dean grad. studies, 1975, dean grad. studies, 1975-83; cons. U. Ariz., 1962. Recipient merit award Dairy Council Greater Kansas City, 1977; General Foods Fund fellow, 1959-60. Mem. Internat. Fedn. Home Econs., Am. Home Econs. Assn., Assn. Adminstrs. Home Econs., Mo. Home Econs. Assn., Am. Vocat. Assn., Mo. Vocat. Assn., Nat. Council Adminstrs. Home Econs., Nat. Assn. Post Secondary Adult Vocat. Home Econs., Mo. State Tchrs. Assn., AAUW, Omicron Nu, Pi Lambda Theta, Delta Kappa Gamma, Sigma Delta Epsilon, Kappa Omicron Phi, Phi Upsilon Omicron, Phi Kappa Phi. Republican. Mormon. Club: Quota Internat. Co-author: (with F. Ehrenkranz) Equipment in the Home, 1973; contbr. articles to profl. jours.

INMAN, TERRY W., oil distribution company executive; b. Sidney, Iowa, Sept. 23, 1940; s. Percy Warren and Mildred Josephine (Campin) I.; m. Patricia Kae Sabo, June 4, 1966; children: Barbara Ann Inman Hanigosky, Dawn Marie, Terry Warren II, Scott Christopher. AA, Cameron State U., Lawton, Okla., 1959; BA in Chemistry, Okla. State U., 1963. Staff chemist, mgr. FMC Corp., Front Royal, Va., 1966-67; in mktg. and mgmt. Mobil Oil Corp., Fairfax, Va., 1967-83; pres., chief exec. officer Clark County Oil Co. subs. Twinman, Inc., Worthington, Ohio, 1963—; v.p., chief fin. officer Fed. Oil Co., Dayton, Ohio, 1986—. Served to capt. U.S. Army, 1963-66, Vietnam. Mem. Am. Soc. Lubrication Engrs. Club: Worthington Hills Country. Avocations: travel, fishing, bridge, reading, lic. comml. pilot. Home: 1240 Clubview Blvd N Worthington OH 43085 Office: Clark County Oil Co subs Twinman 1660 S Yellow Springs St PO Box 1927 Springfield OH 45501

INOHARA, MITSUYA, computer company executive; b. Fujisawa, Kanagawa, Japan, Aug. 19, 1940; came to U.S., 1967; s. Haruo and Chikaka Inohara; m. Kikue Inohara, Oct. 4, 1966; children: Miki, Isamu. BS in Applied Physics, Keio U., Tokyo, 1963; MBA, San Diego State U., 1978. Customer engr. NCR Corp., Tokyo, 1963-67; tech. specialist, mgr. NCR Corp., San Diego, 1967-79; corp. product mgr. NCR Corp., Dayton, Ohio, 1979-83; dir. product mgmt. NCR Corp., Augsburg, Fed. Republic Germany, 1983-85; product mgr. strategic internat. mfg. NCR Corp., Dayton, 1985—. Home: 1715 Park Creek Dr Centerville OH 45459 Office: NCR Corp 1700 S Patterson Blvd Dayton OH 45479

INSLEY, RICHARD WALLACE, lawyer; business executive; b. Tampa, Fla., Sept. 27, 1918; s. Levin Irving and Sadie Bell (Waddell) I.; m. Eleanor Jane Robinson, Oct. 22, 1945; children: Glen Thomas, Anne Insley McCausland. AB, Trinity Coll., Hartford, Conn., 1946; JD, U. Va., 1970; MBA, Harvard U., 1948. Bar: Mich. 1956. Mem. Richard W. Insley, Atty.-at-Law, St. Joseph, Mich., 1950—; pres. Southwestern Developers Inc., St. Joseph, 1960—, also bd. dirs.; pres. Whinco Inc., Pizza Hut franchisee, St. Joseph, 1969—, also bd. dirs.; v.p., sec. Jan Barb, Inc., Holiday Inn franchisee, St. Joseph, 1970—, also bd. dirs. Trustee Barat Coll., Lake Forest, Ill., 1972-82; mem. U.S. Senate Bus. Adv. Bd., Washington. Served to lt. USN, 1942-45. Decorated Silver Star. Mem. ABA, Mich. State Bar Assn., Berrien County Bar Assn. Republican. Episcopalian. Clubs: Point O'Woods Country, Berrien Hills Country (Benton Harbor, Mich.). Home: 278 Ridgeway Saint Joseph MI 49085 Office: 421 Main St PO Box 63 Saint Joseph MI 49085

INZETTA, MARK STEPHEN, lawyer; b. N.Y.C., Apr. 14, 1956; s. James William and Rose Delores (Cirnigliaro) I.; m. Amy Marie Elbert, June 25, 1977; children: Michelle, Margot, Mallory. BBA summa cum laude, U. Cin., 1977; JD, U. Akron, 1980. Bar: Ohio 1980, U.S. Dist. Ct. (no. dist.) Ohio 1980. Legal intern City of Canton, Ohio, 1979-80; assoc. W.J. Ross Co. L.P.A., Canton, 1980-84; real estate counsel Wendy's Internat. Inc., Columbus, Ohio, 1984—; instr. real estate law Stark Tech. Coll., Canton, 1983. Case and comment editor: Akron Law Rev., 1979-80. Instr. religious edn. St. Peter's Cath. Ch.; bd. dirs. Brookside Village Civic Assn., 1985-87, treas., 1986-87; chmn. campaign Earle Wise Appellate Judge, North Canton, Ohio, 1982. Recipient Am. Jurisprudence award Lawyers Coop. Pub. Co., 1978; Dir. of Yr. award North Canton Jaycees, 1982, Presdl. award of honor, 1984; Dist. Dir. award of honor, Ohio Jaycees, 1984. Mem. ABA, Ohio Bar Assn., North Canton Jaycees (bd. dirs. 1981-82, v.p. 1982-83, pres. 1983-84), North Canton C. of C. (bd. dirs. 1983-84). Democrat. Roman Catholic. Home: 1584 Sandy Side Dr Worthington OH 43085 Office: Wendy's Internat Inc 4288 W Dublin-Granville Rd Dublin OH 43017

IORGULESCU, JORGE, international executive, chemical engineer; b. Buenos Aires, July 12, 1935; came to U.S., 1967; s. Nicolas and Ida (Mayer) I.; m. Beatriz Esther Cobenas, July 24, 1969; children: Bernard, Lionel, Andrew. Cert. chemist, LaPlata Nat. Indsl. Sch., Buenos Aires, 1953; MSChemE, LaPlata Nat. U., Buenos Aires, 1959; Program Mgmt. Devel., Harvard U. Sch. Bus., 1970. Tech. mgr. Ducilo S.A. subs. DuPont de Nemours, Buenos Aires, 1959-61; tech. dir. Liquid Carbonic Argentina, Buenos Aires, 1961-67; dir. engring. and prodn. Internat. div. Liquid Carbonic Corp., Chgo., 1967-70, v.p. ops., 1970-83; sr. v.p. internat. Liquid Carbonic Corp., Chgo., 1983-84; pres. Liquid Carbonic Internat. Service Corp., Chgo., 1984—. Mem. ASME, Am. Inst. Chem. Engrs., Am. Mgmt. Assn., Assn. MBA Execs., Council Fgn. Relations, Am. Society Council of the Ams. Avocations: opera, tennis. Home: 504 S Garfield Hinsdale IL 60521 Office: Liquid Carbonic Internat Services 135 S LaSalle St Suite 841 Chicago IL 60603

IORIO, RALPH ARTHUR, automotive company executive; b. Rochester, N.Y., Nov. 21, 1925; s. Andrew and Theresa (Civitillo) I.; m. Ann Marie Ferrante, Sept. 12, 1953; children—Kathleen, Alice, Robert. BEE, Villanova U., 1950. Supt. prodn. engring. Rochester (N.Y.) Products div. Gen. Motors, 1963-67; v.p. engring. ITT Higbie Mfg. Co., Rochester, Mich., 1967-73, v.p. ops., 1973-75, exec. v.p., 1975-81, pres., 1981—; pres. Baylock Mfg. Co., Leonard, Mich., Rochester (N.Y.) Form Machine (subs. ITT Higbie Mfg. Co.), Hisan Co.; v.p. Sterling Stainless Tube Corp.; instr. electronics Rochester Inst. Tech. (N.Y.), 1963-66; bd. dirs. Fulton TI, Birmingham, Eng., Fulton Rohr Hochenheim, Fed. Republic Germany. Bd. dirs Greenfield Health Systems subs. Henry Ford Hosp. Trustee, Henry Ford Satellite Hosp., Sterling Heights, Mich. Served with USN, 1944-46. Mem. Engring. Soc. Detroit. Roman Catholic. Home: 574 Overbrook Rd Bloomfield Hills MI 48013 Office: Higbie Mfg Co 4th & Water Sts Rochester MI 48463

IOTT, GREGORY LAWRENCE, marketing executive; b. Monroe, Mich., June 11, 1951; s. Vern Joseph and Bernice Kathryn (Wittman) I.; m. Debbie A. Meyer, Oct. 13, 1979 (div. Feb. 1982); m. Diane Kay Daubert, July 7, 1984; 1 child, Laura Christine. BA, Mich. State U., 1973. Asst. advt. dir. Prakken Publs., Ann Arbor, Mich., 1973-75; mktg. services mgr. J.J. Keller & Assoc., Neenah, Wis., 1975-82; mktg. dir. Miles Kimball Co., Oshkosh, Wis., 1982—. Bd. dirs. Oshkosh Symphony Assn., 1982—. Mem. Direct Mail Mktg. Assn., Am. Telemarketing Assn., Mich. State U. Adv. Alumni Assn. Roman Catholic. Avocations: bicycling, crosscountry skiing, outdoor activities, music, crafts. Home: 475 Zarling Ave Oshkosh WI 54901 Office: Miles Kimball Co 41 W 8th Ave Oshkosh WI 54901

IOTT, WALLACE D., supermarket chain executive; b. Monroe, Mich., 1915; married. Mgr. br. store A.A. Flors Co., 1939-40; owner, pres. Wally's, 1941-57; pres. State Line Food Market, Inc., 1952-57; pres. Seaway Food Town, Inc., Maumee, Ohio, 1957—, chmn., from 1961, also dir., former chief exec. officer; dir. No. Distbg. Co., Staff Supermarket Assocs., Inc.; bd. dirs. Food Mktg. Inst. Lodge: K.C. Office: Seaway Food Town Inc 1020 Ford St Maumee OH 43537 *

IRELAND, LEE WILSON, school counselor; b. Neosho, Mo., Feb. 26, 1951; s. Paul Wilson and Myra Louise (Million) I.; m. Rayma Lea Reed, Aug. 12, 1972; 1 child, Shonda Ray. BS in Biology, Mo. So. State Coll., 1973; MS in Counseling, Pittsburg State U., 1985. Cert. tchr., Mo. Tchr. sci. Purdy (Mo.) Region 2 Schs., 1973-79; instr. biology Seneca (Mo.) Region 7 Schs., 1979-85, dir. spl. services and elem. counselor, 1985—; assoc. instr. Mo. Fire and Rescue Tng. Inst., Columbia, 1982—; instr. Mo. Emergency Med. Technicians, Neosho, 1980-85. Vol. Neosho Fire Dept., 1969—. Named one of Outstanding Young Men Am., 1982, Fireman of Yr., Neosho Fire Dept., 1985. Mem. Mo. Sch. and Guidance Assn., Mo. Council Adminstrs. in Spl. Edn., Council Exceptional Children, Mo. State Tchrs. Assn., United Comml. Travelers Am. Avocations: photography, farming, carpentry, fishing, football. Home: 1409 Center St Neosho MO 64850 Office: Seneca Region 7 Schs PO Box 469 Seneca MO 64865

IRESTONE, PATRICK PAUL, infosystems specialist; b. St. Paul, June 24, 1950; s. James John and Patricia Ann (Kirkwood) I.; m. Deborah Ann Hirte, Sept. 6, 1969; children: Carly Jean, Kyle Patrick. BA in Mathematics, U. Minn., 1972. Programmer FMC Corp., Mpls., 1972-73; programmer analyst Control Data, Mpls., 1973-74; dir. MIS Medtronic, Inc., Fridley, Minn., 1974-84, Mpls. Star & Tribune, Mpls., 1984—. Mem. Soc. Info. Mgmt., Medtronic Found. Home: 1597 Chatham Ave Arden Hills MN 55112 Office: Mpls Star & Tribune 425 Portland Ave Minneapolis MN 55488

IRPINO, MICHAEL LOUIS, small business owner; b. Chgo., Sept. 19, 1923; s. Dominic and Mary (Chaio) I.; m. Frances Averette, June 20, 1952 (div. 1980). Student, North Park Coll., 1958, Oakton Community Coll., 1985. Sgt. Ill. State Police, 1950-62; pres. Michael's Pub. Inc., Skokie, Ill., 1963—. Served to sgt. USAF, 1943-46. Recipient Appreciation plaque Sky Ranch for Boys, 1970-83; Maryville Sch., 1981. Mem. VFW. Roman Catholic. Lodge: Moose. Avocations: golf, bowling, travel, thoroughbreds. Home: 8626 School St Morton Grove IL 60053 Office: Michael's Pub 8266 Lincoln Ave Skokie IL 60077

IRSAY, JAMES STEVEN, professional football team executive; b. Lincolnwood, Ill., June 13, 1959; s. Robert Irsay and Harriet Pogerzelski; m. Margret Mary Coyle, Aug. 2, 1980; children: Carlie Margret, Casey Coyle, Kalen. B in Broadcast Journalism, So. Meth. U., 1982. With Balt. Colts., from early 1970's; now v.p., gen. mgr. Indpls. Colts; corp. mem. Indiana Sports Corp., Indpls., 1985-87. Composer, performer single Hoosier Heartland, 1985, single and video Go Colts, 1985. Bd. dirs. Noble Ctrs. Retarded Children, Indpls., 1985-87, Motorcycle Drill Team, Indpls. Police Dept., 1985-87. Avocations: weight lifting, guitar, songwriting. Office: Indpls Colts PO Box 24100 Indianapolis IN 46224

IRSAY, ROBERT, professional football club executive, construction company executive; b. Chgo., Mar. 5, 1923; s. Charles J. and Elaine (Nyrtia) I.; m. Harriet Pogorzelski, July 12, 1946; children: Thomas, James. B.S.M.E., U. Ill., 1941. Pres. Robert Irsay Co., Skokie, Ill., 1952-78, Colt Constrn. and Devel. Co., Skokie, Ill., 1978—, Balt. Football Club, Inc., 1972-84, Indpls. Colts, 1984—; dir. Mich. Ave. Nat. Bank, Chgo., 1970-76. Bd. dirs. Clearbrook Ctr. for Handicapped, Rolling Meadows, Ill., 1982-83; bd. dirs. Troubled Children's Found., Hialeah, Fla., 1982-83. Served to lt. USMC, 1941-46, PTO. Home: 156 Sheridan Rd Winnetka IL 60093 *

IRVIN, JOHNNA ANN, social services administrator; b. Hannibal, Mo., Oct. 12, 1934; d. John Henry and Julia Mabel (Shephard) Schadey; m. John A. Bowen, Sept. 24, 1955 (div. 1982); children: John A. Bowen II, Kelly Layne Bowen; m. Gregg Irvin, Mar. 10, 1982. Student in nursing, Hannibal Voc. Sch., 1980. Staff nurse St. Elizabeth's Hosp., Hannibal, 1980-86; owner Levee House, Hannibal, 1986—. Mem. NSPE, Mo. State Bd. Nursing. Baptist. Avocations: trains, football, golf. Home: 263 Lake Apollo Dr Hannibal MO 63401

IRVINE, MAGNUS KEITH, publishing company executive; b. Ipswich, Suffolk, Eng., Aug. 7, 1924; came to U.S., 1952; s. Frederick Robert and Dorothy Stuart Campbell (Gilchrist) I.; m. Marie Aline Hekimian, Apr. 9, 1949; children—Mary Lilian, Marie Dominique, Madeline Maya, John David. Student U. Manchester (Eng.), 1941-42, U. London, 1942, U. Edinburgh (Scotland), 1946-47, The Sorbonne, Paris, 1947-48. Asst. to state dir. Am. Found. for Polit. Edn., N.Y.C., 1956-58; research dir. Ghana Mission to UN, N.Y.C., 1958-69; prin. editor geography Ency. Brit., Chgo., 1969-73; gen. editor encys. Scholarly Press Inc., St. Clair Shores, Mich., 1973-75; pres. Reference Publs. Inc., Algonac, Mich., 1975—. Served with Brit. Royal Navy, 1943-46. Roman Catholic. Author: The Rise of the Colored Races, 1970; gen. editor: Encyclopaedia of Indians of North America, 1974-75, Encyclopaedia Africana Dictionary of African Biography, 1977, Encyclopaedia Africana, 1987—; contbr. articles to numerous encys.

IRWIN, DOUGLAS WADE, auditor; b. Bloomington, Ill., Dec. 3, 1945; s. Lyle Wade and Margie Bernice (Barclay) I.; m. Linda Louise McClure, Sept. 1, 1968; children: Douglas Wade Jr., Penelope Anne. BS, So. Ill. U., 1968, MBA, 1970. Staff acct. Price Waterhouse, St. Louis, 1970; staff acct., mgr. Clifton Gunderson and Co., Kewanee, Ill., 1971-77; ptnr. Kemper CPA Group, Kewanee, 1977-81, Irwin Rollins & Co., Kewanee, 1981-82; pvt. practice acct. Kewanee, 1982-83; pres. Douglas W. Irwin & Co., Ltd., Kewanee, 1984—. Scoutmaster Boy Scouts Am., Kewanee, 1971—, bd. dirs. Prairie council, 1977—, treas., 1978—, mem. Nat. council, rep. Prairie council, Irving, Tex., 1986—. Recipient Silver Beaver award Boy Scouts Am., 1981. Mem. Am. Inst. CPA's, Ill. Soc. CPA's. Republican. Lodge: Rotary (dir. 1984-86, treas. 1986—). Home: 701 E Prospect Kewanee IL 61443 Office: 222 N Main Kewanee IL 61443

IRWIN, GLENN WARD, JR., physician, university official; b. Roachdale, Ind., July 18, 1920; s. Glenn Ward and Elsie (Browning) I.; m. Marianna Ashby; children: Ann Graybill Irwin Warden, William Browning, Elizabeth Ashby Irwin Schiffli. BS, Ind. U., Bloomington, 1942; MD, Ind. U., Indpls., 1944; LLD (hon.), Ind. U., 1986. Diplomate: Am. Bd. Internal Medicine. Intern Meth. Hosp., Indpls., 1944-45; resident in internal medicine Ind. U. Med. Ctr., Indpls., 1945-46, 48-50; mem. faculty Ind. U., Indpls., 1950—, instr. , asst. prof. then assoc. prof., 1950-61, prof. medicine, 1961-86, prof. emeritus, 1986, dean Sch. Medicine, 1965-73, v.p., 1974-86; chancellor Ind. U.-Purdue U., Indpls., 1973-74; sr. assoc. Ind. U. Found.; bd. dirs. Unified Cos. Bd. dirs. United Way, Indpls.; bd. dirs. Indpls. Ctr. Advanced Research, 1975—, Commn. for Downtown, Inc., Goodwill Industries of Central Ind., Indpls., Greater Indpls. Progress Com., Greater Indpls. YMCA, Walther Med. Research Inst., Walther Oncology Ctr., Indpls. Health Inst., Eiteljorg Mus. Western Art and the Am. Indian; elder 2d Presby. Ch. Served to capt. M.C. U.S. Army, 1946-48. Recipient Disting. Alumnus award Ind. U. Sch. Medicine, 1972, Otis R. Bowen Physician County Service award, Benjamin Harrison award, Ind. Acad. award; named Sagamore of the Wabash, Gov. of Ind., 1979. Fellow ACP (gov. for Ind. 1964-70); mem. AMA, Ind. State Med. Assn., Marion County Med. Soc., Ind. Soc. of Chgo., 500 Festival Assn., James Whitcomb Riley Meml. Assn. (bd. govs. 1964-70), Newcomen Soc., Sigma Xi, Alpha Omega Alpha, Beta Gamma Sigma. Clubs: Columbia (Indpls.), Contemporary (Indpls.), Meridian Hills Country, Skyline (bd. dirs.). Lodge: Masons (33 degree), Rotary. Home: 8025 N Illinois Indianapolis IN 46260 Office: Ind Univ-Purdue Univ at Indpls 355 Lansing St Indianapolis IN 46202

IRWIN, LAWRENCE BURTON, accountant; b. Cleve., Mar. 21, 1947; s. Lawrence M. and Barbara L. (Boer) I.; m. Shirley Kay Meece, Feb. 27, 1971; children: Shane, Lesley, Margaret. BS in Acctg., U. Ill., 1969; MBA in Fin., Ohio State U., 1970. CPA, Ill.; lic. real estate broker, Ill. Acct. Arthur Andersen & Co., Chgo., 1971-72; dir. fin. planning Advance Schs., Inc., Chgo., 1972-74; sr. fin. analyst Baxter Travenol, Deerfield, Ill., 1974-76; pres. Burton Group, Schaumburg, Ill., 1976—; real estate broker Burton Investment Properties, Inc., Schaumburg, 1981—; fin. planner Burton Fin. Planning, Inc., Schaumburg, 1985—. Pres. Barrington (Ill.) PTA, 1982; mem. sch. bd. adv. com. Barrington, 1985. Served to lt U.S. Army, 1970-71. Named Eagle Scout, Boy Scout Am., 1960. Mem. Am. Inst. CPAs, Ill. CPA Soc., Barrington (Ill.) C. of C., NW Suburban Assn. of Commerce. Republican. Episcopalian. Home: 206 Otis Rd Barrington IL 60010 Office: Burton Assocs 921 N Plum Grove Rd Schaumburg IL 60173

IRWIN, L(YNN) JAY, III, lawyer; b. Des Moines, Aug. 15, 1953; s. Lynn Jay Jr. and Lucille Mae (Schoen) I.; m. Cynthia Lynn Lizer, May 14, 1983; 1 child, Ashley Anne. Diploma, Kansas State Police Acad., 1974; BA cum laude, Drake U., 1983, JD with honors, 1985. Bar: Iowa, 1986, U.S. Dist. Ct. (no. and so. dists.) Iowa, 1986, U.S. Ct. Appeals (8th cir.) 1986. Law enforcement officer Topeka Police Dept., 1974-76; legal investigator Patterson Law Firm, Des Moines, 1977-82; sole practice Des Moines, 1986—. Vol. United Way of Greater Des Moines, 1978—, Friends of the Des Moines Ballet, 1985—; arbitrator Council of Better Bus. Bur., Washington, 1979—. Mem. ABA, Iowa Bar Assn., Polk County Bar Assn., Assn. Trial Lawyers Am., Iowa Trial Lawyers Assn., Delta Theta Phi, Tau Kappa Epsilon. Republican. Episcopalian. Office: 506 Hubbell Bldg 904 Walnut St Des Moines IA 50309

IRWIN, STEVEN RAY, dentist; b. Kansas City, Mo., Jan. 21, 1950; s. Alfred Coburn and Sylvia Nadine (Leddy) I. BS in Sociology, S.W. Mo. State U., 1972, MBA, 1975; DDS, U. Mo., Kansas City, 1984. Dentist James Elias, DDS, Raytown, Mo., 1984-85; pvt. practice dentistry Grandview, Mo., 1985—; cons. dentist Kansas City Zoo, 1986—. Mem. ADA, Kans. City Dental Soc., Friends of the Zoo. Office: 13013 Fuller Ave Suite C Grandview MO 64030

ISAAC, TOM RICHARD, oil and gas company executive; b. Wadsworth, Ohio, May 26, 1955; s. Lawrence Junior and Donna Virginia (Ullman) I.; m. Jan Elaine Zivick, June 25, 1977; children: Megan Christine, andrea Michelle. BA in Devel. Psychology, Wooster (Ohio) Coll., 1977. Tchr. Wooster City Schs., 1977-78; sales rep. J.M. Huber Corp., Wooster, 1978-79; rig hand Armstrong Drilling, Wooster, 1979-80; ops. mgr. Belden & Blake Corp., North Canton, Ohio, 1980-87, dir. purchasing, 1987—. Mem. mission study com. Reedurban Presby. Ch., Canton, Ohio, 1986. Mem. Soc. Petroleum Engrs., Ohio Oil and Gas Assn. Republican. Avocation: tennis. Home: 5411 Oakcliff St SW Canton OH 44706 Office: Belden and Blake Corp 7555 Freedom Ave NW North Canton OH 44720

ISAACS, ANN REBECCA FABE, educational association administrator, educator, editor; b. Cin., July 2, 1920; d. William and Bessie (Jacoby) Fabe; m. S. Ted Isaacs, July 7, 1939; children: Marjorie Jane, Susan Lynn. BA, U. Cin., 1944; MEd, Xavier U., 1952; postgrad., Ohio State U., 1964, Case Western Res. U., 1968, Case Western Res. U., 1969, Hebrew Union Coll., 1969-75, 79-85; PhD (hon.), NSF, 1977. Psychologist Hamilton County Child Welfare, Cin., 1944-45, Personality Testing Bur., Cin., 1945-49; dir. Personality Devel. Presch., Cin., 1949-57; exec. dir., founder Nat. Assn. for Gifted Children, Cin., 1954-75; pvt. practice counseling Cin., 1954—; chief exec. officer Nat. Assn. for Creative Children and Adults, Cin., 1976—; inservice tchr. trainer numerous schs. and orgns., 1954—; vis. prof., lectr. over 20 univs., 1954—; cons. gifted-talented creative individuals and orgns., 1974—. Author: Crossroads of Talent, 1965, Creativity and Giftedness: An Acrostic for Home and Classroom, 1975, How To Teach Ourselves To Be Good To One Another, 1975, The Creative Cat, 1977, Common Sense Creativity, 1982, How To Be Personally Creative, 1986; founding editor The Gifted Child Quarterly, 1957-75, The Creative Child and Adult Quarterly, 1976—; prin. works include Hallel, Rainbow Snorata, Psalm 8: What Is Man?, numerous others; exhibited in traveling show Smithsonian Mus., 1983; composer of songs; contbr. over 400 articles to profl. jours. Councilperson Amberley Village, Ohio, 1983-86; founder, exec. dir. Cin. Ten, Music for Life; friend of Cin. Zoo; leader Cin. Girl Scouts Am., 1957-67; active Wise Temple Sisterhood, Cin. Named Woman of Yr., City of Cin., 1969. Mem. Nat. Assn. Composers, Cin. Composer's Guild (adv. bd.), Cin. Editor's Assn., Edn. Press. Assn. Am. (bd. govs., Excellence award 1974-76), Music Educator's Nat. Conf., Am. Soc. for Jewish Music, Am. Assn. for the Gifted, Nat. Assn. for Gifted Children (pres. 1954-58), Nat. Assn. for Creative Children and Adults (pres. 1976-80), Brandeis U. Women (life). Jewish. Avocations: gardening, dancing, swimming, sketching, needlework. Home and Office: 8080 Springvalley Dr Cincinnati OH 45236

ISAACS, BURTON EDWARD, lawyer; b. Detroit, Dec. 4, 1934; s. Louis and Ethel (Kramer) I.; m. Sandra Zager, Mar. 20, 1958 (div. 1978); children—Ellen, Craig; m. Judith Roselle Lipson, Nov. 23, 1979. Student Wayne State U., 1953-56; LL.B., Detroit Coll. Law, 1959. Bar: Mich. 1959. With IRS, Detroit, 1958-66; revenue officer, estate tax atty. trust dept. Nat. Bank of Detroit, 1967-69; prin. Rubenstein, Isaacs, Lax & Bordman, Southfield, Mich., 1969—. Mem. ABA (real property, probate and trust, tax and econs. sects.), State Bar of Mich. (legal econs. sect., estate planning and tax sect.). Office: 17220 W Twelve Mile Rd Suite 200 Southfield MI 48076

ISAACS, KENNETH S(IDNEY), psychoanalyst, educator; b. Mpls., Apr. 7, 1920; s. Mark William and Sophia (Rai) I.; m. Ruth Elizabeth Johnson, Feb. 21, 1951 (dec. 1967); m. Adele Rella Brodroghy, May 17, 1969; children—Jonathan, James; stepchildren—John, Curtis, Peter and Edward Meissner. B.A., U. Minn., 1944; Ph.D., U. Chgo., 1956; postgrad., Inst. Psychoanalysis, 1957-63. Intern Worcester State Hosp., Mass., 1947-48; trainee VA Hosp., Chgo., 1948-50; chief psychologist outpatient clinic system Ill. Dept. Pub. Welfare, 1949-56; research assoc., assoc. prof. U. Ill. Med. Sch., Chgo., 1956-63; practice psychoanalysis Evanston, Ill., 1960—; supr. psychiat. residency program Evanston Hosp., Northwestern U., 1972-81; pres. Chgo. Ctr. Psychoanalytic Psychology, 1984-87; cons. to schs., hosps., clinics, pvt. practitioners; pres. Kenisa Drilling Co., Kenisa Securities Co., Kenisa Oil Co. Contbr. articles to profl. publs. Served with AUS, 1943-45, ETO. Mem. Am. Psychol. Assn. (bd. dirs. div. psychoanalysis), AAAS, Chgo. Psychoanalytic Soc., Am. Bd. Psychoanalysis (sec. bd. dirs.), N.Y. Acad. Sci., Sigma Xi.

ISAACS, S. TED, engineering company executive; b. Louisville, July 13, 1914; s. Max and Rose (Kaplan) I., m. Ann Fabe, June 6, 1938; children: Marjorie McKelvey, Susan L. Freund. BS in Chem. Engring., U. Cin., 1936, AA, 1944. Registered profl. engr. , Ohio; cert. sr. grade fluid power tech. Instrument engr. Standard Oil Co. Ohio, Latonia, Ky., 1936-41; instrumentation mgr. Wright Aero. Corp., Lockland, Ohio, 1941-45; sr. process engr. Drackett Co., Cin., 1945-48; pres. The Isaacs Co., Cin., 1948-86; mng. gen ptnr. AFTI Systems, Cin., 1986—; v.p. sales, pres. Indsl. Engring. Corp., Louisville, 1951-55. Contbr. articles to profl. jours. Energy commn. chmn. City Environ. Task Force, Cin., 1970-72. Mem. Instrument Soc. Am. (sr., life, local bd. dirs. 1946-47), Engring. Soc. Cin. (life, pres. jr. chpt. 1947-48), Fluid Power Soc., Metric Assn. (v.p. 1962-65), Sierra Club, Ohio Assn. Railway Passengers. Democrat. Jewish. Avocations: swimming, bridge, spectator sports, music, art. Home: 8080 Springvalley Dr Cincinnati OH 45236 Office: AFTI Systems 1840 Amberlawn Dr Cincinnati OH 45237

ISAACSON, JERRY DAVID, business owner, accountant; b. Chgo., Feb. 26, 1961; s. Calvin and Eileen (Zisook) I. BS, U. Ill., 1983. CPA, Ill. Accountant Laventhol & Horwath, Chgo., 1983; v.p. Gold Merchants, Chgo., 1983-84; pres. Wizards Ice Cream Magic, Chgo., 1984—. Patentee in field. Mem. Am. Inst. CPAs, Music Found. Clubs: East Bank (Chgo.); North Shore (Morton Grove, Ill.). Avocations: sailing, golf, skiing. Office: Wizards Ice Cream Magic 730 N Franklin Chicago IL 60610

ISACKES, RICHARD MORGAN, theatre educator; b. Lexington, Ky., Dec. 6, 1945; s. Charles French and Jean (Knight) I.; m. Beverly Ann Ruddell, Jan. 10, 1982. Student, Oberlin (Ohio) Coll., 1964-67; BA, New Sch. for Social Research, N.Y.C., 1969; MFA, Carnegie Mellon U., 1975. Tchr. Sewickley Acad., Pitts., 1969-72; asst. prof. Bucknell U., Lewisburg, Pa., 1974-76, Boston U., 1978-82; assoc. prof. U. Ill., Champaign/Urbana, 1982—; free lance set designer 1969—; asst. set designer (soap opera) Love of Life, staff set designer Another World. Works include Fedora, N.Y. Lyric Opera Co., Cosi Fan Tutti, Chgo. Lyric Opera, The Woodlanders, Opera Theatre of St. Louis, Two Gentlemen of Verona, Colo. Shakespeare Festival, Boulder. Recipient Hub award Boston Circle Critics, 1983, 85. Mem. United Scenic Artists of Am. Home: Rural Rt 3 Box 24 Champaign IL 61821 Office: U Ill 500 S Goodwin Urbana IL 61801

ISAKSON, STEVEN LOUIS, accountant; b. Mankato, Minn., Nov. 8, 1959; s. Eugene Joseph and Janice Irene (Pettis) I.; m. Jill Elizabeth Stutz, Aug. 21, 1982. BS in Acctg. and Fin., Mankato State U., 1982. CPA, Minn. Staff acct. Morken, Andring & Co., Le Sueur, Minn., 1982-86, Gazzola, Wolf, Etter & Co., North Mankato, Minn., 1986—. Home: 2449 Northridge Dr North Mankato MN 56001 Office: Gazzola Wolf Etter & Co 1120 South Ave North Mankato MN 56001

ISBELL, JANICE MITCHELL, industrial engineer; b. Beaumont, Tex., July 30, 1956; d. Julius Joseph and Janie Mae (Nixon) Mitchell; m. Irvin Lee Isbell, June 6, 1981; 1 child, Irvin Lee Jr. BS ChemE, Washington U., St. Louis, 1980. Indsl. engr. Purex Corp., St. Louis, 1983-85, U.S. Army, St. Louis, 1985—; instr. algebra, basic math Ranken Tech., St. Louis, 1985—. Coach girls' basketball St. Alphonsus Ch. Mem. Am. Helicopter Soc., Nat. Assn. Female Execs., Internat. Tng. Communication (pres. 1986—, publicity chmn. 1983-84), Army Aviation Assn. Am., Fed. Employed Women, Zeta Phi Beta. Democrat. Roman Catholic. Home: 6489 Roberts Ave University City MO 63130 Office: US Army Aviation Systems Command 4300 Goodfellow Blvd Saint Louis MO 63120

ISBELL, KAREN JUNE, consultant; b. Mountain Home, Ark., June 22, 1950; d. Henry H. and Alice I. Isbell (Phipps) I. BS in Psychology and Journalism, Murray State U., 1973. Editor employee publs. Mallinckrodt, Inc., 1973-77; asst. dir. pub. relations St. Louis Bi-State chpt. ARC, 1977-81, dir. pub. relations, 1981-84; account exec. UniCom Corp. Vol. counselor Reproductive Health Services, 1973-84; bd. dirs. Mo. Nat. Abortion Rights Action League, 1980—. Recipient Flair award, local advt. fedn., 1978, 81, 82, 83; named Leader in Communications, St. Louis YWCA. Mem. Internat. Assn. Bus. Communications (awards 1980, 81, 82, 83, dir. St. Louis chpt. 1977—), Pub. Relations Soc. Am. Office: UniCom Corp 505 S Ewing Ave Saint Louis MO 63103

ISBERG, GUNNAR CLIFFORD, city and regional planner; b. Chgo., Feb. 22, 1932; s. Gust Isberg and Gunhild (Brickman) Nelson; m. Carol Lou Sizemore, Sept. 1, 1963; children: Gunnar Boyd, Eric Andrew. BA in Polit. Sci., Roosevelt U., 1962; postgrad., U. Ill. Sch. Law, 1962-64; B in Urban Planning, U. Ill., 1966. Regional planner Twin Cities Met. Council, St. Paul, 1966-71; planning dir. Dakota County, Hastings, Minn., 1971-74; asst. planning dir. City of St. Paul, 1974-76; planning dir. S.M.S.Q. Architects and Planners, Northfield, Minn., 1976-78; pres. I.R.C. Planners, Mpls., 1978-80, Gunnar Isberg & Assocs., Northfield, 1980-86; planning dir. Rochester/Olmsted County, 1987—; mem. energy and natural resources com. Nat. League Cities, 1982—, energy-land use-transp. com. Minn. League Cities, St. Paul, 1980—, Gov.'s Com. on Land Use Law, St. Paul, 1985—. Author planning book Local & Regional Planning in Minnesota, 1975, 2 ed., 1980; contbr. numerous articles to profl. publs. Mem. City Council, Northfield, 1982—, Southeastern Rural Initiatives, Owatonna, Minn., 1985—. Served with USN, 1950-54. Recipient Outstanding Service award Minn. chpt. Soil and Water Conservation Soc. Am., 1980, New Orleans, 1982. Mem. Am. Planning Assn. (pres. Minn. chpt. 1980-81), Minn. Planning Assn. (v.p. 1976-78). Mem. Dem. Farm Labor Party. Methodist. Lodges: Rotary, Masons. Avocations: fishing, skiing, golf, camping. Home: 1300 Washington St Northfield MN 55057 Office: 109 S Water St Northfield MN 55057

ISENBERG, HOWARD LEE, manufacturing company executive; b. Chgo., Dec. 21, 1936; s. Philip and Mildred (Heyman) I.; m. Daryl Holtz, June 17, 1962 (div.); children: Suzanne, Marc; m. Judith Rosen, Aug. 7, 1977; 1 child, Alan. BS, U. Pa., 1958. CPA, Ill. Acct. David Himmelblau Co., Chgo., 1958-60; controller Conley Electronics, Chgo., 1960-63; controller, v.p. Barr Co. div. Pittway Corp., Niles, Ill., 1964-69, pres. Barr Co. div., 1969—; v.p. Pittway Corp., Niles, Ill., 1970—. Bd. advisors Options for People, Chgo., 1982—; treas., trustee Lake Forest (Ill.) Acad., 1986—. Served to 1st lt., U.S. Army, 1959. Mem. Chem. Specialities Mfgs. Assn. Club: International (Chgo.). Home: 686 Lyons Highland Park IL 60035 Office: Pittway Corp Barr Co Div 6100 W Howard St Niles IL 60648

ISENBERG, RAYE SYBIL, social worker; b. Chgo., Apr. 29, 1942; d. Leonard Milton and Lillian Love (Leviten) Havens: m. Sheldon Isenberg, Sept. 13, 1964; children: Joshua Miro, Tira Gavriela, Ariel David. Cert., Inst. Internat. Youth Leaders, Jerusalem, 1960-61; BA in Psychology, U. Chgo., 1967; cert., Gestalt Inst. Chgo., 1974; MSW, U. Ill., 1975. Cert. social worker, Ill. Asst. dir. adolescent unit Ridgeway Hosp., Chgo., 1971-72; project asst. family systems tng. program Inst. Juvenile Research, Chgo., 1972; intern Young Women's Christian Assn. DuPage County, Lombard, Ill., 1973-74; instr. Coll. DuPage, Wheaton, Ill., 1974-75; pvt. practice psychotherapy Lisle and Naperville, Ill., 1975-80; founding ptnr., psychotherapist Isenberg and Assocs., Naperville, 1980—; adj. faculty div. social work edn., George Williams Coll., Downers Grove, Ill., 1975-83; instr. Cen. Continuing Edn., North Central Coll., Naperville, 1982-85, women's adv. bd. continuing edn., 1982-85; bd. dirs. Gestalt Inst. Chgo., Evanston, Ill. Author: (manual) Pro Se Divorce Manual, 1973; producer (video) A Woman's Self Help Clinic, 1974. Sec., bd. dirs. Naperville Women's Resource Project, 1974-76; chmn. bd. dirs. Congregation Beth Shalom, Naperville, 1975-84; sponsor INSIGHTS Community Edn. Series, Naperville, 1985—; judge Ill. High Sch. History Contest, Des Plaines, 1986. Mayor's Office scholar Chgo., 1960, United Synagogues Am. scholar, 1960; named one of Outstanding Young Women Am., 1977. Mem. Nat. Assn. Social Workers (Ill. chpt. Com. on Inquiry 1983-87), Assn. Mental Health Aid Israel, Women in Mgmt. (chairperson spl. events Oak Brook chpt. 1986—), NOW, Naperville C. of C. Avocations: reading, hiking, camping, art, travel. Home: 831 Edgewater Dr Naperville IL 60540 Office: Isenberg & Assocs 552 S Washington St Naperville IL 60540

ISENBERG, STEVEN FREDERICK, physician; b. Indpls., May 30, 1950; s. David Sam and Thelma (Heath) I.; m. Kristine Marie Kohls, Oct. 18, 1969; children: Jason, Mark, Amanda. BS, Ind. U., 1971, MD, 1975. Intern, then resident in otolaryngology Ind. U., 1975-79; practice medicine specializing in otolaryngology Indpls., 1979—. Contbr. articles to profl. jours. Fellow Am. Acad. Otolaryngology, Am. Acad. Facial, Plastic and Reconstructive Surgery; mem. ACS, Alpha Omega Alpha. Home: 9080 Pickwick Dr Indianapolis IN 46260 Office: 5502 E 16th St Indianapolis IN 46218

ISENOGLE, KENNETH FRANKLIN, physician; b. Kokomo, Ind., Nov. 19, 1932; s. Bishop H. and Madge (Walker) I.; m. Luwanna Croxford; 1 child, Tambra Lynn Yates. Student, Ind. U., 1950-53, MD, 1957. Diplomate Am. Bd. Otolaryngology. Resident otolaryngology U. Ind. Hosp., Indpls., 1958-61; pvt. practice Ft. Wayne, Ind., 1961—; pres. Dr. Isenogle and Case, Inc., 1972-81; bd. dirs. Ft. Wayne Surg. Ctr., 1972, No. Ind. Health Systems Agy., 1975-77, Ind. State Health Coordinating Council, 1975-77; bd. dirs., co-founder Ind. Area Profl. Standards Rev.Orgn., Ft. Wayne Occupational Health Ctr., 1983-86. Bd. dirs. Ind. Blue Shield, 1969-75; founder, bd. dirs. Northeast Ind. Found. for med. Care, 1972; bd. dirs., sec. Physician Health Plan of No. Ind. Mem. AMA, ACS, Am. Acad. Otolaryngology and Head and Neck Surgery, Ind. State Med. Assn. (pres. 12th Ind. med. dist. 1968), Ind. Acad. Otolaryngology (pres. 1972), Ft. Wayne Med. soc. (pres. 1971-72, chmn. bd. dirs. 1973). Avocation: golf. Office: 2120 Carew Fort Wayne IN 46805

ISHIDA, YASUO, gynecologist, obstetrician; b. Tokyo, Japan, Aug. 3, 1931; s. Hei-Ichiro and Nami (Akiyama) I.; m. Magdalen C. Daily, 1967 (div. 1974); children: Keiko Cecilia, Yoshiko Theresa; m. Masako Saito, 1981; 1 child, Kenji Michael. BA, U. Oreg., 1958; MD, St. Louis U., 1967. Intern. St. Mary's Hosp., St. Louis, 1967-68; resident in ob-gyn St. Louis Univ. Hosps., 1968-71; practice medicine specializing in ob-gyn St. Louis, 1974—; instr. dept. ob/gyn St. Louis U., 1971-74; instr. dept. biology Webster Coll., St. Louis, 1962-63. Fellow Am. Coll. Ob-Gyn; mem. Internat. Childbirth Edn. Assn., Mo. Med. Soc., St. Louis Med. Soc., St. Louis Gynecol. Soc. Mem. Soc. of Friends. Home: 7446 York Dr Clayton MO 63105 Office: 6744 Clayton Rd Saint Louis MO 63117

ISLES, MARVIN LEE, manufacturing executive; b. Detroit, Jan. 16, 1946; s. Arden Murray and Marilyn Jane (Wingert) I.; m. Susan Kay Janes, Oct. 15, 1964; children: Stacey Lee, Loni Kay, Scott Arden. BSIndslE, Gen. Motors Inst., Flint, Mich., 1969; MBA, Mich. Tech. U., 1971; coop. student, Gen. Motors, Detroit, 1964-68. Engr. Gen. Motors, Detroit, 1968-71; v.p. mfg. Cadillac Products, Sterling Heights, Mich., 1972-79; pres. engineered elastomers div. Gen. Corp., Wabash, Ind., 1979—; mgmt. cons. Hill Assocs., Detroit, 1971-72. Inventor tooling automation for Gen. Motors, 1968, monetary award, 1969. Gen. Motors Grad. fellow, 1970-71. Republican. Episcopalian. Avocations: running, hunting, fishing, photography. Home: 1810 N Dumont Marion IN 46452 Office: Engineered Elastomers div GM One General St Wabash IN 46992

ISRAEL, FRED CARL, library director; b. Kitchener, Ont., Can., Jan. 23, 1933; s. Carl and Marie (Fuhrman) I.; m. L. Kathleen James, June 14, 1958. BA, U. Ottawa, Ont., Can., 1957; B of Library Sci., U. Toronto, Can., 1958. Cataloguer Can. Dept. Agr., Ottawa, Ont., 1958-59; chief librarian Richmond Hill (Ont.) Pub. Library, 1959-64, St. Catharines (Ont.) Pub. Library, 1964-68; dir. Windsor (Ont.) Pub. Library, 1968—; trustee Thames, Ont. Library Service Bd., 1984-85. Mem. Can. Library Assn., Ont. Library Assn. (pres. 1971-72), Council Adminstrs. Large Urban Pub. Libraries (chmn. 1984-86), Chief Execs. Large Pub. Libraries of Ont. (chmn. 1980-81). Club: Torch (Windsor, Ont.) (pres. 1975-76). Lodges: Rotary, KC. Office: Windsor Pub Library, 850 Ouellette Ave, Windsor, ON Canada N9A 4M9

ISRAEL, HOWARD STANLEY, steel company executive; b. Cleve., Aug. 14, 1931; s. Jacob and Gertrude Rosalind (Ausdeutcher) I.; m. Lois Joy Eppstein, Sept. 9, 1956; children—Patricia Jo, Michael Alan. B.S., Ohio State U., 1953. With Consumers Steel Products Co., Cleve., 1953-56, 59-75, mng. ptnr., 1969-75; founder, owner, pres. Tunbridge Steel Co., Cleve., 1976—. Trustee, bd. dirs., v.p. fgn. affairs Cleve. chpt. Am. Jewish Com.; mem. Greater Cleve. Growth Assn., ACLU, Youth Inst. for Peace, Cleve. Mus. Art, Musical Arts Assn., Anti-Defamation League, Smithsonian Instn.; mem. Republican Nat. Com., Am. Israel Pub. Affairs Com., Beachwood Arts Council, Am. Com. for Weizman Inst., Zionist Orgn. Am., Simon Wiesenthal Ctr., Friends of Beachwood Library; George Bush for Pres. campaign worker. Served with U.S. Army, 1956-58. Jewish. Clubs: Temple Men's, B'Nai B'Rith (Cleve.).

ISRAEL, PATRICK, psychiatrist; b. Chgo., Mar. 17, 1922; s. Joseph Leo and Bertha (Simon) I. BS, U. Ill., Chgo., 1946, MD, 1947. Diplomate Am. Bd. Neurology and Psychiatry. Practice medicine specializing in psychiatry Chgo., 1954—; clin. asst. prof. psychiatry U. Ill., Chgo., 1956—; attending psychiatrist Weiss Meml. Hosp., Chgo., 1962—, Barclay Hosp., Chgo., 1970—. Served to 1st lt. M.C., U.S. Army, 1951-53. Fellow Am. Psychiat. Assn.; mem. Ill. Psychiat. Soc., Am. Soc. Clin. Hypnosis. Office: 4640 Marine Dr Chicago IL 60640

ISRANI, KIM, civil engineer; b. Dadu, Pakistan, Dec. 24, 1935; s. Watamal and Vani I.; m. Yashi Israni, May 26, 1964; children: Vijay, Mamta, Sanjay. BS in Engring., Poona U., 1960; MS in Engring., Memphis State U., 1972. Asst. dir. Cen. Water and Power Commn., New Delhi, Ind., 1960-70; civil engr. Pollard Cons., Memphis, 1971-73; design engr. Talbot & Assoc., Orlando, Fla., 1974-75; facilities engr. Dept. Nat. Resources, Des Moines, 1976—. Contbr. articles to profl. jours. Chmn. Indian sect. Internat. Food Fair, Des Moines, 1977-86; dir. Indian dance group Iowa State Fair, Des Moines, 1982-86. Republican. Hindu. Avocations: reading, writing, boating, swimming, foreign travel. Home: 4024 83d St Des Moines IA 50322 Office: Dept Nat Resources Wallace Bldg Des Moines IA 50319-0034

ISSA, ASWAD HASHIM ASIM, minister, educator; b. Detroit, Feb. 19, 1948; s. Roscoe Conquering and Flora Dell (Sanders) Johnson; m. Diane Christine Gray, Aug. 6, 1978. BS, Wayne State U., 1971, MEd, 1977; M of Div., Interdenominational Theol. Ctr., 1981. Ordained to ministry, 1978; cert. tchr. Instr. Detroit Bd. Edn., 1971—; ministerial asst., advisor to youth advisor council, ch. sch. instr. New Calvary Bapt. Ch., Detroit, 1982—; adminstrv. aid to pres. Progressive Nat. Bapt. Conv., Washington, 1983-85, v.p. task force on preparation and initiation of youth into black Christian adulthood, 1983-86; adminstrv. asst. Christian Temple Bapt. Ch., Detroit, 1981-83, chmn. civic action com., 1968-78, 81-83, youth marriage counselor, 1977-78, 81-83. Distbr., dispatcher Richard Austin for Sec. of State com., Detroit, 1971, Coleman Young for Mayor com., Detroit, 1973; chmn. polit. action com. Eastside Detroit Concerned Citizens, 1973-74; del. Mich. Dem. Party, 1973-76; asst. supr. employment and tng. dept. cen. records Summer Youth Employment Program, 1980-81; contract worker Detroit Sr. Citizens Dept., 1982. Recipient Disting. Service award Detroit City Council, 1985, Cert. of Merit award Mich. Edn. Assn., Lansing, 1985. Fellow Fund for Theol. Edn. (Benjamin E. Mays award 1980-81), Dr. Charles W. Butler-New Calvary Bapt. Disting. Ministers (scholarship, award 1979-81); mem. NAACP, Interdenominational Theol. Ctr.-Morehouse Alumnus (treas. 1979-80, Service award 1980), Wayne State U. Alumnus, Kappa Alpha Psi (lt. strategist 1979-81). Avocations: hist. investigations, handicrafts, fixing and repairing, sports, music. Office: New Calvary Bapt Ch 3975 Concord Detroit MI 48207

ISSELHARD, DONALD EDWARD, dentist; b. Belleville, Ill., Apr. 11, 1941; s. Bertram Joseph and Margaret Eda (Dobbins) I.; m. Annette Scanaliato, Mar. 1, 1980; children: Kerstin, Nissa, Michelle, Tara. Student, St. Louis U., 1960-62; BS in Dentistry, U. Ill., Chgo., 1966, DDS, 1970. Gen. practice dentistry Clayton, Mo., 1967-70, Creve Coeur, Mo., 1970—; assoc. instr. Forest Park Community Coll., St. Louis, 1973-77; asst. prof. Washington U., St. Louis, 1975-77; lectr. Continuing Edn. Ctrs. Am., 1977-79. Author: (with others) Anatomy of Orofacial Structures, 1977; contbg. author Comprehensive Rev. of Dental Hygiene, 1986. Fellow Acad. Gen. Dentistry, Dentistry Internat.; mem. ADA, Mo. Acad. Gen. Dentistry, Greater St. Louis Dental Assn., Gateway Practice Devel. Assn. (pres. 1986—). Home: 15471 Shadyford Ct Chesterfield MO 63017 Office: 12401 Olive St Rd Creve Coeur MO 63141

ITIN, SHIRLEY DAWN BESEMER, investment company executive; b. Ithaca, N.Y., Feb. 11, 1936; d. Martin Charles and Josephine Sarah (Palmer) Besemer; m. Thomas William Itin, Jan. 28, 1955; children: Dawn Elizabeth Itin Hebard, Timothy Sean. Student, Cornell U., 1953-55, 57, U. Md., 1960-62. With TWI Internat. Inc., Orchard Lake, Mich., 1968—, sr. v.p., 1981—; pres. First Equity Corp., Orchard Lake, 1983—; v.p. Acrodyne Trading & Contracting Co., Orchard Lake, 1978—, Itin Petroleum Co., Orchard Lake, 1978—. Club: Cornell (Mich.). Office: TWI Internat Inc 7001 Orchard Lake Rd Suite 420C Orchard Lake MI 48033-5354

ITIN, THOMAS WILLIAM, financial consultant for corporate development; b. Mt. Holly, Ohio, Sept. 14, 1934; s. Robert B. Sr. and Carrie (Crouch) I.; m. Shirley Besemer, Jan. 28, 1955; children: Dawn Elizabeth, Timothy Sean. BS, Cornell U., 1957; MBA, NYU, 1959, postgrad., 1959-60. With Mobil Oil Corp., N.Y.C., 1957-62; employee relations advisor Mobil Internat., Europe, North Africa, 1960-62; instr. U. Md.-North African Br., 1960-62; ins. broker Elmhurst, Ill., 1962—; pres., chmn. bd. dirs. Acrodyne Corp., Orchard Lake, Mich., 1963—, TWI Internat., Inc., Orchard Lake, 1968—; chmn. bd. Steel Tree Group, Inc., Colo. Ridge Corp., Itin Oil Co., Dearborn Wheels, Inc., Lilliendahl Corp. Contbr. articles to trade newspapers, mags. Mem. Personnel Mgmt. Council Libya (past pres.), Ski Racing Patrons, Inc. of Mich. (co-founder, past pres.). Club: Cornell (Mich.). Home: Orchard Lake MI 48033 Office: TWI Internat Inc 7001 Orchard Lake Rd Suite 420C Orchard Lake MI 48033

ITNYRE, JOHN FRANCIS, gynecologist, obstetrician; b. Detroit, Oct. 21, 1950; s. John Stouffer and Marguerite Helen (Morgan) I.; m. Cynthia Kay Stringer, May 5, 1973; children: Julia Kay, Laurel Anne. BS magna cum laude, U. Detroit, 1972; MD, Wayne State U., 1977. Diplomate Am. Bd. Ob-Gyn. Intern, then resident in ob-gyn St. Joseph Mercy Hosp., Pontiac, Mich., 1977-81; practice medicine specializing in ob-gyn Med. Arts Group, P.C., Cadillac, Mich., 1981; chief ob-gyn dept. Mercy Hosp., Cadillac, 1984-87. Fellow Am Coll. Ob-Gyn; mem. Wexford Missaukee County Med. Soc. (sec. 1984, v.p. 1985, pres. 1986), Cadillac C. of C. Roman Catholic. Club: Pine Grove Athletic. Avocations: photography, cross country skiing, hiking. Home: 5600 E Blossom Ave Cadillac MI 49601 Office: Med Arts Group PC 520 Cobb St Cadillac MI 49601

IULIANO, JOSEPH D., JR., automations engineer and designer, consultant; b. Cleve., Nov. 28, 1929; s. Joseph D. and Angela M. (Fiorelli) I., m. Janet Y. DeLong, July 9, 1951 (dec. 1970); children: Randy Lee, Kristy Lynn and Kathy Rae (twins); m. Beth Ann McClure, Sept., 24, 1978; 1 stepchild, Richard A. Blessing. AS, Acme Sch. Tool and Die Design, 1955; tool and die journeyman degree, Studebaker Corp., 1956; student in mech. engring., Ind. U., South Bend, 1957-63. Registered profl. engr., Ind., Calif.; cert. mfg. engr. Tooling and machine designer Studebaker Corp., South Bend, 1949-63; automation and design engr. various job shops, South Bend, 1963-65; automation engr. and supr. CTS Corp. Hdqrs., Elkhart, Ind., 1965-70; chief tool and machine engr. Elkhart div. Elkhart div. CTS, 1970-82, security officer, 1983—; mgr. machine quality and gaging electromech. div. CTS, 1982—. Inventor devices and machines for electronics and automotive industries. Chmn. bd. trustees Pleasant Valley Congl. Ch., 1958-60; mgr. Cleveland Twp. Little League, Elkhart, 1965-73. Served with U.S. Army, 1951-53. Mem. Soc. Mfg. Engrs., Robotics/Internat. of Soc. Mfg. Engrs., NSPE, Ind. Soc. Profl. Engrs. Republican. Club: Ski (Elkhart). Lodge: Moose. Avocations: snow skiing, playing tennis, motorcycling, art work, painting. Home: 2611 California Rd Elkhart IN 46514 Office: Elkhart div CTS Corp 1142 W Beardsley Elkhart IN 46514

IVANKOVICH, MICHAEL DAVID, photographer; b. Lansing, Mich., Feb. 17, 1952; s. Daniel James and Leonora Teresa (Thrower) I. BA in graphic arts, Ferris State Coll., 1974; AA in photog. art, Wayne State U., 1982. Photo-fabricator Ford Motor Co., Dearborn, Mich., 1976—; photographer Cruise Mag., Detroit, 1978—. Photographer: (mag.) Saugatuck, Style, 1986, (cover) Mr. U.S.A., Cruise Mag., 1986. Sponsor Mich. Orgn. Human Rights, Detroit, 1986—. Mem. Am. Electroplaters Soc., Assn. Photographers Am. Democrat. Mem. Unity Ch. of Today. Avocation: traveling. Home: 9160 Hazelton Redford MI 48239 Office: 12801 Prospect Dearborn MI 48126

IVENS, VIRGINIA RUTH, veterinary educator; b. Decatur, Ill., July 27, 1922; d. John Raymond and Dessie Lenora (Underwood) I. BS, U. Ill., 1950. Tracer blueprints Caterpillar Mil. Engine Co., Decatur, 1941-45; mem. faculty Coll. Veterinary Medicine, U. Ill., Urbana, 1950—, assoc. prof. veterinary parasitology, 1979—, chmn. curriculum com. dept. veterinary pathobiology, 1976-78; chmn. 9th Ann. Conf. Coccidiosis, 1972. Mem. Am. Soc. Parasitologists (transl. com. 1963-71, 80-85), Soc. Protozoologist, Am. Inst. Biol. Scis., Entomol. Soc. Am., LWV, Sigma Xi, Phi Zeta. Author: Principal Parasites of Domestic Animals in the U.S., 1978, 81, rev. ed. 1987; translator Russian articles on parasitology; contbr. articles to profl. jours. and co-author four monographs. Home: 608 S Edwin St Champaign IL 61821 Office: U Ill 2603 Basic Sci Bldg 2001 S Lincoln Ave Urbana IL 61801

IVERSON, THORVAL SOREN, marketing executive; b. Devils Lake, N.D., Feb. 17, 1959; s. Soren Thorval and Bonita Laura (Kruger) I.; m. Dana Hart, June 23, 1984. BS, N.D. State U., 1981; MBA, Stanford (Calif.) U., 1985. CPA, Calif., N.D. Acctg. systems supr. Hewlett Packard, Palo Alto, Calif., 1981-85; product mgr. Gt. Plains Software, Fargo, N.D., 1985-86, dir. vertical markets, 1986—; pres. adv. council computer sci. dept. N.D. State U., Fargo, 1987. Mem. Am. Inst. CPA's. Republican. Avocations: golf, reading, basketball. Home: 1517 32d St SW Fargo ND 58103 Office: Gt Plains Software 1701 SW 38th St Fargo ND 58103

IVEZAJ, FRANO LEKA, English educator; b. Tuzi, Yugoslavia, Aug. 9, 1958; came to U.S., 1972, naturalized, 1985; s. Lek Pashku and Pashk Kolia (Camaj) I.; m. Sofia Pal Mirakaj, Apr. 12, 1980; 1 child, Kristale Lindita. BA, Detroit Inst. Tech., 1978; MA in Teaching, Wayne State U., 1984. Cert. secondary tchr., Mich. Community liaison Community and Econ. Devel. Dept., Detroit, 1980-83; esl tchr. Ferndale (Mich.) Adult & Community Edn., 1983—; tchr. English Detroit Pub. Schs., 1983—. Sec. St. Paul's Albanian Cath. Ch. Council, Warren, Mich., 1983. Recipient Award of Excellence, Cen. Indsl. Park Citizens Dist. Council, 1981. Mem. MLA, Am. Fedn. Tchrs., Detroit Fedn. Tchrs., Internat. Tchrs. Service, Nat. Council Tchrs. English, Nat. Notary Assn., Wayne State U. Alumni Assn. Avocations: drama, travel, reading, martial arts, soccer. Home: 2167 Logan Dr Sterling Heights MI 48310 Office: Detroit Pub Schs 5057 Woodward Ave Detroit MI 48202

IVKOVICH, RONALD SAMUEL, food company executive; b. McKeesport, Pa., July 23, 1938; s. Samuel and Rose Marie (Kasunic) I.; m. Janice Murphy, June 15, 1963; children: Jill Michele, Cheryl Lynn, Kevin Ronald. B.S., Cornell U., 1961, M.S., 1962. Sales rep. Campbell Soup Co., Syracuse, N.Y., 1965-66; dist. sales supr. Campbell Soup Co., Boston, 1966-67; asst. mgr. food services systems Campbell Soup Co., Camden, N.J., 1967-68; v.p. Food Service div. P & C Food Markets, Syracuse, 1968-75; corp. dir. purchasing I.U. Internat. Viands Corp., Charlotte, N.C., 1975-76; pres. I.U. Internat. Clark & Lewis Co., Jacksonville, Fla., 1976-78, Redi Froz, Inc. div. Scot Lad Foods, South Bend, Ind., 1978-82; v.p. Simon Bros. Inc., South Bend, 1982—. Bd. dirs. Camp Milhouse. Served with AUS, 1962-64. Mem. Midwest Frozen Food Assn., Nat. Frozen Food Assn., Cornell Hotel Assn. Home: 52091 Farmington Square Rd Granger IN 46530 Office: 1901 N Bendix Dr South Bend IN 46619

IVY, CONWAY GAYLE, paint company executive; b. Houston, July 8, 1941; s. John Smith and Caro (Gayle) I.; student U. Chgo., 1959-62; B.S. in Natural Scis., Shimer Coll., 1964; postgrad. U. Tex., 1964-65; M.B.A., U. Chgo., 1968, M.A. in Econs., 1972, postgrad. 1972-74; m. Diane Ellen Cole, May 25, 1973; children—Brice McPherson, Elizabeth Cole. Geol. asst. John S. Ivy, Houston, 1965-72; securities analyst Halsey Stuart & Co. and successor Bache & Co., Chgo., 1973-74, Winmill Securities Inc., Chgo., 1974; econ. and fin. cons., Chgo., 1974-75; dir. corp. planning Gould Inc., Rolling Meadows, Ill., 1975-79; v.p. corp. planning and devel. Sherwin-Williams Co., Cleve., 1979—; pres. Ivy Minerals Inc., Boise, Idaho, 1978—; dir. CorrIm Door Systems Inc. Trustee Cleve. Inst. Music, 1983—, treas., 1987—; trustee Michelson-Morley Centennial Celebration, 1987. Mem. Am. Econs. Assn., N.Y. Acad. Scis., Soc. Mining Engrs., Am. Inst. Mining Engrs., Phi Gamma Delta. Republican. Author of numerous analytical reports for brokerage industry. Office: Sherwin-Williams Co 101 Prospect Ave NW Cleveland OH 44115

IYER, KUMAR V., orthodontist; b. Bombay, Feb. 14, 1951; Came to U.S., 1978; s. Lingam Ganesh and Rukmani Iyer; m. Lakshmi Kumar Manian, Dec. 22, 1980; 1 child, Vinod K. B in Dental Sci., Govt. Dental Coll. and Hosp., 1973; MDS, Nair Hosp. Dentac, 1978; cert. of speciality, Loyola U., Chgo., 1982. Clin. asst. Govt. Dental Coll., Bombay, 1973-74; practice dentistry specializing in orthodontics Bombay, 1974-78; shift supr. Anacomp Micrographics, Des Plaines, Ill., 1978-82; resident Loyola U. Sch. Dentistry, Chgo., 1980-82; orthodontist Dental Assocs. Ltd., Milw., 1982-84, West Allis (Wis.) Dental Group, 1983—; bd. dirs., pres. Orthodontic Care Ctr., Milw., 1984—. Contbr. articles to profl. jours. Mem. ADA, Ind. Dental Assn., Wis. Dental Assn., Greater Milw. Dental Assn., Ind. Orthodontic Assn., Am. Soc. Dentistry for Children. Avocations: reading, travel. Office: Orthodontic Care Ctr 1421 S 108 St West Allis WI 53214

IZENOUR, HARRY EDWARD, artist, art educator; b. Salem, Ohio, June 24, 1940; s. George H. and Betty Mae (Luxeuil) I.; m. Mary Anne Pettit, Nov. 20, 1971; children: Joshua Eric, Amanda Marie, Sarah Adrienne. BFA, Kent State U., 1962; MFA, Ohio U., 1967. Instr. art Salem City Schs., 1962-65; assoc. prof. art Kent State U., Ashtabula, Ohio, 1967—; cons. Ashtabula Arts Ctr., 1967—; exchange prof. U. Warsaw and Art Acad. Warsaw, Poland, 1984; bd. dirs. creative connections Kent State U., 1987—. One man shows include: Case Western Res. U., 1982, Blossom Music Ctr., Akron, Ohio, 1984, Piwna Gallery, Warsaw, 1986, 87. Trustee at large Ashtabula County Arts Council, 1979—; mem. Kosciuszko Found., N.Y.C. Recipient 1st Prize Three Rivers Festival, 1970, Best Show Canton Art Inst., 1971, Jurors Spl. award Butler Inst. Am. Art, 1982. Mem. Am. Assn. Univ. Profs., Internat. Sculptors Assn., New Orgn. for Visual Artists. Home: 1064 Plymouth Rd Ashtabula OH 44004 Office: Kent State U W 13th St Ashtabula OH 44004

JABLONSKI, DALE Z., public relations and advertising executive; b. Detroit, Oct. 16, 1942; s. Norbert S. and Zenona B. (Zielinski) J.; m. Mary Louise Bujak, Feb. 27, 1965; children: Gary, Sandra. BA, U. Detroit, 1965. Communications specialist Chrysler Corp., Detroit, 1965-66; account exec. Editorial Assocs., Detroit, 1966-69; nat. pub. relations and advt. mgr. Realtron Corp., Detroit, 1969; pres. Dale Corp., Troy, Mich., 1969—. Bd. dirs. Mich. Cancer Found., Warren, 1984—. Recipient Golden Pyramid award Internat. Splty. Advt. Assn. Ga., 1981. Mem. Pub. Relations Soc. Am. (Silver Anvil award 1978), Adcraft Club, Sigma Delta Chi. Avocation: boating. Home: 735 Brookwood Walke Bloomfield Hills MI 48013 Office: Dale Corp 2684 Industrial Row Troy MI 48084

JABLONSKI, EDWIN FRANK, manufacturing company executive; b. Mosinee, Wis., Jan. 18, 1925; s. Frank Stanley and Lillian (Sheptoski) J.; m. Dorothy Ann Sobkowiak, Oct. 29, 1955. BBA, U. Wis., 1951. With purchasing and acctg. Marmet Corp., Wausau, Wis., 1951-60; with purchasing and transp. Wausau Metals Corp., 1960-70; pres. Modu-Line Windows, Wausau, 1972-85, Major Industries, Wausau, 1980—; pres. Prime Cons., Wausau, 1983—. Author: (with B. Wohlfahrt) The Art of Tipping: Customs & Controversies, 1984. Bd. dirs. Tippers Internat., Wausau, 1983—. Republican. Roman Catholic. Home: 1222 Single Ave Wausau WI 54401 Office: Major Industries Inc 7111 Stewart Ave Wausau WI 54401

JABLONSKI, JAMES JOHN, accountant; b. Detroit, Dec. 25, 1946; s. Chester and Idell Florence (Chiolero) J.; m. Catherine Josephine Moran, Apr. 21, 1972; children: Pamela L., Kristin M. BS, Wayne State U., 1969. CPA, Mich. Sr. staff acct., mgr. Berger & Wild, CPA's, Troy, Mich., 1968-85; proprietor Jablonski & Co., CPA's, Troy, 1985—. Mem. Am. Inst. CPA's, Mich. Assn. CPA's, Am. Acctg. Assn. Republican. Roman Catholic. Lodge: KC (fin. sec. Sterling Heights, Mich. 1978-85). Avocations: boating, hunting, muskie fishing. Home and Office: 1390 Peachtree Troy MI 48083 Office: Jablonski and Co CPA's 1390 Peachtree Troy MI 48083

JABLONSKI, ROBERT LEO, architect; b. Chgo., Mar. 28, 1926; s. Leo Frank and Rose (Domian) J. BS, U. Ill., 1950. Chief planner Nat. Council YMCA, Chgo., 1957-64; coordinator architecture U. Ill., Chgo., 1964-69, U. Chgo., 1969-70; dir. bldg. program City of Chgo., 1970—. Served with U.S. Army, 1940-46, ETO. Roman Catholic. Avocations: tennis, swimming.

JACKLIN, WILLIAM THOMAS, county official, educator; b. Chgo., Dec. 26, 1940; s. Robert Theodore and Florence Carrie (Dombrow) J.; m. Bonnie Joy Winquist; 1 child, Laura Carrie. BS, Roosevelt U., 1967; MS in Bus., Ind. U., 1968. Assoc. instr. Ind. U., 1967-69; V.p. DuPage Corp., Lombard, Ill., 1970-73; inst. bus. Coll. DuPage, Glen Ellyn, Ill., 1969—; chief dep. auditor DuPage County, 1973, county auditor, 1973—; v.p. DuPage County Employees Credit Union, 1978-79, pres., 1979-80; fiscal officer DuPage Met. Enforcement Group, 1987—. Announcer CRIS Radio for the Blind. Mem. Ill. Prairie Path, DuPage County Rep. Cen. Com.; sec. York Twp. Rep. Orgn., 1978-80; treas. Highland Hills Assn., 1975-78; chmn. DuPage County com Gerald R. Ford presdl. campaign, 1976; mem. fin. mgmt. project com. Ill. Dept. Commerce and Community Affairs, 1980—; bd. dirs. Lombard Hist. Soc., v.p., 1983-87, pres., 1987—; founding co-chmn. Y. Ill. Conservative Coordinating Council. Mem. Inst. Internal Auditors (govt. and pub. affairs com. 1976-82), Nat. Assn. Accts. (assoc. dir.), Am. Acctg. Assn., Ill. Assn. County Auditors (sec.-treas. 1976-78 v.p. 1978-80, pres. 1980-84), Assn. Govt. Accts., Phi Delta Kappa. Christian Scientist. Lodge: Masons (sec. 1979-80). Home: 411 E 17th St Lombard IL 60148 Office: DuPage Ctr 421 N County Farm Rd Wheaton IL 60187

JACKSON, A(MOS) HENRY (HANK), electronic data processing specialist, computer systems educator; b. Mt. Orab, Ohio, July 3, 1944; s. J(ohn) Pierce and Ocie Rebecca (Howlette) J. B.S., SW Mo. State U., Springfield, 1975. Cert. data processor. Programmer, Fasco Industries, Eldon, Mo., 1975-76, Rowlette and Assos. Acctg. Services, Eldon, 1976; programmer EDP coordination Office of Adminstrn., State of Mo., Jefferson City, 1976-78; programmer, analyst info. systems div. Mo. Dept. Revenue, Jefferson City, 1979—. Served with U.S. Army, 1965-68. Mem. Adminstrv. Mgmt. Soc., Data Processing Mgmt. Assn. (Mo., mem. spl. interest group computer personnel), Pi Omega Pi. Mem. Ch. of God. Home: 188 N Summit Dr Lot #12 Holt's Summit MO 65043 Office: Mo Dept Revenue Info Systems Div Harry S Truman Bldg Jefferson City MO 65105

JACKSON, ARLENE L., family therapist; b. Rockford, Ill., July 16, 1943; d. John E. and LaVern R. (Hazzard) J.; divorced; children—Jan Arlene, James Paul. A.A., Rock Valley Coll., 1978; B.A. summa cum laude in Clin. Psychology and Eng. Lit., Beloit Coll., 1979; postgrad. Ill. State U., 1981-82; M.S. in Community Mental Health, No. Ill. U., 1985, postgrad., 1986—. Advocate, coordinator Ill. Status Offender Service, Rockford, 1979-80; dir. Pathways, Inc., Rockford, 1980-81; therapist Family Life Ctr., Rockford, 1982-86; rational interventions therapist, 1986— exec. dir. Youth Services Network, Inc., Rockford, 1982—; prin. J & J Cons., 1986—; cons. in field. Chmn. task forces Youth Services Network, Inc., 1982—; mem. Peace and Justice Commn., Rockford, 1982—; bd. dirs. Knights Community Complex, Rockford, 1984-87. Named One of Outstanding Working Women of Yr. Ill. Bus. and Profl. Women; Bingham fellow Beloit Coll., 1979. Mem. NOW, Nat. Assn. Social Workers, Rockford Network, Nat. Assn. Women Bus. Owners, Rockford C. of C., Phi Beta Kappa, Psi Chi. Unitarian. Avocations: writing poetry; dancing; interior decorating; travel; theater. Office: Youth Services 4402 N Main St Rockford IL 61105

JACKSON, BARBARA JEAN MCKINNEY, psychotherapist, consultant; b. Chgo., May 7, 1944; d. Robert and Corrine (Bolden) McKinney; m. Albert Jackson, June 22, 1974 (div. Sept. 1979); m. John Henry Lee, Sept. 6, 1986. BA in Sociology, U. Ill., 1966; MA in Social Work, U. Chgo., 1969; postgrad., Roosevelt U., 1980-84. Cert. social worker, Ill. Social worker Michael Reese Hosp., Chgo., 1970-74; asst. dean students U. Chgo., 1974-77; asst. prof. Loyola U., Chgo., 1977-79, Roosevelt U., Chgo., 1979-85; pvt. practice psychology Jackson & Assocs., Chgo., 1980—; cons. VA, Chgo., 1984—, Chgo. Mental Health Found., 1984—. Mem. Nat. Assn. Social Workers, Assn. Labor Mgmt. on Alcoholism, Nat. Assn. Black Social Workers (sec. 1971-74), NAACP, Chgo. Urban League, Operation PUSH. Avocations: skating, swimming. Home: 7433 S Chappel Chicago IL 60649

JACKSON, CARL ROBERT, obstetrician, gynecologist; b. Mpls., Jan. 8, 1928; s. Carl J. and Mildred J. (Johnson) J.; m. Ann Flesch, Dec. 26, 1967; children—Amy, Carrie, Tom. B.A., Gustavus Adolphus Coll., 1951; M.D., Jefferson Med. Coll., 1956. Diplomate Am. Bd. Ob-Gyn. Intern St. Mary's Hosp., Duluth, Minn., 1956-57; resident and postdoctoral fellow in ob-gyn U. Wis.-Madison, 1957-61; practice medicine specializing in ob-gyn Madison, 1961—; mem. active staff Madison Gen. Hosp., 1961—, vice chief staff, 1972-74; mem. attending staff Univ. Hosps., Madison; assoc. clin. prof. ob-gyn U. Wis., 1971—, mem. high risk obstetrical team, 1974-75; chmn. Physicians Alliance, Dane County, Wis.; mem. Madison Ob-Gyn Ltd., 1961—; chmn. Madison Med. Ctr., 1979-86. Am. Cancer Soc. fellow, 1960-61. Mem. Am. Coll. Ob-Gyn, Central Assn. Obstetricians and Gynecologists. Republican. Lutheran. Home: 3089 Timberlane Verona WI 53593 Office: Madison Med Ctr 20 S Park St Madison WI 53715

JACKSON, CAROLE CAPMAN, human resources executive; b. Evergreen Park, Ill., Feb. 25, 1951; d. Robert Lawrence and Norma Gene (Benson) C.; m. Donald Charles Jackson, Sept. 24, 1976 (dec. Mar. 1984). BA with honors, U. Ill., Chgo., 1972. Job analyst U. Ill.-Chgo. Circle, 1973-76, personnel coordinator, 1976-80; assoc. personnel dir. U. Ill. Chgo., 1980-83; dir. human resources U. Ill. Hosp., Chgo., 1983—. chmn. United Way Crusade Mercy Campaign Univ. Ill.-Chgo., 1982. Mem. Coll. and U. Personnel Assn., Am. Mgmt. Assn., Am. Soc. Personnel Adminstrn., Am. Soc. Healthcare Human Resource Adminstrn. Home: 2105 Dorval Dr Naperville IL 60565 Office: U Ill Hosp 1740 W Taylor Suite 1400 Chicago IL 60612

JACKSON, CURTIS MAITLAND, metallurgical engineer; b. N.Y.C., Apr. 20, 1933; s. Maitland Shaw and Janet Haughs (Dunbar) J.; m. Cordelia Ann Shupe, July 6, 1957; children: Carol Elizabeth, David Curtis. B.S. in Metall. Engring., NYU, 1954; M.S., Ohio State U., Columbus, 1959, Ph.D. (Battelle staff fellow), 1966. Registered profl. engr., Ohio. Prin. metall. engr. Columbus div. Battelle Meml. Inst., 1954-61, project leader, 1961-67, asso. chief specialty alloys, 1967-77, asso. mgr. phys. and applied metallurgy, 1977—. Chmn. bd.: Wire Jour, 1976-77; dir., 1973-78; Contbr. tech. articles profl. jours. Mem. troop com. Boy Scouts Am., 1975-83 , asst. scoutmaster, 1978-83 ; advisor Order of DeMolay, 1954-57, 78—; mem. ofcl. bd. Methodist Ch., 1957-66. Recipient IR-100 award Indsl. Research Mag., 1976; recipient certificate of appreciation Soc. Mfg. Engrs., 1977, awards Order of DeMolay, 1955, 1978, 83. Mem. Wire Found. (dir. 1974-86), Wire Assn. Internat. (v.p. 1973-76, pres. 1976-77, dir. 1970-78, Mordica Meml. award 1977, J. Edward Donnellan award 1978, Meritorious Tech. Paper award 1981), N.Y. U. Metall. Alumni Assn. (pres. 1966-68), Am. Inst. Mining, Metall. and Petroleum Engrs. (chmn. Ohio Valley sect. 1964-66, chmn. North Central region 1965-66), Am. Soc. Metals, Am. Vacuum Soc., NYU, Ohio State U. alumni assns., Sigma Xi, Alpha Sigma Mu, Phi Lambda Upsilon. Club: NYU. Research on metall. tech. Home: 5088 Dalmeny Ct Columbus OH 43220 Office: 505 King Ave Columbus OH 43201

JACKSON, DAVID MORRIS, dentist, real estate developer; b. Hannibal, Mo., June 10, 1953; s. Russell Morris and Fay Isabell (Thornton) J.; m. Lillian Scuderi, Aug. 14, 1976; children: Jessica, Elizabeth Kate. AA, Hannibal La-Grange Coll., 1973; BS, U. Mo., 1975, DDS, 1981. Gen. practice dentistry Hannibal, 1981—. Bd. dirs. Am. Cancer Soc., Hannibal, 1985—. Mem. ADA, Mo. Dental Assn. (legis. council 1984-86), Great River Dental Study Group (pres. 1984), Delta Sigma Delta (outstanding mem. 1981). Lodge: Kiwanis (bd. dirs. Hannibal club 1984—). Avocation: sailing.

JACKSON, DEBORAH LYNN, lawyer, educator; b. Greensburg, Pa., Nov. 24, 1952; d. Edward and Lorraine (Clark) J. BA in Sociology, U. Pitts., 1974, JD, Cleveland Marshall Coll. Law, 1977. Bar: Ohio 1985, U.S. Dist. Ct. (no. dist.) Ohio 1985. Legal researcher dept. human services Cuyahoga County, Cleve., 1979-83, equal opportunity atty. bd. commrs., 1983—; instr. Cuyahoga Community Coll., Cleve., 1979—. Mem. Bus. Industry and Edn. Council, Cleve. Mem. Ohio Bar Assn., Bar Assn. Greater Cleve., Cuyahoga County Bar Assn., Assn. Trial Lawyers Am., Cleve. Employers Equal Opportunity Assn., NAACP. Republican. Baptist. Avocations: tennis, biking, travel. Home: 462 N Clearview Dr Euclid OH 44123 Office: Cuyahoga County Bd Commrs 1219 Ontario St Cleveland OH 44113

JACKSON, ERNEST HARDING, genealogist, publisher; b. Pollard, Ark., Oct. 13, 1920; s. James William and Minnie Mae (Holcomb) J.; student Harvard U., 1940-41; B.A., U. Albuquerque, 1954; M.A., U. N.Mex., 1955; m. Anna Amalia Hofflund, Aug. 5, 1951. Enlisted U.S. Air Force, 1942, advanced through grades to chief warrant officer, 1968; 35 combat missions, ETO, World War II; assigned to Berlin Air Lift, 1949-50, Spl. Weapons Command, 1951-56; staff supply officer 11th Air Div., Alaskan Air Command, 1956-60; supply officer SAC bases, 1960-68; ret., 1968; asst. prof. English, Rock Valley Jr. Coll., Rockford, Ill., 1968-74. Decorated Air medal with silver and bronze oak leaf clusters, Purple Heart. Mem. Nat. Geneal. Soc., Ill. Geneal. Soc., North Central Ill. Geneal. Soc. (charter mem., past pres.), Winnebago and boone counties Geneal. Soc. (charter mem., pres.), SAR (treas. Ill. soc.), Phi Delta Kappa. Pub.: Jacksoniana - A Jackson Family Newsletter, 1977; compiler, publisher, editor of numerous geneal. publs. Home and Office: 730 Parker Woods Dr Rockford IL 61102

JACKSON, ETHAN, healthcare organization executive. Chmn. Basic Am. Med. Inc., Indpls. Office: Basic Am Med Inc 4000 E Southport Rd Indianapolis IN 46227 *

JACKSON, GREGORY WAYNE, orthodontist; b. Chgo., Sept. 4, 1950; s. Wayne Eldon and Marilyn Frances (Anderson) J.; m. Nora Ann Echtner, Mar. 17, 1973; children: Eric, David. Student, U. Ill., 1968-70; DDS with honors, U. Ill., Chgo., 1974; MSD, U. Wash., 1978. Practice dentistry specializing in orthodontics Chgo., 1978—; instr. orthodontic dept. U. Ill. Coll. Dentistry, Chgo., 1978-81. Coach Little League Baseball, Oak Brook, Ill., 1986. Served to lt. USN, 1974-76. Mem. ADA, Ill. State Dental Soc., Chgo. Dental Soc., Am. Assn. Orthodontists, Midwestern Soc. Orthodontists, Ill. Soc. Orthodontists, Omicron Kappa Upsilon. Evangelical. Club: Oak Brook Polo. Avocations: golf, tennis, skiing. Office: 6435 S Pulaski Rd Chicago IL 60629

JACKSON, H. NOEL, JR., bank executive; b. Moline, Ill., Nov. 6, 1946; s. Homer N. Jackson and Gladys L. (Parker) Meyer; m. Sharon Mae Sackrider, Oct. (, 1970 (div. May 1985); children: Palesa Anne, Jennifer Mae. AA, Blawk Hawk Coll., 1967; BS, No. Ill. U., 1969, MSBA, 1974. CPA, Ill. Vol. U.S. Peace Corps., Maseru, Lesotho, 1969-71; with Harris Bank, Chgo., 1974—; internat. banking officer Harris Bank, 1980, asst. v.p., 1981; asst. treas. Beloit (Wis.) Corp., 1981-82; treas. Presidio Ins. Co., Los Angeles, 1981-82; v.p. Mfrs. Hanover Trust Co., Chgo., 1982—. Vol. fundraiser World Neighbors, 1985—. Mem. No. Ill. U. Alumni Assn. (bd. dirs. 1986—), Delta Psi Omega, Beta Alpha Psi (hon.). Home: 2812 Bel Aire Dr Arlington Heights IL 60004 Office: Mfrs Hanover Trust Co Three First Nat Plaza Chicago IL 60602

JACKSON, JACK HILLMAN, architect; b. Omaha, Feb. 21, 1944; s. Jack Comp and Lila Jeannette (Hillman) J.; m. Janice Jane Miles, Dec. 23, 1967; children: Jack Miles, Kristin Heather. BArch, Kans. State U., 1967. Lic. architect Nebr., Iowa. Architect in tng. San Francisco Bay Naval Shipyard, Vallejo, Calif., 1967-70; ptnr. Jackson-Jackson & Assocs., Omaha, 1970—. Prin. works include First Nat. Bank of York, Nebr., 1981, United Ch. of Christ of Millard, Omaha, 1982, First Interstate Bank, Spencer, Iowa., 1983, St. Joseph Cath. Ch., Springfield, Nebr., 1984. Mem. Landmarks, Inc., Omaha, 1984—. Recipient City Beautification awards Omaha Women's C. of C., 1979. Mem. AIA, Constrn. Specifications Inst., Nebr. State Hist. Soc., Tau Sigma Delta. Republican. Presbyterian. Lodge: Kiwanis (pres. Westside chpt. 1980-81). Avocations: oil painting, old movies, bowling, golf, fishing. Home: 10916 N 62 St Omaha NE 68152 Office: Jackson-Jackson & Assocs 1905 N 81st St Omaha NE 68114

JACKSON, JAMES ALAN, veterinarian; b. Clinton, Ill., Dec. 7, 1952; s. James Robert and Sarah Katherine (Thorp) J.; m. Judith Lynn Patterson, Aug. 9, 1975; children: Valerie Lynn, Bryan Andrew. BS in Pharmacy with honors, U. Ill., Chgo., 1976; DVM with honors, U. Ill., 1980. Veterinarian Colfax (Wis.) Vet. Clinic, 1980-81; research veterinarian Pfizer Inc. Cen. Research, Terre Haute, Ind., 1981-84, sr. research scientist, 1984—. Sec. Wabash Valley Youth for Christ, Terre Haute, 1985—. Mem. AVMA, Am. Assn. Bovine Practitioners, Am. Assn. Swine Practitioners, Am. Assn. Indsl. Veterinarians, Am. Sci. AffiliationSigma Xi (pres. Ind. state chpt. 1988-89). Avocations: walking, tennis, reading, evangelism, racquetball. Home: 4414 Alan Dr Terre Haute IN 47802 Office: Pfizer Inc Cen Research Box 88 Terre Haute IN 47808

JACKSON, JAMES AVELON, JR., criminal justice educator; b. Granite City, Ill., June 5, 1942; s. James Avelon and Ruby Cleona (Lee) J.; B.S., So. Ill. U., 1970; M.A., Sangamon State U., Springfield, Ill., 1973; postgrad. St. Louis U.; children—James Avelon, Jay Allen. Juvenile officer Madison County Sheriff's Office, Edwardsville, Ill., 1970-73; dir., instr. law enforcement program Muscatine (Iowa) Community Coll., 1973-75; asst. prof. Minot (N.D.) State Coll., 1975-76; dir. Inst. for Adminstrn. of Justice McKendree Coll., Lebanon, Ill., 1976-78; coordinator criminal justice and community service programs Southeastern Community Coll., West Burlington, Iowa, 1979-81; assoc. prof., chmn. dept. criminal justice St. Louis Community Coll. at Forest Park, 1981—; pres. Heritage Blade and Arms Inc., Lebanon Cutlery, Inc. Named Tchr. of Yr. St. Louis Community Coll. at Forest Park, 1982-83, 1983-84, 85. Mem. Am. Assn. Univ. Adminstrs., Acad. Criminal Justice Scis., Iowa Criminal Justice Educators Assn. (pres. 1981), Ill. Assn. Criminal Justice Scientists, Midwestern Assn. Criminal Justice Educators (exec. com.), So. Ill. Criminal Justice Educators Assn. (founder), Ill. Community Edn. Assn., Am. Soc. Criminologists, Anglo-Am. Acad., Lambda Alpha Epsilon. Home: 327 E Schuetz Lebanon IL 62254 Office: St Louis Community Coll at Forest Park Saint Louis MO 63110

JACKSON, JAMES DONOVAN, dentist; b. Mitchell, S.D., Feb. 16, 1945; s. James Donovan and Elizabeth Adeline (Breckenridge) J.; m. Cheryl Lynn Watterson, Aug. 27, 1968; children: Scott, Christopher, James. Student, Kalamazoo Coll., 1963-66; DDS, U. Mich., 1970. Research asst. U. Mich. Dental Research Inst., Ann Arbor, Mich., 1967-70; gen. practice dentistry Marquette, Mich., 1970—; cons. dentistry Hemophelia Soc. Mich., Ann Arbor, 1981—, Marquette Pub. Schs. Health Dept., 1974—, No. Mich. U. Sports, 1984—, Upper Peninsula Sports Medicine Assn., Marquett, 1985—. Bd. dirs. Marquette County United Way, 1980-81; varsity tennis coach No. Mich. U., 1984; lay leadership 1st United Meth. Ch., Marquette, 1986. Mem. Am. Dental Soc., Mich. Dental Soc., Chgo. Dental Soc., Superior Dental Soc., U.S. Sport Dentistry Assn. Republican. Avocations: coaching youth sports, ceramics, wood refinishing. Home: 431 E Ridge Marquette MI 49855 Office: Savings Bank Building Marquette MI 49855

JACKSON, JANET MERRILL, accounting instructor; b. Wichita, Kans., Mar. 15, 1956; d. Robert Hamilton and Dorothy Ellen (Burk) J. BBA, Wichita State U., 1979; MS Acctg., Oklahoma State U., 1981. CPA, Kans. Acct. Arthur Young, Tulsa, 1982-84; instr. Wichita State U., 1984—. Mem. Am. Inst. CPA's, Nat. Assn. Accts. Avocations: photography, cooking. Home: 6042 Sullivan Wichita KS 67204 Office: Wichita State Univ Box 87 Wichita KS 67208

JACKSON, JAY MICHAEL, producer, director; b. Lansing, Mich., Sept. 8, 1958; s. Robert H. and Betty Jackson. BA, U. Md., 1980. Sr. media specialist Systems & Applied Sciences Corp., Riverdale, Md., 1981-82; writer, producer On Target Prodns., Washington, 1982-85; producer, dir. for Amatulli & Assocs., Inc., Cin., 1985—; pres. T.R.P. Video Prodns., Cin., 1987—. Composer, producer music video Heaven's Child, 1986; stage mgr. Pres. Reagan 's Inaugural Ball, Kennedy Ctr., 1981. Dramatic Arts scholar Cath. U., Washington, 1975. Mem. Am. Film Inst. (press sec. 1979), Internat. TV Assn., Phi Gamma Delta.

JACKSON, JEFFERY JON, entreprenuer; b. Mobridge, S.D., June 29, 1957; s. Harold Russell and Rosella May (Smith) J.; m. Tamara Kay Anderson, Dec. 5, 1975 (div. Aug. 1980); children: Jon Jeffery, Erica Marie; m. Marie Jean Campbell, June 7, 1982; children: Amanda Lee, Jeffery Jon. Grad., High Sch., Timberlake, S.D., 1975. Desk clk. Wrangler Motel, Mobridge, 1975-82; mgr. Potpourri Drive Inn, Mobridge, 1977; asst. mgr. Wheel Restaurant & Wrangler, Mobridge, 1978-82; mgr., sec./treas., chief exec. officer Wheel Restaurant & Wrangler Motor Inn, Mobridge, 1982-85; pres., chief exec. officer Jackson Enterprises Inc. dba Wrangler Motor Inn, Mobridge, 1985—; ptnr. Moahe Trailer Park; mgr. Jr. Investments; controller Jackson Livestock. Mem. Gov.'s Club, Pierre, S.D., 1985—. Mem. S.D. Innkeepers Assn. (bd. dirs. 1984—), Mobridge C. of C., Mobridge Jaycees. Republican. Lutheran. Club: Mobridge Country. Avocations: reading, flying, golf, hunting, horses. Home: 608 W 8th Ave Mobridge SD 57601 Office: Jackson Enterprises Inc 820 W Grand Crossing Mobridge SD 57601

JACKSON, JESSE LOUIS, clergyman, civic leader; b. Greenville, S.C., Oct. 8, 1941; s. Charles Henry and Helen J.; m. Jacqueline Lavinia Brown, 1964; children: Santita, Jesse Louis, Jonathan Luther, Yusef DuBois, Jacqueline Lavinia. Student, U. Ill., 1959-60; B.A. in Sociology and Economics, N.C. A&T State U., 1964; postgrad., Chgo. Theol. Sem., D.D. (hon.); hon. degrees, N.C. A&T State U., Pepperdine U., Oberlin U., Oral Roberts U., U. R.I., Howard U., Georgetown U. Ordained to ministry Baptist Ch., 1968; founder (with others) Operation Breadbasket joint project So. Christian Leadership Conf., Chgo., 1966; nat. dir. Operation Breadbasket joint project So. Christian Leardership Conf., 1967-71; founder, exec. dir. Operation PUSH (People United to Serve Humanity), Chgo., 1971—; candidate for Democratic nomination for Pres. U.S. 1983-84; chmn. Nat. Rainbow Coalition Inc., Washington; founder PUSH-Excel and PUSH for Econ. Justice; lectr. for high schs., colls., prof. audiences in Am., Europe. Active Black Coalition for United Community Action, 1969. Recipient Presdl. award Nat. Med. Assn., 1969; Humanitarian Father of Year award Nat. Father's Day Com., 1971; Third Most Admired Man in Am. Gallup Poll, 1985; named one of six new leaders on the rise U.S. News World Report. Address: 930 E 50th St Chicago IL 60615 Office: Nat Rainbow Coalition 2100 M St NW Suite 316 Washington DC 20037 *

JACKSON, JUREL V. (DESHAZER), city councilperson; b. Ravenwood, Mo., July 28, 1923; d. George Henry and Nina Slagle DeShazer. BEd, N.W. Mo. State U., 1965, MEd, 1968; specialist in edn., Eastern Ill. U., 1972; postgrad., U. Mo., 1977-78. Cert. tchr. English, Journalism, Psychology, Mo., Ill.; cert. psychol. examiner, Mo., Ill. Reporter Maryville (Mo.) Daily Forum, 1955-62; tchr. lang. arts Savannah (Mo.) R-II Jr. High Sch., 1965-66; tchr. journalism, English Savannah R-II Sr. High Sch., 1966-68; counselor, adminstr. Eastern Ill. U., Charleston, 1968-74; counselor, coordinator spl. services Mexico (Mo.) Jr. High Sch., 1974-84; edn. cons. Maryville, 1984—. Co-author: Tales of Nodaway County, 1977; contbr. articles to Forum mag. Bd. dirs. Shepherd Ctr. Sr. Citizens, Maryville, 1986—; mem. steering com. Leadership Maryville Program, 1985-86; elected mem. city of Maryville Council, 1985—; chmn. Nodaway County Dem. Cen. Com., Maryville, 1984—; Polk Twp. committeewoman in Nodaway County, Maryville, 1984—; sec. 6th Congl. Dist. Dem. Com., 1986—; mem. Com. for Progress, Maryville, 1986—; chmn. 12th Senatorial Dist. Mo. Dem. Com., 1984—. Named Counselor of Yr., Mid-Mo. Guidance Assn., 1984. Mem. NEA (life), AAUW (life, legis. chmn. 1985-86), Nodaway County Ret. Tchrs. Assn. (v.p., program chmn. 1986—), Phi Delta Kappa. Roman Catholic. Lodge: Order of Eastern Star (matron 1957, 74). Avocations: oil painting, travelling, writing. Home: 624 W Thompson St Maryville MO 64468

JACKSON, LAWRENCE ROBERT, labor union administrator; b. Omaha, Apr. 10, 1941; s. Ralph William and Irene (Siepmann) J.; m. Janet M. Tincani; children: Joseph L., Richard E., Lawrence R. II. Student, U. Omaha. Trustee local #50 Am. Fedn. Grain Millers, Omaha, 1964-68, bus. agt. local #50, 1968-69; rep. Am. Fedn. Grain Millers Internat., Omaha, 1969-71, v.p., 1971-83; sec. and treas. Am. Fedn. Grain Millers Internat., Mpls., 1983—; v.p. Food Allied Service Trades, Washington, 1983—, Maritime Trades Dept., Washington, 1983—, Union Label Trades Dept., Washington, 1986—. Bd. dirs. St. Mary's U., San Antonio, 1980-83. Democrat. Roman Catholic. Avocations: boating, golf, fishing, skiing, tennis. Office: Am Fedn of Grain Millers 4949 Olson Memorial Hwy Minneapolis MN 55422

JACKSON, LOLA LEE, horse breeder; b. Lyons, Kans., Oct. 24, 1928; d. Frank Eugene and Lanita Marie (Hamman) Campbell; m. Melvin LeRoy Jackson, June 12, 1955 (dec. July 83); children: Dana, Dennis, Josh, Joel, Jewelee. Student, Wichita U., 1950-55. Postal clk. U.S. Post Office, Wichita, Kans., 1955-65; owner Wichita Heights Motel, 1975-84; owner, breeder Jackson Stables, El Dorado, Kans., 1984—. Author: World of Poetry (Golden Poet of the Yr. 1985, 86, 87). Active Animal Farm Refuge. Mem. Am. Saddle Horse Assn., Hackney Horse Assn., Pinto Horse Assn., Northshore Animal League, Animal Protection Inst. Avocation: writing poetry. Home: Jackson Stables Rural Rt 4 PO Box 47C El Dorado KS 67042

JACKSON, MICHAEL BERNARD, credit and finance executive; b. Dothan, Ala., Oct. 4, 1953; s. Velem Jefferson and Jimmie Lee (Kirkland) J.; m. Loren Sellers, June 10, 1978; children: Leah D., Justin L. BA, Morehouse Coll., 1975. Asst. mgr. Cleve. Trust Co., 1975-78; spl. agt. N.Y. Life Ins. Co., Detroit, 1978-79; field auditor Comml. Services Inc., Madison Heights, Mich., 1979-85; unit mgr. Capital Credit Corp., Southfield, Mich., 1981-82; credit mgr. Abner Wolf Co., Detroit, 1985—; strategic planning advisor Money Enterprises Corp., Detroit, 1985—; cons. in field, Detroit, 1985—; assoc. lease broker Northeastern Leasing Co., Grand Island, N.Y., 1983—. Mem. Nat. Assn. Credit Mgmt., Internat. Assn. Bus. and Fin. Cons., Kappa Alpha Psi. Baptist. Lodge: Fountain. Avocations: bicycling, golfing, photography, personal computers. Home: 18414 Parkside Detroit MI 48221 Office: Abner Wolf Distributors 13901 Joy Rd Detroit MI 48228-2599

JACKSON, REGINALD SHERMAN, JR., lawyer; b. Toledo, Ohio, Oct. 8, 1946; s. Reginald Sherman and Frances (Holland) J.; m. Joanne Marie Warren, Aug. 31, 1968; children—Reginald Sherman III, Michael W., Adam H. BA, Ohio State U., 1968, JD, 1971. Bar: Ohio 1971, U.S. Supreme Ct. 1976. Mem. Fuller, Henry, Hodge & Snyder, Toledo, 1971-76; asst. U.S. atty. no. dist. Ohio, U.S. Dept. Justice, 1976-78; mem. Connelly, Soutar & Jackson, 1978—; adj. prof. trial practice U. Toledo Coll. Law, 1976—. Trustee Toledo Boy's Club, 1981—. Mem. ABA, Ohio Bar Assn., Toledo Bar Assn. (trustee 1978-86, v.p. 1986—). Club: Toledo Country (trustee 1981—). Lodge: Rotary. Home: 2907 River Rd Maumee OH 43537 Office: Connelly Soutar & Jackson 2100 Ohio Citizens Bank Bldg Toledo OH 43604

JACKSON, RICHARD LEWIS, general dentist; b. Oberlin, Ohio, July 12, 1957; s. Robert Lodington and Marjorie Lois (Snapp) J.; m. Kimberly Lynne Doench, June 21, 1986; 1 child, Jennifer Asbury. BA, Miami U., Oxford, Ohio, 1979; DDS, Ohio State U., 1983. Practice gen. dentistry Cin., 1983—. Mem. Mt. Lookout Civic Club, Cin., 1984—, mem. pastor-parish relations com. St. Paul United Meth. Ch., Madeira, Ohio, 1986, choir mem., 1985—. Mem. ADA, Ohio Dental Assn. (chmn. children's dental health month), Cin. Dental Soc. (chmn. children's dental health month com. 1987), J.J.P. Dental Group, Sigma Nu, Psi Omega. Republican. Avocations: sports, music, golf, art, antiques. Office: 1056 Delta Ave Cincinnati OH 45243

JACKSON, RICHARD LEWIS, obstetrician-gynecologist; b. Colfax, Wash., Mar. 1, 1923; s. Thomas Louis and Agnes Grey (Eagle) J.; m. Margarette Helen O'Grady, Nov. 5, 1946; children: Michael T., Patrick L. BS, U. Idaho, 1943; MD, Marquette U., 1946; MS, U. Minn., 1956, PhD, 1956. Cert. Am. Bd. Ob-Gyn. Rotating intern St. Luke's Hosp., Spokane, Wash., 1946-47; resident in gen. practice Sacred Heart Hosp., Spokane, 1947-48; ob-gyn. Atomic Energy Commn., Richland, Wash., 1948-50; ob-gyn. fellow Mayo Found., Rochester, Minn., 1951-56; practice medicine specializing in ob-gyn. Ventura, Calif., 1956-57; ob-gyn. instr. U. Tenn., Memphis, 1957-59; practice medicine specializing in ob-gyn. Mpls., 1960—; asst. clin. prof. U. Minn., Mpls., 1976—. Contbr. articles to profl. jours. Served to maj. USAF, 1952-54. Fellow Am. Coll. Ob-Gyn.; mem. Am. Fertility Soc., Minn. Med. Assn., Minn. Ob-Gyn. Soc., Hennepin County Med. Soc., Sigma Xi. Roman Catholic. Home: 4211 Forest Rd Saint Louis Park MN 55416 Office: 4825 Hwy 55 Minneapolis MN 55422

JACKSON, ROBERT HENRY, physician, medical administrator; b. Norwalk, Ohio, Oct. 5, 1922; s. Samuel Lloyd and Mona Mae (Zuelch) J.; m. Ann Elisabeth Dornback, Sept. 20, 1958; 1 child, Ann Dornback. BS, Western Res. U., 1947; MD, U. Heidelberg, Fed. Republic of Germany, 1953. Rotating intern St. Luke's Hosp., Cleve., 1953-54; fellow in Urology Mayo Clinic, Rochester, Minn., 1954-55; asst. surg. resident Luth. Hosp., Cleve., 1955-56, Perusse Traumatic Surg. Clinic, Chgo., 1956-57; gen. chmn. Internat. Congress on Neoplastic Diseases, Heidelberg, Fed. Republic Germany, 1973. Author: Joseph Colt Bloodgood: Cancer Pioneer, 1971, The Viral Etiology, Immunology, Immunodianosis, Immunotherapy and Immunoprophylaxis of Human Diseases. Mem. Presdl. Task Force, Washington, 1984—, Senatorial Com., Washington, 1984—, Nat. Commn. on Health Manpower, Washington, 1965—. Served to brig. gen. U.S. Army, ETO. Named hon. prof. internat. affairs, recipient Jacob Gould Schurman plaque Cornell U., 1961; U. Heidelberg New Univ. dedicated in his honor. Mem. Mayo Clinic Alumni Assn., AMA (founder sect. neoplastic diseases 1971), Am. Assn. Study Neoplastic Diseases (exec. sec. 1960-73, pres. 1974), Assn. U.S. Army, Res. Officers Assn. (honor roll 1955—), Cleve. Grays, World Med. Assn., Deutsche Medizinische Gesellschaft Von Chgo., Ohio State Med. Assn., Cleve. Acad. Medicine, VFW, U. Heidelberg Med. Alumni in U.S.A., Am. Legion. Club: Cercle D'Etudes sur la Bataille des Ardennes. Avocations: military, woodworking, fishing, boating. Home: 10607 Miles Ave Cleveland OH 44105

JACKSON, ROBERT LEE, II, university administrator; b. Detroit, Apr. 29, 1942; s. Robert L. and Bettye (Armour) J.; m. Betty Jean Darby; children: Robert L. III, Susan M., Nicole E.; stepchildren: Kala Butler, Brandon Darby. AA in Philosophy and Theology, Divine World Sem., 1964; BS in Edn., U. Mich., 1969, MS in Edn., 1971, PhD in Ednl. Research, 1974. Instr. Washtenaw Community Coll., Ann Arbor, Mich., 1969-73; supervising tchr. Washtenaw Intermediate Sch., 1969-70, supr. coordinator psycho-social services, 1970-72, supr. ednl. assessment and evaluation, 1972-74; sr. systems cons. Epic System Inc., Tucson, 1974-76; research dir. Trenton (N.J.) Bd. Edn., 1976-78; dir. office minority edn. Ednl. Testing Service, Princeton, N.J., 1978-83; dir. community edn. Wayne State U., Detroit, 1983-86, assoc. dean, 1986—; probation officer Washtenaw County Juvenile Ct., 1969-70. Contbr. articles to profl. jours. Recipient Indsl. award Metro Detroit YMCA, 1985. Mem. Am. Ednl. Research Assn., Am. Psychol. Assn., Am. Mgmt. Assn., Data Processing Mgmt. Assn. Avocations: reading, painting. Office: Wayne State U Coll of Lifelong Learning 6001 Cass Ave Detroit MI 48202

JACKSON, ROBERT LORING, educator, academic administrator; b. Mitchell, S.D., June 8, 1926; s. Olin DeBuhr and Edna Anna (Hanson) J.; m. Helen M. Baker, June 2, 1951; children—Charles Olin, Catherine Lynne, Cynthia Helen. B.S., Hamline U., 1950; M.A., U. Minn., 1959; Ph.D., 1965. Tchr. math. and sci., pub. schs., Heron Lake, Minn., 1950-52; tchr. math. Lakewood (Colo.) Sr. High Sch., 1952-53, Nouassuer Air Force Sch. Casablanca, Morocco, 1953-54, Baumholder (Germany) Elem. Sch., 1954-55, U. Minn. Univ. Lab. Sch., Mpls., 1955-60; asst. prof. sci. and math. edn. U. Minn., Mpls., 1965-66, assoc. prof., 1966-70, prof., 1970—, head sci. and math. edn., 1980-84, assoc. chmn., dir. undergrad. studies, curriculum and instrn., 1984—; vis. prof. Hamline U., St. Paul, 1958, Mont. State U., Bozeman, 1981, Bethel Coll., St. Paul, 1981, No. Mich. U., Marquette, 1983-84; cons. math. Minn. Dept. edn., St. Paul, 1960-62. Bd. dirs. Minn. Chorale, Mpls., 1973—, pres., 1978-80. Served to pfc. U.S. Army, 1944-46. Decorated Purple Heart; recipient Disting. Teaching award Coll. Edn., U. Minn., 1984. Mem. Minn. Council Tchrs. Math., Nat. Council Tchrs. Math., Council Diagnostic and Prescriptive Math., Math. Assn. Am., Internat. Group for Psychology of Math. Edn., Internat. Platform Assn. Methodist. Co-author book/man. series: Laboratory Mathematics, 1975-76. Home: 2710 N Dale St Apt 101 Roseville MN 55113 Office: U Minn 130 Peik Hall Minneapolis MN 55455

JACKSON, ROBERT WAYNE, internist, rheumatologist; b. Moberly, Mo., Oct. 25, 1955; s. Paul Robert Jackson and Norma Dean (Cole) Mosler; m. Jennifer Ann Wolfe, Sept. 2, 1978; children: Joy Nicole, Jacob Cole, Julie Ann. BS in Biology cum laude, Northeast Mo. State U., Kirsville, 1977; DO in Osteopathic Medicine, Kirksville Coll., 1981. Intern Doctor's Hosp., Columbus, Ohio, 1981-82; resident in internal medicine Kirksville Osteo. Hosp., Columbia, Mo., 1982-84, U. Mo. Health Ctr., Kirksville, 1984-85; felow in rheumatology U. Mo. Health Ctr., Columbia, 1985—; rheumatology cons. Mo. Dept. Social Service, Jefferson City, Mo., 1986. Scholar Nat. Osteo. Coll., 1977, USPHS, 1977-81; research grantee Nat. Osteo. Found. 1984, 85. Mem. ACP (assoc.), Am. Coll. Osteo. Internist (assoc.), Mo. Assn. Osteo. Physicians and Surgeons, Am. Osteo. Assn. Avocations: running, biking, swimming, hunting, fishing. Home: Rt 3 Box 621 West Plains MO 62775 Office: U. Mo Health Sci Ctr MA427 Dept Rheumatology 1 Hospital Dr Columbia MO 65202

JACKSON, ROY GENE, real estate executive; b. Eldon, Mo., Jan. 5, 1939; s. Willard Murrel and Ruby Nadine (Apperson) J.; m. Kilmeny Dunne, Aug. 24, 1968; children: Elizebeth Ashley, Anne Marie, Christopher Brandt. BBA, U. Mo., 1961. Mgt. trainee State Farm Ins., 1963-64; salesman Frank Paxton Co., Kansas City, Mo., 1964-70, v.p., 1976—; salesman Kroh Bros. Devel., 1970-71; asst. mgr. Paxton Properties, Inc., Kansas City, 1971-76. Served to 1st lt. U.S. Army, 1961-63. Mem. Kansas City Home Builders Assn. Republican. Episcopalian. Clubs: Brookridge Country (Overland Park, Kans.). Avocations: flying, golf, fishing. Home: 4047 W 124th Terr Leawood KS 66209 Office: Paxton Properties Inc 9229 Ward Pkwy Kansas City KS 64114

JACKSON, THOMAS DIRK, dentist; b. Pontiac, Mich., May 21, 1945; s. Homer Cornelius and Grace Marie (Scheur) J.; m. Luan Kay Zemmer, Aug. 2, 1969; children: Patricia Lynn, Brent Thomas. BS, U. Mich., 1968; DDS, U. Detroit, 1971. Pvt. practice dentistry Marlette, Mich., 1971—; cons. simplified bite registration, 1985-86. bd. dirs. Teen Ranch Boys Tng. Sch., Marlette, Mich., 1982—, First Baptist Ch., Lapeer, 1977-86; pres. Parents Assn. Kingsbury Sch., Oxford, Mich., 1986—. Mem. ADA, Mich. Dental Assn., Thumb Dist. Dental Soc. (pres. 1980-81). Republican. Clubs: Davison Country, Davison Racquetball. Avocations: golf, downhill skiing. Home: 1256 Briarhill Dr Lapeer MI 48446 Office: Main St Plaza Marlette MI 48453

JACKSON, THOMAS HAMILTON, military officer, computer consultant; b. Houston, June 16, 1945; s. Hiram Thomas Bartlett and Hazel Beatrice (Hagen) J.; m. Lennie Elizabeth Harris, Jan. 29, 1972; 1 child, Susan Elizabeth. BS, U.S. Mil. Acad., 1967; MS in Systems Mgmt., U. So. Calif., Los Angeles, 1982. Commd. 2d lt. U.S. Army, 1967, advanced through grades to lt. col., 1983; comdr. B troop 6th squadron 1st cavalry U.S. Army, Ft. Hood, Tex., 1967-68; staff officer U.S. Army Recruiting Command, Ft. Sheridan, Ill., 1972-75; dep. personnel officer 3d armoured div. U.S. Army, Germany, 1977-80; staff officer soldier support ctr. U.S. Army, Indpls., 1983—. Contbr. articles to mags. Bd. dirs. East Avalon Hills Civic Assn., Indpls., 1984-87; vestryman Ch. of Nativity, 1985-87. Decorated Silver Star with oak leaf cluster, Bronze Star with oak leaf cluster, Purple Heart. Mem. Assn. of U.S. Army. Republican. Club: Skyline. Avocations: gun collecting, personal computing. Home: 6545 Albion Dr Indianapolis IN 46256

JACKSON, THOMAS JAMES, accountant; b. Ashland, Wis., Nov. 21, 1953; s. James Thomas and Sheila Ann (Douglas) J.; m. Dorothy Jackson, May 30, 1975. BS, Ill. State U., 1975; MST, DePaul U., 1978. CPA, Ill. Tax staff Touche Ross, Chgo., 1975-83, tax ptnr., 1983-86, dir. tax ops., 1986—. Mem. Am. Inst. CPA's, Ill. Soc. CPA's, Ins. Tax Conf., Real Estate Securities and Syndication Inst. Clubs: Naperville (Ill.) Country (sec. 1984); Plaza (Chgo.) (bd. govs. 1986—). Avocations: golf, squash. Home: 666 N Lake Shore Dr apt 1207 Chicago IL 60611 Office: Touche Ross & Co 111 E Wacker Dr Chicago IL 60601

JACKSON, WILLIAM GENE, computer company executive; b. Opelika, Ala., Nov. 22, 1946; s. John Willis and Lucy (Jackson) J.; m. Cornelia Turner, Aug. 17, 1969; children—Verzelia Yvett, Gena Nichole, William Gene. B.S. in Mgmt. and Mktg., Syracuse U., 1979, A.A.S. in Mgmt., 1976; postgrad. Pace U. With IBM, 1966—, customer engr. Huntsville, Ala., 1966-72, sr. customer engr., Atlanta, 1972-73, field mgr., Miami, Fla., 1973-75, eastern region ops. analyst Harrison, N.Y., 1975-76, br. mgr., N.Y.C., 1976, region ops. mgr. region 3, Montvale, N.J., 1977-78, employee relations program mgr. personnel, office products div. hdqrs., Franklin Lakes, N.J., 1979, adminstrv. asst. to dir. ops. west, office products div. hdqrs., Franklin Lakes, 1980, IBM corp. service staff, Armonk, N.Y., 1981-82, adminstrv. asst. to pres. customer service div., Franklin Lakes, 1983, region mgr. customer service div., region 7, Southfield, Mich., 1983-84, dir. service support Nat. Service div. Area 4, 1984—. Bd. dirs. spl. affairs Jaycees, Wanaque, N.J., 1978-79. Mem. Am. Mgmt. Assn. Home: 25220 Witherspoon Rd Farmington Hills MI 48018 Office: IBM-NSD Area 4 27800 Northwestern Hwy Southfield MI 48086

JACOB, RICHARD JOSEPH, rubber and plastic manufacturing company executive; b. Detroit, July 25, 1919; s. Ben B. and Nettie (Byron) J.; m. Louise Marks, Apr. 2, 1949; children: Patricia Josephine, Arnold Marks. Student, Butler U., 1938-39, Miami U., 1940-41. Exec. with Mfg. Engring. Co., Detroit, 1945-46; exec. v.p., pres. Cadillac Plastics & Chem. Co., Detroit, 1945-65, dir.; exec. v.p. Dayco Corp., Dayton, Ohio, 1965-68, pres., 1968-73, chmn. bd., chief exec. officer, 1971—; chmn., chief exec. officer Dayco Automotive Aftermarket Co. (div.), Dayton, Ohio; chmn. Dayco Can. Ltd. (subs.), Weston, Ont.; also dir. Dayco Corp., Weston, Ont.; dir. Elder-Beerman Stores Corp., Dayton, FLa. Leasing & Capital Corp., Qartel Corp., Mich. Nat. Corp., Bloomfield Hills; Bank One, Dayton N.A.; Mem. adv. bd. Kettering (Ohio) Med. Center; bd. dirs. Rubber Mfrs. Assn. Hon. trustee Children's Med. Center; trustee Nat. Urban League; bd. overseers Hebrew Union Coll., Cin.; life mem. bd. dirs. Brandeis U. Mem. Dayton Area C. of C., Soc. Plastics Industry, Soc. Plastic Engrs. Clubs: Standard-City (past pres., dir. Detroit); Hundred (Dayton) (chmn.), Racquet (Dayton), Miami Valley Skeet (Dayton), Meadowbrook Country (Dayton); Renaissance (Detroit); Standard-City (Chgo.); Palm Beach (Fla.) Country; Ocean Reef (Key Largo, Fla.); Moraine Country (Kettering); Franklin Hills Country (Franklin, Mich.); Harmonie (N.Y.C.). Home: PO Box 1004 Dayton OH 45401 Office: Dayco Corp 333 W 1st St Dayton OH 45402 *

JACOB, STEVEN EDWARD, manufacturing company executive; b. Detroit, Dec. 7, 1951; s. Herbert H. and Claire L. (Grossman) J.; m. Katherine Frank, May 16, 1981; 1 child, Alexander M. BA, U. Mich., 1973, MBA, 1975. Pres. S.E.J. Enterprises, Madison Heights, Mich., 1977-86, Horizon Sportswear, Madison Heights, 1986—; bd. dirs. Ajax Paving Ind., Madison Heights; gen. ptnr. Bald Mountain West, Madison Heights, 1983—. Jewish. Avocations: racquetball, aerobics, bridge. Home: 32015 N Beverly Ct Birmingham MI 48009 Office: Horizon Sportswear 190 Ajax Dr Madison Heights MI 48071

JACOBI, H. PAUL, dentist; b. Dyersville, Iowa, Nov. 2, 1927; s. Fredrick William and Olga (Kiener) J.; m. Patricia Mary Steele, Aug. 9, 1952; children: Fredrick, Roger, Curt, Kathleen. DDS, Marquette U., 1950. Practice dentistry Neenah, Wis., 1953—; Cons. Sycom, Madison, Wis., 1960-75, Profl. Service Corp., Madison, 1980-86. Author A Dentist's Flight Manuel to Success, 1967, Consumers Dental Bible, 1970. Served to capt. U.S. Army, 1951-53. Fellow Acad. Gen. Dentistry; mem. ADA, Sales Mktg. Execs., Nat. Speakers Assn. Republican. Roman Catholic. Lodge: Rotary, Lions (pres. 1960), Elks (exalted ruler 1962-63). Avocations: hunting, fishing, skiing. Home: 448 Edgewood Ct Neenah WI 54956 Office: Profl Plaza 1215 Doctors Dr Neenah WI 54956

JACOBI, JAN DE GREEFF, school administrator; b. N.Y.C., Oct. 26, 1944; s. Edwin George Jacobi and Marjorie (de Greeff) Litchfield; m. Virginia Powell Newton, July 26, 1986. BA, Stanford U., 1967; MA, Columbia U., 1976. Asst. headmaster, English tchr. The Harvey Sch., Katonah, N.Y., 1973-82; head of lower sch. St. Louis Country Day Sch., 1982—. Avocations: gardening, stargazing, golf. Home: 527 Crescent Saint Louis MO 63122 Office: St Louis Country Day Sch 425 N Warson Rd Saint Louis MO 63124

JACOBI, ROGER EDGAR, arts executive, music educator; b. Saginaw, Mich., Apr. 7, 1924; s. Andrew E. and Olga C. (Schnell) J.; m. Mary Jane Stephans, Aug. 13, 1949; children—Richard William, Martha Jacobi Nale. Mus.B., U. Mich., 1948, Mus.M., 1951; Mus.D. (hon.), Albion Coll., 1980. Cert. tchr., Mich. Tchr. music Ann Arbor (Mich.) Pub. Schs., 1948-56, music dept. chmn., 1959-68; lectr. music U. Mich., Ann Arbor, 1957-59, asst. prof., 1959-63, assoc. prof., 1963-66, prof., 1966—, asst. dean, 1968-71, assoc. dean, 1971; personnel dir., sec. bd. Interlochen Ctr. for Arts, 1956-59, pres., 1971—; cons. Ford Found. Young Composers Project, 1960-62, Juilliard Repertory Project, 1965-67; chmn. music com. Arts Recognition Talent Search Project, Ednl. Testing Service, 1979-80. Named honored alumnus U. Mich. Sch. Music, 1981. Mem. Am. Council Arts, Am. Fedn. Musicians, Am. Sch. Band Dirs. Assn., Coll. Music Soc., Econ. Club Detroit, Internat. Soc. Performing Arts Adminstrs., Music Educators Nat. Conf. (bd. dirs. 1964-68), Music Industry Council, Nat. Assn. Schs. Music, Nat. Fedn. Music Clubs (presdl. citation 1981), Nat. Music Council, Delta Omicron (patron), Phi Mu Alpha Sinfonia. Lutheran. Lodge: Traverse City Rotary (pres. 1982-83, trustee Rotary Charities 1982-83, pres. camps and services 1987—). Author: (with Emil Holtz) Teaching Band Instruments to Beginners, 1966; contbr. articles to profl. jours.

JACOBS, ANDREW, JR., congressman; b. Indpls., Feb. 24, 1932; s. Andrew and Joyce Taylor (Wellborn) J. B.S., Ind. U., 1955, LL.B., 1958. Bar: Ind. Practiced in Indpls. 1958-65, 73-74; mem. 89th-92d congresses from 11th Dist., 1965-73, 94th-97th congresses from 11th Dist. Ind., 1975-83, 98th-99th Congresses from 10th Dist. Ind., 1983—; Mem. Ind. Ho. of Reps., 1958-60. Served with USMC, 1950-52. Mem. Indpls. Bar Assn., Am. Legion. Democrat. Roman Catholic. Office: US House of Reps 1533 Longworth House Office Bldg Washington DC 20515

JACOBS, BURLEIGH EDMUND, foundry executive; b. Milw., Feb. 3, 1920; s. Burleigh Edmund and Ora (Harmon) J.; m. Janet Eloise Grede, Nov. 1, 1942; children: Mary (Mrs. Merrill York), Bruce, Scott, William. B.A., U. Wis., 1942. Joined Grede Foundries, Inc., Milw., 1945; successively works mgr. Iron Mountain Foundry, 1947-49; works mgr. Milw. Steel Foundry, 1950-51, asst. sales mgr., 1952-57, asst. v.p., 1957-60, pres., 1960-73, chmn., chief exec. officer, 1973—; dir. Marshall & Ilsley Bank, Milw., Soo Line R.R. Co. Pres. bd. Met. Milw. YMCA, 1968-70; mem. Greater Milw. Com., 1969—; bd. dirs. Jr. Achievement, 1968-71, Better Bus. Bur. Served with USNR, 1942-45. Recipient Frederick A. Lorenz Meml. medal Steel Founders' Soc. Am., 1970; named Mktg. Man of Yr. Soc. Mfg. Engrs., Milw., 1980. Mem. Steel Founders' Soc. Am. (pres. 1966-69), Am. Foundrymen's Soc. (v.p. 1971-72, pres. 1972-73, Peter L. Simpson gold medal 1983), Cast Metals Fedn. (pres. 1974), Gray and Ductile Iron Founders' Soc. (Gold medal 1973). Conglist. (moderator 1962-64). Club: Bluemound Country (Wauwatosa, Wis.). Home: 1020 Madera Circle Elm Grove WI 53122 Office: Grede Foundries Inc 9898 W Bluemound Rd Milwaukee WI 53226

JACOBS, DAVID SAMUEL, physician, pathologist; b. Detroit, Nov. 7, 1931; s. Harry L. and Rae (Goldman) J.; m. Judy Jacobs, Aug. 16, 1957; children—Diane Sue, Daniel Harry, Thomas Dale, Jonathan Todd. B.S. with distinction, U. Mich., 1953, M.D., 1956. Diplomate Am. Bd. Pathology. Intern, then resident U. Mich., Ann Arbor, 1956-62; resident Mt. Sinai Hosp., Chgo., 1962-63; pathologist Menorah Med. Ctr., Kansas City, Mo., 1963-65; vice chmn. Providence Hosp., Kansas City, Kans., 1964-65, pathologist, dir. labs., 1965-71; pathologist, dir. of labs. Providence-St. Margaret Health Ctr., Kansas City, Kans., 1971—; pres. Pathologists, Chartered, Shawnee Mission, Kans., 1971—; cons. VA Hosp., Leavenworth, Kans., 1972-82; clin. prof. U. Kans. Med. Ctr., Kansas City, 1979, U. Mo.-Kansas City Sch. Medicine, 1978. Author lab. manuals. Contbr. articles to profl. jours. Served as capt. U.S. Army, 1958-60. Fellow ACP, Coll. Am. Pathologists; mem. Am. Soc. Clin. Pathologists, Internat. Acad. Pathology, AMA, Kans. Med. Soc., Am. Assn. Blood Banks, Kansas City Soc. Pathologists, Kans. Soc. Pathologists (pres. 1978-79). Home: 6621 Overhill Rd Shawnee Mission KS 66208 Office: Providence-St Margaret Health Ctr Lab 8929 Parallel Pkwy Kansas City KS 66112

JACOBS, DENNIS WAYNE, architect; b. Kansas City, Mo., Nov. 30, 1946; s. William John and Frances Matilda (Horak) J.; m. Anne Elizabeth Perry, May 2, 1970; children: Scott Douglas, Robert Andrew. BArch, U. Kans., 1969; postgrad., U. Tulsa, 1975-76. Registered architect Kans., Mo., Okla. Architect Nat. Park Service/Hist. Am. Bldg. Survey, Washington, 1969, HTB, Inc., Tulsa, 1971-77, HIGHT/JACKSON/ASSOCS. P.A., Coffeyville, Kans., 1977—. Bd. dirs. Coffeyville Hist. Soc., 1984-87, Salvation Army, Coffeyville, 1985-87. Served to sgt. U.S. Army, 1969-71. Mem. Am. Inst. Architects (Silver Medal 1969), Am. Planning Assn., Kans. Soc. Architects, Nat. Council Archtl. Registration Bds. (cert.). Republican. Presbyterian. Lodge: Rotary (pres. Coffeyville club 1985). Home: 107 Pullins Dr Coffeyville KS 67337 Office: Hight/Jackson Assocs PO Box 756 808 Willow Coffeyville KS 67337

JACOBS, ELMER MATTHEW, appliance company executive; b. Dresden, Kans., Apr. 16, 1937; s. Raymond and Rose (Ritter) J.; m. Viola Leona Brungardt, May 25, 1957; children: Jeanne, Delilah, Debra, Jennifer. Student, Parks Bus. Coll. V.p. Tom Kiel, Inc., Goodland, Kans., 1962-67; pres. Jacobs Appliance, Goodland, 1968—; pres. electronics dept. Northwest Area Vo-Tech. Sch., Goodland, 1976—. Mem. Jaycees. Roman Catholic. Lodge: Kiwanis, Elks, KC (25 Yr. award 1986). Home: 615 Walnut Goodland KS 67735

JACOBS, EVERETT SHERMAN, court system administrator; b. Kansas City, Mo., Feb. 13, 1950; s. Everett Franklin and Carrie Alviena (Gott) J.; Tina Marie Cottle, Aug. 9, 1970; children: Jennifer, Carrie, Danae. BBA, U. Mo., 1976, M Pub. Adminstrn., 1986. Personnel dir. Baker Industries, Kansas City, 1977-79; gen. mgr. Doall Corp., Kansas City, 1979-82; dir. adminstrn. Jackson County Juvenile Ct., Kansas City, 1982—; cons. Act Together, Kansas City, 1983-85. Regional coordinator United Way, Kansas City, 1981. Mem. Am. Mgmt. Assn., Nat. Council Juvenile Judges, Inst. Ct. Mgmt. Mem. Chrisitan Ch. Office: Jackson County Juvenile Ct 625 E 26th St Kansas City MO 64108

JACOBS, FRANCIS ALBIN, biochemist, educator; b. Mpls., Feb. 23, 1918; s. Anthony and Agnes Ann (Stejskal) J.; m. Dorothy Caldwell, June 5, 1953; children: Christopher, Gregory, Paula, Margaret, John. BS, Regis Coll., Denver, 1939; postgrad, U. Denver, 1939-41; PhD, St. Louis U., 1949. Postdoctoral fellow Nat. Cancer Inst., Bethesda, Md., 1949-51; instr. physiol. chemistry U. Pitts. Sch. Medicine, 1951-52, asst. prof., 1952-54; asst. prof. biochemistry U. N.D. Sch. Medicine, Grand Forks, 1954-56; asso. prof. U. N.D. Sch. Medicine, 1956-64, prof., 1964-87, prof. emeritus, 1987—; dir., research supr. Nat. Sci. Research Participation Program in Biochemistry, 1959-63; advisor directorate for sci. edn. NSF. Contbr. articles to profl. jours. Mem. bishop's pastoral council Diocese of Fargo, N.D., 1979-86. Fellow AAAS, N.D. Acad. Sci. (editor 1967, 68); mem. Am. Soc. Biol. Chemists, Am. Inst. Nutrition, Soc. Exptl. Biology and Medicine, Am. Chem. Soc. (chmn. Red River valley sect. 1971), AAAS, AMA, Sigma Xi (pres. chpt. 1965-66, Faculty award for Outstanding Sci. Research U. N.D. chpt. 1982), Alpha Sigma Nu, Phi Lambda Upsilon. Home: 1525 Robertson Ct Grand Forks ND 58201 Office: U ND Sch Medicine Dept Biochemistry and Molecular Biology Grand Forks ND 58202

JACOBS, HAROLD ANTHONY, architect; b. South Holland, Ill., June 8, 1926; s. Hiram and Gertrude (DeGraff) J.; m. Ellen May Funk, June 11, 1949 (div. Aug. 1973); children: Sandra, Cheryl, Tamara, Kim, Tim; m. Peggy Joyce Reagan, Sept. 14, 1974; 1 stepchild, Tammy Dawn. BA in Archtl. Engring., U. Ill., 1951. Archtl. draftsman Swift & Co., Chgo., 1951-53; job capt. Turner & Turner Architects, Hammond, Ind., 1953-54; pvt. practice architecture H.A. Jacobs & Assocs., Architects, South Holland, 1954-57, 68—; prin. Jacobs & Evans, Architects, South Holland, 1957-68. Served with U.S. Army, 1944-46, ETO. Mem. AIA (pres. eastern Ill. chpt. 1969-70), South Holland Bus. Assn. Republican. Methodist. Lodge: Lions. Avocation: sailing. Home: Woodlawn and Bemis 3d Driveway South Crete IL 60417 Office: 16237 Wausau Ave South Holland IL 60473

JACOBS, IRWIN LAWRENCE, diversified corporate executive; b. Mpls., July 15, 1941; s. Samuel and Rose H. Jacobs; m. Alexandra Light, Aug. 26, 1962; children: Mark, Sheila, Melinda, Randi, Trisha. Student pub. schs. Pres., chief exec. officer Jacobs Industries, Inc., Mpls., 1977—; chmn. bd. Fed. Fin. Corp., Mpls., 1976—; chmn. Arctic Enterprises, Inc. (now Minstar, Inc.), Mpls., from 1977, Watkins Products, Winona, Minn., 1978—; owner Grain Belt Properties, 1976—, Countryside Estates, 1978—; v.p. Northwestern Bag Corp., Mpls.; pres. Jacobs Bag Corp., 1977—, Harper-Crawford Bag Co., Charlotte, N.C., 1978—, JYJ Corp., Mpls. Shareholders Co., 1976—, JII Air Service, Inc., Mpls., 1978—, Regional Accounts Corp., Mpls., 1976—, FFC Realty, 1977—, Nationwide Collection Service, Inc., 1977—, Nationwide Accounts Corp., 1977—; chmn. Kodicor, Inc., Mpls., 1979—. Clubs: Minneapolis, Mpls. Athletic, Lafayette Country, Belle Aire Yacht, Oakridge Country. Office: Minstar Inc 1215 Marshall St NE Minneapolis MN 55413 *

JACOBS, JAMES WALTER, county government administrator; b. Champaign, Ill., Jan. 24, 1945; s. Walter F. and Ruby M. (McGuire) J.; m. Janet Sue Butler, Mar. 13, 1971; 1 child, Angela M. Fitton. BA, Eastern Ill. U., 1982. Field person Champaign County, Urbana, 1970-74, dep. supr. assessments, 1974-79, chief dep. supr. assessments, 1979-81, supr. assessments, 1981—. Mem. Internat. Assn. Assessing Officers (cert., profl. designation advisor), Ill. Tax Found. (mem. adv. com. for Ill. real estate assessment study 1985—), Ill. Property Assessment Inst. (bd. dirs. 1986—), Champaign County Assessment Officers' Assn. (various officers), Cert. Ill. Assessing Officers (vice chmn. 1985086, treas. 1984-85). Avocation: golf. Home: 6 Gerald Rd Rantoul IL 61866 Office: Champaign County Office of Assessments 201 E Main Urbana IL 61801

JACOBS, JEFFREY HARRY, broadcasting company executive; b. Evanston, Ill., Sept. 12, 1956; s. Harry D. and Nancy L. (Witte) J.; m. Susan Katherine Comerford, April 16, 1983. BS, DePauw U., Greencastle, Ind., 1978; MBA, Loyola U., Chgo., 1981. Account exec. WWMM Radio, Arlington Heights, Ill., 1980; account exec. WFYR Radio, Chgo., 1980-84, sales mgr., 1984-85; gen. sales mgr. CBS CableConnect, Chgo., 1985-86, gen. mgr., 1986—. Bd. dirs. Chgo. Mental Health Assn., 1985-86. Mem. Broadcast Advt. Club Chgo, Cable TV Adminstrn. and Mktg. Soc., N.Y.C., Sigma Delta Chi. Republican. Roman Catholic. Avocations: tennis, golf, skiing, reading. Home: 1428 Canterbury Ln Glenview IL 60025 Office: CBS CableConnect 8700 W Bryn Mawr Chicago IL 60631

JACOBS, JIM H., fire restoration company executive; b. Loudon, Tenn., July 28, 1939; s. James Albert and Mattie Grace (Shaw) J.; m. Charlene A. Koch, Oct. 23, 1960; children: Karen Ann, Tammy Lynn. Pres. Reliable Carpet Cleaners, Belleville, Ill., 1962-72, Smokecontrol Services, Inc., St. Louis, 1972—. Mem. bd. Freeburg (Ill.) Dist. #77, 1975—. Served with U.S. Army, 1957-60. Mem. Nat. Inst. Fire Restoration (pres. 1984-86, cert restorer), Freeburg Jaycees (mem. 1965-74). Republican. Baptist. Home: Rural Rt #1 Box 15J Freeburg IL 62243 Office: Smokecontrol Services Inc 6827 S Broadway Saint Louis MO 63111

JACOBS, LAURIE ALICE, insurance agency owner; b. Kenosha, Wis., Nov. 24, 1943; d. Steven and Irma Mabel (Rich) Jacobs. Student Carthage Coll., 1962-65. Lic. property and casualty, life health ins. agent, Wis. Sec. Steven Jacobs Agy., Kenosha, Wis., 1965, ind. ins. agent, 1974-79, owner Jacobs, Ins., Kenosha, 1979—; pres. Ins. Women of Kenosha, 1968, 70, 83. Pres., Kenosha County council Girl Scouts U.S.A., 1978-82; bd. dirs. Trinity Luth. Ch., Kenosha, 1974-78; div. chmn. United Way of Kenosha County, 1980-82. Recipient Lamb award Luth. Council of Am., N.Y.C., 1980; named Ins. Woman of Yr. Kenosha Assn. Ins. Women, 1968. Mem. Nat. Assn. Ins. Women, Ind. Ins. Agts. of Am.

JACOBS, LINDA LEE, hospital administrator; b. Lincoln, Nebr., Apr. 18, 1949; d. Jacob and Darleen Rose (Worster) J.; B.S. U. Nebr., 1971. Gastrointestinal asst. Bryan Meml. Hosp., Lincoln, Nebr., 1972-78, chief gastrointestinal asst., 1978-81, supr. gastrointestinal lab., 1981-85, clin. instr. Cooper LaserSonics, 1985-86, cons. trainer CORE Assocs., 1987—, mem. employee adv. com., 1973-74; dir. Jacobs Constrn. Co., Inc., Lincoln. Active Vols. in Probation. Mem. Nat. Soc. Gastrointestinal Assts. (pres. 1980-81, chmn. nominating com. 1981-82, ex officio dir. at large 1981-85, editor jour. 1981-85), Nat. Assn. Female Execs., Am. Soc. Tng. and Devel., Am. Legion Aux., Jr. League, Gamma Phi Beta (corp. bd., pres. 1983-85). Home: 2624

Austin Dr Lincoln NE 68506 Office: CORE Assocs 9202 W 90th Overland Park KS 66212

JACOBS, LOUIS SULLIVAN, architect, engr., planner; s. Morris and Mary Jacobs; B.S. in Architecture and City Planning, Armour Inst. Tech., 1940; M.S. in Indsl. Engring., Ill. Inst. Tech., 1952, Ph.D. in Indsl. Engring., 1958; Sc.D. in Safety, Ind. No. U., 1972, Ph.D. in Human Engring., 1974; M.S. in Profl. Mgmt., 1980. Pres., Louis S. Jacobs & Assos., Architects, Engrs. and Planners, Chgo., 1946—; prof. archtl. engring. Loop Coll., Chgo., 1967-86, coordinator engring., archtl. and tech. services dept. Pub. Service Inst., 1967-75, dept. applied sci., 1975—; prof. indsl. engring. Ill. Inst. Tech., 1948-58, 67; prof. architecture U. Ill., Chgo., 1967; prof. engring. Chgo. Citywide Coll., 1980. Bd. dirs. Old Town Boys Club, 1951—; trustee Chgo. Sch. Architecture Found., 1967. Served as lt. USN, 1942-46. Recipient award of merit Office CD, State of Ill., 1957; citation Gov. State of Ill., Office Emergency Services, 1964; citation for Outstanding public services Office of Pres. U.S., U.S. Emergency Resources Bd., 1967; registered profl. engr., Ill., Del., Calif.; registered indsl. engr., safety engr., mfg. engr., Calif.; registered architect, Ill.; cert. in materials handling, materials mgmt., indsl. hygiene, cert. mfr. engr., Robotics, 1980; cert. materials handling engr., 1957, hazardous control mgr., 1968, mfr. engr., 1968, product safety mgr., 1985, hazardous materials mgr., 1985. Fellow Soc. Am. Registered Architects, Nat. Soc. Profl. Engrs., Systems Safety Soc., Soc. Architects, Ill. Soc. Architects (dir. 1976-78 v.p. 1978-80, pres. 1980-82); mem. AIA, Ill. Soc. Profl. Engrs. (v.p. 1976-83), System Safety Soc. (pres. 1980-85), ASCE, Western Soc. Engrs. (life), Am. Soc. Mil. Engrs., Am. Soc. Safety Engrs., Internat. Materials Mgmt. Soc., Am. Inst. Indsl. Engrs., Soc. for Gen. Systems Research, Standards Engring. Soc., Soc. Mfg. Engrs., Vets. Safety, Constrn. Safety Assn. Am. (v.p. 1976—), Am. Soc. Environ. Engrs. (diplomate), Nat. Safety Mgmt. Soc., Nat. Assn. Fire Investigators, Nat. Fire Protection Assn., Nat. Safety Council, World Safety Orgn. (cert. safety specialist, safety mgr., safety exec. 1986) Mil. Order World Wars, Naval Order U.S., Res. Officers Assn., Tau Beta Pi, Sigma Iota Epsilon, Alpha Phi Mu, Tau Epsilon Phi. Editor: Vector, 1968. Office: 2605 W Pratt Blvd Chicago IL 60645

JACOBS, PAUL ALAN, orthopaedic surgery educator; b. Bklyn., July 25, 1930; s. Leo and Fanny (Samrock) J.; m. Betty Hottenstein, May 30, 1957; children: Debra, Linda, Cynthia, Nancy. BA, Syracuse U., 1951; MD, SUNY Downstate Med. Ctr., N.Y.C., 1954. Intern Kings County Hosp., Bklyn., 1954-55; resident gen. surgeon Henry Ford Hosp., Detroit, 1957-58; res. orthopaedic surgeon Hosp. for Joint Diseases, N.Y.C., 1958-61; instr. orthopaedic surgery Med. Coll. Wis., Milw., 1961-70, asst. clinical prof., 1970-80, assoc. clinical prof., 1980—; asst. clinical prof. kinesiology U. Wis., Milw., 1981—. Contbr. 28 articles to profl. jours. Served to lt. comdr. USNR, 1955-57. Recipient Kleinberg award Hosp. for Joint Diseases, N.Y.C., 1961. Fellow AMA, Am. Acad. Orthopaedic Surgeons, Am. Coll. Orthopaedic Surgeons; mem. Milw. Orthopaedic Soc. (various offices), Musculoskeletal Tumor Soc., Major League Baseball Physicians (pres. 1980). Jewish. Home: 4641 N Lake Dr Milwaukee WI 53211 Office: Milw Orthopaedic Group 1218 W Kilbourn Ave Milwaukee WI 53233

JACOBS, RICHARD DEARBORN, consulting engineer; b. Detroit, July 6, 1920; s. Richard Dearborn and Mattie Phoebe (Cobleigh) J.; divorced; children: Richard, Margaret, Paul, Linden, Susan. BS, U. Mich., 1944. Engr., Detroit Diesel Engine div. Gen. Motors, 1946-51; mgr. indsl. and marine engine div. Reo Motors, Inc., Lansing, Mich., 1951-54; chief engr. Kennedy Marine Engine Co., Biloxi, Miss., 1955-59; marine sales mgr. Nordberg Mfg. Co., Milw., 1959-69; marine sales mgr. Fairbanks Morse Engine div. Colt Industries, Beloit, Wis., 1969-81; pres. R.D. Jacobs & Assocs., cons. engrs., naval architects and marine engrs., Roscoe, Ill., 1981—. Served with AUS, 1944-46. Registered profl. engr., Ill., Mich., Wis., Miss. Mem. Soc. Naval Architects and Marine Engrs. (chmn. sect. 1979-80), Soc. Automotive Engrs., Am. Soc. Naval Engrs., Soc. Am. Mil. Engrs., Soc. Marine Cons., ASTM, Permanent Internat. Assn. Nav. Congresses, Navy League U.S., Assn. U.S. Army, Propeller Club U.S., Nat. Forensic Ctr. Unitarian. Clubs: Country (Beloit); Rockford Polo, Masons. Home: 228 Summit St Poplar Grove IL 61065 Office: 11405 Main St Roscoe IL 61073

JACOBS, RICHARD MARC, podiatrist; b. Worcester, Mass., Oct. 10, 1953; s. Maxwell Saul and Ruth (Jacobson) J. BA in Biology and Anthropology, Case Western Res. U., 1975; BS in Med. Scis., Ill. Coll. Podiatric Medicine, 1981, D Podiatric Medicine, 1981. Diplomate Nat. Bd. Podiatric Med. Examiners. Intern podiatric medicine and surgery Omaha Surgical Ctr., 1981-82; resident St. Vincent Charity Hosp., Cleve., 1982-83, Huron Road Hosp., 1985-86; instr. dept. surgery Ohio Coll. Podiatric Medicine, Cleve., 1984-85; practice medicine specializing in podiatrics Beachwood, Ohio, 1986—; cons. Mt. Sinai Hosp. Podiatric Residency Jour. Club, Cleve., 1986. Mem. Am. Podiatric Med. Assn., Ohio Podiatric Med. Assn., Am. Coll. Foot Surgeons. (assoc.). Jewish. Avocations: racquetball, cycling, traveling, reading, philately.

JACOBS, ROBERT WESLEY, pediatric dentist; b. El Paso, Tex., Feb. 12, 1944; s. Robert William and Elizabeth (Francis) J.; m. Sheryl Lou King, Jan. 21, 1967; children: Robert King, Jennifer Elizabeth, David Andrew. BS in Zoology, U. Okla., 1967; DDS, U. Mo., Kansas City, 1971, diploma in pediatric dentistry, 1975. Practice dentistry specializing in pediatric dentistry Lawrence, Kans., 1975—; chief dental staff Lawrence Meml. Hosp., 1975—; cons. Children's Mercy Hosp., Kansas City, 1975—; pres. Med. Arts Bldg. Inc., Lawrence, 1985—. Bd. dirs. Children's Hour Headstart Program, Lawrence, 1975-80, Trinity Community Services, Lawrence, 1978-82, Centennial Sch. PTA, Lawrence, 1982-85. Mem. ADA, Kans. Soc. Dentistry for Children (pres. 1986-87), Am. Acad. Pediatric Dentistry, Kans. Dental Assn., First Dist. Dental Soc. (pres. 1985-86), Douglas County Dental Soc. (1975-76). Republican. Methodist. Club: Alvamar Country. Lodge: Rotary. Avocations: golfing, personal computers, skiing. Office: 346 Maine Lawrence KS 66044

JACOBS, SUSAN MARIE ANN, systems analyst; b. Belvidere, Ill., Feb. 7, 1961; d. William Dean and Lillian Rose (Hughes) J. AAS in Computer Sci., Rock Valley Coll., 1982; postgrad. in bus. adminstrn., Rockford Coll., 1984—. Applications programmer TDS/CS, Madison, Wis., 1983, programmer analyst, 1984; applications programmer Sundstrand Corp., Rockford, Ill., 1985, systems analyst, 1985—. Mem. Assn. Systems Mgmt. (sr. chmn. 1986), Data Processing Mgmt. Assn. Republican. Roman Catholic. Avocations: snow skiing, softball, volleyball, reading, playing guitar. Home: 850 W Locust St Belvidere IL 61008

JACOBSEN, DEAN WILLIS, advertising executive; b. Omaha, Mar. 21, 1927; s. Louis Martin and Clara Naomi (Cox-Bruning) J.; m. Karyl Joanne Baldwin, July 18, 1955; m. Scott Jerome, Wendy Joanne. Student, Chgo. Art Inst., 1947; AA, North Park Coll., 1949; BS, Millikin U., 1951. Mem. art dept. Leo Burnett Co. Inc., Chgo., 1951-52; advt. mgr. Harris Bros., Chgo., 1952-57; advt. product mgr. Mar. Celotex Corp., Chgo., 1957-61; advt. mgr. U.S. Gyspum Co., Chgo., 1961-65; account exec. Marsteller, Inc., Chgo., 1965-66; dir. chief copy Burlingame Grossman, Chgo., 1966-67; v.p., creative dir. Jack O'Grady Studio, Chgo., 1967-68; exec. v.p., creative dir. Coordinated Advt. Inc., Chgo., 1968-79; pres., chief exec. officer JCI Jacobsen Communications Inc., Palatine, Ill., 1979—, also bd. dirs. Author short stories. Cons. local civ. orgn.; trustee Rep. Presl. Task Force. Served with U.S. Army 1945-47. Recipient Dummer's award Cahner's Pub., Chgo., 1979-86. Mem. Am. Mktg. Assn. Republican. Lutheran. Club: Itasca Country. Avocations: writer, painter, fishing, golf, camping. Office: JCI Jacobsen Communications Inc 800 E Nortwest Hwy Palatine IL 60067

JACOBSEN, ERIC KASNER, consulting engineer; b. N.Y.C., July 21, 1932; s. Henry and Caroline (Kasner) J.; B.S.C.E., U. Iowa, 1956; m. Dorothy H. Caldwell, Mar. 30, 1957; 1 son, Steven. Registered profl. engr., Ill., N.Y., Iowa, Mo., Wis. Structural engr. Stanley Engring. Co., Muscatine, Iowa, 1956-59; asso. dept. mgr. R. W. Booker & Assos., St. Louis, 1959-63; plant mgr. Tri-Cities Terminal div. Nat. Marine Service, Inc., Granite City, Ill., 1963-65; sr. engr. Monsanto Co., 1965-69; chief structural engr. Weitz-Hettalsater Engrs., Kansas City, 1969-72; supr. structural and archtl. engring. Austin Co., Cleve., 1972-78; mgr. Engring. Mining and Metals div., 1978—; cons. engr. structural and archtl. engring., 1960—; owner/mgr. Jacobsen Farms. Recipient Eagle Scout award Boy Scouts Am., 1951;Mem. ASCE, ASME, Chgo. Farmers, Chi Epsilon. Presbyterian. Home: 16 Louise Dr Chagrin Falls OH 44022 Office: 3700 Mayfield Rd Cleveland OH 44121

JACOBSEN, GLENN DALE, general dentistry; b. Humboldt, Iowa, Oct. 25, 1937; s. John Andrew and Millie Jenisene (Gregersen) J.; m. Priscilla Alice Holt, Aug. 27, 1960; children: Cynthia Lynn, Deborah Ann. AA, Eagle Grove Jr. Coll., 1957; BA, Luther Coll., 1959; MS, U. N.D., 1963, PhD, 1965; DDS, U. Iowa, 1976. Instr. Luther Coll., Decorah, Iowa, 1959-61; assoc. prof. anatomy U. N.D., Grand Forks, 1965-66, U. Mo., Columbia, 1966; assoc. prof. anatomy U. Iowa, Iowa City, 1966-73, adj. assoc. prof., 1973-84; pvt. practice dentistry Iowa City, 1984—. Home: 226 Mahaska Dr Iowa City IA 52240 Office: 375 Mormon Trek Blvd Iowa City IA 52240

JACOBSEN, LEIF YNGVE, JR., packaging company executive; b. N.Y.C., Sept. 1, 1936; s. Leif Yngve and Marie Pope (Heiberg) J.; m. Barbara Richards, Sept. 15, 1962 (div. Apr. 1977); children: Kirsten Anne, Keely Erica; m. Anna May Ehn, Oct. 18, 1981. BA, Cornell U., 1955; postgrad., Hope Coll., 1957-60, Ind. U., 1960-61. Dist. mgr. Mobil Oil Corp., Nigeria, Australia, other locations, 1961-69; mktg. mgr. Continental Can Co., N.Y.C., 1969-73; v.p. sales, mktg. Standard Packaging div. Saxton Industries, Clifton, N.Y., 1973-81; dir. mktg. Specialty Papers Co., Dayton, Ohio, 1981-83; pres. Wrap It Packaging Products Inc., Dayton, 1983—; lectr. Ctr. Profl. Advancement, New Brunswick, N.J., 1973-78. Contbr. articles to profl. jours. Deacon Westminster Presbyn. Ch., Dayton. Served with USN, 1955-57. Mem. Nat. Flexible Packages Assn. (bd. dirs. 1975-78), Packing Inst. (chmn. packing materials com. 1977, lectr.). Republican. Lodges: Rotary (chmn. devel. com. 1985-86), Optimist. Avocations: travel, swimming, tennis. Home: 33 Ivanhoe Ave Dayton OH 45419 Office: Wrap It Packaging Products Inc 2801 Far Hills Ave Dayton OH 45419

JACOBSEN, PAUL DOUGLAS, accountant; b. Boone, Iowa, Apr. 28, 1952; s. Egon Christian and Margaret Ann (Peters) J.; m. Nancy Lee Juhl, Aug. 17, 1973; children: Christopher, Joel. AA, Des Moines Area Community Coll., 1972; BS, Iowa State U., 1974. CPA, Iowa. Acct. Whiting Bookkeeping Service, Webster City, Iowa, 1974-79; acct., v.p. Henkel & Assocs., P.C., Boone, 1979—. Treas. Cen. Christian Ch., Boone, 1981-85, deacon. Mem. Am. Inst. CPA's, Iowa Soc. CPA's, Boone Estate and Fin. Planners (v.p. 1985-86, pres. 1986-87), Ames Estate Planning Council, Boone C. of C., Boone Jaycees (former bd. dirs.), Boone Railroad Hist. Soc., Boone County Hist. Soc. Republican. Club: Boone Golf and Country (v.p. 1985-86). Lodge: Rotary (bd. dirs. Boone 1986—), Elks. Avocations: antique cars, golf, bowling, hiking. Office: Henkel & Assocs PC 813 Keeler St Boone IA 50036

JACOBSEN, SONIA MARIE MAASSEL, hydraulic engineer; b. Hankinson, N.D., Dec. 13, 1955; d. Paul Frederick and Ellen Marie (Alberg) Maassel; m. Eric Reynold Jacobsen, May 27, 1978; children: Laura, Heather. BS in Agrl. Engring., U. Minn., 1978; MS in Civil Engring., U. Ill., 1980. Profl. engr., Ill. Design engr. Soil Conservation Service, Champaign, Ill., 1979-81; civil engr. planning Soil Conservation Service, Champaign, 1981-82; constrn. engr. Soil Conservation Service, Lisle, Ill., 1982-86; hydraulic engr. Soil Conservation Service, St. Paul, 1986—. Mem. Am. Soc. Agrl. Engrs., Soil Conservation Soc. Am., Orgn. Profl. Employees Dept. Agriculture. Lutheran. Avocations: cross-country skiing, needlework. Home: 2125 Rosewood Ln N Roseville MN 55113 Office: Soil Conservation Service 316 N Robert St Saint Paul MN 55101

JACOBSEN, THOMAS WINFIELD, manufacturing executive; b. Mpls., June 15, 1924; s. Oscar C. and Marguerite C. (Moon) J.; m. Ruth Marie Doyle, July 7, 1951; children—Daniel Thomas, Christopher Scott. B.A., U. Minn., 1950. Office mgr. Security Envelope Co., Mpls., 1951-55; v.p., gen. mgr. Tension Envelope Corp., Mpls., 1955—. Coordinator Mpls. Aquatennial Assocs., 1964-68. Served with USAAF, 1943-46; PTO. Mem. Mpls. Jaycees (1st v.p. 1960-61; Outstanding Dir. 1962), Mpls. Sales and Mktg. Execs. (Man of Yr. 1972; pres. 1973-74), Envelope Mfrs. Assn., U. Minn. Alumni Assn., Mpls. C. of C. Republican. Lodge: Rotary (sec. 1981-82) (Mpls.). Avocations: music; golf. Home: 5616 Bernard Pl Edina MN 55436 Office: Tension Envelope Corp 129 N 2d St Minneapolis MN 55401

JACOBSOHN, RICHARD HARVEY, marketing professional; b. Chgo., Aug. 12, 1944; s. Howard G. and June S. (Portner) J.; m. Rachel Weiss, Dec. 18, 1966; children: Dara L., Lela S. BS in Econs., U. Pa., 1966; MBA, Northwestern U., 1968. Mgmt. trainee Ford Motor Co., Dearborn, 1966-68; treas. Am. Slicing Machine, Chgo., 1968-72, v.p., 1972-76, pres., 1976—; pres. Redcoach Tours & Travel Ltd., Chgo., 1985—; lectr. Roosevelt U., Chgo., 1976; bd. dirs. Gander Mountain, Inc., Wilmot, Wis. Co-chmn. U. Pa. Secondary Sch. Com., Chgo., 1986-87. Mem. Direct Mktg. Assn., Chgo. Assn. Direct Mktg. (pres.1976-77, Service award 1977). Jewish. Clubs: Standard, Briarwood Country. Avocations: bicycling, golf, squash. Home: 878 Thackeray Highland Park IL 60035 Office: Am Slicing Machine Co 5550 N Elston Ave Chicago IL 60630

JACOBSON, ALLEN FRANK, manufacturing company executive; b. Omaha, Oct. 7, 1926; s. Alma Frank and Ruth Alice (Saalfeld) J.; m. Barbara Jean Benidt, Apr. 18, 1964; children: Allen F., Holly Anne, Paul Andrew. B.S. in Chem. Engring., Iowa State U., 1947. Product engr. tape lab. 3M Co. (Minn. Mining & Mfg. Co.), St. Paul, 1947-50; tech. asst. to plant mgr. 3M Co. (Minn. Mining & Mfg. Co.), Hutchinson, Minn. and Bristol, Pa., 1950-55; tape prodn. supt. 3M Co. (Minn. Mining & Mfg. Co.), Bristol, 1955-59; plant mgr. tape 3M Co. (Minn. Mining & Mfg. Co.), St. Paul, 1959-61, plant mgr. tape and AC&S, 1961-63, tape prodn. mgr., 1963, mfg. mgr. tape and allied products, 1963-68, gen. mgr. indsl. tape div., 1968-70, div. v.p. indsl. tape div., 1970-72, exec. v.p., gen. mgr., 1973-75, v.p. European ops., 1975, v.p. tape and allied products group, 1975-81, exec. v.p. indsl. and consumer sector, 1981-84, pres. U.S. ops., 1984-86, chmn., chief exec. officer, 1986—, dir., 1983—; exec. v.p., gen. mgr. 3M Can., Ltd., 1973-75; dir. Valmont Industries Inc., Valley, Nebr., U.S. West Inc., Denver, No. States Power Co., Mpls., Pillsbury Co., Mpls. Recipient Profl. Achievement citation in engring. Iowa State U., 1983, Marston medal Iowa State U., 1986. Avocations: photography; shooting; gardening; golf; reading. Office: 3M Co 3M Ctr St 220-14W-04 Saint Paul MN 55101

JACOBSON, EARL JAMES, lawyer, tax leasing executive; b. Chgo., May 10, 1940; s. Benjamin L. and Mary (Urman) J.; m. Donna Jean Breen, Mar. 5, 1983; children—Joan, John. B.A., U. Ill., 1961; M.B.A., U. Chgo., 1963; J.D., Loyola U., Chgo., 1980. Bar: Ill. 1980, U.S. Dist. Ct. (no. dist.) Ill. 1980, U.S. Ct. Internat. Trade 1980, U.S. Ct. Customs and Patent Appeals 1980, U.S. Tax Ct., 1985, U.S. Supreme Ct., 1985. Indsl. salesman Honeywell, Xerox, Chgo., 1964-67; dir. mktg. Mastech Computer, Chgo., 1967-71, Datronic Rental Co., Chgo., 1971-81; v.p. Dearborn Computer Co., Park Ridge, Ill., 1981-82; sr. syndication officer Seattle 1st Nat. Bank, Schaumburg, Ill., 1982-83; v.p. fin. and syndication Hartford Fin. Services, Inverness, Ill., 1983-85; v.p. corp. fin. and corp. counsel Lease Investment Corp., Chgo., 1985-86; dir. equity placement, CIS Corp., Syracuse, N.Y., 1986-87; exec. v.p., gen. counsel Tech. Funding, Inc., Deerfield, Ill., 1987—; dir., gen. counsel Info. Systems, Arlington Heights, Ill., 1st Securities, Inc., Chgo., Citifirst, Inc., Chgo. Served with USAF, 1963-69. Mem. ABA, Nat. Assn. Securities Dealers, Equipment Syndication Assn., Ill. State Bar Assn., Chgo. Bar Assn. Club: 20 Plus (Chgo.) (pres. 1980-82). Home: 600 S Dearborn Apt 2102 Chicago IL 60605 Office: Tech Funding Inc 102 Wilmot Rd Suite 500 Deerfield IL 60015

JACOBSON, FRED D., aviation financial analyst; b. Norwich, Conn., May 2, 1946; s. Eli and Anne Edna (Weiss) J.; m. Sandra A. Crothers, July 20, 1975; children: Kevin, Tom, David. BA, Parsons Coll., 1968; MBA, U. Denver, 1969. Sr. analyst Homart Devel., Chgo., 1973-75; supervisory analyst FAA, Des Plaines, Ill., 1976—. Bd. dirs. Little League, Palatine, Ill., 1985-87. Mem. Am. Inst. CPAs. Avocations: investing, traveling. Home: 728 N Williams Dr Palatine IL 60067 Office: FAA 2300 E Devon Ave Des Plaines IL 60018

JACOBSON, GLORIA NADINE, coll. adminstr.; b. Jewell, Iowa, July 12, 1930; d. Christian Frederick and Amanda M. (Englebart) Larson; B.B.A., U. Iowa, 1974; m. Richard T. Jacobson, July 22, 1951; children—Richard Thomas, Douglas L., William Andrew. Mem. adminstrn. staff U. Iowa, Iowa City, 1950—, asst. to the dean Coll. of Pharmacy, 1981—. Mem. Phi Gamma Nu, Kappa Epsilon. Republican. Lutheran. Home: 415 Ridgeview Iowa City IA 52240 Office: U of Iowa Coll of Pharmacy Iowa City IA 52242

JACOBSON, JOAN ELIZABETH, minister; b. Flint, Mich., July 15, 1949; d. William Herbert and Helen (Ruhala) Wolf; m. Don M. Jacobson, May 27, 1978; children: Lara Heather, Heidi Kirsten, Joan Noel. AA, Concordia Coll., 1969; BA, Valparaiso U., 1972; M Div, LSTC, 1978; D Ministry, McCormick Seminary, 1986. Ordained minister, United Ch. Christ, 1979. Deaconess, missionary Trinity Luth. Ch., Cleve., 1972-75; chaplain Tenn. State Women's Prison, Nashville, 1979, Spencer Youth Ctr. Tenn. Dept. Corrections, 1980-81, Luth. Social Services of Ill., Chgo., 1982-83; assoc. minister First Congl. Ch. of Owosso, Mich., 1985—; cons. in field for emotionally disturbed individuals, Owosso, 1983—. Clergy rep. United Way Fund, Shiawassee County, Mich., 1985; bd. dirs. Cath. Social Services, Shiawassee County, 1986—; violinist Shiawassee Strings, 1986. McCormick Theol. Seminary scholar, 1984, Sisterhood of PEO scholar, 1984. Mem. AAUW. Clubs: Owosso Musicale, Mary Guild (bd. dirs. 1986). Office: First Congregational Church 327 N Washington PO Box 452 Owosso MI 48867

JACOBSON, JON MATTHEW, dentist; b. Charlevoix, Mich., June 16, 1942; s. Matthew William Jacobson and Viola Pearl (Raunio) Emery; m. Beverly Jean Hicks, May 30, 1965; children: Katherine, Ross. BS, Alma (Mich.) Coll., 1964; DDS, U. Mich., 1968; MBA, Saginaw (Mich.) Valley State Coll., 1981. Pres. Faucher Dental Group, Saginaw, 1984—. Served to capt. USAF, 1968-71. Mem. ADA, Mich. Dental Assn., Saginaw Valley Dental Assn., Saginaw County Dental Assn. Club: Saginaw. Home: 11210 Dice Rd Freeland MI 48623 Office: Faucher Dental Group 427 N Michigan Saginaw MI 48602

JACOBSON, LLOYD ELDRED, dentist; b. Madison, Minn., Mar. 9, 1923; s. Jacob Elton and Hilda Emily (Larson) J.; m. Ruth Solveig Skinsnes, Jan. 26, 1945; children: Rolf, Kathryn, Heidi. Student, St. Olaf Coll., 1943-44, 46-47, U. Chgo., 1945-46; DDS, U. Minn., 1951. Gen. practice dentistry Kenyon, Minn., 1951—. Chmn. Am. Luth. Ch. Council, Mpls., 1972-74; vol. World Brotherhood Exchange, Bumbuli, Tanzania, 1965; treas. Kenyon Sch. Bd., 1958-60, Kenyon Devel. Corp., 1955-60. Served to 1st lt. USAF, 1943-45. Recipient Outstanding Alumni award St. Olaf Coll., 1972. Mem. Minn. Dental Assn. (treas. 1980-86), S.E. Dist. Dental Soc. (pres. 1979-80, sec.-treas. 1976-79), Rice County Dental Soc. (pres. 1969). Republican. Lodge: Lions (pres. Kenyon club 1952-54, dist. sec.-treas. 1974, Citizen of Yr. award 1986). Avocations: gardening, golfing, stamp collecting. Home and Office: 216 Forest Ave Kenyon MN 55946

JACOBSON, RICHARD BERT, lawyer; b. N.Y.C., Jan. 21, 1945; s. Jack and Dora (Fisher) J.; m. Ellen Morris, Aug. 18, 1968; 1 child, Miriam Emma. BA, Brandeis U., 1966; MA, Harvard U., 1968; PhD, U. Calif., LaJolla, 1971; JD, U. Wis., 1983. Bar: Wis. 1983, U.S. Dist. Ct. (we. dist.) Wis. 1983, U.S. Dist. Ct. (ea. dist.) Wis. 1984, U.S. Ct. Appeals (7th cir.) 1985, U.S. Supreme Ct. 1986. Asst. prof. comparative lit. U. Wis., Madison, 1971-80; law clk. to presiding judge U.S. Bankruptcy Ct. (we. dist.) Wis., Madison, 1983-84; instr. law sch. U. Wis., Madison, 1984; sole practice Madison, 1984-86; ptnr. Borns, Macaulay & Jacobson, Madison, 1986—. Contbr. articles to profl. jours. Am. Council Learned Socs. grantee, 1972, fellow 1978-79. Mem. Inst. Law and Humanities (bd. govs. 1980—), Semiotic Soc. Am. (chmn. nominating com. 1978-80), Assn. Trial Lawyers Am. Democrat. Jewish. Avocations: growing roses, writing fiction, travel. Office: Borns Macaulay & Jacobson 222 S Bedford St Madison WI 53703

JACOBSON, RICHARD DANIEL, accountant; b. Madison, Wis., Apr. 24, 1940; s. Daniel Lethert and Beatrice Marie (Gessler) J.; m. Rebecca Bolton Ratcliff, Aug. 25, 1967; children: Brian, Christine. BBA, U. Wis., 1963. CPA, Ill. Ptnr. Grant Thorton, Chgo., 1963—, mem. exec. com., 1982—. Acctg. editor R.R. Donnelly Handbook, 1973-82. Mem. Am. Inst. CPAs, Ill. CPA Soc. Clubs: Chgo. Athletic, Economic (chmn. membership subcom. 1985—). Office: Grant Thornton Prudential Plaza Suite 600 Chicago IL 60601-6145

JACOBSON, RONALD LEE, hospital executive; b. Webster, S.D., Jan. 11, 1948; s. Milton John and Gertrude Olive (Conklin) J.; m. Carol Louise Fisher, Nov. 2, 1968; children—Brent Ronald, Sara Lynn, Keith Lawrence, Mark Fisher. B.S. in Nursing, S.D. State U., 1970; CAS in Hosp./Health Care Adminstrn., U. Minn., 1978, M.Hosp. Adminstrn., 1981. Dir. nursing Community Meml. Hosp., Elbow Lake, Minn., 1971; dir. nursing services St. Mary's Hosp., Detroit Lakes, Minn., 1971-74; adminstr. Day County Hosp., Webster, S.D., 1974-78, Stevens County Meml. Hosp., Morris, Minn., 1978-84, Stevens Community Meml. Hosp. Inc., 1985—. Mem. Life Span Inc., Mpls., Minn., 1985—; hosp. rep., bd. dirs. Blue Cross Blue Shield Minn. Kellogg Found. grantee, 1980. Mem. Am. Hosp. Assn., Am. Coll. Hosp. Adminstrs., Minn. Hosp. Assn. (trustee 1981—), Morris Area C. of C. (v.p. 1980-81). Republican. Lutheran. Clubs: Shriners, Kiwanis (pres. 1981-82); Coteau Lodge (Webster, S.D.). Home: 13 Westwood Acres Morris MN 56267 Office: 400 E 1st St Morris MN 56267

JACOBSON-WOLF, JOAN ELIZABETH, minister; b. Flint, Mich., July 15, 1949; s. William and Helen Wolf; m. Don M. Jacobson, May 27, 1978; children: Lara Heather, Heidi Kirsten, Joan Noel. AA, Concordia Coll., 1969; BA in Theology, Valparaiso U., 1972; postgrad., Luth. Sem., Mexico City, Phila. and Columbus, Ohio, 1974-76; M in Div., Luth. Sch. Theology, Chgo., 1978; D in Ministry, McCormick Theol. Seminary, 1986. Ordained minister Luth. Ch., 1979; cert. psychiatric chaplain. Deaconess, missionary Trinity Luth. Ch., Cleve., 1972-75; minister youth Bethel Luth. Ch., Middleburg Hts., Ohio, 1976; intern, asst. minister Berwyn (Ill.) United Luth. Ch., 1977-78; campus chaplain Vanderbilt U., Nashville, 1978; minister St. Paul's Luth. Ch., Nashville, 1979-81; chaplain Edison Park Home, Park Ridge, Ill., 1982; minister in residency Riverside Presbyn. Ch., Chgo., 1982-85; assoc. minister First Congl. Ch., Owosso, Mich., 1985—; clin. pastor Beatty Hosp., Ind., 1970, Cherokee State Mental Inst., Iowa, 1971; chaplain Tenn. Women's Prison, 1978-79, Spencer Youth Ctr., 1979-81; community organizer Cleve. Westside Arts Council-Hispanic Murals, Centro Juvenil de Puertoriquenãs and Trinidad Luth. Iglesia. Violinist Flint Summer Theatre Orch., 1965-67, Ann Arbor Symphony, Mich., 1967-69, Valparaiso U. Orch., Ind. 1969-72, Cherokee String Quartet, Iowa, 1971, Cleveland Women's Symphony, 1973-75, Phila. Seminary Ensemble, 1975-76, Oak Park Symphony, Ill., 1977, Nashville Symphony, 1978-80, Shiawassee Strings, 1986—. Mem. Covenant Assn. Mich. Conf. (lic.). Home: 785 Riverbend Dr Owosso MI 48867 Office: First Congl Ch Owosso 327 N Washington Owosso MI 48867

JACOBY, HANS FERDINAND, pharmaceutical consultant; b. Strausberg, Brandenburg, Germany, Dec. 12, 1913; came to U.S. 1936; s. Paul Gustav and Kate (Stern) J.; m. Valborg Oliana, July 21, 1950; children: Paul Magnus, Helen Kay, Ingrid Maria. Pharm. degree, Berlin; chem. degree, Heidelberg, Federal Republic of Germany; B in Pharmacy, U. Mo., Columbia, 1947; M in Chemistry, U. Mo., St. Louis, 1954. Reg. pharmacist. Pharmacist Berlin, 1932-36; German instr. U. Mo., 1937-38; v.p. Midwest Chem. Co., St. Louis, 1938-47; chief chemist K-V Pharmacal, St. Louis, 1938-53; pres. Wilson Keith Pharm. Co., St. Louis, 1953-54, Pvt. Formulae, Inc., St. Louis, 1954—. Leader, Friday Musicale, St. Louis, 1930—. Served as spl. agt. M.I. U.S. Army, 1944-46, ETO. Mem. Am. Chem. Soc., Am. Pharm. Assn., Soc. Pharmacists in Industry (pres. 1958, 80). Home: 12 Pricemont Dr Olivette MO 63132 Office: Pvt Formulae Inc 7603 Forsyth Blvd Saint Louis MO 63105

JACONETTE, JOSEPH RICHARD, radiologist; b. Pontiac, Mich., Aug. 15, 1935; s. Joseph and Theresa (Spatafore) J.; m. Carol Ann Lamont, June 13, 1959; children: Richard, David, Michael, Thomas, William, Susan. Student, U. Mich., 1952-55, MD, 1959. Diplomate Am. Bd. Radiology, Am. Bd. Nuclear Medicine. Resident in radiology Henry Ford Hosp., Detroit, 1960-63, radiologist, 1965-66; radiologist Mt. Carmel Mercy Hosp., Detroit, 1966-75; radiologist Leila Hosp., Battle Creek, Mich., chief of staff, 1986—, vice chief of radiology, 1980—; radiologist Community Hosp., Battle Creek, 1975—. Served with U.S. Army, 1963-65. Mem. AMA (Physician Recognition award), Radiol. Soc. N.Am., Am. Coll. Radiology, Soc. Nuclear Medicine. Roman Catholic. Office: Radiology Cons PC PO Box 1718 Battle Creek MI 49016

JACOVER, JEROLD ALAN, lawyer; b. Chgo., Mar. 20, 1945; s. David Louis and Beverly (Funk) J.; m. Judith Lee Greenwald, June 28, 1970; children—Aric Seth, Evan Michael, Brian Ethan. BSEE, U. Wis., 1967; JD, Georgetown U., 1972. Bar: Ohio 1972, Ill. 1973, U.S. Ct. Appeals (7th cir.) 1974, U.S. Ct. Appeals (Fed. cir.) 1983. Atty. Ralph Nader, Columbus, Ohio, 1972-73, Willian, Brinks & Olds, Chgo., 1973—; lectr. Mallinckrodt Coll., Wilmette, Ill., 1977-78. Mem. Evanston Environ. Control Bd., 1983-86; asst. pack leader Northeast Ill. Council Boy Scouts Am., 1982-84. Mem. Am. Patent Law Assn. (com. chmn. 1980-86, co-editor jour. 1980-81), ABA, Decalogue Soc. Lawyers, Patent Law Assn. Chgo. (treas. 1983-84), Am. Techion Soc. (v.p. 1985-87). Jewish. Club: Nippersink Community (Genoa City, Wis.) (bd. dirs. 1978-86, pres. 1987). Home: 1409 Lincoln St Evanston IL 60201 Office: Willian Brinks & Olds 1 IBM Plaza Suite 4100 Chicago IL 60611

JACOX, JOHN WILLIAM, engineering and consulting company executive; b. Pitts., Dec. 12, 1938; s. John Sherman and Grace Edna (Herbster) J.; 1 child, Brian Erik. BSME, BS in Indsl. Mgmt., Carnegie Mellon U., 1962. Mfg. engr. Nuclear Fuel div. Westinghouse Elec. Co., Pitts., 1962-64; research engr. Continental Can Co. Metal R&D Ctr., Pitts., 1964-65; dataprocessing sales engr., IBM, Pitts., 1965-66; mktg. mgr. nuclear products MSA Internat., Pitts., 1966-72; v.p. Nuclear Cons. Services, Inc., Columbus, Ohio, 1973-84; v.p. NUCON Internat., 1981-84; bd. dirs. NUCON Europe Ltd., London, 1981—; pres. Jacox Assocs., Inc., 1984—; cons., lectr. Nat. Ctr. for Research in Vocat. Edn., 1978-84 ; author, presenter, session chmn. DOE/Harvard Nuclear Air Cleaning Confs., 1974—; lectr. Harvard Sch. Pub. Health Air Cleaning Lab.; co-chmn. program subcom. Tech. Alliance Cen Ohio, 1984-85, vice chmn., chmn.-elect dir. subcom., 1986-87, chmn. bd. trustees, 1986; program com. World Trade Devel. Club; mem. legis. services com. Coop. edn. adv. com. Otterbein Coll., 1978-82. Mem. ASME (code com. nuclear air and gas treatment, main exec. com., chmn. subcom. field test procedures), Am. Nuclear Soc. (pub. info. com.), N.Y. Acad. Scis. (life), Ohio Acad. Sci. (life), Inst. Environ. Scis., Electric Overstress-Electrostatic Discharge Assn., ASHRAE, Inc., Air Pollution Control Assn., Am. Nat. Standards Inst., Columbus Area C. of C. (tech. roundtable 1983), ASTM (F-21), ASM, Air Force Assn. (life), Mensa, Nat. Rifle Assn. (life), Sun Bunch (pres. 1980-81). Club: Capitol. Home: 5874 Northern Pine Pl Columbus OH 43229 Office: 1445 Summit St Columbus OH 43229

JACQUES, LOUIS JAMES, radiologist; b. Cleve., Nov. 11, 1941; s. Richard Henry and Charlotte (Rader) J.; m. Patricia Kay Luckman, Jun 22, 1967; children: Kelly, Richard, Edward, Christine, Elizabeth. BA, Miami U., Oxford, Ohio, 1963; MD, Ohio State U., 1967. Intern Cleve. Clinic, 1967-68, residency internal medicine, 1970-72, residency radiology, 1972-75; dir. radiology Ohio Valley Hosp., Steubenville, Ohio, 1986—; advisor Steubenville Tech. Sch. of Radiology Technicians, 1986—. Served to sr. asst. surgeon USPHS, 1964-66. Mem. Am. Bd. Radiology. Home: 129 HiddenWood Dr Steubenville OH 43952 Office: Ohio Valley Hosp X-Ray Dept 1 Ross Park Steubenville OH 43952

JADEL, JOHN CHARLES, chemical company executive; b. Toledo, Mar. 21, 1930; s. Frank Andrew and Iva Marie (Robb) J.; m. Miriam Elsa Baade, Aug. 30, 1952; children: Pamela Ann, Jeffrey William. AB, Bowling Green State U., 1952; MBA, Ind. U., 1955. Salesman Dow Chem. Corp., St. Louis, 1955-59; mkgt. mgr. Celanese Chem. Co., Los Angeles, Boston, and N.Y.C., 1960-68; gen. mgr. Staley Chemical Co., Boston, 1968-69; sr. v.p. Akzo Chemie Am., Chgo., 1970—; bd. dirs. Hexaquimia S.A., Mexico City. v.p. fin. E. Cen. region Boy Scouts Am., Libertyville, Ill., 1985-87; mem. youth com. New Trier Twp., Winnetka, Ill., 1986—; bd. dirs. Wilmette United Way, 1986—. Served to 1st lt. U.S. Army, 1952-54, Korea. Republican. Clubs: Mich. Shores (Wilmette); Plaza (Chgo.). Office: Axzo Chemie Am 300 S Riverside Plaza Chicago IL 60606

JAEGER, BERNARD, manufacturing company executive; b. St. Joseph, Mich., Oct. 16, 1957; s. Gottlieb and Alma (Bauer) J.; m. Gwendolyn Louise Nelson, Feb. 19, 1984. Student, Andrews U., 1976-78; BBA, Western Mich. U., 1980. Maintenance asst. Lakeshore Die Cast, Baroda, Mich., 1976; v.p., office mgr. D&F Mold Corp. div. Jericho Die Cast, Bridgmen, Mich., 1980-84; v.p. Jericho Die Cast Corp., Bridgman, 1986—; office mgr. Smith Mailer Inc., Los Angeles, 1984-85; tech. sales mgr. Weldan Automation Products, Glendale, Calif., 1985-86. Avocations: stamp collecting, model railroading, golf, racquetball. Home: 12370 Dunes Blvd Sawyer MI 49125 Office: Jericho Die Cast Corp 8080 Jericho Rd Bridgman MI 49106

JAEGER, DEAN ALBERT, music educator; b. Hartley, Iowa, Dec. 28, 1939; s. Henry Louis and Orva Louise (Jipson) J.; m. Karen Ruth Mollet, June 16, 1962; children: Carma Kym, Trent Crosby. BS, Mankato State U., 1968. Cert. elem. tchr., Minn. Tchr. vocal music St. Michael-Albertville (Minn.) Pub. Sch. System, 1968-69; tchr. vocal music Faribault (Minn.) Pub. Sch. System, 1969—, chmn. elem. music dept., 1980—. mem. NEA, Minn. Edn. Assn., Faribault Edn. Assn. (chmn. membership com. 1981-83), Music Educators Nat. Conf., Minn. Music Educators Assn., Minn. Elem. Music Educators (pres. 1982-84). Mem. Assembly of God Ch. Avocations: collecting toy tractors, recreational activities. Office: Faribault Pub Schs-Jefferson 922 Home Pl Faribault MN 55021

JAEGER, FRED KARL, sales executive; b. Racine, Wis., May 16, 1931; s. Fred Franz and Lydia Emma (Kraft) J.; m. Beverly Katherine, Dec. 25, 1955; children: Heidi Lynn, Lisa Marie. Student, U. Wis., Racine, 1950-52; cert. tool and die apprentice, Racine, 1955. Test tech. Walker Mfg. Co., RAcine, 1957-58; plant layout engr. J.I. Case Co., RAcine, 1958-59; plant engr. Bardon Rubber Products Co., Union Grove, Wis., 1959-60; dist. sales mgr. Dumore Co., Racine, 1960-65, Essley Machinery Co., Milw., 1965-69; gen. sales mgr. E.C. Styberg Engrng. Co., Racine, 1969—; pres. sales and mktg. council, Racine, 1981-83. Served with USN, 1955-57. Recipient Disting. Service Pres. Cup, 1982, 83. Mem. Vintage Sports Car Drivers' Assn. (bd. dirs.). Congregationalist. Lodge: Kiwanis (bd. dirs. 1984—). Avocations: vintage automobile racing, music, photography, trap shooting, fishing. Home: 33701 Academy Rd Burlington WI 33105 Office: E C Styberg Engrng Co Inc 1600 Goold St Racine WI 53404

JAEGER, GREGORY RAY, real estate appraiser, computer systems consultant; b. Ft. Thomas, Ky., Oct. 23, 1959; s. Harry R. and Phyllis Jean (Tolwig) J.; m. Rosemary Carbone; 1 child, Jason Michael. BBA, Xavier U., 1980. Systems cons. The Procter and Gamble Co., Cin., 1980-86; pvt. practice real estate appraising Cin., 1986—. V.p. bd. dirs. Cath. Big Bros./Big Sisters, Cin., 1980—, big brother, 1980—. Mem. Internat. Soc. Real Estate Appraisers, Mensa. Republican. Roman Catholic. Avocations: sports, woodworking, working with elderly and children. Home: 1157 Covedale Ave Cincinnati OH 45238

JAEKELS, MICHAEL THOMAS, obstetrician, gynecologist; b. Milw., Mar. 7, 1930; s. Raymond Francis and Teresa A. (Jermain) J.; m. Nancy E. Hirschboeck, June 13, 1959; children: Christopher, Theodore, Mia, Andrew, Julie. BS, Notre Dame U., 1951; MD, Marquette U., 1955. Diplomate Am. Bd. Ob-Gyn. Intern Henry Ford Hosp., Detroit, 1955-56; clin. instr. Med. Coll. Wis., Milw., 1963-79; resident Lewis Meml. Hosp. and Mercy Hosp., Chgo., 1959-62; asst. clin. prof. dept. ob-gyn Med. Coll. Wis., Milw., 1979—, asst. clin. prof. family practice, 1981—; instr. Milw. Area Tech. Coll. Nursing, 1975-86; sec.-treas. St. Michael Hosp. Med. Staff, Milw., 1974-77, chmn. dept. ob-gyn, 1972-76. Served as capt. USAF, 1956-58. Recipient Cert. Appreciation State of Wis. Health Dept., 1970, Teaching award St. Michael Hosp., 1979, Cert. Merit, Med. Coll. Wis., 1982. Fellow Am. Coll. Obstetricians & Gynecologists; mem. Milw. Gynecologic Soc. (pres. 1984-85, sec.-treas. 1982-84), Wis. Soc. Obstetricians & Gynecologists, Mil. County Med. Soc. (del. to State of Wis. Med. Conv. 1980-82). Republican. Roman Catholic. Clubs: Milw. Athletic, North Shore Racquet. Avocations: photography, tennis, squash, cross country skiing. Office: 5631 N Mohawk Milwaukee WI 53217

JAENIKE, VAUGHN, college dean, music educator; b. David City, Nebr., Sept. 30, 1930; s. Carl Albert and Lula (Egly) J.; m. Ruth Louise Lemke, June 27, 1953; children: Fritz, Kurt, Kristen, Katherine, Gretchen. MusB in Edn., U. Nebr., 1952, MusM, 1955, EdD, 1967. Music tchr. pub. schs., Newman Grove, Nebr., 1952-56; jr. high music tchr. Englewood Pub. Schs., Colo., 1956-65; asst. prof. secondary edn. and music edn. U. Nebr., Lincoln, 1967-70, assoc. prof., 1970-72; spl. asst. to pres. U. Nebr. System, Lincoln, 1972-74; dean Coll. Fine Arts, Eastern Ill. U., Charleston, 1974—. Mem. Ill. Humanities Council Bd., 1976-80, exec. com. 1979-80. Grantee Nat. Endowment for the Arts, 1975, 78, Ill. Arts Council, 1974—. Mem. Internat. Council Fine Arts Deans (exec. com. 1979-82), Central Ill. Arts Consortium (pres. 1976-78). Ill. Arts. Alliance (sec. 1982-84, v.p. 1985-87), Charleston Area C. of C. (bd. dirs. 1984). Lutheran. Lodge: Rotary. Avocations: railroading, photography, cartography. Home: 1001 Colony Ln Charleston IL 61920 Office: Dean of Fine Arts Eastern Ill U Charleston IL 61920

JAFAR, JAFAR JEWAD, neurosurgeon; b. Beirut, June 2, 1949; m. Scheherazade, Nov. 9, 1978; 1 child, Layla. Student, Pahlavi U., Shiraz, Iran, 1967-70, MD, 1976. Diplomate Am. Bd. Neurol. Surgery. Intern Pahlavi U. Hosps., 1975-76; resident in basic surgery U. Chgo. Hosps. and Clinics, 1976-77; resident in neurol. surgery U. Chgo., 1977-82; chief resident in neurol. surgery, hon. asst. house physician The Nat. Hosp. for Nervous Diseases, London, 1980; chief resident in neurol. surgery U. Chgo., 1981-82; asst. prof. neurosurgery U. Ill., Chgo., 1982—, dir. stroke research lab., dept. neurosurgery, 1982—, dir. cerebral blood flow lab., dept. neurosurgery, 1982—; chief neurosurgery service W. Side VA Med. Ctr., Chgo., 1982—. Contbr. articles on neurosurgery to profl. jours. Pahlavi U. Sch. Medicine scholar, 1970-75. Mem. Am. Assn. Neurol. Surgeons (cerebrovascular surgery sect.), Congress Neurol. Surgeons, Chgo. Neurol. Soc., Cen. Neurosurg. Soc. Office: U Ill Dept Neurosurgery 912 S Wood St Chicago IL 60612

JAFFE, EUGENE J., oral surgeon, educator; b. Chgo., Mar. 6, 1924; s. Harry J. and Dora (Katz) J.; m. Adelyne Marshak, Oct. 20, 1946; children—Sally, Patti, Francine. Student, Wilson City Coll., 1942-43; D.D.S., Loyola U., 1946. Resident in oral surgery Cook County Hosp., Chgo., 1950-51; pvt. practice oral surgery Chgo., 1952-59, Oak Lawn, Ill., 1969—; asst. prof. oral surgery Loyola U. Sch. Dentistry, 1959-67, U. Ill., 1967—; clin. asst. prof. surgery Lincoln Sch. Medicine, 1967—; mem. attending staff Cook County Hosp., Michael Reese Hosp. and Med. Ctr. Served with USAF, 1946-48. Fellow Internat. Coll. Dentists, Am. Coll. Dentists, Internat. Assn. Oral and Maxillofacial Surgeons, Am. Coll. Oral and Maxillofacial Surgeons, Am. Dental Soc. of Anesthesiology; mem. Am. Assn. Oral and Maxillofacial Surgeons, Chgo. Soc. Oral and Maxillofacial Surgeons (pres. 1964-65), Englewood Dental Soc. (pres. 1968-69). Office: 4435 W 95th St Oak Lawn IL 60453 also: 7625 W 159th St Tinley Park IL 60477 also: 6800 S Rt 83 Darien IL 60559

JAFFE, HAROLD WILLIAM, plastic surgeon; b. Detroit, Mar. 28, 1924; m. Janet Schuster, Sept. 18, 1960; 1 child, Ellen. BA, U. Mich., 1944, MD, 1946. Intern Harper Hosp., Detroit, 1947-48, resident, 1948-49; resident Blodgett Meml. Hosp., Grand Rapids, Mich., 1949-51; preceptee plastic surgeon Dr. Smith & Steffanson, Grand Rapids, 1953-54; resident plastic surgery U. Ill. Research and Edn. Hosp., Chgo., 1954-56; practice medicine specializing in plastic surgery Troy, Mich., 1956—. Served to lt. USNR, 1951-53. Mem. AMA, Am. Soc. Plastic and Reconstructive Surgery, ACS, Plastic Surgery Edn. Found., Mich. Acad. Plastic Surgeons, Mich. State Med. Assn., Cleft Palate Assn. Office: 755 W Big Beaver Rd Suite 246 Troy MI 48084

JAHN, ELLEN ELIZABETH, nurse; b. N.Y.C., Dec. 2, 1951; d. Thomas Raphael and Bertha Elizabeth (McLaughlin) Mawhinney; m. Warren Thomas Jahn, May 25, 1974; children: Warren Thomas Jr., Stephanie Regan. Diploma in nursing, Englewood (N.J.) Hosp. Sch. Nursing, 1971; BS in Nursing, Lewis U., 1979, postgrad., 1979—. Registered nurse; cert. emergency nurse. Staff nurse Englewood Hosp., 1971-74; charge nurse Cen. DuPage Hosp., Winfield, Ill., 1974-79, nurse clinician, Emergency Med. Services coordinator, 1979—. Mem. Ill. Nurse Educators, Emergency Nurse Assn. (edn. com. 1983-85), Chgo. Heart Assn. (instr. basic life support, cardiopulmonary resuscitation 1976—, advanced cardiac life support 1980—), State Nurses Active in Politics in Ill., Sigma Theta Tau Inc. Avocations: tennis, golf, gardening, cooking. Home: 1111 E Roosevelt Rd Wheaton IL 60187 Office: Cen DuPage Hosp 25 N Winfield Rd Winfield IL 60190

JAHN, HELMUT, architect; b. Nurnberg, Germany, Jan. 4, 1940; came to U.S., 1966; s. Wilhelm Anton and Karolina (Wirth) J.; m. Deborah Ann Lampe, Dec. 31, 1970; 1 child, Evan. Dipl. Ing.-Architect, Technische Hochschule, Munich, 1965; postgrad., Ill. Inst. Tech., 1966-67; D.F.A. (hon.), St. Mary's Coll., Notre Dame, Ind., 1980. With P.C. von Seidlein, Munich, 1965-66; with C.F. Murphy Assocs., Chgo., 1967-81, asst. to Gene Summers, 1967-73, exec. v.p., dir. planning and design, 1973-81; prin. Murphy/Jahn, Chgo., 1981—, pres., 1982—, chief exec. officer, 1983—; mem. design studio faculty U. Ill., Chgo., 1981; Elliot Noyes prof. archtl. design Harvard U., Cambridge, Mass., 1981; Davenport vis. prof. archtl. design Yale U., New Haven, 1983. Prin. works include Kemper Arena, Kansas City, Mo., 1974 (Nat. AIA honor award, Bartelt award, Am. Inst. Steel Constrn. award), Auraria Library, Denver, 1975, John Marshall Cts. Bldg., Richmond, Va. 1976, H. Roe Bartle Exhbn. Hall, Kansas City, Mo., 1976, Fourth Dist. Cts. Bldg., Maywood, Ill., 1976, Monroe Garage, Chgo., 1977, Michigan City (Ind.) Library, 1977 (AIA Ill. Council honor award, AIA-ALA First honor award, Am. Inst., Steel Constrn. award), St. Mary's Coll. Athletic Facility, South Bend, Ind., 1977 (AIA Ill. Council Honor award, AIA Nat. honor award, Am. Inst. Steel Constrn. award), Springfield Garage, Ill., 1977, Glenbrook Profl. Bldg., Northbrook, Ill., 1978, Rust-Oleum Corp. Hdqrs., Vernon Hills, Ill., 1978 (Am. Steel Constrn. award), La Lumiere Gymnasium, La Porte, Ind., 1978, Prairie Capital Convention Ctr.-Parking Garage, Springfield, Ill., 1979, W.W. Grainger Corp. Hdqrs., Skokie, Ill., 1979, Xerox Centre, Chgo., 1980, De La Garza Career Ctr., East Chicago, Ind., 1981 (ASHRAE Energy award), Area 2 Police Hdqrs., Chgo., 1981, Oak Brook (Ill.) Post Office, 1981, Commonwealth Edison Dist. Hdqrs., Downers Grove, Ill., 1981 (ASHRAE Energy award), First Source Ctr., South Bend, Ind., 1982, Argonne (Ill.) Program Support Facility, 1982 (Owens-Corning Fiberglass Energy Conservation award), One South Wacker Office Bldg., Chgo., 1982, Addition to Chgo. Bd. of Trade, 1982 (Reliance Devel. Group Inc. award for Disting. Arch., Am. Inst. Steel Constrn. award, Structural Engrng. Assn. Ill. award), Mercy Hosp. Addition, Chgo., 1983, 11 Diagonal St., Johannesburg, Republic of South Africa, 1983, U. Ill. Agrl. Engrng. Sci. Bldg., Champaign, 1984, Learning Resources Ctr., Coll. of DuPage, Glen Ellyn, Ill., 1984, Plaza East, Milw., 1984 (Disting. Architect award Milw. Art Commn.), Shand Morahan Corp. Hdqrs., Evanston, Ill., 1984, 701 Fourth Ave. S., Mpls., 1984, O'Hare Rapid Transit Sta., Chgo., 1984 (Nat. Honor award), State of Ill. Ctr., Chgo., 1985 (Structural Engrng. Assn. Ill. award), Parktown Stands, Johannesburg, 1986, Two Energy Ctr., Naperville, Ill., 1986, Hawthorne Ctr. Office Bldg., Vernon Hills, Ill., 1986, Park Ave. Tower, N.Y.C., 1986, 300 E. 85th St. Apts., N.Y.C.; contbr. to numerous group and solo exhbns. of archtl. drawings and design. Recipient Arnold W. Brunner Meml. Prize in Arch., 1982, Progressive Arch. Design citation, 1977, Progressive Arch. award for Chgo. Central Area Plan, 1985, N.Y. State AIA award. Fellow Architecture Soc./Art Inst. Chgo., Chgo. Archtl. Club; mem. AIA (numerous Chgo. chpt. award 1975—). Roman Catholic. Clubs: Comml. of Chgo., Economic of Chgo., Saddle & Cycle. Office: Murphy/Jahn 35 E Wacker Dr Chicago IL 60601

JAHNS, ARTHUR WILLIAM, educational administrator; b. Milw., Jan. 23, 1929; s. Arthur Victor and Vera (Kranz) J. B.S. in Secondary Edn., U. Wis.-Milw., 1953; M.Ed. in Guidance and Adminstrn., Marquette U., 1964. Tchr., counselor Milw. Pub. Schs., 1959-66, guidance dir., curriculum coordinator, 1967; asst. prin. Burrough Jr. High Sch., Milw., 1967-79; prin. Daniel Webster Middle Sch., Milw., 1980-83, Riverside U. High Sch., 1983—; cons. edn. ptnr. Met. Milw. C. of C., 1984—; ptnr. prin. Milw. Pub. Schs. Corp. Partnership Program, 1983—; cons. secondary edn. U. Wis.-Milw., 1984—. Coordinator, prin. acad. program devel. Riverside U. University Preparatory Program, 1984; ptnr., developer Profl. Partnership program, 1985; participant University-Bus. Cooperative Effort, 1982; coauthor, developer Data Processing Programs Middle School Programming, 1979. Evaluator North Central Assn. for Accreditation, Madison, 1985—; mem. Harvard Grad. Sch. Edn., 1983—; adv. Milw. Inter-High Council, 1965-66; mem. steering com. U. Wis. Milw./Riverside U. High Sch. Partnership in Excellence Program, 1983—. Served to capt. USN, 1953-76. Named Outstanding Educator Marquette U., 1981; recipient Most Outstanding Support and Service award United Negro Coll. Fund, 1984. Mem. Naval Res. Assn. (life) (local pres. 1973-76, Outstanding service award 1976), Res. Officer Assn. (life), Assn. Sch. Curriculum Devel., Wis. Assn. Student Councils (adv.), Milw. Adminstrs. and Suprs. Council (various positions 1974—), U. Wis.-Milw. Alumni Assn. (life), Wis. Farm Bur., Milw. High Sch. Prins. Assn. Republican. Lutheran. Avocations: gardening; business; farming; collecting; music. Home: 3223 North Lake Dr Milwaukee WI 53211 Office: Riverside University High Sch 1615 East Locust St Milwaukee WI 53211

JAKES, GERALD ALLAN, consulting company executive; b. N.Y.C., Dec. 20, 1930; s. Otto Henry and Alice Martha (Voska) J.; m. Emilyn Bixby Larkin, Aug. 7, 1954; children: Linda, David, Cindy. AB, Cornell U., 1953; postgrad., Wharton Sch., Ohio State U., 1982. Sales engr. Reliance Elec. Co., Toledo, 1954-68, dist. mgr., 1968-72, mgr. glass and rubber mktg., 1972-78, mgr. glass worldwide mktg., 1978-82; mgr. mktg. services Glasstech, Inc., Perrysburg, Ohio, 1984-85; pres. Productivity Plus, Toledo, 1982—; cons. Girkins Elec. Co., Toledo, 1984—; mem. strategic mgmt. team Indsl. Printing Co., Toledo, 1985—, strategic mktg. team Toledo Engrng. Co., 1985, sales cost reduction video dept. Dura-Temp, Holland, Ohio, 1986—. Patentee in field; contbr. articles to profl. jours. Mem. IEEE (chmn. publicity com., controls and gen. applications), Am. Mktg. Assn. (exec. mem.), N.Am. Soc. Corp. Planners (regional v.p.), Glass Packaging Inst. (assoc.). Republican. Lutheran. Lodge: Rotary. Avocations: tennis, skiing, guitar, bridge. Home: 5243 Flanders Rd Toledo OH 43623 Office: Productivity Plus 3030 N Reynolds Rd Toledo OH 43615

JAKIEL, JAN J., chamber of commerce executive; b. Buffalo, Jan. 26, 1934; s. Stanley B. and Alvira Z. (Woyski) J.; m. Edith Marie McDonald, June 27, 1969. B.A., SUNY-Buffalo, 1956, M.B.A., 1966. Gen. mgr. Automotive Sales Dealership, Buffalo, 1958-62, Western Electric Co., Buffalo, 1962-69; bus., membership mgr. Buffalo Area C. of C., 1969-73, v.p. ops., 1973-82, v.p. econ. devel., 1982-83; pres. South Bend/Mishawaka Area C. of C., Ind., 1983—; dir., pres., treas. Consumer Credit Counseling, Buffalo, 1976-84; treas., dir. Buffalo Urban League, 1978-84; exec. v.p. ENIDC, Buffalo, 1982-84. Sec., Buffalo Chamber Found., 1978-84; treas. W. N.Y. Polit. Action Com., Buffalo, 1980-84. Served with U.S. Army, 1956-58. Mem. Am. C. of C. Execs., U.S. C. of C., Ind. C. of C. Execs. Assn. (bd. dirs. 1985-86). Clubs: South Bend Country, Morris Park Country (South Bend). Avocations: skiing; golfing; boating. Office: South Bend/Mishawaka Area C of C 401 E Colfax Ave PO Box 1677 South Bend IN 46634

JAKOVICH, ROBERT ANDREW, accountant; b. Camp Atterbury, Ind., Aug. 17, 1953; s. Robert Edward and Mary Ann (Walker) J.; m. Cynthia Ann Hamm, May 28, 1977. BS in Acctg., Dyke Coll., 1976. CPA, Ohio. Credit analyst Nat. City Bank, Cleve., 1976-80; ptnr. Jakovich & Jakovich, Cleve., 1980—. Nat. treas. Serbian Orthodox Ch. of USA, Chgo., 1985—. Mem. Am. Inst. CPA's., Ohio Soc. CPA's. Republican. Avocations: sports, reading, photography. Home: 1594 Woodward Lakewood OH 44107 Office: Jakovich & Jakovich 22972 Lorain Rd Fairview Park OH 44126

JAKUBAS, RICHARD GEORGE, systems company executive; b. Beaconsfield, Eng., July 10, 1949; came to U.S., 1951; s. Bronislaw and Maria (Kwiatkowska) J.; m. Patricia Ann Quinn Lay, Oct. 1985. Student U. Ill.-Urbana, 1967-69, U. Ill.-Chgo., 1969-71; BS in Math., U. Houston, 1974-76. Application engr. Baker Automation System Co., Houston, 1972-76; mgr., application engr. Kobe Systems-BASIC, Houston, 1976-78; corp. devel. mgr. BWT-BASIC, Inc., Houston, 1978-81; v.p. BWT-Data Processors Co., Houston, 1981-82; dir. MIS, Powell Industries, Inc., Houston, 1982-83; regional support mgr. ASK Computer Systems, Inc., Oak Brook Terr., Ill., 1983-87; dir. client support Resource Info. Mgmt. Systems, Inc., 1987—. Inventor software system. Vol. tchr. sch., Prairie du Chien, Wis., 1967. Mem. ASK South Central Regional Users Group (pres. 1982-83). Republican. Avocations: piano, computers, skiing, woodworking, photography. Home: 743 Torrington Dr Naperville IL 60565 Office: Resource Info Mgmt Systems Inc 500 Technology Dr Naperville IL 60540

JAMAR, JOHN PHILIP, engineering company executive; b. Iron Mountain, Mich., Mar. 25, 1961; s. John Woodbridge and Francis Luciel (Edlund) J.; m. Dianna Marie Vykydal, May 19, 1984. BSME, Mich. Tech. U., 1983. Dir. mktg. Cable Constructors, Iron Mountain, 1983—. v.p. First Luth. Ch., Iron Mountain, 1985. Mem. Am. Mgmt. Assn., Delta Sigma Phi, Ducks Unlimited, NRA (life). Republican. Lutheran. Clubs: Sportsman (Meriman). Avocations: hunting, trap shooting, reading. Home: 736 Hamilton Ave Kingsford MI 49801 Office: Cable Constructors Inc 105 Kent St Iron Mountain MI 49801

JAMBOIS, BEVERLY ANN, lawyer; b. Chgo., June 20, 1954; d. William G. and Lorraine V. (Palata) Norman; m. Robert James Jambois, June 9, 1979; 1 child, Stacey Marie. Student, U. Wis., Parkside, 1977-79; BA, U. Wis., Madison, 1981, JD, 1984. Bar: Wis. 1984, U.S. Dist. Ct. (ea. and we. dists.) Wis. 1984. Assoc. Landa Law Offices, Kenosha, Wis., 1984-86, Hansen & Landa, Silver Lake, Wis., 1984-86; sole practice Kenosha, 1986-87; ptnr. Ventura, Dowse, Guttormsen & Jambois, Kenosha, 1987—. Mem. Kenosha Theatre Task Force; bd. dirs. Kenosha Symphony Orch.; mem. citizens' rev. panel United Way, Kenosha Area Devel. Corp. Mem. ABA, State Bar Wis. (chairperson subcom. on participation of women in bar), Kenosha Bar Assn., Assn. Trial Lawyers Am., NOW, Phi Kappa Phi. Office: Ventura Dowse Guttormsen & Jambois 5500 8th Ave Kenosha WI 53140

JAMES, BRAD ALLAN, transportation company executive; b. Ancon, Panama, Aug. 11, 1955; s. Merlin Reese James and Joan Bollenbacher; m. Patricia Ann Ott, Apr. 9, 1983. Student, Wright State U., 1973-75; BSBA, Bowling Green State U., 1977. V.p. sales Craig Transp. Co., Perrysburg, Ohio, 1977-82; pres. Seagate Transp. Co., Rossford, Ohio, 1982—. Mem. Nat. Pub. Transp. Assn. Lutheran. Office: Seagate Transp Co 63 Dixie Hwy Rossford OH 43460

JAMES, ERNEST WILBUR, lawyer; b. N.Y.C., July 21, 1931; s. Ernest Leaman and Lola Marguerita (Clancy) J.; m. Jane Gallagher; children: Ernest Jude, Sean Patrick, Patrick Logan, Sharon Ann; 1 stepchild, Susan Bartsch. BS, U.S. Naval Acad., 1956; MS in Aero. Engring., U.S. Naval Postgrad. Sch., 1964; JD, St. Louis U., 1979. Bar: Mo. 1979. Title examiner Queens County Registrar's Office, N.Y.C., 1949-51; commd. ensign USN, 1956, advanced through grades to comdr., 1971, designated naval aviator, 1958, aviation maintenance mgr., 1956-69, maintenance mgmt. planning engr., 1969-76, ret., 1976; atty., dir. risk mgmt. Bi-State Devel. Agy., St. Louis, 1979-85; ptnr. Haley Fredrickson & Walsh, St. Louis, 1985—; adj. prof. safety Cen. Mo. State U. Active Maryville Homecoming Assn.; vol. fire insp. Maryville Fire Dept. Decorated D.F.C., Air medal (3), Navy Commendation medal. UMTA grantee, 1978. Mem. ABA, Mo. Bar Assn., Met. St. Louis Bar Assn., Met. St. Louis Safety Council, Naval Acad. Alumni Assn., U.S. Naval Inst., Am. Def. Preparedness Assn., Met. St. Louis Bar Assn., VFW. Home: 7416 Foley Dr Belleville IL 62223

JAMES, JOSEPH W., diversified corporation executive; b. Galt, Calif., June 1, 1926; s. William and Josephine James; m. Rachel P. Jaeger, Sept. 30, 1950; children: Helen James MacDonald, Clayton, Christopher, Curtis. BSME, U. So. Calif., 1946; MBA in Indsl. Mgmt., MIT, 1964. Various positions, then dir. product planning Chrysler Corp., 1952-73; pres. Nat. Car Rental System, Inc., Mpls., 1973-81; exec. v.p. Household Internat., Inc., Prospect Heights, Ill., 1981—, also bd. dirs.; bd. dirs. Mack Trucks, Inc., Allentown, Pa. Home: 660 S Circle Ln Lake Forest IL 60045 Office: Household Internat Inc 2700 Sanders Rd Prospect Heights IL 60070 *

JAMES, MARIE MOODY, musician, vocal music educator, clergywoman; b. Chgo., Jan. 23, 1928; d. Frank and Mary (Portis) Moody; m. Johnnie James, May 25, 1968. B Music Edn., Chgo. Music Coll., 1949; MusM, Roosevelt U., 1969, MA, 1976; DD, Internat. Bible Inst. and Sem., Plymouth, Fla., 1985. Ordained to ministry Pentecostal Ch., 1976; cert. vocal music tchr., Ill. Organist Allen Temple A.M.E. Ch., 1941-45; asst. organist Coppin A.M.E. Ch., 1945-49; organist-dir. Progressive Ch. of God in Christ, Maywood, Ill., 1950-60; key punch operator Dept. Treasury, Chgo., 1950-52; tchr. Posen-Robbins Bd. Edn., Robbins, Ill., 1952-59; missionary Child Evangelism Fellowship, Chgo., 1955-63; tchr. vocal music

Englewood High Sch., Chgo., 1964-84; pastor God's House of Love, Prayer and Deliverance, Robbins, 1982—; music counselor Head Start, Chgo., 1965-66; unit leader YWCA, New Buffalo, Mich., 1956-58; minister of music God's House of All Nations, Chgo., 1960-80; exec. dir. House of Love Day Care, Robbins, Ill., 1983-84; dir. music Christian Women's Outreach Ministry, 1984—. Composer, arranger choral music: Hide Me, 1963, Christmas Time, 1980, Come With Us, Our God Will Do Thee Good, 1986. Chmn. Frank and Mary Moody Scholarship Com., 1984—; mem. Robbins Community Council, 1983-85. Coppin A.M.E. Ch. scholar, 1946. Mem. Music Educators Nat. Conf., AFT. Democrat. Clubs: Good News (tchr. 1955-63 Chgo.). Home: 8154 S Indiana Chicago IL 60619

JAMES, MARION RAY, editor, publisher; b. Bellmont, Ill., Dec. 6, 1940; s. Francis Miller and Lorraine A. (Wylie) J.; m. Janet Sue Tennis, June 16, 1960; children—Jeffrey Glenn, David Ray, Daniel Scott, Cheryl Lynne. B.S., Oakland City Coll., Ind., 1964; M.S., St. Francis Coll., Fort Wayne, Ind., 1978. Sports and city editor Daily Clarion, Princeton, Ind., 1963-65; English tchr. Jac-Cen-Del High Sch., Osgood, Ind., 1965-66; indsl. editor Whirlpool Corp., Evansville and LaPorte, Ind., 1966-68, Magnavox Govt. and Indsl. Electronics Co., Fort Wayne, 1968-79; pres., editor, pub. Bowhunter mag. Blue-J Pub. Co., Fort Wayne, 1971—; instr. Ind.-Purdue U., Fort Wayne, 1980—. Author: Bowhunting for Whitetail and Mule Deer, 1975, Successful Bowhunting, 1985; editor: Pope and Young Book World Records, 1975, Bowhunting Adventures, 1977. Recipient Best Editorial award United Community Service Publs., 1970-72; named Alumnus of Yr., Oakland City Coll., 1982, to Hall of Fame, Mt. Carmel High Sch., Ill., 1983. Mem. Outdoor Writers Assn. Am., Fort Wayne Assn. Bus. Editors (Fort Wayne Bus. Editor of Yr. 1969, pres. 1975-76), Alpha Phi Gamma, Alpha Psi Omega, Mu Tau Kappa. Club: Toastmasters (Able Toastmaster award). Home: 11513 Brigadoon Ct Fort Wayne IN 46804 Office: Bowhunter Mag 3720 S Calhoun St Fort Wayne IN 46807

JAMES, MICHAEL EDWARD, management services corporation executive; b. Atlanta, Oct. 10, 1951; s. Walter Simeon and Anne (Pappenheimer) J.; m. Anne Marie Dahlstrom, Aug. 5, 1978; 1 son, Ian Michael. B.A., U. Ga., 1974; postgrad. U. Cin., 1983—. News producer, reporter Sta. WTVC-TV, Chattanooga, 1975-79; news producer Sta. WKRC-TV, Cin., 1979-80; dir. Batesville Mgmt. Services div. Hillenbrand Industries, Ind., 1980-87; dir. mktg. programs Forethought Life Ins. Co., Batesville, 1987—; lectr. in field. Area fund raiser Am. Cancer Soc., 1983—. Mem. Sigma Delta Chi. Republican. Episcopalian. Author: (brochure) Estate Planning (Silver Screen award 1982), 1982; author, copywriter various brochures, audio-visual programs for profl. use, profl. textbooks on mktg. and sales mgmt. Office: Forethought Life Insurance Co Forethought Ctr Batesville IN 47006

JAMES, PHILIP BENJAMIN, physicist, educator; b. Kansas City, Mo., Mar. 18, 1940; s. Benjamin and Catharine (Bagley) J.; m. Sharon Lynn Check, Aug. 28, 1965; children: Eric Benjamin, Kevin Philip, Kirsten Lynn. BS, Carnegie Mellon U., 1961; PhD, U. Wis., 1966. Research assoc. U. Ill., Urbana, 1966-68; prof. U. Mo., St. Louis, 1968—, dept. chmn., 1984—; scientist Viking Mars Project, Pasadena, Calif., 1977-78. Contbr. over 50 articles to profl. jours. Sr. research fellow Nat. Research Council, 1977-78; research grantee NASA, 1979—, Nat. Geographic Soc., 1986—. Fellow Am. Physical Soc.; mem. Am. Geophysical Union, Am. Astronomical Soc., Sierra Club, Sigma Nu. Avocations: philately, skiing, hiking. Office: U Mo Physics Dept Saint Louis MO 63121

JAMES, RICHARD HALE, dentist; b. Emporia, Kans., Apr. 10, 1929; s. William Richard and Vivion S. (Hale) J.; m. Ann Louise Jones, Aug. 11, 1949 (widowed Aug. 1982); children: Louise Ann, William David; m. Jacqueline Louise Murphy, July 23, 1983. BS in Geology, U. Kans., 1952; DDS, U. Mo., Kansas City, 1965. Geologist Phillips Petroleum Co., various locations, 1952-58; cons. geologist James & Hutchinson, Wichita Falls, Tex., 1958-61; practice gen. dentistry Emporia, 1965—; dep. examiner Kans. Dental Bd., 1975-80. Mem. ADA, Kans. Dental Assn., Flint Hills Dental Assn., Lyon County Dental Assn. (pres. 1966-67), Fifth Dist. Dental Soc. (pres. 1972), Soc. for Preservation Oral Health (pres. 1981-82, bd. dirs. 1979-85), U. Mo. Kansas City Dental Alumni Assn. (trustee). Episcopalian. Club: Emporia Country. Avocations: travel, photography, running, cross-country skiing, flying, golf. Home: 1719 Hammond Dr Emporia KS 66801 Office: 201 W 12th Emporia KS 66801

JAMES, WALTER, retired computer information specialist, state official; b. Mpls., June 8, 1915; s. James Edward and Mollie (Gress) Smoleroff; B.Ch.E., U. Minn., 1938, postgrad, 1945-60; m. Jessie Ann Pickens, Dec. 27, 1948; 1 son, Joel Pickens. Process designer Monsanto Chem. Co., St. Louis, 1940-45; instr. math U. Minn., Mpls., 1945-60, extension div., 1950—; researcher computer based applied math. 3M Co., St. Paul, 1960-68; info. systems planner State of Minn., St. Paul, 1968-85; ret., 1985. Mem. Am. Math. Assn., AAAS, Sigma Xi. Contbr. articles to profl. jours. Home: 6228 Brooklyn Dr Brooklyn Center MN 55430

JAMES, WILLIAM W., banker; b. Springfield, Mo., Oct. 12, 1931; s. Will and Clyde (Cowdrey) J.; A.B., Harvard U., 1953; m. Carol Ann Muenter, June 17, 1967; children—Sarah Elizabeth, David William. Asst. to dir. overseas div. Becton Dickinson & Co., Rutherford, N.J., 1956-59; stockbroker Merrill Lynch, Pierce, Fenner & Smith, Inc., St. Louis, 1959-62; with trust div. Boatmen's Nat. Bank of St. Louis, 1962—, v.p. in charge estate planning, 1972—, sr. v.p., 1984—; dir. Heer-Andres Investment Co., Springfield. Mem. gift and bequest council Barnes Hosp., St. Louis, 1963-67, St. Louis U., 1972-78; dir. Mark Twain Summer Inst., St. Louis, 1987—. Served with U.S. Army, 1953-55. Mem. Estate Planning Council St. Louis, Mo. Bankers Assn., Bank Mktg. Assn., Am. Inst. Banking, Harvard Alumni Assn. (bd. dirs. 1987—). Republican. Clubs: Harvard (pres. 1972-73), Mo. Athletic, Noonday (St. Louis). Office: Boatmen's Nat Bank PO Box 7365 Saint Louis MO 63177

JAMESON, JOSEPH ANTHONY, architect, civil engineer; b. Mpls., Sept. 10, 1950; s. Herbert John Sr. and Mary Lou (Smith) J.; m. Patricia Ann Baert, June 19, 1971; children: Jennifer Jean, Jacqueline Marie, Douglas Michael. BArch, U. Minn., 1974, B Civil Engring., 1975. Engr., draftsman L.J. Meisch & Assoc., St. Paul, 1973-78; design engr. Internat. Multi Foods, Mpls., 1978-81; prin. engr. Horner Assocs., St. Paul, 1981; prin. J.A. Jameson Assocs., Ltd., St. Paul, 1981—. chmn. pine wood derby Groveland council Boy Scouts Am., 1985. Mem. AIA, Am. Soc. Civil Engrs. (chmn. structural com. Minn. sect. 1982-83, treas. 1983-85, v.p. tech. services 1985—, Young Engr. of the Yr. 1984), Constrn. Specifications Inst., Am. Concrete Inst. Roman Catholic. Club: Nativity Mens (St. Paul). Home: 1982 James Ave Saint Paul MN 55105 Office: 905 Jefferson Ave Saint Paul MN 55102

JAMES-STRAND, NANCY KAY LEABHARD, advertising executive; b. Oak Park, Ill., July 30, 1943; d. Arthur Ferdinand and Virginia Stella (Albertelli) Leabhard; m. Jack William Strand, July 1, 1971. Student, U. Madrid, 1963-64; BA in Teaching Spanish, U. Ill., 1965. With advt. sales Chgo. Tribune, 1968-69; asst. mgr. Nationwide Advt., Chgo., 1969-78, regional mgr., 1978—. Home: 140 S Grove Oak Park IL 60302 Office: Nationwide Advt 35 E Wacker Dr Chicago IL 60601

JAMISON, ELEANOR A(GNES), social services administrator; b. Larimer, Pa., July 12, 1927; d. John A. and Virginia (Kowalczk) Rice; m. Boris Vugrincic, Aug. 29, 1948 (dec. 1973); children: Kathleen A. Vugrincic, Michael J. Vugrincic. BS, Youngstown (Ohio) State U., 1968; RN, Braddock gen. Hosp. Sch. Nursing. Head nurse Shadyside Hosp., Pitts., 1952-56; obstetrics supr. St. Joseph Hosp., Warren, Ohio, 1956-62; dir. nursing Warren Gen. Hosp., 1962-68; mgr., office nurse E.B. McGovern M.D., Warren, 1969-76; asst. dir. Parkview Hosp., Toledo, 1976-77, St. Luke's Hosp., Maumee, Ohio, 1977-80; 5 St. Vincent Med. Ctr., Toledo, 1980—; cons. PE Industries, Dundee, Ohio, 1980-83. Mem. editorial bd. Hosp. Purchasing News. Mem. speakers bur. Am. Cancer Soc., 1968—, Am. Heart Assn., Toledo, 1968—. Mem. Ohio Soc. Cen. Service (past pres.), N.W. Ohio Cen. Service (past pres.), Am. Soc. Hosp. Cen. Service (past bd. dirs.), Am. Bus. Women's Assn. (past pres.), Assn. Operating Room Nurses, Am. Practitioners in Infection Control, Ohio Fedn. Bus. and Profl. Women, Toledo Bus. and Profl. Women's Club (past pres.), Health Clin. Internat. (pres.), Grey Nuns Assn., Nat. Assn. Female Execs., Mich. Basketweavers. Avocations: leather crafts, ceramic, dancing, music. Office: St Vincent Med Ctr 2213 Cherry St Toledo OH 43608

JAMISON, FREDERICK WILLIAM, data processing executive; b. St. Louis, Oct. 27, 1947; s. Elmer Bryan and Dolores Josephine (Rivers) J.; m. Linda Kae Hickinbotham, Feb. 13, 1971 (div. Nov. 1981); 1 child, Matthew Edward; m. Sharen Marie Wood, June 5, 1982; children: Brian Michael, Tiffany Leigh. BS in Systems and Data Processing, Washington U., 1980. Draftsman McDonnell Douglas Co., St. Louis, 1966-67, Western Electric Co., St. Louis, 1970-72; constrn. engr. Mo. Pacific R.R. Co., St. Louis, 1974-80; data resource mgr. Southwestern Bell Telephone Co., St. Louis, 1980—; tchr. computers Washington U., St. Louis, 1982-83, Meramec Community Coll., St. Louis, 1980-82; cons. data processing mgmt. Southwestern Bell, St. Louis, 1983—. Designer computer systems; patentee in field. Asst. organizer Harriet Wood for Senator, St. Louis, 1986. Served to sgt. U.S. Army, 1967-70, Vietnam. Decorated Bronze Star, Army Commendation medal. Mem. Smithsonian Inst. (assoc.). Lodge: Masons. Avocations: archery, gardening, the outdoors. Office: Southwestern Bell Telephone Co One Bell Ctr Room 22-F-5 Saint Louis MO 63101

JAMISON, KEVIN LEE, lawyer; b. Longbranch, N.J., July 22, 1952; s. Eugene O. and Virginia Jamison; m. Mia Yi, Aug. 6, 1977; children: Kelly Lee, Kenneth Lee. Sole practice Kansas City, 1983—. Contbr. articles to profl. jours. Chmn. Adminstrv. Law Com., Kansas City, 1984. Mem. ABA, Assn. Trial Lawyers Am., Spl. Forces Assn., Assn. U.S. Army. Home: 6413 N Park Gladstone MO 64118 Office: 1807 W 39th Kansas City MO 64111

JAMISON, MARSHALL S., television producer; b. Boston, June 16, 1918; s. Walter Washington and Margaret (Shipman) J.; m. Priscilla Langenbach, June 21, 1939 (div. 1948); 1 child, Patricia Ann; m. Janet Rosa, May 14, 1950; children: Janeen, Joshua, Theresa, Marshall, Janet. Student, New Eng. Conservatory of Music, 1936-37, Yale U., 1938-39. Exec. producer U.S. Steel Hour Theatre Guild Inc., N.Y.C., 1956-58; co-producer Leland Hayward, N.Y.C., 1959-69; dir. ABC-TV, N.Y.C, 1970-71; producer CBS-TV, N.Y.C., 1971-72; exec. producer U. Mid-Am., Lincoln, Nebr., 1974-76; sr. producer U. Nebr. TV, Lincoln, 1976—; writer, producer, dir. TNT Communications, Inc., N.Y.C., 1960-74. Dir.: (Broadway plays) By the Beautiful Sea, The Young and Beautiful, On Borrowed Time, Time Limit, 1953-56; dir., producer That Was the Week That Was, 1963-64. Cons. Rep. Presdl. Conv., Chgo., 1960, coach of speakers, Miami, Fla., 1968, Kansas City, Mo., 1976; coach of speakers Dem. Presdl. Conv., N.Y.C., 1976. Recipient Christopher award Christopher Soc., 1958; numerous Peabody awards, U. Ga. Sch. Journalism, 1953-83, Emmy award TV Acad., 1960; Ohio State award Ohio State U., 1973. Mem. The Players. Avocations: golf, bridge, swimming, gardening. Office: U Nebr TV PO Box 83111 Lincoln NE 68501

JAMISON, ROGER W., pianist, piano educator; b. Marion, Ohio, June 18, 1937; s. Harold Theodore and Martha Louise (Haas) J.; m. Caroline R. Hansley, Jan. 26, 1957; children—Lisa Renee, Eric Karl. B.S., Ohio State U., 1959, M.A. (scholar), 1961; postgrad. Oberlin Conservatory, Oakland U.; student George Haddad, Columbus, Ohio, Mischa Kottler, Detroit. Piano faculty mem. Detroit Conservatory of Music, 1964-68, Cranbrook Schs., Bloomfield Hills, Mich., 1981-84; performer in one-man musical presentation Spirits of Great Composers, 1979—; dir. music Birmingham Temple, Farmington Hills, Mich., 1984—; soloist Brunch with Bach series Detroit Inst. Arts., Detroit Symphony Orch.'s Internat. Brahms Festival; cons. Royal Oak Arts Council; adjudicator Am. Coll. Musicians. Mem. Nat. Guild of Piano Tchrs. (past pres. Oakland-Macomb chpt.) Address: 2300 Bedford Rd Bloomfield Hills MI 48013

JANCIK, CHARLENE A., special education teacher; b. Chgo., Apr. 3, 1949; d. Robert F. and La Vergne M. (Swierczynski) Benza; m. Wayne M. Jancik, Aug., 28, 1976; 1 child, Matthew. AA in Fine Arts, Wright Coll., Chgo., 1974; BA in Elem. Edn., U. Ill., Chgo., 1976, Main Spl. Edn., 1978. Cert. tchr. kindergarten, primary and spl. edn. Learning disabilities tchr. Chgo. Bd. Edn., 1978-81, tchr. trainable mentally handicapped, 1981-86, devel. kindergarten tchr., 1986—; research asst. U. Ill., Chgo., 1976-78; lectr. Weight Watchers, Chgo., 1980-82; asst. dir. Rogers Park Jewish Community Ctr. Day Camp, Chgo., 1982-84. researcher Jour. of Child Devel., 1980. Recipient tuition and fee waiver U. Ill., Chgo., 1978. Mem. Council for Exceptional Children, Assn. for Children with Learning Disabilities, Chgo. Tchrs. Union. Roman Catholic. Home: 5488 N Menard Chicago IL 60630 Office: Penn Sch 1616 S Avers Chicago IL 60623

JANDA, KENNETH FRANK, political science educator; b. Chgo., Nov. 14, 1935; s. John F. and Bessie (Ringl) J.; m. Ann Mozolak, Sept. 2, 1961; children: Susan Ann, Katy Bess. EdB, Ill. State U., 1957; PhD in Govt., Ind. U., 1961. Asst. prof. Northwestern U., Evanston, Ill., 1961-66, assoc. prof., 1966-69, prof., 1969—; dir. Vogelback Computing Ctr. Northwestern U., 1984. Author: Data Processing, 1965, Information Retrieval, 1968, Political Parties, 1980; co-author: Parties and Their Environment, 1982, The Challenge of Democracy: Government in America, 1987. Recipient Alumni Achievement award Ill. State U., 1983. Mem. Am. Polit. Sci. Assn. Office: Northwestern U Dept Polit Sci Evanston IL 60201

JANDA, MARK D., management consultant; b. St. Paul, Feb. 22, 1954; s. Walter M. and Nadine J. (Holst) J.; m. Anne L. Peterson, May 16, 1981; 1 child, Elizabeth Olin. BA, Luther COll., 1975. Mgr. computer systems Rep. Airlines, Mpls., 1975-81; sr. software programmer Rosemont Engring., Mpls., 1981-83; mgr. Peat, Marwick, Main and Co., Mpls., 1983—; cons. Pillsbury, Northwest Info. Services, First Wis. Nat. Bank, Kent (Ohio) State U., Minn. State Senate. Treas. Christ the King Luth. Ch., Bloomington, Minn., 1984—; mem. adv. bd. Dakota City Area Vocat. Tech. Inst., Rosemont, Minn., 1983—. Mem. Assn. System Mgmt. (program com.), Twin Cities Data Base/Data Communications Users Group (bd. dirs. 1983, 85). Avocations: playing trombone in brass quintet, bicycle racing, sailing, cross-country skiing, choral singing. Home: 8981 Darnel Rd Eden Prairie MN 53334 Office: Peat Marwick Main & Co 1700 IDS Ctr Minneapolis MN 53402

JANEČEK, FREDERICK JOSEPH, social worker; b. Charco, Tex., Mar. 7, 1938; s. Joseph and Angela Theresa (Grafe) J.; m. Carol Ann Groshek, July 21, 1973; 1 child, John Frederick. BA, St. Mary's U., San Antonio, 1965, MA, 1979; MSW, U. Wis., Milw., 1979. Diplomate clin. social work, lic. sch. social worker, Wis.; qualified mental retardation profl. Clin. social worker Wis. Dept. Health and Social Services, Madison, 1974—; instr. social work Milw. Area Tech. Coll, 1977-79; clin. social worker Mendota Mental Health Inst., Madison, Wis., 1980-83; dir. Janeček Clinic and Consultation Service, Madison, 1980—. State del. Wis. Dem. Conv., 1983, 85-86. Mem. Nat. Assn. Social Workers (cert., bd. dirs., br. chmn.), Acad. Cert. Social Workers, Am. Fedn. State, County and Mcpl. Employees (chpt. vice chmn. 1984), Czechoslovak Soc. of Wis. (founder, pres.), Polish Heritage Club (bd. dirs. 1985—), German Club, Sons of Confederate Vets., Ceská Katolicka Jednota Texaská, Alpha Delta Mu. Eastern Orthodox. Avocations: travelling, wilderness hiking, reading, local and ethnic history. Home and Office: 5929 Mayhill Dr PO Box 4561 Madison WI 53711-0561

JANECEK, LENORE ELAINE, insurance specialist, consultant; b. Chgo., May 2, 1944; d. Morris and Florence (Bear) Picker; M.A.J. in Speech Communications (talent scholar), Northeastern Ill. U., 1972; postgrad. (Ill. Assn. C. of C. Execs. scholar) Inst. for Organizational Mgmt., U. Notre Dame, 1979-80; M.B.A., Columbia Pacific U., 1982; cert. in C. of C. mgmt. U. Colo., 1982; m. John Janecek, Sept. 12, 1964; children—Frank, Michael. Adminstrv. asst., exec. dir. Ill. Mcpl. Retirement Fund, Chgo., 1963-65; personnel mgr. Profile Personnel, Chgo., 1965-68; personnel rep. Marsh Instrument Co., Skokie, Ill., 1971-73; restaurant mgt. Gold Mine Restaurant and What's Cooking Restaurant, Chgo., 1974-76; pres., owner Secretarial Office Services, Chgo., 1976-78; founder, pres. Lincolnwood (Ill.) C. of C. and Industry, 1978-87; pres. Lenore E. Janecek & Assocs., Lincolnwood, 1987—; rep. 10th dist. U.S. C. of C., 1978—. Mem. mktg. bd. Niles Twp. Sheltered Workshop; pres. Lincolnwood Sch. Dist. 74 Sch. Bd. Caucus; bd. mem., officer, founder Ill. Fraternal Order Police Ladies Aux.; bd. dirs., officer Lincolnwood Girl's Softball League, PTA; bd. dirs. United Way, 1982-83; mem. sch. curriculum com. Lincolnwood Bd. Edn. Recipient Disting. Grad. of Yr. Nat. Honor Soc., 1985. Mem. Am. C. of C. Execs., Ill. Assn. C. of C. Execs., Women in Mgmt. (local officer), Nat. Assn. Female Execs., Am. Notary Soc., Ill. LWV, Nat. Council Jewish Women, Hadassah. Jewish. Home: 6707 N Monticello St Lincolnwood IL 60645 Office: 4433 W Touhy Suite 550 Lincolnwood IL 60646

JANECKE, RONALD BRIAN, jounalist, editor; b. Rock Island, Ill., June 6, 1939; s. Duval Ronald and Bernice Janecke. B.A. in History, Augustana Coll., 1961. Asst. sports editor Moline Dispatch, Ill., 1963-64; asst. mng. editor Moline Dispatch, 1964-66; asst. news editor St. Louis Globe-Democrat, 1966-79, sports editor, 1979-84, assoc. editor, 1984-85; news editor, sports columnist St. Louis Bus. Jour., 1986—. Recipient Con Lee Keliher award Sigma Delta Chi, 1968. Mem. Investigative Reporters and Editors. Democrat. Home: 1851-B S 9th St Saint Louis MO 63104 Office: St Louis Bus Jour 612 N 2d St Saint Louis MO 63102

JANIAK, THOMAS ANTHONY, educator; b. Oak Park, Ill., July 16, 1949. A.S. in Media, Coll. DuPage, Glen Ellyn, Ill., 1971; B.A. in Communications, Sangamon State U., Springfield, Ill., 1973, M.S. in Ednl. Adminstrn., Nat. Coll. Edn., Evanston, Ill., 1979. Media technician Sch. Dist. 201, Cicero, Ill., 1969-71; dir. media, activities, supr. performing arts Argo High Sch. Dist. 217, Summit, Ill., 1973-83; gen. mgr. Cable channel Cablevision of Chgo., 1975-86; project dir. Resource Devel. and Mgmt. Inst. of Chgo., 1980-82, dir. activities, 1984-86; gen. mgr. Sta. WARG-FM; ind. cons. on cable TV, 1980—; prof. mass communications Moraine Valley Community Coll., 1984—, Lewis U., 1987—. Asst. dist. commr. Boy Scouts Am., 1970-72, post advisor, 1972-86, chmn., 1979-80, council mem.-at-large, 1985—; commr. cable, Summit, Ill., 1981—; mem. adv. cable commn., Bridgeview, Ill., 1983—; bd. dirs. Hull House Desplaines Valley Community Center, 1975-76. Mem. ALA, Ill. Library Assn., Am. Assn. Supervision and Curriculum Devel., Assn. Ednl. Communication and Tech., Nat. Assn. Broadcasters, Nat. Assn. Ednl. Broadcasters, Assn. Secondary Sch. Prins., Owassippi Staff Assn. (bd. dirs.). Home: 7806 W 98th St Hickory Hills IL 60457 Office: 7329 W 63rd St Summit IL 60501

JANICAK, PHILIP GREGORY, psychiatry educator; b. Chgo., Aug. 2, 1946; s. Edward and Josephine (Raskauskas) J.; m. Mary Judith Cray, Oct. 16, 1976; 1 child; children: Matthew Cray. BS in Psychology with honors, Loyola U., Chgo., 1969, MD, 1973. Diplomate Am. Bd. Psychiatry and Neurology. Asst. clin. prof. dept. psychiatry Loyola U., Maywood, Ill., 1976-78; research assoc. U. Chgo., 1979-81; asst. prof. U. Ill., Chgo., 1982-85, assoc. prof., 1986—; assoc. dir. cen. research program Ill. State Psychiat. Inst., Chgo., 1984—, chmn. Mental Health Com., 1986; lectr. dept. psychiatry Northwestern U., Chgo., 1984—. NIMH grant co-investigator, 1986. Fellow Am. Psychiat. Assn. Roman Catholic. Avocation: piano.

JANIS, LARRY WILLIARD, educator; b. St. Louis, Dec. 17, 1937; s. Jesse Williard and Mary Helen (McClanahan) J.; m. Patsy Jeanne Rucker, Apr. 29, 1966; 1 dau., Susan Annalee. Student U. Md., 1961-64, Mo. Bapt. Coll., 1965, Forest Park Community Coll., 1966-68; B.S. in Elem. Edn., U. Mo.-St. Louis, 1972; postgrad. U. Alaska-Anchorage, 1972-79; M.Ednl. Adminstrn., U. So. Miss., 1981. Lifetime cert. elem. edn., jr. high sci., high sch. biology, Mo. Dictaphone repairman Dictaphone Corp., 1964-65; customer engr. IBM, 1965-69; custodian Tower Grove Bapt. Ch., 1969-72; tchr. sci., math., art Wasilla Jr. High Sch. (Alaska), 1972-80; tchr. math. and sci. Tower Grove Christian Sch., St. Louis, 1980—; black-light chalk artist for ch./sch. programs. Mem. Wasilla Bicentennial Commn., 1975-76; mem. dist. com. in support presdl. candidate Ronald Reagan, Republican Party, Wasilla, 1976. Served with U.S. Army, 1955-58, USAF, 1960-64. U.S. Govt. edn. grantee, 1974-75, 75-76. Mem. Mo. Assn. Creation. Baptist. Led students to design and build 50-foot hist. totem pole, Wasilla, 1976. Home: 3647 Virginia Saint Louis MO 63118

JANKAS, ROBERT ANTHONY, podiatrist; b. Cleve., Jan. 23, 1956; s. Robert Anthony and Constance (Eberhard) J.; m. Denise Karen Vincent, Aug. 30, 1986; 1 child, Thomas Robert. BS, Ohio State U., 1978; D Podiatric Medicine, Ohio Coll. Podiatric Medicine, 1982. Resident in surgery Flint (Mich.) Gen. Hosp., 1982-83; podiatrist Family Devel. Programs, Inc., Athens, Ohio, 1983-86, Prau Health Services, Inc., Athens, 1986—; courtesy staff O'Bleness Meml. Hosp., Athens, 1983—; cons. staff Vets. Meml. Hosp., Pomeroy, Ohio, 1986—. fund-raiser Ohio U., Athens, 1984-86; mem. organizing com. Spl. Olympics, Athens, 1985-86, Athens area Hike for Hospice, 1986. Mem. Am. Podiatric Med. Assn., Ohio Podiatric Med. Assn., Athens Jaycees (pres. 1985, chmn. bd. 1986), Pi Delta. Home: 68 Pine Aire Village Athens OH 45702 Office: Southern Hills Podiatry Service 400 E State St Athens OH 45701

JANKOWSKI, FRANK DAVID, mechanical engineer; b. Cleve., Nov. 26, 1946; s. Frank Chester and Janet Agnes (Jakubowski) J.; m. Linda Elizabeth Pristas, Aug. 31, 1974. B.S. in Mech. Engring., Ohio U., 1969; M.S. in Mech. Engring., Cleve. State U., 1980; MBA Case Western Res. U., 1985. Registered profl. engr., Ohio, Mech. engr. Babcock & Wilcox, Akron, Ohio, 1969-71, Stone & Webster, Boston, 1971-74, 75; planner Toledo Edison, Ohio, 1974-75; engr. H.K. Ferguson, Cleve., 1975-77; sr. planner Cleve. Electric Illuminating, 1977—; co. rep. generation res. panel East Central Area Reliability Council. Co-author tech. paper. Mem. ASME. Republican. Roman Catholic. Avocations: Cross country skiing, golf. Home: 451 Sandhurst Dr Highland Heights OH 44143 Office: Centerior Energy PO Box 94661 Cleveland OH 44101-4661

JANNINCK, ROBERT FRANK, electronic materials scientist; b. Chgo., Feb. 28, 1935; s. William H. and Rose C. (Wirtz) J.; m. Danielle A. Janninck, June 25, 1966; children: James, Mark. BS in Metallurgy, U. Ill., 1957; MS in Materials Sci., Northwestern U., 1962, PhD in Materials Sci., 1963. Supr. GTE Communication Systems, Northlake, Ill., 1963-86; sr. prin. packaging engr. Siemens, Des Plaines, Ill., 1986—; adj. prof. Elmhurst (Ill.) Coll., 1965-66. Inventor magnetic liquid switch. NSF fellow, 1961. Mem. Internat. Soc. for Hybrid Microelectronics, Internat. Electronic Packaging Soc. Club: Wee C (Elmhurst). Office: Siemens 2000 Nuclear Dr Des Plaines IL 60018

JANOS, JOSEPH ALBERT, chemical company executive; b. Chgo., Jan. 3, 1941; s. Joseph Richard and Anna J. (Lopatkiewicz) J.; m. Joanne DeRaimo, June 19, 1965; children: Jennifer, Joseph Jr., Jeffrey. BS, U. Ill., 1968. CPA, Ill. Sr. acct. Ernst & Ernst, Chgo., 1968-73; asst. controller AAR Corp, Elk Grove Village, Ill., 1973-75; treas., controller Pansophic Systems, Inc., Oak Brook, Ill., 1975-78; controller Charlotte Charles, Chgo., 1978-81; treas. Gt. Lakes Terminal and Transport Corp., Chgo., 1981—. Pres. Lombard (Ill.) United Way, 1983-84, 86-87, St. Pius X Parish Council, Lombard, 1985-87. Mem. Am. Inst. CPA's, Ill. CPA Soc. Roman Catholic. Lodge: Lions (evening club pres. 1981-82). Home: 1019 E Adams St Lombard IL 60148 Office: Gt Lakes Terminal & Transp Corp 1750 N Kingsbury St Chicago IL 60614

JANOUSEK, JOEL EDWARD, physician, radiologist; b. Omaha, Apr. 23, 1950; s. Joseph John and Dorothy Catherine (Chadek) J. BS, Creighton U., 1972; MD, U. Nebr., 1975. Resident in diagnostic radiology Sch. Medicine, U. Kans., 1975-79; staff radiologist St Elizabeth Med. Ctr., Dayton, 1979—. Contbr. articles to profl. jour. Mem. AMA, Am. Coll. Radiology, Radiol. Assn. N.Am. Republican. Roman Catholic. Avocations: skiing, travel, skeet shooting, tennis, racquetball. Office: Med Radiologists Inc 111 W First St Suite 918 Dayton OH 45402

JANOV, BARRY ALLAN, dentist; b. Chgo., Oct. 21, 1935; s. Michael Morris and Idelle Elaine (Cutler) J.; m. Sandra Lee Wolf, Sept. 17, 1964; children—Jill Andrea, Robert Steven. B.S., U. Ill., 1957, D.D.S., 1959. Gen. practice dentistry, Chgo., 1961-75, Des Plaines, Ill., 1975—. Served to capt. U.S. Army, 1959-61. Mem. ADA, Ill. State Dental Soc., Chgo. Dental Soc., Am. Analgesia Soc., Acad. Gen. Dentistry, Acad. History of Dentistry, Antique Radio Club of Ill. (co-founder, v.p. 1980-85), Antique Radio Club of Am., Antique Wireless Assn., Ind. Hist. Radio Soc., Sigma Alpha Mu. Avocations: collecting antique dental and antique radio memorabilia. Home: 1304 Cariann Ln Glenview IL 60025 Office: 2434 Dempster St Des Plaines IL 60016

JANOVER, ROBERT H., lawyer; b. N.Y.C., Aug. 17, 1930; s. Cyrus J. and Lillian D. (Horwitz) J.; B.A., Princeton U., 1952; J.D., Harvard U., 1957; m. Mary Elizabeth McMahon, Oct. 23, 1966; 1 dau., Laura Lockwood. Admitted to N.Y. State bar, 1957, U.S. Supreme Ct. bar, 1961, D.C. bar, 1966, Mich. bar, 1973; practice law, N.Y.C., 1957-65; cons. Office of Edn. HEW, 1965, legis. atty. Office of Gen. Counsel, HEW, 1965-66; asst. gen. atty. Mgmt. Assistance Inc., N.Y.C., 1966-71; atty. Ford Motor Credit Co., Dearborn, Mich., 1971-74; mem. firm Freud, Markus, Slavin, Toohey & Galgan, Troy, Mich., 1974-79; sole practice law, Detroit, 1979—. Bd. dirs. Oakland Citizens League, 1976—, v.p., 1976-79, pres., 1979—; bd. dirs. Civic Searchlight, 1979—. Served to 1st lt. U.S. Army, 1952-54. Mem. Mich. State Bar, Am., N.Y. State, Detroit bar assns., Bar Assn. D.C., Assn. Bar of City of N.Y. Clubs: Univ., Players (Detroit), City (Bloomfield Hills), Harvard (N.Y.C.). Home: 685 Ardmoor Dr Birmingham MI 48010 Office: 21 E Long Lake Rd Suite 202 Bloomfield Hills MI 48013

JANOWAK, MICHAEL C., otolaryngologist, educator; b. Lake Geneva, Wis., July 28, 1948; s. Frank D. and Ida Mae (Flanagan) J.; m. Rosina Janowak; children: Julie, Hollis, Eric, Christopher. MD, Loyola U., Chgo., 1972. Resident in otolaryngology Med. Coll. of Wis., Milw., 1973-77; practice medicine specializing in otolaryngology Oconomowoc, Wis., 1977—; pres. Cen. Otologic, Ltd., Oconomowoc, 1977—; asst. clin. prof. otolaryngology Med. Coll. Wis., Milw., 1977—. Fellow Am. Acad. Otolaryngology, Milw. Soc. Head and Neck Medicine and Surgery (pres. 1986—); mem. AMA, Wis. Med. Assn. Office: 888 Thackeray Trail Oconomowoc WI 53066

JANSEN, CARL ALEXANDER, bank executive; b. Chgo., Jan. 1, 1944; s. Carl Gerhardt and Genevieve M. (Stefanski) J.; m. Barbara Jean Bilanski, Sept. 30, 1967; children: Mark, Michael, Peter. BS in Indsl. Relations, Rockhurst Coll., 1961-65; postgrad., John Marshall Law Sch., 1965-68. Constrn. loan mgr. Baird & Warner Co., Chgo., 1972-82; ops. mgr. real estate div., v.p. Nat. Blvd. Bank, Chgo., 1982—. Mem. Mortgage Bankers Assn. Republican. Roman Catholic. Clubs: Carlton, Rolling Green Country (Arlington Heights, Ill.). Avocations: golf, fishing, sailing. Home: 1422 Chalfont Rd Schaumburg IL 60194 Office: Boulevard Bank Nat Assn 410 N Michigan Ave Chicago IL 60611

JANSEN, LARRY PAUL, controller; b. Jefferson City, Mo., Dec. 18, 1955; s. Carl B. and Irma P. (Ihler) J.; m. Emily Jean Hoelscher, June 24, 1978; children: Eric David, Curtis Allan. BSBA in Accountancy, U. Mo., 1978. CPA, Mo. Auditor State of Mo., Jefferson City, 1978-83, dir. audits Dept. Social Services, 1983-85; internal auditor Mo. State Lottery, Jefferson City, 1985-86, controller, 1986—; speaker in field, 1984—. Mem. Am. Inst. CPA's, Assn. Govtl. Accts. Roman Catholic. Lodge: KC (sec.-treas. Jefferson City 1985-86). Avocations: tennis, golf, fishing, basketball. Home: 234 Eastland Dr Jefferson City MO 65101 Office: Missouri Lottery 1823 Southridge Jefferson City MO 65102

JANSSEN, JULIE ANN, dental hygienist; b. Rockford, Ill., Oct. 6, 1953; d. James Albert and Wilma Amelia (Loenser) Tracy; m. David Brent Janssen, Nov. 16, 1974. AAS, Lakeland Community Coll., 1976. Registered dental hygienist, Ill. Clin. dental hygienist Sullivan, Ill., 1976-78, Springfield, Ill., 1978-86; pub. health dental hygiene advisor State of Ill., Springfield, 1986—; mem. adv. com. So. Ill. U. Sch. Dental Hygiene, Carbondale, 1986—. Mem. exec. council Luth. Ch. Women, 1981—; mem. Jr. League Springfield, 1984—. Mem. Am. Dental Hygienists' Assn., Ill. Dental Hygienists' Assn., Springfield Area Dental Hygienists' Assn., Ill. Pub. Health Assn. Republican. Avocations: aerobics, swimming, skiing, gardening, sewing. Home: 409 Brandywine Rd Springfield IL 62704 Office: Ill Dept Pub Health Region 3 4500 S 6th St Rd Springfield IL 62706

JANSSEN, MARK ANTHONY, financial executive; b. Highland Park, Mich., Apr. 13, 1958; s. Vincent Steven and Virginia Bell (Melchin) J.; m. Kathy Ann Passfield, June 20, 1981; children: Kristopher Robert, Brandon John. B, U. Mich., 1980; MBA, Wayne State U., 1985. Staff auditor Mfrs. Hanover, N.Y.C., 1983, sr. auditor, 1983-84; compliance examiner Mfrs. Hanover, Farmington Hills, Mich., 1981-83, acctg. officer, 1984-86, asst. v.p., 1986—. Mem. Small Bus. Fund Drive United Found., Farmington Hills, 1986, YMCA, Farmington Hills, 1981—, asst. to fund drive, 1984. Mem. Common IBM, Inst. Internal Auditors. Roman Catholic. Avocations: skiing, boating, golf. Home: 4510 Marcello Milford MI 48042 Office: Mfrs Hanover 27555 Farmington Rd Farmington Hills MI 48018

JANSSEN, MARVIN RAY, protective services official; b. Galesburg, Kans., Sept. 24, 1946; s. Merritt Leon Sr. and Florence Loretta (Baird) J.; m. Diana Mae Poor, July 1, 1966; children: Craig Allen, Brent Aaron. AA, Labette Community Coll., 1966; BS, Wichita (Kans.) State U., 1973, MBA, 1981. Cert. law enforcement officer, Kans. Documentation technician Applied Automation, Inc., Bartlesville, Okla., 1968-72; police officer Wichita Police Dept., 1972-76, narcotics detective, 1976-77, police lt., 1977-82, police tng. lt., 1982-87, police capt., 1987—. Contbr. articles to profl. jours. Chmn. bd. elders Countryside Christian Ch., Wichita, 1986. Recipient Gold Valor award Kans. Assn. Chief's of Police, 1981, Silver Valor award Wichita Police Dept., 1981. Mem. Kans. Peace Officer's Assn. (vice chmn. tng. com. 1984—). Republican. Club: Litwin Toastmasters (pres. 1984-85). Avocations: bicycling, woodworking. Office: Wichita Police Dept 455 N Main Wichita KS 67202

JANUARY, LEWIS EDWARD, physician, educator; b. Haswell, Colo., Nov. 14, 1910; s. Frank Puleng and Estella (Miller) J.; m. Virginia Eloise Taylor, Sept 13, 1941; children: Alan Frank, Craig Taylor. B.A., Colo. Coll., 1933, D.Sc. (hon.), 1966; M.D., U. Colo., 1937. Diplomate: Am. Bd. Internal Medicine. Successively intern, resident internal medicine, asst. physician U. Ia. Hosps., 1937-42; mem. faculty U. Iowa Coll. Medicine, 1946—, prof. medicine, 1953-81, emeritus prof., 1981—, asso. chmn. for clin. programs dept. medicine, 1973-81, spl. asst. to chmn., 1981—; also dir. cardiovascular tng. program; mem. staff, dir. heart sta. U. Iowa Hosp., Iowa City, 1946-79; mem. staff VA Hosp., Iowa City.; Mem. Inter-Soc. Commn. for Heart Disease Resources, 1968-71; vis. prof. Ein Shams U., Cairo, Egypt, 1972; mem. cardiovascular tng. com. Nat. Heart and Lung Inst., 1972-74; mem. heart adv. com. Joint Commn. on Accreditation of Hosps., 1974. Author articles in field.; Editorial bd.: Circulation, 1969-74, Am. Heart Jour, 1974-80. Bd. dirs. Community Health, 1966-67, Found. for Joffrey Ballet, 1979—. Served to lt. col., M.C. AUS, 1942-46. Recipient Honors Achievement award Angiology Research Found., 1965; Gold Heart award Am. Heart Assn., 1969; Silver and Gold award U. Colo. Sch. Medicine, 1971; Helen B. Taussig award, 1972; Whitaker Teaching award Iowa Med. Soc., 1977; Internat. Achievement award Am. Heart Assn., 1977; spl. citation for disting. service to internat. cardiology, 1978; Tchr. of Yr. award U. Iowa, 1962, 81; Disting. Alumni award U. Iowa, 1983. Master A.C.P.; fellow Am. Coll. Cardiology, Council Clin. Cardiology (chmn. 1961-63); mem. AMA, Am. Clin. and Climatol. Assn. (council 1973-77), Am. Fedn. Clin. Research, Am. Heart Assn. (dir. 1955-71, pres. 1966-67, internat. program com. 1968-78), Iowa Heart Assn. (dir. 1948-52, heart fund chmn. 1963, pres. 1952-53), Assn. U. Cardiologists (council 1973-76), Am. Soc. Internal Medicine, AAUP, Central Soc. Clin. Research (council 1951-54), Central Clin. Research Club (pres. 1954), Iowa Clin. Med. Soc., Pan Am. Med. Soc. (life), Inter Am. Soc. Cardiology (dir. 1968-76), Internat. Cardiology Fedn. (v.p. 1970-78), Internat. Soc. and Fedn. Cardiology (exec. bd. 1976-78), Sigma Xi, Phi Delta Theta, Nu Sigma Nu, Alpha Omega Alpha. Club: University Athletic (Iowa City) (pres. 1961-64). Home: 3324 Hanover Ct Iowa City IA 52240

JANULIS, RONALD EDWARD, utilities executive; b. East Chicago, Ill., Nov. 12, 1950; s. Edward Lawrence and Leona (Solic) J.; m. Darlene Woolsey, Sept. 18, 1976; children: Paul Benjamin, Nathan Andrew, James Patrick. BA in Speech and Communication, John Carroll U., 1972; MBA, Cleve. State U., 1974. Br. sales mgr. Internat. Telephone & Telegraph Corp., South Bend, Ind. and Cleve., 1973-79; v.p. sales Drum Electronics, Detroit, 1979-82; pres. U.S. Telephone Corp., Detroit, 1982—. Mem. N. American Telecommunications Assn. Republican. Roman Catholic. Lodge: Lions (sec. Chippewa Lake, Ohio club 1978-79). Office: US Telephone Corp 34240 Van Dyke Sterling Heights MI 48077

JANUS, CHRISTOPHER GEORGE, writer; b. Charleston, W.Va., Mar. 25, 1911; s. George and Olympia (Xenopoulos) J.; m. Beatrice Short, May 30, 1940; children: Andronike, Christopher Jr., Lincoln. BS in Philosophy, Harvard U., 1936; postgrad., Oxford (Eng.) U., 1937. Registered rep. Prudential Bache, Chgo., 1955-80; cons. Standard Oil of Ind. (now Amoco), Chgo., 1978-82; prin. Eximport Assocs., Chgo., 1947—. Author: Miss 4th of July, Goodbye, 1986; (short stories) The George Quartette, 1983; co-author: The Search for Peking Man, 1976; pub.: Only for Your Eyes, 1955; Greek Heritage Quar., 1963-65. Econ. asst. U.S. Dept. State, Washington, 1943-44; chief Greek desk, chief Balkan intelligence UNRRA, Cairo, Egypt and Athens, Greece, 1944-45; alt. del. UNRRA Conf., Atlantic City, 1944; del. Time-Life Internat. Indsl. Devel. Cons., San Francisco, 1957, Fgn. Aid and Point Four Seminar, Washington, 1958, First Cultural Delegation from U.S. to People's Republic of China, 1972; trustee Poetry Mag., 1950-82, Athens Coll., 1951-52; mem. com. Mayor's Office for Sr. Citizens and Handicapped, 1981—, Friends of Chgo. Pub. Library, 1978; chmn. All Am. Com. United Rep. Fund of Ill. for Pres. Eisenhower Dinner, 1957-58. Served to lt. USNR, 1953-55. Recipient Services award Mus. Natural History, Beijing, 1979, Adelphi Achievement award Sta. WTTW, Washington, 1957, Spl. Commendation, Govt. of Greece, 1945, Friends of Lit. award for Best Novel, 1986. Mem. Nat. Probation and Parole Assn., Greek War Relief Assn. (chmn. Chgo. chpt. 1941-45). Clubs: Harvard, Overseas Press, Explorer's (New York); Harvard (pres. 1966-68), Caxton, Oxford-Cambridge, Tavern, Arts, Attic (Chgo.). Home: 1420 Sheridan Rd Wilmette IL 60091 Office: PO Box 10334 Chicago IL 60610

JANZEN, ERNST KRIJGERS, orthodontist; b. The Netherlands, Sept. 22, 1932; s. Willem Krijgers and Gerria (Noteboom) J.; D.D.S., Utrecht State U., The Netherlands, 1957; Ph.D., U. Zurich, Switzerland, 1962; D.D.S., Northwestern U., 1965, M.S., 1965; m. Agnes Pot, Jan. 24, 1959; children—Marita, Annette, Nicolette. Came to U.S., 1962, naturalized, 1967. Pvt. practice dentistry, specializing in orthodontics, Northbrook, Ill., 1966—; guest lectr. orthodontics Northwestern U. Served to capt., M.C., Royal Dutch Army, 1957-59. Recipient 1st prize Ann Research Contest, Am. Assn. Orthodontists, 1966, Milo Hellman Research award, 1966. Mem. Am. European, Ill. (exec. bd.) assns. orthodontists, Am. Dental Assn., Dutch Dental Soc. Republican. Presbyn. (trustee). Rotarian. Contbr. articles profl. jours. Home: 2240 Chestnut St Northbrook IL 60062 Office: 1220 Meadow Rd Northbrook IL 60062

JANZEN, NORINE MADELYN QUINLAN, medical technologist; b. Fond du Lac, Wis., Feb. 9, 1943; d. Joseph Wesley and Norma Edith (Gustin) Quinlan; B.S., Marian Coll., 1965; med. technologist St. Agnes Sch. Med. Tech., Fond du Lac, 1966; M.A., Central Mich. U., 1980; m. Douglas Mac Arthur Janzen, July 18, 1970; 1 son, Justin James. Med. technologist Mayfair Med. Lab., Wauwatosa, Wis., 1966-69; supr. med. technologist Dr.'s Mason, Chamberlain, Franke, Klink & Kamper, Milw., 1969-76, Hartford-Parkview Clinic, Ltd., 1976—. Substitute poll worker Fond du Lac Dem. Com., 1964-65; mem. Dem. Nat. Com., 1973—. Mem. Nat. Soc. Med. Technologists (awards com. 1984-87, chmn. 1986—), Wis. Assn. Med. Technologists (chmn. awards com. 1976-77, 84-85, 86-87, treas. 1977-81, pres.-elect 1981-82, pres. 1982-83, dir. 1977-84, 85-87, Mem. of Yr. 1982, numerous service awards, chair ann. meeting 1987-88), Milw. Soc. Med. Technologists (pres. 1971-72; dir. 1972-73), Communications of Wis. (originator, chmn. 1977-79), Southeastern Suprs. Group (co-chmn. 1976-77), LWV, Alpha Delta Theta (nat. dist. chmn. 1967-69; nat. alumnae dir. 1969-71), Methodist. Home: N 98 W 17298 Dotty Way Germantown WI 53022 Office: 1004 E Sumner St Hartford WI 53027

JARBOE, MARK ALAN, lawyer; b. Flint, Mich., Aug. 19, 1951; s. Lloyd Aloysius and Helen Elizabeth (Frey) J.; m. Patricia Kovel, Aug. 20, 1971; 1 child, Alexander. Student, No. Mich. U., 1968-69; AB with high distinction, U. Mich., 1972; JD magna cum laude, Harvard U., 1975. Bar: Minn. 1975, U.S. Dist. Ct. Minn. 1975, U.S. Ct. Appeals (8th cir.) 1975. Law clk. to presiding justice Minn. State Ct., St. Paul, 1975-76; from assoc. to ptnr. Dorsey & Whitney, Mpls., 1976—. Pres. parish council Ch. of Christ the King, Mpls., 1981-83. Mem. Phi Beta Kappa. Republican. Roman Catholic. Home: 4816 W Lake Harriet Pkwy Minneapolis MN 55410 Office: Dorsey & Whitney 2200 1st Bank Pl East Minneapolis MN 55402

JARETT, RHODA RONNIE, computer company executive; b. Boston, Apr. 2, 1930; d. Nathan J. and Etta (Herman) Goldman; m. Irwin M. Jarett, May 28, 1952; children: Andrew Robert, Debra Hope, Alex Scott. Degree med. sec., Chamberlyn Jr. Coll., 1949; student film, So. Ill. U., Edwardsville; student comedy, Webster Coll.; student mktg. and sales, Lincoln Land Community Coll. Mktg. staff Burke Mktg., St. Louis, 1971; buyer Assoc. Dry Goods, Springfield, Ill., 1973-76; mktg. rep. Diane Von Furstenburg, Springfield, Ill. and Ind., 1976-79; dir. adminstrn. Adminstrv. Learning, Springfield, 1979-81; dir. mktg. edn. I.M. Jarett & Assoc., Springfield, 1981-83; dir. mktg., mgr. telemtkg. Fingraph Corp., Springfield, 1983-84; chief exec. officer, cofounder Graphic M*I*S, Inc., Chgo., 1984—. Bd. dirs. YWCA, Springfield; awards and phonothon chmn. United Way Sangamon County, 1976. Mem. Women In Mgmt. (pub. relations chairperson 1985-86, hospitality chairperson 1986—), St. Louis Fedn. (Leadership award 1969), Nat. Assn. Women Bus. Owners (co-founder Springfield chpt. 1986). Am. Soc. Tgn. and Devel. (treas. cen. Ill. 1982-83). Home: 633 S Plymouth Ct Chicago IL 60605

JARKA, LEROY STANLEY, educator; b. Chgo., Apr. 21, 1961; s. Leonard Michael and Loretta Ann (Kaski) J. BA, St. Joseph Coll., Rensselear, Ind., 1983. Cert. secondary tchr., Ill. Tchr. and coach St. Patrick High Sch., Chgo., 1983—. Mem. Ill. Coach's Assn. Roman Catholic. Avocations: reading, playing team sports. Home: 7829 Hiawatha Woodridge IL 60517

JARMUSCH, ROLAND JOHN, pharmaceutical company executive; b. Cleve., Mar. 10, 1945; s. Joseph James and Ursula (Schlegel) J.; m. Mary P. Levin, Oct. 9, 1966; children: Kirsten P., Keith L. BS, U. Ariz., 1967; MBA, Rockhurst Coll., 1985. With Marion Labs., Inc., Phoenix, 1970—; dir. mktg. scientific div. Marion Labs., Inc., Kansas City, Mo., 1982-85, dir. mktg. pharmaceutical div., 1985—; bd. dirs Cliff Winn Realtors, Inc., Scottsdale, Ariz. Served with USN, 1967-70. Mem. Biomed. Mktg. Assn., Sales and Mktg. Execs. Roman Catholic. Avocations: golf, tennis, soccer, softball. Office: Marion Labs Inc 9300 Ward Pkwy Kansas City MO 64114

JAROSZCZYK, TADEUSZ, research engineer; b. Grezow, Poland, Dec. 10, 1938; came to U.S., 1981; s. Alesander and Zofia (Trojanek) J.; m. Dorota-Barbara Pieczara, Sept. 15, 1960; children—Malgorzata, Thomasz-Michal. Prodn. technician, Technicum of Mech. Engring.-Poland, 1956; Mech. Technician, Mil. Officers Sch. in Engring.-Poland, 1960; M.Sc. in Mech. Engring., Mil. Acad. Tech.-Warsaw, 1970; Ph.D., Mil. Acad. Tech., 1975. Process technician Warsaw Tool Assn., Poland, 1956-57; chief repair shop Mil. Service, Poland, 1960-65; mgr. filtration lab. Mil. Acad. Tech., Warsaw, 1970-77; mgr. filtration lab. Radom Inst. Tech., Poland, 1977-79; mgr. filtration and ventilation lab. Central Inst. Occupational Safety & Health, Warsaw, 1979-81; research engr. Nelson Industries, Inc., Stoughton, Wis., 1982—; air and oil filtration expert Polish Central Engrs. Assn., 1975-81. Co-author: Oil, Fuel and Air Filtration for Piston Engines, 1977; Filtration-Principles and Practices, 2d Edit., 1986. Contbr. articles to profl. jours. Inventor in field. Served to lt. col. Polish Army, 1957-77. Recipient 2d Degree Individual award Minister Sci., Higher Edn. and Tech., Warsaw, 1979; 3d Degree award, Minister Nat. Def., Warsaw, 1975. Mem. Soc. Automotive Engrs., Am. Soc. Testing and Materials. Avocations: travel, history. Home: 1231 Furseth Rd Stoughton WI 53589 Office: Nelson Industries Inc Hwy 51 W Box 600 Stoughton WI 53589

JAROSZEWSKI, LEO FRANCIS, hospital administrator; b. South Bend, Ind., Mar. 3, 1939; s. John Stephen and Dorothy (Przybysz) J.; m. Rozanne Zack, June 10, 1961; children: Mark Francis, Lisa Anne. BS, U. Notre Dame, 1961. Commd. 2d lt. USAF, 1961, advanced through grades to lt. col., 1978; hosp. adminstr. USAF, CamRanh Bay, Vietnam, 1970-71, Castle AFB, Calif., 1971-72; med. staff officer USAF Hdqrs., Washington, 1972-76; hosp. adminstr. USAF, George AFB, Calif., 1976-79, Vandenberg AFB, Calif., 1979-81; ret. USAF, 1981; adminstr. hosp. services St. Vincent Med. Ctr., Toledo, 1981—; bd. dirs. Substance Abuse Service Inc., vice chmn. program com. 1984-87. Pres. bd. dirs. St. Mary's Region Sch., Apple Valley, Calif., 1978; founding mem. Sylvania chpt. parents Helping Parents, 1982, treas., 1982-85. Mem. Am. Acad. Med. Adminstrs. (bd. dirs. 1978-80), Ohio Hosp. Assn. (bd. dirs. 1983-86), Soc. Engring. (bd. dirs. 1983-86). Roman Catholic. Lodge: Elks. Office: St Vincent Med Ctr 2213 Cherry St Toledo OH 43608

JARRELL, ROBERT HOMER, management consultant, accounting educator; b. Harrisburg, Ill., July 16, 1923; s. John L. and Catherine (Grace) J.; B.S., U. Ill., 1946; M.S., Ill. Inst. Tech., 1961; m. Elizabeth Jane Beidelman, Feb. 26, 1949; children—Katherine, Michael, Steven, Peter. Accountant, Ill. Farm Supply Co., 1947-50; asst. comptroller Ill. Inst. Tech., 1950-54, comptroller, 1954-62, bus. mgr., 1962-83, lectr. in acctg., 1961-82; treas. Argonne U. Assocs., 1979-83; owner, prin. Robert H. Jarrell & Assocs., mgmt. cons., Naperville, Ill., 1983—. Chmn. edn. div. Ill. Cancer Crusade, Am. Cancer Soc., 1960-63, 65, 66; mem. adv. bd. Salvation Army Settlement, Chgo., chmn., 1975-77; mem. pub. edn. com. Chgo. unit Am. Cancer Soc., vice chmn., 1974-79, chmn., 1979-81; mem. adv. com. Sch. Dist. 203, 1967, 71-72; town clk. Lisle Twp., 1973—; jury commr. 18th Jud. Dist. Ill., 1975—, chmn., 1979—; chmn. Lisle Twp. Republican Orgn., 1976-78; mem. exec. com. Du Page County Central Rep. Com., 1976-78. Mem. Fin. Execs. Inst. (sec. 1964-65), Nat. Assn. Ednl. Buyers (sec.-treas. Ill.-Wis. sect. 1969, chmn. 1971), Nat., Central assns. coll. and univ. bus. officers, Alpha Kappa Psi, Delta Sigma Rho. Republican. Congregationalist. Club: Rotary. Home: 1204 Cardinal Ln Naperville IL 60540

JARRETT, JERRY VERNON, banker; b. Abilene, Tex., Oct. 31, 1931; s. Walter Elwood and Myrtle Elizabeth (Allen) J.; m. Martha Ann McCabe, June 13, 1953; children: Cynthia Ann, Charles Elwood, Christopher Allen, John Carlton. B.B.A., U. Okla., 1957; M.B.A., Harvard U., 1963. Gen. sales mgr. Tex. Coca-Cola Bottling Co., Abilene, 1957-61; exec. v.p. Marine Midland Bank, N.Y.C., 1963-73; exec. v.p. Ameritrust Co., 1973-76, vice chmn., 1976-78, chmn., chief exec. officer, 1978—; chmn., chief exec. officer Ameritrust Corp. Co-author: Creative Collective Bargaining, 1964. Served with USAAF, 1950-54. Mem. Phi Gamma Delta. Home: 2751 Chesterton Rd Shaker Heights OH 44122 Office: Ameritrust Corp 900 Euclid Ave PO Box 5937 Cleveland OH 44101 *

JARRETT, JOHN C., II, obstetrician, gynecologist; b. Cleve., Dec. 25, 1950; s. John Crow and Mary Louise (Gilmore) J.; m. Cynthia L. Jarrett, Aug. 12, 1973 (div. Mar. 1986); children: Jennifer, Jay, Casey. BA, Princeton U., 1973; MD, Case Western Res. U., 1977. Diplomate Am. Bd. Ob-Gyn. Resident in ob-gyn. U. Mich., Ann Arbor, 1977-81; instr. ob-gyn. U. Ill., Chgo., 1981-83, asst. prof. ob-gyn., 1983-84; asst. prof. ob-gyn. Ind. U., Indpls., 1984-85; ob-gyn. Pregnancy Initiation Ctr., Indpls., 1985—, also bd. dirs. Contbr. articles to profl. jours. Fellow Am. Coll. Ob-Gyns.; mem. Am. Fertility Soc., Soc. Reproductive Endocrinologists, Soc. Reproducitve Surgeons, Cen. Assn. Ob-Gyns (Prize award 1983), Alpha Omega Alpha, Am. Diabetes Assn. (Citation 1983). Avocations: running, skiing, biking, carpentry. Home: 10720 Downing Carmel IN 46032 Office: Pregnancy Initiation Ctr 8091 Township Line Rd Suite 110 Indianapolis IN 46260

JARVIS, WALTER LEROY, counselor; b. Omaha, Jan. 28, 1947; s. Clark Boyd and Leta Arlene (Taylor) J.; m. Judith Clair Cusick, June 12, 1970 (dec. Feb. 1980); children: Heather Anne, Rebecca Lynn; m. Sharon Marie Hallett, May 1, 1985; children: Thomas Allen, Anthony Lee. BA in Criminal Justice, U.S. Army Sch. Mil. Intelligence, Balt., 1977; postgrad., U. Nebr., Omaha, 1980—, Bellevue Coll., 1982—. Cert. domestic violence, alcohol and drug abuse, gen. victimology counselor, others, Nebr. Founder, adminstr. Victim-Witness Unit Sarpy County Attys. Office, Papillion, Nebr.; domestic abuse caseworker and counselor family services Sarpy County United Way; counselor Johnson Inst., Mpls.; victim specialist Metro Law Enforcement Agy., 1984—. State Probation Office, Sarpy County Atty.'s Office, Sarpy County Dist. Ct., Sarpy County Ct.; probation officer, victim specialist, State of Nebr., 1982-84; advisor victim rights and services Nebr. Dept. Social Services, 1985—, Pottawatamie County, Iowa County Atty.'s Office, 1987; mem. family services Sarpy County Domestic Abuse Ctr., 1982—; lectr. in field. Author: Victim-Witness Unit Services Dictionary; contbr. articles on domestic abuse to profl. jours. Nebr. founder Adminstr. Victim Witness Unit, 1982—; mem. domestic abuse program United Way, 1981—, Sarpy County Abuse and Neglect Services, 1986—, adv. bd., 1987—. Served to capt. U.S. Army, 1966-73, Vietnam. Decorated Silver Star, Purple Heart with four oak leaf clusters; named Program Counselor Yr., Sarpy County Family Service; U.S. Justice Dept. grantee, 1985, Sarpy County, 1984, 85, 86; recipient Outstanding Contributor to Bellevue Pub. Schs. award, 1983-84; nominee Jefferson award, 1987. Mem. Nebr. Assn. Addiction (counselor), Nat. Orgn. Victim Assistance (mem. elderly victims com., law enforcement com., sexual assault com., victim restitution com., subcom. of victim assistance 1986—), Alcoholism/Drug Counselor Training Insts. Nebr. (cert.), Nat. Assn. State Dirs. of Law Enforcement Trainers (cert.), Mothers Against Drunk Drivers, Nebr. Crime Prevention Assn., Bellevue C. of C., Nebr. Coalition on Victims of Crime (regional v.p. 1984-86, mem. at large 1986—), VFW (nat. polit. action com. 1983-85), Disabled Am. Vets. (life). Lodge: Eagles. Avocation: antiques. Home: 1013 Bert Murphy Blvd Bellevue NE 68005 Office: Sarpy County Atty Office Victim Witness Unit 1210 Golden Gate Dr Papillion NE 68046

JASKIE, WALTER EDWARD, financial planner, accountant; b. Cleve., Jan. 5, 1940; s. Edward Walter and Helen Charolette (Derwis) J.; m. Ann Marie Narduzzi, Aug., 24, 1963; children: Lynn Ann, Karen Elizabeth. BBA, Cleve. State U., 1970, MBA, 1973. CPA, Ohio; cert. fin. planner; registered investment advisor. Internal auditor Ford Motor Co., Cleve., 1968—; pvt. practice acctg. Cleve., 1983—. Served with U.S. Army, 1958-61. Recipient award Bausch and Lomb Optical Co., 1957. Mem. Inst. Cert. Fin. Planners. Home and Office: 14025 Pawnee Trail Middleburg Heights OH 44130

JASMON, ROBERT LAWRENCE, transportation executive; b. Springfield, Ill., Dec. 14, 1936; s. Lawrence G. and Helen L. (McReynolds) J.; m. Norma J. Sexton, Oct. 22, 1955; children: Michael, Mark, Richard, Joseph. BA, Bradley U., Peoria, Ill., 1958. Engring. designer Sangamo Electric Co., Springfield, Ill., 1958-63; fieldman, exec. sec. Tri-State Trucking Assn., Springfield, 1963-65; salesman Charles Bruning div. A-M Corp., Springfield, 1965-68; asst. mgr. Nat. Elect. Contractors Assn., Springfield, 1968-69; purchasing agt. office of Sec. of State State of Ill., Springfield, 1969-72; exec. v.p. Mid-West Trucking Assn., Springfield, 1972—; industry advisor Nat. Gov.'s Conf. Washington, 1984-87; mem. trucking safety task force State of Ill., Springfield, 1987. Mem. exec. com. Sangamon County Rep. Cen. Com., Springfield, 1976—; trustee Capitol Twp., Springfield, 1977—. Mem. Am. Soc. Assn. Execs., Ill. Soc. Assn. Execs. (pres. 1979), Am. Trucking Benevolent Assn. (treas. 1980-86), Springfield Jr. C. of C. (v.p. 1960-61), Springfield C. of C. (transp. com. 1980—). Baptist. Club: Am. Bus. Club. Home: 555 W Elliott Springfield IL 62702 Office: Mid-West Truckers Assn 2715 N Dirksen Pkwy Springfield IL 62702

JASMUND, NORMAN WILLIAM, social worker; b. Detroit, May 5, 1956; s. Norman Lee and Beverly Jean (Hall) J.; m. Kathleen Ann Priest, June 3, 1978; 1 child, Emily Kate. BA in Psychology, Spring Arbor Coll., 1978; MSW, Mich. State U., 1984. Cert. Acad. Cert. Social Workers. Psychiat. med. aide State of Mich. Correction Ctr., Ionia, 1979-84; clin. social worker Dickinson County Counseling Ctr., Kingsford, Mich., 1984—; adj. instr. psychology Bay De Noc Community Coll., Escanaba, Mich., 1985—; cons., specialist Dickinson County Corrections Ctr., Iron Mountain, Mich., 1986—. Named Outstanding Vol., Lansing Vol. Action Agy., 1981. Mem. Nat. Assn. Social Workers. Democrat. Mem. Covenant Ch. Avocations: outdoor sports, banjo, guitar. Home: 208 Iron St Norway MI 49870 Office: Dickinson County Counseling Ctr 715 Pyle Dr Kingsford MI 49801

JASTRAM, STEVEN RICHARD, architect; b. Sioux Falls, S.D., Jan. 28, 1953; s. Richard Louis and Mary Margaret (Hooshagen) J.; m. Vicki Lynn Olson, June 8, 1973; children: Mark, Kristy. BArch, Iowa State U., 1971-75. Registered architect, Iowa, S.D. Intern Beutler & Assocs., Sioux City, Iowa, 1975-77, Koch, Hazard & Assoc., Sioux Falls, S.D., 1977-80; project architect Arch. Inc., Sioux Falls, 1980—. Chmn. sch. bd. Sioux Falls Luth. Sch. Assn., 1980-85. Mem. AIA, S.D. AIA, Sioux Falls Architects Forum, Sioux Falls Jaycees (bd. dirs. 1979-80). Democrat. Lutheran. Home: 2100 S Norton Sioux Falls SD 57105 Office: Arch Inc 335 N Main Sioux Falls SD 57102

JASTRZEBSKI, RONALD JOSEPH, auditor; b. Chgo., Apr. 21, 1959; s. Joseph and Eleanore (Fluder) J.; m. Cheryl Maire B., July 16, 1983; children: Matthew Joseph, Kristin Marie. BBA, Loyola U., Chgo., 1981. CPA, Ill. Acct., auditor State Ill. Commerce Commn., Chgo., 1981-84; cost analyst Gas Research Inst., Chgo., 1984-86; operational auditor Keebler Co., Elmhurst, Ill., 1986—. Mem. Am. Inst. CPA's, Ill. CPA Soc. Roman Catholic. Home: 2335 S 10th Ave North Riverside IL 60546

JAVORNIK, STEVEN VLADO, business systems analyst; b. Buffalo, June 11, 1955; s. Ladislav William and Anne (Stegmaier) J.; m. Kathi Jean King, June 2, 1979; children: Amy, Ross. BS in Bus., Bowling Green State U., 1977, MBA, 1981. Systems analyst Allied-Signal, Fostoria, Ohio, 1981—. Mem. Am. Prodn. and Inventory Control Soc. (v.p. 1984), Nat. Mgmt. Assn. (chmn. 1985), U.S. Chess Fedn. Republican. Methodist. Avocations: family, golf, chess, gardening. Home: 1262 N County Rd #5 Fostoria OH 44830 Office: Allied Corp Box 880 Fostoria OH 44830

JAVOROSKI, LYNN ANNE, architect; b. N.Y.C., Aug. 13, 1943; d. Charles Marshall and Dorothy Fannie (Watova) Kane; m. Robert Steven Javoroski, Feb. 21, 1970; children: Scott David, Thomas Kane. BA in Psychology, Queen's Coll., 1966; MArch, U. Wis., Milwaukee, 1985. Research asst. Abilities, Inc., Albertson, N.Y., 1966-70; architect J/K Architecture, Hustisford, Wis., 1983—. Mem. AIA, Wis. Soc. Architects. Lutheran. Home: N 5106 Butternut Ct Juneau WI 53039 Office: J/K Architecture 130 N Lake St Hustisford WI 35034

JAY, DAVID EDWARD, lawyer, consultant; b. Canton, Ohio, June 15, 1954; s. Alfred Warren and Elaine Lois (Minkow) J. BS, Ohio State U., 1976; JD, U. Akron, Ohio, 1979. Bar: Ohio 1979, U.S. Dist. Ct. (no. dist.) 1980. Assoc. Kramer, Helling & Kramer, Canton, Ohio, 1979-80; sole practice Canton, 1980-83; ptnr. David E. Jay & Assocs., Canton, 1983-85, Jay & Weltman, Canton, 1985—; pres. Jay Fin. Planning, Inc., Canton, 1985—. Chmn. fund raising St. Jude Bike-A-Thon, Canton, 1986. Recipient Gary Shifman Athletic award Canton Jewish Community Ctr., 1972, A.L. Helling Athletic award, 1981. Mem. Ohio State Bar Assn., Stark County Bar Assn., Stark County Trial Lawyers Assn., Internat. Assn. Fin. Planning, Canton Jaycees. Democrat. Jewish. Lodge: Rotary. Avocation: athletics. Home: 5524 Glenhill NE North Canton OH 44721 Office: Jay & Weltman 4884 Dressler Rd NW Canton OH 44718

JAY, STEPHEN JORDAN, physician, researcher, educator; b. Indpls., June 2, 1941; s. Arthur Nottingham and Hilda (Jordan) J.; m. Anne Marie Beegan, July 12, 1969; children—Stephen, Audrey, Matthew, Alan. Student, Wabash Coll., 1959-62; M.D., Ind. U., Indpls., 1966. Diplomate Am. Bd. Internal Medicine. Intern Parkland Hosp., Dallas, 1966-67; resident in medicine Parkland Hosp., 1969-71, fellow in pulmonary medicine, 1971-73; asst. prof. medicine U. Tex. Health Sci. Ctr., Dallas, 1973-74, U. Ky. Med. Ctr., Lexington, 1974-76; assoc. prof., chief pulmonary sect. Wishard Hosp.-Ind. U. Sch. Medicine, 1976-80, prof., asst. dean, 1980—; sr. v.p. acad. affairs and info. services Methodist Hosp. Ind., Indpls., 1980—. Editor Manual of Pulmonary Procedures, 1980, Use and Impact of Computers in Clinical Medicine, 1987; contbr. chpts. to books, articles to profl. jours. Pres. Am. Lung Assn. Ind., 1986-87. Served to lt. USN, 1967-69. Recipient award in recognition excellence of sci. paper Am. Assn. Med. Systems and Informatics, 1983. Fellow Am. Coll. Chest Physicians, ACP; mem. AAAS, Am. Fedn. Clin. Research, Royal Soc. Medicine, AMA, Ind. Thoracic Soc. (pres.), Assn. Am. Med. Colls., Assn. Hosp. Med. Edn. (pres. elect), Sigma Xi, Alpha Omega Alpha. Methodist. Office: Methodist Hosp Ind Inc 1701 N Senate Blvd Indianapolis IN 46202

JAYAPRAKASARAO, KONIJETI, radiologist; b. Ongole, India, Jan. 5, 1946; came to U.S., 1976; s. Veeraraghavulu and Padmavatamma (Talluri) K.; m. Jayaprada Kollipara, May 27, 1973; children: Jayakrishnakamal, Ramdev. PUC, CSR Sarma Coll., Ongole, India, 1962; MD, HKE Socs. Med. Sch., Gulbarga, India, 1968; DMRD, Guntur (India) Med. Coll., 1975. Cert. in radiology and spl. competence in nuclear medicine Am. Bd. Radiology. Resident in radiology Columbus Hosp., Chgo., 1976-79; resident in nuclear medicine Northwest Meml. Hosp., Chgo., 1979-80; staff radiologist, section chief nuclear medicine VA Med. Ctr., Kansas City, Mo., 1981—. Mem. Radiol. Soc. N. Am., Soc. Nuclear Med. Home: 12000 Wenonga Leawood KS 66209 Office: VA Med Ctr 4801 Linwood Blvd Kansas City MO 64123

JAYDOS, ROBERT ANTHONY, architect; b. Chgo., Feb. 5, 1938; s. Anthony Walter and Angeline Rita J.; B.Arch., U. Ill., 1968; children by previous marriage—Robert Anthony, Christine Marie, Shari Anne. Designer, Perkins & Will, Chgo., 1968-69; designer, asst. job capt. Loebl, Schlossman, Bennett & Dart, Chgo., 1969-71; draftsman Graham, Anderson, Probst & White, Chgo., 1971-72; job capt. Marshall Lieb & Assocs., Chgo., 1972-73; pres., design cons. Smith & Jaydos Inc., Elk Grove Village, Ill., owner, operator Jaydos & Assocs., Architects Ltd., Elk Grove Village, 1973-80, pres., 1980—, Jaydos and Assocs., Architects, Ltd. Served with USAF, 1955-59. Mem. Easter Seals Com., 1983. Registered architect, Ill., Nebr., Iowa, Ohio; lic. comml. pilot. Mem. AIA, Nat. Council Archtl. Registration Bds., U. Ill. Alumni Assn. (life), Art Inst. Chgo. Club: Rotary. Office: Jaydos & Assocs Architects Ltd 414 N Orleans Chicago IL 60610

JAYNE, EDWARD RANDOLPH, II, aerospace company executive; b. Kirksville, Mo., Sept. 24, 1944; s. Edward Randolph and Marietta (Jonas) J.; m. Nancy Elizabeth King, June 18, 1966; children: Kathryn Eden, Matthew Randolph. BS, USAF Acad., 1966; PhD, MIT, 1969. Commd. 2d lt. USAF, 1966, advanced through ranks to lt. col., resigned, 1977; staff mem. NSC, Washington, 1976-77; assoc. dir. Office of Mgmt. and Budget, Washington, 1977-80; dir. aerospace planning Gen. Dynamics Corp., St. Louis, 1980-84, v.p. corp. planning, 1984—. Author: Monograph: The ABM Debate-Strategic Defense and National Security, 1969. Bd. dirs. Falcon Found. USAF Acad., Colo., 1984—, Dem. Bus. Council, Washington, 1984—. Serve as lt. col. USAFNG, 1976—. Decorated Silver Star with one oak leaf cluster; White House fellow. Mem. Air Force Assn., N.G. Assn. U.S., Mo. N.G., USAF Acad. Assn. of Grads. Office: Gen Dynamics Corp Pierre LaClede Ctr Saint Louis MO 63105

JAYNES, ROBERT HENRY, JR., military officer; b. Greeneville, Tenn., Feb. 6, 1948; s. Robert Henry and Della Mae (Broyles) J.; m. Peggy Jane Farmer, Dec. 24, 1981. BS, East Tenn. State U., 1970. Pilot 57th assault helicopter co. U.S. Army, Republic of Vietnam, 1972-73; advanced through grades to lt. col. U.S. Army, 1987; co. commdr. U.S. Army, Ft. Jackson, S.C., 1976-78; aviation tng. developer and evaluator for directory evaluation and standardization U.S. Army, Ft. Rucker, Ala., 1978-80; battalion advisor Alaska NG U.S. Army, Kotzebue, 1980-81; exec. officer recruiting battalion U.S. Army, San Juan, P.R., 1981-84; student and staff group leader Command and Gen. Staff Coll. U.S. Army, Ft. Leavenworth, Kans., 1986—; officer-in-charge Allied Officer Hall of Fame U.S. Army Command and Gen Staff Coll., 1984-85; exec. officer U.S. Army Space Initiatives Study, Washington; vice chief of staff U.S. Army Space Council, 1985. Contbr. articles to profl. jours. Mem. Leavenworth Computer Council (pres. 1986—). Decorated Bronze Star. Mem. Assn. U.S. Army, Army Aviation Assn. Am. (v.p. membership 1975-76, v.p. student affairs 1986—), Recreational Equiptment Assn., Scabbard & Blade. Avocations: hunting, fishing, camping, computers, automobiles. Home: 710 Englewood Lansing KS 66043 Office: US Army Command and Gen Staff Coll Fort Leavenworth KS 66027

JEANNERET, JOHN JOSEPH, process engineering executive; b. N.Y.C., Nov. 12, 1958; s. John Joseph Hilderbrand and Irene Margaret (Ferstler) Hunter; m. Yvonne M. Jeanneret, Jan. 1, 1982; children: Derek, Danielle. Student, Purdue U., 1976-78; BSChemE, U. Wis., 1980; MBA, U. Chgo., 1986. Process engr. UOP Inc., Des Plaines, Ill., 1980—. Mem. Am. Inst. Chem. Engrs. Avocations: golf, volleyball, skiing, camping. Home: 1414 Odgen Ave La Grange IL 60525 Office: UOP Inc Drawer C Des Plaines IL 60016

JECK, ROBERT VAN HOUTEN, manufacturing company executive; b. Atlantic, Iowa, Oct. 8, 1931; s. George Van Houten and Gladys (Thomson) J.; m. Beverly Jean Braniff, July 9, 1955; children: Thomas, Tamara, Cynthia. B.S., Iowa State U., 1952; postgrad., London Sch. Econs., 1955-57; M.B.A., Wharton Sch., U. Pa., 1958; A.M.P., Harvard U. Bus. Sch., 1973. With E.I. Dupont de Nemours, Wilmington, Del., 1958-67; pres. div. Amerace Corp., Butler, N.Y., 1968-79; pres., dir. Truck Safety Equipment Co., 1970-77; v.p. corp. Amerace Corp., Butler, N.Y., 1972-79, group v.p. corp., 1972-79; pres. Worthington div. McGraw Edison Co, Basking Ridge, N.J., 1979-85; pres., chief exec. officer ONAN Corp., Mpls., 1985-86; pres. Specialty Metals div. Engelhard Corp., Iselin, N.J., 1986—; v.p. Engelhard Corp., Iselin, N.J., 1986—. Served to lt. USN, 1953-57. Mem. Soc. Automotive Engrs., Motor and Equipment Mfrs. Assn. (chmn., bd. dirs. 1976-79), Soc. Plastics Engrs. Episcopalian. Clubs: Iverness Country (Ill.); Baltusrol Golf (Springfield, N.J.).

JECKLIN, LOIS U., art corporation executive, consultant; b. Manning, Iowa, Oct. 5, 1934; d. J.R. and Ruth O. (Austin) Underwood; m. Dirk C. Jecklin, June 24, 1955; children—Jennifer Anne, Ivan Peter. Student State U. Iowa, 1953-55, 60-61, 74-75. Residency coordinator Quad City Arts Council, Rock Island, Ill., 1973-78; field rep. Affiliate Artists, Inc., N.Y.C., 1975-77; mgr., artist in residence Deere & Co., Moline, Ill., 1977-80; dir. Vis. Artist Series, Davenport, Iowa, 1978-81; pres. Vis. Artists, Inc., Davenport, 1981—; cons. writer's program St. Ambrose Coll., Davenport, 1981, 83, 85; mem. com. Iowa Arts Council, Des Moines, 1983-84; panelist Chamber Music Am., N.Y.C., 1984, Pub. Art Conf., Cedar Rapids, Iowa, 1984; panelist, mem. com. Lt. Gov.'s Conf. on Iowa's Future, Des Moines, 1984. Trustee Davenport Mus. Art, Nature Conservancy Iowa; mem. steering com. Iowa Citizens for Arts, Des Moines, 1970-71; bd. dirs. Tri-City Symphony Orchestra Assn., Davenport, 1968-83; founding mem. Urban Design Council, HOME, City of Davenport Beautification Com., all Davenport, 1970-72. Recipient numerous awards Izaak Walton League, Davenport Art Gallery, Assn. for Retarded Citizens, Am. Heart Assn., Ill. Bur. Corrections, many others; LaVernes Noyes scholar, 1953-55. Mem. Am. Council for Arts, Ptnrs. for Livable Places, Ann. Coll. Univ. Community Arts Adminstrs., Nat. Assembly Local Arts Agys., Crow Valley Golf Club. Republican. Episcopalian. Club: Outing. Lodge Rotary. Home: 2717 Nichols Ln Davenport IA 52803 Office: Vis Artists Inc 106 E 3rd St Suite 220 Davenport IA 52801

JECMEN, JOHN JOSEPH, manufacturing company executive; b. Chgo., Jan. 16, 1916; s. James and Marie (Steker) J.; student DePaul U., 1933-37, Ill. Inst. Tech., 1942; m. Betty R. Malek, June 18, 1938. Chmn. bd. Harris Preble Co., Cicero, Ill., 1933—. Named Man of Achievement, London, Export Exec. of Yr.-World Trade conf., 1982. Mem. adv. council coll. commerce, DePaul U. Mem. NAM, Dist. Export Council, Nat. Assn. Elevator Contractors, Can. Elevator Contract Assn., Ill. Mfrs. Assn., Cicero (Ill.) Mfrs. Assn., Mat. Safety Council, Internat. Bus. Council, Execs. Club Chgo., Chgo. Assn. Commerce and Industry, Briarwood Lakes Community Assn., French-Am. C. of C., Finnish-Am. C. of C., German-Am. C. of C., Mid-Am. Arab C. of C., U.S. C. of C., U.S. Golf Assn., Western Golf Assn., Beta Gamma Sigma (hon.). Club: Butterfield Country (Oak Brook, Ill.). Lodge: Moose. Patentee in field. Home: 210 Briarwood Pass Oak Brook IL 60521 Office: 4608 W 20th St Chicago IL 60650

JEDLICKA, DIANE SCHWEDE, nursing educator; b. Cleve., June 20, 1946; d. Harold Edward and Elsie Margaret (Hatala) Schwede; m. Ronald Louis Jedlicka, May 10, 1975; children: Peter Louis, Dana Marie, Michael Louis. RN, St. Vincent Charity Hosp., 1967; BS in Nursing, Ohio State U., 1972, MS, 1976. Clinic nurse Ohio State U. Hosp., Columbus, 1969, ICU nurse, 1970-72; staff nurse Appalachian Regional Hosp., McDowell, Ky., 1969-70; instr. Grant Hosp. Sch. Nursing, Columbus, Ohio, 1972-80, staff devel. instr., 1980-81; asst. prof. Otterbein Coll., Westerville, Ohio, 1981—; flight nurse Grant Hosp., 1985—; critical care cons. ANCER, 1983—; lectr., cons. Continuing Profl. Edn., 1980-85; lectr. Profl. Med. Edn., Grove City, Ohio, 1979-85; instr. advanced cardiac life support Am. Heart Assn., 1986; basic trauma life support instr. ACS, 1986. Mem. Am. Assn. Critical Care Nurses (critical care RN cert.), Nat. Flight Nurses Assn., Sigma Theta Tau. Home: 475 S Main St Pataskala OH 43062 Office: Otterbein Coll Dept Nursing Westerville OH 43081

JEE, JUSTIN SOONHO, accountant; b. Pusan, Korea, June 29, 1951; came to U.S., 1976; s. Hanwoong and Boksoo (Park) J.; m. Ahyung Lee, May 2, 1976. BS, U. Korea, 1976; BS in Acctg., U. Minn., 1980; MBA, San Diego State U., 1984. CPA, Minn. Tax acct. Midway Nat. Bank, St. Paul, 1981-83; fin. analyst Medical, Inc., Inver Grove Heights, Minn., 1984-87; staff acct. Internat. Trade Adminstrn., Import Adminstrn., U.S. Dept. Commerce, Washington, 1987—; cons. Bus. Devel. Ctr., San Diego, 1984. Mem. Am. Inst. CPA's, Minn. Soc. CPA's, Inst. Cert. Mgmt. Accts. (cert.). Avocations: classical music, poetry.

JEFFE, SIDNEY DAVID, automotive engineer; b. Chgo., May 6, 1927; s. J.I. Jeffe; children: Robert A., Leslie A. B.S. with honors in Mech. Engring., Ill. Inst. Tech., 1950; M.S. with honors in Automotive Engring., Chrysler Inst. Engring., 1952; grad. program for execs., Carnegie-Mellon U., 1968. With Chrysler Corp., 1950-80, v.p. engring. and research, 1976-80; sr. v.p. ops. Sheller Globe Corp., Detroit, 1982-86, sr. v.p. internat. bus. and tech. devel. and implementation, head customer and govt. relations activities, 1986—; exec. dir. Transp. Research Center Ohio, E. Liberty; prof. mech. engring. Ohio State U., 1980-82; sec.-treas. Transp. Research Bd. Ohio, 1980-82; mem. bd. Engring. Sch., Oakland U., 1977—; bd. dirs. Sheller-Ryobi Corp. Author papers in field. Served with AUS, 1945-47. Fellow Engring. Soc. Detroit, Soc. Automotive Engrs. (Russell Springer award 1957, Coll. Fellows 1985—); mem. Tau Beta Pi (Outstanding New Mem. award 1948), Pi Tau Sigma (Outstanding New Mem. award 1948). Unitarian. Clubs: Orchard Lake Country, Detroit Athletic, Ren Cen. Home: 3673 Quail Hollow Bloomfield Hills MI 48013 Office: Sheller Globe Corp 1641 Porter St Detroit MI 48216

JEFFERS, DONALD E., executive recruiter, consultant; b. Louisville, Ill., Aug. 21, 1925; s. Byron V. and Alice B. (Burgess) J.; m. Marion D. Benna, Aug. 14, 1948 (dec.); 1 son, Derek; m. Janice C. Smith, Apr. 21, 1979. B.S. in Accountancy, U. Ill., 1948. C.P.A., Ill., D.C. Sr. accountant Coopers & Lybrand, CPA's, N.Y.C. and Chgo., 1948-56; asst. v.p. Continental Casualty Co., Chgo., 1956-64; dep. comptroller First Nat. Bank Boston, 1965-67; exec. v.p., treas. Interstate Nat. Corp., Chgo., 1967-74; pres., chief exec. officer Interstate Nat. Corp., 1974-85, also dir.; chmn., dir. Interstate Ins. Group and Geo. F. Brown & Sons Inc.; chmn. Jeffers & Assocs., Inc., Chgo., 1985—; former sec., dir. Ill. Ins. Info. Service. Served with inf. AUS, 1943-45. Decorated Purple Heart. Mem. Am. Inst. CPA's, Ill. Soc. CPA's. Clubs: Chicago, Economic (Chgo.). Home: 860 N Lake Shore Dr Chicago IL 60611 Office: 919 N Michigan Ave Chicago IL 60611

JEFFERS, THOMAS ARTHUR, building products company executive; b. Harbor Beach, Mich., Nov. 15, 1938; s. Robert A. and Bernice M. (Brown) J.; A.A., Graceland Coll., Iowa, 1958; B.B.A., U. Mich., 1961, M.B.A., 1962; m. Arlene Joyce Brown, Aug. 8, 1964; children—Daniel, Timothy, Julie, Sandra, Laurie. Jr. to sr. auditor Price Waterhouse, CPAs, 1962-68; asst. controller Wolverine Techs. Inc., Dearborn, Mich., 1968-70, controller, 1970-75, v.p. fin., 1975-80, v.p., treas., 1980—, dir., 1973—. Bd. dirs. S.E. Mich. chpt. Nat. Youth Devel. Found., 1971—, former treas.; minister Reorganized Ch. Jesus Christ Latter-day Saints; bd. dirs. Detroit Internat. Stake Adult Housing Corp., 1978—, pres., 1979—. Served with USAR, 1962-68. Mem. Mich. Assn. C.P.A.s, Am. Inst. C.P.A.s, Am. Mgmt. Assn., Nat. Investor Relations Inst. (past sec. Detroit chpt.), Fin. Execs. Inst. Home: 18961 Blair Ct Allen Park MI 48101 Office: Four Parklane Blvd Dearborn MI 48126

JEFFERSON, ARTHUR, ednl. adminstr.; b. Ala., Dec. 1, 1938; (married); 2 children. B.S., Wayne State U., 1960, M.A. in Polit. Sci, 1963, Ed.D. in Curriculum Leadership, 1973. Asst. region supt. Detroit Public Schs., 1970-71, region supt., 1971-75, interim gen. supt., 1975, gen. supt. schs., 1975—. Mem. Nat., Mich. councils social studies, Assn. Supervision and Curriculum Devel., Am. Assn. Sch. Adminstrs., Mich. Assn. Supervision and Curriculum Devel., Council Basic Edn., Met. Detroit Soc. Black Ednl. Adminstrs., Nat. Alliance Black Sch. Educators, ACLU, NAACP, Wayne State U. Edn. Alumni Assn. (gov. 1968-71), Wayne State U. Alumni Assn. (trustee 1968-71), Phi Sigma Alpha. Home: 19445 Gloucester St Detroit MI 48203 Office: 5057 Woodward Ave Detroit MI 48202

JEFFERSON, JAMES WALTER, psychiatry educator; b. Mineola, N.Y., Aug. 14, 1937; s. Thomas Hutton and Alice (Withers) J.; m. Susan Mary Cole, June 25, 1965; children: Lara, Shawn, James C. BS, Bucknell U., 1958; MD, U. Wis., 1964. Cert. Am. Bd. Psychiatry and Neurology, Am. Bd. Internal Medicine. Asst. prof. psychiatry U. Wis. Med. Sch., Madison, 1974-78, assoc. prof., 1978-81, prof., 1981—; co-dir. Lithium Info. Ctr., Madison, 1975—; dir. Ctr. Affective Disorders, Madison, 1983—. Co-author: Neuropsychiatric Features of Medical Disorders, 1981, Lithium Encyclopedia for Clinical Practice, 1983, 2d edit. 1987, Depression and Its Treatment, 1984, Anxiety and Its Treatment, 1986. Served to maj. U.S. Army, 1968-71. Fellow ACP; mem. Am. Psychiat. Assn., Collegium Internat. Neuropsychopharmacologium, Wis. Acad. Scis., Arts and Letters. Avocations: running, travelling. Office: U Hosp Dept Psychiatry 600 Highland Ave Madison WI 53792

JEFFERSON, MELVIN DORSEY, fire commissioner of Detroit; b. Phila., July 5, 1922; s. Charles and Leona J.; student Temple U.; m. Helen Cuzzens, July 5, 1947; children—Joyce, Melvin. Pres., Superior Beauty and Barber Supply Co., Inc., Detroit; mem. Detroit Bd. Fire Commrs., 1969-74, fire commr., 1974—, exec. commr. Detroit Fire Dept.; mem. Detroit Bd. Suprs.; dir. Johnson Products. Bd. dirs. Econ. Devel. Corp., Coop. Assistance, Boy Scouts Am., North Detroit Gen. Hosp., United Found.; past mem. Detroit Airport Commn.; past bd. dirs., treas. Detroit Urban League. Served to lt. USAF. Mem. NAACP (life), Detroit C. of C. Club: One Hundred. Episcopalian. Office: Office of the Fire Chief 250 W Larnard St Detroit MI 48226 *

JEFFERSON, WAYNE, broadcasting executive; b. Norwalk, Conn., June 12, 1948; s. David and Josephine (Williams) J.; m. Patricia Ann McAllister, Feb. 24, 1979; children—Brandie Michelle, Brian Jordan, Bradley Allen. B.S., NYU, 1971; A.A.S., Bronx Community Coll., 1968. Sr. auditor Price Waterhouse, N.Y.C., 1971-75, CBS, Inc., N.Y.C., 1975-76, mgr. internat. audit, N.Y.C., 1976-79, dir. internal audit, N.Y.C., 1979-82; dir. fin. and adminstrn. CBS/WBBM Radio, Chgo., 1982-85, v.p., gen. mgr. Sta. WBBM-FM, 1985—. Home: 2305 Central Park Ave Evanston IL 60201 Office: WBBM Radio (FM) 630 N Mc Clurg Ct Chicago IL 60611

JEFFERY, CARL RAY, dentist; b. Ft. Wayne, Ind., July 21, 1948; s. Ray Robert and Dorothy Colleen (Smith) J.; m. Susan Marie Rager, Mar. 22, 1970; children: Jennifer, Julie, Jessica. BS, Bowling Green (Ohio) U., 1970; DDS, Ohio State U., 1973. Gen. practice dentistry Van Wert, Ohio, 1973—. Crusade chmn. Am. Cancer Soc., Van Wert; mem. Van Wert City Sch. Bd., Welfare Adv. Bd., Van Wert, Van Wert Rep. Cen. Com. Named one of Outstanding Young Men In Am., 1985. Mem. ADA, Ohio Dental Assn., Van Wert C. of C., Ohio State Alumni Assn., Psi Omega. Republican. Methodist. Club: Van Wert Men's Garden. Home: Rural Rt 4 Box 274 Van Wert OH 45891 Office: 685 Fox Rd Van Wert OH 45891

JEFFREY, PAUL CLESSON, architect; b. Omaha, July 22, 1956; s. Clesson Robert and Justine (Seitz) J.; m. Christine Marie Chonis, June 17, 1978; children: Sarah Elizabeth, Zachary Michael. BArch, U. Nebr., 1978. Registered architect, Nebr. Design asst. Dunbar & Dunn Architects, Omaha, 1978-79; architect Bahr, Vermeer & Haecker, Omaha, 1979—. Mem. Archdiocese of Omaha Liturgy Commn., 1985—, Future Omaha; leader explorers Boy Scouts Am., Omaha, 1985—; vol. Cathedral Arts Project, Omaha, 1986; mem. Leavenworth Homeowner Assn., Omaha, 1985; pres. Leavenworth Neighborhood Assn. Mem. AIA. Republican. Roman Catholic. Club: Omaha. Avocations: carpentry, urban design, squash, volleyball. Home: 1029 S 35th Ave Omaha NE 68105 Office: Bahr Vermeer & Haecker 1209 Harney Omaha NE 68102

JEFFRIES, CHARLES DEAN, scientist, educator; b. Rome, Ga., Apr. 9, 1929; s. Andrew Jones and Rachel Lucinda (Ringer) J.; m. Virginia Mae Alford, Sept. 6, 1953. B.S., N. Ga. Coll., 1950; M.S., U. Tenn., 1955, Ph.D., 1958; postgrad., Purdue U., 1955-56. Techncian Ga. Pub. Health Dept., Rome, 1950-51; instr. microbiology Wayne State U., Detroit, 1958-60, asst. prof., 1960-65, assoc. prof., 1965-70, prof., 1970—, acting chmn. dept., 1972-73, assoc. dermatology, 1968—, asst. dean for curriculum affairs, dir. grad. programs Sch. Medicine, 1975-80; guest researcher Ctr. for Disease Control, USPHS, Dept. Health and Human Services, Atlanta, 1980-81; Fulbright-Hays lectr., Cairo, 1965-66; examiner bacteriology Bd. Basic Scis., State Mich., 1967-72, v.p., 1970-72. Contbr. articles to profl. jours. Councilor Am. Assn. Basic Sci. Bds., 1970-72; mem. sci. adv. bd. Mich. Cancer Found., 1970-79; mem. Am. Inst. Biol. Scis.-EPA adv. panel, 1979-80. Served with AUS, 1951-53. Grantee NIH, 1958-70, NSF, 1959-69. Fellow Am. Acad. Microbiology; mem. Am. Soc. for Microbiology (councilor 1976-78, chmn. med. mycology div. 1977-78), Nat. Registry Microbiologists, Soc. Gen. Microbiology, Soc. Exptl. Biology and Medicine, Internat. Soc. Human and Animal Mycology, Sigma Xi. Home: 22513 Raymond Ave St Clair Shores MI 48082 Office: Dept Immunology and Microbiology Sch Medicine Wayne State U 540 E Canfield St Detroit MI 48201

JEFFRIES, JOHN GALE, business development company executive; b. Cedar Falls, Iowa, July 6, 1956; s. James Henry and Roseann (Nott) J.; m. Mary Lynn Voss, Nov. 12, 1983; 1 child, Ryan James. BS in Engring. Op., Iowa State U., 1978. Mgr. nat. accts. Onan Corp., Mpls., 1979-80; mgr. nat. accts. Century Mfg. Co., Mpls., 1980-81, group sales mgr., 1981-84; mgr. mktg. Wagner Spray Tech., Mpls., 1984-85; prin. Quest Bus. Devel. Group, Inc., Burnsville, Minn., 1985—; cons. Mpls. Aquatennial, 1986—, Mpls. Econ. Devel. Agy., 1986—; speaker Arthur Young Entrepeneur Series, Mpls., 1987—; bd. dirs. Quest Research, Mpls. Recipient Centre award Centre Publs. Ltd., 1985. Mem. Mpls. C. of C. (venture forum group 1986—, facilitator peer group 1986—), Iowa State U. Alumni Assn., Delta Upsilon (cons. 1985). Methodist. Avocations: golf, sailing, racquetball, home improvement, landscaping. Home: 3705 Balsam Ln Plymouth MN 55441 Office: Quest Bus Devel Group Inc 425 Travelers Trail W Burnsville MN 55337

JEFFRIES, PHILIP LEONARD, computer programmer; b. Shelby County, Ind., Oct. 23, 1940; s. Leonard Henry and Mavern (Wickliff) J.; m. Nila Kay Paxton, July 2, 1961; children: Brian Lee, Todd Eric. Student, Purdue U., 1958-59. Computer operator, programmer, systems analyst Farm Bur. Ins., Indpls., 1961-73; systems supr., programmer, mgr. programmimg Service Supply Co., Inc., Indpls., 1973—. Chmn. bd. Shiloh Ch., Greenfield, Ind., 1982-83, chmn. elders, 1986—. Mem. Electronic Data Interchange Nat. Users Group, Consol. Functions Ordinary, Ins. Users Group. Republican. Avocations: traveling, reading, church work, Sunday school teaching. Home: 7496E 300N Greenfield IN 46140 Office: Service Supply Co Inc 603 E Washington St Indianapolis IN 46206

JEFFRIES, ROBERT WAYNE, clinical psychologist; b. Indpls., Aug. 4, 1949; s. Kenneth Robert and Isabelle Joyce (Stafford) J. PhD, Purdue U., 1980. Lic. psychologist, Ind. Behavioral clinician Ind. Boys Sch., Plainfield, 1975-78; clin. psychology intern VA Med. Ctr., Danville, Ill., 1978-80; clin. psychologist Ctr. for Mental Health, Anderson, Ind., 1980—; pvt. practice psychology, Indpls., 1981—. Mem. Am. Psychol. Assn., Ind. Psychol. Assn., Internat. Neuropsychol. Soc., Sigma Chi.

JEGHERS, HAROLD JOSEPH, physician, educator; b. Jersey City, Sept. 26, 1904; s. Albert and Matilda (Gerckens) J.; m. Isabel J. Wile, June 21, 1935; children: Harold, Dee, Sanderson, Theodore. B.S., Rensselaer Poly. Inst., 1928; M.D., Western Res. U., 1932; D.Sc. (hon.), Georgetown U., 1975, Coll. Medicine and Dentistry of N.J., 1976. Intern 5th med. service Boston City Hosp., 1933-34, resident, 1935-37; physician-in-chief Boston City Hosp. (5th Med. Service), 1943-46, cons. physician, 1946-66; instr. to asso. prof. medicine Boston U. Sch. Medicine, 1935-46; prof. and dir. dept. medicine Georgetown U. Sch. Medicine, 1946-56; prof., dir. dept. medicine N.J. Coll. Medicine and Dentistry, Jersey City, 1956-66, emeritus, 1966—; med. dir. St. Vincent Hosp., Worcester, Mass., 1966-78, emeritus, 1979—; prof. med. edn. Office Med. Edn. Research and Curriculum Devel., Northeastern Ohio Univs. Coll. Medicine, 1977-86 ; cons. med. edn. St. Elizabeth Hosp., Youngstown, Ohio, 1977—, Cleve. Health Scis. Library, Case Western Res. U., 1979—, Cleve. Med. Library Assn., 1979-86 ; prof. Tufts U., 1966-74; dir. med. ward service Jersey City Med. Center, 1958-66; dir. Tufts med. service Boston City Hosp., 1969-71; cons. medicine Georgetown U. Sch. Medicine, 1957-59; rep. from A.C.P. to div. med. scis.

NRC, 1950-53. Author articles and sects. in books.; developer: Jeghers Med. Index System. Recipient Laetare award Guild of St. Luke, Boston, 1958; Distinguished Alumni award Case Western Res. U. Sch. Medicine, 1974. Fellow A.C.P., Am. Soc. for Clin. Investigation; mem. A.M.A., Am. Fedn. for Clin. Research, So. Soc. for Clin. Research (v.p. 1948-49), Assn. Am. Physicians, Mass. Med. Soc., Sigma Xi. Office: 1044 Belmont Ave Youngstown OH 44501

JELINEK, KAREL AUGUSTIN, mechanical engineer; b. Prague, Czechoslovakia, Nov. 30, 1935; s. Karel and Marie (Turkova) J.; married; children: Karel V., Daniel A. ME, Czechoslovakia Tech. U., Prague, 1962. Registered profl. engr., Colo., Ohio, Tex. Design engr. Jawa, Prague, 1962-64; asst. prof. Czechoslovakia Tech. U., Prague, 1964-69; design engr. McInnis Ltd., Windsor, Canada, 1969-71, Rupp Inc., Mansfield, Ohio, 1971-72; sr. engr. Armco Inc., Middletown, Ohio, 1972—. Mem. Air Pollution Control Assn., Soc. Automotive Engrs. (com. mem.). Lodge: Optimist. Home: 808 Dover Middletown OH 45044

JELKS, EDWARD BAKER, archeologist, educator; b. Macon, Ga., Sept. 10, 1922; s. Oliver Robinson and Lucille (Jarrett) J.; m. Juliet Elizabeth Christian, Aug. 12, 1944; 1 son. Edward Christian. B.A., U. Tex., 1948, M.A., 1951, Ph.D., 1965. Archeologist Smithsonian Instn., 1950-53, Nat. Park Service, 1953-58; research scientist U. Tex., Austin, 1958-65; assoc. prof. anthropology So. Meth. U., Dallas, 1965-68; prof. anthropology Ill. State U., Normal, 1968-84; prof. emeritus Ill. State U., 1984—; dir. Midwestern Archeol. Research Ctr., 1981-84; active archeol. field research Tex., La., Ill., Va., Mo., Nfld., Micronesia. Co-author: Handbook of Texas Archeology, 1954, Trick Taking Potential, 1974, The Joachim De Brum House, Likiep, Marshall Islands, 1978; author: Archaelogical Explorations at Signal Hill, Newfoundland, 1973. Served with USN, 1942-44. Recipient Outstanding Contributions to Field of Va. Antiquities ann. award, 1982, Clarence H. Webb award, 1984; Smithsonian Instn. research fellow, 1968. Fellow AAAS, Am. Anthropol. Assn.; mem. Tex. Archeol. Soc. (pres. 1957-58), Soc. Profl. Archeologists (pres. 1976-77), Soc. Hist. Archaeology (pres. 1968-69), Am. Soc. for Conservation Archaeology (v.p. 1975-76), Pan Am. Inst. Geography and History (chmn. archaeology work group 1982—), Soc. for Am. Archaeology, Delta Chi. Home: 605 N School St Normal IL 61761

JELLISON, DAVID MICHAEL, real estate development; b. Moorhead, Minn., May 31, 1948; s. Wanda Joyce (Abbott) Olson; m. Susan Leann Geary, Aug. 30, 1969; children: Mindi Sue, Tad David, Kami Joy. BS in Mgmt. Sci., Moorhead State U., 1970. Dist. mgr Am. Campgrounds, Seattle, 1972-74; v.p. Dyna Gym of Minn., Mpls., 1974-77; asst. v.p. United Properties, Mpls., 1977—. Mem. Nat. Assn. Corp. Real Estate Execs., Comml. Indsl. Multiple Listing Service. Republican. Baptist. Home: 2765 Kelly Ave Excelsior MN 55331 Office: United Properties 3500 W 80th St Minneapolis MN 55431

JELLISON, JAMES LOGAN, II, banking executive; b. Chgo., June 3, 1922; s. James Logan and Ethel (Reynolds) J.; Ph.B., DePaul U., Chgo., 1943; B.M.E., Northwestern U., 1948; M.B.A., U. Louisville, 1959; m. Charlotte Jean Scott, Oct. 20, 1951; children—James Logan, Jeanene Lynn, Jennifer Lee. Mgr. mktg. research Gen. Electric Co., Holland, Mich., 1961-85; fin. services rep. D&N Savs. Bank, 1985—. State and County Conv. del. Republican Party; bd. dirs. Ottawa County ARC; chmn. bd. govs. Fountain St. Ch., Grand Rapids, Mich. Served to 1st lt. AUS, 1943-46, ETO. Decorated Bronze Star, Purple Heart; registered profl. engr. Mem. Am. Mktg. Assn., Am. Legion, Elfun Soc., Kappa Sigma. Republican. Home: 729 Lugers Rd Holland MI 49423 Office: 200 Chicago Dr Jenison MI 49428

JELLISON, RICHARD MARION, educator; b. Muncie, Ind., Dec. 26, 1924; s. Carl R. and Leora Melvina (Falkner) J.; m. Kathleen Elizabeth Frick, May 5, 1945; children—Richard G., Stephanie L., Leslie N. B.S., Ball State U., 1948; A.M., Ind. U., 1949, Ph.D., 1953. Instr. history Ind. U., 1952-56; instr. Mich. State U., 1956-58; asso. prof. Eastern Ill. U., 1958-62; prof. Miami U., Oxford, Ohio, 1962—; chmn. dept. history Miami U., 1971—; lectr. U. Berlin, 1966, Siena, Italy, 1968, Budapest, Hungary, 1974. Author: Society, Freedom and Conscience: The American Revolution in Virginia, Massachusetts and New York, 1976; contbr. articles to profl. jours. Served with U.S. Navy, 1942-44, PTO. Colonial Williamsburg summer research fellow, 1958-62. Mem. Am. Hist. Assn., Inst. Early American Culture, Am. Assn. History Medicine, Orgn. Am. Historians, Internat. Soc. History Medicine, Ohio Hist. Soc., Ind. Hist. Soc., S.C. Hist. Soc., AAUP (pres. Miami U. chpt. 1967). Home: 6 Chestnut Hill Oxford OH 45056 Office: Dept History Miami Univ Oxford OH 45056

JENEFSKY, JACK, wholesale executive; b. Dayton, Ohio, Oct. 27, 1919; s. David and Anna (Saeks) J.; m. Beverly J. Mueller, Feb. 23, 1962; 1 child, Anna Elizabeth; 1 stepchild, Cathryn Jean Mueller. BSBA, Ohio State U., 1941; postgrad. Harvard Bus. Sch., 1943; MA in Econs., U. Dayton, 1948. Surplus broker, Dayton, 1946-48; sales rep. Remington Rand-Univac, Dayton, 1949-56, mgr. AF account, 1957-59, br. mgr. Dayton, 1960-61, regional mktg. cons. Midwest region, Dayton, 1962-63; pres. Bowman Supply Co., Dayton, 1963—. Selection adv. bd. Air Force Acad., 3d congl. dist., chmn., 1974-82; chmn. 3d. dist. screening bds. Mil. Acad., 1976-82; coordinator Great Lakes region, res. assistance program CAP, 1970-73. Served from pvt. to capt. USAAF, 1942-46; CBI, maj. USAF, 1951-53; col Res. Mem. Air Force Assn. (comdr. Ohio wing 1957-58, 58-59), Res. Officers Assn. (pres. Ohio dept. 1956-57, nat. council 1957-58, chmn. research and devel. com. 1961-62), Dayton Area C. of C. (chmn. spl. events com. 1970-72, chmn. research com. on mil. affairs 1983—), Miami Valley Mil. Affairs Assn. (trustee 1985—, pres. bd. trustees 1987—), Ohio State U. Alumni Assn. (pres. Montgomery County, Ohio, 1959-60), Nat. Sojourners (pres. Dayton 1961-62). Jewish. Club: Harvard Bus. Sch. Dayton (pres. 1961-62). Lodge: Lions. Home: 136 Briar Heath Circle Dayton OH 45415 Office: Bowman Supply Co PO Box 1404 Dayton OH 45401

JENICKE, GERRY MARIE, graphics printing manager; b. Kansas City, Mo., Oct. 27, 1941; s. George Henry and Frances Mary (Schwartz) Gast; m. A. Wayne Jenicke, June 6, 1964; children: Janel, Jeffrey, Jeremy, Jason, Justin. Grad. high sch., Bucyrus, Kans., 1959. With finished goods div. Hallmark Cards, Inc., Kansas City, Mo., 1959-61, with mfg. div., 1961-65, with photo mech. finishing div., 1965-68; sect. mgr. Hallmark Cards, Inc., Kansas City, 1978-87; sect. mgr. color separation, graphics div. Hallmark Cards, Inc., Kansas City, Mo., 1971-78, 86—. Author tech. manual for graphics div. Del. Other Cultures, Sun Valley, Calif., 1981-84, Friendly Exchange, Guatemala City, 1984-86, host family 1981-86. Democrat. Roman Catholic. Avocation: golf. Home: 12468 Augusta Dr Kansas City KS 66109 Office: Hallmark Cards Inc 25th and McGee Kansas City MO 64141

JENISON, ERIC LEE, gynecologist, gynecologic oncologist; b. Heidelburg, Fed. Republic Germany, Aug. 30, 1950; came to U.S., 1952; s. Merrit C. and Rosemary (Borom) J.; m. Nancy Husk, Aug. 30, 1974; children: Eric, Douglas, Thomas, David. BS, Bowling Green State U., 1971; MD, Med. Coll. Ohio, 1974. Cert. Am. Bd. Ob-Gyn. Rotating intern in surgery Akron (Ohio) Gen. Med. Ctr., 1974-75, resident in ob-gyn, 1975-76, 78-80; fellow in gynecology and oncology Brigham and Women's Hosp. Harvard Med. Sch., Boston, 1981-83; instr. ob-gyn Harvard U., Boston, 1981-83; asst. prof. ob-gyn Northeastern Ohio Univs. Coll. Medicine, Rootstown, Ohio, 1983—; dir. gynecologic oncology Akron (Ohio) Gen. Med. Ctr., 1985—. Am. Cancer Soc. fellow, 1981-83; recipient Pfizer Med. Student Scholarship award, 1973, 1st prize Akron Gen. Med. Ctr., 1980, Gold Apple award Akron Gen. Med. Ctr., 1985. Fellow Am. Coll. Ob-Gyn; mem. AMA, Ohio State Med. Assn., Am. Soc. Clin. Oncologists, Soc. Gynecologic Oncologists (candidate mem.), Summit County Med. Soc., Stark County Med. Soc. Avocation: leisure sports. Home: 970 Pelee Dr Akron OH 44313 Office: 400 Wabash Ave Akron OH 44307

JENKINS, BRUCE ARMAND, manufacturing company executive; b. Lansing, Mich., June 4, 1933; s. George H. Jenkins and Margaret E. (Hoeflinger) Tinlin; m. Peggy A. Unruh, July 22, 1967; children: David, Mark. With Gen. Motors Corp., Lansing, 1953-83, supr. tech. tng., 1984-86; pres. Advanced Tech. Seminars, Inc., Eagle, Mich., 1986—. Author: Automotive Plastics, 1985, Plastics Repair, 1986, Cast Plastic Tooling Techniques, 1986; contbr. numerous articles to profl. jours. Pastor Foursquare Gospel Ch., Eagle, 1983—. Served to 1st lt. U.S. Army, 1950-1961. Republican. Avocations: silver smithing, experimental aircraft. Office: Advanced Tech Seminars Inc PO Box 42 Eagle MI 48822

JENKINS, GEORGE HENRY, photographer, educator; b. Shanghai, China, Oct. 24, 1929 (parents Am. citizens); s. Clarence O. and Efransinia M. (Pomorenkoff) J.; grad. N.Y. Inst. Photography, 1952; student Purdue U., 1952-55; student Ind. U., 1955-58, B.B.A., Ind. No. U., 1972; M.Ed., Wayne State U., 1976, Ph.D., 1985; Ph.D., Columbia Pacific U., 1984; m. Madge Marie Vickroy, Aug. 19, 1967. Photographer, Ft. Wayne (Ind.) Jour.-Gazette, 1952-55; computer programer Gen. Electric Co., Ft. Wayne, 1955-61; data processing mgr. Columbia Record Club subs. CBS, Terre Haute, Ind., 1961-63; adminstrv. coordinator Capital Record Club, Scranton, Pa. and Toronto, Ont., Can., 1963-64; mktg. systems analyst Xerox Corp., Detroit, 1964-66; dir. systems and data processing Nicholson File Co., Anderson, Ind., 1966-69; hosp. adminstr. Wayne County Gen. Hosp., Eloise, Mich., 1969-78; asst. prof. bus. Western Washington U., Bellingham, 1978-80; asst. prof. Lima (Ohio) Tech. Coll., 1980-83; assoc. prof. Findlay (Ohio) Coll., 1983—; freelance photographer, 1969—, writer/producer, 1984—. Chmn. supervisory bd. Eloise Credit Union, 1972-76. Served with USAF, 1948-52. Cert. data processor, data educator, systems profl. Mem. Photog. Soc. Gt. Britian, Photog. Soc. Am., Assn. System Mgmt., Am. Prodn. and Inventory Control Soc., Human Factors Soc., Am. Inst. Indsl. Engrs., Data Processing Mgmt. Assn. of Lima (pres. 1984-85). Presbyterian. Clubs: 8-16 Cine, Detroit Yacht Lodge: Elks. (Van Wert, Ohio). Home: 710 W Main St Cairo OH 45820 Office: Findlay Coll Findlay OH 45840

JENKINS, LAVERE H., management consultant; b. Freedom, Wyoming, Oct. 28, 1930; s. Phillip Eugene and Ida May (Haderlie) J.; m. Rose Ellen Richardson, Aug. 22, 1959; children: Susan, David, Renee, Neil, Brent. BS, Utah State U., 1960. Indsl. engr., field rep. The Boeing Co., Seattle, 1960-69; acct. exec. Consolidated Bus. Services, Inc., Columbus, Ohio, 1969-80; pres., chief exec. officer Fin. Adminstrv. Services, Inc., Zanesville, Ohio, 1981—; cons. in profl. mgmt., 1969—; physical facilities rep. Ch. of Jesus Christ of Latter-Day Sts., Columbus, 1985—. Treas. Tri-Valley Band Boosters Orgn., Dresden, Ohio, 1983-85. Served to sgt. USAF, 1952-56. Mem. Soc. Profl. Bus. Cons. Republican. Mormon. Avocations: wood working, farming, mechanics. Home: 3290 Gorsuch Rd Nashport OH 43830 Office: Fin Adminstrv Services Inc 2809 Bell St Zanesville OH 43701

JENKINS, RAY, retail executive; b. Phila., Feb. 7, 1949; m. Lillian Jenkins, Nov. 11, 1971 (div. Feb. 1975); 1 child, Raymond. BS, Pa. State U., 1971. Buyer Macy's Dept. Store, Newark, 1975-78; regional mgr. Seasonal Industries, Phila., 1978-83; nat. recruiter Stonhard, Mapleshade, N.J., 1983-86; regional mgr. Stonhard, Chgo., 1986-87; group sales dir. Clement Communications, Inc., Concordville, Pa., 1987—. Home: 1110 E Algonquin Rd Schaumburg IL 60173

JENKINS, WALTER KIMBALL, oil company executive; b. Council Bluffs, Iowa, July 25, 1929; s. Walter Lot and Ruth Elizabeth (Kimball) J.; B.S. in Chem. Engring., Iowa State U., 1951; M.B.A., State U. N.Y. at Buffalo, 1960; m. Mary Elizabeth Erler, July 25, 1953; children—Donald, Cindy, Nancy, Pat. Ops. supt. U.S. Indsl. Chem. Co., Tuscola, Ill., 1958-64; acting plant mgr. Apple River Chem. Co., East Dubuque, Ill., 1964-67; ops. mgr. Atlantic Richfield Co., Fort Madison, Iowa, 1967-69; project mgr. Procon Inc., gen. contractor petroleum refineries, Des Plaines, Ill., 1970-72; supervising engr. Union Oil Co., Lemont, Ill., 1972—. Co-chmn. steering com. Douglas County Hosp., 1964; active Boy Scouts Am. Bd. dirs. S.E. Iowa Community Coll.; pres Naperville Council of Chs., 1978. Served as 1st lt. Signal Corps., AUS, 1951-53. Registered profl. engr., Ill. Mem. Tuscola C. of C. (pres. 1963), Am. Inst. Chem. Engrs. (chmn. Joliet sect. 1976). Presbyn. (dir. ch.) Rotarian. Home: 1156 Elizabeth Ave Naperville IL 60540 Office: Union Oil Refinery Lemont IL 60439

JENKINS, WILLIAM ATWELL, univ. chancellor; b. Scranton, Pa., Nov. 18, 1922; s. William A. and Thelma (Atwell) J.; m. Gloria Hyam, Mar. 12, 1944 (div. Aug. 1974); m. Alice Carney, Nov. 1, 1974; children—William Arthur II, Darcy Ann. B.S. in Edn, N.Y.U., 1948; M.S., U. Ill., 1949, Ph.D., 1954. Mem. faculty U. Wis.-Milw., 1953-70, asso. dean, dir. tchr. edn. and grad. studies, 1963-70; vis. prof. edn. U. Hawaii, summer 1969; dean Sch. Edn., Portland (Oreg.) State U., 1970-74; v.p. Fla. Internat. U., Miami, 1974-78; vice chancellor for acad. affairs U. Colo., Denver, 1978-80; chancellor U. Mich.-Dearborn, 1980—; cons. in field. Co-author numerous texts, articles. Sec. Portland Devel. Commn., 1972-73, chmn., 1973-74. Served to 1st lt., C.E. AUS, 1943-46. Mem. Nat. Council Tchrs. English (pres. 1968-69), Nat. Conf. Research and English, Edn. Writers Assn., Wis., Ore. council tchrs. English, Phi Kappa Phi, Phi Delta Kappa, Kappa Delta Phi, Pi Lambda Theta. Home: 551 Golfcrest Dr Dearborn MI 48124

JENKINS, WILMA JEAN, accountant; b. Springfield, Mo., July 22, 1934; d. John Morris and Flossie Mae (Arnold) Vermillion; m. Bill W. Jenkins, Apr. 26, 1952; children: Janet Lynn, Jeffrey Wayne, James Alan. BS in Acctg., Draughons Coll., 1954. Bookkeeper Mo. Electronics, Springfield, 1954-55, Phillips Engraving, Springfield, 1955-57; acct. Systemat Savs. and Loan, Springfield, 1957-59; pvt. practice acctg. Springfield, 1960—. Mem. Nat. Assn. Enrolled Agts., Ind. Acct. Soc. (pres. Springfield chpt. 1972-82, sec. Springfield chpt. 1983-85, bd. dirs. Jefferson City chpt. 1985—, Outstanding Pres. of Yr. 1983), Nat. Soc. Pub. Accts. Republican. Club: Heart of Ozarks (Springfield) (Outstanding Chpt. Pres. 1984). Avocation: word games. Home and Office: 1431 E North Springfield MO 65803

JENNER, ALBERT ERNEST, JR., lawyer; b. Chgo., June 20, 1907; s. Albert E. and Elizabeth (Owens) J.; m. Nadine N., Mar. 19, 1932; 1 dau., Cynthia Lee. J.D., U. Ill., 1930, LL.D., 1979; LL.D., John Marshall Law Sch., 1961, Columbia Coll., 1974, U. Notre Dame, 1975, Northwestern U., 1975, William Mitchell Law Sch., 1976, U. Mich., 1976. Bar: Ill. 1930. Practiced in Chgo., 1930—; sr. partner firm Jenner & Block; counsel, dir. Gen. Dynamics Corp.; spl. asst. atty gen. Ill., 1956-68; counsel Ill. Budgetary Commn., 1956-57; prof. law Northwestern U., 1952-53; chmn. U.S. Supreme Ct. Adv. Com. on Fed. Rules of Evidence, 1965-75; Chmn. Ill. Commn. on Uniform State Laws, 1950-80; mem. Nat. Conf. Commrs. Uniform State Laws, 1952—, pres., 1969-71; mem. Adv. Com. Fed. Rules of Civil Procedure, U.S. Supreme Court, 1960-70, Nat. Conf. Bar Assn. Pres.'s U.S., 1950—, pres., 1952-53; mem. U.S. Loyalty Review Bd., 1952-53; mem. council U. Ill. Law Forum, 1948-51; sr. counsel Presdl. Commn. to Investigate the Assassination of President Kennedy (Warren Commn.), 1963-64; chief spl. counsel to minority Ho. of Reps. Judiciary Com. that conducted impeachment inquiry regarding Pres. Richard M. Nixon.; Law mem. Ill. Bd. Examiners Accountancy, 1948-51. Author and co-author: Illinois Civil Practice Act Annotated, 1933, Outline of Illinois Supreme Court and Appellate Court Procedure, 1935, Smith-Hurd Ill. Annotated Statutes, Volumes on Pleading, Evidence and Practice, 10 edits, 1933-87, also Vols. on Uniform Marriage and Dissolution of Marriage; Mem. permanent editorial bd.: Uniform Commercial Code, 1961—; Contbr. to law revs. and legal publs. on various phases of practice, pleading, evidence, procedure and other legal subjects. Mem. Pres. Lyndon B. Johnson's Nat. Commn. on Causes and Prevention of Violence in U.S., 1968-69; sec. U.S. Navy Meml. Found.; trustee Evanston-Glenbrook Hosp. Arthritis Found., Cerebral Palsey Found., Northwestern U. Library Bd.; mem. presdl. adv. bd. Mus. Sci. and Industry. Recipient Distinguished Service award for outstanding pub. service Chgo. and Ill. Jr. C. of C., 1939, U. Ill. Disting. Alumni award, 1962, Disting. Civic Achievement award Am. Jewish Com., 1973, N.Y. U. Distinguished Citizen's award, 1975; named Chicagoan of Year Chgo. Press Club, 1975; laureate Lincoln Acad. of Ill. Fellow Am. Coll. Trial Lawyers (bd. regents, pres. 1958-59), Internat. Acad. Trial Lawyers, Am. Bar Found.; mem. Ill. Soc. Trial Lawyers, Nat. Assn. Def. lawyers in Criminal Cases, Inter-Am. Bar Assn., Internat. Bar Assn., Am. Bar Assn. (ho. of dels. 1948—, fellow Young Lawyers Sect., state del. 1975-78, chmn. standing com. on fed. judiciary 1965-68, chmn. sect. individual rights and responsibilities 1973-74, mem. council sect. legal edn. 1967-75, bd. govs. 1977-80), Ill. Bar Assn. (pres. 1949-50), Chgo. Bar Assn. (bd. dirs. 1934-47, sec. 1947-49), Assn. Bar City N.Y., Am. Judicature Soc. (pres. 1958-60), Am. Inst. Jud. Adminstrn., Nat. Lawyers Com. for Civil Rights Under Law (dir., nat. co-chmn. 1975-77), Bar Assn. U.S. Ct. Appeals 7th Circuit (bd. govs. 1955-60, Robert Maynard Hutchins Distinguished Service award 1976), Am. Law Inst., Chgo. Council Lawyers, NAACP Legal Def. Fund, Center for Study Dem. Instns. (dir. 1975-79), Order of Coif, Alpha Chi Rho, Phi Delta Phi. Republican. Clubs: Tavern, Midday, Skokie Country, Law, Legal, Chicago. Office: One IBM Plaza Chicago IL 60611

JENNER, WILLIAM ALEXANDER, meteorologist; b. Indianola, Iowa, Nov. 10, 1915; s. Edwin Alexander and Elizabeth May (Brown) J.; A.B., Central Meth. Coll., Mo., 1938; certificate meteorology U. Chgo., 1943; M.Ed., U. Mo., 1947; postgrad. Am. U., 1951-58; m. Jean Norden, Sept. 1, 1946; children—Carol Beth, Paul William, Susan Lynn. Instr. U. Mo., 1946-47; research meteorologist U.S. Weather Bur., Chgo., 1947-49; staff Hdqrs. Air Weather Service, Andrews AFB, Md., 1949-58, Scott AFB, Ill., 1958-84, dir. tng., 1960-84. Mem. O'Fallon (Ill.) Twp. High Sch. Bd. Edn., 1962—, sec., 1964-71, pres., 1971-83, 1985—; pres. St. Clair County Regional Vocat. System Bd., 1986—; mem. O'Fallon Planning Commn., 1973-84, sec., 1979-81, sub-div. chmn., 1978-84; alderman City of O'Fallon, 1984—. Served with AUS, 1942-46. Recipient Disting. Service award O'Fallon PTA, 1968; Disting. Service award City of O'Fallon, 1985; Exceptional Civilian Service award Dept. Air Force, 1984; Jenner Award established by Air Weather Service, 1984. Fellow Am. Meteorol. Soc.; mem. Am. Psychol. Assn., Wilson Ornithological Soc., Am. Philatelic Soc., Am. Philatelic Congress, Am. Meteorol. Soc., AAAS, Nat. Soc. Study Edn., Am. Legion, Phi Delta Kappa, Psi Chi. Clubs: Masons, Shriners, O'Fallon Sportsmen's, Toastmasters Internat. Home: 307 Alma St O'Fallon IL 62269

JENNINGS, EDWARD HARRINGTON, university president; b. Mpls., Feb. 18, 1937; s. Edward G. and Ruth (Harrington) J.; children: William F., Steven W. B.S., U. N.C., 1959; M.B.A., Western Res. U., 1963; Ph.D. (NDEA fellow 1966-69), U. Mich., 1969. Engr. Deering Milliken Co., Spartanburg, S.C., 1959-61, Merck & Co., West Point, Pa., 1963-65; mem. faculty U. Iowa, 1969-75, v.p. fin., 1975-79; vis. prof. U. Der es Salam, Tanzania, 1971-72; pres. U. Wyo., Laramie, 1979-81, Ohio State U., Columbus, 1981—. Co-author: Fundamentals of Investments, 1976; contbr. articles profl. jours. Mem. Am. Fin. Assn., Western Fin. Assn., Midwest Fin. Assn. Lutheran. Office: Ohio State Univ 190 N Oval Mall Columbus OH 43210

JENNINGS, JAMES BLANDFORD, history educator; b. Ironwood, Mich., Jan. 23, 1922; s. Blandford and Anne (Heise) J.; B.E., Ill. State U., 1947, M.Ed., 1948; postgrad. U. Wis., 1950-51, Washington U., 1956, Ripon Coll., 1961, Northwestern U., 1965, Southern Ill. U., Edwardsville, 1970, 71. Instr. polit. sci. and econs. Mc Kendree Coll., Lebanon, Ill., 1948-49; tchr. social studies high sch., Pleasant Hope, Mo., 1950; tchr. history Howe (Ind.) Mil. Sch., 1951-52; tchr. social studies Center Twp. Sch., LaPorte, Ind., 1952-54; tchr. history East High Sch., Aurora, Ill., 1954-67, Maine Twp. High Sch. West, Des Plaines, Ill., 1967-69; instr. history State Community Coll. East St. Louis, 1969—, chmn. humanities, 1972-75; mem. faculty adv. com. Ill. Bd. Higher Edn., 1980-83. Co-chmn. Search for the Am. Dream in East St. Louis, 1976. Served with AUS, 1943-45. Decorated Bronze Star, Purple Heart with 2 oak leaf clusters. Mem. Nat. Forensic League (dist. chmn. 1962-65), Aurora Edn. Assn. (pres. 1961-62), NEA, Ill. Community Coll. Faculty Assn. (editor newsletter 1981-84, treas. 1984—), Am. Hist. Assn., Ill. Hist. Assn., Abraham Lincoln Assn., AAUP, Pi Kappa Delta, Pi Gamma Mu. Home: 7746 Rannells Maplewood MO 63143 Office: 601 James R Thompson Blvd East Saint Louis IL 62201

JENNINGS, JAMES MURRAY, economist, planner; b. Tulsa, Oct. 28, 1924; s. Edward Paul and Eleanor (Easton) J.; m. Aija L. Vilcins, Dec. 24, 1946; children—James M., Linda D. A.A., George Washington U., 1949, B.A., 1950; M.A., U. N.C., 1955; postgrad. Syracuse U., 1953-56. Asst. prof. No. Mich. U., Marquette, 1952-53; grad. fellow Syracuse U. (N.Y.), 1953-56; assoc. prof. geography U. Pitts., 1956-59; dir. area econs. Battelle Meml. Inst., Columbus, Ohio, 1959-65; pres. J.M. Jennings Assocs. Co., Columbus, 1965—. Co-author: Manufacturing in the St. Lawrence Area, 1958, Bringing in the Sheaves, 1986. Chmn. City Planning Commn., Upper Arlington, Ohio, 1971-83; dir. Ohio Basic Econ. Devel. Course, 1982—. Served with U.S. Army, 1943-45. Fellow and hon. life mem. Am. Econ. Devel. Council (bd. regents, cert. econ. developer); mem. Ohio Planning Conf. (pres., 1974-77, dir. 1963—), Mid-Am. Econ. Devel. Council (v.p. 1965), Am. Inst. Cert. Planners (cert. planner), Ohio Devel. Assn. (pres. 1980, dir. 1980—, Ohio Developer of Yr. 1983). Baptist. Home: 1858 Chatfield Rd Columbus OH 43221 Office: James M Jennings Assocs Co 1357 W Lane Ave Columbus OH 43221

JENNINGS, MYRA FERN, savings and loan executive; b. Alton, Ill., Mar. 15, 1941; d. Henry Martin and A. Mae (Nixon) J. A.Acctg., So. Ill. U., 1975, B.S. in Bus. Adminstrn.-Acctg., 1978; grad. diploma Inst. Fin. Edn., 1972 C.P.A., Ill. Teller Citizens Savs. and Loan Assn., East Alton, Ill., 1959-70, treas., 1970—, head acctg. dept., 1969—, dir., 1977—; Organist 1st United Meth. Ch., East Alton, 1982—. Mem. Fin. Mgrs. Soc., Am. Inst. C.P.A.s, Ill. Soc. C.P.A.s, Fin. Inst. Edn. (pres. chpt. 1981-84). Republican. Home: 620 Valley Dr East Alton IL 62024 Office: 700 Berkshire Blvd East Alton IL 62024

JENNINGS, NORMAN RODNEY, data processing executive; b. Pittsburg, Kans., Aug. 14, 1939; s. Frank C. and Edith L. (Gardner) J.; m. Jill Mary Hagi, Feb. 1, 1981; children: Rodney Dean, Mark Andrew. AA in Bus. Adminstrn., Ventura (Calif.) Community Coll., 1962; BS in Mktg., Calif. State U., Chico, 1966. CPCU, 1981. Acct. Texaco Oil Co., Ventura, 1963-64; rep. field claims State Farm Auto Ins., Ventura, 1966-67; mgr. State Farm Auto Ins. Co., Bloomington, Ill., 1975—; programmer State Farm Fire Ins. Co., Bloomington, 1967-69, computer analyst, 1969-73, gen. supt., 1973-75. Mem. Data Processing Mgmt. Assn., CPCU Assn. Avocations: tennis, softball, snow skiing. Home: 3 Tami Ct Bloomington IL 61701 Office: State Farm Ins Co 1 State Farm Plaza B2 Bloomington IL 61701

JENNINGS, STEPHEN GRANT, academic administrator; b. Indpls., Dec. 6, 1946; s. Grant Orville and Helen Zura (MacDonald) J.; m. Sarah Ferguson, Apr. 26, 1969; children: Amy Christina, Meredith Zoe. BA, Trinity U., 1968; MS, Miami U., Oxford, Ohio, 1970; PhD, U. Ga., 1976; diploma, Harvard U., 1982. Asst. dean resident life So. Meth. U., Dallas, 1970-73; asst. dir. housing U. Ga., Athens, 1976; assoc. dean students Tulane U., New Orleans, 1976-80; v.p. student services Furman U., Greenville, S.C., 1980-83; pres. Sch. of Ozarks, Point Lookout, Mo., 1983-87, Simpson Coll., Indianola, Iowa, 1987—; instl. cons. U. Montevallo, Ala., 1983-85; bd. dirs. Centerre Bank, Branson, Mo. Elder Coll. Presbyn. Ch., Sch. of Ozarks, 1983—; bd. dirs. Skaggs Hosp., Branson, 1984—, Presbyn. Children's Services, Farmington, Mo., 1985—. Mem. Am. Council Edn., Am. Assn. Pres. Independent Colls., Council Independent Colls., Nat. Assn. Intercollegiate Athletics (council of pres. 1983—), So. Assn. Colls. and Schs. (visiting teams 1982—), So. Assn. Coll. Student Personnel (pres. 1983). Lodge: Rotary (treas. Branson club 1986—). Avocations: racquet sports, golf, reading. Home: 703 W Ashland Indianola IA 50125 Office: Simpson Coll Pres's Office Indianola IA 50125

JENNINGS, VIVIEN LEE, bookstore management and licensing organization chief executive officer; b. Little Rock, Ark., Mar. 7, 1945; d. Loron and Mildred Louise (Wright) Bolen. B.A., Rhodes Coll., Memphis, 1967. Women's fiction cons. Ballantine Books, Inc., N.Y., 1981-82, Berkeley Pub. Group, N.Y., 1982-83; pres. Rainy Day Books, Inc., Fairway, Kans., 1975—. Editor: nat. weekly bus. letter Boy Meets Girl., 1981-86; exec. editor serialized women's fiction project Day Dreams, 1984. Author: The Romance Wars. Contbr. articles to profl. publs. Featured on nat. pub. radio and nat. tv programs. Mem. Romance Writers Am., Inc. (bd. dirs.), Soc. of Fellows Nelson-Atkins Mus. of Art. Episcopalian. Clubs: Carriage, Cen. Exchange (Kansas City). Home: 5413 Norwood Rd Fairway KS 66205 Office: Rainy Day Books Inc 2812 W 53d St Fairway KS 66205

JENNINGS, WILLIAM PARNELL, real estate broker and developer; b. Evansville, Ind., Feb. 18, 1918; s. John K. and Lillian (Helfrich) J.; m. Elizabeth Nicholls; children: William P. Jr., Judith J. Jennings Barnes, Jeanne M. Jennings Mosher. BS, Ind. U., 1940. Chmn. J&L Realty Inc., Indpls., 1950; ptnr. Jennings & Barnes Co., Indpls. Mem. Ind. Housing Fin. Authority, Am. Soc. Real Estate Counselors, Indpls. Bd. Realtors (pres. 1959-60), Met. Indpls. Bd. Realtors (broker 1950—). Democrat. Office: 5525 Georgetown Rd #E Indianapolis IN 46254

JENS, ARTHUR MARX, JR., insurance company executive; b. Winfield, Ill., June 26, 1912; s. Arthur M. and Jeanette Elizabeth (Vinton) J.; m. Elizabeth Lee Shafer, Aug. 14, 1937; children—Timothy Vinton, Christopher Edward, Jeffrey Arthur. B.S., Northwestern U., 1934; J.D., Kent Coll. Law, Ill. Inst. Tech., 1939. Bar: Ill. 1939. Ins. underwriter, claim mgr. Continental Casualty Co. and Royal Globe Group, Chgo., 1934-39; sec., asst. treas. TWA, Kansas City, Mo., 1939-47; v.p., pres., chmn. bd. Fred S. James & Co. Inc., Chgo., 1947-76, hon. chmn. bd.; dir. Airline Service Corp. and all TWA subs., Comml. Resources Corp.; founder, dir. 6 First Security Banks of DuPage County; chmn. Jenson Corp. Life gov. Central DuPage Hosp.; mem. Ill. Gov.'s Panel on Racing. Mem. Ill. State Bar Assn., ABA, Nat. Assn. Ins. Agts. and Brokers (dir.). Republican. Presbyterian. Clubs: Chgo. Golf (past pres.), Mid-Day (trustee), Chgo. Club Room 19; Thunderbird Country (Palm Springs, Calif.). Contbr. articles to air transp. and ins. jours. Home: 22 W 210 Stanton Rd Glen Ellyn IL 60137 Office: 230 W Monroe St Chicago IL 60606

JENS, ELIZABETH LEE SHAFER (MRS. ARTHUR M. JENS, JR.), civic worker; b. Monroe, Mich., Jan. 25, 1915; d. Frank Lee and Mary (Bogard) Shafer; student Kalamazoo Coll., 1932-34, U. Wis., summer 1935; B.S., Northwestern U., 1936; postgrad. Wheaton Coll., summer 1965; L.P.N., Triton Coll., 1969; m. Arthur M. Jens, Jr., Aug. 14, 1937; children—Timothy V., Christopher E., Jeffrey A. Gray Lady, Hines, (Ill.) Hosp., 1948-49, 51-53; vol. Elgin (Ill.) State Hosp., 1958-72; writer Newsletter Vol. Planning Council, 1960-62; mem. Family Service Assn. Du Page County; vol. coordinator, chmn. bd. dirs., treas. Thursday Evening Club; social club for recovering mental patients Du Page County, 1966—; vol. FISH orgn., 1973-84. Bd. dirs. Du Page County Mental Health Soc., 1962-68, sec., 1963-64, 65-68, chmn. forgotten patient com., 1963-68, chmn. new projects, 1965-68; co-chmn. Glen Ellyn unit Central Du Page Hosp. Assn. Women's Aux., 1959-60; bd. dirs. chmn. com. on pesticides, Ill. Audubon Soc., 1963-73; mem. Ill. Pesticide Control Com., 1963-73, Citizens Com. Dutch Elm Disease, Glen Ellyn, 1960; bd. dirs. Natural Resources Council Ill., 1961-67, sec., 1961-64; bd. dirs. Du Page Art League, 1958-68, chmn. bd., 1961-63, chmn. new bldg. com., 1968-75; bd. dirs. mem. planning com., publicity chmn. Du Page Fine Arts Assn., 1965-67; bd. dirs. Friends Library Glen Ellyn, 1967-68, Rachel Carson Trust for Living Environment 1971-74; bd. dirs. Du Page Mental Health Assn., 1973—, sec., 1973-75, pres., 1980-81, chmn. community liaison, 1981—, chmn. action group, 1976—; mem. Du Page Subarea adv. council Suburban Cook County-Du Page County Health Systems Agy., 1977-83; bd. dirs. Du Page County Comprehensive Health Planning Agy., 1976, DuPage County Bd. of Health, 1987—; citizens adv. bd. to mental health div. Du Page Bd. Health, 1977-87; mem. com. on midlife and older women Ill. Commn. on Status of Women, 1978-85; bd. dirs., publicity chmn., DuPage County Council Vol. Coordinators, 1977-78; bd. dirs., membership chmn. Homemakers Equal Rights Assn. in DuPage County, 1979-84; publicity chmn. Homemakers Coalition for Equal Rights, 1984—, pres. 1986—; mem. DuPage County Health Planning Council, 1984'4 ; now chmn. Grass Roots Com. to Pass Ill. Marital Property Act, 1982—. Hon. mention in Nat. Sonnet contest, 1967; Vol. of Year, Ill. Mental Health Assn., 1975; Service award Ill. Rehab. Assn., 1980; named DuPage County Outstanding Woman Leader in Arts and Culture, W. Suburban YWCA, 1984. Mem. Wilderness Soc., Humane Soc. U.S., W. Suburban Humane Soc., Nat. Trust for Hist. Preservation, Du Page County Hist. Soc., Glen Ellyn Hist. Soc., Nat., Du Page Audubon socs., Nat. Writers Club (monthly meeting chmn. Midwest chpt. 1973-74, 4th award Ann. Mag. Con test 1978), Defenders of Wildlife, Theosophical Soc. Am., Nature Conservancy Ill. (hon.), NAACP, Chgo. Art Inst. (life), Ill. Assn. Mental Health (dir. 1966-68), Amnesty Internat., Pi Beta Phi. Writer column Mental Health and You for Press Publs., 1969—, Life Newspapers, 1982—, Pioneer Newspapers, 1984, Herald Newspapers, 1986—; author: The Jewelled Flower, 1987. Home: 22 W 210 Stanton Rd Glen Ellyn IL 60137

JENSEN, DANIEL LYLE, accounting educator; b. Hutchinson, Minn., Nov. 25, 1940; s. Lyle R. and Alice J.D. (Svendsen) J.; m. Carolyn May Rudy; 1 child, Christian Brogaard. BA, U. Minn., 1962, MS, 1964; PhD, Ohio State U., 1970. CPA, Ohio. Asst. prof. U. Ill., Urbana, 1968-74; assoc. prof. Purdue U., West Lafayette, Ind., 1974-79, prof., 1979-80; Ernst & Whinney prof. acctg. Ohio State U., Columbus, 1980—. Co-author: Advanced Accounting, 1980, Financial Accounting, 1982, Accounting for Changing Prices, 1984; editor: Information Systems in Accounting Education, 1985, Accounting: The Lighter Side, 1986, various other monographs; contbr. over 20 articles to scholarly and profl. jours. Mem. Nat. Assn. Accts., Am. Acctg. Assn., Am. Inst. CPA's, Fin. Execs. Inst. Office: Ohio State U 1775 College Rd Columbus OH 43210

JENSEN, DAVID JOHN, accountant; b. Racine, Wis., Oct. 12, 1957; s. Walter Martin and Marjorie (Nuemann) J. BBA, U. Wis., 1979. CPA, Wis. Staff acct. Botsford, Leslie, Witt Ltd., Racine, 1979-85; pntr. Botsford, Leslie, McClure & Jensen Ltd., Racine, 1986—. Treas. Rep. Party of Racine County, 1983—. Mem. Am. Inst. CPA's, Wis. Inst. CPA's, Am. Orgn. Pub. Accts., Racine-Kenosha CPA Discussion Group, Exptl. Aviation Assn. Avocations: aviation (pvt. pilot), radio controlled helicopter, microcomputers, instrumental music. Home: 3211 Washington Ave #2 Racine WI 53405 Office: Botsford Leslie McClure & Jensen Ltd 840 Lake Ave Racine WI 53403

JENSEN, GWENDOLYN EVANS, college provost, historian, educator; b. Lansdowne, Pa., Feb. 5, 1936; m. Gordon M. Jensen; children: Elizabeth, Donald, Alice. BA in English, U. Hartford, Conn., 1962; MA in History, Trinity Coll., 1963; PhD in History, U. Conn., 1971. Faculty member U. New Haven, West Haven, Conn., 1966-76, dean grad. sch., 1976-83; v.p. acad. affairs Western State Coll., Gunnison, Colo., 1983-86; provost Marietta (Ohio) Coll., 1986—. Contbr. articles to profl. jours. V.P., bd. govs. Conn. Ballet, New Haven, 1976-77. Episcopalian.

JENSEN, JAMES ROBERT, JR., periodontist, educator; b. Mpls., Sept. 22, 1953; s. James Robert and Alvern (Halverson) J.; m. Debra Marie Stanek, Aug. 28, 1982; 1 child, Christopher. BS, Gustavus Adolphus Coll., 1975; BA, U. Minn., 1977, DDS, 1979, MS, 1982. Pvt. practice periodontics Edina, Minn., 1982—; asst. prof. U. Minn., Mpls., 1982—. Mem. ADA, Minn. Dental Assn., Mpls. Dist. Dental Soc., Am. Acad. Periodontics, Minn. Acad. Periodontics. Lutheran. Avocations: hunting, camping, skiing, fishing. Office: 6545 France Ave S Edina MN 55435

JENSEN, JULIE SCHMITZ, city convention and visitors bureau director; b. Lynch, Nebr., Nov. 30, 1956; d. Kenneth Dean and Leona Josephine (Suedbeck) Schmitz; m. Gary Dean Jensen, Mar. 9, 1984. Grad. high sch., Bonesteel, S.D. Exec. sec. office of gov. State of S.D., Pierre, 1975-78; adminstrv. asst. Western S.D. Devel. Corp., Rapid City, 1979; asst. mgr. Conv. and Visitors Bur., Sioux Falls, S.D., 1979-83; dir. Conv. and Visitors Bur., Rapid City, S.D., 1983—; mem. Gov.'s Blue Ribbon Tourism Mktg. Panel, S.D., 1986—; bd. dirs. Rapid City Hospitality Assn., 1984—, Black Hills, Badlands and Lakes Assn., 1985—. chmn. registration S.D. Dem. Conv., Sioux Falls, 1982, Rapid City, 1986; Fundraiser Daschle for U.S. Senate Campaign, S.D., 1985—, Kneip for Gov. Campaign, Rapid City, 1986; bd. dirs. Leadership Rapid City, 1985-86. Mem. Internat. Assn. Conv. and Visitors Burs., Am. Soc. Assn. Execs., Mid-Am. C. of C. Execs. Roman Catholic. Lodge: Zonta (bd. dirs. 1986—). Avocations: reading, sewing, cooking, hiking. racquetball. Home: 955 Penny Ln Rapid City SD 57702 Office: Rapid City Conv and Visitors Bur 444 Mount Rushmore Rd N Rapid City SD 57701

JENSEN, LYNN EDWARD, medical association executive, economist; b. Rock Springs, Wyo., May 27, 1945; s. Glen and Helen (Anderson) J.; m. Carol Jean Lombard, June 10, 1967; children: Chelsea, Kara. BA, Idaho State U., 1967; PhD, U. Utah, 1979. Research assoc. U.S. Dept. Commerce, Washington, 1967, U. Utah, 1971-74, Utah State Planning Office, 1971-74; economist AMA Research Ctr., Chgo., 1974-75, div. dir., 1975-85, v.p. health service policy, 1985—; mem. Robert Wood Johnson Found. Adv. Com., Princeton, N.J., 1983-84, Johnson & Johnson Community Health Program; health adv. com. GAO. Editor-in-chief Intermountain Economic Review, 1972-73; assoc. editor Jour. Bus. and Econ. Stats., 1981—; contbr. articles to profl. jours. Served with U.S. Army, 1968-70, West Germany. Mem.AMA, Assn. Am. Med. Soc. Execs., Am. Soc. Assn. Execs., Am. Econ. Assn., Nat. Assn. Bus. Economists, Methodist. Avocations: jogging; swimming; photography. Home: 4 E Brookwood Ct Arlington Heights IL 60004 Office: AMA 535 N Dearborn St Chicago IL 60610

JENSEN, RICHARD EDWARD, psychologist; b. New Brunswick, N.J., Oct. 1, 1939; s. Otto Carl and Rose Olive (Krautwurst) J. BA, Upsala Coll., 1966; MA, Fairleighe Dickinson U., 1967; PhD, Miami U., Oxford, Ohio, 1973. Diplomate Am. Bd. Psychology. Staff psychologist Mental Health Clinic of Polk County, Lakeland, Fla., 1973-75; chief psychologist FMRS Mental Health Clinic, Beckly, W.Va., 1975-76; chief psychologist, mgr., adminstr. Mental Health Cen. of Western Ky., Paducah, 1976-79; dir. psychology clinic Nova U., Ft. Lauderdale, Fla., 1979-80; assoc. prof. of psychology Mankato (Minn.) State U., 1980—; cons. in field, Mankato, 1984—. Editor (book) Ethical Issues in Clinical Psychology, 1985; author (monograph) Interpersonal Systems Analysis, 1987. Mem. profl. adv. bd. Head Start Program, Paducah, 1978-79; bd. dirs. Beckley Contact Teliministry, 1975-76, Unitarian Universalist Fellowship, Mankato, 1984-86. Mem. Am. Psychol. Assn., Am. Assn. Marriage and Family Therapists (clin.). Avocations: sailing, auxilliary sailing vessels, small boat sailing, poetry writing. Office: Mankato State U Psychology Box 35 Mankato MN 56001-6001 Home: 3561 Kent St Unit 1202 Shoreview MN 55126

JENSEN, RICHARD ELLIS, JR., advertising executive; b. Omaha, Sept. 16, 1953; s. Richard Ellis and Daline Lucille (Green) J.; m. Darlene Marie Reber, June 10, 1977; children: Shannon Nicole, Joshua James. BBA, U. Nebr., Omaha, 1984. Sales rep. Sidles Co., Omaha, 1975-80; account exec. Great Empire Broadcasting, Omaha, 1980-83, Doug Wall Advt., Omaha, 1983-84, Smith, Kaplan, Allen & Reynolds Advt., Omaha, 1984—. Served with U.S. Army, 1972-74, USNG, 1976—. Recipient Meritorious Service award, Nebr. Nat. Guard, 1980, Excellence in Consultation award Nebr. Bus. Devel. Ctr., 1983. Mem. Omaha C. of C. (agrl. mktg. com.), Mid-Am. Direct Mktg. Assn. Club: Maple Village Country (Omaha) (bd. dirs. 1985-86, v.p. adminstrn. 1986-87). Lodges: Optimists (pres. Omaha club 1986-87), Masons. Avocations: golf, bowling, music. Home: 3730 N 95th St Omaha NE 68134 Office: SKAR Advt Agy 111 S 108th Ave Omaha NE 68154

JENSEN, ROGER JOSEPH, engineer; b. Chgo., Mar. 19, 1958; s. Fred Joseph and Agnes C. (Casey) J.; m. Deborah Pahl, Oct. 15, 1983. BS in Chem. Engring., Ill. Inst. Tech., 1980. Registered profl. engr., Ill. Process engr. Western Electric, Chgo., 1980-83, AT&T, Chgo., 1983-85, AT&T Network System, Boston, 1985-86; field support engr. AT&T Internat., Lisle, Ill., 1986—. Recipient Clinton E. Stryker award Ill. Inst. Tech., 1980. Mem. Western Soc. Engrs., Chgo. Jr. Assn. Commerce Industry (bd. dirs. 1983-84). Roman Catholic. Home: 3740 East Ave Berwyn IL 60402

JENSEN, SHIRLEY WULFF, small business owner; b. Kingsbury County, S.D., Jan. 12, 1925; d. Ferdinand and Karen Margaret (Jensen) Wulff; m. Nov. 23, 1975; 1 child, Fred Monroe Smith, Jr. Honor grad., Chillicothe Bus. Coll., 1943. Legal sec. New Port Richey, Fla., 1959-63; ins. agt., mgr., bd. dirs. Farm Mut. Fire Ins. Co. of Kingsbury County, De Smet, S.D., 1972-75; exec. sec. Beresford (S.D.) C. of C. and Beresford Bus and Indsl. Devel. Corp., 1976-78; office mgr., sales asst. Jensen Appliances, Beresford, 1979—. City commr. De Smet, 1974-75; Kingsbury County chmn. Easter Seal Soc., 1973-75; sec. ch. council Emmanuel Luth. Ch., Beresford, mem. S.D. Women's Caucus, Women's Action for Nuclear Disarmament, S.D. Peace and Justice Ctr. Mem. League of Women Voters. Club: Christian Women's, Progress Study. Home and Office: Rt 3 Box 11 Beresford SD 57004

JENSON, CARROLL EUGENE, retired dentist; b. Berthold, N.D., Sept. 1, 1921; s. Canute Theodore and Emma Mathilda (Rhone) J.; m. Sara Marie Kahn, July 27, 1924; 1 child, Peter Christopher. BA, Luther Coll., 1943; DDS, U. Minn., 1951. Practice gen. dentistry Bayport, Minn., 1953-86; bd. dirs. 1st State Bank of Bayport, 1970—, Washington County Cable Corp., Stillwater, Minn. Mayor City of Bayport, 1964-69; chmn. Citizen's Com. for Better Edn., Stillwater, 1953-60; bd. dirs. St. Croix United Way, Stillwater, 1983-85; mem. Ch. Council Library Bd. Served to lt. USNR, 1943-46, 51-53. Mem. ADA (life), Minn. Dental Assn., U. Minn. Century Club (life), Century II Luther Coll. (life), St. Paul Dist. Dental Soc. (v.p. 1970-71), Delta Sigma Delta. Republican. Lodge: Lions (past pres. Stillwater club). Avocations: music, reading, golf, travel. Home: 5 Point Rd Bayport MN 55003

JENTES, WALTER KENNETH, manufacturing company executive; b. Western Port, Md., May 18, 1941; s. Walter and Lydia (Walthert) J.; m. Shirley Dianne Richardson, Nov. 9, 1966; children—Jennifer Lynn, Kenneth Jason. M.S., Cin. U., 1963; B.S. in Acctg., U. Cin., 1973; M.B.A., Xavier U., 1973. Gen. mgr. Whitbeck-Wheeler, Belvidere, Ill., 1965-68; asst. to controller Vulcan Mfg.-Zurn Industries, Cin., 1968-72; plant controller Hillenbrand Industries, Batesville, Ind., 1972-76; v.p. fin. Cin. Time-Gen. Signal, Cin., 1976-86; v.p. ops. PME, Inc., Cin., 1986—, Reading Products, Inc., 1987—; dir. Richardson Realty, Cin., Old Town Investments, Cin. Editor: Direct Costing, 1980. Mem. Nat. Assn. Accts., Am. Prodn. and Inventory Control Soc. Lodge: Masons.

JEPSON, ROBERT SCOTT, JR., international investment banking specialist; b. Richmond, Va., July 20, 1942; s. Robert Scott and Inda (Hodges) J.; B.S., U. Richmond, 1964, M.Commerce, 1975; JD, Gonzaga U., 1986 (hon.), DCS, U. Richmond, 1987; m. Alice Finch Andrews, Dec. 28, 1964; children—Robert Scott, John Steven. With Va. Commonwealth Bankshares, Richmond, 1966-68; v.p. corp. fin. Birr Wilson & Co., Inc., San Francisco, 1968-69; with Calif. Capital Mgmt. Corp., Irvine, 1970-73; pres. Calcap Securities Corp., Los Angeles, 1970-73; v.p., dir. corp. fin. Cantor Fitzgerald & Co., Beverly Hills, Calif., 1973-75; dir. corp. planning and devel. Campbell Industries, San Diego, 1975-77; v.p., mgr. merger and acquisition div. Continental Ill. Bank, Chgo., 1977-82; sr. v.p., group head U.S. Capital Markets Group, 1st Nat. Bank Chgo., 1983—; chmn. bd. Jepson Corp., Chgo., Signet Optical Co., San Diego, Armorlite, Inc., San Marcos, Calif., Emerson Quiet Kool Corp., Woodbridge, N.J., Air-Maze Corp., Bedford Heights, Ohio, Hedstrom Corp., Bedford, Pa., Gerry Sportswear Corp., Denver, Atlantic Industries, Inc., Nutley, N.J., Jepson-Burns Corp., Winston-Salem, N.J., Farwest Garments, Inc., Seattle, Jepson Vineyards Ltd., Ukiah, Calif., Trans-Aero Industries, Inc., Los Angeles; vice chmn. bd. Hill Refrigeration, Trenton, N.J.; asst. prof. fin. Nat. U., 1976. Trustee, Gonzaga U., Spokane, Wash., 1982—; bd. trustees , Hamlin U., St. Paul, Minn., 1987. Served to 1st lt. M.P., Corps, AUS, 1964-66. Mem. Omicron Delta Kappa, Alpha Kappa Psi. Republican. Clubs: Mid-Am., Chgo. Home: 65 Hills and Dales Rd Barrington Hills IL 60010 Office: The Jepson Corp 340 W Butterfield Rd Elmhurst IL 60126

JERDE, ROXANNE GARSKE, marketing executive; b. Grand Forks, N.Dak., May 14, 1953; d. A. Blake and Edith Caroline (Skurdell) Garske; m. Michael Joseph Jerde, Apr. 16, 1977. BBA in Mktg. and Mgmt., U. Iowa, 1975; MBA in Fin. and Organizational Behavior, U. Mo., 1983. Sales mgr. bank cards 1st Nat. Bank, Kansas City, Mo., 1978-80; SBA cons. U. Mo., Kansas City, 1982-83, teaching instr., 1984-85; project mgr. corp. devel. Hallmark Cards, Inc., Kansas City, 1984-86, mgr. creative advt. group, 1986—. Mem. Kansas City Jr. League (hqrs. chmn. 1983-84, tng. chmn. 1986-87), Beta Gamma Sigma, Kappa Kappa Gamma (holiday tour officer 1980-84). Club: Leawood (Kans.) Country. Home: 8841 Cherokee Ln Leawood KS 66206 Office: Hallmark Cards Inc 2501 McGee Kansas City MO 64141-6580

JERELE, JOSEPH JAMES, JR., radiologist; b. Cleve., Mar. 1, 1945; s. Joseph James and Margaret Louise (Meares) J.; m. Linda Sue Wells, June 29, 1973; children—Jordan, Joe, Jacob, Joshua. B.A., Taylor U., 1968; D.O., Kirksville Coll. Osteo. Medicine, 1972. Intern Doctor's Hosp., Columbus, Ohio, 1972-73; emergency room physician Orlando Gen. Hosp., Fla., 1973-74; radiology and nuclear medicine resident Doctor's Hosp., Columbus, 1974-77, sr. attending staff radiologist, 1977—, treas., 1980-81; asst. clin. prof. radiology Ohio U. Athens, 1980—. Contbg. author: X-ray Technology Textbook, 1980. Contbr. book revs. to profl. jours. Recipient Mead Johnson award, 1976. Mem. Am. Osteo. Coll. Radiology (treas. 1982—, bd. dirs. 1982—, cert. radiologist), Am. Osteo. Assn., Ohio Osteo. Assn., Central Ohio Radiol. Assn., Am. Inst. Ultrasound in Medicine, Radiol. Soc. N.Am., Am. Osteo. Coll. Nuclear Medicine (cert. nuclear medicine). Republican. Mem. Grace Brethren Ch. Avocations: triathlons; distance running; soccer; racquetball. Home: 697 Gatehouse Ln Worthington OH 43085 Office: Doctors Hosp 1087 Dennison Ave Columbus OH 43201

JEROME, JERROLD V., insurance company executive. Chmn., pres. Unicoa Corp., Chgo. Office: Unicoa Corp 1 E Wacker Dr Chicago IL 60601 *

JESTER, GUY EARLSCOURT, construction executive, technical consultant and witness; b. Dyersburg, Tenn., Oct. 20, 1929; s. Guy Earlscourt Jester and Thelma (Pate) Wild; m. Roberta Andrews, Dec. 19, 1953 (div. June 1980); children: Mark, Robin, Elaine, Guy Leigh; B.S. in Engring., U.S. Mil. Acad, 1951; M.S. in Civil Engring., U. Ill., 1958, PhD, 1969; postgrad. Columbia U., 1963-65, U.S. Army War Coll., 1968, U. Pitts., 1973; Registered profl. engr., Tex. Commd. 2d lt. U.S. Army, 1951; advanced through grades to col., 1971; dep. dir. and acting dir. Corps of Engrs., Waterways Expt. Sta., 1965-67; div. engr., 9th Inf. Div., 1968-69; office chief research and devel., asst. to chief Research & Devel. and chief info. system, 1968-71; dist. engr. Corps of Engrs., St. Louis, 1971-73; retired, 1973; v.p., bd. dirs. J.S. Alberici Constrn. Co., Inc., St. Louis, 1973—. past vice chmn. bd. transp. St. Louis Regional Commerce and Growth Assn.; v.p., dir. Internat. Waste Energy Systems; chmn. bd. and pres. Assn. for Improvement of Miss. River; chmn. bldg. code rev. com. St. Louis Met. Area, bldg. and indsl. devel. commn. St. Louis County; mem. Confluence St. Louis Task Force; Author: (tech. manual) Soil Structure Interaction in Cuhesive Coil, Vols. I & II, 1979; former sr. warden St. Timothy's Episcopal Ch.; former vice chmn. council Diocese of Mo., Episcopal Ch.; bd. dirs. St. Louis Sch. Pharmacy; adv. com. Dean Engring., U. Ill.; bd. dirs., chmn. philanthropic com. St. Louis Charitable Found.; vice chmn. Profl. Code Com. St. Louis. Recipient Cert. of Appreciation, U.S. Army, C.E., 1974; Spl. Service award, Fed. Exec. Bd., 1972, 73; named St. Louis Constrn. Man of Yr., 1980. Fellow Soc. Am. Mil. Engrs. (past pres., past regional v.p., dir., Appreciation award 1983); mem. ASCE (past pres. St. Louis sect., Presdl. citation 1979), Am. Gen. Contractors (chmn., mem. coms.), Engrs. Club of St. Louis (Merit award 1981), U. Ill. Civil Engr. Alumni Assn. (bd. dirs.), West Point Soc. St. Louis (pres.), Engrs. Club (bd. dirs.), Am. Def. Preparedness Assn. (bd. dirs.), Govt. Contract Mgmt. Assn. Alumni Assn. (bd. dirs.), Sigma Xi, Phi Kappa Phi. Avocations: reading, golf, tennis, bridge. Home: 13093 Greenbough Creve Coeur MO 63146 Office: JS Alberici Constrn Co Inc 2150 Kienlen Ave Saint Louis MO 63121

JESTER, TOD KRUEGER, manufacturing company executive; b. Webb City, Mo., Jan. 31, 1942; s. Paul Marlin and Twila Opal (Krueger) J.; m. Mary Angeline Gleue, Aug. 22, 1964; children: Paul, Lisa, Eric. BSME, U. Mo., Rolla, 1963; MS in Applied Mechanics, U. Ill., 1967. Registered profl engr., Ill. Sr. engr. Union Carbide Corp., Indpls. and Tonawanda, N.Y., 1973-78; dir. engring. UIP Engineered Products Corp., Addison, Ill., 1978-83, pres., 1985—; dir. engring. Groen div. Dover Corp., Elk Grove, Ill., 1983-85; instr. Harper Coll., Palatine, Ill., 1980—; cons. Standard Automatic, Downers Grove, Ill., 1982. Contbr. articles to profl. jours.; inventor limited flexibility joint. Named Engr. of Month Martin Marietta, 1968. Mem. Am. Soc. Mech. Engrs. Republican. Presbyterian. Club: Meadow (Rolling Meadows, Ill.). Office: UIP Engineered Products Corp 145 N Swift Rd Addison IL 60101

JETT, MILDRED SUNDAY, nurse, administrator; b. Bessmer, Ala., July 1, 1947; d. Jimmie and Inez (Norwood) Sunday; m. Arthur Robert Jett, Aug. 15, 1970; children: Nataki Elissar, Kanye Kamau. Diploma in practical nursing, No. Mich. U., 1967; BSN magna cum laude U. Mich., 1975. Lic. practical nurse Providence Hosp., Southfield, Mich., 1968-70; nurse St. Luke's Hosp., Marquette, Mich., 1970-72; lic. practical nurse Univ. Hosp., Ann Arbor, Mich., 1972-74, staff nurse, 1976-77; inservice instr. Kirwood Gen. Hosp., Detroit, 1976-77, dept. head, ednl. dir. hosp. staff devel., 1977-86 ; asst. dir. human resources tng. Wayne State U., Detroit, 1986—; tchr. CPR to sr. citizens; tchr. childbirth edn. Botsford Gen. Hosp., 1986. Served to capt., Nurses Corps, USAR. Mem. Detroit Black Nurses Assn. (2d v.p. 1978-80, 80-82), Am. Nurses Assn., Nat. Black Nurses Assn., Met. Detroit Health Edn. Council, Met. Detroit Coalition for Blood Pressure Control, Mich. Soc. Instructional Tech., Cable Health Coalition, Delta Sigma Theta, Sigma Theta Tau (membership com. 1975-76). Mem. Christian Ch. Office: Wayne State U 5980 Cass Ave ASB# # Room 203 Detroit MI 48202

JETTKE, HARRY JEROME, government official; b. Detroit, Jan. 2, 1925; s. Harry H. and Eugenia M. (Dziatkiewicz) J.; B.A., Wayne State U., 1961; m. Josefina Suarez-Garcia, Oct. 22, 1948; 1 dau., Joan Lillian Jettke Sorger. Owner, operator Farmacia Virreyes/Farmacia Regina, Toluca, Mex., 1948-55; intern pharmacist Cunningham Drug Stores, Detroit, 1955-63; drug specialist, product safety specialist FDA, Detroit, 1963-73; acting dir. Cleve., U.S. Consumer Product Safety Commn., 1973-75, compliance officer, 1975-78, supr., investigations, 1978-82, regional compliance officer, 1982-83, sr. resident, 1983—. Served with Fin. Dept., U.S. Army, 1942-43. Drug specialist FDA. Mem. Am. Soc. for Quality Control (sr., chmn. Cleve. sect. 1977-78, cert. quality technician, cert. quality engr.), Asociación Nacional Mexicana de Estadistica y Control de Calidad, policy com. Cleve. Fed. Exec. Bd., 1985. Roman Catholic. Home: 25715 Yoeman Dr Westlake OH 44145 Office: US Consumer Product Safety Commn One Playhouse Sq 1375 Euclid Ave Cleveland OH 44114

JEWELL, RICHARD BARKLEY, agricultural equipment manufacturing executive; b. Decatur, Ill., Nov. 28, 1945; s. Albert W. and M. Helen (Taggart) J.; m. Cynthea Jensen, Apr. 17, 1970; children—Jennifer Christine, Catherine Elizabeth. B.S. in Acctg., No. Ill. U., 1970; M.B.A., Ill. State U., 1976. Cert. ins. broker. Staff auditor Price Waterhouse & Co., Chgo., 1970-71; acctg. mgr. Am. Hosp. Supply Co., McGaw Park, Ill., 1971-72; spl. project analyst Honeggar & Co., Inc., Fairbury, Ill.; corp. sec. Wheels Leasing, Inc., Fairbury, Ill., 1972-74, JLW Holding Co., Paxton, Ill., 1972-74, Agrl. Comml. Inc., Paxton, 1974-83; controller, corp. sec. Big Wheels Internat. Co., Paxton, 1974—; pres. Video Memories, Inc., Loda, Ill., 1986—; v.p. mktg. Rhino Robots Inc., Champaign, Ill., 1983 exec. v.p., 1983-84; treas. Big Wheels, Inc., 1984—, corp. sec., 1987—; del. Gov.'s First Small Bus. Conf., Ill., 1985, 86, White House Conf. on Small Bus., 1986, fin. task force chmn. Social events chmn. local Am. Cancer Soc. Mem. Am. Prodn. and Inventory Control Soc. (dir.). Methodist. Club: Lakeview Country (Loda). Contbr. articles on robots to publs. Home: POB 305 Loda IL 60948 Office: PO Box 113 Paxton IL 60957

JEWELL, RICHARD DANIEL, dentist; b. Reedsburg, Wis., Feb. 12, 1936; s. Ernest L. and Adele Dorthea (Gall) J.; m. Jeanette Marie Brown, Apr. 15, 1962; children—Todd E., Lisa M. B.A., Luth. Coll., 1958; D.D.S., Marquette Dental Coll., 1962. Practice dentistry, Madison, Wis., 1964—. Served to capt. USAF, 1962-64. Mem. ADA, Dane County Dental Soc., Wis. Dental Assn., Sigma Delta; Lodges: Masons, Elks. Avocations: soap stone carving; stamp collecting; stained glass. Office: 5011 Monona Dr Madison WI 53716

JEWERS, GERALD OLIVER, provincial judge; b. Winnipeg, Man., Can., May 19, 1932; s. Ernest John and Kathleen Victoria (Green) J.; m. Claire Woodcock, Aug. 21, 1954; children: Judith, Robin, Leslie. LLB, U. Man., 1955, LLM, 1957. Assoc. Newman, McLean and Assocs., Winnipeg, 1956-61; ptnr. Fillmore and Riley, Winnipeg, 1961-77; judge County Ct. of Winnipeg, 1977-84, Ct. of Queen's Bench, Winnipeg, Man., 1984—. Mem. Man. Law Reform Commn. Office: Court of Queen's Bench, Law Courts Bldg, Winnipeg, MB Canada R3C 0V8 *

JEWETT, CATHY ANN, elementary principal; b. Middletown, Ohio, Apr. 16, 1946; m. R. F. Jewett, July 21, 1973. BA, Anderson (Ind.) Coll., 1969; MA, Miami U., Oxford, Ohio, 1973. Cert. elem. sch. tchr., counselor, elem. sch. prin. Tchr. Vigo County Schs., Terre Haute, Ind., 1969-72; guidance counselor Ross Local Schs., Hamilton, Ohio, 1973-76, asst. prin., 1976-77, prin., 1977—. Named one of Outstanding Young Women in Am., 1977; recipient Elem. Sch. Recognition program award Ohio Dept. Edn., 1986. Mem. Nat. Assn. Elem. Sch. Prins. (nat. fellow 1985), Ohio Assn. Elem. Sch. Adminstrs., Assn. for Supervision and Curriculum Devel., Nat. Assn. for Edn. of Young Children, Phi Delta Kappa, Delta Kappa Gamma. Presbyterian.

JEWETT, GREGORY LEWIS, research analyst; b. Columbus, Ohio, Apr. 19, 1956; s. Robert Wayne and Marie Sarah (Knol) J. BA, Otterbein Coll., Westervill, Ohio, 1978; MS, Ohio State U., 1980. Ops. research analyst Cooper Tier & Rubber Co., Findlay, OH, 1979—; instr. Findlay Coll., 1981-83. Advisor Jr. Achievement, Findlay, 1982-85; Fellowship Christian Athletes, 1983—; head coach Findlay Coll. Cross Country, 1981-84; asst. coach Findlay Coll. Track and Field, 1981—; track offical Ohio High Sch. Athletic Assn., 1983—. Mem. Assn. Systems Mgmt., Ops. Research Soc. Am. Presbyterian. Avocations: running, various sporting events. Home: 126 Harrington Ave #C Findlay OH 45840 Office: Cooper Tire and Rubber Co Lima and Western Aves Findlay OH 45840

JEZOWSKI, MARIANNE MIKA, computer science and mathematics educator; b. Oklahoma City, June 3, 1943; d. Walter Francis and Ann (Labosh) Mika; m. John Joseph Jezowski, Aug. 14, 1965; 1 child, Michele. B.A., Clarke Coll., 1965; M.Ed., Loyola U.-Chgo., 1977. Math. tchr. Community Consol. Sch. Dist. #15, Palatine, Ill., 1965-69, River Trails Sch. Dist. #26, Mount Prospect, Ill., 1972—. Math. tchr. Coll. of DuPage, Glen Ellyn, Ill., 1984-86. Mem. Ill. Computing Educators Assn. (newsletter editor, bd. govs.), Ill. Edn. Assn., NEA, River Trails Edn. Assn. Roman Catholic. Office: River Trails Jr High Sch 1000 N Wolf Rd Mount Prospect IL 60056

JHAWAR, SHIV RATAN, investment and tax consultant; b. Bikaner, India, Aug. 13, 1948; came to U.S., 1973; s. Dhanraj Harakchand and Ratan Devi (Bajaj) J. B in Commerce with honors, U. Calcutta, India, 1968; MS in Acctg., U. Ill., 1974. Accounts analyst CBS TV, Chgo., 1974-75; pvt. practice investment and tax cons. Chgo., 1975—; lectr. income tax and acctg., India and U.S., 1971-80. Mem. Nat. Soc. Pub. Accts., Am. Acctg. Assn., Inst. Chartered Accts., Chgo. Computer Soc. Avocations: writing, skating, chess, computer programming. Home: 211 S Clark St #2998 Chicago IL 60690-2998 Office: 22 W Monroe St Chicago IL 60602

JIBBEN, LAURA ANN, state agency administrator; b. Peoria, Ill., Oct. 1, 1949; d. Charles Otto and Dorothy Lee (Skaggs) Becker; m. Michael Eugene Hagan, July 7, 1967 (div. Apr. 1972); m. Louis C. Jibben, July 14, 1972. BA in Criminal Justice, Sangamon State U., 1984. Asst. to chief of adminstrn. Ill. Dept. Corrections, Springfield, 1974-77, exec. asst. to dir., 1977-80, dep. dir., 1980-81; mgr. toll services Ill. Tollway Dept., Oak Brook, 1981-86; chief adminstrv. officer Regional Transp. Authority, Chgo., 1986—, also, chmn. pension trust; cons. labor studies Sangamon State U., Springfield, 1981. Recipient Appreciation award VFW, Chgo., 1983. Mem. Nat. Assn. Female Execs., Women's Transp. Seminar, Beta Sigma Phi (treas., v.p., corr. sec. Naperville and Easton, Ill. chpts.). Avocations: reading, camping, boating, gardening.

JICKLING, JOHN WARD, architect; b. Detroit, June 6, 1921; s. Clare Mason and Norma (Carland) J.; m. Barbara Wright Fairman, June 14, 1947; children—Julia, Jennifer, Carol, John, David, Amy. B.Arch., U. Mich., 1948. Architect Swanson Assocs., Bloomfield Hills, Mich., 1948-59; cons. architect Birmingham, Mich., 1960-62; architect Jickling & Lyman, Birmingham, 1963-72; pres. Jickling, Lyman & Powell, Birmingham, 1979—. Prin. works include Mich. Plaza Office Bldg. (Steel Inst. award 1970), Bentley Hist. Library, 1971, A. Alfred Taubman Med. Library, 1976, Gerald R. Ford Presdl. Library (Masonry Inst. award 1981), High Tech. Ctr., Oakland Community Coll. (Detroit chpt. AIA design award 1985). Mem. Traffic and Safety Bd., Birmingham (Mich.), 1970-76; chmn. Planning Bd., Birmingham, 1967-76; trustee Community House, Birmingham, 1983-86, Oakland Parks Found., Oakland County (Mich.), 1983—. Fellow AIA (bd. dirs. 1980-83, Gold medal Detroit chpt. 1983, pres. Detroit 1976-77), Mich. Soc. Architects (pres. 1979-80). Lodge: Lions (pres. 1974-75). Avocations: philately; ornothology; travel. Office: Jickling Lyman & Powell Assocs Inc 909 Haynes Birmingham MI 48009

JILANI, ATIQ AHMED, industrialist; b. Amroha, India, Feb. 1, 1948; s. Siddiq Ahmed and Nasima (Khatoon) J.; m. Khalida Bano Naqvi, Dec. 25, 1975; children: Hussain, Ibrahim. BE, NED Engring. Coll., Karachi U., 1969; MS, Tuskegee Inst., Ala., 1971; cert. in mgmt., Purdue U., 1978, Northwestern U., 1980, U. Pa., 1982. Registered profl. engr., Ill.; cert. mfg. engr.; cert. plant engr. Script writer Karachi (Pakistan) TV, 1967-70; mem. research staff AEC, Tuskegee, Ala., 1970-71; design engr. Lummus Industries, Columbus, Ga., 1971-73; product engr. Borg-Warner Corp., Chgo., 1974-78, mgr. engring. Chgo. Marine Containers div. Sea Containers, Broadview, Ill., 1978-80; v.p., chief operating officer, gen. mgr. Borg-Erickson Corp., Chgo., 1980-85; chmn. bd. dirs. Circuit Systems Inc., 1985—; cons. in industry and agr. UN, including work in South Asia, 1981. Contbr. articles to profl. jours.; patentee (U.S. and internat.) in field agrl. equipment. Mem. Inst. Printed Circuits, Assn. Energy Engrs. (charter), Thinkers Forum (pres. 1967-70). Home: PO Box 3212 Oak Brook IL 60521

JILDEH, RAJA TOUFIC, structural engineer; b. Lansing, Mich., Nov. 17, 1959; s. Toufic N. and Aida (Musallam) J. BSCE, Wayne State U., 1983. Gen. engr. IV Mich. Dept. Transp., Lansing, 1984-85, gen. engr. V, 1985-86, transp. engr. VI, 1986—. Mem. ASCE. Avocations: politics, current events, music. Home: 2305 Seminole Dr Okemos MI 48864 Office: Mich Dept Transp 425 W Ottawa Lansing MI 48909

JIMENEZ, BETTIE EILEEN, small business owner; b. LaCygne, Kans., June 8, 1932; d. William Albert and Ruby Faye (Cline) Montee; m. William R. Bradley, Aug. 21, 1947 (div. Sept. 1950); 1 child, Shirley; m. J.P. Jimenez, Feb. 20, 1951 (div. Nov. 1978); children: Pamela, Joe Jr., Robin Michelle. Student, Ft. Scott Jr. Coll., Paola, Kans., 1979-81. Reporter LaCygne Jour., 1943-45; union recorder I.L.G.W.U., Paola, 1956-57; mgr. Estes Metalcraft, Osawatomie, Kans., 1977-82; owner El Rey Tavern, Osawatomie, 1980-87. Home: 516 Walnut Osawatomie KS 66064

JINKINS, MARK ALLEN, lawyer, accountant; b. Dodgeville, Wis., Apr. 9, 1954; s. Kenneth William and Charlotte Jane (Brun) J.; m. Ann M. Zwicky, Oct. 11, 1980; children: David, Michael. BBA in Acctg. and Mgmt., U. Wis., 1976, JD, 1979. Bar: Wis. 1979, U.S. Dist. Ct. (we. dist.) Wis. 1979, U.S. Dist. Ct. (ea. dist.) Wis. 1980. Sole practice Sturgeon Bay, Wis., 1980; assoc. Pinkert, Smith, Koehn & Weir, Sturgeon Bay, 1981-83; ptnr. Pinkert, Smith, Koehn, Weir & Jinkins, Sturgeon Bay, 1984-86, Pinkert, Smith, Weir & Jinkins, Sturgeon Bay, 1987—. Pres., bd. dirs. HELP of Door County Inc., Sturgeon Bay, 1980-84; bd. dirs. Door County Child Care Services Inc., Sturgeon Bay, 1983—, Door County unit Am. Cancer Soc., 1986—. Mem. ABA, Wis. Bar Assn., Door Kewaunee Bar Assn. (pres., sec.), Door County C. of C. (bd. dirs. 1984-85), U. Wis. Alumni Assn. (local pres., bd. dirs. 1982—). Mem. United Ch. Christ. Club: Sturgeon Bay Yacht (bd. dirs. 1986—). Lodge: Rotary. Avocations: golf, boating, reading. Home: 220 S Hudson St Sturgeon Bay WI 54235 Office: Pinkert Smith Weir & Jinkins PO Box 89 Sturgeon Bay WI 54235

JIRKA, RUDOLF REZSO, association health services executive; b. Torbagy, Pest, Hungary, Jan. 31, 1923; came to U.S., 1963; s. Joseph and Emilia (Lueff) J.; m. Erika Westerman, July 22, 1961. JD, Pazmany Peter U., Budapest, Hungary, 1945; Diploma in Mech. Engring., Armee Blendee, Dalat, Indochina, 1949; BA in Classical Studies, Coll. of Vac, Hungary, 1961; LLD (hon.), Orthodox Cath. U., Chgo., 1972; D of Med. Rehab., Coll. Natural Medicine, Diatalana, Sri Lanka, 1977. Dept. head Hungarian Airlines, Budapest, 1941-44; tech. advisor Service du Material, Indochina and Germany, 1946-54; fitness and health dir. YMCA, Ottawa, Ont., Can., 1955-63, Anderson, Ind., 1963—; cons. Criminal Rehab. Programs, Anderson, 1975; advisor Madison County Superior Ct., Anderson, 1972-80, U.S. Sports Acad., Mobile, Ala., 1985—. Author: Sports medicine and Rehabilitation, 1973. Served to 1st lt. Hungarian Airforce, 1944-46. Decorated Medaille Colonial (France); recipient Merit award France, 1954, Community Service award City of Anderson, 1982. Fellow Health Services Dirs. Soc. (regional v.p. 1962-65); mem. Corrective Therapy Assn., Am. Coll. Sports Medicine. Avocations: music, swimming, gardening, woodworking. Home: 426 W 21st St Anderson IN 46014 Office: Madison County YMCA 28 W 12th St Anderson IN 46015

JIROUSEK, JAMES VICTOR, data processing executive; b. Faribault, Minn., May 5, 1947; s. Victor Frank and Phyllis Joan (Fleckenstein) J.; m. Carol Ann Schimonitz, Aug. 26, 1983. BA in History, U. Minn., 1969. Installer Western Electric, Mpls., 1973-75; billing programmer Northwestern Bell Telephone Co., Omaha, 1978-86, tech. trainer, 1986—; lectr. computers Boy Scouts Am., Bennington, Nebr., 1986. Designer computer programs bill print system, 1983, cash entry system, 1985. Del. DFL Dist. Conv., Mpls., 1978. Served to sgt. USAF, 1969-73. Roman Catholic. Club: Univ. Pep Chess. Avocations: reading, personal computer programming, jogging, racquetball, golf. Office: Northwestern Bell Telephone Co 100 S 19th St Omaha NE 68102

JISCHKE, MARTIN C., university official. Chancellor U. Mo., Rolla. Office: Univ of Mo-Rolla Office of the Chancellor Rolla MO 65401 *

JOB, REUBEN P., clergyman. Bishop Iowa conf. United Methodist Ch. Office: 1019 Chestnut St Des Moines IA 50309 *

JOBE, RONALD LEE, laundry machinery company executive; b. Birmingham, Ala., Jan. 19, 1948; s. Robert Lee and Eloise Dean (Glass) J.; m. Beverly W. Whitehead, Sept. 14, 1968; 1 son, Jason Robert. B.S. in Indsl. Engring., U. Ala., 1970. Methods engr. Butler Mfg. Co., Birmingham, 1973-76; v.p. House of Metals, Inc., Birmingham, 1976-78; v.p. sales and mktg. Arrowhead Grating and Metalworks, Kansas City, Mo., 1978-81; v.p., gen. mgr. Columbia Laundry Machinery Co., Kansas City, 1981—. George C. K. Johnson scholar, 1970. Mem. Am. Inst. Indsl. Engrs. (pres. 1970-71), Ala. Bass Fisherman's Assn. (pres. Tuscaloosa 1971-72), Kansas City C. of C., Alpha Pi Mu (pres. 1969-70). Home: 7919 Hallet Lenexa KS 66215 Office: Columbia Laundry Machinery Co 2210 Campbell Kansas City MO 64108

JODELKA, EDWARD STEFAN, manufacturing company executive; b. Emsdetten, Germany, Sept. 26, 1949; came to U.S., 1951, naturalized, 1966; s. Stefan and Maria (Budnik) J.; B.S. indsl. Edn., Chgo. State U., 1971, postgrad., 1971, 72-73; m. Deborah Lee Boykovsky, July 3, 1971; children—Melissa Lynn, Thomas Edward, David Edward. With Radiant Products Co., Inc., Chgo., 1965-83, v.p. 1978-83; dir. automatic engr. and sales Binks Mfg. Co., Franklin Park, Ill., 1983—; vocat. guidance counselor, sch. programmer, tchr. Cregier Vocat. High Sch., Chgo., 1972-74. Mem. bd. edn. dist. 229 Oak Lawn (Ill.) Community High Sch. Mem. Internat. Entrepreneurs Assn., Am. Entrepreneurs Assn., Am. Mgmt. Assn. Republican. Office: Binks Mfg Co Inc 9201 W Belmont Ave Franklin Park IL 60131

JODSAAS, LARRY E., computer components company executive. Pres. computer systems and services Control Data Corp., Mpls., 1987—. Office: Control Data Corp 8100 34th Ave St Minneapolis MN 55440 *

JOELSON, JACK BERNARD, social work and mental health educator; b. N.Y.C., Dec. 11, 1927; s. Bernard and Bessie (Jaffe) J.; m. Josephine Cannova, Oct. 30, 1947; children: Bernard, Michael, Benjamin. BA, U. Ill., 1948; MSW, Washington U., St. Louis, 1952; PhD, U. Pitts., 1968. Lic. social worker, Ohio. Exec. dir. Black Hawk County Mental Health Ctr., Waterloo, Iowa, 1955-62; field asst. prof. U. Pitts., 1963-66; asst. prof. mental health Case Western Res. U., Cleve., 1966-68, assoc. prof., chmn. mental health specialization, 1968—; social work cons. VA Hosp., Brecksville, Ohio, 1968-70; research dir. Lake County Youth Project, Painesville, Ohio, 1970-72. Mem. Gov.'s Com. on Juvenile Behavior, Iowa, 1958; mem. planning com. Cuyahoga County Mental Health Bd., Cleve., 1983—. Served to 1st lt. U.S. Army, 1952-55. Grantee NIMH U. Pitts., 1962-64, NIMH Case Western Res. U., 1983-85. Mem. AAUP, Nat. Assn. Social Workers (cert.), Am. Assn. Psychiatric Social Workers, Council Social Work Edn., Am. Assn. Social Workers (chmn. Tampa Bay chpt. 1951-52). Democrat. Jewish. Avocations: photography, pingpong. Office: Case Western Res U Sch Applied Social Scis 2035 Abington Rd Cleveland OH 44106

JOERN, CHARLES EDWARD, JR., lawyer; b. Oak Park, Ill., Apr. 27, 1951; s. Charles Edward and Eleanor (Lambert) J.; m. Christine Mary Lake, July 28, 1973; children—Jessica, William, Marisa, Angela. B.A., Knox Coll., 1973; M. Urban Affairs, U. Colo., 1976; J.D., De Paul U., 1980. Bar: Ill. 1980, U.S. Dist. Ct. (no. dist.) Ill. 1980, U.S. Ct. Appeals (7th cir.) 1981. Asst. to planning cons. J. R. Crowley and Assocs., 1973-74; systems analyst U. Colo. sponsored systems analysis of the Aravada, Colo. Bldg. Inspection Div., 1974-75; student intern div. comprehensive health planning Colo. Dept. Health, 1976; law clk. Cook County Legal Assistance Found., Ill., 1978, consumer fraud div. Office Ill. Atty. Gen., 1979-80; assoc. Pope, Ballard, Shepard & Fowle, Ltd., Chgo., 1980—; staff mem. Family in Crisis Conf., Galesburg, Ill., 1973; panel atty. Chgo. Vol. Legal Services Found. Bd. advisers N.C. Outward Bound Sch., Morganton, 1983—; bd. dirs. Richport YMCA, LaGrange, Ill., 1984—. Fellow in pub. affairs U. Colo., 1976. Mem. Ill. State Bar Assn., ABA (litigation sect.), Chgo. Bar Assn. (chmn. child abuse and neglect com. 1985-86), Pi Alpha Alpha. Republican. Roman Catholic. Office: Pope Ballard Shepard & Fowle Ltd 69 W Washington St Chicago IL 60602

JOHANN, WALTER PAUL, marketing executive; b. Far Rockaway, N.Y., Oct. 17, 1946; s. Wilmot Warburton and Virginia M. (Batta) J.; m. Gail Emily Buswell, Mar. 1, 1967; children: Timothy, Jennifer. BA, Iowa Wesleyan Coll., 1968; MBA, SUNY, Albany, 1974. Programmer Mason & Hanger div. Silas MAson Co. Inc., Middletown, Iowa, 1968-69; internal cons. 3M Co., St. Paul, 1974-76, market planning mgr., 1977-78; pres., chief exec. officer Dynamic Strategies, Inc., Forest Lake, Minn., 1979—. Served with U.S. Army, 1969-71, Vietnam. Decorated Bronze Star. Republican. Lutheran. Club: Forest Lake (Minn.) Swim (pres. 1983-86). Avocations: swimming, bicycling, chess, running, karate. Home: 22550 Jason Ave N Forest Lake MN 55025 Office: Dynamic Strategies Inc 1068 S Lake St Forest Lake MN 55025

JOHANNING, RONALD IVAN, electronics executive; b. Richland Ctr., Wis., July 7, 1955; s. William John and Eleanora Kathleen (Lins) J.; m. Georgia Jean Prucha, Sept. 14, 1984. BSME, U. Wis., 1980. Area engr. Mich. Wis. Pipeline, Detroit, 1080-82; pres. Dyna Tech. Services, Madison, Wis., 1982—. Mem. ASME, IEEE, Illumination Enging. Soc., Am. Soc. Heating, Refrigeration and Air Conditioning Execs. Home: Rt 1 Box 739 Rory Rd Poynette WI 53955 Office: Dyna Tech Services Inc 5513 Femrite Dr PO Box 8799 Madison WI 53708

JOHANSON, W.F. WALKER, marketing executive; b. Richmond, Va., Nov. 14, 1945; s. Thomas Alfred Lester and Jane Carden (Walker) J.; m. Kerry Kay Helmick, May 21, 1975; children: Nils, Cooper, Hakon, Riley, Carson. Student, The Cooper Union, 1963; BA in Edn., U. Mich., 1970; grad., Xerox Leadership Seminar, 1972. Customer service supr. Xerox U. Microfilms, Ann Arbor, Mich., 1968-69, mktg. product mgr., 1970-73; v.p. Ashton-Worthington, Balt., 1973; exec. dir., pres. The Nat. Inst. for Orgnl. Research, Ann Arbor, 1973—; mktg. cons. to numerous colleges and univs., 1973—. Author numerous college admissions and fund-raising publs. Bishop Ch. Jesus Christ of Latter-Day Saints, Ann Arbor, 1978-82, mem. stake presidency, 1983-84, pres. stake mission, 1986—. Mem. Am. Mktg. Assn., Sales Promotion Execs. Assn., Council for Advancement and Support of Edn. (numerous awards), Nat. Assn. Coll. Admissions Counselors. Republican. Avocations: family activities, travel, U.S. history, golf. Office: Nat Inst Orgnl Research 2115 Devonshire Pkwy Ann Arbor MI 48104

JOHN, GERALD WARREN, hospital pharmacist; b. Salem, Ohio, Feb. 16, 1947; s. Harold Elba and Ruth Springer (Pike) J.; m. Jean Ann Marie Orris, Nov. 5, 1977; children—Patrick Warren, Jeanette Lynn. B.S.Ph., Ohio No. U., 1970; M.S., U. Md., 1974. Registered pharmacist, Ohio, Md. Staff pharmacist North Columbiana County Community Hosp., Salem, 1970-72; asst. resident in hosp. pharmacy U. Md. Hosp., Balt., 1972-73, sr. resident, 1973-74, chmn. patient care pharmacies, 1974-76; dir. pharmacy Ohio Valley Hosp., Steubenville, Ohio, 1976—; preceptor profl. externship program Ohio No. U. Sch. Pharmacy, 1977—; adj. clin. instr. practical experience program Duquesne U. Sch. Pharmacy, 1976—; mem. bd. govs. Carriage Inn Hospice, 1985—. Named Hosp. Pharmacist of Yr., Md. Soc. Hosp. Pharmacists, 1976, Outstanding Young Man of Am., U.S. Jaycees, 1977. Mem. Am. Soc. Hosp. Pharmacists, Ohio Soc. Hosp. Pharmacists, Am. Pharm. Assn., Jefferson County Acad. Pharmacy, Ohio Pharm. Assn., Southeastern Ohio Soc. Hosp. Pharmacists (pres. 1985-87), Rho Chi. Methodist. Mem. adv. bd. Contemporary Pharmacy Practice, 1977-83.

JOHN, MERTIS, JR., record company executive; b. Detroit, May 22, 1932; s. Mertis and Lillie G. (Robinson) J.; m. Essie M. Wincher, June 16, 1957; 1 son, Darryl E.; m. Olivia M. Fuller, Aug. 6, 1978. A.A., Wayne Coll., 1978. Songwriter for King Records, Cin. and N.Y.C., 1955-67; founder Mertis Music Co., Detroit, 1962—; founder, pres. Meda Record Co., 1981—; co-producer Inside Music, 1977; also musician, songwriter. Served with U.S. Army, 1952-54. Mem. Broadcast Music Assn., Detroit Soc. Musicians and Entertainers (chmn. bd. dirs. 1984—), Am. Fedn. Musicians, Broadcast Music Inc. (corr.). Baptist. Lodge: Masons. Composer over 300 songs; author (poem) Christmas Morn, 1982.

JOHNEY, GLENN ERIC, aerospace engineer; b. Kansas City, Mo., July 15, 1956; s. Eugene Albert and Czerna Bye (Cruce) J. B.S. in Aerospace Engring., U. Mo., Rolla, 1978. Specialist engr. Boeing Mil. Aircraft Co., Wichita, Kans., 1978—; freelance computer programmer Glenn Johney Enterprises, Wichita, Kans., 1984—. Mem. bd. edn. Grace Luth. Ch., Wichita, 1979-80; v.p. Aid Assn. for Lutherans, Wichita, 1985—; bd. dirs. Ind. Living Ctr. South Cen. Kans., 1986—. Mem. AIAA (newsletter editor 1980-81). Avocations: photography; computers; swimming; skiing; travel. Home: 1911 Marion Rd Wichita KS 67216 Office: Boeing Mil Airplane Co 3801 S Oliver St Wichita KS 67210

JOHNS, ANTOINETTE FRANCES, educational administrator; b. Detroit, July 22, 1944; d. Francin James and Annottillie (Turley) Kolvoord; m. William Max Johns, June 19, 1964 (div. 1983); children—Cori Lyne, Heather; m. Leo J. Monster, Sept. 15, 1984. Student Kellog Community Coll., 1964, U. Mich., 1965; B.A. in Elem. Edn. and Spl. Edn., Western Mich. U., 1969, M.A., 1973; cert. sch. psychologist, Western Mich. U., 1974; Ed.D., U. No. Colo., 1977; postgrad. in ednl. adminstrn. U. Minn., 1981. Tchr. mentally retarded Galesburg (Mich.) High Sch., 1968-69, Comstock (Mich.) Elem. Sch., 1969-73; cons. Sci. Research Assocs., Chgo., 1973-75; instr. Western Mich. U., Kalamazoo, 1973-75; coordinator Eastern Service Area, Kalamazoo Intermediate Sch. Dist., Comstock, Mich., 1972-75; instr. U. No. Colo., Greeley, 1975-77; dir. spl. edn. 916 Spl. Intermediate Dist., White Bear Lake, Minn., 1977-83; dir. of Instrn., Minn., 1983—; dir. elem. and secondary instrn., 1986; chmn. East Met. Spl. Edn. Consortium, 1982-83; cons. McKnight Found., 1983, JWK Corp., Washington; chmn. Ramsey County Mental Retardation Adv. Com. Human Services Com.; mem. St. Paul Assn. Retarded Children, Council Exceptional Children. Bush fellow, 1982-83 Gov.'s Citation for Contbn. to Edn., 1987; named Minn. Administr. of Yr., 1987. Mem. Am. Vocat. Assn., Am. Assn. Edn. Severely and Profoundly Handicapped, Minn. Assn. Sch. Adminstrs. (chmn. statewide edn. policy com. 1982-83), Minn. Adminstrs. Spl. Edn., Am. Soc. Tng. and Devel., Minn. Assn. Ednl. office personnel adminstr. of yr. 1987), Kappa Eta Sigma, Phi Delta Kappa, Kappa Delta Pi. Lutheran. Author: Classification Tasks with Mentally Retarded and their Predictor Variables for Success., 1977; co-author research papers. Office: 3300 Century Ave N White Bear Lake MN 55110

JOHNS, MICHAEL RICHARD, regional planner; b. Chgo., Aug. 23, 1952; s. Carl Richard and Josephine Elizabeth (Jacobs) J.; m. Carol Beth Quigley, Aug. 2, 1979; children—Geoffrey Andrew, Rebecca Renee, Daniel Richard. B.A., U. Minn., 1975; M.A., Mankato State U., 1978; postgrad. U. Okla., 1982. Cert. planner. Program asst. spl. projects and program devel. Arrowhead Regional Devel. Comn., Duluth, Minn., 1976-78; state land use planner Iowa Office for Planning and Programming, Des Moines, 1978-79; exec. dir. Green Hills Regional Planning Commn., Trenton, Mo., 1979—; asst. v.p. Green Hills Rural Devel. Inc., Trenton, 1981-86; gen. mgr. Chillicothe-Brunswick(Mo.) Rail Maintenance Authority, Trenton, 1986—. Named one of Outstanding Young Men of Am. U.S. Jaycees, 1981, 82; recipient Creative Writing award Masonic Lodge, Minn., 1970. Mem. Amer. Inst. Cert. Planners, Amer. Planning Assn. (dir. Mo. chpt. 1981-83), Mo. Assn. Councils Govt. Dirs. Com., Amer. Econ. Devel. Council. Roman Catholic. Lodge: Rotary. Contbr. articles to profl. publs. Office: Green Hills Regional Commn 815 Main St Trenton MO 64683

JOHNS, WILLIAM HOWARD, psychiatrist; b. Hamilton, Ohio, Apr. 18, 1941; s. Howard William and Martha (Sleigh) J.; m. Catherine Marie O'Keefe, May 30, 1982; children: Howard William II, Stephanie Marie. AB, Princeton U., 1963; MS in Anatomy, U. Cin., 1968; DO, Kirksville (Mo.) Coll. Osteo. Medicine, 1973; postgrad., Topeka Inst. for Psychoanalysis, 1984—. Instr. anatomy Kirksville Coll. Osteo. Medicine, 1967-73; intern Grandview Hosp., Dayton, 1973-84; resident neurology Cleve. Clinic Hosp., 1974-77; asst. prof. neurology Ohio U. Coll. Osteo. Medicine, Athens, 1977-78; pvt. practice in neurology Dayton, Ohio, 1978-82; resident psychiatry The Menninger Found., Topeka, 1982-85, psychiatrist, 1985—; asst. clinical prof. neurology Wright State U. Med. Sch., Dayton, 1979-82, Ohio U. Coll. Osteo. Medicine, Athens, 1979-82, W.Va. Sch. Osteo. Medicine, Lewisburg, 1979-82. Mem. Am. Psychiat. Assn., Am. Acad. Neurology. Avocations: reading, sports, travelling, family. Home: 517 Danbury Ln Topeka KS 66606 Office: The Menninger Found PO Box 829 Topeka KS 66601

JOHNSON, ANGELA CLAIRE, electrical engineer, reliability engineer; b. Mpls., Mar. 9, 1960; d. Kenneth LeRoy and LaVonna Claudette (Olson) Newstrom; m. Darrell Jean Johnson, Aug. 28, 1982. AA in Math., Anoka-Ramsey Community Coll., 1980; BEE, U. Minn., 1982. Design engr. Rosemount, Inc., Eden Prairie, Minn., 1980-84, AT&T Info. Systems, Denver, 1984-85; sr. reliability engr. Honeywell, Inc., Golden Valley, Minn., 1985—; Gen. mgr., mem. Honeywell Chorus; mem. Honeywell Engineers' Club. Active Minn. chpt. Arthritis Found. Mem. IEEE. Home: PO Box 26252 Saint Louis Park MN 55426 Office: Honeywell Inc 6300 Olson Meml Hwy Mail Sta MN67-2B08 Golden Valley MN 55427

JOHNSON, ARTHUR JOHN, urologist; b. Berwyn, Ill., Jan. 25, 1928; s. Russell Conrad and Vernie Irene (Moseman) J.; m. Jean Louise Douglas, Dec. 29, 1951; children: Robert Arthur, Nancy Louise. MD, U. Mich., 1952; M in Med. Sci., Ohio State U., 1961. Diplomate Am. Bd. Urology. Asst. surgeon Henry Ford Hosp., Detroit, 1961-68, dir. urology, 1968-70; practice medicine specializing in urology Detroit, 1970—; clin. asst. prof. urology Wayne State U., Detroit, 1979—. Contbr. articles to profl. jours. Served to lt. commdr. USN, 1954-58. Grantee Ohio State U., 1958, Am. Cancer Soc., 1959. Presbyterian. Clubs: Bay View Yacht, Grosse Pointe Hunt. Lodge: Rotary. Avocations: competitive sailing, swimming, tennis, music. Home: 828 Pemberton Rd Grosse Pointe Park MI 48230 Office: Harper Hosp Profl Bldg Suite 629 4160 John R St Detroit MI 48201

JOHNSON, BARBARA JANE, sales representative; b. Chgo., Aug. 19, 1946; d. Sidney and Norma Mona Shaffer; B.A. in Sociology and Psychology, U. Ill., 1968; postgrad. M.B.A. program, Roosevelt U., 1971-72; m. Gary Johnson, Aug. 25, 1968; 1 child, Eric Michael. Asst. personnel dir. Associated Mills, Chgo., 1967-69, Scholl Mfg. Co. Inc., Chgo., 1969-71; nurse recruiter Cook County Hosp. Governing Com., Chgo., 1971-73; recruiter Mt. Sinai Hosp., Chgo., 1973-76; sales rep. Stryker Corp., Kalamazoo, 1976-81, area trainer; sales rep. Physio Control, Schaumberg, Ill., 1981—; with Sensormedics Corp., Anaheim, Calif.; founder Chgo. Area Nurse Recruiters; cons. positions as nurse recruiter. Vice pres. Budlong Community Action Group, 1979—; advisor Jr. Achievement, 1969-72; auction com. Edn. TV; trustee Mt. Sinai/Schwab Rehab. Ctr., 1983—. Recipient Lee Stryker sales award, 1979. Mem. Assn. of Operating Room Nurses (sponsor). Recipient first place Recruitment Brochure for Chgo. Area Bus. Communicators, 1975; salesman of year, 1979; first woman to achieve nat. award, 1979.

JOHNSON, BRADLEY WILLIAM, small business owner; b. Woodbury, N.J., Oct. 12, 1950; s. William A. and Betty Loraine (Johnson) J.; m. Kay Jean Johanson, Aug. 10, 1974; children: Johanna Jean. BS in Biology and Gen. Science, U. Minn., Duluth, 1972. Tchr. biology, coach swimming and volleyball Duluth Cen. High Sch., 1972-76; sales rep. Reader's Digest, Deerwood, Minn., 1976—; owner Den of Antiquity, Crosby, Minn., 1984—. Avocations: gun collecting, tennis. Home and Office: Star Rt Box 200 Deerwood MN 56444

JOHNSON, BRUCE EVERETT, medical educator; b. Portland, Oreg., Aug. 2, 1950; s. Everett H. and Lillian E. (Olson) J.; m. Cynda Ann Stolte, July 15, 1972; children: Kevin, Drew. BS, Stanford U., 1972; MD, UCLA, 1976. Intern VA Med. Ctr., Los Angeles, 1976-77; resident U. Kans. Med.

Ctr., Kansas City, 1977-81, asst. prof., 1981-86, assoc. prof., 1986—; med. dir. KU Care Flight. Contbr. articles to profl. jours. Active Am. Field Service Internat. Scholarships. Fellow ACP; mem. AMA, Am. Geriatrics Soc., Soc. Research Edn. Primary Care Internal Medicine, Kansas City Businessmen's Club. Democrat. Lutheran. Avocations: jogging, skiing, collecting, reading. Office: U Kans Dept Medicine Med Ctr Kansas City KS 66103

JOHNSON, BRUCE ROSS, educator; b. La Porte, Ind., May 18, 1949; s. Egbert Johannes Daniel and Ruth Elvera (Johnson) J. B.S., Ball State U., Muncie, Ind., 1971; M.Edn., Valparaiso U., 1975; postgrad. Nat. Coll. Edn., Evanston, Ill., 1974. Cert. elem. sch. tchr., Ind. Vol. tchr. Peace Corps, St. Vincent, W.I., 1971-72; tchr. South Central Sch., Union Mills, Ind., 1972-76, 77—; missionary tchr. Luth. Ch., Liberia, West Africa, 1976-77; vis. educator U. London, 1974, U. Moscow, 1974, U. Paris, 1974. Contbr. articles to newspapers. Pres. People to People Internat., La Porte, Ind., 1981-83, trustee, Kansas City, Mo., 1983—; mem. ch. council Bethany Luth. Ch., La Porte, 1983—; v.p. Friends of La Porte County Library, 1984, pres. 1986—; trustee La Porte County Hist. Soc., 1985—; v.p. Ind. Geneal. Soc., 1981-82; pres. Community Concert Assn., La Porte, 1984; mem. Pan Am. Games Com., 1986-87; mem. steering com. La Porte County Spelling Bee, 1979-85, chmn., 1981, 85; chmn. Miss. Valley council People-to-People, 1983—. Named one of Outsanding Young Men Am., 1985, State finalist NASA Tchr.-in-Space project, 1985. Mem. NEA (life), Ind. State Tchrs. Assn., Phi Delta Kappa. Clubs: Amateur Music (pres. 1982-83) (La Porte), Little Theater (bd. dirs. 1980-83), Lions (bd. dirs. 1983—). Avocations: Performing in musical theater, collecting foreign coins, traveling, gardening. Home: 2012 S Village Rd La Porte IN 46350 Office: South Central Community Schs 9808 S 600 W Union Mills IN 46382

JOHNSON, CARL J., epidemiologist; b. Sims, Ind., July 2, 1929; s. Fred C. and Ena B. Johnson; m. Kathryn Margaret Van Deusen, Oct. 13, 1956; children: Peter, Frederick, Kendrick. BS, Mich. State U., 1953, DVM, 1955; MD, MS, Ohio State U., 1965; MPH, U. Calif., Berkeley, 1969. Diplomate Am. Bd. Preventive Medicine and Pub. Health. Zoo veterinarian Toledo Zool. Park, 1955-58; pathologist Dupont/Haskell Lab. for Toxicology and Indsl. Hygiene, Newark, Del., 1960-62; acting assoc. prof. pathology Cornell U. Sch. Vet. Medicine, Ithaca, N.Y., 1962-63; postdoctoral fellow Ohio State U. Coll. Medicine, Columbus, 1965; sr. asst. surgeon USPHS, Seattle, 1965-66; dist. health officer Seattle-King County Dept. Health, 1966-73; dir. health Jefferson County Health Dept., Lakewood, Colo., 1973-81; prin. investigator, med. cons. Med. Care and Research Found., Denver, 1981-85; med. officer S.D. Dept. Health, Pierre, 1985—; pub. health cons. 6th Army to Ryukyu Islands, 1970; asst. clin. prof. U. Wash. Sch. Pub. Health, 1972-74; assoc. clin. prof. U. Colo. Sch. Medicine, 1973-84; chmn. program devel. bd. Am. Pub. Health Assn., 1980-83; clin. assoc. prof. U. S.D. Sch. Medicine, 1986—. Asst. editor Internat. Perspectives on Pub. Health. Organizer Internat. Physicians for Prevention of Nuclear War, 1980; U.S. del. 1st Internat. Congress, 1981. Served with C.E., U.S. Army, 1946-49. Named Man of Yr., Denver Area Sentinel Newspapers, 1978; grantee NIH, 1970, Nuclear Radiation Research Found., 1981; fellow NIH, 1965. Fellow Am. Coll. Epidemiology, Am. Coll. Preventive Medicine; mem. Internat. Epidemiol. Assn., Health Physics Soc., Soc. Epidemiol. Research, Internat. Radiation Protection Assn., Am. Pub. Health Assn. (chmn. health adminstrn. council 1979-80, co-chmn. joint policy com. 1980-83, governing council 1977-78). Lodge: Rotary. Home: PO Box #983 Pierre SD 57501 Office: 523 E Capitol Pierre SD 57501

JOHNSON, CAROL ANN, chemical engineer; b. Ft. Dodge, Iowa, May 29, 1958; d. John Edward and Lorraine Marie (Matthys) Vohs; m. Jack Rudolph Johnson, Aug. 25, 1979. BS, Iowa State U., 1980. Process engr. Dow Corning Corp., Midland, Mich., 1980-81; sr. process engr. Monsanto Enviro-Chem, Chesterfield, Mo., 1981—. Chmn. membership Monsanto Women's Network, St. Louis, 1986—. Mem. Am. Inst. Chem. Engrs., Iowa State U. Alumni Club (social chmn. 1983, treas. 1984-85, bd. dirs. 1986—). Office: Monsanto Enviro-Chem 14522 S 40 Outer Rd Chesterfield MO 63017

JOHNSON, CARTER FRANCIS, dentist; b. Duluth, Minn., May 3, 1941; s. Russell Mentor and Marian Noel (McCarter) J.; m. Marla Jean Abramson, June 7, 1962 (div. Jan. 1970); children: Jody Lyn, Paige Yvonne; m. Cheryl Louise Larson, Aug. 2, 1980; children: Kelsey Amalie Larson, Ariel Raina Larson. BS, U. Minn., 1963, DDS, 1967. Co-founder, chief of dentistry Pilot City Health Ctr., Mpls., 1968-76; founder Pike Lake Dental Health Ctr., Duluth, Minn., 1973—. Patentee diving board, 1978, window insulation curtains, 1983; builder Pike Lake Profl. Bldg., Duluth, 1976—. Mem. adv. bd. sta. WDTH U. Minn., Duluth, 1982—; mem. bd. Gnesen Community Ctr., 1985—. Mem. Acad. Gen. Dentistry, L.D. Pankey Inst. Alumni Assn., Minn. Acad. Gnathological Research. Office: Pike Lake Dental Health Ctr 3868 Miller Trunk Hwy Duluth MN 55811

JOHNSON, CHARLES E., II, technology company executive; b. Muskegon, Mich., Feb. 22, 1936; s. Paul C. and Anne (Lovelace) Johnson; m. Patricia Bell, Aug. 2, 1958; children: Charles, Julia, Peter. B.A., Colgate Coll., 1958; LL.B., U. Wis., 1961; A.M.P., Harvard U., 1983. Bars: Mich., 1961, Wis. 1961. Group v.p. replacement Sealed Power Corp., Muskegon, 1970-72, group v.p. internat., 1972-82, group v.p. gen. products, 1982-84, exec. v.p., 1984-85, pres., chief operating officer, 1985—, also dir.; dir. First of Am. Bank, Muskegon. Gen. campaign mgr. YFCA, Muskegon, 1978; bd. dirs. Muskegon Bus. Coll., 1984—; trustee Wayland Acad., Beaver Dam, Wis., 1984—. Served with USAR, 1962-68. Named Bus. Leader of Yr., Muskegon C. of C., 1979. Republican. Roman Catholic. Clubs: Century, Muskegon Country. Avocations: boating; golf; tennis. Home: 474 E Circle Dr North Muskegon MI 49445 Office: Sealed Power Corp 100 Terrace Plaza Muskegon MI 49443 *

JOHNSON, CHARLES REED, real estate developer; b. Columbus, Ohio, Oct. 25, 1954; s. Charles White and Lillian (McCain) J.; m. Cynthia O'Quinn, June 6, 1981. BA/BS, Ohio State U., 1982. Assoc. Ball & Galloway, Columbus, 1982-87; exec. v.p. G.W. Banning Assocs. Inc., Worthington, Ohio, 1987—; pres. Charles R. Johnson Co. Inc., Worthington, 1987—; dir. devel. Airborne Commerce Park, Wilmington, Ohio, 1987—. Mem. chmns. club Franklin County Rep. Party. Mem. Nat. Assn. Realtors, Ohio Assn. Realtors, Nat. Found. for Hist. Preservation. Republican. Episcopalian. Clubs: Columbus Maennerchor, Riviera Country. Home: 1567 Sandringham Dr Columbus OH 43220 Office: 685 High St Worthington OH 43085

JOHNSON, CHARLOTTE LEE, librarian; b. Ladysmith, Wis., Dec. 22, 1951; d. Wesley Carl and Ethel Margaret (Lowers) J. BA in Art Edn. and Integrated Liberal Studies, U. Wis., 1974, MLS, 1975. Tchr., librarian Victorian Edn. Dept., Victoria, Australia, 1976-80; freelance artist, photographer Asia, Europe, Can., 1980; asst. phys. scis. librarian Okla. State U., Stillwater, 1981-83; sci. librarian So. Ill. U., Edwardsville, 1983-84, head of user services, 1984—; info. cons. Immunox, Edwardsville, 1984—. Artist (multi-media) Harmony is in the Green, 1986 (Grand prize Artists at the Sta., St. Louis). Library senator So. Ill. U. Senate, Edwardsville, 1983-86; pres. So. Ill. Network of Women, 1987; mem. Friends of St. Louis Art Mus.; bd. dirs. Friends of Lovejoy Library, Edwardsville, 1986—. So. Ill. U. grantee, 1986. Mem. Am. Library Assn., Ill. Library Assn., Assn. of Coll. and Research Libraries, Am. Assn. Univ. Profs. (treas. So. Ill. U. chpt. 1985—, treas. Ill. chpt. 1986—). Office: Southern Illinois U Lovejoy Library Edwardsville IL 62026

JOHNSON, CHRISTINE ANN, nurse; b. Omaha, Nebr., Aug. 23, 1951; d. Ralph James and Marlene (Marlenee) Matney; m. Timothy Carl Johnson, Aug. 1, 1970; children: Erik Carl, Christine Nicole. Cert. practical nurse, Met. Tech. Community Coll., 1973; student, Creighton U., 1987—. Lic. practical nurse; cert. pregnancy exercise instr. EKG technician Bishop Clarkson Meml. Hosp., Omaha, 1971-74, lic. practical nurse, 1978—, instr. pregnancy exercise, 1984-86, instr. sibling preparation, 1985-86, instr. breastfeeding, 1985—; lic. practical nurse Cons. in Cardiology, P.C., Omaha, 1974-78. Sec. United Meth. Women First United Meth. Ch., 1984-85, chmn. 1985-86; mem. Omaha Pub. Schs. Superintendent's Task Force on Human Growth and Devel., 1986. Mem. Psi Chi. Methodist. Home: 4618 N 129 Ave Omaha NE 68164 Office: Bishop Clarkson Meml Hosp 42d at Dewey Omaha NE 68105

JOHNSON, CLARENCE E., diversified manufacturing company executive; b. 1926; married. BBA, Miliken U., 1950. Spl. agt. FBI, prior to 1953; with Borg-Warner Corp., 1953-87, v.p., works mgr. Marvel-Schebler Tillotson div., 1964-67, v.p. mech. div., 1967-68, pres. mech. div., 1968-70, mng. dir. transmission div. (England), 1970-75, pres., gen. mgr. Morse Chain div., 1975-79, corp. v.p., 1979-82, v.p. transmission equipment, 1982-84, pres., chief operating officer, 1984-87, chief exec. officer, 1986-87, also dir. Served with USN, 1944-46. Office: Borg-Warner Corp 200 S Michigan Ave Chicago IL 60604

JOHNSON, CURTIS ALVIN, hospital administrator; b. Ft. Atkinson, Wis., Sept. 3, 1953; s. Norris Alvin and Jayne Maxine (Hake) J.; m. Mary Elizabeth End, Sept. 13, 1980; children: William, Maureen, Kathryn. BBA, U. Wis., Whitewater, 1975; MS, Coll. St. Francis, Joliet, Ill., 1985. CPA, Wis.; lic. nursing home adminstr. Sr. auditor Blue Cross Blue Shield, Milw., 1975-77; controller Howard Young Med. Ctr., Woodruff, Wis., 1977-80; v.p. fin. St. Catherine's Hosp., Kenosha, Wis., 1980-84; pres., v.p. fin. Family Hosp., Milw., 1984-87; adminstr. Northwoods Hosp., Phelps, Wis., 1987—. Recipient Disting. Service award West Side Assn., Milw., 1986. Mem. Healthcare Fin. Mgmt. Assn., Wis. Inst. CPA's., Am. Inst. CPA's. Republican. Roman Catholic. Avocations: furniture restoration, fishing, hunting. Home: Duck Lake Rd Eagle River WI 54521 Office: Northwoods Hosp PO Box 26 Phelps WI 54554

JOHNSON, CURTIS MILTON, educator, ednl. adminstr.; b. St. Paul, Feb. 29, 1928; s. Vivian W. and Emma (Bethke) J.; B.S., St. Cloud State U., 1952; M.A., St. Thomas Coll., 1965; A.B.D., Ohio U., 1974; m. Jewel M. Troyer, July 22, 1949; children—Wendy, Cheryl, Brant, Jay, Dana, Todd. Indsl. arts tchr. Clarkfield (Minn.) Schs., 1952-56; indsl. arts tchr., chmn. dept. Sibley Sr. High Sch., West Saint Paul, Minn., 1956-66; adminstrn. fellowship Ohio U., 1966-67, dir. continuing edn., 1967-69, dir. Ext. Div., 1969-80, dir. internat. edn., 1980-84, asst. prof. engring. graphics, 1976—. Pres., South St. Paul (Minn.) Public Schs. Bd. Edn., 1964-66; chmn. Dakota County (Minn.) Jr. Coll. Com., 1965-66; chmn. Athens Twp. Zoning Commn., 1973-74; dir., pres. Athens County Regional Planning Commn., 1975-87. Served with USCGR, 1946-47. Recipient Nat. Ford Indsl. Arts award, Bush Found. Leadership fellow. Mem. Nat. Univ. Continuing Edn. Assn., Ohio Coll. Assn., Ohio Adult Edn. Assn., Ohio Council on Higher Continuing Edn., Phi Delta Kappa. Rotarian. Home: 8075 SR 56 Athens OH 45701 Office: Ohio Univ 116 Stocker Ctr Athens OH 45701

JOHNSON, CURTIS RAY, dentist, community developer; b. Sioux Falls, S.D., Nov. 7, 1946; s. Hubert Albin and Doris Fern (Peterson) J.; m. Margo Jean Cardin, June 24, 1968; children: Christopher Charles, Eric Jason. BA, Augustana Coll., 1968; DDS, Northwestern U., Chgo., 1972. Gen. practice dentistry Scotland, S.D., 1972—; pres. Scot-Del Devel. Co., Scotland, 1982—; assoc. clin. prof. U. S.D. Sch. Dental Hygiene, Vermillion, 1976-79; bd. dirs. health care consultation com. U.S. Senator Larry Pressler, Sioux Falls, 1984—. Mem. Bd. of Edn. Scotland Sch. Dist. 4-3, 1975-78; mem., vice chmn. Scotland City Council, 1982-86; chmn. Scotland Commn. Econ. Devel., 1986. Mem. ADA, S.D. Dental Found. (bd. dirs. 1982-87, chmn. bd. dirs. 1987—), S.D. Dental Assn., So. Dist. Dental Soc. (pres. 1982-83), Scotland C. of C., Pierre Fauchard Acad., Siouxland Dental Study Club (sec., treas.). Republican. Lutheran. Club: Scotland Golf (pres. 1976-77, bd. dirs. 1975-78). Lodge: Rotary (pres. Scotland 1972-80), Moose. Avocations: golf, fishing. Home: 140 Juniper Scotland SD 57059 Office: 610 Main PO Box 341 Scotland SD 57059

JOHNSON, CYRUS EDWIN, business executive; b. Alton, Ill., Feb. 18, 1929; s. Cyrus L. and Jennie C. (Keen) J.; m. Charlotte E. Johnson; children: Judie M., Renee B. B.S., U. Ill., 1956, M.A., 1959. Dist. traffic mgr. Ill. Bell Telephone Co., Chgo., 1970-71, dist. comml. mgr., 1971-73; v.p. social action Gen. Mills, Inc., Mpls., 1973-78, v.p. dir. corp. personnel, 1978-80, v.p. human resource environment, 1980-81, v.p., dir. facilities and services, 1981—; dir. Ault, Inc., Mpls., Life-Span, Inc., Mpls. Bd. dirs. United Way Mpls. Area, 1975-86; active Nat. YMCA, 1973-79; mem. citizens adv. com. Mpls. Tech. Inst., 1981-84; mem. deans adv. council Coll. Bus., U. Ill., Chgo., 1981-84; past pres. Harvard U. Bus. Sch. Assn., Boston, 1978-79; bd. dirs. Greater Mpls. area Girl Scouts U.S. Served with U.S. Army, 1950-52. Recipient Old Masters Program award Purdue U., 1975; recipient Chgo. Defender Roundtable of Commerce award, 1963. Baptist. Lodges: Rotary; Masons. Office: Gen Mills Inc 9200 Wayzata Blvd Minneapolis MN 55426

JOHNSON, DAVID CURTIS, financial company executive; b. Clinton, Iowa, Oct. 10, 1953; s. Charles Keith Johnson and Nan Jean (Wasta) Heral; m. Patricia Ann Butterbaugh, Feb. 23, 1980; children: Samantha Leigh, Jessica Ann. BS, Coe Coll., 1977. CPA, Ohio. Staff acct. Davison, Boktkin, Koranda and Sieh CPA's, Cedar Rapids, Iowa, 1977, Bell and Van Zee, P.C., CPA's, Cedar Rapids, 1977-80; pvt. practice acct. Wash., 1980-81; v.p. Garlikov and Assocs., Inc., Columbus, 1981—. Author: (book) Risk Management: A Tool in Personal Financial Planning, 1985. Mem. Am. Inst. CPA's (div. personal fin. planning, tchr., discussion leader 1986—), Ohio Soc. CPA's, Iowa Soc. CPA's, Columbus Area Treas. Club. Avocation: boating. Office: Garlikov & Assocs Inc 41 S High St Suite 2710 Columbus OH 43215

JOHNSON, DAVID L., psychologist; b. Cin., Jan. 17, 1950. BS, U. Cin., 1972, MEd, 1974, EdD, 1984. Lic. psychologist, Ohio; Diplomate Am. Bd. Med. Psychotherapists. Staff psychologist Children's Diagnostic Ctr., Hamilton, Ohio, 1976-78, Student Diagnostic Ctr., Cin., 1978-80; cons. psychologist Millcreek Psychiat. Ctr., Cin., 1984, VOCA Corp., Dayton, Ohio, 1985-86; asst. prof. psychology U. Cin., 1980—; cons. psychologist Broadview Devel. Ctr., Broadview Heights, Ohio, 1986, Millcreek Psychiat. Ctr. Children, Cin., 1986-87; trainer in sexuality edn. Longview State Hosp., Cin., 1986; psychologist in behavioral medicine Pain Control Ctr., U. Cin. Hosp. Med. Ctr., 1986. Editor Internat. Jour. Profl. Hypnosis, 1986-87; editorial cons. Jour. Sch. Psychology, 1986; resource reviewer Jour. Sex Edn. and Therapy, 1983—; contbr. numerous articles to profl. jours. Speaker in black history New Hope Baptist Ch., Hamilton, Ohio, 1985, Booker T. Washington Community Ctr., Hamilton, 1986; pro bono services Butler County Headstart Project, Hamilton, 1977-83. Named one of Outstanding Young Men of Am., Outstanding Young Men's Assn., 1983; U. Cin. Provostal grantee, 1986. Mem. Assn. Applied Psychoanalysis, Nat. Acad. Counselors and Family Therapists, Inc., Am. Assn. Family Counselors and Mediators, Inc. (cert.), Am. Psychol. Assn., Am. Assn. Sex Educators, Counselors, Therapists (adv. council Ohio sect. 1985—), Am. Soc. Clin. Hypnosis (bd. dirs. Cin. chpt. 1985-87), Am. Assn. Profl. Hypnosis, Alpha Phi Alpha. Democrat. Episcopalian. Avocations: running, road racing. Home: 5252 Camelot Dr Fairfield OH 45014 Office: 10999 Reed Hartman Hwy Suite 127 Cincinnati OH 45242

JOHNSON, DAVIS, stockbroker; b. Detroit, Feb. 23, 1932; s. Herbert and Carrie (Lee) J.; m. Alphia Johnson, Aug. 10, 1958; 1 child, Cheryl Rene. BS, Wayne State U., 1954. Div. sales mgr. Investor Diversified Service, 1967-83; chmn., chief exec. officer Update Diversified Fin. Service, Oak Park, Mich., 1983—. Home: 19160 Parkside Detroit MI 48220 Office: Update Diversified Fin Service 14500 W 8 Mile Oak Park MI 48237

JOHNSON, DEAN STEVEN, retailer, computer software developer; b. Melrose Park, Ill., Feb. 23, 1955; s. Dale Carlton and Patricia Anne (Robb) J.; m. Sheree Lynn Arnold, Sept. 1, 1979; 1 child, Matthew Phillip. BS in Acctg., Pa. State U., 1977. Acct. Dentsply Internat., York, Pa., 1978-79; asst. trust officer Blue Ball (Pa.) Nat. Bank, 1979-82; owner Petland, Machesney Park, Ill., 1982; majority ptnr. Petland, Cherry Valley, Ill., 1982—; owner Johnson Software, Cherry Valley, 1985—. Recipient Franny award Internat. Franchise Assn., 1984. Home: 2182 Wessman Pkwy Cherry Valley IL 61016

JOHNSON, DENNIS LESTER, consulting firm executive; b. Hampton, Iowa, Oct. 23, 1938; s. Royden Lester and Lorraine Anita (Rhoades) J.; m. Carolyn Louise Campbell, Aug. 18, 1963; children: Dené Lynn, Laurie Anne. B.A., Parsons Coll., 1960. Admissions officer, regional dir., dir. admissions counselors Parsons Coll., Fairfield, Iowa, 1960-67; pres., chmn. bd. Johnson Assocs., Inc., Glen Ellyn, Ill., 1967—; Speaker, lectr. in field. Columnist: Nation's Schools and Colls, 1974—; contbr. articles to profl. jours. Bd. dirs. DuPage Easter Seal Treatment Center, 1975-76, United Cerebral Palsy Greater Chgo., 1977—. Named hon. alumnus Western Md. Coll. 1984. Mem. Am. Assn. Higher Edn., Am. Personnel and Guidance Assn., Soc. Coll. and Univ. Planning, Am. Mktg. Assn. Presbyterian. Clubs: Oak Brook Bath and Tennis; Executives (Chgo.). Home: 1103 Fairview Ave Lombard IL 60148 Office: Suite 20 Bldg A 800 Roosevelt Rd Glen Ellyn IL 60137

JOHNSON, DENNIS WILLIAM, printing company executive; b. Rockford, Ill., Mar. 10, 1938; s. Harry C. and Alice E. (Greenberg) J.; m. Evelyn Jo Stahl, Aug. 12, 1961; children: Tonya, Cary, Rynn. Student Bethel Coll., 1956-58, Rockford Coll., 1958-59; postgrad. Northwestern U., 1985-86. Chief exec. officer H.C. Johnson Press, Inc., Rockford, 1958—; pres. Versatile Ventures, Inc., Rockford, 1966—; chief exec. officer Johnson Graphics, Inc., Dubuque, Ill., Johnson Printing Corp., DeKalb, Ill., Clinic Profl. Weight Control, Rockford; bd. dirs. Camelot World Travel, Inc., Rockford, 1st Community Bank, Rockford, Sta. WQFL Radio, VeQuest Inc., T.J. Cinnamons. Mem. Bd. Suprs. Winnebago County, Rockford, 1965-68; alderman City of Rockford, 1968-83; mem. No. Ill. Law Enforcement Commn., Rockford, 1969-76; bd. dirs. No. Ill. Multiple Sclerosis Bd., 1971-73; Ill. Snow Sculpting Competition, Rockford Mus. Assn.; co-chmn. Winnebago County Bicentennial Commn., 1976-77; chmn. Police and Fire Commn., Rockford; trustee Judson Coll., Elgin, Ill.; bd. dirs. Inst. for Holyland Studies, Jerusalem, Bibles for India, Grand Rapids, Mich., Johnson Found., Rockford, World Home Bible League, South Holland, Ill. Named Outstanding Young Legislator, Rockford Jr. C. of C., 1969. Mem. Printing Industry of Ill., Christian Businessmen's Com., Rockford C. of C. (bd. dirs. 1987—), Gideons. Republican. Mem. Free Ch. Lodge: Rotary. Home: 3134 Talbot Trail Rockford IL 61111 Office: 2801 Eastrock Dr Rockford IL 61125

JOHNSON, DIANE KATHLEEN, database manager; b. Forest City, Iowa, May 1, 1952; d. Glenn Eugene and Emeline Charlotte (Nelson) J. BA, Bethel Coll., 1974; MA, U. Denver, 1975; MBA, U. Iowa, 1986. Reference librarian State Library Iowa, Des Moines, 1975-77, dir. info. services, 1977-81; info. coordinator Pioneer Hi-Bred, Des Moines, 1981-82, info. mgmt. mgr., 1982-85, datebase mgmt. mgr., 1985—. Mem. Des Moines Civic Opera, 1986, Des Moines Civic Ctr., 1986, Des Moines Civic Music, 1986, Des Moines Community Playhouse, 1986, Leadership Iowa, 1986—. Mem. Spl. Library Assn. Democrat. Mem. Evang. Free Ch. Avocations: biking, tennis. Office: Pioneer Hi-Bred Internat 5608 Merle Hay Rd Johnston IA 50131

JOHNSON, DONALD EDWARD, JR., lawyer; b. Denver, Sept. 24, 1942; s. Donald Edward and Miriam Bispham (Chester) J.; m. Charlotte Marie Hassett, Aug. 15, 1964; children—Julie Anna, Jenny Marie. Student Lewis and Clark Coll., 1960-62; B.A. in History, U. Ariz., 1968; J.D., U. Wyo., 1971. Bar: Wyo. 1971, Colo. 1971, U.S. Dist. Ct. Colo. and Wyo., 1971, U.S. Supreme Ct. 1978. Assoc., Hammond and Chilson, Loveland, Colo., 1971-72; dep. dist. atty. 8th Jud. Dist., Loveland, and Ft. Collins, Colo., 1972-80, chief dep. dist. atty., 1977-80; assoc. Allen, Rogers, Metcalf and Vahrenwald, Ft. Collins, 1980-82; ptnr., 1982—; asst. city atty. City of Loveland, 1971-72; asst. mcpl. judge, Loveland, 1972; instr. bus. law Ames Coll., 1972-74; lectr. Regional Homocide Sch., 1977; mem. state tng. com. Colo. Dist. Atty's. Council, 1978-80. Chmn. 45th Republican House Dist., 1977-82; mem. Colo. Rep. Central Com., 1980-85, Larimer County Rep. Central Com., 1980—; mem. Loveland Open Space Adv. Bd., 1977-78; bd. dirs. Loveland United Way, 1977-84, allocations chmn., 1980, pres., 1981-83; bd. dirs. Larimer County Alcohol Services, 1972-78, pres., 1977-78; bd. dirs. Loveland Midget Athletic Assn., sec. 1974-78. Served to sgt. USMC, 1966-68. Mem. ABA (Gold Key award, 1970), Larimer County Bar Assn., Colo. Bar Assn., Wyo. Bar Assn., Nat. Dist. Attys. Assn., Colo. Trial Lawyers Assn. Episcopalian. Lodge: Elks (Fort Collins, Colo.). Author: Criminal Conspiracy—The Colorado District Attorney's Evidence Manual, 1976. Office: Citizens Comml & Savs Bank One Citizens Banking Center Flint MI 48502 *

JOHNSON, DOROTHY PHYLLIS, counselor, art therapist; b. Kansas City, Mo., Sept. 13, 1925; d. Chris C. and Mabel T. (Gillum) Green; B.A. in Art, Ft. Hays. State U., 1975, M.S. in Guidance and Counseling, 1976, M.A. in Art, 1979; m. Herbert E. Johnson, May 11, 1945; children—Michael E., Gregory K. Art therapist High Plains Comprehensive Mental Health Assn., Hays, Kans., 1975-76; art therapist, mental health counselor Sunflower Mental Health Assn., Concordia, Kans., 1976—, co-dir. Project Togetherness, 1976-77, coordinator partial hospitalization, 1978—, out-patient therapist, 1982—; dir. Swedish Am. State Bank, Courtland, Kans., 1960—, sec., 1973-77. Mem. Kans., Am. art therapy assns., Am. Mental Health Counselors Assn., Am. Assn. for Counseling and Devel., Kans. Assn. for Counseling and Devel., Assn. for Humanistic Psychologists, Assn. Transpersonal Psychologists, Assn. Specialists in Group Work, Phi Delta Kappa, Phi Kappa Phi. Contbr. articles to profl. jours. Home: Box 200 Courtland KS 66939 Office: 520 B Washington St Concordia KS 66901

JOHNSON, DOUGLAS, small business consultant; b. Norfolk, Va., Aug. 31, 1952; s. Henry and Nancy Jean (Kurfess) Kowalchick; m. Janis Marie Johnson, Aug. 23, 1980. B.A. in Philosophy (citation), Dartmouth Coll., 1974. Dir. prodn. WQSR Radio, Sarasota, Fla., 1975-78; announcer, personality Embrescia Communications, Cleve., 1978-81; pres. HW Enterprises, Cleve., 1979-83, Concepts, Inc., Lodi, Ohio, 1983—. Author: (plays) Lingua Canis, 1973; The Chalice, 1976; Festival, 1977. Speaker, Citizen's Choice, Cleve., 1982-83; (columnist) Stirring Up the Pot, 1986—. Mem. Christian Ch. Address: 7860 Prouty Rd Lodi OH 44254

JOHNSON, DOUGLAS BLAIKIE, engineer, corporate planning counsel; b. Chgo., Sept. 13, 1952; s. Marvin Melrose and Anne Stuart (Campbell) J.; m. Pamela Jane Tomlinson, Aug. 1, 1975; children—Richard Aaron, Lauren Stuart, Diana Blaikie, Scott Nathaniel. B.S.M.E., U. Nebr., 1974; J.D., Seton Hall U., 1980. Bar: Nebr. 1980, U.S. Dist. Ct. Nebr. 1980; registered profl. engr., Nebr. Project engr. Dupont, Cleve., 1974-75; project engr. Exxon Chems., Linden, N.J., 1975-78, cost engr., 1978-80; sr. engr. InterNorth, Inc., Omaha, 1980-82, market planner, 1982-84, corp. planner, 1984-85, bus. mgr., 1985—. Loaned exec. United Way of Midlands, Omaha, 1982, Midland council Boy Scouts Am., 1984, Jr. Achievement, Cleve., 1974. Mem. ABA, Fed. Energy Bar Assn., Assn. Trial Lawyers Am., Nebr. Bar Assn., Omaha Bar Assn., Sigma Tau, Pi Tau Sigma, Triangle. Republican. Presbyterian. Home: 14705 U Plaza Omaha NE 68137 Office: Enron Resources Co 2600 Dodge St Omaha NE 68131

JOHNSON, EARLE BERTRAND, insurance executive; b. Otter Lake, Mich., May 3, 1914; s. Bert M. and Blanche (Sherman) J.; m. Frances Pierce, 1940 (dec.); children: Earle Bertrand, Victoria, Julia, Sheryl; m. Peggy Minch Rust, Apr. 30, 1972. B.S., U. Fla., 1937, J.D., 1940. With State Farm Ins. Cos., Bloomington, Ill., 1940—; regional agy. dir. State Farm Ins. Cos., 1958-60, regional v.p., 1960-65, v.p., sec. State Farm Mut. Automobile Ins. Co., 1965-80, dir., 1967—; also mem. exec. com.; sr. v.p., treas. State Farm County Mut. Ins. Co. Tex., 1965-80, treas., 1963-80; chmn. State Farm Life Ins. Co., 1970-86, dir., mem. exec. com., 1970—; v.p., mem. exec. com. State Farm Fire & Casualty Co., 1965-80, dir., 1965—; dir. State Farm Investment Mgmt. Corp.; v.p., sec. State Farm Internat. Services, Inc., 1967-81. Mem. Agy. Officers Round Table (exec. coms.), Am., Fla. bar assns., Soc. Former FBI Agts., Life Ins. Mktg. and Research Assn. (dir. 1975-78), Life Underwriter Tng. Council (trustee 1974-77), Phi Alpha Delta, Phi Kappa Tau. Home: 59 Country Club Pl Bloomington IL 61701 Office: State Farm Life Ins Co One State Farm Plaza Bloomington IL 61701

JOHNSON, EDWIN BARNER, mining company executive; b. Ishpeming, Mich., Oct. 21, 1923; s. Edwin William and Blanche (Carlson) J.; m. Lois Millman; children: Scott, Vicki Johnson Caneff, Marsha Johnson Nardi. B.S. in Metallurgy, Mich. Tech. U., Houghton, 1947. Chief metallurgist Cleveland-Cliffs Iron Co., Ishpeming, 1963-64, asst. mgr., 1964-66, mgr. Mich. mines, 1966-71; gen. mgr. mines Cleveland-Cliffs Iron Co., Cleve., 1971-73, v.p. ops., 1973-75, sr. v.p., 1975-83, pres., 1983—, also dir.; dir. Soc. Corp., Cleve., Soc. Nat. Bank, Cleve., U.P. Grnerating Co., Houghton. Mem. Baldwin Wallace Bus. Adv. Council, Berea, Ohio, 1977; trustee Mich. Tech. Fund, Houghton, 1981; mem. Fairview Gen. Hosp., Cleve. Served with U.S. Army, 1942-45. Mem. Am. Iron and Steel Inst., Am. Iron Ore Assn., AIME, Can. Inst. Mining and Metallurgy, Mich. Mfg.

Assn. (bd. dirs.). Republican. Presbyterian. Clubs: Union, Westwood Country. Office: Cleve Cliffs Iron Co Huntington Bldg Cleveland OH 44115 *

JOHNSON, ERIC CARL, software company executive; b. St. Louis, Nov. 21, 1951; s. Charles Leo and Esther Agnes (Rutledge) J.; m. Constance Maria Bearden, Mar. 7, 1981; children: Nicholas Karl, Ryan Patrick. BBA in Mktg. Mgmt., U. Mo., 1974. Account mktg. rep. IBM, St. Louis, 1974-82; mktg. rep. Gen. Software Systems, Inc., St. Louis, 1983-85, v.p./owner, 1985—; cons. St. Louis Med., 1983—. Bd. dirs. Great Forest Park Balloon Race, St. Louis, 1975-86. Mem. Am. Mgmt. Assn., Associated Gen. Contractors, U. Mo. Alumni Assn. Methodist. Avocations: sailing, skiing, travel, home remodeling, wood projects. Home: 15330 Schoettler Estates Dr Chesterfield MO 63017 Office: Gen Software Systems Inc 745 Craig Rd Suite 106 Creve Coeur MO 63141

JOHNSON, ERIC LANCE, steel company executive; b. Toledo, Aug. 27, 1946; s. Karl John and Delores Viola (Durbin) J.; m. Mary Sue Johnson, Aug. 14, 1967 (div. Feb. 1969); m. Judy Lynn Burkett, Sept. 5, 1970; children: Dawn, Lesa, Heather, Rhett. BA, Sinclair Coll., 1974, BBA, 1975; MBA, Ind. U., 1977. Inside salesman Jones & Laughlin Steel, Dayton, Ohio, 1968-70; from salesman to gen. mgr. J.T. Ryerson, Dayton, 1970-78; v.p. Krohn Steel, Springfield, Ohio, 1978-80; pres. and chief exec. officer Burjon Steel, Springboro, Ohio, 1980—, Steel Blanks and Sheets, Franklin, Ohio, 1985—, Springboro Trophy, 1987—. Mem. Springboro Bd. Zoning Appeals, 1986.Served as sgt. USAF, 1964-68. Mem. Dayton 100 Club, Dayton C. of C., Springboro C. of C. (Bus. of Yr. award 1985). Methodist. Avocations: water skiing, tennis, golf, soccer. Home: 441 E Ohio Rt 73 Springboro OH 45066 Office: Burjon Steel Service PO Box 370 350 Sharts Rd Springboro OH 45066

JOHNSON, ERIC PAUL, manufacturing company executive; b. Grand Rapids, Mich., Aug. 9, 1948; s. Paul Harding and Geraldine (Kirchhoff) J.; m. Barbara Corlett; children: Robin, Abigail, Sarah. BS in Engring., U. Mich., 1970, MS in Engring., 1971. Computer application engr. Procter & Gamble Co., Cin., 1971-75; v.p. Corlett-Turner Co., Holland, Mich., 1975—. Served with U.S. Army, 1971-73. Home: 269 Portchester Holland MI 49423 Office: Corlett-Turner Co 2500 104th St Holland MI 49423

JOHNSON, ERNEST MCCABE, human resources executive, consultant; b. Evanston, Ill., May 7, 1944; s. Ernest A. and Ruth Alice (McCabe) J.; m. Linda Sue Millett, Jan. 22, 1966; children—Timothy Ernest, Darin Edward, Elizabeth Linda. B.A., U. Ill., 1970, M.A., 1971. Instr. psychology Parkland Coll., Champaign, Ill., 1970-73; regional psychologist U.S. Office Personnel Mgmt., Phila., 1973-75; personnel psychologist City of Milw., 1975-79; personnel dir. City of Green Bay (Wis.), 1979-83; v.p. human resources Employers Health Ins. Co., 1983—; cons. personnel, Green Bay, 1974—. Bd. dirs. Curative Workshop, Green Bay, 1981-82. Served to sgt. USAF, 1965-69. Mem. Am. Psychol. Assn., Am. Mgmt. Assn. Home: 1013 Redwood Dr Green Bay WI 54304 Office: Employers Health Insurance Co PO Box 1100 Green Bay WI 54344

JOHNSON, ERVIN CLARENCE, lab technician; b. Ruthven, Iowa, Sept. 7, 1940; s. Joseph Clarence Paula Louise (Cuklanz) J.; m. Shirley Juanita Hudson, Feb. 2, 1962; children: Julia Elizabeth, David Craig, Janet Irene. BS in Math., Iowa State U., 1971. Lab technician Mary Greeley Med. Ctr., Ames, Iowa, 1970-71; clin. chemist Fisher Labs., DeKalb, Ill., 1971-72; lab technician Iowa State U., Ames, 1972—. Republican. Lutheran. Avocations: reading, carpentry, tennis. Home: 602 Boone St Sheldahl IA 50243 Office: Iowa State U Ames IA 50010

JOHNSON, FAYRENE, librarian; b. Chgo., Mar. 19, 1957; d. Jimmie Lee and Queen Victoria (Williamson) J. B.A., Lewis U., 1979, postgrad., 1981—. Cert. paralegal. Library supr. Bur Oak Library System, Shorewood, Ill., 1980-81, asst. librarian, 1981, chief librarian, 1981-85; chief librarian Corn Belt Library System, Normal, Ill., 1985—. Co-chmn. Nat. Alliance Against Racist and Polit. Repression, Chgo., 1986—; paralegal tng. instr. Recipient Outstanding Achievement award W.I.N.E. Social Service Orgn., Chgo., 1979. Mem. Am. Correctional Assn., Ill. Library Assn., Nat. Assn. Female Execs. Avocations: reading; singing. Home: 500 Dellwood St Lockport IL 60441 Office: 753 E 79th St Room 209 Chicago IL 60619

JOHNSON, FREDERICK DEAN, II, financial planner; b. Orrville, Ohio, June 24, 1940; s. Frederick Dean and Haulwen (Richey) J.; divorced; children: Frederick D. III, Matthew Lee; m. Patricia Lea Janke, Jan. 5, 1977. BS in Edn., Ashland Coll., 1962; cert., Coll. Fin. Planning, 1979. Pub. sch. tchr. Alliance and Cadiz, Ohio, 1963-64; mfg. rep. Gulf Envelope Co., Houston, Tex., 1964-66; broker, fin. planner Dempsey Tegler & Co., Houston, 1964—; fin. planner Rowles, Winston, Cowen & Co., Cleve.; cert. fin. planner Anchor Nat. Fin. Service, Beachwood, Ohio, 1978—; adj. instr. Cleve. State U., 1979—, Cuyahoga Community Coll., Cleve., 1979—; instr. Chautaugua (N.Y.) Instn., 1984—. Avocations: music, playing jazz piano, reading, travel, art. Home: 3633 Lytle Rd Shaker Heights OH 44122 Office: 23360 Chagrin Blvd Beachwood OH 44122

JOHNSON, GARY KEITH, pediatrician; b. Chgo., Aug. 26, 1951; s. John Edward and Dorothy Lucille (Rudder) J. AB, Dartmouth Coll., 1973; MD, U. Ill., Chgo., 1979, MPH, 1985. Diplomate Am. Bd. Med. Examiners, Am. Bd. Pediatrics. Intern Columbus Hosp., Chgo., 1980, resident in pediatrics, 1980-83; fellow in ambulatory pediatrics Cook County Hosp., Chgo., 1983-85; dir. Ambulatory pediatrics Hurley Med. Ctr., Flint, Mich., 1986—; asst. prof. pediatrics Mich. State U., East Lansing, 1986. Fellow Am. Acad. Pediatrics; mem. Chgo. Pediatric Soc., Am. Acad. Pediatrics (Mich. chpt.), Genesee County Med. Soc., Mich. State Med. Soc., Ambulatory Pediatric Assn., AMA, Am. Pub. Health Assn. Democrat. Presbyterian. Avocations: swimming, bicycling. Home: 3620 Rue Foret Dr Apt #144 Flint MI 48504 Office: Hurley Med Ctr 2 Hurley Plaza Flint MI 48502

JOHNSON, GEORGE, advertising executive; b. Indpls., Feb. 11, 1917; s. George Kirkley and Maud Florence (Peats) J.; m. Ethel Louise Osborne, Oct. 9, 1944 (dec. June 1968); children: Christopher R., Daniel K., Douglas R.; m. Sandra Diane Atwell, June 3, 1972 (div. July 1982); children: Eric D., Andrew L. Student, Ind. U., 1936-37. Reporter Indpls. News, 1939-41, 46-50, St. Louis Star Times, 1950-51; editor R.L. Polk & Co., Detroit, 1953-56; copywriter various agencies, St. Louis, 1957-60; creative dir. French Advt., Inc., St. Louis, 1960-63; freelance writer St. Louis, 1963; pres., creative dir. George Johnson, Advt., St. Louis, 1964—; editor, pub. The Yellow Sheet, St. Louis, 1984—; organize advt. mgmt. workshops; cons. in field. Author: (book) Biography of Richard Nixon, 1961, Biography of Dwight Eisenhower, 1962, Biography of Eleanor Roosevelt, 1962, Biography of Jack Paar, 1962, The Washington Waste-Makers, 1963, The Abominable Airlines, 1964, Your Career in Advertising, 1965, The Pill Conspiracy, 1967. Served to 1st lt. USAAF, 1941-46. Democrat. Avocations: tennis, family. Home: 237 Olive View Dr Manchester MO 63021 Office: 763 New Ballas Rd Room 220 Saint Louis MO 63141

JOHNSON, GEORGE, lieutenant governor, physician; b. Winnipeg, Man., Can., Nov. 18, 1920; s. Jonas George and Laufey Johnson; m. Doris Marjorie Blondal, Dec. 31, 1943; children: Janis, Jennifer, Daniel, Jon, Joann, Gillian. BS, U. Man., Can., 1941, MD, 1950. Practice medicine Gimli, Man., 1950-58; mem. legis. assembly Conservative Govt. Man., Winnipeg, 1958-69, minister of health and pub. welfare, 1958-61, minister of health, 1961-63, minister of edn., 1963-68, minister of health, 1968-69; practice medicine Winnipeg, 1969-79; med. cons. Province of Man. Health Dept., Winnipeg, 1979-86; lt. gov. Province of Man., Winnipeg, 1986—; mem. exec. council Province of Man., Winnipeg, 1958-69. Served to lt. Royal Can. Navy, 1941-45. Fellow Coll. of Family Medicine; mem. Man. Tchrs. Soc. (hon. life), Winnipeg Med. Soc. (hon. life), Manitoba Med. Assn. (hon. life). Lutheran. Club: Kinsmen. Avocations: fishing, golf, sporting events. Office: Legislative Bldg Room 235, Winnipeg, MB Canada R3C 1S4

JOHNSON, GEORGE ROBERT, retired government official; b. Grand Forks, N.D., Sept. 30, 1927; s. Sam A. and Olga (Bjorge) J.; m. Marjorie F. Dorsher, Nov. 24, 1948; children: Sam, Margie, Peter, Kari, Robert. PhB, U. N.D., 1949, postgrad., 1963; postgrad., George Williams Coll., 1950, Oreg. State U., 1950-52, U. So. Calif., 1952-53, George Washington U., 1972. With YMCA, 1941-52; gen. sec. YMCA, Kelso, Wash., 1950-52; research dir. John Danz Found., Seattle, 1952; intern, placement dir. sch. pub. adminstrn. U. So. Calif., Los Angeles, 1952-53; staff fed. personnel programs various orgns., 1953-85. Editor Down's Syndrome News; assoc. editor People With Special Needs/Down Syndrome Report; contbr. articles to profl. jours. Treas. Brown County ARC, 1979-81; mem. Nat. Apostolate Mentally Retarded Persons. Served with U.S. Army, 1946-47. Mem. Classification and Compensation Soc. (founder, pres. 1969-70, Service award 1970), Aberdeen (S.D.) Personnel Assn. (pres. 1980-81), Down's Syndrome Congress (co-founder, Service award 1978), Am. Assn. on Mental Deficiency, Assn. Retarded Citizens, VFW, Am. Legion, Germans from Russia Heritage Soc. Lodge: Sons of Norway. Home: 1409 N 1st St Aberdeen SD 57401 Office: No State Coll PO Box 635 Aberdeen SD 57401

JOHNSON, GEORGE TAYLOR, aircraft company official; b. Kansas City, Mo., Jan. 12, 1930; s. George Dewey and Geneva (Van Leu) J.; B.A., Columbia Coll., 1977; m. Pamela Kay Cole, Aug. 30, 1981; children—Van L., Victoria Johnson-Beineke, Wendell O., Marcella Johnson-Bruce. Enlisted in U.S. Army, 1947, served to 1967; chief instr. rotary wing sect. U.S. Army Transp. Sch., Ft. Eustis, Va., 1965-67; ret., 1967; group leader aerospace publs. Beech Aircraft Corp., Wichita, Kans., 1968-79, adminstr. aerospace logistics programs, 1979-87; staff asst. program mgmt., 1987—. Mem. Community Action Agy., Wichita, 1973-75; founder U.S. Army Black Pilots Reunions, U.S. Army Black Aviators Assn. Served with U.S. Army, 1947-67. Decorated D.F.C., Air medal with V and four oak leaf clusters. Mem. Negro Airmen Internat. (state dir.), Nat. Bus. League, NAACP, Army Aviation Assn. Am., Assn. U.S. Army, Soc. Logistics Engrs., VFW, 9th and 10th Cav. Assn. Baptist. Lodge: Optimist. Home: 202 Miles Ave Valley Center KS 67147 Office: 9709 E Central Wichita KS 67201

JOHNSON, GEORGIA KAY, periodontist, educator; b. Waterloo, Iowa, Aug. 31, 1952; d. Hilbert William and Olga Martha (Lickiss) Tonn; m. William Thomas Johnson; Aug. 25, 1974; children: Aaron Thomas, Jarod William. BS, U. Iowa, 1975, DDS, 1981, MS, 1983. Dental hygienist U.S. Civil Service, Ft. Still, Okla., 1975-77; research asst. U. Iowa, 1981-83; asst. prof. U. Nebr., 1983—. Contbr. articles abstract to research jour. Named one of Outstanding Young Women Am., 1982. Mem. ADA, Am. Acad. Periodontology, Am. Assn. Dental Schs., Internat. Assn. Dental Research, Nebr. Dental Assn., Lincoln Dist. Dental Assn., Nebr. Soc. Periodontology (v.p. 1984-85, pres. 1985-86), Am. Assn. Women Dentist. Republican. Lutheran. Home: 2831 S 74th St Lincoln NE 68506 Office: U Nebr Coll Dentistry 40th and Holdrege St Lincoln NE 68583

JOHNSON, GERALD CARL, controller, accountant; b. Detroit, June 17, 1937; s. Evald Carl and Ruby Aileen (Charboneau) J.; m. Kathleen Roberta McBrady, Aug. 12, 1961; children: Dan (dec.), Suzanne, David, Stephen. BS in Acctg., U. Detroit, 1960; postgrad., U. Mich., 1984—. Mgr. Coopers & Lybrand, Detroit, 1960-71; ptnr. Alam & Co., Detroit, 1971-77; officer Derderian, Kann, Seyferth & Salucci, P.C., Troy, Mich., 1977-79; assoc. Plante & Moran, Southfield, Mich., 1979-82; controller Solar Machine, Romulus, Mich., 1982-83, McKenna Industries, Inc. and subs., Troy, 1983-86, Beznos, Beztak Cos., Farmington Hills, Mich., 1987—. Bd. dirs. Suburban West Community Ctr.; past pres. Woodbrook Homeowners Assn.; past treas. Our Lady of Good Counsel Boy Scouts Am., Plymouth, Mich. Mem. Am. Inst. CPA's, Nat. Assn. Accts. (mem. controllers council), Mich. Assn. CPA's (past chmn. acctg. and auditing procedures and publications coms., co-chmn. U. Mich. fall acctg. conf., mem. fin. instn. relations com.). Roman Catholic. Club: Toastmasters (Plymouth) (past treas.). Avocations: tennis, racquetball, bowling. Home and Office: 10512 Brookwood Plymouth MI 48170

JOHNSON, GLENDORA SHANNON, printing company executive; b. McFarland, Kans., Aug. 17, 1919; d. Arthur and Julia Mary (Mooney) Shannon; m. Clyde W. Talley, Jan. 11, 1937 (div. 1955); m. William Johnson, Nov. 13, 1959. Diploma, Strickler's Bus. Coll., 1937. Gen. adminstrv. mgr. Lago & Whitehead Advt. Agy., Wichita, Kans., 1950-61; adminstrv. asst. to pres. Lawrence Photo Supply, 1961-65; v.p., gen. mgr. Wichita Automotive & Tech. Sch., 1965-69; dir. prodn. services, McCormick-Armstrong Advt. Agy., 1969-84; co-owner-sales mgr. Johnson Printing, 1984—; pres. Adminstrv. Mgmt. Soc., Wichita, 1967-68, Advt. Club of Wichita, 1978-79; co-owner, adminstrv. and fin. mgr. Johnson Printing, 1984—. Pres. Wichita Women's Polit. Caucus. Named Wichita Ad Woman of Yr., 1984. Mem. Bus. and Profl. Women Assn., Nat. Assn. Women Bus. Owners. Democrat. Roman Catholic. Lodge: Zonta (pres. 1970-73). Avocations: bowling, walking, reading, teaching. Home: 423 Topaz Wichita KS 67209

JOHNSON, HARALD VALDIMAR, science education consultant; b. Mountain, N.D., June 5, 1913; s. John Arnason and Inga (Knudson) J.; m. Louise Adelaide Lee, Dec. 15, 1945; 1 child, Jon Lee. BA, U. N.D., 1934; MEd, U. Wash., 1952. Cert. profl. chemist. Lay med. approver, adjudicator VA, Seattle, 1946-48; dir. instructional materials ctr. Lewis County Schs., Chehalis, Wash., 1952-54; sci. tchr., audio-visual coordinator Whittier (Calif.) Union High Sch. Dist., 1954-56; tchr. chemistry, chmn. exptl. analysis and research div. Morningside High Sch. Inglewood (Calif.) Unified Sch. Dist., 1956-73; pvt. practice sci. edn. cons. Gig Harbor, Wash., 1973-86, Elmhurst, Ill., 1986—; chemist Union Oil Calif. Research Ctr., Brea., summer 1955, Fluor Corp. Research Ctr., Whittier, Summer 1956, Calif. Research Corp., La Habra, summer 1958. Author: (with Gene Gretche) Let Your Students Make The Sound, 1956; A Scheme of Semi-Micro Qualitative Cation Analysis with Quantitative Estimations of Selected Elements, 1959, rev. 1972. Served to maj., inf., AUS, 1941-46, ETO. U. Wash. fellow, 1952, Am. Inst. Chemists fellow; recipient Citation Outstanding Teaching Sci., Inst. Advancement Engring., 1970, Cert. Merit, Bd. Dirs. Inglewood Unified Sch. Dist., 1973; recipient NSF grants UCLA, summer 1959, U. Redlands, 1959-60, Harvey Mudd Coll., summers 1967, 70. Fellow Am. Inst. Chemists; mem. Am. Chem. Soc., Calif. Inst. Chemists (charter), Nat. Sci. Tchrs. Assn. (life.), Calif. Assn. Chemistry Tchrs. (bd. dirs. 1971-72), N.Y. Acad. Scis., Icelandic Male Chorus Seattle, Orpheus Male Chorus Tacoma, Bjornson Male Chorus chgo., Phi Delta Kappa. Lodges: Masons, Elks. Home: 2 Atrium Way #601 Elmhurst IL 60126

JOHNSON, HAROLD HAZEN, religious organization administrator; b. Flint, Mich., Feb. 7, 1936; s. Ernest Robert and Alta Mae (Gillam) J.; m. Fe. Jeanne Johnson, May 24, 1980; children: Tammi, Todd, Timothy, Tyler; stepchildren: Douglas, Karelle. BA cum laude, Union Sch., 1958; MDiv, Iliff Sch. Theology, 1961; postgrad., St. Paul Sch. Theology, 1986—. Assoc. minister Montclair Meth. Ch., Denver, 1958-61, Cent. Meth. Ch., Pontiac, Mich., 1961-63; minister DAvisburg (Mich.) Meth. Ch., 1963-67; assoc. minister First Meth. Ch., Warren, Mich., 1967-68; minister Holly (Mich.) Presbyn. Ch., 1968-73; minister First Presbyn. Ch., Ionia, Mich., 1973-75, Alamogordo, N.Mex., 1975-77; minister Unity in Pontiac, Mich., 1979-84; dir. Mich. Assn. Youth Service Bur., Pontiac, Mich., 1979-80, Parent to Parent Coop. Extension, Pontiac, 1980-82; counselor Oakland County Jail, Pontiac, 1982-84; chairperson pastoral studies and skills Unity Sch. Christianity, Unity Village, Mo., 1984—. Club: Toastmasters (Lees Summit, Mo.) (v.p. 1987). Lodge: Lions (dir. 1987—). Avocations: travel, landscaping, golf. Home: 455 Winnebago Dr Lake Winnebago MO 64034 Office: Unity Sch Christianity Unity Village MO 64065

JOHNSON, HAROLD L., risk management executive; b. Ravenna, Nebr., Aug. 3, 1927; s. J. Victor and Theresa E. (Drogseth) J.; m. Anita Eloise Sandager, Aug. 2, 1951; children: Valerie Johnson Wedin, Bruce V. BS with distinction, U. Nebr., 1949; postgrad., U. Omaha, 1950-51, Washington U., St. Louis, 1952; cert., LaSalle Extension U., 1979. With Travelers Ins. Co., Omaha, St. Louis and Houston, Nebr., Mo. and Tex., 1951-62; with State Farm Ins. Cos., Bloomington, Ill., 1962-68, superintendent corp. ins., 1968-70, mgr. corp. ins., 1970-80, dir. risk mgmt., 1980—; council Am. Mgmt. Assn., N.Y.C., 1986—; bd. dirs. Robert Spencer Meml. Found., N.Y.C., Risk Mgmt. Soc. Pub., Inc., N.Y.C. Contbr. articles to profl. jours. Mem. exec. com. Harris County Tex. Reps., Houston, 1960-62; chmn. Rep. Precinct, Houston, 1960-62. Mem. Soc. of Property and Casualty Underwriters, Risk and Ins. Mgmt. Soc. (bd. dirs. Chgo. chpt. 1977-78, v.p. 1979, pres. 1980, bd. dirs. N.Y.C. chpt. 1981-86, v.p. 1986—), Ill. C. of C. (work compensation com. 1974—), Beta Sigma Psi. Republican. Lutheran. Home: 141 Manor Circle Bloomington IL 61701 Office: 112 E Washington Bloomington IL 61701

JOHNSON, HENRY ARNA, mail order company executive; b. Chgo., Mar. 26, 1919; s. John J. and Sigrid (Jorgensen) J.; m. Darlene H. Green, Oct. 11, 1973; children: Nancy, Martin, Roy; step-children: Pamela, James, Kristine. Student, Northwestern U., 1940-43; MBA, U. Chgo., 1964. With mdse. div. Montgomery Ward & Co., Chgo., 1939-49; exec. v.p. Aldens Inc., Chgo., 1949-74; pres. Family Fashions by Avon, Hampton, Va., 1974-76; pres. Spiegel, Inc., Oak Brook, Ill., 1976-85, chief exec. officer, 1976-85, vice chmn., 1985—. Mem. nat. exec. bd. Boy Scouts Am., pres. Area 3 region Boy Scouts Am., pres. Chgo. Area council, 1980-81. Served with USAF, 1943-45. Decorated Air medal; recipient Disting. Citizens award, 1982, Horatio Alger award, 1985. Mem. Direct Mail Mktg. Assn. (dir.), Am. Retail Fedn. (dir.), Nat. Retail Merchants Assn. Clubs: Butterfield Country, Mid-Am., Chgo. Yacht. Office: Spiegel Inc 1515 W 22d St Oak Brook IL 60522

JOHNSON, HOWARD ARTHUR, JR., operations research analyst; b. Indpls., July 25, 1952; s. Howard Arthur Sr. and Joy (Nelson) J.; m. Teresa Thirsk, Aug. 11, 1979. BA in Polit. Sci. and Ops. Research Analysis, U. Kans., 1974; MA in Internat. Studies and Mgmt., U. Wyo., 1984. Ops. research analyst Armament Systems, Inc., Ft. Walton Beach, Fla., 1980-81, EG&G InterTech, Inc., Arlington, Va., 1981-84, dep. to U.S. dir. plans and budgets, Royal Saudi Navy, Saudi Arabian Ministry Def. and Aviation, Riyadh, Saudi Arabia, 1981-82; ops. research analyst FMC Corp., Mpls., 1984-85; ops. research analyst Honeywell, Inc., 1985— sr. prin. systems engr., 1985—; cons. USN, Coronado, 1977-78. Sustaining mem. Rep. Nat. Com., Washington, 1984—. Served to lt. USN, 1974-78. Grad. acad. scholar U. Wyo., 1983-84. Mem. AAAS, Ops. Research Soc. Am., Acad. Internat. Bus., Inst. Mgmt. Scis., Fgn. Policy Research Inst., Mil. Ops. Research Soc., Armed Forces Communications Electronics Assn., Washington Ops. Research Mgmt. Sci. Council, Tau Kappa Epsilon. Home: 3376 Brunswick Ave S Saint Louis Park MN 55416 Office: Honeywell Inc 10400 Yellow Circle Dr Minnetonka MN 55343

JOHNSON, IRENE HARRIS, educational administrator; b. Miami, Fla.; d. Benjamin Franklin and Ollie Lee (Jennings) H.; children: Gordon, Eric, Reginald. BS, Hampton Inst., 1960; MS, Purdue U., 1980, PhD candidate, 1985—. Med. technician Kecoughton VA Hosp., 1960-61; tchr. sci. Dade County Pub. Schs., Miami, Fla., 1961-64; chmn. dept. sci. Richmond (Va.) Pub. Schs., 1964-65; cons. sci. D.C. Pub. Schs., 1965-72; tchr. biology Fairfax County Pub. Schs., Vienna, Va., 1972-77; coordinator minorities sci. program Purdue U., 1977—, dir. tutorial program, Sch. Sci., 1978-80, dir. Summer Outreach Program, 1979-81; cons. coll. relations IBM, Rochester, Minn., 1984—. Chmn. edn. com. NAACP, 1983-84; chmn. Purdue Black Caucus of Faculty and Staff, 1983—. NSF grantee, 1962, 69, 74. Mem. AAAS, Nat. Assn. Negro Women (1st v.p. 1975), Ind. Coalition of Blacks in Higher Edn., Assn. Counseling and Devel., Assn. Multi-cultural Counseling and Devel., Nat. Assn. Student Personnel Adminstrs., Nat. Acad. Adv. Assn., Phi Delta Kappa. Baptist. Avocations: gardening, reading, swimming, matchbook and recipe collecting. Office: Purdue U Sch Sci Math Bldg 948 West Lafayette IN 47907

JOHNSON, JACK JONATHAN, educator; b. Chgo., July 30, 1957; s. Joseph Jackson and Dorothy Anne (Gebert) J. BA, Lake Forest (Ill.) Coll., 1979; Cert. in Data Processing, Control Data Inst., Bensenville, Ill., 1982; postgrad., Keller Grad. Sch. Mgmt., Chgo., 1983-86. Instr. Northwest Bus. Coll., Chgo., 1982-83, Sauk Area Career Ctr., Crestwood, Ill., 1983, Coll. Automation, Chgo., 1983—. Mem. Data Processing Mgmt. Assn. Republican. Roman Catholic. Club: Toastmasters. Home: 1905 W Wilson Ave Chicago IL 60640

JOHNSON, JAMES DUANE, electrical contractor; b. Belvidere, Ill., Apr. 10, 1941; s. Herbert and Edna Louise (Schafman) J.; m. Myrna Irene Thompson, Aug. 29, 1959; children: Cynthia Walters, Michel Johannes. Cert. indsl. electronics, Internat. Correspondence Sch., 1964. Control technician Ingersoll Milling, Rockford, Ill., 1959-67; control engr. Electro Corp., Rockford, 1967-68, Liqui-Trol Corp., Aurora, Ill., 1968-69; salesman Westinghouse Corp., Rockford, Ill., 1969-85; estimating engr. Rockford Electric Power Contractors, 1985—; pres., v.p., treas. Greater Rockford Indsl. Distributors, 1982-85. Pres. Belvidere (Ill.) Youth Baseball Assn., 1983, bd. dirs. 1970-86. Named to Millionaires Club, Westinghouse Corp., 1974 75, 77, 79, 84. Mem. Rock Valley Electric Assn. Republican. Roman Catholic. Clubs: Bel-Mar, Y's Men (treas. 1980-81). Avocations: softball, golfing, swimming, woodworking. Home: 8710 Summerset Dr Belvidere IL 61008 Office: Rockford Electric Power Contractors 5300 Nimtz Rd Loves Park IL 61130

JOHNSON, JAMES FREEMAN, office furniture manufacturing company executive; b. Cedar Rapids, Iowa, Oct. 30, 1932; s. Freeman and Marie Rose Johnson; B.A., Knox Coll., 1954. Salesman, Am. Chicle Co., Minn., 1954-57; advt. mgr., Toronto, Ont., Can., 1962-65; regional sales mgr. Warner Lambert, Chgo., 1969-71; dir. sales, mgr. Europe, Am. Optical Co., South Bridge, Mass., 1971-75; dir. nat. sales Am. Chicle div. Warner Lambert, Morris Plains, N.J., 1976-79; v.p. sales and mktg. The HON Co., Muscatine, Iowa, 1979—. Served with U.S. Army, 1954-56. Home: Route 3 Box 42 Muscatine IA 52761 Office: The HON Co 200 Oak St Muscatine IA 52761

JOHNSON, JAMES ROBERT, restauranteur; b. Marquette, Mich., Oct. 26, 1953; s. Robert Henry and Catherine (Barbiere) J.; m. Joan Marie Tonella, Sept. 5, 1980; 1 child, James Robert Jr. BS in Communications, No. Mich. U., 1977. Owner Casa Calabria, Marquette, 1977—. Tchr. CCD Religious Edn., Marquette, 1976-77, 78-79; sec. Village Devel. Commn., Marquette, 1984—; precinct del. Marquette Dems., 1972. Werner scholar 1975-77. Mem. Village Bus. Assn. (pres. 1984—), Nat. Restaurant Assn., Marquette C. of C., Bd. Realtor, Marquette Coop Brokers (sec. 1977-80). Roman Catholic. Club: Golden Wildcat (bd. dirs.). Avocations: basketball, racquetball. Home: 412 McMillan Marquette MI 49855 Office: 1106 N 3d Marquette MI 49855

JOHNSON, JAYLEN THOMAS, banker; b. Monmouth, Ill., Aug. 17, 1952; s. Clarence Raymond and Josephine Joyce (Brinegar) J. BS in Fin., Ferris State Coll., 1974; grad., Sch. Banking Adminstrn., Madison, Wis., 1981. Teller So. Mich. Nat. Bank, Coldwater, 1969-74, asst. to cashier, 1975-78, asst. auditor, 1978-79, auditor, 1979-86, cashier, 1986-87, asst v.p. and cashier, 1987—. Asst. scoutmaster Boy Scouts Am., Coldwater, 1975-78, leader cubscout roundtable, Branch and St. Joseph Counties, Mich., 1976; co-chmn. fin. institution drive United Way of Branch County, 1982-83; mem., sub-committeeman Coldwater Indsl. Growth Assn., 1983—. Recipient Martin P. Luthy award Mich. Jaycees, 1986, Charles Kulp Jr. Meml. award U.S. Jaycees, 1986; named Eagle Scout Boy Scouts Am., 1968. Mem. Am. Inst. Banking (past 2d v.p., treas., pres.), Coldwater Jaycees (various offices), Lamdba Chi Alpha. Avocations: golf, bowling, racquetball, gardening. Home: 259 N Fiske Rd Coldwater MI 49036 Office: So Mich Nat Bank 51 W Pearl St Coldwater MI 49036

JOHNSON, JEFFREY ROBERT, physician; b. Lincoln, Nebr., July 17, 1948; s. William Fray and Martha Louise (Gilbert) J.; m. Marcia Rea Williams, June 26, 1971; children: Jennifer, Katherine, Jeffrey. BA in Zoology, U. Ark., 1970; MD, U. Tex., 1974; resident in urologic surgery, U. Tex., San Antonio, 1980. Diplomate Am. Bd. Urology. Practice urologic medicine Springfield, Mo., 1980—; cons. urology FeD. Med. Ctr., Springfield, Mo., 1982—. contbr. articles to profl. jours. Bd. dirs. Springfield Little Theater, 1985—; pres. bd. dirs., Springfield Chpt. Kidney Found., 1985-87. Fellow ACS; mem. AMA, Mo. State Med. Soc., Greene County Med. Soc. (treas. 1984, social chmn. 1986), Am. Urology Assn., Sigma Chi, U. Ark. Alumni Assn. (pres. 1984). Episcopalian. Club: Hickory Hills Country (Springfield). Avocation: running. Office: Urology Surgical Assocs Inc 1965 S Fremont #3100 Springfield MO 65804

JOHNSON, JERALD LEE, manufacturing executive; b. Waterloo, Iowa, Dec. 1, 1936; s. Raymond Jesse and Harriet E. (Niedert) J.; m. Mary Lou Graf, July 28, 1956. BA in Math and Physics, U. No. Iowa, 1966. Indsl. engr. John Deere, Waterloo, Iowa, 1966-68, Honeywell Ordinance, Mpls., 1968-69; sr. indsl. engr. Control Data Corp., Mpls., 1969-71; mgr., indsl. engr. Onan Corp., Mpls., 1971-80, dir. mfg. tech. services, 1980—; speaker, seminar leader in field. Served as sgt. USMC, 1955-59. Mem. Inst. Indsl. Engrs. (editor Twin Cities chpt. 1973-74, treas. 1980-81, pres. 1981-83, bd.

dirs. 1983—), Soc. Mfg. Engrs. (sr.). Roman Catholic. Avocation: wine collector. Home: 12173 Cottonwood St NW Coon Rapids MN 55433 Office: Onan Corp 1400 73d Ave NE Minneapolis MN 55432

JOHNSON, JIMMY LEE, tool and die company owner; b. Battle Creek, Mich., June 7, 1945; s. Harry Johnson Jr. and Margaret Fern (Hopkins) Schutte; m. Marsha Lynn Richardson, June 11, 1966; children: Thad Lee, Tory Lynn. AA in Vocat. Tech., Montcalm Community Coll., 1972. Apprentice die maker J.R. Tool & Die, Sheridan, Mich., 1968-72; ind. ins. agt. Greenville, Mich., 1970-76; diemaker, foreman Preferred Tool & Die, Comstock Park, Mich., 1978; owner Bear Tool & Die Co., Greenville, Mich., 1978—; sec. Riversedge Corp. Chmn. Community Action Com., Greenville, 1982—; Webelos leader Cub Scouts, 1978-82; roundtable leader West Mich. Shores council Boy Scouts Am., 1979-82. Served with USNR, 1966-72. Mem. Nat. Fedn. Ind. Businessmen, Mich. Mfrs. Assn., Mich. State C. of C., Greenville Area C. of C. Lodges: Lions (liontamer Greenville club 1983—), Moose. Avocations: refinishing antiques, woodworking, golf, off-roading. Office: Bear Tool & Die Co 720 W Coffren St Greenville MI 48838

JOHNSON, JOEL PETER, design engineer; b. Eau Claire, Wis., Mar. 8, 1960; s. John Clarence and Joyce Irma (Holman) J. BS in Elec. and Computer Engring., U. Wis., 1983. Engr. mfg. mgmt. programmer Gen. Electric Co., San Jose, Calif. and Utica, N.Y., 1983-85; design engr. audio devices Telex Communications, Mpls., 1985—. Patentee programmable function generator, disclosure field. Pres. Dem. Orgn. Progressive Engrs. and Scientists, Madison, Wis., 1982-83; mem. media com. Freeze Voter 1984, San Jose, 1984. Mem. IEEE, Audio Engring. Soc. (assoc.). Avocations: music, tennis, frisbee. Office: Telex Communications 9600 Aldrich Ave S Minneapolis MN 55420

JOHNSON, JOHN ARVID, project engineer; b. Davenport, Iowa, Mar. 24, 1953; s. Arvid and Ellen Sophie (Zahringer) J.; m. Jennie Elizabeth Charron, Dec. 31, 1977; children: Katherine, Joseph, Stephanie. BS, Valparaiso U., 1975; MME, Polytechnic Inst., 1976. Inside sales engr. Northeast Controls, Clifton Park, N.Y., 1976; engr. sales R.S. Stover Co., Marshalltown, Iowa, 1977-82, project mgr., 1982—. Mem. ASME, Am. Soc. Mgmt. Assn., Instrument Soc. Am., Marshalltown Engrs. Club (sec. 1982-85). Republican. Lutheran. Lodge: Optimist. Home: 2014 Skyline Dr Marshalltown IA 50158

JOHNSON, JOHN EDWARD, corporate education and training expert; b. Akron, Ohio, Oct. 8, 1944; s. Byron Thomas and Dorothy (Neal) J.; m. Jane Ferrill, July 17, 1964; 1 child, Todd. BS, Ball State U., 1966, MA in Sociology, 1968, EdD, 1972. Prof. Brunswick (Ga.) Jr. Coll., 1972-77; acad. officer Ind. Commn. Higher Edn., Indpls., 1977-80; exec. dir. Hahn Found. project Ind. Hosp. Assn., Indpls., 1980-82; dir. edn. Community Hosps., Indpls., 1982-86, Kiwanis Internat., Indpls., 1986—; bd. dirs. Kiwanis Capitol Charities, Indpls.; adj. assoc. prof. Ind. U. Sch. Nursing, Indpls., 1980-86. Marshall Mayflower Classic Ladies Profl. Golf Assn., Indpls., 1981-86; transp. commr. U.S. nat. Claypt. Championships, Indpls., 1980-85; chmn. Glynn County Bicentennial Com., Brunswick, Ga., 1975-76. Recipient Honor Citation, Ind. Hosp. Assn., 1982; named one of Outstanding Young Men of Am., 1981. Mem. Am. Soc. Tng. and Devel., Cen. Ind. chpt. Am. Soc. Tng. and Devel. Republican. Lutheran. Lodge: Kiwanis (pres. Indpls. club 1985-86). Avocations: golfing, spectator sports, travelling. Office: Kiwanis Internat 3636 Woodview Trace Indianapolis IN 46268

JOHNSON, J(OHN) GARY, training and development manager; b. Ida Grove, Iowa, May 3, 1958; s. Howard William and Anabel (Lindberg) J.; m. Kimberly Ann Morrison, Sept. 28, 1985. BS, Iowa State U., 1980. Loan officer Farm Credit Banks, Mason City, Iowa, 1980-81; tng. specialist Farm Credit Banks, Omaha, 1981-83, dir. tng., 1983-84, mgmt. devel., tng. cons., 1984-87; compliance and devel. mgr. Comml. Fed. Mortgage Corp./ Comml. Fed. Savs. and Loan Assn., Omaha, 1987—. Mem. Am. Soc. for Tng. and Devel. (program coordinator 1982-83), Iowa State Alumni Assn. Republican. Avocations: skiing, running. Home: 2008 N 53 St Omaha NE 68104 Office: Comml Fed Mortgage Corp 2120 S 72d St Omaha NE 68124

JOHNSON, JORENE KATHRYN, community organization director; b. Rockville Centre, N.Y., Jan. 6, 1931; d. Adam and Kathryn Lillian (Schoen) Freitag; B.F.A., Pratt Inst., 1952; M.P.A., U. Cin., 1975; student Mt. St. Joseph Coll., 1977-78; m. Roland E. Johnson, Oct. 10, 1954; children—Lorin, Melissa. Furniture designer Jacques Bodart, Inc., N.Y.C., 1952-54; interior decorator Albert Parvin Co., Los Angeles, 1955-57, Maria Bergson Assocs., N.Y.C., 1957-61; office mgr., research asst. The Cin. Inst., 1973-74, research mgr., 1974-75; exec. dir. Friends of Cin. Parks Inc., 1975-77; community coordinator College Hill Forum, Cin., 1977-84; sec., insp. Green Twp. Zoning Bd., 1982-84; dir. The Program for Cin., 1984—. Mem. Cin. Mayor's Energy Policy Com., 1982-83; chmn. budget process com. Mayor's Budget Task Force, 1984; vice-chmn. Monfort Heights Civic Assn., 1977, chmn., 1978; mem. Leadership Cin. Class III, 1979-80; mem. planning com. Community Chest, 1982—; mem. planning com. Program for Cin., 1982-83; mem. steering com. Congress of Neighborhood Groups, 1983-85; bd. dirs. Hamilton County Assn. Retarded Citizens, 1983-87. Mem. Internat. Platform Assn., Cincinnatus Assn., Mensa. Home: 5200 Race Rd Cincinnati OH 45247 Office: 230 E 9th St Cincinnati OH 45202

JOHNSON, JOSEPH EGGLESTON, III, physician, educator; b. Elberton, Ga., Sept. 17, 1930; s. Joseph Eggleston Jr. and Marie (Williams) J.; m. Judith H. Kemp, Jan. 21, 1956; children: Joseph Eggleston IV, Judith Ann, Julie Marie. B.A. cum laude, Vanderbilt U., 1951, M.D., 1954. Diplomate Am. Bd. Internal Medicine (bd. govs. 1977-83, exec. com. 1981-83), Am. Bd. Allergy and Immunology. Intern Johns Hopkins Hosp., Balt., 1954-55, resident, 1957-61, physician, 1961-66; mem. faculty Johns Hopkins Med. Sch., Balt., 1961-66, asst. dean, 1963-66; chief infectious diseases U. Fla. Coll. Medicine, Gainsville, 1966-72, assoc. dean, 1970-72; prof., chmn. dept. Bowman Gray Sch. Medicine, Winston-Salem, N.C., 1972-85; dean, prof. internal medicine U. Mich. Med. Sch., Ann Arbor, 1985—; chief med. service N.C. Baptist Hosp., mem. residency rev. com. internal medicine, 1978-83, chmn. residency rev. com. internal medicine, 1983-85; dean Med. Sch., prof. medicine U. Mich., Ann Arbor, 1985—. Contbr. articles to profl. jours. Served to lt. USNR, 1955-57. John and Mary R. Markle scholar, 1962-67; Mead-Johnson postgrad. scholar, 1960-61. Fellow ACP (sci. program com. 1979-85, chmn. sci. program com. 1982-85, chmn. elect bd. govs. 1985, chmn. bd. govs., bd. regents 1985—, gov.-elect N.C. 1981-82, gov. N.C. 1982-86), Am. Acad. Allergy, Royal Soc. Medicine (travelling fellow 1970-71); mem. Am. Fedn. Clin. Research, Assn. Am. Physicians, Infectious Diseases Soc. Am., Soc. Exptl. Biology and Medicine, N.Y. Acad. Scis., Am. Assn. Immunologists, So. Soc. Clin. Investigation, Am. Soc. for Microbiology, Assn. Profs. Medicine (sec.-treas. 1978-81, pres.-elect 1981-82, pres. 1982-83), Am. Clin. and Climatol. Assn., Société Francaise de la Tuberculose et des Maladies Respiratoires, Assn. Program Dirs. in Internal Medicine (exec. council 1980-83), Assn. Am. Med. Colls. (exec. council 1983-85), Council of Acad. Socs. (adminstrv. bd. 1978-85), Federated Council for Internal Medicine (vice chmn. 1981-82, chmn. 1982-83), Phi Beta Kappa, Sigma Alpha Epsilon, Phi Chi, Omicron Delta Kappa, Alpha Omega Alpha. Office: U Mich Med Sch 1301 Catherine Rd Ann Arbor MI 48109-0624

JOHNSON, JULIE WEST, educator, writer; b. Fargo, N.D., Apr. 19, 1947; d. Edmund Elwell and Lillian Lindbergh (Christie) Johnson; m. Lance Jeffrey Rips, Apr. 18, 1976; 1 child, Eve Clare Johnson Rips. BA, Swarthmore Coll., 1969; MA, Stanford U., 1972. Cert. secondary tchr. (life). Editorial asst. New Yorker mag., N.Y.C., 1969-70; English tchr. Notre Dame Acad., Belmont, Calif., 1972-74; tchr.English New Trier High Sch., Winnetka, Ill., 1974—; free-lance writer McDougal, Littell Pubs., Evanston, Ill., 1983—. Author: Literature 9, 1983, 2d rev. edit., 1987, Literature 11, 1984, 2d rev. edit., 1987. Mem. Nat. Council Tchrs. English, Ill. Assn. Tchrs. English, New Trier Tchrs. Assn. Avocations: fiction writing, theater, classical music, cinema. Home: 5410 S Harper Ave Chicago IL 60615 Office: New Trier High Sch 385 Winnetka Ave Winnetka IL 60093

JOHNSON, KATHRYN MARY, sociology educator, researcher, consultant; b. Moline, Ill., July 18, 1952; d. Arthur Gordon and Eleanor C. (Lange) J.; m. Steven Charles Kuemmerle, Oct. 4, 1980; B.S., U. No. Colo., 1975, M.A., 1978; Ph.D., Western Mich. U., 1981. Instr., U. No. Colo., 1976-78, Chapman Coll., 1977-78, Western Mich. U., Kalamazoo, 1979-81; researcher, cons. Ctr. for Social Research, Kalamazoo, 1980-81, Grand Rapids (Mich.) pub. schs., 1979—; asst. prof. sociology Ind. U. N.W., Gary, 1981—. Author: If You Are Raped: What Every Woman Needs to Know, 1984. Contbr. articles to profl. jours. Bd. dirs. Chgo. Abused Women Coalition. Recipient Founder's Day Teaching award Ind. U. N.W., 1983; Ind. U. N.W. Faculty fellow, 1983, 85. Mem. Am. Sociol. Assn., Am. Ednl. Research Assn., North Central Sociol. Assn., NOW, Sociologists for Women in Society. Democrat. Episcopalian. Home: 4059 N Greenview Apt 3N Chicago IL 60613 Office: Ind U NW Dept Sociology Gary IN 46408

JOHNSON, KEITH DONALD, lawyer; b. Mpls., July 18, 1954; s. Dennis Axel and Dorraine Jeannette (Hennen) J. BA, Marquette U., 1976; JD, U. Minn., 1979. Bar: Minn. 1979, U.S. Dist. Ct. Minn. 1980. Assoc. Theodore R. Mellby & Assocs., P.A., Montgomery, Minn., 1979-84; ptnr. Wold, Jacobs & Johnson, Mpls., 1984—. Mem. Assn. Trial Lawyers Am., Minn. Trial Layers Assn., Minn. Bar Assn., Hennepin County Bar Assn., Phi Beta Kappa. Roman Catholic. Office: Wold Jacobs & Johnson Barristers Trust Bldg 247 3d Ave S Minneapolis MN 55415

JOHNSON, KEITH EDWIN, clergyman; b. Chgo., Feb. 21, 1948; s. Edwin Anderson and Margeret Jeanette (Jennings) J. BA, Judson Coll., 1969; grad., Career Acad. Broadcasting, 1970; MA, No. Ill. U., 1971; ThM, MDiv., ThD, Luther Rice U. Dir. admissions Judson Coll., 1968-69; host TV show WXJT-TV, Aurora, Ill., 1969-70; host radio show Impact, LaGrange, Ill., 1970-71; speaker seminar Nationwide Lifestream Program, 1970-72; exec. dir. Teens for Christ, Jacksonville Beach, Fla., 1972—; cons. tchr. U. North Fla., 1978-80, Fla. Jr. Coll., 1978—. Author: God's Policeman, 1979, Family Guidance Series, 1978-82, How to Overcome Stress, 1981, Can We Save Our Children, 1982, Knowing Our Temperaments, 1985, God's Plan for Stress Management, 1985; video series Knowing Your Temperament, 1985. Probation supr. Jacksonville Beach, Fla. Am. Legion grantee, 1976-80, Kiwanis Club grantee, 1979-80. Mem. Internat. Christian Edn. Assn. (advisor), Greater Internat. Teen Challenge Assn. (cons.). Office: 1000 S 350 E Marion IN 46753

JOHNSON, KEITH MORTON, personnel executive, accountant; b. Mpls., Dec. 24, 1943; s. Rodney Morton and Mildred Elizabeth (Peterson) J.; m. Sherry Rae Bonham, Dec. 15, 1972; children: Ryan Michael, Kevin Matthew. AS in Acctg., Grossmont Coll., 1967; BS in Acctg., San Diego State U., 1969. CPA, Calif. Acct. Touche Ross & Co., Mpls., 1969-73; sr. fin. analyst Dayton Hudson, Mpls., 1973-74; dir. acctg. Gen. Mills Corp., Mpls. and Phila., 1974-79; v.p. fin. NCC Industries, Cortland, N.Y., 1979-83; mng. ptnr. Romac Personnel Cons., Mpls., 1983—. Asst. treas. Mpls. Reps., 1975. Served with USN, 1961-64. Mem. Minn. Soc. CPA's, Nat. Assn. Accts. (bd. dirs. 1974-75), Phi Kappa Phi, Beta Alpha Psi. Lodges: Rotary, Kiwanis. Avocation: downhill skiing. Home: 6733 Shingle Creek Dr Brooklyn Park MN 55445 Office: Romac Personnel Cons 3800 W 80th St Suite 1240 Minneapolis MN 55431

JOHNSON, KENNETH DALE, architect; b. Glen Ridge, N.J., Jan. 1, 1946; s. Lowell Everett and Dorothy Mae (Ford) J.; m. Mary Susan Graves, July 13, 1970; children: Nathan Edward, Jessica Marie, Kara Anne. BArch, U. Minn., 1970. Registered architect, Minn. Design architect Horty Elving & Assocs., Mpls., 1970-73; project architect Cottle-Herman Assocs., Mpls., 1973-76; pvt. practice architecture Mpls., 1976-83; design architect D.E. Stanius & Assoc., Duluth, 1983—. Prin. works include the chapel for Bethel Coll. (Minnegasco prize 1969). Mem. Minn. Soc. Architects (bd. dirs. N.E. chpt. 1983-84, pres. 1985-86). Avocations: fishing, camping, skiing, art. Home: 1929 Kent Rd Duluth MN 55812

JOHNSON, KENNETH O., oil company executive. Pres. Derby Refining Co., Wichita, Kans. Office: Derby Refining Co PO Box 1030 Wichita KS 67201 *

JOHNSON, KENNETH ODELL, retired engineering executive; b. Harville, Mo., Aug. 31, 1922; s. Kenneth D. and Polly Louise (Wilson) J.; B.S. in Aero. Engring., Purdue U., 1950; m. Betty Lou Jones, Aug. 5, 1950; children—Cynthia Jo, Gregory Alan. Engr., design, quality and production mgmt. Gen. Lamp Co., Elwood, Ind., 1950-51; mem. staff aircraft gas turbine engine design Allison div. Gen. Motors Corp., Speedway, Ind., 1951-66; mem. turbofan aircraft engines plus marine, indsl. gas turbine engine design mgmt. staff Gen. Electric Co., 1966-86, ret., engring. projects mgr. engring div., Belcan Corp., 1986—. Served to capt. USAF, 1942-45. Fellow AIAA (assoc.). Republican. Methodist. Holder over 20 patents in field. Recipient UDF Pioneer & Extraordinary Service award for unducted fan invention, Gen. Electric Co., 1985 Home: 8360 Arapaho Ln Cincinnati OH 45243 Office: Belcan Corp Engring Div 5420 W Southern Ave Indianapolis IN 46241

JOHNSON, KENNETH STEVEN, radio announcer; b. Chgo., Aug. 10, 1956; s. Ray Marion and Joy (Duvall) J.; m. Kim Kayne Lockwood, Sept. 14, 1980; children: Jeremy, Carly. Student in Radio-TV, So. Ill. U., 1974-80. With various radio stations, Ill., 1974-79; air personality, producer Sta. WTAO, Murphysboro, Ill., 1979-80; morning announcer, prodn. dir. Sta. WWCT, Peoria, Ill., 1980-85; prodn. dir. Sta. WVIC, Lansing, Mich., 1985-86; morning announcer Sta. WWCT, Peoria, 1986—; producer Pro-Media, N.Y.C., 1980-86. Producer numerous novelty songs featured on nationally syndicated Dr. Demento radio show. Recipient 3 Adam awards, Peoria Advt. and Selling Club, 1984, Mich. Addy award Lansing Advt. Club, 1986. Unitarian. Avocations: reading, playing guitar, playing with video.

JOHNSON, KENNETH STUART, publisher and printer; b. Chgo., Aug. 22, 1928; s. William Moss and Lucille (Carsellio) J.; student Wright Jr. Coll., 1949-50, U. Ill., 1951-52; children—Cynthia Diane, Randall, Andrew, Peter. Dir., chmn. Free Press, Inc., Carpentersville, Ill., 1965-83; pres. Johnson Enterprises Inc. Served with U.S. Army, 1946-47. Named Man and Boy of Year, 1963. Mem. Cook County Pubs. Assn. (pres. 1963, dir.), Profl. Journalistic Soc., Nat. Editorial Assn., Sigma Delta Chi. Address: 44 Park Ln Park Ridge IL 60068

JOHNSON, KEVIN BLAINE, lawyer, educator; b. Wichita, Kans., Aug. 28, 1956; s. Howard Blaine and Ruth Signe (Hornlund) J.; m. Suzanne Kay Wright, Aug. 29, 1981. B.A., Wichita State U., 1978; J.D., Washburn U., 1981. Bar: Kans. 1982, U.S. Dist. Ct. Kans. 1982. Sole practice, Overland Park, Kans., 1981-82; asst. dist. atty. Wyandotte, County, Kans., 1982-84; assoc. Law Office of A. B. Fletcher, Wichita, Kans., 1984-86, Law Office of Stan R. Singleton, Derby, Kans., 1986—; prof. law Kans. Newman Coll., Wichita, 1984—. Author: The 11th Kansas Volunteer Cavalry, 1986. Mem. Wichita Citizen Participation Orgn. Council, 1985-86 . Contbr. articles to profl. jours. Drum instr. Sky Ryders Drum and Bugle Corps, Hutchinson, Kans., 1978-81; dir. High Plains Drum Corps, Inc., 1987—. Mem. Assn. Trial Lawyers Am., Wichita Bar Assn. Republican. Lutheran. Home: 1612 Brendonwood Derby KS 67037 Office: PO Box 40 Derby KS 67037

JOHNSON, LARRY EDWARD, manufacturing executive; b. Dayton, Ohio, Oct. 27, 1942; s. Jesse Edward and Margaret (Rayner) J.; m. Kathy Sue Lewis, May 31, 1963; children: Kevin Edward, Mark Rayner. Assoc. Tech. in Indsl. Engring. Tech., U. Dayton, 1974. Sr. tool and process planner Nat. Cash Register, Dayton, Ohio, 1961-72; mgr. indsl. engring. Internat. Harvester, Louisville, 1972-77; gen. mgr. mfg. planning Massey-Ferguson, Detroit, 1977-79; v.p. mfg. Knapheide Mfg. Co., Quincy, Ill., 1979-82; ops. mgr. Miami Industries, Piqua, Ohio, 1982-86, v.p., gen. mgr., 1986—; part-time instr. shop math. Dayton Coop. High Sch., 1969-71, plane geometry NCR Night Sch., Dayton, 1970-72. Chmn. Piqua Track Com., 1985-86; bd. dirs. City Energy Bd., Piqua, 1985—; coach Little League Baseball and Football, Quincy, Ill., 1979-82; elder Westminster Presbyn. Ch., Piqua, 1985—. Mem. Soc. Mfg. Engrs., Indsl. Engring. Soc., Prodn. and Inventory Control Soc., Tau Alpha Pi. Republican. Presbyterian. Avocations: golfing, tennis. Home: 31 Orchard Dr Piqua OH 45356 Office: Miami Industries div Cyclops Industries PO Box 912 Piqua OH 45356

JOHNSON, LESTER LARUE, JR., artist, educator; b. Detroit, Sept. 28, 1937; s. Lester L. and Haroldine M. (Stanley) J. BFA, U. Mich., 1973, MFA, 1974. Prof. drawing and painting, acting sect. chmn. Coll. Art and Design Ctr. for Creative Studies, Detroit, 1975—. Exhibited in group shows at Art Ctr., Richmond, Calif., 1965, Butler Inst., Youngstown, Ohio, 1966, Art Mus. Springfield, Mo., 1966, Internat. Design Ctr., Los Angeles, 1967, Detroit Inst. Arts, 1964-85, Laguna Beach (Calif.) Art Mus., 1970, Smith-Mason Gallery of Art, Washington, 1970, Whitney Mus. Art, 1971, 72, 73, Carnegie Inst., Pitts., 1971-72, Nat. Acad. Design, N.Y.C., 1977, Detroit Focus Gallery, 1983, Mich. Gallery, Detroit, 1984, Kansas City (Mo.) Artists Coalition, Inc., 1985, Cantor/Lemberg Gallery, Birmingham, Mich., 1986, George N'Namdi Gallery, Detroit, 1987; represented in permanent collections Osaka U. Arts, Japan, Detroit Inst. Arts, Flint Inst. Arts, Grand Rapids Mus. Art; prin. works include outdoor urban wall murals, New Detroit, Inc., 1974, New Detroit Receiving Hosp., 1980. Office: Ctr for Creative Studies Coll Art and Design 245 E Kirby Detroit MI 48202

JOHNSON, LINDA L(OU), radio sales executive; b. Smith Center, Kans., Dec. 2, 1954; d. Forrest Jack Bock and Laneta Fern (Gilbert) Bock Karsting; m. Richard Lynn Johnson, Aug. 5, 1973 (div. July 1980); 1 child, Cody Ryan. Degree in fashion merchandising Patricia Stevens Sch., Wichita, Kans., 1973—. Asst. mgr. J. M. McDonald Co., Concordia, Kans. and Holdredge, Nebr., 1979-81; store mgr. Salking & Linoff Inc., Concordia and Sioux City, Iowa, 1982-83; account exec. Sentry Sta. KSEZ, Sioux City, 1983-84; sales mgr. Sta. KGLI, Cardinal Communications, Sioux City, 1984-85, gen. sales mgr. Stas. KGLI/KWSL, 1985—. Mem. Ad Club Sioux City, Nat. Assn. Female Execs. Home: 3728 Jones Sioux City IA 51104 Office: Cardinal Communications 1113 Nebraska Sioux City IA 51105

JOHNSON, LLOYD PETER, banker; b. Mpls., May 1, 1930; s. Lloyd Percy and Edna (Schlampp) J.; m. Rosalind Gesner, July 3, 1954; children: Marcia, Russell, Paul. B.A., Carleton Coll., Northfield, Minn., 1952; M.B.A., Stanford U., 1954. With Security Trust & Savs. Bank, San Diego, 1954-57; vice chmn. charge corp. banking, fiduciary services, internat. banking Security Pacific Nat. Bank, Los Angeles, 1957-84; chmn., pres., chief exec. officer Norwest Corp., Mpls., 1985—; mem. faculty Pacific Coast Banking Sch., 1969-72, chmn., 1979-80; bd. dirs. Minn. Bus. Partnership; mem. Internat. Monetary Conf.; trustee Minn. Mutual Life Ins. Co. Trustee Carleton Coll., Mpls. Soc. Fine Arts; bd. dirs. United Way Mpls., Minn. Orchestral Assn.; mem. U. Minn. Bd. Overseers. Mem. Assn. Res. City Bankers, Calif. Bankers Assn. (pres. 1977-78), Greater Mpls. C. of C. (bd. dirs.), Assn. Bank Holding Cos. Office: Norwest Corp 1200 Peavey Bldg Minneapolis MN 55479-1060

JOHNSON, LOUISE CLAYTON, social work educator; b. Kansas City, Mo., June 15, 1923; d. John Richard and Susan (Thresher) Clayton; m. Charles F. Johnson, Jan. 23, 1944 (div. 1956); children: Nancy J. Emmert, Charlotte. BA, Syracuse U., 1958; MSW, U. Conn., 1962. Group worker Neighborhood Ctr., Utica, N.Y., 1958-60; dir. Waterbury (Conn.) Girls Club, 1962-64; supervising psychiat. social worker Conn. Valley Hosp., Middletown, 1964-68; asst. prof. U. Iowa, Iowa City, 1968-74; prof., dir. social work U. S.D., Vermillion, 1974—; visiting prof. faculty of social work, U. Regina, Sask., Can., 1983; cons. S.D. Dept. Social Services, 1985—. Author: Social Work Practice: A Generalist Approach, 1983, 2d edit., 1986; cons. editor Jour. Social Work Edn., Washington, 1984—; contbr. articles to profl jours., 1972—. Mem. Nat. Assn. Social Workers (edn. chmn., State Social Worker of Yr. 1986), Council on Social Work Edn., Assn. Baccalaureat Program Dirs. (vice chmn.), Delta Kappa Gamma (pres. 1984-86). Baptist. Home: 220 Sycamore Apt 40 Vermillion SD 57069

JOHNSON, LOUISE ELLEN FRENCH, accountant; b. Topeka, Aug. 4, 1960; d. Robert Alison and Irta Louise (Allen) French; m. Daniel Andrew Johnson. BS in Acct. and BBA, U. Kans., 1982. CPA, Kans. Staff auditor Touche Ross, Topeka, 1982-83, sr. tax cons., 1983-86; sr. tax acct. CGF Industries, Inc., Topeka, 1986—. Active Jr. League of Topeka, 1985—; treas. Ct. Appointed Spl. Advocate for Children, Topeka, 1986—; bd. dirs. Vol. Action Ctr., Topeka, 1985—. Mem. Am. Inst. CPA's, Kans. Soc. CPA's, Northeast Kans. Chpt. CPA's, Am. Bus. Women's Assn. (recording sec. 1984, treas. 1985). Republican. Club: Topeka Country. Home: 1601 SW 26th St Topeka KS 66611 Office: CGF Industries Inc 800 Bank IV Tower Topeka KS 66603

JOHNSON, LOWELL C., state legislator; b. Dodge County, Nebr., June 12, 1920; B.S. in Mech. Engring., U. Nebr., 1942; m. Ruth Marion Sloss, June 21, 1943; children—Mark C., Kent R., James S., Nancy L. Farm and property mgmt. exec.; pres. Johnson-Sloss Land Co., North Bend, Nebr.; mem. Nebr. Legislature, 1980—, vice-chmn. legis. appropriations com. Mem. USDA Nat. Adv. Council on Rural Devel.; bd. dirs. Equitable Fed. Savs. Bank, Fremont, Nebr.; former trustee Meml. Hosp. Dodge County; former mem. adv. council Nebr. Dept. Labor; former mem. citizens adv. com. Immanuel Hosp., Omaha; former mem. County Sch. Reorgn. Com.; former field rep. Congressman Charles Thone; pres. bd. dirs. North Bend Sr. Citizens Home. Mem. Am. Legion, Fremont and North Bend C. of C. Clubs: Masons, Shriners, Rotary. Office: PO Box 370 North Bend NE 68649

JOHNSON, LUCIE JENKINS, social worker, educator; b. Elizabethtown, Ky., Feb. 10, 1927; d. Alex Heady and Mary Lee (Igleheart) Jenkins; B.A. magna cum laude, Wake Forest U., 1949; M.S.W., Tulane U., 1953; postgrad. Va. Poly. Inst. and State U., 1974-80; m. Glenn E. Johnson, Oct. 24, 1952; children—Alexander, Rebecca, Catherine, Elizabeth. Psychiat. social worker with families in public/pvt. service, 1952-67; chief psychiat. social worker Youth Services, Va. Dept. Welfare and Instns., Richmond, 1967-69; asst. prof. Va. Commonwealth U., 1969-74; asst. prof., coordinator continuing edn. in social work Wayne State U., Detroit, 1977-81; supr. oncology social work Harper Hosp./Wayne State U., Detroit, 1981-84; supr. med. social work Sinai Hosp. Detroit, 1984—. Mem. Nat. Assn. Social Workers, Acad. Cert. Social Workers, Mich. Soc. Clin. Social Work, Mich. Oncology Social Work Assn., AAUP. Democrat. Presbyterian (elder). Home: 79 Kenwood Rd Grosse Pointe Farms MI 48236

JOHNSON, LUCILLE MERLE BROWN, elementary educator, principal; b. Brown's Town, St. Ann, Jamaica, Nov. 5, 1936; came to U.S., 1970; d. Ezekiel and Christina (Hawthorne) Brown; m. Carl Wesley Johnson, Oct. 26, 1958 (div. 1974); children: Carl Anthony, Michael Ian. BE, Bethlehem Coll., 1957; MEd, Nat. Coll. Edn., 1976, cert. advanced study, 1980. Cert. elem. tchr., Ill. Div. head St. Ann Schs., Jamaica, 1968-69; reading facilitator Sch. Dist. #64, North Chicago, Ill., 1973-76, coordinator tchr. inservice, 1976-80, prin., 1980—; supr. Dist. 64 Yeager Elem. Sch., North Chicago, 1980—. Mem. North Chicago I-SEARCH; sec. Lake County Community Service League, Waukegan/North Chicago, Ill., 1985-86; trustee North Chicago Pub. Library. Mem. Nat. Assn. Elem. Sch. Princs., Nat. Alliance Black Sch. Educators, Lake County Alliance Black Sch. Educators (sec.). Avocations: bowling, dancing, travel. Office: Yeager Elem Sch Morrow and Lewis Ave North Chicago IL 60064

JOHNSON, MARGARET HELEN, welding executive; b. Chgo., June 3, 1933; d. Harold W. and Clara J. (Pape) Glavin; m. Odean Jack Johnson, Nov. 18, 1950; children: Karen Ann, Dean Harold. Student Moody Bible Inst., 1976-78. Vice-pres., sec. Seamline Welding, Inc., Chgo., 1956—, also dir.; trustee SWCEPS, Chgo., 1963—. Author: Living Faith, 1973, 80, Lord's Ladder of Love, 1976, God's Rainbow, 1982; contbr. articles to religion mags. Mem. Republican Presdl. Task Force, 1982-86, trustee, 1986; mem. Lake View Neighborhood Group, Chgo.; mem. Mary Seat of Wisdom Catholic Women's Club, 1970—, Renew facilitator, 1986-87; Sunday sch. tchr., 1985. Mem. ASCAP, Fedn. Ind. Small Bus., Small Group Community (renew co-chairperson 1986-87). Roman Catholic. Home: 6 S Seminary Ave Park Ridge IL 60068

JOHNSON, SISTER MARIE INEZ, librarian; b. Mitchell, S.D., June 2, 1909; d. Charles and Inez L. (Williams) Johnson; B.A. in English, Coll. St. Catherine, 1929, B.S. in L.S., 1939; M.S., in L.S., Columbia, 1940; postgrad. U. Denver, 1951-52, U. So. Calif., 1953-54. Joined Sisters St. Joseph Carondolet, 1926; tchr. elementary schs. St. Paul, 1930-38; librarian Coll. St. Catherine, St. Paul, 1940-42, head librarian, 1942-73. Mem. steering com. U. Minn. Workshop for Librarians, 1956; library cons. survey Mt. Mercy Coll., Cedar Rapids, Iowa, 1963-64; bldg. cons. Fontbonne Coll., St. Louis, 1964—. Mem. Conf. Am. Folklore for Youth, St. Paul Speakers Bur., com. standard catalog for high sch. Cath. Support, Children's Lit. TV Series;

trustee James J. Hill Library, 1970—. Butler Fgn. Study fellow Coll. St. Catherine, 1958. Named Minn. Librarian of Year, 1967. Mem. Am. (various coms.), Cath. (various coms.) library assns. Editor column Cath. Library World, 1954—. Contbr. articles to profl. jours. Address: Coll St Catherine St Paul MN 55105

JOHNSON, MARLENE, lieutenant governor state of Minnesota; b. Braham, Minn., Jan. 11, 1946; d. Beauford and Helen (Nelson) J. BA, Macalester U., 1968. Founder, pres. Split Infinitive, Inc., St. Paul, 1970-82; lt. gov. State of Minn., St. Paul, 1983—; founder, past chmn. Nat. Leadership Conf. Women Execs. in State Govt.; mem. exec. com., midwestern chair Nat. Conf. Lt. Govs. Chmn. Minn. Women's Polit. Caucus, 1973-76; bd. dirs. Nat. Child Care Action Campaign, Minn. Outward Bound Sch., Mpls., Spring Hill Conf. Ctr., Mpls. Recipient Outstanding Achievement award, St. Paul YWCA, 1980, Disting. Citizen citation, Macalester Coll., 1982, Disting. Contributions to Families award Minn. Council on Family Relations, 1986, Minn. Sportfishing Congress award, 1986; named dir. World Press Inst. Mem. Nat. Assn. Women Bus. Owners (past pres.). Office: Office of Lt Gov Room 121 State Capitol Aurora Ave Saint Paul MN 55155 *

JOHNSON, MARTHA CELESTIA KOUTZ, civic organization executive; b. Odessa Twp., Mich., Nov. 17, 1903; d. Charles Jefferson and Charlotte (Musgrove) Koutz; m. Harley D. Johnson, June 8, 1934; children—Alicia Marjorie Johnson Walker, Phyllis Charlene Johnson Carter. Grad. Lansing Bus. U., 1925. Order clk. Lansing Co., Mich., 1926-28; bookkeeper Pingry Tractor and Equipment Co., Grand Rapids, Mich., 1928-33; typist, clk. Dept. Mil. Affairs, State of Mich., Lansing, 1955-56, driver improvement clk., 1957-66; exec. sec. Michigan Pure Water Council, Lansing, 1971—. Pianist Wesleyan Methodist Ch., East Odessa, Mich., 1946-51, Sunday Sch. sec., 1946-51; mem. Heritage Found., Washington, 1975, Rep. Presdl. Task Force, 1982-85, Rep. Nat. Com., 1980, Citizens Clearing House for Hazardous Waste, 1983, Project CURE, 1984; mem. Friends of Mich. Schs., 1963—. Recipient Liberty award Congress of Freedom, 1972-73; cert. of achievement Cen. Ch. of the Nazarene, Lansing, 1975; cert. recognition Hale Found., 1984; spl. tribute State of Mich., 1984. Mem. WCTU, Fedn. of Homemakers, Nat. Health Fedn. (life), Clubs: Safe Water (bd. dirs. 1979-85), Organic Garden (Lansing).

JOHNSON, MARTIN LINN, telecommunications analyst; b. Des Moines, Jan. 22, 1952; s. Robert Louis and Violet Pauline (Glover) J.; m. Cynthia Louise Schoeppel, Dec. 8, 1978. BA, Iowa State U., 1974. Editor newspaper Marion County News, Pleasantville, Iowa, 1978-79; communications systems rep. Northwestern Bell, Des Moines, 1979-82, AT&T, Des Moines, 1982-83; sr. telecommunications analyst Pioneer Hi-Bred, Johnston, Iowa, 1983—. Served with USAF, 1975-78. Mem. Regional System 85 User's Group (sec. 1987—), U.S. Coast Guard Auxiliary (flotilla vice commodore 1986—, instr. Des Moines 1985—). Democrat. Club: Toastmasters (edn. v.p. 1986, pres. 1987—, Competent Toastmaster 1987). Avocations: sailing, bicycling, jogging. Office: Poineer Data Systems 7200 NW 62d Ave Johnston IA 50131

JOHNSON, MARVIN ADOLPH, social service administrator; b. Platte, S.D., Oct. 6, 1931; s. Adolph Joseph and Emily Eleanor (Fotheringham) J.; m. R. Eloise Nelson, Jan. 9, 1954; children: Sonja Ruth, Melinda Ann. BA, Pasadena Coll., 1956; MSW, U. So. Calif., 1958. Cert. social worker. Social worker Luth Child Welfare Assn., River Forest, Ill., 1960-62; chmn. div. social work Luth. Gen. Hosp., Park Ridge, Ill., 1962-86; program mgr. mental health N.W. Community Hosp., Arlington Heights, Ill., 1986—. Served to cpl. U.S. Army, 1954-56. Mem. Nat. Assn. Social Work (treas. 1982-86, pres. 1987), Soc. Hosp. Social Work Dirs., Ill. Assn. Mental and Family Therapy (pres. 1983-84). Avocations: running, art, antiques. Home: 412 S Nawata Mount Prospect IL 60056 Office: NW Community Hosp 800 W Central Rd Arlington Heights IL 60005

JOHNSON, MARVIN FREDERICK, insurance executive; b. Balt., July 19, 1925; s. John Frederick and Jessie (Gadd) J.; m. Grace Verna Rose, Sept. 26, 1946 (dec.); 1 child, Carol Lynn Johnson Rush; m. Dorothea Lee Myers, Aug. 25, 1972; stepchildren—Joy Lee Mitchell, Randall Eric Mitchell, Dennis Alan Mitchell. A.A., U. Balt., 1948, LL.B., 1951. Supt. life and health claims Zurich Ins. Co., Chgo., 1950-58, corp. planning officer, 1970-74; life mktg. dir., life and health claim dir. Allstate Ins. Co., Northbrook, Ill., 1958-69, v.p. internat. ops., 1974-81; ins. mgmt. cons., Chgo., 1969-70, 81—. Author: Life and Health Claim Reference Guide, 1958-59. Contbr. articles to profl. jours. Chmn. stock casualty ins. div. Am. Cancer Soc., Chgo., 1956; div. capt. Northwest Community Hosp. Bldg. Fund, Arlington Heights, Ill., 1956; pres. Balt. Young Men's Democratic Club, 1954. Served with USNR, 1943-46, PTO. Recipient award of Merit Am. Cancer Soc., 1956. Mem. Internat. Claim Assn. (mem. uniform forms com. 1959), Chgo. Claim Assn., C. of C. of U.S. (mem. life ins. com., internat. ins. adv. com.). Republican. Lutheran. Home: 2531 Honeysuckle Ln Rolling Meadows IL 60008

JOHNSON, MARVIN MELROSE, industrial engineer; b. Neligh, Nebr., Apr. 21, 1925; s. Harold Nighram and Melissa (Bare) J.; m. Anne Stuart Campbell, Nov. 10, 1951; children: Douglas Blake, Harold James, Phyllis Anne, Nighram Marvin, Melissa Joan. B.S., Purdue U., 1949; postgrad., Ill. Inst. Tech., 1953; M.S. in Indsl. Engring, U. Iowa, 1966, Ph.D., 1968. Registered profl. engr., Iowa, Mo., Nebr. Quality control supr., indsl. engr. Houdaille Hershey, Chgo., 1949-52; indsl. engr. Bell & Howell, Chgo., 1952-54; with Bendix Aviation Corp., Davenport, Iowa, 1954-64; successively chief indsl. engr., staff asst., supr. procedures and systems Bendix Aviation Corp., 1954-63; reliability engr. Bendix Aviation Corp. (Pioneer Central div.), 1963-64, cons., 1964—; lectr. indsl. engring. State U. Iowa, 1963-64; instr. indsl. engring. U. Iowa, 1965-66; asso. prof. U. Nebr., 1968-73, prof., 1973—; AID adv., mgmt. engring. and food processing Kabul (Afghanistan) U., 1975-76; vis. prof. indsl. engring. U. P.R., Mayaguez, 1982-83; NSF trainee U. Iowa, 1964-67. Editor The Johnson Reporter, 1980—. Served with AUS, 1943-46, ETO. Fellow Am. Inst. Indsl. Engrs.; Mem. Am. Soc. Engring. Educators, Am. Statis. Assn., ASME, Ops. Research Soc. Am., Inst. Mgmt. Sci., Sigma Xi, Tau Beta Pi, Pi Tau Sigma, Alpha Pi Mu. Presbyterian. Home: 2507 Ammon Ave Lincoln NE 68507 Office: 175 Nebraska Hall U Nebr Lincoln NE 68588

JOHNSON, MILTON LEE, civil engineer; b. Lake Mills, Iowa, Dec. 7, 1931; s. Selmer Melvin and Dorothea Adaline (Ruby) J.; m. Mrytle J. Engelby, Mar. 22, 1953; children: Marlys, Emily, Diane, Darrell, Steven. BS in Civil Engring., Iowa State U., 1957. Registered profl. engr., Iowa. Asst. resident engr. Iowa Hwy. Commn., Britt and Decorah, 1957-62; engr. Clayton County, Elkader, Iowa, 1962-80, Wapello County, Ottumwa, Iowa, 1980-87; exec. sec. Nat. Assn. County Engrs., 1987—. Mem. Nat. Assn. County Engrs. (pres. 1977-78, exec. sec. 1979—), Nat. Assn. Profl. Engrs., Am. Soc. Civil Engrs., Iowa County Engrs. Assn. (past pres., Past Pres. award 1969, Engr. of Yr. award 1972, Spl. Service award 1985). Lutheran. Home and Office: 326 Pike Rd Ottumwa IA 52501

JOHNSON, MONTE S., accountant; b. LaCrosse, Wis., May 3, 1958; s. Arthur L. and Joyce G. (Zellmer) J.; m. Mary Catherine McElligott, Sept. 15, 1984. BBA, U. Wis., Eau Claire, 1980. CPA, Minn. Audit mgr., dir. recruiting Touche Ross & Co., Mpls. and St. Paul, 1980—. Bd. dirs. bldg. and grounds com., mem. exec. bd. Falcon Heights United Ch. Christ, 1986, 87; bd. dirs. Minn. Spl. Olympics, 1986, 87. Mem. Am. Inst. CPA's, Minn. Soc. CPA's, Nat. Soc. Accts. for Coops., Nat. Acctg. and Fin. Council, St. Paul Jaycees (various offices, now pres.). Congregationalist. Avocations: sports, traveling overseas. Home: 1599 Bruce Ave Roseville MN 55113 Office: Touche Ross & Co 1600 Amhoist Tower Saint Paul MN 55102

JOHNSON, NOEL MCKINLEY, psychiatrist; b. San Antonio, Mar. 2, 1936; s. Charles Nelson and Florence (McKinley) J.; m. Anita DeArmond, Nov. 28, 1964; children—Michael F., Wendy S. B.A., U. Kans., 1958, Exchange Scholar U. of Exeter, England, 1958-59; M.D. (Regional Scholar), Washington U., St. Louis, 1963. Diplomate Am. Bd. Psychiatry and Neurology. Intern, Ind. U. Med. Center, Indpls., 1963-64; resident in psychiatry Washington U. Med. Sch. Hosp., St. Louis, 1966-69; asst. chief dept. neuro-psychiatry U.S. Army Hosp., Stuttgart, Germany, 1964-66; pvt. practice gen. psychiatry, Springfield, Mo., 1969-72; chief Mental Health Clinic, Student Health Center, U. S.C., Columbia, 1973-76; staff psychiatrist McKinley Student Health Center, U. Ill., Urbana, 1977-79; chief psychiatry service VA Med. Center, Danville, Ill., 1979—; assoc. clin. prof. U. Ill. Coll. Medicine, Champaign-Urbana. Served to capt. U.S. Army, 1964-66. Mem. Am. Psychiat. Assn., Royal Coll. of Psychiatry (Engl.) Corr. Affiliate, Phi Beta Kappa. Office: VA Med Center 1900 E Main St Danville IL 61832

JOHNSON, NORBERT JEFFREY, architect; b. Passaic, N.J., June 3, 1961; s. Robert Oscar and Hannelore (Haselbarth) J. BArch, Ohio State U., 1984. Architect The Bowman Group, Columbus, Ohio, 1984-85, George J. Kontogiannis & Assoc., Columbus, 1985-86, Böhm-NBBJ, Columbus, 1986—; event supr. Nat. Custom Shows, Inc., Worthington, Oh., 1979-82; pres. Rapid Transit Enterprises, Columbus, 1980—; pub. The All Am. Racer mag., 1981-85. Pub. Classic Chrysler Quarterly mag., 1987—. Mem. Nat. Trust Hist. Preservation, Nat. Hot Rod Assn., Spl. Interest Auto Club (pres. 1982-85, cons. 1985). Avocation: drag racing. Home: 1990 Stelzer Rd Columbus OH 43219 Office: Bohm-NBBJ 55 Nationwide Blvd Columbus OH 43215

JOHNSON, NORMA J., specialty wool grower; b. Dover, Ohio, Aug. 30, 1925; d. Jasper Crile and Mildred Catherine (Russell) J.; student Heidelberg Coll., 1943; cert. drafting techniques Case Sch. Applied Sci., 1944; student Western Res. U., 1945-47, Ohio State U., 1951, Muskingum Coll., 1965; A.A., Kent State U., 1979, Buckeye Joint Vocat. Sch., 1979-84; m. Robert Blake Covey, Oct. 7, 1951 (div. 1960); 1 dau., Susan Kay. Instr. arts and crafts Univ. Settlement House, Cleve., 1944; mech. draftswoman Nat. Assn. Civil Aeros., Cleve., 1944-46; mfrs. rep. Nat. Spice House, 1947-49; tchr. econs., home econs., English, math, history, high sch., Tuscarawas County Sch. System, New Philadelphia, Ohio, 1962-69; owner, mgr., operator Sunny Slopes Farm, producer of specialty wools and grains, Dover, Ohio, 1969—. Tchr., Meth. Sunday Sch., 1956-61; chaplain Winfield PTA, 1960; program dir. Brandywine Grange, 1960-62; troop leader Girl Scouts, U.S.A., 1961-70; mem. Tuscarawas County Jail Com., 1981. Recipient cert. of merit Tuscarawas County Schs., 1965, Ohio Wildlife Conservation award Tuscarawas County, 1972, 1st and 3d premiums for handspinning fleece, Ohio State Fair, 1984., 8th and 10th premiums, Mich. Stat Fair, 1985. Mem. Mid States Wool Growers, Am. Angus Assn., Club: Nat. Grange. Bldg. designer, constructor interior facilities for the Scheuerhaus. Home and Office: Route 1 Box 398 Dover OH 44622

JOHNSON, PATRICIA MARTÍNEZ, social worker; b. Leadville, Colo., Apr. 5, 1954; d. Gilbert Edward and Rose (Rael) Martínez; m. Warren Johnson, Dec. 29, 1978. BS in Edn., U. Colo., 1976; MSW, U. Kans., 1983. Lic. clin. specialist social worker, Kans.; cert. sch. social worker, Kans. Eligibility tech. Denver Social Services, 1976-77; youth guidance worker Youth for Christ, Wichita, Kans., Tampa, Fla. and Memphis., 1977-83; sch. social worker Wichita Pub. Schs., 1983—; clin. social worker Family Consultation, Wichita, 1983—; chaplain Booth Meml. Home, Wichita, 1981-85. Republican. Mem. Ind. Charismatic Ch. Avocations: reading, crafts, travel. Home: 3032 S Mount Carmel Wichita KS 67217

JOHNSON, PATRICK JOHN, education educator; b. Detroit, July 31, 1929; s. Thomas Bernard and Ada Mary (Butler) J.; m. Diane D. Demrose, Jan. 30, 1954; children: Michael, Patrick, Steven, Thomas. PhB cum laude, U. Detroit, 1956, MA, 1958; EdD, Wayne State U., 1967. Cert. elem. tchr., Mich. Prin. Lakeview Schs., St. Clair Shores, Mich., 1955-65; instr. Wayne State U., Detroit, 1963-67; assoc. prof. edn. Oakland U., Rochester, Mich., 1967—; cons. in field. Commr. Macomb County, Mich., 1969—; chmn. bd. dirs. Macomb County Library, 1969—; pres. Lake Shore Bd. Edn., St. Clair Shores, 1961-68. Served to sgt. U.S. Army, 1948-52. Recipient Humanitarian award Macomb County Welfare Rights Orgn., 1971. Mem. Mich. Assn. Tchr. Educators (treas. 1985-86). Democrat. Roman Catholic. Avocations: geology, camping. Home: 31918 Jefferson Saint Clair Shores MI 48082 Office: Oakland U Sch Edn 536 O'Dowd Hall Rochester MI 48006-0003

JOHNSON, PAUL OREN, chem. co. exec., lawyer; b. Mpls., Feb. 2, 1937; s. Andrew Richard and LaVerne Delores (Slater) J.; m. Georgene Howalt, July 1, 1961; children: Scott, Paula, Amy. BA, Carleton Coll., 1958; JD cum laude, U. Minn., 1961. Bar: Minn. 1961. Atty. Briggs & Morgan, St. Paul, 1961-62; atty. Green Giant Co., Le Sueur, Minn., 1961-66, asst. sec., 1967-74, sec., 1975-79, v.p., gen. counsel, 1971-79, v.p. corporate relations, 1973-79, mem. mgmt. com., 1976-79; gen. counsel H.B. Fuller Co., St. Paul, 1979-84, sr. v.p., sec., 1980—, mem. mgmt. com., 1981—; bd. dirs. Sta. WCAL-PBS, Northfield, Minn. Council mem. at large Boy Scouts Am., chmn. Republican County Com., 1965; bd. dirs. Minn. State U., 1979-82 , v.p., 1980-82. Served with U.S. Air N.G., 1961. Named One of Outstanding Young Men of Am., Jaycees, 1965. Mem. ABA., Minn. Bar Assn., Ramsey County Bar Assn., Assn. Corp. Secs. Home: Rural Rt 1 Box 112 Nerstrand MN 55053 Office: H B Fuller Co 2400 Energy Pk Dr Saint Paul MN 55108

JOHNSON, PENNY LEIGH, printing company executive; b. Akron, Ohio, Nov. 13, 1952; s. Joseph Pershing Johnson and Betty Joan (Moffett) Adler; m. Charles Edward Foutty, Feb. 14, 1985; children: Tammy, Thomas; stepchildren: Marree Foutty, Valarree Foutty. BBA, Kent State U., 1978. CPA, Ohio. Staff acct. Hausser & Taylor, CPA's, Cleve., 1978-80; acct. Daley and Co. Securities, Cleve., 1980-81; comptroller Dawson Ins., Rocky River, Ohio, 1981-85; treas. Austin Printing Co., Inc., Akron, 1985—; treas., co-founder Ohio Gemini Users Group, Cleve., 1983-85. Fellow Am. Inst. CPA's, Ohio Soc. CPA's. Avocations: raising horses and Australian shepherds, reading, skiing. Home: 1018 N Cleveland-Massillon Rd Akron OH 44313 Office: Austin Printing Co Inc 130 E Voris St Akron OH 44311

JOHNSON, PHYLLIS AUDREY, auditor; b. Darwin, Minn., July 25, 1923; d. John Emmanuel and Emma Elizabeth (Scheidegger) Nelson; B.A., Met. State U., St. Paul, 1973; B.Applied Sci., U. Minn., 1974; diploma U. Wis. Grad. Sch. Banking, 1973; cert. Am. Inst. Banking, 1975; cert. tchr.; lic. real estate sales; m. Ellsworth Orr Johnson, Apr. 6, 1943; children—Elwood Oren (dec.), Christine Marie Johnson Wilbur, Elizabeth Ann Johnson Milne, Eric Christian. Asst. cashier Farmers State Bank, Darwin, 1941-42; asst. cashier State Bank Anoka (Minn.), 1944; cost accountant Red Wing Boat Works (Minn.), 1956-57; banking generalist First Bank Southdale, Edina, Minn., 1960-70; asst. v.p. ops., personnel and purchasing S.W. Fidelity State Bank, Edina, 1970-71; auditor First Nat. Bank Glenwood City (Wis.), 1973—, Hiawatha Nat. Bank, Hagen City, Wis., 1973-86; assoc. bank examiner Office of Comptroller of Currency U.S. Treasury, Mpls., 1986—; employment mgr., personnel officer Bank Shares, Inc., Mpls., 1973-77; mortgage loan officer St. Anthony Park State Bank, St. Paul, 1978-79; pres. DAAV Banking Services, 1984-86; assoc. nat. bank examiner Comptroller of Currency U.S. Treasury, 1986—; instr. bus. mgmt. Mpls. Tech. Inst., 1979-86, mem. adv. com. bus. mgmt. and banking, 1975-86; adv. com. banking program Suburban Hennepin Tech. Inst., White Bear Lake, Minn., 1972-77; speaker in field, 1974—. Precinct chmn. Edina Ind. Republicans, 1970-74; chmn. service unit, mem. coms., leader Edina and Red Wing councils Girl Scouts, 1958-68; sec. Edina United Fund, 1963-64; pres. St. Paul's Lutheran Ch., Mankato, Minn., 1965-67, St. Paul's Luth. Ch., Red Wing, 1950-58, Bethlehem Luth. Ch., Mpls., 1959—. Mem. Am. Mgmt. Assn., Am. Banking Assn., Nat. Assn. Women Bus. Owners, Am. Bus. Women's Assn., Nat. Bus. Edn. Assn., Am. Vocat. Assn., Minn. Bus. Edn. Assn., Minn. Vocat. Assn. Clubs: Normandale Tennis, Winterset, Interlachen Country. Home: 5301 Ayrshire Blvd Edina MN 55436 Office: 920 2d Ave Suite 800 Minneapolis MN 55404

JOHNSON, RAYMOND ALLEN CONSTAN, state auditor of public accounts, accountant; b. Stanton, Iowa, July 25, 1923; s. John E. and Hilda M. (Larson) J. m. Mary Ann Butler, Dec. 28, 1947; children: Cynthia Schram, Constance Rose. BS, Creighton U., 1949. CPA, Nebr. Auditor of pub. accounts State of Nebr., Lincoln, 1971—. Served with USAF, 1943-46. Mem. Am. Inst. CPA's, Nebr. Soc. CPA's, Am. Legion. Republican. Lodges: Elks, Eagles, Masons, Kiwanis. Home: 7541 Old Post Rd #12 Lincoln NE 68506 Office: Auditor Pub Accounts 2303 State Capitol Bldg Lincoln NE 68509

JOHNSON, RHONDA LLOYD, teacher; b. Salem, Ind., Feb. 17, 1958; d. Roger Lee and Evelyn Faye (Williams) L; m. Gary Duane Johnson, June 18, 1983; children: Emily Anne, Zachary Lloyd. BS, Ind. U. S.E., New Albany, 1980. Tchr. Maconaquah Sch. Corp., Bunker Hill, Ind., 1980-83; v.p. Tex-Oil, Inc., Salem, Ind., 1980—; tchr. Tell City (Ind.) Sch. Corp., 1985—, also volleyball coach, 1985-86; Asst. volleyball coach Maconaquah Sch. Corp., 1980-81, cheerleading coach, 1980-83. Mem. NEA, Ind. State Tchrs. Assn. Republican. Am. Baptist. Avocations: swimming, waterskiing, volleyball. Home: 638 20th St Tell City IN 47586

JOHNSON, RICHARD E., association executive. Dir. Cleve. Bapt. Assn. Office: Cleve Bapt Assn 1737 Euclid Ave Suite 240 Cleveland OH 44115 *

JOHNSON, RICHARD EDWIN, dentist; b. Mpls., Dec. 26, 1951; s. Richard Walin and Mary Ann (Kinley) J.; m. Martha Christine Froiland, May 11, 1974. Student, Anoka-Ramsey Community Coll., Coon Rapids, Minn., 1975-77; DDS, U. Minn., 1982. Gen. practice dentistry Anoka, Minn., 1982—. Served with USN, 1971-74. Mem. ADA, Minn. Dental Soc., Mpls. Dental Soc., Ducks Unlimited (chpt. chmn. 1983—), Pheasants Forever. Lutheran. Avocations: hunting, fishing, golf, gardening. Home: 915 Park St Anoka MN 55303 Office: 229 Jackson St Suite 117 Anoka MN 55303

JOHNSON, RICHARD FRED, lawyer; b. Chgo., July 12, 1944; s. Sylvester Hiram and Naomi Ruth (Jackson) J.; m. Sheila Conley, June 26, 1970; children—Brendon, Bridget, Timothy, Laura. B.S., Miami U., Oxford, Ohio, 1966; J.D. cum laude, Northwestern U., 1969. Bar: Ill. 1969, U.S. Dist. Ct. (no. dist.) Ill. 1969, U.S. Ct. Appeals (7th cir.) 1977, U.S. Supreme Ct. 1978, U.S. Ct. Appeals (2d cir.) 1980. Law clk. U.S. Dist. Ct. (no. dist.) Ill., Chgo., 1969-70; assoc. firm Lord, Bissell & Brook, Chgo., 1970-77, ptnr., 1977—; lectr. legal edn. Contbr. articles to profl. jours. Recipient Am. Jurisprudence award, 1968. Mem. Chgo. Bar Assn., Ill. State Bar Assn. Club: Union League (Chgo.). Home: 521 W Roscoe St Chicago IL 60657 Office: Lord Bissell & Brook 115 S LaSalle St Chicago IL 60603

JOHNSON, RICHARD IVAN, academic program director; b. Grafton, N.D., Oct. 30, 1939; s. Ragnar and Edith Irene (Field) J.; m. Dorothy Elaine Anderson, June 4, 1961; children: Beth, Mara, Sara. Student, U. Wis., 1961-62; BA, Concordia Coll., 1961; MA, No. Mich. U., 1967. Analyst, programmmer No. Mich. U., Marquette, 1966-68; asst. prof. computer sci. U. N.D., Grand Forks, 1968-75, chmn. computer sci. dept., 1969-77, assoc. prof., 1975—, acad. cons., 1984—, mgr. user services, 1986—; mem. tech. staff Mitre Corp., Bedford, Mass., 1980-81; cons. Navy Personnel Research and Devel. Ctr., San Diego, 1983-84. Mem. Assn. Computing Machinery, Digital Equipment Computer Users Soc., N.D. Edn. Computing Assn. Lutheran. Office: U ND Computer Ctr Grand Forks ND 58201

JOHNSON, RICHARD KEITH, petroleum/transportation/computer software company executive; b. Hutchinson, Kans., Feb. 24, 1939; s. Glenford Carl and Marjory Eloise (Jackson) J.; m. Shanon Athy, June 27, 1964; children—Reed Athy, Deborah Diane. B.S., Kans. U., 1964. With credit and sales dept. Am. Can Co., Neenah, Wis., 1964-67; prodn. supr. Kay Electronics, Kansas City, Mo., 1967-68; exec. v.p. Robo-Wash, Inc., Kansas City, Mo., 1968-70; leasing mgr. United Telecom, Shawnee Mission, Kans., 1970-72; cons. Lawrence-Leiter, Kansas City, 1972-74; pres. Pronto Systems, Shawnee Mission, 1972—, Trans-Oil, Ltd., Kansas City, 1979—, Computer Programs, Ltd., Kansas City, 1983—. Pres. Johnson County Soccer League, 1982-83, treas., 1979-82. Mem. Am. Petroleum Inst. Lodges: Optimist. Home: 5208 Mansfield Ln Shawnee KS 66203 Office: Trans-Oil Ltd 4303 Speaker Rd Kansas City KS 66106

JOHNSON, RICHARD LEE, sales executive; b. Cin., June 25, 1954; s. Richard Henry and Martha Jean (Carter) J.; m. Dorothy Sue Nead, Mar. 16, 1973; children: Alexander Len, Benjamin James, Cara Sue. BFA, U. Cin., 1973, MFA, 1974. Regional v.p. sales Engler Systems, Cin., 1979-83; pres. Transp. Cons. Services, Dallas, 1983—; nat. sales mgr. K-D Lamp Co., Cin., 1986—; cons. Schlumberger Ltd., Dallas, 1981-83. Editor: (newsletters) The Jour. for Onboard, 1984, Reflections, 1986. Fellow Nat. Truck Equipment Assn., Council of Fleet Specialist, Automotive Service Industry Assn., Automotive Warehouse Distbr. Assn., Automotive Parts and Accessories, River City Fleet Maintenance Council, Transportation Cons. Group (sec. 1982). Republican. Avocations: model railroading, computers, farming. Home: Rural Rt #1 Box 198 Gant Rd Waynesfield OH 45896 Office: K-D Lamp Co 1910 Elm St Cincinnati OH 45210

JOHNSON, RICHARD LOUIS, paper company executive; b. Madison, Wis., May 16, 1916; s. Harry J. and Louise (Nisalk) J.; m. Virginia Eckman, Jan. 1, 1943; children: Gregg E., Timothy D. B.A., U. Wis., 1939, J.D., 1942. Bar: Wis. 1942. Atty. Chief Counsel Office, IRS, Washington, 1943-44; gen. atty, tax mgr., asst. controller Marathon Corp., Menasha, Wis., 1944-55; controller Menasha Corp., 1955-60, pres., 1960-80, chmn. bd., 1980—, also dir.; dir. N.E. Wooden Ware Co., 1st Nat. Bank Menasha, Neenah-Menasha Water Power Co. Trustee Theda Clara Meml. Hosp.; bd. dirs. Bergstrom Art Mus. Mem. Phi Delta Phi. Republican. Presbyterian. Clubs: North Shore Golf; Pelican Bay (Naples, Fla.). Home: 856 Bayview Rd Neenah WI 54956 Office: Menasha Corp PO Box 367 Neenah WI 54956

JOHNSON, RICHARD N., automotive research executive, mechanical engineer; b. Perry, Iowa, Jan. 4, 1942; s. Harding R. and Dorothy M. (Nelson) J.; m. Lila Lee Herron, June 24, 1978 (dec. Oct. 1984); children: Jana, David; m. Karen L. Friedman, May 18, 1986. BS in Applied Math., U. Wis., 1964; MS in Engring. Mechanics, Case Inst., Cleve., 1968; PhD in Engring. Mechanics, U. Wis., 1972; MBA with honors, Roosevelt U., Chgo., 1980. Project mgr. Lewis Research div. NASA, Cleve., 1964-70; teaching asst. U. Wis., Madison, 1970-71; dept. mgr. Gen. Am. Research Div./GATX Corp., Niles, Ill., 1971-82; research mgr. Borg-Warner Research, Des Plaines, Ill., 1982—; cons. Gen. Dynamics, San Diego, 1969, Psych Systems, Virginia Beach, Va., 1979-80. Author: Handbook of Manufacturing High Technology, 1986; co-inventor tire degradation monitor, rubber bond inspection. NASA research grantee, 1970. Mem. Soc. Mfg. Engrs., Robot Industries Assn., ASTM, Sigma Xi. Avocations: computers, model railroads, sailing. Home: 15W755 Shepard Dr Burr Ridge IL 60521 Office: Borg-Warner Research 1200 S Wolf Rd Des Plaines IL 60018

JOHNSON, RICHARD WALTER, investment executive; b. Mpls., Oct. 2, 1928; s. Walter Benjamin and Evelyn (Peterson) J.; children: Richard Walter, William Charles, Nancy Ann, Thomas Gregory, Michael Richard, Jeffrey Wayne. B.B.A. with distinction, U. Minn., 1949. C.P.A., Nebr., Ill. With Arthur Andersen & Co. (C.P.A.'s), 1949-74; mng. partner Arthur Andersen & Co. (C.P.A.'s), Omaha, 1960-74; chmn. bd., chief exec. officer Western Securities Co. of Del., Omaha, 1975—; pres. Modern Equipment Co., Omaha, 1975—. Bd. dirs., exec. com. Jr. Achievement Omaha, 1962—, pres., 1966-67; gen. campaign chmn. Heart of the Midlands United Way, 1972, chmn. pacemaker sect. fund raising campaign, 1964, chmn. corporate standards com., 1966, assoc. gen. chmn., 1968, treas., mem. exec. com., 1969; bd. dirs. Fontenelle Forest Nature Ctr. Assn. Mid-Am. council Boy Scouts of Am., Omaha Symphony Assn., Omaha Big Bros. Assn., Omaha Playhouse Assn.; Trustee Creighton U. Pres.'s Council. Recipient One of Outstanding Young Men in Am. award, 1965. Mem. Am. Inst. C.P.A.'s, Nebr. Soc. C.P.A.'s, Newcomen Soc. N.Am., Omaha C. of C. (chmn. membership relations com. 1962—, bd. dirs. 1965—, mem. exec. com., v.p. 1968), Beta Gamma Sigma, Beta Alpha Psi. Clubs: Masons, Shriners; Garden of the Gods (Colorado Springs); Omaha, Omaha Country; Palm Bay (Miami). Home: 3008 Paddock Rd Omaha NE 68124 Office: 2011 Cuming St Omaha NE 68102

JOHNSON, ROBERT HUGH, financial planner; b. Cleve., Dec. 22, 1934; s. Robert Hugh and Kathleen (McElroy) J.; m. Louise Marie Schulte, July 16, 1960; children—Anne Marie, Jane Ellen, Robert Hugh III, Mary Margaret. B.S., Yale U., 1959; M.B.A., Harvard U. 1961; M.S., Am. Coll., 1983. C.L.U.; chartered fin. cons. Mgr. Container Corp., Chgo., 1961-65; sr. assoc. Hinsdale Assocs., 1966—. Author: Microwave Communications, 1961. Pres. Seton Montessori Sch., Clarendon Hills, Ill., 1965-70; v.p. Am. Montessori Soc., N.Y.C., 1969-70. Named Man of Yr., No. Ill. Gen. Agts., 1968. Mem. Nat. Assn. Life Underwriters, Am. Soc. C.L.U.s, Million Dollar Round Table (chmn. program arrangements 1980), Ill. Life Underwriters (sec.-treas. 1982-84, pres. 1984-85). Roman Catholic. Club: Salt Creek. Avocations: skiing; running; bread baking. Office: The Hinsdale Assocs 119 E Ogden Ave Hinsdale IL 60521

JOHNSON, ROBERT LOUIS, personnel director; b. St. Louis, Aug. 14, 1941; s. Elmer L. and Alice E. (Dickenson) J.; m. Katherine Anne Brooks, May 26, 1963; children: Roberta L., Robert L. Jr. BA, Cen. Meth. Coll., Fayette, Mo., 1963. Cert. sr. profl. in human resources. Dist. scout exec. Boy Scouts Am., Scottsbluff, Nebr., 1963-66; field dir. Boy Scouts Am., Omaha, 1966-70; adminstrv. specialist Peoples Natural Gas Co., Rochester, Minn., 1971; personnel adminstr. Peoples Natural Gas Co., Omaha, 1971-74; indsl. relations mgr. No. Petro Chem. Co., Morris, Ill., 1974-78; dir. human resources Valmont Industries, Inc., Valley, Nebr., 1979—; chmn. bd. Midwest Employers Council, Omaha, 1982-83. Chmn. exploring com. Gamehaven council Boy Scouts Am., Rochester, 1971; chmn. camping com. Mid-Am. council Boy Scouts Am., Omaha, 1985—; chmn. fin. com. Trailways council Girls Scouts U.S., Joliet, Ill., 1977-79; asst. chief, treas. Channahan (Ill.) Vol. Fire Dept., 1974-79; chmn. ch. council United Ch. Christ of Millard, Omaha, 1985. Mem. Am. Soc. Tng. and Devel., Will-Grundy Mfg. Assn. (chmn. labor com. 1977-78), Personnel Assn. Midlands (chmn. legis. com. 1986—). Avocations: model railroading, golf, camping. Home: 1278 South 139th St Omaha NE 68144 Office: Valmont Industries Inc Hwy 275 Valley NE 68064

JOHNSON, ROBERT PAUL, broadcast engineer; b. Bluefield, W.Va., Aug. 18, 1929; s. William W. and Minnie M. (Lewis) J.; m. Pauline Dora Johnson, Mar. 14, 1953; children—Jessica Jean, Christopher Howard. Student Capitol Radio Engring. Inst. 1951; Cert. sr. broadcast engr. Lab. technician Raytheon Mfg. Co., Waltham, Mass., 1954-55, Spl. Techniques Lab. Electronics Corp. of Am., Cambridge, Mass, 1955-58; field engr. Sprague Electric Co., North Adams, Mass., 1958-60; chief engr. Sta. WBEC, Pittsfield, Mass., 1960-66, Sta. WISN/WLPX, Milw., 1966—. Served to staff sgt USAF, 1951-54. Mem. Soc. Broadcast Engrs. Home: 1043 Saratoga Ct Oconomowoc WI 53066 Office: 759 N 19th St Sta WISN Milwaukee WI 53233

JOHNSON, ROBERT WAYNE, agricultural investment executive; b. Peru, Ind., Mar. 14, 1949; s. Russell Eugene and Phyllis Mae (Robins) J.; m. Gale Alice Davidson; May 27, 1972. BS in Agricl. Econs., Purdue U., 1983, MS in Mgmt., 1985. Mgr., sec.-treas. Johnson's Agri-Transport, Inc., 1977-82, Johnson's Egg Farms, Inc., 1970-82; cons. Computer Sharing Corp., 1984-85, John O'Toole & Son, Inc., 1984—; investment mgr. Prudential Agrl. Real Estate Group, Downers Grove, Ill., 1985—; grad. instr. dept. agrl. econs. Purdue U., 1984-85. Active United Way of Cass County, Inc.; elder Presbyn. Ch. USA; ruling elder Bethlehem Presbyn. Ch., Logansport, Ind., 1979-83; scoutmaster Boy Scouts Am., Twelve Mile, Ind., 1973-78; mem. com. to rewrite land-use planning laws of Cass County, Ind., 1979-80. Mem. Am. Soc. Farm Mgrs. and Rural Appraisers, Phi Kappa Phi, Phi Eta Sigma, Alpha Zeta, Sigma Nu. Republican. Lodge: Masons. Avocation: flying. Home: 1311 Brookline Ct Naperville IL 60540 Office: Prudential Agrl Group 1431 Opus Pl Suite 665 Downers Grove IL 60515

JOHNSON, ROGERS BRUCE, chemical company executive; b. Boston, Apr. 8, 1928; s. Rogers Bruce and Dorothy Squires (Aiken) J.; m. Margery Ruth Howe, June 25, 1951; children: Wynn, Carol, Stephen, Herrick. B.A., Harvard U., 1949, M.B.A., 1955. Field salesman Dow U.S.A., Pitts., 1956-61; mgr. molding materials Dow Europe, Zurich, Switzerland, 1961-65; bus. mgr. styrene polymers Dow U.S.A., Midland, Mich., 1965-70; corp. products dir. Dow Chem. Co., Midland, Mich., 1970-76; v.p. supply, distbn. and planning Dow Chem. U.S.A., Midland, Mich., 1976-81, group v.p. adminstrv. services, 1981—; dir. Dow Can., Sarnia, Ont., Can., 1973-77, Dow Pacific, Hong Kong, 1973-77; bd. dirs. Strategic Planning Inst., 1987—. Bd. dirs. Midland Community Tennis Ctr., (Mich.), 1974—, Mich. Citizens' Research Council, 1985—, Strategic Planning Inst., 1987 pres. Midland Community Tennis Ctr. (Mich.), 1975-78, treas., 1972-76, 79-80; pres. Midland County Growth Council, 1985—. Served to 1st lt. USAF, 1951-53. Decorated Bronze Star. Mem. Strategic Planning Inst. (bd. dirs. 1987—). Republican. Office: Dow Chem Co 2020 Dow Center Midland MI 48640

JOHNSON, RON J., wildlife biologist, educator; b. Dayton, Ohio, Sept. 26, 1946; s. Chester E. and Lizzie E. (Thacker) J.; m. Mary McLean Beck, June 18, 1983; 1 child, Lindsay McLean. B.S. with distinction, Ohio State U., 1968, M.S., 1973; Ph.D., Cornell U., 1979. Instr. Ohio State U., Columbus, 1974-75; asst. prof. wildlife sci. U. Nebr., Lincoln, 1979-85, assoc. prof., 1985—; cons. Airport Planning Group Central N.Y., 1978, Gt. Lakes Fisheries, Bayfield, Wis., 1983, Conservation-Tillage Info. Ctr., Washington, 1983—. Author: Who's Who in Great Plains Songbirds, 1985 (Award of Excellence Agrl. Communicators in Edn.); contbr. articles to profl. publs., chpts. to books. Served to 1st. lt. U.S. Army, 1968-71, Vietnam. Recipient Excellence in Programming award U. Nebr., 1983; grantee Research Council, U. Nebr., 1983. Mem. Wildlife Soc., Wilson Soc., Nebr. Acad. Scis., Sigma Xi, Gamma Sigma Delta. Avocations: running; photography; guitar playing. Office: 202 Natural Resources Hall U Nebr Lincoln NE 68583

JOHNSON, RONALD HARRY, business educator; b. Moline, Ill., May 17, 1931; s. Harry Carl and Jane Agatha (Young) J.; B.A. in Bus. Adminstrn., St. Ambrose Coll., 1954; M.A. in Bus. Edn., U. Iowa, 1964; postgrad. U. Santa Clara, 1975, Western Ill. U., 1976, 80; m. Ruth Beverly Ashton, June 10, 1955; children—Michael James, Andrew Ashton, Daniel Ronald. In shipping and receiving positions Sears Roebuck & Co., Moline, 1946-52, salesman, 1952-54; mgr. sporting goods dept., Davenport, Iowa, 1954-57, mgr. automotive dept., Moline, 1957-62, mgr. automotive service, 1962-63; tchr. bus. Central High Sch., Davenport Community Sch. Dist., 1964—. Instr., ARC, 1961—; active Boy Scouts Am., 1965-76, scout master troop 4 Illowa council, 1971-76; swim ofcl. Iowa AAU, 1962—; head scorer 1st Iowa Girls Swim Meet, Iowa Girls High Sch. Athletic Union, 1967; chmn. fin. Sacred Heart Roman Catholic Parish Council, Davenport, 1980-82, v.p. council, 1981-82. Served to cpl. arty. U.S. Army, 1951-52. Mem. Davenport Edn. Assn. (pres. 1968-69, exec. bd. 1969-78), Iowa Edn. Assn. (exec. bd. 1974-78), NEA (rep. del. assembly 1974-78), Gt. River Uniserve Unit (exec. bd. 1982-84), Adminstrv. Mgmt. Soc. (edn. chmn. Quad-Cities chpt. 1970-71, exec. bd. 1970-71, 79-80), Iowa Bus. Edn. Assn. (S.E. Dist. Outstanding Bus. Tchr. award 1969, treas. and mem. exec. bd. 1974-75), Pi Kappa Alpha, Delta Pi Epsilon. Clubs: Sky Cats Flying (treas., exec. bd.), K.C. Home: 2627 Middle Rd Davenport IA 52803 Office: 1020 Main St Davenport IA 52803

JOHNSON, RUTH BEVERLY ASHTON, physical education educator; b. Clinton, Iowa, Sept. 20, 1933; d. Ned Lowell and Gladys Mae (Brooker) Ashton; m. Ronald Harry Johnson, June 10, 1955; children—Michael James, Andrew Ashton, Daniel Ronald. B.A., U. Iowa, 1955; M.A., Northeast Mo. State U., 1977. Dir. swimming program Davenport Parks (Iowa), 1955-68; tchr. Frank L. Smart Jr. High Sch., Davenport, 1955-56; active Lend-A-Hand Swim Program, Davenport, 1956-57; tchr. St. Katherine's Sch., Davenport, 1957-68, Davenport West High Sch., 1968—; coach water polo, competitive swimming and diving, field hockey, synchronized swimming, girls' gymnastics, soccer; nat. synchronized swimming judge, Synchronized Swimming Clinic, 1970, 77; organizer, meet referee Iowa State High Sch. Swimming Meets, 1967; bd. dirs. Iowa Girls High Sch. Athletic Union, 1969-78; mem. Iowa High Sch. Swimming Adv. Com., 1969-85; swimming coach, 1956—. Contbr. writings to publs. in field. Water safety instr., trainer ARC, 1961—, mem. nat. resolutions com., 1965, water safety chmn. Scott County, 1956-71, bd. dirs. Quad City chpt., 1971-77. Mem. NEA, Iowa Edn. Assn. Davenport Edn. Assn., AAHPERD, Iowa Assn. Health, Phys. Edn., Recreation and Dance (treas. 1980-83, pres. 1985, honor award 1986), Am. Swimming Coaches Assn., Iowa High Sch. Swimming Coaches Assn., Synchronized Swimming Coaches Acad., U.S. Synchronized Swimming and Gymnastics Coaches Acad., U.S. Gymnastics Safety Assn., Field Hockey Coaches Acad., U.S. Field Hockey Assn., AAU (nat. bd. govs. 1961-73, women's water polo chmn. 1966-70, synchronized swimming chmn. Iowa chpt. 1970-74, Iowa devel. chmn. 1979-81, Iowa ofcls. chmn. 1982-85, Iowa women's swimming chmn., age group swimming chmn. or gen. swimming chmn. 1956-68), DAR, Phi Beta Kappa, Pi Lambda Theta, Chi Omega. Home: 2627 Middle Rd Davenport IA 52803 Office: West High Sch 3505 W Locust Davenport IA 52804

JOHNSON, RUTH MARIE, national collection agency and computer service company executive; b. St. Paul, Jan. 24, 1917; d. Louis H. and Sylvia Marie (Bricko) Berke; divorced; 1 child, John A. Erickson. Pres., I. C. System, Inc., St. Paul, 1961-84, chmn. bd. dirs., chief exec. officer, 1984—; dir. Am. Nat. Bank, St. Paul, 1978-80. Mem. exec. com. Minn. Leadership Council, St. Paul, 1984; mem. St. Paul Exec. Postal Council, 1979—. Mem. Am. Collectors Assn., Minn. Assn. Commerce and Industry (recipient Hall of Fame award 1983), U.S. SBA, C. of C. Republican. Clubs: North Oaks Country (Minn.), John's Island (Vero Beach, Fla.). Office: I C System Inc 444 E Hwy 96 St Paul MN 55164

JOHNSON, SAMUEL CURTIS, wax company executive; b. Racine, Wis., Mar. 2, 1928; s. Herbert Fisk and Gertrude (Brauner) J.; m. Imogene Powers, May 8, 1954; children: Samuel Curtis III, Helen Powers, Herbert Fisk III, Winifred Johnson Marquart. BA, Cornell U., 1950; MBA, Harvard U., 1952; LLD (hon.), Carthage Coll., 1974, Northland Coll., 1974, Ripon Coll., 1980, Carroll Coll., 1981, U. Surrey, 1985, Marquette U., 1986. With S.C. Johnson & Son, Inc., Racine, 1954—; internat. v.p. S.C. Johnson & Son, Inc., 1962-63, exec. v.p., 1963-66, pres., 1966-67, chmn., pres., chief exec. officer, 1967-72, chmn., chief exec. officer, 1972-79, chmn., 1979-80, chmn., chief exec. officer, 1980—; bd. dirs. Johnson Wax Cos., Eng., Japan, Germany, Switzerland, Can., Australia, France, Egypt, Mex., Deere & Co., Moline, Ill., Mobil Corp., N.Y.C.; chmn. Johnson Worldwide Assocs., Inc.; v.p. Heritage Bank & Trust of Racine. Chmn. The Mayo Found., Johnson's Wax Fund, Inc., Johnson Found., Inc.; trustee Cornell U.; founding chmn. emeritus Prairie Sch., Racine; chmn., bd. dirs. Heritage Racine Corp.; mem. adv. council Cornell U. Grad. Sch. Mgmt.; bd. regents Smithsonian Assn.; mem. Bus. Council. Mem. Chi Psi. Clubs: Cornell (N.Y.C., Milw.); Univ. (Milw.); Racine Country; Am. (London). Home: 4815 Lighthouse Dr Racine WI 53402 Office: S C Johnson & Son Inc 1525 Howe St Racine WI 53403

JOHNSON, SHIRLEY MAY HILL, psychologist; b. Virginia, Minn., Mar. 10, 1947; d. Oliver and Mary (Chitty) Hill; m. George R. Johnson (div. 1985); children: Darien O., Brandon E. BA, Concordia Coll., 1969; MA, Oakland U., 1972. Lic. psychologist, Minn. Psychologist South Wis. Colony and Tng. Sch., Union Grove, 1972-74, Curative Workshop, Milw., 1974-76; psychologist Cen. Mesabi Med. Ctr., Hibbing, Minn., 1977—, counselor employee assistance program, 1985—; instr. Hibbing Community Coll., 1983-85. Democrat. Lutheran. Avocation: racquetball. Office: Mesaba Regional Med Ctr 750 E 34th St Hibbing MN 55746

JOHNSON, SONDRA LEA, accountant; b. Kansas City, Mo., May 11, 1952; d. Albert John Oscar and Dorothy Mae (Hudgens) J. AA, Longview Coll., 1972; BSBA cum laude in Acctg., Cen. Mo. State U., 1974, MBA, 1980. CPA, Mo. Acct. Farmland Industries, Kansas City, 1974-76; acct., auditor Ernst & Whinney, Kansas City, 1976-79, Laventhol & Horwath, Kansas City, 1980-81; corp. acct., mgr. Butler Mfg. Co., Kansas City, 1981-84; audit supr. Grant Thornton Internat., Kansas City, 1984—; specialized instr. nat. continuing edn. tng. program, Grant Thornton Internat., various locations U.S.A.; acctg. instr. Cen. Mo. State U., Warrensburg, 1979-80, Rockhurst Coll., Kansas City, 1981-82. Mem. Nat. Assn. Accts., Am. Inst. CPA's, Mo. Soc. CPA's, Women's C. of C. of Kansas City, Phi Kappa Phi. Democrat. Lutheran. Avocations: travel, collecting ltd. edition figurines, spectator sports, music. Office: Grant Thornton Internat 1101 Walnut Kansas City MO 64106

JOHNSON, STEVEN OLOF, chiropractic physician; b. Little Falls, Minn., Feb. 24, 1955; s. Ralph Linne and Margaret Catherine (Bergren) J.; m. Holly Ann Holmen, Aug. 18, 1979; children: Brittany Jeanette, Brooke Steffany. Cert., Assn. Free Luth. Bible Ash., Mpls., 1975; AS, N. Hennepin Community Coll., 1976; BS, Logan Coll. Chiropractic Medicine, Chesterfield, 1977; Doctorate, Logan Coll. Chiropractic Medicine, 1979. Jr. to sr. intern Logan Coll. Clinic, Chesterfield, 1978-79; gen. practice Upsala (Minn.) Chiropractic Ctr., 1980—; lectr. on nutrition topics Upsala area schs. Cochmn. Planning and Zoning Commn., Upsala, 1983—; treas. Upsala Recreation Bd., Upsala, 1984—. Named one of Outstanding Young Men Am., 1984; recipient appreciation award, Cen. Minn. Boy Scouts Am., Saint Cloud, 1984. Mem. Minn. Chiropractic Assn., Am. Chropractic. Assn., Logan Coll. Alumni Assn. Lutheran. Club: Upsala Booster. Lodge: Lions (pres. Upsala 1985-86). Avocations: bow hunting, water sports, softball, basketball. Home: Box 363 Upsala MN 56384 Office: Upsala Chiropractic Ctr 363 Main St Upsala MN 56384

JOHNSON, SUSAN JEAN, advertising executive; b. Chgo., Oct. 12, 1956; d. John Benjamin and Evelyn (Schaafsma) Hoekstra; m. Gerald Robert Johnson Jr., Oct. 9, 1982. Broadcast coordinator Gielow & Assoc., Grand Rapids, Mich., 1977-80; media coordinator, copywriter Bailen Advt., Grand Rapids, 1981-82; account exec. J.D. Thomas Co., Grand Rapids, 1983—. Mem. pub. relations com. ARC, Grand Rapids, 1986—; co chmn. pub. relations Festival 85, Grand Rapids. Mem. Am. Mktg. Assn., Grand Rapids C. of C. Republican. Clubs: Ad, Econs. (Grand Rapids). Avocations: writing, theatre, music, winter sports. Office: JD Thomas Co 2040 Raybrook SE Grand Rapids MI 49506

JOHNSON, TERESA MARIE, nurse, educator; b. Miami Beach, Fla., July 28, 1953; d. Robert Roy and Evelyh Ophelia (Mullins) Mandrell; m. Barry James Johnson, Aug. 18, 1975 (div. July 1987); children—Lisa Ann, Scott Anthony. A.A., Mo. Bapt. Coll., 1977; B.S. in Nursing, St. Louis U., 1985. Staff nurse St. Elizabeth Hosp., Granite City, Ill., 1974-75, Wood River Twp. Hosp. (Ill.), 1975-78, head nurse intensive care, 1978-79, staff nurse, 1979-80; cardiopulmonary rehab. nurse St. Elizabeth Med. Center, Granite City, 1980-83, pulmonary staff devel. asst., 1983-84, pulmonary clinician, 1984—; mem. Midwestern Nursing Diagnosis Conf. Group, 1984, Patient Edn. Research Interest Group, So. Ill. U., 1985; lectr. in field. Mem. Assn. Rehab. Nurses, Am. Assn. Critical Care Nurses, Sigma Theta. Baptist. Home: 1844 Bremen Ave Granite City IL 62040 Office: Four Doctors Unit St Elizabeth Med Center 2100 Madison Ave Granite City IL 62040

JOHNSON, THERESA ANN, civic organization administrator; b. Chgo., Dec. 17, 1948; d. Joseph and Tabatha (Shutmate) J.; children: Mario L., Melvin. Student, Beloit (Wis.) Coll., 1977. Dist. exec. program aide Boy Scouts Am., Janesville, Wis., 1976-77; exec. dir. Scope Orgn. Chgo. Area Project, Chgo., 1979—; community service worker; bd. dirs. Southeast Devel. Commn.; cons. 300 Club, Chgo., 1986. Active neighborhood festivals, South Chgo., 1986, youth drug prevention edn., Woodstock, Ill., 1982; bd. dirs. S.E. Youth Service Bd., S. Chgo., 1985; community youth advocate in sex edn. Democrat. Baptist. Avocations: writing, reading, art, roller skating, dancing. Office: Scope 9000 S Buffalo Chicago IL 60617

JOHNSON, THOMAS MICHAEL, engineer; b. Parkersburg, W.Va., June 15, 1956; s. Cecil Vivian and Patty Ann Johnson; m. Diane Kay Wagner, Aug. 23, 1975; 1 child, Michael Thomas. AAS, Washington Tech. Inst., Marietta, Ohio, 1976. Reaserch and devel. engr. Skuttle Mfg. Co., Marietta, 1978-83, advt. mgr., 1983—, chief engr., 1984—. Patentee in field. Republican. Home: 103 Kibler Ln Williamstown WV 26187 Office: Skuttle Mfg Co Rt 1 Marietta OH 45750

JOHNSON, THOMAS STUART, lawyer; b. Rockford, Ill., May 21, 1942; s. Frederick C. and Pauline (Ross) J. BA, Rockford Coll. 1964; JD, Harvard U., 1967. Bar: Ill. 1967. Ptnr. Williams & McCarthy, Rockford, 1967—; bd. dirs. John S. Barnes Corp., Rockford, Odin Corp., Rockford. Contbr. articles to profl. jours. Chmn. bd. trustees Rockford Coll., 1986—; chmn. bd. dirs. Ill. Inst. Continuing Legal Edn., Chgo., 1984-86, Emanuel Med. Ctr., Turlock, Cal., 1984—; trustee Swedish Covenant Hosp., Chgo., 1984-86; treas. Lawyers Trust Fund of Ill., Chgo., 1984-86; chmn. bd. Svenson Charitable Found., 1985—; mem. bd. govs., mem. council Regent's Coll., London, 1985—; dir. benevolence bd. Covenant Ch. Am., Chgo., 1984—; chmn. Regent's Found. for Internat. Edn., London; pres. Regent's Found. Internat. Edn., London, 1987—. Served U.S. Army, 1965-67. Fellow Am. Bar Found.; mem. ABA (ho. dels. 1982—, chmn. commn. on advt. 1984—), Ill. Bar Assn. (bd. govs. 1976-82), Am. Judicature Soc. (bd. dirs. 1986—). Republican. Clubs: Rockford Country, University, Rockford City. Home: 913 N Main St Rockford IL 61103

JOHNSON, TIMOTHY PETER, congressman; b. Canton, S.D., Dec. 28, 1946; s. Vandal Charles and Ruth Jorinda (Ljostveit) J.; m. Barbara Brooks, June 6, 1969; children—Brooks Dwight, Brendan Vandal, Kelsey Marie. B.A., U. S.D., 1969, M.A., 1970; postgrad. Mich. State U., 1970-71; J.D., U. S.D., 1975. Bar: S.D. 1975, U.S. Dist. Ct. S.D. 1976. Fiscal analyst Legis. Fiscal Agy., Lansing, Mich., 1971-72; sole practice, Vermillion, S.D., 1975-86; adj. instr. U. S.D., Vermillion, 1974-83; mem. S.D. Code Commn., Pierre, 1982-86; mem. S.D. Ho. of Reps., 1978-82, S.D. Senate, 1982-86; mem.100th Congress from S.D., 1987—. Mem. Vermillion City Planning Commn., 1977, 78; treas. Clay County Democratic Com., Vermillion, 1978. NSF grantee, 1969-70. Mem. S.D. Bar Assn., Clay County Bar Assn., Phi Beta Kappa, Omicron Delta Kappa. Democrat. Lutheran.

JOHNSON, VIVIAN MARIE, nursing adminstrator; b. Chgo., Jan. 20, 1940; d. Edward T. and Vesta C. (Landingham) Crowley; m. Merrill Johnson, Feb. 15, 1958; children: Jeffrey, Jill, Gregg. BSN, No. Ill. U.; MA, Roosevelt U. Cert. emergency nurse, trauma nurse specialist. Supr. McHenry Hosp. (Ill.), 1971-76; instr. trauma nursing St. Joseph Hosp., Elgin, 1976-79, asst. dir. nursing critical care, 1982—; regional nursing coordinator Ill. Dept. Pub. Health Emergency Med. Service, Springfield, 1979-82; nursing cons. Sheridan Mgmt., Waukegan, Ill., 1985—; program coordinator trauma/spl. care symposia; mem. speaker's bur. Co-author: Curriculum for Trauma Nurse Specialist, 1980. Mem. Am. Assn. Critical Care, Emergency Dept. Nurses Assn. (founder Greater N.W. chpt.), Soc. Tchrs. Emergency Medicine (pres. 1980), Sigma Theta Tau, Phi Kappa Theta, Phi Kappa Phi. Roman Catholic. Home: 2404 Timber Trail Crystal Lake IL 60014

JOHNSON, WALLACE HAROLD, lawyer; b. Cleve., Oct. 7, 1939; s. Wallace H. and Esther Johnson; m. Donna Simpson, JUne 9, 1962; children—Kimberly, W. Todd, Vicki, Eric. B.A. in Polit. Sci., Ohio U., 1961; postgrad Rutgers U., 1961; J.D., U. Toledo, 1965. Bar: U.S. Dist. Ct. D.C., 1969, U.S. Ct. Claims, 1974, Ohio 1965, U.S. Supreme Ct. 1968, Nebr. 1975. Trial atty. organized crime and racketeering sect. criminal div. U.S. Dept. Justice, Washington, 1965-69, minority counsel subcom. criminal laws and procedures, 1969-70, assoc. dep. atty. gen., 1970-72; spl. asst. to Pres., White House, 1972-73; asst. atty. gen. land and resources div. U.S. Dept. Justice, 1973-75; ptnr. Kutak, Rock & Campbell, Omaha, 1975—. Recipient Scholastic Achievement award Bur. Nat. Affairs, 1963, Sustained Superior Performance award Atty. Gen., 1971; cert. merit for disting. achievements in law and govt. Ohio U. Alumni Assn. Mem. Omicron Delta Kappa. Republican. Lutheran. Contbr. articles to profl jours. Address: 9905 Devonshire Dr Omaha NE 68114 Office: Kutak Rock & Co 1650 Farnam St Omaha NE 68102

JOHNSON, WENDELL ALLEN, obstetrician-gynecologist; b. Iowa, July 15, 1920; s. Fred Vivian and Irene Maude (Applegate) J.; m. Shirley Joan Chance, Apr. 21, 1945; children: Steven C., Joalyn R. Suzanne L., W. Allen II, Janis A. AA, Creston (Iowa) Jr. Coll., 1939; BA, U. Iowa, 1941, MD, 1944; M in Ob-Gyn, U. Pa., 1958. Diplomate Am. Bd. Ob-Gyn. Resident in pathology Cooper Hosp., Camden, N.J., 1946-47; gen. practitioner Iowa, 1947-52; resident in ob-gyn U. Colo., 1952-53; practice medicine specializing in ob-gyn Denver, 1955-56; commd. ensign USN, 1956, advanced through grades to capt., 1963, ret., 1974; gynecologist U. Ill. Health Service, Urbana, Ill., 1974-80, Park Nicollet Med. Ctr., Mpls., 1981—. Served with USNR, 1943-56. Fellow Am. Coll. Ob-Gyn. Republican. Lutheran. Office: Park Med Ctr 5000 W 39th St Minneapolis MN 55416

JOHNSON, WILLARD VERNER, architect; b. Chgo., May 27, 1938; s. Verner Herman and Lena Ellyn (Newport) J.; m. Lilia Maderang Manalo, Oct. 5, 1968; children: Kenneth Willard, Pamela Ann. Student, U. Ill., 1956-60. Registered architect, Ill., Wis., Mo. Owner Willard Johnson, Architect, Palatine, Ill., 1976-81; staff architect HBE, St. Louis, 1981-84; project architect The Benham Group, St. Louis, 1984-85, Kenneth Balk, Architect, St. Louis, 1985-86; owner Willard V. Johnson, Architect, St. Charles, Mo., 1986—; cons. architecture Casco Corp., St. Louis, 1986. Served as pvt. U.S. Army, 1961-63. Mem. AIA (sec. housing com. 1974, sec. govt. affairs 1975), St. Charles C. of C. Lutheran. Avocation: martial arts. Home and Office: 4039 Providence Dr Saint Charles MO 63303

JOHNSON, WILLIAM BENJAMIN, industrial executive; b. Salisbury, Md., Dec. 28, 1918; s. Benjamin A. and Ethel (Holloway) J.; m. Mary Barb, Dec. 19, 1942; children: Benjamin H., Kirk B., John P., Kathleen M. AB maxima cum laude, Washington Coll., 1940, LLB (hon.), 1975; LLB cum laude, U. Pa., 1943. Bar: Md. 1943, Pa. 1947. Atty. U.S. Tax Ct., 1945-47; asst. solicitor Pa. R.R., 1947-48, asst. gen. solicitor, 1948-51, asst. to gen. counsel, 1951-52, asst. gen. counsel, 1952-59; pres., bd. dirs. REA Express (formerly Ry. Express Agy., Inc.), N.Y.C., 1959-66, chmn. bd. dirs., 1966; pres., chief exec. officer I.C. R.R., Chgo., 1966-68, chmn., chief exec. officer, 1969-72, chmn. exec. com., 1972-76; pres., chief exec. officer Ill. Cen. Industries, Inc., Chgo., 1966-68, chmn., pres., chief exec. officer, 1968-72, chmn., chief exec. officer, 1972-87, chmn. emeritus, 1987—; bd. dirs. Ill. Cen. Gulf R.R., Midas-Internat., Chgo., Pet Inc., St. Louis, Pepsi-Cola Gen. Bottlers, Inc., Chgo., Hussman Corp., Bridgeton, Mo., Pneumo Abex Corp., Boston, Perdue Farms, Salisbury, Md.; bd. dirs., mem. adv. bd. Swiss Air. Bd. dirs. Chgo. Cen. Area Com.; trustee Com. for Econ. Devel.; mem. citizens bd., life trustee U. Chgo.; governing mem. Shedd Aquarium; mem. Northwestern U. Assocs.; bd. overseers U. Pa. Served with Security Intelligence Corps AUS, 1943-45. Mem. ABA, Phila. Bar Assn., ICC Practitioners Assn., Juristic Soc., Conf. Bd., Newcomen Soc. N.Am., Nat. Def. Transp. Assn. (life, past chmn. bd.), Am. Productivity Ctr. (bd. dirs.), Md. Soc. Pa., SAR, Order of Coif, Kappa Alpha, Omicron Delta Kappa. Clubs: Econ. (N.Y.C.); Comml. (Chgo.), Econ., Chgo. (Chgo.); Onwentsia (Lake Forest); Old Elm (Highland Park). Office: IC Industries Inc 111 E Wacker Dr Room 2700 Chicago IL 60601

JOHNSON, WILLIAM DUNCAN, hospital administrator, consultant; b., Kansas City, Kans., June 30, 1932; s. George William and Iva May (Browning) J.; m. Patricia JoAnn Stewart, May 6, 1955; children—Michael Dean, Douglas William. B.A., Kansas City U., 1956. Treas. Midstates Cons., Denver, 1963-65; sr. acct. Lee J. Cooper, C.P.A., Mission, Kans., 1965-70; owner, chief exec. officer Johnson & Assocs., Westwood, Kans., 1970-79, cons., Lenexa, Kans., 1984—; v.p. Mgmt. Concepts Corp., 1984—; adminstr. McDonagh Med. Ctr., Gladstone, Mo., 1979-84. Contbr. articles to trade jours. Pres. Midwest Cardiac Rehab. Ctr., Gladstone, 1979-84; dir. agt. Orange Program for Vietnam Vets., Lenexa, 1981-84; scoutmaster Kaw council Boy Scouts Am., 1969-74; mem. Exec. Forum Jackson County, Kansas City, Mo., 1983-84. Recipient Boss of Yr. award Am. Bus. Women's Assn., Kansas City, 1982, Humanitarian award Vietnam Vets. Am., 1984. Fellow Am. Acad. Homeopathic Medicine; mem. Am. Acad. Preventive Medicine, Nat. Assn. Atomic Vets., Midwest Acad. Preventive Medicine (founder, exec. dir. 1980-84), Kansas City C. of C. (fin. com. 1982-83), North Kansas City C. of C. (ways and means com. 1982). Republican. Lutheran. Club: Brookridge Country (Overland Park, Kans.). Lodge: Order of De Molay. Avocations: hunting; backpacking; golf; black powder gun building; bowling. Home: 13329 W 77th Terr Lenexa KS 66216

JOHNSON, WILLIAM E., JR., hospital executive; b. Mpls., Oct. 11, 1933; s. William E. and Dorothy A. (Peterson) J.; m. Julia Anderson, May 14, 1960; children: Jill, Karen, Steve. BS, U. Minn., 1955, MHA, 1958. Adminstrv. resident Swedish Hosp., Mpls., 1957-58; asst. adminstr. Madison Gen. Hosp., Wis., 1958-64; adminstr. Methodist Hosp., Madison, 1964-74, pres., 1974-82; pres. Meth. Health Services, Inc., Madison, 1982-87; pres. Meriter Health Services, Inc., 1987—. Contbr. articles to profl. jours. Served to 2d lt. U.S. Army, 1956-57. Recipient Merit award Tri-State Hosp. Assembly, 1977. Fellow Am. Coll. Hosp. Adminstrs.; mem. Wis. Hosp. Assn. (cert. in hosp. mgmt.; Harold M. Coon award 1977), Am. Coll. Healthcare Execs. (chmn. 1985), U. Minn. Alumni Found. (pres.-elect program in hosp. and healthcare adminstrn. 1986). Lutheran. Lodges: Masons (33 deg.), Shriners (mem. divan). Avocations: golf, skiing, spectator sports. Home: 6405 Keelson Dr Madison WI 53705 Office: Meriter Health Services Inc 309 W Washington Ave Madison WI 53703

JOHNSON, WILLIAM HERBERT, emergency medicine physician, aerospace physician, retired air national guard officer; b. Elkhart, Ind., Dec. 12, 1928; s. Herbert John and Lorene Wilhemena (Johnson) J.; m. Ann Marie Bacon, Oct. 17, 1964; children—Ernest Michael, Jennifer Lynn. A.B., Augustana Coll., 1951; M.D., Ind. U., 1958. Intern, Indpls. Gen. Hosp., 1958-59; resident in internal medicine Ind. U. Med. Ctr., Indpls., 1960-61; practice medicine specializing in gen. medicine, East Gary, Ind., 1959-60;

asst. surgeon U.S. Steel Co., Gary Works (Ind.), 1959-60; ptnr. Gary Clinic (now Ross Clinic), 1962-69; staff physician student health services Western Mich. U., 1969-74; staff physician Trauma and Emergency Ctr., Bronson Methodist Hosp., Kalamazoo, Mich., 1969—, chmn., 1972-74; asst. clin. prof. medicine Mich. State U. Coll. Human Medicine, East Lansing, 1976—; past mem. staffs Borgess Med. Ctr., Community Hosp. Assn., Leila Y. Post Montgomery Hosp., Three Rivers Hosp.; med. dir. emergency dept., mem. exec. bd. Elkhart (Ind.) Gen. Hosp., Goshen (Ind.) Gen. Hosp.; med. dir. Emergency Med. System, Elkhart County, Ind.; pres. Elkhart Emergency Physicians, Inc. Pres. Corey Lake Improvement Assn., 1978-80. Served with USAF, 1951-53, 61-62; ret. brig. gen. Air N.G., 1962-85. Decorated Air N.G. Meritorious Service award, Legion of Merit; nominee Malcolm C. Grove award USAF Flight Surgeon of Yr., 1971. Fellow Aerospace Med. Assn. (by-laws com., membership com.); mem. Kalamazoo Acad. Medicine, Mich. Med. Soc., AMA Physician's Recognition award 1983), Am. Coll. Emergency Physicians (pres. Mich. chpt. 1976-78, dir.), Calhoun County Med. Soc., Univ. Assn. for Emergency Medicine, Soc. USAF Flight Surgeons (constn., by-laws com.), Alliance of Air N.G. Flight Surgeons (dir., mem. membership com., chmn. nominating com., past pres.), Assn. Mil. Surgeons U.S., Mich. Assn. of Professions, Res. Officers Assn., Air Force Assn. Lutheran. Lodge: Elks. Contbg. editor to books, articles to profl. jours.; contbg. editor, mem. editorial bd. Annals of Emergency Medicine, 1972—; mem. editorial bd. Aviation, Space and Environ. Medicine, 1981—, editor book rev. sect., 1984—. Home and Office: 11451 Coon Hollow Rd Three Rivers MI 49093

JOHNSON, WILLIAM HOWARD, JR., sales executive; b. Chgo., Jan. 24, 1943; s. William H. and Lois C. (Banks) J.; m. Joan C. Cervantes, Dec. 22, 1972 (div. Jan. 1985); children—Kevin L., Marvin E. B.S., Bradley U., 1965. Tchr. pub. schs., Evanston, Ill., 1965; design engr. Conveyor Systems, Inc., Morton Grove, Ill., 1965-67; with IBM Corp., 1967—, dist. sales mgr., Rolling Meadows, Ill., 1984—; dir. edn. tech. div. Nexus, Chgo., 1985—; com. mem. CC&Q, Atlanta, 1985; cons. computer game America Us, 1985. Mem. com. United Negro Coll. Fund, N.Y.C. Recipient Black Achiever award YMCA, Boston, 1979. Mem. Cell Found. Democrat. Methodist. Avocation: tennis. Office: 1701 Golf Rd Rolling Meadows IL 60008

JOHNSON, WILLIAM THEODORE, explorer, treasure hunter; b. Chgo., Dec. 10, 1953; s. Lawrence Paul and Constance Ann (Elfstrom) J. BA, Wheaton Coll., 1977; MA, U. Chgo., 1980. Prof. King Suad U., Riyadh, Saudi Arabia, 1982-83, Al-Bustan, Riyadh, 1983-84; explorer Western Exploration Co., Rockford, Mich., 1985—; program designer, cons. Mari-Wari Community Soc., Kalusangi, Pakistan, 1980-87; v.p. Karachi (Pakistan) Commuter Co., 1984-87; v.p. Commuter Electric Car Co., Riyadh, 1982-84. Author: Coherism: A Political Ideology, 1984; film maker (screen play) The Quest for the Golden Madonna, 1984. Rep. campaign mgr. Mich. Ho. of Reps., Lansing, 1986; mgr. precint del. campaign, Rockford, Mich., 1986; alt. del. Rep. Conv., Detroit, 1986. Home: 127 Pearl St Rockford MI 49341 Office: Western Exploration Co 3925 Ten Mile Rd Rockford MI 49341

JOHNSON, WILLIAM THOMAS, endodontics educator, endodontist; b. Des Moines, Apr. 11, 1949; s. Gaillard Xenton and Alvah (Monson) J.; m. Georgia Kay Tonn, Aug. 25, 1974. B.A., Drake U., 1971; D.D.S., U. Iowa, 1975, cert. endodontics, 1981, M.S., 1981. Diplomate Am. Bd. Endodontics. Resident U. Iowa, Iowa City, 1979-81, asst. prof., 1981-82; pvt. practice endodontics, Des Moines, 1982-83; asst. prof. endodontics U. Nebr., Lincoln, 1983—; pvt. practice dentistry, Cedar Rapids, Iowa, 1977-79. Contbr. articles to profl. jours. Served to capt. U.S. Army, 1975-77; to maj. Iowa N.G., 1977—. Mem. Am. Assn. Endodontists, ADA, Am. Assn. Dental Schs., Delta Sigma Delta. Lutheran. Avocation: photography. Home: 2831 S 74th St Lincoln NE 68506 Office: U Nebr Med Ctr Coll Dentistry 40th and Holdrege St Lincoln NE 68583

JOHNSTON, CHERYL LYNN, marketing professional, consultant; b. Dayton, Ohio, Nov. 29, 1954; d. Walter Kenneth and Emily (Palmer) Heckman; m. Donald David Dooley, Oct. 15, 1977 (div. Apr. 1979); m. Mark Joseph Johnston, July 19, 1981; 1 child, Eric John. BS in Bus. Adminstrn., Wright State U., 1976. Product specialist NCR Systemedia, Dayton, 1977-79; mktg. specialist E.F. MacDonald Co., Dayton, 1979; product mgr. Moore Bus. Forms, Glenview, Ill., 1980-82, Rand McNally & Co., Skokie, Ill., 1982-84; dir. mktg. Adams Bus. Forms, Topeka, 1985-86; mktg. mgr. R&R Direct, Dayton, 1986—; market research analyst Mellon Fin., Oak Brook, Ill., 1980; cons. Monarch Direct, Miamisburg, Ohio, 1984. Lions Cooperative Office Edn. scholar. Avocations: ballet, theatre. Home: 6400 Pine Cone Dr Dayton OH 45449 Office: R&R Direct 129 S Ludlow St Dayton OH 45402

JOHNSTON, CRIS WILLIAM, neuropsychologist; b. LaCrosse, Wis., Mar. 28, 1951; s. Widmer Nelson and Gwendolyn (Hoyt) J.; m. Marcia Lee Holth; children: Reid Arthur, Neil Widmer. AAS, West Wis. Tech. Inst., 1975; BS, U. Wis., La Crosse, 1975; MA, Queens Coll., 1978; PhD, CUNY, N.Y.C., 1983. Licensed cons. psychologist, Minn.; cert. Am. Bd. Profl. Neuropsychology. Cons. Speech-Language Hearing Clinic, Mpls., 1983-86; cons. pediatric neuropsychology U. Minn. Hosps., Mpls., 1985-86; dir. Neurobehavioral Ctr. Children's Hosp., St. Paul, 1987—. editor: Neuropsychology of Eye Movements, 1987; contbr. chpts. to books and articles to profl. jours. Bd. dirs. Minn. Assn. for Children with Learning Disabilities, St. Paul, 1986—. Served with U.S. Army, 1969-71. Minn. Med. Found. grantee, 1984. Mem. Internat. Neuropsychol. Soc., Am. Psychol. Assn., Midwest Neuropsychology Group. Avocation: tennis. Home: 13544 McGinty Rd Minnetonka MN 55343 Office: Neurobehavioral Ctr Childrens Hosp 345 N Smith Ave Saint Paul MN 55102

JOHNSTON, DAVID ALLEN, lawyer; b. Columbia, Mo., Oct. 13, 1958; s. Larry Allen and Gloria (Fenner) J.; m. Mary K. Lucido, Oct. 4, 1986. BS in Bus., U. Mo., 1981, JD, 1984. Bar: Mo. 1984, U.S. Dist. Ct. (we. dist.) Mo. 1984. Law clk. State of Mo., Jefferson City, 1984, U.S. Cts., Springfield, Mo., 1984-87; assoc. Craig A. Van Matre, P.C., Columbia, Mo., 1987—. Election judge Livingston County, Chillicothe, Mo., 1976-81; campaign worker Boone County, Columbia, 1978; vol. pub. sta. KOZK-TV, Springfield, 1985-86. Edna Nelson scholar, 1983; named one of Outstanding Young Men Am., 1985, 86. Mem. ABA, Mo. Bar Assn., Assn. Trial Lawyers Am., U. Mo. Alumni Assn., Order of Coif, Phi Delta Phi. Republican. Roman Catholic. Avocations: racquetball, basketball, running, gardening. Home: 34 Broadway Village Dr Apt E Columbia MO 65201 Office: Craig A Van Matre PC PO Box 1017 Columbia MO 65205

JOHNSTON, DAVID MARK, data processing executive; b. Wyandotte, Mich., Feb. 10, 1956; s. Harold Deloss and Sylvia (Hillgartner) J.; m. Anita Jane Hawkins, MAr. 10, 1979 (div. May 1986). BS in Computer Sci., Oakland U., Rochester, Mich., 1978. Project mgr. Manubank, Southfield, Mich., 1976-81; data processing mgr. Heritage Bank, Taylor, Mich., 1981—; treas. Thrift Spl. Int. Group, Hooksett, N.H., 1984—. Home: 15463 DuPage Taylor MI 48180 Office: Heritage Fed Savs Bank 20600 Eureka Taylor MI 48180

JOHNSTON, JAMES ROBERT, library director; b. Wheaton, Ill., June 3, 1947; s. Robert W. and Elizabeth S. (Townsend) J.; m. Carol Ann Trezza, June 14, 1969; children: Steven J., Julie M. BA, U. Notre Dame, 1969; MLS, Fla. State U., 1973. Head librarian Grande Prairie Library Dist., Hazel Crest, Ill., 1973-76; chief librarian Joliet (Ill.) Pub. Library, 1976—; pres. bd. dirs. Ill. Library Employees Benefit Plan; mem. Bur Oak Library System automation com., Shorewood, Ill.; pres. Ill. Library Employees Benefit Plan, Joliet. Co-author: Illinois Library Trustees Association Booklet "Selecting Consultants", 1986. Mem. Mainstream U.S.A. promotion com., Joliet, interlibrary cooperative subcom. Ill. State Library Adv. Com., 1979-83. Mem. Ill. Library Assn. (Pub. Library sect. 1977-78, legis. devel. com. 1977-82, jr. members. roundtable 1976-77), Beta Phi Mu (Gamma chpt.). Lodge: Kiwanis. Avocations: HO guage model railroading, softball, bowling, golf. Home: 15 Wheeler Ave Joliet IL 60436 Office: Joliet Pub Library 150 N Ottawa St Joliet IL 60436

JOHNSTON, JANIS CLARK, psychologist, consultant; b. South Bend, Ind., Jan. 5, 1947; d. Robert Dale and Lois Treasure (Whitacre) Clark; m. Mark Emmett Johnston, June 14, 1969; children: Ryan Clark, Megan Gale. BA with distinction, Manchester Coll., 1969; MEd, Boston U., 1970, EdD, 1974. Lic. psychologist; cert. sch. psychologist. Psychol. examiner Harvard Pre-Sch. Project, Cambridge, Mass., 1973-74; sch. psychologist Lexington (Mass.) Pub. Schs., 1972-78; therapist and trainer Acorn Employee Assistance Program, Phila., 1979-81; sch. psychologist Oak Park-River Forest (Ill.) High Sch., 1981—; pvt. practice family therapy Oak Park, Ill., 1984—; instr. Boston U., 1974-75; clin. asst. prof. and supr. psychologist Hahnemann Med. Coll. and Hosp., Phila., 1978-81; cons. Acorn, Chgo., 1984—. NDEA Title IV fellow, 1969-72. Mem. Am. Psychol. Assn., Nat. Assn. Sch. Psychologists, Ill. Sch. Psychologists Assn. (region 1 Sch. Psychology Practitioner of Yr. 1984), Psychologists for Social Responsibility, LWV, NOW. Avocations: aerobics, tennis, reading, sewing. Home: 539 N Ridgeland Ave Oak Park IL 60302 Office: Oak Park-River Forest High Sch 201 N Scoville Ave Oak Park IL 60302

JOHNSTON, JOHN WAYNE, educational administrator; b. McAlester, Okla., Oct. 8, 1943; s. Cecil Wayne and Hazel Elena (Robinson) J.; m. Lynda Faith Gee, Feb. 4, 1971 (div.); 1 son, Ian Sean. Student Graceland Coll., 1961-62, William Jewell Coll., 1962-63; B.S. in Journalism, Kans. U., 1964; M.A. in Edn. and Sociology, U. Mo.-Kansas City, 1966; M.A. in Polit. Sci. and Econs., Goddard Coll., 1972; Ph.D. (hon.), Calif. Western U., 1975; Ph.D. in Social Psychology, Internat. U., 1975. Instr. Central Mo. State U., Independence, 1969-72; founder, chancellor The Internat. U., Independence, 1973—; Editor: Internat. U. Press, 1973—. Bd. dirs. Good Govt. League, Independence, Com. for County Progress, Jackson County, Mo. Republican. Mem. Reorganized Church of Jesus Christ of Latter Day Saints (ordained minister). Lodge: Lions (Independence). Author: Divided for Plunder, 1984; Turmoil in the North, 1984, Crisis in Northern Ireland, 1985, The University of the Future, 1985.

JOHNSTON, KURT MALCOLM, packaging company executive; b. Peoria, Ill., Jan. 25, 1954; s. Harold M. Johnston and Anne Marie (Grantham) J.; m. Susan Tolman Basler , Dec. 1, 1984. BS, Mass. Coll. Pharmacy, 1976; MBA, Fordham U., 1980. Registered pharmacist, Maine. Head dept. tablets Lederle Labs., Pearl River, N.Y., 1977-80; fed. sales mgr. Lederle Labs., Washington, 1980-82; hosp. sales mgr. Lederle Labs., Denver, 1982-84; mgr. new products Lederle Labs., Wayne, N.J., 1984-86; pres. Johnston Enterprises, Lake Forest, Ill., 1986-87, Jerome Labs., Des Plaines, Ill., 1987—. Mem. The Propletary Assn., Soc. Cosmetic Chemists, Cosmetics, Toiletries and Frangrances Assn., U.S. Bobsledding Fedn. Republican. Avocations: bobsledding, Nordic & Alpine Skiing, ballooning. Home: 520 E Linden Ave Lake Forest IL 60045 Office: Jerome Labs Inc 95 E Bradrock Dr Des Plaines IL 60018

JOHNSTON, LEE ANN, accountant; b. Canton, Ohio, Nov. 2, 1960; d. Richard Clyde Johnston and Joyce Ann (Burns) Loveman. BA, Mount Union Coll., 1983. CPA, Ohio. Sr. tax cons. Ernst & Whinney, Canton, 1983—. Treas. Siffrin Residential Assn., Canton, 1985—; treas. Stark County Women's Network, Canton, 1986, 87. Mem. Am. Inst. CPA's, Ohio Soc. CPA's. Republican.

JOHNSTON, PETER DEUSTER, architect; b. Burlington, Wis., Apr. 18, 1950; s. Donald Norbeck and Dorothy (von Paumgartten) J.; m. Karolyn Bohnak, May 16, 1981; children: Daniel Q., Stephen J. BArch, U. Wis., Milw., 1976, MArch, 1980. Project architect Heike Design Assocs., Inc., Brookfield, Wis., 1978-84, v.p., 1984—. Author: (book) Jefferson Park Elementary School, 1979. Served with U.S. Army, 1970-71. Roman Catholic. Home: 1338 Breezeland Dr Oconomowoc WI 53066 Office: Heike Design Assocs Inc 13255 W Bluemound Rd Brookfield WI 53005

JOHNSTON, ROBERT BEATTY, financial insurance company executive; b. Moberly, Mo., July 17, 1934; s. Dell Henry and Helen Frances (Beatty) J.; m. Frances J. Berchtold, Dec. 29, 1965; children: Roberta K., James Daniel. Student, Wentworth Mil. Acad. Jr. Coll., U. Kans.; BA, U. Mo. Dist. mgr. Universal C.I.T. Credit Corp., Springfield, Ill., 1956-64; mgr. Midland Guardian Investment, Peoria, Ill., 1965; owner Jon's Ltd., Peoria, 1965-68; mgr. Ill. and Mo. Integon Corp., Winston-Salem, N.C., 1968-72; pres. Am. Fin. Security Corp., Peoria Heights, Ill., 1972—; owner Mgmt. and Research Co. Past pres. Peoria Ch. Golf League; bd. dirs. Greater Peoria Sports Hall of Fame, 1981—. Mem. Ill. Fin. Services Assn. (assoc.), Ill. Ind. Fin. Assn. (assoc.), Old Timers Baseball Assn. (adv. bd. 1986—, former bd. dirs.). Club: Ill. Valley Yacht (Peoria). Lodges: Optimists (sec., treas. Peoria chpt. 1986—), Masons, Shriners. Home: 3528 N Missouri Peoria IL 61603 Office: Am Fin Security Corp 827 E War Memorial Dr Peoria Heights IL 61614

JOHNSTON, ROBERT LEE, banker; b. Logansport, Ind., Dec. 18, 1950; s. Cecil E. and Anna M. (Pfisterer) J.; m. Susan M. Kozusko, Mar. 26, 1972; children—Stefanie Rae, Lindsay Brie. B.S., Ind. State U., 1972. Math. tchr. Kankakee Valley Sch. Corp., Wheatfield, Ind., 1972-73; sales and service rep. Met. Life Ins. Co., Lafayette, Ind., 1973-74; personnel mgr. Wagner Industries, Inc., Plymouth, Ind., 1974-78; human resourses mgr. Universal Cooperatives, Inc., Goshen, Ind., 1978-84; personnel mgr. Am. Nat. Bank, Vincennes, Ind., 1984—; instr. Vincennes U., 1984—. Mem. Emergency Med. System, Goshen, 1983, 84, 85; mem. Vincennes U. Indsl. Adv. Com., 1984—. Mem. Goshen C. of C., Vincennes C. of C., Am. Soc. Personnel Adminstrs., Vincennes Personnel Assn., Valley Mgmt. Assn. Lodge: Elks. Avocations: reading, bicycling, camping, swimming. Home: 522 N 3rd St Vincennes IN 47591-1410

JOHNSTON, ROBERT LEE, dentist; b. Hannibal, Mo., Apr. 10, 1947; s. William Lyles and Rosemary (Morrison) J.; m. Carolyn Joan Bovas, Aug. 15, 1973; Katherine Lea Johnston, Charles William. BA, Drury Coll., 1969; DDS, U. Mo., 1973. Gen. practice dentistry Jefferson City, Mo., 1973—. Fellow Acad. Gen. Dentistry; mem. ADA, Cen. Dist. Dental Soc. (pres.). Baptist. Lodge: Mason. Avocations: woodworking, hunting, fishing. Home: 1916 Greenberry Jefferson City MO 65101 Office: 1111 Madison Jefferson City MO 65101

JOHNSTON, STEPHEN PAUL, electronics executive; b. Detroit Lakes, Minn., Feb. 26, 1951; s. Paul Duane and Audrey Marie (Sauve) J.; m. Lynn Kay Anderson, June 23, 1973 (dec. Oct. 1981). Student, N.D. State U., 1969-70; A in Electronic Engring., Northwestern Electronics Inst., Mpls., 1973. Product devel. C&M Industries, Detroit Lakes, 1973-75; pres. S.J. Electro Systems, Inc., Detroit Lakes, 1975—; adv. bd. small bus. mgmt. Area Vocat. Tech. Inst., Detroit Lakes, Minn., 1981-84. Holder 6 patents. Named fastest growing pvt. co. INC mag. 500 list, 1984, 85, 86, Boss of Yr. Detroit Lakes Jaycees, 1981. Mem. Submersible Wastewater Pump Assn., Sump and Sewage Pump Mfrs. Assn., Pelican River Navigation Restoration Assn. (sec.-treas. 1986—). Roman Catholic. Lodge: Elks. Avocations: building and flying experimental aircraft, boating, motorcycling, travel.

JOHNSTON, W. E., JR., salt mining company executive. Pres. Can. Salt Co., Ltd., Mississauga, Ont. Office: Can Salt Co Ltd, 4 Robert Speck Pkwy, Mississauga, ON Canada L4Z 1S1 *

JOHNSTON, WILLIAM LESLIE, osteopathic physician, educator; b. Sault Ste. Marie, Ont., Can., Feb. 17, 1921; s. Roy Leslie and Eva Pearl (Osborn) J.; m. Margaret MacFarlane, Jan. 1945; children—Merilyn, Gail; m. Anne McCabe, Mar. 18, 1979. D.O., Chgo. Coll. Osteo. Medicine, 1943. Intern, Mass. Osteo. Hosp., Boston, 1944; pvt. practice medicine, Manchester, N.H., 1945-73; mem. faculty Mich. State U. Coll. Osteo. Medicine, East Lansing, 1973—, prof. biomechanics, 1973-81, prof. dept. family medicine, 1981—; cons. staff Lansing Gen. Hosp.; courtesy staff dept. family practice Ingham Med. Hosp. Contbr. numerous articles to profl. publs. Mem. Am. Acad. Osteopathy (cert.; chmn. Conclave of Fellows 1972-74, 1983-84), Am. Osteo. Assn., Mich. Assn. Osteo. Physicians and Surgeons, N.H. Osteo. Assn. (pres.). Home: 830 N Harrison Rd East Lansing MI 48823 Office: Mich State U Coll Osteo Medicine B 216 W Fee East Lansing MI 48824

JOHNSTONE, JOHN KEITH, programmer, analyst; b. Cudahy, Wis., July 30, 1940; s. Lance Van Auken and Angeline Mary (Delopst) J.; m. Judith Ann Stramowski, Sept. 23, 1967; children: Lance Philip, Brett Andrew. AAS, Milw. Area Tech. Coll., 1972, AS in Mech. Tech., 1979, AA in Bus. Adminstrn., 1979. Programmer Caterpillar Tractor Co., Milw., 1964-70, sr. programmer, 1970-75, programmer, analyst, 1975-85; programmer, analyst small power div. RTE Corp., Waukesha, Wis., 1985—. Mem. nat. adv. bd. Am. Security Council, Boston, Va., 1977—; corr. sec. Cudahy Allied Vets. Council, 1982—, Vet. of Yr., 1984. Served with USN, 1958-63. Mem. VFW (post comdr. Dept. Wis., 1982-84, judge adv. Cudahy chpt., 1984—, all-state VFW post comdr 1984), Ducks Unlimited (donor). Presbyterian. Home: 6152 S Illinois Ave Cudahy WI 53110 Office: RTE Corp Small Power Div 1319 E Lincoln Ave Waukesha WI 53186-5317

JOHNSTONE, KAREN SUE, physical therapist; b. Portsmouth, Ohio, Feb. 13, 1938; d. Kermit Thomas and Vera Adaline J. AB, Albion Coll., 1960; MS, DePaul U., 1984. Cert. physical therapist. Staff physical therapist Rehab. Inst., Detroit, 1961-62, supr. physical therapy, 1963-71; dir. Beaumont Hosp., Royal Oak, Mich., 1971—; tech. adv. Detroit Health Service, 1985-86; cons. Vol. Hosp. Am., Tampa, 1985; physical therapist U.S. Wheelchair Team, N.Y.C., 1968-84. Contbr. articles to profl. jours. Mem. Parks and Recreation Commn., Beverly Hills, 1986—. Mem. Am. Physical Therapy Assn., Am. Congress Physical Medicine, Am. Coll. Sports Medicine, Nat. Wheelchair Athletic Assn. Club: Motor City Wheelchairs. Office: William Beaumont Hosp 3601 W Thirteen Mile Royal Oak MI 48072

JOHNSTONE, LESLEY MARIAN, nurse; b. Christchurch, N.Z., May 22, 1946; came to U.S., 1976; d. James Alan and Helen Joan Plessy (Haywood) Jamieson; m. George Henry Johnstone, May 21, 1976; stepchildren: Mary Sue, Sally, Georgia, Robert, Roy. RN diploma, Christchurch (New Zealand) Hosp. Sch. Nursing, 1967; BS in Allied Health Scis., Coll. St. Francis, Ill., 1985. Staff nurse Christchurch Hosp. System, 1971-73, Albert Schweitzer Hosp., Pucallpa, Peru, 1973, Kensington Agy., London, 1973-74, Bindura (Rhodesia) Hosp., 1976, Buffalo (Minn.) Hosp., 1979—; home health nurse More Care Inc., Buffalo, 1984—. Vol. Meals on Wheels, Buffalo, 1979-84; vol. nurse sr. citizens, Rockford, Minn., 1980—; vol. Buffalo area Reps., 1984; sec. Wright County Task Force for Battered Women, 1982-84; publicity chair, 1984-86. Mem. Wright County Horticulture Assn. Republican. Avocations: gardening, reading, knitting, letter-writing, travel. Office: moreCare Inc 1700 Hwy 25 N Buffalo MN 55313

JOINER, GAYLE ANN, nurse; b. Warren, Ohio; d. James Allen Lipscomb and Delores Pauline (Vauple) Swindler; m. Philip Douglas Joiner, Aug. 2, 1980. B.S.N., Kent State U., 1980, M.S.N., 1985. Staff nurse Robinson Meml. Hosp., Ravenna, Ohio, 1980-83, charge nurse spl. care unit, 1983-85, asst. head nurse ICU, 1985-86, clin. mgr. coronary care unit, 1986—. Mem. Am. Assn. Critical Care Nurses, N.Am. Nursing Diagnosis Assn., Sigma Theta Tau. Republican.

JOIST, JOHANN HEINRICH, hematologist, medical researcher, educator; b. Bergisch, Gladbach, West Germany, Jan. 9, 1935; came to U.S., 1972; s. Heinrich and Katharina (Hasbach) J.; m. Nancy Lee Maxeiner, July 25, 1966; children: Bettina Lynn, Catherine Anne, Heidi Elaine. MD, U. Cologne, West Germany, 1962; PhD, McMaster U., Hamilton, Ont., Can., 1977. Lic. physician and surgeon, Mo. Sr. research fellow McMaster U., 1970-72; asst. prof. medicine Washington U., St. Louis, 1972-78; assoc. prof. medicine/pathology St. Louis U., 1978-82, prof. medicine, pathology, 1982—; dir. hemostasis lab. Barnes Hosp., St. Louis, 1972-78; dir. div. hematology-oncology St. Louis U. Med. Ctr., 1978—; mem. hemophilia adv. com. Mo. Div. Health; mem. NIH study sects. and Spl. Research Rev. Com., 1978-87; chmn. med. adv. com. Mo./Ill. region ARC, Mo./Ill. region ARC Blood Services, 1981-84; assembly del. Am. Heart Assn. Council Thrombosis, Dallas, 1982; chmn. Mo. affiliate Am. Heart Assn., mem. research and research peer rev. com., 1984-85; mem. med. sci. adv. com. Nat. Hemophilia Found., 1987; mem. study sects. and spl. research rev. com., 1978-87. Editor: Venous and Arterial Thrombosis, 1979. NIH research fellow, 1964-65, Ont. Heart Assn. research fellow, 1970-72; NIH grantee, 1982. Fellow ACP; mem. Am. Heart Assn., Am. Soc. Hematology, Cen. Soc. Clin. Research, Am. Assn. Pathologists, St. Louis Soc. Internal Medicine. Home: 716 S Central Ave Clayton MO 63105 Office: St Louis U Med Ctr Div Hematology-Oncology 1402 Grand Blvd Saint Louis MO 63104

JOKAY, ALEX, insurance company executive; b. Komarom, Czechoslovakia, Nov. 8, 1927; came to U.S., 1949; s. Nicholas and Elizabeth (Szoboszlay) J.; m. Sharon L. Davis, Sept. 11, 1954; children: Alexander M., Nicholas B. BA, Glenville State Coll., 1953; LLB, Ind. U., 1955. Atty. Lincoln Nat. Life Ins., Ft. Wayne, Ind., 1958-62, asst. gen. counsel, 1962-68, 2d v.p., 1968-72, v.p., 1972-80; exec. v.p. Lincoln Nat. Investment Mgmt. Co., Ft. Wayne, 1980—. Bd. dirs., v.p. Ft. Wayne Philharmon. Soc., 1978-81; bd. dirs. St. Joseph's Hosp., 1977—, Ft. Wayne Fine Arts Found., 1981—. Home: 15622 Canyon Ridge Rd Leo IN 46801 Office: Lincoln Nat Life Ins Co 1300 S Clinton Box 1110 Fort Wayne IN 46801

JOKLIK, GÜNTHER FRANZ, mining company executive; b. Vienna, Austria, May 30, 1928; came to U.S., 1953; s. Karl Friedrich and Helene (Giessl) J.; m. Pamela Mary Fenton, Dec. 22, 1962; children: Carl Duncan, Katherine Pamela, Paul Richard. B.Sc. with 1st class honors, U. Sydney, Australia, 1949, Ph.D., 1953. Exploration geologist Kennecott Corp., N.Y.C., 1954-62, v.p., 1974-79; pres. Kennecott Corp., Salt Lake City, 1980—; exploration mgr. Australia div. AMAX, Inc., Greenwich, Conn., 1963-71, v.p., 1972-73; sr. v.p. metals and mining Standard Oil Co. (parent), Cleve., 1982—; dir. First Security Corp., Salt Lake City; mem. Nat. Strategic Materials Adv. Com., 1984—. Contbr. articles to profl. jours. Fulbright scholar Columbia U., 1953-54. Mem. Internat. Copper Research Assn. (bd. dirs. 1982—), Copper Devel. Assn. (chmn. 1985-87), AIME, Australasian Inst. Mining and Metallurgy, Am. Mining Congress (bd. dirs. 1985—). Clubs: Alta (Salt Lake City); Tokeneke (Darien, Conn.). Avocations: skiing, tennis. Office: Kennecott Corp 10 E South Temple Salt Lake City UT 84133 *

JOLAS, MARY JO, social worker; b. Belleville, Ill., Oct. 19, 1945; d. Myron Fredrick and Irene Eunice (Baumann) Schmitt; m. Ernst Rainer Jolas, Mar. 25, 1967; children: Jennifer Luise, Darrin Rainer. BA, Elmhurst (Ill.) Coll., 1967; MSW, U. Ill., Chgo., 1984. Cert. social worker, Ill. Social worker Ill. Dept. Mental Health, Tinley Park, Ill., 1967-71, Ill. Dept. Children and Family Services, Joliet, Ill., 1977-84; sch. social worker spl. edn. Lincoln Way Area, Frankfort, Ill., 1984—. Deacon St. Peters United Ch. of Christ, Frankfort, 1985-86. Mem. Acad. Cert. Social Workers, Nat. Assn. Social Workers, Ill. Assn. Sch. Social Workers. Avocations: camping, hiking, walking, biking, reading. Office: Lincoln Way Area Spl Edn 110 Hickory St Frankfort IL 60423-1498

JOLIAT, JAY FREDERICK, securities broker, investment advisor, marketing consultant; b. Detroit, Aug. 8, 1956; s. John Francis and Rosemary Jane (La Joie) J.; m. Mary Cathryn Carr, Jan. 11, 1980; children: Jacqueline Nicole, Joseph Michael. BS in Fin., BS in Acctg., Oakland U., 1982. Pres., owner Joliat Custom Builders, Royal Oaks, Mich., 1977-82; account exec. E.F. Hutton & Co., Southfield, Mich., 1982-85; 1st v.p. Dean Witter Reynolds, Inc., Southfield, 1985—; co-chmn.-treas. Cornerstone Advantage Group, Inc., Columbus, Ohio, 1986—. Contbr. articles to profl. jour. Mem. Chartered Fin. Analysts Assn. (cert. 1986). Republican. Roman Catholic. Club: Econ. of Detroit. Avocations: bldg., securities analysis. Home: 16910 Wetherby Birmingham MI 48009 Office: Dean Witter Reynolds Inc 4000 Town Ctr #1900 Southfield MI 48075

JOLIET, LEO JOSEPH, lawyer, real estate title specialist; b. Cleve., June 24, 1925; s. Louis C. and Margaret Mary (Kennedy) J. AB, John Carroll U., 1946; LLB, Western Res. U., 1948. Escrow, title officer Lawyers Title Ins. Corp., Cleve., 1947-84; sr. v.p., chief title officer Midland Title Security, Inc., Cleve., 1984—; lectr. on real estate titles throughout Ohio. Author: (with others) Principles of Ohio Real Estate Titles, 1984. Contbr. articles to legal jours. Recipient various awards Ohio Legal Ctr., Ohio Land Title Assn. Mem. ABA, Ohio State Bar Assn., Cleve. Bar Assn. (various awards), Democrat. Roman Catholic. Club: Mid Day (Cleve.). Avocations: classical music; modern languages, stamp and coin collecting. Home: 1545 Parkwood Rd Lakewood OH 44107 Office: 113 St Clair Ave NE Cleveland OH 44114

JOLLY, DANIEL EHS, dentist; b. St. Louis, Aug. 25, 1952; s. Melvin Joseph and Betty Ehs (Koehler) J.; m. Paula Kay Haas, Oct. 13, 1972; 1 child, Farrell Elisabeth Ehs. BA in Biology and Chemistry, U. Mo., Kansas

City, 1974, DDS, 1977. Resident VA Med. Ctr., Leavenworth, Kans., 1977-78; gen. practice dentistry sect. Newcastle, Wyo., 1978-79; asst. prof. U. Mo., Kansas City, 1979-87; chief restorative dentistry Truman Med. Ctr., Kansas City, 1979-87; dir. dental oncology Trinity Luth. Hosp., 1982-87; clin. assoc. prof., dir. gen. practice residency program Ohio State U. Coll. Dentistry, Columbus, 1987—; bd. dirs. Rinehart Found., U. Mo. Dental Sch., Kansas City, 1985—; cons. Lee's Summit (Mo.) Care Ctr., 1984-87, Longview Nursing Ctr., Grandview, Mo. 1986-87. Author: (manual) Hospital Dental Hygiene, 1984, Hospital Dentistry, 1985; (booklet) Nursing Home Dentistry, 1986, Dental Oncology, 1986. Mem. regional council Easter Seal Soc., Kansas City, 1985—; mem. profl. adv. council Nat. Easter Seal Soc., 1986—. Fellow Acad. Dentistry Internat., Am. Soc. Dentistry for Children, Am. Assn. Hosp. Dentists (com. residency edn.), Acad. Gen. Dentistry (spokesperson on dentistry for handicapped); mem. Internat. Assn. Dentistry for Handicapped., ADA (alternate del. 1985-86), Am. Soc. Geriatric Dentistry, Mo. Dental Assn., (chmn. spl. care dentistry com. 1983-87, del. 1984-87), Greater Kansas City Dental Soc. (chmn. spl patient com., mem. constn. and by-laws com., pub. relations com.), Acad. Dentistry for the Handicapped (bd. dirs. 1984—, mem. research com.), SAR, Omicron Kappa Upsilon. Club: Magna Charta Barons. Avocations: photography, skiing, scuba diving, swimming, sailing. Home: 3429 Riverside Green Dublin OH 43017 Office: Ohio State U Coll Dentistry 305 W 12th Ave Columbus OH 43210

JOLOSKY, RICHARD ALLEN, retail executive; b. Fargo, N.D., Sept. 5, 1934; s. Max Baer and Dora Bessie (Persellin) J.; m. Gaye Louise Lewenshon, July 11, 1954; children: Robert Morris, Nancy Ellen, Shari Beth. BBA, Marquette U., 1960. Buyer Gimbels, Milw., 1960-65; v.p. Meier & Frank, Portland, Oreg., 1965-78, Wal-Mart, Bentonville, Ark., 1978-81; pres. Volume Shoe Co., Topeka, 1981—. Adv. bd. bus. sch. Marquette U., Milw., 1986—; bd. dirs. Portland Jewish Community Ctr., 1972-76, United Way, Topeka, 1986—, Sheltered Living Facility, Topeka, 1986—, Two Ten Shoe Charity, 1986—. Served as cpl. USMC, 1953-56. Avocation: raquetball. Home: 2120 Brooklyn Topeka KS 66611 Office: Volume Shoe Corp 3231 E 6th St Topeka KS 66607

JOLY, CHARLES LEROY, psychology educator; b. Ennis, Tex., Apr. 11, 1924; s. Ambrose V. and Merah Mar (Moyé) J.; children: Elizabeth, John, Matthew, Jennifer, Steven, Alicia Jean Simone, Ann, Meghan. BA, St. Mary's, San Antonio, 1953; MA, Loyola U., Chgo., 1957. Psychologist Cath. Charities, Chgo., 1955-64, Arlington Heights (Ill.) PS, 1964-67, North Surburban Spl. Edn. Dist., Glenview, Ill., 1967—; assoc. prof. psychology Harper Coll., Palatine, Ill., 1970—; bd. dirs. Elk Grove (Ill.) Township Day Care, NW Mental Health Clinic, Arlington Heights, Headstart, Wheeling, Ill., Villa Desiderata, McHenry, Ill. Served with U.S. Mcht. Marine, 1942-46. Home: 34444 Stanley Rd Ingleside IL 60041 Office: Harper Coll Palatine IL 60067

JOMES, MELVIN JENNINGS, electronics executive, consultant; b. Springfield, Ill., Oct. 11, 1931; s. Amos Alferd and Gladys Marie (Cook) J.; m. Anna Belle Stalling, Nov. 4, 1951; children: Melvin Richard, Janice Reneé, Carolyn Jane. BS in Edn. and Bus. with honors, Eastern Ill. U., 1957; MBA in Fin., So. Ill. U., 1977. Computer sales person IBM, 1957-65; coordinator Ill. area John Birch Soc., 1965-68; sales rep. Memorex Corp., St. Louis, 1970-71; br. mgr. Sanders Data Systems, St. Louis, 1972-73; regional mgr. Dearborn Computer Leasing Corp., Park Ridge, Ill., 1973-79; br. mgr. Documation, Inc., St. Louis, 1980-81; sales rep. Storage Tech. Corp., St. Louis, 1981-84; owner, operator Mel-Belle Enterprises, Collinsville, Ill., 1984—. Nat. chmn. Nat. Com. to Repeal 55 MPH, Collinsville, 1979—; lt. gov. candidate Ill. Taxpayers Party , 1982; township chmn. Collinsville Rep. Party, 1986—. Served with USNG, 1952-53, Korea. Mem. VFW (sr. vice comdr. 1972-73), Am. Legion. Republican. Lodges: Masons, Shriners, Elks. Avocations: bowling, deer hunting, boating, monetary reform. Home: 310 Emelie St Collinsville IL 62234 Office: Mel-Belle Enterprises Box 22 Collinsville IL 62234

JONAS, GORDON MARK, manufacturing company executive; b. Bridgeport, Conn., Mar. 29, 1959; s. Gordon Quincy and Norma Elsa (Dittner) J.; m. Cynthia Joy Ellsworth, May 31, 1982. BSME, Lehigh U., 1981. Licensed profl. engr., Minn. Process engr. Sperry Corp., St. Paul, Minn., 1985—. Served to capt. U.S. Army, 1981-85. Republican. Jewish. Avocations: tennis, target shooting, fitness, continuing edn. Home: 604 Maple Park Dr Mendota Heights MN 55118 Office: Sperry Corp PO Box 64942 Roseville MN 55164

JONES, A. CLIFFORD, state senator; b. St. Louis, Feb. 13, 1921; s. Wilbur B. and Irene (Clifford) J.; A.B., Princeton U., 1942; J.D., Washington U., St. Louis, 1948; children—A. Clifford, Irene, Wesley, Janet; m. 2d, Nan Thornton, Nov. 1974. City clk. Ladue (Mo.), 1948-50; mem. Mo. Ho. of Reps., Jefferson City, 1950-58, minority floor leader, 1956-58; mem. Mo. Senate, Jefferson City, 1964—, minority floor leader, 1968-76; pres. Mo. Polaris Corp., Aluminum Truck Bodies, Inc.; sec.-treas. Hewitt-Lucas Body Co., Inc. Pres. Mo. Assn. for Social Welfare, 1953-54; trustee St. Louis Country Day Sch., 1948-50. Served with USNR, 1942-46; ETO, PTO. Recipient award Jaycees of St. Louis, 1952, Globe Democrat award for pub. service, 1958, 65, 69, 76. Mem. Mo., St. Louis (Bicentennial award) bar assns., Am. Legion, John Marshall Club. Republican. Congregationalist. Lodge: Masons (32 deg.). Home: 7 Willow Hill Saint Louis MO 63124 Office: State Capitol Bldg Jefferson City MO 65101

JONES, ABBOTT C., advertising agency executive; b. Lexington, Ky., Aug. 14, 1934; s. John Catron and Lois (Sauters) J.; m. Carol Donahue, June 29, 1957; children: Cynthia, Alison, Hilary. B.A., Principia Coll., 1956; M.B.A., Harvard U., 1958. Salesman Carnation Co., 1959-60; account exec. Benton & Bowles, N.Y.C., 1960-63; with Ogilvy & Mather, N.Y.C., 1963-77; sr. v.p., dir. Ogilvy & Mather, 1973-77; sr. v.p., gen. mgr. Foote, Cone & Belding, N.Y.C., 1977-82; pres. Foote, Cone & Belding, Associated Communications Cos., 1982-86; pres., chief operating officer Foote, Cone, Belding Communications, Inc., 1986—. Served with U.S. Army, 1958-59. Clubs: University, Sky, Harvard Bus. Sch. of Greater N.Y.; Belle Haven (Greenwich, Conn.). Office: 101 Park Ave New York NY 10178 also: Foote Cone & Belding Communications Inc 101 E Erie St Chicago IL 60611

JONES, ANABEL RATCLIFF, anesthesiologist; b. Lafayette, Ind., Sept. 6, 1933; d. Frank William and Mary Rovene (Holt) Ratcliff; A.B., Ind. U., 1955, M.D., 1959; m. Wiley A. Jones, Oct. 4, 1975; 1 son by previous marriage, Warren Lee. Intern, Meth. Hosp., Indpls., 1959-60; resident anesthesiology Ind. U. Med. Center, Indpls., 1960-62; staff anesthesiologist VA Hosp., Indpls., 1962-63; practice medicine, specializing in anesthesiology, Lafayette, 1963—; mem. staff St. Elizabeth Hosp., Home Hosp., Purdue U. Hosp.; instr. Ind. U. Med. Center, Indpls., 1962—. Piano accompanist civic chorus, also combined civic vocal groups; mem. governing bd. Lafayette Symphony Orch., 1971—. Diplomate Am. Bd. Anesthesiology. Mem. Am. Soc. Anesthesiologists, Internat. Anesthesia Research Soc., Ind. Med. Assn., Ind. Soc. Anesthesiologists, AMA, DAR (gen. Lafayette chpt.), Kappa Kappa Kappa, Delta Delta Delta. Methodist. Home: 3301 Cedar Ln Lafayette IN 47905 Office: Life Bldg Lafayette IN 47901

JONES, B. J., attorney; b. Iowa City, Iowa, Sept. 28, 1920; s. M.P. and M.E. Jones; B.S. in Bus. Adminstrn. and Labor Law, State U. Iowa, 1942; M.A., U. Miami, 1946; Ph.D., UCLA, 1948, J.D., 1952; m. Estelle Perry, June 3, 1950 (dec. 1960). Founder, pres., chmn. bd. Exec. Enterprises and Consultants Inc., Miami Beach, Fla., 1953-78; dir. indsl. relations and labor law, v.p. Internat. Harvester, 1946-53; founder, developer, pres., chmn. bd. Paradise Haven Villa, La Jolla, Calif., 1978-84, also Aloha Paradise Haven, Honolulu; founder KCID-TV/AM-FM, Iowa City; personnel dir., asst. city mgr., exec. dir. City of Berkeley (Calif.), 1945-48. Served to maj. USAF, 1942-45. Decorated Purple Heart with 6 clusters, Silver Star, Congressional Medal of Honor with 3 clusters. Mem. Personnel and Indsl. Relations Execs. Assn. (past pres.), Indsl. Relations and Labor Law Execs. Club (Los Angeles, past pres.), Phi Beta Kappa, Phi Delta Theta (past pres.). Clubs: Rotary (past pres.), Kiwanis (past pres.), U. Iowa Athletic, K.C. (4th deg., grand knight), Lions. Author numerous books in field. Office: 715 N Van Buren St Suite 1A Iowa City IA 52240

JONES, BARBARA, pediatrics educator; b. Salt Lake City, Feb. 8, 1828; d. George Merrell and Helen (Skeen) J. AB, Stanford U., 1949; MD, U. Utah, 1952. Diplomate Am. Bd. Pediatrics; ordained priest Episcopal Ch. Instr. pediatrics Washington U., St. Louis, 1955-57, asst. prof., 1958-61; asst. prof. W.Va. U. Sch. Medicine, Morgantown, 1961-63, assoc. prof., 1963-68, prof. pediatrics, 1968-84, from asst. chmn. to assoc. chmn. pediatrics, 1970-82; from asst. chmn. to assoc. chmn. pediatrics West Va. U., 1982-83; chmn. pediatrics U. Kans., Kansas City, 1984—; cons. Nat. Cancer Inst., 1971-73, 75-78, 81-84. Contbr. articles to profl. jours. Vis. scholar Kennedy Inst. Ctr. Bioethics, 1980-81. Mem. Am. Acad. Pediatrics (alt. dist. chmn. dist. III), Am. Pediatric Soc., Soc. Pediatric Research, Am. Soc. Clin. Oncology, An. Soc. Hematology. Episcopalian. Home: 12420 W 85th Terr Lenaxa KS 66215 Office: U Kans Med Sch Dept Pediatrics Rainbow Blvd at 39th Kansas City KS 66103

JONES, BERNARD IRVIN, architectural company executive; b. Estherville, Iowa, Mar. 19, 1933; s. Lawrence Laverne and Beatrice Rebecca (French) J.; m. Jane Ellen Hutchinson, Jan. 19, 1958; children—Tamera Jane, Leslie Anne. A.A., Estherville Jr. Coll., 1953; B.S., Iowa State U., 1957. Registered architect; registered profl. engr.; NCARB cert. Constrn. engr. W.A. Klinger, Inc., Sioux City, Iowa, 1957-58, 60-64; architect, structural engr. James M. Duffy, Sioux City, 1964-68; v.p. DeWild Grant Reckert, Sioux City, 1968-75; pres. FEH Assocs. Inc., Sioux City, 1975-84; owner, prin. Garrison-Jones Architects Inc., Carbondale, Ill., 1984—. Mem., pres. Iowa State Bd. Archtl. Examiners, 1979-84 (GSA Value Engring. Cert.); mem. NCARB Profl. Exam. Com., 1980-84; design juror NCARB Profl. Exam., 1984-86. Served to 1st lt. C.E., U.S. Army, 1958-60. Mem. AIA, Ill. Council Architects (bd. dirs. 1987-88), Constrn. Specifications Inst., Profl. Services Mgmt. Assn. Club: Jackson Country. Avocations: golf; tennis; woodworking. Home: 43 Heritage Hills Carbondale IL 62901 Office: Garrison Jones Architects Inc 1118 W Main St Carbondale IL 62901

JONES, BRUCE DEHAVEN, dentist; b. Detroit, Sept. 14, 1928; s. Lyman Lawrence and Ruth Emily (Kreger) J.; m. Joan Robertson, May 11, 1963; children: Jennifer Lynn, Gordon Lyman. Student, Albion (Mich.) Coll., 1946-48; DDS, U. Mich., 1948-52. Gen. practice dentistry Dearborn, Mich., 1955-57, Trenton, Mich., 1957—; chief cons. Wyandotte (Mich.) Gen. Hosp., 1960-85, dental dir., 1980-85, dir. TMJ Joint Clinic, 1983-85; faculty dental sch. U. Detroit, 1970-74. Contbg. author: Dental Anatomy, 1973. Pres. Trenton Civic Music Assn., 1959-60; mem. Mich. Constitutional Conv., Trenton, 1961, Grosse Ile (Mich.) Council for Edn., 1966-67; chmn. Grosse Ile Tree Com., 1976-80; ruling elder Grosse Ile Presbyn. Ch., 1980-83. Served to lt. (j.g.) USN, 1952-55. Recipient Sch. Bell award Grosse Ile Edn. Assn., 1980. Mem. ADA, Mich. Dental Assn., Detroit Dist. Dental Assn., Am. Acad. Cranio-Mandibular Disorders, Detroit Dental Clinic Club (sec., treas., v.p., pres. 1973-74, trustee found. 1974-81, sec., treas., v.p., pres. 1978-81), Am. Equilibration Assn., Francis Vedder Crown and Bridge Soc., Nat. Wildlife Fedn., Psi Omega. Republican. Presbyterian. Lodges: Kiwanis, Rotary. Avocations: sailing, gardening, music, nature. Home: 20940 Thorofare Grosse Ile MI 48138 Office: 2755 Rutledge Trenton MI 48138

JONES, C. W., banker; b. Murdock, Kans.; s. Claude C. and Ina (Silvius) J.; student Kansas City Jr. Coll., 1942-43, Park Coll., 1943-44; m. Helen Johnson, Sept. 15, 1946; children—Marcia A. (Mrs. James R. Steele III), Mark A., Jeffrey L. With Jones Investment Corp., Independence, Mo., 1955—; pres. Chrisman-Sawyer Bank, now First City Bank, Independence, Mo., 1962—; real estate development builder, 1953—. Life mem. hon. bd. Baptist Hosp., Kansas City. Mem. Am. Bankers Assn., Home Builders Assn., Independent Bankers Assn., Mo. Bankers Assn. Baptist. Office: 201 W Lexington St Independence MO 64051

JONES, CHARLOTTE ENGER, counselor, instructor; b. Aberdeen, S.D., Feb. 11, 1925; d. Harry Wilson and Harriet (Birdsall) E.; m. John Paul Jones, Feb. 4, 1949 (div. 1963); children: Shawn, Leah. BA, U. Iowa, 1947, MA, 1965. Tchr. Allison (Iowa) High Sch., 1947-48; ward clk. U. Iowa, Iowa City, 1949-50, library asst., 1950-51; counselor, instr. Southeastern Community Coll., Keokuk, Iowa, 1967—. Sec. Lee County Mental Health Bd., Keokuk, 1976-78; mem. Art Ctr., Keokuk, 1975-86; mem. Iowa Women's Caucus, 1980-84. U. Iowa fellow, 1964-65. Mem. NEA, Iowa Higher Edn. Assn., Iowa Psychol. Assn. Avocations: fiction writing, history, jazz studies, politics. Home: 203 Washington St Apt 1 Keokuk IA 52632 Office: Southeastern Community Coll Messenger Rd Keokuk IA 52632

JONES, CHRISTOPHER ALLEN, financial executive; b. Flint, Mich., Nov. 29, 1954; s. Robert E. and Joanne J. (Jakeway) J.; m. Wendy J. Wendrick, Nov. 1, 1973; children: Jason A., Karie E. AA, Schoolcraft Coll. 1977, BBA, Eastern Mich. U., 1982. Cost analyst Massey Ferguson, Detroit, 1974-82, Cyclops Corp., Detroit, 1982-83; div. controller AAR Brooks Perkins Co., Livonia, Mich., 1983-84; div. controller robotron div. Midland Ross Corp., Southfield, Mich., 1984—. Mem. Nat. Assn. Accts., Inst. Mgmt. Accts. Avocations: camping, fishing, golf. Home: 400 2d St South Lyon MI 48178 Office: Midland Ross Corp Robotron Div PO Box 5090 Southfield MI 48046

JONES, CLAUDELLA ARCHAMBEAULT, medical institute administrator, educational administrator, consultant, researcher; b. Holgate, Ohio, Sept. 25, 1938; d. Claude Edmund and Marjorie Elizabeth (Warren) Archambeault; m. Christopher Mark Jones; children: Christopher Mark, Daniel Sullivan, Anne Elizabeth. Diploma Mercy Sch. Nursing, Toledo, 1959; NCFD, U. Mich., 1972. R.N., Ohio, Mich. Mem. staff surg. ward St. Charles Hosp., Toledo, 1959; asst. to staff physician Casa Marina Hotel and USCG, Key West, Fla., 1959-60; charge nurse labor and delivery Monroe County Gen. Hosp., Key West, 1959-60; charge nurse emergency room Jackson Meml. Hosp., Miami, Fla., 1960; mem. staff operating room Good Samaritan Hosp., Los Angeles, 1961; charge nurse, medicine, surgery, pediatrics Defiance (Ohio) Hosp., 1961-62; staff nurse, rehab. Tampa Gen. Hosp., 1961-62; float and pvt. duty nurse U. Mich., 1962-64, mem. staff neurosurgery, otology, ophthalmology U. Mich. Med. Ctr., Ann Arbor, 1964-66, head nurse burn unit, 1966-68; mem. project staff Evaluation and Demonstration of a Model Burn Unit, Ann Arbor, 1968-71; dir. burn care technician program U. Mich. Burn Ctr., St. Joseph Mercy Hosp., 1969-71; editor publs. dept. Nat. Inst. for Burn Medicine, Ann Arbor, 1971—, ednl. coordinator, 1971-75, dir. edn., 1975—, adminstr. inst., 1982—; project mgr. Nat. Burn Info. Exchange, 1972—, W.K. Kellogg Found. Gt. Lakes Regional Burn Care Demonstration Project, 1975-77; mgr. Burn Info. Triage System, 1976-78; co-chmn. Rehab. of Burned Patient Seminars, 1975—. Mem. Am. Burn Assn. (Disting. Service award 1978), Assn. Critical Care Nurses, Mich. Nurses Assn., Am. Nurses Assn., Internat. Soc. Burn Injuries. Roman Catholic. Author: (with I. Feller) Nursing the Burned Patient, 1973, Procedures for Nursing the Burned Patient, 1975, Teaching Basic Burn Care, 1975; (with Feller and K.E. Richards) Emergent Care of the Burn Victim, 1977; editor, author: A Decade of Progress in Burn Medicine: NIBM, 1980; Reconstruction and Rehabilitation of the Burned Patient (I. Feller, W.C. Grabb), 1980; editor Am. Burn Assn. newsletter, 1970, NBIE Newsletter, 1980; editor: A Remembrance NIBM, 1987; mem. editorial bd. Dimensions of Critical Care Jour., 1981-82, Burns, Jour. of Burn Care and Rehab., 1982. Office: 1500 E Medical Center Dr Ann Arbor MI 48109

JONES, CLINTON B., university official. Chancellor U. Mich., Flint. Office: Univ of Michigan-Flint Office of the Chancellor Flint MI 48502-2186 *

JONES, D. HARRISON, commercial photographer, filmmaker; b. Indpls., May 31, 1956; s. Edward Harrison and Mary Frances (Curry) J. BA, Wabash Coll., 1978; student, Art Ctr. Coll. Design, 1979-80. Owner, mgr. Harrison Jones Photography, Phoenix, 1980-83; photographer, pres. Questudios, Inc., Phoenix, 1983, Chgo., 1983—; instr. Plaza 3 Comml. Photography Sch., Phoenix, 1981-82. Mem. Advt. Photographers Am. Republican. Methodist. Avocations: fishing, scuba diving, sailing, boating. Office: Questudios Inc 445 W Erie #209 Chicago IL 60610

JONES, DAVID GREGORY, marketing professional; b. Toledo, Feb. 21, 1949; s. Charles Franklin and Esther Irene (Barrett) J.; m. Joan Marie Mauder, Oct. 21, 1972; children: Michael Allen, Matthew Barrett. Student, U. of Toledo, 1967-69; AA, Columbus Tech. Inst., 1970. Sales rep. Sta. WBCO/WBCQ, Bucyrus, Ohio, 1970-83, sales and mktg. mgr., 1983—. Named one of Outstanding Young Men of Am., U.S. Jaycees, 1983, 84, 85. Mem. Uptowne Galion Retail Merchants Assn. (v.p. promotions, bd. dirs. 1975—), Jaycees (Jaycee of Yr. 1982-83, Disting. Service award 1980-81, U.S. Jaycee Ambassador 1986), Bucyrus Area Jaycees (pres. 1984-85, chmn. bd. 1985-86). Republican. Avocations: sports, spending time with family. Home: 605 Ridge Ave Bucyrus OH 44820

JONES, DAVID R., accountant; b. Champaign, Ill., Sept. 10, 1958; s. Norman Thomas and Nevelyn Jane (Childers) J.; m. Donna Jill Schlosser, June 7, 1980. BS in Acctg., Ill. State U., 1980. CPA, Ill. Staff acct. Champion Fed., Bloomington, Ill., 1980-82; auditor Henning, Strouse, Jordan, Bloomington, 1982-86; tax acct. Diamond Star Motors, Bloomington, 1986-87, acctg. br. mgr., 1987—. Treas. First Bapt. Ch., Bloomington, 1980-82. Mem. Am. Inst. CPA's, Ill. CPA Soc., Nat. Assn. Accts. Republican. Club: Exchange (Bloomington). Avocations: tennis, hunting, camping, motorcycling, woodworking. Home: 4 Downing Circle Bloomington IL 61701 Office: Diamond-Star Motors Corp 100 Diamond Star Pkwy Bloomington IL 61701

JONES, DONALD WEIL, superintendent schools; b. Cin., Mar. 20, 1922; s. Harry Herbert and Lauretta Frances (Weil) J.; m. Betty Louise Beyer, Nov. 1, 1947; 1 dau., Judith Lynn Lackey. B.S. in Edn., U. Cin., 1947, Ed.M., 1957; Cert. supt., Ohio. Sr. corr. in pub. relations Wright Aero. Corp., Cin., 1944; exec. YMCA, Cin. and Flint, Mich., 1946-50; owner ins. agy., Hamilton, Ohio, 1951-60; pub. sch. tchr., prin. S.W. Ohio, 1955-68; supt. schs. Guernsey County, Ohio, 1969—; mem. Ohio Supts. Exec. Com. vice pres. Concert Bd.; chmn. bd. Community Theater, 1972; pres. Jr. Achievement, 1972-73; div. chmn. County 175th Anniversary, 1973; pres. Citizen's Scholarship Found., 1976-78. Served with USMCR, 1942-44. Mem. East Central Ohio Schoolmasters (pres. 1971-72), Northeastern Ohio County Sch. Supts. (pres. 1975-76), Am. Assn. Sch. Adminstrs., Buckeye Assn. Sch. Adminstrs., Phi Delta Kappa (pres. elect), South Eastern Ohio, Kentucky, W.Va. Counci for Adminstrv. Leadership (v.p., bd. dirs.), Job Service Employer Com. (v. chmn.). Republican. Methodist (lay leader, chairperson bd. adminstrn.). Clubs: Cambridge Rotary (bd. dirs.), U. Cin. Alumni "C". Contbr. music revs. to newspapers, ednl. articles to gen. mags. Home: Barton Manor Cambridge OH 43725 Office: County Administration Bldg Cambridge OH 43725

JONES, EARL, real estate broker, insurance executive; b. Stephens, Ark., Sept. 30, 1934; s. Ceasar and Pearl (Christopher) J.; m. Edna M. Hollis, Dec. 15, 1953 (div. 1971); children: Donna Lynn, Michelle Marie, Carla Ann; m. Annie Lea Wesley, Apr. 18, 1984. Cert., Mich. State U., 1964; BA, Western State U. for Profl. Studies, 1984, MBA, 1984. Lubrication mechanic Grace Motor Sales, Detroit, 1952-53; various positions Chrysler Corp., Detroit, 1953-60; sales mgmt. Great Lakes Life Ins., Detroit, 1960-65; pres. Earl Jones-Commonwealth Agy., Inc., Detroit, 1965—; real estate broker Detroit, 1971—. Recipient Appreciation awards Detroit C. of C., 1972, 73. Mem. Profl. Ins. Agts. Assn., Ind. Ins. Agts. Assn., Detroit Bd. Realtors, Detroit Real Estate Brokers Assn., Met. Detroit Ins. Club. Methodist. Club: Econ. (Detroit). Lodges: Masons, Shriners. Avocations: farming, horse back riding. Office: 18222 James Couzens Hwy Detroit MI 48235

JONES, E(BEN) BRADLEY, retired steel company executive; b. Cleve., Nov. 8, 1927; s. Eben Hoyt and Alfreda Sarah (Bradley) J.; m. Ann Louise Jones, July 24, 1954; children: Susan Robb, Elizabeth Hoyt Fee, Bradley Hoyt, Ann Campbell. B.A., Yale U., 1950. With Republic Steel Corp., Cleve., 1954-84, v.p. mktg., 1971-74, v.p. comml., 1974-76, exec. v.p., 1976-79, pres., 1979-82, chief operating officer, 1980-82, also dir., chmn., chief exec. officer, 1982-84; chmn., chief exec. officer LTV Steel Co., 1984; bd.dirs. TRW Inc., Nat. City Bank Cleve., Nat. City Corp., Cleve.-Cliffs Inc., NACCO Industries, Inc., Consol. Rail Corp.; trustee 1st Union Real Estate Investments. Trustee, v.p., mem. exec. com. Cleve. Clinic Found.; trustee, exec. com. Univ. Sch., Cleve.; mem. distbn. com. Cleve. Found.; trustee Cleve. Mus. Art; mem. Cleve. Com. for Corp. Support of Edn., Council for Fin. Aid to Edn.; chmn. Cleve. Campaign United Way, 1981. Served with U.S. Army, 1950-53. Mem. Delta Kappa Epsilon. Office: 3401 Enterprise Pkwy Beachwood OH 44122

JONES, EDWARD WITKER, bishop; b. Toledo, Mar. 25, 1929; s. Mason Beach and Gertrude (Witker) J.; m. Anne Shelburne, July 13, 1963; children: Martha, Caroline, David. BA, William Coll., 1951; BD, Va. Theol. Sem., 1954, DD, 1978. Ordained to ministry Episcopal Ch., 1954. Rector Christ Ch., Oberlin, Ohio, 1957-68; exec. asst. to bishop and planning officer Diocese of Ohio, Cleve., 1968-71; rector St. James' Ch., Lancaster, Pa., 1971-77; bishop Episc. Diocese of Indpls., 1977—; lectr. homiletics, 1963-67. Bd. dirs. Ohio Chpt. ACLU, 1964-67, Lorain County Child Welfare Dept., Ohio, 1964-68, Lancaster Tomorrow, 1975-77, Indpls. United Way, 1978-83, Indpls. Urban League, 1982—; bd. visitors DePauw U., 1982-85. Mem. Urban Bishops Coalition. Democrat. Home: Episcopal Church 5008 Derby Ln Indianapolis IN 46226 Office: Diocese of Indianapolis 1100 W 42d St Indianapolis IN 46208

JONES, ELLIS JOHN, business educator; b. New Ulm, Minn., Nov. 13, 1931; s. Ellis Pritchard and Edith Mary (Roberts) J.; m. Janet Ruth Hanson, June 20, 1954; children: Karen Elizabeth, David Ellis. BA, Gustavus Adolphus Coll., 1952; MA, U. Minn., 1955; EdD, U. N.D., 1965. Tchr. bus. Plainview (Minn.) Pub. Sch., Minn., 1955-58; prof. bus. Gustavus Adolphus Coll., St. Peter, Minn., 1958—. Author: (with others) Proofreading Precision, 1982; contbr. articles to profl. jours. Served to sgt. U.S. Army, 1952-54. Mem. Minn. Bus Edn., Inc. (pres. 1964-66, Disting. Service award 1983), Nat. Edn. Assn., Minn. Edn. Assn., Minn. Vocat. Assn., Delta Pi Epsilon (nat. exec. dir. 1966—). Republican. Lutheran. Lodge: Masons. Avocations: raquetball, singing Welsh hymns. Home: 628 W Jefferson Saint Peter MN 56082 Office: Gustavus Adolphus Coll Saint Peter MN 56082

JONES, GARY EDMOND, school system administrator; b. Youngstown, Ohio, Nov. 27, 1938; s. Alvey Edmond and Gladys Louise (Probert) J.; m. Marilyn June Merritt, Nov. 21, 1970; children—Elizabeth Victoria, Merritt Edmond. B.S., Youngstown State U., 1962; M.S., Ind. U., 1967; Ed.D., 1972; postgrad. Valparaiso U., Kent State U. Adminstrv. asst. to supt. schs. Geneva (Ohio) Area City Schs., 1962, tchr., 1964-66; tchr. Calumet Jr. High Sch., Gary, Ind., 1966-68; research analyst, coordinator dropout study Lake Ridge Schs., Gary, 1968, dir. Title I ESEA, 1968-71; prin. Stanbery Freshman Sch., Lancaster, Ohio, 1971-76; prin. Donald E. Gavit Jr. Sr. High Sch., Hammond, Ind., 1976-86; asst. supt. curriculum and instr., Hammond Sch. System, 1986—; mem. policy bd. Ind. Congress on Edn. Bd. dirs. Lake Area Blood Service div.; chmn. Lake County chpt. ARC, Ind.; bd. dirs. Hammond Edn. Found; bd. mgrs. Ind. Congress Parents and Tchrs., mem. council Christ Luth. Ch., Hammond, 1980-82. Served with AUS, 1962-64. Recipient Outstanding Prin. award Ind. Congress Parents and Tchrs., 1985. Mem. Ind. Secondary Sch. Adminstrs. (outstanding secondary sch. adminstr. award 1982), fed. relations coordinator Ind., exec. com.), Nat. Assn. Secondary Sch. Prins., Assn. Supervision and Curriculum Devel. (adv. council), Nat. Soc. Study Edn., Nat. Council Social Studies, Ind. U. Alumni Assn., Am. Legion, Sigma Phi. Clubs: Masons, K.T.

JONES, GERALD GLENN, police officer; b. Pontotoc, Miss., Dec. 1, 1954; s. Flemial Thurman and Ruie (Aycock) J.; m. Shelia Jane Self, Jan. 31, 1975; children: Cynthia Jane, Jonathan Scott. Student, Wood Jr. Coll., Mathiston, Miss., 1973-74; AS, Itawamba Jr. Coll., Fulton, Miss., 1978. Policeman Houlka, Miss., 1976-77, 78-80, Verona, Miss., 1977-78; policeman St. Louis County (Mo.) Police Dept., St. Louis, 1980-82, field tng. officer, 1984—; policeman Memphis (Tenn.) Police Dept., 1982-83. Recipient 3 awards of excellence St. Louis County Police Dept.; named Police Officer of Yr. Lafayette Optimists and St. Louis County Police Dept., 1982. Mem. Phi Theta Kappa. Republican. Baptist. Avocations: writing, painting, fishing, family activities. Home: 253 Lewis Rd Eureka MO 63025 Office: St Louis County Police Dept 7900 Forsyth Blvd Clayton MO 63105

JONES, H. W. KASEY, financial planning executive; b. Burlington, Iowa, Feb. 11, 1942; s. Herbert Warren and Mary Kathryn (Gardner) J.; m. Ellen E. Toon, Mar. 11, 1961 (div. Dec. 1969); children: Kari Lynne, Kevin C., Anthony W. Student, Bradley U., 1960-61. Gen. mgr. sales Wickstrom Chevrolet, Roselle, Ill., 1967-80; v.p. Re-Direct Services, Villa Park, Ill., 1980-81, pres., chief exec. officer, 1982—; also chmn. bd. dirs. Re-Direct Services, Villa Park; founding sponsor, mem. speakers' bureau Nat. Ctr. for Fin. Edn., San Francisco, 1984—. Mem. Internat. Assn. Fin. Planners, Inst.

Cert. Fin. Planners, Profl. Ins. Agts. Ill. Avocations: golf, boating. Home: 940 Indian Boundary Westmont IL 60559 Office: Re-Direct Services 721 E Madison St Villa Park IL 60181

JONES, HENRY VINTON, insurance company executive; b. McKeesport, Pa., July 10, 1938; s. Robert Evan and Norma Winifred (Vinton) J.; m. Carol Anne Stelter, July 23, 1966; children—Bruce Vinton, Stephanie Ruth. A.S., Tampa Coll., 1977; B.S. magna cum laude, Jones Coll., 1979; student Ashland Coll., 1982-84. Casualty underwriter Nat. Union Ins. Co., Pitts., 1960-62; spl. agt. CNA, Erie, Pa., 1962-65; multi-line underwriter Ohio Casualty Co., St. Petersburg, Fla., 1965-75; mgr. Aetna Ins. Co., Columbia, S.C., 1975-81; asst. v.p., dir. casualty underwriting Lumbermen's Mut. Ins. Co., Mansfield, Ohio, 1981-84, sr. mgr. CNA, Chgo., 1984-86; v.p. Gt. Cen. Ins., Co., Peoria, Ill., 1986—. Mem. expansion fund com. Mansfield Gen. Hosp., 1982. Served with AUS, 1956-60. Mem. Soc. Ins. Research. Republican. Lutheran. Home: 917 Shorewood Ct Dunlap IL 61525 Office: Gt Ctn Ins Co 3625 N Sheridan Rd Peoria IL 61604-1434

JONES, JAMES EDWARD, osteopath; b. Poplar Bluff, Mo., Apr. 17, 1939; s. Arthur Lee and Juanita M. (Huffman) J.; m. June Westaver, Apr. 2, 1966; children—James E., Julie Ann. Student N.E. Mo. State U., 1957-61; Western Ill. U., summer 1961; D.O., Kirksville Coll. Osteo. Medicine, 1966. Intern, Normandy Osteo. Hosp., St. Louis, 1966-67; practice osteo. medicine, St. Peters, Mo., 1967—; chief of staff St. Peters Community Hosp., 1982, chief of staff-elect, 1987, also trustee. Mem. AMA, Mo. State Med. Assn., Am. Coll. Gen. Practice, Lincoln/St. Charles County Med. Assn. Republican. Lutheran. Home: PO Box 10 Saint Peters MO 63376 Office: 418 S Church St Saint Peters MO 63376

JONES, JANET LEE, insurance company executive; b. Saginaw, Mich., Sept. 16, 1942; d. Max Loren and Joyce Eleanor (Burlingame) Bowyer; m. Larry Jack Jones, Sept. 8, 1962; children—Melissa J., Audra L., Sarah J. Lic. Ins. Counselor. Claim clk. Frankenmuth Mut., Frankenmuth, Mich., 1965-70; asst. Judd Ins. Agy., Birch Run, Mich., 1970-78; asst. mgr. mktg. Penn Gen. Agy., Saginaw, Mich., 1978-80; mgr. mktg. Ferguson Ins. Agy., Saginaw, Mich., 1980-82; account exec., agt. Universal Underwriters, Birmingham, Mich., 1982-86, regional sales mgr., 1986—. Coach, mgr. Albee Athletic Assn., Burt, Mich., 1979-81; v.p. Little Six Athletic Assn., 1979-81. Fellow Ins. Women Saginaw County, Soc. Cert. Ins. Counselors. Independent. Episcopalian. Home: 6166 Eastknoll Grand Blanc MI 48439

JONES, JEROME B., superintendent schools; b. Balt., July 1, 1947; children—Merrill, Allison. B.A. in Acctg., St. Augustine's Coll., 1959; M.A. in History, Trenton State Coll., 1970; M.A. in Regional Planning, Rutgers U., 1973, Ph.D., 1974. Acting county supt. Essex County, 1975-76; acting asst. commr. edn. N.J. Dept. Edn., 1975-76; supt. Providence Sch. Dept., 1976-81, Stamford Pub. Schs., 1981-83, St. Louis Bd. Edn., 1983—. Mem. Backstoppers (Firemen), 1984—. Recipient Sammy Davis, Jr. award St. Louis Sentinel Newspaper, 1984, Disting. Citzen of Yr. award Mathew-Dickey Boys' Club. Mem. Am. Assn. Sch. Adminstrs., Council of Gt. City Schs., Civic Progress. Office: St Louis City Sch Dist 911 Locust St Saint Louis MO 63101

JONES, JIM I., CAD/CAM company executive; b. Detroit, Apr. 28, 1941; m. Judith G. Easterman, June 15, 1963; children: Jeffrey I., John R., Jamison E. BSEE, GMI Engring. & Mgmt. Inst., 1962; MS Math., Mich. State U., 1963; DEng, U. Detroit, 1970. Project mgr. Gen. Motors, Warren, Mich., 1963-77, supr. tech. assess, 1979-81; mgr. application software CIMLINC, Troy, Mich., 1981-83; mgr. overseas ops. Gen. Motors, Troy, Mich., 1983-85, dir. product mktg., 1985—; cons. graphics Adam Opel, Frankfurt, Fed. Republic Germany, 1977-79. Mem. IEEE. Avocation: sailboat racing. Home: 1236 E Horseshoe Ct Rochester MI 48064

JONES, JIMMIE L., architect; b. Wichita, Kans., Feb. 23, 1947; s. Merle D. and Marietta (Ellinwood) J.; m. Veda Rae Boyd, Nov. 15, 1975; children: Landon, Morgan, Marshall. BArch, U. Ark., 1971. Registered architect, Mo., Kans., Tex., Okla., Ky., Ga. Architect McCreary-Swanson, Tulsa, 1980-81; ptnr. Patterson, Latimer, Jones, Brannon & Assocs., Joplin, Mo., 1982—. Served with U.S. Army, 1971-74, Vietnam. Lodge: Kiwanis. Avocations: tennis, fishing. Home: 505 W 34th Joplin MO 64804 Office: Patterson Latimer Jones Brannon PO Box 2937 Joplin MO 64803

JONES, JOE ELLIS, data processing executive; b. Greencastle, Ind., Oct. 16, 1949; s. Wilbur Ellis and Frances Irene (Wallace) J.; m. Susan Kay Williams, Mar. 7, 1969; children: Jason Todd, Justin Ellis. AA, ITT Tech. Inst., 1969. Engr. Pub. Service Ind., Plainfield, 1969-70, computer programmer, 1970-72, systems analyst, 1972-76, data base analyst, 1976-80, data base coordinator, 1980-84, data mgmt. mgr., 1984—. Active various youth groups, Hendricks COunty, Ind., 1967—. Club: Conservation Bird Dog (v.p. 1980-82) (Amo, Ind.). Avocations: hunting, fishing, children. Home: Rural Rt 2 Box 239 Coatesville IN 46121 Office: Pub Service Ind 1000 E Main St Plainfield IN 46168

JONES, JOHN B., judge; b. Mitchell, S.D., Mar. 30, 1927; s. John B. and Grace M. (Bailey) J.; m. Rosemary Wermers; children—John, William, Mary Louise, David, Judith, Robert. B.S. in Bus. Adminstrn., U. S.D., 1951, LL.B., 1953. Bar: S.D. 1953. Sole practice Presho, S.D., 1953-67; judge Lyman County, Kennebec, S.D., 1953-56; mem. S.D. Ho. of Reps., Pierre, 1957-61; judge S.D. Cir. Ct., 1967-81, U.S. Dist. Ct. S.D., Sioux Falls, 1981—. Mem. ABA, Am. Judicature Soc., S.D. Bar Assn., Fed. Judges Assn., VFW, Am. Legion. Methodist. Lodges: Elks, Lions. Avocation: golf. Home: 1205 W 37th St Sioux Falls SD 57105 Office: US Dist Ct 400 S Phillips St Sioux Falls SD 57102§

JONES, JOHN DAVID, consulting engineer; b. Nanty Glo, Pa., Oct. 4, 1923; s. Joseph Louis and Jennie Gertrude (Beutman) J.; m. Rose Capriola, Dec. 24, 1942; children: James Steven, Lynn Marie, Stephanie Ann. Student, U. Mich., 1949-50; BS in Civil Engring., U. Akron, 1952. Registered profl. engr., Ohio, Pa., Ind., Va., W.Va., Profl. Surveyor, Ohio, Pa. Field engr. AT&T, Cin., 1952-53, City of Akron, 1953-55, Firestone Tire and Rubber Co., Akron, 1955-58; pvt. practice cons. engring. Cuyahoga Falls, Ohio, 1958—; chmn. bd. John David Jones and Assoc., Inc., Cuyahoga Falls, 1970—. Decorated Bronze Star medal, Purple Heart with oak leaf cluster. Past. bd.dirs. Green Cross Gen. Hosp. (now Cuyahoga Falls Gen. Hosp.); elder United Presbyn. Ch.; past. trustee Cuyahoga Valley Christian Acad. Served with U.S. Army, 1942-45. Mem. ASCE, Nat. Soc. Profl. Engrs., Am. Congress on Surveying and Mapping, Profl. Engrs. Ohio, Ohio Assn. Constrn. Engrs., Water Pollution Control Fedn., Am. Water Works Assn., Phi Sigma Tau, Tau Beta Pi. Lodges: Masons, Lions. Club: Univeristy (Akron). Home: 3192 Hudson Dr Cuyahoga Falls OH 44221 Office: 2162 Front St Cuyahoga Falls OH 44221

JONES, JOHN EDWARD, architect; b. St. Louis, Aug. 2, 1938; s. John Eramus and Lucille Isabel (Hudder) J.; m. Gail Iris Berry, Oct. 21, 1967; children: Paula Lynn, Julianne Elaine. Student, Cen. Coll., 1958; BS Archtl. Sci., Washington U., 1962, MArch, 1962. Designer Arthur Standish, East St. Louis, Ill., 1962-63; project architect Winkler-Thompson, Clayton, Mo., 193-66; dir. design Drake Partnership, St. Louis, 1966-69; pres. JonesMayer Architecture, Inc., St. Louis, 1969—. Mem. People to People Del. to China, 1982; chmn. archtl. div. United Way, St. Louis, 1984. Served with NG, 1962-68. Mem. AIA, Profl. Service Mgmt. Assn., Nat. Council Architects Registration Bd., Mo. Council Architects. Episcopalian. Clubs: Mo. Athletic, Greenbrian Hills Country, Town and Country Racquet (St. Louis). Avocation: golf. Office: JonesMayer Architecture Inc 2190 S Mason Rd Saint Louis MO 63131

JONES, KATHERINE ANN, health educator; b. Jackson, Mich., Mar. 22, 1953; d. Harry Irvin and Norma Joanne (Long) J. B.S., Central Mich. U., 1979, M.A., 1984. Grad. intern St. Lawrence Hosp., Lansing, Mich., 1979; health edn. mgr. St. Lawrence Hosp., Lansing, 1979—. Recipient Diabetes Edn. award Mich. Dept. Pub. Health, 1983. Mem. AAHPER and Dance, Soc. Pub. Health Edn. (pres. Great Lakes chpt. 1984-85), Nat. Soc. Pub. Health Edn., Am. Pub. Health Assn., Eta Sigma Gamma. Office: St Lawrence Hosp 1210 W Saginaw St Lansing MI 48915

JONES, KENT, state agricultural administrator; b. Webster, N.D., Apr. 26, 1926; s. John D. and Katherine (Jones) J.; m. Helen L. Johnson, Sept. 10, 1947; children—Deborah, Jeff, Sara, Rebecca. B.S. in Agr., N.D. State U. Farmer, Ramsey County, N.D.; commr. N.D. Dept. Agr., Bismarck, 1981—. Mem. N.D. Ho. of Reps., 1967-69, N.D. State Senate, 1971-79. Served with U.S. Army, 1946-47. Republican. Episcopalian. Lodges: Elks, Masons. Avocations: walking; reading. Office: ND Dept Agr 601 State Capitol Bismarck ND 58505

JONES, LEANDER CORBIN, educator, media specialist; b. Vincent, Ark., July 16, 1934; s. Lander Corbin and Una Bell (Lewis) J.; A.B., U. Ark., Pine Bluff, 1956; M.S., U. Ill., 1968; Ph.D., Union Grad. Sch., 1973; m. Lethonee Angela Hendricks, June 30, 1962; children—Angela Lynne, Leander Corbin. Tchr. English pub. high schs., Chgo. Bd. Edn., 1956-68; vol. English-as-fgn. lang. tchr. Peace Corps, Mogadiscio, Somalia, 1964-66; TV producer City Colls. of Chgo., 1968-73; communications media specialist Meharry Med. Coll., 1973-75; assoc. prof. Black Americana studies Western Mich., U., 1975—, chmn. African studies program, 1980-81, co-chmn. Black caucus, 1983, corr. sec., 1984—; dir. 7 art workshop Am. Negro Emancipation Centennial Authority, Chgo., 1960-63. Mem. Mich. Commn. on Crime and Delinquency, 1981-83; mem. exec. com. DuSable Mus. African Am. History, 1970—; mem. Prisoners Progress Assn., 1977-82, South African Solidarity Orgn., 1978—, Dennis Brutus Def. Com., 1980-83; chmn. Kalamazoo Community Relations Bd., 1977-79; bd. dirs. Kalamazoo Civic Players, 1981-83; pres. Black Theater of Kalamazoo, 1981-83. Served with U.S. Army, 1956-58. Mem. Assn. Study African-Am. History , NAACP (exec. com. Kalamazoo br. 1978-82), Theatre Arts and Broadcasting Skills Ctr. (pres. 1972—), AAUP, Mich. Orgn. African Studies, Nat. Council Black Studies, Popular Culture Assn., 100 Men's Club. Dir. South Side Ctr. of Performing Arts, Chgo., 1968-69, Progressive Theatre Unltd., Nashville, 1974-75; writer, producer, dir. TV drama: Roof Over my Head, Nashville 1975; designer program in theatre and TV for hard-to-educate; developer edn. programs in Ill. State Penitentiary, Pontiac, and Cook County Jail, Chgo., 1971-73. Writer, dir. 10 Score!, 1976, Super Summer, 1978; dir. Trouble in Mind, 1979, Day of Absence, 1981, 85, Happy Ending, 1981, Who's Got His Own, 1983, Take A Giant Step, 1985; producer For Colored Girls Who Have Considered Suicide When the Rainbow is Enuf, 1984; featured at Civic Theater, Kalamazoo, in Great White Hope, 1979, Dutchman, 1980, Moon On a Rainbow Shawl, 1980, Five in the Black Hand Side, 1982, Who's Got His Own, Guys and Dolls, Black Girl, Tambourines to Glory, 1983, Day of Absence, Take a Giant Step, 1985, Soldier's Play, 1986; author: Roof Over My Head, 1975, Africa is for Reel, 1983; exec. producer and host TV series Fade to Black, 1986—. Home: 2226 S Westnedge Ave Kalamazoo MI 49008 Office: Western Mich U Black Americana Studies Kalamazoo MI 49001

JONES, LINDA DEN BESTEN, special education administrator; b. Harvey, Ill., Nov. 17, 1947; d. Neal and Edna Ruth (VerDught) Den Besten; m. Alan Charles Jones, June 1, 1968; children: Amanda, Matthew. BA, Hope Coll., 1968; MEd, DePaul U., 1971; PhD, Loyola U., Chgo., 1979. Tchr. social studies Hudsonville (Mich.) High Sch., 1968-69; tchr. Sch. Dist. 144, Markham, Ill., 1969-71; spl. edn. tchr. Sch. Dist. 155, Calumet City, Ill., 1971-73; spl. edn. supr. Exceptional Children Have Opportunities Joint Agreement, South Holland, Ill., 1973-758; dir. spl. edn. Sch. Dist. 152, Harvey, Ill., 1975—. Author: Guide for Teaching the Learning Disabled, 1975. Named one of Outstanding Young People Am., Harvey Jr. C. of C., 1978. Mem. Council for Exceptional Children (chpt. pres. 1975-76, v.p. 1974-75). Home: 7 Hunter Ct Burr Ridge IL 60521 Office: Sch Dist 152 152d and Mrytle Harvey IL 60426

JONES, NANCYE KNIGHTON, nurse; b. Atascadero, Calif., Dec. 10, 1945; d. Joseph Raymond and Grace Elizabeth (Reed) Knighton; m. Bradford W. Jones, Aug. 22, 1969; children: Christopher David, Amy Elisabeth, Kevin Bradford. RN, West Suburban Med. Ctr., 1966; BA, Wheaton Coll., 1968. Staff nurse U. R.I., Narragansett, 1970-71; charge nurse clinics Planned Parenthood Assn., Grand Rapids, Mich., 1971-74; charge nurse/supr. Cen. DuPage Hosp., Winfield, Ill., 1974-86; staff nurse U. Minn. Hosp., Mpls., 1986-87, Fairview Southdale Hosp., Edina, Minn., 1987—. Mem. Minn. Nurses Assn. Home: 6621 Southcrest Dr Edina MN 55435

JONES, NATHANIEL B., IV, financial consultant; b. Middletown, N.Y., Oct. 18, 1945; s. Christopher Healy and Helen Eva (Bates) J.; m. Judith Ann Operchal, June 27, 1971; children: C. Healy III, Alexander Kirk. BS, Pa. State U., 1967, MS, 1969. Territory mgr. Burroughs Corp., Harrisburg, Pa., 1969-71; asst. treas. Vanderbilt U., Nashville, 1971-77; dir. benefits Pullman Corp., Chgo., 1977-81; v.p. Am. Nat. Bank, Chgo., 1981; sr. v.p. J.H. Ellwood & Assocs., Chgo., 1981—. Fellow Fin. Analyst Fedn.; mem. Chartered Fin. Analyst Fed., Am. Econ. Assn., Am. Fin. Assn., Investment Analyst Soc. Chgo. Home: 35 S Oak St Hinsdale IL 60521 Office: JH Ellwood & Assocs Inc 175 W Jackson Blvd Suite A1827 Chicago IL 60604

JONES, NATHANIEL RAPHAEL, federal judge; b. Youngstown, Ohio, May 13, 1926; s. Nathaniel B. and Lillian J. (Rafe) J.; m. Lillian Graham, Mar. 22, 1974; 1 dau., Stephanie Joyce; stepchildren: William Hawthorne, Rickey Hawthorne, Marc Hawthorne, Pamela Haley. A.B., Youngstown State U., 1951, LL.B., 1955, LL.D. (hon.), 1969; LL.D. (hon.), Syracuse U., 1972. Editor Buckeye Rev. newspaper 1956; exec. dir. FEPC, Youngstown, 1956-59; practiced law 1959-61; mem. firm Goldberg & Jones, 1968-69; asst. U.S. atty. 1961-67; asst. gen. counsel Nat. Adv. Commn. on Civil Disorders, 1967-68; gen. counsel NAACP, 1969-79; judge U.S. Ct. of Appeals, 6th Circuit, 1979—; dir. Buckeye Rev. Pub. Co.; chmn. Con. on Adequate Def. and Incentives in Mil.; mem. Task Force-Vets. Benefits. Served with USAAF, 1945-47. Mem. Ohio State Bar Assn., Mahoning County Bar Assn., Fed. Bar Assn., Nat. Bar Assn., Am. Arbitration Assn., Youngstown Area Devel. Corp., Urban League, Nat. Conf. Black Lawyers, ABA (co-chmn. com. constl. rights criminal sect. 1971-73), Kappa Alpha Psi. Baptist. Clubs: Houston Law (Youngstown); Elks. Office: 432 US Post Office Cincinnati OH 45202

JONES, NINA FLEMISTER, school administrator; b. Madison, Ga., July 30, 1918; d. Sumner L. and Hallie (Hall) Flemister; m. William M. Jones, Sept. 21, 1940; children: William M. Jr, Steven L. BA, Cen. Y.M.C.A. Coll., Chgo., 1938; MEd, Chgo. Tchrs. Coll., 1942; EdD, Loyola U., Chgo., 1975. Tchr. Chgo. Bd. Edn., 1942-59, counselor, asst. prin., 1959-65, prin., 1966-69, dist. supt., 1969-75, asst. supt., 1975-83, sec. bd. examiners, 1983—. Contbr. ednl. and human interest articles to various pubs. Mem. Alpha Kappa Alpha, Alpha Gamma Pi, Pi Lambda Theta. Democrat. Congregational. Avocations: writing, reading, bridge, travel. Home: 9156 S Constance Chicago IL 60617 Office: Bd of Edn 1819 W Pershing Rd Chicago IL 60609

JONES, NORMA LOUISE, educator; b. Poplar, Wis.; d. George Elmer and Hilma June (Wiberg) J. B.E., U. Wis.; M.A., U. Minn., 1952; postgrad, U. Ill., 1957; Ph.D., U. Mich., 1965; postgrad., NARS, 1978, 79, 80; D.A. in Info. Sci., Nova U., 1983. Librarian Grand Rapids (Mich.) Public Schs., 1947-62; with Grand Rapids Public Library, 1948-49; instr. Central Mich. U., Mt. Pleasant, 1954, 55; librarian Benton Harbor (Mich.) Public Schs., 1962-63; asst. prof. library sci. U. Wis., Oshkosh, 1968-70; assoc. prof. U. Wis., 1970-75, prof., 1975—, chmn. dept. library sci., 1980-84, assoc. dir. libraries and learning resources, 1987—; lectr. U. Mich., Ann Arbor, 1954, 55, 61, 63-65, asst. prof., 1966-68. Recipient Disting. Teaching award U. Wis.-Oshkosh, 1977. Mem. ALA (chmn. reference conf. 1975—), Assn. Library and Info. Sci. Educators, Spl. Library Assn., Soc. Am. Archivists, Phi Beta Kappa, Phi Kappa Phi, Pi Lambda Theta, Beta Phi Mu, Sigma Pi Epsilon. Home: 1220 Maricopa Dr Oshkosh WI 54901

JONES, NORMAN M., savings and loan association executive. Chmn., chief operating officer, dir. Met. Fed. Bank FSB, Fargo, N.D. Office: Met Fed Bank FSB 215 N 5th St Fargo ND 58102 *

JONES, PARRIS ALBERT, data processing executive; b. Beaver Falls, Pa., Nov. 4, 1948; s. Parris Albert Sr. and Gertrude Irene (Franklin) J.; m. Daisy Jean Allen, Nov. 2, 1969; children: Tyrone Phillip, LaShawn Marie, Yolanda Marie. Student, Pa. State U., 1966-68; BS in Maths., Geneva Coll., 1973; postgrad., Ohio State U., 1975. Programmer Nationwide Ins. Co., Columbus, Ohio, 1973-77; programmer/analyst United Service Automobile Assn., San Antonio, Tex., 1977; project leader Gold Circle Dept. Stores, Columbus, 1977-78; sr. systems analyst Profl. Tech., Inc., Southfield, Mich., 1978-79; project supr. Upjohn Co., Kalamazoo, 1979—. Fellow Internat. Betta Congress (treas. 1982-87, pres. 1987—, Internat. Grand Champion 1983, 84, Betta Person of Yr. 1983). Avocations: genetical study of the Betta Splendid, dog obedience tng. Home: 1710 Whitby St Portage MI 49081 Office: The Upjohn Co 7000 Portage Rd Kalamazoo MI 49002

JONES, PATRICK LOUIS, federal agency executive; b. Altus, Okla., Oct. 9, 1940; s. Harold William and Laura Margaret (Sperlazza) J.; m. Barbara Ann Wiley, June 29, 1962; children: Kelly Ann, Patrick Louis Jr. BS in Air Sci., Okla. State U., 1962; MBA, U. Utah, 1972; cert. in info. systems analysis and design, Dept. Def. Computer Inst., 1979, cert. automated data processing mgr., 1979, cert. automated info. systems mgmt., 1980. Commd. USAF, advanced through grades to lt. col.; asst. prof. aerospace study Coll. St. Thomas, St. Paul, 1973-76; chief intelligence applications SAC div. USAF, Bellevue, Nebr., 1979-81, chief ABNCP programming div., 1981-83, dir. mobile info. mgmt. systems, 1983-85, dir. info. systems tng., 1985—; Computerized battle staff mgmt. for SAC and Air Force 1. Created MIMS, first Air Force info. mgmt. system written in Ada. Chmn. Griffiss AFB Cub Scouts Am., N.Y., 1978-79; recruiter Combined Fed. Campaign, Bellevue, 1979-86, recruiter ARC blood drives, Bellevue, 1980-86; Met. Reading Council, Omaha, 1984-86; pres. Bellevue West High Sch. Band Boosters, 1985-86; pres. Little League, Griffiss AFB, 1979; coach Little League team, Offutt AFB, 1980. Served to lt. col., USAF, 1977—. Mem. Assn. Computing Machinery, Air Force Assn., Armed Forces Communication and Electronics Assn., Omaha Heath and Zenith User's Group. Republican. Roman Catholic. Clubs: Offutt Officers, Griffiss Officers (bd. govs. 1976-79). Lodge: KC, Order of Daedalions. Avocations: chef, puzzle-solving, skiing, raquetball, fishing. Home: 12804 S 29th Pl Omaha NE 68123

JONES, PHILLIP ERIC, financial executive; b. Manchester, Eng., Feb. 12, 1951; s. Eric and Martha (Shaw) J.; m. Patricia Mulvihill, Sept. 15, 1976; children: Dominique Ann, Nathaniel Kyle, Nicholas Adam. B in Fin., Lancaster U., 1972; postgrad. in Bus. Adminstrn., Cleve. State U., 1984—. Fin. analyst Reed Internat., London, 1972-74; mgr. cost acctg. ITT, London, 1974-76; project adminstr. McDermott Internat. Inc., Dubai, United Arab Emirates, 1976-79, corp. acctg. mgr., 1976-79; dir. fin. and planning Bailey Controls Cleve., 1981-87; corp. controller Prestolite Electric Inc., Toledo, 1987—. Vice chmn. United Way, Lake County, Ohio, 1986; trustee Euclid Gen. Hosp., 1985-87. Roman Catholic. Club: Quail Hollow (Painesville); Riverview (Eastlake). Home: 6938 Cloister Toledo OH 43617 Office: Prestolite Electric Inc 4 Seagate Toledo OH 43692

JONES, REGINALD LORRIN, clinical psychologist, consultant; b. St. Petersburg, Fla., Dec. 12, 1951; s. Daniel George Jones and Susie Beatrice (Lewis) W.; m. Helen Elizabeth Lightfoot, Aug. 18, 1984; children: Tammy Le Vette, Myla Carmel; 1 stepchild, Deneale Elizabeth Hand. BA, Clark Coll., 1973; MA, U. Cin., 1977, PhD, 1980. Lic. psychologist, Ohio. Statistician Atlanta Pub. Schs., 1973-74; psychology trainee U. Cin., 1974-80; team leader, supr. Social Skills Program, Cin., 1980-81; psychologist, unit dir. Day-Mont West, C.M.H.C., Dayton, Ohio, 1981-83; field psychologist advisor Ohio Indsl. Commn., Dayton, 1983—; pvt. practice psychology, Dayton, 1983—; clin. asst. prof. Wright State U., Dayton, 1981—; cons. Adapt Inc., Springfield, Ohio, 1986—, Sickle Cell Awareness Group, Cin., 1986—. V.p., bd. dirs. Sickle Cell Awareness Group, Cin., 1981. Named One of Outstanding Young Men of Am., 1984. Mem. Am. Psychol. Assn., Am. Soc. Clin. Hypnosis, Assn. Black Psychologists, Dayton Assn. Black Psychologists (pres. 1983-84, service award 1986). Democrat. Avocations: African history and culture, gardening. Home: 1724 Salem Ave Dayton OH 45406 Office: Ohio Indsl Commn Rehabilitation 7416 N Main St Dayton OH 45415

JONES, RICHARD CYRUS, lawyer; b. Oak Park, Ill., Oct. 20, 1928; s. Ethler E. and Margaret S. (Stoner) J.; m. Betty Jane Becker; children: Richard C., Carrie, William. PhB, DePaul U., 1960, JD, 1963. Bar: Ill. 1963. Dept. mgr. Chgo. Title & Trust Co., 1947-64; mem. Sachnoff, Schrager, Jones, Weaver & Rubenstein Ltd. and predecessor firms, Chgo., 1964-81; of counsel Sachnoff, Weaver & Rubenstein, Chgo., 1981—; instr. Real Estate Inst., Chgo., 1970—; trustee, sec. Income Properties and Equity Trust, 1974—; trustee, chmn. Ind. Dirs. of Wis. Real Estate Investment Trust, 1980—. Decorated Bronze Star. Mem. ABA, Ill. Bar Assn., Chgo. Bar Assn. (com. chmn. real property law 1970-72, 76—), Chgo. Council Lawyers, Delta Theta Phi. Lodge: Kiwanis. Home: 1044 Forest Ave River Forest IL 60305 Office: 30 S Wacker Dr 29th Floor Chicago IL 60606

JONES, RICHARD JEFFERY, physician, educator; b. Cleve., Apr. 6, 1918; s. Edward Safford and Frances Christine (Jeffery) J.; m. Helen Hart, Oct. 5, 1946; children—Christopher, Ruth, Jeffery, Catherine. A.B., Oberlin Coll., 1938; M.A., U. Buffalo, 1942, M.D., 1943. Diplomate Am. Bd. Internal Medicine. Intern, U. Chgo. Hosps., 1944; resident, 1947-49; assoc. prof. medicine U. Chgo., 1958-76; assoc. prof. clin. medicine Northwestern U., Chgo., 1976—. Author: Chemistry and Therapy of Chronic Cardiovascular Disease, 1961. Editorial bd. Nutrition Revs., 1964-72. Served to lt. USNR, 1944-46, PTO. Recipient Presl. Letter Commendation, Pres. Truman, 1946, vis. assoc. prof. Rockefeller U., 1965. Fellow Am. Heart Assn.; mem. AMA (dir. scientific activites 1976-83, council sec. 1976-83), Central Soc. Clin. Research, Soc. Experimental Biol. and Med. (editorial bd. 1964-74). Unitarian. Home: 4820 S Kenwood Ave Chicago IL 60615 Office: Northwestern Meml Hosp 251 E Chicago Ave Chicago IL 60611

JONES, RICHARD M., business executive; b. Eldon, Mo., Nov. 26, 1926; m. Sylvia A. Richardson, 1950; 3 children. B.S. in Bus. Adminstrn., Olivet Nazarene Coll., 1950, LL.D. (hon.), 1983; grad. Advanced Mgmt. Program, Harvard U., 1973. With Sears, Roebuck & Co., 1950—, store mgr., 1963-68; gen. mgr. Sears, Roebuck & Co., Washington and Balt., 1974; exec. v.p.-East Sears, Roebuck & Co., 1974-80, corp. v.p., 1980, vice chmn. bd., chief fin. officer, 1980-85, pres., chief fin. officer, 1986—; dir. Sears Roebuck Acceptance Corp., Sears Roebuck Found. Chmn. bd. trustees Field Mus. Natural History, Chgo.; bd. govs. Northwestern Univ. Assocs., Chgo., ARC Endowment Fund, Washington. Office: Sears Roebuck & Co Sears Tower Chicago IL 60684

JONES, ROBERT C., symphony orchestra administrator; b. Needham, Mass., July 21, 1943; s. William Arthur and Roberta (Cushman) J.; m. Susan Christine Anderson, Mar. 19, 1966; children: Jeffrey Howard, William Oscar. B.S. in Econs., Portland State U., 1966. Sec.-treas. Musicians Mut. Assn., Local 99, Portland, Oreg., 1969-80; exec. officer Am. Fedn. Musician of U.S. and Can., N.Y.C., 1978-80; v.p., gen. mgr. Minn. Orchestral Assn., Mpls., 1980-83; exec. dir. Indpls. Symphony Orch., 1983—; pres. Northwest Conf. of Musicians, 1976; founding dir. Pacific Northwest Labor Coll., 1977-80; panelist NEA, Washington, 1977-80; dir. Greater Twin Cities Youth Symphonies, Mpls., 1980-83, West Coast Chamber Orch., Portland, 1978-80. Chmn. Met. Arts Commn., Portland, 1977-80; mem. Performing Arts Theatre Task Force, 1979-80; producer Artquake, 1977-80; dir. Arts Celebration, Inc., 1977-80. Mem. Am. Symphony Orch. League, Am. Fedn. Musicians (Oreg. state rep. and legis. dir. 1971-80), Minn. Orchestral Assn. N.Am. Saxaphone Alliance (northwest regional coordinator 1970-80). Democrat. Office: Indpls Symphony Orch 45 Monument Cir Indianapolis IN 46204-2901 *

JONES, ROBERT LYLE, paramedic, educator; b. Washington, Feb. 6, 1959; s. Herman Aven and Dorthy Edith (Fisher) J. B in Gen. Sci., U. Kans., 1982; MA in Adult Edn., U. Mo., 1986. Registered emergency mobile intensive care technician, Mo., Kans. Paramedic team leader Johnson County (Kans.) Med. Action, 1983—; paramedic instr. Med. Ctr. of Independence, Mo., 1983—, Johnson County (Kans.) Community Coll., Overland Park, 1986—; basic cardiac life instr. Am. Heart Assn., Overland Park, Kans, 1979—, adv. cardiac life instr., 1985—. Served to capt. USAR, 1979-87. Mem. Nat. Assn EMT's (trauma life support instr.), Nat. Soc. EMS Adminstrs., Nat. Soc. EMT Paramedics. Republican. Presbyterian. Avocations: bicycling, backpacking, running. Home: 7137 Lowell Dr Overland Park KS 66204 Office: Johnson County Med Action 10975 Elmonte Suite 110 Shawnee Mission KS 66210

JONES, ROBERT WILLIAM, III, dentist; b. St. Paul, Minn., Nov. 12, 1944; s. Robert William Jr. and Marianne Genivieve (Hunt) J.; m. Sandra Lee Balsimo, Apr. 24, 1965; children: Christine Jones Jorissen, Karen, Carla. Student, St. John's U., Collegeville, Minn., 1962-63; BS, U. Minn., 1963-65, DDS, 1965-69. Lic. dentist, Minn., Tex. Staff dentist David Gorde & Assocs., St. Paul, 1971-73; gen. practice dentistry St. Paul, 1983—. Served to capt. USAF, 1969-71. Mem. ADA, Minn. Dental Soc., St. Paul Dental Soc. (pres. speakers bd. 1978). Democrat. Roman Catholic. Club: St. John's Mens (Little Canada, Minn.). Lodge: Rotary (sec. St. Paul 1984). Avocations: watercolor painting, piano playing, golf, softball. Home: 650 E Belmont Ln Saint Paul MN 55117 Office: 914 Lowry Med Arts Saint Paul MN 55102

JONES, ROBERTA LOUISE, psychologist; b. Lansing, Mich., Mar. 7, 1944; d. Robert Edmund and Faith Louise (Manning) Troxell; 1 child, Erik Allen Gilleland. BA in Edn., Ariz. State U., 1966; MEd, Temple U., 1970; PhD, Ohio State U., 1974. Lic. psychologist, Ohio. Kindergarten tchr. Prince George's County, Seabrook, Md., 1967-68; psychologist Diocesan Child Guidance Ctr., Columbus, Ohio, 1974-70, Children's Mental Health Clinic, Columbus, 1979-81; pvt. practice psychology Columbus, 1981-83; psychologist, asst. sattelite dir. Scioto Paint Valley Mental Health Ctr., Circleville, Ohio, 1983—. Mem. Am. Group Psychotherapy Assn. Presbyterian. Office: Scioto Valley Mental Health Ctr 145 Morris Rd Circleville OH 43113

JONES, SANDRA, electronics executive; b. Frankfurt, Fed. Republic Germany, Oct. 5, 1946; d. Irving and Lena (Koönigstein) Zak; m. Charles E. Jones, Dec. 18, 1973; stepchildren: Katherine Jones Mearns, Terry Jones, Cynthia E. Jones. Grad., Charles F. Brush High Sch., 1964. Mgr. ops. J&L Builders, Cleve., 1968-71; v.p. Sabin Machine Co., Cleve., 1971-75; pres. Security Products Col, Cleve., 1975—, also bd. dirs. Mem. Nat. Burglar and Fire Alarm Assn., Security Equipment Industry Assn. (bd. dirs. 85—, v.p. 1986—), Nat. Assn. Wholesalers (trustee 1986—, bd. dels.), Columbus, Ohio Alarm Adv. Council, Lake Erie Burglar and Fire Alarm Assn. Republican. Jewish. Avocations: travel, tennis, scuba diving, skiing, ornithology. Office: Security Products Co 14915 Woodworth Ave Cleveland OH 44110

JONES, SANDRA ANN, health science facility administrator, consultant; b. Indpls., May 18, 1950; d. Quincy Arthur and Bessie Mae (Niven) Day; m. Ronald Edwin Kauffmann, Aug. 15, 1971 (div. 1983); 1 child: Brandon Jay; m. John Karl Jones, Dec. 22, 1984; 1 child, Mary Bess. BFA in Advt. and Mktg., So. Meth. U., 1982; MS, Murray (Ky.) State U., 1974; postgrad., U. Ill., 1986. Ill. statewide facilitator Office Edn., Washington, 1975; pupil personnel sect. Ill. Office Edn., Springfield, 1976; community educator Devel. Services Ctr., Champaign, 1976-78; asst. adminstr. Burnham Hosp., Champaign, 1978—. TV health series host PM Magazine, Champaign, 1980-81. Pres., bd. mem. mktg. commn. Am. Heart Assn., Champaign, 1982-85; crisis nursery chmn. Jr. League, Champaign, 1984. Mem. Am. Mktg. Assn. (exec. bd. mem. 1982-84, treas. 1984-85), Am. Hosp. Assn., Ill. Hosp. Assn. (health facilities and planning council 1983-85, mktg. resource panel 1984—). Republican. Methodist. Clubs: PEO, Symphony Guild (Champaign) (sec. 1982). Avocation: vocal music. Office: Burnham Hosp 407 S 4th Champaign IL 61820

JONES, STANLEY ARDEN, aerial applicator; b. Phillipsburg, Kan., May 20, 1947; s. Vinton and Mildred Evelyn (Yancy) J.; m. Phyllis Jean Jones, June 1, 1966; children: Shawn David, Stacy Daree. AA in Bus., McCook Jr. Coll., 1967. Air traffic controller FAA, Cedar Rapids, Iowa, 1970-74; v.p. Top Hat Aerial, Benkelman, Nebr., 1974-80, pres., 1980—; pres. Top Crop Fertilizer, Benkelman, Nebr., 1979—, Top Hat Flying Service, Benkelman, 1983; sec. Nat. Agrl. Research & Edn. Found., Washington, 1983—. Pres., Dundy County Agrl. Soc., 1982-84; bd. dirs. City Council, Terrytown, Nebr., 1969-70. Recipient Falcon Club award, 1983, Benkelman Good Guy award, 1986. Mem. Nebr. Aviation Trades Assn. (dir. 1976-83, pres. 1984, Pres.'s award 1985, Airman of Yr. aware 1986), Nat. Agrl. Aviation Assn. (dir. 1978-84, treas. 1985, pres. 1986, Outstanding Service award 1983, Allied Industry award 1983). Republican. Methodist. Lodge: Shriners. Address: Top Hat Aerial Applicators Inc Jones Airport Benkelman NE 69021

JONES, STEPHEN GRAF, musician, educator; b. Columbus, Ohio, Oct. 17, 1947; s. James Alfred and Freeda Irene (Graf) J.; m. Teresa Diane Turner, June 19, 1976 (div. Aug. 1979). BS in Music Edn., Ohio State U., 1970; MMus, Wichita (Kans.) State U., 1972; D in Musical Arts, U. Mich., 1978. 3d trumpet Wichita Symphony, 1970-72; prin. trumpet Kalamazoo Symphony, 1972-85; trumpet Wichita Brass Quintet, 1970-72, Kalamazoo, 1972—; prof. trumpet Western Mich. U., Kalamazoo, 1972—; prof. trumpet Western Mich. U., Kalamazoo, 1972—. Contbr. articles to ITG Jour., 1978-85; recording artist Landscapes, 1978, Zupko Masques, 1980, 3 Mosquitos, 1984. Mem. Internat. Trumpet Guild (sec. 1981—). Republican. Lutheran. Avocations: films, arranging music. Home: 2704 Frederick Ave Kalamazoo MI 49008 Office: Western Mich U Sch Music Kalamazoo MI 49008

JONES, SUSAN DIANE, business manager, teacher; b. Elwood, Ind., Aug. 14, 1947; d. William F. and Doris J. (Barnes) Spoo; m. Stephen Michael Jones, Sept. 9, 1967; 1 child, Denise Marie. BS in Edn., Ind. (Kokomo) U., 1970; MA in Edn., Ball State U., 1974. Cert. elem. tchr., Ind. Elem. tchr. Kokomo Ctr. Schs., 1970-73; jr. high sch. tchr. St. Joan of Arc Schs., Kokomo, 1976-80; bus. mgr. Steve Jones Piano Technician, Kokomo, 1979—; English devel. tchr. Ivy Tech. Coll., Kokomo, 1986—. Episcopalian. Club: Toastmasters (v.p. 1976-77). Avocations: sailing, gardening, reading, cross-stich, camping. Address: 2820 Plum Ct Kokomo IN 46902

JONES, TERRY HUNT, rubber products company and hydraulic products company executive; b. La Porte, Ind., Apr. 1, 1943; s. Keith Harris and Wilma Claire (Hunt) J.; m. Frances Marie Rumely; children: Amy, Ethan, Gillian, Haley. Student, Ball State U., Muncie, Ind., 1961-62, Purdue U. of N.C., Westville, Ind., 1969-77, 84-85. V.p. Screw Machine Products Co., Inc., La Porte, 1969—, Jones Enterprise, Inc., La Porte, 1976—; pres. Nephi (Utah) Rubber Products, 1985—. Mem. com. A.J. Rumely for Mayor, La Porte, 1980, John Hiler for Congress, 3d Dist., Ind., 1982-86; mem. La Porte Strategic Planning and Devel. Com., 1985-87; chmn. La Porte council Boy Scouts Am., 1985. Served to 1st lt. U.S. Army, 1966-74. Mem. La Porte Mfrs. Assn. (pres. 1985-87), La Porte C. of C. (bd. dirs. 1985-87). Republican. Baptist. Home: 503 Kingsbury Ave La Porte IN 46350 Office: Screw Machine Products Co Inc PO Box 86 La Porte IN 46350-0086

JONES, THOMAS EVAN, medical product company executive; b. Kansas City, Kans., Jan. 6, 1944; s. Harold E. and Anna Lucille (Peterson) J.; m. Kay Lynette Powell, Aug. 5, 1967; children: Suzanne, Rebecca, Melinda. BSME, U. Kans., 1967; MBA, U. Mo., Kansas City, 1970. Mgr. plant engring. Sealright Co., Kansas City, Kans., 1968-73; v.p. mktg. Puritan-Bennett Corp., Kansas City, Mo., 1973—. Mem. Internat. Oxygen Mfrs. Assn. (bd. dirs. 1987—), Compressed Gas Assn. (bd. dirs. 1984—). Republican. Episcopalian. Clubs: Mission Hills (Kans.) Country, Overland Park (Kans.) Racquet. Avocation: golf. Home: 8849 Cedar Prairie Village KS 66207 Office: Puritan Bennett Corp 10800 Pflumm Rd Lenexa KS 66215

JONES, THOMAS FREDERICK, minister, social services program administrator; b. Jerseyville, Ill., Apr. 26, 1936; s. Frederick Theodore and Mary (Alice) J.; m. Jeannette Walker, Mar. 19, 1960 (div. Sept. 1972); children: Bradley T., Kristina R., Jon A.; m. Reidun Marie Knaust, Aug. 24, 1985. BA, So. Ill. U., 1961; BD, Covenant Theol. Sem., 1965; MA, U. Ga., 1973. Ordained to ministry Presbyn. Ch., 1965. Pastor 1st Reformed Presbyn. Ch., Lookout Mountain, Tenn., 1965-72, Concord Presbyn. Ch., Waterloo, Ill., 1973-76; coord. ch. planting Commn. on Ch. Extension, Carbondale, Ill., 1977-85; pastor Immanuel Presbyn. Ch., Belleville, Ill., 1985—; adj. prof. Covenant Theol. Sem., St. Louis, 1974-76, 80-82; coordinator male discussion group Belleville area Coll., 1983-87; co-dir. Fresh Start Divorce Recovery Seminars, King of Prussia, Pa., 1984—. Contbr. ministry articles to profl. jours. and newsletters. Served with USNR, 1953-61. Avocations: guitar, singing and songwriting recordings, mountain climbing. Home: 197 Rt 3 Waterloo IL 62298 Office: Immanuel Presbyn Ch 225 S High St Belleville IL 62221

JONES, THOMAS HUBBARD, research chemist; b. Batavia, Ill., June 8, 1936; s. O. Lester and Vendela I. (Hubbard) J.; m. Wanda M. Sandeen, Aug. 16, 1958; children: Laura S., Daniel C. AB, Augustana Coll., Rock Island, Ill., 1958; PhD, U. Minn., 1963. Research chemist E.I. DuPont, Parlin, N.J., 1963-69; research chemist and assoc. Richardson Co., Melrose Park, Ill., 1969-82; sr. research chemist Turtle Wax Inc., Chgo., 1984-86, London Chem. Co., Bensenville, Ill., 1986—; cons. Graphcoat, Inc., Holyoke, Mass., 1984. Patentee in field. Mem. Am. Chem. Soc. Office: London Chem Co PO Box 806 240 Foster Ave Bensenville IL 60106

JONES, TREVOR OWEN, automobile supply company executive; b. Maidstone, Kent, Eng., Nov. 3, 1930; came to U.S., 1957, naturalized, 1971; s. Richard Owen and Ruby Edith (Martin) J.; m. Jennie Lou Singleton, Sept. 12, 1959; children: Pembroke Robinson, Bronwyn Elizabeth. Higher Nat. Cert. in Elec. Engring., Aston Tech. Coll., Birmingham, Eng., 1952; Ordinary Nat. Cert. in Mech. Engring., Liverpool (Eng.) Tech. Coll., 1957. Registered profl. engr., Wis.; chartered engr., U.K. Student engr., elec. machine design engr. Brit. Gen. Electric Co., 1950-57; project engr., project mgr. Nuclear Ship Savannah, Allis-Chalmers Mfg. Co., 1957-59; with Gen. Motors Corp., 1959-78, staff engr. in charge Apollo computers, 1967, dir. electronic control systems, 1970-72, dir. advanced product engring., 1972-74; dir. Gen. Motors Proving Grounds, 1974-78; v.p. engring., automotive worldwide TRW Inc., Cleve., 1978-80, group v.p. sales, marketing, planning, bus. develop., 1980—; vice chmn. Motor Vehicle Safety Adv. Council, 1971; chmn. Nat. Hwy. Safety Adv. Com., 1976. Author, patentee automotive safety and electronics. Trustee Lawrence Inst. Tech., 1973-76; mem. exec. bd. Clinton Valley council Boy Scouts Am., 1975; bd. govs. Cranbrook Inst. Sci., 1977. Served as officer Brit. Army, 1955-57. Recipient Safety award for engring. excellence U.S. Dept. Transp., 1978. Fellow Brit. Instn. Elec. Engrs. (Hooper Meml. prize 1950), IEEE (exec. com. vehicle tech. soc. 1977-81), Soc. Automotive Engrs. (Arch T. Colwell paper award 1974, 75, Vincent Bendix Automotive Electronics award 1976); mem. Nat. Acad. Engring., Engring. Soc. Detroit and Cleve. Republican. Episcopalian. Clubs: Birmingham (Mich.) Athletic; Capitol Hill (Washington); Kirtland Country. Home: 18400 Shelburne Rd Shaker Heights OH 44118 Office: TRW Automotive Staff 1900 Richmond Rd Cleveland OH 44124

JONES, VAUGHN PAUL, mental health facility administrator; b. Johnstown, Pa., Apr. 25, 1947; s. Gordon Kenneth and Luella Jane (Seesholtz) J.; m. Margaret Anne Boss, Oct. 20, 1973 (div. July 1985); m. Karen Tolbert, Nov. 22, 1985. BS in Acctg., Ferris State Coll., Mich., 1971; MBA, Capital U., 1985; grad., Columbus (Ohio) Area Leadership Program, 1985-86. Auditor John W. Galbreath, Columbus, 1972-74; mgmt. analyst State of Ohio, Columbus, 1974-76; controller Functional Planning, Inc., Columbus, 1976-82; pres. North Area Mental Health Services, Inc., Columbus, 1982—. Chmn. polit. letterwriting com. State of Ohio, Columbus, 1985; vol. United Way Campaign. Recipient Senatorial citation State of Ohio, Columbus, 1985, House of Reps. citation State of Ohio, Columbus, 1986. Mem. Assn. MBA Execs. Lodge: Rotary (v.p. Capital City West club 1981). Avocation: collecting antique tools. Home: 2328 Arlington Ave Columbus OH 43221 Office: North Area Mental Health Services Inc 5898 Cleveland Ave Columbus OH 43229

JONES, WILLIAM AUGUSTUS, JR., bishop; b. Memphis, Jan. 24, 1927; s. William Augustus and Martha (Wharton) J.; m. Margaret Loaring-Clark, Aug. 26, 1949; 4 children. B.A., Southwestern at Memphis, 1948; B.D., Yale U., 1951. Ordained priest Episcopal Ch., 1952; priest in charge Messiah Ch., Pulaski, Tenn., 1952-57; curate Christ Ch., Nashville, 1957-58; rector St. Mark Ch., LaGrange, Ga., 1958-65; assoc. rector St. Luke Ch., Mountainbrook, Ala., 1965-66; dir. research So. region Assn. Christian Tng. and Service, Memphis, 1966-67; exec. dir. So. region Assn. Christian Tng. and Service, 1968; rector St. John's, Johnson City, Tenn., 1972-75; bishop of Mo. St. Louis, 1975—. Office: Episc Ch 1210 Locust St Saint Louis MO 63103 *

JONES, WILLIAM SOLOMON, JR., physician, surgeon; b. Clifton, Ariz., July 22, 1917; s. William Solomon and Edith Louise (Jackman) J.; m. Mary Rebecca Stimson, June 1, 1945; children: William, Anne, Marcia, Barbara. AB, U. Ariz., 1940; MD, Marquette U., 1943. Diplomate Am. Bd. Otolaryngology. Intern St. Lukes Hosp., Chgo., 1943-44; resident U. Iowa Hosp., Iowa City, 1944-45, 1946-49; practice medicine specializing in otolaryngology, head and neck surgery Menominee, Mich., 1949—; chief of staff St. Joseph-Lloyd Hosp., 1958-60, 1972-74, Marinette (Wis.) Gen. Hosp., 1964-66. Mem. Bd. Edn. Menominee Pub. Schs., 1965-68. Served to lt. (j.g.) USN, 1945-46,PTO, lt. Res. Mem. AMA, ACS, Am. Acad. Otolaryngology, Mich. Med. Soc. (ho. of dels. 1955-56, bd. dirs. 1977-80). Episcopalian. Lodges: Rotary (pres. Menominee 1958-59), Masons, Shriners. Home: 1834 1st St Menominee MI 49858 Office: 1146 10th Ave PO Box 236 Menominee MI 49858

JONISCH, BERNARR, manufacturing company executive. Chief exec. officer Alco Container Corp., Omaha. Office: Alco Container Group 4715 S 132nd St Omaha NE 68114 *

JONS, JULIE JOANNE, publishing executive; b. Garretson, S.D., Nov. 26, 1943; s. Harold August and Esther Geneva (Herreid) J.; m. R. Murray Ogborn, Sept. 10, 1965 (div. Apr. 1980); children: Michael Jon, Elizabeth Anne, Anne Allison. Student, U. Minn., 1961-62, Augustana Coll., Sioux Falls, S.D., 1962-63, No. State Coll., Aberdeen, S.D., 1973-75; BA, U. Nebr., 1980. Editor Nebr. Motor Carriers' Assn., Lincoln, 1980—; pres. Communication Design Specialists, Lincoln, 1985—; adminstr. Nebr. Motor Carriers' Found., Lincoln, 1982-86; desktop pub. cons. Communication Design Specialists Inc., 1986. Editor and writer Nebr. Trucker mag., 1981—. Pres. St. Luke's Hosp. Aux., Aberdeen, S.D., 1973-74. Mem. Internat. Assn. Bus. Communicators (treas. 1982-84), Am. Mktg. Assn. Mem. Unitarian Ch. Club: Prairiewood Golf (Aberdeen) (pres. 1973-74). Lodge: Soroptimists (local sec. 1986—). Avocations: reading, swimming. Office: Communication Design Specialists Inc 521 S 14th #200 Lincoln NE 68508

JONTZ, JAMES (JIM) PRATHER, congressman; b. Indpls., Dec. 18, 1951; s. Leland Dale and Pauline (Prather) J. AB, Ind. U., 1973. Program dir. Lake Mich. Fedn., Chgo.; exec. dir. Ind. Conservation Council, Indpls., 1972-74; mem. Ind. Ho. Reps., Indpls., 1974-84, Ind. State Senate, Indpls., 1984-86, 100th Congress from 5th Ind. dist., Washington, 1987—. Democrat. Methodist. Home: Rural Rt 2 Brookston IN 47923 Office: US Ho Reps Office House Mems 1005 Longworth Office Bldg Washington DC 20515

JORCZYK, EDWARD VINCENT, information systems specialist; b. Bridgeport, Conn., Feb. 15, 1959; s. Edward Rudolph and Eleanor Amelda (Mencel) J. BBA, U. Wis., 1981; MBA, U. Minn., 1985. Cert. systems profl., data processor. Programmer, analyst Gen. Mills, Mpls., 1981-85, applications analyst, 1985-86, info. systems planner, 1986—. Ind. Reps. precinct chairperson, St. Louis Park, Minn., 1986—. Mem. Phi Sigma Epsilon. (pres. 1982-85). Republican. Club: Gen. Mills Employees (pres. 1986—). Avocations: travel, sailing, gardening. Home: 9005 Stanlen Rd Minneapolis MN 55426 Office: General Mills Box 1113 Minneapolis MN 55440

JORDAN, COLEEN MARIE, real estate appraiser; b. Joliet, Ill., Mar. 30, 1953; d. Arthur Joseph and Doroles Florence (Paskvan) Kapella. Student, Lincoln Land Community Coll., 1979-80; BA in Mgmt., Sangamon State U., 1982. Sec. State of Ill., Joliet, 1972-77; dep. cir. ct. clk. 12th Jud. Ill. Cir. Ct., Joliet, 1977-79; sales agt. Century 21, Springfield, Ill., 1983-85; pvt. practice real estate appraising Springfield, 1984—. Mem. Am. Soc. Appraisers, Ill. Bd. Realtors, Springfield Bd. Realtors, Phi Theta Kappa, Alpha Beta Gamma. Avocations: bird watching, jogging. Office: 308 E Lawrence Ave Springfield IL 62701

JORDAN, HOWARD EMERSON, engineer; b. State College, N.Mex., May 14, 1926; s. Howard E. and Elizabeth (Bruden) J.; children: Blair, Julie. BSEE, U. Wis., 1946; MS, Case Western Res. U., 1958, PhD, 1962. With Rayovac Co., Madison, Wis., 1946-52, Reliance Elec., Cleve., 1954—. Author: Energy Efficient Electric Motors and Their Application, 1983; contbg. author: Handbook of Electric Machines, 1987. Served to 1st lt. USAF, 1952-54. Mem. IEEE (sr.), Nat. Electrical Mfrs. Assn. (chmn. motor and generator sect. 1979). Presbyterian. Office: Reliance Electric Co 24701 Euclid Ave Cleveland OH 44117

JORDAN, JIM, association executive; b. Muskogee, Okla., Aug. 29, 1926; s. Tom M. and Ruby M. (Stapleton) J.; m. Betty Lloyd, Nov. 22, 1946; 1 child, James D. Cert. chamber exec., indsl. developer, Mich. Mgr. Agrl.-Area Devel., Muskogee, 1956-62; gen. mgr. C. of C., Muskogee, Okla., 1962-67; v.p. econ. devel. Buffalo Area C. of C., 1967-79; proprietor Jordan Transport Service, Buffalo, 1979-81; exec. v.p. Lansing Regional C. of C., Mich., 1981—. Chmn. 3-County Regional Econ. Devel. Team, gov.'s subcom. on Downtown Lansing Redevelopment; mem. Mich. State U. Japan council; bd. dirs. Joint Labor/Mgmt. council Capital Region Bus. Devel. Corp., Leadership Devel. Acad. Lansing Community Coll. Served with USNR, 1944-46, 1950-52. Mem. Am. C. of C. Execs. Assn., Am. Econ. Devel. Council. Home: 980 Touraine Ave East Lansing MI 48823 Office: 510 W Washtenaw PO Box 14030 Lansing MI 48901

JORDAN, JOHN R., JR., accountant; b. Houston, Jan. 7, 1939; m. Anne Jordan; children—John Jennifer, Stephanie, Anne-Marie, Suzanne. B.A. with highest honors, U. Tex.-Austin, 1961; M.B.A. with high distinction, Harvard Bus. Sch., 1963. With Price Waterhouse, St. Louis, mng. ptnr., mem. policy bd. and finance com. Contbr. articles to profl. jours. Trustee Barnes Hosp., St. Louis; bd. dirs. Washington U. Med. Ctr.; v.p. Cath. Charities, Archdiocese of St. Louis; vice chmn. bd. dirs. Jr. Achievement of Miss. Valley, YMCA of Met. St. Louis; mem. acctg. adv. council U. Tex.-Austin; exec. bd. St. Louis Area council Boy Scouts Am.; fin. com. St. Joseph's Acad.; bd. dirs., v.p. Arts and Edn. Council. Mem. Mo. Soc. C.P.A.s, Am. Inst. C.P.A.s, St. Louis Regional Commerce and Growth Assn. (bd. dirs.), Phi Beta Kappa, Beta Gamma Sigma. Clubs: Bogey, Noonday, Old Warson Country, St. Louis, Harvard Bus. Sch. Avocations: golf; tennis; jogging; photography; reading. Address: Price Waterhouse One Centerre Plaza Saint Louis MO 63101

JORDAN, LEMUEL RUSSELL, hospital administrator; b. Smithfield, N.C., Oct. 21, 1924; s. Thomas and Sophronia Lee (Creech) J.; m. Jean Marrow, Dec. 15, 1951; children: Jean H., Rebecca, Judy. BA, Amherst Coll., 1947; MA, Columbia U., 1949; postgrad. in mgmt., U. N.C., 1949-50, 51-54, Ernest H. Abernathy fellow, 1952-53. Instr. personnel relations U. N.C. Sch. Bus. Adminstrn., 1953-55; asst. dir., asst. prof. hosp. mgmt. Duke U. Med. Ctr., 1955-59; assoc. prof. mgmt. U. Fla. Coll. Bus. Adminstrn., Gainesville, 1959-65; dir. teaching hosps. and clinics J. Hillis Miller Health Ctr., Gainesville, 1959-65; assoc. prof. health and hosp. adminstrn. Coll. Health Related Professions, chmn. grad. program health and hosp. adminstrn., 1963-65; exec. dir., chief exec. officer Bapt. Med. Ctr., Birmingham, Ala., 1965-71, pres., chief exec. officer, 1971-74; pres., chief exec. officer Alton Ochsner Med. Found., New Orleans, 1974-78; chmn. bd., chief exec. officer Eye, Ear, Nose and Throat Hosp. and Clinics, New Orleans, 1976-78; pres., chief exec. officer, bd. dirs. Miami Valley Hosp., Dayton, Ohio, 1978-85; pres., chief exec. officer MedAm. Health Systems Corp., 1982—; adj. prof. U. Ala., Birmingham, 1969-82, Sch. Pub. Health and Tropical Medicine, Tulane U., 1975—, Washington U., St. Louis, 1971—; vis. prof. Kellogg Found., San Salvador, 1964; chmn. Accrediting Commn. Edn. Health Services Adminstrn., 1975-77; adv. com. Robert Wood Johnson Community Hosp.-Med. Staff, Washington, 1974—; guest lectr. Xavier U., Cin., 1978—; adj. assoc. prof. Wright State U. Coll. Medicine, Dayton, 1978—; founder, mem. bd. dirs. VHA Enterprises, adv. com, 1986—. Author papers in field; mem. editorial bd. Healthcare Exec. mag., 1985—. Bd. dirs. Dayton Philharm. Orch., VHA Health Ventures, Voluntary Hosps. Am.; mem. adv. bd. Salvation Army, 1982-85. Served as officer USAAF, World War II, Korea. Named Hon. Alumnus, Duke U., Hon. Alumnus, U. Ala., Hon. Alumnus, George Washington U. Fellow Am. Coll. Hosp. Adminstrs. (chmn. com. article-of-year awards 1969-70); mem. Am. Heart Assn., Am. Hosp. Assn., Am. Mgmt. Assn., Am. Public Health Assn., Nat. League Nursing, Nat. Com. for Quality Health Care (trustee), Assn. Am. Colls (COTH rep.), Dayton Area C. of C. (trustee 1986—), Newcomer Soc., Alpha Kappa Psi (nat. pres. 1959-65, bd. dirs. found. 1965-72, 76—, Disting. Service award 1952, 62-63). Republican. Presbyterian. Clubs: Racquet, Dayton Country (Dayton). Lodge: Rotary. L. R. Jordan Library dedicated at Ida V. Moffett Sch. Nursing, Birmingham, 1975; L. R. Jordan Health Care Mgmt. Soc. founded as nat. ednl. soc., New Orleans, 1978. Office: Miami Valley Hosp 1 Wyoming St Dayton OH 45409

JORDAN, LEO CLAYTON, business executive; b. Louisa, Ky., Nov. 13, 1943; s. Ernest Lowell and Nannie Lee (Wright) J.; m. Margaret Newton, Aug. 21, 1964 (dec. Oct. 1973); 1 child, James R.; m. Elaine G. Beisner, May 7, 1977 (div. Apr. 1981); children: Angela R., Andrew C.; m. Linda Musselman Hartley, Aug. 7, 1982; 1 child, Brian Hartley. BS, Campbellsville Coll., 1964. Gen. acct. Vulcan Tool Co., 1965-72, Tube Products Corp., 1972-74; plant acct. Allied Tech. Inc., 1974-76, div. acctg. mgr., 1976-78, corp. acctg. mgr., 1978-79; controller Lytton Inc., Dayton, Ohio, 1979-85, v.p. fin., 1986—. Mem. Nat. Assn. Accts. (bd. dirs. 1978-79). Republican. Methodist. Avocations: golf, reading, church activities. Home: 1303 Surrey Rd Vandalia OH 45377 Office: Lytton Inc 3970 Image Dr Dayton OH 45414

JORDAN, MICHAEL JEFFERY, professional basketball player; b. Bklyn., Feb. 17, 1963. Student, U. N.C., 1981-84. Player Chgo. Bulls, NBA, 1984—. Recipient Rookie of Yr. award NBA, 1985; named Seagram's NBA Player of Yr., 1987, Most Valuable Player, 1987; named to NBA All-Star team, 1985-87. Mem. NCAA Championship Team, 1982, U.S. Olympic Team, 1984; holder record for most points in a NBA playoff game with 63. Office: c/o David Falk ProServe Inc 888 17th St NW Washington DC 20006 also: c/o Chgo Bulls 1 Magnificent Mile 980 N Michigan Ave Chicago IL 60611 *

JORDAN, ROBERT HADLEY, lawyer, manufacturing company executive; b. Norfolk, Va., Feb. 5, 1959. BSChemE, U. Maine, Orono, 1981; JD, U. Maine, Portland, 1984. Bar: Maine 1984, Minn. 1985, U.S. Patent Office 1985. Patent atty. Minn. Mining and Mfg. Co., St. Paul, 1984—. Advisor Explorer Post, St. Paul, 1985—. Mem. ABA, Minn. Intellectual Property Law Assn. Republican. Avocations: photography, waterskiing. Office: 3M Office of Patent Counsel PO Box 33427 Saint Paul MN 55133-3427

JORDAN, SHARON ANN, clinical social worker, child and family psychotherapist; b. Detroit, July 22, 1953; d. Benneal and Myrtice Marie J. A.B. in Journalism, U. Mich., 1975, M.Urban Planning, 1977, M.S.W., 1979. Intern, research asst. City of Ann Arbor (Mich.), 1976-77; caseworker asst. Ann Arbor Community Center, 1977-78; caseworker aide ARC, 1978-79; parent orientation coordinator U. Mich., 1978, resident dir. housing, 1975-79; adminstrv. intern City of Ann Arbor, 1979; social worker, counselor, staff devel. coordinator U. Mich. opportunity program, 1979-84; clin. social worker U. Mich. Children's Psychiat. Hosp., 1984—. U. Mich. fellow, 1976-77. Mem. Nat. Assn. Social Workers (chairperson Huron Valley chpt.), Acad. Cert. Social Workers, Phi Beta Kappa. Home: 300 N Ingalls Box 50 Ann Arbor MI 48109 Office: U Mich Day Hosp Program NI3 A12 Box 0401 Ann Arbor MI 48109

JORDAN, THURMAN, manufacturing company executive; b. Harrisburg, Ill., Dec. 2, 1936; s. Joseph and Lutishia (Threadgill) J.; m. Teiko Ann Ijichi, Jan. 26, 1963; children—Eric Ichiro, Neal Kiyohiko, Philip Takashi. B.S.B.A., Roosevelt U., Chgo., 1966; M.B.A., U. Chgo., 1982. C.P.A., Ill. Audit mgr. Arthur Andersen & Co., Chgo., 1966-77; corp. controller Signode Corp., Glenview, Ill., 1977-82; v.p., corp. controller Signode Industries, Inc., Glenview, 1982—. Bd. dirs. Evanston United Way, 1978-84, United Way of Suburban Chgo., 1982—, Evanston Art Ctr.; trustee Earn and Learn. Served with Army N.G., 1961-62. Recipient Black Achiever award YMCA, 1977. Mem. United Ch. of Christ. Club: Executive (Chgo.). Office: Signode Industries Inc 3600 W Lake Ave Glenview IL 60025

JORDAN, VIRGINIA GEISEL HOLTON, social worker; b. Hawarden, Iowa, Jan. 9, 1909; d. George Geisel and Madge (Davis) Geisel Holton; m. Paul Hartley Jordan, July 12, 1947 (dec. Nov. 1978); 1 child, Paul Geisel. B Philosophy, U. Chgo., 1934, MA, 1943. Cert. social worker, Ill., Mich. Psychotherapist, writer Inst. Juvenile Research, Chgo., 1943-45, Overseas

Hosp. Service ARC, Luzon, Philippines and Tokyo, 1947-49; mem. staff Mental Hygiene Clinic for Women and Girls Women and Children's Hosp., Chgo., 1947-49; pvt. practice psychotherapy Flint, Mich., 1949—; instr. Washtenaw Community Coll., Ann Arbor, Mich., 1967-75; librarian Library Internat. Relations, Chgo.; lectr. on internat. affairs. Contbr. articles to profl. jours. Recipient Lawrence Mayers Peace award, 1954, 2d prize Midwestern Writers' Conf., 1945, 1st prize, 1947. Fellow Am. Orthopsychiat. Assn. (life, conf. session), Internat. Conf. for Advancement Pvt. Practice in Social Work; mem. Nat. Assn. Social Work (life), People for Promotion Global Understanding, Inst. on Religion in Age of Sci., Am. Assn. for U.N. (organizer Mich. div.), LW (chmn. internat. affairs). Home and Office: 1125 Jordan Ln Grand Blanc MI 48439

JORGENS, THOMAS PHILLIP, regional planner; b. Bertha, Minn., July 14, 1947; s. Joseph Anthony and Anna Marie (Fjeld) J.; B.A., U. Minn., 1969, M.A., 1971; m. Michal Kulenkamp, June 13, 1970; children—Gwendolyn Anna, Amber Blythe. Instr. econs. and history U. Minn., Mpls., 1970-73, researcher, 1974-75; planning dir. Upper Minn. Valley Regional Devel. Commn., Appleton, 1975-79; exec. dir. N.W. Regional Devel. Commn., Crookston, Minn., 1979-86; pres. Meta Dynamics, Inc., Crookston, 1986—; pres. NW Minn. Initiative Fund, 1985—; bd. dirs. Internat. Coalition, 1985—, Crookston Housing and Redevel. Authority, 1985—; exec. vice chmn. Minn. Assn. Regional Commns., 1982-83; mem. Intergovtl. Info. Systems Adv. Council, 1980-83. McMillan fellow, 1972-73. Mem. Am. Planning Assn., Minn. Waterfowl Assn., Ducks Unlimited (bd. dirs. local chpt. 1980-84, chmn. 1985—) , Phi Alpha Theta. Lodge: Lions. Author: The Fiscal Impact of Federal and State Waterfowl Production Areas on Local Units of Government in West Central Minnesota, 1976, A Rural Strategy for Northwest Minnesota, 1985, Integrated Short Rotation Intensive Culture Tree Production and Harvesting as a Cash Crop, 1986. Home: 309 Leonard Ave Crookston MN 56716 Office: 102 N Broadway PO Box 552 Crookston MN 56716

JORGENSEN, DIANE FAY, funeral director; b. Stoughton, Wis., Aug. 10, 1954; d. Philip Ray and Shirley Isabel (Johnson) J. Student, Mt. Mary Coll., 1972-74; Funeral Service (assoc.), Milw. Area Tech. Coll., 1977. Meml. services specialist U.S. Army, Ft. Benning, GA., 1978-81; funeral dir., embalmer Bruni, Nygaard and Ward Funeral Home, Edgerton, Wis., 1981-87; dir. Nat. Cemetery VA Dept. Meml. Affairs, Milw., 1987—. Served with U.S. Army, 1977-81. Mem. Wis. Funeral Dirs. Assn., Nat. Funeral Dirs. Assn., Nat. Assn. Female Execs., Edgerton Jaycettes. Avocation: camping. Home: PO Box 08364 Milwaukee WI 53208 Office: Wood Nat Cemeteryard Funeral Home 5000 W National Ave PO Box 79 Milwaukee WI 53295

JORGENSEN, GERALD THOMAS, psychologist, educator; b. Mason City, Iowa, Jan. 15, 1947; s. Harry Grover and Mary Jo (Kollasch) J.; m. Mary Ann Reiter, Aug. 30, 1969; children—Amy Lynn, Sarah Kay, Jill Kathryn. B.A., Loras Coll., Dubuque, 1969; M.S., Colo. State U., Ft. Collins, 1970, Ph.D., 1973. Lic. psychologist, Iowa. Psychology intern Counseling Ctr., Colo. State U., Ft. Collins, 1971-72, VA Hosp., Palo Alto, Calif., 1927-73; psychologist Loras Coll., 1973-76, Clarke Coll., Dubuque, 1973-76; asst. prof. psychology, Loras Coll., 1976-80, assoc. prof., 1981—, dir. Ctr. for Counseling and Student Devel., 1977-86, assoc. dean of students, 1985-86, dean of students, v.p. for student devel., 1986—; cons. and supervising psychologist Dubuque/Jackson County Mental Health Ctr., 1977—; chairperson Iowa Bd. Psychology Examiners, Des Moines, 1984—, continuing edn. coordinator, 1981. Contbr. articles to profl. jours. Treas. Dubuque County Assn. Mental Health Inc., Dubuque, 1975-82. NDEA fellow, 1969-72. Mem. Am. Coll. Personnel Assn. (chmn. com. VII 1980-82), Am. Assn. Counseling Devel., Am. Psychol. Assn., Iowa Psychol. Assn. (mem. exec. council), Am. Assn. State Psychol. Bds. (exec. com. 1986—), Iowa Student Personnel Assn., Delta Epsilon Sigma, Phi Kappa Phi, Sigma Tau Phi. Democrat. Roman Catholic. Home: 2183 Saint Celia St Dubuque IA 52001 Office: Loras Coll 1450 Alta Vista St Dubuque IA 52004-0178

JORGENSEN, PALLE ERIK TIKOB, mathematician, educator; b. Copenhagen, Denmark, Oct. 8, 1947; came to U.S., 1973, naturalized, 1979; s. Soren A.W. and Gyrit D. (Baden) J.; m. Soon-Min Park, Jan. 4, 1975; children: Anton Y., Greta S., Tina S. AB, U. Aarhus, Denmark, 1968, MS, 1970, PhD, 1973. Asst. prof. math. Stanford (Calif.) U., 1977-79; assoc. prof. U. Aarhus, 1979-83; prof. U. Iowa, Iowa City, 1983—; vis. assoc. prof. U. Pa., Phila., 1982-84. Author: Operator Commutation Relations, 1984, other books on advanced math.; editor: Acta Applicandae Mathematicae, 1983—; contbr. articles to profl. jours. Grantee Danish Research Council, 1976-77, NSF, 1977-79, 82—. Mem. Am. Math. Soc., Danish Math. Soc., Math. Assn. Am., Danish Acad. Sci., Soc. Indsl. and Applied Math. Office: U Iowa Dept Math Iowa City IA 52242

JORGENSEN, RICHARD FREDRICK, insurance executive, city government official; b. Omaha, Apr. 16, 1923; s. Anker Beck Jorgensen and Violet Phyllis (Tyson) Bush; m. Martha Winnifred Irwin, Sept. 3, 1949; 1 child, Eric Paul. Student, Iowa State U., 1946-47, Drake U., 1947-49. CLU; cert. fin. planner; registered health underwriter. Editor Aircraft Dealer mag., Des Moines, 1945-46; dir. air age edn. Iowa Aeronautics Commn., Des Moines, 1948-53; agt. Bankers Life Co., Des Moines, 1953-62; mgr. Union Cen. Life, Des Moines, 1962-67; co-proprietor Jorgensen & Kraeger CLU's, Des Moines, 1967-69; exec. Banker's Life Co. now known as Prin. Fin. Group, Des Moines, 1969—. Patentee in field; contbr. articles to profl. jours. Councilman 3d ward City of Des Moines, 1986—; mem. Mayor's Economy Study Com., 1981, Univ. Place Commerce Co.; past bd. dirs. Neighborhood Housing Services Devel. Corp.; vice chmn. Des Moines Citizen's Sign Com., 1967; mem. council, elder Coll. Ave. Christian Ch.; chmn. Com. to Found Jr. Achievement, Des Moines, 1954-55, Des Moines Riverfront Improvement Commn.; chmn. div. United Way campaign, Des Moines, 1976; mem. bridging com Morris Scholarship Fund, 1983. Served with USAF, 1942-46, maj. res. Recipient Nat. Leadership award Jr. Achievement, Inc., Des Moines, 1978. Fellow Am. Soc. CLU, Inst. Cert. Fin. Planners (past pres. Iowa chpt.); mem. Des Moines Assn. Life Underwriters, Internat. Assn. Fin. Planning (past pres. Des Moines chpt.), Internat. Traders Iowa, Iowa Data Processing Educators Assn., Nat. Assn. Health Underwriters, Nat. Assn. Life Underwriters, Res. Officers Assn. of U.S., The Retired Officers Assn., Iowa Air Force Assn. (past pres.), Des Moines Res. Officers Assn. (past pres.), South Des Moines C. of C. (housing task force com.), Am. Soc. Tng. and Devel., Gen. Agts. and Mgrs. Assn., Greater Des Moines C. of C. Found., Des Moines Estate Planning Council (past pres.), Aerospace Edn. Council Iowa (past pres.), Aircraft Owners and Pilots Assn., Antique Airplane Assn., U.S. Rowing Assn. (assoc. official). Republican. Clubs: East Des Moines, Hawkeye Postcard, Highland Park-Des Moines Bus. (past pres.), Des Moines Rowing (past pres.), Nat. Exchange of Des Moines (past pres.), Friday Forum. Lodges: Order of Daedalians, Quiet Birdmen. Avocations: flying, sculling, rowing. Home: 4005 Kingman Blvd Des Moines IA 50311 Office: Prin Fin Group 711 High St Des Moines IA 50309

JORNDT, LOUIS DANIEL, drug store chain executive; b. Chgo., Aug. 24, 1941; s. Louis Carl and Margaret Estelle (Teel) J.; m. Patricia McDonnell, Aug. 1, 1964; children—Kristine, Michael, Kara. B.S. in Pharmacy, Drake U., 1963; M.B.A., U. N.Mex., 1974. Various mgmt. positions Walgreen Co., Chgo., 1963-68, dist. mgr., 1968-75; regional dir. Walgreen Co., Deerfield, Ill., 1975-79; regional v.p. Walgreen Co., Deerfield, 1979-82, v.p., treas., 1982-85, sr. v.p., treas., 1985—. Bd. dirs. Better Bus. Bur. Chgo., 1982—, Chgo. Assn. Commerce and Industry; nat. chmn. Drake U. Pharmacy Alumni Fund. Mem. Nat. Assn. Corp. Treas., Fin. Execs. Inst. Clubs: Economic (Chgo.); Glen View (Ill.) Golf. Avocations: golf; swimming; reading. Office: Walgreen Co 200 Wilmot Rd Deerfield IL 60015

JORTBERG, RICHARD EDMUND, utility corp. consultant; b. Portland, Maine, June 8, 1923; s. Charles Augustus and Adelaide Cecelia (Mahoney) J.; B.S., U.S. Naval Acad., 1944; M.S., George Washington U., 1971; m. Jo Ann Mundy, June 7, 1952; children—Judith, Patricia, Richard Edmund, Michael. Commd. ensign U.S. Navy, 1944, advanced through grades to capt., 1965; comdr. nuclear attack submarine USS Tullibee, 1959-63, Polaris missile submarine USS Henry L. Stimson, 1965-67, project mgr. deep submergence, Washington, 1969-73, ret., 1973; chief engr. Clinch River Breeder Reactor, Project Mgmt. Corp., 1973-76, gen. mgr. Commonwealth Research Corp., Chgo., 1976-81, dir. nuclear safety Commonwealth Edison Co., Chgo., 1981-84, asst. v.p., 1984-85. cons. nuclear industry, 1986—. . Pres., Canterbury Improvement Assn., 1982-83. Decorated Bronze Star medal, Legion of Merit with cluster, Purple Heart. Mem. Am. Nuclear Soc., Clubs: Executive (Chgo.); Valley Lo Sports (Glenview, Ill.) (bd. dirs.); N.Y. Yacht (N.Y.C.). Roman Catholic.

JOS, C. J., psychiatrist; b. India, May 16, 1943; came to U.S., 1976; m. Tessy C. Jos, May 12, 1969; children: Sapna, Agnes. BS, B in Medicine, U. Mysore, India, 1966; MD, U. Mysore, 1971. Diplomate Am. Bd. Psychiatry and Neurology. Staff psychiatrist VA Med. Ctr., St. Louis, 1979—, supr. psychiatry residents, 1980—; asst. clin. prof. St. Louis U., 1979—; dir. Family Health Services, St. Louis, 1986—. Contbr. articles to profl jours. Research grantee VA Med. Ctr., St. Louis, 1981. Mem. Am. Psychiat. Assn., Ea. Mo. Psychiat. Soc. Roman Catholic. Avocations: tennis, table tennis. Office: VA Med Ctr Saint Louis MO 63125

JOSCELYN, KENT BUCKLEY, research scientist, lawyer; b. Binghamton, N.Y., Dec. 18, 1936; s. Raymond Miles and Gwen Buckley (Smith) J.; B.S., Union Coll., 1957; J.D., Albany Law Sch., 1960; m. Mary A. Komoroske, Nov. 20, 1965; children—Kathryn Anne, Jennifer Sheldon. Bar: N.Y. 1961, U.S. Ct. Mil. Appeals 1962, D.C. 1967, Mich. 1979. Atty., adviser Hdqrs. USAF, Washington, 1965-67; asso. prof. forensic studies Coll. Arts and Scis., Ind. U., Bloomington, 1967-76, dir. Inst. Research in Pub. Safety, 1970-75; head policy analysis div. Hwy. Safety Research Inst., U. Mich., 1976-81, dir. transp. planning and policy, Urban Tech., Environ. Planning Program, 1981-84; partner firm Joscelyn & Treat, P.C., 1981—; cons. Law Enforcement Assistance Adminstrn., U.S. Dept. Justice, 1969-72; Gov.'s appointee as regional dir. Ind. Criminal Justice Planning Agy., also vice chmn. Ind. Organized Crime Prevention Council, 1969-72; commr. pub. safety City of Bloomington, 1974-76. Served to capt., USAF, 1961-64. Mem. Transp. Research Bd. (chmn. motor vehicle and traffic law com. 1979-82), Nat. Acad. Sci., NRC, Am. Soc. Criminology, Am. Assn. Automotive Medicine, Soc. Automotive Engrs., Am. Soc. Pub. Adminstrn., Acad. Criminal Justice Scis., ABA, D.C., Mich., N.Y. State bar assns., Internat. Assn. Chiefs Police (asso.), Nat. Safety Council, Sigma Xi. Editor Internat. Jour. Criminal Justice. Office: 325 E Eisenhower Pkwy Ann Arbor MI 48108

JOSE, PHYLLIS ANN, librarian; b. Detroit, Mar. 15, 1949; d. William Henry and Isobel Eleanor (Mundle) J.; B.A., Mich. State U., 1971, M.A., 1972; M.A. in Library Sci., U. Mich., 1975. Library aide audio-visual div. Dearborn (Mich.) Dept. Libraries, 1973-76, librarian gen. info. div., 1976-77; reference library dir. Oakland County (Mich.) Library, 1977—. Officer Southfield Economic Devel. Corp., 1980—; mem. Southfield Tax Increment Fin. Authority, 1981—; bd. dirs. Southfield Arts Council, 1983—; coordinator Southfield Arts Festival, 1984, 85. Mem. ALA, Mich. Library Assn.(ALA cpht. councilor). Presbyterian. Office: 1200 N Telegraph Rd Pontiac MI 48053

JOSEPH, DONALD LOUIS, management consultant; b. Chgo., Dec. 29, 1942; s. Herbert H. and Florence (Gaertner) J.; B.S. in Engring. Sci., Washington U., St. Louis, 1964; M.B.A., Harvard U., 1966; m. Joyce H. Brand, Dec. 20, 1981. Cert. mgmt. cons. Systems Engr. Teletype Corp., Skokie, Ill., 1966-68; sr. assoc. Brandon Applied Systems, Inc., Chgo., 1968-71; sr. cons. Daniel D. Howard Assoc., Inc., Chgo., 1971-72; dir. mgmt. systems Opelika Mfg. Corp., Chgo., 1972-77; dep. exec. dir. Am. Soc. Clin. Pathologists, Chgo., 1978-80, v.p. fin. and adminstrn., 1980-81; pres. DLJ Assos., Chgo., 1981—; sr. project cons. Stone Mgmt. Corp., 1982-84; bd. dirs. Inst. Mgmt. COns., mgmt. adv. services Shepard, Schwartz & Harris, C.P.A.s, Chgo., 1985—; dir. Office Automation Systems, Hise, Donahue & Assocs., Inc., 1983-84; mem. faculty Elmhurst Mgmt. Program Elmhurst Coll., 1982—. Bd. dirs. Horizon House, Chgo., pres., 1981-82. Mem. Harvard U. Bus. Sch. Assn. Chgo., Am. Soc. Assn. Execs., Chgo. Soc. Assn. Execs., Assn. M.B.A. Execs., Better Govt. Assn., Assn. Systems Mgt., Inst. Mgmt. Cons., Tau Beta Pi, Omicron Delta Kappa. Home: 5733 N Sheridan Rd Chicago IL 60660 Office: Shepard Schwartz & Harris 150 N Wacker Dr Chicago IL 60606

JOSEPH, DWIGHT D., municipal protective services official. Chief of police City of Columbus, Ohio. Office: Office of the Police Chief 120 W Gay St Columbus OH 43215 *

JOSEPH, EARL CLARK, futurist; b. St. Paul, Nov. 1, 1926; s. Clark Herbert and Ida Bertha (Schultz) J.; A.A., U. Minn., 1947, B.A., 1951; m. Alma Caroline Bennett, Nov. 19, 1955; children—Alma (Mrs. Richard Chadner), Earl, Vincent, René. Mathematician/programmer Remington Rand Univac, Arlington, Va., 1951-55, supr., St. Paul, 1955-60, systems mgr. Sperry Univac, St. Paul, 1960-63, staff scientist-futurist, 1963-82; pres. Anticipatory Scis., Inc., 1981—; bd. dirs. Dorn, Swensen & Myer, Inc.; lectr. Coll. St. Thomas, 1985—, Met. State U., 1978—; instr. Walden Univ., 1985—; scholar Scholar Leadership Enrichment Program, Okla. U., 1984; vis. lectr. U. Minn., Mpls., 1971—; mem. Sci. and Mgmt. Adv. Com., U.S. Army, 1972-74. Futurist-in-residence Sci. Mus. of Minn., 1973-82; chmn. bd. Future Systems, 1979-81. Chmn., Met. Young Adult Ministry, 1967-69; mem. Gov.'s Planning Commn. for City Center Learning, 1968. Served with USNR, 1944-46. Disting. lectr. IEEE Computer Soc., 1971-72, 76-82, Assn. Computer Machinery. Mem. IEEE (sr.), Minn. Futurists (founder, dir., past pres.), World Future Soc., Soc. for Gen. Systems Research (founding chpt. pres., bd. dirs. 1978—), Assn. Computer Machinery (gen. chmn. 1975, pres. chpt. 1976-77, 86—), AAAS, Data Processing Mgmt. Assn., Beta Phi Beta. Patents, publs. in field; co-author 50 books; founding editor jour. Futurics; editor Future Trends Newsletter, System Trends Newsletter; adv. editor Jour. Cultural and Ednl. Futures. Home: 365 Summit Ave Saint Paul MN 55102 Office: Anticipatory Scis Inc 245 E 6th St Suite 700 Saint Paul MN 55101

JOSEPH, ILSE HORN, social worker; b. Riesa, German Democratic Republic, Jan. 18, 1921; came to U.S., 1938; d. Saul Louis and Luise Mathilde (Hoeltermann) Horn; m. Gunter Walter Joseph, Jan. 27, 1940; children: Steven George, James Ronald. Pre-med. student, Indiana U., 1938-40. Lic. social worker, Mich.; lic. real estate agt., Mich. Office supr. Artic Refrigeration, Lansing, Mich., 1940-52; office supr. Automotive Supply Ctr., Lansing, 1952-61, owner, mgr., 1961-63; social worker Mich. Dept. Social Services, Eaton and Ingham Counties, 1963-86. Chmn. membership com. Council for Prevention Child Abuse and Neglect, 1981-82; active Sisterhood of Congregation Shaarey Zedek, Lansing; pres. B'Nai B'rith Women's Chpt., Lansing, 1956-58; pres. B'nai B'rith Women's Council of Mich., 1958-60. Recipient Services to Children award Council for Prevention of Child Abuse and Neglect, 1977, award for 20 Yrs. Service to Children American Humane Assn., 1983, cert. of Appreciation, Ingham County Probate Ct., 1986. Mem. Greater Lansing Bd. Realtors. Avocations: writing autobiography for grandchildren, reading, gardening, cooking, traveling. Home: 3801 Inverary Dr Lansing MI 48910

JOSEPH, MARILYN SUSAN, gynecologist; b. Bklyn., Aug. 18, 1946; d. S. Seymour and Maxine Laura (Stern) J.; m. Warren Erwin Regelmann, Dec. 20, 1969; children: Adam Gustave, David Joseph. BA, Smith Coll., 1968; MD cum laude, SUNY Downstate Med. Ctr., Bklyn., 1972. Diplomate Am. Bd. Ob-Gyn, Nat. Bd. Med. Examiners. Intern U. Minn. Hosps., 1972-73, resident in ob-gyn, 1972-76; med. fellow specialist U. Minn., 1972-76, asst. prof. ob-gyn, 1976—, dir. women's clinic, 1984—. Author: Differential Diagnosis Obstetrics, 1978. Fellow Am. Coll. Ob-Gyn (best paper dist. VI meeting 1981); mem. Am. Assn. Gynecol. Laparoscopy, Hennepin County Med. Soc., Minn. State Med. Assn., Mpls. Council Ob-Gyn, Minn. State Ob-Gyn Soc. Jewish. Avocations: cooking bird, watching, travel. Home: 3 Sandpiper Ln North Oaks MN 55127 Office: Boynton Health Service 410 Church St Minneapolis MN 55455-0346

JOSEPH, MONICA ANNA BILCHECK, music educator; b. Orient, Pa., Sept. 3, 1926; d. John and Mary Elizabeth (Blachak) B.; m. Jamele E. Joseph, Aug. 18, 1973. B.Music, Marywood Coll., Scranton, Pa., 1966, M.Music, DePaul U., Chgo., 1970. Tchr. pvt. schs., Trenton, N.J., 1948-50, 56-58, Scranton, Pa., 1950-53, Gary, Ind., 1953-55; adminstr. St. Mary's Sch., Freeland, Pa., 1960-63, Holy Ghost Sch., Jessup, Pa., 1963-66, St. Michael's Sch., Gary, Ind., 1958-60, 66-69; music supr. parochial schs. Diocese Gary, 1969-72; tchr. pub. schs. Waterford and Westwood Heights, Mich., 1972-75; asst. prof. class piano C.S. Mott Community Coll., Flint, Mich., 1975—; pvt. piano tchr. Flint. Monterrey (Mex.) Inst. Tech. Fulbright-Hays grantee, 1970. Mem. Nat. Music Tchrs. Assn., Mich. Music Tchrs. Assn., Flint Music Tchrs. Assn. (pres. 1978-80, Tchr. of Yr. 1981-82), Nat. Fedn. Music, NEA, St. Cecelia Soc. (audition chmn. 1985-86). Roman Catholic. Lodge: Altrusa (pres. 1981-83, 85-86). Home: 6989 Wedgewood Dr Grand Blanc MI 48439 Office: 1025 E Kearsley St Flint MI 48502

JOSEPH, MYRON L., lawyer; b. Cleve., July 11, 1936; s. Lawrence and Florence (Klein) J.; m. Jaye Avery Singer, Aug. 21, 1960; children: Barrie Lynn, Steven Lawrence. BS in Bus. Adminstrn., Northwestern U., 1958; LLB, Case Western Res. U., 1961; LLM in Taxation, Georgetown U., 1967. Assoc. Laikin, Jacobson & Swietlik, Milw., 1961-63; atty. Office of Chief Counsel IRS, Washington, 1963-68; assoc. Chapman & Cutler, Chgo., 1968-71, Meldman Ltd., Milw., 1971-77, Charne, Glassner, Tehan, Clancy & Taitelman, Milw., 1977—; inst. taxation U. Wis., Milw., 1972-80. Contbr. articles to profl. jours. Bd. dirs. St. Francis Hosp. Found., Milw., 1973-76; sec. and bd. dirs. Milw. Jewish Home for Aged, 1982—; bd. dirs. Wis. affiliation Am. Diabetes Assn., Milw., 1986—. Mem. ABA (tax sect.), State Bar Assn. Wis. (bd. dirs. taxation sect. 1977-85, chmn. 1985-86), Milw. Bar Assn. (chmn. tax sect. 1976-77, treas. 1977-80), Estate Counselors Forum, Milw. Estate Planning Council (bd. dirs. 1987—). Republican. Jewish. Club: Ville du Parc Country (Mequon, Wis.). Avocations: tennis, golf. Home: 740 E Fairy Chasm Rd Milwaukee WI 53217 Office: Charne Glassner Tehan Clancy & Taitelman 211 W Wisconsin Ave Milwaukee WI 53203

JOSEPH, SAMUEL KENNETH, education educator, rabbi; b. Phila., Aug. 15, 1949; s. Arthur W. and Judith (Brandes) J.; m. Dori Matje; children: Rachel, Bethami. BS, U. Cin., 1971; MA in Hebrew Letters, Hebrew Union Coll., Cin., 1974; PhD, Clayton U., 1979. Ordained rabbi, 1976. Rabbi Temple Israel, Dayton, Ohio, 1976-79; nat. dir. admissions Hebrew Union Coll., 1979-81, asst. to pres., 1980-81, asst. prof. edn., 1981-84, assoc. prof. edn., 1984—. Author: Jews and The Founding of the Republic, 1985, How to be a Jewish Teacher: An Invitation to Make a Difference, 1987; editor Compass Jour., 1986—; contbr. articles to profl. jours. Bd. dirs. Metro Area Religious Coalition Cin., Jewish Community Relations Council, Black-Jewish Coalition, Interfaith Roundtables. Recipient Tchr. of Yr., Kohl Edn. Found., 1985. Fellow Internat. Ctr. Univ. Teaching Jewish Civilization; mem. Religious Edn. Assn., Assn. Supervision and Curriculum Devel. (nat. supervision commn. 1984-86), Nat. Assn. Temple Educators, Cen. Conf. Am. Rabbis. Avocations: travel, music. Home: 4047 Beechwood Cincinnati OH 45229 Office: Hebrew Union Coll 3101 Clifton Cincinnati OH 45229

JOSEPH, STEPHEN RICHARD, financial systems manager; b. N.Y.C., Feb. 24, 1943; s. Jack J. and Frances (Ginsburg) J.; m. Marie Agnes Lukcso, Aug. 30, 1981; 1 child, Donna. BBA, Pace U., 1964; MBA, Baldwin-Wallace Coll., 1979. CPA, N.Y., Ohio. Semi-sr. auditor Morris, Sherwood & May, N.Y.C., 1964-66; sr. auditor Kaplan Rosen & Co., N.Y.C., 1966-69, Standard Oil Co., Cleve., 1969-74; project mgr. Alyeska Pipeline Co., Anchorage, 1976-77; supr., fin. analyst The Standard Oil Co., Cleve., 1974-79, mgr., transp. systems, 1977-78, mgr acctg. systems, 1978-81, mgr. fin. systems, 1981—; cons. Sohio Alaska Petroleum Co., San Francisco, 1980-81. Mem. Am. Inst. CPA's, Data Processing Mgmt. Assn., Inst. Internal Auditors (committee chmn.), Nat. Inst. Mgmt. Research. (speaker), Homeowners Assn. (v.p., treas. 1982-83), Assn. Systems Mgmt. Home: 1751 Settlers Reserve Way Westlake OH 44145 Office: The Standard Oil Co 200 Public Square Cleveland OH 44114-2375

JOSEPH-FELDMAN, DIANE, appraiser; b. Chgo., May 21, 1933; d. Wilfried Elmer and Rose (Kopca) Davis; ed. Am. Acad. Art, Art Inst. Chgo., Stone-Camryn Sch. Ballet; m. Z. Albert Joseph, 1957 (div. 1969); m. Hy Feldman, Feb. 14, 1979; children—Diana Jill Joseph, John Alan Joseph. Soloist, tchr. ballet Interlochen (Mich.) Nat. Music Camp, 1954-55; soloist in Brigadoon, N.Y.C. Center, 1956, My Fair Lady, other musicals; dancer WGN-TV and Lyric Opera Ballet, Chgo., 1955-58; founder, pres. Heritage Appraisal Service, Inc., Wilmette, Ill., 1971-82; lectr, instr. continuing edn. series antiques Oakton Community Coll. Vol., Hospice of North Shore, Cancer Care Ctr. of Evanston Hosp., Planned Parenthood; bd. mem., Y-Me Breast Cancer Support Group; moderator, Evanston Hosps. Cancer Self-Help Group. Mem. Simon Wiesenthal Center, Democratic Nat. Orgn. Mem. Internat. Soc. Appraisers (rec. and corr. sec. Chgo. chpt.), New Eng. Appraisers Assn., ACLU, NOW, Audubon Soc. Address: 2201 Crestview Ln Wilmette IL 60091

JOSEPHSON, DAVID A., neurologist; b. Gary, Ind., Feb. 24, 1946; s. Sidney N. and Faye W. (Winerlack) J.; m. Jane Cohen, Aug. 17, 1969; 1 child, Andrew. AB with high honors, Ind. U., 1968; MD, Ind. U., Indpls., 1971. Diplomate Am Bd. Psychiatry and Neurolog,. Neurologist Neurology Assocs., Inc., Indpls., 1975—; chmn. dept. neurology Community Hosps., Indpls. Mem. ACP, AMA, Am. Acad. Neurology, Ind. Neurol. Soc. (pres.), Phi Beta Kappa, Alpha Omega Alpha.

JOSEPHSON, JAY LARRY, metal processing executive, accountant; b. Chgo., June 25, 1950; s. Albert and Dorothy (Barmash) J.; m. Lauren Marshall, July 24, 1983; children: Jennifer, Jamie. BS in Acctg. cum laude, No. Ill. U., 1972. CPA, Ill. Acct. Touche Ross & Co., Chgo., 1972-75, Weiss & Co., Northfield, Ill., 1975-78; v.p. fin. Gould Metals, Inc., Schaumburg, Ill., 1978-85; exec. v.p. Tri Star Metals, Inc., Hoffman Estates, Ill., 1985—. Mem. Am. Inst. CPA's, Ill. CPA Soc., Beta Alpha Psi, Beta Gamma Sigma. Club: Mamic (Buffalo Grove, Ill.) (pres. 1978-79). Avocations: golf, tennis, bowling, softball. Home: 2451 N Douglas Ave Arlington Heights IL 60004

JOSEPHSON, PHILIP, fraternal organization administrator; b. Stillwater, Minn., May 26, 1950; s. Alden Clarence and Helen Jeanette (Danielson) J.; m. Jane Carole Pribyl; July 10, 1976; children: Noel, Hans. BS, U. Wis., River Falls, 1972. Asst. exec. dir. Alpha Gamma Rho, Des Plaines, Ill., 1972-75; exec. dir. Alpha Gamma Rho, Kansas City, Mo., 1975. Named Man of Yr. Chgo. Agriculturalists, 1981; recipient Certificate of Achievement Luth. Ch., Prospect Heights, Ill. 1984. Mem. Am. Soc. Assn. Execs., Mo.-Kans. Soc. Assn. Execs., Nat. Interfraternity Conference (bd. dirs. 1984—, cert. 1982), Fraternity Exec. Assn. (pres., bd. dirs. 1980—, Service award 1985—), Bus. and Profl. Assn., Am. Farm Bur. Fedn. Republican. Lodge: Rotary. Avocations: family, snow skiing, golf, racquetball, sports. Office: Alpha Gamma Rho Fraternity 10101 N Executive Hills Blvd Kansas City MO 64153

JOSIAH, TIMOTHY WILLIAM, military officer; b. Bklyn., May 17, 1947; s. William E. and Ruth I. (Whalen) J.; m. Judith A. Saltzman, July 10, 1981. BS, USCG Acad., 1969; JD, U. Md., 1980. Bar: D.C. 1980. Commd. ensign USCG, 1969, advanced through grades to comdr., 1984; chief inspection dept. USCG Marine Safety Office, Balt., 1978—, chief investigations dept., 1978-80; comdg. officer USCG Marine Safety Office, St. Louis, 1985—; chief environ. coordination br. USCG Hdqrs., Washington, 1980-85; advisor assembly marine environ. protection com. U.S. Dels. to Internat. Maritime Orgn., London, 1980-85. Mem. ABA, D.C. Bar Assn., Soc. of Naval Architects and Marine Engrs., Order of Coif. Home: 2379 Westclub Terr Ct Ellisville MO 63011 Office: USCG Marine Safety Office 210 N Tucker Blvd Suite 1128 Saint Louis MO 63101

JOSLYN, DANIEL VANCE, manufacturing company executive; b. Phila., Apr. 22, 1955; s. Ronald J. and Cecelia (Bonbright) J. BS in Indsl. Engring., U. Wis., 1977; MBA, Marquette U., 1981. Indsl. engr. Miller Brewing Co., Milw., 1977-81; corp. engr. Baxter Travenol, Deerfield, Ill., 1981-83; v.p. mfg. Rockline, Sheboygan, Wis., 1983—; cons. in field. Inventor coffee filter dispenser. Bd. dirs. Sheboygan chpt. Big Bros., 1986—. Mem. Mensa. Home: 737 Tomahawk Trail Sheboygan WI 53081 Office: Rockline 813 S Commerce Sheboygan WI 53081

JOSLYN, WALLACE DANFORTH, psychologist; b. Cape Girardeau, Mo., Apr. 13, 1939; s. Lewis Danforth and Margaret Bernice (Gallup) J.; m. Annette Andre, Aug. 27, 1966 (div. Feb. 1969); m. Maureen V. Drescher, May 26, 1979; 1 child, Jonathan David. BA, U. Va., 1961; MS, U. Wis., 1965, PhD, 1967. Lic. psychologist, Iowa. Research asst. Oreg. Regional Primate Research Ctr., Beaverton, 1967-71; clin. psychologist VA Hosp., Knoxville, Iowa, 1972—. Contbr. articles to profl. jours. Fellow NIMH. Republican. Avocations: photography, running, travel, investing. Home:

802 E Competine Knoxville IA 50138 Office: VA Med Ctr Knoxville IA 50138

JOST, PETER, dentist; b. Linz, Austria, June 14, 1955; s. Nikolaus and Katharina (Sattler) J.; m. Laurie Ann Goetz, July 16, 1983; 1 child, Erika Nicole. B in Gen. Studies, U. Mich., Ann Arbor, 1977, DDS, 1981. Dentist Warren (Mich.) Dental Assocs., 1981-84, Dr. E. Ray Stricker, East Detroit, Mich., 1982-85, Dr. Edgar Grieshaber, East Detroit, Mich., 1984-85; pvt. practice East Detroit, Mich., 1985—. Mem. ADA, Mich. Dental Assn., Macomb Dental Soc., Acad. Gen. Dentistry. Roman Catholic. Avocations: softball, jogging, woodwork, reading hist. lit. Office: 18540 E Nine Mile Rd East Detroit MI 48021

JOSTEN, ROY JOSEPH, lawyer; b. Milw., Jan. 31, 1940; s. George John and Adelle L. (Lang) J.; m. Mary Woodruff, June 7, 1969; children—Mark Michael, Theodore Anthony, Alicia Widmer. B.A. magna cum laude, Marquette U., 1963; J.D. cum laude, U. Mich., 1969. Bar: Wis. 1969. Assoc. Whyte & Hirschboeck, S.C., Milw., 1969-72; ptnr. Stewart, Peyton, Crawford & Josten, Racine, Wis., 1972-78; mem. Josten, DuRocher Murphy and Pierce, S.C., Racine, 1978—. Co-founder Civil Legal Services, Inc., Racine, 1975, bd. dirs. 1975-78, pres., 1975-77; mem. adv. bd. Cath. Social Services, Racine, 1974-80, pres., 1975-77; bd. dirs. Racine County Opportunity Ctr., Inc., 1980-84, sec. 1981-84; bd. dirs. Downtown Racine Devel. Corp., 1981-83, pres., 1982-83; bd. dirs. Neighborhood Housing Services Racine, Inc., 1976-78, Racine County Area Found., Inc., 1984—, Catholic Social Services Found., Inc., 1983-85; bd. dirs., pres. Preservation Racine, Inc., 1980-81; mem. adv. bd. Ctr. for Community Concerns, 1984-85. Served with U.S. Army, 1963-66. Mem. ABA, State Bar Wis. (bd. govs. 1983-87), Racine County Bar Assn. Roman Catholic. Club: KC. Assoc. editor Mich. Law Rev., 1968-69. Home: 5501 Valley Trail Racine WI 53402 Office: 927 Main St Racine WI 53403

JOURDAN, MICHAEL ERHARDT, podiatrist; b. Pontiac, Ill., Feb. 15, 1948; s. Clarence Calhoun and Evelyn Mae (Taylor) J.; m. Linda Sue Schroeder, June 19, 1971; children: Cassie, Jennifer, Annie. Student, Ill. State U., 1966-68; DPM, Ill. Coll. Podiatric Med., 1972. Diplomate Nat. Bd. Podiatric Examiners, Am. Bd. Podiatric Surgery. Enlisted U.S. Army, 1972, advanced through ranks to capt.; podiatrist U.S. Army, Ft. Leonardwood, Mo., 1972-76; resigned U.S. Army, 1976; podiatrist Podiatry Assocs. of Wausau, Wis., 1976—. Mem. Am. Podiatry Med. Assn., Wis. State Podiatry Soc. (pres. 1987—), Am. Coll. Foot Surgeons (assoc.). Avocations: running, reading, sports. Office: Podiatry Assocs of Wausau 1445 Merrill Ave Wausau WI 54401

JOY, RICHARD HENRY, association executive, communications consultant, writer; b. Detroit, Oct. 2, 1932; s. William Raymond and Helen Elizabeth (Jamieson) J.; divorced; children—Kenneth R., Karen L., R. Scott. B.A. in Speech, U. Mich., 1954. Dir. liaison, sales, prodn. The Jam Handy Orgn., Detroit, 1956-61; mgr. corp. audio-visual and photographic services Burroughs Corp., 1961-76; cons., writer, dir., 1976—; exec. dir. Audio-Visual Mgmt. Assn., Royal Oak, 1979—. Served to 1st lt. AUS, 1954-56. Recipient "The Bennie" award Printing Industries of Am., 1973; Disting. Achievement award Ind. Audio-Visual Assn., 1974; CINE Golden Eagle, 1985. Mem. Detroit Producers Assn. Presbyterian. Clubs: U. Mich. of Detroit, High Noon Old Pro League. Editor/producer Village Vision for Presbyterian Village, Inc. Producer/writer/dir. numerous sales and ednl. motion pictures, slide presentations, speeches, articles, brochures, and videotape presentations. Home and Office: 3633 Crooks Rd #4 Royal Oak MI 48073

JU, SEMMY, educational administrator; b. Peking, People's Republic of China, Sept. 11, 1945; came to U.S., 1970; B of Archtl. Engring., Chung-Yuan Christian Coll. Sci. and Engring., Chung-Li, Republic of China, 1969; M of Regional Planning, U. Mass., 1972. Planner, office phys. planning and constrn. U. Chgo., 1972-79; assoc. dir. office budget and planning No. Ill. U., DeKalb, 1979—, project dir. remodeling Coll. of Law, 1979-82, project dir. planning and constrn. Student recreations Ctr., 1979-85. Mem. AIA (assoc.), Soc. Coll. and Univ. Planning, Am. Planning Assn. Avocations: tennis, volleyball. Home: 114 Ilehamwood Dr DeKalb IL 60115 Office: No Ill U Office of Budget and Planning DeKalb IL 60115

JUAREZ, ANGELO DAVID, marketing executive; b. Chgo., Feb. 9, 1930; s. Hillary Martin and Mary (Mazzola) J.; m. Jean Marian Orel, Nov. 1, 1952; children: Marc, Marian, Steven. BA, Governors State U., University Park, Ill., 1977. Research analyst Chgo. Daily News, 1953-60; dir. mktg. Chgo. Sun-Times, 1960-80, The Columbus (Ohio) Dispatch, 1981—; freelance mktg. specialist Chgo., 1980-81. Served to maj. gen. U.S. Army, 1951-53, Korea, comdg. gen. Res. 1980—. Mem. Am. Mktg. Assn., Internat. Newspaper Promotion Assn., Newspaper Research Council, Sr. Res. Comdrs. Assn., Res. Officers Assn. Roman Catholic. Home: 2278 Harvest Ln Crete IL 60417 Office: The Columbus Dispatch 34 S Third St Columbus OH 43215

JUBY, MICHAEL LEROY, investment company executive; b. El Dorado, Kans., Sept. 8, 1957; s. Harold L. and Patricia L. (Orton) J.; m. Kathrina Belle Stotts, Dec. 15, 1979; children: Michael Andrew, Adam Wesley. BS in Bus., Emporia (Kans.) State U., 1979. CPA, Kans. Tax mgr. Regier, Carr & Monroe, Wichita, Kans., 1979-85; chief fin. officer Wells Investments, Hutchinson, Kans., 1985—; sec., treas. E. R. Wells Enterprises, Colorado Springs, Colo., 1985—; sec., treas., bd. dirs. Longneckers, Inc., Hutchinson, 1987—. Mem. Hutchinson Acctg. Assn. Republican. Methodist. Club: Prairie Dunes. Avocations: running, racquetball. Home: 2518 E 45th Hutchinson KS 67502 Office: Wells Investments One Compound Dr Hutchinson KS 67502

JUDAH, ROBERT EASTON, dentist; b. Stinesville, Ind., July 14, 1938; s. Robert Easton and Abbie (Ator) J.; m. Gloria Jean Elmore, Feb. 19, 1966; children: Amy Lynn, Robert Easton III. BS, Ind. U., 1960, MS, 1963, DDS, 1969. Tchr. Triton Cen. High Sch., Fairland, Ind., 1963-65; gen. practice dentistry Fairland, 1969—; faculty, practitioner Ind. U. Sch. Dentistry, Indpls., 1982—. Dist. chmn., scoutmaster, tng. chmn. Gemini dist. Boy Scouts Am., 1978—; organizer Triton Youth Athletic Assn., Fairland, 1979. Recipient cert. of appreciation and commendation Ind. Dept. Nat. Resources enforcement div., 1981, Dist. Award of Merit Boy Scouts Am., 1985. Mem. Nat. Wildlife Fedn. (life), Nat. Rifle Assn. (life), Nat. Muzzle Loader Rifle Assn. (assoc.). Democrat. Club: Sugar Creek Conservation (Fairland) (pres. 1971-73). Lodge: Masons. Home: Rt 2 Box 604 Fairland IN 46126 Office: PO Box 192 Fairland IN 46126

JUDD, DOROTHY HEIPLE, educator; b. Oakwood, Ill., May 27, 1922; d. Eldridge Winfield and Mary Luciel (Oliphant) Heiple; B.A., Ind. U., 1944; M.Ed., U. Toledo, 1971; Ed.S., Troy State U., 1976; Ed.D., No. Ill. U., 1981; m. Robert Carpenter Judd, Sept. 19, 1964; children by previous marriage—Patricia Ann Konkoly, Catherine Rafferty, Deborah Brown, Nancy Lee Arrington; stepchildren—Dianna Kay Judd Carlisi, Nancy Carol Judd Wilber, Linda Judd Marinaccio Pucci. Head lang. arts dept. Eisenhower Jr. High Sch., Darien, Ill., 1961-70; instr. devel. edn. Owens Tech. Coll., Perrysburg, Ohio, 1971-73; instr. edn. Troy State U., Montgomery, Ala., also right-to-read coordinator State of Ala., 1975-76; core dept. chair Community Consol. Sch., Dist. 15, Palatine, Ill., 1977-79; asst. prof. curriculum and instrn. No. Ill. U., 1979-83; asst. prof. edn. Southeastern La. U., Hammond, 1984—; pres. R.C. Judd & Assos., Bloomingdale, Ill., 1980-86; pres. Edn. Tng. Service, Inc., Glandale Heights, Ill., 1986—. Mem. Assn. Ednl. Data Systems, Assn. Supervision and Curriculum Devel., Assn. Tchr. Edn., Internat. Council Computers in Edn., Internat. Reading Assn., Nat. Council Social Studies, Nat. Council Tchrs. of English, Pi Lambda Theta. Author: Mastering the Micro, 1984. Contbg. editor Ednl. Computer mag., 1981-84, Electronic Edn., 1984—, Acad. Technology, 1987—; contbr. articles to profl. jours. Home: 1990 Flagstaff Ct Glendale Heights IL 60139

JUDD, JAMES ALLEN, accountant; b. Oconto Falls, Wis., Aug. 10, 1947; s. Harvey John and Marie Elizabeth (Housner) J.; m. Darlene Janel Johnson, June 3, 1972; children: Brian James, Kevin John. BBA in Acctg., U. Wis., 1970. Staff acct. Ronald Mattox and Assocs., Madison, Wis., 1969-71; mgr. fidelity bond claims Cumis Ins. Soc., Madison, 1971-72; v.p. Suby, Von Haden and Assocs., S.C., Madison, 1972—. Pres. Wis. Spl. Olympics, Inc., Madison, 1986—; games official South Cen. Wis. Spl. Olympics, Madison, 1978—. Mem. Am. Inst. CPA's, Wis. Inst. CPA's. Avocations: youth baseball and ice hockey, tennis. Home: 7801 Old Sauk Rd Verona WI 53593 Office: Suby Von Haden & Assocs SC 901 S Whitney Way Madison WI 53711

JUDD, JAMES JUSTICE, physical education educator; b. North Baltimore, Ohio, Dec. 29, 1937; s. Kenneth Wilbur and Elsia (Nigh) J.; m. Bea Mae Carpenter, June 11, 1961; children—James C., J. Todd. B.S., Findlay Coll., 1962; M.Ed., Bowling Green State U., 1965. Tchr. Otsego (Ohio) Local Schs., 1962-64, Ottawa-Glandorf (Ohio) Pub. Schs., 1964-65, Spencerville (Ohio) High Sch., 1965-68; instr. phys. edn., wrestling coach, golf coach Southwestern Mich. Coll., Dowagiac, 1968—; head coach Mich. Hawks, semi-profl. football team, 1971-72; mem. Region XII wresting com. Nat. Jr. Coll. Athletic Assn. Mem. Econ. Devel. Corp. Dowagiac, 1976—; councilman, City of Dowagiac, 1982-86, mayor protem, 1984. Served with paratroopers U.S. Army, 1956-58. Coached winning wrestling team Nat. Acad. All-Am. Team Championship, 1973. Mem. Mich. Mcpl. League, Ohio Edn. Assn., U.S. Team Handball Fedn., Am. Tae Kwan Do Assn., Nat. Jr. Coll. Athletic Assn. Wrestling Coaches' Assn., Mich. Mcpl. League (fin. and taxation com. 1983-85), Jr. C. of C. Lodges: Elks, K.P. Home: 318 E Division St Dowagiac MI 49041 Office: Southwestern Mich Coll Cherry Grove Rd Dowagiac MI 49041

JUDD, RALPH EDWARD, data processing executive; b. Cheboygan, Mich., Mar. 26, 1938; s. Dwight Francis and Grace Ann (Chimner) J.; m. Alice Ann Cooley, May 27, 1961; children: Timothy, Gordon, Linda. BBA, Wayne State U., 1972. Sr. programmer Kelly Services, Troy, Mich., 1965-67; data processing mgr. Dura Corp., Southfield, Mich., 1967-69; software cons. Computer Services, Southfield, Mich., 1970-73; prin. analyst City of Detroit, 1973-78; ops. mgr. 36 Dist. Ct., Detroit, 1978—. nominee 17th Congrl. Dist., Detroit, 1972. Served to cpl. USMC, 1956-59. Mem. Assn. Urban Cons. (bd. dirs. 1974-75), Data Processing Mgrs. Assn., Assn. Systems Mgmt., SAAA. Democrat. Roman Catholic. Clubs: MCC-MAC Athletic (bd. dirs. 1978-82). Lodge: KC. Avocation: running. Office: 36 Dist Ct 421 Madison Detroit MI 48226

JUDGE, CHARLES JOSEPH, dentist, consultant, researcher; b. Cin., Oct. 31, 1940; s. Robert Thomas and Marie (Barlow) J. m. Kathleen Cain, May 5, 1973; children: Charles, Marc. Grad., Xavier U., 1961; DDS, Loyola U., Chgo., 1965. Dental surgeon Meth. Home, Cin., 1969-78; pvt. practice dentistry, Cin., 1965—. Mem. Clifton Town Meeting, Cin., 1965—, Clifton Bus. Assn., 1965—. Recipient Am. Coll. Surgery Merit award, 1965, R.C.A. Corp. Merit award, 1958, J.D. Squire award, 1973; named to Hon. Order Ky. Cols., 1983. Mem. Greater Cin. Dental Study Club (sec. 1975-78, pres. 1980), Cin. Dental Assn. (chmn. access councilmen 1983-85), Ohio Dental Soc. (councilman 1983-85), Am. Dental Soc. (advisor, councilman 1983-85), Pub. Dental Service Soc. (pres. 1980-82, clinician and advisor 1965-79, trustee 1979—), Acad. Gen. Dentistry, Cin. C. of C., Xavier U. Alumni Assn., Loyola U. Alumni Assn., Arctic Explorers, Blue Key, Psi Omega. Republican. Roman Catholic. Clubs: Camera (pres.), One Hundred of Cin. Lodge: Kiwanis. Avocations: photography, electronics, computers, travel, hunting. Office: 3349 Whitfield Ave Cincinnati OH 45220

JUDISCH, DOUGLAS MACCALLUM LINDSAY, theology educator; b. St. Paul, Apr. 25, 1946; s. Paul Christoph and Grace Amelia (Lindsay) J. BA, Concordia Sr. Coll., 1967; M Div., Concordia Sem., 1971; PhD, U. St. Andrews, Scotland, 1979; diploma, U. Salamanca, Spain, 1983. Ordained to ministry Luth. Ch., 1974. Vicar St. Johns Ch., McClusky, N.D., 1969-70; vis. preacher St. Columba's Ch., East Kilbride, Scotland, 1971-74; asst. prof. Concordia Theol. Sem., Ft. Wayne, Ind., 1974-82, assoc. prof. Old Testament exegesis, 1982—; vis. prof. Concordia Sem., St. Catherines, Ont., Can., 1976-79; vis. pastor St. Columba's Ch., East Kilbride, 1974—. Author: An Evaluation of Claims to the Charismatic Gift, 1978, Isagogical Notes on the Pentateuch, 1985; co-author, The Concordia Psalter, 1980; editor Heraldo de Cristo; asst. editor Concordia Theol. Quar.; contbr. articles to numerous jours. Archdeacon Redeemer Luth. Ch., Ft. Wayne, 1978—; acting advisor hispanic studies Concordia Theol. Sem., Ft. Wayne, 1985—. Grad. scholar, Luth. World Fedn., 1971-74, postdoctoral scholar, Aid Assn. for Luths., 1980, sabbatical scholar, Luth. Brotherhood, 1983. Mem. Soc. Bibl. Lit., Oriental Inst., Am. Schs. Oriental Research (life), Bibl. Archaeology Soc., Evang. Theol. Soc., Internat. Orgn. for Study of Old Testament., Scottish Tartan Soc. Club: Clan Lindsay. Office: Concordia Theol Sem Fort Wayne IN 46825

JUDKINS, DEAN R., health care facility administrator; b. Columbus, Ohio, June 21, 1949; s. Alva R. and Phyllis (Greenwood) J.; m. Stephanie H. Buttle, Feb. 19, 1977; children: Brian Christopher, Andrew Stephen, Sarah Elizabeth. BA, Ohio U., 1971; MHA, Ohio State U., 1980. Sr. adjudicator VA, Roanoke, Va., 1973-78; mgmt. trainee Bethesda Hosp., Cin., 1980-81, mgr. med. staff services, 1981-82, asst. v.p., 1982-83; v.p. ops., sec. Ambulatory Med. Care, Milford, Ohio, 1983—, also bd. dirs. Pres. Mt. Washington Presbyn. Ch., Cin., 1981-82, deacon, 1982-85, chmn. planning com., 1985—. Served with U.S. Army, 1971-73. Mem. Am. Hosp. Assn. Republican. Presbyterian. Avocations: golf, biking, hiking, reading, woodworking. Home: 6885 Burhaven Ln Cincinnati OH 45230 Office: Ambulatory Med Care Inc 935 St Route 28 Milford OH 45150

JUDSON, JOHN PAUL, cardiovascular and thoracic surgeon; b. Washington, July 14, 1939; s. John H. and Joyce Mary (Duffield) J.; m. Ann Marie Ull, June 20, 1964; children—Ruth, Andrea, Sarah, Christopher, Therese. B.S. in Chemistry, Villanova U., 1961; M.D., Georgetown U., 1965. Diplomate Nat. Bd. Med. Examiners, Am. Bd. Surgery, Am. Bd. Thoracic Surgery. Resident in surgery Yale-New Haven Hosp., 1965-71, instr. surgery Yale U., 1970-71; surgeon, pres. Surgical Assocs. of Blacksburg, Va., 1971-77; resident in cardiac surgery U. Utah, Salt Lake City, 1977-79; fellow in cardiac surgery Mayo Clinic, Rochester, Minn., 1979-80; chief cardiovascular surgery Tex. Tech U., Lubbock, 1980-82; surgeon, pres. Berrien Cardiovascular Surgery, Benton Harbor, Mich., 1982—; research asst. VA Hosp., Washington, 1963; chief dept. surgery Montgomery County Hosp., Blacksburg, 1971-75, chief of staff-elect, 1976-77; mng. ptnr. Profl. Assocs., 1973-77; mem. profl. adv. com. Beverly Home Health Care of St. Joseph, Mich., 1984; mem. med. adv. com. Hospice at Home, Inc., 1984; pres. Berrien County Heart Unit, Benton Harbor, Mich., 1984—; mem. staff Southwest Mich. Health Care Assn.; Meml. Hosp., St. Joseph; Watervilet Community Hosp., Mich.; Burgess Med. Ctr., Kalamazoo. Contbr. articles to profl. jours.; lectr., speaker, presenter profl. assns., socs. Fellow Am. Coll. Surgeons, Med. Soc. Va., Med. Soc. Am. Coll. Surgeons, Am. Soc. Abdominal Surgery, Southeastern Surg. Congress, So. Med. Soc., Flying Physicians Assn., Am. Coll. Chest Physicians, Soc. Thoracic Surgeons. Roman Catholic. Avocations: aviation.

JUDSON, LYMAN SPICER VINCENT, speech pathologist, educator; b. Plymouth, Mich., Mar. 27, 1903; s. Ernest W. and Fannie Louise (Spicer) J.; m. E. Ellen MacKechnie, 1933 (dec. 1964); m. S. Adele H. Christensen, 1968. AB in Biol. Scis., Albion Coll., 1925; postgrad., S.E. Mich. U., 1926, U. Iowa, 1929-30, U. So. Calif., 1927, Harvard, 1942, U. San Francisco, Palma, Mallorca, Spain, 1967; M.S., U. Mich., 1929; Ph.D., U. Wis., 1933. Chmn. dept. sci. Las Vegas (Nev.) High Sch., 1925-27; instr. speech, studio dir. Sta. KUSD U.S.D., 1927-28; instr. speech U. Mich., 1928-29; research assoc. speech pathology U. Iowa, 1929-30; chmn. dept. speech Ala. Poly. Inst., Auburn, 1930-31; assoc. prof. speech U. Ill., 1933-35; prof. speech Kalamazoo Coll., 1936-42; chief motion picture and visual edn. divs. Pan Am. Union OAS, 1946-50; chmn. dpet. speech, dir. pub. relations Babson Coll. Bus. Adminstrn., 1950-55; asst. to pres. Alfred U., 1955-57; dir. devel. Ripon Coll., 1957-63; lectr. U. Wis., 1963-64; prof. speech Minn. U., Winona, 1964-71; TV cons. Johnson Found., 1963-64; devel. and long-range planning cons., 1965—; chmn. bd., treas. Am. Fine Arts Found., Rochester, Minn., 1964—. Author: Electrodynamic Recorder, 1930, Objective Studies on the Influence of the Speaker and the Listener, 1930, Combining the Breathing Undae of Speaker and Listener, 1932, Preliminary Study of the Offerings of Speech-Content Courses in the Technical Colleges of the United States, 1932, The Vegetative Versus the Speech Use of Biological Systems, 1932, Basic Speech and Voice Science, 1933, The Fundamentals of the Speaker-Audience Relationship, 1934, Modern Group Discussion, 1935, Manual of Group Discussion, 1936, Public Speaking for Future Farmers, 1936, After-Dinner Speaking, 1937, Winning Future Farmers Speeches, 1939, The Student Congress Movement, 1940, The Monroe Doctrine and the Growth of Western Hemisphere Solidarity, 1941, Voice Science, 1942, rev. edit., 1965, The Judson Guides to Latin America, including: Let's Go to Colombia, 1949, Let's Go to Guatemala, 1950, Let's Go to Peru, 1951, Your Holiday in Cuba, 1952, Report of Command Information Bureau 47 on Operation Inland Seas, 1959, The Interview, 1966, The Business Conference, 1969, Vincent Judson: The Island Series, 1973, Solution: PNC and PNCLAND, 1973, The AQUA Declaration, 1976, Happy 60th Birthday, 1982, The Shadow(s), 1983. Propr. Boston Athenaeum.; Mem. Explorers Scout bd.; cabinet mem., bd. mem., exec. com. mem., treas. Twin Lakes council Boy Scouts Am., 1972-73; sustaining mem. Rochester Civic Theater. Served to comdr. UNSR, 1942-65. Fellow Am. Geog. Soc.; mem. Inter-Am. Soc. Anthropology and Geography, Soc. Am. Archeology, Am. Soc. Agrl. Scis., Am. Acad. Polit. and Social Scis., Pub. Relations Soc. Am., Rochester Art Center, Judson Latin Am. Collection, Smithsonian Instn., Walker Art Center, Archeol. Inst. Am. (pres. Winona-Hiawatha Valley chpt.), AAAS, Am. Micros. Soc., Navy League, Service Corps Ret. Execs., Sigma Xi (Mayo Found. chpt.), Alpha Phi Omega, Delta Sigma Rho (nat. sec., nat. editor), Tau Kappa Alpha, Pi Kappa Delta, Sigma Delta Chi, Sigma Chi. Methodist. Clubs: Rotary; Explorers (N.Y.C.); Cosmos (Washington). Home: Rochester Towers 207 SW 5th Ave Rochester MN 55904

JUDY, BERNARD FRANCIS, newspaper editor; b. Grove City, Pa., Mar. 20, 1920; s. Francis Xavier and Catherine Veronica (Toomey) J.; m. Jane Elizabeth Urey, Apr. 3, 1945; children—Kathleen, Cynthia, Jill, Mark. B.S. in Commerce, Grove City Coll., 1941; A.B. in Econs, Washington and Lee U., Lexington, Va., 1947; M.S. in Journalism, Columbia, 1948. Mem. staff Toledo Blade, 1948—, assoc. editor, 1969-73, editor, 1973-85, editor-in-chief, 1985—; v.p., dir. Toledo Blade Co. Served with USAAF, 1942-44; CIC AUS, 1945. Mem. Am. Soc. Newspaper Editors, Phi Beta Kappa, Sigma Delta Chi. Roman Catholic. Home: 3405 Kenwood Blvd Toledo OH 43606 Office: Toledo Blade Co 541 Superior St Toledo OH 43660

JUELICH, RICHARD JAMES, construction equipment executive; b. St. Paul, July 4, 1950; s. Richard Jerome and Rosella Mary (McCormick) J.; m. Renee C. Yaritz; children: Rochelle, Catherine, Richard. BSCE, U. Minn., 1972; JD, William Mitchell Coll. Law, 1977. Bar: Minn.; registered profl. engr., Minn. Chief engr. Am. Hoist & Derrick Co., St. Paul, 1975-80, v.p. engring., 1980-83, v.p. marine and energy products, 1983—. Patentee in field. Recipient Outstanding Engring. Project award NSPE, 1977. Mem. Internat. Standards Orgn., Minn. Bar Assn., ASCE.

JUENEMANN, SISTER JEAN, hospital administrator, nun; b. St. Cloud, Minn., Nov. 19, 1936; d. Leo A. and Teresa M. (Oster) Juenemann. Diploma St. Cloud (Minn.) Sch. Nursing, 1957; student Coll. St. Benedict, 1957-59; B.S. cum laude in Nursing, Seattle U., 1967; M.H.A., U. Minn., 1977. Joined Order of St. Benedict, Roman Catholic Ch., 1959; asst. head nurse orthopedics St. Cloud Hosp., 1960-62; dir. nursing service St. Michael's Hosp., Richfield, Utah, 1962-63; dir. nursing service Queen of Peace Hosp., New Prague, Minn., 1963-65, 67-77, asst. adminstr., 1967-77, chief exec. officer, 1977—; speaker at confs. Chmn. Community Com. for Prevention Chem. Abuse, New Prague, 1975-80; bd. dirs. St. Cloud (Minn.) Hosp., 1979—. Named participant Itasca Seminar on Leadership, Mpls. Found., 1979; Bush Found. summer fellow Cornell U., U. Calif., Berkeley, 1982. Fellow Am. Coll. Healthcare Execs.; mem. Am. Hosp. Assn., Cath. Hosp. Assn., AAUW (past pres. New Prague chpt.), Women's Health Leadership Trust, Sigma Theta Tau.

JUERGENS, WILLIAM GEORGE, judge; b. Steeleville, Ill., Sept. 7, 1904; s. H.F. William and Mathilda (Nolte) J.; m. Helen A. Young, Dec. 14, 1929 (dec. Feb. 1966); children: Jane Juergens Hays, William G.; m. Charlotte Louise Mann, Mar. 18, 1967. A.B., Carthage Coll., 1925, LL.D., 1970; J.D., U. Mich., 1928; S.J.D. (hon.), William Woods Coll., 1977. Bar: Ill. bar 1928. County judge Randolph County, 1938-50; judge 3d Jud. Circuit Ct. Ill., 1951-56; judge U.S. Dist. Ct. So. Dist. Ill. (formerly Eastern Dist. Ill.), 1956—, chief judge, 1965-72, U.S. sr. dist. judge, 1972—; Adv. bd. Inst. Juvenile Research, Ill., 1945-56. Recipient 1st Ann. Honor Alumnus award Carthage Coll., 1961; George Washington Honor Medal award Freedoms Found. at Valley Forge, 1978. Mem. Fed., Ill., Randolph County bar assns., Bar Assn. 7th Fed. Circuit, Nat. Lawyers Club. Republican. Presbyn. Clubs: Masons (32 deg.), Shriners. Home: 1836 Swanwick St Chester IL 62233 Office: U S Dist Ct First Nat Bank Bldg Chester IL 62233

JUERGENSMEYER, JOHN ELI, lawyer; b. Stewardson, Ill., May 14, 1934; s. Irvin Karl and Clara Augusta (Johannaber) J.; m. Elizabeth Ann Bogart, Sept. 10, 1963; children—Margaret Ann, Frances Elizabeth. B.A., U. Ill., 1955, J.D., 1963; M.A., Princeton U., 1957, Ph.D., 1960. Bar: Ill. 1963. Mem. faculty extension div. U. Ill., 1961-63, U. Hawaii, 1958-60; mem. firm Kirkland, Brady, McQueen, Martin & Schnell, Elgin, Ill., 1963-64; founder, sr. ptnr. Juergensmeyer, Zimmerman, Smith & Leady, Elgin, 1964-81, Juergensmeyer & Assocs., 1981—; mgr., owner Tollview Office Complex, 1976—; asst. pub. defender Kane County, 1964-67, asst. states atty., 1976-78; spl. asst. atty. gen. State of Ill., 1978-85; hearing officer Ill. Pollution Control Bd., 1971-74; commr. U.S. Nat. Commn. on Libraries and Info. Scis., 1982—; lectr. Inst. for Continuing Legal Edn., Ill Bar Assn., 1971-73; trustee ALA Endowment Fund, 1979-84; assoc. prof. Judson Coll., Elgin, 1963—. Chmn. Hiawatha Dist. Boy Scouts Am.; v.p. Elgin Family Service Assn., 1967-71; sec. Lloyd Morey Scholarship Fund, 1967-73; commr. Elgin Econ. Devel. Commn., 1971-75; chmn. Elgin Twp. Republican Central Com., 1978-80; adv. bd. Ill. Youth Commn., 1964-68; bd. dirs. Wesley Found. of U. Ill., 1971-75; pres. adv. bd. Elgin Salvation Army, 1973-75. Served to capt. Intelligence Service, USAF, 1958-60. Recipient Anti-Pollution Echo award Defenders of the Fox River, Inc., 1971, Cert. Merit, Heart Fund, 1971, Outstanding Young Man award Jr. C. of C., Elgin, 1967; Princeton U. fellow, 1955-56, Merrill Found. fellow, 1956-58. Mem. Assn. Trial Lawyers Am., ABA, Ill. Bar Assn. (chmn. local govt. com. 1974-75, editor local govt. law newsletter 1973-74), Chgo. Bar Assn. (chmn. local govt. com. 1975-76), Kane County Bar Assn., Am. Arbitration Assn. (arbitrator), Am. Polit. Sci. Assn., Izaak Walton League, Fed. Bar Assn., Phi Beta Kappa, Phi Alpha Delta, Alpha Kappa Lambda. Author: President, Foundations, and the People-to-People Program, 1965. Contbr. to publs. in field. Methodist. Club: Union League (Chgo.). Lodges: Masons, Shriners, Elks, Rotary (pres. 1977-78). Office: 707-A Davis Rd Elgin IL 60120

JUGEL, RICHARD DENNIS, data processing management executive; b. Winside, Nebr., July 25, 1942; s. Donald Jerome and Ilene Mae (Christensen) J.; m. Marlene Ann Meyer, Jan. 15, 1966; children: Lisa Ann, Lynn Marie. Student, Valparaiso U., 1960-61, Wayne State Coll., 1963. Mgr., dir. Info. Mgmt. Tech., Fargo, N.D., 1968-70; system engr., sales Electronic Data Systems, Dallas, 1970-75; data processing officer Mut. of Omaha, 1975-83; exec. v.p. NewAm. Tech., Inc., Omaha, 1983-85; pres. Richard D. Jugel & Co., Omaha and Fargo, N.D., 1985—; bd. dirs. Mgmt. Info. Solutions, Inc., Houston, 1985—; cons. Distributed Info. Systems Corp., Dallas, 1984—. Emergency coordinator USMC Affiliated Radio Service, Omaha. 1978-82; active disaster communications ARC, Omaha, 1980—. Mem. Data Processing Mgmt. Assn., Nebr. Amateur Radio Emergency Services. Republican. Lutheran. Clubs: AK-SAR-BEN Amateur Radio (life, pres. 1980) (Omaha). Avocations: photography, music, target shooting, writing. Home: 8014 Taylor Circle Omaha NE 68134 Office: 4510 13th Ave SW Fargo ND 58121-0001

JUHL, DANIEL LEO, manufacturing and marketing firm executive; b. Sioux City, Iowa, Aug. 18, 1935; s. Burnett Andrew and Margret Anne (Osinger) J.; m. Colleen Ann Eagan, Dec. 20, 1958; children: Gregory, Michael, Jennifer. Student, U. S.D., 1956; BSME, UCLA, 1959; postgrad., Harvard U., 1976. Design engr. Edler Industries, Newport Beach, Calif., 1959-61; v.p. mfg. Raymark Corp. (now Rayteck Corp.), Trumbull, Conn., Can. and Europe, 1961-80; v.p. ops. Easco/KD Tools, Lancaster, Pa., 1980-83; mgr. ops. S.K. Wellman Corp., Bedford Heights, Ohio, 1983-86; gen. mgr. N.Am. Systems, Bedford Heights, 1986-87; pres. Stanhope Products Co., Brookville, Ohio, 1987—; indsl. mgmt. cons.; pres. Stanhope Products Co., Brookville, Ohio, 1967—. Contbr. numerous articles to trade jours.; patentee high temperature lightweight plastic insulation. Fund raiser United Way, 1980-85. Mem. Soc. Automotive Engrs. (chmn. com. 1977), Soc.

Plastics Industry. Lodge: Elks. Avocations: traveling, sports, woodworking. Office: Stanhope Products Co 379 Albert Rd Brookville OH 45309

JUILLERAT, ERNEST EMANUEL, JR., safety professional; b. Portland, Ind., Dec. 2, 1921; s. Ernest Emanuel and Anna Liza Etta (Stanley) J.; m. Mary Frances Knakal, Nov. 18, 1945; children—Mary Anne Juillerat Koepfler, Martha Grace. B.B.A., Capitol City Coll., 1951; postgrad. W.Va. State Coll., 1959-61. With Union Carbide Corp., Institute, W.Va., 1947-61; mgr. fire analysis dept. Nat. Fire Protection Assn., Boston, 1961-70; asst. exec. dir. Nat. Sch. Bds. Assn., 1971-73; asst. dir. safety and fire protection dept. pub. safety Northwestern U., Evanston, Ill., 1973—; cons. in field; lectr. in field. Bd. dirs. Bel Canto Found., 1979—, Northwestern Library Council, 1972—. Served with USCG, 1942-46; PTO. Decorated Silver Star. Mem. Am. Soc. Safety Engrs., Nat. Fire Protection Assn., Nat. Safety Council, Campus Safety Assn., U.S. Naval Inst., Am. Legion. Republican. Presbyterian. Clubs: Masons, Shriners. Author: Campus Fire Safety, 1978; contbr. articles to profl. jours. Home: 628 Colfax St Evanston IL 60201 Office: 1819 Hinman Ave Evanston IL 60201

JULIAN, TIMOTHY RAY, minister, music educator; b. Kokomo, Ind., Oct. 3, 1956; s. John Franklin and Nancy Ann (Hostetler) J.; m. Melody Ann Romack, Dec. 31, 1976; children: Aaron Timothy,, Jonathan Allen. BA, Anderson (Ind.) Coll., 1980; M of Music Edn., Wichita (Kans.) State U., 1984. Cert. music tchr., Ind., Ohio. Music tchr. Eastern Howard Sch., Greentown, Ind., 1981-82; minister of music and youth East Foulke Church of God, Findlay, Ohio, 1984—. Home: 712 Charles Ave Findlay OH 45840

JUNE, RICHARD PAUL, dentist; b. Cleve., Jan. 13, 1948; s. Phillip Joseph and Dolores Marie (Beck) J.; m. Susan Prell, Dec. 20, 1974 (dev. 1977); 1 child, Heather Ann; m. Laura Jean McCarthy, July 27, 1979; children: Jody Marie, Kelly Danielle. BS in Zoology, John Carroll U., 1970, postgrad., 1970-71; DDS, Loyola U., Maywood, Ill., 1975. Resident in dentistry Chgo. West-Side VA Hosp., 1975-76; assoc. Grove Dental Assoc., Bolingbrook, Ill., 1975-78; gen. practice dentistry Henry, Ill., 1976—; clin. instr. Ill. Valley Community Coll., 1984-86. Pres. Marshall-Putnam County chpt. Am. Cancer Soc., Henry, 1985—, Marshall County Bd. Health, Lacon, Ill., 1986; bd. dirs. Lake Wildwood Assn., Varna,Ill., 1983-86. Mem. ADA, Ill. State Dental Soc., Chgo. Dental Soc. (assoc.), Peoria Dist. Dental Soc., Am. Fedn. Musicians. Republican. Roman Catholic. Club: Creve Coeur (Peoria). Avocations: tennis, boating, water skiing, landscaping, carpentry. Home: 38 April Ct Lake Wildwood Varna IL 61375 Office: 309 Edward St Henry IL 61537

JUNGQUIST, PAUL JEROME, accountant; b. Mpls., Sept. 16, 1961; s. Jerome Kenneth and Rose Irene (Chisholm) J.;. BBA in acctg., Notre Dame, 1984. CPA, Minn. Staff acct. Grant Thornton, Mpls., 1984—. Mem. Am. Inst. CPA's, Minn. Soc. CPA's. Roman Catholic. Avocations: sports, reading, traveling. Home: 5547 E Danube Rd Fridley MN 55432 Office: Grant Thornton 500 Pillsbury Ctr Minneapolis MN 55402

JUNKINS, JOANN, dental group executive; b. Oskaloosa, Iowa, Aug. 14, 1936; d. Lawrence Nicholas and Helen Maxine (Dusenberry) Vander Linden; m. Larry James Junkins, Dec. 18, 1955 (div. Aug. 1971); children: Dennis L., Debra Suzanne. Diploma, Lacey Consol., New Sharon, Iowa, 1954. Typist Meredith Pub., Des Moines, 1954-55; sec. Messer, Hamilton, Cahill, Iowa City, 1955-58, U. Iowa, Iowa City, 1958-62, Dan Nevaiser, Madison, Wis., 1969-77, Wm. Krell, Madison, 1977; exec. dir. Am. Acad. Dental Group Practice, Madison, 1977-86, Dental Group Mgmt. Assn., 1985—; real estate broker J.J. Realty, Madison, 1973—. Avocations: traveling, reading, softball, bowling. Home and Office: Dental Group Mgmt Assn 2425 Ashdale Dr #35 Austin TX 78758 Home and Office: 3 Lakewood Gardens Ln Madison WI 53704

JUNKUS, JUSTIN JOSEPH, computer company executive; b. Chgo., May 12, 1947; s. Justin Bernard and Valerie T. (Kukutis) J.; m. Marilyn June Peterson, June 6, 1970; children: Kristin, Suzanne, Kimberly. BSE, U. Ill., Chgo., 1969; MBA, Loyola U., Chgo., 1975. Devel. engr. Western Electric Co., Chgo., 1969-74; product cons. Western Electric Co., Warrenville, Ill., 1974-76; industry analyst AT&T Corp., Basking Ridge, N.J., 1976-81; staff mgr. AT&T Corp., Lisle, Ill., 1982-85; nat. account mgr. Ill. Bell, Oak Brook, Ill., 1981-82; v.p. mktg. RR James Services, Ltd., Elgin, Ill., 1985—. Mem. U. Ill. Engr. Alumni Assn. (bd. dirs. 1982-86). Republican. Roman Catholic. Avocations: travel, fishing, woodworking. Home: 1056 Fox Valley Dr Aurora IL 60505 Office: RR James Services Ltd 75 Market St Suite 14B Elgin IL 60123

JUNTUNEN, CHARLES EDWIN, transportation company executive; b. Bottineau, N.D., Aug. 26, 1937; s. Edwin T. and Gweneath L. (Guenther) J.; m. Karen M. Wentsel, Dec. 22, 1963; children: Amy, Adam. BS in Bus. Administrn., U. N.D., 1959, MS, 1963. CPA, Minn., N.D. Ptnr. Arthur Young & Co., Mpls., 1963-83; chief fin. officer Overland Express, Inc., Indpls., 1983-86; chief fin. officer Transport Am., Mpls., 1986—, also bd. dirs. Served to capt. U.S. Army, 1960-63. Mem. Am. Inst. CPA's, Fin. Execs. Inst., Minn. Soc. CPA's, Decathlon Assn. Lodge: Masons. Avocations: skiing, hunting. Office: Transport Am Inc 10700 Lyndale Ave S Bloomington MN 55420

JUREK, KENNETH RUDOLPH, television producer; b. Cleve., Jan. 19, 1950; s. Walter Rudolph and Ilona (Novasat) J.; m. Laureen Evelyn Hoggatt, June 23, 1973 (div. 1981); m. Joan Marie Dollard, May 26, 1984. BS, Ohio U., 1971; MA, Kent State U., 1973. V.p. Quality Services, Inc., Stow, Ohio, 1974-76; account exec. KPGN-TV, Denver, 1973-74; instructional TV supr. Cuyahoga Community Coll., Cleve., 1976-80, prof., dept. head audio-visual tech., 1980-81; dir. video communications services Mgmt. Recruiters Internat., Inc., Cleve., 1981—; prof. John Carrol U., University Heights, Ohio, 1982—. Author: (book) Finding A Job In Non-Broadcast Video, 1986, also screenplays and telescripts; contbr. articles to profl. jours. Recipient Twyla Conway Video award Greater Cleve. Radio-TV Comml., 1976, 77, Assn. Visual Communications award, 1985, 86. Mem. Internat. TV Assn. (treas. 1977-78, v.p. 1982-83, pres. Cleve. chpt. 1983-84). Avocations: photography, antiques, travel. Office: Mgmt Recruiters Internat Inc 1127 Euclid Ave Suite 1400 Cleveland OH 44115

JUREK, THOMAS FRANCIS, broadcast consultant; b. Chgo., Aug. 2, 1949; s. Arthur Francis and Lottie (Glodek) J.; m. Rosemarie Stalec, Oct. 22, 1977; 1 child, Ann Marie. BA in Communications, St. Joseph's Coll., 1971. Owner, mgr. Sta. WFDT Radio, Columbia City, Ind., 1973-75, Sta. WRIN Radio, Rensselaer, Ind., 1975-86; pres. DJ Service, Rensselaer, 1983-86; owner, mgr. Sta. WLQI Radio, Rensselaer, 1983-86; gen. mgr. Sta WMCL, McLeansboro/Mount Vernon, Ill., 1986—; broadcast cons.; mem. NW Ind. Regional Planning, Hammond, 1974-75, 86—. Author: Small Market Radio, 1986. Campaign mgr. Smith for State Senate, Rensselaer, 1982-84; publicity chmn. Cousin Jasper Festival, Rensselaer, 1981-84; dir. mktg. adoption services Cath. Charities St. Louis, 1987—. Republican. Roman Catholic. Lodges: Rotary, Shriners (publicity dir. Grand Prairie club 1985-86, Appreciation award 1985), Masons (publicity chmn. Rensselaer club 1982-84), Elks (publicity chmn. Columbia City club 1973-74). Avocations: video recording, reading for the blind. Office: 11420 Surfside Saint Louis MO 63138

JUREWICZ, DENNIS ANTHONY, chemical company executive; b. Buffalo, Jan. 11, 1941; s. Arthur and Stephania (Siekierski) J.; m. Christina Marie Ludwig, Nov. 4, 1961; children: Dennis Jr., Michelle, Douglas. BS in Chem. Engring., SUNY, Buffalo, 1968; MS in Mgmt., Frostburg (Md.) State Coll., 1973. Engr. Bettis Atomic Power Lab, West Mifflin, Pa., 1967-69; project leader Celanese Fibers Co., Cumberland, Md., 1969-72; project engr. Armour-Dial, Montgomery, Ill., 1972-74; plant engr. Ashland Chem. Co., Hammond, Ind., 1974-79; environ. affairs mgr. Sherex Chem. Co., Mapleton, Ill., 1979—; vice. chmn., bd. dirs. Ill. Environ. Regulatory Group, Springfield, 1985—. Chmn. Families Opposed to Contaminating Uses of Soil, Pekin, Ill., 1984-86. Mem. Am. Inst. Chem. Engrs., Air Pollution Control Assn. Republican. Roman Catholic. Club: Good Govt. of Erie County (bd. dirs. 1962-66)(Buffalo). Avocations: reading, walking, computers. Home: 4553 Forest Hill Dr Pekin IL 61551 Office: Sherex Chem Co PO Box 9 Mapleton IL 61547

JURGENS-TOEPKE, PAMELA MARIE, dentist; b. Chgo., Dec. 3, 1958; d. Donald Joseph and Mary Alice (Winn) Jurgens; m. Timothy Toepke, Nov. 17, 1984; 1 child, Carly. BS, U. Ill., Urbana, 1980; DDS, U. Ill., Chgo., 1984. Pvt. practice dentistry Frankfort, Ill., 1984—; instr. U. Ill., Chgo., 1984—; cons. dept. of pub. aid State of Ill. Mem. disaster team for Cook County. Mem. ADA, Chgo. Dental Assn., Ill. Dental Soc. Avocations: sewing, jewelry making, child rearing, jogging, aerobics. Home: 516 S Oak Park Ave Oak Park IL 60304 Office: 55 E Washington #3003 Chicago IL 60602

JURICH, ANTHONY PETER, marriage and family therapist, educator; b. Mineola, N.Y., July 9, 1947; s. Peter Paul and Clara Mary (Kaftanski) J. BS, Fordham U., 1969; MS, Pa. State U., State College, 1971, PhD, 1972. Lic. marraige and family therapist, sex therapist. Instr. Pa. State U., 1970-72; asst. prof. Kans. State U., Manhattan, 1972-76, assoc. prof., 1976-80, prof., 1980—; clin. dir. marriage and family therapy Kans. State U. Family Ctr., Manhattan, 1978—. Author: Adolescent Moral Development, 1979; New Prespectives in Marriage and Family Therapy, 1982; contbr. numerous articles to profl. jour. Fellow Am. Assn. Marriage and Family Therapy (research com. 1981-85); mem. Nat. Council on Family Relations (vice chmn. therapy 1983-86), Am. Assn. Sex Therapists, Am. Family Therapy Assn. Avocations: sports, softball, football, racquetball, theater. Home: 118 McCain Ln Apt 338 Manhattan KS 66502

JURICH, JULIE ANN, family and child therapist; b. Toledo, June 18, 1946; d. Anthony and Lillian Agnes (Tomes) Vavrik; m. Anthony P. Jurich, June 18, 1971 (div. Dec. 1979). BS, Ohio State U., 1968; MEd, MS, Penn. State U., 1970; PhD, Kans. State U., 1978. Cert. marriage family therapist, Kans.; cert. sex therapist, Kans. Elem., secondary guidance counselor Tyrone (Pa.) Area Sch Dist., 1970-72; social services asst. Irwin Army Community Hosp., Fort Riley, Kans., 1972-77; family and child therapist Irwin Army Community Hosp., Fort Riley, 1977—. Contbr. articles to profl. jours. Mem. Am. Assn. Marriage and Family Therapists, Soc. Pediatric Psychology, Am. Assn. Sex Educators and Counselors, Am. Psychol. Assn., Am. Assn. for Counseling and Devel. Home: 2125 N 125 Circle Omaha NE 68164 Office: Operation Bridge 701 N 114th St Omaha NE 68154

JURKOVICH, MIKE, dentist, medical technologist; b. Kansas City, Kans., May 21, 1954; s. Joseph F. and Bernice J. Jurkovich; m. Joann M. Anderson, Apr. 27, 1974 (div. Nov. 1981); 1 child, Laurie Ann; m. Barbara S. Allison, May 14,1983; 1 child, Michael Christopher. BS in Med. Tech., U. Kans., Lawrence, 1976; DDS, U. Mo., 1983. Supr. lab. Kans. U. Med. Ctr., Kansas City, 1976-77, Shawnee Mission Med. Ctr., Shawnee, Kans., 1978-79; resident in gen. dentistry St. Francis Hosp., Honolulu, 1983-84; fellow in hosp. dentistry Am. Assn. Hosp. Dentists, New Orleans, 1984; gen. practice dentistry Overland Park, Kans., 1984—. Author, editor: Clinic Manual, 1983. Mem. ADA, Kans. Dental Assn., 5th. dist. Dental Soc., Am. Assn. Dental Schs. (rep. S. Cen. region 1982-83), Mo. C of C. Democrat. Roman Catholic. Office: 6300 Glenwood #13 Overland Park KS 66202

JUST, EDWARD LOUIS, advertising and public relations executive; b. Cleve., June 20, 1927; s. Frank and Anna (Kuhar) J.; m. Patricia Lucille Zaletel, July 14, 1956; children: John, Peter. BBA, Cleve. State U., 1950. Asst. advt., sales promotion mgr. Towmotor Corp., Cleve., 1951-55; acct. exec. Bayless-Kerr Co., Cleve., 1955-62; indsl. acct. mgr. Lando, Inc., Erie, Pa., 1962-63; v.p., br. mgr. Dix & Eaton, Inc., Erie, 1964-71; sr. exec. v.p. Dix & Eaton, Inc., Cleve., 1972-81; pres. Just & Co., Cleve., 1982—. Served with U.S. Army, 1945-46. Mem. Greater Cleve. Growth Assn., Nat. Machine Tool Builders Assn. (gold award 1980), Council Smaller Bus. Enterprises, Cleve. Advt. Club (Best Objectives Oriented Advt. 1960, 61, Best Single Advt. 1976), Erie Advt. Club (Best Sales Lit. 1984). Lodge: Kiwanis. Home: 29131 Lincoln Rd Bay Village OH 44140 Office: Just & Co PO Box 40312 Bay Village OH 44140

JUST, LESLEY LYNN, registered nurse; b. Prairie du Chien, Wis., May 1, 1957; d. Robert Francis and Joanne Rae (Haupt) Welsch; m. John Stanley Just, Aug. 28, 1982; 1 child, Jessica Nicole. Student, U. Minn., Duluth, 1975-78; BS in Nursing, Viterbo Coll., 1982. Nurse's aide St. Francis Nursing Home, LaCrosse, Wis., 1980-82; med. and cardiac RN St. Francis Med. Ctr., LaCrosse, 1982-83, RN in psychiatry, 1983—, acting nurse, clinician psychiatry, 1987; mem. nursing quality assurance com., 1986—; ad hoc com. Clin. Ladder, 1986. Vol. Mat G. Polinsky Rehab. Ctr., Duluth, Minn., 1978, ARC Adopt-a-Grandparent Program, LaCrosse, 1978—. Mem. Gamma Omicron Beta. Roman Catholic. Avocations: travel, swimming, bicycling, tennis. Home: 623 McIntosh Rd LaCrescent MN 55947 Office: St Francis Med Ctr 700 West Ave S LaCrosse WI 54601

JUSTAK, SUSAN, nurse; b. Hammond, Ind., Nov. 3, 1953; d. John Stephen and Helen Marie (Mihalov) Markovich; m. Jeffrey Eugene Justak, Apr. 29, 1972; children—Jeffrey Jerome, Christine Marie. R.N., St. Margaret Hosp., 1979; A.A.S., Purdue U., 1980, student, 1985—. Staff nurse St. Margaret Hosp., Hammond, 1979—. Mem. Emergency Dept. Nurses Assn. (cert.). Democrat. Roman Catholic. Home: 1447 Poplar Ln Munster IN 46321 Office: St Margaret Hosp 5454 Hohman Ave Hammond IN 46320

JUTTING, LESLIE NEIL, insurance executive; b. Milbank, S.D., Feb. 12, 1946; s. John Louis and Vera Mae (Govers) J.; m. Marcie S. McDaniel, July 27, 1968; children: Susan M., Michelle M., Neil J., Tamra E. Student, S.D. State U. Mgr. camera dept. Haywoods Jewelry, Watertown, S.D., 1971-75; dist. rep. A.A.L., Sioux Falls, S.D., 1975-79; asst. gen. agent Aid Assn. for Lutherans, Roanoke, Va., 1979-82; gen. agent Aid Assn. for Lutherans, Aberdeen, S.D., 1982—. Mem. Aberdeen Assn. Life Underwriters (pres. 1986-87), S.D. State Fraternal Congress (pres. 1976-77), S.D. State Fraternal Ins. Counselors (pres.). Avocations: fishing, hunting, phtography, golf. Home: 1729 S 7th St Aberdeen SD 57401 Office: AAL 23 6th Ave SW Aberdeen SD 57401

KABANCE, GALEN C., special education teacher; b. Topeka, Mar. 26, 1936; s. James Frank and Marguerite (Boettcher) K.; m. Rose E. Moore, Apr. 22, 1957; children: Kyle, Teresa, Jeffrey, Wesley. BS in Geology and Math., Wichita State U., 1958; MS in Edn. and Guidance Counseling, Kans. State Tchrs. Coll., 1965; EdS, Pittsburg (Kans.) State U., 1975. Cert. edn. counselor, tchr., spl. edn. tchr. behavior disorders. Math. and sci. tchr. Denison (Kans.) High Sch., 1960-62, Mayetta (Kans.) High Sch., 1962-64; counselor, tchr. Belle Blaine (Kans.) High Sch., 1965-66; counselor Pittsburg High Sch., 1966-78; dir. Wis. area Starks Meat Co., Watertown, 1978-80; behavior disorders tchr. Parsons (Kans.) Middle Sch., 1980—; dir. adult edn. Pittsburg, 1970-77. Served as 1st lt. U.S. Army, 1959-69; commdr. NG, 1960-65. Recipient football scholarship Wichita State U., 1954-58, summer sch. fellowship NSF, 1966. Mem. Kans. Guidance Assn. (treas.), Nat. Edn. Assn. Methodist. Avocations: ceramics, camping, football, coaching, building. Home: Route 3 Box 173 Pittsburg KS 66762

KABES, SHARON ELAINE, education educator; b. Denver, Sept. 11, 1944; d. Leslie Lennis Craig and Peggy Joy (Kranich) Truetken; m. David Edwin Kabes, Sept. 3, 1966; children: Wendy Sharlen, Randy Allen. BS, Colo. State U., 1965, MS, 1974; postgrad., U. N.D. Tchr. West Mesa High Sch., Albuquerque, 1966-68; instr. biology Colo. Coll., Colorado Springs, 1975-76; tchr. Lafayette High Sch., Red Lake Falls, Minn., 1977-86; adminstrv. intern Cen. High Sch., Grand Forks, N.D., 1986-87; grad. teaching asst. U. N.D. Dept. Edn., Grand Forks, 1986—; curriculum coordinator Pine to Prairie Vocat. Ctr., Red Lake Falls, 1978-79; cons. in field, 1986-87. Mem. Red Lake Falls Civic Assn., 1984—; county rep. Dem. Caucus, Red Lake County, Minn., 1982; elder First Presbyn. Ch., Red Lake Falls, 1979-82. Mem. Nat. Assn. Secondary Sch. Prins., Minn. Assn. Secondary Sch. Prins., U. N.D. Ednl. Leadership Orgn., Phi Delta Kappa. Avocations: skiing, aerobics, clarinet, oil painting, tennis. Home: 511 St John's Ave SE Red Lake Falls MN 56750

KABLER, MICHAEL LEE, school psychologist, educator, consultant; b. Ripley, Ohio, Sept. 24, 1943; s. Howard L. and Mary Helen (Schuman) K.; m. Diane Ellen Wells, Aug. 17, 1968; children: Heather Lee, Heidi Anne. BS, Ohio State U., 1966, MA, 1968, PhD, 1976. Lic. psychologist, Ohio, profl. sch. psychologist, Ohio. Tchr. Westerville (Ohio) Pub. Schs., 1966-69, dir. pupil services, 1985-87, asst. supt. secondary edn., 1987—; psychologist Franklin County (Ohio) Pub. Schs., 1970-72, chief sch. psychologist, 1972-74; ednl. cons. Ohio Dept. Edn., Columbus, 1976-77, coordinator program rev. 1977-79, cons. sch. psychol. services, 1982-84; asst. prof. Ohio State U., Columbus, 1980-82, adj. asst. prof. 1982—; chmn. Ohio Sch. Psychology Exam Com. Author: (with Dardig and Heward) Leaders Manual: Sign Here, 1977, (with Crisci, Garwood and Wendt) The Ohio School Psychologists Association Handbook on Law, 1978; asssoc. editor The Directive Tchr. mag., Spl. Services in the Schs. Jour.; contbr. articles to profl. jours. Adminstr. multihandicapped unit Ohio State Sch. for Blind, Columbus, 1984-85. Ohio Dept. Edn. grantee, 1980, Spencer Found. grantee, 1981. Mem. Am. Psychol. Assn., Council Exceptional Children, Ohio Sch. Psychologists Assn., Nat. Assn. Pupil Personnel Adminstrs., Nat. Assn. Sch. Psychologists, Assn. Pupil Personnel Adminstrs., Ohio Assn. Pupil Personnel Adminstrs., Phi Delta Kappa. Office: Westerville Pub Schs 336 S Otterbein Ave Westerville OH 43081

KACHORIS, PAUL JOHN, psychiatrist; b. Gary, Ind., June 29, 1938; s. John Apostolou and Sevaste (Voulis) K.; m. Jean Louise Elsass, Oct. 22, 1967; children: John, Kathryn, Gregory. AB in Sci., Ind. U., 1961, MD, 1964. Diplomate Am. Bd. Pediatrics, Am. Bd. Psychiatry and Neurology, Am. Bd. Child Psychiatry. Intern Parkland Meml. Hosp., Dallas, 1964-65; pediatric resident Children's Meml. Hosp., Chgo., 1967-69, fellow child psychiatry, 1969-71; adult psychiatry resident Ill. State Psychiat. Inst., Chgo., 1971-73; staff physician Ill. State Psychiatric Inst., Chgo., 1973-76; staff physician Inst. for Juvenile Research, Chgo., 1973-76, dir. psychiatrists to pediatrics liaison, 1973-80; dir. child psychiatric in-patient unit Old Orchard Hosp., Skokie, Ill., 1980—; med. dir. Old Orchard Hosp., Skokie, 1986—; psychiatric sch. cons. Barrington (Ill.) Schs., Niles East High Sch., Skokie, Niles North High Sch., Skokie, Niles West High Sch., Morton Grove, Ill.; psychiatric cons. to police dept. Northbrook and Winnetka, Ill. Chmn. Hosp. Child Protection Coalition, Chgo., 1976-80, youth affairs steering com. St. Peter/Paul Greek Orthodox Ch.; mem. task force on child abuse Ill. Psychiatric Soc., 1979-80. Served to capt. USAF, 1965-67. Named Dr. of Yr. Child Protection Coalition, 1985. Mem. Am. Psychiatric Assn., Am. Acad. Child Psychiatrists, Am. Bd. Pediatrics, Am. Soc. Adolescent Psychiatry, Ill. Council Child Psychiatry. Office: Old Orchard Hosp 636 Church St Evanston IL 60201

KACVINSKY, RAYMOND CARL, marketing executive; b. Ashland, Wis., June 14, 1949; s. Paul Walter and Eva Marie (Lindahl) K.; m. Mary Anne Kinney, Aug. 14, 1971; children: Gregory Paul, Sarah Marie, Katherine Colleen. B in Indsl. Engring., U. Wis., 1971, MBA, 1972. Cert. Mgmt. Acct. Mgmt. cons. Alexander Grant & Co., Madison, Wis., 1977-79; mgr. research and devel. Roy's Dairy, Monroe, Wis., 1979-81; strategic planning analyst Marathon Electric Mfg. Corp., Wausau, Wis., 1973-75, product mgr., 1975-77, asst. to pres., 1981-82, mktg. mgr., 1982—; spkr. value engring. seminars U. Wis., Madison, 1977-81, adhoc prof. acctg., 1974-77, 82-85. Instr. Jr. Achievement, Wausua, 1981-86. Recipient Honeywell award U. Wis., 1971. Mem. Nat. Acctg. Assn., Inst. Mgmt. Acctg., U. Wis. Alumni Assn., Phi Kappa Phi, Tau Beta Pi, Beta Comma Sigma. Clubs: YMCA Century. Avocations: golf, racquetball, cross country skiing. Home and Office: 1610 Woodland Ridge Rd Wausau WI 54401

KACZMAREK, HENRY ANTHONY, engineering company executive; b. Elizabeth, N.J., July 18, 1921; s. Anton S. and Katherine (Bera) K.; m. Margaret Loretta Hewitt, July 8, 1961. Student, Devry Tech. Inst., Chgo., 1949-51. Engr. Republic Aviation, Farmingdale, N.Y., 1939-49, R.W. Neill Co., Chgo., 1949-67; chief engr. Marquardt Ind. Products Co., 1967-68; v.p. Larry McGee Co., Chgo., 1968-74, pres., 1974—. Served with USAF, 1942-45, ETO. Mem. Am. Assn. Railroads, Am. Legion (sr. v.p. Chgo. 1957). Club: Radio Control (Chgo.). Office: Larry McGee Co 4937 W Fullerton Chicago IL 60639

KADLUB, LEONARD ALLEN, controller; b. Cleve., Aug. 25, 1951; s. Joseph F. and Idella L. (Barber) K.; m. Joanne M. Babika, Feb. 20, 1971; children: Michael J., Jeffrey A. BBA, Cleve. State U., 1973. CPA, Ohio. Acct. Curtis Industries, Eastlake, Ohio, 1972-73; acct., fin. analyst, controller Picker Internat., Highland Heights, Ohio, 1973-79; div. controller Bethandale, Mentor, Ohio, 1979—; pvt. practice acctg., Wickliffe, Ohio, 1978-84. mem. various coms. Our Lady of Mt. Carmel Ch., Wickliffe, 1981—. Mem. Nat. Assn. Accts. (bd. dirs 1975-79, Mem. of Yr. Cleve. East Chpt. 1975-76). Republican. Roman Catholic. Avocations: golf, bowling, racquetball. Office: Bethandale 8229 Tyler Blvd Mentor OH 44060

KADONSKY, WILLIAM JAMES, corporate systems analyst; b. Marshfield, Wis., July 29, 1954; s. George Frank and Elizabeth Eleanore (Kalson) K.; m. Carol Jean Marie Schuh, Aug. 16, 1975; children: Christine, David, Robert. Student, U. Wis., Wausau, 1972-73; BA, U. Wis., 1975; postgrad., U. Md., 1977. Spl. research analyst Dept. of Def., Fort Mead, 1975-79; systems analyst Wausau (Wis.) Ins. Cos., 1979-81; corp. systems analyst, 1983-85, corp. bus. systems analyst, 1986—; corp. bus. systems analyst Kimberly-Clark Co., Neenah, Wis., 1985-86. Active Marathon County Hist. Soc., Wausau, 1986, Wausau Civic Symphony, 1972-73. Mem. Am. Affairs Inst. (exec. commn. 1978-79). Democrat. Roman Catholic. Avocations: geneology, white water canoeing, family and ch. activities. Home: 615 Town Line Rd Wausau WI 54401 Office: Wausau Ins Cos 2000 Westwood Dr Wausau WI 54401

KAEDING, GEORGE FREDERICK, controller; b. Chgo., July 9, 1933; s. Fred John and Marie Lillian (Menard) K.; m. Louise Allen Sprowl, June 18, 1960; children: Peter, James, Marie. BSBA, Bradley U., 1955. Personnel mgr. Phoenix Trimming Co., Chgo., 1958-70, controller, 1970—, sec., treas., 1974—. Mem. Northtown Indsl. Mgmt. Council, Chgo., 1958-70. Served with USAF, 1951-55, USN, 1955-57. Recipient Service award Northtown Indsl. Mgmt. Council, 1966. Republican. Methodist. Lodge: Elks. Avocations: boating, automobiles, making movies, bicycling, motorcycling. Office: Phoenix Trimming Co 910 Skokie Blvd Northbrook IL 60062

KAEHR, ROBERT EUGENE, librarian, educator; b. Bluffton, Ind., July 2, 1942; s. William Edward and Vendetta Edna (Hupp) K.; m. Winnifred Helen Bertha Suski, Aug. 14, 1965; children: Renee Helen, Thomas Ryan. BS, Huntington Coll., 1964; MS, No. Ariz. U., 1972; MLS, George Peabody Coll. for Tchrs., Nashville, 1976. Tchr. Edon (Ohio) Sch. Dist., 1964-65, Huntington (Ind.) Sch. Corp., 1965-68, Window Rock (Ariz.) Sch. Dist., 1968-76; librarian, asst. prof. library sci. and dir. library services Huntington Coll., 1976—; chmn. planning small coll. com. Office Mgmt. Studies. Book reviewer Christian Librarian, Fortress Press. Mem. Assn. Christian Librarians, Tri-Area Library Services Authority (v.p. exec. bd.), Beta Phi Mu. Mem. United Brethren Ch. Office: Huntington Coll 2303 College Ave Huntington IN 46750

KAEMMERLEN, CATHY JUNE, dancer, educator; b. Pasadena, Tex., Sept. 3, 1949; d. Cyril Joseph and Martha (Ziebutski) K.; m. Robert Martin Gaare, Dec. 28, 1974; children: Michael Anders, Sara Catherine, Eric Haldan. BA, U.N.C., 1971; MFA, U. Wis., 1973. Dance faculty SUNY, Buffalo, 1974; dance artist/tchr. Fine Arts Ctr., High Sch. of the Arts, Greenville, S.C., 1974-76; movement specialist S.C. Arts Commission, 1977—, NEA, 1977—, Performing Tree, Los Angeles, 1977—, Wis. Arts Bd., 1981—; dance faculty Chapman Coll., Orange, Calif., 1979; solo performer various locations, 1976—. Choreographer: (solo children's shows) Wiggles, Jiggles, Twists and Turns, 1977, More Wiggles, 1978, Salt and Pepper, 1979, Dancing Tales/Tattling Tales, 1986, (with Bob Kann) Peppered Biscuits, 1987. NEA fellow, 1976; Wis. Arts Bd. grantee, 1981, 82, 83, 87. Home: 705 Yorkshire Rd Neenah WI 54956

KAESER, JOHN LOUIS, dentist; b. Marion, Ill., May 14, 1932; s. John Frederick and Elsa Flora (Weber) K.; m. S. Romelle, Dec. 24, 1954; children: Diane, Steven, David. BS, U. Ill., 1954, DDS, 1956. Gen. practice dentistry Marion, 1958—; v.p. Community Savs. and Loan, Marion. Served to capt. USAF, 1956-58. Mem. ADA, Ill. Dental Assn. Home: 1903 W Cherry Marion IL 62959 Office: 301 N Van Buren Marion IL 62959

KAFANTARIS, GEORGE E., restaurateur; b. Kardamyla, Chios, Greece, Nov. 20, 1937; came to U.S., 1951; s. Elias G. and Koula (Pagonis) K.; m. Maria G. Chlorou, Oct. 8, 1958; children: Elias G., Koula G., Constantine G. Student, Mich. State U.; Assoc. Bus., Lansing (Mich.) Community Coll. Chief clk. Mich. Dept. Corrections, Lansing, 1962-82; owner, mgr. Parthenon Restaurant, Lansing, 1977—. Active Am. Hellenic Ednl. Prog. Assn. Served with USN, 1956-60. Mem. Nat. Restaurant Assn., Mich. Restaurant Assn., Mich. Beverage Assn., Lansing Regional C. of C., Lansing Conv. Bur. Greek Orthodox. Home: 1009 Chris J Dr Lansing MI 48917 Office: Parthenon Restaurant and Lounge 227 S Washington Sq Lansing MI 48933

KAFKA, GENE F., academic counselor; b. Beemer, Nebr., Apr. 2, 1942; s. Stephen and Mildred (Vogeltanz) K.; Deborah Jean Steele, Aug. 29, 1964; children: Tom, Bob, Sue. BA in Edn., Wayne (Nebr.) State U., 1963; MS, Omaha U., 1966; EdD, U. Nebr., 1975. Cert. Nat. Bd. Cert. Counselors. Tchr. Council Bluffs (Iowa) Schs., 1963-65; counselor Coucil Bluffs High Sch., 1966-67; counselor, administr. U. Nebr., Omaha, 1967—; cons. Bromell-Tabot Sch., Omaha, 1982—. Lodge: Optimists (pres. North Omaha chpt. 1975-76). Avocations: gardening, welding, automobile body work. Home: 9323 N 29th St Omaha NE 68112 Office: U Nebr Omaha 60th and Dodge St Omaha NE 68182

KAGAN, GEORGE IRWIN, dentist; b Brookline, Mass., Aug. 8, 1939; s. Abraham and Sylvia (Coleman) K. BS in Biol. Psychology, U. Chgo., 1961, BS in Dentistry, 1963; DDS, U. Ill., 1965. Technician Cook County Sch. Nursing, Chgo., 1964-65; intern U. Chgo., 1965-66; staff dentist Chgo. Bd. Health, 1966-68, Stickney Twp. Pub. Health Dist., Burbank, Ill., 1969; dental health care provider State of Ill., 1969-79; gen. practice dentistry, Chgo., 1968—; table clinician Chgo. Dental Soc., 1980—, Ariz. State Dental Soc., Phoenix, 1983-85. Served to capt. USAR, 1965-67. Fellow Acad. Gen. Dentistry, Royal Soc. Health; mem. Chgo. Dental Soc., Royal Coll. Dental Surgeons Ont. (licentiate), Ill. State Dental Soc., ADA. Club: Ill. Railway Museum (Union). Avocations: railroading, restoration of classic autos, motorsports, touring. Office: 1525 E 53d St #516 Chicago IL 60615

KAGANN, JOEL ALLAN, municipal court administrator, municipal and county government official; b. Chgo., Sept. 16, 1936; s. Joseph J. and Eleanor E. (Priess) K.; m. Laurie C. Klauser, July 1, 1967; children: Joseph Edward, Carol Eleanor. Student, U. Ill., Chgo., 1954-56; cert. in criminal justice, St. Joseph Coll., 1958. Sgt. police Golf (Ill.) Police Dept., 1955-57, Hanover Park (Ill.) Police Dept., 1957-60; chief police Woodridge (Ill.) Police Dept., 1961-71, capt. police, 1977-78; adminstrv. asst. DuPage Cir. Ct., Wheaton, Ill., 1973-77, exec. asst., 1978—; vice chmn. Ill. State Police Emergency Radio System, Springfield, Ill., 1968-73, Crescent Criminal Justice Ag., Wheaton, 1975-77; chmn., vice-chmn. DuPage Law Enforcement Com., Wheaton, 1968-75; chmn. court com. DuPage Criminal Justice Ag., Wheaton, 1978-79; mem. com. Judicial Mgmt. Adv. Council, Ill. Supreme Ct., 1978—. Mayor Village Woodridge, 1973-77, clk. 1979-81; mem. exec. com. Lisle (Ill.) Township Rep. Orgn., 1984-86; pres. Woodridge Spl. Events Com., 1984-87. Named Outstanding Resident Village Woodridge, 1984; recipient Community Recognition award Village Woodridge, 1984. Mem. DuPage Chiefs Police (charter, sec. 1963-73), Ill. Assn. Chiefs Police (life, exec. bd. 1965-71), West Suburban Chiefs Police (sec., treas. 1965-66), Internat. Assn. Chiefs Police (life, asst. sgt. arms 1967-69), Ill. Police Assn. (life), Woodridge Hist. Soc. (treas. 1985—). Republican. Roman Catholic. Lodges: Lions (pres. 1970-71, 1987-88), KC (adv. 1965—), Moose. Office: 18th Jud Cir Ct 201 Reber St Wheaton IL 60189-0707

KAGEL, RONALD OLIVER, chemist; b. Milw., Jan. 16, 1936; s. Harold Adolph and Lorraine Erna (Miller) K.; m. Lois Jeanne Kaercher, Dec. 27, 1959; children: Jennifer Ann Kagel St. Onge, Kathryn Marie Kagel Ennis, Sharon Emily. BS, U. Wis., 1958; PhD, U. Minn., 1964. With analytical labs. Dow Chem., Midland, Mich., 1977-79, mgr. environ. quality dept., 1979-81, dir. environ. quality dept., 1981-85, environ. dir. Advanced Tech. Applications div., 1985—; mem. indsl. adv. council Ill. Inst. Tech., Chgo., 1985—. Co-author: Infrared Spectra of Inorganic Compounds, 1971; contbr. articles to profl. jours. Recipient cert. Appreciation EPA, 1977. Fellow Am. Inst. Chemists; mem. Am. Chem. Soc. (cert., Appreciation cert. 1981), Chem. Mfg. Assn. (task force group leader 1976-85), Synthetic Organic Chems. Mfg. Assn. (environ. quality com. 1981-86), Coalition for Responsible Waste Incineration (chmn., bd. dirs. 1987—), NRC (sub coms. 1968, 75), AAAS, Optical Soc. Am. (chmn. com. 1975-77), Coblentz Soc. (bd. dirs. 1973-77), Soc. for Applied Spectroscopy (chmn. com. 1975-82), N.Y. Acad. Scis., Alpha Chi Sigma, Phi Lambda Upsilon, Sigma Xi. Lutheran. Home: 4 Hannah Ct Midland MI 48640 Office: Dow Chem Co Advanced Tech Applications Research Bldg 734 Midland MI 48667

KAGLER, WILLIAM GEORGE, supermarket and food manufacturing consultant; b. Scranton, Pa., June 4, 1932; s. George M. and Marion B. (Lewis) K.; m. Gail A. Whitehead, Sept. 12, 1959; children: Kim Noel, Kristin Amy, Kerri Lu. BS in Journalism, Syracuse U., 1954; postgrad., Columbia U., 1958, U. Pa., 1959-60, U. Cin., 1963. Pub. relations counsel The Kroger Co., Cin., 1964-66, dir. pub. relations, 1966-71, v.p. corp. affairs, personnel and human resources, 1971-74, corp. v.p., 1974-77, group v.p., 1977, sr. v.p., 1977-83, pres., 1983-86; bd. dirs. The 5th 3d Bank, Cin., Union Cen. Life Ins. Co., The Ryland Group, Inc. Bd. dirs. Found. State Legislatures; group chmn. pub. service div. United Appeal, Cin., 1979; trustee Good Samaritan Hosp., 1980—; mem. nat. corps. com. United Negro Coll. Fund, N.Y.C., 1980—; fin. chmn. Hamilton county Clarence J. Brown for Gov. com., Cin., 1982. Served with CIC U.S. Army, 1955-57. Am. Polit. Assn. Congl. fellow, 1963-64. Clubs: Queen City (bd. dirs. 1982—); Commonwealth (sec. 1983—); Comml. Office: Kagler & Assocs Columbia Plaza Suite 1500 250 E Fifth St Cincinnati OH 45202

KAH, GARY HENRY, writer, consultant; b. Dayton, Ohio, July 11, 1959; s. Heinrich and Irmgard Marie (Gekeler) K.; m. Audrey Marie Liechty, May 30, 1981; 1 child, Alyssa Laurén. BA in Econs., German and Bus. Adminstrn., Anderson Coll., 1982. Trade specialist Europe and Mid East Ind. Dept. Commerce, Indpls., 1981-85; writer Indpls., 1985—; mem. steering com. Ind. Emerging Med. Cos. Conf., Indpls., 1984, Ind. Emerging Electronics Cos. Conf., Indpls., 1984-85; internat. trade and fin. cons. Computer Control Systems, Inc., Bargersville, Ind., 1985. Author: The Coming World Crisis, 1987; author, editor; Indiana Coal Export Mission, 1982; producer: (video) Indiana Coal Export Mission, 1982. Mem. planning com. German/Am. Tricentennial Commn., Indpls., 1983; gen election sheriff Indpls. Reps., 1983; counselor Youth Group Ch. at the Crossing, Indpls., 1982-84, evangelistic outreach dir. Singles Group, 1985-86; rep. Affirmative Action com. Ind. Dept. Commerce, Indpls., 1984; candidate Nat. Def. Exec. Res., Washington, 1984—. Recipient Ind. Cardinal Soc. award Ind. State Treas., 1980, A.C. Wall Street Jour. award, 1981, Gov.'s Commendation State of Ind., 1983, Meritorious Hoosier award Ind. Sec. of State, 1984. Mem. Ch. of God. Avocations: racquetball, baseball, internat. travel, ch. activities. Office: PO Box 55687 Indianapolis IN 46205

KAH, RALPH EDWARD, obstetrician-gynecologist; b. Middletown, Ohio, Apr. 26, 1933; s. Ralph Edward and Zelma May Sargent K.; m. Mary Margaret Finney, June 20, 1957 (div. June 1960); 1 child, Kathryn Lee; m. Deeann Haney, July 14, 1962. AB, MA, Miami U., Oxford, Ohio, 1955; MD, Ohio State U., 1959, MMS, 1964; PhD, Calif. COast U., 1978. Cert. Am. Bd. Ob-Gyn. Intern Ohio State U. Hosps., 1959-60, resident in obgyn., 1960-64; ptnr. Gynecologic Cons. Inc., Middletown, Ohio, 1966-84; pvt. practice ob-gyn. Middletown, 1984—; lectr. nursing edn. Miami U., Oxford, 1972—; asst. clin. prof. ob-gyn. Wright State U., 1976—. Mem. adv. com. Planned Parenthood Assn. Served with U.S. Army, 1964-66. Mem. AMA, Ohio State Med. Assn., Butler County Med. Soc., Am. Coll. Ob-Gyns., Am. Fertility Soc., Cin. Ob-Gyn. Soc., Am. Assn. Gyn. Laparoscopists, Pan-Am. Surgical Soc., Dayton Ob-Gyn. Soc., Am. Endocrine. Soc., Gynecologic Urology Soc., Gynecologic Laser Soc., Am. Cancer Soc., Flying Physicians, Am. Soc. Liposuction Sugery. Republican. Episcopalian. Home: 3209 Milton Rd Middletown OH 45044 Office: 4492 Marie Dr Middletown OH 45044

KAHAN, MITCHELL DOUGLAS, art museum director; b. Richmond, Va., May 1, 1951; s. Abraham and Shirley (Abrams) K. BA, U. Va., 1973; MA, Columbia U., 1975; M of Philosophy, CUNY, 1978, PhD, 1983. Mus. aide Nat. Mus. Am. Art, Washington, 1978; curator Montgomery (Ala.) Mus. Fine Art, 1978-82, N.C. Mus. Art, Raleigh, 1982-86; dir. Akron (Ohio) Art Mus., 1986—; cons. La. World's Exposition, New Orleans, 1983-84. Author: Art Inc.: American Paintings in Corporate Collections, 1979, Roger Brown, 1981, Minnie Evans, 1986. Columbia U. fellow, 1973, Smithsonian Inst. fellow, 1976-78, CUNY grad. research fellow, 1978, Nat. Endowment for Arts fellow, 1987. Mem. Coll. Art Assn., Intermus. Conservation Assn. (trustee 1986—). Home: 733 West Market St Apt 707 Akron OH 44303 Office: Akron Art Mus 70 E Market St Akron OH 44308

KAHAN, SHELDON ALAN, window manufacturing executive; b. Cleve., June 6, 1960; s. Bernard and Geraldine A. (Greenberg) K.; m. Brenda Marcia Ostrow, Aug. 16, 1983; 1 child, Meredith Faye. BA in Pub. Relations, Ohio State U., 1982. Project dir. Kenneth Danter & Co., Columbus, Ohio, 1982-93; unit mgr. GC Services Inc., Cin., 1983-84; regional sales mgr. Thermal Industries, Inc., Cin., 1984—; cons. GL Sizemore & Assocs., Cin., 1986—. Mem. Nat. Assn. Remodeling Industry (bd. dirs. 1984—), Nat. Assn. Home Builders. Jewish. Avocations: tennis, golf. Home: 17 Mapleview Ct Cincinnati OH 45246 Office: Thermal Industries Inc 4884 Duff Dr Cincinnati OH 45236

KAHANOVSKY, LUIS, physical therapist; b. Buenos Aires, Argentina, Apr. 17, 1934; came to U.S., 1972; s. Naum and Vera (Sacsagansky) K.; m. Elizabeth Ann Bogdan, Jan. 24, 1974. Diploma in physical therapy, U. Buenos Aires, 1965. Staff physical therapist U. Hosp., Buenos Aires, 1965-67; dir. orthopedic rehab. Pirovano Hosp., Buenos Aires, 1967-71; staff physical therapist Henry Ford Hosp., Detroit, 1972-77; pres., dir. Farmington Physical Therapy, Farmington Hills, Mich., 1977—. Mem. Am. Physical Therapy Assn., Physical Therapists in Pvt. Practice Inc. (exec. dir., treas. 1982-85), United Soc. Physiotherapists N.Y. (past v.p., past pres., Devotion to Profl. Standards award 1984). Republican. Jewish. Avocations: raising dogs, swimming, horse back riding.

KAHLENBECK, HOWARD, JR., lawyer; b. Fort Wayne, Ind., Dec. 7, 1929; s. Howard and Clara Elizabeth (Wegman) K.; m. Sally A. Horrell, Aug. 14, 1954; children: Kathryn Sue, Douglas H. BS with distinction, Ind. U., 1952, LLB, U. Mich., 1957. Bar: Ind. 1957. Ptnr. Krieg, DeVault, Alexander & Capehart, Indpls., 1957—; sec., bd. dirs. Maul Tech. Corp. (formerly Buehler Corp.), Indpls., Am. Monitor Corp., Indpls., Am. Interstate Ins. Corp. Wis., Milw., Am. Interstate Ins. Co. Ga., Am. Underwriters Group, Inc., Indpls.; bd. dirs. Pafco Gen. Ins. Co. Served with USAF, 1952-54. Mem. ABA, Ind. Bar Assn., Indpls. Bar Assn., Alpha Kappa Psi, Delta Theta Phi, Beta Gamma Sigma, Delta Upsilon Internat. (sec., bd. dirs. 1971-83, chmn. 1983-86, trustee found. 1983—). Lutheran. Home: 6320 Old Orchard Rd Indianapolis IN 46226 Office: Krieg DeVault Alexander & Capehart 2800 Indiana National Bank Tower Indianapolis IN 46204

KAHLER, LEE DANIEL, manufacturers sales executive; b. Kansas City, Mo., Mar. 19, 1959; s. Peter Delbert and Helen Francis (Best) K.; m. Cheryl Susan Bialowas, June 22, 1985. BSBA, Kansas State U., 1982. Sales rep. 3M Bus. Machines, Kansas City, 1982-83; sales rep. Maidenform, Toledo, 1983-84, Kansas City, 1984—. Recipient Top Salesman award, 1986. Republican. Avocations: tennis, music, snow skiing, fishing, stereo. Home and Office: 1400 NW 74th St Kansas City MO 64118

KAHN, CHARLES FREDERICK, JR., lawyer; b. Milw., Apr. 19, 1949; s. Charles Frederick and Louise Ann (Hartmann) K.; m. Elizabeth Martha Brauer, Dec. 28, 1975. B.A., George Washington U., 1971; J.D., U. Wis., 1974. Bar: Wis. 1975, U.S. Dist. Ct. (ea. and we. dists.) Wis. 1975, U.S. Supreme Ct. 1983. Staff atty. Wis. Indian Legal Services, Keshena, 1975-76; trial atty. misdemeanor and felony divs. Legal Aid Soc. Milw., 1976-78, chief staff atty. juvenile div., 1978; ptnr. Kahn & Levine, 1979-83; sr. atty. Charles Kahn & Assocs., Milw., 1983-86, ptnr., shareholder Kahn and Flynn, S.C., Attys. at Law, 1987—; spl. prosecutor pro tem Milw. County, 1981-82; counsel for Bd. of Attys. Profl. Responsibility, 1981—; cir. ct. commr., parttime 1983—; mng. v.p. Colby-Abbot Bldg. Co., 1980—; vis. lectr. dept. criminal justice U. Wis.-Milw., 1982-85; moderator, speaker, panelist profl. seminars and convs.; testimonial witness Wis. Senate and Assembly, 1981, 83. Contbr. writings to profl. pubs. Bd. dirs. Parents Anonymous of Greater Milw., 1980-84; vice chmn. Milw. County North Shore Unit, Democratic Party of Wis., 1982-84; mem. Gov.'s Exec. Trade Delegation to Israel, 1985. Recipient Pro Bono award Posner Found., 1983; named Outstanding Young Lawyer 1980, Milw. Jaycees. Mem. ABA, Milw. Bar Assn., Wis. Acad. Trial Lawyers, Bar Assn. 7th Fed. Cir., ACLU, Am. Jewish Com., Bldg. Owners and Mgrs. Assn. (bd. dirs. polit. action com. 1983-84), Milw. Young Lawyers Assn. (chmn. criminal justice com. 1980-81), Met. Milw. Assn. Commerce, Nat. Audubon Soc., Wis. Environ. Decade. Club: Photo Club of Schlitz Audubon Ctr. Home: 3043 N Summit Ave Milwaukee WI 53211 Office: Kahn and Flynn SC 759 N Milwaukee St Suite 500 Milwaukee WI 53202

KAHN, DAVID VICTOR, lawyer; b. Oak Park, Ill., June 17, 1930; s. Albert Z. and Sarah G. (Berkson) K.; m. Ruth Israelit, Apr. 19, 1959; children: Jonathan, Ethan, Suzanne. AB, U. Chgo., 1949, JD, 1952. Ptnr. Altheimer & Gray, Chgo., 1959—. Served to capt. USAF, 1953-57. Mem. Am. Jewish Congress (nat. sr. v.p., pres. midwest region 1980-85, trustee 1982—). Home: 1000 Lake Shore Plaza #10 Chicago IL 60611 Office: 333 N Wacker Dr 26th Fl Chicago IL 60606

KAHN, JAN EDWARD, manufacturing company executive; b. Dayton, Ohio, Aug. 29, 1948; s. Sigmond Lawrence and Betty Jane K.; m. Deborah Ann Deckinga, Nov. 28, 1975; children: Jason Edward, Justin Allen, Julie Ann. BS in Metall. Engring., U. Cin., 1971. Mgmt. trainee U.S. Steel Corp., Gary, Ind., 1971-72; plant metallurgist Regal Tube Co., Chgo., 1972-74, gen. foreman, 1974-76, supt., 1976-77, mgr. tech. service, 1978-80, materials mgr., 1980-81; mgr. quality control Standard Tube Co., Detroit, 1977-78; dir. ops. Boye Needle Co., Chgo., 1981-82, v.p. ops., 1982-83, v.p., gen. mgr., 1984-85, pres., 1985—. Mem. Am. Soc. Metals, AIME, ASTM, Ravenswood Indsl. Council (bd. dirs. 1983-84, pres. 1985), Hand Knitting Assn. (chmn. 1986—). Republican. Mem. Christian Reformed Ch. Club: Triangle. Home: 9135 S Mulligan Oak Lawn IL 60453 Office: Boye Needle Co 4343 N Ravenswood Chicago IL 60613

KAHN, JOEL IRA, industrial engineer, business educator; b. Chgo., Aug. 4, 1952; s. Sidney and Phyllis Frances (Cohn) K.; m. Susan Frances Jaet, May 29, 1977; 1 child, Philip Michael. BSME, Ill. Inst. Tech., 1973; MS in Indsl. Engring., U. Cin., 1978, MS in Quantitative Analysis, 1981, PhD in Indsl. Engring., 1986. Registered profl. engr., Ohio. Engr. Procter & Gamble, Cin., 1974-80, group mgr., 1980-83, sect. mgr., 1983—; adj. prof. U. Cin., 1982-85, No. Ky. U., Highland Heights, 1986. Vol. Multiple Sclerosis Soc., Cin., 1980-86. Mem. Inst. Indsl. Engring. (pres. Cin. chpt. 1982), Inst. Mgmt. Sci. Avocations: reading, microcomputers. Home: 475 Hilltop Ln Cincinnati OH 45215 Office: Procter & Gamble PO Box 599 Cincinnati OH 45201

KAHN, MARK LEO, arbitrator, educator; b. N.Y.C., Dec. 16, 1921; s. Augustus and Manya (Fertig) K.; B.A., Columbia U., 1942; M.A., Harvard U., 1948, Ph.D. in Econs., 1950; m. Ruth Elizabeth Wecker, Dec. 21, 1947 (div. Jan. 1972); children—Ann Mariam, Peter David, James Allan, Jean Sarah. Asst. economist U.S. OSS, Washington, 1942-43; teaching fellow Harvard U., 1947-49; dir. case analysis U.S. WSB, Region 6-B Mich., 1952-53; mem. faculty Wayne State U., Detroit, 1949-85, prof. econs., 1960-85, prof. emeritus, 1985—, dept. chmn., 1961-68, dir. indsl. relations M.A. Program, 1978-85; arbitrator union-mgmt. disputes, specializing in airline industry. Bd. govs. Jewish Welfare Fedn. Detroit, 1976-82; bd. dirs. Jewish Home for Aged, Detroit, 1978—. Served to capt. AUS, 1943-46. Decorated Bronze Star. Mem. Indsl. Relations Research Assn. (pres. Detroit chpt. 1956, exec. sec. 1979—; exec. bd. 1986-88), AAUP (past chpt. pres.), Nat. Acad. Arbitrators (bd. govs. 1960-62, v.p. 1976-78, chmn. membership com. 1979-82, pres. 1983-84), Soc. Profls. in Dispute Resolution (v.p. 1982-83, pres. 1986-87). Co-author: Collective Bargaining and Technological Change in American Transportation, 1971; contbr. articles to profl. jours. Home and Office: 4140 2d Ave Detroit MI 48201

KAHN, SANDRA S., psychotherapist; b. Chgo., June 24, 1942; d. Chester and Ruth (Goldblatt) Sutker; m. Jack Murry Kahn, June 1, 1965; children: Erick, Jennifer. BA, U. Miami, 1964; MA, Roosevelt U., 1976. Tchr. Chgo. Pub. Schs., 1965-67; pvt. practice psychotherapy, Northbrook, Ill., 1976—. Host Shared Feelings, Sta. WEEF-AM, Highland Park, Ill., 1983—; author: The Kahn Report on Sexual Preferences, 1981. Mem. Ill. Psychol. Assn., Chgo. Psychol. Assn. (bd. dirs.). Jewish. Office: 2970 Maria Ave Northbrook IL 60062

KAHN-FEUER, LOIS HENNING, psychotherapist; b. Chgo., Aug. 16, 1943; d. Alexander M. and Marian I. (Mesigal) Henning; m. Max Feuer; children: Samantha Kahn, Jason Kahn, Aaron Kahn, Marcia Feuer, Paul Feuer. BS, Boston U., 1965; MS, So. Ill. U., 1983. Prin., therapist Amber Counseling Service, St. Paul, 1983-85; therapist Kiel Clinic, St. Paul, 1985-87, Affiliated Psychol. Services, Inc., Mpls., 1987—, Youth Service Bur., Roseville, Minn., 1987—; cons. Minn. State High Sch. League, Anoka, 1986—, Hazelton-Cork Sports Edn., Mpls., 1987—. Bd. dirs. Talmud Torah St. Paul, 1983-86, v.p., 1987. Mem. Minn. Psychol. Assn., Phi Kappa Phi.

KAHNKE, WILLIAM PAUL, accountant; b. Mankato, Minn., Jan. 12, 1961; s. Eugene Sebastian and Mary Ann (Templin) K. BA in Acctg. summa cum laude, Coll. St. Thomas, St. Paul, 1983. CPA, Minn. Sr. staff acct. Johnson, West & Co., St. Paul, 1983—; acctg. tutor Coll. St. Thomas, 1982-83. Recipient Govtl. Incentive award Fed. Hwy. Adminstrn., 1980, St. Paul Mayor's award Jaycees, 1983; Tozer Found. scholar Coll. St. Thomas, 1982. Mem. Am. Inst. CPA's, Minn. Soc. CPA's, Soc. Advancement of Mgmt., Delta Epsilon Sigma, Omicron Delta Epsilon. Roman Catholic. Avocations: golf, swimming, bicycling, hiking. Home: 1870 Duck Pond Dr West Saint Paul MN 55118 Office: Johnson West & Co 1400 Pioneer Bldg Saint Paul MN 55101

KAHNWEILER, WILLIAM MARK, management consultant, trainer; b. Chgo., May 4, 1950; s. Louis S. and Ruth M. (Markus) K.; m. Jennifer Boretz, June 17, 1973; children—Lindsey Meg, Jessie Beth. B.A., Washington U., St. Louis, 1972, M.Ed., 1973; Ph.D., Fla. State U., 1979. Program adminstr. Adolescent Counseling Ctr., Amherst (Mass.) High Sch., 1973-76; instr., cons., researcher, therapist Fla. State U., Fla. Correctional Inst., Tallahassee, 1976-79; asst. prof. Miami U., Oxford, Ohio, 1979-80; mgmt. trainer, cons. Gen. Electric Co., Cin., 1980-83; mgmt. cons. Hay Mgmt. Cons., Cin., 1983—; cons. indsl., fin., service and health care orgns.; cons. to sch. systems, 1976-79; adj. prof. U. Cin., Miami U., 1980—. Mem. Am. Psychol. Assn. (div. indsl. and organizational psychology), Am. Soc. Tng. and Devel., Phi Beta Kappa. Club: Athletic (Cin.). Contbr. articles to profl. jours.

KAHRL, ROBERT CONLEY, lawyer; b. Mt. Vernon, Ohio, June 2, 1946; s. K. Allin and Evelyn Sperry (Conley) K.; m. LaVonne Elaine Rutherford, July 12, 1969; children: Kurt Freeland, Eric Allin, Heidi Elizabeth. AB, Princeton U., 1968; MBA, JD, Ohio State U., 1975. Bar: Ohio 1975, U.S. Ct. Appeals (6th cir.) 1976, U.S. Dist. Ct. (no. dist.) Ohio 1977, U.S. Ct. Appeals (9th cir.) 1979, U.S. Ct. Appeals (fed. cir.) 1984, U.S. Ct. Appeals (D.C. cir.) 1986. Law clk. to presiding judge U.S. Ct. Appeals (6th cir.), Cleve., 1975-76; assoc. Jones, Day, Reavis & Pogue, Cleve., 1976-84, ptnr., 1985—. Chmn. vis. com. Coll. Arts and Scis. Cleve. State U., 1985—. Served to lt. USN, 1968-72. Mem. ABA, Order of Coif, Am. Guild Organists. Republican. Presbyterian. Club: Cleve. Athletic. Home: 7624 Red Fox Trail Hudson OH 44236 Office: Jones Day Reavis & Pogue 901 Lakeside Ave Cleveland OH 44114

KAHRS, STEVEN ARTHUR, systems analyst; b. Chgo., Jan. 11, 1959; s. Thomas George and Sylvia J. (Cunningham) K. BA in Philosophy, Northwestern U., 1981. Actuarial intern Combined Ins., Northbrook, Ill., 1981-82; actuarial tech. Combined Ins., Northbrook, 1982-83, tech. specialist, 1983; programmer analyst Combined Ins., Chgo., 1984-86, systems analyst, 1986—. Sec., St. Nicholas Parish Council, Evanston, Ill., 1986-87, mem. lay ministry, 1985—, v.p., 1987—. Fellow Life Mgmt. Inst. Roman Catholic. Avocations: bicycling, sailing, writing. Home: 715 Mulford St Evanston IL 60202 Office: Combined Ins 5050 Broadway Chicago IL 60640

KAIRIES, JAMES WALTER, steel company executive; b. Mpls., Nov. 12, 1942; s. Walter Henry and Doris Elizabeth (Riley) K.; m. Bridget Kathleen O'Harrow, June 28, 1975; children: Katie, Allsion. BA, Carleton Coll., 1965; MA, Johns Hopkins U., 1967. Sales rep. Cargill Inc., Cin., 1971-72; sales projects mgr. Cargill Inc., Guadalajara, Mex. and N.Y.C., 1972-73; regional mgr. Cargill Inc., Omaha, 1973-75; asst. v.p. Cargill Inc., Mpls., 1975-82; rep. dir. C. Tennant Sons & Co. N.Y., Tokyo, 1982-85; pres. Cargill Steel and Wire, East Chicago, Ind., 1985—. Advisor Jr. Achievement, Mpls., 1978-80; co-chmn. United Way, Mpls., 1981; mem. adv. council Johns Hopkins U., Washington, 1985—. Served to 1st lt. U.S. Army, 1967-70, Vietnam. Decorated 2 Bronze Stars, Silver Star, Purple Heart, 2 Air Medals, Cross of Gallantry (Rep. Vietnam); H.B. Eahart fellow Relm Found., Ann Arbor, Mich., 1965-67. Mem. Steel Service Ctr. Inst. Republican. Roman Catholic. Clubs: Olympia Fields (Ill.) Country, Tokyo Am. (chmn. mem. relations com. 1983-85), Fgn. Correspondent (Tokyo).

KAISER, FREDERICK HENRY, electronics executive; b. Chgo., July 13, 1941; s. Frederick Henry and Lydia (Busch) K.; m. Klara Korossy, Apr. 3, 1965; children: Frederick, Christopher, Kathryn. BS, U.S. Naval Acad., 1963. Commd. ensign USN, 1963, advanced through ranks to lt., served in Vietnam, resigned, 1968; mktg. rep. IBM, Chgo., 1969-70; account mgr. Accuray Corp., Columbus, Ohio, 1971-73; regional sales mgr. Dieterich Standard, Boulder, Colo., 1973-80; pres. Kaiser Technology, Crystal Lake, Ill., 1981—. Mem. Instrument Soc. Am., Mfrs. Agts. Nat. Assn. Avocations: weightlifting, camping, water sports. Home: 685 Tamarisk Terr Crystal Lake IL 60014 Office: Kaiser Technology Inc 800 McHenry Ave Crystal Lake IL 60014

KAISER, HERBERT HARLAN, real estate insurance executive; b. Monticello, Ill., Nov. 23, 1900; s. Harry E. and Lucy Jeanette (Harlan) K.; m. Dorothy Elizabeth Dennis, Apr. 27, 1929; 1 child, Herbert Harlan Jr. Student, U. Ill., 1919-21, Cambridge U., Eng., 1921-22, Dartmouth Coll., 1921-22; BS in Econs., U. Pa., 1923-24; student, Columbia U. Law Sch.; LLB, U. Ill. Law Sch. Pres. Kaiser Abstract Co. and subs., Monticello, Ill., Elizabeth Harlan, Inc. Mem. Ill. Land Title Assn. (past pres.), Piatt County Bar Assn. (past pres.), Piatt County Hist. Soc. (past pres.). Avocations: music, opera, foreign travel. Home: 315 S Buchanan St Monticello IL 61856 Office: Kaiser Abstract Co 110 N Charter St Monticello IL 61856

KAISER, K. CHRISTOPHER, accountant; b. Stratford, Ont., Can., June 8, 1955; s. Ward Louis and Lorraine Eva (Macke) K.; m. Karen Ann Macioce, July 20, 1985. BA, Otterbein Coll., 1977. CPA. Controller, treas. Candlelite Builders, Columbus, 1983-84; staff acct. audit dept. Deloitte Haskins & Sells, Columbus, Ohio, 1977-83; sr. cons. Deloitte Haskins & Sells, 1984-85, mgr. emerging bus. dept., 1985—. Vol. Fundraiser United Way, Columbus Mus. Art. Mem. Am. Inst. CPAs, Nat. Assn. Accts., Ohio Soc. CPAs. Avocations: sailing, woodworking, softball, volleyball. Home: 5653 Tamarack Blvd Columbus OH 43229 Office: 155 E Broad St Columbus OH 43213

KAISER, PAUL JACOB, consulting engineer, retired county official; b. Calumet, Mich., Dec. 5, 1925; s. William Lewis and Elizabeth Theresa (Marston) K.; m. Bette Ruth Hore, July 28, 1951; children—William G., Catherine M. Kaiser Bolton, Susan E. B.S. in Civil Engring., Mich. Tech. U., 1953. Registered profl. engr., Mich. Project engr. Houghton County Road Commn., Hancock, Mich., 1946-50; county hwy. engr. Baraga County Road Commn., L'Anse, Mich., 1950-51; engr., supt. C.G. Bridges Constrn. Co., Escanaba, Mich., 1951-52; county hwy. engr. mgr. Van Buren County Road Commn., Lawrence, Mich., 1953-85, ret., 1985; now cons. engr. Mem. regional exec. bd. Boy Scouts Am., 1980—. Served with C.E., U.S. Army, 1943-46. Mem. Nat. Assn. County Engrs., Am. Road and Transp. Builders Assn., Mich. Engring. Soc., County Road Assn. Mich., Am. Legion. Republican. Presbyterian. Contbr. articles to profl. jours. Home: 51693 351/2th St Paw Paw MI 49079

KAISER, RAYMOND LEROY, business office procedures educator; b. Strasburg, Ohio, Dec. 23, 1929; s. George Edward and Anna Marie (Shear) K.; m. Anna Mae Gerber, July 17, 1952; children—James Robert, Patricia Ann, Terry Lee. B.S. in Edn. cum laude, Kent State U., 1955, M.E. in Edn., 1960. Cert. tchr., Ohio. Acct., Arthur G. McKee Co., 1950-52; tchr. bus. edn. Baltic (Ohio) High Sch., 1954-60; tchr. acctg. typing, shorthand, bus. English, bus. math. and vocat. acctg. Washington High Sch., Massillon, Ohio, 1960—. Mem. Ohio Edn. Assn., Ohio Vocat. Educators Assn., Kappa Delta Pi. Republican. Mem. Nazarene Ch. Clubs: Ashland Pioneer Coin and Investment Guild, Masons, Grange.

KAIYALETHE, JOHN KURUVILLA (K.K.), minister; b. Erath, India, May 24, 1936; came to U.S., 1962; s. Kuruvilla Korula and Rachel (Yohannan) K.; m. Tamara Fogel, Sept. 3, 1963; children: Nara, David, Michal. Diploma in Theology, Zion Biblr Coll. and Sem., Mulakuzha, India, 1957; ThD, Kingsway Coll. and Sem., 1986. Pastor India; campus pastor, counselor U. Minn.; evangelist, conf. speaker; nat. dir. edn. and Sunday schs. India; v.p. U. Minn. Council Religious Advisors. Pres. Internat. Student Fellowship; mem. Pres. adv. com. Commn. Campus Unrest. Avocations: photography, travel.

KAKOS, STEVE JAMES, dentist; b. Chgo., Jan. 8, 1933; s. James P. and Bertha (Papadopoulis) K.; m. Dena Peterson, June 30, 1963 (div. June 1980); children: Pamela, James S. DDS, U. Ill., 1958. Gen. practice dentistry Chgo., 1958—. Mem. ADA, Ill. Dental Assn., Chgo. Dental Assn., Hellenic Dental Soc. (founder 1963). Greek Orthodox. Home: 815 Nebel Ln Des Plaines IL 60018 Office: 2715 N Central Ave Chicago IL 60639

KALAL, ROBERT JAMES, data processing executive; b. Cleve., Apr. 28, 1946; s. Joseph James and G. Alice (Morse) K.; m. Linda Lee Talmadge, May 14, 1978; 1 child, Katherine Frances. BA in Computer and Info. Sci., Ohio State U., 1981. Engring. assoc. Ohio Bell Telephone Co., Cleve., 1968-73; analyst, cons. U. Assocs., Columbus, Ohio, 1973-77; bldg. supt. St. Thomas More Neman Ctr., Columbus, 1973-77; lead analyst quality assurance The Ohio Coll. Library Ctr., Columbus, 1977-79; mgr. application systems Instrn. and Research Computer Ctr., Ohio State U., Columbus, 1979—; cons. data processing for ch. orgns., Columbus, 1973—. Chmn. elect bd. trustees Maple Grove Presch., Columbus, 1986; chmn. bd. trustees Maple Grove Presch., Columbus, 1986—; lay ch. ministries St. Thomas More Newman Ctr., 1970—; mem. Diocesan Pastoral Council, Roman Catholic Diocese of Columbus, 1976. Served to sgt. USAF, 1964-68. Mem. Inst. Cert. Computer Profls. (cert. in data processing), Cen. Ohio Assn. Computing Machinery. Democrat. Roman Catholic. Avocations: coastal oceanography, church activities. Home: 100 Nottingham Rd Columbus OH 43214 Office: Ohio State U 1971 Neil Ave Columbus OH 43210

KALE, SATISH LAKSHMAN, mechanical engineer; b. Bombay, Maharashtra, India, Nov. 6, 1952; came to U.S., 1973; s. Lakshman S. and Kumudini L. Kale; m. Alka S. Joshi, Jan. 5, 1978; 1 child, Santosh. BSME, U. Bombay, 1973; MS in Indsl. Engring., Ill. Inst. Tech., 1974, MSME, 1977; postgrad., Northwestern U. Sch. Bus., Chgo., 1977—. Registered profl. engr., Ill., Ind. Design engr. H.K. Porter, Chgo., 1974-75; product engr. Blackstone Mfg. Co., Chgo., 1975-76; sr. product engr. Ortman Fluid Power, Hammond, Ind., 1976-80, Miller Fluid Power, Bensenville, Ill., 1980—. Fellow Ill. Inst. Tech., 1975-77. Mem. Nat. Fluid Power Assn., Fluid Power Soc. Avocations: chess, bridge, reading. Home: 25 Wildwood Trail Palos Park IL 60464 Office: Miller Fluid Power 800 N York Rd Bensenville IL 60106

KALEE, ROBERT JOHN, dentist; b. Grand Rapids, Mich., Jan. 30, 1937; s. John C. and Gertrude (Kriekard) K.; m. Marilyn Karel, Jan. 31, 1958 (div. Apr. 1985); children: Cheryl, Debra, Karel; m. Judith Kay Vander Plaats. Student, Hope Coll., 1954-57; DDS, U. Mich., 1961. Staff Pine Rest Christian Hosp., Grand Rapids, 1961-62; gen. practice dentistry Jenison, Mich., 1961—; staff Hudsonville (Mich.) Rest Home, 1982—. Bd. dirs. Jenison Pub. Schs., 1965-72, Evang. Lit. League, Grand Rapids, 1970-84; tchr. surgical dentistry, Chiapas, Mex., 1974, 76, 78, 80, 83. Served to capt. U.S. Army, 1962-64. Mem. ADA, Am. Straight Wire Orthodontic Assn., Mich. Dental Assn., W. Mich. Dental Soc., Kent County Dental Soc., Jenison Businessmens Assn. (bd. dirs. 1964-70). Republican. Home: 1328 Bent Tree Dr Hudsonville MI 49426 Office: 7610 Cottonwood Dr Jenison MI 49428

KALENAK, JOHN, physician; b. Nanty Glo, Pa., June 22, 1921; s. Mike and Anna Kalenak; m. Mary Fatula, Jan. 29, 1949. BS, Longisland U., 1947; DO, Coll. Osteopathic Medicine and Surgery, 1955. Practice osteopathic medicine Grand Rapids, 1955—. Office: 3755 Remembrance NW Grand Rapids MI 49504

KALET, SYDNE JO, communications company sales executive; b. Buffalo, Mar. 24, 1946; d. Sidney Ralph and Caryl Jane (Cohen) K. B.S. in Speech, NYU, 1967. Profl. actress, N.Y.C., 1967-69; office adminstr. Nat. Hockey League, N.Y.C., 1969-76; owner, designer SK Designs, Ortonville, Mich., 1976-81; salesperson So. Pacific Communications, Birmingham, Mich., 1981-82; dist. sales mgr. US Sprint, Southfield, Mich., 1983—. Mem., past rec. sec. Lakeland Players, Waterford, Mich., 1979—; patron Detroit Inst. Arts. Mem. Internat. Orgn. of Wo/Men in Telecommunications, (past treas.), Armed Forces Communications and Electronics Assn., Nat. Assn. Female Execs., Profl. Women in Sales. Jewish. Avocations: community theatre; singing; reading; physical fitness. Home: 7043 Hillside Dr Clarkston MI 48016 Office: US Sprint Communications 3000 Town Ctr #300 Southfield MI 48075

KALIFF, WILLIAM JOYCE, rancher; b. York, Nebr., Aug. 21, 1925; s. Rudolph Ludwig and Myrtle Naomi (Seng) K.; m. Helen Barbara Crabtree, Dec. 17, 1950; children: William S., Melanie Sue, Heather Elizabeth. Student, U. Nebr., 1942-43; BS in Engring., U.S. Mil. Acad., 1946. Commd. 2d lt. U.S. Army, 1946, advanced through grades to capt., 1952, resigned, 1954; asst. mgr. farming R. L. Kaliff Ranch Co., York, Nebr., 1954-61, pres., 1968—; dist. mgr. Equitable Life Assurance Soc., 1961-64. Republican. Presbyterian. Home: 1717 S Garland Grand Island NE 68801 Office: R L Kaliff Ranch Co Box 218 York NE 68467

KALKOWSKI, LAWRENCE ALBIN, secondary educator; b. Spencer, Nebr., Nov. 29, 1934; s. Albin Anton and Rose (Sedivy) K.; m. Kay Lynn Schoneberg, Aug. 6, 1960; children: Jeffrey, Timothy, Christopher, John. BE, U. Nebr., 1961, MA, 1970. Cert. speech communications. Tchr. Rock County High Sch., Bassett, Nebr., 1961—; bd. dirs. Consolidated Investors; rancher Boyd County, Nebr. Bd. dirs. Cornhusker Archery, Bassett, Natural Resources Dist., Upper Elkhorn Nebr. Served with U.S. Army, 1957-59. Recipient awards NDEA Inst., 1965, 67. Mem. NEA, Nebr. State Edn. Assn., Rock County Edn. Assn., Rock County High Sch. Tchrs. Assn., Nebr. Speech Assn. Roman Catholic. Lodge: KC. Avocations: hunting, wildlife conservation. Home: Sunrise Terr Bassett NE 68714

KALLEWAARD, MARY CATHERINE, advertising executive; b. Detroit, Nov. 28, 1947; d. Irving Nicholas and Gwendolyn (Hinderliter) Fisher; m. Thomas R. Kallewaard, June 28, 1969; children: John Andrew, Jane Erin. BA, U. Mich., 1969. From copywriter to account exec. Arbor Advt. Inc., Ann Arbor, Mich., 1969-80; owner The Written Image, Manchester, Mich., 1982—. Pres. pro tem Village Council, Manchester, 1982—; sec. Village Planning Commn., Manchester, 1981—; trustee Township Library Bd., Manchester, 1981-82. Recipient Mich. Addy award Lansing Advt. Club, 1985, 2d pl. Mich. Addy Lansing Advt. Club, 1979, Cert. Merit Zeta Tau Alpha Fraternity, 1975. Mem. Manchester C. of C. (pres. elect 1986—). Avocation: gardening. Home: 202 N Macomb St Manchester MI 48158 Office: The Written Image 200 Riverside Dr Manchester MI 48158

KALLICK, SONIA BELLE, nurse, high school teacher; b. Chgo., Mar. 11, 1933; d. Sven and Belle (Damtjernhaug) Aamot; m. Charles Arthur Kallick, Dec. 23, 1956; children: Steven, Karen, Ingrid. RN, Cook County Sch. Nursing, 1953; BS, U. Ill., Chgo., 1956; MA, Lewis U., 1977. RN, Ill.; cert. tchr., Ill. From staff nurse to head nurse Cook County Hosp., Chgo., 1953-56; elem. tchr. Lemont (Ill.) Sch. Dist. 113, 1964-77; high sch. tchr. Lemont Dist. 210, 1977—. Newspaper columnist, 1973-85; author: A Walking Tour of Lemont, 1976. Trustee Chgo. Mural Group, 1976—, Lemont Hist. Soc., 1973—, v.p., 1975-78; v.p. Friends of the Ill. and Mich. Canal, 1982-86, trustee, 1986—. Recipient Citizens' award, Lemont Bicentennial com., 1976. Mem. Nat. Assn. English Instrs., Assn. Concerned Scientists, Am. Nurses Assn.

KALLNER, NORMAN GUST, management information systems manager; b. Rockford, Ill., Apr. 28, 1950; s. Gust and Vera May (Brinkmeyer) K.; m. Mary Ann Wikoff, July 30, 1976; 1 child, Stephanie Ann. Student, U. Ill., 1968-70, No. Ill. U., 1975-79. Programmer Woodward Gov. Co., Rockford, 1970-73, Rock Valley Coll., Rockford, 1973-74; programmer/analyst Kysor of Byron (Ill.), 1974-76; systems programmer Rockford Bd. Edn., 1976-80; systems programmer Harris Corp., Quincy, Ill., 1980-84, mgmt. info. systems tech. support mgr., 1984-86, prin. software, data base analyst, 1986—; cons. Outboard Marine Corp., Beloit, Wis., 1979-80. Treas. Our Redeemer Luth. Ch., Quincy, 1986, 87; asst. leader Girl Scouts U.S., Quincy, 1986. Avocation: woodworking. Home: 1520 S 28th St Quincy IL 62301 Office: Harris Corp PO Box 4290 Quincy IL 62305

KALMER, WILLIAM JOHN, insurance sales executive; b. Milw., Feb. 24, 1943; s. Phillip Henry and Margaret Anne (Buckett) K.; m. Diane L., July 26, 1974; children: William J. II, Anne L., Timothy P., Mary E. BA, Marquette U., 1966. CLU; chartered fin. cons. Sales exec. Conn. Mut. Ins., Milw., 1968—; v.p. Clark/Bardes Orgn., Milw., 1985—. Mem. Am. Coll. Life Underwriters, Million Dollar Round Table, Nat. Assn. Life Underwriters, Assn. for Advanced Life Underwriting. Republican. Roman Catholic. Clubs: Milw. Athletic, Tripoli Country. Avocations: scuba diving, golf, sky diving, racquetball. Home: 13585 Dunwoody Dr Elm Grove WI 53122 Office: 611 N Broadway Suite #411 Milwaukee WI 53202

KALT, MELVYN BARRY, judge; b. Detroit, Aug. 12, 1941; s. Charles and Pearl (Sperber) K.; m. Paula Ann Marks, May 28, 1967; children: Julie, Brian. BS, U. Mich., 1963; PhD in Chemistry, Wayne State U., 1967; JD cum laude, Detroit Coll. Law, 1973. Bar: Mich. 1973, U.S. Supreme Ct. 1979. Sr. research chemist M&T Chems., Detroit, 1967-74; atty. U.S. Army Corps of Engrs., Detroit, 1974-79, dist. counsel, 1979-82; adminstrv. law judge HHS, Detroit, 1982—. Contbr. book revs. to profl. jours.; patentee in field. Mem. Fed. Bar Assn. (exec. com. Detroit chpt. 1981-84), Assn. Adminstrv. Law Judges, Fed. Adminstrv. Law Judges Conf. Avocation: computers. Office: 25900 Greenfield Suite 430 Detroit MI 48237

KALTHOFF, JAMES W., clergyman; b. Marshall, Mo., Feb. 13, 1938; s. James William Sr. and Elsie (Osborn) K.; m. Vickie Kaye Jump, July 20, 1961; children: John Martin, Kassandra Kaye, James Paul. BTh, Concordia Sem., Springfield, Ill., 1963. Ordained to ministry Luth. Ch. Mo. Synod. Pastor Our Savior Luth. Ch. and St. Paul's Ch., Muscatine and Wapello, Iowa, 1963-66, Our Savior Luth. Ch., Sedalia, Mo., 1966-71, Faith Luth. Ch., Jefferson City, Mo., 1971—; cir. counselor Luth. Ch. Mo. Synod, 1968-71, 81-85, 2d v.p. Mo. dist., 1985—, bd. dirs. Mo. dist., 1985—, chmn. Family Life com., 1973-75, chmn. Pastor's Conf., 1977-83; pastoral counselor Mo. dist. Luth. Women's Missionary League, 1984—; speaker (radio show) Word of Faith, 1975—. Contbr. articles to profl. jours. Recipient Effective Ministry award Concordia Sem., 1978. Mem. Nat. Right to Life, Mo. Lutherans for Life (bd. govs. Meml. Hosp.). Avocations: reading, writing, tennis. Office: Faith Luth Ch 2027 Industrial Dr Jefferson City MO 65101

KALVER, GAIL ELLEN, dance company manager; musician; b. Chgo., Nov. 25, 1948; d. Nathan Eli and Alice Martha (Jaffe) K. BS in Music Edn., U. Ill., 1970; MA in Clarinet, Chgo. Musical Coll., Roosevelt U., 1974. Profl. musician, Chgo., 1970-77; assoc. mgr. Ravinia Festival, Highland Park, Ill., 1977-83; gen. mgr. Hubbard Street Dance Co., Chgo., 1984—; bd. dirs., sec. Chicago Dance Art Coalition, 1984—; bd. dirs. Ill. Arts Alliance, Sheffield Winds, Chgo., 1982—; mem. dance panel Ill. Arts Council, Chgo., 1983-85; mem. grants panel Chgo. Office Fine Arts, 1985; cons. music Nat. Radio Theatre, Chgo., 1983—. Editor: Music Explorer (for music edn.), 1983-86. Office: Hubbard St Dance Co 218 S Wabash Ave Chicago IL 60604

KALYAN-RAMAN, KRISHNA, neurologist; b. Madras, India, June 2, 1935; came to U.S., 1965; s. Natesan and Savithri Kalyan-Raman; m. Uma Parvathi, Feb. 6, 1963; children: Kartik, Chitra. MBBS, Madras U., 1958; MD in Internal Medicine, Delhi U., India, 1962; DM in Neurology, Madras U., 1971. Diplomate Am. Bd. Psychiatry and Neurology. Intern G.G. Hosp., Madras, 1957-58; resident in neurology E. J. Meyer Meml. Hosp., Buffalo, 1965-66, Montreal (Can.) Neurologic Inst., 1967-68; clin. asst. prof. neurology SUNY, Buffalo, 1971-72, asst. prof. neurology, 1972-75, assoc. prof. neurology, 1976; assoc. prof. neurology U. Ill., Peoria, 1976-83, prof. clin. neurology, 1983—; dir. Muscular Dystrophy Assn. Clinic, Peoria, 1979—. Contbr. articles to profl. jours. Recipient Golden Apple award U. Ill., 1977, 78; Citation of Merit, Muscular Dystrophy Assn. Am., 1969, 79. Fellow ACP, Am. Acad. Neurology; mem. Neurol. Soc. India, Am. Assn. EMG & Electrodiagnosis (assoc.). Office: U Ill Coll Medicine Dept Neurosciences 530 NE Glen Oak Ave Peoria IL 61637

KAMAREI, HOSSEIN, business educator; b. Tehran, Iran, Apr. 21, 1945; came to U.S., 1973; s. Khalil and Ozra (Javadian) K.; m. Zahra Behdadfar, July 20, 1978; children: Kusha, Donna. BA in Bus. Adminstrn., Tehran Bus. Coll., 1972; MBA, Ind. U., 1975, PhD in Econs. and Bus., 1985. Assoc. instr. econs. Ind. U., Bloomington, 1977-80, assoc. instr. math., 1981-82; lectr. in econs. Butler U., Indpls., 1981-82; lectr. in stats. and bus. math. Ind. U., South Bend, 1983-85, asst. prof. quantitative bus., 1985—. Served with Iranian Literacy Corps, 1964-65. Internat. student scholar Ind. U., 1977; summer faculty fellow Ind. U., 1986. Mem. Am. Econ. Assn., Am. Statis. Assn., Decision Scis. Inst., Soc. for Indsl. and Applied Math., Omicron Delta Epsilon. Islam. Avocations: reading, translation, sports. Home: 450 Traverse Ct Mishawaka IN 46545 Office: Ind U Div Bus and Econs 1700 Mishabaka Ave South Bend IN 46634

KAMENETZKY, RICARDO DANIEL, engineer; b. San Lorenzo, Argentina, Mar. 7, 1954; came to U.S., 1976; s. Mario and Sofia (Iurcovich) K.; m. Deborah Jean Morrison, Sept. 6, 1978; children: Elena, Julia. BS in Indsl. Engring., U. Buenos Aires, 1975; MS in Indsl. Engring., U. Pitts., 1977, PhD in Indsl. Engring., 1981. Engineer Tintaprest S.A., Buenos Aires, 1976; cons. Buenos Aires Bauen Hotel, 1978-79; mgmt. research analyst Alcoa, Pitts., 1981-84; indsl. engring. supr. Davenport (Iowa) Works div. Alcoa, 1985—; advisory bd. St. Ambrose Coll. Inst. Indsl. Engring., Davenport, 1986—. Contbr. articles to profl. jours. Health Care Mgmt. Ctr. fellow U. Pa., 1980. Mem. Inst. Indsl. Engrs., Inst. Mgmt. Scis., Omega Rho Soc. (v.p. Pitts. chpt. 1977). Avocations: volleyball, tennis, running, cross country skiing. Home: 2728 Sycamore Terr Bettendorf IA 52722 Office: Alcoa PO Box 3567 Davenport IA 52808

KAMIKOW, NORMAN B., publishing company executive; b. Chgo., Dec. 25, 1943; s. Howard M. and Ethel (Morris) K.; divorced; children: Jeffrey R., David A.; m. Susan B. Chaplik, Aug. 16, 1987. BA in Journalism, Drake U., 1967. Account exec. Chgo. Tribune, 1967-69; account exec., dir. sales devel. Branham Newspapers, Chgo., 1969-72; asso. Chgo. mgr. Seventeen mag., 1972-76; Midwest advt. dir. Penthouse Internat., Chgo., 1976-82; pres. Kamikow & Co., Pubs.' Reps., 1982-85, also bd. dirs.; exec. v.p. Gerber/Kamikow Pubs.' Reps., 1985—, also bd. dirs.; pres. Decks, Inc., 1984—, also bd. dirs.; bd. dirs. D.E.K. Properties, Power Advt.; guest lectr. U. Ill. Mem. Chgo. Advt. Club, Nat. Assn. Pubs. Reps., Direct Mktg. Assn. Clubs: Plaza, East Bank, Agate of Chgo.; Variety of Ill. Office: 1309 Rand Rd Arlington Heights IL 60004

KAMILARIS, LORI ANN, nurse; b. Toledo, Dec. 27, 1958; d. Donald Carl and Kathryn Elizabeth (Whaley) Dugan; m. George Andreas Kamilaris, June 12, 1982; 1 child, Sarah Marie. BS in Nursing, Capital U., 1976-80. Registered nurse. Staff nurse St. Charles Hosp., Oregon, Ohio, 1980—. United Methodist. Avocation: ch. activities. Home: 240 Chantilly Rue E Northwood OH 43619

KAMIN, KAY HODES, lawyer; b. Chgo., July 3, 1940; d. Barnet and Eleanor (Cramer) Hodes; m. Malcolm S. Kamin, June 12, 1963; children—Kim Alison, Kyle Barret. BA, Vassar Coll., 1961, MA, U. Chgo., 1962, PhD, 1970; JD cum laude, Northwestern U., 1981. Bars: Ill. 1981, U.S. Dist. Ct. (no. dist.) Ill. 1981. Cert. tchr., Ill. History tchr. Lincoln Park High Sch., Chgo., 1963-67; social studies coordinator U. Chgo., 1968-69; assoc. prof. edn. Rosary Coll., River Forest, Ill., 1970-76; jud. law clk. Ill. Appellate Ct., Chgo., 1981-83; assoc. Mayer, Brown & Platt, Chgo., 1983-85; v.p., gen. counsel Glencorp Inc., 1985—, also bd. dirs. Co-author: Contract Law, 1983. Contbr. articles to profl. jours. Pres., Chgo. Council for Social Studies, 1967-69; gov. life. mem. Chgo. Art Inst., 1974—, pres. soc. for contemporary art, 1974-76; pres. Sedoh Found., 1986—; bd. dirs. Whigmore Soc. Northwestern U. Law Sch. Grad. fellow U. Chgo., 1967-70, fellow Newberry library. Mem. Chgo. Bar Assn., Ill. Bar Assn., ABA, Chgo. Council Lawyers. Club: Arts, John Evans (Northwestern U.). Avocations: golf, jogging, skiing, art collecting. Office: Glencorp Inc 1496 Waukegan Rd Glenview IL 60025

KAMINSKI, ROBERT STANLEY, fastner company executive; b. Youngstown, Ohio, Feb. 3, 1936; s. Stanley and Agnes (Javorsky) K.; m. Mary Ann Bell, Feb. 9, 1957; children—Robert M., Janice M., David M. B.E. in Chem. Engring., Youngstown U., 1961. Plant mgr. Ammet, New Castle, Pa., 1961-63; sr. engr. Brush Beryllium, Elmore, Ohio, 1963-65; dept. supt., 1965-71; dept. mgr., 1971-73, div. mgr., Brush Wellman, Cleve., 1973-75; v.p. ops. S.K. Wellman, Bedford, Ohio, 1975-81, Janesville Products, Norwalk, Ohio, 1981-83; pres. Continental Midland, Park Forest, Ill., 1983-86; chief exec. officer, pres. Continental/Midland Inc, Park Forest, 1986—. Mem. Am. Inst. Chem. Engrs., Jaycees. Lodge: KC. Avocations: golf; Little League coaching; Sunday School teaching. Home: 3500 Parthenon Way Olympia Fields IL 60461 Office: Continental/Midland 25000 S Western Ave Park Forest IL 60466

KAMINSKY, ALBERT ABRAHAM, jeweler, watchmaker; b. Toronto, Ont., Can., Jan. 18, 1921; came to U.S., 1922-23; s. Morris Isaac and Anna Altah (Eichenthal) K.; m. Alice Patricia Harris, Apr. 15, 1952; children: Gary Earl, Deborah Ann, Steven Mark. Cert. master watchmaker. Ptnr. Kaminsky Jewelers, Fostoria, Ohio, 1945-87, Findlay, Ohio, 1964-83, owner, pres., 1983—. Mem. Bd. Health, Fostoria, 1960. Served as staff sgt. USAF, 1942-45, ETO. Mem. Horological Inst. Am., Am. Watchmakrs Inst. Democrat. Jewish. Lodges: Masons, Shriners. Avocations: literature, music, swimming, restoration of antique watches. Home: 1804 Hilton Ave Findlay OH 45840 Office: Kaminsky Jewelers 414 S Main St PO Box 964 Findlay OH 45839

KAMM, CAROL ANN, software design engineer; b. Detroit, Jan. 5, 1959; d. Vernon Charles and Kathryn Lucille (Dutil) K.; m. James Wesley Howe, Oct. 13, 1984. BS in Computer Engring., U. Mich., Ann Arbor, 1982. Research asst. ISDOS Project U. Mich., Ann Arbor, 1980-83; data systems analyst Boeing Computer Services, Wichita, Kans., 1983-84; product designer Holland Systems, Ann Arbor, 1984-85; technical product mgr. Network Technologies Internat., Inc., Ann Arbor, 1985—. Mem. Assn. for Computing Machinery. Avocations: antiques, music, reading, wine, gardening. Office: Network Technologies Internat Inc 315 W Huron Ann Arbor MI 48103

KAMPEN, EMERSON, chemical company executive; b. Kalamazoo, Mar. 12, 1928; s. Gerry and Gertrude (Gerlofs) K.; m. Barbara Frances Spitters, Feb. 2, 1951; children—Douglas S., Joanie L. Kampen Dunham, Laura L. Kampen Shiver, Emerson III, Deborah L. Kampen Smith, Cynthia S., Pamela E. B.S. in Chem. Engring., U. Mich., 1951. Chem. engr Gt. Lakes Chem. Corp., West Lafayette, Ind., 1951-62, plant mgr., 1962-67, v.p., 1968, sr. v.p., 1969-71, exec. v.p., 1972-73, pres., 1977—, chief exec. officer, 1977—; pres., chief exec. officer GLCD, Inc., Ark., also bd. dirs.; chmn. bd. subs. cos. E/M Corp., Hydrotech Chem. Corp., Gt. Lakes Chem. (Europe) Ltd.; pres. Ark. Chems.; pres., dir. GLC (Internat.) Inc., GHC (Properties) Inc.; bd. dirs. WIL Research Labs., Inc., Oilfield Service Corp. Am., Lafayette Life Ins. Co., Lafayette Nat. Bank, Inland Splty. Chem. Corp., Huntsman Chem. Corp., Salt Lake City, Pub. Service Ind., Plainfield; chmn. bd. dirs. Enzyme Tech. Corp., Ashland, Ohio; mem. listed co. adv. com. Am. Stock Exchange. Mem. corp. advising group Nat. Huntington's Disease Assn., N.Y.C.; commr. Ind. United Way Centennial Commn.; trustee Ind. U., Bloomington; bd. dirs. Jr. Achievement Greater Lafayette, Inc., Lafayette Art Assn. Found. Inc., Purdue Research Found., West Lafayette, Lafayette Symphony Found. Served to capt. USAF, 1953. Recipient Bronze medal Wall Street Transcript, 1980, 86, Gold medal Wall Street Transcript, 1983, 85, Man of Yr. award Nat. Huntington's Disease Assn., 1984; co-recipient Gold medal Wall Street Transcript, 1984; named 5th Most Involved Chief Exec. Officer, Chief Exec. mag., 1986. Fellow Am. Inst. Chemists; mem. Am. Indsl. Health Council (bd. dirs.), Soc. Chem. Industry (bd. dirs.), Nat. Assn. Mfrs. (bd. dirs.), Chem. Mfrs. Assn., Ind. C. of C. (bd. dirs.), Greater Lafayette C. of C. Clubs: Lafayette Country, Skyline (Indpls.). Lodges: Elks, Rotary. Avocations: golf; family events. Home: 168 Creighton West Lafayette IN 47906 Office: Gt Lake Chem Corp US Hwy 52 NW PO Box 2200 West Lafayette IN 47906 *

KAMSTRA, DENNIS ALVIN, health care facility administrator; b. Graceville, Minn., Nov. 24, 1949; s. Alvin J. and Shirley Marie (Strootman) K.; m. Joyce Olea Omland, Aug. 28, 1971; children: Jennifer, Greg. AS, Bur. Criminal Apprehension, Mpls.; student, U. Minn., Morris. Cert. Emergency Med. Technician, Minn.; lic. hosp. adminstr., Minn., lic. long-term care adminstr., Minn. Conservation officer State of Minn., Clarkfield, 1972-73; dep. sheriff Yellow Medicine County, Clarkfield, 1973-75; city adminstr. City of Clarkfield, 1975-76; hosp. adminstr. Clarkfield Hosp. and Home, 1976-84; owner, pres. Christian Nursing and Living Ctrs., Willmar, 1985—; pres. P&K Mgmt., Inc., Willmar, 1985—; health care cons. City of Miltona, Minn., 1980-81; chmn. State Apartment Owners Conf., 1987—. Pres. Ambulance Squad, Clarkfield, Minn., 1980-84; del. to Rep. Conv., Mpls., 1979-80. Mem. Minn. Assn. Homes for Aging, Minn. Hosp. Assn., Minn. Assn. Health Care Facilities, Health Systems Agy. Six (pres. 1982), State Nursing Home Assn. (mem. governing bd. 1987—). Lutheran. Avocations: outdoor sports, woodworking, chess. Home: 1221 SW 18th St Willmar MN 56201 Office: Christian Nursing Ctr 1801 Willmar Ave Willmar MN 56201

KANDAH, WALID FUAD, osteopathic physician; b. Ramallah, Jordan, July 18, 1952; came to U.S., 1957; naturalized, 1957; s. Fuad Saliba and Helen Fuad (Kazaleh) K.; m. Randa Zanayed, July 17, 1983. B.S., U. Mich., 1974; D.O., Kansas City Coll., 1980. Diplomate Am. Bd. Family Practice, Nat. Bd. Examiners in Osteo. Medicine. Intern, Mt. Clemens (Mich.) Gen. Hosp., 1980-81; resident in family practice St. Joseph Hosp., Flint, Mich., 1981-83; emergency dept. physician Ionia County (Mich.) Meml. Hosp., 1982-83, Hills and Dales Gen. Hosp., Cass City, Mich., 1981-83, Sinai Hosp. of Detroit, 1983-84, Garden City Hosp., 1984-86, Botsford Gen. Hosp., 1986—; clin. instr. family practice Mich. State U., East Lansing, 1981-83. Mem. Am. Acad. Family Physicians, Am. Osteo. Assn., Am. Coll. Emergency Physicians, Am. Assn. Occupational Medicine, Mich. Acad. Family Physicians, Mich. Assn. Osteo. Physicians and Surgeons, Psi Sigma Alpha. Republican. Home: 37546 River Bend Farmington Hills MI 48024

KANE, ANDREW WILLIAM, psychologist; b. Faribault, Minn., Nov. 3, 1944; s. Harry and Mary (Millunchick) K.; m. Karen Plaks, Oct. 12, 1975 (div. Aug. 29, 1986); children: Elisabeth Sarah, Daniel Howard. BA in Psychology, U. Minn., 1966; MS in Clin. Psychology, U. Wis., Milw., 1968, PhD in Clin. Psychology, 1971. Lic. psychologist, Wis. Clin. intern VA Hosp., Wood, Wis., 1968-69; founding exec. dir. The Counseling Ctr. of Milw., 1970-78; pvt. practice psychology Milw., 1978—; clin. cons. The Thompson Group, Milw., 1979—; adj. prof. Wis. Sch. Profl. Psychology, 1982—, chmn. com. on Faculty, Policies and Procedures, mem. curriculum com., long-range planning com.; cons. dept. psychiatry and mental health scis. Med. Coll. Wis., 1979-80, assco. clin. prof. 1979—; cons. Milw. County Mental Health Complex, 1979-80; mem. allied health profl. staff Milw. Psychiat. Hosp., 1979—; mem. ind. allied health profl. staff dept. medicine St. Anthony Hosp., Milw., 1986—; mem. habilitation and maintenance com. State Health Policy Council, 1980—; mem. legis. com. State Council on Mental Health, 1985—, mem. allied health profl. staff dept. Psychiatry Good Samaritan Hosp., 1986—, mem. mental health protection and advocacy com., Wis. Coalition on Advocacy, 1987—. Co-author: The Alternate Services, 1975; contbr. articles to profl. jours. Recipient Citizenship award Mut. Trust Life Ins., 1975. Fellow Am. Orthopsychiat. Assn.; mem. Wis. Psychol. Assn. (pres. 1983-84, chmn. task force on sexual misconduct by psychotherapists 1985—, Disting. Profl. Contbn. to the Practice of Psychology in the Pub. Interest 1987), Am. Psychol. Assn., Soc. Clin. and Cons. Psychologists, Soc. Psychologists in Addictive Behaviors, Am. Psychology Law Soc., Milw. Area Psychol. Assn. (pres. 1982-83). Avocations: audio visual equipment, tennis, children. Home: 2726 E Newberry Blvd Milwaukee WI 53211 Office: 2815 N Summit Ave Milwaukee WI 53211

KANE, JOHN EDWARD, manufacturing company executive; b. Terre Haute, Ind., July 23, 1943; s. James Joseph and Isabelle Catherine (McKinney) K.; m. Joyce Marie Croenne, Apr. 24, 1965; children: Laura Ann, Stephanie Lynn, Kevin Michael. BS in Mgmt., Ind. State U., 1973. Data processing mgr., programmer Hulman & Co., Terre Haute, 1967-71; sr. systems analyst Ind. State U., Terre Haute, 1971-74; corp. mfg. systems analyst Hyster Co., Danville, Ill., 1974-77; systems project leader Henry Pratt Co., Aurora, Ill., 1977-79; mgr. adminstrv. systems Rockwell Internat., Troy, Mich., 1979—. Mem. Data Processing Mgmt. Assn. Republican. Roman Catholic. Office: Rockwell Internat 2135 W Maple Rd Troy MI 48084

KANE, KENDALL KENT, pathologist; b. Washington, Sept. 30, 1932; s. Thomas Leiper and Marguerite (Mussey) K.; m. Barbara Heath, Apr. 11, 1961 (div. 1971); children: John, Lei, Kathryn; m. Gay Louise Krieger, Aug. 14, 1981; 1 child, Delayne. BA, Princeton U., 1955; MD, Columbia U., 1960. Chief clin. microbiology Walter Reed Gen. Hosp., Washington, 1966-67, acting chief clin. chemistry, 1967-68; asst. to assoc. pathologist St. Luke's Hosp. Ctr., N.Y.C., 1968-77; dir. lab. Equitable Life Assurance Soc., N.Y.C., 1975-77; assoc. pathologist Good Samaritan Hosp., Dayton, Ohio, 1977—; dir. Walter Reed Sch. Med. Tech., 1967-68; asst. attending physician pathology dept. St. Luke's Hosp. Ctr., N.Y.C., 1968-71, attending physician, 1976; instr. pathology Coll. Physicians and Surgeons Columbia U., N.Y.C., 1970-73, asst. clin. prof., 1973-77; assoc. clin. prof. Wright State U., Dayton, 1977—. Mem. editorial bd. Annals Clin. and Lab. Sci., 1980—; contbr. articles to profl. jours. Fellow Assn. Clin. Scis. (pres. 1983-84), Am. Soc. Clin. Pathologists; mem. AMA, Ohio Soc. Pathologists, Montgomery County Med. Soc., Am. Assn. Blood Banks, Ohio Assn. Blood Banks, Acad. Medicine Wright State U., Berkeley Scientific Labs. Users Group, Phi Beta Kappa, Sigma Xi. Libertarian. Avocations: birding, computers. Home: 814 Harman Ave Dayton OH 45419 Office: Good Samaritan Hosp 2222 Philadelphia Dr Dayton OH 45406

KANE, STEVEN EDWARD, human resources executive; b. Milw., Sept. 7, 1949; s. Edward Thomas and Marion Jean (Regan) K.; children: Clifford, Stacy. BS in Indsl. Relations, Cornell U., 1972, MBA, 1973; JD, U. Akron, 1977. Bar: Ohio 1977, Tex. 1977. Labor relations staff BF Goodrich, Akron, Ohio, 1973-77; cons. Modern Mgmt., Bannockburn, Ill., 1978; dir. employee relations Am. Hosp. Supply, Evanston, Ill., 1979-85; v.p. human resource adminstrn. Baxter Travenol Labs., Deerfield, Ill., 1986—. Mem. ABA, Ohio Bar Assn., Tax. Bar Assn. Home: 831 Garfield Ave Libertyville IL 60048 Office: Baxter-Travenol Labs Inc 1 Baxter Pkwy Deerfield IL 60015

KANE, WILLIAM MATTHEW, obstetrician, gynecologist; b. Bridgeport, Conn., Oct. 5, 1927; s. William Matthew and Mary (Fekete) K.; m. Shirley Rita Steeves, Aug. 26, 1950; children—William, Claire, Daniel, Mary Kathleen, Susan, John. A.B., Holy Cross Coll., 1950; M.D., George Washington U., 1954. Diplomate Am. Bd. Ob-Gyn. Rotating intern St. Vincents Hosp., Bridgeport, Conn., 1954-55, resident in ob-gyn, 1955-57; resident in ob-gyn St. Francis Hosp., Bridgeport, 1957-59; practice medicine specializing in ob-gyn, Trumbull, Conn., 1959-61, The Eddy Clinic, Hays, Kans., 1961-78, Canterbury Women's Clinic, Hays, 1978—. Bd. dirs. United Fund, Hays, 1968-70; dist. chmn. Coronado Council Wheatland Dist. Boy Scouts Am., Hays; chmn. fund drive Hays Pub. Library. Served with U.S. Army, 1946-47. Mem. AMA, Kans. Med. Soc., Kans. Ob-Gyn Soc. (pres.1972-73), Am. Fertility Soc., Am. Coll. Ob/Gyn. Club: Smoky Hill Country (Hays) (bd. dirs.). Avocations: fishing; sailing; magic; photography. Office: 2503 Canterbury Rd Hays KS 67601

KANGER, DAVID WAYNE, petroleum retailing company executive; b. Springfield, Ill., Jan. 30, 1946; s. John James Kanger and Mary Anne (Mesich) Neitzelt; m. Deborah Anne Freeman, Jan. 24, 1970; children: James Scott, David Andrew. Student Danville Jr. Coll., 1964-67; BA in Biology, Elmhurst Coll., 1969; postgrad. Nat. Coll. Edn., 1986—. Mgr. Bill's Shell Service, Lisle, Ill., 1967-72; ptnr. Oak Hill Shell, Lisle, 1979-84, Maple Grove Automotive, Downers Grove, Ill., 1980-83; owner, operator Dave's Shell Auto Care, Lisle, 1972-84; pres. K-Kar Service Ctrs., Lisle, 1984—; pres., chmn. bd. dirs. D & D Kwik Marts, Inc., Lisle, 1984—. Scoutmaster West Suburban council Boy Scouts Am., 1979-87, leadership tng. com., 1982-87, 1st asst. scoutmaster, 1985. Served with U.S. Army, 1969-71, Vietnam. Recipient Top Performance award Shell Oil Co., 1972-86, Dealer of Yr. award Shell Oil, 1980. Mem. Lisle C. of C., Nat. Rifle Assn. Republican. Lodge: Lions (v.p. 1975-79). Avocations: big game and upland hunting, backpacking, canoeing, reloading. Home: 1520 Chicago Ave Downers Grove IL 60515 Office: K-Kar Service Ctrs Inc 1117 Maple Ave Lisle IL 60532

KANIA, WALTER, psychologist; b. Cleve., Apr. 4, 1933; s. Joseph and Rose Kania; m. Ann Isabel Stiers, Dec. 18, 1954; children: Regan, Lanette, Jill. Student, Miami U., Oxford, Ohio, 1950-52; BS, Ohio State U., 1954; MDiv, Tex. Christian U., 1961; PhD, Mich. State U., 1965. Lic. psychologist; ordained clergyman. Asst. prof. psychology Bethany (W.Va.) Coll., 1965-66, Ohio State U., Mansfield, 1966-71; pvt. practice clin. psychology Mansfield, 1971—. Pastor United Campus Ministry, East Lansing, Mich., 1961-65.Served to capt. USAF, 1954-58. Mem. Am. Psychol. Assn., Ohio Psychol. Assn. Republican. Congregationalist. Home: 581 Cliffside Dr Mansfield OH 44904 Office: Am Mgmt & Personnel Cons Inc 666 Park Ave W Mansfield OH 44906

KANNE, MICHAEL STEPHEN, judge; b. Rensselaer, Ind., Dec. 21, 1938; s. Allen Raymond and Jane (Robinson) K.; m. Judith Ann Stevens, June 22, 1963; children: Anne, Katherine. Student, St. Joseph's Coll., Rensselaer, 1957-58; BS, Ind. U., 1962, JD, 1968; postgrad., Boston U., 1963, U. Birmingham, Eng., 1975. Bar: Ind. 1968. Assoc. Nesbitt and Fisher, Rensselaer, 1968-71; sole practice Rensselaer, 1971-72; atty. City of Rensselaer, 1972; judge 30th Jud. Cir. of Ind., 1972-82, U.S. Dist. Ct. (no. dist.) Ind., Hammond, 1982-87, U.S. Ct. Appeals, Chgo., 1987—; lectr. law St. Joseph's Coll., 1975—; faculty Nat. Inst. for Trial Advocacy, South Bend, Ind., 1978—. Bd. dirs. Sagamore council Boy Scouts Am., 1979—; trustee St. Joseph's Coll., 1984—. Served to 1st lt. USAF, 1962-65. Recipient Disting. Service award St. Joseph's Coll., 1973. Mem. Fed. Judges Assn., Fed. Bar Assn., Am. Judicature Soc., Ind. State Bar Assn. (bd. dirs. 1977-79, Presdl. citation 1979), Jasper County Bar Assn. (pres. 1972-76), Law Alumni Assn. Ind. U. (pres. 1980). Roman Catholic. Club: Nat. Lawyers (Washington). Avocation: woodworking. Home: 605 Milroy Ave Rensselaer IN 47978 Office: US Ct Appeals 219 S Dearborn St Chicago IL 60604

KANOWSKY, LOUIS SYLVESTER, controller; b. Evansville, Ind., Jan. 31, 1957; s. Louis Henry and Agnes Milburn (Wimsatt) K.; m. Susan Elaine Ulrich, June 2, 1979; children: Brian Matthew, John Patrick. BSBA, U. Evansville, 1979; postgrad. in bus. adminstrn., Ind. U., Indpls., 1985—. CPA, Ind. Staff acct. Burks, Vernon & Co., CPA's, Evansville, 1978-79; auditor Arthur Andersen & Co., Indpls., 1979-84; mgr. cash receipts Blue Cross-Blue Shield, Indpls., 1984-86, div. controller, 1986—. Program dir. Jr. Achievement, Evansville, 1977-79; vol. adviser Jr. Achievement-Cen. Ind., Indpls., 1979; vol. solicitor Jobnet Ptnrs. 2000, Indpls., 1985. Mem. Am. Inst. CPA's, Ind. CPA Soc. (scholar 1978-79), Inst. Cert. Mgmt. Accts. Roman Catholic. Home: 6883 Grampian Way Indianapolis IN 46254 Office: Blue Cross Blue Shield of Ind 120 W Market St Indianapolis IN 46204

KANTOFF, JOYCE, court probation officer; b. Chgo., Apr. 13, 1945; d. Morton H. and Selma (Shapiro) K.; m. Apr. 3, 1973 (div. Jan. 1977). B.S., Loyola U., 1968. Field worker Juvenile Ct. Cook County, Chgo., 1968-79; complaint screener probation officer, 1981—. Mem. Anti-Vivesection Soc., Defenders of Wildlife, Greenpeace, Ctr. for Environment Edn., Nature Conservatory, Animal Protection Fund, Whale Protection Fund, World Wildlife Fund., African Wildlife Fund, Lincoln Park Zoo, Seal Rescue Fund. Democrat. Jewish. Office: 1100 S Hamilton St Chicago IL 60612

KANTOR, NEIL MICHAEL, osteopathic physician; b. N.Y.C., July 4, 1940; m. Felice M. Zimmerman, June 20, 1965; children—Robert Joseph, Sheryl Beth, Michelle Jayne, Adam Scott. B.A., NYU, 1961; D.O., Phila. Coll. Osteo. Medicine, 1965. Diplomate Am. Bd. Pediatrics, Am. Bd. Neonatal-Perinatal Medicine, Am. Bd. Neonatology, Am. Bd. Osteo. Pediatricians. Intern, Doctor's Hosp., Columbus, Ohio, 1965-66; resident in pediatrics Grandview Hosp., Dayton, Ohio, 1966-68; practice osteo. medicine specializing in pediatric critical care and neonatology, Dayton, 1968-75, 83—, Jacksonville, Fla., 1975-81, Omaha, 1981-83; chmn. dept. pediatrics Grandview Hosp., Dayton, 1971-75; chmn. dept. pediatrics Jacksonville Gen. Hosp., 1975-78, fellow in neonatal-perinatal medicine Univ. Hosp., Jacksonville, 1975-78, assoc. dir. regional neonatal intensive care ctr., 1979-81; med. dir. neonatal intensive care nursery Jacksonville Children's Hosp., 1979-81; dir. pediatric critical care medicine div. St. Joseph Hosp., Omaha, 1981-83; dir. nurseries regional perinatal ctr. Miami Valley Hosp., Dayton, 1983—; clin. instr. dept. pediatrics Wright State Sch. Medicine, Dayton, 1974-75; asst. prof. U. Fla., Jacksonville, 1978-81; assoc. prof. Creighton U., Omaha, 1981-83; adj. clin. prof. Univ. Osteo. Med. and Health Scis., Des Moines, 1982—; assoc. clin. prof. Wright State U. Sch. Medicine, Dayton, 1983—; clin. prof. Ohio U. Coll. Osteo. Medicine, 1983—; med. cons. pediatrics State of Ohio Aid Dependent Children, 1971-75; med. cons. neonatalogy State of Fla. Children's Med. Services, Health and Rehab. Services, 1976-81; med. cons. United Cerebral Palsy Duval County, Jacksonville, 1979-81; med. cons. Nebr. Dept. Child and Maternal Welfare, 1981—; cons. Am. Bd. Neonatology, Am. Bd. Osteo. Pediatricians. Bd. dirs. Speech and Hearing Council Met. Dayton, 1971-75; mem. med. adv. com. Am. Diabetes Assn., Montgomery County, Dayton, 1973-75; mem. com. Prevention Lead Poisoning, State of Ohio, 1975-76; mem. med. adv. bd. Tay-Sach's Screening Program, Jacksonville, 1976-77; mem. Fla. Infant Screening Adv. Council, 1978, Genetic Adv. Council, 1978; mem. med. adv. com. March of Dimes, 1981-83, legis. action com. Western Ohio Pediatric Soc., 1986—; bd. dirs. Hillel Acad., Dayton, 1972-73, Beth Israel Synagogue, Omaha, 1982-83. Recipient Resident Tchr. award Grandview Hosp., 1972; award Recognition Am. Reyes Syndrome Assn., 1982; numerous research grants. Fellow Am. Acad. Pediatrics; mem. Am. Osteo. Assn., Ohio Osteo. Assn., Am. Coll. Osteo. Pediatricians (sr. mem., dir., pres. 1985-86), Greater Plains Orgn. Perinatal Care. Author: (with R.D. Garrison) neonatal Transport Handbook, 1979; (with T. Chiu, R.D. Garrison) Houseofficers Manual for Intensive Care Unit, 1978, 1983; editor (with A. Tolaymat, S. Deering) Training Modules in Pediatrics, 1980; editorial cons. Jour. Am. Osteo. Assn., 1976—; mem. editorial bd. Health Values, 1982—; contbr. articles to profl. jours.

KANTOR, PAUL BERL, researcher, consultant; b. Washington, Nov. 27, 1938. AB, Columbia U., 1959; PhD in Physics, Princeton U., 1963. Research assoc. Brookhaven, Upton, N.Y., 1963-65; vis. asst. prof. SUNY, Stonybrook, 1965-67; physics asst. prof. Case Western Res., Cleve., 1967-70, assoc. prof., 1970-72; pres. Tantalus, Inc., Cleve., 1976—. Contbr. articles to profl. jours. Pres. Ormond Rd. Assn., Cleve., 1977—; disting. vis. scholar OCLC, 1987. Mem. Am. Phys. Soc., N.Y. Acad. Scis., Am. Statis. Assn., Am. Soc. Info. Home: 3257 Ormond Rd Cleveland OH 44118 Office: Tantalus Inc 2140 Lee Rd Suite 218 Cleveland OH 44118

KANTZER, KENNETH SEALER, clergyman; b. Detroit, Mar. 29, 1917; s. Edwin Frederick and Clara (Sealer) K.; m. Ruth Forbes, Sept. 21, 1939; children: Mary Ruth Wilkinson, Richard Forbes. AB, Ashland Coll., 1938; DD (hon.), Ashland Theol. Sem., 1981; MA, Ohio State U., 1939; BD, MST, Faith Theol. Sem., 1943; PhD, Harvard U., 1950; postdoctoral, U. Goettingen, Fed. Republic Germany, 1954-55; DD (hon.), Gordon Coll., 1979; HHD (hon.), John Brown U., 1981. Ordained to ministry Evang. Free Ch., 1950. Instr. Bible, history Kings Coll., New Castle, Del., 1941-43; instr. Hebrew Gordon Coll./Sem., Boston, 1944-46; instr. Bible, prof. bibl. and systematic theology, chmn. div. Bible, philosophy and religious edn. Wheaton (Ill.) Coll., 1946-63; dean, v.p. grad. studies, prof. bibl. and systematic theology Trinity Evang. Div. Sch., Deerfield, Ill., 1963-78, prof. bibl. and systematic theology, 1984—; editor in chief Christianity Today, Carol Stream, Ill., 1978-82, sr. editor, dean research inst., 1984—; pres. Trinity Coll., Deerfield, 1982-83, chancellor, 1983—; bd. dirs. Columbia (S.C.) Bible Coll., John Brown U., Siloam Springs, Ark., The Evang. Alliance Mission, Wheaton; pres., bd. dirs. Inst. Advancement of Christian Scholarship, 1987—. Editor: Evangelical Roots, 1978, Perspectives in Evangelical Theology, 1979, Applying the Scriptures, 1987; contbr. numerous articles to profl. jours., chpts. to books. Sec. Inst. for Advancement Christian Scholarship Ednl. Found., Chgo., 1978—; bd. dirs. Heritage Christian Sch., Lincolnshire, Ill., 1984—, Pioneer Ministries, Carol Stream, 1980—. Named Tchr. of Yr., Wheaton Coll., 1962; Hopkins scholar Harvard U., 1944. Mem. Evang. Theol. Soc. (pres.), Evang. Philos. Soc. Republican. Home: 1752 Spruce Highland Park IL 60035 Office: Trinity Coll 2077 Half Day Rd Deerfield IL 60015

KANZAKI, GEORGE AKAKI, industrial engineer, educator; b. Summit, N.J., Oct. 6, 1912; s. Kishiro and Sayeda Kanzaki; m. Katharina Ruehl, Feb. 15, 1955; children: Heikro, Tyrone. BSME, Stevens Inst. Tech., Hoboken, N.J., 1934; MS in Indsl. Engring., Arizona State U., 1961; MA, U. Iowa, 1975, PhD, 1980. Registered profl. engr.; cert. mfg. engr. Commd. USAF, 1945, advanced through grades; materials estimator USAF, Nellis AFB, Nevada, 1948-50; mgmt. engring. supr. USAF, Langley AFB, Va., 1950-68; ret. USAF, 1968; indsl. engr. U.S. Army Mgmt. Engr. Tng. Activity, Rock Island (Ill.) Arsenal, 1968-86; prof. indsl. engring. St. Ambrose U., Davenport, Iowa, 1986—; adj. prof. Fla. Inst. Tech., Rock Island, 1976—; asst. prof. U. Iowa, Iowa City, 1984-85. Author, editor: U.S. Army handbook on Mfg. Technology, 1980; contbr. article to profl. jours. Sr. advisor U.S. Congl. Adv. Bd., 1984, 86. Mem. Inst. Indsl. Engrs. (sr.), Soc. Mfg. Engrs., Machine Vision Assn. (sr.), Robotic Inst. Am. (charter), Computer and Automated Systems Assn. (charter), Robotic Internat. Club: Rock Island Arsenal Officers. Home: 4327 Royal Oaks Dr Davenport IA 52806 Office: St Ambrose U 518 W Locust St Davenport IA 52803

KAO, WEN-HONG, electrochemist, researcher; b. Taipei, Taiwan, Republic of China, Mar. 15, 1954; came to U.S., 1979; s. Yung-Han and Hsien (Huang) K.; m. Shu-Jen Fang, Mar. 18, 1979; children: Yvonne S., Peter S., Jonathan J. BS, Nat. Tsing Hua Univ., Taiwan, 1976; PhD, Ohio State U., 1984. Lead scientist Ray-O-Vac Corp., Madison, Wis., 1984—. Contbr. articles to profl. jours.; patentee in field. Postdoctoral fellow Ohio State U., 1984. Mem. Am. Chem. Soc., Electrochem. Soc. USA. Office: Ray-O-Vac Corp 630 Forward Dr Tech Ctr Madison WI 53711

KAO, WILLIAM CHISHON, dentist; b. Santiago, Chile, July 10, 1952; s. John S. and Mary Kao; m. Susic M. Moy, June 3, 1978; children: Jonathan, Kristen. BS with high honors, U. Ill., Chgo., 1974, BS in Dentistry with honors, 1976, DDS with honors, 1978. Comprehensive inst. U. Ill. Coll. Dentistry, Chgo., 1978-80; dentist, assoc. Dental Bldg., Oak Lawn, Ill., 1978-83; pvt. practice Carol Stream, Ill., 1978-82; dentist Preventive Dental Group, Glendale Heights, Ill., 1982-86; pvt. practice Roselle, Ill., 1986—. Mem. Chgo. Dental Soc., Ill. State Dental Soc., ADA (presiding chmn. ltd. attendance clinic at midwest convention 1980), U.S. Dental Inst. Avocation: tennis. Office: 1150 W Lake St Roselle IL 60172

KAPILA, VED PARKASH, engineer, surveyor, builder; b. Lopon, India, Dec. 27, 1932; s. Baboo Ram and Amravati (Vasishta) K.; came to U.S., 1963; naturalized, 1977; student Punjab U., India, 1949-51; diploma in civil engring Civil Engring. Sch., Lucknow, Ind., 1951-53; B.S. in Civil Engring., U. Mich., 1964, M.S. in Civil Engring., 1965; M.B.A., Wayne State U., 1970, value engring. orientation, 1970; m. Pushpa Pipat, Nov. 18, 1952; children—Shashi, Rajnish, Rita, Renu. Engring. sect. officer Punjab State Public Works Dept., India, 1953-63; design, engr. Ayres, Lewis, Norris & May, Ann Arbor, Mich., 1964-65; Obenchain Corp., Dearborn, Mich., 1965-66; v.p., chief civil and structural engr. O. Germany, Inc., Warren, Mich., 1966-76; dir. project services and chief planning and scheduling, chief quality assurance, chief client purchasing Hoad Engrs., Inc., Ypsilanti, Mich., 1976-78; pres. Kapila Constrn. Co., Inc., Kapila Contracting Co., Inc., Kapila & Assocs., 1968—. Registered profl. engr. Mich., Ga., Va., Punjab State (India); registered land surveyor, Mich.; licensed builder, Mich.; certified Nat. Council Engring. Examiners. Mem. ASCE, Am. Congress Surveying and Mapping, Am. Concrete Inst., Am. Inst. Steel Constrn., Mich. Soc. Registered Land Surveyors, Am. Soc. Quality Control, Soc. Am. Value Engrs., Nat. Soc. Profl. Engrs. Office: 31333 Thirteen Mile Rd Farmington HIlls MI 48018

KAPLAN, ALEX H., psychiatrist; b. Hull, Eng., Sept. 25, 1912; came to U.S., 1914; s. Nathan and Dora (Bogdanoff) K.; m. Ada Marie Leibson, June 7, 1936; children: Dale H. Carriero, Lawrence Paul, Robert Alan. BS, CCNY, 1932; MD, St. Louis U., 1936. Diplomate Am. Bd. Psychiatry, Am. bd. Psychonalysis. Resident in psychiatry Grasslands Hosp., Valhalla, N.Y., 1937-39, Rockland State Hosp., Orangeburg, N.Y., 1939-43; asst. prof. psychiatry Washington U. Sch. Med., St. Louis, 1955-70, assoc. prof., 1970-77, prof., 1977—; acting dir. St. Louis Child Guidance Clinic, 1955-58; psychiatrist-in-chief St. Louis Jewish Hosp., 1959-66; med. dir. St. Louis Psychoanalytic Found., 1965-72, assoc. med. dir., 1972-82. Contbr. articles to profl .jours. Served to lt. M.C. USNR, 1943-46. Fellow Am. Psychiat. Assn., Am. Psychoanalytic Assn. (treas. 1971-77, pres. 1977-79); St. Louis Psychoanalytic Soc. (pres. 1966-68, 82-84), Am. Coll. Psychoanalysts (pres. 1987), Eastern Mo. Psychoanalytic Soc. (pres. 1958-59). Democrat. Avocation: tennis. Home: 11 Winding Brook Ln Saint Louis MO 63124 Office: Wash Univ Med Sch 4524 Forest Ave Saint Louis MO 63108

KAPLAN, BRUCE LEONARD, osteopath; b. Bklyn., Mar. 12, 1949; s. Benjamin and Helen (Geller) K.; m. Stacey Linda Kaplan, June 17, 1973. BSEE, Tufts U., 1971; DO, Coll. Osteo. Medicine and Surgery, Des Moines, 1975; postgrad., Wayne State U. Sch. Medicine, 1979. Diplomate Am. Bd. Med. Examiners; cert. Am. Bd. Internal Medicine, Am. Bd. Rheumatology. Intern Detroit Osteo. Hosp., Highland Park, Mich., 1975-76, resident in internal medicine, 1976-78; fellow in rheumatology and clin. immunology Dept. Internal Medicine Wayne State U., Detroit, 1978-80; gen. practice rheumatology Southfield, Mich., 1980—; active staff Wayne State U. Complex Hosps., Bi County Hosp.; chief dept. rheumatolgy Providence Hosp., v.p. staff Rehab. Inst.; others. Contbr. articles to profl. jours. Mem. Am. Osteo. Assn., Am. Coll. Osteo. Internists, Am. Rheumatism Assn., Mich. Rheumatism Soc., Mich. Assn. Osteopaths and Surgeons, Macomb County Osteo. Soc., Sigma Sigma Phi. Jewish. Office: 22250 Providence Dr Southfield MI 48075

KAPLAN, ETHAN ZADOK, urban planning executive; b. Pontiac, Mich., May 9, 1935; s. Morris J. and Certie (Bock) K.; B.A., U. Chgo., 1955, M.A., 1958; postgrad. Washington U. at St. Louis, 1960-62; m. Jane B. Breese, Dec. 23, 1958; children—Mark, Alan. Sr. planner St. Louis County Planning Com., 1962-66, prin. planner, 1967-69; chief advanced planning City Alexandria, Va., 1966-67; research planner Health and Welfare Council St. Louis, 1969-75; pvt. cons., 1975-78; exec. dir. Southeast Kans. Regional Planning Commn., 1978—. Served with AUS, 1958-60. Mem. Am. Inst. Cert. Planners, Nat. Con. Social Welfare, Am. Planning Assn., Am. Sociol. Assn. Home: 630 S Evergreen St Chanute KS 66720

KAPLAN, FRED MARTIN, architect; b. Chgo., Feb. 7, 1948; s. James E. and Muriel Jane (Isenson) K.; m. Nancy Lee Frank, June 8, 1969; children: Keri Lynn, Kenneth Lere. BArch, BS in Environ. Design, U. Okla., 1972. Registered architect, Ill., Ohio, Ind., Colo. Draftsman Cable-Kamerman, Hillside, Ill., 1972-74, Thelander & Nelson, Chgo., 1974-75; architect Altman Saichek, Chgo., 1975-77; assoc. architect Grunsfeld & Assoc., Chgo., 1977-81; prin. Fred Kaplan Architect, Northbrook, Ill., 1981-85; ptnr. Kaplan Mangurten Architecture, Deerfield, Ill., 1985—; mem. Nat. Trust for Hist. Preservation, Washington, 1978, Heritage Soc., 1986—. Bd. dirs. Med. Research Inst. Council, Chgo., 1973—. Served with USAR, 1971-77. Recipient Cert. of Merit, Big 8 Emergency Housing Exhbn., Okla. State U., 1971. Fellow Soc. Am. Registered Architects. Jewish. Club: Northmoor Country (Highland Park, Ill.) (bd. dirs. 1979—). Avocations: travel, golf. Office: Kaplan Mangurten 1141 Lake Cook Rd Suite F Deerfield IL 60015

KAPLAN, GERSON H., psychiatrist; b. Chgo., Feb. 16, 1930; s. Hayman B. and Dora (Bariff) K.; m. Ruth Trugman, May 8, 1957; children: Douglas, Andrew, Bruce, Susan. BA, Stanford U., 1951; MD, Northwestern U., 1955. Diplomate Am. Bd. Psychiatry. Pvt. practice psychiatry Chgo., 1963—. Mem. AMA, Am. Psychiat. Assn. Jewish. Office: 111 N Wabash Suite 1119 Chicago IL 60602

KAPLAN, HOWARD GORDON, lawyer; b. Chgo., June 1, 1941; s. David I. and Beverly Kaplan. BS, U. Ill., 1962; JD, John Marshall Law Sch., Chgo., 1967. Bar: Ill. 1967, D.C. 1980, N.Y. 1982, Wis. 1983, U.S. Supreme Ct. 1971; CPA, Ill. Acct., Chgo., 1962-67; sole practice, Chgo., 1967—; ptnr. Angell, Kaplan & Zaidman, 1975—; asst. prof. Chgo. City Colls., 1967-78. Author papers in field. Mem. ABA, Ill. Bar Assn., Chgo. Bar Assn., Bar Assn. 7th Circuit, Decalogue Soc., Am. Inst. CPA's, Ill. Soc. CPA's. Clubs: Chgo. Athletic Assn., Standard, Bryn Mawr Country (Chgo.); Friars (Los Angeles). Lodge: B'nai B'rith. Office: 180 N LaSalle St 28th Floor Chicago IL 60601

KAPLAN, LAURA KAY, marketing executive; b. Chippewa Falls, Wis., Apr. 12, 1958; d. Robert Raymond and Frances Darlene (Schnabel) K. BFA, Drake U., 1980. Mktg. rep. Mademoiselle mag., N.Y.C., 1977-80; asst. to pres. Hutson Advt., La Crosse, Wis., 1979; account exec. Gerdes Advt., Des Moines, 1979-80; account exec., sr. writer Colle & McVoy Advt., Mpls., 1981-82; mktg. mgr. Jostens, Inc., Mpls., 1982-86; dir. sales Mary Kay Cosmetics, Inc., Bloomington, Minn., 1986—; cons., lectr. Author: They Never Said It Would Be Like This, 1984; contbr. articles to profl. jours. Mem. Walker Art Ctr., Mpls., Inst. Arts; loaned exec. United Way of Mpls., 1985. Named Outstanding Mem. AD/2 Twin Cities, 1982; Drake Art scholar, 1976-80; recipient Best Visual Merchandising award Jewelers of Am., 1986. Mem. Am. Advt. Fedn., Art Dirs., Copywriter's Club, Jewelers of Am., Am. Mgmt. Assn., Women in Communications, Redheads Club Internat., Mpls. C. of C. (mem. tourism com. 1980-82), Drake Alumni Assn., Chi Omega Alumni Assn. (fin. advisor 1986—). Republican.

KAPLAN, SHEILA, university official. Chancellor U. Wis.-Parkside, Kenosha. Office: Univ of Wis-Parkside Box Number 2000 Kenosha WI 53141-2000 *

KAPOLNEK, GREGORY ALLEN, controller; b. Detroit, Aug. 14, 1959; s. Frank Stephen and Celine Veronica (Jablonski) K. BBA, U. Mich., Dearborn, 1981. CPA, Mich. Staff acct. Baditoi, Segroves & Co., P.C., Southfield, Mich., 1982-85; controller Galaxy Precision Machining Co., Inc., Plymouth, Mich., 1985—; mem. audit com. St. Mel's Fed. Credit Union, Dearborn Heights, Mich., 1983; chmn. creditors com. Production Tech, Inc., Troy, Mich., 1986—; bd. dirs. Galaxy Industries and subs., Plymouth. Mem. Am. Inst. CPA's (Elijah Watt Sells cert. 1982), Mich. Assn. CPA's (William A. Paton award 1982). Office: Galaxy Precision Machining 41150 Joy Rd Plymouth MI 48170

KAPOOR, TARUN, restaurateur; b. Bangalore, India, May 23, 1955; came to U.S., 1976; s. Om Prakash and Vimla (Puri) K.; m. Sandra Ann Kaiser, Aug. 21, 1982. Diploma, Inst. Hotel Mgmt., New Delhi, India, 1975; BS, U. Wis. Stout, Menomonie, 1977; MBA, Mich. State U., 1978. Ptnr. K&M Cons., Marshall, Minn., 1979-83; gen. mgr., cons. Hyatt Regency, New Delhi, 1983; pres. Kebab, Inc., Mpls., 1984—; cons. in field, Marshall, 1979—; assoc. prof. S.W. State U., Marshall, 1979-86. Mem. Midwest Assn. Hosp. Educators. Avocations: travel, reading. Office: Kebab Inc 1 Main at Riverplace Minneapolis MN 55414

KAPP, JOHN CHARLES, brewing company sales ececutive; b. Ft. Dodge, Iowa, June 17, 1943; s. John Leonard and Ellen Leone (Davidson) K.; m. Martha Jane Enyart, Aug. 14, 1969; children: John Jay, Debra Dana. AA, Ventura Coll., 1963; BBA, Calif. State U., Chico, 1965. Asst. state mgr. Miller Brewing Co., San Francisco, 1966; area mgr. Miller Brewing Co., Dallas and Phoenix, 1966-72; trade relations and draft mgr. Miller Brewing Co., Dallas, 1972-73; regional sales mgr. Miller Brewing Co., Chgo., 1973-74; regional mgr. Miller Brewing Co., San Francisco, N.Y.C., New Orleans, Chgo., 1974-86; dir. field sales south Miller Brewing Co., Milw., 1986—. Mem. bus. mgmt. adv. council Calif State U., Chico, 1985; bd. dirs. United Cerebral Palsy Assn. SE Wis. Served to sgt. USAFR, 1965-71. Mem. Delta Sigma Phi. Roman Catholic. Club: Commonwealth. Avocations: tennis, home computers, reading. Home: 1509 E Standish Pl Bayside WI 53217-1960 Office: Miller Brewing Co 3939 W Highland Blvd Milwaukee WI 53208

KAPP, SHERMAN RANDOLPH, construction company owner; b. Chillicothe, Ohio, July 21, 1951; s. Arthur Marion and Betty Alice (Parks) K.; m. Rita Kay Robinson, July 15, 1972; children: Tiffany Marie, Tyler Matthew. Assoc. in Civil Engring. cum laude, Clark Tech. Coll., 1976. Estimator Kaffenbarger Constrn., Springfield, Ohio, 1976-80, office mgr., v.p., 1980-85; pres. Kapp Constrn., Springfield, 1985—. Mem. adv. bd. Salvation Army, Springfield, 1981—. Mem. Bldg. Industry Assn. (pres. 1984-86), Nat. Assn. Home Builders, Springfield C. of C. Office: Kapp Constrn 98 Bechtle Ave Springfield OH 45504

KAPPEL, PETER FRANK, dentist; b. Dickinson, N.D., Aug. 1, 1923; s. Joseph J. and Mary Elizabeth (Sigl) K.; m. Marie Wanda Wojtowicz; children: Kathryn, Peter Jr., Suzanne. Student, St. Thomas Coll., 1941-43, U. Chgo., 1944; DDS, U. Minn., 1947. Gen. practice dentistry White Bear Lake, Minn., 1947—. Mem. ADA, Minn. dental Assn., St. Paul Dist. Dental Soc. (v.p. 1960-61), White Bear Lake C. of C. Roman Catholic. Lodge: KC. Avocations: photography, cross country skiing, bird watching, golf. Home: 1994 Oak Knoll Dr White Bear Lake MN 55110

KAPPES, PHILIP SPANGLER, lawyer, laboratory equipment company executive; b. Detroit, Dec. 24, 1925; s. Philip Alexander and Wilma Fern (Spangler) K.; m. Glendora Galena Miles, Nov. 27, 1948; children: Susan Lea, Philip Miles, Mark William. B.A. cum laude, Butler U., 1945; J.D., U. Mich., 1948. Bar: Ind. 1948, U.S. Supreme Ct. 1970. Sole practice Indpls., 1948—; assoc. Armstrong and Gause, 1948-49; assoc. law offices C. B. Dutton, 1950-51; ptnr. Dutton, Kappes & Overman, 1952-85, of counsel, 1983-85; ptnr. Lewis Kappes Fuller & Eads, 1985—; ptnr. Labeco Properties; Creston Group; chmn. bd., sec., dir. Lab. Equipment Co., Mooresville, Ind.; sec., dir. Labsonics, Inc., Premier Distbg. Co., Labthermics, Inc.; instr. bus. law Butler U., 1948-49, chmn. bd. govs., 1965-66. Bd. dirs. Crossroads Am. council Boy Scouts Am., 1965—, v.p. fin., mem. exec. com then pres. 1977-79; bd. dirs. Fairbanks Hosp., Indpls., 1986—; trustee Butler U., 1987—, Children's Mus., Indpls., 1969—, pres. bd. trustees, 1984-85. Mem. Am. Judicature Soc., ABA (ho. of dels. 1970-71), Ind. Bar Assn. (ho. dels. 1959—, mem. chmn. pub. relations exec. com. 1966-69, sec. 1973-74, bd. mgrs. 1975-77), Indpls. Bar Assn. (treas., 1st v.p. 1965, pres. 1970, bd. mgrs. 1968-71, 75-77), Indpls. Legal Aid Soc., Indpls. Jr. C. of C. (past 1st v.p., dir.), Butler U. (past pres.), Mich. alumni assns., Phi Delta Theta, Tau Kappa Alpha. Republican. Presbyterian (deacon, elder, past pres. bd. trustees). Lodges: Masons (33 degree, most wise master Indpls. chpt. Rose Croix 1982-84), Shriners, Meridian Hills Country, Lawyers, Gyro (pres. 1966), Mystic Tie (worshipful master 1975). Home: 624 Somerset Dr Indianapolis IN 46260 Office: 1210 One American Sq Indianapolis IN 46282-0003

KAPTUR, MARCIA CAROLYN, congresswoman; b. Toledo, June 17, 1946. B.A., U. Wis., 1968; M. Urban Planning, U. Mich., 1974; postgrad., U. Manchester, (Eng.), 1974. Urban planne; asst. dir. urban affairs domestic policy staff White House, 1977-79; mem. 98th-100th Congresses from 9th Dist. Ohio, 1983—. Bd. dirs. Nat. Ctr. Urban Ethnic Affairs; adv. com. Gund Found.; exec. com. Lucas County Democratic Com.; mem. Dem. Women's Campaign Assn. Mem. Am. Planning Assn., Am. Inst. Cert. Planners, NAACP, Urban League, Polish Mus., U. Mich. Urban Planning Alumni Assn. (bd. dirs.), Polish Am. Hist. Assn. Roman Catholic. Clubs: Lucas County Dem. Bus. and Profl. Women's, Fulton County Dem. Women's. Office: US House of Representatives 1228 Longworth House Office Bldg Washington DC 20515 *

KAPUR, KAILASH CHANDER, industrial engineering educator; b. Rawalpindi, Pakistan, Aug. 17, 1941; s. Gobind Ram and Vidya Vanti (Khanna) K.; m. Geraldine Palmer, May 15, 1969; children—Anjali Joy, Jay Palmer. B.S., Delhi U., India, 1963; M.Tech., Indian Inst. Tech., Kharagpur, 1965; M.S., U. Calif.-Berkeley, 1968, Ph.D., 1969. Registered profl. engr., Mich. Sr. research engr. Gen. Motors Research Labs., Mich., 1969-70; sr. reliability engr. TACOM, U.S. Army, Mich., 1978-79; mem. faculty Wayne State U., Detroit, 1970—, assoc. prof. indsl. engring. and ops., 1973-79, prof., 1979—; vis. prof. U. Waterloo, Can., 1977-78; vis. scholar Ford Motor Co., Mich., summer 1973. Author: Reliability in Engineering Design, 1977; assoc. editor Jour. Reliability and Safety, 1982—; contbr. articles to profl. jours. Grantee Gen. Motors Corp., 1974-77, U.S. Army, 1978-79, U.S. Dept. Transp., 1980-82. Mem. IEEE (sr.), Ops. Research Soc. Am. (sr.), Inst. Indsl. Engrs. (assoc. editor 1980—). Home: 1371 Club Dr Bloomfield Hills MI 48013 Office: Wayne State U Dept Indsl Engring Detroit MI 48202

KAPUSTA, KATHLEEN MARIE, social services administrator; b. Cleve., Aug. 15, 1952; d. John Ted and Therese Marie (Dombrowski) Betlejewski; m. John Peter Kapusta, June 5, 1976; children: Mark Adam, Scott John. BA in Sociology, John Carroll U., 1974; M in Social Sci. Adminstrn., Case Western Reserve U., 1976. Lic. ind. social worker, Ohio. Social worker Parma (Ohio) Community Gen. Hosp., 1976-79, dir. social services, 1982—; psychiat. social worker Cleve. VA Med. Ctr., Brecksville, Ohio, 1979-82; cons. Mt. Alverna Home, Parma, 1978-86; instr. Cuyahoga Cummunity Coll., Parma, 1978-83. Mem. Am. Hosp. Assn. Social Work Dirs., N.Am. Employee Assistance Assn., Ohio Hosp. Assn. Social Workers (bd. dirs. 86-87), N.E. Ohio Hosp. Social Work Dirs. Assn. (pres., sec., treas. 1983-85), Assn. Labor Mgmt. Adminstrs. and Cons. on Alcoholism. Roman Catholic. Avocations: camping, gardening, hand crafts. Home: 6622 Beechwood Dr Independence OH 44131 Office: Parma Community Gen Hosp 7007 Powers Blvd Parma OH 44129

KARACA, AHMET RAHMI, plastic and reconstructive surgeon; b. Istanbul, Turkey, Jan. 30, 1947; came to U.S., 1971; s. Macit Remzi and Neriman Karaca; m. Zerrin Zehra Yenigun, Oct. 21, 1978; children: Esra, Bora. MD, U. Istanbul, 1971. Intern Grace Hosp., Detroit, 1971-72, resident in surgery, 1972-76; resident in plastic surgery Wayne State U. Hosp., Detroit, 1976-78; practice medicine specializing in plastic and reconstructive surgery Troy, Mich., 1978—. Fellow ACS; mem. Am. Soc. Plastic and Reconstructive Surgeons, Mich. State Med. Soc., Oakland County Med. Soc. Office: 1579 W Big Beaver B Troy MI 48084

KARAGON, JAMES J., social worker, history educator; b. Michigan City, Ind., Jan. 14, 1944; s. james Nicholas and Carrie Irene (Wyttenbach) K.; m. Mary Catherine McEachen,Apr. 19, 1969. BA, Western Mich. U., 1967, MA, 1973; Cert. Specialist in Aging, Wayne State U., 1984, postgrad., 1986—. Social worker State of Mich., Detroit, 1969—; adj. tchr. history Wayne Community coll., Detroit, 1969—, Madonna Coll., Detroit, 1984—; instr. Wayne State U., Detroit, 1975; chmn. sect. 504 rehab. act Dept. Social Services, Detroit, 1982—. Mem. Concerned Citizens Cass Corridor, Detroit, 1984, Mich. Coalition for Fair Budget, Detroit, 1984—; vol. counselor Coalition Temporary Shelter, Detroit, 1985-86. Mem. Orgn. Am. Historians, Mich. Hist. Soc., Farmington Hist. Soc. (v.p. 1980-81), Mus. African-Am. History. Democrat. Greek Orthodox. Avocation: running.

KARALES, STEPHEN PETER, manufacturing and franchising business executive, consultant; b. Cleve., Jan. 31, 1946; s. Peter and Stella (Vlahos) K., m. JoAnn Rogers, July 15, 1984. BS, Ohio State U., 1969; MBA, Case Western Res. U., 1971; assoc. degree in real estate, Cuyahoga Community Coll., Cleve., 1978, AA in Food Service Mgmt., 1980; PhD in Bus. Mgmt., Dorman Young Inst., N.Y.C., 1980. Regional med. sales mgr. Beckman Instruments, Inc., Fullerton, Calif., 1970-76; nat. mktg. dir. Century 21 Internat., Inc., Costa Mesa, Calif., 1976-79; v.p. real estate devel. McDonald's Corp., Cleve., 1979-81; v.p. franchise devel. Physicans Weight Loss Ctrs. Am., Inc., Akron, Ohio, 1981-84; v.p. mktg. and franchise devel. Sparkle Wash Internat., Inc., Cleve., 1984—, also bd. dirs.; cons. franchise devel. Internat. Franchise Archtl. Design Corp., Cleve., 1978-86; pres., cons. franchise devel. Karales Mgmt. Corp., Cleve., 1978-86; bd. dirs. Christina Corp., Columbus, Ohio. Author: A Plan For Your Future In Franchising, 1979 (outstanding Award for Excellellance for Creative Design 1979); also articles. Bd. dirs. Realtors Polit. Action Com., Columbus, 1978-80, Nat. Hist. Soc. Bi-Centenial Com., Cleve., 1975-76, Strongsville (Ohio) Community Action Com.1976. Served with M.C., U.S. Army, 1967-69. Named one of Outstanding Young Men of Am., 1976, 77, 78; named to Hon. Order of Ky. Cols., 1986; recipient Outstanding Award of Excellence for Franchise Sales and Mktg., Sales and Mktg. Inst., 1980, Outstanding Franchise Devel. award Dorman Young Inst., 1980. Mem. Sales and Mktg. Execs. (bd. dirs. 1977-78, outstanding bus. leader 1980), Internat. Orgn. Planning Execs. (bd. dirs. 1978-79), Sales and Mktg. Mgmt. Assn. (bd. dirs. 1980-81, Excellence for Mktg. award 1982), Internat. Franchise Assn., Nat. Realtors Mktg. Inst. (Outstanding Marketers Achievement 1980), Strongsville Jaycees (bd. dirs. 1972-73, v.p. 1973-75, pres. 1976, Outstanding Jaycee of Yr. 1972, Outstanding Community Service award 1974). Republican. Greek Orthodox. Lodges: Rotary (bd. dirs. Cleve. club 1978-79, named Outstanding Businessman of Cleve. 1977; recipient Outstanding Young Businessman award 1977, Fgn. Exchange grantee 1977); Ahepa (bd. dirs. 1978-79). Home: 11040 Westwind Ct Cleveland OH 44136 Office: Sparkle Wash Internat Inc 26851 Richmond Rd Cleveland OH 44146

KARAMCHANDANI, BALRAM CHETANDAS, food company executive; b. Karachi, Pakistan, Aug. 2, 1944; s. Chetandas J. and Devi C. Karamchandani; m. Kamini Ramchand Tulsiani, Mar. 3, 1972; children: Shaun, Ashish, Kunal. B MechE, U. Baroda, India, 1967, postgrad., 1968; MS in Indsl. Engring., U. Ark., 1970; MBA, Kent State U., 1980. Indsl. engr. Day & Zimmerman, Texarkana, Tex., 1970-74, Morton Frozen Foods, Russellville, Ark., 1974-75; mgr. indsl. engring. Morton Frozen Foods, Crozet, Va., 1975-77; mgr. indsl. engring. Stouffer Frozen Foods, Solon, Ohio, 1977-79, asst. plant mgr., 1979-81, dir. indsl. engring. and prodn. planning, 1981—. Mem. Am. Inst. Indsl. Engrs. (sr., bd. dirs. 1970-74). Republican. Hindu. Avocation: golf. Home: 37045 Valley Forge Dr Solon OH 44139 Office: Stouffer Foods Corp 5750 Harper Rd Solon OH 44139

KARASIK, MYRON SOLOMON, information systems venture management company executive; b. N.Y.C., June 3, 1950; s. Jack and Bertha Clara (Shapiro) K.; M.S.E.E., Purdue U., 1972; M. Mgmt. with distinction (Austin scholar), Northwestern U., 1975; m. Sara Louise Lieber, Aug. 29, 1976; children: Ruth Jacqueline, Jacob Edwin. Mem. tech. staff, acting supr. Bell Telephone Labs., Piscataway, N.J., 1972-73; cons. Deloitte Haskins & Sells, Chgo., 1975-78; v.p. adminstrn. J.P. Walsh, Inc., Chgo., 1979; prin. cons., mgr. info. services MWS Cons., Inc., Chgo., 1980; partner Veatch, Rich & Nadler, Chartered, 1980-83; pres. Coldframe, Inc., Chgo., 1984—. Chmn. Project 200 com. Congregation Emanuel, 1980, v.p. Brotherhood, 1980. C.P.A., Ill.; cert. mgmt. cons., systems profl. Mem. IEEE (software quality assurance standards group), Am. Inst. C.P.A.s, Ill. Soc. C.P.A.s (MAS com. 1982—), Assn. for Computing Machinery, Data Processing Mgmt. Assn. Republican. Jewish. Designer expenditure control system for maj. fgn. govt.; developer software quality assurance methodology (regression testing); author software products; contbr. articles to profl. jours. Office: 180 N LaSalle St Suite 700 Chicago IL 60601

KARAVOLOS, LUCAS, utilities company administrator; b. Pireaus, Greece, Mar. 19, 1946; came to U.S., 1955; s. Michael George and Evangelia (Glyptis) K.; m. Irene Tetonis, Jan. 28, 1973; children: Michael, Gelena. BBA, Baruch Coll., 1974; postgrad., Pace U., 1975-78; mgmt. devel. program, Ohio State U., 1982. CPA, Ohio. Sr. acct. Chase Manhattan Bank, N.Y.C., 1969-73, Crowell Internat., N.Y.C., 1973-74; forecast analyst Am. Elec. Power Co., N.Y.C., 1974-77; rate case coordinator Columbus, Ohio, 1977—. Treas. Greek Orthodox Youth Orgn., Bklyn., 1963-64; staff organizer Annehurst Civic Assn., Westerville, Ohio, 1982-85. Served as sgt. U.S. Army, 1966-68, Vietnam. Mem. Am. Inst. CPA's. Avocations: swimming, tennis, chess, gardening. Home: 1055 Harbor View Dr Westerville OH 43081

KARAZIM, LINDA ANN, educator; b. Toledo, June 29, 1949; s. Theodore Robert and Gloria Norma (Zaborowski) Staszak; m. Thomas James Karazim, Aug. 26, 1972; children: Todd, Andrew. BE, U. Toledo, 1973, MEd, 1975, DEd, 1987. Substitute tchr. Toledo Pub. Sch., 1970-73; grad. assist. U. Toledo, 1981-82; tchr. Evergreen Local Schs., Metamora, Ohio, 1974—; right to read instr. Ohio Dept. Edn., Metamora, 1975-80; curriculum adv. bd. mem. Evergreen Schs., Metamora, 1982—, evaluator in English competency, 1985—, co-chmn. N. Cen. evaluation for Evergreen High Sch., 1983-84. Contbr. articles to profl jours. Mem. Martha Holden Jennings Scholar, 1976-77. Named Tchr. of Yr. Evergreen Future Tchrs., 1978. Mem. Evergreen Edn. Assn., Phi Delta Kappa. Roman Catholic. Avocations: needlepoint, reading, dancing, sewing, baking. Home: 2347 Crossbough Toledo OH 43614 Office: Evergreen High Sch 1-14544-6 Metamora OH 43540

KARELS, MARY CHRISTINE, accountant; b. Ortonville, Minn., July 3, 1959; d. Valentine Simon and LolaMae Catherine (Strei) K. BS summa cum laude, S.W. State U., Marshall, Minn., 1980. CPA, Minn. Staff auditor Robert G. Englehart & Co., Burnsville, Minn., 1981, Deloitte Haskins & Sells, Mpls., 1981-84; mgr. fin. acctg. Iowa Meth. Med. Ctr., Des Moines, 1985—. Mem. Am. Inst. CPA's, Minn. Soc. CPA's, Healthcare Fin. Mgmt. Assn. Roman Catholic. Avocations: pianist, softball, volleyball, travelling. Home: 1233 SW Park Des Moines IA 50315 Office: Iowa Meth Med Ctr 1200 Pleasant St Des Moines IA 50308

KARG, DANIEL WILLIAM, engineering company executive; b. Akron, Ohio, June 23, 1953; s. James F. and Joanne L. (McTaggart) K. BS in Prdn. Mgmt., Personnel Mgmt., Miami U., Oxford, Ohio, 1975; AAS in Fire Protection Tech., U. Akron, 1986. Indsl. engr. Akron Packaging, Cuyhoga Falls, Ohio, 1976-77; project engr. Ridge Tool Co., Elyria, Ohio, 1977-79; staff mfg. engr. Norton Co., Stow, Ohio, 1979-80; mgr. assembly Karg Corp., Tallmadge, Ohio, 1980-81, mgr. engring., 1981—. Patentee in field. Vol. firefighter Copley Twp., Ohio, 1976—; exploring chmn. Boy Scouts Am., Akron, 1978; vice chmn. ARC disaster service, Akron, 1980—. Mem. Soc. Mfg. Engrs., Soc. Fire Protection Engrs. Club: Amateur Radio Relay League. Lodge: Rotary. Office: Karg Corp 241 Southwest Ave PO Box 197 Tallmadge OH 44278

KARJALA, JEANETTE ARLENE, business educator; b. Wadena, Minn., Feb. 21, 1942; d. Edwin Arthur and Hilja Liisa (Marjamaa) K. BA in Edn., W. Washington U., 1964, MA in Edn., 1974; PhD, U. N.D., 1986. Cert. secondary vocat. tchr. Bus. tchr. W.F. West High Sch., Chehalis, Wash., 1964-74, Wenatchee (Wash.) High Sch., 1974-80; part-time instr. various colls., Wash. and N.D., 1979-80, 82-83; asst. prof. bus. Minot (N.D.) State Coll., 1983-86, St. Cloud (Minn.) State U., 1986—. John C. Peterson Meml. scholar U. N.D., 1983-84. Mem. Am. Bus. Communications Assn., Wash. Bus. Edn. Assn. (sec.-treas. 1968-69, 76-77), Wash. Vocat. Assn. of Am. Vocat. Assn. (recording sec. 1977-78), Bus. and Profl. Women (treas. 1986), Minot State Coll. Edn Assn. of NEA (v.p. 1985-86), Phi Delta Kappa (historian 1985-86), Delta Pi Epsilon (treas. Alpha Nu chpt. 1981-82, pres. Alpha Nu chpt., 1982-83), Delta Kappa Gamma Soc. (pres. Wenatchee 1977-79, chair Minot 1984-86, masters studies scholarship, 1973-74, doctoral studies scholarship 1980, Catherine Nutterville Scholarship, 1983). Avocations: playing piano, reading, singing. Office: St Cloud State U Coll Bus Edn Office Adminstrn Dept Saint Cloud MN 56301

KARLAN, MARC SIMEON, facial plastic surgeon, consultant; b. N.Y.C., Sept. 10, 1942; s. Henry Milton and Alexandria (Stambler) K.; m. Lynn Hoggatt, May 29, 1983; children—Laura, Dean, Alexander. B.A. magna cum laude, Tufts Coll., 1964; M.D., U. Pa., 1968; postdoctoral (Physicians and Surgeons fellow) Columbia U., 1970-73. Diplomate Am. Bd. Otolaryngology. Intern, Montefiore Hosp. and Med. Center, Bronx, N.Y., 1968-69; resident in otolaryngology Presbyn. Hosp., N.Y.C., 1970-73; vis. lectr. Med. Coll. Va., 1973-75; asst. prof., then assoc. prof. dept. surgery, dept. communicative disorders Grad. Sch. Arts and Scis., Coll. Engring. U. Fla. Sch. Medicine, Gainesville, 1975-79; vis. fellow U. Zurich (Switzerland), 1979-80; assoc. prof. surgery Northwestern U. Med. Sch., Chgo., 1980—; bd. dirs. Northwestern Med. Faculty Found., 1982-83; cons. FDA Bur. Med. Devices, NIH, Ill. Med. Legal Affairs; dir. research Milton Med. Co. Contbr. articles to profl. jours. Served to maj. U.S. Army, 1973-75. Recipient Tchr. Investigator award NIH, 1976-80. Mem. AMA, Ill. State Med. Soc., Am. Acad. Facial Plastic Surgery (chmn. research com., mem. awards and edn. coms., recipient Ira Tresley award for outstanding research 1977), Am. Acad. Cosmetic Surgery, Am. Acad. Otolaryngology, Assn. Research in Otolaryngology, Soc. of Univ. Otolaryngologists, Sigma Chi. Jewish. Office: 446 E Ontario Suite 1001 Chicago IL 60611

KARLBERG, MARY ANN, small business owner; b. Gatewood, Mo., Feb. 21, 1939; d. Evert Sherman and Nancy Ann (Arnold) Redus; m. Boyd Holdcroft, Mar. 12, 1960 (div. Nov. 1974); children: Boyd, Barry; m. Stig Karlberg (div. Sept. 1985). Student pub. schs., Gatewood, Mo.; student high sch., Couch, Mo. Cert. cosmetologist, lic. real estate broker. Teller, bookkeeper United Bank Loves Park, Ill., 1962-63; owner, operator beauty shop, Rockford, Ill., 1971-74; broker, salesman Whitehead, Inc., Rockford, 1971-74; ptnr. v.p. Karlberg Enterprises, Rockford, 1976-85; owner, mgr. Karlberg European TanSpa, Inc., Rockford, 1982—; importer JK Soltron tanning equipment, 1982-85. Avocations: architectural renovation, importing. Office: Karlberg European TanSpa Inc 4734 E State St Rockford IL 61108

KARLINS, NATHANIEL LOUIS, radiologist; b. Webster, S.D., Feb. 25, 1950; s. Walter Howard and Luvay Pearl (Nesheim) K.; m. Linda Mae Burns, Feb. 14, 1986; 1 child, Walter Nathan. BS, U. So. Dakota, 1973; MD, Washington U., St. Louis, 1975. Intern Cleve. Metro Gen. Hosp., 1975-76; resident in radiology Univ. Hosps. Cleve., 1976-79; staff radiologist Cuyahoga County Hosp., Cleve., 1979—; asst. prof. Case Western Res. U., Cleve., 1979—. Bd. dirs. Lyric Opera Cleve., 1985—. Mem. Am. Coll. Radiology, Radiol. Soc. N.Am., Am. Inst. Ultrasound in Medicine, Cleve. Acad. Medicine, Cleve. Radiol. Soc., U. S.D. Sch. Medicine Alumni Council, Phi Beta Kappa, Photographic Soc. Am. Democrat. Unitarian. Avocations: opera, history. Office: Cuyahoga County Hosp 3395 Scranton Rd Cleveland OH 44109

KARLSON, BEN EMIL, kitchen design company executive; b. Hedemora, Sweden, Aug. 27, 1934; came to U.S., 1954, naturalized, 1960; s. Emil W.J. and Ester Linnea (Hellman) Karlsson; student bus. mktg. Alexander Hamilton Inst., N.Y.C., 1967, Am. Inst. Kitchen Designers, 1972; grad. Dale Carnegie Inst., 1972; m. Susan Jo Kaupert, Feb. 7, 1958; children—David, Kristine, Thomas. Salesman, Edward Hines Lumber Co., Chgo., 1954-63; v.p., gen. mgr. Lake Forest Lumber Co. (Ill.), 1963-67; pres. Karlson Home Center, Inc., Evanston, Ill., 1967—, Poggenpohl-Midwest/USA, Inc., Evanston, Atag USA Corp., Evanston; dir. tng. U.S. Poggenpohl, Herford, W. Ger., 1981-86 ; pres. Bank Lane Investors, Lake Forest, 1971-72; founder chmn. Evanston Home Show, 1973, 74; judge, Nat. Design Contest, 1974; showroom design cons., Ill., Poggenpohl Kitchens Germany; speaker in field; lectr. on kitchen bus. and design at univs. and convs. Mem. steering com. Covenant Meth. Ch., Evanston, 1968-69; bd. dirs. Evanston Family Counseling Service, 1973-75, Evanston United Community Services, 1974-75, mid-Am. chpt. No. region ARC, 1974; chmn. bus. div. Evanston United Fund, 1974, gen. campaign chmn., 1975. Recipient awards for community service. Cert. kitchen designer. Mem. Am. Inst. Kitchen Designers (pres. 1975-76), Soc. Cert. Kitchen Designers, 1987— (bd. govs., sec. 1987—), Evanston C. of C. (dir. 1973-74, v.p. 1975, pres. 1976), Westmoreland C. of C., Nat. Fed. Ind. Bus., Mid-Am. Swedish Trade Assn. Club: Evanston Rotary (pres. 1984-85). Contbr. kitchen designs to nat. mags. Home: 2311 Central Park Ave Evanston IL 60201 Office: 1815 Central St Evanston IL 60201

KARMAN, KENNETH ALLEN, controller; b. St. Louis, July 20, 1943; s. Allen V. and Ivy M. (Myer) K.; m. Patricia C. Baumann, Mar. 28, 1964 (div. 1979); m. Carolyn J. Wheeler, May 24, 1980; children: Ronald L. Squires II, Ryan L. Squires. BBA, U. Mo., St. Louis, 1972; MS in Accountancy, Western Ill. U., 1979. CPA, Mo., Ill. Audit staff Ernst & Whinney, St. Louis, 1972-76; asst. controller Broadcast Products div. Harris Corp., Quincy, Ill., 1976-78; instr. Western Ill. U., Macomb, 1978-80; mgr. acctg. Foster & Gallagher, Inc., Peoria, Ill., 1980-83, controller, 1983-87, v.p., 1987—; mem. Acctg. Adv. Bd. ICC; bd. dirs. 1st Chillicothe (Ill.) Corp. Served to staff sgt. USAF, 1966-70. Named one of Outstanding Young Men in Am., 1975. Mem. Am. Inst. CPA's, Mo. Soc. CPA's, U. Mo. St. Louis Alumni Assn. (life), Beta Alpha Psi. Lodge: Lions (sec. Chillicothe club 1983-84, bd. dirs. 1984—, pres. 1987—). Avocations: boating, gardening, antiques, antique automobiles. Home: 1213 W Pine Chillicothe IL 61523 Office: Foster & Gallagher Inc 6523 N Galena Rd Peoria IL 61632

KARNES, DAVID, U.S. senator; b. Omaha, Dec. 12, 1948; m. Elizabeth Karnes; children: Korey, Kalen, Mary Karalyn, Laurel. BA, U. Nebr., 1971, postgrad.; JD, U. Wis., 1974. Spl. asst. sec. HUD, Washington, 1981-82, undersec., 1982-83; spl. counsel Fed. Home Loan Bank Bd., Washington, 1983; sr. v.p., gen. counsel Scoular Co., 1983-86; U.S. senator from Nebr., Washington, 1987—. Office: Office of the United States Senate Office of Senate Members Washington DC 20510 *

KARNES, EVAN BURTON, II, lawyer; b. Chgo.; s. Evan Burton and Mary Alice (Brosnahan) K.; m. Bridget Anne Clerkin, Oct. 9, 1976; children—Kathlen Anne, Evan Burton III, Molly Aileen. A.B., Loyola U., Chgo., 1975; J.D., DePaul U., 1978; student in trial advocacy program, U. Calif. Hastings Coll. Law, 1979. Bar: Ill. 1978, U.S. Dist. Ct. (no. dist.) Ill. 1978, U.S. Ct. Appeals (7th cir.) 1978, U.S. Supreme Ct. 1983. Trial atty. Chgo. Milw. St. Paul & Pacific R.R., Chgo., 1978-81; litigation dept. Baker & McKenzie, Chgo., 1981-87; sr. litigation counsel, Levin & Ginsburg Ltd., Chgo., 1987—. Mem. Chgo. Bar Assn., Def. Research Inst., Nat. Assn. R.R. Trial Counsel, Ill. Trial Lawyers Assn., Assn. Trial Lawyers of Am., Blue Key (sec. Loyola U. chpt. 1974-75), Pi Sigma Alpha, Phi Alpha Delta. Club: Union League (Chgo.). Office: Levin & Ginsburg Ltd 180 N LaSalle St 22d Floor Chicago IL 60601

KARNS, ESTHER MAE, psychologist; b. Union City, Ind., May 21, 1932; d. Zelmer Carlton and Wanda Evalena (Short) Weyrick; m. Willard Dale Karns, Mar. 7, 1952; children: Connie Jean, Denise Diane, Cynthia Marie. BS in Elem. Edn., Miami U., Oxford, Ohio, 1964, MS in Sch. Psychology, 1972. Cert. elem. tchr., Ohio; lic. psychologist, Ohio. Tchr. New Lebanon (Ohio) Schs., 1964-66, Eaton (Ohio) Schs., 1966-72; intern sch. psychologist Montgomery County Schs., Dayton, Ohio, 1972-73; sch. psychologist Preble County Schs., Eaton, 1973—. Bd. dirs. Preble County Mental Health Assn., 1980-85; mem. Preble County Hist. Soc., 1980—. Mem. Southwestern Ohio Sch. Psychologist Assn. (bd. dirs. 1978-80, treas. 1984—), Ohio Sch. Psychologist Assn., Nat. Assn. Sch. Psychologists, NEA, Ohio Edn. Assn. Home: 212 E Wadsworth St Eaton OH 45320

KARON, BERNARD LOUIS, librarian, educator; b. St. Paul, Aug. 19, 1942; s. Irvine and Ruth (Mark) K.; m. Jaylene Abramovitz, Sept. 12, 1965; children: Michelle, Jacqueline, Edward, David. BS, U. Minn., 1964, MLS, 1965. Jr. librarian U. Minn., Mpls., 1965-67, librarian, 1967-71, asst. prof., 1971-74, asst. prof., chief cataloger, 1975—; cons. library Talmud Torah, St. Paul, 1979—. Author: Cataloging and Classification, 1979; contbr. articles to profl. jours. Bd. dirs. Talmud Torah, St. Paul, 1975-83. Mem. Am. Library Assn., Church and Synagogue Library Assn., Online Audiovisual Cataloguers (vice chmn. 1986—), Library Council (vice chmn. 1979-83, chmn. 1983-87), Original Cataloguers Group (chmn. 1984-87). Jewish. Avocations: wine, gourmet restaurants. Home: 1781 Summit Ln Mendota Heights MN 55118 Office: U Minn 160 Wilson Library Minneapolis MN 55455

KARPICKE, JOHN ARTHUR, systems engineer, experimental psychologist; b. Saginaw, Mich., Nov. 26, 1945; s. Herbert August and Eleanor Louise (Stafford) K.; m. Susan Gail Denyes, Aug. 5, 1972; children—Jeffrey Denyes, Jennifer Denyes. B.S., Mich. State U., 1972; Ph.D., Ind. U., 1976. NIH postdoctoral fellow in psychobiology Fla. State U., Tallahassee, 1976-77; asst. prof. psychology Valparaiso (Ind.) U., 1977-81, research fellow, 1978, 79, 80; mem. tech. staff human factors group Bell Telephone Labs., Indpls., 1981-82; mem. tech. staff system architecture group AT&T Consumer Products Labs., Indpls., 1983-84; mem. tech. staff functional systems design and software group AT&T Consumer Products Labs, Indpls., 1984-85, disting. mem. tech. staff advanced cellular technologies design group, 1985, advanced Voice Techs. group, Indpls., 1986—. Served with USNR, 1969-71; Vietnam. NIMH research grantee, 1979-80; recipient Disting. Tech. Staff award AT&T, 1985. Mem. AAAS, N.Y. Acad. Scis. Contbr. numerous articles to psychology jours. Office: 6612 East 75th St PO Box 1008 Indianapolis IN 46206

KARPIEL, DORIS CATHERINE, state legislator; b. Chgo., Sept. 21, 1935; d. Nicholas and Mary (McStravick) Feinen; m. Harvey Karpiel, 1955 (div.); children—Sharon, Lynn, Laura, Barry. A.A., Morton Jr. Coll., 1955; B.A., No. Ill. U., 1976. Real estate sales assoc. Bundy-Morgan BHG; coordinator Bloomingdale Twp. Republican Presdl. Hdqrs., Ill., 1960, 64, 68; former pres. Bloomingdale Twp. Rep. Orgn.; mem. Twp. Ofcls. of Ill.; trustee Bloomingdale Twp., 1974-75, supr., 1975-80; precinct committeewoman Bloomingdale Twp. Rep. Central Com., 1972, chmn., 1978-80; mem. Ill. Ho. of Reps., 1979-82, Ill. State Senate from 25th Dist., 1984—. Mem. Am.

Legislators Exchange Council, Rep. Orgn. Schaumberg Twp.; former sec. Dupage County Suprs. Assn.; former sec. Dupage County Twp. Ofcls.; mem. Dupage County Women's Rep. Orgn., Meml. Hosp. Guild, Am. Cancer Soc. Mem. LWV, DuPage Bd. Realtors, Pi Sigma Alpha. Clubs: Bloomingdale Roselle and Streamwood Country, University Women's, St. Walters Women's. Office: Ill State Capitol Bldg Springfield IL 62706 Other Address: 127 W Lake St Bloomingdale IL 60108

KARR, GERALD LEE, agrl. economist, state senator; b. Emporia, Kans., Oct. 15, 1936; s. Orren L. and Kathleen M. (Keller) K.; B.S., Kans. State U., 1959; M.S. in Agrl. Econs., So. Ill. U., 1962, Ph.D. in Econs., 1966; m. Sharon Kay Studer, Oct. 18, 1959; children—Kevin Lee, Kelly Jolleen. Livestock mgr. Eckert Orchards Inc., Belleville, Ill., 1959-64; grad. asst. So. Ill. U., Carbondale, 1960-64; asst. prof. econs. Central Mo. State U., Warrensburg, 1964-67; asst. prof. agrl. econs., head dept. Njala U., Sierra Leone, West Africa, 1967-70; asst. prof. agrl. econs. U. Ill., Urbana, 1970-72; asso. prof. agrl. econs., chmn. dept., mgr. coll. farms Wilmington (Ohio) Coll., 1972-76; farmer, Emporia, Kans., 1976—; mem. Kans. Senate, 1981—; research advisor Bank of Sierra Leone, Freetown, summer 1967; agrl. sector cons. Econ. Mission to Sierra Leone, IBRD, 1973. Mem. Am. Agrl. Econs. Assn., Lyon County Farmer Union, Lyon County Farm Bur., Lyon County Livestock Assn., Omicron Delta Epsilon, Farm House. Contbr. articles to profl. jours. Democrat. Methodist. Club: Kiwanis.

KARR, JOHN F., sports executive; b. Detroit, Apr. 13, 1929; s. Eino E. and Helen K.; married; children—John E., Karen, Christopher, Susan. B.S., Wayne State U., 1952; M.B.A., Ind. U., 1953. Formerly with Burroughs Corp., Trane Co., Arthur D. Little, Inc., Goodyear Tire & Rubber Co.; with Cole Nat. Corp., Cleve., 1968-78; v.p. fin. and adminstrn., dir., to Cole Nat. Corp., 1978; pres., dir. Northstar Met Center/Mgmt. Corp., Bloomington, Minn., 1978—. Served in U.S. Army, 1946-48. Office: Minn North Stars 7901 Cedar Ave S Bloomington MN 55420

KARR, JOSEPH PETER, podiatrist; b. Chgo., Sept. 7, 1925; s. Vendelin Stephan and Irene (Bielik) Karkoška; m. Marilyn Isabelle Calder, Sept. 1, 1951; children: Joseph Jr., Michael, Paul, Kenneth. D of Surgical Chiropody, Chgo. Coll. Chiropody and Pedic Surgery, 1951; D of Podiatric Medicine (hon.), Ill. Coll. Podiatric Med., 1973. Lic. podiatrist, Ill. Podiatrist Chgo., 1951—; alumni advisor Dr. William M. Scholl Coll. of Podiatric Medicine, Chgo., 1986—. Author: (pamphlet) A Method To Alleviate and Cure the Painful Heel Syndrome, 1978. Served with USCGR, 1943-46. Mem. Am. Podiatric Med. Assn., Ill. Podiatry Soc., Ill. Podiatry Edn. Group, Am. Legion. Roman Catholic. Avocations: philosophy, travel, home movies, family. Home: 10624 Kildare Ave Oaklawn IL 60453 Office: 4008 W 57th Pl Chicago IL 60629

KARR, MICHAEL B., real estate and financial consultant; b. Russia, Aug. 30, 1920; came to U.S., 1923, naturalized, 1930; s. Sam and Dina (Flanzbaum) Karpoff; student Cornell U., 1941; B.S., Ohio State U., 1943, postgrad. Grad. Sch. Agrl. Econs. and Real Estate; Dr. Bus. Appraisal, Pacific Western U., 1978; m. Pauline W. Medert, Sept. 1973; children—Lisa B., Keith M., Melissa B., Elisabeth S. Real estate broker, 1940—; pres., chief exec. officer numerous corps., 1945—; instr. real estate Bliss Coll., Columbus, 1973-75; vis. lectr. real estate appraisal Franklin U., Columbus, 1974; past pres. Columbus Recreation and Parks Commn. Past pres. Columbus and Franklin County Met. Park Dist., Vision Center Central Ohio, Franklin County Forum; past pres., past dir. bds. and commns. sect. Ohio Parks and Recreation Assn.; trustee Columbus Zool. Assn.; past trustee Franklin County unit Am. Cancer Soc.; chmn. bd. Columbus Charity Solicitation Bd.; mem. adv. bd. Ohio Capital Planning and Improvement Bd.; past chmn. Ohio Underground Parking Commn.; mem. Columbus Dist. adv. council SBA; mem. hon. alumni com. Ohio State U. Sch. Natural Resources; past pres. Sight Savers Columbus. Named Ky. col., 1970. Mem. Nat. Inst. for Real Estate Cons.'s, Am. Soc. Appraisers, Frat. Order Police Assocs., Frat. Order Dep. Aux., Columbus Maennerchor. Republican. Jewish. Clubs: Columbus Elks (life), Masons, Shriners (pres. Morgan Horse patrol 1981, Shrine Jesters Ct. #8), Agonis, Columbus Downtown Lions (past pres.), Athletic of Columbus, Press of Ohio, Columbus Feed (past sec.-treas.). Home: 3411 Sunningdale Way Columbus OH 43221 Office: 1230 S High St Columbus OH 43206

KARR, WILLIAM LEE, land surveyor; b. Alexandria, Va., June 24, 1951; s. Raymond A. and Margaret E. (Richards) K.; m. Patricia A. Brotherton, Nov. 14, 1970 (div.); children—William R., Matthew T.; m. Carol A. Kolad, Apr. 11, 1987. B.S., Mich. Tech. U., 1975. Lic. land surveyor, lic. forester. Survey mgr. Estes park Surveyors, Colo., 1977-79, Granger Engring., Sault Ste. Marie, Mich., 1979-81; prin., pres. Northwoods Land Surveying, Inc., Sault Ste. Marie 1981—; dir. Easter Upper Peninsula Regional Planning com., 1981—; sec. Mich. Bd. Registration for Land Surveyors, 1985-86, chmn., 1986—; vice chmn. Profl. Engrs., 1986—; Chippewa County Surveyor, Mich., 1983—. Mem. Soc. Am. Mil. Engrs. (pres. 1983-84), Mich. Soc. Registered Land Surveyors (Upper Peninsula chpt. rep. to state bd. 1980-83), Am. Congress Surveying and Mapping, Nat. Soc. Profl. Surveyors. Democrat. Baptist/Methodist. Lodge: Kiwanis (local pres. 1982-83, Disting. past pres. award 1983). Avocations: hunting; canoeing; gardening. Home: 806 Court St Sault Ste Marie MI 49783 Office: Northwoods Land Surveying Inc 125 Arlington St Suite 1 Sault Sainte Marie MI 49783

KARRE, DAVID JEFFREY, library administrator; b. Buffalo, Oct. 11, 1949; s. Milton Edward and Marjorie Thelma (Hughes) K.; m. Mary Ann Pawelski, Sept. 26, 1975; children: Meghan Sara, Bryan David. BA, SUNY, Buffalo, 1972, MLS, 1975, MBA, 1981. Asst. dir. Niagara Falls (N.Y.) Pub. Library, 1975-85; dir. N. Cen. Library Coop., Mansfield, Ohio, 1985—; vis. lectr. SUNY, Buffalo, 1981-85; chmn. Asst. Commr.'s Task Force on Fed. Library Service in N.Y., 1982-84. Author: Government Publications for Small and Medium-Sized Libraries: A Core Collection, 1984. Mem. Am. Library Assn., Ohio Library Assn. (sec. audio-visual roundtable 1987), N.Y. Library Assn. (pres. govt. documents roundtable 1980-82, chmn. pubs. editorial bd. 1982-85), Beta Phi Mu (pres. Beta Delta chpt. 1978-79). Democrat. Lodge: Masons. Home: 1764 Lexview Circle Mansfield OH 44907 Office: North Cen Library Coop 27 N Main St Mansfield OH 44902

KARROW, ROBERT WILLIAM, JR., librarian; b. Milw., Aug. 5, 1945; s. Robert William and Martha Mabel (Schultz) K. m. Lee Ann Zilversmit, June 26, 1970; children: Katherine Ann, David Louis. BS, U. Wis., Milw., 1968; MSLS, U. Wis., 1971. Map cataloger Newberry Library, Chgo., 1971-74, acting curator of maps, 1974-75, curator maps, 1975—. Editor: Checklist of Printed Maps of the Middle West to 1900, 1981; contbr. articles to profl. jours. Council on Library Resources fellow, 1977-78. Mem. ALA, Chgo. Map Soc. (pres. 1983-84), Internat. Soc. History of Cartography. Club: Caxton (Chgo.). Home: 639 Lyman Oak Park IL 60304 Office: Newberry Library 60 W Walton St Chicago IL 60610

KARSON, ALLEN RONALD, aerospace company executive; b. Chgo., June 18, 1947; s. Bruno Stanley and Rose Jean (Nowakowski) Kasprzyk; m. Bonnie Jean Pazdziora, Sept. 1, 1968. BS in Acctg., Bradley U., 1970; postgrad. DePaul U., 1972. CPA, Ill. Corp. controller Time Industries, Inc., Chgo., 1973-77; controller U.S. ops. Indal, Inc., Toronto, Ont., Can., 1977; v.p. fin. affairs Rentco Internat., Inc., subs. Fruehauf Corp., The Hague, The Netherlands, 1977-83; pres., chief exec. officer Ideal Aerosmith, Inc., Cheyenne, Wyo., 1983-84, East Grand Forks, Minn., 1984—. Apptd. hon. consul of The Hague, 1985; pres. Bus. Devel. Bd., East Grand Forks, Minn., East Grand Forks Devel. Authority, 1986—. Mem. Am. Inst. CPA's, Ill. Soc. CPA's, Minn. Soc. CPA's, Planning Execs. Inst., Nat. Assn. Accts. (bd. dirs. Netherlands chpt. 1981-83). Roman Catholic. Lodge: Elks. Office: Ideal Aerosmith Inc Hwy 2 East Grand Forks MN 56721

KARST, GARY GENE, architect; b. Barton County, Kans., Sept. 2, 1936; s. Emil and Clara (Nuss) K.; m. Loretta Marie Staub, Nov. 30, 1957; children: Kevin Gene, Sheri Lynn, Stacey Marie. BArch, Kans. State U., 1960. Registered profl. architect., Kans., Mo. Staff architect Horst & Terrill Architects, Topeka, 1960-64; ptnr. Horst, Terrill & Karst Architects, Topeka, 1965—, dir. design, 1965-73, sec., 1973-78, v.p., treas., 1978—; design architect Ruhnau, Evans, Brown & Steinman Architects, Riverside, Calif., 1964-65; mem. Capital City Redevel. Agy., Topeka, 1981—, adv. bd. Kans. State U. Dept. Architecture, Manhattan, 1985—. Prin. works include Emporia (Kans.) High Sch., 1972 (Kans. Soc. Architects award 1975), S.W. Bell Telephone Co. Equipment Bldg., 1974 (Bell System award 1976), Durland Hall-U. Engring. Bldg., 1981 (Kans. Soc. Architects award 1983), Kans. State Prison Medium Security Facility, 1983 (Kans. Soc. Architects award 1985). Mem. Future Heritage Topeka, Inc., 1986—. Weigel scholar Kans. State U., 1958-60. Mem. AIA, Kans. Soc. Architects (pres. 1981-82), Council Edn. Facilities Planners. Lodge: Optimists (pres. Topeka breakfast club 1970-71) (lt. gov. Kans. dist. 1981-82). Avocations: woodworking, photography, sculpting. Home: 3535 MacVicar Topeka KS 66611 Office: Horst Terrill & Karst Architects 2900 MacVicar Topeka KS 66611

KARTJE, JEAN VAN LANDUYT, college dean; b. Great Lakes, Ill., Aug. 14, 1953; d. John Emil and Alice Louise (Graikowski) Van Landuyt; m. John Karl Kartje, Mar. 10, 1979. B.A. in Psychology and English, Barat Coll., 1975; postgrad. U. Chgo., 1975-76, So. Ill. U., 1976-77; M.A. in Mgmt., Webster U., 1985. Dir. residence Barat Coll., Lake Forest, Ill., 1977-80, dean students, 1981—, also psychology instr.; employee Hotel Therme, Bad Vals, Switzerland, 1980-81. Mem. steering com. ann. awards YWCA Lake County, 1983; mem. Lake County Council on Women's Programs, 1982—. Mem. Assn. Campus Activities Adminstrs., Alumnae Assn. Barat Coll. (dir. at large 1984-85, student relations chair 1985—), Chicagoland Deans' Assn. Democrat. Roman Catholic. Avocations: reading; gardening; traveling. Home: W210 West Shore Dr Mundelein IL 60060 Office: Barat Coll 700 E Westleigh Rd Lake Forest IL 60045

KARTSONIS, PAUL DAVID, advertising executive; b. Kansas City, Mo., July 19, 1959; s. Paul Murray and Jeannene E. (Evans) K.; m. Barbara Jo Baker, May 12, 1984. Co-owner Sudden Comfort Furniture Mfg. and Retail Co., Harrisonville, Mo., 1981-83; pres. Paul Kartsonis and Assocs., Harrisonville, 1981-84; account exec. Batz Hodgson Neuwoehner, Inc., St. Louis and Kansas City, Mo., 1984-85; owner Kartsonis & Assocs., Kansas City, 1985—; bd. dirs. Preventics, Inc. Pres., bd. dirs. Nat. Com. of One, 1985-86. Served with USN, 1977-81. Mem. Advt. Club of Kansas City (1 Silver award, 3 Bronze awards 1986), Assn. of Young Execs. (pres., bd. dirs.), Kansas City Art Advt. Club (3 Omni Merit awards 1986), Greater Kansas City C. of C., VFW. Republican. Lodges: Rotary, Optimists. Office: Kartsonis and Assocs 10401 Holmes Suite 450 Kansas City MO 64131

KARTUSH, JACK MICHAEL, otologist; b. Detroit, May 18, 1952; s. Sam and Jean (Klein) K.; m. Christine Ann Ostrowski, June 21, 1984; 1 child, Alison. BS, Mich. State U., 1974; MD, U. Mich., 1978. Resident in gen. surgery St. Joseph Hosp., Ann Arbor, 1978-80; resident in otolaryngology U. Mich. Hosp., Ann Arbor, 1980-84, fellow in otology and neurotology, 1984-85; asst. prof. otology U. Mich., Ann Arbor, 1985-87; staff physician, dir. otology VA Hosp., Ann Arbor, 1984-87; staff physician specializing in facial paralysis Greater Detroit Otologic Group, Farmington Hills, Mich., 1987—; nat. lectr. on facial paralysis. Contbr. articles to profl. jours. and textbooks. Nat. Hearing Assn. grantee, 1984, Deafness Research Found. grantee, 1986. Fellow Am. Acad. Otolaryngology (facial paralysis study group); mem. AMA, Am. Neurotology Soc. Office: Greater Detroit Otologic Group 27555 Middlebelt Farmington Hills MI 48018

KARTY, JACK Z., financial management consultant; b. St. Louis, Oct. 16, 1929; s. Julius Lee and Mary (Hoffman) K.; m. Carol Steinberg, Dec. 30, 1956; children: Robert Arthur, Richard Joel. BS in Commerce, St. Louis U., 1951; MBA, Washington U., St. Louis, 1957. CPA, Mo. Cons. computer systems Sperry Rand Univac, St. Louis, 1955-56; acct. Price Waterhouse, CPA's, St. Louis, 1956-58; systems analyst, internal auditor McDonnell Douglas Co., St. Louis, 1958-59; controller Mo. Research Labs., Inc., St. Louis, 1959-65; fin. ops. auditor May Dept. Stores, St. Louis, 1965-66; asst. controller Universal Match Corp., St. Louis, 1967-69; asst. corp. controller Diversified Industries, Inc., St. Louis, 1970-71; controller, treas., dir. ins. Consol. Grain and Barge Co., St. Louis, 1972-84; v.p. fin. and adminstrn. DeBruce Grain, Inc., Kansas City, Mo., 1984-86; cons. fin. mgmt. St. Louis and Kansas City, 1987—. Served to 1st lt. USAF, 1952-54. Named assoc. in risk mgmt. Ins. Inst. Am., Malvern, Pa., 1984. Mem. Fin. Execs. Inst., Am. Inst. CPA's. Home: 9870 Greenery Ln Saint Louis MO 63132

KARWISCH, GEORGE AUGUST, JR., clinical psychologist; b. Cin., July 30, 1936; s. George August Sr. and Rose Anna (Ash) K.; m. Linda Lee Vanoli, Dec. 28, 1963; children: Stephanie, Eric, Kirsten. BS cum laude, Xavier U., Cin., 1964, MA in Clin. Psychology, 1965; PhD in Clin. Child Psychology, Purdue U., 1971. Lab. technician USI Chemicals, Cin., 1956-64; psychologist Longview State Hosp., Cin., 1964-66; coordinator adolescent program, asst. dir. psychology dept. Larue Carter Hosp., Indpls., 1970—; cons. psychologist Regional Mental Health Ctr., Kokomo, Ind., 1970-1982; asst. prof. sch. medicine Ind. U., Indpls., 1971—. Chmn. bd. edn. St. Gabriel Parish, Indpls., 1973-79. Mem. Am. Psychol. Assn., Ind. Psychol. Assn. (chmn. ethics com. 1974-79, elections chmn. 1986), Midwestern Psychol. Assn. Roman Catholic. Club: Southeastern Ohio Coin & Gun Club (founder and pres. 1959-67). Home: 6014 Penway Circle Indianapolis IN 46224 Office: Larue Carter Hosp 1315 W 10th St Indianapolis IN 46224

KARZEN, JUDITH H(ANELIN), musician, educator, lecturer; b. Chgo., June 10, 1940; d. Herman Elliot and Leah Jacobson Hanelin; m. Michael Karzen, Aug. 7, 1960; children: Harriet, Rachel, Aviva. MusB, Roosevelt U., 1962; MusM with honors, DePaul U., 1979. Dir. music Temple Beth Israel, Chgo., 1962—; tchr. music Chgo. Pub. Schs., 1979-82; choir dir. North Suburban Synagogue Beth El Temple Sholom, 1983-86; choral dir. for high holy days Temple Sholom, Chgo., 1983—; artistic dir. Halevi Choral Soc., Chgo., 1983—; dir. music Solomon Schechter Day Schs., Chgo., 1986; lectr. various groups, cons. in field. Mem. Guild of Temple Musicians (pres. 1976-86, newsletter editor), Am. Choral Dirs. Assn. Jewish. Office: Temple Beth Israel 3939 W Howard St Skokie IL 60076

KASER, RICHARD TODD, communications executive; b. Dover, Ohio, Aug. 29, 1952; s. Richard I. and Mary (Miller) K.; m. Victoria Cox, June 29, 1974; 1 child, Adaline. BS in Journalism summa cum laude, Ohio U., 1974; MA in Internat. Communications, Ohio State U., 1976. Public info. officer State of Ohio, Columbus, 1974-75; mgr. sales promotion Columbia Nat. Corp., Columbus, 1976-77; sales promotional specialist Chem. Abstracts Service, Columbus, 1977-79, advt. mgr., 1979-83, corp. communications mgr., 1983—. Mem. fin. com. Cen. Ohio Council Internat. Visitors, Columbus, 1985—. Mem. Nat. Fedn. Abstracting and Info. Services (chmn., newsletter editor adv. bd. 1985—), Phi Kappa Phi. Democrat. Episcopalian. Avocations: jogging, swimming, antiques, books, writing. Office: Chem Abstracts Service 2540 Olentangy River Rd Columbus OH 43210

KASHANI, JAVAD HASSAN-NEJAD, physician; b. Meshed, Iran, Aug. 30, 1937; came to U.S., 1971; s. Ali-Akbar and Kobra F. Kashani; m. Soraya Rezvani, Mar. 23, 1962; children: Fred, Donna. BS, Meshed Med. Coll., 1960; MD, Meshed Med. Sch., 1969. Diplomate Am. Bd. Psychiatry and Neurology, Can. Bd. Psychiatry. Intern St. Ann's Hosp., Chgo., 1972; resident Northwestern U., Chgo., 1972-75; fellow U. Mo., Columbia, 1976-77, prof. medicine, psychiatry and pediatrics, 1985—; dir. children's services Mid-Mo. Mental Health Ctr., Columbia, 1981—. Avocation: oil painting. Office: Dept of Psychiatry 3 Hospital Dr Columbia MO 65201

KASICH, JOHN R., congressman; b. McKees Rocks, Pa., May 13, 1952. B.A., Ohio State U., 1974. Administrv. asst. Ohio State Senate, 1975-77; mem. Ohio Legislature, 1979-82, 98th-100th Congresses from 12th Dist. Ohio, 1983—. Office: House of Representatives Office of House Members Washington DC 20515 *

KASPAR, JOSEPH CLIFFORD, child psychologist; b. Chgo., Sept. 12, 1932; s. Joseph John and Anna Virginia (Gralla) K.; m. Dolores Ann Kucera, Aug. 23, 1958; children: Cynthia Ann Kaspar Fabricius, Christopher Joseph. BS, U. Ill, 1953; MA, DePaul U., Chgo., 1955; PhD, U. Chgo., 1961. Diplomate in Clin. Psychology; registered clin. psychologist. Staff psychologist Children's Meml. Hosp., Chgo., 1960-63, chief psychologist, 1963-75; chief psychologist Hutchings Psychiatric Ctr., Syracuse, 1975-77; exec.dir. Doyle Ctr. and Day Sch., Loyola U., Chgo., 1977—; assoc. prof. clin. psychology Loyola U., 1980—; adv. bd. Child and Adolescent Service Dept. Mental Health, 1984—. Author: the Therapeutic Dialogue, 1964, Brain Damage and Behavior, 1965; cons. editor: The Clinical Neuropsychologist, 1986—; contbr. articles to profl. jour. Served with USN, 1954-56. Mem. Am. Psychol. Assn., Am. Bd. Profl. Psychology (examiner 1969—), Internat. Neuropsychol. Soc. Roman Catholic. Avocation: literature, music, history. Office: Doyle Ctr Loyola U 1043 W Loyola Ave Chicago IL 60626

KASPAR, PAUL TIMOTHY (TIM), financial analyst; b. Oak Park, Ill., Dec. 18, 1949; s. Paul Arthur and Marian (Fitzgibbon) K.; m. Deborah Lee Untiedt, Dec. 1, 1973; children: Erin Brye, Lindsay Michelle. BBA, St. Mary's Coll., Winona, Minn., 1971; MBA in Fin., DePaul U., 1976. Chartered fin. analyst. Analyst, portfolio mgr. Minn. Mut., St. Paul, 1976-85; portfolio mgr. Peregrine Capital Mgmt., Mpls., 1985—. Served with USAR, 1972. Mem. Twin Cities Soc. Security Analysts. Republican. Roman Catholic. Avocations: woodworking, cross country skiing, aerobics. Home: 22 Doral Rd Dellwood MN 55110 Office: Peregrine Capital Mgmt 512 Nicollet Mall Minneapolis MN 55402

KASPER, MICHAEL ANTHONY, accounting executive; b. Chgo., May 22, 1946; s. Alexander Joseph and Anne Dorothy (Jakovich) K.; m. Mary Patricia Page, Apr. 3, 1976; children: Michael, Anne Marie. BS in Bus. and Econs., Ill. Inst. Tech., 1969; MBA, U. Ill., 1975. CPA, Ill. Cost analyst Motorola, Inc., Schaumburg, Ill., 1975-78; plant controller Broco Products Co., Beloit, Wis., 1978-84; mgr. adminstrn. Enzyme Bio-Systems, Beloit, 1984—. Commr. Belvidere (Ill.) Park Dist., 1980-81; mem. Rock County (Wis.) Employer Com., 1987. Served with U.S. Army, 1969-73. Gen. R.E. Wood Found. scholar, 1964. Mem. Am. Inst. CPA's, Ill. CPA Soc., Wis. CPA Soc., Am. Legion. Roman Catholic. Lodge: Rotary. Office: Enzyme Bio-Systems Ltd 2600 Kennedy Dr Beloit WI 53511

KASPEREK, JOHN JOSEPH, JR., accountant; b. Hammond, Ind., Apr. 1, 1957; s. John Joseph Sr. and Dolores (Novak) K.; m. Beverly Louise Smith, Oct. 1, 1983. BS in Bus., Ind. U., Gary, 1979. Sr. auditor Thomas Havey & Co., CPA's, Chgo., 1979-86; pvt. practice acctg. Burnham, Ill., 1986—. Treas. Village of Burnham, 1985—. Mem. Am. Inst. CPA's, Ill. CPA Soc. Democrat. Roman Catholic. Lodge: Lions (treas. Calumet City, Ill., 1985-86, 2d v.p. 1986—). Home and Office: 2608 Goodrich Ave Unit 1 Burnham IL 60633

KASPERSON, RICHARD WILLET, pharmaceutical company executive; b. Grand Haven, Mich., June 1, 1927; s. Ernest Richard and Elizabeth (Willet) K.; m. Mary Lucinda Wanner, Nov. 9, 1957; children: David Arthur, Ernest Richard. BA, Mich. State U., 1949; JD, Northwestern U., 1958. Bar: Ill. 1958. With FTC, 1958-62; v.p. corp. regulatory affairs Abbott Labs., North Chicago, Ill., 1962—; mem. Ill. Food, Drug, Cosmetic and Pesticides Studies Commn., 1965-72; mem. Pres.'s Pvt. Sector Survey, 1982. Served to lt. USN, 1950-54. Pres. Northeast Ill. Council Boy Scouts Am., 1987. Mem. ABA, Ill. Bar Assn., Calorie Control Council (sec.), Food and Drug Law Inst. (trustee). Republican. Clubs: Capitol Hill (Washington), Skokie (Ill.) Country. Home: 954 Western Ave Northbrook IL 60062 Office: Abbott Labs Abbott Park D-387 North Chicago IL 60064

KASPRZYK, RICHARD CLEMENS, insurance agent; b. Chgo., Jan. 2, 1941; s. Clemens S. and Aldona R. (Lewandowski) K.; m. Dana Eve Patka, Mar. 29, 1969. BS in Bus., Marquette U., 1964; MBA in Mktg., Loyola U., Chgo., 1974. Mgr. F. W. Means & Co., Chgo., 1964-70; agt. Bankers Life, Chgo., 1974-81, mng. agt., 1974-81; owner Quality Ins., Naperville, Ill., 1981—. Served to capt. U.S. Army, 1964-70. Mem. DuPage Life Underwriters (Quality awards 1977, 79, 82). Democrat. Roman Catholic. Home and Office: 25 W 124 Jane Ave Naperville IL 60540

KASS, DAVID RICHARD, pension actuary; b. Bklyn., Nov. 16, 1931; s. Harry M. and Vivian S. Kass; m. Carole J. Black, June 4, 1956; children—Ruth, Michael, Sara. A.B. magna Cum Laude, Princeton U., 1952; With Mut. of N.Y., N.Y.C., 1954-69, assoc. group actuary, 1965-68, asst. v.p., 1969; v.p. E. M. Klein & Assocs., Cleve., 1969-70; founder, pres. Kass, Germain & Co., Shaker Heights, Ohio, 1970-83, v.p. Kass, Germain div. Johnson & Higgins Co. of Ohio, 1983-85; pres. David R. Kass & Co., 1986— . Served with U.S. Army, 1952-54. Fellow Soc. Actuaries; mem. Am. Acad. Actuaries (charter), Midwest Pension Conf., Am. Pension Conf. Office: 25550 Chagrin Blvd Beachwood OH 44122

KASSEBAUM, NANCY LANDON, U.S. Senator; b. Topeka, July 29, 1932; d. Alfred M. and Theo Landon; children: John Philip, Linda Josephine, Richard Landon, William Alfred. BA in Polit. Sci, U. Kans., 1952; MA in Diplomatic History, U. Mich., 1956. Mem. Maize (Kans.) Sch. Bd.; mem. Washington staff Sen. James B. Pearson of Kans., 1975-76; mem. U.S. Senate from Kans., 1979—, mem. fgn. relations com., commerce, sci. and transp. com., budget com., select com. on ethics. Republican. Episcopalian. Office: US Senate 302 Russell Senate Office Bldg Washington DC 20510

KASTANTIN, JOSEPH THOMAS, accounting educator; b. Ottumwa, Iowa, Aug. 30, 1947; s. Brony Frank and Virginia Mae (Smith) K.; m. Jane A. Mondanaro, Sept. 16, 1966 (div. Jan. 1971); children: Anthony Joseph, Leilani Michelle; Linda Krause, Sept. 21, 1974; 1 child, Andrew Thomas. AA, El Paso Community Coll., 1974; BS, Marian Coll., 1976; MBA, Butler u., 1979. CPA, cert. mgmt. acct. Enlisted U.S. Army, 1966, advanced through grades to sgt. 1st class, 1975, resigned, 1978; controller Top Value Fabrics, Carmel, Ind., 1978-79; bus. mgr. Ray Hutson Chevrolet, La Crosse, Wis., 1979-80; mgr. Frank Uhler Assocs. CPAs, La Crosse, 1980-82; pres. Horizon Designs, Inc., Kearney, Nebr., 1982-83; cons. Small Bus. Devel. Ctr., La Crosse, 1984—; bd. dirs. Vis. Nurses Assn. Contbr. articles to profl. jours. Pres. Western Wis. Regional Arts, La Crosse, 1986-87. Decorated Bronze Star, 1972. Mem. Am. Inst. CPAs, Wis. Inst. CPAs, Nat. Assn. Acctg., Am. Acctg. Assn. Republican. Congregationalist. Avocations: author, jogging, Charles Dickens. Home: 614 N 23d St La Crosse WI 54601 Office: U Wis 1725 State St La Crosse WI 54601

KASTEN, ROBERT W., JR., U.S. senator; b. Milw., June 19, 1942; s. Robert W. and Mary (Ogden) K.; m. Eva Jean. B.A., U. Ariz., 1964; M.B.A., Columbia U., 1966. With Genesco, Inc., Nashville, 1966-68; dir., v.p. Gilbert Shoe Co., Thiensville, Wis., 1968-75; mem. Wis. Senate, Madison, 1972-75, mem. joint fin. com., 1973-75, chmn. joint survey com. on tax exemptions, 1973-75; mem. 94th-95th congresses from 9th Wis. Dist., U.S. Senate, 1980—; mem. 100th Congress Com., appropriations com., budget com., commerce, sci. and transp. com., small bus. com. Mem. Milw. Soc. for Prevention of Blindness; regional dir. Milw. Coalition for Clean Water. Served to 1st lt. USAF, 1967-72. Named Jaycee of Yr., 1972; named Legis. Conservationist of Yr. Nat. Wildlife Fedn., 1973, Conservationist of Yr. Wis. Wildlife Fedn., 1986; One of Best Legislators Senate Rep. Class of 1980, Nat. Jour., 1986. Mem. Nat. Audubon Soc., Sigma Nu, Alpha Kappa Psi. Office: US Senate 110 Hart Senate Office Bldg Washington DC 20510

KASTEN, ROGER NEIL, JR., data processing executive; b. St. Georges Parish, Bermuda, U.K., Mar. 15, 1959; came to U.S., 1961, naturalized, 1959; s. Roger Neil and CoNette Lee (Nofzinger) K.; m. Leah Ann Peterson, Aug. 21, 1982; 1 child, Joel Parker. BS in Geology, Wichita State U., 1986. Apprentice baker Ketteman's Bakery, Wichita, Kans., 1973-75; mechanic Hillcrest Co., Wichita, 1975-77; salesman Kellogg-Buck Furniture Co., Wichita, 1977-79; lighting technician Am. Electric Co., Wichita, 1979-80; asst., geologist Goodin Trust Petroleum Co., Wichita, 1980-81; staff petroleum geologist D.R. Lauck Oil Co., Inc., Wichita, 1981-86; regional sales mgr. Newer Tech., Wichita, 1986—. Ricks scholar, 1982. Campaign mgr. for Barbara Pomeroy Kans. Gubernatorial Primary, 1986. Mem. Am. Assn. Petroleum Geologists (energy and minerals divs.), Kans. Geol. Soc., Wichita Area C. of C. (state legis. com. 1984—, water resources com. 1984—), Jaycees (bd. dirs. 1983-84, v.p. 1984-85), Sigma Gamma Epsilon (pres. 1981-82). Republican. Mem. Disciples of Christ Christian Ch. Avocations: kayaking, real estate,"high end" audiophile equipment. Home: 1985 S Longford Wichita KS 67207 Office: Spectrum Engring/Newer Tech 251 Whittier Wichita KS 67207

KASTENBAUM, ABRAHAM, social worker; b. N.Y.C., June 22, 1906; s. Harry and Sarah (Strahl) K.; m. Naomi Berman, Aug. 7, 1947. BSEd, NYU, 1933, MSEd, 1936; MSW, U. Minn., 1952. Cons. on aging Community Health and Welfare Council of Hennepin County, Mpls., 1970-72;

producer, host, moderator Sr. Citizen's Forum Sta. KMSP-TV 9, Mpls., 1973—. Active Minn. Bd. on Aging, St. Paul, 1978—. Served with U.S. Army, 1943-45, ETO. Recipient Outstanding Community Service award Minn. Dept. Human Services, 1986, Outstanding Profl. Community Involvement award Am. Coll. Health Care Adminstrs., 1986, Success Over 60 award Sr. Options Health Futures Inst., 1985, Good Neighbor award WCCO Radio-Northwest Airlines, 1985, Spl. Services to Older Minnesotans Minn. Bd. on Aging, 1982, Justice award Hennepin County Bar Assn., 1975-76, The Better Life award Am. Nursing Home Assn., 1975. Mem. Nat. Council on the Aging, Nat. Assn. Social Workers (cert.), Minn. Gerontol. Soc., Am. Assn. Jewish Ctr. Workers, Am. Soc. Aging, Mid-Am. Congress on Aging., Minn. Press Club. Office: KMSP-TV 9 6975 York Ave S Minneapolis MN 55435

KASTENMEIER, ROBERT WILLIAM, congressman; b. Beaver Dam, Wis., Jan. 24, 1924; s. Leo Henry and Lucille (Powers) K.; m. Dorothy Chambers, June 27, 1952; children: William, Andrew, Edward. LL.B., U. Wis., 1952. Bar: Wis. 1952. Dir. br. office claims service War Dept., Philippines, 1946-48; practiced in Watertown 1952-58, justice of the peace, 1955-58; mem. 86th-100th congresses from 2d Dist. Wis., mem. com. on judiciary, chmn. subcom. house jud. com. Served from pvt. to 1st lt., inf. AUS, 1943-46. Mem. Wis. Bar Assn. Office: 119 Martin Luther King Jr Blvd Suite 505 Madison WI 53703 also: 2328 Rayburn House Office Bldg Washington DC 20515

KASTER, LEONARD ALBERT, mechanical engineer; b. Chgo., May 12, 1947; s. Albert John and Helen (Munson) K.; m. Kay Starner, July 3, 1976; children: Erica Lynn, Mark Edward. BS in Mech. Aerospace Engring., Ill. Inst. Tech., 1970; MBA, Lewis U., 1984. Registered profl. engr., Ill. Sales engr. Moog Inc., Chgo., 1977-81, N.L. Rucker, Chgo., 1981-82, Rexroth, Chgo., 1982-83; regional application engr. Parker Hannifin, Des Plaines, Ill., 1984-86; porduct liability cons. Triodyne, Skokie, Ill., 1975-82; pvt. practice cons., Palos Hills, Ill. 1982—. Mem. ASME (assoc.), Soc. Automotive Engrs. Roman Catholic. Avocations: skiing, raquetball, golf, fishing. Home: 8457 Sun Valley Dr Palos Hills IL 60465 Office: Parker Hannifin 500 S Wolf Rd Des Plaines IL 60016

KASTNER, MICHAEL JAMES, dentist; b. Huntington, Ind., Oct. 20, 1954; s. James H. and Barbara A. (Bartrom) K.; m. Kimberly A. Ricke, June 18, 1983. BS, Manchester Coll., 1977; DDS, Ind. U., Indpls., 1981. Gen. practice dentistry Toledo, 1981—. Mem. ADA (Cert. of Recognition for Vol. Service in a Fgn. Country 1987), Acad. Gen. Dentistry, Ohio Dental Assn., Toledo Dental Soc., Mensa. Roman Catholic. Avocations: photography, basketball, tennis, martial arts, camping. Home: 5747 Hunting Creek Rd Toledo OH 43615

KASTUL, JEAN ANNE, program director; b. Milw., July 30, 1950; d. Harry R. and Helen W. (Strobel) Gessner; m. Jeff A. Kastrul, July 17, 1976; children: Emily, Ryan. BS, Carroll Coll., 1972. Elem. tchr. ElmBrook Schs., Brookfield, Wis., 1972-78; crisis counselor Task Force on Battered Women, Milw., 1978-83; parent Teen Shelter Care House, Waukesha, Wis., 1979-80; dir. vol. services YWCA, Milw., 1983-85; dir. nat. vol. program Endometriosis ASsn., Milw., 1984; dir. tng. YWCA Greater Milw., 1985—; speaker Woman to Woman Conf., Milw., 1985086; cons. YWCA, Milw., 1983-84; bd. dirs. Task Force on Battered Women, 1983. Co-author Trainers in Tng., 1985; editor OUTCRY, 1978-83. Mem. Friends of Shorewood (Wis.) Library, 1985—, Whitefish Bay PTA, 1986—; vol. Shorewood and Whitefish Bay (Wis.) Schs., 1982—; bd. dirs. Family After Sch. Program. Mem. Am. Soc. Tng. and Devel., Milw. Council Adult Edn., Vol. Action Ctr., Assn. Vol. Adminstrn. Democrat. Presbyterian. Club: Book of Shorewood. Avocations: reading, interior decorating, antiques, music. Home: 5944 N Santa Monica Blvd Whitefish Bay WI 53217 Office: YWCA 2211 E Kenwood Milwaukee WI 53211

KASUM, JAMES KENNETH, computer science educator; b. Milw., Sept. 2, 1943; s. Anton and Katherine Susan (Boden) K.; m. Mary Margaret Pahler, May 30, 1970; children—Kelly, Kathleen, Christine. B.S. in Math., U. Wis.-Milw., 1966, M.S. in Math., 1968, Ph.D. in Math., 1974, M.S. in Engring., 1985. Asst. prof. Cardinal Stritch Coll., Milw., 1971-82, assoc. prof., 1984—, chmn. grad. program ednl. computing, dir. computer services, 1984—; asst. prof. U. Wis.-Milw., 1982-84; cons. Owensboro Pub. Schs., Ky., 1976, Computrek Bus. Systems, Milw., 1978, Oster Mfg. Co., Milw., 1982. Cons. computer curriculum numerous area schs., 1983—. Wis. Alumni Research Found. grantee, 1972. Mem. Math. Assn. Am., Nat. Council Tchrs. Math., Wis. Math. Council (exec. council 1980-82), Assn. Computing Machinery, Milw. Ednl. Computing Assn. (pres. 1986-87), Phi Kappa Phi, Delta Chi Sigma, Delta Epsilon Sigma. Roman Catholic. Avocations: cycling; swimming; music. Home: 416 E Fox Dale Ct Fox Point WI 53217 Office: Cardinal Stritch Coll 6801 N Yates Rd Milwaukee WI 53217

KATAYAMA, K. PAUL, endocrinologist, gynecologist; b. Tokyo; m. Alyce Coyne; children: Christopher T., Ellen Y. MD, U. Tokyo, 1962, PhD, 1971. Instr. ob/gyn Johns Hopkins U., Balt., 1970-74, asst. prof., 1974-75; assoc. prof. Med. Coll. Wis., Milwaukee, 1975—; vis. prof. Nippon Med. Sch., Tokyo, 1982; dir. dept. reproductive endocrinology Union Meml. Hosp., Balt., 1982-83; dir. in vitro fertilization program Waukesha (Wis.) Meml. Hosp., 1983—. Contbr. over 40 articles to profl. jours. Mem. Am. Coll. Obstetricians and Gynecologists, Endocrine Soc., Am. Fertility Soc., Pacific Coast Fertility Soc., Milw. Gynecol. Soc. Home: 1185 Gray Fox Dr Waukesha WI 53186 Office: Advanced Inst Fertility 725 American Ave Waukesha WI 53188 also: 2000 W Kilbourne Milwaukee WI 53233

KATCHER, MURRAY L., pediatrician. SB, MIT, 1967; PhD, U. Wis., 1972, MD, 1975. Resident in pediatrics U. Wis., Madison, 1975-78, asst. prof. pediatrics, 1978-86, assoc. clin. prof., 1986—; maternal and child health physician State of Wis., Madison, 1985—.

KATE, CHRISTINE JANE, educator; b. Massillon, Ohio, Nov. 12, 1955; d. Paul H. and Esther J. (Waltz) K. B.S. in Edn., Kent State U., 1977; M.S. in Edn., U. Akron, 1981. Supr. cert., Ohio; vocat. cert., Ohio; high sch. cert., Ohio. Tchr. home econs. McKinley Sr. High Sch., Canton, Ohio, 1977, Hartford Jr. High Sch., Canton, 1977—; cons. Global Connections Resource, 1986. Mem. Assn. for Supervision and Curriculum Devel., Ohio Assn. Supervision and Curriculum Devel., Internat. Home Econs. Assn. (chmn. for Ohio), Am. Home Econs. Assn. Ohio Home Econs. Assn. (nominating com., program and conv. planning com., chmn. internat. sect.), Am. Vocat. Assn., Ohio Vocat. Assn. (chmn. membership com., pres. home econs. div. 1986-87), Am. Home Econs. Educators Assn., Nat. Assn. Vocat. Tech. Edn. Tchrs., Stark County Home Econs. Assn., Kappa Omicron Phi, Kappa Delta Pi. Home: Route 1 Strasburg OH 44680 Office: Hartford Jr High Sch 1824 3d St SE Canton OH 44707

KATELEY, RICHARD, real estate consultant; b. Niagara Falls, N.Y., June 1, 1944; s. Lawson M. and Mary T. Kateley. BA, U. Tex., 1966; MA, U. Chgo., 1973. Chief adminstrv. asst. office of lt. gov. State of Ill., Chgo., 1973-77; exec. v.p. and bd. dirs. Real Estate Research Corp., Chgo., 1977—. Co-author: America's High-Rise Office Buildings, 1986, Emerging Trends in Real Estate, 1986; contbr. articles to profl. jours. Bd. dirs. The Woodlawn Orgn., Chgo., 1985; mem. Gov.'s Film Fin. Task Force, 1986—. Fulbright fellow, 1971. Mem. Urban Land Inst., Econ. Club Chgo., Am. Polit. Sci. Assn., Lambda Alpha Internat. Democrat. Club: University (Chgo.). Home: 1366 N Dearborn Chicago IL 60610 Office: Real Estate Research Corp 72 W Adams St Chicago IL 60603

KATES, SAMUEL SIMON, lawyer, labor arbitrator; b. Cleve., Nov. 10, 1901; s. Harry and Sarah (Rosenberg) K.; m. Dorothy Davis, July 16, 1929; children—Robert D., Alix Kates Shulman. L.L.B., Cleve. Law Sch. Baldwin Wallace U., 1925. Bar: Ohio 1925. Sole practice, Cleve., 1925-51; ptnr. Hertz & Kates, 1951-74, Hertz, Kates, Friedman & Kammer, Cleve., 1974-85; sole practice labor arbitration, 1985—. Contbr. articles on aspects of arbitration to profl. jours. Mem. Cleve. adv. bd. SSS, 1942-45. Mem. Nat. Acad. Arbitrators, ABA (hon.), Ohio State Bar Assn. (hon.), Greater Cleve. Bar Assn. (hon., exec. com. 1936-39), Cuyahoga County Bar Assn. (hon.). Office: Hertz Kates Friedman & Kammer 1020 Leader Bldg Cleveland OH 44114

KATHREIN, MICHAEL LEE, leasing company executive, real estate company executive; b. Chgo., Nov. 26, 1953; s. Joseph A. and Mildred M. Kathrein; married, 1981; children: Jane Emily, Joseph Andrew. BS in Acctg., U. Nebr., 1978; M Mgmt., Northwestern U., 1985. CPA, Ill.; lic. real estate broker. Tax specialist Touche Ross & Co., Chgo., 1978-84; corp. controller, v.p. Lettuce Entertain You Enterprises, Chgo., 1984-86; pres., chief exec. officer Kathrein Leasing Co., Chgo., 1983—; also bd. dirs; pres., chief exec. officer Empire Real Estate Investment Co., Chgo., 1986—; also bd. dirs.; speaker Nat. Speakers Bur., N.Y.C., 1985—; cons. The Fla. Investor, Inc., Cocoa, 1986—. Author: (how-to book) Real Estate Comparative Analysis, 1986. Dir. revenue Crusade of Mercy, United Way, Chgo., 1980. Mem. Am. Inst. CPA's, Cert. Mgmt. Accts. Assn. (cert.), Cert. Internal Auditors Assn. (cert.), Nat. Assn. Realtors, Northwestern U. Alumni Assn., Mensa. Avocations: flying, lecturing. Home: 6242 N Greenview Chicago IL 60660-1822

KATONA, JOSEPH WILLIAM, engineering executive; b. Detroit, Jan. 20, 1929; s. Joseph and Marie (Flora) K.; m. Barbara Lee Knapp, Aug. 21, 1954; children: Paula Ann, David Joseph. Grad. high sch., Lincoln Park, Mich., 1946; student mech. engring., Lawrence Inst. Tech., 1960-63. Draftsman Bowen Products, Ecorse, Mich., 1945-48; draftsman/foreman Mills Products, Detroit, 1949-51; plant supt., chief engr. Mills Products, Walled Lake, Mich., 1953-70; v.p. engring. Mills Products, Farmington, Mich., 1971—. Patentee in field. Served to cpl. U.S. Army, 1951-53, Korea. Home: 2222 Paulette Walled Lake MI 48088 Office: Mills Products Inc 33106 W 8 Mile Rd Farmington MI 48024

KATTERHENRY, KEVIN ROBERT, real estate broker; b. St. Mary's, Ohio, Mar. 11, 1956; s. Robert E. and Anne E. (Hay) K.; m. Karen L. Bruns, July 7, 1973 (div. July 1986); children: Lisa Kay, Nicholos John, Nanette Maria. B Bus. Mgmt., Wright State U., 1979; cert. broker, Realtors Inst., 1986. Mgr. Burger King, St. Mary's, 1977-80, Ponderosa, Dayton, Ohio, 1980-83; real estate assoc. Frank & Mackenbach, St. Mary's, 1983-85; co-owner, real estate broker McCullough Realty, Inc., St. Mary's, 1985—. Mem. Nat. Assn. Realtors, Nat. Assn. Land Appraisers, Realtors Inst.(cert. broker), Ohio Assn. Realtors (Profl. of Yr. 1985, Pres.'s Sales Club 1986). Republican. Roman Catholic. Lodges: Optimists (local v.p. 1985-86), Rotary, Eagles. Avocations: boating, water skiing, snow skiing. Home: 141 Lago Vue Southmoor Shores Saint Marys OH 45885 Office: McCullough Realty Inc PO Box 81 Saint Mary's OH 45885

KATUBIG, CORNELIO P., pathologist; b. Dagupan, Pangasinan, Philippines, Nov. 15, 1939; came to U.S., 1964; s. Cornelio C. and Barbara P. Katubig; m. Carmencita Rivera, June 14, 1964; children: Cornelio John, Christina, Catherine. MD, U. of the East, Philippines, 1963. Diplomate Am. Bd. Pathology. Intern Oakwood Hosp., Dearborn, Mich., 1964-65; resident in internal medicine Huron Rd. Hosp., Cleve., 1965-66; resident in pathology Cleve. Met. Hosp., 1966-71; staff pathologist Aultman Hosp., Canton, Ohio, 1971-72; chief of lab. Marion (Ill.) Mem. Hosp., 1972—, VA Med. Ctr., Marion, 1974—. Contbr. articles to profl. jours. Mem. AMA, Am. Coll. Pathologists, Am. Soc. Clin. Pathologists, Ill. Med. Soc. Roman Catholic. Lodge: KC (Marion). Avocations: tennis, golf, skiing, jogging. Home: 305 Lakeview Rd Marion IL 62959 Office: 1009 W Cherry St Marion IL 62959

KATZ, ALLEN MARTIN, executive recruiter; b. New Hunstanton, Eng., Feb. 9, 1954; came to U.S., 1954; s. Samuel and Miriam (Meyers) K.; m. Irmgard Geiss, Sept. 30, 1978; 1 child, Christopher Allen. Diploma, Devry Tech. Inst., Chgo., 1974. Tech. specialist Fisher Sci., Itasca, Ill., 1974-77; exec. recruiter Electronic Search, Arlington Heights, Ill., 1978-84; exec. recruiter 1st Search, Inc., Chgo., 1984—, also corp. officer; cons., Chgo., 1977-78. Author: Get That Electronics Job, 1983. Active Irving Park (Ill.) YMCA. Mem. IEEE, Nat. Assn. Personnel Cons., Internat. Assn. Scientologists (life). Scientologist. Avocations: telecommunications, fishing, self-help projects, children's edn. Home: 9025 Kostner Skokie IL 60076 Office: 1st Search Inc 4200 W Peterson Suite 100 Chicago IL 60646

KATZ, DAVID ALLAN, lawyer, business consultant; b. Toledo, Nov. 1, 1933; s. Samuel and Ruth (Adelman) K.; m. Joan G. Siegel, Sept. 4, 1957; children: Linda Katz Beren, Michael S., Debra L. BBA, Ohio State U., 1955, JD summa cum laude, 1957. Bar: Ohio 1957. . Ptnr. Spengler, Nathanson, Heyman, McCarthy & Durfee, Attys., Toledo, 1957-86, mng. ptnr., 1986—; dir., corp. sec. Seaway Food Town, Inc., Maumee, Ohio, 1980—; sec. Apollo Industries, Inc., Toledo, 1982—; dir., sec. Wabash-Lagrange Steel Co., Toledo, Meilink Industries, Inc., Toledo. Pres. Temple B'nai Israel, Toledo, 1970-73, Jewish Welfare Fedn., Toledo, 1977-79, Toledo Bar Assn. Found., 1983—; trustee St. Vincent Med. Ctr., 1987—; trustee St. Vincent Med. Ctr. Found., vice chmn. 1986—; v.p. Jewish Edn. Service N.Am, 1985—. Mem. Toledo Bar Assn. (sec. and trustee 1972-78), Ohio State Bar Assn., ABA. Office: Spengler Nathanson Heyman et al 1000 Nat Bank Bldg Toledo OH 43604

KATZ, DAVID JOSEPH, architect; b. Gary, Ind., July 25, 1926; s. Isadore and Jeanette (Janofsky) K.; m. Byrna Baran, Jan., 1951 (div. 1963); children: Marcia, Kenneth, Janis; m. Mardi Sue Engel, Jan. 26, 1973. BArch, U. Ill., 1949. Pvt. practice architecture Crown Point, Ind., 1951—. Bd. dirs. Court House Found., Crown Point, Ind., 1973—, Save Our Station, Hobart, Ind., 1984—. Mem. AIA, Nat. Council Archtl. Registration, Ind. Soc. Architects. Democrat. Lodges: B'Nai B'Rith, Civitan (pres. Merrillville, 1959—, gov. midwest dist. 1962). Avocation: tennis. Office: 106 W Clark St Crown Point IN 46307

KATZ, ELAINE RONSHEIM, office manager; b. Cin., June 15, 1934; d. Howard Myron and Maryleonne (Heyn) Ronsheim; m. James B. Katz, Sept. 11, 1955 (dec. June 1983); children: Andrew, Michael, Sherrie. BA summa cum laude, Ohio State U., 1956; MA in Edn., Case-Western U., 1958; postgrad., Ursuline Coll., 1978—. Tchr. Cleve. Bd. Edn., 1956-59; office mgr. Solomon, Sholiton & Marcotty, MDs, Inc., Cleve., 1984—. Vol., mem. Women's Auxiliary Bd. Mt. Sinai Hosp., 1970-84; former mem. elem. PTA bd., pres., 1973-74; former mem. high sch. PTA bd., pres., 1978-79; mem. exec. com., sec. Citizens' Adv. Com. Bd., 1975-77; pres. Orange Community Arts Council, 1976-77; sec. Orange Antique Show Com., 1975-78; chmn. com. to study high sch. program, 1975-76; mem. Fedn. of Orange Communities, 1976—; mem. Sch. Bd. of The Temple; Trustee Pike Civic League, 1977-80, sec., 1978-79, vice chmn., 1979-80;mem. Orange City Schs. Bd. Edn., 1979-87, pres., 1981, 86. Mem. Ohio Sch. Bds. Assn., Phi Beta Kappa. Jewish. Home: 28850 Gates Mills Blvd Pepper Pike Blvd OH 44124 Office: Solomon Sholiton & Marcotty MDs 26900 Cedar Rd Suite 310 Beachwood OH 44122

KATZ, LEWIS ROBERT, legal educator; b. N.Y.C., Nov. 15, 1938; s. Samuel and Rose (Turoff) K.; m. Jan Karen Daugherty, Jan. 14, 1964; children: Brett Elizabeth, Adam Kenneth, Tyler Jessica. AB, Queens Coll., 1959; JD, Ind. U., 1963. Bar: Ind 1963, Ohio 1971. Ptnr. Snyder, Bunger, Cotner & Harrell, Bloomington, Ind., 1963-65; instr. U. Mich. Law Sch., Ann Arbor, 1965-66; asst. prof. Case Western Res. U. Law Sch., Cleve., 1966-68, assoc. prof., 1968-71, prof., 1971—, John C. Hutchins prof. law, dir. Ctr. for Criminal Justice, 1973—; criminal justice agys. cons. Author: The Justice Imperative: Introduction to Criminal Justice, 1979, (with O.C. Schroeder, Jr.) Ohio Criminal Law, 1974, Justice Is The Crime, 1972, Ohio Arrest Search and Seizure, 1985, 2d edition, 1987. Recipient Disting. Tchr. award Case West Res. U. Law Alumni Assn.; Nat. Defender Project of Nat. Legal Aid and Defender Assn. fellow, 1968. Mem. ABA. Home: 2873 N Park Blvd Cleveland Heights OH 44118 Office: Case Western Res U Law Sch Cleveland OH 44106

KATZ, MYER, industrial metals company executive, educator, biologist, historian; b. Winona, Minn.; s. William Udell and Anna Sara (Schochett) K.; B.E. in Biol. Sci. and History, U. Wis.; M.A. in Biol. Scis., George Washington U.; postgrad. U. Wis., U. Minn., U. Chgo., Am. U., Western Wis. Tech. Inst. Sec.-treas., Katz Indsl. Metals, Inc., La Crosse, Wis., 1959—; exec. v.p. Gateway Plastics Corp., La Crosse, 1965-69; instr. bus. mgmt. Western Wis. Tech. Inst., La Crosse, 1969-71; instr. Am. history and gen. scis. Central High Sch., La Crosse; research biologist and writer U.S. Dept. Agr., Washington, U.S. Dept. Interior, Washington; office mgr. Wis. Dept. Hwys., Madison; guest lectr. U. Wis. Library Sch., 1972-73; lectr. local, state and Jewish history to various sch., civic and ch. groups in Wis., 1980-87; editorial writer La Crosse Tribune, 1977-87, spl. features writer, 1980-87. Pres., La Crosse Public Library Friends, 1969-71; mem. Mayor's Bicentennial Commn., La Crosse, 1975-76, chmn. heritage div., 1975-76; mem. U. Wis. Bicentennial Commn.; mem. La Crosse City and County Historic Sites Commn., 1973-78, chmn., 1973-78; bd. curators Swarthout Hist. Mus., 1975—; bd. dirs. Congregation Sons of Abraham, La Crosse, 1974-76, La Crosse Public Library, 1968-72; bd. dirs. Mississippi River Sci. and Industry Center, La Crosse, 1979-86, hist. adv., 1979-86; bd. dirs. Wis. Libraries Friends, 1969-72; del. Wis. Gov.'s Conf. on Libraries, 1978; bd. advisers Riverside U.S.A., 1982—. Served with U.S. Army Mil. Welfare, field dir. ARC. Recipient Bronze Plaque award La Crosse County Hist. Soc., 1976; award of Recognition Luther Rice Soc., George Washington U., 1972; Blue Ribbon for meritorious contbns. to Am. Bicentennial Year, 1976; nat. award of Commendation, Am. Assn. State and Local History, 1977; award of Merit, State Hist. Soc. Wis., 1974; 1st citizen award City of La Crosse, 1980, disting. service award Phi Delta Kappa, 1981, achievement award Hist. Preservation Soc. Am., 1980, recognition award George Washington U., 1972. Mem. Am. Bibl. Archeol. Soc., Wis. Archeol. Soc., Coalition for Regional Environ. Studies, Washington Biol. Soc., AAAS, Wis. Soc. Jewish Learning, Wis. Acad. Scis., Arts and Letters, Am. Ornithologists Union, Nat. Audubon Soc., Smithsonian Instn., Cousteau Soc., Hist. Preservation Alliance of La Crosse, La Crosse Writers Club, U. Wis. Alumni Assn., George Washington U. Alumni Assn., La Crosse County Hist. Soc. (dir. publs. 1973-77, pres. 1975-76, museum dir. 1973-75), Wis. State Hist. Soc. (spl. commendation 1976), John Quincy Adams Assocs., George Washington Univ., Tau Alpha Omega. Lodge: B'nai B'rith. Author: History of Jews and Judaism in La Crosse Area (State award), 1974; Pictorial History of Mayors of La Crosse, 1974; History of Rabbinate of La Crosse, 1979; History of Onalaska, Wis., 1974; The Caves of Barre Mills, Wis., 1975; History of Hebrew Chirography, The Hirshheimer Saga, 1976, Echoes of Our Past, 1985, Biography of Thomas Stoddard, 1986; contbr. articles on local and state history to scholarly publs. Home: 1525 State St La Crosse WI 54601 Office: 2535 E Ave S La Crosse WI 54601

KATZ, RICHARD, architect; b. Chgo., Dec. 19, 1948; s. Jules and Esther (Zuckerstein) K.; m. Susan Rae Ehrlich, Aug. 28, 1977; 1 child, Rachel Elaine. BArch in Design, U. Ill., Chgo., 1974. Registered architect, Ill., Wis. Prin. R. Katz and Assocs., Inc., Oak Park, Ill., 1980—; cons. various law firms, 1980—; faculty mem. Triton Coll., River Grove, Ill., 1986. Mem. research ctr. Frank Lloyd Wright Home and Studio Found., Oak Park, Ill., 1987. Mem. AIA, Constrn. Specifications Inst., Am. Numismatic Assn. Jewish. Avocations: numismatics, travel. Office: R Katz & Assocs 1103 Westgate 304 Oak Park IL 60301

KATZ, SIDNEY F., obstetrician-gynecologist; b. Detroit, Sept. 5, 1928; m. Sally R. Katz. BS, Wayne State U., 1949; MD, U. Mich., Ann Arbor, 1953. Diplomate Am. Bd. Ob-Gyn. Pvt. practice Dearborn, Mich. Served as capt. USAF, 1954-56. Fellow Am. Coll. Ob-gyn., ACS, Mich. Soc. Gynecologists, So. Mich. Surgical Soc. Office: 4407 Roemer St Dearborn MI 48126

KATZ, STEPHEN ERIC, psychiatrist; b. Topeka, Dec. 23, 1948; s. Jerome Bertram and Alma (Mindel) K.; m. Judith Holiner, May 23, 1971 (div. 1977); m. Jan K. Peimann, June 7, 1980; children: Eric, Natalie, Rachel. MD, U. Kans., Kansas City, 1976. Diplomate Am. Bd. Psychiatry and Neurology. Resident Karl Menninger Sch. Psychiatry, Topeka, 1976-81; staff psychiatrist Meml. Hosp., Topeka, 1979—, St. Francis Hosp., Topeka, 1981—, C.F. Menninger Meml. Hosp., Topeka, 1981—; supr. Karl Menninger Sch. Psychiatry, 1981—; investigator drug research, C.F. Menninger Hosp., 1983—, cons., 1984—, chmn. and founder psychopharmacology com., 1984—. Seeley fellow Menninger Sch. Psychiatry, 1979-80. Democrat. Jewish. Avocations: reading, constructing hi-fi loudspeakers, photography, astronomy, music. Home: 3310 Alameda Dr Topeka KS 66614 Office: Menninger Found 5800 W 6th Topeka KS 66606

KATZEL, JEANINE ALMA, journalist; b. Chgo., Feb. 20, 1948, d. LeRoy Paul and Lia Mary (Arcuri) Katzel; B.A. in Journalism, U. Wis., 1970; M.S. in Journalism, Northwestern U., 1974. Publs. editor U. Wis. Sea Grant Program, Madison, 1969-72; editor research div. agrl. sch. U. Wis., Madison, 1972; research editor Prism mag. AMA, Chgo., 1972-73; free lance writer, 1974-75; lit. editor Plant Engring. mag. Tech. Pub. Co., Barrington, Ill., 1975-76, news editor, 1976-77, asso. editor, 1977-79, sr. editor, 1979—; sr. editor Plant Engring mag Cahners Pub., Des Plaines, Ill., 1987—. Judge assoc. ann. competition Engring. Coll. Mag., 1978-83, 85—. Recipient Elsie Bullard Morrison prize in Journalism, U. Wis., 1969; Peter Lisagor award in bus. journalism, 1983. Mem. Women in Communications, Am. Soc. Bus. Press Editors (pres. Chgo. chpt. 1977-78), Soc. Profl. Journalists, Soc. Fire Protection Engrs., Am. Inst. Chem. Engrs., Am. Chem. Soc., Nat. Audubon Soc., Nat. Fire Protection Assn. (tech. com. on fire pumps), Am. Soc. Safety Engrs., Internat. Soc. Fire Service Instrs., No. Ill. Computer Soc., AAUW, Phi Kappa Phi. Home: 16 Boxwood Ln Cary IL 60013 Office: 1350 E Touhy Ave PO Box 5080 Des Plaines IL 60018

KATZKE, AUGUST FLOYD, engineer; b. New Salem, N.D., Feb. 3, 1930; s. Henry August and Anna (Rotschiller) K.; m. Carola Clara Thornberg, June 13, 1953 (dec. Sept. 1983); children: Mary, Craig, Patricia, Evelyn, Holly, Sharon, David; m. Ellen Margaret Prigge, July 7, 1984. BSME, N.D. State U., 1954. Registered profl. engr., Minn. Engr. microswitch div. Honeywell Inc., Freeport, Ill., 1954-56; engr. Toro Mfg., Windom, Minn., 1956-64, Jostens Inc., Owatonna, Minn., 1964-67, Owatonna Mfg. Co., 1967-72; v.p. Tafco Equipment Co., Blue Earth, Minn., 1972—, also bd. dirs.; bd. dirs. Gem Mfg. Co., Blue Earth. Served to sgt. U.S. Army, 1951-53, Korea. Mem. Am. Legion, Blue Earth C. of C. Lutheran. Lodge: Lions (pres. Blue Earth 1983-84). Avocations: fishing, farming, hiking. Home: Rural Rt 3 Box 99 Blue Earth MN 56013 Office: Tafco Equipment Co Hwy 16 W Industrial Blue Earth MN 56013

KATZMAN, ELLEN JO, community center administrator; b. Indpls., June 16, 1957; d. Abraham and Riva L. (Tuch) K. B.S. in Criminal Justice, Ind. U., 1980, M.S.W., 1982. Youth and young adult dir. Jewish Community Ctr., Indpls., 1982-85, program dir., 1985—; Dor L' Dor Israel seminar participant, 1984. Jewish Welfare Fedn. Scholar, 1981-82. Recipient Louis Kraft award, 1986. Mem. Nat. Council of Jewish Women, Orgn. for Rehab. Through Tng. (v.p. 1983-84), Assn. Jewish Ctr. Workers, Jewish Welfare Fedn. (co-chairperson young women's div.). Office: Jewish Community Ctr 6701 Hoover Rd Indianapolis IN 46260

KAUFMAN, EDWARD PHILLIP, psychotherapist; b. Bronx, N.Y., Aug. 8, 1939; s. Harry Oscar and Terry Rose (Saeperstein) K.; m. Adele Mae Weltman, June 24, 1962; children: Elizabeth Ann, Daniel Mark. BA, U. Ill., 1962, MSW, 1964. Cert. social worker, child psychotherapist. Social acting dir. admissions children's services Chigo. Read Mental Health Hosp., 1964-66; adminstr., clin. supr. Jewish Children's Bur., Chgo., 1966-85; pvt. practice psychotherapy Chgo., 1969—; clin. supr., adminstrv. cons. St. Mary's Services, Chgo., 1977-84, cons. spl. edn. dept. Glenbrook High Sch., Northbrook, Ill., 1978-81; cons. various child welfare agys. and schs., Chgo., 1977—; mem. faculty Inst. Psychoanalysis, Chgo., 1982—; lectr. in field. Mem. Mayor's Commn. on Vandalism, city of Highland Park, Ill., 1978-79; bd. dirs. Highland Park Youth Commn., 1980—. Mem. Assn. Child Psychotherapists (treas. 1977-79, exec. com. 1983-85), Ill. Soc. Clin. Social Work, Nat. Assn. Social Workers, Nat. Registry Clin. Social Workers. Avocations: photography, scuba diving, tennis. Home: 825 Edgewood Rd Highland Park IL 60035 Office: 111 N Wabash Suite 1704 Chicago IL 60602 also: 1893 Sheridan Rd Highland Park IL 60035

KAUFMAN, HARVEY ISIDORE, neuropsychologist; b. Virginia, Minn., May 13, 1937; s. Carl and Marcia (Borkon); m. Glenda Kaufman, Oct. 16, 1971; children: Jason Alexis, Justin Bram. BA, U. Minn., Duluth, 1959, BA cum laude, 1960; MA, U. Minn., Mpls., 1961; PhD, Marquette U., 1967. Diplomate Am. Bd. Neuropsychology, Am. Bd. Med. Psychotherapists. Psychology supr. Winnebago (Wis.) Mental Health Inst., 1971-75; dir. outpatient services Fond du Lac Care Ctr., Fond du Lac, Wis., 1975-81; neuropsychologist Sharpe Clinic, Fond du Lac, 1983—, St. Mary's Hosp., Milw., 1986—. Fellow dept. neurology U. Wis. Med. Sch., 1981-82. Fellow Am. Bd. Med. Psychotherapist; mem. Am. Psychol. Assn., Wis. Psychol. Assn.,

Nat. Acad. Neuropyschologists, Am. Soc. Clin. Hypnosis, Internat. Soc. Clin. Hypnosis, Internat. Neuropsychol. Soc. Home: 409 Berkley Place Fond du Lac WI 54935 Office: Sharpe Med Ctr 92 E Division St Fond du Lac WI 54935

KAUFMAN, JEROME BENZION, neurosurgeon; b. Waterloo, Iowa, July 22, 1934; s. Louis and Dorothy (Rosenbloom) K.; m. Judith Ellen Lasker, June 29, 1967; children: David, Jonathan, Jefferey. BA, Wayne State U., 1955, MD, 1961; postgrad., U. Madrid. Diplomate Am. Bd. Neurol. Surgery. Rotating intern Michael Reese Hosp. and Med. Ctr., Chgo., 1961-62; resident in internal med. Michael Reese Hosp. and Med. Ctr., Chgo., 1962-63; resident in gen. surgery VA Hosp., Bronx, 1965-66, resident in neurology, 1966, resident in neurosurgery, 1967, from sr. to chief resident neurosurgery, 1969-70; resident neurosurgery Neurol. Inst. N.Y., Columbia Presbyn. Hosp., 1968; resident neuropathology Mt. Sinai Hosp. and Med. Sch., N.Y.C., 1968; chief resident neurosurgery City Hosp., Elmhurst, N.Y., 1969; chmn. dept. neurosurgery Carle Clinic Assoc. and Found. Hosp., Urbana, Ill., 1972—; cons. neurosurgery McKinley Hosp., Urbana, Burnham City Hosp., Champaign, Mercy Hosp., Urbana; asst. instr. internal medicine Chgo. Med. Sch., 1963; clin. assoc. prof. neurosurgery U. Ill. Coll. Medicine, Urbana, 1982—. Contbr. articles to profl. jours. Served to capt. USAF, 1963-65. Fellow ACS, Am. Assn. Neurol. Surgeons (Continuing Edn. award in Neurosurgery 1980, 83), Internat. Coll. Surgeons (vice gov.), N.Y. Acad Scis.; mem. AMA (Physicians Recognition award 1980, 82), Ill. Med. Soc., Champaign County Med. Soc., Congress of Neurol. Surgeons, Cen. Neurosurg. Soc., Assn. Mil. Surgeons of U.S., Chgo. Neurol. Soc. Home: 2104 Zuppke Dr Urbana IL 61801 Office: 602 W University Ave Carle Clinic Assn Urbana IL 61801

KAUFMAN, JULIAN ROWE, physician; b. Louisville, Ky., Aug. 12, 1910; s. Louis and Ann (Rowe) K.; m. Ellen Caplin; children: Lois, Don, Michael, Stuart. MD, U. Louisville, 1936. Diplomate Am. Bd. Internal Medicine, Am. Bd. Allergy and Immunology. Intern St. Louis County Hosp., Clayton, Mo., 1936-37; resident in gen. medicine U. Pa. Grad. Hosp., Phila., 1939-40, U. Wis. Gen. Hosp., Madison, 1940-41; clin. prof. medicine Med. Coll Ga., Augusta, 1939-42; practice medicine specializing in allergy Fort Wayne, 1942—. Served to capt. USMC, 1942-46. Fellow Am. Coll. Physicians, Am. Coll Allergists, Am. Acad. Allergy. Jewish. Home: 5405 Old Mill Rd Fort Wayne IN 46807 Office: 3030 Lake Fort Wayne IN 46807

KAUFMAN, KENTON RICHARD, mechanical engineer; b. Mitchell, S.D., Feb. 19, 1952; s. Richard and Leona Wilma (Herbst) K.; m. Nancy Ann Brockel, June 3, 1978. BS, S.D. State U., 1974, MS, 1976. Registered profl. engr., N.D. With Caterpillar Tractor Co., Peoria, Ill., summer 1974; grad. research asst. S.D. State U., Brookings, 1975-76; asst. prof. N.D. State U., Fargo, 1976-86, grad. teaching fellow, 1985-86; vis. scientist, Mayo Clinic, Rochester, Minn., 1986—; cons. UN Indsl. Devel. Orgn., Vienna, Austria, summer 1983. Contbr. articles to profl. jours. F.O. Butler scholar, 1971, 3M Co. scholar, 1972, Ralston Purina scholar, 1973; Bush Leadership fellow, 1986; grantee Internat. Harvester Co., Allis Chalmers Co. fellow, U.S. Dept. Agr. fellow. Mem. Orthopedic Research Soc., Nat. Strength and Conditioning Assn., Sigma Xi, Alpha Epsilon, Tau Beta Pi, Phi Kappa Phi, Gamma Sigma Delta. Lutheran. Home: 2700 56th St NW Bldg 2 Unit 4 Rochester MN 55901 Office: Biomechanics Lab C007 Guggenheim Mayo Clinic Rochester MN 55905

KAUFMAN, LAWRENCE CLARK, city administrator; b. Oklahoma City, Mar. 21, 1950; s. Clark Ernest and Barbara Jo (Landsberger) K.; m. Deborah Anne Deckard, Sept. 26, 1972 (div.); m. Vickie Lynn Bourne, Dec. 12, 1985. B.S. in Pub. Adminstrn., Southwest Mo. State U., 1972. Adminstrv. asst. City of Independence (Mo.), 1972-76, community devel. dir., 1976-78, asst. to city mgr., 1978—. Mem. Internat. City Mgmt. Assn. (assoc.), Mo. City Mgmt. Assn., Am. Pub. Works Assn., Am. Soc. for Pub. Adminstrn., Nat. Corvette Owners Assn. (charter), Nat. Corvette Restorers Soc. Contbr. articles to profl. jours. Office: 111 E Maple St Independence MO 64050

KAUFMAN, LESLIE MICHAEL, marketing executive; b. St. Louis, Aug. 9, 1946; s. Hyman and Betty (Margulis) K.; m. Marilyn Sue Slein, Jan. 18, 1970; children: Lisa Victoria, Laura Carolyn. Student, London Sch. Econs., 1966-67; BA, U. Wis., 1968; MBA, U. Chgo., 1974. Dir. sales devel. Western Pub. Co., Racine, Wis., 1969-79; exec. v.p., chief ops. officer Progressive Industries, Dayton, Ohio, 1979-81; dir. mktg. Sigma-Aldrich Corp., St. Louis, 1981-85; v.p. mktg. Dir. Mail Corp. Am., St. Louis, 1985—. Mem. Dir. Mktg. Assn., Phi Beta Kappa. Jewish. Avocations: tennis, publishing. Home: 3 Rio Vista Saint Louis MO 63124 Office: Dir Mail Corp Am 1533 Washington Ave Saint Louis MO 63103

KAUFMAN, SUZANNE DRYER, art educator, artist; b. Indpls., Oct. 10, 1927; d. Gerald and Iola (Callier) Mahalowitz; m. Joseph G. Dryer, Oct. 18, 1948 (div. 1964); children—Janet Dryer Perez, Jeffrey (dec.), Joel. Student, Purdue U., 1944-46; B.A., Rockford Coll., 1965; M.A., No. Ill. U., 1968. Cert. tchr., Ill. Asst. editor William H. Block & Co., "Block's Booster", Indpls., 1946-49; tchr. art Rockford (Ill.) Sch. Dist., 1965-70; instr., asst. prof., assoc. prof., prof. art Rock Valley Coll., Rockford, Ill., 1970—; lectr. Rockford Coll.; art critic New Art Examiner, Rockford Register Star, WREX-TV; cons. A.C.T.S. Inc., Glencoe, Ill.; judge for juried art competitions; lectr. in field; over 400 art works in pub. and pvt. collections, 14 one man shows, 53 group and invitational exhibits, 31 juried exhibits. Initiator gift fund and presentation Lindisfarne Gospels from Rockford Coll. to Holy Island, Eng., 1970; mem. visual arts panel Ill. Arts Council, 1975; mem. Mayor's Urban Design Rev. Com., Rockford, 1974-76, sculpture com. for Rockford Symbol, 1974-77; co-founder Rockford Gifted Child Assn.; v.p., sec. Rockford Art Assn. bd., 1972-82; mem. Rockford Hosp. Vols. bd., 1959-64; bd. dirs., v.p., sec. chmn. center mgmt. com. Jewish Community Center, 1960-65; vol. Highland Park Hosp., 1955-59; mem. Ind. Jewish Community Relations bd., 1948-52; chmn. Indpls. Jewish Community Center adult activities, 1950-52. Recipient Outstanding Vol. of Yr. award Sinnissippi Lung Assn., 1983, 84; 10 Yr. Service award Rockford Art Assn., 1982; numerous service awards from Rockford Meml. Hosp., Highland Park Hosp., Temple Beth El Sisterhood; 15 Yr. Service award Rock Valley Coll.; named Disting. Alumnus of Yr., No. Ill. U., 1985, also award for outstanding profl. achievement Dept. Art Alumni, 1985. Mem. Coll. Art Assn., Community Coll. Humanities Assn., Community Coll. Faculty Assn. Home: 240 Lovesee Rd Roscoe IL 61073 Office: 3301 N Mulford Rd Rockford IL 61101 Studio: Stone Hollow Studio 3318 N Main St Rockford IL 61103

KAUFMAN, VICKIE L., accountant; b. Kansas City, Mo., Jan. 11, 1953; d. Clifford Eugene Keith and Peggy Lou (Jones) Rusk; m. Lawrence C. Kaufman, Dec. 12, 1985; 1 child, Monica Lea. BBA, U. Mo., Kansas City, 1975. CPA, Mo. Auditor Peat, Marwick, Kansas City, 1973-77; acct. Kenworth Truck Co., Kansas City, 1978-81; city auditor City of Independence, Mo., 1981-86; dir. internal compliance Ferrell Co., Inc., Liberty, Mo., 1986—. Chmn. Am. Cancer Soc. Dick Howser Golf Classic, Independence, 1987. Mem. Am. Inst. CPA's, Mo. Soc. CPA's (continuing edn. com. 1987). Avocations: skiing, reading, movies, acrobics. Home: 11303 Winner Rd Independence MO 64052 Office: Ferrell Co Inc One Liberty Plaza Liberty MO 64068

KAUFMAN, WILLIAM WAYNE, veterinarian; b. Lima, Ohio, Mar. 25, 1949; s. William Edward and Clara Juan (Evans) K.; m. Mary Elizabeth Lehman, Sept. 14, 1969; children: Elizabeth Anne, Emily Blythe. BS in Agriculture, Ohio State U., 1970, DVM, 1975; diploma in Vet. Radiology I, Royal Coll. of Vet. Surgeons, London, 1976. Surg. intern The Royal Vet. Coll., London, 1975-77; assoc. veterinarian Fair Oaks Vet. Hosp., Lima, 1977-79; veterinarian Fair View Vet. Hosp., Lima, 1979—; bd. dirs. Animal Health Studies Inst., Lima; cons. pet therapy Oakwood Forensic Ctr., Lima, 1983—; mem. staff, bd. dirs. Equestrian Therapy, Lima, 1983—. Chmn., mem. citizens adv. bd. Oakwood Forensic Ctr., Lima, 1983—; mem. exec. com. Near West Side Neighborhood Assn., Lima, 1987. Recipient Meritorious Service award Lima-Allen County Humane Soc., 1980, Vol. Service award Oakwood Forensic Ctr., 1986, 87. Mem. Am. Vet. Med. Assn., Ohio Vet. Med. Assn., Brit. Small Animal Vet. Assn., Brit. Equine Vet. Assn., Ohio State U. Alumni Assn., Am. Animal Hosp Assn., Am. Assn. Equine Practitioners, N.Y. Acad. Scis. Methodist. Lodge: Rotary. Avocations: reading, walking, travel, tennis, camping. Home: 1434 W Market St Lima OH 45805 Office: Fair View Vet Hosp 2920 Bellefontaine Rd Lima OH 45804

KAUFMANN, URLIN MILO, English educator; b. Cleve., Aug. 27, 1934; s. Albert Walter and Alda Winona (Aiken) K.; m. Helen Elizabeth Olson, Sept. 1, 1956; children: Felice, Laurie, Andrew. BA, Greenville (Ill.) Coll., 1956; MA, U. Ill., 1957; PhD, Yale U., 1960. Instr. North Park Coll., Chgo., 1961-62; instr. U. Ill., Urbana, 1962-63, asst. prof., 1963-67, assoc. prof. English, 1967—. Author: The Pilgrim's Progress and Traditions in Puritan Meditation, 1967, Paradise in the Age of Milton, 1978, Heaven: A Future Finer Than Dreams, 1981. Pres. Light and Life men's aux. Free Meth. Ch. N.Am., Winona Lake, Ind., 1985—; bd. dirs. Empty Tomb, Inc., Urbana-Champaign, 1980—. Mem. MLA Am., Conf. on Christianity and Lit. (treas. 1962-64). Democrat. Home: 13 Concord Ln Urbana IL 61801 Office: U Ill 608 S Wright St Urbana IL 61801

KAUTZ, RICHARD CARL, chemical and feed company executive; b. Muscatine, Iowa, Aug. 1, 1916; s. Carl and Leah (Amlong) K.; m. Mary Elda Stein, Dec. 24, 1939; children: LindaKautz Osterkamp, Judith Kautz Curb, John Terry, Thomas R., Susan E. Kautz Teeple, Sarah J. Kautz Aavang, Mary Catherine Kautz Huff, Jennifer W. Kautz Kreger. Student, U. Ariz., 1936-37; BS with high distinction, U. Iowa, 1939; DHL, George Williams Coll., 1973. Supr. in fin. dept. Gen. Electric Co., 1939-43; with Grain Processing Corp. and Kent Feeds, Inc., Muscatine, 1943—, chmn. bd. dirs., mem. exec. com., 1966—; mem. adv. com. Export-Import Bank U.S., 1984—. Mem. citizens com. Rock Island dist. U.S. Army Engrs.; chmn., pres. bd. trustees, mem. Herbert Hoover Presdl. Library Assn., 1976—; chmn. nat. bd. dirs. YMCA, 1970-73, mem. exec. com. and bd. dirs.; mem. exec. com. World Alliance YMCA's, 1973—, mem. pres.'s com., exec. com.; mem. Bd. Trustees YMCA's; trustee YMCA Retirement Fund, Ctr. for Study of Presidency, 1977—; bd. dirs., mem. exec. com., chmn. Bus.-Industry Polit. Action Com., 1977—. Mem. NAM (bd. dirs., chmn. exec. com. 1977, chmn. fin. com. 1978, vice chmn. 1975, chmn. 1976), Iowa Mfrs. Assn. (bd. dirs.), Muscatine C. of C., DeMolay Legion of Honor, Beta Gamma Sigma (dirs. table), Sigma Chi (named Significant Sig.). Presbyterian. Clubs: Union League (Chgo.); Met., Capitol Hill (Washington); Marco Polo, Met., Canadian (N.Y.C.); U. Iowa Pres.'s, Univ. Athletic (Iowa City); Des Moines, Lincoln (Des Moines). Lodges: Masons, Shriners, Elks, Rotary. Home: Rural Route 4 Box 201 Muscatine IA 52761 Office: Grain Processing Corp 1600 Oregon St Muscatine IA 52761

KAVANAGH, KEVIN PATRICK, insurance company executive; b. Brandon, Man., Can., Sept. 27, 1932; s. Martin and Katherine Power K.; m. Elisabeth M. Mesman, July 1963; children: Sean K., Jennifer T. B in Communications, U. Man., 1953. With Great-West Life Assurance Co., 1953—; v.p. mktg. (U.S.) Great-West Life Assurance Co., Denver, 1973-75; v.p. group ops., head office Great-West Life Assurance Co., Winnipeg, Man., 1975-78, sr. v.p. group ops., 1978, pres., 1978—, chief exec. officer, 1979—; bd. dirs. Power Fin. Co. Former bd. dirs. Man. div. Can. Cancer Soc.; bd. govs. Man. Mus. Man and Nature; bd. dirs. Winnipeg Symphony Orch. Mem. Men's Club Winnipeg (exec. com.), Conf. Bd. Can. Clubs: Manitoba, Winnipeg Winter, Toronto. Office: Great-West Life Assurance Co, 100 Osborne St N, Winnipeg, MB Canada R3C 3A5 *

KAVANAUGH, PAUL FRED, lawyer; b. St. Louis, Mo., Aug. 24, 1959; s. Eldon J. and Virginia M. (Wallace) K.; m. Deborah L. Smith, Aug. 24, 1985. BA, Westminster Coll., 1981; JD with distinction, U. Mo., Kansas City, 1984. Bar: Mo. 1984, U.S. Dist. Ct. (we. dist.) Mo. 1984, Army Ct. Mil. Rev. 1984. Commd. 1st lt. U.S. Army, 1981, advanced through grades to capt., 1985; criminal def. atty. U.S. Army, Leavenworth, Kans., 1984-87; assoc. Lantz Welch, P.C., Kansas City, Mo., 1987—. Editor U. Mo. Kansas City Law Rev., 1982. Contbr. articles to profl. jours. Mem. ABA, Kansas City Met. Bar Assn., Assn. Trial Lawyers Am., Mo. Assn. Trial Attys., Am. Soc. Law and Medicine, Order of Bench and Robe, Phi Kappa Phi, Delta Theta Phi. Democrat. Roman Catholic. Club: Kansas City. Avocations: biking, running. Home: 3805 NW 73d St Kansas City MO 64151

KAVANAUGH CONLISK, JEAN TORTICILL TOOHEY, real estate company executive; b. Davenport, Iowa, July 23, 1934; d. John Lawrence and Jean Torticill (Murphy) Toohey; m. Thomas E. Kavanaugh, May 24, 1985 (div. Jan. 1980); children: Mike, James, Anne, Dan, Paul; m. G. Michael Conlisk, Apr. 23, 1983. BS, Marquette U., 1956; MA, Western Mich. U., 1980. Pub. relations/mass communications executive U.S. Census Bur. Kalamazoo County, Kalamazoo, Mich., 1980; broker asst. Chuck Jaqua Realtor, Kalamazoo, 1980-81; owner JKC Property Mgmt., Kalamazoo, 1982-83, R.E. Broker Vacation Places Ltd., Kalamazoo and South Haven, Mich., 1984—. Com. mem. Jr. League, Kalamazoo, 1978—, Service Club Kalamazoo, 1979—. Recipient Good Citizenship award Am. Legion, 1950. Mem. Southwestern Mich. Bd. Realtors, Soc. Real Estate Appraisers, Am. Assn. Univ. Women, Alpha Sigma Nu. Club: Tuesday Book Rev. (Kalamazoo) (pres. 1984—). Avocations: piano, tennis, bicycling, cross country skiing. Home: 15342 77th St South Haven MI 49090 Office: 546 Phoenix South Haven MI 49090

KAVKA, STEPHEN J., plastic surgeon; b. Chgo., June 15, 1941; s. Selig J. and Grace E. (Kramer) K.; m. Dorothy Cooperman, Apr. 24, 1965; children: Amy, Rebecca, Jennifer. BS, U. Chgo., 1961, MD, 1965. Diplomate Am. Bd. Plastic Surgery. Practice medicine specializing in plastic surgery Chgo., 1972—. Fellow ACS; mem. Am. Soc. Plastic and Reconstructive Surgeons, Midwest Assn. Plastic Surgeons, Chgo. Soc. Plastic Surgeons. Office: 233 E Erie St Suite 709 Chicago IL 60611

KAVLIE, GAYLORD JEROME, surgeon; b. Fairbault, Minn., Aug. 5, 1953; s. Hampton Almor and Ethel Lorraine (Schroeder) K.; m. Cynthia Kay Lennick, Aug. 18, 1973; children: Lisa, Lucas, Laura. BS, N.D. State U., 1975; BS in Medicine, U. N.D., 1977, MD, 1978. Cert. Am. Bd. Surgery. Resident gen. surgery Sacred Heart Hosp., Yankton, S.D., 1979-84, VA Hosp., Sioux Falls, S.D., 1979-84; gen. surgeon Mid-State Clinic, Harvey, N.D., 1984-85, Mid Dakota Clinic, Bismarck, N.D., 1985—; clin. assoc. dept. anatomy U. S.D., Vermillion, 1979-81, dept. surgery, Yankton, 1979-84; clin. assoc. prof. dept. surgery U.N.D., Bismarck, 1985—. Fellow Am. Soc. Abdominal Surgeons; mem. AMA, Christian Med. Soc., ACS (candidate group). Republican. Lutheran. Avocation: hunting. Home: 931 N 12th St Bismarck ND 58501 Office: Mid Dakota Clinic 401 N 9th St Bismarck ND 58501

KAWITT, ALAN, lawyer; b. Chgo., 1937. J.D., Chgo.-Kent Coll. Law, 1965; postgrad. Lawyers Inst. John Marshall Law Sch., 1966-68. Bar: Ill. 1966, U.S. Dist. Ct. (no. dist.) Ill. 1967, U.S. Ct. Appeals (7th cir.) 1971, U.S. Supreme Ct., 1971. Sole practice, 1970—. Mem. Am. Arbitration Assn. (arbitrator), Trial Lawyers Assn., Ill. Bar Assn., Ill. Trial Lawyers Assn., Chgo. Bar Assn., Decalogue Assn. Lawyers (coms. bankruptcy and reorgn., tort law, admiralty and maritime law, civil practice, mil. law). Office: 30 W Washington St Chicago IL 60602

KAY, ALBERT JOSEPH, textile executive; b. Cleve., June 3, 1920; s. Simon and Eszter (Rozensweig) K.; m. Irene Pramisloff, June 11, 1944; children: Leslie Andrzejewski, Stephen Kay, Adrienne Gallagher. Student, Cuyahoga Community Coll., 1961. Sales rep. The Carnegie Textile Co., Cleve., 1938-68, v.p., gen. mgr., 1968—. Pres. Mayfield High Sch. PTA, 1968-69; former pres. Mayfield Boys Baseball League; past sect. chmn. United Way; founder Mayfield Heights Bicentennial Com., Mayfield Area Recreation Council; mem. Citizens Com for Edn., 1968; chmn. Citizens for Honest Govt., 1965; past pres. Friends of Hillcrest Library; council mem. City Mayfield Heights, 1969—, council pres., 1981-85; campaign co-chmn. Aveni for State Rep., Ohio, 1975; mem. exec. com. Hillcrest Dem. Caucus, Acad. Booster's Club; former chmn. planning and zoning commn. City of Mayfield Heights. Served with U.S. Army, 1943. Recipient Community Service award Nat. Exchange Club, 1984, Outstanding Service award Mayfield Heights C. of C., 1979, Citizenship award VFW, 1976. Mem. Internat. Assn. Wiping Cloth Mfrs. (bd. dirs. 1981-85, Outstanding and Dedicated Service award 1985), Am. Assn. Retired Persons. Democrat. Jewish. Club: Jewish War Vets. (Cleve.) (comdr. 1946-48). Lodge: Masons. Avocations: polit. activity, piano. Home: 1835 Beham Dr Mayfield Heights OH 44124 Office: The Carnegie Textile Co 1734 Ivanhoe Rd East Cleveland OH 44112

KAY, ARLAN KEPPY, architect; b. Davenport, Iowa, Mar. 8, 1943; s. Ralph Henry and Irma Amanda (Keppy) K.; m. Lori Meier, Aug. 22, 1964; children: Heidi Kaarin, Erik Andrew, Kietra Chantal. BArch, Iowa State U., 1966. Registered architect, Wis. Draftsman Louis C. Kingscott, Madison, Wis., 1963-67; designer, drafter Ames Torkelson & Assocs., Madison, 1967-70; architect Marshall Erdman, Madison, 1971-73, Krueger/Shutter, Madison, 1973; architect, dir. Design Coalition, Madison, 1972-75; architect, owner Arlan Kay & Assocs., Madison and Oreg., Wis., 1974—; vice chmn. State of Wis. Architects Exam Bd., Madison, 1983—. V.p. Wis. Citizens for Arts, Madison, 1984-85. Mem. AIA, Wis. Soc. Architects (treas. 1973), Nat. Council Archtl. Registration Bds. (vice-chair region 4, examination writer nat. architects exam 1986-87, exam planning com. 1987—). Democrat. Lutheran. Lodge: Rotary (pres. Oreg. club 1981-82). Avocations: photography, bicycle touring, wine making. Home: 5685 Lincoln Rd Oregon WI 53575 Office: 110 King St Madison WI 53703

KAY, DONNA IRENE, newspaper publisher; b. Cambridge, Ohio, Jan. 24, 1920; d. James Clark and Nettie Alice (Cunningham) Booth; m. Wendell Earl Kay, Aug. 31, 1946 (dec. Nov. 1979); children: David William, Richard Dale, Timothy Clark. AS in Bus. Adminstrn., Youngstown (Ohio) U., 1939. Jr. interviewer Ohio State Employment Service, Warren, 1939-42; exec. sec. Copperweld Steel, Warren, 1942-45; bus. mgr. and asst. to pub. Phoenix Publs., Niles, Ohio, 1956-81, pub., 1981—. Sec., bd. dirs. Trumbull County ARC, Warren, 1985-86; bd. dirs. Tri-County Easter Seal Soc., Youngstown, 1983—, adv. bd. Trumbull County Chpt., Warren, 1983—; bd. dirs. Pvt. Industry Council, Niles, 1983—, Eastern Ohio Lung Assn., Youngstown, 1986-87. Mem. Nat. Newspaper Assn., Ohio Newspaper Assn., Niles Area C. of C. (bd. dirs. 1984—, Disting. Service award 1985). Republican. Methodist. Lodges: Altrusa (pres., bd. dirs. Warren chpt. 1968—, 2d vice gov. internat. chpt.), Order of Eastern Star. Avocations: golf, reading, travel. Home: 1237 Niles Cortland Rd Niles OH 44446 Office: Phoenix Publs Inc 35 W State St Niles OH 44446

KAY, JERALD, child psychiatry educator, researcher; b. Washington, Mar. 26, 1945; s. Max and Miriam (Schwartz) K.; m. Rena Lynn Victor, Aug. 17, 1968; children: Sarah Jennifer, Rachel Hannah, Jonathan Emile. BA, Washington U., 1967; MD, U. Md., 1971; diploma, Cin. Psychoanalytic Inst., 1984. Diplomate Am. Bd. Psychiatry and Neurology. Instr. child psychiatry U. Cin. Coll. Medicine, 1971-77, asst. prof. child psychiatry, 1977-82, assoc. prof. child psychiatry, 1982—; dir. med. student edn. U. Cin. Dept. Psychiatry, 1975-82, dir. residency tng., 1982—. Contbr. articles on child and adult psychiatry, psychoanalysis, ethics, psychiatric edn. to profl. jours. Recipient Golden Apple Teaching award U. Cin. Coll. Medicine, 1979. Fellow Am. Psychiat. Assn. (chmn. med. studies edn. com. 1982-86, council med. edn., career devel. 1986—, mem. com. on psychotherapy, program com.); mem. Am. Acad. Child, Adolescent Psychiatry, Am. Assn. Directors of Psychiatry Residency Tng. (pres.-elect 1987—). Avocations: playing jazz drums, tuba, reading. Home: 4192 Rose Hill Ave Cincinnati OH 45229 Office: U Cin Coll Medicine Dept Psychiatry 231 Bethesda Ave Cincinnati OH 45267-0559

KAY, PETER PATRICK, plastic and reconstructive surgeon, cranio maxillo facial specialist; b. Kroonstad, South Africa, Apr. 14, 1949; came to U.S., 1977; s. Patrick Anthony Barrington and Elizabeth Margaret (Rooke) K.; m. Melinda Marie Harrison, Oct. 21, 1985. B in Medicine, BCHir, U. Witwatersrand, Johannesburg, South Africa, 1974. Diplomate Am. Bd. Otolaryngology, Am. Bd. Plastic Surgery. Intern Johannesburg (South Africa) Gen. Hosp., 1975, sr. house officer orthopedics, 1976; resident in gen. surgery Cleve. Clinic Found., Cleve., 1977-79; resident in otolaryngology, 1979-82, resident in plastic surgery, 1982-84; fellow in craniofacial surgery Hosp. for Sick Children, Toronto, Can., 1985; plastic and reconstructive surgeon Mayo Clinic, Rochester, Minn., 1985-86, cons. div. plastic surgery, asst. prof., 1987—; sr. cons. div. plastic surgery Scott & White, Temple, Tex., 1985-86; asst. prof. Tex. A&M U., Temple, 1985-86. Served to 2d lt. M.C. South African Army, 1967. Crile travelling scholar Cleve. Clinic Found., 1984. Fellow Royal Coll. of Surgeons Can., Royal Coll. Surgeons Edinburgh (G.B. Ong medal 1986); mem. AMA, Am. Cleft Palate Assn. Roman Catholic. Avocations: short wave radio listening, classical music, travel, african politics. Home: 310 8th Ave SW Rochester MN 55902 Office: Mayo Clinic Div Plastic Surgery Rochester MN 55905

KAYE, RICHARD WILLIAM, utility company executive; b. Chgo., May 14, 1939; s. Albert Louis and Helen (Beckman) K.; m. Betty Ann Terry, Aug. 7, 1964; children: Ronald, William, Richard, Timothy. AB, Cornell U., 1960; MBA, Columbia U., 1962. Various fin. positions Inland Steel Co., Chgo., 1964-81; dir. info. services No. Ind. Pub. Service Co., Hammond, Ind., 1981-86, dir. econ. analysis, 1986—. Advisor Calumet Coll., Whiting, Ind., 1985—. Served to lt. (j.g.) USNR. Mem. Am. Mgmt. Assn., Cornell U. Alumni Assn., Columbia U. Alumni Assn. Lodge: Rotary. Avocations: tennis, golf. Home: 2801 Cherrywood Ln Hazel Crest IL 60429 Office: No Ind Pub Service Co 5265 Hohman Ave Hammond IN 46325

KAYE, ROBERT CHARLES, physician; b. East Chicago, Ind., Aug. 2, 1947; s. Frank and Helen Kaye; m. Cheryl Ann Peifer, Aug. 21, 1970; children: Leslie Suzanne, Bradley Robert. BS in Pharmacy, Purdue U., 1970; MD, Ind. U., 1974. Diplomate Am. Bd. Family Practice. Resident physician Santa Monica (Calif.) Hosp. Med. Ctr., 1974-77; practice family medicine Rensselaer, Ind., 1977—; chief of staff Jasper County Hosp., Rensselaer, Ind., 1984—. Mem. AMA, Ind. State Med. Assn., Am. Acad. Family Practice, Ind. Acad. Family Practice, Jasper County Med. Soc. (pres. 1984—). Home: Rural Rt #3 Box 174A Rensselaer IN 47978 Office: 1103 E Grace St Rensselaer IN 47978

KAYLARIAN, VICTOR HARRY, osteopathic physician; b. Springfield, Mass., Sept. 28, 1944; s. Victor Zadig and Perina (Messerlian) K. BS, Northeast Mo. State U., 1968; DO, Phila. Coll. Osteo. Medicine, 1976. Diplomate Am. Bd. Internal Medicine. Intern Botsford Gen. Hosp., Farmington, Mich., 1976-77; resident in internal medicine Cleve. Clinic Found., 1977-80; emergency room physician Hillcrest Hosp., Cleve., 1980-81; assoc. prof. medicine U. Osteo. Medicine, Des Moines, 1981—, chmn. dept. medicine, 1984—; pres. faculty U. Osteo. Medicine, 1985-86. Served to lt. comdr. USN, 1968-72, with Res., 1972-80. Named Disitng. Naval Grad., 1969. Mem. Am. Osteo. Assn., ACP, Am. Soc. Internal Medicine, Am. Diabetes Assn. Avocations: sailing, amateur radio, skiing. Home: 6479 James Francis Pl Johnston IA 50131 Office: U Osteo Medicine 3200 Grand Ave Des Moines IA 50312

KAYLOE, JUDITH CAROLYN, psychotherapist; b. Bronx, N.Y., Aug. 9, 1941; d. Isadore C and Myra (Simon) Rubin; m. Alvin Kayloe, June 15, 1967; children—Lili, Jordan, Rachel. B.A. in Psychology, Wittenberg U., 1969; M.A. in Clin. Psychology, U. Dayton, 1976; postgrad. Kent State U. Care agy. counselor, psychotherapist, 1977—. Contbr. articles to profl. jours. Mem., exec. com. citizens council Fedn. Community Planning, 1980—; instr. local community colls., community edn. Recipient Richter Fund award, Jewish Found. Edn. Girls, 1974-75. Mem. Am. Psychol. Assn., Ohio Assn. Counseling Devel. Cleve. Psychol. Assn., Internat. Assn. Psycho-Social Rehab., Chi Sigma Iota, Kappa Delta Pi. Democrat. Jewish. Founder FIND program for after-care of psychiat. patients. Home: 19482 Albion Rd Strongville OH 44136 Office: Far West Center 29133 Health Campus Dr Westlake OH 44145

KAYNE, JON BARRY, industrial psychologist; b. Sioux City, Iowa, Oct. 20, 1943; s. Harry Aaron and Barbara Valentine (Daniel) K.; m. Bunee Ellen Price, July 25, 1965; children: Nika Jenine, Abraham; m. 2d Sandra Kay Fossbender, Jan. 5, 1985; 1 child, Shay-Marie Kathryn. BA, U. Colo., 1973; MSW, U. Denver, 1975; PhD, U. No. Colo., 1978. With spl. services Weld County Sch. Dist. 6, Greeley, Colo., 1975-77; forensic diagnostician Jefferson County (Colo.) Diagnostic Unit, 1977-78; assoc., dir. mktg. 1 Dow Ctr., assoc. prof. psychology Hillsdale (Mich.) Coll., 1978—; pres. Jon B. Kayne, P.C., Hillsdale, 1980—; chmn. bd. dirs., chief exec. officer Am. Internat. Mgmt. Assocs., Ltd., Denver, 1984—. Chmn. bd. dirs. Domestic Harmony, 1979-82; dir. religious sch., Greeley, 1975-77; candidate for sheriff of Boulder County, 1974. Served with USAR, 1962. Mem. Am. Psychol. Assn., Am. Soc. Clin. Hypnosis, Am. Statis. Assn., Internat. Neuropsychol. Soc., Mich. Soc. Investigative and Forensic Hypnosis (chmn. bd., pres. 1982), N.Y.

Acad. Scis., Phi Delta Kappa, Psi Chi, Alpha Gamma Sigma. Home: Bellevue Coll Galvin Rd at Harvell Dr Bellevue NE 68005

KAYS, ARNOLD ROBERT, manufacturing company executive; b. Covington, Ohio, Dec. 6, 1924; s. Vallis P. and Ruth N. (Rothrock) K.; m. Nellie Kathren Gray, Feb. 24, 1945; children: Sharon Ann, William Vallis, Ruth Jean. BS in Mech. Engring., Rose Poly. Inst., 1944. Registered profl. engr., Ind. Elec. engr. Seeger Refrigeration Co., Evansville, Ind., 1945-51; elec. engr. Am. Kitchens div. AVCO, Connersville, Ind., 1951-56, mgr. elec., mech. depts., 1956-59; project engr. Design and Mfr. Corp., Connersville, 1959-82; mgr. research and devel. Design and Mfg. Corp., Connersville, 1982—; also bd. dirs.; chmn. dishwasher engring. com. Nat. Elec. Mfrs. Assn., N.Y.C., 1957-59, Assn. Home Appliance Mfrs., Chgo., 1969-87. Edn. officer U.S. Power Squadrons, Raleigh, N.C., 1982-85. Mem. NSPE, Ind. Soc. Profl. Engrs. (sec., treas. 1975), Industry Adv. Underwriters Lab. (mem. council dishwashers 1970—). Baptist. Club: Connersville Country. Avocations: golf, boating. Home: 804 Village Creek Dr Connersville IN 47331 Office: Design & Mfg Corp 2000 Illinois Ave Connersville IN 47331

KAYTON, LAWRENCE, psychiatrist; b. Chgo., Apr. 12, 1938; s. Basil and Belle Kayton; m. Sandra D. Kayton, Apr. 6, 1984; children: Todd, Cheryl, Sarahbeth, Seth. BA, U. Ill., 1960; MD, U. Ill., Chgo., 1963. Diplomate Am. Bd. Psychiatry and Neurology. Intern U. Mich. Hosps., Ann Arbor, 1963-64; resident in psychiatry Michael Reese Med. Ctr., Chgo., 1964-69; practice medicine specializing in psychiatry Chgo., 1969—; dir. tng. Michael Reese Med. Ctr., Chgo., 1969-76; clin. dir. psychiatry MacNeal Meml. Hosp., Berwyn, Ill., 1985—; assoc. clin. prof. psychiatry Loyola U. Med. Ctr., 1986—; research dir. schizophrenia project Michael Reese Med. Ctr., 1969-76; sr. cons. adolescent psychiatry Ill. State Psychiat. Inst., 1969-83; assoc. clin. prof. psychiatry Loyola U. Med. Ctr., Maywood, Ill., 1986—. Contbr. articles on schizophrenia to profl. jours. Served to maj. Med. Service Corps, 1967-69, Korea. Fellow Am. Psychiat. Assn.; mem. AAAS, Am. Soc. Adolescent Psychiatry, Alpha Omega Alpha, Phi Beta Kappa. Avocation: racquetball. Office: 111 N Wabash Chicago IL 60602

KAZAN, ROBERT PETER, neurosurgeon; b. Chgo., Mar. 29, 1947; s. Peter Joseph and Genevieve (Pauga) K.; m. Janet Rae Hoiland, June 21, 1975. BS, Loyola U., Chgo., 1969, MD, 1973. Diplomate Am. Bd. Neurol. Surgeons; lic. physician Ill., Minn. Intern in surgery Mayo Clinic, Rochester, Minn., 1973-74, resident in neurosurgery, 1974-78; neurosurg. cons. West Suburban Neurosurg. Assocs., Hinsdale, Ill., 1978—; clin. asst. prof. neurosurgery U. Ill., Chgo., 1983—; various teaching appointments West Suburban Hosp. Dept. Surgery, Chgo. Med. Soc. Midwest Conf., Northwestern U.; staff neurosurgeon Hinsdale Hosp. Contbr. articles to profl. jours. Fellow ACS; mem. AMA, Chgo. Med.Soc., Ill. Med.Soc., Mayo Clin Neurosurg. Soc., Congress of Neurosurg. Surgeons, Am. Assn. Neurol. Surgeosn, Cen. Neurosurg. Soc. Republican. Roman Catholic. Home: 120 Lakewood Circle Burr Ridge IL 60521 Office: West Suburban Neurosurg Assocs 20 E Ogden Hinsdale IL 60521

KAZIMIERCZUK, MARIAN KAZIMIERZ, electrical engineer, educator; b. Smolugi, Poland, Mar. 3, 1948; came to U.S., 1984; s. Stanislaw and Stanislawa (Tomaszewska) K.; m. Alicja Nowowiejska, July 5, 1973; children: Andrzej, Anna. MS, Tech. U. of Warsaw, Poland, 1971, PhD, 1978, DSc, 1984. Instr. elec. engring. Tech. U. of Warsaw, Poland, 1972-78, asst. prof., 1978-84; project engr. Design Automation, Inc., Lexington, Mass., 1984; vis. prof. Va. Poly. Inst., Blacksburg, 1984-85, Wright State U., Dayton, Ohio, 1985—. Contbr. numerous articles to profl. jours.; patentee in field. Recipient Univ. Edn. and Tech. award Polish Ministry of Sci., 1981, 84, 85, Polish Acad. Sci. award 1983. Mem. Assn. Polish Engrs., Polish Soc. Theoretical and Applied Elec. Scis. Roman Catholic. Home: 35 Old Yellow Springs Rd Apt F Fairborn OH 45324 Office: Wright State U Dept Elec Systems Engring Dayton OH 45435

KAZMIERZAK, MITCHELL JOSEPH, landscape architect; b. South Bend, Ind., Nov. 20, 1923; s. Joseph John and Lillian Lewosia (Kukla) K.; m. Eleanor Juliann Jagodzinski, Mar. 1, 1945; children: David Alan, Michael Lee. Student, Notre DAme U., 1940-41; cert., Nat. Landscape Inst., Calif., 1946-47, South Bend Bus. Coll., H.R. Block Tax Sch. Cert. landscape architect. Prin. Mitchell and Sons, South Bend, 1947—; cons. landscape South Bend, 1947—; ptnr. Frepan Floral. Dir. religion edn. CCD, youth minister St. John the Bapt., South Bend, 1983-87. Served to sgt. U.S. Army, 1943-46, PTO. Mem. Ind. Assn. Nurserymen (bd. dirs., past pres., edn. com.). Avocation: oil painting. Home: 23436 Lawrence St South Bend IN 46628 Office: Mitchell and Sons 23405 Ardmore Trail South Bend IN 46628

KAZRAGYS, LINDA KAYAN BUBLIS, teacher; b. East Chicago, Ind., Nov. 26, 1946; d. Bert Charles and Iram Aldonna (Matuck) Bublis; m. Vitas Joseph Kazragys, June 22, 1968; children: Amanda, Julianna, Adam. BSE, Ball State U., 1968; MSE, Purdue U., 1984. Elem. tchr. East Chicago Pub. Schs., 1968-70, 73-78; dir. nursery sch. St. John the Bapt. Sch., Whiting, Ind., 1978-83, elem. tchr. Dicoese of Gary, 1983—, Cath. youth moderator, mem. home and sch. com. Dir. adult edn. Girl Scouts Calumet County, Highland, Ind., 1982-84. Recipient St. Anne's award Girl Scouts of Calumet Council, Gary, Ind., 1972, Thanks Badge, Highland, Ind., 1978. Mem. Nat. Cath. Educators Assn. Democrat. Avocations: traveling, outdoor activities, reading, art, music. Home: 2028 Lake Ave Whiting IN 46394 Office: St John the Bapt Sch 1844 Lincoln Ave Whiting IN 46394

KAZYAK, RONALD DUANE, auditor; b. Bay City, Mich., Dec. 8, 1960; s. Michael Edward and Marion (Prihan) K. AA, Delta Coll., 1981; BS, Cen. Mich. U., 1983; MBA, Western Mich. U., 1987. CPA, Mich. Sr. auditor Yeo & Yeo, Kalamazoo, 1983-86; corp. auditor The Upjohn Co., Kalamazoo, 1986. Mem. Am. Inst. CPA's, Mich. Assn CPA's. Roman Catholic. Club: SW Mich. Gun. Avocations: hunting, fishing, weightlifting, reading, skiing. Home: 1547 Concord Pl #3-B Kalamazoo MI 49009 Office: The Upjohn Co 7000 Portage Rd Kalamazoo MI 49001

KEANEY, WILLIAM REGIS, engineering and construction services executive, consultant; b. Pitts., Nov. 2, 1937; s. William Regis Sr. and Emily Elizabeth (Campi) K.; m. Sharon Lee Robinson, Feb. 23, 1956; children: William R., James A., Robert E., Susan Elizabeth. BBA in Mktg. and Internat. Mktg., Ohio State U., 1961. Sales engr. Burdett Oxygen Co., Cleve., 1961-64, A.O. Smith Co., Milw., 1964-66; pres. W.R. Keaney & Co., Columbus, Ohio, 1966-71, Power Equipment Service Corp., Columbus, 1971-80, Gen. Assocs. Corp., Worthington, Ohio, 1980—; cons. Mannesmann, Houston, 1984-85, TVA, Knoxville, 1984-86, Power Authority of N.Y., White Plains, 1985-86, Utility Power Corp., Atlanta, 1985-86; mem. various task forces in the field. Vol. Cen. Ohio Lung Assn., Columbus, 1984-86. Mem. Am. Welding Soc., Welding Research Council. Democrat. Methodist. Club: Mil. Vehicle Collectors (Ohio). Lodge: Masons. Avocations: antique cars, genealogy, camping, photography. Home: 1314 Oakview Dr Worthington OH 43085 Office: Gen Assocs Corp PO Box 762 Worthington OH 43085

KEARBY, PAUL DOYLE, minister; b. Oklahoma City, Nov. 30, 1955; s. John C. and Elaine F. (Pollard) K.; m. Teresa A. Smith, Dec. 31, 1977; children: Laura Beth, Stephen Paul. BS in Bibl. Studies, Okla. Christian Coll., 1979. Assoc. minister Mayfair Ch. of Christ, Oklahoma City, 1978-79; minister Wayne (Okla.) Ch. of Christ, 1979-81, Ch. of Christ, Alva, Okla., 1981-82, Cherry Hill Ch. of Christ, Joliet, Ill., 1982-84; chaplain Joliet Correctional Ctr., 1982-84; minister Ch. of Christ, Valparaiso, Ind., 1984—; chaplain Westville (Ind.) Correctional Inst., 1985-86; missionary work Austria, Hungary and Yugoslavia, 1977-78; tchr., co-dir. Lariet Creek Christian Camp, Okla., 1979-82; tchr, counselor Rockford (Ill.) Christian Camp, 1982—; teaching house parent Shults-Lewis Child and Family Care Agy., Valparaiso, 1984-86. Author: Historical Outlines of Old Testament Characters, 1979, Accepting God's Power, 1981, Detours, Dead Ends and Dry Holes, 1982, Marriage, Divorce and Remarriage, 1985; co-host radio program, 1981-82; featured columnist The Paul's Valley Dem., 1980, The Alva Rev. Courier, 1981-82. Named one of Outstanding Young Men of Am., 1982, 83. Club: Exchange (Joliet). Lodge: Rotary (bd. dirs. Alva club 1982). Avocations: writing, golfing, softball. Home: 363-2 E County Rd 300 S Valparaiso IN 46383 Office: Valparaiso Ch of Christ 1155 Sturdy Rd Valparaiso IN 46383

KEARNS, MARY LOU, coroner, nurse; b. Chgo., May 5, 1944; d. Joseph Michael and Mary (Comiskey) Kearns; 1 son, Joseph Michael. R.N., St. Anne's Hosp., 1965; B.S., No. Ill. U., 1976; M.P.H., U. Ill.-Chgo., 1981. R.N. Staff nurse med. and trauma units, Cook County Hosp., Chgo., 1965-66; coronary and intensive care nurse Delnor Hosp., St. Charles, Ill., 1966-67; trauma nurse specialist, head nurse and in-service instr. Cook County Hosp., 1967-72; hosp. care program coordinator Chgo. Med. Found., State of Ill., 1972-73; emergency room nurse St. Joseph Hosp., Elgin, Ill., 1974-75; nursing supr. Community Hosp., Geneva, Ill., 1976; coroner of Kane County, Geneva, 1976—; lectr. in field. Contbr. articles to med. and nursing jours. Dem. Candidate U.S. Ho. Reps. 14th Dist. Ill., 1986. Named Ill. Outstanding Women of Yr., 1978; recipient Resolution of Commendation Ill. Nurses Assn., 1977. Fellow Am. Acad. Forensic Sci.; pres. Kane County Chiefs Assn. (pres. 1983), Ill. Coroners Assn. (v.p. 1983, pres. elect 1984), Internat. Coroners and Med. Examiners, Nat. Women's Polit. Caucus. Democrat. Roman Catholic. Home: 603 S 13th Ave Saint Charles IL 60174 Office: Kane County Govt 719 Batavia Ave Geneva IL 60134

KEARNS, MERLE GRACE, county official; b. Bellefonte, Pa., May 19, 1938; d. Robert John and Mary Catharine (Fitzgerald) Grace; m. Thomas Raymond Kearns, June 27, 1959; children—Thomas, Michael, Timothy, Matthew. B.S., Ohio State U., 1960. Tchr. St. Raphael Elem. Sch., Springfield, Ohio, 1960-62; substitute tchr. Mad River Green dist., Springfield, 1972-78; instr. Clark Tech. Coll., Springfield, 1978-80; commr. Clark County, Ohio, 1981—; pres. bd. county commrs., 1982, 83, 86, 87, v.p., 1985. Bd. dirs. Springfield Symphony, 1980-86, Arts Council, 1980-85; mem. exec. com. Springfield Republicans, 1984—. Ohio State U., scholar, 1957-59; named Woman of Yr. Springfield Pilot Club, 1981. Mem. Abilities Unltd. Network, County Commrs. Assn. of Ohio (bd. dirs. 1985—, welfare adv. com. 1984—), Southwest Commrs. of Ohio (pres. 1985, sec., v.p. 1983-84), LWV (bd. dirs. 1964—, pres. 1975-78), Omicron Nu. Roman Catholic. Avocations: reading; golf. Home: 2664 Brookdale Dr Springfield OH 45502 Office: Bd Clark County Commrs 31 N Limestone St Springfield OH 45502

KEARNS, MICHAEL JAMES, television photographer; b. Stevens Point, Wis., Feb. 10, 1951; s. Dennis Joseph and Irene Loretta (Malek) Wanserski; m. Beverly Kay Kearns, July 21, 1979. BS, U. Wis., Stevens Point, 1976. New photographer Sta. WSAU-TV, Wausau, Wis., 1976-78; news photographer Sta. WISC-TV, Madison, Wis., 1978-81; photographer, eassignment editor Sta. WLUK-TV, Green Bay, Wis., 1981—. Sound editor (ednl. film) 99 Bottles: Responsibility in Drinking, 1976 (Hon. Mention award N.Y. Film Festival, 1981). Served with U.S. Army, 1970-72. Mem. Nat. Press Photographers Assn. Democratic. Roman Catholic. Avocations: golf, running, tennis, picture framing. Home: 1417 W Lorain Ct Appleton WI 54914

KEATING, MICHAEL JOSEPH, lawyer; b. St. Louis, June 8, 1954; s. John David and Patricia Ann (Sullivan) K.; m. Maureen Ann Moder, Aug. 28, 1981; children: Sarah Kathleen, Brendan Michael. A.B., Washington U., St. Louis, 1976; J.D., St. Louis U., 1979. Bar: Mo. 1979, Ill. 1980. Law clk. Mo. Ct. Appeals, St. Louis, 1979-80, U.S. Dist. Ct. (ea. dist.) Mo., St. Louis, 1980-81; assoc. Bryan, Cave, McPheeters & McRoberts, St. Louis, 1981-83; corp. atty. Emerson Electric Co., St. Louis, 1983-85, sr. atty., 1985-87, asst. gen. counsel product liability, 1987—. Mem. St. Louis U. Law Jour., 1977-79, mng. editor, 1978-79. Mem. ABA (chmn. subcom. on product liability compliance program litigation sect. 1984—), Sigma Alpha Epsilon, Phi Delta Phi, Pi Sigma Alpha. Roman Catholic. Club: Mo. Athletic (St. Louis). Home: 891 Totem Woods Ct Saint Louis MO 63021 Office: Emerson Electric Co PO Box 4100 8000 W Florissant Saint Louis MO 63136

KEATON, WILLIAM RICHARD, manufacturing engineer; b. Chgo., Sept. 29, 1955; s. Albert William and Dorothy Mae (Agnos) K.; m. Robin Sue Lussow; 1 child, Susan Christine. BS in Engring. Ops., Iowa State U., 1977. Various mfg. engring. positions GTE Automatic Electric Corp., Northlake, Ill., 1977-81; sr. mfg. engr. GTE Corp., Genoa, Ill., 1981—. Patentee photoresist exposure method. Dir. Genoa-Kingston (Ill.) United Way, 1983—, pres., 1984; sec. Genoa Planning Comm., 1986—; mem. adv. bd. Kishwaukee Jr. Coll., 1987—. DeKalb County Indsl. Mgmt. Club (mem. nominating com. 1987). Lodge: Lions (bd. dirs. Genoa club 1984—). Avocations: golf, fishing, skiing. Home: Rt 1 Box 215 Genoa IL 60135

KEATS, GLENN ARTHUR, manufacturing company executive; b. Chgo., July 1, 1920; s. Herbert J. and Agnes H. (Streich) K.; m. Olga Maria Loor Hurtado, Feb. 13, 1946; children—Maria Susana Keats Eggemeyer, Allwyn Dolores Keats Gustafson. BS in Commerce, Northwestern U., 1941. Sales exec. Keats-Lorenz Spring Co., Chgo., 1947-56; controller, auditor Plantaciones Ecuatorianas, S.A., Guayaquil, Ecuador, 1956-58; co-founder, sec.-treas. Keats Mfg. Co., Evanston, Ill., 1958—; bd. dirs. Bullock Keats, Ltd., Eng. Sec. Hispanic Soc. Chgo., 1965—. Served to lt. comdr. USN, 1941-47. Mem. Spring Mfrs. Inst., Northwestern U. Alumni Assn., Sigma Nu. Republican. Lutheran. Club: Evanston Golf. Home: 368 Woodland Rd Highland Park IL 60035 Office: 1227 Dodge Ave Evanston IL 60202

KEATS, ROGER ALAN, state senator, business executive; b. Cleve., Aug. 12, 1948; s. Robert L. and Margaret Anne (Achelpohl) K.; B.A., U. Mich.; M.A., U. Ill. Mem. Ill. Ho. of Reps., 1976-79; mem. Ill. Senate, 1979—. Served with armor br. U.S. Army, 1972-74, USAR, 1976—. Republican. Evangelical. Office: State Capitol Springfield IL 62706

KECK, ROBERT CLIFTON, lawyer; b. Sioux City, Iowa, May 20, 1914; s. Herbert Allen and Harriet (McCutchen) K.; m. Ruth P. Edwards, Nov. 2, 1940 (dec.); children: Robert, Laura E. Simpson, Gloria E. Sauser; m. Laryne E. Geroge, June 20, 1987. A.B., Ind. U., 1936; J.D., U. Mich., 1939; L.H.D., Nat. Coll. Edn., 1973. Bar: Ill. 1939. Since practiced in Chgo; mem. firm Keck, Mahin & Cate, 1939—, partner, 1946—; sec., dir. Methode Electronics, Inc.; bd. dirs. Schwinn Bicycle Co. Chmn. bd. trustees Nat. Coll. Edn., 1955—; trustee Sears Roebuck Found., 1977-79. Served with USNR, 1943-45. Fellow Am. Coll. Trial Lawyers; mem. ABA, Fed. Bar Assn., Ill. Bar Assn., Chgo. Bar assn. Seventh Fed. Circuit (past pres.), Phi Gamma Delta. Republican. Methodist. Clubs: Westmoreland Country (Wilmette); Economic, Chicago, Metropolitan; Biltmore Forest Golf (Asheville, N.C.); Glen View (Golf, Ill.). Lodge: Masons. Office: Sears Tower 83rd Floor Chicago IL 60606

KEDDLE, DAVID GLEN, library administrator; b. Howell, Mich., Jan. 27, 1951; s. Glen Joseph and Burla Alfreda (Doherty) K.; m. Cynthia Louise Conley, Jan. 12, 1980; children: Jenny Sue, Michael David. AA in Bus. and Library, Lansing Community Coll. (Mich.), 1972. Dir. John W. Chi Meml. Med. Library, Ingham Med. Ctr., Lansing, 1973—. Sec. Livingston County Rep. Com., 1974-78. Mem. Lansing Area Library Assn. (pres. 1979-80), Med. Library Assn., Capital Area Library Network (bd. dirs. 1981—), Mich. Health Scis. Libraries Assn. (chmn. 1974-79, bd. dirs. 1977-80, state council bd. 1984-86, chmn. union list of serials 1986-87, ad hoc com. electronic mail 1985, grants com. 1986-87), Spl. Library Assn., ALA, Mich. Library Assn., Holt Jaycees (chpt. and newsletter editor 1984-85, individual devel. v.p., pres. 1985-86, chmn. bd. 1986-87; named Jaycee of Yr. 1984-85). Methodist. Office: Ingham Med Ctr Med Library 401 W Greenlawn Ave Lansing MI 48910

KEDO, PAUL NICHOLAS, information systems manager; b. Chgo., July 16, 1949; s. Nicholas Alexander and Helen (Norek) K. BFA, U. Iowa, 1971; MFA, Northwestern U., 1974, MBA, 1983; postgrad., DePaul U., 1986—. Advt. mgr. Creative Interiors, Chgo., 1971-72; data processing mgr. Bell and Howell Video, Northbrook, Ill., 1975-80; programmer, analyst GATX Corp., Chgo., 1980-81; info. systems mgr. IC Industries, Chgo., 1981—. Mem. Data Processing Mgmt. Assn., Assn. Computing Machinery. Avocation: flying. Office: IC Industries 111 E Wacker Dr Chicago IL 60601

KEEHN, SILAS, banker; b. New Rochelle, N.Y., June 30, 1930; s. Grant and Marjorie (Burchard) K.; m. Marcia June Lindquist, Mar. 26, 1955; children: Elisabeth Keehn Lewis, Britta, Peter. A.B. in Econs, Hamilton Coll., Clinton, N.Y., 1952; M.B.A. in Fin, Harvard U., 1957. With Mellon Bank N.A., Pitts., 1957-80; v.p., then sr. v.p. Mellon Bank N.A., 1967-78, exec. v.p., 1978-79, vice chmn., 1980; v.p. Mellon Nat. Corp., 1979-80, vice chmn., 1980; chmn. bd. Pullman, Inc., Chgo., 1980; pres. Fed. Res. Bank Chgo., 1981—. Charter trustee Hamilton Coll.; trustee Rush-Presbyn.-St. Luke's Med. Center; mem. Northwestern U. Assocs.; bd. dirs. United Way/Crusade of Mercy, United Way Chgo.; mem. governing bd. Ill. Council on Econ. Edn. Served with USNR, 1953-56. Mem. Chgo. Council on Fgn. Relations (dir.), Chgo. Assn. Commerce and Industry (dir.). Clubs: Chgo; Commercial (Chgo.), Economic (Chgo.) (bd. dirs.); Fox Chapel Golf (Pitts.); University (Chgo.); Links (N.Y.C.); Rolling Rock (Ligonier, Pa.); Bankers, Indian Hill. Office: Fed Res Bank of Chgo 230 S LaSalle St Chicago IL 60690

KEELING, RICHARD MICHAEL, data processing executive; b. Guildford, Eng., Aug. 15, 1957; s. Michael David and Joanna Margaret (Day) K.; m. Cynthia Anne Larson, May 23, 1981. BS, Sussex U., Falmer, Eng., 1980. Sr. research asst. U. Mo., Columbia, 1981-82; data processing mgr., asst. company sec. St. Louis Steel Casting, Inc., 1984—; purchasing agent St. Louis Steel Castings, Inc. Avocations: music, literature, fantasy gaming. Office: St Louis Steel Casting 100 Mott St Saint Louis MO 63111

KEENAN, FREDERICK, investment and property management executive; b. Evanston, Ill., Apr. 27, 1944; s. Phillips and Emily Lora (Wylie) K.; m. Katharine Howe French, Dec. 20, 1969; children: Whitney, Emily. AB, Brown U., 1966; MBA, U. Pa., 1972. Account exec. Chapman Direct Mktg., N.Y.C., 1972-76; sr. account exec. N.W. Ayer, N.Y.C., 1976-78; account supr. Chapman Direct Mktg., N.Y.C., 1978-79; direct mail mgr. Garden Way Assocs., Norwalk, Conn., 1979-80; mng. ptnr. Wylie Resources Ltd., Lake Forest, Ill., 1980—; bd. dirs. DD&B Stiles, Waukegan, Ill.; sales assoc. L. Phelps Real Estate, Chgo., 1983—. Served to lt. USN, 1966-72. Republican. Avocations: sailing, skiing. Office: Wylie Resources Ltd PO Box 664 Lake Forest IL 60045

KEENER, DOUGLAS MARTIN, metallurgic and nondestructive testing research analyst; b. Ashland, Ohio, July 27, 1946; s. Guy Franklin and Harriet Estel (Abrams) K.; m. Suzanne Elizabeth Michael, Sept. 3, 1967; 1 child, Scott Michael. AS in Metallurgy, Mansfield (Ohio) Sch. Tech., 1966. Technician Timken Research Co., Canton, Ohio, 1966-69, research technician, 1969-75, sr. research technician, 1975-80, tech. analyst, 1980-83, sr. tech. analyst, 1983-85, sr. research analyst, 1985—. Mem. Am. Soc. Nondestructive Testing. Lodge: KC. Avocations: woodworking, camping, fishing. Office: Timken Co 1835 Dueber Canton OH 44706

KEENEY, MARISA GESINA, psychologist; b. Amarillo, Tex., Dec. 11, 1927; d. James Lesley and Anna Gesina (Reimers) K. BA, Trinity U., 1949; MRE, Princeton Sem., 1952; PhD, Mich. State U., 1966. Lic. psychologist, Mich. Edn. dir. Mt. Lebanon Presbyn. Ch., Pitts., 1952-56, First Presbyn. Ch., Ann Arbor, Mich., 1956-63; univ. counselor II Wayne State U. Counseling Service, Detroit, 1966-72, univ. counselor III, 1972—, asst. dir., 1984—; chair Wayne State U. Commn. on the Status of Women, 1974-76. Pres., bd. dirs. United Campus Ministries, Wayne State U., 1983-84; pres., bd. dirs. Ecumenical Campus Ctr., U. Mich., 1984-85. Recipient proclamation recognition for chairing Wayne State U. Commn. on the Status of Women, 1977, Outstanding Service award U. Mich. Ecumenical Campus Ctr., 1987. Mem. Am. Psychol. Assn., Mich. Psychol. Assn. (founding chair women's issues com. 1984—), AAUP, Ecumenical Assn. for Internat. Understanding (bd. dirs. 1987), Delta Kappa Gamma (pres., v.p., treas. 1971-76, Internat. Women's Yr. award 1976). Avocations: travel, crafts. Office: Wayne State U Counseling Services 334 Mackenzie Hall 5050 Cass Ave Detroit MI 48202

KEESEE, ROGER N., family entertainment company executive. Pres., chief exec. officer Six Flags Corp., Chgo. Office: Bally Mfg Corp 8700 W Bryn Mawr Chicago IL 60631 *

KEGAN, DANIEL L., lawyer; b. Chgo., Mar. 3, 1944; s. Albert I. and Esther O. Kegan; m. Cynthia L. Scott; children: Amelia Scott Kegan, Benjamin Scott Kegan. BS, Swarthmore Coll., 1965; MS, PhD, Northwestern U., 1971, JD, 1984. Bar: Ill., 1984; registered psychologist, Calif., Ill., Mass. Dir. instl. evaluation Hampshire Coll., Amherst, Mass., 1973-77; cons. Synergy Works, Oakland, Calif., 1978; pres. Elan Assocs., Evanston, Ill., 1979—; ptnr. Kegan & Kegan Ltd., Chgo., 1984—, designer Greenlight software, 1986—; mem. faculty Ill. Inst. Tech., Chgo., 1982—, Pepperdine U., Malibu, Calif., 1980-81. Contbr. articles to profl. jours. Alumni interviewer Swarthmore (Pa.) Coll., 1971—; chmn. fin. com. Watergate Community Assn., Emeryville, Calif., 1981. Walter P. Murphy fellow Northwestern U., 1965. Mem. ABA (council and computer group 1981—), Am. Psychol. Assn., Computer Law Assn., Orgn. Devel. Network, Assn. Media Psychology, Copyright Soc. U.S.A., Boston Computer Soc. Club: The Rest of Us. Avocations: Macintosh computers, reading, outdoor activities, aquatics. Office: Kegan & Kegan Ltd 79 W Monroe #1320 Chicago IL 60603-6949

KEHLMEIER, RICHARD HENRY, architect; b. Columbus, Ohio, June 20, 1922; s. Henry and Clara (Roedell) K.; m. Janet Ach, May 12, 1951 (div. 1972)); m. Margaret L. Fought, Nov. 4, 1983. BArch, U. Cin., 1952. Registered architect, Ohio. Commd. USAF, 1941, advanced through grades to sgt., 1946, resigned, 1952, with Res., 1952-54; architect Fosdick & Hilmer, Cin., 1955-71, Bauer, Stark & Lashbrook, Toledo, 1971—. Served to 1st lt. USAF. Mem. AIA, Constrn. Specifications Inst. (pres. 1986, Edn. award 1986). Avocations: fishing, camping. Home: 203 Merton Holland OH 43528 Office: Bauer Stark & Lashbrook 1600 Madison Ave Toledo OH 43624

KEHOE, PETER HERBERT, optometrist; b. Galesburg, Ill., July 30, 1959; s. Herbert Peter and June Carolyn (Melick) K.; m. Melissa Sue Thomas, June 19, 1982; children: Vincent, Alexandra, Kathryn. Student, Ind. U., 1977-79; BS, OD, Ill. Coll. Optometry, 1984. Owner Galesburg (Ill.) Vision Assocs. & Kehoe Optical, 1979—, Val-Pak of Cen. Ill., Galesburg, 1984—. Mem. Am. Optometric Assn., Ill. Optometric Assn., Optometric Extension Prgram (assoc.), Galesburg Area C. of C. (bd. dirs. 1986). Lodge: Lions (bd. dirs. 1987—, chamber bd. 1987—). Avocations: flying, golf, racquetball, entrepreneur. Home: 789 N Broad Galesburg IL 61401 Office: 4 L Plaza PO Box 911 Galesburg IL 61402

KEHOE, SUSAN, communications and training company executive, consultant; b. Cleve., Dec. 5, 1947; d. John William and Mary Margaret (Swicia) Kehoe; m. Gerald Nicholas, May 15, 1970 (div.); children—Patricia, Mark. B.A., U. Detroit, 1970; M.A., Oakland U., 1980, Ph.D., 1983. Cert. secondary tchr., Mich. Trainer ESL Utica Community Schs., Mich., 1974-78; coordinator program Oakland Univ., Rochester, Mich., 1980-83; adj. prof. mktg. Wayne State Univ., Detroit, 1983-85, U. Mich., Ann Arbor, 1984-85; pres., owner The Kehoe Group, Birmingham, Mich., 1983—; trainer, program designer Gen. Motors, Detroit, 1984—; trainer, cons. Nat. Steel, Ecorse, Mich., 1984—; trainer, speech coach AM Gen., Livonia, Mich., 1984—; presenter Nat. Reading Conf., 1981, 83, Internat. Reading Assn., 1982, Am. Edn. Research Assn., 1982, Conf. on Coll. Composition, 1984; mktg. com. Detroit Symphony Orch. Mem. Pub. Relations Soc. Am. (membership chair). Club: Econ. of Detroit. Avocations: art, travel, music. Home: 3858 Lincoln West Birmingham MI 48010 Office: PO Box 242 Franklin MI 48025

KEIL, M. DAVID, international association executive; b. Hinsdale, Ill., Jan. 22, 1931; s. Milton Derby and Lydia Anne (Landwehr) K.; m. Marilyn Jean Martin, May 15, 1976. B.S.J., Northwestern U., Evanston, Ill., 1952. Brand mgr. Armour & Co., Chgo., 1953-60; sr. v.p. Young & Rubicam, Chgo., 1960-74, Sandy Corp., Detroit, 1974-75, D'Arcy-MacManus & Masius, Chgo., 1976-80; pres., mng. dir. Audit Bur. Circulations, Schaumburg, Ill., 1980—. Bd. dirs. Off the Street Club, Chgo., 1974-84, Robert Crown Ctr. for Health Edn., Hinsdale, Ill., 1980-84; sec. gen. Internat. Fedn. Audit Burs. Circulation, 1986—. Lutheran. Club: Hinsdale Golf (Ill.). Avocations: sports; reading; travel. Office: Audit Bur of Circulations 900 N Meacham Rd Schaumburg IL 60173-4968

KEIL, ROBERT MATTHES, chemical company executive; b. Bloomefield, N.J., Apr. 5, 1926; s. Wiiliam August and Myra (Maguire) K.; m. Betty Jane Apgar, May 3, 1952; children: Barbara Lynn, Nancy Lee. B.S., Syracuse U., 1948. Gen. mgr. olefin plastics Dow Chem. U.S.A., Midland, Mich., 1969-

76, v.p. consumer goods and services, 1976-78, v.p. mktg., 1978-79, exec. v.p., 1979-80; fin. v.p. Dow Chem. Co., Midland, Mich., 1980-82, exec. v.p., 1982—, dir., 1981—; dir. Dowell Schlumberger, Houston, Dow Corning Corp., Midland, Mich., Comerica bank, Midland; chmn. Dow Chem. Que. Ltd., 1978-82. Pres. Midland Community Ctr., 1976-77. Served to lt. U.S. Army, 1943-46, 51-52. Office: Dow Chem Co 2030 Willard H Dow Center Midland MI 48674

KEINATH, STEVEN ERNEST, polymer science educator, researcher; b. Saginaw, Mich., Sept. 10, 1954; s. Ernest Frederick and Verna Alma (Ill) K. BS in Chemistry and Physics, Saginaw Valley State Coll., 1976; MS in Polymer Sci., U. Mass., 1978; MBA, Saginaw Valley State Coll., 1981; MEd, Cen. Mich. U., 1985. Research asst. chemistry dept. Saginaw Valley State Coll., Univ. Ctr., Mich., 1974-76; asst. to dir. instrumentation polymer sci. dept. U. Mass., Amherst, 1978; sr. research asst. Mich. Molecular Inst., Midland, 1978-84, ind. researcher, 1984-85, instr., 1985—; asst. editor MMI Press, Midland, 1981-82; adminstr. grants and contracts Mich. Molecular Inst., Midland, 1983-84; cons. Quantum Composites, Inc., Midland, 1983—, Gordon & Breach Sci. Publ., N.Y., 1986—. Editor: Molecular Motion in Polymers by ESR, 1980, Order in the Amorphous "State" of Polymers, 1987; contbr. 15 articles in various polymer sci. jours. Mem. Am. Chem. Soc. (editor local sect. publ. The Midland Chemist 1984—), AAAS, N.Y. Acad. Scis., Internat. Union Pure and Applied Chemistry, North Am. Thermal Analysis Soc., Am. Soc. for Composites, Sigma Xi. Lutheran. Avocations: stamp and first day cover collecting, reading, theatre, canoeing, cross-country skiing. Office: Mich Molecular Inst 1910 W St Andrews Rd Midland MI 48640-2696

KEISER, PAUL DAVID, communications executive; b. Bklyn., July 3, 1955; s. Sidney Solomon and Mildred (Saffron) K.; m. E. Christine Brown, Sept. 27, 1986. BA in Journalism and Polit. Sci., Indiana (Pa.) U., 1977. Reporter Lebanon (Pa.) Daily News, 1977-78; pub. affairs asst. Contel, Hershey, Pa., 1978-81; pub. affairs coordinator Contel, St. Mary's, W.Va., 1982; dir. pub. relations Ill. Consol. Communications, Inc., Mattoon, 1982—. Chmn. pub. relations com. Ill. Telephone Assn.; bd. dirs. Accent on Edn., Mattoon, 1983-86, Coles County Assn. for Retarded, Charleston, Ill., 1986, treas., 1986—. Recipient Family Festival Merit award Community Relations Report, 1984, Gold medal Springfield (Ill.) Advt. Club, 1985, Advt. award Springfield Advt. Assn., 1985. Mem. Pub. Relations Soc. Am., Am. Mktg. Assn., U.S. telephone Assn. (pub. relations com. 1985—), Internat. Assn. Bus. Communicators (sec./treas. heart of Ill. chpt. 1986—). Avocations: tennis, reading, fitness. Home: 21-D Prairie Ave Mattoon IL 61938 Office: Consol Communications Inc 121 S 17th St Mattoon IL 61938

KEISER, ROSS EDWARD, psychologist; b. Fostoria, Ohio, Apr. 21, 1951; s. George E. and June Adele (von Juensch) K.; m. Susan Elizabeth Bragg, Oct. 30, 1976 (div. June 1979); m. Elizabeth Francis Murray, July 24, 1980; children: Anselm Josef, Otto Christian. MusB, Bowling Green State U., 1973, MusM, 1974, M in Rehab. Counseling, 1978; MA, Loyola U., Chgo., 1981, PhD, 1982. Registered psychologist, Ill.; lic. cons. psychologist, Minn., cert. rehab. counselor, Minn. Psychologist Parkside Human Services, Park Ridge, Ill., 1982-84, Mental Health Ctr., Hamilton, Mont., 1984; pvt. practice psychology Victor, Mont., 1984-85, Bemidji, Minn., 1986—; asst. prof. Bemidji State U., 1985—. Mem. Am. Psychol. Assn., Soc. Personality Assesment. Lodge: Rotary, Moose. Avocations: music, fishing, canoeing. Office: 1819 Bemidji Ave Bemidji MN 55601

KEITH, BRIAN DUNCAN, petroleum geologist, consultant; b. El Paso, Tex., Nov. 29, 1943; s. Stanton Baker and Elizabeth (Abernathy) K.; m. Jean Elizabeth Scott, Dec. 17, 1966; children—Colin McLean, Ian Andrew, Arlyn Elizabeth, Logan Charles. B.A., Amherst Coll., 1965; M.S., Syracuse U., 1971; Ph.D., Rensselaer Poly. Inst., 1974. Cert. profl. geologist, Ind. Exploration geologist Chevron Oil Co., Oklahoma City, 1969-71; research scientist Amoco Prodn. Co., Tulsa, 1974-78; geologist Ind. Geol. Survey, Bloomington, 1978-86, head basin analysis sect. 1987—; cons. Amoco Exploration Tng., Tulsa, 1981-86; asst. prof. Ind. U., Bloomington, 1982—; assoc. instr. Gerry Exploration, Inc., Troy, N.Y., 1984—. Editor: Trenton of Eastern North America, 1985, Midwestern Geology, 1987—. Contbr. articles to profl. jours., maps and State of Ind. publs. NSF trainee, 1967; research grantee Sigma Xi, 1972, Am. Assn. Petroleum Geologists, 1972, Pub. Service of Ind., 1978. Mem. Soc. Econ. Paleontologists and Mineralogists, Ind.-Ky. Geol. Soc., Am. Assn. Petroleum Geologists, Ind. Acad. Sci. Democrat. Avocation: science fiction. Office: Ind Geol Survey 611 N Walnut Grove Ave Bloomington IN 47405

KEITH, CARL WALTER, newspaper editor; b. Mar. 13, 1927; s. Harvey Schwartz and Frances (John) K.; m. Nadine Keith, Sept. 15, 1973; children—Eric, Kile. B.A., U. Nebr., 1950. Reporter Beatrice Daily Sun, Nebr., 1950-53; wire editor Hastings Tribune, Nebr., 1953-54; news editor Lead Daily Call, S.D., 1954-57, Scottsbluff Star-Herald, Nebr., 1957-60; night mng. editor Omaha World-Herald, 1960—; instr. U. Nebr., Lincoln, 1965-68. Served with U.S. Army, 1944-47, 50-51. Unitarian. Club: Omaha Press (bd. dirs. 1972). Home: 415 Oakland Ave Council Bluffs IA 51501 Office: Omaha World-Herald World Herald Sq Omaha NE 68102

KEITH, DAMON JEROME, judge; b. Detroit, July 4, 1922; s. Perry A. and Annie L. (Williams) K.; m. Rachel Boone, Oct. 18, 1953; children: Cecile Keith, Debbie, Gilda. S.B., W.Va. State Coll., 1943; LL.B., Howard U., 1949; LL.M., Wayne State U., 1956; hon. degrees, U. Mich., Howard U., Wayne State U., Mich. State U., N.Y. Law Sch., Detroit Coll. Law, W.Va. State Coll., U. Detroit, Atlanta U., Lincoln U. Bar: Mich. 1949. Atty. Office Friend of Ct., Detroit, 1952-56; sr. ptnr. firm Keith, Conyers Anderson, Brown & Wahls, Detroit, 1964-67; mem. Wayne County Bd. Suprs., 1958-63; chief U.S. judge Eastern Dist. Mich., 1967-77; judge U.S. Ct. Appeals for 6th Circuit, Detroit, 1977—; Mem. Wayne County (Mich.) Bd. Suprs., 1958-63; chmn. Mich. Civil Rights Commn., 1964-67; pres. Detroit Housing Commn., 1958-67; commnr. State Bar Mich., 1960-67; mem. Mich. Com. Manpower Devel. and Vocat. Tng., 1964, Detroit Mayor's Health Advisory Com., 1969. Contbr. to legal jours. Trustee Med. Corp. Detroit; trustee Interlochen Arts Acad., Cranbrook Sch.; mem. Citizen's Advisory Com. Equal Ednl. Opportunity Detroit Bd. Edn.; vice pres. United Negro Coll. Fund Detroit; 1st v.p. emeritus Detroit chpt. NAACP; mem. com. mgmt. Detroit YMCA, Detroit council Boy Scouts Am., Detroit Arts Commn. Served with AUS, World War II. Recipient Alumni citation Wayne State U., 1968, Citizen award Mich. State U., numerous others; Spingarn medalist, 1974; named 1 of 100 Most Influential Black Ams. Ebony Mag., 1971, 77. Mem. Am. (council sect. legal edn. and admission to bar), Nat., Mich., Detroit bar assns., Nat. Lawyers Guild, Am. Judicature Soc., Alpha Phi Alpha. Baptist (deacon). Club: Detroit Cotillion. Office: UC Court Appeals 240 Fed Bldg Detroit MI 48226 *

KEITH, FRANCIS EDWARD, dentist; b. Des Moines, Sept. 20, 1930; s. Ralph Elden and Martha Helen Keith; m. Nan Elizabeth Stevens, Mar. 8, 1952; children: Kristine Elizabeth Weinheimer, Steven Edward, Rebecca Elaine Potts. DDS, U. Iowa, 1957. Gen. practice dentistry Des Moines, 1957—. Contbr. articles to profl. jours. Trustee Des Moines Library, pres. 1985—; v.p. Iowa Health Council, 1986—. Recipient Silver Beaver award Boy Scouts Am., 1970. Fellow Am. Coll. Dentists; mem. ADA (del. 1980—, chmn. subcom. Council on Fed. Dental Services 1984— of Council Govtl. Affairs), Iowa Dental Assn. (treas. 1986—), Des Moines Dist. Dental Soc. (v.p. 1986—), Pierre Fouchard Acad. Republican. Methodist. Lodge: Sertoma (past pres. Des Moines chpt.). Home: 617 E Sheridan Ave Des Moines IA 50313 Office: 2601 E 14th St Des Moines IA 50316

KEITH, MICHAEL WARREN, hand surgeon; b. Tokyo, May 14, 1948; s. Michael Eugene Keith and Cynthia (Mizushima) Troncales; m. Catherine Bruce, June 7, 1968; children: Ellen, Alison. AB, Case Western Res. U., 1969; MD, Ohio State U., Columbus, 1973. Diplomate Am. Bd. Surgery. Asst. prof. Coll. Medicine Case Western Res. U., 1979-85; asst. prof. dept. orthopedics and dept. biomed. engring. Case Western Res. U., 1985—; advisor rehab. div. Cleve. Indsl. Commn., 1985—. Contbr. articles to profl. jour. Fellow ACS, Am. Acad Othropedic Surgeons; mem. Am. Soc. Surgery of Hand. Office: Case Western Res U 2074 Adelbert Rd Cleveland OH 44106

KEITH, SUSAN ELIZABETH, financial planner; b. Keokuk, Iowa, Apr. 15, 1959; d. Teddy Jr. and Delores Ann (Curless) K. B Bus. Mktg., Western Ill. U., MBA. Instr. mktg. Western Ill. U., Macomb, 1982-84; fiscal analyst McDonnell Douglas Astronautics, St. Louis, 1984—. Vol. USO, St. Louis, 1984, Better Bus. Bur., 1985, McDonnell Douglas Vol. Services Orgn., St. Louis, 1985, Leukemia Soc., 1986. Recipient Two-On-Two award, 1986, Tow-On-The-Town award, 1986; named one of Outstandin Young Women Am. Mem. Nat. Agra-Mktg. Assn., Am. Mktg. Soc., Western Ill. U. Alumni Assn., Mortar Bd., U.S. Amateur Confedn. Roller Skating, Phi Kappa Phi, Sigma Kappa, Alpha Mu Alpha. Republican. Avocations: photography, swimming. Home: 950 Rue de LaBanque E Saint Louis MO 63141 Office: McDonnell Douglas Astronautics Saint Louis MO 63141

KEITH, TIMOTHY ZOOK, psychology educator; b. Providence, May 7, 1952; s. Charles Herbert and Julia Mercer (Zook) K.; m. Mary Anne Forbes, Aug. 16, 1975; children: Davis Henry, Scott Forbes, William Howe. BA, U. N.C., 1974; MA, East Carolina U., 1978; PhD, Duke U., 1982. Licensed psychologist, Iowa, N.C. Lead psychologist Montgomery County Schs., Troy, N.C., 1978-80; sch. psychologist Durham (N.C.) City Schs., 1981-82; asst. prof. U. Iowa, Iowa City, 1982-85, assoc. prof., 1985—; Research cons. Iowa Dept. Corrections, 1985-86, Iowa Dept. Edn., Des Moines, 1983—. Contbr. articles to profl. jours.; author (videotape) Sch. Psychologist's Applications of Computers in Edn., 1984; editorial adv. bd. Sch. Psychology Rev., 1985—. Iowa Measurement Research Found. grantee, 1984-85; U. Iowa grantee, 1983-84, 85-86. Mem. Nat. Assn. Sch. Psychologists, Am. Psychol. Assn. (sch. psychology div. 1985, membership com. 1985, ednl. psychology div. 1987), Am. Ednl. Research Assn., Iowa Sch. Psychologists Assn., Iowa Ednl. Research and Evaluation Assn., Ednl. Excellence Network, Phi Delta Kappa (research rep. 1985-86), Sigma Xi. Episcopalian. Home: 612 Normandy Dr Iowa City IA 52240 Office: U Iowa N280 Lindquist Ctr Iowa City IA 52242

KEITHLEY, JOSEPH FABER, electronic engineering manufacturing company executive; b. Peoria, Ill., Aug. 3, 1915; s. Giles E. and Elizabeth F. (Faber) K.; m. Nancy Jean Pearce, Jan. 17, 1948; children: Joseph Pearce, Elizabeth Margaret, Roy Faber. SB, MIT, 1937, SM, 1938. Registered profl. engr., Ohio. Mem. tech. staff Bell Telephone Labs., N.Y.C., 1938-40; engr., Naval Ordnance Lab., Washington, 1940-45, MASSA Labs., Cleve., 1945-46; pres., chmn. bd. Keithley Instruments, Inc., Cleve., 1946-73, chmn. bd., 1973—; mem. vis. com. Case Western Res. U. Sch. Mgmt., 1979—, elec. engring. and computer sci. dept. MIT, 1980—. Patentee station selecting system, method and apparatus for measuring and analyzing transient pressures in body of water, circuit interrupter. Recipient Disting. Civilian Service award U.S. Navy, 1945. Fellow IEEE (IECI Achievement medal 1976, Instrumentation and Measurement Soc. award 1983, Centennial medal 1984). Clubs: Union Club of Cleve., Mayfield Country. Avocation: photography. Home: 2780 Chesterton Rd Shaker Heights OH 44122 Office: Keithley Instruments Inc 28775 Aurora Rd Cleveland OH 44139

KELEHER, JAMES P., priest. Ordained priest, Roman Catholic ch., 1958. Bishop Belleville, Ill., 1984—. Office: Catholic Ctr 220 W Lincoln St Belleville IL 62221

KELEHER, PETER DOWNS, financial consultant; b. Sept. 4, 1935; s. Jerome Louis and Jeanne (Wehrle) K.; m. Lila Jean Blitsch, Sept. 17, 1960; children: Leardon, Peter Jr., Elizabeth, Mary. BA, Rutgers U., 1957; postgrad., Loyola U., Chgo. Owner Keleher Group, Naperville, Ill., 1969—; pres. Land Investment Dynamics, Ltd., Naperville, 1974—; pres. Grocer's Express, Inc., Naperville, 1987—; fin. advisor City of Naperville, 1985—. Treas. Samaritan Interfaith Counseling Naperville, 1979—; precinct committeeman Dupage County, Ill., 1960-66; campaign com. Ogilvie for Gov. Served to capt. USNR, 1958-84. Mem. Mich. Assn. Realtors (exchange div.), Nat. Assn. Tax Practitioners, Fla. Real Estate Exchangers Assn., Wis. Exchangers Assn., Naperville C. of C., Res. Officer's Assn., Naval Res. Assn. Clubs: Cress Creek Golf and Country, Naperville Racquet; Cotillion Dance. Avocations: tennis, computers, golf, sailing. Home: 1536 Towhee Ln Naperville IL 60565 Office: Keleher Group 475 River Bend Rd Naperville IL 60540

KELLAMS, DWIGHT EUGENE, accountant; b. Tell City, Ind., Jan. 10, 1959; s. Gene Lloyd and Dolores Jean (Saalman) K.; m. Saundra Jean Fowler, May 1, 1982. BS, Ind. U., 1981. CPA, Ind. Staff acct. Crowe, Chizek & Co., South Bend, Ind., 1981-83; asst. controller Vonnegut Indsl. Products, Inc., Indpls., 1983-87; sr. acct. fed. tax GTE-MTO, Inc., Westfield, Ind., 1987—. Mem. Am. Inst. CPA's, Ind. CPA Soc. Methodist. Avocations: cycling, downhill skiing, water skiing. Home: 9633 N Highgate Circle Indianapolis IN 46250 Office: GTE-MTO Inc 19845 N US 31 Westfield IN 46074

KELLAMS, JEFFREY JERONE, psychiatrist; b. Washington, Ind., Nov. 24, 1944; s. John and Alice E. (Keith) K.; m. Connie Lee York, May 26, 1979; 1 child, Christopher. BA, U. Indpls., 1967; MD, U. Ind., 1971. Cert. Am. Bd. Psychiatry and Neurology. Practice medicine specializing in psychiatry Greenwood and Indpls., Ind., 1975—; med. dir. Valle Vista Hosp., Greenwood, 1984—; assoc. prof. psychiatry Ind. U., Indpls., 1975—. Contbr. articles to profl. jours. Mem. AMA, Soc. Biol. Psychiatry, Am Psychiat. Assn. Methodist. Office: 896 E Main St Greenwood IN 46143

KELLER, CHARLOTTE EVELYN, restaurant owner, consultant; b. Chgo., Feb. 26, 1932; d. Charles Spellman and Ethel Ruth (Ritchey) Greene; m. Ralph Joseph Keller, Sept. 12, 1953; children: Robert, Susan, Robin, David. Grad., High Sch., Hyde Park, Chgo., Ill., 1950. Sec. USAF, Chgo., 1950-53; civic worker Lansing, Mich., 1953—; owner, operator Charlotte's Web Gift Shop, Williamston, Mich., 1975-82, Keller's Restaurant and Ice Cream Parlor, Williamston, 1982—; developer, owner Keller's Plaza, Williamston, 1982—. Author: Childrens Stories, 1949. Active Lansing Gen. Hosp., 1956—; organizer polit. campaign, Meridian Twp., Mich., 1978; chairperson Discover Williamston Day, 1981, 86, Mich. Sesquicentennial, Williamston, 1986-87. Republican. Roman Catholic. Avocations: profl. artist, photographer, swimming, sailing, flying. Home: 4470 Greenwood Okemos MI 48864 Office: Kellers Plaza 126 E Grand River Williamston MI 48895

KELLER, DAVID COE, department store executive; b. Warren, Ohio, Jan. 30, 1921; s. David Claude and Minnie Corlin (Furgerson) K.; m. Gladys Marie Carstens, Jan. 6, 1945; 1 dau., Anne Marie (Mrs. Scot McCormick). B.B.A., Cleve. State U., 1943. Staff acct. Touche Ross & Co., Cleve., 1946-49; asst. controller M. O'Neil Co. (dept. store), Akron, Ohio, 1950-56; controller, treas., dir. F.N. Arbaugh Co. (dept. store), Lansing, Mich., 1956-59; v.p., treas., dir. Wurzburg Co. (dept. store), Grand Rapids, Mich., 1959-72; chief financial officer, v.p., treas. Wieboldt Stores Inc., Chgo., 1972-82, pres., chief exec. officer, 1982-86, chief operating officer, 1986; pres., owner Fasionfull, 1986—. Bd. dirs. Jr. Achievement Grand Rapids, 1961-69; dir. Civic Fedn., Chgo., 1974—. Served with USMCR, 1943-45. Named Grand Rapids Boss of Year Am. Woman's Clubs, 1969. Mem. Ill. Retails Mchts. Assn. (treas. 1977—, bd. dirs., exec. com., chmn. bd. 1985—), State St. Council (bd. dirs., exec. com.), Tau Kappa Epsilon. Club: Mason (Shriner). Office: Wieboldt Stores Inc 1 N State St Chicago IL 60602

KELLER, DAVID WAYNE, systems analyst; b. Louisville, Ky., Aug. 26, 1960; s. Donald Wallace and Lois (Miller) K.; m. Kandy Luann Raper, June 23, 1984. BS in Computer Sci., Ball State U., 1982; MBA in Mktg. and Mgmt., Ind. U. Sch. Mgmt., 1987. Systems analyst Eli Lilly and Co., Indpls., 1982-83, project leader, 1984—. Avocations: golf, racquetball, guitar, softball. Home: 11505 Hartford Ln Noblesville IN 46060

KELLER, ELIOT AARON, broadcast executive; b. Davenport, Iowa, June 11, 1947; s. Norman Edward and Millie (Morris) K.; m. Sandra Kay McGrew, July 3, 1970; 1 dau., Nicole. B.A., U. Iowa, 1970; M.S., San Diego State U., 1976. Corr. Sta. WHO-AM/FM/TV, Des Moines, 1969-70; newsman Sta. WSUI, Iowa City, Iowa, 1968-70; newsman, corr. Sta. WHBF-AM/FM/TV, Rock Island, Ill., 1969; newsman Sta. WOC-AM/FM/TV, Davenport, Iowa, 1970; freelance newsman and photographer Iowa City, 1969-77; pres. KRNA, Inc., Iowa City, 1971—, mem. exec. com., 1982—; gen. mgr. Sta. KRNA, 1974—; dir. KRNA, Inc., 1971—; adj. instr. dept. communications studies U. Iowa Iowa City 1983, 84. Mem. Radio-TV News Dirs. Assn., Broadcast Fin. Mgmt. Assn. Jewish. Home: 609 Keokuk Ct Iowa City IA 52240 Office: KRNA Inc 2105 Act Circle Iowa City IA 52240

KELLER, HAL LLOYD, electronics company executive; b. Muncie, Ind., Jan. 8, 1940; s. William Carey and Edna Irene (Kaster) K.; children: Donn Ryan, Randall Denny. BA, Ball State U., 1971; BEE, Purdue U., 1973; PhD in Mktg., N.Am. U., 1982. Gen. mgr. Wm. Keller Constrn. Co., Muncie, 1958-63; pres. Product Specialties div. Lancaster Colony Corp., Columbus, Ohio, 1965-75; sales promotion dir. Product Specialties, Muncie, 1975-78; pres. Forbes, Inc., Bellwood, Ill., 1978—. Chmn. fund raising com. Alexian Bros. Hosp., Elk Grove Village, Ill., 1985—; chmn. vendor com., bus. council Ill. Masonic Med. Ctr., Chgo., 1985—. Served with U.S. Army, 1963-65. Recipient Key to City, Louisville, Ky., 1964, Lighting award Elec. Assn., Chgo., 1984, 85. Mem. Exec. Hosp. Engring. Assn. Republican. Home: 712 N LaGrange Rd LaGrange Park IL 60525 Office: Forbes Inc 2600 W Van Buren Bellwood IL 60104

KELLER, HAROLD WILLIAM, chemical company executive; b. Grand Forks, N.D., Aug. 24, 1922; s. Charles Earl and Margaret Ann (Carlson) K.; student U. N.D., 1940-42, 46-48; m. S. Betty Larsen, Oct. 31, 1947; children—Charles William, Kenneth Earl. Asst. dir. research Ill. Water Treatment Co., Rockford, 1952-68, service mgr., 1968-69, mgr. market devel., 1969-72; v.p. Techni-Chem, Inc., Cherry Valley, Ill., 1972-77, pres., 1977—, also owner, corp. exec., dir. Served with USAAF, 1942-46. Mem. Am. Chem. Soc., Am. Oil Chemists Soc., Am. Inst. Chem. Engrs., Am. Soc. Sugar Beet Tech., Lambda Chi Alpha. Home: 7633 Lucky Ln Rockford IL 61108 Office: 6853 Indy Dr Belvidere IL 61008

KELLER, JEANNE ALLIE, social worker; b. Chgo., Nov. 1, 1948; d. Chester and Emma Evelyn (Todd) K.; 1 son, Kenyon Todd. Student So. Ill. U., 1966-67, DePaul U., 1968; B.A., Roosevelt U., 1971; M.A., Gov. State U., 1975. Registered social worker, Ill. Social worker Chgo. Assn. Retarded Children, 1972; program coordinator Clair-Christian Ctr., Chgo., 1972-73; social worker Westside Parents Exceptional Children, Chgo., 1973-76; dist. coordinator Chgo. Police Dept., 1977—; notary pub., Ill., Lawndale Peoples Planning and Action Conf., Chgo.; bd. dirs. Westside Assn. Community Action, Brotherhood Against Slavery Addiction; mem. Little Village Community Council. Mem. Sigma Gamma Rho (1st anti-basileus 1973-75). United Methodist. Home: PO Box 867 Chicago IL 60690 Office: 10th Dist Beat Representative Program 2434 S Pulaski Rd Chicago IL 60623

KELLER, JOHN JAY, oral surgeon; b. Lincoln, Nebr., Sept. 8, 1945; s. John and Lillian E. (Baker) K.; Marian O. Sicklebower, June 10, 1967: Polly, Matthew, Paige. DDS, U. Nebr., 1969. Diplomate Am. Bd. Oral and Maxillofacial Surgery. Commd. USN, 1969, advanced through ranks to commdr., 1974, resigned, 1974; resident Great Lakes Naval Hosp., Waukegan, Ill., 1974-78; pres. SOMA, Ltd., Sheboygan, Wis., 1978—; clin. instr. Med. Sch. Milw., 1984—. Contbr. articles to profl. jours. bd. dirs. Salvation Army, Sheboygan, 1985—; mem. exec. coms. various hosps., 1978—. Fellow Am. Assn. Oral Maxillofacial Surgeons, Am. Soc. Dental Anesthesiology; mem. Wis. Dental Assn., Sheboygan Dental Soc. (pres. 1985-86), Wis. Thoroughbred Owners & Breeders Assn. (bd. dirs. 1985—). Club: Sheboygan Country (bd. dirs. 1986—), Wis. (Milw.). Lodge: Masons, Shriners, Rotary. Avocations: golf, travel, riding. Home: 1328 N 3d Sheboygan WI 53081 Office: SOMA Ltd 1407 N 8th St Sheboygan WI 53081

KELLER, JOHN MILTON, gynecologist/obstetrician, educator; b. Phila., Jan. 12, 1922; s. Frederick E. and Ruth (Lock) K.; m. Ruth C. Stranford, Apr. 28, 1929; children—John Frederick, Brian Keith. B.A., W. Va. U., 1943; M.D., Jefferson Med. Coll., 1946. Diplomate Am. Bd. Ob-Gyn. Resident in ob-gyn St. John's Hosp., Bklyn., 1951-54; clin. fellow Am. Cancer Soc., SUNY, Bklyn., 1954-55; attending obstetrician/gynecologist Williston, N.D., 1955-62, Geisinger Med. Ctr., Danville, Pa., 1962-69; assoc. prof. Abraham Lincoln Sch. Med., U. Ill., Chgo., 1969-70, U. Health Scis., Chgo. Med. Sch., 1971-74; prof. univ. health scis. Chgo. Med. Sch., 1974-80; assoc. clin prof. Peoria Sch. Medicine, U. Ill., 1982—; clin. prof. Creighton U. Sch. Medicine, 1983—; attending chief ob-gyn Fairbury (Ill.) Hosp., 1980-84; sr. attending Colposcopy Clinic, St. Francis Hosp., Peoria, 1981-84; attending ob-gyn St. Elizabeth Hosp., Bryan Meml. Hosp., Lincoln Gen. Hosp., Nebr., 1984—; obstetrician-gynecologist Health Am., Lincoln, 1984—. Served with M.C., U.S. Army, 1947-49. Geisinger Med. Ctr. grantee, 1968; U. Ill. grantee, 1971-72. Mem. ACS, Am. Coll. Ob-Gyn, Am. Soc. Colposcopy, Am. Inst. Ultrasound in Medicine, Chgo. Gynecol. Soc., AMA, Nebr. Med. Soc., Lancaster County Med. Soc. Republican. Lutheran. Club: Masons (32 deg.), Shriner. Contbr. articles to profl. jours. Office: 17th & N Sts Lincoln NE 68508

KELLER, KENNETH CHRISTEN, advertising executive; b. Toledo, Feb. 17, 1939; s. Theodore G. and Edna L. (Christen) K.; m. Mary Carolyn Folsom, Sept. 10, 1960; children—Kathryn Elizabeth Keller Oulevey, David Folsom Keller. Student Ohio State U., 1957-59. Part-time staff announcer Sta. WMNI, Columbus, Ohio, 1958-59, Sta. WTVN, Columbus, 1959, Sta. WBNS-TV, Columbus, 1959; staff announcer Sta. WRFD, Worthington, Ohio, 1959-61; staff announcer, news supr., program dir. Sta. WOSU, Columbus, 1961-65; on-air talent Sta. WBNS, Columbus, 1962-65; copywriter Joe Hill & Assocs., Columbus, 1965-66; creative dir. Myers, Ault & Assocs., Columbus, 1966-70; co-owner, account exec. Angeletti, Wise & Keller, Columbus, 1970-72; co-owner TRIAD, Columbus, 1972-86, owner, 1986—, v.p., dir. creative services, 1972-85, pres., 1985—; owner Radio City Music Hole. Bd. dirs. Friends of WOSU, 1981—, sec. bd., 1982-83, v.p. and pres.-elect, 1983-85, pres., 1985-87; apptd. by Franklin County Commrs. to bd. dirs. Cen. Ohio Mktg. Council, 1986—. Lyricist, co-composer Best Radio Comml. award Internat. Assn. Fairs and Expns., Ohio State Fair, 1978, 81. Mem. AFTRA (pres. chpt. 1978). Home: 270 Park Blvd Worthington OH 43085 Office: TRIAD 6525 Busch Blvd Columbus OH 43229

KELLER, KENNETH HARRISON, university president; b. N.Y.C., Oct. 19, 1934; s. Benjamin and Pearl (Pastor) K.; m. Dorothy Robinson, June 2, 1957 (div.); children: Andrew Robinson, Paul Victor; m. Bonita F. Sindelir, June 19, 1981; 1 son, Jesse Daniel. A.B., Columbia U., 1956, B.S., 1957; M.S. in Engring., Johns Hopkins U., 1963, Ph.D., 1964. Asst. prof. dept. chem. engring. U. Minn., Mpls., 1964-68; assoc. prof. U. Minn., 1968-71, prof., 1971—, assoc. dean Grad. Sch., 1973-74, acting dean Grad. Sch., 1974-75, head dept. chem. engring. and materials sci., 1978-80, v.p. acad. affairs, 1980-85, pres., 1985—; cons. in field; mem. cardiology adv. com. NIH, 1982-86. Editor chem. engring. sect.: Jour. Bioengring, 1975-79. Mem. adv. com. program for Soviet emigre scholars, 1974-82; bd. govs. Argonne Nat. Lab., 1982-85; bd. dirs. Walker Art Ctr., Mpls. Inst. Fine Arts. Served from ensign to lt. USNR, 1957-61. NIH Spl. fellow, 1972-73. Mem. Am. Soc. Artificial Internal Organs (pres. 1980-81), Am. Inst. Chem. Engrs. (Food and Bioengring. award 1980), Internat. Soc. Artificial Organs, N.Y. Acad. Scis., Am. Council for Emigré s in the Professions (dir. 1972-80), Mpls. C. of C. (bd. dirs.), Phi Beta Kappa, Sigma Xi (nat. lectr. 1978-80). Office: U Minn 202 Morrill Hall 100 Church St SE Minneapolis MN 55455

KELLER, ROBERT CHARLES, state agency administrator; b. St. Louis, Oct. 29, 1947; s. Robert Lyle and Marguerite Gertrude (Bepler) K.; children: Robert C. Jr., Scott Daniel. BSME, U. Mo., 1969. Registered profl. engr., Mo. Assoc. engr. Boeing Co., Wichita, Kans., 1969-70; engr. McDonnell-Douglas, St. Louis, 1970-73; design engr. State of Mo., Jefferson City, 1973-77, asst. dir. div design and constrn., 1977—; project engr. Chas J.R. McClure Assn., St. Louis, 1977. Bd. govs. Meml. Community Hosp., Jefferson City, 1979—; mem. adminstrv. bd. First United Meth. Ch., Jefferson City, 1982—. Mem. ASME, Am. Soc. Heating, Refrigerating and Air Conditioning Engrs., Nat.Soc. Profl. Engrs., Mo. Soc. Profl. Engrs., Am. Pub. Works Assn., Pi Tau Sigma, Tau Beta Pi. Methodist. Office: State of MO Design and Constrn Div PO Box 809 Jefferson City MO 65102

KELLER, RONALD WAYNE, osteopath; b. Ottumwa, Iowa, Nov. 5, 1947; s. Joseph William and Mary Lavon (McIntosh) K.; m. Mary Jane Bergener, Aug. 1971 (div. Apr. 1979); m. Blanche Belliston, May 22, 1981; children: Kelli, Stephanie, Ronald Jr., Erin, Kathy, David, Jon. Student, U. Mo., 1965-68; BS, Northeast Mo. U., 1973; DO, Kirksville Coll. Osteo. Medicine,

1977. Commd. U.S. Army, 1969, advanced through grades to capt., 1977; served as medic U.S. Army, Vietnam, 1969-72; intern in osteo. medicine U.S. Army Tripler Am. Hosp., Honolulu, 1977-78; flight surgeon U.S. Army, Ft. Huachuca, Ariz., 1978-82; resigned U.S. Army, 1982; gen. practice osteopathy Memphis, Mo., 1982—; pres. med. staff Scotland County Hosp., Memphis, Mo., 1983-86; bd. dirs. Showne Software, Memphis. Decorated Bronze Star. Mem. Mo. Osteopathy Assn. (N.E. Mo. del. 1985—). Republican. Mormon. Lodge: Scotland County Rotary (bd. dirs. 1983-86, pres. 1987—). Avocations: running, hunting, geneology, gardening. Home: Rt 3 Box 107D Memphis MO 63555 Office: Keller Med Clinic Rt 3 Box 10 Memphis MO 63555

KELLER, VERN DENNIS, construction company executive, accountant; b. Scottsbluff, Nebr., Jan. 20, 1950; s. Robert and Martha (Meier) K.; m. Kathleen Joy Baum, Nov. 25, 1978; children: Scott Corbin, Brett Jordan. BS in Bus. Adminstrn., Kearney State Coll., 1972. Acct. Colossal Cattle Co., Minatare, Nebr., 1972-74; office mgr. Am. Beef Packers, Minatare, 1974-76; owner, mgr. U&I, Ltd., Scottsbluff, 1976-78; v.p., treas. Dominion, Inc., Scottsbluff, 1978—. Patentee in field. Congregationalist. Lodge: Elks. Home: 1202 Larkspur Dr Scottsbluff NE 69361 Office: Dominion Inc Hwy 26 Scottsbluff NE 69361

KELLER, WILLIAM WAITE, business owner; b. Madison County, Ohio, Nov. 27, 1918; s. Charles Franklin and Ethel Greeley (Phellis) K.; m. Eileen Catherine Miller, Mar. 13, 1948; children: Thomas, Patricia Eileen. BS in Pharmacy, Cin. Coll. of Pharmacy, 1938. Ptnr. Keller Co., Mechanicsburg, Ohio, 1946-81; chief, exec. officer Keller-Sorbol Co., Inc., Mechanicsburg, 1981-86. Sec., treas. Goshen Meml. Park, Mechanicsburg, 1961-87, Episcopal Ch., Mechanicsburg, 1946-71, Vestry Episcopal Ch., Mechanicsburg, 1946-87; scoutmaster Boy Scouts Am., Mechanicsburg, 1945-87; comdr. Am. Legion, Mechanicsburg, 1949, 67, VFW, Mechanicsburg, 1948-87. Served as cpl. U.S. Army, 1941-45. Decorated Purple Heart, Combat Medic Badge, 10 battle stars. Republican. Episcopalian. Lodges: Lions (founder, organizer 1952, pres. Mechanicsburg chpt. 1961-62), Masons. Avocations: travel, golf.

KELLER-COHEN, DEBORAH, linguistics educator; b. Detroit, Dec. 24, 1948; d. Harry Alex and Thelma Betty (Pollock) Keller; m. Evan Howard Cohen, June 6, 1971; 1 child, Jedd Isaac. AB with distinction, U. Mich., 1970; MA, U. Colo., 1971; PhD, SUNY, Buffalo, 1974. Cert. tchr., Mich. Asst. prof. linguistics U. Mich., Ann Arbor, 1974-80, assoc. research scientist Ctr. Human Growth and Devel., 1980—, assoc. prof., 1980—, assoc. research scientist English Language Inst., 1981—, dir. English Composition bd., 1985—; cons. Mich. Bell Telephone, Detroit, 1985—. Rackham Faculty fellow U. Mich., 1977. Mem. Linguistic Soc. Am. (chmn. status of women in linguistics com. 1976-77, program com. 1984-86). Avocations: swimming, weaving. Office: U Mich English Composition Bd 1025 Angell Hall Ann Arbor MI 48109-1003

KELLEY, BARBARA CARTIER, information specialist, artist; b. Ludington, Mich., May 15, 1928; d. Warren Raphael Cartier and Mary Josephine (Hendry) C.; m. Roger F. Kelley, Apr. 22, 1950 (div.); children—Brian, Stephen, Susan, Peter. Student, St. Mary-of-the-Woods Coll., 1945-47; B.S., Mich. State U., 1950; M.L.S., U. Mich., 1978. Info. specialist Market Opinion Research, Detroit, 1978—. Patron Birmingham/Bloomfield Art Assn., Surface Design Assn., Founders Soc., Detroit Inst. Arts, Am. Craft Council; Friends of Detroit Pub. Library, Bloomfield Twp. Library; mem. allocations com. United Way of Mich.; mem. adv. bd. Women United Found. Mem. Spl. Library Assn. Roman Catholic. Home: 1040 Stratford Ln Bloomfield Hills MI 48013 Office: Market Opinion Research 243 W Congress Detroit MI 48226

KELLEY, DOUGLAS EATON, military officer; b. Cleve., July 17, 1960; s. Robert Ernest Vinson and Elizabeth Caroline (Kirsheman) K.; m. Mary Josephine Horlacher, May 7, 1983; children: Katherine Elizabeth, Caroline Josephine. BA in Psychology, The Citadel, 1982; MA in Mgmt. and Supervision, Cen. Mich. U., 1986; grad., Squadron Officers Sch., 1987. Cert. missile combat crew evaluator. Commd. USAF, 1982, advanced through grades to capt., 1986; dep. missile combat crew commdr., dep. flight commdr. 741st Strategic Missile Squadron, Minot AFB, N.D., 1983, missile combat crew commdr., 1985-86; missile combat crew instr. 91st Strategic Missile Wing, Minot AFB, N.D., 1984-85, missile combat crew evaluator, 1986-87; airborne missile ops. officer 4th Airborne Command and Control Squadron, Dept. of Army, Ellsworth AFB, S.D., 1987, comdr. airborne missile combat crew, 1987—. Mem. Air Force Assn., Missile Ops. Assn., Missile Competition Assn. Republican. Episcopalian. Avocations: music, record collecting, sports, personal fitness. Home: Ellsworth AFB SD 57706 Office: 9308A Coolidge Dr Ellsworth AFB SD 57706

KELLEY, EDGAR ALAN, education educator; b. Bath, Mich., Aug. 1, 1940; s. Clarence E. and Cora (Bollinger) K.; B.A., Mich. State U., 1961, M.A., 1965, Ph.D., 1970; m. Marie Elaine Foerch, Aug. 10, 1963; 1 son, Wesley Lynn. Tchr., Ovid Elsie (Mich.) Area Schs., 1961-67; sch. adminstr. Colon (Mich.) Community Schs., 1967-69; asst. prof. edn!. adminstrn. and secondary edn. Tchrs. Coll., U. Nebr., Lincoln, 1970-74, assoc. prof. ednl. adminstrn., curriculum and instrn., 1974-79, prof., 1979-84; prof., chmn. dept. ednl. leadership Western Mich. U., Kalamazoo, 1984—; dir. Mich. Acad. Prin. Prep., 1986—. Recipient Disting. Teaching award U. Nebr., 1979. Mem. Assn. Supervision and Curriculum Devel. (exec. bd. 1978-83), Nat. Assn. Secondary Sch. Prins. (Disting. Service award, chmn. task force effective sch. environment 1982—), Nebr. Assn. Supervision and Curriculum Devel. (Disting. Service award 1979, 83), Nat. Soc. Study Edn., Nebr. Council Sch. Adminstrs. (Disting. Service award 1983), Am. Assn. Sch. Adminstrs., Nat. Orgn. Legal Problems in Edn., Phi Delta Kappa (Outstanding Young Leaders in Edn. award 1981). Editor: Catalyst, 1977-82; co-editor UCEA monograph series 1983-86; contbr. articles to profl. jours. Home: 6875 Glen Creek SE Caledonia MI 49316 Office: Western Mich U 3312 Sangren Hall Kalamazoo MI 49008

KELLEY, FRANK JOSEPH, state government official; b. Detroit, Dec. 31, 1924; s. Frank Edward and Grace Margaret (Spears) K.; m. Nancy Courtier; children: Karen Ann, Frank Edward II, Jane Francis. Pre-law certificate, U. Detroit, 1948, J.D., 1951. Bar: Mich. 1952. Gen. practice law Detroit, 1952-54, Alpena, 1954-61; atty. gen. Mich. Lansing, 1962—; Instr. econs. Alpena Community Coll., 1955-56; instr. pub. adminstrn., Alpena County, 1956; atty. city real estate law U. Mich. Extension, 1957-61. Mem. Alpena County Bd. Suprs., 1958-61; pres. Alpena Community Services Council, 1956; chmn. Gt. Lakes Commn., 1971; Founding dir., 1st sec. Alpena United Fund, 1955; founding dir., 1st pres. Northeastern Mich. Child Guidance Clinic, 1958; pres., bd. dirs. Northeastern Mich. Cath. Family Service, 1959. Mem. ABA, 26th Jud. Circuit Bar Assn. (pres. 1956), State Bar Mich., Nat. Assn. Attys. Gen. (pres. 1967), Internat. Movement Atlantic Union, Alpha Kappa Psi., K.C. (4 deg., past legal adv.). Office: 525 W Ottawa Law Bldg 7th Floor Lansing MI 48913 *

KELLEY, GLENN E., state supreme court justice; b. St. Edward, Nebr., Apr. 25, 1921; m. Margaret A. Kelley, July 25, 1946; children: Glenn A., David P., Anne L. B.S., No. State Coll., 1944; LL.B., U. Mich., 1948. Bar: Minn. 1948. Sole practice 1948-69; judge Minn. Dist. Ct. 3d Jud. Dist., Winona, Minn., 1969-81; assoc. justice Minn. Supreme Ct., St. Paul, 1981—. Served to 1st lt. USAAF, 1942-45. Mem. Nat. Assn. R.R. Trial Counsel, Am. Judicature Soc., Minn. Bar Assn., ABA. Office: Minnesota Supreme Court State Capitol Saint Paul MN 55155

KELLEY, JOSEPH FRANK, allergist; b. Salem, Ohio, Dec. 3, 1927; s. Joseph Martin and Ella (Smith) K.; m. Ann Higley, June 22, 1957; children: David Martin, Elizabeth Smith. AB, Dartmouth Coll., 1948; MD, Case Western Res. U., 1953. Intern Univ. Hosp., Cleve., 1953-54, resident, 1956-58, 59-60; allergies and immunology fellow Univ. Hosp., Ann Arbor, Mich., 1958 59; gen. practice medicine Univ. Hosps., Cleve., 1960-67; staff Cleve. Clinic Found., 1967—, chmn. dept. allergy and immunology, 1977—. Served to capt. USAFR. Fellow Am. Acad. Allergy and Immunology, Am. Coll. Allergists, Am. Assn. Cert. Allergists; mem. AMA, Ohio State Med. Assn., Cleve. Acad. Medicine, Ohio Soc. Allergy and Immunology (pres. 1981-82), Cleve. Allergy Soc. (pres. 1973-74, 80-81), Midwest Forum on Allergy (sec., treas. 1985—). Republican. Home: 22700 Calverton Rd Shaker Heights OH 44122 Office: Cleve Clin Found 9500 Euclid Ave Cleveland OH 44106

KELLEY, PATRICIA LOU, social work educator; b. Mpls., Jan. 11, 1935; d. Oral Robert and Gladys (Alexander) Neal; m. Verne Robert Kelley, Aug. 20, 1960; children: Elizabeth, Carolyn. BA, Carleton Coll., 1956; MSW, U. Minn., 1959; PhD, U. Iowa, 1981. Lic. social worker, Iowa. Caseworker Family Service Agy., Milw., 1959-60, Cedar Rapids, Iowa, 1962-65; clin. social worker Mental Health Ctr., Spencer, Iowa, 1967-70; psychiat. social worker U. Iowa, Iowa City, 1960-62, asst. dir. psychology tng. clinic, 1970-75, asst. prof. social work, 1975-81, assoc. prof., 1981—; cons. Mental Health Ctr., Iowa City, 1972-74, VA Hosp., Knoxville, Iowa, 1979-81; supr. family therapy tng. program Menniger Found., Des Moines, 1982-85. Contbr. articles on social work and family therapy to profl. jours.; mem. editorial bd. Jour. Ind. Social Work, 1985—. Dem. committeeman, Iowa City, 1980-84; bd. dirs. Johnson County United Way, Iowa City, 1982—. Consortium of Internat. Assns. grantee Mid-West U., 1982; Old Gold fellow U. Iowa, 1982. Mem. Am. Assn. Marriage and Family Therapy (pres Iowa div. 1986—), Nat. Assn. Social Workers (del. Nat. Assembley 1981), Council on Social Work Edn., Nat. Acad. Cert. Social Workers. Democratic. Unitarian. Home: 376 Koser Ave Iowa City IA 52240 Office: U Iowa 308 North Hall Iowa City IA 52242

KELLEY, VENITA JANE, banker; b. Kansas City, Mo., July 12, 1943; d. Charles Gordon and Martha Jane (Russell) Richter; m. Joseph William Kelley, Dec. 9, 1961; children: William Shawn, Stephen F. AAS, Penn Valley Coll., 1977; AA, Maple Woods Coll., 1979; BS summa cum laude, Avila Coll., 1980, MBA, 1982. Ops. mgr. Dean Witter, Kansas City, 1968-75; programmer Fed. Res. Bank, Kansas City, 1977; sr. ops. analyst Commerce Bank, Kansas City, 1979-81; sr. v.p. Unimark, Inc., Overland Park, Kans., 1981—. Mem. Nat. Assn. Accts., Assn. Equipment Lessors, Mensa. Avocations: golf, travel, reading. Office: Unimark Inc 9400 Reeds Rd Overland Park KS 66207

KELLEY, WENDELL J., utilities executive; b. Champaign, Ill., May 2, 1926; s. Victor W. and Erma (Dalrymple) K.; m. Evelyn Kimpel, June 12, 1947; children: Jeffrey, David, Alan, Stephen, John. B.S. in Elec. Engring, U. Ill., 1949. Registered profl. engr., Ill. With Ill. Power Co., Decatur, 1949—; mgr. personnel Ill. Power Co., 1959-61, v.p., 1961-66, pres., 1966-76, chmn. and pres., 1976—, also dir.; dir. Magna-Millikin Nat. Bank, Decatur, Electric Energy, Inc., Joppa, Ill., Magna Mortgage Co., St. Louis, Franklin Ins. Co., Springfield, Ill., Assn. Edison Illuminating Cos., N.Y.C., Magna Group, Inc., Belleville, Ill. Chmn. Mid-Am. Interpool Network, 1969-71, vice chmn., 1975-77, past mem. exec. com.; bd. dirs. Edison Electric Inst., Washington, 1974-77, 80-83; trustee Millikin U., Decatur; past trustee Nat. Electric Reliability Council, vice chmn., 1975-77, chmn., 1978-80; past mem. Ill. Council on Econ. Edn., citizens com. U. Ill., U. Ill. Found.; past mem. adv. council St. Mary's Hosp., Decatur, pres., 1972-73; past mem. Shults-Lewis Children's Home, Valparaiso, Ind. Served with USAAF, 1944-45. Recipient Alumni Honor award Coll. Engring., U. Ill., 1974, Alex Van Praag, Jr. Disting. engring. award, 1983. Fellow IEEE (past chmn. central Ill. sect., Centennial medal and cert. 1984); mem. Nat. Soc. Profl. Engrs., Elec. Engring. Alumni Assn. U. Ill. (past pres., Disting. Alumnus award 1973), Ill. State C. of C. (chmn. 1973-74, past dir.), U. Ill. Alumni Assn. (past dir.), Nat., Ill. socs. profl. engrs., Eta Kappa Nu. Mem. Ch. of Christ (elder). Home: 65 Dellwood Dr Decatur IL 62521 Office: 500 S 27th St Decatur IL 62525

KELLEY-MARSHALL, SHERRY, development company consultant; b. Harlan, Ky., May 15, 1953; d. Charles Edward Kelley and Clara Dorothy (Browning) Foster; m. Danny Roy Marshall, Sept. 4, 1976. BA, Earlham Coll., 1975. Dir. pub. relations Miami Purchase Assn. for Hist. Preservation, Cin., 1975-78; program planner Regional Council of Govt., Cin., 1978-81; devel. officer Dept. Neighborhoods, Cin., 1981-85; field officer Great Lakes dist. Neighborhood Reinvestment Corp., Cin., 1985—; event planner Gen. Electric Centennial, Evendale, Ohio, 1978; cons. City of Forest Park, Ohio, 1983-85. Author: (book) Madisonville Coordinating Committee: A Study in Neighborhood Action, 1983. Founder, trustee Invest in Neighborhoods, Cin., 1981; founder, bd. dirs. A Day in Eden Festival, Cin., 1983; v.p. Neighborhoods USA, Cin., 1984, pres., 1985, 86; trustee New Life Youth Services, 1984—; com. chmn. Madisonville Community Council, 1981—. Named Most Creative City Employee Congress of Neighborhoods, 1981, 82, 83; Community Service award Neighborhoods USA, 1984, Pub. Service award Human Relations Commn., 1985. Mem. Cin. C. of C. (Leadership Cin. award 1986), E-Club Coll. Athletic Alumni Assn., Withrow Alums. Mem. Soc. of Friends. Clubs: Women's City. Avocations: hot air ballooning, raquetball. Home: 4317 Watterson Cincinnati OH 45227 Office: Neighborhoods Reinvestment Great Lakes Dist 2368 Victory Pkwy Cincinnati OH 45206

KELLISON, DONNA LOUISE GEORGE, accountant, educator; b. Hugoton, Kans., Oct. 16, 1950; d. Donald Richard and Zepha Louise (Lowry) George. BA in Elem. Edn. with honors, Anderson (Ind.) Coll., 1972; MS in Elem. Edn., Ind. U., 1981. CPA; Ind.; lic. tchr., Ind. Tchr. elem. Maconaquash Sch. Corp., Bunker Hill, Ind., 1972-73; office mgr. Eskew & Gresham, CPA's, Louisville, Ky., 1973-78; para-profl. Blue & Co., Indpls., 1979-83, tax compliance specialist, 1983-84, tax sr., 1984-86, tax supr., 1986-87, tax mgr., 1987—. Vol. Children's Clinic, Indpls., 1985—. Mem. Network Women in Bus., Am. Inst. CPA's, Ind. CPA Soc. Presbyterian. Club: Toastmasters (Indpls.) (sec. 1986). Home: 9318 Embers Way Indianapolis IN 46250 Office: Blue & Co PO Box 80069 Indianapolis IN 46280-0069

KELLOGG, ROLAND THOMAS, process engineer; b. Paterson, N.J., Jan. 30, 1945; s. Roland Guthrie and Alice Marie (Bahrenburg) K.; m. Michele Sue Benedict, Apr. 1, 1966; children: Ronald, Gina, Melissa. B Indsl. Engring., Gen. Motors Inst., 1968. Prodn. control auditor New Departure Hyatt div. Gen. Motors Corp., Sandusky, Ohio, 1968-69, process engr., 1970-77, sr. process engr., 1978—. Mem. Soc. Mfg. Engrs. Methodist. Lodge: Elks. Home: 2820 Park Ln Sandusky OH 44870 Office: Gen Motors Corp New Departure Hyatt Div 2509 Hayes Ave Sandusky OH 44870

KELLOW, JAMES HARRY, transportation company executive; b. Hot Springs, Ark., June 30, 1939; s. Russell Peter and Margaret Elizabeth (Henry) K.; m. Nancy Elaine Womack, Sept. 21, 1974; 1 child, Patrick Clifton. AA, U. Md., 1964; BBA, Memphis State U., 1966, MA, 1969. Asst. dir., sr. research assoc. Bur. Bus. and Econ. Research Memphis State U., 1970-72; dep. dir. Memphis Housing Authority, 1972-77; dir. fin. and adminstrn. Port of Corpus Christi, Tex., 1977-79; pres. Louisville and Jefferson County Riverport Authority, 1979-84; exec. dir. Detroit and Wayne County Port Authority, 1984-86, Gt. Detroit Fgn. Trade ZOne, Inc., 1986—; co-gen. mgr. Detroit Windsor Port Corp., 1986—; bd. dirs. Am. Assn. Port Authorities, Internat. Great Lakes Ports. Mem United Way Corpus Christi, 1979, chmn. allocation com., 1979; mem. Leadership Detroit, 1985—, Mich. Dist. Export Council, 1985—; treas. Bd. Commrs., Glenview, Ky., 1984. Mem. Inland Rivers Ports and Terminals (1st v.p. 1984), Nat. Assn. Fgn. Trade Zones, Mich. Indsl. Devel. Assn., Detroit Econ. Club. Episcopalian. Club: Propeller Port of Detroit (v.p. 1987—). Avocations: model railroading, golf. Home: 765 Balfour Grosse Pointe Park MI 48230 Office: Detroit Wayne County Port Auhtority 100 Rennaissance Suite 2020 Detroit MI 48243

KELLY, ARTHUR LLOYD, management and investment company executive; b. Chgo., Nov. 15, 1937; s. Thomas Lloyd and Mildred (Wetten) K.; B.S. with honors, Yale U., 1959; M.B.A., U. Chgo., 1964; m. Diane Rex Cain, Nov. 25, 1978; children: Mary Lucinda, Thomas Lloyd, Alison Williams. With A.T. Kearney, Inc., 1959-75, mng. dir., Dusseldorf, W.Ger., 1964-70, v.p. for Europe, Brussels, 1970-73, internat. v.p., London, 1974-75, ptnr., dir., 1969-75, mem. exec. com., 1972-75; pres., chief operating officer, dir. LaSalle Steel Co., Chgo., 1975-81; pres., chief exec. officer, dir. Dalta Corp., Chgo., 1982—; mng. ptnr. KEL Enterprises Ltd., Chgo., 1983—; vice chmn., bd. dirs. ARCH Devel. Corp., Chgo., 1986 ; dir. Snap-on Tools Corp., Kenosha, Wis., Twin Disc Inc., Racine, Wis., Georgetown Industries, Inc., Charlotte, N.C., Cimlinc, Inc., Elk Grove Village, Ill., Crosspoint Venture Ptnrs., Palo Alto, Calif., Bankhaus Trinkaus & Burkhardt KGaA, Dusseldorf, Fed. Republic of Germany, Reditronics Ltd., Jersey, Channel Islands. Chmn. vis. com. div. phys. scis. U. Chgo., also mem. council Grad. Sch. Bus.; mem. adv. council Ditchley Found., Oxford, Eng.; bd. dirs. Chgo. Council Fgn. Relations (mem. exec. com.), Am. Council on Germany, N.Y.C. Mem. Young Pres.'s Orgn., Beta Gamma Sigma. Clubs: Chgo., Racquet, Casino (Chgo.), Brook, Yale (N.Y.C.). Office: 135 S La Salle St Suite 1117 Chicago IL 60603

KELLY, DEBORAH JEANNE, communications manager; b. Topeka, June 4, 1950. BA, Washburn U., 1983. Communications cons. Southwestern Bell, Topeka, 1973-82; market support specialist ATT Info Systems, Topeka, 1983-84; telecommunications mgr. State of Kansas Dept. Social and Rehab. Services, Topeka, 1984—; cons. in field, Topeka, 1984. Home: 1701 SW Arrowhead Topeka KS 66604

KELLY, JAMES CRAIG, pet food company executive; b. Medina, Ohio, Nov. 10, 1957; s. William Henry and Ruth (Willey) K. BSBA, Witteberg U., 1980. Sales rep. Bil-Jac Foods, Inc., Medina, 1980-82, v.p., 1982—, also bd. dirs.; bd. dirs. Dexters Internat., Columbus, Ohio, 1987. Recipient Silver Patron award The Alliance Repertory Co., Hollywood, Calif., 1987. Republican. Methodist. Avocations: sports, music, travel. Home: 5274 Applecreek Dr Centerville OH 45429 Office: Bil-Jac Foods Inc 2015 Granger Rd Medina OH 44256

KELLY, JANICE HOWLETT, accountant, educator; b. St. Louis, July 11, 1938; d. Johnie and Gladys (Morris) Howlett; m. Douglas Earnest Kelly, July 22, 1957; children: Pamela Diane, Patricia Elaine. BS, Chgo. State U., 1973; MS in Acctg., Roosevelt U., 1979. Trust auditor Harris Trust and Savs. Bank, Chgo., 1973-78; trust acct. Continental Ill. Nat. Bank, Chgo., 1979-80; acct. Harris-Stowe State Coll., St. Louis, 1980-81; prof. acctg. St. Louis Community Coll.-Forest Park, 1981—. Vol. acct. United Negro Coll Fund Annual Telethon, St. Louis, 1982-87. Mem. NEA (treas. jr. coll. dist. 1986—), Am. Inst. CPA's, Mo. Soc. CPA's, Nat. Assn. Black Accts. (Achievement award 1981), Am. Acctg. Assn. Office: St Louis Community Coll Forest Park 5600 Oakland Ave Saint Louis MO 63110

KELLY, JAY THOMAS (TOM KELLY), major league baseball club manager; b. Graceville, Minn., Aug. 15, 1950; s. Joseph Thomas and Anna Grace (Heisenbottle) K.; m. Mary Sara Harland, Jan. 20, 1973; children: Sharon Clare, Thomas John. Student, Mesa (Ariz.) Jr. Coll., 1968-69. Profl. baseball player Minn. Twins, Mpls., 1968-77, coach, 1982-86, mgr., 1987—; mgr. Toledo Farm Club, 1978-82. Mem. Assn. Profl. Baseball Players, U.S. Trotting Assn. Avocation: harness racing. Home: 57 Kierst St Parlin NJ 08859 Office: Minn Twins Hubert H Humphrey Metrodome 501 Chicago Ave S Minneapolis MN 55415

KELLY, JERRY BOB, social services administrator; b. Chgo., Feb. 6, 1942; s. Robert Lee and Mildred Florence (Griffin) K.; BS in Acctg., Roosevelt U., 1968; m. Diane Joyce Wilburn, Nov. 29, 1969; children—Jerold Robert, Joycelyn Renée. Lic. real estate salesman and life ins. producer, Ill. Br. mgr. Chgo. Econ. Devel. Corp., 1970-77; acct. Weather Bloc Mfg. Co., Chgo., 1967-68; programmer Morton Salt Co., Chgo., 1968-69; ptnr. Smith Distbrs., 1977-79; mgr. fin. and adminstrn. Suburban Cook County Area Agy. on Aging, Chgo., 1979-85; exec. dir. Lawndale Bus. and Local Devel. Corp., Chgo., 1985—. Treas. Day Care Crisis Council Met. Chgo., 1973-76, appreciation award; 1st v.p. West Side Health Planning Orgn., 1974-76, appreciation award; treas. Met. Chgo. chpt. Nat. Caucus and Ctr. on Black Aged. Served with AUS, 1964-67. Recipient appreciation award Chgo. Black Caucus, Am. Fedn. Tchrs., Chgo. Bd. Election Commrs., Comprehensive Health Planning Orgn. Chgo. Mem. Assoc. Photographers Internat. Baptist. Club: Elks (2d v.p. Ill.-Wis., past grand exalted ruler). Research on redevel. plans for East Garfield. Home: 1415 N Mayfield Ave Chicago IL 60651 Office: 1111 S Homan Ave Chicago IL 60624

KELLY, JONATHAN RICHARD, psychiatrist; b. Middlebury, Vt., Jan. 19, 1949; s. Francis William and Mary Rose (Mackovjak) K.; m. Katherine Elizabeth Butler, July 5, 1974; children: Mary Claire, Paul, Anne. BS in Biology, St. John Fisher Coll., Rochester, N.Y., 1971; MD, SUNY, Syracuse, 1975. Diplomate Am. Bd. Psychiatry and Neurology, Am. Bd. Forensic Psychiatry. Intern Strong Meml. Hosp., Rochester, 1975-76, resident in psychiatry, 1976-79; fellow forensic psychiatry Rush-Presbyn. St. Luke's Hosp., Chgo., 1979-80, faculty psychiatrist, 1980—, asst. prof. psychiatry, 1980—, forensic psychiatrist, 1980—. Mem. AAAS, Am. Psychiat. Assn., Am. Acad. Psychiatry and the Law, Am. Acad. Forensic Scis. Office: Rush Presbyn St Luke's Hosp 1720 W Polk St Chicago IL 60612

KELLY, JOSEPH FRANCIS, theology educator; b. N.Y.C., Aug. 13, 1945; s. James Patrick and Marion Rita (Gleason) K.; m. Ellen Marie Murray, Aug. 17, 1968; children: Robert, Amy, Alicia. BA, Boston Coll., 1967; MA, Fordham U., 1970, PhD, 1973. Instr. theology Molloy Coll., Rockville Ctr., N.Y., 1969-72; from asst. to assoc. prof. John Carroll U., Cleve., 1972-82, prof., 1982—. Author: Why There Is A New Testament, 1986; editor: Scriptores Hiberniae Minores, 1974, Perspectives on Scripture, 1976. NEH fellow, Andrew W. Mellon Found. fellow. Mem. N.Am. Patristic Soc., Medieval Acad. Am., Am. Soc. Ch. History. Democrat. Roman Catholic. Avocations: piano playing, running. Office: John Carroll U University Heights OH 44118

KELLY, JOSEPH RAYMOND, JR., accountant; b. St. Louis, Sept. 25, 1943; s. Joseph Raymond and Loretta Vey (Wilker) K.; m. Stephanie Corcoran; 1 child, Christine Marie. Cert. bus. adminstrn., Washington U., St. Louis, 1967; BS in Mgmt., So. Ill. U., 1968. Treas., gen. mgr. J.R. Kelly, Inc., St. Louis, 1970-71; investigator Cir. Atty.'s Office, St. Louis, 1971; adminstrv. asst. Mayor's Office, St. Louis, 1971-74, dir. emergency employment program, 1974; dir. pub. service employment program St. Louis Agy. on Tng. and Employment, 1974-81; acct. St. Louis Dept. Health and Hosps., 1982—. Served to sgt. U.S. Army, 1968-70. Decorated Nat. Def. medal, Army Commendation medal. Mem. St. Louis City Employees Fed. Credit Union (sec. 1978-84, pres. 1984—). Democrat. Roman Catholic. Avocations: coin collecting, football, viewing satellite TV. Home: 4106 Upton Ct Saint Louis MO 63116 Office: Dept Health and Hosps 634 N Grand Saint Louis MO 63103

KELLY, JOSEPHINE KAYE, social worker; b. Grand Rapids, Mich., May 30, 1944; d. Clark Everet Peterson and Dorothy Jane (Mudd) Schaefer; m. Raymond Luke Kelly, July 19, 1969; children: William Lawrence, Kenneth James. BA with honors, Grand Valley State Coll., 1967; postgrad., Western Mich. U., 1984—. Exec. dir. Voluntary Action Ctr., Grand Rapids, 1970-77; project coordinator Area Agy. on Aging, Grand Rapids, 1977-79; program coordinator Aquinas Coll., Grand Rapids, 1979-80; psychiat. social worker Kent Oaks Psychiat. Unit, Grand Rapids, 1980—; Registered social worker. Trustee Chester Twp., 1984—, mem. canteen services unit, 1984—; mem. planning bd. St. Mary's Hosp., Grand Rapids, 1981-82; mem. lay adv. bd. Cath. Info. Ctr., Grand Rapids, 1983-85, pres., 1984-85; pres. Council on Aging of Kent County, Grand Rapids, 1979-80, mem. 1977-81; mem. transp. adv. commn. Coopersville (Mich.) Area Pub. Schs., 1977-81; sec. Conklin Food Coop., 1977-80; bd. dirs. Women's Resource Ctr., Grand Rapids, 1977-79, steering com., 1972-73. Mem. Am. Soc. Pub. Adminstrn., Am. Legion (aux.), Mich. Beefalo Breeders Assn. (sec./treas. 1982-84), Am. Beefalo World Registry, Vol. Mgmt. Assn. Western Mich. (founder, 1st pres. 1975-76), Conklin Brotherhood Assn. Republican. Roman Catholic. Avocations: computers, reading, genealogy, sewing. Home: 3616 Coolidge St Conklin MI 49403 Office: Kent Oaks Psychiat Unit 1330 Bradford NE Grand Rapids MI 49503

KELLY, MARGARET BLAKE, auditor, state official; b. Crystal City, Mo., Sept. 17, 1935; d. Emory and Florine (Stovesand) Blake; m. William Clark Kelly; children: Kevin, Tom, John. BSBA, U. Mo., 1957; MBA, S.W. Mo. State U., 1975; D in Bus. Adminstrn. (hon.), S.W. Bapt. U., 1986. CPA, Mo. Acct. Williams-Keepers, Columbia and Jefferson City, Mo., McNabb, Westermann, Mitchell & Branstetter, Springfield, Mo., Fox & Co., Springfield; county auditor Cole County, Mo., 1982-84; state auditor State of Mo., Jefferson City, 1984—. Recipient Faculty-Alumni Gold Medal award U. Mo., 1985. Mem. Am. Inst. CPA's, Assn. Govt. Accts., Nat. State Auditors Assn., Nat. Assn. State Auditors, Comptrollers, and Treas., Am. Soc. Women Accts. Republican. Baptist. Lodge: Zonta. Office: Mo State Auditor's Office 224 State Capitol Box 869 Jefferson City MO 65101

KELLY, MICHAEL EVANS, health science association executive; b. Flint, Mich., Nov. 2, 1948; s. Raymond John Jr. and Katherine (LeVasseur) K.; m. Linda Kaye Wilkins, Oct. 11, 1975; children: Johanna Marie, James Michael. BA in Govt., U. Notre Dame, 1970; postgrad., U. Mich., 1978—. Exec. dir. 7th Dist. Mich. Reps., 1972-75; producer, writer Beck-Ross Communications, Flint, 1975-77; dir. Home Learning Ctr., Flint, 1977-81; gen. mgr. Kelly & Sons, Inc., Flint, 1981-85; exec. dir. Mich. Chiropractic Council, Lansing, 1985—; trustee polit. action com. Mich. Chiropractic Council. Columnist Flint Editorial, 1985—; producer, writer Sta. WFBE, Flint, 1977—; contbr. articles to profl. jours. Del. Mich. Rep. State Conv., 1967-86, mem. state cen. com., 1972-75; mem. polit. action com. BID, MCC; trustee Bldg. Industry Devel. Polit. Action Com.; bd. dirs. Family Service Agy., Flint, 1972-82, Flint Bluegrass Festival Ltd., 1979—. Served with U.S. Army, 1970-72. Recipient Spl. Service award Flint United Way, 1982, Disting. Service award Wayne County Govt., 1986, Spl. Service award Am. Polit. Items Collectors, 1986. Mem. Builders Assn. Met. Flint. Roman Catholic. Lodge: Sons of Desert. Avocations: collecting polit. Americana. Home: 3314 Dillon Rd Flushing MI 48433 Office: Mich Chiropractic Coucil 200 N Capitol Ave Suite 410 Lansing MI 48933

KELLY, PATRICIA T., management and training executive; b. St. Louis, May 26, 1949; d. Frank J. Graf and Edna E. (Becker) Graf Frasca; m. Sheppard W. Kelly, May 19, 1979; 1 child, Ryan W. EdB, S.E. Mo. State U., 1971; EdM, U. Mo., 1974. Counselor Risco (Mo.) R II, 1974-78; owner Banbury Cross, Dexter, Mo., 1976-78; staff specialist Ill. State Police Acad., Springfield, 1978—. Mem. Nat. Assn. Women in Careers, Am. Soc. Tng. and Devel., Internat. Assn. Chiefs of Police, Internat. Women in Law Enforcement, Ill. Women in Law Enforcement. Mem. United Ch. Christ. Avocations: tennis, golf, racquetball. Address: care of Edna Frasca 1018 Oran Dr Saint Louis MO 63137 Office: Ill State Police Acad 3700 E Lake Shore Dr Springfield IL 62707

KELLY, PATRICK F., federal judge; b. Wichita, Kans., June 25, 1929; s. Arthur J. and Reed (Skinner) K.; m. Joan Y. Cain, Jan. 3, 1953; children: Deanna Kelly Riepe, Patrick F. B.A., Wichita U., 1951; LL.B., Washburn Law Sch., 1953. Bar: Kans. Individual practice law Dunn & Hamilton, 1955; from asso. to partner firm Kahrs & Nelson, 1955-59; partner firm Frank & Kelly, 1959-68, Render, Kamas & Kelly, 1968-76; individual practice law Patrick F. Kelly (P.A.), Wichita, 1976-80; judge U.S. Dist. Ct., Dist. of Kans., Wichita, 1980—. Trustee Wichita State U., 1969-74, chmn., 1972-74; chmn. Midway chpt. ARC, 1967. Served with JAGC USAF, 1953-55. Fellow Am. Coll. Trial Lawyers; mem. Am. Bar Assn., Kans. Bar Assn., Kans. Trial Lawyers Assn., Am. Arbitration Assn. (arbiter), Internat. Soc. Barristers, Am. Bd. Trial Advocates. Office: US Dist Court US Courthouse 232 Federal Bldg Wichita KS 67202 *

KELLY, ROBERT DONALD, accounting company exec., cons.; b. Chgo., Sept. 14, 1929; s. Donald Francis and Irene Sarah (Gardner) K.; B.S. in Indsl. Engring., Iowa State U., 1951; M.S., Purdue U., 1955, Ph.D., 1957; m. Kay R. Black, Apr. 25, 1959; children—Kim Robert, Kris Donald, Candis Elizabeth. Faculty, Purdue U., West Lafayette, Ind., 1953-57; asso., prin., then partner, dir. Kearney Mgmt. Cons., Chgo., 1957-79; partner internat. personnel Arthur Andersen, Chgo. and Geneva, Switzerland, 1979—; dir. Allied Farm Equip., Duff Truck Line, Smith, U.S. Chmn. bd. trustees Clarendon Hills Presbyn. Ch., 1969-72, chmn. bd. deacons, 1966-69; pres. Bd. Edn. Hinsdale Sch. Dist., 1975-83; trustee Coll. DuPage Bd., 1985—. Served with USAF, 1951-53. Cert. mgmt. cons.; lic. indsl. psychologist, Ill. Mem. Am. Acctg. Assn., Am. Inst. Mgmt. Cons., Am. Compensation Assn., Am. Psychol. Assn., Am. Inst. Indsl. Engrs., Sigma Xi. Presbyterian. Clubs: Univ., Econs. Contbr. articles to profl. jours. Home: 120 S Elm St Hinsdale IL 60521 Office: 69 W Washington St Chicago IL 60602

KELLY, ROBERT DUANE, publishing company executive; b. Los Angeles, Oct. 16, 1933; s. Lawrence Bernard and Ruth Marie (Reddinger) K.; BS, U. So. Calif., 1959; m. Anne Margaret Halpin, Apr. 4, 1964; children: Kathleen, Patricia. Mgmt. trainee Foote, Cone & Belding, advt. agy., Los Angeles, 1959-62; assoc. nat. advt. dir. Wall Street Jour., N.Y.C., 1962-74; midwest regional mgr. Chilton Pub. Co., Chgo., 1974-77; western sales mgr. Southern Progress Corp., Chgo., 1977—. Treas., bd. dirs. Western Springs (Ill.) Community Ctr. Served with U.S. Army, 1954-56. Mem. Nat. Agri Mktg. Assn. Midwest (past pres.), Farm Harvest Assn. (past pres.), U. So. Calif. Midwest Alumni Club. (past pres.). Republican. Roman Catholic. Office: So Progress Corp 10 S Riverside Plaza Chicago IL 60606

KELLY, ROBERT VINCENT, JR., metal company executive; b. Phila., Sept. 29, 1938; s. Robert Vincent and Catherine Mary (Hanley) K.; m. Margaret Cecilia Taylor, Feb. 11, 1961; children: Robert V. III, Christopher T., Michael J., Tasha Marie. BS in Indsl. Mgmt., St. Joseph's U., Phila., 1960; postgrad., Roosevelt U., 1965-66. Gen. foreman prodn. Republic Steel Corp., Chgo., 1963-68; supt. prodn. Phoenix Steel Corp., Phoenixville, Pa., 1969-73; gen. supt. ops. Continental Steel Corp., Kokomo, Ind., 1973-77; gen. mgr. Mac Steel div. Quanex Corp., Jackson, Mich., 1977-81; corp. v.p. Quanex Corp., Houston, 1979-82; pres. steel and bar group Quanex Corp., Jackson, 1982—; pres. La Salle Steel Co., Hammond, Ind., 1985—, Arbuckle Corp., Jackson, 1984—. Leader, com. mem. Boy Scouts Am., Jackson. Served to lt. USN, 1960-63. Mem. Am. Mgmt. Assn. (pres.), Inst. Indsl. Engrs., Assn. Iron and Steel Engrs., Am. Soc. for Metals, USN Inst. Clubs: Jackson Country. Avocations: hiking, camping, sailing, scouting. Home: 1734 Metzmont Dr Jackson MI 49203 Office: Quanex Corp Steel and Bar Group 1 Jackson Sq Jackson MI 49201

KELLY, TIMOTHY MICHAEL, computer company executive; b. Rochester, N.Y., Sept. 26, 1953; s. Edward F. and Mary Ellen (Coughlin) K.; m. Sharon Lynn Villa, July 17, 1976. B.S. in Econs., Boston Coll., 1975. Ter. mgr. Burroughs Corp., Rochester, 1975-77; regional mgr. Infortext, Chgo., 1977-79, nat. accounts mgr., 1979-80, nat. sales mgr., 1980-81, exec. v.p., 1981—. Bd. dirs. Youth Football League, Arlington Heights, Ill., 1982. Mem. Am. Mgmt. Assn. Avocations: skiing; youth football. Home: 1110 W Maude Ave Arlington Heights IL 60004 Office: Infortext 1067 E State Pkwy Schaumburg IL 60195

KELLY, WILLIAM BERNARD, data processing executive; b. Highland Park, Mich., Apr. 30, 1955; s. Joseph Henry and Catherine (Shannon) K.; m. Kirsten Frank; Aug. 20, 1983. BBA, Eastern Mich. u., 1976; MBA, U. Detroit, 1985. Sr. acct. Am. Fed. Savs., Southfield, Mich., 1977-78, programmer/analyst, 1978-80; programmer/analyst Detroit Osteo. Hosp. Corp., Oak Park, Mich., 1980-81; programmer/analyst, systems analyst, project mgr. Merit Systems, Inc., Troy, Mich., 1981-84, sr. account mgr., 1984—. Mem. Data Processing Mgrs. Assn. Roman Catholic. Avocations: tennis, racquetball, golf, sailing. Home: 1319 Somerset Grosse Pointe Park MI 48230 Office: Merit Systems Inc 5800 Crooks Rd Troy MI 48098

KELLY, WILLIAM JAMES, dentist; b. Binghamton, N.Y., June 1, 1936; s. William James and Mary (Schmitt) K.; m. Lenore Mary Bastian, July 26, 1960; children: Mary Susan, William III. DDS, U. Pa., 1961; MS in Dentistry, St. Louis U., 1967. Diplomate Am. Bd. Dental Electrosurgery. Mem. faculty St. Louis U., 1964-70; gen. practice dentistry St. Louis, 1970—; dental faculty So. Ill. U., Edwardsville, Ill., 1974—. Served to lt. comdr. USN, 1961-70. Fellow Am. Coll. Dentistry, Acad. Gen. Dentistry; mem. Am. Dental Assn., St. Louis Dental Assn. (bd. dirs. 1979-83), Am. Assn. Dental Research., Am. Electrosurgery Acad. (pres. 1983), Meremal Valley Dental Study Club (treas. 1983—). Republican. Avocations: skiing, sailing, fishing. Home: 13662 Van Courtland Saint Louis MO 63131 Office: Concord Dental Group 12000 Tesson Ferry Saint Louis MO 63128

KELLY, WILLIAM R., employment agency executive; b. 1905; married. Grad., U. Pitts., 1925. With Kelly Services, Inc., 1946—; chmn. Kelly Services, Inc., Troy, Mich., 1965—; also bd. dirs. Kelly Services, Inc. Office: Kelly Services Inc 999 W Big Beaver Rd Troy MI 48084 *

KELMAN, STEPHEN JAY, chiropractor; b. Louisville, Feb. 11, 1944; s. Ben and Billie Ethel (Hark) K.; A.A., U. Louisville, 1968; D.Chiropractic magna cum laude, Palmer Coll. Chiropractic, 1971; m. Delores Sue Callaway, Feb. 11, 1968; children—Jason David, Rachel Leah. Dir., Chiropractic Arts Center, Fort Wayne, Ind., 1971-72; owner, Three Rivers Chiropractic Center, Ft. Wayne, Ind., 1972—; guest examiner, Ind. State Bd. Chiropractic Examiners, 1985—. Bd. dirs. Allen County chpt. Am. Cancer Soc., 1976-79. Rep., Ft. Wayne Jewish Fedn., 1975-79, 80-81, 87—; bd. dirs. N.E. Subarea adv. council No. Ind. Health Systems Agy., 1977-82; bd. dirs. B'nai Jacob Synagogue, 1973-76, 78-79, 80-82, 84—, pres. Men's Club, 1978-79; advisor B'nai B'rith Youth Orgn., 1972-79. Served with U.S. Army, 1964-66. Recipient Service awards Ind. State Chiropractic Assn., 1974, 75, 81; Service award B'nai Jacob Synagogue, 1980; Merit award B'nai B'rith Youth Orgn., 1981; Ky. Col. Mem. Am. Chiropractic Assn. (alt. state del. 1977-83), Ky. Assn. Chiropractors, Ky. Chiropractic Soc., Ind. State Chiropractic Assn., Inc. (dir. 1973-81, 2d v.p. 1977-78, 1st v.p. 1978-79, pres. 1979-80, sec. 1982-83, chmn. council on ins. 1981-84, peer rev. chmn. 1981-86, legal com. chmn. 1983—, chiropractor of Yr. award 1982), Allen County Chiropractic Soc. (pres. 1973-75), Palmer Coll. Alumni Assn. Ind. (pres. 1984-87), Delta Delta Pi, Pi Tau Delta. Jewish. Lodge: B'nai B'rith. Home: 7408 Kingsway Dr Fort Wayne IN 46809 Office: 3310 E State Blvd Fort Wayne IN 46805

KELSEY, CAROL JOSEPHINE, patient care computer systems administrator; b. Thief River Falls, Minn., Mar. 31, 1938; d. Ervin Gerhard and Olga (Boardson) Engevik; m. Donald Gale Kelsey, Aug. 25, 1962; children: Mark David, Heather Ann, Michael John. BS, U. Minn., 1960; postgrad. in learning and human devel., Coll. St. Thomas, 1987—. Asst. head nurse Miller Hosp., 1960-61; staff nurse Kaiser Found. Hosp., Oakland, Calif., 1961; instr. inservice Charles T. Miller Hosp., St. Paul, 1962-68; staff nurse U. Minn. Hosps., Mpls., 1969; supr., staff nurse United Hosp., St. Paul, 1968-77, dir. nursing edn., 1977-85; dir. patient care and clin. systems HealthOne Corp., Mpls., 1985—; v.p. Nat. Star Products User's Group, 1986. Mem. neighborhood adv. com. HHH Job Corps., St. Paul, 1983-86. Mem. Am. Soc. Health Care Edn. and Tng. (pres. Minn. chpt. 1983-84, Outstanding Mem. 1985), Nat. Computer Users Group, Sigma Theta Tau. Democrat. Lutheran. Avocations: reading, singing. Home: 1347 Simpson Saint Paul MN 55108

KELTY, PAUL DAVID, physician; b. Louisville, Oct. 2, 1947; s. William Theadore and Mary Frances (Hinton) K.; m. Connie Darlene Wilkerson, Apr. 16, 1983. B.E.E., U. Louisville, 1970; M.S., Ohio State U., 1971; M.D., U. Louisville, 1978. Mem. tech. staff Bell Labs., Whippany, N.J., 1970-72; design engr. Gen. Electric Co., Louisville, 1972-74; intern St. Mary's Med. Center, Evansville, Ind., 1978-79, resident in ob-gyn, 1979-82; practice medicine, specializing in ob-gyn, Corydon, Ind., 1982—; clin. instr. Dept. Ob-Gyn U. Louisville (Ky.) Sch. Medicine, 1987— . Mem. AMA, Am. Fertility Soc., Am. Inst. Ultrasound in Medicine, N.Y. Acad. Scis., Sigma Xi, Phi Kappa Phi, Tau Beta Pi, Sigma Tau, Sigma Pi Sigma, Eta Kappa Nu, Gamma Beta Phi, Omicron Delta Kappa. Roman Catholic. Home: 2000 Edsel Ln Corydon IN 47112 Office: Highway 135 N and 337 NW Corydon IN 47112

KELVIN, FREDERICK MAXWELL, radiologist; b. Leeds, England, May 9, 1943; s. Ernest and Ida (Schaier) Kohut; m. Anne Templeton Getty, May 20, 1979; children: Elizabeth, David. MB BS, U. London, 1966. Asst. prof. radiology Duke U. Med. Ctr., Durham, N.C., 1975-80, assoc. prof. radiology, 1980-85; staff radiologist Meth. Hosp. of Ind., Indpls., 1985—. Author: (with R. Gardiner) Clinical Imaging of the Colon and Rectum, 1986; also articles on gastrointestinal Radiology. Fellow Royal Coll. Radiologists; mem. Royal Coll. Physicians, Soc. Gastrointestinal Radiologists. Jewish. Avocations: golf, tennis, jogging, classical music. Home: 255 Royal Oak Ct Zionsville IN 46077 Office: Radiologic Specialists of Ind 1709 N Senate Blvd Indianapolis IN 46202

KELZ, ROBERT JOSEPH, utilities executive; b. Detroit, Mar. 3, 1956; s. William and Genevieve (Raczak) Klesczewski; m. Marcia A. Milewski, June 5, 1981. BS in Bus., Oakland U., 1978; postgrad., Wayne State U., Lawrence Inst. Tech. Acctg. clk. Hygrade Food Div., Mt. Clemens, 1978-80; service rep. Mich. Bell Telephone Co., Southfield, 1980-83, assoc. analyst, 1983-85, systems analyst, 1985-86, staff supr., 1986—. Lodge: Rotary (bd. dirs. Camp Rotary 1985—), Elks. Avocations: vintage cars, theater. Home: 21776 Colony Park Circle Southfield MI 48076 Office: Mich Bell Telephone Co 23777 Southfield Pl Southfield MI 48075

KEMINK, JOHN LAWRENCE, otolaryngology educator, surgeon; b. Muskegon, Mich., Sept. 4, 1949; married; 1 child, Lauren Francis. BA, Hope Coll., 1971; MD, U. Mich., 1975. Resident in gen. surgery UCSF, 1975-77; resident in otolaryngology U. Mich., Ann Arbor, 1977-81, fellow in otology, neurotology, skull base surgery, 1981-82, instr., 1981-82, asst. prof., 1982-86, assoc. prof., 1986—. Contbr. articles to profl. jours; chpts. to books. Fellow Am. Acad. Otolaryngology, Am. Neurotology Soc.; mem. AMA, Mich. Otolaryn. Soc. (program dir. 1984-86, exec. council 1984-86), Soc. Univ. Otolaryngologists. Office: U Mich Hosps Dept Otolaryngology 1500 E Medical Ctr Dr Ann Arbor MI 48109

KEMP, HILDA THIGPEN, educator; b. Henderson, N.C., Oct. 16, 1927; d. Zeno E. and Carrie B. (Wilkins) Thigpen; m. Jerahn T. Kemp, June 7, 1952 (div.); children—Jerahn T. III, Jeannette, Jon. B.S., St. Paul's Coll., 1950; M.S., Ind. U., 1970. Tchr., N.C. Pub. Schs., 1951-52, Palmer Inst., Sedalia, N.C., 1952-53, Warrenton, Ga., 1953-55; tchr. Monroe County Community Schs., Bloomington, Ind., 1969—. Mem. NEA, MCCSC (chairperson found., discussion council), Ind. Tchrs. Assn., Monroe County Edn. Assn. (discussion council), Delta Sigma Theta. Episcopalian. Club: Order Eastern Star. Home: PO Box 1184 Bloomington IN 47402

KEMP, JOHN BERNARD, retired state secretary of transportation; b. Scobey, Mont., Aug. 14, 1918; s. John Bert and Margaret Antoinette (Little) K.; m. Kathryn Elinor Lally, July 22, 1944 (dec. Dec. 31, 1950); children: Kathryn JoAnn Kemp Lehmann, John Daniel, Mary Elizabeth Kemp Titus; m. Elizabeth Joan Berscheid, Feb. 7, 1970; stepchildren: Susan Louise Stacey, Elizabeth Ann Stacey Cicha. Student, No. Mont. Coll., 1935-36; BA in Econs. and Sociology, Mont. State U., 1940; BS in Gen. Engring., Iowa State U., 1947, MS in Engring. Valuation and Econs., 1949. Registered profl. engr., Iowa, Kans. Instr. engring., vet.'s counselor Iowa State U., Ames, 1946-48; civil engr. U.S. Corps Engrs., 1948-49; hwy. engr. U.S. Bur. Pub. Rds. and Fed. Hwy. Adminstrn., St. Paul, 1949-52; planning engr., dist. engr., div. engr. U.S. Bur. Pub. Rds. and Fed. Hwy. Adminstrn., Bismark, N.D., 1952-63; div. engr. U.S. Bur. Pub. Rds. and Fed. Hwy. Adminstrn., Frankfort, Ky., 1963-67; chief systems and locations div. U.S. Bur. Pub. Rds. and Fed. Hwy. Adminstrn., Washington, 1967-68; regional fed. hwy. adminstr. U.S. Bur. Pub. Rds. and Fed. Hwy. Adminstrn., Kansas City, Mo., 1968-79; sec. transp. State of Kans., Topeka, 1979-87. Pres. N.D. Easter Seal Soc., 1957-60. Served to lt. USNR, 1942-46. Named one of Am.'s Top Ten Pub. Works Leaders of Yr., Am. Pub. Works Assn., 1982; recipient Silver medal award U.S. Dept. Commerce, 1965, Bronze medal award Fed. Hwy. Adminstrn., 1969, Gold medal award U.S. Dept. Transp., 1971, Bronze medal award U.S. Dept. Transp., 1979, Disting. Alumni award U. Mont., 1985. Fellow ASCE; mem. Am. Soc. Pub. Adminstrs., Nat. Soc. Profl. Engrs., Kans. Engring. Soc. Lodge: Lions (pres. Bismark chpt. 1960). Home: 8004 El Monte Prairie Village KS 66208

KEMP, RONALD NUBURN, psychologist; b. Cyril, Okla., July 23, 1936; s. Luther Nuburn and Lois Mary (Scoggins) K.; m. Lou Thelen Peterson, Aug. 3, 1957; children: Ronald N. Jr., Luther Harrold, Wesley Don. BA, Okla. Bapt. U., 1958; MDiv., Southwestern Sem., 1962; MA, Sam Houston State U., 1970; DMin., Midwestern Sem., 1981. Lic. psychologist, Mo.; ordained to ministry Bapt. Ch., 1956. Pastor Brock Bapt. Ch., Weatherford, Tex., 1960-62, Second Bapt. Ch., Huntsville, Tex., 1962-65; specialist on alcoholism Tex. Dept. Corrections, 1967-69; coll. chaplain S.W. Bapt. U., Bolivar, Mo., 1969-76; ctr. supr. Christian Psychol. and Family Services, Springfield, Mo., 1976-79; copr. officer Assn. for Counseling and Consultation, Springfield, 1980-85; dir. Family Inst. of the Ozarks, Springfield, 1985—. Fellow Internat. Council Sex Edn. and Parenthood; mem. Mo. Assn. Marriage and Family Therapy (pres. 1986—), Am. Assn. Pastoral Counselors, Mo. Psychol. Assn. (assoc.), Assn. Clin. Pastoral Edn. (clinical), Am. Assn. Marriage and Family Therapy (clinical). Lodge: Optimists. Home: PO Box 196 Bolivar MO 65613 Office: Family Inst of Ozarks 1722-w S Glenstone Suite 200 Springfield MO 65804

KEMPE, ROBERT ARON, venture management executive; b. Mpls., Mar. 6, 1922; s. Walter A. and Madge (Stoker) K.; m. Virginia Lou Wiseman, June 21, 1946; children: Mark A., Katherine A. BS in Chem. Engring., U. Minn., 1943; postgrad. metallurgy, bus. adminstrn., Case Western Res. U., 1946-49. Various positions TRW, Inc., Cleve., 1943-53, div. sales mgr., 1953; v.p. Metalphoto Corp., Cleve., 1954-63, pres., 1963-71, pres. Allied Decals, Inc., affiliate, Cleve., 1963-68; v.p., treas. Horizons Research Inc., 1970-71; pres. Reuter-Stokes, Inc. (subs. of GE Corp.), 1971-87; pres. Kempe Everest Co., Hudson, Ohio, 1987—; bd. dirs. Horizon Research Inc., Bicron Corp., Centrak Corp. Served to lt. (j.g.) USNR, 1944-46, PTO. Mem. Am. Nuclear Soc. (vice chmn. No. Ohio sect.), Sigma Chi. Club: Chemists (N.Y.C.); Country of Hudson (Ohio). Contbr. articles to profl. jours. Patentee in field. Home: 242 E Streetsboro St Hudson OH 44236 Office: Kempe Everest Co 10 W Streetboro St Hudson OH 44236

KEMPER, DAVID WOODS, II, banker; b. Kansas City, Mo., Nov. 20, 1950; s. James Madison and Mildred (Lane) K.; m. Dorothy Ann Jannarone, Sept. 6, 1975; children: John W., Elizabeth C., Catherine B. B.A. cum laude, Harvard U., 1972; M.A. in English Lit., Oxford, Worcester Coll., 1974; M.B.A., Stanford U., 1976. With Morgan Guaranty Trust Co., N.Y.C., 1975-78; v.p. Commerce Bank of Kansas City, Mo., 1978-79; sr. v.p. Commerce Bank of Kansas City, 1980-81; pres. Commerce Bancshares, Inc, 1982-86, pres. and chief exec. officer, 1986—, also dir.; chmn. Commerce Bank of St. Louis, 1985—; bd dirs. BMA, Kansas City, Mo., Fed. Res. Bank of St. Louis. Contbr. articles on banking to profl. jours. Bd. dirs. Mo. Botanical Garden, St. Louis Symphony Orch. Mem. Assn. Res. City Bankers. Clubs: Kansas City Country, University, River (Kansas City); St. Louis, Racquet (St. Louis). Office: Commerce Bancshares Inc Commerce Bank Bldg 1000 Walnut St Kansas City MO 64199 also: Commerce Bancshares Inc Commerce Bank Bldg 8000 Forsyth Clayton MO 63105 also: Commerce Bank of St Louis NA 8000 Forsyth Saint Louis MO 63105

KEMPER, JAMES MADISON, JR., banker; b. Kansas City, Mo., Oct. 10, 1921; s. James M. and Gladys (Grissom) K.; m. Mildred Lane, Mar. 30, 1948 (dec. Dec. 1986); children: Laura Lane, David Woods, Jonathan McBride, Julie Ann. B.A., Yale U., 1943. With Commerce Trust Co. (now Commerce Bank of Kansas City), Kansas City, 1946—; asst. cashier Commerce Trust Co. (now Commerce Bank of Kansas City), 1946-49, v.p., dir., 1949-55, exec. v.p., 1955, pres., 1955-64, chmn., 1964; chmn. bd., pres. Commerce Bank of Kansas City, 1964-66, chmn. bd., 1966-83, dir., 1983—; chmn., pres. Commerce Bancshares, Inc., Kansas City, Mo., 1966-86, chmn., chief exec. officer, 1986—, chmn. bd., 1986—; pres., chmn. Tower Properties, Inc.; dir. Owens-Corning Fiberglas Corp., Toledo. Office: Commerce Bancshares Inc Commerce Bank Bldg 1000 Walnut PO Box 13686 Kansas City MO 64106

KEMPER, JONATHAN, bank executive; b. Kansas City, Mo., July 23, 1953; s. James Madison Kemper Jr.; m. Nancy Lee Smith; 1 child, Charlotte Lee. AB, Harvard U., 1975, MBA, 1979. Asst. bank examiner Fed. Res. Bank, N.Y.C., 1975-76; asst. treas. Second Dist. Securities, N.Y.C., 1976-77; account officer Citicorp, Chgo., 1981-83; v.p. Commerce Bank of Kansas City, Mo., 1983-84, sr. v.p., 1984-85, pres., 1985—, also bd. dirs.; bd. dirs. Tower Properties, Greater Kansas City Community Found., Inroads, Inc. Office: Commerce Bank of Kansas City 1000 Walnut St Kansas City MO 64106

KEMPER, WALKER WARDER, JR., dentist, educator; b. Indpls., Aug. 26, 1924; s. Walker Warder Sr. and Margaret Louise (Mast) K.; m. Janet Morene Cottingham, June 10, 1950 (div. Oct. 1973); children—Walker Warder III, Todd Geller; m. Stephanie Ann Brean, June 24, 1978; stepchildren—Jeffrey L., Michael L., Scott L. B.S., Butler U., 1949; D.D.S., Ind. U., 1953, M.Sci. Dentistry, 1965. Clin. instr. Ind. U., Indpls., 1953-65; practice dentistry specializing in prosthodontics, Indpls., 1953—; dentistry prof., Ind. U., 1979—; chief dental sect. St. Vincent Hosp. and Health Care Ctr., 1976-86, exec. com., 1976-86; mem. Ind. State Bd. Dental Examiners, 1971-77; dental dir. Marquette Manor Retirement Home, Indpls., 1975—. Active in Ind. U. Century Club, Indpls., 1968—, Butler U. Pres.'s Club, 1966—; bd. dirs. Little Read Door Cancer Soc., 1970-74. Served to staff sgt. USAF, 1943-46. Mem. East African Hunters Assn. (hon.), ADA, John F. Johnston Soc. (pres. 1982, exec. com. 1977-86), Ind. State Dental Assn., Indpls. Dist. Dental Assn. (pres. 1970-71), Am. Coll. Dentists (pres.-elect Ind. sect.), Am. Acad. Crown and Bridge, Am. Acad. Dental Medicine, Safari Club Internat. (prt. (pres. 1982-83 Ind. chapt.), Adult Firecrafter, Phi Delta Theta, Omicron Kappa Upsilon, Psi Omega. Republican. Methodist. Clubs: Meridian Hills Country, Columbia (Indpls.). Avocations: big game hunting; fishing; scuba diving; swimming; skiing; golf. Home: 7574 N Morningside Dr Indianapolis IN 46240 Office: 8402 N Harcourt Rd Suite 404 Indianapolis IN 46260

KEMPERS, ROGER DYKE, physician, educator; b. Puebla, Mexico (parents Am. citizens), Feb. 29, 1928; s. John R. and Mable R. (VanDyke) K.; m. Marcia Ann DenHerder, June 17, 1950; children—Mary Christine, Thomas Robert, Steven Edward. A.B. cum laude, Hope Coll., 1949; M.D., Wayne State U., 1954; M.S. in Ob/Gyn., U. Minn., 1960. Diplomate Am. Bd. Ob/Gyn. (examiner 1980—). Fellow in ob-gyn. Mayo Grad. Sch. Medicine, 1957-60; cons. ob/gyn Mayo Clinic, 1961—; prof. ob/gyn Mayo Med. Sch., 1977—, dir. edn. dept. ob-gyn, 1970-83, dir. div. reproductive endocrinology, 1985—, mem. curriculum com., 1969-80, mem. admissions com., 1973-78; assoc. mem. thesis com. U. Minn., Mpls., 1975-80. Coauthor: (with Edward E. Wallach) Modern Trends in Infertility and Conception Control, vol. I, 1979, Vol. II, 1982, Vol. III, 1985; editor-in-chief Fertility and Sterility, 1975—; assoc. editor Ob/Gyn Survey & Postgraduate Ob/Gyn, 1979—; contbr. chpts. to books and articles to profl. jours.; sci. exhibitor Vagaries of Endometriosis. Ruling elder First Presbyn. Ch.; bd. dirs. United Way, Children's Home Soc., 1965—. Served to capt. MC, U.S. Army, 1955-57. Mem. Central Assn. Ob/Gyn, Am. Fertility Soc. (program chmn. 1975, pres.-elect 1986-87), Am. Coll. Ob/Gyn (scientific program com. 1980-84, sci. program chmn. 1985, chmn. ann. clin. meeting 1986, chmn. site selection com. 1986-87), Continental Gynecol. Soc., Minn. Ob/Gyn Soc., Ob/Gyn Travel Club, Am. Gynecol. and Obstet. Soc., AMA, Minn. State Med. Assn., Zumbro Valley Med. Soc., ACS, Sigma Xi. Club: Rochester (Minn.) Rotary. Home: 1205 6th St SW Rochester MN 55902 Office: Mayo Clinic 200 1st St SW Rochester MN 55905

KEMPSKI, RALPH A., bishop; b. Milw., July 16, 1934; s. Sigmund Joseph and Cecilia Josephine (Chojnacki) K.; m. Mary Jane Roth, July 30, 1955; children—Richard, Joan, John. B.A., Augsburg Coll., 1960; M.Div., Northwestern Luth. Theol. Sem., 1963; D.Div., Wittenberg U., Springfield, Ohio, 1980. Pastor Epiphany Luth. Ch., Mpls., 1963-68; pastor St. Stephen Luth. Ch., Louisville, Ky., 1968-71, Our Saviour Luth. Ch., West Lafayette, Ind., 1971-79; bishop Ind.-Ky. Synod Luth. Ch. Am., Indpls., 1979—; bd. dirs. Luth. Sch. Theology Chgo., 1979—, Wittenberg U., Springfield, Ohio, 1979—; governing bd. Nat. Council of Chs. Christ U.S.A., N.Y.C., 1981—. Avocations: gardening, reading, camping, travelling, flying. Office: Lutheran Church 9102 N Meridian St Indianapolis IN 46260

KEMPTON, ALAN GEORGE, microbiologist; b. Toronto, Can., Aug. 21, 1932; s. Albert Edward and Velma Pearl (Williams) K.; m. Suzanne Philp, Aug. 13, 1955; children—Alan Scott, Kathryn Suzanne. B.S.A., U. Toronto, Ont., Can., 1954, M.S.A., 1956; Ph.D., Mich. State U., 1958. Research officer Agr. Can., Swift Current, Sask., Can., 1958-60; chemist U.S. Army, Natick, Mass., 1960-64; chief bacteriologist Can. Packers Ltd., Toronto, Ont., Can., 1964-66; prof. biology U. Waterloo, Ont., 1966—; cons. food industry. Bioadsorption patentee; contbr. articles to profl. jours. Fellow AAAS; mem. N.Y. Acad. Scis., Soc. Indsl. Microbiology, Can. Soc. Microbiologists, Can. Coll. Microbiologists. Home: 117 Moccasin Dr, Waterloo, ON Canada N2L 4C2 Office: U Waterloo, University Ave, Waterloo, ON Canada N2L 3G1

KENDALL, DAVID LAWRENCE, automotive company executive; b. Grand Rapids, Mich., Feb. 4, 1947; s. Larry Trimble and Ann Marie (Rose) K.; m. Ellen Kristen Larson, Sept. 5, 1970; children: Matthew David, Erin Elizabeth. BA, Mich. State U., 1969; MBA, Western Mich. U., 1970. Sales analyst Am. Motors Corp., Southfield, Mich., 1973-75, mgr. short range mktg., 1975-78, coordinator forecasting, 1978-82, supr. market research, 1982-83, mgr. U.S., Can. pricing, 1983-86, mgr. world pricing, 1986—. Mem. Detroit Area Bus. Economists. Republican. Presbyterian. Club:

Nomads, Inc. (bd. dirs. 1975-77). Home: 29555 Pond Ridge Rd Farmington Hills MI 48018

KENDALL, GEORGE P., JR., insurance company executive; b. 1935. Student, Cornell U.; MBA, Northwestern U. With Washington Nat. Ins. Co., Evanston, Ill., 1967—, securities analyst, 1967-70, asst. treas., 1970-72, treas., 1972-74, v.p., treas., 1974-75, sr. v.p., treas., 1975-76, exec. v.p., 1976-83, now vice chmn. bd. dirs. Office: Washington Nat Ins Co 1630 Chicago Ave Evanston IL 60201 *

KENDALL, STEVEN WALTER, marketing executive; b. Chgo., Oct. 18, 1947; s. Walter and Josephine (Andrews) Krist; m. Susan Gardes Kendall, May 25, 1974; children: Kimberly Ann, Kristen Jeanne. BS in Commerce, De Paul U., 1969; MBA, Ohio State U., 1972. Product mgr. Mercury div. Brunswick Corp., Fond Du Lac, Wis., 1973-75; product mgr. consumer div. Brunswick Corp., Skokie, Ill., 1975-78, mktg. mgr. consumer div., 1978-81; dir. mktg. Brandt Inc., Watertown, Wis., 1981-86; v.p. mktg. Dukane Corp., St. Charles, Ill., 1986—; cons. investment Gardes Investments Ltd., Columbus, Ohio, 1974—; bd. dirs. Nu-Air Inc., San Diego, Interstate Filter Inc. Fund raiser Reps. of Waukesha (Wis.) County, 1982-86; advisor Jr. Achievement. Mem. Am. Mktg. Assn., Am. Mgmt. Assn. Roman Catholic. Home: 38W054 Horseshoe Dr Batavia IL 60510 Office: Dukane Corp 2900 Dukane Dr Saint Charles IL 60174

KENDALL, WILLIAM FRANKLIN, manufacturing engineering executive; b. Atlanta, Oct. 25, 1948; s. Clarence Nolan and Katie M. (Boyd) K.; m. Penny A. McIntire, Aug. 18, 1974; children: Shelley, Abigail. AS in Mech. Design, Inst. Tech., Morrison, Ill., 1969. Design engr. Penberty/Houdaille, Prophetsville, Ill., 1969-76; mech. engr. Raynor Mfg., Dixon, Ill., 1976-80, dir. engring., 1980-83, v.p. engring., 1983—. Mem. Nat. Assn. Garage Door Mfg., Door and Operator Dealers Assn. Lodge: Moose. Avocations: home restoration, golf, carpentry. Office: Raynor Mfg Dixon IL 61021

KENDZIOR, ROBERT JOSEPH, fast food chain marketing executive; b. Chgo., Mar. 24, 1952; s. Joseph W. and Josephine R. Kendzior. B.Arch., Ill. Inst. Tech., 1975. Account supr. Burger King Corp., Rogers Merchandising, Inc., Chgo., 1975-77; account exec. Walgreen Corp., Eisaman, Johns & Laws Advt., Inc., Chgo., 1977-78; dir. mktg. Midwest and Southeast regions, Dunkin Donuts Am., Inc., Park Ridge, Ill., 1978—. Recipient Most Valuable Promotion award PepsiCo, 1984. Mem. Triangle Fraternity, Chgo. Advt. Club. Office: Dunkin Donuts of Am Midwest Regional Hdqtrs 1550 N Northwest Hwy Park Ridge IL 60068

KENEFICK, JOHN COOPER, railroad executive; b. Buffalo, Dec. 26, 1921; s. John L. and Charlotte (Cooper) K.; m. Helen Walker Ryan, Aug. 19, 1973; 1 dau., Mary; stepchildren: Elizabeth, John, Mary, Nancy Ryan. B.S., Princeton U., 1943. With Union Pacific R.R., Omaha, 1947-52; v.p. ops., then exec. v.p. Union Pacific R.R., 1968-70, chief exec. officer, 1970-71, pres., 1971—, chmn. bd., chief exec. officer, 1982-86; vice chmn. Union Pacific Corp., 1986-87; with N.Y. Central R.R., 1946, 54-68, Denver Rio Grande & Western R.R., 1952-54; bd. dirs. Valmont Industries, FirsTier, Inc. Bd. dirs. Creighton U., Omaha, Clarkson Hosp.; trustee Princeton U. Served to lt. (j.g.) USNR, 1943-46. Mem. Omaha C. of C. (past pres.). Clubs: Omaha Country, Omaha; Links (N.Y.C.), Sky (N.Y.C.). Home: 410 Fairacres Rd Omaha NE 68132 Office: Union Pacific RR Co 1416 Dodge St Omaha NE 68179

KENITZER, RUSSELL EUGENE, advertising executive, accountant; b. Beaver Dam, Wis., Dec. 23, 1958; s. Eugene Melvin and Juanita Dawn (Bodin) K.; m. Deborah Lynn Price, June 13, 1981; children: Rebecca Lynn, Joshua Adam. BBA, U. Wis., Eau Claire, 1981. CPA, Wis. Jr., sr. acct. Touche Ross & Co., Milw., 1981-84; mgr. budgets and costs Time Ins., Milw., 1984-86; mgr. acctg. Hoffman York & Compton, Inc., Milw., 1986—. Deacon St. Lukes Evang. Luth. Ch., Greendale, Wis., 1985—. Mem. Wis. Inst. CPA's, U. Wis. Eau Claire Alumni Assn. Lodges: Wis. Ct. Chevaliers, Nathan Hale. Avocations: sports, classical music. Home: 2901 W Hilltop Ln Franklin WI 53132 Office: Hoffman York & Compton Inc 330 E Kilbourn Ave Milwaukee WI 53202

KENNAUGH, RALPH CHRISTOPHER, radiation oncologist, entrepreneur; b. Johannesburg, Transvaal, Republic of South Africa, Apr. 25, 1947; s. Hartwell Alexander and Marion (Rhodes) K.; m. Jennifer Fripp, Dec. 12, 1970 divorced; children: Alex, Megan. B in Medicine and BChir, U. Cape Town, Republic of South Africa, 1970. Diplomate Am. Bd. Radiology. Intern in med. surgery Frere Hosp., East London, Republic South Africa, 1971; resident trauma unit Groote Schuur Hosp., Cape Town, Republic South Africa, 1972, resident in radiaton oncology, 1974-78; med. officer, med. surgeon Frere Hosp., East London, Republic South Africa, 1973-74; asst. radiation oncologist Cancer Control Agy., Vancouver, B.C., Can., 1978-80; asst. prof. therapeutic radiology U. Colo., Denver, 1980-84; dir. radiation oncology Riverside Meth. Hosp., Columbus, Ohio, 1984—, chmn. c.o.c., 1985—; pvt. practice specializing in medicine, Columbus, 1984—; pres. Manx Found., Columbus, 1985—, GAAA, Columbus, 1986—, Hosp. Inns Inc., Columbus, 1986—, Manx Assocs. Inc., Columbus, 1986—. Contbr. articles to profl. jours. Mem. Am. Soc. Therapeutic Radiology and Oncology, Am. Coll. Radiology, Ohio State Med. Assn., Radiology Soc. Club: Le Chaiwe. Avocation: sports cars. Office: Riverside Meth Hosps 3535 Olentangy River Rd Columbus OH 43214

KENNEALY, LORI MARIE, gas company executive; b. St. Croix Falls, Wis., Jan. 20, 1960; d. Jerome Joseph and LaVonne Marie (Haar) K. BBA, U. Wis., Eau Claire, 1982. Records adminstr. Del Webb Corp., Phoenix, 1982-83; supr. records Wis. Gas Co., Milw., 1983—. Mem. Assn. Info. and Image Mgmt. (pres. 1985-86), Assn. Records Mgrs. and Adminstrs. (treas. 1985-86). Office: Wis Gas Co 626 E Wisconsin Ave Milwaukee WI 53202

KENNEDY, CHARLES ALLEN, lawyer; b. Maysville, Ky., Dec. 11, 1940; s. Elmer Earl and Mary Frances Kennedy; m. Patricia Ann Louderback, Dec. 9, 1961; 1 child, Mimi Mignon. A.B., Morehead State Coll., 1965, M.A. in Edn., 1968; J.D., U. Akron, 1969; L.L.M., George Washington U., 1974. Bar: Ohio 1969. Asst. cashier Citizens Bank, Felicity, Ohio, 1961-63; tchr. Triway Local Sch. Dist., Wooster, Ohio, 1965-67; with office of gen. counsel Fgn. Agr. and Spl. Programs Div., U.S. Dept. Agr., Washington, 1969-71; ptnr. Kauffman, Eberhart, Cicconetti & Kennedy Co., Wooster, 1972-86, Kennedy and Cicconetti, Wooster, 1986—. Mem. ABA, Fed. Bar Assn., Assn. Trial Lawyers Am., Ohio State Bar Assn., Ohio Acad. Trial Lawyers, Wayne County Bar Assn., Phi Alpha Delta, Phi Delta Kappa. Republican. Club: Exchange (Wooster). Lodges: Lions, Elks. Home: 1770 Burbank Rd Wooster OH 44691 Office: Kennedy and Cicconetti 558 N Market St Wooster OH 44691

KENNEDY, CHERYL LYNN, museum director; b. Pekin, Ill., Nov. 25, 1946; d. Paul Louis and Ann Marie (Bingham) Wieburg; m. Roger Nicholas Kennedy, Feb. 7, 1966; children: Kurt Alan, Kimberly Ann. Grad. high sch., Pekin, Ill. Prin., and profl. quilter Mahomet, Ill., 1976-81; program coordinator Early Am. Mus., Mahomet, 1981-85, dir. mus., 1985-86; dir. mus. and edn., 3 parks Champaign County Forest Preserve, Mahomet, 1986—; co-chair Ill. quilt documentation project Early Am. Mus. and Land of Lincoln Quilt Assn., 1986—. Creator and presenter (slide programs) Our Founding Mothers, 19th Century Life. Historian Meth. Local History Com., Mahomet, 1984-86. Mem. Midwest Mus. Council, Am. Assn. Museums, Am. Assn. State and Local History Museums, Cong. Ill. Hist. Socs. and Museums (dir. regionII), Ill. Heritage Assn., Ill. State Hist. Soc., Champaign County Hist. Soc., Nat. Quilt Assn. and Am. Quilt Soc., Antique Quilt Study Group and the Quilt Conservancy. Avocations: quilting, women's history, walking. Home: Rural Rt 3 Box 52 Mahomet IL 61853 Office: Early Am Mus PO Drawer 669 Mahomet IL 61853

KENNEDY, CORNELIA GROEFSEMA, judge; b. Detroit, Aug. 4, 1923; d. Elmer H. and Mary Blanche (Gibbons) Groefsema; m. Charles S. Kennedy, Jr.; 1 son, Charles S. III. B.A., U. Mich., 1945, J.D. with distinction, 1947; LL.D. (hon.), No. Mich. U., 1971, Eastern Mich. U., 1971, Western Mich. U., 1973, Detroit Coll. Law, 1980, U. Detroit, 1987. Bar: Mich. bar 1947. Law clk. to Chief Judge Harold M. Stephens, U.S. Ct. of Appeals, Washington, 1947-48; asso. Elmer H. Groefsema, Detroit, 1948-52; partner Markle & Markle, Detroit, 1952-66; judge 3d Judicial Circuit Mich., 1967-70; dist. judge U.S. Dist. Ct., Eastern Dist. Mich., Detroit, 1970-79; chief judge U.S. Dist. Ct., Eastern Dist. Mich., 1977-79; circuit judge U.S. Ct. Appeals, 6th Circuit, 1979—. Mem. Commn. on the Bicentennial of the U.S. Constitution (presdl. appoinment). Recipient Sesquicentennial award U. Mich. Fellow Am. Bar Found.; mem. ABA, Mich. Bar Assn. (past chmn. negligence law sect.), Detroit Bar Assn. (past dir.), Fed. Bar Assn., Am. Judicature Soc., Nat. Assn. Women Lawyers, Am. Trial Lawyers Assn., Nat. Conf. Fed. Trial Judges (past chmn.), Fed. Jud. Fellows Commn. (bd. dirs.), Fed. Jud. Ctr. (bd. dirs.), Phi Beta Kappa. Office: US Ct of Appeals (6th cir) 744 Fed Bldg US Courthouse 231 W Lafayette St Detroit MI 48226

KENNEDY, D. P., provincial judge. Judge Ct. of Queen's Bench, Winnipeg, Man., Can. Office: Court of Queen's Bench, Law Courts Bldg, Winnipeg, MB Canada R3C OV8 *

KENNEDY, DAVID BURL, physician; b. Indpls., Jan. 26, 1950; s. Robert Dean and Esther Evelyn (Stephani) K.; m. Barbara Anne Ehrgott, Jan. 6, 1973; children—Elizabeth Anne, Jeffrey Townsend. B.S., Ind. U., 1972, M.D., 1975. Diplomate Am. Bd. Psychiatry and Neurology. Intern, resident Ind. U. Med. Ctr., Indpls., 1975-78; cons. psychiatrist Psychiat. Clinics of Ind., Anderson, 1977, Four County Mental Health Ctr., Logansport, Ind., 1980-86; med. dir. Tipton Psychiat. Program, Tipton County Meml. Hosp., 1986—; staff psychiatrist Regional Mental Health Ctr., Kokomo, Ind., 1978-80; pres. David B. Kennedy, M.D., Inc. and Kennedy Clinics, Indpls. and Kokomo, 1980—; asst. clin. prof. psychiatry Ind. U. Sch. Medicine, Indpls., 1978—; mem. adv. bd. Profl. Communications, Inc., Teaneck, N.J., 1984. Mem. AMA, Ind. State Med. Assn., Marion County Med. Soc., Am. Psychiat. Assn., Ind. Psychiat. Soc., Phi Beta Kappa. Club: Columbia, Skyline (Indpls.). Avocations: boating; computers. Office: 4954 E 56th St Indianapolis IN 46220

KENNEDY, EUGENE CULLEN, writer, psychology educator; b. Syracuse, N.Y., Aug. 28, 1928; s. James Donald and Gertrude Veronica (Cullen) K.; m. Sara Connor Charles, Sept. 3, 1977. AB, Maryknoll Coll., 1950; STB, Maryknoll Sem., 1953, MRE, 1954; MA, Cath. U. Am., 1958, PhD, 1962. Instr. psychology Maryknoll Sem., Clarks Summit, Pa., 1955-56, Cath. U., Washington, 1959-60; prof. psychology Maryknoll Coll., Glen Ellyn, Ill., 1960-69, Loyola U., Chgo., 1969—; cons. Menninger Found., 1965-67; mem. profl. adv. bd. Chgo. Dept. Mental Health; dir. King Kullen Grocery Co. Author 40 books, including: Himself! The Life and Times of Richard J. Daley, 1978 (Carl Sandburg award 1978), Father's Day, 1981 (Soc. of Midland Authors fiction award 1981, Friends of Lit. award 1981, Carl Sandburg award 1981), Queen Bee, 1982, The Now and Future Church, 1984; (with Sara Charles) Defendant, 1985; author TV play: I Would Be Called John, PBS, 1987; also articles, book reviews. Trustee U. Dayton, Ohio, 1977-86. Recipient Thomas More medal, 1972, 78, Wilbur award Religious Pub. Relations Council. Fellow Am. Psychol. Assn. (div. pres. 1975-76); mem. Soc. Sci. Study Religion, Authors Guild. Democrat. Roman Catholic. Home: 1300 Lake Shore Dr Chicago IL 60610 Office: Loyola U Dept Psychology 6525 N Sheridan Chicago IL 60626

KENNEDY, GARY ALLEN, dentist; b. Gallipolis, Ohio, Dec. 8, 1956; s. Lawrence Evert and Eva Luise (Knight) K. BS, Marshall U., 1979; DDS, Ohio State U., 1983. Gen. practice dentistry Russells Point, Ohio, 1983—. Mem. Ohio Dental Assn., ADA, Mad River Valley Dental Soc., Point Amusement (com. mem.). Office: 303 E Main St Box 848 Russells Point OH 43348

KENNEDY, GEORGE D., chemical company executive; b. Pitts., May 30, 1926; s. Thomas Reed and Lois (Smith) K.; m. Valerie Putis; children: Charles Reed, George Danner, Jamey Kathleen, Susan Patton, Timothy Christian. BA, Williams Coll., 1948. With Scott Paper Co., 1947-52, Champion Paper Co., 1952-65; pres. Brown Co., 1965-71; exec. v.p. Internat. Minerals & Chem. Corp., Northbrook, Ill., 1971-78, pres., 1978-86, chmn., 1986—, chief exec. officer, 1983—, also bd. dirs.; chmn., com. mem., bd. dirs. Brunswick Corp.; bd. dirs., mem. exec. com. Kemper Corp. V.p., bd. dirs. N.E. Ill. council Boy Scouts Am.; chmn. Children's Meml. Hosp.; bd. dirs. McGaw Med. Ctr. Northwestern U.; trustee Chgo. Symphony; mem. Chgo. Com., Mid-Am. Com., Com. for Econ. Devel.; mem. bus. adv. council Carnegie-Mellon U. Grad. Sch. Indsl. Adminstrn.; trustee Nat. Com. Against Drunk Driving. Mem. Chgo. Assn. Commerce and Industry (bd. dirs.), Chgo. Council Fgn. Relations (bd. dirs.), Am. Mining Congress (vice chmn. bd. dirs.). Clubs: Board Room, N.Y. Athletic (N.Y.C.); Larchmont (N.Y.) Yacht; Sleepy Hollow Country (Scarborough, N.Y.); Skokie Country (Glencoe, Ill.); Comml. (Chgo.). Office: Internat Minerals & Chem Corp 2315 Sanders Rd Northbrook IL 60062

KENNEDY, JAMES EDWARD, JR., controller, accountant; b. Columbus, Ohio, May 17, 1961; s. James Edward Kennedy and Sandra Susan (Sachs) Kennedy Smith. BS in Acctg., U. Ky., 1983. CPA, Ohio. Sr. asst. cons. Deloitte Haskins & Sells, Columbus, 1983-86; controller Pizzuti, Inc., Columbus, 1986—. Mem. Am. Inst. CPA's, Delta Tau Delta (sec. 1982). Republican. Methodist. Club: Scioto Country (Columbus). Avocations: golf, basketball, platform tennis, volleyball. Home: 2893 Ravine Way Dublin OH 43017 Office: Pizzuti Inc 250 E Broad St Suite 1900 Columbus OH 43215

KENNEDY, LARRY EUGENE, communications executive; b. Macomb, Ill., July 30, 1936; s. Darrell Eugene and Lorena Magdalene (Thompson) K.; m. Karen Kay Cooper Hall, Apr. 25, 1958 (div.); children: Rick Eugene, Kimberly Kay; m. Lenore Julianne Peters, July 29, 1970; 1 child, Julianne Elizabeth. BS, Northwestern U., 1958, MA, 1962. Tchr., drama dir. Janesville (Wis.) Sr. High Sch., 1958-61, West Leyden High Sch., Northlake, Ill., 1961-67; tchr., dir. forensics and debate Highland Park (Ill.) High. Sch., 1967-80; pres. Kennedy Communication Cons., Evanston, Ill., 1980—. Mem. Am. Soc. Tng. and Devel., Ill. Tng. and Devel. Assn., Chgo. Sales Tng. Assn. (bd. dirs. 1984—), Nat. Forensic League. Office: Kennedy Communication Cons 8846 Forestview Evanston IL 60203

KENNEDY, MICHAEL JAMES, microbiologist, researcher; b. Wayne, Mich., Mar. 14, 1958; s. James Edward Kennedy and Adrienne Eve (Branecki) Kennedy Star; m. Laura Ann Ramage, Aug. 18, 1979; children: Alyssa Lauren, Andrea Michelle. BS, Eastern Mich. U., 1980, MS, 1984. Microbiologist research service and infectious diseases sect. VA Med. Ctr., Ann Arbor, Mich., 1980-82; research microbiologist dept. microbiology and immunology U. Mich., Ann Arbor, 1982-84; biologist/biochemist II microbiology and nutrition research The Upjohn Co., Kalamazoo, 1984—; research microbiologist extraterrestrial research div. NASA, Ames Research Ctr., Moffett Field, Calif., 1983-84. Contbr. numerous articles to profl. jours. Mem. Am. Soc. for Microbiology, Am. Soc. for Photobiology, Soc. for Intestinal Microbial Ecology and Disease, Internat. Soc. for Human and Animal Mycology, Explorers Club, Planetary Soc., Sigma Xi (Grad. Student Research award 1982), Beta Beta Beta (Nat. Hon. Soc. for Biol. Scis. award 1983). Democrat. Baptist. Avocations: family, church, scuba diving, camping. Office: The Upjohn Co 7922-190-MR Kalamazoo MI 49001

KENNEDY, SCOTT CLARENCE, dentist; b. Topeka, Aug. 14, 1950; s. Howard Unger and Frances Louise (Field) K.; m. Kathleen Louella James, Jan 8, 1972; children: Kristen, Molly. Student, Kans. State U., 1970-71; DDS, U. Mo., Kansas City, 1975. Pvt. practice dentistry Topeka, 1975—. Sec., treas. Kans. Dental Political Action Com., 1981-83. Mem. ADA (spl. com. on young dentists 1986-87), Kansas Dental Assn. (legis. com. 1983-84, chmn. 1984-86, sec. 1986—), Topeka Dist. Dental Soc. (sec., treas. 1983-84, v.p. 1985-86, pres. 1985-86). Office: 1002 Garfield Topeka KS 66604

KENNEDY, WALTER JEFF, JR., lawyer; b. Kansas City, Kans., May 18, 1928; s. Walter Joseph and Emily (Knecht) K.; m. Norma Jeanne Buie, June 4, 1949 (dec. Mar. 1984); children—Kathleen Kim, Nancy Jo.; m. Geraldine N. Rieke, May 30, 1986. A.A., Kansas City Jr. Coll., 1952; A.B., Kans. U., 1954, J.D., 1956. Bar: Mo. 1956, Kans. 1956, U.S. Ct. Appeals (8th and 10th cirs.), U.S. Ct. Claims, 1971, U.S. Tax Ct., 1959, U.S. Dist. Ct. (we. dist.) Mo. 1956, U.S. Dist. Ct. Kans. 1956, U.S. Supreme Ct. 1970. Assoc. Davis, Thompson, Fairchild & Van Dyke, Kansas City, Mo., 1956—; sole practice, El Dorado, Kans., 1957-61; mem. legal staff Farmland Industries, Kansas City, Mo., 1961-63; assoc. Hoskins, King, McGannon, Hahn & Hurwitz, Kansas City, Mo., 1963-68, ptnr., 1968—. Served with USN, 1945-50; PTO. Mem. ABA, Mo. Bar Assn., Mo. Bar Assn. Corp. (banking and bus. orgns. com. 1984-86), Kans. Bar Assn., Lawyers Assn. Kansas City, Kansas City Bar Assn. Club: Milburn Country (Overland Park, Kans.). Author articles. Office: Commerce Trust Bldg Suite 1100 Kansas City MO 64106

KENNELLY, HEIDI A., respiratory therapist; b. Connersville, Ind., Nov. 24, 1954; d. Ruth A. (Hermann) Asleson; m. Kevin Kennelly, June 4, 1976; 1 child, Kory Charles. BS, Mercer U., 1976; Assoc. Respiratory Therapy, Madison Area Tech. Coll., 1979. Registered respiratory therapist, 1980. Respiratory therapist St. Vincent Hosp., Green Bay, Wis., 1979-86; with cardiopulmonary lab. St. Vincent Hosp., Green Bay, 1985-86; respiratory therapist St. Joseph Hosp., Milw., 1986—; CPR instr., Green Bay, 1980-86, Milw., 1986—. Mem. Am. Assn. Respiratory Care, Wis. Assn. Respiratory Care. Avocations: walking, swimming, skiing. Home: N100 W16825 Revere Ln Germantown WI 53022

KENNELLY, JOHN JEROME, lawyer; b. Chgo., Dec. 11, 1918; s. Joseph Michael and Anna (Flynn) K.; m. Mary Thompson, Mar. 21, 1949. Ph.B., Loyola U., Chgo., 1939, LL.B., 1941. Bar: Ill. 1941, U.S. Dist. Ct. (no. dist.) Ill. 1941, U.S. Ct. Appeals (7th cir.) 1946, U.S. Supreme Ct. 1956. Sole practice, Chgo., 1946—. Served with USN, 1941-46. Fellow Internat. Acad. Trial Lawyers (past chmn. aviation sect.); mem. Chgo. Bar Assn. (bd. mgrs. 1965-67), Ill. State Bar Assn., ABA (aviation com. chmn. 1981-82), Inter-Am. Bar Assn., Ill. Trial Lawyers Assn. (pres. 1968-69), AIAA, Assn. Trial Lawyers Am., Am. Judicature Soc., Law Sci. Acad. Am., World Assn. Lawyers, Am. Coll. Trial Lawyers, Internat. Acad. Law and Sci., Internat. Soc. Barristers, Am. Soc. Internat. Law, Am. Bar Found. Clubs: Butterfield Country (Hinsdale, Ill.); Beverly Country (Chgo.). Author: Litigation and Trial of Air Crash Cases, 1969; contbr. articles to profl. jours. Office: 111 W Washington St Suite 1449 Chicago IL 60602

KENNER, JOHN ROBERT, social worker, administrator, therapist; b. Detroit, Sept. 23, 1954; s. Wilmer Allen and Mary Eloise (Robinson) K.; m. RAchael Annette Evans, Aug. 27, 1983; children: Camille Annette, Jonathan Robert. BSW, U. Detroit, 1976; MSW, Wayne State U., 1979. Cert. social worker, Mich. Crisis counselor Project Headline Eastwood Community Clinic, Detroit, 1975; med. social worker Sickle Cell Progress, Inc., Detroit, 1976-77; child care worker Meth. Children's Home Soc., Detroit, 1978; clin. social worker Life Stress Ctr. Health Care Inst., Detroit, 1979-80, Ambulatory Mental Health Service, Detroit, 1980-83; outpatient coordinator Renaissance West Community Mental Health Ctr., Detroit, 1983-87; clin. social worker VIB Northville (Mich.) Regional Psychiatric Hosp., 1987—; pvt. practice social work Boone-Kenner Assocs., Detroit, 1979-84, Evening Hours Clinic, Detroit, 1984—; chmn. Progressive Young Adult Ctr., Detroit, 1981-85. Mem. Nat. Assn. Social Workers (bd. dirs. 1981-84), Am. Soc. Notaries,Alpha Phi Alpha (asst. sec. 1986-87, v.p. 1987—). Republican. Roman Catholic. Avocations: classical music, opera, ballet, golf, reading. Home: 2106 Oakman Blvd Detroit MI 48238 Office: Northville Regional Psychiatric Hosp 41001 7 Mile Northville MI 48167

KENNEY, CHARLES SAMUEL, lawyer; b. Bay City, Mich., July 26, 1917; s. Samuel Charles and Kathern C. (McClellan) K.; B.C.S., Cleary Coll., 1937; B.S., Eastern Mich. U., 1940; J.D., Wayne State U., 1951; m. Ellen G. Hilbert, Oct. 8, 1944; children—Barbara (Mrs. William M. Silvis), Peter C., William S., Scott S. Admitted to Mich. bar, 1952; tchr. Woodland (Mich.) High Sch., 1940-42; auditor Mich. State Accident Fund, 1945-52; partner firm Archer, Kenney, & Wilson, Dearborn, Mich., 1952—. Pres., Western Wayne Homeowners Assn., 1966, Woodland Tchrs. Assn., 1941. Served with U.S. Army, 1942-45. Mem. Dearborn (pres. 1965), Mich., Am. bar assns., Am. Coll. Probate Counsel, Delta Theta Phi. Presbyn. (deacon 1972—). Home: 8909 Beck Rd Plymouth MI 48170 Office: 20390 W Outer Dr Dearborn MI 48124

KENNEY, JOHN PATRICK, dentist; b. Joliet, Ill., July 8, 1946; s. John Edward and Nellie (Fratia) K.; m. Catherine McGehee, June 1, 1968. BS in Mktg., Christian Bros. Coll., 1968; DDS, Loyola U., Maywood, Ill., 1977, cert. in pediat. dentistry, 1979; MS in Oral Biology, Loyola U., Chgo., 1979. Diplomate Am. Bd. Forensic Odontology. Supr. passenger services Am. Airlines, Chgo., 1968-72; practice dentistry specializing in pediatric dentistry Park Ridge, Ill., 1980—; asst. prof. pediat. dentistry Northwestern U., Chgo., 1983—; forensic odontologist Cook County Med. Examiner, Chgo., 1984—, Kane County (Ill.) Coroner, Geneva, 1984—; cons. forensic odontologist Am. Airlines, Chgo., 1979, Midwest Express Airlines, Milw., 1985. Contbr. articles to profl. jours. Fellow Am. Acad. Forensic Scis; mem. ADA, Internat. Orgn. for Forensic Odonto-stomatology (v.p. 1984—), Ill. State Dental Soc., Chgo. Dental Soc., Am. Acad. Pediat. Dentists, Ill. Soc. Pediat. Dentists, Am. Soc. Forensic Odontology, Am. Bd. Forensic Odontology. Lodge: Kiwanis (pres. 1983-84, Disting. Pres. 1984). Office: 101 S Washington Park Ridge IL 60068-4290

KENT, BARBARA DALY, social worker; b. York, Maine, Mar. 15, 1941; d. William Everett and Hazel Evelyn (Quinn) Daly; m. Michael Harold Kent, Nov. 26, 1959 (div. Nov. 1967); children: Michael Louis, David William. AA, Lewis and Clark Community Coll., 1974; med. asst. cert., Carnegie Inst. Med. Tech., 1960; psychiat. aid. cert., Alton (Ill.) State Hosp., 1966; BS, So. Ill. U., 1976. Registered social worker, Ill. Researcher, author Tri-City Area United Way, Granite City, Ill., 1977-78; counselor crisis intervention Macoupin County Mental Health Ctr., Carlinville, Ill., 1978—; psychiat. staff Meml. Med. Ctr. St. John's Hosp., Springfield, Ill., 1982—; mem. guidelines com. for case mgmt. for services for chronically mentally ill State Ill. Dept. Health and Developmental Disability, Chgo., 1985—. Mem. So. Ill. U. Alumni Assn. Avocations: camping, travel. Home: Rural Rt 1 Box 71 Plainview IL 62676 Office: Macoupin County Mental Health Ctr 100 N Side of Square Carlinville IL 62626

KENT, ELIZABETH NOEL, editor; b. Greensboro, N.C., Dec. 6, 1940; d. William Alfred and Rosa Elouise (Baughn) K. B.S., Ga. So. Coll., 1962; M.A., Ball State U., 1983. Tchr. English, Bd. Edn. Savannah, Ga., 1962-67; tchr. English, Stenography Div., Fort Harrison, Ind., 1974-77; edn. specialist Directorate of Tng. and Doctrine, Dept. Army, Fort Harrison, Ind., 1977-79, editor, 1979-83, chief editor, 1983-86; instr. English Vincennes U., 1979-86; realtor Realty World Sargent and Assocs., 1986—; communication cons., lectr. on communication and English to profl. groups. Served to capt. U.S. Army, 1967-74. Recipient Sustained Superior Performance award U.S. Army, 1976, Spl. Act award for superior editing, 1985. Mem. Fed. Women's Program, Federally Employed Women, Nat. Assn. Female Execs., Am. Legion, DAV, Women's Army Corps Assn., Met. Indpls. Bd. Realtors, Bus. and Profl. Women. Anglican Catholic. Avocation: reading. Home: 11430 Wolf Ln Indianapolis IN 46229 Office: Sargent and Assoc Realtors 4712 N Franklin Rd Indianapolis IN 46226

KENT, GEORGE GLAU, wheat farmer; b. Denver, July 30, 1926; s. Jesse Clarence and Wilhelmina S. (Struve) GLau; m. Edythe Geraldine Fenner, June 4, 1948 (div. June 1962); 1 child, Kitty Chili; m. Cheryl M. Underhill, Oct. 9, 1981. BBA, U. Denver, 1958, MA, 1966. Cert. tchr., Colo. Prodn. worker Cascade Plywood Corp., Lebanon, Oreg., 1948-51; cattle farmer Greenbrier, Ark., 1951-54; tchr. Denver Pub. High Schs., 1959-62; owner Kent Farm, Hemingford, Nebr., 1966—. Mem. Wheat Growers Assn. Democrat. Avocations: polit. studies, exposure of myths, pilot. Address: Kent Farm HC 60 Box 65 Hemingford NE 69348

KENT, JAMES H., food products company executive; b. 1923. With Grain Processing Corp., Muscatine, Iowa, 1945—, v.p., 1960-66, pres., 1966—, also bd. dirs. Office: Grain Processing Corp 1600 Oregon St Muscatine IA 52761 *

KENT, ROBERT JOHN, accountant; b. Kalamazoo, Mar. 2, 1947; s. W. Wallace and Laverne A. (Fredlund) K.; m. Raenell Kay Seeds, July 15, 1972; children: Robert Jr., T. Bradley. BBA in Acctg., Western Mich. U., 1969; BA in Hotel Mgmt., Mich. State U., 1972. CPA, Mich., Calif., Ill. Staff acct. Harris, Kerr, Forster and Co., San Francisco, 1972-76; audit supr., cons. Harris, Kerr, Forster and Co., Chgo., 1976-78; audit mgr. Alexander Grant and Co., Kalamazoo, 1978-84, Siegfried, Crandall, Vos and Lewis

P.C., Kalamazoo, 1985—. Contbr. articles to profl. mags. Trustee Kalamazoo Valley Community Coll., 1982—, treas., 1985—. Mem. Am. Inst. CPA's, Mich. Assn. CPA's, Mich. Community Coll. Assn. (bd. dirs. 1982—, sec., exec. com. 1986—). Episcopalian. Lodges: Rotary (sec. Gull Lake area 1987—).

KEOGH, JEANNE MARIE, librarian; b. Toledo, Sept. 20, 1924; d. Thomas Leroy and Agnes Mary (Wenzler) K. BA, Mary Manse Coll., 1946; BLS, Western Res. U., 1947. Asst. librarian tech. dept. Toledo Pub. Library, 1946-54; tech. librarian Libbey Owens Ford Co., Toledo, 1954-83; librarian Libbey Owens Ford Co. (now subs. Pilkington Group), Toledo, 1983—. Established library Riverside Hosp. Nursing Sch., Toledo, 1950-51; gray lady ARC, Toledo, 1966-70; mem. Transp. Safety Info. com., 1972—; mem. fin. com. Mary Manse Coll., Toledo, 1972-75; chmn. bd. Ecumenical Library Toledo, 1976—. Mem. Ohio Library Assn., Cath. Library Assn., Spl. Libraries Assn. (chmn. 1960-70, 72-74, scholarship com. 1968-74, chmn. Detroit conf. hospitality com. 1970, chmn. metals/materials div. 1977-78, metals/materials div. Honors award 1987), Mary Manse Coll. Alumni Assn. (bd. dirs. 1971-76, pres. 1972-73). Club: Quota (Toledo). Office: Libbey Owens Ford Co 1701 E Broadway Toledo OH 43605

KEOUGH, JAMES GILLMAN, JR., minister; b. Reading, Pa., June 2, 1947; s. James Gillman Sr. and Mora (Deturck) K.; m. Dawn Eileen Wiest, Sept. 17, 1976; children: Cynthia Ann, James Michael, Wendy Sue, Danielle Lynn, Erin Mae, Bevin Leigh. BA in History Edn., Messiah Coll., Grantham, Pa., 1970; MDiv, Lancaster (Pa.) Theol. Sem., 1973; D of Ministry, Ashland (Ohio) Theol. Sem., 1980. Ordained to ministry United Ch. Christ, 1973. Minister St. Luke's United Ch. Christ, Kenhorst, Pa., 1972-75, Congl. Ch., Winchester, Va., 1975-78, 1st Congl. Ch., Newton Falls, Ohio, 1978-82, Cen. Congl. Ch., Middleboro, Mass., 1982-85; sr. minister 1st Congl. Ch., Pontiac, Mich., 1985—. Author: Teaching Prayer in the Local Parish, 1980. Mem. adv. council Pontiac Schs., 1987—; pres. Somebodycares, Pontiac, 1983—. Mem. Nat. Assn. Congl. Christian Chs., Southeast Mich. Congl. Ministerium, Pontiac Ministers Assn. Republican. Lodge: Kiwanis. Avocations: reading, hiking, fishing. Home: 3062 St Jude Dr Drayton Plains MI 48020 Office: 1st Congl Ch 65 E Huron St Pontiac MI 48059

KEPLEY, BENJAMIN FRANKLIN, oral and maxillofacial surgeon, educator; b. Detroit, June 20, 1937; s. Benjamin Franklin and Martha Mae (Crawford) K.; m. Sandra Lee Basch, Sept. 11, 1961; children: Franklin Kyle, Damon Kirk. DMD, U. Louisville, 1962. Diplomate Am. Bd. Oral and Maxillofacial Surgery. Asst. dir. oral and maxillofacial surgery residency program Naval Hosp., Oakland, Calif., 1976-79, chief of dental service, Pensacola, Fla., 1979-82; clinic dir. Naval Dental Clinic, San Diego, 1982-84; dir. oral and maxillofacial surgery residency program Naval Hosp., Great Lakes, Ill., 1984—; clin. assoc. prof. Loyola U., Chgo., 1984—, VA Hosp., North Chicago, 1984—. Recipient Humanitarian medal U.S. Navy, 1976. Fellow Am. Assn. Oral and Maxillofacial Surgeons, Internat. Coll. Dentists; mem. Am. Dental Soc. of Anesthesiology, ADA, Ky. Dental Assn. Avocations: physical fitness, golf. Home: 1213 Green Tree Ct Libertyville IL 60048 Office: Naval Hosp Oral Surgery Dept Great Lakes IL 60088

KER, (ALICE) ANN STEELE, music educator, composer, organist, choir director; b. Warsaw, Ind., Nov. 10, 1937; d. George Arthur and Winifred Pauline (Foster) Steele; m. Charles Arthur Ker, Sept. 8, 1957 (div.); children: Kelly Lynne, Karen Elizabeth, Kristin Ann. Student, DePauw U., 1955-57, Butler U., 1957-58; BME, Ind. U., 1974; MA, Notre Dame U., 1987. Organist 1st Presbyn. Ch., Warsaw, 1969-79; dir. music Cen. Christian Ch., Huntington, Ind., 1980; mem. faculty Huntington Coll., 1975—; dir. music Redeemer Luth. Ch., Warsaw, 1980—; festival condr. Luth. Circuit Festival Chorus; co-founder, bd. mem. No. Ind. Opera Assn.; mem. Lakeland Community Concert Assn., concert critic, bd. mem., 1976-80. Composer: Hear This!, 1973, Triptych, 1980, Three Men on Camelback, 1982, One Glorious God, 1982, For Me, O Lord, 1983, Softly, 1983, Ways to Praise, 1983, The House of the Lord, 1984. Active Kosciusko Community Hosp. Aux., 1975—. Winner 1st place composition competition St. Francis Coll., 1974. Mem. Internat. League Women Composers, Am. Guild Organists (bd. dirs. 1978-81), Am. Choral Dirs. Assn., Nat. Guild Piano Tchrs., Am. Musicol. Soc., Music Tchrs. Nat. Assn., Women in Music. Republican. Home: 1607 N Springhill Rd Warsaw IN 46580 Office: Huntington Coll Music Dept Huntington IN 46750

KERAN, DOUGLAS CHARLES, natural resources consultant, educator; b. Mpls., Nov. 12, 1943; s. Philip Leroy and Charlotte Virginia (Hoaglund) K.; m. Julie Doris Godtland, May 12, 1979; children: Douglas, Kevin, Shane, Brianna. BS, U. Minn., 1965; MA, St. Cloud U., 1976; PhD, Pacific West U., 1987. Researcher, U. Minn. Cedar Creek Natural History Area, 1964-65; dir. Crow Wing Natural History Area, Brainerd, Minn., 1969-73; instr. fisheries and wildlife Brainerd Tech. Inst., 1973—; pres. Kerdolian, Inc., Brainerd, 1981—, wildlife cons., 1980—; night sch. instr. Brainerd Tech. Inst., 1973—. Served with USCG, 1965-69. Named Outstanding Reservist in Minn., Res. Forces Component, 1972; Profl. Environ. Quality award, 1984; Minn. Nongame Wildlife Program grantee, 1982—. Mem. Nat. Wildlife Soc., Raptor Research Found., N. Central Wildlife Soc., Minn. Wildlife Soc., Kestrel Karetakers, Am. Fisheries Soc., Minn. Ornithological Union, Minn. Wildlife Assistance Coop. Lutheran. Club: Bee Nay She Council (Brainerd). Contbr. articles to profl. jours. Home: 2266 Whispering Woods Ln N Brainerd MN 56401 Office: 300 Quince St Brainerd MN 56401

KERBER, CHARLES, farm production supplies cooperative executive; b. 1935; married. Grad., Ind. U., 1957. Pres., dir. Ind. Farm Bur. Coop. Am. Inc., Indpls., 1981—. Office: Ind Farm Bur Coop Assn Inc 120 E Market St Indianapolis IN 46204 *

KERBESHIAN, JACOB, child psychiatrist, consultant; b. Cambridge, Mass., Jan. 21, 1944; s. Jacob and Mary (Marderosian) K.; m. Lynn Marie Anderson, Feb. 4, 1967; children: Marie, Jack, Neva, Sarah. AB, Harvard Coll., 1966; MD, U. Rochester, 1970. Diplomate Am. Bd. Psychiatry and Neurology. Intern in pediatrics Cleve. Met. Hosp., 1970-71; resident in psychiatry U. Rochester, 1971-73, fellow in child psychiatry, 1973-75; child psychiatrist Grand Forks (N.D.) Clinic, 1977—; dir. psychiatry United Hosp., Grand Forks, 1977—; cons. in field. Contbr. articles to profl. jour. Mem. gov's commn. on Children and Adolescents at Risk, N.D., 1986. Served to maj. USAF, 1975-77. Mem. AMA, Am. Acad. Child and Adolescent Psychiatry, Am. Psychiat. Assn. Assn. Third Dist. Med. Soc. (pres. 1986-87), N.D. Psychiat. Soc. (pres. 1984-86). Episcopalian. Home: 1620 Belmont Rd Grand Forks ND 58201 Office: Grand Forks Clinic 1000 S Columbia Rd Grand Forks ND 58201

KERBIS, GERTRUDE LEMPP, architect. m. Walter Peterhans (dec.); m. Donald Kerbis (div. 1972); children: Julian, Lisa, Kim. B.S., U. Ill.; M.A., Ill. Inst. Tech.; postgrad., Grad. Sch. Design, Harvard U., 1949-50. Archtl. designer Skidmore, Owings & Merrill, Chgo., 1954-59, C.F. Murphy Assocs., Chgo., 1959-62, 65-67; pvt. practice architecture Chgo., 1967—; lectr. U. Ill., 1969; prof. William Rainey Harper Coll., 1970—, Washington U., St. Louis, 1977, 82; archtl. cons. Dept. Urban Renewal, City of Chgo.; mem. Northeastern Ill. Planning Commn., Open Land Project, Mid-North Community Orgn., Chgo. Met. Housing and Planning Council, Chgo. Mayor's Commn. for Preservation Chgo.'s Hist. Architecture; bd. dirs. Chgo. Sch. Architecture Found., 1972-76; trustee Glessner House Found., Inland Architect Mag.; lectr. Art Inst. Chgo., U. N.Mex., Ill. Inst. Tech., Washington U., St. Louis, Ball State U., Muncie, Ind., U. Utah, Salt Lake City. Prin. archtl. works include U.S. Air Force Acad. dining hall, Colo., 1957, Skokie (Ill.) Pub. Library, 1959, Meadows Club, Lake Meadows, Chgo., 1959, O'Hare Internat. Airport 7 Continents Bldg, 1963; prin. developer and architect: Tennis Club, Highland Park, Ill., 1968, Watervliet, Mich. Tennis Ranch, 1970, Greenhouse Condominium, Chgo., 1976, Webster-Clark Townhouses, Chgo., 1985; exhibited at Chgo. Hist. Soc., 1984, Chgo. Mus. Sci. and Industry, 1985, Paris Exhbn. Chgo. Architects, 1985; represented in permanent archtl. drawings collection Art Inst. Chgo. Recipient award for outstanding achievement in professions YWCA Met. Chgo., 1984. Fellow AIA (dir. Chgo. chpt. 1971-75, chpt. pres. 1980, mem. nat. com. architecture arts and recreation 1972-75, com. on design 1975—, head subcom. inst. honors nomination); mem. AAUP, ACLU, U. Ill., Ill. Inst. Tech. alumni assns., Art Inst. Chgo., Chgo. Council Fgn. Relations, Chgo. Women in Architecture (founder), Planned Parenthood Assn., Chgo. Network, Lincoln Park Zool. Soc., Chgo. Arts Club., Lambda Alpha. Club: Cliff-Dwellers (Chgo.). Office: Lempp Kerbis Architects 172 W Burton Pl Chicago IL 60610

KERCH, STEVEN JAMES, journalist; b. Freeport, Ill., July 18, 1956; s. James Franklin and Mary Jane (Morrow) K. BA in Journalism, U. Wis., 1978. Design editor Suburban Tribune, Hinsdale, Ill., 1979-81; reporter Chgo. Tribune, 1982-84, real estate writer, 1984—. Bd. dirs. Literacy Vols. of Chgo. Mem. Nat. Assn. Real Estate Editors (bd. dirs.). Home: 1753 W Columbia Ave Chicago IL 60626 Office: Chicago Tribune 435 N Michigan Ave Chicago IL 60611

KERES, KAREN LYNNE, English educator; b. Evanston, Ill., Oct. 22, 1945; d. Frank and Bette (Pascoe) K.; B.A., St. Mary's Coll., 1967; student U. Notre Dame, 1967-68; M.A., U. Iowa, 1969. Asst. to editor U. Chgo. Press, 1968; assoc. prof. humanities, fine art William Rainey Harper Coll., Palatine, Ill., 1969—; cons. bus. communications. Mem. MLA, Ill. Assn. Tchrs. English, Am. Fedn. Tchrs., Nature Conservancy, Mensa. Home: 222 Fairfield Dr Island Lake IL 60042 Office: William Rainey Harper Coll Dept Liberal Arts Palatine IL 60067

KERICH, JAMES PATRICK, manufacturing company executive; b. Wichita, Kans., May 25, 1938; s. Bernard William and Helen Marie (Hendrickson) K.; m. Julia Jean Grosjean, June 28, 1958; children—Marie Suzanne, Julie Ann, Wendy Kathryn. Student Kans. U. Dir. ops. Skyline Corp., Elkhart, Ind., 1974-79, v.p., officer, 1982—; ptnr. gas and oil ops. Okla. Farming, 1981—; pres. ON TV, Detroit, 1979-81; sports negotiator, cons., investor Pay TV, Chgo., Detroit and Dallas, 1981-82; cons. Buford TV, Chgo., 1981, Golden West Broadcasting, Los Angeles, 1981. Republican. Roman Catholic. Clubs: South Bend Country; Sugar Mill Country (New Smyrna Beach, Fla.). Lodge: Elks. Home: 1525 Greenleaf Blvd Elkhart IN 46514 Office: Skyline Corp 2520 By Pass Rd Elkhart IN 46514

KERLAGON, RAYMOND LEE, telephone company executive; b. St. Louis, Dec. 15, 1945; s. Lawrence Raymond and Lola Louise (Isgrig) K.; A. Sci.-and Commerce in Econs., St. Louis U., 1971, M.B.A., 1976; B.S. in Bus. Adminstrn., Washington U., 1974; m. Jane Arlene Schnuriger, Nov. 6, 1965; children—Sherri Lynn, Michael James. Spl. rep. Southwestern Bell Telephone Co., St. Louis, 1965-69, communications cons., 1977, phone power specialist, 1977, account exec., 1977-79, staff specialist promotions and motivation, 1979-80, industry mgr., 1980-81, staff mgr. competitive tactics, 1981, staff mgr. sales devel., 1981—; field sales rep. Xerox Corp., 1969-72; sr. customer service rep. Monsanto, 1972-74, voice communications analyst, 1974-76; zone mgr. Ford Motor Co., 1976-77; adj. prof. Meramec Community Coll.; faculty investments and fin. mgmt. Webster U. Troop capt. Greater St. Louis council Girl Scouts U.S.A., 1974; mem. curriculum adv. com. St. Louis Community Coll., 1983—; asst. mgr. Ballwin Baseball, 1980-82. Recipient Dist. Profl. award Southwestern Bell, 1979. Mem. Nat. Assn. Securities Dealers. Baptist. Contbr. to profl. jours. and booklets. Home: 15494 Strollways Dr Chesterfield MO 63017 Office: 12800 Publications Dr Suite 404 Saint Louis MO 63131

KERMEEN, SHARON KAY, social services worker; b. Caledonia, Mich., Dec. 2, 1938; d. Wayne Earl and Crystal Doreen (Johnson) K. Grad. high sch., Middleville, Mich. Typist, clk. social aid bur. Barry Co., Hastings, Mich., 1957-69; clerical supr. Mich. Dept. Social Services, Hastings, 1969-70, eligibility examiner, 1970-72, assistance payments worker, 1972—. Mem. cast Hastings Civic Players, 1963. Mem. Mich. State Employees Assn. (sec. treas., v.p.), United Auto Workers, Hastings Bus. and Profl. Women's Club)corr. sec., 2d v.p.). Methodist. Avocations: traveling, ceramics, photography, knitting, reading. Home: 321 S Broadway Middleville MI 49333

KERN, THOMAS LEE, manufacturing company executive; consultant; b. Cleve., July 23, 1946; s. Elroy J. and Carol L. (Scheuerman) K.; m. Dorothy Weitzel, Jan. 27, 1967; children—Michelle, Lynette, Bryan, Christine. B.S.B.A., Bowling Green State U., 1968. Machinist, Hartland Machine, Norwalk, Ohio, 1962-66; machinist-assembler Printainer Corp., Norwalk, 1966-68; gen. foreman Clevite Corp., Milan, Ohio, 1968-69, indsl. engr., 1969-70; v.p., gen. mgr. Poly-Foam Internat., Fremont, Ohio, 1970-72, pres., chief exec. officer, 1972—; ptnr. Hartland Auto Stores, Clyde, Ohio, 1973—; pres. Top Distbrs., Clyde, 1978—; pres., chief exec. officer GMH Enterprises, Inc., Fremont, 1986—; sec., bd. dirs. Aunt Maggies, Inc., Norwalk, Ohio, 1986—; bd. dirs. PFI Transport, Fremont. Recipient W. C. Coleman award Coleman Co., Wichita, Kans., 1983. Mem. Warehouse Distbrs. Assn. Republican. Presbyterian. Home: 179 Saint Thomas Dr Fremont OH 43420 Office: Poly Foam Internat Inc 600 Hagerty Dr Fremont OH 43420

KERNS, GERTRUDE YVONNE, psychologist; b. Flint, Mich., July 25, 1931; d. Lloyd D. and Mildred C. (Ter Achter) B.; B.A., Olivet Coll., 1953; M.A., Wayne State U., 1958; Ph.D., U. Mich., 1979. Sch. psychologist Roseville (Mich.) Pub. Schs., 1958-68, Grosse Pointe (Mich.) Pub. Schs., 1968—; pvt. practice psychology, 1980—; instr. psychology Macomb Community Coll., 1959-63. Mem. Mich., Am. psychol. assns., Mich., Nat. socs. sch. psychologists, NEA, Psi Chi. Home: 28820 Grant St Saint Clair Shores MI 48081 Office: 63 Kercheval Suite 205 Grosse Pointe MI 48236

KERR, ANDREW, JR., physician, educator; b. Wilkinsburg, Pa., Dec. 30, 1914; s. Andrew and Mary (Keister) K.; m. Ann Burnham Jackson, Apr. 5, 1940 (div. 1963); children: Katherine, Andy, Ward; m. Mary VanCleve Quincy, May 20, 1963. AB, Colgate U., 1937; MD, Harvard U., 1941. Instr. medicine Tulane U., New Orleans, 1948-50; asst. prof. medicine La. State U., New Orleans, 1950-55; assoc. prof. SUNY, Syracuse, 1955-60; clin. prof. Med. Coll. Ga., Augusta, 1960-61; clin. asst. prof. U. Rochester, N.Y., 1961-67; prof. N.E. Ohio Coll. Medicine, Akron, 1974-87, prof. emeritus, 1987—; asst. chief medicine VA Hosp., Syracuse, 1955-60; chief medicine VA Hosp., Augusta, 1960-61, Batavia, N.Y., 1962-67; chmn. dept. medicine Akron City Hosps., 1967-75. Served to capt. M.C., U.S. Army, 1945-46, ETO. Avocations: gardening, fox hunting. Home: 7431 Valley View Hudson OH 44236

KERR, DAVID MILLS, state legislator; b. Pratt, Kans., May 4, 1945; s. Fred H. and Eleanor Mills (Barrett) K.; m. Mary Patricia O'Rourke, Aug. 24, 1979; children: Ryan, Daniel. BA, Kans. State U., 1968; MBA, U. Kans., 1970. Auditor Trans World Airlines, Kansas City, Mo., 1970-72, mgr. fin., 1972-76; pres. Agronomics Internat., Hutchinson, Kans., 1976-84; mem. Kans. State Senate, Topeka, 1984—; bd. dirs. Kans. tech. Enterprises Corp.; vice chmn. com. Senate Econ. Devel., 1986. Mem. Advanced Tech. Commn., Topeka, 1985; chmn. Task Force on Capitol Markets And Tax, Topeka, 1986. Named Kans. Exporter of Yr., Internat. Trade Inst., 1981. Mem. Kans. C. of C. (bd. dirs. 1983—). Republican. Presbyterian. Avocations: traveling, hunting, fishing. Home: 6 Golf Green Dr Hutchinson KS 67502 Office: Recovery Systems Inc Box 2620 Hutchinson KS 67502

KERR, ELIZABETH MARGARET, educator, author; b. Sault Ste Marie, Mich., Jan. 25, 1905; d. John Arthur and Katherine Dorothy (Hirth) Kerr. BA, U. Minn., 1926, MA, 1927, PhD, 1941. Instr. English, Tabor Coll., Hillsboro, Kans., 1929-30, U. Minn., Mpls., 1930-37, 38-43, Coll. of St. Catherine, St. Paul, 1937-38; asst. prof. Rockford (Ill.) Coll., 1943-45; instr. Milw. State Coll., 1945-55; assoc. prof. U. Wis., Milw., 1956-59, prof., 1959-70, prof. emeritus English, 1970—. Author: Bibliography of the Sequence Novel, 1950, Yoknapatawpha: Faulkner's Little Postage Stamp of Native Soil, 1969, William Faulkner's Gothic Domain, 1979, William Faulkner's Yoknapatawpha: "A Kind of Keystone in the Universe", 1984. MLA research grantee, 1942, Summer Salary Support grantee U. Wis., Milw., 1959, 1961. Mem. MLA, Dickens Studies, Soc. for Study So. Lit. Democrat. Congregationalist. Home: Fairhaven 435 Starin Rd Whitewater WI 53190

KERR, JOSEPH KENT, lawyer; b. Kittanning, Pa., Oct. 26, 1946; s. Joseph Kent and Virginia Rita (Marazzi) K. BS, Xavier U., 1968; JD, U. Cin., 1971. Lic. real estate broker, Ohio, Ill., Tex., Fla. Sr. atty. McDonald's Corp., Chgo., 1973-79; gen. atty. Montgomery Ward, Chgo., 1979-86; gen. counsel First Nat. Realty and Devel. Co., Inc., Chgo., 1986—; mgr. Springdale Realty Investors, Ltd., 1982-83; pres. Sheridan Park Realty, Inc., Chgo., 1978-84. Author: Legal Checklists, 3d edit., 1986. Served to capt. U.S. Army, 1972. Mem. ABA, Ill. Bar Assn., Ohio Bar Assn., I.C.S.C. Democrat. Roman Catholic. Avocations: photography, sailing. Office: First Nat Realty and Devel 910 W Van Buren Chicago IL 60607

KERR, NANCY KAROLYN, pastor, mental health consultant; b. Ottumwa, Iowa, July 10, 1934; d. Owen W. and Iris Irene (Israel) Kerr; student Boston U., 1953; A.A., U. Bridgeport, 1966; B.A., Hofstra U., 1967; postgrad. in clin. psychology Adelphi U. Inst. Advanced Psychol. Studies, 1968-73; m. Richard Clayton Williams, June 28, 1953 (div.); children—Richard Charles, Donna Louise. Pastoral counselor Nat. Council Chs., Jackson, Miss., 1964; dir. teen program Waterbury (Conn.) YWCA, 1966-67; intern in psychology N.Y. Med. Coll., 1971-72; research cons., 1972-73; coordinator home services, psychologist City and County of Denver, 1972-75; cons. Mennonite Mental Health Services, Denver, 1975-78; asst. prof. psychology Messiah Coll., 1978-79; mental health cons., 1979-81; called to ministry Mennonite Ch., 1981, pastor Cin. Mennonite Fellowship, 1981-83, adv. ch. curriculum, 1981, coordinator campus peace evangelism, 1981-83, mem. Gen. Conf. Peace and Justice Reference Council, 1983-85; instr. Associated Mennonite Bibl. Sems., 1985; teaching elder Assembly Mennonite Ch., 1985-86; pastor Pulaski Mennonite Ch., 1986—; mem. Tri-County Counseling Clinic, Memphis, Mo., 1980-81; spl. ch. curriculum Nat. Council Chs., 1981; mem. Central Dist. Conf. Peace and Justice Com., 1981—. Mem. Waterbury Planned Parenthood Edn., 1964-67; mem. MW Children's Home Bd., 1974-75; bd. dirs. Boulder (Colo.) ARC, 1977-78; mem. Mennonite Disabilities Respite Care Bd., 1981-86. Mem. Am. Psychol. Assn., Am. Assn. Mental Deficiency, Soc. Psychologists for Study of Social Issues, Am. Acad. Polit. and Social Scientists, Davis County Ministries Ass. Office: Pulaski Mennonite Ch Box 98 Pulaski IN 52584

KERR, RICHARD WILLIAM, machine products company executive; b. Cleve., Apr. 15, 1926; s. Charles Lawson and Cora Baker (Kizer) K.; m. Rita Marie Gibbons, July 4, 1952; children: Marianne, Charles Lawson II. V.p. then pres. Kerr Lakeside Inc., Euclid, Ohio, 1949—; pres. Delker Mfg. Inc., Euclid, 1958—, Krel Corp., Euclid, 1968—; Pres. Nat. Screw Machine Products Assn., Brecksville, Ohio, 1981. Assoc. Euclid Gen. Hosp., 1971—, Ohio Wesleyan U., Delaware, Ohio, 1973—. Served with USN, 1944-45. Lodge: Rotary (bd. dirs. 1977—, sec. 1986). Avocations: golf, curling, bridge. Office: Kerr Lakeside Inc 26841 Tungsten Rd Euclid OH 44132

KERR, WILLIAM ANDREW, lawyer, educator; b. Harding, W.Va., Nov. 17, 1934; s. William James and Tocie Nyle (Morris) K.; m. Elizabeth Ann McMillin, Aug. 3, 1968. A.B., W.Va. U., 1955, J.D., 1957; LL.M., Harvard U., 1958; B.D., Duke U., 1968. Bar: W.Va. 1957, Pa. 1962, Ind. 1980. Assoc. McClintic, James, Wise and Robinson, Charleston, W.Va., 1958; assoc. Schnader, Harrison, Segal and Lewis, Phila., 1961-64; asst. prof. law Cleve. State U., 1966-67, assoc. prof. law, 1967-68; assoc. prof. law Ind. U., Indpls., 1968-69, 72-74; prof. Ind. U., 1974—; asst. U.S. atty. So. Dist. Ind., Indpls., 1969-72; exec. dir. Ind. Jud. Ctr., 1974-86; dir. research Ind. Pros. Attys. Council, 1972-74; mem. Ind. Criminal Law Study Commn., 1973—, sec., 1973-83; reporter speedy trial com. U.S. Dist. Ct. (so. dist.) Ind., 1975-84; trustee Ind. Criminal Justice Inst., 1983-86; dir. Indpls. Lawyers Commn., 1975-77, Ind. Lawyers Commn., 1980-83; mem. records mgmt. com. Ind. Supreme Ct., 1983-86. Bd. dirs. Ch. Fedn. Greater Indpls., 1979-87. Served to capt. JAGC, USAF, 1958-61. Decorated Air Force Commendation medal; Ford Found. fellow Harvard Law Sch., 1957-58; recipient Outstanding Prof. award Students Ind. U. Sch. Law, 1974, Disting. Service award Ind. Council Juvenile Ct. Judges, 1979, Outstanding Jud. Edn. Program award Nat. Council Juvenile and Family Ct. Judges, 1985. Mem. Ind. State Bar Assn., Indpls. Bar Assn., Phila. Bar Assn., W.Va. Bar Assn., Nat. Dist. Attys. Assn., Am. Judicature Soc., Fed. Bar Assn. (Outstanding Service award Indpls. chpt. 1975), Order of Coif, Phi Beta Kappa. Office: 735 W New York St Indianapolis IN 46202

KERRIGAN, WALTER W., II, financial planner; b. Pitts., May 6, 1953; s. Walter W. and Doris E. (Ward) K.; m. Susan F. Jagniszak, Apr. 8, 1978; 1 child, Kelly F. BA, U. Pitts., 1978. Cert. fin. planner. Chief exec. officer Inst. Fin. Planning, Farmington Hills, Mich., 1981—. Mem. Internat. Assn. Fin. Planners (bd. dirs. Southeast Mich. chpt. 1984—, co-founder, pres., chmn. bd. dirs. Metro Detroit Soc. chpt. 1985-86), Nat. Assn. Personal Fin. Advisors, Inst. Cert. Fin. Planners, Am. Arbitration Assn. (comml. panel arbitrators). Republican. Presbyterian. Office: Inst Fin Planning 31878 Northwestern Hwy Farmington Hills MI 48018

KERSCHNER, SHARON LYNNE, product manager; b. Cleve., Feb. 23, 1956; d. Emery Joseph and Anna Rita (Molitoris) Torok; m. Charles Kenneth Kerschner, June 28, 1986. Office services mgr. Am. Heart Assn., Cleve., 1978-79, asst. to exec. dir., 1979-80; program coordinator Tremco Inc., Cleve., 1980-81, distbn. specialist, 1981-83, adminstrn. mgr., 1983-84; product mgr. Stanadyne/Moen Group, Elyria, Ohio, 1985—. Mem. leadership devel. com. Fedn. Cath. Community Services, Diocese of Cleve., 1985—. Mem. Am. Mgmt. Assn., Nat. Assn. Female Execs. Roman Catholic. Avocations: golf, skiing. Office: Stanadyne/Moen Group 377 Woodland Ave Elyria OH 44036

KERSEY, ALFRED LEON, data center manager; b. Brookville, Ind., Sept. 13, 1947; s. Hubert and Margie (Isaacs) K., m. Rebecca Lee Swango, Dec. 7, 1949; children: Angela Lynn, Benjamin Leon. Cert., Vocat. Versailles, 1971; AS, U. Cin., 1980. Ops. supr. Blue Cross S.W. Ohio, Cin., 1972-79; ops. mgr. U.S. Shoe Corp., Cin., 1979-83; data ctr. mgr. Hill-Rom Co., Inc., Batesville, Ind., 1983—; data processing bd. Southeastern Ind. Vocat. Sch., Versailles. Den leader Boy Scouts Am., Lawrenceburg, Ind., 1985—, Weblows leader, 1986-87; mem. Overall Econ. Devel. for Southeastern Ind. Served with U.S. Army, 1966-68, Vietnam. Decorated Bronze Star. Mem. Data Processing Mgmt. Assn. Republican. Methodist. Clubs: Lakeside Archery (pres. 1982-84), Hidden Valley Lake Bass (sec., treas. 1978-81). Avocations: competitive archery, bow hunting, boating, photography. Home: 49 Beechwood Cir Lawrenceburg IN 47025 Office: Hill Rom Co Inc Hwy 46 Batesville IN 47006

KERSHAW, STEVEN MICHAEL, computer programming technician; b. Spencer, Iowa, Feb. 3, 1958; s. Kenneth B. and Shirley A. (Michaels) K.; m. Cheryl A. Grider, May 1987. Student, U. Nebr., 1976-78; AS, DeKalb Community Coll., Clarkston, Ga., 1980; student, Ga. State U., 1980; BS, Purdue U., Indpls., 1982; postgrad., Wichita (Kans.) State U., 1987—. Tutor Glendale Learning Ctr., Indpls., 1981-82; contract programmer Disciple Data Inc, Indpls., 1982; software developer Programs for the 80's, Indpls., 1982-83; data base programmer Data Chem, Indpls., 1983-84; data base program analyst Software Architects, Wichita, Kans., 1984-86; quality assurance inspector software Boeing Mil. Airplane Corp., Wichita, 1986—. Chmn. bd. dirs. Sedgwick County REACT, Wichita, 1985-86, pub. relations com., 1986, team capt., 1985. Named one of Outstanding Young Men Am., U.S. Jaycees, 1985. Mem. Sigma Pi Alpha. Republican. Mem. Christian Ch. Avocations: C.B. radio, singing, camping, Tae Kwon Do.

KERSTETTER, GUINEVERE ANNE, financial analyst, accountant; b. Phila., Nov. 24, 1944; d. William Megargee and Mary (Helman) Cotton; m. Chester Paul Kerstetter, Aug. 21, 1971; children: Julia Anne, Larissa S., Olivia K. BS summa cum laude, West Chester (Pa.) U., 1982. CPA, Pa., Kans. Staff acct. Jerome S. Ross, CPA, Newton Square, Pa., 1982-84, Mize Houser & Co., Topeka, 1984-86; analyst fin. ops. Calif. Inn Mgmt., Inc., Lawrence, Kans., 1986—. Recipient West Chester U. Outstanding Acctg. Student award Pa. Inst. CPA's, Harrisburg, 1983. Mem. Am. Inst. CPA's, Kans. Soc. CPA's, Am. Woman's Soc. CPA's, Am. Assn. Univ. Women (treas. 1987). Republican. Episcopalian. Avocations: reading, golf, travel. Home: 2100 Inverness Dr Lawrence KS 66046 Office: Calif Inn Mgmt Inc 1611 Saint Andrews Dr Lawrence KS 66046

KERWIN, GERALD CHARLES, television station executive; b. Cleve., Mar. 15, 1938; s. Myron Louis and Gertrude Lillian (Schultz) K.; m. Kay Marie Martin, Jan. 9, 1965; children: Timothy, Todd. BA, Ohio Wesleyan U., 1960; MS, Syracuse (N.Y.) U., 1964. Advt. mgr. Nat. City Bank, Cleve., 1964-69; account exec. Sta. WJW-TV, Cleve., 1969-73, Sta. WKYC-TV, Cleve., 1973-79; v.p. Marschalk Co., Cleve., 1979-84; sta. mgr. Sta. WCLQ-TV, Cleve., 1984—.

KERWIN, JOSEPH HUNT, dentist; b. St. Louis, July 13, 1955; s. William and Geraldine (Black) K.; m. Catherine Toalson, May 26, 1979; children: Rachel Rose, Kelly Elizabeth. BS in Edn., U. Mo., 1977; DDS, U. Iowa, 1983. Registered med. technologist, Am. Soc. Clin. Pathologists. Med. technologist U. Mo. Hosps. and Clinics, Columbia, 1977-79; resident St. Anthony's Hosp., Oklahoma City, 1983-84; gen. practice dentistry Marshfield, Mo., 1984—. Mem. Am. Dental Soc., Acad. Gen. Dentistry (trustee 1986), Springfield Dental Study Club (pres. 1986), Parkcrest Orthodontic Study Club, Omicron Kappa Upsilon, Kappa Delta Pi. Lodge: Rotary (sec. Marshfield club 1986—). Avocations: swimming, boating, water skiing, jogging. Home: 1078 Cedarbrook Marshfield MO 65706 Office: 403 S Marshall Marshfield MO 65706

KERYCZYNSKYJ, LEO IHOR, lawyer, county official, educator; b. Chgo., Aug. 8, 1948; s. William and Eva (Chicz) K.; m. Alexandra Irene Okruch, July 19, 1980. B.A., DePaul U., 1970, B.S., 1970, M.S. in Public Service, 1975; J.D., No. Ill. U., 1979; postgrad. U. Ill.-Chgo., 1980-82. Bar: Ill. 1981, U.S. Dist. Ct. (no. dist.) Ill. 1981, U.S. Ct. Appeals (7th cir.) 1981, U.S. Tax Ct. 1981, U.S. Ct. Claims, 1982, U.S. Ct. Mil. Appeals 1982, U.S. Ct. Internat. Trade 1982, U.S. Ct. Appeals (fed. cir.) 1983, U.S. Supreme Ct. 1984. Condemnation officer Cook County Treasurer's Office, Chgo., 1972-75, adminstrv. asst., 1975-77, dep. treas., 1977—; adj. prof. DePaul U., Chgo., 1979—; bd. dirs. First Security Fed. Savs. Bank Chgo.; Capt. Ukrainian Am. Democratic Orgn., Chgo., 1971. Recipient Outstanding Alumni award Phi Kappa Theta, 1971. Mem. ABA, Ill. State Bar Assn., Ill. Trial Law Assn., Chgo. Bar Assn., Theta Delta Phi. Ukrainian Catholic. Home: 2324 W Iowa St Apt 3R Chicago IL 60622 Office: Cook County Treas Office 118 N Clark St Rm 212 Chicago IL 60602

KESLAR, KENNETH FRANKLIN, military officer; b. Cleve., Jan. 11, 1959; s. William Franklin and Rosemarie (Krmpotich) K.; m. Donna Lee Hetzel, May 30, 1981; children: Kenneth Franklin II, Daniel Edward, Dennis Michael. BS in Engring., USAF Acad., 1981. Commd. 2d lt. USAF, 1981; student pilot USAF, Williams AFB, Ariz., 1981-82, instr. pilot, 1982-84, class comdr., 1985; advanced through grades to capt. USAF, 1985; C 141 pilot and exec. officer USAF, McGuire AFB, N.J., 1985—. Asst. scoutmaster Boy Scouts Am., Bedford Heights, Ohio, 1983—. Mem. Air Force Assn. Republican. Baptist. Avocation: woodworking. Home: 5677 Vickie Ln Bedford Heights OH 44146

KESLER, DARREL J., research scientist, educator; b. Portland, Ind., Sept. 21, 1949; s. D. Gordon and Lucille M. (Bullock) K.; m. Cheryl Scaletta, May 26, 1973; children: Cheralyn Elizabeth, Darrel Phillip Adam. BS, Purdue U., West Lafayette, Ind., 1971, MS, 1974; PhD, U. Mo., 1977. Research asst. U. Mo., 1974-77; asst. prof. U. Ill., Urbana, 1977-81, assoc. prof., 1981—; biochemist Abbott Labs., North Chicago, 1983-84; cons. research scientist Roussel UCLAF, 1985, Hoffman-LaRoche, Nutley, N.J., 1985, CEVA Labs, Overland Park, Kans., 1986-87. Contbr. articles to sci. jour. Mem. AAAS, Am. Soc. Animal Sci. (Midwest Outstanding Young Scientist award 1983), Controlled Release Soc. Roman Catholic. Home: 22 Lake Park Rd Champaign IL 61821 Office: U Ill 1301 W Lorado Taft Dr Urbana IL 61801

KESLER, JAY LEWIS, university administrator; b. Barnes, Wis., Sept. 15, 1935; s. Elsie M. Campbell Kesler; m. Helen Jane Smith; children: Laura, Bruce, Terri. Student, Ball State U., 1953-54; BA, Taylor U., 1958, LHD (hon.), 1982; Dr. Divinity (hon.), Barrington Coll., 1977, Asbury Theol. Sem., 1984; HHD (hon.), Huntington Coll., 1983; LHD, John Brown U., 1987. Dir. Marion (Ind.) Youth for Christ, 1955-58, crusade staff evangelist, 1959-60, dir. Ill.-Ind. region, 1960-62, dir. coll. recruitment, 1962-63, v.p. personnel, 1963-68, v.p. field coordination, 1968-73, pres., 1973-85, also bd. dirs.; pres. Taylor U., Upland, Ind., 1985—; bd. dirs. Christianity Today, Evang. Council for Fin. Accountability, Evangelicals for Social Action, Prison Fellowship Internat.; mem. bd. reference Christian Camps, Inc., Christian College Coalition, Nat. Educators Fellowship; mem. adv. bd. Christian Bible Soc., Internat. Council on Bibl. Inerrancy; co-pastor First Bapt. Ch. Geneva, Ill., 1972-85; mem. faculty Billy Graham Schs. Evangelism; lectr. Staley Disting. Christian Scholar Lecture Program. Speaker on Family Forum (daily radio show); mem. adv. com. Campus Life mag.; author: Let's Succeed With Our Teenagers, 1973, I Never Promised You a Disneyland, 1975, The Strong Weak People, 1976, Outside Disneyland, 1977, I Want a Home with No Problems, 1977, Growing Places, 1978, Too Big to Spank, 1978, Breakthrough, 1981, Parents & Teenagers, 1984, Family Forum, 1984, Making Life Make Sense, 1986, Parents and Children, 1986; contbr. articles to profl. jours. Office: Taylor Univ Office of the President Reade Ave Upland IN 46989

KESLER, STEPHEN EDWARD, economic geology educator; b. Washington, Oct. 5, 1940; s. Thomas Lingle and Margaret Alice (Menges) K.; m. Judith Alphield Eliason, Aug. 22, 1965; children: Sarah Margaret, David Stephen. BS with honors, U. N.C., 1962; PhD, Stanford U., 1966. Asst. prof. econ. geology La. State U., Baton Rouge, 1966-70; assoc. prof. U. Toronto, Ont., Can., 1970-77; prof. U. Mich., Ann Arbor, 1977—; vis. scientist Instituto Geográfico Nacional, Guatemala, 1966-69, Consejo de Recursos Minerales, Mexico City, 1974-75; geol. assessor Dirección General de Minas, Santo Domingo, 1983-84; cons. exploration for metallic and nonmetallic mineral deposits. Author: Our Finite Mineral Resources, 1975; (with others) Economic Geology of Central Dominican Republic, 1984; assoc. editor Econ. Geology 1981—; mem. editorial bd. Jour. Geochem. Exploration, 1984—; contbr. articles to profl. jours. Trustee Soc. Econ. Geology Found. Fellow Geol. Soc. Am.; mem. Soc. Econ. Geologists (program chmn. 1981, councillor 1983-86), Assn. Exploration Geochemists (councillor 1981-84), Soc. Mining Engrs. of AIME (program chmn. 1977). Lutheran. Office: Univ Mich Dept Geol Scis Ann Arbor MI 48109

KESMODEL, CHARLES MYOHL, JR., small business owner; b. Balt., Nov. 2, 1931; s. Charles Myohl and Margaret Belle (Wood) K.; m. Wilma Jane Martin, Sept. 7, 1956; children: Charles, Mark, Amy, Matthew. BBA, Marshall U., 1958. With mktg. mgmt. Union Oil Co. Calif., Schaumburg, Ill., 1958-77; v.p. Murphy Oil Co., Lafayette, Ind., 1977-79, also bd. dirs.; pres. Grovertown (Ind.) Truckstop, 1979—, also chmn. bd. dirs.; pres. Cammco, Inc., Culver, Ind., 1985—, also chmn. bd. Served with USN, 1951-55. Named to Hon. Order Ky. Cols., 1976. Mem. Nat. Assn. Truck Stop Operators, Ill. Truck Stop Assn., U.S. Senatorial Club, Culver C. of C. (bd. dirs. 1983), VFW (All State Comdr. 1986, post comdr. 1985-86, post trustee 1986-87), Am. Legion. Republican. Lutheran. Club: Petroleum (Indpls.) (pres. 1975). Avocations: boating, fishing, gardening.

KESSELER, ROGER LOUIS, controller; b. Grayling, Mich., Sept. 27, 1936; s. George Jerome and Loretta Helena (Sorenson) K.; m. Phyllis Joan Ziebell, Aug. 10, 1957; children: Lisa Ann, Lori Ann, Michael Louis, Maureen Kay. BBA, Cen. Mich. U., 1958. Acct. The Dow Chem. Co., Midland, Mich., 1958-71; div. controller, mgr. employee relations The Dow Chem. Co., Freeport, Tex., 1971-79; mgr. corp. reporting The Dow Chem. Co., Midland, 1979-81, corp. controller, 1981—. Fin. chmn. Midland County Rep. Orgn., 1980-87; bd. dirs. Midland County Cancer Soc., 1982-87, Midland Hosp. Assn., 1984-87, Cen. Mich. U. Devel. Fund, Mt. Pleasant, Mich., 1985-87. Served as capt. USAR, 1958-66. Recipient Alumni Recognition award Alumni Assn. Cen. Mich. U., 1982; named Outstanding Alumni, Cen. Mich. U. Acctg. Soc., 1984. Mem. Nat. Assn. Accts. Roman Catholic. Office: Dow Chem Co 2030 Willard H Dow Ctr Midland MI 48674

KESSINGER, JAN HENDERSON, publisher; b. Junction City, Kans., Feb. 20, 1951; s. Edward L. and Mona E. (Henderson) K.; BJ, U. Kans., 1973; postgrad. Pepperdine U., 1982-84, Rockhurst Coll., 1985—; m. Jeanne E. Snow, May 2, 1975; children: Carrie Elizabeth, Courtney Kristin, Julie Henderson. Assoc. editor Junction City Republic, 1973; buyer Gibson's Discount Center, Lawrence, Kans., 1974-75; dept. mgr. Venture Stores, Kansas City, Mo., 1975-76; Western div. mgr. The Packer, Vance Pub., Anaheim, Calif., 1976-84, pub. ProNet-The Packer Produce Network, Overland Park, Kans., 1984-87, assoc. pub. The Packer, 1987—. Bd. dirs., pres. Westport Ballet, Kansas City, Mo. Mem. Nat. Agrl. Mktg. Assn., Produce Mktg. Assn., United Fresh Fruit and Vegetable Assn., Nat. Agrimktg. Assn., Mensa. Presbyterian. Club: Boulevard. Home: 8404 W 115th St Overland Park KS 66210 Office: Vance Pub Overland 7950 College Blvd Overland Park KS 66210

KESSLER, CLEMM CROMWELL, management consultant; b. Hartford, Conn., Mar. 12, 1941; s. Clemm Cromwell and Elizabeth (Graf) K.; m. Patricia Jane Catherman, Aug. 31, 1963; children: Dawn Elizabeth, Danielle Ursula. BA, Bucknell U., 1963; MS, Case Western Res. U., 1965, PhD, 1967. Asst. to assoc. prof. U. Nebr., Omaha, 1967-77; dir. mgmt. devel. Pacesetter Corp., Omaha, 1977-78, v.p. personnel, 1978-80; ptnr. Kessler, Kennedy & Assocs., Omaha, 1980—. Mem. Nebr. Psychol. Assn., Midwestern Psychol. Assn., Am. Psychol. Assn. Home: Route 2 Glenwood IA 51534 Office: Kessler Kennedy & Assocs 6818 Grover St Omaha NE 68106

KESSLER, CRAIG J., accountant; b. Detroit, Dec. 11, 1956; s. Richard L. and Patricia A. (Mc Cann) K.; m. Lynda K. Kessler, Sept. 15, 1981; 1 child, Christopher James. BSBA, U. Mo., 1979. CPA. Staff acct. Baird Kurtz and Dobson, Springfield, Mo., 1979-81, sr. acct., 1982-84, mgr., 1985—. Mem. Am. Inst. CPA's, Mo. Soc. CPA's. Avocations: golf, tennis, softball, racquetball. Home: 3504 S Nettleton Springfield MO 65807 Office: Baird Kurtz and Dobson PO Box 1276 SSS Springfield MO 65805

KESSLER, LAURIE GAIL, accountant; b. Springfield, Ill., June 17, 1958; d. Dale Edward and Elizabeth Ann (Stilley) Farmer; m. William Kurt Kessler, Feb. 28, 1987. BS in Acctg., Ind. U., 1983. CPA, Ind. Sr. accountant Whipple and Co., Indpls., 1983—. Mem. Am. Inst. CPA's, Ind. CPA Soc. Home: 9308 Budd Run Dr Indianapolis IN 46250 Office: Whipple & Co 9302 N Meridian St Suite 300 Indianapolis IN 46260

KESSLER, LAWRENCE W., scientist, scientific instrument company executive; b. Chgo., Sept. 26, 1942; s. Michael C. and Sue (Sniader) K.; m. Francesca Agramonte, Nov. 30, 1985;hildren: Jeffrey, Bret, Cory, Brandy. BSEE, Purdue U., 1964; MS, U. Ill., 1966, PhD, 1968. Mem. research staff Zenith Radio Corp., Chgo., 1968-74; pres. Sonoscan, Inc., Bensenville, Ill., 1975—; adj. prof. info. engring., U. Ill., Chgo.; organizer 7th Internat. Symposium Acoustical Imaging and Holography, 1976, 16th Internat. Symposium on Acoustical Imaging, June 1987; mem. statutory adv. com. FDA, 1973-75. Editor: Procs. Ultrasonics Symposium, IEEE, Inc. 1970; Acoustical Holography, Vol. 7, 1977, Vol. 16, 1988; contbr. articles to tech. jours. Patentee acoustical microscopy, Bragg diffraction imaging, also liquid crystal device. Fellow Acoustical Soc. Am.; sr. mem. IEEE (sec.-treas. sonics and utrasonics div. 1969-71, pres. div. 1971-73, nat. lectr. 1981-82)); mem. Am. Inst. Ultrasound in Medicine, Am. Soc. Non-destructive Testing, Sigma Xi, Etta Kappa Nu. Home: 543 Rutgers Ln Elk Grove Village IL 60007 Office: Sonoscan Inc 530 E Green St Bensenville IL 60106

KESSLER, LYNN GRIFFITH, communications administrator; b. Greensburg, Pa., July 30, 1947; s. Jack E. and Alice G. (Griffith) K.; m. Donna M. Dawson, Jan. 30, 1971; children: Jennifer, Michael. BSBA in Acctg., Tri-State Coll., Angola, Ind., 1969; MBA, St. Francis Coll., Ft. Wayne, Ind., 1980. Acct. CTS Corp., Elkhart, Ind., 1969-70; various positions GTE, Ft. Wayne, Ind., 1970-78, tax mgr., 1978-81, gen. acctg. mgr., 1981-83, staff supr., 1983—. Sec., treas., dir., vice chmn. Three Rivers Ambulance Authority, Ft. Wayne, 1982—; chmn. sch. budget com. Taxpayers Research Authority, Ft. Wayne, 1985—. Republican. Methodist. Lodge: Masons. Home: 1602 Buckskin Dr Fort Wayne IN 46804

KESSLER, PHYLLIS ANN, health services administration executive; b. Detroit, July 21, 1932; d. Paul Gerhart and Mary J. Louise (Stoerman) Gerndt; m. Robert Harold Merchant, Apr. 23, 1951 (dec. Mar. 1975); children: Robert, Susan, James; m. Robert Paul Kessler, June 14, 1980. Student, Madonna Coll., 1982-86. Statistician, typist Gen. Motors Corp., Detroit, 1958-64; exec. dir. Dearborn Heights (Mich.) Human Services Ctr., Inc., 1970—; trustee Garden City (Mich.) Osteopathic Hosp., 1975—; bd. dirs. Garden Nursing Corp., 1982—. Writer, dir., producer ednl. T.V. series What Will the Neighbors Think, 1986. Task force mem. Gov.'s Task force Promogation of Rules for Pub. Act 335-340, Lansing, Mich., 1975; Gov.'s Task Force Drug Abuse Prevention Edn., Lansing, 1978. Mem. Mich. Alcohol Addiction Assn., Dearborn Heights C. of C. (Woman of Yr. 1979), Amerigard Corp. (corp. mem.), League of Women Voters (founding pres. Dearborn Heights chpt. 1964). Democrat. Methodist. Avocations: golf, bridge, gardening, photography. Home: 23525 Tireman Dearborn Heights MI 48127 Office: Dearborn Heights Human Services Ctr 5928 Telegraph Rd Dearborn Heights MI 48127

KESSLER, RODNEY ARTHUR, accounting company financial consultant; b. Roswell, N.Mex., June 8, 1953; s. Charles W. and June (Mathis) K.; m. Pamela T. Bowers, May 22, 1976; children: Katherine G., Timothy B. BS in Acctg., U. Kans., 1975. CPA, Kans., Mo. Audit mgr. Touche Ross, Kansas City, Mo., 1975-84, 87—, N.Y.C., 1984-86. Author acctg. manuals. Bd. dirs. and chmn. fin. Craft Learning Ctr., Kansas City, 1980-83; bd. dirs. and treas. Big Bros. and Sisters Kansas City, 1982-84. Mem. Am. Inst. CPA's, Fin. Mgrs. Soc. Clubs: University, Kansas City Country. Home: 4904 W 69th St Prairie Village KS 66208

KESSLER, WILLIAM EUGENE, hospital administrator; b. St. Louis, Dec. 15, 1944; s. Joseph John and Margaret Mary (Burns) K.; m. Patricia Christine Wilson, Nov. 9, 1968; children: Christina, William, John, Timothy, Jennifer, Catherine, Joseph, Daniel. BS in Commerce, St. Louis U., 1966, MHA, 1968. Various positions St. John's Hosp., St. Louis, 1963-67; adminstrv. resident St. Mary's Hosp., Grand Rapids, Mich., 1967-68; exec. dir. St. Anthony's Hosp., Alton, Ill., 1971—; speaker profl. and community settings, 1972—; preceptor St. Louis U., 1980—; bd. dirs. Hosp. Assn. Met. St. Louis, 1975-85. Contbr. articles to profl. jours., 1972—. Admissions advisor U.S. Mil. Acad., 1973—; treas., bd. dirs. Cath. Childrens' Home Alton, 1981—; v.p. Diocesan Bd. Edn. Diocese of Springfield, Ill., 1981-82, pres. 1982-84, mem. 1986—; mem. Diocesan Council, 1987—; chmn. ARC, Alton, 1984-85; bd. dirs. Am. Cancer Soc., Alton, 1984—. Served to capt. U.S. Army, 1968-71. Paul Harris fellow Alton Jaycees, 1979; recipient Army Commendation medal. Fellow Am. Coll. Healthcare Execs.; mem. Am. Hosp. Assn. (Ho. of Dels. 1984—), Ill. Hosp. Assn. (exec. com. 1981-86, chmn. 1984-85), Cath. Health Assn. U.S.A., (bd. dirs. 1987—), St. Louis U. Hosp. Adminstrn. Alumni Assn. (pres. 1978-79), Southwestern Ill. Indsl. Assn. (exec. com. 1983—). Club: Stadium (St. Louis). Lodge: Rotary (pres. Alton chpt. 1981-82, Paul Harris fellow 1985). Avocations: photography, sports, family travel. Home: 1216 N Hanser Ln Godfrey IL 62035 Office: St Anthony's Hosp St Anthony's Way Alton IL 62002

KESTEN, JACK LEONARD, architect; b. N.Y.C., Nov. 4, 1935; s. Herman and Bessie (Peckerman) K.; m. Elaine Adele Lapofsky, May 18, 1976. Cert. in Architecture, Cooper Union for Advancement of Sci. and Art, 1955; B.Arch., MIT, 1958. Registered architect, N.Y., N.J., Mo. Staff architect William B. Tabler, F.A.I.A., N.Y.C., 1958-66; job capt. William Lescaze, F.A.I.A., N.Y.C., 1966-67; project mgr. Pomerance and Breines, Architects, N.Y.C., 1968-69; prin. architect Vollmer Assocs., N.Y.C., 1969-70; project architect Morris Lapidus Assocs., N.Y.C., 1970-71; project mgr., job capt., rep. field The Gruzen Partnership, N.Y.C., 1971-78; project architect, design architect HBE Corp., St. Louis, 1978-86, Campbell Design Group, St. Louis, 1986—. Prin. works include residence for Hon. V.P. Nelson A. Rockefeller, Pocantico Hills, N.Y., Yorkville Subway Sta., N.Y.C., renovation of Commodore Hotel to Grand Hyatt Hotel, N.Y.C., U.S. Atty. Office Bldg. Met. Correctional Ctr., N.Y.C., cell block revisions Attica Correctional Facility, N.Y., York Coll. Lab. Facilities, Jamaica, N.Y., South Park Hosp., Shreveport, La., new and remodeled hosps. in Ariz., Bermuda, Colo., Ga., Maine, Mass., N.J., N.Y., S.C., S.D., Tex., W.Va., HBE Corp. Hdqrs., St. Louis, Adam's Mark Hotel, St. Louis, Retirement Community, Sun City, Ariz. Emil Schweinburg postgrad. scholar, 1955, Nat. Bd. Fire Underwriters scholar, 1957. Mem. AIA (St. Louis chpt.), Mo. Council Architects, MIT Club. Avocations: sailing, photography, spectator ice hockey, tennis, bicycling. Home: 1771 Canyon View Ct Chesterfield MO 63017

KETCHAM, WARREN ANDREW, psychologist, educator; b. Manistee, Mich., June 28, 1909; s. Perry Warren and Anna Ella (Ulrich) K.; m. Edna May Wearne, Nov. 23, 1962. BM, U. Mich., 1932, MA, 1947, PhD, 1951. Licensed psychologist Mich., Tex. Tchr. Reed City (Mich.) Pub. Schs., 1934-36, Melvindale (Mich.) Pub. Schs., 1936-38; supr. Dearborn (Mich.) Pub. Schs., 1938-43; sch. psychologist Ferndale (Mich.) Pub. Schs., 1950-53; prof., sch. psychologist U. Mich., Ann Arbor, 1953-77, prof. emeritus, 1978—; pvt. practice clin., indsl., orgnl. psychology Mich. and Tex., 1964—; cons. Am. Sch., Guatemala City, Guatemala, 1958-80. Served to sgt. U.S. Army, 1943-45, PTO. Fulbright Scholar Leeds U., 1959; U. Mich. Hinsdale scholar, 1951. Fellow Am. Psychol. Assn.; mem. Am. Soc. Clin. Hypnotists, Mich. Soc. Clin. Psychologists, Mich. Psychol. Assn., Nat. Registered Health Service Providers in Psychology. Home and Office: 6518 Heritage West Bloomfield MI 48033

KETCHUM, MICHAEL JEREMY, health insurance company executive; b. Lansing, Mich., Sept. 3, 1932; s. Jay C. and Lola M. (Power) K.; m. Simmey Lynn Dietrich; children—Sarah, Julie. B.S., Mich. State U., 1959. Enrollment rep. Mich. Hosp. Service (Blue Cross), 1959-61; hosp. relations dir. Ill. Hosp. and Health Service (Blue Cross), 1961-63; enrollment mgr., project planning mgr., competition and distbn. analyst Mich. Med. Service (Blue Shield), 1963-66; with Ohio Med. Indemnity Mut. Corp. (Blue Shield), 1966-84, sr. v.p., 1969-72, pres., 1972-84; chmn. bd. Community Mut. Ins. Co. (Blue Cross-Blue Shield), 1984-87, chmn. emeritus, cons., 1987—; bd. dirs., mem. audit com. BCS Fin. Corp., Chgo.; chmn. bd. dirs. Community Nat. Assurance Co., Community Life Ins. Co., Health Care Mut. Assn.; exec. dir. Plan Investment Fund, Inc.; dir. Community Life Ins. Co., Exec. & Employee Benefit Plans, Inc., Ins. Fedn. Ohio, Systems Re Ltd., Nassau, Bahamas, Health Plans Capital Services Corp., Chgo. Bd. dirs. United Way of Franklin County, Columbus; mem. regional bd. of Citizens Fed. Savs. & Loan Assn. Served with USNR, 1952-56. Mem. Columbus, Worthington (Ohio) chambers commerce. Clubs: Dublin-Worthington Rotary, Ohio State U. Pres.'s. Office: Community Mut Ins Co 6740 N High St Worthington OH 43085

KETTEMAN, DANIEL EDWARD, dentist; b. Oak Grove, Mo., June 13, 1955; s. James Edward and Elizabeth Winifred (Flynn) K. BS in Biology and Psychology, Baker U., 1977; DDS, U. Mo., Kansas City, 1981. Gen. practice resident VA Adminstrn., Leavenworth, Kans., 1981-82; practice gen. dentistry Palmyra, Mo., 1982—; bd. dirs. Mo. Dental Polit. Action Com., 1984—; sec.-treas. Great River Dental Study Club, Hannibal, Mo., 1983-85. Chmn. Girl Scout Fund Drive, Palmyra, Mo., 1985. Mem. ADA, Palmyra C. of C., Alpha Delta Sigma, Alpha Psi Omega. Methodist. Lodge: Kiwanis (pres. Palmyra club 1986—). Avocations: water skiing, racquetball, music. Home: 1515 S Main Palmyra MO 63461 Office: PO Box 326 Palmyra MO 63461

KETTER, JAMES PATRICK, accountant; b. St. Joseph, Mo., May 20, 1956. BBA, Marquette U., 1978. CPA, Mo., Kans. Acct., audit mgr. Melvin Ketter, P.C., St. Joseph, 1976-84; audit mgr. Coopers & Lybrand, Kansas City, Mo., 1985-86; mgr. acctng. and auditing Reda, Thomas & Seigel, Overland Park, Kans., 1986—. Mem. Friends of Art, Kansas City, 1986; Friends of Symphony, Kansas City, 1986. Mem. Am. Inst. CPA's, Mo. Soc. CPA's, Kansas Soc. CPA's, Beta Gamma Sigma, Alpha Sigma Nu. Roman Catholic. Lodge KC. Avocations: classical literature, church music, tennis, racquetball, bicycling. Home: 5400 W 80th Prarie Village KS 66208 Office: Reda Thomas Seigel Corporate Woods Bldg 24 Overland Park KS 66210

KETTLER, THOMAS DALE, realtor; b. Cuba City, Wis., Aug. 29, 1944; s. Dale Orville and Julia Mary Patricia (Boyle) K.; m. Susanne Margot Klingler, July 13, 1968; children—John Thomas, Christine Susanne. B.A., Marquette U., 1972. Real estate sales assoc. Rite Realty Corp. Milw., 1974-77, sales mgr., 1977-78; v.p., gen. mgr., 1978-80; owner, pres. Ketco Corp., Rite Realty, Milw., 1980—. Served with USN, 1966-72. Mem. Milw. Bd. Realtors, Wis. Realtors Assn., Nat. Assn. Realtors. Roman Catholic. Avocations: Boy Scout Leadership, traveling; reading; golfing; gardening. Office: Rite Realty 5910 W Forest Home Ave Milwaukee WI 53220

KETTLESON, DAVID NOEL, orthopaedic surgeon; b. St. Paul, Dec. 20, 1938; s. John Benton and Dorothy S. (Elkins) K.; m. Karen Nordstrom, Aug. 25, 1961; children: Maria, Daniel, Laura. BA, U. Minn., 1960, BS, MD, 1964. Diplomate Am. Bd. Orthopaedic Surgery. Intern St. Mary's Hosp., Duluth, Minn., 1964-65; resident in othopaedic surgery U. Minn. Hosp., Mpls., 1965-69; v.p., sec., treas. Orthopaedic Surgery, Inc., Omaha, 1971—; chmn. dept. orthopaedics Immanuel Med. Ctr., Omaha, 1978-82. Served to maj. USAF, 1969-71. Mem. AMA, Mid Cen. States Orthopaedic Soc., Mid Am. Orthopaedic Soc., Nebr. Orthopaedic Soc. (sec. 1974-85), Scoliosis Research Soc. Republican. Presbyterian. Avocations: hunting, springer spaniels, collecting decoys. Office: Orthopaedic Surgery Inc 290 Embassy Plaza Omaha NE 68114

KEULER, ROLAND LEO, shoe company executive; b. Kiel, Wis., Aug. 28, 1933; s. Joseph N. and Christina (Woelfel) K.; m. Shirley A. Johst, June 22, 1957; children: Suzanne Marie, Catherine Ann, David Richard, Carolyn Marie, Brian John and Barbara Jean (twins). B.A., Marquette U., 1959. C.P.A., Wis. Acct. Arthur Andersen & Co. (C.P.A.'s), Milw., 1959-65; sec.-treas. Napco Graphic Arts, Inc., Milw., 1965-70; controller Weyenberg Shoe Mfg. Co., Milw., 1970-72; treas. Weyenberg Shoe Mfg. Co., 1972-; sec. Weyenburg Shoe Mfg. Co., 1986—; project bus. cons. 1977-84. Served with AUS, 1954-56. Mem. Am., Wis. insts. C.P.A.s, Beta Gamma Sigma, Beta Alpha Psi. Home: 720 W Fairfield Ct Glendale WI 53217 Office: Weyenberg Shoe Mfg Co 234 E Reservoir Ave PO Box 1188 Milwaukee WI 53201

KEY, MARTIN L., surgeon; b. Hamburg, Iowa, Oct. 30, 1943; s. Melvin L. and Linda F. (Hawthorne) K.; m. Carolyn J. Schwartz, Dec. 28, 1963; children: Shannon M., Marla L., MacLane C. Key. Student, Drake U., 1964-65, BS, 1968; MD, U. Iowa, 1971. Diplomate Am. Bd. Surgery. Resident in family practice Spartanburg (S.C.) Gen. Hosp., 1971-72; gen. practitioner Sainte Genevieve (Mo.) Meml. Hosp., 1972-77; resident in surgery Lincoln Med. Edn. Found., 1977-81; attending surgeon Hot Spring County Meml. Hosp., 1981-82, Cass County Meml. Hosp., Atlantic, Iowa, 1982—, Clarinda (Iowa) Meml. Hosp., 1985—. Bd. dirs. Iowa Am. Cancer Soc., Des Moines, 1985—. Served with USN, 1961-64. Fellow ACS; mem. AMA. Republican. Avocations: golf, reading. Home: 2806 Chestnut St Atlantic IA 50022 Office: 1500 E 10 St Atlantic IA 50022

KEYES, EDWARD LAWRENCE, JR., electric company executive; b. N.Y.C., Apr. 19, 1929; s. Edward Lawrence and Emily (Shepley) K.; 1 dau., Elisabeth Elliott. B.A. cum laude, Princeton, 1951. Asst. to pres. Emerson Electric Co., St. Louis, 1961-64; asst. v.p. adminstrn. Emerson Electric Co., 1964-66; v.p. adminstrn. Emerson Electric Co. (Emerson Motor div.), 1966-67; exec. v.p., dir. Emerson Electric Co. (Day-Brite Lighting div.), 1967-70; pres. Emerson Electric Co. (Builder Products div.), 1970, Emerson Electric Co. (Chromalox Comfort Conditioning div.), 1970-71; pres. Emerson Electric Co. (Day-Brite Lighting div.), 1971-73, dir. div., group v.p. corporate, 1973-74, exec. v.p. ops., 1974-77, pres. co., 1977-86, also dir.; dir. 1st Nat. Bank Clayton, Central Trust (Jefferson City), Mo. Bd. dirs. St. John's Hosp., St. Louis. Served to 1st lt. USAF, 1951-56. Mem. Bldg. Products Exec. Conf. (dir.). Republican. Roman Catholic. Clubs: Cottage (Princeton); St. Louis Country (St. Louis), Racquet (St. Louis); Log Cabin. Home: 33 Deerfield Rd Saint Louis MO 63124 Office: Emerson Electric Co 8000 W Florissant Ave Saint Louis MO 63136 *

KEYS, CHRISTOPHER BENNETT, psychology; b. N.Y.C., Mar. 18, 1946; s. William Walters and Margaret (Forman) K.; m. Elizabeth Jaffer, Sept. 14, 1969; children: Benjamin, Daniel. BA, Oberlin Coll., 1968; MA, U. Cin., 1971, PhD, 1973. Registered psychologist, Ill. Asst. prof. U. Ill., Chgo., 1973-78, assoc. prof., 1978—; psychologist adminstr. Ill. Inst. for Devel. Disabilities, Chgo., 1984—; dir. criminal justice tng. program U. Ill., Chgo., 1980-81; dir. program START Evaluation U. Ill., Chgo., 1973-70; visiting research assoc. Ctr. for Ednl. Policy & Mgmt. U. Oreg., Eugene, 1979-80. Mem. editorial bd. Am. Jour. Community Psychology, 1982-85, Jour. of Applied Behavioral Sci., 1982—; contbr. articles to profl. jours. Recipient Pub. Service award Cook County, 1974, Disting. Service award AIA, 1980. Mem. Am. Psychol. Assn. (community psychology program dirs., 1985-87, chair tng. council 1985-87, Midwest coordinator div. community psychology, 1982-84, Excellent Conference Presentation 1985), Midwestern Psychological Assn., Soc. for Psychol. Study of Social Issues. Home: 533 N Cuyler Ave Oak Park IL 60302 Office: U Ill Dept Psychology Box 4348 Chicago IL 60680

KEYS, ELIZABETH JAFFER, clinical psychologist; b. Hartford, Conn., May 2, 1946; d. Maurice H. and Blanche (Susman) Jaffer; m. Christopher Bennett Keys, Sept. 14, 1969; children: Benjamin, Daniel. BA, Oberlin Coll, 1968; MA, U. Cin., 1971, PhD, 1976. Lic. psychologist, Ill. Staff psychologist DuPage County Health Dept., Wheaton, Ill., 1972-74; staff psychologist counseling service U. Ill. at Chgo., 1976—; cons. non-profit ednl./service orgns., 1969—. Contbr. articles to profl. jours. Mem. Am. Psychol. Assn., Assn. Psychol. Type, Phi Beta Kappa. Avocation: travel. Home: 533 N Cuyler Ave Oak Park IL 60302 Office: Counseling Service U Ill at Chgo 721 S Wood St Chicago IL 60612

KHALIL, TAWFIK BOSHRA, research engineer; b. Cairo, Jan. 1, 1940; came to U.S., 1968; s. Boshra and Meriam (Attia) K.; m. Barbara Andrea Karam, Feb. 24, 1968; 1 child, Laura. BSME, Ain Shams U., Cairo, 1963; MSME, Carleton U., Ottawa, Ont., Can., 1968; PhD in Applied Mechanics, U. Calif., Berkeley, 1973. Instr. Ain Shams U., 1963-66; research asst. Carleton U., 1966-68; analytical engring. United Aircraft Co., Montreal, Que., Can., 1968-69; research assoc. U. Calif., Berkeley, 1969-73; adj. asst. prof. Wayne State U., Detroit, 1982—; staff research engr. Gen. Motors Corp., Warren, Mich., 1973—. Contbr. articles to profl. jours. Mem. ASME, Am. Soc. Automotive Engrs., Motor Vehiclel Mfr. Assn. (occupant simulation sub com. 1979—), Sigma Xi. Republican. Mem. Coptic Orthodox Ch. Home: 5208 Clarendon Crest Ct Bloomfield Hills MI 48013 Office: Gen Motors Research Lab 30500 Mound Rd Warren MI 48090-9055

KHAMIS, EDWARD ALBERT, pharmaceutical executive; b. Chgo., Jan. 29, 1952; s. Albert Ezra and Ann (Perzigian) K. BS in Edn., Sociology and Psychology, Milton Coll., 1975; MS in Human Resources and Mgmt. Devel., Nat. Coll. Edn., 1983. Planning specialist, orgnl. supr. Walgreen Co., Deerfield, Ill., 1975-78; personnel asst. AllState Ins. Co., Northbrook, Ill., 1978-81; personnel mgr. McGraw Edison, Elk Grove Village, Ill., 1981-83; mgr. human resources LyphoMed, Inc., Melrose Park, Ill., 1983-84, dir. human resources, 1984-86, v.p. human resources, 1986—. Soloist Skokie Valley Concert Choir, Skokie, Ill., 1978-84; actor Devonshire Community Theater, Skokie, 1981—; v.p. fin. Light Opera Works, Evanston, Ill., 1981-83; precinct capt. Skokie Reps., 1979-83. Mem. Am. Soc. Personnel Adminstrn., Midwest Indsl. Assn. (exec. com.), No. Ill. Indsl. Assn., Greater O'Hare Assn., How Military Sch. Alumni Assn. (bd. dirs.). Episcopalian. Avocations: operatic singing, racquetball, philately. Office: LyphoMed Inc 2020 Ruby St Melrose Park IL 60601

KHAN, KALIM ULLAH, project engineer, consultant; b. Kanpur, India, Feb. 9, 1937; naturalized Am. citizen; s. Abdul Hai and Salamat (Begam) K.; m. Florence Dedes, Sept. 5, 1954 (dec.). Diploma engring. Aligarh Muslim U., (India), 1959; M.E., Goethe Inst. (W.Ger.), 1963; cert. Vickers Hydraulic Inst., 1971. Engr., M-A-N, A.G., Mainz-Gustavsburg, W.Ger., 1961-63; designer U.S. Industries, Inc., Chgo., 1964-65; project engr. Grotnes Metalforming Systems, Inc., Chgo., 1965-83; cons. engr. Wm. Wrigley Jr. Co., Chgo., 1983-84; sr. cons. engr. Barnes & Reinecke, Inc., Elk Grove Village, Ill., 1984—; dir. engring., cons. Khan Hydraulic Engring., Inc., Wheeling, Ill., 1985—. Mem. ASME, Soc. Automotive Engrs., SAE, Soc. Am. Mil. Engrs., Republican. Moslem. Clubs: Rotary, Engineering. Home: 850 Mark Ln Suite 221 Wheeling IL 60090

KHAN, M. ALI, municipal air quality control administrator; b. India, Apr. 28, 1940; came to U.S., 1968, naturalized, 1971; m. Zarina Ansari, July 4, 1968; 1 child. B.Engring., India, 1965; M.S. in Engring., U. Miss., 1970. Registered profl. engr., Ill., Ind. Research asst. U. Miss., Oxford, 1968-70; engr. Air Quality Control, East Chicago, Ind., 1971-72, asst. dir., 1972—. Mem. Air Pollution Control Assn., IEEE, Am. Planning Assn. Avocations: tennis; hiking. Office: Dept Air Quality Control City of East Chicago 4525 Indianapolis Blvd East Chicago IN 46312

KHAN, MOHAMMED VAHID HUSAIN, physician; b. Hyderabad, India, Oct. 31, 1927; came to U.S., 1958; s. Mohammed Ameen and Amina (Begum) K.; m. Georgia Kelley, Sept. 2, 1960; children: Talat M., Sarwat A., Irshad H., Farhat A., Nurul A. FSc, Osmania U., 1945; B of Medicine and BS, Dow Med. Coll., Karachi, Pakistan, 1955; D of Tropical Medicine and Hygiene, London Sch. Hygiene and Tropical Medicine, 1962. Civil Hosp., Karachi, 1955-56; med. officer Govt. of Bahrain, 1957-58; intern Cook County Hosp., Chgo., 1959; resident internal medicine Mo. Pacific Hosp., St. Louis, 1960; edn. council Fgn. Med. Grads., 1964; gen. practice medicine Nat. Health Service, London, 1962-63; med. officer Preston Hall Chest Hosp., Maidstone, Kent, Eng., 1964-65; resident internal medicine Wyckoff Heights Hosp., Bklyn., 1965-68; practice medicine specializing in internal medicine, Lake Grove, N.Y., 1968-78, Smithtown, N.Y., 1968-78; assoc. attending physician Smithtown Gen. Hosp., 1968-78; civilian med. officer internal medicine U.S. Gen. Leonard Wood Army Hosp., Fort Leonard Wood, Mo., 1978-79; staff physician VA Med. Ctr., St. Louis, 1979-82; mem. attending staff internal medicine St. Charles Hosp., Port Jefferson, N.Y., 1968-78; staff assoc. attending internal medicine Mather Hosp., Port Jefferson, 1968-78; assoc. attending internal medicine St. John's Smithtown (N.Y.) Hosp., cons. Pilgrim State Hosp., Brentwood, N.Y., 1969; cons. examiner State of N.Y., Bur. Disability Determinations, 1974. Mem. Republican Presdl. Task Force, 1985. Suffolk Acad. Medicine fellow, 1969-78; N.Y. Cardiol. Soc. assoc. fellow, 1973. Fellow Royal Soc. Tropical Medicine; mem. Brit. Med. Assn., AMA, Am. Soc. Internal Medicine, Am. Soc. Tropical Medicine, Islamic Med. Assn. U.S.A. and Can., N.Y. State Soc. Internal Medicine, Mo. State Soc. Internal Medicine. Islam. Home and Office: 4432 Louisiana Ave Saint Louis MO 63111

KHINDUKA, SHANTI KUMAR, university administrator, educator; b. Jaipur, Rajasthan, India, Dec. 22, 1933; came to U.S., 1964; s. Ram C. and Koka D. Khinduka; m. Manorama Khinduka, May 5, 1955; children: Abha, Seema. BA, Rajasthan U., 1953; MSW, Lucknow U., India, 1955, U. So. Calif., 1961; PhD, Brandeis U., 1968. Asst. prof. Lucknow U., 1955-64; assoc. social affairs office UN, N.Y.C., 1965; from assoc. to prof., asst. dean St. Louis U., 1967-74; prof. social work, dean Washington U., St. Louis, 1974—. Editor: Social Work in India, 2d edit., 1965; co-editor: Social Work in Practice, 1976; chmn. edit. bd. Jour. Social Service Research, 1976—; contbr. articles to profl. jours. Bd. dirs. Council on Social Work Edn., 1978-81, commn. accreditation, 1984—; bd. dirs. United Way of St. Louis, 1982—, Mo. Goodwill Industries, 1987—. Mem. Nat. Assn. Social Workers (chmn. symposium planning com. 1978-79, chmn. publ. com. 1985—), Nat. Conf. Social Welfare (bd. dirs. 1979-82). Avocations: reading, travel. Home: 354 Cooperstown Dr Chesterfield MO 63017 Office: Washington U G Warren Brown Sch Social Work Campus Box 1196 Saint Louis MO 63130

KHO, EUSEBIO, surgeon; b. Philippines, Dec. 16, 1933; s. Joaquin and Francisca (Chua) K.; came to U.S., 1964; A.A., Silliman U., Philippines, 1955; M.D., State U. Philippines, 1960; fellow in surgery, Johns Hopkins, 1965-67; m. Grace C. Lim, May 24, 1964: children—Michelle Mae, April Tiffany, Bradley Jude, Jaclyn Ashley, Matthew Ryan. Intern in surgery Balt. City Hosp., 1964-65, resident in gen. surgery, 1965-67; research asso. pediatric surgery U. Chgo. Hosps., 1967-68; resident in gen. surgery, then chief resident U. Tex. Hosp., San Antonio, 1968-70; hosp. surgeon St. Anthony Hosp., Louisville, 1970-72; practice medicine specializing in surgery, Scottsburg, Ind., 1972—; chmn. dept. surgery Scott County Meml. Hosp., 1973—; cons. surgeon Washington County Meml. Hosp., Salem, Ind., also Clark County Meml. Hosp., Jeffersonville, Ind., 1973—; courtesy surgeon Suburban Hosp., Louisville, 1973—; gen. surgeon U.S. Army Hosp., Louisville, 1980—. Served to lt. col. M.C., USAR, 1980—. Diplomate Am. Bd. Surgery. Fellow A.C.S., Am. Soc. Abdominal Surgeons; mem. Am. Coll. Internat. Physicians (founding mem., trustee 1974—), AMA (Physician's Recognition award 1969, 72), Ind., Ky., Philippine med. assns., Internat. Coll. Surgeons, Soc. Philippine Surgeons in Am. (life), Assn. Philippine Practicing Physicians in Am. (life), Assn. Mil. Surgeons of U.S., Res. Officers Assn. of U.S., Mark Ravitch Surg. Assn., Bradley Aust Surg. Soc., N.Y. Acad. Scis. Presbyterian. Clubs: Optimists, Masons. Home: 14 Carla Ln Scottsburg IN 47170 Office: 137 E McClain Ave Scottsburg IN 47170

KHOSH, MARY SIVERT, psychologist; b. Akron, Ohio, July 28, 1942; d. Floyd Calvin and Mattie Paul (Milwee) Sivert; m. John G.H. Khosh, Sept. 1, 1961; children: Sheila June, Deanna June, Lisa June, Lora June. BA, U. Akron, 1966, MS, 1970; PhD, Kent State U., 1976; MBA, Baldwin-Wallace Coll., 1983. Career counselor Baldwin-Wallace Coll., Berea, Ohio, 1974-75, asst. dir. counseling and advising ctr., 1975-76, assoc. dir. counseling and advising ctr., 1976-78, dir. articulation project, 1976-77, dir. counseling and advising ctr., 1978-80, dir. career counseling and field experience, 1980-83; pvt. practice indsl. and organizational psychology Cleve., 1977—; mgmt. psychologist, cons. Ohio Psychol. Cons. to Industry Inc., Shaker Heights, 1983-84); mem. adj. faculty Baldwin-Wallace Coll., 1983—; cons. in field. Contbr. articles to profl. jours. V.p. S.W. Gen. Hosp. Jr. Bd., Berea, 1969; guest organist Akron United Meth. Ch., 1961; mem. S.W. Gen. Hosp. Med. Wives, 1966-76, pres. 1968-70. Mem. Am. Psychol. Assn., Ohio Psychol. Assn., Cleve. Psychol. Assn. (trustee 1984-85, v.p. 1985-86), Cleve. Cons. Psychol. Assn., Am. Soc. Personnel Adminstrn., Am. Soc. Tng. and Devel., Fairview Gen. Hosp. Women's Aux. Democrat. Methodist. Home: 19484 Tawny Brook Strongsville OH 44136 Office: Khosh & Assocs 7261 Engle Rd Suite 202 Cleveland OH 44130

KHOSHO, FRANCIS KALO, biologist, researcher; b. Mangeshi, Iraq, July 1, 1950; s. Kalo and Shone H. Khosho; m. Bernadette T. Khosho, Jan. 26, 1978; children: Andrew, Shannon. BSc, Sulamania U., 1974; MA, Sangamon State U., 1980. Researcher So. Ill. U., 1980—. Contbr. articles to med. jours. Mem. Electron Microscopy Soc. Am., Cen. States Electron Microscopy Soc. Avocations: coaching YMCA soccer, outdoor activities. Home: 66 Bonniebrook Chatham IL 62629 Office: So Ill U Sch Medicine 801 N Rutledge Springfield IL 62704

KIBBY, CLAUDE ANSON, supervisor distributive processing technology; b. Scott City, Kans., Aug. 1, 1949; s. Halcon Vee and Ruth Elenor (Stinson) K.; m. Diane Ellen Westerfield, Dec. 28, 1973; children: Nathan, Rachel. BS in Youth Leadership, Brigham Young U., 1971. Cert. ltd. tchr., Calif. Co-owner, dir. The Dance Factory, Modesto, Calif., 1972-75; asst. dir. Franklin & Downs, Modesto, 1975-76; prodn. mgr. The Coleman Co. Inc., Wichita, Kans., 1976-79; system programmer Farmland Data Services, Hutchinson, Kans., 1979-83, mgr. systems and communications, 1984—; system programmer Mut. Omaha, 1983-84. Scoutmaster Boy Scouts Am., Hutchinson, 1984-85, com. mem., 1984—. Mem. Imperial Soc. Tchrs. Dance (assoc.). Republican. Mormon. Avocations: running, music, hiking, camping. Home: 1209 E 27th Ave Hutchinson KS 67502-5025 Office: Farmland Data Services 1600 N Lorraine Hutchinson KS 67501

KIDDER, CORBIN SHERWOOD, transit consumer advocate; b. Madison, Wis., May 8, 1922; s. Charles Joseph and Donna Mary (Kutchin) K.; m. Kathleen Kidder, Aug. 8, 1947 (div. June 1969); children: Paul, Deborah, Faith, Ellen, Jonathan; m. Ann Loring Woodworth Meissner, Oct. 28, 1979. BS, Pa. State U., 1950; postgrad., U. Minn., 1950-53. Data applications analyst Sperry Corp., St. Paul, 1960-64, quality engr., 1965-75, quality audit instr., 1976-81. Vice chair Adv. Com. Transit, Mpls., 1979-85; participant Urban Mass Transit Adminstrn. Consumer Affair Conf., Arlington, Va., 1980, Ann Arbor, Mich., 1982; dist. sec., mem. cen. com. Dem. Farm Labor Party-sec. Minn. SD 65. Served to 1st lt. U.S. Army, 1943-46, 1st lt. Res. 1946-81. Mem. Am. Soc. Quality Control, Nat. Assn. Transit Consumer Orgn. (bd. dirs. 1981—), Minn. Transp. Mus., Travelers Protective Assn. Avocations: computers, politics, photography, graphics. Home and Office: 442 Summit Ave #2 Saint Paul MN 55102

KIDDER, THOMAS MICHAEL, otolaryngologist; b. Los Angeles, Oct. 2, 1942; s. Edwin Ralph and Margaret Irene (Collins) K.; m. Eileen Elizabeth, June 26, 1965; children: Terese Marie, Steven Mark. BS in Biology, Marquette U., 1964, MD, 1968. Diplomate Am. Bd. Otolaryngology. Intern Columbia Hosp., Milw., 1968-69; residency in otolaryngology Med. Coll. Wis., Milw., 1969-73, assoc. prof. clin. surgery, 1984—; practice medicine specializing in otolaryngology Milw., 1975—; chief of staff St. Luke's Hosp., Milw, 1984-86. Served to lt. comdr. USN, 1973-75. Fellow ACS, Am. Acad. Otolaryngology (instr.); mem. AMA, Am. Soc. Head and Neck Surgery, Am. Cancer Soc. (bd. dirs. Milw. 1986—), Milw. Acad. Medicine. Roman Catholic. Avocations: sailing, cycling, woodcarving, photography. Home: 4019 E Allerton Ave Cudahy WI 53110 Office: 2901 W K-K River Pkwy Suite 201 Milwaukee WI 53215

KIECOLT-GLASER, JANICE KAY, psychologist; b. Oklahoma City, June 30, 1951; d. Edward Harold and Vergie Mae (Lively) Kiecolt; m. Ronald Glaser, Jan. 18, 1980. BA in Psychology with honors, U. Okla., 1972; PhD in Clin. Psychology, U. Miami, 1976. Lic. psychologist, Ohio. Clin. psychology intern Baylor U. Coll. Medicine, Houston, 1974-75; postdoctoral fellow in adult clin. psychology U. Rochester, N.Y., 1976-78; asst. prof. psychiatry Ohio State U. Coll. Medicine, Columbus, 1978-84, assoc. prof. psychiatry and psychology, 1984—, active various coms.; presenter confs. on various mental health and social behavioral topics. Mem. editorial bd. Brain, Behavior and Immunity jour., 1986—; reviewer Health Psychology jour., Jour. Behavioral Medicine, Jour. Cons. and Clin. Psychology, Jour. Personality and Social Psychology, Psychiatry Research jour., Psychosomatic Medicine jour.; ad hoc reviewer NIH; contbr. articles to profl. jours., also chpts. to books. NIMH grantee, 1985—. Mem. Am. Psychol. Assn., Soc. Behavioral Medicine (program com. 1985, New Investigator award 1984), Acad. Behavioral Medicine Research, Phi Beta Kappa. Avocation: jogging. Office: Ohio State U Coll Medicine Dept Psychiatry 473 W 12th Ave Columus OH 43210

KIEDROWSKI, (PETER) JAY, state finance commissioner; b. Mpls., Aug. 20, 1949; s. Peter Joseph and Genievive Barbara (Andrewski) K.; m. Iris Ann Miller, Apr. 29, 1972; children: Alison Iris, Peter Raymond, Elizabeth Ann. BS MechE, U. Minn., 1971, MA in Pub. Affairs, 1973; exec. devel. cert., Northwestern U. Program analyst U.S. Dept. Transp., Washington, 1972; researcher Minn. State Senate, St. Paul, 1973-77; budget dir. City of Mpls., 1978-81, asst. city mgr.-fin., 1982; dep. commr. fin. State of Minn., St. Paul, 1983-85, commr. fin., 1985—; participant Salzburg (Austria) Sem., 1981; bd. dirs. Workers Compensation Reins. Assn., St. Paul, 1985—; chmn. bd. Rural Fin. Adminstrn., St. Paul., 1986; lectr. U. Minn. Humphrey Inst., Mpls., 1978—. Contbr. research studies, reports, articles to govt. publs. Chmn. bd. Project for Pride in Living, Mpls., 1986; mem. Citizen's League, Mpls., 1973—, Minn. Bd. Investment Adv. Council, St. Paul, 1985—; bd. dirs. U. Minn. Athletic Alumni Club, Mpls., 1982-83. Recipient Disting. Community Service award Minn. Jaycees, Mpls., 1980, Leadership Mpls. award Mpls. C. of C., 1981. Mem. Govt. Fin. Officers Assn., Nat. Assn. State Budget Officers (exec. com. 1985-86). Democrat. Roman Catholic. Avocations: racquetball, piano, sailing, coaching basketball.

KIEFER, DAVID JOHN, systems analyst; b. Rockford, Ill., Mar. 12, 1959; s. Norbert Anthony and Elizabeth Jane (Cera) K.; m. Constance Laura Swenson, Jan. 18, 1985. BA, Rockford Coll., 1981, Rockford Coll., 1984. Programmer/analyst Winnebago County, Rockford, 1981-84; systems analyst Swedish Am. Hosp., Rockford, 1984—; mem. supervisory com. Swedish Am. Federal Credit Union, 1985-87. Mem. Data Processing Mgmt. Assn. (bd. dirs. 1984—, sec. 1985-86, treas. 1987), U.S. Cycling Fedn., League of Am. Wheelmen. Avocations: bicycling, sailing, photography. Office: Swedish Am Hosp 1400 Charles St Rockford IL 61108

KIEFER, RODNEY MICHAEL, corporate communications executive; b. Menasha, Wis., Feb. 25, 1943; s. Rodney Joseph and Janet Linda (Johnson) K.; m. Frances Irene Golden, Mar. 7, 1970; 1 child, Karen. BJ, U. Wis., 1967. Asst. pub. info. Wis. Pub. Service, Green Bay, 1967-78, supr. pub. info., 1978-80, asst. dir. corp. communications, 1980-81, dir. corp. communications, 1981—; chmn. adv. subcom. U.S. Com. Energy Awareness, 1986—; mem. exec adv. com. Edison Electric Inst., 1984-85. Contbg. editor (play) Einstein the Man, 1978. Bd. dirs. United Way, Brown County, Wis., 1976. Club: Fox Valley Ad (pres. 1974) (Appleton, Wis.). Home: 3567 Champeau Rd Rural Rt 15 Green Bay WI 54301 Office: Wis Pub Service PO Box 19001 Green Bay WI 54307-9001

KIEFER, WILLIAM LEE, computer marketing executive; b. St. Louis, Aug. 19, 1946; m. Joyce Ann Cwiklowski, Aug. 15, 1970; children: Jason Lee, William Andrew. AA, St. Louis Community Coll., 1971; BS, U. Mo., St. Louis, 1975. Ins. agt. Liberty Mut. Ins. Co., St. Louis, 1973-75; Dem. dir. elections City of St. Louis, 1975; mktg. specialist GAF Corp., Lincolnwood, Ill., 1976-79; with Microdata Corp., St. Louis, 1979-83, Honeywell, Inc., St. Louis, 1983-85, Harris computer systems div., 1985-86, Computervision Corp., St. Louis, 1986—. Dem. ward committeeman City of St. Louis, 1976-79, mem. ward steering com., 1974-79, campaign mgr., 1974-76. Served with USMC, 1965-69. Mem. Am. Inst. Design and Drafting, Soc. Mfg. Engrs. (program chmn. St. Louis chpt. 1987), Assn. Integrated Mfg., St. Louis Jaycees, North Park Neighborhood Assn. (chmn.), VFW, Am. Legion, U. Mo.-St. Louis Alumni Assn. (v.p.), Alumni Alliance U. Mo. System, U. Mo.-St. Louis Bus. Alumni Assn. (pres. 1980-81). Roman Catholic. Club: St. Louis Engrs. Home: 9472 Yorktown Dr Saint Louis MO 63137

KIEFT, GERALD NELSON, mechanical engineer; b. Chgo., Dec. 29, 1946; s. Ralph and Alice (Nelson) K.; m. Linda Louise Fank, Oct. 28, 1967; children: Gerald Nelson II, Dawn Michelle. BSME, Midwest Coll. Engring., Lombard, Ill., 1971. Sr. designer Clark Equipment Co., Aurora, Ill., 1971-73; project engr. Elgin (Ill.) Sweeper Co., 1974-86, GPI Industries, St. Charles, Ill., 1986—. Inventor in field. Company chmn. United Way Campaign, Elgin, 1977. Presbyterian. Home: 42 W 192 Silver Glen Rd Saint Charles IL 60174 Office: GPI Industries 1840 Production Dr Saint Charles IL 60174

KIEHL, JAMES MICHAEL, financial officer; b. Shamokin, Pa., Nov. 14, 1945; s. Earl Sylvester and Pearl (Fashtak) K.; m. Catherine Christine Amato, Mar. 18, 1970; children: James M. II, Kristin Lorraine. AS in Bus., McCann Sch. Bus., 1973; BBA, Pa. State U., 1974. CPA, Pa. Staff acct. Peat, Marwick, Mitchell & Co., Harrisburg, Pa., 1974-77; sr. internal auditor CNA Ins., Reading, Pa., 1977-78, Sentry Ins. and Mut. Co., Stevens Point, Wis., 1978-80; v.p. fin. Reed Industries, Atlanta, 1980-82, v.p. beverage products group, 1982-84; v.p., controller SNE Corp., Wausau, Wis., 1984—. Served with USN, 1967-71. Mem. Am. Inst. CPA's, Pa. Inst. CPA's. Club: Wausau. Lodge: Kiwanis. Avocation: photography. Home: 900 Frontenac Stevens Point WI 54481 Office: SNE Corp 910 Cleveland Ave Wausau WI 54401

KIEL, FREDERICK ORIN, lawyer; b. Columbus, Feb. 22, 1942; s. Fred Otto and Helen Louise (Baird) K.; m. Vivian Lee Naff, June 2, 1963; 1 child, Aileen Vivian. AB magna cum laude, Wilmington Coll., 1963; JD, Harvard U., 1966. Bar: Ohio 1966, U.S. Supreme Ct. 1972. Assoc. Peck, Shaffer & Williams, Cin., 1966-71, ptnr., 1971-80; ptnr. Taft, Stettinius & Hollister, Cin., 1980—; lectr. Contbr. articles on mcpl. bond fin. to profl. jours. Mem. Wilmington Coll. Alumni Council, 1984-86, v.p. 1986—; arbitrator Mcpl. Securities Rulemaking Bd.; mem. Anderson Township Govtl. Task Force, 1986—. Recipient Bond Atty.'s Workshop Founder's award, 1982. Mem. Nat. Assn. Bond Lawyers (dir. 1979-84, pres. 1982-83, hon. dir. 1984—, editor The Quarterly Newsletter 1982—; workshop steering com. 1976, 83, 85), Ohio State Bar Assn., Cin. Bar Assn. Republican. Clubs: Queen City, Terrace Park Country, Queen City Mcpl. Bond. Office: Taft Stettinius & Hollister 1800 First Nat Bank Ctr 425 Walnut St Cincinnati OH 45202

KIELHOFER, JOHN DALE, sales executive, pilot; b. Chgo., Dec. 17, 1955; s. Gene Dale and Janice Elizabeth (Buslee) K.; m. Barbara Sue Bernhardt, July 2, 1981; children—Carrie Leigh Clark, Kenneth Andrew Clark, Barbara Janice. Assoc. in Mktg. Mgmt., Oakton Community Coll., Morton Grove, Ill., 1977. Part owner, apprentice Neumann-Buslee & Wolfe, Des Plaines, Ill., 1971-79, sales exec., 1977-79; sales exec. Ingredient Tech., Des Plaines, 1979-84, H.B. Taylor & Co., Chgo., 1987—; pres. Another Era, Ltd., Bloomingdale, Ill., 1984-86, Bloomin T's Ltd., Bloomingdale, Ill. Com. mem. Cub Scouts Am., 1983; bd. dirs. Notre Dame High Sch. Alumni Assn.; v.p. Old Town Bloomingdale Mchts. Assn., 1984-85, pres., 1985-86. Recipient award for meritorious service Notre Dame High Sch. Fathers Club, Niles, Ill., 1972, 73, 74. Mem. Am. Assn. Cereal Chemists, Chgo. Perfumery Soap and Extract Assn., Inst. Food Technologists, Bloomingdale C. of C. (assoc. dir. 1985, bd. dirs. 1985-87), Aircraft Owners and Pilots Assn., Exptl. Aircraft Assn. Republican. Roman Catholic. Club: Oak Brook Polo, Oakton Flying of Morton Grove (founding pres. 1975-76). Home: 570 Northport Dr Elk Grove Village IL 60007 Office: H B Taylor & Co 4830 S Christiana Chicago IL 60632

KIELMAN, RICHARD CHARLES, hospital administrator, management educator; b. Sioux Falls, S.D., Mar. 15, 1946; s. Herman and Viola Frances Geneva (Oihus) K.; m. Cheryl Rae Prins, Jan. 25, 1969 (div. Sept. 1983); children—Christopher Charles, Tamra Lynn. B.S., U. S.D., 1968, M.B.A., 1971. Instr., Benedictine Coll., Atchison, Kans., 1972-75, chmn., asst. prof., 1975-77; dir. edn. Meml. Hosp., Fremont, Nebr., 1977-78, dir. support service, 1978-80, v.p., 1980—; mgmt. instr. Met. Community Coll., Omaha, 1979—. Bd. dirs. Health Planning Council of the Midlands, Omaha, 1980-81. Served to 1st lt. U.S. Army, 1968-70. Mem. Am. Soc. Hosp. Planning, Am. Acad. Med. Adminstrs., Am. Coll. Healthcare Execs., Nebr. Hosp. Assn. Republican. Club: Sertoma (Fremont, Nebr.).

KIELY, BARBARA ANN, financial executive; b. Clinton, Iowa, May 8, 1949; d. John Henry Kiely and Helen Louise (Pace) (Kiely) Wolfe; m. Eugene John Berens Jr., Aug. 2, 1975. BA, Luther Coll., 1971; MBA, Loyola U., Chgo., 1976. CPA, Ill. Internal auditor Montgomery Ward & Co., Inc. subs. Marcor Inc., Chgo., 1976-79; dir. internal audit IDC Services, Inc., Chgo., 1979-82; chief fin. officer Zwiren & Wagner Advt., Chgo., 1983-85; chief exec. officer H & K Fin. Services, Inc., Chgo., 1985—, also chmn. bd. dirs. Mem. Am. Inst. CPA's, Nat. Assn. Women Bus. Owners, Assn. Ind. Comml. Producers (assoc.), Ill. CPA Soc., Execs. Club Chgo., Chgo. Soc. Women CPA's (bd. dirs., treas.), Women in Film. Avocations: skiing, tennis, travel. Home: 651 W Sheridan #6D Chicago IL 60613 Office: H & K Fin Services Inc PO Box 138116 Chicago IL 60613

KIELY, DENNIS LEE, physician; b. Grayling, Mich., June 3, 1950; s. Robert Burton and Betty Mae (Bloom) K.; m. Chelo Mae Merritt, Nov. 13, 1982; 1 child, Timothy Allen. A.S., Delta Coll., 1970; B.S., Mich. State U., 1974, D.O., 1977. Registered histologist Am. Soc. Clin. Pathologists. Intern, Bay Osteo. Hosp., Bay City, Mich., 1977-78; resident in pediatrics Chgo., 1978-79; gen. practice osteo. medicine Pub. Health Dept., Mt. Pleasant, Mich., 1982-83, The Community Clinic, Weidman, Mich., 1984—; gen. practice osteo. medicine, Midland, Mich., 1983-84; med. dir. Branch County Clinic, Coldwater, Mich., 1984; med. cons. Tri-County Center, Midland, 1983-84, 1016 House (drug rehab.), Midland, 1983-84. Com. mem. Lake Huron Area Council Boy Scouts Am., Weidman, 1985; scout master, asst. scout master Paul Bunyan Council Boy Scouts Am., 1961-68 (recipient Eagle, God, Country awards). Mem. Am. Osteo. Assn., Osteo. Gen. Practioners of Mich., Am. Coll. Osteo. Pediatricians (assoc.). Presbyterian. Avocations: hunting, camping, fishing, horseback riding. Home and Office: 3180 First St PO Box 215 Weidman MI 48893

KIEPER, DAVID GLENN, data processing executive, data processing consultant; b. Antigo, Wis., Aug. 10, 1959; s. Glenn Theodore Martin and Margaret Ruth (Hunter) K.; m. Peggy Ann Kielcheski, Aug. 16, 1980. BS in Chemistry, U. Wis., Green Bay, 1979. Systems programmer U. Wis., Green Bay, 1979-81, systems mgr., 1981-84, asst. dir., 1984—; cons. in software Telefile Computer Products, Inc., Irvine, Calif., 1981-86, mgr. software research and devel., 1986—. Mem. Telexchange Computer Users Group (chartered, mgr. program library 1983-85, vice chmn. 1986, chmn. 1987). Republican. Lutheran. Office: U Wis 2420 Nicolet Dr Green Bay WI 54302

KIEREN, BARRY FRANCIS, computer systems project leader; b. Detroit, Mar. 12, 1952; s. Roger Charles and Kathleen (O'Day) K.; m. Joan Martha Teschendort, Oct. 27, 1979; children: Andreé C., Anne M. Grad. in bus. adminstrn., U. Minn., 1978. Mgmt. info. systems specialist Hennepin County, Mpls., 1974-81; sr. systems mgr. First Bank of Mpls., 1981-83; systems officer First Bank Systems, Mpls., 1983—; cons. in field. Pres., bd. dirs. Minn. Dance Theatre and Sch., Mpls., 1986; bd. dirs. Hennepin Ctr. for Arts, Mpls., 1986. Mem. Assn. System Mgrs. Avocations: sailing, skiing, hunting. Home: 5629 Fremont S Minneapolis MN 55419 Office: First Bank Systems 120 S 6th St Minneapolis MN 55480

KIERSCHT, CHARLES M., financial company executive; b. Des Moines, Iowa, 1939. Grad., U. Iowa. Pres., chief operating officer, dir. Kemper Fin. Services, Inc., Chgo.; pres., dir. Kemper Growth Fund, Chgo., Kemper Income and Capital Preservation, Chgo., Kemper Investors Life Ins. Co., Chgo., Kemper Money Market Fund, Chgo., Kemper Mcpl. Bond Fund,

Chgo., Kemper Summit Fund, Chgo., Kemper Total Return Fund, Chgo. Office: Kemper Fin Services Inc 120 S LaSalle St Chicago IL 60603 *

KIESOW, LINDA F., data processing executive; b. Rock Island, Ill., July 5, 1953; d. Oscar R. and Helen F. (Junk) McElroy; m. James Thomas Kiesow, May 26, 1973. B.Bus. in Acctg., Western Ill. U., 1979; M.B.A., U. Iowa, 1985. Cert. data processor. Produce mgr. Carthage Super Valu, Ill., 1974-75; aggregate sample analyst Valley Quarry, St. Augustine, Ill., 1975-76; data processing mgr. Moline Consumers Co., Ill., 1979-87; ops. supr. Alcoa, Davenport, Iowa, 1987—. Fulbright scholar Western Ill. U., Macomb, 1977; Coll. Bus. Scholar, Western Ill. U., 1978; Acctg. Dept. scholar Western Ill. U., 1978. Mem. Acctg. Soc. (mem. banquet com. chmn., v.p. 1977-78), Nat. Assn. Female Execs., Data Processing Mgmt. Assn., Assn. of Inst. for Cert. of Computer Profls., Alpha Lambda Delta, Phi Kappa Phi. Republican. Baptist. Avocations: reading; sports. Home: 4907 48th Ave Moline IL 61265 Office: Alcoa PO Box 3567 Davenport IA 52808

KIHNE, JOHN FRANKLIN, educator; b. Grafton, N.D., Dec. 5, 1950; s. Joseph R. and Holmfridur (Asmundson) K.; m. Susan Amelia Hoffman, Aug. 14, 1971; children—Jason Alexander, Nancy Jo. B.S. in Edn. U. N.D., 1973. Tchr. indsl. arts Turtle Mountain Community Sch., Belcourt, N.D., 1973-77; tchr. indsl. arts Mandan (N.D.) High Sch., 1977—, asst. coach in cross country, track, 1980—. Served to 1st lt. USAR, 1973-81. Mem. N.D. Indsl. Arts Assn. (Tchr. of Yr. award 1982), Am. Indsl. Arts Assn., N.D. Vocat. Assn., Am. Vocat. Assn., N.D. Edn. Assn., NEA, Am. Legion. Democrat. Roman Catholic. Lodges: Elks, Moose. Home: 1202 3rd St NE Mandan ND 58554 Office: 905 8th Ave NW Mandan ND 58554

KIKOL, JOHN CHARLES, financial executive; b. Cleve., Jan. 26, 1944; s. John J. and Margaret (Hromoga) K., m. Barbara Jelinek, June 14, 1969; children—Todd, Carri, Courtney. B.B.A., Ohio U., 1966; J.D., Cleve. State U., 1970. Bar: Ohio, 1970. With Central Nat. Bank, Cleve., 1966-69, The Hannan Co., Cleve., 1969-71; exec. v.p., sec., counsel CleveTrust Advisors Inc., Cleve., 1971-74, pres., dir., 1974-82; pres. CleveTrust Realty Investors, Cleve., 1974—, trustee, 1982—; bd. govs., chmn. ins. com. Nat. Assn. Real Estate Investment Trusts, Washington; bd. dirs. MacDonald Money Fund, N.Y., MacDonald Money Tax-Free Fund, N.Y. Mem. Nat. Assn. Over-the-Counter Cos. (bd. dirs. 1984—), Nat. Assn. Security Dealers (corp. adv. bd. 1983-86, market surveillance com. 1984-87, info. com. 1987—). Office: 1020 Ohio Savings Plaza Cleveland OH 44114

KIKTA, PAUL CHARLES, human resources executive; b. Endicott, N.Y., Feb. 20, 1944; s. Paul and Edith T. (Chonka) K.; div.; children: Paulette Marie, Jon-Paul. BA in Speech and English, SUNY, Fredonia, 1969; postgrad., Harvard U., 1980, Sterling Inst., 1981. Dir. alumni affairs SUNY, Fredonia, 1969-77; communications mgr. bearings div. TRW Corp., Cleve., 1977-79, mgr. human resources replacement parts div., 1980-82, mgr. placement and tng. world hdqrs., 1982-84, dir. human resources automotive worldwide sector, 1984—; asst. to v.p. Penn-Dixie Steel Corp., 1979-80. Served with U.S. Army. Avocations: scouting, golf, philately. Home: 12525 Edgewater Dr Apt 325 Lakewood OH 44107 Office: TRW Inc 1900 Richmond Rd Cleveland OH 44124

KILBORN, RICHARD C., insurance company executive; b. Hammond, Ind., May 17, 1929; s. Charles Albert and Mildred (Thielman) K.; m. Roberta Jane Taylor, Jan. 1, 1951; children: Carol Luke, Charles F., Karen J. BS, Ind. U., 1951. Adminstrv. asst. Mut. Med. Ins., Inc. (Blue Shield Ind.), Indpls., 1955-58, asst. exec. v.p., 1958-66, exec. v.p., 1966-67, pres. and chief exec. officer, 1967-85; pres. and chief operating officer Associated Ins. Cos., Inc. (Blue Cross and Blue Shield of Ind.), Indpls., 1985—; corp. v.p. Blue Cross and Blue Shield Joint Ops., Indpls., 1973-82; bd. dirs. Blue Cross and Blue Shield Assn., Chgo., Am. Fletcher Corp., BCS Fin Corp.; bd. dirs. Regional Mktg., Inc., vice chmn., 1981-85, pres. 1985—; bd. dirs. Health Maintenance, Inc., vice chmn., 1982-85, pres. 1982—; bd. dirs. Assocs. Life Ins. Co., vice chmn., 1982-85, pres. 1985—; chmn. bd. dirs. Key Benefits Adminstrs., Inc. Mem. Senator Quayle's Health Adv. Com., 1985-86, com. health scis. and tech. Indpls. Growth Project, 1985-86, Indpls. Corp. Community Council; vice chmn. Marion County Assn. Retarded Citizens, Indpls., 1983; chmn. Indpls. Pvt. Industry Council, Indpls., 1984-86; bd. dirs. United Way Greater Indpls. Mem. Indpls. C. of C. Republican. Episcopalian. Clubs: Indpls., Athletic, Skyline (Indpls.). Lodges: Rotary, Masons, Shriners. Avocations: boating, skiing, snow mobiling, traveling, golfing. Home: 212 Carringan Point Nobelsville IN 46060 Office: Associated Ins Companies Inc 120 W Market St Indianapolis IN 46204

KILDEE, DALE E., congressman; b. Flint, Mich., Sept. 16, 1929; s. Timothy Leo and Norma Alicia (Ullmer) K.; m. Gayle Heyn, Feb. 27, 1965; children: David, Laura, Paul. B.A., Sacred Heart Sem., 1952; tchr.'s cert., U. Detroit, 1954; M.A., U. Mich., 1961; postgrad. (Rotary Found. fellow), U. Peshawar, Pakistan, 1958-59. Tchr. U. Detroit High Sch., 1954-56, Flint Central High Sch., 1956-64; mem. Mich. Ho. of Reps., 1964-74, Mich. Senate, 1975-76, 95th-100th congresses from 7th Mich. Dist., 1977—. Mem. Am. Fedn. Tchrs., Urban League, Phi Delta Kappa. Lodges: K.C; Optimists. Home: 1434 Jane St Flint MI 48506 Office: US House of Representatives 2432 Rayburn House Office Bldg Washington DC 20515 also: 1176 Robert T Longway Blvd Flint MI 48503 *

KILE, MARILYN JANET, social worker, consultant; b. St. Louis, Oct. 14, 1951; d. James Raymond and Loretta Coletta (Haefner) K.; m. Randall Lee Rasmussen, May 24, 1975; children: Elizabeth, Michael. BA, Moorhead State U., 1973; MSSW, U. Wis., 1976. Psychiat. social worker No. Pines Guidance Clinic, Cumberland, Wis., 1976-80; pvt. practice clin. social work Ft. Atkinson, Wis., 1981-85; coordinator health awareness programs U. Wis., White Water, 1985—. Co-author: BodyRights, 1986. Coordinator NOW, Ft. Atkinson. Mem. Nat. Assn. Social Work. Office: U Wis Whitewater Student Health Ctr Whitewater WI 53190

KILEY, DAVID ALLEN, retail company executive; b. Cleve., Mar. 27, 1941; s. John James and Rosa Lillian (Murley) K.; m. Sherry Lynn Schilling; children: Douglas, Diane, Debra. BA, Ohio State U., 1965. Asst. buyer Lazarus Dept. Store, Columbus, Ohio, 1966-68, buyer, 1969-71; mgr. mdse. Ziegler Dept. Store, Medina, Ohio, 1971-78, gen. mgr. mdse., 1979-83, exec. v.p., 1984—, pres., chief operating officer, 1985—. Bd. advisors Wayne Coll., Wooster, Ohio, 1978-79; mem. steering com. Boy Scouts Am., Chippewa dist., Medina, 1980. Mem. Ohio Mens Wear Assn. (sec., v.p. 1982-85), Medina C. of C. (pres. retail div. 1972). Republican. Methodist. Lodge: Kiwanis (pres. 1982-83). Avocations: woodworking, photography, herbal gardening. Home: 7373 Wolff Rd Medina OH 44256 Office: Ziegler Store Inc 23 Public Sq Medina OH 44256

KILGORE, JOE MOFFATT, editor; b. Clifton, Tex., Sept. 9, 1916; s. Walter Louis and Mary Alice (Gallagher) K.; B.J. magna cum laude, Temple U., 1950; M.S.J., UCLA, 1951; m. Cathryn McCormick, Feb. 4, 1965; 1 dau., Linda Kilgore Brandon. Mng. editor Three Sons Publ. Co., Northbrook, Ill., 1961—; realtors assoc. Glenbrook & Assocs., Wauconda, Ill. Mem. Constl. Amendment Conv., 1977. Served with USN, 1939-46. Mem. Nat. Assn. Realtors, Lake County Bd. Realtors. Address: Rural Rt #3 Carterville IL 62918

KILKEARY, NAN M., communications specialist; b. Evergreen Park, Ill., Sept. 17, 1943; d. Robert M. and Barbara E. (Bailey) Lundberg; m. William P. Kilkeary, Dec. 17, 1966 (div. Aug. 1978); children—Timothy T., Christopher K. B.S., U. Ill., 1965; postgrad. U. Chgo., 1974-75. Editor, UPI Broadcast, Chgo., 1966-67, 69; asst. mgr. press relations CNA, Chgo., 1971-74; account supr. Harshe-Rotman & Druck, Chgo., 1974-76; dir. communications Allstate, Northbrook, Ill., 1976-81; v.p. communications Investors Diversified Services, Mpls., 1981-82; dir. communications Montgomery Ward, Chgo., 1982-85; pres. Kilkeary Communications, 1985—; sr. v.p. mktg. communications and strategic planning Wieboldt Stores, Inc., Chgo., 1986—; owner, mgr. O'Rourke's Pub., Chgo., 1966-75. Author: The Good Communicator, 1987; contbr. articles to profl. jours. Founder, Ill. Housewives for ERA, Evanston, Ill., 1972; bd. dirs. New City YMCA. Recipient Golden Trumpet, Publicity Club Chgo., 1975, 79, 80, Shaunessy award, 1979, 80; Pres. award Internat. Assn. Bus. Communicators, 1979. Mem. Pub. Relations Soc. Am. (silver anvil 1977, 79), Nat. Investor Relations Inst. (chpt. dir. 1975-80), Women in Communications. Democrat. Unitarian. Club: Carleton. Office: 500 Skokie Blvd Northbrook IL 60062

KILLERMANN, ROSEMARY DONOVAN, research company executive; b. Chgo., Apr. 24, 1929; d. Timothy V. and Mabel (Hederman) Donovan; divorced Feb. 1965; children: Adam, Mark, Lisa, Stephen, Kevin, Jeffrey, Susan. Student, Fla. So. Coll., 1947-48, U. Wis., 1949-50, Northwestern U., 1951-52. V.p. Intercon Research, Evanston, Ill., 1965—. Mem. Licensing Exec. Soc., Soc. Auto Engring. Club: Rockies (Ft. Collins, Colo.). Home: 1304 Hillside Dr Fort Collins CO 80524 Office: Intercon Research 1219 Howard St Evanston IL 60202

KILLIAN, LYNNE ELIZABETH, psychologist; b. Duluth, Minn., Nov. 29, 1956; d. John Norman and Jeannette Alice (LaMar) Green; m. Michael Patrick Killian, Sept. 25, 1982; 1 child, Rachel Lynne. BA, U. Minn., Duluth, 1979; MA, U. Mo., Kans. City, 1980. Lic. psychologist, Minn. Instr. U. Mo., Kansas City, 1979-80; psychologist Polinsky Med. Rehab. Ctr., Duluth, 1981—, dept. dir., 1982—. Author: Physical Management of Industrial Injuries, 1987. Mem. Minn. Lic. Psychologists. Lutheran. Home: 6892 Arrowhead Rd Duluth MN 55811 Office: Polonsky Med Rehab Ctr 530 E 2d St Duluth MN 55811

KILLIAN, WILLIAM FRANCIS, periodontist, air force officer; b. Balt., Sept. 8, 1943; s. William Frank and Elizabeth Mary (Schmidt) K.; m. Melanie Cecelia Reese, June 8, 1968; children—William F., Brian D., Ashley E. B.A., Loyola Coll., Balt., 1965; D.D.S., U. Md.-Balt., 1969; M.S., U. Tex.-Houston, 1976. Commd. 2d lt. U.S. Air Force, 1966, advanced through grades to col., 1984; chief gen. dentistry USAF Hosp., Fairchild AFB, Wash., 1971-73; resident in periodontics Wilford Hall Med. Ctr, San Antonio, 1973-76; chief periodontics USAF Clinic, Charleston AFB, S.C., 1976-79, Hickam AFB, Hawaii, 1979-83, USAF Med. Ctr., Scott AFB, Ill., 1983—; cons., 1983—. Mem. Am. Acad. Periodontology, ADA, Omicron Kappa Upsilon, Beta Beta Beta, Gorgas Dental Honor Soc. Republican. Roman Catholic. Avocation: woodworking. Home: 807 Meadowlark Dr O'Fallon IL 62269 Office: USAF Med Ctr Scott AFB IL 62225

KILLIAN, WILLIAM PAUL, manufacturing company executive; b. Sidney, Ohio, Apr. 26, 1935; s. Ray and Erie K.; m. Beverly Ann Buchanan, Sept.7, 1957; children: William, Katherine, Michael. B in Chem. Engring. with honors, Ga. Inst. Tech., 1957; M in Engring. Adminstrn. with honors, U. Utah, 1968. Chem. engr. Esso, Baton Rouge, La., 1957-58; mgr. research and devel. mfg. engring., then plant mgr. Thiokol Corp., Brigham City, Utah, 1958-68; mgr. corp. project mgmt. Masonite Corp., Chgo., 1968-70, mgr. new bus. ventures, 1970-73; mgr. strategic planning chem. and metall. group Gen. Electric Co., Pittsfield, Mass. and Columbus, Ohio, 1973-77; v.p. corp. planning and devel. Hoover Universal Inc., Ann Arbor, Mich., 1977-85; v.p. corp. devel. Johnson Controls Inc., Milw., 1985-87, v.p. corp. devel. and strategy, 1987—. Mem. Corp. Planning Council, Machinery and Allied Products Inst. Mem. Assn. for Corp. Growth (pres. Wis. chpt.), Planning Forum, Machinery and Allied Products Inst., Mensa, Tau Beta Pi, Omicron Delta Kappa, Phi Kappa Phi, Pi Delta Epsilon, Phi Eta Sigma. Clubs: North Shore Racquet, Mequon Racquet, Le Club. Home: 9637 N Courtland Dr Mequon WI 53092 Office: Johnson Controls Inc 5757 N Green Bay Ave PO Box 591 Milwaukee WI 53201

KILLINGBECK, JANICE LYNELLE (MRS. VICTOR LEE KILLINGBECK), journalist; b. Flint, Mich., Nov. 11, 1948; d. Leonard Paul and Ina Marie (Harris) Johnson; B.A., Mich. State U., 1970; postgrad. Delta Coll., 1971-72; m. Victor Lee Killingbeck, Sept. 26, 1970; children—Deeanna Dawn, Victor Scott. Tourist counselor Mich. Dept. State Hwys., Clare, 1969; copy editor Mich. State News, East Lansing, 1969-70; gen. reporter Midland (Mich.) Daily News, 1970; tchr. Saginaw (Mich.) Public Schs., 1971; public relations teller 1st State Bank of Saginaw, 1971-75; crew leader spl. census in Buena Vista Twp., Detroit Regional Office, U.S. Bur. Census, 1976, interviewer ann. housing survey-standard met. statis. areas, 1977-78, interviewer on-going health surveys, 1979—, Nat. Crime Survey, 1985-86; editor AMEN newsletter United Meth. Women, Saginaw, 1984-87, Bridgeport-Birch Run Weekly News, 1986—. Mem. Women in Communications, Sigma Delta Chi. Methodist. Home: 4946 Hess Rd Saginaw MI 48601 Office: 130 Broad St PO Box 388 Cheansaning MI 48616

KILLPACK, JAMES ROBERT, banking exec.; b. Persia, Iowa, Aug. 11, 1922; s. James Marion and Dorothy (Divelbess) K.; m. Norma Hewett, June 11, 1949; children—James, John, Steven. B.S., Miami U., Oxford, Ohio, 1946. C.P.A., Ohio. With Peat, Marwick, Mitchell & Co., Cleve., 1946-58; treas. Ferro Corp., Cleve., 1958-66; fin. v.p. Island Creek Coal Co., Cleve., 1966-68; dir.corp. planning Eaton Corp. (formerly Eaton Yale & Towne Inc.), Cleve., 1968-69; v.p. corp planning Eaton Corp. (formerly Eaton Yale & Towne Inc.), 1969, v.p. adminstrn., 1970, v.p. fin., 1970-78, exec. v.p. fin. and adminstrn., 1978-79; dir. Nat. City Bank, Cleve., from 1979, vice chmn., 1979, pres., 1979-84; dir. Nat. City Corp., Cleve., 1979—, vice chmn., 1979-80, pres., 1981-86, chmn., chief exec. officer, 1986—; dir. Sherwin-Williams Co., Weatherchem Corp. Served with AUS, 1942-45. Mem. Fin. Execs. Inst. (dir. Cleve. chpt., pres. 1970-71), Am. Inst. C.P.A.'s. Mem. Christian Ch. Clubs: Tavern (Cleve.), Union (Cleve.), Pepper Pike Country, The Country; Shaker Country (Shaker Heights, Ohio); John's Island (Fla.); Rolling Rock (Pa.). Home: 13515 Shaker Blvd Suite 8-B Cleveland OH 44120 Office: Nat City Corp 1900 E 9th St Cleveland OH 44114

KILPATRICK, LORI SUE, computer engineer; b. Joliet, Ill., Dec. 24, 1958; d. Ronald John and Dorothy Jean (Gregory) Menozzi; m. David Michael Kilpatrick, May 30, 1981. BS in Computer Engring., U. Ill., 1980; MS in Computer Sci., U. Mo., Rolla, 1986. Assoc. elec. engr. McDonnell Aircraft Co., St. Louis, 1981-82, electronics engr., 1982-85, coll. recruiter, 1982—, sr. electronics engr., 1985-86, lead electronics engr., 1986—. Named Teammate of Distinction, McDonnell Douglas Corp., St. Louis, 1984. Republican. Avocations: golf, gardening. Home: 4066 90th Ave Florissant MO 63034 Office: McDonnell Douglas Corp PO Box 516 Saint Louis MO 63134

KILROY, WILLIAM TERRENCE, lawyer; b. Kansas City, Mo., May 24, 1950; s. John Muir and Katherine Lorainne (Butler) K.; m. Marianne Michelle Maurin, Sept. 8, 1984. B.S., U. Kans., 1972, M.A., 1974; J.D., Washburn U., 1977. Bar: Mo. 1977. Assoc. firm Shughart, Thomson & Kilroy, Kansas City, Mo., 1977-81, mem., dir., 1981—. Contbr. articles to profl. publs. Mem. Kansas City Citizens Assn., 1980—. Mem. Lawyers Assn. Kansas City, Kansas City Bar Assn. (chmn. civil rights com. 1984, chmn. 1986), Mo. Bar Assn., ABA. (subcom. on arbitration, labor law sect. 1977—), Greater Kansas City C. of C. Republican. Methodist. Club: University. Home: 6016 Central St Kansas City MO 64113 Office: Shughart Thomson & Kilroy 120 W 12th St 12 Wyandotte Plaza Kansas City MO 64105

KILSTOFTE, IRWIN HELGE, architect; b. Sandstone, Minn., Mar. 11, 1927; s. Helge Berntsen Kilstofte and Agnes Marie Frokjer; m. Patricia Ann Rodeghier, Sept. 17, 1955 (div. 1978); children: Peter, Paul, Daniel; m. Marilyn Annette, Nov. 2, 1985. Registered profl. architect. Trainee Hubert Swanson Architects, Mpls., 1953-55, Abbett and Griswold Architects, Mpls., 1955-58; pres. Irwin H. Kilstofte Architect, Wayzata, 1958-61, Kilstofte and Vosejpka Inc., Wayzata, 1961-70, Kilstofte Assocs. Inc., Wayzata, 1970—. Contbr. articles on geodesic structures to profl. jours. Served with USN, 1945-46. Republican. Lutheran. Lodge: Rotary (bd. dirs. 1986). Avocations: sailing, skiing, tennis. Office: Kilstofte Assocs Inc 305 Minnetonka Ave S Wayzata MN 55391

KIM, DAVID YOUNG, psychiatrist; b. Seoul, Korea, Apr. 23, 1945; came to U.S., 1974, naturalized 1980; s. Hyun-oo and Janran (Jung) K.; m. Jennifer Park, Mar. 17, 1971; children: Emily, Park. BS, U. Korea, Seoul, 1967, MD, 1971. Diplomate Am. Bd. Psychiatry and Neurology. Resident in psychiatry Nassau County Med. Ctr., East Meadow, NY., 1974-77; asst. clin. prof. Med. Coll. Wis., 1980; practice medicine specializing in psychiatry, Racine, Wis., 1980—; clin. dir. Mental Health Mgmt., Racine, 1984—; chmn. dept. psychiatry St. Luke's Hosp., Racine, 1984—; instr. SUNY, Stony Brook, 1976-77. Bd. dirs. Bell City Learning Ctr., Racine, 1982. Recipient Excellence in Clin. Practice award State of Wis., 1978. Mem. Am. Psychiat. Assn., Wis. Med. Soc. Republican.

KIM, KWAN S(UK), economist, educator, consultant; b. Pusan, Korea, Oct. 8, 1936; came to U.S., 1959, naturalized, 1970; s. Joon W. and Bok Hee (Yoo) K.; m. Gloria Jean Letourneau, Mar. 19, 1966; children—Kevin Christopher, Malaika Nicole. B.A., Seoul (Korea) Nat. U., 1959; M.A. in Polit. Sci., U. Minn., 1961, Ph.D. in Econs., 1967. Research economist North Star Research and Devel. Inst., Mpls., 1964; econometrician Pillsbury Co., Mpls., 1964-66; instr. U. Minn., Mpls., 1966-67; asst. prof. econs. U. Notre Dame (Ind.), 1967-75, assoc. prof., 1975-86, prof., 1986—; vis. lectr. U. Nairobi (Kenya), 1971-73; vis. prof. U. Dar es Salaam (Tanzania), 1975-77; econ. policy adviser AID, Washington, 1979-81; vis. prof. Universidad Autonoma de Nuevo Leon (Mexico), 1982; econ. adviser Nacional Financiera, Mexico, 1984; vis. prof. Delft Inst. Mgmt. Sci., The Netherlands, 1984; vis. prof. Am. Grad. Sch. Internat. Mgmt., 1987; cons. AID, 1983. Recipient Merit award AID, 1980; Asian Research Inst. fellow Pan-Asia Inst., Washington, 1970-71; Rockefeller Found. grantee, 1971-73, 75-77. Mem. Am. Econ. Assn., Econometric Soc. N.AAm. Econ. and Fin. Assn. Roman Catholic. Club: Atari Computer (South Bend, Ind.). Author: Industrial Policy and Development in South Korea, 1985, (co-author) Papers on the Political Economy of Tanzania, 1979; Korean Agricultural Research, 1982; Debt and Development in Latin America, 1985; contbr. numerous articles to profl. jours. Home: 414 Napoleon Blvd South Bend IN 46617 Office: U Notre Dame Decio 110 Dame IN 46556

KIM, MOON HYUN, physician, educator; b. Seoul, Korea, Nov. 30, 1934; s. Jae Hang and Kum Chu (Choi) K.; m. Yong Cha Pak, June 20, 1964; children: Peter, Edward. M.D., Yonsei U., 1960. Diplomate: Am. Bd. Ob-Gyn. (examiner 1979—). Sr. instr. Ob-Gyn Yonsei U., Seoul, 1967-68; intern Md. Gen. Hosp., Balt., 1961-62; resident in Ob-Gyn Cleve. Met. Gen. Hosp., 1962-66; fellow in reproductive endocrinology U. Wash., Seattle, 1966-67, U. Toronto, Ont., Can., 1968-70; asst. prof. Ob-Gyn, also chief endocrinology and infertility U. Chgo., 1970-74; asso. prof. Ob-Gyn Ohio State U., Columbus, 1974-78; prof. Ohio State U., 1978—, chief div. reproductive endocrinology, 1974—, vice chmn. dept. ob-gyn. Contbg. author books; contbr. articles to profl. jours. Recipient McClintock award U. Chgo., 1975; named Prof. of Yr. Ohio State U., 1976; recipient Clin. Teaching award, 1980. Fellow Am. Coll. Ob-Gyn; mem. Am. Gynecol. and Obstetric Soc., Korean Med. Assn., Am. Fertility Soc., Chgo. Gynecol. Soc., Endocrine Soc., Soc. Study Reprodn., Soc. Gynecol. Investigation. Home: 4331 Donington Rd Columbus OH 43220 Office: Ohio State U Hosps 1654 Upham Dr MH-533 Columbus OH 43210 also: 410 W 10th Ave N-613 Columbus OH 43210

KIM, SOOJAA LEE, polymer scientist; b. Milyang, Kyongsangnam-do, Korea, Mar. 9, 1944; came to U.S., 1967; d. Keun Jin and Kyong-Jo (Chung) Lee; m. Dong Kwang Kim, June 10, 1972; children: Eugene, Norman. BS, Seoul (Korea) Nat. U., 1966; MS, SE Mass. U., 1969; PhD, N.C. State U., 1973. Mem. research staff Nat. Indsl. Research Inst., Seoul, 1966-67; postdoctoral fellow Lehigh U., Bethlehem, Pa., 1973-77, research scientist, 1978; assoc. scientist Goodyear Tire and Rubber, Akron, Ohio, 1978—. Mem. Am. Chem. Soc., Soc. for Plastics Engrs. Home: 4194 Big Spruce Dr Akron OH 44313 Office: Goodyear Tire and Rubber 142 Goodyear Blvd Akron OH 44316

KIM, YOUNG CHUL, radiologist; b. Republic of Korea, Jan. 16, 1943; came to U.S., 1971; s. Sang Yeol Kim and Hung Soo Park, m. Pil Joo Lee, Oct. 23, 1970; children: Ruth, Christine, Paul. MD, Kyungpook Nat. U., Taegu, Rep. of Korea, 1967. Diplomate Am. Bd. Radiology, Am. Bd. Nuclear Medicine. Intern Jamaica Hosp., Queens, N.Y., 1971-72; resident Meth. Hosp., Bklyn., 1972-75; with nuclear medicine dept. Western Pa. Hosp., Pitts., 1976-77; dir. nuclear medicine and ultra sound U. Louisville, 1977-80, Medina (Ohio) Radiology Group, Inc., 1980—; ultra sound cons. V.A. Hosp., Louisville, 1977-80. Author: (handbook) Nuclear Medicine in Vivoimaging, 1979; contbr. articles to profl. jours. Ordained deacon, chmn. deacons Korean Baptist Ch. Cleve., 1980. Served to capt. Rep. of Korea Army, 1967-70. Mem. AMA, Radiol. Soc. N.Am., Soc. Nuclear Medicine, Am. Inst. Ultrasound in Medicine, Am. Coll. Radiology. Avocations: photography, tennis, chess, fishing. Office: Medina Radiology Group Inc 990 E Washington St Medina OH 44256

KIM, YUNG DAI, research scientist; b. Seoul, Korea, Mar. 24, 1936; came to U.S., 1957, naturalized, 1971; s. Ik S. and Jung H. (Juhn) K.; m. Young S. Chyung, June 17, 1967; children—Jean Ok, Sue Ok. Ph.D., U. Minn., 1968. Vis. scientist Kettering Research Lab., Yellow Springs, Ohio, 1968-69; NIH fellow Northwestern U., Evanston, Ill., 1969-71; NIH research fellow U. Pa., Phila., 1971-73; immunochemist Worthington Biochem. Co., Freehold, N.J., 1973-74; sr. scientist Abbott Labs., North Chicago, Ill., 1974—. Mem. Am. Assn. Immunologists, Am. Chem. Soc., Sigma Xi, Phi Lambda Upsilon. Contbr. articles to profl. jours.; patentee in field. Home: 75 N Rolling Ridge Lindenhurst IL 60046 Office: Abbott Labs North Cancer Researcl Lab D90C Chicago IL 60064

KIM, ZAEZEUNG, allergist, immunologist, educator; b. Hamhung, Korea, Feb. 21, 1929; came to U.S., 1967; s. Suh and Suyeo (Hahn) K.; m. Youngju Kim, June 2, 1961; children: Keungsuk, Maria. Student, Hamhung Med. Coll., Korea, 1946-50; MD, Seoul U., Korea, 1960; PhD in Immunology, U. Cologne, Fed. Republic of Germany, 1968. Diplomate Am. Bd. Allergy and Immunology. Intern Seoul Nat. U. Hosp., 1960-61, resident in medicine, 1961-63; resident in medicine Heidelberg U. Hosp., Fed. Republic of Germany, 1963-64; research fellow Max-Planck Inst., Cologne, 1965-67; fellow in hematology U. Tex., Houston, 1967-68; resident in allergy and immunology Temple U. Hosp., Phila., 1968-69; fellow in medicine Ohio State U., Columbus, 1969-71; instr. medicine Med. Coll. Wis., Milw., 1972-75, asst. prof., 1975-78, assoc. clin. prof., 1978—; practice medicine specializing in allergy and immunology Racine, Wis. Contbr. articles to profl. jours. Fellow Am. Acad. Allergy and Immunology, Am. Coll. Allergists; mem. AMA. Home: 4521 N Wildwood Ave Milwaukee WI 53211 Office: 1300 S Green Bay Rd Racine WI 53406

KIMBALL, KURT FREDERICK, city manager; b. Detroit, July 4, 1950; s. Fred Earl and Thelma Mary (Scheiwe) K.; m. Randy Rae Kroft, June 19, 1971; children: Tamara Leigh, Karilyn Rae. BA, U. Mich., 1971, M of Pub. Policy, 1974. Adminstrv. asst. City of Grand Rapids (Mich.), 1974-77, exec. asst., 1977-80, performance mgmt. adminstr., 1980-82, asst. city mgr., 1982-87, city mgr., 1987—. Vol. United Way of Kent County, Mich., 1974-76. Mem. Internat. City Mgmt. Assn., Am. Soc. Pub. Adminstrn., Mich. City Mgmt. Assn., West Mich. City Mgmt. Assn. (treas. 1984-86, pres. 1986-87). Office: City of Grand Rapids 300 Monroe Ave NW Grand Rapids MI 49503

KIMBERLIN, TRACY KELLY, hotel executive; b. Sullivan, Mo., Nov. 15, 1951; s. Clyde Eugene and Hazel Marie (Dace) K.; m. LaDonna Marie Kitchen, Aug. 8, 1976 (div. Apr. 1979); m. Belinda Ipock, Sept. 4, 1983 (div. Sept. 1985); 1 child, Michael Toby. BS in Edn., Southwest Mo. State U., 1975. Dir. sales Sheraton Inn, Springfield, Mo., 1975-76, gen. mgr., 1976-85; gen. mgr. Ramada Hotel Hawthorn Park, Springfield, 1985-87; exec. dir. Springfield Conv. and Visitors Bur., 1987—; adv. bd. Springfield Conv. and Visitor's Bur., 1981-86, Ozark Mktg. Council, Branson, Mo., 1983-87. Mem. Mo. Hotel/Motel Assn. (bd. dirs. 1983-86), Springfield Hotel/Motel Assn. (v.p. 1979-83, pres. 1980-81). Baptist. Avocations: flying, softball, golf. Office: Springfield Conv and Visitors Bur 320 N Jefferson PO Box 1687 Springfield MO 65805

KIMBLE, JAMES A., management consultant, accountant; b. Owosso, Mich., June 6, 1937; s. Gaylord Browning and Iva I. (Ansted) K.; children from previous marriage: Kim, Katherine, Kerri, Charles; m. Anne Park, June 13, 1970; 1 child, Jeffrey. B.B.A., U. Toledo, 1959. v.p. The PM Group-Toledo, Inc., 1961—; mgmt. cons., Toledo, 1978—. Pres. Citizens for Metroparks, Toledo, 1976-77; v.p., commr. Met. Park Dist., 1977-86, pres. Metroparks, Toledo, 1986—; chmn. July spl. events Toledo Sesquicentennial, 1987 . Recipient Treasury Card IRS, 1976. Mem. Soc. Profl. Bus. Cons. (bd. dirs. 1977-80, cert.), Inst. Cert. Profl. Bus. Cons., Black & Skaggs Assocs. Republican. Avocation: fishing; travel; photography; genealogy. Office: The PM Group Toledo Inc 3150 Republic Blvd N Toledo OH 43615

KIMBREW, JOSEPH, municipal official. Fire chief City of Indpls., 1986—. Office: Office of the Fire Chief 2501 City-County Bldg 555 N New Jersey Indianapolis IN 46204 *

KIMBROUGH, WILLIAM WALTER, III, psychiatrist; b. Cleve., Sept. 26, 1928; s. William Walter and Minerva Grace (Champion) K.; student Cornell U., 1945-46; B.S., U. Mich., 1948, M.D., 1952; m. Jo Ann Greiner, July 6, 1953; children—Elizabeth, Douglas. Intern, Ohio State U. Health Center, Columbus, 1952-53; resident U. Chgo. Clinics, 1955-56, Ypsilanti (Mich.) State Hosp., 1956-59; asso. psychiatrist U. Mich. Health Service, Ann Arbor, 1959-61; practice medicine specializing in psychoanalytic psychiatry, Ann Arbor, 1961—; cons. atty. gen. U.S., 1958—, Center for Forensic Psychiatry, 1974—, Brighton Found. for Alcoholism, 1961—, Washtenaw County (Mich.) Community Mental Health Services, 1978—, Mich. Dept. Social Services, 1978—; clin. dir. Livingston County (Mich.) Community Mental Health Services, 1983—, Mich. Dept. Corrections, 1985—. Served to col. USPHSR, 1953-87. Recipient Physicians Recognition awards AMA, 1972-86. Fellow Am. Acad. Psychiatry and Law, Am. Soc. Psychoanalytic Physicians; mem. Am. Acad. Psychotherapists, Am. Psychiat. Assn., Ann Arbor Psychiatric Assn., Am. Acad. Psychiatrists in Alcoholism and Addiction (founding mem.), Mich. Psychiat. Assn., N.Y. Acad. Sci., AAAS, Hon. Order Ky. Cols., Sigma Alpha Epsilon, Phi Rho Sigma. Clubs: Ann Arbor Town, Ann Arbor Racquet, Univ., Travis Pointe Country (Ann Arbor); Little Harbor (Harbor Springs, Mich.). Home: 520 Hillspur Rd Barton Hills Village MI 48105 Office: 400 Maynard St Ann Arbor MI 48104

KIMES, ROBERT HILLMER, interior designer; b. Freeport, Ill., June 4, 1927; s. Thomas Albert and Marion E. (Hillmer) K.; m. Fawn Gray, Dec. 28, 1950; children—Bradford, E., Tracy M., Grant T. B.S., Knox Coll., 1950. Mgr. Bldg. & Design Ctr., Freeport, 1953-60; owner, mgr. Robert Kimes Designs, Freeport, 1956—. Pres. Greater Downtown Freeport, 1968-69; bd. dirs. YMCA, Freeport, 1983—. Served with USN, 1945-46. Recipient Liberty Bell award ABA, 1968. Mem. Am. Soc. Interior Designers (bd. dirs. 1973-74, v.p. 1977). Republican. Methodist. Lodge: Rotary (Freeport) (v.p. 1984-85, pres. 1985-86). Home: Hickory Hill Freeport IL 61032 Office: Robert Kimes Designs 9 N Chicago Ave Freeport IL 61032

KIMM, JAMES WILSON, cons. engr.; b. Huron, S.D., Sept. 26, 1925; s. Arthur A. and Mary (Fry) K.; B.S., U. Iowa, 1950; m. Dorothy A. Madsen, Aug. 16, 1952; children—Mary L., Jill A., Tobias J. Pub. health engr. Iowa State Dept. Health, Des Moines, 1950-55; head san. engring. report sect. Stanley Engring. Co., Muscatine, Iowa, 1955-61; pres. Veenstra & Kimm, Inc., Engrs. and Planners, West Des Moines, Iowa, 1961—, West Des Moines Devel. Corp. Served with AUS, 1943-45. Named Engr. Distinction, Engrs. Joint Council. Mem. Am. Water Works Assn. (Fuller award), Iowa Engring Soc., Nat. Soc. Profl. Engrs., C. of C., Cons. Engrs. Council Iowa, Water Pollution Control Fedn. (dir.), Tau Beta Pi, Chi Epsilon. Presbyterian (elder). Contbr. articles and papers to profl. jours. Home: 3932 Ashworth Rd West Des Moines IA 50265 Office: 300 West Bank Bldg 1601 22d St West Des Moines IA 50265

KIMURA, JAMES HIROSHI, biochemistry educator; b. Kona, Hawaii, Oct. 29, 1944; s. Robert Takenori and Adelaide Yoshi K.; m. Pamela Sue Simmons, Apr. 26, 1975; children—Melissa Hanako, Daniel Takenori. B.S., U. Hawaii, Honolulu, 1971; Ph.D., Case Western Res. U., 1976. Postdoctoral fellow Case Western Res. U., Cleve., 1976. Nat. Inst. Child Health and Human Devel., Bethesda, Md., 1976-78; NIH staff fellow Nat. Inst. Dental Research, Bethesda, 1978-80, NIH sr. staff fellow, 1980-81; asst. prof. dept. orthpedic surgery and biochemistry Rush Med. Coll., Chgo., 1981-84, assoc. prof. biochemistry, 1984—. Mem. editorial bd. Jour. Biol. Chemistry, 1984—. Mem. Am. Soc. Biol. Chemists, AAAS, Orthopaedic Research Soc. Home: 632 S Clarence Oak Park IL 60304 Office: Rush Med Coll Dept Biochemistry 1653 W Congress Pkwy Chicago IL 60612

KIMURA, JUN, medical educator, neurologist; b. Kyoto, Japan, Feb. 25, 1935; came to U.S., 1962; s. Tomihiko and Hamako (Akera) K.; m. Junko Kubata, Oct. 10, 1965; children—Ken, Ray, Joe. Student, U. Kyoto, 1953-61, M.D., 1961. Diplomate Am. Bd. Psychiatry and Neurology (examiner). Intern U.S. Naval Hosp., Yokosuka, Japan, 1961-62; resident in medicine and neurology Univ. Hosps., Iowa City, Iowa, 1962-66; instr. dept. neurology Univ. Hosps., 1968-69, assoc. prof., 1972-77, chief div. clin. electrophysiology, 1976—, prof., 1977—, mem. com. on Criteria Document for Occupational Exposure to Carbamyl. Author: Electrodiagnosis in Diseases of Nerve and Muscle: Principles and Practice, 1983; mem. editorial bd. Archives of Neurology, 1981; assoc. editor Muscle and Nerve, 1986; Electroencephalography and Clin. Neurophysiology, 1984, Neurology, 1985; contbr. articles to profl. jours. Fulbright travel scholar, 1962-67; grantee Med. Research Council Can., Multiple Sclerosis Soc. Can., Nat. Multiple Sclerosis Soc., Japan Soc. for Promotion of Sci. Fellowship. Mem. AMA, Am. Assn. Electromyography and Electrodiagnosis (sec.-treas. 1981-84, pres. 1985-86, examiner, dir.), Am. Electroencephalographic Soc., Am. Acad. Neurology, Am. Acad. Clinical Neurophysiology (exec. bd.), Am. Soc. for Clinical Evoked Potentials (bd. dirs.), Am. Neurol. Assn., Sigma Xi. Buddhist. Club: Clin. Neurophysiology Travel. Home: 1 Gilmore Ct Iowa City IA 52240 Office: Div Clin Electrophysiology 0181 RCP Univ Hosps Iowa City IA 52242

KINCAID, ARTHUR ROY, lawyer; b. Gardner, Kans., Apr. 24, 1911; s. Roy Porter and Sadie (Arnold) K.; m. Marion King, May 23, 1942; 1 dau., Carol Ann. A.B., William Jewell Coll., 1932; LL.B., U. Kansas City, 1941. Bar: Mo. 1941. Ptnr. firm Hale, Kincaid, Waters, and Allen, P.C., Liberty, Mo., 1944—, sr. mem., 1976—, pres., 1979—; mem. Mo. Ho. of Reps., 1937-42; city atty., Liberty, 1944-50. Chmn. bd. Liberty Pub. Works, 1960-70. Served to pvt. U.S. Army, 1943. Mem. ABA, Mo. Bar Assn., Clay County Bar Assn. Democrat. Mem. Christian Ch. Club: Rotary (Liberty). Home: 726 W Mississippi St Liberty MO 64068 Office: Hale Kincaid Waters Allen 17 W Kansas St Liberty MO 64068

KINCAID, JAMES, JR., controller; b. Lebanon, Pa., Dec. 20, 1954; s. James Sr. and Betty (Asper) K.; m. Kathleen Marie Lynch, June 5, 1981; children: Melissa, Jennifer. BS in Bus. Adminstrn., Drexel U., 1977. CPA, Pa. Sr. acct. Touche Ross & Co., Harrisburg, Pa., 1977-80; sr. auditor Harsco Corp., Camp Hill, Pa., 1980-82, dir. auditing, 1982-85; controller Reed Minerals div. Harsco Corp., Highland, Ind., 1985—. Mem. Am. Inst. CPA's, Pa. Inst. CPA's, Fin. Acctg. Found., Alpha Beta Psi, Beta Gamma Sigma, Phi Kappa Phi. Lutheran. Home: 2443 Capri Dr Schererville IN 46375 Office: Reed Minerals div Harsco Corp 8149 Kennedy Ave Highland IN 46322

KINCAID, MARY ELIZABETH, author, illustrator; b. Cleve., June 4, 1923; d. George Walter and Elizabeth (Phillips) Getz; m. William Harold Kincaid, Dec. 26, 1945; children: Judith Elizabeth, Jay Alexander, Rebecca Lee. BA, U. Mich., 1944. Author-illustrator fgn. lang. comic strip Contes Francais various Am. newspapers, 1962-66; author, designer, dir. audiovisual film Lang. Strips, 1973-76; co-author bilingual radio series French Minutes 1973-76; cons., speaker audiovisual fgn. lang. instructional techniques. Contbr. articles to mags. and newspapers. Recipient award Mich. Council Arts, 1975-76, award Soc. Tech. Communication. Home: 3550 Woodland Rd Ann Arbor MI 48104

KINDER, IRA GEORGE, farm manager; b. Catlin, Ill., May 31, 1912; s. David Osborn and Nora Bell (Church) K.; m. Helen Louise Hayes, July 4, 1942; children: Suzanne, Sharon, Richard. BS in Agr., U. Ill., 1934. Soil erosion engr. U.S. Dept. Interior, Dixon Springs, Ill., 1934-35; civilian conservation corps camp supr. USDA, Dixon Springs, Ill., 1936-37; supr., agronomist USDA, Durand, Ill., 1938; conservationist USDA, Danville, Ill., 1938-68; farm mgr. First Nat. Bank, Danville, Ill., 1968-78, G. H. R. Kinder Inc., Catlin, 1979—; mem. Prime Farmland Preservation Catlin Township, 1972—, stripmining reclamation com. Soil and Water Conservation Dist., Ill., 1982—; stripmining law lobbyist, Washington, 1974. Contbr. to book Khaki Pants and Hobnail Boots, 1984, stripmining articles to local newspapers, 1972—. mem. Catlin Township Bd. Edn., 1956-66; chmn. Catlin Township Zoning Bd. Appeals, 1972—, Vermillion (Ill.) County Conservation Dist., 1971-75. Served as major U.S. Army, ETO. Decorated Bronze Star (3). Lodges: Shriners, Masons. Home: PO Box 1 605 W Vermillion Catlin IL 61817 Office: G.H.R. Kinder Inc PO Box 629 Catlin IL 61817

KINDER, RICHARD PAUL, quality assurance engineer; b. Louisville, Aug. 24, 1958; s. Clyde White and Violet (Nicklies) K.; m. Debra Ann Ross, Aug. 16, 1981. BS in Indsl. Engring., Purdue U., 1981. Registered profl. engr., Ind. Sr. indsl. engr. aide ICI Americas, Charlestown, Ind., 1981-82, indsl. engr. "B", 1982-83, quality engr., 1983—. Mem. Inst. Indsl. Engrs. (sr., v.p. chpt. 18, 1985—). Presbyterian. Lodge: Lions. Home: Rural Rt 1 Charlestown IN 47111 Office: ICI Americas Hwy 62 Charlestown IN 47111

KINDINGER, PAUL EUGENE, state director of agriculture; b. Adrian, Mich., Nov. 5, 1946; s. Robert Paul and Evelyn Clara (Heldt) K. BS in Agrl. Econs., Mich. State U., 1970, MS in Agrl. Econs., 1971; PhD in Agrl. Econs., Cornell U., 1975. Dir. commodity research Mich. Farm Bur., Lansing, 1975-79; chief mktg. div. Mich. Dept. Agr., Lansing, 1979-81, asst. dir., 1981, dir., 1983—; asst. dir. coop. extension service Mich. State U., East Lansing, 1981-83. Mem. Nat. Assn. State Depts. Agr. (bd. dirs. 1986), Mid-Am. Internat. Agri-Trade Council (pres. 1986), Midwest Assn. of State Depts. of Agriculture (pres. 1986), Mich. State U. Alumni Assn. Avocations: running, golf, tennis, photography, traveling. Home: 12895 Oneida Woods Trail Grand Ledge MI 48837 Office: Mich Dept Agr PO Box 30017 Lansing MI 48909

KINDLEBERGER, CHARLES POOR, III, city planner; b. Balt., July 27, 1940; s. Charles Poor II and Sarah (Miles) K.; m. Joan H. Rasch, Apr. 19, 1970; 1 child, Lisa Rachael. Systems analyst City of New Haven, Conn., 1967-70; head of advance planning St. Louis County, Clayton, Mo., 1970-76; dir. planning, Community Devel. Agy. City of St. Louis, 1976—; pres. Applied Video Tech., St. Louis, 1981—. Author: (directory) Interactive Video, 1984, 87; contbr. numerous articles on urban info. systems. Served to 1st lt. inf. U.S. Army, 1963-65, Korea. Mem. Am. Inst. Cert. Planners, Am. Planning Assn. (pres. St. Louis sect. 1973), Urban and Regional Info. Systems Assn. (pres. elect 1986). Democrat. Unitarian. Home: 5118 Westminster Pl Saint Louis MO 63108 Office: St. Louis Community Planning Agy 411 N 10th St Saint Louis MO 63101

KINDRICK, ROBERT LEROY, educator; b. Kansas City, Mo., Aug. 17, 1942; s. Robert William and Waneta LeVeta (Lobdell) K.; B.A., Park Coll., 1964; M.A., U. Mo., 1967; Ph.D., U. Tex., 1971; m. Carolyn Jean Reed, Aug. 20, 1965. Instr., Central Mo. State U., Warrensburg, 1967-69, asst. prof., 1969-73, asso. prof., 1973-78, prof. English, 1978-80, head dept. English, 1975-80; dean Coll. Arts and Scis., also prof. English, Western Ill. U., Macomb, 1980-84; v.p. acad. affairs, prof. English, Emporia State U., Kans., 1984-87, Eastern Ill. U., Charleston, 1987—. Chmn. bd. dirs. Mo. Com. for Humanities, 1979-80. U. Tex. fellow, 1965-66; Am. Council Learned Socs. travel grantee, 1975; Nat. Endowment for Humanities summer fellow, 1977; Mediaeval Acad. Am. grantee, 1976; Mo. Com. Humanities grantee, 1975-76; Assn. Scottish Lit. Studies grantee, 1979. Mem. Mo. Assn. Depts. English (pres. 1978-80), Mo. Philological Assn. (founding pres. 1975-77), Medieval Assn. Midwest (councillor 1977—), Ill. Medieval Assn. (founding exec. sec. 1984—), Mid-Am. Medieval Assn., Rocky Mountain MLA, Assn. Scottish Lt. Studies, Mo. Assn. Depts. English, Early English Text Soc., Société Rencesvals, Medieval Acad. N.Am. (exec. sec. com. on ctrs. and regional assns.), Internat. Arthurian Soc., Sigma Tau Delta, Phi Kappa Phi. Club: Rotary. Author: Robert Henryson, 1979; A New Classical Rhetoric, 1980; editor: Teaching the Middle Ages; contbr. articles to profl. jours. Home: PO Box 556 Charleston IL 61920 Office: Eastern Ill U Office of Provost Charleston IL 61920

KINDS, HERBERT E(UGENE), educator; b. Cleve., Feb. 25, 1933; s. Levander and Esther (Johnson) K. B.S. (Tyng scholar), Williams Coll., 1951-55; postgrad. Harvard U., 1955-58, Case Western Res. U., 1972, 80-81. Instr. Natchez (Miss.) Jr. Coll., 1958-68, registar, 1967, dean, 1968; tchr. Cleve. Pub. Schs., 1968—; owner Kinds Tutorial Service, 1972—; instr. med. sci. Cuyahoga Community Coll., 1975-81, instr. chemistry. Deacon Mt. Herodon Bapt. Ch.; mem. Cleve. City Club, 1968, Comdr.'s Club for Disabled Am. Vets.; nat. assoc. Smithsonian Instn. Mem. Math. Assn. Am., Am. Chem. Soc., Am. Fedn. Tchrs., Internat. Platform Assn., Phi Beta Kappa. Clubs: Williams of N.Y., Williams of Northeastern Ohio. Home: 9023 Columbia Ave Cleveland OH 44108

KINER, CAROL ANN, home economist; b. Chgo., July 22, 1954; d. Daniel Charles and Doris Elaine (Balling) K.; m. David Allen Howerton, Oct. 2, 1982. B.S. with honors, U. Ill., 1976, M.Ed. with highest honors, 1979. Tchr. home econs. Fenton High Sch., Bensenville, Ill., 1976-81; cons. home econs. Ill. Bd. Edn., Springfield, 1981-82; nat. mktg. services mgr. Forecast for Home Econs. mag., Scholastic, Inc., Chgo., 1982—. Mem. Am. Home Econs. Assn. (nat. resolutions com., new achiever award 1986), Chgo. Home Economists in Bus. (chmn.), Am. Vocat. Assn., Nat. Assn. Vocat. Home Econs. Tchrs., Ill. Home Econs. Assn., Ill. Vocat. Assn., Ill. Vocat. Home Econs. Tchrs. Assn. (Outstanding mem. 1985), Home Econs. Edn. Assn., U. Ill. Home Econs. Alumni Assn., Phi Upsilon Omicron, Kappa Delta Pi. Lutheran.

KING, ARTHUR GUSTAVE, gynecologist/obstetrician; b. Cambridge, Mass., Aug. 1, 1906; s. Myron Louis and Sophie (Snow) K.; m. Marthe Leftovith, July 24, 1931; children: Angie King Rogers, Deborah King Wroth. AB cum laude, Harvard U., 1926, MD cum laude, 1930; MS, Tulane U., 1933. Diplomate Am. Bd. Ob-Gyn. Practice medicine specializing in ob-gyn Cin., 1936—; sr. attending staff Jewish Hosp., Cin., 1936—; chief of staff Catherine Booth Hosp., Cin., 1950-65; asst. clin. prof. Coll. Medicine U. Cin., 1936-71, cons. ob-gyn, 1971—. Author: Cincinnati Obsterical and Gynecological Society, 1876-1976, 1976; contbr. articles to profl. med. and history jours. Served to col. U.S. Army, 1942-44, PTO. Decorated Bronze Star. Fellow Am. Coll. Ob-Gyn (founding); mem. Cen. Assn. Obstetricians and Gynecologists, Retired Officers Assn. (life), Harvard Club Cin., Am. Assn. for the History of Medicine. Avocations: travel, hist. research. Home: 554 Evanswood Pl Cincinnati OH 45220 Office: 2825 Burnet Ave Cincinnati OH 45219

KING, BRADLEY EDHOLM, dentist; b. Bismarck, N.D., Oct. 13, 1954; s. Robert Ernest and Doris (Edholm) K.; m. Jean Danelle Christ, Sept. 8, 1984; 1 child, Amanda. BS, N.D. State U., 1977; DDS, U. Minn., 1981. Pvt. practice dentistry Bismarck, N.D., 1981—; dentist African Inland Mission, Kijabe, Kenya, 1980. Pres. Intervarsity Christian Fellowship, Fargo, N.D., 1976-77; chmn. Voyageur Cove Ministries, Pick City, N.D., 1983—. Mem. ADA, Mo. Slope Dental Assn. (chmn. polit. action com., 1985—), Am. Endodontic Soc., Bismarck C. of C. Episcopalian. Avocations: international travel, hunting, fishing, bicycling, backpacking. Home: 719 N 1st St Bismarck ND 58501 Office: 405 E Broadway #208 Bismarck ND 58501

KING, BUDDE BENNETT, engineer; b. Chgo., Oct. 21, 1949; s. Cecil Franklin and Winifred Gertrude (Budde) K. BS, Ill. Inst. Tech., 1971, MBA, 1973. Bus. planning ops. mgr. Internat. Harvester Co., Chgo., 1974-77; gen. mgr. Budde King Photography, Westchester, Ill., 1977-84; sr. project specialist Barnes & Reinecke, Inc., Elk Grove, Ill., 1984-85, sr. engring. specialist, 1985, project mgr., 1985—. Mem. Nat. Contract Mgmt. Assn., Am. Def. Preparedness Assn., Soc. Am. Valve Engrs., Soc. Logistics Engrs., Soc. Automotive Engrs., Assn. U.S. Army, Air Force Assn. of the U.S., Navy League of the U.S., U.S. Marine Corps League (assoc.), Sigma Iota Epsilon. Republican. Home: 1914 Gardner Rd Westchester IL 60153 Office: Barnes & Reinecke Inc 2375 Estes Ave Elk Grove IL 60007

KING, CHARLES ROSS, physician; b. Nevada, Iowa, Aug. 22, 1925; s. Carl Russell and Dorothy Sarah (Mills) K.; m. Frances Pamela Carter, Jan. 8, 1949; children—Deborah Diane, Carter Ross, Charles Conrad, Corbin Kent. Student, Butler U., 1943; B.S. in Bus., Ind. U., 1948, M.D., 1964. Diplomate Am. Bd. Family Practice. Dep. dir. Ind. Pub. Works and Supply, 1949-52; salesman Knox Coal Corp., 1952-59; rotating intern Marion County Gen. Hosp., Indpls., 1964-65; family practice medicine Anderson, Ind., 1965—; sec.-treas. staff Community Hosp., 1969-72, pres. elect, dir., chief medicine, 1973—, bd. dirs., 1973-75; sec.-treas. St. John's Hosp., 1968-69, chief medicine, 1972-73, chief pediatrics, 1977—; dir. Rolling Hills Convalescent Ctr., 1968-73; pres. Profl. Ctr. Lab., 1965—; vice chmn. Madison County Bd. Health, 1966-69, chmn., 1986—; chmn. bd. dirs. First Nat. Bank Madison County, Anderson. Bd. dirs. Family Service Madison County, 1968-69, Madison County Assn. Mentally Retarded, 1972-76; chmn. bd. dirs. Anderson Downtown Devel. Corp., 1980—. Served with AUS, 1944-46. Recipient Dr. James Macholtz award Spl. Olympics, 1986—. Fellow Royal Soc. Health, Am. Acad. Family Practice (charter); mem. AMA (Physician's Recognition award 1969, 72, 75, 78, 81, 84, 87), Ind. Med. Assn., Pan Am. Med. Assn., Am. Acad. Gen. Practice, Madison County Med. Soc. (pres. 1970), 8th Dist. Med. Soc. (sec.-treas. 1968), Anderson C. of C. (bd. dirs. 1979-82), Indpls. Mus. Art (corp. mem.), Phi Delta Theta (pres. Alumni Assn. 1952), Phi Chi. Methodist. Club: Anderson Country (bd. dirs. 1976-79). Home: 920 N Madison Ave Anderson IN 46011 Office: 1933 Chase St Anderson IN 46014

KING, CLARENCE CARLETON, health administrator; b. Asheville, N.C., June 12, 1956; s. Clarence Carleton King and Betty Ann (Barker) Haddon; m. Janet Susan Kerley. BBA, Ga. State U., 1978; MHA, Duke U., 1980. Adminstr. projects coordinator Shallowford Hosp., Atlanta, 1978; cons. Duke-Watts Family Medicine, Durham, N.C., 1979-80; adminstr. So. Med. Ctr., Cario, Ill., 1980-82, Crawford Meml. Hosp., Robinson, Ill., 1982-86; v.p. devel. Carle Care, Inc., Champaign, Ill., 1986—; bd. dirs. Community Health Services, Cairo. Mem. Am. Coll. Healthcare Execs., Healthcare Fin. Mgmt. Assn., Am. Hosp. Assn. Baptist. Avocations: cars, basketball. Office: Carle Care Inc 602 W University Urbana IL 61801

KING, DARYL KEITH, mining engineer; b. Wray, Colo., Apr. 12, 1945; s. Gordon William and Alberta (Wessel) K.; m. Kathleen Lynn Schuerman, Jan. 3, 1970; children: Matthew Ryan, Andrea Lynn, Rebecca Renee. Degree in mining, Colo. Sch. of Mines, 1968. Registered profl. engr., Ohio, Tenn. Environ. equipment sales engr. Link-Belt div. FMC, Colmar, Pa., 1968-70; ops. engr. Cen. Silica sub. Olgeby Norton, Zanesville, Ohio, 1970-76; plant mgr. Millwood Sand sub. Olgeby Norton, Mt. Vernon, Ohio, 1976-77; mgr. quary ops. Marquette Co., Nashville, 1977-82; pres., co-founder K&W Engring. Assocs., Nashville, 1982-84; v.p. TAMMSCO, Inc., Tamms, Ill., 1984—; bd. dirs. Avatar Industries, Franklin, Tenn. Home: Rt 3 Box 237C Jackson MO 63755 Office: TAMMSCO Inc Box J Tamms IL 62988

KING, DAVID MERVIN, investment management company executive; b. nr. Ottawa, Kans., July 3, 1927; s. Alvin Jesse and Gertrude Beatrice (Jones) K.; B.S., Emporia (Kans.) State U., 1950; m. Bernice Arlene Owen, June 11, 1950; 1 dau., Elizabeth A. Salesman, Mut. Life of New York, Wichita, Kans., 1950; mgr. Colby (Kans.) C. of C., 1952-54; self employed, 1954-56; dist. mgr. King Merritt & Co. Investments, Colby, 1956-60; v.p., regional mgr. Westam. Securities, Inc., Hays, Kans., 1960-78; v.p. Investment Mgmt. and Research Co., 1978—; pres. David M. King and Assos., Ltd., King Fin. Services Corp.; partner Berdeak Assocs. Served with USMCR, 1945-46, 50-52. Mem. Internat. Assn. Fin. Planners, Inst. Cert. Fin. Planners (pres. 1978), Internat. Bd. Standards and Practices Cert. Fin. Planners (chmn. bd. 1985—), Hays C. of C. Republican. Presbyterian. Lodges: Masons, Rotary. Home: 3007 Tam O'Shanter Dr Hays KS 67601 Office: David M King & Assocs Ltd 103 W 13th St Hays KS 67601

KING, DONALD THEODORE, financial specialist, educator; b. Chgo., Mar. 31, 1948; s. Michael D. and Vernal M. (Miller) K.; m. Cathie M. Gunty, May 3, 1975; children: Kevin, David, Steven. BS in Math., Ill. Inst. Tech., 1970; MS in Taxation, De Paul U., 1979. CPA, Ill. Revenue agent IRS, Chgo., 1973-78; tax prin. Arthur Young & Co., Chgo., 1978-85; fin. planner JMG Fin. Group, Oakbrook Terr., Ill., 1985—; instr. De Paul U., Chgo., 1982—. Sec. St. Bernadette Sch. Bd., Evergreen Park, Ill. 1986—. Served with U.S. Army, 1970-72, Vietnam. Mem. Am. Inst. CPA's (tax div.), Ill. CPA Soc. (chmn. tax regulation com. 1984-86, chmn. tax legis. com. 1986-87, vice-chmn. tax exec. com. 1987—), Internat. Assn. Fin. Planners. Roman Catholic. Office: JMG Fin Group Ltd One Oakbrook Terr #312 Oakbrook Terrace IL 60181

KING, EDWARD ALVIN, city official; b. Pratt City, Ala., Sept. 4, 1919; s. Fred Elijah and Phyllis Ann (Robertson) K.; A.B., Del. State Coll., 1943; M.S.W., Atlanta U., 1947; m. Beatrice Pitts, Nov. 14, 1980; children by previous marriage—Linda Ann, Antone J. Scrivens, Daniel Scrivens. Dir. group work, community relations Grand Rapids (Mich.) Urban League, 1947-53; community relations specialist Boston Urban League, 1953-57; supr. Pitts. Human Relations Commn., 1957-63; exec. dir. Dayton (Ohio) Human Relations Council, 1963—; instr. U. Dayton, 1968-71. Bd. dirs. Johnson C. Smith Sch. Theology, 1975—; sr. elder Trinity United Presbyn. Ch., 1973—. Served with AUS, 1943-46. Recipient Public Service awards Rotary Club, 1973, Kiwanis Club, 1979, U. Dayton, 1979, Optimist Club, 1974, Dayton Bd. Edn., 1980. Mem. Internat. Assn. Ofcl. Human Rights Agys., Nat. Assn. Human Rights Workers, NAACP, Alpha Phi Alpha. Club: Kiwanis (dir. 1976-80). Home: 1828 Ruskin Dr Dayton OH 45406 Office: Dayton Human Relations Council 40 S Main St Suite 721 Dayton OH 45402

KING, FRED LEE, radiologist, author; b. Queen City, Mo., Aug. 9, 1931; s. Fred and Lillian D. (Campbell) K.; m. Anita Marie White, Aug. 12, 1956; children—Vincent, Christopher, Phyllis. B.S., N.E. Mo. State U., 1959; D.O., Kirksville Coll. Osteo. and Surgery; LL.B., LaSalle Extension U., Chgo., 1967. Cert. Roentgenology Am. Osteo Coll. Radiology. Practice gen. medicine and radiology Laughlin Hosp., Kirksville, Mo., 1961-83, Samaritan Meml. Hosp., Macon, Mo., 1983-86; practice medicine specializing in radiology, 1986—. Author: weekly newspaper column" Nostalgia", 1983—; contbr. articles to med. jours. Served with USN, 1951-55; Mem. Am. Osteo. Assn., Mo. Osteo. Assn., Am. Osteo. Coll. Radiology, Northeast Mo. Osteo. Assn., Republican. Lodge: Masons. Avocations: writing; antique collecting; history; old radio tapes. Home: 508 Sunset Dr Macon MO 63552 Office: Old Highway 36 E Macon MO 63552

KING, GEORGE RALEIGH, manufacturing company executive; b. Benton Harbor, Mich., May 13, 1931; s. Maurice Peter and Opal Ruth (Hart) King; m. Phyllis Stratton, Apr. 10, 1950; children—Paula King Zang, Angela King Moleski, Philip. Student Adrian Coll., 1950-51. Cert. purchasing profl. exec. status. With Kirsch Co., Sturgis, Mich., 1951—, data processing trainee, 1951-53, data processing mgr., 1953-59, asst. purchasing agt., 1959-62, purchasing agt., 1962-68, asst. dir. purchasing, 1968-71, dir. purchasing, 1971—. Author: Rods & Rings, 1972. Elder, 1st Presbyterian Ch., Sturgis, 1970; pres. Sturgis Civic Players, 1972. Recipient citation Boy Scouts Am., 1966, Jr. Achievement, 1967; nominated candidate for adminstr. Fed. Procurement Policy, Reagan Adminstrn., Washington, 1980. Mem. Am. Purchasing Soc. (pres. 1979-81), Nat. Assn. Purchasing Mgmt., Southwestern Purchasing Assn. Clubs: Klinger Lake Country, Exchange (pres. Sturgis 1959, dist. gov. dist and nat. clubs 1961). Masons, Elks. Home: 906 S Lakeview Sturgis MI 49091 Office: Kirsch Co 309 N Prospect St Sturgis MI 49091

KING, JAMES DOUGHERTY, osteopath; b. Fayette, Mo., July 12, 1949; s. Joseph Gray and Helen Morrison (Dougherty) K.; m. Marcia Kay Shelton, Jan. 23, 1971; 1 child, Andrew. AB, U. Mo., 1971; DO, Kirksville Coll., 1975. Intern Davenport (Iowa) Osteopathic Hosp., 1975-76, resident in internal medicine, 1976-79; practice internal medicine Davenport, 1979—. Sectional leader United Way Campaign, Davenport, 1986; bd. dirs. Quad City Health Plan, Davenport, 1982-85; Quad City Osteopathic Found., Davenport, 1985-86. Mem. Am. Osteopathic Assn., Am. Coll. Osteopathic Internists, Iowa Osteopathic Med. Assn. (del. Hous of Reps., 1985-86). Methodist. Club: Crow Valley Country (Bettendrof, Iowa). Lodge: Noon Optimist. Avocations: golf, racquetball, fishing, woodwork. Home: 4410 N Cedar Davenport IA 52806 Office: 3801 Marquette St Suite 304 Davenport IA 52806

KING, JAMES HOWARD, industrial engineer; b. Urbana, Ill., Dec. 19, 1952; s. William Clifford and Mable Ruth (O'Brien) K.; m. Virginia Lynn LeMaster, May. 10, 1977; children: Lisa, Christen. BS in Indsl. Engring., Ohio U., 1971-76. Indsl. engr. Unverferth-McCurdy, Kalida, Ohio, 1977, Buckeye Steel, Columbus, Ohio, 1977-78, McGraw Service, Columbus, 1978-84, Mac Tools, Washington Court House, Ohio, 1985—. Mem. Am. Soc. Metals, Inst. Indsl. Engrs. (sr.). Avocation: farming. Home: 9865 State Rd 323 Mount Sterling OH 43143 Office: Mac Tools S Fayette St Washington Court House OH 43160

KING, JEROME, process and automation systems specialist; b. Chgo., Mar. 7, 1952; s. Ferd Schmitt and Angelina (Sciortino) K.; m. Joy Lee Blankenhagen, Aug. 13, 1982. Student, Northwestern U., 1970-71; BS in Engring., Ill. Inst. Tech., 1978; MS in Mgmt., Aurora (Ill.) U., 1983. Mech.

engr. Fermi Nat. Accelerator Lab, Batavia, Ill., 1977-81; sr. project engr. Armour-Dial, Aurora, 1980-81; mgr. project engring. Lever Bros., Chgo., 1981-84; mgr. food and consumer goods projects Indsl. Automation Systems div. Allen Bradley Co., Highland Heights, Ohio, 1984—. Contbr. articles to profl. jours. Mem. ASME. Avocations: guitar, landscaping, gardening, skiing, hiking. Home: 9518 Catalpa Circle Mentor OH 44060 Office: Allen Bradley Co Indsl Automation Systems Div 625 Alpha Dr Highland Heights OH 44143

KING, JERRY WAYNE, research chemist; b. Indpls., Feb. 19, 1942; s. Ernest E. and Miriam (Sanders) K.; m. Bettie Maria Dunbar, Aug. 8, 1965; children: Ronald Sean, Valerie Raquel, Diana Lynn. BS, Butler U., 1965; PhD, Northeastern U., 1973; fellow, Georgetown U., 1973-74. Research chemist Union Carbide Corp., Bound Brook, N.J., 1968-70; asst. prof. dept. chemistry Va. Commonwealth U., Richmond, 1974-76; research scientist Arthur D. Little, Inc., Cambridge, Mass., 1976-77; research assoc. Am. Can Co., Barrington, Ill., 1977-79; research scientist CPC Internat., Summit-Argo, Ill., 1979-86; research chemist NRRC-ARS div. USDA, Peoria, Ill., 1986—; guest lectr. various sci. groups, meetings, 1964-87. Contbr. articles on chromatography and super-critical fluids to sci. jours. Corp. grantee, 1975-77; NSF fellow, 1973-74. Mem. IFT, AAAS, Am. Chem. Soc., Soc. Plastic Engrs., Va. Acad. Scis. Home: 1820 Sunnyview Dr Peoria IL 61614 Office: No Regional Research Ctr ARS/USDA 1815 N University St Peoria IL 61604

KING, JOHN JOSEPH, manufacturing company executive; b. Toledo, Jan. 12, 1924; s. Walter and Frances (Gwozd) Kawecka; m. Joy G. Mohler, Jan. 28, 1950; children: Catherine M., Carolyn S., David J., Michael R., Mark A.R. BSME magna cum laude, U. Toledo, 1957, MS in Indsl. Engring., 1961. Registered profl. engr., Ohio. Draftsman, Tecumseh Products Co., 1941-42; die designer Bingham Stamping Co., 1942-46; tool designer Spicer Mfg. Co., 1946-47; product designer Am. Floor Surfacing Co., 1947-50; founder, mgr. engr. Kent Industries, 1950-52; mech. engr. Owens Ill. Inc., Toledo, 1953-63; mgr. research and devel. Permaglass Inc., Genoa, Ohio, 1963-69; founder, pres. Ashur Inc., Rossford, Ohio, 1969—, also chmn. bd. dirs. Patentee in field. Mem. Am. Ceramic Soc., Soc. Mfg. Engrs., Phi Kappa Phi, Tau Beta Pi. Republican. Roman Catholic. Clubs: Devils Lake Yacht, Ukranian Am. Citizens. Lodge: KC. Home: 1111 W Elm Tree Rd Rossford OH 43460 Office: Ashur Inc 1117 Elm Tree Rd Rossford OH 43460

KING, JOSEPH CLEMENT, physician; b. Colorado Springs, Colo., Aug. 20, 1922; s. Charles Clement and Gladys (Ascher) K.; B.S., Tulane U., 1944, M.D., 1946; m. Margie Freudenthal Leopold, Apr. 2, 1947; children—Leopold Ascher, Jocelyn King Tobias. Instr. zoology Tulane U., 1941-42; rotating intern Michael Reese Hosp., Chgo., 1946-47, resident in internal medicine, 1947-50; assoc. with Dr. Sidney Portis, Chgo., 1950-51; practice medicine specializing in internal medicine, Chgo., 1953-77, Palm Springs, Calif., 1977-79; attending staff Louis A. Weiss Hosp., Chgo., 1953-77, hon. staff, 1979—; attending staff Desert Hosp., 1977-79; med. dir. Life Extension Inst., Chgo., 1979-80; dir. employee health services Continental Ill. Nat. Bank, Chgo., 1980-87; exec. cons. health care mgmt. Coopers & Lybrand, Chgo., 1987—; asst. to assoc. clin. prof. internal medicine Northwestern U. Med. Sch., Chgo., 1954-67; clin. asst. prof. medicine Abraham Lincoln Sch. Medicine U. Ill., 1973-77; clin. asst. prof. preventive medicine and community health Northwestern U. Med. Sch., 1980—; asst. prof. preventive medicine Rush Med. Coll. Served to capt. M.C., AUS, 1944-46, 1951-53. Diplomate Am. Bd. Internal Medicine. Fellow ACP; mem. Chgo. Soc. Internal Medicine, Chgo. Med. Soc., Am., Ill. med. assns., Am. Heart Assn., Chgo. Heart Assn. (bd. govs.), Am. Rheumatism Assn., Assn. Bank Med. Dirs., Am. Cancer Soc. (v.p. Chgo. unit), Cen. States Acad. Occupational Medicine, Central States Occupational Med. Assn. (bd. govs.), Am. Occupational Med. Assn., Tulane Med. Alumni Assn. (past dir., midwest adv. bd.), Medic Alert, Ill. State C. of C. (health care cost mgmt. task force), Phi Beta Kappa, Beta Mu, Alpha Omega Alpha. Club: Med. Dirs. Chgo. (pres.). Contbr. numerous articles in field to med. jours. Office: Coopers & Lybrand 203 N LaSalle St 25th floor Chicago IL 60601

KING, LAWRENCE EDWARD, lawyer, corporate professional; b. Cin., Jan. 4, 1948; s. Lawrence E. and Dora M. (Kugel) K.; m. Barbara M. Bollin, Sept. 7, 1974; children: Sarah, Steven. BSEE, Purdue U., 1970; JD, U. Toledo, 1974. Bar: Ohio 1975, U.S. Dist. Ct. (no. dist.) Ohio, 1982. Atty. Toledo Edison Co., 1975-77; corp. atty. Sheller-Globe Corp., Toledo, 1977-82, corp. atty., asst. sec., 1982—. Dir. Toledo/N.W. Ohio Foodbank. Mem. Am. Soc. Corp. Secs., Ohio State Bar Assn., Toledo Bar Assn. Home: 7311 Oak Hill Dr Sylvania OH 43560 Office: Sheller-Globe Corp 1505 Jefferson Toledo OH 43624

KING, MORRIS KENTON, dean med. sch.; b. Oklahoma City, Nov. 13, 1924; s. C. Willard and Lenore (Miesse) K.; m. June Ellen Greenfield, June 21, 1953; children—Michael, Douglas, John, David, Thomas. B.A., U. Okla., 1947; M.D., Vanderbilt U., 1951. Intern Barnes Hosp., St. Louis, 1951-52; resident Barnes Hosp., 1954-55, Vanderbilt U. Hosp., 1953-54; mem. faculty preventive medicine Washington U., St. Louis, 1958—; prof. Washington U., 1967—; dean Washington U. (Sch. Medicine), 1965—. Served with USNR, 1943-46. Mem. Central Soc. Clin. Research, Infectious Diseases Soc. Am. Home: 7017 Kingsbury St Saint Louis MO 63130 Office: 660 S Euclid St Saint Louis MO 63110

KING, PATRICK JAMES, marketing executives; b. Chgo., July 13, 1930; s. Edward J. and Gladys (Reising) K.; m. Elizabeth C. Grimm, Oct. 22, 1960; children: Patrick M., Daniel J., Eileen E. BSS, St. Mary's Coll., 1953. Sales rep. Inland Steel div. Standard Oil Co., Chgo., 1955-56; reseller sales rep. Standard Oil Co., Chgo., 1956-58; sales rep. Milw. Electric Tool Co., 1958-60; nat. merchandising mgr. Motorola Communcations & Electronics, Chgo., 1960-69; div. gen. mgr. ITT, N.Y.C., 1969-73; gen. mgr. Electra Co. div. Masco Corp., Indpls., 1973-77; pres. King Mktg. Systems, Inc., Indpls., 1977—. Served to lt. (j.g.) USN, 1953-55, Korea. Mem. Electronic Reps. Assn. (pres. 1983-85, Disting. Service award 1985). Roman Catholic. Clubs: Indpls. Athletic, Hillcrest Country. Avocation: tennis. Home: 7850 N Illinois Indianapolis IN 46260 Office: King Mktg Systems Inc 8650 Commerce Pkwy Indianapolis IN 46268

KING, PATRICK JOSEPH, art dealer, gallery owner and consultant; b. St. Joseph, Mo., Nov. 8, 1951; s. William Clifford and Joann Phyllis (Kneib) K. Student, Mo. Western U., 1970-71; BFA, Kansas City (Mo.) Art Inst., 1974; postgrad., Parson's Sch. Design, N.Y.C., 1976. Asst. curator Herron Sch. Art, Indpls., 1978-80; asst. dir. Editions Ltd. Gallery, Indpls., 1980-82; art dealer and owner Patrick King Contemporary Art, Indpls., 1982—; pres. Metro Arts Pubs., Indpls., 1985—; visual arts editor Arts Insight mag., Indpls., 1978-80; arts writer New Art Examiner mag., Chgo., 1979-81. Editor: (exhibition catalogues) Fiber Structures, 1979, Am. Artists/Indpls., 1983, Passion Leads, 1984, Mary Beth Edelson, 1985. V.p. St. Joseph Hist. Assn., Indpls., 1981-83. Roman Catholic. Avocation: music. Office: 427 Massachusetts Ave Indianapolis IN 46204

KING, PAUL MAX, college administrator; b. Logan County, Ohio, Apr. 17, 1929; s. Alva Jay and Lulu Marie (Keenen) K.; m. Lois Irene Marquart, Oct. 11, 1952; children—Bruce Marquart, Timothy Paul, John Eric. B.S., Bluffton Coll., 1957; C.L.U., Am. Coll., 1977. With sales dept. Nationwide Ins. Co., Bluffton, Ohio, 1957-60, with sales mgmt., Bowling Green, Ohio, 1960-75; investment estate planning Bluffton Coll., Ohio, 1975-78, dir. devel., 1978—; ins. cons. M.M.A.S., Bluffton, 1977—; dir. Goodville Mut. Casualty Co., New Holland, Pa., 1977—; pres. Bluffton Slaw Cutter, 1983—. Writer, editor estate planning mag. Spirit, 1981—. Served with USAF, 1951-55. Mem. Estate Planning Council, Bluffton C. of C. Republican. Mennonite. Lodge: Optimist. Avocations: flying; skiing; woodwork. Home: 9220 Bixel Rd Bluffton OH 45817 Office: Bluffton Coll College Ave Bluffton OH 45817

KING, PETER JOHN, healthcare financial executive; b. Dayton, Jan. 10, 1948; s. Victor Charles and Helen Marie (Condron) K.; m. Mary Ann Franklin, May 13, 1972; children: Anna, David. BS, Miami U., Oxford, Ohio, 1972. CPA, Ohio. Staff acct. Deloitte, Haskins & Sells, Dayton, 1972-76; controller McCullough-Hyde Hosp., Oxford, Ohio, 1976-77; asst. v.p. fin. The Jewish Hosp. Cin., 1977—. Bd. dirs. Cath. Big Bros. and Sisters, Cin., 1984—. Fellow Health Care Fin. Mgmt. Assn. (bd. dirs. 1986—); mem. Am. Inst. CPA's. Avocations: sports, coaching. Office: Jewish Hosp Cin 3200 Burnet Ave Cincinnati OH 45229

KING, RALEIGH WAYNE, beauty school executive; b. Camden, N.J., Oct. 18, 1945; s. Travis Greer and Eva Virginia K.; student U. Md., 1969-71, Belleville Area Coll., 1972-74. Instr., Coiffure Sch. Beauty Culture, Belleville, Ill., 1978-79, dir., 1979—; educator Revlon-Realistic, 1981—; stylist Roux Inc., 1983; co-chmn. Sch. Continuing Cosmetology Edn., So. Ill. U., 1983. Bd. dirs. Ill. Assn. Cosmetology Schs., 1981; permanent mem. Ill. Hair Fashion Com.; chmn. cosmetology adv. council Belleville Area Coll. Served with USAF, 1965-76. Mem. Nat. Hairdressers and Cosmetologists Assn. (pres. affiliate 40 1979-83, 85—), Ill. Hairdressers and Cosmetologists Assn. (2d v.p. 1981-82, 5th v.p. 1982-83), Sigma Alpha Chi Alumni (life). Home: Ash Creek Manor 209 S Old Hwy 158 O'Fallon IL 62269 Office: Coiffure Sch Beauty Culture 402 E Main St Belleville IL 62220

KING, RANDOLPH DAVID, publishing executive, real estate executive; b. Oak Park, Ill., Apr. 19, 1954; s. Perry Benjamin and Elaine Agnes (McManus) K.; m. Carrie Dawn Millar, Oct. 19, 1981; 1 child, Kyle Randolph. BS, S Ill. U., 1976; MBA, Marshall U., 1977. Sales service mgr. Crain Communications, Chgo., 1977-78; mgr. new bus. Laven, Fuller & Perkins, Chgo., 1978-79; media dir., acct. supr. Fensholt, Chgo., 1979-81; mgr. midwest regional sales Cahners Publ., Des Plaines, Ill., 1981—; pres. Marshall, Southern & York, Inc., Chgo., 1985—; dir. communications campaign World of Flat Cable, 1981. Mem. N.W. Real Estate Bd. Mem. Advt. Council (standards com.), Electronics Industries Assn. (distributor products div.), Theta Zeta Alumni Assn. (pres. 1982-83). Avocations: karate, target pistol.

KING, RUDOLPH HENRY, office products company executive; b. Evanston, Ill., Oct. 26, 1934; s. Arthur Charles King and Marian (Keitel) King Bishop; m. Nancy Jo Flanagan, June 29, 1956; children—Cynthia Lynn King Dell, Sharon King Wencel, Jennifer. B.A., Brown U., 1956. Sales trainee Ryerson Steel Co., Chgo., 1956-58; salesman Mead Papers, Chgo., 1958-65; v.p., gen. mgr. Boise Cascade, Chgo., 1965-67; sales mgmt. staff Mead Papers, 1967-71; pres. Wis. Office Supply Co., Madison, 1971—; dir., sec.-treas. Wis. Graphic Forms, Madison, 1971—; dir., v.p. Bus. Graphics, Madison, 1971—, AD Madison, 1982—; dir. M&I Bank of Jamestown, Madison, 1978—. Bd. dirs. Chgo. Boys Club, 1969-71, Orchard Ridge Community Assn., Madison, 1976-78. Served with U.S. Army, 1956-57, 60-61. Mem. Sales and Mktg. Execs. Assn. (pres. 1979-80, Best Club Internat. award 1980), Pi Sigma Epsilon. Republican. Presbyterian. Avocations: athletics; reading; gardening; cooking. Home: 42 Oak Creek Trail Madison WI 53717 Office: Wis Office Supply Co 3120 Syene Rd Madison WI 53713

KING, THOMAS HOWARD, financial systems manager; b. Pitts., Mar. 27, 1955; s. Thomas Walter and Marlene Q. (Schmitt) K.; m. Cheryl Lyn Scott, Sept. 5, 1981. BS in Bus. Adminstrn., The Pa. State U., 1977; MS in Indsl. Adminstrn., Carnegie-Mellon U., 1985. CPA. Sr. acct. Deloitte, Haskins & Sells, Pitts., 1977-81; mgr. Price Waterhouse, Pitts., 1981-83; mgr. fin. ops. Union Pacific Railroad, Omaha, 1985-86, mgr. fin. systems, 1986—. Arhtur C. Carter scholar Am. Acctg. Assn., 1984. Mem. Am. Inst. CPA's, Nebr. Soc. CPA's, Pa. Soc. CPA's. Republican. Methodist. Avocations: photography, theater, bicycling, raquetball. Home: 15364 Nicholas St Omaha NE 68154 Office: Union Pacific Railroad 1416 Dodge St Omaha NE 68179

KING, WAYNE WELDON, information center administrator; b. Saginaw, Mich., July 12, 1936; s. Weldon Fredrick and Lula Margaret (Dunn) K.; m. Betty Lou Ann Miley, July 1, 1955; children: Sherrill Ann, Kim Marie, Kathy Ann; m. 2d Phyllis Ann King (dec. 1970). Dir. Mich./Can. Bigfoot Info. Ctr., Caro, 1977—. Home and Office: Mich/Can Bigfoot Info Ctr 152 W Sherman St Caro MI 48723

KING, (JACK) WELDON, photographer; b. Springfield, Mo., Jan. 19, 1911; s. Clyde Nelson and Mary Blanche (Murphy) K.; B.A., Drury Coll., 1934, Mus.B., 1934. Chief still photographer African expdns. including Gatti-Hallicrafters Expdn., 1947-48, 12th Gatti Expdn., 1952, Wyman Carroll Congo Expdn., 1955, 13th Gatti Expdn., 1956, 14th Gatti Expdn., 1957; also freelance photog. expdns., Africa, 1960, 66, 76-77; trips for GAF Corp. to S.Am., 1962, 63, 77-78, Australia and N.Z., 1972-73; Alaska, 1982, Europe, 1983, also numerous assignments throughout contiguous states U.S. Served as photographer with Coast Arty. Corps, U.S. Army, 1941-42; PTO; Japanese prisoner of war, 1942-45. Decorated numerous service ribbons and battle stars. Mem. Space Pioneers, Am. Theatre Organ Soc., Humane Soc. U.S., Friends Animals, Animal Protection Inst. Am., African Wildlife Leadership Found., World Wildlife Fund, Am. Defenders of Bataan and Corregidor, Am. Ex-Prisoners War, Lambda Chi Alpha. Democrat. Roman Catholic. Contbr. to numerous art books including Africa is Adventure, 1959, also French and German edits.; Primitive Peoples Today, 1956; Africa: A Natural History, 1965; South America and Central America, 1967; Animal Worlds, 1963; Living Plants of the World, 1963; The Earth Beneath Us, 1964; Living Trees of the World; The Life of the Jungle, 1970; Living Mammals of the World. Contbr. photographs to mags., encys., textbooks. Address: 1234 E Grand Ave Springfield MO 65804

KING, WILLIAM CARL, transportation executive; b. Lake City, Fla., May 23, 1944; s. William G. and Ruth O. (Barker) K.; m. Mary Lee Bray, June 24, 1966 (div. 1980); children: Julie Ann, Jeffrey Carl; m. Christine Nora Schieck, Aug. 14, 1981. BBA, Western Mich. U., 1966; MBA, Baldwin Wallace Coll., 1978. With purchasing ddiv. Pontiac (Mich.) Motor Co., 1966-69; dir. planning dept. Kelsey Hayes, Romulus, Mich., 1969-74; dir. materials, mgmt. info. system Bendix, Elyria, Ohio, 1974-77; gen. mgr. Bendix HUS Ltd., London, Ontario, Can., 1977-80; v.p., gen. mgr. Bendix FMD, Troy, N.Y., 1980-84; group v.p. Allied Automotive, Southfield, Mich., 1985—. Bd. dirs. Jr. Achievement, Albany, N.Y., 1980-82, officer, 1982-85. Mem. Soc. Automotive Engrs., Am. Prodn. Inventory Control Soc., Omicron Delta Kappa, Delta Chi. Republican. Methodist. Club: Farmington Hills (Mich.) Country. Lodge: Elks. Home: 41610 Fallbrook Ct Northville MI 48167 Office: Allied Automotive PO Box 5029 Southfield MI 48086

KING, WILLIAM H., bank company executive. BS, Ind. State U., 1960. Chmn. bd. dirs., chief exec. officer Second Nat. Bank, Richmond, Va., also bd. dirs. Served to 2d lt. USNG, 1961-67. Office: The Second Nat Bank of Richmond 8th & Promenade Richmond IN 47374 *

KINGERY, JOHN RUSSELL, engineering executive; b. Mpls., Apr. 30, 1955; s. Raymond George and Phyliss Elsie (Pickett) K.; m. Jean Marie Helmberger, July 22, 1978; 1 child, Katherine Louise. BSME, U. Minn. Inst. Tech., 1977. Design engr. Deere and Co., Waterloo, Iowa, 1977-78; design engr. The Toro Co., Bloomington, Minn., 1978-80, sr. design engr., 1980-81; sr. mech. engr. Micro Component Tech., Shoreview, Minn., 1981-84; program mgr. Micro Component Tech., Shoreview, 1984—. Ruling elder, deacon Knox Presby. Ch., Mpls., 1982-85. Mem. Soc. Automotive Engrs. Avocation: restores old cars. Home: 8759 Bentwood Dr Eden Prairie MN 55344 Office: Micro Component Tech 3850 N victoria St Shoreview MN 55164

KINGMAN, JOSEPH RAMSDELL, III, banker; b. Mpls., Dec. 8, 1927; s. Joseph Ramsdell and Margaret Perry (Morris) K.; m. Kathleen Popesh, Aug. 4, 1977; children: James B., Kate P. B.A., Amherst Coll., 1949. With 1st Nat. Bank of Mpls., 1950-61, Imperial Fin. Services, 1962-63; with 1st Nat. Bank of Mpls., 1963-82, vice chmn., to 1982; pres., chief operating officer Am. Nat. Bank & Trust Co., St. Paul, 1983—. Bd. dirs. Met. Econ. Devel. Assn.; bd. dirs. Center for Humanism, Awareness and Research Tng., St. Paul Chamber Orch. Served with U.S. Army, 1950-52. Mem. Am. Bankers Assn. Clubs: Minneapolis, St. Paul Athletic, Minnesota. Office: Am Nat Bank & Trust Co 5th & Minnesota St Saint Paul MN 55101 *

KINGSLEY, JAMES GORDON, college president; b. Houston, Nov. 22, 1933; s. James Gordon and Blanche Sybil (Payne) K.; m. Martha Elizabeth Sasser, Aug. 24, 1956; children: Gordon Alan, Craig Emerson. A.B., Miss. Coll., 1955; M.A., U. Mo., 1956; B.D., Th.D., New Orleans Bapt. Theol. Sem., 1960, 65; H.H.D., Mercer U., 1980; postgrad., U. Louisville, 1968-69, Nat. U. Ireland, 1970, Harvard U., 1976. Asst. prof. Miss. Coll., 1956-58; instr. Tulane U., 1958-60; asst. prof. William Jewell Coll., Liberty, Mo., 1960-62; prof. lit. and religion William Jewell Coll., 1969—, dean, 1976-80, pres., 1980—; asso. prof. Ky. So. Coll., Louisville, 1964-67, prof., 1967-69. Author: A Time for Openness, 1973, Frontiers, 1983; contbr. articles to profl. jours. LaRue fellow, 1976. Mem. English Speaking Union, Council Ind. Colls. (bd. dirs.), Am. Assn. Pres. Ind. Colls. and Univs. (bd. dirs.), Am. Assn. Higher Edn., Bapt. Hist. Soc. Baptist. Clubs: Kansas City, Univ. Lodge: Rotary. Home: 510 E Mississippi St Liberty MO 64068 Office: William Jewell Coll Liberty MO 64068

KINLEY, SHIRLEY J., university administrator; b. Harrisburg, Ill., Jan. 19, 1942; d. John Paul and Ruby Fern (Thomas) Whittington; m. James E. Kinley, June 11, 1960; 1 child, Douglas Lee. BA, Sangamon State U., 1979, MA in Fin. and Human Resource Mgmt., 1981. Office supr. State of Ill. Dept. Mental Health, Springfield, 1960-64, office mgr., 1967-69; office mgr. Met. Life, McMinnville, Tenn., 1965-66; office supr. counseling and testing dept. So. Ill. U., Carbondale, 1966-67, asst. dean Coll. Bus. and Adminstrn., 1984—; asst. to pres. Sangamon State U., Springfield, 1969-84. Mem. adv. bd. Rochester (Ill.) Schs., 1968-83; bd. mem. High Sch. Bus. Edn. Assn., Rochester, 1970-83, Rochester Little League, 1975-77; sec. Rochester PTA, 1972-75; den mother Cub Scouts Am., Rochester, 1972-74. Outstanding Alumni award Sangamon State U., 1985. Mem. Ill. Employment and Tng. Assn. Avocations: swimming, skiing, golf, piano, organ. Home: 2710 Sunset Dr Carbondale IL 62901 Office: So Ill Univ Coll Bus Adminstrn Rehn Hall Room 114 Carbondale IL 62901

KINNEARY, JOSEPH PETER, U.S. judge; b. Cin., Sept. 19, 1905; s. Joseph and Anne (Mulvihill) K.; m. Byrnece Camille Rogers, June 26, 1950. B.A., U. Notre Dame, 1928; LL.B., U. Cin., 1935. Bar: Ohio 1935, U.S. Supreme Ct 1960. Pvt. practice in Cin. and Columbus, 1935-61; asst. atty. gen. Ohio, 1937-39; 1st asst. atty. gen. 1949-51, spl. counsel to atty. gen., 1959-61; U.S. atty. So Dist. Ohio, 1961-66; judge U.S. Dist. Ct., So. Dist. Ohio, 1966—, chief judge, 1973-75; lectr. law trusts Coll. Law, U. Cin., 1948. Delegate Democratic Nat. Conv., 1952. Served to capt. AUS, World War II. Decorated Army Commendation ribbon. Mem. Phi Delta Phi. Roman Catholic. Home: 2440 Northwest Blvd Columbus OH 43221 Office: U S Dist Ct 319 US Courthouse 85 Marconi Blvd Columbus OH 43215 *

KINNEY, BEVERLY SEEMAN, elementary teacher; b. Toledo, Dec. 1, 1936; d. Arnold George Seeman and Luella M. (Genson) Lawrence; m. John Philip Kinney, May 17, 1957; children: Jeffrey, John. BEd, U. Toledo, 1962; MEd, U. Cin., 1972; M in Instrn. Econ. Edn., U. Del., 1983. Cert. elem. tchr., Ohio. Tchr. Toledo City Schs., 1962, Princeton City Schs., Glendale, Ohio, 1968—; consumer coordinator Greater Cin. Ctr. Econ. Edn. U. Cin., 1983—. Author: Children in the Marketplace, 1984. Leader Divorce Workshops for Children, Lebanon, Ohio, 1983—; coordinator CROP WALK for Hunger, Lebanon, 1983—. Named Tchr. of Yr., Ohio Dept. Edn., 1986. Mem. Ohio Gifted and Talented Assn. Lutheran. Avocations: jogging, camping. Home: 840 Stubbs Mill Rd Lebanon OH 45036 Office: Robert E Lucas Sch 3900 Cottingham Dr Sharonville OH 45241

KINNEY, EARL ROBERT, food executive; b. Burnham, Maine, Apr. 12, 1917; s. Harry E. and Ethel (Vose) K.; m. Margaret Velie Thatcher, Apr. 23, 1977; children: Jeanie Elizabeth, Earl Robert, Isabella Alice. A.B., Bates Coll., 1939; postgrad., Harvard U. Grad. Sch., 1940. Founder, North Atlantic Pack Co., Bar Harbor, Maine, 1941; pres. North Atlantic Pack Co., 1941-42, treas., dir., 1941-64; with Gorton Corp. (became subs. Gen. Mills, Inc. 1968), 1954-68, pres., 1958-68; v.p. Gen. Mills, Inc., 1968-69, exec. v.p., 1969-73, chief fin. officer, 1970-73, pres., chief operating officer, 1973-77, chmn. bd., 1977-81; pres., chief exec. officer IDS Mut. Fund Group, Mpls., 1982—; dir. Nashua Corp., Deluxe Check Printers, Inc., Kenner Parker Toys Inc., Crystal Brands, Inc., Hannaford Bros. Co., Portland, Maine, Union Mut. Life Ins. Co., Portland Jackson Lab., 11 Sun Co. Trustee Bates Coll., also chmn. alumni drives, 1960-64. Office: IDS New Dimensions Fund Inc 1000 Roanoke Bldg Minneapolis MN 55402

KINNEY, JOHN FRANCIS, clergyman; b. Oelwein, Iowa, June 11, 1937; s. John F. and Marie B. (McCarty) K. Student, St. Paul Sem., 1957-63, N.Am. Coll., Rome, 1968-71; J.C.D., Pontifical Lateran U., 1971. Ordained priest Roman Catholic Ch., 1963. Assoc. pastor Ch. of St. Thomas, Mpls., 1963-66; vice chancellor of St. Paul and Mpls. Diocese 1966-73; assoc. pastor Cathedral, St. Paul, 1971-74, chancellor, 1973; pastor Ch. of St. Leonard, St. Paul, from 1974; titular bishop of Caorle and aux. bishop Archdiocese of St. Paul and Mpls., 1977-82; bishop Diocese of Bismark, N.D., 1982—. Mem. Canon Law Soc. Am. Roman Catholic. Office: Chancery Office 420 Raymond St PO Box 1575 Bismarck ND 58501 *

KINNEY, JOSEPH ALLEN, trade association director, consultant; b. Joplin, Mo., Mar. 8, 1949; s. Lawrence W. and Betty R. (Brixey) K.; m. Andree Vary, Oct. 22, 1984. BS, Ill. State U., 1972; MA, U. Pa., 1974; M in Pub. Adminstrn., Syracuse U., 1974. Mng. auditor U.S. Gen. Acctg. Office, Washington, 1974-76; legis. asst. U.S. Senate, Washington, 1976-78, exec. asst., 1978-80; dir. staff Nat. Govs. Assn., Washington, 1980-84; exec. dir. Nat. Safe Workplace Inst., Chgo., 1986—, also bd. dirs.; pres. Strategic Communications, Inc., 1986; founder The "Real" Chgo. Program for Fgn. Journalists, Nat. Safe Workplace Inst. Contbr. articles to profl. jours. Served with USMC, 1967-69, Vietnam. Mem. Chgo. Council Fgn. Relations, Japan-Am. Soc. Lutheran. Home: 5059 N Sheridan Chicago IL 60640 Office: 33 N Dearborn Suite 1501 Chicago IL 60602

KINNIE, ROBERT H., retail company executive. Chmn., pres., chief exec. officer Can. Safeway, Ltd., Winnipeg, Man. Office: Canada Safeway Limited, 313 Pacific Ave, Winnipeg, MB Canada R3A OM2 Other Address: Mac Donalds Consolidated Ltd, 840 Cambie St, Vancouver, BC Canada V6B 4S8 *

KINSEL, MICHAEL LESLIE, museum director; b. Council Bluffs, Iowa, May 5, 1947; s. Leslie Henry, Jr. and Stella Julia Sophia (Pedersen) K. B.A., Augustana Coll., 1969; postgrad. Luth. Sch. Theology, Chgo., 1969-73. Asst. to dir. devel. Luth. Sch. Theology, Chgo., 1970-73; dir. devel. Suomi Coll., Hancock, Mich., 1973; account exec. Knaphurst Co., Chgo., 1973-74; dir. Omaha History Mus. (formerly Western Heritage Mus.), Omaha, 1974-87, pres. Kinsel & Assocs., 1987—. Part-time instr. Lifelong Learning Ctr., Creighton U., Omaha; fund-raising cons. Chmn. Douglas County Mental Health Adv. Bd., Mem. Am. Assn. Mus., Am. Assn. State and Local History, Internat. Council Mus., Nat. Soc. Fund-Raising Execs., Lewis and Clark Found., Mus. Council Greater Omaha, U.S. Constn. Bicentennial Commn. Nebr., U.S. Constn. Bicentennial Commn. Omaha, Western History Assn., Nat. Trust Hist. Preservation, Mountain-Plains Mus. Conf., Omaha Com. Fgn. Relations, Nebr. Mus. Roundtable, Nebr. History Network, Omaha Sister City Assn., Omaha Westerners, Omaha Bacchanalian Soc. Republican. Lutheran. Clubs: Omaha Press, Park Avenue. Lodge: Rotary.

KINSER, MICHAEL DEAN, dentist; b. Middletown, Ohio, Apr. 14, 1951; s. Ralph Dean and Helen Joyce (Fairchild) K.; m. Teresa Gail Rose, june 29, 1974; children: Erica Lynn, Kristin Courtney. BA, Miami U., Oxford, Ohio, 1973; DDS, Ohio State U., 1976. Electrician C.E. Kinser & Sons, Inc., Middletown, 1966-76; gen. practice dentistry Middletown, 1977—; instr., advisor, dentist dental assisting class Middletown High Sch., 1977—; advisor Dental Emergency Fund for Area Children, Middletown, 1982—. Advisor Middletown Vocat. Edn. Adv. Council, 1978-82. Mem. ADA, Ohio Dental Assn., Keely Dental Soc., Ohio State U. Alumni Assn., Ohio State U. Coll. Dentistry Alumni Assn., Delta Sigma Delta. Republican. Mem. Church of God. Lodge: Optimist. Avocations: softball, basketball, water skiing. Home: 509 Ken Ridge Dr Middletown OH 45042 Office: 3719 Roosevelt Blvd Middletown OH 45044

KINSMAN, ROBERT DONALD, art museum administrator; b. Bridgeport, Conn., Sept. 13, 1929; s. Cummings Sanborn and Sarah Elizabeth (Barton) K.; m. Patricia Ann Mulreed, Oct. 3, 1953. B.S., Columbia U., 1958, M.A. in Art History, 1966, A.B.D. in Art History. Asst. curator Nat. Gallery Art, Washington, 1961-62; instr. art history Mary Washington Coll., U. Va., Fredericksburg, 1962-63; curator contemporary art Detroit Inst. Arts, 1963-65; asst. prof. art history and dir. duPont Art Galleries, Mary Washington Coll., 1966-68; asst. prof. art history SUNY, Albany, 1968-77; dir. Sheldon

Swope Art Gallery, Terre Haute, Ind., 1978-85, Met. Mus. and Art Ctr., Coral Gables, Fla., 1985-86. Contbr. articles to profl. jours. Bd. dirs. Arts Illiana, Inc., 1981-85. Served with U.S. Army, 1951-53. Mem. Am. Assn. Museums, AAUP, Coll. Art Assn. Am.

KINTNER, ROBERT ROY, chemistry educator; b. Weeping Water, Nebr., Apr. 3, 1928; s. Elmer Hayes and Rae Imogene (Swartwout) K.; m. Helen Ruth Remmers, Aug. 31, 1952; children: Timothy Roy, Melinda Rae Kintner Hooper, SueLynn Reneé. BS in Chem. Tech., Iowa State U., 1953; PhD in Organic Chemistry, U. Wash., 1957; postdoctoral research U. Calif., Santa Cruz, 1987—. Prof. chemistry Augustana Coll., Sioux Falls, S.D., 1957—; vis. prof. chemistry, U. Wash., Seattle, 1959; U. Nebr., Lincoln, 1980-81, U. Md., Munich, 1985-87; cons., co-prin. investigator Augustana Research Inst., Sioux Falls, 1978-80. Author: (with others) Chemistry of the Carbonyl Group, 1966; contbr. articles to profl. jours. Served to cpl. USMC, 1946-49. Petroleum Research Fund faculty fellow U. Wash., Seattle, 1964-65; NSF faculty fellow U. Calif.-Santa Cruz, 1971-72. Mem. ASTM (faculty fellow),Am. Chem. Soc. (pres. Sioux Valley sect. 1965-66), S.D. Acad. Sci. (pres. 1970), Sigma Xi, Phi Lambda Upsilon. Lutheran. Avocations: hiking, camping, biking, nutrition, youth ministries. Office: Augustana Coll Chemistry Dept Sioux Falls SD 57197

KIPPERT, ROBERT JOHN, JR., lawyer; b. Detroit, Aug. 29, 1952; s. Robert John Sr. and Jeanne Marcella (DeYonker) K.; m. Dorothy Marie Cunningham, Oct. 28, 1978; 1 child, Cristie. BBA, U. Mich., 1974; JD, Wayne State U., 1977. Bar: Mich. 1979. Tax staff acct. Arthur Young and Co., Bloomfield Hills, Mich., 1977-78; tax staff sr. mgr. McEndarfer, Hoke & Bernhard, Bloomfield Hills, 1978-84; tax supr. Cen. Transport, Inc., Sterling Heights, Mich., 1984-85; tax atty. Chrysler Fin. Corp., Troy, Mich., 1985. Mem. ABA, Mich. Bar Assn., Oakland County Bar Assn., Macomb County Bar Assn., Am. Inst. CPA's, Mich. Assn. CPA's. Republican. Roman Catholic. Avocations: softball, basketball officiating. Home: 14983 Annapolis Sterling Heights MI 48078 Office: Chrysler Fin Corp 901 Wilshire Dr Troy MI 48084

KIPPLEY, JOHN FRANCIS, audiovisual writer and producer, social services executive; b. Mpls., Nov. 6, 1930; s. Frank F. and Hazel E. (Forth) K.; m. Sheila K. Matgen, Apr. 27, 1963; children: Jennifer, Mary, Margaret, Karen, Christopher. BA in Philosophy, St. Paul (Minn.) Sem., 1952; MA in Indsl. Relations, U. Minn., 1956; MA in Theology, U. San Francisco, 1967; M Applied Theology, Grad. Theol. Union, Berkeley, Calif., 1970. Cons. bus. and mktg. various, 1956-62; religious educator 1963-69, educator coll. theology, 1970-74; pres. Couple to Couple League, Cin., 1974—. Author: Birth Control and The Marriage Covenant, 1970; (with others) The Art of Natural Family Planning, 1971, last rev. edit., 1985; also articles. Roman Catholic. Office: Couple to Couple League PO Box 111184 Cincinnati OH 45211

KIRALY, PHILIPPA JANET, writer; b. Haslar, Eng., June 21, 1935; d. Douglas Arnold Newbery and Janet Dorothy (James) Young; m. William Seymour Kiraly, June 11, 1960; stepchildren: Wendy, Daniel; 1 child, Tessa. Grad. high sch., Eng. RN, Eng. Freelance journalist Cleve., 1980. Mem. adv. bd. Cleve. Philharmonic Orchestra, 1985—; trustee Fairmount Ctr. for the Performing Arts, Cleve., 1977-80, The Dance Ctr., Cleve., 1980-82. Ohio Arts Council fellow, 1985. Fellow Music Critics Insts., Music Critics and Editors Inst.; mem. Music Critics Assn., Nat. Fedn. Press Women. Avocations: people, travel, camping, music, reading. Home and Office: 3389 E Monmouth Rd Cleveland Heights OH 44118

KIRBY, BRENDA RUTH, educator; b. Marston, Mo., Jan. 31, 1948; d. Howard David and Dorothy Louise (White) K. BA, Coll. of Sch. of Ozarks, 1970. Tchr. New Madrid (New Madrid) R-1 Sch. Dist., 1970—. Seller (computer data disks) Word Attack. Active Dem. Nat. Com. Mem. Mo. State Tchrs. Assn. Democrat. Baptist. Avocations: reading French and English, computers, swimming. Home: Box 296 Dunklin St Marston MO 63866 Office: New Madrid County R-1 Sch Dist New Madrid MO 63869

KIRBY, DOROTHY MANVILLE, social worker; b. Burke, S.D., Oct. 23, 1917; d. Charles Vietz and Gail Lorena (Coonen) Manville; m. Sigmund Kirby, July 11, 1941 (div. 1969); children; Paul Howard, Robert Charles. BA, Wayne State U., 1970, MSW, 1972. Cert. social worker, Mich. Pvt. practice social work Allen Park, Mich., 1973—; conduct seminars on stress, personal effectiveness and communication for various orgns., hosps. and bus. Subscription chmn. Allen Park Symphony Orchestra, 1985-86. Mem. Am. Group Psychotherapy Assn., Nat. Assn. Social Workers (clin.), Nat. Assn. Marriage and Family Counseling, Mich. Assn. Marriage and Family Counseling (sec. 1982), LWV (pres. Allen Park 1965-66). Presbyterian. Lodge: Soroptimists. Avocation: playing violin. Home and Office: 15720 Wick Rd Allen Park MI 48101

KIRBY, JACK, technology educator; b. Stoughton, Wis., Dec. 1, 1929; s. Henry John and Alta Mae (Herron) K.; m. Nancy Elizabeth Knudsen, Sept. 5, 1953; children: James, Keith, David, Katherine. Student, Luther Coll., 1947-48; BS, U. Wis., Platteville, 1954; MS, U. Wis., Stout, 1958; EdD, U. Mo., 1965. Tchr. Mineral Point (Wis.) High Sch., 1954, Wautoma (Wis.) High Sch., 1954-55; tchr., dept. chmn. Muskego (Wis.) High Sch., 1957-63; prof. tech. edn., chmn. dept. indsl. tech. U. Wis., Platteville, 1965—. Contbr. articles to profl. jours. Mem. Gov.'s Council on Aeronautics, Madison, Wis., 1983—. Served with U.S. Army, 1955-56. Fellowship grantee U.S. Office Edn., U. Wis., Platteville, 1966-67. Mem. Am. Vocat. Assn., Wis. Tech. Edn. Assn. (pres. 1979-82), Internat. Tech. Edn. Assn., Council for Ind. Arts State Assn. Officers (pres. 1984-87), Council on Tech. Tchr. Edn. (treas. 1977-79). Methodist. Clubs: Golf and Country (Platteville) (pres. 1970-72), Univ. Fliers (pres. Platteville chpt. 1980-84). Avocations: golf, basketball, flying, traveling. Home: 1245 Union St Platteville WI 53818 Office: U Wis Platteville 1 Univ Plaza Platteville WI 53818

KIRBY, JOE F., insurance company executive; b. 1953. BA, Augustana Coll., Rock Island, Ill., 1975; postgrad., U. S.D.- Vermillion, 1978. With Western Surety Co., Sioux Falls, S.D., 1978-, now chmn. Office: Western Surety Co 101 S Phillips Sioux Falls SD 57192*

KIRBY, JOE P., insurance company executive. Pres. Western Surety Co., Sioux Falls, S.D. Office: Western Surety Co 101 S Phillips Sioux Falls SD 57192 *

KIRBY, JULIE MAE, accountant; b. Galesburg, Ill., July 1, 1959; d. Kenneth G. and Doris M. (Cash) Hartz; m. Jay T. Kirby, June 20, 1981; 1 child, Jaime M. BA in Acctg., Monmouth Coll., 1980. CPA, Ill.; CLU. Sr. tax analyst State Farm Life Ins. Co. subs. State Farm Mut. Automobile Ins. Co., Bloomington, Ill., 1980—. Fellow Life Mgmt. Assn.; mem. Am. Soc. CPA's, Ill. Soc. CPA's. Avocations: piano, sewing, reading. Home: Rural Rt 13 Box 336 Bloomington IL 61701 Office: State Farm Life Ins Co B-1 One State Farm Plaza Bloomington IL 61710

KIRBY, ROBERT STEPHEN, lawyer; b. Rochelle, Ill., Aug. 4, 1925; s. Stephen F. and Eulalia E. (Coleman) K.; m. Carolyn C. Clark, June 10, 1950; children: Kathleen, Robert, James, Thomas, Julie. B.S., U. Ill., 1948; postgrad., U. Wis.-Madison, 1948; J.D., U. Ill., 1950. Bar: Ill. 1950, U.S. Dist. Ct. (no dist.) Ill. 1950, U.S. Ct. Appeals (7th cir.) 1953, U.S. Supreme Ct. 1956. Ptnr. Frisch & Fox, Chgo., 1950-52; with Ill. Cen. R.R. Co., Chgo., 1952-69, gen. atty., 1961-66, asst. gen. solicitor, 1966-69; with IC Industries, Inc., Chgo., 1969—, sr. v.p., gen. counsel, sec., 1981-84, exec. v.p. law and adminstrn., gen. counsel, sec., 1984-85, exec. v.p. law and adminstrn., corp. sec., 1986—; bd. dirs. IC Products Co., LaSalle Properties, Inc.; mem. adv. bd. Northwestern U. Sch. Law Corp. Counsel Ctr. Bd. dirs. Washington Sq. Health Found., Inc., Chgo. Served with USMC, 1943-45. Mem. Chgo. Bar Assn., Northwestern U. Assocs., Delta Kappa Epsilon, Phi Delta Phi. Clubs: Mid-America (Chgo.); Skokie Country (Glencoe, Ill.); Quail Ridge (Boynton Beach, Fla.). Office: IC Industries Inc 111 E Wacker Dr Chicago IL 60601

KIRBY, RUSSELL STEPHEN, research analyst; b. New Haven, June 8, 1954; s. Frank Eugene and Emily (Baruch) K.; m. Elizabeth Margaret Ivens, July 9, 1977; children: Rachel Anne, Amelia Jeanne. BA, U. Wis., 1974, MS, 1977, PhD, 1981. Lectr. U. Wis., Madison, 1980, 82-83; research analyst 3 Wis. Ctr. for Health Stats., Madison, 1981-83, research analyst 5, 1983-85, research analyst 6 maternal and child health statistician, 1985—. Contbr. articles to profl. jours. Mem. Assn. Am. Geographers (life), Am. Pub. Health Assn., Agrl. History Soc. (life), So. Hist. Soc. (life), Wis. Assn. Perinatal Care (cert. Appreciation 1986). Avocations: camping, writing book reviews, computer cartography and graphics, used books. Home: 1254 Rutledge St Madison WI 53703 Office: Wis Ctr Health Stats PO Box 309 Madison WI 53701

KIRCHER, DUDLEY PAUL, forest products company executive; b. Dayton, Ohio, Nov. 12, 1934; s. Ralf Charles and Mary Virginia (Paul) K.; m. Carole A. Jacobs; children—Christopher, Stacy, Ralf Edward. B.A., Ohio U., 1957; M.B.A., Harvard U., 1960. Cons. Logistics Mgmt. Inst., Washington, 1963-65; cons., assoc. Booz, Allen & Hamilton Assocs., Washington, 1965-69; v.p. Kircher, Helton & Collett Inc., Dayton, Ohio, 1969-72; v.p., dir. Dayton Devel. Council, 1972-79; v.p. Mead Corp., Dayton, 1979—; dir. Gem Savs. Assn., Dayton, Van Dyne Crotty, Dayton, Greater Dayton Pub. TV. Dir. Dayton Mus. Natural History, 1971—, U.S. Aviation Hall of Fame, Dayton, 1978—; Republican candidate for U.S. Congress, 3rd Dist. Ohio, 1978. Named Mktg. Man of Yr., Am. Mktg. Assn., 1975, Man of Yr., Air Force Assn., Dayton, 1976, Outstanding Pub. Servant, Sta. WKEF-TV, Dayton, 1976. Mem. Dayton Area C. of C. (pres. 1974-78). Episcopalian. Clubs: Moraine Country (bd. dirs. 1970-85), Dayton Racquet (bd. dirs. 1976—). Home: 530 Walnut Springs Dr Dayton OH 45419 Office: Mead Corp Courthouse Plaza NE Dayton OH 45463

KIRCHNER, JOHN HOWARD, psychologist; b. Passaic, N.J., Dec. 28, 1933; s. John Howard and Anita Gladys (Smith) K.; m. Nora Ilse Kuehne, June 16, 1956; 1 child, John Douglas. AB, U. Ill., 1955; MA, Northwestern U., 1956, 60, PhD, 1964. Diplomate Am. Bd. Profl. Psychologist. Tchr. Evergreen Park (Ill.) High Sch., 1956-57, Maine Twp. High Sch., Park Ridge, Ill., 1959-61; assoc. prof. Ill. State U., Normal, Ill., 1964-71; chief psychologist Wood County Mental Health Clinic, Bowling Green, Ohio, 1971-75; exec. dir., chief psychologist Gt. River Mental Health Ctr., Muscatine, Iowa, 1975-79, Jasper County Mental Health Ctr., Newton, Iowa, 1979-84; psychologist Des Moines Child Guidance Ctr., 1984—; cons., psychologist VA Hosp., Knoxville, Iowa, 1980-84, Area Comprehensive Evaluation Services, Des Moines, 1984-86, Orchard Place, Des Moines, 1987—. Contbr. articles to profl. jours. Served with U.S. Army, 1957-59, 61-62. Mem. Am. Psychol. Assn., Iowa Psychol. Assn., Phi Beta Kappa, Phi Delta Kappa. Avocation: fgn. langs. Home: 524 22d Ave SW Altoona IA 50009 Office: Des Moines Child Guidance Ctr 1206 Pleasant St Des Moines IA 52804

KIRCHNER, RICHARD JAY, educator; b. Schenectady, Feb. 17, 1930; s. Richard Jacob and Leah (Williams) K.; B.S., U. Wis., 1952, M.S., 1955, postgrad., 1956; Ed.D., Mich. State U, 1962; m. Barbara Ann Crane, Feb. 2, 1952; children—Richard Alec, Barbara Jayne, Carolyn Diane, Robert Jay, Kathleen Kay. Instr. wrestling and track coach St. Cloud (Minn.) Tchrs. Coll., 1955-56; asst. prof., coaching staff Central Mich. U., Mt. Pleasant, 1956-62, prof. recreation, chmn. dept., 1962—, with Office of Dean sch. edn., health and human services, 1987—, chmn. pres.'s adv. com.; camp program dir., camp dir. Elkton-Pigeon-Bayport Sch. Camp, Caseville, Mich., 1962; municipal recreation dir. Petoskey (Mich.), 1963, cons., 1964-74; vice chmn. citizens adv. com. Recreation Services div. Mich. Dept. Conservation, 1966-67. Pres. Mt. Pleasant Intermediate Sch. PTA, 1968-69; chmn. tech. planning com. Mt. Pleasant Recreation Commn. Served to capt. USMCR, 1952-54. Mem. AAHPER (v.p. Mich. 1966-67, v.p. Midwest dist. 1973-74), Nat Recreation and Parks Assn., Am. Assn. Leisure and Recreation (nat. pres. 1976-77, nat. accreditation council 1978-83, vice chmn. 1979-81, chmn. 1981-83), Am. Camp Assn., Mich. Soc. Arts, Sci. and Letters, Mich. Soc. Gerontology, Outdoor Edn. and Camping Council (charter), Mich. Recreation and Parks Assn. (v.p. 1968-70), Phi Eta Sigma, Phi Epsilon Kappa, Phi Delta Kappa. Home: 6953 Riverside Dr Mount Pleasant MI 48858

KIRCHSTEIN, JAMES EDWARD, electronics engineer, consultant; b. Madison, Wis., Mar. 28, 1931; s. Frank Henry and Helen Elenor (Callaway) K.; m. Nancy Jeanne Mathews, June 26, 1976; children—Betty Lou, Vicki Lynn, Helen Susan, James Esteban, Lydia Ann, Mathew James, Daniel Warren, Eva Marie. B.S.E.E., U. Wis., 1958. Lic. comml. pilot. Exec. dir. Sauk Prairie Radio, Sauk City, Wis., 1964-67; pres. Am. Music Corp., Sauk City, 1967, Seven Sounds Pub., Sauk City, 1970; dir. elec. media U. Wis., Madison, 1968-82; sr. elec. engr. dept. adminstrn. Bur. Engring., State of Wis., Madison, Madison, 1982—. Explorer advisor, 1968-70. Served with USN, 1950-54; Korea. Mem. Audio Engring. Soc., Soc. Motion Picture Engrs., Aircraft Owners and Pilots Assn. Mem. United Ch. of Christ. Clubs: August Derleth Soc. (pres. 1987—); Sauk Prairie Optimist (pres. 1969). Developer spl. acoustical ceiling for sound rec.; created largest catalog of ethnic music in world, 1961-72. Home: 3830 STH 78th Mount Horeb WI 53572

KIRK, BALLARD HARRY THURSTON, architect; b. Williamsport, Pa., Apr. 1, 1929; s. Ballard and Ada May (DeLaney) K.; m. Vera Elizabeth Kitchener, Mar. 13, 1951; children: Lisa Lee, Kira Alexandria, Dayna Allison, Courtlandt Blaine. BArch, Ohio State U., 1959. Pres. Kirk Assocs., Architects, Columbus, Ohio, 1963—; Mem. Ohio Bd. Bldg. Standards, Columbus, 1973-78; pres. Nat. Council Architect Registration Bds., Washington, 1984-85, Ohio Bd. Examiners Architects, Columbus, 1973-78; bd. dirs. Nat. Archtl. Accrediting Bd., Washington, 1986—. Mem. AIA. Republican. Mem. Brethern Ch. Home: 2459 Tremont Rd Columbus OH 43221 Office: Kirk Assoc Architects PO Box 21366 Columbus OH 43221

KIRK, GERALD E., electric company executive; b. St. Louis, Oct. 26, 1941; s. Howard E. and Josephine (Quagliata) K.; m. Dolly S. Minnix, Jan. 27, 1962; 1 child, Tara Lynn. Grad. high sch., St. Louis County, 1959. V.p. Guarantee Electrical Co., St. Louis. Mem. Am. Sub Contractors Assn., Am. Soc. Profl. Estimators. Office: Guarantee Electrical Co 4161 Gravois Saint Louis MO 63116

KIRK, HAROLD LAVERNE, utility company executive; b. McCune, Kans., Dec. 24, 1928; s. Glenn H. and Bertha L. (Painter) K.; m. D. Arlene Bates, Nov. 2, 1951; children: Lucinda Lee, Anna Marie, Harold L. II. BS in Commerce and Engring., Kans. State Coll., 1951. Cert. indsl. developer. Ptnr. McCune Tire and Appliance, 1953-55; special risk underwriter Western Ins. Co., Ft. Scott, Kans., 1955-58; adminstrv. asst. Mid Am., Inc., Parsons, Kans., 1958-63; mng. dir. Clinton (Iowa) Devel. Co., 1963-74; project planner The Austin Co., Kansas City, Mo., 1974-83; mgr. indsl. devel. Mo. Pub. Service Co., Kansas City, 1983—; advisor Clinton Community Coll., 1965-74; cons. in field. Author: 5 "W"s For "Spec" Buildings, 1966; contbr. articles to profl. jours. Advisor Boy Scouts Am., Kans. and Iowa, 1951-83. Served with U.S. Army, 1951-53. Mem. Am. Econ. Devel. Council, Indsl. Devel. Research Council (profl. assoc.), Soc. Indsl. Realtors (assoc.), So. Indsl. Devel. Council, Mo. Indsl. Devel. Council, Iowa Profl. Developers Assn., Kans. State Coll. Alumni Assn. Baptist. Club: Toastmasters. Lodges: Rotary, Lions. Avocations: golf, painting, art, history. Home: 2000 W 86th Terr Leawood KS 66206 Office: Mo Pub Service Co 10750 E 350 Hwy PO 11739 Kansas City MO 64138

KIRK, MELDON CLARK, financial executive; b. Gentry, Ark., Oct. 29, 1932; s. Martin Luther and Josephine (McElligott) K.; m. Carrie Mae Klinkenberg, July 25, 1952; children: Stephen, David, Lawrence. BBA, U. Mo., 1961, MBA, 1966. Cons. supr. Peat, Marwick, Mitchell & Co., N.Y.C., 1966-71; treas. Mid. W. Service Co., Chgo., 1971-74; assoc. exec. dir. Am. Library Assn., Chgo., 1974-78; dir. adminstrn. and services Midwest Research Inst., Kansas City, Mo., 1978-85, exec. dir. fin. and treas., 1985—; cons. Surfaces Research and Application, Lenexa, Kans., 1986—; bd. dirs. Ill. Stock Transfer Co., Brookside Corp. Bd. dirs. Heart of Am. United Way, Kansas City, 1985-86. Served to sgt. U.S. Army, 1952-55. Mem. Am. Mgmt. Assn., Fin. Execs. Inst. Republican. Methodist. Avocations: bridge, reading. Office: Midwest Research Inst 425 Volker Blvd Kansas City MO 64110

KIRK, MILDRED THOMAS, educator; b. St. Louis, Apr. 1, 1927; d. Robert and Annie Laura (Poole) Thomas; B.S., U. Mo., 1975; m. Isaac Wilson Kirk, Apr. 10, 1948; 1 son, Isaac Douglas. Acctg. clk. Southwestern Bell Telephone Co., St. Louis, 1950-75; tchr. Buder Sch., St. Louis, 1976-83; tchr. Shenandoah Valley Sch., Chesterfield, Mo., 1983-84, Barretts Sch., Des Peres, Mo., 1984-85. Mem. Assn. Supervision and Curriculum Devel., NEA, U. Mo. Alumni Assn., Nat. Writers Club. Lutheran. Author: A Different Kind of Birthday, 1980. Home: 5919 Evergreen St Saint Louis MO 63134

KIRK, WEIR RICHARD, health services executive; b. Terre Haute, Ind., Feb. 18, 1920; s. C. Weir and Etta Barbara (Zimmerman) K.; m. Marvel B. Dickson, June 13, 1951; children: Vicki Marie, Jeanine Gayle, Patti Richelle, Terri Sue, Richard Brian, Michael Wayne. BS in Edn., Ind. State Teachers Coll., 1940, MS, 1953. Adminstr. Crawford Meml. Hosp., Robinson, Ill., 1962-64, Riley County Hosp., Wharton Manor, Manhattan, Kans., 1953-62; dir. membership Am. Coll. Hosp. Adminstrs., Chgo., 1964-82; exec. dir. Assn. Mental Health Adminstrs., Chgo., 1984—; dir. devel. credentialing Am. Coll. Healthcare Execs., Chgo., 1985. Author: Your Future in Hospital Administration, 1963, Aim For a Job in a Hospital, 1968, Your Future in Hospital Work, 1971, Your Future in Hospital and Health Services Administration, 1976, Exploring Careers in Health Services Administration, 1982; contbr. articles to profl. jours. Mem. Community Chest Pub. Relations Com., Lafayette, Ind., 1942-43, mem. com. on youth Oak Park (Ill.) Twp. chmn., 1973; coordinator Post-War Planning Comm., Jeffersonville, Ind., 1943-44; mem. pub. info. com. Allen County Cancer Soc., Ft. Wayne, Ind., 1948-49; prodn. mgr. Community Theater, Terre Haute, 1951-52; bd. dirs. Riley County Mental Health, 1954-60, pres., 1958-60; active Boy Scouts Am., West Lafayette, Ind., River Forest, Ill., Irvine, Tex., 1942—; bd. dirs. Crawford County Tuberculosis and Health Assn., Robinson, Ill., 1963-64, Bethesda Luth. Home, Watertown, Wis., 1965-83; mem. Bd. Health, Oak Park, Ill., 1986—; mem. alumni adv. council Ind. State U., Terre Haute, 1977-80, Univ. Futures Forum, 1979-80, acad. planning workshop, 1977; mem. bd. health Oak Park, Ill., 1986—. Served to sgt. U.S. Army, 1944-46, ET), to lt. (hon.) USN, 1982—. Recipient Disting. Alumni award Ind. State U., 1983, Humanitarian award Nat. Assn. Health Services Execs., 1983; honoree Weir Richard Kirk Day, City of Chgo., Sept. 16, 1986. Fellow Am. Coll. Hosp. Adminstrs.; mem. Am. Hosp. Assn., Nat. Com. Health Credentialing Agencies, Kans. Hosp. Assn., Blue Cross Relations Com. Luth. Hosp. Assn. Kans., Ill. Hosp. Assn., Profl. Exam. Service (founding)(bd. dirs. 1971-77). Lodges: Rotary (bd. dirs. Manhattan chpt. 1958-61), Optimists (bd. dirs. Terre Haute chpt. 1950-52, pres. 1952-53). Office: Assn Mental Health Adminstrs 840 N Lake Shore Dr Chicago IL 60611

KIRK, WILLIAM GERARD, psychology educator; b. Chgo., July 2, 1941; s. Knox Paul and Genevieve (Burke) K.; m. Linda Griffin, Feb. 19, 1966; children: Sara, Garrett, Jonathon, Molly. BA, Qunicy (Ill.) Coll., 1966; MA, Ill. State U., Normal, 1967; PhD, U. Kans., 1978. Diplomate Am. Acad. Behavioral Medicine; registered psychologist, Ill. Sch. psychologist East Ill. Area Spl. Edn., Mattoon, Ill., 1967-69; clin. psychologist Effingham County (Ill.) Mental Health Hosp., 1969-71; research grad asst. U. Kans., 1971-74; clin. intern in psychology Zeller Zone Ctr., Peoria, Ill., 1974-75; prof. psychology Eastern Ill. U., Charleston, 1975—; cons. psychologist Behavioral Medicine Intervention Systems, Tampa, Fla., 1982-83, Ctr. East Alcohol and Drug Council, Mattoon, 1985—, Catholic Charities, Springfield, Ill., 1984—. Contbr. articles to profl. jour. Mem. Am. Psychol. Assn., Ill. Assn. Suicidology., Psi Chi. Roman Catholic. Home: 1811 Meadow Lake Dr Charleston IL 61920 Office: Eastern Ill U Charleston IL 61920

KIRKE, ROBERT JAMES, investment banker; b. Des Moines, Feb. 21, 1936; s. Bernard Michael and Pearl L. (Laverty) K.; BS, Iowa State U., 1957; m. Loral B. Baker, Nov. 21, 1959; children—Kelly Gerard (dec.), Elizabeth (dec.), Matthew, Kathryn. Asst. mdse. mgr. Montgomery Ward & Co., Chgo., pres., owner Shaw, McDermott & Co., Des Moines, 1960—. Pres. St. Augustin Bd. Edn., Des Moines. Mem. Iowa Investment Bankers Assn. (past pres.). Republican. Roman Catholic. Clubs: Embassy, Wakonda, Cyclone. Home: 3240 Terrace Dr Des Moines IA 50312 Office: 518 First Bldg Des Moines IA 50309

KIRKEL, DAVID LEE, chemical executive; b. Berwyn, Ill., Nov. 20, 1949; s. Leo and Mildred Rose (Zajebal) K.; m. Jualynn Mai Pham, Aug. 8, 1981; stepchildren: Cynthia Parrish, David Parrish. BS in Chemistry, Bradley U., 1971. Chemist Alberto Culver, Melrose Park, Ill., 1971-73; engr. Seaquist Valve Co., Cary, Ill., 1973-76; sales rep. Witco Chem., Chgo., 1976-78, Teknor Apex Co., Chgo., 1978-82; pres. Poly-Pro, Inc., Indian Head Park, Ill., 1982—. Patentee, inventor of hair care products. Mem. Indian Head Park Planning Comm., 1986. Mem. Soc. Plastics Engrs. Republican. Avocations: golf, coin and stamp collecting, model railroading, old cars.

KIRKENMEIER, THOMAS EDWARD, investment counselor; b. Detroit, Nov. 29, 1955; s. Milton Thomas and Betty Jane (Welch) K.; m. Constance Marie Miloch, May 8, 1982; children: Eric, Evan. BS in Fin., U. Ill., 1977; MBA, DePaul U., 1980. CPA, Ill., chartered fin. analyst. Investment officer No. Trust Co., Chgo., 1977-82; investment mgr. Brown Bros. Harriman, Chgo., 1982—. Mem. Fin. Analyst Fedn., Investment Analysts Soc. Chgo. (com. mem. 1984—). Republican. Protestant. Avocations: reading, sports. Home: 339 S 6th Ave La Grange IL 60525

KIRKEVOLD, RANDY JON, engineer, state agency administrator; b. Fargo, N.D., Feb. 28, 1955; s. Charles Arthur and Thelma Viola (Hagen) K.; m. Doreen Kay Brudvig, May 29, 1981. BS in Constrn. Mgmt., N.D. State U., 1979. Engr./mgr. N.D. State Hwy. Dept., Fargo, 1982—. Lutheran. Home: 111 28th Ave N Fargo ND 58102 Office: ND State Hwy Dept 503 38th St S Fargo ND 58103

KIRKHAM, JAMES ALVIN, business executive; b. Sumner County, Tenn., June 18, 1935; s. Shirley Barnes and Ouida Redempta (Bursby) K.; m. Shirley Ann Clouse, Sept. 3, 1954; children—Denise Anne, James Alvin II, Hughe Allan. Welder, Ind. Wire Co., 1952-54; truck driver Arthur Lowe Cigar & Candy Co., 1954-56; time study Insley Mfg. Co., 1957; salesman Am. Chicle Co., 1958-59; mgr. Ace Battery, Inc., Indpls., 1960-67, pres., 1967—; v.p. L P Industries, Inc., Indpls., 1977—; ptnr. TKT Leasing, Indpls., 1978—, LDJ Leasing, Indpls., 1979—. Bd. dirs. English Ave. Boys Club, State 4-H Horse and Pony Orgn.; pres. PTO, Clark Twp. Sch. Dist.; v.p. Johnson County 4-H Fairboard; active Boy Scouts Am.; chmn. fund raising equestrian events 10th Pan Am. Games. Recipient Golden Boy award Indpls. Boys Club Alumni Assn., 1970; named Outstanding Show Mgr., Ind. State Fair, 1971. Mem. U.S. C. of C., Ind. Motor Truck Assn., Indpls. Motor Truck Assn., Indpls. C. of C. Clubs: Ind. Pony Exhibitors, Ind. Pony of Am., Ind. Shetland Pony Breeders, Ind. Saddle Horse Assn., Am. Hackney, Am. Horse Show Assn., Masons, Shriners, Moose. Home: 1213 N Mathews Rd Greenwood IN 46143 Office: 2166 Bluff Rd Indianapolis IN 46225

KIRKLAND, ALFRED YOUNGES, judge; b. Elgin, Ill., 1917; s. Alfred and Elizabeth (Younges) K.; m. Gwendolyn E. Muntz, June 14, 1941; children: Pamela E. Kirkland Jensen, Alfred Younges, James Muntz. BA, U. Ill., 1941, JD, 1943. Bar: Ill. 1943. Assoc. Mayer, Meyer, Austrian & Platt, Chgo., 1943; sr. ptnr. Kirkland, Brady, McQueen, Martin & Callahan and predecessor firms, Elgin, 1951-73; spl. asst. atty. gen. State of Ill., 1969-73; judge 16th Cir. Ct. Ill., 1973-74; judge U.S. Dist. Ct. (no. dist.) Ill., 1974-79, sr. judge, 1979—; mem. Council Practicing Lawyers U. Ill. Law Forum, 1969—, mem. adv. bd., 1972-73, adv. council continuing legal edn., 1959-62; chmn. Ill. Def. Research Inst., 1965-66. Outdoor editor: Elgin Daily Courier-News, Kewanee Star-Courier; fishing editor: Midwest Outdoors Mag. Pres. Elgin YMCA, 1963. Served to 2d lt. AUS, 1943-46. Fellow Am. Coll. Trial Lawyers, Am. Bar Found.; mem. ABA (ho. of dels. 1967-70), Ill. State Bar Assn. (pres. 1968-69), Chgo. Bar Assn., Kane County Bar Assn. (pres. 1961-62), Elgin Bar Assn. (pres. 1951-52), Am. Judicature Soc. (bd. dirs. 1967—), Ill. Bar Found. (bd. dirs. 1961-69), Ill. Def. Counsel (bd. dirs. 1966-69), Soc. Trial Lawyers, Legal Club Chgo., Law Club Chgo., Internat. Assn. Ins. Counsel, Fed. Ins. Counsel, Assn. Ins. Counsel, Outdoor Writers Assn. Am. (gen. counsel 1978—), Assn. Gt. Lakes Outdoor Writers (v.p., bd. dirs.), Ill. C. of C. (bd. dirs. 1969-70), Phi Delta Phi, Sigma Nu. Republican. Congregationalist. Clubs: Elgin Country (pres. 1956), Cosmopolitan. Lodges: Elks, Moose. Home: 10N944 Leith Ct Elgin IL 60123

KIRKLAND, DAVID LEE, real estate executive, investment banker; b. Yakima, Wash., Jan. 27, 1947; s. John Turner and Lela Faye (Swopes) K.; m. Ligaya Cunamay Reyes, Mar. 3, 1978; children: Louisa, Larissa. BA, Boston U., 1968; grad., Southwestern Grad. Sch. Banking, 1980. Officer trainee Citicorp, Agana, Guam, 1972-73; v.p. Centerre Bancorp., St. Louis, 1973-81; ptnr. Amshel, Jacksonville, Fla., 1981-83; sr. v.p. Love Cos., St. Louis, 1983—; bd. dirs. Economy Fed. Savs., St. Louis, Love Funding Co., Washington. Bd. pres. Youth in Need, 1979-80; bd. pres. Providence Program, St. Louis, 1985-86; mem. bd. overseers Lindenwood Coll., St. Charles, Mo; bd. dirs. Punta Gorda Isles, 1987—. HUD fellowship, 1971. Office: Love Cos 515 Olive St Saint Louis MO 63101

KIRKLAND, THOMAS RAY, industrial engineer; b. Heidelberg, Fed. Republic Germany, July 26, 1959; s. Marlyn E. and Patricia A. (Thorson) K.; m. Melissa S. Edwards, Oct. 18, 1980; children: Benjamin T., Megan K. AA, Bethel Coll., 1979; cert. indsl. engring. tech., Red Wing (Minn.) Tech. Inst., 1982. Assoc. mfg. engr. Litton Microwave, Plymouth, Minn., 1982-84; indsl. engr. Liberty Diversified Industries, New Hope, Minn., 1984—. Treas. Rockford (Minn.) Alliance Ch., 1983—. Recipient Silver medal, blueprint reading, Vocat.-Indsl. Clubs Am., 1981, Gold medal, 1982. Mem. IIE, Minn. Soc. Indsl. Engrs. (exec. v.p. 1985-86, pres. 1986-87, editor Pro-File newsletter 1983-85). Club: Vocat.-Indsl. of Am. (Red Wing) (pres. 1981-82). Avocations: music, cross-country skiing, computer programming, church youth work.

KIRKMAN, JAMES (JIM) WATSON, mayor; b. Norton, Kans., Dec. 26, 1910; s. Robert Allan and Velma Amy (Castor) K.; m. Edith Mae Burlingame, June 30, 1935; children: James Watson, Michael Elliott. Student, U. Nebr., 1933. Adv. mgr. sports editor North Platte (Nebr.) Telegraph, 1926-66, pub., 1965-75; prof. U. Nebr., LIncoln, 1975-76; exec. dir. Mid-Nebr. Community Found., North Platte, 1980-84. Mayor City of North Platte, 1984—; active North Platte Community Playhouse, Great Plaines Regional Med. Ctr., Nebr., Pvt. Industry Council, State of Nebr., Lincoln County Red Cross Bd., Heart Bd.; community activities, North Platte; appointed to Great Navy of Nebr. by Gov. J. James Exon, 1972, by Gov. Bob Kerry, 1986. Named to Cody Scouts for Community Service to North Platte, 1961, Boss of Yr., North Platte Jaycees, 1971, Master Editor Pubs., Nebr. Press Assn., 1976. Mem. Daily Pubs. Assn. Nebr. (past pres.), Congress of Parents and Tchrs. (hon. life), Outstanding Services to Nebr. Advt. Mgr.'s Assn. (hon. life), North Platte C. of C. Club: Ambassadors of North Platte. Lodges: Elks, Rotary. Avocations: golfing, tennis. Home: 315 S Oak North Platte NE 69101 Office: Office of the Mayor 211 W 3d North Platte NE 69101

KIRKPATRICK, ANNE SAUNDERS, systems analyst; b. Birmingham, Mich., July 4, 1938; d. Stanley Rathbun and Esther (Casteel) Saunders; m. Robert Armstrong Kirkpatrick, Oct. 5, 1963; children: Elizabeth, Martha, Robert, Sarah. Student, Wellesley Coll., 1956-57, Laval U., Quebec City, Can., 1958, U. Ariz., 1958-59; BA in Philosophy, U. Mich., 1961. Systems engr. IBM, Chgo., 1962-64; systems analyst Commonwealth Edison Co., Chgo., 1981—. Treas. Taproot Reps., DuPage County, Ill., 1977-80; pres. Hinsdale (Ill.) Women's Rep. Club, 1978-81. Club: Wellesley of Chgo. (bd. dirs. 1972-73). Home: 524 N Lincoln Hinsdale IL 60521 Office: Commonwealth Edison Co 72 W Adams Room 1122 Chicago IL 60603

KIRKPATRICK, CHARLES BISHOP, computer systems specialist; b. Frankfort, Ind., June 10, 1928; s. Frank Austin and Mary Adeline (Bishop) K.; m. Phyllis Mary LaPour, Apr. 26, 1954; children: Thomas L., Carol S., David C., Donald F. BSME, Purdue U., 1950; MBA, Northwestern U., 1955; Assoc. in Applied Sci. (hon.), Schoolcraft Coll., 1975. Cost acct. fin. staff Ford Motor Co., Dearborn, Mich., 1955-57, fin. analyst internat. staff, 1958-63, supr. warranty sect. internat. staff, 1963-65, systems project mgr. fin. staff, 1966-70, supr. staff systems sect. fin. staff, 1970—. Chmn. troop com. Boy Scouts Am., Birmingham, Mich., 1970-79; treas., trustee Schoolcraft Coll., Livonia, Mich., 1961-64; trustee, editor Bloomfield (Mich.) Village Assn., 1974-77. Served to lt. (j.g.) USN, 1950-53, Korea. Republican. Episcopalian. Club: Birmingham Athletic. Lodge: Masons. Avocations: squash, tennis. Home: 3136 Morningview Terr Birmingham MI 48010 Office: Ford Motor Co PO Box 1899 Room 1165 WHQ Dearborn MI 48121

KIRKPATRICK, ROBERT HUGH, marketing executive; b. Kingston, N.Y., Mar. 3, 1954; s. Oscar Hugh and Ann (Page) K.; m. Debra Cook, Oct. 25, 1986. BA in Polit. Sci. with high honors, SUNY, Oneonta, 1977; M in Pub. and Pvt. Mgmt., Yale U., 1979. Mgr. mktg. Cummins Engine Co., Columbus, Ind., 1980-81, mgr. mktg. ops., 1982-83, dir. electronics mktg., 1984-86; dir. bus. devel. Service Products Co. subs. Cummins Engine Co., Columbus, Ind., 1987—; cons. in field, New Haven, Conn., 1978-79. Trustee SUNY, Albany, N.Y., 1975-76; pres. Columbus Arts Guild, 1981-82; treas. Sans Souci, Inc., Columbus, 1983-85. Club: Yale (Indpls. treas. 1981-85). Home: 3973 N Wood Lake Dr Columbus IN 47201 Office: Cummins Engine Co Box 3005 Columbus IN 47202

KIRKSEY, AVANELLE, nutrition educator; b. Mulberry, Ark., Mar. 23, 1926. BS, U. Ark., Fayetteville, 1947; MS, U. Tenn., Knoxville, 1950; PhD, Pa. State U., 1961; postdoctoral, U. Calif., Davis, 1976. Assoc. prof. Ark. Polytechnic U., Russellville, 1950-55, 1950-55; research asst. Pa. State U., University Park, 1956-58, fellow Gen. Foods, 1958-60; assoc. prof. Purdue U., West Lafayette, Ind., 1961-69, prof. nutrition, 1970-85; disting. prof. Purdue U., West Lafayette, 1985—; prin. investigator nutrition project in rural Egypt. Contbr. articles to profl. jours. Recipient Borden award Am. Home Econs. Assn., 1980. Mem. Am. Inst. Nutrition, N.Y. Acad. Scis., Phi Kappa Phi, Sigma Xi. Home: 400 N River Rd Apt 1708 West Lafayette IN 47906 Office: Purdue U Dept Foods and Nutrition West Lafayette IN 47907

KIRKSEY, ROBERT FREDERICK, air force officer; b. Blytheville, Ark., Feb. 16, 1959; s. Roy Lee and Olive Esther (Wahl) K.; m. Pamela Kay Rector, June 6, 1981; 1 child, Brittany Elizabeth. BA, U. Ark., 1981; MS of Adminstn., Cen. Mich. U., 1986. Commd. USAF, 1981, advanced through grades to capt.; from deputy missile combat crew commander to missile combat crew commander USAF, Minot AFB, N.D., 1982-86, missile procedures trainer operator, 1986—, protocall officer, 1982, security mgr. 91 SMW/DOT, 1986-87, chief DOTM tng., 1987—. Named one of Outstanding Young Men Am., 1985. Mem. Air Force Assn., Arnold Air Soc. (outstanding sr. 1981). Avocations: volleyball, softball, basketball, reading, swimming, hunting. Home: 120-2 Chevy Chase Minot AFB ND 58704 Office: 91 SMW/DOT Bldg 475 Minot AFB ND 58705

KIRSCH, JEFFREY SCOTT, securities executive; b. Chgo., Nov. 11, 1947; s. Norton M. and Estelle (Kaufman) K.; m. Jodi Lynn Spak, May 20, 1985; 1 child, Alexandra J. BBA, Babson Coll., 1970. V.p. Auto Gard Inc., Chgo., 1970—; securities dealer Chgo. Bd. Option Exchange, 1973—, mem. arbitration com., 1978-79, mem. system and facilities com., 1980-81; pres. Kirsch Inc., Chgo., 1981—; mng. ptnr. Fromex, Chgo., 1981—. Bd. dirs. Young Men's Jewish Council, Chgo., 1978. Mem. Automotive Parts and Accessories Assn., Babson Coll. Alumni Com. Club: Standard (Chgo.). Avocations: boating, tennis, polo, racquetball, windsurfing. Home: 442 Wellington Chicago IL 60657 Office: First Option Chgo 440 S LaSalle St Chicago IL 60605

KIRSCHBAUM, LEROY ROBERT, business systems analyst; b. Granite Falls, Minn., Jan. 2, 1948; s. Arnold Robert and Luella Idella (Gatchell) K.; m. Susan Lynn Ankrom, July 8, 1973; children: Krista, Kara, Eric. BA, Union Coll., Lincoln, Nebr., 1970; MA, Andrews U., Berrien Springs, Mich., 1972. Math, sci. tchr. Whispering Pines Sch., Old Westerbury, N.Y., 1972-73; jr. programmer Firestone Tire & Rubber, Akron, Ohio, 1973-75, programmer, 1975-77, analyst, programmer, 1977-79, application analyst programmer, 1979-82, bus. systems analyst, 1982—. Free-lance illustrator, 1978—. Chmn. Mayfair Jr. Acad. Sch. Bd., Uniontown, Ohio, 1985-86; counsellor Pathfinders, Akron, 1986; bd dirs. Akron First Seventh Day Adventist Ch., 1975-84. Home: 861 Griggy Rd Mogadore OH 44260 Office: Firestone Tire & Rubber 1200 Firestone Pkwy Akron OH 44317

KIRSCHENBAUM, STUART EDWARD, podiatrist; b. Bklyn., Jan. 23, 1945; s. Albert Barry and Eleanor K.; B.S., Mich. State U., 1965; D.P.M., N.Y. Coll. Podiatric Medicine, 1970; m. Janice Beardslee, July 27, 1967; children—Jennifer Robin, Storm Tyler. Resident in foot surgery Grand Community Hosp., Detroit, 1970-71; gen. practice podiatry, Detroit, 1970—; founder, pres. Foot Surgeons of Detroit, P.C., 1970—; chief podiatry services, trustee Monsignor Clement Kern Hosp. for Spl. Surgery, 1979-81; nat. lectr. in foot surgery; bd. dirs. Mich. Foot Health Found.; bd. dirs. Detroit Jr. Action Youth Services; mem. adv. bd. Am. Assn. Improvement of Boxing; Profl. and amateur boxing judge Mich. Athletic Commn.; judge World Boxing Assn.; judge U.S. Amateur Boxing Fedn., World Boxing Council, World Athletic Assn., U.S. Boxing Assn., N. Am. Boxing Fed., Internat. Boxing Fedn.; chairperson Mich. Athletic Bd. Control, 1982—; mem. World Congress of Ring Ofcls.; second opinion cons. Blue Cross & Blue Shield Assn., Mich. Blue Cross & Blue Shield, Prudential Ins. Co. am., Aetna Life Ins. Co. Diplomate Am. Bd. Podiatric Surgery, Nat. Bd. Podiatry Examiners. Fellow Royal Soc. Health, Am. Coll. Foot Surgeons, Am. Soc. Podiatric Dermatology, Am. Soc. Hosp. Podiatrists, Am. Soc. Podiatric Medicine; mem. Am. Podiatric Med. Assn., Mich. Podiatric Med. Assn. (ethics com.), Mich. Pub. Health Assn., Am. Pub. Health Assn. (chmn. substance abuse: categorical podiatric health concerns com.), Am. Med. Writers Assn., Am. Coll. Sports Medicine (chmn. boxing com.), Acad. Podiatric Medicine, World Med. Assn., Am. Soc. Podiatric Sports Medicine, Am. Acad. Podiatric Acupuncture, World Boxing Historians Assn., U.S. Amateur Boxers and Coaches Assn., Am. Running and Fitness Assn., Internat. Platform Assn., Internat. Vet. Boxers Assn. (podiatry cons.), Acad. clin. Electrodynography, Am. Physicians Fellowships for Medicine in Israel, Am. Podiatric Med. Writers Assn., Mich. Assn. Profl. Boxing Ofcls. (charter), Assn. Boxing Commns., Author publs. on foot surgery and sports medicine. Home: 27080 Wellington Rd Franklin MI 48025 Office: 8300 Mack Ave Detroit MI 48214 Office: 8319 Grand River Detroit MI 48204

KIRSHBAUM, RONALD MICHAEL, business executive; b. Chgo., Apr. 20, 1938; s. Charles C. and Frances (Walker) K.; m. Adrienne C. Kaufman, Aug. 22, 1965; children—Benjamin, Jonathan, Sarah, Daniel. B.A. cum laude, Northwestern U., 1960; M.S. in Indsl. Mgmt., MIT, 1962. Mktg. research analyst Swift & Co., Chgo., 1962-64; asst. product mgr. Alberto Culver Co., Melrose Park, Ill., 1964-65, product mgr., 1965-67, group product mgr., 1967-69, dir. mktg., 1969-73, gen. mgr. Household/Grocery div., 1973-77, v.p., gen. mgr. Food Service div., 1977-84, v.p., gen. mgr. Food Service and Splty. Products dir., 1984—; bus. cons. Served with U.S. Army, 1962-68. Jewish. Home: 154 Green Bay Rd Highland Park IL 60035 Office: Alberto Culver Co 2525 Armitage Ave Melrose Park IL 60160

KIR-STIMON, WILLIAM, clinical psychologist; b. Chgo., June 5, 1910; s. Morris and Mollie (Hodas Kirk) K.-S.; m. Phyllis Carl, June 30, 1938; children: Joan, Vicki, Lynn; m. Margit Fleischner, Mar. 23, 1973; children: Steve, Karen, Leah, Joshua. PhB, U. Chgo., 1932; MA, Northwestern U., 1939, PhD, 1955. Lic. psychologist, Ill. Mem. faculty Columbia Coll., Chgo., 1942-57, Pestalozzi-Froebel Teaching Coll., Chgo., 1943-48, Ind. U.-Gary, 1956-58, DePaul U., Chgo., 1958-60; pres. William Kir-Stimon, PhD and Assocs. Ltd., Flossmoor, Ill., 1953—; asst. prof. Purdue U.-Hammond, Ind., 1955-57; dir. counseling Services Rehab. Inst. Chgo., 1957-66. Author: Inside the Open Cage, 1984; editor: Psychotherapy and The Memorable Patient, 1986; contbr. book chapts. and articles to profl. jour. Mem. mental health coalition South Suburban Cook County, 1978-85. Mem. Ill. Psychol. Assn., Am. Acad. Psychotherapists, Chgo. Personnel Guidance Assn., Am. Personnel and Guidance Assn., Am. Psychol. Assn., Ill. Rehab. Assn. (bd. dirs. 1965-68), Internat. Soc. Study Time, Ill. Personnel and Guidance Assn., Chgo. Psychology Club., Nat. Rehab. Assn., Midwestern Psychol Assn., Soc. Clin. and Exptl. Hypnosis, Am. Soc. Clin. Hypnosis, Internat. Soc. Hypnosis, N.Y. Acad. Scis., Am. Ednl. Research Assn. Phi Beta Kappa, Phi Delta Kappa. Office: 3235 Vollmer Rd Flossmoor IL 60422 also: 708 Church Evanston IL 60201

KISCADEN, LAURA LINNÉA, psychologist; b. Mpls., Nov. 3, 1950; d. Robert Albert and Eleanor Esther (Hultman) K.; m. Roger Russell Alm, Oct. 14, 1983. BA in Psychology, Moorhead (Minn.) State U., 1972; MS Counseling & Guidance, U. N.D., 1974. Licensed psychologist, Minn. Counselor Cen. Tech. Community Coll., Hastings, Nebr., 1974-76; counselor, dir. career ctr. Anoka-Ramsey Community Coll., Coon Rapids, Minn., 1976-77; counselor Normandale Community Coll., Bloomington, Minn., 1979; career devel. specialist State Dept. Edn., St. Paul, 1978, 80-83, sex equity specialist, 1984—; Cons. in field, 1978—. Dept. edn. del. Minn. Women's Consortium; counselor, speaker Washington COunty Family Violence Network; bd. dirs. Explorer Scouts, St. Paul, 1980-83. N.D. Bd. Higher Edn. scholar, 1973-74; named Outstanding Young Woman of Am., Fuller & Dees, 1976. Mem. Am. Assn. for Career Devel. (regional dir. 1982), NOW (pres. Hastings chpt. 1975-76), St. Paul C. of C. (youth and edn. task force 1981-83). Avocation: music. Office: Minn State Dept Edn 550 Cedar St Saint Paul MN 55101

KISER, BONNIE BEA, educator; b. Fort Wayne, Ind., Feb. 3, 1945; d. Andrew U. and Marian M. (Carr) Smith; m. John T. Kiser, Oct. 5, 1968; 1 son, J. Christopher. B.S., Findlay Coll. (Ohio), 1963; M.S. Ind. U.-Fort Wayne, 1983. Cert. tchr. Calif., Ind. Sci. tchr. Carey Schs. (Ohio), 1967-68; math./sci. tchr. Oklahoma City Schs., 1968-69, Corona-Norco Unified Schs., Corona, Calif., 1969-78; math. tchr. Windsor Schs. (Mo.), 1971-72; math./sci. gifted tchr. East Allen County Schs., Fort Wayne, Ind., 1978—; lectr. in field. Sponsor, Civic Theatre, Fort Wayne. Mem. NEA, Nat. Council Tchrs. Math., Ind. State Tchrs. Assn., East Allen Edn. Assn., Ind. Assn. for Gifted, Phi Delta Kappa. Methodist.

KISH, LESLIE, emeritus educator, research statistician; b. Poprad, Hungary, July 27, 1910; came to U.S., 1926, naturalized, 1936; s. Albert and Serena (Spiegel) Kiss; m. Rhea Helen Kuleske, Mar. 3, 1947; children: Carla Elene, Andrea Stefanie. B.S. in Math cum laude, CCNY, 1939; M.A. in Math. Stats., U. Mich., 1948, Ph.D. in Sociology, 1952. Sect. head U.S. Bur. Census, 1940-41; statistician Dept. Agr., 1941-47; mem. faculty U. Mich., 1951—, prof. sociology, 1960-81, prof. emeritus, 1981—, Henry Russel lectr., 1981; sampling head of the U. Mich. (Survey Research Center), 1951—; program dir., research scientist Inst. Social Research, 1963—, dir. sampling program fgn. statisticians, 1962-81; vis. prof. in statistics London Sch. Econs., 1965, 69, 72-73; cons. World Fertility Survey, UN, WHO. Author: Survey Sampling, 1965; Statistical Design for Research, 1987; contbr. numerous articles to profl. jours., chpts. to books. Served with USAAF, 1942-45. Recipient Distinguished faculty award U. Mich., 1975. Fellow Am. Statis. Assn. (v.p. 1973-75, pres. 1977), Internat. Statis. Inst., Internat. Assn. Survey Statisticians (v.p. 1977-79, pres. 1983-85), Am. Sociol. Assn., Royal Statis. Soc. (hon. fellow), AAAS, Am. Acad. Arts and Scis.; mem. Population Assn. Am., Inter-Am. Statis. Inst., Phi Beta Kappa, Sigma Xi. Home: 702 Sunset Rd Ann Arbor MI 48103 Office: Inst Social Research U Mich Ann Arbor MI 48106

KISHPAUGH, ALLAN RICHARD, mechanical engineer; b. Dover, N.J., Aug. 31, 1937; B.S. in Mech. Engring., N.J. Inst. Tech., 1967; m. Maryann M. Bizub, July 31, 1965. Engring. technician Stapling Machines Co., Rockaway, N.J., 1956-65; design engr. Airoyal Engring. Co., Livingston, N.J., 1965-66; project engr. Simautics Co., Fairfield, N.J., 1966-67; design engr. Pyrofilm Resistor Mfg. Co., Cedar Knolls, N.J., 1967-68; sr. engr., project mgr. Packaging Systems div. Standard Packaging Corp., Clifton, N.J., 1968-77; sr. machine design engr. Travenol Labs., Round Lake, Ill., 1977-79; dir. engring. TEC, Inc., Alsip, Ill., 1979-80; mgmt. cons., machine developer, Palos Heights, Ill., 1980—; owner Ark Internat., 1981—. Councilman, Borough of Victory Gardens (N.J.), 1969-71, council pres., 1971, police commnr., 1970-70, chmn. fin. com., 1970; pres. Pompton River Assn., Wayne, N.J., 1976-77; mem. Wayne Flood Control Commn., 1976-77; past deacon, elder, Sunday sch. tchr. and supt. local Presbyn. chs. Served with Air N.G., 1960-61, 62-65, with USAF, 1961-62. Registered profl. engr., N.J., Ill. Mem. ASME (vice chmn. N.J. sect. 1973-74, numerous other regional offices, food, drug and beverage com. 1983—), Nat. Soc. Profl. Engrs., Midwest Soc. Profl. COns. (bd. dirs. 1986—), Ill. Soc. Profl. Engrs. (chpt. officer 1984—), Chgo. Assn. Commerce and Industry, Midwest Soc. Profl. Cons. (bd. dirs. 1986—). Patentee mechanism for feeding binding wire, wirebound box-making machine, method packaging granular materials, others in field. Address: 6118 W 123d St Palos Heights IL 60463

KISOR, HENRY DU BOIS, editor, critic, columnist; b. Ridgewood, N.J., Aug. 17, 1940; s. Manown and Judith (Du Bois) K.; m. Deborah L. Abbott, June 24, 1967; children: Colin, Conan. B.A., Trinity Coll., 1962; M.S. in Journalism, Northwestern U., 1964. Copy editor Wilmington News-Jour. (Del.), 1964-65; copy editor Chgo. Daily News, 1965-73, book editor, 1973-78; book editor Chgo. Sun-Times, 1978—; adj. prof. Medill Sch. Journalism Northwestern U., Evanston, Ill., 1979-82. Bd. dirs. Chgo. Hearing Soc., 1975-76. Nat. Endowment for Humanities seminar fellow, 1978; recipient Pulitzer prize nomination in criticism Columbia U., 1981; Stick-o-Type award Chgo. Newspaper Guild, 1981, 85; Outstanding Achievement award Ill. UPI, 1983, 85; 1st place, columns div. Ill. AP, 1985. Mem. Nat. Book Critics Circle. Office: Chicago Sun-Times 401 N Wabash Ave Chicago IL 60611

KISPERT, DONALD EUGENE, engineering executive; b. Clinton, Ind., Sept. 1, 1928; s. Ortie Curtis and Euphemia (Broatch) K.; B.S. in Civil Engring., Ind. Inst. Tech., 1951; m. Nancy Marie Berghoff, Aug. 27, 1950; children—Robert Calvin, Donna Jean, Linda Sue. Field project engr. E.I. DuPont Co., Ind., Ga., N.J., 1951-54, 55-56; constrn. supr. Socony Mobil Oil Co., New Goshen, Ind., 1954-55; field supt. Fruin-Colnon Constrn. Co., Indpls., 1956-59; design engr. Clyde Williams & Assoc., Indpls., 1956-59, E.R. Hamilton & Assos., 1959-60; bldg. and maintenance mgr. R.R. Donnelley & Sons Co., Warsaw, Ind., 1960-70, group mgr. engring., 1970-78, 84—, quality and services group mgr., 1978-82, materials group mgr., 1982-84. Bd. dirs. Warsaw YMCA, 1965-72. Served with U.S. Army, 1946-48. Licensed profl. engr., Ind. Mem. Nat., Ind. socs. profl. engrs. Republican. Presbyterian. Clubs: Optimists, Masons. Home: 1933 E Clark St Warsaw IN 46580 Office: RTE 30 W Warsaw IN 46580

KISS, JANOS, music educator, composer, condr.; b. Hungary, Mar. 21, 1920; s. Andras and Maria (Laszlo) K.; came to U.S., 1956, naturalized, 1973; teaching diploma Bela Bartok Conservatory of Music, Budapest, 1954; conducting diploma People's Ednl. Inst., Budapest, 1956; Franz Liszt Acad. Music, Budapest, 1954-56; student music edn. sci. Western Res. U., 1960-64; m. Josephine Anna Recse, July 27, 1963. Tchr. brasses Cleve. Music Sch. Settlement, 1964-79; chmn. music dept. St. Luke Sch., Lakewood, Ohio, 1966-70; dir. orch., composer in residence, tchr. instruments Western Res. Acad., Hudson, Ohio, 1967-72; tchr., composer in residence St. Edward High Sch., Lakewood, Ohio, 1968-74; composer in residence Luth. High Sch., Rocky River, Ohio, 1973-76; chmn. music dept. Holy Family Sch., Parma, Ohio, 1974-82, St. Ann's Sch., Cleveland Heights, 1974-75; co-founder, condr., music dir. West Suburban Philharmonic Orch., 1969—; hon. mem. Zoltan Kodaly Acad. and Inst., Chgo. Mem. Am. Soc. Univ. Composers, Nat. Assn. Composers U.S.A., Music Tchrs. Nat. Assn., Ohio Music Tchrs. Assn., Cleve. Fedn. Musicians, Am. Music Center, ASCAP, Bela Bartok Soc. Am. Composer: Black Rose of the Alamo, 1964; Spring-At-Last!, 1970; String Bass Concerto, 1970; Flute Concerto, 1970; Concerto for Trombone, 1971; On the Wing, for flute and guitar, 1972; Josepha, quintet for alto recorder with violin, viola, cello and harp, 1973; Concerto for B-Flat Clarinet, with orch., 1974; Celebration and Challenge, for wind ensemble with electronics, 1974; Western Legend, rhapsody for harp and orch., 1975; Twilight Mist, for string quartet and organ, 1975; Impression, for trumpet and piano, 1975; Adagio for Viola, with two violins, cello and harp, 1975; Silent Presence, tone poem for clarinet, viola and organ, 1975; winter's Sonnet, flute-harp-organ, 1975; Ballet for Harps, 1975; Concerto for violoncello and orch., 1976; Lexington '76, Bicentennial Rhapsody for Orch., 1976; Divertimento, solo violin, solo viola, solo string bass, harp and chamber ensemble, 1977; Episode for oboe, french horn, bassoon and harp, 1977; In Homage for harp ensemble, 1977; Suite in Stilo Antico for orch. with harpsichord, 1977; Salute-in Retrospect, cimbalom solo with orch., 1977; Chorale Prelude, organ, 1977; Via Lactea (The Galaxy), symphonic fantasy, 1978; Rhapsody for Cimbalom and Orch., 1978; Dance of Colors on the Black Hills of South Dakota, for harp ensemble, 1978; Sinfonia Atlantis, for orch., 1979; Canzone da Sacra for string quartet, 1979; Let Me Be Near for voice and orch., 1980; Las Vegas (The Meadows), cimbalom solo with orch., 1980; Ave Maria for voice and organ, 1980; Benedictus Dominus for orch. and mixed voices, 1981; Mount of Atlantis clarinet solo with synthesizer and orch., 1981; Agnus Dei for orch. and mixed voices and organ, 1981, mixed voices and harp, 1982, trumpet solo, 1984, In the Forests of Atlantis, 1983, In Memory of Frances Villon, 1984, Sequoia Five, 1984, Messengers from Atlantis for cello and harp, 1984, Here I Stand for mixed voices and orch., 1984, Josepha flute and Harp with string ensemble, 1986, XVII Century Songs of Hungary for bassoon quartet, 1986, Invocation for solo violin and chamber orch. with harp, 1987.

KISSEL, WESLEY ALLEN, mental health facility administrator, psychiatrist; b. San Diego, Nov. 29, 1927; s. Norman Alfred Kissel and Ethel W. (Trim) Volz; m. Mary Elizabeth Wendelboe, July 3, 1954; children: Steven, Virginia, Margaret, Carolyn. AB in Psychology, Stanford U., 1949, MD, 1954. Diplomate Am. Bd. Psychiatry and Neurology. Intern Rochester (N.Y.) Meml. Hosp., 1953-55; resident in psychiatry Ind. U. Med. Ctr., Indpls., 1957-60; clin. dir. psychiatry Marion County Gen. Hosp., Indpls., 1960-65; practice medicine specializing in psychiatry Indpls., 1961-85; staff psychiatrist South Cen. Community Mental Health Ctrs., Inc., Bloomington, Ind., 1985, med. dir., 1986—; chmn. psychiatry Marion County Gen. Hosp., 1960-66; from instr. to asst. prof. psychiatry Ind. U., 1960—. Mem. Ind. State Correction Bd., Indpls., 1978—. Served to capt. M.C., USAF, 1955-57. Fellow Am. Psychiat. Assn., Ind. Psychiat. Soc. (pres. 1972-73); mem. AMA, Ind. State Med. Assn., Owen-Monroe County Med. Soc. Republican. Methodist. Avocations: contract bridge, swimming, piano, organ. Office: South Cen Community Mental Health Ctrs Inc 645 S Rogers St Bloomington IN 47401

KISSICK, LUTHER CLEVELAND, JR., retired air force officer, freelance writer; b. Mount Hope, Kans., Feb. 21, 1919; s. Luther Cleveland and Irma LouAnna (Fisher) K.; m. Phyllis Anne Traver, Nov. 13, 1946. Student, Kans. State U., 1941; BA in Polit. Sci., Syracuse U., 1957; MA in Internat. Relations, USAF Inst., 1958. Enlisted USAF, 1941; commd. 2d. lt. AUS, 1942; advanced through grades to col. USAF, 1963; air combat intellegence officer 23d Fighter Group 14th Air Force, Republic of China, 1942-45; chief J-2 policy Hdqrs. Far East Command/UN Command, Tokyo, 1954-57; comdr. Def. Liasion Ministry of Nat. Def., London, 1963-66; ret. USAF, 1969; commodity specialist Goodbody & Co., Tampa, Fla., 1969-70; internat. mktg. profl. Fla. Citrus, Tampa, 1971-72; account exec. B.C. Christopher, Hutchinson, Kans., 1973-76; freelance writer, cons. Mount Hope, 1977—. Author: Guerrilla One, 1982. Organizer U.S. wheat mktg. program to China Wheat Growers Assn., Hutchinson and Mt. Hope, 1976-80. Decorated Bronze Star (2), Purple Heart, Legion of Merit (2), Air Medal, Chinese Wings. Mem. Flying Tigers, Ret. Officers Assn., RAF Club. Lodge: Masons. Avocations: fishing, hunting, golfing, gardening, farming. Home and Office: Rural Rt 1 Box 54 Mount Hope KS 67108

KIST, NICOLAAS CHRISTIAAN, consulting engineer; b. S.I., N.Y., Aug. 8, 1928; s. Herman Jacob and Ernestine Clara (Nickenig) K.; m. Nancy Prichard Jones, Apr. 24, 1954; children—Cornelia Helena, Johanna Claire, Susanna Maria. M.S. in Civil Engring., Technische Hogesch., Delft, Netherlands, 1953. Registered profl. engr., Ill. Jr. and field engr. Chgo. Bridge and Iron, Chgo., 1957-59, project mgr., Italy, 1959-60, constrn./sales/engring. service mgr., Netherlands, 1960-67, internat. engr. standards coordinator, Oak Brook, Ill., 1967-68, asst. dir. corp. nuclear quality assurance, 1968-72; pres. N.C. Kist & Assocs., Inc., Naperville, Ill., 1972—; speaker, cons. in quality assurance/quality improvement; internat. speaker quality auditing. Served to lt. (j.g.) USN, 1953-57. Mem. Am. Soc. Quality Control (regional councilor 1981-85), Am. Arbitration Soc. (arbitrator 1979), ASME, ASCE, Royal Soc. Engrs. (Netherlands). Republican. Methodist. Avocations: backpacking, art history, travel, observing nature. Home: 900 E Porter Ave Naperville IL 60540 Office: N C Kist & Assocs Inc 127-A S Washington Naperville IL 60540

KISTLER, CHARLES JAMES, JR., osteopathic physician and surgeon; b. Warren, Ohio, Dec. 17, 1944; divorced; 1 child, Brittany Lee. BS in Microbiology, Ohio State U., 1967; DO, Coll. Osteopathic Medicine and Surgery, Des Moines, 1971. Intern Osteo. Gen. Hosp., North Miami Beach, Fla., 1971-72; pvt. practice med. Kistler & Paolucci, North Miami Beach and Ft. Lauderdale, Fla., 1972-79; emergency room physician M.E.F., Inc., Marysville, Ohio, 1979-80; sr. staff physician Town St. Med. Ctr., Columbus, Ohio, 1980—; emergency room physician Community Hosp. South Broward, Hallendale, Fla., 1972-79; med. dir. Columbus Ctr. for Human Services, 1982—; utilization review officer Manor Care, Westerville, Ohio, 1980—. Named Boss of Yr. Ohio Osteo. Assts. Assn., 1983. Mem. Ohio Osteo. Assn., Am. Osteo. Assn., Am. Coll. Osteo. Medicine, Gen. Family Medicine and Surgery, Columbus Acad. Osteo. Medicine. Roman Catholic. Avocations: sprint car, formula one and sports car racing, auto bldg., skiing, bicycling, sports. Office: Town St Med Ctr 867 W Town St Columbus OH 43222

KISTLER, THOMAS CARL, computer information systems specialist; b. Garrett, Ind., Aug. 24, 1947; s. Kenneth Otto and Dorothy Pearl (Boner) K.; m. Pamela Kay Lockwood, June 21, 1969; children: Sarah Marie, Emily Suzanne. BS, Ball State U., 1972, postgrad., 1981-84. Asst. mgr. Val Corp., New Castle, Ind., 1973-75; cen. sta. mgr. Winchester Alarm Co., Muncie, Ind., 1976-81, data processing mgr., 1981-84; analyst Dana Corp., Hagerstown, Ind., 1984—; pres. Kistler & Assocs., Muncie, 1985—. Co-chmn. supervisory com. Munseetown Credit Union, 1982-84. Served with U.S. Army, 1966-68, ETO. Mem. Nat. Rifle Assn., Nat. Audubon Soc. Methodist. Club: Commonwealth of Calif. Lodge: Masons. Avocations: photography, target shooting, travel. Home: 2809 Pleasant Dr Muncie IN 47302-8914 Office: Dana Corp PO Box 500 Hagerstown IN 47346

KITCH, LINDA MARIE, accountant; b. Flint, Mich., Aug. 19, 1961; d. Daniel Lee and Carole Ann (Haynes) Pulliam; m. Steven Curtis Kitch, Nov. 26, 1983. BS, Ind. State U., 1983. CPA, Ind. Supr. Coopers & Lybrand, Indpls., 1983—. Named one of Outstanding Young Women Am., 1983. Mem. Am. Inst. CPA's, Ind. CPA Soc., Indpls. Jaycees (treas. 1987—). Republican. Lutheran. Office: Coopers & Lybrand 2900 One American Sq Indianapolis IN 46282

KITCHENS, JAY BARTLEY, financial planner; b. Coshocton, Ohio, Jan. 16, 1950; s. James Edgar and Nina (Jane) K.; m. Marjorie A. Moody, Sept. 15, 1972; 1 child, Andrew J.; m. Patricia A. Spencer, Feb. 16, 1978; children: Alicia R., Sabrina D. BBA, Ohio U., 1972. Asst. state mgr. Kemper Group, Marietta, Ohio, 1972-81; fin. planner Century Fin. Services of NE Ohio, New Philadelphia, Ohio, 1982—; speaker in field. Contbr. articles to profl. jours. Mem. council Emanual Luth. Ch., New Philadelphia, 1985—. Named one of Outstanding Young Men. in Am., 1976. Mem. Internat. Assn. Fin. Planners, Nat. Assn. Life Underwriters, Tuscarawas Life Underwriters Assn. (v.p. 1987), Tuscarawas County C. of C. Lodge: Lions (bd. dirs. local club 1987—). Home: 516 Lockport Ave SW New Philadelphia OH 44663 Office: Century Fin Services NE Ohio Rt 2 Box 2085 New Philadelphia OH 44663

KITLAS, RONALD ALLAN, food industry executive; b. Detroit, Oct. 18, 1953; m. Marie T. Sperber, Oct. 16, 1982. AB magna cum laude, U. Detroit, 1975; JD, Detroit Coll. Law, 1980. Bar: Mich. 1980. Adminstrv. asst. U.S. Ho. of Reps., Ann Arbor, Mich., 1975-76; govt. relations atty. Kellogg Co., Battle Creek, Mich., 1981-82, mgr. corp. services, 1982-83, dir. indsl. relations, 1983-84, dir. personnel services, 1984—. State coordinator Unemployment Compensation Alert Network, Mich., 1982; bd. dirs. Indsl. Mich. com., Lansing, 1982; trustee Workers Compensation Funds, Lansing, 1984-86; commr. Mich. Employment Security Commn., Detroit, 1986—; vice-chmn. Calhoun County ARC, Battle Creek, 1980—. Mem. Mich. Bar Assn. Republican. Roman Catholic. Club: Athelstan. Avocations: photography, piano. Home: 2405 W Gull Lake Dr Richland MI 49083 Office: Kellogg Co One Kellogg Square Battle Creek MI 49016

KITSCHA, HECTOR, manufacturing executive; b. Laredo, Tex., Apr. 8, 1930; s. Emilio and Gloria (Martinez) K.; m. Marcia Schneider, July 22, 1950; children: Glory Kitscha Fentz, David, Joy Kitscha Rogala, John. BSEE, Milw. Sch. Engring., 1952. Registered profl. engr., Wis. Devel. supr. Cutler-Hammer Inc., Milw., 1959-67, dir. mfg. devel., 1967-69, dir. devel., 1969-74; v.p. power control Eaton Corp., Milw., 1974-79, v.p. indsl. control and power distbn.-worldwide, 1979—; corp. bd. mem. Milw. Sch. Engring., 1977—. Contbr. numerous articles to profl. jours.; patentee motor control design. Pres. Safari Club Conservation Fund, Tucson, 1981-82. Named an Outstanding Alumnus, Milw. Sch. Engring., 1978. Mem. Am. Mgmt. Assn., Nat. Elec. Mfrs. Assn., Mgmt. Resource Assn., Engrs. Soc. Milw., Milw. World Trade Assn. Office: Eaton Corp 4201 N 27th St Milwaukee WI 53216

KITSIS, ARLEN THOMAS, confectionary company executive; b. Mankato, Minn., Jan. 16, 1935; s. Louis and Florence (Marcus) K.; m. Tybelle Scherling, June 17, 1956; children—Steven, Mindy, Edward. A.A., U. Minn., 1956. Vice pres. sales Shari Candies, Inc., Mankato, 1956-66, exec. v.p., 1966-76, owner/pres., 1984—; pres. confectionary div. CFS Continental, Chgo., 1976-84. Bus. chair chpt. Am. Cancer Soc., 1975-78; mem. exec. com. City of Hope, 1980-85. Recipient Golter award City of Hope, 1976. Mem. Mankato C. of C. (Minn. Viking Chair 1965-80), Nat. Candy Wholesalers Assn. Trustee, B'nai Emet Synagogue, 1981-83. Republican. Jewish. Club: Golden Valley Country, Oak Ridge Country (Mpls.). Lodges: B'nai B'rith (pres. 1958-80), Shriners. Avocations: golf; music; sports; travel. Home: 6601 Parkwood Rd Edina MN 55436 Office: Shari Candies 5780 Lincoln Dr Edina MN 55436

KITT, WALTER, psychiatrist; b. N.Y.C., Dec. 18, 1925; s. Elias and Mary (Opiela) K.; m. Terry Escorcia, May 15, 1957 (dec. 1974); 1 child, Gregory; m. Sally Anderson Chappell, June 22, 1977. Student, CCNY, 1942-44; AB magna cum laude, Syracuse (N.Y.) U., 1948; MD, Chgo. Med. Sch., 1952. Diplomate Am. Bd. Psychiatry and Neurology. Resident Neuropsychiat. Inst., Chgo., 1953-56; practice medicine specializing in psychiatry Chgo., 1956-64, Munster, Ind., 1963-80; psychiatrist Lakeside VA Med. Ctr., Chgo., 1981-87, acting chief psychiat. services, 1986—; asst. prof. clin. psychiatry U. Ill. Med. Ctr., Chgo., 1958-64, Northwestern U., Chgo., 1974—; chmn. div. psychiatry Our Lady of Mercy Hosp., Dyer, Ind., 1970-72. Served with U.S. Army, 1944-46, PTO. Mem. AMA, Am. Psychiat. Assn., Chgo. Med. Soc., Ill. Med. Soc., Soc. Med. Decison Making. Home: 3750 N Lakeshore Dr Chicago IL 60613 Office: Lakeside VA Med Ctr 333 E Huron St Chicago IL 60611

KITTELSON, JOHN EDWARDS, insurance field underwriter; b. Beresford, S.D. July 19, 1936; s. Helmey and Ella (Grunning) K.; m. Marcia Lea Gunderson, June 28, 1959; children—John Olaf, Susan Marie. B.S. in Math., Augustana Coll., 1961; postgrad. N.W. Mo. State U., 1973; grad. U.S. Air Force Command and Staff Coll., 1969. Registered health underwriter. System simulation designer System Devel. Corp., Santa Monica, Calif., 1961-63; engring. mgr. Raven Industries, Inc., Sioux Falls, S.D., 1963-68, mgr. mktg. and sales, 1969-72; field underwriter N.Y. Life Ins. Co., Sioux Falls, 1973—; admission liaison officer U.S. Air Force Acad., Colorado Springs, 1975—, liaison officer comdr. for S.D., 1981-86; fighter pilot, dir. pub. affairs U.S. Air Force, Calif. Air N.G., S.D. Air N.G., 1955-84; col. USAFR, 1984—, state preparedness liaison officer for S.D., 1986—. Pres. Nordland Fest Assn., Inc., Sioux Falls, 1983; bd. dirs. Nordland Heritage Found., Sioux Falls, 1982-86, Nordland Fest Assn., Inc., Sioux Falls, 1983—, S.D. Children's Home Soc., Sioux Falls, 1981-86; mem. council First Luth. Ch., Sioux Falls, 1978-81, dir. parish edn., 1978-81; mem. S.D. Com. on Employers Support of Guard and Res., Sioux Falls, 1982-85; chmn. U.S. Sen. Pressler's Selection Com. for Mil. Acad. Nominations, Sioux Falls, 1978-82; mem. center com., Bergland Sr. Citizens Ctr., Sioux Falls, 1977—. Fellow Augustana Coll.; mem. Air Force Assn. (v.p. S.D. 1983-84, pres. 1984-86), Res. Officer Assn. (pres. S.D. 1979-80, Reservist of Yr. 1981, nat. councilman 1984—), N.G. Assn. (exec. com. S.D. 1980-82), Estate Planning Council (bd. dirs. 1980-82), Nat. Assn. Life Underwriters (nat. council 1986-87), Sioux Falls Life Underwriters (treas. 1982-83, sec. 1983-84, v.p. 1984-85, pres. elect 1985-86, pres. 1986-87), Sioux Falls Area C. of C. (bd. dirs. 1980-83, chmn. aviation com. 1978-80, chmn. mil. and vets. affairs com. 1983-85). Lodges: Rotary Internat., Optimists Internat. (Disting. lt. gov. 1968; pres. Sioux Falls 1966-67; lt. gov. Dakota-Man.-Minn. 1967-68), Elks. Home: 2012 S Holly Sioux Falls SD 57105 Office: 141 N Main Suite 308 Sioux Falls SD 57102

KITTLE, CHARLES FREDERICK, surgeon; b. Athens, Ohio, Oct. 24, 1921; s. Frederick F. and Ida (Falls) K.; m. Jeane Mignon Groenier, 1945 (div. 1973); children: Candace Mignon, Bradley Dean, Leslie Jeane, Brian David; m. Ann Catherine Bates, 1981. A.B. with honors, Ohio U., Athens, 1942, LLD, 1967; M.D. with honors, U. Chgo., 1945; M.S. in Surgery, U. Kans., 1950. Diplomate Am. Bd. Surgery, Am. Bd. Thoracic Surgery (mem. bd. 1967-75, chmn. 1973-75). Intern U. Chgo. Clinics, 1945-46; resident gen. and thoracic surgery U. Kans. Med. Center, 1948-52; spl. tng. radio-isotopes for med. use Oak Ridge Inst. Nuclear Studies, 1950, cons. med. div., 1950-55; mem. faculty U. Kans. Sch. Medicine, 1950-66; asso. prof. surgery, lectr. history medicine 1959-66; cons. thoracic surgery VA Hosp., Wadsworth, Kans., 1954-57; cons. gen. surgery VA Hosp., 1957-60; attending gen. surgery VA Hosp. Kansas City, Mo., 1954-66, Wichita, Kans., 1955-62; prof. surgery, head sect. thoracic and cardiovascular surgery U. Chgo. Clinics, 1966-72; prof. surgery, dir. thoracic surgery sect. Rush Med. Sch. and Presbyn.-St. Luke's Hosp., 1973—; dir. Rush Cancer Center, 1978-86; attending surgery Cook County Hosp., 1966—, McNeal Hosp., Berwyn, Ill.; cons. Municipal Tb Sanatorium, Chgo., 1968-74, Hines VA Hosp., Maywood, Ill., 1973—; spl. research cardiovascular surgery, control of blood flow. Served as lt. (j.g.) USNR, 1946-48. Clin. fellow Am. Cancer Soc., 1950-52; Markle scholar med. scis., 1953-58. Mem. AAAS, Am. Assn. History Medicine, Am. Assn. Thoracic Surgery, Am. Coll. Cardiology (bd. govs. Kans. 1963-66, Ill. 1968—), Chgo. Surg. Soc. (pres. 1972-73), A.C.S. (bd. govs. 1965-68), Am. Heart Assn. (chmn. program com. cardiovascular surgery 1965-68, exec. com. cardiovascular surgery council 1962-74, chmn. council 1972-74), Am. Physiol. Assn., Central Surg. Soc., Chgo. Med. Soc., Am. Surg. Assn., Internat. Cardiovascular Soc. (sec. 1965-71), Internat. Soc. Surgery, Soc. Med. Hist. (pres. Chgo. 1983-85), N.J. Thoracic Surgery Soc., Ill. Thoracic Surgery Soc. (pres. 1983-84), Soc. Clin. Surgery, Soc. Surg. Oncology, Soc. Vascular Surgery, Soc. Univ. Surgeons (pres. 1966-67), Soc. Thoracic Surgery, Phi Beta Kappa, Sigma Xi, Alpha Omega Alpha. Home: 856 S Laflin Chicago IL 60607 Office: Rush Med Coll 1725 W Harrison St Chicago IL 60612

KITTLESON, MICHAEL OWEN, long term care facility administrator; b. Galesville, Wis., June 8, 1942; s. Victor Lorrain and Eileen Helen (Osgood) K.; m. Vicki Lynn Hestekind-Kittleson, June 17, 1961; children: Kevin Lee, Karmen Michelle, Jason Gordon. BBA, U. Wis., Milw., 1974; MA in Health and Human Services Adminstrn., St. Mary's Coll., Winona, Minn., 1984. Cert. nursing home adminstr.; registered sanitarian. Field supr. Wis. Dept. Agr., Madison, 1964-74; hosp. and nursing home surveyor Wis. Dept. Health and Social Services, Madison, 1974; adminstr. Lincoln Village Convalescent Ctr., Racine, Wis., 1974-76, Lincoln Luth. Home, Racine, 1976-77; adminstr., chief exec. officer Grand View Care Ctr., Blair, Wis., 1977—; mem. adj. faculty U. Wis., Eau Claire, 1977—, mem. health care adminstrn. adv. com., 1977—; preceptor health care adminstrn. U. Wis., Eau Claire, 1977—. Contbr. articles to profl. jours. Mem. Blair Indsl. Corp., 1985—; clk., v.p. Blair Sch. Bd., 1979-85, negotiating team, 1980-85. Mem. Am. Health Care Assn. (Better Life award 1982), Wis. Assn. Nursing Homes (v.p. exec. com. 1980-85, treas. 1986, fin. mgmt. com. 1982—), Nat. Fire Protection Assn., Nursing Home Adminstrs. Examing Bd. (chmn. 1985—, internal audit com. 1986, by-laws com. 1986), Wis. Assn. Nursing Home Service Corp., Wis. Assn. Sch. Bds. (personnel com. 1984-85), Blair C. of C. (bd. dirs. 1985—). Lutheran. Lodge: Lions. Avocations: reading, sports, hunting, fishing, farming. Home: PO Box 202 Blair WI 54616 Office: Grand View Care Ctr Inc PO Box 27 Blair WI 54616

KITTO, JOHN BUCK, JR., mechanical engineer; b. Evanston, Ill., Dec. 22, 1952; s. John Buck and Marie (Comstock) K.; m. Cecilia Higgins, Aug. 17, 1974; children: Christopher Daniel, Andrew Comstock. BSME, Lehigh U., 1975; MBA, U. Akron, 1980. Reg. profl. engr., Ohio, Pa. Sr. engr. Babcock & Wilcox Co., Alliance, Ohio, 1975-80, research engr., 1980-81, program mgr., 1981—. Editor (book) Heat Exchangers for Two, 1983, Two-Phase Heat Exchanger, 1985; patentee in field. Active Trinity Episcopal Ch., Alliance, 1977. Mem. Am. Soc. Mech. Engrs. (chmn. local chpt. 1983-84), Am. Inst. Chem. Engrs., Assn. Energy Engrs., NSPE (Young Engr. of Yr. award 1986), Nat. Fire Protection Assn. Republican. Episcopalian. Avocations: reading, hiking, board games. Home: 1150 7th St NE North Canton OH 44720 Office: Babcock & Wilcox Co Research and Devel Div 1562 Beeson St Alliance OH 44601-2196

KITTOCK, CLAUDIA JEAN, educator; b. Rochester, Minn., May 3, 1952; d. Garth William and Betty Louise (Kline) Evarts; m. Richard Carl Kittock, Dec. 23, 1978; 1 child, Tyler Richard. AA, Rochester (Minn.) Community Coll., 1972; BA, Gustavus Adolphus Coll., 1974; MA, U. Minn., 1977, PhD, 1986. Cert. elem. and secondary tchr., Minn. Vocal dir. Byron (Minn.) H.S., 1974-76, Rockford (Minn.) High Sch., 1977-81; behavior specialist St. Francis (Minn.) High Sch., 1981-85; edn. instr. Gustavus Adolphus Coll., St. Peter, Minn., 1985-86; behavior specialist Forest View Elem. Sch., Forest Lake, Minn., 1986-87; prof. psychology Cambridge Community Coll., Forest Lake, 1987—; cons. Minn. Gifted and Talented Assn., 1983—. Mem. Minn. Music Educators, Minn. Educators of the Emotionally Disturbed, Council of Research in Music Edn., AAUW. Avocations: skiing, swimming, biking. Office: Cambridge Community Coll Hwys 95 and 70 Forest Lake MN 55025

KITTS, JEFFREY BRAD, air force officer; b. Radford, Va., Feb. 14, 1956; s. Myron Bradford and Bessie Jane (Dove) K.; m. Carmen Socorro Torres, May 15, 1982; children: Marty, Christi, Trinity, Justin. BA in Econs., Va. Mil. Inst., 1978. Commd. 2d lt. USAF, 1978, advanced through grades to capt., 1982; dep. missile crew comdr. 66 Strategic Missile Squad, Ellsworth AFB, S.D., 1978-80, missile crew comdr., 1980-82; officer codes control 44 Strategic Missile Wing, Ellsworth AFB, S.D., 1982-84; missile procedures trainer operator 91 strategic missile wing, Minot AFB, N.D., 1984-85, chief missile procedures trainer, 1985-86, instrl. systems mgr., 1986—. Named one of Outstanding Young Men in Am., 1985. Mem. Air Force Assn., Antique Automobile Club Am. Republican. Roman Catholic. Clubs: Marriage Encounter/Resource Couple. Avocations: photography, camping, hiking, woodworking, automobile repair. Home: 113-1 Sirocco Dr Minot Air Force Base ND 58704 Office: 91 SMW D05 Minot AFB ND 58704

KITZ, STEVEN LEONARD, mechanical engineer; b. Chgo., Oct. 20, 1953; s. Leonard John and Beverly Rose (Bailey) K.; m. Betty Jo Lab, Apr. 4, 1981. BS in Mech. Engring., Ill. Inst. tech., 1980. Registered profl. engr. With Johnson & Johnson, Park Forest South, Ill., 1974-76; mech. engr. Goodyear Tire and Rubber Co., Akron, Ohio, 1977—. Patentee in field. Mem. ASME, Robotics Internat./Soc. Mfg. Engrs. (sr.). Club: Sports Car of Am. Avocations: boating, biking, tinkering. Home: 12652 Williamsburg NW Uniontown OH 44685 Office: Goodyear Tire & Rubber Co 1144 E Market St Akron OH 44316

KITZAN, WARREN WALTER, accountant, real estate developer; b. Richardton, N.D., Mar. 2, 1946; s. Walter and DeLores (Kungel) K.; m. Janice Kay Reetz, June 13, 1966; children: Cory, Melanie. BSBA in Acctg., U. N.D., 1967. CPA, N.D. Acct., auditor Haskins & Sells, Portland, Oreg., 1967-69, Hoerner & Kovash, Dickinson, N.D., 1969-70; v.p., cashier and trust officer Liberty Bank, Dickinson, 1970-77; broker assoc. Joe LaDuke Real Estate Investments, Dickinson, 1977; owner Century 21 Investors Realty, Inc., Dickinson, 1978-85; sole practice acctg. Dickinson, 1986—; broker assoc. Century 21 Morrison Realty, Inc., Bismarck, N.D., 1987—. Author, editor Century 21 Policy Procedure & Tng. Manual, 1983. Mem. Am. Inst. CPA's, N.D. Soc. CPA's, Nat. Assn. Realtors, N.D. Assn. Realtors,N.D. Apt. Owners Assn., West River Apt. Owners Assn. (treas. 1985). Lodge: Elks. Home: 629 10th Ave W Dickinson ND 58601 Office: Century 21 Morrison Realty Inc 2917 Stetson Dr Bismarck ND 58501

KIVA, DONALD JOHN, data processing executive; b. Marquette, Mich., Nov. 23, 1939; s. Matthew J. and Mabel L. (Hambly) K.; m. Marjeanne R. Creeger, Aug. 15,1964; children: Jeffrey, Gregg, Scott. BA, Northern Mich. U., Marquette, 1962; MBA, U. Detroit, 1970. Project mgr. Montgomery Ward, Chgo., 1971-82, MGIG, Milw., 1982-83; dir. info. systems No. Ill. Med. Ctr., McHenry, 1983-84; dir. mgmt. info. services Evans Transp. Co., Itasca, Ill., 1984—. Episcopalian. Lodge: Masons. Avocation: tennis. Home: 1400 Mill Creek Dr Buffalo Grove IL 60089 Office: Evans Transp Co 450 E Devon Itasca IL 60143

KIVETT, MARVIN FRANKLIN, anthropologist; b. Nebr., Mar. 10, 1917; s. Thomas and Murl (Mark) K.; m. Caroline Ritchey, Sept. 12, 1941; 1 son, Ronald Lee. AB, U. Nebr., 1942, MA, 1951. Archeologist Smithsonian Inst., 1946-49; mus. dir. Nebr. Hist. Soc., Lincoln, 1949-63, adminstrv. dir., 1963-85; dir. Nebr. State Hist. Found., Lincoln, 1965—. Editor: Nebr. History, 1963-85; contbr. articles to profl. jours. Served with AUS, 1942-46. Home: 5425 Franklin St Lincoln NE 68506 Office: Nebr State Hist Found 100 N 56 NE Suite 415 Lincoln NE 68504

KIVLAND, CYNTHIA MARIE, development consultant, counselor; b. Cleve., Feb. 6, 1953; d. Edward Joseph and Anne (Volchko) Guzi; m. Michael Joseph Kivland, Sept. 14, 1975; children: Kelly Anne, Chelsey Louise, Michael Paul. BS, U. Ill., 1975; MEd, No. Ill. U., 1986. Asst. adminstr. Meadows, Inc., Rolling Meadows, Ill., 1975-78; human resources consultant Person to Person, Inc., Crystal Lake, Ill., 1985—; educator, trainer McHenry County Coll., Crystal Lake, 1985-86; therapist, educator Baum Counseling Service, Elgin, Ill., 1985-86; parent-family communication specialist various schs., orgns., No. Ill.; internat. cons. Author several manuals on stress, weight and family counseling, 1985—. Mem. Mental Health Resource League (bd. dirs. 1986—), Bus. and Profl. Womens' Club, Nat. Assn. Social Work, Am. Assn. Counseling and Guidance, Phi Kappa Phi, Kappa Delta Phi. Avocations: spending time with children, gardening, walking, swimming, sightseeing. Home and Office: 6704 Concord Trail Crystal Lake IL 60014

KIZER, BERT L., management consultant; b. Montpelier, Ohio, Oct. 27, 1930; s. Weldon William and Nina Dell (Oberlander) K.; m. Patricia Jean Minard, Apr. 10, 1971; 1 son, Geoffrey Minard. B.S. in Bus. Adminstrn., Miami U., Ohio, 1952. With sales and mktg. depts. Mead Corp., Dayton, Ohio, 1956-65; mgr. paperboard ops. Scholle Container Corp., Northlake, Ill., 1965-66; owner, pres. Bert L. Kizer & Assocs., Inc., Hinsdale, Ill., 1966—. Mem. Hinsdale Village Caucus, 1977-80. Served to lt. (j.g.), U.S. Navy, 1952-55. Mem. TAPPI. Republican. Presbyterian. Clubs: Edgewood Valley Country (LaGrange, Ill.), Woods Swim and Tennis (Burr Ridge). Home: 1148 Laurie Ln Burr Ridge IL 60521 Office: 930 York Rd Suite 202 Hinsdale IL 60521

KIZILOS, APOSTOLOS P., electronics company executive; b. Athens, Greece, May 10, 1935; s. Peter and Marina (Laskos) K.; m. Betty Mae Ahola, June 7, 1958; children: Peter, Paul, Mark. BS in Mech. Engring., MIT, 1957, MS, 1958; MFA, U. Iowa, 1971. Prin. research engr. Honeywell, Inc., Mpls., 1961-70; ombudsmen systems and research ctr. Honeywell, Inc., Mpls., 1971-76, human resources devel. mgr., 1976-80, human resource devel. cons., 1981-83, dir. orgnl. devel., 1983—; lectr. U. Minn., Mpls., 1979. Author: Dwarf's Legacy, 1976; contbr. book revs. Mpls. Sunday Tribune, 1969-75; patentee in field. interviewer Bush Found., Mpls., 1982—. Bush Found. fellow, 1970. Dem. Farm Labor. Greek Orthodox. Home: 2841 Mayfield Rd Wayzata MN 55391 Office: Honeywell Systems and Research Ctr 3660 Technology Dr Minneapolis MN 55418

KIZMAN, SUSAN LEE, food company executive; b. Chgo., Apr. 27, 1947; d. William Fred and Vivian Ann (Brandenburg) Herod; m. Joseph J. Kizman, Jr., Dec. 28, 1968 (div. July 1973); children—Michael, Wendy. Student Wright Coll., 1965-66, Triton Coll., 1980, 82, Roosevelt U., 1983-86. Coordinator exec. edn. IBM Corp., Chgo., 1968-69; sec., v.p. mktg. Bresler's 33 Flavors, Inc., Chgo., 1973-75, adminstrv. asst., 1975-77, dir. adminstrv. services, 1977-85, v.p., 1979-85; exec. v.p. Mama Tish's Enterprises, Ltd., 1985—. Mem. Women in Mgmt., Nat. Assn. Female Execs., Roundtable for Women in Food Service. Lutheran. Home: 8507 W Gregory St Chicago IL 60656 Office: 5245 N Rose St Rosemont IL 60018

KIZZIER, DONNA LORRAINE, educator; b. Beatrice, Nebr., Jan. 16, 1951; d. Willard Henry and Emma (Johnson) McAlister; m. Roy James Kizzier, Dec. 19, 1971; children—Nicole, Ryan. B.S., U. Nebr., 1972, M.E., 1978, Ed.D., 1985. Bus. instr. Hildreth (Nebr.) Pub. Schs., 1973-75; bus. tchr., vocat. coordinator Lexington (Nebr.) Sr. High Sch., 1973-75; instr. bus. Kearney (Nebr.) State Coll., 1975-81, prof. bus., 1982—, asst. provost, 1985-87; prof. edn. U. Nebr., Lincoln, 1987—; adminstrv. intern Lincoln (Nebr.) Pub. Schs. and Nebr. Dept. Edn., summer 1981; cons. Bd. dirs. Kearney Campfire Assn., 1982—; tchr. Sunday sch. Methodist Ch., 1976-78. Recipient Dean's Council Research award Kearney State Coll., 1983. Mem. Women in Mgmt. Assn. Central Nebr. (pres. 1980), Nat. Bus. Edn. Assn., Nebr. Bus. Edn. Assn. (conf. dir. 1983), Am. Vocat. Assn., Nebr. Vocat. Assn., Soc. Data Educators, Nat. Assn. Tchr. Educators, Delta Pi Epsilon (state pres. 1982, nat. council rep. 1983—, nat. rep. 1983—, nat. award 1987), Phi Delta Kappa. Club: Shrine Aux. Home: 2010 W 35th St Kearney NE 68847 Office: U Nebr 529A Nebraska Hall Lincoln NE 68588-6515

KJESBO, ADRIAN DAVIS, engineer; b. Eau Claire, Wis., June 1, 1949; s. Royal Winston and Ivadell Ione (Ruff) K.; m. Vickie Joyce Solberg, June 14, 1969; children: Carrie Ann, Megan Marie. Student, U. Wis., Eau Claire, 1968-69, U. Philippines, Clark AFB, 1970; BS in Indsl. Tech., U. Wis., Menomonee, 1974; postgrad., Mankato State U., 1974-76. Engr. Geo. A. Hormel & Co., Austin, Minn., 1974-76, Fremont, Nebr., 1976-77; engr. Litton Microwave Cooking Products, Sioux Falls, S.D., 1977-80, engring. mgr., 1980—. Treas. Brandon (S.D.) Bapt. Ch., 1978; chmn. Park and Recreation Bd., Brandon, 1980. Served as sgt. USAF, 1968-72. Democrat. Club: Investment Oppportunities (local treas. 1980-82). Avocations: investing, automobiles. Home: 109 S Yellowstone Dr Brandon SD 57005 Office: Litton Microwave Cooking Products 600 E 54th St N Sioux Falls SD 57105

KLABACHA, MARTIN EDMUND, plastic and reconstructive surgeon; b. Chgo., Dec. 3, 1951; s. Thaddeus Martin and Stella Carolyn (Jurkowski) K.; m. Peggy Ann Pryor, Oct. 4, 1976; children: Kristen, Thaddeus, Jonathon. BS, U. Notre Dame, 1973; MD, Loyola U., 1976. Diplomate Am. Bd. Otolaryngology, Am. Bd. Plastic Surgery. Plastic and reconstructive surgeon Lakeland Med. Assocs., Woodruff, Wis., 1985—. Author five publs. Recipient Pierce award Chgo. Laryngologic Orgn., 1980. Mem. AMA, Am. Acad. Head and Neck Surgery. Avocation: golf. Home: 9321 Timberline Dr Minocqua WI 54548 Office: 222 Maple St Woodruff WI 54568

KLAEREN, ALVIN PAUL, architect; b. Elmhurst, Ill., Aug. 28, 1928; s. John Lawrence and Elfriede Wilhemina (Gerhardt) K.; m. Carla Eileen Fladung, June 14, 1969; 1 child, Christopher. BS in Archtl. Engring., Chgo. Tech. Coll., 1951; postgrad., Ill. Inst. of Tech., 1956-57. Registered architect, Ill.; cert. Nat. Council Archtl. Registration Bds., 1977. Draftsman W. Scott Armstrong, Chgo., 1953-54, George Fred Keck & William Keck, Chgo., 1955-59, Charles Stade, Park Ridge, Ill., 1959-61, Olin & Kosover, Chgo., 1961-64, Nerad & Carlsen, Clarendon Hills, Ill., 1964-66, 68-74; project architect Fugard Orth & Assoc., Hinsdale, Ill., 1966-68, 76-82, Fields, Goldman & Magee, Oak Brook, Ill., 1974-76, Donohue Hetherington & Assoc., Itasca, Ill., 1982—. Served with U.S. Army, 1951-53. Mem. AIA (corp.), Am. Water Ski Assn. (participant tournaments 1958-87), Ill. Water Ski Fedn. (pres. 1963-65). Played semi-profl. football for Elmhurst (Ill.) Travelers, 1947-50, 1953-60. Home: 747 Spring Rd Elmhurst IL 60126 Office: Donohue Hetherington & Assoc 250 E Devon Ave Suite 150 Itasca IL 60143

KLAM, ROGER NAJEEB, obstetrician; b. Indpls., Mar. 29, 1943; s. Najeeb Klam; m. Gayle Guenther, Dec. 8, 1965; children: Sherry, Christina, Yvonne. MD, Tulane Med. Sch., 1967. Intern Thoas D. Dee Hosp., Ogden, Utah, 1967-68; resident in ob-gyn So. Bapt. Hosp., New Orleans, 1968-71; staff ob-gyn dept. Carbondale (Ill.) Clinic, 1973—; clinical assoc. prof. So. Ill. U.; bd. dirs. Ill. Caucus in Teenage Pregnancy. Pres. YMCA, Carbondale, 1982-83; bd. dirs. United Way, Carbondale, 1980-86. Served with U.S. Army, 1971-72. Fellow Am. Coll. Ob-Gyn; mem. Am. Med. Soc., Ill. Med. Soc. (del.), Ill. Gynecology Soc., Am. Soc. for Laser Medicine and Surgery, Inc., Perinatal Assn. Ill. (pres. 1984-85), Jackson County Med. Soc. (pres. 1976-77), Ill. Assn. Child and Maternal Health (pres. 1983-84). Aovcations: horseback riding, golf, flying. Home: 36 Pinewood Carbondale IL 62901 Office: Carbondale Clinic 2601 W Main Carbondale IL 62901

KLAMERUS, KAREN JEAN, pharmacist, educator; b. Chgo., Aug. 10, 1957; d. Robert Edward and Jane Mary (Nawoj) K.; m. Frederick P. Zeller. BS in Pharmacy, U. Ill., 1980; PharmD, U. Ky., 1981. Registered pharmacist Ky., Ill. Staff pharmacist Haggin Meml. Hosp., Harrodsburg, Ky., 1980-81, Regional Med. Ctr., Madisonville, Ky., 1982; critical care liasion, 1982; clin. pharmacist resident U. Nebr., Omaha, 1983; clin. pharmacist cardiothoracic surgery U. Ill., Chgo., 1983—, clin asst. prof. dept. pharmacy practice, 1983-86, asst. prof., 1986—, departmental affiliate dept. pharmaceutics, 1986—; cons. Dimensional Mktg. Inst., Chgo., 1983—, Channing, Weinbergs' Co., Inc., N.Y.C., 1983—. Mem. rev. bd. Am. Jour. Hosp. Pharmacy, Clin. Pharmacy, Drug Intelligence and Clin. Pharmacy. Mem. Heart Assn. DuPage County (bd. dirs.), Am. Assn. Colls. Pharmacy, Am. Coll. Clin. Pharmacy, Am. Heart Assn., Am. Soc. Hosp. Pharmacists, No. Ill. Soc.

Hosp. Pharmacists, Rho Chi. Avocations: computers, sports, gardening, sewing. Office: U Ill Chgo 833 S Wood St Room 244 Chicago IL 60612

KLANCER, RICHARD GEORGE, savings and loan executive; b. Sheboygan, Wis., Feb. 8, 1937; s. Victor Joseph and Frances (Cigalle) K. BA, U. Wis., Oshkosh, 1964; postgrad., Northwestern U., 1969-70. Promotions mgr. Rotary Internat., Evanston, Ill., 1965-68; v.p. Gt. Am. Fed. Savs., Oak Park, Ill., 1968—; bd. dirs. Gt. Oaks Mortgage Corp., Oak Park. Served with USN, 1957-60. Mem. Am. Soc. Personnel Adminstrs., Fin. Insts. Mktg. Assn., U.S. League Savs. and Loans (nat. personnel com. 1982, 83), Oak Park/River Forest C. of C. (bd. dirs. 1983—). Avocations: bridge, travel, gardening, computers. Office: Gt Am Fed Savs 1001 Lake St Oak Park IL 60301

KLANDERMAN, JOEL DEAN, securities broker; b. Waukesha, Wis., Oct. 27, 1947; s. Walter Dean and Wanda Henrietta (Stelsel) K.; m. Karla Gene Kwitek Hofferber, Nov. 6, 1971 (div. Jan. 1983); 1 child, Krista Lynn; m. Marysue Crouch, June 22, 1985. Student, St. Paul Bible Coll., 1966-68. Salesman Les Stumpf Ford, Appleton, Wis., 1974-76; dist. sales mgr. Johnson Pub., Loveland, Colo., 1976-77; gen. sales mgr. Sta. WHBY-WAPL Radio, Appleton, 1978-82, Blocher Outdoor Adv., Appleton, 1982; gen. mgr. Sta. WFCL Radio, Clintonville, Wis., 1983; registered rep., resident mgr. B.C. Ziegler & Co., Inc., Fond du Lac, Wis., 1984—. Advisor Sea Scouts Boy Scouts Am., Appleton, 1978-79, Boy Scouts Am., Appleton, 1980-81; mem. Festival of Light Com., Appleton, 1981-82; chmn. Fox Cities Coalition to Prevent Shoplifting, 1981-82; adv. bd. DECA Appleton Pub. Sch., 1982; capt. profl. div. United Way Fund Dr., 1987—; elder 1st Presbyterian Ch., discipleship com., profl. div. chmn. United Way drive, 1987. Recipient Eagle Scout award also 2 Palm awards, 1962. Mem. Appleton Downtown Retail Assn., Kaukauna Bus. Assn., Little Chute Bus. Assn., Menasha Bus. Assn., Neenah Bus. Assn., Northside Bus. Assn., W. Coll. Ave. Retail Assn., Fox Cities C. of C. (chmn. crime control com. 1982, ambassador 1981-82). Ordained elder 1st Presbyn. Ch. Lodge: Rotary. Avocations: reading, swimming, golfing, fishing, traveling. Home: 208 Morningside Dr Fond du Lac WI 54935 Office: BC Ziegler & Co 24 E 1st St Fond du Lac WI 54935

KLAPPER, NORMAN DANIEL, information systems executive; b. West Palm Beach, Fla., July 11, 1956; s. Max and Sophia (Brodsky) K.; m. Kristin Lee Johannessen, May 10, 1980; children: Sarah Elizabeth, Aaron Daniel. BS, Ind. U., 1979. CPA, Ind.; cert. data processor, Ind. Staff acct. Carter, Kirlin & Merrill, P.C., Indpls., 1979-80; acctg. analyst Western Electric Co., Inc., Indpls., 1980-81; systems analyst Standard Oil Co., Lebanon, Ind., 1981-84; product mgr. Image Bus. Systems, Carmel, Ind., 1984-85; dir. mgmt. info. systems Girardot, Strauch & Cox, P.C., Lafayette, Ind., 1985—. Mem. Am. Inst. CPA's, Ind. Soc. CPA's, Data Processing Mgmt. Assn., EDP Auditors Assn. Jewish. Club: Lafayette Country (com. chmn. 1987). Avocations: tennis, golf, flying. Home: 2104 Edgewood Dr West Lafayette IN 47906 Office: Girardot Strauch & Cox PC 316 Main St Lafayette IN 47901

KLARE, GEORGE ROGER, psychology educator; b. Mpls., Apr. 17, 1922; s. George C. and Lee (Launer) K.; m. Julia Marie Price Matson, Dec. 24, 1946; children: Deborah, Roger, Barbara. Student, U. Nebr., 1940-41, U. Minn., 1941-43, U. Mo., 1943; B.A., U. Minn., 1946, M.A., 1947, Ph.D., 1950. Instr. U. Minn., 1948-50; staff psychologist Psychol. Corp., N.Y.C., 1950-51; research assoc. U. Ill., 1952-54; asst. prof. dept. psychology Ohio U., Athens, 1954-57; assoc. prof. Ohio U., 1957-62, prof., 1962-79, disting. prof., 1979—, chmn. dept., 1959-63, acting dean Coll. Arts and Sci., 1965, 85-86, dean, 1966-71, media coordinator, 1972-75, acting assoc. provost for grad. and research programs, 1986-87; research assoc. Harvard U., 1968-69; vis. prof. State U. N.Y. at Stony Brook, 1971-72, U. Iowa, 1979-80; staff mem. N.Y.C. Writers Conf., 1956-57; cons., lectr. Nat. Project Agr. Communication, 1957-59, Com. on World Literacy and Christian Lit., 1958-62; exec. asst., sr. research engr. Autonetics, 1960-61; cons. Resources Devel. Corp., 1962-65, Boston Pub. Sch., 1968, D.C. Heath Co., 1971, Western Electric, 1973, Westinghouse, 1975, Human Resources Research Orgn., 1978-79, U.S. Navy, 1975, Armed Services Readability Research, 1975, Center for Ednl. Experimentation, Devel. and Evaluation, 1978-79, 81, U.S. Army, 1979, Bell System Center for Tech. Edn., 1975-80, Time, Inc., 1977-79, AT&T, 1979-81; lectr. Open Univ., Eng., 1975, NATO Conf. Visual Presentation of Info., The Netherlands, 1978. Author: (with Byron Buck) Know Your Reader, 1954, The Measurement of Readability, 1963, (with Paul A. Games) Elementary Statistics: Data Analysis for the Behavioral Sciences, 1967, A Manual for Readable Writing, 1975, 4th edit., 1980, How to Write Readable English, 1985; editorial bd.: Info. Design Jour, 1979—, Instructional Science, 1975—, Reading Teacher, 1981-82, Reading Research and Instruction, 1985-87. Served to 1st lt. USAAF, 1943-45. Decorated Air medal, Purple Heart; Fulbright travel grantee U.S.-U.K. Ednl. Commn. to Open U., 1977-81. Fellow Am. Psychol. Assn.; mem. Nat. Reading Conf. (invited address 1975, Oscar Causey award for outstanding contbns. to reading research 1981), Internat. Reading Assn., Am. Ednl. Research Assn., Phi Beta Kappa, Delta Phi Lambda, Psi Chi, Phi Delta Kappa. Home: 5 Pleasantview Dr Athens OH 45701

KLARE, JULIA MARIE, writer, consultant; b. Colony, Kans., Feb. 5, 1922; d. Guy Vaughn and Bernice (McCoy) Price; m. Roland Eugene Matson, Sept. 29, 1942 (dec. Jan. 1945); m. George R. Klare, Dec. 24, 1946; children: Deborah Klare Fox, Roger Price, Barbara. Student, Kansas City Jr. Coll., 1938-39, U. Mo., 1940-41; BS in Edn., Kansas City Tchrs. Coll., 1942; MA in Psychology, U. Minn., 1947. Lic. psychologist, Ohio. Psychologist Athens (Ohio) County Mental Health Ctr., 1960-62; instr. psychology dept. Ohio U., Athens, 1962-65, 69-76, coordinator study skills, 1974-78; cons., ptnr. Clarity, Athens, 1978-87; freelance writer Athens and Jensen Beach, Fla., 1987—; instr. Suffolk County Community Coll., Selden, N.Y., 1972. Author numerous poems. Active State Bd. United Campus Ministry in Higher Edn. in Ohio, 1965-71, Community Mental Health Bd. for Athens, Hocking and Vinton Counties, Ohio; sec. United Campus Ministry Ohio U., Athens, 1960-65, pres. 1976-77. Recipient 1st and 4th prizes Save Our Starving Poets contest Writers Grapevine, Columbus, Ohio, 1986. Mem. Nat. Assn. for Applied Poetry. Democrat. Presbyterian. Avocations: collecting glass paperweight antiques, swimnastics, reading. Home and Office: Clarity 5 Pleasantview Dr Athens OH 45701 also: 1258 NE 14th Ct Jensen Beach FL 34957

KLARFELD, NATHAN, dentist; b. St. Louis, Sept. 3, 1950; s. Ely and Frania (Finklestein) K.; m. Lori Anne Silvers, July 23, 1972; 1 child, Adam Bennett. BA, Washington U., 1971; DDS, U. Mo., Kansas City, 1975. Pvt. practice dentistry Overland Park, Kans., 1975—; clin. instr. U. Mo. dental sch., Kansas City, 1975-77; clin. advisor Westport Free Health Clinic, Kansas City, 1975-79. asst. editor Dental Assisting Mag., Waco, Tex., 1979-81, staff columnist, 1981—; contbr. articles to profl. jours. Served to maj. U.S. Army. Res., 1981-86. Mem. Am. Assn. Pub. Health Dentists (Outstanding Student Project 1974). Democrat. Jewish. Avocations: running, tennis. Home: 8009 Rosewood Prairie Village KS 66208 Office: 10983 Granada Overland Park KS 66211

KLASS, MARC WAYNE, manufacturing executive; b. Chgo., June 2, 1951; s. Jack J. and Minette (Bastain) K.; m. Lynn Irving, June 5, 1977. BS cum laude, No. Ill. U., 1973; MBA, U. Chgo., 1978. CPA, Ill. Audit staff Alexander Grant & Co., Chgo., 1973-76; acctg. mgr. Libby, McNeill & Libby, Chgo., 1976-77; asst. controller Howard Nat. Corp., Chgo., 1977-79; v.p. Key Industries, Inc., East Peoria, Ill., 1979—; bd. dirs. Irving-Klass Graphics, Inc., Peoria, 1982—. Bd. dirs. Northmoor Hills Homeowners Assn., Peoria, Synagogue Agudas Achim, Peoria. Mem. Am. Inst. CPA's. Avocations: sports, weight lifting, conditioning. Home: 6019 Sherwood Peoria IL 61614 Office: Key Industries Inc 215 Taylor St Peoria IL 61611

KLAUS, ANDREW PETER, cardiologist; b. Columbus, Ohio, Nov. 7, 1941; s. Emmett John and Mary Louise (Wochos) K.; m. Jean Ann Poling, June 19, 1965; children—David, Jennifer, Kevin. B.S., Northwestern U., 1963, M.D., 1966. Diplomate Am. Bd. Internal Medicine, subsplty. bd. cardiology. Intern, resident Ward Med. Service, Barnes Hosp., St. Louis, 1966-68; fellow in cardiology Johns Hopkins Hosp., Balt., 1970-72; physician, chief of cardiology, dir. cardiac catheterization lab., dir. CCU, Frederick C. Smith Clinic and Community Meml. Hosp., Marion, Ohio, 1972-75; founding ptnr. Cardiology, Inc., Columbus, Ohio, 1975—; clin. instr. in cardiology Ohio State U. Coll. Medicine, Columbus, 1972-81, clin. asst. prof. medicine, 1981—; dir. cardiac noninvasive lab. Mount Carmel Med. Ctr., 1980—; chmn. clin. research rev. com. Mt. Carmel Hosp., 1978—; chief cardiology, dir. CCU, Mount Carmel East Hosp., 1979—. Contbr. articles to profl. jours. Served as surgeon USPHS, 1968-70. Fellow Am. Coll. Cardiology, Am. Heart Assn. (Council on Clin. Cardiology, pres., bd. dirs. Central Ohio chpt.); mem. Alpha Omega Alpha, Phi Beta Kappa. Republican. Avocations: golf; boating. Home: 4839 Stonehaven Dr Columbus OH 43220 Office: 777 W State St Columbus OH 43222

KLAUS, RICHARD MOORE, equipment company executive; b. Olney, Ill., Sept. 8, 1927; s. Frank Charles and Kathleen (Moore) K.; m. Carolyn Guelker, June 5, 1954; children: Martha, Linda, William. BSME, U. Cin., 1951; MBA, Xavier U., 1960. Registered profl. engr., Ohio. Design engr. OPW Corp., Cin., 1954-58; chief engr. Dover Corp., Cin., 1958-63; founder, pres. Automatic Equipment Corp., Cin., 1963—; adj. tchr. metallurgy Ohio Coll. Applied Sci., Cin., 1962-64; exec. v.p. Railway Expn. Co., Inc. Editor: Through the Heart of Ohio, 1973; inventor automatic gasoline dispensing nozzle. Pres. Westwood Town Hall Performing Arts Ctr., Beautiful Woodlawn Bus. Assocs., chmn. pubs. com.; bd. dirs. Cin. Sci. Ctr.; pres. Mus. Health Sci. and Industry, 1983. Served with AUS. Recipient Nat. Design Competition award (3) Material in Design Engring. mag., Disting. Service award Cin. Recreation Commn. Mem. NSPE, Engring. Soc. Cin., Cin. C. of C. (transp. com.), Cin. Hist. Soc., Cin. chpt. Nat. Ry. Hist. Soc. Presbyterian. Lodge: Kiwanis. Home: 3230 Epworth Ave Cincinnati OH 45211 Office: 2974 Graves Ln Cincinnati OH 45241

KLAUSEGER, JUDITH LEE, marketing research director; b. Chgo., Mar. 19, 1959; d. Rita G. Krolak; m. Frank Paul Klauseger, Oct. 24, 1981. BA in Mktg., Loyola U., 1981. Research analyst Vance Pub., Lincolnshire, Ill., 1982-83, sr. research analyst, 1982-83, project mgr., 1983-85, research dir., 1985—. Mem. Mktg. Research Assn. Republican. Roman Catholic. Office: Vance Pub Co 400 Knights Bridge Pkwy Lincolnshire IL 60069

KLAUSMEYER, JAMES WILLIAM, real estate appraiser; b. Detroit, July 25, 1935; s. Leonard Frederick and Ada (Senseman) K.; m. Diane Elizabeth Paradis, Mar. 18, 1959 (div. Jan. 1968); children: Susan Elizabeth, Ellen Ada; m. Caroll Wynn Crane, Dec. 24, 1971; 1 stepchild, Charles Robert Bates. BS in Engring., U. Mich., 1960; postgrad. in bus. adminstrn., Calif. State Coll., Los Angeles, 1961-65, Lansing Community Coll., 1985-87. Dist. sales mgr. Hoffman Electronics, Redwood City, Calif., 1963-68; asst. prof. bus. Calif. State Coll., San Jose, 1967-69; founder Embark Inc., Pontiac, Mich., 1970-73; owner, proprietor James W. Klausmeyer Realty, Highland, Mich., 1976—; nat. edn. dir. Partridge & Assocs., Pontiac, 1980-81; dep. assessor-appraiser City of Novi, Mich., 1982—; proprietor, lectr. Novi Community Edn., 1984—; lectr. Mich. State Assessors Bd., Lansing, 1987—. Mem. Rep. Nat. Com. (sustaining), 1978—. Mem. Nat. Assn. Realtors, Nat. Assn. Home Builders, Internat. Assn. Assessing Officers, Mich. Assessors Assn. Methodist. Avocation: hunting, fishing. Home: PO Box 144 4033 Loch Dr Highland MI 48031 Office: City of Novi 45225 W Ten Mile Novi MI 48050

KLEBBA, RAYMOND ALLEN, banker; b. Chgo., Apr. 16, 1934; s. Raymond Aloysius and Marie Cecelia (Tobin) K.; m. Barbara Ann Gurbal, Oct. 7, 1961; children: Anne, Daniel, Mary, Theresa. Student, Loyola U., Chgo., 1954-56; cert. property mgr., Inst. Real Estate Mgmt., 1970. Corr., rep. Western R.R. Assn., Chgo., 1956-61; pres. Midland Warehouse, Chgo., 1961-68; v.p., gen. mgr. Strobeck, Reiss Sch. Mgmt. Co., Chgo., 1968-70, real estate mgr. and broker, 1970-83; v.p. mktg. Mid-Am. Nat. Bank, Chgo., 1983—, also bd. dirs. Mem. Bank Mktg. Assn., Chgo. Bd. Realtors (vice chmn. comml. and indsl. leasing property mgmt. council), Inst. Real Estate Mgmt. (chmn. chpt. of yr. com. 1975-76). Lodges: Rotary, Moose. Avocations: bowling, golf, gardening, treasure hunting, fishing. Home: 395 Dundee Rd Glencoe IL 60022 Office: Mid-Am Nat Bank Prudential Plaza Chicago IL 60601

KLECZKA, GERALD D., congressman; b. Milw., Nov. 26, 1943; m. Bonnie Scott, 1979. Ed., U. Wis.-Milw. Mem. Wis. Assembly, 1968-74; mem. Wis. Senate, 1974-84, 98th-99th Congresses from 4th Wis. dist., 1984—. Del., Democratic Nat. Conv. Served with Air N.G., 1963-69. Mem. Polish Nat. Alliance, Wilson Park Advancement Assn., Polish Assn. Am., South Side Businessmen's Club, Milw. Soc. Office: 226 Cannon House Office Bldg Washington DC 20515

KLEFFNER, GREGORY WILLIAM, accountant; b. St. Louis, Nov. 21, 1954; s. Francis R. and Charlotte P. (Petersen) K.; m. Peggy A. Flavin, July 15, 1977; 1 child, Patricia Elaine. BSBA, Washington U., 1977. Staff Arthur Andersen & Co., St. Louis, Mo., 1977-79; sr. acct. Arthur Andersen & Co., St. Louis, 1979-81, mgr., 1981—. Mem. Am. Inst. CPA's, Mo. Soc. CPA's, St. Louis County Econ. Devel. Assn. (loan rev. com. 1986-87), Am. Y-Flyer Yacht Racing Assn. (sec.-treas 1984—). Avocation: sailing. Home: 489 Redwood Forest Dr Saint Louis MO 63021 Office: Arthur Andersen & Co 1010 Market St Saint Louis MO 63101

KLEIMAN, BERNARD, lawyer; b. Chgo., Jan. 26, 1928; s. Isadore and Pearl (Wikoff) K.; m. Gloria Baime, Nov. 15, 1986; children—Leslie, David. B.S., Purdue U., 1951; J.D., Northwestern U., 1954. Bar: Ill. bar 1954. Practice law in assn. with Abraham W. Brussell, 1957-60; dist. counsel United Steel Workers Am., 1960-65, gen. counsel, 1965—; partner Kleiman, Cornfield & Feldman, Chgo., 1960-75; prin. B. Kleiman (P.C.), 1976-77, Kleiman and Whitney (P.C.), 1978—; Mem. collective bargaining coms. for nat. labor negotiations in basic steel, aluminum and can mfg. industries. Contbr. articles to legal jours. Served with U.S. Army, 1946-48. Mem. Am., Ill., Chgo., Allegheny County bar assns. Office: 1 E Wacker Dr Chicago IL 60601 also: 5 Gateway Center Pittsburgh PA 15222

KLEIN, BARBARA ANN, accountant. BS, U. Ill., 1979. CPA, Ill., Mo. Staff acct. Arthur Andersen, St. Louis, 1980-82; sr. acct. Grant Thornton, Chgo., St. Louis, 1982—. Bronze Tablet scholar, 1979. Mem. Am. Inst. CPA's, Mo. Soc. CPA's. Roman Catholic. Avocations: travel, Italian lang. and lit., photography. Office: Grant Thornton 500 Washington Ave Suite 1200 Saint Louis MO 63101

KLEIN, CARL FREDERICK, research scientist, technology forecaster; b. Milw., June 20, 1942; s. Paul and Rose Katharine (Ruos) K.; m. Mary Jean Uscham, Nov. 23, 1969; children: Christine Jean, Matthew Frederick, John Paul, James Andrew. BSEE, U. Wis., 1965, MSEE, 1967. Registered profl. engr., Wis. Design and devel. engr. Louis Allis, Milw., 1965; sr. research engr. Johnson Controls, Inc., Milw., 1971-79, sr. research scientist, 1979-80, mgr. tech. forecasting, 1980-82, research sect. leader, 1982—; instr. Marquette U., Milw., 1967-72. Contbr. articles to profl. jours.; patentee in field. Mem. IEEE, World Future Soc., AAAS, Am. Assn. Artificial Intelligence, Eta Kappa Nu. Methodist. Avocations: tennis, skiing, piano, trumpet. Home: 5740 S Lochleven New Berlin WI 53151 Office: Johnson Controls Inc 507 E Michigan St Milwaukee WI 53201

KLEIN, CERRY MARTIN, operations research educator, consultant; b. Kansas City, Mo., Dec. 11, 1955. BS, Northwest Mo. State U., Maryville, 1977; MS, Purdue U., West Lafayette, 1980, PhD, 1983. Tchr. Cen. Sch. Dist. #1, Kansas City, 1977-78; prof. U. Mo. Columbia, 1984—; cons. in field. contbr. articles to profl. jour. Counselor Big Bros., Maryville, 1975-77. Research fellow U. Mo., 1986, David Ross fellow Purdue U., West Lafayette, 1982,83. Mem. Ops. Research Soc. Am., Soc. Indsl. and Applied Maths, Math. Programming Soc., Pi Mu Epsilon, Sigma Xi. Democrat. Mem. Christian Ch. Avocations: paleontology, raquetball, basketball, bicycling, astronomy. Home: 712 Medina Dr Columbia MO 65202 Office: U Mo Columbia 121 Elect Engr Bldg Columbia MO 65211

KLEIN, CHARLES HENLE, lithographing co. exec.; b. Cin., Oct. 5, 1908; s. Benjamin Franklin and Flora (Henle) K.; student Purdue U., 1926-27, U. Cin., 1927-28; m. Ruth Becker, Sept. 23, 1938; children—Betsy (Mrs. Marvin H. Schwartz), Charles H., Carla (Mrs. George Fee III). Pres., Progress Lithographing Co., Cin., 1934-59, Novelart Mfg. Co., Cin., 1960—; dir. R.A. Taylor Corp. Founding mem. Chief Execs. Forum. Clubs: Losantiville Country, Queen City, Bankers (Cin.). Home: 6754 Fairoaks Dr Amberley Village Cincinnati OH 45237 Office: 2121 Section Rd Amberley Village Cincinnati OH 45237

KLEIN, CHARLES MOSHER, radiologist; b. Cleve., June 24, 1932; s. Matthew George and Jean Isabel (Mosher) K.; m. Barbara Ann Barr, Aug. 20, 1955; children: Janet Ellen, James Mosher. BS, Case Western Res. U., 1954, MD, 1958. Intern St. Luke's Hosp., Cleve., 1958-59; resident in radiology U. Mich., Ann Arbor, 1959-62; ptnr. Drs. Peck, Means, & Straub, Toledo, 1964-68; radiologist Toledo Radiol. Assocs., Inc., 1968—, pres., 1975-77. Served to lt. comdr. USNR, 1962-64. Fellow Nat. Cancer Inst., 1961-62. Fellow Am. Coll. Radiology (alt. councilor-at-large 1984—); mem. AMA (mem. hosp. med. staff sect. com. 1982-83,), Ohio State Med. Assn. (pres. 1982-83), Radiol. Soc. N.Am., Ohio State Radiol. Soc. (sec. 1980-82). Mem. United Ch. of Christ. Club: Torch (pres. Toledo chpt. 1971-72). Avocations: tennis, travel, reading. Office: Toledo Radiol Assocs Inc 3939 Monroe St Toledo OH 43606

KLEIN, CRAIG A(LLEN) (MIKE), real estate developer; b. Cin., Jan. 9, 1949; s. Robert B. and Betty Ann (Morrow) K.; m. Linda Sherry Keller, June 7, 1975; children: Christa Marie-Lynn, James Craig. Grad., U. Cin., 1975; cert. shopping ctr. mgr., U. Ga., 1976; cert. constrn. mgr., U. Ky., 1979. Cert. real estate broker. Asst. advt. mgr. Thriftway Supermarkets, 1963-71; property mgr. Marvin Warner Corp., 1972-73; leasing agt. Arthur Rubloff, 1973-74; dir. acquistion and devel. NAMADCO, 1974-81; owner C.A.K. Cons., Cin., 1981—, Plaza Venture I, Ltd., Cin., 1984—; cons. James Keller, Inc., Cin., 1981—, G.M. Horton Corp., South Bend, Ind., 1981-82, Towne Properties, Cin., 1983-84, Vantage Corp., Cin., 1984-85; seminar instr. Xavier U., Cin., 1978. Served with U.S. Army, 1971-72. Mem. Internat. Council Shopping Ctrs. (seminar instr. 1974—), Am. Legion. Methodist. Lodge: Kiwanis. Avocation: golf. Office: CAK Cons 44 Eswin St Suite C Cincinnati OH 45218

KLEIN, GEORGE DEVRIES, geologist; b. Den Haag, Netherlands, Jan. 21, 1933; came to U.S., 1947, naturalized, 1955; s. Alfred and Doris (deVries) K.; m. Chung Sook Kim Chung, May 23, 1982. BA, Wesleyan U., 1954; MA, U. Kans., 1957; Ph.D., Yale U., 1960. Research sedimentologist Sinclair Research Inc., 1960-61; asst. prof. geology U. Pitts., 1961-63; asst. prof. to assoc. prof. U. Pa., 1963-69; prof. U. Ill., Urbana, 1970—; vis. fellow Wolfson Coll. Oxford U., 1969; vis. prof. geology U. Calif., Berkeley, 1970; vis. prof. oceanography Oreg. State U., 1974, Seoul Nat. U., 1980, U. Tokyo, 1983; CIC vis. exchange prof. geophys. sci. U. Chgo., 1979-80; chief scientist Deep Sea Drilling Project Leg 58, 1977-78; continuing edn. lectr.; asso. Center Advanced Studies U. Ill., 1974, 83. Author: Sandstone Depositional Models for Exploration for Fossil Fuels, 3d edit, 1985, Clastic Tidal Facies, 1977, Holocene Tidal Sedimentation, 1976; mem. editorial bd. Geol. Soc. Am. Bull., 1973-74, assoc. editor, 1975-81; cons. editor: McGraw-Hill Ency. of Sci. and Yearbook, 1977—; chief cons. adv. editor: CEPCO div. Burgess Pub. Co, 1979-81; series editor: Geol. Sci. Monographs, Internat. Human Resources Devel. Corp. Press, Inc., 1981-87; mem. editorial bd. Sedimentary Geology, 1985— Elsevier; mng. editor Sedimentology, Earth Sci. Revs., 1987—. Recipient Outstanding Paper award Jour. Sedimentary Petrology, 1970; Erasmus Haworth Disting. Alumnus award in geology U. Kans., 1980; Outstanding Geology Faculty Mem. award U. Ill. Geology Grad. Student Assn., 1983; NSF grantee. Fellow AAAS, Geol. Soc. Am. (chmn. div. sedimentary geology 1985-86), Geol. Assn. Can.; mem. Am. Geophys. Union, Am. Inst. Profl. Geologists, Soc. Exploration Geophysicists, Soc. Econ. Paleontologists and Mineralogists, Internat. Assn. Sedimentologists, Am. Assn. Petroleum Geologists, Sigma Xi. Office: Dept Geology Univ Ill 245 Natural History Bldg 1301 W Green St Urbana IL 61801-2999

KLEIN, JAMES WALTER, paper mill executive; b. Appleton, Wis., Apr. 30, 1940; s. George R. and Josephine Ann (Fetterer) K.; m. Mary Frances Vandercook, Aug. 11, 1962; children—Kathleen, Jennifer, Jeffrey. Student, St. Norbert Coll., 1958-59; B.S., U. Minn., 1962, M.S., 1969. Mgmt. trainee Container Corp. Am., Chgo., 1969-70, mill mgr., 1970-74; mill mgr. Clevepak Corp., Dallas, 1974-75, asst. pres. mill div., 1975-76; v.p., gen. mgr. Wis. Paperboard Corp., Milw., 1976-86; v.p. Newark Boxboard Co., 1986—. Served to capt., C.E., U.S. Army, 1962-68. Homolite Forestry scholar, 1962. Mem. Soc. Am. Foresters, TAPPI, Am. Mgmt. Assn., Paper Industry Mgmt. Assn., Nat. Rifle Assn., Xi Sigma Pi. Club: YMCA. Home: 9914 Huntington Dr Mequon WI 53092 Office: 1514 E Thomas Ave Milwaukee WI 53211

KLEIN, JERRY EMANUEL, insurance and financial planning; b. Cin., Apr. 4, 1933; s. Milton H. and Ida S. (Dunsker) K.; m. Arlene Ruth Rosen, July 3, 1957 (dec. Nov. 1974); children—Marjorie, Bradley, Amy; m. Nancy Cohen Hahn, Aug. 7, 1982. B.Mech. Engring., Cornell U., 1956; M.B.A., Ohio State U., 1959. C.L.U.; chartered fin. cons., 1984. Fin. engring. Avco Electronics, Cin., 1959-61; spl. agt. Northwestern Mut. Life of Milw., Cin., 1961—. Vice chmn. Am. Jewish Com., 1978; pres. Social Health Assn., 1964-66, Jewish Vocat. Service, 1978-80, Cancer Family Care, 1981-83; chmn. fin. com. Jewish Fedn., 1981-83, treas., mem. exec. com., 1981-84; bd. dirs. Children Psychiat. Ctr., Jewish Family Service, Jewish Vocat. Service, Cinti Jewish Fedn.; chmn. HILB Scholarship Com., 1985-87. Served to 1st lt. USAF, 1956-58. Recipient Kate S. Mack award Jewish Fedn., 1975. Mem. Million Dollar Round Table (life), Nat. Assn. Life Underwriters, Assn. C.L.U.s. Jewish. Office: Northwestern Mut Life of Milw 635 W 7th St Suite 202 Cincinnati OH 45203

KLEIN, MICHAEL DAVID, pediatric surgeon; b. Cleve., Jan. 17, 1944; s. Barney and Lillian (Deitch) K.; m. Margaret G. Sharpe, April 20, 1979; children—Alisa, Andrew, Elizabeth. A.B. U. Chgo., 1965; postgrad. Princeton U., 1965-66; M.D. Case Western U., 1971. Cert. Nat. Bd. Med. Examiners; diplomate Am. Bd. Surgery. Intern, U. Wash. Hosps., Seattle, 1971-72; asst. resident Harvard Surg. Service, Deaconess Hosp., Boston, 1972-74, chief resident, 1976-77; sr. asst. resident, research assoc. Children's Hosp. Med. Ctr., Boston, 1974-76; instr. surgery Harvard Med. Sch., 1976-77; assoc. chief resident, chief resident Children's Hosp. of Mich., Detroit, 1977-79, dir. surg. edn., 1983-84, assoc. chief pediatric gen. surgery, 1984—; asst. prof. surgery and pediatrics U. N.Mex., 1979-80; asst. prof. surgery U. Mich. Med. Sch., 1980-83; assoc. prof. surgery Wayne State U., Detroit, 1983—; adj. pres. chrm. and metalurgical engring. Fellow ACS, Am. Acad. Pediatrics; mem. Assn. Acad. Surgery, Am. Pediatric Surg. Assn., Cen. Surg. Assn., Mich. Pediatric Surg. Soc. (pres. 1980—), AAAS, Am. Soc. for Artifical Internal Organs, Am. Soc. for Parenteral and Enteral Nutrition, Detroit Surg. Assn., Soc. Univ. Surgeons. Home: 1049 Kensington Grosse Pointe Park MI 48230 Office: Children's Hosp of Mich 3901 Beaubien Detroit MI 48201

KLEIN, MICHAEL SHERMAN, manufacturing executive; b. Evanston, Ill., Feb. 8, 1951; s. Mathias Anthony and Audrey Jean (Sherman) K.; m. Gwenda Jeannette Howell, Nov. 29, 1975; children: Michael, Karen, Kevin, Derek. BA in Econs., Duke U., 1973; MBA, Lake Forest Sch. Mgmt., 1984. Budget analyst First Union Nat. Bank, Raleigh, N.C., 1973-74, br. mgr., 1974-75; various sales positions customer service Klein Tools, Inc., Chgo., 1975-79, v.p. adminstrn., 1979-82, pres., chief operating officer, 1982—, also bd. dirs.; bd. dirs. Tool Ins. Co. Ltd., Bermuda, RTW Internat., Inc., Chgo. Fund raising vol. Loyola Acad., Wilmette, Ill., 1978—; softball coach Deerfield (Ill.) Youth Baseball Assn.; vice chmn. capital campaign Holy Cross Parish, Deerfield, 1986. Mem. Young Pres.'s Assn., Am. Mgmt. Assn. (bd. dirs. Chgo. chpt. 1985—, program chmn. 1986-87, Mfg. Council 1985—), Hand Tools Inst. (com. chmn. 1984—). Republican. Roman Catholic.

Club: Thorngate Country (Deerfield). Avocations: tennis, golf, reading. Office: Klein Tools Inc 7200 McCormick Blvd Chicago IL 60645

KLEIN, PAULA SCHWARTZ, public relations and development executive; b. Chgo., Oct. 16, 1941; d. Arthur A. and Rosalyn (Davidson) Schwartz; student Mich. State U., 1959-60; B.A., Governors State U., 1974, M.A., 1975; m. Sanford David Klein, Dec. 18, 1960 (div. 1981); children—Gregory Scott, Julie Ann. Mem. editorial staff Okinawa Morning Star, Machinato, 1960-63; exec. dir. Bloom Twp. Com. on Youth, Chicago Heights, Ill., 1975-81; dir. fund devel. and pub. relations South Chgo. Community Hosp., 1981-84; v.p. South Chgo. Health Care Found., 1982-84; dir. devel. and pub. relations Chgo. Crime Commn., 1985—. Mem. Calumet Area Indsl. Commn. Mem. Nat. Soc. Fund Raising Profls., Nat. Assn. Prevention Profls., So. Suburban Youth Service Alliance, Criminal Def. Consortium, Nat. Assn. Hosp. Devel., Twp. Ofcls. Ill., Youth Network Council, Sierra Club. Jewish. Home: 2100 Lincoln Park West Chicago IL 60614 Office: Chgo Crime Commission 79 W Monroe St Chicago IL 60603

KLEIN, RICHARD EARL, mechanical engineering educator, consultant; b. Stratford, Conn., Feb. 11, 1939; s. Albert Wilhelm and Ellen Moeller (Kristensen) K.; m. Marjorie Ann Maxwell, Sept. 1, 1963; children—Victoria Ellen, Timothy Maxwell. B.S. in Mech. Engring., Pa. State U., 1964, M.S. in Mech. Engring., 1965; Ph.D. in Mech. Engring., Purdue U., 1968. Asst. prof. mech. engring. U. Ill., Urbana, 1968-71, assoc. prof., 1971—; cons. dynamic systems, automatic control systems to firms. Served with USAR, 1956-63. Mem. ASME, IEEE, AAAS, Nat. Rifle Assn. (life), Sigma Xi. Presbyterian. Patentee electro hydraulic steering device, assigned to Caterpillar Tractor Co., 1972. Author: (with L.D. Metz), Man and the Technological Society, 1973. Contbr. articles to engring. jours. Home: Rural Route 1 Box 182 Dewey IL 61840 Office: 1206 W Green St Room 354 Urbana IL 61801

KLEIN, ROBERT EDWARD, publishing company executive; b. Cin., Dec. 27, 1926; s. Albert and Elisabeth (Muschnau) K.; m. Nancy Minter, May 28, 1958; children: Robert Schuyler, Elisabeth Susan. AB, Kenyon Coll., 1950; MBA, Cornell U., 1952; AM, U. Chgo., 1969, PhD, 1983. With Sealy Inc., Chgo., 1964-66; chief exec. officer Market Power, Inc., Chgo., 1966-69; with McGraw Hill Co., Chgo., 1969—, dist. mgr. Housing mag., 1980, now dist. mgr. Modern Plastics mag., Modern Plastics Internat. mag.; cons. U.S. Dept. Justice, 1967-71, Time/Life Books, 1980; lectr. in Soviet history Barat Coll., 1970-72; lectr. in history Mallinckrodt Coll., 1983-85; assoc. dept. history Northwestern U., Evanston, Ill., 1986—. Author: J.F.C. Fuller and The Tank, 1983, Christian Opposition to Hitler, The Underground Christian Church in The Soviet Union. Served with U.S. Army, 1944-46, PTO. Grolier scholar, 1952. Mem. Am. Legion, Am. Hist. Assn., Beta Theta Pi. Republican. Episcopalian. Clubs: Westmoreland Country (Wilmette, Ill.); Cornell. Lodge: Masons. Avocations: writing, lecturing. Home: 633 Park Dr Kenilworth IL 60043 Office: McGraw Hill Co 645 N Michigan Ave Chicago IL 60611

KLEIN, SHEFFIELD, symphony orchestra manager; b. New Brunswick, N.J., Feb. 22, 1918; s. Julius and Ida (Schneider) K.; m. Gisela H. Stetter, Jan. 12, 1964; children—Michael, Susanna, Randi. Student CCNY, 1936-41; B.S., Columbia U., 1946, M.A., 1947, Ed.D., 1956. Dir. instrumental music Battle Creek (Mich.) Schs., 1950-54; dir. sch. sales World Book Ency., Chgo., 1958-77; gen. mgr. Sioux City Symphony (Iowa), 1979—; music instr., Atlantic City, 1947-50, Tchrs. Coll. Columbia U., 1954-56. Served as fighter pilot USAAF, 1941-46; maj. USAFR ret. Decorated Air medal. Mem. Am. Symphony Orch. League, Met. Orch. Mgrs. Assn., Phi Mu Alpha. Lodge: Rotary. Author: Community Music, 1957. Home: 3805 Chippewa Ct Sioux City IA 51104 Office: 370 Orpheum Bldg Sioux City IA 51101

KLEIN, SHERWIN J., packaging company executive; b. Chgo., Mar. 19, 1943; s. Morris and Gertrude (Comiss) K.; m. Lynda Carol Leavitt, Oct. 18, 1964; children: Eric, Steven, Kimberly. Student, U. Ill., Chgo., 1960-61, Roosevelt U., 1962-63, Ill. Inst. Tech., 1963-64. Quality control mgr. Capitol Packaging Co., Melrose Park, Ill., 1963-64, research and devel. leader, 1964-66, research and devel. mgr., 1966-71, dir. tech. sales and services, 1971-76; corp. v.p. sales and mktg. Accra Pac Group, Elkhart, Ind., 1976—, also bd. dirs. Pres. Churchill Homeowners Assn., Niles, Ill. Mem. ASTM, Am. Mgmt. Assn., Soc. Cosmetic Chemists, Chem. Specialties Mfg. Assn. Democrat.

KLEIN, WILLIAM DAVID, lawyer; b. St. Cloud, Minn., Oct. 30, 1954; s. Wilfred George and Rita Christina (Gottwalt) K.; m. Rebecca Lynn Ready, May 26, 1979; 1 child, Michaela Laine. BA summa cum laude, St. Olaf Coll., 1976; JD magna cum laude, U. Mich., 1979. Bar: Minn. 1979, U.S. Dist. Ct. Minn. 1979, U.S. Claims Ct. 1983, U.S. Tax Ct. 1985. Law clk. Minn. Supreme Ct., St. Paul, 1979-80; assoc. Gray, Plant, Mooty, Mooty, & Bennett P.A., Mpls., 1980-84, ptnr., 1985—. Mem. ABA, Minn. State Bar Assn., Hennepin County Bar Assn. Office: Gray Plant Mooty Mooty & Bennett 33 S 6th St Suite 3400 Minneapolis MN 55402

KLEINGARTNER, LARRY, agricultural association executive; b. Kulm, N.D., Mar. 14, 1945; s. William Fred and Elsie (Riebhagen) K.; m. Nancy Lee Brand, Sept. 2, 1978; children—Jessie Lee, Brita Paula, Anika Rae. A.A., Bismarck Jr. Coll., 1965; B.A., Jamestown Coll., 1967; M.A., U. Hawaii, 1974. Vol., U.S. Peace Corps, Maharastra, India, 1968-71; dir. mktg. N.D. Dept. of Agr., Bismarck, N.D., 1975-79; exec. dir. Nat. Sunflower Assn., Bismarck, 1980—. Contbr. articles on agr. to profl. jours. V.p. New Horizons Fgn. Adoption Services, Bismarck, 1983—; bd. dirs. Bismarck Mandan Civic Chorus, 1980; Sunday sch. tchr. Lord of Life Luth. Ch., Bismarck, 1978—, council mem. 1984—. Nat. Def. Lang. fellow, 1972-74. Avocations: cross-country skiing; horseback riding; music. Home: 2876 Woodland Pl Bismarck ND 58501 Office: Nat Sunflower Assn PO Box 2533 Bismarck ND 58502

KLEINMAN, BURTON HOWARD, real estate investor; b. Chgo., Nov. 19, 1923; s. Eli I. and Pearl (Cohan) K.; m. Shirley A. Freyer, Sept. 6, 1950 (div. Oct. 1969); children: Kim, Lauri. BS in Engring., U.S. Naval Acad., 1948. Commd. ensign USN, 1948, resigned, 1949; v.p. C.F. Corp., Chgo., 1958-80, pres., 1980-85; owner B.H. Kleinman Co., Northfield, Ill., 1955—; ptnr. Middlefork Enterprises, Northfield, 1968—. Bd. dirs. United Way Northfield, 1970-72, North Shore Mental Health Assn., 1978-82. Mem. Northfield C. of C. (bd. dirs. 1976-81). Republican. Unitarian. Clubs: Deerfield Singles (pres. 1974-75), Winnetka Tennis Assn., Ridge & Valley Tennis. Avocations: tennis, scuba diving, sailing. Home: 570 Happ Rd Northfield IL 60093 Office: BH Kleinman Co 456 Frontage Rd Northfield IL 60093

KLEINSCHMIDT, GARY ARTHUR, investment executive; b. Chgo., June 25, 1953; s. Wilfred James Kleinschmidt and Elaine Jennet (Fischer) Dieterle; m. Cynthia Louise Versluis, Mar. 1, 1986. BS, Bradley U., 1975, MA, 1976. Registered rep. Dain Bosworth, Davenport, Iowa, 1976-80, investment officer, 1980-81, assoc. v.p., 1981-83, v.p., 1983—. Caucus rep. Scott County Rep. Party, 1978. Lodge: Rotary. Avocation: boating. Home: 2245 E 32d St Davenport IA 52807 Office: Dain Bosworth 202 W 3d St Davenport IA 52801

KLEINSORGE, CLINTON ARTHUR, management consulting company executive; b. St. Louis, May 12, 1947; s. Clarence Jerome and Laura Virginia (Fuchs) K.; m. Kathleen Muldowney, Feb. 1, 1975. Student Forrest Park Community Coll., 1968-70. Computer operator Wagner Electric Co., St. Louis, 1965-67, programmer/analyst Internat. Shoe Co., St. Louis, 1967-69; project mgr. ITT Hamilton Life Ins. Co., St. Louis, 1969-71; sr. programmer/analyst Market Devel. Corp., St. Louis, 1971-75; mgr. new devel. Comml. State Life Ins. Co., St. Louis, 1975-77; br. mgr. Analysts Internat. Corp., St. Louis, 1977-83, mktg. dir. 1983-84; br. mgr. Applied Info. Devel., St. Louis, 1984—; bd. dirs. Fed. Systems. Recipient Pres.' Quar. Efficiency award 1981 (2), 82-83, Summit Club award Analysts Internat. Corp., 1984. Mem. Am. Prodn. and Inventory Control Soc., Nat. Assn. Accts., Data Processing Mgmt. Assn., Assn. for Systems Mgmt. (cert.), St. Louis Regional Commerce and Growth Assn. Lodge: Rotary. Home: 1456 Gettysburg Landing Saint Charles MO 63303

KLEIT, STUART ALLEN, nephrologist, physician, educator, dean; b. Passaic, N.J., July 29, 1933; s. Morris W. and Ruth (Gelman) K.; m. Cynthia A. Levenson, Aug. 31, 1958; children: Andrew N., David H. Student, Williams Coll., Williamstown, Mass., 1951-53; DDS, U. Pa., 1957; MD, U. Fla., 1961. Intern Ind. U. Hosps., Indpls., 1961-62; chief resident Ind. U. Hosps., 1964-65; resident physician Shands Teaching Hosp., Gainesville, Fla., 1962-63; fellow in renal medicine Shands Teaching Hosp., Gainesville, 1963-64; asst. prof. medicine, chief renal sect. Ind. U. Sch. Medicine, Indpls., 1967-71, assoc. prof. medicine, chief renal sect., 1971-74, prof. medicine, chief renal sect., 1974—, acting dir. univ. hosp., 1984-85, assoc. dean clin. affairs, 1985—; chmn. Edn Stage Renal Disease Network, Ind., 1978-79. Contbr. articles to profl. jours. Trustee Nat. Kidney Found., N.Y.C., 1972—, pres., 1978-80; chmn. Nat. Kidney and Urologic Disease Adv. Bd., NIH, 1987—; bd. dirs., treas. Am. Blood Commn., Washington, 1974-78. Served to lt. comdr. USNR, 1965-67. Recipient Cert. of Merit, Am. Acad. Dental Medicine, 1961, Martin K. Wagner award Nat. Kidney Found., 1984, Legion of Merit award Ind. Kidney Found., 1986; NIH fellow, 1963-64. Fellow ACP (council of subspecialties 1981-82); mem. AMA, Internat. Soc. Nephrology, Am. Soc. Nephrology, Soc. Artificial Internal Organs. Avocations: golf, stamps, history. Office: Ind U Sch Medicine 1120 South Dr Indianapolis IN 46223

KLEJMENT, ANNE, church historian; b. Rochester, N.Y., Apr. 27, 1950; d. Z. Henry and Alice (Wegner) K. BA cum laude, Nazareth Coll., 1972; MA, SUNY, Binghamton, 1974, PhD, 1981. Asst. prof. Am. Cath. social hist. Coll. of St. Thomas, St. Paul, 1983—. Author: The Berrigans: A Bibliography, 1979, Dorothy Day and The Catholic Worker: A Bibliography and Index, 1986. SUNY Found. fellow, 1976-77. Mem. Am. Cath. Hist. Assn., Am. Soc. Ch. History, Orgn. Am. Historians, Cath. Hist. Soc. Office: Coll of St Thomas Dept History Box 4188 Saint Paul MN 55105

KLEMAN, JEROME ARTHUR, hospital laboratory manager; b. Delphos, Ohio, Jan. 27, 1948; s. Charles L. and Ruth V. (Dunlap) K.; m. Wilma Jean Hunt, June 21, 1969; children: Christina M., Tiffany R., Tammy L., Kevin L. Diploma, Cleve. Jr. Coll., 1967. Registered med. technologist; cert. clin. technologist. Lab. mgr. Union City Meml. Hosp., Ind., 1967—. Officer, Randolph County Vols. in Probation, Winchester, Ind., 1969-81; chmn. Union City Republican Com., 1983. Mem. Am. Assn. Med. Technologists, Ind. Soc. Med. Technologists (bd. dirs. 1972-78), Ind. Assn. Blood Banks, Union City Jaycees, Union City Ind.-Ohio C. of C. (bd. dirs.). Roman Catholic. Lodges: K.C. (4th degree, dist. dep. 1979-81, state health service chmn. 1981-82). Avocations: gardening, golf, tennis. Home: 1239 Beverly St Union City IN 47390 Office: Union City Meml Hosp 900 N Columbis St Union City IN 47390

KLEMER, ROBERT WADSWORTH, retired textile company executive; b. Faribault, Minn., Aug. 21, 1910; s. Frank Henry and Eleanor Myrtle Klemer; m. Anna Margaret Danielson, July 15, 1936; children—Susan, Anne, Mary. Student, U. Minn., 1928-30; B.S., Phila. Coll. Textiles and Sci., 1932. Supt. Faribault Woolen Mill Co., Faribault 1940-49, pres., 1949-77, chmn., 1977-85, bd. dirs., 1985—. Bd. dirs. emeritus Faribault YMCA; mem. Faribault Bd. Edn., 1948-53. Served to capt. U.S. Army, 1942-46. Recipient Service To Mankind award Sertoma Club. Mem. Nat. Wool Mfrs. Assn. (dir., v.p.), Am. Textile Mfrs. Inst. (dir. wool div.), Minn. Assn. Commerce and Industry (dir.), C. of C. of Faribault, Phi Psi. Republican. Congregationalist. Clubs: Lions, Faribault Country.

KLEMKE, JUDITH ANN, mortgage banking executive; b. Berwyn, Ill., July 22, 1950; d. John Stanley and Mildred Lucille (Baldwin) K.; m. Keith Michael Kurzeja, Nov. 6, 1976. B.S., U. Ill., 1972. With Ben Franklin Savs., Oak Brook, Ill., 1973-74, asst. v.p., Skokie, Ill., 1975; asst. v.p. 1st Fin. Savs. & Loan Assn., Downers Grove, Ill., 1975-76, v.p., 1977-80, sr. v.p., 1981-82; v.p. First Family Mortgage Corp., Lisle, Ill., 1980—. Mem. Am. Mortgage Bankers Assn., Ill. Mortgage Bankers Assn., Nat. Assn. Female Execs., Am. Soc. Profl. and Exec. Women, AAUW, Bus. and Profl. Women, U. Ill. Alumni Assn. (life), Alpha Gamma Delta. Home: 18 W 206 Lathrop Villa Park IL 60181 Office: 2900 Ogden Ave Lisle IL 60532

KLEMM, JAMES LOUIS, systems analyst; b. South Bend, Ind., Oct. 30, 1939; s. Paul Otto and (Margaret) Grace (Taylor) K.; m. Barbara Elaine Whitten, June 3, 1965 (div. 1976); children—Paul Andrew, Sarah Ruth; m. 2d, Martha Ruth Ritchie, Aug. 1, 1981. B.S., U. Chgo., 1961; M.S., Purdue U., 1963; Ph.D., Mich. State U., 1970. Grad. asst. in math. Purdue U., 1961-65; asst. prof. math. Indiana U. of Pa., 1965-67; grad. asst. Mich. State U., 1967-70; asst. prof. engring. analysis U. Cin., 1970-77; sr. pubs. specialist NCR Corp., Dayton, Ohio, 1977-80, systems analyst, 1980-81, sr. prin. systems analyst, 1981-83, cons. analyst, 1983-86, Orlando, Fla., 1986—. NSF grantee, 1971-72. Methodist. Mem. AAAS, Sigma Xi.

KLEMM-GRAU, H(ARRIET) ELAINE, psychotherapist; b. South Haven, Mich.; d. William Wheaton and Charlotte W. (Neumann) Richards; m. Robert H. Klemm, Feb. 1, 1921 (dec. Dec. 1972); children: David, Douglas, John Stephen, Colleen, Amy, Julianne; m. Wallace Edward Grau, Nov. 2, 1921; children: Gregory, Charles, Bruce, Bryan. B in Psychology, U. Wis., Kenosha, 1972; M in Social Work, U. Wis., Milw., 1974. Mgr. Neurol. Clinic, Lansing, Mich., 1946-51; mgr., psychotherapist Met. Clinic, Racine, Mich., 1976-77; psychotherapist, clinic dir. Family Social and Psychotherapy Services, Racine, 1977-82; psychotherapist Lakeside Family Therapy, Racine, 1982—; pres. Hickory Hollow Devel., Racine, 1981—. Mem. Nat. Assn. Social Workers, Northside Bus. Profl. Assn. Democrat. Roman Catholic. Avocations: fishing, bridge, stamp collecting, knitting, reading. Office: Lakeside Family Therapy Services 4810 Northwestern Ave Racine WI 53402

KLEPERIS, JOHN VICTOR, aerospace executive, former air force officer; b. Jaunrauna, Latvia, June 19, 1935; came to U.S., 1950, naturalized, 1955; s. Otto and Elza Otilija (Zarins) K.; m. Margaret Dean, Dec. 28, 1957; children—John V., Jr., Richard W. B.A. in Math., U. Conn., 1957; M.S. in Materials Engring., Air Force Inst. Tech., 1964. Registered profl. engr., Ohio. Commd. 2d lt. U.S. Air Force, 1957, advanced through grades to col., 1977; dir. program mgmt. Andrews Air Force Base, Md., 1976-77; dir. simulator SPO, Aeronautical Div., Wright Patterson Air Force Base, Ohio, 1977-79, dir. SPO cadres, 1979-80, dir. F-15 projects, 1980-82, dir. tactical planning, 1982-84; retired, 1984; dir. advanced concepts Sci. Applications Internat. Corp., Dayton, Ohio, 1984—. Decorated Legion of Merit, D.F.C., Bronze Star, Air medal (8). Mem. Air Force Assn., Am. Def. Preparedness Assn., Soc. Old Crows, Sigma Phi Epsilon, Tau Beta Pi. Republican. Avocations: Gourmet cooking; sports cars. Home: 2399 Meadowgreen Dr Beavercreek OH 45431 Office: Sci Applications Internat Corp 1321 Research Park Dr Dayton OH 45432

KLEPITSCH, FRANK JOHN, architect; b. Chgo., Sept. 1, 1957; s. Frank Joseph and Maria (Stern) K. BS, U. Ill., 1979. Registered architect, Ill. Architect Shaw & Assocs., Inc., Chgo., 1979-81; dir. design Lester B. Knight & Assocs., Chgo., 1981—. Mem. AIA (Cert. of Merit 1986), Soc. Am. Registered Architects (Award of Excellence 1986, Nat. Merit award 1986). Office: Lester B Knight & Assocs Inc 549 W Randolph Chicago IL 60606

KLERKX, MARTIN ALAN, information management executive; b. Detroit, Dec. 1, 1942; s. Walter Martin and Sylvia Imogene (Greene) K.; B.S., Mich. State U., 1964; m. Ruth Ann Bouchard, Dec. 27, 1982; children by previous marriage—Gregory William, David Walter. Staff systems analyst Mich. Consol. Gas Co., Detroit, 1968-69; systems cons. Univ. Computing Co., Detroit, 1969-72; mgmt. cons. Ernst & Whinney, 1972-73; info. systems dir. Mich. Judicial Data Center, 1973-81; mgmt. cons. Peat Marwick Mitchell & Co., 1981-82; gen. mgr. Info. Systems div. TIC Internat., Indpls., 1982-83; dir. info. services agy. City of Indpls. and Marion County, 1984-86; project supr. Guardian Industries Corp., Northville, Mich., 1986—. Served with USN, 1964-68. Mem. Am. Mgmt. Assn., Soc. Mgmt. Info. Systems, Naval Inst. Methodist. Home: 22313 Solomon Blvd Apt #207 Novi MI 48050 Office: Guardian Industries Corp 43043 W Nine Mile Rd Northville MI 48167

KLESNER, JOSEPH LEE, political science educator; b. Ft. Madison, Iowa, Sept. 27, 1958; s. John E. and Darlene B. (Fraise) K.; m. Kimberlee A. Twohill, Nov. 14, 1981. BA, Cen. Coll., Pella, Iowa, 1980; postgrad., U. Va., 1981; SM, Mass. Inst. Tech., 1983, postgrad., 1987. Lectr. pub. adminstrn. Northeastern U., Boston, 1984-85; instr. polit. sci. Kenyon Coll., Gambier, Ohio, 1985—. Contbr. chpt. to book, articles to profl. jours. Fulbright grantee, 1983-84. Mem. Am. Polit. Sci. Assn., Midwest Polit. Sci. Assn., Internat. Studies Assn., Latin Am. Studies Assn. Roman Catholic. Avocations: gardening, basketball, softball. Home: 102 W Woodside Dr Gambier OH 43022 Office: Kenyon Coll Dept Polit Sci Gambier OH 43022

KLETTKE, WILLIAM AUGUST, financial executive; b. Bloomington, Ill., Oct. 28, 1952; s. William Herman and Dorothy Lucille (Miller) K.; m. Catherine Jean Capodice, Apr. 19, 1980. BA in Psychology and Sociology, Baker U., 1974; BS in Acctg., Ill. State U., 1975; M in Mgmt., Northwestern U., 1985. CPA, Ill. Surp. acctg. Enterprise Paint co., Wheeling, Ill., asst. controller, controller; v.p. adminstrn. Enterprise Paint co., Wheeling, v.p. fin.; v.p. fin. ERO Industries, Chgo., 1987—. Mem. creditor com. Wickes Creditors Commn., Los Angeles, 1983-1985; trustee Midco waste site EPA Super Fund, 1985-1987. Mem. Am. Inst. CPA's, Ill. Soc. CPA's, Nat. Assn. Accts. Republican. Lutheran. Avocations: reading, fishing, hiking, chess, photography. Home: 6117 Wyndwood Dr Crystal Lake IL 60014 Office: 8130 N Lehigh Morton Grove IL 60653

KLICAR, FRANK MARK, film producer; b. Chgo., Dec. 10, 1941; s. Frank George and Frances Catherine (Pozgay) K.; m. Margaret Ann Cruse, Oct. 18, 1975. BS in Zoology, Roosevelt U., 1964. Pres. Megamark Films, Downers Grove, Ill., 1968—; cons. pub. affairs Forest Preserve Dist. of DuPage County, Ill., 1970-79. Producer, cinematographer: (films) Passage to Spain, 1983, China-The Dragon Awakes, 1986. Served to comdr. USN, 1964-67, Vietnam. Mem. Internat. Motion Picture and Lectrs. Assn. (bd. dirs. 1985—), Internat. Fedn. Tourism Writers, Naval Reserve Assn., Naperville (Ill.) Astron. Assn. Avocations: astronomy, skiing. Office: Megamark Films 19 W 456 Deerpath Ln Lemont IL 60439

KLIEGMAN, PAULA GOLDEN, social worker; b. Chgo., Mar. 23, 1937; d. Herman H. and Ethel (Kamfner) Golden. BA, Northwestern U., 1958; AM, U. Chgo., 1960. Cert. social worker. Social worker La Rabida Hosp., Chgo., 1960-66, Child and Family Services, Chgo., 1963-66; social worker, assoc. chief social services Dept. Psychiatry Michael Reese Hosp., Chgo., 1966—; cons. Cicero (Ill.) Family Services, 1980-82; tchr. Inst. Psychoanalysis, Chgo., 1976-79. Contbr. articles on parenting to profl. jours. Mem. Nat. Assn. Social Workers, Assn. Child Psychotherapists (treas. 1978-79), Am. Orthopsychiat. Assn. Avocations: riding horses, dressage. Home: 1607 E 50th Pl Chicago IL 60615 Office: 111 N Wabash #822 Chicago IL 60602

KLIEWER, HENRY B., educator, farmer, lay minister; b. Henderson, Nebr., Sept. 1, 1904; s. Peter J. and Susanna (Buller) K.; A.B., York Coll., Nebr., 1931; A.M., U. Nebr., 1939; postgrad. Kans. State U., Emporia, 1953-67; m. Eva Peters, Aug. 18, 1927; children—Marion Waller, Lowell Joyce, Herald James, Ruth Elaine. Tchr. rural schs., Nebr., 1923-29; tchr. Henderson High Sch., 1931-35, prin., 1935-39; supt. Henderson Public Schs., 1939-48; prin. Hillsboro (Kans.) High Sch., 1948-55; supt. Unified Sch. Dist. 410, Hillsboro, 1955-69, Corn (Okla.) Bible Sch., 1969-72; instr. Bible, Tabor Coll., Hillsboro, 1972-75; ordained minister Mennonite Brethren Ch., 1943, pastor, Henderson, also Corn, 1969-72; sec. Mennonite Aid Plan, Dist. 25, Hillsboro, 1978—, chmn. Mennonite Brethren Bd. Publs., 1954-57; mem. Parkside Homes, Inc.; coordinator Parkside Fund Drive. Mem. Hillsboro C. of C., Nebr. Tchrs. Assn., Kans. Tchrs. Assn., Am. Assn. Sch. Adminstrs., NEA. Club: Kiwanis (pres. Hillsboro 1976-77, lt. gov. Div. V, Kans. dist. 1979-80). Home and Office: 110 N Adams St Hillsboro KS 67063

KLIGERMAN, CHARLES, psychoanalyst; b. Phila., Apr. 22, 1916; s. Nathan and Edith (Cutler) K.; m. Honore Sue Schlesinger, June 7, 1956; children: Daniel, Rachel Naomi, Peter Nathan. AB, Dartmouth Coll., 1937; MD, U. Chgo., 1941; cert., Chgo. Inst. for Psychoanalysis, 1952. Diplomate Am. Bd. Psychiatry and Neurology. Instr. psychiatry U. Chgo., 1950-52; mem. staff and council Chgo. Inst. for Psychoanalysis, 1958-86; lectr. U. Chgo., 1958-78; tng. analyst Chgo. Inst. for Psychoanalysis, 1957—. Coauthor: Psychosomatic Specificity, 1968; contbr. over 20 articles to profl. jours. Served as capt. AUS, 1943-46, ETO. Fellow Am. Psychiat. Assn.; mem. Am. Psychoanalytic Assn. Jewish. Avocations: quartet and chamber violin, tennis, travel, art history. Home: 5803 Blackstone Ave Chicago IL 60637 Office: 180 N Michigan Ave Chicago IL 60601

KLIMEK, EDWARD MARK, pediatrician, educator; b. Warren, Ohio, May 17, 1950; s. Joseph and Ruth Marie (Blystone) K.; m. Nancy Rae Kearbey, June 12, 1976; children: Joseph Eugene, Stephanie Lynn. BS in Biology, Youngstown State U., 1972; postgrad., 1972-73; DO, Coll. Osteo. Medicine and Surgery, Des Moines, 1976. Diplomate Nat. Bd. Examiners Osteo. Physicians and Surgeons, Am. Osteo. Bd. Pediatrics (bd. cert.). Rotating intern Grandview Hosp., Dayton, Ohio, 1976-77; resident in pediatrics Chgo. Osteo. Hosp., 1977-79, chief pediatric resident, 1978-79, asst. prof. pediatrics, 1979-85, assoc. prof. pediatrics, 1985—, assoc. chmn. dept. pediatrics, 1984—, resident trainer, program dir. dept. pediatrics, 1984—; sec., treas. staff Chgo. Osteo. Hosp., Olympia Fields Osteo. Med. Ctr., 1981-82, vice chief of staff, 1982-83; acting chmn. dept. pediatrics Chgo. Coll. Osteo. Medicine, 1984-85; mem. staff, 1979—; mem. staff Olympia Field Osteo. Med. Ctr., 1979—; mem. exec. staff Chgo. Coll. Osteo. Medicine, 1981—. Contbr. articles to profl. jours. Named Resident of Yr. Chgo. Coll. Osteo. Medicine, 1979, Outstanding Educator, 1984; recipient 1st place writing award Am. Coll. Osteo. Pediatrics, 1979. Mem. Student Osteo. Med. Assn., Am. Osteo. Assn., Ill. Assn. Osteo. Physicians and Surgeons, Am. Coll. Osteo. Pediatricians (sr., residency insp.). Baptist. Avocations: photography, stamp collecting. Office: Olympia Fields Osteo Med Ctr 20201 S Crawford Ave Olympia Fields IL 60411

KLINCK, BRUCE DEE, operations director; b. Toledo, Ohio, Nov. 24, 1940; s. Norman Earl and Minnie Mary K.; student U. Toledo, 1958-59, Owens Tech. Coll., 1975-78; m. Carole Faye Henson, Oct. 7, 1961; children—Bruce Allen, Lisa Michelle. Sample maker, photo specialist Owens Ill. Glass Co., Toledo, 1959-63; with Toledo Police, 1963-84, with selective enforcement units, 1967-73, with planning and research unit, 1974-84; cons./specialist crowd control, pre-planning mass crowd events, indsl. and retail security, 1979—, on constrn. and remodelling of police facilities. Recipient 1st place award Internat. Chiefs of Police Facilities Workshop, 1978. Mem. Ohio Police Planners Assn., Nat. Assn. Police Planners (charter mem.). Democrat. Lutheran. Office: Five Seagate 408 N Summit St Toledo OH 43604

KLINE, BRUCE EDWARD, health science facility administrator; b. Woodstock, Ill., Aug. 23, 1944; s. Bruce Leffingwell and Kneldrith Eileen (Harden) K.; m. Linda Sue Wallis, Aug. 20, 1964 (dec. Aug. 1969); Leora Kathleen Martin, Dec. 27, 1970; children: April A., Jonathan D. AA, Cen. Coll., McPherson, Kans., 1964; BS, Greenville (Ill.) Coll., 1968; MS, Wichita (Kans.) State U., 1977; D in Psychology, Wright State U., 1982. Lic. psychologist, Ohio. Intern Green Meml. Hosp., Green Hall, Ohio, 1980, Clark County Community Mental Health Ctr., Ohio, 1981-82; resident in psychology Sch. Profl. Psychology Consortium, Wright State U., 1983; high sch. tchr. Unified Dist. 418, McPherson, Kans., 1968-75; prof. Sterling Coll., Kans., 1976-80; clin. dir. Mingenback Family Life Ctr., McPherson, 1977-80; dir. psychology Millcreek Psychiat. Hosp., Cin., 1983—; pvt. practice Kline and Assocs., Dayton, Ohio, 1983—; dir. Ctr. Exceptional Children and Adults, Dayton, 1985—; research assoc. Menninger Found. Hosp., Topeka, 1977—. Co-author: Awareness and Change, 1981; contbr. articles to profl. jours. Mem. Am. Psychol. Assn., Ohio Psychol. Assn., World Fedn. Mental Health, World Council Gifted Children, Nat. Assn. Gifted Children, Ohio Assn. Gifted Children, Nat. Register of Health Care Providers. Methodist. Home: 4601 Carlyle Circle Kettering OH 45429 Office: 529 E Stroop Kettering OH 45429

KLINE, GERALD RAY, research physicist; b. Marshalltown, Iowa, Jan. 8, 1945; s. Franklin Carlyle and Flossie Mae (Van Gorp) K.; m. Carol Rae Andreessen, Feb. 13, 1971. BA, William Jewell Coll., 1967. With Ames (Iowa) Lab., 1967-82, with Rare Earth Info. Ctr, 1967-69, asst. physicist x-ray diffraction, 1969-71, asst. physicist neutron diffraction, 1971-76, assoc. physicist neutron diffraction, 1976-79, assoc. physicist solar energy research, 1979-82; assoc. physicist Microelectronics Research Ctr., Ames, 1982—. Contbr. articles to profl. jours.; inventor acoustic resonator and method for making same. Mem. Sigma Pi Sigma. Office: Microelectronics Research Ctr 1925 Scholl Rd Ames IA 50011

KLINE, JAMES EDWARD, lawyer; b. Fremont, Ohio, Aug. 3, 1941; s. Walter J. and Sophia Kline; m. Mary Ann Bruening, Aug. 29, 1964; children: Laura Anne, Matthew Thomas, Jennifer Sue. BS in Social Sci., John Carroll U., 1963; JD, Ohio State U., 1966. Bar: Ohio 1966. Assoc. Eastman & Smith, Toledo, 1966-70; ptnr. Eastman, Stichter, Smith & Bergman, 1970-84, Shumaker, Loop & Kendrick, 1984—; corp. sec., Sheller-Globe Corp. 1977-84; bd. dirs. Bostleman Corp., Diversified Material Handling, Inc., Security Funding, Inc., Essex Devel. Group. Trustee Kidney Found. of Northwestern Ohio, Inc., 1972-81, pres., 1979-80; bd. dirs. Crosby Gardens, Toledo, 1974-80, pres., 1977-79; trustee Toledo Symphony Orch., 1981—; bd. dirs. Toledo Zool. Soc., 1983—, Toledo Area Regional Transit Authority, 1984—, Home Away From Home, Inc. (Ronald McDonald House NW Ohio), 1983—. Fellow Ohio Bar Found.; mem. ABA, Ohio State Bar Assn. (corp. law com. sec. 1973-76, vice chmn. 1977-82, chmn. 1977-82, 83-86), Toledo Bar Assn., Nat. Assn. Corp. Dirs., Toledo Area C. of C. Roman Catholic. Clubs: Inverness, Toledo. Home: 5958 Swan Creek Dr Toledo OH 43614 Office: 1000 Jackson Blvd Toledo OH 43624

KLINE, MABLE CORNELIA PAGE, educator; b. Memphis, Aug. 20, 1928; d. George M. and Lillie (Davidson) Brown; 1 dau., Gail Angela Page. Student LeMoyne Coll.; B.S.Ed., Wayne State U., 1948, postgrad. Tchr., Flint, Mich., 1950-51, Pontiac, Mich., 1953-62; tchr. 12th grade English, Cass Tech High Sch., Detroit, 1962—, coordinator Summer Sch. High Sch. Proficiency Program. Life mem. YWCA, NAACP. Mem. NEA (life), Assn. Supervision and Curriculum Devl., Am. Fedn. Tchrs., Nat. Council Tchrs. English, Internat. Platform Assn., Wayne State U. Alumni Assn., Delta Sigma Theta. Episcopalian. Home: 1101 Lafayette Towers W Detroit MI 48207 Office: 2421 2d Ave Detroit MI 48207

KLINE, RAYMOND CURTIS, manufacturing company executive; b. Kansas City, Mo., Oct. 7, 1931; s. Raymond Irving and Mary Agnes (Redeker) K.; m. Dorothy Gene Wymore, Oct. 1, 1955; children: Karen Ann, Randall Irving. BSEE, Finlay Engring. Coll., Kansas City, Mo., 1951; student in bus., Rockhurst Coll., 1958-61. Registered profl. engr., Mo. Engr. Union Wire Rope, Kansas City, Mo., 1951-61; gen. foreman maintenance Armco Inc., Kansas City, 1961-66, supr. maintenance and cost control, 1966-70, sr. engr., 1970-85; mfg. mgr. Schroer Mfg. Co., Kansas City, 1985—. Active Jackson County (Mo.) Com., 1973-75, Church Choir, Raytown, Mo. Served with U.S. Army, 1952-54. Recipient Spl. Recognition award Jr. Achievement, Kansas City, 1969, spl. award Steel Mag., 1969. Mem. Am. Inst. Plant Engrs. (pres. 1958-86, Engr. of Yr. 1972), Internat. Mgmt. Club (pres. 1966-84, Spl. Recognition award 1981, R. C. Rhoades award 1983), Am. Prodn. and Inventory Control Soc., Tau Kappa Epsilon. Republican. Roman Catholic. Lodge: KC. Avocations: golf, tennis, bowling, photography. Home: 7501 Overton Raytown MO 64138 Office: Schroer Mfg Co 2221 Campbell Kansas City MO 64108

KLINE, ROBIN SANDERS, rehabilitation executive; b. Norfolk, Va., Apr. 16, 1953; d. George Harding and Sylvia (Wudel) Sanders; m. Ted Arnold Kline, May 25, 1974; 1 child, Jay Arnold. B.S., U. Wis., 1974; M.S., DePaul U., 1979. Dir. rehab. Goodwill Industries, Des Moines, 1974-79; exec. dir. Boone County Developmental Disabilities Council, Boone, Iowa, 1979-80; ctr. dir. Assn. Retarded Citizens of Polk County, Des Moines, 1980-82; extended employment coordinator, program evaluation coordinator Opportunity Workshop, Minnetonka, Minn., 1982—. Surveyor, Commn. on Accreditation Rehab. Facilities, Tucson, 1978—. Mem. Nat. Rehab. Assn., Iowa Rehab. Assn., Minn. Rehab. Assn., Vocat. Evaluation and Work Adjustment Assn., Minn. Rehab. Assn. Avocations: camping; canoeing; computers. Office: Opportunity Workshop Inc 5500 Opportunity Ct Minnetonka MN 55343

KLINENBERG, EDWARD LEE, communications company executive; b. Chgo., Mar. 21, 1942; s. Jerome Jacob and Muriel (Abrams) K.; B.A. in English, U. Mich., 1963; postgrad. U. Paris, 1964-65; children—Eric Martin, Danielle Elyse. Public info. dir. Chgo. unit Am. Cancer Soc., 1966-67; account exec. Stral Advt. Co., Chgo., 1967-69; pres. Precise Communications, Inc., Chgo., 1969—; leader seminars, speaker in field. Bd. dirs., v.p. public relations Hull House Assn., Chgo., 1977—; bd. dirs. Internat. Visitors Center Chgo., 1975-77; pres. Old Town Triangle Assn., 1975-77. Served with AUS, 1965-66. Mem. Chgo. Council Fgn. Relations (dir. 1969-76), Com. on Fgn. and Domestic Affairs (exec. com. 1978—). Office: 233 E Erie St Chicago IL 60611

KLING, GEORGE ALBERT, radiologist; b. Mt. Clemens, Mich., May 25, 1934; s. Albert Peter and Dorothy Mae (Elson) K.; m. Judith Ann Nickel, Aug 18, 1956; children: Victoria E., Cynthia E., Jeffrey G. MD, U. Mich., 1958. Diplomate Am. Bd. Radiology. Intern Harper Hosp., Detroit, 1958-59, resident, 1959-62; pres. L. Reynolds Assoc., PC, Detroit, 1975—; chief dept. radiology Harper-Grace Hosp.; mem. staff Children's Hosp.; assoc. prof. radiology Wayne State U., chmn. dept. radiology, 1984—. Contbr. articles to Am. Jour. Roentgenology. Served with M.C., U.S. Army, 1966-68. Decorated Bronze Star. Fellow Am. Coll. Radiology; mem. AMA, Mich. State Med. Soc., Wayne County Med. Soc., Am. Roentgen Ray Soc. (mgr.), Mich. Radiol. Soc. (past sec., treas.), Detroit Gastrointestinal Soc., Detroit Acad. Medicine (sec., treas. 1986), Bockus Internat., Profl. Conv. Mgmt. Assn. Club: Detroit Athletic. Home: 208 Moran Grosse Pointe Farms MI 48236 Office: 3990 John R St Detroit MI 48201

KLING, JOHN ANTHONY, computer systems executive; b. Orange, N.J., May 16, 1938; s. John Joseph and Madeline Ruth (Marcelle) K.; m. Sharon Jewelle LaForest, Aug. 19, 1961; children: Larry John, Darren Scott. AA, Triton Coll., 1975; BA, Elmhurst Coll., 1981. Cert. data processor, Ill. Programmer, analyst Motorola C & E, Inc., Chgo., 1965-69; sr. systems analyst Alberto-Culver, Melrose Park, Ill., 1969-71; sr. project mgr. Victor Comptometer, Chgo., 1971-75; mgr. systems devel. Kroehler Mfg. Co., Naperville, Ill., 1975-79; mgr. applications systems Duchossois Industries, Inc., Elmhurst, Ill., 1979—; v.p. Chamberlain Employee Fed. Credit Union, Elmhurst, 1980—; cons. Computerland, Elmhurst, 1986; bd. dirs., founder Pat-Bus. Assocs., Inc., 1987. Bd. dirs. Elmhurst United Way, 1983-85. Served with USAF, 1957-61. Lutheran. Lodge: Lions (candy day chmn. Elmhurst 1986, bd. dirs. Elmhurst 1984-86, v.p. Elmhurst 1986-87, Myron Luhrsen Meml. award 1985). Avocations: golf, swimming, stamp collecting, bike riding. Home: 185 Evergreen St Elmhurst IL 60126 Office: Duchossois Industries Inc 845 Larch Ave Elmhurst IL 60126

KLING, SANDRA SCHOENBERG, civic organization director; b. Winnipeg, Manitoba, Can., Dec. 25, 1932; came to U.S., 1944; d. Joseph Samuel and Yhetta (Tritt) Perlman; m. Harry W. Schoenberg, Aug. 1, 1954 (div. 1978); children: Mark Schoenberg, Jennifer Schoenberg-Schaeffer, Richard Schoenberg; m. Merle Kling, 1978. BA, Sarah Lawrence Coll., 1954; M in Govt. Adminstrn., U. Pa., 1969; PhD, Bryn Mawr Coll., 1974. Asst. prof. sociology Washington U., St. Louis, 1973-81, asst. prof. dept. psychiatry Sch. Medicine, 1981-83; assoc. prof. sociology Hofstra U., Hempstead, N.Y., 1983-85; exec. dir. Citizens for Modern Transit, 1985—. Author: Neighborhoods That Work, 1980; contbr. articles to profl. jours. Mem. Am. Sociol. Assn. (program chmn. community sect. 1982), Midwest Sociol. Soc. (chmn. pubs. com. 1981), Eastern Sociol. Assn., Sociologists for Women in Society. Democrat. Jewish. Home: 20 N Kings Hwy Saint Louis MO 63108

KLING, TIMOTHY GEORGE, physician; b. Newton, Iowa, Apr. 8, 1944; s. Henry Leonard Kling and Marianna (Dunn) Schell; m. Marilyn Kay Heady, Aug. 8, 1965; children: Timothy Andrew, Nathan David. BS, U. Iowa, 1966, MD, 1971. Diplomate Am. Bd. Ob-Gyn. Resident in ob-gyn U. Iowa., Iowa City, 1974; gen. practice medicine specializing in ob-gyn Macomb, Ill., 1974—; dir. ob-gyn McDonough Hosp., Macomb, 1977, 79, 83; chief med. staff, 1978. Contbr. articles to profl. jours. U. Iowa Coll. Medicine scholar Oxford, Eng., 1971. Fellow Am. Coll. Ob-Gyn; mem. AMA, Am. Fertility Soc., Ill. Med. Soc., Macomb Area C. of C. (pres. 1986-87), Am. Shetland Sheepdog Assn. (bd. dirs. 1984—). Republican.

KLINGBERG, WILLIAM G(ENE), JR., manufacturing executive; b. St. Louis, Dec. 19, 1943; s. William G. and Barbara Jean (Hendrickson) K.; m. Adele R. Martello, Dec. 30, 1977; children: Robert, Lucas. BS MechE, W.Va. U., 1966. Regional mgr. The Duriron Co., Dayton, Ohio, 1968-83; v.p., sales mgr. Peabody Barnes Inc. subs. Peabody Internat. Corp., Mansfield, Ohio, 1983—. Bd. dirs. Jr. Achievement, Mansfield, 1986. Mem. Submersible Wastewater Pump Assn. Republican. Presbyterian. Avocations: tennis, sports cars. Home: 1554 Brookpark Dr Mansfield OH 44906 Office: Peabody Barnes Inc 651 N Main St Mansfield OH 44902

KLINK, BRIAN JEFFERY, bank marketing executive; b. Lincoln, Ill., Aug. 9, 1957; s. Darrell Ellsworth and Cynthia (Denbo) K.; m. Tamera Lee Burwell, Jan. 27, 1979; children: Jeffery Winston, Karissa Lee, Kristina Roseann. BS, Western Ill. U., Macomb, 1979, MBA, 1981. Product analyst Citicorp Savs. Ill., Chgo., 1981-82, sr. product analyst, 1982-84; product devel. mgr. The Marine Corp., Milw., 1984-87; mgr. Fed. Res. Bank, Chgo., 1987—. Mem. Bank Mktg. Assn., Assn. MBA Execs., Internat. Assn. Fin. Planners. Republican. Methodist. Club: Toastmaster. Avocations: all sports, fin. investments. Home: 21W240 Walnut Glen Ellyn IL 60137 Office: Fed Res Bank of Chgo 230 S LaSalle Chicago IL 60603

KLINKHAMMER, STEPHEN PHILLIP, health care administrator; b. Racine, Wis., Oct. 10, 1954; s. Phillip Henry and Faythe Rita (Newton) K.; m. Rita Helen Bencriscutto, May 6, 1978; children: Justin, Adam, Jordan, Zachary. Student, U. Wis., Parkside, 1976-78, Gateway Tech. Inst., Racine, Wis., 1982-83; Assoc. in Nursing, Gateway Tech. Inst., Kenosha, Wis., 1981; BS in Mgmt., Cardinal Stritch Coll., Milw., 1985—. RN, Wis.; cert. alcohol and drug abuse counselor. Counselor Innovative Youth Services Racine Inc., 1976-77; dir. Alcohol and Other Drug Abuse Spanish Ctrs., Racine, 1977-79; RN intensive care unit St. Mary's Med. Ctr., Racine, 1981-86; dir. home care Burlington Outreach subs. Coordinated Health and Mgmt. Services, Milw., 1986; dir. devel. Coordinated Health and Mgmt. Services, Brown Deer, Wis., 1986—. Contbg. author: Everything We Had: Oral History of the Vietnam War, 1981; contbr. articles on Vietnam veterans and post traumatic stress syndrome to profl. jours. Bd. dirs. Racine Veteran's Assn., 1981—. Served with M.C. USN, 1972-76, as 2d lt. Nurse Corps USAR, 1986—. Recipient Outstanding Contbns. to the Community by a Vietnam veteran award Pres. Jimmy Carter, 1980. Mem. VFW (post surgeon 1983—), Wis. Assn. Concerned Veterans (v.p. 1986—, dir. health care com. 1978-86, bd. dirs. 1979-81), Nat. Assn. Concerned Veterans (cons. 1979-81), state coordinator 1979-81), Am. Assn. Critical Care Nurses, Smithsonian Inst. Assocs. Roman Catholic. Avocations: profl. pianist, musician, model shipbuilding. Home: 2920 Jean Ave Racine WI 53404

KLIPFELL, JOHN MARTIN, III, controller; b. Cleve., Sept. 2, 1949; s. John Martin Jr. and Sophie Josephine (Prusick) K.; m. Cheryl Ann Maresh, Sept. 7, 1970; children: John, Elizabeth. CPA, Ohio. Staff acct. Battelle & Battelle CPA's, Dayton, Ohio, 1971-74; internal auditor Am. Greetings Corp., Cleve., 1975-76, dir. corp. acctg., 1976-82, asst. controller, 1982-83, corp. controller, 1983—. Mem. St. Vincent De Paul Soc., Strongsville, Ohio, 1985—. Mem. Am. Inst. CPA's, Nat. Assn. Accts. Roman Catholic. Office: Am Greetings Corp 10500 American Rd Cleveland OH 44144

KLITGAARD, HOWARD MAYNARD, university administrator, consultant; b. Harlan, Iowa, Oct. 16, 1924; s. Andrew Christan and Gladys (Maude) K.; m. Anna Plzakova, Nov. 17, 1945; children—Andrew, Margaret, Michael, Patricia, Diana. B.A., State U. Iowa, 1949, M.S., 1950, Ph.D., 1953. Instr. physiology Marquette U., Milw., 1953-61, asst. chmn. physiology, 1961-66, chmn. basic scis., 1978—; assoc. chmn. physiology Med. Coll. Wis., Milw., 1966-67, vice chmn. physiology, 1967-78; cons. VA Ctr., Wood, Wis., 1957-86. Contbr. articles to profl. jours. Script writer video tapes on boating safety. Comdr. U.S. Power Squadron, Milw., 1984. Served with U.S. Army, 1943-46; ETO. Mem. Am. Physiol. Soc., Endocrine Soc., Soc. Exptl. Biology in Medicine, Sigma Xi, Omicron Kappa Upsilon (hon.). Club: South Shore Yacht (Milw.). Office: Marquette Univ 604 N 16th St Milwaukee WI 53233

KLOBUTCHER, JEROME ALVIN, gynecologist/obstetrician; b. Kankakee, Ill., Nov. 19, 1954; s. Lawrence Matthew and Lucy Joan (Sczukauskas) K.; m. Judith Ann Governile, Sept, 2, 1979; children: Kathryn Elizabeth, Michael Jerome, Andrew Joseph. BS in Biology, Loyola U., Chgo., 1976; MD, Loyola U., Maywood, 1979. Diplomate Nat. Bd. Ob-Gyn. Intern, then resident in ob-gyn Loyola U. Med. Ctr., Maywood, 1979-83; practice medicine specializing in ob-gyn Northwest Ob-Gyn Assoc. Ltd., Park Ridge, Ill., 1983—. Artist numerous paintings. Lobbyist Ill. State Med. Soc. Capital Bldg., Springfield, 1986, Suburban O'Hare Commn. Capital Bldg., 1986, petition seeker, Park Ridge 1988; tribal chief 1986-87, Indian Princesses YMCA,. Mem. AMA, Am. Coll. Ob-Gyn, Cook County Med. Soc., Ill. State Med. Soc. Roman Catholic. Avocations: sports, painting, inventing games. Office: Northwest Ob-Gyn Assoc Ltd 2 Talcott Rd Park Ridge IL 60068

KLOCK, STEVEN WAYNE, electrical engineering technician; b. Deadwood, S.D., Apr. 16, 1954; s. Earl Leroy and Irma Helena (Neamy) K.; m. Robin Ann Barney, June 25, 1982; children: Tana, Renee, Thomas, Stephanie. Cert., Denver Inst. Tech., 1974; student, S.D. Sch. Mines and Tech., 1980—. Test tech. Magnetic Peripherals Inc., Rapid City, S.D., 1974-76, group leader, 1976-81, engring. tech., 1981—. Mem. S.D. Emergency Med. Technician Assn. Democrat. Avocations: computers, restoring early Mustangs. Office: Magnetic Peripherals Inc 222 Disk Dr Rapid City SD 57701

KLODT, GERALD JOSEPH, office products executive; b. Ottumwa, Iowa, Feb. 6, 1949; s. Edward William and Isabelle Margaret (Herrmann) K.; m. Menzi Louise Behrnd, May 26, 1979. BFA, U. Iowa, 1971, MA, 1972; MFA, U. Ill., 1974, U. Wis., 1979. Designer Tevcin, Inc., Perry, Iowa, 1972-75; assoc. designer William Stumpf & Assocs., Middleton, Wis., 1975-77; prof. design U. Wis., Madison, 1977-84; engr. Fel-Pro Energy Inc., Lake Geneva, Wis., 1982-83; pres., chief exec. officer Klodt & Assocs., Madison, 1977—; v.p. research and devel. W.T. Rogers Co., Madison, 1984—; cons. engr. Linton Assocs., Chesieres, Switzerland, 1984; project dir., engr. U.S. Dept. Energy, Madison, 1980-83; bd. dirs. Kool-View Inc., Madison. Author: Earth Sheltered Housing, 1985; patentee office accessories, creator The Klodt Collection. Bd. dirs. Energy Idea Exchange, Madison, 1978-80; mem. Wis. State Resources Advisory Panel, 1978-80; leader, educator Am. Youth Found., Camp Miniwanca, Mich., 1977. Mem. Kappa Sigma. Home: 3409 Stevens St Madison WI 53705

KLODZINSKI, JOSEPH ANTHONY, data communications executive, consultant; b. Chgo., Aug. 19, 1942; s. Joseph Fabian and Haline Ann (Bieganski) K.; m. Mary Margaret Osten, Nov. 19, 1966; children: Joseph II, Catherine Ann, Patricia Ann. BBA, Loyola U., Chgo., 1964; MEd, Boston U., 1968; MBA, Northwestern U., 1971. Packaging engr. Westvaco, Chgo., 1969-72; regional mgr. MacMillan, Chgo., 1972-74; fin. applications cons. IC Systems Corp., Schaumburg, Ill., 1974-77; mgmt. info. systems salesman Honeywell, Chgo., 1977-80; mgmt. info. systems and communications cons. Intertel, Chgo., 1980-82; Midwest dist. mgr. UDS/Motorola, Chgo., 1982—. Contbr. articles to profl. jours. Mem. parish council Ch. of Holy Spirit, Schaumburg, 1980-85. Served to capt. U.S. Army, 1965-69, Vietnam. Decorated Bronze Star; named Pacesetter, Honeywell Mktg. Mgmt., 1978, Top Sales Mgr., IC Systems Corp., 1975-76, Top Sales Mgr., MacMillan, 1974; fellow Lions Clubs Internat. Found., 1984. Mem. Am. Numismatic Assn. of Australia (life), co-founder Australian Numismatic Assn. (Sydney), Oceanic Navigation Research Soc. Roman Catholic. Lodges: K.C., Elks, Lions (pres. Schaumburg 1980-82, DG cabinet No. Ill. zone chmn. 1982-86, dep. dist. gov. 1986—, DG awards 1983-86). Home: 1419 Chalfont Dr Schaumburg IL 60194 Office: UDS/Motorola 3801 W Lake Ave Glenview IL 60025

KLOECKL, JANE MARIE, speech and language clinician; b. Melrose, Minn., May 7, 1955; d. Clarence Joseph and Pauline Christine (Donnay) Ettel; married, July 13, 1985. BA in Elem. Edn., S.W. State U., 1977; BA in Speech Pathology and Audiology, St. Cloud State U., 1978. Tchr., speech clinician Willmar (Minn.) Pub. Schs., 1978-85, Glencoe (Minn.) Pub. Schs., 1985—. Mem. Parent Advocacy for Ednl. Rights, Glencoe, 1978—; counselor Camp Courage, Willmar, 1984-85. Mem. NEA, Willmar Edn. Assn. (bd. dirs. negotiations 1984-85), Minn. Edn. Assn., Crow River Edn. Assn. (unified bargaining com. 1985—). Roman Catholic. Avocations: volleyball, aerobics, biking, swimming. Office: Glencoe Pub Schs Lincoln Elem Sch 16th and Pryor Arlington MN 55336

KLOEHN, RALPH ANTHONY, plastic surgeon; b. Milw., Dec. 18, 1932; s. Ralph Charles and Virginia Mary (kosak) K.; m. Mary Theresa Landers, Nov. 4, 1961; Children: COlleen, Gregory, Kristine, Patricia, Timothy, Philip, Michelle. BS, Marquette U., 1954, MD, 1958. Diplomate Am. Bd. Plastic Surgery. Rotating intern Charity Hosp. La., New Orleans, 1958-59; gen. surgery resident Marquette U. Hosps., Milw., 1961-65; resident in plastic and maxillofacial surgery Galveston, Tex., 1965-68; fellowship in plastic and reconstructive surgery African Med. Research FOund., Nairobi, Kenya, 1968-69; practice medicine specializing in plastic surgery Milw., 1969—. Contbr. articles to profl. jours. Served to lt. USNR, 1959-61. Fellow ACS, Internat. Coll. Surgeons; mem. AMA, Am. Soc. Aesthetic Plastic Surgery, Am. Soc. Plastic and Reconstructive Surgery, Singleton Surgical Soc., Am. Soc. Maxillofacial Surgeons. Republican. Roman Catholic. Avocations: photography, sports fishing. Home: 1305 Helene Dr Brookfield WI 53005 Office: Affiliated Cosmetic and Plastic Surgeons 2323 N Mayfair Rd Suite 503 Milwaukee WI 53226

KLOPFENSTEIN, BRUCE CARL, communications educator; b. Tiffin, Ohio, July 31, 1957; s. Carl Grover and Esther Mae (Willoughby) K.; m. Debra Ann Zam, May 18, 1985. BA, Bowling Green State U., 1979; MA, Ohio State U., 1981, PhD, 1985. Teaching asst. Ohio State U., Columbus, Ohio, 1979-84; news reporter Sta. WTVN-AM, Columbus, 1981-83; research cons. Battelle Meml. Inst., Columbus, 1983-84; research assoc. Online Computer Library Ctr., Dublin, Ohio, 1984-85; research analyst Sta. WOSU-AM-FM-TV, Columbus, 1983-85; asst. prof. mass communications Bowling Green (Ohio) State U., 1985—; dir. Ohio Cable TV Network Study, Ohio Mcpl. League and Ohio Cable TV Assn., Columbus, 1983; mem. grad. faculty Bowling Green State U., 1985—; mem. adj. faculty Franklin U., 1981-83. Contbr. articles, book chpts., papers in field. Recipient Walter B. Emery award Ohio State U. Dept. Communication, 1984. Mem. Internat. Communication Assn., Am. Soc. Info. Sci., Am. Mktg. Assn., Speech Communication Assn., Am. Assn. Pub. Opinion Research, Broadcast Edn. Assn. Mem. United Ch. Christ. Home: 324 Pearl St Bowling Green OH 43402 Office: Bowling Green State U Radio TV and Film Dept Bowling Green OH 43403-0235

KLOPFER, ERIC LESLIE, data processing executive; b. Dayton, Ohio, Oct. 9, 1947; s. Leslie Edward and Loretta Florence (Wendling) K.; m. Claudia Gail Karns, Mar. 6, 1976; children—: Eric Neil, Samantha Erin; 1 child by previous marriage: Christopher Leslie. A.A. in Libral Arts, Sinclair Community Coll., 1978; B.S. in Data Processing, Rockwell U., 1982. Cert. data processor, systems profl. Analyst/programmer Reynolds & Reynolds, Dayton, Ohio, 1969-77; systems analyst NCR Corp., Dayton, 1977; programmer/analyst Allied Tech., Dayton, 1977-78; mgr. data processing Ledex, Inc., Dayton, 1978—; dir. computer services. Mem. Data Processing Mgmt. Assn., Assn. for Cert. of Computer Profls., Assn. System Profls., Assn. Systems Mgmt. Address: 968 Rayberta Dr Vandalia OH 45377

KLOPFLEISCH, CRAIG OLEN, marketing executive; b. Celina, Ohio, Mar. 24, 1949; s. Carl Louis and Odessa Ann (Duncan) K.; m. Nancy Ann Otis, Aug. 14,1976; stepchildren: Thomas Lloyd Cole, Julie Elizabeth Cole. BA, Capital U., 1971; M of Internat. Mgmt., Am. Grad. Sch. of Internat. Mgmt., Glendale, Ariz., 1977. Dir. student activities Capital U., Columbus, Ohio, 1971-73; tng. mgr. Celina Group, 1973-76; div. mktg. mgr. Hilti, Inc., San Francisco, 1977-80; group product mgr. Hilti, Inc., Tulsa, 1980-83; new product devel. mgr. Royston (Ga.) Corp., 1983-84; v.p. mktg., bd. dirs., sec. C. Montaj, Inc., Celina, 1985—; pres., bd. dirs. Cimakon Electronics Corp. Heyde-Mangold Trust fellow, 1971. Lutheran. Lodge: Rotary (fin. chmn. Celina chpt. 1986). Avocations: sailing, woodworking, stained glass, photography. Home: 661 N Main St PO Box 635 Celina OH 45822-0635 Office: The Ashley House 125 W Fayette St Celina OH 45822

KLOSKA, RONALD FRANK, financial executive; b. Grand Rapids, Mich., Oct. 24, 1933; s. Frank B. and Catherine (Hilaski) K.; m. Mary F. Minick, Sept. 7, 1957; children—Kathleen Ann, Elizabeth Marie, Ronald Francis, Mary Josephine, Carolyn Louise. Student, St. Joseph Sem., Grand Rapids, Mich., 1947-53; Ph.B., U. Montreal, Que., Can., 1955; M.B.A., U. Mich., 1957. Staff accountant Lybrand Ross Bros. & Montgomery, Niles, Mich., 1957; staff to sr. accountant Lybrand Ross Bros. & Montgomery, 1960-63; treas., v.p. Skyline Corp., Elkhart, Ind., 1963-67; exec. v.p. finance, treas. Skyline Corp., 1967-74, pres., 1974—, also dir.; dir. Midwest Commerce Banking Co., Elkhart. Bd. trustees Cath. Charities, Ft. Wayne/South Bend, Ind. Served to 1st lt. AUS, 1957-60. Mem. Am. Inst. C.P.A.s, Mich. Soc. CPA's, Ind. Soc. C.P.A.'s. Roman Catholic. Club: South Bend Country. Home: 1329 E Woodside St South Bend IN 46614 Office: Skyline Corp 2520 By Pass Rd Elkhart IN 46514

KLOSTERMAN, LINUS HENRY, controller; b. Highland, Ill., May 21, 1954; s. Arthur A. and Regina C. (Rehkemper) K.; m. Susan M. Kuhl, Oct. 23, 1976; children: Barbara J., Thomas A., Debra R., Philip H. B, So. Ill. U., Edwardsville, 1975. CPA, Ill. Staff acct. R.C. Fietsam & Co. CPA's, Belleville, Ill., 1975-78; v.p., sec., dir. O'Neal Petroleum Inc., Belleville, 1978-87; controller Highland (Ill.) Mfg. & Sales, 1987—; cons. Strata Corp., Columbus, Ohio, 1983—. Mem. St. Dominic Bd. Edn., Breese, Ill., 1985—. Mem. Am. Inst. CPA's, Ill. CPA Soc. Roman Catholic. Lodge: Optimists. Home: 190 N 7th Breese IL 62230

KLOTZ, CHARLES ROBERT, diversified industry executive; b. Wheeling, W.Va., Oct. 10, 1938; s. Helen (Kerringer) K. B.M.E., Fenn Coll., 1962; M.S. in Mech. Engring., Calif. Inst. Tech., 1963; postgrad. Case Western Res. U., 1966-67, Cleve. State U., 1982-83. Propulsion engr. N.Am. Aviation, Downey, Calif., 1962; research engr. Calif. Inst. Tech., Pasadena, 1963; staff engr. Chrysler Space Corp., New Orleans, 1964; prin. research engr. Boeing Co., New Orleans, 1964; pres., prin. scientist C.R. Klotz & Co., Washington, 1965; staff engr. Lear-Siegler, Inc., Cleve., 1965-66; chmn. bd., chief exec. officer Midwest Controls Corp., Cleve., 1967-76; pres. Klotz Aerospace, Klotz Bank, Klotz Consol., Klotz Controls, Klotz Internat., Klotz Law Orgn., 1976—; cons. to various corps.; adv. to Govt. France, French Navy. ASHRAE scholar, 1961; Earle C. Anthony scholar, 1962-63; U.S. Steel Found. fellow, 1963-64; Charles W. Bingham fellow, 1966-67. Mem. ASME, Air Force Assn., Am. Security Council, U.S. Naval Inst., Sigma Xi, Tau Beta Pi, Pi Mu Epsilon. Office: 4241 W 50th St Cleveland OH 44144

KLOTZ, HAROLD ANDREW, JR., electrical engineer, engineering educator; b. Red Bud, Ill., Apr. 1, 1956; s. Harold A. and Ann M. (Sander) K. BSEE, So. Ill. U., Edwardsville, 1978; MSEE, Washington U., St. Louis, 1981; DSc, Wash. U., St. Louis, 1986. Elec. engr. McDonnell Douglas Astronautics Co. div. McDonnell Douglas Corp., St. Louis, 1978—; asst. prof. elec. engring. Washington U., St. Louis, 1985—. Active St. Paul United Ch. of Christ, Columbia, Ill., 1970—; mem. People Against Landfills, St. Clair County, Ill., 1985—. elec. engring. student award St. Louis Elec. Bd. Trade, 1978. Mem. IEEE, AIAA, So. Ill. U.-Edwardsville Engrs. Alumni Assn., Pi Mu Epsilon. Avocations: photography, music, computers. Home: Rural Rt #1 Box 188 East Carondelet IL 62240 Office: McDonnell Douglas Astronautics Co PO Box 516 Saint Louis MO 63166

KLOTZER, CHARLES LOTHAR, publisher, journalist, editor; b. Berlin, Nov. 1, 1925; s. Salo Klotzer and Meta Meyer; m. Rose Libby Finn, June 7, 1953; children: Miriam, Daniel, Ruth. BA, Wash. U., 1954; postgrad., St. Louis. Mng. editor Troy (Ill.) Tribune, 1948-51; editor Jewish Light, St. Louis, 1954-55; dir. pub. relations and advt. Fruin Colnon, St. Louis, 1955-60; founder, editor and pub. Focus Midwest, St. Louis, 1960-84, St. Louis Journalism Rev., 1970—. Served as cpl. U.S. Army, 1951-53. Mem. Soc. Profl. Journalists, St. Louis Press Club, Investigative Reporters and Editors. Jewish. Home: 884 Berick Saint Louis MO 63132 Office: 8380 Olive Blvd Saint Louis MO 63132

KLOUBEC, RICHARD W., state representative; b. 1931; m. Andrew Kloubec, 1958. BA, N.D. State U., 1952. State rep. N.D. Dist. 51, Bismarck, 1973—, speaker of the house, 1987—. Served with AUS. Office: Office of the State Speaker 3233 16th Avenue S #202 Fargo ND 58103 *

KLUG, GERARDO ALBERTO, obstetrician-gynecologist; b. Crespo, Entre Rios, Argentina, Apr. 6, 1943; came to U.S., 1973; s. Santiago and Guillermina (Mildenberger) K.; m. Cheryl Ann VanRaaphorst, Mar. 28, 1980; children: Andrea Guillermina, Stephanie Monica. BS, Colegio San Jose Esperanza, Sante Fe, Argentina, 1962; MD, U. Cordoba, Argentina, 1971. Diplomate Am. Bd. Ob-gyn. Intern Oakwood Hosp., Dearborn, Mich., 1973, resident in ob-gyn, 1974-77; practice medicine specializing in ob-gyn Dearborn, 1977—. Fellow Am. Coll. Ob-Gyn, InterAm. Coll. Physicians and Surgeons; mem. AMA, Wayne County Med. Soc., Mich. State Med. Soc., Am. Assn. Gynecol. Laparoscopists. Republican. Roman Catholic. Avocations: tennis, model airplanes. Home: 407 S Waverly Dearborn MI 48124 Office: Assoc Physicians 24555 Haig Taylor MI 48180

KLUG, PEGGY JEAN, insurance company executive; b. Cedar Rapids, Iowa, July 30, 1957; d. Duane A. and Edna M. (Irons) Johnson; m. Christopher M. Klug. BS, Iowa State U., 1981. CPA, Ill. Sr. auditor Iowa Auditors of State, Des Moines, 1981-82; jr. acct. Shand, Morahan & Co., Inc., Evanston, Ill., 1982-83, sr. acct., 1983-84, supr., 1984-85, asst. mgr., 1985—. Vol. Evanston Homeless Shelter, 1984—. Mem. Ill. CPA Soc. Presbyterian. Avocations: softball, racquetball, volleyball, reading, gardening. Home: 2426 Noyes St Evanston IL 60201 Office: Shand Morahan & Co Inc Shand Morahan Plaza Evanston IL 60201

KLUGE, WILLIAM FREDRICK, rope company executive; b. Chgo., Oct. 22, 1952; s. William Fredrick and Pauline (Green) K.; m. Joanne Marie Sorce, Aug. 19, 1978; 1 child, Kevin William. Student, Western Ill. U., 1970-74. With pub. services Brookfield (Ill.) Zoo, 1967-73; shipping clk. Brad Harrison Co., Countryside, Ill., 1974-77; sales trainee Am. Marine Products, Burr Ridge, Ill., 1977-78; v.p. Am. Cotton Yarns, Westmont, Ill., 1978-83; pres. Phoenix Rope and Cordage Co. Inc., Joliet, Ill., 1983—. Sports reporter for local newspaper. Presbyterian. Avocations: sports, reading, collectables, plants. Office: Phoenix Rope and Cordage Co Inc 280 Alessio Dr Joliet IL 60434

KLUNZINGER, THOMAS EDWARD, writer, reapportionment specialist; b. Ann Arbor, Mich., Sept. 11, 1944; s. Willard Reuben and Katherine Eileen (McCurdy) K.; B.A. cum laude in Advt., Mich. State U., 1966. Copywriter Campbell-Ewald Advt. Co., Detroit, 1966-70; travel cons. Moorman's Travel Service, Detroit, 1973-74; media dir. Taylor for Congress campaign, East Lansing, Mich., 1974; communications specialist House Republican Staff, Lansing, Mich., 1975-80; trustee Meridian Twp., Ingham County, Mich., 1980-84; vice chmn. Econ. Devel. Corp., 1982-84; compliance officer The Eyde Co., Lansing, 1985—. Mem. Ingham County Republican Com., 1976—, sec., 1987-88, Mich. Rep. State Com., 1981-85. Mem. Dramatists Guild, Am. Numismatic Assn., Mich. Numismatic Soc., Zero Population Growth, Mensa. Author: Chester!, 1981; Heavy Lady, 1983; Double Standards, 1985; A Villa in Unadilla, 1985, Incumbering Blues, 1987. Address: PO Box 16231 Lansing MI 48901

KLUSMAN, MARVIN, food products company executive. Chmn. Cass-Clay Creamery, Inc., Fargo, N.D. Office: Cass-Clay Creamery Inc 1220 Main Ave Box 2947 Fargo ND 58108 *

KLUTE, ALLAN ALOYS, physicist, economist, consultant; b. St. Louis, July 19, 1916; s. Aloys J. Henry and Noelie Constance (Jeep) K. A.B., Washington U., St. Louis, 1949, postgrad., 1949-50. Supr. technics office Aero. Chart and Info. Center, St. Louis, 1951-72; pvt. practice as economist and investor, Imperial, Mo., 1972—; investment cons. Active St. Louis Council on World Affairs, UN Assn., Conservation Fedn. Mo. Served to 2d lt. USAAF, 1942-45; prisoner-of-war, Germany, 1944-45. Decorated Air medal, Purple Heart; recipient organizational excellence award USAF, 1970. Mem. Am. Assn. Individual Investors, Mil. Order World Wars, Air Force Assn. Co-developer system of mapping surface of moon.

KLUZA, JEROME JOHN, management consultant; b. Detroit, Jan. 5, 1942; s. John Michael and Elizabeth Florence (Jasinski) K.; m. Marie Carmella Vecchione, Oct. 14, 1978; children: John Jerome, Anne Elizabeth. BS in Indsl. Mgmt., Wayne State U., 1965; MS in Mgmt. Sci., Rensselaer Poly. Inst., 1967. Tng. specialist Tex. Instruments Inc., Attleboro, Mass., 1967-72; sr. program dir. Am. Mgmt. Assn., N.Y.C., 1973-74; supr. tng. and devel. Internat. Paper Co., N.Y.C., 1974-78; mgr. tng. and devel. Dow Chem. Co., Miami, Fla., 1978-81; mgr. mgmt. devel. Rexnord Inc., Brookfield, Wis., 1981-87; pres. Corp. Tng., Brookfield, Wis., 1987—; cons. Arabian Am. Oil Co., Dhahran, Saudi Arabia, 1974; adj. faculty mem. Fordham U., N.Y.C., 1977-78, Bryant Coll., Providence, 1969-70. Editor: American Society of Training and Development. Co-founder Milw. chpt. Couple to Couple League, 1983—. Mem. Sigma Xi, Delta Sigma Rho. Republican. Roman Catholic. Avocations: personal computers, telecommunications, teaching natural family planning. Home: 3140 Old Lantern Dr Brookfield WI 53005 Office: Corp Tng PO Box 1088 Brookfield WI 53008

KLUZNIK, KURT, landscape design building executive; b. Cleve., Sept. 7, 1953; s. Stephen L. and Mary (Parker) K. Provisional registered profl. landscape architect, Ohio. Pres. Yardmaster Inc., Painesville, Ohio, 1971—. Mem. Soc. for Mktg. Profl. Services, Ohio Nurseryman's Assn., Ohio Landscapers Assn., Am. Assn. Nurserymen, Assoc. Landscape Contractor's Assn., Bldg. Industry Assn. Avocation: boating. Office: Yardmaster Inc 1447 N Ridge Rd Painesville OH 44077

KLYKYLO, WILLIAM MICHAEL, psychiatrist; b. Bay City, Mich., Nov. 28, 1948; s. Henry John and Rena Elizabeth (Vicini) K.; m. Dorothyann Feldis, Sept. 1, 1976; children: Michael John. AB, U. Mich., 1970, AM, 1973, MD, 1975. Cert. Am. Bd. Psychiatry and Neurology. Intern Oakwood Hosp., Dearborn, Mich., 1975-76; resident U. Cin., 1976-78, clin. fellow, 1978-80, asst. prof., 1980—; clin. asst. prof. Ohio State U., Columbus, 1980-81; assoc. dir. psychiatry Children's Hosp., Cin., 1980—; cons. CCDD, Cin.; dir. child psychiatry fellowship program U. Cin., 1984—. Contbr. articles to profl. jours. Mem. Finneytown Civic Assn., Cin., 1984—, Dem. Congl. Campaign Com., 1982—, So. Poverty Law Ctr., Montgomery, Ala., 1982—. Mem. AAAS, Am. Acad. Child Psychiatry, Am. Psychiat. Assn., Am. Coll. Psychiatry (Laughlin fellow 1980), Cin. Council Child Psychiatry, Cin. Council Child Psychiatry (pres. 1987-88), Physicians for Social Responsibility, U. Mich. Alumni Assn., Am. Radio Relay League, Med. Amateur Radio Council, Phi Beta Kappa. Democrat. Roman Catholic. Club: Cin. F.M. (pres. 1979-80). Home: 7633 Pineglen Dr Cincinnati OH 45224 Office: Childrens Hosp Med Ctr Elland and Bethesda Aves Cincinnati OH 45229

KLYMAN, CASSANDRA MORLEY, psychoanalyst; b. N.Y.C., Jan. 1, 1938; d. Frank Britton and Wanda Delores (Zielinski) Brooks; m. Calvin, June 26, 1960; children: Marc, Robert. BA, Barnard Coll., 1958; MD, U. Mich., 1962. Diplomate Am. Bd. Psychiatry and Neurology. Intern Children's Hosp., Detroit, 1962-63; resident in psychiatry Sinai Hosp., Detroit, 1963-66; sr. attending psychiatrist Sinai Hosp.; practice medicine specializing psychiat. medicine Bloomfield Hills, Mich., 1966—; asst. clin. prof. Wayne State U., 1975—. Contbr. articles to profl. jours. Fellow Am. Psychiat. Assn., Am. Acad. Psychoanalysis; mem. Am. Psychoanalytic Soc. (assoc.), Mich. Psychiat. Soc., Internat. Psychoanalytic Soc.. Jewish. Club: Barnard. Avocations: tennis, travel, movies. Home: 3060 Chickering Ln Bloomfield Hills MI 48013

K'MET, JAMES ALLEN, cabinet manufacturing company owner; b. Chgo., Feb. 20, 1938; s. Paul A. and Anna (Tobolik) K.; m. Vivian E. DeSalvo, June 13, 1959; children: Darlene Cozzi, Dean (dec.), Lisa, Christine. Carpenter Chgo., 1956-65, salesman constrn. products, 1965—; owner Harwood Cabinet Co., Harwood Heights, Ill., 1982—. Author (quarterly bus. newsletter) Kmet Kronical, 1969—. Juvenile worker Village of Harwood Heights, 1959-61. Mem. Nat. Kitchen and Bath Assn. (cert. kitchen designer 1982), N.W. Builders Assn. Democrat. Roman Catholic. Lodge: Rotary. Avocation: woodworking. Home and Office: Harwood Cabinet Co 4936 N Oconto Ave Harwood Heights IL 60656

KNABUSCH, CHARLES THAIR, manufacturing company executive; b. Detroit, Nov. 25, 1939; s. Edward M. and Henrietta (Muelhisen) K.; m. June Ellen Heck, June 30, 1962; children: Charles Jr., Debora, Michael, Christopher. AB, Cleary Coll., Ypsilanti, Mich., 1962. Pres., chief exec. officer La-Z-Boy Chair Co., Monroe, Mich., 1961—. Mem. Nat. Assn. Furniture Mfrs. (pres. 1981). Office: La-Z-Boy Chair Co 1284 N Telegraph Rd Monroe MI 48161

KNACK, THOMAS MICHAEL, psychologist; b. Saginaw, Mich., June 24, 1950; s. Francis Robert Knack and June Rose (Bowerman) Willing; m. Susan Lynne Skalla, Aug. 22, 1980; children: Laura Elyse, Marissa Christina. BA, U. Mich., 1972, EdS, 1975, MA, 1976, PhD, 1978; cert., Western Mich. Biofeedback Inst., 1978. Lic. psychologist, Mich. Tchr. Gabriel Richard High Sch., Riverview, Mich., 1972-74; psychologist Birch Run (Mich.) Schs., 1975, Child Guidance Clinic, Saginaw, 1976-79, Planning for Living, Bay City, Mich., 1979-81; psychologist, co-dir. Mid-Mich. Psychol. Services, Saginaw, 1981-83; pvt. practice psychology Saginaw, 1983—; cons. Saginaw County Juvenile Ct., 1976—, Saginaw County Child Devel. Ctr., Inc., 1979—, Tuscola County Dept. Social Services, Caro, Mich., 1979—, Underground R.R. Women's Shelter, 1979—. Contbr. to McCarthy Screening Psychol. Test, 1978. Bd. dirs. READ Assn. Saginaw County, 1977-79. Mem. Am. Psychol. Assn., Mich. Psychol. Assn., Mich. Soc. Clin. Psychologists, Mid-Mich. Psychologists, Inc. (pres. 1977-79), U. Mich. Alumni Club Saginaw (bd. govs. 1985-87). Democrat. Roman Catholic. Club: U. Mich. Alumni (bd. govs. Saginaw 1985-86). Avocations: bikeriding, water skiing, football. Office: 2076 Hemmeter Rd Saginaw MI 48603

KNAFLA, ROY THOMAS, systems programmer, consultant; b. Shreveport, La., July 23, 1960; s. Roy Thomas and Linda Jane (Bartlett) K. BA in Computer Sci., U. Minn., Duluth, 1983. Systems programmer UNISYS, Roseville, Minn., 1984—; cons. in field. Avocations: golf, hunting, fishing, motorcycling, weight lifting. Home: 13316 Linwood Forest Circle Champlin MN 55316 Office: UNISYS Corp 2276 Highcrest Rd Roseville MN 55113

KNAK, ROGER DALE, firefighter; b. Hillsboro, Kans., Nov. 11, 1958; s. Eldon Willard and Hilda (Funk) K.; m. Linda Jean Barnes, Oct. 27, 1979. AS, Dodge City (Kans.) Community Coll., 1979. Paramedic, firefighter Ford County Fire Dept., Dodge City, 1978—; instr. firefighting and emergency med. tech. recert. classes. fund-raiser Muscular Dystrophy, Dodge City, 1981—, mem. Ch. Sanctuary Choir, Dodge City, 1984—; organizer Toys for Tots program, Dodge City, 1985. Named Eagle Scout, Boy Scouts Am., 1974, one of Outstanding Young Men Am., 1985; recipient cert. of recognition Muscular Dystrophy Assn., 1983. Mem. Internat. Assn. Firefighters Local 2736 (sec., treas. 1981-83, pres. 1983-85), Kans. State Council Firefighters (trustee 1982-85, western v.p. 1985—), Kans. Soc. Fire Service Instrs. Republican. Methodist. Club: Kennel (bd. dirs. Dodge City). Lodges: Masons (jr. deacon). Avocations: fishing, hunting, camping, woodworking. Home: 2204 Ave A Dodge City KS 67801 Office: Ford County Emergency Services 1st and Water Sts Dodge City KS 67801

KNAPIK, RICHARD PATRICK, electrical engineer; b. Cleve., Mar. 16, 1934; s. Michael Thomas and Helen Margaret (Estock) K.; m. Elizabeth Ann Erich, Aug. 3, 1957 (div. Nov. 1981); m. Patricia Anne Gillespie, June 26, 1982; children: Jean Ann, Katherine Mary, Michael Francis, Patricia Ann. AA in Electronic Engring., DeVry Inst. Tech., 1959; cert. in teaching, Kent State U., 1975. Cert. tchr., Ohio. Sr. elec. designer Addressograph-Multigraph, Euclid, Ohio, 1959-65; asst. chief controls engr. Motch & Merryweather, Euclid, 1965-70; tchr. and varsity football coach Brooklyn (Ohio) Bd. Edn., 1971-78; elec. engr. Eaton Corp., Saginaw, Mich., 1978-85; staff engr. Honda Am. Mfg., Marysville, Ohio, 1985—. Author: Vocational Electrical, 1971, Machine Standards, 1981. Served with USN, 1952-56. Republican. Roman Catholic. Avocation: sports coaching. Office: Honda Am Mfg 24000 US Rt 33 Marysville OH 43040

KNAPP, BRIAN ALLEN, hospital administrator; b. Rochester, N.Y., Feb. 15, 1955; s. Dale Gordon and Aileen Nancy (Suter) K.; m. Carla Marie Nelson, Aug. 3, 1985; 1 child, Kevin Nelson. BS in Biology, Bucknell U., 1977; MHA, Duke U., 1979; MBA, Coll. St. Thomas, 1986. Adminstrv. fellow Fairview Community Hosps., Mpls., 1979-80, asst. dir., mgr. affiliated div., 1980-81, asst. dir. mgmt. services Brim & Assoc. subsidiary, 1981-82, dir. mgmt. services, 1982; asst. adminstr. Fairview Ridges Hosp., Burnsville, Minn., 1982—. Mem. Duke U. Hosp. and Health Adminstrn. Alumni Assn., Burnsville C. of C. Lutheran. Avocations: golf, running, reading. Office: Fairview Ridges Hosp 210 E Nicollet Blvd Burnsville MN 55337

KNAPP, DONALD ROY, musician, educator; b. Mpls., Dec. 26, 1919; s. Roy Cecil and Nellie Anette (Johnson) K.; m. Loretto C. Downes, June 5, 1960 (dec. 1975); m. Kimberly J. Carr, May 9, 1977 (div. 1980); 1 child, Deidre. Student Met. Sch. Music, Voss Bus. Coll. Percussionist Sauter-Finegan Band, N.Y.C., 1962-64, Shubert Theater, Chgo., 1970-75, Arie Crown Theater, Chgo., 1975-77, mus. show Annie, N.Y.C., 1978-82, Lyric Opera of Chgo., 1955-57; prof. percussion Met. Sch. Music, Chgo., 1945-48; instr. percussion Roy C. Knapp Sch. Percussion, Chgo., 1948-52; played in Broadway musicals including original prodns. of West Side Story, Hello Dolly, Guys and Dolls, Gypsy, Kismet, Cabaret, Can Can, Fiddler on the Roof. Served with USN, 1941-45, PTO. Mem. Chgo. Fedn. Musicians (bd. dirs. 1983-84), Musicians Union of Greater N.Y.C., Musicians Union of Los Angeles. Republican. Lodges: Masons, K.T., Shriners (band). Home: 2828 Pine Grove Chicago IL 60657

KNAPP, GREGORY ALLEN, utilities executive; b. Webb City, Mo., July 16, 1951; s. Charles and Elizabeth (Canady) K.; m. Paula Elizabeth Semrad, Nov. 6, 1971; children: Brian, Steven, Allison. BS in Acctg., Mo. So. State Coll., Joplin, 1973; MBA, South West Mo. State U., Springfield, 1985. CPA, Mo., Kans. Sr. acct. Peat, Marwick, Mitchell & Co., Kansas City, Mo., 1973-76; internal auditor Kansas City Power & Light Co., 1976-78; dir. auditing Empire Dist. Electric Co., Joplin, 1978-83, controller, asst. treas., 1983—. Mem. Am. Inst. CPA's, Mo. Soc. CPA's (pres. S.W. chpt. 1987-88), Internat. Childbirth Edn. Assn. (treas. 1978-81). Office: The Empire Dist Electric Co PO Box 127 Joplin MO 64802

KNAPP, K. BRAD, dentist; b. Lakewood, Ohio, June 26, 1955; s. Ralph Frank and Gloria Dean (Loesch) K.; m. Cynthia Louise Corlett, July 29, 1978; 1 child, Kelly Danielle. Student, Ohio Weslyan U., 1973-75; BA, Case Western Res. U., 1977, DDS, 1982; postgrad., Cleve. State U., 1977-78. Gen. practice dentistry Cleve., 1982—. Mem. ADA, Ohio Dental Assn., Cleve. Dental Assn., Delta Sigma Delta, Doan Study Club. Home: 5436 A Cascade Ct Willoughby OH 44094 Office: 401 Osborn Med Bldg Cleveland OH 44115

KNAPP, KEVIN DOUGLAS, bank executive; b. Gibson City, Ill., Dec. 13, 1960; s. Robert Douglas and Mary Elizabeth (Taylor) K.; m. Christine Marie Stinde, May 3, 1986. BBA, Western Ill. U., 1983; MBA, Keller Grad. Sch. Mgmt., 1985. Auditor Chem. Bank, Chgo., 1984-85, project mgr., 1985—. Mem. Am. Inst. CPA's, Ill. CPA Soc. Presbyterian. Home: 575 W Madison #3503 Chicago IL 60606 Office: Chem Card Services Corp 300 S Riverside Plaza Chicago IL 60606

KNAPP, MICHAEL GERALD, osteopath; b. Normandy, Mo., Apr. 20, 1953; s. Gerald Wilbur and Helen Gertrude (Fitzgerald) K.; m. Kathleen Ann Heimann, June 27, 1981; children: Bradley Charles, Spencer Gerald. DO, Kirksville Coll. Osteo. Medicine, 1980. Practice gen. medicine Shady Cove, Oreg., 1981-82; practice emergency medicine Oak Hill Hosp., Joplin, Mo., 1982—; chmn. dept. gen. practice Oak Hill Hosp., Joplin, 1982-83, chmn. emergency room com., dir. med. edn., 1982—; adj. faculty mem. Okla. Coll. Osteo. Medicine, Tulsa, 1984-86. Mem. med. control com. Joplin Emergency Med. Services, 1982—. Mem. Am. Osteo. Assn., Am. Coll. Osteo. Emergency Physicians, Am. Coll. Gen. Practitioners, Am. Acad. Osteopathy, Mo. Assn. Osteo. Physicians and Surgeons (dist. pres. 1985-86). Republican. Lutheran. Avocations: ornithology, camping, hunting, skiing. Home: 3515 Ivy Ln Joplin MO 64804 Office: Oak Hill Hosp 932 E 34th St Joplin MO 64804

KNAPP, MILDRED FLORENCE, social worker; b. Detroit, Apr. 15, 1932; d. Edwin Frederick and Florence Josephine (Antaya) K.; B.B.A., U. Mich., 1954, M.A. in Community and Adult Edn. (Mott Found. fellow 1964), 1964, M.S.W. (HEW grantee 1966), 1967. Dist. dir. Girl Scouts Met. Detroit, 1954-63; planning asst. Council Social Agencies Flint and Genessee County, 1965; sch. social worker Detroit public schs., 1967—; field instr. grad. social workers. Mem. alumnae bd. govs. U. Mich., 1972-75, scholarship chmn., 1969-70, 76-80, chmn. spl. com. women's athletics, 1972-75, class agt. fund raising Sch. Bus. Adminstrn., 1978-79; mem. Founders Soc. Detroit Inst. Art, 1969—, Friends Children's Museum Detroit, 1978—, Women's Assn. Detroit Symphony Orch., 1982—; trustee Children's Mus. Recipient various certs. appreciation. Mem. Nat. Assn. Social Workers, Acad. Cert. Social Workers, Nat. Community Edn. Assn. (charter), Outdoor Edn. and Camping Council (charter), Mich. Sch. Social Workers Assn. (pres. 1980-81), Detroit Sch. Social Workers Assn. (past pres.), Detroit Assn. U. Mich. Women (pres. 1980-82), Detroit Fedn. Tchrs. Methodist. Clubs: Detroit Boat, Detroit Women's City. Home: 702 Lakepointe Grosse Pointe Park MI 48230 Office: 4300 Marseilles Detroit MI 48224

KNAPP, WILLIAM BERNARD, cardiologist; b. Paterson, N.J., Oct. 26, 1921; s. Joseph and Mary (Cannon) K.; m. Jeannette C. Zarnowiecki, Jan. 31, 1948; children: William, Thomas, Bernadette, Richard, Suzanne. Attending physician Cook County Hosp., Chgo.; assoc. clin. prof. medicine Loyola U., Chgo.; chmn. medicine Little Co. of Mary Hosp., 1960-80; chmn. Holy Cross Hosp., Suburban Hosp., Hinsdale, Ill., 1976-81; practice medicine specializing in cardiology; chmn. S.W. Hosp. Planning, Chgo. Bd. dirs. Retirement Village, Civic Assn., Geneva Lake, Wis., 1970—; dir. water safety patrol, Geneva Lake, 1970—. Served with U.S. Army, 1943-46. Recipient Research award Ill. Inst. Medicine; Professorial Chair named in honor Loyola U., Chgo., 1985 . Fellow Am. Coll. Cardiology; mem. N.Am. Soc. Pediatric Physiology, AMA, ACP, Ill. Med. Soc., Chgo. Med. Soc., Inst. Medicine Chgo. Roman Catholic. Clubs: Butterfield Country (Oak Brook, Ill.); Big Foot Country; Beverly Country (Chgo.); Tracer; Whitehall. Office: 3900 W 95th St Evergreen Park IL 60642

KNAPSTEIN, JOHN WILLIAM, psychologist; b. New London, Wis., June 20, 1937; s. John Joseph and Irene Frances (Poepke) K.; m. Betty Ann Wilhelm, Nov. 25, 1966; John Karl, Susan Elise, Eric Steven. BA, St. John's U., Collegeville, Minn., 1959; MA, Marquette U., 1961; PhD, Tex. Tech U., 1970. Tchr. Hortonville (Wis.) High Sch., 1959-60; counselor Vocat. and Adult Sch., Racine, Wis., 1961-62; psychologist VA Hosp., St. Louis, 1970-72, Hines, Ill., 1972—. Deacon Diocese of Joliet, Ill., 1982—; bd. dirs., officer Community Service Council of No. Will County, Romeoville, Ill., 1979—. Served to capt. USAF, 1962-66. Marquette U. scholar, 1960. Mem. Am. Psychol. Assn., Nat. Rehab. Assn., Am. Assn. for Counseling and Devel., Nat. Career Devel. Assn., Nat. Rehab. Counseling Assn. Roman Catholic. Lodge: KC. Avocations: gardening, reading, computers. Home: 120 Pamela Dr Bolingbrook IL 60439-1347 Office: Psychology Service VA Hosp Hines IL 60141

KNAUF, WAYNE R., accountant; b. Marshfield, Wis., May 4, 1947; s. Donald Richard and Jane M. (Brown) K.; m. Marcia A., Dec. 20, 1985; children: Kelley, Stephanie, Amy Nicole, Kersten. BS, Marquette U., 1969. CPA. Share holder, mgr. Braun & Preboske, Rhinelander, Wis., 1976-82; pvt. practice acctg. Rhinelander, 1983—. Served with USNG, 1969-75. Mem. Am. Inst. CPAs, Wis. Inst. CPAs. Lodge: Lions. Home: 6500 Round Lake Rd Rhinelander WI 54501 Office: 6A N Brown Box 821 Rhinelander WI 54501

KNAUP, PETER HARVEY, real estate developer; b. Beaver Dam, Wis., Apr. 25, 1947; s. Glen B. and Olive J. (Harvey) K.; m. Christine Barstow July 5, 1975; children: Clarence, Jennifer. Student, MAdison Bus. Sch., Mpls. Bus. Sch., Mackinac Coll. Pres. Knaup Homes Inc., Beaver Dam, Port Supply and Property Mgmt. Ltd., Beaver Dam. HUD grantee 1984-86. Mem. Am. Legion. Lodge: Elks. Office: Port Supply and Property Mgmt 300 N Spring St Beaver Dam WI 53916

KNAUS, JOANNE MILLICIENT, interior designer; b. Sharon, Pa., Nov. 11, 1936; d. Anthony and Anna (Buzon) Lopuh; m. Robert Lucius Knaus, Feb. 14, 1970 (dec. Oct. 1979). Cert., Chgo. Acad. Art, 1959. Asst. interior designer Watson & Boaler, Chgo., 1959-60, with planning and styling dept. Simmons Co., Chgo., 1960; asst. interior designer Lubliner & Himmel, Chgo., 1960-61; head designer styling Whitaker-Guernsey, Chgo., 1962-67; prin. Joanne Lopuh Designer, Chgo., 1967-73; head contract designer Childs-Dreyfus, Chgo., 1973—; tchr. Art Inst. Chgo., 1967-68, Harrington Inst., Chgo., 1968-69. Mem. Am. Soc. Interior Designers. Avocations: piano, language, fitness. Home: 40 E Cedar Chicago IL 60611

KNAUSS, DALTON L., electronic components manufacturing company executive; b. Imboden, Ark., 1928. Grad., DeVry Coll., 1951; Student, Ill. Inst. Tech. Chmn., chief exec. officer, dir. Square D Co., Palatine, Ill.; dir. Kemper Corp. Office: Square D Co 1415 S Roselle Palatine IL 60067

KNAUSS, KEITH DAVID, labor educator; b. Emmaus, Pa., Dec. 26, 1945; s. Samuel Paul Sr. and Viola Helen (Heil) K.; m. Paula Nan Auburn, Nov. 23, 1973. BA, Pa. State U., 1967; MA, U. Minn., 1974. Instr. labor edn. service U. Minn., Mpls., 1971-72; coordinator div. labor studies Ind. U., South Bend, 1972—, assoc. prof., 1978—. Author: (with others) A Basic Guide to Federal Labor Law, 1981; contbr. articles to profl. jours. Served with U.S. Army, 1969-71, Vietnam. Mem. AFL-CIO (del. North Cen. Ind. council 1973—), Am. Fedn. Tchrs. Local 2002 (treas. 1973—), Univ. and Coll. Labor Edn. Assn. (chair profl. council 1978-79), Workers Edn. Local 189 (treas. 1972-75). Office: Ind U South Bend Labor Studies 1700 Mishawaka PO Box 7111 South Bend IN 46634

KNAWA, JAMES, comptroller; b. Chgo., July 3, 1957; s. Stanley J. and Arlene F. (Tomaszek) K.; m. Kathleen A. O'Connor, Oct. 10, 1981; children: Beth A., Daniel J. BBA, St. Xavier Coll., 1979; MBA, Lewis U., 1984. Controller Montgomery Ward, Chgo., 1979-80; acct. N.Y. Blower Co., Willowbrook, Ill., 1980-83; comptroller Robinson Inc., Chgo., 1983—; asst. prof. bus. Moraine Valley Coll., Palos Hills, Ill., 1984—; cons. Knawa and Co., Orland Park, Ill., 1984—. Youth instr. Worth Twp. Youth Orgn., Alsip, Ill., 1979-80; youth instr. Tinley Park (Ill.) Park Dist.,1983, (same position) Westhaven (Ill.) Park Dist., 1984. Mem. Nat. Assn. Accts. Roman Catholic. Home: 15421 Sunflower Ct Orland Park IL 60462 Office: Robinson Inc 135 S La Salle St Chicago IL 60603

KNEAREM, KEITH L., horticulturalist; b. Wilmington, Del., Oct. 15, 1958; s. James L. and Mary Louise (Perella) K.; m. Joanne M. Reynolds, Nov. 14, 1981; children: Tiffany Anne, Heather Marie, Holly Elizabeth. BS in Hort., Pa. State U., 1981. Owner Blue Valley Nursery, Olathe, Kans., 1982—; instr. Johnson County Community Coll., Overland Park, Kans., 1986. Mem. Kans. Assn. Nurserymen (cert.), Western Assn. Nurserymen., Am. Assn. Nurserymen. Presbyterian. Home: 15485 Quivira Rd Olathe KS 66062

KNEEN, JAMES RUSSELL, health care administrator; b. Kalamazoo, Dec. 16, 1955; s. Russell Packard and Joyce Elaine (Knapper) K.; m. Peggy Jo Howard, Aug. 4, 1979; children: Benjamin Russell., Katherine Elaine. B.A., Alma Coll., 1978; M.H.A., U. Mo., 1982. Systems analyst Bronson Meth. Hosp., Kalamazoo, 1976-79; adminstrv. resident Meth. Hosp. Ind., Indpls., 1981-82; div. dir. psychiat. care services Parkview Meml. Hosp., Ft. Wayne, Ind., 1982—. Bd. dirs. Washington House Alcoholism Treatment Ctr.; bd. dirs., sec.-treas. Parkview Regional Outreach, 1985—. Mem. Allen County Mental Health Assn., Am. Coll. Healthcare Execs., Am. Hosp. Assn. Office: 2200 Randallia Dr Fort Wayne IN 46805

KNEEN, RUSSELL PACKARD, health care executive; b. Fall River, Mass., July 30, 1923; s. Russell Packard and Lucy Sanford (Smith) K.; m. Joyce Elaine Knapper, Aug. 4, 1951; children: John, James, Andrew, Robert. BA, Boston U., 1949. CPA, Mich. Ptnr. Lawrence Scudder & Co., Kalamazoo, Mich., 1955-68; ptnr. Alexander Grant, Kalamazoo, 1968-80, mng. ptnr., 1980-82; pres. Bronson Healthcare Group, Kalamazoo, 1982-84, chmn., 1983—, chief exec. officer, 1984—; bd. dirs. IBA Health and Life Assurance Co., Kalamazoo, Physician's Health Plan, Kalamazoo, First Fed., 1983—, Caymich, 1984—; trustee Bronson Meth. Hosp., Kalamazoo. Campaign treas. Congressman Garry Brown, Kalamazoo, 1966-78; pres. planning commn. Kalamazoo Hosps., 1975-78; mem. fin. com. Kalamazoo

Inst. Arts, 1975-82. Served with U.S. Army, 1943-45. Mem. Am. Inst. CPA's, Nat. Assn. Accts., Mich. Assn. CPA's, Mich. Hosp. Assn. (mem. com. on assn. governance and strategic planning 1985—), Kalamazoo C. of C. (pres. 1964-66). Avocation: golf. Home: 1209 Edgemoor Kalamazoo MI 49008 Office: Bronson Healthcare Group One Healthcare Plaza Kalamazoo MI 49007

KNELSON, NELDA LORAIN RIFE, mental health technician; b. Pierce County, N.D., June 16, 1915; d. Herbert Edward and Katie Marie (Christianson) Rife; m. Henry W. Knelson, Sept. 16, 1931 (dec.); children: John Henry, Nelda May (Mrs. James W. Daley), James Douglas. Student, Sauk Valley Coll., 1968-75; PhD (hon.), U. Internat. Found. Mental Health Sci., 1985. Numerous positions various orgns., Dixon, Ill., 1937-47; survey worker, real estate salesperson Hurd Realtors, Dixon, 1948-50; mental health supr. and technician Dixon Devel. Ctr., 1964-83. Author: (poetry) Out of the Inkwel, 1959, Out of the Fire, 1960, Out of The Mist, 1968; (juvenile book) Tiger the Autobiography of a Cat, 1975. Active Girl Scouts U.S. and Boy Scouts Am.; mem. Lee County (Ill.) Hist. Soc.; pres. Lee County Home Extension, 1957-59; trustee Rep. Presdl. Task Force. Mem. Women in the Arts (charter), World Wildlife Fund., Smithsonian Assocs. Home: 2016 W 1st St Dixon IL 61021

KNEPPER, EUGENE ARTHUR, realtor; b. Sioux Falls, S.D., Oct. 8, 1926; s. Arlie John and May (Crone) K.; B.S.C. in Acctg., Drake U., Des Moines, 1951; m. LaNel Strong, May 7, 1948; children—Kenton Todd, Kristin Rene. Acct., G.L. Yager, pub. acct., Estherville, Iowa, 1951-52; auditor R.L. Meriwether, C.P.A., Des Moines, 1952-53; acct. govt. renegotiation dept. Collins Radio Co., Cedar Rapids, Iowa, 1953-54; head acctg. dept. Hawkeye Rubber Mfg. Co., Cedar Rapids, 1954-56; asst. controller United Fire & Casualty Ins. Co., Cedar Rapids, 1956-58; sales assoc. Equitable Life Assurance Soc. U.S., Cedar Rapids, 1958-59; controller Gaddis Enterprises, Inc., Cedar Rapids, 1959-61; owner Estherville Laundry Co., 1959-64; sales assoc., comml. investment div. mgr. Tommy Tucker Realty Co., Cedar Rapids, 1961-74; owner Real Estate Investment Planning Assocs., Cedar Rapids, 1974—; controlling ptnr. numerous real estate syndicates; cons. in field, fin. speaker; guest lectr. Kirkwood Community Coll., Cedar Rapids, Mt. Mercy Coll., Cedar Rapids, Cornell Coll., Mt. Vernon; creative financing instr. Iowa Real Estate Commn.-Iowa Assn. Realtors. Patron Cedar Rapids Symphony, 1983—, treas., mem. exec. com., bd. dirs.; bd. dirs. Oak Hill-Jackson Outreach Fund, 1970-83, pres., 1973-74; bd. dirs. Consumer Credit Counseling Service Cedar Rapids-Marion Area, 1974-80, pres., 1974-80. Served with USNR, 1945-46. Recipient Storm Manuscript award, 1976. Mem. Nat. Assn. Realtors (state mcpl. legis. com., subcom. on multi-family housing), Iowa Assn. Realtors (pres. comml. investment div. 1973, 80; state legis. com., savs. and loan formation feasibility com., mcpl. and county legis. com.), Nat. Assn. Accountants, Nat. Inst. Real Estate Brokers (membership chmn. Iowa 1972-73, regional v.p.), Real Estate Securities and Syndication Inst. (small group investment council, steering com. 1985, vice chmn. regional officers and state officers devel. com.; gov. Iowa div.), Cedar Rapids Bd. Realtors, Internat. Platform Assn., Internat. Inst. Valuers. Methodist. Clubs: Cedar Rapids Optimist (past chmn. boys work com.); Eastern Iowa Execs. (dir., pres. 1981-82). Contbr. articles to profl. jours. Home: 283 Tomahawk Trail SE Cedar Rapids IA 52403 Office: 1808 IE Tower Cedar Rapids IA 52401

KNIGHT, CHARLES FIELD, electrical equipment manufacturing company executive; b. Lake Forest, Ill., Jan. 20, 1936; s. Lester Benjamin and Elizabeth Anne (Field) K.; m. Joanne Parrish, June 22, 1957; children: Lester Benjamin III, Anne Field, Steven P., Jennifer Lee. B.S. in Mech. Engring., Cronell U., 1958; M.B.A., Cornell U., 1959. Mgmt. trainee Goetzewerke A.G., Burscheid, W. Ger., 1959-61; pres. Lester B. Knight Internat. Corp., 1961-63; exec. v.p. Lester B. Knight & Assocs., Inc., Chgo., 1963-67; pres. Lester B. Knight & Assocs., Inc., 1967-69, pres., chief exec. officer, 1969-73; vice chmn. bd. Emerson Electric, St. Louis, 1973; sr. vice chmn. bd., corp. exec. officer Emerson Electric Co., 1973, vice chmn. bd., 1973-74, chmn. bd., 1974—, chief exec. officer, 1973—, pres., 1987—, dir.; dir. Southwestern Bell Telephone Co., Mo. Pacific Corp., Ralston Purina Co., First Union Bancorp., Trans. World Corp. Mem. Civic Progress, 1973; bd. dirs. United Way Greater St. Louis; bd. Arts and Edn. Council; bd. dirs. Barnes Hosp.; trustee Washington U., St. Louis. Mem. Sigma Phi. Clubs: St. Louis Country; Log Cabin (St. Louis), Racquet (St. Louis); Glen View Golf (Ill.); Chicago. Office: Emerson Electric Co 8000 W Florissant Ave Saint Louis MO 63136 *

KNIGHT, CLARENCE LAWRENCE, U.S. postal service executive; b. Thompson, Ga., Aug. 18, 1943; s. James and Minnie (Ivory) K.; m. Jacqueline Coleman, Jan. 10, 1964 (div. Jan. 1984); children—Sheldon G., Erik C.; m. Betty J. Warren, Nov. 1, 1986. Grad. high sch., Detroit; student Lawrence Inst., 1969-70; cert. Rets Electronic Sch., Detroit, 1970; Student Wayne Community Coll., 1972-74. Mail flow controller U.S. Postal Service, Allen Park, Mich., 1975-77, mail processing supr., 1977-79, master instr., Oak Brook, Ill., 1980, regional postal ops. analyst, Chgo., 1980-82, regional maintenance officer, 1983-86, mgr. Maintenance engring. support, 1986—, Grand Rapids div., 1986—; acting mgr. plant maintenance, St. Louis, 1982-83, acting dir. mail processing dept., Allen Park, 1985; chmn. affirmative action program, U.S. Postal Service, Chgo., 1984—. Adminstrv. asst. Boy Scouts Am., Downers Grove, Ill., 1980; assoc. Smithsonian Inst., Washington, 1984; pres. Mendota Block Club, Detroit, 1967. Mem. Am. Mgmt. Assn., Nat. Assn. Postal Suprs. (pres. 1977-78, corr. sec. Mich. br. 1978-79, Am. Mgmt. Assn. (assoc.). Recipient Cert. of Recognition 1981, Letter of Appreciation 1981, Cert. of Achievement 1982, Cert. of Appreciation 1984). Lutheran. Lodges: Wolverine (degree team 1978), Masons (32 degree), Shriners. Avocations: fishing; painting; bowling; boating.

KNIGHT, JAMES GORDON, computer products executive; b. Los Angeles, June 15, 1945; s. Paul Ellis and Pauline (Rayburn) K.; m. Sharon Marie Dunlap, May 28, 1970; children: Robert E. Piker, Thomas H. Piker, Carrie L. Grad. in tool design, Chastain Inst., 1973; grad. in electronics, DeVry Inst., 1976. Computer aided design, printed circuit bd. designer Gen. Electric, Gen. Purpose Control, Bloomington, Ill., 1973-78, computer aided design specialist, 1978-83; engr. computer aided design/computer aided makeup Litton, Advanced Circuitry Div., Springfield, Mo., 1983-85, mgr. CAD/CAM, 1985-86; mgr. pre-prodn. dept. Litton, Advanced Circuitry Div., Springfield, 1986—; chmn. Scitex Internat. User Group, Bedford, Mass., 1984—. Mem. Nat. Computer Graphics Assn. (charter), Bloomington Atari Systems Inthusiates. Republican. Baptist. Avocations: pool, photography, woodworking, canoeing. Home: 3339 W Weaver Springfield MO 65807 Office: Litton Advanced Circuitry Div 4811 W Kearney Springfield MO 65803

KNIGHT, JOHN LORD, tool manufacturing company executive; b. Chgo., Mar. 16, 1936; s. William Windus and Elsie (Stranahan) K.; m. Sharon Dempsey, Sept. 24, 1958 (div. Aug. 1962); children—Katherine, Deborah; m. Darlene Bock, May 9, 1963 (div. Sept. 1983); children—John Lord, Angela, Robert; m. Beverly Larson, June 16, 1984. B.A., Colo. Coll., 1958; M.B.A., Harvard U., 1962. With devel. dept., tech. div. Libbey Owens Ford Glass Co., Toledo, 1958-60; various mgmt. positions Dana Corp., Ind. and Mich., 1962-70; pres., chief exec. officer Viking Drill & Tool, Inc., St. Paul, 1970—. Charter trustee Colo. Coll., Colorado Springs. Mem. Soc. Mfg. Engrs., Metal Cutting Tool Inst. (dir.), Cutting Tool Mfrs. Am. (dir.). Republican. Mem. Evangelical Free Ch. Home: 13 Evergreen Rd North Oaks MN 55110 Office: Viking Drill & Tool Inc PO Box 65278 355 State St Saint Paul MN 55165

KNIGHT, ROBERT EDWARD, banker; b. Alliance, Nebr., Nov. 27, 1941; s. Edward McKean and Ruth (McDuffee) K.; B.A., Yale U., 1963; M.A., Harvard U., 1965, Ph.D., 1968; m. Eva Sophia Youngstrom, Aug. 12, 1966; Asst. prof. U.S. Naval Acad., Annapolis, Md., 1966-68; lectr. U. Md., 1967-68; fin. economist Fed. Res. Bank of Kansas City (Mo.), 1968-70, research officer, economist, 1971-76, asst. v.p., sec., 1977, v.p., sec., 1978-79; pres. Alliance (Nebr.) Nat. Bank, 1979—, now also chmn.; pres. Robert Knight Assocs., banking and econ. cons., Alliance, 1979—; mem. faculty Stonier Grad. Sch. Banking, 1972—, Colo. Grad. Sch. Banking, 1975-82, Am. Inst. Banking, U. Mo., Kansas City, 1971-79, Prochnow Grad. Sch. Banking, U. Wis. Trustee, 1984-85, Knox Presbyn. Ch., Overland Park, Kans., 1965-69; bd. regents Nat. Comml. Lending Sch., 1980-83; chmn. Downtown Improvement Com., Alliance, 1981-84; trustee U. Nebr. Found.; bd. dirs. Stonier Grad. Sch. Banking, Box Butte County Devel. Commn., Nebr. Com. for Humanities, 1986—; mem. fin. com. United Meth. Ch., Alliance, 1982-85, mem. adminstrv. bd., 1987—; Box Butte County Industrial Devel. Bd., 1987—; mem. Nebr. Com. for the Humanities, 1986—; ambassador Nebr. Diplomats. Woodrow Wilson fellow, 1963-64. Mem. Am. Econ. Assn., Am. Fin. Assn., So. Econ. Assn., Nebr. Bankers Assn. (com. state legis. 1980-81, com. comml. loans and investments 1986-87), Am. Inst. Banking (state com. for Nebr. 1980—), Am. Bankers Assn. (econ. adv. com. 1980-83, community bank leadership council), Western Econ. Assn., Econometric Soc. Clubs: Rotary, Masons. Contbr. articles to profl. jours. Home: Drawer E Alliance NE 69301 Office: Alliance Nat Bank Alliance NE 69301

KNIGHT, ROBERT MONTGOMERY, basketball coach; b. Massilon, Ohio, Oct. 25, 1940; s. Carroll and Hazel (Menthorne) K.; m. Nancy Lou Knight, Apr. 17, 1963; children: Timothy Scott, Patrick Clair. B.S., Ohio State U., 1962. Asst. coach Cuyahoga Falls (Ohio) High Sch., 1962-63; freshman coach U.S. Mil. Acad., West Point, N.Y., 1963-65; head basketball coach U.S. Mil. Acad., 1965-71, Ind. U., Bloomington, 1971—; speaker clinics in field; condr. tng. clinics for coaches and players. Trustee Naismith Meml. Basketball Hall of Fame. Served with U.S. Army. Recipient Big Ten Coach-of-Year award, 1973, 75, 76, 81; named Nat. Coach of Year AP and Basketball Weekly, 1976; recipient appreciation plaque from team, 1979; coach U.S. team to gold medal 1984 olympics; coached Ind. U. team to NCAA Championship, 1976, 81, 87. Mem. Nat. Assn. Basketball Coaches (bd. dirs.). Methodist. Coached team to NCAA Championship, 1976, 81. Office: Indiana Univ Basketball Office Assembly Hall Bloomington IN 47405 *

KNIGHT, ROBERT PERKINS, sales executive; b. Evanston, Ill., Oct. 10, 1924; s. Francis M. and Helen (Perkins) K.; m. Andrea Saladine, Mar. 12, 1949; children—Robert P. Jr., Susan, Margaret. Student Hotchkiss Sch., 1942; A.B. in Econs., Yale U., 1948. C.P.C.U. 1954. Asst. v.p. Marsh & McLennan Inc., Chgo., 1956-62, v.p., 1962-70, sr. v.p., 1970-86; sr. v.p. prodn.; ret., 1986; past pres. Evanston Charitable Assn., Chgo. Trustee Northland Coll., Ashland; chmn. bd. trustee Wis. Winnetka Congl. Ch.; bd. dirs. Children's Meml. Hosp., former bd. dirs. Duncan YMCA; United Charities, Mental Health Soc. Chgo., Inroads. Served to sgt. USAF, 1942-45. Mem. Nat. Assn. Ins. Brokers (former dir.), Ill. Assn. Ins. Brokers, Soc. C.P.C.U. Republican. Congregational. Clubs: Economic, University, Chicago Yacht, Commonwealth (Chgo.); Indian Hill (Winnetka).

KNIGHT, RONALD ALLEN, mathematics educator, researcher; b. Miami, Ariz., Aug. 29, 1937; s. Coy Francis and Ruby Olean (Sanders) K.; m. Belle Arnold Knight, Apr. 5, 1961; children: Ronald Allen, Steven Michael. BS in Math., Brigham Young U., 1960, MS in Math., 1962; PhD in Math., Okla. State U., 1971. Instr. Brigham Young U., Provo, Utah, 1962-63; asst. prof. math. NE Mo. State U., Kirksville, Mo., 1965-69, 71-74, assoc. prof., 1974-84, prof., 1984; research paper referee several profl. jours. Author: Introduction to the Elementary Functions, 1969; contbr. articles to profl. jours., 1971—. Title IV grantee NSF, 1970-71, numerous research grants NE Mo. State U., 1974-84. Mem. Am. Math. Soc., Math. Assn. Am., Soc. Indsl. and Applied Math. Republican. Mormon. Avocation: genealogy. Office: NE Mo State U. Math and Computer Sci Div Kirksville MO 63501

KNIGHT, WILLIAM WILTON, JR., entrepreneur, investor, consultant; b. Emmettsburg, Iowa, Jan. 24, 1922; s. William Wilton and Ellen (Peterson) K.; m. Helen Patten, Dec. 12, 1948 (div. Dec. 1974); 1 child, Karen Lynn; 1 stepchild, Charles Crane; m. Jean Stegall, Nov. 1, 1980. Diploma, Lyons Twp. Jr. Coll., 1941; BS, U. Ill., 1947. Licensed comml. pilot FAA. Service engr. Internat. Harvester Co., Melrose Park, Ill., 1947-48; sales engr., v.p. Patten Industries, Elmhurst, Ill., 1948-83; pvt. practice investment cons. Palos Heights, Ill., 1983—. Mem. adv. bd. Am. Security Council. Served to maj. USMCR, 1942-59, PTO, Korea. Decorated D.F.C. (2) Air medal (7). Mem. Marine Corps Res. Officer's Assn., Res. Officer's Assn. U.S., Mil. Order of World Wars, U. Ill. Alumni Assn., Rep. Nat. Com. (sustaining), Air Force Assn., Aircraft Owners and Pilots Assn., NRA, Am. Legion. Republican. Protestant. Avocations: flying, sports.

KNIGHTON, HARRY SEVILLE, electronics technician, association executive; b. Columbus, Ohio, July 23, 1915; s. Ervin William and Elsie Alice (Dixon) K.; m. Elsie Louise Webb, July 2, 1937. Electrician, Wheeling Steel Corp., Portsmouth, Ohio, 1934-43; electronic technician Empire Detroit Steel, Portsmouth, 1945-80. Editor: The Mycophile, 1963-86. Dist. commr. Scioto Area council Boy Scouts Am., 1953-55; mem. Salvation Army Adv. Bd., Portsmouth, 1983—. Served as staff sgt. U.S. Army, 1943-45; PTO. Recipient Ohio State Conservation Achievement award Dept. Natural Resources, 1983. Mem. North Am. Mycological Assn. (exec. dir. 1967—, nat. chmn. Forays 1963—, Contbns. to Amateur Mycology award 1965). Methodist. Avocations: naturalist; stamp collector. Home: 4345 Redinger Rd Portsmouth OH 45662

KNILANS, MICHAEL JEROME, merchant; b. Columbus, Ohio, Mar. 3, 1927; s. Alfred Sidney and Bernice (Meyers) K.; m. Anne Eberhardt, June 15, 1947; children—Michael, Kyleen, Christine, Timothy, Suzanne. B.S., Ohio State U., 1949. With Big Bear Stores Co., Columbus, 1942—; mdse. mgr. Big Bear Stores Co., 1952-61, v.p., 1961-70, exec. v.p., 1970-76, pres., 1976—, also dir.; dir. Topco Assos., Inc. Pres. Central Ohio council Boy Scouts Am., Served with USNR, 1944-46, PTO. Mem. Food Mktg. Inst. (dir.), Ohio Council Retail Mchts. (treas.), Better Bus. Bur. (pres. 1978), C. of C. Republican. Lutheran (chmn. congregation 1968). Clubs: Masons, Shriners, Jesters, Rotary (pres. 1981—). Home: 1119 Kingsdale Terr Columbus OH 43220 Office: Big Bear Inc 770 W Goodale Blvd Columbus OH 43212

KNIPP, RICHARD HENRY, building contractor; b. Tipton, Mo., Nov. 14, 1914; s. Carl Henry and Rosa Elizabeth (Hartmen) K. Owner Knipp Constrn. Co., Columbia, Mo., 1940—; v.p. Cen. Mo. Abstact and Title Co.; v.p. Glenview Drug Co., Columbia, 1965; trustee Mo-Kan Teamsters Pension Trust Fund, 1971—. Mem. Columbia City Council, 1963-73, 79-81, Columbia Planning and Zoning Commn., 1981-89. Mem. Kansas City Builders Assn., Assoc. Gen. Contractors Am. Roman Catholic. Club: Country of Mo., Columbia Country. Lodges: Lions, Elks, KC. Home: 210 W Forest Ave Columbia MO 65203 Office: Richard Knipp Assoc 1204 Pannell St Columbia MO 65201

KNIPP SR., ALAN LEONARD, data services executive; b. Chgo., May 23, 1947; s. Leonard E. and Joan E. (Jansen) K.; m. Kathryn Knipp; children: Alan Jr., Lisa Marie, Laura Marie. Cert., Internat. Data Processing Inst., Chgo., 1966; student, Triton Coll., River Grove, Ill., 1977. Bus. analyst Quasar div. Motorola Corp., Frnaklin Park, Ill., 1967-69, programmer/analyst, 1969-79; system analyst Centel Data Services, Chgo., 1979, project mgr., 1979-86, staff mgr. planning, 1986—; planning analyst/cons. Centel Cable TV, Chgo., Centel Data Services, Chgo., 1985—, Centel Bus. Systems, Chgo., 1985—, Central Telephone Co., Chgo., 1985—. Contbr. articles to profl. jours. Head youth football coach Leyden Twp. (Ill.), Elmhurst (Ill.), Hanover Park (Ill.), 1966-84; pres. George Halas Football League, Suburban Chgo., 1976-78; chmn. Hanover Park Youth Commn., 1981-83; mem. U.S. Power Squadron. Mem. SHARE. Roman Catholic. Avocations: sports, magic, music, fishing, camping. Office: Centel Data Services 8745 W Higgins Chicago IL 60631

KNITTEL, ROBERT EDWARD, social and health programs consultant; b. St. Louis, July 22, 1923; s. George Ernest and Paula Marie (Fischer) K.; student St. Louis U., 1941-42, 45-46; B.J., U. Mo., 1948; Ph.D. in Anthropology, So. Ill. U., 1967; m. Elizabeth Rita Geers, June 5, 1948; children—George Randall, David Allen, Rita Marie. Asst. mgr. Doubleday Book Shop, St. Louis, 1948-50, mgr., New Orleans, 1950-52, Clayton, Mo., 1952-54; community relations cons. Housing Rehab. project City of St. Louis, 1954-56; community cons. Community Devel. Services So. Ill. U., 1956-57, asst. dir., 1957-59, dir., 1959-65, asst. dir. research, 1965-67, community cons. area services studies, 1967-68, research asso., 1969-74; coordinator Gulfstream Area Agy. on Aging, Palm Beach, Fla., 1974-75; asso. prof. dept. regional and community affairs U. Mo., 1975-79; pvt. practice social and health programs consulting, St. Louis, 1979—; owner, mgr. Grass-Hooper Press. Active Boy Scouts Am., Murphysboro, Ill., 1963-71; chmn. bd. St. Andrews Parochial Sch., Murphysboro, 1968. Served with U.S. Navy, 1943-46. Fellow Am. Anthrop. Assn., Soc. Applied Anthropology; mem. AAAS, Soc. Med. Anthropology, So. States Anthropl. Assn., Mo. Playwrights Assn. (pres. 1981). Author: Walking in Tower Grove Park, 1978, rev. edit., 1983. Author play: Prometheus (recipient Mo. Council for the Arts Playwrighting contest award), 1978. Editor: A Missouri Playwrights Anthology, 1981. Home and Office: 4030 Connecticut St Saint Louis MO 63116

KNÖBEL, DAVID HAROLD, lawyer, financial advisor; b. Beaufort, S.C., Sept. 5, 1951; s. William Harold and Joan (Purdy) K. BA in Polit. Sci., Calif. State U., Long Beach, 1974; postgrad., Nat. U., San Diego, 1980; JD, Western State U., Fullerton, Calif., 1982. Bar: Ind. 1983, U.S. Dist. Ct. (no. and so. dists.) Ind. 1983, U.S. Tax Ct. 1983, U.S. Ct. Mil. Appeals 1983. Pvt. practice fin. advisor Norco, Calif., 1980—; sole practice law Merrillville, Ind., 1983—; instr. Am. Coll. Paralegal Studies, Detroit, 1984; cons., advisor SCORE, Gary, Ind., 1984—; bd. dirs. Poma, Inc., Merrillville. Pres., v.p. Marlon Home Assn., Cedar Lake, Ind., 1984—. Served as 1st lt. USMCR, 1975-77. Mem. ABA, Ind. Bar Assn., Lake County Bar Assn., Assn. Trial Lawyers Am., Ind. Trial Lawyers Assn. Club: Vintage Chevrolet and Car (Calif.). Lodge: K.C. Avocations: antique auto restoration, scuba diving. Home: 995 3d St Norco CA 91760 Office: 1000 E 80th Pl Suite 519N Merrillville IN 46410

KNODELL, ROBERT JAMES, mfg. co. exec.; b. Chgo., May 28, 1932; s. Homer Edward and Mildred Jenette (Miller) K.; student Morton Jr. Coll., 1962-65; m. Jean Marie Klean, Jan. 29, 1955; children—James, Sandra, Richard. Lab. tech. Indsl. Bio-Test Labs., Northbrook, Ill., 1962-70; service sta. dealer Standard Oil of Ind., Brookfield, Ill., 1971-77; service tech. Hobart Corp., Broadview, Ill., 1977—; also freelance writer. Bd. dirs. Library Bd., Brookfield, 1977-81; Dem. precinct capt., 1965—; precinct coordinator, 1982—. Mem. Chgo. Council on Fgn. Relations, Am. Enterprise Inst. for Pub. Policy Research. Democrat. Presbyterian. Club: Kiwanis (past pres. Brookfield chpt.). Home: 9317 Jackson Ave Brookfield IL 60513 Office: 2747 S 25 Ave Broadview IL 60153

KNODT, DIETMAR OTTO WILHELM, architect; b. Marburg, West Germany, June 23, 1936; came to U.S., 1958; s. Wilhelm K.F.P. and Gertrud L. (Hofmann) K.; m. Ann Armstrong, Feb. 18, 1967; children: Michael Christian, Kirsten Ann. Student, Grinnell Coll., 1959; BArch, Ohio State U., 1963. Lic. architect Ohio, Fla., Ky., Vt., N.Y. Draftsman Ted H. Prindle & Assocs., Columbus, 1963-67; project mgr. Brubaker/Brandt, Inc., Columbus, 1967-70; prin. Knodt/Maddox, Inc., Dublin, Ohio, 1970—. Recipient Boss of Yr. award Archtl. Secs. Assn., 1979. Mem. AIA, Builders Exchange of Ohio (mem. jury, Craftsmanship award 1980), Nat. Trust of Hist. Preservation (officer 1986—), Ohio State U. Alumni Assn. (life), Columbus C. of C. Club: Maennerchor, Sawmill Athletic (Columbus). Office: Knodt/Maddox Inc 5186 Blazer Parkway Dublin OH 43017

KNOEBEL, SUZANNE BUCKNER, cardiologist, medical educator; b. Ft. Wayne, Ind., Dec. 13, 1926; d. Doster and Marie (Lewis) Buckner. A.B., Goucher Coll., 1948; M.D., Ind. U.-Indpls., 1960. Diplomate: Am. Bd. Internal Medicine. Asst. prof. medicine Ind. U., Indpls., 1966-69, assoc. prof., 1969-72, prof., 1972-77, Krannert prof., 1977—; asst. dean research Ind. U., Indpls., 1975—; assoc. dir. Krannert Inst. Cardiology, Indpls., 1974—; asst. chief cardiology sect. Richard L. Roudebush VA Med. Ctr., Indpls., 1982—. Fellow Am. Coll. Cardiology (v.p. 1980-81, pres. 1982-83); mem. Am. Fedn. Clin. Research, Assn. Univ. Cardiologists. Office: Ind U Sch Medicine 1100 W Michigan St Indianapolis IN 46223

KNOEDEL, DIANA LYNN, physician assistant; b. Cedar Rapids, Iowa, Nov. 10, 1956; d. Norman Raymond and Donna Jean (Kennedy) Bahndorf; m. David Edwin Knoedel, May 12, 1984. BS in Zoology, U. Iowa, 1978, BS in Medicine, 1981. Physician asst. pediatric cardiology dept. U. Iowa, Iowa City, 1981—; vol. physician asst. Free Med. Clinic, Iowa City, 1981-85. Mem. Am. Assn. Physician Assts., Iowa Physician Asst. Soc., Am. Heart Assn. Democrat. Avocations: collecting and refinishing antiques, snow skiing, walking. Office: U Iowa Hosp W139 GH Iowa City IA 52242

KNOEDLER, THOMAS BERNARD, computer analyst and programmer; b. Springfield, Ill., Jan. 20, 1952; s. Joseph Bernard and Rose Louise (Geier) K.; B.A. in Math. Systems, Sangamon State U., 1974, M.A. in Math. Systems/Computer Sci., 1981. Mgmt. analyst, programmer II, Sangamon State U., Springfield, 1977—. Mem. Assn. Computing Machinery, L5 Soc., Planetary Soc., U.S. Chess Fedn. (life). Roman Catholic. Club: Springfield Chess (v.p.). Office: PAC 595 Shepherd Rd Springfield IL 62708

KNOLL, GLENN FREDERICK, nuclear engineering educator; b. St. Joseph, Mich., Aug. 3, 1935; s. Oswald Herman and Clara Martha (Bernthal) K.; m. Gladys Hetzner, Sept. 7, 1957; children: Thomas, John, Peter. B.S., Case Inst. Tech., 1957; M.S. in Chem. Engring., Stanford, 1959; Ph.D. in Nuclear Engring., U. Mich., 1963. Asst. research physicist U. Mich., Ann Arbor, 1960-62; asst. prof. nuclear engring. U. Mich., 1962-67, asso. prof., 1967-72, prof., 1972—, chmn. dept. nuclear engring., 1979—, also mem. bioengring. faculty.; Vis. scientist Institut für Angewandte Kernphysik, Kernforschungszentrum Karlsruhe, Germany, 1965-66; sr. vis. fellow dept. physics U. Surrey, Guildford, Eng., 1973; summer cons. Electric Power Research Inst., Palo Alto, Calif., 1974; cons. in field. Author: Radiation Detection and Measurement, 1979, Principles of Engineering, 1982; mem. editorial bd. Nuclear Instns. and Methods in Physics Research. Recipient excellence in research award Coll. Engring., U. Mich., 1984; Fulbright travel grantee, 1965-66; NSF fellow, 1958-60, Sci. Research Council sr. fellow, 1973; vis. fellow Japan Soc. Prom. Sci., 1987. Fellow Am. Nuclear Soc., IEEE (editorial bd. Trans. on Medical Imaging); mem. Am. Soc. Engring. Edn. (Glenn Murphy award 1979), Sigma Xi, Tau Beta Pi. Patentee in field. Office: U Mich Dept Nuclear Engring 119 Cooley Bldg Ann Arbor MI 48109

KNOPMAN, DAVID S., neurologist; b. Phila., Oct. 6, 1950. AB, Dartmouth Coll., 1972; MD, U. Minn., 1975. Diplomate Am. Bd. Psychiatry and Neurology. Intern Hennepin County Med. Ctr., 1975-76; resident U. Minn., 1976-79; asst. prof. neurology U. Minn., Mpls., 1980-86, assoc. prof. neurology, 1986—; dir. Alzheimer's Disease Clinic, U. Minn. Hosp., Mpls., 1983—. Office: U Minn Dept Neurology Minneapolis MN 55455

KNORR, JOHN CHRISTIAN, music and entertainment executive, band leader, show producer; b. Crissey, Ohio, May 24, 1921; s. Reinhold Alfred and Mary (Rieth) K.; m. Jane Lucy Hammer, Aug. 10, 1922; children: Gerald William, Janice Grace Knorr Wilcox. Student Ohio No. U., 1940-41. Violin soloist with Helen O'Connell, 1934-35; reed sideman Jimmy Dorsey, Les Brown and Sonny Dunham orchs., 1939-48; mem. theater pit orchs. and club shows, Ohio, 1949-57; leader Johnny Knorr Orch, Toledo, 1958—; mgr. Centennial Terr.; owner Johnny Knorr Entertainment Agy.; band leader, show producer. Recordings: Live at Franklin Park Mall, 1973, Let's Go Dancing, 1979, Encore, 1984, (TV spl.) An Era of Swing, 1973, Live at Centennial Terrace, 1986. Trustee Presbyn. Ch. Served to cpl. AUS, 1944-45. Recipient outstanding dance band citations, Chgo., 1966, Des Moines, 1968, Las Vegas, 1969, Nat. Ballroom Operators Assn., Omaha, 1970, Entertainment Operators Assn., 1973; named Grand Duke of Toledo, King of the Hoboes, 1975. Mem. Am. Fedn. Musicians, Am. Legion. Clubs: Exchange, Circus Fans Am. Lodges: Masons, Shriners, Ind. Order Foresters. Home and Office: 1751 Fallbrook Rd Toledo OH 43614

KNOTT, CAROL REDE, interior designer; b. Weston, W.Va., Mar. 18, 1930; d. Marion Wyllys and Mary Warren Rede; student Rollins Coll., 1948-49; B.A., Northwestern U., 1966; m. Richard F. Knott, Nov. 26, 1949; children—Diana Despard, Richard F., Thomas Read, Sally Oliver. Designer, Betty Lotz Interiors, Winnetka, Ill., 1966-73; owner Carol R. Knott Interior Design, Kenilworth, Ill., 1973—; tchr. Wilmette Park Dist. Mem. Am. Soc. Interior Designers (dir.), Chgo. Designers Club, Colonial Dames, Desc. Signers Declaration of Independence. Republican. Episcopalian. Clubs: Farmington Country (Charlottesville, Va.); Mchts. and Mfrs. (Chgo.). Office: 430 Green Bay Rd Kenilworth IL 60043

KNOTT, DAVID LEE, journalism educator; b. Dale, Ind., Mar. 20, 1939; s. Hilary Francis and Eunice M. (Heichelbech) K.; m. Mary Ann Wolf, July 27, 1963; children: Ann M., Alan L., Daniel C. BS, Ind. State U., 1961, MS, 1965; MA, Ball State U., 1971; EdD, U. Toledo, 1981. Tchr. English and journalism Washington High Sch., Indpls., 1961-70; grad. teaching asst. Ball State U., Muncie, Ind., 1970-71, asst. prof. journalism, coordinator Daily News, 1976-87, assoc. prof. journalism, 1987; instr. journalism U. Toledo, 1971-76. Mem. Soc. Profl. Journalists (pres. N.W. Ohio chpt. 1973-74), Coll. Media Advisers (pres. 1985—, editor Coll. Media Rev., 1984—), Ind. Collegiate Press Assn. (exec. sec. 1977—), Gold Key, Kappa Tau Alpha. Democrat. Roman Catholic. Avocations: piano, gardening. Home: 4201 Coventry Dr Muncie IN 47304 Office: Ball State U Dept Journalism Muncie IN 47306

KNOTT, DELORIS CATHERINE, bank executive; b. Carrollton, Mo., Mar. 22, 1946; d. Raymond Fredrich Heinrich and Betty Catherine (Fuller) Herberger; m. James William Simms, Feb. 26, 1967 (dec. Feb. 1969); m. C. Robert Knott, Mar. 24, 1979; 1 child, Tyler Austin. BBA with honors, Cen. Mo. State U., 1971. Lic. real estate sales rep., Mo. Buyer retail fashion Famous Barr May Dept. Stores, St. Louis, 1971-76, Burdines Federated Dept. Stores, Miami, Fla., 1976-78, Meier-Frank May Dept. Stores, Portland, Oreg., 1978-79; real estate sales rep. Knott-Wagaman, Bogard, Mo., 1979—; v.p., sec. The Knott Holding Co., Carrollton, 1980—; exec. v.p. The Farmers Bank, Carrollton, 1979ú, also bd. dirs.; named as contact for women bus. owners, SBA, Kansas City, Mo., 1984. Vol. United Way, Belville, Ill., 1977, swimming pool com. City of Carrollton, 1979, ARC, Quantico, Va., 1968. Named one of Outstanding Women Am., Gen. Fedn. Women's Club, 1977. Mem. Am. Mktg. Assn. Cen. Mo. State U. (charter officer 1970). Club: Women's (Carrollton). Avocations: skiing, reading. Home: 1104 N Main Carrollton MO 64633 Office: Farmers Bank One W Washington Ave Carrollton MO 64633

KNOTT, WILEY EUGENE, customer support manager; b. Muncie, Ind., Mar. 18, 1938; s. Joseph Wiley and Mildred Viola (Haxton) K.; B.S. in Elec. Engring., Tri-State U., 1963; postgrad. Union Coll., 1970-73, Ga. Coll., 1987—; 1 child, Brian Evan. Assoc. aircraft engr. Lockheed-Ga. Co., Marietta, 1963-65; tech. publs. engr. Gen. Electric Co., Pittsfield Mass., 1965-77, sr. publs. engr., 1977-79, group leader, 1967-79; specialist engr. Boeing Mil. Airplane Co., Wichita, Kans., 1979-81, sr. specialist engr., 1981-84, logistics mgr., 1984-85, customer support mgr., 1985—; part-time bus. cons., 1972—. Active Jr. Achievement, 1978-79, Am. Security Council, 1975—, Nat. Republican Senatorial Com., 1979-86 , Nat. Rep. Congressional Com., 1979—, Rep. Nat. Com., 1979—, Rep. Presdl. Task Force, 1981-86 , Joint Presdl./Congl. Steering Com., 1982-86, Rep. Polit. Action Com., 1979-86. state advisor U.S. Congl. Adv. Bd., 1981-86; adviser Jr. Achievement, 1978-79. Served with AUS, 1956-59. Mem. Am. Def. Preparedness Assn. (life), Am. Mgmt. Assn., Soc. Logistics Engrs., U.S. Golf Assn. PGA Inner Circle, Fraternal Order Police (assoc.), Air Force Assn. (life), Boeing Mgmt. Club, Nat. Audubon Soc. Methodist. Lodge: Old Crows.

KNOUSE, CHARLES ALLISON, osteopathic physician, pathology educator; b. Plattsburg, Mo., Mar. 14, 1921; s. Charles Albert and Alice Susan May (Trout) K.; m. Iris Christine Ehrenreich, May 21, 1944; children—Thea Christine Knouse Price, Charles Allison, Karen Elizabeth Knouse Brungardt, John Arthur. Grad., Emmettsburgh Jr. Coll., Iowa, 1941; student, U. Chgo., 1941-42; D.O., Kansas City Coll. Osteopathy and Surgery, 1949. Diplomate Nat. Bd. Examiners Osteo. Physicians. Gen. practice medicine Howard City, Mich., 1950-55; asst. to editor Am. Osteo. Assn., Chgo., 1955; gen. practice Seattle, 1956; resident Hosps. Kansas City Coll. Osteopathy and Surgery, 1958-61; mem. faculty Kirksville Coll. Osteopathy and Surgery, Mo., 1961-65; mem. staff Kirksville Osteo. Hosp. 1961-65; prof. pathology, chmn. dept. U. Health Scis., Kansas City, Mo., 1965-68; chmn. dept. pathology Meml. Osteo. Hosp., York, Pa., 1968-78; prof. pathology Ohio U. Coll. Osteo. Medicine, 1978—, dir. lab. services; gen. clinician Ohio U. Osteo. Med. Ctr. (formerly Ohio U. Med. Assocs. Clinic); mem. vis. faculty W.Va. Sch. Osteo. Medicine, 1975-78, U. New Eng. Coll. Osteo Medicine; cons. pathology Nat. Bd. Examiners for Osteo. Physicians and Surgeons. Contbr. articles to osteo. jours. Moderator, chmn. bd. elders 1st Christian Ch., Athens, Ohio. Served with U.S. Mcht. Marine, 1942-44, U.S. Army, 1944-46, ETO. U. Chgo. scholar, 1941. Fellow Am. Osteo. Coll. Pathologists; mem. Am. Osteo. Assn. (lab. surveyor hosp. accreditation, editorial cons. pubs.), Ohio Osteo. Assn., Am. Acad. Osteopathy, AAUP, Am. Assn. Automotive Medicine, Am. Med. Writers Assn., Physicians for Social Responsibility, Psi Sigma Alpha. Mem. Christian Ch. (Disciples of Christ). Home: 85 S May Ave Athens OH 45701 Office: Ohio U Coll Osteo Medicine Grovesnor Hall Athens OH 45701

KNOWLES, ROY CANEDY, child psychiatrist, educator; b. Aberdeen, S.D., Dec. 8, 1913; s. Roy Otis and Sarah Leora (Canedy) K.; m. Geraldine Margaret Nash, Aug. 18, 1943; children: Richard, Margaret, Judith, Kathleen. BA, U. Ala., 1936; MD, Albany Med. Coll., 1940. Diplomate Am. Bd. Psychiatry and Neurology, Am. Bd. Child Psychiatry. Pvt. practice gen. medicine Little Falls, N.Y., 1942-48; resident in psychiatry Menninger Sch. of Psychiatry, Topeka, 1948-52; dir. Mental Health Ctr., Sioux Falls, S.D., 1952-64; practice medicine specializing in psychiatry Sioux Falls, 1964-70; med. dir. Wilder Services to Children, St. Paul, 1970-79; prof. child psychiatry S.D. Sch. Med., Sioux Falls, 1979-87, prof. emeritus, 1987—; cons. Luth. soc services S.D. Children's Home, Sioux Falls, 1954-64, 79-84; clin. prof. Dept. Psychiatry Med. Sch., Minn., 1972-79; lectr. in field. Contbr. articles to profl. jours. Mem. Gov.'s Com. on Aging, S.D., 1959-60, Bd. of Edn., Sioux Falls, 1966-69; bd. dirs. United Way, Sioux Falls, 1960-63. Recipient Fischer award Sioux Empire Mental Health Assn., 1981. Fellow Am. Psychiatric Assn.; mem. AMA (life), Am. Group Psychotherapy Assn., Am. Assn. Child and Adolescent Psychiatry, S.D. Mental Health Assn. (bd. dirs. 1952-69, Watson award 1970), C. of C. (edn. com. 1960). Avocations: travel, fishing. Home: 2825 Ridgeview Way Sioux Falls SD 57105 Office: Dept Psychiatry 800 E 21st Sioux Falls SD 57101

KNOWLTON, AUSTIN E. (DUTCH KNOWLTON), professional sports team executive. BS, Ohio State U. Owner Knowlton Constrn. Co., ARGA Co.; majority owner Cin. Reds (Major Leagues), 1970's; chmn. bd. The Cin. Bengals (NFL). Office: Cin Bengals 200 Riverfront Stadium Cincinnati OH 45202 *

KNOWLTON, RICHARD L., food and meat packing company executive; b. 1932; married. B.A., U. Colo., 1954. With George A. Hormel & Co., Austin, MInn., 1948—; mgr. meat products div. and route car sales George A. Hormel & Co., Austin, Minn., 1967-69; asst. mgr. George A. Hormel & Co. (Austin plant), 1969; gen. mgr. George A. Hormel & Co., Austin, 1974, v.p. ops., 1974, group v.p. ops., 1975-79; pres., chief operating officer George A Hormel & Co., Austin, 1979; chmn., pres., chief exec. officer George A. Hormel & Co., Austin, 1981—, dir.; dir. Nat. Livestock and Meat Bd., Hormel Found. Bd., First Nat. Bank of Austin, First Bank Mpls., Can. Packers. Trustee U. Minn. Mem. Am. Meat Inst. (chmn., dir.), Minn. Bus. Partnership (dir.). Office: George A Hormel & Co 501 16th Ave NE Austin MN 55912

KNOX, ARTHUR LLOYD, investment banker; b. Perkins, Okla., May 12, 1932; s. Myrl Frank and Margaret (Grant) K.; B.S., Okla. State U., 1955; m. Earlene Lois Luff, Feb. 19, 1955; children—Arthur Earl, Angela Marie. With Lincoln (Nebr.) Steel Corp., 1957-84, exec. v.p., chief operating officer, 1979-81, pres., 1981-84; sr. v.p. Commerce Capital Inc., 1984—; ptnr. Reinox Devel., 1984—; ptnr. 2LK Horse & Cattle Co., K&L Leasing Co., Knox Rentals; bd. dirs. Cornhusker Bank, Lincoln; adv. bd. Nebr. Dept. Econ. Devel., 1979-83; del. White House Conf. Small Bus., 1974—. Chmn., Lancaster County Young Reps., 1966-67, Nebr. Fedn. Young Reps., 1967-68, Lancaster County Rep. Com., 1972-76; asst. chmn. Nebr. Rep. Party, 1979-80; mem. Rep. Nat. Com., 1980-84; co-chmn. Gov. Charles Thone Campaign, 1978, Gov. Kay Orr Campaign, 1986; mem. adv. com. Nebr. Small Bus. Adminstrn., 1986, Nebr. Econ. Devel. Commn., 1987; bd. dirs. Lower Platte S. Natural Resources Dist., 1974—; presdl. elector for Nebr., 1976—. Served with AUS, 1955-57. Recipient various Rep., Jaycee awards. Mem. Am. Welding Soc., Nebr. Assn. Commerce and Industry, Associated Industries Lincoln, Lincoln C. of C. (dir. 1981—), Farmhouse. Presbyterian. Club: Elephant. Lodge: Rotary (bd. dirs.). Home: 920 Pine Tree Ln Lincoln NE 68521 Office: 646 NBC Ctr Lincoln NE 68508

KNOX, JAMES MARSHALL, lawyer; b. Chgo., Jan. 12, 1944; s. Edwin John and Shirley Lucille (Collett) K.; m. Janine Lenar, July 18, 1964; children—Erik M., Christian S. B.A., U. Ill., 1968; M.A. in L.S., Rosary Coll., 1973; J.D., DePaul Coll. of Law, 1979. Bar: Ill. 1979, U.S. Dist. Ct. (no. dist.) Ill. 1979, U.S. Ct. Appeals (7th cir.) 1980. Assoc., Fishman & Fishman, Ltd., Chgo., 1979—. Vestryman St. Mark's Episc. Ch., Evanston, Ill., 1980-83; dir. Child Devel. Ctrs., Inc., Chgo. Mem. ABA, Ill. State Bar Assn., U. Ill. Alumni Assn. (dir. 1986—). Republican. Home: 1305 Lincoln Evanston IL 60201 Office: Fishman & Fishman Ltd 134 N LaSalle Suite 1016 Chicago IL 60602

KNOX, JANICE ANN, data processing executive; b. Chgo., Mar. 18, 1948; d. James W. and Lucy Olivia (Williams) Knox; married; 1 child, Heather Olivia Belcher. B.A. in Math., Northeastern Ill. U., 1971; postgrad. Northwestern U. With First Nat. Bank Chgo., 1971—, programming instr., 1973-76, systems mgr., 1976-82, systems officer, 1979-82, systems application mgr., 1982-87, data security mgr. 1987—; asst. v.p., 1984— ; programming instr. Malcolm X Coll., Chgo., 1974; tng. specialist urban skills City Colls. Chgo., 1978-83. Bd. dirs., treas. Beacon Neighborhood House, 1983-84; bd. dirs., chmn. state coordinating com. NAACP, 1983-85, mem. exec. bd. Chgo. Southside br., 1983—, 1st v.p. women's aux., 1981-83; mem. NAACP'S Affirmative Action Task Force, 1985—; mem. edn. com. Anti-Defamation League B'Nai B'Rith, 1983-84. Grantee NSF, 1964-65. Mem. Assn. Computing Machinery, Pansophic Users Learning and Sharing Exchange, Assn. Systems Mgmt. (profl.), Info. Systems Security Assn., Inc. Lodge: B'nai B'rith. Office: 1 First Nat Plaza Suite 0272 Chicago IL 60670

KNOX, JON BRUCE, cultural organization administrator; b. New London, Conn., Jan. 23, 1939; s. Frank Judd and Anna (Ware) K.; m. Susan Jean Busse, June 1961; children: Sharon, Barbara, Susan. Community program dir. Pasadena (Calif.) YMCA, 1961-65; community program and camp dir. Tacoma YMCA, 1965-69; exec. Puyallup Valley Br., Tacoma, 1969-72; program dir. Joliet (Ill.) YMCA, 1972-76, met. program dir., 1976-81, gen. dir., 1980-81; dir. Briggs Family Ctr., Joliet, 1979-81; assoc. gen. dir. Briggs Family Ctr., 1980-81; bus. mgr. program resources YMCA, Elk Grove, Ill., 1981-84; exec. dir. Internat. Mgmt. Council of YMCA, Des Plaines, Ill., 1984—; mem. nat. exec. com. Y-Indian Guide Program, 1975-76; mem. Nst. Y-Indian Guide conv. Com., 1976-78; trainer YMCA Positive Parenting; instr. YMCA-AMA Essentials of Mgmt. Course. Field mgr. Youth for Understanding, Washington, 1979—; nat. bd. dirs. United Cerebral Palsy, 1985—, Will County, Ill., 1978—, pres., 1983-85; organizer, bd. dirs. Friends United Cerebral Palsy, Joliet, 1982—. Mem. Inst. Cert. Profl. Mgrs. (regent 1984—), Assn. Profl. Dirs. (cert.). Republican. Mem. United Ch. of Christ. Avocations: camping, travel, history. Office: Internat Mgmt Council YMCA 2250 E Devon Suite 318 Des Plaines IL 60018

KNOX, TRUDY, psychologist, consultant; b. Cape Girardeau, Mo., Aug. 11, 1926; d. Raymond Kenneth and Gertrude (McCann) K.; m. Joseph Russel Bagby, Feb. 14, 1962 (div. July 1969); children: Kenneth, Laurel, James. BS, Northwestern U., 1948; MA, U. Fla., 1951; EdD, U. Ark., 1973. Lic. psychologist, Ill., Ohio. Psychologist Columbus State Sch. State of Ohio, 1952-57, Scioto Village State of Ohio, Delaware, 1957-62; psychologist, cons. Granville, Ohio, 1962—; adj. faculty Ohio State U., Newark, Columbus, 1974—. Pub. book and cassette program The Music Is You by R. Perez, 1983; contbr. articles to prof. jours. Co-founder Columbus Met. Club, 1975. Mem. Am. Psychol. Assn., Am. Group Psychotherapy Assn., Tri-State Group Psychotherapy Soc., Ohio Psychol. Assn., Ohio Speakers Forum (founder, charter pres. 1980-81, Trudy Knox award 1986), Nat. Speakers Assn., Meml. Soc. Columbus (pres. 1986—). Home and Office: 168 Wildwood Dr Granville OH 43023

KNUDSON, GORDON STUART, accountant; b. Colfax, Wis., Nov. 9, 1945; s. Hogan Henry and Oliana (Johnson) K.; m. Kathryn Marie Valaske, Aug. 4, 1973 (div. May 1987); children: Lisa, Kent, Kari. BS, U. Wis., Eau Claire, 1969; postgrad., Georgetown U., 1970-71, U. Md., 1971-72. CPA, Wis. Mgr. ops. First Wis. Nat. Bank, Eau Claire, 1973-76; cashier First Nat. Bank, Hudson, Wis., 1976-78; controller, purchasing agt. Sterling Plastics Corp., St. Paul, 1978-79; acct. Andersen and Seiberlich, Stillwater, Minn., 1979-80, McGladrey Hendrickson & Co., Stillwater, 1980-81, Olson Knutson & Co. S.C., Hudson, 1981-83; pvt. practice acctg. Hudson, 1983—. Bd. dirs. Hudson Sch. Dist., 1981-82; leader Cub Scouts Am., 1986—. Served with USN, 1969-73. Mem. Am. Inst. CPA's, Wis. Inst. CPA's, Minn. Soc. CPA's, Am. Legion. Republican. Lutheran. Lodge: Lions (treas. Hudson 1987). Avocations: flying, golf, gardening, bowling.

KNUDSON, MARK BRADLEY, medical corporation executive; b. Libby, Mont., Sept. 24, 1948; s. Melvin R. and Melba Irene (Joice) K.; m. Susan Jean Voorhees, Sept. 12, 1970; children—Kirstin Sue, Amy Lynn. B.S., Pacific Luth. U., 1970; Ph.D., Wash. State U., 1974. Asst. prof. U. Wash., Seattle, 1977-79; physiologist Cardiac Pacemakers, Inc., St. Paul, 1979-80, mgr. research, 1980-82, dir. applied research, 1983; pres., chmn. bd. SenTech Med. Corp., St. Paul, 1983-86; pres. Arden Med. Systems Inc. subs. Johnson & Johnson, 1987—; lectr. in field. NIH fellow, 1975-76. Mem. AAAS, Am. Heart Assn. Republican. Lutheran. Contbr. articles to profl. jours.; patentee in field. Office: PO Box 64302 Saint Paul MN 55164

KNUEPPELHOLZ, ANTJE MITOYO, financial company executive; b. Ann Arbor, Jan. 14, 1958; s. Joachim and Ethel (Nakama) K. BBA, Ea. Mich. U., Ypsilanti, 1980; M in Taxation, Walsh Coll., 1982. CPA, Mich. Acct. Arthur Andersen & Co., Detroit, 1981-85; v.p. planning First Continental Fin. Corp. Am., Birmingham, Mich., 1985—. Mem. Am. Inst. CPA's, Mich. Assn. CPA's, Am. Assn. Individual Investors. Club: Stoic Soc., Ea. Mich. U. (Treas. 1979-80). Avocations: photography, traveling. Office: First Continental Fin Corp 380 N Woodward Suite 100 Birmingham MI 48011

KNUEVEN, ROBERT JOSEPH, finance executive; b. Cin., Mar. 19, 1939; s. Walter Valentine and Dorothy (Honekamp) K.; m. Diane Collette Brisson, June 28, 1968; children: Robert Jr., Laura, Vincent, Joel. BSBA, Xavier U., 1961, MBA, 1972. CPA, Ohio. Mgr. Ernst & Whinney, Cin., 1963-76; asst. adminstr. fin. Deaconess Hosp., Cin., 1977-79; mgr. Arthur Anderson, Cin., 1979-80; v.p. fin. Mercy Hosp., Hamilton, Ohio, 1981—. Bd. dirs. Beechwood Home, Cin., 1982—; 1st. v.p. Hospice of Miami Valley, Hamilton, Ohio., 1986. Served to. 1st lt. U.S. Army, 1961-63, with res. 1963—. Mem. Soc. Advancement Mgmt. (pres. Cin. chpt. 1979-80, treas. Cin. chpt. 1986), Health Care Fin. Mgmt. (pres. 1984-85, Reeves Silver award 1985), Res. Officer Assn., Assn. U.S. Army. Roman Catholic. Lodge: KC. Home: 742 McClelland Rd Milford OH 45150 Office: P.O. Box 418 Hamilton OH 45012

KNUTESON, MILES GENE, broadcasting executive; b. Wisconsin Rapids, Wis., Aug. 18, 1952; s. Kenneth Thomas and Myrtle Lucille (Knoll) K.; m. Christine Marie Coleman, Aug. 18, 1979; 1 child, Katherine Marie. BS, U. Wis., Stevens Point, 1974. News reporter Sta. WHBY, Appleton, Wis., 1974-77, account exec., 1977-79; gen. sales mgr. Sta. WAPL, Appleton, 1979-80, Stas. WHBY and WAPL-FM, Appleton, 1980-81, Sta. WGEE, Green Bay, Wis., 1981-83; v.p., gen. mgr. Stas. KIOA and KDWZ-FM, Des Moines, 1983—. Sec. adv. bd. Salvation Army, Appleton, 1977-83, chmn. adv. bd., 1981-83, mem. adv. bd. Des Moines, 1986—. Recipient Pub. Affairs award N.W. Broadcast News Assn., 1976, Sch. Bell award Wis. Edn. Assn. Council, 1976. Mem. Des Moines Radio Broadcasters Assn. (v.p., sec., chair). Lutheran. Home: 509 45th St Des Moines IA 50265 Office: KIDA/KDWZ Radio 215 Keo Way Des Moines IA 50309

KNUTSEN, ALAN PAUL, pediatrician, allergist, immunologist; b. Mpls., July 21, 1948; s. Donald Richard aand Shirley Marie (Erickson) K.; m. Patricia Gaye Low, Dec. 21, 1974; children: Laura Joelle, Brian A., Benjamin C., Elizabeth G., Katharine M. BA, U. Calif., Riverside, 1971; MD, St. Louis U., 1975. Resident pediatrics St. Louis U. Med. Ctr., 1975-78; asst. prof. St. Louis U., 1980—; co-dir. allergy/immunology St. Louis U. Med. Ctr., 1985—; fellow allergy Duke U. Med. Ctr., Durham, N.C., 1978-80; mem. credentials com. St. Louis U. Med. Ctr., 1980—, infectious disease com., 1980—; dir. diagnostic pediatric immunology lab, 1983—; cons. NIOSH, 1984. Contbr. articles to profl. jours. Mem. Am. Acad. Allergy/Immunology (seminar com.), Southwestern Allergy Assn., Mo. State Allergy Assn., Soc. Pediatric Research, Phi Beta Kappa, Alpha Omega Alpha. Democrat. Presbyterian. Home: 327 S Elm Webster Groves MO 63119 Office: St Louis U Pediatric Research Inst 1465 S Grand Saint Louis MO 63104

KNUTSON, JANET, elementary teacher; b. Beloit, Wis., Feb. 1, 1947; d. Marvin Lester and Sylvia Janet (Meuler) Hefti; m. David Wayne Knutson, Aug. 9, 1969. BA, Luther Coll., Decorah, Iowa, 1969; MS, U. Wis., Whitewater, 1974. Cert. elem. teacher, elem. guidance and counselor, Wis. Tchr. Converse Elem. Sch., Beloit, 1969-70, Hackett Elem. Sch., Beloit, 1970-85, Wright Environ. Sch., Beloit, 1985—; instr. environ. teaching methods Beloit Coll., 1985-87. Author: (teaching units) Big Hill Park, 1984, Wis. Makeit and Takeit, 1985; co-author: (teaching unit) Mound Builders Archeogical Unit, 1987. Pres., bd. dirs. YWCA, Beloit, 1978-82; co-founder Beloit Girls Softball Orgn., 1980; co-coordinator Beloit Girls Softball program, 1980-87; coach, chmn. Beloit Spl. Olympics, 1980-86. Recipient Beloit Tchr. of Month award Kiwanis Club, Beloit, 1979, Coach of Yr. award Spl. Olympics, Beloit, 1982, 86, Educator of Yr. award YWCA, Beloit, 1983, Outstanding Educator award Rock County Dept. Land Conservation, 1983. Mem. Wis. Assn. Environ. Edn., Wis. Interscholastic Athletic Assn. (officiated regional championships 1986), Alpha Delta Kappa. Lutheran. Avocations: cross country skiing, volleyball. Home: 927 8th St Beloit WI 53511 Office: Wright Environ Sch 1033 Woodard Beloit WI 53511

KNUTSON, STEVEN JOHN, architect; b. Mitchell, S.D., Mar. 13, 1951; s. Herman Lee and Hope (Daugherty) K.; m. Shirley Rose Sogge; children: Travis, Chad. BArch, U. Minn., 1979. Registered architect, Minn., Ohio. Project architect A.J. Berream Assocs., Mpls., 1973-81, Hills/Gilbertson Architects, Mpls., 1981-83; owner Wolfgram/Knutson Architects Ltd., Mpls., 1983—. Pres. South Athletic Council, South Mpls., 1983—, Keewatdin Park Neighborhood Council, South Mpls., 1981—. Recipient Service Recognition award Longfellow/Nokomosis Community Council, Mpls., 1984, Cert. of Appreciation, Mpls. Parks and Recreation Bd., 1985. Mem. AIA, Minn. Soc. Architecture. Lutheran. Home: 5104 37th Ave S Minneapolis MN 55417 Office: Wolfgram/Knutson Architects Ltd 3960 Minnehaha Ave S Minneapolis MN 55406

KO, WEN-HSIUNG, electrical engineering educator; b. Shang-Hong, Fukien, China, Apr. 12, 1923; came to U.S., 1954, naturalized, 1963; s. Sing-Ming and Sou-Yu (Kao) K.; m. Christina Chen, Oct. 12, 1957; children: Kathleen, Janet, Linda, Alexander. B.S. in E.E. (Tan-Ka-Kee fellow), Nat. Amoy U., Fukien, China, 1946; M.S., Case Inst. Tech., 1956, Ph.D., 1959. Engr., then sr. engr. Taiwan Telecommunication Adminstrn., 1946-54; mem. faculty Case Inst. Tech., Cleve., 1956—; prof. elec. engring. Case Inst. Tech., 1967—, prof. elec. and biomed. engring., 1970—, dir. engring. design center, 1970-83; cons. Conoflow Corp., IBM, Diamond Alkali, NIH, 1966-76. Fellow IEEE; mem. Instrument Soc. Am., Bio-Med. Engring. Soc., Sigma Xi, Eta Kappa Nu. Home: 1356 Forest Hills Blvd Cleveland Heights OH 44118 Office: Case Western Res U Electronics Design Center Cleveland OH 44106

KOBAK, ALFRED JULIAN, JR., obstetrician-gynecologist; b. Chgo., Feb. 10, 1935; s. Alfred J., and Rose B. (Baron) K.; m. Sue B. Stein, May 3, 1959; children—William, Steven, Jane, Deborah. B.S., U. Ill., 1957, M.D., 1959. Diplomate Am. Bd. Ob-Gyn. Intern Michael Reese Hosp., Chgo., 1959-60; resident Cook County Hosp., 1960-62, 64-65; practice medicine specializing in ob-gyn., Valparaiso, Ind., 1965—; mem. med. staff Porter Meml. Hosp., Valparaiso, 1965—, pres., 1981-82; asst. clin. prof. ob-gyn Ind. U.; clin. instr. ob-gyn Rush Med. Sch., Chgo.; pres. Ob-Gyn Assocs., Valparaiso, 1970—. Bd. dirs. Northwest Ind. Jewish Fedn., 1970-84, Pines Village. Served to capt. USAF, 1962-64. Fellow ACS, Internat. Coll. Surgeons, Am. Coll. Ob-Gyn.; mem. AMA, Am. Fertility Soc., Ind. Med. Assn., Central Assn. Obstetricians and Gynecologists, Porter County Med. Soc. (pres. 1979, 86), Physicians Med. Alliance Ind. (bd. dirs.). Republican. Clubs: Valparaiso Country. Contbr. articles to med. jours. Office: 1101 E Glendale Valparaiso IN 46383

KOBAK, SHARON TORREANO, osteopath, psychiatrist; b. Chgo., Jan. 20, 1943; d. Dominic and Berniece (Bednarz) Torreano; m. Mathew W. Kobak, Jan. 2, 1976 (dec. Jan. 1985); 1 child, Caroline. BA, St. Xavier Coll., 1964; DO, Chgo. Coll. Osteo. Medicine, 1973. Diplomate Am. Bd. Psychiatry and Neurology. Intern Pontiac (Mich.) Osteo. Hosp., 1973-74; resident in psychiatry Chgo. Med. Sch., 1974-77; psychiatrist Chgo. Osteopathic Med. Ctr., 1977-80, Family Service and Mental Health Ctr. of S. Cook County, Chicago Heights, 1980—; cons. Oak Forest (Ill.) Hosp., 1980—, Lakeside VA Hosp., Chgo., 1982—; adj. asst. prof. Chgo. Osteopathic Coll. Med., 1980—. Judge Chgo. Pub. Sch. Sci. Fair, 1983—. Mem. Am. Ostepathic Assn., Am. Psychiatric Assn., Ill Psychiatric Soc. Club: Quadrangle (Chgo.). Home: 916 Braemar Rd Flossmoor IL 60422 Office: Oak Forest Hosp 15900 Cicero Ave Oak Forest IL 60452

KOBAYASHI, ROGER HIDEO, pathology and microbiology educator; b. Honolulu, May 21, 1947; s. Roy T. and Setsuko (Ebesugawa) K.; m. Ai Lan Doan, May 21, 1974; children: Lisa, Timothy. MS in Physiology, U. Hawaii, 1975; MD, U. Nebr., 1975. Diplomate Am. Bd. Allergy and Immunology, Am. Bd. Pediatrics, Nat. Bd. Med. Examiners. Asst. prof. pediatrics U. Nebr. Med. Ctr., Omaha, 1980-84, asst. prof. medical microbiology, 1980-85, dir. pediatric allergy and immunology, 1980—, assoc. prof. pediatrics, 1984—, assoc. prof. pathology and microbiology, 1985—; bd. dirs. Am. Lung Assn. Nebr., Asthma and Allergy Found. Am., Am. Lung Assn. Nebr., cons. physician Children's Hosp., 1980—; cons. physician Vis. Nurses Nebr., 1985—; mem. U. Nebr. Chancellor's Com. Rural Health, 1982—. Recipient Enzon Inc. 1986-87, Sondoz Inc. 1986-87, Schering Co. 1987-88, Sondoz Inc. 1987-88; research award Mead-Johnson, 1983-84, NIH, 1982. Fellow Am. Acad. Pediatrics, Am. Acad. Allergy and Immunology; mem. Am. Fedn. Clin. Research, Am. Soc. Microbiology, Nebr. Fly Fishing Assn. Avocations: fly fishing, wine collecting, tennis, med. econs. Home: 9942 Lafayette Ave Omaha NE 68114 Office: U Nebr Med Ctr Div Immunology and Allergy 42d and Dewey Omaha NE 68105

KOBER, ARLETTA REFSHAUGE (MRS. KAY L. KOBER), ednl. adminstr.; b. Cedar Falls, Iowa, Oct. 31, 1919; d. Edward and Mary (Jensen) Refshauge; B.A., State Coll. Iowa, 1940; M.A., U. No. Iowa; m. Kay Leonard Kober, Feb. 14, 1944; children—Kay Mary, Karilyn Eve. Tchr. high schs., Soldier, Iowa, 1940-41, Montezuma, Iowa, 1941-43, Waterloo, Iowa, 1943-50, 65-67, co-ordinator Office Edn. Waterloo Community Schs., Waterloo, Iowa, 1967—; head dept. co-op. career edn. West High Sch., Waterloo, 1974—. Mem. Waterloo Sch. Health Council; nominating com. YWCA, Waterloo; Black Hawk County chmn. Tb Christmas Seals; ward chmn. ARC, Waterloo; co-chmn. Citizen's Com. for Sch. Bond Issue; pres. Waterloo PTA Council, Waterloo Vis. Nursing Assn., 1956-57, Kingsley Sch. PTA, 1959-60; v.p. Waterloo Women's Club, 1962-63, pres., 1963-64, trustee bd. clubhouse dirs., 1957—; mem. Gen. Fedn. Women's Clubs, Nat. Congress Parents and Tchrs.; Presbyterian world service chmn. Presbyn. Women's Assn.; bd. dirs. Black Hawk County Republican Women, 1952-53, United Services of Black Hawk County, Broadway Theatre League, St. Francis Hosp. Found. Mem. AAUW (v.p. Cedar Falls 1946-47), NEA, LWV (dir. Waterloo 1951-52), Black Hawk County Hist. Soc. (charter), Delta Pi Epsilon (v.p. 1966-67), Delta Kappa Gamma. Club: Town (dir.) (Waterloo). Home: 1046 Prospect Blvd Waterloo IA 50701 Office: 503 W 4th St Waterloo IA 50702

KOBLENZER, MARGARET ETHRIDGE, clinical social worker; b. Huntington, N.Y., June 27, 1954; d. Mark Foster and Margaret Burns (Furbee) Ethridge; m. Warren Dale Koblenzer, Aug. 11, 1979; 1 child, Katherine

Burns. B.A., Ohio Wesleyan U., 1977; M.S. in Social Adminstrn., Case Western Res. U., 1980. Lic. independent social worker. Clin. social worker Catholic Service League, Akron, Ohio, 1980-81; psychiat. social worker Akron Child Guidance Ctr., 1981-84; ind. social worker Psychotherapy Assocs., Akron, 1983—. Bd. trustees Blick Clinic for Devel. Disabilities, Akron, 1986-89; allocation com. mem. United Way Summit County. Mem. Nat. Assn. Social Workers, Acad. Cert. Social Workers, Jr. League of Akron, Kappa Kappa Gamma. Democrat. Episcopalian. Club: Portage Country (Akron). Office: 3200 W Market St Akron OH 44313

KOBLER, FRANK JOHN, psychology educator emeritus; b. Chgo., Apr. 6, 1915; s. Joseph and Elizabeth (Bollman) K.; m. Carolyn King, 1942; children: Claudia, Mark, Mary, Katherine, Roxanne, Michael, Charles, Carol. PhB, DePaul U., 1936; MA, Niagara U., 1937; PhD, U. Chgo., 1942. Diplomate Am. Bd. Psychology. Psychologist Inst. for Juvenile Research, Chgo., 1940-42; chief civilian psychologist U.S. War Dept., Chgo., 1942-43; prof. psychology, dir. grad. clin. training Loyola U., Chgo., 1946-85, prof. emeritus psychology, 1985—. Author: Case Book in Psychopathology; contbr. articles to profl. jours. Cons. VA, Chgo., 1950—, Archdiocese of Chgo., 1964-84; Commr. City of Chgo., 1965-85; chmn. Ill. State Psychology Examining Bd., Springfield, 1970-75. Served to lt. U.S. Army, 1943-45. Fellow Am. Psychology Assn. (William James award 1980); mem. Ill. Psychology Assn., Am. Bd. Profl. Psychologists (trustee 1970-77). Roman Catholic. Home: 7667 W Norwood St Chicago IL 60631 Office: Loyola U 6525 N Sheridan Rd Chicago IL 60626

KOBRIGER, ANNETTE MARIE, nutritionist, consultant; b. Phila., May 13, 1944; d. Cecil Paul and Anna Victoria (Lisowski) Kosko; m. Robert Nicholas Kobriger, May 13, 1970; 1 child, Carolyn Ann (dec.). BS, Pa. State U., 1966; MPH, U. Minn., 1972; postgrad., U. Mo., 1983—. Registered dietitian, Mo., Wis., Ala. Nutritionist Wis. Dept. Health and Social Services, Green Bay, 1968-72; perinatal nutritionist Northeast Wis. Perinatal Ctr., Green Bay, 1975-79; asst. prof. U. Ala., Tuscaloosa, 1979-80; nutrition specialist Mo. Dept. Health, Jefferson City, 1981—; instr., coordinator Northeast Wis. Tech. Inst., Green Bay, 1972-73; dietary cons. Appleton (Wis.) Extended Care Ctr., 1973-75; cons. community nutrition U. Wis., Green Bay, 1974-75; cons., educator, Marquette U., Milw., 1977-78; distbr. Success Motivaiton Inst. Co-author: (with R. Mathissen and M. Egan) Neonatal Nutrition Manual, 1987. Adv. bd. Shelter Care, Inc., Tuscaloosa, 1979, Northeast Wis. Tech. Inst., Green Bay, 1968-74; co-treas. Candlelighters, U. Mo. Med. Ctr., Columbia, 1982-86. Abbey Sutherland scholar, 1963; grantee U.S. Children's Bur., 1967. Mem. Am. Dietetic Assn. (chmn. pub. health nutrition practice group 1986—), Nat. Perinatal Assn., Mo. Perinatal Assn., Mo. Pub. Health Assn. (chmn. food and nutrition com. 1986—). Roman Catholic. Avocations: physical fitness, writing, gardening. Home: 2220 Brandy Ln Jefferson City MO 65101

KOBS, ANN ELIZABETH JANE, nursing administrator, consultant; b. Clinton, Iowa, Feb. 13, 1944; d. Francis Hubert and Leora Elizabeth (Sodeman) Boeker; m. Dennis Raymond Kobs, Oct. 15, 1966; children—Michael, Peter, Amy. Diploma, Mercy Hosp. Sch. Nursing, 1965; B.S. in Nursing, Marycrest Coll., 1978; M.S. in Nursing Adminstrn., No. Ill. U., 1981. Staff charge nurse Mercy Hosp., Davenport, Iowa, 1965-66; clin. instr. Marycrest Coll., Davenport, 1967; cons. to physicians in pvt. practice, Rock Island, Ill., 1973-75; pre-reviewer for continuing edn. and career counselor in residence Ill. Nurses Assn., Chgo., 1978-80; career devel. cons. Ill. Hosp. Assn., Oak Brook, 1980-81, staff specialist nursing, 1981-83, dir. nursing, Naperville, 1983-84; dir. nursing surg./maternal-child health Alexian Bros. Med. Ctr., Elk Grove Village, Ill., 1984-87; cons. Premier Hosps. Alliance, Inc., 1987; dir. nursing services Rochelle (Ill.) Community Hosp., 1987—; lectr. No. Ill. U., 1981-87, St. Xavier Coll., 1987. Mem. City Beautification Commn. Rock Island, 1972-76, also sec., vice-chmn. Mem. Am. Soc. Nursing Services Adminstrs. (sec., vice-chmn.), Am. Soc. Nurse Execs., Ill. Orgn. Nurse Adminstrs. (mem. exec. com., chmn. Task Force on Sunset Ill. Nursing Act 1984—), Nat. League Nursing (sec.), Ill. League Nursing, Women's Health Exec. Network, Nat. Assn. Female Execs., Sigma Theta Tau. Roman Catholic. Editor: Ill. Nurses Assn. Directory of Baccalaureate Degree Completion Programs for RNs in Ill., 1979; writer, producer, dir.: Nursing: Opportunities Unlimited, 1980.

KOCH, ALBERT ACHESON, acctg. co. exec.; b. Atlanta, May 16, 1942; s. Albert H. and Harriet M. (Acheson) K.; B.S. cum laude, Elizabethtown Coll., 1964; m. Bonnie Royce, June 6, 1964; children—Bradford Allen, David Albert, Robert Acheson, Donald Leonard. With Ernst & Whinney, 1964—, nat. dir. client services nat. office, Cleve., 1977-81, mng. partner Detroit office, 1981—; mem. adv. com. on replacement cost implementation SEC, 1976. Bd. dirs. Harper-Grace Hosps., 1982—, Radius Health Services, 1984—, New Detroit, 1985—, Elizabethtown Coll., 1981—, Met. Detroit YMCA, 1982—, Mich. Colls. Found., 1981—, Detroit Symphony Orch., 1983—. Served to 1st lt. Fin. Corps, USAR, 1966-72. Recipient Elijah Watt Sells Gold Medal award Am. Inst. C.P.A.s, 1965, Educate for Service award Elizabethtown Coll., 1966. Fellow Life Mgmt. Inst.; mem. Am. Inst. C.P.A.s, Mich. Assn. C.P.A.s. Clubs: Bloomfield Hills Country, Orchard Lake Country, Detroit, Detroit Athletic, Renaissance, Econ. Detroit (dir. 1981—). Co-author: SEC Replacement Cost Requirements and Implementation Manual, 1976. Office: 200 Renaissance Center Suite 2300 Detroit MI 48243

KOCH, CHARLES G., diversified business executive; b. Wichita, Kans., 1935; ed. MIT. Chmn., chief exec. officer Koch Industries, Inc., Wichita; bd. dirs. Squibb Corp., First Nat. Bank of Wichita. Bd. dirs. Inst. Humane Studies, Cato Inst., Citizens For A Sound Economy, Wesley Found.; bd. trustees Wichita Collegiate Sch.; mem. Mont Pelerin Soc., Met. Wichita Council. Office: Koch Industries Inc PO Box 2256 Wichita KS 67201

KOCH, DANIEL KURTZON, lighting company executive; b. Evanston, Ill., May 28, 1947; s. David and Slyvia (Kurtzon) K.; m. Kamla Devi Bhatty, Nov. 25, 1978; 1 child, Adam Joginder. BA, U. Wis., 1969; MA, U. Hawaii, 1977. Vol. Peace Corps, Borneo, 1969-71; tchr. ESL Hawaii and Mex., 1972-74; instr. linguistics U. Hawaii, Honolulu, 1975-78; pres. Morris Kurtzon, Inc., Chgo., 1978—, also bd. dirs.; cons. Albany Park Com. Ctr., Chgo., 1986. Mem. adv. council Malcolm X Coll., Chgo., 1984—; pres. Fitch Park Condominium Assn., Chgo., 1984; co-chmn. Indian Boundry Area Council, Chgo., 1985. Served as liaison officer Saranak Borneo Scouts, 1970-71. Mem. Ill. Engring. Soc., Chgo. Lighting Club. Clubs: Wis. Union (v.p. 1967), Downtown Sports. Lodge: Masons. Avocations: physical fitness, sailing, collecting books, micronesian navigation.

KOCH, DONALD LEROY, geologist, state agency administrator; b. Dubuque, Iowa, June 3, 1937; s. Gregory John and Josephine Elizabeth (Young) K.; m. Celia Jean Swede, July 5, 1962; children: Kyle Benjamin, Amy Suzanne, Nathan Gregory. BS, U. Iowa, 1959, MS in Geology, 1967, postgrad., 1971-73. Research geologist Iowa Geol. Survey, Iowa City, 1959-71, chief subsurface geology, 1971-75, asst. state geologist, 1975-80, state geologist and dir., 1980-86; state geologist and bur. chief Geol. Survey Bur., Iowa City, 1986. Contbr. articles to profl. jours. Fellow Iowa Acad. Sci. (bd. dirs. 1986—); mem. Geol. Soc. Iowa (pres. 1969-86), Iowa Groundwater Assn. (pres. 1986), Sigma Xi. Lodge: Rotary. Avocations: bicycling, camping, chess, numismatics. Home: 1431 Prairie du Chien Rd Iowa City IA 52240 Office: Geol Survey Bur 123 N Capitol St Iowa City IA 52242

KOCH, GARY EDWARD, government administrator; b. Jacksonville, Ill., Sept. 24, 1950; s. Byron Edward and Paula Elizabeth (Scoggins) K.; m. Valerie Jean Ludden, Dec. 8, 1979; 1 child, Laura Elizabeth. BA, Ill. Coll., Jacksonville, 1972; MA, Sangamon State U., 1973, MA, 1985. Reporter State Jour.-Register, Springfield, Ill., 1973; legis. aide Ill. Ho. Reps., 1973-74; pub. info. officer Ill. Dept. Local Govt. Affairs, Springfield, 1974-79, Ill. Dept. Commerce and Community Affairs, Springfield, 1979-82; exec. dir. Legis. Local Acctg. Task Force, Springfield, 1982-84; dep. dir. local govt. fiscal programs Office State Comptroller, Springfield, 1984—; mem. State Comptroller's Local Govt. Adv. Bd., 1984—; spokesman Gov.'s Adv. Commn. on Taxes, 1978-79, mem. Gov.'s Task Force on Reorgn. State Govt., 1978-79. Editor Local Govt. Report, Local Govt. Bull.; co-editor: Simplified Financial Management Manual for Illinois Park Districts, 1976. Mem. Ill. Press Assn., Pub. Relations Soc. Am., Internat. Assn. Bus. Communicators, Scott County Hist. Soc., Springfield Jaycees, Sangamon State Alumni Assn. (bd. dirs.), Springfield Soc. Ill. Coll. (past pres.). Democrat. Lutheran. Home: 2206 Makemie St Springfield IL 62704 Office: 325 W Adams 4th Floor Springfield IL 62706

KOCH, ROBERT MARTIN, industrial executive; b. Chgo., Oct. 21, 1930; s. Martin and Pearl (Unison) K.; m. Anita Ernst, Dec. 6, 1952; children—Susan Ellen, Cathy Lynn, Robert Ernst (dec.), Jeffrey John. Student U. Ill.-Chgo., 1948-50; B.A. cum laude, Augustana Coll., 1952. Engr., sales engr., asst. mgr. Sears Roebuck & Co., Moline and Chgo., Ill., 1952-55; engr., gen. foreman, prodn. mgr. Advance Transformer Co., Chgo., 1955-62; ops. and plant mgr. Grand Sheet Metal Products Co. Melrose Park, Ill., 1962-65; v.p., exec. v.p., gen. mgr., pres. Standard Transformer Co., Warren, Ohio, 1965-72; dir. and v.p. ops. Bastian Blessing and Rego divs. Golconda Corp., Grand Haven, Mich. and Chgo., 1972-83; v.p. mfg. Fort Lock Corp., River Grove, Ill., 1983—. Home: 2805 Weller Ln Northbrook IL 60062

KOCH, ROBERT WARREN, foods manufacturing executive; b. Chgo., Jan. 5, 1927; s. Otto C. and Florence G. (Brown) K.; m. Florence Mary Rooney, 1949 (dec. 1961); children—Robert Warren, Jr., Kathleen P.; m. Anne M. Donnelly, 1963; children—Mark Uhler, Amy D. B.S. in Bus. Adminstrn., Northwestern U., 1949, postgrad., 1950-57. Acct., Busby & Oury, C.P.A.s, Chgo., 1949-50; with Food Materials Corp., Chgo., 1950—, v.p., 1955-56, exec. v.p., 1956-58, pres., 1958-72, 85—, chmn., 1972-84; v.p. Culver Legion, Culver Mil. Acad. Served with AC, U.S. Army, 1946-47. Mem. Flavor & Extract Mfrs. Assn. (past pres.), Sigma Nu Alumni Assn. (v.p., sec.-treas. 1975-85). Club: Chgo. Yacht. Home: 2137 N Cleveland Ave Chicago IL 60614 Office: 2711 W Irving Park Rd Chicago IL 60618

KOCH, WILLIAM JOSEPH, advertising and public relations agency executive; b. Celina, Ohio, June 6, 1949; s. George Albert and Helen Marie (McKovich) K.; B.A., U. Akron, 1974; m. Susan Margaret Griffith, June 14, 1969; children—Brian William, Dana Marie. Draftsman, Summit County Engr.'s Office, Akron, Ohio, 1968-72; public info. officer Ohio Dept. Transp., Ravenna, 1972-75; asst. dir. mktg. and public relations Metro Regional Transit Authority, Akron, 1975-78; sr. account exec. Meeker-Mayer Agy., Akron, 1978-83; v.p. Meeker-Mayer Pub. Relations, 1983-84; exec. v.p., chief exec. officer, David A. Meeker & Assocs., Inc./Pub. Relations, 1984-87, mgr. pub. affairs Tricil Environ. Services, Inc., Akron, 1987—. Trustee All-Am. Soap Box Derby, Inc., 1978—. Mem. Public Relations Soc. Am., Akron Press Club. Democrat. Roman Catholic. Clubs: Jaycees (senator, Disting. Service award 1983). Home: 3325 Bancroft Rd Akron OH 44313 Office: 1789 Theiss Rd Akron OH 44313

KOCHAR, MAHENDR SINGH, physician, educator, administrator, researcher, writer; b. Jabalpur, India, Nov. 30, 1943; came to U.S., 1967; s. Harnam Singh and Chanan Kaur (Khaturia) K.; m. Arvind Kaur, 1968; children: Baltej, Ajay. MB, BS, All India Inst. Med. Scis., New Delhi, 1965; MSc, Med. Coll. Wis., 1972, MBA, U. Wis., Milw., 1987. Intern, All India Inst. Med. Scis. Hosp., New Delhi, 1966, Passaic (N.J.) Gen. Hosp., 1967-68; resident in medicine Allegheny Gen. Hosp., Pitts., 1968-70; fellow in clin. pharmacology Milw. VA Med. Center, 1970-71, attending physician, 1973; fellow in nephrology and hypertension Milwaukee County Gen. Hosp., 1971-73, attending physician, 1973—; attending physician St. Michael Hosp., Milw., 1974—, dir. hemodialysis unit, 1975-80; clin. asst. prof. medicine and pharmacology and toxicology Med. Coll. Wis., Milw., 1973-75, asst. prof., 1975-78, assoc. prof., 1978-84, prof. 1984—; assoc. dean grad. med. edn., 1987—; attending physician St. Joseph's Hosp., Milw., 1975—; cons. nephrology Elmbrook Meml. Hosp., Brookfield, Wis., 1976—; chmn. medicine Northpoint Med. Group, Milw., 1974-75; dir. Milw. Blood Pressure Program, 1975-78; dir. Hypertension Clinic, Milwaukee County Downtown Med. and Health Services, 1975-79; chief hypertension sect. VA Med. Center, Milw., 1978—, assoc. chief staff for edn., 1979—; exec. dir. Med. Coll. Wis. Affiliated Hosps. Inc., Milw., 1987—. Diplomate Am. Bd. Internal Medicine and Nephrology, Am. Bd. Family Practice. Fellow A.C.P. Cardiology, Am. Acad. Family Physicians, Royal Coll. Physicians Can., Am. Coll. Clin. Pharmacology; mem. Am. Acad. Med. Dirs., AMA, Royal Coll. Physicians (London), Internat. Soc. Nephrology, AAAS, Am. Fedn. Clin. Research, Am. Heart Assn., Am. Soc. Nephrology, Am. Soc. Internal Medicine, Am. Med. Writers Assn., Am. Diabetic Assn., council Biology Editors, Milw. Acad. Medicine, Mensa. Author: Hypertension Control, 1978, 2nd rev. edit., 1985; editor: Textbook of General Medicine, 1983. Clubs: Milw. Internist, Highland Tennis. Home: 18630 LeChateau Dr Brookfield WI 53005 Office: Clement Zablocki VA Med Ctr 5000 W National Ave (14-A) Milwaukee WI 53295

KOCHEN, MANFRED, information science and computer researcher, educator; b. Vienna, Austria, July 4, 1928; s. Max and Pepi (Figur) Kochen; m. Paula Landerer, Aug. 15, 1954; children—David Jay, Mark Neil. B.S., MIT, 1950; M.S., Columbia U., 1951, Ph.D., 1955. Programmer, analyst Inst. Advanced Study, Princeton, N.J., 1953-55; mathematician Biot & Arnold, N.Y.C., 1950-53, Paul Rosenberg Assocs., Mount Vernon, N.Y., 1953-55; lectr. Columbia U., N.Y.C., 1950-51; mgr., scientist, mem. tech. staff IBM Research Ctr., Yorktown Heights, N.Y., 1956-64; assoc. prof. U. Mich., Ann Arbor, 1965-70, prof. info. sci. Med. Sch., 1980—, adj. prof. computers and info. systems Bus. Sch., 1980—, chmn. sociotechnol. systems area PhD Program in Planning, 1984—; pres. Wise Corp.; vis. research assoc. Harvard U., 1973-74; vis. prof. Rockefeller U., 1980-81; cons. Rand Corp., RCA, United Aircraft Co., Library of Congress, cons. in field. Author 8 books including: The Growth of Knowledge, Information for Action, Decentralization; contbr. articles to profl. jours. Ford Found. fellow, 1955-56. Fellow AAAS; mem. Am. Math. Soc., Am. Phys. Soc., Am. Soc. Info. Sci. (award of merit 1974). Home: 2026 Devonshire Rd Ann Arbor MI 48104 Office: Univ Mich MHRI Ann Arbor MI 48104

KOCORAS, CHARLES PETROS, federal judge; b. Chgo., Mar. 12, 1938; s. Petros K. and Constantina (Cordonis) K.; m. Grace L. Finlay, Sept. 22, 1968; children: Peter, John, Paul. Student, Wilson Jr. Coll., 1956-58; B.S., Coll. Commerce, DePaul U., 1961; J.D., DePaul U., 1969. Bar: Ill. 1969. Assoc. Bishop & Crawford, 1969-71; asst. atty. Office of U.S. Atty. No. Dist. Ill. U.S. Dept. Justice, 1971-77; judge U.S. Dist. Ct., Chgo., 1980—; chmn. Ill. Commerce Commn., Chgo., 1977-79; ptnr. Stone, McGuire, Benjamin and Kocoras, Chgo., 1979-80; instr. trial practice, evening div. John Marshall Law Sch., 1975—; various positions IRS, Chgo., 1962-69. Served with Army N.G., 1961-67. Mem. Chgo. Bar Assn., Fed. Criminal Jury Instruction Com. Seventh Circuit, Beta Alpha Psi. Greek Orthodox. Office: US Courthouse 219 S Dearborn St Chicago IL 60604 *

KODNER, LESLEY, flooring contracting company executive; b. Chgo., Oct. 20, 1917; s. Louis and Ollie Kodner; m. Denise Friedman, June 17, 1945; children—David, Peter. Student Northwestern U., 1943-45. Lic. judge Am. Kennel Club. Reporter, Chgo. Herald Am., Chgo., 1940-43, Chgo. Sun Times, 1943-45; from salesman to pres. Morton Floors, Inc., Lincolnwood, Ill., 1946-75, chmn. 1982—. Served to sgt. U.S. Army, 1941-43. Mem. Profl. Flooring Installers (past pres.), Chgo. Chpt. of Am. Subcontractors Assn. (past v.p., pres. Chgo. chpt.). Clubs: Metropolitan (Chgo.), Mchts. and Mfrs. Lodges: Masons (comdr. in chief Chgo. chpt. Scottish rite), Shriners. Office: Morton Floors Inc 6525 N Proesel St Lincolnwood IL 60645

KOEBEL, CARL EDWARD, health department official; b. Fremont, Ohio, Mar. 17, 1943; s. Ivan A. and Mary L. (Miller) K.; m. Monette L. Fehnrich, Nov. 26, 1967 (div. April 1985); m. Mary Anne Wagner, Sept. 13, 1986; children: Michelle Lee, David A. A, Bowling Green State U., 1975. Registered sanitarian, Ohio. Sanitarian Sandusky County Health Dept., Fremont, Ohio, 1966-70; chief sanitarian Erie County Health Dept., Sandusky, 1970-79; dir. environ. health Ottawa County Health Dept., Port Clinton, Ohio, 1979—. Contbr. articles to profl. jours. Mem. Ottawa Planning Commn., Port Clinton, 1979—; bd. dirs. Ottawa County Humane Soc., Port Clinton, 1980-82. Served with U.S. Army N.G., 1975-86. Mem. Nat. Environ. Health Assn., Ohio Environ. Health Assn. (pres. 1983-84, Ohio Outstanding Sanitarian 1978, Ivan Baker Mem. Recognition award 1982), Ohio Pub. Health Assn. Democrat. Lutheran. Club: Port Clinton Yacht. Lodge: Kiwanis (pres. Pt. Clinton 1985, Disting. Pres. 1985, chmn. Key Club div. Ohio Dist. 1986, chmn. of Yr. 1986). Avocation: music. Office: Ottawa County Health Dept 315 Madison St Port Clinton OH 43452

KOEGEL, SHIRLEY ANN, small business owner; b. Ft. Wayne, Ind., Mar. 23, 1941; d. Carl Otis and Hazel Maude (Bellis) Boroff; m. James Kenneth Koegel, Dec. 19, 1959; children: Julie, June, Jill, Janet. Cert., U. Mo., 1982. Sec. Schlatter Hardware, Ft. Wayne, 1959-60; with collections dept. Sears and Roebuck Co., Ft. Wayne, 1969-70; Kelly girl Preferred Painters, Ft. Wayne, 1979, sec., bookkeeper, 1979-80, corp. sec., 1980-81, v.p., 1981-82; pres., owner Top of the Ladder, Ft. Wayne, 1982—; tchr. Success Motivation, Inc. Goal Courses, Ft. Wayne, 1985. Mem. Nat. Assn. of Women in Constrn. (pres. 1985-87), Women Bus. Owners (cert., bd. dirs. 1983-85), Ft. Wayne C. of C. (small bus. council), The Council. Republican. Methodist. Avocations: reading, snowmobiling, traveling. Home: 14306 Winters Rd Roanoke IN 46783 Office: Top of the Ladder Inc 301 W State Blvd Fort Wayne IN 46808

KOEHLER, SCOTT BRIAN, accountant; b. Hudson, Wis., May 31, 1958; s. Hugh Duane and Maureen Rose (Roberts) K.; m. Lisa Ann Metze, Sept. 5, 1981; 1 child, Sarah. BA, U. Wis., 1979, MS, 1984. CPA, Wis. Tax auditor State of Wis., Milw., 1980-82; tax mgr. Ernst & Whinney, Milw., 1985—. Contbr. articles to profl. jours. Recipient Excellence in Teaching award U. Wis., 1983-84. Mem. Am. Inst. CPA's, Wis. Inst. CPA's. Presbyterian. Office: Ernst & Whinney 735 N Water St Milwaukee WI 53202

KOEHN, WILLIAM JAMES, lawyer; b. Winterset, Iowa, Mar. 24, 1936; s. Cyril Otto and Ilene L. (Doop) K.; m. Francia C. Leeper, Sept. 6, 1958; children—Cynthia Rae, William Fredric, James Anthony. B.A., U. Iowa, 1958, J.D., 1963. Bar: Iowa 1963, U.S. Ct. Appeals (8th cir.) 1971, U.S. Ct. Appeals (10th cir.) 1972, U.S. Ct. Appeals (2d cir.) 1972, U.S. Ct. Appeals (5th cir.) 1977, U.S. Supreme Ct. 1971. Ptnr., Davis, Hockenberg, Wine, Brown and Koehn, Des Moines, 1963—. Bd. editors Iowa Law Rev., 1961-63. Co-founder Big Bros.-Sisters of Greater Des Moines, 1969, pres., 1976-77; chmn. Des Moines Friendship Commn., 1970-71; bd. dirs. Greater Des Moines YMCA, 1983—; co-chmn. Des Moines Bicentennial Commn., 1975-76. Served to lt. USNR, 1958-61. Named Best Lawyer in Am. Naiffh & Smith Bus. Litigation Sect., 1983-87. Mem. Iowa State Bar Assn. ABA (environ. litigation com.), Polk County Bar Assn., Def. Research Inst., Order of Coif. Republican. Home: 607 Country Club Blvd Des Moines IA 50312 Office: 2300 Financial Ctr Des Moines IA 50309

KOENE, WAYNE GEORGE, educator, radio broadcasting executive; b. Kiel, Wis., Sept. 22, 1937; s. George Henry and Norma Louise (Laux) K.; m. Mary Ann Hanseter, July 17, 1965 (div. June 1982); children: Noreen M., David J.; m. Helen Kratz Bloch, Oct. 19, 1984. BS, U. Wis., Madison, 1960, MS, 1963. Cert. ednl. adminstrn., agrl. edn., vocat. edn., cheese-making, Wis. Vocat. agr. instr. Glenwood City High Sch., 1961-66; farm editor Sta. WBAY-TV, Green Bay, Wis., 1966-67, food sci. instr. Moraine Park Tech. Inst., Fond du Lac, Wis., 1967-69, div. chmn., 1969-87; farm dir. Sta. KFIZ, Fond du Lac, 1978—; adj. faculty U. Wis. at Stout, Menomonie, 1973-79; adv. bd. AVI Pub. Co., Westport, Conn., 1967-74. Contbr. articles on agr. to profl. jours. Pres. Fond du Lac County Agrl. agencies, pres. Kiel Future Farmers Alumni Assn., 1978-79; bd. dirs. Fond du Lac Area Agribus. Council, 1980-84. Served to maj. USAR, 1960-82. Recipient Tchr. of Tchrs. bronze and silver awards Nat. Vocat. Agr. Instrs. Assn., 1970, 75, State Winner Sound Off for Agr. award Nat. Vocat. Agr. Instrs. Assn., 1978, 79. Mem. Wis. Assn. of Vocat. Agr. Instrs. (pub. relations chmn. 1961-76, 30-Minute Club award 1963, 64, 69, 71, 74), Am. Vocat. Assn., Wis. Vocat. Assn. (George P. Hambrecht award 1987, Exemplary Educator award 1987), Wis. Agr. Coordinators Assn. (pres. 1977-78), Nat. Assn. Farm Broadcasters, Nat. Environ. Tng. Assn., U. Wis. Alumni Assn. Lodges: Kiwanis (pres. 1977-78; Disting. Service award). Avocations: reading non-fiction books, photography, travel, collecting records and books, geneaology. Home: 40 S Pioneer Pkwy Fond du Lac WI 54935 Office: KFIZ Radio 235 N National Ave PO Box 1167 Fond du Lac WI 54935

KOENIG, JEROME, retired psychologist; b. Mpls., Oct. 6, 1930. BA, Coll. of St. Thomas, 1952, MEd, 1958; MA, U. Minn., 1961, EdS, 1965. Lic. cons. psychologist, Minn., sch. psychologist, Minn., sch. counselor, Minn. Tchr., counselor Minn. Pub. Schs., 1952-59; counselor, supr. human services Sch. Dist. 279, Osseo, Minn., 1959-86. Editor Minn. Research Project Summaries, 1968; contbr. articles to profl. jours, chpt. to book. Mem. Minn. Psychol. Assn., Am. Assn. Counseling and Devel. Lodge: KC. Home: 6033 79th Ave N Brooklyn Park MN 55443

KOENIG, KARL ERIC, research group leader; b. Washington, Dec. 27, 1947; s. Earl T. and Iris F. (Woodhouse) K.; m. Jo Ann Weber, Feb. 18, 1984. AS, San Antonio Jr. Coll., 1968; BS in Chemistry, U. Tex., 1970; PhD, U. So. Calif., Los Angeles, 1974. Postdoctoral fellowship UCLA, Los Angeles, 1974-76; research chemist Monsanto, St. Louis, 1976—. Served to capt. USAF, 1972-74. Mem. ACS, Mo. Whitewater Assn. (pres. 1983—). Avocations: whitewater canoeing, flying, scuba diving, bridge, volleyball. Home: 809 Renee Ln Creve Coeur MO 63141 Office: Monsanto 800 N Lindbergh Blvd T4G Saint Louis MO 63167

KOENIG, KARL JOSEPH, oil company executive; b. Washington, Oct. 1, 1955; s. Raymond Alexander and Mary Elizabeth (Kammerer) K. BSCE with highest distinction, U. Va., 1977, MBA, 1983. Registered profl. engr., Ohio, Va. Acquisitions and planning mgr. retail mktg. real estate The Standard Oil Co., Cleve., 1983—. Mem. ASCE (Outstanding Civil Engring. Student award 1977), Tau Beta Pi, Chi Epsilon. Roman Catholic. Home: 27832 Aberdeen Rd Bay Village OH 44140 Office: Standard Oil Co 200 Public Square 18-I-3206 Cleveland OH 44114

KOENIG, PATTI JEAN, social worker; b. Ann Arbor, Mich., July 12, 1941; d. Paul J. and Rose Mary (Greca) K. BA, Oakland U., 1963; MSW, Wayne State U., 1986. Cert. social worker, substance abuse counselor, Mich. Field dir. Girl Scouts U.S., Albuquerque, 1967-68; camp adminstr. Girl Scouts U.S., Terre Haute, Ind., 1969; field advisor Girl Scouts U.S., Pontiac, Mich., 1972-78; vol. Peace Corps, El Salvador, 1969-72; therapist, prevention coordinator LA CASA, Detroit, 1978—; coach LA CASA Boxing Team, 1980. V.p., campership com. chmn., coop. funding com., Walled Lake (Mich.) Agy. Council , 1975-78. Recipient Cert. of Appreciation Girl Guides, El Salvador, 1971, Spl. Service award Comite Patroitico Mexicana de Pontiac, 1974, Outstanding Contributions award Puerto Rican Club, Pontiac, 1975, Vol. award Detroit Pub. Schs., 1985-86. Mem. Nat. Assn. Social Workers, Detroit Inst. Alcohol and Research Tng. Avocations: sewing, knitting, gardening, photography. Home: 758 4th St Pontiac MI 48055 Office: LA CASA 4124 W Vernor Detroit MI 48055

KOENIG, SHARON ANN, banker; b. Appleton, Wis., Dec. 2, 1947; d. Joseph A. and Dolores Iva (Bergner) Gregorius; m. Stanley Louis Koenig, Aug. 7, 1971; children: Bryan Louis, Lisa In Hee. Student, Carthage Coll., 1966-68; BA, U. Wis., 1971. Residential mortgage loan processor, underwriter First Wis. Nat. Bank Madison, 1971-80, mgr., officer residential mortgage dept., 1980-83, comml. mortgage loan officer, 1983-86, coordinator, officer mortgage and SBA, 1986—. Officer, rep. Nakoma Neighborhood Assn., Madison, 1984-86; vice chmn. Families by Adoption South Cen. Wis., Madison, 1985-87, chmn. 1987—. Mem. Madison Bd. Realtors, Wis. Mortgage Bankers Assn., Nat. Mortgage Bankers Assn. Avocations: camping, hiking, water sports, downhill skiing, travelling. Home: 4206 Manitou Way Madison WI 53711 Office: First Wis Nat Bank Madison One S Pinckney St Madison WI 53711

KOENINGS, CHARLES PETER, social worker; b. West Bend, Wis., Oct. 16, 1953; s. Christ Peter and Elizabeth Agatha (Bahr) K.; m. Judith Griesbach, Sept. 8, 1984. B.S., U. Wis., Milw., 1975, M.S.W., 1977. Cert. sch. social worker. Day camp counselor Neighborhood House Milw., summer 1975; sch. social worker Coop. Ednl. Service Agy. 9, Green Bay, Wis., 1977-82; social worker Big Bros./Big Sisters Met. Milw., Inc., 1982-85, Oconomowoc Devel. Tng. Ctr., 1985—; coach basketball and soccer teams. Home: W 169 N 8757 Sheridan Dr Menomonee Falls WI 53051 Office: 36100 Genesee Lake Rd Oconomowoc WI 53066

KOENKE, DOUGLAS WILLIAM, dentist; b. Mt. Clemons, Mich., Jan. 16, 1955; s. Melvin William and Betty Jean (Bates) K.; m. Martha Ann Van Buskirk, Oct. 17, 1981; children: Heather Elizabeth, Stephanie Renee, Trisha

Lynn. BS in Microbiology, U. Mich., 1977; DDS, U. Detroit, 1981. Gen. practice dentistry Detroit, 1981—. Republican. Baptist. Avocations: photography, hunting, travel. Office: 18525 Moross Detroit MI 48224

KOEPKE, DON LORENZ, manufacturing company executive; b. Rice Lake, Wis., Apr. 27, 1938; s. Lawrence Herman and Genevieve Marie (Kavanaugh) K.; m. Marion Ruth Zordel, Nov. 21, 1959; children: Julie Ann, Susan Lee, Douglas Lorenz. Student, Monmouth (Ill.) Coll., 1958. V.p. Koepke Sand and Gravel Co., Appleton, Wis., 1954-60; pres. Concrete Pipe Corp., Appleton, 1960-82, Visions Unlimited of Am., Inc., Appleton, 1983—; bd. dirs. Valley Nat. Bank, Appleton. Mem. Mayor's Citizens Adv. Commn., Appleton; telethon chmn. Rawhide Boy's Ranch, New London, Wis.; bd. dirs. United Cerebral Palsy, Oshkosh, Wis. Served to 2d lt. U.S. Army. Mem. Concrete Pipe Assn. Wis. (pres. 1972), Wis. Assn. Tng. and Devel., Wis. Profl. Speakers Assn. Lodges: Rotary, Elks. Avocations: restoring old cars, fishing, hunting, trap shooting, pub. speaking. Home and Office: Rt #2 Broadway Dr Appleton WI 54915

KOEPKE, DONALD HERBERT, real estate salesman; b. Milw., Sept. 19, 1923; s. Herbert Hugo and Lillie (Kirchen) K.; B.A. in Bus., Valparaiso U., 1949; B.S. in Mech. Engring., Purdue U., 1951; m. Mary Ruth Brudi, June 16, 1951; children—Debora, Andrew, Thomas. Vice pres. dealer relations Valeer Industries, Inc., Mundelein, Ill., 1974-76; dir. engring. Respiratory Care, Inc., Arlington Heights, Ill., 1976-80; pres. Sorbets, Inc., Hampshire, Ill., 1980-83; pres. Liquorland Enterprises, Inc., Elgin, Ill., 1962-84, also dir.; chief engr. Rinn, Inc., Elgin, 1984-86; with real estate sales dept. Country Oaks Realty, Elgin, 1986—. Active Elgin Choral Union. Served with U.S. Army, 1943-46. Cert. mfg. engr. Mem. Elgin Bd. Realtors, Soc. Automotive Engrs., Soc. Mfg. Engrs. Republican. Lutheran. Club: Anvil. Lodge: Lions. Contbr. articles to profl. jours.; patentee in field. Home: 532 N Melrose Ave Elgin IL 60123 Office: Country Oaks 374 McLean Blvd Elgin IL 60123

KOEPPEN, RAYMOND BRADLEY, lawyer; b. Valparaiso, Ind., July 9, 1954; s. Raymond Carl August and Thelma Gleda (Moore) K.; m. Debra Gail Ray, Dec. 21, 1985. BS, Ball State U., 1976; MA, Kent (Ohio) State U., 1983; JD, Valparaiso U., 1983. Bar: Ind. 1984, Fla. 1984. Assoc. Sachs & Hess, P.C., Hammond, Ind., 1984-85, Lucas Holcomb Medrea, Merrillville, Ind., 1985; city atty. City of Valparaiso, 1985—. Mem. com. Valparaiso Popcorn Festival, 1985-87; mem. Valparaiso Econ. Devel. Corp., 1986, 87, mem. Valparaiso C. of C.; bd. dirs. Boys and Girls Club of Porter County, 1986—. Greek Ministry of Culture and Sci. scholar, 1975; Fulbright scholar U.S. Ednl. Found., 1976. Mem. ABA, Ind. State Bar Assn., Nat. Inst. Mcpl. Lawyers, Ind. Mcpl. Lawyers Assn., Porter County Bar Assn., Fla. Bar Assn., Phi Alpha Theta, Pi Gamma Mu, Beta Theta Pi. Democrat. Presbyterian. Avocations: running, basketball, reading. Home: 2306 Shannon Valparaiso IN 46383 Office: David A Butterfield Law Offices 11 E Lincolnway Valparaiso IN 46383

KOETTING, ROBERT A., optometrist; b. St. Louis, Nov. 1, 1925. Student St. Louis U., 1943; O.D., So. Coll. Optometry, 1947. Pvt. practice optometry, practice limited to contact lenses, St. Louis, 1962-86; asst. adj. prof. Ill. Coll. Optometry, 1983-86, U. Mo., St. Louis, 1985-86; assoc. prof., adj. clin. faculty So. Coll. Optometry, 1981-82; lectr. in field. Contbr. articles to profl. jours. Patentee in field. Mem. editorial staff Contact Lens Forum, Contact Lens Spectrum, Optometric Mgmt. Adv. Bd., St. Louis Area Council on Aging, 1982-84. Named Optometrist of Yr., Mo. Optometric Assn., 1978; recipient Grand Honors, Nat. Eye Research Found., 1980, Boys Town of Mo. Service award, 1983. Fellow Southwest Contact Lens Soc.; mem. Am. Acad. Optometry, Am. Optometric Assn. (pres.-elect, Contact Lens Person of Yr. 1986), Am. Soc. Contact Lens Specialists (sec.), Better Vision Inst. (bd. dirs.), Heart of Am. Contact Lens. Soc. (pres. 1967-68, Optometrist of Yr. 1967), Internat. Soc. Contact Lens Research (council), Nat. Eye Research Found. (bd. dirs.), St. Louis Optometric Soc. (pres. 1983-84), Sociedad Americana Ofthalmologia y Optometria, Internat. Soc. Contact Lens Specialists, Nat. Acad. Practice, Beta Sigma Kappa. Lodges: Rotary, Toastmasters. Home: 1034 S Brentwood Saint Louis MO 63117

KOEVENIG, BRIAN PAUL, paint manufacturing manager, chemist; b. Oregon, Ohio, June 8, 1956; s. Paul Henry and Beverly Rose (Ramp) K.; m. Linda Louise Junod, Sept. 17, 1983. BA in Chemistry, U. Toledo, 1982. Lab. technician Dolphin Paint and Chem., Toledo, Ohio, 1978-79, tech. dir., 1979-86; mgr. research and devel. Titan Finishes Corp., Detroit, 1986; tech. dir. Structural Coatings and Chemicals, Inc., Wayne, Mich., 1986—. Mem. Am. Chem. Soc., Am. Inst. Chemists, Am. Soc. for Quality Control, Pi Kappa Alpha (pres. 1978-79). Republican. Lutheran. Lodge: Masons. Avocations: chess, snow skiing, piano, photography. Home: 8092 Sundon Rd Lambertville MI 48144 Office: Structural Coatings & Chemicals Inc 5645 Cogswell Rd Wayne MI 48184

KOFORD, STUART KEITH, electronics executive; b. North Hollywood, Calif., Oct. 25, 1953; s. Kenneth Harold and Theresa (Sutton) K.; m. Gail Anne Joerger, Dec. 28. 1985. BSME, Mich. Tech. U., 1976. Sr. engr. Motorola, Schaumburg, Ill., 1977-79; engring. project mgr. Amphenol, Cicero, Ill., 1979-80, mgr. research and devel., 1980-82; mgr. engring. Amphenol, Broadview, Ill., 1982—; pres. Koford Engring., Addison, Ill., 1982. Contbr. articles to profl. jours. Mem. IEEE (program com. Electronic Components Conf. 1979—), Soc. Plastic Engrs., ASME, Electronic Connector Study Group (program chmn. 1982-84). Republican. Roman Catholic. Avocation: slot car racing. Home: 19W 281 Paul Revere Ln Oak Brook IL 60521 Office: Koford Engring 415 Belden Ave Addison IL 60101

KOGLIN, NORMAN ALFRED, architect; b. Chgo., May 5, 1928; s. Alfred Ernst and Elizabeth Maria (Faselt) K.; m. Bernice E. Morrell, May 22, 1982; children—Eric Norman, Andrew Mc Clean, Lisa, Susan Jane. B.S. in Architecture, U. Ill., 1951. Architect Skidmore, Owings & Merrill, architects, Chgo., 1957-61; partner Tigerman & Koglin, architects, Chgo., 1961-64; asso. partner C.F. Murphy & Assos., architects, Chgo., 1965-67; pres. Norman A. Koglin Assos., Ltd., Chgo., 1967—; Served with C.E. U.S. Army, 1951-53. Mem. AIA. Clubs: Economic, Monroe, Mid-Day, Sports Car of Am. (Chgo.). Office: 111 W Monroe St Chicago IL 60603

KOH, TONG CHUI, anesthesiologist; b. Kuala Lumpur, Malaysia, Jan. 20, 1946; came to U.S., 1971.; s. Pooi Kee and Poh Lam (Ong) K.; m. Siew Ai, May 5, 1971; children: Yee Ming, Yip Kheon, Yip Khoon. Grad., Victoria Inst., 1958-64; MBBS, U. Malaysia, 1971. Diplomate Am. Bd. Anesthesiology. Pvt. practice anesthesiology Brookfield, Wis., 1974—. Mem. State Med. Soc. Club: Westmoor Country (Milw.). Avocation: badminton, golf. Home: 125 Stockton Ct Brookfield WI 53005

KOHFELD, CAROL WEITZEL, political science educator; b. Balt., June 16, 1940; d. William Frederick and Margaret (Roeder) Weitzel; children: D. Kurt, Karen E. BS in Zoology, Wheaton Coll., 1962; MA in Govt., So. Ill. U., 1973; PhD in Polit. Sci., Washington U., 1976. Tchr. Champaign (Ill.) Sr. High Sch., 1962-66, Ft. Knox (Ky.) Dependent Sch., 1967-68; instr. St. Louis U., 1974-75; asst. prof. U. Houston, 1976-78; prof. polit. sci. U. Mo., St. Louis, 1977—; officer Decker and Assocs., Inc., Clayton, Mo., 1983—; bd. dirs. Pub. Research Assocs., Clayton, 1985—. Mem. editorial bd. Am. Jour. Polit. Sci., 1984—; contbr. articles to profl. jours. Research grantee NSF, 1978, Nat. Inst. Justice grantee, 1983-86. Mem. Am. Polit. Sci. Assn., Midwest Polit. Sci. Assn. (various coms.), Am. Soc. Criminology. Democrat. Avocations: sports, sailing. Home: 6623 San Bonita Clayton MO 63105 Office: U Mo Dept Polit Sci Saint Louis MO 63121

KOHL, RICK ALLEN, accountant, educator; b. Milw., Nov. 12, 1952; s. John Joseph and Carol Jean (Haack) K.; m. Julie Ann Rafferty, Oct. 24, 1975 (div. Sept. 1981); m. Patricia Jean Blankenmeyer, June 1, 1985. BBA, U. Wis., Milw., 1977. CPA, Wis. Sr. accountant Kerber Eck & Braeckel, Milw., 1978-82; ptnr. Nickel & Assocs., Menomonee Falls, Wis., 1986—; instr. Milw. Area Tech. Coll., 1982—. Bd dirs. Menomonee Falls YMCA, 1987. Mem. Am. Inst. CPAs, Wis. Inst. CPAs, Menomonee Falls C. of C. (ambassador 1982—). Republican. Roman Catholic. Avocations: reading, racquetball, golf, traveling. Office: Nickel & Assocs N89 W15909 Appleton Ave Menomonee Falls WI 53051

KOHL, RONALD NESTER, accountant; b. St. Louis, 1946; m. Diane G. Kohl; 1 child, Kristopher R. BS, U. Mo., 1968, MBA, 1969. CPA, Mo., Iowa. Ptnr. Rubin, Brown, Gornstein & Co., Clayton, Mo.; lectr., instr. various constrn. and real estate confs. and meetings. Contbr. articles to profl. jours. Pres. bd. trustees The Coll. Sch.; bd. dirs. Nat. Found. Ileitis and Colitis, Inc., St. Louis. Mem. Mo. Soc. CPA's (pres. St. Louis chpt.), Home Builders Assn. (mag. columnist), Assoc. Gen. Contractors St. Louis. Office: Rubin Brown Gornstein & Co 230 S Bemiston Saint Louis MO 63105

KOHLER, JEFFREY JOSEPH, accountant; b. St. Louis, Aug. 17, 1961; s. Rodger Gary and Mary Katherine (Wunderlich) K.; m. Linda Diane Schmit, May 5, 1984; 1 child, Matthew Ryan. BSBA, Rockhurst Coll., 1983. Staff acct. Rubin, Brown, Gornstein & Co., St. Louis, 1983-86; acctg. analyst real estate Gen. Am. Life Ins. Co., St. Louis, 1986—. Mem. Am. Inst. CPA's, Mo. Soc. CPA's. Roman Catholic. Avocations: softball, reading, music, travel. Home: 9557 Dulles Ct Saint Louis MO 63123 Office: Rubin Brown Cornstein & Co 230 S Bemiston Saint Louis MO 63105

KOHLER, RUSSELL EDWARD, chaplain, priest; b. Monroe, Mich., Nov. 12, 1943; s. Vernon A. "Barney" and Mary Elizabeth (Kellison) K. AB, Sacred Heart Sem., Detroit, 1968; grad., U. Detroit; grad. in theology, St. John's Provincial Sem. Ordained priest Roman Catholic Ch., Apr. 1973. Pastor St. Aloysius Ch., Detroit, 1974-80; chaplain Sinai Hosp., Harper-Grace Hosp., Detroit, 1982—; Exec. dir. Pope John XXIII Hospice, Detroit, 1975—; dir. St. Patrick's Pediatric Retreat, Irish Hills, Mich., 1979—. Founder The XXIII Club; bd dirs. Endurance Pediatric Pilgrimages, Discovery: Arts with Youth in Therapy. Mem. Internat. Pediatric Hospice Found. (pres. 1985—). Lodge: Lions, KC, Order of Hibernians. Home: 3977 2d Ave Detroit MI 48201

KOHLER, STEVEN ALAN, lawyer; b. Highland Park, Mich., Jan. 2, 1951; s. Robert C. Kohler and Edith (Sussman) Fried; m. Barbara R. Friedman, July 21, 1979; 1 child, Aaron Kohler. BA, Wayne State U., 1973; JD, Detroit Coll. Law, 1981. Bar: Mich. 1984, U.S. Dist. Ct. (ea. dist.) Mich. 1984, U.S. Ct. Appeals (6th cir.) 1984, Fla. 1985. Social worker Mich. Dept. Social Services, Royal Oak, Mich., 1974-80; ptnr. Meklir, Schreier, Nolish & Friedman, P.C., Southfield, Mich., 1984-87, Matz & Rubin, P.C., Birmingham, Mich., 1987—. State of Mich. Dept. Edn. scholar, 1970. Mem. ABA, Mich. Bar Assn., Fla. Bar Assn., Oakland County Bar Assn., Assn. of Trial Lawyers Am., Mich. Trial Lawyers Assn. Democrat. Jewish. Lodge: Order of DeMolay (master councilor Mosaic chpt. 1967-68). Avocations: reading, travel, sports. Home: 4949 Broomfield Ln West Bloomfield MI 48322 Office: Matz & Rubin PC 30600 Telegraph Rd Suite 2363 Birmingham MI 48010

KOHLER, STEVEN LENZ, editor; b. St. Louis, Feb. 4, 1947; s. Theodore Nicholas and Pauline (Lenz) K.; m. Kathy Geist, June 21, 1968 (dec. Oct. 1969); m. Peggy Sue Knight, Oct. 13, 1973; 1 child, Roxanne Elizabeth. Student, Antioch Coll., 1965-68; BA, Washington U., St. Louis, 1970. Chief photographer U. Kans. Med. Ctr., Kansas City, 1970-75; editor Farmington (Mo.) Press, 1975-82; writer U. Mo. Press, Columbia, 1982-84; editor Fishing & Hunting Jour., St. Louis, 1985—. Author: Two Ozark Rivers, 1984 (Art. Dirs. Merit award 1985); contbr. articles to mags. Mem. Outdoor Writers Assn. Am. Democrat. Episcopalian. Avocations: photography, canoeing, fishing.

KOHLI, CHANDER MOHAN, neurosurgeon; b. Mandibaudin, India, May 14, 1940; came to U.S., 1966; s. Sardarilal and Ram Piyari (Anand) K.; m. Karen Lee Prindle, Dec. 21, 1968; children: Aneal, Nisha. Pre-med student, Hindu Coll., Delhi, India, 1957-58; MBBS, All India Inst. of Med. Scis., New Delhi, 1962. Diplomate Am. Bd. Neurol. Surgery, COngress Neurol. Surgeons. Intern, then resident Elyria (Ohio) Meml. Hosp., 1966-68; resident in neurosurgery Univ. Hosp. Edmonton, Alta., Can., 1968-69, Mercy Hosp., Pitts., 1969-72; staff neurosurgeon St. Elizabeth Hosp., Youngstown, Ohio, 1972—; Mem. Council Surg. Edn., Youngstown, 1977—; chief dept. neurosurgery St. Elizabeth Hosp., 1979—; asst. prof. Northeast Ohio Univ. Coll. Medicine, Rootstown, 1979—; asst. dir. surgery St. Elizabeth Hosp., 1984-86. Contbr. articles to profl. jours. Fellow ACS; mem. Am. Assn. Neurosurgeons, AMA, Ohio Neurol. Soc., Ohio Med. Soc., Northeast Ohio Neurosurg. Soc., Soc. Neuroscis., Am. Pain Soc., Mahoning County Med. Soc., India Assn. Greater Youngstown (chmn. bd. trustees 1976-77, 82-84, mem. exec. com. 1976-78, Man of Yr. award 1984). Republican. Hindu. Avocations: bridge, camping, computers, photography, chess. Office: 540 Parmalee Ave Suite 410 Youngstown OH 44510

KOHN, KAREN JOSEPHINE, graphic designer, exhibition designer; b. Muskegon, Mich., Jan. 8, 1951; d. Herbert George and Catherine Elizabeth (Johnson) K.; m. Robert Joseph Duffy Jr. , July 10, 1982; 1 child, Megan Kathleen. B.F.A., cum laude, U. Mich., 1973; M.F.A., Sch. Art Inst. Chgo., 1975. Free lance designer, Chgo., 1976-77; designer Stevens Exhibits, Chgo., 1977-78; artist-in-residence Chgo. Council on Fine Arts, 1978-79; designer Chgo. Hist. Soc., 1979-81; dir. design Chgo. Hist. Soc., 1981-84; prin. Karen Kohn & Assocs., Chgo., 1985—. Designer Chicago History quar. mag., 1979-84 (4 awards Am. Assn. Mus. 1982, 83, 85), poster for Holabird & Root Exhbn., 1980 (award Am. Assn. Mus. 1982), invitation Ill. Toys Exhbn., 1982 (award Am. Assn. Mus. 1983), poster Chgo. Furniture Exhbn., 1984. Mem. Am. Assn. Mus., Nat. Assn. Mus. Exhibitors (Midwest regional rep. 1983-84), Soc. Typog. Arts, Chgo. Mus. Communicators.

KOHN, MARY LOUISE BEATRICE, nurse; b. Yellow Springs, Ohio, Jan. 13, 1920; d. Theophilus John and Mary Katharine (Schmitkons) Gaehr; A.B., Coll. Wooster, 1940; M.Nursing, Case Western Res. U., 1943; m. Howard D. Kohn, 1944; children: Marcia R., Marcia K. Epstein. Nurse, 1943-44, Atlantic City Hosp., 1944, Thomas M. England Gen. Hosp., U.S. Army, Atlantic City, 1945-46, Peter Bent Brigham Hosp., Boston, 1947, Univ. Hosps., Cleve., 1946-48; mem. faculty Frances Payne Bolton Sch. Nursing Case Western Res. U., 1948-52; vol. nurse Blood Service, ARC, 1952-55; office nurse, Cleve., part time 1955—; free-lance writer. Bd. dirs. Aux. Acad. Medicine Cleve., 1970-72, officer, 1976—; mem. Cleve. Health Mus. Aux.; mem. women's com. Cleve. Orch., 1970; women's council WVIZ-TV. Mem. Am., Ohio nurses assns., alumni assns. Wooster Coll., Frances P. Bolton Sch. Nursing (pres. 1974-75), Assn. Operating Rm. Nurses, Antique Automobile Assn. Am., Western Res. Hist. Soc., Am. Heart Assn., Cleve. Playhouse Aux., Internat. Fund for Animal Welfare, Cleve. Animal Protective League, U.S. Humane Soc., Friends of Cleve. Ballet, Smithsonian Instn., Council World Affairs, Orange Community Arts Council. Clubs: Cleve. Racquet, Women's City, Women's of Case-Western Res. U. Sch. Medicine. Author: (with Atkinson) Berry and Kohn's Introduction to Operating Room Technique, 5th edit., 1978, 6th edit., 1986. Asst. editor Cleve. Physician, Acad. Medicine Cleve., 1966-71. Home: 28099 Belcourt Rd Cleveland OH 44124

KOHN, MITCHELL BARRY, architectural lighting consultant; b. Chgo., Sept. 2, 1952; s. Harold and Bunny (Gordon) K.; m. Barbara Rosenberg, May 31, 1975; children: Lindsay Brooke, Evan Seth. BFA, Carnegie-Mellon U., 1974. Product mgr. Lightolier Inc., Jersey City, 1975-77; mgr. lighting design services Herman Miller Inc., Zeeland, Mich., 1977-81; pvt. practice archtl. lighting cons. Highland Park, Ill., 1981—. Contbr. articles to profl. jours. Mem. Illuminating Engring. Soc. (pres. West Mich. sect. 1981-83, bd. dirs. Chgo. sect. 1984-86, Award of Merit, 1981, 84), Internat. Assn. Lighting Designers. Avocations: travelling, skiing, golfing. Office: 2256 Linden Ave Highland Park IL 60035

KOHN, NORMAN VITA, neurologist; b. Cleve., Sept. 26, 1951; s. Howard M. and Orietta (Vita) K.; m. Lisa Salkovitz, Mar. 11, 1979; children—Isaac V., Russell J. S.B., MIT, 1972; M.D., Yale U., 1976. Diplomate Am. Bd. Psychiatry and Neurology. Resident in medicine Case Western Res. U., Cleve., 1976-77; resident in neurology U. Chgo., 1977-80, neuroimmunology fellow, 1980-82; practice medicine specializing in neurology, Chgo., 1982—; mem. staff Mt. Sinai Hosp., 1980—; chmn. neurology dept., 1984—. clin. asst. prof. U. Chgo. Mem. Am. Acad. Neurology, Am. Assn. Electromyography and Electrodiagnosis. Office: Mt Sinai Hosp California Ave at Ogden Chicago IL 60608

KOHNKE, JAMES HENRY, data processing executive; b. St. Paul, June 5, 1948; s. Henry James and Wanda Marie (Cook) K.; m. Lois Ann Fields, Nov. 22, 1969; children: Eric James, Jeffrey Robert. Student, Inver Hills Community Coll., 1970-75; AS, St. Petersburg Jr. Coll., 1977; BBA, U. So. Fla., 1980; MBA, Mankato State, 1986. Inspection engr. product assurance dept. Sperry Corp., Oldsman, Fla., 1975-76, engr. program quality dept., 1976-77, engr. product reliability, 1977-80; analyst def. pricing dept. Sperry Corp., St. Paul, 1980-85, program mgr. navsea standard products dept., 1985—. Served to sgt. N.G., 1974-75. Democrat. Roman Catholic. Avocations: golf league, camping, reading. Home: 7912 Conroy Way Inver Grove Heights MN 55075 Office: Sperry Corp PO Box 64525 Saint Paul MN 55164

KOHOUTEK, FRANK LEO, JR., educator, athletic coach; b. LaMoure, N.D., May 31, 1931; s. Frank Leo and Margaret Mabel (Sandeen) K.; m. Joan Peggy Case, Aug. 9, 1953; children—Linda, Frank Leo, Kathleen, Karen. B.S., Jamestown Coll. (N.D.), 1954; M.Ed., U. N.D., 1964. Cert. tchr., N.D., Minn.; cert. coach, Minn. Tchr., coach Drayton High Sch. (N.D.), 1956-60, Newfolden High Sch. (Minn.), 1960-65, Sebeka High Sch. (Minn.), 1965-70, Wadena High Sch. (Minn.), 1970—. Mem. Minn. State Softball Adv. Council, 1980-83; Coach Minn. State Champion Softball Team, 1979, Minn. State Tournament Softball Team, 1980, 81. Served with U.S. Army, 1954-56. Mem. U.S.-China Peoples Friendship Assn., NEA, Minn. Edn. Assn., Minn. State Softball Coaches (pres. 1982), Minn. State High Sch. Coaches, Assn. for Girls Sports, Inc., Nat. Wood Carvers Assn. Methodist. Lodge: Masons, Lions (pres. 1965). Home: 121 Colfax Ave SW Wadena MN 56482

KOHRS, LLOYD FREDERICK, electrical engineer; b. St. Charles, Mo., Sept. 6, 1927; s. William August and Lolita Kathrine (Nolle) K.; m. Diana Joyce Button, Mar. 14, 1960; 1 stepchild, Randall Grant Pemberton; 1 child, Charmaine Lynette Kohrs Seavy. BSEE, Washington U., 1950. Test conductor McDonnell Aircraft, St. Louis, 1950-55; mgr. space propulsion Aerojet Gen. Corp., Sacramento, Calif., 1955-67; mgr. propulsion Hughes Aircraft, El Segundo, Calif., 1967-69; chief propulsion engr. McDonnell Douglas Astronautics, St. Louis, Mo., 1969-73; mgr. space shuttle program McDonnell Douglas Astronautics, St. Louis, 1973-83, mgr. DSP Laser Crosslink program, 1983—. Served with U.S. Army, 1945-46. Recipient Disting. Pub. Service medal NASA, 1982. Mem. Am. Inst. Aeronautics and Astronautics (Wyld Propulsion award 1982). Democrat. Avocations: travel, fine arts, theater, photography. Home: 3 Pretoria Ct Saint Charles MO 63303 Office: McDonnell Douglas Astronautics Co PO Box 516 Saint Louis MO 63166

KOHTZ, RICHARD LEE, manufacturing company procurement executive, electrical engineer; b. Pekin, Ill., Jan. 21, 1952; s. Robert Arther and Shirley Jeanne (Wolf) K.; m. Paula Jean Burland, Apr. 20, 1985. BSEE, U. Ill., 1976. Trainee mfg. mgmt. program Gen. Electric Co., Milw. and Louisville, 1976-78; field liason rep. Gen. Electric Co., Los Angeles, 1978-80; buyer computers, test equipment, semiconductors Gen. Electric Co., Cin., 1981-83; mgr. elec. components procurement aircraft engine electronic control ops. Gen. Electric Co., Ft. Wayne, Ind., 1984, mgr. procurement, 1985—. Gen. Electric campaign organizer Fine Arts Fund, Cin., 1982; account mgr. United Way, Cin., 1984. Mem. IEEE, Eta Kappa Nu. Democrat. Lutheran. Lodge: Elks. Avocations: golf, raquetball, pocket billiards, reading, travel. Home: 8832 Village Grove Dr Fort Wayne IN 46804 Office: Gen Electric Co 2000 Taylor St Fort Wayne IN 46804

KOHUT, NESTER CLARENCE, social scientist; b. Saskatoon, Sask., Can., Nov. 24, 1925; s. Frank and Dora K.; m. Marguerite Eiche, Apr. 3, 1961; children: Michael, Gregory, Judith, Timothy. BS, U. Manitoba, 1950, LLB, 1959; MA, Cath. U. Am., 1958; EdD, U. Sarasota, 1979. Probation officer Cook County Juvenile Ct., Chgo., 1962-67; child care supr. Ill. Dept. Mental Health, Chgo., 1967-68; welfare caseworker Cook County Dept. Pub. Aid, Chgo., 1969-70; exec. dir. Wis. State Council Home and Family, Madison, 1970-71; founder Am. Family Communiversity, Chgo., 1965—. Author: A Manual on Marital Reconciliation, 1963, Therapeutic Family Law, 1968, Divorce for the UnBroken Marriage, 1973. Rep. Legisl. candidate, Dane County, Wis., 1972. Served with Can. Navy, 1944-45. Recipient Community Service award Chgo. Community Coms., 1965. Home: 838 N Harlem Ave River Forest IL 60305 Office: Am Family Communiversity 5242 W North Ave Chicago IL 60639-4430

KOIVO, ANTTI JAAKKO, electrical engineering educator, researcher; b. Ilmajoki, Finland, Apr. 9, 1932; s. Niilo J. and Elma S. (Lahti) K.; m. Anne Pihlak, Apr. 19, 1969; children: Lilli S., Allan Th. Diploma engring., Finland Inst. Tech., 1956; PhD in Elec. Engring., Cornell U., 1963. Design engr. Stroemberg OY, Helsinki, Finland, 1957-60; from asst. to full prof. Purdue U., Lafayette, Ind., 1965—. Contbr. articles on robotics, modelling and control to profl. jours.; numerous conf. presentations. Office: Purdue U Dept Elec Engring West Lafayette IN 47907

KOIVULA, STEVEN JOHN, insurance accounting executive; b. Waukegan, Ill., July 19, 1949; s. Einar Arnold and Bertha Marie (Vanka) K.; m. Julie Ann Carlsen, May 29, 1971 (div. May, 1984); 1 child, Kirsten Ann; m. Nona Ellen Wolfram, Sept. 2, 1984. BA, Augustana Coll., 1971; MBA, No. Ill. U. CPA, Ill. Instr. No. Ill. U., Dekalb, 1973-74; sr. auditor Ernst & Whinney, Chgo., 1974-78; acctg. mgr. CNA Ins. Cos., Chgo., 1978—. Treas. Fox Valley chpt. ARC, St. Charles, Ill., 1980-85, Kane County (Ill.) Defenders, 1984—. Mem. Am. Inst. CPA's, Ill. CPA's Soc. Republican. Lutheran. Avocations: fishing, sports. Office: CNA Ins Cos CNA Plaza Chicago IL 60685

KOJICH, DONALD, editor; b. Gary, Ind., Oct. 19, 1959; s. John Kojich; m. Betty Ann Ralston, Nov. 27, 1985; 1 child, Philip Andrew. BA in Broadcasting, Purdue U., 1982. Media relations coordinator Chgo. Blitz, 1983-84; sports info. asst. Ea. Ill. U., Charleston, 1984-86, publications editor, 1986—. Mem. Red Cloud Athletic Assn., Chgo., 1982-84. Named Hoosier scholar State of Ind., 1978-82; recipient Henderson-Mellinger scholarship Mellinger Ednl. Found., 1978-82; named one of Outstanding Young Men Am., 1985. Mem. Coll. Sports Info. Dirs. Am., Purdue U. Alumni Assn. Club: Culver (Ind.) Legion. Avocations: photography, golf, travel. Home: 1013 W Hayes St Charleston IL 61920 Office: Eastern Ill U Old Main Room 109 Charleston IL 61920

KOKALIS, SOTER GEORGE, chemistry educator, financial investments consultant; b. East Chicago, Ind., Jan. 29, 1936; s. George S. and Katherine (Duron) K. BS in Chemistry, Purdue U., 1958; MS in Chemistry, U. Ill., 1960, PhD in Chemistry, 1962. Asst. prof. chemistry Washington U., St. Louis, 1962-64, U. Ill., Chgo., 1964-67; assoc. prof. Chgo. State Coll., 1967-69, William Raney Harper Community Coll., Palatine, Ill., 1969—; cons. adv. placement chemistry E.T.S./Coll. Bd., Trenton, N.J., 1982—, cons. taxes H.R. Block Co., Des Plaines, 1982-85, Land of Lincoln Tax Service, Hoffman Estates, Ill., 1985—. Contbr. articles on chemistry and sci. for gifted students to profl. jours. Leader St. Hubert's Cath. Parish Bible Study, Hoffman Estates, Ill. 1983-86. Grantee DuPont Chem. Co., 1960-61, Ethyl Chemical Corp, 1961-62. Mem. Am. Coll. Sports Medicine, Am. Chem. Soc. (com. chmn. 1986), Ill. Police Fedn., Phi Delta Kappa. Democrat. Club: Chgo. Health (Schaumburg, Ill.). Lodges: KC, Square and Compasses. Avocations: camping, hiking, reading. Home: 1476 Dennison Rd Hoffman Estates IL 60195-3434 Office: W R Harper Community Coll Algonquin Rd Palatine IL 60067

KOKES, DIANE MARIE, publishing executive; b. Omaha, Apr. 16, 1957; d. Gary Howard and Loralyn Marie (Beeler) K. BFA, Northern Ill. U., 1980. Artist Hammond Litho, Northfield, Ill., 1975-76; prodn. supr. Standard Rate and Date Service, Inc., Wilmette, Ill., 1980—. Mem. Women in Design (v.p. Chgo. chpt. 1985—, mem. dir., program dir., pub. relations dir.), Nat. Acad. TV Arts and Scis., Soc. Typographic Arts. Roman Catholic.

KOKKELENBERG, LAWRENCE DOMENIC, psychologist; b. Chgo., Dec. 1, 1943; s. Edward Charles and Caroline (Totera) K. BA, St. Procopius Coll., 1967; MSW, U. Ill., Chgo., 1969; PhD, Union Grad. Sch., Cin., 1977. Cert. social worker, Ill. Pres., founder Ctr. Bus. Devel.,

McHenry, Ill., 1966-69, Lakeshore Services, Northbrook, 1976-84, Contractors Leasing, Northbrook, Ill., 1981—; v.p. D.L. Ward Assocs., Chgo., 1973—; exec. v.p. Creative Cons. Inc., Colorado Springs, Colo., 1980—, Nat. Mgmt. Inst., Dallas, 1983—. Served with USAF, 1967-73. Mem. Am. Soc. Tng. and Devel., Nat. Assn. Social Workers, Nat. Speakers Assn. Republican. Avocations: skiing, scuba, motorcycling, whitewater canoeing, jogging. Home and Office: Ctr Bus Devel 2409 Villa Ln McHenry IL 60050-2961

KOKORON, NICKOLAS STEVEN, accountant; b. Chgo., Apr. 4, 1947; s. Nickolas Vincent and Eva (Bleizeffer) K.; m. Barbara Darlene Zadny, July 14, 1978; children—Heather, Nickolas J., Bradley J. B.S., Ill. Inst. Tech., 1970. Auditor, Price Waterhouse & Co., Chgo., 1970-72; controller Pansophic Systems Inc., Oak Brook, Ill., 1972-74; ptnr. Kokoron, Monco & Co., Arlington Heights, Ill., 1974—; lectr.; dir. Vogel Tool & Die Co., Stone Park, Ill. Commr. River Trails Park Dist. Author: Managing the Small Professional Practice, 1986. Mem. Am. Inst. C.P.A.s, Ill. Soc. C.P.A.s. Club: Rolling Meadows Social (officer 1979-84). Lodge: Masons. Home: 1112 Dogwood Ln Mount Prospect IL 60056 Office: Kokoron Monco & Co 1845 E Rand Rd Arlington Heights IL 60004

KOLA, LENORE ATHENA, social work educator; b. Cleve., June 29, 1939; d. Klime and Athina (Vasil) K. AB, Ohio U., 1963; AM, Boston U., 1964, PhD, 1970. Lic. clin. psychologist, Mass., Ohio. Regional coordinator div. alcoholism Dept. Pub. Health, Boston, 1969-74; dir. clin. service Mass. Health Research Inst., Boston, 1974-75; assoc. prof. social worker Case Western Res. U., Cleve., 1975—; grant proj. dir. Nat. Inst. on Alcohol Abuse and Alcoholism Tng., Case Western Res. U., 1975-82, NIAAA Research Tng., 1976-81; project dir. Nat. Occupational Program, 1981-82; mem. Council on Social Work Edn. Contbr. articles on alcoholism and the elderly, women, and adolescents to profl. jours. Mem. Nat. Assn. Social Workers, Assn. Labor and Mgmt. Adminstrs. and Cons. on Alcoholism, Pi Gamma Mu, Psi Chi. Avocation: sailing. Office: Case Western Res U Sch Applied Social Scis 2035 Abington Rd Cleveland OH 44106

KOLB, EDGAR CHRISTIAN, mechanical engineer; b. Lebanon, Ill., May 3, 1937; s. Edgar J. and Aurelia E. (Karch) K.; m. Darlene Marlowe Mitchell; Nov. 26, 1960; children: Wesley Roy, Christina Julene. BSME, Ind. Inst. Tech., 1958. Engr. Phelps Dodge, Ft. Wayne, Ind., 1959-61; assoc. engr., project engr. Micro Switch, Freeport, Ill., 1961-66, sr. and prin. engr., 1967-72, product design supr., 1973-76, project mgr., 1976-84, engring. mgr., 1984—; sr. design engr. Gen. Electric Co., Bloomington, Ill., 1966-67. Patentee multi-position rotary actuating mechanism, 1970, adjustable mechanism for control devices, 1976. Served to staff sgt. USAR. Named Boss of Yr. Freeport Jaycees, 1985. Republican. Lutheran. Home: 1145 W Logan St Freeport IL 61032 Office: Micro Switch 11 W Spring St Freeport IL 61032

KOLB, JOHN CARL, family therapist, clergyman; b. Bay City, Mich., Apr. 6, 1943; s. Carl Henry Edwin and Renate Marie (Krieger) K.; m. Malinda Marie Hartman, June 5, 1966; children: Rebecca Marie, Debra Renee, Charles Walter. BA, Concordia Sr. Coll., 1964; MDiv, Concordia Sem., St. Louis, 1968; MST, Christian Theol. Sem., Indpls., 1972; student McCormick Theol. Sem., 1975-76. Ordained to ministry, Luth. Ch., 1968. Pastor Emanuel Luth. Ch., Arcadia, Ind., 1968-72; pres. Hamilton County (Ind.) Mental Health Assn., 1971-72; pastoral resident Luth. Gen. Hosp., Park Ridge, Ill., 1972-73; mental health therapist Northwestern Meml. Hosp. and Northwestern Inst. Psychiatry, Chgo., 1973-76; pastoral care fellow, chaplain Evanston (Ill.) Hosp., 1974-75, social worker, group therapist, asst. team leader Refocus Program, 1976-78; family therapist Luth. Child and Family Services, Indpls., 1978—; pastor Hosanna Luth. Ch., Oaklandon, Ind., 1980—; vis. prof. Concordia Theol. Sem., Ft. Wayne, 1984-86; pastoral advisor Ind., Ky Dist. Luth. Laymen's League; chmn. Ind. Dist. of LCMS Pastors and Wives Retreat Com.; pres. Trinity Luth. Parent Tchr. League, 1982-84. Contbr. articles to religious publs. Garret Theol. Sem. fellow, 1974-75. Mem. Am. Assn. Pastoral Counselors (pastoral affiliate). Home: 2613 Sheffield Dr Indianapolis IN 46229 Office: Luth Family Counseling 1525 N Ritter St Indianapolis IN 46219

KOLBERG, CURTIS LEE, truck equipment manufacturing executive; b. Rockford, Ill., Aug. 28, 1959; s. Robert L. and LaVerne A. (Provost) K. BSBA, Drake U., 1981. Sales and service coordinator Atwood Mobile Products, Rockford, Ill., 1981-82; sales adminstr. Milw. Cylinder, Beaver Dam, 1982-84; product mgr. Milw. Cylinder, Beaver Dam, Wis., 1984—. Mem. Am. Trucking Assn. (maintenance council), Nat. Truck Equipment Assn., BEaver Dam C. of C. Republican. Roman Catholic. Club: Old Hickory Golf and Country (Beaver Dam). Home: 112 Mary St Beaver Dam WI 53916 Office: Milw Cylinder 950 Green Valley Beaver Dam WI 53916

KOLBERG, JOHN F., lawyer; b. Columbus, Ohio, Mar. 27, 1957; s. Gerald D. and Carolyn A. (Emch) K.; m. Sharon M. Steilberg, Aug. 31, 1985. BA, U. Dayton, 1979, JD, 1982. Bar: Ohio 1983, U.S. Dist. Ct. (so. dist.) Ohio 1985. Adj. prof. U. Dayton, Ohio, 1984-85; assoc. Baver, Messham & Bookwalter Co., Miamisburg, Ohio, 1984—. Mem. ABA, Ohio Bar Assn., Dayton Bar Assn., Assn. Trial Lawyers Am., Sports Lawyer's Assn., Ohio Bar Coll. Avocations: baseball, baseball memorabilia. Office: Baver Messham & Bookwalter Co 202 E Central Miamisburg OH 45342

KOLDA, THOMAS JOSEPH, college executive; b. Chgo., Dec. 1, 1939; s. Amos Joseph and Cecilia Marie (Baxa) K.; B.A., Coe Coll., 1961; M.A., 1984, Ph.D. in Adminstrn. and Mgmt., Columbia Pacific U., 1986; m. Gail Judith Kettler, June 30, 1962; children—Brian Joseph, Jeffrey Thomas. Dir devel./pub. relations Mt. Mercy Coll., Cedar Rapids, Iowa, 1965-69; v.p. devel. St. Mary's Coll., Orchard Lake, Mich., 1969-71; dir. devel. Roman Catholic Diocese, Tucson, 1971-74; dir. devel./community relations St. Mary's Hosp., Milw., 1974-75; dir. devel./pub. relations The Pontifical Coll. Josephinum, Columbus, Ohio, 1975-77; dir. trusts and estates Ohio State U. Devel. Fund, Columbus, 1977-85; v.p. devel. Coe Coll., Cedar Rapids, Iowa, 1985-87; dir. trusts and estates Marquette U., Milw., 1987—. Commr., Perry Twp. (Ohio) Zoning Bd. Cert. fund raising exec. Mem. Nat. Soc. Fund Raising Execs. (past pres. Central Ohio chpt.), Council Advancement and Support Edn., Lambda Chi Alpha. Roman Catholic. Club: Kiwanis (bd. dirs., pres. Worthington-Linworth, Ohio). Home: 2055 Underwood Pkwy Elm Grove WI 53122 Office: Marquette Univ 1212 W Wisconsin Ave Milwaukee WI 53233

KOLEHOUSE, DONALD MICHAEL, investment banker; b. Grand Rapids, Mich., June 26, 1957; s. Donald Dale Kolehouse and Donna Marie (Coolsen) Sterken; m. Darlene Lisa Palchak, Dec. 17, 1982; children: Kristin Leigh, Donald Michael II. AA, Grand Rapids Jr. Coll., 1977; BBA summa cum laude, Western Mich. U., 1978. CPA, Mich. Audit and tax supr. Seidman & Seidman, Grand Rapids, 1978-83; v.p. fin. Daverman Assocs., Inc., Grand Rapids, 1983-86; dir. investment banking H.B. Shaine & Co., Inc., Grand Rapids, 1986-87; pres. Lemmon & Kolehowe, Inc., Grand Rapids, 1987—; bd. dirs. West Michigan Venture Capital Group. Bd. dirs., v.p. Grand Rapids Jaycees, 1985—. Mem. Am. Inst. CPA's, Mich. Assn. CPA's. Clubs: Grand Rapids Econ.; West Mich. Venture Capital Group. Avocations: fishing, hunting, sailing, skiing. Home: 3581 Watergate SW Wyoming MI 49509 Office: Lemmon & Kolehouse Inc 107-D Waters Bldg Grand Rapids MI 49503

KOLENBRANDER, HAROLD MARK, college administrator, consultant; b. Sibley, Iowa, Oct. 7, 1938; s. Dirk J. and Nellie (Van Heukelom) K.; m. Laurie L. Bouma, Aug. 28, 1958; children—Kimberly, Kirk, Kerri. B.A., Central Coll., 1960; Ph.D., U. Iowa, 1964. From asst. prof. to prof. chemistry Central Coll., Pella, Iowa, 1964-71, chmn. chemistry dept., 1967-71, provost, dean coll., 1975-86; dean acad. planning Grand Valley State Coll., Allendale, Mich., 1971-75; pres. Mt. Union Coll., Alliance, Ohio, 1986—; cons. Council Ind. Colls., Washington, 1979—; cons. evaluator N. Central Assn. Colls., Chgo., 1980—, commr.-at-large, 1982-86. Contbr. articles to profl. jours. NIH fellow, 1961-64, 69-70. Mem. Am. Assn. Higher Edn., Royal Soc. Chemistry, Biochem. Soc. Club: Rotary (pres. 1980). Avocation: personal computing. Home: 1304 S Union Ave Alliance OH 44601 Office: Mount Union Coll Office of the President Alliance OH 44601

KOLESAR, EDWARD STEVEN, JR., educator; b. Canton, Ohio, June 24, 1950; s. Edward Steven Sr. and Margaret Mary (Skolosh) K.; m. Elinor Kropac, Oct. 7, 1976; children: Lauren Marie, Elizabeth Anne. BSEE, U. Akron, 1973; MBA, Midwestern U., 1976; MSEE, Air Force Inst. Tech., 1978; PhD, U. Tex., 1985. Co-op engring. student Hoover Co., North Canton, Ohio, 1970-72; elec. engr. Electronics Systems Div., Hanscom AFB, Mass., 1973-77; biomed. engr. Sch. Aerospace Medicine, San Antonio, 1979-82; asst. prof. Air Force Inst. Tech., Dayton, Ohio, 1985—; cons. engr. scientific adv. bd. USAF, Washington, 1981, Johns Hopkins U., Balt., 1983, Ardex Inc., Austin, 1985. Patentee gas contamination detection device, 1985. Judge Sci. Clubs Am., San Antonio, 1979-82, Dayton, 1985—. Served to maj. USAF, 1985—. Named one of Outstanding Young Men in Am., U.S. Jaycees, 1982. Mem. IEEE (sr.), Air Force Inst. Tech. Assn. of Grads., Air Force Assn. Republican. Roman Catholic. Avocations: woodworking, philatelist. Home: 3630 Navara Dr Beavercreek OH 45431

KOLESON, DONALD RALPH, college dean, educator; b. Eldon, Mo., June 30, 1935; s. Ralph A. and Fern M. (Beanland) K.; children—Anne, David, Janet. B.S. in Edn., Central Mo. State U., 1959; M.Ed., So. Ill. U., 1973. Mem. faculty So. Ill. U., Carbondale, 1968-73; dean tech. edn. Belleville (Ill.) Area Coll., 1982—. Mem. Am. Vocat. Edn. Assn., Am. Welding Assn., Nat. Assn. Two-Year Schs. of Constrn. (pres. 1984-85). Clubs: Masons; Shriners, Jesters.

KOLET, STEVEN ALEXANDER, military officer; b. Danville, Pa., Mar. 7, 1946; s. Steve Kolet and Adele (Ladonis) McHenry; m. Carole Ruth Young, July 5, 1969 (div. May 1985); children: Alisha, Ryan; m. Adrian Dana, Sept. 6, 1985. BS in Aeronautical Engring., USAF Acad., 1969; MS in Astronautical Engring., Air Force Inst. Tech., 1976. Commd. USAF, 1969, advanced through grades to maj.; crew sta. engr. USAF, Wright Patterson AFB, Ohio, 1977-78, cockpit engr., 1978-80; instr. pilot USAF, Griffiss AFB, N.Y., 1980-81, officer controller, 1981-83; chief aerospace physiology USAF, Ellsworth AFB, 1983-86; with aerospace physiology med. ctr. USAF, Wright Patterson AFB, 1986—; mem. faculty Wright State U., Fairborn, Ohio, 1987—. Mem. Human Factors Soc., Aerospace Med. Assn. Club: Radio Aero Modeler. Avocation: outdoor sports, model aviation. Office: Med Ctr Wright Patterson AFB OH 45433

KOLF, JAMES, home health care service manager; b. Detroit, July 22, 1948; s. John A. and Mary M. (Whalen) K.; m. Marie Anne Mace, Nov. 25, 1970; children: Heather Anne, Rebecca Lynn, Kelly Marie. BS, Wayne State U., 1970, postgrad., 1972-73. Cert. tchr., Mich. Tchr. St. Raymond Sch., Detroit, 1970-73; pharm. sales Eaton Labs., Norwich, N.Y., 1973-74; ter. mgr. Baxter Travenol Labs., Deerfield, Ill., 1974-75, field tng., 1976-81; med. edn. coordinator Mt. Carmel Hosp., Detroit, 1975-76; gen. mgr./antibiotic/TPN specialist Home Health Care Am., Newport Beach, Calif., 1981—; gen. mgr. New Eng. Critical Care, 1987—. PTO grantee, 1971. Mem. Assn. Hosp. Med. Edn., Sigma Pi (sec. 1967-68), 200 Club, 400 Club. Republican. Roman Catholic.

KOLINEK, ROBERT BRETT, marketing executive; b. Chgo., Sept. 20, 1954; s. Jerry W. and Renee C. K. BS in History, U. Wis., 1975; postgrad. in econ. studies U. Chgo., 1976. With Helen Brett Enterprises, Inc. and R.B.K. Enterprises, Ltd., Chgo., 1976—, exec. v.p., 1980—; pres. Petro-Tech Expos., Ltd., trade show mgmt. co. oil and gas industry, Chgo., 1981—. Mem. Nat. Assn. Exhbn. Mgrs. (chmn. new memberships, treas. 1982, sec. 1983), Internat. Technol. Exchange (bd. dirs.); asst. exec. dir. Nat. Caterer's Assn. Winner NAIA Vault Championship, horizontal bar Championship. Ill. champion, 1973. Office: Helen Brett Enterprises Inc 1 Quincy Ct Chicago IL 60304

KOLKER, RICHARD LEE, lawyer; b. LeMars, Iowa, Apr. 17, 1939; s. Lawrence Francis and Genevieve Josephine K.; m. Janet Kay Shabino, Aug. 29, 1964; children—Martin, Audra, Anthony. B.A. in Econs., St. Mary's Coll., Winona, Minn., 1961; J.D., U.S.D., Vermillion, 1964. Bar: S.D. 1964, U.S. Dist. Ct. S.D. 1965, U.S. Tax Ct. 1980. Sole practice, Groton, S.D., 1964; ptnr. Maloney, Kolker, Fritz, Hogan & Johnson, Groton, 1965—; dep. states atty. Brown County, S.D., 1967-71, state atty., 1971-72; mem. S.D. Ho. of Reps., 1973-74; appointed to State Council for Legal Services, 1980, Gov.'s Adv. Com. on Outdoor Recreation, 1986—; chairperson Blue Ribbon com. S.D. Supreme Ct., 1985. Republican. Roman Catholic. Home: 807 N First Groton SD 57445 Office: Maloney Kolker Fritz et al 101 N Main Groton SD 57445

KOLL, RICHARD LEROY, chemical company executive; b. Muscatine, Iowa, Mar. 16, 1925; s. Charles C. and Emma (Schafer) K.; m. Patricia Ann Grunder, Jan. 2, 1955; children: Craig, Christine, Cary. B.S. in Mech. Engring., U. Iowa, 1951. Plant mgr. Grain Processing Corp., Muscatine, Iowa, 1971-72, v.p., 1972-77, sr. v.p., 1977—. Served with USMC, 1944-46. Clubs: University Athletic (Iowa City); Geneva Golf and Country. Lodge: Elks. Home: 1317 Oakland Dr Muscatine IA 52761 Office: Grain Processing Corp 1600 Oregon St Muscatine IA 52761

KOLLARITSCH, FELIX PAUL, accounting educator; b. Graz, Austria, June 7, 1925; came to U.S., 1950, naturalized, 1956; s. Carel and Cornelia (Nemerad) K.; m. Martha Jane Moore, Aug. 27, 1951; children—Paul Walter, Carl Richard. M.B.A., Hochschule fuer Welthandel, Vienna, Austria, 1950, Ph.D., 1952. C.P.A., Ind. Pub., indsl. accountant 1952-54; asst. prof. Ill. Wesleyan U., Bloomington, 1954-56; asso. prof. Butler U., Indpls., 1956-62; prof. accounting Ohio State U., Columbus, 1962—; chmn. dept. Ohio State U. Author: Opinions, Scholastic Rankings and Professional Progress of Accounting Graduates, 1968, Cost Systems for Planning, Decisions, and Controls, 1979; Contbr. articles to profl. jours. Mem. Am. Inst. C.P.A.s, Am. Acctg. Assn., Fin. Execs. Inst., Beta Alpha Psi, Beta Gamma Sigma. Home: 2801 Canterbury Rd Columbus OH 43221

KOLLES, BERTRAND ALOY, optometrist; b. Pierz, Minn., Sept. 25, 1931; s. Albert Karl and Sophia (Wiedenbach) K.; m. Irene Marie Kuelbs, Dec. 29, 1956; children: Mary, Julie, Joseph, Brett, Camille. BS, Ill. Coll. Optometry, Chgo., 1953, DO, 1954. Ptnr. Dr.'s Kolles and Kennedy, Roseville, Minn., 1958-81; pvt. practice optometry Dr. Kolles and Assocs., New Brighton, Minn., 1981—. Inventor corneal gauge, 1974, orthokeratology method, 1976; contbr. articles to profl. jours. Fellow Internat. Orthokeratology Sect.; mem. Am. Optometric Assn., Minn. Optometric Assn., Met. Optometric Soc. Republican. Roman Catholic. Home: 965 Lydia Ave Roseville MN 55113 Office: Dr Kolles & Assocs 2655 N Innsbruck Dr New Brighton MN 55112

KOLLINS, MICHAEL JEROME, automotive engineer, historian; b. St. Clairsville, Ohio, Mar. 20, 1912; s. Michael Arthur and Mary Ann (Peck) K.; student Coll. City Detroit, 1928-32; m. Julia Dolores Advent, Jan. 16, 1934; children—Michael Lewis, Richard, Laura. Chief sect. service engring. and tech. data Studebaker-Packard Corp., Detroit, 1945-55; mgr. tech. services Chrysler Corp., Detroit, 1955-64, mgr. warranty adminstrn., 1964-68, mgr. Highland Park Service center, 1968-75; pres. Kollins Design & Engring., Detroit, 1975—. Pres., Oakland (Mich.) U. Chorus, 1969-71, Home Owners Assn. of Eastover Farms No. 1, 1981—; trustee Nat. Automotive Hist. Collection, 1982—; bd. dirs. Capuchin Charity Guild, 1983—; active Birmingham (Mich.) Chorale, Meadowbrook (Mich.) Festival Chorus; mem. adv. bd. Am. Security Council, 1972—. Served with USN, 1942-45. Mem. U.S. Auto Club (vice-chmn. tech. com. 1971-82, dir. cert. com. 1983—), Am. Automobile Assn. (contest bd.), Soc. Automotive Engrs., Soc. Automotive Historians, Engring. Soc. Detroit (industry ambassador 1972—). Contbr. articles to profl. publs. Designer racing cars, 1932-39, sports cars, spl. luxury vehicles, 1951—, automotive performance and safety devices, 1946—. Home: 821 Highwood Dr Bloomfield Hills MI 48013 Office: Kollins Design & Engring PO Box 214 Bloomfield Hills MI 48013

KOLNICKI, KENNETH JOHN, accountant, financial investment consultant; b. Chgo., Dec. 12, 1948; s. John F. and Antoinette (Candolph) K.; divorced; children: Michael, Kristine, Karyn. BS, U. Ill., 1970. CPA, Ill. Mgr. Wolf & Co., CPA's, Chgo., 1970-75; managing ptnr. Kolnicki, Nuzzo, Trapani & Co., Oak Brook, Ill., 1975—. Mem. Am. Inst. CPA's, Ill. CPA Soc. (real estate com.). Roman Catholic. Club: Italo-Am. Club (bd. dirs. 1984—), Bianco Lodge (v.p. 1980—). Office: Kolnicki Nuzzo Trapani & Co 1211 W 22d St Oak Brook IL 60521

KOLOTKIN, RICHARD ALAN, psychologist; b. Bklyn., Feb. 14, 1950; s. Kalman and Sydell (Kempner) K. BA in Psychology magna cum laude, Wesleyan U., Middletown, Conn., 1972; PhD in Clin. and Community Psychology, U. Minn., 1978. Lic. cons. psychologist, Minn.; lic. psychologist, N.D. Teaching asst. dept. psychology U. Minn., Mpls., 1972-76; research asst. dept. psychology U. Minn., Mpls., 1973, 1976-77; instr. dept. psychology U. Minn., Mpls., 1974-76; clin. fellow dept. psychiatry Harvard U. Mass. Gen. Hosp., Boston, 1976-77, intern, 1976-77; pvt. practice psychology Moorhead (Minn.) State U., Fargo, N.D., 1978—; cons. Lakeland Mental Health Ctr., Fergus Falls, Minn., 1981, West Cen. Region Juvenile Ctr., Moorhead, 1981—, Fargo Forum, 1982, 85, Northwestern Mut. Life Ins., 1984-85, N.D. Council on Arts, 1985, Fargo Clinic, 1985, Dakota Hosp., Fargo, 1983-84, Fargo Pub. Schs., 1982, IRS, Fargo, 1982, VA Hosp., Fargo, 1981, Am. Crystal Sugar, Moorhead, 1981; clin. instr. dept. neurosci. U. N.D., Grand Forks, 1978-85, clin. asst. prof. dept. neurosci., 1985-86, clin. assoc. prof. dept. neurosci., 1986—; asst. prof. dept. psychology Moorhead State U., 1977-83, assoc. prof., 1983—; dir. Life Skills Assocs., Fargo, 1982—. Contbr. articles to profl. jours.; editorial reviewer: Behavior Therapy, 1981, Behavior Assessment, 1982. Recipient Walkley prize, 1972; fellow NIH, 1972; grantee Bush Found., 1982, Moorhead State U., 1980, 1979, NIH, 1972. Mem. Am. Psychol. Assn., Assn. Advancement Behavior Therapy (Cert. Merit, 1980), Red River Assn. Behavior Therapy (pres. 1980). Avocations: racquetball, skiing, bicycling. Home: 906 N 8th St Fargo ND 58102 Office: Moorhead State U Psychology Dept Moorhead MN 56560

KOMMEDAHL, THOR, plant pathology educator; b. Mpls., Apr. 1, 1920; s. Thorbjorn and Martha (Blegen) K.; m. Faye Lillian Jensen, June 4, 1924; children—Kris Alan, Siri Lynn, Lori Anne. B.S., U. Minn., 1945, M.S., 1947, Ph.D., 1951. Instr. U. Minn., St. Paul, 1946-51, asst. prof. plant pathology, 1953-57, assoc. prof., 1957-63, prof., 1963—; asst. prof. plant pathology Ohio Agrl. Research and Devel. Ctr., Wooster, 1951-53, Ohio State U., Columbus, 1951-53; cons. botanist and taxonomist Minn. Dept. Agr., 1954-60. cons. editor McGraw-Hill Ency. Sci. and Tech., 1972-78; editor-in-chief Phytopathology, 1964-67; editor: Procs. IX Internat. Congress Plant Protection, 2 vols., 1981, corn disease newsletter, 1970-76; sr. editor: Challenging Problems in Plant Health, 1982, Plant Disease Reporter, 1979; Contbr. articles to profl. jours. Guggenheim fellow, 1961; Fulbright scholar, 1968. Fellow AAAS, Am. Phytopathol. Soc. (pres. 1971, publs. coordinator 1978-84, disting. service award 1984); mem. Am. Inst. Biol. Scis., Bot. Soc. Am., Council Biology Editors, Internat. Soc. Plant Pathology (councilor 1971-78, sec.-gen. and treas. 1983-88), Mycol. Soc. Am., Minn. Acad. Sci., N.Y. Acad. Scis., Soc. Scholarly Publs., Weed Sci. Soc. Am. (award of excellence 1968). Baptist. Home: 1666 Coffman St #322 Saint Paul MN 55108 Office: U Minn 495 Borlaug Hall 1991 Buford Circle Saint Paul MN 55108

KOMMRUSCH, FREDRICK GUSTAV, information system specialist; b. Milw., Dec. 15, 1938; s. Fredrick Gustav and Rosalie Agnes (Piechura) K.; m. Judith Ann Kumbier, Nov. 24, 1966. BS in Applied Math and Physics, U. Wis., Milw., 1966, postgrad., 1967-73. Programmer Astronautics, Milw., 1966-69; programmer, analyst Badger Meter, Milw., 1969; sr. systems analyst Allen Bradley, Milw., 1969—; Author: Fuel Management For Jet Aircraft, 1967. Club: Bagatelle Card (Milw.) (sec.-treas.). Avocations: photography, geneology. Home: 5670 N Paradise Ln Glendale WI 53209 Office: Allen Bradley Co 1201 S 2d St Milwaukee WI 53204

KOMP, BARBARA ANN, technical writer; b. La Porte, Ind., Nov. 3, 1954; d. Gerald Lee and Betty Mae (Schelin) K. B.A. in Elem. Edn., Ball State U., 1977; student Mech. and Elec. Engring. Tech., Purdue U., 1984-86, Ind. Vocat. Tech. Coll., 1986—. Quality control insp. Foreman Mfg. Co., Rolling Prairie, Ind., 1978-80; quality control insp. Weil-McLain Co., Michigan City, Ind., 1980-81, jr. quality control engr., 1981-84, tech. writer, 1984—. Advisor Jr. Achievement, Michigan City, 1982—. Mem. Am. Soc. Quality Control (cert., membership chmn. 1981-83, treas. 1984-85), Soc. for Tech. Communication (Tech. Manual Achievement Award 1986). Avocations: writing childrens' stories, jazz aerobics, photography, skin care zones. Office: Weil-McLain A Marley Co Blaine St Michigan City IN 46360

KONDELIK, JOHN P., library administrator; b. Chgo., Jan. 28, 1942; s. John P. Kondelik and M. Kathleen (Vaught) Henderson; m. Marlene Rosenthal, May 14, 1967; 1 child, Vicki. B.A., U. Fla., 196'; M.S.L.S., Fla. State U., 1966; postgrad., U. Mich. Acquisitions librarian Fla. Presbyn. Coll., St. Petersburg, 1966-68; cataloger Eckerd Coll., St. Petersburg, 1968-74; dir. libraries Olivet Coll., Mich., 1974-83; dir. Irwin Library Butler U., Indpls., 1984—; trustee Mich. Library Consortium, Lansing, 1974-83, mem. exec. com., 1981-82; exec. com. Cen. Ind. Library Services Authority, 1987—. Contbr. articles to profl. jours. Mem. ALA, Ind. Library Assn. (exec. com. coll. and univ. div. 1987—). Avocations: book and stamp collecting; fishing; golf. Office: Butler U Irwin Library 4600 Sunset Ave Indianapolis IN 46208

KONEN, ROBERT DAVID, dentist; b. Sheboygan, Wis., Sept. 9, 1954; s. Clemens Julius Jr. and Loraine Lenora (Lenz) K. BS, U. Wis., 1978; DDS, Marquette U., 1983. Assoc. dentist Dental Clinic, Madison, Wis., 1983-84; gen. practice dentistry Baraboo, Wis., 1984—; tchr. Madison Area Tech. Coll., 1983—. Commr. Baraboo Parks and Recreation Com., 1986; mem. Friends of Downtown Baraboo, 1986, Friends of Baraboo Zoo, 1986. Mem. ADA, Wis. Dental Assn., Acad. Gen. Dentistry, Wis. Dental Soc., Chgo. Dental Soc., Sauk-Juneau-Adams County Dental Soc., Am. Straight Wire Orthodontic Assn., U. Wis. Alumni Assn., Baraboo C. of C., Baraboo Jaycees, Psi Omega. Lutheran. Lodge: Kiwanis. Avocations: softball, bowling, running, aerobics, golf. Home: 819 2d Ave #2 Baraboo WI 53913 Office: 101 4th St Baraboo WI 53913

KONG, JULIE CHAN, nutrition educator; b. Chgo., Nov. 7, 1958; d. Bing S. and Chiu C. Chan; m. John Kong Jr. BS in Nutrition and Med. Dietetics with honors, U. Ill., Chgo., 1980; MEd, Loyola U., Chgo., 1985. Clinical dietitian Northwestern Mem. Hosp., Chgo., 1980-84; teaching asst. U. Ill. Chgo., 1984-85, teaching assoc., 1985—. Author: (with others) Treatment and Care Guide for Head and Neck Surgical Patients, 1984; developer computer edn. tng. manual; contbr. articles to newspapers, profl. jours. Chairperson awards com. Coll. Alumni Bd., Coll. Associated Health Professions, U. Ill., 1985—; mem. student affairs com. U. Ill., 1985, admissions com. U. Ill., Chgo. Mem. Am. Dietetic Assn., Ill. Dietetic Assn., Chgo. Dietetic Assn. (co-chairperson subcom. in revision of diet manual), Am. Soc. Enteral and Parenteral Nutrition. Office: U Ill Hosp and Med Ctrs Dept Dietetics and Nutrition 808 S Wood St Chicago IL 60612

KONIE, JOSEPH C., orthodontist; b. Chgo., Jan. 6, 1932; s. Joseph and Sophie (Malkiewicz) Konieczny; m. Marion C. Kukankos, Dec. 26, 1981. BS, U. Ill., Chgo., 1955, DDS, 1957, MS, 1963. Instr. U. Ill. Coll. Dentistry, Chgo., 1960-61; practice dentistry specializing in orthodontics Oak Lawn, Ill., 1963—. Sec. med. field Poland's Millenium of Christianity, Chgo., 1966. Served to capt. USAF, 1957-59. Mem. ADA, Ill. Dental Soc., Chgo. Dental Soc., Am. Assn. Orthodontists, Midwestern Assn. Orthodontists, Chgo. Soc. Orthodontists (bd. dirs. 1972). Roman Catholic. Clubs: Beverly Country, Dental Arts of Chgo. Home: 6730 W Navajo Dr Palos Heights IL 60463 Office: 9501 S Central Oak Lawn IL 60453

KÖNIG, PETER, pediatrician, educator; b. Cluj, Romania, Feb. 14, 1938; came to U.S., 1976; s. Rudolf and Irina (Grünwald) K.; m. Lea Schiffer, Sept. 30, 1965; 1 child, Orly. Student, Timisoara Med. Sch., Romania, 1954-59; MD, Hebrew U., Jerusalem, 1966; PhD, U. London, 1974. Resident Bikur Cholim Hosp., Jerusalem, 1970-71, staff, 1974-76; fellow in pulmonary diseases Brompton Hosp., London, 1971-74; asst. prof. child health U. Mo., Columbia, 1976-80, assoc. prof. child health, 1980-84, prof. in child health, 1984—. Fellow Am. Acad. Allergy; mem. Am. Thoracic Soc., Acad. Allergy, Soc. Pediatric Research, Chilean Asthma Found., Sigma Xi. Home: 916 Rollingwood Dr Columbia MO 65203 Office: U Mo Child Health 1 Hospital Dr Columbia MO 65212

KONIGSBERG, IRA, film and literature educator; b. N.Y.C., May 30, 1935; s. Sidney and Mary (Silverman) K.; m. Nancy Joan Smith, Sept. 7, 1958 (div. Aug. 20, 1979); children: Peter Eugene, Anna Rebecca; m. Nancy Hilary Goldman, Feb. 24, 1985; 1 stepchild, Sasha Bagchi. BA, CCNY, 1956; MA, Columbia U., 1957; PhD, Stanford U., 1961. Asst. prof. English Brandeis U., Waltham, Mass., 1961-68; assoc. prof. English U. Mich., Ann Arbor, 1968-74, prof. English, 1974—. Editor: The Classic Short Story, 1971, Criticism in the Poststructuralist Age, 1981; co-editor: Critical Thinking, 1969; author: Samuel Richardson and the Dramatic Novel, 1968, Narrative Technique in the English Novel: DeFoe to Austin, 1985, The Complete Film Dictionary, 1987; contbr. articles to profl. jours. Served with U.S. Army, 1956-57. U. Vienna Fulbright-Hays lectureship 1966-67; U. Mich. Rackham fellow 1974, 76, 79; U. Mich. Rackham grantee 1981, 83, 85-86. Mem. MLA, Am. Film Inst., Am. Soc. Eighteen Century Studies. Home: 1901 Frieze Ave Ann Arbor MI 48104 Office: U Mich English Dept Ann Arbor MI 48109

KONIKOW, ROBERT BERNARD, writer, editor, consultant; b. Boston, Apr. 9, 1914; s. Moses Joseph and Rose (Bernard) K.; m. Ella Klaiman, Sept. 4, 1938; children: Robert Moses, Tobi Harriet (Mrs. Curtiss Hoffman). AB in Math. cum laude, Harvard U., 1932. With various govt. agys. 1940-43; free-lance writer Washington, 1946-56; editor Advt. & Sales Promotion, Chgo., 1956-69; creative dir. Abelson-Frankel, Chgo., 1969-71; free-lance writer Chgo., 1971—; tchr. writing and editing U. Chgo., 1959-60, Northwestern U., 1961-63, Downers Grove (Ill.) Adult Evening Sch., 1963-68. Author: Discover Historic America, 1973, Sight 'n Sound Techniques for Sales Meetings and Sales Presentations, 1973, How to Participate Profitably in Trade Shows, 1976; (with Frank E. McElroy) Communications for the Safety Professional, 1975, Exhibit Design, 1984, Point of Purchase Design, 1985, Exhibit Design 2, 1986. Pres. Downers Grove Friends of the Library, 1968-71, 1983-87; Chgo. Film Council, 1968-71; treas. Community Concert Assn., 1967-69, Midwest Seminar on Videotape and Film, 1972-76, pres. 1977-78. Served with AUS, 1943-45. Mem. DuPage Apple Users Group (pres. 1984-86, bd. dirs. 1986—). Club: Harvard (Chgo.). Home and Office: 4528 Sterling Rd Downers Grove IL 60515

KONKEL, KURT FREDERICK, orthopedic surgeon; b. Milw., Mar. 21, 1945; s. Robert John and Elda Clara (Altpeter) K. m. Maureen Curtis, June 8, 1968; children: Theresa, Jennifer, Corine, Karen. BS, Marquette U., Milw., 1966; MD, U. Wis., Madison, 1970. Intern U. Utah Hosps. and Clinics, Salt Lake City, 1970-71; resident in gen. surgery and orthopedics U. Wis., Madison, 1971-73; resident in orthopedics Miami Valley Hosp., Dayton, Ohio, 1973-75; orthopedic surgeon Falls Med. Group, Menomonee Falls, Wis., 1977—, Hartford (Wis.) Parkview Clinic, 1985—; med. dir. phys. therapy Hartford Hosp., 1981—, bd. dirs. 1981-85, chief of staff, 1985-86. Commr. Pike Lake Protections and Rehab., hartford, 1983, sec., 1985-86. Served with USNR, 1975-77. Named Commodore Nat. Butterfly Assn., 1985. Fellow Am. Bd. Orthopedic Surgeons. Republican. Roman Catohlic. Lodge: Lions. Avocations: sailing, skiing, hunting. Home: 3464 Lake Dr Hartford WI 53027 Office: Falls Med Group SC N84 WI6889 Menomonee Ave Menomonee Falls WI 53051

KONLE, MARY CAROLINE, educator; b. Morgantown, W.Va., Nov. 28, 1923; d. John Malcolm and Mary Barriere (Tomlinson) Orth; m. Robert Louis Konle, June 30, 1945; children—Dale Reed Konle, Kathleen Konle Schneider; m. William R. Bungle, 1987. Student Morris Harvey Coll., 1940-42; B.A., W.Va. U., 1944; M.S. in Guidance, U. Wis.-Milw., 1961, postgrad., 1961-82; Ed.D., Marquette U., 1976; postgrad. Inst. Norte Americano, San Luis Potosi, Mex., summer 1981. Tchr. cert., Wis. Tchr. schs., Harpers Ferry, W.Va., 1944-45, Trenton, N.D., 1945-46; tchr. phys. edn. Bradenton (Fla.) High Sch., 1946-47; elem. tchr. New Berlin (Wis.) Pub. Schs., 1956-69; tchr. New Berlin High Sch., 1969-77; reading specialist Glen Park Middle Sch., New Berlin, 1978-85, Southwest High Sch., San Antonio, 1986-87; co-founder, dir. Friendship Center Reading Camp, Dodgeville, Wis., 1970—. Contbg. mem. Am. Friends Service Com., 1947-82; mem. dirs. Am. Youth Hostels, Milw., 1978-81; adv. Am. Field Service, 1970-74. Recipient service award Am. Youth Hostels, 1953. Mem. Internat. Reading Assn., Wis. Reading Assn., Assn. Supervision and Curriculum Devel., NEA, Wis. Edn. Assn., New Berlin Edn. Assn., Common Cause, World Federalist Assn., Servas, Audubon Soc., Kappa Delta Pi. Quaker. Home: 12418 W Rosemary St New Berlin WI 53151

KONNAK, JOHN WILLIAM, surgery educator; b. Racine, Wis., June 28, 1937; s. William Frank and Ruth Viola (Cape) K.; m. Betty LaFleur, June 9, 1962; 1 child, William. BS, U. Wis., 1959, MD, 1962. Diplomate Am. Bd. Urology. Intern Phila. Gen. Hosp., 1962-63; asst. resident Harbor Gen. Hosp., Torrance, Calif., 1965-66; resident U. Mich. Hosp., Ann Arbor, 1966-69, attending staff mem., 1969—; prof. surgery U. Mich. Med. Sch., Ann Arbor, 1982—. Served with USPHS, 1963-65. Fellow ACS; mem. Cen. Surg. Assn., Am. Urol. Assn., Transplantation Soc. Mich. (pres. 1981-83), Alpha Omega Alpha. Republican. Avocation: scuba diving. Home: 2906 Park Ridge Ann Arbor MI 48103 Office: U Mich Med Ctr 1500 E Medical Center Dr Ann Arbor MI 48109

KONOPINSKI, VIRGIL JAMES, industrial hygienist; b. Toledo, Ohio, July 11, 1935; s. Mack and Mary Veronica (Jankowski) K.; m. Joan Mary Wielinski, June 27, 1964; children—Ann Marie, Carol Sue, Peter James. B.S. in Chem. Engring., U. Toledo, 1956; M.S. in Chem. Engring., Pratt Inst., Bklyn., 1960; M.B.A., Bowling Green State U., 1971. Registered profl. engr., Ohio, Ind., Calif.; cert. indsl. hygienist; cert. safety profl. Assoc. engr. Owens Illinois, Toledo, 1956, 60; real estate developer, Grand Rapids, Ohio, 1961; chem. engr. USPHS, Cin., 1961-64; sr. environ. engr. Vistron Corp., Lima, Ohio, 1964-67; environ. specialist, asst. to dir. environ. control Owens Corning Fiberglas, Toledo, 1967-72; gen. mgr. Midwest Environ. Mgmt., Maumee, Ohio, 1972-73; staff specialist, indsl. hygienist Williams Bros. Waste Control., Tulsa, Okla., 1973-75; dir. div. indsl. hygiene and radiol. health Ind. State Bd. Health, Indpls., 1975—, dir. IOSHA indsl. hygiene, 1975-83; cons., lectr. Served with USNR, 1956-59. Mem. Am. Indsl. Hygiene Assn., Am. Conf. Govtl. Indsl. Hygienists, Am. Soc. Safety Engrs., U.S. Naval Inst., Toledo Zool. Soc. Republican. Roman Catholic. Contbr. articles to profl. jours. Home: 60 Irongate Dr Zionsville IN 46077 Office: 1330 W Michigan Indianapolis IN 46206

KONOPKA, MARY ANN STEPHANY, container mfg. co. exec.; b. Chgo., Jan. 30, 1933; d. Thomas Stephen and Mary Irene (Plucinski) Poltorak; m. Louis Steven Konopka, Nov. 22, 1964 (dec. 1976); stepchildren: Linda Marie Konopka Orseno, Lorraine Louise Konopka Capra. With Continental Group, Inc., West Chicago, Ill., 1952—, project control supr., 1978-83, supr. inventory control, 1983—. Mem. Am. Inventory and Prodn. Soc., Nat. Assn. Female Execs., Am. Soc. Profl. and Exec. Women, U.S. CB Radio Assn. Democrat. Roman Catholic. Club: Northwest Internat. Trade. Home: 526 E Pomeroy St West Chicago IL 60185 Office: Continental Group Inc 1700 Harvester Rd West Chicago IL 60185

KONSTANS, DOROTHY JANICE, school psychologist, special educaion coordinator; b. Chgo., Apr. 21, 1936; d. James T. and Winifred M. (Hayhurst) Hume; m. Constantine Kontans, Feb. 28, 1959; children: Chris T., Randall J., Russell D. AB, Ripon (Wis.) Coll., 1958; MA, U. Chgo., 1961. Registered psychologist, Ill. Psychologist Silver Cross Hosp., Joliet, Ill., 1961-62; sch. psychologist Dist. 303, St. Charles, Ill., 1963-73; sch. psychologist, spl. edn. coordinator Dist. 301, Burlington, Ill., 1973—. Mem. Am. Psychol. Assn., Nat. Health Service Providers, Ill Sch. Psychologists Assn., Phi Beta Kappa. Methodist. Home: PO Box 527 Saint Charles IL 60174 Office: Dist 301 PO Box 396 Burlington IL 60109

KONYHA, LARRY DEAN, printing franchise owner; b. Detroit, Aug. 24, 1956; s. Lawrence Lewis and Martha Deane (Moore) K.; m. Kim Marie Frost, Mar. 17, 1979; children: Kevin Micheal, David Robert. AS in Printing, Ferris State Coll., 1976, BS in Tech. Edn., 1978. Printer Ford Motor Co., Dearborn, Mich., 1978-79; tech. rep. Itek Graphic Products, Southfield, Mich., 1979-80; sr. tech. rep. Am. Speedy Printing Ctrs., Inc., Birmingham, Mich., 1981—. Mem. Internat. Franchise Assn. Republican. Wesleyan. Avocations: hunting, fishing. Office: Am Speedy Printing Ctrs Inc 32100 Telegraph Ste 110 Birmingham MI 48010

KONZELMANN, HENRY JOSEPH, pediatrician; b. Elizabeth, N.J., Aug. 11, 1935; s. Henry Joseph and Marianne Jahn K.; B.S. in Biology, Holy Cross Coll., 1956; M.D., Georgetown U., 1960; married; children—Suzanne, Kathleen, Henry, Robert, Daniel, Agnes, John. Intern, Harrisburg (Pa.) Hosp., 1960-61; resident in pediatrics U. Md., Balt., 1963-66; practice medicine specializing in pediatrics, Springfield, Ill., 1966—; chmn. pediatrics dept. St. John's Hosp.; assoc. clin. prof. pediatrics So. Ill. U. Med. Sch. Bd. dirs. Med. Found. Central Ill. Served with USPHS, 1961-63. Diplomate Am. Bd. Pediatrics. Mem. AMA, Am. Acad. Pediatrics, Ill. Med. Soc., Sangamon County Med. Soc. Conservative Republican. Roman Catholic. Home: 1520 W Lake Dr Springfield IL 62707 Office: 2657 W Lawrence Ave Springfield IL 62704

KOO, PETER HUNG-KWAN, immuno-biochemist, educator; b. Shanghai, China; came to U.S., 1959, naturalized, 1975; s. Yung-Foo and Shun-Wa (Ko) K.; m. S. Alice Ho, Dec. 23, 1967; children: David G., Christopher G. BA, U. Wash., 1964; PhD, U. Md., 1970. Research assoc. Johns Hopkins U., 1970-74, asst. prof. oncology and radiology, 1975-77; staff fellow NIH, Bethesda, Md., 1974-75; asst. prof., assoc. prof. microbiology/immunology Northeastern Ohio Univs. Coll. Medicine, Rootstown, 1977—; adj. assoc. prof., depts. chemistry and biology Kent (Ohio) State U. Research, publs. in field. Deacon, 1st Christian Ch. of Kent, 1978-85, mem. fin. com., 1982-84, bd. dirs., 1982—; chmn. profl. edn. com. Am. Cancer Soc., 1985, chmn., 1985—, v.p., 1987—, bd. dirs., v.p., chmn. profl. edn. com. Portage County (Ohio) chpt. Recipient Cystic Fibrosis Care Fund award 1979, 82; NIH grantee, 1978-82, Am. Cancer Soc. grantee, 1979, 82, United Way Health Found. grantee, 1982, MEFCOM Found. grantee, 1983—, NSF grantee, 1984—. Mem. N.Y. Acad. Scis., Am. Assn. Immunologists, Johns Hopkins Med. Surg. Assn., AAAS, Am. Chem. Soc., Am. Soc. for Microbiology, Ohio Acad. Sci., Sigma Xi. Office: Northeastern Ohio Univs Coll Medicine Rootstown OH 44272

KOOISTRA, PAUL DAVID, seminary administrator; b. Duluth, Minn., Oct. 11, 1942; s. David and Laura (Bowman) K.; m. Janet Carlson, June 27, 1964; children: Paul Jr., Shary, Jennifer. BA, U. Minn., 1964; MDiv, Columbia Sem., Decatur, Ga., 1967; PhD, U. Ala., 1980. Ordained to ministry Presbyn. Ch., 1967. Minister of edn. Pinelands Presbyn. Ch., Miami, 1967-69, Seminole Presbyn. Ch., Tampa, Fla., 1969-73; prof. christian edn. Belhaven Coll., Jackson, Miss., 1973-75; prof. edn. Reformed Theol. Sem., Jackson, 1975-85; pres. Covenant Theol. Sem., St. Louis, 1985—. Mem. Assn. Profs. and Researchers in Religious Edn., Kappa Delta Pi, Phi Delta Kappa. Republican. Home and Office: Covenant Theol Sem 12330 Conway Rd Saint Louis MO 63141

KOOISTRA, WILLIAM HENRY, clinical psychologist; b. Grand Rapids, Mich., May 20, 1936; s. Henry P. and Marguerite (Brinks) K.; m. Jean Heynen, Aug. 24, 1957 (div. Dec. 1984); children: Kimberly Lynn, William Peter, Kristin Jean, Allison Carol; m. Carol Sue Smitter, Mar. 9, 1985. BA, Calvin Coll., 1957; PhD, Wayne (Mich.) State U., 1963. Diplomate Am. Bd. Profl. Psychology. Intern psychology Lafayette Clinic, Detroit, 1961-62; chief psychologist Pine Rest Christian Hosp., Grand Rapids, Mich., 1964-67; clin. psychologist Kooistra, Jansma, Elders, Teitsma & DeJonge, Grand Rapids, 1967—; instr. Wayne State U., 1959-63, Hope Coll., Holland, Mich., 1964, Calvin Coll., Grand Rapids, 1964-81. Mem. adv. bd. Acad. Psychology Bulletin, 1980—. Founder Project Rehab, Grand Rapids, 1968, bd. dirs., 1969—, pres., 1972-74; mem. Kent County Dem. Exec. Com., 1969-73, 79-82, 86—. Mem. Am. Psychol. Assn. (council rep. 1982-85), Am. Soc. Psychologists in Pvt. Practice (sec. 1973-75), Mich. Psychol. Assn.(pres. 1979), Mich. Soc. Forensic Psychology, Grand Rapids Area Psychol. Assn (pres. 1968). Avocations: golf, tennis, sailing. Home: 2946 Cascade Rd SE Grand Rapids MI 49506 Office: 3330 Claystone SE Grand Rapids MI 49506

KOON, CARL DANIEL, information systems executive; b. Watseka, Ill., Sept. 11, 1942; s. Carl Dwight and Helen Madge (Arbuckle) K.; m. Patricia Brannon, Apr. 29, 1966 (div. Dec. 1980); children—Kathleen Gayle, Mary Patricia, Erin Colleen; m. 2d, Mary Carolyn Hiner DeMyer, Jan. 24, 1981; stepchildren—Catherine Jane Wright, Karen Margaret Wright. Student computer sci., Purdue U., 1966-69. Mgr. info. systems Ind. Bell Telephone Co., Indpls., 1967-83; dir. mktg. info. systems Ameritech Communications Inc., Chgo., 1983-85; dir. planning Ameritech Services Inc., Arlington Heights, Ill., 1985-86; dist. mgr. Ind. Bell, 1987— . Sports host Nat. Sports Festival, Indpls., 1982; pres. Westlane Little League, Indpls., 1981-82; awards chmn. Nat. Rowing Championships, Indpls., 1983; coach Catholic Youth Orgn., Indpls., 1970-75. Served with USAF, 1962-66. Democrat. Roman Catholic. Home: 7763 Spring Mill Indianapolis IN 46260 Office: Ind Bell 220 N Meridian Indianapolis IN 46204

KOONCE, EILEEN MARY, industrial designer, drafter; b. Chgo., Dec. 12, 1955; s. Norbert William and Marilyn Josephine (LaRocco) Graunke; m. Peter Michael Koonce, Dec. 28, 1974; 1 child, Adam Ross. AAS in Library Sci., Coll. DuPage, 1974; AAS in Archtl. Tech., So. Ill. U., 1978. Drafter GTE Automatic Electric, Inc., Northlake, Ill., 1978, JC Penney, Schaumburg, Ill., 1978-80; systems planner Philips Communications, Arlington Heights, Ill., 1980-83; quotations mgr. Major Control Products, Cary, Ill., 1983-85; drafter and designer Swiderski Electronics, Elk Grove Village, Ill., 1985—. Ill. State Scholar, 1973-74.

KOONTZ, RAYMOND, security equipment company executive; b. Asheville, N.C., 1912; m. Carol Hamlin; 1 son, Cary Hamlin. With Maguire Industries Inc., 1936-46; with Diebold Inc., Canton, Ohio, 1947—, treas., 1947-51, exec. v.p., treas., 1951-52, pres., chief exec. officer, 1952-78, chmn. bd., chief exec. officer, 1978-82, chmn. bd., 1982—. Mem. Newcomen Soc. N.Am. Clubs: Canton (Canton, O.), Brookside (Canton, O.); Union (Cleve.); Congress Lake (Hartville, Ohio); Green Boundary (Aiken, S.C.). Home: 2601 Foxhills Dr NW Canton OH 44708 Office: Diebold Inc 818 Mulberry Rd SE Canton OH 44711

KOOPMAN, RICHARD NELSON, engineer; b. Buffalo, N.Y., Nov. 26, 1945; s. Richard John Walter and Nellie Elkins (Wisbrock) K.; m. Mary Margaret Blume, July 17, 1970; Anthony Blake, Laura Nicole. BS in Mech. Engring., Washington U., 1968; MS in Mech. Engring., U. Minn., 1969, PhD, 1975. Engr. Honeywell, Inc., Mpls., 1973-75, Argonne (Ill.) Nat. Lab, 1975-80; mem. tech. staff Bell Labs, Naperville, Ill., 1980-85; staff dir. McDonald's Corp., Oakbrook, Ill., 1985—; sec., bd. dirs. Grave Mill Corp., Hinsdale, Ill., 1981—. Contbr. articles to profl. jours. Served with U.S. Army, 1969-71. Mem. Am. Soc. Mech. Engrs. (section chmn. 1980-81, nat. rep. 1982—), Hinsdale Jaycees (treas. 1980-83), Tau Beta Pi, Omicron Delta Kappa, Pi Tau Sigma. Mem. United Ch. of Christ. Office: McDonald's Corp McDonald's Plaza Oak Brook IL 60521

KOPAC, MILAN JAMES, microsurgery consultant, cell biologist; b. Ravenna, Nebr., Mar. 12, 1905; s. James and Mary B. (Skala) K. BS, U. Nebr., 1927, MS, 1929, DSc (hon.), 1962; PhD, U. Calif., Berkeley, 1934. Investigator Dry Tortugas Marine Lab., 1933-35, 37; nat. research fellow NYU, 1934-35, research assoc. biology, 1934-38; vis. asst. prof., 1938-43, asst. prof., 1944-46, assoc. prof., 1947-49, prof. biology, 1949-73, prof. emeritus, 1973—, head all-univ. dept. biology, 1963-70, dir. Robert Chambers Lab. Microsurgery, 1968-77; specialist in microsurgery; vis. instr. U. Nebr., 1934, vis. prof. biology, 1962; mem. physiology fellowships panel NIH, 1962-66; chmn. Gordon Research Conf. Cancer, 1964; sci. adv. com. Damon Runyon Mel. Fund Cancer Research, 1950-73, chmn., 1966-69, sci. dir., 1967-69; adv. com. instnl. grants Am. Cancer Soc., 1963-66. Cons. editor: Mechanisms of Cell Division, 1951, Cancer Cytology and Cytochemistry, 1956; contbr. over 200 articles to books, tech. and sci. jours. Served to 2d lt., inf., USAR, 1927-37. Fellow N.Y. Acad. Scis. (councilor, v.p. 1958, pres. 1960, trustee 1960-62; Gold Medal award 1969); mem. Am. Soc. Cytology (founder), Harvey Soc. (life), Am. Assn. Cancer Research, Sigma Xi (pres. NYU chpt. 1953-55). Home: 521 Brookside Dr Lincoln NE 68528

KOPE, MARTIN GREGORY, agency administrator; b. Detroit, June 20, 1933; s. John Joseph and Elsie Elizabeth (Tatina) K.; m. Beverly Rae Kunde, Aug. 21, 1954 (dec. Nov. 1958); m. Sally Ann Bosz-Roser, Dec. 13, 1959; children: Kimberly, Michael, Lynn, Kathryn. BA, Capitol U., Columbus, Ohio, 1955; MDiv, Capital U. Theol. Sem., 1959; AS in Mgmt., Wayne State U., 1969; MS, DePaul U., 1983. Pastor Christ Luth. Ch., Haysville, Ind., 1959-64, Peace Luth. Ch., Evansville, Ind., 1964-68; rehab. specialist United Community Services of Met. Detroit, 1969-71; assoc. dir. Goodwill Industries of Greater Detroit, 1971-77, dir. human services, 1977-84, v.p., 1984—; human services cons. Wayne Regional Interagy. Coordinating Com., Detroit, 1984—. Founding pres., bd. dirs. Housing for Exceptional People, Detroit, 1972—; com. chmn. Wayne County Life Services System, Detroit, 1983—. Recipient Spl. Honor and Recognition award Housing for Exceptional Citizens, 1984, Ednl. grant Rehab. Services Adminstrn., 1968. Mem. Nat. Rehab. Assn., Nat. Assn. Rehab. Facilities, Mich. Assn. Retarded Citizens (exec. com. 1974-77). Office: Goodwill Industries of Greater Detroit 3132 Trumball Detroit MI 48216

KOPEL, DAVID, psychologist, educator; b. Czestachowa, Poland, Feb. 22, 1910; came to U.S., 1913, naturalized, 1924; s. Joseph and Shandel Mary (Motel) K. B.S., Northwestern U., 1930, MS, 1934, PhD, 1935; postgrad., Wiener Psychoanalytischen Vereinigung, Austria, 1948-49, U. Chgo., 1950-52, Psychoanalytic Psychology Study Group, 1955-70. Diplomate: Am. Bd. Profl. Psychology (clin. psychology). Research and teaching asst. Northwestern U., 1933-34, psychologist, instr., 1934-38; sch. psychologist Evanston (Ill.) Pub. Schs., 1935-37; tchr. psychology and edn. Chgo. State U. (formerly Chgo. Tchrs. Coll.), 1938-43, 49—, dir. Grad. Sch., 1954-61, coordinator internat. summer study tours, prof. psychology and edn., 1958-76, emeritus, 1976—; supt. U.S. Dependents Schs. System, Austria, 1946-47; specialist tchr. edn. U.S. Allied Commn., Austria, 1947-49; summer faculty Columbia U., 1938, Alameda (Calif.) Guidance Center, 1941, Ohio State U., 1942, U. Ill., 1950; cons. Gary (Ind.) and Chgo. Pub. Schs., Chgo. Psychol. Inst., Temple Sholom; dir. Northwestern U. Psycho-Edn. Clinic, Chgo., 1950-51; pvt. practice psychotherapy, 1952—. Author: (with Paul A. Witty) Diagnostic Child Study Record and Manual, 1936, Reading and the Educative Process, 1938, Mental Hygiene and Modern Education, 1939; contbr.: Progress in Clinical Psychology, 1953; co-editor: Ill. Schs. Jour., 1966-68; contbr. articles to profl. jours. Served to 1st lt. AUS, 1943-46; to lt. col., Res. 1949-63. Decorated Army Commendation and campaign medals. Fellow Am. Psychol. Assn.; mem. Ill. Psychol. Assn. (treas.), Am. Orthopsychiat. Assn., AAUP (pres. Chgo. chpt.), Internat. Reading Assn. (pres. Chgo. chpt.), Internat. Soc. Gen. Semantics (pres. Chgo. chpt.), Chgo. Psychol. Assn. (pres.), Psychoanalytic Psychol. Study Group (co-convener, chmn.), Internat. House Assn., U. Chgo. (bd. dirs.). Home and Office: 6700 S Oglesby Ave Apt 2101 Chicago IL 60649

KOPERSKI, ROSEANN ELIZABETH, insurance agency executive; b. Toledo, Ohio, Mar. 8, 1947; d. Anthony John and Stella Elizabeth (Guziolek) Rogowski; m. Kenneth James Koperski, Aug. 20, 1966; children—Karleen Marie, Kristin Marie, Kelly Ann. Client service rep. W.F. Roemer Ins., Inc., Toledo, 1965-83, asst. v.p. comml. lines underwriting, 1983—. Mem. Profl. Ins. Agts. Assn., Ins. Women Toledo (welfare chmn. 1973-74). Roman Catholic. Home: 3863 Almeda Dr Toledo OH 43612 Office: WF Roemer Ins Inc 3912 Sunforest Ct Toledo OH 43623

KOPIDLANSKY, VICTOR RAYMOND, lawyer; b. Manitowoc, Wis., Dec. 15, 1931; s. Albert M. and Mary A. (Radey) K.; m. Diana Meredith Chrobak, July 9, 1960; children: Lisa, Mark, Cynthia, Erik. BA, St. Norbert Coll., 1956; cert., U. Copenhagen, 1959; MMS, U. Notre Dame, 1960; JD, John Marshall Law Sch., 1964. Bar: Ill. 1964. Mgr. Texaco, Inc., Chgo., 1959-64; asst. to treas. Texaco, Inc., N.Y.C., 1965; atty. Motorola Inc., Chgo., 1965-68; internat. atty. Motorola Inc., Geneva, 1968-74; v.p., gen. atty. Motorola Inc., Pheonix, 1974-77; corp. v.p., asst. gen. counsel Motorola Inc., Schaumburg, Ill., 1977—. Author Book of Priors of the English-German Nation of the Sorbonne, 1958. Served to staff sgt. USAF, 1950-53, ETO. Fulbright scholar. 1958-59. Mem. ABA, Chgo. Bar Assn., Delta Epsilon Sigma. Republican. Roman Catholic. Avocations: skiing, boating. Home: 381 Meadow Ln Palatine IL 60067 Office: Motorola Inc 1303 E Algonquin Rd Schaumburg IL 60196

KOPISCHKE, MARK S., controller; b. Mpls., May 28, 1955; s. Rudolph Alfred and Grace Elizabeth (Jewison) K.; m. Deborah Ann Schilling, Dec. 27, 1985. AA, Rochester (Minn.) State Jr. Coll., 1975; BS, Mankato (Minn.) State U., 1978. CPA, Minn. From sales tax acct. to tax supr. Gelco Corp., Eden Prairie, Minn., 1978-80; from staff acct. to acctg. dir. Interregional Services Corp., Mpls., 1980-84; controller Farm Credit Leasing Services Corp., Mpls., 1984—. Mem. Am. Inst. CPA's, Minn. CPA Soc., Nat. Soc. Accts. for Coops. Roman Catholic. Avocations; golf, raquetball.

KOPP, RONALD SINCLAIR, lawyer; b. Canton, Ohio, May 21, 1954; s. Cecil Gene and Sue Ann (Sinclair) K.; m. Jean Elizabeth Hicks, July 3, 1982; children: Meghan Elizabeth, Molly Sinclair. AB cum laude, Miami U., 1976; JD, Ohio State U., 1979. Assoc. Roetzel & Andress, Akron, Ohio, 1979-86, ptnr., 1986—; gen. counsel Akron Beacon Jour. Charity Fund. Commr. Urban Design Commn., Akron, 1984—; mem. Summit County Hist. Soc., 1982—, Leadership Akron, 1986—; co-organizer United Way, Akron, 1986; deacon Disciples of Christ Ch., Akron. Mem. ABA, Ohio Bar Assn., Akron Bar Assn. (chmn. continuing legal edn. com.), Soc. Mfg. Engrs., Robotics Inst. Republican. Club: Akron City. Avocations: running, bicycling, golf, fishing. Office: Roetzel & Andress 75 E Market St Akron OH 44308

KOPP, WILLIAM LOUIS, physician, educator; b. Chgo., Nov. 7, 1925; s. Louis Henry and Louise (Vasconcelles) K.; m. Alice Martin; children: Thomas M., Douglas E. BS, U. Mich., 1951, MD, 1954, MS, 1962. Asst. assoc. prof. VA Hosp. U. Wis., Madison, 1962-70; physician Dean Med. Ctr., Madison, 1970—; chief internal medicine St. Mary's Hosp., Madison, 1977-79. Contbr. articles to profl. jours. Served to capt. U.S. Army, 1955-57. Fellow ACP, Am. Acad. Allergy; mem. Cen. Soc. Clin. Research, Dane County Med. Soc. (pres. 1986—), Phi Beta Kappa. Avocations: music, photography, jogging. Home: 6 Yellowstone Ct Madison WI 53705 Office: Dean Med Ctr 1313 Fish Hatchery Rd Madison WI 53715

KOPRIVICA, DOROTHY MARY, management consultant, real estate and insurance broker; b. St. Louis, May 27, 1921; d. Mitar and Fema (Guzina) K. B.S., Washington U., St. Louis, 1962; cert. in def. inventory mgmt. Dept. Def., 1968. Mgmt. analyst Transp. Supply and Maintenance Command, St. Louis, 1954-57, Dept. Army Transp. Materiel Command, St. Louis, 1957-62; program analyst Dept. Army Aviation System Command, St. Louis, 1962-74, spl. asst. to comdr., 1974-78; ins. broker D. Koprivica, Ins., St. Louis, 1978—; real estate broker Century 21 KARE Realty, St. Louis, 1978—. Mem. Bus. and Profl. Women (pres. 1974-75). Eastern Orthodox. Lodge: Order Eastern Star.

KOPSTAIN, CLEMENT CRAIG, university executive; b. Berwyn, Ill., Nov. 28, 1938; s. Clement Joseph and Priscilla Ann (Parsons) K.; m. Judith Anna Stoneberg, Jan. 12, 1963; children—Lori Kristine, Eric Craig. B.S. in Bus. Adminstrn., Roosevelt U., 1969; Cert. in Advanced Mgmt., U. Chgo., 1970; M.A., Northwestern U., 1978. Corp. trust adminstr. Continental Ill. Nat. Bank, Chgo., 1962-64; asst. personnel dir. Vapor Corp., Niles, Ill., 1964-72; mgr. compensation and staffing Honeywell Corp., Arlington Heights, Ill., 1972-74; assoc. dir. Northwestern U., Evanston, Ill., 1974-78; mgr. Deloitte Haskins & Sells, Chgo., 1978-84; dir. engring. placement Northwestern U., 1985—; pvt. practice counseling, Mt. Prospect, 1985—; vice chmn. Task Force on Correctional Industries, State of Ill., 1972-74; cons. USN, 1978. Author: Basic Intelligence Tng. and Evaluation, 1982. Pres. Wheeling High Sch. Career Adv. Council, Ill., 1972-75; bd. dirs., corp. sec. Pace Inst., Chgo., 1973-75. Served to cmdr. USNR. Recipient John Howard award John Howard Assn., 1970. Mem. Naval Res. Assn., Res. Officers Assn., Phi Delta Kappa, Beta Gamma Sigma. Lutheran. Lodge: Elks (treas. 1959-60). Home: 623 N Elmhurst Ave Mount Prospect IL 60056

KOR, EVA, realtor; b. Portz, Romania, Jan. 31, 1935; d. Alexander and Jaffa (Hersch) Mozes; m. Michael Kor, Apr. 27, 1960; children: Alexander, Rina. Student, Ind. State U., 1979—. Draftsperson Ewing Miller Architecture, Terre Haute, Ind., 1960-61, 65-77, Constrn. Engring. Service, Terre Haute, 1969-77; real estate salesperson Johnson-Barcus Inc., Terre Haute, 1977-79, Calico Realty, Terre Haute, 1979-82, Williams and Assocs., Terre Haute, 1982—. Founder, exec. dir. Children of Auschwitz Nazi Deadly Lab. Experiment Survivors (C.A.N.D.L.E.S.) Orgn. for Auschwitz Twins, Terre Haute, 1983-86, ednl. dir. 1983—, initiator, dir. C.A.N.D.L.E.S. mock trial and inquest of Josef Mengele, Jerusalem and Terre Haute, 1985; organizer, dir. ICH Holocaust Conf. on Prejudice, Terre Haute, 1981-82; organizer Hadassah-Freedom Petition for Soviet Jews, Terre Haute, 1976-77.

Recipient Jewish Activism award Jewish News & Views, N.Y., 1985. Mem. Nat. Assn. Realtors. Democrat. Avocations: history, activism. Office: CANDLES 24 W Lawrin Blvd Terre Haute IN 47803

KORANDA, BRIAN KENNETH, psychologist; b. Baudette, Minn., June 10, 1955; s. Kenneth E. and Margaret D. (Alich) K.; m. Louise Quackenbush, June 2, 1979; children: David A St. Denis, Ellen M., Michael B. AA, Crosier Jr. Coll. Sem., 1975; BA, Moorhead (Minn.) State U., 1979; MA, U. N.D., 1980, postgrad., 1980. Lic. psychologist, Minn. Instr. U. Minn., Crookston, 1981-84; psychologist, sr. case mgr. Northwestern Apts., Crookston, 1980-85; psychologist Faribault, Martin, Watonwon Human Service Bd., Blue Earth, Minn., 1985-86, Counseling Assn. S. Minn., Blue Earth, 1986—. Mem. Am. Psychol. Assn. (assoc.). Democrat. Roman Catholic. Avocations: carpentry, stamp collecting, gardening. Home: 204 W 5th Blue Earth MN 56013 Office: Counseling Assocs care of United Hosp Moore St Blue Earth MN 56013

KORBECKI, GREGORY ALAN, system programmer; b. Chgo., Dec. 9, 1955; s. Thomas A. Korbecki and Isabell (Sabaj) K.; m. Rebecca Lynn Hill, Aug. 18, 1979; children: Eric Allen, Sara Lynn. BS in Computer Sci., So. Ill. U., 1978; MS in Info. Systems (with honors), Roosevelt U., 1987. Sr. system programmer Kraft Inc., Glenview, Ill., 1978-80; system programmer A, Volvo-White Truck Corp., Libertyville, Ill., 1980-82; tech. system specialist Zurich Am. Ins., Schaumburg, Ill., 1982-84; system programmer Unocal Refining and Mktg., Schaumburg, 1984—. Mem. Computer Measurement Group, Share Inc. MVS Performance Group. Office: Unocal Refining and Mktg 1650 E Golf Rd W-85 Schaumburg IL 60196-1088

KORBER, KENNETH EDWARD, physician assistant, consultant, medical writer; b. Queens, N.Y., Nov. 30, 1955; s. Francis Xavier and Margaret Adele (Titus) K.; m. Marcia Ann Kozikowski, Nov. 8, 1986. BS in Biology, SUNY, 1978; MHS, Yale U., 1985; cert. microsurg. techniques, Harvard Med. Sch., 1981. Clin. research asst. L.I. Orthopedic Specialists, Smithtown, N.Y., 1980-85; research asst. (pathology) Yale U. Sch. Medicine, New Haven, 1984-85; research assoc. (surgery) Washington U. Sch. Medicine, St. Louis, 1985—; tech. dir. microsurgery lab. Washington U. plastic surgery div., St. Louis, 1985—. Author: Handbook of Microsurgery in the Research Lab, 1987; cons. editor Microsurgery, 1987—; assoc. editor Lab. Microsurgery, 1985—; co-author articles in profl. jours.; mem. editorial bd. Assn. Surg. Technologists. Mem. Soc. Microsurg. Specialists. Roman Catholic. Avocations: bonsai horticulture, tennis, photography, golf. Home: 4019 E Westminster Pl Saint Louis MO 63108 Office: Washington U Sch Medicine Clin Sci Research Bldg Box 8109 Saint Louis MO 63110

KORBITZ, BERNARD CARL, oncologist-hematologist, medical educator, medical-legal consultant; b. Lewistown, Mont., Feb. 18, 1935; s. Fredrick William and Rose Eleanore (Ackmann) K.; m. Constance Kay Bolz, June 22, 1957; children—Paul Bernard, Guy Karl. B.S. in Med. Sci., U. Wis.-Madison, 1957, M.D., 1960, M.S. in Oncology, 1962; LL.B., LaSalle U., 1972. Asst. prof. medicine and clin. oncology, U. Wis. Med. Sch., Madison, 1967-71; dir. medicine Presbyn. Med. Ctr., Denver, 1971-73; practice medicine specializing in oncology, hematology, Madison, 1973-76; med. oncologist, hematologist Radiologic Ctr. Meth. Hosp., Omaha, 1976-82; practice medicine specializing in oncology, hematology, Omaha, 1982—; sci. advisor Citizen's Environ. Com., Denver, 1972-73; mem. Cancer Com. Bergan Mercy Hosp., Omaha, 1982—; Meth. Hosp., Omaha, 1977—; dir. Bernard C. Korbitz, P.C., Omaha, 1983—; bd. dirs., pres. Korbitz Langdon, P.C. Contbr. articles to profl. jours. Webelos leader Denver area Council, Mid. Am. Council of Nebr. Boy Scouts Am.; bd. elders King of Kings Luth. Ch., Omaha, 1979-80; mem. People to People Del. Cancer Update to People's Republic China, 1986, Eastern Europe and USSR, 1987; mem. U.S. Senatorial Club, 1984, Republican Presdl. Task Force, 1984. Served to capt. USAF, 1962-64. Fellow ACP, Royal Soc. Health; mem. Am. Soc. Clin. Oncology, Am. Coll. Legal-Medicine, Am. Soc. Internal Medicine, AMA, Nebr. Med. Assn., Omaha Med. Society, Omaha Clin. Soc., Phi Eta Sigma, Phi Beta Kappa, Phi Kappa Phi, Alpha Omega Alpha. Avocations: photography fishing, travel. Home: 9024 Leavenworth St Omaha NE 68114 Office: 8300 Dodge St Suite 226 Omaha NE 68114

KORCZAK, EDWARD STANLEY, association executive; b. Chgo., July 12, 1945; s. Stanley and Helen (Dzik) K.; m. Linda Marie Venzon, May 30, 1969; children—Jori, Dana; m. Jacqueline Mandy Utt, Oct. 16, 1977; children—Grant, Dirk. B.A., Northeastern Ill. U., 1973; postgrad. Harper Coll., 1973-76; Assn. Mgmt. Degree, U. Notre Dame/U.S. C. of C., 1977. With Charles Pfizer Co., Chgo., 1963-67; sales mgr. Kaynar Mfg. Co., Chgo., 1967-69; asst. exec. dir. Profl. Photographers Am., Des Plaines, Ill., 1969-78; exec. dir. Retail Floorcovering Inst., Inc., Chgo., 1978—. Bd. dirs. Floor Covering Industry Edn. Found.; pres. Nat. Council for Small Bus. Devel., Chgo., 1974-75; council mem., com. chmn. Resurrection Luth. Ch., 1981-84, 87-90. Served with U.S. Army, 1965-67. Mem. Am. Soc. Assn. Execs., Chgo. Soc. Assn. Execs., U.S. C. of C. Republican. Lutheran. Office: 13-154 Merchandise Mart Chicago IL 60654

KORENBLAT, PHILLIP ERWIN, allergist, immunologist; b. Little Rock, June 23, 1935; married; Arlene Korenblat; 3 children. B in Med. Sci., U. Ark., Fayetteville, 1956; MD, U. Ark., Little Rock, 1960. Diplomate Am. Bd. Internal Medicine, Am. Bd. Allergy and Immunology. Intern Jewish Hosp. of St. Louis, 1960-61, residency, 1963-65, attending physician, allergy cons., 1966—, also mem. med. exec. and med. staff councils; fellow Scripps Clinic and Research Found., La Jolla, Calif., 1965-66; practice medicine specializing in allergy and immunology Associated Med. Specialists, Inc., St. Louis, 1966—; attending physician, allergy cons. Barnes Hosp., St. Louis, 1970—; assoc. clin. prof. med. Washington U., St. Louis, 1981—, postgrad. allergy program dir., 1978—. Co-editor: Allergy: Theory and Practice, 1984. Bd. dirs. Jewish Community Ctr. Assn., St. Louis; mem. fin. com. The Jewish Fedn., St. Louis. Served to capt. U.S. Army, 1961-63. Fellow Am. Acad. Allergy (chmn. credentials com.), Mo. Allergy Assn. (pres. 1981-82), Am. Coll. Allergy; mem. AMA, Soc. Internal Medicine. Club: Internists (St. Louis) (pres. 1975). Home: 11249 Tureen Dr Saint Louis MO 63141 Office: Associated Med Specialists Inc 10287 Clayton Rd Saint Louis MO 63124

KORGESKI, GREGORY PAUL, clinical psychologist; b. Scranton, Pa., May 15, 1954; s. Frank Alexander and Shirley Josephine (Fitch) K.; m. Elaine Jeanne Madigan, July 15, 1978; 1 stepson, Michael L. Madigan. BS, U. Scranton, 1976; PhD, U. Minn., 1981. Lic. cons. psychologist, Minn. Psychologist Washington County Human Services, Oakdale, Minn., 1981-86; dir. counseling ctr. Hamline U., St. Paul, 1983-86; psychologist Kiel Clinic, St. Paul, 1986; sr. clin. psychologist Met. Clinic of Counseling, Mpls., 1986—; cons. Kiel Mgmt. Counsellors, 1985. Recipient Richard Elliott award U. Minn., 1982. Vol. supr. Walk-In Counseling Ctr., Mpls., 1979—, bd. dirs., 1986—. Mem. Am. Psychol. Assn., Minn. Psychol. Assn. Contbr. articles to profl. jours. Office: Met Clinic of Counseling Inc 625 Highway 10 Blaine MN 55434

KORNEL, LUDWIG, educator, physician, scientist; b. Jaslo, Poland, Feb. 27, 1923; came to U.S., 1958, naturalized, 1970; s. Ezriel Edward and Ernestine (Karpf) K.; m. Esther Muller, May 27, 1952; children—Ezriel Edward, Amiel Mark. Student, U. Kazan Med. Inst., USSR, 1943-45; M.D., Wroclaw (Poland) Med. Acad., 1950; Ph.D., U. Birmingham, Eng., 1958. Intern Univ. Hosp., Wroclaw, 1949-50, Hadassah-Hebrew U. Hosp., Jerusalem, 1950-51; resident medicine Hadassah-Hebrew U. Hosp., 1952-55; Brit. Council scholar, Univ. research fellow endocrinology U. Birmingham, 1955-57, lectr. medicine, 1956-57; fellow endocrinology U. Ala. Med. Ctr., 1958-59, successively asst. prof., assoc. prof., prof. medicine, 1961-67; dir. steroid sect. U. Ala. Med. Center, 1962-67, assoc. prof. biochemistry, 1965-67; postdoctoral trainee in steroid biochemistry U. Utah, 1959-61; prof. medicine U. Ill. Coll. Medicine, Chgo., 1967-71; dir. steroid unit Presbyn.-St. Lukes Hosp., Chgo., 1967—; assoc. biochemist Presbyn.-St. Lukes Hosp., 1967-70, sr. biochemist on sci. staff, 1970-71, attending physician, 1967-71; prof. medicine and biochemistry Rush Med. Coll., 1970—; sr. attending physician, sr. scientist Rush-Presbyn.-St. Lukes Med. Cen., 1970—; hon. guest lectr. Polish Acad. Sci., Warsaw, 1965; vis. prof. Kanazawa (Japan) U., 1973, 82. Mem. editorial bd. Clin. Physiology and Biochemistry, 1982; co-editor: Yearbook of Endocrinology, 1986—; contbr. articles on endocrinology and steroid biochemistry to profl. jours. Recipient Physicians Recognition award AMA, 1969, 73, 76, 81, Outstanding New Citizen award Citzenship Council Met. Chgo., 1970. Fellow Am. Coll. Clin. Pharmacology and Chemotherapy, Nat. Acad. Clin. Biochemistry (bd. dirs. 1982-86), Royal Soc. Health; mem. AMA, AAAS, AAUP, Endocrine Soc., Am. Fedn. Clin. Research, N.Y. Acad. Scis., Am. Physiol. Soc., Cen. Soc. Clin. Research, Am. Acad. Polit. and Social Scis., Fedn. Am. Socs. for Exptl. Biology (nat. corr. 1975—), Sigma Xi. Home: 6757 N LeRoy Ave Lincolnwood IL 60646 Office: Rush Presbyn St Lukes Med Ctr 1753 W Congress Pkwy Chicago IL 60612

KORNHAUS, DEBORAH ANN, savings and loan executive; b. Kansas City, Mo., Nov. 8, 1954; d. Lawrence David and Vera Mae (Rowe) Winsky; m. John Patrick Kornhaus, June 2, 1979; 1 child, Ashley Lynne. BS, Kans. State U., 1976. CPA, Kans. Staff acct. Grant Thornton, Kansas City, 1976-78; supr. Touche Ross & Co., Kansas City, 1978-81; v.p. fin. Colonial Savings, Shawnee Mission, Kans., 1981—. Vol. Campaign to Reelect Bob Dole, Johnson County, Kans., Am. Cancer Soc., Johnson County, Campaign for Excellence Shawnee Mission Sch. Dist., 1987. Recipient Leadership Overland Park award Johnson County Community Coll. and Overland Park C. of C., 1986. Mem. Am. Inst. CPA's, Fin. Mgrs. Soc., Kans. Soc. CPA's, Econ. Devel. Com. for Kans., Overland Park C. of C. (mem. Pres. Club). Republican. Roman Catholic. Avocations: tennis, aerobics, jogging. Office: Colonial Savings 4000 Somerset Shawnee Mission KS 66208

KOROLY, MICHAEL VINCENT, gynecologist obstetrician; b. Akron, Ohio, Jan. 26, 1949; s. Michael and Dorothy Anna (Zurz) K.; m. Susan Kay Deavers, Aug. 28, 1971. BS in Pharmacy, Ohio No. U., 1972; DO, U. Health Sci., 1978. Diplomate Am. Bd. Ob-Gyn. Intern Normandy Hosps., St. Louis, 1978-79; resident JFK Hosps., Stratford, N.J., 1979-83; practice medicine specializing in ob-gyn Cuyahoga Falls, 1983—; chmn., chief executive officer Applied Biotechs. Inc., Akron, Ohio, 1986—; chmn. ob-gyn Cuyahoga Falls Gen. Hosp., 1983-86; asst. clin. prof. Ohio U., Athens, Ohio 1983—, U. Health Sci., Kansas City, Mo. 1983—; adj. asst. prof. Inst. Biomed. Engring., U. Akron. Contbr. articles to profl. jour.; inventor Koroly artificial Heart. Mem. Ohio Ballet, Akron Symphony, Akron Art Inst.; trustee Precious Parents, Inc., Akron, 1984—. Mem. Am. Coll. Osteopathic Ob-Gyn (sr.), Am. Osteopathic Assn. (Nat. Osteopathic Found. grantee 1981-83), Internat. Soc. Artificial Organs, Am. Soc. Artificial Internal Organs, Ohio State Med. Assn., Akron Obstet. Soc. Republican. Clubs: Portage Country (Akron). Office: 2808 Front St Cuyahoga Falls OH 44221

KOROSE, MARSHA SOBY, military officer; b. Lackawanna, N.Y., Aug. 16, 1952; d. Richard Edward and Mary Louise (Glass) Soby; m. Robert John Korose, Feb. 11, 1978. BS in Biology, Fla. State U., 1974; postgrad., Tex. A&M U., 1975-76; MS in Meteorology, St. Louis U., 1985. Commd. 2d lt. USAF, 1975, advanced through grades to maj., 1986, atmospheric forecaster Cheyenne Mountain region NORAD, 1976-78, solar forecaster, 1978-79, satellite analyst Guam Joint Typhoon Warning Ctr., 1979-81, aerial reconnaissance weather officer, 1981-83; chief readiness support Environ. Tech. Applications Ctr. Scott AFB, Ill., 1985—. Decorated Air medal with one bronze oak leaf cluster. Mem. Am. Meteorol. Soc. (treas. 1975-76, 77-78, 85-86, sec. 1979-83, speaker, chair speakers bur. 1985-87), Chi Epsilon Pi. Avocations: tng., showing dressage horses. Office: USAF Environ Tech Applications Ctr Scott AFB IL 62225

KORSAK, MICHAEL THOMAS, educator; b. Chgo., Nov. 24, 1952; s. Norbert Thomas and Adeline (Muslak) K. B.S.Ed., Chgo. State U., 1973, M.S.Ed., 1976; postgrad. St. Xavier Coll., 1976-81, U. Chgo., 1978, Nat. Coll. Edn., 1982. Indsl. edn. instr. Carl Sandburg High Sch., Orland Park, Ill., 1974-81; lectr. Chgo. State U., 1981; dept. chmn. Victor J. Andrew High Sch., Tinley Park, Ill., 1981—; part-time instr. Moraine Valley Coll., 1981—; cons. Tech. Edn. Research Corp., 1974. Pres. Hurley Homeowners Civic Assn., Chgo., 1976. Recipient Award of Merit Am. Vocat. Assn., 1982. Mem. Nat. Assn. Secondary Sch. Prins., Phi Delta Kappa, Epsilon Phi Tau. Roman Catholic. Home: 3726 W 68th Pl Chicago IL 60629 Office: 171st and 90th Aves Tinley Park IL 60477

KORSVIK, WILLIAM JAMES, banker, consultant; b. Chgo., Sept. 9, 1917; s. Oscar J. and Anna (Shine) K.; m. Janet Ruth Greene, Mar. 5, 1949; children: Sherry, Holly, Scott, Heather. BSBA, Northwestern U., 1949; MBA, U Chgo., 1955; grad., Grad. Sch. Banking U. Wis., 1951. With The First Nat. Bank Chgo., 1935-49, asst. cashier, 1949-56, asst. v.p., 1957-61, v.p. research, 1962-74, v.p. internat. banking, 1974-78, sr. v.p. internat. banking, 1979-82; assoc. dir. Grad. Sch. Banking, U. Wis., 1953-83; assoc. sec. fed. adv. council FRS, 1956—; cons. Kellogg Grad. Sch. Mgmt. Northwestern U., 1983—; dir. First Am. Savs. and Loan, Benton, Ill.; chmn. bd. dirs. Life Savs. Assn. Am., Melrose Park, Ill., 1986-87. Contbg. columnist Chgo. Tribune, 1974-80. Life trustee Chgo. Theol. Sem. Served with U.S. Army, 1942-45. Democrat. Congregationalist. Clubs: Econ., Univ., Bankers. Home: 1738 Central Ave Wilmette IL 60091

KORTE, RALPH, construction company executive. B.S. in Bus. Adminstrn., So. Ill. U. Founder Ralph Korte Constrn. Co., St. Louis, 1958, now chmn. bd.; dir. Mark Twain St. Louis Bank. Pres. So. Ill. U. Found., Edwardsville, 1982-83; pres. Cahokia Mound council, Boy Scouts Am., 1980-81, N. Central Regional bd. dirs.; exec. bd. St. Louis Regional Commerce and Growth Assn.; bd. dirs. New Age Coll. for Living, Webster Groves, Mo., St. Joseph's Hosp., Highland, Ill. Recipient Alumnus of Yr. award So. Ill. U., 1978; Silver Beaver award, 1984. Mem. Assoc. Gen. Contractors Am. (nat. bd. dirs.), So. Ill. Builders Assn. (past pres.), World Bus. Council, Young Pres.'s Orgn., Highland C. of C. (past pres.). Home: 7 Briarwood Highland IL 62249 Office: Ralph Korte Constrn Co Inc 700 St Louis Union Station #300 Saint Louis MO 63103-2251

KORTEBEIN, STUART ROWLAND, orthopaedic surgeon; b. Evanston, Ill., Apr. 17, 1930; s. Rowland J. and Grace K.; m. Alice C. Johnson, July 10, 1954; children: William, David. AA, North Park Coll., 1950; BS, Wheaton Coll., 1952; postgrad., North Park Theol. Sem., 1952-53; MD, Loyola U., 1957; JD, Jefferson Coll. Law, 1983. Diplomate Nat. Bd. Med. Examiners, Am. Bd. Orthopaedic Surgery. Intern Akron (Ohio) Gen. Hosp., 1957-58, resident, 1961-64; resident Hines (Ill.) VA Hosp., 1960, Northwestern U., Chgo., 1964; practice medicine specializing in orthopedic surgery Arlington Heights, Ill., 1965—; chief dept. orthopedic surgery U.S. Naval Hosp., Great Lakes, Ill., 1987; attending surgeon Northwest Community Hosp., Arlington Heights, 1969—, chief orthopedics, 1976; assoc. surgeon Shriners Hosp., Chgo., 1968; v.p. Magnetrans Research and Devel. Corp., 1972-84, Window Well Protectors, Inc., McHenry, Ill., 1983-86; coordinator med. cons. Compusoft Corp., Darien, Ill., 1984—; instr. emergency medicine technician course Harper Coll., 1973-84; vis. instr. police self-def. tactics Oakton Community Coll., 1984—. Water safety instr. ARC, 1949-54; aux. police officer City of Rolling Meadows, Ill., 1985—; bd. dirs. Chicagoland Drug Prevention Program, 1971-84; deacon North Haven Covenant Ch., Cuyahoga Falls, Ohio, 1963; choir dir. First Bapt. Ch., Twenty Nine Palms, Calif., 1959-60. Served to lt., M.C., USNR, 1958-60. Mem. ACS, Am. Acad. Orthopaedic Surgeons, Physicians Martial Arts Assn., Soc. Black Belts Am., AMA (Physicians Recognition award 1970-88), Christian Med. Soc., Ill. State Med. Soc., Chgo. Med. Soc., Chgo. Bar Assn. (student 1982-84), Ill. Trial Lawyers Assn., Assn. Trial Lawyers Am., Fraternal Order of Police, Hakko-Ryu Jitsu Fedn., Jiu Jitsu Black Belt Fedn. Am. (pres. Ill. rep. 1971-74), Oikiru-Ryu Ju Jitsu (Sandan instr. 1977-85). Home and Office: 357 S Belmont Ave Arlington Heights IL 60005

KORTY, DAVID JOSEPH, transportation company executive; b. Patterson, N.J., Aug. 10, 1950; s. Raymond Victor and Agnes Gertrude (Vaughan) K.; m. Kay Ann Whitley, June 25, 1977; children: Jonathan Joseph, Andrea Bess. BS in Indsl. Mgmt., Purdue U., 1972; MBA, U. Indpls., 1983. Cert. prodn. and inventory mgr. Prodn. supr. Essex Wire Co., Elwood, Ind., 1972-73; prodn. scheduler Amos Plastics, Edinburg, Ind., 1973-75; prodn. planner Shellar-Globe, Portland, Ind., 1975-76; purchase parts mgr. Farm Fans, Inc., Indpls., 1976-84; planning and inventory coordinator Comml. Filters, Lebanon, Ind., 1984-86; inventory control supr. Am. Trans Air, Indpls., 1986—. Pres. Young Dems. Purdue, West Lafayette, Ind., 1971-72; del. Dem. State Conv., Indpls., 1972; Dem. precinct committeeman, New Whiteland, Ind., 1978. Mem. Am. Prodn. and Inventory Control Soc., Assn. MBA Execs., MBA Alumni Assn. Avocations: jogging, camping. Home: 617 Oakland Way New Whiteland IN 46184 Office: Am Trans Air 2141 S High School Rd Indianapolis IN 46491

KORVER, GERRIT ROZEBOOM (GERRY), purchasing executive; b. Orange City, Iowa, June 17, 1952. BA, Northwestern Coll., 1977. Purchasing mgr., textiles/ops. K-Products, Inc., Orange City, 1978—. Bd. dirs. Northwestern Coll. Nat. Alumni Bd., Orange City, 1986—. Mem. Nat. Assn. Purchasing Mgmt. (cert.). Avocation: athletics. Home: 401 5th St SE Orange City IA 51041 Office: K-Products Inc Industrial Air Park Orange City IA 51041

KOSA, SAMUEL JOHN, rubber manufacturing company executive, consulting engineer; b. Youngstown, Ohio, June 4, 1947; s. Victor and Anna Marie (Blotor) K.; m. Barbara Ann Popa, Sept. 4, 1971; children—Katherine Marie, Laura Ann. B.Engring. in Civil Engring., Youngstown State U., 1971, postgrad., 1973, 75. Registered profl. engr., Ohio, Pa., N.Y., Iowa. Engr., J.N. Cernica & Assocs., Youngstown, 1965-72; v.p., ptnr. Concrete Testing Services, Inc., Youngstown, 1969-74; chief engr. Inter-Lock Steel Co., Sharon, Pa., 1972; underground support engr. Comml. Shearing, Inc., Youngstown, 1972-74; project engr. Hale & Kullgren, Inc., Akron, Ohio, 1974; cons. engr. Samuel J. Kosa & Assocs., Canton, Ohio, 1974—; chief civil/structural engr. C.F. Simmers div. Pollock Research & Design, Inc., Canfield, Ohio, 1974-76; instr. Youngstown State U., 1976-77; project engr. Firestone Tire & Rubber Co., Akron, 1977-86; sr. engr. Goodyear Tire & Rubber Co., Akron, 1986—. Mem. Nat. Soc. Profl. Engrs., Ohio Soc. Profl. Engrs., ASCE (pres. Youngstown br. 1975-76), Mahoning Valley Tech. Socs. Council (vice-chmn. 1976-77). Republican. Byzantine Catholic. Home: 6191 Constance Circle NW Canton OH 44718-1009 Office: Goodyear Tire & Rubber Co 1144 E Market St Akron OH 44316-0001

KOSCIERZYNSKI, RONALD JOHN, educator; b. Detroit, July 18, 1947; s. William Joseph and Jean Mary (Sloncz) K.; m. Barbara Renata, Aug. 19, 1972; children—John Joseph, Anne Marie, Mark Michael, Teresa Rose. A.T., Macomb County (Mich.) Community Coll., 1968; B.S.Ed., Wayne State U., 1970, M.Ed., 1973, Ed.D., 1979. Tchr. electronics Utica (Mich.) Community High Sch., 1972—, chmn. indsl. arts dept., 1981-86, chmn. system-wide indsl. edn., 1975-79; instr. Macomb County Community Coll., 1977-81; tchr. electronics Hazel Park (Mich.) Adult Edn., 1972-77. Served with AUS, 1970-72. Fin. dir. Our Lady Queen of Apostles Parish, 1978-80. Recipient Paul M. Shilling Disting. Service award Mich. Indsl. Edn. Soc., 1981. Mem. AMVETS (AMVET of yr. Mich., 1982, cmdr. dist. 1 Mich. 1982-83, fin. officer 1984-85, judge advocate 1985-86, 2nd vice commdr. for programs 1986-87, sr. vice comdr. 1987-88), Mich. Indsl. Edn. Soc. (membership dir. 1981-84, treas., 1977-80), Am. Indsl. Arts Student Assn. (chmn. orgnl. com. 1984-87), Am. Polish Engring. Assn., Am. Vocat. Assn., Electricity Electronics Tchrs. Mich., Mich. Occupational Edn. Assn., Mich. Trade and Tech. Educators, Nat. Assn. Indsl. and Tech. Tchrs. Educators, Vocat. Indsl. Clubs Am., Phi Delta Kappa. Club: K.C. Contbr. articles to profl. jours. Office: Utica High Sch 47255 Shelby Rd Utica MI 48087

KOSER, GARY RICHARD, civil engineer; b. Milw., Nov. 18, 1950; s. Lawrence E. and Grace M. (Willing) K. BSCE, U. Wis., Milw., 1973, postgrad; postgrad., Northwestern, Marquette U. Registered profl. engr., Wis. Assoc. engr. Barton-Aschmann Assocs., Evanston, Ill., 1973-74, Computerized Structural Design, Milw., 1974-76; regional mgr. Holguin & Assocs., El Paso, Tex., 1976-79; gen. mgr. ECOM Assocs., Milw., 1979—; pres. ECOM Assocs., Milw., 1986—. Contbr. articles to profl. jours. Chmn. bldg. program Immanuel Luth. Ch., 1982-84, sec. bd. edn., 1980-85. Mem. ASCE (sec. tech. council computer practices), NSPE, Am. Mgmt. Assn., Model A Ford Club Am. (sec. 1985-86, nat. dir. 1985—, pres. Wis. chpt. 1981, 87, Mem. of Yr. 1974, 87). Home: 13645 Sevene Ln Brookfield WI 53005 Office: ECOM Assocs Inc 8634 W Brown Deer Rd Milwaukee WI 53224

KOSHETAR, PAUL, JR., information systems planner; b. Phila., Jan. 9, 1945; s. Paul and Mary Koshetar; m. Marilyn J. Wilkes, Sept. 18, 1971; children: Tara Lyn, Paul Wilkes. Grad., Officer Candidate Sch, 1966; BS, Pa. State U., 1972; MS in Systems Mgmt., U. So. Calif., 1977; grad. in mil. edn., Air Command and Staff Coll., Maxwell AFB, Ala., 1981. Enlisted U.S. Army, 1965, various staff positions, 1965-66, commd. 2d lt., 1966, advanced through grades to lt. col., 1983; facility chief data processing 59th Ordnance Group U.S. Army, Pirmasens, Fed. Republic of Germany, 1974-75, comdg. officer 636th Ordnance Corps., 1976-77; exec. officer Tech. Escort U.S. Army, Edgewood, Md., 1977-79; organizational strategic planner U.S. Army Chem. Sch., Anniston, Ala., 1979-80; mgr. combat supply system U.S. Army, Ft. McPherson, Ga., 1981-83; info. systems strategic planner U.S. Army, Atlanta, 1984-86; ret. U.S. Army, 1986; info. systems strategic planning cons. Deloitte Haskins & Sells, Chgo., 1986—; cons. fed. govt. projects Deloitte Haskins & Sells. Mem. Assn. Systems Mgmt., Assn. MBA Execs., Assn. of U.S. Army. Republican. Methodist. Avocations: golf, jogging. Home: 6416 Berkshire Ct Lisle IL 60532 Office: Deloitte Haskins & Sells 200 E Randolph Dr Chicago IL 60601

KOSHICK, JOHN CHARLES, theatrical management firm executive; b. Milw., Aug. 13, 1955; s. John Stanley and Charlotte Cecilia (Herro) K.; m. Jean Marie Wall, Oct. 4, 1986; 1 child, Cathrine Rose. Student, U. Wis.-Milw. Lic. booking agt. Concert promoter Utopia Prodns., Milw., 1973-76, Internat. Talent Assn., N.Y.C., 1976-78; co. mgr. Broadway nat. tour Passion of Dracula, N.Y.C., 1978; gen. mgr. Gordon Crowe Prodns., N.Y.C., 1978-79; pres. Jack Koshick Mgmt., Milw., 1980—, Koshick Bros. Concerts, 1986-87; personal mgr. Badfinger Rock Act, Liverpool, Eng., 1980—; tour mgr. Searchers Rock Act, London, 1983; talent coordinator Festa Italiana, Milw., 1985-86. Democrat. Melkite. Avocations: karate, juggling, song writing, immigration work. Office: Jack Koshick Mgmt PO Box 54 Hales Corners WI 53130

KOSICK, HOWARD ALLEN, accountant, finance executive; b. Chgo., Feb. 3, 1954; s. Raymond M. and Helen (Ozga) K.; m. Mary Jane Lacke, Aug. 21, 1976; children: Robert, David, Jill. BA, U. Ill., 1976. CPA, Ill. Sr. acct. Price Waterhouse, Chgo., 1976-81; mgr. corp. accts. Household Mfg., Northbrook, Ill., 1981-82, fin. analysis mgr., 1982-85; controller Halsey Taylor/Structo div., Freeport, Ill., 1985-86; fin. dir. Halsey Taylor/Thermos div., Freeport, Ill., 1986—. Mem. Am. Inst. CPA's, Ill. CPA Soc., Nat. Assn. Accts. Republican. Roman Catholic. Avocations: golf, handball. Home: 746 Sante Fe Dr Freeport IL 61032 Office: Halsey Taylor/Thermos Route 75 East Freeport IL 61032

KOSLOSKE, JACK CLEMENT, financial planner; b. Neenah, Wis., Oct. 30, 1939; s. Clement F. and Beatrice A. (Staniak) K.; m. Margaret A. Stumpf, May 5, 1962; children: Carolee, Chayne. BBA, U. Wis., Oshkosh, 1969. CPA, Wis.; cert. fin. planner. Acct. Wipfli Ulrich & Co., Wausau, Wis., 1969-72; controller L.F. Strassheim Co., Bowling Green, Ky., 1972-73, Impact 7, Rice Lake, Wis., 1973-74; gen. mgr. Oxford Structures, 1974-81; fin. planner 1st Affiliated Securities, Appleton, Wis., 1981—; bd. dirs. Bull's Eye Credit Union, Wisconsin Rapids, Wis., 1975-82; registered investment advisor Fin. Success Advisors, Appleton, 1986—. Served with USN, 1959-63. Mem. Am. Inst. CPA's, Wis. Inst. CPA's., Internat. Assn. Fin. Planning (v.p. NE Wis. chpt. 1985—), Inst. Cert. Fin. Planners (pres. NE Wis. chpt. 1985—). Lodge: Rotary. Avocations: golf, bird hunting. Home: 36 Apache Ct Appleton WI 54914 Office: 1st Affiliated Securities 54 Park Pl Appleton WI 54915

KOSS, BETTY JEAN, dentist; b. Indpls., Sept. 27, 1925; s. Harry Albert Sr. and Alice E. (Walden) K. AB in Zoology, Butler U., 1946; DDS, Ind. U., 1951. Practice dentistry specializing in pedodontics Indpls., 1951-82, Bourbon, Ind., 1977-84, Mentone, Ind., 1984-87. Mem. Ind. State Council on Nutrition, 1951-64; pres. Ind. Pub. Health Found., 1983-87; gov. dist. VI, Zonta internat., 1974-76; charter pres. Hoosier Dachshund Club, 1961; treas. Lake Tippecanoe Property Owners Assn., 1986—. Named Sagamore of Wabash, Gov. of Ind., 1976; recipient Alumni Achievement award, Butler U., 1981. Fellow Internat. Coll. Dentists, Am. Acad. Pedodontics; mem. Indpls. Dist. Dental Soc. (pres. 1981-82), Am. Assn. Women Dentists (pres. 1962-63), Ind. State Soc. Pedodontics (pres. 1960-62). Republican. Baptist. Avocations: bridge, fishing, boating, stamp collecting. Home: RR2 Old Mill Pl Leesburg IN 46538

KOSS, GREGORY ALAN, architect; b. Tallahassee, Fla., Dec. 19, 1952; s. John Peter and Jacquelyn Elizabeth (Moore) K.; m. Mary Beth Botzum, Aug. 4, 1973; children—Jennifer, Jonathan. B.A. in Architecture, U. Mich., 1975, M.Arch. with distinction, 1976. Cert. AIA, Nat. Council Archtl. Registration Bds. Plan examiner City of Dayton (Ohio), 1976; project architect Kleski & Assocs., Dayton 1977-78; project mgr. The Austin Co., Cleve., 1979-83, mgr. design and engring., 1983-84; mgr. design build group Picker Internat., 1984-87; project dir. Middough Assocs. Inc., 1987—. Mem. AIA, Architects Soc. Ohio. Roman Catholic. Office: Middough Assocs Inc 1901 E 13th St Cleveland OH 44114-3599

KOSS, JOHN CHARLES, consumer electronics products manufacturing company executive; b. Milw., Feb. 22, 1930; s. Earl L. and Eda K.; m. Nancy Weeks, Apr. 19, 1952; children: Michael, Debra, John Charles, Linda, Pamela. Student, U. Wis., Milw., 1952; D.Eng. (hon.), Milw. Sch. Engring. Founder Koss Corp., TV leasing co., Milw., 1953; owner, operator Koss Corp., 1953-58, pres., 1972-81, chmn. bd., chief exec. officer, 1974—; creator home-stereophone, 1958; dir., Metalcraft. Bd. dirs., past pres. Jr. Achievement S.E. Wis.; bd. dirs. Milw. Symphony. Served with Air Force Band USAF, 1950-52. Named Entrepreneur of Yr. Research Dirs. Assn. Chgo., 1972, Mktg. Man of Yr. Milw. chpt., 1972; named to Audio Hall Fame, 1979; Mktg. Exec. of Yr. Sales and Mktg. Execs., 1976; recipient Debby award Soc. Audio Cons.'s, 1975. Mem. Chief Execs. Orgn., Inst. High Fidelity (pres. 1968). Republican. Baptist. Clubs: Milw. Country, University; Les Ambassadeurs (London). Office: Koss Corp 4129 N Port Washington Ave Milwaukee WI 53212

KOSS, MARY LYNDON PEASE, psychology educator; b. Louisville, Sept. 1, 1948; s. Richard Charles and Carol (Bade) Pease; m. Paul G. Koss, Aug. 3, 1968; children: John Bade, Paul Shanor. AB, U. Mich., 1970; PhD, U. Minn., 1972. Lic. psychologist, Ohio. Asst. prof. psychology St. Olaf Coll., Northfield, Minn., 1973-76; prof. psychology Kent (Ohio) State U., 1976—; vis. prof. dept. psychiatry U. Ariz. Med. Sch., Tucson, 1987—. Grantee NIMH, 1978-88, Nat. Inst. Justice, 1985—. Mem. Am. Psychol. Assn., Eastern Psychol. Assn., Midwestern Psychol. Assn., Ohio Psychol. Assn. Democrat. Unitarian.

KOSTECKE, B. WILLIAM, utilities executive; b. Caro, Mich., Aug. 1, 1925; s. Steve and Stella (Telewiek) K.; m. Lo Rayne M. Smith, Mar. 25, 1950; children: Diane, Keith. B.S., U.S. Mcht. Marine Acad., 1947, Mich. State U., 1951. Controller Miller Brewing Co., Milw., 1963-66, treas., chief financial officer, 1966-70, pres., 1970-72; v.p., treas., dir. Wis. Gas Co., Milw., from 1972; v.p., treas., sec., dir. WICOR, Inc., Milw. Gen. chmn. Milw. Nat. Alliance Businessmen, 1972; bd. dirs. Milw. County council Boy Scouts Am., Milw. Better Bus. Bur., Wis. Council on Econ. Edn., Wis. Soc. for Prevention of Blindness; trustee Citizens Govtl. Research Bur. Recipient Dean Mellencamp award U. Wis., Milw., 1967, Outstanding Profl. Achievement award Kings Point Alumni Assn., 1972. Mem. Financial Execs. Inst., Am. Gas Assn. Clubs: Blue Mound Golf and Country; University (Milw.). Home: 10708 N Fairway Circle Mequon WI 53092 Office: 626 E Wisconsin Ave Milwaukee WI 53201

KOSTERE, KIM MARTIN, psychologist; b. Detroit, Jan. 22, 1954; d. Walter Thomas and Shirley Marian (Goebel) K. BA, Mercy Coll., 1977; MA, Ctr. Humanistic Studies, Detroit, 1983, postgrad., 1986. Therapist Metro T.A.G., Livonia, Mich., 1978-81, Highland Waterford Ctr., Waterford, Mich., 1981-83; psychologist Square Lake Counseling Ctr., Bloomfield Hills, Mich., 1983—; co-founder, dir. Ontario (Can.) NLP Inst., 1979-80. Co-author: Get The Results You Want, 1987. Democrat. Roman Catholic.

KOSTOLANSKY, DAVID JOHN, mechanical engineer; b. Charleroi, Pa., Feb. 4, 1943; s. Joseph Paul and Anne Louise (Biress) K.; m. Mary Margaret Biondi, Nov. 27, 1965; children: David, Paul, Julianne, Margaret. BSME, U. Notre Dame, 1964. Design engr. Lee-Norse Co., Charleroi, 1964-65; sales, services rep. Cleve. Electric Illuminating Co., 1965-67; mech. engr. Union RR Co., Monroeville, Pa., 1967-72; v.p. Briggs & Turivas, Inc., Dennison, Ohio, 1972-77; v.p. engring. Shaefer Equipment Inc., Warren, Ohio, 1977-86, v.p. sales, 1986—. Rep. United Way, Warren, 1983-84; mem. exec. bd. Boy Scouts Am. Warren, 1981—, v.p. 1985—. Mem. ASME, Am. Soc. for Metals, Am. Mgmt. Assn., RR Supply Assn., Pitts. Ry. Club. Democrat. Roman Catholic. Clubs: Kennedy (sec. 1985—), Notre Dame (Warren). Lodge: Elks. Avocations: tennis, sailing. Home: 9008 Briarbrook Dr NE Warren OH 44484 Office: Schaefer Equipment Inc Phoenix Rd Warren OH 44483

KOSTRZEWA, JOSEPH GERALD, oil company executive; b. Saginaw, Mich., Apr. 22, 1941; s. Joseph J. and Anna M. (Budzinski) K.; m. Kathleen Ann Perry, June 2, 1963; children: Ann, Mary, David, Sue. BS, Ferris State U., 1965. CPA. Tax mgr. Arthur Andersen, Chgo., 1965-72; ptnr. Seidman & Seidman, Traverse City, Mich., 1972-76; exec. v.p. Traverse Corp., Traverse City, 1976-80; pres. Traverse Oil, Traverse City, 1980-83; chmn. Federated Nat. Resources, Traverse City, 1983—; advisor to pres. Munson Med. Ctr., Traverse City, 1985—; bd. dirs. Wright K. Tech., Saginaw, Mich., Old Kent Bank, Traverse City, Fed. Nat. Reserve, Traverse City. Trustee Nat. Cherry Festival, Traverse City, 1983, Northwestern Mich. COll., Traverse City, 1984. Mem. Independent Petroleum Assn. Am. (bd. dirs. 1985—), Mich. Oil & Gas Assn. (bd. dirs. 1984). Republican. Roman Catholic. Avocations: sailing, golf. Home: 2885 Holiday Pines Traverse City MI 49685 Office: Federated Nat Resources Corp 13561 W Bay Shore Dr Traverse City MI 49684

KOSTYRA, EUGENE MICHAEL, province official; b. Winnipeg, Man., Can., June 19, 1947; s. Albert and Jean (Swetz) K.; m. Jeri McKee, Feb. 1, 1985. Electrician, Man. Hydro Co., Winnipeg, Can., union rep. Can. Union Pub. Employees; minister of fin. Province of Man., Winnipeg, 1983-86 , minister of the crown Govt. of Man., Winnipeg, 1981—. Mem. New Democratic Party. Office: Govt of Manitoba, Ministry of Fin Legis Bldg, 103-450 Broadway, Winnipeg, MB Canada R3C 0V8

KOSZEWSKI, BOHDAN JULIUS, medical educator; b. Warsaw, Poland, Dec. 17, 1918; Came to U.S., 1952; s. Mikolaj and Helena (Lubienski) K.; children: Mikolaj Joseph, Wanda Marie, Andrzej Rohdan. MD, U. Zurich, Switzerland, 1946; MS, Creighton U., 1956. Resident in pathology U. Zurich, 1944-46, resident in internal medicine, 1946-50, assoc. in medicine, 1950-52; intern St. Mary's Hosp., Hoboken, N.J., 1953; practice medicine specializing in internal medicine Omaha, 1953—; mem. staff St. Joseph's Hosp., Luth Med. Ctr., Mercy and Meth. Hosps.; instr. internal medicine Creighton U., 1956-57, asst. prof., 1957-65, assoc. prof. internal medicine, 1965—; cons. hematology Omaha VA Hosp., 1957—. Author: Prognosis in Diabetic Coma, 1952; contbr. numerous articles to profl. jours. Served with Polish Army, 1940-45. Fellow ACP, Am. Coll. Angiology (gov. Nebr. chpt.); mem. AAAS, AMA, Am. Fedn. Clin. Research, Am. Soc. Hematology, Internat. Soc. Hematology, Polish-Am. Congress Nebr. (pres. 1960-68). Home and Office: 4502 S 42d St Omaha NE 68107

KOTLARCZYK, JOHN JOSEPH, accountant; b. Chgo., June 15, 1945; s. Joseph and Stephanie Joan (Pasieka) K.; m. Christine Cynthia Jasinski, May 18, 1968; children: John Joseph Jr., David Paul. BS in Acctg., U. Ill., Chgo., 1967. CPA, Ill. Audit mgr. Price Waterhouse, Chgo., 1967-73; audit supr. Alexander Grant & Co., Chgo., 1973-75; sr. v.p. fin. Soiltest, Inc. subs. Cenco Inc., Chgo., 1975-81; v.p. fin. ATM Network Mgmt. Corp., Downers Grove, Ill., 1981-82; pvt. practice mgmt. cons. Bolingbrook, Ill., 1982-84; v.p., corp. controller Atlas Van Lines, Inc., Evansville, Ind., 1984-86; v.p., chief fin. officer Overland Express, Inc., Indpls., 1986—, also bd. dirs. Treas., com. chmn. Boy Scouts Am., Bolingbrook, 1977-83. Mem. Am. Inst. CPA's, Ill. Soc. CPA's, Ind. Soc. CPA's. Roman Catholic. Lodge: Lions (club treas. 1983-84). Avocations: reading, golf, tennis, jogging. Home: 1191 Cottonwood Ct Carmel IN 46032 Office: Overland Express Inc 1631 W Thompson Rd PO Box 7025 Indianapolis IN 46207

KOTOSKE, DONALD EDWARD, osteopathic physician and surgeon; b. South Bend, Ind., Oct. 6, 1930; s. Michael Edward and Louise Josephine (Gallo) K.; m. Anne Helen Sergio, Nov. 7, 1953; children: David, Kathleen, Thomas, Karen, Lisa. BS, Notre Dame U., 1952; DO, Chgo. Coll. Osteo. Medicine and Surgery, 1968. Diplomate Am. Bd. Osteo. Medicine. With mktg. dept. Pharm. Industry Eaton Labs., Norwich, N.Y., 1952-64; intern South Bend Osteo. Hosp., 1968-69; gen. practice osteo. medicine South Bend, 1970—; chief of staff South Bend Osteo. Hosp., 1974-75, chmn. gen. practice dept., 1977-78. Mem. RYFF-PAC, Washington, 1986—. Fellow Am. Coll. Gen. Practice. Club: Notre Dame (South Bend). Avocations: radio and TV writing, acting, nationwide pub. speaking. Office: 4104 S Miami South Bend IN 46614

KOTSOGIANNIS, NIKKI, senior systems analyst; b. Chgo.; d. Russell and Bess Kotsogiannis. BS in Quantitative Methods, U. Ill., Chgo., 1981; MBA, DePaul U., 1985—. Assoc. programmer Sears, Roebuck & Co., Chgo., 1981-82, programmer, 1982-84, systems programmer, 1984-85, tech. programmer, 1985-86, sr. systems analyst, 1986—. Mem. Sts. Constatine and Helen Choir, Palos Hills, Ill. Mem. Hellenic Profl. Soc., United Young Adult League (bd. dirs.).

KOTTMEIER, JAMES ALAN, communication and meeting consultant, executive; b. Cedar Rapids, Iowa, Sept. 9, 1944; s. William Henry and Hildegarde Caroline (Rabus) K.; m. Cheryl Chase, Aug. 28, 1984; 1 child, James Blair. BSBA, U. Minn., 1971. Design draftsman Collins Radio Corp., Cedar Rapids, 1962-64; sr. designer Strom Engring. Corp., Hopkins, Minn., 1966-67; asst. plant mgr. GAF Corp., Mpls., 1971-80; mktg. bus. mgr. Control Data Corp., Mpls., 1971-80, meeting mgr., 1984—, tng. cons., 1977-81; pres., ptnr., Twin Cities Unltd., Travel and Meeting Services. Contbr. articles to profl. jours. Musician-drummer RUMC Players, Richfield, Minn., 1978—. Served with U.S. Army, 1966-68. Mem. Minn. Metting Planners Internat. (pres.). Methodist. Home: 2000 W 86th St Bloomington MN 55431 Office: Twin Cities Unltd 6425 Nicollet Ave S Suite 116 Minneapolis MN 55423

KOTVIS, STEPHEN PAUL, marketing professional; b. Milw., May 24, 1956; s. Bernard Marvin Kotvis and Flora Jo (Larson) Bierdz; m. Camille Maria Gibson, Sept. 3, 1983. BA in Social Psychology cum laude, Park Coll., 1977; MSW, M in City and Regional Planning, Ohio State U., 1981. Sr. research analyst Metro Human Services Commn., Columbus, 1979-82, dir. research, 1982-83; sr. planner Pub. Demographics Midwest, Inc., Mpls., 1983-86, project mgr., 1986—; sr. mktg. analyst, cons. Grey Advt., Mpls., 1985-86; cons. Peter M. Hale Advt., Mpls, 1986—, AM Creative Advt., Mpls, 1986—, Beaumont-Bennett Assocs., 1986-87. Counselor Suicide Prevention Service, Columbus, Ohio, 1978; mem. Citizens League, Mpls., 1983-87; ward rep. capital long term improvement com., City of Mpls., 1984-86. Served with USAF, 1974-78. Recipient Outstanding Vol. Service award City of Mpls., 1985, 86. Mem. Am. Mktg. Assn., Am. Planning Assn., Am. Inst. Cert. Planners, Am. Soc. Competitor Intelligence Profls. Democrat. Club: YMCA (Mpls.). Avocations: photography, volleyball, tennis, bicycling. Home: 2024 Queen Ave S Minneapolis MN 55405 Office: Pub Demographics Midwest Inc 529 S 7th Suite 507 Minneapolis MN 55415

KOUCHOUKOS, NICHOLAS THOMAS, surgeon; b. Grand Rapids, Mich., Dec. 26, 1936; s. Thomas Paul and Antoinette (Karver) K.; m. Judith Buell, Aug. 24, 1966; children—Nicholas Thomas, Robert Buell, Thomas Paul. Student (James B. Angell scholar), U. Mich., 1954-57; M.D. cum laude, Washington U., 1961. Intern Barnes Hosp., Washington U. Med. Ctr., St. Louis, 1961-62; asst. resident in surgery Barnes Hosp., Washington U. Med. Ctr., 1962-65, chief adminstrv. resident, 1965-66; sr. clin. trainee in surgery USPHS, 1966-67; asst. in surgery Sch. Medicine Washington U., St. Louis, 1961-65; instr. surgery Sch. Medicine Washington U., 1965-67, John M. Shoenberg prof. cardiovascular surgery, 1984—; research fellow surgery Sch. Medicine, U. Ala., Birmingham, 1967-68; instr. surgery Sch. Medicine, U. Ala., 1967-69, advanced trainee thoracic and cardiovascular surgery, 1968-70, asst. prof. surgery, 1969-71, assoc. prof., 1971-74, prof., vice-dir. div. thoracic and cardiovascular surgery, 1974-81, clin. prof., 1981-84; cardiovascular surgeon-in-chief Jewish Hosp. of St. Louis, 1984—; mem. cardiovascular research study com. Am. Heart Assn., 1977-79; surgery study sect. USPHS, Bethesda, Md., 1977-80; ad hoc cons. Specialized Centers in Research Arteriosclerosis, Nat. Heart and Lung Inst., Bethesda, 1971-72, mem. ad hoc rev. com. for collaborative studies on coronary artery surgery, 1973-75, surgery A study sect., 1976-77; mem. merit rev. bd. in cardiovascular studies VA, Washington, 1976-78. Editorial bd. Jour. Cardiac Rehab., 1979-84, Current Topics in Cardiology and Circulation, 1977-80, Cardiology Update, 1979—, Annals Thoracic Surgery, 1980—, Cardiosat, 1984—. Fellow Southeastern Surg. Congress, Am. Coll. Cardiology (finalist Young Investigators award 1962), ACS; mem. Am. Assn. Thoracic Surgery, AAUP, AMA, Am. Surg. Assn., Assn. Clin. Cardiac Surgeons, Assn. Academic Surgery, Internat. Surg. Soc., St. Louis Met. Med. Soc., John Kirklin Soc., Soc. Thoracic Surgeons, St. Louis Thoracic Surg. Soc., So. Thoracic Surg. Assn., So. Surg. Assn., Soc. Univ. Surgeons, Soc. Vascular Surgery, Internat. Cardiovascular Soc., Phi Beta Kappa, Alpha Omega Alpha. Home: 25 Picardy Lane Saint Louis MO 63124 Office: 216 S Kings Hwy Saint Louis MO 63110

KOUCKY, JOHN RICHARD, metallurgical engineer, manufacturing executive; b. Chgo., Sept. 21, 1934; s. Frank Louis and Ella (Harshman) K.; m. Beverly Irene O'Dell, Aug. 16, 1958; children: Deborah, Diane. BS in MetE., U. Ill., 1957; MBA, Northwestern U., 1959. Metallurgist, asst. plant mgr. Fansteel Metall. Corp., North Chicago, Ill., 1957-64; supr. production engring. cen. foundry div. Gen. Motors Corp., Saginaw, Mich., 1964-67; asst. gen. mgr. Marion (Ind.) Malleable Iron, 1967-68; mgr. production engring. tech., plant mgr. Wagner Castings Co., Decatur, Ill., 1968-79, v.p. engring., bd. dirs., 1983—; v.p., gen. mgr. Pa. mall iron div. Gulf & Western, Lancaster, 1979-82. Served to 1st lt. U.S. Army, 1957-58. Mem. Am. Soc. Metals (local chmn. 1958—), Am. Foundrymans Soc. (local vice chmn. 1968—), Ductile Iron Soc. (nat. bd. dirs. 1983—), Iron Castings Soc., Soc. Automotive Engrs., U. Ill. Dept. Metallurgy and Mining Alumni Assn. (bd. dirs. 1983—, Loyalty award 1986). Republican. Clubs: Decatur, Decatur Tennis (pres. 1976-78), Decatur Raquet. Avocations: tennis, golf, bridge, gardening. Home: 834 Stevens Creek Ct Decatur IL 62526 Office: Wagner Castings Co 825 Lowbar PO Box 1319 Decatur IL 62525

KOUMOULIDES, JOHN THOMAS ANASTASIOS, historian, educator; b. Greece, Aug. 23, 1938; came to U.S., 1956, naturalized, 1969; s. Anastasios Lazaros and Sophia (Theodosiadou) K. A.B., Montclair State Coll. (N.J.), 1960, A.M., 1961; Ph.D., U. Md., 1968; postgrad., Fitzwilliam Coll., Cambridge (Eng.) U., 1965-67; postgrad. vis. fellow, 1971-72. Grad. asst. U. Md., 1961-63; asst. prof. history Austin Peay State U., Clarksville, Tenn., 1963-65, Vanderbilt U., summer 1968; mem. faculty Ball State U., Muncie, Ind., 1968—; prof. history Ball State U., 1975—; vis. tutor Campion Hall, Oxford U., 1980-81. Author: Cyprus and the Greek War of Independence, 1821-1829, 2d edit, 1974, Byzantine and Post-Byzantine Monuments at Aghia in Thessaly, Greece: The Art and Architecture of the Monastery of Saint Panteleimon, 1975; co-author: Churches of Agia in Larissa, Greece; also monographs, articles and revs.; editor: Greece in Transition: Essays in the History of Modern Greece, 1821-1974, 1977, Greece: Past and Present, 1979, Hellenic Perspectives: Essays in the History of Greece, 1980, Greece and Cyprus in History, 1960-1985, 1986, Cyprus in Transition 1960-85, 1986, Greek Connections: Essays on Culture and Diplomacy, 1987; co-editor: Byzantine Perspectives: Essays in Byzantine History and Culture, 1986. Recipient Archon Chartophylax of the Ecumenical Patriarchate of Constantinople, 1979, Acad. of Athens prize, 1985; research grantee Ball State U., (6 awards) 1969-86, research grantee Am. Philos. Soc., 1973, 79, research grantee Am. Council Learned Socs., 1969, 71, Fulbright-Hays research awardee Greece, 1977-78, 1987-88, Dumbarton Oaks research grantee, 1982-86; vis. fellow Wolfson Coll., Oxford U., 1983-84; guest scholar Woodrow Wilson Internat. Ctr. for Scholars, 1982. Mem. Am. Hist. Assn., Archaeol. Inst. Am., AAUP, Modern Greek Studies Assn., Soc. Promotion Hellenic Studies, Brit. Hist. Assn., Cambridge U. Hist. Assn., Cambridge Philol. Assn., Cambridge U. Soc., Oxford U. Soc., Byzantine Soc., Phi Alpha Theta, Alpha Tau Omega. Greek Orthodox.

KOUNKEL, TERYLE LEE, engineer; b. LeMars, Iowa, June 15, 1946; s. Walter A. and Eunice G. (Gotto) K.; m. Jane A. Carter, Nov. 30, 1968; children: Ayn, Matthew, Jonathan. BSME, Iowa State U., 1968. Mech. engr. Alcoa, Davenport, Iowa, 1968-76, div. engr., 1976-78; chief mech. engr. Berkley & Co., Spirit Lake, Iowa, 1978-84, mgr. mfg. engring., 1984-86, engring. mgr., 1986—. Councilman City of Riverdale, Iowa, 1972-77; mem. bicentennial commn. Riverdale, 1976, sanitary landfill commn., Scott County, Iowa, 1977, adv. council Spirt Lake High Sch., 1986; bd. dirs. Dickinson County Credit Union, Spirit Lake, 1980-82. Mem. Soc. Mfg. Engrs. (sec. 1983-84, treas. 1984-85, program chmn. 1985-86, chmn. 1986-87). Lutheran. Avocations: water skiing, fishing, wallyball, little league baseball, volleyball.

KOURAJIAN, STEVEN CHARLES, optometrist; b. Jamestown, N.D., Oct. 1, 1957; s. Charles and Marcia Mathilda (Skroch) K.; m. Debra Kay Keller, July 26, 1985. Student, Jamestown Coll., 1975-76, Pacific U., 1976-78; OD, Pacific U., 1981. Gen. practice optometry Harvey, N.D., 1981—. Pres. Prairie Concert Assn., Harvey, N.D., 1982-84. Mem. N.D. Optometric Assn., N. Star Harvey Optometric Soc., Harvey C. of C. (bd. dirs. 1982-85), Harvey Jaycees (v.p. 1982-84, pres. 1984-85, treas. 1986—). Republican. Roman Catholic. Lodges: Eagles, Kiwanis (local bd. dirs. 1983-86). Home: 1011 Allen Ave #4 Harvey ND 58341 Office: 907 1/2 Lincoln Ave Harvey ND 58341

KOURAKIS, EMANUEL MICHAEL, osteopath; b. Chgo., Aug. 26, 1934; s. Manoussos Emanuel and Evangelia (Manoussakis) K.; m. Themis Ianthe Soter, Aug. 27, 1959; children; Stephen Michael, Thomas Michael, Anna Michelle. BS, De Paul U., Chgo., 1956; DO, Coll. Osteopathic Medicine and Surgery, Des Moines, 1963. Diplomate Am. Bd. Internal Medicine, Am. Bd. Nuclear Medicine. Intern Detroit Osteo. Hosp., 1963-64; resident Grandview Hosp., Dayton, Ohio, 1964-67; osteoapthic physician specializing in internal medicine Milw.; bd. dirs. Northwest Gen. Hosp., Milw., 1981—. Mem. Am. Osteopathic Assn., Am. Coll. Osteopathic Internists Physicians and Surgeons, Soc. Osteo. Physicians and Surgeons (Milw. dist.), Wis. Assn. Osteo. Physicians and Surgeons. Mem. Greek Orthodox. Avocations: photography, chess, archery. Home: 2789 N 122d St Wauwatosa WI 53222 Office: 4025 N 92d St Milwaukee WI 53222

KOURI, LOUIS PETER, restaurateur; b. Peoria, Ill., Aug. 2, 1927; s. Thomas Fadul and Marianne (Mrad) K.; m. Delores May Anthony, June 29, 1955; children: Thomas, Steve, Dan, Ken, James. Owner Lariat Club, Peoria, 1970—. Served to corp. U.S. Army, 1952-54, Korea. Republican. Roman Catholic. Home: 720 Skyview Dr East Peoria IL 61611 Office: Lariat Club 2232 W Glen Ave Peoria IL 61614

KOUTROULIS, ARIS GEORGE, artist, educator; b. Athens, Greece, May 14, 1938; came to U.S., 1953; s. George Aris and Julia (Eftimiades) K.; m. Mary Ann Schmid, 1964 (div. 1973); m. Jill Warren, July 4, 1982; 1 dau., Georgina. B.F.A., La. State U., 1961; Master Printer, Tamarind Lithography Workshop, Los Angeles, 1964; M.F.A., Cranbrook Acad. Art, Bloomfield Hills, Mich., 1966. Chmn. bd. Willis Gallery, Detroit, 1970-71; pres. Common Ground of the Arts, Detroit, 1969-72; guest artist Ox-Bow Summer Sch. Art, Saugatuck, Mich., 1973, co-dir., 1975; assoc. prof. art Wayne State U., 1966-75; head painting dept. Ctr. Creative Studies, Detroit, 1975-81, chmn. Fine Arts Dept., 1981—; exhibited one-man shows, Hanamura Gallery, Detroit, 1966, Montgomery Mus. Fine Arts, Ala., 1966, Va. Poly. Inst., 1968, Baton Rouge Gallery, 1968, Wayne State U., 1969, Mich. Council for Arts, 1969, Gertrude Kasle Gallery, Detroit, 1970, Detroit Artists Market, 1973, Klein-Vogel Gallery, Detroit, 1974, Detroit Inst. Arts, 1976, Gloria Cortella Gallery, N.Y.C., 1977, Gallery Renaissance, Detroit, 1980, Haber-Theodore Gallery, N.Y.C., 1980; OK Harris Gallery, N.Y.C., 1980, 81, 82, 83, 85, 87, Mich. Traveling Exhbn., 1981, Cantor/Emberg Gallery, Birmingham, Mich., 1982, Dubins Gallery, Los Angeles, 1984, Nimbus Gallery, Dallas, 1986; exhibited group shows Decorative Arts Ctr., N.Y.C., 1973, Detroit Inst. Arts, 1974, Bykert Gallery, N.Y.C., 1974, Bklyn. Mus., 1977, Brooks Meml. Art Gallery, Memphis, 1977, La. State U. Gallery, 1978, Tyler Sch. Art, Temple U., 1978, Mus. Fine Arts, Springfield, Mass., 1978, Van Doren Gallery, San Francisco, 1978, Consulate Gen. Greece, N.Y.C., 1978, Landmark Gallery, N.Y.C., 1978, Cranbrook Mus. Art, Bloomfield Hills, Mich., 1979, Detroit Inst. Arts, 1980, Mus. Fine Arts Tampa, 1987, 51st nat. mid-yr. exhbn. Butler Inst. Am. Art, Youngstown, Ohio, 1987; represented in pub. collections including Mus. Modern Art, Nat. Gallery Art, Detroit Inst. Arts, Los Angeles County Mus. Art, Cranbrook Mus. Art, Detroit Engring. Soc., Detroit Pub. Library, U. Mich. Art Mus., Anglo-Am. Mus., Amon Carter Mus. Western Art, Ft. Worth, UCLA Grunwald Graphic Arts Found., Ball State U. Art Mus.; represented in corp. collections; commd. Standard Oil Corp., San Ramon, Calif., Arbor Drugs, Inc., Focus Gallery, Bracewell/Patterson, Washington, Mich. Found. for Arts, Detroit Engring. Soc., Art for Detroit, City of Detroit, WDIV-TV4, Detroit, Tampa Mus. Collection. Address: Center for Creative Studies Dept Fine Arts 245 E Kirby St Detroit MI 48202

KOUTSOHILIS, KOSTAS KIRIAKOS, restaurateur; b. Rhodos, Greece, Feb. 10, 1916; came to U.S., 1956; s. Kiriakos Kostas and Besty Angia (Anestiannis) K.; m. Kalipio Kotas Theodare, May 15, 1955; children: Kiriakos Kostas, Avenia Kostas, Mache Kostas. B in Bus. Mgmt., Athens U., Greece, 1945. Pres. Venice Restaurant Inc., Daytona Beach Shores, Fla., 1956—, Kiriakos Enterprises, St. Louis, 1970—. Served to lt. col. Greek Air Force, 1946-51. Recipient Best Restaurant award Fla. Restaurant Assn., 1983, 84, 85. Mem. Am. Hellenic Ednl. Progressive Assn. Greek Orthodox. Avocations: tennis, golf. Home: 9615 Aerouista Ct Saint Louis MO 63123

KOVAC, JOHN NICHOLAS, transportation executive, military logistic manager; b. Bridgeport, Conn., Apr. 24, 1950; s. Nicholas Paul and Gertrude Margaret (Ulbrick) K.; m. Patricia Ruth Clark, Sept. 14, 1974; children: Jason Robert, Nicholas John. BS in Indsl. Mgmt., Lowell (Mass.) Technol. Inst., 1972; MBA, George Washington U., 1977. Cert. rail ops. specialist. Officer communications and security USN, Pentagon, Washington, 1973-75; program analyst Fed. R.R. Adminstrn., Dept. Transp., Washington, 1976-77; staff analyst nat. freight car utilization program Assn. Am. R.R.s, Washington, 1977-78; operating asst. Santa Fe Railway Co., Chgo., 1978, asst. mgr. equipment, 1985—; insp. transp., asst. trainmaster Santa Fe Railway Co., Newton, Kans., 1979-85. Cubmaster Boy Scouts Am., Newton, 1982-83, merit badge counselor, La Grange, Ill., 1983—. Served to lt. comdr. USNR, 1971—. Recipient Eagle Scout award Boy Scouts Am., Trumbull, Conn., 1964. Mem. Nat. Def. Transp. Assn., Delta Nu Alpha, Kappa Sigma. Republican. Lodge: Kiwanis (v.p. Lowell Circle K club 1971-72). Avocations: sailing, camping. Home: 500 S Stone La Grange IL 60525 Office: Santa Fe Railway Market Devel and Research 80 E Jackson Chicago IL 60604

KOVACIK, NEAL STEPHEN, hotel and restaurant executive; b. Toledo, Mar. 2, 1952; s. Albert Joseph and Phyllis (Lesinski) K.; m. Denise Reichert, Apr. 20, 1974 (div. June 1976). Student, Bowling Green State U., 1971-72, U. Toledo, 1973-74, Owens Tech. Coll., 1975. Dir. food and beverages Motor Inn of Perrysburg, Ohio, 1976-78; v.p. food and beverage ops. Bennett Enterprises, Perrysburg, 1978-82, v.p. hotel and restaurant ops., 1982—. Recipient Food and Beverage Dir. of Yr. award Holiday Inns, Inc. and Internat. Assn. Holiday Inns, 1976. Mem. Northwestern Ohio Restaurant Assn. (bd. dirs. 1980-84), Toledo Hotel and Motel Assn. Democrat. Roman Catholic. Avocations: art, wildlife photography. Home: 9640 Monclova Rd Monclova OH 43542 Office: Bennett Enterprises Corp 27476 Holiday Ln Perrysburg OH 43551

KOVACS, GAIL LOUISE PATEK, hospital administrator, nurse, biologist; b. Cleve., Feb. 17, 1949; d. Louis Cornelius and Veronica Rose (Skerl) Patek; m. John Joseph Kovacs, June 24, 1972 (div.); 1 child, Jeffrey Joseph. BA in Biology cum laude, Ursuline Coll., 1971; RN, Cleve. Met. Sch. Nursing, 1975; MBA magna cum laude, Cleve. State U., 1982. Med. technologist Cleve. Clinic Found., 1971-72; immunology research asst. Case Western Res. U., Cleve., 1972-73; staff nurse Mt. Sinai Hosp., Cleve., 1975-76; staff nurse Cleve. Met. Gen. Hosp., 1976, infectious disease nurse, 1976-78; assoc. dir. supply services Univ. Hosps of Cleve., 1978-79, asst. dir. material mgmt., 1979, administrv. assoc., 1979-80, assoc. dir. material mgmt., 1980-84, asst. gen. mgr. adminstrn., 1984—; lectr. mgmt., epidemiology and material mgmt. Recipient Paul Widman Meml. award Ctr. Health Affairs/Greater Cleve. Hosp. Assn., 1985; Cleve. Found. grantee, 1980-81. Mem. Am. Coll. Health Care Execs., Health Care Adminstrs. Assn. N.E. Ohio, Healthcare Fin. Assn., Transplantation Soc. of N.E. Ohio, Health Care Fin. Mgmt. Soc., Health Care Material Mgmt. Soc. (v.p.; Presdl. citation 1985), Internat. Material Mgmt. Soc., Soc. for Hosp. Purchasing and Material Mgmt., N.E. Ohio Soc. for Health Care Material Mgmt., Beta Gamma Sigma. Roman

Catholic. Home: 1450 Blossom Park Ave Lakewood OH 44107 Office: Univ Hosps of Cleveland 2074 Abington Rd Cleveland OH 44106

KOVACS, STEPHEN ANDRAS, manufacturing executive; b. Szarvas, Hungary, Mar. 6, 1955; s. Andras and Gabriella Klara (Koritar) K.; m. Theresa Travis, Dec. 30, 1977. BS, U. Louisville, 1977, MS, 1978; MBA, Xavier U., 1986. Engr. Procter & Gamble, Cin., 1978-81, group leader, 1981-85, tech. brand mgr., 1985—. Mem. Am. Inst. Chem. Engrs. Republican. Lutheran. Avocations: basketball, travel, reading. Home: 10139 Bolingbroke Dr Cincinnati OH 45241 Office: Procter & Gamble Co 11520 Reed Hartman Hwy Cincinnati OH 45241

KOVATCH, DENISE BEEBE, domestics company executive; b. Cleve., Mar. 19, 1952; d. Dermont L. and Marie J. (Jankovich) Beebe; m. Stephen J. Kovatch, Feb. 28, 1975. BS in Home Econs., Ohio U., 1974. Regional sewing inst. Singer Sewing Co., Fairview Park, Ohio, 1975-79; buyer domestics May Co., Cleve., 1979-87; regional sales mgr. Perfect Fit Industries, Inc., Cleve., 1987—. Roman Catholic. Avocations: running, gardening, designing and sewing clothes.

KOVELESKI, KATHRYN DELANE, educator; b. Detroit, Aug. 12, 1925; d. Edward Albert Vogt and Delane (Bender) Vogt; B.A., Olivet (Mich.) Coll., 1947; M.A., Wayne State U., Detroit, 1955; m. Casper Koveleski, July 18, 1952; children—Martha, Ann. Tchr. schs. in Mich., 1947—; tchr. Garden City Schs., 1955-56, 59—, resource and learning disabilities tchr., 1970—. Mem. NEA, Mich. Edn. Assn., Garden City Edn. Assn., Bus. and Profl. Women (pres. Garden City 1982-83, Woman of Yr. 1983-84). Congregationalist. Clubs: Wayne Lit. (past pres.), Sch. Masters Bowling League (v.p. 1984-87), Odd Couples Bowling League (pres. 82-83). Office: 33411 Marquette St Garden City MI 48135

KOVICH, NICHOLAS JOSEPH, chemical engineer, investment analyst; b. Kansas City, Kans., Mar. 12, 1956; s. Nick and Mary Jeanne (DuChanois) K.; m. Karen Jean Briner, Oct. 23, 1982. BS Chem. Engring. cum laude, U. Kans., 1979, MBA in Fin., 1981. Chartered fin. analyst, Okla. Tech. service project engr. Amoco Oil Co., Kansas City, Mo., 1981-82; asst. v.p., sr. investment analyst Waddel & Reed, Kansas City, 1982—. Mem. Fin. Analyst Fedn., Inst. Chartered Fin. Analysts, Kans. City Soc. Fin. Analysts, Milhaven Homes Assn. (bd. dirs. 1987—), U. Kans. Alumni Assn., Milhaven Homes Assn. (bd. dirs. 1987—). Avocations: reading, biking, swimming, photography, model railroading. Office: Waddell & Reed Inc 1 Crown Ctr PO Box 418343 Kansas City MO 64141-9343

KOWALCZEWSKI, DOREEN MARY THURLOW, communications company executive; b. London, May 5, 1926; came to U.S., 1957, naturalized, 1974; d. George Henry and Jessie Alice (Gray) Thurlow; B.A., Clarke Coll., 1947; postgrad. Wayne State U., 1959-62, Roosevelt U., 1968; m. Witold Dionizy Kowalczewski, July 26, 1946; children—Christina Julianna, Janet Alice, Stephen Robin. Agy. supr. MONY, N.Y.C., 1963-67; office mgr. J.B. Carroll Co., Chgo., 1967-68; mng. editor Sawyer Coll. Bus., Evanston, Ill., 1968-71; mgr. policyholder service CNA, Chgo., 1971-73; EDP coordinator Canteen Corp., Chgo., 1973-75; mgr. documentation and standards LRSP, Chgo., 1975-77; data network mgr. Computerized Agy. Mgmt. Info. Services, Chgo., 1977-86; founder, chmn. Tekman Assos., 1982—; assoc. Austin Cons., 1986—. Pres., Univ. Park Assn., 1980-84. Mem. Nat. Assn. Female Execs., Women in Info. Processing, Chgo. Orgn. Data Processing Educators, Women in Mgmt., Mensa. Home: 8923 Southview Brookfield IL 60513

KOWALCZYK, PAUL ALAN, civil engineer; b. Phila., Feb. 5, 1947; s. Andrew Paul and Bertha Florilla (Burnham) K.; m. Mary Jane Gresser, June 17, 1972; children: Andrew, Katherine, Benjamin, Sarah. BS, U.S. Mil. Acad., 1970; MS in Profl. Mgmt., Fla. Inst. Tech., 1979. Registered profl. engr., Colo. Commd. 2d lt. U.S. Army, 1970, advanced through grades to capt., resigned, 1979; project engr. U.S. Army Engring. Dist., Seoul, Korea, 1974-75; project mgr. U.S. Army Corps of Engrs., Rock Island, Ill., 1976—. Soccer coach NE Family YMCA, Bettendorf, Iowa, 1981-82; treas. Boy Scouts Am., Bettendorf, 1983-85, com. mem. 1986. Mem. Soc. Am. Mil. Engrs. (sec. 1977-78), Phi Kappa Phi. Roman Catholic. Avocations: biking, camping, skiing, reading, woodworking. Home: 1111 Pinehill Rd Bettendorf IA 52722 Office: US Army Corps of Engrs Clock Tower Bldg Rock Island IL 61204

KOWALSKI, ANTHONY JUDE, III, real estate developer, construction company executive; b. Chicago Heights, Ill., Aug. 27, 1952; s. Anthony J. II and Olivia V. K. BA, DePaul U., 1976. Lic. real estate broker, Ill. Property mgr. Carl Johnson & Co., Chgo., 1977-78; pres. Innovative Investments, Chgo., 1978-82; v.p. Springer Constrn. Services Inc., Chgo., 1980—; cons. Harbor Mgmt. Inc., Chgo., 1977-78. Mem. Urban Land Inst. Home: 220 E 21st St Chicago Heights IL 60411 Office: Springer Constrn Services Inc 2023 W Potomac Chicago IL 60622

KOWALSKI, KATHLEEN JOYCE, accountant; b. Garden City, Mich., Dec. 19, 1956; d. Jay Buford and Gladys Irene (Bassett) Cox; m. John Robert Kowalski, Feb. 13, 1976 (div. Nov. 1981); children: Kristine Lynn, Michael John. BBA, Detroit Coll. Bus., 1985. CPA, Mich. Bookkeeper Triple R Boring, Livonia, Mich., 1978-79; tax preparer H & R Block, Dearborn, Mich., 1979-80; staff auditor Sallan, Zack, Knoblock & Miller, Southfield, Mich., 1980-82; sr. acct. Collis, Kopmeyer & Co., CPA, Birmingham, Mich., 1983-85; faculty Detroit Coll. Bus., Dearborn, 1986—; owner Kathleen J. Kowalski, P.C., Lincoln Park, Mich., 1986—. Mem. Am. Inst. CPA's, Am. Women's Soc. CPA's, Mich. Assn. CPA's, South Metro Detroit Assn. CPA's. Avocation: clarinet, singing, dancing. Home and Office: 1713 Fort St Lincoln Park MI 48146

KOZAK, LAWRENCE EDWARD, mechanical engineer; b. Chgo., Dec. 15, 1949; s. Edward John and Irene Ann (Sebonia) K.; m. Marlene Louise Galante, Apr. 16, 1977. BSME, U. Ill., 1971; MBA, Loyola U., 1977. Registered profl. engr., Ill. Supr. tech. staff Commonwealth Edison Co., Chgo., 1977-79, prin. engr., 1979-81, sr. mktg. engr., 1981-82; power engr. UOP Inc., Des Plaines, Ill., 1982-83; project engr. Eisenmann Corp., Crystal Lake, Ill., 1983—. Mem. ASME, NSPE, Ill. Soc. Profl. Engrs. Roman Catholic. Avocation: apple orchard mgmt. Home: 13 Cambridge Ln Lincolnshire IL 60015 Office: Eisenmann Corp 150 E Dartmoor Dr Crystal Lake IL 60014

KOZAK, ROGER LEE, university administrator; b. Lake Andes, S.D., Oct. 15, 1945; s. John Henry and Louise Frances (Jaeger) K.; m. Patricia Ann Patocka, June 7, 1970. BS, So. State U., 1969; MA, U. S.D., 1970, EdS, 1972, EdD, 1979. Tchr. Yankton (S.D.) Middle Sch., 1970-71; prof. So. State U., Springfield, S.D., 1971-74; researcher Higher Edn. Governing Bd., Pierre, S.D., 1974-79; v.p. adminstrn. U. S.D., Vermillion, 1979—; cons. City of Vermillion, 1980-82, Black Hills State Coll., Spearfish, S.D., 1982-83. Co-author: State Planning System, 1979. Mem. Nat. Assn. Coll. and Univ. Bus. Officers, Cen. Assn. Coll. and Univ. Bus. Officers, Nat. Assn. Instl. Researchers, Coll. and Univ. Environment, Phi Delta Kappa. Roman Catholic. Lodge: Rotary (bd. dirs. Vermillion chpt. 1985-86). Avocations: sailing, golf, woodworking. Home: 928 Ridgecrest Dr Vermillion SD 57069 Office: U SD Slagle 129 414 E Clark Vermillion SD 57069

KOZANDA, KENNETH J., controller, finance executive; b. Chgo., Dec. 29, 1956; s. Stanley A. and Sylvia C. (Helaszek) K.; m. Corine K. Anderson, Sept. 8, 1979. BS in Acctg., No. Ill. U., 1978; MBA in Fin., DePaul U., 1981. CPA, Ill. Tax acct. Arthur Andersen, Chgo., 1978-79; Dir. Fin. Analysis Gatx Corp., Chgo., 1979-84; controller Stein Roe & Farnham, Chgo., 1984—; cons. Ansam Electric, Chgo., 1979—, ADK Fin. Services, Chgo., 1985—. Mem. Am. Inst. CPA's, Ill. Soc. CPA's. Republican. Roman Catholic. Home: 5806 S Corona Dr Palatine IL 60067 Office: Stein Roe & Farnham 1 S Wacker Suite 3300 Chicago IL 60606

KOZBERG, STEVEN FREED, psychologist; b. Mpls., Apr. 30, 1953; s. Martin L. and Lois (Bix) K. B.A., Macalester Coll., 1975; M.A., U. Minn.-Duluth, 1978; Ph.D., U. Wis.-Madison, 1981. Lic. cons. psychologist, Minn. Research asst. dept. counseling and guidance U. Wis.-Madison, 1978-79, teaching asst., 1980-81, research asst. Guidance Inst. for Talented Students, 1979-80; counseling psychologist, asst. prof. psychology Carleton Coll., Northfield, Minn., 1981—. Mem. Am. Psychol. Assn., Am. Assn. Counseling and Devel., Minn. Psychol. Assn. (exec. council), Minn. Assn. for Counseling and Devel., Soc. for Research on Adolescence, Sigma Xi, Phi Kappa Phi. Home: 6400 Barrie Rd Apt 606 Edina MN 55435 Office: Carleton Coll Northfield MN 55057

KOZBIAL, RICHARD JAMES, education professional; b. Toledo, Nov. 11, 1933; s. Phillip and Bernice Bronislawa (Durka) K.; m. Jane Ardys Verny, July 8, 1961 (dec. Nov. 1983); children: Ardys Jane, Beth Lynne. EdB, U. Toledo, 1957, EdM, 1976. Tchr. Toledo Pub. Schs., 1956-58, 1962-84, intern tchr. cons., 1984—; tchr. Van Dyke Sch. Dist., Warren, Mich., 1958-62; mem. textbook selection coms., Toledo Pub. Schs.; instr. student tchr. tng. programs Toledo U. 1962-84, Bowling Green State U. 1962-84, Mich. State U. 1958-59. Author Spelling Curriculum Guide Toledo Pub. Schs., 1968; producer (TV programs)WQTE Famous Ams. Born in Feb., Israel. Mem. Toledo Mus. Art; vestry mem. Trinity Episcopal Ch., 1984—. Named Outstanding Young Educator Toledo C. of C., 1965-66; Jennings Found. scholar, 1979-80; recipient Miss Peach award Toledo Blade, 1963. Mem. Am. Fedn. Tchrs., Ohio Fedn. Tchrs., Toledo Fedn. Tchrs., Internat. Inst., Inc. (life, bd. dirs. 1985—), Assn. Two Toledos, Toledo U. Alumni Assn., Am. Assn. Retired Persons, Phi Delta Kappa, Kappa Delta Pi. Democrat. Avocations: singing, swimming, walking, gardening, travel. Home: 3823 Grantley Rd Toledo OH 43613 Office: Intern Office Toledo Pub Schs 1901 W Central Ave Toledo OH 43606

KOZELKA, EDWARD WILLIAM, seed and feed company executive; b. Monona, Iowa, July 19, 1912; s. William Frank and Elizabeth (Tayek) K.; student Loras Coll., 1929-31; m. Beulah Annette Gunderson, Feb. 24, 1941; 1 dau., Gail Kathleen. Gen. mgr. Hall Roberts' Son, Postville, Iowa, 1932-46, v.p., gen. mgr., 1946-75, treas., 1975—; salesman Schiedel Real Estate, Postville, 1984—; dir. Postville State Bank, Postville Telephone Co. Mem. Postville City Council, 1960-61; pres. Postville Hist. Soc., 1975-78; treas. Upper Explorerland Resource, Conservation and Devel. Com., 1969—; chmn. Upper Explorerland Regional Planning Commn., 1971-80; chmn. N.E. Iowa River Basin Com., 1976-79; mem. Iowa Policy Adv. Council on Water Quality, 1976-82; mem. citizens adv. council Dept. Transp., 1977—; mem. NE Iowa Water Resource Bd., 1986—, planning and fin. com. Postville Hosp., 1959-60; chmn. bldg. com. Postville Hosp., 1960-61; co-chmn. fund raising com. Postville Good Samaritan Center, 1968; bd. dirs. Big 4 Fair, 1946-74; mem. adv. council Area Aging Com., 1983—. Recipient Disting. Service award Jaycees, 1966; hon. future farmer FFA. Mem. Iowa Seed Dealers Assn. (pres. 1972), Iowa Grain and Feed Assn., Western Seed Dealers Assn. Republican. Roman Catholic. Clubs: Kiwanis, Postville Comml. Home: 205 Williams St W Postville IA 52162 Office: PO Box 396 Postville IA 52162

KOZICKI, DANIEL RAYMOND, dentist; b. Chgo., May 15, 1951; s. Raymond Joseph Kozicki and Sabina Elaine (Zielinski) Wolski; m. Vivian Linda Lamastus, June 22, 1974; children: Daniel Raymond, William Robert, Raymond Joseph. BS in Biology with honors, U. Ill., Chgo., 1973, BS in Dentistry with honors, 1976, DDS with honors, 1978. Sr. comprehensive instr. U. Ill. Coll. Dentistry, Chgo., 1978-79; gen. practice dentistry Chgo., 1978—. Cubmaster Chgo. area council Boy Scouts Am., 1986—. James scholar U. Ill., Chgo., 1969. Mem. ADA, Ill. Dental Soc., Chgo. Dental Soc., Omicron Kappa Upsilon, Phi Eta Sigma. Republican. Roman Catholic. Club: Dental Arts (Chgo.). Office: 4114 W 63d St Chicago IL 60629

KOZINA, THOMAS JOSEPH, gynecologist, obstetrician, educator; b. Milw., June 25, 1930; s. Frank Joseph and Arlene Emily (Skochpol) K.; 1 child, Joan Worachek. BS, Marquette U., 1952, MD, 1957. Diplomate Am. Bd. Ob-Gyn. Intern St. Mary's Hosp., Milw., 1957-58, resident in ob-gyn, 1958-60; resident in ob-gyn Mt. Sinai Hosp., Milw., 1960-61; practice medicine specializing in ob-gyn Milw., 1961-78; dir. resident edn. St. Francis Hosp., Milw., 1976-78; assoc. prof. Med. Coll. Wis., Milw., 1978—; chmn. dept. ob-gyn St. Francis Hosp., 1970-78; dir. ob-gyn edn. in family practice Med. Coll. Wis., 1979—. Contbr. articles to profl. jours. Bd. dirs. St. Francis Hosp., 1981-83, Franklin (Wis.) State Bank, 1982—, Mchts. & Mfrs. Bank Holding, Milw., 1984—. Fellow Am. Coll. Ob-Gyn; mem. AMA, Am. Assn. Gynecol. Laparoscopists, Soc. Tchrs. Family Practice, Milw. Gynecol. Soc., St. Francis/Trinity/St. Luke's Ind. Physician's Assn., Inc. (pres. 1987—), Am. Shetland Sheepdog Assn. (nat. show chairperson 1981-84). Clubs: Combined Splty. Greater Milw. (pres. 1972-80). Avocations: breeding and showing dogs, golf. Home: 8432 W Ryan Rd Franklin WI 53132 Office: 3237 S 16 St Milwaukee WI 53215

KOZIOL, RICHARD DANIEL, municipal building and zoning director; b. Chgo., June 16, 1935; s. Frank Albert and Phyliss (Cygnar) K.; m. Gerrie Lou Lyster, Apr. 12, 1958 (div. May 1984); children: Ken, Karen Koziol Keth, Linda Koziol Dickens. cert. bldg. official Council Am. Bldg. Officials. Bldg. inspector Village of Skokie, Ill., 1962-67; dir. bldg. and zoning Village of Downers Grove, Ill., 1967-68, Village of Glenview, Ill., 1968—. Leader Boy Scouts Am., Rosemont, Ill., 1966-72. Served to master sgt. U.S. Army, 1957-61. Mem. Internat. Conf. Bldg. Officials, Nat. Fire Protection Assn., Bldg. Officials and Code Adminstrs. Internat., Ill. Council Code Adminstrs. (pres. 1982-83), Suburban Bldg. Officials (pres. 1981, William F. Bartell Meml. award 1984), N.W. Bldg. Officials (pres. 1973). Roman Catholic. Clubs: Radio Control Model (Chgo.), Model Aeronautics (Washington). Avocations: sailing, bicycling, canoeing, water skiing, cross country skiing. Home: 2944 W Neva Chicago IL 60634

KOZLOWSKI, ROBERT A., food services company executive; b. 1925. Student, Wayne State U., 1949. With Canteen Corp., Chgo., 1949—, v.p., 1972-74, v.p. vending, 1974-76, sr. v.p., gen. mgr. food vending, 1976-83, exec. v.p., 1983-84, pres., chief exec. officer, 1984—, also bd. dirs. Served with USMC, 1944-46. Office: Canteen Corp 1430 Merchandise Mart Chicago IL 60654 *

KOZLOWSKI, RONALD STEPHAN, librarian; b. Chgo., Oct. 18, 1937; s. Stephan James and Helen Marie Beck (Tancula) K.; m. Barbara Hartlein, Aug. 8, 1964; children: Ann, Keith, Ellen, Brent. B.S. in Edn, Ill. State U., 1961; M.A. in L.S, Rosary Coll., 1968. Audiovisual librarian Triton Jr. Coll., River Grove, Ill., 1968-69; br. librarian Evansville (Ind.) Pub. Libraries, 1969-70, asst. dir., 1971-74; head reference and acquisitions dept. Ind. State U., Evansville, 1970-71; dir. West Fla. Regional Library, Pensacola, 1974-77, Louisville Free Public Library, 1977-83, Pub. Library Charlotte and Mecklenburg County, N.C., 1983-86; exec. dir. Cuyahoga County Pub. Library, Cleve., 1986—; del. White House Conf. on Libraries. Mem. ALA, Ohio Library Assn. Office: Cuyahoga County Public Library 4510 Memphis Ave Cleveland OH 44144

KOZOKOFF, NEIL JAMES, lawyer; b. Cleve., Aug. 29, 1955; s. Norman Jack and Phyllis Rosalyn (Gombiner) K. AB, Colgate U., 1977; JD, Case Western Res. U., 1981. Bar: Ohio 1981, U.S. Dist. Ct. (no. dist.) Ohio 1981, U.S. Ct. Appeals (6th cir.) 1982; Ill. 1985. Assoc. Guren, Merritt, Cleve., 1981-84, Benesch, Friedlander, Cleve., 1984, Rudnick & Wolfe, Chgo., 1984—; gen. ptnr. KPH Partnership, Cleve., 1982—, Metro A, Cleve., 1984—, Melrose St. Syndicate, Chgo., 1987—. Mem. ABA, Chgo. Bar Assn. Democrat. Jewish. Avocations: bldg. restoration, archtl. drawings, music. Home: 910 Lake Shore Dr Chicago IL 60611 Office: Rudnick & Wolfe 30 N LaSalle Chicago IL 60602

KOZOLL, CHARLES EVANS, academic director; b. Milw., Apr. 12, 1938; s. Harry H. and Becky (Sharp) K.; m. Joan Pass, Aug. 10, 1970; children: Richard Howard, Scott Frederick. BS, U. Mich., 1960; MA, Boston U., 1962; diploma in edn., Makerere Coll., Kompalo, Uganda, 1963; PhD, Columbia U., 1969. Sr. assoc. Bank State Coll. Edn., East Harlem, N.Y., 1968-69; sr. edn. analyst ABT Assocs., Inc., Cambridge, Mass., 1969; assoc. dir. so. region edn. bd. Adult Basic Edn., Atlanta, 1970-72; assoc. dean adult edn. U. Ga., Athens, 1972-74; assoc. dir. continuing edn. U. Ill., Champaign, 1974—; cons. in field; lectr. various states, 1971-75; program evaluation cons. Nat. Assn. Pub. Continuing Adult Edn., Washington, 1972-78; cons. with local orgns., 1986. Author: TimeLine, 1982, Time Management for Coaches, 1985, Plan for Success, 1985, (video tape) Time Management A Daily Excercise, 1986. Mem. Internat. and Am. Oil Chemist's Soc., U.S. Civil Service Commn., Phi Delta Kappa. Home: 1108 Plymouth Dr Champaign IL 61820 Office: U Ill Continuing Edn Pub Services 302 E John Suite 202 Champaign IL 61820

KRAATZ, ROLAND LEE, utility company executive; b. Evanston, Ill., May 18, 1943; s. Arthur William Kraatz and Dorothy Loraine (Strauss) Keyes; m. Gloria Jean Hohisel, Sept. 4, 1965. B.S. in Elec. Engring., Bradley U., 1965; M.B.A., U. Chgo., 1971. Registered profl. engr., Ill. Engr., Commonwealth Edison Co., Maywood, Ill., 1965-68, Joliet, Ill., 1969-71, Chgo., 1971-82, dir. econ. research, 1982-85, dir. rates, 1985—. Mem. IEEE (sr.), Western Soc. Engrs. Home: 1857 Mission Hills Ln Northbrook IL 60062

KRABBENHOFT, KENNETH LESTER, radiologist, educator; b. Sabula, Iowa, Jan. 7, 1923; s. Lester Henry and Bessie Grant (Thompson) K.; m. Gloria Darlene Eriksen, June 17, 1944; children: Kenneth Lester, Douglas Harold, Karen Ann Krabbenhoft Graham. BA, State U. Iowa, 1943, MD, 1946. Diplomate: Am. Bd. Radiology. Intern Harper Hosp., Detroit, 1946-47, resident in radiology, 1949-52, assoc. radiologist, 1952-57, radiologist, 1957—; practice medicine specializing in radiology Birmingham, Mich., 1957—; prof., chmn. dept. radiology Wayne State U., Detroit, 1969-84; chief radiology Detroit Receiving Hosp.-Univ. Health Center, 1980-84; cons. radiologist VA Hosp., Allen Park, Mich., Children's Hosp. Mich., Crittenton Gen. Hosp., Herman Kiefer Hosp., Nat. Cancer Inst.; mem. Nat. Cancer Adv. Bd., 1970-73; pres. Affiliated Radiologists, Inc., Detroit, 1973-85 , Detroit Gen. Hosp. Research Corp., 1974-82; mem. Environ. Radiation Exposure Adv. Com., 1975-78; trustee Am. Bd. Radiology, 1970—, sec., exec. dir., 1981—; treas. Am. Bd. Med. Specialists, 1981-85; alt. del. Internat. Congress Radiology. Cons. editor: Am. Jour. Roentgenology, 1975-81. Served to lt. (j.g.), M.C. USNR, 1947-49. Nat. Cancer Inst. grantee, 1971-75; Nat. Cancer Inst. Specialized Cancer Center grantee, 1973-75. Fellow Am. Coll. Radiology; mem. Detroit Acad. Medicine, Detroit Med. Club, AMA (vice chmn. sect. council 1969-71), Mich., Wayne County med. socs., Mich. Radiol. Soc. (pres. 1969-70), Am. Radium Soc., Am. Roentgen Ray Soc. (silver medal 1962), AAAS, Radiol. Soc. N.Am., Inter-Am. Coll. Radiology, Friends of Detroit Public Library, Founders Soc. Detroit Inst. Art, State Hist. Soc. Iowa, Mich. Hist. Soc., Lost Lakes Woods Assn., Sigma Xi, Alpha Omega Alpha. Clubs: Masons, Detroit. Exhibited portable radioactive istopes for radiography at Smithsonian Inst., 1964-67. Home: 52 Oxford Rd Pleasant Ridge MI 48069 Office: 300 Park St Suite 440 Birmingham MI 48009

KRABILL, ROBERT ELMER, osteopathic physician; b. Wayland, Iowa, June 4, 1934; s. Robert H. and Amanda (Wyse) K.; m. Ellen Savage, Sept. 1, 1963; children: Keith Andrew, Angela Kay, Valerie Ann, Kelly Dawn. BS, Iowa Wesleyan Coll., 1961; DO, Kirkville (Mo.) Coll. Osteo. Medicine, 1966. Diplomate Am. Bd. Family Practice. Intern Cuyahoga Falls (Ohio) Gen. Hosp., 1966-67, mem. staff, 1967—; gen. practice osteo. medicine Uniontown, Ohio, 1967—; sec., treas. gen. practice dept. Cuyahoga Falls Gen. Hosp., 1985-86. Named one of Outstanding Young Men of Am., U.S. Jaycees, 1969. Mem. Am. Osteo. Assn., Ohio Osteo. Assn., Am. Coll. Gen. Practitioners Osteo. Medicine and Surgery. Mennonite. Home: 3733 N Vista NW Uniontown OH 44685 Office: 13017 Cleveland Ave NW Uniontown OH 44685

KRAEMER, ELIZABETH EMERSON, clinical psychologist, educator; b. Lynchburg, Va., Mar. 1, 1936; d. Cameron and Leona (Greene) King; children—Mark Karl, Kristina Marie, Katherine Ann, Teresa Kelle. A.B., U. Mo., 1970, M.A., 1971, Ph.D., 1978. Asst. dir. Psychol. Clinic, U. Mo., Columbia, 1974-75; clin. psychologist Mark Twain Mental Health Ctr., Kirksville, Mo., 1975-78; dir., pvt. practice clin. psychology Profl. Counseling Services, Kirksville, 1978—; mem. faculty Northeast Mo. State U., 1978—. Bd. dirs. ARC, 1979-82, Kirksville Crisis Line, 1978-83, Transisition Care Ctr., 1980-82. Mem. Am. Psychol. Assn., Phi Beta Kappa. Democrat. Roman Catholic. Office: 404 S Franklin St Suite 3 Kirksville MO 63501

KRAEMER, PAUL WILHELM, utilities executive; b. Mpls., Dec. 28, 1920; s. John C. and Rose (Schoenstuhl) K.; m. Doris Carter, Jan. 2, 1946; children: Bruce, Fred (dec.). B.S. in Chem. Engring, U. Minn., 1942; B.S. in Law, William Mitchell Coll. Law, 1957. With Minn. Gas Co., 1947—, v.p. ops., 1958-66, exec. v.p., 1966-67, pres., chief exec. officer, 1967-81, chmn. bd., 1981—, dir., 1965—, mem. exec. com., 1966—; dir. Investors Group of Cos., N.Am. Life & Casualty Co. Contbr. articles to profl. jours. Trustee emeritus William Mitchell Coll. Law; v.p., bd. dirs. Greater Mpls. Met. Housing Corp.; trustee, chmn. Dunwoody Indsl. Inst. Served to lt. USNR, 1942-46. Recipient Operating award of merit Am. Gas Assn., 1959; named Engr. of Year Mpls. Engrs. Club, 1968. Mem. Engrs. Club, Am. Gas Assn. (fin. com., dir.). Clubs: Masons (Mpls.), Mpls. (Mpls.), Minikahda Country (Mpls.); Delray Dunes Country (Fla.).

KRAESZIG-MULCAHY, KARLA MARIA, optometrist; b. Indpls., Oct. 29, 1951; d. Harry E. and Lillian (Lieland) Kraeszig; m. James George Mulcahy, Oct. 11, 1980; 1 child, James Lionel. BS, Ind. U., 1973, OD, 1975. Optometrist Arner & Kraeszig, Rockford, Ill., 1976-82; owner, optometrist Dr. Karla Kraeszig-Mulcahy, Byron, Ill., 1982—; mem. Vol. Optometric Services to Humanity, 1980—. Mem. Am. Optometic Assn. (contact lens sect., Ill. chairperson profl. enhancement program 1984—), Ill. Optometric Assn. (v.p. orgn. 1985—), Phi Beta Kappa, Omega Epsilon Phi.

KRAFCISIN, MICHAEL HARRY, radio station manager; b. Chgo., Mar. 4, 1958; s. Michael J. and Josephine L. (Szela) K. Student, Loyola U., Chgo., 1976-77. Ops. mgr., programmng cons. The FM 100 Plan, Chgo., 1976-82, Bonneville Broadcasting System, Palatine, Ill., 1982-84; dir. client services Bonneville Broadcasting System, Northbrook, Ill., 1985; gen. mgr. Sta. WSEX-FM, Arlington Heights, Ill., 1986—. Ill. State scholar, 1976. Roman Catholic. Home: PO Box 847 Barrington IL 60011-0847 Office: Sta WSEX-FM 120 W University Dr Arlington Heights IL 60004-1892

KRAFT, MARY ELLEN HARKINS, librarian, media specialist, photographer; b. Akron, Ohio, Feb. 11, 1934; d. Edwin Daniel and Anne Henrietta (Reid) Harkins; m. Robert Francis Kraft, Nov. 24, 1956; children: Robert Edwin, Steven Michael, Timothy John. BA in English, Hanover Coll., 1955; MS in Edn., Butler U., 1975. Cert.. librarian/media specialist. Librarian/media specialist Noblesville (Ind.) Schs., 1973—. Author poems; photographer Dance Mag., 1983. Mem. Friends of Photography, Carmel, Calif., 1982-87, Indpls. Mus. Art, Indpls., Indpls. Art League; patron Hamilton County Theatre Guild, Noblesville, 1964—. Mem. ALA, Assn. for Ind. Media Educators (Young Hoosier award com. 1980-86, media com. 1986-87). Avocations: photography, poetry, piano, travel. Home: 5610 E 161st St Noblesville IN 46060 Office: Hinkle Creek Elem Sch 595 S Harbour Dr Noblesville IN 46060

KRAFVE, ALLEN HORTON, management consultant; b. Superior, Wis., Jan. 26, 1937; s. Richard Ernest and Frances Virginia (Horton) K.; m. Lois Anne Reed, Aug. 15, 1959; children—Bruce Allen, Anne Marie, Carol Elizabeth. B.S. in Mech. Engring., U. Mich., 1958, M.B.A., 1960, M.S. in Mech. Engring., 1961. Asst. prof. mech. engring. San Jose State U. (Calif.), 1961-65; various positions including quality control mgr. Ford Motor Co., Dearborn, Mich., 1965-77; engring. mgr. Kysor/Cadillac, Cadillac, Mich., 1977-82; mgmt. cons., Lake City, Mich., 1982—; bd. dirs. NOC Industries, Cadillac; pres. Lark Homes, Inc., 1979—. Co-author: Reliability Considerations in Design, 1962, internat. conf. paper, 1961. Bd. dirs. Crooked Tree council Girl Scouts U.S.A., Traverse City, Mich., 1983. Mem. ASME, Soc. Automotive Engrs., Am. Soc. Quality Control, Am. Soc. Engring. Edn. Republican. Methodist. Home: 145 Duck Point Dr Lake City MI 49651 Office: Allen H Krafve Cons 2604 Sunnyside Dr Cadillac MI 49601

KRAIBERG, LINDA ARLENE, fine arts educator; b. St. Louis, Oct. 28, 1948; d. Lloyd and Edith Fern (Pierce) Fannon; m. Leo C. Kraiberg, Dec. 21, 1985; 1 child, Kimberly Gayle. BA in Edn., Webster U., 1979. Cert. tchr., Mo. Elem. sch. tchr. Parkway Schs., St. Louis, 1979-80; adminstrv. asst. Cancer Info. Program, St. Louis, 1980-82; substitute tchr. St. Louis Pub. Schs., 1982-83, art tchr., 1983—; dental asst. Carlo J. Rumbolo, DMD, St. Louis, 1981-83. Judge poster contest Internat. Reading Assn. , 1987;

cooperating tchr. poster contest Six Flags Over Mid-AM., 1986, 87. Mem. Am. Fedn. Tchrs., St. Louis Tchrs. Union.

KRAIG, BRUCE ZACHARY, history and humanities educator; b. N.Y.C., Sept. 23, 1939; s. Abe and Zaira (Astafijew) K.; m. Barbara Adams, Nov. 1960 (div. 1975); children: Robert A., Michael B., Theodore D.; m. Janice Ione Thompson, Aug. 21, 1984. Student, Heidelberg U., Fed. Republic Germany, 1959-60; BA, U. Calif., Berkeley, 1962; MA, U. Pa., 1963, PhD, 1969; postgrad., U. Leeds, Eng., 1966-68. Asst. prof. history Eastern Ill. U., Charleston, 1968-70; prof. history and humanities Roosevelt U., Chgo., 1971—, dir. honors program, asst. dean faculties,, 1977-81; asst. dir. archeol. excavations Dept. Environment and Deserted Village Group, London and Belfast, Northern Ireland, 1964, 66, 68; dir. archeol. excavations Pa. State Mus., Harrisburg, 1965; cons. Scott, Foresman & Co., Glenview, Ill., 1980—. Author: (with others) Stonehenge: The Indo-European Heritage, 1978, The Formation of Civilization, 1979, Mexican-American Plain Cooking, 1982, Our World: Eastern Hemisphere, 1983, World History, 1987; food columnist, editor Oak Park (Ill.) News, 1978-80, Wednesday Jour. Oak Park and River Forest (Ill.), 1980—, also bd. dirs., 1982-86; columnist Forest Park Rev., 1980—; contbr. articles to hist., ednl. and ch. jours., food articles to Chgo. Sun-Times, Chgo. Reader; producer and host radio and TV programs; co-author (film) The Rock That Glowed, 1987. Sec. Oak Park Environment Commn., 1981-85. Recipient Lt. Gov.'s award State of Pa., 1963, 66. Mem. Am. Hist. Assn., Soc. Med. Archaeology (Colt Fund grant 1967-68), Deserted Village Research Group, Royal Archeol. Inst., Council British Archaeology. Democrat. Home: 636 N Harvey Ave Oak Park IL 60302

KRAINIK, ARDIS, opera company executive; b. Manitowoc, Wis., Mar. 8, 1929; d. Arthur Stephen and Clara (Bracken) K. BS cum laude, Northwestern U., 1951, DFA (hon.), 1984, postgrad., 1953-54; LHD (hon.), DePaul U., 1985, Loyola U., 1986, U. Wis., 1986; DFA (hon.), St. Xavier Coll., 1986. Tchr. drama, pub. speaking Horlick High Sch., Racine, Wis., 1951-53; exec. sec., office mgr. Lyric Opera, Chgo., 1954-59; asst. mgr. Lyric Opera, 1960-76, artistic adminstr., 1976-80, gen. mgr., 1981—; bd. dirs. No. Trust Co. Mezzo soprano appearing with, Chgo. Lyric Opera, 1955-59, Cameo Opera Co., Chgo.; appeared in: Artists Showcase, NBC-TV, recitals throughout area. Recipient Commendatore Italian Order Merit, 1984, Ill. Order Lincoln, 1985, Alumni Merit award Northwestern U., 1986. Mem. Ill. Arts Alliance, Internat. Assn. Opera Dirs., Opera Am. (bd. dirs), Mortar Bd., Phi Kappa Lambda. Christian Scientist. Clubs: Economic, Commercial (Chgo.). Office: c/o Lyric Opera of Chgo 20 N Wacker Dr Chicago IL 60606

KRAKER, DAVID NELSON, accountant; b. Zeeland, Mich., Sept. 24, 1961; s. Howard Nelson and Harlene Faye (Arens) K. AA, Grand Rapids (Mich.) Jr. Coll., 1981; BBA, U. Mich., 1983. CPA, Mich. Staff acct. Seidman & Seidman, Grand Rapids, 1983-85, sr. acct., 1985—. Adv. Jr. Achievement, Grand Rapids, 1983-85. Mem. Am. Inst. CPA's, Mich. Assn. CPA's, Grand Rapids Jaycees. Avocations: photography, travel, sports. Office: Seidman & Seidman 99 Monroe NW Suite 800 Grand Rapids MI 49503

KRAKOWSKI, RICHARD JOHN, lawyer, public relations executive; b. Meppen, W.Ger., Apr. 3, 1946; came to U.S., 1951, naturalized, 1962; s. Feliks and Maria (Chilinski) K. M.B.A., DePaul U., 1979; J.D., John Marshall Law Sch., 1983. Bar: Ill. 1984. Personnel dir. Andy Frain, Inc., Chgo., 1973-78; pub. relations dir. Chgo. Health Systems Agy., 1978-84; assoc. firm Mangum, Smietanka & Johnson, Chgo., 1984—; lectr. in field. Fundraising and pub. relations dir. Cabrini-Green Sandlot Tennis program, Chgo., 1979-83; sustaining mem. Republican Nat. Com., 1981—. Served to capt. U.S. Army, 1969-72. Mem. ABA, Ill. Bar Assn., Chgo. Bar Assn., Chgo. Council Fgn. Relations, Advocates Soc., Lyric Opera Guild. Roman Catholic. Club: Publicity (Chgo.). Co-author: Health Care Financing and Policy Making in Chicago and Illinois, 1982. Home: 65 E Scott St Apt 12C Chicago IL 60610 Office: 35 E Wacker Dr #2130 Chicago IL 60601

KRALL, JANICE MARIE, health service executive, consultant; b. Eveleth, Minn., Aug. 19, 1950; d. Edward John and Rose Marie (Korcha) K.; m. Richard Charles Shannon, June 13, 1981. BA in Med. Record Adminstrn., Coll. St. Scholastica, Duluth, Minn., 1972; student in nursing home adminstrn., U. Wis., 1982. Dir. med. records Mendota Mental Health Inst., Madison, 1972-75; med. record cons. div. of health Bur. Quality Compliance, Madison, 1975—; instr. Moraine Park Tech. Inst., Fond du Lac, Wis., 1980-81; guest lectr. Sch. of Allied Health Professions, Milw., 1984—. Editor: (newsletter) The Special, 1984-86. Mem. St. Bernards Social Concerns Commn., Madison, 1985—; chmn. Koinonia Com., Dale Heights Ch., Madison, 1986—. Mem. Am. Med. Record Assn. (cert., del. Wis. 1976-86), Wis. Med. Record Assn. (pres. 1986-87), Madison Area Med. Record Assn. (pres. 1981-82). Roman Catholic. Avocations: scuba diving, camping, sewing, cooking, pottery. Home: 3649 Mathias Way Verona WI 53593 Office: Bur Quality Compliance 1 W Wilson PO Box 309 Madison WI 53701

KRALL, JOSEPH PATRICK, business machine company executive; b. Cambridge, Ohio, Aug. 10, 1931; s. Joseph and Anne Rita (Crevey) K.; m. Marlene Diane Gibson, May 23, 1958; children: Michelle Anne, Angelia J. BS, Muskingum Coll., 1953; postgrad., U. Miami, 1955, Ohio State U., 1957, 60. Cost estimator RCA, Cambridge, 1961-65; mgr. cost estimating Collins Radio, Cedar Rapids, Iowa, 1965-66; mgr. cost estimating NCR Corp., Cambridge, 1968-70, mgr. mfg. engr., 1970-73, program mgr., 1973-78, product mgr., operations program mgr., 1978—. Served to cpl. USMC, 1953-55. Mem. Cambridge C. of C. Roman Catholic. Avocations: tennis, hunting, fishing. Home: 64225 Morrison Rd Cambridge OH 43725 Office: NCR 800 Cochran Ave Cambridge OH 43725

KRAMER, ALEX JOHN, dentist; b. Aurora, Ill., Dec. 21, 1939; s. Roy Edward and Frances (Astromskis) K.; m. Phyllis Rose Gonsky, July 15, 1967 (div. Sept. 1978); m. Brenda Jean Schillinger, Sept. 12, 1981; children: Ian Alexander, ELizabeth Katherine. Student, Marquette U., 1957-60; DDS, U. Ill., Chgo., 1964. Gen. practice dentistry Montgomery, Ill., 1966—. Mem. exec. bd. Two Rivers Boy Scouts Am., St. Charles, Ill., 1969-79. Served to lt. USNR, 1964-66. Mem. ADA, Am. Assn. Maxillofacial Orthopedics, Ill. State Dental Assn., Chgo. Dental Soc., Aurora Dental Soc., Fox Valley Dental Soc., Am. Acad. Gnathological Orthopedics, Am. Soc. Gen. Dentistry, Dentafacial Orthopedics Study Club Mo., Am. Assn. Functional Orthodontics, Internat. Acad. Orthomolecular and Preventive Medicine., U. Ill. Alumni Assn., Pershing Rifles Hon. Mil. Frat., Psi Omega. Republican. Methodist. Club: Aurora (Ill.) Country. Lodge: Optimists. Avocations: boating, skiing, diving, fishing, hiking. Home: 68 Garfield Oswego IL 60543 Office: 115 N Main St Montgomery IL 60538

KRAMER, BARRY ALLEN, hospital planning adminstrator; b. St. Louis, July 19, 1949; s. Roy Harry and Alberta (Knieste) K.; m. Patricia Ann Coop, Oct. 27, 1979; children: Todd Alan, Holly Michelle. BA, Westminster Coll., Fulton, Mo., 1971; MS in Pub. Health, U. Mo., 1972; M of Pub. Adminstrn., U. Kans., 1977. Health educator Topeka/Shawnee County Health Dept., Topeka, Kans., 1972-76; health planning project reviewer Kans. Dept. Health and Environment, Topeka, 1976-81; dir. planning Shawnee Mission (Kans.) Med. Ctr., 1981—; pres. Topeka City Employees' Credit Union, 1975. Bd. dirs. Kansas City (Mo.) Homesharing Council, 1984-86. Named one of Outstanding Young Men of Am., 1975. Mem. Am. Coll. Health Care Execs., Soc. Hosp. Planning and Mktg., Am. Pub. Health Assn., Kansas City Regional Soc. Health Care Planners and Marketers (bd. dirs. 1983). Republican. Presbyterian. Lodge: Masons (master 1978). Home: 14715 W 91st St Lenexa KS 66215 Office: Shawnee Mission Med Ctr 9100 W 74th St Shawnee Mission KS 66201

KRAMER, CHARLES HENRY, psychiatrist; b. Oak Park, Ill., May 31, 1922; s. Charles Henry and Martha (Ball) K.; m. Jeannette Ross, Sept. 15, 1945; children: Dan, Judy, Doug, Greg, Chip, David. B.S., U. Ill., 1944, M.D., 1945; grad., Inst. Psychoanalysis, Chgo., 1967. Diplomate: Am. Bd. Psychiatry and Neurology. Intern Cook County Hosp., Chgo., 1945-46, U. Ill. Hosp., Chgo., 1946-47; resident Chanute AFB Hosp., Ill., 1951-53, Elgin (Ill.) State Hosp., 1953-54, Inst. Juvenile Research, Chgo., 1955-59; pvt. practice medicine and surgery Palatine, Ill., 1947-51; pvt. practice psychiatry Oak Park, 1954—; founder Family Inst. Chgo., 1968, pres., 1968-86; dir. family studies Inst. Psychiatry, Northwestern Meml. Hosp., 1975-86; prof. psychiatry and behavioral scis. Northwestern U. Med. Sch., 1975—; founder, pres. Plum Grove Nursing Home, 1953-83, Kramer Found., 1961—, Kramer Enterprises, 1980—; cons. mental health orgns. Author: Basic Principles of Long-Term Patient Care, 1976, Becoming a Family Therapist, 1980; cons. editor: Jour. Psychotherapy and the Family, Family Systems Medicine. Served with U.S. Army, 1943-45; Served with USAF, 1951-53. Recipient Better Life awards Ill. and Am. Nursing Home Assns., 1970. Fellow Am. Psychiat. Assn. (life); mem. Chgo. Psychoanalytic Soc., Ill. Council Child Psychiatry, Ill. Psychiat. Soc., Am. Family Therapy Assn. (incorporator, founding dir.), Am. Assn. Marriage and Family Therapy (approved supr.), Sigma Xi. Club: Chgo. Yacht. Home: 417 N Kenilworth Oak Park IL 60302 Office: 666 Lake Shore Dr #1530 Chicago IL 60611

KRAMER, DANIEL LOUIS, controller; b. St. Louis, July 6, 1962; s. Vernon Louis and Geraldine Lorretta (Boelhauf) K. BBA, Loyola U., New Orleans, 1984. CPA, Mo., La. Sr. cons. Ernst & Whinney, St. Louis, 1984-86; corp. controller Feld Chevrolet Co., St. Louis, 1986—. Mem. Am. Inst. CPA's, Mo. Soc. CPA's, La. Soc. CPA's. Office: Feld Chevrolet Co 11200 St Charles Rock Rd Bridgeton MO 63044

KRAMER, JACK A., accountant; b. Chgo., May 25, 1950; s. Gerald J. and Beatrice (Solomon) K.; m. Helene Rae Bartlett, Nov. 3, 1979; children: Adam, Jaime. BS in Acctg., U. Ill., 1972. CPA, Ill. Staff acct. Berman & Berman, Ltd., Chgo., 1971-78, ptnr., 1978-85; ptnr. Checkers, Simon & Rosner, Chgo., 1985—. Bd. dirs. Young Men's Jewish Council, Chgo., 1982—. Mem. Am. Inst. CPA's, Ill. Soc. CPA's, Real Estate Securities and Syndication Inst., Jr. League Chgo. (fin. adv. com. 1986—). Office: Checkers Simon & Rosner One S Wacker Dr Suite 2400 Chicago IL 60606

KRAMER, JOEL ROY, journalist, newspaper executive; b. Bklyn., May 21, 1948; s. Archie and Rae (Abramowitz) K.; m. Laurie Maloff, 1969; children—Matthew, Elias, Adam. B.A., Harvard U., Cambridge, 1969. Editor-in-chief Harvard Crimson; reporter Sci. Mag., Washington, 1969-70; free lance writer Washington, 1970-72; from copy editor to news editor, exec. news editor, asst. mng. editor Newsday, L.I., N.Y., 1972-80; exec. editor Buffalo Courier-Express, 1981-82, Star Tribune, Mpls., St. Paul, 1983—; bd. dirs. Harvard Crimson Inc., 1969—. Co-recipient Pulitzer prize for Pub. Service, Newsday " The Heroin Trail", 1973; Best Legal Writing on Large Daily award N.Y. Bar Assn., 1974. Mem. Am. Soc. Newspaper Editors, AP Mng. Editors Assn. Office: Star Tribune 425 Portland Ave Minneapolis MN 55488

KRAMER, MARY ANN EGAN, dentist; b. Oak park, Ill., Mar. 13, 1957; d. Thomas Joseph and Julia Mae (Curtin) Egan; m. Jesse James Kramer, July 2, 1983; 1 child, Jesse. BSN, U. Ill., Chgo., 1979, BS in Dentistry, 1982, DDS, 1984. Nurse Rush Presbyn. St. Lukes Hosp., Chgo., 1979-84; supervising dentist Harper Coll., Palatine, Ill., 1984, instr. pharmacology, 1985—; gen. practice dentistry Dental Concepts Westmont, Ill., 1984—, Dental Concepts Westchester, Ill., 1985—; dental advisor West Suburban Dental Hygiene Soc., 1985-86. Mem. Chgo. Dental soc., Sigma Theta Tau. Republican. Roman Catholic. Avocations: piano, tennis. Office: Dental Concepts 3075 Wolf Rd Westchester IL 60153

KRAMER, MILT LOUIS, teacher, mayor; b. Elkader, Iowa, Feb. 19, 1937; s. Milton M. and Anna Mae H. (Eberhardt) K.; m. D. Joanne Doerring, July 18, 1959; children: Kerry Jo Johnson, Jill Ellen Davidson. BA, Luther Coll., 1959; postgrad., U. No. Iowa, 1966, 69, 71, 82, Iowa State U., 1979, Drake U., 1986-87. Cert. tchr., Iowa. Instr. social studies, dept. chairperson Fayette (Iowa) High Sch., 1959-63, West Delaware Schs., Manchester, Iowa, 1963—. City councilman City of Manchester, 1970-73, mayor, 1973—; v.p. Manchester Enterprises, 1984—; numerous bds. and commns. Named one of Outstanding Young Men Am., 1972. Mem. NEA, Iowa State Edn. Assn., West Delaware Edn. Assn. (pres. 1973-74), N.E. Iowa Edn. Assn. (pres. 1976-77), Jaycees (Outstanding Young Educator award, 1969, Disting. Service award, 1973, Outstanding Citizen award, 1976). Lutheran. Home: 1008 Doctor St Manchester IA 52057 Office: Mayor's Office 208 E Main Manchester IA 52057

KRAMER, PAMELA KOSTENKO, librarian; b. Chgo., Mar. 5, 1944; d. Barry Michael and Helene (Ullrich) Kostenko; m. Claude Richard Kramer, Aug. 17, 1966. A.B., U. Ill., 1966; M.A.L.S., Rosary Coll., 1973. Tchr. English United Twp. High Sch., E. Moline, Ill., 1966-70, audiovisual librarian, 1970-76; instr. Marycrest Coll., Davenport, Iowa, 1973-75; librarian United Twp. High Sch., E. Moline, 1976-81, librarian, audio visual dept. head, 1981-86; librarian Libertyville (Ill.) High Sch., 1986—. Trustee River Bend Library System, 1986-87. Author audiovisual software revs. for Previews mag. Sch. Library Jour., 1973—. Edmund J. James scholar, 1962-66. Mem. ALA, Women in Edn. Adminstrn., Ill. Library Assn., Ill. Assn. Ednl. Communications and Tech., NEA, Ill. Edn. Assn., Classroom Tchrs. Assn., Ill. Assn. Tchrs. English, Ill. Assn. Media in Edn., Am. Assn. Sch. Librarians, Assn. Supervision and Curriculum Devel., Delta Kappa Gamma, Beta Phi Mu. Home: 3441 60th St Apt 5C Moline IL 61265 Office: Libertyville High Sch 708 W Park Ave Libertyville IL 60048

KRAMER, ROY HOWARD, financial executive; b. N.Y.C., July 25, 1960; s. Richard Melvyn and Elaine (Feingold) K.; m. Martha Rachel Barker, Nov. 3, 1985; 1 child, Marissa Rachel Barker. BS in Acctg., U. Mo., 1982. CPA, Mo. Staff acct. Mayer Hoffman McCann, kansas City, Mo., 1982-83; sr. tax acct. Arthur Andersen & Co., St. Louis, 1983-85; fin. officer Prewitt-Moore, St. Louis, 1985—; cons. Creve Coeur Ins., St. Louis, Mo.; v.p., sec. James Shelton, Inc., N.Y.C. Mem. Am. Inst. CPA's, St. Louis Lotus Users Group, Mo. Soc. CPA's. Democrat. Jewish. Avocations: music, travel, golf. Home: 1139A Knollwood Pkwy Dr Saint Louis MO 63042

KRAMER, WILLIAM DEAN, banking consultant, accountant; b. Atkinson, Nebr., Aug. 1, 1957; s. Sylvester John and Frances Gertrude (Kaup) K.; m. Marie Annette Stewart, May 27, 1978. BS in Acctg., Minot State Coll., 1983. CPA, N.D. Real estate salesman Century 21, Minot, N.D., 1979-81; sr. acct. Gate City Fed. Bank, Fargo, 1983-85; asst. v.p., cons. Dakota First Services, Inc., Fargo, 1985-87; with Prudential Home Mortgage Co., Mpls., 1987—. Served with USAF, 1975-79. Mem. Am. Inst. CPA's, N.D. Soc. CPA's, Inst. Internal Auditors. Roman Catholic. Club: Southgate Racquet (Fargo). Avocations: skiing, racquet sports, woodworking, reading. Home: 14114 Park Ave S Burnsville MN 55337

KRAMER, WILLIAM SWALLOW, pediatric dentistry educator; b. Butte, Nebr., Jan. 10, 1922; s. Sylvester John and Mabel Louise (Swallow) K.; m. Mary Louise Neal, Mar. 18, 1944; children: Kathryn Ann, Steven, David, Mark. BS, U. Nebr., 1946, DDS, 1948, MS, 1954. Diplomate Am. Bd. Pedodontics. Instr. dentistry U. Nebr., Lincoln, 1948-52, prof. of dentistry, 1954-58, prof. pediatric dentistry, 1958—, chmn. dept., 1958-80; pvt. practice Holdrege, Nebr., 1952-54; vis. prof. 10 univs.; lectr. U.S., Mex., Can.; examiner Am. Bd. Pedodontics, 1962-69, exec. sec., 1971-80. Author 15 profl. papers. Served to cpl. U.S. Army, 1942-44. Dental Asst. Utilization grantee, USPHS, 1962-68. Fellow Am. Acad. Pediatric Dentistry (pres. 1970-71; mem. ADA, (cons.), Am. Soc. Dentistry for Children, Sigma Xi, Omicron Kappa Upsilon (sec., treas. Supreme Chpt. 1970-86, Wm. S. Kramer award of Excellence established at all U.S. dental schs. 1986). Avocations: tennis, running, oil painting. Home: 5124 Ventura Fremont NE 68025 Office: U Nebr Coll Dentistry 40th & Holdrege Lincoln NE 68583-0740

KRANTZ, BEATRICE V., ednl. adminstr.; b. Chgo.; d. Andrew S. and Beatrice K.; B.A., Lake Forest Coll.; M.A. in Public Law, Columbia U.; postgrad. Northwestern U., 1944-60, U. Ill., 1960-62, No. Ill. U., 1964, Ill. Inst. Tech., 1969. Formerly adminstrv. asst. to lawyer, Chgo.; tchr. social studies Deerfield (Ill.) Shields High Sch.; tchr. govt., econs. and history High Sch. Dist. 218, Blue Island, Ill., 1936-47; asst. county supt. schs., dir. tchr. personnel and placement Cook County Schs., Chgo., 1947-51, asst. supt. secondary edn., scholarships, guidance, 1967-70, asst. supt. in charge West area Ednl. Service Region, Cook County, 1970—; adminstrv. asst. to supt. Dist. 88, Du Page County, 1951-59, dean of girls, Elmhurst, Ill., 1960-66; ednl. cons., 1974—. Past mem. exec. com. Heart Assn. W. Cook Regions for County. Recipient Distinguished Alumni award Lake Forest Coll., 1976. Mem. NEA, Am. Assn. Sch. Adminstrs., No. Ill. Supts. Round Table, Pan Hellenic Assn., Delta Kappa Gamma, Alpha Xi Delta. Research in field. Office: 1032 Washington Blvd Oak Park IL 60302

KRANTZ, STEVEN GEORGE, mathematics professor, writer; b. San Francisco, Feb. 3, 1951; s. Henry Alfred and Norma Olivia (Crisafulli) K.; m. Randi Diane Ruden, Sept. 7, 1974. B.A., U. Calif.-Santa Cruz, 1971; Ph.D., Princeton U., 1974. Asst. prof. UCLA, 1974-81; assoc. prof. Pa. State U., University Park, 1981-84, prof., 1984-86; prof. dept. math. Washington U., St. Louis, 1986—; cons. John Wiley and Sons, N.Y.C., 1980—, Wadsworth Pub., Belmont, Calif., 1978—. Author Function Theory of Several Complex Variables (monograph), 1982. Author numerous research articles. Recipient Disting. Teaching award UCLA Alumni Found., 1979; Crown-Zellerbach Corp. fellow, 1971, NSF fellow, 1971-74; NSF research grantee, 1974—. Mem. Am. Math. Soc. Avocation: bicycling. Office: Washington U St Louis Dept Math Saint Louis MO 63130

KRANZ, ROY JOSEPH, academic administrator; b. Grand Island, Nebr., Feb. 29, 1936; s. Roy Edward and Marie Catherine (Boehl) K.; m. Mary Kathleen Murphy, Aug. 6, 1955; children: Loretta, Janet, Roy, Victoria, Julie, Cathy, Audra. BS in Bus. Adminstrn., Creighton U., 1957; MEd, Kearney (Nebr.) State U., 1975. Editor, mgr. Crawford (Nebr.) Tribune, 1962-64; owner, broker Circle K Realty Ins., Grand Island, 1964-65; personnel services supr. Mason-Hanger, Silas Mason, Grand Island, 1965-68; bus. and office instr. Cen. Community Coll., Grand Island, 1968-75, chmn. bus. and office, 1975—; creator, trainer telemarketing firms, Nebr. Author: Personal Resource Development, 1986, Professional Selling--A Practical Approach, 1980. Active St. Mary's Sch. Bd., Grand Island, 1970-76, Hall County Hist. Soc., Grand Island. Hon. mention Canon Nat. Photography Contest, 1986. Mem. Am. Assn. for Tng. and Devel. Roman Catholic. Club: Liederkranz (Grand Island). Lodge: Elks. Avocations: writing, photography, music. Home: 233 S Locust Grand Island NE 68801 Office: Cen Community Coll PO Box C Grand Island NE 68801

KRAPAUSKAS, JEANNE, art educator; b. Chgo., Feb. 10, 1955; d. Paul Charles and Angela (Bertucci) Ciaccio; m. Virgil Krapauskas, June 27, 1982. BA, Barat Coll., 1977; MEd, Nat. Coll. Edn., 1980. Tchr. art Victor J. Andrew High Sch., Tinley Park, Ill., 1977—, sponsor art and photography club, 1977-87; cons. Apple Computers, Chgo., 1986—, Sch. Chgo. Art Inst., 1984—; keynote speaker Ill. Alliance Arts, 1983. Exhibitor: (computer art) Lithuanian Art Exhbn., 1983 (1st place award); (photography) Lithuanian Photography Exhbn., 1984 (2d place award), Camera Cove, 1983 (1st place award), Cedar Park Cemetery Photography Contest, 1981 (2d place award). Roman Catholic. Avocations: travel, opera. Home: 15411 Treetop Dr Orland Park IL 60462 Office: Victor J Andrew High Sch 171st & 90th Ave Tinley Park IL 60477

KRATZ, MILDRED SANDS, artist; b. Pottstown, Pa.; d. M. Stanley Q. and Ann (Hohl) Sands; m. Lowell F. Kratz (div.); children—Melissa and Melinda (twins); m. Richard Keith Johnson, Sr. Grad. high sch., Pottstown. One-woman shows include: Gallery Madison 90, N.Y.C., Piccolo Mondo, Palm Beach, Fla., Little Gallery, Phila; exhibited in group shows, U.S. and Can.; represented in permanent collections: Reading Mus., General Mills. Recipient Senatorial Citation, Pa. Senate, 1976. Author: American Artist, Palette Talk, Prints, 40 Watercolorists and How They Work. Trustee Ohio Watercolor Soc., 1987; profl. judge, juror, lectr. nat. art groups. Recipient 100 awards, 6 gold medals in nat. competition; elected to Watercolor U.S.A. Honor Soc., 1986. Mem. Pottstown Area Artists (co-founder, pres. 1963), Am. Watercolor Soc., Ohio Watercolor Soc., Am. Artist Prof. League, Allied Artists, Nat. Arts Club, Phila. Watercolor Club. Avocation: skiing; tennis. Home and Office: 2988 Silverview Dr Silver Lake OH 44224

KRAUS, FREDERICK THIER, pathologist; b. Oklahoma City, May 1, 1930; s. William Albert and Harriet (Hill) K.; m. Madeleine Veron, Apr. 11, 1959; children: Grant, Madeleine, Caroline. AB, William and Mary Coll., 1951; MD, Washington U., 1955. Diplomate Am. Bd. Pathology. Instr. Washington U., St. Louis, 1961-62; assoc. pathologist St. Luke's Hosp., St. Louis, 1962-73; lab. dir. St. John's Mercy Med. Ctr., St. Louis, 1974—; prof. vis. staff Washington U. Sch. Medicine, St. Louis, 1982—. Contbr. 40 articles to pathology jours. Served to capt. U.S. Army, 1959-61. Mem. AMA, Internat. Acad. Pathology, Am. Soc. Clin. Pathologists, Am. Coll. Obstetricians and Gynecologists (assoc.), Arthur Purdy Stout Soc. (trustee 1984-86). Avocations: running, fishing, tennis. Home: 714 S Price Rd Saint Louis MO 63124 Office: Saint John's Mercy Med Ctr Pathology 615 S New Ballas Rd Saint Louis MO 63141-8221

KRAUSE, CHESTER LEE, publishing company executive; b. Iola, Wis., Dec. 16, 1923; s. Carl and Cora E. (Neil) K. Grad. high sch. In contracting bus, 1946-52. Chief exec. officer Krause Publs., Inc., Iola, pub. 16 hobby periodicals, 1952—. Co-editor: Standard Catalog of World Coins. Mem. Assay Commn., 1961; chmn. bldg. fund drive Iola Hosp., 1975-80; Mem. Village Bd., 1963-72. Served with AUS, 1943-46. Mem. Am. Numis. Assn. (medal of merit, Farren Zerbe award), Central States Numis. Assn. (medal of merit), Canadian Numis. Assn. Club: Lion. Home: 290 E Iola St Iola WI 54945 Office: 700 E State St Iola WI 54945

KRAUSE, GEORGE ROBERT, radiologist; b. Cleve., Oct. 30, 1910; s. David and Clara (Gradis) K.; widowed; children: Elliott, David, James. AB, Case Western Res. U., 1931, MD, 1935. Diplomate Am. Bd. Radiology. Intern, then chief resident in radiology Met. Gen. Hosp., Cleve., 1935-40; radiologist St. John's Hosp., Cleve., 1940; staff radiologist Mt. Sinai Hosp., Cleve., 1946-58, chief radiology, 1958-77; chief radiology U.S. Vets. Hsop., Cleve., 1977—. Contbr. articles to profl. jours. Served to lt. col. Med. Corps, AUS, 1940-46. Recipient Disting. Service award Cleve. Acad. Medicine, Disting. Service award Case Western Res. U. Fellow Am. Coll. Radiology; mem. Acad. Medicine (sec.-treas. 1951-54), Ohio State Radiol. Soc. (pres. 1955-56, Disting. Service award), Radiol. Soc. North Am. (councillor), Am. Roentgen Ray Soc. Republican. Jewish. Club: Lake Forest Country (Hudson, Ohio). Avocations: reading, golfing, travelling. Home: 22655 Chagrin Blvd Cleveland OH 44122 Office: VA Med Ctr 10700 East Blvd Cleveland OH 44106

KRAUSE, JAMES WILLIAM, management consultant; b. Fergus Falls, Minn., May 21, 1930; s. William Otto and Esmere (Tomhave) K.; m. Roselyn Sonniette Olson, Aug. 15, 1959; children—Paul Frederick, Alan James, John William. B.A., Concordia Coll., 1951; J.D., U. Minn., 1954; postgrad. U. Harvard Grad. Sch. Bus. Adminstrn., 1966-67. Bar: Minn. 1954, N.D., 1954; C.L.U. Trust officer, 1st Bank N.D., Fargo, 1954-58; head bus. and econs. dept., assoc. prof. Concordia Coll., Moorhead, Minn., 1958-61; practice law, Fargo and Moorhead, 1958-61; legal counsel Lutheran Brotherhoods Ins., Mpls., 1961-66, sr. v.p. adminstrn. and investments, 1967-77; pres. Luth. Brotherhood Securities Corp., 1970-77; prin. Saks, Inc., Mpls., 1975—; dir., exec. com. Luth. Brotherhood Ins. Co., 1967—; pres. N. Central Mgmt. Assocs. Inc., 1977—; Pres. Minn. Higher Edn. Coordinating Bd., 1980-82, bd. dirs., 1978-82. Recipient Bush Leadership award Bush Found., 1966. Mem. North Central Mgmt. Assn. (pres. 1978—); pres. Conf. and Tng. Ctrs., Inc. 1986—, Minn. Bar Assn., Minn. Bd. Continuing Legal Edn., Soc. Advancement Mgmt., Am. Mgmt. Assn., Assn. for Corp. Growth (planning forum). Clubs: Minnesota; Harvard Bus. Sch. Minn. Office: N Central Mgmt Assocs Inc 5300 Glenwood Ave Minneapolis MN 55422

KRAUSE, JUSTIN GARDNER, osteopath; b. Cin., May 29, 1923; s. Albert Paul and Vadna (Gardner) K.; m. Glenna Bonita (dec.); children: Justin G., Paula K., Cecelia Sue, Elizabeth Jane, Patti Ann; m. Lois Jackquelin Fowler, Dec. 17, 1969; 1 child, Matthew Fowler. Student, Carnegie Tech., 1941-42, Miami U., Oxford, Ohio, 1942, U. Cin., 1945-46; DO, Kansas City Coll. Osteo. Medicine, 1950. Diplomate Am. Bd. Family Practice, Am. Bd. Gen. Practice. Gen. practice osteo. medicine Kansas City, 1950—; coroner Greene County, Ohio, 1964—. Served to sgt. U.S. Army, 1942-45, ETO. Decorated Bronze Star. Fellow Am. Acad. Family Practice, Amer. Acad. Forensic Sci. Democrat. Methodist. Avocations: photography, golf, boating. Home: 3838 S Greenbrier Fairborn OH 45287

KRAUSE, LAURA LEE, financial analyst; b. Detroit, Jan. 13, 1960; d. Ronald Stewart and Rozella (Bruce) Halliday; m. Michael Joseph Krause, Nov. 9, 1985. BBA, U. Mich., Dearborn, 1982. CPA, Mich. Fin. analyst

Fred Sanders, Detroit, 1983; auditor Grant Thornton & Co., Southfield, Mich., 1983-86; fin. analyst investor relations Fretter, Inc., Livonia, Mich., 1986—. Mem. Am. Inst. CPA's, Mich. Assn. CPA's. Avocations: golf, tennis. Office: Fretter Inc 35901 Schoolcraft Livonia MI 48150

KRAUSE, MAUREEN THERESE, educator; b. Evanston, Ill., June 17, 1947; d. Walter William and Eileen Ann (Gill) K.; m. David Lawrence Francoeur, July 28, 1978. BA, Northwestern U., 1969; student, Inst. Advanced Studies, Stanford U., 1969; MA, Ohio State U., 1970, PhD, 1980. Teaching assoc. in German, Ohio State U., Columbus, 1970-74, 77-78, 79-80, instr., 1980-81; sr. transl. aide Battelle Columbus Labs., 1974-77; asst. prof. in German, Rose-Hulman Inst. Tech., Terre Haute, Ind., 1981-85, assoc. prof., 1985—; mem. editorial staff New German Critique, 1981; bibliographer Soc. German-Am. Studies, 1979-82. Vol. Am. Cancer Soc., 1982—; instl. del. Arts Illiana, 1983; active Vigo County Hist. Soc., 1981-84, Audubon Soc., 1983-84; sponsor U.S. Com. for Friendship with German Dem. Republic. Recipient Deptl. Disting. Teaching award Ohio State U., 1971; Ohio State U. fellow, 1970; Fulbright grantee, 1983. Mem. Am. Assn. Tchrs. of German, Am. Council Teaching of Fgn. Langs., Hoffmann-Gesellschaft (Ger.), MMLA, MLA, German Studies Assn., Am. Translators Assn., U.S. Com. for Friendship with the GDR. Office: Rose Hulman Inst Tech Terre Haute IN 47803

KRAUSE, ROBERT ALAN, accountant; b. Detroit, Apr. 26, 1956; s. Duane K. and MaryAnn (Bayer) K. BSBA in Acctg. with high distinction, Valparaiso U., 1978; MBA with distinction, U. Mich., 1983. CPA, Mich., Ill. Sr. auditor Ernst & Whinney, Detroit, 1978-81; sr. acct. Nathan, Ettinger & Shewach, P.C., Southfield, Mich., 1981-82, Arthur Andersen & Co., Chgo., 1983-85; project. mgr. fin. reporting Baxter Internat. Inc. (formerly Baxter Travenol Labs., Inc.), Deerfield, Ill., 1985-86, mgr. corp. reporting, 1986—. Participant Vol. Income Tax Assistance Program, Detroit and Chgo., 1978—; treas. Christ the King Luth. Ch., Grosse Pointe Woods, Mich., 1981-83. Mem. Am. Inst. CPA's, Mich. Assn. CPA's, Ill. Soc. CPA's, Nat. Assn. Accts. (officer 1981-83, 85), Fin. Mgmt. Assn., Beta Gamma Sigma. Lutheran. Avocations: spectator sports, golfing, stamp collecting, reading. Home: 1147 Russellwood Ct Buffalo Grove IL 60089 Office: Baxter Internat Inc One Baxter Pkwy Deerfield IL 60015

KRAUSE, WILLIAM RICHARD, industrial arts educator; b. Chgo., May 7, 1949; s. Richard Joseph and Mary (Reczek) K.; m. Roberta Ann Schmidt, July 8, 1972; children—Thomas Joseph, Amanda Elizabeth. B.S., Western Ill. U., 1971; M.Ed., U. Ill., 1976, Advanced Cert. Edn., 1980. Cert. tchr., adminstr., Ill. Tchr., Proviso Twp. (Ill.) High Schs., 1971—; instr. Triton Jr. Coll., 1974-75; prin. Olde Tyme Toys Co., 1976-78. Mem. Oak Brook (Ill.) Civic Assn., 1978—, Oak Brook Library Assn., 1978—, Oak Brook Community Caucus, 1980—, Ben Fuller Assn., Oak Brook, 1981—; treas. Brook Forest Community Assn., 1982-86, pres., 1986—; trustee York Twp. Youth Commn., 1984—; pres. Oak Brook Little League, 1985—; elected to dist. 53 Bd. Edn. ., Oak Brook, 1986. Mem. Am. Vocat. Assn., Ill. Vocat. Assn., Am. Indsl. Arts Assn., Ill. Indsl. Edn. Assn., Chgo. Area Roundtable. Club: Oak Brook Racquet. Contbr. articles to indsl. arts jours. Home: 9 Lambeth Ct Oak Brook IL 60521 Office: Wolf and Harrison Sts Hillside IL 60162

KRAUSEN, ANTHONY SHARNIK, surgeon; b. Phila., Feb. 22, 1944; s. B.M. and Kay S. (Sharnik) K.; m. Susan Elizabeth Park, Sept. 6, 1970; children—Nicole, Allison. Student Germantown Acad., 1949-61; B.A., Princeton U., 1965; M.D., U. Mich., 1969. Intern, Presbyn. Med. Center, Denver, 1969-70; resident St. Joseph Hosp., Denver, 1970-71, Barnes Hosp., St. Louis, 1972-76; with Milw. Med. Clinic, 1976—, head dept. facial plastic surgery, 1984—; mem. staffs Columbia, St. Michael, Children's, St. Mary Hosps., Milw. Pres. Contemporary Art Soc., Milw. Art Mus., 1983, bd. dirs. Friends of Art. Served with U.S. Army Nat. Guard, 1970-76. Fellow Am. Acad. Facial Plastic and Reconstructive Surgery, Am. Acad. Otolaryngology, Soc. Univ. Otolaryngologists, A.C.S.; mem. Nat. Neurofibromatosis Soc. (med. advisor Wis. chpt. 1985—), Wis. Otolaryngological Soc. Clubs: Ivy (Princeton, N.J.); Ausblick Ski (Milw.). Office: 3003 W Good Hope Rd Milwaukee WI 53209

KRAUSS, ALAN ROBERT, physicist; b. Chgo., Oct. 3, 1943; s. Paul and Shirley (Shapiro) K.; m. Julie Emelie Roasdo, Aug. 28, 1965; 1 child, Susan. B.S., U. Chgo., 1965; postgrad., Columbia U., 1965-66; M.S., Purdue U., 1968, Ph.D., 1972. Research assoc. U. Chgo., 1971-74; staff physicist Argonne Nat. Lab., (Ill.), 1974—; cons. Dept. Energy, 1979, USAF, 1985-86. Contbr. articles on microcomputer applications, quantum physics and surface emission to sci. jours.; patentee (2). Served with USAF, 1985-86. Recipient research award DOE, 1979, Outstanding Research award DOE, 1984. Mem. Am. Phys. Soc., Am. Vacuum Soc. (publicity chmn., adv. com. plasma sci. andtech. div. 1980—, newsletter editor, exec. com. Ill. chpt.), Sigma Xi, Sigma Pi Sigma. Club: Downers Grove Camera (sec. 1979-81, treas. 1982-83). Office: Argonne Nat Lab 9700 S Cass Ave Argonne IL 60439

KRAUSS, DAVID ARTHUR, psychologist; b. Springfield, Ohio, July 10, 1947; s. Gerald Martin and Bonita (Strauss) K.; m. Amy J. Jacobs, May 31, 1971; children: Benjamin Michael, Leah Danielle. BA, Case Western Reserve U., 1969, MA, 1974; PhD, Kent State U., 1979. Lic. psychologist, Ohio. Pvt. practice psychology South Euclid, Ohio; cons. hosp. chem. dependency program. Author, editor: Phototherapy in Mental Health, 1983; contbr. articles to profl. jours. Mem. Am. Psychol. Assn., Am. Orthopsychiat. Assn., Nat. Register of Health Service Providers in Psychology. Avocations: photography, music writing and performing, backpacking, men's issues, parenting. Office: 2120 S Green Rd South Euclid OH 44121

KRAVETZ, RUSSELL STUART, psychiatrist; b. Lexington, Ky., July 22, 1930; s. Louis and Florence (Byer) K.; m. Maxine Stolar, Nov. 2, 1986; children: Dayna Ilene, Todd Michael. BS, U. Cin., 1950, MD, 1954. Diplomate Am. Bd. Psychiatry and Neurology. Rotating intern Cin. Gen. Hosp., 1954-55, jr. resident dept. internal medicine, 1957-58, asst. resident dept. psychiatry, 1958-60, clin. fellow psychosomatic medicine dept. psychiatry, 1960-61, clinician dept. internal medicine and psychiatry, outpatient dept., 1961—, asst. attending psychiatrist, 1961—; practice medicine specializing in psychiatry Cin., 1961—; asst. dir. psychiat. clinic City Cin. Mcpl. Ct., 1961-62; asst. clin. prof. dept. psychiatry U. Cin. Coll. Medicine, 1967-73, assoc. clin. prof., 1973—; attending staff dept. psychiatry Jewish Hosp., Cin.; active staff dept. Neuropsychiatry Christ Hosp., Cin. Trustee Cen. Psychiat. Clinic, 1973—, Glen Manor Home for Aged. Served as lt. M.C., USNR, 1955-57. Mem. AMA, Cin. Acad. Medicine, Cin. Soc., Am. Psychiat. Assn., Ohio Psychiat. Assn., Ohio Acad. Neurology and Psychiatry, Phi Beta Kappa, Alpha Omega Alpha. Office: 2607 Burnet Ave Cincinnati OH 45219

KRAVIS, DAVID SCOTT, food company executive; b. Bklyn., Jan. 9, 1951; s. Samuel Joseph and Beryl (Gittelman) K.; m. Lynn Barbara Ferszt, May 26, 1979. B.S., Va. Poly. Inst., 1973; postgrad. Bus. Sch., U. Cin., 1975-78. Staff engr. Procter & Gamble Co., Cin., 1973-77, group leader, 1977-78; group leader ITT Continental, Rye, N.Y., 1978-80, mktg. mgr., 1980-81, mgr. research and devel., 1981-82; dir. research and devel. Bunge Edible Oil Corp., Kankakee, Ill., 1982-86; dir. research and Devel. Bunge Corp., 1986—. Mem. Ill. Public Action Council, 1983—. N.Y. Regents scholar, 1969. Mem. Inst. Shortening and Edible Oils, Inst. Food Technologists (exec. com. food engring. div. 1984—), Am. Inst. Chem. Engrs., Am. Oil Chemists Soc. (found. bd. dirs. 1984—, sec. 1986-87), Am. Assn. Cereal Chemists, Am. Inst. Baking (sci. adv. council 1984—), Research and Devel. Assocs., Am. Mgmt. Assn., Alpha Chi Sigma. Republican. Patentee meaty flavored deep-fat frying compositions; contbr. articles to profl. jours. Home: 2748 2d Private Rd Flossmoor IL 60422 Office: PO Box 192 Kankakee IL 60901

KRAVITZ, LARRY PHILIP, dentist; b. Plainfield, N.J., July 1, 1950; s. Elmer Howard and Irene Esther (Burkons) K.; m. Karen Ann Brooker, June 16, 1985; 1 child, Michael Eliot. BS cum laude, U. Miami, 1972; DDS cum laude, Ohio State U., 1975. Gen. practice dentistry Mentor-on-Lake, Ohio, 1976—. Mem. ADA, N.E. Ohio Dental Soc. (exec. bd. 1981—), Shelby Am. Automobile Club, Alpha Omega (exec. bd. 1983—), Omicron Kappa Upsilon. Jewish. Clubs: Aqua Amigos Scuba Diving, Elysium Ice Skating (exec. bd. 1981-84). Lodge: Knights of Pythias. Avocations: auto restoration, ice skating, golfing, tennis, skiing. Office: 7925 Munson Rd Mentor-on-the-Lake OH 44060

KRAWCZYK, DANIEL JOSEPH, property manager; b. Mpls., Apr. 28, 1959; s. Eugene Stephen and Harriet Ellen (Wigand) K.; m. Judy Ann Hill, Aug. 13, 1983. Grad. high sch., St. Anthony, Minn., 1976. Property mgr. Rixmann Cos., Edina, Minn., 1983-85, Hirsch Newman Co., Mpls., 1985—. Mem. Minn. Multi Housing Assn., Minn. Manufactured Housing Assn., Inst. Real Estate Mgmt., Ducks Unlimited. Republican. Roman Catholic. Avocations: camping, hunting, fishing, snowmobiling, boating. Home: 18075 Weaver Lake Dr Maple Grove MN 55369 Office: Hirsch Newman Co 3010 Plaza VII Tower 45 S 7th St Minneapolis MN 55402-1607

KREAGER, EILEEN DAVIS, bursar; b. Caldwell, Ohio, Mar. 2, 1924; d. Fred Raymond and Esther (Farson) Davis. B.B.A., Ohio State U., 1945. With accounts receivable dept. M & R Dietetic, Columbus, Ohio, 1945-50; complete charge bookkeeper Magic Seal Paper Products, Columbus, 1950-53, A. Walt Runglin Co., Los Angeles, 1953-54; office mgr. Roy C. Haddox and Son, Columbus, 1954-60; bursar Meth. Theol. Sch. Ohio, Delaware, 1961-86; adminstrv. cons. Fin. Ltd., 1986—; ptnr. Coll. Administrv. Sci., Ohio State U., 1975-80; seminar participant Paperwork Systems and Computer Sci., 1965, Computer Systems, 1964, Griffith Found. Seminar Working Women, 1975; pres. Altrusa Club of Delaware, Ohio, 1972-73. Del. Altrusa Internat., Montreal, 1972, Altrusa Regional, Greenbrier, 1973. Assoc. Am. Inst. Mgmt. (exec. council of Inst., 1979); mem. Am. Soc. Profl. Cons., Internat. Platform Assn., Ohio State U. Alumna Assn., AAUW, Kappa Delta. Methodist. Clubs: Ohio State U. Faculty, Delaware Country. Home: PO Box 214 Worthington OH 43085

KREBS, DAVID ALAN, accountant; b. Columbus, Ohio, Aug. 29, 1958; s. Albert J. and Helen M. (Kelley) K.; m. Jean K. Kucheman, May 7, 1983. BS in Bus. Acctg., Miami (Ohio) U., 1976-80. CPA, Ohio. Sr. acct. Coopers & Lybrand, CPA's, Columbus, 1980-84, Acceleration Corp., Columbus, 1984-85; pres. Krebs & Knapp, Pub. Accts., Inc., Columbus, 1985—. Treas., dir. Man-to-Man, Woman-to-Woman, Columbus, 1985—. Named Outstanding Young Man Am., Jaycees, 1980, 82, 85. Mem. Am. Inst. CPA's, Nat. Assn. Accts., Pub. Accts. Soc. Ohio, Ohio Soc. CPA's, Delta Upsilon (dir., counselor Miami chpt. 1982—, treas., trustee Internat. 1983—). Republican. Roman Catholic. Club: CoServe (pres. 1986). Lodges: Kiwanis (pres. Univ. chpt. 1980-86, KC (chancellor 1984-85). Avocations: bowling, volleyball, jogging, hiking, softball. Home: 45 Glenmont Ave Columbus OH 43214 Office: Krebs & Knapp Pub Accts Inc 487 E Mound St Columbus OH 43215

KREBS, KAY ELLYN, marketing executive, small business owner; b. Browntown, Wis., Aug. 27, 1946; d. John T. and Ruth M. (Anderson) K. BS, U. Wis., 1970; MBA, U. Chgo., 1980. Mktg. mgr. Kimberly-Clark Corp., Neenah, Wis., 1977-81, research dir., 1981-84, dir., new products, 1984-86; owner Kay Krebs & Assocs., Oshkosh, Wis., 1986—; advisor new products lab. U. Chgo. Sch. Bus., 1986. Inventor and patentee surgical drape, 1971. Foster parent Winnebago County, Oshkosh, Wis., 1971-75; dir. Barbershop Chorus, Neenah, 1986. Mem. Beta Gamma Sigma, Phi Kappa Phi. Avocations: barbershop singing, woodworking, skiing, bicycling, hiking. Home and Office: 5130 I Ah May Tah Oshkosh WI 54901

KREBS, ROBERT DUNCAN, transportation company executive; b. Sacramento, May 2, 1942; s. Ward Carl and Eleanor Blauth (Duncan) K.; m. Anne Lindstrom, Sept. 11, 1971; children: Robert Ward, Elisabeth Lindstrom, Duncan Lindstrom. B.A., Stanford U., 1964; M.B.A., Harvard U., 1966. Asst. gen. mgr. So. Pacific Transp. Co., Houston, 1974-75; asst. regional ops. mgr. So. Pacific Transp. Co., 1975-76; asst. v.p. So. Pacific Transp. Co., San Francisco, 1976-77; asst. to pres. So. Pacific Transp. Co., 1977-79, gen. mgr., 1979, v.p. transp., 1979-80, v.p. ops., 1980-82, pres., 1982-83, also dir.; pres., chief operating officer Santa Fe So. Pacific Corp., 1983—, also dir. Trustee Glenwood Sch. for Boys, John G. Shedd Aquarium, Northwestern Meml. Hosp., Chgo.; mem. Northwestern U. Assocs., bd. dirs. Phelps Dodge Corp. Mem. Stanford U. Alumni Assn., Phi Beta Kappa, Kappa Sigma. Republican. Episcopalian. Clubs: Onwentsia (Lake Forest, Ill.); Pacific Union, World Trade, Bohemian, Chicago. Office: Santa Fe So Pacific Corp 224 S Michigan Ave Chicago IL 60604

KREBSBACH, MARK C., rancher; b. Warwick, N.D., May 13, 1951; s. Ralph M. and Carolyn (Thorstad) K.; m. Connie L. Hanson, June 18, 1973; children: Dezerie, Kaila. BS in Animal Sci., N.D. State U., 1973, BS in Agrl. Edn., 1974. Instr. Lake Region Jr. Coll., Devils Lake, N.D., 1974-77; rancher Arrowhead Angus, Warwick, 1977—. Mem. N.D. Jaycees (pres. 1986, Outstanding Young Farmer 1981). Lutheran. Home and Office: PO Box 57 Rural Rt 1 Warwick ND 58381

KREGER, CHRISTINE L., health care administrator; b. Somerset, Pa., May 22, 1947; d. Thomas W. and Genevie (Everhart) K. BA in Psychology, Cleve. State U., 1979; MBA, Case Western Res. U., 1986. Work leader med. secretaries Cleve. Clinic Found., 1976; adminstrv. asst. Cleve. Clinic, 1977-78, divisional adminstr., 1979—. Recipient Woman of Excelence award YWCA Career Achievement, 1982. Mem. N.E. Ohio Hosp. Adminstr. Assn. Office: Cleveland Clinic Foundation 9500 Euclid Ave Cleveland OH 44106

KREGER, ELWYN LORAIN, mortgage underwriter; b. Clear Lake, S.D., June 30, 1924; s. Fred E. and Sarah B. (Anderson) K.; m. Kay B. Parks, Aug. 7, 1965; 1 child, Scott F. BS in Acctg., U. S.D., 1947. Asst. v.p. Conservative Mortgage Co., Mpls., 1960-69; asst. chief underwriting dept. VA, Mpls., 1969-78; sr. v.p. chief underwriter and credit officer Knutson Mortgage Co., Mpls., 1978—. Mem. Mortgage Bankers Assn. Republican. Methodist. Avocations: writing cookbook geared to heart disease prevention, gardening. Home: 8619 Rich Rd Bloomington MN 55437 Office: Knutson Mortgage Co 8400 Normandale Lake Blvd Bloomington MN 55437

KREHBIEL, J. H., JR., electronics company executive; b. 1906. With Molex, Inc., Lisle, Ill., chmn. bd. dirs., 1957—. Office: Molex Inc 2222 Wellington Ct Lisle IL 60532 *

KREHBIEL, WAYNE LEROY, accountant; b. Moundridge, Kans., July 3, 1930; s. Herman Gustav and Anna Marie (Albright) K.; m. Betty Jean Westerman, Nov. 4, 1950 (div. July 1978); children: Diane Rene, Duane Robert, Dawn Rochelle; m. Patricia Sue Dillingham, Apr. 19, 1980. BBA in Acctg. CPA, Ill. Controller Cebrehm Oil Co., Mt. Vernon, Ill., 1956-66; mng. ptnr. Krehbiel & Assocs., CPA's, Mt. Vernon, 1966—; pres. Orion Petro Corp., Mt. Vernon, 1984—. Served to sgt. USMC, 1951-59. Mem. Am. Inst. CPA's, Ill. Soc. CPA's (pres. so. chpt. 1973, named CPA of Yr. 1977), Ind. Petroleum Assn. Am. Republican. Methodist. Lodges: Elks, Moose, Rotary (pres. Mt. Vernon 1965), Shriners (pres. Jefferson County 1971). Avocations: golf, tennis. Home: 14 Westbrook Mount Vernon IL 62864 Office: Krehbiel & Assocs 125 N 11th Mount Vernon IL 62864

KREIDER, GARY LYNN, accountant, banker; b. Richmond, Ind., Feb. 17, 1949; s. Kenneth Karl and Treva Naomi (Weist) K.; A.B., Earlham Coll., 1971; M.B.A., Ind. U., 1973; children by previous marriage: Scott Alan, Jason Michael; m. Beverly Jean Johnson Delhagen, June 7, 1984. C.P.A. Staff acct., then sr. acct. George S. Olive & Co., Indpls., 1973-77; asst. controller Second Nat. Bank of Richmond (Ind.), 1977-79, v.p., controller, 1979—. Rose City Ambassador (pub. relations com. of C. of C.), 1980—. Am. Water Works scholar, 1967-71; Ind. U. assistantship, 1971-73. Mem. Ind. Soc. C.P.A.s, Nat. Assn. Accts. (chpt. dir. 1978-79, 84-85), Richmond Jaycees (named Outstanding Officer 1978-79, adminstrv. v.p. 1981-82), Am. Inst. C.P.A.s. Republican. Home: RR1 Box 297 Fountain City IN 47341 Office: 800 Promenade St Richmond IN 47374

KREIFELS, FRANK ANTHONY, lawyer, corporation executive; b. Omaha, Nov. 26, 1951; s. Robert Frank and Mary Ellen (Basan) K.; 1 child, Katherine Joy. BBA in Fin., Creighton U., 1974, MBA in Fin. and Acctg., 1975; J.D., Hamline U., 1977. Bar: Minn. 1978, U.S. Dist. Ct. Minn. 1978, Nebr. 1983. Staff atty. NCR-Comten Inc., St. Paul, 1978-80; gen. counsel, sec. Agriventure Corp., Foxley & Co., Foxley Cattle Co., Herd Co., Flavorland Industries (and all affiliates), Omaha, 1980-85; mem. Ellsworth Law Firm, Omaha, 1985-87, exec. v.p., gen. mgr. Dale Beggs Devel. Co. (and all affiliates), 1987—; cons. Small Bus. Adminstrn., Omaha, 1974; corp. lobbyist Foxley Cattle Co./Herd Co., Omaha, 1981-85; appointed Neb. state reporter Am. Agrl. Law Update, 1985—. Campaign coordinator Nebr. Republican Party, 1982, 84. Smith. Recipient Cert. of Merit, Small Bus. Adminstrn., 1974. Mem. ABA, Am. Corp. Counsel Assn., Am. Agrl. Law Assn., Nebr. State Bar Assn., Phi Alpha Delta. Roman Catholic. Clubs: Omaha Barrister's, Omaha Westroads. Home: 10206 Ohio Dr Omaha NE 68134 Office: Dale Beggs Devel Co 5332 S 138th St Suite 300 Omaha NE 68137

KREIL, CURTIS LEE, research chemist; b. Milw., Aug. 22, 1955; s. Hugo Harvey and Sofia (Patelski) K. AA, U. Wis. Ctr., West Bend, 1975; BS in Chemistry, U. Wis., Madison, 1977; PhD in Chemistry, U. Calif., Los Angeles, 1983. Tech. prodn. asst. DIMAT Inc., Cedarburg, Wis., 1973-75; research asst. U. Wis., Madison, 1975-77; research fellow Columbia U., N.Y.C., 1976; research asst. U. Calif., Los Angeles, 1977-82; sr. research chemist 3M, St. Paul, 1983—; chmn. photochemistry chpt. 3M Tech. Forum, St. Paul, 1984-85. Contbr. articles to profl. jours.; inventor electron beam adhesion-promoting treatment of polyester film base for silicone release liners, electron beam adhesion promoting treatment of polyester film base. Served to 1st lt. Civil Air Patrol. Recipient Merck Index award Merck & Co., 1977; grad. fellow NSF, 1977-80. Mem. Am. Chem. Soc., Aircraft Owners' and Pilots' Assn., Exptl. Aircraft Assn., 3M Aviation Club (pres. 1985-86), Phi Beta Kappa. Avocations: scuba diving instr., backpacking, rock climbing, comml. piloting. Office: 3M 208-1-01 3M Ctr Saint Paul MN 55144

KREIN, WILLIAM A., electronics company executive; b. Springfield, Mass., July 6, 1940; s. Gustave A. and Frieda E. (Klaiber) K.; m. Lee C. Ericson, June 22, 1963; children: Todd, Marta, Derek. BS MechE, Worcester Poly. Inst., 1962; MBA in Fin., Babson Inst., 1964. Mfg. engr. Gen. Electric Co., Schenectady, N.Y., 1966-72; staff analyst Gen. Electric Co., N.Y.C., 1972-74; mgr. fin. and adminstrn., service engr. div. Gen. Electric Co., Schenectady, 1974-80; v.p. controller Zenith Electronics Corp., Glenview, Ill., 1980—; mem. adv. council Worcester (Mass.) Poly. Inst., 1986—. Bd. dirs. United Way of Suburban Chgo., Hinsdale, Ill., 1985—, United Way of Northbrook, Ill., 1981-86, United Cerebral Palsy Assn., Schenectady, 1976-79; elder Grace Luth. Ch., Northbrook, 1976-79. Served to 1st lt. U.S. Army. Mem. Fin. Execs. Inst. Lutheran. Avocations: flying, golf, antique collecting. Office: Zenith Electronics Corp 1000 Milwaukee Ave Glenview IL 60025

KREINBRINK, MARK JAMES, construction engineer; b. Lima, Ohio, July 30, 1961; s. Harold James and Patricia Jean Marie (Schroeder) K. BSCE, U. Cin., 1984; MS in Engring., U. Mich., 1985. Registered profl. engr., Ohio. Field engr. J.A. Jones Constrn. Co., Vick, La., 1981-83; office engr. J.A. Jones Constrn. Co., Lima, 1983-84; asst. supt. Turner Constrn. Co., Columbus, Ohio, 1985—. Mem. ASCE, Am. Concrete Inst. Democrat. Roman Catholic. Home: 5422 Bermuda Bay #1C Columbus OH 43220

KREISER, FRANK DAVID, real estate exec.; b. Mpls., Sept. 20, 1930; s. Harry D. and Olive W. (Quist) K.; student U. Minn., 1950-51; m. Patricia Williams, Aug. 23, 1973; children—Sally, Frank David, Susan, Paul, Mark, Patti, Richard. Founder, owner Frank Kreiser Real Estate, Inc., Mpls., 1966—, pres., 1979—; partner, founder B & K Properties Co., Mpls., 1976—; chmn. bd., founder Transfer Location Corp., Atlanta, 1979—. Served with U.S. Army, 1948-50, Korea. Certified resdl. specialist and resdl. broker. Mem. Nat. Assn. Realtors, Mpls. Bd. Realtors (dir. 1972), St. Paul Bd. Realtors, Dakota County Bd. Realtors, Minn. Assn. Realtors, Realtors Nat. Mktg. Inst., Employers Relocation Council. Lutheran. Club: Decathlon Athletic. Address: 5036 France Ave S Minneapolis MN 55410

KREISMAN, JEROLD JAY, psychiatrist; b. St. Louis, Dec. 28, 1947; s. Erwin and Frieda Marion (Pokres) K.; m. Judith Irene (Korn), Aug. 9, 1970; children—Jennifer Laine, Brett Joshua. B.S., B.A., Washington U., 1969; M.D., Cornell U., 1973. Diplomate Am. Bd. Psychiatry and Neurology. Intern, Denver Gen. Hosp., 1973-74; resident St. Elizabeth's Hosp./NIMH, Washington, 1974-76, St. Louis U., 1976-77; practice medicine specializing in psychiatry; mem. staff St. John's Mercy Med. Ctr.; asst. clin. prof. St. Louis U., 1982—. Served with USPHS, 1974-76. Mem. AMA, Am. Psychiat. Assn., Am. Group Psychotherapy Assn., Internat. Psychogeriatric Assn., Am. Soc. Adolescent Psychiatry, Assn. Acad. Psychiatry, Eastern Mo. Psychiat. Soc. (pres. 1985-86), Mo. Psychiatric Assn. (pres. 1986-87), Phi Beta Kappa. Jewish. Office: 621 S New Ballas St Suite 4018 Saint Louis MO 63141

KREITER, KATHY JEANNE, corporate travel executive; b. Detroit, Oct. 24, 1955; d. William Stewart and Mary Augusta (Bennett) Young; m. John Clarence Kreiter, Oct. 4, 1980. AA, Ball State U., 1977, BS, 1978, postgrad., 1987—. Cert. travel counselor. Travle agt. Jo-Mar Travel, Inc., Plymouth, Ind., 1978-82; supr., travel counselor Zimmer, Inc., Warsaw, Ind., 1982—. Mem. Nat. Passenger Traffic Assn., Ohio Valley Passenger Traffic Assn., Phi Gamma Nu, Delta Theta Tau. Republican. Presbyterian. Avocations: swimming, walking, skiing, reading, jazzercise. Home: 2803 Sharon St Winona Lake IN 46590 Office: Zimmer Inc Rt 7 Box 191 Warsaw IN 46580

KREITLER, THOMAS EDWARD, engineer; b. Monticello, Ill., June 10, 1948; s. Ralph Edward and Frances (Thomas) K.; m. Roseann Frances Virgil, June 24, 1983. BS in Indsl. Engring., Ill. State U., 1971. Regional sales mgr. Valmont Energy Systems, Valley, Nebr., 1980-81; plant mgr. Garner Industries, Lincoln, Nebr., 1981-83, sales mgr., 1983-84; mgr. quality engring. tooling Brunswick, Lincoln, 1984-86; owner, operator Command Engring., Lincoln, 1987—. Patentee in field. Recipient Govs. Sailing Cup, 1982. Mem. Soc. Mfg. Engrs. (sr.), Am. Welding Soc., Lincoln Inventors Assn. (pres. 1987—), Nebr. Water Resources Assn. Roman Catholic. Lodge: Elks. Avocations: sailing, photography, tennis, fishing. Home: 662 W Lakeshore Dr Lincoln NE 68528 Office: Command Engring 251 Capitol Beach Blvd Lincoln NE 68528

KREJCSI, CYNTHIA ANN, textbook editor; b. Chgo., Dec. 28, 1948; d. Charles and Dorothea Bertha (Hahn) .; m. Daniel Neil Ehlebracht, May 16, 1986. B.A., North Park Coll., 1970. Prodn. editor Ency., Brit. Chgo., 1970-71, style editor, 1971-72 ; asst. editor Scott, Foresman & Co., Glenview, Ill., 1972-77, assoc. editor, 1977, editor, 1978-84, sr. editor, 1984—; sr. editor Benefic Press, Westchester, Ill., 1977-78. Mem. Nat. Assn. Female Execs., Chgo. Council on Fgn. Relations, Field Mus. Natural History, Chgo. Women in Pub., Internat. Reading Assn. Office: Scott Foresman & Co 1900 E Lake Ave Glenview IL 60025

KRELL, KEITH VINCENT, endodontist; b. Houston, Aug. 12, 1948; s. Emmett Warren and Katie Eveline (Lusk) K.; m. Virginia Diane Dillport, Aug. 17, 1971; children: Rayda Kathryn, Nathan Emmett. BA, Washington U., St. Louis, 1970; MA, U.S. Internat. U., San Diego, 1975; DDS, U. Iowa, 1981, MS, 1983. Diplomate Am. Bd. Endodontics. Asst. prof., undergrad. clin. dir. U. Iowa, Iowa City, 1983-86, assoc. prof., 1986—; dir. grad. program in endodontics U. Iowa, 1986—; site reviewer NIH, Washington, 1986—, cons. 1985—. Contbr. articles to profl. jours. Served to maj. U.S. Army N.G., 1978—. Mem. ADA, Am. Assn. Endodontists (research award 1983), Am. Assn. Dental Schs., Am. Soc. Dentistry Children, Pulp Biology Group, Am. Fund Dental Health (dental teaching fellowship 1981-83), Omicron Kappa Upsilon. Avocations: fishing, guitar, scouting. Home: 515 Normandy Dr Iowa City IA 52240 Office: U Iowa Coll Dentistry Dept Endodontics Iowa City IA 52242

KREMSNER, FRANK FRED, real estate executive; b. Chgo., Nov. 7, 1917; s. Richard and Anna (Blaskovits) K.; grad. high sch. Warehouse foreman Campbell Soup Co., Chgo., 1945-52, Wright Sales, 1952-54; with Goldblatt Bros. Dept. Store, Chgo., 1954-80, v.p., dir. ops., 1968-80; owner, pres. Rensmerk Co., 1981—; broker Century 21, Beacon Realty, 1982—. Served with AUS, 1942-45. Mem. Nat. Guild Profl. and Bus. Graphologists (pres. 1973-77), Internat. Material Mgmt. Soc., Field Mus. Natural History, First Burgenlaender Soc., Soc. of the Little Flower, Am. Legion. Home and Office: 7749 S Kenneth Ave Chicago IL 60652

KREN, MARGO, art educator, artist. BS, U. Wis., 1966; MA, Kans. State U., 1969; MFA, U. Iowa, 1979. Instr. art Kans. State U., Manhattan, 1971-80, asst. prof., 1980—; represented by Seghi Gallery, St. Louis, Ben Pickard Gallery, Oklahoma City, Jennifer Pauls Gallery, Sacramento; guest artist workshop Tarkio (Mo.) Coll., 1983; artist residency Ragdale Found., Lake Forest, Ill., 1986, Va. Ctr. for Creative Arts, Sweet Briar, 1987; vis. artist Wichita (Kans.) State U., 1986. Contbr. articles and artwork to New Art Examiner, numerous others, 1981—; one-woman shows include Mulvane Art Ctr., Topeka, 1981-83, Pittsburg (Kans.) State U., 1981, Fort Hays (Kans.) State U., 1982, Reuben Saunders Gallery, Wichita, Kans., 1983, 85, Avila Coll., Kansas City, Mo., 1984, Albrecht Art Mus., St. Joseph, Mo., 1986, Southwestern Coll., Winfield, Kans., 1986, North Hennepin Community Coll., Mpls., 1986, U. Minn., Morris, 1986, Wichita State U., 1986, William Jewell Coll., Liberty, Mo., 1987, St. Louis Community Coll., 1987, Hutchinson (Kans.) Art Assn., 1987; exhibited in group shows at Swen Parson Gallery, De Kalb, Ill., 1981, Kellas Gallery, Lawrence, Kans., 1982, Lawrence Art Ctr., 1983, South Bend (Ind.) Art Ctr., 1985, Downey Mus., Los Angeles, 1985, Spiva Art Ctr., Joplin, Mo., 1986, 10th Ann. Nat. Invitational Drawing Exhbn., Emporia, Kans., 1986, Karl Oskar Gallery, Kansas City, 1986, Emporia State U., 1986; represented in permanent collections El Paso (Tex.) Mus. Art, Hosp. Trust Tower, Providence, Mut. Benefit Life Ins. Co., Kansas City, Nebr. Wesleyan U., Lincoln, Western Mich. U., Kalamazoo, Albrecht Art Mus. Recipient Faculty Research Award Kans. State U., 1980, 85; grantee Nat. Endowment for Arts and Kans. Art Commn., 1981, Nat. Endowment for Arts, 1982-83. Mem. Kans. Arts Commn. (visual artists panelist 1984-85, Artist in Edn. panelist 1984-86), Kansas City Artist Coalition (pres. 1982-83). Home: 823 Bertrand Manhattan KS 66502 Office: Kans State U Dept Art Manhattan KS 66506

KRENZ, JON CHARLES, dentist; b. Mendota, Ill., Oct. 23, 1954; s. Robert John and Marilyn Jean (Walton) K. BS in Zoology, Western Ill. U., 1976; postgrad., No. Ill. U., So. Ill. U., 1977-78; DMD, Tufts U., 1981. Gen. practice dentistry Krenz Dental Clinic, Mendota, 1981—. Mem. ADA, Am. Endodontic Soc., Acad. Gen. Dentistry, Chgo. Dental Soc. Methodist. Home and Office: 704 Indiana Ave Mendota IL 61342

KRENZER, GAIL CLAIRE (OVERHOLT), pediatric psychologist; b. Omaha, July 27, 1944; d. Donald McLeran and Claire Luella (Abbott) Overholt; m. Vernon William Krenzer, June 18, 1966; children: Douglas William, Jeffrey Donald, Andrew Richard. BS with distinction, U. Nebr., 1966, MEd, 1969, cert. in sch. psychology, 1978, PhD, 1980. Cert. tchr., Nebr.; lic. psychologist, Nebr. Tchr. English Tecumseh (Nebr.) Jr. Sr. High Sch., 1966-67; tchr., guidance counselor Cen. High Sch., Omaha, 1967-71; tchr. adult edn. Omaha Pub. Schs., 1973-76; sch. psychologist Millard Pub. Schs., Omaha, 1979-85; pvt. practice in pediatric psychology Omaha, 1981—; psychologist Services for Crippled Children, Omaha, 1979-83; instr. U. Nebr., Omaha, 1977-79, 82-83, adj. prof., 1985—. Den mother, com. chmn. Boy Scouts Am.; mem. parent adv. com. Talented and Gifted Edn.; unit orgn. chmn. LWV; mem. Christian edn. bd. Countryside Community Ch.; bd. dirs. Meyer Children's Rehab. Inst., 1980-86, Creche Child Care Ctr., 1984-86, Hattie B. Monroe Home, U. Nebr. Med. Ctr.; trustee Goodwill Industries Nebr., 1984—. U. Nebr. career scholar, 1965-66. Mem. Am. Psychol. Assn. (devel. psychology div.), Nebr. Psychol. Assn. (chmn. legis. com.), Nat. Assn. for Edn. of Young Children, Omaha Assn. for Edn. Young Children, Pi Beta Phi Alumni Assn., Phi Delta Kappa. Democrat. Club: Loveland Community (Omaha). Home and Office: 8305 Hickory St Omaha NE 68124

KRENZLER, ALVIN IRVING, judge; b. Chgo., Apr. 8, 1921. A.B., Case Western Res. U., 1946, LL.B., 1948; LL.M., Georgetown U., 1963. Bar: Ohio 1948. Practice law Cleve., 1948-68; judge Cuyahoga County Ct. Common Pleas, Ohio, 1968-70, Ohio Ct. Appeals, Cleve., 1970-81; Judge U.S. Dist. Ct. (no. dist.), Ohio, 1981—; counsel, dir. Ohio Narcotics Investigation, 1953-55; asst. atty. gen. State of Ohio, 1951-56; trial atty. office chief counsel IRS, Washington, 1960-63. Chmn. Cuyahoga County Bd. Mental Retardation, 1967-70; trustee Cleve. State U., 1967-70, Mt. Sinai Hosp., Cleve., 1973-82; chmn. Ohio Criminal Justice Supervisory Commn., 1975-83. Mem. ABA; MEM. Greater Cleve. Bar Assn.; mem. Cuyahoga County Bar Assn., Fed. Bar. Assn. Office: U S Dist Ct 400 U S Courthouse 201 Superior Ave Cleveland OH 44114

KRESE, MICHAEL JOSEPH, marketing company executive; b. Chgo., June 19, 1956; s. Stanley Leopold and Antonia (Agnich) K.; m. Linda May Brink, Sept. 8, 1979; 1 child, Jennifer Lynn. BBA, Valparaiso (Ind.) U., 1978. Sales rep. Gen. Electric Co., Milw., 1979-83; sales mgr. Bill Casey Electric Sales, Wauwatosa, Wis., 1983-84; pres. M.J. Krese Co., Wauwatosa, 1984—. Mem. Mfg.'s Agts. Nat. Assn., Electric League Milw. Avocations: family, golf, exercise, skiing, boating. Home and Office: 522 N 104th St Wauwatosa WI 53226

KRESL, MILES L., paper company executive; b. Berwyn, Ill., June 29, 1939; s. Miles L. and Helen M. (Novak) K.; m. Joan F. Kresl, Oct. 15, 1966; children: David J., Adam J., Laura J. BBA in Acctg., Milton Coll., 1963. Cost acct. Badger Paper Mills, Peshtigo, Wis., 1963-66, acctg. mgr., 1966-80, sec., treas., 1980—. Served with USCG, 1963-69. Roman Catholic. Home: Rt 2 Box 130 Laura Ln Peshtigo WI 54157 Office: Badger Paper Mills Inc 200 W Front St Peshtigo WI 54159

KRESS, THOMAS GEORGE, manufacturing company executive; b. Dubuque, Iowa, May 11, 1931; s. Henry L. and Jane (Schadle) K.; m. Lou Ann Kuehnle, Sept. 6, 1952; children—Kristine, Elizabeth, Kathleen, Susan, Thomas George, Andrew, Julianna, Matthew, Michael. B.A., Loras Coll., 1953; M.B.A., Northwestern U., 1961; grad., Advanced Mgmt. Program, Harvard, 1971. Cost analyst Gen. Electric Co., Chgo., 1956-62; div. controller Sheller Mfg. Corp., Keokuk, Ia., 1962-64; asst. corp. controller Sheller Mfg. Corp., Detroit, 1964-66; corp. controller Sheller Globe Corp., Toledo, 1967-72, treas., 1972-74, v.p. treasury, 1974-84, v.p. mgmt. info. and telecommunications systems, 1984-85, v.p. finance, 1986; v.p., gen. mgr. indsl./comml. div. The DeVilbiss Co., Toledo, 1986—; v.p., chief fin. officer Champion Spark Plug Co., Toledo, 1987—. Served with U.S. Army, 1953-55. Mem. Financial Execs. Inst., Nat. Assn. Accountants. Clubs: Toledo, Inverness. Home: 4731 Rose Glenn St Toledo OH 43615 Office: 900 Upton Ave Toledo OH 43661

KRESTA, JIRI ERIK, research chemist, consultant, educator; b. Kosice, Czechoslovakia, Apr. 19, 1934; came to U.S., 1969; s. Alfons Kresta and Josefa (Ciglova) Krestova. M in Chem. Engring., Inst. Chem. Tech., Prague, 1957, MS, 1964; DSc, Czechoslovak Acad. of Scis., 1967. Research assoc. Research Inst. Synthetic Rubber, Gottwaldov, Czechoslovakia, 1957-62; research scientist Research Inst. Macromol Chems., Brno, Czechoslovakia, 1962-69; research assoc. Wayne State U., Detroit, 1969-71; research prof. U. Detroit, 1971—; cons. Chemapex Inc., Warren, Mich., 1983. Editor, author books; contbr. numerous articles to profl. jours. Mem. Am. Chem. Soc., Soc. Plastics Engring, N.Y. Acad. Scis., Young Reps. Home: 4097 Frazho Warren MI 48091

KRESTEL, ROBERT D., bank executive. Chmn., pres., chief exec. officer First of Am. Bank, Detroit. Office: First of Am Bank-Detroit N A 645 Griswold Detroit MI 48226 *

KRETA, MARLENE THERESA, management company executive; b. Detroit, June 2, 1944; d. Marion G. (Goetschy) Davis; children: Scott Alexander, Jason Michael Alexander, Marlene Theresa. Student, Highland Park (Mich.) Jr. Coll., St. Clair (Mich.) Community Coll., Northwestern Mich. Coll. Sec., office mgr. Am. Credit Indemnity, Detroit, 1962-65; office mgr. Great Lakes Bowling Corp., Detroit, 1965-67; legal sec., office mgr. Sanilac County Prosecutor, Sandusky, Mich., 1968-71; exec. asst. Owosso (Mich.) State Savs. Bank, 1973-74; legal asst. Running, Wise & Wilson, Traverse City, Mich., 1974-79; adminstrv. asst., office mgr. Land Coordinator Great Lakes Niagaran, Traverse City, 1979-82; cons. Magnum Mgmt., Traverse City, 1982—; speaker Magnum Mgmt., Traverse City, 1982—; instr. Northwestern Mich. Coll., Traverse City, 1983—, cons., 1986; instr. Career Legal Secretarial Inst. Rutgers Law Inst., 1986, adj. prof., 1987; dir. Nat. Inst. for Continuing Legal Edn., 1987. Editor: The Quill, 1979-83 (Nat. award 1979-83), The Official Record, 1984-85 (Nat. award 1984, 85). Mem. Mich. Assn. Legal Secs. (corr. sec. 1982-84, officer 1982-85), Grand Traverse County Legal Secs. (pres., v.p., gov., nals rep. 1978—, Legal Sec. of Yr. award 1980-81), Nat. Assn. Female Execs. (bd. dirs. 1983—), Mich. Assn. Petroleum Landmen. Home: 12909 Sunset Dr Traverse City MI 49684 Office: Magnum Mgmt PO Box 2227 Traverse City MI 49685

KRETCHMER, VALERIE SANDLER, real estate corporation officer, consultant; b. N.Y.C., May 19, 1953; d. Sidney and Nellie (Klein) Sandler; m. Keith Kretchmer, Aug. 29, 1976; children: Joanna, Andrea. BA, Washington U., St. Louis, 1970-74; MPA, NYU, 1974-76. Project planner Community Improvement Agy., New Orleans, 1976-77; sr. analyst Real Estate Research Corp., Chgo., 1978-81; asst. v.p. VMS Realty, Inc., Chgo., 1982-85; prin. Valerie S. Kretchmer Assocs., Chgo., 1985—. Mem. Urban Land Inst., Am. Planning Assn., Chgo. Real Estate Council. Home: 2707 Walnut Ave Evanston IL 60201 Office: Valerie S Kretchmer Assocs Inc 2707 Walnut Ave Evanston IL 60201

KREUTZER, PAUL, JR., interior designer; b. Sharon, Pa., Jan. 22, 1954; s. Paul and Maria (Schuster) K. A. in Specialized Tech., Art Inst. Pitts., 1973. With Hume's Carriage House, Youngstown, Ohio, 1974-84, buyer, 1978-79, sr. staff designer, 1979-84; propr. Paul Kreutzer Interiors, 1984—. Ch. council Honterus Evang. Luth. Ch., Youngstown, 1986-87, ch. treas., 1986-87. Mem. Am. Soc. Interior Designers (assoc., chair profl. devel. Ohio North chpt. 1985). Lutheran. Clubs: Alliance Transylvanian Saxons (U.S. group leader 8th internat. youth rally 1984) (Cleve.); Youngstown Saxon Br. 30 (asst. fin. sec. 1984-86), Youngstown Saxon Culture Group (v.p. 1977, 84, pres. 1985-87, trustee 1976, youth advisor 1970-71, news corr. 1974, 80, 81, 82), Youngstown Area C. of C. Home and Office: 198 Wychwood Ln Youngstown OH 44512

KREUTZKAMPF, JUNE ELIZABETH, social studies and home economics educator; b. Estherville, Iowa, June 13, 1940; d. Albert Olaf Theodore and Pearl Pauline (Wede) K. B.S., Iowa State U., 1962, M.S., 1970; Ph.D., U. Minn., 1978. Tchr. pub. schs. Hawarden, Maquoketa and Jefferson, Iowa, 1962-69; asst. prof. SUNY-Buffalo, 1971-74; vis. asst. prof. Brigham Young U., Provo, Utah, 1975-76; asst. prof. Peru State Coll., Nebr., 1979-80; asst. prof., chmn. dept. home econs. U. Minn.-Duluth, 1980-84, coordinator social studies program, 1984-86—, assoc. prof. dept. instructional sci., 1986—. Bd. dirs. Spirit Mountain Recreational Area Authority, Duluth, 1983—. Mem NEA, AAUW, Am. Edn. Research Assn., Nat. Council Social Studies, Assn. Tchr. Educators, Assn. for Supervision and Curriculum Devel., Phi Delta Kappa, Omicron Nu, Kappa Omicron Phi, Alpha Delta Kappa, Beta Sigma Phi. Democrat. Methodist. Avocations: traveling, reading, sewing, photography. Home: 312 Hawkins St Duluth MN 55811 Office: U Minn 221 Bohannon Hall Duluth MN 55812

KREYKES, KATHLEEN KAY, media services executive; b. Iowa City, June 28, 1952; d. Howard Baker and Katharine Eloise (Jennison) Waddell; m. Rodney Dale Kreykes, July 18, 1981. BA, U. Iowa, 1974, MA, 1975. Dir. media services Marshalltown (Iowa) Community Coll., 1975—, pres. faculty senate, 1981-82, 85-86, dir. student orientation, 1986—, acting dean instrn., 1986. Mem. Iowa Higher Edn. Instructional Resources Consortium (exec. dir. 1985—), Iowa Assn. Communication Tech. (bd. dirs. 1987-89), Iowa Ednl. Media Assn. (chmn. pub. relations com. 1986-88), NEA, Assn. Edn. Communication Tech., Iowa State Edn. Assn., Pi Lambda Theta,. Avocations: travel, gardening, bicycling. Home: 2510 S 6th St E36 Marshalltown IA 50158 Office: Marshalltown Community Coll 3700 S Center St Marshalltown IA 50158

KRIAUCIUNAS, ROMUALDAS, psychologist; b. Panevezys, Lithuania, Jan. 21, 1936; came to U.S., 1950; s. Mykolas and Roze (Sukyte) K.; m. Grazina Virginija Pauliukonis, July 21, 1962; children: Aidas V., Aras M., Alidas P. BA, Roosevelt U., Chgo., 1956, MA, 1962; PhD, Washington U., St. Louis, 1967. Lic. psychologist, Mich., Ill.; cert. marriage counselor, Mich. Clin. psychologist Ill. Dept. Mental Health, Manteno, Anna and Kankakee, Ill., 1962-69; dir. tng. Ingham Community Mental Health Ctr., Lansing, Mich., 1969—; asst. to assoc. clin. prof. Coll. Human Medicine Mich. State U., East Lansing, Mich., 1975—; pvt. practice psychology, Lansing, 1972—. Pres., bd. dirs. Youth Camp Dainava, Manchester, Mich., 1981-84; bd. dirs. Fedn. Ateitis, Chgo., 1981—. Served with U.S. Army, 1958-62. Mem. Am. Psychol. Assn., Mich. Psychol. Assn., Mich. Assn. for Better Speech and Hearing (pres. bd. dirs. 1981). Roman Catholic. Avocations: travel, canoeing, camping, chess, writing. Home: 1816 Tecumseh River Dr Lansing MI 48906 Office: Ingham Community Mental Health Ctr 407 W Greenlawn Ave Lansing MI 48910

KRICK, FREDERICK MARLOWE, biology educator; b. Des Moines, May 20, 1960; s. George Frank and Marlene Faye (Eaton) K. AA, Des Moines Area Community Coll., 1980; BA, Drake U., 1982, MA, 1986. Grad. teaching asst. Drake U., Des Moines, 1982-84; lab. technician, instr. biology Des Moines Area Community Coll., Ankeny, Iowa, 1985—. Active judge com. Hawkeye Sci. Fair, Des Moines, 1983-87. Mem. Beta Beta Beta, Alpha Epsilon Delta, Tau Kappa Epsilon. Republican. Presbyterian. Avocations: piano, hunting, fishing, camping, leathercraft. Home: 7207 SW 48th Ave Des Moines IA 50321 Office: Des Moines Area Community Coll 2006 S Ankeny Blvd Bldg 4 Ankeny IA 50021

KRICK, KENNETH A., transportation executive; b. Lancaster, Pa., May 13, 1934; s. Thomas B. and Marguerite (Aukamp) K.; m. Rita Killian, May 26, 1956; children: Kenneth, John, Tracy, David. BS in Acctg., Franklin and Marshall Coll., Lancaster, 1952; postgrad. in Advanced Mgmt., Harvard U., 1983. CPA, Pa. V.p. fin. Fuller Co., Bethlehem, Pa., 1975-78, pres., chief operating officer, 1978-82, chmn., chief exec. officer, 1982-86; group v.p. GATX Corp., Chgo., 1983-86; pres., chief exec. officer Gen. Am. Transp. Co., Chgo., 1987—; bd. dirs. Can. Gen. Transit, Montreal, ANCAF, Mexico City. Served to capt. USAF, 1956-59. Mem. Am. Inst. CPA's, Nat. Freight Transp. Assn. Clubs: Saucon Valley (Bethlehem); Edgewood Valley, Metropolitan (Chgo.). Avocations: tennis, reading. Home: 4738 Howard Ave Western Springs IL 60558 Office: Gen Am Transp Corp 120 S Riverside Plaza Chicago IL 60606

KRIEBEL, DENISE A.T., personnel director; b. Balt., Sept. 30, 1952; d. William George and Dorothy Elizabeth (Seibert) Trimble; m. James Edward Kriebel, July 5, 1975; children: James W., Matthew E., David A. BA in Psychology and Sociology, Anderson Coll., 1974; MA, Ball State U., 1984. Adminstrv. asst. Conn. Gen., Balt., 1974-75; claimstaker Ind. Employment Security Div., Anderson, Ind., 1975-76; employment interviewer Ind. Employment Security Div., Muncie, Ind., 1976-82; dir. personnel services Anderson (Ind.) Coll., 1982—. Mem. Am. Soc. Personnel Adminstrn., Coll. and Univ. Personnel Assn., Internat. Mgmt. Council (sec. 1986—). Republican. Mem. Ch. of God. Office: Anderson Coll 1100 E 5th St Anderson IN 46012

KRIEG, LON RAY, osteopathic physician; b. Mpls., Feb. 25, 1955; s. Harry Edward Jr. and Eunice Arlene (Erickson) K.; m. Jan Lynn Severance, Sept. 4, 1976; children: Morgan Rachel, Kelsey Lynn. AA, Rochester Community Coll., 1975; B of Elected Studies, U. Minn., 1977; DO, Kirksville (Mo.) Coll. Osteo. Medicine, 1982. Diplomate Nat. Bd. Med. Examiners. Mem. staff Rice County Dist. One Hosp., Faribault, Minn., 1983—; dep. med examiner Goodhue County, 1984—. Team physician Kenyon (Minn.) Jr.-Sr. High Sch., 1983—. Mem. Am. Osteo. Assn., Am. Acad. Osteo. Sports Medicine, Am. Coll. Gen. Practitioners, Minn. Osteo. Med. Soc., Goodhue County Med. Soc., Kirksville Coll. Osteo. Medicine Alumni, U. Minn. Alumni Assn. Republican. Lutheran. Avocations: hunting, fishing, golf, flying, softball. Home: 529 Spring St Kenyon MN 55946 Office: Kenyon Med Clinic PA 104 Third St Kenyon MN 55946

KRIEGER, MICHAEL PARIS, neurologist; b. Bay City, Mich., Sept. 13, 1942; s. Maurice Harold and Elinor L. (Kuttner) K.; m. Sherry A. Saunders, Feb. 14, 1983; children—William Harvey, Elizabeth Maurine. A.B., Dartmouth Coll., 1964; M.D., N.Y. Med. Coll., 1968. Diplomate Am. Bd. Psychiatry and Neurology. Resident in internal medicine Meadowbrook Hosp., Long Island, N.Y., 1969-70; resident in neurology Walter Reed Army Med. Ctr., Washington, 1970-73; chief neurology sect. Walson Army Hosp., Ft. Dix, N.J., 1973-75; clin. neurologist, mng. ptnr. Neurol. Assocs. N. Central Ohio Inc., Mansfield, 1975-83; pres., practice medicine specializing in neurology Neurol. Services Inc., Mansfield, 1983—; med. dir. Peoples Hosp. Sleep Disorder Lab., 1986—; chief of staff Peoples Hosp., 1987; cons. neurology, epilepsy Rehab. Ctr. N. Central Ohio, Mansfield, 1967-86. Bd. dirs. Multiple Sclerosis Soc., Mansfield, 1976-78. Served to maj. U.S. Army, 1970-75. Mem. Clin. Sleep Soc., Am. Acad. Neurology, Am. Soc. Internal Medicine, Ohio State Med. Assn., Richland County Med. Soc., Am. Legion. Club: Mens Garden (Mansfield). Avocations: gardening; skiing. Office: Neurol Services Inc 661 Park Ave E Mansfield OH 44905

KRIEKAARD, JOHN EDWARD, II, designer; b. Grand Rapids, Mich.; s. John Edward and Lillian Virginia (Stanton) K.; m. Diane Petrakis, May 31, 1986. Grad., Kendal Sch. Design, Grand Rapids, Mich., 1970, Aquinas, Grand Rapids, 1975. Designer, ad artist Isreal's Design for Living, Grand Rapids, 1973-75; designer, sales DeKorne Furniture, Grand Rapids, 1975-76; designer Business Interiors, Grand Rapids, 1976-77; internat. design mgr. Westinghouse Furniture System, Grand Rapids, 1977-82; owner, designer Designarts, Alto, Mich., 1982—; design cons. Herman Miller, Zealand, Mich., 1986—, Westinghouse Furniture System, Grand Rapids, 1986—, Haworth, Holland, Mich., 1986—. Avocations: painting, sculpture, photography, sailing, skiing.

KRIEKEMANS, ALBERT PAUL JOZEF KAREL, chemical executive, marketing consultant; b. Munster, Westfalen, Fed. Republic of Germany, Sept. 24, 1957; came to U.S., 1981; s. Karel Albert Christiane Kriekemans. B in Chem. Engring., KIHL, Limburg, Belgium, 1979. Sales engr. Donaldson N.V., Leuven, Belgium, 1979-81; indsl. engrs. De Neef Chemie N.V., Heistoldberg, Belguim, 1981; gen. mgr. De Neef Am. Inc., St. Louis, 1981-84, v.p., 1984—. Home: 3600 Genk, Reinpadstraat 66 Belgium, Federal Republic of Germay Office: De Neef Am Inc 122 N Millstreet Saint Louis MI 48880

KRIER, CURTIS GENE, accounting and finance consultant; b. Mpls., Aug. 11, 1948; s. Curtis George and Jeanne (Dale) K.; m. Nancy D. Carlson, Sept. 1980. B.A., U. Minn., 1970, B.S.B., 1978; M.B.A., Mankato State U. (Minn.), 1978. Cert. Am. Inst. Banking. Asst. to bank ops. officer 3d Northwestern Nat. Bank, Mpls., 1972-75; staff acct. Robert G. Engelhart & Co., Burnsville, Minn., 1978-79, House & Nezerka, C.P.A.s, 1979-80; controller Calc-Type, Inc., Mpls., 1980-81; pres. Curtis G. Krier & Co., acctg. and fin. cons., Edina, Minn., 1981-86; v.p. fin. Data Recording Tech. Corp., Mpls., 1986—. Mem. Nat. Assn. Accts. (sec. bd. dirs. Mpls. Viking chpt. 1982-84). Home: 9211 Lake Riley Blvd Chaska MN 55318 Office: Data Recording Tech Corp 690 Mendelssohn Ave Minneapolis MN 55427

KRINDLE, RUTH, provincial judge; b. Winnipeg, Man., Can., Feb. 6, 1943; d. Harold and Gwendolyn Marion (Henderson) K. LLB, U. Man. Bar: Man. 1968. Sole practice Man., 1968-70; prosecutor Province of Man. Dept. Atty. Gen., Winnipeg, 1970-75; chmn. Man. Labor Bd., Winnipeg, 1967-77; ptnr. Tolton and Krindle Barristers, Winnipeg, 1977-80; judge County Ct. of Winnipeg, 1980-84, Ct. of Queen's Bench, Winnipeg, 1984—. Office: Court of Queen's Bench, Law Court Bldg, Winnipeg, MB Canada R3C OV8 *

KRISHNAN, AHALYA, psychologist, researcher; b. Tiruppur, Madras, India, Feb. 24, 1931; came to U.S. 1959; d. Jayeendrachar and Jayalaksmi; m. Narayanan, Sept. 15, 1958 (dec. Nov. 1961); 1 child, Vani; m. Rama Krishnan, June 16, 1965. BA, Madras State U., 1955; MS with high honors, U. Wis., Platteville, 1969; PhD, Kent State U., 1975. Cert. counselor. Hindi tchr. Holy Angels Convent, India, 1950-56, Ministry Home Affairs, Govt. of India, 1956-59; econ. asst. Indian Embassy, Washington, 1960-65; statis. asst. World Bank, Washington, 1965-67; research asst. Kent (Ohio) State U., 1974-75; part-time instr. Youngstown (Ohio) State U., 1969-73, prof. psychology, 1975—. Recipient Disting. Prof. award Youngstown State U., 1983. Mem. Am. Psychol. Assn., Midwestern Psychol. Assn. (local rep. 1975—), Am. Ednl. Research Assn., Indian Assn. Greater Youngstown. Home: 7979 Forest Lake Dr Youngstown OH 44512 Office: Youngstwon State U 410 Wick Ave Youngstown OH 44555

KRISHNAN, RUTH SORENSEN, physical therapist; b. Esther, Iowa, Aug. 1, 1958; d. Leo Ardet and Alice Marie Sorensen; m. Santosh Sorensen Krishnan, Aug. 21, 1982. BS, U. Iowa, 1982, cert. in physical therapy, 1984. Cert. physical therapist. Physical therapist Moline (Ill.) Pub. Hosp., 1984-86, Mercy Hosp., Davenport, Iowa, 1986—; lectr. Moline Diabetic Assn., 1984, Cardiac Club, Moline, 1985, Quad-Cities Renal Ctr., Moline, 1985; presentor posture screening booth, Fitness Festival, Davenport, 1986. Vol. Com. to Re-elect Lane Evans, Moline,1984, LWV, Moline, 1984. Recipient Bill Pearson award, Nat. Assn. Am. Bus. Clubs, 1983-84; Iowa State U. scholar, 1976-78, U. Iowa scholar, 1981-83. Mem. Am. Physical Therapy Assn. (presentation annual conf. 1984), Ill. Chpt. Am. Physical Therapy Assn. (mem. orthopaedics, neurology & geriatrics spl. section.). Lodge: Danish Sisterhood. Avocations: cross country skiing, bicycling, reading, travel. Home: 709 36th Ave East Moline IL 61244 Office: Mercy Hosp W Central Pk at Marquette Davenport IA 52804

KRIST, DONALD EUGENE, insurance association executive; b. Topeka, June 26, 1926; s. George M. and Florence (McInerny) K.; m. Marilyn McClurkin, May 29, 1948; children: Lisa Ann, James Eric. BA, Drake U., 1951. Cert. assn. exec. Pub. relations dir. U.S. Jr. C. of C., 1953-55, Meredith Cos., 1955-60; exec. v.p. Iowa Consumer Fin. Assn., 1960-66, Profl. Ins. Agts. Iowa, West Des Moines, 1973—; owner, mgr. Donald Krist & Assocs., Inc., Des Moines, 1966-73; instr., lectr. pub. relations Drake U., Des Moines, 1957-70. Editor: Iowa Ins. Interpreter mag., 1973—. Served with USN, 1943-46. Recipient Outstanding Achievement award Iowa 1752 Club, 1980. Mem. Am. Soc. Assn. Execs. (Mgmt. Achievement award 1976), Iowa Soc. Assn. Execs., Smithsonian Instn. Assocs. Clubs: Des Moines, Des Moines Press (pres. 1959). Home: 800 52d Ct West Des Moines IA 50265 Office: Westgate Plaza 1000 73d St Suite 12 Des Moines IA 50311

KRIST, JAMES ERIC, insurance company executive; b. Des Moines, Feb. 25, 1959; s. Don E. and Marilyn (McClurk) K.' m. Lisa J. Brubaker, May 25, 1985. BBA in Fin. Econs., U. Iowa, 1982; MBA, Drake U., 1985. Cert. ins. counselor. Account exec. Hawkeye Bancorp., Des Moines, 1982-83; asst. v.p. Profl. Ins. Agts. Iowa, Des Moines, 1983-84, v.p. edn. and research, 1984—. Contbr. articles to profl. jours. Mem. Soc. Cert. Ins. Counselors, Soc. Profl. Ins. Agts. Execs., Assocs. Bus. Club (pres. 1983-84). Republican. Presbyterian. Avocations: swimming, skeet and trap shooting, photography, motorcycling. Home: 1443 20th St West Des Moines IA 50265 Office: Profl Ins Agts Iowa 1000 73d St Suite 12 Des Moines IA 50311

KRISTAL, DAVID MARTIN, orthodontist; b. Milw., Mar. 7, 1949; s. Morris and Bessie (Rudberg) K.; m. Barbara Joy Linde, Aug. 19, 1973; 1 child, Stephanie Aleeza. BA, Northwestern U., 1971; DDS, Case Western Res. U., 1975; Cert. in Orthodontics, Fairleigh Dickinson U., 1978. Practice dentistry specializing in orthodontia Columbus, Ohio, 1978—. Mem. ADA, Am. Assn. Orthodontists, Columbus Dental Soc., Alpha Omega (pres. 1986-87). Home: 2737 Brentwood Rd Columbus OH 43209 Office: 5350 E Main St Columbus OH 43213

KRIT, ROBERT LEE, development executive; b. Chgo., Apr. 6, 1920; s. Jacob and Tania (Etzkowitz) K.; B.S. in Commerce, DePaul U., 1946; A.B.A., N. Park Coll., 1939; children—Melissa, Margaret, Justin. Dir. Chgo. Herald Am. Mercy Fleet charity drives, 1940-41; asst. exec. dir. cancer research found. U. Chgo., 1947-48; state campaign dir. Am. Cancer Soc., Inc., Chgo., 1948-63; dir. med. devel. U. Chgo., 1963-67; v.p. devel. U. Health Scis./Chgo. Med. Sch. (formerly Chgo. Med. Sch.), 1967—. Moderator, NBC-TV series Tension in Modern Living, Drug Abuse, Aging and Retirement, Health and Devel. Children, Cancer, Bridge For Tomorrow, Healthy Life Style, NBC Ednl. Exchange; host producer TV series Med. Looking Glass, Relevant Issues in Health and Medicine, Coping, Su Salud, Spanish TV series, Chgo. Med. Sch. Reports, radio series; chmn. Ill. Comm. for Nat. Health Agys. Fed. Service Campaigns; mem. adv. bd. Central States Inst. for Addiction Services; v.p. Drug Abuse Council of Ill.; bd. dirs. Lawson YMCA, United Way Lake County, Ill. Found. Dentistry for the Handicapped; vice chmn. North Chgo. Citizens Against Drug & Alcohol Abuse. Served to 1st lt. USAAF, 1942-46. Fellow Inst. Medicine Chgo. (cochmn. com. on public info., editorial bd. Procs.; Disting. Service award); mem. Chgo. Soc. Fund Raising Execs. (pres. 1964-65), Chgo. Assn. Commerce and Industry (health-in-industry com.), Nat. Acad. TV Arts and Scis. Home: 3513 Lake Ave Apt 406 Wilmette IL 60091 Office: 200 E Randolph Dr Suite 7938 Chicago IL 60601

KRITSAS, ZOE PANAS, nurse; b. Mazatlan, Sinaloa, Mex., Sept. 5, 1933; came to U.S., 1957; d. John D. and Helen (Kutrumpusi) Panas. B.A., U. So. Calif., 1951; B.S., U. Guadalajara, 1953; R.N., Triton Coll., Maywood, Ill., 1979. Cert. obstet. nurse; disaster nurse ARC. Sec.-treas. Am. consulate, Guadalajara, 1952-55; coordinator State Fair, Govt. of Jalisco (Mex.), 1950-51; mem. staff Hosp. Service League, Chgo., 1968—; nurse Resurrection Hosp., Chgo. Author children's stories. Active ARC; interpretor Cook County Ct. Systems, 1981-82; chmn. Community Health Services No. Cook County Republican. Greek Orthodox. Office: Resurrection Hosp Chicago IL 60631

KRIVO, DAVID ALAN, industrial supply company executive; b. Chgo., June 23, 1950; s. Albert A. and Marcia (Goldberg) K.; m. Patti E. Tyser, June 15, 1974; children: Ariel Sara, Eliza Florence, Sydney Ava. Chief exec. officer Krivo Indsl. Supply Co., Chgo., 1972—, corp. v.p., 1977-86, exec. v.p., 1986—. Active Jewish United Fund. Mem. Nat. Indsl. Distbrs. Assn., Cen. States Indsl. Distbrs. Assn., Ill. Indsl. Distbrs. Assn. Democrat. Home: 4410 Bobolink Terr Skokie IL 60076 Office: Krivo Indsl Supply Co 1618 W Fullerton St Chicago IL 60614

KRIVOSHA, NORMAN, chief justice state supreme court; b. Detroit, Aug. 3, 1934; s. David B. and Molly K.; m. Helene Miriam Sherman, July 31, 1955; children: Terri Lynn, Rhonda Ann. B.S., U. Nebr., 1956, J.D., 1958; LL.D., Central Mich. U., 1983, Creighton U., 1985. Bar: Nebr. Ptnr. firm Ginsburg, Rosenberg, Ginsburg & Krivosha, Lincoln, Nebr., 1958-78; chief justice Nebr. Supreme Ct., Lincoln, 1978—; city atty. City of Lincoln, 1969-70; gen. counsel Lincoln Electric System, 1969-78, Lincoln Gen. Hosp., 1969-78; mem. Uniform Law Commn., 1973—. Pres. Lincoln council Camp Fire Girls; pres. Congregation Tifereth Israel, Lincoln; pres. central states region United Synagogue Am., v.p., 1983—; bd. dirs. Lincoln YMCA; Nebr. chmn. Israel Bonds; chmn. fund drive Lincoln Jewish Welfare Fedn.; mem. Lincoln Charter Revision Commn.; bd. dirs. Ramah Commn., Camp Ramah, Wis. Recipient Outstanding Jewish Leader award State of Israel Bonds, 1978. Mem. ABA, Nebr. Bar Assn. (chmn. com. on procedure), Lincoln Bar Assn., Am. Trial Lawyers Assn., Nebr. Assn. Trial Attys. (sec. 1961-64, v.p. 1964-65), Am. Soc. Hosp. Attys., Am. Pub. Power Assn. (chmn. legal sect.), Lincoln C. of C. (bd. dirs.), Sigma Alpha Mu (nat. pres. 1980-83). Home: 2835 O'Reilly Dr Lincoln NE 68502 Office: Nebr Supreme Ct Suite 2214 State Capitol Bldg Lincoln NE 68509 *

KRIZ, ROBERT J., allergist, educator; b. N.Y.C., Mar. 21, 1945; s. John and Stella (Barczak) K.; m. Linda Ann Byrne, Dec. 18, 1977; children: Karyn, John, Laura, Joseph. BA magna cum laude, Queens Coll., 1965; MD, N.Y.U., 1969. Diplomate Am. Bd. Internal Medicine. Asst. clin. prof. U. Wis., Madison, 1980—. Served to maj. USAF, 1971-73. Mem. AMA, Am. Coll. Physicians, Am. Acad. Allergy and Immunology, Am. Thoracic Soc., Phi Beta Kappa. Roman Catholic. Avocations: computers, piano. Office: Allergy & Immunology Group 1 S Park St Suite 600 Madison WI 53715

KRIZSA, THOMAS FREDERICK, controller; b. Cin., June 26, 1948; s. Louis John and Marion Elizabeth (Speckert) K.; m. Kathleen Ann Heider, Aug. 16, 1969; children: Thomas F. Jr., Angela Marie, Stephanie Rose. B in Math., Bellarmine Coll., 1970; postgrad. studies in edn., Northern Ky. U., 1971-73; postgrad. studies in acctg., Franklin U., 1976-78. CPA, Ohio. Gen. acctg. supr. Revlon-Realistic, Cin., 1981-83, controller, 1983-84; asst. controller Revlon Profl. Products, Jacksonville, 1984-85; corp. controller Cornerstone Mfg., Orange Park, Fla., 1985—; bd. dirs. Pulstar Corp. Gainesville, Fla.; instr. Becker CPA Rev., Jacksonville, Fla., 1985—. Mem. Ch. Athletic Group for Kids, Cin., 1980-83, soccer and basketball coordinator, v.p., 1982, pres. 1983. Mem. Fla. Inst. CPA's (industry govt. edn. com.), Ohio Soc. CPA's, Am. Inst. CPA's. Roman Catholic. Avocations: swimming, basketball, golf. Home: 6250 Kingoak Dr Cincinnati OH 45248 Office: Xetron Corp 40 W Crescentville Rd Cincinnati OH 45246

KROCH, CARL ADOLPH, retail executive; b. Chgo., June 21, 1914; s. Adolph and Gertrude (Horn) K.; m. Jeanette Kennelly, Aug. 12, 1939. B.A., Cornell U., 1935. With Kroch's Bookstores, Inc., 1935-54, pres., dir., 1949-54; pres. Brentano's Bookstores, Inc., 1950-54; pres., dir. Kroch's & Brentano's, Inc., Chgo., 1954-86, chmn., 1986—; pres. Booksellers Catalog Service, Inc.; ptnr. Cin. Reds Baseball Team; bd. dirs. Nat. Blvd. Bank Chgo., Boulevard Bancorp. Author: American Booksellers and Publishers: A Personal Perspective, 1981. Bd. dirs. Northwestern Meml. Hosp., Ill. Humane Soc., USO; presdl. councillor Cornell U. Served to lt. USNR, 1942-45. Mem. Am. Booksellers Assn., Ill. Retail Mchts. Assn., Better Bus. Bur. Chgo., Wine and Food Soc., Beta Theta Pi. Clubs: North Shore Country (Glenview, Ill.); Caxton, Mid-Am., Chgo. Yacht, Tavern, University (Chgo.); Lake Zurich (Ill.) Golf. Home: 3240 N Lake Shore Dr Chicago IL 60657 Office: 29 S Wabash Ave Chicago IL 60603

KROEGEL, JAMES, marketing executive; b. Deerfield, Ill., Aug. 16, 1954; s. John and Alice (Gray) K. BS, U. Ill., 1976. Mktg. mgr. Duo-Dent Corp., Glenview, Ill., 1976-78; mktg. coordinator Swift Adhesives, Chgo., 1978-83; mktg. dir. Comml. Investment Council, Chgo., 1983—. Team capt. team Am. walk March of Dimes. Chgo., 1982. Mem. Am. Soc. Assn. Execs. Avocations: pvt. pilot. sailing, scuba diving, photography. Home: 1112 Elmwood Ave Deerfield IL 60015 Office: Comml Investments Council 430 N Michigan Ave Chicago IL 60611

KROETCH, PATRICIA ANN ROBINSON, educational diagnostician, educator; b. Tucson, Feb. 16, 1935; d. Lloyd Madison and Edith Beatrice (Kellogg) Robinson; m. George Duane Kroetch, July 3, 1955; children—Gregory, Sheron, Erika. Student San Jose State Coll., 1952-55; B.S. in Elem. Edn., Dominican Coll., Racine, Wis., 1956; M.Ed., S.D. State U., 1968. Elem. tchr. cert., Wis., S.D.; elem. adminstrn. cert., S.D. Tchr., Horicon (Wis.) pub. schs., 1956-57, Elk Mound Consol. Sch., Elk Mound, Wis., 1958-59; elem. tchr. Douglas Sch. System, Ellsworth AFB, S.D., 1964-80, Title I diagnostician, 1980-83, prin. elem. sch., 1983—; instr. S.D. State U., Brookings, 1979. Bd. dirs. Black Hills Waldorf Sch., 1981. AAUW scholar, 1965. Mem. Nat. Council Tchrs. Math., Internat. Reading Assn., Assn. Supervision and Curriculum Devel., Collegial Assn. for Devel. and Renewal of Educators, Delta Kappa Gamma, Alpha Delta Kappa. Republican. Episcopalian. Home: 1011 Franklin St Rapid City SD 57701 Office: Douglas School System Ellsworth AFB SD 57706

KROFT, GUY JOSEPH, provincial judge; b. St. Boniface, Man., Can., May 27, 1934; s. Charles and Heloise (Cohn) K.; m. Hester Lee, June 10, 1956; children: Jonathan Barry, Deborah Faith, David Joseph, Sarah Lynn. BA, U. Man., 1955, LLB, 1959. Judge Ct. of Queen's Bench, Winnipeg, Man. Office: Court of Queen's Bench, Law Courts Bldg, Winnipeg, MB Canada R3C 0V8 *

KROGH, HARRY M., department store company executive; b. 1929. Student, McCook Jr. Coll., 1949, Nebr. Wesleyan U., 1951, U. Denver, 1954. Mgr. adminstrv. services Arthur Andersen & Co., Chgo., 1954-68; mgr. mfg. controls Peat Marwick Mitchell & Co., 1968-70; dir. fin. and adminstrn. Boise (Idaho) Cascade Corp., 1970-72; v.p. fin. Bendix Home Systems, Boise, 1973-74; with Interco Inc., St. Louis, 1974—, v.p. fin. Florsheim Shoe div., 1974-80, now pres. Served with USAF, 1951-53. Office: Interco Inc 101 S. Hanley Rd Saint Louis MO 63105 *

KROGSTAD, WILBUR DONALD, JR., electrical engineer, land surveyor; b. Lebanon, Mo., July 8, 1944; s. Wilbur Donald and Caroline Eleanor (Bowman) K.; m. Freida Mae Sanning, Dec. 20, 1969; children—Cynthia Jean, Judith Ann. BSEE, U. Mo., Rolla, 1967; M in Pub. Adminstrn., U. Mo., Columbia, 1987. Registered profl. engr., land surveyor, Mo. San. engr. Clean Water Commn., Jefferson City, Mo., 1967-69; design engr. Lake of the Ozark Regional Planning Commn., Camdenton, Mo., 1971-72; cons. engr. Mo. Engring. Corp., 1972-74; design engr. Div. Design and Constrn., Mo. Office of Adminstrs., Jefferson City, 1974-77, chief design engr., 1977—. Active Holts Summit Civic Assn. Served with U.S. Army, 1969-71. Mem. Nat. Soc. Profl. Engrs., Mo. Soc. Profl. Engrs. (bd. dirs.), Mo. Assn. Registered Land Surveyors. Republican. Methodist. Office: Mo Office of Adminstrn Box 809 Jefferson City MO 65102

KROHA, BRADFORD KING, electronics manufacturing corporation executive; b. Rochester, N.Y., Dec. 16, 1926; s. George Frederic and Neva Alice (Smy) Kroha; m. Nona Jane Hobbs, June 15, 1979; children by previous marriage: Nancy, Judy, Sally, Jane, Robert. B.E.E., Yale U., 1947; B.S. in Indsl. Adminstrn., 1948; postgrad., Harvard U. Grad. Sch. Bus. Adminstrn., 1952. Gen. mgr. Can. Motorola Ltd., Toronto, Ont., 1969-72; dir. internat. subs. Motorola Inc., Schaumburg, Ill., 1972-77, asst. gen. mgr. communications internat. div., 1977-79, v.p., gen. mgr. European communications div., 1979-85; v.p., dir. communications sector sourcing Motorola Inc., 1985—. Served with USNR, 1944-46. Republican. Presbyterian. Club: Barrington Hills Country (Ill.). Home: 82 Paganica Rd Barrington Hills IL 60010 Office: Motorola Inc 1301 E Algonquin Rd Schaumburg IL 60196

KROKAR, JAMES PAUL, history educator; b. Chgo., July 17, 1948; s. Louis Joseph and Mary Theresa (O'Connell) K.; m. Christine Larsen, Sept. 4, 1982. BA, DePaul U., Chgo., 1969; MA, Ind. U., 1971, PhD, 1980. Edit. asst. Am. Hist. Rev., Bloomington, Ind., 1977-80; archives assoc. Ind. U., Bloomington, Ind., 1980-81; asst. prof. history dept. DePaul U., Chgo., 1981—. Gen. editor Common Studies textbooks; contbr. articles to profl. jours. Served as sgt. U.S. Army, 1970-72, Germany. Woodrow Wilson Found. fellow, 1969, IREX fellow, 1974; research council grantee DePaul U., Chgo., 1985. Mem. Am. Hist. Assn., Am. Assn. Advancement Slavic Studies, Am. Assn. Southeast European Studies, Ill. Assn. for Advancement History. Avocation: reading. Office: Depaul Univ Dept History Chicago IL 60614

KROLL, PHILIP DORIAN, psychiatrist; b. Detroit, Apr. 25, 1941; s. Benjamin and Mary (Ogoroskin) K.; m. Syma Lipschutz, Sept. 1, 1980; children: Kara Kantor, Rebecca Kantor. BA, Brandeis U., 1963; MD, U. Mich., 1968. Diplomate Am. Bd. Psychiatry and Neurology. Intern Wayne County Gen. Hosp., 1967-68; resident in psychiatry Lafayette Clinic, Detroit, 1968-71; from instr. to asst. prof. psychiatry U. Mich., Ann Arbor, 1973—; dir. alcohol treatment unit VA Hosp., Ann Arbor, 1975—. Contbr. articles on alcoholism to profl. jours. Served to maj. USAF, 1971-73. Mem. Am. Psychiat. Assn., Am. Acad. Psychiatrists in Alcohol and the Addictions, Am. Med. Soc. on Alcoholism and Other Dependencies, Nat. Council on Alcoholism. Avocations: running, sailing. Office: VA Hosp 2215 Fuller Rd Ann Arbor MI 48105

KRONOUR, DAVID R(ICKY), management counsultant; b. Dayton, Ohio, Dec. 1, 1953; s. Carl Cyril and Ruby Mae (Foreman) K.; m. Linda Lorraine Lannigan, June 23, 1979; 1 child, Starr Lynette. BS in Bus., Wright State U., 1976. Office mgr. C.C. Kronour Digging and Trucking Corp., Dayton, 1977-78, pres., 1978—. Author: Building Up America, 1985. Creator Bldg. Up Am., Dayton, 1983, Bldg. Up Am. Meml. at Wright State U., 1985, Bldg. Up Am. Documentary, 1987; mem. Eagle Scouts. Mem. Wright State U. Alumni Assn., Dayton Inventors Club. Republican. Baptist. Avocations: reading, research, swimming. Home: 4257 Lamont Dr Kettering OH 45429

KRONSCHNABEL, GEORGE JAMES, brass company executive; b. Kimberly, Wis., Feb. 11, 1925; s. George J. and Ellen (Hardy) K.; m. Betty Michel, Aug. 21, 1948; children: William, Mary, Ann, Jim, Rita, Jane, Peter, Ellen, Paul, Ted. BS, St. Thomas Coll., 1949; postgrad., Syracuse U., 1963. V.p. Michael Sales Co., St. Paul, 1949-52; sales promotion mgr. Union Brass Co., St. Paul, 1952-53, sales mgr., 1954-57, v.p., sales, 1958-62, v.p. sales and mktg., 1963—, also bd. dirs.; bd. dirs. Viking Properties, St. Paul. Served with USN, 1942-46, ATO, PTO. Republican. Roman Catholic. Club: Town and Country. Avocations: golf, fishing, athletics. Home: 1425 Summit Ave Saint Paul MN 55105 Office: Union Brass Co 501 W Lawson Ave Saint Paul MN 55117

KROON, JOHN C., physicist; b. Holland, Netherlands, May 30, 1939; came to U.S., 1974, naturalized, 1983; s. Gerardus and Duifje (van deNes) K.; m. Marian Barry, Aug. 28, 1965; children: Stephanie, Lisa. BS, U. Ottawa, Ont., 1966; MS, U. Ottawa, 1968, PhD, 1971. Physicist Chalk River (Ont.) Nuclear Lab. Atomic Energy Can. Ltd., 1971-72; mgr. research and devel. Reuter-Stokes, Inc., Cleve., 1974-86, pres., 1986—. Contbr. articles to profl. jours.; patentee in field. Mem. Am. Nuclear Soc., IEEE (sr.). Home: 690 Oakwood Ave Sheffield Lake OH 44054 Office: Edison Park Twinsburg OH 44087

KROTEE, MARCH LEE, physical education educator; b. Riverside, Calif., July 4, 1943; s. Walter Rowland and Alfreda (Pennywell) K.; m. Leslie Latshaw, Aug. 21, 1965; children: March, Robert. BA, West Chester State U., 1965; MA, U. Md., 1967; PhD, U. Pitts., 1971. Teaching asst. U. Md., College Park, 1965-67; tchr. phys. edn. Pitts. Pub. Schs., 1967-68; instr. Carnegie-Mellon U., Pitts., 1968-71; asst. prof. George Mason U., Fairfax, Va., 1972-75; assoc. prof. U. Minn., Mpls., 1975—; Fulbright prof. Kenyatta U., 1984-85; cons. Pres.'s Council on Phys. Fitness, Washington, 1984—; chmn. edn. and sports com. Ptnrs. of Ams., Minn., 1975—. Author: THe Theory and Practice of Physical Activity, 1979, Personalized Weight Training, 1984, The Theory and Practice of Badminton, 1985; author/editor: International Dimensions of Comparitive Physicial Education and Sport, 1986; editor: The Dimensions of Sport Sociology, 1979. Mem. Fulbright Hayes State Com. Edn., Minn., 1983—; mem. com. Spl. Olympics, Minn., 1975—, water safety com. ARC, Mpls., 1975—, citizens com. Plymouth (Minn.) Community Ctr., 1983—, Dist. 284 Sports Com., Plymouth and Wayzata, Minn., 1981-83. Fellow Research Consortium; mem. AAHPERD, Nat. Assn. Sport and Phys. Edn. (pres. sport sociology com. 1975-77), Nat. Strength Tng. Coaches Assn. (bd. dirs. 1982—), N.Am. Soc. Sport Sociology, Internat. Soc. Comparative Phys. Edn. and Sport. Republican. Lutheran. Avocations: reading, stock market, sports. Home: 305 Merrimac Ln Plymouth MN 55447 Office: U Minn Div Phys Edn 218 Cooke Hall Minneapolis MN 55455

KROTZ, EDWARD WILLIAM, supermarket executive; b. Lincoln, Ill., Feb. 19, 1925; s. Frank C. and Dora J. Krotz; m. Cecilia D. Shay, July 20, 1952; children: Frank, Edward William Jr., Mark, Sheila, Keith. BS, U. Ill., 1948, MBA, 1981. Lic. real estate broker, Ill. Sales engr. Sparkler Mfg. Co., Mundelein, Ill., 1953-55; v.p., ptnr. F. Krotz Food Co., Taylorville, Ill., 1955-86, pres., owner, 1986—; v.p. Bloomington Eastgate Corp., 1980-86, pres., 1986—; mem. adv. bd. J.M. Jone Retail, 1976-79. Served to lt. USN, 1943-46, 50-52. Mem. Nat. Assn. Retail Grocers, Ill. Retail Grocers Assn., Food Mktg. Inst., VFW. Democrat. Roman Catholic. Lodges: KC, Eagles, Elks. Home: 2344 Hawthorne Dr Decatur IL 62521 Office: PO Box 99 Taylorville IL 62568

KROUPA, DOUGLAS CRAIG, information systems analyst; b. Pensacola, Fla., Dec. 18, 1954; s. Bohumil Jr. and Diane Marie (Simek) K.; m. Jean Daria Coleman, Feb. 10, 1979; 1 child, Adam. BS, Loras Coll., DuBuque, Iowa, 1976. Info. systems analyst AT&T Network Systems, Lisle, Ill., 1977—. Mem. Data Processing Mgmt. Assn. (program dir. 1985-86, bronze service award 1985, v.p. 1987). Avocations: coaching youth soccer, church choir, exploring. Office: AT&T Network Systems 2600 Warrenville Rd Lisle IL 60532

KROUSE, ANN WOLK, publishing executive; b. Chgo., Feb. 4, 1945; d. Barnett David and Shirley (Schwartz) Wolk; m. Paul Carl Krouse, Aug. 8, 1964; children: Amy Renee, Beth Diane, Joseph David, Katie Sue. Student, U. Miami, Fla., 1962. Ops. mgr. Playboy Club, Chgo., 1963-64; v.p. Ednl. Communications, Inc., Lake Forest, Ill., 1967—; bd. dirs. URT Industries, Inc., Hialeah Gardens, Fla., Peaches Entertainment Corp., Hialeah Gardens. Pub., co-editor (book) Who's Who Among Black Americans, 1976— (Outstanding Reference Book, 1976). Bd. dirs. scholarship found. Ednl. Communications, Inc., 1970—; mem. Jewish United Fund, 1970—, Mothers Against Drunk Driving, 1985—. Mem. Nat. Sch. Pub. Relations Assn., Ednl. Press Assn., Direct Mail Mktg. Assn., Lake Forest Open Lands Assn. Office: Ednl Communications Inc 721 N McKinley Rd Lake Forest IL 60045

KRUCKS, WILLIAM, electronics manufacturing executive; b. Chgo., Dec. 26, 1918; s. William and Florence (Olson) K.; m. Lorraine C. Rauland, Oct. 23, 1947; children: William Norman, Kenneth Rauland. B.S., Northwestern U., 1940; postgrad., Loyola U., Chgo., 1941-42. Auditor Benefit Trust Life Ins. Co., Chgo., 1940-42; chief tax accountant, asst. to comptroller C.M., St.P.&P. R.R., Chgo., 1942-56; asst. comptroller, dir. taxation, asst. treas. C. & N.W. Ry., Chgo., 1956-58; treas. C. & N.W. Ry., 1968-75; asst. treas. N.W. Industries, Inc., 1968-72; chmn. bd., chief exec. officer, pres. Rauland-Borg Corp.; chmn. bd., pres. Rauland-Borg (Can.) Inc.; dir ATR Mfg. Ltd., Kowloon, Hong Kong. Bd. dirs. Civic Fedn. Chgo. Mem. Nat. Tax Assn., Tax Execs. Inst., Ill. C. of C., Internat. Bus. Council Mid Am. Republican. Methodist. Clubs: Tower; Execs. (Chgo.), Union League (Chgo.), Internat. Trade (Chgo.). Home: 21 Indian Hill Rd Winnetka IL 60093 Office: 3535 W Addison St Chicago IL 60618

KRUEGER, ALAN DOUGLAS, communications company executive; b. Little Rock, Dec. 24, 1937; s. Herbert C. and Estelle B. Krueger; m. Betty Burns, Apr. 4, 1975; children: (by previous marriage) Scott Alan, Dane Kieth, Kip Douglas, Bryan Lee. Student, U. Ill., 1956, Wright Coll., 1957-58. Project engr. Motorla, Inc., Chgo., 1956-64; service mgr., field tech. rep. Motorola, Inc., Indpls., 1964-67; pres. Communications Maintenance, Inc., Indpls., 1967-68, Communications Unlimited, Inc., Indpls., 1968—. Methodist. Club: Elks. Home: Rural Rt 2 Box 119 Franklin IN 46131 Office: Communications Unlimited Inc 4032 Southeastern Ave Indianapolis IN 46203

KRUEGER, BONNIE LEE, editor, writer; b. Chgo., Feb. 3, 1950; d. Harry Bernard and Lillian (Soyak) Krueger; m. James Lawrence Spurlock, Mar. 8, 1972. Student Moraine Valley Coll., 1970. Adminstrv. asst. Carson Pirie Scott & Co., Chgo., 1969-72; traffic coordinator Tatham Laird & Kudner, Chgo., 1973-74; traffic coordinator J. Walter Thompson, Chgo., 1974-76; prodn. coordinator, 1976-78; editor-in-chief Assoc. Pubs., Chgo., 1978—; editor-in-chief Sophisticate's Hairstyle Guide, 1978—, Sophisticates Beauty Guide, 1978—, Complete Woman, 1981—; pub., editorial services dir. Sophisticate's Black Hair Guide, 1983—. Mem. Statue of Liberty Restoration Com., N.Y.C., 1983; campaign worker Cook County State's Atty., Chgo., 1982; poll watcher Cook County Dem. Orgn., 1983. Mem. Soc. Profl. Journalists, Nat. Assn. Female Execs., Am. Health and Beauty Aids Inst., Sigma Delta Chi. Lutheran. Clubs: Sierra, Cousteau Soc. Office: Complete Woman 1165 N Clark St Chicago IL 60610

KRUEGER, CHARLES ALVIN, finance and accounting educator; b. Marshfield, Wis., Oct. 28, 1951; s. Alvin Carl and Marion Edith (Gosse) K.; m. Scheree Lea Smith, May 21, 1977; children: Nikalas Charles, Daccia Lea. BS, U. Wis., Stevens Point, 1974; MBA, U. Wis., Oshkosh, 1977. CPA, cert. internal auditor. Underwriter Sentry Ins., Stevens Point, 1972-77, internal auditor, 1977-79, acctg. mgr., treas., 1979-80; sr. internal auditor Am. Family Ins., Madison, Wis., 1981-82; asst. prof. fin. and acctg. U. Wis., Madison, 1982—. Author (monograph) Ratio Analysis, 1986, numerous articles. Sec. Bethlehem Endowment Found., Sun Prairie, Wis., 1984—. Mem. Am. Inst. CPA's, Nat. Assn. Accts., Inst. Internal Auditors, Wis. Inst. CPA's, Soc. Ins. Trainers and Educators. Lutheran. Home: 6763 Peaceful Ct Sun Prairie WI 54481 Office: U Wis 432 N Lake St Madison WI 53590

KRUEGER, JOHN RICHARD, human resources executive, psychologist; b. Richfield, Minn., June 10, 1948; s. Glen F. and Mary Jane (Barke) K.; m. Patricia Mary Vos Krueger; Aug. 22, 1970; children: Molly Jane, Sarah Anne, Kathryn Leigh, Mark John. BA, St. Johns U., Collegeville, Minn., 1970; MS, St. Cloud (Minn.) State U., 1972. Lic. psychologist, Minn. Counseling psychologist St. Cloud VA, 1970-74; unit supr. St. Cloud Children's Home, 1974-78, program dir., 1978—. Bd. dirs. United Way St. Cloud, 1979-83; chmn. bd. dirs. Samaritans Suicide Prevention Ctr, St. Cloud, 1978-79; pres. bd. dirs. St. John's U. Nat. Alumni Bd., 1982—; bd. dirs. Sartell (Minn.) Bd. Edn., 1983—; trustee Great River Regional Library System, St. Cloud, 1980-83; del. Minn. Sch. Bds. Assn. Legis. Del. Assembly, St. Paul, 1983-84; bd. dirs. Sartell (Minn.) Bd. Edn., 1981—. Mem. Minn. Council Residential Treatment Ctrs. (bd. dirs. 1980—), Cen. Minn. Group Health Plan (bd. dirs. 1985—), Stearns-Benton Spl. Edn. Cooperative (bd. dirs. 1983—). Roman Catholic. Avocations: golf, hunting, racquetball, collecting wildlife art. Home: 040477 County Rd #1 Rice MN 56367 Office: St Cloud Children's Home 1726 7th Ave S Saint Cloud MN 56301

KRUEGER, LESTER EUGENE, psychology educator; b. Chgo., Nov. 6, 1939; s. Carl and Helen (Milanowski) K.; Ph.D., Harvard U., 1969. Asst. prof. CCNY, 1969-72, assoc. prof., 1973-74; asst. prof. psychology Ohio State U., Columbus, 1974-76, assoc. prof., 1976-80. prof., 1980—. Served with U.S. Army, 1957. NIH grantee, 1970-76; NIMH grantee, 1979-80. Fellow Am. Psychol. Assn.; mem. Psychonomic Soc., Midwestern Psychol. Assn., AAUP, Sigma Xi. Cons. editor Memory and Cognition; assoc. editor Perception and Psychophysics; contbr. articles to profl. jours. Home: 2036-D Northwest Blvd Columbus OH 43212 Office: 404B W 17th Ave Columbus OH 43210

KRUEGER, MARTY L., controller; b. Algoma, Wis., Jan. 27, 1957; s. Leon F. and June I. (Lardinois) K. BBA, U. Wis., Oshkosh, 1979. CPA, Wis. Acct. Clifton, Gunderson & Co., Oshkosh and Neenah, Wis., 1979-84; controller Norland Corp., Ft. Atkinson, Wis., 1984—. Mem. Am. Inst. CPA's, Wis. Soc. CPA's. Roman Catholic. Avocations: softball, watching sports. Home: 326 Kent Ln Apt 203 Madison WI 53713 Office: Norland Corp Rt 4 Norland Dr Fort Atkinson WI 53538

KRUEGER, MICHAEL PAUL, information systems specialist; b. Sheboygan, Wis., Feb. 17, 1950; s. Robert Paul and Marion B. (Quasius) K.; m. Nancy Corrine Schroeder, Aug. 26, 1972; children: Jami, Bryan, Andrea. BS, U. Wis., 1973; MBA, Marquette U., 1984. Systems analyst Kohler Co., Wis., 1973-79; mgr. mgmt. info. systems Allen-Bradley Co., Highland Heights, Ohio, 1979—. Mem. Am. Prod. and Inventory Control Soc. Avocations: golf, soccer coaching, baseball. Home: 17995 Birch Hill Dr Chagrin Falls OH 44022 Office: Allen Bradley Co 747 Alpha Dr Highland Heights OH 44143

KRUEGER, NORMAN LELAND, physician; b. Bagley, Iowa, Dec. 5, 1915; s. Charles William and Helen Young (McLellan) K.; B.A., McPherson Coll., 1941; M.D., U. Iowa, 1950; m. Alma McLamb, June 26, 1948; children—Jean, Charles. Intern, St. Francis Hosp., Wichita, Kans., 1950-51, resident in pathology, 1954-55; resident in internal medicine, VA Hosp., Wood, Wis., 1955-57; practice medicine, Casey, Iowa, 1957—; clin. instr. Marquette U., 1955-57. Served with USN, 1942-45. Mem. Iowa Med. Soc., AMA, AAAS, Am. Coll. Angiology, Am. Assn. Physicians and Surgeons, Alpha Kappa Kappa. Republican. Mem. Church of the Brethren. Office: Hayes Bldg Casey IA 50048

KRUEGER, RANDY RAY, safety specialist; b. Monticello, Iowa, Aug. 22, 1955; s. Jerry J. and Jean Marie (CLark) K. BS, U. Dubuque, 1979. Dir. safety D.C. Taylor Co., Cedar Rapids, Iowa, 1982—. Contbr. articles on roofing safety to profl. jours. Mem. various coms. on safety. Mem. Am. Soc. Safety Engr., Nat. Safety Council. Republican. Presbyterian. Home: Rural Rt 1 Monticello IA 52310 Office: DC Taylor Co 1620 East Ave NE Cedar Rapids IA 52406

KRUG, DONALD JOSEPH, social services administrator; b. Dayton, Ohio, May 14, 1952; s. Paul Edward and Mildred Elizabeth (Stoff) K.; m. Susan B. Hack, July 21, 1975. B in Urban Planning, U. Cin., 1975; MBA, Xavier U., 1981. Planning technician Transp. Coordinating Com., Dayton, Ohio, 1975-77; mgr. Council on Aging, Cin., 1977-82; exec. dir. Easy Riders, Cin., 1982—. Speaker for various causes. Named Citizen of the Day WLW Radio, 1981. Mem. AMA, Nat. Soc. Fund Raising Execs., Passenger Assistance Technicians. Democrat. Roman Catholic. Avocations: chess, computer programming, fishing, astronomy. Home: 5532 Palomino Dr Cincinnati OH 45238 Office: Easy Riders Inc 2400 Reading Rd Cincinnati OH 45202

KRUG, JOHN CARLETON (TONY), college administrator, library consultant; b. Evansville, Ind., Nov. 27, 1951; s. John Elmer and Mary Ellen

(Moore) K.; m. Anna Marie Waters, July 3, 1983. B.A., Ind. State U., 1972, M.L.S., 1973; Ph.D., So. Ill. U.-Carbondale, 1985. Lic. minister Baptist Ch. Exec. dir. Olney (Ill.) Carnegie Pub. Library, 1973-74; assoc. dean Wabash Valley Coll., Mt. Carmel, Ill., 1974-84; mem. Com. for U.S. Depository State Plan, Springfield, Ill., 1982-84; dir. libraries Maryville Coll., St. Louis, 1984—; sec. pro-tem Ill. Basin Coal Mining Manpower Council, Mt. Carmel, 1974-79; mem. governing bd. exec. com. Higher Edn. Ctr. Cable TV, 1986—. Author: Libraries Using/Planning for Microcomputers, 1986; also computer programs. Vice pres. bd. dirs. Wabash Area Vocat. Enterprises, Mt. Carmel, 1979-81; mem. bd. edn. Wabash Community Unit, Mt. Carmel, 1980-83; mem. exec. com. Community Edn. and Arts Assn., Carbondale, 1983-84; mem. visual arts adv. com. Ill. Arts Council, Chgo., 1982-84; pastor Hopewell United Meth. Ch., Bridgeport, Ill., 1976-77; lic. minister Terre Haute 1st Bapt. Ch. (Ind.), 1972—; elder Gateway Christian Ch., 1986—; bd. dirs. Fair Haven Christian Sch., 1986—. Conf. speaker Kans. State U., 1982. Mem. ALA, Mo. Library Assn., Nat. Assn. for Preservation and Perpetuation of Storytelling, So. Ill. Learning Resources Consortium (del.), St. Louis Regional Library Network (del. 1985—), St. Louis Med. Librarians Assn., Evang. Ch. Library Assn., Ch. and Synagogue Library Assn., Gateway Storytelling Guild. Mem. Christian Ch. Home: 121 Solley Dr Winchester MO 63021 Office: Maryville College 13550 Conway Rd Saint Louis MO 63141

KRUG, JUDITH FINGERET, association administrator; b. Pitts., Mar. 15, 1940; d. David and Florence (Leiber) Fingeret; m. E. Herbert Krug, Oct. 12, 1963; children: Steven, Michelle. BA in Polit. Theory, U. Pitts., 1961; MA, U. Chgo., 1964. Reference librarian John Crerar Library, Chgo., 1962-63; cataloger dental sch. library Northwestern U., Chgo., 1963-65; research analyst ALA, Chgo., 1965-67; dir. Office Intellectual Freedom, ALA, Chgo., 1967—; exec. dir. Freedom to Read Found, Chgo., 1969—; mem. com. on pub. understanding about the law ABA, Chgo. 1985—. Editor: Newsletter on Intellectual Freedom, 1970—, Freedom to Read Foundation News, 1972—; exec. producer (film) The Speaker, 1977 (Silver Cindy award 1978, Silver Screen award 1979). Recipient Irita Van Doren Book award Am. Booksellers Assn., 1976, Robert B. Downs award U. Ill., Champaign-Urbana, 1978, Carl Sandburg Freedom to Read award Friends of Chgo. Pub. Library, 1983. Mem. ALA, Phi Beta Kappa (assoc., exec. commn. 1980—). Office: Am Library Assn Office for Intellectual Freedom 50 E Huron St Chicago IL 60611

KRUG, SAMUEL EDWARD, JR., psychologist; b. Chgo., Nov. 15, 1943; s. Samuel Edward Sr. and Evelyn Catherine (LaVelle) K.; m. Marion Ethel Besch, June 29, 1968; children: Mark, Michael, David, Timothy. AB, Coll. of the Holy Cross, 1965; MA, U. Ill., 1968, PhD, 1971. Lic. psychologist, Ill., Ariz. Dir. Inst. for Personality and Ability Testing, Champaign, Ill., 1966-84; pres. MetriTech, Inc., Champaign, 1984—; cons. psychologist various bus. and profl. orgns., municipalities and U.S. Armed Forces. Author: (psychol. test) IPAT Depression Scale, 1976, numerous books on psychol. assessment in medicine; contbr. 65 articles to profl. jours. Fellow Soc. Personality Assessment, Am. Psychol. Assn. Home: 2208 Galen Dr Champaign IL 61821 Office: MetriTech Inc 111 N Market St Champaign IL 61820

KRUGEL, LEONARD STEPHEN, accountant; b. Detroit, Jan. 23, 1947; m. Michele Paulette, Sept. 7, 1969; children: Howard, Jaime, Bradley. BS, Wayne State U., 1969. CPA, Mich. Cons. Lapeer County, Lapeer, Mich., 1981, Monroe County, Monroe, Mich., 1983, Saginaw County, Saginaw, Mich., 1985, Ionia County, Ionia, Mich., 1986—; cons. Salvation Army, Detroit, 1984—, bus. mgr., 1986—. Mem. Am. Inst. CPAs, Mich. Assn. CPAs (subcom. chmn. profl. ethics and unauthorized practice com. 1981—). Democrat. Mem. Shaarey Zedek Ch. Home: 29138 Shenandoah Farmington Hills MI 48018

KRUGER, FRED WALTER, university administrator, mechanical engineering educator; b. Chgo., Dec. 17, 1921; s. Fred and Magdalen (Lotz) K.; m. Esther Marie Foelber, Aug. 23, 1947; children—Paul Walter, John Robert, Thomas Herman. Student, Valparaiso U., 1940-42; B.S. in Elec. Engring, Purdue U., 1942-43, B.S. in Mech. Engring, 1947; M.S. in Mech Engring, Notre Dame U., 1954. Registered profl. engr., Ind. Mem. faculty Valparaiso U., 1947—, prof., 1959—, chmn. dept. mech. engring., 1955-65, dean Coll. Engring., 1965-72, v.p. bus. affairs, 1974-87, prof. emeritus, 1987—; cons. McDonnell Aircraft Co., Caterpillar Tractor Co., Argonne Lab., No. Ill. Gas Co.; mem. Ind. Bd. Registration for Profl. Engrs., 1957—. City councilman Valparaiso, 1972—; mem. City Plan Commn., 1977-83. Served to lt. USNR, 1943-46. Mem. Am. Soc. M.E., Am. Soc. Engring. Edn., Tau Beta Pi. Lutheran. Home: 1058 Linwood Ave Valparaiso IN 46383

KRUGER, RICHARD HUNT, beverage company executive; b. Springfield, Mass., Oct. 13, 1953; s. Leon Moses and Anita Joan (Katz) K.; m. Judith Ann Mosse, Oct. 16, 1977; children: Erica Mosse, Daniel Brian. BA, U. Va., 1975; MBA, Syracuse U., 1977. Brand asst. Procter & Gamble, Cin., 1977-79; brand mgr. Sterling Drug Co., N.Y.C., 1979-81; v.p. mktg. Beatrice/Esmark, Chgo., 1981-85; dir. mktg. Allnet Communications, Chgo., 1985-87, Hinckley & Schmitt Inc., Chgo., 1987—; guest lectr. Syracuse (N.Y.) U., 1980. Trustee Wilbraham and Monson (Mass.) Acad., 1984; bd. dirs., bus. com. Boca Raton (Fla.) Symphony, 1984. Avocations: golf, cooking. Home: 1666 Old Briar Rd Highland Park IL 60035 Office: Hinckley & Schmitt Inc 6055 S Harlem Ave Chicago IL 60638

KRUGER, SCOTT BRIAN, sales and marketing representative; b. Anderson, Ind., Dec. 1, 1962; s. Gerald Lavern and Judith Kay (Johnson) K. AS in Electronic Engring., ITT Tech., Indpls., 1983. Sales rep., promoter exhbns. and shows Baseball Card World, Chesterfield, Ind., 1981—. Recipient Customer Service award Sports Collectors Digest, 1984, 85. Mem. Nat. Fedn. Ind. Bus. Republican. Avocations: softball, golf, skiing, fishing. Office: Baseball Card World 319 Anderson Rd Chesterfield IN 46017

KRUGER, WILLIAM ARNOLD, consulting civil engineer; b. St. Louis, June 13, 1937; s. Reynold and Olinda (Siefker) K.; B.C.E., U. Mo.-Rolla, 1959; M.S., U. Ill., 1968; m. Carole Ann Hofer, Oct. 17, 1959. Civil engr. City of St. Louis, 1959; with Clark, Dietz & Assocs., and predecessors, Urbana, Ill., 1961-79, sr. design engr., 1963-67, dir. transp. div., 1968-79; civil engr. div. hwys. Ill. Dept. Transp., Paris, 1979-83; part-owner ESCA Cons., Inc., Urbana, 1983—; instr. Parkland Coll., Champaign, 1972; mem. Ill. Profl. Engrs. Examining Com., 1982—. Served with C.E., AUS, 1959-61. Registered profl. engr., Ill., Mo., Fla., Miss., N.Y., Iowa, Del., Ohio, Ind. Mem. Nat. Ill. (chpt. pres. 1974, state chmn. registration laws com. 1973, 78) socs. profl. engrs., Ill. Assn. Hwy. Engrs., ASCE (br. pres. 1982-83), Am. Pub. Works Assn. (sect. dir. 1974-77, 80), Inst. Transp. Engrs., Ill. Registered Land Surveyors Assn., Soc. Am. Mil. Engrs., Nat. Council Engring. Examiners, ASTM, Urbana C. of C., U. Mo.-Rolla Acad. Civil Engrs., U. Mo.-Rolla Alumni Assn., Theta Tau, Tau Beta Pi, Chi Epsilon, Pi Kappa Alpha. Club: Champaign Ski. Home: 1811 Coventry Dr Champaign IL 61821 Office: 1606 Willow View Rd Urbana IL 61801

KRUIDENIER, DAVID, newspaper executive; b. Des Moines, July 18, 1921; s. David S. and Florence (Cowles) K.; m. Elizabeth Stuart, Dec. 29, 1948; 1 child, Lisa. B.A., Yale U., 1946; M.B.A., Harvard U., 1948; LL.D., Buena Vista Coll., 1960, Simpson Coll., 1963. With Mpls. Star and Tribune, 1948-52; with Des Moines Register and Tribune, 1952-85, pres., pub., 1971-78, chief exec. officer, 1971-85, chmn., chief exec. officer, 1982-85; vice chmn. bd. Cowles Media Co., 1973-83, chief exec. officer, 1983-86, chmn., 1985. Pres. Gardner and Florence Call Cowles Found.; trustee Drake U., Menninger Found., Des Moines Art Ctr., Walker Art Ctr., Civic Ctr. Greater Des Moines, Grinnell Coll. Served with USAAF, 1942-45. Decorated Air medal with three clusters, D.F.C. Mem. Am. Newspaper Pubs. Assn., Council on Fgn. Relations, Newspaper Advt. Bur. (bd. dirs.), Sigma Delta Chi, Beta Theta Pi, Beta Gamma Sigma. Clubs: Des Moines, Mpls, Mill Reef. Home: 3409 Southern Hills Dr Des Moines IA 50321 Office: 715 Locust St Des Moines IA 50304 also: 425 Portland Minneapolis MN 55488

KRUKEWITT, RONALD WESLEY, loan officer; b. Urbana, Ill., Jan. 7, 1946; s. Donald Rudolf and Helen Elizabeth (Tibbets) K.; m. Sharon Kay Pedersen, May 6, 1967; children: Brent David, Douglas William. BS in Bus., Eastern Ill. U., 1971. Field rep. Charleston (Ill.) Prodn. Credit Assn., 1971-73, asst. v.p., 1980-85; farmer Homer, Ill., 1972-79; asst. v.p. Vermilion County Prodn. Credit Assn., Danville, Ill., 1974-80; loan officer Boatmen's Nat. Bank of Charleston, 1985—. Coach Charleston Recreation Dept., 1980-84, Youth Baseball, Charleston, 1985-86; bd. dirs. Coles County United Way, Charleston, 1986—. Served to sgt. USMC, 1965-68, Vietnam. Mem. Charleston Area C. of C. (bd. dirs. 1982-85). Lodge: Kiwanis (treas. 1986—). Avocations: golf, football, baseball, softball. Home: 821 Biggs Dr Charleston IL 61920 Office: Boatmen's Nat Bank of Charleston 418 6th St Charleston IL 61920

KRULEWICH, EDWARD BARNETT, mechanical engineer; b. Chgo., May 17, 1941; s. Harry and Jean (Ratner) K.; m. Arlene Eunice Milsk, Aug. 21, 1960; children: Ellen, Debra, Daniel, Mitchell. BSME, Ill. Inst. Tech., Chgo., 1963. Registered profl. engr., Ky. Mech. engr. Gen. Electric, Louisville, 1963-67; devel. engr. Am. Standard, New Brunswick, N.J., 1968-72; prin. design engr. Gen. Electric, Louisville, 1973-80; sr. engr. NIBCO, Inc., Elkhart, Ind., 1980-84; project engr. Universal Nolin, Conway, Ark., 1984-85; sr. staff engr. Admiral, Galesburg, Ill., 1985—. Mem. ASME, Soc. Plastics Engrs. Home: 1650 N Broad Galesburg IL 61401 Office: Admiral Monmouth Blvd Galesburg IL 61401

KRULL, DANA LANCE, accountant; b. Goshen, Ind., Sept. 22, 1944; s. David G. and Myrtle L. (Reed) K.; m. Sherry L. Burd, Apr. 20, 1968; children: Douglas, Brian, Amanda. BS, Manchester Coll., 1966. CPA, Ill., Ind. Acct. Pinecrest Manor, Mt. Morris, Ill., 1966-67, Timbercrest Home, North Manchester, Ind., 1967-68; sr. acct. Ernst & Ernst, Indpls., 1968-72; ptnr. Gilbert, Naragon & Co., North Manchester, 1972-76; sole practice in acctg. Pierceton, Ind., 1976-86. Mem. Am. Inst. CPA's, Ind. Assn. CPA's, North Manchester Jaycees (pres. 1975), Pierceton C. of C. (pres. 1980-81). Avocations: golf, tennis. Home: 502 S 1st Pierceton IN 46562 Office: State Rd 13 South Pierceton IN 46562

KRULL, JEFFREY ROBERT, library director; b. North Tonawanda, N.Y., Aug. 29, 1948; s. Robert George and Ruth Otilie (Fels) K.; m. Alice Marie Hart, Apr. 12, 1969; children: Robert, Marla. BA, Williams Coll., Williamstown, Mass., 1970; MLS, SUNY, Buffalo, 1974. Cert. profl. librarian, N.Y., Ohio, Ind. Traffic mgr. New Eng. Telephone Co., Burlington, Vt., 1970-71; tchr. Harrisburg (Pa.) Acad., 1971-72; reference librarian Buffalo and Erie County Pub. Library, 1973-76; head librarian Ohio U., Chillicothe, 1976-78; dir. Mansfield-Richland County Pub. Library, Ohio, 1978-86, Allen County Pub. Library, Ft. Wayne, Ind., 1986—; exec. com. Ft. Wayne Area Library Service Authority, 1986—. Trustee Ohionet, Columbus, 1984-86. Mem. ALA, Ohio Library Assn. (bd. dirs. 1985-86), Ind. Library Assn., Beta Phi Mu. Home: 8915 Sunburst Lane Fort Wayne IN 46804 Offices: Allen County Pub Library 900 Webster St PO BOx 2270 Fort Wayne IN 46801

KRUMBEIN, ELIEZER, psychologist, consultant, educator; b. Bklyn., July 4, 1926; s. Abraham and Sarah (Milberg) K.; m. Elaine Rochelle Frohman, June 18, 1950; children: Deborah Hannah Krumbein Dworin, Judith Esther Krumbein Stein, Aaron. SB in Psychology cum laude, Harvard U., 1946; MA in Counseling, Northwestern U., 1956, PhD in Counseling Psychology, 1960. Lic. psychologist, Ill.; registered sch. psychologist, Ill. Asst. nat. dir. dept. interreligious cooperation Anti-Defamation League, Chgo., 1948-49; dir. religious edn. North Shore Congregation Israel, Glencoe, Ill., 1949-56; dir. spl. services to bus. and industry U. Chgo., 1957-60; dir. edn., asst. prof. Transp. Ctr., Northwestern U., Evanston, Ill., 1960-65; assoc. prof. edn. U. Ill., Chgo., 1965-82, assoc. prof. emeritus, 1982—; pres. Krumbein & Wolff Co., Highland Park, Ill., 1975—; psychologist Lincoln Ctr. Clin. Service, Highland Park, 1975—; vis. prof. Hebrew U. Jerusalem Med. Sch., 1969. Elected mem. bd. edn. Sch. Dist. 108, Highland Park, 1962-68. Mem. Am. Psychol. Assn., Ill. Psychol. Assn., Am. Ednl. Research Assn., Phi Delta Kappa. Democrat. Jewish. Avocations: painting, jogging, swimming, tinkering. Home: 1004 Sheridan Rd Highland Park IL 60035 Office: 1866 Sheridan Rd Suite 320 Highland Park IL 60035

KRUMHOLZ, RICHARD A., physician; b. Wilkes-Barre, Pa., Nov. 5, 1935; s. Manuel and Ella (Weber) K.; m. Sylvia Krumholz; children: Harlan, Susan, Lynne, Julie; m. Cheryl S. Kelley, Sept. 11, 1985; 1 child, Jill. Student, U. Pitts., 1953-55; BS, U. Dayton, 1956; MD, St. Louis U., 1960. Practice medicine specializing in allergy and pulmonary diseases Dayton, Ohio, 1965—. Served with USAF, 1963-65. Home: 5805 Shiloh Springs Rd Dayton OH 45426 Office: Allergy and Pulmonary Ctr Ohio 700 Talbot Tower 118 W First St Dayton OH 45402

KRUMM, DANIEL JOHN, manufacturing company executive; b. Sioux City, Iowa, Oct. 15, 1926; s. Walter A. and Anna K. (Helmke) K.; m. Ann L. Klingner, Feb. 28, 1953; children: David Jonathan, Timothy John. B.A. in Commerce, U. Iowa, 1950; postgrad., U. Mich., 1955; D.B.A. (hon.), Westmar Coll., Le Mars, Iowa, 1981; D. Comml. Sci. (hon.), Luther Coll., Decorah, Iowa, 1983. With Globe Office Furniture Co., Mpls., 1950-52; with Maytag Co., Newton, Iowa, 1952—; v.p. Maytag Co., 1970-71, exec. v.p., 1971-72, pres., treas., 1972-74, chief exec. officer, 1974-86, chmn., chief exec. officer, 1986—; pres., chief exec. officer Maytag Co. Ltd., Toronto, 1970—; dir. Centel Corp., Chgo., Snap-On-Tools Corp., Kenosha, Prin. Fin. Group, Des Moines. Mem. bd. of visitors U. Iowa Coll. Bus. Adminstrn.; mem. steering com. for Iowa endowment 2000 campaign; pres., trustee Maytag Co. Found.; past chmn. Iowa Natural Heritage Found.; bd. govs. Iowa Coll. Found.; chmn. bd. dirs. Grand View Coll., Des Moines, Des Moines Symphony Assn., U. Iowa Found., Vocat. Rehab. Workshop for Handicapped Citizens of Jasper County (Iowa), NAM; chmn. Iowa Venture Capital Fund, Iowa Bus. Council; mem. com. for econ. devel. Iowa Peace Inst. Served with USNR, 1944-46. Recipient Oscar C. Schmidt Iowa Bus. Leadership award, 1983; Disting. Achievement award U. Iowa Alumni Assn; named Iowa Bus. Leader of the Yr., 1986. Mem. Am. Mktg. Assn. (past pres. Iowa), Elec. Mfrs. Club, Newton C. of C. (community service award 1980), Maytag Mgmt. Club. Republican. Lutheran. Club: Newton Country. Office: Maytag Corp Newton IA 50208

KRUMREY, WILLIAM M., state agency administrator; b. Chgo., Aug. 17, 1944; s. Melvin E. and Margaret (Ripp) K.; m. Elizabeth Ann Fowler, Aug. 13, 1966; 1 child, Michael W. BS, So. Ill. U., 1966, So. Ill. U., 1974; MS, So. Ill. U., 1977. Cert. pub. housing exec. Mgr. material control Nat. Mobile Homes, Anna, Ill., 1973-74, asst. mfg. mgr., 1974-75; exec. dir. Massac County Housing Authority, Metropolis, Ill., 1975—; pres. Massac County Health Improvement Assn. Bd. dirs. Metropolis Boy Scouts Am., 1980-83. Served to capt. U.S. Army, 1966-70, Republic of Germany and Korea. Mem. Ill. Assn. Housing Authorities (bd. dirs. 1977-86), Egyptian Council Housing Ofcl. (pres. 1977-78), Nat. Assn. Housing and Devel. Ofcls., Pub. Housing Authorities Dir. Assn. Methodist. Lodge: Rotary (pres. Metropolis 1979-80). Avocations: boating, fishing, skiing. Office: Massac County Housing Authority PO Box 528 Metropolis IL 62960

KRUMSKE, WILLIAM FREDERICK, JR., marketing educator, business consultant; b. Chgo., Dec. 17, 1952; s. William Frederick and Harriet Marie (Piwowarczyk) K.; BS, Ill. Inst. Tech., 1974; MS in Bus. Adminstrn., No. Ill. U., 1978; PhD in Mktg., U. Ill.-Urbana-Champaign, 1987. Salesman, warehouse mgr. Lus-Ter-Oil Beauty Products, Palos Heights, Ill., 1972-74; pub. relations dir. Crouching Lion Inn, Alsip, Ill., 1974; mgr. food and beverage Inn Devel. & Mgmt., Chicago Heights, Ill., 1974-75; v.p., dir. mktg. DeKalb (Ill.) Savs. and Loan Assn., 1975-81; sr. v.p. mktg. Regency Fed. Savs. and Loan Assn., Naperville, Ill., 1981-83; mktg. and research cons., Champaign, Ill., 1983-87; asst. prof. mktg. DePaul U., Chgo., 1987—; cons. in field Oakbrook Terrace, Ill., 1987—; dir. Rock Valley Network, Inc., Rockford, Ill., 1981-82; instr. Coll. Bus., No. Ill. U., 1978-83; mktg. mgr. Jordan Gallagher for State's Atty. campaign, 1976. AMA Doctoral Consortium fellow, 1986, Walter H. Stellner fellow in Mktg., 1985-87; recipient David Kinley Grad. Fellowship award, 1986, William J. Hendrickson award, 1980. Mem. Am. Mktg. Assn., Ill. Savs. and Loan League (mktg. com. 1977-81, chmn. 1979-80), Savs. Instns. Mktg. Soc. Am. 1976-83, Quill and Scroll, Beta Gamma Sigma. Lutheran. Contbr. articles to profl. jours. Home: 17W710 Butterfield Rd Apt 201 Oakbrook Terrace IL 60181 Office: DePaul Univ Coll Bus Dept Mktg 25 E Jackson Blvd Chicago IL 60604

KRUPA, ROBERT STANLEY, data processing executive; b. Detroit, Oct. 14, 1928; s. Leonard John and Catherine (Valentine) K.; m. Maxine Loraine Baker, May 17, (dec. Nov. 1985); m. Ruth Anne Alverson, Aug. 16, 1986; stepchildren: Larry, Todd, Troy. Asst. planning mgr. Kelvinator, Grand Rapids, Mich., 1964-68; with material control dept., buyer Evart (Mich.) Products Co., 1968-70, data processing tech., 1970-80, data processing surp., 1980-86, supr. systems analysis ops., 1986—. Funds raiser Evart Reps., 1984. Served with USN, 1946-48. Avocations: camping, travel, nature photography. Home: 21775 Monroe Rd Morley MI 49336 Office: Evart Products Co PO Box 518 Evart MI 49631

KRUPANSKY, BLANCHE, judge; b. Cleve., Dec. 10, 1925; d. Frank and Ann K.; m. Frank W. Vargo, Apr. 30, 1960. A.B., Flora Stone Mather Coll., 1943-47; J.D., Case Western Res. U., 1948, LL.M., 1966. Bar: Ohio 1949. Gen. practice law 1949-61, 82-83; asst. atty. gen. State of Ohio; asst. chief counsel Ohio Bur. Workmen's Compensation; judge Cleve. Mcpl. Ct., 1961-69; judge Common Please Ct. Cuyahoga County, 1969-77, Ct. Appeals Ohio 8th Appellate Dist., 1977-81; justice Supreme Ct. Ohio, 1981-83; judge 8th Dist. Ct. Appeals, 1983—; vis. com. Case Western U. Law Sch., 1974-78, bd. govs., 1975-76. Recipient Outstanding Jud. Service award Supreme Ct. Ohio, 1972-76; Law Book scholar award Cuyahoga Women's Polit. Caucus, 1981; recipient outstanding contbn. to law award Ohio Assn. Civil Trial Attys., 1982, Disting. Alumna award, 1982, Disting. Service award Women's Space, 1982, award Democratic Women's Caucus, 1983, award Women's Equity Action League Ohio, 1983; named Woman of Achievement Inter-Club Council Cleve., 1969; inducted into Ohio Women's Hall of Fame, 1981. Mem. Nat. Assn. Women Lawyers, Nat. Assn. Women Judges, Ohio Bar Assn., Bar Assn. Greater Cleve., Cuyahoga County Bar Assn., Cleve. Women Lawyers, LWV, Ohio Cts. of Appeals Assn., Ohio Assn. Attys. Gen., Ohio Appellate Judges Assn., Soc. of Benchers. Republic. Roman Catholic. Club: Woman's City (Woman of Achievement award 1981) (Cleve.). Office: Ohio Ct Appeals 8th Appellate Dist Cuyahoga County Court House 1 Lakeside Ave Cleveland OH 44113

KRUPANSKY, ROBERT BAZIL, U.S. judge; b. Cleve., Aug. 15, 1921; s. Frank A. and Anna (Lawrence) K.; m. Marjorie Blaser, Nov. 13, 1952. B.A., Western Res. U., 1946, LL.B., 1948; J.D., Case Western Res. U., 1968. Bar: Ohio bar 1948, also Supreme Ct. Ohio 1948, Supreme Ct. U.S 1948, U.S. Dist. Ct. No. Dist. Ohio 1948, U.S. Circuit Ct. Appeals 6th Circuit 1948, U.S. Ct. Customs and Patent Appeals 1948, U.S. Customs Ct 1948, ICC 1948. Pvt. practice Cleve., 1948-52; asst. atty. gen. State of Ohio, 1951-57; mem. Gov. of Ohio cabinet and dir. Ohio Dept. Liquor Control, 1957-58; judge Common Pleas Ct. of Cuyahoga County, 1958-60; sr. partner Metzenbaum, Gaines, Krupansky, Finley & Stern, 1960-69; U.S. atty. No. Dist. Ohio, Cleve., 1969-70; U.S. dist. judge No. Dist. Ohio, 1970-82; judge U.S. Ct. Appeals (6th cir.), Ohio, 1982—; spl. counsel Atty. Gen. Ohio, 1964-68; adj. prof. law Case Western Res. U. Sch. Law, 1969-70. Served to 2d lt. U.S. Army, 1942-46; col. USAF Res. ret. Mem. Am., Fed., Ohio, Cleve., Cuyahoga County bar assns., Am. Judicature Soc., Assn. Asst. Attys. Gen. State Ohio. Office: US District Court 250 US Court House Cleveland OH 44114 *

KRUSE, WILLIAM G., bank executive. Chmn., chief exec. officer First Nat. Bank, Dubuque, Iowa. Office: First Nat Bank Locust at 7th Dubuque IA 52001 *

KRUTH, LAWRENCE FRANCIS, steel fabricating company executive; b. Sharpsburg, Pa., Nov. 13, 1953; s. Lawrence Herman and Emma (Bennardo) K.; m. Linda Kay Ankeny, Sept. 10, 1977; children—James Andrew, Adam David. B.S. in Civil Engring. Tech., U. Pitts.-Johnstown, 1976. Registered profl. engr., Pa., Mich. Engr., Franklin Assocs., Inc., Somerset, Pa., 1976-80; staff engr. Master Engrs. Corp., Pitts., 1980-81; sr. engr. Raymond Kaiser Engrs., Pitts., 1981-84; contracts mgr. H&G Steel Fabricating, Inc., Grand Ledge, Mich., 1984; project mgr. Douglas Steel Fabricating, Inc., Lansing, Mich., 1984—. Mem. ASCE. Republican. Lutheran. Club: Internat. Apple Core (Santa Clara, Calif.). Avocations: computer programming; computer graphics; computer aided drafting; design and engring. Home: 614 Belknap St Grand Ledge MI 48837 Office: Douglas Steel Fabricating Inc 1312 S Waverly Rd Lansing MI 48909

KRUTTER, FORREST NATHAN, lawyer; b. Boston, Dec. 17, 1954; s. Irving and Shirley Krutter. BS in Econs., MS in Civil Engring., MIT, 1976; JD cum laude, Harvard U., 1978. Bar: Nebr. 1978, U.S. Supreme Ct. 1986. Antitrust counsel Union Pacific R.R., Omaha, 1978-86; gen. counsel large risk div. Berkshire Hathaway Ins. Group, Omaha, 1986—. Co-author: Impact of Railroad Abandonments, 1976, Railroad Development in the Third World, 1978; author: Judicial Enforcement of Competition in Regulated Industries, 1979; contbr. articles Creighton Law Rev. Mem. ABA, Assn. Transp. Practitioners, Phi Beta Kappa, Sigma Xi. Office: Berkshire Hathaway Ins Group 3024 Harney St Omaha NE 68131

KRUYER, JOSEPH FRANCIS, architect; b. South Bend, Ind., July 5, 1924; s. George Peter and Clara Anna (Grater) K.; m. Irene Marie Andrzejewski, Apr. 19, 1947; children: Deborah Joan, Joseph F. Jr., Robert J. BArch, U. Notre Dame, 1948. Registered architect, Ind., Mich., Ill., Ohio; lic. real estate broker, Ind. Chief architect Colpaert Homes, Inc.A, South Bend, 1948-60; assoc. Maurer & Maurer Architects, South Bend, 1960-64, Donlon & Lofgren Assocs., Mishawaka, Ind., 1964-67; chief architect Charles W. Cole & Son, South Bend, 1967-69; prin. Joseph F. Kruyer, AIA, South Bend, 1969—; bd. dirs. Sobiesk Fed. Savs. & Loan, South Bend, chmn. bd., 1982-85. Mayor's appointee South Bend-St. Joseph County Bldg. Authority, 1959-60; bd. dirs. Gibault Home for Boys, Terre Haute, 1972—, chmn. bd. 1974-76. Served with USMC, 1943-45, PTO. Mem. AIA, Ind. Soc. Architects, No. Ind. Soc. Architects, Constrn. Specifications Inst. Roman Catholic. Lodges: Lions (pres. South Bend 1974-75), KC (grand knight, 1963-65, named Knight of the Yr. 1976, Cath. Layman of Yr. 1977, state dep. Ind. 1972-74). Avocations: stamp collecting, fishing, travel. Home and Office: 18785 Arapaho Ln South Bend IN 46637

KRYN, RANDALL LEE, public relations exec.; b. Chgo., Oct. 12, 1949; s. Chester N. and Beatrice K. Kryn. A.A., Morton Coll., 1970; B.S. in Journalism, No. Ill. U., 1973. Writer and researcher William M. Young & Assocs., Oak Park, Ill., 1977; asst. public relations dir. Oak Park Festival, 1978; founder Oak Park Ctr. of Creativity, 1978, pres., 1978—, public relations dir., 1978—; founder, dir. Reality Communication, Oak Park, 1976—; dir. publicity campaigns for communication related orgns., 1976—. Legis. aide to rep. 21st dist. Ill. Gen. Assembly, 1980-83; Republican candidate for Ill. State Senate, 1982; chmn. 7th Congl. Republican Council, 1986—; 7th Congl. Dist. Ill. Young Reps., 1982-86. Recipient Golden Trumpet award Publicity Club of Chgo., 1979; named One of 48 Outstanding Young Men of Am. from Ill., Ill. Jaycees, 1980; ambassador for Canberra, Australia, 1982. Mem. Public Relations Soc. Am., Seward Gunderson Soc. (co-founder 1978), Mensa. Author: James Bevel; The Strategist of the 1960s Civil Rights Movement. Home and Office: 1030 Wenonah St Oak Park IL 60304

KRZYZAK, DONALD ANTHONY, dentist; b. Chgo., July 12, 1934; s. Anthony Leonard and Sophie Josephine (Wlezien) K.; m. Carol Ann Pradzinski, Sept. 6, 1958; children: Jacqueline, Kathleen, Brian, Darlene. BA, U. Ill., 1956, BS, 1959, DDS, 1961. Gen. practice dentistry Chgo., 1961—; chmn. pub. relations Chgo. Dental Soc., 1979-80; gen. chmn. Chgo. Dental Soc., 1986, chmn. pub. relations 1982-83; cons. Delta Dental Plan Ill., Chgo., 1983-86. Mem. St. Emily's Choir, Mt. Prospect, Ill., 1980-86, St. Raymond's Choir, Mt. Prospect, 1969-79, pres. 1973-75. Served to capt. U.S. Army, 1961-63. Mem. ADA, Am. Coll. Dentists, Internat. Coll. Dentists, Acad. Dentistry Internat., Ill. State Dental Soc., Dental Arts Club (pres. 1982-83), U. Ill. Dental ALumni Assn. (pres. 1985-86), U. Ill. Alumni Assn. (bd. dirs. 1984-86), Chgo. Dental Soc. (pres. N.W. side br. 1978-79). Roman Catholic. Lodge: Lions. Avocations: gardening, golf, cooking. Home: 124 S Waverly Pl Mount Prospect IL 60056

KUA, PAUL L., manufacturing company executive; b. Quanzhou, Fujian, People's Republic of China, Jan. 20, 1954; s. Boon Kiok and Chuy Goo (Lim) K.; m. Jolia K. Law, May 27, 1984; 1 child, Valerie S. BA in Econs., Pomona Coll., 1978; MBA in Fin., UCLA, 1982. Asst. buyer Duty Free Shopper, Hong Kong, 1978-79, buyer, 1979-80; Treasury analyst Hewlett-Packard Co., Palo Alto, Calif., 1982-83; system adminstr., sr. acct. Hewlett-Packard Co., Hong Kong, 1983-84; fin. mgr. S.C. Johnson & Son, Inc., Hong Kong, 1984-86; bus. devel. mgr. S.C. Johnson & Son, Inc., Racine,

Wis., 1986—; task force mem. Price Waterhouse Internat., Los Angeles, 1980-82. Contbr. (book) Accounting Terminology in Use in the People's Republic of China and the USA, 1985. Inst. Internat. Edn. Direct Placement scholar, 1974. Mem. Am. Inst. CPA's, Wash. Soc. CPA's, Hong Kong Soc. Accts., Hong Kong Mgmt. Assn., Mensa, Beta Gamma Sigma. Office: SC Johnson & Son Inc 1525 Howe St Mail Station 072 Racine WI 53403

KUBE, MICHAEL ROBERT, lawyer; b. Cleve., Aug. 29, 1941; s. Mike and Herta Kube; m. Mary Jump, June 29, 1963; children—Scott, Julie. B.A., Baldwin-Wallace Coll., 1963; J.D., Case Western Res. U., 1967. Bar: Ohio 1967. Ptnr. Kube & Weinberger, Cleve., 1984—. Mem. Ohio Acad. Trial Attys. (pres. 1987—), Cleve. Acad. Trial Attys. (pres. 1980). Address: 118 St Claire NE Suite 103 Cleveland OH 44114

KUBEK, RALPH A., management consultant, accountant; b. Chgo., Nov. 11, 1955; s. Bruno Joseph and Viola J. Kubaszewski; m. Karen Ann Meale, June 18, 1977; children: Nicole Marie, William Joseph. BS in Acctg., DePaul U., Chgo., 1977; MBA in Systems Mgmt., DePaul U., 1982. CPA, Ill.; cert. mgmt. cons., Ill. Staff account supr. Veatch, Rich & Nadler, Northbrook, Ill., 1976-81, cons., 1981-82, dir. mgmt. adv. services, 1983-85, ptnr. in charge mgmt. adv. services, 1985—; mem. IEEE working group on standards for software verification plans. Chmn. adv. council Palatine (Ill.) Sch. Dist. 15, 1985-86; mem. Village of Palatine Planning Commn., 1987—. Mem. Am. Inst. CPA's, Ill. CPA Soc., Inst. Mgmt. Cons., Am. Prodn. and Inventory Control Soc., Palatine C. of C. (bd. dirs. 1986—), Delta Mu Delta. Lodge: Rotary. Avocations: golf, racquetball, reading, computers. Office: Veatch Rich & Nadler 425 Huehl Rd Northbrook IL 60062

KUBE-MCDOWELL, MICHAEL PAUL, novelist; b. Phila., Aug. 29, 1954; s. John Franklin and Lilian Patricia (Deich) McD.; m. Karla Jane Kube, Dec. 12, 1975; 1 child, Matthew Tyndall. BA with high honors, Mich. State U., 1976; MS in Edn., Ind. U., 1981. Cert. tchr., Ind. Sci. tchr. Middlebury (Ind.) Community Sch., 1976-83; writer Elkhart (Ind.) Truth, 1982-84; book reviewer South Bend (Ind.) Tribune, 1981—; screenwriter Laurel TV, Inc., N.Y.C., 1985-86; instr. Miles Labs., Elkhart, 1978-80, Goshen (Ind.) Coll., 1984-85; freelance writer, Lansing, Mich., 1978—. Author: Emprise, 1985, Enigma, 1986, Empery, 1987, Thieves of Light, 1987, Odyssey (Isaac Asimov's Robot City I), 1987. Presdl. Scholar Dist. Tchr. White House Commn. on Pub. Schs., 1985. Mem. Sci. Fiction Writers Am., Writer's Guild Am., Nat. Space Soc., Elkhart County Media Assn., Planetary Soc. Avocations: guitar, viola, photography, basketball, bicycling. Office: PO Box 506 Okemos MI 48864-0506

KUBIAK, THEODORE JOSEPH, health science facility administrator; b. Cleve., Aug. 28, 1945; s. Theodore Christopher and Evelyn Mae (Scharf) K.; children: Tanya Marie, Glenn James. AS, Cuyahoga Community Coll., 1973; BA, Viterbo Coll., 1985. Physicians asst. Family Medicine Inc., Richmond, Ind., 1973-78, Davis Ellis, MD, Rushville, Ind., 1978-81; dir. indsl. medicine Skemp Grand View La Crosse (Wis.) Clinic, 1981-85; dir. occupational medicine Shyboygen (Wis.) Clinic, 1985—; advisor physician's asst. program Ind. U., 1974-78. Sec., treas. La Crosse Indsl. Safety Council, 1984-85; mem. Sheboygan Safety Council, 1985—. Fellow Ind. Acad. Physicians Assts. (pres. 1977-78); mem. Am. Acad. Physician's Assts. in Occupational Medicine. Lodge: Rotary. Avocations: stained glass, motorcycling, bowling. Home: 1031 A N 8th Sheboygan WI 53081 Office: Sheboygan Clinic 2414 Kohler Meml Dr Sheboygan WI 53081

KUBICKI, CHARLES JOSEPH, development company executive; b. Kansas City, Mo., Nov. 4, 1939; s. Julian Francis and Rita Louise (Dauben) K.; m. Mary Margaret Shaffer; children: Charles Jr., Cris, Holly, Michael, David Brian. Student, U. Cin., 1962. V.p. Gallewstein Bros., Cin., 1960-79; pres. Cin. United Developers, 1979—. Chmn. bd. dirs. Midwest Com., Edgewood, Ky., 1982—. Republican. Roman Catholic. Club: Kenwood Country (Cin.). Home: 9400 Cunningham Rd Cincinnati OH 45243 Office: 11626 Deerfield Rd Cincinnati OH 45242

KUBICZEK, EDWARD JOHN, computer programmer, analyst; b. Detroit, Oct. 13, 1943; s. Louis and Stella (Jagoda) K. BS, Wayne State U., 1966. Programmer Blue Cross/Blue Shield Ins. Co., Detroit, 1970-73; programmer/analyst City of Detroit, 1973—. Mem. Sr. Accts. and Analysts and Appraisers Assn. (union dept. rep. Detroit 1976—). Avocations: golf, bowling, travel. Home: 19029 W Warren Detroit MI 48228 Office: City of Detroit 528 City-County Bldg Detroit MI 48226

KUBIK, MATTHEW, architectural technology educator; b. Michigan City, Ind., Dec. 2, 1950; s. Francis Joseph and Frances Drury (Roberts) K.; children from previous marriage: Nora Carver-Kubik, Alice Carver-Kubik; m. Sharon Corrigan, Aug. 23, 1986; children: Joel Mandel, Sara Mandel Kubick, Robert Aronesti Kubick. Diploma, Archtl. Assn. Sch. Architecture, London, 1977; AB, U. Notre Dame, 1973, BArch, 1975. Lic. architect, Ind., Ill.; cert. Nat. Council Archtl. Registration Bds. Artist Chgo., 1974-75; architect Kingscott, Assocs., Kalamazoo, Mich., 1977-78, Frankel and Assocs., Chgo., 1978-79, Skidmore, Owings & Merrill, Chgo., 1979-81; pvt. practice architecture Michigan City, 1981-83, Ft. Wayne, Ind., 1983—; asst. prof. Ind. U.-Purdue U., Ft. Wayne, 1983—. Prin. works include Brooklin Condominiums, and The Cottages. Chmn. sesquicentennial steering com., Michigan City, 1981-84; chmn. sign rev. bd. Ft. Wayne, 1984—. Mem. AIA (bd. dirs. Ft. Wayne chpt. 1985-86, pres. 1987), Ind. Soc. Architects (bd. dirs. 1987). Episcopalian. Club: Notre Dame (Michigan City) (pres. 1982-83). Home: 311 Colfax Michigan City IN 46360 Office: Ind U-Purdue U 2101 Coliseum Blvd Fort Wayne IN 46805

KUBISEN, STEVEN JOSEPH, JR., chemical company manager; b. Iowa City, June 21, 1952; s. Steven Joseph Sr. and Laverne Marie (Ziegler) K.; m. Jean Ann, Nov. 29, 1986. AB, Cornell U., 1974; PhD, Harvard U., 1978. Sr. research chemist Union Carbide Corp., Bound Brook, N.J., 1978-81, project scientist, 1981-84, group leader, 1984-86; dir. polymer tech. Akzo Coatings, Troy, Mich., 1986—. Patentee in field. Mem. Am. Chem. Soc., Sigma Xi. Avocations: sailing, investments, bicycling. Home: 3186 Greenspring Ln Rochester Hills MI 48309 Office: Akzo Coatings 650 Stephenson Hwy Troy MI 48083

KUBISTAL, PATRICIA BERNICE, secondary school principal; b. Chgo., Jan. 19, 1938; d. Edward John and Bernice Mildred (Lenz) Kubistal. AB cum laude, Loyola U. of Chgo., 1959, AM, 1964, AM, 1965, PhD, 1968; postgrad. Chgo. State Coll., 1962, Ill. Inst. Tech., 1963, State U. Iowa, 1963, Nat. Coll. Edn., 1974-75. With Chgo. Bd. Edn., 1959—, tchr., 1959-63, counselor, 1963-65, adminstrv. intern, 1965-66, asst. to dist. supt., 1968-69, prin. spl. edn. sch., 1969-75, prin. Simpson Sch., 1975-76, Brentano Sch., 1975-87, Roosevelt H.S., 1987—; supr. Lake View Evening Sch., 1982—; lectr. Loyola U. Sch. Edn., Nat. Coll. Edn. Grad. Sch., Mundelein Coll.; coordinator Upper Bound Program of U. Ill. Circle Campus, 1966-68. Book rev. editor of Chgo. Prins. Jour., 1970-76, gen. editor, 1982—. Active Crusade of Mercy; mem. com. Ill. Constnl. Conv., 1967-69; mem. Citizens Sch. Com., 1969-71; mem. edn. com. Field Mus., 1971; ednl. advisor North Side Chgo. PTA Region, 1975; gov. Loyola U., 1961—. Recipient Outstanding Intern award Nat. Assn. Secondary Sch. Prins., 1966, Outstanding Prin. award Citizen's Shc. Com. of Chgo., 1986; named Outstanding History Tchr., Chgo. Pub. Schs., 1963, Outstanding Ill. Educator, 1970, one of Outstanding Women of Ill., 1970, St. Luke's-Logan Sq. Community Person of Yr., 1977; NDEA grantee, 1963, NSF grantee, 1965, HEW Region 5 grantee for drug edn., 1974, Chgo. Bd. Edn. Prins.' grantee for study robotics in elem. schs.; U. Chgo. adminstrv. fellow, 1984; Chgo. Bd. Edn. Prins.' grantee for study robotics in elem. schs. Mem. Ill. Personnel and Guidance Assn., NEA, Ill. Edn. Assn., Chgo. Edn. Assn., Am. Acad. Polit. and Social Sci., Chgo. Prins. Club (pres. aux.), Nat. Council Adminstrv. Women, Chgo. Council Exceptional Children, Chgo. Council Fgn. Relations, Chgo. Urban League, Loyal Christian Benevolent Assn., Kappa Gamma Pi, Pi Gamma Mu, Phi Delta Kappa, Delta Kappa Gamma (parlimentarian 1979-80, Lambda state editor 1982—, mem. internat. communications com.), Delta Sigma Rho, Phi Sigma Tau. Home: 5111 N Oakley Ave Chicago IL 60625 Office: Roosevelt High Sch 3436 W Wilson Chicago IL 60625

KUBLY, A(LVIN) RAY, seed company executive, agronomist; b. Watertown, Wis., May 22, 1924; s. Rudolf and Anna (Richard) K.; m. Ruth Audrey Wegwart, Sept. 4, 1948; children: Roger Ray, Joan Kristine, Carol Ann, Mary Lee. BS in Agr., U. Wis., 1952. Cert. profl. agronomist. Dist. sales mgr. Cargill, Inc., Mpls., 1952-59, Teweles Seed Co., Milw., 1959-61; v.p., gen. sales mgr. Dairyland Seed Co., West Bend, Wis., 1961—. Chmn. bd. dirs. Immanuel Luth. Ch., Watertown, Wis., 1967-69; pres. Watertown Unified Sch. Dist., 1966-81, Coop. Service Ednl. Agy., Waupun, Wis., 1971-76. Served to 2d lt. USAF, 1944-45, prisoner of war, 1944; ETO, ret. lt. col. USAFR. Decorated Purple Heart, Air medal. Mem. Agronomy Soc., Wis. Soybean Assn. (bd. dirs. 1971-76), RDA (exec. sec.-treas. 1987—), Retired Officer's Assn. (life), Res. Officers Assn. (life), Ex-Prisoner of War Assn. (life), VFW, Am. Legion, DAV (life), Air Force Assn. (life), U. Wis. Agrl. Alumni Assn. Lodge: Elks. Home: 1204 Amber Ln Watertown WI 53094 Office: Dairyland Seed Co Inc PO Box 958 West Bend WI 53095

KUBO, GARY MICHAEL, advertising agency executive; b. Chgo., Aug. 15, 1952; s. Robert S. and Hideko K.; m. Harriet Davenport, June 14, 1975. BS, Ill. State U., 1974. Research project dir. Foote, Cone & Belding Communications, Chgo., 1974-76, account research supr., 1976-79, research mgr., 1979-80; assoc. research dir. Young & Rubicam, Chgo., 1980-83; ptnr., group research dir. Tatham, Laird & Kudner Advt., Chgo., 1983—. Mem. Advt. Research Found., Am. Mktg. Assn. Home: 2587 Oakton Ct Lisle IL 60532

KUBY, BARBARA ELEANOR, personnel executive, management consultant; b. Medford, Mass., Sept. 1, 1944; s. Robert William and Eleanor (Frasca) Asdell; m. Thomas Kuby, July 12, 1969. BS in Edn./Psychology, Kent State U., 1966, MEd, 1987. Tchr. Nordonia/Euclid (Ohio) Pub. Schs., 1966-76; mgr. tng. and devel. United Bldg. Facilities, Manama, Bahrain, 1979-81, Norton Co., Akron, Ohio, 1981-85; v.p. Kuby and Assocs. Inc., Chagrin Falls, Ohio, 1973—; corp. dir. human resource devel., employee relations TransOhio Savs. Bank, Cleve., 1985—; adj. faculty, cons. Buffalo State U., 1972—, Lake Erie Coll., Cleve., 1985—; lectr., cons. Cleve. State U., 1978—, Inst. for Fin., Chgo., 1986—; program dir. Ctr. Profl. Adv., East Brunswick, N.J., 1978—. cons., lectr. Girls Scouts Am., Cleve., 1981—; cons. Vocat. Info. Program, Cleve., 1970-85, Women Starting Over for Success, Cleve., 1986. Mem. Am. Mgmt. Assn., Am. Soc. for Tng. and Devel., Orgnl. Devel. Network, Gestalt Inst. of Cleve. Avocations: travel, gardening, photography. Home: 7236 Chagrin Rd Chagrin Falls OH 44022

KUCERA, DANIEL WILLIAM, college president, bishop; b. Chgo., May 7, 1923; s. Joseph F. and Lillian C. (Petrzelka) K. B.A., St. Procopius Coll., 1945; M.A., Catholic U. Am., 1950, Ph.D., 1954. Joined Order of St. Benedict, 1944; ordained priest Roman Cath. Ch., 1949; registrar St. Procopius Coll. and Acad., Lisle, Ill., 1945-49, St. Procopius Coll., Lisle, 1954-56; acad. dean, head dept. edn. St. Procopius Coll., 1956-59, pres., 1959-65; abbot St. Procopius Abbey, Lisle, 1964-71; pres. Ill. Benedictine Coll. (formerly St. Procopius Coll.), Lisle, 1971-76; chmn. bd. trustees Ill. Benedictine Coll. (formerly St. Procopius Coll.), 1976-78; aux. bishop of Joliet, 1977-80; bishop of Salina Kans., 1980-83; archbishop of Dubuque Iowa, 1983—; Chaplain Czech Cath. Union; weekend asst. St. Louise de Marillac Parish, 1955-64. Contbr. articles to religious pubs. Lodge: K.C. (4 deg.). Address: Archdiocese of Dubuque PO Box 479 Dubuque IA 52001

KUCHAR, WILLIAM RUDOLPH, mechanical designer, architectural design consultant; b. Grand Forks, N.D., May 30, 1955; s. Rudolph Joseph and Donna Mae (Yeager) K.; m. Kimberley Ann Monson, June 4, 1977; children—Michael, William, David, Joseph. Student U. N.D., 1974-75, State Sch. Sci., Wahpeton, N.D., 1976-78, N.D. State U., 1979-80. Surveyor, K.B.M. Consultants, Grand Forks, 1972-73; mech. designer Mobility Inc., Mpls., 1980-84, Food Engring. Co., Mpls., 1984-85, Marley Pump Co., Mission, Kans., 1985—; cons. Merrill Lynch, Mpls., 1984-86. Roman Catholic. Lodge: Elks. Home: 8813 Gallery Rd Lenexa KS 66215 Office: Marley Pump Co 5800 Foxridge Dr Mission KS 66202

KUCHARO, DONALD DENNIS, JR., manufacter's representative; b. Des Moines, Mar. 25, 1946; s. Donald Dennis and Billie Wenonah (Stanford) K.; m. Carole Lee Toran, Sept. 11, 1971; children—Brian Neal, Bradley Alan. B.S.E.E., U. Iowa, 1969. Sales rep. Montgomery Elevator Co., Moline, Ill., 1970-73; v.p. Donald D. Kucharo Co., Davenport, Iowa, 1973-82, pres., 1982—; safety cons., leader product seminars. Mem. Soc. Mfg. Engrs. Republican. Unitarian. Club: Lindsay Park Yacht. Home: 2753 Nichols Ln Davenport IA 52803 Office: PO Box 727 Bettendorf IA 52722

KUCHTA, JOHN ALBERT, chemical company executive; b. Chgo., June 3, 1955; s. John and Janet Mary (Ivancak) K.; B.S. in Math., Northwestern U., 1982. Work coordinator Continental Ill. Nat. Bank & Trust Co., Chgo., 1974-78; lab. technician Kasar Labs., Chgo., 1975-76, supr. quality control, 1976-77; supr. weights and measures Bell Chem. Co., Chgo., 1977-78, quality control chemist, 1978-82, asst. ops. mgr., 1982—. Active Best Off Broadway Theatre, Music On Stage Theatre, Des Plaines Theatre Guild; music arranger community theatre. Mem. Am. Soc. Quality Control, Am. Prodn. and Inventory Control Soc., N.Y. Acad. Scis., Alpha Sigma Lambda. Roman Catholic. Home: 8023 N Wisner St Niles IL 60648 Office: 411 N Wolcott Ave Chicago IL 60622

KUDLATA, LEONARD JAMES, publishing company executive; b. Chgo., July 7, 1933; s. James Fred and Mildred (Kuchar) K.; m. Karen Ann Maschhoff, Sept. 12, 1959; children: Jeffrey, Randy. BA, U. Ill., 1957. Trainee Standard Rate & Data Service, Skokie, Ill., 1957-59; dist. mgr. Standard Rate & Data Service, Skokie, 1060-71, sales mgr., 1971-76, pub., 1977-83; pres. Standard Rate & Data Service, Wilmette, Ill., 1984—. Served as cpl. U.S. Army, 1953-55. Mem. Am. Bus. Press, Mag. Pubs. Assn., Internat. Newspaper Advt. Mktg. Execs. Republican. Lutheran. Club: Knollwood (Lake Forest, Ill.). Avocations: fishing, hunting, tennis. Home: 1261 S Oak Knoll Dr Lake Forest IL 60045 Office: Standard Rate & Data Service 3004 Glenview Rd Wilmette IL 60091

KUDRYK, OLEG, librarian; b. Rohatyn, Ukraine, Dec. 14, 1912; came to U.S., 1949, naturalized, 1954; s. Theodosius and Olga (Spolitakevich) K.; m. Sophie H. Dydynski, Feb. 5, 1944. Diploma, Conservatory Music, Lviv, 1934; LL.M., U. Lviv, 1937, M.A. in Econ. Sci., 1938; postgrad., U. Vienna, 1945-46; M.A. in L.S., U. Mich., 1960; Ph.D. in Polit. Sci., Ukranian Free U., Munich, 1975. Mgr., legal advisor Coop. Agrl. Soc., Chodoriv, Ukraine, 1938-39; mgr. Import-Export Corp., Cracow, Poland, 1940-44; tchr. Comml. Sch., Ulm, Germany, 1946; adminstr. UNRRA and Internat. Refugee Orgn., Stuttgart, Germany, 1947-49; asst. treas., mgr. Self-Reliance Fed. Credit Union, Detroit, 1953-60; rep., cons. Prudential Ins. Co., Detroit, 1955-60; catalog librarian Ind. U., Bloomington, 1960-63, head order librarian, 1963-70, head acquisitions librarian, 1971-82, spl. projects librarian, asst. to assoc. dean, 1982—; lectr. Ukranian Free U., 1975—; guest lectr. Ind. U. Sch. Library and Info. Sci., 1965—. Contbr. articles to profl. jours. Grantee Ind. U. Office Research and Advanced Studies Internat. Programs, 1972. Mem. Ukranian Library Assn. Am. (v.p. 1972-75, exec. bd. 1975—), AAUP (chpt. treas., exec. bd. 1976—), ALA, Assn. Coll. Research Libraries, Am. Econ. Assn., Am. Acad. Polit. and Social Scis., Shevchenko Sci. Soc. Home: 409 Clover Ln Bloomington IN 47401 Office: Ind U Library Bloomington IN 47405

KUEHL, RICHARD JOHN, chemical company executive; b. Chgo., July 30, 1930; s. John Christen Fredrick and Josephine Louise (Schmidt) K.; m. Ina Lea Judy, Dec. 20, 1951; children—Diane Louise, Dale Richard, Kathryn Lee. B.E.E., Rose Poly. Inst., 1950. Sales engr. Allis Chalmers, St. Louis, 1950-57; project engr. Dow Chem. U.S.A., Baton Rouge, 1957-67, plant supt., 1967-70, prodn. mgr., Sarnia, Ont., Can., 1970-74, purchasing mgr., Midland, Mich., 1974-82, project mgr., Bay City, Mich., 1983—; cons. Pres. Reagan's Pvt. Sector Survey on Cost Control (Grace Commn.), 1982, Nat. Inst. Bldg. Scis., Washington, 1982-83. Served as 1st lt. C.E., U.S. Army, 1951-53. Clubs: Men of Music (pres. 1976-79). Home: 600 Harper Ln Midland MI 48640 Office: Dow Chem USA 4675 E Wilder Rd Bay City MI 48707

KUEHL, RONALD BOYD, marketing executive; b. Arnprior, Can., Aug. 19, 1953; s. Gerald Boyd and Lois Evelyn (Raycroft) K.; m. Mary Ellen Buese, May 28, 1976; children: Jonathon Michael, Jared Ashley. Student, N.Am. Baptist Coll., Edmonton, Alta.; BA in Administrn., Econs., Tabor Coll. Asst. mgr. Continental Bank of Can., Belleville, Ontario, 1976-77; dir. mktg. Nova Media, Regina, Sask., 1977-79, Can. Broadcast COrp., Swift Current, Sask., 1979-84; dir. mktg. Tabor Coll., Hillsboro, Kans., 1984-85, dir. instl. advancement, 1985—; cons. Internat. Ctr. for Learning, Ventura, 1980-85, Gospel Light Pubs., Ventura, 1983-85, various others. Adv. Progressive Conservative Party, Swift Current, Sask., 1980-83; mem. council advancement and support edn. Kans. Ind. Coll. Fund; mem. adv. bd. Dynamics of the Bibl. World. Recipient Award of Excellence, Council Advancement and Support Edn., 1985. Mem. Mktg. for Nonprofit Orgn., Christian Edn. Commn., Swift Current C. of C. (bd. dirs. 1981-83). Mennonite. Club: Sask. Roughrider Football (area rep., 1982-83). Avocations: golf, travel. Home: 608 East F St Hillsboro KS 67063 Office: Tabor Coll 400 S Jefferson Hillsboro KS 67063

KUEHN, JOHN ALLAN, economic consultant; b. St. Louis, Mar. 18, 1941; s. John and Bernice (Schuette) K.; m. Alice Foy, Apr. 15, 1967; children: John, Karen, Becky, James. BA, Cath. U. Am., 1963; MS, U. Mo., 1966, PhD, 1970. Agrl. economist USDA, Columbia, Mo., 1966-78, project leader, economist, 1978-86; assoc. prof. Dept. Agrl. Econs. U. Mo., Columbia, 1979-86, Dept. Community Devel. U. Mo., Columbia, 1980-86; pres. Econ. Futures, Hartsburg, Mo., 1986—; adj. prof. U. Mo. Contbr. articles to profl. jours. Mem. St. Peter's Liturgy Com., Jefferson City, Mo. Served with U.S. Army, 1968-69, Vietnam. Mem. Am. Soc. Univ. Dirs. Internat. Agrl. Programs, So. Regional Sci. Assn. Avocation: fishing. Home and Office: Rt 1 Box 248B Hartsburg MO 65039

KUEHN, JOHN LAMPERT, psychiatrist; b. Toledo, Nov. 8, 1930; s. Adelbert John G. and Emma Marie (Neff) K.; m. Jane Kleinmann (dec. June 1986); children: Elisabeth, William, John, Robert, Margaret, Edward. AB, Ohio Wesleyan U., 1952; MD, Ohio State U., 1957; diploma, Menninger Sch. Psychiatry, 1964. Diplomate Am. Bd. Psychiatry and Neurology. Research asst. in pharmacology Washington U., St. Louis, 1952-57; psychiatrist Ind. U., Bloomington, 1964-66; resident psychiatrist Peace Corps project U. Hawaii, Hilo, 1966; dir. counseling and health service La. State U., Baton Rouge, 1966-75; med. dir. Central Stark Mental Health Ctr., Canton, Ohio, 1976-79; v.p. psychiatry Canton Med. Edn. Found., Canton, 1979-82; social psychiatry cons. N.E. Ohio Psychiatric Inst., Akron, 1982—; sr. cons. Blick Clinic for Devel. Disability, Akron. Served to capt. M.C., USNR, 1953—. Fellow Am. Psychiat. Assn. Lutheran. Avocation: classical music. Home: 3375 Hood Rd Medina OH 44256 Office: NE Ohio Psychiat Inst 340 S Broadway Akron OH 44308

KUEHNL, PHYLLIS ROSE KANGAS, psychologist, educator; b. Toledo, Sept. 17, 1944; d. George S. and Katherine (Gaitanes) Kangas; m. George Andre, June 6, 1965 (div. July 1969); m. Thomas Franklin Kuehnl, Nov. 25, 1970; children: Todd Christopher, Eric Stephen; stepchildren: Greg, Karen, Michael, Kristy. BE, U. Toledo, 1966, MEd, 1968, PhD, 1974. Lic. psychologist, Ohio. Tchr. physical edn. and health DeVilbiss Sch., Toledo, 1966-67; counselor Penta High Sch., Perrysburg, Ohio, 1968-69, U. Toledo, 1969-70; instr. psychology Sinclair Community Coll., Dayton, Ohio, 1970-73; dir. SBH unit Day Mont West Community Mental Health Ctr., Dayton, 1974-76; pvt. practice psychology Centerville, Ohio, 1976—; adj. prof. Ohio U. Med. Sch., Athens, 1979-86, U. Dayton, 1985-86; cons. psychologist Common Pleas Ct. Montgomery County, Dayton, 1980-86; rep. psychologist Wright State U., Daytpn, 1986—. Mem. Am. Psychol. Assn., Ohio Psychol. Assn., Miami Valley Psychol. Assn. (newsletter editor 1985-86, pres. 1986—), Milton Erickson Soc. (pres. 1985-86). Republican. Club: Walnut Grove Country (Dayton) (bd. dirs. women's orgn. 1986). Avocations: golf, tennis, dance, soccer, bridge. Office: 44 Marco Ln PO Box 564 Centerville OH 45459

KUEKER, VIOLET LOUISE, educator; b. East St. Louis, Ill., June 27, 1929; d. Marcellus C. and Mildred M. (Meyer) Hartman; m. Edmund E. Kueker, Mar. 31, 1951. Student MacMurray Coll., 1947-49; BS in Edn., So. Ill. U., 1951; MEd, U. Ill., 1957. Home econs. tchr. Zeigler (Ill.) High Sch., 1951-52, Waterloo (Ill.) Pub. High Schs., 1952—. Past mem. N. Cen. Evaluation Team; past mem. Ill. Vocat. Evaluation Team. Recipient Outstanding Tchr. award Waterloo High Sch., 1982. Mem. NEA (life), AAUW, Am. Home Econs. Assn., Nat. Assn. Vocat. Home Econs. Tchrs., Am. Vocat. Assn., Ill. Coop. Vocat. Edn. Coordinators Assn., Ill. Home Econs. Assn., (pres. dist. V 1981-82), Ill. Vocat. Home Econs. Tchrs. Assn. (chair region V, 1983-85), Ill. Vocational Assn., Monroe County Homemakers Extension Assn., Monroe County Fair Assn., Monroe County Hist. Soc., Petersrown Heritage Soc., Delta Kappa Gamma. Mem. United Ch. of Christ. Clubs: Evening Women's Guild. Office: Bellefontaine Dr Waterloo IL 62298

KUEMMEL, DAVID ANTHONY, city public works commissioner; b. Milw., Nov. 2, 1932, s. Joseph A. and Lydia (Rueter) K.; m. Marie C. Lewis, July 17, 1954; children: Peter, Jeanne, Paul, Cathrine, Virginia, Rachel, Andrew, Phillip. BS in Civil Engring., Marquette U., 1954; MS in Civil Engring., U. Wis., Milw., 1960. Registered profl. engr. From civil engr. I to civil engr. IV Dept. Pub. Works City of Milw., 1954-66, traffic control engr. V, 1966-72, asst. supt., 1972-83, commr., 1983—. Chmn. Milw. Marriage Encounter, 1978-80. Served with U.S. Army, 1954-56. Recipient Annual Alumni award Puis XI High Sch., Milw., 1983, Career Guidance award Soc. Women Engrs., 1979, Profl. Achievement award Marquette U. Engring. Alumni, 1987. Fellow ASCE, Inst. Transp. Engrs.; mem., Am. Pub. Works Assn. (exec. council), Engrs. and Scientists of Milw. (IT exec. council), Milw. Mcpl. Engrs. Assn. Roman Catholic. Avocations: roses, photography. Office: City of Milw Dept Pub Works 841 N Broadway Room 516 Milwaukee WI 53202

KUENNE, BERNARD J., accountant; b. Medford, Wis., Oct. 15, 1941; s. Arthur L. and Theresa J. (Poehnelt) K.; m. Kay C. Kerr, Feb. 23, 1974; children: Ruth, Daniel, Ben, Neal. Assoc., North Cen. Tech. Inst., 1962. CPA Wis. Inst. CPA's, Milw., 1975—, state chmn., 1985-87. Treas. Taylor County March of Dimes (Nat. Fund Raiser award 1980-84), Medford, 1966-72, chmn., 1972—; chmn. Immanual Bd. Edn., Medford, 1976-82. Mem. Am. Inst. CPA's, Wis. Inst. CPA's (north cen. chpt.). Club: Toastmaster (treas. 1983, pres. 1984-86) (Medford). Lodge: Lions (treas. 1976, sec. 1986-87). Home and Office: PO Box 165 Medford WI 54451-0165

KUENZI, CURT WILLIAM, chemical engineer; b. Milw., Dec. 11, 1956; s. William Alden and Barbara Ruth (Struening) K.; m. Katherine Ann Blanch, June 21, 1980; children: Katie Ann, Christopher William. BS in Chem. Engring., Iowa State U., 1981. Co-op engr. Dow Corning, Midland, Mich., 1978-80; process engr. 3M, St. Paul, 1981-82, advanced process engr., 1982-86, sr. process engr., 1986—. Mem. Am. Inst. Chem. Engrs. Lutheran. Avocations: softball, volleyball, motorcycles, automobile restoration. Home: 8495 Cottage Trail Inver Grove Heights MN 55075 Office: 3M Ctr Bldg 236-1S-04 Saint Paul MN 55144

KUENZLI, GWEN LEE, communication skills educator, speech pathologist; b. Bucyrus, Ohio, Nov. 30, 1936; d. Charles Alexander and Mildred Gertrude (Hall) Naus; m. David Paul Kuenzli, June 6, 1958; children: Brent, Leigh, Douglas. BFA, Ohio U., 1958, MFA, 1959; postgrad., Bowling Green State U., Ohio, 1975-76, 1986. Lic. speech pathologist, Ohio. Speech pathologist Syracuse (N.Y.) Pub. Schs., 1959-60, Worthington (Ohio) Schs., 1961-62; substitute tchr. hearing impaired Findlay (Ohio) Schs., 1971-78; speech and hearing cons. Hancock Bd. Health, Findlay, 1977-80; profl. staff communication skills ctr. Ohio No. U., Ada, 1979-80; asst. prof. Findlay Coll., 1980—, dir. honors program, 1983—; dir. Supporting Skills System, Findlay, 1983-86, Speech Lab., Findlay, 1980—; dir. speech pathology services Home Health Agy., Blanchard Valley Hosp., Findlay, 1980-84; cons. Bilingual Multicultural Ctr., Findlay, 1985—. Editor: Registry of Ohio Clin. Services, 1985-86. Mem. exec. bd. Hancock Family Services, Findlay, 1983—. Mem. Am. Speech and Hearing Assn. (clin. cert.), Ohio Speech and Hearing Assn. (chmn. legis. com. 1986—), Ohio Speech Communication Assn., Aphasiology Assn. of Ohio, (mem. exec. bd. 1982—), Cen. States Speech Assn. (reader, women's caucus 1985—), Writing Ctrs. Assn., William Shakespeare Club (pres. 1979). Methodist. Lodge: Zonta. Home: 5163 Rd #79 Rawson OH 45881 Office: Findlay Coll 1000 N Main Street Findlay OH 45840

KUEPFER, M. CHARLES, food products company executive; b. Canton, Ohio, Feb. 13, 1931; s. Matthew Charles and Mildred Marion (Miller) K.; m. Marcia Jane Hays, June 7, 1953; children: Kristi Lynn, David Michael, Teri

Jane. BSME, Case Inst. Tech., Cleve., 1953. Registered profl. engr., Ohio, Mich. Test engr. Cummins Engine Co., Columbus, Ind., 1955-57; chief engr. electric heat Arvin Industries, Columbus, 1957-61; mgr. product engring. lab. Clark Equipment Co., Battle Creek, Mich., 1961-80, quality engr., 1980-86; pres. The Cookie Bin, Inc., Kalamazoo, 1986—. Patentee in field. Bd. dirs. Goodwill Industries, Battle Creek, 1972-78, pres. 1975; curriculum adv. bd. Kellogg Community Coll., Battle Creek, 1974-80. Served with USCG, 1953-55. Mem. Soc. Autimotive Engrs. (bd. dirs. engring. activity bd. 1977-80, chmn. farm constrn. and indsl. machine activity 1979). Baptist. Office: The Cookie Bin Inc 7684 Sprinkle Rd Park Sq Commons Kalamazoo MI 49002

KUETTNER, KLAUS EDUARD, biochemistry educator; b. Bunzlau, Germany, June 25, 1933; came to U.S., 1962, naturalized, 1969; s. Gerhard Paul and Elfriede (Oelze) Küttner; m. Yolanda Adler, Aug. 25, 1975. B.S., Minden, Fed. Republic Germany, 1956; M.S., U. Freiburg, Fed. Republic Germany, 1958; Ph.D., U. Berne, Switzerland, 1961. Research assoc. Presbyterian St. Luke's Hosp., Chgo., 1964-66; instr. biol. chemistry U. Ill. Coll. Medicine, Chgo., 1964-65; asst. prof. dept. biochemistry Rush Med. Coll., Rush Presbyn.-St. Luke's Med. Ctr., Chgo., 1971-72, assoc. prof. dept. orthopedic surgery and biochemistry, 1972-77, prof. biochemistry and orthopedics, 1980—, chmn. dept. biochemistry, 1980; chmn. chemistry, physiology and structure of bones and teeth Gordon Research Conf., 1978; editorial adv. bd. Joun. Orthopedic Research, 1981—; organizer, chmn. Internat. Workshop Conf. on Articular Cartilage Biochemistry, Wiesbaden, Fed. Republic Germany, 1985; bd. dirs. WHO Ctr. Rheumapathologie, Mainz, Fed. Republic Germany, 1986—; chmn. Proteoglycan Gordon Research Conf., 1984; co-chmn. fellowship subcom. Nat. Arthritis Found., 1981-82. CIBA fellow, Basel, Switzerland, 1961-62; AEC fellow, 1962-64. Recipient Carol Nachman prize for Rheumatology Research, 1987. Mem. Am. Soc. Biol. Chemists, Am. Soc. Cell Biology, Am. Chem. Soc., Am. Acad. Orthopedic Surgeons (adv. com. mem. research, Orthopedic Research Soc. Internat. Assn. Dental Research. Office: Rush Presbyterian St Luke's Med Ctr Dept Biochemistry 1653 W Congress Pkwy Chicago IL 60612

KUFELDT, GEORGE, biblical educator; b. Chgo., Nov. 4, 1923; s. Henry and Lydia (Dorn) K.; m. Kathryn Rider, July 24, 1943 (dec. July 1956); children: Anita Kay Kufeldt Shelton, Kristina Sue Kufeldt Schmidt; m. Claudena Eller, June 21, 1957 (dec. Sept. 1978); m. Lydia Borgardt, Aug. 12, 1980. AB, Anderson Coll., Ind., 1945, ThB, 1946, MDiv, 1953; PhD, Dropsie U., 1974. Ordained to ministry Ch. of God, 1949. Pastor Ch. of God, Homestead, Fla., 1948-50, Ch. of God, Cassopolis, Mich., 1954-57, Ch. of God, Lansdale, Pa., 1957-61; prof. O.T. and Hebrew, Anderson Coll., 1961—. Contbr. to Wesleyan Bible Commentary, vol. II, 1968, Nelson's Expository Dictionary of the Old Testament, 1980. Dropsie U. fellow, 1961, 63; Land of the Bible Workshop grantee NYU, 1966. Mem. Soc. Bibl. Lit., Nat. Assn. Profs. of Hebrew, AAUP. Lodge: AHEPA (pres.). Home: 907 N Nursery Rd Anderson IN 46012 Office: Anderson Coll Sch of Theology Anderson IN 46012

KUGLER, RUSSELL D(UANE), agricultural products executive; b. Culbertson, Nebr., May 21, 1927; s. Carl B. and Pearl M. (Bright) K.; m. G. Diane Manning, Oct. 19, 1952; children: John, Michael. BBA, U. Nebr., 1951. Salesman Continental Oil Co., Scottsbluff, Nebr., 1951-53; pres. Kugler Co., McCook, Nebr., 1954—. Mem. Community Hosp. Found., McCook, Culbertson City Council. Served as sgt. AUS, 1946-47, Korea. Mem. Nat. Fertilizer Solutions Assn., Nebr. Petroleum Marketers (bd. dirs. 1970-71), Sigma Chi, VFW. Republican. Methodist. Club: Petroleum (Denver). Lodges: Elks, Masons. Home: 1603 Norris Ave McCook NE 69001 Office: The Kugler Co W 3d and C McCook NE 69001-1748

KUHAR, JUNE CAROLYNN, retired fiberglass manufacturing company executive; b. Chgo., Sept. 20, 1935; d. Kurt Ludwig and Dorothy Julia (Lewand) Stier; m. G. James Kuhar, Feb. 5, 1953; children: Kathleen Lee, Debra Suzanne. Student William Rainey Harper Coll., Chgo. Engaged in fiberglass mfg., 1970—; sec.-treas. Q-R Fiber Glass Industries Inc., Elgin, 1970—. Mem. Multiple Sclerosis Soc., Nat. Fedn. Ileitis and Colitis, Bus. and Profl. Women N.W., Bus. and Profl. Woman's Club (pres. 1984—), Women in the Arts (charter). Home: 2303 Meadow Dr Rolling Meadows IL 60008 Office: 701 N State St Elgin IL 60120

KUHAR, TIMOTHY MARTIN, accountant; b. South Bend, Ind., June 4, 1965; s. Joseph S. and Gladys E. (Wiekewicz) K. BS in Acctg., St. Joseph Coll., Rensselaer, Ind., 1977. CPA, Ind. Cost acct. Pilgrim Farms, Inc., Plymouth, Ind., 1977-79, plant acct., 1980-81, treas., 1982—. Bd. dirs. RumVillage Neighbor Assn., South Bend, 1986. Mem. Ind. Soc. CPA's, Am. Inst. CPA's. Roman Catholic. Avocations: jogging, camping, softball. Home: 1726 S Catalpa South Bend IN 46613 Office: Pilgrim Farms Inc 1430 Western Ave Plymouth IN 46563

KUHEL, JAMES JOSEPH, information systems analyst; b. Cleve., Apr. 12, 1934; s. Charles and Ann (Mauer) K.; m. Irene Francis Babski, May 12, 1956; children: Lynn, James, Timothy. Grad. high sch., Cleve., 1952. Sales tng. mgr. Bruning div. A.M. Internat., Chgo., 1956-72; regional mgr. OCE Industries Inc., Cleve., 1972-75; pres. Micro Inc., Cleve., 1976-81; territory mgr. A.B. Dick Record Systems Operation, Cleve., 1981-87, mgr. nat. distbr. sales, 1987—. Author: How to Sell Systems in Business, 1969. Served with U.S. Army, 1954-56. Mem. Bus. Equipment Mfrs. Assn. (Man in the Booth 1968), Assn. Info. Image Mgmt. (v.p. 1986—), Soc. Reproduction Engrs. (edn. chmn. 1960-61), Internat. Reprographic Assn. Republican. Roman Catholic. Avocations: basketball, walking. Home: 22691 Briscoe Dr Rocky River OH 44116 Office: AB Dick Record Systems Operation 6750 Miller Rd Brecksville OH 44141

KUHL, RICHARD (RICK) ALLEN, architect; b. Holdrege, Nebr., Oct. 23, 1949; s. Ernest Earl and Patricia Louise (Childress) K. BArch, U. Nebr., 1976, MArch, 1978. Intern architect Design Group, Lincoln, Nebr., 1974-80; architect Bahr Vermeer & Haecker, Lincoln, 1980-82; project architect ADK Assocs., Inc., Lincoln, 1982-87, Nat. Archtl. Services Inc., Lafayette, Ind., 1987—; part time faculty U. Nebr., Lincoln, 1978—. Commr. mgmt. YMCA, Lincoln, 1985—; bd. trustees Christ Meth. Ch., Lincoln, 1986; mem. Leadership Lincoln, 1986—. Regent's scholar U. Nebr., 1975-76; recipient Rho Chi Medal award U. Nebr., 1978, Faculty award U. Nebr., 1978. Mem. AIA (sec., treas. Lincoln chpt. 1986—, cons. research corp. Washington 1976). Democrat. Methodist. Avocations: woodworking, running, bicycling. Office: Nat Archtl Services Inc 401 S Earl Ave Lafayette IN 47903

KUHLMAN, KIMBERLY ANN, clinical dietician; b. Toledo, Ohio, June 30, 1954; d. James Gilbert and Jane Marie (Konczal) Schramm; m. Carl Edwin Kuhlman Jr., May 23, 1981; children: Eric, Christopher. BS in Pub. Health, U. Toledo, 1977; BS in Dietetics, Bowling Green State U., 1978. Dietetic intern Good Samaritan Hosp., Cin., 1979; dietitian, tchr. The Toledo Hosp., 1980, clinical dietitian, 1981-83, nutrition support dietitian, 1983-86; dietitian Alcohol Treatment Ctr., Toledo, 1986-87; clin. dietitian Coop. Care Unit, Toledo Hosp., 1987—; guest lectr. Toledo Pub. Schs., 1983-84; instr. Health Aware program Toledo Hosp. Community Health Project, 1980-83. Author: Home Parental Nutrition Fact Sheet, Pediatric Nutrition Instruction Booklet. Mem. The Toledo Art Mus.; treas. Presch. Nutrition Council Northwest Ohio, Toledo, 1986—. Mem. Toledo Dietetic Assn. (chmn. regulations com. 1986—, chmn. membership com. 1984-85, co-chmn. membership com. 1983-84), Am. Soc. Parenteral and Entral Nutrition, Dietitians in Critical Care Practice Group, Am. Dietetics Assn., Eta Gamma Sigma. Lutheran. Avocations: reading, knitting. Home: 3903 Beverly Dr Toledo OH 43614

KUHLMANN, FRED L., brewery consultant, lawyer, baseball executive; b. St. Louis, Apr. 24, 1916; s. Fred A and Meta (Borrenpohl) K.; m. Mildred E. Southworth, July 11, 1941; children: Marilyn Kuhlmann Brickler, Fred M. AB, JD, Washington U., 1938; LLM, Columbia U., 1942. Bar: Mo. 1938. Ptnr. Stolar, Kuhlmann, Heitzmann & Eder, 1956-67; gen. counsel Anheuser-Busch Inc., St. Louis, 1967-70, v.p., gen. counsel, 1971-74, sr. v.p. adminstrn. and services, 1974-77, exec. v.p., 1977-84; exec. v.p. Anheuser-Busch Cos., Inc., St. Louis, 1979-84, vice chmn. bd., 1979—, also bd. dirs.; exec. v.p., chief operating officer St. Louis Nat. Baseball Club Inc., 1984—, also bd. dirs.; Bd. dirs. Mfrs. Ry. Co., Concordia Pub. House, St. Luke's Health Corp. Contbr. articles to legal pubs. Bd. dirs. Civic Ctr. Corp., Anheuser Busch Cos., Inc., St. Louis Nat. Baseball Club, Inc.; mem. St. Lukes Health Corp. Mem. ABA, Mo. Bar Assn., St. Louis Bar Assn., Mfrs. Ry. Co., Concordia Pub. House, Order of the Coif, Phi Beta Kappa. Clubs: St. Louis, Bellerive Country. Home: 6 Coach N Four Frontenac MO 63131 Office: 250 Stadium Plaza Saint Louis MO 63102

KUHN, DAVID ALAN, lawyer; b. Cleve., Ohio, May 7, 1929; s. Irwin Albert and Margaret (Janke) K.; m. Jacqueline McColloch, July 2, 1955; children—David McColloch, Douglas Alan. A.B., Kenyon Coll., 1951; J.D., Case Western Res. U., 1954. Bar: Ohio 1954. Asst. to sec. Warner & Swasey Co., Cleve., 1956-59; staff atty. Oglebay Norton Co., Cleve., 1959-70, asst. sec., 1970-80, sec., counsel, 1980—. Trustee Kenyon Coll., 1983—. Mem. ABA, Cleve. Bar Assn., Ohio State Bar Assn., Am. Soc. Corp. Secs., Kenyon Coll. Alumni Assn. (pres. 1974; named Outstanding Alumnus 1976-77), Delta Tau Delta. Served to capt. USAF, 1954-56. Clubs: Cleve. Yachting (sec. 1983—), Cleve. Athletic. Republican. Home: 337 Morewood Pkwy Rocky River OH 44116 Office: Oglebay Norton Co 1100 Superior Ave Cleveland OH 44114

KUHN, JEFFREY PAUL, actuary; b. Phila., Jan. 3, 1945; s. Alfred and Nina Margurite (De Angeli) K.; m. Nancy Roberta Hensley, July 30, 1966; 1 child, Kathrine De Angeli. BS, U. Cin., 1966, postgrad., 1967. Actuarial student Western-So. Life, Cin., 1967-71, actuarial assoc., 1972-74, asst. actuary, 1975-79, assoc. actuary, 1980-85, 2d v.p., assoc. actuary, 1985—. Fellow Soc. Actuaries; mem. Am. Acad. Actuaries. Avocations: reading, sports, gardening. Home: 574 Old US 52 New Richmond OH 45157 Office: Western-So Life 400 Broadway Cincinnati OH 45157

KUHN, ROBERT JOSEPH, dentist; b. West Union, Iowa, Feb. 11, 1954; s. Arnold Alois and Theresa J. (Schmelzer) K.; m. Tamara Sue Ayers, May 28, 1977; children: Michael, Timothy. BS, U. Iowa, 1976, DDS, 1980. Gen. practice dentistry Newton, Iowa, 1980—. Mem. ADA, Iowa Dental Assn., Jasper County Dental Soc. (pres. 1984-85), Newton Jaycees (bd. dirs. 1984-87). Club: Jasper County I (Newton) (v.p. 1985-86). Lodge: Kiwanis (pres.-elect Newton Morning club 1986-87, pres. 1987-88). Avocations: fishing, biking, cross-country skiing. Home: 324 W 3d St S Newton IA 50208 Office: 320 E 3d St N Newton IA 50208

KUHN, RONALD JOSEPH, computer Systems engineer; b. Ft. Wayne, Nov. 11, 1957; s. Raymond Jerome and Delores Jean (Gaither) K.; m. Brenda Gail Lucker, June 22, 1985. BS in Applied Math., Western Mich. U., Kalamazoo, 1980. Corp. systems engr. Control Upjohn, Kalamazoo, 1980—. Mem. Assn. Computer Mgmt.

KUHN, THEODORE FRANK, economist, educator; b. Indpls., Sept. 7, 1953; s. Theodore R. and Theresa A. Kuhn; m. Lisa K. Price. BA, Ind. U., 1975; postgrad., U. Pa., 1975-76; MA, U. Tex., 1978. Research economist Pub. Utility Commn. Tex., Austin, 1977-80; cons. economist R.W. Beck & Assocs., Indpls., 1980—; asst. instr. U. Tex., Austin, 1976-78; adj. instr. Butler U., Indpls., 1983—. Mem. Am. Econ. Assn., Phi Beta Kappa, Phi Kappa Phi, Alpha Sigma Phi. Avocations: piano, keyboard, tennis, bicycling. Home: 4014 Monaco Dr #E Indianapolis IN 46220 Office: RW Beck & Assocs 5920 Castleway W Dr Indianapolis IN 46250

KUHN, TIMOTHY EDWARD, pharmacist, consultant; b. Bay City, Mich., July 25, 1951; s. Francis Gerald and Pauline Marie (Brissette) K.; m. Colleen Ann Taberski, Sept. 12, 1975; children: Amy Marie, Ryan Timothy. BS, Ferris State Coll., 1974. Cert. pharmacist, Mich. Pharmacy intern Gen. Hosp., Bay City, Mich., 1972-74; pharmacist mgr. Union Prescription Ctr., Bay City, 1978-79; pharmacist Bay Med. Ctr., Bay City, 1974-78, pharmacist supr., 1979—; pharmacy educator Delta Coll., Univ. Ctr., Mich., 1980-84; adv. bd. Hosp. Purchasing Service, Middleville, Mich., 1983-85, Bay Med. Edn., Bay City, 1983—; cons. pharmacist Standish (Mich.) Hosp., 1985—. V.p. Am. Cancer Soc. Bay County, Mich., 1982-83, pres. 1983-85. Mem. Am. Soc. Hosp. Pharmacists, Mich. Pharmacists Assn., Bay County Pharamcist Assn. (pres. 1982-84, Recognition award 1984). Democrat. Roman Catholic. Avocations: golf, investments. Home: 1490 Evelyn Rd Bay City MI 48708 Office: Bay Med Ctr Pharmacy Dept 1900 Columbus Ave Bay City MI 48708

KUHR, LEONARD GERARD, manufacturing company executive, accountant; b. Chgo.; s. Leonard Anthony Kuhr; m. Barbara Straube, Oct. 13, 1979. BBA in Acctg., Loyola U., Chgo., 1979; MS in Taxation, DePaul U., 1981. CPA, Ill. Mgr. taxation Am. Hosp. Supply Co., Evanston, Ill., 1978-85; mgr. internat. tax Coopers & Lybrand, Chgo., 1986; dir. internat. tax Baxter Travenol Labs Inc., Deerfield, Ill., 1987—. Mem. Am. Inst. CPA's, Ill. Soc. CPA's, Tax Execs. Inst., Chgo. Tax Club. Avocations: golf, racquetball. Office: Baxter Travenol Labs Inc 1 Baxter Pkwy OF6-4E Deerfield IL 60015

KUIPERS, JACK, mathematician, educator, consultant; b. Grand Rapids, Mich., Mar. 27, 1921; s. Bernard Jacob and Grace (Werkema) K.; m. Lois Belle Holtrop, Mar. 25, 1948; children—Benjamin Jack, Emily Louise, Joel Corneal, Alison Jane, Lynne Marie. A.B., Calvin Coll., 1942; B.S.E.E., U. Mich., 1943, M.S.E., 1958, Info. and Control Engr.'s degree, 1966; postgrad. U. Calif.-Santa Barbara, 1967-70. Asst. to dir. research Electric Sorting Machine Co., Grand Rapids, 1946-50; project engr. Flight Reference and Autopilot Systems, Lear, Inc., Grand Rapids, 1950-53, sr. project engr., analytical design, 1954-59; chief engr. instrument div. R.C. Allen Bus. Machines, In., Grand Rapids, 1953-54; sr. physicist Instrumentation and Control Div. Cleve. Pneumatic Industries, Grand Rapids, 1959-62; lectr. Horace B. Rackman Sch. of Grad. Studies, U. Mich., Ann Arbor, 1962-67, research engr. NASA Apollo Applications Inst. of Sci. and Tech., 1962-67; prof. math. Calvin Coll., Grand Rapids, 1967—; cons. in aerospace tech., math. models. Served with U.S. Army, 1942-46. Mem. Math. Assn. of Am., IEEE, Sigma Xi. Mem. Christian Reformed Ch. Patentee: SPASYN, electromagnetic tracking device and other devels. in field; frequent guest lectr.; contbr. articles to profl. jours. Home: 3085 Baker Park Dr SE Grand Rapids MI 49508 Office: Calvin Coll Dept Math Grand Rapids MI 49506

KUIPERS, PETER WILLIAM, orthodontist; b. Mitchell, S.D., Feb. 27, 1942; s. William and Vesta Edna (Feiok) K.; m. Lorraine Delha Williamson, Oct. 1969 (div. Aug. 1975); m. Marilyn Esther Sellars, Mar. 26, 1976; stepchildren: Anne Michelle Case Urban, Linda Lee Case LaSalle. BS, U. Minn., 1967, DDS, 1969, PhD, 1972. Lic. orthodontist, Minn. Assoc. prof. U. Balt. Sch. Dentistry, 1972-74; practice dentistry specializing in orthodontics Bloomington, Minn., 1974—. Mem. ADA, Am. Assn. Orthdontics. Republican. Avocations: golf, hunting, thorough bred horses. Office: 8900 Penn Ave S Bloomington MN 55431

KUKLA, EDWARD RICHARD, rare books and special collections librarian, lecturer; b. Detroit, Jan. 31, 1941; s. Stanley Frank and ClaraBelle (Morton) K. BA, Wayne State U., 1962; MA, U. Mich., 1963, M.L.S., 1973. Teaching fellow U. Mich., Ann Arbor, 1963-66; asst. instr. Mich. State U., 1970-72; media mobile librarian State Library Mich., 1972; asst. librarian rare books and manuscripts Greenfield Village and Henry Ford Mus., Dearborn, Mich., 1974-78; rare books and spl. collections librarian Wash. State U., Pullman, 1979-86; head spl. collections dept., Mpls. Athenaeum librarian Mpls. Pub. Library, 1987—; educator, lectr. rare books, history of books and printing, book collecting. Recipient Mich. Jr. Acad. Sci., Arts, and Letters membership, 1958. Mem. ALA, Assn. Coll. and Research Libraries, U. Mich. Sch. Library Sci. Alumni Assn., Am. Contract Bridge League, Am. Cut Glass Assn., Am. Swedish Inst., Ampersand, Mpls. Soc. Fine Arts, Minn. Library Assn., Phi Beta Kappa, Sigma Delta Pi, Beta Phi Mu. Clubs: U. Mich. Union. Author: Un estudio critico sobre Altazor de Vicente Huidobro, 1963; The Scholar and the Future of the Research Library Revisited, 1973; The Struggle and the Glory: A Special Bicentennial Exhibition, 1976. Home: 2439 3d Ave S Apt C-11 Minneapolis MN 55404-3518 Office: Mpls Pub Library/Info Ctr 300 Nicollet Mall Minneapolis MN 55401-1992

KUKRAL, DAVID ALLEN, accountant; b. Cleve., June 27, 1960; s. Kenneth Elmer and Elaine Winfred (Rogers) K. BBA in Acctg., John Carroll U., 1982. CPA, Ohio. Office mgr. APSCO, Inc., Valley View, Ohio, 1982-83; acct. Western Res. Savs. Bank, Cleve., 1983-85, Gangloff, Kemme & Supelail, Cleve., 1985-86, Mathews, Gallovic, Granito & Co., Mentor, Ohio, 1986—. Mem. Am. Inst. CPA's, Ohio Soc. CPA's.

KULCZYCKI, MICHAEL TERRY, marketing professional; b. Chgo., May 29, 1952; s. Michael C. and Diane K. Kulczycki; m. Susan A. Richards, June 15, 1974; children: David M., Julie K. AB in Communications, U. Notre Dame, 1974; M in Mgmt., Northwestern U., 1987. Asst. pub. relations Weiss Meml. Hosp., Chgo., 1974-76; asst. dir. pub. relations Augustana Hosp., Chgo., 1976-80; dir. communications Hosp. Research and Ednl. Trust, Chgo., 1980-85; dir. mktg. Healthcare Fin. Mgmt. Assn., Oak Brook, Ill., 1985—. Editor: The Hospital's Role in Caring for the Elderly: Leadership Issues, 1983. Mem. Internat. Assn. Bus. Communicators (Spectra award 1983, 85), Am. Mktg. Assn. (planning com. Kotler awards 1984-85), Acad. Hosp. Pub. Relations (McEachern award 1979), Soc. Tech. Communications (Merit award Chgo. chpt., Cert. Achievement, Disting. Tech. Communication award 1984), Chgo. Hosp. Pub. Relations Soc. (sec. 1976-77), Welfare Pub. Relations Forum (Helen Cody Baker award), Chgo. Jaycees. Roman Catholic. Club: Notre Dame (Chgo). Home: 1100 S Grove Oak Park IL 60304 Office: Healthcare Fin Mgmt Assn 1900 Spring Rd 500 Oak Brook IL 60521

KULECK, CATHARINE KNIGHT, developmental psychologist; b. Mpls., Oct. 15, 1947; d. Robert Preston and Agnes Vinall (Oleson) Vindall; m. Kirby Charles Knight, Sept. 12, 1971 (dec. Nov. 1981); m. Walter Julius Kuleck, Jan. 2, 1983. BA, St. Cloud State (Minn.) Coll., 1969, MS, 1973; PhD, Ariz. State U., 1982. Edn. dir. Tri County Action Program, St. Cloud, 1971-73; speech-lang. pathologist Therapy Assocs., St. Paul, 1973-75, Vis. Nurse Service, Mesa, Ariz., 1975-78; instr. psychology Mesa Community Coll., 1979-81; v.p. Cognitive Processes, Inc., Cleveland Heights, Ohio, 1983—; pres. The Hennepin Group, Inc., Cleveland Heights, 1985—; cons. various bus. and indsl. orgns., 1983—; adj. prof. Cleve. State U., 1983—. Contbr. articles to profl. jours. Co-founder Cleve. Venture Club, 1983; mem. Greater Cleve. Growth Assn., 1983—. Post Doctoral fellow Nat. Inst. Child Health and Devel., 1983-86; research grantee Spencer Found., 1984-87. Mem. Am. Psychology Assn., Soc. Research in Child Devel. Lutheran. Club: Mid Day. Avocations: pure bred dogs, cello. Home: 3631 Fairmount Blvd Cleveland Heights OH 44118 Office: The Hennepin Group Inc 3631 Fairmount Blvd Cleveland Heights OH 44118

KULECK, WALTER JULIUS, psychologist, consultant; b. Phila., Aug. 25, 1945; s. Walter J. and Alma Kuleck; m. Carol S. Edmonson, June 15, 1968 (div.); 1 child, Julian James; m. Catharine C. Knight, Jan. 2, 1983. BS in Aero. Engring., MIT, 1967, MS in Aero. Engring., 1968; MA in Psychology, U. Mich., 1974, PhD (Ctr. for Creative Leadership fellow), 1976. Lic. psychologist, Ohio. Engr., Vertol div. Boeing, Phila., 1966-71; parts and accessories mgr. West Chester (Pa.) Honda, 1971-72; NIMH trainee, asst. research dir. Inst. for Social Research, U. Mich., Ann Arbor, 1972-76; postdoctoral fellow Ctr. for Creative Leadership, Greensboro, N.C., 1976-77; staff psychologist William, Lynde & Williams, Inc., Painesville, Ohio, 1977-83; pres. Cognitive Processes, Inc., Cleveland Heights, Ohio, 1983—; founding prin. ProTrane, Detroit, 1984-85; cons. psychologist The Creative Thinking Ctr., Hudson, Ohio, 1983-85, MacArthur Found. Human Devel. Consortium; dir. Innovative Health Systems, Inc., 1984—, v.p. mktg. 1986—; mgmt. psychologist; creativity cons. Bd. dirs. Ch. Growth Ctr., Inc., 1986—. Mem. Am. Psychol. Assn., Cleve. Venture Club (founder), Ruger Collectors' Assn. Republican. Lutheran. Club: Solon Sportsman's (Ohio). Contbr. articles to profl. jours. Office: 3631 Fairmount Blvd Cleveland Heights OH 44118

KULI, AMIEL MICHAEL, airline executive; b. Akron, Ohio, Aug. 5, 1942; s. Amiel Michael and Margaret Emma (Brady) K.; m. Carolyn Elizabeth Phinney, Sept. 26, 1964; children—Michelle Marie, Michael Steven (dec.). Student AG Aviation Acad., Reno, Nev., 1967-68, Akron U., 1969-70, Kent State U., 1971-72. Airline transport pilot, jet capt. Airborne Express, Wilmington, Ohio, 1976-78, chief pilot, dir. flight ops., 1978-79, dir. ops., 1979, v.p. air contract ops., 1979-80, v.p. ops., 1980-83, v.p. govt. affairs, 1983-86; v.p. Air Park Devel.; pres. Sound Suppression, Inc., 1985—; pres. Escort Air, Inc., Akron, Ohio, 1973-76; chief pilot Forest City Enterprises, Cleve., 1970-73. Served with USN, 1960-64, Cuba. Decorated Cuba Crisis medal. Mem. Quiet Birdmen, Nat. Street Rod Assn., Nat. Assn. Fgn. Trade Zones, Connecting Rods Car (pres. 1986—), Am. Legion, VFW (nat. com. 1976). Methodist. Avocations: automobiles; motorcycles; water skiing. Office: Airborne Express Inc 145 Hunter Dr Wilmington OH 45177

KULICH, BETTY ALICE, home economics educator; b. Columbus, Ohio, Jan. 15, 1952; d. Russell and Virginia Lee (Jaynes) Rodgers; m. Richard Alexander Kulich, Jan. 20, 1973; 1 child, Carrie Ann. BS in Home Econs., Ohio State U., 1974, MS in Early Childhood Edn., 1980. Cert. home economist, tchr., Ohio. Home econs. tchr. and job tng. child care services and multi-area instr. Columbus (Ohio) Pub. Schs., 1974—; pub. relations spokesman Ohio Vocat. Legis. Network, 1978-80. Active Future Home Makers Am., Home Econs. Related Occupations, 1974—. Author curriculum guide, multi-media presentation. Recipient Outstanding Service award Redeemer's Ch., Columbus, Ohio, 1978. Mem. NEA, Ohio Edn. Assn., Columbus Edn. Assn. (union bldg. rep. 1981-86), Cen. Ohio Tchrs. Assn., Nat. Vocat. Assn., Ohio Vocat. Assn., Columbus Home Econs. Assn. (pres. 1979-80), Alpha Delta Kappa. Office: 546 Jack Gibbs Columbus OH 43215

KULICH, ROMAN THEODORE, finance administrator; b. Benton Harbor, Mich., Mar. 1, 1953; s. Roman and Helen (Gadumski) K.; m. Janet Kay Zuhl, Sept. 14, 1974; children: Andrew Joseph, Stephanie Ann. BBA magna cum laude, Mich. State U., 1974. CPA, Mich. Sr. auditor Ernst & Ernst, Detroit, 1975-77; controller Sinai Hosp. of Detroit, 1977-81, dir. finance, 1981-84; dir. finance Health Alliance Plan, Detroit, 1984-86, v.p. adminstrn. and finance, 1986—. Tiscornia Found. Scholarship winner, St. Joseph, Mich., 1971. Fellow Health Care Fin. Mgmt. Assn. (bd. dirs. Ea. Mich. chpt. 1986—); mem. Am. Inst. CPA's, Mich. Assn. CPA's. Club: Renaissance (Detroit). Avocations: family activities, reading. Home: 29080 Forest Hill Dr Farmington Hills MI 48018 Office: Health Alliance Plan 2850 W Grand Blvd Detroit MI 48202

KULISH, NANCY MANN, psychologist, researcher; b. Chgo., Aug. 18, 1938; d. Fred and Marian (Ofner) M.; m. Harold Kulish, Mar. 31, 1968; children: Melinda, Jonathan. BA, U. Calif., Berkeley, 1960; PhD, U. Mich., 1965. Lic. psychologist, Mich. Chief psychologist out patient dept. Detroit Psychiat. Inst., Detroit, 1965-69; adj. clin. prof. U. Detroit, 1966—; chief psychologist Northland Clinic, Southfield, Mich., 1971—; clin. instr. Wayne State U. Med. Sch., Detroit, 1982—; research assoc. U. Mich. Psychology Clinic, Ann Arbor, 1982—; cons. Detroit Edison Co., 1983-85. Contbr. articles to profl. jours. Mem. Am. Psychol. Assn., Mich. Psychol. Assn., Mich. Psychoanalytic Soc. (program chmn. friends of soc. 1979-81), Mich. Soc. Psychoanalytic Psychologists (sec. 1981-83). Democrat. Jewish. Avocations: skiing, tennis, cooking, classical music. Office: 29260 Franklin #104 Southfield MI 48034

KULLBOM, TERRENCE LEE, oral surgeon, educator; b. Council Bluffs, Iowa, May 22, 1940; s. Marion Albert and Ellen Mae (Campbell) K.; m. Nancy Lee Guthrie, Sept. 7, 1964 (div. May 1979); children: Nick, Kelly, Matthew; m. Julie Rae Martens, Oct. 30, 1981; 1 child, Kristine. BA, Augustana Coll., Sioux Falls, S.D., 1962; DDS, U. Iowa, 1966; MS, U. Nebr., 1973. Diplomate Am. Bd. Oral and Maxillofacial Surgeons. Practice dentistry specializing in oral and maxillofacial surgery Council Bluffs, 1973—; asst. prof. U. Nebr., Omaha, 1979—; assoc. prof. Creighton U., Omaha, 1979-81. Contbr. articles to profl. jours. Mem. adv. com. Iowa Western Coll., Council Bluffs, 1977-80, corp. fundraising Brownell Talbot Sch., Omaha, 1982; chmn. profl. div. United Fund Midlands, Council Bluffs, 1982-83. Served to capt. USAF, 1966-68. Grantee Am. Soc. Oral Surgeons, 1971, U. Nebr., 1971; named Employer of Yr., Omaha Dist. Dental Soc., 1982. Fellow Am. Coll. Oral and Maxillofacial Surgeons; mem. ADA, Iowa Soc. Oral Surgeons (pres. 1977, sec. 1986—, legis. chmn. 1986—), Omaha Dist. Dental Soc. (adv. com. 1981-82). Republican. Presbyterian. Lodge: Masons. Avocations: fishing, 4-wheeling, snow mobiling. Home: 108 S 51st St Omaha NE 68132 Office: 201 Ridge St Suite 308 Council Bluffs IA 51501

KULOW, KEITH RAYMOND, pediatrician; b. Hubbard, Ohio, Apr. 5, 1942; s. Raymond John and Nelle May (Wahler) K.; m. Elizabeth Kathryn Haag, Jan. 6, 1968; children: Karl Stephen, Kevin William. BS in Biology, Capital U., 1964; MD, Ohio State U., 1968. Diplomate Am. Bd. Pediatrics. Intern in pediatrics Columbus (Ohio) Children's Hosp., 1968-69, resident in pediatrics, 1971-73; practice medicine specializing in pediatrics, pres. Newark (Ohio) Pediatrics, Inc., 1973—; bd. dirs. Area VIII Profl. Standards Rev. Orgn., Zanesville, Ohio, 1980-82; chief of pediatrics Licking Meml. Hosp., Newark, 1982-84; speaker Reynolds & Reynolds, Dayton, Ohio, 1987—. Bd. dirs. 648 Bd. Mental Retardation, Newark, 1977-79; v.p. Cath. Social Services, Newark, 1980-82. Served to capt. U.S. Army, 1969-71, Vietnam. Decorated Bronze Star. Fellow Am. Acad. Pediatrics (mem. exec. com. Ohio chpt.); mem. AMA, Ohio State Med. Assn., Cen. Ohio Pediatric Soc. (sec., treas., v.p., pres. 1984-86), Licking County Med. Soc. (sec., treas. 1976-77, pres. 1981-82). Republican. Presbyterian. Club: Century (Newark). Avocations: fishing, gardening, golf, tennis, snorkeling. Office: 1634 W Church St Newark OH 43055

KULPRATHIPANJA, SANTI, chemist; b. Thailand, Sept. 18, 1944; came to U.S., 1968; s. Henglee and Morsul (Gor) Lim; B.S., Chulalongkorn U., 1968; M.S., East Tex. State U., 1970; Ph.D., Iowa State U., 1974; m. Apinya Prasertsintu, Nov. 25, 1974; children—Sathit, Ames, Ann. Research asso. M.I.T., Cambridge, 1975-78; research asso. Mass. Gen. Hosp., Boston, 1976-78; research asso. Harvard Med. Sch., 1977-78; sr. research chemist UOP, Inc., Des Plaines, Ill., 1978-81, research specialist, 1981-85; research specialist Allied-Signal Inc., Des Plaines, 1985—. Mem. Am. Chem. Soc., Soc. Nuclear Medicine, Chgo. Soc. Chromatography, Chgo. Catalysis Club, Phi Lambda Upsilon. Contbr. more than 20 articles to tech. jours. Numerous patents in field of separations. Home: 3920 Winston Dr Hoffman Estates IL 60195 Office: Signal Research Ctr 50 E Algonquin Rd Des Plaines IL 60017

KULUMANI, SAMBAMOORTHY MUTHUSWAMY, accountant; b. Tiruchirapalli, Tamil Nadu, India, Jan. 17, 1951; came to U.S., 1983; s. Muthuswamy Subbuswamy and Lakshami (Rukmani) K.; m. Vidya Sambamoorthy. B in Commerce, Nat. Coll., Tiruchirapalli, 1970. CPA, Ill. Audit clerk Krishnasamy & Jegianathan, Tirucru, India, 1970-74; qualified asst. R.G.N. Price & Co., Madras, India, 1974-75; internal auditor Canara Bank, Goa, India, 1975-77; sec., acct. Salgaocar Shipping Co., Goa, 1978-79; internal auditor Y.B.A. Kanoo, Saudi Arabia, 1979-83; Medicare auditor Aetna Life Ins. Co., Rosemont, Ill., 1984—. Mem. Am. Inst. CPA's, Ill. CPA Soc., Inst. Chartered Accts. India (assoc.), Inst. Co. Secs. India (assoc.). Avocations: stamp collecting, reading Leo Tolstoy and Somerset Maugham books, writing poetry. Home: 15 Sunset Ct Bensenville IL 60106 Office: Aetna Life & Casualty 10600 Higgins Rd Rosemont IL 60018

KUMAR, MARY LOUISE, physician, educator; b. Chgo., Jan. 23, 1941; d. Donald Martin and Esther (Acton) Morrison; m. Unni P. K. Kumar, June 15, 1968; children: Krishna, Shanta, Ravi, Maya. BA, U. Colo., 1962; MD, Case Western Res. U., 1967. Intern, resident Cleve. Met. Gen. Hosp., 1967-70, chief resident, 1970-71, instr. pediatrics, 1971-75, asst. prof., 1975-85; assoc. prof. Case Western Reserve Sch. Medicine, Cleve., 1985—. Office: Cleve Met Hosp 3395 Scranton Rd Cleveland OH 44109

KUMAR, SHAILENDRA, mechanical engineer, consultant; b. Agra, India, July 2, 1941; s. Ram Babu and Sushila (Gupta) K.; m. Shashi Kala Gupta, Jan. 16, 1967; children: Sanchay, Pankaj (Bobby), Neil. AS in Sci. and Math., Agra Coll., 1961; BSME, Am. Inst. Engring. & Tech., 1965; MS in Engring. Mgmt., George Washington U., 1967. Registered profl. engr., Wis. With various cons. engring., archtl. engring., contracting engring. firms, Ill., Mich., N.Y., D.C., 1965-82; founder, pres., cons. Shail & Assocs., Inc./ Energetic Bldg. Systems, Flossmoor, Ill., 1982—, also bd. dirs. Contbr. articles to profl. jours.; designer over 100 constrn. projects. Fellow Instn. Diagnostic Engrs. (founding mem.); mem. ASME, ASHRAE, Am. Inst. Plant Engrs. (cert.), Assn. Energy Engrs. (cert.), Am. Soc. Profl. Engrs. Hindu. Home: 18701 S Cypress Ave Country Club Hills IL 60477 Office: PO Box 421 Flossmoor IL 60422-0421

KUMAR, SUDHIR, biochemistry and neurology educator, researcher; b. Anjhi, India, Sept. 16, 1942; came to U.S., 1965; s. Sita Ram and Sarla (Agarwal) K.; m. Nilima Jain, Jan. 5, 1969; children: Avanti, Anjali. BS in Biology, U. Rajasthan, Jaipur, India, 1959, MS in Biochemistry, 1961; PhD in Biochemistry and Neurochemistry, U. Lucknow, India, 1966; postdoctoral Baylor Med. Sch., 1965-67. Sr. research scientist N.Y. State Res. Inst. of Neurochemistry, Wards Island, 1967-69; chief biochemist Meth. Hosp., Bklyn., 1969-73; research biochemist V.A. Hosp., Bklyn., 1973-75; dir. perinatal lab Christ Hosp., Oak Lawn, Ill., 1975-82; asst. prof. biochemistry and neurology Rush Med. Coll., Chgo., 1976-79, assoc. prof. 1979-83; dir., pres. clinical diagnostics Oak Forest, Ill., 1982—; prof. Rush Med. Coll. Chgo., 1983—; cons. scientist V.A. Med. Center, Hines, Ill., 1977-80; bd. dirs. Edn. Services, Inc., Flossmoor, Ill.; expert UNESCO and Tokten program Govt. of India, 1986-87. Editor: Biochemistry of Brain, 1980, Perinatal Medicine Vol. 1, 2, and 3, 1979-82, Advances in Brain Biochemistry, 1984; contbr. articles to profl. jours.; patentee in field. Pres. Lucknow U. Alumni Assn., 1976-78, 83-84; nat. v.p. Assn. Indians in Am., 1983-86, pres. Ill. chpt., 1983-86; bd. dirs. Festival of India, Ill., 1984-86. Recipient Outstanding New Citizen award Citizenship Council of Chgo., 1983; Research fellow C.S.I.R. 1962-65, fellow UNESCO & INSERM, 1971-73, Dreyfus Found. Research fellow, 1971-73; Travel grant Am. Inst. of Nutrition, 1981. Fellow N.Y. Acad. Scis., Nat. Acad. Clin. Biochemists, Royal Inst. Chemistry; mem. Am. Soc. Biol. Chemists, Am. Soc. Clin. Nutrition, Am. Soc. Neurochemistry, Soc. Pediatric Research, Am. Soc. Microbiology, Nat. Acad. Clin. Biochemists, Sigma Xi. Jain-Hindu. Club: Flossmoor Country. Lodge: Rotary. Avocations: stamp and coin collecting, tennis, travel. Home: 18901 Springfield Flossmoor IL 60422 Office: Clin Diagnostics 16405S Frontage Rd Oak Forest IL 60452

KUMINSKI, ARTHUR JOHN, mechanical engineer; b. Cleve., July 13, 1940; s. John Bernard and Stella Kuminski; m. Joanne Carol Bisesi; children: Carla Anne, John Philip. BSME, Cleve. State U., 1967. Plant engr. Universal Grinding Corp., Cleve., 1963-73; sr. mfg. engr. Tenna Corp., Cleve., 1973-76; design engr. Cert. Chem. and Equipment, Cleve., 1976-79; project engr. Kirby Co., Cleve., 1979-83, Invacare Corp., Elyria, Ohio, 1983-86; product engr. Leece-Neville div. Sneller-Globe, Cleve., 1987—. Democrat. Roman Catholic. Avocations: tropical fish, golf.

KUMMER, FRED S., institution management company executive; b. 1929. Student, U. Mo., 1952. Engr. William Ittner & Co., 1952-56; with Buckley Constrn. Co., Inc., 1957-59, Kummer Constrn. Co., Inc., from 1959; now pres., treas. HBE Corp., St. Louis. Office: H B E Corp 11330 Olive St Box 27339 Saint Louis MO 63141 *

KUMMERLE, HERMAN FREDERICK, electronics company executive, chemical engineer; b. N.Y.C., Apr. 25, 1936; s. Herman O. and Edyth K. (Osburg) K.; m. Joan D. Bell, June 1, 1957 (dec. July 1985); children: Anne R. Trachsel, Katherine L. Greenhill; m. Evelyn Hummon Holton, Mar. 1, 1986. BSChemE magna cum laude, NYU, 1957; MSChemE, U. Toledo, 1967. Registered profl. engr., Ohio. Research engr. Union Carbide Corp., Niagra Falls, N.Y., 1957-61; process engr. Maumee Chem. Co., Toledo, 1962-65; sr. engr., group leader Owens Ill., Toledo, 1965-67, chief chem. engring., 1967-72, mgr. devel. and engring. services, 1972-76, adminstrn. mgr. corp. tech., 1976-79, mgr. energy tech., 1979-84; v.p. tech. and operating services Ann Arbor (Mich.) Cirs., 1985—; mem. tech. rev. team Ohio Dept. Energy, Columbus, 1977-80; mem. environ. and energy subcom. Toldeo Econ. Planning Council, 1979-81. Contbr. articles to profl. jours.; patentee in field. Chmn. bd. dirs. Toledo Met. Mission, 1977-78; mem. exec. com. Toledo Area Council of Chs., 1977-78; bd. dirs. Friendly Ctr., Inc., Toldeo, 1973-76, 80-82; chmn. bd. trustees Toledo Dist. UMC, 1980-82. Served to capt. U.S. Army, 1961-62. Mem. Am. Inst. Chem. Engrs. (various offices), NSPE, Ohio Soc. Profl. Engrs., Toledo Soc. Profl. Engrs., Gas Research Inst. (gas firing reseach task force 1982-83), Glass Packaging Inst. (chmn. energy task force 1976-83), Tau Beta Pi, Phi Kappa Phi, Phi Lambda Upsilon, Sigma Xi. Methodist. Avocations: photography, tennis, bridge. Home: 5139 Olde Ridge Rd Sylvania OH 43560 Office: Ann Arbor Circuits 424 W Washington Ann Arbor MI 48103

KUMP, LARRY D(OUGLAS), public employee labor leader; b. Chambersburg, Pa., Jan. 27, 1948; s. Willis Theodore and Betty Ann (Steinbach) K.; m. Carolyn Anne Daniels, Dec. 3, 1976 (div. Sept. 1979); children: David Christopher, Sarah Elizabeth. Student Hagerstown Jr. Coll., 1965-68; BS, Frostburg State Coll., 1970; postgrad., U. Md., 1974, Ind. U., 1980. Chief exec. asst. to senate minority leader Pa. Senate, 1972; labor relations rep. Md. Classified Employees Assn., 1972-78; exec. dir. Ind. State Employees Assn., Indpls., 1978—; guest lectr. labor relations Ind. U., 1981—; vol. arbitrator Better Bus. Bur., 1982—; Rep. candidate for Md. Ho. of Dels., 1974; Rep. vice precinct committeeman, Indpls., 1981; mem. Marion County exec. com. Libertarian party, 1982-83; elder Mormon Ch. Named hon. Ky. col., 1984; Nat. Merit scholar. Mem. Assembly Govtl. Employees (pres. cen. region, nat. bd. 1978-85), Ind. Council for Econ. Edn., Ind. Mental Health Assn. (mem. pub. policy com.), Ind. Fiscal Policy Inst., Am. Arbitration Assn. (arbitrator). Home: 1517 E Ruth Dr Ravenswood IN 46240-3154 Office: Ind State Employees Assn 5 E Market St Suite 1326 Indianapolis IN 46204-3011

KUN, JOYCE ANNE, secondary teacher; b. Salem, Ohio, Oct. 20, 1946; d. Robert Malvern Slutz and Helen Roberta (Williams) Short; m. James Joseph Kun, June 10, 1978; 1 child, Jessica Erin. BS in Edn., Ohio U., 1969; MA in Tech., Kent State U., 1980. Cert. tchr., Ohio. Tchr. Ridgewood Local, West Lafayette, Ohio, 1970-71, Norton (Ohio) High Sch., 1971—. Mem. NEA, Ohio Indsl. Tech. Edn. Assn., NE Ohio Indsl. Tech. Edn. Assn. (officer 1972-78), Norton Tchrs. Assn., Epsilon Pi Tau. Lutheran. Lodges: Norton Grange, Barberton Moose. Avocation: bowling, golf, flower gardening. Home: 3500 Greenwich Rd Norton OH 44203 Office: Norton High Sch 4108 Cleveland-Massilon Rd Norton OH 44203

KUNDERT, ALICE E., school system administrator; b. Java, S.D., July 23, 1920; d. Otto J. and Maria (Rieger) K. Elementary tchr.'s cert., No. State Coll., Aberdeen, S.D., state tchr. cert. Tchr. elementary grades 1939-43, 48-54; clk., mgr., buyer Gates Dept. Store, Beverly Hills, Calif., Clifton Dress Shop, Hollywood, Calif., 1943-48; dep. supt. schs. Campbell County, S.D., 1954; county cts. clk. 1955-60, register deeds, 1955-69; town treas. Mound City, 1965-69; auditor State of S.D., Pierre, 1969-79; sec. of state 1980-87; coordinator sch. programs of S.D. Edn. and Cultural Affairs dept. Bicentennial U.S. Constn. and State Centennial, 1987—. Leader 4-H Club, 1949-53, county project leader in citizenship, 1963-64; sec. Greater Campbell County Assn., 1955-57; organizer, leader Mound City Craft and Recreation Club, 1955-60; chmn. Heart Fund, March Dimes, Red Cross, Mental Health drs.; mem. S.D. Gov.'s Study Commn., 1968—; mem. state and local adv. com. region VIII Office Econ. Opportunity; bd. mem., chmn. Black Hills Recreation Lab., 1956-61; exec. sec. Internat. Leaders Lab., Ireland, 1963; Polit. co. vice chmn. Republican Com., 1964-69, sec-treas. fin. chmn., 1968; mem. State Rep. Adv. Com., 1966-68; state and nat. counselor Teen Age Rep. Club Campbell County, 1964—. Named Outstanding Teenage Rep. adv. in nation, 1970, 71, 76; Recipient Disting. Alumni award No. State Coll., 1975. Home: 407 N Van Buren St Pierre SD 57501 Office: Office Sec of State State Capitol Bldg Pierre SD 57501

KUNEY, JACK RAY, retail executive; b. Adrian, Mich., Nov. 11, 1933; s. Lavon Blair and Yvonne H. (Johnson) K.; m. Carol C. Slowinski, Nov. 27, 1956; children: Kelly, Kevin, Karen, Pamela. BS, Mich. State U., 1955. Gen. mdse. mgr. J.C. Penney Co., Wayne, N.J., 1973-77, fashion mdse. mgr/, 1977-78; store mgr. J.C. Penney Co., Carsile, Pa., 1978-81; regional mdse. mgr. J.C. Penney Co., Pitts., 1981-84; store mgr. J.C. Penney Co., Cin., 1984—. Lodges: Kiwanis (v.p. Uniontown, Ohio chpt.), Masons. Home: 5932 Creekview Milford OH 45150 Office: JC Penney Co Eastgate Mall Cincinnati OH 45245

KUNIN, KALMAN CLARENCE, obstetrician and gynecologist; b. N.Y.C., June 9, 1920; s. Alex and Clara (Schneiderman) K.; m. Roberta Shine, Dec. 9, 1945; children: Jay Stuart, Dale Elizabeth, Richard David. BS, McGill U., Montreal, Can., 1941, MD, 1943; postgrad. in medicine, U. Pa., 1946-47. Diplomate Am. Bd. Ob-Gyn. Intern Royal Victoria Hosp., Montreal, 1943; resident in ob-gyn Hillcrest Hosp., Tulsa, 1947-48, Mt. Sinai Hosp., Cleve., 1948-51; practice medicine specializing in ob-gyn Youngstown, Ohio, 1951—; chmn. ob-gyn dept. Western Res. Care System, Youngstown, 1982-86; assoc. prof. ob-gyn, Neoucom, Rootstown, Ohio, 1982-86. Contbr. articles to med. jours. Recipient Pollock award Planned Parenthood, Youngstown, 1981. Fellow Am. Coll. Ob-Gyn, Am. Coll. Sugeons; mem. Cleve. Soc. Ob-Gyn, Youngstown Soc. Ob-Gyn (pres. 1968-79). Jewish. Clubs: Squaw Creek Country (Vienna, Ohio); Fripp Island Club (S.C.). Avocations: golf, flying. Home: 4137 Sampson Rd Youngstown OH 44505 Office: North Side Med Ctr 500 Gypsy Ln Youngstown OH 44501

KUNIN, MYRON, hair care company executive. Chmn., pres. Regis Corp., Edina, Minn., also dir. Office: Regis Corp 5000 Normandale Rd Edina MN 55436 *

KUNKEL, ROBERT LOUIS, psychiatrist; b. Cin., May 30, 1930; s. Theodore and Sophia (Kenning) K.; m. Maria A. Manganello, June 30, 1984; children: Robert L. Jr., Jerome A., Paul J., Mary C. BA, Athenaeum of Ohio, 1951; MEd, Xavier U., Cin., 1951; MD, U. Cin., 1961. Cert. Am. Bd. Psychiatry and Neurology. Instr. psychiatry U. Cin., 1965-69, asst. prof., 1969-70, assoc. clin. prof., 1979—; practice medicine specializing in psychiatry Cin., 1970—; cons. Wm. Mitchell Ctr., Cin., 1984—; co-med. dir. Emerson A. North Hosp., Cin., 1981-83; sec. dept. psychiatry Good Samaritan Hosp., Cin., 1971-73. Served to capt. U.S. Army, 1952-55. Fellow Am. Psyhiat. Assn.; mem. Ohio Psychiat. Assn. (co-editor newsletter 1981-84), Cin. Psychiat. Assn. Office: 2600 Euclid Ave Cincinnati OH 45219

KUNKLER, ARNOLD WILLIAM, surgeon; b. St. Anthony, Ind., Nov. 18, 1921; s. Edward J. and Selma (Hasenour) K.; m. Muriel Helen Burns, May 22, 1954; children: Lisa, Arnold William, Carolyn, Christine, Phillip, Kevin. A.B., Ind. U., 1943, M.D., 1949. Diplomate Am. Bd. Surgery. Intern, Ind. U. Med. Ctr., Indpls., 1949-50; asst. resident in surgery, fellow vascular surg. research Ind. U. Med. Ctr., 1950-54, resident in surgery, 1954-55, faculty, 1955—, clin. prof. surgery, 1976—; individual practice medicine specializing in gen. surgery, Terre Haute, Ind., 1955—; dir. med. edn. Terre Haute Regional Hosp., 1970-79; staff Terre Haute Center Med. Edn., Terre Haute Regional Hosp. Contbr. articles to profl. jours. Pres. Terre Haute Med. Edn. Found., 1972-73, 78-81, bd. dirs., 1967-86; pres. community adv. council Terre Haute Center Med. Edn., 1976-80; treas. Wabash Valley Community Blood Program, 1974-78 ; trustee Terre Haute Regional Hosp., 1978-84 , chmn. bd., 1981-84. Served with U.S. Army, 1943-46, ETO. Fellow ACS (pres. Ind. chpt. 1980-81); mem. Terre Haute C. of C., Ind. Med. Assn. (com. med. edn. 1986—), Vigo County Med. Soc., AMA, Pan Am. med. assns., Pan Pacific Surg. Assn., Midwest Surg. Assn., Aesculapian Soc. Wabash Valley, Soc. Abdominal Surgeons, Ind. Soc. Chgo. Democrat. Roman Catholic. Club: Country of Terre Haute. Home: 3515 Ohio Blvd Terre Haute IN 47803 Office: 4333 S 7th St Terre Haute IN 47802

KUNST, OTTO JOHN NICHOLAS, diagnostic radiologist; b. Rockville Centre, N.Y., May 9, 1946; s. Otto and Taimi Gertrude Maria (Aalto) K.; m. Laurel Ann Bassett, July 4, 1981; 1 stepson, Douglass Edward Gaus. Student, U. Miami, 1963-67, MD, 1971. Cert. diagnostic radiologist Am. Bd. Radiology. Intern U. Miami (Fla.) Affiliated Hosps., 1971-72; resident Jackson Meml. Hosp., Miami, 1972-75; asst. prof. radiology W.Va. U. Med. Ctr., Morganstown, 1977-79, clin. asst. prof. radiology, 1979—; radiologist Wheeling (W.Va.) Hosp., 1979-81; med. dir. dept. radiology Potters Med. Ctr., East Liverpool, Ohio, 1981—; radiologist Medina (Ohio) Radiology Group, Inc., 1987—. Co-author: Asbestos Related Disease, 1982. Served to maj. USAF, 1975-77. Mem. AMA, Am. Coll. Radiology, Am. Inst. Ultrasound in Medicine, Am. Acad. Thermology, Acad. Neuro-muscular Thermology, Phi Kappa Phi, Alpha Omega Alpha. Republican. Lutheran. Avocations: chess, swimming, coin and stamp collecting, church activities. Office: Medina Community Hosp 990 E Washington St Medina OH 44256

KUNTZ, JOHN KENNETH, religion educator; b. St. Louis, Jan. 20, 1934; s. John Frederick and Zula Belle (Reed) K.; m. Ruth Marie Stanley, July 7, 1962; children: David Kenneth, Nancy Ruth. BA, Grinnell Coll., 1956; BD, Yale U., 1959; PhD, Union Theol. Sem., 1963. Ordained to ministry, 1961. Tutor in O.T., Union Theol. Sem., N.Y.C., 1961-63; instr. Bibl. history Wellesley (Mass.) Coll., 1963-65, asst. prof., 1965-67; asst. prof. religion U. Iowa, Iowa City, 1967-70, assoc. prof., 1970-76, prof., 1976—, chmn. grad. studies Sch. Religion, 1980-83, chmn. lectures com., 1983—; active admissions com. U. Iowa Coll. Liberal Arts, 1985—, U. Iowa Study Abroad Com., 1985—. Author: The Self-Revelation of God, 1967, The People of Ancient Israel, An Introduction to Old Testament Literature, History and Thought, 1974; contbr. articles to profl. jours. Minister South Bethel United Meth. Ch., Tipton, Iowa, 1974-79. Recipient Huber Faculty Research award Wellesley Coll., 1966, Old Gold Faculty Research award U. Iowa, 1970, 79; Nat. Endowment Humanities grantee, 1971, 84; Alexander von Humboldt (Germany) fellow, 1971-72, 73, 79. Mem. Iowa Meth. Conf. Bd. Ministry, Am. Acad. Religion, Soc. Bibl. Lit., Am. Schs. Oriental Research, Cath. Bibl. Assn., Council Grad. Studies in Religion (sec.-treas.), Phi Beta Kappa. Democrat. Home: 321 Koser Ave Iowa City IA 52240 Office: U Iowa 313 Gilmore Hall Iowa City IA 52242

KUNTZ, MARY M. KOHLS, corporate treasurer; b. Chgo., Nov. 25, 1928; s. George William and Myrtle Hansen K.; m. Earl Jeremy Kuntz, July 28, 1957; children: Karen A., Bradford G. Student, Northwestern U., 1946-50. Pvt. practice acctg. Chgo., 1951-63; owner Chgo. Tax Service, 1954-63; controller Gen. Bus. Services, Chgo., 1960-68; v.p., treas. Gen. Tele-Communications, Inc., Chgo., 1968—. Leader Girl Scouts Am., 1968-71; pres. Wilmette (Ill.) PTA, 1971-75. Mem. Assn. Telemessaging Services Internat., Nat. Soc. Pub. Accts., Chgo. Soc. Clubs. Clubs: Women's Club of Wilmette (bd. dirs. 1975). Office: Gen Tele-Communications Inc 69 W Washington St Chicago IL 60602

KUNZ, DAVID NELSON, medical equipment company executive; b. Flint, Mich., Apr. 4, 1951; s. Nelson Wilton and Marjorie Marie (Hughes) K.; m. Janet Lynn Boddy, June 8, 1974; children: Rebekah Lynn, Benjamin David. BSME, U. Mich., 1973; MS in Bioengineering, U. Wyo., 1981. Prin. engr. Holley Carburetor Div., Warren, Mich., 1974-78; mgr. product devel. Stryker Corp., Kalamazoo, Mich., 1981-85; v.p. engring. Joerns Healthcare, Stevens Point, Wis., 1985—; cons. Environ. and Resources Techs., Brookfield, Conn., 1978-80. Mem. Ch. of Nazarene. Avocations: hunting, fishing, wildlife art. Home: 942 W Bayview Dr Mosinee WI 54455 Office: Joerns Healthcare Inc 5555 Joerns Dr Stevens Point WI 54481

KUNZE, MARY HELEN MONSEN, hospital administrator; b. Milw., Mar. 17, 1938; d. Maynard Adolph and Milda Frances (Seidl) Monsen; m. Peter Kurt Kunze, Jan. 21, 1961; children—Christopher Peter, Joseph Maynard, Elizabeth Irmgard, Anne Ludmilla. M.B.A., J.L. Kellogg Grad. Sch. Mgmt., Northwestern U., 1984. Adminstr. pediatrics dept. Med. Coll. Wis., Milw., 1976-80; dir. pediatric adminstrn. Milw. Children's Hosp., 1976-80, v.p. ambulatory services, 1980-85, v.p. acad. and external affairs, 1985— ; dir. Guadalupe Clinic, Milw., 1978—, Coalition Community Health Ctrs., Milw., 1980—. Bd. dirs. Health Care for the Homeless, 1984—, Robert Wood Johnson Found., 1984—; chmn. bd. trustees, bd. dirs. Ronald McDonald House. Mem. Ambulatory Assn. Roman Catholic. Clubs: Elm Grove Women's, Zonta, Tempo. Home: 1065 Lower Ridgeway Elm Grove WI 53122 Office: 1700 W Wisconsin St Milwaukee WI 53233

KUNZE, RALPH CARL, savings and loan executive; b. Buffalo, Oct. 31, 1925; s. Bruno E. and Esther (Graubman) K.; m. Helen Hites Sutton, Apr. 1978; children by previous marriage: Bradley, Diane Kunze Cowgill, James. BBA, U. Cin., 1950, postgrad., 1962-63; grad., Ind. U. Grad. Sch. Savs. and Loan, 1956, U. Calif., 1973. With Mt. Lookout Savs. & Loan Co., Cin., 1951-63, sec., mng. officer, 1958-63; with Buckeye Fed. Savs. & Loan Assn., Columbus, Ohio, 1963-77, exec. v.p., sec., 1967-70, pres., sec., vice chmn. bd. dirs., 1970-77; pres., chief operating officer, dir. Gate City Savs. and Loan Assn., Fargo, N.D., 1977-81; pres., chief exec. officer, dir. United Home Fed., Toledo, 1981—, also chmn. bd. dirs., 1985—; trustee Ohio Savings and Loan League. Mem. Toledo Com. 100, fin. com. Toledo Zoo; pres. Toledo Neighborhood Housing Services, 1981-83, United Way Franklin County, Ohio, 1977, also chmn. personnel com.; past pres. Ohio Soc. Prevention Blindness; campaign cabinet Toledo United Way; bd. dirs. Revitalization Corp. Toledo, 1983-84; trustee Kidney Found. Northwestern Ohio, Luth. Social Services, Wesley Glen Retirement Meth. Ctr., Toledo, 1974-77. Served with USNR, 1944-45. Mem. U.S. League Savs. Instns. Toledo Area C. of C. (bd. trustees), Lambda Chi Alpha. Club: Toledo. Lodges: Masons (32 deg.), Shriners. Home: 2606 Emmick Dr Toledo OH 43606 Office: 519 Madison Ave Toledo OH 43604

KUNZEMAN, JOHN WILBUR, state agency adminstrator; b. Beardstown, Ill., Mar. 27, 1948; s. Wilbur H. and Betty Ann (Bennett) K.; m. Susan L. King, OCt. 25, 1969 (div. Apr. 1978); 1 child, Kimberly Dawn. BS in Bus., Bradley U., 1970, MBA in Fin., 1971. Staff Ill. State Senate, Springfield, 1972-77, dir. appropriations, 1981—; chief fiscal officer Ill. Dept. Rehab. Services, Springfield, 1977-78; exec. dir. Ill. Pub. Aid. Commn., Springfield, 1978-79; dep. dir. Ill. Econ. Commn., Springfield, 1979-81. Republican. Lutheran. Avocation: golf. Home: 10 Twilight Ln Springfield IL 62707 Office: Ill State Senate 309 State House Springfield IL 62705

KUONI, JANE, home economics consultant, food stylist; b. Oconomowoc, Wis.; d. John Hans Christiansen and Dora Van Buskirk; widowed; children: Charles F. III, Todd. BS, Milw.-Downer Coll., 1944. Home economist Oscar Mayer, Madison, Wis., 1944-45, Kroger Food Found., Cin., 1946-47, Gen. Mills, Mpls., 1947-49; home econs. cons. Chgo., 1949—. Trustee Lawrence U., Appleton, Wis., 1981—. Mem. Am. Home Econs. Assn., Chgo. Home Econimists in Bus., Chgo. Architecture Found., Chgo. Profl. Photographers Assn. Home and Office: 111 E Chestnut 34C Chicago IL 60611

KUPER, ORLIN L., heat transfer manufacturing executive; b. Sioux Falls, S.D., Nov. 20, 1948; s. Luverne W. and Laura J. (Schoffelman) K.; m. Dianne Kay Struk, Apr. 14, 1972;children: Jaime Ellen, Jessica Laura. BSME, S.D. State U., 1967-72. Supr. Westinghouse Corp., Cin., 1963-76; sr. service engr. Electric Machinery, Mpls., 1976-79; facilities ngr. McCord Co., Canton, 1979-84, mgr. product design, 1984—. Recipient Energy award Dept. Energy, U.S. Govt., Washington, 1984. Mem. ASHRAE. Republican. Home: 2307 Harriet Lea Sioux Falls SD 57103

KUPLEN, ALBERT CLIFTON, lawyer, former insurance company executive, consultant; b. Crawford County, Kans., May 4, 1915; s. Albert and Goldie (Markey) K.; m. Ruth Caroline Laney, Feb. 13, 1937; children—Albert Clifton, Gregory Edward. Student Kans. State Coll., Pittsburg, 1933-35; J.D., U. Mo.-Kansas City, 1939. Bar: Mo. 1939, U.S. Supreme Ct. 1939. Assoc., Heckle Bros., Kansas City, Mo., 1939; sole practice, Kansas City, Mo., 1940-43, Lees Summit, Mo., 1946-47; claims atty. Western Ins. Cos., Fort Scott, Kans., 1947-67, asst. sec., 1967-72, asst. v.p., 1972-73, v.p. claims, claims atty., 1973-81; cons. in field; dir. Western Casualty & Surety Co., Western Firm Ins. Co.; mem. Kans. Gov.'s Adv. Com. on Workers Compensation, 1963-69. Served with JAGC, U.S. Army, 1943-46, Res., 1946-53. Mem. Mo. Bar Assn., Central Claims Execs. Assn. Episcopalian. Club: Ft. Scott Country. Home and Office: 1394 Marblecrest Dr Fort Scott KS 66701

KUPPLER, KARL JOHN, hospital administrator; b. Painesville, Ohio, June 22, 1955; s. Herman Gustav and Audrey Jean (Dumbeck) K.; m. Susan Marie Kompes, Aug. 18, 1979; children: Jason Karl, Ryan John. B.S. in Econs. and Bus., Allegheny Coll., 1977; M.S. in Hosp. and Health Services Adminstrn., Ohio State U., 1979. Grad. adminstrv. assoc. Ohio State U. Hosps., 1978-79; adminstrv. asst. Trumbull Meml. Hosp., Warren, Ohio, 1979, asst. exec. dir., 1979—. Loaned exec. United Way of Trumbull County, 1983—; mem. bldg., planning and zoning commn. of Cortland, Ohio. USPHS grantee, 1979. Mem. Am. Coll. Hosp. Adminstrs., Forum Health Service Adminstrn. (chmn. program com. 1982-83, pres. 1984-85), Jaycees of Warren. Lutheran. Lodge: Lions (treas. 1982-83, sec. 1983-85, pres. 1985-86). Home: 281 Corriedale Dr Cortland OH 44410 Office: 1350 E Market St Warren OH 44482

KUPST, MARY JO, psychologist, researcher; b. Chgo., Oct. 4, 1945; d. George Eugene and Winifred Mary (Hughes) K.; m. Alfred Proctor Stresen-Reuter Jr., Aug. 21, 1977. BS, Loyola U., 1967, MA, 1969, PhD, 1972. Postdoctoral fellow U. Ill. Med. Ctr., Chgo., 1971-72; research psychologist

Children's Meml. Hosp., Chgo., 1972—; practice clin. psychologist, Chgo., 1975—, McHenry, Ill., 1987—; assoc. prof. pediatrics & psychiatry, Northwestern U. Med. Sch., Chgo., 1980—. Editor: (with others) The Child with Cancer, 1980; contbr. articles to profl. jours. Mem. Am. Psychol. Assn., Ill. Psychol. Assn. Avocations: swimming, farming. Home: 7920 Howe Rd Ringwood IL 60072 Office: Dept Child Psychiatry Childrens Meml Hosp 2300 Childrens Plaza Chicago IL 60014

KURANZ, KYLE ALAN, communication executive; b. Aurora, Ill., May 22, 1940; s. Alfred Loren and Elsie Virginia (Peterson) K.; m. Bernice Elaine Orethun, July 31, 1965; children: Julie, Michelle, Kristine, Ann. BS in Edn., No. Ill. U., 1965; postgrad., Rockford (Ill.) Coll., 1984—. Artist Barber-Colman Co., Rockford, 1965-69, art dir., 1969-73, art supr., 1973-82, mgr. communications dept., 1982—; freelance artist, Rockford, 1965—. Contbr. articles to profl. jours. Youth leader Christ Our Savior Ch., Roscoe, Ill., 1979—; bd. dirs. Alcare Drug Abuse Ctr., Rockford, 1985—; mem. Congregations in Mission, Rockford, 1985—, Rockford Hist. Soc., 1985—. Named Craftsman of Yr., Craftsmen Rock River, 1973-74, 84-85, Craftmen 6th Dist., 1985-86. Mem. Internat. Assn. Craftsmen (pres. Rock River Valley 1971-73, 82-84, pres. 6th dist. soc. 1977-78)/. Republican. Lutheran. Club: Rock River Valley (pres. 1982-84). Avocations: reading, nature studies, fishing. Home: 11596 Crockett Rd Roscoe IL 61073 Office: Barber Colman Co PO Box 2940 Loves Park IL 61132

KURAS, RANDALL SCOTT, engineer; b. Chgo., Apr. 10, 1947; s. Gilbert Harry and Dorothy Elaine (Winkler) K.; m. Terry Lee Price, Aug. 1,1970 (div. June 1971); m. Pamela Fredd, Dec. 4, 1971; Philip Allen, Leslie Dianne. Student in engring., Carthage Coll., 1965-67; BS in Civil Engring., U. N.Mex., 1970; cert. in engring., Corps of Engrs., 1972; postgrad., U. Utah, 1973-74. Registered profl. engr., Ill., Wis. Project engr. Aluminum Co. Am., Port Comfort, Tex., 1974-75; project mgr. McClure Engr. Assocs., Grayslake, Ill., 1975-79; city engr. City of Prospect Heights, Ill., 1979-85; village engr. Village of Libertyville, Ill., 1985—; cons. RSK Cons., Gurnee, Ill., 1984—; pres. Omni Interests, Libertyville, 1977—; instr. Coll. of Lake County, Grayslake, 1980—. Served to 1st lt. U.S. Army, 1970-74. Lutheran Acad. scholar Luth. Ch. Carthage Coll., 1966. Mem. Am. Pub. Works Assn., Ill. Soc. Profl. Engrs. (sec. Lake County chpt. 1978-79, Young Engr. award 1978), Am. Water Works Assn. Republican. Lutheran. Avocations: carpentry, woodworking, photography. Home: 36586 Traer Terr Gurnee IL 60031-1345 Office: Village of Libertyville 200 E Cook Ave Libertyville IL 60048

KURATKO, DONALD F., business educator, consultant, funeral director; b. Chgo., Aug. 27, 1952; s. Donald W. and Margaret M. (Browne) K.; m. Deborah Ann Doyle, Dec. 28, 1979; 1 child, Christina Diane. B.A. in Econs., John Carroll U., 1974; M.S. in Mortuary Sci. and Adminstrn., Worsham Coll., 1975; M.B.A. in Mktg.-Mgmt., Ill. Benedictine Coll., 1979; D.B.A. in Small Bus. Mgmt., Nova U., 1984. Lic. funeral dir., Ill. Tchr., chmn. bus. dept. Immaculate Conception High Sch., Elmhurst, Ill., 1975-78; prof. bus. Ill. Benedictine Coll., Lisle, 1979-83; prof., coordinator small bus.-mgmt. and entrepreneurship Ball State U., Muncie, Ind., 1983—; funeral dir. Kuratko Funeral Home, North Riverside, Ill., part-time, 1975—; cons. Kendon Associates, Riverside, 1983—; dir. Ind. Cert. Devel. Corp., Indpls.; cons. Small Bus. Devel. Ctr., Muncie C. of C., 1985. Author: Management, 1984; Effective Small Business Management, 1986. Mem. editorial bd. Mid-Am. Bus. Jour., 1985—. Contbr. articles in field to profl. jours. Mem. Small Bus. Council, Muncie, 1984—. Named Tchr. of Yr., Immaculate Conception High Sch., Elmhurst, 1977, Prof. of Yr., Ill. Benedictine Coll., 1981, 83, Prof. of Yr., Ball State U., Muncie, 1984, 85, 86, 87, Outstanding Young Hoosier, Ind. Jaycees, 1985, one of Outstanding Young Men of Am., 1983, 84, named one of Outstanding Young Faculty, Ball Stae U. 1987. Mem. Nat. Acad. Mgmt., Internat. Council for Small Bus., Midwest Bus. Adminstrn. Assn., Midwest Case Writers Assn. Roman Catholic. Avocations: weightlifting; jogging. Home: 3500 S Robinwood Dr Muncie IN 47304 Office: Ball State U Coll Bus Muncie IN 47306

KURE, PATRICIA ANN, police social worker; b. Oak Park, Ill., Feb. 28, 1952; d. Fred Matthew and June Dorothy (Malkin) K. BS in Psychology and Sociology, Elmhurst (Ill.) Coll., 1974; MS in Guidance and Counseling, U. Wis., Whitewater, 1975. Police social worker Wheaton (Ill.) Police Dept., 1976-78; social worker Bensenville (Ill.) Home Soc., 1978-79; police social worker New Berlin (Wis.) Police Dept., 1979—; instr. police sci. Waukesha County Tech. Inst., Wis., 1982—, group facilitator, 1983—; hostage negotiator New Berlin Police Dept., 1982—. Bd. dirs. Family Service Waukesha County, 1983—, sec., 1984-86, treas., 1986—. Mem. Wis. Juvenile Officer Assn., Waukesha County Juvenile Officers Assn. Avocations: gardening, bicycling, camping, canoeing, reading. Office: New Berlin Police Dept 17165 W Glendale Dr New Berlin WI 53151

KURIT, NEIL, lawyer; b. Cleve., Aug. 31, 1940; s. Jay and Rose (Rainin) K.; m. Doris Tannenbaum, Aug. 9, 1964 (div.); m. Donna Chernin, Aug. 24, 1986. BS, Miami U., Oxford, Ohio, 1961; JD, Case Western Res. U., 1964. Bar: Ohio 1964. Prin. Kahn, Kleinman, Yanowitz & Arnson Co., L.P.A., Cleve., 1964—. Co-author Handbook for Attorneys and Accountants, Jewish Community Fedn. Endowment Fund. Trustee, v.p. Montefiore Home, 1983-87; trustee Jewish Community Fedn. Cleve., 1983-86. Mem. ABA, Ohio State Bar Assn. Home: 2870 Courtland Blvd Shaker Heights OH 44122 Office: Kahn Kleinman Yanowitz & Arnson Co LPA 1300 Bond Ct Bldg Cleveland OH 44114

KURKOWSKI, RICHARD MICHAEL, accountant; b. Chgo., June 15, 1949; s. Walter C. and Dolores (Kukla) K.; m. Dolores T. Spatz, June 17, 1972; (div. 1980); children—Michael, Richard. B.S., U. Ill., 1971, M.A.S., 1972. C.P.A., Ill. Audit supr. Arthur Young & Co., Chgo., 1972-77; fin. analyst Uarco, Inc., Barrington Ill., 1977-78; mgr. McDonald's Corp., Oak Brook, Ill., 1978-81; controller, treas. Spencer Stuart & Assocs., Chgo., 1981—. Mem. Am. Inst. C.P.A.s, Ill. Soc. C.P.A.s. Office: Spencer Stuart & Assocs 401 N Michigan Ave #2500 Chicago IL 60611

KURTICH, JOHN WILLIAM, architect, film-maker, educator; b. Salinas, Calif., Oct. 18, 1935; s. John Joseph and Elizabeth (Lyons) K.; B.A. in Theatre and Cinematography, UCLA, 1957; B.Arch., U. Calif.-Berkeley, 1966; M.S. in Architecture and Urban Design (William Kinne fellow, Fgn. Travelling fellow), Columbia U., 1968. Film-maker SMP, Architects, San Francisco, 1960-61; film-maker, archtl. draftsman McCue & Assocs., San Francisco, 1962-66; freelance film-maker, designer Friedberg, N.Y., 1968; instr. Sch. of Art Inst. Chgo., 1968-70, asst. prof., 1970-74, assoc. prof., 1974-82, prof., 1982—, chmn. dept. design and communication, 1977—, chmn. undergrad. div., 1987—, area head interior architecture; staff architect Am. Excavations, Samothrace, Greece, 1970—; archtl. cons. Fed. Res. Bank Chgo., 1978. Served with USNR, 1957-60. Recipient Architecture medal Alpha Rho Chi, 1966; grantee NEA, 1972, Woman's Bd. Art Inst. Chgo., 1973, Union Independent Colls. Art, 1974, Fulbright-Hays (Eng.), 1976, Fulbright-Hays (Jordan), 1981. Fellow Royal Soc. Arts (London); mem. AIA (corp. mem.), Soc. Archtl. Historians, Nat. Com. for Interiors, Chgo. Archtl. Club. Multi-media productions include: Hellas, Columbia U., N.Y.C., 1968, Art Inst. Chgo., 1971, 79; Muncie: Microcosm of America (NEA grant), Muncie, Ind., 1972; Legend of the Minotaur, Art Inst. Chgo., 1973; The Seasons, Shapes, Contrasts, Art Inst. Chgo., 1977, 1983, 84. Home: 2054 N Humboldt Blvd Chicago IL 60647 Office: Sch of Art Inst Chgo Dept Design and Communication Columbus Dr and Jackson Blvd Chicago IL 60603

KURTIDES, EFSTRATIOS STEPHEN, physician; b. Kilkis, Greece, July 4, 1930; came to U.S. 1955, naturalized 1963; s. Theodore and Agapy (Papadopoulos) K.; m. Elli Hamali, Aug. 17, 1958; children—Pauline, Theodore, Carl, John. Diploma Gymnasium, Kilkis, Greece; M.D., Aristotle U., Thessaloniki, Greece, 1954. Diplomate Am. Bd. Internal Medicine, Am. Bd Hematology. Instr., research fellow Northwestern U. Med. Sch., Chgo., 1961-63; assoc. in medicine, attending physician Northwestern Univ. and Evanston Hosps., Chgo. and Evanston, 1963-66, asst. prof. and sr. attending physician, 1966-76; assoc. prof., chmn. St. Joseph Hosp., Chgo., 1977-79; prof., chmn. Evanston Hosp., Ill., 1979—; bd. dirs. Evanston Hosp., 1980—, Northwestern Infirmary, Student Health Service, 1979—. Contbr. articles to med. jours. Mem. Sch. Bd. Caucus Dist. 65, Evanston, 1963-68. Named Physician of Yr., Evanston Hosp., 1966, 72, 73, 80; recipient Silver Plaque, Evanston Hosp. Medical Staff, 1977. Fellow ACP; mem. AMA, ACS (commn. cancer 1987), Am. Soc. Hematology, AAAS, Am. Soc. Internal Medicine, Am. Hosp. Assn. (rep. nat. commn. cancer 1987—), N.Y. Acad. Scis., Alpha Omega Alpha. Greek Orthodox. Club: Mich. Shores (Wilmette, Ill.). Avocations: reading; debate; backgammon; bicycling. Office: Dept Medicine Evanston Hosp 2650 Ridge Ave Evanston IL 60201

KURTZ, CHARLES JEWETT, III, lawyer; b. Columbus, Ohio, May 13, 1940; s. Charles Jewett, Jr. and Elizabeth Virginia (Gill) K.; m. Linda Rhoads, Mar. 18, 1983. BA, Williams Coll., 1962; JD, Ohio State U., 1965. Bar: Ohio 1965. Law clk. to presiding justice Ohio State Supreme Ct., Columbus, 1965-67; assoc. Porter, Wright, Morris & Arthur, Columbus, 1967-71, ptnr., 1972—. Mem. ABA, Columbus Bar Assn., Def. Research Inst., Columbus Def. Assn. (pres. 1976), Ohio Civil Trial Attys. Assn. Clubs: University, Columbus Country, Capital. Office: Porter Wright Morris & Arthur 41 S High St Columbus OH 43215

KURTZ, HAROLD PAUL, hospital administrator; b. Milw., May 21, 1936; s. Henry John and Minnie Christina (Olson) K.; m. Grace Jahn, June 16, 1963; children—Steven, David. B.A., Wartburg Coll., 1958; M.S., U. Wis., 1961. Journalist, Post-Crescent, Appleton, Wis., 1961-63; dir. pub. relations Lutheran Gen. Hosp., Park Ridge, Ill., 1963-73, Med. Coll. Wis., Milw., 1973-77, Children's Hosp., St. Paul, 1977—. Author: Public Relations for Hospitals, 1969; Public Relations and Fund Raising for Hospitals, 1981; (with M. Burrows) Effective Use of Volunteers, 1971. Editor: Toward a Creative Chaplaincy, 1973. Bd. dirs. Bd. Edn., Dist. 621, Mounds View, 1985—, treas., 1986—; bd. dirs. Spl. Intermediate Sch. Dist. 916, 1986—, United Hosp. Edn. and Research Inst., St. Paul, 1978-84, Minn. Internat. Health Vols., 1984-86. Recipient Community Service citation Wartburg Coll., 1970; named Boss of Yr., Internat. Assn. Bus. Communications. Mem. Chgo. Hosp. Pub. Relations Soc. (pres. 1971-72), Wartburg Coll. Alumni Assn. (bd. dirs. 1962-66). Lutheran. Home: 1465 17th Ave NW New Brighton MN 55112 Office: Children's Hosp 345 N Smith Ave Saint Paul MN 55102

KURTZ, JAMES EUGENE, freelance writer, publisher's representative; b. Altoona, Pa., June 28, 1928; s. Harry F. and Mildred (Sipes) K. Hon. DD, Ridgedale Theol. Sem., Chatanooga, 1975; hon D of Div., N.Am. Bible Coll., Dodge City, Kans., 1978. Editorial writer Altoona Tribune, 1962-64; minister Jackson Park Ch., Chgo., 1964-67; advt. mgr. Pacific Flush Tank Co., Chgo., 1968-78; freelance news corr. Chgo., 1978-82; freelance corr. Joliet, Ill., 1985—; pub.'s rep. Antioch Pub., Joliet, 1986—. Editor Opinion mag., 1980; contbr. articles to popular mags. Home: PO Box 3169 Joliet IL 60434

KURTZ, KAREN BARBARA, editor, writer; b. Ft. Dodge, Iowa, July 21, 1948; d. Clifford Wenger and Eleanor Marie (Ulrich) Swartzendruber; m. Mark Allen Kurtz, June 25, 1977. AA, Hesston Coll., 1968; BA in Edn., Goshen (Ind.) Coll., 1970; MA in Elem. Edn., Ind. U., 1975. Lifetime cert. elem. tchr. First grade tchr. Fairfield Community Sch., Goshen, 1970-79; asst. editor and advt. copywriter Barth and Assocs., Middlebury, Ind., 1986-87; free-lance writer Kurtz Lens and Pen, Goshen, 1979—. Author: Paper Paint and Stuff, 1984; asst. editor: Heritage Country Mag., 1986-87; contbr. articles to various mags. Ch. bd. dirs. Goshen City Ch. of Brethren, 1977, also chmn. stewardship dr., coordinator art in the ch. Mem. NEA, Ind. State Tchr.'s Assn., Fairfield Educators Assn. Republican. Club: Bayview. Avocations: collecting antique dolls, traveling, aviation.

KURTZ, LINDA FARRIS, social work educator; b. Kansas City, Mo., Jan. 19, 1939; d. C. Raymond and Marian Ruth (Kypke) Johnson; m. Carl E. Farris, Aug. 11, 1967 (dec. Oct. 1979); m. Ernest Kurtz, Aug. 23, 1980. BA, Washburn U., 1961; MSW, U. Pitts., 1964; D in Pub. Adminstrn., U. Ga., 1983. Social worker Mercy Hosp., Chgo., 1964-66, United Charities, Chgo., 1966-67, Ga. Mental Health Inst., Atlanta, 1967-78; asst. prof. U. Ga., Athens, 1978-84, U. Chgo., 1984-86; assoc. prof. Ind. U., Indpls., 1986—. Contbr. articles to profl. jours. Mem. Nat. Assn. Social Workers (cert.), Ind. Assn. Social Work Educators, Council Social Work Edn., Com. Advancement Social Work with Groups, Pi Alpha Alpha. Roman Catholic. Home: 5857 Brockton Dr Indianapolis IN 46220 Office: Ind U Sch Social Work 902 W New York St Indianapolis IN 46223

KURTZ, MARVIN ALPHAEUS, health science facility administrator; b. Wooster, Ohio, Dec. 18, 1946; s. Irvin Culp and Vera Nancy (Yoder) K.; m. Linda Darnell Smith, Feb. 21, 1976; 1 child, Kelli Renee Bredeweg. BA, Goshen (Ind.) Coll., 1969; MBA, Ind. U., 1977. CPA, Ind. Various acctg. positions Health and Hosp. Corp., Indpls., 1969-77; dir. fiscal services Elkhart (Ind.) Gen. Hosp., 1977-80, v.p. fin., 1980-86; v.p. fin., treas. Luth. Hosp. Ft. Wayne, Ind., 1986—. Mem. Am. Coll. Healthcare Execs., Am. Inst. CPA's, Ind. Healthcare Financial Mgmt. Assn. (bd. dirs. 1984-86, sec. 1986-87, dir., treas. 1987—, Follmer award 1984), Ind. Soc. CPA's. Avocations: camping, snow skiing, water skiing. Home: 3236 Copper Hill Run Fort Wayne IN 46804 Office: Luth Hosp Ft Wayne 3024 Fairfield Ave Fort Wayne IN 46807

KURTZ, RICHARD, otolaryngology; b. Chgo., June 5, 1934; s. Henry Zachary and Esther Evelyn (Lapin) K.; m. Geraldine A. Prince, July 14, 1957; children: Lynda C., Mary B., Henry S. BS, Ind. U., 1955; MD, Ind. U., Indpls., 1958. Diplomate Am. Bd. Otolaryngology. Intern Indpls. Gen. Hosp., 1958-59; resident in otorhinolaryngology Northwestern U., Chgo., 1959-62; practice medicine specializing in otorhinolaryngology Indpls., 1962—; chmn. dept. otolaryngology Winona Hosp., Indpls., 1987. Pres. bd. Indpls. speech and hearing ctr. United Way, 1978. Served to capt. U.S. Army, 1962-64. Fellow Am. Acad. Otolaryngology, Am. Soc. Cosmetic Surgery; mem. AMA, Ind. State Soc. Otolaryngology (pres. 1979), Marion County Soc. Otolaryngology (sec. 1980-86). Jewish. Avocation: computer tech. Office: 3351 N Meridian St Indianapolis IN 46208

KURTZ, WINIFRED MARY, club woman; b. Washington, Iowa, Aug. 28; d. Charles Sanford and Gertrude Josephine (Swift) Ragan; student Washington Jr. Coll., 1949-50, St. Ambrose Coll., Davenport, Iowa, 1950; m. Robert Kurtz, Sept. 12, 1951; 1 son, Michael R. Hostess, waitress Grand Lake Lodge, Colo., 1946; desk clk. Cosmopolitan Hotel, Denver, 1946; cashier Sears Roebuck & Co., Kansas City, Mo., 1947; tchr. Pleasant Hill Sch., Washington County, Iowa, 1950-51, Riverside Sch., Brighton, Iowa, 1952-53. Pres. dist. 11, Diocesan Council Cath. Women, 1972-74, 76-78, parish rep., 1970—, mem. nominating com., 1983; mem. legis. commn. Davenport Diocesan Council, 1983-84, 3d v.p., 1987—; Sunday sch. tchr. St. Joseph's Ch. East Pleasant Plain, Iowa, 1960-70, v.p. Altar and Rosary Soc., 1980-81; mem. entertainment com. Washington Care Ctr.; sec. Writers Round Table, 1966-80; asso. Citizens for Decency through Law, 1974—; pres. Pleasant Plain (Iowa) Sch. PTA, 1966-68; state historian Daus. Am. Colonists, 1966-68, state corr. sec., 1968-70, state 1st vice regent, 1972-74, state regent, 1974-76, 81-83, chmn. nat. def., 1976-78, vice-chmn. flag U.S.A., 1976—, chmn. state nominating com. 1982, mem. state nominating com., 1983-84, del. state assembly, 1983; state chmn. flag of U.S.A., DAR, 1976-78, nat. vice chmn. flag U.S.A., 1976-80, chpt. regent, 1971-73, 80-83, del. state conv., 1983, chmn. constn. com. Washington chpt. 1984—, chmn. Am. Indian Com., Washington chpt., 1985-87, bicentennial commn., 1985-87; mem. state nominating Dau. Am. Colonists, 1986; mem. Iowa Button Club. Republican. Home: Route 2 Brighton IA 52540

KURUMETY, SURYARAO, radiologist; b. Amadalavalasa, Andhra Pradesh, India, July 10, 1935; came to U.S., 1974; s. Damodaram and Mangaraju (Mandavilly) K.; m. Kamala Kancherla, Oct. 19, 1956; children: Suseela, Ravi Kumar, Sudharani, Usharani. Intermediate in scis., Andhra U., India, 1952; B. of Medicine, B. of Surgery, Madras U., India, 1970. Diplomate Am. Bd. Radiology. Radiologist Community Hosp., Marlette, Mich., 1982-84, St. Mary's Hosp., Saginaw, Mich., 1984-86; chief radiology Community Hosp., Caro, Mich., 1986—. Served to comdr., Med. Service Corps, USNR, 1975-82. Mem. AMA (Physician Recognition award 1984), Mich. State Med. Soc., Am. Coll. Radiology, Radiol. Soc. No.Am., Susruta Radiology Soc., East Cen. Mich. India Assn., Detroit Telugu Assn. Avocations: gardening, reading. Office: Community Hosp Dept Radiology Caro MI 48723

KURUP, VISWANATH PARAMESWARAN, microbiologist; b. Thattayil, India, Jan. 20, 1936; came to U.S., 1968; d. Parameswaran K. and Kunjulekshmi K. (Amma) Nair; m. Indira V. Kurup, Nov. 2, 1962; children: Mini, Manoj, Vinod. BS, Fergusson Coll., Poona, India, 1957; MS, U. Poona, 1959; PhD, U. Delhi, India, 1967. Mycologist Med. Coll., Trivandrum, Kerala, India, 1959-63, 67-68; post-doctoral fellow Ohio State U., Columbus, 1968-70; microbiologist St. Anthony Hosp., Columbus, 1970-73, VA Med. Ctr., Milw., 1973—; asst. prof. Med. Coll. Wis., Milw., 1973-77, assoc. prof., 1977-86, prof., 1986—; Fulbright vis. prof. to Finland, 1984. Contbr. numerous articles to profl. jours.; chpts. to books. Fund collector Leukemia Soc., Wis., 1983. Grantee NIH, VA, 1973—. Fellow Am. Acad. Microbiology; mem. Am. Acad. Allergy and Immunology, Internat. Soc. Human and Animal Mycology, Am. Soc. Microbiology, Mycol. Soc. Am. Home: Brookridge Dr Brookfield WI 53005 Office: VA Med Ctr Research Service 151 5000 W National Ave Milwaukee WI 53295

KURUTZ, ANDREW STEPHEN, industrial design; b. N.Y.C., May 18, 1952; s. Andrew Michael and Josephine Marie Theresa (Pottfay) K. BS in Indsl. Design, Phila. Coll. Art, 1974. Designer Gen. Motors Corp., Warren, Mich., 1973; draftsman Wenczel Tile Co., Trenton, N.J., 1974; designer Lenox China Inc., Trenton, 1974-76, Capitol Display Inc., Port Reading, N.J., 1976-77; sr. indsl. designer Am. Greetings Corp., Cleve., 1977-86; designer Libbey Glass, Toledo, 1986—. Designer Turbine Luxury Car Gen. Motors Corp., 1973, Subaru Brat Pick-Up Truck, 1975. Mem. Milestone Car Soc. Roman Catholic. Avocations: futuristic cityscape illustrator, display/merchandiser designer, graphic designer, jogger, classical music. Home: 3838 Sylvania Ave #302 Toledo OH 43623 Office: Libbey Glass PO Box 919 940 Ash St Toledo OH 43693

KURYLO, DIANE IRENE, advertising executive; b. Detroit, Feb. 3, 1955; d. Bohdan and Maria (Zhuk) Kurylo; m. Peter A. Kovalyshyn, May 25, 1980; children: John B., Andrea M. BA, Mich. State U., 1976; MA, Wayne State U., 1984. Program asst. Sta. WKBD-TV, Southfield, Mich., 1976-79; supr. Gen. Motors Corp., Flint, Mich., 1979-82; pub. relations writer Mt. Clemens (Mich.) Gen. Hosp., 1982-85; pres. Image Mgmt., Inc., Warren, Mich., 1985—. Editor: (manual) Credit: What You Don't Know Will Hurt You, 1986. Mem. Mich. Hosp. Pub. Relations Assn. (award of excellence for brochures 1985), Warren C. of C. (mktg. com. 1986). Byzantine Catholic. Avocations: reading, writing, travel. Office: Image Mgmt 23328 Sherwood Warren MI 48091

KURZEJA, WAYNE SAMUEL, real estate broker; b. Chgo., Jan. 29, 1946; s. Stanley Benny and Josephine Mary (Bovelli) K.; m. Mary Lou Czaja, Nov. 11, 1972. BA, ABS, Nat. Coll. Edn., Evanston, Ill.; OPM, Harvard U.; postgrad., John Marshall Law Sch. Lic. real estate broker. Advt. asst. to v.p. Dominick's Foods, Northlake, Ill., 1964-72; pres., chief exec. officer Advt. Service Co., Barrington, Ill., 1972-83.

KURZWEIL, ALAN DENNIS, social worker, marriage and family therapist, consultant; b. N.Y.C., May 27, 1950; s. Raffael and Hilda Molly (Meisel) K.; m. Paula Lee Backstrom, Oct. 24, 1971; children: Jeffrey Michael, Justin Henry. BA in Psychology, Allegheny Coll., 1971; MSSA, Case Western Reserve, 1976. Diplomate Clin. Social Work; lic. ind. social worker, Ohio. Theraeputic activities worker Polk (Pa.) State Sch., 1972-74; planning intern Geauga County Mental Health Bd., Chardon, Ohio, 1974-75; clin. social worker intern Akron Child Guidance Ctr., Barberton, Ohio, 1975-76; clin. social worker Western Reserve Human Services, Akron, Ohio, 1976—; pvt. practice marriage and family therapist Fairlawn, Ohio, 1983—; co-dir. Stages, Fairlawn, 1984—. Mem. health and physical edn. com. Akron Jewish Ctr., 1983—; coach Akron Indoor Soccer, 1986-87. Mem. Nat. Assn. Social Workers (dist. sec. 1980-82, dist. treas. 1982-86, mental health chairperson 1980—, dist. v.p. 1986-88), Registry Clin. Social Workers. Democrat. Jewish. Clubs: NW Akron Soccer (asst. coach 1986), Summit County Slow Pitch (team capt. 1984-86). Avocations: softball, raquetball, hiking, jogging, travel. Home: 1547 Kingsley Ave Akron OH 44313 Office: Fairlawn Med Bldg 3094 W Market St Suite 120 Fairlawn OH 44313

KUSEY, JULIUS, educator; b. Omer, Mich., July 1, 1931; s. Toney F. and Rose A. (Tellish) K.; B.S., Central Mich. U., 1957; M.S. in Art Edn., U. Wis., Madison, 1964. Tchr. art Rochester (Mich.) Community Sch. Dist., 1957—, kindergarten-through 12th grades art coordinator, 1975-81, art cons., 1957—; bd. dirs. Rochester Arts Commn., 1979-80. Sch. chmn. United Found., Rochester, 1959—; mem. Oakland County (Mich.) Cultural Councl, 1980—. Served with M.C., U.S. Army, 1952-55. Recipient Silver C Club award Central Mich. U., 1982, 25 Yrs. Continuous Teaching award Rochester Community Schs., 1982. Mem. Mich. Art Edn. Assn. (Elem. Art Tchr. of Yr. award 1971, Mich. Art Educator of Yr. 1983, pres. 1980-82, 82-84), Mich. Edn. Assn., Nat. Art Edn. Assn. (State Art Educator award Western region 1984), Am. Crafts Council, Internat. Soc. Edn. Through Art, Am. Hort. Soc., Am. Primrose Soc. Democrat. Roman Catholic. Office: 522 W Fourth St Rochester MI 48063

KUSTRA, ROBERT PAUL, dentist; b. Milw., Aug. 14, 1933; s. Leopold Martin and Irene Frances (Chmielewski) K.; m. Susan Lutter, June 23, 1965; children: Jennifer Lynn, Robert Paul Jr., Christopher George, Rebecca Ann. DDS, Marquette U., 1957. Gen. practice dentistry Janesville, Wis., 1959-60, Milw., 1960-62, Oak Creek, Wis., 1962—. Bd. dirs. Wis. Bd. Health, Franklin. Served to capt. U.S. Army, 1959. Recipient Jefferson award Am. Inst. Pub. Service, 1983. Mem. Wis. Soc. Dentistry for Children (Service award 1982). Republican. Roman Catholic. Avocations: spectator sports, skiing, travelling, map collecting. Home: 8710 W Hawthorne Ln Franklin WI 53132 Office: 9585 S Howell Ave Oak Creek WI 53154

KUTLER, BENTON, dentist, educator; b. Council Bluffs, Iowa, May 21, 1920; s. Harry and Sarah K.; m. Harriet Dorothy Lorkis, June 25, 1944; children: Laura, Robert, David, Howard, Bruce. BA, U. Iowa, 1942; DDS, Creighton U., 1945. Gen. practice dentistry Omaha, 1945—; asst. prof. Coll. Medicine U. Nebr., Omaha, 1945—, asst. prof. coll. dentistry, 1980—. Assoc. editor Chronicle; contbr. articles to profl. jours. Pres. Nebr. Found. Visually Handicapped. Served to lt. USN, 1945-46, 1952-54. Fellow AAAS, Acad. Gen. Dentistry, Internat. Coll. Dentistry; mem. ADA, Soc. Dentistry for Children, Am. Assn. Endodontists, Omaha Dist. Dental Soc. (pres. 1969-70), Nebr. Acad. Gen. Dentistry (past pres.), Pierre Fauchard Acad., Nat. Fed. Jewish Men's Clubs (area gov.), Sigma Xi. Club: Ak-Sar-Ben Gold Inlay. Lodge: Rotary (bd. dirs. 1983-86), Lions (dist. gov., chmn. Nebr. Sight Conservation Found.). Avocations: flying, reading. Home: 9909 Essex Dr Omaha NE 68114 Office: 321 Doctors Bldg 4239 Farnam Omaha NE 68131

KUTNICK, JACK D., dentist, consultant; b. Detroit, Dec. 7, 1918; s. Samuel and Ida (Dworkin) K.; m. Ann G. Rosenfeld, July 16, 1942; children: Steven, Peter, Sheldon. DDS, U. Detroit, 1942. Gen. practice dentistry Detroit, 1942—; nat. and internat. lectr. all phases of dentistry. Contbr. articles to profl. jours. Mem. Comprehensive Health Planning Council, Oakland County, 1975-79. Served to maj. dental corps U.S. Army, 1942-46. Fellow Acad. Gen. Dentistry (master), Acad. Dentistry Internat.; mem. Mich. Acad. Gen. Dentistry (pres. 1975-79), Detroit Dental Clinic Club (pres. 1972-74), B'nai B'rith. Democrat. Jewish. Avocation: sr. citizens affairs. Home: 29420 Farmbrook Villa Ct Southfield MI 48034 Office: 15 E Kirby Detroit MI 48202

KUTTY, KESAVAN, medical educator; b. Chittilenchery, India, June 1, 1949; came to U.S., 1973; s. Raman T.K. and Thankammal C.P. Menon; m. Claire Ann Birmingham, Sept. 15, 1981; 1 child, Ramani Latha. MedB, BS, Armed Forces Med. Coll., Poona, India, 1972. Diplomate Am. Bd. Internal Medicine, Am. Bd. Pulmonary Disease. Intern, resident Luth. Med. Ctr., Bklyn., 1973-76, chief resident, 1976-77; fellow in pulmonary disease Zablocki VA Med. Ctr., Milw., 1977-79; asst. prof. medicine Med. Coll. Wis., Milw., 1980-85, assoc. prof., 1985—; assoc. academic chmn. medicine, attending physician St. Joseph Hosp., Milw., 1981—; dir. respiratory therapy VA Med. Ctr., Milw., 1981—; cons. Good Samaritan Hosp., Northwest Gen. Hosp., New Berlin Meml. Hosp., Milw. Patnaik scholar Chief of Air Staff Medalist Armed Forces Med. Coll., 1968-69. Fellow Am. Coll. Physicians, Am. Coll. Chest Physicians; mem. Am. Thoracic Soc.,Am. Assn. Physicians from India (bd. dirs. Wis. chpt. 1985—), Wis. Thoracic Soc. (sec.-treas 1985-

87, pres. 1987—). Home: W140 N7866 Lilly Rd Menomonee Falls WI 53051 Office: St Josephs Hosp 5000 W Chambers St Milwaukee WI 53210

KUZNIAR, JOSEPH ALPHONSE, interior designer, lighting consultant; b. Chgo., Aug. 7, 1946; s. Stanley and Meta (Jedresak) K. Student Acad. of Lighting Arts, Chgo., 1965-66, Chgo. Acad. Fine Arts, 1965-68. Cert. residential lighting cons. Dir. store planning Homemakers Furniture, Schaumburg, Ill., 1973-76, Nelson Bros. Furniture, Ill. and Wis., 1977-78, Darvin Furniture, Orland Park, Ill., and Chgo., 1979-82; interior designer Kuzniar's and Assocs. Interior Design, Chgo., 1978—; interior design cons. Darvin Furniture and Nelson Bros. Furniture. Mem. Am. Soc. Interior Designers (assoc.), Interior Design Soc. Ill., Inst. of Bus. Designers. Roman Catholic. Avocations: church organist. Home: 523 S Lincoln St Addison IL 60101

KVIDERA, ALLEN P., periodontist, educator, researcher; b. Des Moines, Iowa, Feb. 2, 1948; m. Judy Kvidera; 3 children. BS, U. No. Iowa, 1970; DDS, U. Iowa, 1976, cert. in periodontology, 1978, PhD, 1985. Adj. faculty periodontics U. Iowa, Iowa City, 1978-80, 1986—; practice dentistry specializing in periodontics Davenport, Iowa, 1981—. Mem. ADA, Am. Acad. Periodontology, Am. Assn. Dental Research, Iowa Soc. Periodontology (pres. 1983-84). Home: 3526 Jersey Ridge Rd Davenport IA 52807

KWIAT, DONNA JEAN, interior designer; b. Chgo., May 29, 1957; s. Eugene V. and Evelyn Jean (Jachec) K. Student, Kent State U., 1975-76; BS in Design, U. Cin., 1981. Cert. interior designer. Contract interior designer Armco, Inc., Middletown, Ohio, 1981-82; office planner The Timken Co., Canton, Ohio, 1982-85, sr. office tech. analyst, 1986—. Cons. United Way Facilities Relocation, Canton, 1984. Recipient first prize Cleve. Press Ideal Room Contest, 1979. Mem. Am. Soc. Interior Designers, Network, Inc., U. Cin. Alumni Assn., Humane Soc. Club: Toastmasters. Avocations: tennis, physical fitness, music, piano, sewing. Home: 4805 South Blvd #3 Canton OH 44718 Office: The Timken Co 1835 Dueber Ave Canton OH 44706

KYLE, GEORGE WILLIAM, nuclear systems project engineer, consultant; b. Westerly, R.I., Aug. 9, 1945; s. Albert Groves and Dorothy Ella (Hill) K.; m. Miriam Angela Dupree, Feb. 1970. A.A. in Personnel Mgmt., A.S. in Data Processing, Southwestern Coll., 1976; B.G.S. in Computer Sci., Roosevelt U., 1982. Data systems tech., chief petty officer U.S. Navy, various locations, 1963-83; supr. plant computers Clinton Power Station, Ill. Power Co., Clinton, 1983, supr. nuclear info. systems, 1983-85, nuclear controls and instrumentation systems project engr., 1985—; owner, cons. Kyle Enterprises, Clinton, 1983—. Recipient 2nd Place Business award Bank of Am., 1976; Disting. Service award Arthritis Found., 1981; Appreciation award Mid-Pacific Roadrunners Club, 1982. Mem. Internat. Platform Assn., Alpha Gamma Sigma (pres. 1975). Club: Mid-Pacific Roadrunners. Lodge: Masons. Avocations: running, leatherwork, scuba diving. Home: 1 Nancy Ln RR 2 Box 156 Clinton IL 61727 Office: Ill Power Co Clinton Park Station 6 Mile E Rt 54 Clinton IL 61727

KYLE-RENO, SHELIA ANN, lawyer; b. Owensboro, Ky., Sept. 13, 1951; d. Herman William and Evelyn Maxine (Johnson) Kyle; m. Charles Edward Reno, Feb. 7, 1974; 1 child, La Mer Kyle-Reno. B.A., Wright State U., 1978; J.D., U. Dayton, 1983. Bar: Ohio 1983. Computer operator Owensboro Mcpl. Utilities, 1971-73; community organizer City Mgrs. Office, Owensboro, 1972-73; hotline coordinator Ky. Wesleyan U., Owensboro, 1971-73; law extern U.S. Magistrates, Dayton, 1981-82; law clk. Henley Vaugh Becker, Wald, Dayton, Ohio, 1982-83; atty. Legal Aid Soc. of Dayton, 1983—, EEO officer, 1983—, coordinator Contract Atty. Program, 1985—, mng. atty. family law unit, 1985—, coordinator client services, 1985—, acting exec. dir., 1986—. Pres. Womens Polit. Caucus, Dayton, 1980; mem. People for Am. Way, 1982. Key to City, City of Owensboro, 1971. Mem. ABA, Ohio Bar Assn., Dayton Bar Assn., Am. Acad. Trial Lawyers, Ohio Acad. Trial Lawyers, Miami Valley Assn. Women Attys., ACLU, NOW, Phi Alpha Delta. Democrat. Home: 5565 Hummock Rd PO Box 26425 Dayton OH 45426 Office: Legal Aid Soc Dayton 117 S Main St Suite 515 Dayton OH 45402

KYLES, CALVIN EUGENE, manufacturing company marketing executive; b. Lake Charles, La., Oct. 26, 1937; s. William and Hattie (Hagger) K.; student McNeese State Coll., 1957; B.B.A., Tex. Southern U., 1977; m. Girtha Lee Little John, Jan. 5, 1965; 1 dau., Yolanda Yvette. With Riverside Gen. Hosp., Houston, 1964-77, asst. adminstr., 1974-76, project dir. met. health founds. health maintenance orgn. feasibility study, 1974-76; system engr. Automated Health Services div. McDonnell Douglas Co., St. Louis, from 1977, now mktg. specialist. Pres., young adults NAACP, Lake Charles, 1959-61; scoutmaster Boy Scouts Am., 1959-61; pres. PTA Elementary Sch., Houston, 1974-77; mem. citizens participating com. City of Florissant (Mo.). Served with AUS, 1961-63. Recipient Parent Year award Fairchild Elementary sch., 1977; named Teammate of Distinction, McDonnell Douglas Co. Pres. sr. choir St. John Bapt. Ch., Houston. Home: 2085 Teakwood Manor Dr Florissant MO 63031 Office: 5775 Campus Pkwy Hazelwood MO 63042

KYRIAZOPOULOS, DIMITRIOS GEORGE, mathematics educator; b. Roino, Greece, Apr. 23, 1931; came to U.S., 1959; s. George and Eleni (Gavrilos) K.; m. Mary Vetsinouris, Apr. 7, 1983; children: Kiki, Patty, Joanna. BA, U. Okla., 1963; MEd, DePaul U., 1969; MS, Ill. Inst. Tech., 1970; PhD, Walden U., 1974. Instr. Indsl. Engr. Coll., Chgo., 1963-64; mgmt. Gestetner Corp., Chgo., 1964-65; sr. prof. math. Devry Inst. Tech., Chgo., 1965—. Mem. 24th Dist. Police Bd., Chgo., 1980-84; nat. supreme chmn. United Hellenic Voters, 1974-86; tchr. Greek and dancing, YMCA Community Coll., 1964-70. Mem. Math. Assn. Am., Am. Univ. Profs. Assn., United Hellenic Youth of Am. (founder 1979, pres. 1979-85). Republican. Home: 1218 W Byron Addison IL 60101 Office: DeVry Inst Tech 3300 N Campbell Chicago IL 60101

KYSELA, FRANCIS JOSEPH DANIEL, IV, dentist; b. Cleve., Jan. 31, 1930; s. Francis Joseph III and Ruth Clare (Denton) K.; m. Shirley Ann Ruby, Aug. 20, 1955; children: Francis Joseph V, Jerome Garwin. Student, John Carroll U., 1948-50, Marquette U., 1950-51; DDS, Marquette U., 1955. Gen. practice dentistry Cleve., 1955—. Fulbright Found. scholar Centro Escolar U., Philippines, 1955, Fulbright Found. scholar U. of East, Philippines, 1956; Fulbright U.S. Govt. grantee, Philippines, 1955-56. Fellow Acad. Gen. Dentistry; mem. ADA, Cleve. Dental Soc. (bd. dirs. 1972-78), Ohio Dental Assn., Cleve. Mus. Art, Les Amis Du Vin (dir. 1977—), Wine and Food Soc. (cellermaster 1983—), Chaine De Rotisseur (dir. food and wine 1977-82, vice conseilleur gastronomique), Delta Sigma Delta (pres. 1977-78). Republican. Roman Catholic. Clubs: Cleve. Yachting, Cleve. Print. Lodges: Morc Station 14 (commodore 1971-72), Rotary. Avocations: wine, food, sailing, gardening, art collecting. Home: 19790 Beachcliffe Blvd Rocky River OH 44116 Office: 4406 Rocky River Dr Cleveland OH 44135

LABADIE, DWIGHT DANIEL, lawyer; b. Pontiac, Mich., Dec. 16, 1940; s. Francis Edwin and Blanche Burdine (Yoakum) L.; m. Barbara L. Boyden, Sept. 5, 1964; children—Dwight D. Jr., Barbara L., Monique. BA, Kalamazoo Coll., 1963; JD cum laude, Wayne State U., 1971. Bar: Mich. 1971, U.S. Dist. Ct. Mich. 1971. Claim rep. Aetna Casualty Co., Detroit, 1964-68; workmen's compensation rep. Chrysler Corp., Highland Park, Mich., 1968-72; assoc. Davidson, Gotshall, Detroit, 1972-78; ptnr. Kohl, Secrest, Wardle, Lynch, Clark & Hampton, Farmington Hills, Mich., 1972—; atty. Detroit Workers Disability Compensation Council, 1981-83; lectr. Oakland U., Pontiac, 1984. Author newsletter, Current Law Notes, 1981—. Mem. State Bar Mich. (worker's compensation sect., negligence sect.), Nat. Rifle Assn. Club: Econ. Detroit, Cruise of Am. (Chgo.). Avocations: boating, sailing, hunting, scuba diving. Home: 1193 Roslyn Rd Grosse Point Woods MI 48236 Office: Kohl Secrest Wardle Lynch Clark & Hampton 30903 Northwestern Hwy Farmington Hills MI 48018

LABARBERA, ANDREW RICHARD, physiology and ob-gyn educator; b. Teaneck, N.J., Oct. 6, 1948; s. Mario Richard and Georgine (Mart) LaB. B.S. cum laude, Iona Coll., 1970; M.Phil., Columbia U. Coll. Physicians and Surgeons, 1974, M.A., 1974, Ph.D., 1975. Instr. dept. biology Iona Coll., 1970; NIH predoctoral trainee, 1971-75; staff assoc. Ctr. Reproductive Scis., Columbia U., N.Y.C., 1975-77; research fellow Mayo Grad. Sch. Medicine, Rochester, Minn., 1977-80; asst. prof. physiology Northwestern U. Med. Sch., Chgo., 1980-86, assoc. prof. physiology 1986—, asst. prof. ob-gyn, 1985-86, assoc. prof. ob-gyn, 1986—; dir. R.I.A. labs. Ctr. for Endocrinology, Metabolism and Nutrition, 1980-85; also dir. in vitro fertilization labs Prentice Women's Hosp. and Maternity Ctr., 1985—. Contbr. articles to profl. jours. Bd. dirs. West Wellington Condominium Assn., 1984-85; pres. Sangamon Loft Condominium Assn., 1985—. Recipient New Investigator award Am. Diabetes Assn., 1982; grantee Population Council, 1972-75, Northwestern U., 1980-81, USPHS-NIH, 1982—, U.S. Dept. Agr., 1986—. Mem. AAAS, Am. Inst. Biol. Sci., Am. Physiol. Soc., Am. Soc. Zoologists, Chgo. Assn. Reproductive Endocrinologists, Am. Fertility Soc., Endocrine Soc., Soc. Expl. Biology and Medicine, Soc. Study of Reproduction (chmn. info. mgmt. com. 1983-85, chmn. membership com. 1987—), Tissue Culture Assn., Lyric Opera Guild, Chgo. Symphony Soc., Art Inst. Chgo., Field Mus. Natural History, Sigma Xi, Beta Beta Beta. Avocation: music. Home: 913 W Van Buren 4D Chicago IL 60607 Office: Prentice Women's Hosp and Maternity Ctr 333 E Superior St Chicago IL 60611

LABATE, DAVID FREDERICK, financial analyst; b. Akron, Nov. 12, 1953; s. Frederick and Lenora (Long) LaB.; m. Frances Ann Paridon, June 4, 1976 (div. Dec. 1979); 1 son, Christopher Michael. B.S., U. Akron, 1975; M.B.A., 1979. Claims investigator Hartford Ins. Co., Akron, 1976-78; pricing analyst TLT Babcock Inc., Fairlawn, Ohio, 1978-79, fin. analyst, 1979-80; supr. gen. acctg. Lawson Co., Cuyahoga Falls, Ohio, 1980, fleet adminstr./fin. analyst, 1980-82, mgr. fin. analysis and fleet adminstrn., 1983-86, mgr. fin. reporting and acctg., 1986—. Roman Catholic. Home: 461 Loomis Ave Cuyahoga Falls OH 44221 Office: The Lawson Co 210 Broadway E Cuyahoga Falls OH 44222

LABBE, RONALD H., sales executive; b. New Bedford, Mass., May 3, 1950; s. Richard J. and Claire B. (Rainville) L.; 1 child, Michelle Deanne. BA, Jacksonville U., 1975. Sales rep. Burroughs Corp., Jacksonville, Fla., 1975-76, DAP Inc., Jacksonville, 1976-77; territory mgr. DAP Inc., Columbus, Ohio, 1977-79; dist. sales mgr. DAP Inc., Dayton, Ohio, 1979-82, regional sales mgr., 1982-85, dir. mgmt. devel. and tng., 1985—. Served with USN, 1968-72. Mem. Alpha Kappa Psi. Democrat. Roman Catholic. Avocations: golf, racquetball, aerobics. Office: DAP Inc PO Box 277 Dayton OH 45401

LABEAU, MARK HENRI, osteopath; b. Chgo., Aug. 19, 1951; s. Henri William and Elaine A. (Truchan) LaB. BS in Biology, Northeastern Ill. U., Chgo., 1974; DO, Coll. Osteopathic Medicine, Des Moines, Iowa, 1978; student, Art. Inst. Chgo., 1984—. Physician, instr. Chgo. Osteo. Med. Sch. and Hosp., 1980-81; osteo. physician Brandon Med. Assn., Chgo., 1981-83; gen. practice osteo. medicine Chgo., 1982-86, Rhema Med. Assn., Chgo., 1986—; clin. instr. Chgo. Osteo. Med. Sch., 1981—. Mem. AMA, Ill. Med. Soc., Chgo. Med. Soc., N.Y. Acad. Sci., Am. Assn. Fitness and Running, Am. Osteo. Assn., Ill. Osteo. Assn. Physicians and Surgeons, Am. Acad. Osteopthy, Osteo. Cranial Acad., Am. Osteo. Assn. Sports Medicine., Chgo. Sch. Massage Therpy (hon.). Roman Catholic. Clubs: Pine Point Ski, East Bank Health, Lincoln Park Volleyball, Lake Shore Ski (Chgo.). Avocations: fine arts, music composition, exercise. Office: 46 E Oak Suite 401 Chicago IL 60611

LABEDZ, BERNICE R., state legislator; b. Omaha, Sept. 19, 1919; m. Stanley J. Labedz, May 9, 1942; children—Terry, Jan, Toni, Frank. Student pub. schs. Former businesswoman, mem. Nebr. State Dept. Revenue, then mayoral, senatorial asst., pub. relations dir.; mem. Nebr. State Legislature, 1976—. Recipient community service awards. Office: Nebr State Capitol Bldg Lincoln NE 68509 Other: 4417 S 40th St Omaha NE 68107

LABELLE, CHARLES EARL, engineering manager; b. Laurium, Mich., Apr. 28, 1927; s. Charles E. and Sigrid A. (Jacobson) LaB.; children: Charles E. III, Renee J. Rewitzer. BSME, Mich. Tech. U., 1952; postgrad., Alexander Hamilton U., 1959. Registered profl. engr., Wis. Experimental engr. Clinton Engines, Maquoketa, Iowa, 1955-57; project engr. Thomas Industries, Sheboygan, Wis., 1957-63, engr. mgr., 1974—; design engr. Aro Inc., Tullahoma, Tenn., 1963-66; aircraft engine devel. engr. Continental Motors, Muskegon, Mich., 1966-70; research and devel. engr. Roper Corp., Bradley, Ill., 1970-74. Patentee in field. Served with USNR, 1945-46. Mem. ASME, Am. Soc. Testing Engrs., Soc. Automotive Engrs., Mich. Tech Alumni Club. Avocations: golf, woodworking, computing. Home: Rt 2 Box 592 Oostburg WI 53070

LABER, RICKY LEE, accounting executive; b. Port Huron, Mich., Aug. 16, 1957; s. Frederick and Patricia Geraldine (Gougeon) L.; m. Brenda Ruth Krell, Aug. 6, 1977; children: Justin Michael, Lindsey Ruth. BS in Bud. Adminstrn., Cen. Mich. U., 1979. CPA, Mich. Staff Ernst % Whinney, Jackson, Mich., 1979-81, sr., 1981-83, mgr., 1983-86, sr. mgr., 1986—. Treas. Jackson Jaycees, 1986, v.p. individual devel., 1985. Mem. Am. Inst. CPAs, Nat. Assn. Accts. (treas. local chpt. 1986-87), Mich. Assn. CPAs. Republican. Baptist. Avocations: golfing, stamp collecting, rocketry. Office: Ernst & Whinney One Jackson Sq Suite 900 Jackson MI 49201

LABIT, JAMES RICHARD, engineering manager; b. Washington, Mo., June 3, 1946; s. Emmanual Joseph and Mary Jane (Leber) L.; m. Barbara Ann Siess, June 7, 1969; children: James Andrew, Ann Katherine. BSME, U. Mo., Rolla, 1969, MS in Engring. Mgmt., 1979. Registered profl. engr., Mo., Calif., Can. Engr. Wagner Electric Corp., St. Louis, 1969-71, mgr. mfg., 1971-78; dir. engring. Nat. Marine Service, St. Louis, 1978-85; mgr. adminstrn. Fed. Res. Bank, St. Louis, 1985—. Mem. Adv. Bd. Community Coll. Dist., St. Louis, 1979-84. Mem. NSPE, Mo. Soc. Profl. Engrs., Soc. Engring. Mgmt., Soc. Naval Architects and Marine Engrs., Soc. Mfg. Engrs. Clubs: Propeller of U.S. (various offices), Toastmasters Intl. (St. Louis). Avocations: profl. musician, golf, sailing, mountain climbing.

LABRIOLA, ROSE ANN, nurse, hospital administrator, consultant; b. Chgo., Sept. 25, 1955; d. Saverio Carmen and Wilma Angelina (Aiello) Fortini; m. Joey Dean Labriola, Jan 4, 1975; 1 child, Deana Ann. BS, St. Xavier Coll., 1977, MS, 1984. RN. Staff nurse St. Francis Hosp., Blue Island, Ill., 1977-79, head nurse, 1979-80, charge nurse, 1980-83; clin. coordinator Parkview Orthopedics, Palos Hts., Ill., 1983-85; clin. dir. Silver Cross Hosp., Joliet, Ill., 1985—; cons. in sports medicine, Tinley Park, Ill., 1984—. Chairperson Am. Heart Assn., 1985—. Mem. Ill. Nurses Assn., Am. Assn. Critical Care Nurses (chairperson southside Chgo. area chpt., pres. 1979—, cert. intensive care), Am. Coll. Sports Medicine, Am. Legion. Avocations: softball, volleyball. Home: 16450 Manchester Tinley Park IL 60477

LABSVIRS, JANIS, economist, emeritus educator; b. Bilska, Latvia, Mar. 13, 1907; s. Karlis and Kristina L.; Mag.Oec., Latvian State U., 1930; M.S., Butler U., 1956; Ph.D., Ind. U., 1959. Tchr., Latvia, 1930-36; dir. dept. edn. Fedn. Latvian Trade Unions, 1936-37; v.p. Kr. Baron's U., Extension, Riga, Latvia, 1938-40, also exec. v.p. Filma, Inc., 1939-40; with UNRRA and Internat. Refugee Orgn., Esslingen, Germany, 1945-50; asst. prof. econs. Ind. State U., Terre Haute, 1959-62, assoc. prof., 1963-68, prof., 1969-73, prof. emeritus, 1973—; head dept. public and social affairs Latvian Ministry for Social Affairs, 1938-40; dir. Sch. of Commerce and Gymnasium, Tukums, Latvia, 1941-44. Danforth grantee, 1961; Ind. State U. research grantee, 1966. Mem. Am. Latvian Assn., Am. Assn. Advancement Slavic Studies, Assn. Advancement Baltic Studies, Am. Econ. Assn., Royal Econ. Soc. Lutheran. Author: Local Government's Accounting and Management Practices, 1947; A Case Study in the Sovietization of the Baltic States: Collectivization of Latvian Agriculture 1944-1956, 1959; Atminas un Pardomas, 1984; Karlis Ulmanis, 1987; contbr. articles profl. jours. Home: 3313 Hovey St Indianapolis IN 46218

LACEY, DANIEL DAMIAN, public relations executive, author; b. Wilkes-Barre, Pa., Apr. 30, 1950; s. Harold E. and Florence J. (Godlewski) L.; m. Margaret Mary Mulvey, Dec. 1, 1978. AS in Journalism, Luzerne County Community Coll., 1980; student, Wilkes Coll., Ohio U. Editor bus. sect. Scranton (Pa.) Times, 1979-81; editor Sunday bus. sect. Miami (Fla.) Herald, 1981; editor morning bus. sect Cleve. Press, 1982; assoc. editor Personnel Adminstr., Alexandria, Va., 1983; account exec. Dix and Eaton, Cleve., 1984-86; pres. Lacey and Co., North Olmstead, Ohio, Los Angeles, 1986—. Editor: (with others) Work in the 21st Century, 1984; contbr. articles to profl. jours. Mem. Am. Film Inst., Soc. Profl. Journalists (com. profl. devel. 1986—), Greater Cleve. Council of Smaller Enterprises, Sierra Club (exec. com. Pa. chpt. 1979-80). Roman Catholic. Home: 17615 Archdale Ave Lakewood OH 44107 Office: Lacey & Co 25000 Great Northern Corp Ctr Suite 300 North Olmstead OH 44070

LACEY, HOWARD RAYMOND, food technologist; b. Fitchburg, Mass., Mar. 18, 1919; s. Clarence Frederick and Sarah Lovisa (Hancock) L.; m. Dorothy Louise Daulton, Aug. 23, 1947; children—Howard R., Janet H. Lacey Wanink. B.S. in Chemistry, U. Mass., 1942. Processed foods inspector USDA, various locations, 1942-46; tech dir. P.J. Ritter Co. (now Curtice-Burns, Inc.), Bridgeton, N.J., 1946-67; gen. mgr., v.p. mfg. Brooks Foods (now Curtice-Burns, Inc.), Mt. Summit, Ind., 1967-74, tech. dir., 1974-85; pres. Lacey Assocs., Inc., 1985—; cons. Cape May Canners, N.J., Party Tyme Corp., N.Y.C.; instr. Better Process Control Sch., Purdue U., West Lafayette, Ind., 1981—. Inventor 100% corn sweetner added to catsup, improved method for firming diced red peppers, Stannous chloride added to asparagus. Asst. mgr. Little League Baseball, Bridgeton, N.J., 1958-61; merit badge counselor Boy Scouts Am., 1957-67; contbg. mem. U.S. Senatorial Club (Republican), Washington, 1978—, Rep. Nat. Com., 1982—. Recipient New Foods award Canner/Packer Mag., Bridgeton, 1957-67. Mem. Inst. Food Tech. (nat., Hoosier chpt., quality assurance sect.), Phi Tau Sigma. Club: Toastmasters (Bridgeton). Lodges: Masons, Elks. Avocations: tennis; reading; bicycling.

LACH, ALMA ELIZABETH, food and cooking writer, consultant; b. Petersburg, Ill.; d. John H. and Clara E. (Boeker) Satorius; diplome de Cordon Bleu, Paris, 1956; m. Donald F. Lach, Mar. 18, 1939; 1 dau., Sandra Judith. Feature writer Children's Activities mag., 1954-55; creator, performer TV show Let's Cook, children's cooking show, 1955; hostess weekly food program on CBS, 1962-66, performer TV show Over Easy, PBS, 1977-78; food editor Chgo. Daily Sun-Times, 1957-65; pres. Alma Lach Kitchens Inc., Chgo., 1966—; dir. Alma Lach Cooking Sch., Chgo.; lectr. U. Chgo. Downtown Coll., Gourmet Inst., U. Md., 1963, Modesto (Calif.) Coll., 1978, U. Chgo., 1981; resident master Shoreland Hall, U. Chgo., 1978-81; food cons. Food Bus. Mag., 1964-66, Chgo.'s New Pump Room, Lettuce Entertain You, Bitter End Resort, Brit. V.I., Midway Airlines, Flying Food Fare, Inc., Berghoff Restaurant, Hans' Bavarian Lodge, Unocal '76; columnist Modern Packaging, 1967-68, Travel & Camera, 1969, Venture, 1970, Chicago mag., 1978, Bon Appetit, 1980, Tribune Syndicate, 1982. Recipient Pillsbury award, 1958; Grocery Mfrs. Am. Trophy award, 1959, certificate of Honor, 1961; Chevalier du Tastevin, 1962; Commanderie de l'Ordre des Anysetiers du Roy, 1963; Confrerie de la Chaine des Rotisseurs, 1964; Les Dames D'Escoffier, 1982. Mem. U. Chgo. Settlement League, Am. Assn. Food Editors (chmn. 1959). Clubs: Tavern, Quadrangle (Chgo.). Author: A Child's First Cookbook, 1950; The Campbell Kids Have a Party, 1953; The Campbell Kids at Home, 1953; Let's Cook, 1956; Candlelight Cookbook, 1959; Cooking a la Cordon Bleu, 1970; Alma's Almanac, 1972; Hows and Whys of French Cooking, 1974. Contbr. to World Book Yearbook, 1961-75, Grolier Soc. Yearbook, 1962. Home and Office: 5750 Kenwood Ave Chicago IL 60637

LACH, CHRISTINE MARIE, real estate appraiser; b. Chgo., June 12, 1956; d. Walter T. and Violet A. (Ranieri) L.; m. Eric W. Hinds. BS in Fin., U. Ill., 1978. Appraisal trainee Home Savs. Assn., Houston, 1978-79; data collector Cole-Layer-Trumble, Houston, 1979; asst. v.p. Real Estate Research Corp., Chgo., 1986—; appraiser Allison-Bullitt-Hutchins, Inc., 1979-86. Mem. AAUW (pres. Montrose br. 1980-81). Home: 316 E Quincy St Riverside IL 60546 Office: Real Estate Research Corp 72 W Adams St Chicago IL 60603

LACHAPELLE, CLARK FRANCIS, dentist; b. Mpls., Apr. 8, 1936; s. Adrian Joseph and Eleanor (Schmitt) LaC.; m. Yvonne Marie Markgraf, Apr. 4, 1959; children: Jennifer Rae, Andrea Lee. BS with distinction, U. Minn., 1958, DDS, 1960; advanced dental internship, Madigan Gen. Hosp., 1960-61. Dentist USA Dental Corp., Tacoma, 1960-61, Milw., 1961-63; clin. instr. U. Minn. Dental Sch., Mpls., 1963-67; gen. practice dentistry Burnsville, Minn., 1963—; part owner, cons. Aspen Capital Group, Inc. Commr. Burnsville Indsl. Commn., 1969-80; campaign dir. City of Burnsville, 1966, 68, commr. 1969-80. Served to capt. U.S. Army, 1960-63. Mem. ADA, Acad. Gen. Dentistry, Mpls Dental Soc., St. Paul Dental Soc., Bloomington Study Club, Am. Soc. Dentistry for Children (pres. 1970-71), Omicron Kappa Upsilon. Republican. Roman Catholic. Clubs: Mendakota Country, Burnsville Athletic. Avocations: golf, kit car builder, skiing, world wide travel. Home: 13409 1st Ave Burnsville MN 55337 Office: Ridge Point Med Bldg #205 14050 Nicollet Ave Burnsville MN 55337

LACHAT, MICHAEL RAY, Christian ethics educator; b. Chgo., Sept. 5, 1948; s. Nicholas John and Iva Louise (Petrey) La C. BA magna cum laude, Nebr. Wesleyan U., 1970; MDiv magna cum laude, Harvard U., 1973, PhD, 1980. Visiting asst. prof. Liberal Studies St. John's U., Collegeville, Minn., 1980-82; asst. prof. Christian ethics Meth. Theol. Sch. in Ohio, Delaware, 1982-86, assoc. prof., 1986—; mem. Ethics and Econs. Council, Columbus, Ohio, 1982—; del. Ohio State U. Commn. on Interprofl. Edn. and Ppractice, Columbus, 1983—; cons. bioethics com. Riverside Meth. Hosp., Columbus, 1985—; lectr. Nebr. Wesleyan U., 1985. Editor Troeltsch and Modern Theology, 1986; contbr. articles to profl. jours. precinct committeeman, chmn. membership drive Delaware County Dem., 1982—; bd. dirs. People In Need, Inc., Delaware, Ohio, 1982-84. Mem. Am. Acad. Religion, Soc. for Christian Ethics, Sierra Club, Phi Kappa Phi. Lodge: Moose. Avocations: fishing, weightlifting, folk music, camping. Home: 1333-A E Towne Ln Delaware OH 43015 Office: Meth Theol Sch in Ohio 3081 Columbus Pike Delaware OH 43015

LACHENAUER, ALESIA MARIE, graphic designer; b. Detroit, Dec. 2, 1961; d. Richard Paul and Barbara Ann (Stickney) L. Student, Northwestern Mich. Coll., 1980-82, Grand Valley State Coll., 1983-85. Framer pictures Frames Unltd. Grand Rapids (Mich.), 1985; keyliner, designer Utley Bros., Inc., Troy, Mich., 1985-87; designer Billy Whitelaw and Talented Friends, Detroit, 1987—. Democrat. Lutheran. Avocations: painting, music, movies. Home: 2114 Clawson Royal Oak MI 48073

LACKEY, GWYNETH ELDRED, magazine editor; b. Chgo., Apr. 21, 1956; d. Melvin Willard and Louana Mae (Engelhart) L.; m. Stephen Michael Rynkiewicz, Nov. 27, 1976 (div. Feb. 1980). BA, U. Wis., 1976. News editor Instns. Mag. (name now Restaurants and Instns.), Chgo., 1976-77; editor Chain Report, Chgo., 1977-81; head dept. communications Howe (Ind.) Mil. Sch., 1984-85; corr. South Bend (Ind.) Tribune, 1984-86; editor Electronic House mag., Mishawaka, Ind., 1985—. Pres. Friends of the El, Chgo., 1979; leader Girl Scouts Am., Elgin, Ill., 1979-81. Democrat. Episcopalian. Clubs: RENEW (Elgin) (pres. 1982-83); Corfu (Chgo.) (v.p. 1979-82). Avocation: sports cars. Home: 103 Old Stable Ln Mishawaka IN 46545 Home: Cedar Lake Rd Howe IN 46746 Office: Electronic House Mag 524 E McKinley Ave Mishawaka IN 46545

LACKEY, JEFFERY IRVIN, manufacturing executive; b. Indpls., Jan. 2, 1944; s. Clyde Irvin and Geneva Winnie (Collier) L.; m. Barbara Joan Rudy, June 14, 1969; children: Jil Ileen, Jay Irvin. BS in Physics, Rose Hulman Inst. Tech., Terre Haute, Ind., 1966; MSE in Engring. Mechanics, U. Mich., 1971, postgrad., 1971-73. Cert. Quality Engr., Reliability Engr. Devel. engr. BF Goodrich, Akron, Ohio, 1966-69, sr. research and devel. engr., 1974-81; research assoc. BF Goodrich, Brecksville, Ohio, 1981-86; mgr. statistical systems BF Goodrich, Akron, 1986; research asst. U. Mich., 1969-74; mgr. statis. methods Uniroyal Goodrich, Akron, 1986—. Contbr. papers to profl. jour. Judge Northease Ohio Sci. Fair, Akron, 1986. Hwy. Safety Research Inst. fellow, Ann Arbor, Mich. 1970-71. Mem. Am. Soc. Quality Control (sr.), Soc. Experimental Mechanics, Quarter Century Wireless Assn. (sec. treas. 1984-86). Avocations: amateur radio, gardening, cake decorating. Home: 1186 Temple Trails Stow OH 44224 Office: Uniroyal Goodrich Tire Co 600 S Main St Akron OH 44397

LACKRO, PAUL WILLIAM, III, plant metallurgist; b. Langley AFB, Va., July 21, 1945; s. Paul William Jr. and Marie (Goettel) L.; m. Elizabeth Mask, Jan. 25, 1969; children: Andrea, Christopher. BS, Drexel U., 1980. Technician Foote Mineral Co., Exton, Pa., 1969-80, tech. analyst, 1980-83;

process metallurgist Foote Mineral Co., Keokuk, Pa., 1983-84, plant metallurgist, 1985—. Served to 1st lt. U.S. Army, 1965-68, Vietnam. Decorated Bronze Star with oak leaf cluster. Mem. Am. Soc. Quality Control, The Metall. Soc., Am. Legion. Avocations: astronomy, music, chess, golf, swimming. Home: #1 Greenbrier Ct Keokuk IA 52632 Office: Foote Mineral Co Comml St Keokuk IA 52632

LACOURSIERE, ROY B., psychiatrist; b. Windsor, Ont., Can., Aug. 9, 1937; s. Lionel and Cecile (Robinet) L.; m. Marilyn E. Marshall, Sept. 9, 1961 (div. Apr. 1974); children: Jacqueline, Joan, Colette; m. Joanna Durrance, Sept. 25, 1982; 1 stepchild, Eric. BA with honors, U. Windsor, 1962; MD, McGill U., Montreal, Can., 1966. Diplomate Am. Bd. Psychiatry and Neurology, Diplomate Am. Bd. Forensic Psychiatry. Intern then resident Menninger Sch. Psychiatry, Topeka, Kans., 1966-71; dir. community service office Menninger Found., Topeka, 1971-74; chief chem. problems treatment unit VA Hosp., Topeka, 1975—, cons. psychiatry, 1972-74; practice medicine specializing in forensic psychiatry Topeka, 1973—; vis. prof. Washburn U. Law Sch., Topeka, 1974—; mem. Shawnee Community Alcohol/Drug Adv. Com., Topeka, 1980-85. Author: The Life Cycle of Groups, 1980; contbr. articles to profl. jours. Vestry, St. David's Episc. Ch., Topeka, 1985—. Fellow Am. Psychiat. Assn., ACP, Royal Coll. Physicians and Surgeons Can.; mem. Am. Acad. Psychiatry and Law, Am. Acad. Forensic Scis. Avocations: travel, reading. Home: 34 Pepper Tree Ln Topeka KS 66611 Office: VA Hosp Topeka KS 66622

LACOURT, LUIS, oral and maxillofacial surgeon; b. Rio Piedras, P.R., May 5, 1944; s. Luis and Elizabeth (Lopez) L.; m. Annie Sanchez, July 7, 1968; childern: Luis E., Carlos I. BS, U. P.R., 1964, DDS, 1968. Diplomate Am. Bd. Oral and Maxillofacial Surgery. Intern VA Hosp., San Juan, P.R., 1968-69; oral and maxillofacial surgeon U. P.R. Hosp., San Juan, 1970-73; practice dentistry specializing in oral and maxillofacial surgery San Juan City Hosp., 1973-78, chief dental services, 1974-78; practice dentistry specializing in oral and maxillofacial surgery Marion, Ohio, 1978—. Fellow Am. Assn. Oral and Maxillofacial Surgery; mem. ADA, Marion Acad. Dentistry (pres. 1983). Roman Catholic. Lodge: Kiwanis. Avocation: golf. Home: 1625 Oxford Rd Marion OH 43302 Office: 285 Mt Vernon Ave Marion OH 43302

LACY, HERMAN EDGAR, management consultant; b. Chgo., June 21, 1935; s. Herman E. and Florence L.; children: Frederick H., Carlton E., Douglas H., Jennifer S., Victoria J., Rebecca M. BS in Indsl. Engring., Bradley U., 1957; MBA, U. Chgo., 1966. Cert. mgmt. cons. Plant mgr., indsl. engring. supr. Hammond Organ Co., Chgo., 1961-66; mgr. corp. indsl. engring. Consol. Packaging Corp., Chgo., 1966-68; mgr. mgmt. cons. Peat, Marwick, Mitchell & Co., Chgo., 1966-70; dir. ops. Wilton Enterprises, Inc., Chgo., 1970-77; v.p., gen. mgr. Intercraft Industries Corp., Chgo., 1978-79; pres. Helmco Cons., Inc., Glenview, Ill., 1979—; instr. Roosevelt U., Oakton Coll., Harper Coll. Served to capt. USAF, 1957-61. Mem. Inst. Indsl. Engrs. (past pres., founder North suburban Ill. chpt.), Am. Mgmt. Assn., Nat. Council Phys. Distbn. Mgmt., Soc. Mfg. Engrs., Inst. Mgmt. Cons. Office: Helmco Cons Inc 1920 Waukegan Rd Glenview IL 60025

LACY, RAYMOND A., commodities firm executive, consultant; b. Kansas City, Mo., Nov. 23, 1942; s. Anthony L. and Mary Ann (Kusan) L.; m. Helen E. Lawless, Nov. 20, 1965; children: Timothy, Robert, Mark, Suzanne. AS, Donnelly Coll., 1962; BS, U. Kans., 1965. CPA, Kans. Auditor Touche, Ross & Co., Kansas City, Mo., 1965-71; mgr. corp. acctg. Iowa Beet Processores, Dakota City, Nebr., 1971-74; v.p., asst. sec. REFCO, Inc., Chgo., 1974—. treas. Saddle Brook Home Owners Assn., Oak Brook, 1982-84, Highland PTA, Downers Grove, Ill., 1982-84, Hamerschmidt PTA, Lombard, Ill., 1978-79, Boy Scouts Am., Lombard, 1982-86. Mem. Am. Inst. CPAs, Nat. Assn. Accts. (dir. Sioux City chpt. 1972-74). Republican. Roman Catholic. Avocation: golf. Home: 183 Saddle Brook Dr Oak Brook IL 60521 Office: REFCO Inc 111 W Jackson Chicago IL 60604

LADAGE, KENNETH CHARLES, broadcasting executive; b. Springfield, Ill., Sept. 3, 1944; s. henry Isaac and Mary Amelia (Kvitkauska) L.; m. Judith Ann Fredrickson, Aug. 27, 1967; children: Alexander Charles, Megan Elizabeth. BS, U. Ill., 1967. Program dir. Sta. WICD-TV, Champaign, Ill., 1967-73, Sta. WOWT-TV, Omaha, 1973-78; dir. program ops. Sta. WRTV-TV, Indpls., 1978—. Exec. producer (TV program) Battle for Breath, 1982 (Birmingham Film Festival award 1982), The World Comes to In, 1984 (Ohio State award 1985). Fund raiser Indpls. Opera Co., 1983. Mem. Nat. Assn. TV Program Dirs. (IRIS award 1976, 85), U. Ill. Alumni Assn. of Indpls., Sigma Phi Epsilon Alumni Assn. (pres. 1970-73). Democrat. Lutheran. Club: Indpls. Advt. Avocations: golf, jogging, reading, tennis, swimming. Office: Sta WRTV-TV 1330 N Meridian Indianapolis IN 46206

LADAGE, WANDA LEE MAXSON, nursing educator; b. Elm Grove Twp., Kans., Dec. 5, 1929; d. Irvin Ray and Geneva Irene (Duncan) M.; m. Jack C. Goodwin, Aug. 14, 1947; children—Penny Bennett, Paula Van Nice, Kim McMunn, Mona Garrett; m. 2d, Dwayne Curtis Ladage, May 19, 1979. A.D.Nursing, Labette Community Coll., 1972; B.S.N., Kans. State Coll., Pittsburg, 1976; M.S., Pittsburg State U., 1979, Ed.S., 1980; Ph.D., Kans. State U., 1985. Staff nurse Coffeyville (Kans.) Meml. Hosp., 1972-74, house supr., 1974-76; dir. edn. Parsons (Kans.) State Hosp. & Tng. Ctr., 1976-77; nursing instr. Labette Community Coll., Parsons, Kans., 1977-81, dir. nursing edn., 1981—. Mem. adv. bd. and pharmacy bd. Elm Haven Nursing Home; active Am. Diabetes Assn., others. Named Student Nurse of Yr., Labette Community Coll., 1972; Employee of Yr., Coffeyville Meml. Hosp., 1975. Mem. Labette County Farm Bur., Ogan. for Advancement Assoc. Degree Nursing (chairperson Kans. Chpt.), Sigma Theta Tau. Democrat. Mem., Ch. of the Brethren. Club: Katy Golf Assn. Lodge: Order Eastern Star.

LADD, KENNETH PAUL, clergyman, counselor; b. Delphos, Ohio, Aug. 3, 1938; s. Lawrence Andrew and Velma (May) L.; m. Kay Elaine Saunders, July 15, 1961; children—Kristine Lynn (dec.), Kevin Lee, Kim Leann, Karin Lynette. B.A., Huntington Coll., 1962; M.Div., United Thwol. Seminary, 1966; Ph.D., U. Beverly Hills, 1983. Cert. tchr., Ohio. Ordained to ministry United Methodist Ch., 1966; pastor Antioch Christian Ch., Ottoville, Ohio, 1958-59, Goblesville Cir. Evangel. United Brethren Ch., Huntington, Ind., 1960-62, Salem Evangel. United Brethren Ch., Bettsville, Ohio, 1962-65, First Evangel. United Brethren Ch., Wauseon, Ohio, 1965-67, St. Paul's United Meth. Ch., Bloomville, Ohio, 1967-68; chaplain Maumee Youth Camp, Liberty Center, Ohio, 1968-80; dir. Counseling Center, Wauseon, 1980—; pastor Taylor United Meth. Ch., Delta, Ohio, 1980, Beulah United Meth. Ch., Winameg, Ohio, 1981—. Bd. dirs. Valley Oak Council Camp Fire Youth, 2d v.p.; chmn. Ohio Youth Commn. Chaplains; bd. dirs. Four County Mental Health Bd. Mem. Ohio State Chaplains Assn. (1st v.p.), Wauseon Ministerial Assn. (past pres.), Am. Assn. Counseling and Devel., Am. Personnel and Guidance Assn., Am. Mental Health Counselors Assn., Am. Assn. Profl. Hypnotherapists, Ohio Mental Health Counselors Assn., Ohio Assn. Counseling and Devel., Hope (bd. dirs.), Fellowship Christian Magicians, Internat. Brotherhood of Magicians, Soc. Am. Magicians. Contbr. chpts. to books; author courses of study for use with alienated youth; developer workshops under fed. grant. Home: 234 E Superior St Wauseon OH 43567 Office: 120 W Chestnut St Wauseon OH 43567

LADD, SIDNEY LARRY, pharmacist; b. Muskegon, Mich., Apr. 2, 1932; s. Sidney Archibald and Louisa True (Olson) L.; m. Marlene Ann Haliburda, Sept. 2, 1956 (div. July 1979); children: Walter C., Dee Ann, Nancy Jean, Carol Ann; m. Linda Burton Cavender, Aug. 16, 1982. BS in Pharmacy, Ferris State Coll., 1954. Pharmacist Simpson Pharmacy, Muskegon, 1954-59, D.C. Johnson, Muskegon, 1959-60; prin. Ladd Pharmacy, Muskegon, 1960—. Bd. dirs. Mona Lake Improvement Assn., Muskegon, 1985. Mem. W. Mich. Pharmacy Assn. (bd. dirs. 1956-57). Republican. Roman Catholic. Club: Mona Lake Boat (commodore 1982, bd. dirs. 1986). Lodges: Elks, Vikings. Avocations: cabinet making, boating, art. Home: 1162 Ransford Ln Muskegon MI 49441 Office: Ladd Pharmacy 4230 Henry St Muskegon MI 49441

LADEHOFF, LEO WILLIAM, metal products manufacturing executive; b. Gladbrook, Iowa, May 4, 1932; s. Wendell Leo and Lillian A. L.; m. Beverly Joan Dreessen, Aug. 1, 1951; children: Debra K., Lance A. B.S., U. Iowa, 1957. Supt. ops. Square D Co., 1957-61; mfg. mgr. Fed. Pacific Electric Co., 1961; v.p. ops. Avis Indsl. Corp., 1961-67; pres. energy products Group Gulf & Western Industries, Inc., 1967-78; chmn. bd., pres., chief exec. officer, dir. Amcast Indsl. Corp., Ohio, 1978—; bd. dirs. Krug Internat., Inc., GF Bus. Equipment Co., Soc. Bank N.A., Hobart Bros., Troy, Ohio. Mem. Dayton Area Progress Council. Served with USAF, 1951-54, Korea. Mem. Am. Foundrymen's Soc., Soc. Automotive Engrs., Iron Castings Soc., Dayton Area C. of C., Dayton One Hundred Club, Newcomen Soc., U. Alumni Alumni Assn., Alpha Kappa Psi. Republican. Clubs: Moraine Country, Dayton Racquet. Home: 4501 Troon Trail Dayton OH 45429 Office: Amcast Indsl Corp 3931 S Dixie Ave Kettering OH 45439

LADLY, FREDERICK BERNARD, health services company executive; b. Toronto, Ont., Can., July 14, 1930; s. John Bernard and Olivia Montgomery (Fenimore) L.; m. Sharon Mary Davidson; children: Patricia, Elizabeth, Katherine, Martha, Sarah, Meghan. B.A., U. Toronto, 1951. Gen. mgr. internat. ops. Can. Packers Inc., Toronto, 1973, v.p., 1974-78, dir., 1975-84, exec. v.p., 1978-84; pres., chief exec. officer Extendicare Health Services Inc., Toronto, 1984—; chmn., chief exec. officer United Health, Inc., Milw., 1984—; bd. dirs. Crownx Inc., Toronto, 1986—. Clubs: Toronto Lawn Tennis, Beaver Valley Ski.

LADRIGAN, JAMES DEE, communications executive; b. Cin., Mar. 6, 1947; s. Frank James and Dorothy Jane (Taylor) L.; m. Patricia Ann Krzynowek, Jan. 24, 1970 (div. June 1979); children: Timothy James, Sean Alden; m. Sompon Charletyam, June 12, 1982. Student, Edgecliff Coll., 1972, Univ. Cin., 1977-81. Installation mgmt. Cin. Bell. Telephone, 1978-80, bus. office mgmt., 1980, mem. divestment task force, 1980-82; v.p. MRC Telecommunications, Cin., 1984—. Active Rep. Nat. Com. Served to sgt. USMC, 1965-72. Mem. World Trade Club. Methodist. Club: Mercedes Benz of Am. (Cin.). Avocations: world travel, fishing. Home: 598 Wooster Pike Terrace Park OH 45174

LAFATA, JOSEPH SAMUEL, accountant; b. St. Louis, Aug. 6, 1958; s. Samuel Joseph and Josephine Anita (De Caro) L.; m. Lynette Ann Murphy, May 3, 1986. BSBA, U. Mo., 1980. CPA/. Jr. acct. Bournstein & Bender, CPA's, St. Louis, 1981-82; staff acct. Bournstein & Assocs., CPA's, St. Louis, 1982-83; mgr. Robert E. Wright & Co., PC, St. Louis, 1983-86; sr. tax acct. Brown, Smith, Wallace, Librach, Seltzer & Gordon CPAs, St. Louis, 1986—. Fellow Am. Inst. CPA's, Mo. Soc. CPA's; mem. Am. Mgmt. Assn. Office: Brown Smith Wallace Librach & Gordon 168 N Meramec Clayton MO 63105

LAFATA, SALVATORE (SAM), health care administrator; b. Detroit, Jan. 31, 1945; s. Victor and Rose (Licavoli) L.; m. Patricia Kinney, Aug. 7, 1971 (div. July 1980); Amy Elizabeth, Sarah Ann, Kathleen Marie; m. Donna M. Baranek, Sept. 11, 1981; 1 child, Elizabeth Suzanne. Student, Ctr. Creative Studies, Detroit, 1963-67; BA, Mercy Coll. Detroit, 1976. Asst. adminstr. J.L. Posch, M.D., Detroit, 1971-76; customer relations mgr. Kinney Bros. Wall Coverings, Oakland, Calif., 1977-79; adminstr. Hand Therapy Services, Detroit, 1979-81; adminstr., owner Ctr. Evaluation and Rehab., Inc., Warren, Mich., 1981—. Served with U.S. Army, 1967-70. Mem. Warren C. of C. Roman Catholic. Lodge: Rotary. Home: 24370 Santa Ana Warren MI 48093 Office: Ctr for Evaluation and Rehab Inc 11012 E 13 Mile Rd Warren MI 48093

LAFEVER, HOWARD NELSON, plant breeder, geneticist, educator; b. Wayne County, Ind., May 13, 1938; s. Samuel L. and Flossie B. (Ellis) L.; m. Kay M. Schutz, Aug. 30, 1958; children—Julie, Jeff. B.S., Purdue U., 1959, M.S., 1961, Ph.D., 1963. Instr. Wis. State U., LaCrosse, 1963; assoc. prof. Purdue U., West Lafayette, Ind., 1963; research geneticist USDA-Agrl. Research Service, Starkville, Miss., 1963-65; plant breeder, prof. agronomy Ohio State U., Ohio Agr. Research and Devel. Ctr., Wooster, 1965—; cons. Ohio Found. Seeds, Croton, 1967—, Rohm & Haas Corp., Phila., 1975-78. Patentee Ruler, Titan, Adena wheats plus 10 other small grain varieties; contbr. numerous articles to profl. jours. Grantee John Deere, 1982-84, Eli Lilly, 1984, 85, Quaker Oats, 1984, 85—. Mem. Am. Soc. Agronomy (bd. dirs. 1982-84, assoc. editor 1982-85), Assn. Ofcl. Seed Certifying Agys., Ohio Seed Improvement Assn. (dir. 1968-83, grantee 1975-85). Presbyterian. Club: Gnat Boxers (Wooster) (treas. 1983-84). Avocations: woodworking; golf. Home: 2739 Heyl Rd Wooster OH 44691 Office: Ohio State U-Ohio Agrl Research and Devel Ctr 1680 Madison Ave Wooster OH 44691

LAFF, CHARLES RUDER, health care executive, financial consultant; b. Chgo., Mar. 17, 1942; s. Milton M. and Bertha (Ruder) L.; divorced; children: Michael, Joshua. BS in Accountancy, U. Ill., 1963. CPA, Ill. Treas. Budget Rent-a-Car, Chgo., 1965-71, v.p., fin. treas., 1971-73; v.p. InterContinental Service, Chgo., 1973-75; pres. In Home Health Care, Morton Grove, Ill., 1975—; fin. cons., Northbrook, Ill., 1976—, Pub. Funding Corp., Morton Grove, 1982—. Contbr. article to publs. Mem. Am. Inst. CPA's, Nat. Assn. for Home Care (membership com.), Ill. Soc. Home Health Agys. (reimbursement com.). Republican. Jewish. Home: 2764 Wilshire Ln Northbrook IL 60062

LAFLEUR, AVIS ANN, accountant; b. Thief River Falls, Minn., Mar. 30, 1932; d. Cleve and Sena (Johnson) Bergum; m. Robert F. LaFleur, Aug. 2, 1950; children: Mitchell, Mark, Jon. BS, Nat. Coll., Rapid City, S.D., 1978. CPA, S.D. Pvt. practice acctg. Rapid City, 1983—. Mem. Am. Inst. CPA's, S.D. Soc. CPA's. Republican. Lodge: Zonta. Avocations: bridge, reading. Home: 3218 Iris Dr Rapid City SD 57702 Office: 2040 W Main # 309 Rapid City SD 57702

LA FOLLETTE, DOUGLAS J., secretary state of Wisconsin; b. Des Moines, June 6, 1940; s. Joseph Henry and Frances (Van der Wilt) LaF. B.S., Marietta Coll., 1963; M.S., Stanford U., 1964; Ph.D., Columbia U., 1967. Asst. prof. chemistry and ecology U. Wis.-Parkside, 1969-72; mem. Wis. Senate 1973-75; sec. state State of Wis., Madison, 1975-79, 83—. Author: Wisconsin's Survival Handbook, 1971. Mem. Council Econ. Priorities; mem. Lake Michigan Fed., Wis. Environ. Decade, 1971, S.E. Wis. Coalition for Clean Air, Democratic candidate for U.S. Congress, 1970, Democratic candidate for Wis. lt. gov., 1978. Recipient Environ. Quality EPA, 1976. Mem. Am. Fedn. Tchrs., Fedn. Am. Scientists, Phi Beta Kappa. Office: Office Sec State PO Box 7848 Madison WI 53707

LAFOUNTAIN, LESLIE JOSEPH, language educator; b. Belcourt, N.D., July 3, 1959; s. Joseph F. and Shirley M. (Gunville) LaF. Student, State Sch. Sci., Wahpeton, N.D., 1977-78; BS, N.D. State U., 1984. Cert. tchr., N.D. Resource tchr. Ojibwa Indian Sch., Belcourt, 1984-85; language resource trch. Dunseith (N.D.) Day Sch., 1985—; advisor Indian club Dunseith Day Sch., 1985-86. Chmn. Turtle Mountain Indian Hist. Soc., N.D., 1981—; v.p. Save the Children Fedn., Dunseith, N.D., 1985-86; mem. steering com. H.O.P.E. Orgn./War Against Alchohol and Drug Abusers, Belcourt, 1986. Named One of Outstanding Young Men of Am., 1985. Mem. N.D. Indian Affairs Commn. (rep. 1985-86). Democrat. Roman Catholic. Avocations: native Am. arts and crafts, traveling, horse back riding. Home: Box 893 Dunseith ND 58329

LA FOUNTAIN, WILLIAM LOUIS, psychotherapist, writer; b. Chgo., Apr. 2, 1928; s. William Louis and Lucille (Roos) La F.; children: Ellen, Joan, Janet. BA, Valparaiso (Ind.) U., 1950; MDiv, Luth. Sch. Theology, Chgo., 1954. Pastor Ascension Ch., Pontiac, Mich., 1956-61; exec. dir. Luth. Student Found., Athens, Ohio, 1961-66, Luth. Student Fedn., Champaign, Ill., 1966-72, Family Counseling Service, Aurora, Ill., 1972-81; pvt. practice psychotherapy Aurora, 1982—. Author: Setting Limits, 1981, Parents in Crisis, 1987. Pres. Mental Health Assn., Athens, 1964; mem. Human Rights Commn., Aurora, 1976-77. Mem. Am. Assn. for Marriage and Family Therapy (clin.), Am. Assn. Family Counselors and Mediators. Office: 403 W Galena Blvd Aurora IL 60506

LAFRAMBOISE, LYLE BERNARD, architect, engineer; b. Ft. Yates, N.D., Sept. 4, 1934; s. Joseph Emmett LaFramboise and Floreine Vivian (Patchen) Walling; m. Karen J. Davis, Apr. 23, 1966; children: Jon, Sarah, Clifford, Benita, Brian, Eva, Casey, Emmaline, Lynnette, Janice, KayeLynn, Thomas, Jill, Kerry, Michael. BSCE, U. Utah, 1971. Registered profl. engr., S.D., N.D., Mont., Utah, Ariz. Party chief J.A. Terteling, Boise, Idaho, 1967-69, Brown Constrn., Salt Lake City, 1970; project coordinator H. Fagg & Assocs., Billings, Mont., 1971-72; gen. mgr. Standing Rock Housing Corp., McLaughlin, S.D., 1972-76; project coordinator Dana Larson Roubal, Pierre, S.D., 1976-81; pres., owner Eagle 2000 Engring. and Design, Inc., Pierre, 1981—. Chmn. Pierre Indian Parent Com., 1982-85, Black Hills Indian Council, Rapid City, S.D., 1982-85. Served with U.S. Army, 1956-58. Mem. NSPE, S.D. Soc. Civil Engrs., S.D. Minority Contractors Assn. (chmn. 1984-85), Am. Indian Council Architects and Engrs. Democrat. Mormon. Lodge: Elks. Avocations: golf, chess. Home: 603 Circle Dr Rapid City SD 57701 Office: Eagle 2000 Engineering and Design Inc 201 Main Suite G Rapid City SD 57701

LAFRENIERE, PETER ALAN, dentist; b. Ishpeming, Mich., June 24, 1958; s. Rudolph John and Patricia Lael (Beauchcine) L. BS, U. Mich., 1980, DDS, 1984. Practice gen. dentistry Negaunee, Mich., 1984—. Mem. ADA, Acad. Gen. Dentistry. Democrat. Lutheran. Avocations: photography, art, music. Home: 117 Heritage Dr Negaunee MI 49866 Office: 200 Marquette St Negaunee MI 49866

LAGES, JOHN DAVID, economist, educator; b. Denver, Jan. 25, 1936; s. Charles Richard and Ruth (Lewis) L.; m. Pamela Nisen, Nov. 18, 1961; children: Jane Elizabeth, Christopher Rowland. AB cum laude, Cen Meth. Coll., 1957; MA, U. Mo., 1958; PhD, Iowa State U., 1967. Instr. econs. Iowa State U., Ames, 1958-59; asst. prof. bus. adminstrn. Coll. of Pacific, Stockton, Calif., 1959-60; mem. faculty S.W. Mo. State U., Springfield, 1963—, prof. econs., 1971—; bd. dirs. Ozarks Labor Union Archive; vice chmn. bd. City Utilities of Springfield, 1979-81; cons. in field. Author: (with C. Ketch) Religious-Economic Survey of Springfield, Mo., 1966, Manpower Demand Survey of Selected counties of Missouri, 1967; The Tourist Industry in Missouri: An Analysis, 1986; Ozarks Union Archive Newsletter, 1985—. Chmn. Springfield Archives devel. com. Bd. Hist. Sites; mem. Mayor's Energy Task Force, 1982-83. Iowa State U. Manpower Research Inst. postdoctoral fellow, 1967. Mem. Am. Econs. Assn., Mo. Acad. Sci., Midwest Econs. Assn., Athenaeum Soc., Ill. Labor Hist. Soc., AAUP, Pi Gamma Mu, Phi Mu Alpha, Sigma Epsilon Pi, Omicron Delta Epsilon. Office: SW Mo State U 901 S National St Springfield MO 65804

LAGOS, JAMES HARRY, lawyer, small business advocate; b. Springfield, Ohio, Mar. 14, 1951; s. Harry Thomas and Eugenia (Papas) L.; m. Nike Daphne Pavlatos, July 3, 1976. BA cum laude, Wittenberg U., 1970; JD, Ohio State U., 1972. Bar: U.S. Supreme Ct. 1976, U.S. Ct. Appeals (6th cir.) 1979, U.S. Dist. Ct. (so. dist.) Ohio 1973, U.S. Tax Ct. 1975, Ohio Supreme Ct. 1973. Asst. pros. atty. Clark County, Ohio, 1972-75; ptnr. Lagos & Lagos, Springfield, 1975—; mem. Springfield Small Bus. Council, past chmn., 1977—; del. Ohio Small Bus. Council, 1980—, past chmn., vice chmn. ; del. Ohio Nat. Small Bus. United, v.p., 1982—; del. Small Bus. Nat. Issues Conf., 1984, Ohio Gov.'s Conf. Small Bus., 1984, resource person regulatory and licensing reform com., 1984. Bd. dirs., pres. Greek Orthodox Ch., 1974—; mem. diocese council Greek Orthodox Diocese of Detroit, 1985-86; past chmn. Clark County Child Protection Team, 1974-82, Clark County Young Rep. Club, past pres., sec., treas., 1968-76, chmn. Ohio del. White House Conf. Small Bus., 1985-86. Served to staff sgt. with Ohio Air NG, 1970-76. Recipient Dr. Melvin Emanuel award West Central Ohio Hearing and Speech Assn., 1983, Medal of Saint Paul the Apostle Greek Orthodox Archdiocese of North and South Am., 1985; Disting. Service award Springfield-Clark County, 1977; named one of Outstanding Young Men of Am., 1978. Mem. Am. Hellenic Inst. (bd. dirs. 1985, pub. affairs com. 1979—), Am. Hellenic Endl. Progressive Assn. (past treas.), C. of C. (past bd. dirs.), Jaycees (past chmn. several coms. 1977—, Spoke award 1974), ABA, Ohio State Bar Assn., Springfield Bar and Law Library Assn. (past sec., exec. com. 1973—), West Cen. Ohio Hearing and Speech Assn. (bd. dirs., pres., v.p. 1973-84), Alpha Alpha Kappa, Phi Eta Sigma, Tau Pi Phi, Pi Sigma Alpha. Home: 2023 Audubon Park Dr Springfield OH 45504 Office: Lagos & Lagos 31 E High St Suite 500 Springfield OH 45502

LAGOSKI, CHARLES WILLIAM, physician; b. Chgo., May 25, 1949; s. Charles Edward and Marie Victoria (Bylinowski) L.; m. Diane Marie McMullin, Aug. 11, 1973; children: Megan, Emily, Laura. BS, Loyola U., 1971; DO, Chgo. Coll. Osteo. Medicine, 1979. Osteopath Saunders Med. Group, Avon, Ill., 1980-83, Med. Block, River Falls, Wis., 1984-85, Brown County Family Health Ctr., Mt. Sterling, Ill., 1985—; coroners physician Brown and Schuyler County, Ill., 1985—; preceptor Chgo. Coll. Osteo. Medicine, 1986. Pres. Am. Cancer Soc., Mt. Sterling, 1986; mem. St. Mary Sch. Bd., Mt. Sterling, 1986. Mem. AMA, AM. Osteo. Assn., Ill. Med. Soc., Schuyler County Med. Soc., Am. Heart Assn. Roman Catholic. Avocations: aviation, fishing, jogging. Office: Brown County Family Health Ctr 206 SW Cross Mount Sterling IL 62353

LAGRANGE, MICHAEL JUDE, operations analyst; b. Louisville, Nov. 5, 1958; s. Wayne Patrick and Dorothye Rose (Lutgring) LaG.; m. Marcella Cobb, May 30, 1981; 1 child, Elise Monique. Traffic coordinator Am. Comml. Barge Line, Jeffersonville, Ind., 1981-84, research analyst, 1984-87, ops. analyst, 1987—. Vol. Dem. campaigns Clark County, Ind., 1976—. Recipient Speaker's award Ky. Youth Assembly, 1976, Ind. Youth Assembly, 1977, Roger Graham Meml. award CYO, Indpls., 1977. Mem. Jeffersonville Jaycees. Democrat. Roman Catholic. Club: Propeller of Am. Avocations: hunting, fishing, sports. Home: 27 Wildwood Rd Jeffersonville IN 47130 Office: Am Comml Barge Line Co 1701 E Market St Jeffersonville IN 47130

LA GRANT, LAURENCE JOHN, internal auditor; b. Mt. Clemens, Mich., Mar. 23, 1947; s. Harry and Ida Ann (Cryderman) L.; m. Margaret Anne Clark, June 27, 1970. BA, Wayne State U., 1969, MBA, 1984. Sr. programmer Mich. Credit Union League, Southfield, Mich., 1972-73; project leader Chrysler Corp., Detroit, 1973-76, 1978-83, EDP auditor, 1983—; systems specialist Rockwell Internat. Corp., Troy, Mich., 1976-78. Mem. Inst. Internal Auditors, Assn. MBA's, Beta Gamma Sigma. Office: Chrysler Corp CIMS 417 27 32 12000 Chrysler Dr Highland Park MI 48288-1919

LAHAM, SANDRA LEE, behavioral consultant; b. Grand Rapids, Mich., Mar. 26, 1950; d. George Salim and Mildred Helen (Mitchell) L. BA, Western Mich. U., 1972, MA, 1974; PhD, W.Va. U., 1978. Instr. behavior psychology U. Mo., St. Louis, 1973-75; instr., teaching fellow W.Va. U., Morgantown, 1975-78; behavior psychologist Macomb Intermediate Schs., Mt. Clemens, Mich., 1978-79, cons. behavior, 1979—; guest lectr. Wayne State U., Detroit, 1981, Oakland U., Rochester, Mich., 1986. Author: Users Guide to ABC, 1983, Writing Behavior Programs, 1985; editor: The Adaptive Behavior Curriculum vol. 1 and 2, 1981-82. Mem. Am. Psychol. Assn., Assn. Behavior Analysis, Assn. Persons with Severe Handicaps, Council Exceptional Children. Home: 1477 Oakbrook E Rochester MI 48063 Office: Macomb Intermediate Sch Dist 44001 Garfield Rd Mount Clemens MI 48044

LAHN, MERVYN LLOYD, trust company executive; b. Hanover, Ont., Can., June 24, 1933; s. Charles Henry and Emma (Leifso) L.; B.A., Waterloo Coll., 1954; LL.D. (hon.), Wilfrid Laurier U., 1978; m. Myra Ann Helen Smith, Sept. 17, 1960; children—J. Geoffrey, Pearce A., Margaret Ann. With Waterloo Trust & Savs. Co., 1955-68, asst. gen. mgr., treas., 1967-68; asst. gen. mgr. midwestern Ont. region Can. Trustco Mortgage Co., Can. Trust Co., London, Ont., Can., 1968-72, dep. gen. mgr., 1972-73, sr. v.p., gen. mgr., 1973-74, exec. v.p., 1974-78, pres., chief operating officer, 1978-79, pres., chief exec. officer, 1979-87, chmn., chief exec. officer, 1987— , also dir.; dir. Allpack Ltd., Cadillac Fairview Corp. Ltd., Dana Corp., Hayes-Dana, Inc., John Labatt Ltd., Can. Trustco Mortgage Co., Can. Trust Co., Union Enterprises, Ltd., John P. Robarts Research Inst.; mem. adv. bd. London Salvation Army, 1976-86, Theatre London, 1981—, Orch. London, 1977—, Merrymount Children's Centre; mem. adv. com. Sch. Bus. Adminstrn., U. Western Ont. Conservative. Lutheran. Clubs: London Hunt & Country, London, Toronto, Westmont Golf and Country. Office: Canada Trust Mortgage Co, 275 Dundas St, London, ON Canada N6B 3L1

LAHR, JOHN WILLIAM, optometrist; b. Lafayette, Ind., June 11, 1950; s. Willard Keith and Verly Marion (Westfall) L.; m. Mary Jo Geffert, Sept. 11, 1976; children: Brian, Jennifer, Suzanne. BS, Ind. U., 1972, OD, 1974. Assoc. Dr. Earl Doelle, Grand Rapids, Minn., 1974-75; assoc. Dr. G. T. Gibbons, Cambridge, Minn., 1975-77; pres. Cambridge (Minn.) Eye Clinic, 1977—. Cons. Grand Rapids Vocat. Tech. Inst., 1974-75, Cambridge State Hosp., St. Cloud Vocat. Tech. Inst., 1979—, Sandstone Fed. Corr. Inst.,

1982—; dir. mktg. America's Doctors of Optometry, Tracy, Minn., 1982—. Fellow Am. Acad. Optometry; mem. Am. Optometric Assn., Minn. Optometric Assn. (pres. 1987—), Met. Dist. Optometric Soc., Cambridge C. of C. Republican. Methodist. Club: Rum River Pilots. Home: 707 Sunset Ln Cambridge MN 55008 Office: 120 E 1st Ave Cambridge MN 55008

LAHRMAN, DON EUGENE, orthodontist; b. Ft. Wayne, Ind., Mar. 12, 1932; s. Clarence F. and Orpha (Krauter) L.; m. Carolyn Lou Steinbacher, Aug. 29, 1953; children: Lisa Lynn, Don Eugene II. BS, Ind. U., 1954, DDS, 1957, MS in Orthodontics, 1965. Practice dentistry specializing in orthodontics Ft. Wayne, 1962—; instr. dentistry Ind. U., Ft. Wayne, 1965-68. Author: Clinical Dento-Facial Biometry In Norma Frontalis, 1965. Served to capt. AUS, 1957-59. Mem. Isaac Knapp Dental Soc. (del. 1967-73, pres. 1971-72), Ind. Dental Assn., ADA, Great Lakes Soc. Orthodontists (pres. 1986-87), Am. Assn. Orthodontists (chmn. council on orthodontic health care 1984-86), Am. Profl. Practice Assn., Ind. Acad. Dental Practice Adminstrn., Found. Orthodontic Research, Am. Cleft Palate Assn., Fedn. Dentaire Internat., Izaac Walton League, Ft. Wayne C. of C. Republican. Lutheran. Home: 2933 Covington Lake Dr Fort Wayne IN 46804 Office: 2426 E State Blvd Fort Wayne IN 46805 also: 6215 Covington Rd Fort Wayne IN 46804

LAI, JENG YIH, surgeon; b. Rep. China, Dec. 5, 1941; came to U.S., 1968; s. Ting-Zo and See-Mae (Lee) L.; m. Su Kao, July 19, 1944; children: Stephen, Christina, Monica. MD, Nat. Taiwan U., 1967. Diplomate Am. Bd. Surgery, Am. Bd. Thoracic Surgery. Intern St. Francis Gen. Hosp., Pitts., 1968-69, resident in gen. surgery, 1969-73; fellow in cardiovascular surgery Rush-Presbyn.-St. Luke's Med. Ctr., Chgo., 1973-74; resident in cardiovascular and thoracic surgery St. Paul Hosp., Dallas, 1974-76; fellow in cardiovascular surgery Tex. Heart Inst., Houston, 1976-77; surgeon cardiovascular and thoracic surgery St. Francis Regional Med. Ctr., Wichita, Kans., 1977—; pvt. practice specializing in cardiovascular and thoracic surgery Wichita, 1981-86; clin. asst. prof. in surgery U. Kans., Wichita. Bd. dirs. Wichita Indochinese Ctr., 1985-86. Served as lt. surgeon China Army, 1967-68. Fellow Am. Coll. Surgeons, Denton A. Cooley Cardiovascular Soc.; mem. AMA, Am. Heart Assn., Med. Soc. Kans., Sedgwick County Med. Soc., Wichita Asian Assn. (pres. 1985-86). Avocations: tennis, traveling, reading. Home: 8501 Killarney Pl Wichita KS 67206

LAIB, HELEN WIEDEMER, surgeon; b. San Juan, P.R., Mar. 15, 1948; d. Arthur Paul and Dorothy Marie (Davis) W.; m. David Steven Laib, Sept. 5, 1981; 1 child, Andrew Christopher. BS, U. Wis., 1970; MD, Baylor Coll. of Medicine, 1973; postdoctoral, U. Ill., Chgo., 1979. Diplomate Am. Bd. Surgery. Intern Baylor Affiliated Hosps., Houston, 1973-74; resident gen. surgery Cook County Hosp., Chgo., 1974-79, gen. surgeon, 1980-86, clin. chief surgery adult emergency services, 1984-86; practice specializing in surgery Rockford, Ill., 1986—; asst. prof. surgery U. Ill., Chgo., 1980—. Contbr. articles to profl. jours. Recipient Young Investigator award Am. Diabetes Assn., 1980. Fellow ACS, Am. Coll. Emergency Physicians; mem. AMA, Ill. Med. Assn., Winnebago County Med. Soc. Home: 4804 Innsbruck Dr Rockford IL 61111 Office: 2500 N Rockton Suite 419 Rockford IL 61103

LAIKIN, GEORGE JOSEPH, lawyer; b. Milw., June 21, 1910; s. Isadore and Bella (Schoene) L.; m. Sylvia Goldberg, Jan. 20, 1935; children: Michael B., Barbara (Mrs. Dan L. Funkenstein). B.A., LL.B., U. Wis., 1933. Bar: Wis. 1933, D.C. 1944, Ill. 1945, Calif. 1972, N.Y. 1980; Cert taxation specialist, Calif. Pvt. practice law Milw., 1933-42; spl. asst. to U.S. Atty.-Gen., Tax Div., Dept. Justice, Washington, 1942-45; pvt. practice law Wis., 1945, Milw., Washington, Chgo., 1945—, Los Angeles, 1972—; pres. Laikin & Laikin, S.C., Milw., 1980—; gen. counsel Milw. Assn. Life Underwriters, 1953-85, Wis. Assn. Life Underwriters, 1955-85; gen. counsel, dir. Schwerman Trucking Co., Milw., 1959-84, Continental Bank and Trust Co., Milw., 1963-70; counsel, dir. Mirisch Motion Pictures, Hollywood, Calif., 1960—; gen. counsel, dir. Empire Gen. Life Ins. Co., Los Angeles, 1963-77; chmn. bd., gen. counsel Univ. Nat. Bank, Milw., 1971-76; gen. counsel, dir. U.S. Life Ins. Co., Hinsdale, Ill., 1971-76; gen. counsel Liberty Savs. and Loan Assn., Milw., 1979—; spl. atty. M & I Marshall & Ilsley Bank, Milw., 1973—; also writer, lectr. in field. Contbr. articles to profl. publs. Chmn. Spl. Gifts and Bequests Com., Marquette U., 1967-70; pres. Wis. Soc. Jewish Learning, 1967-71; mem. Milw. Estate Planning Council. Mem. ABA, Wis. Bar Assn., Ill. Bar Assn., Calif. Bar Assn., Bar Assn. D.C., Assn. Trial Lawyers of Am., Nat. Assn. Criminal Def. Lawyers. Clubs: Milw. Athletic, Milw. Yacht; Standard of Chgo.; Carmel Yacht of Haifa (Israel). Home: 1610 N Prospect Ave Milwaukee WI 53202 Office: 825 N Jefferson St Milwaukee WI 53202

LAINE, DEBRA ANN, utilities executive; b. St. Cloud, Minn., Aug. 9, 1959; d. Warren Lerone and Margaret Louise (Johnson) Rydell; m. Burton Oscar Laine, Jan. 3, 1981. BS, U. Wis., Menomonie, 1981; MEd, U. Minn., 1984. Licensed tchr., Minn. Community edn. dir. Esko (Minn.) Pub. Schs., 1981-83; acting county extension agt. U. Minn., Duluth, 1983; mktg., tng. coordinator No. Minn. Utilities (formerly ICG Utilities), Cloquet, Minn., 1984-87; cons., owner Laine Resources, Cloquet, 1987—. Vol. Agrl. Extension Service, Carlton, Minn., 1981—; cons. United Meth. Ch., 1985—. Mem. Am. Home Econs. Assn. (bd. dirs. 1982-85), Home Econs. in Bus., Am. Soc. Tng. and Devel., Arrowhead Home Econs. Club (hostess 1983-86), Milaca Jaycees (Hall of Fame 1986), Arrowhead Rabbit Breeders Assn. (sec. 1984-85). Avocations: flower gardening, horseback riding, rabbit breeding and showing. Home: 383 Laine Rd Cloquet MN 55720 Office: Laine Resources 383 Laine Rd Cloquet MN 55720

LAING, GLYNIS JOHNS, nurse, hospice administrator; b. Cleve., Sept. 8, 1949; d. Garfield and Shirley Mae (Jones) Johns; m. David Allen Laing, June 12, 1971; children: Steven Paul, Jeffrey Michael. BS in Nursing, Kent (Ohio) State U., 1974, MA, 1978; PhD, Tex. Women's U., Denton, 1983. RN, Ohio. From staff nurse to asst. head nurse Mt. Sinai Hosp., Cleve., 1974-76; instr. Huron Rd. Hosp., Cleve., 1977-79; asst. prof. nursing Lake Erie Coll., Painesville, Ohio, 1984; dir. of hospice Luth. Med. Ctr., Cleve., 1985—; tech. advisor El Campo Centro, Columbia, 1980—. Contbr. articles to profl. jours. Mem. spl. task force Am. Cancer Soc., Cleve., 1985—. Recipient Disting. Service award Eta Sigma Gamma, 1980. Mem. Am. Nurses Assn., Nat. League Nursing, Ohio Hospice Orgn. (bd. dirs. 1986—). Episcopalian. Avocations: biking, reading, family activities. Office: Luth Med Ctr 2609 Franklin Blvd Cleveland OH 44113

LAING, JOAN RAE, psychologist; b. Delta, Iowa, Dec. 10, 1938; d. George and Dorothea (Walker) Jones; m. Earl John Laing, Aug. 12, 1961 (div. July 1979); children: Catherine, John, Patricia. BA with honors, Cen. Coll., Pella, Iowa, 1958; MA, U. Iowa, 1960; MS, Iowa State U., 1977, PhD, 1979. Lic. psychologist, Iowa. Teaching asst. U. Iowa, Iowa City, 1958-60; tchr. Iowa Pub. Schs., 1960-63; research asst. U. Iowa, Iowa City, 1964-67; intern in psychology U. Cin., 1978-79; psychologist Vassar Coll., Poughkeepsie, N.Y., 1979-80; research psychologist Am. Coll. Testing, Iowa City, 1980—. Editor: Newsnotes, Assn. for Measurement and Evaluation in Counseling and Devel., 1984-87, mem. editorial bd., 1986—; mem. editorial bd. Jour. of the Nat. Assn. for Women Deans, Adminstrs. and Counselors, 1983-87; contbr. numerous articles to profl. jours. Mem. Friends Iowa City Pub. Library, 1980—. Mem. Assn. for Measurement and Evaluation in Counseling and Devel. (mem. exec. council), Am. Psychol. Assn., Iowa Psychol. Assn., Assn. on Handicapped Student Service Programs in Post-Secondary Edn., Nat. Assn. for Women Deans, Adminstrs. and Counselors. Episcopalian. Avocations: travel, reading, music, hiking. Office: Am Coll Testing Program PO Box 168 Iowa City IA 52243

LAINSON, HARRY ACKLEY, JR., manufacturing company executive; b. Fairbury, Nebr., Aug. 7, 1912; s. Harry Ackley and Celia W. (Jennings) L.; m. Gretchen Helen Hollman, Jan. 2, 1938; children—Margaret Helen Lainson Hermes, Mary Catherine Lainson Olsen. A.B., Hastings Coll., 1934, LL.D, 1982; LL.B., Whitworth Coll., 1965. Warehouseman, Dutton-Lainson Co., Hastings, Nebr., 1932-34, advt. mgr., 1934, warehouse mgr., 1935, sec., 1936, traffic mgr., personnel mgr., 1937-48, v.p., gen. mgr., 1948-50, pres., 1950-74, chmn., 1960—, chmn., chief exec. officer, 1974—; pres. Midland Corp., Jaden Mfg. Co.; dir. City Nat. Bank, Lincoln Telephone and Telegraph Co., Lincoln TeleCom, Alarm Systems Nebr. Mem. Civil Service Commn., Hastings; mem. Gov.'s Task Force, 1981; trustee Hastings Mus.; bd. dirs. Hastings Carnegie Library; mem. shell com. Dept. War; past pres. bd. trustees Hastings Coll.; nat. bd. dirs. SBA; founder, incorporator Nebr. Ind. Coll. Found. Mem. NAM, Assoc. Industries Nebr. (bd. dirs.), Am. Ordnance Assn. (life), Navy League U.S. (dir., state pres.). Republican. Presbyterian. Club: Lochland Country (Hastings). Lodge: Masons. Home: 229 University Blvd Hastings NE 68901 Office: 2d and St Joseph Ave Hastings NE 68901

LAINSON, PHILLIP ARGLES, dental educator; b. Council Bluffs, Iowa, Feb. 11, 1936; s. Donald Wesley and Olive Ione (Stageman) L.; m. Mary Margaret Tangney, June 18, 1960; children—David, Michael, Elizabeth. B.A., U. Iowa, 1960, D.D.S., 1962, M.S., 1968; Dental Intern Cert., USAF Malcom Crow Hosp., 1963. Diplomate Am. Bd. Peridontology. Instr. dept. periodontics U. Iowa, Iowa City, 1965-69, asst. prof., 1969-71, assoc. prof., 1971-75, prof., 1975—, head dept. periodontics, 1976—; cons. in periodontics VA Hosp., Knoxville, Iowa, 1967—, Iowa City, 1976—, Central Regional Dental Testing Service, Topeka, Kans., 1977-81, Commn. on Dental Accreditation, Chgo., 1984—. Contbr. articles to profl. jours. Editor newsletter Midwest Soc. Periodontology, 1982-85. Assoc. editor Iowa Dental Jour., 1974-76. Chmn., Bd. in Control of Athletics U. Iowa, 1984-86. Served to capt. USAF, 1962-65, Iowa Army N.G., 1973—. Am. Coll. Dentists fellow, 1976. Mem. Iowa Soc. Periodontology (pres. 1987-88), U. Dist. Iowa Dental Assn. (pres. 1979-80), Midwest Soc. Periodontology (v.p. 1985-86, pres. 1987—), Am. Acad. Periodontology, Internat. Assn. Dental Research, Am. Dental Assn., Am. Assn. Dental Schs., Sigma Xi, Omicron Kappa Upsilon. Republican. Roman Catholic. Lodge: Rotary. Avocations: sailing; fishing; biking; tennis. Home: 16 Ridgewood Ln Iowa City IA 52240 Office: U Iowa Coll Dentistry Iowa City IA 52242

LAITY, RONALD LEONARD, consulting engineer; b. Hancock, Mich., July 16, 1927; s. Leonard Benjamin and Ida Sophia (Baakko) L.; B.S. in Elec. Engring., Mich. Technol. U., 1953; m. Leola Gladys Upton, Nov. 26, 1948; children—Kathryn, Teresa, Matthew. With Commonwealth Assos. Inc., Jackson, Mich., 1953-83, sr. staff engr. power and indsl. systems div., asst. treas., 1972-83; v.p., coordinator of projects Wolf Wineman Engrs., Inc., Southfield, Mich., 1984-86; pvt. practice cons. engr., Jackson, 1987. Served with USAF, 1945-47. Mem. Nat. Soc. Profl. Engrs., Mich. Soc. Profl. Engrs., IEEE, Engring. Soc. Detroit, Tau Beta Pi, Eta Kappa Nu. Presbyterian. Home and Office: 3239 McCain Rd Jackson MI 49203

LAJOIE, WILLIAM RICHARD, professional baseball team executive; b. Wyandotte, Mich., Sept. 27, 1934; s. Thomas Napoleon and Ladyne Edith (Fulmer) L.; m. Gloria Ann Stanik, Feb. 2, 1957; children: William, Jeffrey, Julie. B.S., Western Mich. U., 1956; postgrad., Eastern Mich. U., 1960-65. Profl. baseball player Balt., Los Angeles, Kansas City, Minn., 1955-64; tchr. Detroit Pub. Schs., 1965-73; baseball scout, mgr. Detroit Tigers, 1969-73, scouting dir., 1974-78, v.p., 1978-83, v.p., gen. mgr., 1983—. Co-author: Baseball The Major League Way, 1975. Recipient Mgr. of Yr. award Appalachian League, 1969; co-recipient Gen. Mgr. of Yr. award ESPN, 1984. Congregationalist. *

LAKIN, DUANE EDWARD, industrial psychologist; b. St. Joseph, Mo., Feb. 22, 1948; s. Edward Daniel and Margaret Evelyn (Gregory) L.; m. Melanie Catherine Gimbut, Mar. 16, 1969; 1 child, Jennifer Elizabeth. B.A. in Psychology, U. Minn., 1970, Ph.D. in Psychology in Schs. Tng. Program, 1978. Evaluation dir. Lake Minnetonka Mental Health Ctr., Minn., 1974-78; cons. psychologist, v.p. Mgmt. Psychologists, Inc., Chgo., 1978-80; pres. Lakin Assocs., Chgo., 1980—. Composer: (song book) Get It Together, 1970; author book chpt., articles. V.p. adv. bd. Sisters of St. Joseph, LaGrange, Ill., 1984—. Mem. Am. Psychol. Assn., Am. Prodn. and Inventory Control Soc. Club: Execs. of Chgo. Home: 2105 Willow Run Wheaton IL 60187 Office: Lakin Assocs 20 N Wacker Dr Suite 1828 Chicago IL 60606

LALLA, SANDRA JO, accountant; b. Chicago Heights, Ill., Oct. 10, 1961; d. Joseph S. and Shirley Irene (Krueger) Nardi; m. Kenneth Michael Lalla, June 15, 1985. BS in Acctg., U. Ill., 1983. CPA, Ill. Acct. Ernst & Whinney, Chgo., 1983-85; mgr. gen. acctg. Richard D. Irwin, Inc., Homewood, Ill., 1985—. Mem. Am. Inst. CPA's, Ill. CPA Soc. Roman Catholic. Avocations: softball, bowling, volleyball. Office: Richard D Irwin Inc 1818 Ridge Rd Homewood IL 60430

LALLY, ANN MARIE, former educational administrator; b. Chgo., Sept. 23, 1914; d. Martin J. and Della (McDonnell) Lally; A.B., Mundelein Coll., 1935; A.M., Northwestern U., 1939, Ph.D., 1950; postgrad. Chgo. Tchrs. Coll., Chgo. Art Inst., 1935-36. Tchr., Amundsen High Sch., 1935, Lindblom and Von Steuben high schs., Chgo., 1936-38; chmn. art dept. Schurz High Sch., 1938-40; supr. art Chgo. Pub. Elementary Schs., 1940-48, dir. art Chgo. Public Schs., 1948-57; prin. John Marshall High Sch., 1957-63; supt. Dist. 16, Chgo. Pub. Schs., 1963-64, Dist. 5, 1964-80; lectr. Wright Jr. Coll., 1948; instr. creative drawing Chgo. Acad. Fine Art, 1941; instr. interior design Internat. Harvester Co., 1946-48; lectr. in edn. DePaul U., 1952-74; lectr. in edn. and art U. Chgo., 1956-59; lectr. edn. Chgo. Tchrs. Coll., 1960-62. Trustee Pub. Sch. Tchrs. Pension and Retirement Fund Chgo., 1957-71, sec.-treas., 1960-65, pres., 1965-70. charter mem. women's bd. Loyola U.; charter mem. women's bd. Art Inst., Chgo.; mem. Ill. Div. Individual Liberties Task Force, 1987—. Mem. Am., Ill. assns. sch. adminstrs., N.E.A. (life), Ill. Edn. Assn., Dist. Supts. Assn. (pres. 1973-75), Ill. Women Adminstrs. Assn. (award 1979), Nat. Council Adminstrv. Women in Edn. (profl. relations chmn. 1958-62), Assn. Supervision and Curriculum Devel., Chgo. Area Women Adminstrs. in Edn. (award for outstanding adminstrn. 1981), Nat. Art Edn. Assn. (mem. council 1956-60), Western Arts Assn. (pres. 1956-58), Internat. Soc. Edn. in Art, Ill. Art Edn. Assn. (pres. 1955), LWV of Chgo., Chgo. Art Educators Assn. (a founder; past v.p., sec. and treas), Ill. Club Cath. Women (dir., 1981—, rec. sec. 1982-86), Chgo. Pub. Sch. Art Soc., Chgo. Hist. Soc., AAUW (Chgo. chmn. elem. and secondary edn. 1966—, dir.-at-large 1962-66, 78-80), Chgo. Area Reading Assn. (dir. 1963-69), Nat., Ill. assns. secondary sch. prins., Artists Equity Assn., Chgo., Council on Fgn. Relations, Mundelein Coll. Alumnae Assn. (past pres., chmn. bd., Magnificat medal 1964), Pi Lambda Theta, Delta Kappa Gamma (chmn. legacy com. 1987—). Club: Chgo. Woman's. Contbr. articles to art and ednl. jours. Home: 307 Trinity Ct Evanston IL 60201

LALUK, MARTA MARIA, architect; b. Cleve., June 10, 1958; d. Phillip and Susanna Jenine (Oryshkewych) Telishewsky; m. Michael Alexander Laluk. BS, BArch, Kent (Ohio) State U., 1981; MArch, U. Pa., 1982. Designer dept. facilities and planning U. Pa., Phila., 1981-83; architect William Dorsky Assocs., Beachwood, Ohio, 1983-85, R.P. Madison Internat., Cleve., 1985—; archtl. studio juror Kent State U., 1985, 86; designer urban design charette City of Cleve., 1983. Active Girl Scouts U.S., Cleve., 1964—. Mem. AIA. Republican. Roman Catholic. Club: Ski (Brandywine, Ohio). Office: RP Madison Internat 2930 Euclid Ave Cleveland OH 44115 Mailing Address: 6781 Queensway North Royalton OH 44133

LAMALFA, JOACHIM JACK, clinical psychologist; b. Milw., Aug. 10, 1915; s. Salvatore and Josephine (Foti) L.; m. Constance Zarcone, Dec. 27, 1944; children: Constance Joanne, John Cibik, Jacquelyn Grace, Houston Lee Browne. BS, Marquette U., 1938; MS, U. Wis., 1941; PhD, U. Mich., 1949. Lic. psychologist, Wis. Research asst. U. Mich., Ann Arbor, 1946-47; psychiat. intern Milw. County Hosp. for Mental Diseases, 1947-49; instr. psychology Marquette U., Milw., 1951-52; pvt. practice psychology Milw., 1949—; founder dept. psychology Milw. County Hosp. for Mental Diseases, 1947, Marquette U. Dept. Psychology, 1947; founder, chmn. St. Michael's Hosp. Mental Health Clinic, 1952. Author: (with Henry Viet) Psychosis with Cerebral Arteriosclerosis as Affected by Adrenal Cortical Extract. Mem. AAAS, Am. Psychol. Assn., Wis. Psychol. Assn., Soc. Clin. Psychologists, Milw. Psychol. Assn., Nat. Register Health Service Providers in Psychology, Phi Kappa Phi, Phi Delta Kappa. Republican. Roman Catholic. Home: 7821 N Lake Dr Fox Point WI 53217 Office: 115 W Silver Spring Whitefish Bay WI 53217

LA MANTIA, JOSEPH JOHN, illustrator; b. Chgo., Jan. 6, 1947; s. Joseph Sr. and Nellie (Sulluca) La M.; m. Merridee Shaw, Jan. 30, 1982; 3 children. BA in Art Edn., U. Ill., Chgo., 1971. Art therapist Madden Mental Health, Maywood, Ill., 1971-73; freelance jeweler Boston, 1976-78, freelance illustrator, 1978-84; illustration tchr. Boston Archtl. Ctr., 1980-84; freelance illustrator Bloomington, Ind., 1984—. Illustrator Print-Regional Design Annual (cert. of Design Excellence 1985, 87), Bloomington Post Card Series (Award of Excellence Art Dirs. Club Ind. 1985), ABA Pamphlet (Award of Excellence Art Dirs. Club Ind. 1987); co-illustrator (book) Images of Deviance and Social Control, 1985. Mem. Art Dirs. Club Ind., 1986. Avocations: carpentry, gardening, cooking. Home and Studio: 820 W Howe St Bloomington IN 47401

LAMAR, HAROLD, JR., optometrist; b. Reading, Pa., Oct. 24, 1943; s. Harold Lamar and Ann (Terefenko) R.; m. Karen Elaine Kostin, Dec. 16, 1967; children: Kristianna, Leslie. Student, Gen. Motors Inst., 1961-63; BS in Indsl. Engring., Western Mich. U., 1967; OD, Pacific U., 1979. Practice optometry Fenton, Mich., 1980—; pres. Squall Line Outfitting Co., Fenton, 1985—, bd. dirs. Genesee County Head Start. Served to capt. USAF, 1968-74. Republican. Lutheran. Lodge: Rotary (bd. dirs. Fenton 1985—), Lions. Avocations: running, skiing, sailing. Home: 2478 Grove Park Rd Fenton MI 48430 Office: 521 N Leroy St Fenton MI 48430

LAMAR, WILLIAM FRED, chaplain, educator; b. Birmingham, Ala., Jan. 4, 1934; s. William Fred Sr. and Everette (Kelley) L.; m. Roberta Anton, Sept. 17, 1955 (dec.); 1 child, Jonathan Frederick; m. Martha Anne Lee, June 7, 1985. BA, U. Ala., 1954; BD, Vanderbilt U., 1957; PhD, St. Louis U., 1972; D Min., Eden Theol. Sem., 1974. Minister United Meth. Ch., Bynum, Ala., 1959-61, Fultondale, Ala., 1961-65; campus minister U. Mo., Rolla, 1965-74; chaplain, prof., dir. overseas missions DePauw U., Greencastle, Ind., 1974—; ednl. cons. electric utilities, 1974—; advisor overseas vol. program UMC Ind., Indpls., 1980—. Author: (book) Role of the College Chaplain at the Church-Related College, 1984; designer electric utility computer programs, 1979-85. Vice chmn. County Welfare Bd., Rolla; bd. dirs. Sr. Vol. Program Action, Greencastle, 1977-80. Served to 1st lt. U.S. Army, 1957-59. Recipient Award of Honor, Ind. Gov.'s Voluntary Action, 1976, Cross of Jerusalem, Episcopal Diocese of Guatemala, 1979; Danforth fellow, 1971-72. Mem. Nat. Campus Ministry Assn. (chmn. sci. and ethics network), Nat. Assn. Coll. Chaplains, Assn. Religion in Intellectual Life. Home and Office: 103 DePauw Ave Greencastle IN 46135

LAMB, GORDON HOWARD, music educator, university executive; b. Eldora, Iowa, Nov. 6, 1934; s. Capp L. and Ethel L. (Hayden) L.; m. Nancy Ann Painter; children: Kirk, Jon, Phillip. B in Music Edn., Simpson Coll., 1956; M of Music, U. Nebr., 1962; PhD, U. Iowa, 1973. Choral dir. Iowa pub. schs., Tama/Paullina, Sac City, 1957-68; asst. prof. music U. Wis., Stevens Point, 1969-70, U. Tex., 1970-74; prof., dir. div. music U. Tex., San Antonio, 1974-79, prof., v.p. acad. affairs, 1979-86; pres. Northeastern Ill. U., Chgo., 1986—. Author: Choral Techniques, 1974; editor: Guide for the Beginning Choral Director; contbr. articles to scholarly and profl. jours.; composer numerous pieces choral music. Served with U.S. Army, 1957-58. Mem. Am. Assn. Higher Edn., Assn. Urban Univs. (bd. dirs.), Am. Assn. State Colls. and Univs., Am. Choral Dirs. Assn. (life, chmn. nat. com. 1970-72). Office: Northeastern Ill Univ Office of the President 5500 N St Louis Ave Chicago IL 60625-4699

LAMB, POSE MAXINE, education educator; b. Pitts., Oct. 31, 1927. BS in Edn., Ohio State U., 1948, MA in Edn., 1952, PhD in Edn., 1960. Cert. tchr., Ind.; specialist in lang. acquisition, linguistics. Classroom tchr. Bexley (Ohio) Pub. Schs., 1949-57; tchr. lab. sch. Ball State U., Muncie, Ind., 1957-62; instr. Purdue U., Lafayette, Ind., 1962—, also chmn. elem. edn. Author: Linguistics in Proper Perspective, 2d edit., 1977, Guiding Children's Language Learning, 1972, Reading: Foundations and Instructional Strategies, 1980. Mem. AAUW, Internat. reading Assn., Nat. Council Tchrs. English, Assn. Childhood Edn., Am. Ednl. Research Assn., Delta Kappa Gamma, Alpha Delta Kappa, Pi Lambda Theta. Home: 172 W Navajo West Lafayette IN 47906 Office: Purdue U Dept Edn West Lafayette IN 47907

LAMB, REINHOLD PHILIPP, finance educator; b. Windsor, Ont., Can., June 5, 1958; came to U.S., 1979; s. Philipp and Hildegard (Sorg) L.; m. Deborah Ann Johnson, Jan. 2, 1982. BBA, Geneva Coll., 1981; MBA in Fin. with honors, Roosevelt U., 1984. Lectr. U. Wis., Oshkosh, 1984—. Mem. Midwest Fin. Assn. Republican. Baptist. Avocations: collecting sports memorabilia, golfing, racquetball. Office: U Wis Algoma Ave Oshkosh WI 54901

LAMBE, DEAN RODNEY, writer; b. Seattle, Oct. 31, 1943; s. William Emil and Clara Francis (Pennock) L.; m. Julie Ann Gaisford, Aug. 27, 1966. BA, Whitman Coll., 1965; PhD, Duke U., 1976. Asst. prof. Marietta (Ohio) Coll., 1970-77; cons. Suomi Software, Vincent, Ohio, 1976-86. Author: The Odysseus Solution, 1986. Pres. Washington County (Ohio) Bd. Health, 1982—. Fellow Woodrow Wilson Found., 1965. Mem. Sci. Fiction Writers Am. (co-chair grievance com.). Democrat. Avocation: electronics. Home: State Route 676 PO Box 14 Watertown OH 45787

LAMBERSON, LEONARD ROY, educator; b. Stanwood, Mich., Nov. 18, 1937; s. Roy L. and Lucy M. (Marco) L.; m. Yvonne Molnar, Dec. 14, 1974; children: Jonathan, Leslie, Debra. BME, Gen. Motors Inst. Engring. and Mgmt. Inst., 1961; MS in Indsl. Engring., N.C. State U., 1962; PhD, Tex. A&M U., 1968. Registered profl. engr., Mich. Prodn. foreman Chevrolet Motor Div., Flint, Mich., 1961-64; asst. prof. Gen. Motors Inst. Engring. and Mgmt. Inst., Flint, 1964-65, assoc. prof., 1968-70; asst. prof. Tex. A&M U., College Station, 1965-68; assoc. prof. Wayne State U., Detroit, 1970-80, prof. indsl. engring., chmn. dept., 1980—. Co-author: Reliability in Engineering Design, 1977. Mem. Inst. Indsl. Engrs. (Div. award 1985), Am. Soc. Quality Control (Craig award 1978, Disting. Service award 1980), Am. Soc. Engring. Edn. Avocation: fishing. Home: 21438 Meridian Rd Grosse Ile MI 48138 Office: Wayne State U 5050 Anthony Wayne Detroit MI 48202

LAMBERT, ALLEN THOMAS, banker; b. Regina, Sask., Can., Dec. 28, 1911; s. Willison Andrew and Sarah (Barber) L.; m. Marion Grace Kotchapaw, May 20, 1950; children: William Allen, Anne Barber. Ed. Victoria pub. high schs. With Toronto Dominion Bank, 1927-78, asst. gen. mgr., 1953-56, gen. mgr., 1956, v.p., bd. dirs., 1956-60, pres., 1960-72, chmn. bd. dirs., 1961-72, chmn. bd. dirs., chief exec. officer, 1972-78; bd. dirs. R. Angus Alta., Ltd., Western Internat., Raritan River Steel Co., Dome Mines, Ltd., Dome Petroleum Ltd., Royal Trustco, Ltd., Rolls-Royce Industries Can., Ltd., Falconbridge Ltd., Inspiration Resources Corp., Royal LePage Ltd., The Holden Group; chmn. bd., dir. Trilon Fin. Corp., Lonvest Corpl., Hudson Bay Mining and Smelting Co., Ltd. Served with Royal Canadian Navy, 1943-45. Mem. United Ch. Can. Clubs: Toronto, Toronto Golf, Toronto Hunt, Granite, York (Toronto). Office: London Life Ins, 255 Dufferin Ave, London, ON Canada N6A 4K1

LAMBERT, CARL FREDERICK (NICK), risk management executive; b. Kansas City, Mo., Sept. 29, 1932; s. Carl Frederick and Genevieve Elizabeth (Corbin) L.; m. Mary Jo Lee, Dec. 2, 1961 (div. Feb. 1977); children: Corbin F., Bryan J. Student U. Va., 1950-53. Commd. 2d lt. USAF, 1956, advanced through grades to maj., 1967, resigned, 1968; life ins. salesman and mgr., regional dist. mgr. Equitable Life Assurance Soc., Lakeland, Fla., 1968-72; v.p. Consol. Investors Life Assurance Co., Coral Gables, Fla., 1972-76; mgr. safety and compliance Hannah Marine Corp., Lemont, Ill., 1977-82; mgr. loss control/loss prevention Canonie, Inc., Muskegon, Mich., 1982-85; pres. Cons. Risk Mgmt. Services, Muskegon, 1985—. Mem. Am. Soc. Marine Artists, Midwest Watercolor Soc. Club: Propeller of U.S. (1st v.p. Port of Chicago 1982-83). Home: 575 Lake Forest Ln Apt L-10 Muskegon MI 49441 Office: 559 E Western Ave Muskegon MI 49443

LAMBERT, JOSEPH BUCKLEY, chemistry educator; b. Ft. Sheridan, Ill., July 4, 1940; s. Joseph Idus and Elizabeth Dorothy (Kirwan) L.; m. Mary Wakefield Pulliam, June 27, 1967; children: Laura Kirwan, Alice Pulliam, Joseph Cannon. B.S., Yale U., 1962; Ph.D. (Woodrow Wilson fellow 1962-63, NSF fellow 1962-65), Calif. Inst. Tech., 1965. Asst. prof. chemistry Northwestern U., Evanston, Ill., 1965-69; assoc. prof. Northwestern U., 1969-74, prof. chemistry, 1974—, chmn. dept., 1986—, dir. integrated sci. program, 1982-85; vis. assoc. Brit. Mus., 1973, Polish Acad. Scis., 1981. Author: Organic Structural Analysis, 1976, Physical Organic Chemistry through Solved Problems, 1978, The Multinuclear Approach to NMR Spectroscopy, 1983, Archaeological Chemistry III, 1984, Introduction to Organic

Spectroscopy, 1987; audio course Intermediate NMR Spectroscopy, 1973, Recent Advances in Organic NMR Spectroscopy, 1987; contbr. articles to sci. jours. Recipient Nat. Fresenius award, 1976; Alfred P. Sloan fellow, 1968-70; Guggenheim fellow, 1973; Interacad. exchange fellow (U.S.-Poland), 1985. Fellow Japan Soc. for Promotion of Sci., Brit. Interplanetary Soc., AAAS; mem. Ill. Acad. Sci. (life), Am. Chem. Soc., Royal Soc. Chemistry, Soc. Archaeol. Scis. (pres. 1986-87), Phi Beta Kappa, Sigma Xi. Home: 1956 Linneman St Glenview IL 60025 Office: Dept Chemistry Northwestern U 2145 Sheridan Rd Evanston IL 60208

LAMBERT, LECLAIR GRIER, writer, lecturer, state government education administrator; b. Miami, Fla., s. George F. and Maggie (Grier) L.; B.S., Hampton Inst., 1959; postgrad. Harvard U., 1959, U. Munich (Germany), 1965-66. Researcher, copy reader Time-Life Books, 1961-64; tchr. biology and Eng. lit., secondary level U.S. Dependent's Schs. Overseas, Tripoli, Libya, 1964-65; biology editor of high sch. textbooks Holt, Rinehart & Winston, N.Y.C., 1966-69; biology editor and writer Ency. Britannica, N.Y.C., 1969; copy editor Russian sci. monographs The Faraday Press, N.Y.C., 1970-71; writer Med. World News, N.Y.C., 1971; pub. relations writer Nat. Found./March of Dimes, White Plains, N.Y., 1972; lectr. community and human relations, Black cultural heritage at local schs. and colls., 1977-87; dir. edn. programs Minn. Ho. Reps., 1987—; radio commentator Sta. KEEY, 1975-80; reporter Twin Cities Courier, Mpls., 1976-86; free lance writer and designer of brochures and pamphlets, 1974—; dir. communications St. Paul Urban League, 1972-80, asst. to exec. dir., 1977-80, 85-86; exec. dir. African Am. Mus. Art and History, 1980-86; info. officer Mpls. Urban League, 1978-79, 85. Founder, bd. dirs. Summit-University Free Press, 1974—; bd. dirs. Help Enable Alcoholics to Receive Treatment, 1977—; adv. bd. Concordia Coll. Minority Program, 1979-85, U. Minn. Black Learning Resource Center, 1980-83; mem. Twin Cities Cable Arts Consortium, Roy Wilkins Meml. Com., St. Paul; mem. state meml. com. Martin Luther King; mem. Ethiopian Famine Relief Com.; mem. rev. com. Twin Cities Mayors' Public Art Awards, 1981; co-founder West Suburban Annual Black History Month Celebration Com., 1983—; mem. St. Paul Civic Ctr. Authority Bd., 1985—; sgt.-at-arms Minn. Ho. of Reps., 1987—. Served to 1st lt., Chem. Corps., U.S. Army, 1959-61. Recipient Community Martin Luther King Communications award, 1978, Spl. Recognition award Mpls. St. Acad., 1983; Spl. Achievement award Roosevelt High Sch., 1985, Liberty Square Tenants' Spl. Recognition award, 1986. Mem. Pub. Relations Soc. Am., Twin Cities Black Journalists Assn., African-Am. Mus. Assn. (nat. legis. edn. com. 1983, exec. council, Midwest region rep. 1984-87). Club: Minn. Press. Author: Reflections of Life-Poems, Prose and Essays, 1981, A Learning Journey Through Black History, 1982; editor, writer: Minnesota's Black Community, 1977; editor Art in Development: A Nigerian Perspective, 1983. Office: 120D State Capitol Saint Paul MN 55155

LAMBERTY, LEONARD KENNETH, physician; b. Scribner, Nebr., July 10, 1941; s. Earlyon John and Gladys Meta (Havekost) L.; m. Eleanor Grace Barton, Dec. 21, 1963; children: David, Michael, Suzanne, Nancy. BS, U. Nebr., 1963, MD, 1966. Diplomate Am. Bd. Family Practice. Intern Deaconess Hosp., Spokane, Wash., 1966-67; physician Southwest Nebr. Med. Ctr., McCook, 1970-72; pvt. practice specializing in family practice Decorah, Iowa, 1972-76; physician Wadena (Minn.) Med. Ctr., 1977—; physician Luther Coll., Decorah, 1972-75; med. cons. Wadena County, 1980—; mem. med. services rev. bd. Minn. Dept. Labor and Industry, St. Paul, 1983—. Mem. Wadena County Child Protection Team, 1979—; flutist Wadena Area Band, 1985—. Served to lt. comdr. USN, 1967-70. Mem. AMA, Am. Acad. Family Physicians, Minn. Acad. Family Physicians (bd. dirs. 1979-83). Republican. Lutheran. Avocations: woodworking, fishing, photography, music. Home: Rural Rt 3 Box 46 Wadena MN 56482 Office: Wadena Med Ctr 4 NW Deerwood Wadena MN 56482

LAMBRECHT, GORDON LEE, personel director; b. Kensal, N.D., Feb. 20, 1936; m. Kathleen Ann Korsmo, June 5, 1961; children: Mark, Jeffrey, Jason. BS, N.D. State U., 1965. Program specialist N.D. Job Service, Bismark, 1966—. Chmn. Govs. Council Employment Handicapped, 1981-87, mem. Council Devel. Disabilities Handicapped, 1984—, Council Human Resources, 1984—, Bismarck Mayor's Com. Handicapped, 1986—; chmn. credit com. Job Service Credit Union, 1984—. Served to sgt. U.S. Army, 1955-57. Named Internat. Peace Gardener Gov. Bismarck, 1984. Mem. Internat. Assn. Personnel Employment Security (Outstanding Employee 1st Place Merit award 1987), N.D. Pub. Employees Assn., Am. Legion (chaplin 1986—). Roman Catholic. Lodges: Elks, Eagles. Home: 708 Crescent Ln Bismarck ND 58501

LAMBRECHTS, EMILE DAUMONT, dentist; b. St. Louis, June 5, 1920; s. Emile Daumont and Julia Cecelia (Walsh) L.; m. Mary Jane Catherine McCartney, Apr. 22, 1947; children: James Michael, Emile Daumont II, Mary Ann Carol, Robert John. DDS, St. Louis U., 1945. Gen. practice dentistry Florissant, Mo., 63031. Exec. sec. St. Apallonia Guild, 1961, mem. 1961—; chmn. bd. Bellevue Acres Village, St. Louis County, 1965-67, health commr., 1967-68, tax collector, 1969; bd. dirs. Christian Bros. Coll., 1969-71. Served with U.S. Army, 1945-46, lt. (j.g.) USN, 1946-48. Recipiuent Merit award St. Appallonia Guild, 1980. Mem. Mo. State Dental Soc. Laboratory Assn. (chmn. 1980—), St. Louis Dental Soc. (chmn. info. com. 1975-80). Roman Catholic. Club: Media (St. Louis). Lodges: Kiwanis, KC. Avocations: hunting, fishing, farming. Home: 17 Jenny Cliffe Ln Chesterfield MO 63007 Office: 1723 S Florissant Florissant MO 63031

LAMBRECHTS, JOHN PAUL, accountant; b. Portsmouth, Va., Feb. 18, 1957; s. Herman I. and Mary Ann (Alexandrowicz) L.; m. Cindy Lou Gerbeth, Aug. 9, 1980; 1 child, Afton Ashley. BS in Acctg., Manchester Coll., 1979; MSBA, Ind. U., South Bend, 1982. CPA, Ind. Fin. analyst Wheelhorse, South Bend, 1979-81; internal auditor Nat. Standard, Niles, Mich., 1981-82, corp. acctg. mgr., 1984-87; cons. corp. fin. reporting The Upjohn Co., Kalamazoo, Mich., 1987—; auditor McGladrey, Hendrickson & Pullen, Elkhart, Ind., 1982-84. Cons. Jr. Achievement, South Bend, 1986, advisor, Niles, 1982. Mem. Am. Inst. CPA's, Nat. Assn. Accts.(bd. dirs. 1983-84). Democrat. Roman Catholic. Avocations: soccer, tropical fish, sports cars. Home: 130 Candlewyck Apt 508 Kalamazoo MI 49001 Office: The Upjohn Co 7000 Portage Rd Kalamazoo MI 49001

LAMBROS, THOMAS DEMETRIOS, U.S. judge; b. Ashtabula, Ohio, Feb. 4, 1930; s. Demetrios P. and Panagoula (Bellios) L.; m. Shirley R. Kresin, June 20, 1953; children: Lesley P., Todd T. Student, Fairmount (W.Va.) State Coll., 1948-49; LL.B., Cleveland-Marshall Law Sch., 1952. Bar: Ohio bar 1952. Partner firm Lambros and Lambros, Ashtabula, 1952-60; judge Ct. Common Pleas, Jefferson, Ohio, 1960-67, U.S. Dist. Ct., No. Dist. Ohio, Cleve., 1967—; mem. faculty Fed. Jud. Center. Contbr. articles legal publs. Mem. exec. bd. N.E. Ohio council Boy Scouts Am.; pres. Ashtabula county chpt. National Found. Served with U.S. Army, 1954-56. Recipient Disting. Service award Ashtabula Jr. C. of C., 1962; Outstanding Young Man of Ohio award Ohio Jaycees, 1963; Man of Yr. award Delta Theta Phi, 1969; Outstanding Alumnus award Cleveland Marshall Coll. of Law, 1974. Fellow Internat. Acad. Law and Sci.; mem. ABA, Ohio Bar Assn., Ashtabula County Bar Assn. (past pres.), Atty. Gen. Advocacy Inst. Innovator of summary jury trial. Office: US Dist Ct 106 US Courthouse Cleveland OH 44114 *

LAMENDOLA, FRANK PHILIP, nurse, educator; b. Kingston, N.Y., Feb. 4, 1949; s. Philip James and Antoinette T. (Taverna) L. Diploma, Cen. ISLIP (N.Y.) State Hosp. Sch. Nursing, 1970; BS in Nursing, Rush U., 1976; MS in Nursing, U. Ill., 1979; cert. Nurse Practitioner, Coll. St. Catherine, 1984. Nursing supr. Rush-Presbyn.- St. Lukes Med. Ctr., Chgo., 1976-78, practitioner, tchr., 1978-79; hospice staff nurse Bethesda Hosp., St. Paul, 1979-80; hospice head nurse No. Meml. Med. Ctr., Robbinsdale, Minn., 1980-82, hospice staff nurse, 1982-85; health edn. dir. Aspen Med. Group, Mpls. and St. Paul, 1985—; candidate screener RNS-CARE, Mpls., 1984-85. Mem. Minn. Nurses Assn. (third dist. pub. affairs dir. 1984-86), Coalition for Terminal Care, Soc. for Pub. Health Educators. Clubs: Twin Cities Men's Chorus (founder 1981, chmn. long range plan 1985-86). Avocations: singing, hiking, reading. Home: 3845 Oakland Ave S Minneapolis MN 55407 Office: Aspen Med Group 7920 Cedar Ave S Bloomington MN 55420

LAMFERS, JEAN A., lawyer; b. St. Paul, June 28, 1959; d. Herbert Frank Sr. and Lois Jean (Bartig) Sakalaucks; m. Jeffrey Lynn Lamfers, June 19, 1982. BS in Journalism, U. Kans., 1981; JD, Washburn U., 1986. Bar: Kans. 1986, U.S. Dist. Ct. Kans. 1986. Anchorwoman Sta. WIBW-TV, Topeka, 1981-83; law clk. Nat. Assn. Broadcasters, Washington, 1985; now with Media Profl. Ins., Kansas City, Mo.; vice chmn., defamation com. torts and ins. practice sect. ABA. Contbr. chpt. on Kans. to book 1987 Media Law 50 State Survey. Mem. ABA (Forum Com. on Communication Law), Kans. Bar Assn., Kansas City Met. Bar Assn., Alpha Phi (pres. corp. bd. Lawrence 1985—). Avocation: photography. Office: Media Profl Ins 1001 E 101st Terr Kansas City MO 64131

LAMINEN, DALE WILLIAM, technical information engineer; b. Cloquet, Minn., Oct. 31, 1939; s. William Toivo and Veronica Barbara (Beaupre) Lamminen; m. Mary Ann Feldhaus, May 13, 1959; children: Pamela, Carmella, Karen. With engring. tech. info. div. Sperry Univac, St. Paul, 1960-63, supr., 1963-75, mgr., 1975—. Project leader Pierce County 4-H, Wis., 1975—. Named Friend of 4-H, Pierce County, 1976, 82. Mem. Assn. Image and Info. Mgmt. Congregationalist. Avocations: hunting, horsemanship, cattle farming. Home: 63 Viking View Rd Spring Valley WI 54767 Office: Sperry Univac Box 3525 Saint Paul MN 55165

LAMKIN, MARTHA DAMPF, lawyer; b. Talladega, Ala., May 20, 1942; d. Keith J. and Neva (Magness) Dampf; m. E. Henry Lamkin Jr., Aug. 28, 1968; children: Melinda Magness, Matthew Davidson. BA in summa cum laude, Calif. Baptist Coll., 1964; MA in English and Am. Lit., Vanderbilt U., 1966; JD, Ind. U., 1970. Bar: Ind. 1970. Assoc. Joseph D. Geeslin, Indpls., 1971-72, Lowe, Gray, Steel & Hoffman, Indpls., 1979-82; field office mgr. U.S. Dept. Housing and Urban Devel., Indpls., 1982-87; exec. dir. govtl. affairs Cummins Engine Co., Inc., Columbus, Ind., 1987—. commr., sec., chmn. Indpls. Human Rights Commn., Indpls., 1971-79; commr. Indpls. Housing Authority, 1979-82; chmn., exec. council S.K. Lacy Exec. Leadership, Indpls., 1986-87; chmn. Ind. Leadership Celebration, Indpls., 1985-87; sec. Gov.'s Mansion Commn., Indpls., 1981—; bd. dirs. Great Indpls. Progress Commn., 1986-87, Indpls. Symphony Orchestra, 1983—, Indpls. Project, 1986—; bd. dirs., v.p. Indpls. Zoo, 1980—; chmn. bd. trustees Christian Theol. Sem., Indpls., 1983—; mem. exec. com. Mayor's Task Force on Housing, 1987—. Recipient Presdl. Rank award 1985, Mental Health Initiative Gov. Ind., 1986, Matrix award Women in Communication, 1987. Mem. ABA, Ind. Bar Assn., Indpls. Bar Assn., State Assembly Women (pres. 1977-79), Indpls. Jr. League. Republican. Mem. Christian Ch. Office: Cummins Engine Co Inc PO Box 3005 Columbus IN 47202-3005

LAMMERT, LELAND VAL, communications company executive, author, consultant; b. Portland, Oreg., Jan. 6, 1955; s. Valentine Frank and Louise Marie (Gerfe) L.; B.S.E.E., U. Mo., 1976; M.S.E.E., So. Meth. U., 1979; Ph.D., Calif. Western U., 1982; m. Nancy Jane Wright, May 6, 1978. Design engr. Tex. Instruments, Sherman, Tex., 1977-79; sr. systems engr. Emerson Electric, St. Louis, 1979-82; pres. Omnitec Corp., St. Louis, 1980—, System Research Assocs., St. Louis, 1982-84, Omnitec Ventures Corp., 1983—; propr. Orion Systems, Creve Coeur, Mo., 1981-83; v.p. MLD Computer Services, St. Louis, 1982-86; exec. dir. Triad Found., 1985—; pres. Interactive Video Productions, 1986—. Mem. Ind. Computer Cons. Assn. (pres. St. Louis chpt.), IEEE, ACM, Am. Entrepreneurs Assn., Nat. Soc. Profl. Engrs., Mo. Soc. Profl. Engrs., Sigma Xi. Contbr. articles to profl. jours., various tech. training programs. Address: PO Box 12747 Saint Louis MO 63141

LA MOTHE, ESTHER ELIZABETH, english educator; b. Cass City, Mich., Dec. 16, 1946; d. Arlington Earl and Marion Elizabeth (Leishman) Gray; m. Roger Joseph LaMothe, Aug. 9, 1969; children: Joseph Arlington, Robert Charles. BA, Cen. Mich. U., 1969, MA, 1972. Lic. real estate agt., Mich. Tchr. English and speech, head English dept. Vandercook Lake Pub. Schs., Jackson, Mich., 1969—; advisor quiz bowl Vandercook Lake Pub. Schs., 1976—, acad. game, 1979—, coordinator creative writing, 1979—. Contbr. articles to newspapers. Bd. dirs., treas. Jackson Child Care Ctr., 1976-84; active latchkey adv. com. Jackson Pub. Schs., 1984, gifted/talented com., 1986-87. Creative writing workshop grantee Kellogg Corp., 1983; recipient creative writing awards Mich. Youth Fine Arts Council, 1983. Mem. Mich. Council Tchrs. English, Mich. Assn. for Academically Talented, NEA, Mich. Edn. Assn. (local v.p., sec. 1969—), Les Amis du Vin. Republican. Avocations: crossword puzzles, reading, traveling, wine. Home: 5885 Marengo Jackson MI 49201 Office: Vandercook Lake High Sch 1000 Golf Ave Jackson MI 49201

LA MOTHE, ROGER JOSEPH, utility executive; b. Sault Ste Marie, Mich., Jan. 3, 1942; s. Joseph Herman and Myerl Adeline (Smith) La M.; m. Esther Elizabeth Gray, Aug. 9, 1969; children: Joseph Arlington, Robert Charles. Rate analyst Consumers Power Co., Jackson, Mich., 1972-73, gen. rate analyst, 1973-75, sr. rate analyst, 1975-78, supr. rate analyst, 1975-78, 1978-84, rate adminstrn. supr., 1984—; pres., v.p., treas. Pro-gro Investments, Jackson, 1980—. Wine judge Mich. State Fair, Detroit, 1986-87; troop com. Boy Scouts Am., Jackson, 1986—; bd. dirs. Mich. Theatre Preservation Assn., Jackson, 1975-83; v.p Jackson County Rose Festival, 1985—. Mem. Mensa. Club: Les Amis du Vin (dir. 1974—, Dir. of Yr. 1984). Lodge: Lions (v.p. Jackson 1985—, pres., sec. Eyeopeners 1984—). Avocation: amateur radio, bicycling. Home: 5885 Marengo St Jackson MI 49201 Office: Consumers Power Co 212 W Michigan Ave Jackson MI 49201

LAMOTHE, WILLIAM EDWARD, food company executive; b. Bklyn., Oct. 23, 1926; s. William John and Gertrude (Ryan) LaM.; A.B., Fordham U., 1950; m. Patricia Alexander, June 24, 1950. With Kellogg Sales Co., 1950-60, product devel. coordinator, 1958-60; asst. to pres. Kellogg Co., Battle Creek, Mich., 1960-65, v.p., 1962-70, v.p., corporate devel., 1965-70, sr. v.p. corporate devel., 1970-73, pres., chief operating officer, 1973-79, pres., chief exec. officer, 1979-80, chmn. bd., chief exec. officer, 1980—, also dir. Office: Kellogg Co PO Box 3599 Battle Creek MI 49016-3599 *

LAMOTTE, JOHN VINCENT, JR., city planner; b. Chgo., Mar. 25, 1954; s. John Vincent and Paula Ann (Sommers) LaM. BS in Urban Planning, U. Utah, 1977; MS Urban and Regional Planning, U. Wis., 1980. Planner Des Plaines, Ill., 1977-78; project coordinator Columbia County, Wis., 1979-80; city planner Chgo. Econ. Devel. Commn., 1981-82; program dir. Chgo. Dept. Econ. Devel., 1982-83; dir. planning Perkins & Will, Chgo., 1983-87; v.p. planning Lohan Assocs., Chgo., 1987—. Vol. mediator Neighborhood Justice Ctr.; chmn. Albany Park Planning Com.; bd. dirs. Ravenswood Manor Improvement Assn., N. River Commn., Lawrence Area Devel. Corp. Mem. Am. Planning Assoc. (chmn Chgo. Met. sect.), Am. Inst. Cert. Planners (cert.), Nat. Council for Urban Econ. Devel., Comml. Real Estate Orgn., Chgo. High Tech Assn. Roman Catholic.

LAMOTTE, WILLIAM MITCHELL, insurance brokerage company executive; b. Phila., Sept. 3, 1938; s. Ferdinand and June (Mitchell) LaM.; B.A., Princeton U., 1961; m. Elizabeth Ewing, Sept. 16, 1961; children—William Mitchell, Anne Hilliard, Nicole. Underwriter, Chubb & Son, N.Y.C., 1961-62; various assignments Johnson & Higgins Pa., Inc., Phila., 1962-69, pres. Johnson & Higgins Wilmington, Del., 1969-75, pres. Johnson & Higgins Mo. Inc., St. Louis, 1975-77, Johnson & Higgins Ill. Inc., Chgo., 1977—, dir. parent firm. Vice pres. Boys Clubs Wilmington, 1974-75; bd. dirs. St. Louis Zoo Friends Assn., 1976-77, Lincoln Park Zool. Soc., 1981—; bd. dirs. Chgo. Boys and Girls Clubs, 1983—, pres., 1984. Clubs: Corinthian Yacht (Phila.); Chicago, Chgo. Yacht, Indian Hill. Home: 109 Greenbay Rd Hubbard Woods IL 60093 Office: Johnson & Higgins Ill Inc 101 S Wacker Dr Chicago IL 60606

LAMOUREUX, GERARD WILLIAM, container manufacturing company executive; b. Chgo., July 27, 1946; s. Donald Benjamin and Anna Rita (Williamson) L.; B.S. in Mech. Engring. Tech., Purdue U., 1970; m. Gloria Jean Kempa, Feb. 13, 1971; children—Gerard Joseph, Jennifer Ann, Brian Gerard. Design draftsman Whiting Corp., Harvey, Ill., 1967-69; plant engr. DeSoto, Inc., Chicago Heights, Ill., 1970-74; maintenance mgr. Panduit Corp., Tinley Park, Ill., 1974-75; plant engr., plant supt. Container Corp. Am., Dolton, Ill., 1975-79, plant engr., Anderson, Ind., 1979-84, sr. staff engr., Carol Stream, Ill., 1984-86, project engr. Jefferson Smurfit Corp. and Container Corp. Am., Carol Stream, 1986—. Mem. mech. adv. bd. Thornton Community Coll., South Holland, Ill., 1975-79. Mem. South Holland United Fund-Crusade of Mercy Com., 1976-78; bd. dirs. Madison County Jr. Achievement, 1980-83. Mem. Am. Inst. Plant Engrs., Madison County Mgmt. Club (v.p. 1984), TAPPI (exec. com. Chgo. sect. 1987-88), Anderson Jaycees, Anderson YMCA, Christian Fellowship Businessmen, Full Gospel Businessmen's Fellowship Internat., Purdue U. Alumni Assn., South Holland Jaycees (pres. 1978-79, state dir. 1976-77). Roman Catholic. Home: 505 Longmeadow Circle Saint Charles IL 60174 Office: 450 E North Carol Stream IL 60188

LAMPING, WILLIAM JAY, lawyer; b. Detroit, Aug. 27, 1954; s. William Jay and Marilyn Alice (Welsand) L.; m. Kathryn Szczepanik, July 18, 1981; children: Elizabeth, Jacqueline. BS, U. Mich., 1976; JD, Wayne State U., 1979. Bar: Mich. 1979, U.S. Dist. Ct. (ea. dist.) Mich. 1979, U.S. Ct. Appeals (6th cir.) 1981. Research asst., Wayne State U. Law Sch., Detroit, 1978-79; clk. Wayne County Cir. Ct., Detroit, 1979-80; assoc. Kiefer, Allen, Cavanagh & Toohey, Detroit, 1980-82; ptnr. Fieger, Fieger & Lamping, Southfield, Mich., 1982-84, William J. Lamping, P.C., Birmingham, Mich., 1984-86, Vestevich, Dritsas, McManus, Evans, Payne & Vicko, P.C., Bloomfield Hills, Mich., 1986—; ptnr. Woodward Fin. Services Group, Birmingham, 1984—; arbitrator Better Bus. Bur., Detroit, 1981. Mem. steering com. Ann Arbor Tenants Union, Mich., 1976. Nat. Merit scholar U. Mich., Ann Arbor, 1972. Mem. ABA, State Bar Mich., Assn. Trial Lawyers Am., Mich. Trial Lawyers Assn. Democrat. Roman Catholic. Lodge: Optimists. Home: 34209 Banbury Farmington Hills MI 48018 Office: Vestevich Dritsas McManus et al 800 W Long Lake Rd Suite 200 Bloomfield Hills MI 48013

LAMPIRIS, LEWIS NICK, dentist; b. N.Y.C., Apr. 3, 1952; s. Nicholas and Koula (Karras) L. BA cum laude, CUNY, 1973; DDS, Temple U., 1977. Gen. practice dentistry Chgo., 1981—. Served to capt. U.S. Army, 1977-81. Greek Orthodox. Office: 646 N Michigan Ave Suite 408 Chicago IL 60611

LANDAZURI, COLLEEN ANN, public health nurse; b. Fond du Lac, Wis., Sept. 8, 1950; d. James Edward and Elizabeth Ann (Masloff) Flood; m. Gabriel Landazuri, Oct. 26, 1974; children: Dario James, Patrick Xavier, Alexander Gabriel. BS in Nursing, Marquette U., 1972, postgrad., 1976-77. Staff nurse Nursing Bur., Milw. Health Dept., 1972-75, Lady Pitts program nurse, 1975-76, dist. supr., 1976-80, dir. prenatal edn. and assessment program, 1980—; fed. nurse trainee, 1976-77, coordinator interdisciplinary dental and nursing student program Marquette U. Sch. Dentistry, 1976-77. Mem. Greater Milw. Com. for Unmarried Parent's Services, 1980—, vice co-chairperson., 1985, chairperson, 1986; mem. critical health problems curriculum adv. com. Milw. Pub. Schs., 1980-86, chmn., 1982-84; mem. adv. com., sch. aged parents program Lady Pitts Ctr., 1980—; mem. adv. com. Family Hosp. Teen Pregnancy Service, 1984—, nurse adv. com. March of Dimes, 1985-86; choir mem. St. Catherine's Ch. Mem. Sherman Park Community Assn., Orgn. Twin-Blessed Mothers (sec. 1984), Sigma Theta Tau. Roman Catholic. Club: North Shore Jrs. Woman's. Home: 3368 N 44th St Milwaukee WI 53216 Office: 841 N Broadway Suite 228 Milwaukee WI 53202

LANDERS, RAY DANIEL, musician, author, composer, lecturer, educator; b. Kissimmee, Fla., Nov. 17, 1942; s. John Silvey and Jewel Oline (Fain) L.; Mus.B., Sherwood Conservatory of Music, 1964; Mus.M., Northwestern U., 1966; Mus.D., Ind. U., 1974. Assoc. instr. Sch. Music, Ind. U., 1966-71; instr. dept. music Chgo. State U., 1971-75, asst. prof., 1975-79, assoc. prof., 1979-80; founder, dir. Suzuki Music Acad. of Chgo., 1975-86, Chicagoland Suzuki Music Festival, 1981-86, Chgo. Summer Suzuki Inst., 1982-86; mem. faculty Am. Suzuki Inst., U. Wis., 1976—, Westminster Choir Coll. Conservatory, 1986—; founder, bd. dirs. Andrews Internat. Music Festival, 1986—; advisor Suzuki Music Assn. Greater Chgo., 1986—; pianist, clinician, U.S., Can., Europe, Australia; participant Tchaikovsky Internat. Competition, Moscow, 1970, Vianna da Motta Competition, Lisbon, 1971, Rockefeller Competition for Excellence in Am. Music, Chgo., 1978; performed concertos with Sherwood Symphony Orch., Chgo. Chamber Orch., Ind. U. and Gold Coast orchs; also numerous raido and TV interviews and performances. Mem. Music Educators Nat. Conf., Music Tchrs. Nat. Assn., Ill. State Music Tchrs. Assn., Suzuki Assn. Americas (chmn. publ. com., former nat. bd. dirs.). Composer numerous mus. compositions. Author: The Talent Education School of Shihichi Suzuki-An Analysis, The Importance of Arts in Am., Second Piano Accompaniments for Teachers and Students, Is Suzuki Education Working in America? also articles and recordings. Office: Suzuki Mus Assn Chgo 3000 W 179 Pl Hazel Crest IL 60429

LANDERS, RUSSELL DEAN, insurance company executive; b. Charles City, Iowa, Nov. 5, 1949; s. Ardean Henry and Inez Margaret (Rodman) L.; m. Becky Lea Landers, Aug. 23, 1969; children: Ryan Dean, Amy Lynn, Michael Dean. AAS, Ellsworth Coll., 1969; BA, U. North Iowa, 1973. Tchr. music Waterloo (Iowa) Schs., 1974-78; broker farm real estate Doanne Agrl. Service, St. Louis, 1978-80; broker comml. real estate Land Pac Brokers, Waterloo, 1980-82; mgr. ins., inventory A.L. Williams Assocs., Waterloo, 1982—. Dir., player Brass Choir Zion Luth. Ch., Waterloo, 1987. Republican. Avocation: pvt. pilot.

LANDFIELD, BARBARA JENSWOLD, editor, bookseller; b. Duluth, Minn., July 27, 1921; d. John Darrah and Marion M. (Townsend) Jenswold; m. Sidney Landfield, Feb. 27, 1945 (dec. Apr. 1977); children—Bruce, Susan, Scott, Robert. Student Mills Coll., 1939-40; B.A., U. Mich., 1943. Reporter, City News Bur., Chgo., 1943-44; asst. editor World Book Ency., Chgo., 1945-47; assoc. editor Am. Educator Ency., Lake Bluff, Ill., 1960-66; owner The Book Post, Duluth, Minn., 1971—; editor Lake Superior Mag., Duluth, 1983—. Co-author: The Other Side of the Sheet, 1965. Mem. Kappa Kappa Gamma. Home: 2234 Woodland Ave Duluth MN 55803 Office: 325 Lake Ave S Duluth MN 55802

LANDINI, RICHARD GEORGE, university president, English educator; b. Pitts., June 4, 1929; s. George R. and Alice (Hoy) L.; m. Phyllis Lesnick, Nov. 26, 1952; children—Richard, Gregory, Matthew, Cynthia, Vincent. A.B., U. Miami, 1954, M.A., 1956; Ph.D., U. Fla., 1959; D.Civil Law, Quincy Coll., 1985; LLD, U. Miami, 1980, Baiko Jo Gakuin Coll., Japan, 1987. From asst. prof. to prof. English Ariz. State U., 1959-70, dean, 1968-70; prof. English, acad. v.p. U. Mont., 1970-75; pres. Ind. State U., 1975—, prof. English, 1975—; bd. dirs., sec., Ind. Corp. for Sci. and Tech., 1984—. Contbr. articles on lit. and higher edn. to profl. jours. Served with U.S. Army, 1948-51. Mem. Phi Beta Kappa, Phi Delta Kappa, Phi Alpha Theta, Phi Kappa Phi. Roman Catholic. Office: Ind State U President's Office Terre Haute IN 47809

LANDIS, GEORGE HARVEY, psychotherapist; b. Newton, Kans., Dec. 12, 1918; s. Melvin D. and Erie Emma (Byler) L.; student Baker U., 1937-38; B.A., John Fletcher Coll., 1941; M.S.W., U. Nebr., 1948. Diplomate Registry of Clin. Social Workers; m. Lois I. Donaldson, Sept. 26, 1943; children—Judy Carol Landis Forsman, Richard G. Caseworker, Family Service of Omaha, 1948-50; psychotherapist Midwest Clinic, Omaha, 1950—, Served with U.S. Army, 1941-46. Mem. Acad. Cert. Social Workers, Registry Clin. Social Workers. Home: 4628 Hascall St Omaha NE 68106 Office: 105 S 49th St Omaha NE 68132

LANDIS, SALLY LOU, furniture manufacturers representative, restaurant executive; b. Youngstown, Ohio, Oct. 13, 1950; d. Eugene Louis and Mary Grace (Murphy) Dougherty. Interior designer Strouss Dept. Stores, Youngstown, 1973-74, dir. 3 design studios, 1975-77, upholstery, occasional buyer, 1978-81; furniture sales rep. Bruard's Inc., Ohio and Ky. ters., 1982—, Furniture Imports Inc., State of Ohio, 1982—, Hickory Ridge Furniture Inc., State of Ohio, State of Ky., 1984—, Progressive Furniture Inc., State of Ohio, 1986—; owner Cornerburg Pizza franchise, 1984—. Mem. Cleve. Home Furnishings Reps. Assn., Nat. Assn. Female Execs. Democrat. Roman Catholic. Avocations: interior design, golfing, gourmet cooking. Office: PO Box 3155 Youngstown OH 44512

LANDMAN, LOUIS CHARLES, chemical company executive; b. St. Paul, Aug. 31, 1914; s. Philip Albert and Julia Florence (Smith) L.; m. Mae Catherine Claffey, Oct. 22, 1938; children: L. Charles Jr., Mary Louise Landman Nixon. BA, Coll. St. Thomas; LLD, St. Mary's Coll., Winona,

Minn., 1969. Pres. Nat. Chems. Inc., Winona, 1949-79, sr. exec. officer, 1979—. Served to lt. USN, 1944-47. Republican. Roman Catholic. Avocation: golf. Home: 627 Market St Winona MN 55987 Office: Nat Chems Inc 105 Liberty St Box 32 Winona MN 55987

LANDMARK, DANIEL MICHAEL, farmer; b. Montevideo, Minn., July 22, 1947; s. Harold F. and Petra O. (Nydhal) L.; m. Audrey K. Rasmussen, Nov. 29, 1980 (div. Nov. 1982). BS, Southwest State U., Marshall, Minn., 1979; postgrad., Granite Falls (Minn.) Area Vocat.-Tech. Sch., 1986-87. Farmer Granite Falls, 1967—. Mem. Yellow Medicine County Farm Bur. Democrat-Farm-Laborer. Avocations: photography, golf, audio and video recording. Home and Office: Rt 1 Box 142 Granite Falls MN 56241

LANDMESSER, HAROLD LEON, tool distributor consultant; b. Mt. Clemons, Mich., Mar. 12, 1917; s. A.R. and Ottilie (Berlin) L.; m. Grace Rae Valmore, Apr. 27, 1940 (dec. Aug. 1981); children: Frederick, Lawrence; m. Geraldine Gretchine Schaupner, Feb. 12, 1982. Student, U. Detroit, 1936. Salesman Snap-On Tools Corp., Detroit, 1936-40, field salesman, 1940-42, asst. mgr., 1942-56, mgr., 1956-61; owner Landmesser Tools Co., Pontiac, Mich., Chgo., 1962-82; cons. Landmesser Tools Co., Pontiac, 1982—. Lodge: Elks (Pontiac). Home: 3605 Lakefront Pontiac MI 48054 Office: Landmesser Tools Co 960 S Cass Lake Rd Pontiac MI 48054

LANDOLT, RUDOLPH F., insurance company executive; b. 1922. BA, Pa. State U., postgrad. With Lumbermen's Mut. Casualty Co., Lake Zurich, Ill., 1949—, sr. exec. v.p., 1978-81, now pres.; pres., also bd. dirs. Am. Motorists Ins. Co., Long Grove, Ill. Served with AUS, 1942-45. Office: Lumbermens Mut Casualty Co Kemper Center Long Grove IL 60049 *

LANDON, DONALD DEAN, sociology educator; b. Council Bluffs, Iowa, May 23, 1930; s. Lee Edward and Lucille (Eliason) L.; m. Shirley Johnson, May 4, 1952 (div. Apr. 1971); m. Lea Crim, Jan. 23, 1972; children: Mark, Scott, Larry, Jon, Mary, David. AA, Graceland Coll., 1950; BA, U. Mo., Kansas City, 1962; MA, U. Mo., 1966; PhD, U. Kans., 1977. Minister Reorganized Ch. Jesus Christ of Latter Day Sts., 1951-60; radio minister Reorganized Ch. Jesus Christ of Latter Day Sts., Independence, Mo., 1960-65, commn. edn., 1965-70; prof. sociology Southwest Mo. State U., Springfield, 1970-84, head dept. sociology, anthropology and social work, 1984—. Author: To Be the Salt of the Earth, 1966, For What Purposes Assembled, 1969; contbr. articles to sociology jours. Mem. Am. Sociological Assn., Midwest Sociological Assn., Law and Soc. Assn., Am Bar Found. (visiting scholar, 1982-83). Mem. Christian Ch. Avocations: golf, backpacking, gardening. Home: 3538 E Carol Dr Springfield MO 65804 Office: SW Mo State U Sociology Dept Springfield MO 65804

LANDOW, MICHELE KARLA, accounting educator; b. Lockport, N.Y., Aug. 21, 1953; d. Robert and Ada (Riemer) L.; m. Glenn Steele Price, July 31, 1982. BSBA, Valparaiso (Ind.) U., 1975; MBA, U. Chgo., 1980. Sr. tax staff Arthur Andersen & Co., Chgo., 1975-79, tax mgr., 1979-83; edn. mgr. Arthur Andersen & Co., St. Charles, Ill., 1983-86, sr. edn. mgr., 1986—. Mem. Am. Inst. CPA's, Ill. Soc. CPA's, Chgo. Women's Soc. CPA's, Am. Soc. Tng. and Devel. Avocations: remodeling, church activities. Office: Arthur Andersen & Co 1405 N 5th Ave Saint Charles IL 60174

LANDRETH, JOHN CHARLES, auditor; b. Chgo., Apr. 14, 1957; s. Oliver Vincent and Edith (Hillman) L.; m. Patricia Jane Collins, Sept. 11, 1982; 1 child, David Oliver. BAcctg., De Paul U., 1979, postgrad., 1987—. CPA, Ill. Staff acct. Arthur Andersen & Co., Chgo., 1979-81; sr. auditor United Ins. Am., Chgo., 1981-84; dir. internal audit dept. Northwestern Meml. Hosp., Chgo., 1984—. Mem. Am. Inst. CPA's, Healthcare Internal Auditors Group (regional coordinator 1986—, instr. 1987), Healthcare Fin. Mgmt. Assn., Inst. Internal Auditors. Republican. Avocations: photography, golf, tennis, backgammon. Home: 1026 S Cleveland Park Ridge IL 60068 Office: Northwestern Meml Hosp 259 E Erie Room 601 Chicago IL 60068

LANDRY, MARK EDWARD, podiatrist, researcher; b. Washington, May 24, 1950; s. John Edward and Daphne (Fay) L.; m. Mary Ann Kotey, Sept. 7, 1974; children: John Ryan, Christopher John, Jessica Marie. D in Podiatry, Ohio Coll. Podiatric Medicine, 1975; MS in Edn., U. Kans., 1982. Diplomate Am. Bd. Podiatric Surgery. Gen. pratice podiatry Kansas City, Mo., 1977—; clin. asst. prof. U. Health Scis., Kansas City, 1979—; clin. assoc. prof. Coll. Podiatric Medicine and Surgery, U. Osteo. Medicine and Health Scis., Des Moines, 1985—; clin. instr. Sch. Medicine, U. Mo., Kansas City, 1987—; founder, dir., Kansas City Podiatric Residency Program, Kansas City, 1982—; chmn. podiatry staff Univ. Hosp., Kansas City, 1979—. Contbr. articles to profl. jours. Cons. Mid-Am. Track and Field Assn., Lenexa, Kans., 1978—; com. chmn. Boy Scouts Am., Overland ParK, Kans., coach Johnson County Soccer League, 1983-86. Served to 1st lt. USAF, 1975-77. Recipient Pres.'s award Ohio Sch. Podiatric Medicine, 1975; USAF scholar Armed Forces Health Professions, 1973-75. Fellow Am. Coll. Foot Surgeons, Acad. Podiatric Sports Medicine; mem. Mid-Am. Masters Field and Track Assn., British Podiatry Assn. (hon.). Republican. Roman Catholic. Clubs: Holy Cross Social (pres. 1983-84), Athletic (Overland Park). Avocations: swimming, running, weight tng. Home: 8120 W 99th St Overland Park KS 66212 Office: 8600 W 95th #201 Overland Park KS 66212

LANDSKE, DOROTHY SUZANNE, state senator; b. Evanston, Ill., Sept. 3, 1937; d. William Gerald and Dorothy Marie (Drewes) Martin; m. William Steve Landske, June 1, 1957; children—Catherine Suzanne Hudson, Jacqueline Marie Stoops, Pamela Florence Landske Snyder, Cheryl Lynn, Eric Thomas. Student St. Joseph's Coll., Ind. U., U. Chgo. Receptionist Cedar Lake Med. Clinic (Ind.) 1959-62; owner, operator Sues Bridal House, 1967-75; dep. clk.-treas., Cedar Lake, 1975; chief dep. twp. assessor Center Twp., Crown Point, Ind., 1976-78, twp. assessor, 1979-84, mem. Ind. Senate, 1984—. Vice chmn. Lake County Republican Central Com., 1978—; Lake County rep. to 5th Congl. Dist.; mem. Women's Week panel Purdue U.-Calumet. Mem. Council State Govts., Nat. Order Women Legislators. Roman Catholic. Office: 7325 W 143rd Ave Cedar Lake IN 46303

LANDSKRONER, LAWRENCE, lawyer; b. N.Y.C., June 9, 1927; s. Jack and Jean (Hershofsky) L.; m. Florence Alberta Blaiwes, July 2, 1957; children—Leigh, Lynn, Kathy, Jack. Student Dennison U., 1945, Union Coll., 1945, Miami U., Oxford, Ohio, 1946; LL.B., Vanderbilt U., 1950, J.D., 1979. Diplomate Nat. Bd. Trial Advocacy; bar: Ohio 1950. Sole practice, Cleve., 1950-52; gen. counsel Region 2 UAW, W. Pa., No. Ohio, 1970-81; sr. ptnr. Landskroner & Phillips, Cleve., 1952—; spl. counsel to atty. gen. State of Ohio, Cleve., 1970—; acting judge Arbitration Common Pleas Ct., Am. Arbitration Assn.; part-time lectr. law Case Western Res. U. Law Sch., Cleve. State U. Law Sch.; moot ct. judge Case Western Res. Law Sch.; gen. counsel Fraternal Order of Police of Ohio, 1975—; lectr. Contbr. articles to legal jours. Bd. dirs. Legal Aid Soc., Cleve., 1978-85; bd. dirs. Cleve. Met. Gen. Hosp., 1974-86, No. Ohio March of Dimes, Cleve., 1977—, Kolff Found., Cleve., 1979-80. Served with USNR, 1945-46. Mem. Assn. Trial Lawyers Am. (lectr. 1960—), Ohio Bar Assn., Cuyahoga County Bar Assn., Cleve. Bar Assn., Ohio Trial Lawyers Assn., Vanderbilt Alumni Assn. (pres. No. Ohio 1975-81, Inner Circle Advocates 1985). Club: Lakeside Yacht (Cleve.) (vice commodore 1965, trustee).

LANE, ARDEN RICHARD, sales and marketing executive, consultant; b. Chgo., July 4, 1935; s. Richard Henry Lane and Evelyn (Gates) Rod; m. Marie E. Spence, Feb. 16, 1974; 1 child, Suzanne. BA in Mktg., Northwestern U., 1960. Resident store mgr. Jewel Food Stores, Chgo., 1954-64; v.p. sales Dominion Foods, Evanston, Ill., 1964-70; nat. sales mgr. Pompeian, Inc., Balt., 1970-73; sales mgr. Lindsay (Calif.) Internat., 1973-74; v.p. sales, mktg. A.J. Funk Co., Elgin, Ill., 1974—; advt. cons. Food Market News, Chgo., 1980—. Rep. precinct capt., Arlington Heights, Ill., 1965-68. Mem. Grocery Mfrs. Sales Execs. (bd. dirs. 1976-83, pres. 1981, disting. service award 1981), Merchandising Exec. Club (bd. dirs. 1983). Methodist. Avocations: sailing, golf, racquetball, swimming. Home: 188 Betty Dr Inverness IL 60010

LANE, DAVID WILSON, advertising executive; b. Alva, Okla., Dec. 9, 1939; s. Samuel Walter and Mayme Myrle (Anderson) L.; m. Karen Sue Stallman, June 16, 1963; children: Laura, Darla, Jennifer. AA, Hutchinson (Kans.) Jr. Coll., 1959; BA, Okla. City U., 1961. Acct. exec. Watson Assocs., Hutchinson, 1961-62, owner, 1962-65; prin. Lane Ltd., Hutchinson, 1965-71; pres. Lane & Leslie Advt. Agy., Hutchinson, 1971-79, Wichita, Kans., 1979—; trustee Affiliated Advt. Agencies Internat., Denver, treas., 1985-86. Office: Lane & Leslie Advt Agy 221 S Broadway Wichita KS 67202

LANE, JUDITH ANN, teacher; b. Ft. Worth, Tex., July 12, 1944; d. Harry Timmons and Charlsie Grace (Hogue) Harmount; m. Bobby Jan Lane, Nov. 18, 1966; children: Kent Timmons, Molly Melissa. BA in English and History magna cum laude, Tex. Christian U., 1966; postgrad., Wright State U., 1974, Miami U., Oxford, Ohio, 1982, U. Cin., 1982-86. Cert. tchr., Ohio, Tex. Tchr., sr. class advisor L.D. Bell High Sch., Hurst, Tex., 1966-69; learning disabled tchr. Kettering (Ohio) Bd. Edn., 1974-77; tchr. learning disabled Carlisle (Ohio) Local Bd. Edn., 1980; tchr. social studies D. Russel Lee Vocat. Sch., Hamilton, Ohio, 1981—, faculty adv. com., 1982-84; coordinator Ohio's Yr. of Reflections, 1986-87. leader Girl Scouts Am., Franklin, 1979-81; coach Hunter Youth Recreation Assn., Franklin, 1979—; mem. chorus Middletown Symphony, 1979-83; chmn. Franklin Soccer Parents Club, 1986; mem. external task force Butler County Levy Com., 1987—. Martha Holden Jennings Found. scholar, 1986—; Taft Inst. Two-Party Govt. scholar, 1987. Mem. Nat. Council for Social Studies, Ohio Council for Social Studies, Greater Cin. Council for Econ. Edn., Mortar Bd., Phi Alpha Theta (pres.), Kappa Alpha Theta (v.p. 1983-84). Republican. Episcopalian. Club: Promises (program chmn. 1979-83). Avocations: racquetball, needlework. Office: D Russel Lee Vocat Sch 3603 Hamilton-Middleton Rd Hamilton OH 45011

LANE, RONALD, dentist; b. Flint, Mich., Aug. 17, 1958; s. Hovie Curtis Jr. and Caroline Ruth (Wallace) L.; m. Diane Marie Ruzicka, Aug. 7, 1981; 1 child, Christopher Paul. BS in Chemistry, U. Mich., 1980; DDS, U. Detroit, 1984. Pvt. practice dentistry Ortonville, Mich., 1984—. Mem. ADA, Acad. Gen. Dentistry, Mich. Dental Assn. Democrat. Avocations: running, softball, bowling. Office: 830 M-15 Box 110 Ortonville MI 48462

LANE, STEPHEN JOHN, financial analyst, financial planner; b. Fairbury, Ill., June 26, 1949; s. Seth William Lane and Naomi Lavonne (Barnhart) Bossong; m. Suzanne Marie Schulz, July 19, 1975; children: Robert S., Stephanie S. BS, Ind. State U., 1972. CPA, Ohio, Ill.; cert. fin. planner. From controller trainee to store controller Sears Roebuck & Co., Chgo., 1972-81, acctg. group controller, 1981-83, acctg. ctr. controller, 1983-84, adminstrv. group internal controller, 1984, fin. analyst, 1984—. Mem. Am. Inst. CPA's. Club: Arrowhead Health (Wheaton, Ill.). Avocations: white water rafting, reading.

LANE, WILLIAM NOBLE, III, financial executive; b. Evanston, Ill., Aug. 2, 1943; s. William Noble and Marjorie Elizabeth (Hamilton) L.; children: Campbell, Heather, Carl. A.B., Princeton U., 1965. Salesman, Wallace Press, Inc., 1965-66; mgr. corp. planning Gen. Binding Corp., Northbrook, Ill., 1966-72; vice chmn. Gen. Binding Corp., 1978-82, chmn., 1983—; pres. Northwestco, Inc., Chgo., 1972-78; chmn. bd., pres. Lane Industries, Inc., Northbrook, 1978—; chmn. bd. Lake View Trust & Savs. Bank, Chgo., N.W. Nat. Bank Chgo., Pioneer Bank & Trust Co., Northbrook Trust & Savs. Bank; dir. Hydraulic Component Services, Inc., Otis Assos. (architects), Schwaab, Inc. Trustee Rush Presbyn. St. Luke's Med. Center, Chgo., Lake Forest (Ill.) Acad., Chgo. Zool. Soc.; bd. govs. United Republican Fund Ill.; mem. Northwestern U. Assos.; econ. adv. council Princeton U.; bd. dirs. Irving Park YMCA, Chgo. Mem. Explorers Club. Episcopalian. Clubs: Winter (Lake Forest), Onwnetsia (Lake Forest); Princeton (N.Y.C.); Port Royal Beach (Naples, Fla.); Commonwealth (Chgo.), Univ. (Chgo.), Econ. (Chgo.); Adventurers. Office: Gen Binding Corp 1 GBC Plaza Northbrook IL 60062 *

LANE, WILLIAM W., automobile company executive; b. 1929. With Gen. Motors Corp., 1953—, dist. mgr. Oldsmobile div., 1953-55, office mgr. car distbn., 1955-56, dist. mgr. Milw. Oldsmobile div., 1956-59, mgr. bus. mgmt., 1959-60, asst. zone mgr. Omaha div., 1960-63, asst. zone mgr. Indpls. div., 1963-66, asst. zone mgr. Milw. div., 1967-69, zone mgr. Atlanta div., 1969-72, zone mgr. Detroit div., 1972-73, regional mgr. SW div., 1973-77, asst. gen. sales mgr. Oldsmobile div., 1978-80, asst. gen. sales mgr. Eastern div., 1980-81, gen. sales mgr. Pontiac Motor div., 1981-84, gen. sales and service mgr. Pontiac Motor div., 1984-85, v.p., mgr. Oldsmobile div., 1985—. Served with USAF, 1951-53. Office: Gen Motors Corp 3044 W Grand Blvd Detroit MI 48202 *

LANG, CURTIS ELDON, dentist; b. St. George, Utah, Nov. 24, 1948; s. Eldon Snow and Norma (Esplin) L.; m. Karen Ronning, Dec. 21, 1974; children: Chelsea, Jessica, Nelson. AA, Dixie Jr. Coll., 1970; BA, U. Utah, 1972; DDS, Northwestern U., 1976. Gen. practice dentistry Courtview Dental Ctr., Sycamore, Ill., 1976—. Bd. dirs. Two Rivers Boy Scout Council, St. Charles, Ill., 1985, Kishwaukee Jr. Coll., Malta, Ill., 1985. Fellow Acad. Gen. Dentistry; mem. ADA, Am. Assn. Functional Orthodontics, Quad City Assn. Study Orthodontics (pres. 1986), Fox River Valley Dental Soc. (v.p. 1986), Sycamore C. of C. Republican. Mormon. Club: Ambassadors. Lodge: Rotary (pres. 1978-79). Avocations: gardening, golf, fishing. Home: Rural Rt 2 Airport Rd Sycamore IL 60178 Office: Courtview Dental Ctr 134 W State St Sycamore IL 60178

LANG, DOUGLAS RICHARD, pharmacist, hospital administrator; b. St. Louis, Aug. 14, 1956; s. Richard Thomas and Marilyn Ruth (Maurer) Lang Vitale; m. JoAnn Embry, Mar. 9, 1979; children—Joshua Ryan, Erin Dyan. A.A. in Life Scis., St. Louis Community Coll., 1977; B.S. in Pharmacy, St. Louis Coll. Pharmacy, 1981. Registered pharmacist, Mo. Staff pharmacist satellite coordinator St. Louis U. Hosp., 1981-84, asst. dir. pharmacy, 1984—; clin. instr. health careers St. Louis Coll., 1984-86. Mem. Am. Soc. Hosp. Pharmacists, Mo. Soc. Hosp. Pharmacists, St. Louis Soc. Hosp. Pharmacists (treas. 1983-84, pres. 1985-86), Kappa Psi (Outstanding Sr. award St. Louis chpt. 1981, Man of Yr. award 1984, pres. grad. chpt. 1983—, John Zahradka Past Regent award 1984). Office: Saint Louis U Hosp 1325 S Grand Blvd Saint Louis MO 63104

LANG, JOE ALLEN, lawyer; b. Memphis, Oct. 7, 1944; s. Harry and Eula Fern (Deyoe) L.; m. Teresa Ann Richards, Mar. 23, 1985. BA, Sterling Coll., 1966; MA, Emporia State U., 1972; JD, Washburn U., 1977. Bar: Kans. 1977, U.S. Dist. Ct. Kans. 1977, U.S. Ct. Appeals (10th cir.) 1979. Tchr. Luray and Fairfield High Schs., Luray and Langdon, Kans., 1966-74; research atty. Kans. Supreme Ct., Topeka, 1977-79; asst. atty. City of Wichita, Kans., 1980—; com. chmn. Nat. Inst. Mcpl. Law Officers, Washington, 1985—. Del. Kans. Rep. Conv., 1976, 84; deacon First Presbyn. Ch., Wichita, 1983-85; Rep. precinct commiteeman, 1986—. Served with U.S. Army, 1967-69, Vietnam. Mem. ABA, Kans. Bar Assn., Wichita Bar Assn., City Atty. Assn. Kans. (com. chmn., bd. dirs.). Presbyterian. Avocations: photography, stamp collecting, skiing, ham radio. Home: 1836 N Reca Wichita KS 67212 Office: City of Wichita Law Dept 455 N Main 13th Floor Wichita KS 67202

LANG, RICHARD LEWIS, orthodontist, educator; b. Chgo., Jan. 25, 1951; s. Lewis and Lilian Alice (Wilkinson) L. BS in Math, Loyola U., Chgo., 1972; DDS, Loyola U., Maywood, 1976, MS in Oral Biology, cert. of specialty, 1980. Gen. practice dentistry Palatine, Ill., 1976-80; pvt. practice orthodontics Elmhurst, Ill., 1980—; asst. prof. Loyola U. Sch. Dentistry, Maywood, 1979—; lectr. in field; cons. St. Paul Ins. Co., Ill. Dental Service, Am. Jour. Orthodontics, 1983—. Named one of Outstanding Coll. Athletes of Am., 1972; mem. Loyola U. Hall of Fame, 1983. Mem. ADA, Ill. Dental Soc., Chgo. Dental Soc. (sec. mediation com. 1983, vice chmn. 1984, chmn. 1985, peer rev. com. 1986), Midwest Soc. Orthodontics, Am. Soc. Functional Orthodontics, West Suburban Study Guild, West Suburban Orthodontic Study Club, Delta Sigma Delta (faculty advisor 1981—), Loyola U. Alumni Assn. (v.p. 1981—), Elmhurst C. of C. and Industry, Am. Equilibrium Soc. Roman Catholic. Lodge: Lions (treas. Elmhurst 1981-84). Home: 2500 Windsor Mall Park Ridge IL 60068 Office: 135 Robert T Palmer Dr Elmhurst IL 60125

LANG, THOMAS EDWARD, advertising and marketing professional; b. St. Louis, Oct. 1, 1939; s. Edward Bernard and Helen Maria Lang; divorced; children: Ellen Maria, Amy Borden. BS in Journalism, So. Ill. U., 1962. Test market mgr. Lever Bros. Co., St. Louis, 1962-65; advt. mgr. Monsanto Co., St. Louis, 1965-72; acct. supr. Direct Mail Corp., St. Louis, 1972-74; co-owner, mgr. Shoss, Lang & Assocs., St. Louis, 1975-77; pres. Lang & Smith Group, St. Louis, 1978—; bd. dirs. Boy's Town of Mo., St. James, Sanford Brown Coll., St. Louis. Bd. dirs. St. Louis Aviation Mus., 1987. Mem. St. Louis Exhibitors Show Assn., (bd. dirs. 1987—), Bus. and Profl. Adv. Assn. Republican. Roman Catholic. Avocations: photography, swimming, travel, horseback riding. Office: Lang & Smith Group Inc 1177 N Warson Rd Saint Louis MO 63132

LANGE, DENIS KENT, commercial artist; b. Ashland, Ohio, June 12, 1955; s. Roy Franklin and Harriet Irene (Johnson) L.; m. Vallorie Whitwell, May 15, 1982 (div. Mar. 1985); m. Barbara Ann McNaull, Mar. 29, 1986; stepchildren: Jamison K. Tobias, Michael J. Tobias, Anthony J. Tobias. Assoc. Applied Sci., Colorado Mountain Coll., 1975; airbrush illustrator cert., Dynamic Graphic Edn. Found., Peoria, Ill., 1985. Mktg. mgr. asst. White Westinghouse, Mansfield, Ohio, 1977-78; freelance designer Lange Design, Ashland, 1978-81, 85—; creative dir. Heritage Press, Ashland, 1981—. Illustrator book covers Bookcrafters, Inc. Mem. Brethren Ch. Avocations: music, bicycles, radio controlled cars and planes. Home: 1545 County Rd 995 Rt 4 Ashland OH 44805 Office: Heritage Press Inc 1601 Cottage St Ashland OH 44805

LANGE, FREDERICK EDWARD, computer information systems scientist; b. Johnstown, Pa., Oct. 21, 1946; s. Frederick Edward and Jean Louise (Huebner) L.; m. Karen Ann Mawson, Mar. 15, 1975; 1 child, Sharon Ann. BA in Social Scis., Cleve. State U., 1969, MA in Econs., 1978. Cert. secondary tchr., Ohio. Vol. Peace Corps, Liberia and Micronesia, 1969-73; tchr. Cleve. Pub. Schs., 1973-74; dir. Westside Inst. Tech., Cleve., 1974-81; systems analyst Case Western Res. U., Cleve., 1982-83; systems engr. Profl. Support, Inc., Brecksville, Ohio, 1983—; bd. dirs. Zoe, Inc., Cleve. Editor: Fuel Efficiency and Safety, 1979. Mem. Richmond Heights (Ohio) Civic League, 1986, Northeast Ohio Returned Vol. Assn., Cleve., 1978—. Mem. Am. Econs. Assn., Data Processing Mgmt. Assn., Instrument Soc. Am. (Dedicated Service award 1980), Javelin Assn. (fleet capt. 1982-83, sec. 1987). Avocations: sailing, gardening. Home: 4850 Lindsey Ln Richmond Heights OH 44143 Office: Profl Support Inc 8221 Brecksville Rd Brecksville OH 44141

LANGE, FREDERICK EMIL, retired lawyer; b. Washington, May 24, 1908; s. Emil F. and Jane (Austin) L.; A.B., U. Nebr., 1928; J.D., M.P.L., Washington Coll. Law, 1932; m. Leila M. Benedict, Sept. 11, 1930; children—Frederick Emil, Jr., David W., James A. (deceased). Admitted to D.C. bar, 1932, Minn. bar, 1943; examiner U.S. Patent Office, 1929-35; patent lawyer Honeywell, Inc., 1935-63, mgr. Mpls. patent dept., 1954-63; partner firm Dorsey, Marquart, Windhorst, West & Halladay, Mpls., 1965-73; individual practice law, Mpls., 1973-78; ptnr. Kinney & Lange, P.A., Mpls., 1978-86; spl. lectr. patent law U. Minn., 1949-51, Minn. Continuing Legal Edn., 1976. Bd. trustees 1st Unitarian Soc., 1970-71; chmn. Minn. br. World Federalists, 1958-60, nat. exec. com., 1958-64; bd. dirs. Group Health Plan, Inc., 1967-78, 1st v.p., 1975-78; bd. dirs. St. Paul Civic Symphony Assn., 1976-81, Environ. Learning Center, 1977-79. Minn. Funeral and Meml. Soc. Recipient Distinguished Service award U. Nebr., 1968. Mem. ABA, Minn. Bar Assn. (ho. of dels. 1987—), D.C. Bar Assn., Hennepin County Bar Assn., Am. Patent Law Assn., Minn. Patent Law Assn. (pres. 1954-55), Am. Judicature Soc., Sigma Nu Phi (lord high chancellor 1984-87). Holder U.S. patents. Home: 1235 Yale Pl Apt 201 Minneapolis MN 55403

LANGE, SCOTT LESLIE, communications company executive, voice professional; b. Chgo., July 10, 1946; s. Harry W. and Evelyn (Udell) L.; m. Linda A. Shoenthal, Mar. 30, 1969; 1 child, Stephen H. BS in Speech, Northwestern U., 1968. Prodn. mgr., announcer WCOG Radio, Greensboro, N.C., 1971-72; writer, producer, dir. ARC, Washington, 1973-78; mgr. audio-visual services Am. Bankers Assn., Washington, 1978-79; writer, producer, dir. AT&T Communications, Washington, 1979-82, Cin., 1982-84; pres. Lange Communications, Cin., 1984—. Writer, producer, dir. numerous films, videotapes, radio and TV pub. service announcements, slide programs. Served with U.S. Army, 1968-71, Vietnam. Recipient Cert. Outstanding Creativity, U.S. TV Commls. Festival, 1973, 75, Gold Quill of Excellence award Internat. Assn. Bus. Communicators, 1981. Mem. AFTRA, Internat. TV Assn. (pres. D.C. chpt. 1981, Golden Reel of Merit award 1978, Golden Reel of Excellence award 1980), Soc. Motion Picture and TV Engrs. Jewish. Avocations: film and videotape collector, music enthusiast. Home and Office: Lange Communications 2692 Montchateau Dr Cincinnati OH 45244

LANGE, THOMAS EDWARD, lawyer; b. Evergreen Park, Ill., June 29, 1959; s. Richard E. and Danielle (Patacco) L.; m. Tami Anne Tavis, June 13, 1981; children: Brian Richard, Kevin Lee. BBA, U. Notre Dame, 1981, JD, 1986. CPA, Ill. Auditor, tax acct. Ernst & Whinney, Chgo., 1981-83; assoc. Whyte & Hirschboeck, Milw., 1986—. Kiley scholar U. Notre Dame, 1986. Mem. Am. Inst. CPA's, Wis. Inst. CPA's. Roman Catholic. Home: 1313 E Kensington Blvd Shorewood WI 53211 Office: Whyte & Hirschboeck SC 2100 Marine Plaza Milwaukee WI 53202

LANGE, THOMAS FRANCIS, dentist; b. Dubuque, Iowa, Aug. 18, 1950; s. Arnold Lawrence and Catherine Emella (Salzmann) L. BBA, U. Wis., 1972; BS, U. Minn., 1980, DDS, 1982. Advt. sales rep. Honolulu Mag., 1974-76; media dir. J. Framer Advt. Inc., Honolulu, 1974-76; copywriter, media dir. R. Cohn Advt. Inc., Chgo., 1972-74; advt. mgr. U. Wis.-Eau Claire Newspaper, 1970-72; gen. practice dentistry Appleton, Wis., 1982—. Mem. ADA, Wis. Dental. Assn., Acad Gen. Dentistry. Avocations: art, design, nutrition, exercise, reading. Home: 2470 W Glendale Ave Loft F Appleton WI 54914

LANGENBERG, DONALD NEWTON, physicist, educational administrator; b. Devils Lake, N.D., Mar. 17, 1932; s. Ernest George and Fern (Newton) L.; m. Patricia Ann Warrington, June 20, 1953; children: Karen Kaye, Julia Ann, John Newton, Amy Paris. B.S., Iowa State U., 1953; M.S., UCLA, 1955; Ph.D. (NSF fellow), U. Calif. at Berkeley, 1959; D.Sc. (hon.), U. Pa., 1985, MA (hon.), 1971. Electronics engr. Hughes Research Labs., Culver City, Calif., 1953-55; acting instr. U. Calif. at Berkeley, 1958-59; mem. faculty U. Pa., Phila., 1960-83; prof. U. Pa., 1967-83; dir. Lab. for Research on Structure of Matter, 1972-74; vice provost for grad. studies and research 1974-79; chancellor U. Ill.-Chgo., 1983—; maitre de conference associe Ecole Normale Superieure, Paris, France, 1966-67; vis. prof. Calif. Inst. Tech., Pasadena, 1971; guest researcher Zentralinstitut für Tieftemperaturforschung der Bayerische Akademie der Wissenschaften and Technische Universität München, 1974; dep. dir. Nat. Sci. Found., 1980-82. Recipient John Price Wetherill medal Franklin Inst., 1975, Disting. Contribution to Research Adminstrn. award Soc. Research Adminstrs., 1983, Disting. Achievement Citation, Iowa State Alumni Assn., 1984, Significant Sig award Sigma Chi, 1985; fellow NSF, 1959-60, Alfred P. Sloan Found., 1962-64; Guggenheim Found., 1966-67. Fellow AAAS, Am. Phys. Soc., Sigma Xi; mem. Nat. Acad. Univ. Research Adminstrn. Research and publs. on solid state and low temperature physics including electronic band structure in metals and semicondrs., quantum phase coherence and nonequilibrium effects in supercondrs. Home: 3750 N Lake Shore Dr Chicago IL 60613 Office: U Ill Chgo Box 4348 Chicago IL 60680

LANGENBERG, FREDERICK CHARLES, business executive; b. N.Y.C., July 1, 1927; s. Frederick C. and Margaret (McLaughlin) L.; m. Jane Anderson Bartholomew, May 16, 1953; children: Frederick C., Susan Jane. BS, Lehigh U., 1950, MS, 1951; PhD, Pa. State U., 1955; postgrad. execs. program, Carnegie-Mellon U., 1962. With U.S. Steel Corp., 1951-53; vis. fellow MIT, 1955-56; with Crucible Steel Corp., Pitts., 1956-68, v.p. research and engring., 1966-68; pres. Trent Tube div. Colt Industries, Milw., 1968-70; exec. v.p. Jessop Steel Co., Washington, Pa., 1970, pres., 1970-75, also bd. dirs.; pres., bd. dirs. Am. Iron and Steel Inst., Washington, 1975-78; chmn. bd., chief exec. officer Interlake Corp., Oak Brook, Ill., 1978—, also bd. dirs.; bd. dirs. Carpenter Tech., Reading, Pa., CNW Corp., Chgo. and Northwestern Transp. Co., Peoples Energy Corp. Contbr. articles to tech. jours.; patentee in field. Served with USNR, 1944-45. Named Oak Brook Bus. Leader of Yr., 1986; Alumni fellow Pa. State U., 1977. Fellow Am.

Soc. Metals (disting. life mem. 1982, trustee, Pitts. Nite lectr. 1970, Andrew Carnegie lectr. 1976; David Ford McFarland award Penn State chpt. 1973); mem. AIME, Assn. Iron and Steel Engrs., Metals Powder Industry Fedn., Phi Beta Kappa, Sigma Xi, Tau Beta Pi. Clubs: Duquesne, St. Clair Country (Pitts.); Univ., Congl., Burning Tree, Carlton (Washington); Chgo. Golf, Chgo., Butler Nat. Golf, Commercial (Chgo.); Laurel Valley, Rolling Rock (Ligonier, Pa.). Home: 22 Bradford Ln Oak Brook IL 60521

LANGENDERFER, RANDALL LEE, auditor; b. Toledo, Ohio, Nov. 17, 1957; s. Harvey Paul and Genevieve Rose (Simon) L.; m. Melanie Jean Penko; children: Elizabeth, Amy. Student, DePauw U., 1976-77; BBA, Bowling Green State U., 1980; MBA, Bowling Green (Ohio) State U., 1986. Acct. Steyer, Huber & Assocs., Defiance, OH, 1980; revenue acct. Marathon Oil, Findlay, Ohio, 1981-82, systems analyst, 1983-86, EDP auditor, 1986—. Vol. Findlay Area Youth For Christ, 1982-84; fin. sec. local ch., 1984-86. Named one of Outstanding Young Men Am., 1985. Democrat. Mem. United Brethren. Home: 3015 Heatherdowns Dr Findlay OH 45840 Office: Marathon Oil Co 539 S Main St Findlay OH 45840

LANGER, ALVIN, obstetrician-gynecologist, educator; b. Chgo., Oct. 20, 1934; s. Joseph and Sally Berniece (Kardon) L.; m. Sheila Ann Herbstman, July 1, 1962; children: Betty Suzanne, Diane Marie. BS in Medicine, U. Ill., Chgo., 1956, MD, 1958. Diplomate Am. Bd. Ob-Gyn. Intern U. Okla. Hosps., Oklahoma City, 1958-59; resident in ob-gyn U. Ill. Research and Edn. Hosps., Chgo., 1959-62; practice medicine specializing in ob-gyn Waukegan, Ill., 1964-65; obstetrician, gynecologist Permanente Med. Group, Santa Clara, Calif., 1965-70; from asst. to assoc. prof. ob-gyn N.J. Med. Sch., Newark, 1970-76; prof. ob-gyn Northeastern Ohio U., Rootstown, 1976—; acad. dir. ob-gyn Aultman Hosp., Canton, Ohio, 1976—; acad. council Northeastern Ohio U., 1979-82, 83—; med. adv. com. March of dimes Northeastern Ohio, Cleve., 1986—; trustee Planned Parenthood Stark County, Canton, 1978—. Co-editor: Perinatology Case Studies, 1979, 85, Extrauterine Pregnancy, 1986; contbr. chpts. to ob-gyn textbooks; contbr. articles to profl. jours. Served to capt. USAF, 1962-64. Recipient Genetics Services grant Ohio Dept. Health, 1982—. Fellow Am. Coll. Obstetricians-Gynecologists, ACS; mem. AMA, Assn. Profs. Ob-Gyn, Am. Fertility Soc., Am. Assn. Human Genetics, Sigma Alpha Mu, Phi Delta Epsilon (dist. gov. 1983—). Jewish. Avocations: music, spectator sports. Office: Aultman Hosp 2600 6th St SW Canton OH 44710

LANGER, FREDERICK WILLIAM, accountant; b. Milw., Dec. 27, 1951; s. Herman S. and Phyllis (Cohn) L.; m. Janet Rebecca Lenahan, May 20, 1974; 1 child, Matthew. BBA, U. Wis., 1974. CPA, Wis. Fin. analyst Snap-On-Tools, Kenosha, Wis., 1974-75; treas., audit ptnr. Scribner Cohen & Co. Service Corp., Milw., 1975—. Mem. Am. Inst. CPA's, Wis. Inst. CPA's. Office: Scribner Cohen & Co Sc 1840 N Farwell Ave Milwaukee WI 53202

LANGER, JACK FRED, pharmacist; b. Milw., June 2, 1922; s. Walter S. and Norma A. (Abeles) L.; m. Shirley Lee Abrams, Oct. 28, 1948; children: Julie Ann, Jeffrey Scott, Daniel Bruce. BS, U. Wis., 1943. V.p. Langer Labs., Milw., 1946-66; pres. Jack F. Langer Pharmacy, Inc., Milw., 1966—. Served to sgt. U.S. Army, 1944-46. Mem. Wis. Pharm. Assn., Am. Pharm. Assn., Nat. Assn. Retail Drugists. Jewish. Lodge: Masons. Avocations: travel, photography. Office: Jack Langer Pharmacy and Gifts 3567 S Howell Ave Milwaukee WI 53207

LANGER, LEONARD O., JR., radiologist, educator; b. Mpls., Oct. 16, 1928; s. Leonard Otto and Louise (Buro) L.; m. Rollie Helen Segal, Sept. 13, 1952; children: Maren, Sara, Elizabeth, Kristen. BA summa cum laude, U. Minn., 1950, BS, 1951, MD, 1953. Diplomate Am. Bd. Radiology. Intern Salt Lake County Hosp., Salt Lake City, 1953-54; resident in radiology U. Mich. Hosp., 1956-59; instr. radiology U. Pitts. Med. Sch., 1959-60; from instr. to assoc. prof. radiology U. Minn. Med. Sch., Mpls., 1961-66; radiologist Suburban Radiology Cons., Mpls., 1966-78, 84—; prof. U. Wis. Med. Sch., Madison, 1978-84; clin. assoc. prof. radiology U. Minn. Med. Sch., Mpls., 1966-78; clin. prof. radiology U. Wis. and U. Minn., 1984—; cons. clin. genetics div. U. Wis. Med. Sch., 1984—, skeletal dysplasia program, U. Minn. Med. Sch., 1984—; mem. com. Internat. Nomenclature of Constitutional Diseases of Bone, Paris, 1969—. Author: Bone Dysplasias, 1974; contbr. over 87 articles to profl. med. jours. Served to capt. USAF, 1953-56. Fellow Am. Coll. Radiology; mem. Internat. Skeletal Soc. (cons. editor Skeletal Radiology 1976—), Soc. Pediatric Radiology, Radiological Soc. N.Am., Little People Am. (hon. life, med. adv. bd., 1966—). Democrat. Unitarian. Avocations: swimming, skiing, tennis. Home: 1235 Yale Pl 710 Minneapolis MN 55403 Office: Suburban Radiologic Cons Ltd 4801 W 81st St Minneapolis MN 55437

LANGER, STEVEN, cons. personnel mgmt. and indsl. psychology; b. N.Y.C., June 4, 1926; s. Israel and Anna (Glaisner) L.; B.A. in Psychology, Calif. State U., Sacramento, 1950; M.S. in Personnel Service, U. Colo., 1958; Ph.D., Walden U., 1970; m. Elaine Catherine Brewer, Dec. 29, 1979; children—Bruce, Diana, Geoffrey. Asst. to personnel dir. City and County of Denver, 1956-59; personnel dir. City of Pueblo (Colo.) 1959-60; personnel cons. J.L. Jacobs & Co., Chgo., 1961-64, adminstrv. mgr., 1966-68; sales selection mgr. Reuben H. Donnelly Corp., Chgo., 1964-66; pres.,Abbott, Langer & Associates, Crete, Ill., 1967—; vis. prof. mgmt. Loyola U., Chgo., 1969-71; community prof. behavioral scis. Purdue U., Calumet campus, Hammond, Ind., 1973-75. Registered psychologist, Ill. Mem. Midwestern Psychol. Assn., Ill. Psychol. Assn. (chmn. sect. indsl. psychologists 1971-72), Chgo. Psychol. Assn. (pres. 1974-75), Am. Soc. Personnel Adminstrn. (chmn. research award com. 1966-69), Am. Compensation Assn., Chgo. Compensation Assn. (sec. 1976-77), Mensa (pres. Chgo. chpt. 1972-74). Unitarian. Contbr. numerous reports and articles on indsl. psychology and personnel mgmt. to profl. publs. Home: 309 Herndon St Park Forest IL 60466 Office: 548 1st St Crete IL 60417

LANGER, SUSANNE M., cosmetologist; b. Red Wing, Minn., Aug. 19, 1955. Diploma Cosmetology, Ritter St. Paul Coll., 1974; grad., Bruno's, 1978. Instr. Ritter's St. Paul Coll., 1974-75; asst. mgr., mgr. Scot Lewis Inc., Bloomington, Minn., 1975-79; edn. dir. My Kind of Place, St. Paul, 1979-80; pres., co-owner Someone's Looking (formerly Charpentier's Inc.), St. Paul, 1980-86; owner Charpentier's Inc., St. Paul, 1986—; styles dir. women's sect. Minn. Cosmetology Edn. Com. Fundraiser, chairperson Battered Women's Shelter, St. Paul, 1984, Children's Home Soc., St. Paul, 1985; vol. St. Paul Food SHelves Food Dr., 1985; vol., model United Arts Fashion Show, 1986; vol. fundraiser pub. TV Action Auction. Recipient numerous hairstyling awards. Mem. Nat. Cosmetologists Assn., Minn. Hairdressers and Cosmetologists Assn., St. Paul Cosmetologists Assn. (dir. 1981-83, pres. 1983-85), Hair Am., Minn. Hair Fashion Com. Avocations: singing, cross country skiing, traveling. Home: 400 Selby Ave Saint Paul MN 55102 Office: Someone's Looking Inc 151 Endicott Arcade Saint Paul MN 55101

LANGERMAN, WAYNE RICHARD, data processing executive; b. Estherville, Iowa, Dec. 17, 1952; s. Marcus John and Kathryn Jean (Henriksen) L. BS in Econs., Iowa State U., 1975. Programmer First Data Resources, Omaha, 1975-76; programmer, analyst Olivette, Omaha, 1976-78, Fed. Land Bank, Omaha, 1978-79; systems analyst AT&T, Omaha, 1979—; cons. Omaha Software, 1976-79. Mem. Assn. Computing Machinery. Avocations: planting trees, investments. Office: AT&T Network Systems Dept 1722 PO Box 37000 Omaha NE 68137

LANGHOFF, PETER WOLFGANG, physicist; b. N.Y.C., Jan. 19, 1937; s. Joachim and Frieda A. (Damm) L.; m. Judith Dianna Perrotta, June 30, 1962; children: Lisa M., Kristen D., Allison K. BS in Physics, Hofstra U., 1958; PhD in Physics, SUNY, Buffalo, 1965; postgrad., Officer's Candidate Sch., 1970-71. Research physicist Cornell Aero. Labs, Buffalo, 1962-65; research fellow Harvard U., 1967-69; asst. prof. chemistry Ind. U., Bloomington, 1969-73, assoc. prof., 1973-77, prof., 1977—; chmn. program in chem. physics 1977-83; prof. chem. and faculty assoc., Supercomputer Computations Research Inst., Fla. State U., Tallahassee, 1985-86; tech. dir. Solar Reactor Techs., Inc. 1986—; cons. MIT Lincoln Lab., 1967-69, Lawrence Livermore (Calif.) Lab., 1977-83; inst. fellow Brandeis U., 1961; vis. research scientist dept. chemistry Harvard U., 1970, Harvard Colls. Obs., 1971, Stanford U., 1975; Stanford Ames Faculty fellow dept. aeros. and astronautics, Stanford U., 1976; vis. fellow Joint Inst. for Lab. Astrophysics Nat. Bur. Standards and U. Colo., Boulder, 1976-77; sr. NRC resident research assoc. NASA Ames Research Ctr., Mountain View, Calif., 1978-79; vis. fellow theoretical chemsitry U. Sidney, Australia, 1981; prof. associè U. Paris, Orsay Cedex, 1981; vis. prof. U. B.C., 1983; vis. research scientist Max Planck Inst. for Physics and Astrophysics, Munich, Fed. Republic of Germany, 1980—. Contbr. articles to profl. jours. Served to capt. U.S. Army, 1965-67. Grantee Petroleum Research Found., 1971—, NASA, 1978—, NSF, 1980—, Doe, 1985—. Mem. Am. Phys. Soc., Am. Chem. Soc. Home: 4890 Inverness Woods Rd Bloomington IN 47401 Office: Ind U Dept Chemistry Bloomington IN 47405

LANGLOIS, ROBERT JEROME, manufacturing executive; b. Manitowoc, Wis., May 12, 1929; s. I.J. and R.M. (Pionkowski) L.; m. Ione J. Henning, June 6, 1953; children: Jeffrey, Kim, Jeanine, Michelle, Anthony, Andrew, Christopher. BSEE, Marquette U., 1957. Registered profl. engr., Wis. Dir. personnel and indsl. relations, v.p. mktg. Paragon div. AMF Inc., Two Rivers, Wis., 1959-77; exec. v.p., then pres. RCL div. AMF Inc., Manchester, N.H., 1977-81; pres. Burger Boat Co., Inc., Manitowoc, Wis., 1983—, also bd. dirs.; pres. Burger Sales and Service Co., West Palm Beach, Fla., 1983—. Served to sgt. U.S. Army, 1948-52. Recipient Achievement award, 1971, Performance award, 1975, AMF, Inc. Mem. IEEE, Am. Soc. Quality Control (sr.), Northeast Wis. Indsl. Assn. (bd. dirs.). Republican. Roman Catholic. Avocations: fishing, jogging. Office: Burger Boat Co Inc PO Box 7 1811 Spring St Manitowoc WI 54220

LANGONE, DENNIS CHARLES, dentist, psychotherapist; b. San Diego, Aug. 20, 1947; s. Frank Charles Langone and Mary Ellen (Gleason) Gregoire; m. Frances Gene Mendenhall, Mar. 19, 1969 (div.); 1 child, Elissa Claire; m. Marguerite Kay Martin, Apr. 10, 1976; children: Ericka, Danielle. BS, Loyola U., Los Angeles, 1969; DDS, Creighton U., 1975; MS, U. Nebr., 1986. Lic. dentist in Nebr., Iowa, Calif. Gen. practice dentistry Malvern, Iowa, 1975-81, Omaha, 1981—. Awarded Red Belt Karate, Internat. Council Martial Arts Edn., 1983. Mem. Am. Orthodontic Soc., Aircraft Owners and Pilots Assn. Roman Catholic. Avocation: sailing, flying (lic. pvt. and comml.pilot, ground flight instr.), writing, scuba diving. Home: 10322 N St Omaha NE 68127 Office: Mockingbird Family Dentistry 10731 Mockingbird Dr Omaha NE 68127

LANGREN, CARL WESGAARD, corporate treasure r; b. Sioux City, Iowa, Sept. 11, 1955; s. Donald Richard and Mary Frances (Johnson) L.; m. Jane Diane Deitchler, June 16, 1979 (div. Dec. 1984). B in Bus. Sci. with highest honors, U. Iowa, 1977. CPA. Staff acct. McGladrey Hendrickson and Pullen, Iowa City, 1977-79; tax mgr. McGladrey Hendrickson and Pullen, Des Moines, 1979-83; treas. DFM Corp., West Des Moines, Iowa, 1983—. Mem. Am. Inst. CPA's, Iowa Soc. CPA's. Republican. Avocations: skiing, photography. Home: 4650 NW Lovington Des Moines IA 50310 Office: DFM Corp 1200 35th St Suite 109 West Des Moines IA 50265

LANGRILL, LAWRENCE NELSON, radiation physicist, instrumentation engineer; b. Detroit, Nov. 4, 1949; s. Harold Pershing and Mary Edna (Hert) L.; m. Jean Louise Gillette, Sept. 1, 1973; children: Rebekah, Martha, Deborah, Benjamin. BS in Physics, Oakland U., 1975; MSEE, Mich. State U., 1986. Med. physics resident Henry Ford Hosp., Detroit, 1975-77, physics fellow, 1977-79; radiation physicist Midland (Mich.) Hosp., 1979—. Contbr. articles to profl. jours. Mem. Am. Assn. Physicists in Medicine. Republican. Mem. Assembly of God Ch. Avocations: singing with church groups, playing guitar, electronic design, camping. Office: Midland Hosp Ctr 4005 Orchard Dr Midland MI 48670

LANGSLEY, PAULINE ROYAL, psychiatrist; b. Lincoln, Nebr., July 2, 1927; d. Paul Ambrose and Dorothy (Sibley) Royal; m. Donald G. Langsley, Sept. 9, 1955; children: Karen Jean, Dorothy Ruth Langsley Runman, Susan Louise. BA, Mills Coll., 1949; MD, U. Nebr., 1953. Cert. psychiatrist, Am. Bd. Psychiatry and Neurology. Intern Mt. Zion Hosp., San Francisco, 1954; student health psychiatrist U. Calif., Berkeley, 1957-61, U. Colo., Boulder, 1961-68; assoc. clin. prof. psychiatry U. Calif. Med. Sch., Davis, 1968-76; student health psychiatrist U. Calif., Davis, 1968-76; assoc. clin. prof. psychiatry U. Cin., 1976-82; pvt. practice psychiatry Cin., 1976-82; cons. psychiatrist Federated States of Micronesia, Pohnpei, 1984-87. Trustee Mills Coll., Oakland, 1974-78. Fellow Am. Psychiat. Assn.; mem. AMA, Am. Med. Womens Assn., Acad. Medicine Cin., Ohio State Med. Assn. Home: 9445 Monticello Ave Evanston IL 60203

LANGSTON, JACK MILES, pharmaceutical company executive; b. Mexico City, Jan. 23, 1932; came to U.S., 1944; s. Maurice Charles and Ruth Virginia (Etheridge) L.; m. Jeanne Marie Schaefer, June 5, 1954 (div. Feb. 1982); children: Gregory Miles, Geoffrey Steven. BS, Purdue U., 1953. Registered pharmacist, Ind. Div. sales mgr. Upjohn Internat., Mexico City, 1956-58; dir. sales Eli Lilly and Co., Sâu Paulo, Brazil, 1958-62; mgr. internat. mktg. Eli Lilly and Co., Indpls., 1963-64, internat. symposia mgr., 1973—; dir. mktg. Eli Lilly and Co., Basingstoke, Eng., 1964-67, Mexico City, 1967-73; pres., chief exec. officer Lexigrow Internat., Indpls., 1981—. Pres. Windridge Assn., Indpls., 1987. Served with U.S. Army, 1953-55. Mem. Sigma Delta Chi (pres. 1952-53). Avocations: writing, gardening, tennis, sailing. Home: 5353 Chipwood Ln Indianapolis IN 46226 Office: Eli Lilly and Co Lilly Corporate Ctr Indianapolis IN 46285

LANGWORTHY, AUDREY HANSEN, state legislator; b. Grand Forks, N.D., Apr. 1, 1938; d. Edward H. and Arla (Kuhlman) Hansen; m. Asher C. Langworthy Jr., Sept. 8, 1962; children: Kristin H., Julia H. BS, U. Kans., 1960, MS, 1962. Tchr. jr. high sch. Shawnee Mission Sch. Dist., Johnson County, Kans., 1963-65; councilperson City of Prairie Village, Kans., 1981-85; mem. Kans. State Senate, 1985—; del. Midwestern Conf. State Legislatures, 1985; alt. del. Nat. Conf. State Legislatures, 1985-87, del., 1987—; mem. subcom. Latin Am. com. State/Fed. Assembly. City co-chmn. Kassebaum for U.S. Senate, Prairie Village, 1978; pres. Jr. League Kansas City, Mo., 1977, Kansas City Eye Bank, 1982-85; bd. dirs. Greater Kansas City ARC, 1975—, pres., 1984; nat. bd. govs. ARC, 1987—. Recipient Outstanding Vol. award Community Services Award Found., 1983, Confidence in Edn. award Friends of Edn., 1984. Mem. Nat. Rep. Legislator's Assn., LWV, AAUW, English-Speaking Union, U. Kans. Alumni Assn., Kappa Kappa Gamma. Lutheran. Avocations: hunting, running, family. Home: 6324 Ash Prairie Village KS 66208

LANIAUSKAS, MARIUS MINTAUTAS, dentist; b. Cleve., Dec. 2, 1954; s. Simonas and Stase (Degutis) L.; m. Egle Aniceta Giedraitis, June 18, 1977; children: Matas, Simas, Lukas, Vaiva. BS, Case Western Reserve U., 1977, DDS, 1980. Resident in gen. denstistry Cleve. Met. Gen. Hosp., 1980-81; clin. instr. Case Western Reserve U., Cleve., 1981-86, sr. clin. instr., 1986—; practice dentistry Cleve., 1981—. Pres. local chpt. Dainava Youth Camp, Cleve., 1983—, bd. dirs. Manchester, Mich. chpt., 1984—. Mem. ADA, Ohio Dental Assn., Cleve. Dental Soc., Acad. Advanced Dental Edn. Roman Catholic. Club: Zaibas Athletic (Cleve.). Avocations: golf, fishing, volleyball, photography. Home: 25514 Chatworth Dr Euclid OH 44117 Office: 13224 Shaker Sq Cleveland OH 44120

LANIK, CRAIG CARLTON, dentist; b. Akron, Ohio, May 8, 1957; s. Emil Andrew and Gaynor Elizabeth (Dorrien) L. BS in Zoology, Kent State U., 1979; DDS, Ohio State U., 1983. Dentist John C. Kline, DDS, Akron, 1983-86; gen. practice dentistry Uniontown, Ohio, 1986—. Fellow ADA; mem. Ohio Dental Assn., Akron Dental Soc. Democrat. Avocations: skiing, hunting, basketball, racquetball. Office: 12033 Cleveland Ave Uniontown OH 44685

LANK, DARLENE LYNETTE, accountant; b. Ellsworth, Kans., July 30, 1956; d. Erwin L. and Elsie A. (Stueder) Wenz; m. Terry T. Lank, June 2, 1979; children: Travis J., Nicole R. BS in Acctg., Emporia (Kans.) State U., 1978. Staff acct. Fox & Co., Wichita, Kans., 1979-82, Peterson, Peterson & Goss, Wichita, Kans., 1983-86; pvt. practice acctg. Claflin, Kans., 1986—. Treas. St. Peter Luth. Ch., Holyrood, Kans., 1987. Mem. Am. Inst. CPA's, Kans. Soc. CPA's. Republican. Lutheran. Avocations: ch. organ playing. Home and Office: Rural Rt 1 Box 174 Claflin KS 67525

LANKSTON, ROBERT JASON, mechanical engineer; b. Bridgeport, Ill., Mar. 19, 1927; s. Jason Franklin and Elva Grace (Foss) L.; m. Evelyn Bailey, July 1, 1950; children—Kathy, Jeffrey, Nancy, Richard. B.S. in Mech. Engring., U. Ill., 1950. Registered profl. engr., Ill., Kans. Sales engr. Chgo. Pneumatic Tool Co., 1950-52; project engr. Taylor Forge Inc., Chgo., 1952-64, chief engr., Paola, Kans., 1964-67; mgr. engring. Taylor Forge Engring. div. Gulf & Western, Paola, 1967-84, Taylor Forge Engineered Systems, Inc., Paola, 1984—; mem. pressure vessel research com. Welding Research Council, N.Y.C., 1970—. Patentee in field. Contbr. articles to profl. jours. Served with USN, 1945-46. Mem. ASME, Am. Welding Soc., Am. Soc. Metals. Lodge: Lions (treas. 1962-64). Avocation: ham radio. Home: 4876 Black Swan Dr Shawnee KS 66216 Office: Taylor Forge Engineered Systems 1st and Iron Sts Paola KS 66071

LANPHAR, WILLIAM LAVERNE, investment company executive; b. Detroit, Feb. 17, 1929; s. Melvin Fletcher and Corinne Otilla (Wirth) L.; m. Jane Carol Nagelkirk, Mar. 22, 1952; children: William Dyke, Lindsay Carol, Christine Mary. BA in Advt., Mich. State U., 1951; JD, Northwood Inst., 1978. Exec. trainee Lanphar's, Inc., Detroit, 1954-57, asst. v.p. land processing and real estate mgmt., 1958-62, v.p., 1963-72; pres., chief op. officer Lanphar's, Inc., 1973—. Chmn. bd., trustee Starr Commonwealth for Boys, Albion, Mich., 1955-79; chmn. fin. and exec. coms., trustee Northwood Inst., Midland, Mich., 1960—. Served to lt. USN, 1952-54, Korea. Mem. Real Estate Securities and Sydications Inst. (bd. dirs. 1977), The Syndications Corp. (registered securitiy agt. 1978—), Pewters Collector Club of Am. Republican. Avocations: golf, tennis, swimming, collecting pewter, selling antiques. Home: 26477 Old Homestead Farmington Hills MI 48018 Office: Lanphars Inc 27102 Grand River Detroit MI 48240

LANSMON, KATHRYN ELIZABETH, utilities executive; b. Cape Girardeau, Mo., June 5, 1953; d. James Robert and Edith (Matthews) L. BS in Edn., Southeast Mo. State U., 1975, MA in Edn., 1978. Group mgr. operator services Southwestern Bell Telephone Co., St. Louis, 1978-79, force mgr. operator services, 1979-80, mgr. operator services, 1980-82, staff mgr. operator services, 1985—; mgr. tng. instr. Southwestern Bell Telephone Co., Dallas, 1982-85. Home: 524 Spring Glen Dr Ballwin MO 63021 Office: Southwestern Bell Telephone Co 1 Bell Ctr 8-X-01 Saint Louis MO 63101-3099

LANTER, DAVID MICHAEL, communications executive; b. Kansas City, Mo., July 23, 1949; s. Harlan DeBolt and Frances Theresa (Schubert) L.; m. Kathleen Ann Murray, Dec. 18, 1970; children: Rebecca Ann, Shawn Patrick. BA, Rockhurst Coll., 1971—. Advt. copywriter Western Auto, Kansas City, 1969-73, assoc. editor, 1973-75; editor Black & Veatch, Kansas City, 1975-78, communications dir., 1978—. adult leader Boy Scouts Am., Kansas City, 1986; mem. Kansas City Riverfront Task Force, 1986. Mem. Internat. Assn. Bus. Communicators, Greater Kansas City C. of C. Republican. Roman Catholic. Home: 8109 Fontana Prairie Village KS 66208 Office: Black & Veatch Engrs-Architects 1500 Meadow Lake Pkwy Kansas City MO 64114

LANTZ, DAVID LAWRENCE, economist; b. Bloomington, Ind., Nov. 23, 1956; s. Thomas Wendell and Nancy Martina (Rummel) L.; m. Sally Ming Farmer, Aug. 4, 1979; children: Sarah Michelle, Jason Thomas, Joshua Alexander. BA, Butler U., 1979; M in Pub. Affairs, Ind. U., 1981. Program analyst Ind. Legis. Services Agy., Indpls., 1981-83; dir. research Hoosiers for Econ. Devel., Indpls., 1983-87; sr. research assoc. Ind. Fiscal Policy Inst., Indpls., 1987—; cons. Ind. Infrastructure Inc., Indpls., 1986—. Contbr. articles to prof. jour. Vol. Wheeler Rescue Mission, Indpls., 1985—; vice precinct committeeman Marion County Reps., Indpls., 1986-87. Mem. Regional Sci. Assn., Ind. U. Alumni Assn. (bd. dirs. sch. pub. and environ. affairs). Presbyterian. Club: Toastmaster. Home: 7802 Cannonade Dr Indianapolis IN 46217 Office: Hoosiers Econ Devel 1150 Meridian St Suite 1005 Indianapolis IN 46217

LANTZ, ERIC JOHN, radiologist; b. Rochester, Minn., Nov. 7, 1951; s. Charles Emil and Doris (Greenwood) L.; m. Jane Ellen Paul, Sept. 24, 1977; children: Eric B., Laura J., Stephen K. BA summa cum laude, Hamline U., 1973; MD, Mayo Med. Coll., 1977. Cert. Am. Bd. Radiology. Resident Mayo Grad. Sch. Medicine, Rochester, 1977-81; staff radiologist Mayo Clinic, Rochester, 1981—, St. Mary's Hosp., Rochester, Meth. Hosp., Rochester. Contbr. articles to profl. jours. Mem. AMA, Radiol. Soc. N.Am., Am. Roentgen Ray Soc. Methodist. Avocations: photography, sports, botany. Home: 652 20 St NE Rochester MN 55904 Office: Mayo Clinic Rochester MN 55905

LANTZ, RICHARD DALE, building materials company official; b. Berne, Ind., Oct. 29, 1951; s. Dale Bernell and Ruby Maxiene L.; m. Debra Sue Spichiger, July 29, 1972; children—Krista, Jessica, Gregory. B.S., Ind. U., 1974. Sales rep. Owens Corning Fiberglas, Oklahoma City, 1974-76, sr. sales rep., Tulsa, 1976-77, supply mgr., Oklahoma City, 1977-78, Cin., 1978-81, br. mgr., Chgo., 1981-84, mktg. mgr., Toledo, 1984—. Mennonite. Home: 2548 Wealdstone Toledo OH 43615

LANTZSCH, HANS EDWIN, school superintendent; b. Krogis, Germany, Aug. 7, 1923; s. Rheinhold Edwin and Louise (Ettmeier) L.; came to U.S., 1927, naturalized, 1934; B.A., Central Mich. U., 1948; M.A., U. Mich., 1950; postgrad. Wayne State U., 1952-63; m. Dora Jablinskey, June 19, 1948; children—James Edwin, Susan Elizabeth, Thomas Paul. Asst. and acting supt. Ecorse (Mich.) Pub. Schs., 1948-67; supt. Trenton (Mich.) Pub. Schs., 1967-71, Gerrish Higgins Sch., Roscommon, Mich., 1971—. Dir. Community Resources Workshop, Mich. State U., 1955-72; asst. dir. NSF Chemistry Inst., Mont. State Coll., 1958. Chmn. sch. liaison Met. Detroit Sci. Fair, 1957-68; mem. com. Wayne County Intermediate Sch. Dist. Occupational Edn., 1969-71; mem. Com. for Educating New Supts. in Mich., 1973-83. Trustee, Mich. Council for Econ. Edn., 1965-68; mem. exec. bd. Down River Learning Disability Ctr., Wyandotte, Mich., 1966-71. Served with AUS, 1943-46. Decorated Bronze Star. Mem. Am. Assn. Sch. Adminstrs. (life, del. assembly 1981, 82, 83, 87), Mich. Edn. Assn. (life), No. Mich. Supts. Assn. (pres. 1977-78), Phi Delta Kappa (life). Office: Gerrish Higgins Bd Edn Roscommon MI 48653

LAPELLE, DIANE MCDONNELL, banker; b. Chgo., June 22, 1952; d. George F. and Mary M. (Merrick) McDonnell; m. William J. Lapelle, June 19, 1976. BA, U. Notre Dame, 1974. Mem. staff ops. and mgmt. services Continental Ill. Nat. Bank, Chgo., 1974-76, cash position sr. analyst, 1976-79, mgr. cash position, 1979, ops. officer, 1980, mgr. cash position and ops. control, 1981, 2d v.p., 1982-85, mgr. relationship money ctr. banks, 1985-86, v.p., 1986—. Mem. Assocs. St. Joseph Hosp., Chgo., 1979—. Club: Notre Dame (bd. govs. 1986—). Office: Continental Ill Nat Bank 231 S LaSalle St Chicago IL 60697

LAPIN, ANDREW WILLIAM, lawyer; b. Chgo., Feb. 2, 1953; s. Robert Allan and Elaine (Muhlrad) L.; m. Debra Nan Goldberg, July 7, 1979; children: Lauren Elise, Marisa Anne. BA, Ind. U., 1975; JD, John Marshall Law Sch., 1978. Bar: Ill. 1978, U.S. Dist. Ct. (no. dist.) Ill. 1978. Sole practice, Chgo., 1978-79, 81-87; assoc. Tash & Slavitt, Ltd., Chgo., 1979-81; of counsel Siegan, Barbakoff & Gomberg, Cngo., 1987—. Bd. dirs. Am. Soc. for Technion, Chgo. Chpt. Israel Inst. Tech. Mem. ABA, Chgo. Bar Assn. (real property com., real property fin. subcom.), Ill. Bar Assn. Office: Siegan Barbakoff & Gomberg 20 N Clark Suite 1000 Chicago IL 60602

LAPIN, HARVEY I., lawyer; b. St. Louis, Nov. 23, 1937; s. Lazarus L. and Lillie L.; m. Cheryl A. Lapin; children: Jeffrey, Gregg. BS, Northwestern U., 1960, JD, 1963; LLB in Taxation, Georgetown U., 1967. Bar: Ill. 1963, Fla. 1980, Wis. 1985. Cert. tax lawyer, Fla. Bar. Atty., Office Chief Counsel, IRS, Washington, 1963-65; trial atty. Office Regional Csl., IRS, Washington, 1965-68; assoc., then ptnr. Piffer & D'Angelo, Chgo., 1968-75; pres. Harvey I. Lapin, P.C., Chgo., 1975-83; mng. ptnr. Lapin, Hoff, Spangler & Greenberg, 1983—; instr. John Marshall Law Sch., 1969—; facility adv. lawyers asst. program Roosevelt U., Chgo.; mem. cemetery adv. bd. Ill. Comptroller, 1974—. C.P.A., Ill. Mem. Chgo. Bar Assn., Ill. Bar Assn., ABA, Fla. Bar Assn., Wis. Bar Assn. Jewish. Asst. editor Fed. Bar Jour., 1965-67; contbg. editor Cemetery Business and Legal Guide; contbr. articles to trade assn. jours. Office: Lapin Hoff Spangler & Greenberg 115 S LaSalle St Chicago IL 60603

LA PLATA, GEORGE, federal judge; b. 1924; m. Frances Hoyt; children: Anita J. La Plata Rard, Marshall. AB, Wayne State U., 1951; LLB, Detroit Coll. Law, 1956. Sole practice 1956-79; judge Oakland County (Mich.) Cir. Ct., Pontiac, 1979-85, U.S. Dist. Ct. (ea. dist.) Mich., Ann Arbor, 1985—; prof. Detroit Coll. Law, 1985-86. Trustee William Beaumont Hosp., 1979—, United Found., 1983—. Served to col. USMC, 1943-46, 52-54. Mem. ABA, Oakland County Bar Assn., Hispanic Bar Assn. Lodge: Optimists. Office: US Dist Ct 200 E Liberty Suite 400 Ann Arbor MI 48104 *

LAPOINTE, KITTIE VADIS, choreographer, ballet school director, educator; b. Chgo., June 4, 1915; d. Samuel Joseph and Katie (Parbst) Andrew; m. Arthur Joseph LaPointe, Dec. 17, 1938 (dec. Apr. 1985); children: Janice Deane, Suzanne Meta. Studies with, Marie Zvolanek, Chgo., 1921-28, Laurent Novi Koff, Chgo., 1928-35, Edward Caton, Chgo., 1928-35; student, Royal Danish Ballet, Copenhagen, 1926. Dancer Chgo. Civic Opera, 1929-32, Century of Progress, Chgo., 1933-34, Stone-Camryn Ballet, Chgo., 1934-35, Mary Vandas Dancers, Chgo., 1935-38, Balaban-Katz Theaters, Chgo., 1935-36; tchr., choreographer Studio of Dance Arts, Chgo., 1952-68, Herrstrom Sch., Chgo., 1968-72; dir. LaBallet Petit Sch., Chgo., 1972—. Soloist in Michael Fokine's Co., 1935. Mem. Danish Sisterhood (pres. 1962-65, 72-75, mid-west dist. pres. 1972-74), Chgo. Outdoor Art League (sec. 1975-79). Avocations: sewing costumes, writing. Home: 2940 Eastwood Ave Chicago IL 60625 Office: Le Ballet Petit Sch of Dance 4630 N Francisco Chicago IL 60625

LAPOSKY, BEN FRANCIS, comml. artist; b. Cherokee, Iowa, Sept. 30, 1914; s. Peter Paul and Leona Anastasia (Gabriel) L. Free-lance comml. artist, oscillographic designer, 1938; creator electronic abstractions, Oscillons, 1952; one-man shows include: USIA, France, 1956; group shows include: Cybernetic Serendipity, London, 1968; Computer Art, N.Y.C., 1976; Computer Art Internat., Lawrence Hall of Sci., U. Calif., Berkeley, 1979; others; contbr. articles to art jours. Recipient Gold Medal award N.Y. Art Dirs. Club, 1957. Subject of article Arts Mag., June 1980. Home and Office: 301 S 6th St Cherokee IA 51012

LAPP, CHARLES JOSEPH, physician; b. Detroit, Jan. 10, 1927; s. Willard Ross and Hattie Louise (Kay) L.; m. June Vera Labatt, June 11, 1951; children—Cynthia, Christopher, Linda, Pamela, Charles, Jr. B.S., Wayne State U., 1949, M.D., 1952. Diplomate Am. Bd. Family Practice. Intern, Detroit Meml. Hosp.; ptnr. family practice, Glendale, Ariz., 1953-54; gen. practice medicine Luna Pier, Mich., 1954-55, Utica, Mich., 1957—; anesthesiologist Weiss, Palaus, Atler, Lapp, Toledo, Ohio, 1955-57; asst. clinical prof. Dept. Family Practice Wayne State Coll. Medicine; coroner, Macomb County. Served to seaman lc USNR, 1944-46. Mem. AMA, Mich. State Med. Soc., Macomb County Med. Soc., Acad. Family Practice. Republican. Lutheran. Avocations: photography; electronic experimenting; auto repair. Home: 8830 Suncrest Sterling Heights MI 48078 Office: Charles J Lapp MD PC 7817 McClellan Utica MI 48087

LAPP, JAMES MERRILL, clergyman, marriage and family therapist; b. Lansdale, Pa., July 20, 1937; s. John E. and Edith (Nice) L.; m. Nancy Sevartzentruber, Mar. 1, 1936; children: Cynthia Ann, J. Michael, Philip Alan. B.A., Eastern Mennonite Coll., 1960; B.D., Goshen Bibl. Sem., 1963; D.Min., Drew U., 1981. Ordained to ministry Mennonite Ch., 1963. Pastor Belmont Mennonite Ch., Elkhart, Ind., 1961-63; paster Perkasie Mennonite Ch., Pa., 1963-72, Albany Mennonite Ch., Oreg., 1972-81; dir. campus ministries Goshen Coll., Ind., 1981—; tchr. Christopher Dock Mennonite High Sch., Lansdale, Pa., 1963-70; moderator Pacific Coast Conf. of Mennonite Ch., Oreg., 1977-79, Mennonite Gen. Assembly, Lombard, Ill., 1985-87. Contbr. articles to Mennonite Ch. publs. Mem. Am. Assn. Marriage and Family Therapy (cert.). Democrat. Avocation: gardening; baking. Home: 210 Oak Ln Goshen IN 46526 Office: Goshen Coll Goshen IN 46526 *

LAPRE, KATHRYN MARY, computer scientist; b. Manchester, N.H., May 3, 1939; d. Clayton Gerald and Margaret May (Flood) Hobbs; m. Robert Henry Lapre, Sept. 30, 1959 (div.); children: Donna Marie, Robert James, Michael Jon. BA magna cum laude, providence Coll., 1972, MBA, 1976, Cert. in Data Processing, 1977. With Raytheon Co., 1961-69; programmer analyst Kay Windsor, New Bedford, Mass., 1969-70; programmer analyst Providence Pile Fabric, Fall River, Mass., 1970-72; systems analyst Citizens Bank, Providence, 1972-74; project leader, lead analyst R.I. Hosp. Trust Nat. Bank, Providence, 1974-77; instr. bus. and computer sci. Providence Coll., 1977-81; research and devel. systems coordinator U. Fla. Gainesville, 1981-82, adj. instr.; mgr computer services GMI Engring. and Mgmt. Inst., Flint, Mich., 1982-84; dir. computer ctr. Denison U., Granville, Ohio, 1984—; Bd. dirs. Camp Fire Girls, 1972-73; active Explorer Scouts, 1982-84, chmn. Post 407, 1983-84. Author: Getting Started in BASIC, 1980. Served with USAF, 1957-58. Mem. Assn. Systems Mgmt. (sec. 1979-80), Assn. Women in Computing. Home: 57813 Moull St Newark OH 43055 Office: Denison U Computer Ctr Fellows Hall Granville OH 43023

LAQUA, JOHN FRANCIS, JR., accountant; b. Langdon, N.D., Mar. 16, 1958; s. John Francis and Marlys (Kutter) LaQ.; m. Tamara Jo Farrell, Aug. 14, 1987. BSBA, U. N.D., 1981. CPA, Minn. Staff acct. McGladrey Hendrickson, Mpls., 1981-84; sr. auditor Deloitte Haskins & Sells, Mpls., 1984-86; sr. corp. acct. Deluxe Check Printers, Inc., Shoreview, Minn., 1986—. Mem. Am. Inst. CPA's, Minn. Soc. CPA's, U. N.D. Club, U. N.D. Letterman's Club, Beta Alpha Psi. Lodge: Elks. Avocations: running, downhill skiing, hunting, fishing, tennis. Office: Deluxe Check Printers Inc 1080 W County Rd F Shoreview MN 55126-8201

LA RAUS, ROGER ALAN, teacher; b. N.Y.C., July 8, 1939; s. Julius and Fritzie (Deixler) LaR.; m. Lynda Levin; children: David, Rob, Peter. BA in Sociology and Anthropology, Carleton Coll., 1961; MA in Edn., Northwestern U., 1968, PhD in Edn., 1976. Tchr., adminstr. Evanston/Skokie (Ill.) Schs., 1964—; pres. Different Speakers Bur., Evanston, 1980—; bd. dirs. Chgo. Leadership Conf., Oakbrook, Ill., 1986. Author: Planet Earth, 1976, Citizenship Decision Making, 1978, Our Home, Our Earth, 1980, The Challenge of Freedom, 1985. Pres. North Shore Sch. Jewish Studies, Skokie, 1985—. Named "Someone You Should Know" Harry Porterfield CBS TV, Chgo., 1978, "Bizarre but Effective" Tom Brokaw NBC T.V., 1978, Tchrs. of Am. History award Daus. of the Colonial Revolution, 1979. Mem. Northwest Suburban Ill. Assn. for Supervison and Curriculum Devel. (pres. 1984-85), Ill. Council for the Social Studies (v.p. 1980-81), Nat. Council for the Social Studies (Japan study fellowship 1980). Avocations: kayaking, sculpting. Home: 814 Reba Pl Evanston IL 60202 Office: Evanston/Skokie Dist 65 Schs 1314 Ridge Ave Evanston IL 60201

LARGENT, ALFRED JOSEPH, power company official; b. Cadillac, Mich., June 19, 1930; s. Alfred Clay and Cecilia M. (Long) L.; m. Caroline C. Weber, June 17, 1950; children: Edward, Robert, Linda, Sherri. Grad. Traverse City (Mich.) pub. and parochial schs., DeForrest Radio and Electronics Sch., Internat. Corr. Schs. With Traverse City Light & Power Co., 1948-87, beginning as meter reader, successively polyphase meter reader, line crew, journeyman lineman, 1948-68, supt. transmission and distbn., 1968-87; mem. Grand Traverse County Bd. Commrs., 1968-82. Active Boy Scouts Am., Community Chest, Walking Blood Bank. Mem. Mich. Assn. Commrs., Mich. Elec. Assn. Democrat. Roman Catholic. Club: K.C. Home: 857 Kinross St Traverse City MI 49684 Office: 400 Boardman Ave Traverse City MI 49684

LARK, JAMES DAVID, lawyer, restaurant owner; b. Detroit, Dec. 27, 1930; s. Frank Walter and Armalene Elizabeth (Gignac) L.; m. Mary Irene Satory, Oct. 15, 1960; children: Jarratt David, Adrian Maura, Eric Ian, Kurt Karl, James David II. BS, U. Detroit, 1952; JD, LLB, Georgetown U., 1955. Bar: D.C. 1955, Mich. 1956. Sole pracice law West Bloomfield, Mich., 1955—; treas. Kaufman & Broad, Southfield, Mich., 1957-60; ptnr. real estate Binder & Lark, West Bloomfield, 1960—; owner The Lark Restaurant, West Bloomfield, 1981—. Editor assn. and adminstrn. law sects. Georgetown Law Jour., 1953-55; contbr. articles on food and travel to jours. including Food & Wine, AAA Mich. Living, Gastronome. Nat. treas. Students for Stevenson Sparkman, Washington, 1952; active various charities. Served with USN, 1955-57. Mem. ABA, Mich. Bar Assn., Nat. Assn. Home Builders, Nat. Restaurant Assn., Mich. Restaurant Assn., Internat. Chili Soc. (mem. nat. adv. bd., chmn. Mich. chpt.), Confrerie de la Chaine des Rotisseurs (Maitre de Table mem.). Republican. Roman Catholic. Club: Hunters Creek (Metamora, Mich.). Avocations: travel, hunting, fishing. Office: The Lark Restaurant 6430 Farmington Rd West Bloomfield MI 48033

LARKY, SHELDON GLEN, lawyer; b. Detroit, Sept. 16, 1941; s. Irving and Lucille C. (Ziegler) L.; m. Barbara T., Apr. 25, 1965; children: Adam, Howard. BA, U. Mich., 1964; postgrad. Wayne State U., 1964-65; JD, U. Detroit, 1969. Bar: Mich. 1970, U.S. Dist. Ct. (ea. dist.) Mich. 1970, U.S. Ct. Apls. (6th cir.) 1972. Claims adjuster Liberty Mut. Ins. Co., Chgo., Detroit, 1962-64; personnel dir. ITT Continental Baking Co., Detroit, 1964-69; law clk. to presiding justice 6th Jud. Cir. Ct. Mich., Pontiac, 1969-70; ptnr. Leib & Leib, Southfield, Mich., 1970-76; v.p. Hiller, Larky, Hoekenga & Amberg, P.C., Southfield, 1976-87, sole practice, 1987—. Contbr. articles to profl. jours. Mem. ABA, Mich. Bar Assn. (chmn. com. on character and fitness 1980-82, com. on plain English 1981-83, sec. profl. liability ins. com. 1985—, profl. devel. task force com. 1985-87), Oakland County Bar Assn. (dir. 1974-84, pres. 1983-84, editor Laches 1974-82, chmn. law office mgmt. and econs. com. 1986-87), Nat. Conf. Bar Pres., Am. Judicature Soc. Home: 14730 Talbot St Oak Park MI 48237 Office: 30600 Telegraph Rd Suite 2160 Birmingham MI 48010

LAROCHE, ROBERT EUGENE, finance company executive; b. Washington, Ind., Dec. 26, 1926; s. Henry Arther and Donna Alma (Armes) LaR.; m. Kathleen Grace Wood, Nov. 17, 1973; children from previous marriage: Michele Marie LaRoche Mutzke, Debrah Verlene LaRoche Vaughan. Student, Washington U., 1944-47. Vice pres. Borg-Warner Acceptance Corp., Chgo., 1959-67; pres. Borg-Warner Acceptance Corp., 1967-72, chmn. bd. dirs., 1972—; v.p. Borg-Warner Corp., 1975—; dir. Marina Bank, Chgo., Borg-Warner Acceptance Can., Ltd., Borg-Warner Acceptance Corp., Australia, Borg-Warner Acceptance Ltd., London, Borg-Warner Financieringsmaatschappij B.V., Amsterdam, Borg-Warner Finanzierungs GmbH, W. Germany, S.A. Borg Warner Acceptance Corp. N.V., Brussels. Served with inf. U.S. Army, 1944-45. Address: Borg-Warner Acceptance Corp 225 N Michigan Ave Chicago IL 60601

LARRABEE, GENE ROSS, health care executive; b. Hammond, Ind., Nov. 30, 1947; s. James F. and Kathryn J. (Eggers) L.; B.A., U. Iowa and Winona (Minn.) State U., 1970; postgrad. U. Toledo, 1970-71; M.H.A., Governors State U., Park Forest South, Ill., 1972; children—Brent E.J., Kirk F.J., Aaron A.R. Unit adminstr. Elisabeth Ludeman Mental Retardation Center, Park Forest, Ill., 1972-73; adminstr. RN Convalescent Home, Berwyn, Ill., 1973-74; adminstr. Niles Manor Nursing Center, Niles, Ill., 1974; adminstr. Park Rehab. Center, Euclid, Ohio, 1974-82, chmn. bd., 1982—; pres. Primus Inter Pares Health Cons., Inc., 1982—; pres. Medi-Pro Employment Services, Inc., 1981—; pres. Consultronics Corp., Euclid, 1975—; v.p. Euclid Park Nursing Center Pharmacy, Euclid, 1975—, Hermetic Chem. Labs., Inc., Euclid, 1976—; mem. seminar faculty Ohio U.; treas. St. Anthony's Continuing Care Center, Rock Island, Ill., 1978-79; mem. Gov.'s Commn. on Ohio Health Care Costs, 1983. Mem. Ohio Acad. Nursing Homes (bd. dirs. 1980-86, chmn. legal com., mem. legis. com. 1980-81, treas. 1980-81, pres. 1981-83, 86, mem. geriatric polit. action com., pres. 1981-83), Am. Coll. Nursing Home Adminstrs., Am. Health Care Assn., Ohio Health Care Assn., N.E. Ohio Nursing Home Assn., Am. Assn. Rehab. Facilities. Home: 5191 B Liberty Ln Willoughby OH 44094 Office: 20611 Euclid Ave Euclid OH 44117

LARRIMORE, RANDALL WALTER, manufacturing company executive; b. Lewes, Del., Apr. 27, 1947; s. Randall A. and Irene (Faucett) L.; m. Judith Cutright, Aug. 29, 1970; children: Jacob, Alex. BS, Swarthmore (Pa.) Coll., 1969; MBA, Harvard U., 1971. Product mgr. Richardson-Vick, Wilton, Conn., 1971-75; sr. engagement mgr. McKinsey & Co., N.Y.C., 1975-80; pres. Pepsi-Cola Italia, Rome, 1980-83, Beatrice Home Specialties, Inc., Skokie, Ill., 1983—. Home: 830 Sheridan Rd Winnetka IL 60093 Office: Beatrice Home Specialties Inc 5555 Howard St Skokie IL 60077

LARRISON, THEODORE ROBERT, consultant and drug dependency therapist; b. Peru, Ind., Sept. 15, 1944; s. Glen Ballard and Roberta Elliott (Baker) L.; m. Darlene Ruth Ritter, June 21, 1964; children: David Charles, Rebecca Elizabeth, Matthew Robert. BA in Sociology, Goshen (Ind.) Coll., 1968; postgrad., Wesley Theol. Sem., Washington, 1968-69; MS in Adult Edn., Ind. U., 1983. Cert. in pub. mgmt., Ind., alcoholism counselor, Ind. Missionary Soc. of Friends, Jamaica, 1969-72; counselor Whites Inst., Wabash, Ind., 1972-74; dir. contbr. relations Indpls. Goodwill Industries, 1974-75; dir. vol. services Elkhart (Ind.) Probation Dept., 1975-78; profl. trainer Nat. Ctr. for Voluntary Action, Washington, 1977-80; exec. dir. Youth Village, Inc., Elkhart, 1978-80; staff therapist So. Hills Counseling Ctr., Jasper, Ind., 1980—. Contbr. articles to profl. jours., mags. pres. Elkhart County Council on Volunteerism, Elkhart, 1976-78; v.p. bd. dirs. Ind. Juvenile Justice Task Force, Indpls., 1979-85; pres. bd. dirs. Hoosier Hills Prisoner and Community Together, Nat. Assn. Drug Abuse P!roblems, Paoli, Ind., 1981-84. Kellogg Found. grantee, 1976. Mem. Nat. Assn. Alcoholism and Drug Abuse Counselors, Ind. Counselors Assn. on Drug and Alcohol Abuse. Mennonite. Lodge: Optimists (chmn. community services 1986). Office: So Hills Counseling Ctr PO Box 245 Jasper IN 47546

LARSEN, GRACE MARY, bank executive; b. Milw., Aug. 18, 1940; d. Sylvester and Anne Gertrude (Zimny) Paradowski; m. Thor Eric Larsen, July 8, 1971. BA with honors, Alverno Coll., 1981; MS in Mgmt., Cardinal Stritch Coll., 1986. Clk. Marine Nat. Exchange Bank, Milw., 1962-64, systems analyst, 1965-74, ops. officer, 1975-79, asst. v.p., 1980-84, v.p., 1985—; mem. ops. com. Tyme, Inc., Milw., 1976-78, Milw. County Clearinghouse, Milw., 1980-82. Mem. Nat. Assn. Bank Women. Republican. Roman Catholic. Avocations: camping, sports, gardening, poetry, classical music. Home: 2181 E Spruce Ct Oak Creek WI 53154 Office: Marine Nat Exchange Bank PO Box 2071 111 E Wisconsin Ave Milwaukee WI 53202

LARSEN, LEONARD CHRISTIAN, social worker; b. Elgin, Ill., Feb. 8, 1929; s. Carl Ingvard and Louise Marie (Gertsen) L.; m. Delores Agnes Juhl Larsen, June 7, 1953; children: Kristine, Jean, Joan. BA, St. Olaf Coll., 1951; MSW, U. Ill., 1953; LLD (hon.), Wartburg Coll., 1983. Lic. social worker. Social worker Jacksonville (Ill.) State Hosp., 1952-53; psychiat. social work officer U.S. Army, San Francisco, 1953-55; dir. casework Beloit, Ames, Iowa, 1955-59; br. dir. Luth. Social Services, Waterloo, Iowa, 1959-71; dir. profl. services Luth. Social Services, Des Moines, 1971-77, exec. dir., 1977—; cons. Iowa dist. Am. Luth. Ch., 1973-86, Iowa synod Luth. Ch. in Am., 1973-86, Equitable Life Ins. Co., Des Moines, 1976-86. Served to lt. U.S. Army, 1953-55. Mem. Nat. Assn. Social Workers (chpt. pres. 1985), Social Work Licensing Bd. (vice-chmn., 1986-87), Coalition of Execs. (bd. dirs. 1986-87, bd. social ministry orgns. 1988). Lutheran. Office: Luth Social Services 3116 University Ave Des Moines IA 50311

LARSEN, MARK LEIF, construction executive, accounting and management executive; b. Elgin, Ill., Sept. 20, 1956; s. Donald Ernst and Corinna (Gessa) L. BSBA, U. Ill., 1978. Field engr. Thorleif Larsen & Son, Inc., Itasca, Ill., 1978-79, project mgr., estimator, 1979-81, v.p. adminstrn., 1981—; pres. GM Acctg./Mgmt. Services, Inc., Itasca, 1983; exec. bd. dirs. Mason Contractors Assn. of Greater Chgo., 1987—. Trustee apprenticeship and tng. program Bricklayers Local 21, Chgo., 1987—. Republican. Clubs: Medinah (Ill.) Country; Chgo. Athletic Assn. Home: 287 Pembridge Ln Schaumburg IL 60195 Office: Thorleif Larsen & Son Inc 801 W Thorndale Ave Itasca IL 60143

LARSEN, ROBERT LEONARD, insurance company executive; b. Chgo., Sept. 2, 1937; s. Leonard Angus and Alice Mary (Welsh) L.; m. Joan Campagna, June 23, 1962 (div. June 1984); children: Lisa Marie, Robert L. Jr., Scott Christopher, Matthew James; m. Cheryl Janson, Sept. 8, 1984; 1 child, Jessica Rebeccah. Student, DePaul U., 1955-61. CLU. Exec. v.p. Assn. Group Ins. Adminstrs., Washington, 1963; v.p. R.K. Tongue Co., Inc., Balt., 1963-72; pres. Ins. Adminstrn. Ctr., Inc., Park Ridge, Ill., 1972—; bd. dirs. Wilson Enterprises, Elk Grove Village, Ill., Pharm. Ins. Ltd., Bermuda; cons., advisor to wholesale distbn. industry. Served to cpl. USMC, 1956-58. Mem. Nat. Assn. Life Underwriters, Ill. Life Underwriters Assn., Chgo. Life Underwriters Assn., Internat. Assn. Fin. Planners. Republican. Roman Catholic. Club: Anvil (East Dundee, Ill.). Office: Ins Adminstrn Ctr Inc 1480 Renaissance Dr Park Ridge IL 60068

LARSON, ANDRÉ PIERRE, museum director; b. Little Fork, Minn., Nov. 10, 1942; s. Arne B. and Jeanne F. (Kay) L.; m. Mary Hueschen (div. 1977); 1 child, Nathan; m. Linda S. Hansen; 1 child, Nikolas. MM, U. S.D., 1968; PhD, W.Va. U., 1974. Dir. The Shrine to Music Mus., U. S.D., Vermillion, 1972—; prof. music U.S.D., 1972—. Contbr. articles to profl. jours. Mem. Am. Musical Instrument Soc. (pres. 1979-87, editor newsletter 1976—). Republican. Unitarian. Avocations: travel, reading. Home: 325 Linden Vermillion SD 57069

LARSON, ANDREW ROBERT, lawyer; b. Pine County, Minn., Feb. 25, 1930; s. Gustaf Adolf and Mary (Mach) L.; B.A., U. Minn., 1953, B.S. Law, St. Paul Coll. Law, 1956; LL.B., William Mitchell Coll. Law, 1958; m. Evelyn Joan Johnson, Sept. 12, 1953 (div. 1980); children—Linda Suzanne, Mark Andrew; m. Barbara Louise Drager Coen, May 4, 1987; stepchildren: Mark Anthony Coen, Mary Coen, Susan Coen, Peter Coen, Teresa Coen. Bar: Minn. 1958. With Armour & Co., 1953-56, Minn. Dept. Taxation, 1956-58; individual practice law, Duluth, Minn., 1958—; municipal judge Village of Proctor, part-time 1961-74; dir., sec. various bus., real estate corps.; pres. Larson, Huseby and Brodin, Ltd.; v.p., sec. Sea Jay Corp. Arbitrator Minn. Bur. Mediation Services. chmn. Duluth Fair Employment and Housing Commn., 1965-76; vice chmn. Mayor's Arena Auditorium Com., Duluth, 1964-65; active United Way; mem. State Bd. Human Rights, 1967-73; Midwest regional rep. nat. standing com. on legislation United Cerebral Palsy, 1967-71, bd. dirs. nat. assn., 1971-72; bd. dirs. United Day Activity Ctr., 1969-76, Am. Cancer Soc., 1973-75, Light House for Blind, 1975-79, 80—, Environ. Learning Ctr., 1978-81; mem. Greater Downtown Council. Recipient Humanitarian Service award United Cerebral Palsy, 1965, I Care award Republican party, 1964, Disting. Service award local chpt. Jaycees, 1965. Mem. Minn. Bar Assn., Minn. Jud. Council, Am. Arbitration Assn., Nat. Fedn. Ind. Businessmen, Nat. Assn. Accts., Fresh Water Soc., Blue Army, Count Nuno Soc. (sec.), U.S. C. of C., Minn. Arrowhead Assn., Western Lake Superior Recreation Assn., Boat Owners Assn. U.S., Nat. Wildlife Fedn., Minn. Pub. Radio, Beta Phi Kappa. Republican. Roman Catholic. Clubs: 242 Yacht, Duluth Keel. Lodge: Kiwanis. Home: 3002 E Superior St Duluth MN 55812

LARSON, BRETT ALLEN, biology educator; b. Gainesville, Fla., Dec. 17, 1955; s. Alfred Joseph and Barbara (Allen) L. Student, Auburn U., 1974; BS, U. Ga., Athens, 1977; PhD, U. Oreg., Eugene, 1983. Postdoctoral fellow U. Calif., Berkeley, 1983-86; asst. prof. biology Wichita (Kans.) State U., 1986—. NIH fellow, 1983-86; U. Ga. Regents scholar, 1976-77. Mem. Am. Soc. Zoologists, AAAS, Genetics Soc. Am., Am. Fisheries Soc., Genetics Soc. Am., Sigma Xi (grantee 1980-81). Democrat. Methodist. Avocations: running, tennis, racquetball, swimming, backpacking. Home: 7627 E 37th N Apt 2408 Wichita KS 67226 Office: Wichita State U Dept Biol Scis Wichita KS 67208

LARSON, BRIAN FOIX, architect; b. Eau Claire, Wis., July 6, 1935; s. Albert Foix and Dorothy Jean (Thompson) L.; m. Mildred Anne Nightswander, Feb. 13, 1961; children: Urban Alexander, Soren Federick. BArch, U. Ill., 1959. Registered architect, Wis. Architect-in-tng. Geometrics, Inc., Cambridge, Mass., 1959-60, Bastille Halsey Assoc., Boston, 1960-62; ptnr. Larson, Playter, Smith, Eau Claire, 1962-72; v.p. Larson, Hestekins, Smith, Ltd., Eau Claire, 1962-80, Ayres Assocs., Eau Claire, 1980—; sec. Wis. Bd. Archtl. Examiners, 1985—. Prin. works include One Mill Plaza, Laconia, N.H. (Honor award New Eng. Regional Council AIA 1974), Eau Claire County Courthouse, Wis., (Honor award Wis. Soc. Architects 1978). Mem. Hist. Bldg. Code Adv. Com., Wis., 1985. Mem. AIA, Wis. Soc. Architects (pres. 1983), Soc. Archtl. Historians. Home: 215 Roosevelt Ave Eau Claire WI 54701 Office: Ayres Assocs 1320 W Clairemont Ave Eau Claire WI 54702

LARSON, CLAUDE STANLEY, physician; b. Sioux Falls, S.D., Dec. 29, 1915; s. Charles O. and Selma (Person) L.; m. Edith Camilla Hallburg, June 5, 1941; children: Gayle, Camille, Mary. BA, Augustana Coll., Sioux Falls, 1937; BS, Northwestern U., 1941, MD, 1942. Diplomate Am. Bd. Radiology. Fellow Lahey Clinic, Boston, 1942-43, 45; pvt. practice radiology Smith Clinic, Corpus Christi, Tex., 1946-48; radiologist Med. X-Ray Ctr., Sioux Falls, 1948-71; field rep. on cancer Am. Coll. Surgeons, Chgo., 1972-74; med. cons. Social Security Adminstrn., Chgo., 1974—. Served as lt. M.C. USNR, 1943-45. Fellow Am. Coll. Radiology; Radiol. Soc. N.Am., Am. Roentgen Ray Soc. Republican. Home: 175 E Delaware Pl #4811 Chicago IL 60611

LARSON, CLIFFORD EMIL, marketing educator, corporate consultant; b. Rice Lake, Wis., May 31, 1928; s. Casper Paul and Augusta Louise (Kinn) L.; m. Winifred Esther Wentorf, June 19, 1954; children—Karl C., David R., Ann L., Jane E. B.B.A., U. Wis., 1950, M.B.A., 1951, Ph.D., 1957. Bd. dirs. TIME Ins. Corp., Milw., 1973-78, TEKRA Corp., New Berlin, Wis., 1983—, H.C. Prange Co., Sheboygan, Wis., 1983—; dean coll. bus. admin. U. Wis.-Oshkosh, 1969-84, prof. mktg., 1969—; pres. Bethel Home, Oshkosh, 1984—, bd. dirs., 1980—. Bd. dirs. Oshkosh Symphony, 1980—, pres. 1980-82; mem. Milw. Symphony State Adv. Bd., 1980-82, Adv. Bd., Oshkosh, 1979—; bd. dirs. Work Adjustment Services, Inc., Wis. Citizens for Arts, Inc., 1985—. Mem. Assembly Collegiate Sch. Bus. (accreditation chmn., various chairs 1973-84), Am. Mktg. Assn., Fin. Execs. Inst. Midwest Mktg. Assn., Beta Gamma Sigma (bd. govs. 1976-80), Mu Kappa Tau. Republican. Congregationalist. Avocations: model railroading; railroad history; sailing; cross-country skiing. Home: 940 Windward Ct Oshkosh WI 54901 Office: U Wis Coll Bus Adminstrn Oshkosh WI 54901

LARSON, DALE ALAN, solid fuel safety technician; b. Eau Claire, Wis., Sept. 19, 1953; s. Lawrence Christian and Mary Elaine (Anderson) L.; m. Bonita Louise Buttenhoff, Feb. 14, 1978; children—Dustin Levi, Dalton Jon. Grad. North High Sch., Eau Claire, 1971. Optical lab. technician Benson Optical Co., Eau Claire, 1976-81; prin. Mr. Sweep Inc., Lake Hallie, Wis., 1978—; agent Buttenhoff Ins. Co., Eau Claire, 1982—; cons. solid fuel safety to consumers. Served with U.S. Army, 1971-74; Germany. Mem. Nat. Chimney Sweep Guild (cert., Wis. state rep. 1983—), Wis. Guild Chimney Sweeps, Wood Heating Alliance, Energy Alternatives Inst. (cert.), Wood Heat Edn. Research Found. (cert.), Ind. Safety Commn. (cert.). Home: 5707 Lakeshore Dr Chippewa Falls WI 54729

LARSON, DAVID CHRISTOPHER, lawyer, judge; b. Spencer, Iowa, Sept. 4, 1955; s. Leonard and Margaret Roxanne (Proctor) L.; m. Carol Ann Kuntz, Sept. 17, 1983. BS in Constrn. Engring., Iowa State U., 1978; JD, Creighton U., 1981. Bar: Iowa 1981, U.S. Patent Office 1981, U.S. Dist. Ct. (no. dist.) Iowa 1981, U.S. Ct. Appeals (8th cir.) 1981. Law clk. Henderson & Sturm, Omaha, 1981; ptnr. Stoller & Larson, Spirit Lake, Iowa, 1981-84; sole practice, 1984—; alt. dist. assoc. judge Iowa Jud. Dist. 3A, 1983—. Mem. Iowa State Bar Assn. (com. on patents, trademarks and copyrights 1982—), Dist. 3A Bar Assn. (pres. 1983-84), Dickinson County Bar Assn. (chmn. Am. citizen com. 1982-83, pres. 1983-84), ABA, Iowa Patent Law Assn., Iowa Great Lakes C. of C. (ambassador 1982—). Republican. Methodist. Club: Okoboji Yacht (trophy chmn. 1984—). Lodges: Kiwanis (fin. com. chmn. 1983, bd. dirs. 1984, pres.-elect 1986, pres. 1987), Masons. Home: Rural Rt 5520 Spirit Lake IA 51360 Office: PO Box 246 Spirit Lake IA 51360

LARSON, DAVID EDMUND, orthopaedic surgeon; b. Mpls., Dec. 10, 1942; s. Lawrence Myrlin and Phyllis (Ells) L.; m. Cheryl Berry; children: David Wesley, Chad Michael. BA, Dartmouth Coll., 1964; MA, George Washington U., 1969; MD in Orthopaedics, U. Minn., 1974. Cert. Am. Bd. Orthopaedic Surgery, 1975. Surg. intern Milwaukee County Hosp., 1969-70; residency in orthopaedics U. Minn. and VA Hosps., Mpls., 1970-74; pvt. practice Alexandria (Minn.) Orthopaedic Assocs., 1974—. Fellow Am. Acad. Orthopaedic Surgery; mem. AMA, Minn. Med. Assn., Mid-Minn. Associated Physicians (pres., bd. dirs. 1986—), Park Region Med. Soc. Home: Rt 3 Box 209 Alexandria MN 56308 Office: Alexandria Orthopaedic Assocs PA 1500 Irving Alexandria MN 56308

LARSON, DAVID GEORGE, educator; b. River Falls, Wis., May 23, 1961; s. Charles Jeffers and Aralda Rose (Thayer) L. BS in Indsl. Edn., U. Wis., Menomonie, 1983, postgrad., 1984. Tchr. Waupaca (Wis.) Sch. Dist., 1984—. Mem. Wis. Edn. Assn., Future Farmers Am. Alumni (v.p. 1985-86). Episcopalian. Lodge: Masons. Avocation: outdoor activities. Home: E 3429-A S Apple Tree Ln Waupaca WI 54981

LARSON, DAVID KEITH, information systems executive; b. Springfield, Ill., Oct. 5, 1949; s. Herschel Seward and Clara Emily (Larson); m. Janice Eileen Burnett, July 22, 1972; children: Allan, Douglas. BA in Econs., Sangamon State U., 1974, MA in Bus. Adminstrn., 1983. Asst. project leader Ill. Dept. Transp., Springfield, 1974-77, project leader, 1977-79, logical design mgr., 1979-82, network planning and design mgr., 1982-85, mgmt. systems mgr., 1985—; part-time instr. Lincoln Land Community Coll., Springfield, 1982—. Served with USNG, 1968-74. Named One of Outstanding Young Men of Am. Baptist. Avocation: camping. Home: 1837 S College Springfield IL 62704 Office: Ill Dept Transp 2300 S Dirksen Pkwy Springfield IL 62764

LARSON, EARL RICHARD, judge; b. Mpls., Dec. 18, 1911; s. Axel R. and Hannah (Johnson) L.; m. Cecill Frances Carlgren, Dec. 30, 1939; children: Jane, Earl R. BA, U. Minn., 1933, LLB, 1935. Bar: Minn. 1935. Judge U.S. Dist. Ct. Minn., Mpls., 1961-77, sr. judge, 1977—. Served to lt. USNR, 1943-46. Recipient Outstanding Achievement award U. Minn., 1978. Office: U S Dist Ct 661 U S Courthouse 110 S 4th St Minneapolis MN 55401

LARSON, EMILIE G., retired educator; b. Northfield, Minn., Apr. 28, 1919; d. Melvin Cornelius and Frieda (Christiansen) L.; A.B., St. Olaf Coll., 1940; M.A., Radcliffe Coll., 1946; student U. Chgo., 1951-52. Tchr. Hanska (Minn.) High Sch., 1940-42, Two Harbors (Minn.) High Sch., 1942-43; tchr. J.W. Weeks Jr. High Sch., Newton, Mass., 1946-56, guidance counselor, 1956-79; counselor Warren Jr. High Sch., Newton, 1979-81. Deacon, Univ. Luth. Ch., 1979; bd. dirs. Bus. History and Econ. Life Program, Inc., Northeastern U. Mem. AAUW (state v.p. for program devel., topic chmn. Mass. div. 1975-76; corp. rep., area rep. for internat. relations Minn. div. 1984-86), Mass., Newton tchrs. assns., St. Olaf Coll. Alumni Assn. (dir. 1982-85), PEO, Virginia Gildersleeve Internat. Fund for Univ. Women Inc. (membership com., bd. dirs.), Pi Lambda Theta. Lutheran. Contbr. articles to profl. jours. Address: 1008 W 1st St Northfield MN 55057

LARSON, GAYLEN NEVOY, financial executive; b. Leland, Ill., Jan. 24, 1940; s. Nevoy Leslie and Genevieve Gladys (Champlain) L.; m. Joanne E. Matthew, Sept. 3, 1960; children—Mark, Andrea, Paul. B.S., No. Ill. U., 1962. C.P.A., Ill. Sr. mgr., partner Deloitte Haskins & Sells, Chgo., 1961-79, partner, 1974-79; group v.p., controller Household Internat., Inc., Prospect Heights, Ill., 1979—; mem. emerging issues task force Fin. Acctg. Standards Bd. Pres. Golf View Homeowners Assn., 1971, Flint Lake Interested Property Owners, 1979, 80. Mem. Am. Inst. C.P.A.s (chmn. fin. cos. audit guide com., auditing standards adv. council), mem. acctg. standards exec. com., fin. instn. task force acctg. loan fees and expenses. Ill. C.P.A. Soc., Fin. Execs. Inst. (chmn. nat. com. corporate reporting), Fin. Execs. Research Found. (trustee). Republican. Presbyterian. Club: Barrington Hills Country. Office: 2700 Sanders Rd Prospect Heights IL 60070

LARSON, GREGORY EUGENE, architect, artist; b. Emporia, Kans., Sept. 15, 1951; s. Wallace Eugene and Joan Ellen (Beck) L.; m. Delia Lynne Krehbiel, Aug. 2, 1975; children: Stephanie Dawn, Carrie Renee. BArch, Kans. State U., 1974. Lic. architect, Kans. Architect Platt, Adams, Braht & Assocs., Wichita, Kans., 1974-79; project architect Hallmark Cards Inc., Kansas City, Mo., 1979—. Mem. AIA, Tau Sigma Delta (treas. Omicron chpt. 1973-74). United Methodist. Avocations: art, hiking, camping, cycling, golfing. Home: 5309 W 80th St Prairie Village KS 66208 Office: Hallmark Cards Inc 2440 Pershing Suite 500 Kansas City MO 64108

LARSON, JACQUELINE FAY, media specialist; b. Gate, Calif., Nov. 6, 1940; d. Joseph F. and Neta Elizabeth (Hill) McPherron; m. Donald Lee Larson, Feb. 23, 1963; children—Gregory Paul, Kimberly Ann, Jill Marie. B.S., N.W. Mo. State U., 1965; M.S. in Edn., Ft. Hays State U. (Kans.), 1982. Library asst. Clarinda Pub. Library, Iowa, 1964-65; bookmobile librarian Mpls. Pub. Library, 1966-67; librarian Unified Sch. Dist. 273, Beloit, Kan., 1968—; com. mem. North Central Eval. Team, Belleville and Oberlin, Kans., 1982, 83; speaker in field. Contbr. articles to profl. jours. Vol. Multiple Sclerosis, Am. Cancer Soc., ARC; chmn. self-evaluation com. for high sch. ednl. evaluation, 1985-86. Mem. Kans. Assn. Sch. Librarians (sec. 1978-80), ALA, Am. Assn. Sch. Librarians, Young Adult Services, Kans. Assn. Ednl. Communications Tech., Phi Delta Kappa. Lutheran. Lodge: Eagles. Home: 213 N Campbell St Beloit KS 67420 Office: Beloit Jr-Sr High Sch 1711 N Walnut St Beloit KS 67420

LARSON, JERRY EUGENE, information systems manager, educator; b. Kansas City, Kans., July 6, 1945; s. Charles Raymond and Wilma Evoi (Buckley) L.; m. Leslie Wing Armstrong, Dec. 30, 1967; children: Christopher, Melissa, Amy. BA, U. Kans., 1967. Programmer/analyst Hallmark Cards, Kansas City, Mo., 1968-73; data processing mgr. Wyandotte County Dist. Cts., Kansas City, Kans., 1974-79; cons. DASD Corp., Shawnee, Kans., 1980-82; prin., bus. systems mgr. Knight-Ridder Fin. Info. Group, Leawood, Kans., 1984—; instr. Johnson County Community Coll., Overland Park, Kans., 1981—. Mem. Assn. Systems Mgmt. Republican. Presbyterian. Home: 11530 Rosehill Overland Park KS 66210 Office: Knight-Ridder Fin Info Group 2100 W 89th Leawood KS 66206

LARSON, JERRY L., state supreme court justice; b. Harlan, Iowa, May 17, 1936; s. Gerald L. and Mary Eleanor (Patterson) L.; m. Linda R. Logan; children: Rebecca, Jeffrey, Susan, David. B.A., State U. Iowa, 1958, J.D., 1960. Bar: Iowa. Partner firm Larson & Larson, 1961-75; dist. judge 4th Jud. Dist. Ct. of Iowa, 1975-78; justice Iowa Supreme Ct., 1978—. Office: Office of the Iowa Supreme Ct Des Moines IA 50319

LARSON, LUCY LUDWIG, accounting educator; b. Mpls., Jan. 30, 1940; d. Lester John and Margaret (Gardner) Ludwig; m. Raymond Henry Larson, Mar. 24, 1961; 1 child, Mark Frederick. BA in German, U. Minn., 1964; MBA in Acctg., St. Cloud State U., 1972. CPA, Minn. From instr. to asst. prof. acctg. St. John's U., Collegeville, Minn., 1972-81, assoc. prof., 1984—; instr. St. Cloud (Minn.) State U., 1982-84. Treas. Chamber Music Soc. St. Cloud, 1982—. Mem. Am. Inst. CPA's (Elijah Watt Sells award 1984), Minn. Soc. CPA's (Pres's award 1984), Am. Acctg. Assn. Avocations: reading, operas. Home: 401 Birch St Saint Joseph MN 56374 Office: St John's U Dept Acctg Collegeville MN 56321

LARSON, MARIAN GERTRUDE, catalog sales company executive; b. Madison, Wis., Aug. 22, 1927; s. Guy Henry and Gertrude Francis (Everett) L. B.A., U. Wis., 1948; M.B.A., U. Chgo., 1982. Mgr. continuity, Sta. WISC, Madison, 1948-53; copy chief Spiegel, Inc., Chgo., 1953-58, editor-in-chief women's, 1958-62, catalog mgr., domestics and shoes, 1962-76, group catalog mgr. hardlines, 1976-79, v.p. advt., Oak Brook, Ill., 1979—; pres. Spiegel Pub. Co., Oak Brook, 1979—. Bd. dirs. Hinsdale United Way; alumni bd. U. Chgo. Grad. Sch. Bus. Mem. Chgo. Advt. Club, Nat. Assn. Women Bus. Owners, Direct Mktg. Assn. Office: Regency Towers Oak Brook IL 60521

LARSON, MILO HILLARD, restaurant owner and manager; b. Mpls., Nov. 7, 1928; s. Alvin and Mina (Wrethrich) L.; m. Patricia Jane Cain, July 8, 1950; children: Mark, Paul, John. Grad high sch., Blackduck, Minn. Mgr. Oklee (Minn.) Elevator Co., 1951-67; supr. Northland Chem. Co., East Grand Falls, Minn., 1967-70; owner, mgr. Third Base Inc., Brooks, Minn., 1970—. Office: Third Base Inc Brooks MN 56715

LARSON, ROBERT CRAIG, real estate executive; b. Mpls., June 15, 1934; s. Eugene and Frances (Wescott) L.; m. Lucy Ann Ballinger, June 20, 1957 (div. 1981), m. Karen Chase, Sept. 5, 1981; children: Elizabeth, Eric, Kathryn. B.A., Carleton Coll., Northfield, Minn., 1956. Various staff positions Inland Steel Co., Chgo., 1956-67; gen. mgr. Inland Steel Container Co., Cleve., 1967-70; v.p. Inland Steel Devel. Co., Washington, 1970-74; gen. mgr. Georgetown Inland Corps., Washington, 1970-74; sr. v.p. Taubman Co., Washington, 1974-78; pres. Taubman Co., Bloomfield Hills, Mich., 1978—, dir., 1978—; pres. Met. Affairs Corp., Detroit. Vice chmn. Nat. Urban League, N.Y.C.; trustee Christian Century Found., Chgo.; dir. Ctr. Community Change, Washington; bd. govs. Cranbrook Acad. Art, Bloomfield Hills, Mich.; trustee Children's Hosp. of Mich., Detroit, Citizens Research Council of Mich., Detroit; bd. dirs. Detroit Econ. Growth Corp, Detroit Symphony Orch., Inc., 1987—. Recipient Man of Yr. award Washington Urban League, 1983. Mem. Nat. Realty Com. (chmn. 1986—), Urban Land Inst., Internat. Council Shopping Ctrs. Democrat. Clubs: Bloomfield Open Hunt (Bloomfield Hills); City Tavern (Washington); Birmingham Athletic (Mich.); Renaissance (Detroit); World Trade (San Francisco). Avocations: travel, tennis, contemporary art, sailing.

LARSON, SALLY JOAN, consumer consultant; b. Wausau, Wis., May 9, 1948; d. Rufus John and Adeline (Kraege) Rodemeier; m. Gerald C. Larson, June 29, 1968. AA in Office Mid-Mgmt., Nicolet Coll. and Tech. Inst., 1979; BSBA, U. Wis., Superior, 1982. Installment loan sec. Manitowoc (Wis.) Savings Bank, 1969-71; sec. to asst. credit mgr. Mueller Climatrol, Milw., 1971-73; fin. aids sec. Nicolet Coll. and Tech. Inst., Rhinelander, Wis., 1973-74; exec. sec. Nicolet Coll. and Tech. Inst., Rhinelander, 1974-86, affirmative action officer, 1982-86; consumer cons. Wis. Pub. Service, Rhinelander, 1986—; spl. interim tchr. Nicolet Coll. and Tech. Inst., 1979—; tchr. U. Wis.-Stout, Rhinelander, 1985. Mem. bd. visitors U. Wis., Superior, 1984—; mem. advocate team U. Wis. system, 1986—; community coordinator Northwise Network, Rhinelander, Minocqua, 1986; trustee 1st Congl. Ch., Rhinelander, 1984-87. Mem. Soc. Consumer Affairs Profls. Avocations: golf, quilting, photography. Home: 116 N Pelham Rhinelander WI 54501 Office: Wis Public Service Corp 111 E Davenport St Rhinelander WI 54501

LARSON, SANFORD JOHN, neurosurgeon, educator; b. Chgo., Apr. 9, 1929; s. Leslie S. and Bertha (Doezma) L.; m. Jacquelyn McKay, Aug. 28, 1957; children: Nancy, Michael, Mary. BA, Wheaton Coll., 1950; MD, Northwestern U., 1954, PhD in Anatomy, 1957. Diplomate Am. Bd. Neurol. Surgery, 1965. Intern Passavant Meml. Hosp., Chgo., 1954-55; resident neurosurg. program Northwestern U., Chgo., 1955-57, 1959-61; clin. asst. in surgery Northwestern U., Chgo., 1961-62; fellow in post-doctoral research USPHS, 1961-62; dir. neurosurg. edn. Cook County Hosp., Chgo., 1962-63; assoc. prof., chmn. Med. Coll Wis., Milw., 1963-68, prof. neurosurgery, dept. chmn., 1968—; neurosurgeon, chief neurosurg. services VA Med. Ctr., Milw., 1963—; attending neurosurgeon, chief neurosurg. service Milw. County Med. Complex, 1963—; attending neurosurgeon, dir. neurosurgery services Luth. Meml. Hosp., Milw., 1980—; cons. Milw. Children's Hosp., 1963—, Columbia Hosp., Milw., 1963—, Shriners Hosp. for Crippled Children, Chgo., 1965—, Elmbrook Meml. Hosp., Brookfield, Wis., 1969—, Community Meml. Hosp., Menomonee Falls, Wis., 1972—. Author: Electroanesthesia: Biomedical and Biophysical Studies, 1975, Impact Injury of the Head and Spine, 1983, Mechanisms of Head and Spine Trauma, 1986; contbr. chpts. to books in field and numerous articles to profl. jours. Served to maj. Med. Service Corps, USAF, 1957-59 PTO. Fellow ACS; mem. AMA, Wis. Neurosurg. Soc., Milw. Surg. Soc., Milw. Acad. Medicine, Soc. Univ. Surgeons, Soc. Neurol. Surgeons, Am. Spinal Injury Assn., Am. Paraplegia Soc., Am. Assn. Neurol. Surgeons (chmn. AANS/CNS joint sect. of spinal disorders, joint sect. on trauma 1979-83), Am. Assn. Anatomists, Am. Soc. for Stereotactic and Functional Neurosurgery (bd. dirs. 1977-81, v.p. 1979-80, by-laws com. 1980), Cen. Neurosurg. Soc., Cervical Spine Research Soc., Congress Neurol. Surgeons, Internat. Med. Soc. Paraplegia, Internat. Soc. for the Study of the Lumbar Spine, Research Soc. Neurol. Surgeons, Alpha Omega Alpha. Club: Cajal. Home: 4385 Continental Dr Brookfield WI 53005 Office: Med Coll Wis 8700 W Wisconsin Ave Milwaukee WI 53226

LARSON, SIGRID JAN, social worker; b. Concordia, Kans., Nov. 20, 1936; d. Marvin Enoch and Josephine E. (Pullis) L.; m. Roscoe W. Morris, June 12, 1960 (div. July 1976); children: Evan M., Alec A. BA in Anglo-Am. Intellectual History, U. Calif., Santa Barbara, 1960; MSW, Calif. State U., San Diego, 1970. Counselor Devereux Ranch Sch., Goleta, Calif., 1957-59; child welfare worker Dept. Pub. Welfare, San Diego, 1960-62; supervising probation officer Hillcrest Home, San Diego, 1963-65; social worker San Diego County Adoptions, 1970-71; field instr. MSW program U. Calif., Berkeley, 1972-75; psychiat. social worker Trinity Sch., Ukiah, Calif., 1975; vis. asst. prof. Calif. State U., Chico, 1975-76; asst. prof. social work U. Kans., Lawrence, 1976-79; research coordinator Menninger Found., Topeka, 1979-82, clin. social worker, 1982-85, dir. family edn. and support, 1985—, also workshop dir., 1979—, cons., 1975; cons. New Morning Group Homes, Ukiah, Calif. Contbr. numerous articles to profl. jours., also presentations. Avocations: collecting antique beads, East Indian cooking. Office: The Menninger Found Box 829 Topeka KS 66601

LARSON, STEVEN EDWARD, mechanical engineer; b. Albany, Ga., Oct. 20, 1954; s. John F. and Jacqueline (Morehouse) L.; m. Melissa Hayes, Oct. 25, 1980. BS in Engring., So. Ill. U., 1977; MS in Mech. Engring., U. Ill., Chgo., 1985. Registered profl. engr., Ill. Engr. U.S. EPA, Rockford, Ill., 1977-78; applications engr. Liquid Carbonic Corp., Chgo., 1978-79; project engr. Maremont Corp., Chgo., 1979-83; mech. engring. group leader Motorola, Inc., Schaumburg, Ill., 1983—. Mem. Am. Soc. Mech. Engrs., Ill. Soc. Profl. Engrs., Soc. Automotive Engrs. (assoc.), So. Ill. U. Alumni Assn. (life), U. Ill. Alumni Assn. (life). Club: Die Hard Cub Fan. Avocations: physical fitness, spectator sports, golf, Nordic skiing, camping. Office: Motorola Inc 4000 Commercial Dr Northbrook IL 60062

LARSON, TIMOTHY DENNIS, dentist; b. St. Louis, Sept. 14, 1953; s. Earl William and Melissa May (Lavender) L.; m. Carol Janice Goldstein, May 23, 1976; 1 child, Jenna Michelle. BA, U. Mo., Columbia, 1975; DDS, U. Mo., Kansas City, 1980. Gen. practice dentistry St. Charles, Mo., 1980—. Mem. ADA, Acad. Gen. Dentistry, Am. Endodontic Soc., Jaycees. Mem. United Church of Christ. Avocations: travel, photography, fishing, hunting. Home: #5 River Valley Ct Saint Charles MO 63303 Office: 1600 Heritage Landing #210 Saint Charles MO 63303

LARSON, WILLIAM JOHN, safety engineer; b. Benton, Ill., Mar. 8, 1923; s. Thure Alfred and Ruth Esther (Anderson) L.; student U. Nebr., 1943-44; E.E., U. Mich. and Mich. State U., 1945; B.S.M.E., Ill. Inst. Tech., 1948; m. Ruth Virginia Cannon, Mar. 17, 1945; children—Barbara Lee Larson Biskie, John Philip. Coop. student to safety engr. Hartford Accident & Indemnity Co., 1941-43, 46-57; safety engr. Argonne (Ill.) Nat. Lab., 1957-71, safety engring. supr., 1971—, supr. fire protection and safety engr., 1972-87 ; safety cons. 1987—; compliance officer Dept. of Labor, 1971; safety cons. and instr. Republican precinct committeeman, 1965-71; vol. Joliet Area Community Hospice, 1983—. Served with Signal Corps, AUS, 1943-46. Cert. safety profl.; registered profl. engr. Calif. Mem. Ill. Engring. Council, Am. Soc. Safety Engrs., Indsl. Conf., Nat. Safety Council (exec. com. research and devel. sect., chmn. research and devel. sect. 1984-85 4 Cameron awards). Mem. Evangelical Covenant Ch. Adv. bd. Am. Soc. Safety Engrs. Jour., 1967-75, chmn., 1972-75; contbr. numerous articles to safety jours. Home: 2212 Mayfield Ave Joliet IL 60435 Office: Argonne National Lab 9700 S Cass Ave Argonne IL 60439

LARUE, ROBERT LEONARD, architect; b. Indpls., Apr. 22, 1925; s. George Robert and Minnie (Patterson) LaR.; m. Jewell E. LaRue; children: Collette Jaye, Denise Kaye. BArch, U. Ill., 1951. Draftsman, designer Fran Schroeder Assocs., Indpls., 1954-56, Wright Porteous & Lowe, Inc., Indpls., 1956-60; ptnr. Wright-Porteous-Lowe, Indpls., 1964—; Mem. Ind. State Rev. Bd. for Hist. Places, Indpls., 1982; bd. dirs. Indpls. Hist. Preservation Com., Indpls., 1980—, Hist. Landmarks, Indpls., 1983. Bd. dies. Flanner House, Indpls. Served to sgt. USAF, 1943-46. Recipient Excellence in Devel. award Met. Devel. Com., Indpls., 1981, 83. Mem. AIA. Presbyterian. Avocation: golf. Office: Wright Porteous & Lowe Inc 20 N Meridian Indianapolis IN 46204

LASATER, DAVID B., evangelist; b. Kansas City, Mo., Feb. 18, 1948; s. Fon and Sarah (Smith) L.; m. Susan Owen, May 16, 1980; children: Jennie Rebecca, Aaron David, Phillip Michael. AA, Casper (Wyo.) Jr. Coll., 1968; BA, Okla. Christian Coll., 1972; postgrad., Abilene (Tex.) Christian U. Evangelist Hoffman Heights Ch. of Christ, Aurora, Colo., 1974-77, College Street Ch. of Christ, Dinuba, Calif., 1977-80, Morrie Ave Ch. of Christ, Cheyenne, Wyo., 1980-81; evangelist Ch. of Christ, Lazbuddie, Tex., 1981-83, Naperville, Ill., 1984—; missionary Ch. of christ, Logan, Utah, 1974-77. Editor religious jour., 1982. Chaplain Naperville Police Chaplain's Assn., 1984—. Named one of Outstanding Young Men Am., 1981, 83, 85. Republican. Lodge: Rotary Internat. (sgt. at arms Dinuba 1978-80). Avocations: painting, sculpting, golf. Home: 1809 Lisson Rd Naperville IL 60540

LASATER, DONALD E., banker; b. St. Louis, Dec. 8, 1925; s. Jacques and Kathryne (Haessel) L.; m. Mary E. McGinnis, Apr. 4, 1951; children—Kevin Michael, Timothy Patrick, Thomas Brady, Laura Clark, John Robert. Student, S.E. Mo. State Coll., 1942-43, U. Iowa, 1943; LL.B., U. So. Calif., 1948; student, Nat. Trust Sch., 1960. Bar: Mo. bar. Practice law St. Louis, 1949-54; asst. pros. atty. St. Louis County, 1955-56; counselor 1957-58; with Merc. Trust Co., St. Louis, 1959—; v.p. trust dept. Merc. Trust Co., 1965-67, dir., pres., 1967-70, chmn. bd., 1970—; dir. Ill. Power Co., Gen. Am. Life Ins. Co., St. Louis, Interco Inc. Mem. exec. com. St. Louis Area council Boy Scouts Am.; Bd. dirs. Barnes Hosp., St. Louis, Jr. Achievement Miss. Valley; trustee Washington U., St. Louis. Served with USNR, 1943-45. Mem. Mo. Bar Assn., Bar Assn. St. Louis, Am. Bankers Assn. (legis. council). Republican. Roman Catholic. Clubs: Noonday, St. Louis, Bogcy, Old Warson Country. Home: 751 Cella Rd Ladue MO 63124 Office: PO Box 524 Saint Louis MO 63166

LASKO, STEVEN ROBERT, mechanical designer, consultant; b. Cleve., Oct. 9, 1946; s. Steve and Mary Julia (Segedey) L.; m. Denise Marie Knowles, Oct. 8, 1977. Student, Cleve. Art Inst., 1968; cert. in machine design, Cleve. Engring Inst., 1970. Jr. designer electronic terminal connectors div. ITT, Cleve., 1972-75; product designer Compact Air Prodn., Cleve., 1975-76; mechanical designer Charles Lowe Co., Cleve., 1976-77, Essex Internat., Cleve., 1977-78, Lewis Machine Co., Cleve., 1978-86. Author: (book) Oils Well Ends Well, 1963. Republican. Presbyterian. Avocations: model railroading, antique auto models, literature.

LASKOWSKI, EDWARD LEONARD, electrical engineer, manufacturing company executive; b. Cleve., Mar. 13, 1943; s. Leonard Adam and Mary Barbara (Droba) L.; m. Carole Jean Zidlicky, Aug. 12, 1972; children: David, Jennifer. BEE, U. Detroit, 1966; MS in Elec. Engring., Ohio State U., 1968; D of Engring., Cleve. State U., 1978. Registered profl. engr., Ohio. Sr. research engr. Gen. Electric Co., Cleve., 1968-79; mgr. advt. devel. Bendix Automation Co., Solon, Ohio, 1979-84; mgr. computer integration systems Cleve. Pneumatic Co., 1984-85; v.p. engring. Namco Controls, Mentor, Ohio, 1985—. Patentee in field. Mem. IEEE, Soc. Mfg. Engrs. Avocations: photography, treatre organs, travel. Home: 6154 Winchester Dr Seven Hills OH 44131 Office: Namco Controls 8303 Tyler Blvd Mentor OH 44060

LASLEY, THOMAS J., educator; b. Delaware, Ohio, July 23, 1947; s. Thomas J. and Anna F. (Cooper) L.; m. Janet L. Olney, Apr. 21, 1973; children—Julianne Marie, Elizabeth Ann. B.S., Ohio State U., 1969, M.A., 1972, Ph.D., 1978. Cert. tchr. and administr., Ohio. Tchr., Upper Arlington, Ohio, 1969-75; research assoc. Ohio State U., 1975-77; cons. Ohio Dept. Edn., 1977-80, asst. dir. tchr. edn. and cert., 1980-83; assoc. prof. U. Dayton (Ohio), 1983—; cons. on sch. research and disruptive student behavior. Mem. Am. Ednl. Research Assn., Assn. Supervision Curriculum Devel., Phi Delta Kappa. Co-author: Biting the Apple, 1980; Handbook of Schools with Good Discipline, 1982; editor Jour. Tchr. Edn.; numerous articles. Office: U Dayton Chaminade Hall Dayton OH 45469

LASSERS, ELISABETH, psychiatrist; b. Offenbach, Germany, Mar. 17, 1920; d. Robert and Dora (Metz) S.; m. Willard J. Lassers, June 30, 1946; 1 child, Deborah. BS, U. Ill., Chgo., 1947, MD, 1949; trainee, Ctr. for Handicapped Children U. Ill., Chgo., 1959-60; student, Family InNst. Chgo., 1970-72. Diplomate Am. Bd. Pediatrics, Am. Bd. Psychiatry, Am. Bd. Child Psychiatry. Intern Mt. Sinai Hosp., Chgo., 1949-50; fellow in pediatric neurology Cook County Hosp., Chgo., 1950-51, resident in pediatrics, 1951-52; resident in pediatrics U. Ill. Research and Ednl. Hosps., Chgo., 1955-56; med. dir. Ill. Children's Hosp. Sch., Chgo., 1951-53; pvt. practice pediatrics Chgo., 1956-59; assoc. in pediatrics Northwestern U., 1960-63; assoc. attending physician Michael Reese Hosp., Chgo., 1957-63; pediatrician, med. dir. Dysfunctional Child Ctr. Michael Reese Hosp., Chgo., 1960-63; resident in psychiatry, fellow child psychiatry U. Chgo. Hosps. and Clinics, 1963-67; child psychiatrist U. Ill. Coll. Medicine, Chgo., 1967-71; chief sect. child psychiatry Ill. Masonic Med. Ctr., Chgo., 1971-75; pvt. practice psychiatry Chgo., 1970—; cons. child psychiatry Ill. Masonic Med. Ctr., Chgo., 1975—; lectr. psychiatry U. Chgo., 1971-79, professorial lectr. psychiatry, 1979—; pt. time clinical instr. pediatrics U. Ill. Coll. Medicine, 1955-59; clinical asst. prof. psychiatry and pediatrics U. Ill., Chgo., 1971—. Contbr. articles to profl. jours. Mem. subcom. on community mental health, govs. commn. to revise the mental health code, Chgo., 1975-77, Ill. Council Child Psychiatry; sec.-treas., bd. dirs. Chgo. Council Child Psychiatry, 1972-76; bd. dirs. Nat. Commn. Correctional Health Care, Chgo., 1984—. Mem. Am. Acad. Pediatrics, Am. Psychiatric Assn., Am. Acad. Child Psychiatry, Am. Soc. for Adolescent Psychiatry, Am. Med. Women's Assn. Jewish. Avocations: reading, travelling, swimming, theater. Home: 1509 E 56th St Chicago IL 60637 Office: 151 N Michigan Ave Chicago IL 60601

LASSILA, KENNETH EINO, physicist, educator; b. Hancock, Mich., Apr. 27, 1934; s. Eino Isaac and Anja Helmi (Heikkinen) L.; m. Jean Hannah Day, Mar. 17, 1957 (div. Nov. 9, 1982); children—Kathrin, Erik, Kirsten. B.S., U. Wyo., 1956; M.S., Yale U., 1959, Ph.D., 1962. Postdoctoral assoc. Case Western Res. U., Cleve., 1961-63, Stanford (Calif.) U., 1966; asst. prof. Iowa State U., Ames, 1963-64, 66-67, assoc. prof., 1967-69, prof. physics, 1969—, sr. physicist Ames Lab., 1969—, spokesman high energy theory, 1978-84; sr. research assoc. U. Helsinki (Finland), 1964-66, docent, 1973—. Contbr. articles to profl. jours. Fulbright research scholar U. Helsinki, 1965, Fulbright lectr. U. Oulu (Finland), 1972; NORDITA prof. Finland, 1973. Fellow Am. Phys. Soc.; mem. Finnish Phys. Soc. Lutheran. Office: Iowa State U Dept Physics Ames IA 50011

LASSITER, LEWANZER, obstetrician-gynecologist; b. N.Y.C., Nov. 3, 1948; d. Herbert Gabriel and Helen Juanita (Lassiter) Oliver, m. Reginald Douglas Moore, Feb. 11, 1980; 1 child, Monica Moore. BS, Rollins Coll., 1970; MD, Loyola U., Chgo., 1976. Diplomate Am. Bd. Ob-Gyn. Resident St. Joseph Hosp., Chgo., 1976-80; with health service corps. HEW, Washington, 1980-82; pvt. practice ob-gyn. Chgo., 1982—; asst. dir. med. edn. St. Joseph Hosp., Chgo., 1986—. Fellow Am. Coll. Ob-Gyn.; mem. AMA, Ill. State Med. Soc., Chgo. Med. Soc. Office: 1525 E 53rd St #808 Chicago IL 60615

LASSUS, JON FRANCIS, oil company executive; b. Fort Wayne, Ind., May 21, 1937; s. Elmer F. and Madeline (Boedeker) L.; m. Kathleen McCoy, Aug. 22, 1959; children—Jon R., Michelle, Todd, Gregory. B.A., Xavier Coll., Cin., 1960. Exec. v.p. Lassus Bros. Oil, Inc., Fort Wayne, 1965-72, pres., chief exec. officer, 1972—; pres. Lasco Leasing Co., Inc., 1974—, Handy Dandy Food Stores, Inc., 1982—, Anthony Wayne Vending Co., Inc., 1980—; v.p. Century Dynamics, 1975—; dir. Summit Bank, Wayne Pipe & Supply Co. Bd. dirs. Jr. Achievement Fort Wayne, St. Francis Coll., YMCA, Better Bus. Bur., ARC, Catholic Social Service, Public TV Fort Wayne; past pres. Covington Lake Assn.; mem. council parish St. Patrick's Catholic Ch., also past pres. Mem. Fort Wayne C. of C., Ind. Oil Marketers, N.E. Ind. Oil Men's Club, Bus. Forum, Young Pres. Orgn., St. Joseph Hosp. Health Found. Clubs: Fort Wayne Country (past dir.), Mad Anthonys. Lodge: Rotary (past dir.). Home: 3216 La Balme Trail Fort Wayne IN 46804 Office: Lassus Bros Oil Inc 4600 W Jefferson Blvd Fort Wayne IN 46804

LASTER, RALPH WILLIAM, JR., insurance company executive, accountant; b. Hutchinson, Kans., Oct. 4, 1951; s. Ralph William Sr. and Peggy Edith (O'Connell) L.; m. Jerri Laster, May 26, 1971; children: Tarissa Marie, Damian Michael. BSBA, Emporia (Kans.) State U., 1974. Staff acct. Deloitte, Haskin & Sells, Kansas City, Mo., 1974-76, Mize, Houser, Mehlinger & Kimes, Topeka, 1976-78; ptnr. Gregg, Prichard & Laster CPA's, Winfield, Kans., 1978-81; v.p., chief fin. officer, sec. Am. Investors Life Ins. Co., Inc., Topeka, 1981-84, exec. v.p., chief fin. officer, sec., 1985—, also bd. dirs.; v.p. chief fin. officer, sec., treas. Am. Vestob Fin. Corp., Topeka, also bd. dirs. AmVestors Fin. Corp., Topeka, Nat. Investment Corp., Topeka. Republican. Methodist. Home: 4825 Cochise

Topeka KS 66614 Office: Am Investors Life Ins Co Inc 415 SW 8th Ave Topeka KS 66603

LASTOVICA, FRANK RUDOLPH, JR., architect; b. Omaha, Apr. 23, 1953; s. Frank Rudolph and Dorothy Mae (Karpisek) L.; m. Karen Elizabeth Duke, Oct. 15, 1982; 1 child, Christine Elizabeth. BArch, U. Nebr., 1975. Registered architect, Nebr. V.p. Richard D. Nelson Co., Omaha, 1975-84, Purdy & Slack Architects P.C., Omaha, 1984—; guest speaker Omaha Schs. Through Jr. League of Omaha, 1985—. Mem. AIA (pres. Omaha chpt. 1986). Republican. Methodist. Lodges: Rotary, Masons. Avocations: skiing, tennis, volleyball, wood working, art glass. Home: 2729 N 129th Circle Omaha NE 68164 Office: Purdy & Slack Architects 1065 N 115th St Suite 200 Omaha NE 68154

LASWELL, GEORGE ROBERT, health care administrator, consultant; b. Ft. Monmouth, N.J., Sept. 23, 1946; s. Harry Taylor and Bernice Dorice (Harrison) L.; m. Dixie Lee Buoy; 1 child, Katherine. BS, U.S. Mil. Acad., 1968; MA, U. Colo., 1973; MBA, Murray State U., 1978. Commd. 2d lt. U.S. Army, 1968, advanced through grades to maj., 1977; maj. USAR, 1977—; exec. adminstr. dept. anesthesiology Michael Reese Hosp., Chgo., 1978—. Decorated Bronze Star with four bronze oak leaf clusters. Mem. Am. Acad. Med. Adminstrs., Nat. Rifle Assn., Internat. Game Fish Assn. Avocations: fishing, hunting. Office: Michael Reese Hosp Med Ctr Lake Shore Dr at 31st St Chicago IL 60616

LASWELL, LUCIEN KROLL, sales executive; b. Decatur, Ill., Oct. 10, 1939; s. Lucien Collins and Catherine (Kroll) L.; divorced; 1 child, Kayla Helene Hahn. Student, U. Wis., 1957-60, Rockford Coll., 1962-64. Casting buyer Barber Colman Co., Rockford, Ill., 1961-70; sales engr. State Line Foundries, Roscoe, Ill., 1970-71; v.p. sales Micro Industries, Rock Falls, Ill., 1971—. Served as sgt. U.S. Army, 1961-64. Mem. Am. Diecast Inst., Soc. Diecast Engrs. Roman Catholic. Avocations: boating, waterskiing. Home: Rural Rt 1 Byron IL 61010 Office: Micro Industries Inc 200 W 2d St Rock Falls IL 60171

LASWELL, LYNN EDWARD, accountant, consultant; b. Granite City, Ill., June 26, 1952; s. Arthur Ernest and Ruth Elenora (Mefford) L.; m. Harriet Jane Martin, June 23, 1973; children: Kristen Lynne, Kelly Beth. Student, So. Ill. U., 1971-73; BBA, Ill. Coll., 1975. CPA, Ind., Ill. Controller Ill. Midstates, Belleville, 1978-83; asst. controller Nat. Western, Austin, Tex., 1983-84; fin. reporter and analyst Coll. Life, Indpls., 1984-86; internal auditor Indpls., 1986—; v.p. Ill. Assn. Life Ins. Cos., Springfield, 1982-83. Fellow Life Mgmt. Inst.; mem. Am. Inst. CPA's, Ind. CPA Soc. (ins. com. 1987), Ill. CPA Soc., Nat. Assn. Accts., Inst. Internal Auditors. Avocations: roses, photography, reading. Home: 8021 Sandi Ct Indianapolis IN 46260 Office: State Life Ins Co 141 E Washington Indianapolis IN 46204

LATER, JEFFREY PHILLIP, marketing professional; b. Evanston, Ill., July 13, 1957; s. George Phillip and Peggy (Behrens) L. BS in Bus., Miami U., Oxford, Ohio, 1979. Sales rep. Belden Corp., Raleigh, N.C., 1979-81; sales rep. II Belden Corp., Phila., 1981-83; mktg. specialist Belden Electronic Wire & Cable, Richmond, Ind., 1983-84, mgr. mktg. communications, 1984—. Loaned exec. United Way, Richmond, 1984. Mem. Miami U. Alumni Assn. (Young Alumni award 1985), Whitewater Valley Alumni Assn. (pres. 1985), Richmond C. of C. Republican. Roman Catholic. Avocations: golf, running, swimming. Office: Belden Electronic Wire & Cable PO Box 1980 Richmond IN 47375 Home: 250 S 48th St Richmond IN 47374

LATIF, SAMI MOHAMMAD, dentist; b. Jerusalem, June 29, 1953; (father U.S. citizen); s. Mohammad M. and Zohra (Tamimi) L.; m. Zeineb H. Latif. BS in Biology, NE Mo. State U., 1974; MA in Physiology, Ball State U., 1976; DMD, So. Ill. U., 1984; BSEE, Ohio State U., 1986. Gen. practice dentistry Columbus, Ohio, 1984—. Mem. Arab Am. Anti Descrimination League, 1986. Mem. ADA, Acad. Gen. Dentistry, Ohio Dental Soc., Columbus Dental Soc., Arab Am. Inst. Muslim. Avocations: travel, tennis, golf, reading, photography. Home: 7870 Ridpath Rd Grove City OH 43123 Office: 1151 S High St Columbus OH 43206

LATIMER, THOMAS HUGH, trade association executive; b. Memphis, Oct. 30, 1932; s. Ira Helser and Imogene Henrietta (Atcheson) L.; m. Mildred Irene Moore, Oct. 11, 1957; children: Carol Ann Latimer Dennis, Michael Lee, Linda Sue Latimer Nonnemann. AB, U. Chgo., 1951; post-grad., U. Miami Law Sch., 1951-52, John Marshall Law Sch., 1952-53, Northwestern U., 1954-56. Acctg. tchr. Automation Inst., Chgo., 1964-66; acctg. mgr. Cory Corp., Chgo., 1966-67; mktg. adminstr. Stromberg Datagraphics, San Diego, Calif., 1967-68; exec. v.p. Ill. Small. Businessmen's Assn., Chgo., 1968—, Am. Fedn. Small. Bus., Chgo., 1971—; exec. v.p. Nat. Council for Labor Reform, 1968—; exec. v.p. Ill. Right To Work Com.; moderator, del. State House Conf. on Small Bus., 1983, 85. Pres. Conservative Caucus of Ill., 1983—, named Outsanding State Coordinator, 1982; v.p. Ethnic Am. Council, Chgo., 1984—; co-founder Coalition for Peace Through Strength. Mem. Nat. Assn. Accts. (editor Chgo. chpt. newsletter 1967-68), Ill. C. of C. (small bus. council 1980-84), SAR. Republican. Lutheran. Avocations: photography, swimming. Home: 3238 Adams Lansing IL 60438 Office: Am Fedn Small Bus 407 S Dearborn Chicago IL 60605

LA TOURETTE, JOHN ERNEST, university official; b. Perth Amboy, N.J., Nov. 5, 1932; s. John Crater and Charlotte Ruth (Jones) LaT.; m. Lillie M. Drum, Aug. 10, 1957; children—Marc Andrew, Yanique Renee. B.A., Rutgers U., 1954, M.A., 1955, Ph.D., 1962. Instr. Rutgers U., 1960-61; asst. prof. econs. SUNY, Binghamton, 1961-65; assoc. prof. SUNY, 1965-69, prof., 1969-76, chmn. dept. econs., 1967-76, acting provost for grad. studies and research, 1975-76; dean Grad. Coll., vice provost for research Bowling Green State U., 1976-79; provost, v.p. No. Ill. U., DeKalb, 1979-86; pres. No. Ill. U., 1986—; vis. prof. Karlsruhe (W. Ger.) U., 1974; research prof. Brookings Inst., 1966-67; vis. scholar Ariz. State U., 1969, 70; lectr. Econs. Inst., U. Colo., 1966; dir. NSF Departmental Sci. Devel. Grant, 1970-75. Contbr. articles to profl. jours. Served to capt. USAF, 1955-58. Ford Found. grantee, 1963; SUNY Found. grantee, 1963, 65, 70. Mem. Am. Econ. Assn., Can. Econ. Assn. Home: 901 Woodlawn Dr De Kalb IL 60115 Office: Pres's Office 307 No Ill U De Kalb IL 60115

LATTA, DELBERT L., congressman; b. Weston, Ohio, Mar. 5, 1920; m. Rose Mary Kiene; children: Rose Ellen Kuebeck, Robert Edward. A.B., LL.B., Ohio No. U. Bar: Ohio bar 1944. State senator Ohio, 3 terms; mem. 86th-99th congresses from 5th Ohio Dist. Republican. Office: 2309 Rayburn House Office Bldg Washington DC 20515 *

LATTANZIO, RICK JAMES, data processing company official; b. Chgo., May 12, 1953; s. Glenn and Maryann (Crivello) L.; m. Christine Marie Migala, June 12, 1976. B.S., Wright Coll., 1975. Field sales mgr. Pitney Bowes, Arlington Heights, Ill., 1975-78; dir. mktg. Vaxar, Inc., Des Plaines, Ill., 1978-80; regional mgr. Computer Sharing, Chgo., 1980-84; v.p., gen. mgr. CoAms, Inc., Chgo., 1984—. Mem. Chgo. Commerce and Industry.

LATZ, WILLIAM MICHAEL, accountant; b. Logansport, Ind., Oct. 14, 1944; s. John William and Mary Katherine (Broderick) L.; m. Diane Marie Wolfangle, May 16, 1970; 1 son, Kenneth Michael. B.S. in Bus., Ind. U., 1972. C.P.A., Ind.; lic. pilot. Staff acct. Michael C. Latz & Assocs., Indpls., 1968-72; ptnr. Nyikos & Latz, CPAs, Indpls., 1972-81, Ashby, Brown, Latz, Maudlin & Co., Indpls. and Anderson, Ind., 1981-83; pres., chief exec. officer, tax ptnr. Latz & Maudlin, Inc. CPAs, Indpls. and Fairmount, Ind., 1983—; dir. KML Enterprises, Inc., Plainfield, Ind. Served with U.S. Army, 1966-68; Viet Nam. Mem. Am. Inst. C.P.A.s, Ind. C.P.A. Soc., Aircraft Owners and Pilots Assn. Republican. Roman Catholic. Office: 8750 Purdue Rd Indianapolis IN 46268

LATZER, RICHARD NEAL, investment company executive; b. N.Y.C., Jan. 6, 1937; s. Paul John and Alyce A. Latzer; B.A., U. Pa., 1959, M.A., 1961; m. Ellen Weston, Sept. 5, 1965; children—Steven, David. Security analyst Mut. Benefit Life Ins. Co., Newark, 1963-66; portfolio mgr. Equitable Life Ins., Washington, 1966-68; securities analyst Investors Diversified Services, Mpls., 1968-69, dir. cert. and ins. investments, 1969-77, v.p. cert. and ins. investments, 1977-84; v.p. cert. and ins. investments IDS Fin. Services, Inc., 1984-86, IDS Fin. Corp., 1987—; v.p. investments, IDS Reins. Co., 1986—; asst. treas. Investors Syndicate Life Ins. & Annuity Co., Mpls., 1969-72; v.p. IDS Life Ins. Co., Mpls., 1973-80, v.p. investments, 1980—; v.p. Investors Syndicate of Am., 1973-77, v.p. investments, 1977-84; v.p. Investors Syndicate Title & Guaranty Co., 1977-83, investment officer IDS Life Ins. Co. of N.Y., 1977—; v.p. investments IDS Life Capital Resource Fund I, Inc., 1981—, IDS Spl. Income Fund, Inc., 1981—, Am Enterprise Life Ins. Co., 1986—, Reinsurance Co. 1986—; IDS Life Series Fund, 1986—; IDS Life Managed Fund, Inc., 1986—, IDS Property Casualty, 1987—; v.p. IDS Realty Corp., 1987—; pres., chmn. bd., bd. dirs. Real Estate SErvices Co., 1986—; IDS Life Moneyshare Fund, Inc., 1981—; IDS Cert. Co., 1984—; chmn. bd., dir. IDS Real Estate Services Co., 1983-86; v.p. Fireman's Fund Am. Life Ins. Co., 1985-86; dir. Investors Syndicate Devel. Corp., Mpls., 1970—, Nuveen Realty Corp., Mpls., 1976-80. Served to lt., USN, 1960-63. Chartered fin. analyst. Mem. Twin City Soc. Security Analysts, Inst. Chartered Fin. Analysts. Home: 6835 Harold Ave Golden Valley MN 55427 Office: 3000 IDS Tower Minneapolis MN 55402

LAUBER, CHRISTINE ANN, accountant; b. Chgo., Oct. 4, 1945; d. Joseph W. Lauber and Agatha M. (Wilhelm) Mootz; m. Ronald A. Schubert, June 13, 1971 (div. Jan. 1986); children: Jessica B., Peter W. Student, Northwestern U., 1963-65; BS in Bus., Ind. U., South Bend, 1970, MSBA, 1973. CPA, Ind. Office mgr. J.C. Lauber Co., South Bend, 1966-70; mgr. McGladrey Hendricksen, South Bend and Elkhart, Ind., 1970-80, John Z. Olcott CPA, South Bend, 1980-82; pvt. practice acctg. South Bend, 1982—. Treas. campaign com. Tom Westfall, South Bend, 1987; bd. dirs. Friends of the Unemployed, South Bend, 1983—; officer Estate Planning Council, 1985—. Mem. Am. Inst. CPA's (MAS com. 1985—), Ind. Assn. CPA's (bd. dirs. 1984-87, MAS com. 1981-84), Nat. Assn. Accts. (chpt. pres. 1980-81, nat. bd. dirs. 1982-84, regional officer 1985—). Roman Catholic. Office: 1402 Mishawaka Ave South Bend IN 46615

LAUBER, JACK MOORE, history educator; b. Archbold, Ohio, Oct. 8, 1934; s. William Burke and Velma Mae (Moore) L.; m. Margaret Jean Carlson, Aug. 7, 1964; children—Chad William, Megan Margaret. B.S., Bowling Green State U., Ohio, 1959, M.A., 1960; Ph.D., U. Iowa, 1967. Instr. Ohio State U., Columbus, 1964-67; asst. prof. history U. Wis.-Eau Claire, 1967-69, assoc. prof., 1969-77, prof., 1977—, dept. chmn., 1982—. Contbr. articles to profl. jours. Served with USN, 1953-57. Mem. Am. Hist. Assn., Am. Assn. for Advancement Slavic Studies, Phi Alpha Theta. Avocations: reading; chess. Office: U Wis Dept History Eau Claire WI 54701

LAUBER, PETER HERMANN, psychotherapist, consultant; b. Glen Cove, N.Y., Feb. 26, 1944; s. Hermann and Emma Katherine (Hill) L.; m. Cheryl Anne Pump, Jan. 30, 1965; children: Deborah Susan, Steven Mark. AB, Wheaton Coll., 1966; MSW, Wayne State U., 1968, PhD, 1975. Cert. social worker, Mich.; cert. marriage therapist, Mich. Clin. social worker VA Hosp., Allen Park, Mich., 1968-73; sch. social worker Wayne-Westland Schs., Mich., 1973-75; prof. social work John wesley Coll., Owosso, Mich., 1975-79; pvt. practice psychotherapy Owosso, 1979—. Elder Community Evang. Presbyn. Ch., Owosso, 1985—. Mem. Am. Assn. Marital and Family Therapy, Nat. Assn. Social Workers, No. Am. Assn. Christians in Social Work (pres. 1977-80, v.p., bd. dirs. 1984—). Avocation: camping. Home and Office: 1327 Summit St Owosso MI 48867

LAUDER, NORMA J., corporate finance executive; b. Springfield, Ill., June 17, 1949; d. Joseph T. and Elizabeth A. (Maher) Thompson; m. David C. Lauder, Oct. 23, 1971. BS in Acctg., U. Ill., 1971. CPA, Ill. Mem. tax staff Arthur Andersen & Co., Chgo., 1971-76, tax mgr., 1976-82, ptnr., 1982-85; v.p. dir. taxes Beatrice Cos. Inc., Chgo., 1985-86; sr. v.p., dir. taxes First Chicago Corp., Chgo., 1986—. Bd. dirs. Music of the Baroque, Chgo., 1983—; dir. fin. com. Cath. Charities, Chgo., 1984—; mem. vis. adv. com. DePaul U. Sch. Accountancy. Fellow Leadership Greater Chgo., 1987-88. Mem. Am. Inst. CPA's, Ill. CPA Soc. Roman Catholic. Clubs: Monroe, University (Chgo.). Home: 322 Hambletonian Dr Oak Brook IL 60521 Office: First Chicago Corp Mail Suite 0308 Chicago IL 60670-0308

LAUDICK, BONNIE BROUWER, therapeutic recreation specialist, consultant; b. Ft. Wayne, Ind.; d. Lester Jay Brouwer and Geraldine Smith; children: William, Robert. BS, Ind. U., 1965, MS, George Williams Coll., 1986. Dir. recreation therapy and phys. edn. Ill. Children's Hosp. Sch., Chgo., 1965-68; day supr., activity therapy Henry Horner Children's Ctr., Chgo. Read Mental Health Ctr., Chgo., 1975-76; dir. recreational therapy and spl. services Orangegrove Rehab. Hosp., Garden Grove, Calif., 1976-78; cons. activity therapy Hosp. Affiliates Internat., Inc., Nashville, 1980-81, Hosp. Corp. Am., Nashville, 1982—; dir. activity therapy Riveredge Hosp., Forest Park, Ill., 1978—; speaker local, state and nat. confs. therapeutic recreation assns. Contbr. articles to profl. jours. Mem. Forest Park Community Edn. Adv. Council, 1981-82. Recipient Outstanding Service award Nat. Cystic Fibrosis Found., 1973, 74, 75, Top Fundraiser award, 1971, 72, 73; Outstanding Achievement in Activity Therapy award Hosp. Affiliates Internat., Inc., 1979, Outstanding Dept. award, 1980. Mem. Nat. Recreation and Parks Assn., Nat. Therapeutic Recreation Soc. (joint commn. on accreditation hosps. com. 1981, 82, co-chmn., 1983—, mem. mental health com. 1982), Ill. Parks and Recreation Assn. (mem. awards com. 1981-82, bd. dirs. 1987), Ill. Therapeutic Recreation Sect. (bd dirs. 1981—, sec.-treas. 1983—, pres. 1987, Outstanding Program award 1980), West Suburban Juvenile Officers Assn.(sec. 1982—). Office: 8311 W Roosevelt Rd Forest Park IL 60130

LAUDIG, LARRY BRYANT, engineer; b. Poland, Ind., June 2, 1938; s. Wayne Raymond and Helen Maxine (Greenlee) L.; m. Kathleen Sue Montz, Oct. 1, 1966; children: Larry, Elizabeth, Matthew. BS in Engring., U.S. Naval Acad., 1960; MS in Math., Purdue U., 1974; MBA in Fin., St. Francis Coll., 1984. Commd. ensign USN, 1960, advanced through grades to lt., disability ret., 1965; mathematician U.S. Naval Avionics, Indpls., 1966-67; sr. staff engr. Magnavox, Ft. Wayne, Ind., 1967—; chmn. bd. dirs. N.Am. Philips Fed. Credit Union, Ft. Wayne. Mem. Magnavox Mgmt. Club, U.S. Naval Acad. Alumni Assn. Methodist. Club: Toastmasters (pres. Ft. Wayne chpt. 1973, area gov. 1974, Disting. Toastmaster award 1986). Avocations: golf, bridge, gardening. Home: Rural Rt 1 Yoder IN 46798 Office: Magnavox 1313 Production Rd Fort Wayne IN 46808

LAUENSTEIN, ANN GAIL, librarian; b. Milw., Nov. 8, 1949; d. Elmer Lester Herbert and Elizabeth Renatta (Bovee) Zaeske. B.A., U. Wis.-Madison, 1971, M.A., 1972. Asst. librarian U. Wis.-Wausau, 1972-73; cataloger, librarian MacMurray Coll., Jacksonville, Ill., 1973-76; corp. librarian Anheuser-Busch Co., Inc., St. Louis, 1976—; facilitator Anheuser-Busch Quality Circle, St. Louis, 1984—; Sec. Friends of Kirkwood Library, 1986—. Mem. Spl. Libraries Assn. (network liason 1981-83, chmn. employment com. 1983-84, chmn. hospitality com. 1984-85), St. Louis Regional Library Network (council 1981-83), St. Louis Online Users Group, AAUW (editor jour. 1981-84, publicity chmn. 1985-87, scholar 1984), Women in Bus. Network (adv. panel 1980-82, 86-87, programs planner 1987).Avocation: stamp collecting. Office: Anheuser-Busch Co Inc One Busch Pl Saint Louis MO 63118

LAUER, ROBERT A., accounting firm executive; b. Akron, Ohio, Dec. 17, 1943; s. Claude F. and June E. (Ade) L.; m. Penny Earl, July 17, 1970; children: Alisha, Sarah. B in Indsl. Engring., Ohio State U., 1967, MBA, 1968. CPA, Ohio. Ptnr.-in-charge info. cons. Arthur Andersen & Co., Cleve., 1984—. Mem. exec. bd. Greater Cleve. Council Boy Scouts Am., 1985, v.p. Explorer program, 1987. Mem. Am. Prodn. Inventory Soc., Council on Logistics Mgmt., Leadership Cleve. Club: Cleve. Athletic. Office: Arthur Andersen & Co. 1717 E 9th St Cleveland OH 44114

LAUER, ROBERT JOHN, electrical engineer, manufacturing executive; b. Toledo, June 24, 1921; s. Fred John and Albina (Ernst) L.; m. Phyllis Mary Grothjan, Nov. 2, 1945 (div. June 1981); children: Robert, Jeanne, Thomas, Janice, Christopher, Carolyn, Peter; m. Mary Ann Walter, Dec. 14, 1985. Student, DeSales Coll., 1940; BS, U.S. Naval Acad., 1944, postgrad. in electronics, 1951. Commd. ensign USN, 1944, advanced through ranks to lt., 1951, resigned, 1953; elec. engr. A. Bentley & Sons, Toledo, 1953-62; elec. engr. Haughton Elevator Co., Toledo, 1962-66, v.p. engring., 1966-79; v.p. engring. Schindler Elevator Co., Toledo, 1979—; cons. elevator field, 1985—. Contbr. articles to profl. jours.; patentee in field. Mem. Landmarks Com., Toledo, 1983-86; committeeman Boy Scouts Am., Toledo, 1957-60. Mem. NSPE, Ohio Soc. Profl. Engrs., Toledo Soc. Profl. Engrs., Nat. Mgmt. Assn., Am. Mensa, Toledo C. of C. Republican. Roman Catholic. Clubs: Inverness. Avocations: golf, bridge, woodcarving, history, travel. Home: 3825 Sulphur Spring Rd Toledo OH 43606 Office: Schindler Elevator Corp 671 Spencer St Toledo OH 43609

LAUER, ROBERT LEE, food company executive; b. Crook, Colo., Oct. 25, 1933; s. Martin F. and Mary A. (Hofsetz) L.; m. Mary Redman, Aug. 25, 1956; children: Anne, Lisa, John. B.S. in Journalism and Pub. Relations, Bowling Green State U., 1956. Mgr. Procter & Gamble, Cin., 1962-69; account supr. Harshe-Rotman & Druck, Los Angeles, 1969-70; mgr. corp. relations Clorox Co., Oakland, Calif., 1970-77; dir. pub. affairs S.C. Johnson & Son, Racine, Wis., 1977-81; v.p. corp. affairs Sara Lee Corp. (formerly Consolidated Foods Corp.), Chgo., 1981—. Bd. dirs. Chgo. Equity Fund Inc., Second Harvest Nat. Food Bank Network, Pub. Affairs Council, Washington. Mem. Pub. Relations Soc. Am., Econ. Club Chgo. Clubs: University, Executives (Chgo.); Commonwealth (San Francisco). Office: Sara Lee Corp 3 First Nat Plaza Chicago IL 60602

LAUFFENBURGER, DAVID LIND, psychologist; b. Warren, Penn., Sept. 19, 1945; s. Alfred Lee and Harriet Rachel (Lind) L.; m. Linda Janelle Meeker, Nov. 1, 1969 (div. Dec. 1978); m. Susan K. Toole, Apr. 18, 1987; 1 child, Brian. BA, Thiel Coll., Greenville, Pa., 1967; MA, Miami U., Oxford, Ohio, 1973. Lic. psychologist, Ohio. Psychologist Cin. Pub. Sch., 1969-71, Glenview Sch. for Boys, Cin., 1971-73; psychology asst., then psychologist Miami Valley Childrens's Ctr., Hamilton, Ohio, 1973-78; psychologist Children's Mental Health, Xenia, Ohio, 1978-81; supr. psychologist, dir. children's program Miami County Mental Helth, Troy, Ohio, 1981—. Mem. Ohio Psychol. Assn. Avocations: music, reading, woodworking, photography, sports. Home: 4994 Cakes Rd Trotwood OH 45426 Office: Miami County Mental Health 1059 N Market St Troy OH 45373

LAUFMAN, LESLIE RODGERS, hematologist, oncologist; b. Pitts., Dec. 13, 1946; d. Marshall Charles and Ruth (Petrauskas) Rodgers; m. Harry B. Laufman, Apr. 25, 1970 (div. Apr. 1984); children: Hal, Holly. BA in Chemistry, Ohio Wesleyan U., 1968; MD, U. Pitts., 1972. Diplomate Am. Bd. Internal Medicine and Hematology. Intern Montefiore Hosp., Pitts., 1972-73, resident in internal medicine, 1973-74; fellow in hemotology and oncology Ohio State Hosp., Columbus, 1974-76; dir. med. oncology Grant Med. Ctr., Columbus, 1977—; practice medicine specializing in hemotology and oncology Columbus, 1977—; bd. dirs. Columbus Cancer Clinic. Contbr. articles to profl. jours. Mem. AMA, Am. Women Med. Assn. (sec./treas. 1985-86, pres. 1986—), Am. Soc. Clin. Oncologists, Oncology Assocs. Am., Southwest Oncology Group, Nat. Surg. Adjuvant Project for Breast and Bowel Cancers. Avocations: tennis, piano, sailing, hiking, travel. Office: 340 E Town St 8-300 Columbus OH 43215

LAUGHLIN, TERRY XAVIER, management consultant; b. Oskaloosa, Iowa, Dec. 7, 1936; s. John Dwight and Beryle Beatrice (Bible) L.; m. Marilyn Jean Bendig, May 14, 1966. B.B.A., U. Notre Dame, 1960; LL.B., Blackstone Sch. Law, 1967; Ps.D., Coll. Metaphysics, 1971. Real estate broker, Ill., 1965-66; div. mgr. Britannica Schs., Chgo., 1966-68; pres. Laughlin Assocs., Inc., Roselle, Ill., 1968—. Mem. Am. Soc. Profl. Cons., N.W. Suburban Assn. Commerce and Industry. Republican. Roman Catholic. Clubs: Ventura 21 (Roselle, Ill.); KC; Toastmasters (v.p.). Home: 56 N Salt Creek Rd Roselle IL 60172

LAUMANN, DENNIS JAMES, manufacturing company executive; b. Milw., Aug. 16, 1941; s. Carl August and Helen Dorothy (Brodel) L.; m. Duane Mary Lasecki, June 26, 1967 (div. Sept. 1974); 1 child, David James; m. Janice Audrey Bahr, June 28, 1975; 1 child, Michelle Denise. BS, U. Wis., Milw., 1972. Lab. technician A.O. Smith Corp., Milw., 1968-72; plant mgr. Benson Mfg., Menomonee Falls, Wis., 1972-74; cons. Standard Bus. Research, Chgo., 1974-78; v.p. mfg. Sub-Zero Freezer Co., Madison, Wis., 1978—; chmn. bd. dirs. D.J. Leasing, Madison. Served with USN, 1960-66. Republican. Lutheran. Avocations: golf, swimming, bridge. Home: 2133 Liberty Dr Cottage Grove WI 53527 Office: Sub-Zero Freezer Co Inc 4717 Hammersley Rd Madison WI 53711

LAUN, ANNE A., advertising media planner; b. Van Wert, Ohio, Jan. 8, 1957; d. Charles Raymond and Maria De Etta (Gossman) Atkinson; m. Craig Michael Laun, Aug. 12, 1978; 1 child, Emily Caroline. BS, Miami U., Oxford, Ohio, 1979. Advt. asst. Cleve. Inst. of Electronics, 1979-80; account coordinator Griswold-Eshleman, Cleve., 1980-83; media buyer Griswold, Inc., Cin., 1983-84; media planner, buyer Northlich, Stolley, Inc., Cin., 1984—. Mem. Cin. Advt. Club, Cin. C. of C. (mem. bus. industry directory com. 1986), Sigma Kappa (v.p. alumni chpt. 1985—, alumnae relations com. 1977-79). Avocations: needle work, sewing, music (flute, piano and voice). Office: Northlich Stolley Inc 200 W 4th St Cincinnati OH 45202

LAUR, JOSEPH MICHAEL, therapist; b. Milw., Feb. 23, 1952; s. Joseph Edwin and Ruth Bernadette (Beiswehger) L.; m. Susan Marie Wisniewski, Oct. 1, 1977 (div. July 1983); children: Melanie Brooke, Sean Joseph; m. Mary Kay Howie. BFA, U. Wis., 1975. Cert. Rolfer. Head masseur YMCA, Milw., 1975-76, health club dir., 1975-77; resident rolfer Cambridge House, Milw., 1977-82; rolfer Milw. Wellness Clinic, 1980-84; ind. rolfer Milw., 1984-86; ptnr. Saatkamp, Laur & Assocs., Milw., 1986-87; founder Joe Laur and Assocs., Milw., 1987—; co-founder Madison Holistic Health Ctr., 1979-85; mem. Milw. Wellness Council, 1987—. Chairperson Recreation and Open Space Com., Mequon, Wis., 1981-86; campaign coordinator John Anderson for Pres., 9th congl. dist., 1980; co-founder Wis. Wellcare Assocs. Nat. Merit scholar, 1970. Avocations: log bldg., forestry, woodworking. Home: 12501 N Circle Dr Mequon WI 53092 Office: Joe Laur and Assocs 200 W Silver Spring Suite 300 Milwaukee WI 53217

LAUREL, DEBORAH SPRING, personnel management consultant; b. Washington, Feb. 9, 1948; d. Seymour Solon and Merle (Plockie) Levine; m. G. Don L. Robbins; 1 child, Jennifer Laurel Main. BA in English Lit. with honors, Clark U., 1971; MA in English Lit., U. Wis., 1973. Pres. Apple Corps Ltd., Madison, Wis., 1972-81; personnel officer Wis. State Govt., Madison, 1976-85; pres. Laurel and Assocs., Madison, 1985—; ad hoc instr. U. Wis. Mgmt. Inst., Madison, 1974—; instr. Cardinal Stritch Coll., Madison, 1985—; cons. govt. agys., Madison, 1974-85. Playwrite: Empty Space Blues, 1972, Women Alone Together, 1973, Zounds There's A Sound, 1974; (poem) A Collection, 1968 (Hoyt Poetry award 1968). Chmn., trainer State Employee's Combined Campaign, Dane County, Madison, 1978-86. Recipient Gov's. award State Employee's Combined Campaign, Madison, 1984; Nat. Endowment for Arts grantee, 1974, 75. Mem. Am. Soc. Tng. Devel. (v.p. 1986—), Am. Mgmt. Assn., Wis. Women in Bus., Phi Beta Kappa. Jewish. Avocations: running, swimming, theater, music, gardening. Home: 917 Vilas Ave Madison WI 53715 Office: Laurel and Assocs 917 Vilas Madison WI 53715

LAURENCE, PHILIP HENRY, dentist; b. Danville, Ill., July 15, 1923; s. Albert Fredrick and Frances Lorinda (Swanson) L.; m. Norma Jean Stebbins, Dec. 9, 1950; children: Anne Laurence Little, Jean Laurence Buss, Kathryn Laurence Szott, John P. DDS, U. Ill., Chgo., 1950. Staff dentist Ill. Dept. Pub. Health, Springfield, 1950-51; pvt. practice Danville, 1951—. Served as 1st lt. U.S. Army AC, 1943-46, PTO. Mem. ADA, Ill. State Dental Soc., Danville Dist. Dental Soc. (pres. 1955), Soc. for Occlusal Studies, Internat. Dental Health Found., Am. Endodontic Soc. Republican. Methodist. Club: Danville Country. Avocations: clock building, sailing, camping. Home: 1431 Woodridge Danville IL 61832 Office: 917 N Walnut Danville IL 61832

LAURENCE, RICHARD ROBERT, history educator; b. Knoxville, Tenn., Apr. 22, 1937; s. Robert A. and Sally (Claxton) L.; m. Gertraud Fuehrer, July 6, 1961; children: Daniel Robert, Sonya Christina, Alfred James. BA, U. Tenn., 1959; postgrad., Middlebury Coll., 1959; MA, Stanford U., 1962, PhD, 1968. Instr. dept. humanitites Mich. State U., 1966-68, asst. prof., 1968-76, assoc. prof., 1976-82, prof., 1982—, asst. chmn., 1985—. Contbg. author: Doves and Diplomats, 1978, Focus on Vienna 1900, 1982, Biographical Dictionary of Internationalists, 1983, Biographical Dictionary of Modern Peace Leaders, 1985; others. Fulbright scholar U. Vienna, 1959-60;

Woodrow Wilson fellow, Stanford U. fellow, Austrian Govt. research fellow; grantee NEH, 1979. Mem. Am. Hist. Assn., Council Peace Research in History, Mich. Acad. Sci., Arts and Letters, German Studies Assn. Home: 1572 Cahill Dr PO Box 4842 East Lansing MI 48823 Office: Mich State U Dept Humanities East Lansing MI 48824

LAURENSON, ROBERT MARK, mechanical engineer; b. Pitts., Oct. 25, 1938; s. Robert Mark and Mildred Othelia (Frandsen) L.; m. Alice Ann Scroggins, Aug. 26, 1961; children: Susan Elizabeth Laurenson Matchael, Shari Lynn. Student, Drury Coll., 1956-58; BS in Mech. Engring., Mo. Sch. Mines, 1961; MS in Mech. Engring., U. Mich., 1962; PhD in Mech. Engring. (NASA tng. grantee), Ga. Inst. Tech., 1968. Registered profl. engr., Mo. Dynamics engr. McDonnell Douglas Corp., St. Louis, 1962-64, sr. dynamics engr., 1968-71, group engr., 1971-74, staff engr., 1974-75, tech. specialist, 1975-78, sr. tech. specialist, 1978-81, sect. chief, 1981-85, prin. tech. specialist, 1985—; participant 14th Midwestern Mechanics Conf., 1975; lectr. engring. mechanics St. Louis U., part-time 1969-71; adj. assoc. prof. U. Mo.-Rolla Grad. Engring. Ctr., St. Louis, 1980—; participant Symposium on Dynamics and Control of Large Flexible Spacecraft, Blackburg, Va., 1977; mem. panel Am. Astronauticla Soc. Symposium on Dynamics and Control of Nonrigid Spacecraft, UCLA, 1974. Contbr. articles to profl. jours.; reviewer profl. jours. Vestryman Episcopal Ch., 1972-76, sr. warden, 1976, usher chmn., 1978-80, Sunday sch. tchr., 1980-84, chmn. every mem. canvas, 1983, mem. steering com., 1983—, chmn. steering com., 1987—, mem. search com., 1984-85; mem. Commn. on Ministry, Diocese of Mo., 1985—. Mem. ASME (structures materials com. aerospace div. 1975-84, com. chmn. 1979-81, session organizer, chmn. ann. meeting , 1975, participant ann. meeting, 1986; mem. exec. com. aerospace div. 1980-85, sec.-treas. 1981-82, vice-chmn. 1982-83, chmn. 1983-84, mem. conf. organizing com., session chmn. Structures, Structural Dynamics and Materials Conf., 1977, chmn. tech. program, 1978, gen. co-chmn., 1979, gen. chmn., 1981, chmn., 1981-82, session chmn., 1985, adv. com., 1978-82, participant, 1979, 83, 86; mech. engring. evaluator Accreditation Bd. Engring. and Tech., 1985—, organizer symposium on microgravity fluid mechanics 1986, mem. planning com. edn. conf., 1986; editor: Advances in Aerospace Structures, 1982, Proceedings, 1986), AIAA (sr., gen. chmn. dynamics specialist conf. 1981, session chmn. 1987), Sigma Xi, Pi Tau Sigma, Tau Beta Pi, Phi Kappa Phi, Sigma Phi Epsilon. Home: 349 Beaver Lake Dr Saint Charles MO 63303 Office: McDonnell Douglas Corp Box 516 Saint Louis MO 63166

LAURENT, STEPHAN (FAESI), choreographer, artistic director, ballet teacher; b. Lausanne, Vaud, Switzerland, June 24, 1948; came to U.S., 1973; s. Hugo Max and Annette Eva Faesi; m. Martha Anne Denton, Nov. 10, 1973; children: Christopher Michael, Daniel Monroe, Emma Laurence. Baccalaureat es Lettres, Gymnase du Belvedere, Lausanne, 1964; BFA, So. Meth. U., 1974, MFA summa cum laude, 1979. Dancer, Ballet Royal de Wallonie, Charleroi, Belgium, 1974-75, Scapino Ballet, Amsterdam, the Netherlands, 1975-77; guest artist, various ballet cos. in Europe and U.S., 1972-82; ballet master Ballet Del Monte Sol, Santa Fe, 1978, Repertory Dance Co., Dallas, 1978-79; asst. prof. dance U. Wis.-Milw., 1979-82; artistic dir. Des Moines Ballet Co., 1982—; dance critic Feuille d'Avis de Lausanne, Switzerland, 1968-72; cons. Wis. Arts Bd., 1980-84, Iowa Arts Council, 1982—, Affiliated Arts Agys., Mpls., 1982—; coach Swiss team Internat. Ballet Competition, Varna, Bulgaria, 1976. Choreographer: Journey Into Elsewhere, 1980; The Nutcracker, 1982, Coppelia, 1984, The Hunchback of Notre-Dame, 1984 (commn. Iowa Arts Council 1984), Cinderella, 1986, Catulli Carmina, 1987, others. Canton of Zurich Scholar, 1973-77; Steo Found. grantee, Zurich, 1977; recipient Iowa Outstanding Artistic Achievement award, 1986. Office: Des Moines Ballet Co 4333 Park Ave Des Moines IA 50321

LAURES, GERALD MATHEW, financial executive; b. McHenry, Ill., Dec. 17, 1947; s. Erwin T. and Elaine F. (Heimer) L.; m. Anne Marie Pasquarelli, July 24, 1976; children: Christopher J., Stephanie T. BBA, John Carroll U., 1970; MBA, Northwestern U., 1972. CPA, Ill. Auditor Arthur Andersen & Co., Chgo., 1972-75; mgr. planning Masonite Corp., Chgo., 1975-82; controller Woodland Services Co., Chgo., 1982—. Mem. Am. Inst. CPA's, Ill. Soc. CPA's. Home: 1151 Walden Ln Deerfield IL 60015 Office: Woodland Services Co 20 N Wacker Dr Chicago IL 60606

LAURICH, DENNIS GARY, dentist; b. Highland Park, Mich., Dec. 3, 1953; s. Ludwig and Martha (Seppa) L.; m. Jill Quackenbush, Aug. 18, 1978; children: Andrew Foster, Matthew Charles. DDS, U. Mich., 1978. Gen. practice dentistry Livonia, Mich., 1978—. Mem. ADA, Mich. Dental Assn., Detroit Dist. Dental Soc. (pres. western component 1986—). Avocations: master's swimming, tennis, travel. Home: 4524 Walden Birmingham MI 48010 Office: 29105 W 8 Mile Rd Livonia MI 48152

LAURIDSEN, EARL BENTON, manufacturing executive; b. Hamilton, Ohio, Oct. 10, 1942; s. Karl Etlar and Virginia Mae (Johnston) L.; m. Laura Jean Lauridsen, July 1, 1967; children: Kendra, Karla, Krista. BA, Anderson Coll., 1966; MBA, Baldwin Wallace Coll., 1983. Tchr. Cleve. Pub. Schs., 1966-86; ptnr. St. Clair Cut Off and Mfg. Co., Cleve., 1974—, Ski-Way Machine Products Co., Euclid, Ohio, 1973—; sales rep. Uarco Inc., Cleve., 1969-73. Trustee Mentor (Ohio) Community Ch. of God, 1974-84, elder, 1984—. Mem. Nat. Tooling and Mfg. Assn., Am. Soc. Metals, Soc. Automotive Engrs. Republican. Club: Mentor Heisley Racquet. Avocations: tennis, woodworking, golfing, gardening. Home: 8239 Munson Rd Mentor OH 44060 Office: Ski Way Machine Products Co 24460 Lakeland Blvd Euclid OH 44132-1402

LAURITZEN, BRUCE RONNOW, banker; b. Omaha, June 21, 1943; s. John Ronnow and Elizabeth Ann (Davis) L.; m. Kimball McKay Bowles, Nov. 26, 1965; children: Margaret, Blair, Clarkson. AB, Princeton U., 1965; MBA, U. Va., 1967. With First Nat. Bank Omaha, 1967—, 2d v.p., 1972, v.p., 1972-83, exec. v.p., 1983-87, pres., 1987—, also bd. dirs., mem. exec. com., 1968—; pres. Farmers Savs. Bank, Shelby, Iowa, 1969-82, Harlan County Bank, Alma, Nebr., 1972—, Landmands Nat. Bank, Audubon, Iowa, 1972—, Sibley (Iowa) Ins. Agy., 1972—, Sibley State Bank, 1972—, First Nat. Bank, Elm Creek, Nebr., 1974-77, Landmands Ins. Agy., Kimballton, Iowa, 1974—, K.B.J. Enterprises, Iowa, 1975—, Viking Corp., Iowa, 1975—, Lauritzen Corp., Nebr. and Iowa, 1985—, Emerson (Iowa) State Bank, 1980-84; vice chmn. Crawford County Bank, Denison, Iowa, 1976—; chmn. MCV Acceptance Corp., Omaha, 1986—; treas. First Nat. Leasing Inc., Omaha, Banclease Inc., Omaha, First of Omaha Savs. Co. Pres., dir. Clarkson Meml. Hosp., Omaha; bd. dirs. Creighton U., Omaha; trustee Joslyn Art Mus., Omaha, Nebr. Ind. Coll. Found., Lincoln. Mem. Young Pres. Assn. (edn. chmn. 1985—), Omaha C. of C. (bd. dirs. Devel. Found. 1986—; named Outstanding Young Omahan, 1978). Republican. Episcopalian. Clubs: Omaha Country, Omaha, Omaha Press; Univ. Cottage (Princeton, N.J.); Minnesouri Angling (Alexandria, Minn.). Avocations: skiing, golf, hunting, tennis. Home: 608 Fairacres Rd Omaha NE 68132 Office: First Nat Bank of Omaha One First National Ctr Omaha NE 68102

LAURITZEN, JOHN RONNOW, banker; b. Mpls., Mar. 28, 1917; s. Max R. and Margaret (Flannery) L.; m. Elizabeth Ann Davis, Nov. 4, 1939; children: Bruce Ronnow, Ann Davis (Mrs. Ray Pape). Student, Princeton, 1937-38, U. Minn., 1939, U. Wis. Sch. Banking, 1947-49. With First Nat. Bank, Omaha, 1943—, v.p., 1949-61, pres., 1967-70, chmn. bd. dirs., chmn. exec. com., 1971—, also bd. dirs.; pres., chmn. bd. dirs. Emerson State Bank, Iowa, First State Bank, Loomis, Nebr., Washington County Bank, Blair, Nebr., Farmers & Mchts. State Bank, Bloomfield, Nebr., Burt County State Bank, Tekamah, Nebr., Harlan County Bank, Alama, Nebr., Farmers Savs. Bank, Shelby, Iowa, 1st Nat. of Nebr., Inc., Lauritzen Corp., Omaha, Emerson Ins. Agy., Inc., Blair Ins. Agy., Inc., Burt County Ins. Agy., Inc., Farmers & Mchts. Co. of Bloomfield, Farmers & Ranchers Service Co., Fin. Service Co., Lauritzen Corp., Omaha. Clubs: Omaha, Omaha Country, Univ. Cottage, Alexandria Golf; Island Country (Marco Island, Fla.); Eagle Creek Golf (Naples, Fla.). Home: 6621 Underwood Omaha NE 68132 Office: First Nat Bank of Omaha 16th & Dodge Sts Omaha NE 68102

LAUSON, HENRY DUMKE, medical educator; b. New Holstein, Wis., Aug. 20, 1912; s. Henry Detlef and Lydia (Dumke) L.; m. Eleanor Catchis, Sept. 4, 1936 (dec. 1975); m. Ruth Louise Eckart Laun, Aug. 27, 1977; stepchildren: Jonathan Laun, Bertha Laun Maalouf, William. BS, U. Wis., 1936, PhD, 1939, MD, 1940. Intern U. Kans. Hosp., Kansas City, 1940-41; resident Henry Ford Hosp., Detroit, 1941-42; instr. physiology NYU, N.Y.C., 1942-46; assoc. physician Rockefeller Inst. Med. Research, N.Y.C., 1946-50; assoc. prof. physiology Cornell U., 1950-55; prof., chmn. Albert Einstein Coll. Medicine, Bronx, N.Y., 1955-78; prof. emeritus Albert Einstein Coll. Medicine, 1978—. Contbr. articles to profl. jours. Mem. Internat. Soc. Nephrology, Am. Physiol. Soc., Am. Soc. for Clin. Investigation, Harvey Soc., Am. Soc. Nephrology, Am. Fedn. Clin. Research, Soc. Exptl. Biology and Medicine, Phi Beta Kappa, Alpha Omega Alpha.

LAUT, PHILIP ROLAND, writer, publisher, educator; b. Flushing, N.Y., May 1, 1942; s. Philip and Elizabeth Edith (Jackson) L.; m. Jeanne Miller, Sept. 27, 1986. BS, USCG Acad., 1964; MBA, Harvard U., 1970. Commd. USCG, 1964; communications officer USCG Cutter Humboldt, Boston, 1964-65; commanding officer USCG Cutter Cape Horn, Woods Hole, Mass., 1965-66, USCG Cutter Point Gammon, Danang, Vietnam, 1967-68; resigned USCG, 1968; fin. analyst Digital Equipment Corp., Maynard, Mass., 1970-72; controller engring. dept. Digital Equipment Corp., Maynard, 1972-76; publisher, writer Trinity Pubs., Cin., 1976—; bd. dirs. Associated Integrative Rebirthers, Cin. Author, publisher: Money Is My Friend, 1979, Rebirthing—The Science of Enjoying All of Your Life, 1983. Decorated Navy Commendation medal with Combat "V," Combat Action Ribbon, Cross of Gallantry with Palm. Home: 2625 Perkins Ln Cincinnati OH 45208 Office: Trinity Publications PO Box 8269 Cincinnati OH 45208

LAUTER, CARL BURTON, internist, immunologist, allergist, infectious disease specialist; b. Detroit, Dec. 30, 1939; s. Reuben David and Sadie (Kaplowitz) L.; m. Jain Beth Mogill, Dec. 21, 1975; children: Shira Lynn, Rebekah Dana, Jonathan Norton. BA in Chemistry, Wayne State U., 1962, MD, 1965. Diplomate Am. Bd. Internal Medicine, Am. Bd. Allergy and Clin. Immunology, Am. Bd. Infectious Diseases. Asst. prof. medicine Wayne State U., Detroit, 1973-78, assoc. prof. medicine, 1978—; dir. med. edn. Grace Hosp., Detroit, 1973-78; vice chief medicine William Beaumont Hosp., Royal Oak, Mich., 1980-83, chief medicine, 1983—; specialist in infectious diseases. Editorial manuscript reviewer several med. jours.; contbr. articles to profl. jours. Served to capt. USAF, 1967-69. Fellow Infectious Disease Soc. Am., Am. Coll. Physicians, Am. Coll. Clin. Pharmacology, Mich. Allergy Soc. (exec. com. 1984—); mem. Am. Acad. Allergy. Jewish. Avocations: reading, music, family activities. Office: William Beaumont Hosp 3601 W 13 Mile Rd Royal Oak MI 48072

LAUTERBACH, CARL GERSHOM, psychologist; b. Sac City, Iowa, Dec. 22, 1924; s. Paul Adam and Ada Elizabeth (Johnson) L.; m. Mary Cameron McIntyre, Sept. 7, 1947; children: Scott Lawrence, Nancy Elizabeth, Mary Carla. Student, Ind. U., 1943-44; BA, U. Iowa, 1949; PhD, Iowa State U., 1952. Diplomate Am. Bd. Profl. Psychology; cert. clin. psychologist, Ind. Enlisted as pvt. U.S. Army, ETO, 1943-45; commd. 2d lt. U.S. Army, 1950, advanced through grades to lt. col., 1966; clin. psychologist various U.S. Army Hosps., 1952-57; chief clin. psychologist Madigan Gen. Hosp., Tacoma, Wash., 1957-59, Walter Reed Gen. Hosp., Washington, 1959-63, 1967-68; research clin. psychologist U.S. Mil. Acad., West Point, N.Y., 1965-67; retired U.S. Army, 1968; prof. psychology, dir. research ctr. Marywood Coll., Scranton, Pa., 1969-74; chief psychologist South Beach Psychiat. Ctr., Staten Island, N.Y., 1975-78; assoc. prof. clin. psychology Ind. U., Indpls., 1978-81; staff psychologist VA Med. Ctr., Marion, Ind., 1981—; instr. psychology U. Ga. Extension Service, Ft. Benning, 1955; clin. psychologist Loudoun County Mental Hygiene Clinic, Reesburg, Va., 1960-63, Craig House, Beacon, N.Y., 1965-67; cons. VA Hosp. Wilkes-Barre, Pa., 1974-75. Author: Adaptation of Siblings of Mentally Retarded Child, 1974; contbr. articles to profl. jours. Bd. dirs. Marion Urban League, 1982—; trustee Temple Congl. Ch., Marion, 1984—. Mem. Am. Psychol. Assn., Cen. Ind. Psychol. Assn., Ind. Psychol. Assn. (reader, evaluator), Ind. Mental Health Assn., Grant County Mental Health Assn., Sigma Xi, Psi Chi, Phi Delta Kappa. Democrat. Club: Exchange (Marion). Avocations: reading, classical music, golf, bridge, camping. Home: 119 N D St Marion IN 46952 Office: VA Med Ctr 38th St Marion IN 46952

LAUVER, LYNN D., lawyer; b. Wichita, Kans., Feb. 25, 1943; s. Philip John and Margie Grace (McDougal) L.; m. Edith Martha Herrmann, Feb. 14, 1964; children: Enriquo, Robert, Norman, Diana. BA, Memphis State U., 1976; MA, Wichita State U., 1983; JD, Washburn Law Sch., 1983. Bar: Kans. 1983, U.S. Dist. Ct. Kans. 1983. Enlisted U.S. Army, 1960, advanced through grades to sgt. 1st class ret., 1980; assoc. Patton & Patton, Topeka, 1983-87; sole practice Topeka, 1987—. Mem. ABA, Am. Trial Lawyers Assn., Am. Bankruptcy Inst., Kans. Trial Lawyers Assn. Home: Rural Rt 1 13532 NW 50th St Rossville KS 66533 Office: 3601 SW 29th St Suite 215 Topeka KS 66614

LA VAQUE, THEODORE JOSEPH, psychologist; b. Merrill, Wis., June 24, 1940; s. Theodore Joseph and Mildred Rose (Young) La V.; m. Barbara Jean Moody, June 9, 1962; 1 child, Danielle Denyse. BS, U. Wis., 1963; MS, N.Mex. Highlands U., 1965; PhD, Iowa State U., 1972. Asst. prof. psychology U. No. Iowa, Cedar Falls, 1967-72, U. Ill., Chgo., 1972-75; pvt. practice psychology Downers Grove, Ill., Green Bay, Wis., 1975—; coordinator pain/stress clinic Mercy Ctr. for Health Care Services, Aurora, Ill., 1978-84. Contbr. articles to profl. jours. Mem. Brown County Soc. Clin. Cons. Psychologists, Soc. Clin. and Cons. Psychologists, Inc., Wis. Psychol. Assn., Biofeedback Soc. Am. Avocations: boating, skiing. Office: 211 S Monroe Ave Green Bay WI 54301

LAVELLE, GEORGE A., manufacturing company executive. Chmn., pres. Lavelle Co., Fargo, N.D. Office: Lavelle Co 115-31st St S Box 2583 Fargo ND 58108 *

LAVENUTA, FERDINAND, physician; b. Bklyn., Apr. 15, 1939; s. Ben and Roslyn (Babkes) L.; m. Erin Ann Beary, July 3, 1965; 1 child, Elizabeth Ann. BA, NYU, 1959, MD, 1963. Diplomate Am. Bd. Otolaryngology. Intern Meth. Hosp.-Bklyn., 1963-64; resident in otolaryngology The N.Y. Hosp., N.Y.C., 1964-69; practice medicine specializing in otolaryngology Dakota Clinic Ltd., Fargo, N.D., 1972—, also bd. dirs. Served to comdr. USN, 1969-72. Fellow Am. Acad. Otolaryngology; mem. AMA. Roman Catholic. Office: Dakota Clinic Ltd 1701 S Univeristy Dr Fargo ND 58108

LAVERY, MICHAEL JOSEPH, bank executive; b. Quincy, Ill., June 19, 1946; s. Joseph Elwood and Anita Catherine (Fischer) L.; m. Karen Suzanne Schlipman, Aug. 3, 1968; children: Michelle K., John M., Kristin A., Mark E., Matthew R. BBA, U. Iowa, 1969. Sales Shell Oil Co., Hinsdale, Ill., 1969-72; v.p., loan officer Gem City Savs., Quincy, Ill., 1972-84; div. pres. Am. Savs. Bank, Quincy, 1985—; mem. rural revitalization conf. Fed. Home Loan Bank Chgo., Macomb, Ill., 1981. Pres. Quincy Park Dist., 1982-83; mem. Pub. Works Commn., Quincy, 1985; bd. dirs. Neighborhood Housing Services, Quincy, 1983-86, Quincy Mus. Sci. and Industry, 1984-87; mem. Quincy Notre Dame Found., 1987—; charter mem., chmn. Tree Commn.-City of Quincy, 1987. MMem. Quincy Bd. Realtors (affiliate). Roman Catholic. Club: Exchange (Quincy) (pres. 1982-83). Lodge: KC. Office: Am Savs Bank 730 Maine Quincy IL 62306

LAVIN, JUSTIN PAUL, JR., obstetrician, gynecologist, perinatologist; b. Haverhill, Mass., Aug. 4, 1947; s. Justin Paul Sr. and Pauline (Ford) L.; m. Louise Joan Miller, Aug. 18, 1974; children: Sean, Brian, Andrew, Eric. BA, U. Pa., 1969, MD, 1975. Resident in ob-gyn U. Pa. Hosp., Phila., 1975-79; fellow maternal and fetal medicine U. Cin. Med. Ctr., 1979-81; prof. ob-gyn N.E. Ohio U. Coll. Med., Rootstown, 1981—; co-dir. Akron (Ohio) Regional Perinatal Ctr., 1981—; chief obstetrics Akron City Hosp., 1982—. Author: Obstetrics for the House, 1984; contbr. articles to profl. jours. Fellow Am. Coll. Ob-Gyn, Soc. Perinatal Obstetricians; mem. Am. Inst. Medicine Ultrasound, Ohio Med. Soc., Summit County Med. Soc., Akron Ob-Gyn Soc. Club: Fairlawn Country. Avocations: skiing, tennis, computers. Home: 2166 Ridgewood Rd Akron OH 44313 Office: Akron City Hosp 525 E Market St Akron OH 44309-2090

LAVIN, LEONARD H., personal care products company executive; b. 1919, Chgo.; married. BA, U. Wash., 1940. With Lucien Lelong, 1940-46; v.p. sales, gen. mgr. Halgar, Inc., 1946-51; with Leonard H. Lavin Co., 1951-55; with Alberto-Culver Co., Melrose Park, Ill., 1955—, now. chmn., pres., chief exec. officer, also bd. dirs. Served to lt. commdr. USNR, 1941-45. Office: Alberto-Culver Co 2525 Armitage Ave Melrose Park IL 60160 *

LAVIN, LOUISE MILLER, psychiatric nurse; b. Altoona, Pa., May 20, 1947; d. Stanley and Evelyn (Wilner) Miller; m. Justin Paul Lavin Jr., Aug. 18, 1974; children: Sean, Brian, Drew, Eric. BS in Nursing with distinction, U. Rochester, 1969; MS in Nursing, U. Pa., 1971. Registered nurse, Ohio, Pa. Nurse Orthopädische Klinik, U. Heidelburg, Fed. Republic Germany, 1969; instr. nursing staff devel. Inst. Pa. Hosp., Phila., 1970; clin. specialist, dir. nursing edn. Phila. Psychiat. Ctr., 1971-73; psychiat. clin. specialist Med. Coll. Pa., Phila., 1973-79; instr. nursing grad. div. U. Pa., Phila., 1975-79; instr. psychiat. nursing grad. div. U. Cin., 1979-81; pvt. practice psychiat. nursing therapy Akron, Ohio, 1983—. Active Fairlawn Elem. Sch. PTA, Akron, 1981—. Mem. Am. Nurses Assn. (charter mem. council advanced practitioners in psychiat. and mental health nursing), Ohio Nurses Assn., Childbirth Edn. Specialists (cert.), Pi Lambda Theta (hon.), Sigma Theta Tau (hon.). Avocations: camping, skiing, swimming, needlework, music. Home: 2166 Ridgewood Rd Akron OH 44313 Office: 1745 W Market St Akron OH 44313

LAVINE, MICHAEL DAVID, diagnostic radiology; b. Brookline, Mass., Nov. 29, 1948; s. Henry and Harriet Pauline (Miller) L.; m. Lorette Pauline, Oct. 30, 1977; children: Erica Jamie, Adrienne Mary. BA, Marietta Coll., 1970; MD, NYU, 1974. Cert. Am. Coll. Radiology. Resident NYU Med. Ctr., N.Y.C., 1974-78; attending physician Radiology Assocs., Ft. Pierce, Fla., 1978-82, Radiology Ctr., S.C., Flossmoor, Ill., 1982-84; attending physician, dir. radiology Suburban Heights Med Ctr, Chicago Heights, Ill., 1984—. Fellow Am. Coll. Radiology; mem. Radiologoc Soc. N.Am. Home: 1718 Pinehurst Ln Flossmoor IL 60422 Office: 333 Dixie Hwy Chicago Heights IL 60411

LAVOLL, GUNNBJORG BERIT, psychiatrist; b. Luster, Norway, Apr. 1, 1945; came to U.S., 1973; d. Lars and Johanna (Wendelbo) L.; m. Robert R. Edger. MD, Royal Coll. Surgeons, 1971. Resident in psychiatry Northwestern Meml. Hosp., Chgo., 1973-76; fellow in child and adolescent psychiatry Michael Reese Hosp., Chgo., 1976-78; staff psychiatrist Children's Meml. Hosp., Chgo., 1978-80; practice medicine specializing in psychiatry Chgo., 1978—; assoc. Northwestern U., Chgo., 1978—. Mem. Am. Psychiat. Assn., Am. Acad. Child Psychiatry, Ill. Council Child Psychiatry (bd. dirs. 1978—), Ill. Psychiat. Assn. (chair com. on women's issues 1987). Home: 3122 N Sheridan Rd Chicago IL 60657 Office: Lavoll and Edger SC 230 N Michigan Suite 3100 Chicago IL 60601

LAVORATO, LOUIS A., state judge. Judge Iowa Supreme Ct., Des Moines, 1986—. Office: Office of the Supreme Court Des Moines IA 50319§

LAW, DAN UDALL, educator, coach; b. Maryville, Mo., Aug. 18, 1948; s. Junior Benjamin and Betty Jo (Gordon) L.; m. Elizabeth Ann Schnur, May 15, 1975. BS in Edn., NW Mo. State U., 1975, MS in Edn., 1982. Tchr. Grand Community Schs., Boxholm, Iowa, 1974-76, Swea City (Iowa) Schs., 1976-77, Martensdale (Iowa)-St. Mary's Schs., 1977-79, S.E. Polk Schs., Runnells, Iowa, 1979—. Served with U.S. Army, 1968-70. Mem. NEA, Iowa Edn. Assn., Ducks Unlimited. Republican. Roman Catholic. Club: Pheasants Forever (Colo, Iowa). Avocations: hunting, fishing, boating. Home: 1019 Scott Felton Rd Indianola IA 50125 Office: SE Polk Community Schs 8325 NE University Runnells IA 50237

LAW, DAVIS JOSEPH, humanities educator; b. Elsie, Nebr., Mar. 10, 1923; s. Joseph Davis and Lucy Aliene (Williams) L.; m. Dorothy Ora Teichert, Aug. 18, 1951; children: Kenna, Joseph, Kathleen, Dianne, Douglas, Kristine. B of Music Edn., U. Nebr., 1952; MA, U. Wyo., 1960. Tchr. music Thomas County High Sch., Thedford, Nebr., 1951-61; prof. humanities Ellendale (N.D.) State Tchrs. Coll., 1961-71, U. N.D., Williston, 1971—. Choir dir. 1st Union Ch., Williston, 1971—. Served with AUS, 1943-45. Fellow Inst. Internat. Affairs, 1959, Am. Studies, 1972, Inst. Southwest Asia, 1975. Mem. NEA, AAUP, VFW, Am. Legion. Presbyterian. Lodges: Masons, Order Eastern Star (worthy grand patron 1987—). Office: U ND Dept Humanities PO Box 1326 Williston ND 58801

LAW, STEPHEN EDWARD, packaging executive; b. St. Paul, June 1, 1957; s. Edward and Patricia (Reid) L.; m. Kathryn Raths; 1 child, Doreen. BA, U. Oreg., 1979. Safety dir. Flour City Press Pack, Mpls., 1980-84, health and safety dir., 1984-86, human resource dir., 1986—; cons. Flom Corp., Mpls., Washington; speaker Minn. Safety Council. Contbr. articles to Flour City Gazzette, 1980—, Paperbox Assn. Newsletter, 1985. Mem. Planned Parenthood, N. Como Ch. Mem. Paper Industry Mgmt. Assn. (Achievement award), Broadway Bus. Assn. Presbyterian. Club: Toastmaster Internat., St. Paul Hiking. Avocations: racquetball, tennis, running, volleyball, basketball. Home: 21 Maywood Pl Saint Paul MN 55117 Office: Flour City Press Pack 500 Stinson Blvd Minneapolis MN 55413

LAWBAUGH, EMANUEL SYLVESTER, IV, educator, lawyer; b. St. Marys, Mo., Mar. 31, 1935; s. Emanuel Sylvester III and Halita Joan (Bartlett) L.; m. Verna Catherine Tucker, Dec. 29, 1956 (dec.); children: Kathleen Ann, Steven Richard, James William, Christine Marie; m. Sonja Ann Semiginowski, Dec. 27, 1977. BS, Regis Coll., 1957; MEd, U. Mo., 1962; EdD, U. Miss., 1972; JD, U. Ark., 1983. Bar: Nebr. 1984, S.D. 1984. Commd. capt. USMC, 1963, advanced through grades to lt. col., 1974; plans officer Marine Corps Edn. Ctr., Quantico, Va., 1976-78; comdg. officer Marine Wing Command Squadron, Okinawa, Japan, 1978-80; marine corps dir. Def. Elec. Analysis Ctr., Annapolis, Md., 1980-81; retired USMC, 1981; dean admissions & fin. aid Yankton (S.D.) Coll., 1984; sole practice Yankton, 1984-85; dir. devel. Buena Vista Coll., Storm Lake, Iowa, 1985—; prof. orgnl. behavior U. Va., Quantico, Va., 1976, mgmt. Pepperdine U., Malibu, Calif., 1977-78. Author: Survey of Marine Corps Education; contbr. articles to profl. jours. Trustee Buena Vista Work Activity Ctr., Storm Lake, Iowa, 1986—; mem. Sch. Bd. Quantico Dept. Schs., 1973-76. Decorated Purple Heart, Bronze Star, Vietnam Honor medal, Def. Meritorious Service medal. Mem. ABA, Nebr. Bar Assn., S.D. Bar Assn., Marine Corps Assn. (Fitness award 1980), ARC (Service award 1975, 76), Jaycees (v.p.). Republican. Roman Catholic. Lodge: Kiwanis (sec. Storm Lake chpt. 1986—). Avocations: travel, swimming, basketball, reading, coin collecting. Home: 516 Swallum Dr Storm Lake IA 50588 Office: Buena Vista Coll College & W 4th St Storm Lake IA 50588

LAWLER, NOEL FRANCIS, manufacturing and financial executive; b. Chgo., Dec. 25, 1944; s. Walter Francis and Margaret Florence (Henry) L.; m. Marilyn Bernice Tischer, Aug. 28, 1965; children: Michael Patrick, Kevin Walter. AA in Applied Sci., Richard J. Daley Jr. Coll., Chgo., 1975; BBA, Roosevelt U., 1977. Mgr. computer ops. Option Clearing Corp., Chgo., 1972-75; dir. data processing Heritage Bank, Chgo., 1973-77; mgr. cons. Consumer Systems, Oak Brook, Ill., 1977-80; mgr. mgmt. info. systems Hollister, Inc., Libertyville, Ill., 1980-81; dir. bus. devel. CGA Computer, Inc., Des Plaines, Ill., 1981-85; pres. Nomar, Inc., Worth, Ill., 1985—. Office: Nomar Inc 5146 W 115th St Worth IL 60482

LAWLESS, RONALD, English educator; b. Chgo., Sept. 7, 1960; s. Mable (Rolack) Lawless. BA, Columbia Coll., Chgo., 1982; MS, No. Ill. U., 1987. With Sta. WFBN-TV, Chgo., 1982-84; account exec. Sta. RKO, Chgo., 1984-85, Sta. ABC, Houston, 1985-86; instr. English City Coll. Chgo., 1986—. Judge Bd. Election, Chgo., 1983—; chairperson Inner City Self Ctr., Chgo., 1986—. Democrat. Roman Catholic. Club: DECA. Avocations: football, baseball, hockey, reading, traveling.

LAWRENCE, ALVIN PATRICK, plant engineer; b. Essex, Ont., Can., Mar. 17, 1927; came to U.S., 1947; s. William Harrison and Adelia (Mueller) L.; m. Madge Maurie Surratt, June 10, 1951; children: Susan Carol, Sally Kay, Alvin Patrick Jr. ASEE, Cen. Tech. U., 1960. Commd. AUS, 1947, advanced through grades to capt., retired, 1957; plant engr. Midland Mfg., Kansas City, Kans., 1960-64, Nat. Distillers, Memphis, 1965-73; plant mgr. Offset Spring Co., Memphis, 1965, Tecumseh Products, Paris, Tenn., 1978; facilities engr. Wurlitzer Co., Holly Springs, Miss., 1973-78; spl. projects engr. Arvin N.Am. Automotive, Dexter, Mo., 1979—; cons. OSHA, Midsouth region, 1975. Probation officer Shelby County Juvenile Ct., Memphis,

1969-73; Rep. precinct and voting poll ofcl., Memphis and Tenn., 1966-78. Mem. Am. Inst. Plant Engrs. (treas. 1972, Achievement award 1972), IEEE. Republican. Methodist. Club: Jack Miner's Boys (Kingsville, Ont.). Lodges: Elks, Odd Fellows. Avocations: boating, fishing, hunting, birdwatching, bridge. Home: Box 305 Rt 1 Springville TN 38256 Office: Arvin NAm Automotive 1207 Arvin Rd Dexter MO 63841

LAWRENCE, CONRAD ARTHUR, cinematographer, writer; b. Madison, Wis., Oct. 27, 1954; s. Richard Mortimer and Ardys Virgene (Severson) L. BA in Communication Arts, U. Wis., 1980. Asst. producer, studio mgr. Cinemon Film Prodns., Madison, Wis., 1980-82; freelance gaffer Wis., 1980-81; cameraman Sta. WMTV-TV, Madison, 1981; freelance lighting dir. So. Wis., 1981-83; cameraman, dir. Rustad-Wickham Video Studios, Madison, 1983-85; freelance cinematographer throughout Midwest, 1985—; freelance actor, Midwest, 1986—. Recipient Addy award Madison Advt. Fedn., 1984, 85, Clio award for Media Promotion and Broadcasting Internat. Clio Awards Adv. Bd., 1985. Lutheran. Avocations: parachute jumping, water skiing, canoeing. Home and Office: 4421 Rolla Ln Madison WI 53711

LAWRENCE, DAVID, JR., newspaper editor, publisher; b. N.Y.C., Mar. 5, 1942; s. David Sr. and Nancy Wemple (Bissell) L.; m. Roberta Phyllis Fleischman, Dec. 21, 1963; children: David III, Jennifer Beth, Amanda Katherine, John Benjamin, Dana Victoria. BS, U. Fla., 1963; postgrad. advanced mgmt. program bus. sch., Harvard U., 1983; LHD (hon.), Siena Heights Coll., Adrian, Mich., 1985; HHD (hon.), Lawrence Inst. Tech., Detroit, 1986. Reporter, news editor St. Petersburg (Fla.) Times, 1963-67; news editor Style/Washington Post, 1967-69; mng. editor Palm Beach (Fla.) Post, 1969-71, Phila. Daily News, 1971-75; exec. editor Charlotte (N.C.) Observer, 1975-76, editor, 1976-78; exec. editor Detroit Free Press, 1978-85, pub., chmn., 1985—. Bd. dirs. Children's Hosp., Detroit, 1985—, Grosse Pointe (Mich.) Acad., Founders Soc. Detroit Inst. Arts, Found. Am. Communication, Detroit Renaissance, Detroit Zoological Soc.United Found., Mich. Council Arts, Wayne State Journalism Inst. for Minorities. Named Disting. Alumnus U. Fla., 1982; recipient Nat. Human Rights award Am. Jewish Com., 1986. Mem. Am. Newspaper Pub. Assn., Am. Soc. Newspaper Editors (bd. dirs.), , Sigma Delta Chi. Club: Detroit, Renaissance, Econ. of Detroit (bd. dirs.). Office: Detroit Free Press 321 W Lafayette Blvd Detroit MI 48231

LAWRENCE, EDMUND P., JR., neurosurgeon; b. Buffalo, Sept. 18, 1946; s. Edmund P. and Ruth (Jone) L.; m. Morgan A., July 11, 1972; 1 child, Max P. BS in Chemistry, Washington and Lee U., 1968; MD, Vanderbilt U., 1972. Diplomate Am. Bd. Neurol. Surgery. Intern, then resident in neurosurgery Northwestern U., Chgo., 1974-79; chmn. dept. neurol. surgery St. Vincent's Hosp. and Med. Ctr., Toledo, 1984-87; practice medicine specializing in neurosurgery Toledo, 1987—; bd. dirs. neurol. ICU, St. Vincent's Hosp., Toledo. Contbr. numerous articles and research papers to profl. jours; exhibited paintings at Ravinia Founders Day Art Competition, Chgo., 1976. Mem. founders soc. Detroit Inst. Art, Toledo Mus. Art, 1979—. Recipient Eleanor Clarke Research award Northwestern U. Sch. Medicine, 1975. Mem. AMA, Ohio State Med. Assn., Toledo Acad. Medicine. Episcopalian. Avocation: painting, martial arts instruction. Office: 2213 Cherry St Toledo OH 43608

LAWRENCE, JAMES LESTER, college dean and official; b. N.Y.C., Oct. 22, 1941; s. Ernice B. and Telete Zorayda (Lester) L.; B.A., Tex. Christian U., 1963, M.A., 1965; Ph.D., U. Maine, 1968. Asst. prof. biology Hartwick Coll., Oneonta, N.Y., 1968-70, asst. dean faculty, 1970-71, asst. v.p., assoc. dean of coll., 1971-74, v.p. ednl. affairs, dean coll., 1974-75; dean of coll. Huron Coll., S.D., 1979-81; sr. v.p., dean of coll. Marycrest Coll., Davenport, Iowa, 1981—; mem. student life council Colls. Mid-Am., Sioux Falls, S.D., 1979-81, mem. deans' council, Sioux Falls, 1979-81, chmn., 1981; mem. adv. bd. Huron Coll./Huron Regional Med. Ctr. Sch. Nursing, 1979-81, mem. com. accreditation, 1980-81; mem. Council Ind. Colls. Nat. Cons. Network, Washington, 1980—; mem. program rev. panel Quad-Cities Grad. Study Ctr., Rock Island, Ill., 1981—; presenter workshops and seminars. Contbr. articles and poetry to profl. publs. Fulbright fellow, 1972-73; Helene Wurlitzer Found. grantee, 1975. Bd. dirs. Community Chorale, Oneonta, N.Y., 1974-78, Huron Symphony, 1979-81, Community Theatre, Huron, 1980-81, Glimmerglass Opera Theatre, Cooperstown, N.Y., 1976-78, Davenport Med. Ctr., Iowa, 1985—; vestryman Grace Ch., Huron, 1980-81, chmn. religious edn. com., 1980-81; mem. Friends of Art, Davenport Art Mus., 1984—. Mem. Davenport C. of C. (edn. com. 1981-83, small bus. council 1986—, steering com.), Huron C. of C. (edn. com. 1980-81), Am. Assn. Higher Edn., Am. Assn. Acad. Deans, Council Advancement Exptl. Learning, Nat. Assn. Advisers for Health Professions. Democrat. Episcopalian. Avocations: writing, cooking, singing. Home: 112 Slavens Manor Bettendorf IA 52722 Office: Marycrest Coll 1607 W 12th St Davenport IA 52804

LAWRENCE, JOHN KIDDER, lawyer; b. Detroit, Nov. 18, 1949; s. Luther Ernest and Mary Anna (Kidder) L.; m. Jeanine Ann DeLay, June 20, 1981. A.B., U. Mich., 1971; J.D., Harvard U., 1974. Bar: Mich. 1974, D.C. 1978, U.S. Supreme Ct. 1977. Assoc., Dickinson, Wright, McKean & Cudlip, Detroit, 1973-74; staff atty. Office of Judge Adv. Gen., Washington, 1975-78; assoc. Dickinson, Wright, McKean, Cudlip & Moon, Detroit, 1978-81; ptnr. Dickinson, Wright, Moon, VanDusen & Freeman, Detroit, 1981—. Patron, Founders Soc. Detroit Inst. Arts, 1979—; mem. founds. com. Detroit Symphony Orch., 1983—. Served with U.S. Navy, 1975-78. Mem. ABA, State Bar Mich., D.C. Bar Assn., Am. Judicature Soc., Internat. Bar Assn., Detroit Com. on Fgn. Relations, Am. Hist. Assn., Phi Eta Sigma, Phi Beta Kappa. Democrat. Episcopalian. Club: Detroit. Office: Dickinson Wright Moon et al 800 1st National Bldg Detroit MI 48226

LAWRENCE, JOHN SHELTON, philosophy educator; b. Amarillo, Tex., Mar. 30, 1938; s.William Byron and Alta (Davis) L.; m. Nancy Caroline Cummings, June 10, 1961; children: Jennifer, Eric. BA, Stanford U., 1960; student, Princeton U., 1960-61; PhD, Tex. U., 1964. Asst. prof. U. Denver, 1964-66, Morningside Coll., Sioux City, Iowa, 1966—. Author: Fair Use and Free Inquiry, 1980, Electronic Scholar, 1984; co-author America Monomyth, 1977. Unitarian. Home: 3320 Chalet Ct Sioux City IA 51106 Office: Morningside Coll Philosophy Dept Sioux City IA 51106

LAWRENCE, JOHN WARREN, business and broadcasting executive; b. Kalamazoo, Mar. 25, 1928; s. William Joseph and Borgia Marie (Wheeler) L.; m. Joanne Myrtle McDonald, Oct. 27, 1956; children: Joni Lawrence Knapper, Jane Lawrence Brogger, John Warren Jr., Jeffrey Michael. BS, Western Mich. U., 1949; MBA, U. Mich., 1950. Gen. mgr. Ill. Envelope, Inc., Kalamazoo, 1958-66, pres., 1958-80, chmn. bd., 1980-85; sec.-treas. Superior Pine Products Co., Fargo, Ga., 1967—; pres. Channel 41, Inc., Battle Creek, Mich., 1972—; chmn. MCE, Inc., Kalamazoo, 1980—; founder, chmn. bd. Lawrence Prodns., Inc., Battle Creek, 1985—; bd. dirs. Old Kent Bank of Kalamazoo. Trustee Commonwealth Schs., Albion, Mich., 1969-83; vice chmn., trustee Borgess Med. Ctr., Kalamazoo, 1982—; trustee Gull Lake Sch. Found., Richland, Mich., 1983—; bd. dirs. United Way of Mich., 1976-80; chmn. bd. trustees Nazareth Coll., Kalamazoo, 1979—. Served to lt. (j.g.) USNR, 1952-55. Recipient Mich. Citizen's award Greater Mich. Found., 1963. Roman Catholic. Clubs: Park (Kalamazoo); Gull Lake Country (Richland, Mich.). Office: 157 S Kalamazoo Mall Suite 250 Kalamazoo MI 49007

LAWRENCE, RALPH WALDO, manufacturing company executive; b. Mineola, N.Y., Sept. 10, 1941; s. Ralph Waldo and Gertrude (Ingles) L.; m. Judith Alice Frost, June 20, 1964; children: Susan, Carolyn. BA, W.Va. Wesleyan Coll., 1963; M in Pub. Adminstrn., Western Mich. U., 1979. Pres. Lawrence Mfrs., Columbus, Ohio, 1970-85; chief automated info. systems contract services Systems Automation Ctr., Columbus, 1980-87, chief plans and mgmt. div., 1987—. Served to capt. U.S. Army, 1963-66. Mem. Data Processing Mgmt. Assn. (pres. Columbus chpt. 1987, program dir. Columbus chpt. 1985). Republican. Presbyterian. Lodge: Masons. Avocations: golf, sailing. Home: 10201 Covan Dr Westerville OH 43081 Office: Systems Automation Ctr PO Box 1605 Columbus OH 43216-5002

LAWRENCE, WILLIAM CHARLES, psychologist, educator; b. Downingtown, Pa., Oct. 5, 1922; s. Robert M. and Irma M. (Miles) L.; m. Marilyn E. Rice, Aug. 23, 1973; children: Brian, Daniel, Kathleen. BA, U. Tenn., 1949, MA, 1951; PhD, NYU, 1954. State psychologist State of Tenn., Knoxville, 1951-52; asst prof. U. Tenn., 1952-53; teaching fellow NYU, 1953-54; assoc. prof. Eastern Mich. U., Ypsilanti, 1954-56, v.p., 1956-68; pvt. practice Southfield, Mich. and Sarasota, Fla., 1968—; cons. Mich. Bell. Telephone, Detroit, 1965-67, Detroit Assocs., Southfield, 1985-86, Punta Gorda (Fla.) Police Dept., 1984-86, FDA Task Force, Washington, 1964-66. Served to capt. USAF, 1942-46. Fellow Am. Ortho Psychiat. Asst.; mem. Am. Psychol. Assn., Mich. Psychol. Assn., Fla. Psychol. Assn., Am. Acad. Stress Disorders. Avocations: pvt. flying, boating, reading, photography. Home: 601 N Owl Dr Sarasota FL 34236 Office: 26555 Evergreen Suite 1712 Southfield MI 48076

LAWS, CHARLES EDWARD, academic administrator; b. Quincy, Ill., Feb. 4, 1936; s. Leon Edward and Helen Erie (Hagen) L.; m. Carol Ann Johnson, Mar. 28, 1959; children: Lisa Marie, Gretchen Ann. BS, Northwestern U., 1954-58; ME, U. Ill., 1959-63, EdD, 1975-78. Tchr. hist. Moline (Ill.) Sr. High, 1958-67; dean liberal studies, student services and community services U. Parallel, Moline, 1967-81; pres. Black Hawk Coll., Moline, 1981—. Vol. budget com. United Way, Quad Cities, 1970, 80's; mem. Rock Island County Council on Addiction, Quad Cities, 1970. Mem. Ill. Council Econ. Edn., Nat. Council Instrnl. Adminstrs., Ill. Quad Cities C. of C., Phi Delta Kappa. Lutheran. Clubs: Dynamon Stock (sec., pres.), "M" Mens Assn. (pres., sec., treas) (Moline). Avocations: golf, handicrafts. Office: Black Hawk Coll 6600 34th Ave Moline IL 61265

LAWS, ROBERT E., diversified company executive; b. 1927; married. BA, Ind. U., 1949, MA, 1955. With Indpls. Morris Planning Corp., 1949-59, Economy Fin. Corp., 1959-69; with ITT Consumer Services Corp., N.Y.C., 1969—, v.p., 1973—, now chmn., pres., chief exec. officer, also bd. dirs.; also sr. v.p. parent co. ITT Corp. Office: ITT Consumer Services Corp 320 Park Ave New York NY 10022 *

LAWSON, DAVID JERALD, bishop; b. Princeton, Ind., Mar. 26, 1930; s. David Jonathon and Bonnetta A. (White) L.; m. Martha Ellen Pegram, July 16, 1950; children—John Mark, Karen Sue Lawson Strang. A.B., U. Evansville, 1955; M.Div., Garrett Theol. Sem., 1959; D.D., U. Evansville, 1977. Ordained to ministry United Methodist Ch. Pastor, Tell City United Meth. Ch., Ind., 1956-67, Beach Grove United Meth. Ch., Indpls., 1967-72; dist. supt. So. Ind. Conf., 1972-76, conf. council dir., 1976-82; pastor Carmel United Meth. Ch., Ind., 1982-84; bishop United Meth. Ch., Sun Prairie, Wis., 1984—; trustee North Central Coll., Naperville, Ill., 1984—, Meth. Health Service, 1984—, Cedar Crest Home, Janesville, Wis., 1984—, Christian Community Home, Hudson, Wis., 1984—. Author monograph: Administrative Spirituality. Contbr. articles to profl. jours. Mem. Wis. Coordinating Com., Nicaragua, 1984, Community Dept. of Instnl. Chaplains of State, City Traffic Commn., Ind., Marion County Bd. Zoning Appeals, Ind. Democrat. Lodge: Lions (membership sec. Indpls. 1967-72). Home: 5113 Comanche Way Madison WI 53704 Office: United M E Ch 750 Windsor St Suite 303 Sun Prairie WI 53590 *

LAWSON, JAMES EARL, osteopath; b. Detroit, June 4, 1945; s. Gerald James and Janet Virginia (Owen) L.; m. Lois Ann Levitt, June 29, 1968 (div. Sept. 1975); 1 child, Matthew Owen; m. Mary Ann Spencer, June 10, 1978 (div. Dec. 1982); 1 child, David James; m. Marian Judith Marcero, May 8, 1986. BS in Zoology, U. Mich., 1967; DO, Kirksville (Mo.) Coll. Osteo. Medicine, 1971. Cert. Am. Osteo. Bd. Internal Medicine. Chief exec. officer BioMed. Applications of Detroit, 1978—; med. dir. Inst. for Health Maintenance, Southfield, Mich., 1981-83; pres. Met. Nephrologists, Detroit, 1981—; mem. med. rev. bd. End Stage Renal Disease Network. Team mem. Youth at Risk, Detroit, 1986. Mem. Am. Osteo. Assn., Mich. Assn. Osteo. Physicians and Surgeons, Wayne County Osteo. Assn., Am. Coll. Osteo. Internists, Nat. Kidney Found., Am. Soc. Nephrology, Renal Physicians Assn., Am. Heart Assn., Physicians for Social Responsibility, Am. Med. Athletics Assn. Club: Motor City Striders. Avocation: running. Office: 101 Hutzel Profl Bldg 4727 Saint Antoine Detroit MI 48201

LAWSON, JOSEPH FREDERICK, construction company owner; b. Mason, W.Va., Aug. 28, 1952; s. Raymond Paul and Mary Ann (Striggle) L.; m. Carol Jane Peters, May 10, 1970 (div. Feb. 1983); 1 child, Jason; m. Kathleen A. Waddell, Aug. 27, 1983; 1 child, Laura. Carpenter C.P. Constrn. Co., Lancaster, Ohio, 1970-75; foreman, head carpenter C.P. Constrn. Co., Lancaster, 1975-78; pvt. practice bldg. Lancaster, 1978-83; pres., owner J. Rick Lawson Constrn. Co., Lancaster, 1983—. Coordinator Cameo Concerts, Lan Fest, Lancaster, 1985. Mem. Nat. Assn. Realtora, Lancaster Bd. Realtors, Nat. Assn. Home Builders, Lancaster Assn. Home Builders (v.p. 1984-85, pres. 1986-87, Fairfield County C. of C. Republican. Roman Catholic. Avocations: fishing, drafting, boating, auto racing, people watching. Home: 300 Hartford Dr Lancaster OH 43130

LAWSON, KENNETH RICHARD, state trooper, association executive; b. Greenfield, Mass., June 9, 1950; s. John Edmund and Ruby Harriet (Hutchinson) L.; m. Barbara Ann Webb; children—Michael K., Jennifer K., Jason K., Kimberly R. B.A. in Theology, Union Coll., 1976. Minister Seventh-day Adventist Ch., Wis., Mo., 1976-80; state trooper III, Wis. State Patrol, Madison, 1980—. Founder, pres. Friends of Missing Children, Madison, 1982—. Served with U.S. Army, 1970-72. Recipient Wis. State Patrol Outstanding Service award Ind. Ins. Agts. Wis., 1981. Avocations: amateur radio, outdoor sports. Home: PO Box 14402 Madison WI 53714 Office: Friends of Missing Children PO Box 8848 Madison WI 53708

LAWSON, MATTHEW S., securities industry executive; b. New Fairfield, Conn., Aug. 8, 1946; m. Mary Coryn, Jan. 2, 1978. A.B., Hamilton Coll., 1968; M.B.A. with honors, U. Chgo., 1985. Account exec. Foote, Cone & Belding Advt., Inc., Los Angeles, 1969-71, account dir., 1971-72; corp. pub. affairs mgr. Mazda Motors Am., Inc., Los Angeles, 1972-74; v.p. Eisaman, Johns and Laws Advt. Inc., Los Angeles, 1975-76; dep. news sec. to Gov. Ronald Reagan Presdl. Campaign, 1976, 80; dir. corp. communications Computer Scis. Corp., El Segundo, Calif., 1977-82; dir. investor relations Gould Inc., Rolling Meadows, Ill., 1982-85, dir. strategic planning, 1985-86; v.p. instl. equity sales County Securities Corp., 1987—. Mem. Calif. Republican Central Com., 1969-71; dir. Calif. Rep. Assembly, 1969-73; communications dir. for Lt. Gov. John Harmer, 1974. Mem. IEEE, N.Y. Soc. Security Analysts, Nat. Investor Relations Inst., Soc. Automotive Engrs., Chgo. Sci. Analysts, The Planning Forum. Club: Meadow. Home: 1505 E Central Rd Arlington Heights IL 60005 Office: 33 N Dearborn St Chicago IL 60602

LAWSON, PATRICIA JEAN, college administrator; b. Lafayette, Ind., Mar. 11, 1939; d. Charles Ephrem and Alice Maxine (Hoagland) Krecek; m. Michael Alan Lawson, June 20, 1957; children: Deborah, Jeffrey, Tracy, Steven. Student, Purdue U., 1978-80, 86—. Exec. sec. Ross div. TRW, Lafayette, 1965-69; adminstrv. sec. FFR Coop., Battleground, Ind., 1970-75; grad. sec. Purdue U., West Lafayette, Ind., 1975-76, office mgr., 1976-84, adminstrv. asst. to dean, 1984—. Mem. Purdue Women's Causus, West Lafayette, 1982—, Purdue Day Care Com., 1983. Mem. Profl. Secs. Internat. (sec., membership chmn. 1984-86, rep. to C. of C. legis. com. 1986, cert.), Bus. and Profl. Women (officer, com. chmn. 1982-86). Roman Catholic. Club: YWCA (Lafayette). Lodges: Eagles, Moose. Avocations: reading, motor sports, basketball, volleyball. Home: 4262 Sunburst Trail 520 Lafayette IN 47905 Office: Purdue U Office of Dean Agr AGAD 114 West Lafayette IN 47907

LAWSON, PETER WALLACE, psychologist; b. Mpls., Aug. 11, 1940; s. Ansel Hamilton and Lora Carolyn (Wallace) L.; m. Vija Rumpe, June 11, 1965; 1 child, Mara; m. 2d, Carole Anne Dahmes, Dec. 14, 1977; children: Jennifer Buckley, Thomas Buckley, Kristin. Student, Dartmouth Coll., 1958-60; BA, U. Minn., 1965, MA, 1968; PhD, Wash. State U., 1982. Lic. psychologist. Counseling intern Minn. State Services for Blind and Visually Handicapped, St. Paul, 1967-68; counseling psychologist Lakewood Community Coll., White Bear Lake, Minn., 1968—; vol. Parent-Advisor Com. Minn. Assn. for Children and Adults with Learning Disabilities, St. Paul, 1984—; research cons. Sharing Life in the Community, St. Paul, 1979. Author: (with others) Big Gray Career/Student Handbook, 1977. Assembly del. Minn. Annual United Meth. Ch. Conf., St. Cloud, 1985, 86. Served to sgt. U.S. Army, 1960-63. Mem. NEA, Minn. Edn. Assn., Minn. Assn. for Counseling and Devel., Minn. College Personnel Assn. Democrat. Avocations: camping, travel. Home: 969 Monterey Dr Shoreview MN 55126 Office: Lakewood Community Coll 3401 Century Ave White Bear Lake MN 55110

LAWSON, THOMAS WALTER, motor company executive; b. Schentady, N.Y., Sept. 23, 1935; s. Thomas Elbert and Aria (Ormsby) L.; m. Dona Jean Jacobson, June 23, 1962; children: Thomas W. II, David Kinsley. B Scis. and Arts, Wayne State U., 1966, MBA, 1969; postgrad., U. Mich., 1981-83, Coll. for Fin. Planning, 1984-87. Cert. fin. planner, real estate broker; registered investment advisor; lic. builder/contractor, Mich. Mgr. computer ctr. Ford Motor Co., Livonia, Mich., 1962—; real estate broker Phoenix Co., Ann Arbor, Mich., 1979—; part-time instr. Schoolcraft Coll., Livonia, 1969—, Cleary Coll., Livonia, 1969—. Served with USAF, 1954-58. Mem. Nat. Realtors Assn., Inst. Cert. Fin. Planners, Cleary Coll. Alumni Assn. (trustee 1983-84). Republican. Avocation: furniture rebuilding. Home: 6629 Fleming Creek Dr Ann Arbor MI 48105

LAWSON, WARREN GLENN, state national guard adjutant general; b. Fairfield, Iowa, Aug. 2, 1933; s. Vernon C. and Wilma Aletha (Rabel) L.; m. Barbara Lee Gardner, Aug. 4, 1955; children: Lance Andrew, Laura Lee. BS in Commerce, Iowa U., 1955; MA in Personnel and Indsl. Mgmt., U. Nebr., 1965; grad., U.S. Naval War Coll., 1967, U.S. Army War Coll., 1973. Commd. 2d lt. U.S. Army, 1955, advanced through grades to maj. gen., 1975, retired, 1979; dep. adjutant gen. Iowa Army N.G., Des Moines, 1979-85, adjutant gen., 1985—. Mem. Assn. U.S. Army (pres. Des Moines chpt. 1982-84), N.G. Assn. U.S., Am. Security Agy., Am. Legion. Methodist. Lodge: Rotary. Home and Office: Iowa NG Pub Def Dept 7700 NW Beaver Dr Camp Dodge Johnston IA 50131-1902

LAWSON, WILLIAM HOGAN, III, electrical motor manufacturing executive; b. Lexington, Ky., Feb. 3, 1937; s. Otto Kirsky and Gladys (McWhorter) L.; m. Martha G. Grubb, Aug. 24, 1963; children—Elizabeth, Cynthia. B.S. in Mech. Engring, Purdue U., 1959; M.B.A., Harvard U., 1961. Gen. mgr. service div. Toledo Scale Corp., 1964-68; exec. v.p., chief ops. officer Skyline Corp., Elkhart, Ind., 1968-85; chmn. bd. dirs., chief exec. officer Franklin Elec. Co., Inc., Bluffton, Ind., 1985—, also bd. dirs.; bd. dirs. JSJ Corp., Skyline Corp., Durakool Corp., Prog. Office Tech. Corp., Oil Dynamics Inc.; instr. U. Toledo, 1966-67. Served with U.S. Army, 1961-63. Mem. Harvard U. Bus. Sch. Assn., Orchard Ridge C. of C. Republican. Presbyterian. Home: 14915 Powderhorn Rd Fort Wayne IN 46804 Office: 400 E Spring Rd Bluffton IN 46714

LAWTHERS, JUDITH ANN, radiologic technologist; b. Akron, Ohio, May 31, 1954; s. James Troupe Baston and Betty Jean (Moore) Pettitt; m. Larry Gene, Sept. 18, 1971 (div. July 1984); children: Yvonne Marie, Jason Paul; m. Robert Edward Jr., May 25, 1985. Grad. high sch., Akron, 1977; student, Timken Mercy Med. Ctr. Sch. Radiologic Tech., 1978-80. Nurse aide Nursing Home, Akron, 1969-71; nurse aide Timken Mercy Med. Ctr., Canton, 1972-74, radiologic technologist in surg. radiography, 1980-84; radiologic technologist in portable, gen. radiography Massillon (Ohio) Community Hosp., 1980-83, inservice edn. radiography, 1982-83; radiologic technician Cuyahoga Falls (Ohio) Gen. Hosp., 1983-86; acting supr. radiol. tech. Med. Clinic Ctr., North Canton, Ohio, 1985-86; radiologic technician in mammography Diagnostic Imaging, Akron, 1986—. Mem. Am. Soc. Radiologic Technologists. Democrat. Mem. Ch. of Christ. Avocations: sewing, skiing, cake decorating. Home: 1214 Inman St Akron OH 44306 Office: Diagnostic Imaging Inc 20 S Broadway Akron OH 44308

LAWTON, JOHN MILLER, dentist; b. Hancock, Mich., Dec. 20, 1943; s. Robert Augustus and Jane Inez (Miller) L.; m. Karla Jean McCray, June 21, 1969; children: Daniel, Kimberly, Teri. DDS, Ind. U., 1969. Gen. practice dentistry Hancock, 1969. Mem. USCG Auxiliary, 1975—, flotilla comdr., 1986—. Mem. ADA, Am. Soc. Dentistry for Children, Mich. Dental Assn., Copper County Dental Assn., Isle Royal Natural History Assn. (life), Houghton County Hist. Soc. (life), Psi Omega. Methodist. Lodges: Rotary (sec. Hancock 1975, treas. Hancock 1976-78), Elks. Avocations: boating, swimming, jogging. Home: 326 Mason Ave Hancock MI 49930 Office: 1550 W Quincy St Hancock MI 49930

LAWTON, RUTH FRANCES, social services administrator, consultant; b. Flint, Mich., Mar. 5, 1951; d. Thomas Andrew and Frances Eva (Chisholm) L. BS, Mich. State U., 1973; MSW, U. Mich., 1985—. cert. gerontologist, social worker, home economist. Home economist Flint (Mich.) Community Schs., 1973-75, Genesee County Coop. Extension, Flint, 1975, 76-78, Flint Community Schs., 1976; social worker Victoriuos Christian Youth, Flint, 1979-81; agy. exec. Diversion Adolescent Foster Care, Flint, 1981—; agy. exec. Diversion of Ohio, Findlay, 1982—; cons. Diversion Alternatives in Youth Placement, Flint, 1981—. Author/editor: (books) The Key to Lapeer County Community Services, 1973, Community Services Directory for Genesee County, 1976; author consumer edn. brochures, 1976. Bd. dirs. Hospice of Flint, 1977; deacon 1st Presbyn. Ch., Flint, 1982-83. Mem. Am. Home Econs. Assn., Mich. Home Econs. Assn. (bd. dirs., pres. 1986—), Nat. Assn. Social Workers, Mich. Assn. Social Workers, LWV (Flint bd. dirs. 1981), Delta Zeta. Republican. Avocations: needlepoint, sewing. Home: 2502 Green Acres Grand Blanc MI 48439 Office: Diversion Foster Care Inc 653 S Saginaw Flint MI 48502

LAWYER, VIVIAN JURY, lawyer; b. Farmington, Iowa, Jan. 7, 1932; d. Jewell Everett Jury and Ruby Mae (Schumaker) Brewer; m. Verne Lawyer, Oct. 25, 1959; children—Michael Jury, Steven Verne. Tchr.'s cert. U. No. Iowa, 1951; B.S. with honors, Iowa State U., 1953; J.D. with honors, Drake U., 1968. Bar: Iowa 1968, U.S. Supreme Ct. 1986. Home econs. tchr. Waukee High Sch. (Iowa), 1953-55; home econs. tchr. jr. high sch. and high sch., Des Moines Pub. Schs., 1955-61; sole practice law, Des Moines, 1972—; bd. dirs. Micah Corp.; chmn. juvenile code tng. sessions Iowa Crime Commn., Des Moines, 1978-79, coordinator workshops, 1980; assoc. Law Offices of Verne Lawyer, Des Moines, 1981—; co-founder, bd. dirs. Youth Law Center, Des Moines, 1977—; mem. com. rules of juvenile procedure Supreme Ct. Iowa, 1981—, adv. com. on costs of ct. appointed counsel Supreme Ct. Iowa, 1985—; trustee Polk County Legal Aid Services, Des Moines, 1980-82; mem. Iowa Dept. Human Services and Supreme Ct. Juvenile Justice County Base Joint Study Com., 1984—; mem. Iowa Task Force permanent families project Nat. Council Juvenile and Family Ct. Judges, 1984—; mem. substance abuse com. Commn. Children, Youth and Families, 1985—. Editor: Iowa Juvenile Code Manual, 1979, Iowa Juvenile Code Workshop Manual, 1980; author booklet in field, 1981. Mem. Polk County Citizens Commn. on Corrections, 1977. Iowa Dept. Social Services grantee, 1980. Mem. ABA, Iowa Bar Assn., Polk County Bar Assn., Polk County Women Attys. Assn., Assn. Trial Lawyers Am., Assn. Family Counseling in Juvenile and Family Cts., Purple Arrow, Phi Kappa Phi, Omicron Nu. Republican. Home: 5831 N Waterbury Rd Des Moines IA 50312 Office: 427 Fleming Bldg Des Moines IA 50309

LAXTON, DONALD KENNETH, lawyer, financial planner; b. Berwyn, Ill., Jan. 23, 1956; s. Kenneth William and Mary I. (Thomas) L. BA, Northwestern U., Evanston, 1977; JD, U. Ill., 1980. CLU, ChFC. Asst. state's atty. Kane County, Geneva, Ill., 1979; fin. planner Equitable Fin. Services, Northbrook, Ill., 1981—. Precinct committeman Dundee Twp. Reps., Carpentersville, Ill., 1974—; chmn. by-laws com. Dist. 220 Sch. Bd. Caucus, Barrington, Ill., 1982-83; vice chmn. Dundee Twp. Cen. Com., 1986—. Mem. ABA, Ill. Bar Assn., Chgo. Bar Assn., Internat. Assn. Fin. Planners, Am. Soc. CLU's, Nat. Assn. Life Underwriters, Phi Alpha Delta, Theta Delta Chi (sec. Northwestern U.). Lutheran. Home: PO Box 1265 Barrington IL 60011 Office: Equitable Fin Services 5 Revere Dr #500 Northbrook IL 60062

LAY, DONALD POMEROY, judge; b. Princeton, Ill., Aug. 24, 1926; s. Hardy W. and Ruth (Cushing) L.; m. Miriam Elaine Gustafson, Aug. 6, 1949; children: Stephen Pomeroy (dec.), Catherine Sue, Cynthia Lynn, Elizabeth Ann, Deborah Jean, Susan Elaine. Student, U.S. Naval Acad., 1945-46; BA, U. Iowa, 1948, JD, 1951; LLD (hon.), Mitchell Coll. Law, 1985. Bar: Nebr. 1951, Iowa 1951, Wis. 1953. Assoc. Kennedy, Holland, DeLacy & Svoboda, Omaha, 1951-53, Quarles, Spence & Quarles, Milw., 1953-54, Eisenstatt, Lay, Higgins & Miller, 1954-66; judge U.S. Ct. Appeals (8th cir.), 1966-80, chief judge, 1980—; faculty mem. on evidence Nat. Coll. Trial Judges, 1964-65; mem. U.S. Jud. Conf., 1980—. Mem. editorial bd.: Iowa Law Rev., 1950-51; contbr. articles to legal jours. Pres. Douglas

County (Nebr.) Dystrophy Assn., 1964; bd. dirs. Hattie B. Monroe Home, Omaha, 1961-67. Served with USNR, 1944-46. Recipient Hancher-Finkbine medal U. Iowa, 1980. Fellow Internat. Acad. Trial Lawyers; mem. ABA, Nebr. Bar Assn., Iowa Bar Assn., Wis. Bar Assn., Am. Judicature Soc. (bd. dirs. 1976—, exec. bd. 1979—), Law Sci. Acad. (v.p. 1960), Assn. Trial Lawyers Am. (bd. govs. 1963-65, Jud. Achievement award), U. Iowa Alumni Assn. (pres. Omaha-Council Bluffs chpt. 1958), Order of Coif, Delta Sigma Rho (Significant Sig award 1986), Phi Delta Phi, Sigma Chi. Presbyterian. Office: PO Box 75908 Saint Paul MN 55175

LAY, THORNE, geosciences educator; b. Casper, Wyo., Apr. 20, 1956; s. Johnny Gordon and Virginia Florence (Lee) L. BS, U. Rochester, 1978; MS, Calif. Inst. Tech., 1980, PhD, 1983. Research assoc. Calif. Inst. Tech., Pasadena, 1983; asst. prof. geosciences U. Mich., Ann Arbor, 1984—; cons. Woodward Clyde Cons., Pasadena, 1982-84. Contbr. articles to scientific jours. NSF fellow, 1978-81, Guttenberg fellow Calif. Inst. Tech., 1978, Lilly fellow Eli Lilly Found., 1984. Fellow Royal Astronomical Soc.; mem. Am. Geophys. Union, Soc. Exploration Geophysicists. Home: 3673 Partridge Path St Apt 6 Ann Arbor MI 48108 Office: U Mich Dept Geological Scis 1006 CC Little Bldg Ann Arbor MI 48109

LAYBOURN, HALE, insurance company executive; b. Cedar Rapids, Iowa, July 20, 1923; s. Harold Hale and Reba S. (Strudevant) L.; B.S.B.A., U. Wyo., 1949; m. Barbara G., Dec. 21, 1947; children—Lillian Louise Laybourn Casares, Constance Grace Laybourn Harb, Deborah Hayle Laybourn Davis, Paul James, Richard Tod, Dorothy M. Asst. bus. mgr. Cheyenne (Wyo.) Newspapers, Inc., 1949-50; fiscal and personnel officer, dir. hosp. facilities Wyo. Dept. Health, 1950-60; dir. internal ops. Blue Cross and Blue Shield, Cheyenne, Wyo., 1960-65; pres. Blue Cross N.D., Fargo, 1965-86; pres., chief exec. officer Dental Service Corp., Vision Service, Inc., 1976-86; Coordinated Ins. Service, 1982—; chmn. bd. No. Plains Life Ins. Co., 1983-86, chmn. bd., pres., 1986—; v.p. Care Plan HMO; bd. dirs. Nat. Blue Cross Assn., 1973-77; chmn. Dist. X Plan Pres's., 1970-73; dir. West Fargo State Bank. Pres., Fargo-Moorhead Civic Opera Co., 1968-81, chmn. bd., 1981—; chmn. United Fund, Fargo, 1972. Served with inf. U.S. Army, 1942-45. Mem. Fargo C. of C. (pres. 1977). Republican. Episcopalian. Clubs: Elks, Kiwanis. Office: 4510 13th Ave SW Fargo ND 58121

LAYDEN, DONALD WILLIAM, JR., lawyer; b. Bklyn., Dec. 2, 1957; s. Donald William and Barbara (Tepper) L.; m. Mary Jo DeWalt, Aug. 8, 1981; children: Christopher, Jacob. BA in Econs., Marquette U., 1979, JD cum laude, 1982. Bar: Wis. 1982, U.S. Dist. Ct. (ea. dist.) Wis. 1982. Assoc. Quarles & Brady, Milw., 1981—; lectr. securities regulation Marquette U., Milw., 1983—. Chmn. exploring north sect., exec. bd. Boy Scouts Am., Milw., 1983—; chmn. fin. com. St. Sebastian Parish, Milw., 1984—; mem. securities merit rev. com. Wis. Commr.'s Office, Madison, 1986—. Recipient Award of Merit Boy Scouts Am., 1982, Bronze Big Horn award Boy Scouts Am., 1986. Mem. ABA, Wis. Bar Assn., Milw. Bar Assn., Phi Kappa Theta. Roman Catholic. Club: Milw. Athletic. Avocations: reading, photography, softball, backpacking. Office: Quarles & Brady 411 E Wisconsin Ave Milwaukee WI 53202-4497

LAYMAN, BUDDY HAROLD, agricultural products company executive; b. Winchester, Ohio, Mar. 27, 1933; s. Harold Leslie and Icy Belle (Prather) L.; m. Betty Louise Melvin, July 28, 1951; children: Gary, Dona, Sharon, Alan. Grad. high sch., Hamersville, Ohio, 1951. Designer Allis-Chalmers, Norwood, Ohio, 1951-66; owner Good Buddy Seeds, Mt. Orab, Ohio, 1980—. Patentee in field. Deacon Ch. of Christ, Hamersville, 1958-73; v.p. Sandy Shores Condominium Assn., Daytona Beach Shores, Fla., 1983—. Republican. Avocations: softball, basketball, golf. Home: 1236 Sodom Rd Hamersville OH 45130 Office: Good Buddy Seeds PO Box 306 Mount Orab OH 45154

LAYMAN, MARK RICHARD, infosystems specialist; b. Lancaster, Ohio, Jan. 22, 1958; s. Richard Floyd and Bonnie Louise (Steed) L.; m. Brenda Lee Jones, June 9, 1979; children: Jonathan Mark, Daniel Mark. BS in Computer Sci., Ohio State U., 1980. Info. systems designer Western Electric Co., Columbus, Ohio, 1980-81, mem. staff info. systems, 1981-83; mem. staff info. systems AT&T, Columbus, 1984-85, software dept. chief, 1985—. Mem. Nat. Soc. Profl. Engrs., Assn. Computing Machinery, Ohio Acad. Sci. (judge sci. fair Ohio Weslyan U. 1984, 85, 87). Republican. Methodist. Avocations: photography, camping, music, family. Home: 1142 Hilton Dr Reynoldsburg OH 43068 Office: AT&T Network Systems Dept 45540 6200 E Broad St Columbus OH 43213-1550

LAYMON, JOHN L. (I.O.), manufacturing executive; b. Frankfort, Ind., May 7, 1917; s. John L. and Estella Mable (Sprunger) L.; m. Ruth Viola Keller, Apr. 28, 1940; children: Anita Ruth Laymon Lamos, Susan Jane Laymon Jones, Thomas John. Student, Purdue U. and Ind. U., Ft. Wayne, 1959; grad., Gen. Electric Co. Mgmt. Tng. Program, Ft. Wayne, 1962-64. Registered profl. engr., Ind. Indsl. engr. Gen. Electric Co., Ft. Wayne, 1935-48; mgr. prodn. and materials, sr. mfg. engr. gen. purpose motor dept. Gen. Electric Co., Linton and Shelbyville, Ind., 1948-64; mgr. mfg. engring. and services Franklin Electric Co., Bluffton, Ind., 1964-68; corp. mgr. mfg. engring. Hobart Mfg. Co., Troy, Ohio, 1968-78; v.p. mfg. and plant mgr. Rexair, Inc., Cadillac, Mich., 1978—. Author: Predetermined Time Standards System, Synchronous Flow Manufacturing, How to Attain 100% in a Day Work Plant. Served with U.S. Army, 1943-46, PTO. Mem. Mfrs. Assn., Personnel Assn. Republican. Clubs: Gideons (v.p. 1985), Christian Bus. Men (pres. 1983) (Cadillac). Avocations: golf, fishing, travel. Home: 1613 Sunnyside Dr Cadillac MI 49601 Office: Rexair Inc 230 7th St Cadillac MI 49601

LAYSTROM, RICHARD ARTHUR, manufacturing executive; b. Chgo., May 27, 1923; s. Hilding Albert and Erma S. (Schwartz) L.; m. Rita Mae Servoss, Jan. 20, 1951; children: Robert, Barbara, James. BS in Indsl. Engring., Ill. Inst. Tech., 1947. Pres. Laystrom Mfg. Co., Chgo., 1947—. Served as pvt. U.S. Army, 1944-46, ETO. Club: Bob-O-Link (Highland Park, Ill.). Home: 2605 Crestwood Ln Deerfield IL 60015 Office: Laystrom Mfg Co 3900 W Palmer Chicago IL 60015

LAZAR, LAWRENCE WILLIAM, manufacturing engineering company, educator; b. Chgo., July 7, 1954; s. William A. and Hazel R. (Mattiolli) L.; m. Caroline Susan Mayer, May 21, 1977; 1 child, Katharine. BSME, Milw. Sch. Engring., 1981, MS in Engring. Mgmt., 1984. Registered profl. engr. Engr. Falk Corp., Milw., 1981-82; sr. proj. engr. McGraw-Edison Co., Milw., 1982-84, mgr. mfg. engring., 1984—; coll. instr. Milw. Sch. Engring., 1978—. Inventor switchgear mechanism, 1984. Served with USN, 1972-77. Recipient Outstanding Achievement award Milw. Sch. Engring., 1981. Mem. Soc. Mfg. Engrs. (sr.), Tau Alpha Pi. Avocations: golf, fishing, camping. Home: 1530 S 74 St West Allis WI 53214 Office: McGraw Edison Co 2800 9th Ave S Milwaukee WI 53172

LAZAR, LEE ALAN, transportation company executive, hospital services company executive; b. Pitts., Dec. 29, 1951; s. Bernard and Ethel L.; m. Karen Laine, Sept. 3, 1978; children—Stephen, Wendy. B.A., George Washington U., 1973; J.D., Washington U. St. Louis, 1976. Bar: Pa. 1976. Assoc. Kuhn, Engle & Stein, Pitts., 1976-79; labor counsel Leaseway Transp. Corp., Cleve., 1979-80, gen. mgr. personnel leasing div., 1980-86, dir. adminstrn. transp. resource mgmt. group, 1986—; pres. Stendy Corp. and Deliverex of Cleve., 1987—. Contbr. articles to profl. jours. Home: 1811 Edenhall Dr Lyndhurst OH 44124 Office: 2201 Naiman Pkwy Cleveland OH 44139

LAZAR, MARDA GOLDFINE, cosmetics company executive; b. Chgo., Jan. 12, 1956; d. Judd Arnold and Audree (Lazarus) Goldfine; m. Andrew P. Lazar, Apr. 18, 1982; 1 child, Michael Goldfine. B.F.A., Ariz. State U., 1977; student U. Iowa, 1973-75, Hispanic Inst., Burgos, Spain, 1975. Lic., real estate, Ill. Cosmetic, indsl., corp. designer Frederick Vallarta & Assocs., Chgo., 1978; toy, indsl., package designer Playskool, Inc., Chgo., 1978-79; space utilization analyst Baxter Travenol Labs., Inc., Deerfield, Ill., 1979-82, exec. staff asst. to dir., 1982-83; pres. DermaLab Ltd., Bensenville, Ill., 1983—, also dir.; chmn. publicity Crusade of Mercy, Baxter Travenol, 1981-82; womens bd. dirs. Lambs Farm, Libertyville, 1982—. Mem. Ind. Cosmetic Mfrs. Assn., Gamma Phi Beta. Jewish. Club: Northmoor Country. Lodge: B'nai B'rith. Avocations: running, travel, gourmet cooking, golf, art. Office: DermaLab Ltd 400 Country Club Dr Bensenville IL 60106

LAZERSON, EARL EDWIN, university president; b. Detroit, Dec. 10, 1930; s. Nathan and Ceil (Stashefsky) L.; m. Ann May Harper, June 11, 1966; children from previous marriage: Joshua, Paul. B.S., Wayne State U., Detroit, 1953; postgrad., U. Leiden, Netherlands, 1957-58; M.A., U. Mich., 1954, Ph.D., 1982. Mathematician Inst. Def. Analyses, Princeton, N.J., 1960-62; asst. prof. math. Washington U., St. Louis, 1962-65, 66-69; vis. asso. prof. Brandeis U., 1965-66; mem. faculty So. Ill. U., Edwardsville, 1969—; prof. math. So. Ill. U., 1973—, chmn. dept. math. studies, 1972-73; dean So. Ill. U. (Sch. Sci. and Tech.), 1973-76, univ. v.p., provost, 1977-79, pres., 1980—. Bd. dirs., mem. exec. com. So. Ill. U. Edwardsville Found.; mem. exec. com. Higher Ednl. Council St. Louis; bd. dirs. St. Louis Regional Commerce and Growth Assn., Am. Assn. State Colls. and Univs., St. Louis Technol. Ctr., St. Louis Symphony Soc., St. Louis Com. on Fgn. Relations; trustee KETC-TV; chmn. Leadership Council Southwestern Ill.; mem. Southwestern Ill. Council Econ. Devel.; rep. Div. Urban Affairs, Nat. Assn. State Univs. and Land Grant Colls.; trustee Jefferson Nat. Expansion Meml. Assn.; mem. Miss. Bridge Panel. Recipient St. Teaching Excellence award Standard Oil Found., 1970-71. Mem. Am. Math. Soc., Math. Assn. Am., London Math. Soc., Soc. Mathematique France, AAUP, Am. Assn. Higher Edn., Fulbright Alumni Assn., Sigma Xi. Home: 219 S Charles St Edwardsville IL 62025 Office: So Ill Univ at Edwardsville Office of the Pres Edwardsville IL 62026-1001

LAZZARA, DENNIS JOSEPH, dentist, orthodontist; b. Chgo., Mar. 14, 1948; s. Joseph James and Jacqueline Joan (Antonini) L.; m. Nancy Ann Pirhofer, Dec. 18, 1971; children—Kristin Lynn, Bryan Matthew, Matthew Dennis, Kathryn Marie, David Brady. B.S., U. Dayton, 1970; D.D.S., Loyola U., 1974. M.S. in Oral Biology, 1976, cert. orthdontics, 1976. Practice dentistry specializing in orthodontics, Geneva, Ill., 1976—; sec. dental staff Community Hosp., Geneva Hosp., 1978-80, v.p., 1980-82, pres., 1982-84, exec. com., 1982-84. Recipient Award of Merit, Am. Coll. of Dentists, 1974, Harry Sicher honorable mention Council on Research, Am. Assn. Orthodontists, 1977. Mem. Am. Assn. Orthodontists, Midwestern Soc. of Orthodontists, Ill. Soc. Orthodontists, ADA, Fox River Valley Dental Soc. (bd. dirs. 1983-86), Blue Key Nat. Honor Soc. Roman Catholic. Avocations: sailing, golf. Office: 1725 South St Box 575 Geneva IL 60134

LEA, ALBERT ROBERT, manufacturing executive; b. Melrose, Mass., May 27, 1921; s. Robert Wentworth and Lillian (Ryan) L.; m. Joyce Winona Padgett, May 17, 1943 (div.); children: Patricia, Jennifer, Anne, Melissa Lea; m. Helen Clay Jones, May 12, 1961; children: Albert Robert, Robbert Wentworth II. AB, Amherst Coll., 1943; student Harvard Grad. Sch. Bus. Adminstrn., 1943. Exec. v.p. Ashcraft Inc., Kansas City, 1957-67, 83-86, pres., 1967-83, also dir.; pres. The Lea Co., 1986—. Trustee Westminster Coll., Fulton, Mo., 1983—. Served as lt. Supply Corps, USNR, 1943-46. Mem. Phi Gamma Delta. Clubs: Mission Hills Country, University (Kansas City); Met. (N.Y.C.). Home: 625 W Meyer Blvd Kansas City MO 64113 Office: 605 W Meyer Blvd Kansas City MO 64113

LEACH, DONALD PAUL, institute executive; b. Mount Vernon, N.Y., Mar. 17, 1945; s. Alfred Grahame and Anne Marie (Hantz) L.; m. Nancy Lynne Davis, Jan. 30, 1967; children: Donald Paul, Brian, Deborah. BS, Cedarville Coll., 1968; MBA, U. Dayton, 1974. Acct., mem. corp. staff Top Value Enterprises, Dayton, Ohio, 1969-72; tax analyst, corp. staff Philips Industries, Inc., Dayton, 1972-73; tax mgr. Danis Industries Corp., Dayton, 1973-76, asst. v.p., 1976-78, v.p., treas. constrn. products group, 1978-82; v.p., treas. Moody Bible Inst., Chgo., 1982—; instr. acctg. Sinclair Community Coll., Dayton, 1974-82. Mem. fin. com. Dayton Christian Schs., 1981-82; trustee Washington Hts. Bapt. Ch., Dayton, 1981-82, supt., 1977-80; deacon Faith Bapt. Ch., Winfield, Ill., 1984-87; treas. Alumni Council of Cedarville (Ohio) Coll., 1983-88, chmn., 1983-87; pres. Dayton Tax Club, 1977-78. Served with U.S. Army, 1967. Mem. Nat. Assn. Accountants, Inst. Internal Auditors, Christian Ministries Mgmt. Assn. Home: 1481 Fanchon St Wheaton IL 60187 Office: Moody Bible Inst 820 N La Salle St Chicago IL 60610

LEACH, JAMES ALBERT SMITH, congressman; b. Davenport, Iowa, Oct. 15, 1942; s. James Albert and Lois (Hill) L.; m. Elisabeth Foxley, Dec. 6, 1975; 1 child, Gallagher. B.A., Princeton U., 1964; M.A., Johns Hopkins U., 1966; student, London Sch. Econs., 1966-68. Mem. staff Congressman Donald Rumsfeld, 1965-66; U.S. Fgn. Service officer 1968-69, 70-73; spl. asst. to dir. OEO, 1969-70; mem. U.S. del. Geneva Disarmament Conf., 1971-72, UN Gen. Assembly, 1972, UN Natural Resources Conf., 1975; pres. Flamegas Companies Inc., Bettendorf, Iowa, 1973-76; chmn. bd. Adel Wholesalers, Inc., Bettendorf, 1973-76; mem. 95th-99th congresses from 1st Dist. of Iowa, U.S. Adv. Commn. Internat. Ednl. and Cultural Affairs, 1975-76. Chmn. Iowa Republican Directions '76 Com. Episcopalian. Office: 1514 Longworth Bldg Washington DC 20515 *

LEACH, MARK FERRETER, microbiologist; b. Gadsden, Ala., Mar. 4, 1958; s. Leonard Calvin and Dorothy (Waddell) L.; m. Esther Elizabeth Wood. BS in Microbiology, U. Ala., 1980, MS in Microbiology, 1983. Research technician U. Ala., Tuscaloosa, 1982-83; research assoc. Upjohn Co., Kalamazoo, 1984—. Deacon First Bapt. Ch., Portage, Mich., 1984. Named one of Outstanding Young Men of Am., 1985. Mem. Am. Soc. Microbiology, Sigma Xi. Republican. Avocations: golf, tennis, running, volleyball, reading. Home: 7905 Julie Dr Portage MI 49081 Office: Upjohn Co 301 Henrietta St Kalamazoo MI 49007

LEACH, RONALD LEE, manufacturing company executive; b. Athens, Ohio, Aug. 22, 1934; s. Ralph and Lelia Celesta (Woodruff) L.; m. Marilyn Rose Dreger, Sept. 3, 1956; children: Cynthia Diane, Mark Ronald, Douglas Ralph. B.S., Ohio U., 1958. With Ernst & Ernst, Cleve., 1960-70, mgr., 1967-70; asst. to v.p. and controller Eaton Corp., Cleve., 1970-72, asst. controller fin. acctg., 1972-77, corp. controller, 1977-78, v.p., controller, 1979-81, v.p. acctg., 1981—, dir., officer several subs. Mem. exec. adv. bd. bus. adminstrn. Ohio U., 1978—; treas. Lakeview Ch. of God, Parma, Ohio, 1968-84, trustee, 1969—, chmn. bd., 1984—; trustee, treas. Univ. for Young Ams., 1981—. Served with USAF, 1958-60. Mem. Fin. Execs. Inst. (dir. NE Ohio chpt. 1979-80, v.p. 1980-81, pres. 1981-82), Fin. Execs. Inst. (com. corp. reporting 1979—), Greater Cleve. Growth Assn., Am. Inst. C.P.A.s, Ohio Soc. C.P.A.s, Am. Acctg. Assn., Nat. Assn. Accts., Nat. Elec. Mfgrs. Assn., Beta Alpha Psi, Pi Gamma Mu, Beta Gamma Sigma. Republican. Club: Clevelander. Office: Eaton Corp Eaton Center Cleveland OH 44114

LEACH-CLARK, MARY AGNES, educator, counselor of handicapped; b. Wichita, Kans., Aug. 5, 1931; d. Frank N. and May Jean (Hollow) Leach; m. Courtney Clark, June 12, 1954 (div.); children—David Courtney, Bruce Colin, Anne Clark Nelson, Jeffrey Charles. B.S. in Edn., U. Kans., 1954; M.Ed. in Counseling, Wichita State U., 1978. Lic. counselor, Kans., Colo. Tchr. gifted Dist. 110, Overland Park, Kans., 1954-56; activity dir. Booth Meml. Hosp., Wichita, 1978; tchr. personal and social adjustment classes, Wichita, 1979-81; therapist aidance devel. programs, 1980—; elem. sch. counselor Dist. 259, Wichita, 1986—; dist. resource cons. Kans. Resource Tng. Systems, 1986-87; instr. interior design AIM's Community Coll., Greeley, Colo., 1983; art curriculum coordinator Creative Arts Ctr., Greeley, 1983; instr. interior design and piano improvisation Wichita State Free U., 1983-85 ; interior design instr. Marcus Ctr., Wichita State U., 1984—, also workshop dir. interior design Small Bus. Devel. Ctr., 1985—; home bound spl. edn. tchr. Wichita Pub. Schs. Dist. 259, 1983—; developmental program tchr. in classrooms Adolescent Psychiat. Unit, St. Francis Hosp., Wichita, 1984. Vol., dir. Off-Broadway Lewis St. Troupers, Downtown Sr. Ctr., 1984—. Interior design cons. Kaleidiscope Segment KAKE TV. Mem. Am. Assn. Counseling and Devel., Amer. Personnel and Guidance Assn., Kans. Mental Health Counselors, Kans. Personnel and Guidance Assn., Kans. Author's Club, Alpha Chi Omega. Office: Box 2034 Wichita KS 67208

LEACOX, WILLIAM BRAMMER (LEE WILLIAMS), stockbroker; b. Coon Rapids, Iowa, Mar. 9, 1918; s. Glen F. and Neta (Brammer) L.; m. Winifred Duncan, Mar., 1935; children—Paul, Suzanne; m. 2d, Laura Beth Mahorney, Aug. 28, 1953; children—Paula Beth, Brent, Scott. Student Northwestern Mo. U., 1935-36, U. No. Iowa, 1938-39. Band leader, 1937-52; entertainment rep., 1952-59; with Harold Helme Investment Co., Omaha, 1960-65; v.p. Robert E. Schweser Co., Omaha, 1965-67; mng. dir. Piper, Jaffray & Hopwood, Omaha, 1968—. Vol. Mid-Am. council Boy Scouts Am. Served to sgt. U.S. Army 1944-46. Mem. Omaha-Lincoln Fin. Analysts. Republican. Clubs: Omaha Press, West Omaha Cosmopolitan (past pres.), Oak Hills Country, Masons, Scottish Rite, Downtown Kiwanis, Shriners (Omaha); Elks (Shenandoah). Home: 10751 Berry Plaza Omaha NE 68127 Office: 910 N 96th St Suite 200 W Omaha NE 68114

LEADERS, HOMER GURNEY, engineer; b. Portage, Mich., Mar. 21, 1925; s. Homer G. and Cora Lenora (Dustin) L.; m. Jaunita Ruth Burnett, Aug. 27, 1948 (div. Nov. 1954); 1 child, Guy Wayne; m. Arija Rungis, June 21, 1955; children: Ernest Allen, Sandra Kay , Brenda Lee. BEE, Internat. Coorespondence Sch., Kalamazoo, 1952; MBA, Alexander Hamilton Inst., Hartford City, Ind., 1967. Service mgr. Newhouse Printer Supply, Kalamazoo, 1959-63; forman gen. maintenance 3M Co., Hartford City, 1963-69; plant engr. 3M Co., Freeport, Ill., 1970-78; plant mgr. 3M Co., Pine City, Minn., 1978—; plant. mgr. Cleveland Container, Eaton, Ind., 1969; pres. Leaders Enterprises, St. Cloud, Minn., 1984—, Leaders, Inc., LeSueur, Minn., 1985—. Mem. adv. com. Pine City Vocat. Tech. Served with USN, 1943-47. Decorated Purple Heart. Mem. Am. Mgmt. Assn., Instrument Soc. Am., Am. Inst. Petroleum Engrs., Am. Legion, VFW. Republican. Methodist. Lodge: Masons. Avocations: flying, hunting, fishing. Home: PO Box 521 445 W 8th St Rush City MN 55069 Office: 3M Co 400 2d St Pine City MN 55063

LEAHY, JOHN AUSTIN, pastor; b. Cleve., May 27, 1931; s. Joseph F. and Helen F. (Roberts) L. MA in History, John Caroll U., 1960, MEd, 1961; postgrad., Case Western Res. U., 1978. Prof. Borromeo Coll., Wickliffe, Ohio, 1960-64; prin., dir. St. Vincent High Sch., Akron, Ohio, 1964-65; supt. elem. schs. Diocese of Cleve., 1965-73, ednl. cons., 1973-83; dir. Parmadale, Parma, Ohio, 1970-83; pastor St. Bartholomew Ch., Middleburg Heights, Ohio, 1983—. TV commn. Middleburg Heights, 1986—; bd. dirs. Cath. Counseling Ctr., Cleve., 1969—, trustee, 1973—. Mem. Nat. Cath. Edn. Assn. Home and Office: St Bartholomew Ch 14865 Bagley Rd Middleburg Heights OH 44130

LEAKE, FRANK, gynecologist; b. Sandusky, Ohio, Mar. 4, 1925; s. Vere Henry and Helen Elizabeth (Nutzki) L.; m. Jan Zellner, Aug. 1, 1953; children: Diane E., Jonathan F. BA, Johns Hopkins U., 1950, MD, 1954. Diplomate Am. Bd. Ob-Gyn. Resident in ob-gyn Johns Hopkins U. Hosp., Balt., 1954-60; practice medicine specializing in ob-gyn Sandusky, 1960—; instr. ob-gyn Johns Hopkins U., 1955-60. Served with U.S. Army, 1943-46, ETO. Decorated Purple Heart with oak leaf cluster, Bronze Star with oak leaf cluster. Fellow Am. Coll. Ob-Gyn; mem. AMA. Office: 3004 Hayes Ave Sandusky OH 44870

LEAMAN, STEPHEN JAMES, finance company executive; b. Waynesboro, Pa., June 18, 1947; s. James Hershey and Louise Henrietta (Reese) L.; m. Gill Russell, Feb. 14, 1975. BSME, U.S. Naval Acad., 1969. Commd. ensign USN, 1969, advanced through grades to lt. comdr., 1969, resigned, 1975; supt. DuPont Co., Memphis, 1975-81; sr. product mgr. Progressive, Cleve., 1981-82, v.p. mktg., 1982-83, pres. fin. services div., 1984-86, pres. fin. services group, 1987—; bd. dirs. Prog. Casualty, Prog. Gulf ; bd. dirs., pres. United Fin., Prog. Am. Life, Classic and Prog. County Mut. Serves as lt. comdr. USNR, 1977—. Burke scholar USN, 1969. Mem. Young Pres. Orgn.(asst. sec. Cleve. chpt. 1987—), U.S. Naval Inst., U.S.A. Rugby Football Union (com. mem. 1984—), Midwest Rugby Football Union (chmn. Ref. Soc. 1986—). Home: 198 E Washington St Chagrin Falls OH 44022

LEASE, ELAINE ALBERTA, marketing executive; b. Lima, Ohio, Oct. 27, 1947; d. Roland William and M. Jean (Newcomb) Stroh; m. Dennis F. Hartnagle, July 5, 1969 (dec. June 1974); 1 child, William Michael (dec.); m. Jerry R. Lease, July 19, 1975 (div. Oct. 1980). BS in French, Miami U., Oxford, Ohio, 1969; BSBA in Mktg., Franklin U., 1985. Cert. mktg. exec., U. Pitts. Regional account sales rep. Lease Equipment/Kubota, Greenville, Ohio, 1975-78; export coordinator Dencoa Internat., Columbus, Ohio, 1978-79; internat. sales asst. McGraw-Edison Service, Columbus, 1979-81; export sales rep. Sherex Chem., Dublin, Ohio, 1981-85; internat. mktg. dir. Multipress Inc., Columbus, 1985-86; sales, mktg. mgr. MedServe Systems Inc., Worthington, Ohio, 1986—; cons. internat. bus. Vacalon Systems, Pickerington, Ohio, 1979-80; mktg. advisor Oradent Internat., Columbus, 1981—; property mgr. Elaine A. Lease Enterprises, Reynoldsburg, Ohio, 1984—. Creative designer sales bulletins, 1984, 86; author (instructional booklet) Procedure for Sherex Forwarder, 1985. Mem. Woman's Assn. of Columbus Symphony, 1975—; scholarship founder Miami U. Pres.'s Club, Oxford, 1983—. Recipient scholarship Future Tchrs. Am., 1965-67, Am. Legion Auxiliary, 1965, Ohio State Life Ins. Co., 1984, "E" award U.S. Dept. Commerce, 1979. Mem. Am. Mktg. Assn., Nat. Machine Tool Builders Assn., World Trade Devel. Club, Am. Mgmt. Assn., Columbus Area C. of C., Columbus Council on World Affairs, Miami U. Alumni Assn., Tau Pi Phi, Kappa Phi (pres. Oxford chpt. 1968-69). Club: Music (sec. 1972-73) (Greenville). Lodges: Order Eastern Star, Rainbow Girls (pres. 1964). Avocations: Miami U. and Ohio State U. football, golf, travel, photography, reading. Home: 7433 Marlan Ave Reynoldsburg OH 43068 Office: MedServe Systems Inc 7870 Olentangy River Rd Suite 103 Worthington OH 43085

LEASE, THOMAS CHARLES, perodontist; b. Salem, Ohio, Nov. 9, 1941; s. Donald Earl and Evelyn Louise (Horch) L.; 1 child, Dawn Dee. BA, Ohio State U., 1963, DDS, 1967; M Sci. Dentistry, Ind. U., 1971. Gen. practice dentistry Creve Coeur, Mo., 1971—. Served to lt. comdr. USNR, 1967-69. Mem. ADA, Am. Acad. Periodontology, Mo. Dental Assn., Mo. Soc. Periodontists, Midwest Soc. Periodontology, Greater St. Louis Dental Soc. Avocations: fishing, snow skiing. Home: 1411 Bald Eagle Rd Glencoe MO 63038 Office: 443 N New Ballas Rd Creve Coeur MO 63141

LEATHERWOOD, MARK ALAN, small business owner; b. Columbus, Ohio, Apr. 7, 1951; s. Coit Gale and N. Ann (Rogers) L.; m. Catherine Ann Wellman, June 11, 1983. BS, U.S. Naval Acad., 1973; MBA, Ohio State U., 1985. Commd. lt. USN, 1973, resigned, 1978; nuclear power student USN, Bainbridge, Md. and West Milton, N.Y., 1973-75; div. officer USN, New London, Conn., 1975-77, asst. engr., 1977-78; co-founder, v.p. Capt. Steamer, Inc., Ashville, Ohio, 1978-81; service line mgr. Chemlawn Corp., Columbus, 1981-85; co-owner Leatherwood & Assocs., Ashville, 1985—; chmn. adv. bd. Camrasco USA, London, 1985. Author technical manuals on carpet cleaning, 1981—. Chmn. pastor-parish relations com. Hedges Chapel, Ashville, 1985-86. Mem. Mensa, Beta Gamma Sigma. Republican. Methodist. Avocations: property restoration, golf, running, reading. Home: 309 E Main St Ashville OH 43103

LEAVITT, JEFFREY STUART, lawyer; b. Cleve., July 13, 1946; s. Sol and Esther (Dolinsky) L.; m. Ellen Fern Sugerman, Dec. 21, 1968; children—Matthew Adam, Joshua Aaron. A.B., Cornell U., 1968; J.D., Case Western Res. U., 1973. Bar: Ohio 1973. Assoc. Jones, Day, Reavis & Pogue, Cleve., 1973-80, ptnr., 1981—. Contbr. articles to profl. jours. Trustee Bur. Jewish Edn., Cleve., 1981—, v.p. 1985—, Fairmount Temple, Cleve., 1982—, v.p. 1985—, Citizens League Greater Cleve., 1982—, pres., 1987—; sec. Kulas Found., 1986—. Mem. ABA (employee benefits coms. 1976—), Midwest Pension Conf. Jewish. Home: 25961 Annesley Rd Beachwood OH 44122 Office: Jones Day Reavis & Pogue North Point 901 Lakeside Ave Cleveland OH 44114

LEAVITT, JUDITH ANN, information specialist; b. Washington, Iowa, Nov. 21, 1947; d. David Elwood and Ada Beth (Denison) Kleese; m. David Russell Leavitt, Aug. 30, 1969; children: Joseph, John. BA with honors and distinction, U. Iowa, 1970; MLS, Ind. U., 1977. Periodicals and catalog librarian Ball State U., Muncie, Ind., 1979-81; supr. info. ctr. Collins div. Rockwell Internat., Cedar Rapids, Iowa, 1982—. Author: Women in Management, 1980, 82, Dual Career Families, 1982, American Women Managers & Adminstrators, 1985, Local Area Networks, 1986, Telecommuting, 1986, Women in Management and Administration, 1988. Named Woman of Yr., Cedar Rapids YWCA, 1985. Mem. Spl. Libraries Assn., Women Library Workers Assn., Iowa Library Assn., LWV, Beta Phi Mu. Democrat. Unitarian. Club: Toastmasters (past pres. local chpt.). Avocation: travel. Home: 1223 38th St NW Cedar Rapids IA 52405 Office: Rockwell Internat 400 Collins Rd NE Cedar Rapids IA 52498

LEAVITT, MARTIN JACK, lawyer; b. Detroit, Mar. 30, 1940; s. Benjamin and Annette (Cohen) L.; m. Janice C. (McCreary) Leavitt; children: Michael J., Paul J., David A. LLB, Wayne State U., 1964. Bar: Mich. 1965, Fla. 1967. Assoc. Robert A. Sullivan, Detroit, 1968-70; officer, bd. dirs. Law Offices Sullivan & Leavitt, Northville, Mich., 1970—, pres., 1979—; bd. dirs. Premiere Video, Inc., Tyrone Hills of Mich., others. Served to lt. comdr., USNR, 1965-68. Detroit Edison Upper Class scholar, 1958-64. Mem. ABA, Mich. Bar Assn., Fla. Bar Assn., Transp. Lawyers Assn., ICC Practitioners. Jewish. Clubs: Meadowbrook Country, Huron River Hunting & Fishing, Chgo. (bd. dirs.) Traffic, Savoyard, Rolls Royce Owners. Home: 20114 Longridge Northville MI 48167 Office: 22375 Haggerty Rd PO Box 400 Northville MI 48167

LEAVY, RICHARD LAWRENCE, psychology educator; b. Phila., May 12, 1949; s. Sidney and Diana (Cohen) L.; m. Christine Lynn Jones, Apr. 2, 1977; children: Aaron, Catherine. BS in Psychology, U. Pitts., 1971; MA, U. Mass., 1973, PhD, 1976. Lic. psychologist, Ohio. Asst. prof. psychology St. Mary's Coll., Notre Dame, Ind., 1976-80; asst. prof. psychology Ohio Wesleyan U., Delaware, Ohio, 1980-84, assoc. prof., 1984—; psychologist Delaware Counseling Services, 1984—. Contbr. articles to profl. jours. Mem. Am. Psychol. Assn., Soc. Psychologists in Addictive Behaviors. Office: Ohio Wesleyan U Delaware OH 43015

LEBAMOFF, IVAN ARGIRE, lawyer; b. Ft. Wayne, Ind., July 20, 1932; s. Argire V. and Helen A. (Kachandov) L.; m. Katherine S. Lebamoff, June 9, 1963; children—Damian I., Jordan L., Justin A. A.B. in History, Ind. U., 1954, J.D., 1957. Bar: Ind. 1957, U.S. Ct. Dist. Ct. (no. and so. dists.) 1958, U.S. Supreme Ct. 1963. Sole practice Ft. Wayne, Ind., 1957-68; ptnr. Lebamoff, Ver Wiebe & Snow, Ft. Wayne, Ind., 1968-71; mayor City of Ft. Wayne, 1972-75; sole practice Lebamoff Law Offices, Ft. Wayne, 1975—; U.S. commr. No. Dist. Ind., 1957-62; fgn. service officer USIA Dept. Commerce, Bulgaria, 1963; vis. prof. dept. urban affairs Ind. U.-Purdue, Ft. Wayne, 1976-77. Chmn. Allen County Democratic Com., 1968-75, Ft. Wayne Dept. Parks and Recreation, 1984—; nat. pres. Macedonian Patriotic Orgn. of U.S. and Can., 1983—. Served with USAF, 1958-64. Mem. Allen County Bar Assn., Ind. Bar Assn., Am. Trial Lawyers Assn., Ind. Trial Lawyers Assn. Eastern Orthodox. Lodge: Kiwanis, Masons. Home: 205 E Packard Ave Fort Wayne IN 46806 Office: Lebamoff Law Offices 918 S Calhoun St Fort Wayne IN 46802

LEBEAU, JOSEPH E., chemical company executive; b. Virginia, Minn., July 23, 1941; s. Joseph and Mary (Valentini) LeB.; m. Terisita Schwartz, Nov. 30, 1974; children: Darin, Matthew. BS in Zoology, Mich. State U., 1964, DVM, 1966, MS in Pharmacology, 1970. Diplomate Am. Bd. Toxicology. Veterinarian, biomed. researcher Dow Corning, Midland, Mich., 1970-73; res. specialist, toxicology Dow Chem., Midland, Mich., 1973-74, group leader, toxicology, 1974-75, research mgr., toxicology, 1976-79, dir. preclin. research, 1979-82, dir. health and environ. scis., 1982—. Contbr. articles to profl. jours. Mem. Dow hdqrs. polit. action com., Midland, 1984-86. NIH postdoctoral fellow Mich. State U. grad. sch., 1968-70. Mem. Soc. of Toxicology (chmn. animals in research com. 1984-87), Am. Assn. for Lab. Animal Sci. (past pres.), Am. Vet. Sci. Assn., Indsl. Vet. Assn., Internat. Soc. for Study of Xenoblotics, Pharm. Mfg. Assn. Roman Catholic. Club: Midland Country. Avocations: sailing, boating, hunting, skiing. Office: Dow Chem Co 1803 Building Midland MI 48674

LEBLANC, JOAN MARIE, social worker; b. Plaquemine, La., Mar. 20, 1952; d. Joseph Jr. and Josephine Marion (Smith) LeB.; 1 child, Lachanté, Leneé. AA, Sauk Valley Jr. Coll., 1972; BA, Western Ill. U., 1974. Registered social worker, Ill. Social worker Dixon (Ill.) Devel. Ctr., 1974-83, Howe Devel. Ctr., Tinley Park, 1983-84, Dept. Children and Family Services, Rock Falls, Ill., 1984—. Baptist. Club: Altrusa (Sterling, Ill.). Home: 606 Monroe Dixon IL 61021

LEBLANC, JOHN KEITH, manufacturing company executive; b. Collinsville, Ill., July 1, 1945; s. John Dolton and Mary Jane (Flenniken) LeB., m. Jean Marie Bartlett, Sept. 9, 1966; children: John David, Joel Kirk. BS in Mgmt. Sci., So. Ill. U., Edwardsville, 1974, MBA in Internat. Bus. Mgmt., 1976. Quality control lab supr. Owens-Ill., Alton, 1974-76; supt. mfg. Obear-Nester Glass, East St. Louis, Ill., 1976-78; mgr. finished products Kerr Glass Co., Huntington, W.Va., 1978-80; asst. plant mgr. Kerr Glass Co., Dunkirk, Ind., 1980-81; plant mgr. Donaldson Co., Inc., Frankfort, Ind., 1981—; adj. prof. mgmt. sci. Ball State U., Muncie, Ind., 1980—. Author (handbook) Quality Control, 1978. Trustee Frankfort Pub. Schs., 1987—; mem. adv. bd. Ind. Vocat. Tech. Coll. Region IV, Lafayette, 1983—; bd. dirs. Frankfort Housing Authority, 1985—. Served as sgt. USAF, 1965-69, Vietnam. Decorated Bronze Star with V device. Mem. Soc. for Advancement of Mgmt., Ops. Mgmt. Assn., Nat. Eagle Scout Assn., Beta Gamma Sigma, Sigma Iota Epsilon. Republican. Baptist. Lodge: Rotary (bd. dirs. Frankfort club 1986—). Avocations: cert. basketball official Ind., Ohio, W.Va., Ky., Ill.; golf, tennis, softball. Home: 1159 Kelly Frankfort IN 46041 Office: Donaldson Co Inc State Rd 28 W Frankfort IN 46041

LEBLANC, L. JAMES, JR., manufacturing company executive; b. Rochester, Minn., May 5, 1947; s. Leo James Sr. and Ann M. (Held) LeB.; m. Judith Ann Wirth. BS, St. Louis U., 1971. V.p. Panduit Corp., Chgo., 1981-86, Atcor, Inc., Chgo., 1986—. Mem. Mayor's Leadership Council, St. Charles, Ill., 1986—; pres. Aintree Community Assn., St. Charles, 1986—.

LEBOVITZ, PHIL STANLEY, psychiatrist, psychoanalyst; b. Memphis, Nov. 11, 1940; s. Dave and Miriam (Phillips) L.; m. Donna Joyce Rudnick, June 20, 1964; children: Miriam, Aaron. BA, Columbia U., 1962; MD, Baylor U., 1966. Diplomate Am. Bd. Psychiatry and Neurology. Intern Baylor Affiliated Hosps., Houston, 1966-67; resident U. Minn. Hosp., Mpls., 1967-70; staff mem. student health service Northwestern U., Evanston, Ill., 1972-79; assoc. in psychiatry Northwestern U. Med. Sch., Chgo., 1972-86; clin. asst. prof. U. Health Scis. Chgo. Med. Sch., North Chgo., Ill., 1986—. Served to lt. comdr. USN, 1970-72. Mem. Am. Psychiatric Assn., Am. Soc. Adolescent Psychiatry, Am. Psychoanalytic Assn. (affiliate). Avocations: photography, sailing, golf. Home: 1128 Green Bay Rd Glencoe IL 60022

LECHNER, GEORGE WILLIAM, surgeon; b. Denver, July 30, 1931; s. Frank Clifford and Hazel Mae (Elkins) L.; m. Betty Jane Baumbach, Aug. 3, 1952; children: Kathleen Ann, Elaine Marie, Carol Jean, Patricia Louise, James Richard. Student, U. N.Mex., 1948-49; BA, Pacific Union Coll., 1952; MD summa cum laude, Loma Linda U., 1956. Diplomate Am. Bd. Surgery. Intern Pontiac (Mich.) Gen. Hosp., 1956-57; resident in surgery Harper Hosp., Detroit, 1957-58, Wayne State U. Hosp., 1961-64; instr. surgery Wayne State U., 1963-64; practice medicine specializing in gen., vascular and bariatric surgery Kettering, Ohio, 1964—; dir. surgery sect. 3 Kettering Med. Ctr., Dayton, 1967—, also mem. staff; assoc. clin. prof. surgery, assoc. developer. gen. surgery residency, dir. emergency medicine residency Wright State U., 1975-78, also chmn. residency devel. com.; mem. staff Sycamore Med. Ctr.; adj. faculty Kettering Coll. Med. Arts; pres. Kettering Med. Room Corp. Active Big Bros./Big Sisters; bd. elders Seventh-Day Adventist Ch., Kettering; trustee, mem. exec. com. Kettering Med. Ctr., 1971-74; pres. Spring Valley Acad., 1973-75, trustee 1973-78. Served with AUS, 1958-61, Japan. Recipient C.V. Mosby award for acad. excellence, 1956; ACS fellow. Mem. AMA, AAAS, Midwest Surg. Assn., Dayton Surg. Soc., Ohio and Montgomery County Med. Socs., Am. Coll. Emergency Physicians, Soc. Tchrs. Emergency Medicine, Univ. Assn. Emergency Med. Services. Republican. Lodge: Rotary. Home: 1928 Burnham Ln Kettering OH 45429 Office: Leiter Rd Miamisburg OH 45342

LECKLIDER, ROBERT WALTER, architect; b. Greenville, Ohio, Nov. 22, 1922; s. David Walter Lecklider and Ruth Hershey; m. Mary Helen Schmalenberger, Mar. 26, 1950; children: Todd D., Mark A., Amy R. BArch, Miami U., Oxford, Ohio, 1950. Registered architect, Ohio. Job capt. Yount/Sullivan, Dayton, Ohio, 1950-57; jr. ptnr. Yount/Sullivan/Lecklider, Dayton, 1957-66; ptnr. Sullivan/Lecklider/Jay, Dayton, 1966-76; sr. ptnr. Lecklider/Jay Architects, Dayton, 1976—; instr. Sinclair Community Coll., Dayton, 1954-57. Prin. works include Cox Internat. Airport, Dayton, Charles F. Kettering Meml. Hosp., Kettering, Ohio, Sinclair Community Coll., Millett Hall, Wright State U., Dayton, Reynolds-Reynolds Computer Bldg., Dayton, Mead Data Cen. Computer Facilities, Dayton, Cedarville (Ohio) Coll. Library, numerous others. Mem. Miami Valley Regional Planning Commn., Dayton, 1969-71; chmn. Planning Commn., Kettering, 1971; bd. dirs. Met. YMCA, Dayton, 1970-79. Served to staff sgt. C.E., U.S. Army, 1943-45. Recipient E.H. Berry award in Architecture, Cin. Architecture Soc., 1950, Beautification award City of Dayton, 1968, Excellence in Design award Ohio Prestressed Council Assn., Columbus, 1976, Singerman award Camp Kern YMCA, Oregonia, Ohio, 1978. Mem. AIA (pres. Dayton chpt. 1958-59), Ohio Soc. Architects (pres. 1975-76), Constrn. Specifications Inst. (pres. Dayton chpt. 1979-80, awards chmn. Great Lakes region 1983-87). Clubs: Engineers. (library chmn. 1958), Crestwood (Dayton) (pres. 1972-73). Lodge: Rotary. Avocations: woodworking, skiing, bicycling. Home: 704 Brubaker Dr Kettering OH 45429 Office: Lecklider/Jay Architects 110 E 2d St Dayton OH 45402

LECLAIR, J. MAURICE, transportation company executive; b. June 19, 1927; s. Francois and Rose-Anna (Chass'38) LeC.; m. Pauline H'38roux, Nov. 22, 1952; children: Suzanne, Marie, Francois, Manon, Nathalie, Guy. AB, McGill U., MD. Dean of medicine U. Montreal, Que., Can., 1962-65; dep. minister Health and Welfare Dept. of Can., Ottawa, 1970-74; with Can. Nat., Montreal, 1979—, corp. v.p., 1979-81, sr. corp. v.p., 1981, pres., chief exec. officer, 1981-85, chmn., chief exec. officer, 1985—; now also chmn. Grand Trunk Corp., Detroit. Office: Grand Trunk Western R R Co 131 W Lafayette Blvd Detroit MI 48226 *

LE CLERE, JOSEPH EARL, optometrist; b. Tell City, Ind., Aug. 6, 1950; s. Earl and Gloria Marie (Etienne) L.; m. Leanne Elizabeth Ringeman, July 5, 1980; children: Lauren Marie, Steven Joseph, Kristen Elizabeth. Student, U. Evansville, 1968-69; BS, Ind. State U., 1972; OD, Ind. U., 1977. Practice optometry Tell City, Ind., 1977—. Pres. Perry County unit Am. Cancer Soc., Tell City, 1978, Tell City Hist. Soc., 1981-83, Tell City Jaycees, 1981-82, United Way Perry County, Tell City, 1985. Recipient Disting. Service award Tell City Jaycees, 1984. Mem. Tell City C. of C. (bd. dirs.). Roman Catholic. Lodge: KC. Office: 715 Main PO Box 457 Tell City IN 47586

LECUREUX, KENNETH WAYNE, corporate treasurer; b. Saginaw, Mich., Sept. 21, 1950; s. Donald L. and Lavon M. (Mason) L.; m. Janet M. Spicer, Oct. 5, 1973; 1 child, Jonathan. BS in Acctg., Mich. State U., 1973. CPA, Mich. Ptnr. Foulds & LeCureux, CPA, Saginaw, 1973-85; treas., chief fin. officer Bierlein Cos., Saginaw, 1985—, bd. dirs. Trustee Mich. Community Blood Ctrs.; bd. dirs. ARC, Saginaw, 1985, Valley Blood Program, Saginaw, 1987. Mem. Am. Inst. CPA's, Mich. Assn. CPA's. Clubs: Saginaw Country, Germania.

LEDDICK, GEORGE RUSSELL, counseling and educational psychologist; b. Newman, Calif., April 6, 1948; s. Kenneth L. and Margaret R (McIntosh) L.; B.A., DePauw, U., 1970; M.A., Fisk U., 1977; Ph.D., Purdue U., 1980. Cert. clin. mental health counselor. Instr. Purdue U., West Lafayette, Ind., 1979-80; asst. prof. edn., coordinator counseling Ind.-Purdue U., Ft. Wayne, 1980—. Fellow, Internat. Council Sex Edn. and Parenthood; mem. Am. Assn. Marriage and Family Therapy (clin.), Am. Psychol. Assn., Am. Assn. for Counseling and Devel. (past pres.), Ind. Assn. Counseling and Devel. (past pres.), Ind. Counselor Edn. and Supervision, Ind. Specialists in Group Work (past pres.), Assn. Counselor Edn. and Supervision (chmn. supervision com.), Am. Mental Health Counselors Assn., Phi Delta Kappa. Author: (with others) Handbook of Counseling Supervision; mem. editorial bd. Jour. Specialists in Group Work, Clin. Supr.; contbr. articles to profl. jours., other publs.

LEDERMAN, REGINA PLACZEK, nurse educator; b. Bronx, N.Y., Feb. 23, 1940; d. Kurt and Selma Placzek; m. Edward Lederman, Aug. 20, 1960; children: Terence Daniel, Mark Andrew. Diploma nursing, Mt. Sinai Hosp. Sch. Nursing, 1960; BS in Nursing Edn., Columbia U., 1963; MNEd in Nursing, Tchrs. Coll., 1965; PhD in Behavioral Scis. Edn., U. Mich., 1977. Asst. prof. nursing Skidmore Coll., 1967-68; staff assoc. Nat. League for Nursing, 1969; asst. prof. nursing U. Mich., Ann Arbor, 1971-75, assoc. prof. nursing, 1975-79, prof. nursing, 1979-81; prof. nursing, project dir. U. Wis., Madison, 1981—, Helen Denne Schulte prof. nursing, 1985—. Author: Psychosocial Adaptation in Pregnancy, 1984. USPHS grantee 1975—. Fellow Am. Acad. Nursing, Soc. For Research in Child Devel.; mem. AAAS, N.Y. Acad. Scis., Am. Soc. Psychosomatic Obstetrics and Gynecology, Midwest Nursing Research Soc. (Outstanding Nurse Researcher award 1983), Singa Theta Tau. Home: 3 Kewaunee Ct Madison WI 53705 Office: U Wis Sch Nursing 600 Highland Ave K6/346 Madison WI 53792

LEDFORD, K. HAROLD, electronics executive; b. Lakewood, Ohio, July 20, 1935; s. Kenneth Harold and Angela Marie (Wagner) L.; m. Rosalinda E. Kendall, June 1, 1957 (div. Jan. 1981); children: Sally-Lee Maria, Dale Benedict, Christian Matthais, Karl Dominick, Jane Chantal, Erik Francis; m. Leatrice E. Friedel, Jan 4, 1982. AA, Community Coll. of the Air Force, 1970. Enlisted USAF, 1953, advanced through ranks to chief master sgt., 1976; avionics support program mgr. F-111 Program Office, Dayton, Ohio, 1971-74, F-15 Program Office, Dayton, 1974-77; avionics support program mgr. F-16 Program Office, Dayton, 1977-78, aircraft program mgr., 1978-82, ret., 1982; bus. devel. mgr. Emerson Electric Co., Dayton, 1983-85, exec. program mgr., 1985—. Mem. Air Force Assn. (exec. dir. Dayton Wright Meml. chpt. 1982—), Dayton C. of C. Republican. Roman Catholic. Lodge: KC (staff dir. 1975—). Avocations: golf, photography, stamp collecting. Home: 9620 Whaler Wharf Centerville OH 45459

LEE, BENSON PEI-SING, health care technology entrepreneur, health care company executive; b. N.Y.C., May 11, 1941; s. Richard Tuh-Yu Lee and Julie Tse-Fung (Chang) Lauh; m. Vicki Anne Parker, July 25, 1944; 1 child, Melissa Elisabeth. BEE, Cornell U., 1964; postgrad., NYU, 1964-68. Systems engr. IBM Corp., N.Y.C., 1964-67; planning cons. corp. hdqrs. IBM Corp., Armonk, N.Y., 1967-68; mgr. health care Westinghouse Electric Corp., Pitts., 1968-71; pres., chief exec. officer Datalogics, Inc., Cleve., 1971—, Intersci., Inc., Cleve., 1971—; bd. dirs. Hathaway Brown Corp., Cleve. Mem. health issues com. Fedn. Community Planning, Cleve., 1971—; trustee Cornell Research Fedn., Inc., Ithaca, N.Y., 1979—, Cornell U., 1985—, Cleve. Tomorrow Ctr. for Venture Devel., 1980—. Mem. Assn. for Corp. Growth (sec. 1986-87), The Planning Forum. Republican. Episcopalian. Clubs: Lakeside Y, Cornell (bd. dirs.), NYU, Club of N.E. Ohio. Avocations: sailing, starting new businesses.

LEE, CHENG-FEW, finance educator; b. Tao-Yuen, Taiwan, Jan. 29, 1939; s. Wan-Chen and Chi-Mei (Chang) L.; m. Schwinne Chwen Tzen, Oct. 20, 1966; children—John C., Alice C. B.S. in Econs., Nat. Taiwan U., 1962; M.S. in Stats., W.Va. U., 1970; Ph.D. in Econs., SUNY-Buffalo, 1973. Mem. staff Bank of China, Taipei, Taiwan, 1963-68; asst. prof. U. Ga.-Athens, 1973-76; assoc. prof. fin. U. Ill.-Champaign, 1976-78, prof., 1978-82, Ill. Bus. Edn. prof., 1982—; research advisor Fed. Res. Bank of Chgo., 1984-86, World Bank, 1986—. Author: Financial Analysis and Planning, 1985, Urban Econometrics, 1986; editor Advances in Financial Planning and Forecasting, 1983—, Advances in Quantitative Analysis of Fin. and Acctg., Readings in Investments, 1980, Readings in Financial Analysis and Planning, 1983; assoc. editor Jour. Fin. and Quantitative Analysis, 1977-83; co-editor The Fin. Review, 1985—. Wharton Sch. Ins. Research Inst. grantee, 1978, Chgo. Merc. Exchange grantee, 1980. Mem. Am. Econs. Assn., Am. Fin. Assn., Am. Statis. Assn., Western Fin. Assn. Home: 601 Shurts St Urbana IL 61801 Office: U Ill Dept Fin 1206 S 6th St Champaign IL 61820

LEE, CHUNG-SENG, physician; b. Ping-Tung, Republic of China, June 8, 1944; s. Ming-Shiang and Hong-Yen (Tsai) L.; m. Shuishih Sage Chang, Mar. 31, 1973; children: Yvonne, Michael. MD, Nat. Taiwan U., Taipei, 1969. Diplomate Am. Bd. Internal Medicine. Resident Nat. Taiwan U. Hosp., Taipei, 1970-72; intern City Hosp. Ctr., Elmhurst, N.Y., 1972-73; resident Highland Hosp., Rochester, N.Y., 1973-74; postdoctoral fellow Strong Meml. Hosp., Rochester, 1974-77; instr. U. Rochester, N.Y., 1974-77; chief med. services VA Med. Ctr., Ft. Wayne, Ind., 1977-81; mem. med. staff St. Joseph Med. Ctr., Ft. Wayne, 1981—, Parkview Meml. Hosp., Ft. Wayne, 1981—. Home: 5728 Prophets Pass Fort Wayne IN 46825 Office: 3217 Lake Ave Fort Wayne IN 46805

LEE, DANIEL ANDREW, osteopathic physician, optometrist; b. Bklyn., Aug. 20, 1951; s. Jack W. and Lily (Ho) L.; m. Janet Lynne Eng, June 14, 1975 (div. Sept. 1985); children: Jason Matthew, Brian Christopher. BS in Psychobiology, SUNY, Stony Brook, 1973; BS in Biology, Westminster Coll., 1973; OD, Pa. Coll. Optometry, 1977; DO, Ohio U., 1984. Cert. in low vision proficiency. Instr. Mohawk Valley Community Coll., Rome, N.Y., 1978-80; pvt. practice optometry, Utica, N.Y., 1978-80, Chauncey, Ohio, 1981-84, Dayton, Ohio, 1984—; intern Grandview Hosp., Dayton, 1984, mem. staff, 1984-85, ophthalmology resident, 1985—; cons. Rome Sch. Dist., Cen. Assn. for Blind, Utica, Kernan Sch. for Multiple Handicapped, Utica; speaker various profl. orgns. and confs.; mem. curriculum adv. com. Deer Creek Curriculum Rev. Conf., 1982. Contbr. articles to profl. jours. Mem. adv. bd. ARC, Rome, 1977-80; mem. Mohawk Valley Chinese Cultural Assn., Rome, 1977-80, Dayton Area Chinese Assn., 1985—; nominated People to People Optometry Delegation to People's Republic of China, 1985, India, 1986. Served with USAF, 1977-80, to lt. comdr. USNR, 1981—. Fellow Am. Acad. Optometry; mem. Am. Osteo. Assn. (student rep. nat. com. on colls. 1984), Ohio Osteo. Assn., Am. Acad. Ophthalmology, Dayton Area Chinese Assn., Gold Key, Beta Beta Beta. Episcopalian. Avocations: hunting, fishing, martial arts, photography, playing mandolin. Home: 434 Grand Ave Apt 36D Dayton OH 45405 Office: Grandview Hosp 405 Grand Ave Dayton OH 45405

LEE, DAVID CHANG, physician; b. Seoul, Republic of Korea, Sept. 14, 1940; s. Young C. Lee and Hae W. (Kim) Kim; m. Margaret C. Park, Sept. 10, 1965; children: Edward, Grace, George. MD, Yon-Sei Sch. Med., Seoul, 1965. Diplomate Am. Bd. Otolaryngology. Intern Howard med. Ctr., Washington, 1965-66; resident gen. surgery Roger's Meml. Hosp., Washington, 1966-67; resident otolaryngology St. Louis City Hosp., 1967-70, U. Md. Hosp., Balt., 1970-71; staff physician Ft. Howard (Md.) Vets. Hosp., 1971-73; asst. prof. U. Ill., Chgo., 1973—. Fellow ACS, Am. Acad. Otolaryncology and Head and Neck Surgery; AMA. Presbyterian. Avocations: Tae Kwon Do (black belt), golf. Office: 5320 W 159th St Oak Forest IL 60452

LEE, DELORES WASHINGTON, airport police communications supervisor; b. St. Louis, Jan. 31, 1941; d. Clifford E. and Sarah H. Washington; m. Harold N. Lee, Aug. 9, 1964 (div. Oct. 1980); 1 child, Kimberly Renee. AA, Forest Park Community Coll., 1975; BS, Washington U., St. Louis, 1978. Librarian St. Louis Pub. Library, 1959-64, St. Louis Mcpl. Sch. Nursing, 1964-78; planning technician Community Developing Agy., St. Louis, 1978-81; supr. airport police communications Lambert Airport, St. Louis, 1981—; library cons. Annie Malone Children's Home, St. Louis, 1983-84. Author: Dispatcher's Manual, 1983. Home: 5115 Northland Saint Louis MO 63113 Office: Lambert Airport Police Dept PO Box 10212 Saint Louis MO 63145

LEE, DO IK, research scientist; b. Chinnampo, Republic of Korea, Mar. 6, 1937; came to U.S., 1962, naturalized, 1976; s. Hyun Joo and Sang Duk; m. Ilhae Kim, July 25, 1970; 1 son, Albert. BS in Chem. Engring., Seoul Nat. U., 1959; MS in Chem. Engring., Columbia U., 1964, Sc.D. in Engring., 1967. Research asst. Columbia U., N.Y.C., 1962-67; research engr. Dow Chem. Co., Midland, Mich., 1967-72, research specialist, 1972-75, sr. research specialist, 1975-79, assoc. scientist, 1979-82, sr. assoc. scientist, 1982—. Contbr. articles to profl. jours.; patentee in field. Served to 1st lt. Korean Air Force, 1958-61. Mem. Am. Inst. Chem. Engrs., Am. Chem. Soc., TAPPI (Coating and Graphic Arts Div. award 1978, 86—, Charles W. Engelhard Medallion), AAAS, Korean Scientists and Engrs. in Am., Sigma Xi. Home: 5109 Nakoma Dr Midland MI 48640 Office: Dow Chem USA Midland MI 48640

LEE, DONALD ALLEN, small business owner; b. Sebring, Ohio, Dec. 30, 1922; s. Bricely O. Lee and Anna J. (Birch) L.; m. July 8, 1942; children: Sharon, Dennis, Richard. Grad. high sch., Sebring, 1941. Welder, electrician Babcock-Wilcox Alliance Machine, Ohio, 1941-63; prin. Lee's Appliance, Sebring, 1963-72; Prin. Norge Town Dry Cleaner, Austintown, Ohio, 1972-83, Norge Village Dry Cleaner, Alliance, Ohio, 1968—. Mem. Ohio Dry Cleaners Assn., Small Businessmen's Assn. Republican. Mem. Ch. of Christ. Avocations: organist, pilot. Home: 185 E Vermont Ave Serbring OH 44672 Office: Norge Village 195 E State St Alliance OH 44601

LEE, FRED, radiologist; b. Buffalo, July 23, 1930; s. Wallace and Mary Lan Fong (Wong) L.; m. Ethel Margaret, Aug. 4, 1955; children: Alexa, Suzanne, Fred Jr., Amy B., Andrew C. BA, U. Buffalo, 1952, MD, 1956. Intern U. Chgo., 1956-57; researcher Harvard Med. Sch., Boston, 1957; resident radiology Peter Bent Brigham, Boston, 1957-60; asst. prof. U. Rochester, N.Y., 1962-64; instr. radiology U. Mich., Ann Arbor, 1964—; assoc. radiologist St. Joseph Mercy Hosp., Ann Arbor, 1964—. Served to capt. USMC, 1960-62. Named Michiganian of Yr. Detroit News 1987, Alpha Omega Alpha scholar, 1956; St. Joseph Mercy Hosp. grantee, 1985-86, Blue Cross Blue Shield grantee, 1986. Mem. AMA, Am. Coll. Radiology, Am. Inst. Ultrasound in Medicine. Avocations: walking, running, yoga, family, Charles Dickens. Home: 1926 Day St Ann Arbor MI 48104 Office: St Joseph Mercy Hosp Ann Arbor MI 48106

LEE, GILBERT BROOKS, retired ophthalmology engineer; b. Cohasset, Mass., Sept. 10, 1913; s. John Alden and Charlotte Louise (Brooks) L.; m. Marion Corrine Rapp, Mar. 7, 1943 (div. Jan. 1969); children: Thomas Stearns, Jane Stanton, Frederick Cabot, Eliot Frazar. Asst. psychologist Civil Service, Psychophysics of Vision, U.S. Naval Submarine Base, New London, Conn., 1950-53; research assoc. Project Mich., Vision Research Labs., Willow Run, 1954-57; research assoc. dept. ophthalmology U. Mich., Ann Arbor, 1958-72, sr. research assoc., 1972-75, sr. engring. research assoc. ophthalmology, 1975-82, part-time sr. engr. ophthalmology, 1982—. Contbr. articles to profl. jours.; local organizer, moderator (TV program) Union of Concerned Scientists' Internat. Satellite Symposium on Nuclear Arms Issues., 1986. Precinct del. Dem. County Conv., Washtenaw County, 1970, 74; treas. Dem. Party Club, Ann Arbor, Mich., 1971-72, 74-79, vice chmn. nuclear arms control com., 1979; chmn. Precinct Election Inspectors, 1968-75. Served to capt. AUS, 1942-46, 61-62. Mem. Optical Soc. Am., AAAS, Fedn. Am. Scientists, N.Y. Acad. Sci., Assn. Research in Vision and Ophthalmology, Nation Assocs., ACLU. Home: 901 Edgewood Pl Ann Arbor MI 48103

LEE, JACK (JIM SANDERS BEASLEY), broadcast exec.; b. Buffalo Valley, Tenn., Apr. 14, 1936; s. Jesse McDonald and Nelle Viola (Sanders) Beasley; m. Barbara Sue Looper, Sept. 1, 1961; children—Laura Ann, Elizabeth Jane, Sarah Kathleen. Student, Wayne State U., 1955-57; B.A., Albion Coll., 1959. Announcer Sta. WHUB-AM, Cookeville, Tenn., 1956; news dir., program dir. Sta. WALM-AM, Albion, Mich., 1957-59; radio-TV personality WKZO-Radio-TV, Kalamazoo, 1960-62; prodn. dir. Stas. WKMH-WKNR, Detroit, 1962-63; gen. mgr. Sta. WAUK-AM-FM, Waukesha, Wis., 1963-65; asst. program mgr. WOKY, Milw., 1965-70; program mgr. WTMJ-WKTI, Milw., 1970-76; gen. mgr. WEMP-WMYX, Milw., 1976—; pres. Jack Lee Enterprises, Ltd.; instr. dept. mass communication U. Wis.-Milw., 1972-81; adviser Nat. Baha'i Info. Office; maj. CAP, 1964—. Bd. dirs. Milw. Summerfest; bd. dirs. Variety Club Wis. Served with U.S. Army, 1959, 61-62. Decorated Army Commendation medal; Billboard radio program dir. finalist, 1975. Mem. AFTRA, Omicron Delta Kappa, Alpha Epsilon Rho. Home: W 183 N 8521 Lawrence Ct Menomonee Falls WI 53051 Office: Sta WEMP-AM 11800 W Grange Ave Hales Corner Milwaukee WI 53130

LEE, JAMES, social services administrator; b. Eutaw, Ala., Mar. 11, 1925; s. James Polk and Classie (Ryans) L.; m. Joann Jones, June 24, 1951; children: Hilary, Denise. BSW, Wayne State U., 1977, MSW, 1978. Lic. social worker, Mich. Juvenile group leader I Wayne County Youth Home, Detroit, 1969-76, juvenile group leader II, 1976-78, dept. mgr., 1982—; supr. juvenile group leaders D.J. Healy Children's Ctr., Detroit, 1978-82. Served with USN, 1943-46. Mem. Mich. Juvenile Detention Assn. (treas. 1973-77, Child Care Worker of Yr. 1975). Avocations: bowling, spectator sports. Office: Wayne County Youth Home 1333 E Forest Detroit MI 48207

LEE, JERRY WAYNE, lawyer; b. Columbus, Ohio, Nov. 3, 1944; m. Judith Ann Skulski, Nov. 27, 1965; children—Bryan D., Kirsten N. B.S. in Edn., Bowling Green State U., 1966, M.A., 1968; J.D., U. Toledo, 1978. Bar: Ohio 1978, U.S. Dist. Ct. (no. dist.) Ohio 1979, U.S. Supreme Ct. 1982. Tchr. Otsego Local Schs., Tontogany, Ohio, 1966-67; teaching asst. Bowling Green

State U., Ohio, 1967-68; instr. speech Ohio No. U., Ada, 1968-74; jud. clk. Wood County Ct. Common Pleas, Bowling Green, 1978-79; assoc. Reddin, Reddin & Lee, Bowling Green, 1979-81, ptnr., 1981—; v.p. Research and Devel. Co., Toledo, 1974-75, Wood County Title Agy., Inc., 1983—; instr. Am. Inst. for Paralegal Studies, Inc.; judge pro tem Bowling Green Mcpl. Ct. Bus. editor U. Toledo Law Rev., 1977-78. Contbr. articles to profl. jours. Asst. den leader Toledo Area Cub Scouts Am., 1973-74, asst. troop leader Boy Scouts Am., 1976-81; past pres., trustee Autistic Community of N. W. Ohio, Whitehouse, 1976—, Bowling Green PeeWee League, Inc., 1978-82; mem. Wood County Democratic Exec. Com., Bowling Green, 1979—; trustee Indsl. and Devel. Corp. Bowling Green, 1985—; vice-chmn. Bowling Green Housing Commn., 1981-82; chmn. Bowling Green Cable Vision Com., 1982-83; mem. city council, Bowling Green, 1983, mem. cablevision com., 1984—; trustee Wood county chpt. Am. Diabetes Assn., Bowling Green, 1984—, chmn. bd. of trustees Ohio affiliate; bd. dirs. Wood County unit Am. Cancer Soc., 1984—; pres. bd. of trustees Wood County Mental Health Ctr., Inc., 1985—. Recipient Resolution for Community Service Univ. Circle, Bowling Green State U. Alumni Assn., 1984. Mem. Ohio State Bar Assn., Ohio Trial Lawyers Assn., ABA, Assn. Trial Lawyers Am., Wood County Bar Assn., Bowling Green C. of C. (chmn. econ. devel. com.), Jaycees (bd. dirs. 1979-80, Phi Alpha Delta. Democrat. Clubs: Falcon, Bowling Green Country. Lodges: Kiwanis (bd. dirs. 1985—), Optimists (bd. dirs. 1979). Home: 226 Sandridge Rd Bowling Green OH 43402 Office: Reddin Reddin & Lee 136 N Main St Bowling Green OH 43402

LEE, JOEL MARVIN, publisher, librarian; b. San Antonio, Aug. 13, 1949; s. Lewis C. and Charlotte (Lippman) L. AB in English, Oberlin Coll., 1971; MA, U. Chgo., 1972. Asst. librarian Lake Forest (Ill.) Coll., 1972-77; headquarters librarian ALA, Chgo., 1977-86, sr. mgr. info. tech. publ., 1986—. Assoc. editor ALA World Encyclopedia, 1980, 86; editor-in-chief Who's Who in Library and Information Services, 1982; co-editor As Much To Learn As To Teach, 1979; contbr. articles to various pubs. Mng. trustee 860 Lake Shore Dr. Trust, Chgo., 1984-86. Mem. ALA, Spl. Libraries Assn., Am. Soc. for Info. Sci. Jewish. Avocations: opera, home video, microcomputers, telecommunication.

LEE, KANG H., obstetrician, gynecologist; b. Republic of Korea, May 5, 1942; m. Inja Kang, Dec. 7, 1968; children: Eddie, Michael. MD, Yonsei U. Sch. Med., Seoul, Republic of Korea, 1968. Diplomate Am. Bd. of Ob-Gyn. Intern Christ Hosp., Cin., 1969; resident Henry Ford Hosp., Detroit, 1971-74; chmn. ob-gyn Meml. Med. Cen. W. Mich., Ludington, 1974—. Fellow Am. Coll. Ob-Gyn; mem. AMA, Mich. Med. Soc., Am. FertilitySoc., Am. Assn. Gynecol. Laparascopist. Lodge: Rotary. Avocation: painting. Home: 1114 N Sherman St Ludington MI 49431 Office: 12 Atkinson Dr Ludington MI 49431

LEE, KYO RAK, radiologist; b. Seoul, Korea, Aug. 3, 1933; s. Ke Chang and Ok Hi (Um) L.; came to U.S., 1964, naturalized, 1976; M.D., Seoul Nat. U., 1959; m. Ke Sook Oh, July 22, 1964; children—Andrew, John. Intern, Franklin Sq. Hosp., Balt., 1964-65; resident U. Mo. Med. Center, Columbia, Mo., 1965-68; instr. dept. radiology U. Mo., Columbia, 1968-69, asst. prof., 1969-71; asst. prof. dept. radiology U. Kans., Kansas City, 1971-76, assoc. prof., 1976-81, prof., 1981—. Served with Republic of Korea Army, 1950-52. Diplomate Am. Bd. Radiology. Recipient Richard H. Marshak award Am. Coll. Gastroenterology, 1975. Fellow Am. Coll. Radiology; mem. Radiol. Soc. N.Am., Am. Roentgen Ray Soc., Assn. Univ. Radiologists, Kans. Radiol. Soc., Greater Kansas City Radiol. Soc., Wyandotte County Med. Soc. Presbyterian. Contbr. articles to med. jours. Home: 9800 Glenwood St Overland Park KS 66212 Office: U Kans 39th St and Rainbow Blvd Kansas City KS 66103

LEE, MARGARET NORMA, artist; b. Kansas City, Mo., July 7, 1928; d. James W. and Margaret W. (Farin) Lee; Ph.B., U. Chgo., 1948; M.A., Art Inst. Chgo., 1952. Lectr., U. Kansas City, 1957-61; cons. Kansas City Bd. Edn., Kansas City, Mo., 1968-86; guest lectr. U.Mo.-Columbia, 1983, 85, 87; one-woman shows Univ. Women's Club, Kansas City, 1966, Friends of Art, Kansas City, 1969, Fine Arts Gallery U. Mo. at Columbia, 1972, All Souls Unitarian Ch. Kansas City, Mo., 1978; two-Woman show Rockhurst Coll., Kansas City, Mo., 1981 exhibited in group shows U. Kans., Lawrence, 1958, Chgo. Art Inst., 1963, Nelson Art Gallery, Kansas City, Mo., 1968, 74, Mo. Art Show, 1976, Fine Arts Gallery, Davenport, Iowa, 1977; represented in permanent collections Amarillo (Tex.) Art Center, Kansas City (Mo.) Pub. Library, Park Coll., Parkville, Mo. Mem. Coll. Art Assn. Roman Catholic. Contbr. art to profl. jours.; author booklet. Home and studio: 4109 Holmes St Kansas City MO 64110

LEE, MARVA JEAN, counselor, physical educator, family life education consultant; b. Cleveland, Miss., Feb. 16, 1938; d. Henry Davis and Willie Mae (Caver) Hardy. B.S., George Williams Coll., 1960; M.A., Northeastern Ill. U., Chgo., 1972; M.Edn., Loyola U., Chgo., 1978. Child care worker Inst. Juvenile Research, Chgo., 1960-61; phys. educator Chgo. Bd. Edn., 1961-69; instr. George Williams Coll., Downers Grove, Ill., 1969-73; phys. educator Chgo. Bd. Edn., 1973-86, counselor, 1986—, workshop leader family life edn., 1983—. Chmn. Chgo. Pub. Sch. campaign United Negro Coll. Fund, Chgo., 1981, 82, chmn. profl. women's aux., 1983—; bd. dirs. Chgo. com. NAACP Legal Defense and Edn. Fund, 1980—; sec. bd. dirs. Treshan Youth Found., Chgo., 1977—; mem. Com. to Elect/Re-elect Roland Burris State Comptroller, 1978—, Com. to Elect Harold Washington Mayor Chgo., 1982-83. Named Outstanding Vol., Mid-Am. chpt. ARC, Chgo., 1976, Outstanding Vol., United Negro Coll. Fund, N.Y.C., 1982; recipient Image award Fred Hampton Found., 1979. Mem. AAHPER and Dance, Ill. Assn. Health, Phys. Edn. and Recreation (mem. exec. com. Chgo. dist.), Ill. Council Family Relations, Alpha Kappa Alpha. Avocations: community vol.; community fundraiser; travel. Home: 8300 S Peoria St Chicago IL 60620 Office: Sol R Crown Community Acad 2128 S St Louis St Chicago IL 60623

LEE, MORDECAI, state legislator, political scientist; b. Milw., Aug. 27, 1948; s. Jack Harold and Bernice (Kamesar) L.; m. Storm Garrison, Apr. 15, 1984; stepchildren—Benjamin, Alyssa, Alexandra. B.A., U. Wis., 1970, M.P.A., Syracuse U., 1972, Ph.D., 1975. Guest scholar Brookings Instn., Washington, 1972-74; legis. asst. to Congressman Henry Reuss, Washington, 1975; asst. prof. polit. sci. U. Wis.-Whitewater and Parkside, 1976; mem. Wis. Ho. Reps., 1977-82; mem. Wis. Senate, 1982—; adj. prof. govt. U. Wis.-Milw. Democrat. Jewish.

LEE, MYOUNG CHONG, neurologist, educator; b. Chunchou, Korea, July 27, 1940; came to U.S., 1964; m. Sung Bok Cho, Feb. 28, 1969; children: Jean Hee, Diana Kyn. MD, Yousei U., Seoul, Republic of Korea, 1964. Diplomate Am. Bd. Psychiatry and Neurology. Intern St. Francis Hosp., Pitts., 1964-65; resident Hartford (Conn.) Hosp., 1965; resident in neurology U. Minn. Hosp., Mpls., 1966-69; assoc. prof. medicine U. Minn., Mpls., 1976—. Fellow Am. Acad. Neurology, Am. Heart Assn. Home: 1200 Orono Oaks Dr Long Lake MN 55356 Office: U Minn Hosp Minneapolis MN 55455

LEE, MYUNG J., physician; b. Inchon, Republic of Korea, Apr. 10, 1943; came to U.S., 1972; s. Kang Min and Bong Ann (Song) L.; m. Jin Hee Kim, Feb. 19, 1972; children: John, Natalie, Najean. MD, Seoul (Korea) Nat. U., 1967. Diplomate Am. Bd. Internal Medicine, Am. Bd. Allergy and Immunology. Physician Biederman-Lee Allergy Clinic, Cin., 1978—. Served to capt. Air Force, 1968-71, Korea. Mem. AMA, Am. Acad. Allergy and Immunology. Office: Biederman-Lee Allergy Clinic 24 W Third St Cincinnati OH 45202

LEE, OSCAR, strategic planning executive; b. Tegucigalap, Honduras, Mar. 13, 1953; came to U.S., 1966; s. Oscar W. and Haydee (Chiu) L.; m. Rosa Wei-Chih Yuan, July 4, 1984. BS in Mgmt. Sci., Case Western Res. U., 1978; MBA, Baldwin-Wallace Coll., 1981. Programmer Gen. Electric Co., Cleve., 1976-79; asst. analyst Ohio Bell Co., Cleve., 1979-82; cons. internat. systems Alltel Corp., Hudson, Ohio, 1982-84; systems analyst Alltel Corp., Hudson, 1984-86, mgr. strategic planning, 1986—, product mgr. data services, 1987—; systems cons. Saudi Arabian Royal Commn., Yanbu, Saudi Arabia, 1982-84, sr. cons. Mobile Telephone Systems, Co., Kuwait, 1986. Chmn. social events Chinese Assn. Greater Cleve., 1985; active Cleve. Growth Assn.; mem. exec. council Baldwin-Wallace Coll. MBA Assn., Berea, Ohio. Mem. Am. Mgmt. Assn., Info. Group, Planning Forum, Orgn. Overseas Chinese, On-Leong Benevolent Assn. Avocations: photography, martial arts, fine arts. Home: 1583 E 36th St Cleveland OH 44114 Office: Alltel Corp 2000 Highland Rd Twinsburg OH 44087

LEE, RANDALL RAY, religious publishing executive, assistant pastor; b. Wisconsin Rapids, Wis., Jan. 13, 1956; s. Raymond M. and Marilyn L. (Boycks) L. BA in Religion with honors, Valparaiso U., 1978; M Div., Christ Sem.-Seminex, 1982, STM, 1983; ThM, Luth. Sch. Theology at Chgo., 1985. Asst. pastor Bethel Luth. Ch., St. Louis, 1982-83; asst. dir. devel. Christ Sem.-Seminex, Chgo., 1983-84; asst. pastor The Ch. of St. Luke, Chgo., 1984—; editor Luth. Perspective, Chgo., 1985—; chief exec. officer Evang. Luths. in Mission, Chgo., 1985—; dir. communications Assn. Evang. Luth. Chs., Chgo., 1984—. Mem. Associated Ch. Press. Republican. Avocations: gourmet cooking, organ, travel. Office: Evang Luths in Mission PO Box 578555 Chicago IL 60657-8555

LEE, RICHARD FRANK, general and home building contracting company executive; b. Richland Center, Wis., Nov. 19, 1941; s. Clarence Arlington and Vivian Clare (Postel) L.; m. Judith Ann Jordan, July 9, 1966; children: Jeffrey Alan, Jennifer Ann. BS, Wis. State U., 1964. Lic. fire instr. 1, Wis. Mgr., Janeff Credit Corp., Madison, Wis., 1965-66; with A.B.C. Builders, Madison, 1966—, owner, pres., 1976—. Mem. Fitchburg (Wis.) Vol. Fire Dept., 1970-83. Served with Wis. Air N.G., 1964-70. Mem. Builders Assn., Nat. Ski Patrol. Lutheran. Lodges: Optimists, Masons, Scottish Rite, Shriners. Home: 2762 Marledge St Madison WI 53711 Office: 6213 Monona Dr Madison WI 53716

LEE, ROBERT, manufacturing company executive; b. Inchon, Korea, Dec. 4, 1949; s. Catherine Chung; m. Sandra Lee Schultz, June 10, 1972; children: Travis, Shana. BA in Indsl. Design, U. Ill., Chgo., 1973; MBA, U. So. Miss., 1976. Treasury rep. Westinghouse Electric Corp., Chgo., 1976-77; sr. mfg. devel. engr. Baxter Travenol Labs. Inc., Round Lake, Ill., 1977-81; dir. mfg. Renal Systems Inc., Mpls., 1981-85, Scimed Life System Inc., Mpls., 1985-86; program mgr. Endotronics Inc., Coon Rapids, Minn., 1986—. Inventor microporous hollow fiber membrane assembly, 1982, separation device, 1983. Served to capt. USAR. Office: Endotronics Inc 8500 Evergreen Blvd Coon Rapids MN 55433

LEE, ROBERT HUGH, business consultant, educator; b. Honolulu, Jan. 3, 1950; s. Hugh Sebastian and Margaret Carol (Bennett) L.; m. Lois Ann Brown, Jan. 31, 1981. BA in Communications, Coll. St. Francis, 1972; MBA, No. Ill. U., 1977. Pres., owner Robert Hugh Lee Pub., Lockport, Ill., 1973-76; pres. Robert Hugh Lee, MBA and Assocs., DeKalb, Ill., 1978—; lectr., tchr. bus. strategy, mktg. and fin. at several univs. in Midwest. Dem. candidate Clk. of Cir. Ct., McLean County, Ill., 1980, candidate for Treas. DeKalb County, Ill., 1986; Dem. ward capt. cen. com., Blackhawk County, Iowa, 1982-85. Avocations: chess, reading, dog tng., carpentry. Home: 1512 Somonauk Rd #79 DeKalb IL 60115 Office: PO Box 801 DeKalb IL 60115

LEE, ROBERT WAYNE, research facility administrator; b. Artesia, N.Mex., May 30, 1952; s. Robert E. and Vivian A. (Blackwelder) L.; m. Kay Kountz, Mar. 29, 1976; 1 child, Kelsey Elizabeth. BS, N.Mex. State U., 1975; MS, Tex. Tech. U., 1976; PhD, N.Mex. State U., 1980. Asst. prof. Kans. State U., Garden City, 1981-84; feedlot nutritionist Purina Mills, Inc., St. Louis, 1984-85; dir. research Brookover Ranch Research Ctr., Garden City, 1986—. Mem. Am. Soc. Animal Sci., Am. Registry Profl. Animal Scientists, Am. Meat Sci. Assn., Plains Nutrition Council, Kans. Livestock Assn. Republican. Methodist. Avocations: hunting, fishing, racquetball. Home: 3675 Blutstem Rd Garden City KS 67846 Office: Brookover Ranch Research Ctr Box 917 Garden City KS 67846

LEE, SHIU TAO, statistician; b. Taichung, Taiwan, Mar. 19, 1940; came to U.S. 1967, naturalized 1975; d. Su and Yei Nu (Liu) Hung; m. Chun-Cheng Lee, Jan. 8, 1967; children: Eming R., Cincy H. BA, Taiwan Normal U., 1965; M in Stats., N.C. State U.-Raleigh, 1970, postgrad. 1971-72. Tchr. Taichung, Taiwan, 1958-61; tchr. high sch. English, Taipei, Taiwan, 1965-66; statis. analyst N.C. State Govt., Raleigh, 1973-74; programmer/analyst Power & Light Co., Raleigh, 1974-75; scientist N.C. Power & Light Co., Raleigh, 1975-76; statistician NIOSH, Cin., 1976—; cons. in field. Contbr. articles to profl. jours. Recipient Cash award NIOSH, 1985. Mem. AAAS, Am. Statis. Assn., Internat. Environ. Protection Assn. (chairperson U.S. chpt. occupational safety and health group 1987), Taiwanese Women's Club (pres. 1984-85). Home: 10285 Gentlewind Dr Cincinnati OH 45242 Office: Nat Inst Occupational Safety and Health 4676 Columbia Pkwy Cincinnati OH 45226

LEE, SIU-LEUNG, chemist; b. Hong Kong, Nov. 17, 1943; s. Kun-Hor and Suet-Chun (Loo) L.; m. Theresa S. Wai, Oct. 1, 1973; children: Joan Wai-Chung, Adrienne Wai-Wah. BS, Chinese U. Hong Kong, 1969; PhD, Purdue U., 1974; post doctoral, Yale U., 1974-75. Staff scientist Yale U., New Haven, Conn., 1975-77; asst. prof. Tex. A&M U., Coll. Station, 1977-82; sr. research scientist Corning (N.Y.) Glass Works, 1982-84, Battelle Meml. Inst., Columbus, Ohio, 1984—. Contbr. articles to profl. jours.; patentee in field. Mem. Am. Chem. Soc., Am. Assn. Advancement Sci., Rho Chi, Phi Lambda Upsilon. Home: 3959 Ritamarie Dr Columbus OH 43220 Office: Battelle Meml Inst 505 King Ave Columbus OH 43201

LEE, SOO K., pediatrician; b. Korea, Mar. 1, 1940; s. Kun D. and Kae S. (Kim) L.; m. Seung Ja Seo, June 9, 1966; children: Greg, Young, Janet. MD, Kyungpook Nat. U., 1965; PhD, Columbia Pacific U., 1985. Intern, resident in pediatrics Michael Reese Hosp., Chgo., 1969-72; fellow in pediatric nephrology LaRabida Hosp.- U. Chgo., 1972-74; attending pediatric physician Cook County Hosp., Chgo., 1974-76; practice medicine, specializing in pediatrics, Joliet, Ill., 1976—; instr. pediatrics U. Ill., 1974-76. Med. cons. Parent Power, 1976-80. Served to capt. M.C., Korean Army, 1966-69. Mem. Am. Acad. Pediatrics, AMA. Roman Catholic. Office: 210 N Hammes Ave Joliet IL 60435

LEE, STEVEN, dentist; b. Jamaica, N.Y., Jan. 5, 1950; s. Wee Lim and Bo Yuk (Luke) L.; m. Linda Sue Petersen, Apr. 15, 1980: children: Joey Michele, Michael Taylor. AA, Normandale Jr. Coll., 1970; BS, U. Minn., 1975, DDS, 1977. Clin. dir., mem. planning com. Health Etcetera, Mpls., 1980—; gen. practice dentistry W. St. Paul, 1980—; mem. dental quality assurance com. Health Consortium, Mpls., 1986—. Coach gymnastics Mini-Hops, Bloomington (Minn.) Gymnastics, Lincoln High Sch., Kennedy High Sch., 1968-77, White Bear High Sch., White Bear Lake, Minn., 1981-86. Served to lt. USN, 1977-80. Recipient coaching awards, Minn. State High Sch. League, 1981-86; named one of Outstanding Young Men of Am., 1985. Mem. ADA, Minn. Dental Assn., Minn. Therapeutic Massage Network (therapist 1986—), Minn. Coaches Assn., Sci. Mus. of Minn. Assn., Soc. for Creative Anachronism. Baptist. Avocations: aikido, gymnastics, racquetball, fishing, ballroom dancing. Office: Health Etcetera 1518 E Lake St Minneapolis MN 55407

LEE, STEVEN GIN-KWANG, chemist; b. San Francisco, Jan. 14, 1956; s. Henry Hing and Shui Wan (Yee) L.; m. Vivian Wang, Jan. 20, 1984. BS, U. Calif., Berkeley, 1977; MS, U. Calif., Riverside, 1981, PhD, 1983. Postdoctoral research assoc. N.C. State U., Raleigh, 1984; sr. chemist Mobay Corp., Kansas City, Mo., 1984—. Mem. Am. Chem. Soc., Agrochems. div. Am. Chem. Soc., Sigma Xi. Club: Asian (Kansas City). Avocations: gardening, financial investments, travelling. Home: 16712 E 51st St Ct Independence MO 64055 Office: Mobay Corp Div Agrl Chemistry PO Box 4913 Hawthorn Rd Kansas City MO 64120

LEE, TERRANCE RILEY, educator; b. Jamestown, N.D., June 16, 1940; s. Riley Ever and Ina Lois (Didier) L. B.A., St. Cloud State U., 1966; M.A.T. in Chemistry, U. Wis., 1973. Tchr. Cromwell Wright Pub. Sch., Cromwell, Wis., 1967-68, Owen Pub. Schs., Wis., 1968-69, Winter Pub. Schs., Wis., 1969—. Democrat. Lodges: Masons, Shriners. Avocations: folk music; stamps. Home: Rural Route 1 Box 44 Winter WI 54896

LEE, THOMAS EDWARD, accountant, financial consultant; b. Milw., July 17, 1954; s. James Elmer and Katlyn Janet (Cafmeyer) L. BSBA, St. Louis U., 1976; postgrad., Washington U., St. Louis, 1986—. Staff acct. Nolan & Wolff, St. Louis, 1976-77, Bohlmann & Co., St. Louis, 1977-79; sr. internal auditor Unidynamics Corp., St. Louis, 1979-84; comptroller, data processing mgr. Wachter Constrn. Co., St. Louis, 1984-85; pvt. practice acctg., income tax, mgmt. cons., and fin. analysis St. Louis, 1984—. Recipient Consulting award U.S. Small Bus. Adminstrn. St. Louis Dist., 1976, Award for Excellence Chgo. Tile Inst., 1975. Mem. U.S. Amateur Hockey Assn. (instr. 1978-83), Alpha Delta Gamma (pres. 1978-83, nat. steward 1975, nat. bd. dirs. 1975-76, nat. rep. 1976, Benjamin Aranda award 1976), Gateway Alumni Assn. (pres. 1978-83), Data Processing Mgmt. Assn. (mem. student chpt. Washington U.), Assn. for Systems Mgmts. (Hon. Mention in Papers Competition 1987), Alpha Kappa Psi. Republican. Roman Catholic. Avocations: sports, ice hockey, snow skiing, golf, outdoors. Address: 331 George Ave PO Box 26631 Kirkwood MO 63122

LEE, TIEN SHUEY, chemical firm executive; b. Yunnan, China, Nov. 11, 1925; came to U.S., 1954; s. Chien and In-Ho (Wang) L.; m. Laura Teng, Aug. 31, 1963; children: Everett, Lawrence. BS, Chung-Cheng Inst. Tech., China, 1948; MA, U. Oregon, 1956; PhD, Purdue U., 1963. Instr., asst. prof. Chung-Cheng Inst. Tech., Republic of China, 1948-54; research assoc. Harshaw Chem. Co., Cleve., 1963-66; sr. staff chemist Union Carbide Corp., Cleve., 1966-74; mgr. research and devel. Gould, Inc., Rolling Meadows, Ill., 1976-79; task mgr. Argonne (Ill.) Nat. Lab., 1979-85; pres. Sci. Resources, Inc., Palatine, Ill., 1985—. Contbr. articles to profl. jours.; patentee in field. Mem. Electrochem. Soc. (chmn. Cleve. sect. 1972, George Heise medal 1973),Nat. Assn. Corrosion Engrs., Am. Chem. Soc., Sigma Xi, Phi Lambda Epsilon. Avocations: reading, music, travel. Office: Sci Resources Inc 1058 Whytecliffe Rd Palatine IL 60067

LEE, WAYNE CYRIL, author; b. Lamar, Nebr., July 2, 1917; s. David Elmer and Rosa Belle (Deselms) L.; m. Pearl May Sheldon, Mar. 17, 1948; children—Wayne Sheldon, Charles Lester. Rural mail carrier, Lamar, 1951-77; instr. Writer's Digest Sch., 1976—; author non-fiction: Scotty Philip, the Man Who Saved the Buffalo, 1975; Trails of the Smoky Hill, 1980; author fiction: Shadow of the Gun, 1981; Guns at Genesis, 1981; Putnam's Ranch War, 1982; The Violent Trail, 1984; War at Nugget Creek, 1985; Massacre Creek, 1985; The Waiting Gun, 1986; Hawks of Autumn, 1986; many others. Served with Signal Corps, U.S. Army, 1945. Named Historian of Year, High Plains Preservation of History Commn., 1981. Mem. Western Writers Am. (pres. 1970-71), Nebr. Writers Guild (pres. 1974-76), Nebr. State Hist. Soc. Found. (dir. 1975—). Republican. Mem. Christian Ch. Club: Toastmasters (pres. 1964-65, 72-73) (Imperial, Nebr.). Home and Office: Lamar NE 69035

LEE, WILLIAM CHARLES, federal judge; b. Fort Wayne, Ind., Feb. 2, 1938; s. Russell and Catherine (Zwick) L.; m. Judith Anne Bash, Sept. 19, 1959; children—Catherine L., Mark R., Richard R. A.B., Yale U., 1959; J.D., U. Chgo., 1962. Bar: Ind. 1962. Ptnr., Parry, Krueckeberg & Lee, Fort Wayne, 1964-70; dep. pros. atty. Allen County, Fort Wayne, 1963-69, chief dep., 1967-69; U.S. atty. No. Dist. Ind., Fort Wayne, 1970-73; ptnr. Hunt, Suedhoff, Borror, Eilbacher & Lee, Fort Wayne, 1973-81; U.S. Dist. judge No. Dist. Ind., Fort Wayne, 1981—; instr. Nat. Inst. Trial Advocacy. Co-chmn. Fort Wayne Fine Arts Operating Fund Drive, 1978; past bd. dirs., v.p. Fort Wayne Philharm. Orch., Fort Wayne Fine Arts Found., Hospice of Fort Wayne, Inc.; past bd. dirs. Fort Wayne Civic Theatre, Neighbors; past bd. dirs., pres. Legal Aid of Fort Wayne, Inc.; past mem. Trinity English Lutheran Ch. Council; trustee Fort Wayne Community Schs., 1978-81, pres., 1980-81; trustee Fort Wayne Mus. Art, 1984—. Griffin scholar, 1955-59; Weymouth Kirkland scholar, 1959-62. Fellow Am. Coll. Trial Lawyers, Ind. Bar Found.; mem. ABA, Allen County Bar Assn., Ind. State Bar Assn., Fed. Bar Assn., Seventh Cir. Bar Assn. Republican. Lutheran. Office: US Dist Ct 243 Fed Bldg 1300 S Harrison St Fort Wayne IN 46802 *

LEE, WILLIAM JOHNSON, lawyer; b. Oneida, Tenn., Jan. 13, 1924; s. William J. and Ara (Anderson) L.; student Akron U., 1941-43, Denison U., 1943-44, Harvard U., 1944-45; J.D., Ohio State U., 1948. Bar: Ohio 1948, Fla. 1962. Research asst. Ohio State U. Law Sch., 1948-49; asst. dir. Ohio Dept. Liquor Control, chief purchases, 1956-57, atty. examiner, 1951-53, asst. state permit chief, 1953-55, state permit chief, 1955-56; asst. counsel, staff Hupp Corp., 1957-58; spl. counsel City Attys. Office Ft. Lauderdale (Fla.), 1963-65; asst. atty. gen. Office Atty. Gen., State of Ohio, 1966-70; adminstr. State Med. Bd. Ohio, Columbus, 1970-85, also mem. Federated State Bd.'s Nat. Commn. for Evaluation of Fgn. Med. Schs., 1981-83; Mem. Flex 1/Flex 2 Transitional Task Force, 1983-84; pvt. practice law, Ft. Lauderdale, 1965-66; acting municipal judge, Ravenna, Ohio, 1960; instr. Coll. Bus. Adminstrn., Kent State U., 1961-62. Mem. pastoral relations com. Epworth United Meth. Ch., 1976; chmn. legal aid com. Portage County, Ohio, 1960; troop awards chmn. Boy Scouts Am., 1965; mem. ch. bd. Melrose Park (Fla.) Meth. Ch., 1966. Mem. Am. Legion, Fla., Columbus, Akron, Broward County (Fla.) bar assns., Delta Theta Phi, Phi Kappa Tau, Pi Kappa Delta. Served with USAAF, 1943-46. Editorial bd. Ohio State Law Jour., 1947-48; also articles. Home: 4893 Brittany Ct W Columbus OH 43229

LEE, YONG H., plastic surgeon; b. Seoul, Republic of Korea, July 10, 1936; came to U.S., 1970; s. Jong Young and Milliam (Lim) L.; m. Jung Kill Kim, June 15, 1965; children: Samuel S., Esther S., Helen E. BS in Engring., Yonsei U., Seoul, 1957; MD, Yonsei U., 1961. Intern, then resident Won Ju Union Christian Hosp., Republic of Korea, 1961-66; intern Trumbull Meml. Hosp., Warren, Ohio, 1970-71; resident in surgery Union Meml. Hosp., Balt., 1971-72, The Grace Hosp., Detroit, 1972-74; resident in plastic surgery Allentown (Pa.) Hosp. Assn., 1974-76; attending physician Good Samaritan Hosp., N.Y.C., 1976-77, Trumbull Meml. Hosp., Warren, 1977—. Served to maj. Rep. Korea Army. Fellow Am. Coll. Surgeons.; mem. Am. Soc. Plastic and Reconstructive Surgeons, Ohio Valley Plastic and Reconstructive Surgeons, Trumbull County Med. Soc., Am. Assn. Hand Surgeons. Methodist. Avocations: photography, tennis. Home: 8516 Hunters Trail Warren OH 44484 Office: 1924 E Market St Warren OH 44484

LEEHEY, PETER JOHN, lawyer; b. Iowa City, Mar. 9, 1959; s. Paul J. and Donna L. (Munson) L.; m. C. Mary Copper, June 26, 1982. AA, Ellsworth Community Coll., 1979; B Gen. Studies, U. Iowa, 1981, JD, 1984. Assoc. Lynch, Lynch & Fenchel, Algona, Iowa, 1984-85, Shelton Law Firm, Chariton, Iowa, 1985—; asst. county atty. Lucas County, Chariton, 1985—. Mem. ABA, Iowa State Bar Assn. (young lawyers sect. com. on alternatives to resolving disputes 1986—, mock trial com. 1987—), Lucas County Bar Assn., Assn. Trial Lawyers Am., Assn. Trial Lawyers Iowa (membership com. 1985—), Algona Jaycees (pres. 1985). Roman Catholic. Lodge: Kiwanis (bd. dirs. Chariton 1987—). Avocations: running, golf, rugby. Home: 724 N Grand Chariton IA 50049 Office: Shelton Law Firm 1920 Court Chariton IA 50049

LEENHOUTS, LILLIAN SCOTT, architect; b. Milw., June 2, 1911; d. Ronald and Viola May (Zimmerman) Scott; m. Willis Cornelius Leenhouts, July 21, 1943; 1 child, Robin. BArch, U. Mich., 1936. Registered profl. architect, Wis., Ill. Draftsman Harry Bogner/Architect, Milw., 1936-42, various cos., various locations, 1942-45; prodn. illustrator Fairchild Aircraft, Hagerstown, Md., 1945; ptnr., architect W.&L. Leenhouts, Architects, Milw., 1945—; lectr. in field. Mem. Mayor's Beautification Com. Milw. 1965; organizer Architects River Com., Milw., 1968; mem. pres. adv. bd. Alverno Coll., Milw., 1977-81. Fellow AIA, Soc. Women Engrs.; mem. Profl. Dimensions (Sacajawea award 1986), Theosophical Soc. Milw. (pres. 1980). Avocations: bicycling, photography. Home: 1204 E Concordia Ave Milwaukee WI 53212 Office: 3332 N Dousman St Milwaukee WI 53212

LEESON, JANET CAROLINE TOLLEFSON, cake specialties company executive; b. L'Anse, Mich., May 23, 1933; d. Harold Arnold and Sylvia Aino (Makikangas) Tollefson; student Prairie State Coll., 1970-76; master decorator degree Wilton Sch. Cake Decorating, 1974; grad. Cosmopolitan Sch. Bus., 1980; m. Raymond Harry Leeson, May 20, 1961; 1 son, Barry Raymond; children by previous marriage—Warren Scott, Debra Delores. Mgr., Peak Service Cleaners, Chgo., 1959; co-owner Ra-Ja-Lee TV, Harvey, Ill., 1961-66; founder and head fgn. trade dept. Wilton Enterprises, Inc., Chgo., 1969-75; tchr. cake decorating J.C. Penney Co., Matteson, Ill., 1975; office mgr. Pat Carpenter Assocs., Highland, Ind., 1975; pres. Leeson's Party Cakes, Inc., cake supplies and cake sculpture, Tinley Park, Ill., 1975—; lectr. and demonstrator cake sculpture and decorating; lectr. small bus. and govt. Sec., Luth. Ch. Women; active worker Boy Scouts Am. and Girl Scouts

U.S.A., 1957-63; bd. dirs. Whittier PTA, 1962-70; active Bremen Twp. Republican party. Recipient numerous awards for cake sculpture and decorating, 1970—. Mem. Internat. Cake Exploration Soc. (charter, Outstanding Mem. Ill. 1984), Retail Bakers Am., Chgo. Area Retail Bakers Assn. (1st pl. in regional midwest wedding cake competition 1978, 80, 1st pl. nat. 1982, others), Am. Bus. Women's Assn. (chpt. publicity chmn., hospitality chmn. 1982-83, named Woman of Yr. 1986), Ingalls Meml. Hosp. Aux, Lupus Found. Am. Lutheran. Home: 6713 W 163d Pl Tinley Park IL 60477 Office: Leeson's Party Cakes Inc 6713 W 163d Pl Tinley Park IL 60477

LEFEVER, MAXINE LANE, educator, consultant; b. Elmhurst, Ill., May 30, 1931; d. Thomas Clinton Lane and Georgia Marie (Hampton) L.; m. Orville Joseph Lefever, Aug. 18, 1951 (div.). Student Ill. Wesleyan U., 1949-51; BA, Western State Coll., 1958; MS, Purdue U., 1964, postgrad., 1965. Elem. sch. tchr. Leaf River (Ill.) Pub. Schs., 1953-54, Mancos (Colo.) Pub. Schs., 1954-56; elem./jr. high sch. tchr. Cortez (Colo.) Pub. Schs., 1956-60; instr. bands, Purdue U., Lafayette, Ind., 1965-79, asst. prof., 1980—; cons. numerous festivals and contests; pres. music/ednl. travel corp., 16 years. Hon. mem. U.S. Navy Band; recipient citation of excellence Nat. Band Assn.; Star of Order of Merit, J.P. Sousa Found. Mem. Ind. Music Educators Assn., Music Educators Nat. Conf., Nat. Band Assn. (v.p., exec. sec.), Coll. Band Dirs. Nat. Assn., Percussion Arts Soc., John Philip Sousa Found.(v.p.,exec. sec.), Big Ten Band Dirs. Assn., Alpha Lambda Delta, Delta Omicron, Tau Beta Sigma, Kappa Kappa Psi (hon.), Phi Sigma Kappa (hon.). Contbr. articles to profl. jour.; composer percussion ensembles. Home: PO Box 2454 2924 Wilshire St West Lafayette IN 47906 Office: Purdue Univ Bands West Lafayette IN 47907

LEFEVRE, CAROL BAUMANN, psychologist; b. Pierron, Ill., Nov. 26, 1924; d. Berhard Robert and Eunice Leone Hoyt (Heston) Baumann; m. Perry Deyo LeFevre, Sept. 14, 1946; children: Susan LeFevre Hook, Judith Ann LeFevre-Levy, Peter Gerret. AA, Stephens Coll., 1944; MA in Sociology, U. Chgo., 1948, MST, 1965, PhD in Human Devel., 1971. Registered psychologist, Ill. Tchr. Chgo. Theol. Sem. Nursery Sch., 1962-63, U. Chgo., Lab. Sch., 1965-66; asst. prof. psychology St. Xavier Coll., Chgo., 1970-74, assoc. prof., 1974-86, acting chmn. dept. psychology, 1970-71, chmn. dept. psychology, 1971-77, asst. dir. Inst. Family Studies, 1973-82, dir., 1982-85; intern in clin. psychology with Adlerian pvt. practitioner, Chgo., 1973-75; pvt. practice clin. psychology, Chgo., 1975—; mem. staff Logos Inst. Chgo. Theol. Sem., 1973-76; speaker in field. Author, researcher on subjects including returning women grad. students' changing self-conceptions, women's roles, inner city children's perceptions of sch., aging and religion. Pub. Health Service tng. grantee NIMH, 1969. Mem. Am. Psychol. Assn., Ill. Psychol. Assn., Chgo. Psychol. Assn., Gerontol. Soc., N.Am. Soc. Adlerian Psychology, Phi Beta Kappa. Mem. United Ch. of Christ. Home: 1376 E 58th St Chicago IL 60637 Office: 400 Ravinia Pl Orland Park IL 60462

LEFEVRE, DONALD KEITH, electrical engineer; b. Casper, Wyo., Feb. 12, 1956; s. Lorin Durward and Margery Phyllis (Green) L.; m. Susan Lesley Nichols, May 31, 1975; children: Justin, Michelle, Mark, Kristen, Gregory. BS in Physics, BSEE, S.D. Sch. Mines and Technology, 1978; MSEE, U. Utah, 1985. Sr. engr. Sperry Def. Systems, Salt Lake City, 1978-84; chief engr. Anderson Scientific, Rapid City, S.D., 1984-86; assoc. prof. elec. engring. S.D. Sch. Mines and Technology, Rapid City, 1986—; pres. Wesha Technologies, Inc., Rapid City, 1987—. Patentee in field. Mem. bd. advisors Black Hills Bus. Innovation Ctr., Rapid City, 1986—. Mem. IEEE, Soc. Physics Students (pres. 1977), Eta Kappa Nu, Tau Beta Pi, Sigma Pi Sigma, Pi Mu Epsilon. Republican. Roman Catholic. Lodge: KC. Home: 4911 S Canyon Rd Rapid City SD 57702 Office: Wesha Technologies Inc Box 1688 3824 Jet Dr Rapid City SD 57709

LEFEVRE, HARVARD STANLEY, engineering company executive; b. Stephenson, Mich., Oct. 3, 1920; s. Louis and Delia (Gardner) L.; m. Mary Lee Moore, Apr. 10, 1943; children—Linda, Terese, Stephen. Student U.S. Army Air Force Tech. Sch., 1943, San Angelo Army Air Field Bombardier Sch., 1943, Sch. Bus. Adminstrn., U. Mich., 1952; exec. tng. Alexander Hamilton Inst., 1955. With King Engring. Corp., Ann Arbor, Mich., 1941—, exec. v.p., 1956-67, pres., 1967—, acting chmn. bd., 1970-76, chmn. bd., 1976—, treas., 1970—, also dir. Served with USAAF, 1942-46. Mem. Engring. Soc. Detroit, Soc. Mfg. Engrs., Am. Mgmt. Assn., Ann Arbor Mfrs. Assn., Ann Arbor C. of C. (dir. 1976—), Ann Arbor Personnel Assn. Roman Catholic. Patentee gas dispersoid separator. Home: 801 Mount Pleasant St Ann Arbor MI 48103 Office: King Engring Corp 3201 S State St Ann Arbor MI 48106

LEFF, ROBERT MARK, psychologist; b. N.Y.C., Apr. 26, 1941; s. Samuel and Sally (Flank) L. BA, NYU, 1962; MA, U. Pa., 1964, PhD, 1967. Lic. psychologist, Wis. Psychology intern Mass. Mental Health Ctr., Boston, 1966-67; clin. psychologist Wis. Children's Treatment Ctr., Madison, 1967-72; chief psychologist Wis. Children's Treatment Ctr., Madison, 1972-73; clin. instr. dept. psychiatry U. Wis., Madison, 1968-77; assoc. dir. research Mendota Mental Health Ctr., Madison, 1973-76, Tng. Adolescent for Community Living unit chief, 1976—. Editor CTC Jour. 1969-72, CAC Jour. 1973-74, Mendota Memo Instl. Newsletters, 1986—; producer, editor (film) Home and Community Treatment-Activating Family Change, 1976; contbr. articles to profl. jours. Avocations: art, aviation, fishing. Office: Mendota Mental Health Inst 301 Troy Dr Madison WI 53704

LEFKIADES, MICHAEL, business owner; b. Thessaloniki, Greece, Feb. 9, 1931; came to U.S., 1952; s. Thrasivoulos and Eleni (Arzoglou) L.; m. Dorothy Jean Kuligowski, Aug. 16, 1952; children: Gary Alan, Thomas Michael. BA, Anatolia Coll., Thessaloniki, 1950. Prin. Meditterranean Systems Inc., Saginaw, Mich., 1964—. Mem. adv. council to U.S. Senate for Small Bus. Affairs, Washington, 1980—; del. White House Confernce on Small Bus., Washington, 1986. Recipient Outstanding Achievement for Small Bus. Affairs award White House, 1986. Mem. Saginaw C. of C., Am.-Hellenic Ednl. Progressive Assn. (pres. Saginaw Valley chpt. #216). Democrat. Greek Orthodox. Club: Bay City Country. Home: 2942 Thunderbird Dr Bay City MI 48706 Office: 1841 N Michigan Ave Saginaw MI 48602

LEFKOVITZ, THOMAS, lighting company treasurer; b. Bklyn., Nov. 26, 1944; s. Sidney and Helen (Aaron) L.; m. Lisa Sharon Sue Valenti, Jan. 26, 1969; children: Jeffrey Thomas, Keili Elizabeth. BS, Ohio State U., 1966; MBA, U. Mo., 1969. Sec., treas. Midwest Chandelier Co., Kansas City, Kans., 1969—. Served with USMC, 1966-70. Republican. Jewish. Office: Midwest Chandelier Co 100 Funston Rd Kansas City KS 66115

LEFOND, DENNIS CHARLES, university administrator, marketing specialist; b. Cleve., Apr. 13, 1948; s. Stanley John and Anne (Newman) L.; m. W. Anne McKee, Dec. 27, 1975; children: Susan Anne, Elizabeth Anne. BA, Wittenberg U., 1970; MA, Case Western Res. U., 1975, PhD, 1979; cert., Gestalt Inst. Cleve., 1976. Asst. dir. housing Eastern Mich. U., Ypsilanti, 1980-83, lectr. dept. leadership and counseling, 1984—, exec. mgr. residence halls, 1983-85, dir. mktg. research, 1985—; mem. mktg. coms. Eastern Mich. U.; asst. dir. Upward Bound Program, Baldwin Wallace Coll., Berea, Ohio, 1975-76, area coordinator, 1976-79, asst. dean of students, 1979. Mem. Am. Mktg. Assn., Direct Mktg.Assn., Market Research Assn. Club: Toastmasters (pres. Huron Valley chpt. 1986). Avocations: trathlete, jogging. Home: 4860 Woodside Ypsilanti MI 48197 Office: Eastern Mich U Ypsilanti MI 48197

LEFTON, JEFF SCOTT, economic development specialist; b. St. Louis, May 6, 1957; s. Robert Eugene and Marlene Rea (Shanfeld) L. BS in Psychology magna cum laude, Tufts U., 1979; MBA in Fin., Washington U., St. Louis, 1985. Pres. Jeff Lefton Magical Entertainment, St. Louis, 1969—; asst. dir. fin. services St. Louis County Econ. Council, 1984—. Mem. entrepeneurship task force Confluence St. Louis, 1985; bldg. rep. De Boliviere Pl. Condominium Assn., St. Louis, 1986. Mem. Inventors Assn. St. Louis (bd. dirs. 1985—, treas. 1986—), Active Core Execs., Regional Commerce Growth Assn. (resource action com. 1986—). Avocations: hockey, tennis, baseball, listening to jazz. Office: PO Box 11521 Saint Louis MO 63105 Office: St Louis County Econ Council 130 S Bemiston Suite 800 Saint Louis MO 63105

LEGEL, MICHAEL L., financial manager; b. Denver, Colo., Mar. 7, 1957; s. Herman L. and Ruth K. (Peterson) L.; m. Margaret Ann Raycraft, Mar. 1, 1980. Student, Rock Valley Jr. Coll., 1975-77, U. Ariz., 1977-78; BS in Acctg., Ill. State U., 1979; postgrad., Northwestern U., 1985—. CPA, Ill. Acct. Coopers & Lybrand, Chgo., 1979-81; auditor Mid Con Corp., Lombard, Ill., 1981-85, fin. mgr., 1985—. Mem. Am. Inst. CPA's, Ill. CPA Soc., Inst. Internal Auditors. Roman Catholic. Lodge: Moose. Home: 1440 Thornwood Dr Downers Grove IL 60516 Office: Mid Con Corp 791 E 22d St Lombard IL 60148

LEGG, CALEB NORRIS, training developer, self instructional teacher; b. Indpls., May 26, 1953; s. Frank Edward and Minnie Alve (Wright) L.; m. Kathryn Ann Schranz, Oct. 4, 1982. BS in Indsl. Mgmt., Purdue U., 1972; BS in Labor Studies, Ind. U., 1986. Service rep. Ind. Bell, Indpls., 1976-78, sales mgr., 1978-82, staff assoc., 1982—. Mem. Inco Choir, Indpls., 1985; mem. communications com. Pan Am. Games, Indpls., 1986. Mem. Minorities in Engring., Ptnrs. 2000, Old Northside Inc. (v.p. 1986—). Roman Catholic. Club: Toastmasters Internat. (local pres. 1984-85). Avocations: photography, architectural restorations, traveling.

LEGG, LOUIS EDWARD, JR., lumber company executive; b. Coldwater, Mich., Jan. 21, 1928; s. Louis Edward and Dorothy A. (Wood) L.; m. Joan Mary Donkin, June 21, 1953; children: Louis III, Thomas C. BS, Mich. State U., 1950. Chmn. bd. Lansing Lumber Co., Holt, Mich., 1952—, Marion (Ind.) Lumber Co., 1968—, Legg Lumber, Coldwater, 1972—, Mfg. Homes, Inc., Marshall, Mich., 1972—, Battle Creek (Mich.) Lumber, 1985—, Allegan (Mich.) Lumber Co., 1982—; dir. Mfg. Bank Lansing, 1967—; trustee workmen's compensation fund Lumber & Bldg., Detroit, 1979—. Dir. Edward Sparrow Hosp., Lansing, 1967—; pres. Lansing YMCA, 1968; trustee Thoman Found., Lansing, 1968; chmn. State Bldg. Commn., 1970-82. Mem. Mich. State C. of C. (bd. dirs. 1985-90). Republican. Episcopalian. Club: Lansing Country (Mich.). Lodge: Rotary (pres. Lansing chpt. 1978-79). Office: Lansing Lumber Co 4000 E Holt Rd Holt MI 48842

LEGGETT, ROBERTA JEAN (BOBBI LEGGETT), association executive; b. Kankakee, Ill., Nov. 30, 1926; d. Clyde H. and Sybil D. (Billings) Karns; m. George T. Leggett, Aug. 25, 1956. Sec. Cardov div. Chemetron Corp., Chgo., 1951-60; sec., asst. mgr. Ravisloe Country Club, Homewood, Ill., 1961-65; sec. Nationwide Paper Co., Chgo., 1966-68; exec. dir. Am. Bd. Oral and Maxillofacial Surgery, Chgo., 1969—. Mem. Chgo. Soc. Assn. Execs., Conf. Med. Soc. Execs. of Greater Chgo., Profl. Secs. Internat. Methodist. Office: 211 E Chicago Ave Suite 836 Chicago IL 60611

LEGGITT, DOROTHY, educator; b. Oblong, Ill., Feb. 19, 1903; d. Clarence C. and Louise Frances (Muchmore) L. Diploma, Eastern Ill. State U., 1923, LHD (hon.), 1977; PhB, U. Chgo., 1930, MA, 1933, postgrad., intermittently, 1937-62. Tchr. rural schs., Jasper & Crawford Counties, Ill., 1920-22; tchr. high sch., Glen Ellyn, Ill., 1923-35; lectr., prof. No. Ill. State U., DeKalb, 1936-37; tchr. social studies, counselor Clayton (Mo.) pub. schs., 1937-52; tchr. Decatur (Ill.) pub. schs., 1952-54, Park Ridge (Ill.) pub. schs., 1954-61; reading specialist Joliet (Ill.) Jr. Coll., 1961-62, Niles West High Sch., Skokie, Ill., 1962-63; reading cons. Kenosha High Sch., Kenosha, Wis., 1963-65; head study skills dept. Palm Beach (Fla.) Jr. Coll., 1965-73, prof. emeritus, 1973—; summer lectr. various colls. and univs.; field rep. grad. edn. and social sci. depts. U. Chgo. Author: Basic Study Skills and Workbook, 1942; contbr. articles to profl. jours. Mem. found. bd. Eastern Ill. U. Recipient Walgreen Found. award in social, econ. and polit. instns., 1948, Scholarship award Pi Lambda Theta, 1948, Distinguished Alumni award Eastern Ill. U., 1974. Mem. Newberry Library Assn. (assoc.), Ill. Edn. Assn., AAUW, Internat. Platform Assn. Office: Grand Ohio Venture 211 E Ohio St Chicago IL 60611 Mailing Address: PO Box 1432 Chicago IL 60690

LEGINSKI, JANET, systems analyst; b. Oak Park, Ill., Jan. 23, 1949; s. Ignatius Peter and Ruth Elaine (Molenda) L. Student, Roosevelt U., 1969-79, Loop Coll., 1986. Sec. Borg-Warner Corp., Chgo., 1968-70, programmer, 1970-80, programming supr., 1980-83, sr. systems analyst, 1983—; pres. Femline Designs, Bridgeview, Ill., 1981—. Avocations: writing, gardening, art, body-building. Home: 6907 Roberts Rd Bridgeview IL 60455 Office: Borg Warner Corp 200 S Michigan Chicago IL 60604

LEGLER, PAUL KEVIN, lawyer; b. Lisbon, N.D., Oct. 2, 1955; s. Victor Wilbert and Marlys B. (Timm) L.; m. Julie M. Wild, Sept. 12, 1979; children: Alison, Mark. B.A., U. N.D., 1976; J.D., U. Minn., 1979. Bar: Minn. 1979, N.D. 1981, U.S. Dist. Ct. Minn. 1980, U.S. Dist. Ct. N.D. 1981, U.S. Ct. Appeals (8th cir.) 1982. Staff atty. Western Minn. Legal Services, Willmar, 1979-81; sole practice, Fargo, N.D., 1981—; instr. Moorhead State U., Minn., 1983—. Mem. Assn. Trial Lawyers Am., Minn. State Bar Assn., N.D. State Bar Assn., Cass County Bar Assn., Clay County Bar Assn., Phi Beta Kappa. Democrat. Presbyterian. Home: 1542 S 8th St Fargo ND 58103 Office: 2501 13th Ave S Fargo ND 58103

LEGRADY, DAN CARL, pharmacy educator; b. Oak Park, Ill., Aug. 15, 1948; s. Carl Francis and Ella Mary (Mezaros) LeG.; m. Loralei Rose Saraniec, July 4, 1981. BSc, U. Ariz., 1972; PharmD., U. Minn., 1976. Staff pharmacist St. Joseph Hosp., Phoenix, 1972-74; asst. dir. Rush-Presbyn. St. Luke's Hosp., Chgo., 1976-78, adj. scientist, instr., 1978-80; post doctoral fellow Northwestern U., Chgo., 1981-83; asst. prof. Creighton U., Omaha, 1984—; study recruitment Creighton U., 1984—, statistical cons., 1985—. Contbr. articles to profl. jours. Vol. Cedar Riverside Peoples Ctr., Mpls., Pharm House, Mpls., 1976. Mem. Am. Soc. Hosp. Pharmacists, Am. Statistical Assn., Kappa Psi, Rho Chi. Avocations: philately, running, tennis, swimming, rocketry. Office: Creighton U 24th and California Criss III Room 482 Omaha NE 68178

LEGUEY-FEILLEUX, JEAN-ROBERT, political scientist, educator; b. Marseilles, France, Mar. 28, 1928; came to U.S., Aug. 1949; s. E. Feilleux and Jeanne (Leguey) Feilleux Levassort; m. Virginia Louise Hartwell, Sept. 19, 1953; children—Michele, Monique, Suzanne, Christiane. M.A., Ecole Superieure de Commerce, France, 1949; Diplome Superieur d'Etudes Coloniales, U. d'Aix-Marseille, France, 1949; M.A., U. Fla., 1951; Ph.D., Georgetown U., 1965. Lectr. Sch. Foreign Service Georgetown U., Washington, 1957-66; dir. research Inst. World Polit. Georgetown U., 1960-66; asst. prof. St. Louis U., 1966-70, assoc. prof., 1970—, chmn. polit. sci. dept., 1983—; vis. scholar Harvard Law Sch., Cambridge, Mass., 1974-75; chmn. Fulbright Commn. for France Inst. Internat. Edn., N.Y.C., 1974-76; vis. researcher UN, N.Y.C., 1981. Author (with others): Law of Limited International Conflict, 1965. Contbr. chpt. to Implications of Disarmament, 1977. Contbr. articles to profl. jours. Author testimony Pres.'s Commn. on 25th Anniversary of UN, 1970. Recipient Medaille d'Or Institut Comml., France, 1949, Fulbright award U.S. State Dept., 1950, Cert. Disting. Service Inst. Internat. Edn., 1976; named Outstanding Educator Nutshell Mag., 1982. Mem. UN Assn. (mem. nat. council chpt. and div. pres. 1972-73, steering com. 1973-75), Am. Biog. Inst. (named to Hall of Fame, 1986), Internat. Human Rights Task Force (chmn. 1975-81), Character Research Assn. (pres. 1980-83), Georgetown U. Gold Key Soc., Alpha Sigma Nu, Phi Alpha Theta, Pi Sigma Alpha, Delta Phi Epsilon, Pi Delta Phi. Roman Catholic. Home: 6139 Kingsbury Ave Saint Louis MO 63112 Office: Saint Louis U Political Science Dept 221 N Grand Blvd Saint Louis MO 63103

LEHMAN, BARRY ALAN, minister; b. Jersey Shore, Pa., Aug. 4, 1948; s. Harold Keller and Dora (Moldawsky) L.; m. Valerie Anne Nocek, Apr. 22, 1972; 1 child, Elizabeth Anne. BA in Govt., Lehigh U., 1970; MDiv., Moravian Sem., 1975. Ordained to ministry Moravian Ch., 1974. Youth minister Rosemont Luth. Ch., Bethlehem, Pa., 1972-73; pastor Grace Moravian Ch., Center Valley, Pa., 1974-77, Covenant Moravian Ch., York, Pa., 1977-84, Watertown (Wis.) Moravian Ch., 1984—; synod del. Moravian Ch. North, Bethlehem, 1974, 78, 86; chmn. broadcast commn. York County Council Chs., 1979-84; vice chmn. bd. Moravian Ch. Camp, Hope, N.J., 1982-84; mem. Mt. Morris Program Moravian Ch. West, Madison, Wis., 1984-86; mem. bd. Watertown Counseling Ctr., 1985—. Author: Moravian study guide on AIDS; contbr. articles to profl. jours.; producer (radio series) Waging Peace, 1983; (cable TV series) Faith Alive, 1983-84. Mem. Moravian Western Christian Edn. Commn., 1986—; chmn. Moravian Western Video and Media Commn., 1986—. Mem. Watertown Clergy Roundtable, Wis. Conf. of Chs. Broadcast Commn. Democrat. Avocations: audio/visuals, video prodn., computers, music. Office: Watertown Moravian Ch 510 Cole St Watertown WI 53094

LEHMAN, DAVID WALTER, medical practice management executive; b. Cleve., Feb. 5, 1956; s. Walter A. and Ruth V. (Miller) L.; m. Mary Kay Moore, June 11, 1983. BA, Case Western Res. U., 1978, MBA, 1979. CPA, Ohio. Acct. in-charge Walthall & Drake CPA's, Cleve., 1979-84; bus. mgr. pathology Univ. Hosps. Cleve., 1984—; v.p., bus. mgr. Univ. Pathologists Cleve., 1984—; bus. mgr. Univ. Med. Labs., Cleve., 1985—. Mem. Am. Inst. CPA's, Med. Group Mgmt. Assn., Ohio Soc. CPA's, Ohio Med. Group Mgmt. Assn., Soc. Bibl. Lit. and Am. Acad. of Religion. Republican. Lodges: Masons (worshipful master Bedford chpt. 1982-83). Avocations: music, theater, ballet, golf, softball. Home: 78 Southwick Dr Bedford OH 44146-2624 Office: Univ Pathologists Cleve 2083 Adelbert Rd Cleveland OH 44106

LEHMAN, DENNIS DALE, chemistry educator; b. Youngstown, Ohio, July 15, 1945; s. Dale Vern and Coryn Eleanor (Neff) L.; m. Maureen Victoria Tierney, July 19, 1969 (div. Mar. 1981); children—Chris, Hillary; m. Kathleen Kim Kuchta, May 15, 1983. B.S., Ohio State U. 1967; M.S., Northwestern U., 1968, Ph.D., 1972. Prof. chemistry Chgo. City Colls., 1968—, Northwestern U., Evanston, Ill., 1974—; lectr. biochemistry Northwestern U. Med. Sch., Chgo., 1979—; cons. Chgo. Bd. Edn. Mem. Am. Chem. Soc., AAAS, Sigma Xi. Club: Lake Forest Swim. Author: Chemistry for the Health Sciences, 1981, 6th edit., 1985; Laboratory Chemistry for the Health Sciences, 1981, 2d. edit., 1985. Home: 3940 Elm Ln Wadsworth IL 60083 Office: Northwestern U Dept Chemistry Evanston IL 60208

LEHMAN, JOHN FREDERICK, advertising agency executive; b. Chgo., June 8, 1941; s. Edward Henry and Grace (Solway) L.; m. Patricia Whyte, Oct. 13, 1967; children—John Karl, Pamela Christine. B.A., Notre Dame U., 1963; M.A., U. Mich., 1972. Tchr. Whitehall Dist. Sch., Mich., 1972-79; owner, mgr. Gate of Horn Art Gallery, Whitehall, 1973-76; pres. Storyboard, Inc., Madison, Wis., 1980—; advt. dir. INSUL-CRETE Co., Inc., McFarland, Wis., 1983-85. Author: (poems) Quick Blue Gathering, 1977. Founder Muskegon Area Tchrs. of English, Mich., 1978. Served to capt. Med. Service Corps, U.S. Army, 1963-69. Decorated Bronze Star. Mem. Madison Advt. Fedn., Sales and Mktg. Execs. Madison, Am. Mktg. Assn. Home: 315 N Ingersoll Madison WI 53703 Office: Storyboard Inc 615 E Washington Ave Madison WI 53703

LEHMAN, SHERELYNN, psychotherapist; b. Cleve., June 27, 1941; d. Marvin and Esther (Morgenstern) Friedman; m. Theodore Gary Falcon, Aug. 19, 1962 (div. Apr. 1971); 1 child, Michael Aaron Falcon; m. Paul James Lehman, Apr. 21, 1974 (div. Nov. 1984); 1 child, Jonathan Paul. BS, Ohio U., 1963; postgrad., UCLA, 1970-72; MA, Loyola U., Los Angeles, 1974. Cert. sex therapist; lic. marriage, family and child counselor. Instr. psychology Cuyahoga Community Coll., Cleve., 1977-82; pvt. practice marriage, family and sex therapy Cleve., 1978—; instr. psychology St. Thomas of Villanova, Miami, Fla., 1980-81; clin. mem. Gender Team Case Western Res. U., Cleve., 1983—. Author: Love Me, Love Me Not: How to Survive Infidelty, 1985; TV personality A.M. Cleve., sta. WKYC, 1981—; talk show host sta. WJW, Cleve., 1983-85. Fellow Internat. Council of Sex Edn. and Parenthood; mem. Am. Assn. for Marriage and Family Therapy (clin.), Nat. Com. on Values and Sexuality (v.p.), Am. Assn. Sex Educators, Counselors and Therapists (adv. bd., nat. pub. relations com.), Am. Assn. TV and Recording Artists, Assn. for Retarded Citizens, Assn. for Children with Learning Disabilities, Phi Beta Kappa, Pi Gamma Mu, Kappa Delta Pi, Alpha Lambda Delta. Avocations: racquetball, traveling, playing the commodity and stock markets. Office: 3619 Park E Suite 213 S Beachwood OH 44122

LEHNERT, KAREN KAY, industrial information systems engineer; b. Lincoln, Nebr., June 20, 1959; d. Richard R. and Edna F. (Lammers) Nelson; m. Dieter Hans Lehnert, July 10, 1982; 1 child, Kristin. BS in Indsl. Engring., U. Cin., 1982; postgrad., Case Western Res. U., 1984-85. Indsl. engr. Packard Electric Gen. Motors, Warren, Ohio, 1978-82, Technicare Johnson & Johnson, Solon, Ohio, 1982-84; mgmt. engr. HBO & Co., Cleve., then Akron, Ohio, 1984—. Mem. Inst. Indsl. Engrs., Healthcare Info. Mgmt. Systems Soc., Am. Bus. Women's Assn. Home: 2017 Wren Haven Dr Hudson OH 44236 Office: HBO & Co 525 E Market St Akron OH 44309

LEHR, GLENN CARLTON, dentist; b. Grand Rapids, Mich., Apr. 16, 1934; s. Glenn Cecil and Nella (Van Ian Waarden) L.; m. Maria Rhodes, Jan. 25, 1959; children—Glenn Christopher, Michael David, Victoria Alice. B.A., U. Nebr.-Omaha, 1962; D.D.S., U. Mich., 1968. Gen. practice dentistry, Manchester, Mich., 1968-83; pres. Am. Dental Health, Ypsilanti, Taylor, Jenison, Grand Rapids and Battle Creek, Mich., 1982—, Diversified Dental Services, Ypsilanti, 1983—. Pres. Assn. Performing Arts; Athletic Boosters; bd. dirs. Emmanual Ch.; chmn. United Way, 1981-82; mem. exec. bd. Wolverine council Boy Scouts Am. Served to capt. USAF, 1955-64. Mem. Am. Dental Soc., Mich. Dental Soc., Chgo. Dental Soc., Detroit Dental Soc., Vedder Crown and Bridge Soc., Bunting Periodontal Study Club, Am. Acad. Group Practice, Manchester C. of C. (pres. 1974), Am. Soc. Preventive Dentistry (bd. dirs.). Republican. Lodge: Optimists. Home: 19220 Sanborn Manchester MI 48158 Office: Am Dental Health 3825 Carpenter Ypsilanti MI 48197

LEHR, MAX I., dentist; b. Russia, Aug. 25, 1908; came to U.S., 1923; s. Isaac and Bella (Curshan) L.; m. Nannette G. Hymanson, Oct. 18, 1947; children: Judith Lehr Smith, Les I. DDS, Northwestern U., 1935. Gen. practice dentistry Oak Park, Ill., 1936—. Served to maj. USAF, 1943-45, PTO. Decorated Bronze Star. Mem. ADA, Ill. Dental Soc., Chgo. Dental Soc., Assn. Mil. Surgeons, Pierre Fauchard Acad., Fédération Dentaire Internationale, Jewish War Vets. of U.S., Am. Legion, Alpha Omega. Club: Northwestern of Chgo. Lodge: B'nai B'rith.

LEIB, JOHN KENNETH, engineering manager; b. Columbia, S.C., Nov. 10, 1943; s. John Kenneth and Dorothy Romain (Corish) L.; m. Karen Susan Wiedman, Oct. 21, 1967; children: Mark Andrew, Kenneth John, Nicole Marie, Katherine Elizabeth. BEE, U. Dayton, Ohio, 1966, MS in Engring. Mgmt., 1971. Engr. NCR, Dayton, Ohio, 1966-71, Bendix Corp., Dayton, Ohio, 1971-72, RCA, Findlay, Ohio, 1972-74; mgr. NCR, Wichita, Kans., 1974—. Republican. Roman Catholic. Avocations: piano, sports, reading biographies. Home: 2211 Cardinal Dr Wichita KS 67204 Office: NCR 3718 N Rock Rd Wichita KS 67226

LEIBIG, RICHARD A., food products manufacturing company executive. Pres. Moorman Mfg. Co., Quincy, Ill. Office: Moorman Mfg Co 1000 N 30 th St Quincy IL 62301 *

LEIBOVICH, SAMUEL JOSEPH, biochemist, researcher; b. Southport, Eng., June 21, 1948; s. Mendel and Ruth (Riseman) L.; m. Susan Deborah Scheiner, July 11, 1976; children—Esther, Dahlia. B.Sc. with honors, U. Manchester (Eng.), 1968, Ph.D., 1971. Postdoctoral fellow U. Wash., Seattle, 1972-74; sr. scientist The Weizmann Inst. Sci., Rehovot, Israel, 1974-80; assoc. prof. dept. oral biology Northwestern U., Chgo., 1980—. Served to cpl. Israeli Army, 1980. Mem. AAAS, Am. Soc. Cell Biology, N.Y. Acad. Sci., Sigma Xi. Jewish. Contbr. articles to profl. jours. Home: 9101 Pottawattami Dr Skokie IL 60076 Office: Northwestern U Dept Oral Biology 311 E Chicago Ave Chicago IL 60611

LEIBRECHT, JOHN J., bishop; b. Overland, Mo., Aug. 3, 1930. Student, Cath. U., Washington. Ordained priest, Roman Cath. Ch., 1956. Bishop Springfield-Cape Girardeau, Mo., 1984—. Address: PO Box 1957 SSS Springfield MO 65805 *

LEIBZEIT, MERLIN ELROY, restaurant franchise owner; b. Plymouth, Wis., Nov. 10, 1920; s. Henry Gottleib and Ella (Dassow) L.; m. Erna Julia Holdorf, Nov. 26, 1941; children: Larry, Beverly, Dennis (dec.), Betty, Steven. Owner Dairy Queen Prodn. Co., Hilbert, Wis., 1940-57, Dairy Queen, Appleton, Wis., 1950—, Merlin's Coupon Magic, 1981—. Served with U.S. Army, 1944-46, ETO. Mem. Internat. Fedn. of Dairy Queen Store Owners (pres. 1971-77, 79), Wis. Dairy Queen Store Owners Assn. (pres. 1971-76). Republican. Lutheran. Avocations: world travel, photography. Home and Office: 525 W Pershing St Appleton WI 54911

LEIDEL, EDWIN M., JR., priest; b. Balt., Oct. 13, 1938; s. Edwin M. and Gertrude (Stablefeldt) L.; m. Ira Pauline Voigt, June 20, 1964; children: Andrew, James. BS, U. Wis., 1961; M of Div., Nashotah House Sem., 1964. Rector St. Stephen's Ch., Racine, Wis., 1965-70; assoc. rector Christ Ch., Milw., 1970-75; rector St. Timothy's Ch., Indpls., 1975-80, 82-86, Christ Ch. Cathedral, Darwin, Australia, 1981-82, St. Christopher's Ch., St. Paul, 1986—. Contbr. articles to profl. jours. Served to lt. USN, 1960-62. Episcopalian. Home: 715 Forest Dale Rd Saint Paul MN 55112 Office: St Christophers Episc Ch 2300 N Hameline Ave Saint Paul MN 55113

LEIDER, ALLAN R., communications company executive; b. LaCrosse, Wis., Jan. 15, 1953; s. Robert E. and Florence H. (Geldaker) L.; m. Terri L. Niehaus, July 4, 1979. AA in Architecture, Parkland Coll., 1976; BS in Mass Communications, U. Wis., LaCrosse, 1979. Dist. mktg. mgr. Teleprompter, LaCrosse, 1979-81; gen. mgr. Group W Cable, Winona, Minn., 1982-83; region bus. mgr. Group W Cable, Mahwah, N.J., 1983-85; gen. mgr. Marcus Communications, Winona, 1986—; bd. dirs. Sta. KQAL, Winona. Filmmaker, editor Hare Who Lost Spectacles, 1979. Founder Coalition for Common Sense, Winona, 1985; sec. Minn. Community Involvement Program, Winona, 1986; mem. Winona Civic Assn., 1987. Served with USAF, 1972-75. Mem. Nat. Cable TV Assn., Winona C. of C. Lodge: Kiwanis (pres. Winona 1982). Avocations: photography, camping. Home: 540 W Broadway Winona MN 55987 Office: Marcus Communications 127 W 4th Winona MN 55987

LEIDTKE, BYRON TODD, dentist; b. Canton, Ohio, Aug. 15, 1936; s. Homer James and Thelma (Charlene) L.; m. Sue Elizabeth Hoskin, June 1, 1963; children: Amy, Morgan. BS, Ohio State U., 1961, DDS, 1963; Cert., Am. Straight Wire Orthodontic Assn., 1984. Gen. practice dentistry Sunbury, Ohio, 1965-67; chief of clinic Chillocothe (Ohio) Correctional Inst., 1967; gen. practice dentistry Delaware, Ohio, 1967—; asst. clin. prof. dentistry Ohio State U., 1980, tchr. dental occlusion, 1980—. Served to capt. USAF, 1963-65. Mem. ADA, Ohio Dental Assn., Cen. Ohio Dental Soc. (peer review panel 1973—), Am. Assn. Functional Orthodontics, Am. Straight Wire Orthodontics Assn., Cen. Ohio Acad. Dental Practice Mgmt. Lodge: Sertoma (sec. Delaware, Ohio 1974, pres. 1976, treas. 1977). Avocations: bicycling, tennis, fishing, mycology. Home: 238 N Franklin St Delaware OH 43015 Office: 226 N Liberty St Delaware OH 43015

LEIGH, GARY DEAN, lawyer; b. Danville, Ill., Jan. 14, 1955; s. Donald Dean and Myra Elizabeth (Stipp) L. B.A., U. Miami, 1978; J.D., John Marshall Law Sch., 1981. Bar: Ill. 1981, Calif. 1981, U.S. Dist. Ct. (no. dist.) Ill. 1981, U.S. Dist. Ct. (no. dist.) Calif. 1982, U.S. Dist. Ct. (so. dist.) Calif. 1982, U.S. Ct. Appeals (7th cir.) 1981, U.S. Ct. Appeals (9th cir.) 1982. Ptnr. Fisher, Leigh & Assocs., 1984-86; assoc. Leonard M. Ring & Assocs., Chgo., 1981-83, Susan E. Loggans & Assocs., Chgo., 1983—, Loggans & Reiter, 1984—. Contbr. articles to profl. jours. Mem. Assn. Trial Lawyers Am. (advanced trial advocacy cert. 1983), Ill. Trial Lawyers Assn. (products liability com. 1981—), Calif. Trial Lawyers Assn., Chgo. Bar Assn. (trial techniques sect. 1981—), Ill. State Bar Assn., ABA (tort and ins. practice sect. 1981—). Home: 1247 N State Pkwy Chicago IL 60610 Office: Susan F Loggans & Assocs 615 N Wabash Ave Chicago IL 60611

LEIGHTON, GEORGE NEVES, judge; b. New Bedford, Mass., Oct. 22, 1912; s. Antonio N. and Anna Sylvia (Garcia) Leitao; m. Virginia Berry Quivers, June 21, 1942; children: Virginia Anne, Barbara Elaine. A.B., Howard U., 1940; LL.B., Harvard U., 1946; LL.D., Elmhurst Coll., 1964, John Marshall Law Sch., 1973, Southeastern Mass. U., 1975, New Eng. U. Sch. Law, 1978. Bar: Mass. 1946, Ill. 1947, U.S. Supreme Ct. 1958. Partner Moore, Ming & Leighton, Chgo., 1951-59, McCoy, Ming & Leighton, Chgo., 1959-64; judge Circuit Ct. Cook County Ill., 1964-69, Appellate Ct. 1st Dist., 1969-76; U.S. dist. judge No. Dist. Ill., 1976-86; sr. dist. judge U.S. Dist. Ct., 1986—; Mem. council sect. legal edn. and admissions to bar ABA, chmn. council, 1976; adj. prof. John Marshall Law Sch., Chgo.; commr., mem. character and fitness com. for 1st Appellate Dist., Supreme Ct. Ill., 1955-63, chmn. character and fitness com., 1961-62; mem. joint com. for revision jud. article Ill. and Chgo. bar assns., 1959-62; joint com. for revision Ill. Criminal Code, 1959-63; chmn. Ill. adv. com. U.S. Commn. on Civil Rights, 1964; mem. pub. rev. bd. UAW, AFL-CIO, 1961-70; Asst. atty. gen. State of Ill., 1950-51; pres. 3d Ward Regular Democratic Orgn., Cook County, Ill., 1951-53; v.p. 21st Ward, 1964. Contbr. articles to legal jours. Bd. dirs. United Ch. Bd. for Homeland Ministries, United Ch. of Christ, Grant Hosp., Chgo.; trustee U. Notre Dame, 1979-83, trustee emeritus, 1983—; bd. overseers Harvard Coll., 1983—. Served to capt., inf. AUS, 1942-45. Decorated Bronze Star.; Recipient Civil Liberties award Ill. div. ACLU, 1961; named Chicagoan of Year in Law and Judiciary Jr. Assn. Commerce and Industry, 1964. Fellow Am. Bar Found.; mem. Howard U. Chgo. Alumni Club (chmn. bd. dirs.), John Howard Assn. (dir.), Chgo., Ill. bar assns., NAACP (chmn. legal redress com. Chgo. br.), Nat. Harvard Law Sch. Assn. (council), Phi Beta Kappa. Office: Dirksen Fed Bldg 219 S Dearborn Chicago IL 60604

LEIGHTON, KIM GREGORY, infosystems specialist; b. St. Louis, May 13, 1952; s. James Leland and Rosemary Dolores (Schroll) L. BA in Biology, U. Mo., 1974, MBA, 1976, MS in Mgmt. Info. Systems, 1986. CPA, Mo. Auditor Ernst & Whinney, St. Louis, 1976-79; sr. auditor Anheuser-Busch Cos., St. Louis, 1979-81; fin. analyst Seven-Up Co., St. Louis, 1981-82, mgmt. info. systems field coordinator, 1982-85; asst. controller Amedco, Inc., Chesterfield, Mo., 1985-86, dir. acctg. and adminstrn., 1986-87, dir. infosystems and tech., 1987—; cons. Cen. Med. Ctr., St. Louis, 1979-80, Seven-Up Co., 1985-86. Mem. Backers of St. Louis Reportory Theatre, Friends of St. Louis Art Mus., Friends of St. Louis Zoo, Mo. Botanical Garden. Mem. Am Inst. CPA's, Inst. Econometric Research, U. Mo. at St. Louis Alumni Assn., Beta Gamma Sigma, Beta Alpha Psi. Republican. Roman Catholic. Avocations: tennis, music, movies, reading, nautilus. Home: 535 Fee Fee Hills Hazelwood MO 63042 Office: Amedco Inc 14323 S Outer Forty Rd Chesterfield MO 63017

LEIGHTON, RICHARD K., accounting company executive; b. Jasper, Ind., Aug. 18, 1945; s. Harold Robert and Catherine M. (Schuler) L.; m. Anne Margurite Feltman, Aug. 10, 1968; children: Michele, Christine, Jennifer. BS, Ind. U., 1967. Ptnr. Robert M. Finn & Co., Indpls., 1967-81, King Main Hurdman, Indpls., 1982-86; prin. Richard K. Leighton & Co., Carmel, Ind., 1987—. Author: (with others) Government Accounting and Auditing, 1987. Bd. dirs. Marquette Manor, Indpls., 1981-83, Voice of Good News, Inc., Indpls., 1982—, Ind. Justice Task Force, Indpls., 1984-86. Served with U.S. Army, 1967-73. Mem. Am. Inst. CPA's, Ind. CPA Soc. (bd. dirs. 1982-83). Republican. Roman Catholic. Clubs: Meridian Hills Country, Skyline (Indpls.). Lodge: Sertoma (pres. Carmel/Clay chpt. 1986-87). Avocations: reading, golf, tennis. Home: 12832 Andover Dr Carmel IN 46032 Office: 2000 E 116th St Carmel IN 46032

LEINBERGER, JOAN SCHMIDT, mental health business manager; b. Bay City, Mich., Nov. 28, 1942; d. Alvin H. and Linda K. (Kernstock) Schmidt; m. Kenneth Edgar Leinberger, Oct. 14, 1961; children: Kelly Jean, David Alan. AS, Bay de Noc Community Coll., 1971; BS, No. Mich. U., 1973, MS, 1977. Sec. The Dow Chem. Co., Midland, Mich., 1960-61, 62-68, Briggs Mfg., Warren, Mich., 1961-62; purchasing asst. Rust Engring., Escanaba, 1973; substitute tchr. Gladstone (Mich.) Area Schs., 1974-76; coll. instr. Bay de Noc Community Coll., Escanaba, 1974-76; bus. mgr. George D. Maniaci Ctr., Escanaba, 1976—. Planning commr. Escanaba City Planning Commn., 1985—; bd. dirs. Delta County Community Concert Assn., Escanaba, 1985—, mem. 1982—; mem. William Bonifas Fine Arts Ctr., Escanaba, 1987; bd. dirs., sec. Pub. Service Employees Fed. Credit Union, Escanaba, 1986—. Mem. AAUW (v.p. 1985-86, program edn. chair 1986-87), Am. Soc. Pub. Adminstrn., Phi Kappa Phi. Lutheran. Avocations: cross country skiing, camping, bowling. Office: George D Maniaci Ctr 2920 College Ave Escanaba MI 49829

LEINBERGER, PAUL DANIEL, management consultant; b. Lake Forest, Ill., Oct. 10, 1947; s. Hugo and Ruth Margerita (Lundquist) L.; m. Susan Harris, Sept. 16, 1984. B in Urban Planning, U. Ill., 1970, M in Urban Planning, 1971; PhD, Wright Inst., 1979. Sr. planner Urban Investment and Devel. Co., Chgo., 1971-73; prof. of Planning Gov.'s State U., University Park, Ill., 1973-76; sr. ptnr. Meridian Group, Berkeley, Calif., 1978-82; dir. planning and fin. Levi Strauss & Co., San Francisco, 1982-85; pres. Execuserve, Inc., St. Paul, 1986—; chmn. Roosevelt Ctr. for Am. Policy Studies, Washington, 1985—. Author: Organization Man Revisited, 1987. Mem. exec. com. Nat. Retiree Vol. Ctr., Mpls., 1987; bd. dirs. Nat. Council Aging, Washington, 1987. UCLA research fellow, 1976-77. Mem. United Ch. Christ. Avocations: running, racketball, bicycling, tennis, hiking. Home: 2335 Buford Ave Saint Paul MN 55108 Office: Execuserve Inc 610 Meritor Tower 444 Cedar St Saint Paul MN 55101

LEINENWEBER, HARRY DANIEL, lawyer, district court judge; b. Joliet, Ill., June 3, 1937; s. Harry Dean and Emily Theresa (Lennon) L.; m. Lynn Martin, Jan. 7, 1987; children: Jane Dunn, John Dunn, Thomas More, Stephen Becket, Justin Lennon. AB, U. Notre Dame, 1959; JD, U. Chgo. 1962. Bar: Ill. 1962, U.S. Dist. Ct. (no. dist.) Ill. 1967. Atty. City of Joliet, 1963-67; asst. states atty. Will County, Joliet, 1968-70; mem. Ill. Ho. of Reps., Springfield, 1973-83, chmn. judiciary com., 1981-83; ptnr. Dunn, Leinenweber & Dunn, Ltd., Joliet, 1979-86; judge U.S. Dist. Ct. (no. dist.), Chgo., 1986—; bd. dirs. Will County Legal Assistance, 1982-86. Precinct com. Will County Reps., 1966-86, bd. dirs., 1984-86; bd. dirs. Am. Cancer Soc., New Lenox, Ill., 1980-85, Good Shepherd Manor, Momence, Ill., 1981—; del. Rep. Nat. Conv., Detroit, 1980. Mem. Ill. Bar Assn., Will County Bar Assn. (bd. dirs. 1984-86), Ill. Trial Lawyers Assn., Am. Interprofl. Inst. Roman Catholic. Office: US Dist Ct 219 S Dearborn St #1778 Chicago IL 60604

LEINIEKS, VALDIS, classics educator; b. Liepaja, Latvia, Apr. 15, 1932; came to U.S., 1949, naturalized, 1954; s. Arvid Ansis and Valia Leontine (Brunaus) L. B.A., Cornell U., 1955, M.A., 1956; Ph.D., Princeton U., 1962. Instr. classics Cornell Coll., Mount Vernon, Iowa, 1959-62, asst. prof. classics, 1962-64; assoc. prof. classics Ohio State U., 1964-66; assoc. prof. classics U. Nebr., Lincoln, 1966-71, prof. classics, 1971—, chmn. dept. classics, 1967—, chmn. program comparative lit., 1970-86, interim chmn. dept. modern langs., 1982-83. Author: Morphosyntax of the Homeric Greek Verb, 1964; The Structure of Latin, 1975; Index Nepotianus, 1976; The Plays of Sophokles, 1982. Contbr. articles to profl. jours. Mem. AAUP, Am. Classical League, Classical Assn. Middle West and South, Am. Philol. Assn. Republican. Home: 2505 A St Lincoln NE 68502 Office: U Nebr Dept Classics Lincoln NE 68588

LEININGER, ELMER, emeritus chemistry educator; b. Milw., Apr. 19, 1900; s. Philip Henry and Louise (Hardtke) L.; B.S., Carroll Coll., 1923; postgrad. U. Wis., 1923-24; M.S., Mich. State U., 1931; Ph.D., U. Mich., 1941; m. Hazel Ann MacNamara, Dec. 30, 1924 (dec. June 1961); 1 dau., Mary Louise (Mrs. Robert Reed); m. 2d, Byrnice L. Dickinson, 1964. Instr. chem. Mich. State U., 1924-30, prof. chemistry, head analytical chemistry sect. 1930-65, prof. emeritus, 1965—; chem. cons., 1965—. Sec., dir. Geneva Lake Civic Assn., 1968-76, 79—; bd. dirs., moderator Pilgrim Ch. Mem. Am. Chem. Soc. (chmn., councilor Mich. sect.), Am. Philatelic Soc., Sigma Xi, Alpha Chi Sigma, Phi Lambda Upsilon. Republican. Clubs: Lake Geneva Country; Green Valley (Ariz.) Country. Editorial adv. bd. Analytical Chemistry. Contbr. articles to profl. jours. Address: S Lake Shore Dr Rural Route 1 Box 70 Lake Geneva WI 53147

LEININGER, MADELEINE MONICA, nursing educator, administrator, researcher, anthropologist; b. Sutton, Nebr., July 13, 1925; d. George and Irene Leininger. BS in Biology, Scholastic Coll., 1950, LHD, 1976; MS in Nursing, Cath. U. Am., 1953; PhD in Anthropology, U. Wash., 1965. RN. Instr., mem. staff, head nurse med.-surg. unit, supr. psychiat. unit St. Joseph's Hosp., Omaha, 1950-54; assoc. prof. nursing, dir. grad. program in psychiat. nursing U. Cin. Coll. Nursing, 1954-60; research fellow Nat. League Nursing, Eastern Highlands of New Guinea, 1960-62; research assoc. U. Wash. Dept. Anthropology, Seattle, 1964-65; prof. nursing and anthropology, dir. nurse-scientist PhD program U. Colo., Boulder and Denver, 1966-69; dean sch. nursing, prof. nursing, lectr. anthropology U. Wash., Seattle, 1969-74; dean coll. nursing, prof. nursing U. Utah, Salt Lake City, 1974-80; Anise J. Sorell prof. nursing Troy (Ala.) State U., 1981; prof. nursing, adj. prof. anthropology, dir. Ctr. for Heatlh Research, dir. transcultural nursing offerings Wayne State U., Detroit, 1981—; adj. prof. anthropology U. Utah, 1974-81; disting. vis. prof. at 29 univs., U.S. and overseas, 1970—. Author: 22 books including Nursing and Anthropology: Two Worlds to Blend, 1970, Contemporary Issues in Mental Health Nursing, 1973, Caring: An Essential Human Need, 1981, Reference Sources for Transcultural Health and Nursing, 1984, Basic Psychiatric Concepts in Nursing, 1960, Care: The Essence of Nursing and Health, 1984, Qualitative Research Methods in Nursing, 1985, Care: Discovery and Clinical-Community Uses, 1987; editor or co-editor 18 books on nursing; contbr. 200 articles to profl. jours.; 30 chpts. to books. Recipient Outstanding Alumni award Cath. U. Am., Washington, 1969, Award of Recognition, Am. Assn. Colls. of Nursing, 1976, Nurse of Yr. award Dist. 1 Utah Nurses Assn., 1976, Utah Nurses Assn. Literary award, 1978, Trotter Disting. Pub. Lectr. award U. Tex., Disting. Faculty Recognition award, 1985, Bd. Govs. U. Tex., Outstanding Faculty Scholar award Wayne State U., 1985, Gershenson Research award Wayne State U., 1986, Award for acad. excellence AAUW-Detroit; named Detroit Woman of Yr., AAUW, 1987. Fellow Am. Anthropol. Soc. (exec. com. 1980-84), Am. Acad. Nursing, Am. Nurses Assn.; mem. Am. Assn. Humanities, Am. Applied Anthropol. Soc., Transcultural Nursing Soc. (founder, pres. 1974-80), Cultural Community Group Assn. (ethics, humanities heritage study group), Nat. Research Care Confs. (leader human care research), Sigma Xi, Pi Gamma Mu, Sigma Theta Tau (Lectr. of Yr. 1987—), Delta Kappa Gamma, Alpha Tau Delta. Office: Wayne State U 5557 Cass St Detroit MI 48202

LEISE, FRED, music company administrator; b. Washington, Sept. 15, 1949; s. David and Phyllis Rhea (Fleitman) L. B.S. in math., U. Md.-College Park, 1974. Asst. to gen. mgr. Buffalo Philharm., 1976-77; mgr. Albany Symphony, N.Y., 1977-80; gen. mgr. Waverly Consort, N.Y.C., 1981-82; bus. mgr. Music of the Baroque, Chgo., 1982-84, dir. fin., 1984-86, asst. gen. mgr., 1987— ; dir. Ill. Arts Alliance Chgo., 1984—, Ill. Arts Action Coalition, Chgo., 1984—, Ill. Arts Action Coalition, Chgo., 1984-87; mem. Ill. Arts Alliance Found., 1987—; mem. choral panel NEA, 1987; dir., treas. Chgo. Music Alliance, 1986—. Dir. N.Y.C. Gay Men's Chorus, 1981-82; mem. Windy City Gay Chorus, Chgo., 1983—, dir., 1983. Mem. Am. Symphony Orch. League. Avocations: choral singing; rare book collecting. Home: 900 W Ainslie St Chicago IL 60640 Office: Music of the Baroque 343 S Dearborn Chicago IL 60604

LEISER, THOMAS EDWARD, financial officer; b. Eau Claire, Wis., Nov. 3, 1938; s. Wilbur R. and Catherine Z. (Zehring) L.; m. Nancy Peterson, June 9, 1962; children: Anne M., David W. BBA, U. Wis., 1960. CPA, Minn. Acct., ptnr. Arthur Andersen & Co., Mpls. and St. Paul, 1960-77; chief fin. officer W.D. Larson Cos., Mpls. and St. Paul, 1978-80, Wintz Transp. Co., St. Paul, 1981-82, 1 Potato 2, Inc., Mpls., 1983—. Served with U.S. Army, 1962-64. Mem. Am. Inst. CPA's, Minn. Soc. CPA's. Office: 1 Potato 2 Inc 5640 International Pkwy New Hope MN 55428

LEISNER, ANTHONY BAKER, publishing company executive; b. Evanston, Ill., Sept. 13, 1941; s. A. Paul and Ruth (Solms) L.; B.S., Northwestern U., 1964, M.B.A., 1983; children—Justina, William, Sarah. Salesman, Pitney Bowes Co., 1976-77; with Quality Books Inc., Northbrook, Ill., 1968—, v.p., 1972—, gen. mgr., 1979—; adj. faculty Lake Forest (Ill.) Sch. Mgmt., 1983—, Kellogg Grad. Sch. Mgmt. Northwestern U., Evanston, Ill. Pres. bd. dirs. Lake Villa (Ill.) Public Library, 1972-78; bd. dirs. No. Ill. Library Systems, 1973-78; chmn. Libertarian Party Lake County (Ill.), 1980-81; probation officer Lake County CAP, 1981. Mem. ALA, Ill. Library Assn. (Gerald L. Campbell award 1980), Am. Booksellers Assn., Acad. Mgmt., Am. Mktg. Assn., Internat. Platform Assn., World Future Soc., World Isshin Ryu Karate Assn. Author: Official Guide to Country Dance Steps, 1980; also articles. Home: 1174 Cherry St Winnetka IL 60093 Office: Quality Books Inc 918 Sherwood Dr Lake Bluff IL 60044

LEISTICO, MILDRED FAE, information processing consultant; b. Hobart, Okla., July 4, 1947; d. Walter D. and Ethel Marie (Koehn) Goossen; m. Melvin Allen Leistico, May 17, 1975; 1 child, Sean Duane. Student Wichita Bus. Coll., 1965-66. Sec. Farmers Ins. Group, Wichita, Kans., 1965-66; asst. cashier Nat. Life & Accident Ins., Enid, Okla., 1966; typist Dow Chem. Co., Freeport, Tex., 1967; supply clk. Kans. U. Med. Ctr., Kansas City, 1968; statis. sec. Centerre Bank of Kansas City (Mo.) (formerly Columbia Union Nat. Bank), 1969-70, 73-79, analyst, 1979-80, info. processing mgr., 1980-86; cons. mktg. and implementation Frank Brennan & Assocs., 1986; cons. seminars and placement WPS Inc., Mission, Kans., 1987—; sec. First Nat. Bank, Lake Jackson, Tex., 1970-71; statis. typist Arthur Andersen & Co., Kansas City, Mo., 1972; mem. adv. bd. Fort Osage Vo-Tech., 1983—. Asst. editor: Christ For Me, Inc., 1980—, photographer, 1986—. Mem. Assn. Info. Systems Profls. (bd. dirs. 1982-83, 84-85, v.p. membership 1983-84), Internat. Platform Assn. Office: WPS Inc 5700 Broadmoor Mission KS 66202

LEISTNER, MARY EDNA, educator; b. Evanston, Ill., Apr. 13, 1929; d. Joseph W. and Edna C. (Moe) Cox; m. Delbert L. Leistner, Sept. 30, 1950; children: David, Martha, Joseph. BS in Chemistry, Purdue U., 1950; MEd, Miami U., Oxford, Ohio, 1964. Tchr. sci. and math. Cen. Jr. High Sch., Sidney, Ohio, 1962-66; tchr. chemistry, biology, advanced chemistry Sidney High Sch., 1966—; mem. high sch. chemistry test com. Nat. Sci. Tchrs. Assn. Am. Chem. Soc., 1983-85. Mem. exec. com. Ohio Dist. Luth. Women's Missionary League, Columbus, 1978-82, pres. Miami Valley zone, 1985-87; pres. Redeemer Ladies Soc., Sidney, 1980—. Mem. Nat. Sci. Tchrs. Assn. (Cadre 100 award), Western Ohio Sci. Tchrs. Assn. (pres. 1972-73), Sci. Edn. Council Ohio (dist. rep. exec. bd. 1984-86, treas. 1986—), Sidney Edn. Assn. (treas. 1980-82, 85-86). Republican. Lutheran. Office: Sidney High Sch 1215 Campbell Rd Sidney OH 45365

LEITCH, JAY ANDREW, agriculture science educator; b. Fergus Falls, Minn., Sept. 20, 1948; s. Andy Caldwell and Carol Margerette (Ank) L.; m. Diane Jean Tollerude, Apr. 10, 1968; 1 child, Philip Jerome. AA, Fergus Falls (Minn.) State Jr. Coll., 1972; BA, Moorhead State U., 1974; MS, N.D. State U., 1976; PhD, U. Minn., 1981. Assoc. prof. N.D. State U., Fargo, 1981—; cons. state, fed. agys., 1981—; scientific advisor Dept. U.S. Army, Arlington, Va., 1985-86; sr. economist Dept. Interior, Washington, 1985-87; assoc. dir. N.D. Water Resources Research Inst., Fargo., 1987—. Contbr. numerous articles on natural resources to profl. jours. Mem. Citizens Adv. Com., Moorhead, 1983-85, Leadership Moorhead Planning Com., 1986-87. Served with USN, 1968-71, Vietnam, with Res., 1971—. Numerous research grants from various state, federal, pvt. agys. Mem. Soc. Wetland Scientists, Am. Agrl. Econs. Assn., Assn. Environ. and Resource Economists, Can. Water Resource Assn., Water Resources Assn., Nat. Rifle Assn., VFW. Republican. Presbyterian. Clubs: Toastmasters, Moorhead Rod and Gun. Avocations: travel, regional history, outdoor sports, woodworking. Home: 2314 N River Dr Moorhead MN 56560 Office: ND State U Dept Agrl Econs Fargo ND 58105

LEITNER, YORAM BENJAMIN, otolaryngologist; b. Haifa, Israel, Mar. 12, 1953; came to U.S., 1957; s. Amos J. and Eva (Bialostotzky) L.; m. Cathy Sue Woodring, Aug. 12, 1974; children: Elizabeth Jeanne, Amanda Leah, Diana Miriam. BA, Oberlin Coll., 1973; MD, NYU, 1977. Diplomate Am. Bd. Otolaryngology. Resident in Otolaryngology U. Va. Hosp., Charlottesville, Va., 1977-82; physician The Wichita Clinic, 1982—; teaching residents family practice Wesley Med. Ctr., Wichita, 1985—, Saint Francis Regional Med. Ctr., 1984—. Fellow ACS; mem. Alpha Omega Alpha. Avocation: restoration early model corvette convertible. Office: The Wichita Clinic 3311 E Murdock Wichita KS 67208

LEITZKE, JACQUE HERBERT, corporation pres., psychologist; b. Watertown, Wis., Dec. 25, 1929; s. Herbert Wilbert and Ruth Valberg (Stavenow) L.; m. Mary Annis Lacey, June 20, 1950 (div. Nov. 1963); children: Keith Alan, Sari Dawn, Thora Jacquelynne. BS, U. Wis., Madison, 1955; MA, Kent State U., 1958. Lic. psychologist, Wis., Ill., N.Y. Sch. psychologist BCG, N.Y.C., 1959-61; clin. psychologist Winnebago County Guidance Ctr., Neenah, Wis., 1961-64; sch. psychologist Waukegan City (Ill.) Sch. Dist. 61, 1965-66; clin. psychologist Wis., Ill., 1967-78; corp. pres., chief exec. officer Psychometrics Internat. Corp., Watertown, 1979—. Author: Definitively Incorporeal Human Intelligence Itself;originator intelligence test Abecedarian Measure of Human Intelligence, 1979. Trustee Human Intelligence Research Found. Served with USAF, 1948-51. Mem. Am. Psychol. Assn., Mensa. Avocations: oil painting, formula one aficionado (Gran Prix racing). Home: 1153 Boughton St 808 Watertown WI 53094 Office: Psychometrics Internat Corp PO Box 247 Watertown WI 53094

LEJEUNE, DENNIS EDWARD, financial trader; b. Chgo., Feb. 25, 1942; s. Edward George and Eileen Marie (Donnellan) L.; m. Barbara Katharine Benson, July 24, 1965; children—Angela Marie, Katharine Kelly, Amy Eileen. B.B.A., U. Notre Dame; postgrad., Northwestern U. Internat. banking officer Provident Nat. Bank, Phila., 1971-73; fgn. exchange trader Harris Trust & Savs. Bank, Chgo., 1966-71, asst. v.p., 1973-74, v.p., mgr. IMM div., 1974-80, sr. v.p., mgr. investment dept., 1980-81, exec. v.p., 1981-86; dir. internat. fin. services Stotler & Co., Chgo., 1986—. Tchr., St. Faith, Hope & Charity Ch., Winnetka, Ill., 1977-81. Served with U.S. Army, 1964, USAR, 1964-70. Mem. Forex Assn. N.Am. (sec. 1976-80), Bond Club Chgo. (dir., treas.), Dealer Bank Assn., Pub. Securities Assn. (dir. 1983-85). Republican. Roman Catholic. Clubs: University, Glen Lake Yacht. Avocations: sailing; golf; swimming; ancestry; sailing. Office: Stotler & Co Bd Trade Bldg Chicago IL 60604

LEKAN, BRIANA MARKER, photographer; b. Columbus, Ohio, Oct. 9, 1955; d. Daniel Lee and Charlotte (Holley) Marker; m. Thomas James Lekan, Aug. 12, 1978; 1 child, Danelle Kara Lekan. BA in Art Edn., Ohio State U., 1978. Lic. forensic photographer. Forensic photographer Cuyahoga County, Cleve., 1978-82; free-lance photographer Cin., 1985—; photographer Clev. Basic Police Sch., 1978-82, Cuyahoga County Coroner's Office, 1978-81. Club: AMA Aux. (Columbus, Ohio). Avocations: hiking, painting. Home: 8200 Miami Rd Cincinnati OH 45243

LEKBERG, ROBERT DAVID, chemist; b. Chgo., Feb. 2, 1920; s. Carl H. and Esther (Forsberg) L.; m. Sandra Sakal, Oct. 19, 1970; children by previous marriage: Terry Lee, Jerrald Dean, Roger Daryl, Kathleen Sue, Keith Robin. AA, North Park Coll., 1940; BS, Lewis Inst., 1943. Chemist Glidden Co., Hammond, Ind., 1940-43, Wilson Packing Co., Calumet City, Ill., 1943-45, Libby, McNeil & Libby, Blue Island, Ill., 1945-47; chief chemist Dawes Labs., Chgo., 1947-50; owner, pres. Chemlek Labs. Inc., Alsip, Ill., 1950—, Chemlek Labs. Can. Ltd., Windsor, Ont., 1960-66; lobbyist Ill. Indsl. Council. Editor: Indsl. Dist. Assn. Newsletter, 1975—; patentee chem. processes, pollution control. Violinist Chgo. Civic Symphony, 1940-42, N.W. Ind. Symphony, 1976—, Chicago Heights Symphony, 1959—, Southwest Symphony, 1970—; officer with U.S. Power Squadron. Mem. Ill. Mfrs. Assn., Ill. Indsl. Council, Chgo. Feed Club. Republican. Club: Dolton Yacht (past commodore). Home: 6624 Linden Dr Oak Forest IL 60452 Office: Chemlek Labs Inc 4040 W 123d St Alsip IL 60658

LELAND-YOUNG, JANET KAYE, psychiatric social worker; b. Saginaw, Mich., Dec. 6, 1954; d. Ward Coville and Betty Jane (Browne) Leland; m. Paul R. Stuhmer, Mar. 22, 1977 (div. Dec. 1980); m. Loren J. Leland-Young, June 5, 1982; 1 child, Amanda Robin. BA, Mich. State U., 1977, MSW, 1981. Cert. social worker, Mich. Assoc. prof. Mich. State U., Lansing, 1976-77; instr. Lansing Community Coll., 1979—; therapist Sanctuary, Royal Oak, Mich., 1981-82, Cath. Social Services, Pontiac, Mich., 1982-84; residential dir. Battered Women's Shelter, Pontiac, 1984; pvt. practice psychiat. social work Detroit, 1986; cons. Mich. State U., 1977-81, Ingham County (Mich.) Women's Commn., 1979, Council for Children at Risk, Detroit, 1981; expert witness Ingham County Prosecutor, 1981. Author: Rape Research and Analysis, 1977. Bd. dirs. Listening Ear Crisis Ctr., East Lansing, Mich., 1979. Recipient Cert. Appreciation, NOW, 1979, Cert. Appreciation, Council Against Domestic Assault, 1979. Mem. Nat. Assn. Social Workers, Acad. Cert. Social Workers. Avocations: reading mysteries, decorating.

LEMBERGER, LOUIS, pharmacologist, physician; b. Monticello, N.Y., May 8, 1937; s. Max and Ida (Seigel) L.; m. Myrna Sue Diamond, 1959;

children: Harriet Felice, Margo Beth. B.S. magna cum laude, Bklyn. Coll. Pharmacy, L.I. U., 1960; Ph.D. in Pharmacology, Albert Einstein Coll. Medicine, 1964, M.D., 1968. Pharmacy intern VA Regional Office, Newark, summer 1960; postdoctoral fellow Albert Einstein Coll. Medicine, 1964-68; intern in medicine Met. Hosp. Center, N.Y. Med. Coll., N.Y.C., 1968-69; research assoc. NIH, Bethesda, Md., 1969-71; clin. pharmacologist Lilly Lab. for Clin. Research, Eli Lilly & Co., Indpls., 1971-75; chief clin. pharmacology Lilly Lab. for Clin. Research, Eli Lilly & Co., 1975-78, dir. clin. pharmacology, 1978—, clin. research fellow, 1982—; asst. prof. pharmacology Ind. U., 1972-73, asst. prof. medicine, 1972-73, assoc. prof. pharmacology, 1973-77, assoc. prof. medicine, 1973-77, prof. pharmacology, 1977—, prof. medicine, prof. psychiatry, 1977—, mem. grad. faculty, 1975—; adj. prof. clin. pharmacology Ohio State U., 1975-86; physician Wishard Meml. Hosp., 1976—; cons. U.S. Nat. Commn. on Marijuana and Drug Abuse, 1971-73, Can. Commn. Inquiry into Non-Med. Use Drugs, 1971-73; guest lectr. various univs., 1968—. Author: (with A. Rubin) Physiologic Disposition of Drugs of Abuse, 1976; contbr. numerous articles on biochemistry and pharmacology to sci. jours.; editorial bd.: Excerpta Medica, 1972—, Clin. Pharmacology and Therapeutics, 1976—, Communications in Psychopharmacology, 1975-81, Pharmacology, Internat. Jour. Exptl. and Clin. Pharmacology, 1978—, Drug and Alcohol Abuse Research, 1979—, Drug Devel. Research, 1980-87, Trends in Pharmacol. Scis, 1980-85. Post adviser Crossroads of Am. council Boy Scouts Am., 1972-77. Served with USPHS, 1969-71. Fellow A.C.P., AAAS, Am. Coll. Neuropsychopharmacology, Am. Coll. Clin. Pharmacology; mem. Am. Soc. Pharmacology and Exptl. Therapeutics (com. div. clin. pharmacology 1972-78, chmn. com. 1978-83, council 1980-83, chmn. long-range planning com. 1984-86, pres. 1987—), Am. Soc. Clin. Pharmacology and Therapeutics (chmn. sect. neuropsychopharmacology 1973-80, chmn. fin. com. 1976-83, v.p. 1981-82, pres. 1983-84, dir. 1975-81, 84-87), Am. Soc. Clin. Investigation, Collegium Internat. Neuro-Psychopharmacologicum, Am. Fedn. Clin. Research, Central Soc. Clin. Research, Soc. Neuroscis., Sigma Xi, Alpha Omega Alpha, Rho Chi. Office: Eli Lilly and Co Wishard Meml Hosp Lilly Lab Clin Research Indianapolis IN 46202

LEMIEUX, JOSEPH HENRY, manufacturing company executive; b. Providence, Mar. 2, 1931; s. Mildred L. Lemieux; m. Frances Joanne Schmidt, Aug. 11, 1956; children: Gerald Joseph, Craig Joseph, Kimberly Mae Lemieux Wolff, Allison Jo. Student, Stonehill Coll., 1949-50, U. R.I., 1950-51; BBA summa cum laude, Bryant Coll., 1957. With Owens-Ill., Toledo, 1957—, various positions with glass container div. and closure and metal container group; exec. v.p. Owens-Ill. Owens-Ill., Inc., Toledo, 1984, pres. pkg. ops., 1984, pres., chief operating officer, 1986—, also bd. dirs.; chmn. bd. dirs. Health Care & Retirement Corp. Am.; bd. dirs. Ohio Citizens Bank, Toledo. Vice chmn. bd. govs. Edison Indsl. Systems Ctr. U. Toledo, 1986. Served to staff sgt. USAF, 1951-55. Named one of Outstanding Young Men Am., Jaycees, 1965. Mem. Glass Packaging Inst. (chmn. 1984-86), Packaging Edn. Found. (bd. dirs.). Roman Catholic. Clubs: Toledo, Shadow Valley Tennis, Inverness (Toledo). Avocations: golf, tennis. Office: Owens-Ill Inc One Seagate Toledo OH 43666

LEMIRE, JEROME ALBERT, lawyer, geologist; b. Cleve., June 4, 1947; s. George A. and Matilda (Simon) L.; m. Sandra Marsick, Oct. 1, 1976; children—Laura, Lesley, Thomas. B.S. in Geology, Ohio State U., 1969, M.S. in Geology, 1973, J.D., 1976. Bar: Ohio 1976; cert. fin. planner. Geologist United Petroleum Co., Columbus, Ohio, 1976-77; assoc. Brownfield, Bowen & Bally, Columbus, 1977-79; land mgr. POI Energy Inc., Cleve., 1979-81; cons., Jefferson, Ohio, 1981-83; v.p. Carey Resources Inc., Jefferson, 1984-86; pres. Lemire & Assocs. Inc., Jefferson, 1986—. cons., 1986—. Vice chmn. Tech. Adv. Council, Columbus, 1984—. Served to 1st lt. U.S. Army, 1970-72. Mem. ABA, Ohio Bar Assn., Am. Assn. Petroleum Geologists, Am. Assn. Petroleum Landman, Inst. Cert. Fin. Planners. Democrat. Roman Catholic. Home: 838 State Route 46 N Jefferson OH 44047

LEMKE, CORRINE LARUE, university grants official; b. Sabin, Minn., May 25, 1934; d. Oswald Edward and Ida M. (Krabbenhoft) L. B.A. in Philosophy, Moorhead State U., 1972. Notary pub., Minn. With WDAY radio and TV sta., Fargo, N.D., 1953-67; fin. aid grant coordinator Moorhead State U., 1967—, mem. task force study of changing student mix, 1983-84. Vol. Comstock Hist. House, Moorhead. Recipient cert. Gov. Minn., 1976, 10 yr. service award Moorhead State U., 1980, letter of commendation U.S. Dept. Edn., 1983. Mem. Minn. Assn. Fin. Aid Adminstrs., Minn. Assn. Student Fin. Aid Adminstrs., Minn. Hist. Soc., State Hist. Soc. Wis., Concordia Hist. Inst. of St. Louis, Phoenix Soc. of Moorhead, Concordia Coll. Alumni Assn., Moorhead State U. Alumni Assn. Lutheran. Author pvt. family history publs. Home: 128 Pierce Trailer Ct Moorhead MN 56560 Office: Moorhead State U Moorhead MN 56560

LEMKE, MICHAEL ALOIS, finance executive; b. Milw., Mar. 23, 1951; s. Richard Michael and Dorothy Clara (Kaml) L.; m. Doris Barbara Schmilewski, May 19, 1973; children: Steven, Jessica. BBA with honors, U. Wis., Milw., 1974. CPA, Wis. Auditor Deloitte Haskins & Sells, Milw., 1974-76; sr. fin. analyst Cutler Hammer, Milw., 1976-79; treas. ABCO Dealers, Inc., Milw., 1979—, v.p. fin. adminstrn., 1987—. Asst. cub master Brookfield council Boy Scouts Am., 1984-85; treas., trustee Immanuel Luth. Ch., Milw., 1982-83, chmn. audit com., 1982, 85. Milw. Soc. Engrs. scholar, 1969. Mem. Am. Inst. CPAs (Elija Watts Sells award, 1974), Wis. Inst. CPAs., Beta Gamma Sigma. Avocation: woodworking. Home: W161 N5037 Hickory Tree Ln Menomonee Falls WI 53051

LEMME, BARBARA HANSEN, psychologist, educator; b. Oak Park, Ill., Sept. 28, 1947; d. George Flogstad and Evelyn June (Nissen) Hansen; m. Ronald Dale Lemme, July 29, 1978; 1 child, Rebecca Kristen. BA, U. Kans., 1969, MA, 1970; EdD, Nova U., 1980. Lic. psychologist, Ill. Instr. psychology Coll. DuPage, Glen Ellyn, Ill., 1970-79, dean social and behavioral scis., 1979-80, prof. psychology, 1981—, honors coordinator, 1985—; lectr. various civic groups. Trustee Coll. DuPage Found., 1976-82; mem. DuPage Sr. Citizens Council. Mem. Am. Psychol. Assn., Midwestern Psychol. Assn., Ill. Psychol. Assn., Am. Soc. Aging, Nat. Collegiate Honors Council, Wheaton Jr. Women's Club (chmn. ways and means 1983-84, treas. 1985-86, bd. dirs. 1986-87, nominating chmn. 1986-87). Democrat. Presbyterian. Avocations: travel, country antiques, crafts, bridge. Office: Coll DuPage 22d St and Lambert Rd Glen Ellyn IL 60137

LEMMONS, JAMES CURTIS, manufacturing company executive; b. Jonesboro, Ark., July 8, 1948; s. Charles Norman Lemmons and Betty Jo (Knotts) Albertina; m. Dianne Louise Feller, Apr. 24, 1983. BS in Indsl. Engring., U. Ill., 1972; MBA, DePaul U., 1976. Mfg. engr. Elkay Mfg. Co., Broadview, Ill., 1972-78; plant mgr. Dayton-Ogden Corp., Ogden, Utah, 1978-83; dir. mfg. engr. Elkay Mfg. Co., 1983; v.p. ops. Fed. Signal Corp., University Park, Ill., 1983—. Clubs: Fedn. Fly Fisherman (West Yellowstone, Mont.); Amateur Trap-Shooting Assn. (Vandalia, Ohio). Avocations: trap shooting; fly fishing; alpine skiing. Home: 337 Hampton Pl Hinsdale IL 60521 Office: Fed Signal Corp 2645 Federal Signal Dr University Park IL 60466

LEMON, CHESTER EARL (CHET), professional baseball player. Centerfielder Detroit Tigers, 1982—; mem. 1984 World Series Championship team. Gold Glove winner. Office: Detroit Tigers Tiger Stadium Detroit MI 48216 *

LEMUS, FRATERNO, neurologist; b. Quetzaltenango, Guatemala, Dec. 5, 1948; came to U.S., 1974; s. Emilio and Isabel (Mazariegos) L.; m. Clare J. Ciannamea, Sept. 3, 1977; children: Lorena Elizabeth, Natalie Ann, Stephanie Noel. MD, Univ. de San Carlos, Guatemala City, 1973. Diplomate Am. Bd. Psychiatry and Neurology. Resident neurology tng. program Mt. Sinai Med. Ctr. and Affiliated Hosps., Chgo., 1974-77, chief resident, 1977; practice medicine specializing in neurology Orland Park, Ill.; chmn. Div. Neurology St. Mary of Nazareth Med. Ctr., Chgo., 1981—. Mem. AMA, Am. Acad. Neurology. Office: 1600 Ravinia Pl Orland Park IL 60462

LENARD, MICHAEL JOHN, postal clerk, philatelist; b. Wausau, Wis., July 5, 1943; s. Alexander T. and Genevieve M. (Stoltz) L.; m. Tangie Jean Rusch, Nov. 2, 1974; children—Andrew James, April Jan. Student Marathon County U. Wis., 1963-65. With Wausau Homes, Inc., 1965-66; postal clk., U.S. Postal Service, Wausau, 1966—. Served with USMC, 1967. Recipient First Place and Grand awards stamp shows, 1973—. Mem. Am. Philatelic Soc., Croatian Philatelic Soc. Democrat. Mem. Ch. Jesus Christ of Latter-day Saints. Expert on Yugoslavian stamps. Home: 1514 N 3d Ave Wausau WI 54401

LENCZYCKI, JULIE MARIE, interior designer; b. Kalamazoo, Mar. 11, 1958; d. Charles Dewayne and Judith Marie (Durham) Roberts; m. Andrew Tad Lenczycki, Sept. 1, 1984. BS, Western Mich. U., 1981. Detailer, drafter Borrough's Div. LSI, Kalamazoo, 1982-86; interior designer Mich. Office Environments, Kalamazoo, 1986—. Alumnea advisor Phi Mu Frat., Kalamazoo, 1986. Mem. Am. Soc. Interior Designers (assoc.), Austin Lake Catamaran Assn. Avocations: sailing, skiing, renovation of old homes. Home: 5057 Long Lake Dr Portage MI 49002 Office: Mich Office Environments 5123 Portage Rd Kalamazoo MI 49002

LENDER, MENAHEM, physician, educator; b. Afula, Israel, Apr. 3, 1941; came to U.S., 1976; s. Baruch L.; m. Pirhia Midroni, 1963; children: Hadar Y., Dafna. Student, Hadassah Med. Sch., Israel; MD, Hebrew U., Jerusalem, 1970. Diplomate Am. Bd. Internal Medicine, Am. Bd. Endocrinology and Metabolism, Am. Bd. Nutrition. Resident in internal medicine Share Zedek Hosp., Jerusalem, 1970-75; dir. hosp. services Ministry of Health, Jerusalem, 1975-76; resident in endocrinology VA Hosp., Hines, Ill., 1976-78, staff physician, 1978—; assoc. prof. medicine Loyola U., Maywood, Ill., 1977—; lectr. medicine U. Health Scis., Chgo. Med. Sch., North Chicago, Ill., 1982—. Contbr. numerous chpts. to books, articles to med. jours. Served to capt. Israeli Med. Corps, 1959-62. Fellow ACP, Am. Coll. Nutrition (cert.); mem. N.Y. Acad. Scis., Chgo. Endocrine Club. Home: 909 Park Ave River Forest IL 60305 Office: VA Hosp 5th Ave and Roosevelt Rd Hines IL 60141

LENDT, HAROLD HANFORD, manufacturing representative; b. Boone, Iowa, Jan. 2, 1922; s. Howard Wesley and Hulda Victoria (Tweedt) L.; m. Verna A. Jessen, Nov. 10, 1946 (div. June 1962); children: Cindy Tuttle, Carol Woodbury, Larry. Student, Augustana Coll., 1946-47; BBA, U. S.D., 1948. Salesman Louden Machinery Co., Fairfield, Iowa, 1953-60, Omaha Mut., St. Paul, 1960-62; maintenance supr. Dayton Hudson Corp., Mpls., 1962-79, Towle Real Estate, Mpls., 1979-82; owner, mgr. Harold Lendt Co., St. Paul, 1975—. Trustee Presdl. Task Force, Washington, 1981; mem. Rep. Com., Washington, 1974-81. Served to sgt. U.S. Army, 1942-44, ETO. Recipient Merit award Rep. Task Force, Washington. Home: 2010 Merriam Ln Saint Paul MN 55104 Address: PO Box 40231 Saint Paul MN 55104

LENEAU, PETER WILLARD, controller; b. Mpls., Jan. 19, 1954; s. Thomas Jean and Evelyn (Schwantes) LeN.; m. Claudia Marie Guimond, Oct. 22, 1977; children: Michele, Kyle. BS in Pub. Acctg., St. Cloud (Minn.) State U., 1975. CPA, Minn. Staff acct. Main Lafrentz CPA's, Mpls., 1975-77; mgr. Goldfein Silverman CPA's, Mpls., 1977-83; system analyst Q E D Inc., Mpls., 1983; controller Norhaven Inc., St. Paul, 1983—. Treas. 26th St Project, Mpls., 1984—, St. Paul ARC, 1985-86; mem. fin. com. local ch., Brooklyn Ctr., Minn., 1987. Mem. Am. Inst. CPA's, Minn. Soc. CPA's. Office: Norhaven Inc 276 N Snelling Ave Saint Paul MN 55104

LENHART, MILTON JOHN, obstetrician-gynecologist; b. Youngstown, OH, Feb. 6, 1932; s. Milton Stephen and Anna (Vansuch) L.; m. Roberta Rubenstahl, Nov. 28, 1959; children: Milton George, Denise Marie, Lisa Ann, Lorraine Eleanor. BS, Ohio State U., 1953, MD, 1957. Practice medicine specializing in ob-gyn. Youngstown, Ohio, 1964—; Chief ob-gyn. Youngstown Hospital Assn., 1979-84, attending physician 1964—; courtesy staff St. Elizabeth's Med. Ctr., Youngstown, 1964—. Pres. St. Edward's Home and Sch. Assn., Youngstown, 1976. Served to lt. USNR, 1958-60. Mem. AMA, Ohio State Med. Assn., Mahoney County Med. Soc. (counsil 1986), Cleve. Ob-Gyn. Soc., Youngstown Ob-Gyn. Soc. Roman Catholic. Lodge: Rotary (social chmn. Youngstown 1985). Avocations: photography, gardening, travel. Home: 2225 Fifth Ave Youngstown OH 44504 Office: 435 Gypsy Ln Youngstown OH 44504

LENHART, NED ALLAN, accountant; b. Fairfield, Iowa, Aug. 6, 1957; s. Kermit Arthur and Charlotte Mae (Coen) L.; m. Laurie Ann Wulf, Aug. 18, 1984. BA, Iowa Wesleyan Coll., 1980; MBA, Mankato State U., 1982. CPA, Mo. Instr. bus. Iowa Wesleyan Coll., Mt. Pleasant, 1982-84; instr. acctg. William Woods Coll., Fulton, Mo., 1984-86; budget analyst State of Mo., Jefferson City, 1986-87, asst. div. dir. Dept. Revenue, 1987—. Fellow Am. Inst. CPA's, Mo. Soc. CPA's, Assn. Govtl. Accts. Republican. Methodist. Avocations: golfing, boating, woodworking.

LENIHAN, DERMOT PATRICK, public health administrator; b. London, Eng., Aug. 26, 1948; came to U.S., 1955; s. Thomas D. and Lucy (Fay) L.; m. Sharon L. Bonow, Sept. 24, 1972. BS, U. Ill., Urbana, 1974; MS, U. Ill., Chgo., 1976. Dir. of research Health Systems Agy. of Kane, Lake and McHenry Counties, Inc., Cary, Ill., 1976-80; dir. info. systems Chgo. Health Systems, 1980-83; dep. commr. Chgo. Health Dept., 1983—; cons. and lectr. U.S. Dept. Health, USPHS, 1978, U. Ill., 1979, Chgo. Med. Sch., 1979, Roosevelt U., 1985; mem. plan devel. com. Chgo. Health Systems Agy., 1984-86. V.p. issues com. Lake View Citizens Council, Chgo., 1985-86. Mem. Am. Pub. Health Assn., Ill. Pub. Health Assn., Am. Health Planning Assn., Am. Assn. Hosp. Planners. Home: 3750 N Wayne Chicago IL 60613 Office: Chgo Dept Health Daley Ctr Plaza 50 W Washington St Chicago IL 60602

LENK, MICHAEL, research and development engineer; b. Grossburgwedel, Fed. Republic Germany, Apr. 29, 1960; s. Reinhard and Ingrid (Pinkepank) L.; m. Laurie Kay Kraus, Nov. 22, 1980; children: Amanda Michelle. BSME, Purdue U., 1982. Research and devel. engr. Champion Spark Plug Co., Toledo, 1980—. Inventor low engine oil sensing, 1985, low engine oil sensing switch, 1986. Advisor Jr. Achievement, 1983-84. Mem. ASME (assoc.), Am. Welding Soc. (assoc.), Laser Inst. Am. Republican. Lutheran. Avocations: sports, camping, coin collecting. Home: 2045 E Crest Toledo OH 43614 Office: Champion Spark Plug Co 900 Upton Ave Toledo OH 43661

LENN, SENKA J., banker, lawyer; b. Gary, Ind., July 19, 1955; d. Violet (Bjelivuk) Miletic. BS, U. Colo., 1977; JD, Case Western Reserve U., 1982. Bar: Ohio 1983. Assoc. Chattman, Garfield Friedlander & Paul, Cleve., 1982-84; mgr. investor reporting and servicing transfers Transohio Savs. Bank, Cleve., 1986—. Vol. atty. Legal Aid Soc., Cleve., 1982, Divorce Equity, Cleve., 1984-86. Mem. Jr. League, Case Western Reserve U. Law Review. Clubs: Women's City (Cleve.), 13th St. Racquet (Cleve.). Avocations: sports, theater, reading, fgn. films and langs. Office: Transohio Savs Bank 1250 Superior Ave NE Cleveland OH 44114

LENNES, GREGORY, manufacturing and financing company executive; b. Chgo., Aug. 5, 1947; s. Lawrence Dominic and Genevieve (Karoll) L.; m. Maryann Meskers, July 27, 1968; children: Robert, Sandra, Ryan. BA, U. Ill., 1969, MA, 1971, postgrad., 1971-73. Corp. archivist Navistar Internat. Corp. (formerly Internat. Harvester Co.), Chgo., 1973-80, records mgr., 1980—, asst. sec., 1980—; sec. Navistar Fin. Corp., Schaumburg, Ill., 1980—, Navistar Internat. Transportation Corp., 1987—. Editor: Historical Records in the Farm Equipment Industry, 1977. Mem. Am. Soc. Corp Secs., Assn. Records Mgrs. and Adminstrs., Soc. Am. Archivists, Midwest Archives Conf., Assn. Info. and Image Mgmt. Home: 14637 Atlantic Ave Dolton IL 60419 Office: Navistar Internat Corp 401 N Michigan Ave Chicago IL 60611

LENNES, SCOTT RICHARD, health association company executive; b. Marshal, Minn., Aug. 4, 1959; s. Richard Norman and Sandra Dawn (Korger) L.; m. Lori Ann Dummer, May 31, 1980. BS, St. Cloud State U., 1981. CPA, minn. Mgr., acct. Larson, Allen, Weishair and Co., Mpls., 1981-85; owner, v.p. fin. Health Dimensions, Inc., Cambridge, Minn., 1985—. Mem. Am. Inst. CPA's, Minn. Soc. CPA's, Care Providers Minn., Cambridge Jaycees, Beta Gamma Sigma, Phi Kappa Phi. Office: Health Dimensions Inc 115 N Dellwood Cambridge MN 55008

LENNON, DANIEL FRANCIS, insurance company executive; b. Mt. Clemens, July 6, 1946; s. Jacob John and Margaret (Ayer) L.; m. Dolores Fisher, Jan. 25, 1975; children: Thomas, Henry, Matthew. BS in Gen. Engring., U.S. Mil. Acad., 1969. CLU. Commd. 2d lt. U.S. Army, 1969, advanced through grades to capt., resigned, 1974; sales rep. Liberty Mut. Ins. Co., Smithtown, N.Y., 1975-77; supr. Blue Cross/Blue Shield Ind., Indpls., 1977-79; mgr. Regional Mktg. Inc., Indpls., 1979-82, dir., 1982—; risk mgr. Pan Am. games X, Indpls., 1986—. Author: (software system) Group Adminstrv. System, 1981. Instr. Jr. Achievement, Indpls., 1986. Republican. Roman Catholic. Home: 7339 Cape Cod Circle Indianapolis IN 46250 Office: Regional Mktg 333 N Alabama Suite 300 Indianapolis IN 46204

LENNON, SHERYL ROSENBERG, accountant; b. Detroit, Aug. 23, 1955; d. Herbert Hirsh and Florence (Wolkin) Rosenberg; m. Mark William Lennon, May 1, 1983. BS in Acctg., Wayne State U., 1977; MBA, U. Detroit, 1985. CPA, Mich. Sr. acct. Jack Martin and Co., P.C., Birmingham, Mich., 1975-80; dep. dir. Acctg. Aid. Soc., Detroit, 1980-81; supr. acctg. Southeastern Mich. Transportation, Detroit, 1981-84; sr. internal auditor Gen. Dynamics, St. Louis, 1984-86, Volkwagen of Am., Troy, Mich., 1986—. Tax reviewer IRS Vol. Income Tax Assistance, Detroit, 1975-85. Mem. Am. Inst. CPA's, Mich. Assn. CPA's, Inst. Internal Auditors, B'nai B'rith Accts. Group, LaPeer County Bd. Realtors. Jewish. Club: X Factor (Royal Oak, Mich.) (treas. 1986—). Avocations: scuba diving. Home: 402 E St Clair Almont MI 48003 Office: Volkswagen of Am 888 W Big Beaver Rd Troy MI 48007-3951

LENNOX, DONALD D(UANE), automotive and housing components company executive; b. Pitts., Dec. 3, 1918; s. Edward George and Sarah B. (Knight) L.; m. Jane Armstrong, June 11, 1949; children: Donald D., J. Gordon. BS with honors, U. Pitts., 1947. CPA, Pa. With Ford Motor Co., 1950-69; with Xerox Corp., 1969-80; corp. v.p. and sr. v.p. info. tech. group Xerox Corp., Rochester, N.Y., 1969-73, group v.p. and pres. info. tech. group, 1973-75, group v.p., pres. info. systems group, 1975-80; sr. v.p., sr. staff officer Xerox Corp., Stamford, Conn., 1973-74; sr. v.p. ops. staff Navistar Internat. Corp., Rochester, 1980-81, exec. v.p., 1981-82, pres., chief operating officer, 1982, pres., chief exec. officer, 1982, chmn., chief exec. officer, 1983-87; chmn., chief exec. officer Schlegel Corp., Rochester, 1987—, also bd. dirs. Trustee St. John Fisher Coll. Served with AC USN, 1942-45. Decorated D.F.C. with 2 gold stars, Air medal with 4 gold stars. Mem. Rochester Area C. of C. (pres. 1979), Order of Artus, Soc. Automotive Engrs., Beta Gamma Sigma. Republican. Clubs: Country of Rochester, Genesee Valley; Econ. (Chgo.).

LENON, RICHARD ALLEN, chemical corporation executive; b. Lansing, Mich., Aug. 4, 1920; s. Theo and Elizabeth (Amon) L.; m. Helen Johnson, Sept. 13, 1941; children: Richard Allen, Pamela A., Lisa A. B.A., Western Mich. Coll., 1941; postgrad., Northwestern U., 1941-42. Mgr. finance div. Montgomery Ward & Co., Chgo., 1947-56; v.p. finance Westinghouse Air Brake Co., 1963-67, treas., 1965-67; v.p., treas. Internat. Minerals & Chem. Corp., Skokie, Ill., 1956-63; group v.p. finance and adminstrn. Internat. Minerals & Chem. Corp., 1967-68, exec. v.p., 1968-70, pres., 1970-78, chmn., 1977-86, chmn. exec. com., 1986—; dir. Am. Standard Co., Bankers Trust Co., Fed. Paper Bd. Co., Allied-Signal Inc., Allis-Chalmers Co., Internat. Minerals & Chem. Corp. Served to lt. comdr. USNR, 1942-47. Clubs: University (Chgo.); Glen View (Ill.). Home: 803 Solar Ln Glenview IL 60025 Office: Internat Minerals and Chem Corp 2315 Sanders Rd Northbrook IL 60062

LENOX, ARLENE NADINE, manufacturing company executive; b. Wichita, Kans., Aug. 28, 1932; d. Alfred E. and Eva M. (Buttrick) Arnett; m. Bill G. Lenox, May 13, 1965 (div. July 1972); children: Michael Bolinger, Karen Bolinger Shingler, Troy Lenox. Sec. and gen. mgr. Plaza Towel Holder Co., Wichita, 1956-72, v.p. and treas., 1972-82, pres. and gen. mgr., 1982-84; pres. and gen. mgr. Lenox Mfg., Inc., Wichita, 1984—. Mem. Kans. Lodging Assn., Wichita Lodging Assn., North Wichita Bus. Assn., Wichita C. of C., Midwest Genealogy Soc., Topeka Genealogy Soc. Presbyterian. Avocations: genealogy, swimming, bowling, walking. Home: 7600 N Broadway Wichita KS 67219 Office: Lenox Mfg Inc 1845 N Broadway PO Box 4737 Wichita KS 67204

LENT, ROBERT WILLIAM, counseling psychologist; b. Bklyn. Apr. 1, 1953; s. Jack Harvey and Gladys (Unger) L. B.A., SUNY-Albany, 1975; M.A., Ohio State U., 1977, Ph.D., 1979. Lic. psychologist. Teaching assoc. Ohio State U., Columbus, 1976-77; psychology intern Mpls. VA Hosp., 1977-78; psychology intern Ohio State U., 1978-79; asst. prof. student counseling bur., U. Minn., 1979-84, assoc. prof., 1984-85; asst. prof. counseling psychology Mich. State U., East Lansing, 1985-86, assoc. prof., 1986—. Vol. counselor Walk-in Counseling Ctr., Mpls., 1977-78. Mem. Am. Psychol. Assn., Am. Assn. Counseling and Devel., Phi Beta Kappa. Co-author profl. publs., tng. films; co-editor Handbook of Counseling Psychology. Office: Mich State U Dept Counseling and Psychology 513 Erickson East Lansing MI 48824

LENTZ, GORDON FRANKLIN, muffler franchise company executive; b. Milan, Mich., Apr. 16, 1936; s. Leonard Leo and Clarice Hubba (Albright) L.; m. Gloria Jean Plummer, Oct. 4, 1958; children—Brad, Jeff, Greg. B.A., Wayne State U. Sales rep. Bankers Life & Casualty Co., Southfield, Mich., 1961-65; gen. agt. Wayne Nat. Life Ins. Co., Detroit, 1965-66; sales engr. Dexion Inc., Warren, Mich., 1966-72; franchisee Tuffy Muffler, Kalamazoo, Mich., 1972-83; pres., chief exec. officer Lentz U.S.A. Mufflers, Kalamazoo, 1983—. Served with AUS, 1959-61. Mem. Ind. Muffler Dealers Assn. (v.p. 1978-85). Congregationalist (moderator 1978).

LENTZ, LINDA KAY, learning disability educator, school psychologist; b. Dayton, Ohio, Aug. 13, 1936; d. Harry E. and Mary E. (Swinger) Denlinger; m. Paul Dean Lentz, May 5, 1955; children: Lisa Kay Heaton, David Paul. BS, U. Dayton, 1981, MS, 1985; MEd, Wright State U., 1987. Cert. tchr., Ohio. Tchr., owner Springboro (Ohio) Pre-sch., 1974-83; tchr. learning disabilities Franklin (Ohio) City Schs., 1983-87, sch. psychologist intern, 1987—. Mem. Springboro Bd. Edn., 1981-84; chairperson Help through Edn. Leads to Prevention, Springboro, 1982-85. Recipient Community Involvement award Springboro Jaucees, 1983, Disting. Service award Springboro Jaycees, 1984, William Holden Jennings Scholar award U. Dayton, 1986-87. Mem. Nat. Assn. Sch. Psychologists, Nat. Assn. for Children with Learning Disabilities, Ohio Assn. for Children with Learning Disabilities, Ohio Assn. for Counseling and Devel. Methodist. Avocations: reading, swimming, water skiing, pursuing ednl. endeavors. Home: 2921 E State Rt 73 Waynesville OH 45068

LENZ, ROBERT THOMAS, business educator; b. New Albany, Ind., May 12, 1947; s. Robert Lee and Ruth Day (Kist) L.; m. Marla Kay Clark, Aug. 21, 1977; children: Abigail Clark, Gregory Thomas. BS with high distinction, Ind. U., 1969, DBA, 1978; MBA, U. Louisville, 1972. Process control engr. Gen. Electric Co., Bloomington, Ind., 1971-73, mgr. quality control, 1973-74; asst. prof. bus. Ind. U.-Indpls., 1978-81, assoc. prof. bus. adminstrn., 1982—, chmn. exec. MBA-CIP program, 1985-87, assoc. dean, 1987—; resident dir. Tilburg Program, Program in Western European Studies, John F. Kennedy Inst., U. Tilburg (Netherlands), 1984; bd. dirs. Guarantee Auto Stores, Inc.; vis. assoc. prof. strategic mgmt. Sanford U., 1987. Contbr. articles, mem. editorial rev. bd. Strategic Mgmt. Jour., Acad. of Mgmt. Rev.; contbr. articles to profl. jours. Recipient Teaching Excellence award MBA Career in Progress Student Adv. Com., 1978-80, 82-86, Amoco Found. Teaching Excellence award; grantee Strategy Research Ctr., 1983. Mem. Acad. Mgmt. (exec. com., bus. policy and planning div. 1985-87), Beta Gamma Sigma, Sigma Iota Epsilon. Methodist. Club: Econs. (Indpls.). Office: Indiana U 801 W Michigan St Suite 3024 Indianapolis IN 46223

LEON, ARTHUR SOL, research cardiologist, exercise physiologist; b. Bklyn., Apr. 26, 1931; s. Alex and Anne (Schrek) L.; m. Gloria Rakita, Dec. 23, 1956; children: Denise, Harmon, Michelle. BS in Chemistry with high honors, U. Fla., 1952; MS in Biochemistry, U. Wis., 1954, MD, 1957. Intern Henry Ford Hosp., Detroit, 1957-58; fellow in internal medicine Lahey Clinic, Boston, 1958-60; fellow in cardiology Jackson Meml. Hosp.-U. Miami (Fla.) Med. Sch., 1960-61; dir. clin. pharmacology research unit Hoffmann-La Roche Inc.-Newark Beth Israel Med. Ctr., 1969-73; from instr. to assoc. prof. medicine Coll. Medicine and Dentistry N.J., Newark, 1967-73; from assoc. prof. to prof. Lab. Physiol. Hygiene div. of epidemiology U. Minn. Sch. Pub. Health, also Grad. Sch., Med. Sch., Mpls., 1973—, dir. applied physiology and nutrition, 1973—; mem. med. eval. team Gemini and Apollo projects NASA, 1964-67. Author numerous articles in field. Trustee Vinland Nat. Sports Health Ctr. for Disabled, 1978—. Served as officer M.C. U.S. Army, 1961-67, col. Res. 1978—. Recipient Anderson award AAHPER, 1981; Am. Heart Assn. fellow, 1960-61. Fellow Am. Coll. Cardiology, Am. Coll. Chest Physicians, Am. Coll. Cin. Pharmacology, N.Y. Acad. Sci., Am. Coll. Sports Medicine (trustee 1976-78, 82-83, v.p. 1977-79, pres. Northland chpt. 1975-76); mem. Am. Physiol. Soc., Am. Soc. Pharmacology and Exptl. Therapeutics, Am. Inst. Nutrition, Am. Heart Assn. (v.p. Hennepin County div. 1980-81, pres. 1982-83), Am. Coll. Nutrition, Am. Fedn. Clin. Research, Minn. Lung Assn. (trustee 1978-81), Phi Beta Kappa, Phi Kappa Phi. Jewish. Home: 5628 Glen Ave Minnetonka MN 55345 Office: U Minn Sch Pub Health Div Epidemiology 611 Beacon St SE Minneapolis MN 55455

LEONARD, ALAN THOMAS, psychologist; b. Vermontville, Mich., Oct. 21, 1917; s. Archie George and Mabel Groves (Cook) L.; m. Anne Bertha Bosma Cronick, Oct. 12, 1954; children: Karen Anne, Charles Herbert. Student, U. Vienna, Austria, 1945; BS, Wayne State U., 1946, MA, 1948; PhD, Columbia U., 1983. Lic. psychologist, Mich. Chief psychologist Grand Rapids (Mich.) Child Guidance Clinic, 1948-58; pvt. practice psychology Muskegon, Mich., 1958—; cons. State of Mich. 1958—, numerous govtl. agys., 1958—. Host Pub. Radio and TV series on mental health and edn., Grand Rapids, Muskegon, 1956-58. Served to sgt. U.S. Army, 1943-45, ETO. Fellow Am. Orthopsychiat. Assn.; mem. Am. Psychol. Assn., Am. Rehab. Assn., Mich. Psychol. Assn., Mich. Med. Soc. Avocations: golf, coin collecting, flying helicopters. Home: 302 3d St North Muskegon MI 49445 Office: 435 Whitehall Rd North Muskegon MI 49445

LEONARD, BERNARD MICHAEL, accountant; b. Chgo., June 26, 1947; s. Bernard Justin and Margaret June (Debiase) L.; m. Patricia Ann Faragia, Aug. 29, 1970 (div. Aug. 1978); children: Michael Bernard, Daniel James; m. Susan Jean Keesen, Aug. 23, 1980. AA, Triton Coll., 1969; student, No. Ill. U., 1969-71. CPA, Ill. Staff acct. Accts. Associated, Chgo., 1967-71; prin. Leonard & Co., Elmwood Park, Ill., 1971—; pres. Tax Line, Inc., Elmwood Park, 1983—, also bd. dirs.; bd. dirs. Remsco, Inc., Arlington Heights, Ill.; co-founder Success Planners Inst.; nat. speaker on taxation, success planning, motivational tng.; enrolled to practice before IRS. Trustee Goodwill Industries, Chgo., 1986; mem. acctg. adv. com. Triton Coll., River Grove, Ill., 1983. Mem. Am. Inst. CPA's, Ill. CPA Soc., Nat. Soc. Pub. Accts., Italo-Am. Nat. Union. Roman Catholic. Avocations: writing music, racquetball, collecting coins. Office: 7234 W North Ave Elmwood Park IL 60635

LEONARD, JAMES FRANCIS, professional sports agent; b. Chgo., July 28, 1952; s. John Edward and Eleanor Mary (Dever) L.; m. Patricia Marie Bigoness, Aug. 13, 1977; children: James, Robert, Nicholas. BA, North Cen. Coll., 1974; MBA, No. Ill. U., 1980. Cert. secondary tchr., Ill. Acct. Walgreen's, Deerfield, Ill., 1973; tchr. math. St. Francis High Sch., Wheaton, Ill., 1974-76; tchr. bus. A.A. Stagg High Sch., Palos Hills, Ill., 1976—, Elmhurst (Ill.) Coll., 1979—; cons. Coll. Sororities, Elmhurst, 1980—; comptroller student fund North Cen. Coll., Naperville, Ill., 1972-74; mem. curriculum com., Palos Hills, 1983—. Mem. Assn. MBA, Nat. Educators Assn., Ill. Educators Assn., Ill. High Sch. Assn., Nat. Fedn. Interscholastic Officials Assn., South Suburban Officials Assn., Unified Met. Profl. Services. Republican. Roman Catholic. Avocation: officiating high sch. and coll. football and baseball. Home: 40 Birchdale Dr Lockport IL 60441 Office: Amos Alonzo Stagg High Sch 111th & Roberts Rd Palos Hills IL 60465

LEONARD, LISA ANN, immunologist; b. Schenectady, N.Y., Feb. 3, 1959; d. Richard Mayne and Blythe (Igoe) L.; m. Richard L. Timm, Sept. 20, 1986. BS in Microbiology, Colo. State U., 1982; MS in Immunology, Albany Med. Coll., 1986. Research asst. Becton Dickinson Immunodiagnostics, Orangeburg, N.Y., 1982-83; mgr. ops. Diagnostic Reagent Tech., Teaneck, N.J., 1983-85; research assoc. Mayo Clinic, Rochester, Minn., 1986—. Bd. dirs. Rochester Internat. Assn., 1986; mem. corp. com. Rochester Art Ctr., 1986—. Mem. N.Y. Acad. Sci., AAUW, Am. Soc. Clin. Pathologists, Am. Soc. for Microbiology, Schenectady Jr. League. Avocations: curling, sailing, tennis, horticulture. Office: Mayo Clinic Plummer 442-A Rochester MN 55905

LEONARD, PAUL R., lieutenant governor; b. Dayton, July 3, 1943; s. Paul R. and Ida L. B.S. with honors in Journalism, Ohio U., 1965; J.D., Chase Coll. Law, Cin., 1969. Bar: Ohio. Labor relations rep. Gen. Motors Corp., 1966-69; asst. prosecuting atty. Montgomery County, Ohio, 1969-72; mem. Ohio Ho. of Reps., 1972-80; mayor City of Dayton, Ohio, 1981-86; lt. gov. State of Ohio, Columbus, 1987—; adj. prof. polit. sci. Wright State U., Dayton; mem. com. Econ. Devel., State and Fed. Relations. Mem. bd. dirs. Dayton Urban League; mem. Miami Valley Cancer Consortium. Named to Ohio U. Alumni Hall of Fame, recipient Medal of Merit; First Annual award Dayton Pub. Sch. System's Outstanding Graduates; Outstanding Community Leader award Knights of Columbus Council. Mem. Nat. Lt. Govs. Assn., Dem. Lt. Govs. Assn. (exec. com.). Leading advocate for fire safety legislation and reforming laws to help the mentally ill in Ohio. Home: 2815 Lake Shore Pl Dayton OH 45420 Office: Statehouse Columbus OH 43215 *

LEONARD, RICHARD PHILLIP, fireplace company executive; b. Milw., Dec. 19, 1934; s. Phillip S. and Cecilia (Kalamajka) L.; m. Karen Maria Sandberg, Nov. 7, 1959; children: Scott, Susan, Jon. Student, Wis. State Tchrs. Coll., 1954-55. Pub. relations rep. Miller Brewing Co., Milw., 1957-61; v.p. G & S Supply Co., Wauwatosa, Wis., 1961-65; sales rep. Best Block Co., Menomonee Falls, Wis., 1965-73; v.p. Unitized Homes, Inc., Muskego, Wis., 1973-74; pres. Fireplace Systems, Ltd., New Berlin, Wis., 1974—. Bd. dirs. Malone Meml. Charity Celebrity Golf Tournament, Waukesha, Wis., 1986. Served as pvt. U.S. Army, 1955-57. Mem. Met. Builders Assn. Milw., Home Improvement Council Milw. Roman Catholic. Lodge: Rotary (pres. 1985-86, Rotarian of Yr. 1983). Avocations: golf, painting, travel, hosting fgn. students. Home: Rt 6 S90 W31295 Wigwam Dr Mukwonago WI 53149 Office: Fireplace Systems Ltd 14967 W National Ave New Berlin WI 53151

LEONARD, THOMAS EDWARD, science educator; b. Chgo., July 11, 1934; s. John Howard and Thelma Phoebe (Van Fossen) L.; m. Natalie Ruth Hahn, Sept. 8, 1956; children: Jonathan Thomas, Stephen Edward, Joanne Ruth. PhD, U. Iowa, 1982. Cert. secondary tchr., Wis. Analytical chemist Stauffer Chem., Weston, Mich., 1956-60; forensic scientist State of Wis., Madison, 1960-63; sci. educator Concordia Coll., Mequon, Wis., 1963—; cons. forensic sci., Milw., 1963—. Editor: (book) Drinking and Driving, 1961. Fulbright scholar, 1983. Mem. Am. Chem. Soc., Nat. Sci. Tchrs. Assn. Republican. Lutheran. Home: 7225 W Vienna Ct Milwaukee WI 53216

LEONARD, THOMAS SIMON, tax accountant; b. Chgo., Aug. 27, 1961; s. John J. and Susan M (Gildea) L.; m. Marian T. Haberkorn, Aug. 14, 1987. BS in Acctg., Bradley U., 1983; MS in Taxation, DePaul U., 1987. CPA, Ill. Staff acct. Coleman, Epstein & Berlin, Chgo., 1984-85; tax analyst Sara Lee Corp., Chgo., 1985—. Mem. Ill. CPA Soc., Am. Inst. CPA's. Avocations: running, reading, school. Office: Sara Lee Corp 3 First Nat Plaza Chicago IL 60602-4260

LEONARDI, JOHN FRANCIS, JR., lawyer, real estate consultant; b. Highland Park, Ill., Sept. 18, 1938; s. John Francis and Gabrielle Dorothy (Walsh) L.; m. Annette Marie Ketchum, 1962 (dec. Feb. 1977); children: John F. III, Marisa Louise; m. Emily Marie Simpson, Dec. 12, 1978. BBA, Marquette U., 1960; JD, John Marshall, 1964-68. Dir. mktg. Pioneer Nat. Tile, Waukegan, Ill., 1968-73; co-owner Mid. Am. Tile Co., Waukegan, Ill., 1973-84; pvt. practice cons. investments Libertyville, Ill., 1984—. Instr. Youth Fishing Program, Lake County Forest Preserve, Libertyville, 1986—. Served to 1st lt. U.S. Army, 1960-64. Mem. Lake County Bd. Realtors (bd. dirs. 1979-80), Lake County Home Builders Assn. (bd. dirs. 1975-79), Lake County Bar Assn. (bd. dirs. 1974-75), Ducks Unlimited (dinner commn. Waukegan 1984—). Roman Catholic. Avocations: fishing, outdoor print collecting, hunting. Home: 1120 Sandstone Dr Libertyville IL 60048

LEONG, PERRY THOMAS, chemical engineer; b. St. Louis, Sept. 30, 1956; s. James On Cook and Janet Van (Ho) L. BS in Chem. Engring., Washington U., St. Louis, 1979, MBA, 1984. Research engr. Dow Chem. USA, Freeport, Tex., 1979-80; engr. Monsanto, St. Louis, 1980-83, sr. process engr., 1983-87, sr. prodn. supr., 1987—. Mem. Am. Inst. Chem. Engrs. Republican. Avocations: computers, photography.

LEONHARDT, RONALD DAVID, research association executive; b. Medford, Wis., Aug. 3, 1947; m. Margaret Mary Hamel, Dec. 30, 1971; children: Matthew, Luke, Elizabeth, Peter. BA, U. Wis., 1969, JD, 1975. Legis. atty. Wis. Legis. Ref. Bur., Madison, 1975-79; assoc. Cook & Franke, S.C., Milw., 1980-82; dir. Milw. Legis. Ref., Milw., 1982—. Mem. State Bar Wis., research clearing house Met. Milw. Roman Catholic. Office: Legis Ref Bur 200 E Wells St Milwaukee WI 53202

LEONIDA, DOMINGO DOMINIC JOSEPH, physician; b. Honolulu, July 3, 1927; s. Fernando Gabriel and Fortunata (Ragas) L.; B.S., Marquette U., 1951; M.S., U. Cin., 1953, M.D., 1959; M.P.H., U. Mich., 1962; post-grad. (fellow) Computer Sci., U. Ill., 1978-80; m. Madelaine Ching Hua Kao, Aug. 7, 1954; children—Mark Huaming Patrick, Clara HuaCin Catherine. Intern, Mercy Hosp., Toledo, 1959-60; resident U. Mich. Hosp., Ann Arbor, 1961-62; research biochemist U.S. Indsl. Chem.-Nat. Distillers Corp., Cin., 1955-56; epidemiologist Ohio Dept. Health, Columbus, 1962-64, chief chronic diseases, 1964-65; fellow Physicians Alcohol Studies Inst., Rutgers U., New Brunswick, N.J., 1964; med. dir. immuniz activities and grants, epidemiologist N.Y. Dept. Health, Albany, 1965-67; med. dir. Skokie (Ill.) Health Dept., 1967-69, Kenosha (Wis.) Health Dept., 1969-71; with Caterpillar Tractor Co., 1971-73; family practice, indsl. practice medicine, Lincoln, Ill., 1973—; instr. Coll. Medicine, Ohio State U., 1963-64, spl. edn. Ill. State U., 1973-74, Coll. Medicine, U. Ill., Peoria, 1971-77; clin. asst. prof. occupational medicine Coll. Medicine, U. Ill., Chgo., 1980—; mem. staff Meth. Hosp., Peoria, Pekin (Ill.) Hosp., Warner Hosp., Clinton, Ill. Chmn. camping health and safety coms. Kenosha council Boy Scouts Am., 1970-71. Served with inf. U.S. Army, 1946-48; lt. M.C., USN, 1960-61; lt. col. M.C., Army Res. N.G., 1978—; comdr. USNR, 1984—. Mental health profl., Hamilton, Ohio. Fellow Am. Coll. Preventive Medicine, Am. Acad. Family Practice; mem. AAAS, Ecol. Soc. Am., AMA, Ill. State, Logan County Med. Socs., Am. Heart Assn. (Chgo. br.), N.Y. Public Health Assn. Roman Catholic. Contbr. articles to med. jours. Home and Office: 42 Northbrook St Lincoln IL 62656 Office: OWCP 230 S Dearborn St Chicago IL 60604

LEOPANDO, ODDED VELOSO, special vehicle company executive; b. Buenavista, Bohol, Philippines, Nov. 6, 1945; came to U.S., 1973; s. Oscar del Rosario and Remedios Javier (Veloso) L.; m. Fe Yabut Baluyut, Mar. 1, 1969; children: Michael, Michelle. BSMechE, Mapua Inst. Tech., Manila, 1965; MBA, U. Detroit, 1986. Plant engr. Chrysler Corp., Detroit, 1973-74; plant and facilities engr. Crane Co., Inc., Chgo., 1975-77; mgr., mfg. engr. Allis Chalmers Corp., Harvey, Ill., 1977-79; plant mgr. Massey-Ferguson, Inc., Detroit, 1979-82; exec. v.p. Cars & Concepts, Inc., Brighton, Mich., 1982—; bd. dirs. C & C, Inc., Brighton; instr. Mapua Inst. Tech., Manila, 1966-72. Mem. NSPE, Soc. Automotive Engrs., Beta Gamma Sigma (membership award 1987). Club: Economic (Detroit). Avocations: music, reading, fishing, tennis, golf. Home: 11420 Spicer Dr Plymouth MI 48170 Office: Cars & Concepts Inc 12500 E Grand River Ave Brighton MI 48116

LEOPOLD, JERRY LEE, optometrist; b. Colby, Kans., Dec. 29, 1952; s. Dale Melville and Linnie Irene (Gilbert) L.; m. Deanna Rose Allmon, May 18, 1980. Student B.S., U. Houston, 1974, O.D., 1976. Optometrist, Drs. Aplin & Leopold, P.A., McPherson, Kans., 1976—. Chmn. Cobb for Treas. Campaign, McPherson, 1984; chmn. bd. dirs. McPherson County Diversified Services, 1978, 79, 84, 85, 86, treas., 1981-83. Mem. Kans. Optometric Assn. (bd. dirs. 1986—, zone pres. 1982-85, chmn. polit. action com. 1982-85, mem. assistance to grads. and undergrads. com. 1982-85, chmn. ins. com. 1985), Am. Optometric Assn. (coordinator State polit. action com. 1985—). Republican. Methodist. Lodges: Optimists (project chmn. 1977-86); Elks (dist. dep. grand exalted ruler 1984-85, exalted ruler 1982-84, 86-87, Elk of Yr. 1985, bd. dirs. tng. ctr. for handicapped, treas., 1986-87), Masons, Shriners (McPherson). Home: 1009 Heatherwood Pl McPherson KS 67460 Office: 1233 Main St PO Box 306 McPherson KS 67460

LEOPOLD, ROBERT BRUCE, lawyer; b. Toledo, Ohio, June 25, 1949; s. James A. and Florence B. (Barnett) L.; m. Cathryn Lucy Hagler, Nov. 2, 1978; 1 child, Maureen Ann. A.B., in Polit. Sci., Ind. U., 1971; J.D., Valparaiso U., 1974. Bar: Ill., Ind. 1975. Dep. prosecutor Lake County, Ind., 1975-76; assoc. Cohen, Cohen & Bullard, East Chicago, Ind., 1977-78; sole practice law, Munster, Ind., 1978—. Pres., Westlake Unit of Northwest Ind. div. Am. Heart Assn., 1982-85. Mem. ABA, Ind. Bar Assn., Ill. Bar Assn., Assn. Trial Layers of Am., Delta Theta Phi. Address: 9335 Calumet Ave Suite D Munster IN 46321

LEOPOLD, VIVIAN ARTHUR, osteopath; b. Trenton, Nebr., Sept. 6, 1896; s. David Wilcox and Bertha (Stoller) L.; m. Mildred E. Birney, Nov. 24, 1915 (dec. Jan. 1986); children: Dwight, Dick. DO, Kirksville (Mo.) Coll., 1925. Diplomate Am. Bd. Proctology. Practice osteopathic medicine Garden City, Kans., 1925—; fellow in hypnosis Am. Inst. Hypnosis and Hypnoanalysis. Author video tapes on age regression and hypnosis, pamphlets on various topics of office procedures. Recipient Disting. Citizen award Garden City, 1985. Fellow Am. Inst. Hypnosis and Hypnoanalysis; mem. Kans. State Assn. Osteo. Medicine (hon. life; past pres.), Kans. State Bd. Health (life; past pres.), Am. Osteo. Assn., Am. Coll. Osteo. Proctology, Western States Proctology Assn. Republican. Methodist. Lodges: Kiwanis (50 yr. mem., pres. Garden City), Masons (50 yr. mem.). Avocation: hypnosis. Home: 919 Davis Garden City KS 67846 Office: PO Box 914 Garden City KS 67846

LEPONTOIS, JOAN IRENE, social worker; b. Cleve., Oct. 16, 1942; s. Henry Alfred and Martha (Greene) LeP. BA with honors, Miami U., Oxford, Ohio, 1964; MA, U. Chgo., 1970; MSW, Loyola U., Chgo., 1985. Social worker City of Cleve., 1964; therapist Sonia Shankman Orthogenic Sch. U. CHgo., 1965-66; therapist William Healy Sch., Chgo., 1966-69; program coordinator Inst. Juvenile Research, Chgo., 1969-71; social worker Michael Reese Hosp., Chgo., 1971-80, Children's Meml. Hosp., Chgo., 1980—; mem. faculty Sch. Allied Health Scis., Chgo., 1978-80, Rush-Presbyn. Hosp., Chgo., 1979-80, McArthur Symposiums, Chgo., 1981-82. Avocation: fiction writing. Home: 5232 N Glenwood Chicago IL 60640 Office: Children's Meml Hosp Dept Social Work Chicago IL 60614

LEPSETZ, STEVEN GARY, accountant; b. Detroit, June 19, 1950; s. Joseph and Bertha (Sher) L.; m. Alice Louise Liepman, Sept. 25, 1977; children: Neal, Deborah. B in Bus., Wayne State U., 1972, M in Bus., 1976. CPA, Mich. Acct. Farquharson, Pointon & Pitser, Southfield, Mich., 1972—; tax preparer Accts. Aid Soc., Detroit, 1980. Author: Tax Aspects of Closely Held Corporations, 1971. Counselor Active Corp Execs. of SBA, Detroit, 1972—. Mem. Am. Inst. CPA's, Mich. Assn. CPA's, Nat. Assn. Investment Clubs (pres. accts. unit 1971, trustee Detroit council 1971), Southfield Jaycees (v.p. 1980). Avocations: sailing, chess. Home: 20050 Winchester Southfield MI 48076 Office: Farquharson Pointon & Pitser 26600 Telegraph Rd Suite 212 Southfield MI 48034

LERCH, JEFFREY WALTER, obstetrician-gynecologist; b. Chgo., Dec. 14, 1948; s. Abraham and Rissel (Lutwak) L.; m. Barbara Sharon Schwartz, June 20, 1971; children: Brian, Sheryl. BA, U. Ill., Chgo., 1970; MD, Loyola U., Maywood, Ill., 1974. Diplomate Am. Bd. Ob-Gyn. Resident in ob-gyn Loyola U. Hosp., Maywood, Ill., 1974-77; practice medicine specializing in ob-gyn. Northwest Physicians for Women, S.C., Hoffman Estates, Ill., 1974—; clin. instr. Loyola U. Stritch Sch. Medicine, Maywood, 1974—; staff mem. at large Humana Hosp., Hoffman Estates, 1982-84, treas. med. staff, 1983-84, chmn. ob-gyn. dept., 1984—, exec. com. 1982—. Fellow Am. Coll. Ob-Gyn; mem. AMA, Ill. State Med. Soc. (hosp. med. staff sect. 1986—), Am. Fertility Soc., Am. Assn. Gynecologic Laparoscopists. Republican. Jewish. Avocations: baseball, ice hockey, science fiction, collecting miniature automoblie models. Office: NW Physicians for Women SC 1575 N Barrington Rd Hoffman Estates IL 60154

LERE, JOHN COVEY, accounting educator; b. Mpls., Sept. 8, 1945; s. John Edwin and Neva M. (Covey) L.; m. Dee Ray, June 20, 1970. BS, U. Ill., 1967; M in Profl. Acctg., U. Tex., 1969; PhD, U. Wis., 1976. CPA, Ill. Teaching asst. U. Tex., Austin, 1967-68; instr. bus. Winston Churchill Coll., Pontiac, Ill., 1968-70; asst. prof. Ill. State U., Normal, 1970-73; lectr., teaching asst. U. Wis., Madison, 1973-76; asst. prof. U. Minn., Mpls., 1976-83; prof. acctg. St. Cloud (Minn.) State U., 1983—. Author: Pricing Techniques for the Financial Executive, 1974; contbr. articles to profl. jours. Mem. Am. Inst. CPA's, Am. Acctg. Assn., Nat. Assn. Accts. Methodist. Avocations: reading, model r.r.'s, cross-country skiing. Home: 1024 Highview Dr New Brighton MN 56301 Office: St Cloud State U Coll Bus Saint Cloud MN 55112

LERITZ, THOMAS RICHARD, computer systems executive; b. St. Louis, Oct. 16, 1936; s. Joseph Daniel and Mary Agnes (Lyons) L.; m. Mary Cecelia Evrard, June 18, 1966; children: Ann, Marie, Thomas, William. BS in Polit. Sci., St. Louis U., 1958. Cert. data processor, Mo. Systems supr. Am. Investment, St. Louis, 1961-71; systems mgr. Moog Automotive, St. Louis, 1971-77; mgr. data processing Pfizer Genetics, St. Louis, 1977-80; dir. info. systems SKF Automotive Products, St. Louis, 1980—; instr. Washington U., St. Louis, 1971-74. Contbr. articles on systems to profl. jours. Sec. Young Rep. Club, St. Louis, 1964; Scout com. chmn. Boy Scouts Am., Creve Coeur, Mo. 1984-85. Served with U.S. Army, 1958-59. Mem. Assn. Systems Mgmt. (pres. 1973-74, div. dir. 1974-75, Merit award 1972, Achievement award 1975). Roman Catholic. Lodges: K.C., Elks. Avocations: golf, fishing. Office: SKF Automotive Products 2320 Marconi Saint Louis MO 63110

LERMINIAUX, KEITH JULES, lawyer; b. Detroit, Aug. 3, 1954; s. Armille M. and Gertrude J. (Rouke) L.; m. Janet M. Jacobson, Aug. 11, 1979; 1 child, Ryan J. BS, Mich. State U., 1976; JD, U. Detroit, 1979. Bar: Mich. 1979. Assoc. Cummings, McClorey, Livonia, Mich., 1979-80, Vandeveer Garzia, Detroit, 1980—. Mem. ABA, Mich. Bar Assn., Lawyer Pilot Bar Assn. Roman Catholic. Avocations: jogging, waterskiing, racquet sports, flying. Home: 18621 Williams Ct Livonia MI 48152 Office: Vandeveer Garzia 333 W Fort Suite 1600 Detroit MI 48226

LERNER, DENNIS BRUCE, insurance salesman; b. Detroit, Apr. 30, 1947; s. Ben and Beatrice (Gendel) L.; m. Connie Ferrel, Sept. 14, 1969 (div. Dec. 1979); 1 child Jeffery H.; m. Nancy A. Balwin, Feb. 28, 1983. BS in Mktg., Ferris State Coll., 1970. Sales rep. Fidelity Union Life, Big Rapids, Mich., 1969-70, Mass. Mut. Life, Big Rapids, 1977—; com. mem. adv. system Mass. Mut. Life, Springfield, Mass., 1984—. Bd. dirs. Mecosta County Humanities Council, Big Rapids, 1980—, Mecosta County Economic Devel. Council, 1980—, Ferris State Coll. Devel. Council, 1983—, Indsl. Devel. Corp., Big Rapids, 1983—. Served with Mich. N.G., 1969-76. Mem. Million Dollar Round Table (life), Nat. Assn. Life Underwriters, Grand Rapids Assn. Life Underwriters., Ferris State Alumni (bd. dirs. 1986—). Jewish. Avocations: golf, tennis. Home: 14655 Wigwam Big Rapids MI 49307 Office: Lerner & Assocs 125 E Pine Big Rapids MI 49307

LERNER-CONNAGHAN, GAIL LEIGHTY, mental health nurse clinician; b. Burlington, Iowa, Feb. 24, 1947; d. Marcus Rankin and Patricia Lee (Freedman) Leighty; m. Gary Sanford Lerner, Mar. 30, 1969 (div. Jan. 1979); children: Jack Ivan, Sara Janine; m. Kevin Henry Connaghan, Aug. 11, 1984. BS in Nursing, U. Mo., 1970; MS in Psychology, Avila Coll., 1983. Registered nurse; cert. clin. specialist. Staff nurse Research Med. Ctr., Kansas City, Mo., 1970; head nurse The Children's Mercy Hosp., Kansas City, 1970-72, asst. clin. nurse specialist, 1972-77; staff nurse Shwnee Mission Med. Ctr., Merriam, Kans., 1977-81; mental health nurse clinician Matrix, Inc., Kansas City, 1978—. Mem. Am. Nurses Assn., Internat. Transactional Analysis Assn. (clin. cert.). Democrat. Jewish. Avocations: gardening, reading, racquetball. Office: Matrix Inc 7447 Holmes Kansas City MO 64131

LESCH, THOMAS MICHAEL, small business owner; b. Mansfield, Ohio, Mar. 20, 1947; s. Joseph Peter and Lillian Jean (Wentz) L.; m. Sandra Kay Freiheit, Sept. 14, 1968; children: Michelle, Brian. BBA, Ohio U., 1969. Indsl. engr. North Electric Co., Galion, Ohio, 1969-71, foreman, 1971-72; indsl. relations mgr. North Electric Co., Kenton, 1972-73; gen. mgr., v.p. Brandt Distbg. Co. Inc., Mansfield, 1973-84; pres. P&J Rentals, Mansfield, 1984—. Mem. Nat. Fed. Ind. Bus., Mansfield C. of C. Republican. Roman Catholic. Club: Westbrook Country. Lodge Moose. Avocation: sports. Home: 1195 Butternut Ct Mansfield OH 44906 Office: P&J Rentals Inc 260 N Trimble Rd Mansfield OH 44906

LESH, MICHAEL JOSEPH, accountant; b. Hamburg, Ark., Sept. 22, 1929; s. Michael Lesh and Mary (Herlevic) Wallesh; m. Georgiann Agnes Egloff, June 16, 1951; children: Mark Kenneth, Carolyn Lesh Rowley, Mary Kathryn (dec.). BS, U. Ill., 1955. CPA, Ill. Supr. auditing Peat, Marwick, Mitchell & Co., Chgo., 1955-62; asst. controller Chgo. & Eastern Ill. R.R. Co., Chgo., 1962-66; cons. project dir. Booz, Allen & Hamilton, Chittagong, Bangladesh and Tehran, Iran, 1966-69; mgr. budgets and cost acctg. Atchison, Topeka & Santa Fe R.R. Co., Topeka, 1969-74, asst. to v.p. acctg., 1984—; controller Santa Fe Energy Co. div. Santa Fe Natural Resources, Chgo., Amarillo, Tex., 1974-84. Sustaining mem. Nat. Rep. Com., 1981—. Roman Catholic. Avocations: reading, bridge, golf, travel. Home: 5823 SW Turnberry Ct Topeka KS 66614 Office: Atchison Topeka & Santa Fe Ry Co 920 Quincy St Topeka KS 66628

LESHKEVICH, MICHAEL JTONE, stockbroker; b. Detroit, Nov. 9, 1956; s. Antony and Mildred (Lesniak) L.; m. Mary Jo. Mercurio, Apr. 20, 1985. Grad., Edsel Ford High Sch., 1970-74. Ins. salesman A. L. Williams and Assoc., Troy, Mich., 1981-84; stockbroker Fahnestock & Co., Inc., Dearborn, Mich., 1984—; Mem. Support the Am. Made Product (treas. 1986—). Mem. Mich. Big Game Hunters Assn. (treas.). Republican. Mem. Free Methodist Ch. Avocations: hunting, fishing. Home: 2011 Pelham Rd Dearborn MI 48124 Office: Fahnestock & Co Inc 23400 Michigan Ave #110 Dearborn MI 48124

LESKI, DAN R., advertising executive; b. Chgo., Feb. 3, 1951; s. Edwin Paul and Marion Theresa (Broda) Leszczynski; m. Joanne Marie Zale, May 24, 1975. BS in Journalism, Northwestern U., 1972, MS in Journalism, 1973. Mktg. asst. Canon USA, Elmhurst, Ill., 1973-75; communications mgr. UOP Air Correction, Des Plaines, Ill., 1976-77; advt. mgr. TRW United Greenfield, Northbrook, Ill., 1978-79; acct. supr. McKinney/Mid Am., Chgo., 1980-84, HCM, Chgo., 1984—. Mem. Bus./Profl. Advt. Assn. (Chgo. chpt., Cert. Excellence Tower award 1975). Roman Catholic. Avocations: golf, snorkeling, folk guitar, travel. Office: HCM 1 E Wacker Dr Chicago IL 60601

LESKOVAR, KARL HEINZ, accountant; b. Wildon, Austria, Mar. 12, 1951; came to U.S., 1954; s. Karl Albert and Hildegard (Schmidtke) L.; Ann E. Trebilcock, Apr. 2, 1976; 1 child, Matthew Karl. BA, Mich. State U., 1973, MBA, 1977. CPA, Mich. Cost and budget analyst Gen. Tire Rubber Co., Ionia, Mich., 1973-75; instr. acctg. Mich. State U., East Lansing, 1975-76; sr. acct. Crowe, Chizek and Co., CPA's, South Bend, Ind., 1976-79; ptnr. Beene, Garter and Co., CPA's, Grand Rapids, Mich., 1979—; cons. ABC Builders and Contractors, Grand Rapids, 1985—. Editor Because It's Your Business newsletter. Cons. advisor Concerned Citizens for Equal Rights for the Deaf, Grand Rapids, 1982—. Mem. Am. Inst. CPA's, Internat. Assn. Fin. Planners, Inst. Cert. Fin. Planners, Mich. Assn. CPA's. Republican. Lutheran. Avocations: running, gardening, skiing, travel. Home: 6066 Meyers Lake Rd Rockford MI 49341 Office: Beene Garter & Co CPAs 50 Monroe Suite 600 Grand Rapids MI 49503

LESLIE, ROBERT WENDELL, business executive; b. Lincoln, Nebr., June 28, 1933; s. Oliver Wendell and Hazel Rosetta (Barnett) L.; m. Janet, June 5, 1957; children: Steven, David, Mark. BA, Nebr. Wesleyan U., 1957; MA, U. Nebr., 1960. Tchr., coach schs. in Nebr. and Calif. 1957-66; with Jostens Inc., Mpls., 1966—; v.p. sales, then v.p., div. mgr. Jostens Inc., 1971-72, pres., 1977—. Served with USNR, 1953-55. Republican. Presbyterian. Office: Jostens Inc 5501 Norman Ctr Dr Minneapolis MN 55437 *

LESSENDEN, EDITH ANN FLEMING, writer, monologist; b. Garden City, Kans., Jan. 21, 1922; d. Arthur Milo and Edith Ann (Hambleton) Fleming; m. Chester Merral Lessenden, June 1, 1943; children—Sandra L. Lessenden; Marged L. Amend, Eve L. Supica, Mark Charles. A.B., Kans. U., 1946, M.A., 1952. Editor-writer Med. Aux. News, Kans., 1958-60, Allegro, Topeka Symphony, 1970-86; writer, dir. musical revues; contbr. articles to various publs. Organizer, chmn. Symphony League, Topeka, 1966-70, bd. dirs., 1966—; bd. dirs. Kans. Med. Aux., 1958—, pres., 1964-65; bd. dirs. AMA Aux., 1970-77, fund-raiser, 1973-75, regional v.p. 1975-77. Recipient Charles Marling award Topeka Symphony Soc., 1984. Mem. Nat. League Am. Pen Women (Roller award 1985, pres. Topeka br. 1986—), Kans. Authors Club, P.E.O. (chpt. pres. 1959-60, coop. bd. pres. 1961-62), Mortar Bd. Republican. Methodist. Clubs: Minerva (pres. 1963-64), Western sorosis (pres. 1980-81). Avocations: French conversation; sewing; needlepoint; reading.

LESSIN, DEBRA JEAN, accountant; b. Phila., July 1, 1954; d. Robert Leonard and Shirley (Glassman) L. BBA, U. Wis., 1976; MS in Taxation, DePaul U., Chgo., 1982. Sr. acct. Price Waterhouse & Co., Chgo., 1976-79; tax mgr. Walter Heller & Co., Chgo., 1979-84; pres. D.J. Lessin and Assocs, Inc., Chgo., 1984—. Treas. Sheffield Neighborhood Assn., Chgo., 1985—, bd. dirs. Chgo. Filmmakers, 1987—. Mem. Am. Inst. CPA's, Ill. CPA's Soc., Beta Gamma Sigma, Beta Alpha Psi (sec. 1976). Jewish. Avocations: cooking, fitness, photography. Office: D J Lessin & Assocs Inc 444 N Wells #504 Chicago IL 60610

LESTER, LINDA LEE, accountant; b. Kadoka, S.D., Mar. 24, 1949; d. William M. and Ruth I. (Searby) Capp; m. Robert J. Lester, Dec. 26, 1966; children: Kimberly, Paul, Heather. BA in Acctg., U. No. Iowa, 1979. CPA, S.D. Staff acct. Dunmire, Short & Co., Rapid City, S.D., 1979-82, McGladrey, Hendrickson & Pullen, Rapid City, 1982-85; pvt. practice acctg. Rapid City, 1985—. Treas. Kandaras for Commr. Com., Rapid City, 1986. Mem. Am. Inst. CPA's, S.D. Soc. CPA's (vice chair edn. com. 1985-86), Black Hills Chpt. CPA's, Am. Bus. Women's Assn. (treas. Rapid City centennial chpt. 1982-83), Women's Network (treas. 1987—). Lutheran. Club: Toastmasters. Avocations: reading, golf, photography. Office: PO Box 5575 Rapid City SD 57709

LESTER, ROGER HARLAN, manufacturing company executive; b. Guernsey, Iowa, Jan. 25, 1941; s. Carl L. and Daisy S. (Kluber) L.; m. Shirley Kay Brown, Oct. 24, 1958; children: Denise Kay, Caryl Sue, Timothy Brian, Debra Lynn. BA, Grace Bible Inst., 1964; BA in Psychology, U. Nebr., Omaha, 1968, postgrad., 1968-73. Advt. mktg. mgr. Inland Mfg. Co., Omaha, 1958-77; pres. Clean Air Specialists Inc., Omaha, 1977—. pres. Fine Arts Support Team Northwest High Sch., Omaha, 1982-84; youth dir. Park Lane Baptist Ch., Omaha, 1966—. Republican. Club: Awana (commdr. 1967—) (Omaha). Home and Office: 5709 Whitmore St Omaha NE 68152-2363

LESTER, SANDRA KAY, social worker; b. Kalamazoo, Sept. 18, 1944; d. LeRoy Clifford and Maxine Blenn (Stafford) Butcher; m. Edward Bernard Lester, Sept. 1, 1978; children—Kevin Craig, Julie Kathleen, Nicholas, Edward. B.S., Western Mich. U., 1970, postgrad., 1979—. Case mgr. Mich. Dept. Social Services, Kalamazoo, 1971, interagency foster care liaison, 1973-77, recruiter, trainer for foster care, 1977-80, purchase of service contract specialist, 1980-83, employment and tng. counselor, 1983—, contract mgr., 1984-86, weatherization/home repair specialist, 1986—; instr. Kalamazoo Valley Community Coll., 1976-77. Bd. dirs. Continuing Edn. for Young Families, 1981; pres., bd. dirs. Regional Interagency Council for Developmentally Disabled, 1973-76. Mem. Network, Internat. Platform Assn., Internat. Personnel Mgmt. Assn., Am. Soc. Aging. Democrat. Lutheran. Home: 3822 Mt Olivet St Kalamazoo MI 49004 Office: 322 Stockbridge St Kalamazoo MI 49001

LESTZ, JEFFREY SCOTT, financial service company executive; b. Chgo., Nov. 25, 1956; s. Sidney and Bertha (Singer) L.; m. Peggy Jean Griffin, Dec. 19, 1975. Student, So. Ill. U., 1974-75. Sales rep. Met. Life, Carbondale, Ill., 1975-77, Country Cos. Ins., Murphysboro, Ill., 1977-78; dist. mgr. Aetna Life & Casualty, St. Louis, 1978-81; sr. v.p. A.L. Williams Co., Carbondale, Ill., 1981—. Author: (with others) Victory from Debt, 1983. Republican. Avocations: bicycling, reading, collecting antiques. Office: AL Williams Co 705 W Main Carbondale IL 62901

LETO, GLENN KEITH, educator; b. Chgo., Sept. 8, 1946; s. Samuel and Ann (Dulek) L. B.S., No. Ill. U., 1968, M.S., 1972. Biology tchr. Barrington High Sch. Dist. 220, Barrington, Ill., 1970—; cons. Mus. Sci. and Industry, Chgo., 1985-86, Tech. Pub. Co., Barrington, 1984-85, State of Ill. Dept. Edn., Springfield, 1979, 1984-87. Author: (with others) Biology, 1985; coauthor tng. manual force and motion, 1986. Am. Assn. Physics Tchrs. grantee, 1982, 86, State of Ill. grantee, 1983; Kellogg Found. fellow, 1983, 84. Mem. Nat. Sci. Tchrs. Assn., Nat. Assn. Biology Tchrs., Sigma Xi. Avocations: photography, computer applications, hiking. Home: 10013 Hillshire Dr W Richmond IL 60071 Office: Barrington High Sch 616 W Main St Barrington IL 60010

LETO, JOHN ANTHONY, trucking firm executive; b. Des Moines, Sept. 19, 1962; s. Paul Joseph and Elsa Mae (Domres) L. Student Grand View Coll., 1981-83, Drake U., 1983-85, Iowa State U., 1986—. Treas. City Wide Cartage Inc., Des Moines, 1975-84, pres., 1984-86. Republican. Roman Catholic. Avocations: photography; golf; bowling. Home: 4453 88th St Urbandale IA 50322 Office: City Wide Cartage Inc 1617 NE 51st Ave Des Moines IA 50313

LETSON, ALAN DOUGLAS, ophthalmologist, vitreo-retinal surgeon, educator; b. C.Z., Apr. 6, 1951; s. Holton Charles and Betty Jean (Mellinger) L.; m. Susan Reade, Aug. 2, 1975; children—Robert Alan, Charles Venning. B.A., Miami U., 1973; M.D., Case Western Res. U., 1977. Diplomate Am. Bd. Ophthalmology. Intern, St. Luke's Hosp., Cleve., 1977-78; resident Ohio State U., Columbus, 1978-81, fellow in vitreo-retinal surgery, 1981-82; practice medicine specializing in vitre-retinal surgery, Columbus, Ohio, 1982—; clin. instr. Ohio State U., 1978-82, clin. asst. prof., 1982—, clin. research, 1978—; cons. Dayton VA Hosp., 1982-84. Contbr. articles to sci.-ophthalmic jours. Mem. med. adv. com. Nat. Soc. to Prevent Blindness, 1982—; Ohio Diabetes Task Force, chmn. subcom. on vision care. Recipient AMA Physicians' Recognition award, 1981, 83, Ophthalmology Tchr. of Yr. award, 1986. Fellow Am. Acad. Ophthalmology; mem. AMA, Ohio Ophthal. Soc. (liaison to Ohio Diabetes Control Program), Ohio State Med. Assn., Columbus Ophthal. and Otolaryn. Soc. Home: 1810 Waltham Rd Upper Arlington OH 43221 Office: 393 E Town St Suite 228 Columbus OH 43215

LETT, ALLISON, research developer, professional fundraiser; b. Cin., Sept. 6, 1958; d. Allen Downey and Jacqueline (Light) L. AA, Pine Manor Coll., 1977; BA, U. Cin., 1980. Mgr. Magic Lantern, Bridgton, Maine, 1977; head booker Allied Artists, Boston, 1977-78; mgr. Hyde Park Theater, Cin., 1978-79; mgr. research br. Kelly Services, Cin., 1980-83; br. mgr. Metro Temporaries, Cin., 1984; research devel. officer Cin. Zoo, 1984-87; research grant mgr. dept. surgery Good Samaritan Hosp., Cin., 1987—; grants coordinator Cin. Playhouse, 1984—; dir. fundraising May Festival, Cin. 1985. Vol. Nixon/Ford local campaign, Cin., 1972, Com. to Elect Kelly Farnish, Cin., 1983. Mem. Nat. Soc. Fundraising Execs. Republican. Methodist. Office: Cin Zoo 3400 Vine St Cincinnati OH 45220

LEUBITZ, DAVID C., dentist; b. Akron, Ohio, Jan. 28, 1947; s. Eli P. and Rose Susan (Umansky) L.; m. Sherri Joy Slavin, Mar. 13, 1983. Student, Akron U., 1967; DDS, Washington U., St. Louis, 1972. Gen. practice dentistry Akron, Ohio, 1972—. Author: Blue Book, 1976, Arapaho II, 1979. Mem. adv. bd. Great Trail Council, Akron, 1986, mem. exec. bd., 1976-83. Mem. ADA, Am. Dental Soc., Ohio Dental Assn., Alpha Omega (officer 1978-80). Avocations: Boy Scouts, stamp collecting. Office: 1778 Goodyear Blvd Akron OH 44305

LEUENBERGER, JAMES MONROE, advertising/public relations executive; b. Decorah, Iowa, Oct. 23, 1946; s. Clinton Monroe and Mary (Silhacek) L.; m. Glenda Gay Fike, Feb. 28, 1970; children—Jeffrey, Jennifer, Jeremy. B.S., Iowa State U., 1968, M.S., 1970. 4-H youth agt., Winneshiek County, Iowa, 1968; dir. info. Nat. Holstein Assn., Brattleboro, Vt., 1970-75; dir. advt./pub. relations 21st Century Genetics Coop., Shawano, Wis., 1975—. Dir. World Dairy Expo. Served with Vt. N.G., 1968-74. Named Disting. Pres., Shawano Optimist Club, 1980, Editor of Outstanding A.I. Newsletter, Nat. Assn. Animal Breeders, 1979. Mem. Coop. Editorial Assn., Internat. Assn. Bus. Communicators, Nat. Dairy Shrine (dir., sec.), Nat. Post-Sec. Agr. Student Orgn. (dir.). Democrat. Roman Catholic. Club: Optimist. Home: 305 Prospect Circle Shawano WI 54166 Office: RFD 2 Shawano WI 54166

LEUNG, JANNY CHUN, computer systems specialist; b. Hong Kong, May 24, 1950; came to U.S., 1970; d. Edmund K.H. and Monica P.F. (Long) Lee; m. Bernie T.M. Leung, July 4, 1975; children: Serena B.L., Audrey B.S. BA, U. Nebr., 1973, MBA, 1975; AAS, Cen. Community Coll., Columbus, Nebr., 1981. Paralegal Nebr. Pub. Power Dist., Columbus, 1976-78, programmer, analyst, 1978-81; analyst Becton Dickinson, Columbus, 1981-84; mgr. computer systems Reed, Veach, Wurdeman & Assocs., Columbus, 1984—; cons., translator Mgmt. and Engring. Group, Columbus, 1980—. Mem. AAUW (treas. 1984), Nebr. Soc. Profl. Engring. Aux. (v.p. 1986, sec. 1984), Data Processing Mgmt. Assn. (chmn. com. 1985), DEC Users Group. Roman Catholic. Avocations: stained glass windows, writing. Home: 4721 Hill Crest Dr Columbus NE 68601

LEUNG, RODERICK CHI-TAK, architect; b. Kumming, Peoples Republic of China, Aug. 12, 1949; s. Pe Ban and Kit Chong (Fung) L.; m. Julia Dexter Clark, Sept. 5, 1982; children: Emily, Rebecca. BArch, U. Minn., 1975; MArch, MIT, 1978. Architect Skidmore, Owing & Merrill, Chgo., 1975-83, John Portman & Assocs., Atlanta, 1983-84, Cooper Carry & Assocs., Atlanta, 1984—. Mem. AIA Chgo., AIA Atlanta, MIT Alumni Assn.

LEUNG, TERENCE HON-YIN, dentist; b. Kowloon, Hong Kong, Aug. 24, 1953; s. Tat Shing and Oi Wah (Yuen) L. BA, SUNY, Buffalo, 1978; D of Dental Medicine, Washington U., St. Louis, 1984. Asst. inst.sch. dental medicine Washington U., St. Louis, 1984-86; gen. practice dentistry St. Louis, 1986—. Mem. ADA, Greater St. Louis Dental Assn., Acad. Gen. Dentistry. Avocations: tennis, fishing, reading, music, golf. Home: 12387 N Cross Creek Cove Creve Coeur MO 63141

LEUPOLD, TREVA ELLEN, psychotherapist; b. Grand Rapids, Minn., Jan. 21, 1945; d. John Ward and Anna Lillian (McGlade) Ozbun; m. Thomas Carl Leupold, Aug. 8, 1970; children: Kimberly, Jason. BA, Coll. St. Teresa, 1967; MSW, U. Hawaii, 1969. Therapist treatment and foster care Dept. Health and Social Services, Milw., 1967-72; social worker Milw. Pub. Schs., 1977-82; pvt. practice psychotherapy Wauwatosa, Wis., 1982—. Mem. religious edn. com. St. Sebastian's Ch., Milw., 1985—; program mem. Research Clearing House, Milw., 1986-87. New Membership award Wis. Fedn. of Women's Clubs, 1977. Mem. Nat. Assn. Social Workers, Nat. Registry Clin. Social Workers (cert.), Mental Health Assn., Menninger Found., Wis. PTA (pres. Washington Sch., Wauwatosa, 1984-85, v.p. Wauwatosa East High Sch., 1987-88). Democrat. Roman Catholic. Club: Wauwatosa Jr. Woman's (pres. 1979-80). Avocations: tennis, piano, needlework, cooking. Home: 6264 Upper Pkwy N Wauwatosa WI 53213 Office: Associated Psychiat and Cons Services 2300 N Mayfair Rd Wauwatosa WI 53226

LEUSER, ROBERT H., printing company executive. Pres. Charles P. Young, Chgo. Office: Charles P Young-Chgo 320 S Jefferson St Chicago IL 60606 *

LEUTHER, MICHAEL DOYLE, research biochemist; b. St. Louis, Feb. 15, 1948; s. Elmer Carl and Doyle Price (Bennett) L.; m. Regalia Jean Simons, Mar. 29, 1969 (div.); 1 child, Danielle Renea; m. Kathlee Mae Schnabel, Sept. 20, 1981. BA in Biology, U. Mo.-St. Louis, 1970; PhD in Biochemistry, St. Louis U., 1983. Product mgr. monoclonal hepatitis diagnostics A.D.D. Abbott Labs., Abbott Park, Ill., 1981-85; product mgr. hepatitis/AIDS diagnostic products research and devel., Abbott Diagnostics Div. Abbott Labs., Abbott Park, 1981—, sect. head AIDS and hepatisis diagnostice products research and devel., 1987—; lectr. AIDS and hepatitis, Abbott Labs. Speakers Bur., 1986—. Contbr. articles to profl. publs. Served to capt. USAF, 1971-75. Decorated Unit Merit Citation; named Citizen of Month, St. Louis Bd. Police Commrs., Dec. 1968; recipient Presdl. award of achievement, Abbott Labs., 1983. Mem. Sci. Research Soc., AAAS, Sigma Xi. Republican. Presbyterian. Home: 17574 W Winnebago Dr Wildwood IL 60030 Office: Abbott Labs 9ZR - AP1O Abbott Park IL 60064

LEVAK, BARBARA ANN, educator; b. Lorain, Ohio, June 29, 1949; d. Martin Michael and Olga (Mihalsky) L. B.S. cum laude, Bowling Green State U., 1971; M.Ed., Ohio State U., 1983; tng. Adelphi U. Nat. Tng. Inst., 1981. Cert. tchr., Ohio. Tchr., Fremont (Ohio) City Schs., 1971-73; tchr. Reynoldsburg (Ohio) City Schs., 1973—, bldg. coordinator English dept., 1978—, curriculum coordinator, 1984—mem. Sch. and Dist. Think Tank, 1981—; mem. Prin.'s Adv. Com., 1979-81; mem. Supt.'s Adv. Com., 1980-81. Mem. Reynoldsburg Com. for Prevention of Substance Abuse, 1981; mem. resource bd. Spl. Wish Found. Grantee Tchr. Center of Franklin County, 1982. Mem. Reynoldsburg Edn. Assn. (exec. com.), Ohio Edn. Assn., NEA, Assn. Supervision and Curriculum Devel., Central Ohio Assn. Curriculum Devel. and Supervision, Bowling Green State U. Alumni Assn., Phi Delta Kappa. Eastern Orthodox. Home: 5880 Parliament Dr Columbus OH 43213 Office: 2300 Baldwin Dr Reynoldsburg OH 43068

LEVAN, ARTHUR BERNARD, obstetrician-gynecologist; b. Chgo., Dec. 31, 1912; s. Samuel Albert and Sarah (Salk) L.; m. Elfriede Horst, May 29, 1944 (dec. July 1979); children: Kathryn, Peter. BS, U. Ill., Champaign and Chgo., 1934; MD, U. Ill., Chgo., 1936, MS in Pathology, 1937. Diplomate Am. Bd. Ob-Gyn. Chmn. dept. ob-gyn Resurrection Hosp., Chgo., 1956-58, Holy Family Hosp., Des Plaines, Ill., 1964—; staff Luth. Gen. Hosp., Park Ridge, Ill.; clin. assoc. in ob-gyn, U. Ill. Chgo. Served to maj. U.S Army Med. Corps., 1941-46. Fellow ACS, Am. Coll. Ob-Gyn; mem. AMA, Chgo. Gynecol. Soc. Avocations: golf, swimming, horsemanship. Office: 494 Lee St Des Plaines IL 60016

LEVANDOWSKI, BARBARA SUE, educational administrator; b. Chgo., Mar. 16, 1948; d. Earl F. and Ann (Klee) L.. BA in Edn. and Spanish, North Park Coll., 1970; MS in Elem. Edn., No. Ill. U., 1975, EdD, 1979. Cert. elem. tchr.; cert. secondary tchr. Tchr. Round Lake (Ill.) Sch. Dist., 1970-75; tchr. Schaumburg (Ill.) Sch. Dist., 1975-87, asst. prin., 1977—; curriculum cons. Spring Grove (Ill.) Sch. Dist., 1980-81; instr. various courses, Schaumburg, 1984-86; presenter various confs. Mem. editorial bd. Ill. Sch. Research and Devel. Jour., 1981—; contbr. articles to profl. jours. Mem. staff Round Lake Park Dist., 1973—. Recipient numerous awards for excellence in teaching, Those Who Excel award State of Ill., 1979; fed. grantee. Mem. Am. Biog. Inst. Research Assn. (research bd. dirs. 1985—, publs. com. 1983), Assn. for Supervision and Curriculum Devel. (inservice presenter 1984-86), Ill. Assn. for Supervision and Curriculum Devel. (chairperson. research com. 1982), Ill. Prin. Assn., Phi Delta Kappa. Home: 426 Normandie Ln Round Lake IL 60073 Office: 1100 Laurie Ln Hanover Park IL 60103

LEVANG, CURTIS ARVID, psychologist, consultant; b. Wadena, Minn., June 11, 1954; s. Norman Tilin and Ethel Fern (Nungesser) L.; m. Elizabeth Rizzo, Mar. 27, 1982. BS in Psychology, Evangel Coll., 1977; MA in Counseling and Psychol. Services, St. Mary's Coll., 1981; MA Clin. Psychol., The Fielding Inst., 1985, PhD Clin. Psychol., 1986. Lic. psychologist, Minn. Psychologist Hennepin County, Plymouth, Minn., 1977—; psychologist Met. Clinic Counseling, Mpls., 1984—. Fellow Am. Psychol. Assn., Minn. Psychol. Assn.; mem. Biofeedback Soc. Am. Mem. Assembly of God Ch. Avocations: golfing, jogging, sailing, traveling, collecting Bossom figure heads. Home: 4010 Bayside Rd S Maple Plain MN 55359 Office: Hennepin County Adult Corrections 1145 Shenandoah Ln Plymouth MN 55447

LEVANTROSSER, FREDERICK CARL, civil engineer, natural gas expert; b. Detroit, Apr. 20, 1938; s. Frederick Rudolph and Grace Emma (Schroeder) L.; m. Barbara Jane Chaplin, July 1, 1961; children: Laura Beth, Sandra Kay, Debra Sue. BCE magna cum laude, Wayne State U., 1960, MCE, 1967; MBA, Mich. State U., 1973, cert. in advanced mgmt., 1973. Registered profl. engr., Mich., Ohio, Calif. Civil engr. Gen. Motors Corp., Detroit, 1958-61; interface surveillance engr. The Boeing Co., Seattle, 1961-63; sr. civil engr. Giffels & Assocs., Detroit, 1963-64; civil engr. Ford Motor Co., Dearborn, Mich., 1964-76, mgr. utilities and fuel conservation, 1977, chief civil and structural engr., 1978-80, environ. chief, 1981, energy rate control specialist, 1982-87; expert witness on natural gas transp., 1982—; speaker on natural gas transp. issues, 1985—; cons. Project Bus., Jr. Achievement, Detroit, 1984-86, Project Self-reliance, State of Mich., Lansing, 1986. Author: Metrication in the Construction Industry, 1973. Founding mem. Down River Community Council, Allen Park, Mich., 1965; campaign chmn. G.N. Richards for Councilman, Allen Park, 1972; rep. Allen Park Council of Chs., 1966-72. Fellow ASCE (nat. conv. coodinator 1985); mem. Assn. Energy Engrs., Phi Beta Kappa, Chi Epsilon (cons. engrs. award). Lutheran. Club: St. Paul Luth. (Dearborn) (fin. chmn. 1983, v.p. 1985, pres. 1986). Lodges: Masons, Shriners. Avocations: swimming, collecting works of Frank Lloyd Wright. Home: 22834 Park Dearborn MI 48124 Office: Ford Motor Co 614 World Hdqrs Dearborn MI 48121

LEVER, MICHAEL, clinical psychologist; b. Milw., May 12, 1942; s. Jack Allen and Cecelia (Grodinsky) L.; m. Leah Lande, June 19, 1966. BA, Marquette U., 1964, MS, 1968, PhD, 1972. Lic. psychologist, Wis. Psychologist DePaul Hosp., Milw., 1972-77, chief psychologist, 1977-80; practice psychoanalytic psychology Milw., 1977-80, Milw. Devel. Ctr., Milw., 1980-82, Associated Mental Health Services Inc., Milw., 1982—. Mem. Am. Psychol. Assn. (div. psychotherapy), Nat. Register Health Service Providers in Psychology, Am. Soc. Clin. Hypnosis, Acad. Family Therapy. Avocations: fishing, cards, reading. Office: AHMS Inc 250 W Coventry Ct #101 Milwaukee WI 53217

LEVERINGTON, JOHN JAMES, family therapist; b. New Hampton, Iowa, Oct. 27, 1951; s. Thomas Rex and Elda Louise (Bahe) L.; m. Rebecca Jean Leistikow, Jan. 13, 1973; children: Sarah Beth, Shawn David. BA, U. Iowa, 1973, MSW, 1978; cert., Multnomalh Sch. of Bible, 1974. Mem. child care staff Youth for Christ, Portland, Oreg., 1974-77; family therapist Families Inc., Cedar Rapids, Iowa, 1978—; dir. tng. Families Inc., Cedar Rapids, 1984—; pvt. practice family therapy Cedar Rapids, 1980—. Contbr. articles to profl. jours. Mem. Am. Assn. Marriage and Family Therapists, Nat. Assn. Social Workers. Avocations: jogging, photography, skiing, fishing. Home: 1350 Westland Rd NW Cedar Rapids IA 52405 Office: Families Inc PO Box 130 West Branch IA 52358

LEVI, DAVID RIES, accountant, financial planner; b. Chgo., Oct. 18, 1960; s. Richard R. and Nancy R. (Roseman) L.; m. Laurie Belzer, Sept. 5, 1982. BBA in Acctg., U. Iowa, 1982. CPA, Minn. Mgr. tax and fin. planning Schweitzer, Rubin, Gottlieb & Karon, Mpls., 1982—. Contbg. editor Mpls. Star, Mpls. Tribune, 1986. Mem. Minn. Soc. CPA's (mem. tax conf. com., fed. taxation com., state taxation com., estate and fin. planning conf.), Mpls. Jaycees. Jewish. Avocations: aerobics, reading, music, cycling. Office: Schweitzer Rubin Gottlieb Karon 1420 Twin City Fed Tower Minneapolis MN 55402

LEVI, EDWARD HIRSCH, former attorney general U.S., university president emeritus; b. Chgo., June 26, 1911; s. Gerson B. and Elsa B. (Hirsch) L.; m. Kate Sulzberger, June 4, 1946; children: John, David, Michael. Ph.B., U. Chgo., 1932, J.D., 1935; L.H.D.; J.S.D. (Sterling fellow 1935-36), Yale U., 1938; LL.D., U. Mich., 1959, U. Calif. at Santa Cruz, Jewish Theol. Sem. Am., U. Iowa, Brandeis U.; Lake Forest Coll., U. Pa., Dropsie U., Columbia U., Yeshiva U., U. Rochester, U. Toronto, Yale U., U. Notre Dame, Denison U., U. Nebr., U. Miami, Boston Coll., Brigham Young U., Duke U., Ripon Coll., Georgetown U.; L.H.D., Hebrew Union Coll., DePaul U., Loyola U., Kenyon Coll., Bard Coll., Beloit Coll.; D.C.L., N.Y. U. Bar: Ill. U.S. Supreme Ct. 1945. Asst. prof. U. Chgo. Law Sch., 1936-40, prof. law, 1945-75, dean, 1950-62; provost univ. U. Chgo., 1962-68, univ. pres., 1968-75, pres. emeritus, 1975—; Karl Llewellyn Distinguished Service prof. (on leave) U. Chgo. Law Sch., from 1975, Glen A. Lloyd Disting. Service prof., 1977-85, Glen A. Lloyd Disting. Service prof. emeritus, 1985—; atty. gen. U.S., 1975-77; Thomas Guest prof. U. Colo., summer 1960; Herman Phleger vis. prof. Stanford Law Sch., 1978; lectr. Salzburg (Austria) Seminar in Am. Studies, 1980; spl. asst. to atty. gen. U.S., Washington, 1940-45; 1st asst. war div. Dept. Justice, 1943, 1st asst. antitrust div., 1944-45; chmn. interdeptl. com. on monopolies and cartels, 1944; counsel Fedn. Atomic Scientists with respect to Atomic Energy Act, 1946; counsel subcom. on monopoly power Judiciary Com., 81st Congress, 1950; trustee Aerospace Corp., 1978-80; Mem. research adv. bd. Com. Econ. Devel., 1951-54; bd. Social Sci. Research Council, 1959-62, Council Legal Edn. and Profl. Responsibility, 1968-74; chmn. 1969-73; mem. Citizens Commn. Grad. Med. Edn., 1963-66, Commn. Founds. and Pvt. Philanthropy, 1969-70, Pres.'s Task Force Priorities in Higher Edn., 1969-70, Sloan Commn. Cable Communications, 1970, Nat. Commn. on Productivity, 1970-75, Nat. Council on Humanities, 1974-75, dir. Continental Ill. Holding Corp. Author: Introduction to Legal Reasoning, 1949, Four Talks on Legal Education, 1952, Point of View, 1969; editor: (with J. W. Moore) Gilbert's Collier on Bankruptcy, 1936, Elements of the Law, (with R. S. Steffen), 1950. Hon. trustee U. Chgo.; trustee Internat. Legal Ctr., 1966-75, Woodrow Wilson Nat. Fellowship Found., 1972-75, 77-79, Inst. Psychoanalysis Chgo., 1961-75, Urban Inst., 1968-75, Mus. Sci. and Industry, 1971-75, Russell Sage Found., 1971-75, Aspen Inst. Humanistic Studies, 1970-75, 77-79, Inst. Internat. Edn. (hon.), 1969; public dir. Chgo. Bd. Trade, 1977-80; bd. overseers U. Pa., 1978-82; chmn. bd. Nat. Humanities Ctr., 1979-83, trustee, 1978—; bd. dirs. MacArthur Found., 1979-84, William Benton Found., 1980—, Martin Luther King Jr. Fed. Holiday Commn., 1986. Decorated Legion of Honor (France); recipient Learned Hand medal Fed. Bar Council, 2nd. cir., 1976, Fordham-Stein award Fordham U., 1977, Brandeis medal Brandeis U., 1978. Fellow Am. Acad. Arts and Scis. (nat. pres. 1986—), Am. Bar Found.; mem. Am. Philos. Soc., Fed. (hon. award 1975), Am., Ill. (award of honor 1983), Chgo. (Centennial award 1975) Bar Assns., Am. Law Inst. (council), Am. Judicature Soc., Supreme Ct. Hist. Soc., Phi Beta Kappa, Order of Coif. Clubs: Century (N.Y.C.); Chgo. Comml. Quadrangle Mid-Am. (Chgo.); Columbia Yacht. Office: U Chgo 1116 E 59th St Chicago IL 60637

LEVIN, CARL, U.S. senator; b. Detroit, June 28, 1934; m. Barbara Halpern, 1961; children: Kate, Laura, Erica. B.A., Swarthmore Coll., 1956; J.D., Harvard U., 1959. Mem. firm Grossman, Hyman & Grossman, Detroit, 1959-64; asst. atty. gen., gen. counsel Mich. CRC, 1964-67; chief appellate defender for city of Detroit 1968-69; mem. firm Schlussel, Lifton, Simon, Rands & Kaufman, 1971-73, Jaffe, Snider, Raitt, Garratt & Heuer, 1978-79; mem. City Council Detroit, 1970-73, pres., 1974-77; mem. U.S. Senate from Mich., 1979—; past instr. Wayne State U., U. Detroit. Mem. Mich. Bar Assn., D.C. Bar. Democrat. Office: 459 Russell Senate Bldg Washington DC 20510

LEVIN, CHARLES LEONARD, state justice; b. Detroit, Apr. 28, 1926; s. Theodore and Rhoda (Katzin) L.; children—Arthur, Amy, Fredrick. B.A., U. Mich., 1946, LL.B., 1947; LL.D. (hon.), Detroit Coll. of Law, 1980. Bar: Mich. bar 1947, N.Y. bar 1949, U.S. Supreme Ct. bar 1953, D.C. bar 1954. Practiced in N.Y.C., 1948-50, Detroit, 1950-66; partner firm Levin, Levin, Garvett & Dill, Detroit, 1951-66; judge Mich. Ct. Appeals, Detroit, 1966-73; justice Mich. Supreme Ct., 1973—; mem. Mich. Law Revision Commn., 1966. Trustee Marygrove Coll., 1971-77, chmn., 1971-74; mem. vis. coms. to Law Schs., U. Mich., U. Chgo., 1977-80, Wayne State U. Mem. Am. Law Inst. Office: 1008 Travelers Tower Southfield MI 48076

LEVIN, DANIEL NEAL, psychologist; b. Madison, Wis., Feb. 15, 1954. BA, U. Wis., 1975, MS, 1978, PhD, 1982. Licensed psychologist, Wis. Research assoc. Dept. Neurology U. Wis., Madison, 1983-84; psychologist Affiliated Psychol. Resources, Madison, 1983—; cons. Abaris Ctr., Beloit, 1984-85, HospiceCare, Inc., Madison, 1984—, Luth. Social Services, Madison, 1985—, Am. Cancer Soc., 1986—. Contbr. articles to profl. jours. Mem. adv. bd. Hospice Care, Inc., Madison, 1985—; bd. dirs. Jewish Social Services, Madison, 1986. Mem. Am. Psychol. Assn., Soc. Behavioral Medicine. Office: Affiliated Psychol Resources 617 N Segoe Rd Madison WI 53705

LEVIN, DEBBE ANN, lawyer; b. Cin., Mar. 11, 1954; d. Abram Asher and Selma Ruth (Herlands) L. BA, Washington U., St. Louis, 1976; JD, U. Cin.,

1979; LLM, NYU, 1983. Bar: Ohio 1979. Staff atty. U.S. Ct. Appeals 6th Circuit, Cin., 1979-82; assoc. Schwartz, Manes & Ruby Co., LPA, Cin., 1983—; lectr. tax conf. U. Cin., 1984-86, adj. prof. coll. of bus., 1987. Editor: U. Cin. Law Review, 1972-79. Recipient Judge Alfred Mack prize U. Cin., 1979. Mem. ABA, Ohio Bar Assn., Cin. Bar Assn., Cin. Bus. & Profl. Women's Club, Order of Coif. Jewish. Office: Schwartz Manes & Ruby Co LPA 2900 Carew Tower Cincinnati OH 45202

LEVIN, FRED MICHAEL, psychoanylist, psychiatrist; b. Chgo., July 15, 1942; s. Harry and Pearl (Eisenstein) L.; m. Sachiko Tanaka, Sept. 16, 1966; children: David A., Daniel K. BA, Dartmouth Coll., 1964; MD, Northwestern U., 1968. Diplomate Am. Bd. Med. Examiners; cert. Am. Bd. Psychiatry and Neurology. Intern Michael Reese Hosp., Chgo., 1969, resident in psychiatry, 1974; lectr. Northwestern U., Evanston, Ill., 1974-76, asst. prof. psychiatry, 1976—; mem. faculty Inst. for Psychoanalysis, Chgo., 1981—; clin. dir. Sieegel Inst., Michael Reese Hosp., Chgo., 1974—; pvt. practice psychiatry Chgo., 1974—; vis. prof. Kitazato U. Med. Sch., Tokyo, 1976, 85, U. Manitoba, Winnipeg, Can., 1986. Mem. editorial bd. Analytic Press, Inc., 1981—; contbr. chpts. to books, articles to profl. jours. Mem. Am. Psychoanalytic Assn. (lectr. Chungdu, Republic of China, 1983, arrangements com. 1976—, cert.), Chgo. Psychoanalytic Soc. (program com. 1976—), Phi Delta Epsilon. Jewish. Avocations: jogging, tennis, stamp collecting. Home: 200 E Delaware Apt 19A Chicago IL 60611 Office: 111 N Wabash Suite 1315 Chicago IL 60602

LEVIN, JANE SUSAN, psychologist; b. N.Y.C., Aug. 30, 1948; s. Lawrence M. and Frances M. (Minowitz) L. BA, Queens Coll., 1970; MA in Edn., Washington U., St. Louis, 1975, PhD, 1981. Lic. cons. psychologist. Clin. assoc. Washington U., St. Louis, 1975-84; post-doctoral fellow Mo. Inst. Psychiatry, St. Louis, 1982-84; clin. dir. Lesbian and Gay Community Services, Mpls., 1984-85, Northland Therapy Ctr., Mpls., 1985—; adj. assoc. prof. St. Mary's Coll., Mpls., 1985—; cons. Pride Inst., Eden Prairie, Minn., 1986—, The Wayside House, Mpls., 1986—, Model Women's Treatment Program, St. Paul, 1986—; trainer Bur. Criminal Apprehension, St. Paul, 1985-86. Contbr. articles to profl. jours. v.p., bd. dirs. Crossroads Counseling Ctr., St. Louis, 1975-76; midwest organizer March on Washington for Lesbian/Gay Rights, Washington, 1979; organizer Take Back the Night, St. Louis, 1982; co-founder Community Liaison for Edn. and Research, St. Louis, 1981-84; author funding grants United Way of Hennepin County, Mpls., 1984. Mem. Am. Psychol. Assn. (task force co-chairperson), Assn. Lesbian and Gay Psychologists, Assn. for Women in Psychol. Jewish. Avocations: playing the violin, birdwatching, weightlifting. Office: Northland Therapy Ctr 800 S 10th St Minneapolis MN 55404

LEVIN, JERRY WAYNE, food company executive; b. San Antonio, Apr. 18, 1944; s. Bernard H. and Marion (Bromberg) L.; m. Carol Lee Motel, Dec. 18, 1966; children—Joshua, Abby. B.S.E.E., U. Mich., 1966, B.S.E. in Math., 1966; M.B.A., U. Chgo., 1968. With Tex. Instruments, Dallas, 1968-72; with Marsh & McLennan, Chgo., 1972-74; with The Pillsbury Co., Mpls., 1974—, exec. v.p. corporate devel., treas., 1985—, exec. v.p. corp. devel., chmn. Haagen-Dazs div., 1987—; bd. dirs. Apogee Enterprises, Inc. Bd. dirs. St. Paul Chamber Orch., 1982, Met. Econ. Devel. Assn., Mpls., 1983, Mpls. Fedn., 1982. Mem. Internat. Assn. Corp. Growth (bd. dirs. 1981-83), Corp. Profl. Assn. (bd. dirs. 1982-83). Club: Mpls.; Oak Ridge Country (Hopkins, Minn.); Lafayette (Wayzata, Minn.). Home: 4260 Chimo E Deephaven MN 55391

LEVIN, JON, bookstore executive; b. Lindsborg, Kans., Dec. 16, 1935; s. Joseph A. and Amy E. (Nelson) L.; m. Lila J. Orme, Aug. 19, 1956; children—Jeffrey, Steve, Susan. B.S. in Bus. Adminstrn., Kans. State U., 1957. Book mgr. Varney's Bookstore, Inc., Manhattan, Kans., 1957-74, gen. mgr., 1974—; dir. Citizens Bank, Manhattan. Pres. United Way, Manhattan, 1969-70; bd. dirs. Red Cross, Manhattan, 1978; trustee Leadership Kans., Topeka, 1984-76. Served to 2d lt. U.S. Army, 1960-62. Recipient Outstanding Service award United Cerebral Palsy of Kans., 1969, 70. Mem. Designated Cert. Store Profl. Prof., Assn. Coll. Stores, Kans. Retail Council (bd. dirs. 1982—); Manhattan C. of C. (bd. dirs.). Republican. Presbyterian. Club: Rotary (bd. dirs. 1970-71). Avocation: golf. Office: Varney's Bookstore Inc 623 N Manhattan Ave Manhattan KS 66502

LEVIN, JULES DARRELL, neurosurgeon; b. Milw., Jan. 14, 1915; s. Joseph Victor and Toby Anna (Rymeland) L.; m. Beverly Lubotsky, June 17, 1945; children: Ronald, Ellen Rachel, Bruce. BA with honors, U. Wis., 1936, MD, 1938. Diplomate Am. Bd. Neurolo. Surgery. Practice medicine specializing in neurol. surgery Milw., 1948—; assoc. clin. prof. Med. Coll. Wis., 1958—. Contbr. articles to med. jours. Served to capt. M.C., U.S. Army, 1944-46. Recipient Med. Arts Humanitarian award State of Israel Bonds, 1976. Fellow: Am. Coll. Surgeons; mem. AMA, Wis. Med. Soc. (pres. 1978-79, Disting. Service Neurol. Surgery award 1984), Milw. County Med. Soc. (pres. 1972-73), Am. Assn. Neurol. Surgeons, Congress Neurol. Surgeons, Am. Acad. Neurology, Royal Soc. Medicine (assoc.), Am. Legion. Jewish. Club: Athletic (Milw.). Lodges: Rotary (pres. local club 1980-81), Masons, Consistory, Shriners. Home: 1530 W Spruce Ct River Hills WI 53217 Office: 324 East Wisconsin Ave Milwaukee WI 53202

LEVIN, KERRY, neurologist; b. Chgo., Apr. 11, 1951; s. Howard and Saralee (Greenblatt) L. BA, Johns Hopkins U., 1973, MD, 1977. Diplomate Am. Bd. Psychiatry and Neurology. Resident Case Western Res. U. Hosp., Cleve., 1977-79; resident in neurology U. Chgo. Hosp., 1979-82; fellow in electromyography Mayo Clinic, Rochester, Minn., 1982-83; asst. prof. neurology U. Mass. Hosp., Worcester, 1983-84; staff neurologist Cleve. Clinic, 1984—. Mem. Am. Assn. Electromyography and Electrodiagnosis (com. mem. 1986—). Office: Cleve Clinic Dept Neurology 9500 Euclid Ave Cleveland OH 44106

LEVIN, LESLEY JEANNE, corporate executive; b. Cleve., Nov. 26, 1946; d. Sol and Rose Ann (Bostwick) Baker; m. Mark Milton Levin, June 27, 1971; children: Sara R., Joshua B. BA, Ind. U., 1969; MS, Case Western Reserve U., 1973. Cert. social worker. Social worker Kaiser Hosp., Cleve., 1978-80, Family Counseling Agy., Crete, Ill., 1980-81, Palos Community Hosp., Palos Heights, Ill., 1981-82; dir. social services Olympia Fields (Ill.) Osteo., 1982-85; program mgr. Compcare, Chgo., 1985; cons. Personal Performance Cons., St. Louis, 1985—; pvt. practice psychotherapist, Park Forest, Ill., 1981-85. Contbr. articles to profl. jours. Recipient Women in Leadership award Coro Found., 1986. Mem. Nat. Assn. Social Workers, Am. Assn. Marriage and Family Therapist, Assn. Hosp. Social Work Dirs. (sec. 1985), South Suburban Continuity Care (pres. 1985), Women's Am. ORT (v.p. 1978-79). Avocations: quilting, bicycling, gardening, walking, swimming. Home: 11857 McKelvey Gardens Dr Maryland Heights MO 63043 Office: Personal Performance Cons 211 N Lindbergh Saint Louis MO 63141

LEVIN, MYRON JAME, physician, educator, consultant; b. Los Angeles, Mar. 6, 1912; s. Ben S. and Elsie (Jame) L.; m. Anita Dresner, July 7, 1940; children—Harold D., Marilyn Jean. B.S., U. Ill., 1935, M.S. in Bacteriology, 1937, M.D., 1937. Diplomate Am. Bd. Anesthesiology. Intern, Woodlawn Hosp., Chgo., 1937-38; resident in anesthesiology Hines VA Hosp. (Ill.), 1949-51, asst. chief anesthesiology, 1951-72, cons., 1951—; dir. anesthesiology Am. Hosp., Chgo., 1956-70; chmn. anesthesiology Gottlieb Meml. Hosp., Melrose Park, Ill., 1961-78, cons., 1978—; sr. attending anesthesiology, chmn. dept. Pain Mgmt. Clinic, Cook County Hosp., Chgo., 1981—; clin. assoc. prof. anesthesiology U. Ill. Coll. Medicine, Chgo., 1951-75; clin. prof. anesthesiology Chgo. Med. Sch., 1975—, acting chmn. anesthesiology, 1980-81; cons. VA Hosp., North Chicago, Ill., 1979—; field rep. Joint Commn. on Accreditation of Hosps., 1976-78. Contbr. articles to profl. jours., chpts. to books. Served to capt. M.C., AUS, 1942-46. Fellow Am. Coll. Anesthesiologists, Internat. Coll. Surgeons; mem. AMA, Chgo. Med. Soc., Ill. State Med. Soc., Am. Soc. Anesthesiologists, Ill. Soc. Anesthesiologists, Chgo. Soc. Anesthesiologists (pres. 1956-57). Lodges: Masons, Shriners. Home: 1280 Rudolph Rd #3H Northbrook IL 60062 Office: Cook County Hosp Dept Anesthesiology 1835 W Harrison St Chicago IL 60612

LEVIN, PATRICIA OPPENHEIM, educator; b. Detroit, Apr. 5, 1932; d. Royal A. and Elsa (Freeman) Oppenheim; A.B. in History, U. Mich., 1954, Ph.D., 1981; M.Ed., Marygrove Coll., 1973; m. Charles L. Levin, Feb. 21, 1956; children—Arthur David, Amy Ragen, Fredrick Stuart. Substitute tchr. Oak Park (Mich.) Schs., 1955-67; substitute tchr. Detroit Pub. Schs., 1960-67, reading and learning disabled tchr., cons., 1967-76; guest lectr. Marygrove Coll., 1974-76, coordinator spl. edn., 1976-86; adj. prof. Oakland U., 1987—; adj. prof., conf. presenter. Mem. Mich. regional bd. ORT, 1965-68; v.p. women's aux. Children's Hosp. Mich.; bd. dirs. women's com. United Community Services, 1968-73; women's com. Detroit Grand Opera Assn., 1970-75; mem. coms. Detroit Symphony Orch., Detroit Inst. Arts; torch drive area chmn. United Found., 1967-70. Mem. Friends of Detroit Pub. Library, NAACP (life), Internat. Reading Assn., Nat. Council Tchrs. of English, Assn. Supervision and Curriculum Devel., Nat. Assn. Edn. of Young Children, Assn. Children and Adults with Learning Disabilities, Mich. Assn. Children with Learning Disabilities (edn. v.p., exec. bd.), Council Exceptional Children, Assn. Gifted and Talented Children Mich., Mich. Assn. Emotionally Disturbed Children, Orton Soc., Phi Delta Kappa, Pi Lambda Theta. Home: 30840 Running Stream #1 Farmington Hills MI 48018

LEVIN, PAUL FREDERICK, lawyer; b. Cambridge, Mass., Feb. 2, 1947; s. Spencer Ely and Ruth (Rubinsky) L.; m. Joan M. Meltzer, June 11, 1970; children: Marshall Aaron, Sarah Abigail. BA, Case Western Res. U., 1969; JD, Columbia U., 1972. Bar: N.Y. 1973., Ohio 1974, U.S. Dist. Ct. (no. dist.) Ohio 1975, U.S. Ct. Appeals (6th cir.) 1978, U.S. Supreme Ct. 1978. Atty. Aims Group, N.Y.C., 1972-74; asst. dir. law City of Cleve., 1975-79; assoc. Gaines, Stern, Schwarzwald and Robiner, Cleve., 1979-81; ptnr. Schwarzwald, Robiner, Wolf and Rock, Cleve., 1981—. Trustee, pres. Sussex Community Assn., Shaker Heights, Ohio, 1983—; trustee Shaker Youth Ctr., Shaker Heights, 1987—. Mem. ABA, Ohio Bar Assn. (sch. law com. 1975—), Ohio Council Sch. Bd. Attys., Greater Cleve. Bar Assn., Cuyahoga County Bar Assn., Cuyahoga County Law Dir. Assn., Case Western Res. U. Alumni Assn. (trustee 1987—), Zeta Beta Tau. Home: 3661 Sutherland Rd Shaker Heights OH 44120 Office: 616 Bond Ct 1300 E 9th St Cleveland OH 44114

LEVIN, ROBERT DAVID, physician; b. Memphis, Dec. 10, 1943; s. Jack and Sarah (Stagman) L.; m. Pamela Joy Gilford, June 13, 1976; children: Nickolai, Douglas. BS in Chemistry, Calif. Inst. Tech., 1965; MD, U. Chgo., 1969. Diplomate Am. Bd. Internal Medicine, Am. Bd. Med. Oncology. Asst. prof. Rush U. Rush Presbyn.-St. Luke's Med. Ctr., Chgo., 1977—; attending physician Mt. Sinai Med. Ctr., Chgo., 1977—; chief med. oncology Am. Internat. Hosp., Zion, Ill., 1986—. Chmn. physician's edn. com. Chgo. chpt. Am. Cancer Soc., 1982—. Served to capt. USAF, 1969-71. Mem. AMA, Am. Soc. Hematology, Am. Soc. Clin. Oncology. Jewish. Office: Am Internat Hosp 1911 27th St Zion IL 60099

LEVIN, SANDER (MARTIN), congressman; b. Detroit, Sept. 6, 1931; s. Saul and Bess (Levinson) L.; m. Victoria Schlafer, 1957. B.A., U. Chgo., 1952; M.A., Columbia U., 1954; LL.B., Harvard U., 1957. Supr. Oakland County Bd. Suprs., Mich., 1961-64; mem. Mich. Senate, 1965-70; fellow Kennedy Sch. Govt., Inst. Politics, Harvard U., Cambridge, Mass., 1975; asst. adminstr. AID, Washington, 1977-81; with Schwartz, O'Hare & Levin, 1957-64, Jaffe, Snider, Raitt, Garrett & Heuer, 1971-74, Beer & Boltz, 1975-77; mem. 98th-99th Congresses from 17th Mich. dist., Washington, 1983—; adj. prof. law Wayne State U., Detroit, 1971-74. Chmn. Mich. Democratic Com., 1968-69. Office: 17117 W 9 Mile Rd Southfield MI 48075

LEVIN, STEPHEN DEAN, accountant; b. Chgo., June 19, 1955; s. Jacob Louis and Betty Ann (Ascher) L.; m. Diane Lynn Garton, Dec. 1, 1985. BS in Acctg., Bradley U., 1976; MS in Taxation, DePaul U., 1985. CPA, Ill. Acct. Kupferberg, Goldberg & Neimark, Chgo., 1977—. Bd. dirs. Young Leadership div. Jewish United Fund, Chgo., 1984-85, 87—; treas. Forum Square Condominium Assn., Glenview, Ill., 1982-86. Mem. Am. Inst. CPA's, Tau Epsilon Phi Alumni Assn. (founder, pres. 1977-82). Avocations: tennis, golf. Home: 90 Marquette Rd Highland Park IL 60035 Office: Kupferberg Goldberg & Neimark 111 E Wacker Dr #1400 Chicago IL 60601

LEVINE, BERYL JOYCE, state supreme court justice; b. Winnipeg, Man., Can., Nov. 9, 1935; came to U.S., 1955; d. Maurice Jacob and Bella (Gutnik) Choslovsky; m. Leonard Levine, June 7, 1955; children: Susan Brauna, Marc Joseph, Sari Ruth, William Noah, David Karl. B.A., U. Man., Winnipeg, 1965; J.D. with distinction, U. N.D., 1974. Assoc. Vogel, Branther, Kelly, Knutson, Weir & Bye, Ltd., Fargo, N.D., 1974-85; justice N.D. Supreme Ct., Bismarck, 1985—, chmn. jud. planning com. Bd. dirs. Fargo Youth Commn., 1974-77, Hospice of Red River Valley, Fargo; chmn. Gov.'s Commn. on Children at Risk, 1985. Named Outstanding Woman in N.D. Law, U. N.D. Law Women's Caucus, 1985. Mem. Cass County Bar Assn. (pres. 1984-85), N.D. State Bar Assn., Burleigh County Bar Assn., Order of Coif. Office: ND Supreme Ct Bismarck ND 58505

LEVINE, ELLIOT MARK, obstetrician-gynecologist, educator; b. Chgo., Aug. 14, 1952; s. Sam Theodore and Florence Phyllis (Grossman) L.; m. Debra Jo Vorhies, June 22, 1986. BS, U. Wis., 1974; MD, Chgo. Med. Sch., 1978. Cert. Am. Bd. Ob-Gyn. Practice medicine specializing in ob-gyn Chgo., 1982—; dir. undergrad. med. edn. in ob-gyn Ill. Masonic Med. Ctr., Chgo., 1982—, dir. gynecol. laser surgery, 1983—; gynecol. cons. Loyola Sexual Dysfunction Clinic, Maywood, Ill., 1983—; lectr. Merck, Sharp & Dohme, 1985—. Contbr. articles to profl. jours. Fellow Am. Coll. Ob-Gyns; mem. Cen. Assn. Ob-Gyns, Chgo. Med. Soc., Midwest Bio-Laser Inst. Jewish. Avocations: tennis, bicycling, chess, music, cooking. Home: 2856 W Estes Chicago IL 60645 Office: 166 E Superior Suite 301 Chicago IL 60611

LEVINE, FREDERICK HUGH, cardiovascular surgeon; b. N.Y.C., May 9, 1943; s. Alexander Benjamin and Thelma (Marcus) L.; m. Patricia Beverly Zimmerman, July 3, 1965; children—Shira, Hallie. A.B., Columbia U., 1964; M.D., Harvard U., 1968. Diplomate Am. Bd. Surgery, Am. Bd. Thoracic Surgery. Intern and resident in surgery Mass. Gen. Hosp., Boston, 1968-75, resident in cardiovascular and thoracic surgery, 1976; instr., asst. prof. surgery Mass. Gen. Hosp., Harvard Med. Sch., Boston, 1977-81; chmn. dept. cardiovascular and thoracic surgery Sinai Hosp. of Detroit, 1981—; assoc. clin. prof. surgery Wayne State U., Detroit, 1981—. Contbr. articles to med. jours. Served to lt. comdr. USPHS, 1970-72. NIH grantee, 1977-81. Mem. Assn. for Acad. Surgery, AMA, N.Y. Acad. Scis., Am. Heart Assn., Am. Coll. Cardiology, ACS, Soc. Thoracic Surgeons, Soc. Univ. Surgeons, Am. Assn. for Thoracic Surgery, Internat. Cardiovascular Soc. Jewish. Office: Sinai Hosp of Detroit 6767 W Outer Dr Detroit MI 48235

LEVINE, HOWARD L., otolaryngologist; b. Cleve., Mar. 22, 1944; s. Sam and Edith (Stein) L.; m. Susan Cahn, June 24, 1967; children: Natalie, Wilton, Rebecca. BA, U. Pa., 1966; MD, Northwestern U., 1970. Diplomate Am. Bd. Otolaryngology, Am. Bd. Head and Neck Surgery. Intern., straight surg. resident U. Hosps., Cleve., 1970-72; resident in otolaryngology Northwestern U., Chgo., 1972-75; sr. staff mem. dept. otolaryngology and communicative disorders The Cleve. Clinic Hosp., 1975—; cons. staff mem. dept. otolaryngology div. surgery St. Vincent Charity Hosp., Cleve., 1978—; asst. clin. prof. otolaryngology div. surgery Case Western Res. U., Cleve., 1980—; mem. numerous coms. Cleve. Clinic Found. including pediatric surgery com. Ctr. Children and Youth 1983—, head and neck task force cancer ctr. com. 1979—, hosp. task force com. 1983—, edn. governing group 1983—, physicians edn. council 1983—, chmn. 1983—, program dir. dept. otolaryngology and communicative disorders 1976-83, vice chmn. div. edn. 1984—; mem. ethicon facial plastic surgery adv. panel 1980—; presenter in field. Author: (with K. Alperin and M. Groves) Tracheostomy Car Manual, 1982; contbr. numerous chpts. to books, articles to profl. jours. Mem. young leadership div., physicians cabinet, chaplaincy com., Jewish Community Fedn., missions com. 1983, leadership devel. task force 1983—, corp. fund raising campaign com. Cleve. Ballet, 1977, mem. Council Jewish Physicians 1984—, trustee 1985, trustee Jewish Family Service 1981—, program service com. 1982, refugee resettlement service 1982, fin. com. 1982, fee com. 1982, nominating and leadership devel. com. 1983—, pub. affairs com. 1983—, pub. relations com. 1983—, adv. bd. residential facilities and services to the adult mentally retarded 1985. Fellow ACS (mem. com. on trauma 1979-80), Am. Acad. Facial Plastic and Reconstructive Surgery (mem. future plans com. 1978—, pubs. com. 1981—), Am. Acad. Ophthalmology and Otolaryngology, Am. Soc. Head and Neck Surgery; mem. AMA, Ill. State Med. Soc., Chgo. Med. Soc., Acad. Medicine Cleve. (mem. trauma and emergency care com. 1979-80), Ohio State Med. Soc., Northeastern Ohio Otolaryngology and Maxillofacial Surgery Soc. (program chmn. 1977-78, sec.-treas. 1978-79, pres. 1979-80), Soc. Ear, Nose and Throat Advances in Children, Soc. Univ. Otolaryngologists, Am. Acad. Otolaryngology Head and Neck Surgery (facial nerve paralysis study group, acad.'s tchrs. sect. in otolaryngology 1985, task force on new materials 1980—, home study course task force 1983—, self-instructional package faculty 1985), Soc. Head and Neck Surgeons, Am. Laryngol., Rhinol. and Otological Soc., Phi Delta Epsilon (nat. placement com. 1980—, com. intern/resident liaison 1976—). Club: Oakwood (Cleve.). Avocation: tennis, reading, classical music, cross country skiing. Office: Cleve Clinic Found 9500 Euclid Ave Cleveland OH 44106

LEVINE, HOWARD MARVIN, obstetrician, gynecologist; b. N.Y.C., Apr. 24, 1933; s. Benjamin and Esther (Brody) L.; m. Alice Esta Edelman, June 12, 1954; children: Linda Krause, Steven Brody, Douglas Becker. AB, NYU, 1953; MD, U. Louisville, 1957. Diplomate Am. Bd. Ob-Gyn. Intern Mt. Sinai Hosp., N.Y.C., 1957-58; resident in ob-gyn Albert Einstein Coll. Medicine, Bronx Mcpl. Hosp. Ctr., N.Y.C., 1958-62; practice medicine specializing in ob-gyn Mpls., 1964—; assoc. clin. prof. U. Minn., 1985—. Served as capt. USAF, 1962-64. Fellow Am. Coll. Ob-Gyn, ACS, Am. Geriatrics Soc., Internat. Coll. Surgeons, Am. Soc. Colpolscopy and Cervical Neoplasia. Home: 11215 57th Ave N Plymouth MN 55442 Office: 920 Med Arts Bldg Minneapolis MN 55402

LEVINE, JAMES, conductor, pianist, artistic director; b. Cin., June 23, 1943; s. Lawrence M. and Helen (Goldstein) L. Studied piano, with Rosina Lhevinne and Rudolf Serkin; studied conducting with Jean Morel, Fausto Cleva and Max Rudolf, studied theory and interpretation with Walter Levin; student, Juilliard Sch. Music; hon. degree, U. Cin. Piano debut with Cin. Symphony, 1953; conducting debut at Aspen Music Festival, 1961; Met. Opera debut, 1971; Chgo. Symphony debut at Ravinia Festival, 1971; regularly appears throughout U.S. and Europe as condr. and pianist, including Vienna Philharm., Berlin Philharm., Chgo. Symphony, Phila. Orch., Boston Symphony, N.Y. Philharm., Wagner Festival at Bayreuth; made Bayreuth debut in new prodn. of Parsifal, 1982; condr. Salzburg Festival premiere Schönberg's Moses and Aron, 1987; condr. Met. premier prodns. of Verdi's I Vespri Siciliani, Weill's The Rise and Fall of the City of Mahogonny, Stravinsky's La Rossignol, Oedipus Rex, Berg's Lulu, Mozart's Idomeneo and La Clemenza di Tito, Gershwin's Porgy and Bess; subject of documentary for Pub. Broadcasting System. Office: PO Box 698 Canal St Sta New York NY 10013

LEVINE, JEFFERY ROBIN, insurance executive; b. Detroit, Apr. 27, 1955; s. Abe Louis and Elaine Sandra (Gaum) L.; m. Annise Lynn Swartz, July 1, 1982; 1 child, Ashley Nicole. BA in Journalism, Mich. State U., 1977. Dir. pub. relations Am. Income Life, Southfield, Mich., 1977-84; prin. Jeff Levine Agy., Inc., Oak Park, Mich., 1984—; cons. Metro Detroit Sr. Citizens Services, 1982-86, United Dental Assocs., Detroit, 1985-86. Contbr. articles to newspapers. Mem. Nat. Assn. Life Underwriters, Greater Detroit Assn. Life Underwriters, Mich., A. Philip Randolph Inst. (coalition of trade unionists), AFL-CIO (Detroit Chpt., mem. Frontlash 1978, del. Mich. council), Histadrut. Democrat. Jewish. Home: 35447 Bunker Hill Farmington Hills MI 48018 Office: 25900 Greenfield #259 Oak Park MI 48237

LEVINE, JEFFREY LURIE, real estate executive, lawyer; b. Springfield, Ohio, June 1, 1951; s. Martin A. and Harriett (Lurie) L.; m. Ellen Martha Kepnes, June 2, 1974; children—Jeffrey Kyle, Peter Kepnes. B.S., Miami U., Ohio, 1973; J.D., Capital U., 1976. Bar: Ohio 1976, Fla. 1985. Vice-pres., counsel Levine Realty Co., Springfield, 1976-83, pres., 1983—; prin. Convest Mgmt. Corp., Columbus, Ohio; mng. ptnr. Main Assocs., Springfield, Southwest Realty Assocs., Springfield; owner So. Properties; officer, dir. Assoc. Real Estate Investors, Inc., Springfield, Levine Investment Co., Springfield; pres. Real Estate Ctr. Assocs., Inc., Springfield; exec. v.p. Feesavers, Inc., Springfield; ptnr. Second Equity Co., Springfield; bd. dirs. Huntington Nat. Bank, Springfield, Fin. Land Corp., Springfield, Core Renewal Corp., Springfield. Mem. fin. adv. com. Mercy Med. Ctr.; trustee Friends of Mercy, United Way Clark County, 1980; trustee, chmn. fin. com. Ridgewood Sch.; mem. exec. com. Springfield Arts Ctr., also chmn. devel. com.; mem. exec. bd. Clark County chpt. ARC, also chmn. personnel com.; trustee Ridgewood Sch. Mem. ABA, Ohio Bar Assn., Fla. Bar Assn., Springfield Bar and Law Library Assn., Springfield Real Estate Bd., Ohio Assn. Realtors, Internat. Council Shopping Ctrs., Nat. Assn. Realtors. Republican. Jewish. Clubs: Springfield Country, University (Springfield). Lodge: Rotary (Springfield). Avocations: tennis; skiing. Office: 501 W High St PO Box 1848 Springfield OH 45501

LEVINE, JOEL HOWARD, radiologist; b. Chgo., Dec. 7, 1930; s. Albert and Estelle Lea (Eisenberg) L.; m. Ann-Mari Johannson, June 23, 1959; children: Beatrice Desiré, Todd Michael, Ann-Tina, Thomas. BS in Medicine, U. Ill., Chgo., 1955, MD, 1956. Diplomate Am. Bd. Radiology. Intern Cook County Hosp., Chgo., 1956-57; resident in radiology Northwestern U., Chgo., 1961-64; practice medicine specializing in radiology Unimed, Ltd., Highland Pk., Ill.; staff radiologist Hyde Pk. Community Hosp., Chgo., Cen. Community Hosp., Chgo., Franklin Community Hosp., Chgo., Bethesda Community Hosp., Chgo., Glendale Heights (Ill.) Community Hosp. Served to capt. USAF, 1959-61. Mem. AMA, Ill. State Med. Soc., Chgo. Med. Soc., Am. Coll. Radiology, Radiol. Soc. N.A. Jewish. Avocation: philately. Home: 17856 Tipton Homewood IL 60430 Office: Unimed Ltd 555 Vine Highland Park IL 60035

LEVINE, LAURENCE ARVIN, otolaryngologist; b. Bklyn., Feb. 15, 1941; m. Edith A. Levine; children: Debra Nancy, Rebecca Michelle. BA, Hofstra U., 1962, MA, 1963; DDS, NYU, 1967; MD, Union U., 1971. Diplomate Am. Bd. Otolaryngology, Nat. Bd. Dental Examiners, Nat. Bd. Medical Examiners. Intern in oral surgery Bellevue Hosp., N.Y.C., 1967-68; intern in gen. surgery The Jewish Hosp. of St. Louis, 1971-72, resident in gen. surgery, 1972-73, assoc. dir., asst. attending physician, 1977-79, otolaryngologist-in-chief, spl. cons. dept. phys. medicine and rehabilitation, 1979—, also active various coms.; resident in otolaryngology Wash. U., St. Louis, 1973-77; cons. staff St. Louis City Hosp., 1978-75, 84-85; VA Hosp. St. Louis, 1980—; Charter Hosp., St. Louis, 1985—; cons. physician med. div. St. Louis Met. Police Dept., 1984—; asst. otolaryngologist Barnes Hosp., St. Louis, 1977—, active various coms., 1977—; assoc. prof. Wash. U., St. Louis, 1986—. Served to lt. M.C., USNR. NIH fellow, 1973-77; Bi-State Regional Med. grantee, 1972-73, Lidosporin Otic Solution grantee Burroughs Wellcome Co., 1981-82Lilly research grantee Eli Lilly & Co., 1982-85. Fellow ACS, Am. Acad. Otolaryngology-Head and Neck Surgery, Inc.; mem. AAAS, AMA, Mo. State Med. Assn., St. Louis Met. Med. Soc., The Centurions of Deafness Research Found. Southeast Cancer Study Group-Head Neck Task Force, Ear Nose and Throat Club St. Louis, Internat. Soc. Photoscopy (founder), Voice Found., Bellevue Hosp. Oral Surgery Alumni Assn. Home: 4910 Forest Park Suite 212 Saint Louis MO 63108 Office: Jewish Hosp at Wash U Jewish Hosp Saint Louis MO 63108

LEVINE, LAWRENCE DAVID, manufacturing executive, consultant; b. Washington, D.C., June 28, 1932; s. Mack and Edith (Kaplan) L.; m. Orabeth Ruderman, June 17, 1956; children: Jill Debra Shirley, Jonathan Daniel, Theodore Samuel. BS, U.S. Coast Guard Acad., 1954; MBA, Northeastern U., 1968. Commd. ensign USCG, 1954, advanced through grades to lt., 1958, resigned, 1959; capt. USCGR, 1975—; cons. Arthur D. Little Inc., Cambridge, Mass., 1966-70; mgr. mfg. engring, shop ops. Gen. Electric, Chgo., 1970-78; dir. Ingersoll. Engrs., Rockford, Ill., 1978-81; v.p. Ogden Corp., Cleve., 1982-84; pres. The Lawrence Group, Northbrook, Ill., 1985-86, Onsrud Machine Corp., Wheeling, Ill., 1986—. Contbr. articles to profl. jours. Mem. Mfg. Mgmt. Assocs. (bd. dirs. 1985—), Numerical Control Soc. (nat. bd. dir. 1970-74, chmn. Yankee chpt. 1969-70). Jewish. Avocations: tennis, photography, foreign travel, bicycling. Office: Onsrud Machine Corp 110 W Carpenter Ave Wheeling IL 60090

LEVINE, ROBERT SIDNEY, orthopaedic surgeon; b. Detroit, Aug. 1, 1942; s. Joseph and Bertha (Berhowitz) L.; m. Faye Paula Chernihov, May 7, 1970; children: Aviva Rebecca, Rachel Ann. BA, U. Mich., 1963; MD, Wayne State U., 1968. Diplomate Am. Bd. Orthopaedic Surgery. Intern St. Joseph Mercy Hosp., Pontiac, Mich., 1968-69, resident in orthopaedic surgery, 1969-70, attending staff, 1973—; resident in orthopaedic surgery

Wayne State U. Affiliated Hosps., Detroit, 1970-73; clin. instr. Wayne State U., 1973-77; jr. assoc. staff Detroit Gen. Hosp., 1973-77, attending staff, 1980—; attending staff Pontiac Gen. Hosp., 1973—; clin. asst. prof. Wayne State U., 1977—; attending staff Harper Hosp., Detroit, 1980—; affiliate cons. staff Detroit Gen. Hosp., 1977-80; cons. staff Oakland County (Mich.) Med. Care Facility, 1976—, Rehab. Inst. Detroit; adj. assoc. prof. bioengring. Wayne State U., 1976—; med. dir. Bioengring. Ctr. Wayne State U., 1977—; chief dept. orthopedic surgery St. Joseph Mercy Hosps., 1985—, mem. edn. com. 1974-76, mem. utilization rev. com. 1974-75, chmn. utilization rev. com. 1975—; mem. infection control com. Pontiac Gen. Hosp. 1974-75; mem. Stapp Car Crash Adv. Com. 1976—. Contbr. articles profl. jours. Fellow ACS, Am. Acad. Orthopaedic Surgery; mem. AMA, Am. Assn. Automotive Medicine (bd. dirs. 1981-84), Am. Soc. Biomechanics, Detroit Acad. Orthopaedic Surgery, Detroit Surg. Assn., Detroit Surg. Soc., Mich. Orthopaedic Soc., Mich. Med. Soc. (alternate del. 1981-83, del. 1983—) , Mid-Am. Orthopaedic Soc., Oakland County Med. Soc. (med. legal liaison com. 1978—, chmn. ad hoc hwy. safety com. 1980-81), Soc. Automotive Engrs., Wayne State U. Med. Alumni Assn. (bd. govs. 1974-83, pres. 1977-78). Republican. Jewish. Lodge: B'nai Brith (pres. health care unit Oakland County 1986—). Avocations: teaching, researching. Home: 761 Falmouth Dr Bloomfield Hills MI 48013 Office: 1711 N Woodward Suite 101 Bloomfield Hills MI 48013

LEVINE, STEVEN ALAN, appraiser, consultant; b. Cin., Aug. 28, 1951; s. E. Pike and Beverly Rae (Friedman) L. BA with honors, U. Cin., 1975; postgrad., George Washington U., 1975-77. Appraiser Real Estate Evaluators and Cons., Cin., 1969-75; program asst. U.S. Renegotiation Bd., Washington, 1975; appraiser D.C. Govt., Washington, 1976-77; emergency mgmt. specialist Fed. Emergency Mgmt. Agy., Washington, 1977-80; v.p. Am. Res. and Appraisal Ctr., Cin., 1980-82; prin. Steven A. Levine & Assocs., Cin., 1982—; cons. U.S. Army, 1982—. Author: The Renegotiation of Defense Contracts, Military Installation Real Property Management, Property Tax Relief Measures for the Elderly, Minimal Repair Program Handbook. Coordinator Henry Jackson for Pres., Washington, 1976; mem. Forum for Urban Studies, Washington, 1977; mem. Common Cause, Washington, 1975-78. Served to sgt. USAF, 1969-75. Named to Hon. Order Ky. Cols., Louisville, 1979; named lt. col. aide-de-camp Staff of Gov. of Ga., Atlanta, 1979, lt. col. aide-de-camp Staff of Gov. of Ala., Montgomery, 1983. Mem. Am. Assn. Cert. Appraisers (sr.), Nat. Assn. Realtors, Am. Soc. Pub. Adminstrn. Jewish. Avocations: running, classical music, reading. Home: 1 Lytle Pl #701 Cincinnati OH 45202 Office: Steven A. Levine & Assocs 7536 Reading Rd Suite 6 PO Box 37652 Cincinnati OH 45222

LEVING, JEFFERY MARK, matrimonial lawyer; b. Chgo., July 2, 1951; s. Al and Rebecca Leving; B.S., So. Ill. U., 1974; J.D., Chgo.-Kent Coll. Law, 1979. Bar: Ill. 1979, U.S. Dist. Ct. (no. dist.) Ill. 1979, U.S. Ct. Appeals (7th cir.) 1980. Fed. tax law editor Commerce Clearing House, Chgo., 1979-80; staff atty. Chgo. Vol. Legal Services, 1980-81; sole practice, Chgo., 1981—; contbr. to drafting of Ill. Joint Custody law; testified as proponent of Grandparent Visitation Bill (H.B.1574) in Ill. Ho. Reps. Judiciary com.; guest speaker various radio and TV programs. Mem. Advs. for Shared Custody; panelist Fatherhood Forum Conf. Mem. Chgo. Bar Assn. (matrimonial law com.), Ill. Bar Assn. (commendation and recognition 1983), Fathering Support Services, Decalogue Soc. Democrat. Jewish. Office: 105 W Madison Suite 1008 Chicago IL 60603

LEVINSON, CHARLES BERNARD, architect, educator, real estate developer; b. Youngstown, Ohio, Dec. 15, 1912; s. Al and Goldye (Davis) L.; m. Doris Mombach, Nov. 10, 1940; children: Ronnie Ann (Mrs. John Shore), Barbara Jean (Mrs. Ronald Stern), Suzanne (Mrs. Ralph Stern). BS in Architecture, U. Cin., 1934. Draftsman Gulf Refining Co., 1934-35; designer Hunt and Allen, 1935-36; pvt. practice architecture Cin., 1936-39, 40—; ptnr. Steelcraft Mfg. Co. div. Prefabricate Bldg. and Bldg. Products, 1940-44, v.p., 1945-51, exec. v.p., 1951-66, pres., 1966-69; v.p. then pres. Bldg. Products div. Knapp Bros. Mfg. Co., 1949-65, Leesburg Realty Co., 1952-76; sec./treas. then v.p./sec. ABCO Tool and Die Co., 1953-70; v.p., sec. Oceanautic Mfg. and Research Co., 1968-70; prof. U. Cin. Coll. Design Archtl. Art, 1970-85; vis. prof. architecture U. Wis., 1973-76, Coll. of the Desert, Palm Springs, Calif., 1976. V.p. Big Bros. Am., Cin., 1957, mem. spl. projects com., 1965, bd. dirs., 1956-66; bd. trustees Big Bros. Assn. Cin., pres., 1953-54, Bob Hope Cultural Ctr., Palm Desert, Calif., 1986—, Cin. Ballet Co.; mem. Nat. Com. Children and Youth, Nat. Com. for Employment of Youth, vice chmn., 1969, bd. dirs. 1962-68; mem. ad hoc adv. steering com. White House Conf. on Children and Youth, 1966-70; bd. dirs. Better Housing League of Cin., 1950—, Jewish Community Ctr., Cin., 1955—, Home for the Jewish Aged, Cin., 1955—, Palm Springs Friends of Los Angeles Philharmonic Orch., 1986—; numerous other civic activities. Mem. AIA, Ohio Soc. Architects. Republican. Jewish. Clubs: Queen City (Cin.), Losantiville Country (Cin.), Desert Island Country (Rancho Mirage, Calif.). Home: 2355 Bedford Ave Cincinnati OH 45208 Office: 1212 Sycamore St Cincinnati OH 45210

LEVINSON, RALPH, psychologist; b. N.Y.C., July 25, 1948; s. Samuel and Martha (Blum) L.; m. Victoria Dianne Burgin, Aug. 14, 1982; children: Lara Julia, Jacob Benjamin. MFA, Art Inst. Chgo., 1975; PhD, U. Ill., Chgo., 1983. Registered clin. psychologist, Ill. Pvt. practice art therapy cons. Chgo., 1973—; clin. psychologist Group Psychol. Services Ltd., Chgo. and Evanston, Ill., 1983—, Charles I. Doyle Ctr. Loyola U., Chgo., 1983—; instr. art therapy dept. U. Ill., Chgo., 1982—; asst. clin. prof. psychology dept. Loyola U., 1983—. Author: Artists in the Classroom, 1978; co-author: Photography in the Classroom, 1976. Mem. Am. Psychol. Assn., Am. Art Therapy Assn. (registered), Ill. Art Therapy Assn. (pres.). Democrat.

LEVITAN, KENNETH MARK, psychiatrist; b. Chgo., Dec. 4, 1946; s. Leonard and Esther (Newman) L.; m. Marla Barnow, Aug. 4, 1974; children: Samuel, Emily, Aaron. BS, U. Ill., 1969; MD, U. Ill., Chgo., 1973; postgrad., Chgo. Ins. Psychoanalysis, 1974—. Resident in psychiat. Michael Reese Hosp., Chgo., 1973-76; practice psychiat. Chgo., 1976—. Mem. Am. Psychiatric Assn., Ill. Psychiatric Soc., Am. Psychoanalytic Soc. (assoc.), Chgo. Psychoanalytic Soc., Chgo. Soc. Adolescent Psychiatry. Clubs: Michael Reese Hosp. Staff, Highland Park Hosp. Staff. Office: 180 N Michigan Ave #1010 Chicago IL 60601

LEVITAN, VALERIE FASSLER, fraternal organization executive; b. Phila., Aug. 18, 1932; d. Joseph Lionel and Regina (Sekler) Fassler; m. Peter Wallfield Levitan, Dec. 20, 1950 (div. Nov. 1972); children: Daniel Fassler, Regine Levitan McRae. BEd, U. Pa., 1954, postgrad, 1954, 65-66. Coowner, adminstr. Levitan Sch., Phila., 1950-69; exec. dir. Soroptimist Internat. Am., Phila., 1970-79, Zonta Internat., Chgo., 1979—; dir. pubs. various orgn. manuals; author, presenter Category I status application Econ. and Social Org. UN, 1985. Pres. Cong. Kol Ami, Chgo., 1986-87, pres., 1987. Recipient Merit award Alumnae Assn. Phila. High Sch. for Girls, 1970, Achievement award, Zonta Internat., 1985, Am.'s Citizen Vol. award, U.S. Savs. Bond, 1982. Mem. AAUW, Am. Soc. Assn. Execs., Am. Assn. World Health (bd. dirs. 1986—), UN Assn. (bd. dirs. 1986—, pres. USA Ill. and greater Chgo. area), Nat. Vol. Orgn. for Ind. Living of Aging (grantee 1976-77, chmn. 1986-86), Nat. Council Aging (bd. dirs. 1984-86), League of Women Voters. Democrat. Jewish. Lodge: Zonta Chgo. Waterfront. Avocations: reading, painting, cooking, visiting museums. Office: Zonta Internat 557 W Randolph St Chicago IL 60606

LEVITAS, JOHN ROBERT, orthopedic surgeon; b. Green Bay, Wis., Dec. 18, 1924; s. Isaac Edward and Gloria Faye (Zucker) L.; m. Marcia Corinne Siegel, June 19, 1951; children—Cynthia, Paul, Lori, Edward. Student U. Wis., 1942-44; B.S., Northwestern U., 1948, M.D. 1949. Diplomate Am. Bd. Orthopedic Surgery. Intern, Cook County Hosp., Chgo., 1948-50; resident Cin. Jewish Hosp.-1950-52, U. Cin., 1954-57; practice medicine, specializing in orthopedic surgery, Louisville, 1957-59, Cin., 1959—; mem. staffs Cin. Jewish Hosp., Cin. Children's Hosp., Holmes Hosp., Univ. Hosp., Providence Hosp.; asst. clin. prof. orthopedic surgery U. Cin. Served with M.C., USAF, 1952-54. Fellow ACS, Am. Acad. Orthopedic Surgeons. Home: 6745 E Beechlands St Cincinnati OH 45237 Office: 400 Melish Ave Cincinnati OH 45229

LEVITT, JOHN LAWRENCE, health program administrator; b. Chgo., June 20, 1951; s. Herbert Paul and Babette (Stein) L. BA, Miami U., Oxford, Ohio, 1973; AM, U. Chgo., 1978, PhD, 1981. Cert. social worker, Ill., assoc. addictions counselor, Ill. Supr. social work med. ecology unit Luth. Gen. Hosp., Park Ridge, Ill., 1980-84; coordinator eating disorders program Old Orchard Psychiat. Hosp., Skokie, Ill., 1984; dir. HELP eating disorders programand Ptnrs. in Psychiatry program Forest Hosp., Des Plaines, Ill., 1984—; mem. med.-profl. staff Forest Hosp. 1983-85, sr. mem. 1985—; mem. med.-profl. staff, allied health provider Old Orchard Psychiatric Hosp., 1984—. Contbr. articles to profl. jours. Mem. Nat. Assn. Social Workers (cert.), Am. Assn. Marriage and Family Therapy (clin.), Council on Social Work Edn., Social Work Group for the Study of Behavioral Methods, Assn. for the Advancement of Behavior Therapy, Am. Assn. Eating Disorders Counselors (charter). Ill. Soc. Clin. Social Work, Ill. Assn. Suicidology. Avocations: English, Irish and Welsh folk music, poetry, drawing. Home: 9377 Bay Colony Dr #2N Des Plaines IL 60016 Office: Partners in Psychiatry 1695 Elk Blvd Des Plaines IL 60016

LEVITT, RICHARD SANDER, finance company executive; b. Des Moines, May 8, 1930; s. Ellis Isaac and Nelle (Seff) L.; B.A., U. Iowa, 1952, J.D., 1954; m. Jeanne Strauss, July 2, 1952; children: Randall, Mark, Beth, Jay. With Norwest Fin. Sevices, Inc., Des Moines, 1954—; vice chmn., Norwest Corp.; dir. Meredith Corp., Mass Mdsers., Inc. bd. dirs. Simpson Coll., U. Iowa Found. Mem. Am. Fin. Services Assn. Democrat. Jewish. Clubs: Wakonda; Embassy; Des Moines; Oakridge Country (Mpls.). Home: 3141 Dean Ct #1201 Minneapolis MN 55416 Office: Norwest Nin Inc 206 8th St Des Moines IA 50309

LEVY, ARNOLD S(TUART), real estate company executive; b. Chgo., Mar. 15, 1941; s. Roy and Esther (Scheff) L.; m. Eva Cichosz, Aug. 8, 1976; children—Adam, Rachel, Deborah. B.S., U. Wis., 1963; M.P.A., Roosevelt U., 1970. Dir. Neighborhood Youth Corps, Chgo., 1966-68; v.p. Social Planning Assn., Chgo., 1968-70; planning dir. Office of Mayor Chgo., 1970-74; dep. dir. Mayor's Office Manpower, Chgo., 1974-75; sr. v.p. Urban Investment & Devel. Co., Chgo., 1975—; pres. Ritz-Carlton of Chgo., 1984—, Urban Hotels, 1986—, Logan Sq. Bldg. Corp, Market St. Bldg. Corp., UIDC of Washington, Inc.; lectr. at univs. Pres. Ark, Chgo., 1970-72, Parental Stress Services, Chgo., 1978-79; del. Mid-Term Democratic Nat. Conf., Memphis, 1978; v.p. Inst. Urban Life, Chgo., 1983—. Club: Carlton (Chgo.). Home: 535 Park Ave Glencoe IL 60022 Office: Urban Investment & Devel Co 333 N Wacker Dr Chicago IL 60606

LEVY, DEBORAH LOUISE, psychologist; b. Mpls., Nov. 3, 1950; d. Walter Julius and Hilma Benice (Cohn) L. BA, U. Chgo., 1972, PhD, 1976. Clinical intern N.Y. Hosp., Bloomingdale, 1976-77; postdoctoral fellow Menninger Found., Topeka, Kans., 1977-79; research scientist Ill. State Psychiat. Inst., Chgo., 1979—; Bd. dirs. 7720 Inc., Chgo. Contbr. articles to numerous publs. Recipient Research Scientist Devel. award NIMH, Washington, 1981-86. Mem. AAAS., Am. Psychopathological Assn., Am. Psychol. Assn., Soc. for Neurosci., Sigma Xi. Avocations: skiing, traveling. Office: Ill State Psychiat Inst 1601 W Taylor St Chicago IL 60612

LEVY, HERMAN ABRAHAM, internist; b. Chgo., Aug. 4, 1908; s. Joseph and Elizabeth (Sternberg) L.; m. Sadel Rita Prosterman, Nov. 25, 1932; children: Charles G., Gerald E., Marcia R. Levy Wingard. BS in Medicine, Loyola U., Chgo., 1930, MD, 1932. Diplomate Am. Bd. Internal Medicine. Intern Cook County Hosp., Chgo., 1932-33, resident in pathology, 1933-34; practice medicine specializing in allergic diseases Chgo., 1934—; electrocardiographer Bethany Meth. Hosp., Chgo., 1962—; asst. emeritus prof. medicine, U. Ill., Chgo., 1986—. Contbr. articles on hypoparathyroidism to profl. jours. Served to 1st lt., U.S. Army, 1932-34. Fellow Am. Coll. Allergy, Am. Acad. Allery, Am. Coll. Physicians, Am. Geriatric Soc., Internat. Soc. Medicine. Jewish. Avocation: music.

LEVY, JERRE, psychobiology educator; b. Birmingham, Ala., Apr. 7, 1938; s. Jerome Milton and Marie (Ullman) L.; m. Thomas Andrew Nagylaki, Jan. 30, 1969; children: Marie Basch, Todd Basch. BA, U. Miami, 1962, MS, 1966; PhD, Calif. Inst. Tech., 1970. Postdoctoral fellow U. Colo., Boulder, 1970-71, Oreg. State U., 1971-72; asst. to assoc. prof. U. Pa., Phila., 1972-77; assoc. prof. to prof. U. Chgo., 1977—. Cons. editor Jour. Exptl. Psychology: Human Perception and Peformance, 1972-84; assoc. editor Brain and Cognition, 1982—; editorial bd. Human Neurobiology, 1985—; contbr. articles to profl. jours. and books. Grantee Spencer Found. 1979—, NIMH, 1979—. Mem. Internat. Neuropsychol. Symposium. Avocations: reading, traveling. Home: 1441 E 54th St Chicago IL 60615 Office: Univ Chgo 5848 S University Ave Chicago IL 60637

LEVY, MARK EARL, data processing manager; b. Chgo., Nov. 2, 1957; s. Ralph Jay and Sandra (Holstein) L. AA in Data Processing, Oakton Community Coll., 1978. Sr. system programmer Stiffel Lamp Co., Chgo., 1979, Northwest Community Hosp., Arlington Heights, Ill., 1979-80; data processing mgr. Am. Heritage Industries, Waukegan, Ill., 1980-84; systems mgr. Midwest Stock Exchange, Chgo., 1984-85, Travenol Labs., McGaw Park, Ill., 1985—. Mem. Digital Equipment Computer Users Soc. Avocations: photography, electronics, bicycling.

LEVY, MARTIN BERYL, physical therapist, rehabilitation consultant, educator; b. N.Y.C., June 17, 1927; s. William Harold and Ethel Marie (Ament) L.; m. Helen E. Lipkin, June 6, 1954; children—Elizabeth, Patricia. B.S. NYU, 1951, M.A., 1956. Lic. phys. therapist, Ohio. Staff therapist Inst. Phys. Medicine and Rehab., N.Y.C., 1955, for pvt. physician, Cedarhurst, L.I., N.Y., 1956; coordinator rehab. Drake Meml. Hosp., Cin., 1957-83; dir. rehab. Community Multi-care Ctr., Fairfield, Ohio, 1983—; phys. therapy cons., mem. adv. com. home health services Cin. Health Dept. Served to 2d lt. USAF, 1952-53. Mem. Am. Phys. Therapy Assn. Jewish. Home: 840 Yorkhaven Rd Cincinnati OH 45240 Office: Community Multi-Care Ctr 908 Symmes Rd Fairfield OH 45014

LEVY, MARTIN IRA, oral and maxillofacial surgeon; b. N.Y.C., Mar. 1, 1940; s. Irving and Lillian (Kamenetsky) L.; m. Honora Lee Hoffert, Sept. 20, 1970; children: Jodi Cara, Todd Aaron. Student, Hofstra U., 1963-66; DDS, U. Detroit, 1970. Practice dentistry specializing in oral surgery Farmington, Brighton and Dearborn, Mich., 1971-86, Garden City, Mich., 1986—; dir. oral and maxillofacial surgery dept. Providence Hosp., Southfield, Mich., 1980-87; asst. clin. prof. dept. oral and maxillary surgery Detroit Receiving Hosp., dept. surgery Wayne Med. Sch. Served to cpl. USMC, 1959-63. Recipient Gold Foil award Am. Acad. Gold Foil Operators, 1970. Fellow Am. Coll. Oral and Maxillofacial, Internat. Coll. Oral and Maxillofacial Surgery, Am. Soc. Oral and Maxillofacial Surgery; mem. Am. Dental Soc. Anesthesiology, Alpha Omega. Republican. Jewish. Avocations: tennis, golf, hockey, softball, baseball. Office: 27513 W Warren Rd Garden City MI 48135

LEVY, MAURICE DOUGLAS, surgeon; b. N.Y.C., Dec. 3, 1942; s. Marcus and Anna Levy; m. Nicole Marraché, Oct. 22, 1972; children: Marc, David. BS, NYU, 1963, MD, 1966. Intern Erie County Med. Ctr., Buffalo, 1966-67, resident in surgery, 1971-75; staff surgeon VA Med. Ctr., Topeka, 1982—. Served to capt. USAF, 1968-70. Office: 2200 Gage Blvd #112 Topeka KS 66622

LEVY, STANLEY ROY, educational administrator; b. Bklyn., July 19, 1934; s. Abraham and Rose (Weinberger) L.; m. Joan Weinberg, June 15, 1963; children: Scott, Marcia. BA, U. Mich., 1955, MA, 1959, PhD, 1964. Assoc. dean students U. Ill., Urbana, 1968-73, asst. vice chancellor, 1973-76, assoc. vice chancellor, 1976-78, acting vice chancellor, 1978-79, vice chancellor, 1979—. Bd. dirs. Arrowhead Council Boy Scouts Am., 1983, United Way of Champaign County, 1976-85; active Champaign County Crimestoppers, 1986—. Served to 1st lt. U.S. Army, 1955-57, Germany. Mem. Am. Assn. Higher Educ., Nat. Assn. Student Personnel Adminstrs. (v.p. 1976-78), N. Cen. Assn. Schs. and Colls. (cons., evaluator 1979—). Jewish. Lodges: B'nai Brith, Rotary. Home: 3006 Meadowbrook Ct Champaign IL 61821 Office: 601 E John St Champaign IL 61820

LEW, ALBERT YEE-HONG, accounting educator; b. Canton, Republic of China; came to U.S., 1968; s. Tak Wong and Mei-Lin (Lam) L. BS in Acctg., San Jose State U., 1972; MBA, U. Utah, 1973; M Accountancy, Va. Poly. Inst. & State U., 1976; PhD, U. Nebr., 1984. CPA, Ark. Instr. U. Nebr., Lincoln, 1980-83; asst. prof. Wright State U., Dayton, Ohio, 1983—. Contbr. articles to profl. jours. Mem. Am. Inst. CPA's, Nat. Assn. Accts. (dir. manuscripts, 1986—), Am. Acctg. Assn. Office: Wright State Univ Dept Accountancy Dayton OH 45435

LEWANDOWSKI, JOHN J., materials science educator; b. Pitts., Dec. 17, 1956; s. John Francis and Mildred (Fidell) L.; m. Amy Ellen Cook, Aug. 27, 1983. BS in Metallurgy and Materials Sci., Carnegie-Mellon U., 1979, ME, 1981, PhD, 1984. NATO postdoctoral fellow U. Cambridge, Eng., 1984-85, Alcan research fellow, 1985-86; prof. Case Western Res. U., Cleve., 1986—; cone. Pete Wieser & Assocs., Cleve., 1986—. Contbr. articles to profl. jours. Named one of Outstanding Young Men of Am., 1986. Fellow Cambridge Philosophical Soc.; mem. Am. Soc. Metals (chmn. student affairs com. Cleve. chpt. 1986—, Metall. scholar 1979), The Metall. Soc.-Am. Inst. Mining Engrs. Republican. Roman Catholic. Avocations: running, bicycling, racquet sports, travel. Home: 3636 Traynham Rd Shaker Heights OH 44122 Office: Case Western Res U Dept Materials Sci and Engring 10900 Euclid Ave Cleveland OH 44106

LEWELLYN, ELIZABETH SUE, education educator, consultant; b. Frankfort, Ind., Feb. 5, 1936; d. Paul Marcellus and Helen Irene (Wingler) Crum; m. Wallace Delbert Lewellyn, Aug. 28, 1977; 1 child, James Martin Stone. B in Elem. Edn., Ind. U., 1960, MS in Elem. Edn., 1970. Cert. tchr., Ind., Ohio. Elem. tchr. Elmhurst (Ill.) Schs., 1960-61, Pipe Creek Schs., Bunker Hill, Ind., 1961-62, Maconaquah Sch., Bunker Hill, 1962-64, Munster (Ind.) Schs., 1964-77; educator cons. Grove City, Ohio, 1977—; student tchr. advisor Purdue U., Ind. U., St. Joseph U., Ball State U., St. Joseph Coll. Vol. Children's Hosp., Columbus, Ohio, 1977—, Profl. Golf Assn. Meml. Tournament, Muirfield, Ohio, 1978—, U.S. Sr. Open Golf Tournament, Columbus, 1986. Named Outstanding Elem. Tchr. Am., Munster Schs., 1972, Outstanding Leader in Elem. and Secondary Edn. award Munster Schs., 1976, Golf Digest Hole in One Assn., 1986. Mem. Am. Assn. Univ. Women (rep. edn. found. com. 1985-86), Columbus Women's Golf Assn. (chairperson rules com. 1985-86), Ind. U. Alumni Assn. Presbyterian. Clubs: Foxfire Golf (Ohio) (pres. 1985-86), U. Women's Investment. Lodge: Elks. Avocations: reading, gardening, crafts, golf, travel. Address: 5385 Hoover Rd Grove City OH 43123

LEWIN, WALTER, psychiatrist; b. Hamburg, Germany, Aug. 25, 1930; came to U.S., 1939; s. Hans and Eva (Jendersic) L.; m. Grace Marie Bogart, June 9, 1956; children: Margaret, Thomas, William, James. BA, U. Kans., 1952; MD, Kans U., 1956. Cert. Am. Bd. Psychiatry. Intern City Meml. Hosp., Winston Salem, N.C., 1956-57; fellow Menninger Sch. Psychiatry, Topeka, 1959-62; dir. outpatient and day patient services Prairie View Hosp., Newton, Kans., 1962-67; med. dir. Johnson County Mental Health Ctr., Shawnee Mission, Kans., 1967-69; practice psychiatry Shawnee Mission Psychiat. Group, 1969—; clin. asst. prof. psychiatry, Kans. Med. Ctr., Kansas City, 1967—; psychiat. cons. to German Consulate, Chgo., 1969—; assoc. med. dir. Toral Health Care, Kansas City, 1981—. Bd. dirs. Kansas City Ballet, 1973-76, 78-79. Served to capt. U.S. Army, 1957-59. Fellow Am. Orthopsychiat. Assn.; mem. AMA, Am. Psychiat. Assn., Kans. Psychiat. Assn., Johnson County Med. Soc. Republican. Episcopalian. Avocations: swimming, hiking, reading, traveling. Home: 6331 Beverly Dr Mission KS 66202 Office: Shawnee Mission Psychiat Group 8901 W 74 St Shawnee Mission KS 66204

LEWIS, CALVIN FRED, architect, educator; b. Chgo., Mar. 27, 1946; s. Howard George and Fern Teresa (Voelsch) L.; m. L. Diane Johnson, Aug. 24, 1968; children: Nathan, Miller, Cooper, Wilson. B of Architecture, Iowa State U., 1969. Architect Charles Herbert and Assocs., Des Moines, 1970-86; prin. Herbert Lewis Kruse Blunck Architects, Des Moines, 1987—; instr. architecture Iowa State U., Ames, 1981, 84—; architect, lectr. Talented and Gifted Scholars Conf. Drake U., 1986, Wis. Am. Inst. Architecture, Madison, 1985, Inter Market Sq., Mpls., 1985, Nat. Tile Conf., Los Angeles, 1987. Contbr. articles to profl. jours. Recipient Best in Design award Time Mag., 1982; named one of Top Young Architects in Country, Met. Home mag., 1983. Mem. AIA (30 design awards 1972—), Des Moines Architects Council. Congregationalist. Avocations: sports, photography. Office: Herbert Lewis Kruse Blunck Architects 202 Fleming Bldg Des Moines IA 50309

LEWIS, CHARLES SIDNEY, wholesale company executive; b. Detroit, Nov. 23, 1926; s. Sam Charles and Miriam (Goldsmith) L.; m. Marcia Gilbert, Oct. 25, 1953; children: Scott, Nancy. B of Bus. Adminstrn., U. Mich., 1948. Acct. S.L. Moss, Detroit, 1949-50; pres. Sam Lewis Co., Troy, Mich., 1950—. Jewish. Club: Franklin (Mich.) Hills Country (bd. dirs. 1978-84, asst. sec.-treas. 1981-84). Avocation: golf. Home: 2015 Waldon's Ct West Bloomfield MI 48322 Office: Sam Lewis Co 1146 E Big Beaver Rd Troy MI 48083

LEWIS, DALE ARTHUR, insurance company executive; b. Detroit, Jan. 29, 1947; s. Robert Dale and Vernetta (Dibler) Steinmetz L.; m. Cynthia Anne Kopczyk, Apr. 21, 1971; children—Andrew D., Lisa A., Brian A. C.L.U., Chartered Fin. Cons. Agt., Aid Assn. for Lutherans, Appleton, Wis., 1971-73, bus. ins. adminstr., 1977-80; supr. Conn. Mut. Life, Detroit, 1973-75; 2d v.p. Fed. Home Life Ins. Co., Farmington Hills, Mich., 1980-87; pres. Decorating Systems-Great Lakes; sec.-treas. Decorating Den of Battle Creek (Mich.); mem. Calhoun County Estate Planning Council, 1980-84. Sustaining mem. Republican Nat. Com. Served with U.S. Army, 1966-68. Mem. Am. Soc. C.L.U.s (Gold Key Soc.) (pres. S. Mich. chpt.), Battle Creek C. of C., Nat. Assn. Life Underwriters, DAV (life), Midwest Tng. Dirs. Assn. (pres. 1984-85). Lutheran. Home: 30140 Mullane Dr Famington Hills MI 48018 Office: Alexander Hamilton Life Ins Co PO Box 1776 Famington Hills MI 48018

LEWIS, DARLENE DOROTHY, manufacturing company executive; b. Milw., May 4, 1938; d. William John and Agnes Mary (Funk) Gengler; m. Lynn Ernest Lewis, May 29, 1961; children: Tracy Lee, Kelley Jean. Cert. mgmt., Marquette U., 1982. Sales asst. Kimberly Clark, Neenah, Wis., 1956-65; sr. v.p. Cheney Co., New Berlin, Wis., 1970-87, pres., 1987—, also sec., 1980—. Mem. Assn. Sales and Mktg. Execs. (Exec. of Yr. 1986). Republican. Clubs: Westmoor Country (Brookfield, Wis.), Tumblebrook Country (Waukesha, Wis.). Avocations: running, interior design, aerobics. Home: 1411 N Jenkins Dr Oconomowoc WI 53066 Office: Cheney Co 3015 S 163d St New Berlin WI 53131

LEWIS, DAVID, tax specialist; b. Clinton, Ind., Sept. 25, 1953; s. Earl Jehu and Pauline (Deener) L. AS in Acctg. with high honors, Ind. Vocat. Tech. Coll., 1974; BS/MBA candidate, Columbia Pacific U., 1986—; cert. fin. planner candidate, Coll. Fin. Planning, Denver. Office mgr. Johnson Welding, Terre Haute, Ind., 1974-78; auditor State of Ind., Indpls., 1978-82; acctg. mgr. Village Furniture, Lafayette, Ind., 1982-84; tax specialist Hugh V. Banta P.C., Rockville, Ind., 1984—. Chmn. audit com. Freedom Bapt. Assn., 1985; deacon Marshall (Ind.) Bapt. Ch., 1986-87, trustee 1985-86, supt., 1982-85, youth dir., 1982-85. Mem. Nat. soc. Pub. Accts., Ind. Soc. Pub. Accts. Republican. Avocations: tennis, reading, bible study. Home: PO Box 335 Rockville IN 47872 Office: Hugh V Banta PC 206 Howard Ave Rockville IN 47872

LEWIS, DAVID PAUL, accountant, auditor; b. Erie, Pa., June 1, 1956; s, Norbert Ronald and Patricia (Anthony) L. BS in Acctg., Pa. State U., 1978; postgrad., Cleve. Marshall Coll. Law, 1987. CPA, Ohio. Internal auditor Roadway Express, Akron, Ohio, 1978-81, Broadview Savs. & Loan, Cleve., 1981-82, U.S. Truck Lines, Cleve., 1982-85; audit mgr. Nat. City Bank, Cleve., 1986—. Mem. ABA (student), Am. Inst. CPA's, Ohio Soc. CPA's. Republican. Roman Catholic. Avocations: athletics, music, Italian food, Pa. State U. football. Home: 1227 Goldfinch Trail Stow OH 44224 Office: Nat City Bank 1900 E 9th St Cleveland OH 44114

LEWIS, DAVID WAYNE, plant engineer; b. Wurtzberg, Fed. Republic Germany, Mar. 12, 1955; came to U.S., 1956; s. Richard Marshall and Dorothy Marie (Nance) L.; m. Linda Susan Daniel, June 30, 1973; children: Lynette Suzanne, Leann Michelle. BS, Rose-Hulman Inst. Tech., 1977; MBA, Ind. Cen. U., 1985. Registered profl. engr., Ind. Plant engr. Western Electric, Indpls., 1977-83, AT&T, Indpls., 1983—; tchr. Indpls. Bapt. Coll.,

1984. Served to capt. U.S. Army, 1977-81. Mem. NSPE, Am. Inst. Plant Engrs., Constrn. Specifications Inst. Republican. Baptist. Avocations: golf, fishing. Home: 3280 S New Jersey St Indianapolis IN 46227 Office: AT&T 6612 E 75th St PO Box 1008 Indianapolis IN 46206

LEWIS, EDWARD ALAN, religious organization adminstrator; b. Brazil, Ind., July 22, 1946; s. Edward and Ruth Margaret (Eberwein) L. B in Music Edn., Grace Coll., 1969; M in Divinity, Grace Sem., 1973. Asst. to pastor, youth dir. Grace Brethren Ch., Winona Lake, Ind., 1969-73; nat. dir. youth ministries Grace Brethren Ch. Christian Edn., Winona Lake, 1973-85; dir. personnel Grace Brethren Fgn. Missions, Winona Lake, 1982—; exec. dir. Grace Brethren Ch. Christian Edn., Winona Lake, 1985—. Mem. Grace Brethren Ch., Winona Lake, 1969—, exec. mem. denominational youth com., 1984—. Mem. Grace Sem. Alumni Assn. (pres. 1984-85), Ind. Dist. Ministerium, Nat. Ministerium Assn. Avocations: music, piano, singing, jogging, travel. Home and Office: PO Box 365 Winona Lake IN 46590

LEWIS, EVELYN, communications and public relations executive; b. Goslar, Germany, Sept. 19, 1946; came to U.S. 1952, naturalized 1957; d. Gerson Emanuel and Sala (Mendlowicz) L. B.A., U. Ill.-Chgo., 1968; M.A., Ball State U., 1973, Ph.D., 1976. Research analyst Comptroller, State Ill., Chgo., 1977-78; lectr. polit. sci. dept. Loyola U., Chgo., 1977; asst. to commr. Dept. Human Services, Chgo., 1978-81; group mgr. communications Arthur Anderson & Co., Chgo., 1981-84; dir. communications and pub. relations Heidrick and Struggles, Inc., Chgo., 1984—. Mem. Children of the Holocaust, Chgo., 1982. Mem. Internat. Assn. Bus. Communicators, Publicity Club Chgo., Nat. Assn. Female Execs., B'nai Brith. Jewish. Club: Metropolitan (Chgo.). Avocations: writing, poetry, bicycling, hiking. Office: Heidrick and Struggles Inc 125 S Wacker Dr Chicago IL 60606

LEWIS, GARY FLOYD, advertising executive; b. New Castle, Pa., July 28, 1931; m. Nancy S. Loresch, May 6, 1960; children: Douglas, Geoffrey, Susan. BA in Journalism, Pa. State U., 1953; grad. mktg. mgmt. program, Harvard U., 1972. Supr. advt. and sales promotion U.S. Steel, Pitts., 1957-65; mgr. mktg. projects U.S. Steel, N.Y.C., 1965-69; mgr. mktg. services Internat. Nickel, Huntington, W.Va., 1969-77; mgr. mktg. ops. Herman Miller, Holland, Mich., 1977-78; mgr. promotion group Steelcase, Grand Rapids, Mich., 1978-80; pres. Lewis Mktg., Holland, 1980—; cons. 1st Nat. Bank of Am., Holland, 1983—. Author: World Cruise, 1957, Consortium Advertising, 1978. Bd. dirs. Holland Tulip Time, 1984—. Served to lt. USN, 1953-57. Mem. Am. Mktg. Assn., Bus. and Profl. Advt. Club (v.p. 1975-77, Outstanding Advt. Program 1975), Holland C. of C. (promotion com. 1982-86), Pa. State Alumni Assn. (regional dir. 1966-67). Republican. Presbyterian. Clubs: Holland Country, Grand Rapids Advt. Avocations: golf, tennis, sport cars. Office: Lewis Mktg PO Box 2002 Holland MI 49422

LEWIS, GERALD DAVID, music educator; b. Elkhart, Ind., Dec. 14, 1922; s. Russell Kinkaid and Ruth Elnora (Horein) L.; m. Marjorie Louise Lewis, June 17, 1951; children—Julia, Scott, Jacqueline. B.S., Juilliard Sch. Music, N.Y.C., 1950; M.M., U. So. Calif., 1954. Violinist, St. Louis Symphony and Sinfoniette, 1950-53, Los Angeles Philharm., 1953-57; tchr. South Bend (Ind.) Community Schs., 1960-70; concertmaster South Bend Symphony, 1960-70; assoc. prof. orch. dir., violin theory Gustavus Adolphus Coll., St. Peter, Minn., 1970—; tchr. New Eng. Music Camp, Oakland, Maine, summers 1978—; past sec. Minn. String Task Force. Served with U.S. Army, 1943-46. Decorated Bronze Star. Mem. Am. Fedn. Musicians, Music Educators Nat. Conf., Am. String Tchrs. Assn. (Gold Merit award Ind. chpt. 1964). Home: 418 N 3d St Saint Peter MN 56082 Office: Gustavus Adolphus Coll Saint Peter MN 56082

LEWIS, JAMES CLARENCE, academic administrator, income property manager; b. Coleman, Mich., Jan. 30, 1945; s. Clarence Victor and Doris Jean (Wilson) L.; m. Nancy Marie Clark, Dec. 14, 1968; 1 child, Christopher James. BA in Communications, Mich. State U., 1967. Account exec. Burroughs Corp., Lansing, Mich., 1967-68, Mich. Broadcasting Corp., Jackson, 1970-73; admissions rep. Saginaw (Mich.) Bus. Inst., 1973-74; account exec. Tri-Medea Corp., Bay City, Mich., 1974-78; dir. admissions Great Lakes Jr. Coll. Bus., Saginaw, 1978-82, v.p. mktg., 1982—; cons. various pvt. schs., Mich., 1981—. Dist. chmn. Boy Scouts Am., 1985; active Manpower Planning Council, Saginaw County, 1982-83. Served to sgt. U.S. Army, 1968-70, Vietnam. Mem. Am. Assn. Coll. Registrars and Admissions Officers, Mich. Assn. Coll. Registrars and Admissions Officers, Mich. Assn. Coll. Admissions Counselors. Lodge: Optimists (lt. gov. 1983, Optimist of Yr., Saginaw club 1982). Avocation: hunting. Home: 532 Rustic Saginaw MI 48604 Office: Great Lakes Jr Coll Bus 310 S Washington Saginaw MI 48607

LEWIS, JAMES MICHAEL, electronics engineer; b. Ft. Wayne, Ind., Sept. 6, 1947; s. James Trueman and Ruth Margaret (Luyben) L.; m. Sandra Kay Rediger, Mar. 1, 1969; children—Shane, Mindelle. B.S. in Elec. Engring. Tech., Purdue U., Ft. Wayne, Ind., 1979. Inventory control supr. Stanscrew Dist. Ctr., Garrett, Ind., 1971-74; estimator Mid. Am. Electronics, Auburn, Ind., 1974-76; with Dana Corp., Auburn, 1976—, plant engr., 1982—. Sound technician Bible Baptist Ch., Auburn, Ind., 1982—; basketball coach Faith Christian Acad., Auburn, 1982-83. Republican. Home: 0811-CR28 Corunna IN 46730 Office: Dana Corp 5th and Brandon Sts Auburn IN 46706

LEWIS, JAMES VICTOR, accountant; b. Eau Claire, Wis., Oct. 8, 1949; s. Sanford James and Doris Ann (Radtke) L.; m. Susan Jane Schutts, Aug. 8, 1970; children: Adam Terry, Carey Michelle. BBA, U. Wis., Eau Claire, 1970; MBA, Coll. St. Thomas, St. Paul, 1978. Staff acct. Haskins & Sells, Milw., 1970-72; sec., treas. Wilkerson Guthmann & Johnson, Ltd., St. Paul, 1972—. Treas. Bennett Fin. Com., St. Paul, 1982-85; treas., bd. dirs. Gustavus Adolphus Luth. Ch., St. Paul, 1987; bd. dirs. Little Lakes Little League, St. Paul, 1982-87. Mem. Am. Inst. CPA's, Minn. Soc. CPA's (ethics com. 1979-81, audit com. 1982), Internat. Assn. Fin. Planners, Hastings (Minn.) C. of C. (legis. com. 1984-85), Shoreview Jaycees (treas., bd. dirs. 1984-85). Republican. Lutheran. Lodges: Kiwanis (bd. dirs. Hastings 1985), Optimists (treas., bd. dirs. St. Paul 1984-85). Home: 4441 Foothill Trail Vadnais Heights MN 55110 Office: Wilkerson Guthmann & Johnson Ltd 1300 Norwest Ctr Saint Paul MN 55101

LEWIS, JOSEPH DAVID, physician, surgeon, educator; b. Orange, N.J., Oct. 7, 1937; s. Joseph and Ada Elizabeth (Jones) L.; m. Judith Irene Stanier, June 25, 1960; children—Jean Evelyn, Joan Elizabeth, Joseph David II, Janet Elaine. A.B., Oberlin Coll., 1959; M.D., U. Tenn. 1962. Diplomate Am. Bd. Surgery. Intern Buffalo Gen. Hosp., 1963; resident Marquette U. Affiliated Hosps., Milw., 1966-70; from instr. to assoc. prof. surgery Med. Coll. Wis., Milw., 1970-78; assoc. clin. prof., 1978—; surgeon Gen. Clinic of West Bend, Wis., 1978—; area med. dir. Wisc. div. Am. Cancer Soc., Madison, 1979—. Contbr. articles to profl. jours. Served to surgeon USPHS, 1964-66. Fellow ACS (chpt. pres. 1981-82); Wis. Surg. Soc. (bd. dirs. 1981-84), Milw. Acad. Surgery (pres. 1987—), Wis. Med. Soc. (county soc. pres. 1986—), Milw. Surg. Soc., Central Surg. Assn. Avocations: skiing, golf. Home: 668 Highland View Dr West Bend WI 53095 Office: Gen Clinic of West Bend 279 S 17th Ave West Bend WI 53095

LEWIS, JOSEPH WILLIAM, manufacturing company executive; b. Adrian, Minn., Mar. 18, 1935; s. William Joseph and Eleanor Mary (Masgai) L.; m. Mary Ellen Donnelly, Aug. 24, 1957; children: Patrick, James, Daniel, Lori. BSME, U. Minn., 1958. Sales engr. Johnson Controls, Inc., Milw., 1958-67, branch mgr., 1969-75, midwest region mgr., 1976-77, v.p. and gen. mgr. systems engring. and construction div., 1977-84, v.p. and gen. mgr. systems and services div., 1984-86, v.p. controls group, 1986—; bd. dirs. Automated Systems, Brookfield, Wis. Bd. dirs. Elmbrook Hosp., Brookfield, 1981—, Friends of Mus., Milw., 1984—, UWM Found., Wheaton Franciscan Services Inc., Milw. Clubs: Wisconsin (Milw.), S. Shore Yacht (Milw.). Avocations: sailing, golf. Home: 2200 Glen Cove Ln Brookfield WI 53005 Office: Johnson Controls Inc 507 E Michigan St Milwaukee WI 53201

LEWIS, LARRY LYNN, college official, minister; b. Mexico, Mo., Jan. 27, 1935; s. Artie Francis and Mary Lue (Whiteside) L.; m. Betty Jo Cockerell, Feb. 28, 1964; children—Janet Lynn, Christy Ann, Mark Ray. A.A., Hannibal-LaGrange Coll., 1954; B.A., U. Mo., 1956; B.D., Southwestern Bapt. Sem., 1960, M.R.E., 1960; D.Ministry, Luther Rice Sem., 1978. Ordained to ministry Southern Bapt. Conv., 1954; pastor Parsons Bapt. Ch., Columbus, Ohio, 1961-66, Delaware Valley Bapt. Ch., Willingboro, N.J., 1966-71; dir. religious edn. Bapt. Conv. Pa./South Jersey, Harrisburg, Pa., 1971-74; pastor Tower Grove Bapt. Ch., St. Louis, 1974-81; pres. Hannibal-LaGrange Coll., Hannibal, Mo., 1981—; minister edn., youth Tri-Village Bapt. Ch., Columbus, 1961-62; pub. sch. tchr. Columbus Pub. Sch., 1962-63; ch. growth cons. Bapt. Sunday Sch. Bd., Nashville, 1971-74; pres. Tower Grove Christian Sch., 1978-81; pres. Mo. Bapt. Pastors Conf., 1979; v.p. Southern Bapt. Pastors Conf., Southern Bapt. Conv., 1980. Bd. dirs. Hannibal YMCA. Author: The Bus Ministry, 1971; (with others) Outreach with Church Buses, 1973; Organize to Evangelize, 1980. Editor: Walking with God, 1972. Contbr. articles to various ch. mags. Mem. Mo. Edn. Assn., Hist. Hannibal Assn., Hannibal C. of C. (pres. 1985). Lodge: Hannibal Rotary. Avocation: farming. Home: 3035 Muir St Hannibal MO 63401 Office: Pres Hannibal-LaGrange Coll 2800 Palmyra Rd Hannibal MO 11999

LEWIS, LAURINE ANNE, small business owner; b. Willmar, Minn., Dec. 29, 1956; d. Henry William and Avis Ida (Schmidt) L. BA in English, Carleton Coll., 1979. Legal asst. Stacker, Ravich & Simon, Mpls., 1981; alterations sewing Sew Biz Tailoring, Inc., Mpls., 1981-83; owner, mgr. Sew Biz Tailoring, Inc, Mpls., 1983—. Presbyterian. Office: Sew Biz Tailoring Inc 75 S Fifth St Minneapolis MN 55402

LEWIS, PHILIP, education company executive; b. Chgo., Oct. 23, 1913; s. Solomon and Fannie (Margolis) L.; m. Geraldine Gisela Lawenda, Sept. 1, 1947; 1 child, Linda Susan. B.S., DePaul U., Chgo., 1937, M.A., 1939; Ed.D., Columbia Tchrs. Coll., 1951. Chmn. dept. edn. Chgo. Tchrs. Coll.; also asst. prin., tchr. South Shore High Sch., Chgo., 1940-51; prin. Herman Felsenthal Elementary Sch., Chgo., 1955-57; dir. Bur. Instructional Materials, Chgo. Pub. Schs., 1957-63, Bur. Research Devel. and Spl. Projects, 1963-67; pres. Instructional Dynamics Inc., Chgo., 1967—; nat. cons. TV and instructional techniques, 1955—; ednl. cons. to accrediting bur. Health Edn. Schs., 1971—; chmn. adv. com. U.S. Office Edn., Title VII, 1964-67. Author: Educational Television Guidebook for Electronics Industries Association, 1961, also numerous articles.; mem. editorial bd. Nation's Schs. and Colls; multimedia tech. editor: Tech. Horizons in Edn; cons.: Jour. Ednl. Tech. and Communications; producer ednl., multimedia, tng. and mental health and human devel. materials. Served to lt. comdr. USNR, 1942-45. Mem. Soc. Programmed and Automated Learning (pres. 1960-65), NEA (v.p. dept. audiovisual instrn., chmn. commn. on tech. standards dept. audiovisual instrn. 1965-85), Nat. Assn. Ednl. Broadcasters, Am. Legion, Council for Ednl. Facilities Planners (editorial adv. bd. 1972-80) Ill. C. of C. (edn. com. 1970-77), Chgo. Assn. Commerce and Industry (chmn. edn. com. 1970-80), Nat. Audio-Visual Assn. (profl devel. bd. 1969-76, chmn), Phi Delta Kappa. Club: Chicago Press. Lodges: Masons (32 deg.), Shriners, Rotary. Home: 2 E Oak St Apt 3201 Chicago IL 60611 Office: 3200 W Peterson Ave Chicago IL 60659

LEWIS, ROBERT, therapist, educator; b. Wisconsin Rapids, Wis., Jan. 3, 1932; s. Laurence G. and Lois M. (Kellogg) L.; m. Kathleen J., Sept. 4, 1955; children: Craig Alan, David Paul. BA, U. Wis., 1956; M Div., Moravian Theol. Sem., 1956; MA, U. Minn., 1966, PhD, 1969. Asst. prof. Augsburg Coll., Mpls., 1968-69; assoc. prof. U. Ga., Athens, 1969-73, Pa. State U., University Park, 1973-77; prof. family studies Ariz. State U., Tempe, 1977-80; chmn. dept., prof. family studies Purdue U., West Lafayette, Ind., 1981—. Editor: Assessing Marriage, 1981, Men in Difficult Times, 1981, Men's Changing Roles in the Family, 1986, Men in Families, 1986; assoc. editor (jours.) Family Relations, 1985, Lifestyles, 1983, J. Marriage and Family, 1975-81. Co-chmn. Purdue U. United Way Campaign, W. Lafayette, 1984-85; mem. Community Orgn. for Drug Abuse, Mental Health and alcohol, Phoenix, 1980-81; bd. dirs. New Directions, West Lafayette, 1981-85, Family Service Agy., W. Lafayette, 1983-85. Nat. Inst. Drug Abuse grantee, 1979-81, 85-89. Mem. Nat. Council Family Relations (v.p. 1986—), Ind. Council on Family Relations (pres. 1985—), Groves Conf. Marriage/Family, Northfield Jaycees (sec., Disting. Service award 1963). Moravian. Lodge: Lions. Avocations: photography, scuba driving, swimming. Office: Purdue U Dept Child Devel/Family Studies West Lafayette IN 47907

LEWIS, ROBERT ALAN, musician; b. Oshkosh, Wis., Jan. 23, 1936; s. Barton Evan and Dorothy Marie (Sprister) L.; m. Myrna Kay Mayette, Jan. 6, 1962 (div.); 1 dau., Laura Marie. Mus.B., U. Wis., 1957, Mus. M., 1958. Profl. musician trumpet and flugel horn, Chgo., 1961—; recorded over 6000 commercials, records, films; co-leader Ears-Jazz of All Eras; leader Forefront Trumpet Ensemble; soloist Chgo. Symphony Orch.; music dir. Miss Peggy Lee. Served with U.S. Army, 1959-60. Nat. Endowment Arts grantee, 1974, 75. Mem. ASCAP, Nat. Assn. Rec. Artists, Nat. Trumpet Guild, Nat. Jazz Educators, Jazz Inst. Chgo. Composer for trumpet (15 etudes), others.

LEWIS, ROBERT DAVID, ophthalmologist, educator; b. Thomasville, Ga., Aug. 27, 1948; s. Ralph N. and E. Margaret (Klaus) L.; m. Frances Elizabeth Golys, Aug. 29, 1970. BS, St. Louis Coll. Pharmacy, 1971; MD, St. Louis U., 1975. Diplomate Am. Bd. Ophthalmology; registered pharmacist. Intern, Cardinal Glennon Hosp. Children, St. Louis, 1975-76; resident St. Louis U., 1976-79; practice medicine specializing in ophthalmology, St. Louis, 1979—; dir. pediatric ophthalmology St. Louis U., 1980-82, 85, asst. prof., 1980—; dir. pediatric ophthalmology Cardinal Glennon Hosp. for Children, St. Louis, 1980-82, 85; mem. adv. bd. Delta Gamma Found. for Visually Handicapped Children. Recipient St. Louis U. Award for Teaching, 1982. Fellow ACS, Am. Coll. Emergency Physicians; mem. AMA, Mo. Med. Assn., St. Louis Med. Soc., Am. Acad. Ophthalmology, Assn. for Research in Vision and Ophthalmology, Contact Lens Assn. Ophthalmology, Internat. Assn. Ocular Surgeons, Am. Intraocular Implant Soc. Office: 10004 Kennerly Rd Saint Louis MO 63128 also: #16 Hampton Village Saint Louis MO 63109

LEWIS, ROGER F., healthcare executive, lawyer; b. Chgo., Mar. 21, 1936; s. Louis I. and Evelyn (Kraut) L.; children: Stephanie, Noelle. BS, U. Ill., 1957; JD, Northwestern U., 1960. Bar: Ill. 1960, D.C. 1960. With U.S. Govt., Washington, 1960-67; sole practice Washington, 1967-71, Chgo., 1971-74; sr. counsel Baxter Travenol, Deerfield, Ill., 1974-83, corp. v.p., 1983—. Governing mem. Shedd Aquarium, Chgo., 1984—. Mem. D.C. Bar Assn., Chgo. Bar Assn., Anti Defamation League (mem. exec. com.). Lodge: B'nai Brith. Office: Baxter Travenol Labs Inc One Baxter Pkwy Deerfield IL 60015

LEWIS, RUSSELL EUGENE, architect; b. Marshall, Tex., Dec. 8, 1950; s. Eugene Jr and Julia Lorine Lewis; m. Patricia Ann Reid, Oct. 1, 1973; children: Brandon, Kristopher. AB, Wash. U., St. Louis, 1973; MA, Wash. U., 1976. Registered architect, Mo., Kans., Ill. Grad. architect Rather & Roth Architects, St. Louis, 1973-77; project architect Peckham Guyton Albers & Viets, St. Louis, 1977-84; pres. By Design, Inc., St. Louis, 1984—; instr. St. Louis Community Coll., Kirkwood, Mo., 1985—; also mem. adv. com. Active Citizens for Modern-Transit, St. Louis, 1986; mem. Kirkwood Planning & Zoning Comm., 1982-86. Mem. AIA, Nat. Council Archtl. Registration Bds., Nat. Orgn. Minority Architects, Regional Commerce and Growth Assn. Baptist. Office: 906 Olive Suite 908 Saint Louis MO 63101

LEWIS, SALLY BUTZEL (MRS. LEONARD THEODORE LEWIS), civic worker; b. Detroit, June 29, 1912; d. Leo Martin and Caroline (Heavenrich) Butzel; B.A., Vassar Coll., 1934; m. Leonard Theodore Lewis, Apr. 4, 1935; 1 son, Leonard Theodore. Mem. Women's City Club of Detroit, 1932-67, dir., 1935-38; dir., chmn. community services com. Village Woman's Club of Birmingham-Bloomfield dir. Franklin-Wright Settlement, Inc., Detroit, 1939—, pres. 1959-60; trustee Oakland County Children's Aid Soc., 1950-64, Oakland U. Found., 1973-82; mem. exec. com. Detroit Fedn. Settlements, 1961; mem. steering com., women's orgn. United Fund, 1960-61; mem. Oakland planning div. United Community Services, Met. Detroit, 1959-70; membership chmn. Bloomfield Art Assn., Birmingham, Mich.; mem. scholarship com. Meadow Brook Sch. Music, Meadow Brook Festival, Rochester, Mich.; treas. Cranbrook Music Guild, Inc., 1959, dir., 1958-63, sec., 1960-61; mem. women's com. Cranbrook Art Acad. and Mus., Bloomfield Hills; exec. com. Meadow Brook Festival, Rochester, Md., 1969-76. Mem. Nat. Council Jewish Women, Am. Jewish Com., Women's Assn. Detroit Symphony, Friends Detroit Symphony. Clubs: Women's Nat. Farm and Garden, Village, Ibex. Home: 1763 Alexander Dr Bloomfield Hills MI 48013

LEWIS, STEPHEN BLAINE, lawyer; b. Indpls., July 16, 1952; s. Ted B. and Phyllis J. (Keyser) L.; m. Katheryn L. Ruff, May 10, 1980. B.A., DePauw U., 1974; J.D., Ind. U., 1977. Bar: Ind. 1978, U.S. Dist. Ct. (no. dist.) Ind. 1978, Ill. 1980, U.S. Dist. Ct. (no. dist.) Ill. 1980. Law clk. Ind. Nat. Bank, Indpls., 1975-78, counsel, 1978-80; counsel Continental Bank, Chgo., 1980-82, Borg-Warner Corp., Chgo., 1982—; counsel Continental Bank, Chgo., 1980-82, Borg-Warner Corp., Chgo., 1982-85; assoc. gen. counsel Heller Fin. Inc., 1986—. Bd. dirs., pres. aux. bd. North Ave. Day Nursery, Chgo., 1983—; dir. aux. bd. Henrotin Hosp., Chgo., 1983—, Northwestern Meml. Hosp.; bd. dirs., treas. Legal Clinic for Disabled, Chgo., 1984-86; mem. exec. bd. Chgo. Area council Boy Scouts Am., 1984—. Mem. ABA (chmn. internat. lawyers young lawyers div. 1984—), Chgo. Bar Assn. (dir. young lawyers sect. 1985-86, mem. exec. council 1984—, chmn. law explorers com. 1984-85), Ill. State Bar Assn., Ind. State Bar Assn. Club: Union League of Chgo. Lodge: Masons. Home: 875 N LaSalle St #2-S Chicago IL 60610 Office: Heller Fin Inc 200 N LaSalle St Chicago IL 60601

LEWIS, STEVEN ROBERT, dentist; b. Columbus, Ohio, Feb. 23, 1949; s. Robert Elliott and Marilyn (Purdum) L.; m. Marcia Marsh, Dec. 16, 1972; children: Lauren, Kyle, Alex. BS in Biology, Bowling Green U., 1971; DDS, Ohio State U., 1975. Clin. dentist Cin. Bd. Edn., 1975-78; pvt. practice gen. dentistry Cin., 1976—; treas., founding bd. mem. Midwest Dental Plans Inc., Cin., 1984—; dental dir. Health Power Health Plan, 1986—. Mem. ADA, Ohio Dental Assn., Cin. Dental Soc. Republican. Presbyterian. Club: N.W. Cin. Exchange (v.p., 1982, pres. 1983, youth chmn. 1984—); Wyo. Golf. Avocations: golfing, basketball, softball, home repair, football. Home: 726 Stout Ave Wyoming OH 45215 Office: 7120 Pippin Rd Cincinnati OH 45239

LEWIS, VICTOR LAMAR, JR., plastic and reconstructive surgery educator; b. Evanston, Ill., Sept. 22, 1942; s. Victor Lamar and Anne (Ward) L.; m. Jayne Martin, Dec. 2, 1972; children: Victor Lamar, Michael Martin. BA, Yale U., 1964; MD, Northwestern U., 1968. Diplomate Am. Bd. Surgery, Am. Bd. Plastic Surgery. Assoc. in surgery Northwestern U., Chgo., 1977-79, asst. prof. surgery, 1979—; chief of staff Rehab. Inst. Chgo., 1985—; chief plastic surgery Lakeside VA Hosp., Chgo., 1977—. Contbr. articles to profl. jours. Served to lt. comdr. USN, 1975-77. Grantee Plastic Surgery Edn. Found., 1986. Mem. Chgo. Soc. Plastic Surgery (v.p. 1986—). Club: Saddle and Cycle (Chgo.). Office: 251 E Chicago Ave Chicago IL 60611

LEWITAS, ALVIN ROY, health services company executive; b. Bklyn., Oct. 17, 1941; s. Jack and Rita (Spilke) L.; m. Holly Lynn McCown, Mar. 31, 1983; children: David, Alison. BA, U. Md., 1967; MBA, George Washington U., 1970. Adminstrv. asst. Michael Reese Hosp., Chgo., 1970-72; exec. v.p. Mile Sq. Health Ctr., Chgo., 1972-76; pres. Lewitas & Co., Inc., Chgo., 1976-86, Total Home Health Care, Chgo., 1983—; cons. Dysfunctioning Child Ctr., Chgo., 1972—; bd. dirs. MWB, Inc. Bd. dirs. U. Chgo. Cancer Research Ctr., 1985—. Served with USAF, 1962-66. Mem. Am. Coll. Healthcare Execs. Home: 40 E Cedar St Chicago IL 60611 Office: Total Home Health Care 1050 N State St Chicago IL 60610

LEY, CONNIE J., university administrator; b. Beaver Falls, Pa., June 25, 1944; d. Edward M. and Jean E. (Schriver) L. BS, Ind. U. Pa., 1966; MS, Pa. State U., 1975, PhD, 1979. Cert. home economist. Tchr. high schs. Pitts., 1966-74; grad. asst. Pa. State U., State College, 1974-75, instr., 1975-79; asst. prof. U. Nebr., Lincoln, 1979-84; assoc. prof., chmn. dept. home econs. Ill. State U., Normal, 1984—. Contbr. articles to profl. jours. Recipient Outstanding Tchr. award U. Nebr., Lincoln, 1984. Mem. Am. Home Econs. Assn., Am. Vocat. Assn., Am. Vocat. Edn. Research Assn. (sec. 1983-85, v.p. 1985, pres. 1986, research grantee 1980). Office: Ill State U Dept Home Econs Normal IL 61761

LEY, ROLAND GERALD, accountant; b. Watkins, Minn., May 19, 1932; s. Norbert Henry and Mathilda (Koelzer) L.; m. Rose Anne Thiesen, Sept. 2, 1955; children: Stephen, Thomas, Katherine, Karen, Patricia, Jonathan. BA, St. John's U., Collegeville, Minn., 1953; MBA, Northwestern U., 1956. Audit staff Arthur Young & Co., Chgo., 1956-61, audit mgr., 1962-68, audit ptnr., 1968—, ptnr. in charge audit dept., 1984—. Author: (book) Phaze II & You, 1973; gen. editor (book) Hospital Economic Controls, 1974. Chmn. Ill. CPA's for Polit. Action, Chgo., 1980-84. Served as cpl. U.S. Army, 1950-53. Mem. Better Govt. Assn. (bd. dirs. 1970—, pres. 1982-83), Ill. CPA Soc. (bd. dirs. 1982-83), Am. Inst. CPA's (utilities com. 1982-84). Republican. Roman Catholic. Clubs: Union League (fin. com.), Rolling Green Country (treas.). Home: 1534 Circle Ln Palatine IL 60067 Office: Arthur Young & Co One IBM Plaza Chicago IL 60611

LEYH, GEORGE FRANCIS, association executive; b. Utica, N.Y., Oct. 1, 1931; s. George Robert and Mary Kathleen (Haley) L.; m. Mary Alice Mosher, Sept. 17, 1955; children—Timothy George, Kristin Ann. B.C.E., Cornell U., 1954; M.S. (Univ. fellow), 1956. Structural engr. Eckerlin and Klepper, Syracuse, N.Y., 1956-59; asso. dir. engring. Martin Marietta Corp., Chgo., 1959-63; structural engr. Portland Cement Assn., Chgo., 1963-67; dir. mktg. Concrete Reinforcing Steel Inst., Chgo., 1967-75; exec. v.p. Am. Concrete Inst., Detroit, 1975—; editor jour. Am. Concrete Inst., 1975—. Mem. Planning Commn., Streamwood, Ill., 1960-68; chmn. Lake Bluff (Ill.) Citizens Com. for Conservation, 1972. Recipient Bloem Disting. Service award Am. Concrete Inst., 1972. Mem. ASCE, Am. Soc. Assn. Execs., Am. Mgmt. Assn., Nat. Inst. Bldg. Scis., Am. Ry. Engring. Assn., Am. Nat. Standards Inst. (dir. 1986—), Am. Soc. for Concrete Constrn. (dir. 1984—), Phi Kappa Phi. Clubs: North Cape Yacht, Lake Bluff Yacht (dir. 1969-74, commodore 1973). Home: 1327 Lone Pine Rd Bloomfield Hills MI 48013 Office: Am Concrete Inst 22400 W Seven Mile Rd Detroit MI 48219

L'HOMMEDIEU, ROGER HART, emergency department administrator; b. Ann Arbor, Mich., Nov. 5, 1952; s. Roger Hart and Violet Ann (Pankowski) L'H.; m. Susan Lee Alderman, June 21, 1975; children: Timothy Ross, Daniel Adam. BS in Pharmacy, Ohio State U., 1976; MD, Med. Coll. Ohio, 1979. Cert. in emergency medicine Am. Bd. Emergency Medicine. Resident Emergency Medicine Residency Program, Toledo, 1979-81, chief resident, 1981-82; staff physician emergency dept. Robinson Meml. Hosp., Ravenna, Ohio, 1982-83, dir. emergency med. services, 1982—; asst. prof. emergency medicine Northeastern Ohio Coll. Medicine, Rootstown, 1983—. Fellow Am. Coll. Emergency Physicians; mem. AMA, Ohio State Med. Assn., Portage County Med. Soc., Alpha Omega Alpha, Rho Chi. Republican. Avocation: snow skiing. Office: Robinson Meml Hosp Emergency Dept 6847 N Chestnut St Ravenna OH 44266

LI, JAMES TUNG CHIEH, physician; b. N.Y.C., Dec. 7, 1953; s. George and Sylvia (Young) L.; m. Susan Rector, June 30, 1955; 1 child, Daniel. BA, Princeton U., 1974; MD, PhD, Duke U., 1981. Resident in medicine Duke U., Durham, N.C., 1981-84; fellow in allergy Mayo Clinic, Rochester, Minn., 1984-85, sr. assoc. cons., 1985-87; cons. allergic diseases, internal medicine, 1987—. Mem. AMA, Am. Coll. Physicians, Am. Acad. Allergy and Immunology (Pres.'s Grant-in Aid award 1985). Office: Mayo Clinic 200 1st St SW Rochester MN 55905

LI, NORMAN L., state ofcl.; b. Hong Kong, Mar. 11, 1947; came to U.S., 1971; s. Po On and Lena (Lam) L.; 1 son, David T. B.A., Nat. Taiwan U., 1971; M.A., Central Mo. State U., 1974; m. Judy Cheng, May 8, 1976. Internat. mktg. dir. Tataicheong Co. Ltd., Hong Kong, 1970-72; mgr. New Moon of Merrillville Inc., 1974-79; trade specialist Ill. Dept. Commerce and Community Affairs, Chgo., 1979-82; mng. dir. Ill. Far East Bur., Hong Kong, 1982—; leader state trade missions to China, Hong Kong, Korea, Singapore, Taiwan; developer trade promotion agreement between Ill. and Taiwan, 1979, between Ill. and Liaoning, China, 1983. Mem. Am. C. of C. in Hong Kong. Home: 430 Quail Dr Naperville IL 60565

LI, STEPHEN KU-CHING, architect; b. Taipei, Taiwan, Republic of China, Sept. 10, 1948; came to U.S., 1974, naturalized, 1982; s. Jun-te and Yue-hsia (Chou) L.; m. Annie Ho, Dec. 6, 1975. B.Arch, Chung Yuan Coll., 1972; M.Arch, Ill. Inst. Tech., 1976. Registered architect, Calif., Ill., Wis., Ind. Designer, Martin Oil Service Co., Alsip, Ill., 1975-77; draftsman Schiller & Frank, Wheeling, Ill., 1977; designer Perkins & Will, Chgo., 1977-79; job capt. L.B. Knight & Assocs., Chgo., 1979-81; mgr. J.A. Iacopi & Assocs.,

Northbrook, Ill., 1981-83; owner, mgr. K.C. Li & Assocs., Roselle, Ill., 1983—. Mem. AIA. Avocations: tennis, soccer.

LIAO, SHUTSUNG, biochemist; b. Tainan, Taiwan, Jan. 1, 1931; s. Chi-Chun Liao and Chin-Shen Lin; m. Shuching Liao, Mar. 19, 1960; children: Jane, Tzufen, Tzuming, May. BS in Agrl. Chemistry, Nat. Taiwan U., 1953, MS in Biochemistry, 1956; postgrad., Ill. Inst. Tech., Chgo., 1956-57; PhD in Biochemistry, U. Chgo., 1961. Research assoc. Ben May Lab. Cancer Research, U. Chgo., 1960-63, instr. biochemistry and molecular biology, 1963-64, asst. prof., 1964-69, assoc. prof., 1969-71; prof. biochemistry and molecular biology Ben May Inst., 1972—; cons. various nation and internat. confs., agys., founds. and workshps. Editor Jour. Steroid Biochemistry, The Prostate; assoc. editor Cancer Research; contbr. over 140 articles to profl jours. V.p. Chgo. Formosan Fed. Credit Union, 1977-79; trustee Taiwanese United Fund in U.S., 1981—; mem. adv. com. Taiwan-U.S. Cultural Exchange Ctr., 1984—. Recipient Sci.-Tech. Achievement prize Taiwanese-Am. Found., 1983; NIH grantee, 1962—, Am. Cancer Soc. grantee, 1974—. Mem. Am. Soc. Biological Chemists, Endocrine Soc., N. Am. Taiwanese Profs. Assn. (pres. 1980-81, exec. dir. 1981—). Home: 5632 S Woodlawn Chicago IL 60637 Office: U Chgo Ben May Inst 5841 S Maryland Chicago IL 60637

LIAPIS, GUS HARRY, electronics company executive; b. Price, Utah, Mar. 27, 1950; s. Harry Paul and Ann (Papazaharis) L.; m. Sharon Kay Long, Aug. 19, 1972; children: Philip, Scott, Stephanie, Zachary. BSEE, U. Utah, 1973, BS in Bus. Adminstrn., 1975, MSEE, 1978; postgrad., Coll. Eastern Utah, 1968-70. Design engr. U. Utah Expt. Sta., Salt Lake City, 1971-75; project design engr. Evans & Sutherland, Salt Lake City, 1975-78, engr. tech. mktg., 1978-80, rep., program mgr., mem. mgmt. group, 1980-84; mgr. program mgmt. Systems Research Lab., Dayton, Ohio, 1984-85, mgr. bus. group, 1985-87, program dir., 1987—; cons. Delta Electronics, Salt Lake City, 1980-84. Pres. Research Park Softball League, Salt Lake City, 1975-78; bd. dirs. softball Salt Lake County Recreation Dept., Salt Lake City, 1982-84; mem. Dayton Art Inst., 1984-85, Utah del. launching USS Salt Lake City, Norfolk, Va., 1984; mgr. Patterson Park Little League, Dayton, 1984—; mem. com. Dayton Philharm. Orch., 1984—; cub master Boy Scouts Am., Dayton, 1986—. Mem. Soc. Info. Displays, IEEE (vice chmn. Salt Lake City chpt. 1971-72), Nat. Assn. Def. Preparedness. Greek Orthodox. Lodge: Elks. Avocations: reading, travel. Home: 269 Northview Rd Dayton OH 45419

LIBAUER, LARRY NORMAN, manufacturing executive; b. Balt., May 20, 1937; s. Lee and Bertha (Solomon) L.; children: Sheri l., Lynda M. BS, U. Maryland, 1960; MBA, U. Chgo., 1965; LLB, La Salle U., 1973. Personnel mgr. MSL Steel Co., Chgo., 1965-67; mgr. indsl. relations MSL Plastics Co., Franklin Park, Ill., 1967-69, Ekco Housewares Co., Chgo., 1969-71; dir. indsl. relations Ekco Housewares Co., Franklin Park, 1971-80, div. v.p.human resources, 1980-84, corp. v.p. human resources, 1984—; instr. in mgmt. Ill. Inst. Tech., Chgo., 1966-75; lectr. Northwestern U., Evanston, Chgo., 1976-86, sr. lectr. 1987—; cons. in field. Labor relations officer City of Morton Grove, 1974-83; arbitrator Am. Arbitration Assn., Chgo., 1984—, Better Bus. Bur. Greater Chgo., 1983-84; mem. Bus. Adv. Council, Northwestern U., Evanston and Chgo., 1979-81. Served to staff Sgt. USAF, 1960-65. Mem. Am. Soc. Personnel Admsinstrn., Tooling and Mfrs. Assn., Cookware Mfrs. Assn., Midwest Indsl. Mfrs. Assn., Employer's Assn. Greater Chgo. Republican. Avocation: sailing. Home: 7928 W Davis St Morton Grove IL 60053 Office: Ekco Housewares Inc 9234 W Belmont Ave Franklin Park IL 60131

LIBBE, SCOTT MICHAEL, comptroller; b. Toledo, Apr. 22, 1956; s. William C. and Mary A. (Meyer) L.; m. Jane A. Poenicke, June 17, 1978; children: Katherine E., Laura E., Sarah E. BBA, U. Cin., 1978. CPA, Ohio. Staff acct. Arthur Young & Co., Cin., 1978-80, Toledo, 1980-82; audit and taxation supr. Spartan Chem. Co., Inc., Toledo, 1982-85, comptroller, 1985—. Mem. Am. Inst. CPA's, Ohio Soc. CPA's, Black Swamp Carvers. Republican. Lutheran. Club: Black Swamp Wood Carvers (Toledo). Avocation: wood carving. Office: Spartan Chem Co Inc 110 N Westwood Toledo OH 43607

LIBBEE, DOROTHY ALBERTA, grain and seed company executive; b. Brookfield, Mo., May 20, 1928; d. Albert Daniel and Daisy Pearl (Harris) Mustapha; m. Rex Thomas Lewis, Feb. 14, 1947 (div. 1955); 1 child, Dannette Jill; m. Guy Wynne Libbee, Apr. 4, 1973. Cert., Chillicothe Bus. Coll., 1946; student, Draughon Bus. U., 1954. Legal sec. Davis, Kitt & Lintner, Chillicothe, 1946-48; corp. sec. Lipscomb Grain and Seed Co., Springfield, Mo., 1954—, 1986—; corp. sec. Lipscomb Bros., Inc., 1986—. Democrat. Baptist. Lodge: Royal Neighbors Am. Avocations: camping, antique post cards. Home: 2147 E Division Springfield MO 65803 Office: Lipscomb Grain & Seed Co PO Box 1125 700 W Wall Springfield MO 65805

LIBBY, JUDITH LYNN, lawyer; b. Elgin, Ill., Oct. 20, 1948; d. Jules Leon and Virginia Marie (Marshall) L.; B.A. in English Lit., Roosevelt U., 1970; J.D. with highest distinction (Scholar), John Marshall Law Sch., 1977; m. Richard J. Coffee, II; children: David Patrick, Brent William. Bar: Ill. 1977. Tchr. humanities Craigmore High Sch., Smithfield, South Australia, Australia, 1971-73; assoc. firm Taussig, Wexler & Shaw, Ltd., Chgo., 1977-78; chief counsel Ill. Dept. Ins., Springfield, 1978-80; ptnr. Libby & Coffee Law Office, Springfield, 1981-84; implementation dir. Ill. Coalition Against Sexual Assault, 1984-85; asst. defender Office of State Appellate Defender, Springfield, 1986—. Mem. Chgo. Bar Assn. Office: State Appellate Defender Ill 300 E Monroe Suite 102 Springfield IL 62701

LIBBY, STEPHEN CRAIG, engineer; b. Winterset, Iowa, May 22, 1950; s. Harold Clarence and Zelma (Harrell) L.; m. Gunda Sue Wheeler, June 13, 1970; children: Chad Michael, Ryan Matthew. BA in Polit. Sci., Simpson Coll., 1974. Craft technician Northwestern Bell Telephone, Des Moines, 1969-77, revenue supr., 1977-80, design engr., 1980-82, power engr., 1982-85, equipment engr., 1985—. Pres. Indianola (Iowa) Little League, 1982. Mem. Telephone Pioneers Am., Ind. Athletic Boosters. Republican. Methodist. Avocations: coaching sports, swimming. Office: Northwestern Bell Telephone Co 925 High St Des Moines IA 50309

LIBERMAN, LEE MARVIN, utility executive; b. Salt Lake City, July 12, 1921; s. Benjamin L. and Sylvia (Goldflam) L.; m. Jeanne Hirsch, Oct. 19, 1946; children: Alise, James, Celia; m. Ann Medler, Aug. 21, 1982. B.S. in Chem. Engring., Yale U., 1942. Registered profl. engr., Mo. With Laclede Gas Co., St. Louis, 1945—; exec. v.p. Laclede Gas Co., 1968-70, pres., 1970—, chief exec. officer, 1974—, chmn., 1976—, also dir.; bd. dirs. Boatmen's Bancshares, Boatmen's Nat. Bank, Angelica Corp., Falcon Products Co., INTERCO Inc., Instituform Mid-Am. Inc., CPI Corp. Mem. Civic Progress, Inc.; chmn. Regional Commerce and Growth Assn.; co-chmn. St. Louis Regional Health Care Corp.; past pres. Family and Children's Service St. Louis; bd. dirs. Art and Edn. Council; chmn. St. Louis Symphony Soc.; chmn. campaign United Way, 1987; past chmn. bd. Jewish Hosp. Served with USAAF, 1944-45. Named St. Louis Man of Yr., 1986. Mem. Nat. Soc. Profl. Engrs., Mo. C. of C., Regional Commerce and Growth Assn. (chmn.). Office: Laclede Gas Co 720 Olive St Saint Louis MO 63101

LICHTEN, EDWARD MARK, gynecologist and obstetrician; b. Akron, Ohio, July 8, 1947; m. Gail Marie Zimmerman, Aug. 18, 1968; children: Jason Brett, Stephanie Renee. BS, U. Akron, 1868; MD, Ohio State U., 1972, cert., 1976. Diplomate Am. Bd. Ob-Gyn. Resident ob/gyn Ohio State U. Hosps., 1972-76; practice medicine specializing in ob-gyn Southfield, Mich., 1984—. Office: 4400 Town Center #290 Southfield MI 48075

LICHTENFELD, MELVIN ALLEN, pharmacist; b. Gary, Ind., June 13, 1927; s. Albert Isidore and Sidell (Korenthal) L.; m. Elaine Kaplan, Apr. 6, 1952; children—Dean Howard, Jan Rae, Michelle Ann, Bruce Harvey. B.S. in Pharmacy, Purdue U., 1951. Staff pharmacist Walgreen Drug Co., Gary, 1951-52; pharmacist, mgr. Hobart Drugs, Hobart, Ind., 1952-60; owner, pharmacist Mel's Pharmacy, Gary, 1960-70; chief pharmacist, dir. pharmacy Ross Med. Pharmacy, Merrillville, Ind., 1970—; corp. sec. Merrillville Health Ctr. Pharmacy, 1970—; regional dir. Bank of Indiana, Merrillville, 1984—. Author: Man Power in Pharmacy, 1976. Recipient Bowl of Hygeia A.H. Robins Co., 1980. Mem. Nat. Assn. Retail Druggists (Leadership award 1980), Am. Pharm. Assn., Ind. Pharmacist Assn. (pres. 1978-79), Lake County Pharmacist Assn. (pres. 1961-62), Merrillville C. of C. Club: Lofs Golf Assn. (Crown Point Ind.). Lodges: Masons, Lions, B'nai B'rith. Avocations: golf, racquetball, photography, travel. Home: 3037 Sunrise Dr Lofs Crown Point IN 46307

LICHTENSTEIN, IRVIN YALE, mortgage banking company executive; b. Columbus, Ohio, Dec. 21, 1924; s. Samuel and Bessie Lichtenstein; m. Mitzi Lee Shaucet, Aug. 31, 1947; children—Hindi Lee, Jeffrey Alan. Student Ohio State U., 1942-43, 46-47. With Yerke Mortgage Co., Columbus, Ohio, 1954—, v.p., 1960-73, exec. v.p., 1973—; instr. post licensing courses Columbus Bd. Realtors; speaker numerous seminars conducted by local newspapers; expert commentator local TV stas. on residential mortgage financing; speaker on specialty, FHA and VA govt. insured mortgages. Served to sgt. AC, U.S. Army, 1943-45. Decorated Air medal with 2 oak leaf clusters. Mem. Columbus Bd. Realtors, Mortgage Bankers Assn. (pres. 1963). Republican. Jewish. Club: Winding Hollow Country (Columbus). Lodge: B'nai B'rith. Office: 145 E Rich St Columbus OH 43215

LICHTENSTEIN, NATHAN H., lawyer; b. Chgo., June 12, 1953; s. Henry and Mary (Mayerowicz) L.; m. Aviva Shelly Zackai, Nov. 20, 1977; children—Sarah, Elana, Rachel. B.A., Northwestern U., 1974; J.D., DePaul U., 1977; LL.M., John Marshall U., 1981. Bar: Ill. 1977, Fla. 1977, U.S. Dist. Ct. (no. dist.) Ill. 1977. Assoc. Goldgehn, Leonardo, Goldgehn & Isaacson, Chgo., 1977-83; ptnr. Greenberg, Keele, Lunn & Aronberg, Chgo., 1984—. Mem. Ill. State Bar Assn., Decalogue Soc. Lawyers, Am. Jewish Congress (governing council 1983—), Commn. on Law and Social Action. Office: Greenberg Keele Lunn & Aronberg One IBM Plaza Chicago IL 60611

LICHTY, WARREN DEWEY, JR., lawyer; b. Colorado Springs, Colo., Dec. 17, 1930; s. Warren D. and Margaret (White) L.; m. Margaret Louise Grupy, Dec. 8, 1962. Student Chadron State Coll., 1948-50; BS in Law, U. Nebr., 1952, JD, 1954. Bar: Nebr. 1954, U.S. Dist. Ct. Nebr., 1954, U.S. Ct. Appeals (8th cir.) 1973, U.S. Supreme Ct. 1979. Spl. agt. CIC, 1955-58; county judge Dawes County, Nebr., 1958-61; spl. asst. atty. gen. Nebr. Dept. Justice, Lincoln, Nebr., 1961-69; asst. atty. gen., chief counsel Nebr. Dept. Roads, Lincoln, 1969—; lectr. law Chadron State Coll., 1959-60; mem. com. on eminent domain and land use, transp. research bd. Nat. Acad. Sci.-NRC. Bd. dirs. Scottish Rite Found. Nebr., 1981—, DeMolay Found. Nebr., 1980—, Nebr. Masonic Home Corp., 1979—. Served with U.S. Army, 1954-58. Mem. Nebr. Bar Assn., Lincoln Bar Assn., Am. Assn. State Hwy. and Transp. Ofcls. (subcom. on legal affairs), Am. Legion. Republican. Episcopalian. Clubs: Hiram (past pres.), Nebr. (Lincoln). Lodges: Masons (33 deg.; grand master Nebr. 1979, vice chmn. conf. Grand Masters of N.Am., 1980), Shriners, Royal Order of Scotland, Philalithes Soc., Elks. Home: PO Box 2559 Lincoln NE 68502 Office: PO Box 94759 Lincoln NE 68509

LIEB, CHARLES FRANCIS, manufacturing company executive; b. Beaver, Pa., Mar. 12, 1948; s. Charles Francis Sr. and Ruth Lillian (Davis) L.; m. Kathleen Diann Lewis; children: Emily Susan, Alison Yung. BS, Lehigh U., 1970, MBA, 1971. With Westinghouse Electric Corp., Grand Rapids, 1978-80; mgr. purchases Westinghouse Elevator Co., Gettysburg, Pa., 1978-80; mgr. warehouse ops. Westinghouse Furniture Systems, Grand Rapids, 1980-81, dir. purchases, 1981-83, mgr. customer resources, 1983-85, v.p., 1985—. Bd. dirs. ARC, Grand Rapids, 1986—, Boy Scouts Am., Grand Rapids, 1986—. Republican. Avocations: pub. speaking, profl. reading, golf. Home: 397 Greenbrier Dr Grand Rapids MI 49506 Office: Westinghouse Electric Corp 4300 36th St Grand Rapids MI 49508

LIEBENOW, ROLAND RUDOLPH, insurance company medical director; b. Jefferson County, Wis., Sept. 17, 1922; s. Rudolph F. and Elma L. (Loper) L.; B.S., U. Wis., Madison, 1944, M.D., 1948; m. Martha E. Anderson, May 5, 1950; children—Linda S., Ronald M., Kurt S. Intern, Colo. Gen. Hosp., Denver, 1948-49; gen. practice medicine, Stevens Point, Wis., 1949-50; practice medicine specializing in medicine and surgery, Lake Mills, Wis., 1950-67; asso. med. dir. Northwestern Mut. Life Ins. Co., Milw., 1967-82; v.p., med. dir. CUNA Mut. Ins. Group, 1982—. teaching asst. in anatomy Med. Sch., U. Wis., 1944, research asst. in pharmacology, 1946-47; mem. med. staffs Deaconess Hosp., Milw., Watertown Meml., Ft. Atkinson Meml. hosps.; pres. exec. com. Marquardt Manor Nursing Home, Watertown, Wis., 1972-74; pres. med. staff St. Mary's Hosp., Watertown, 1959; vice chief of staff Ft. Atkinson (Wis.) Meml. Hosp., 1967; clin. asst. prof. Med. Coll. Wis., 1976-84. Chmn. troop com. Sinnissippi council Boy Scouts Am., 1965-76; vice chmn. bd. elders Lake Mills Moravian Ch., 1972-75; appointed to Wis. State Task Force on Alzheimer's Disease, 1984; mem. exec. bd, Four Lakes Council Boy Scouts Am., 1987— Served to capt. M.C., U.S. Army, 1953-55. Named Alumnus of Year, Lake Mills Alumni Assn., 1972. Diplomate Am. Bd. Family Practice; cert. Bd. Life Ins. Medicine. Fellow Am. Acad. Family Practice, Human Values Inst.; mem. Jefferson County Med. Assn. (pres. 1959-60), Wis. State Med. Soc. (mem. ho. of dels. from Jefferson County 1980-87, mem. fed. legislation com. 1981-87, mem. com. aging 1982-87, chmn. extended care facilities 1983—), AMA, Wis. Acad. Arts and Scis., Assn. Life Ins. Med. Dirs., Am. Council Life Ins. (legis. com., med. sect.), Aerospace Med. Assn., U. Wis. Med. Alumni Assn. (bd. dirs. 1985—), Soc. for Prospective Medicine, Am. Legion, Phi Kappa Phi. Republican. Clubs: Northwestern Mut. Stamp (pres. 1972-76), Philatelic Classics Soc., Masons, Rotary. Co-author monograph on chloroform, 1951. Home: 309 Lakeview Ave Lake Mills WI 53551 Office: 5910 Mineral Point Rd Madison WI 53705

LIEBER, TODD MICHAEL, English educator; b. Phila., Nov. 30, 1944; s. Sylvan and Thelma (Wiser) L.; m. Lorianne Baily, June 24, 1967 (div. 1981); 1 child, Terry. BA, Duke U., 1966; PhD, Case Western Res. U., 1969; MFA, U. Ariz., 1983. Asst. prof. Simpson Coll., Indianola, Iowa, 1969—, assoc., 1975, prof., 1986. Author: Endless Experiments, 1973; contbr. articles and short stories to mags. NDEA fellow, 1966-69; Nat. Endowment for Arts grantee, 1987. Mem. Associated Writing Programs, Phi Beta Kappa. Home: 789 Jesup St Indianola IA 50125 Office: Simpson Coll Indianola IA 50125

LIEBERGEN, GARY JOSEPH, hotel executive; b. Green Bay, Wis., Nov. 22, 1950; s. Joseph Alvin and Josephine Veronica (Brey) L.; m. Adrienne Allyn Hess, Sept. 18, 1976; children: Adam, Justin, Stephanie. BS, U. Wis., Green Bay, 1972. CPA, Wis. Staff auditor Arthur Andersen & Co., Milw., 1972-75, sr. auditor, 1975-77; mgr. Arthur Andersen & Co., Kansas City, Mo., 1977-85; v.p. fin. Sunway Hotel Group, Kansas City, 1985-86, sr. v.p., 1987—; bd. dirs. Sunway Investments, Sunway Hotel Mgmt., Kansas City. Treas., bd. dirs. Guadalupe Ctr., Inc., Kansas City, 1979-84. Served with U.S. Army, 1972-78. Fellow Am. Inst. CPA's; mem. Mo. Soc. Pub. Accts., Wis. Soc. Pub. Accts. Republican. Roman Catholic. Avocations: golf, racquetball. Home: 10828 Barton Overland Park KS 66210 Office: Sunway Hotel Group 800 W 47th St Kansas City MO 64112

LIEBERMAN, DAVID JOSEPH, physician, administrator, educator; b. Phila., Feb. 2, 1928; s. Wolf Meyer and Anne (Elman) L. Student, Temple U., 1946; M.D., Jefferson Med. Coll., Phila., 1950; postgrad., U. Pa., 1952-53, 66; M.P.H., Harvard U., 1966. Lic. physician Pa., N.Y., Mich. Rotating intern Phila. Gen. Hosp., 1950-52; ship surgeon Grace Line, N.Y.C., 1952-53, U.S. Lines, N.Y.C., 1960; resident in gen. surgery Albert Einstein Med. Ctr., Phila., 1953-56; tour physician Harlem Globetrotters Basketball Exhbn. World Tour, 1956; practice medicine specializing in gen. surgery Albert Einstein Med. Ctr., No. div., 1956-59, Temple U. Sch. Medicine, Phila., 1956-59; assoc. surgeon Rush Hosp. for Diseases of Chest, 1956-59; chief surg. services Warren State Hosp., Pa., 1960-64; physician Pa. Dept. Health, Bur. Field Services, 1964-65; asst. dir. health dist. Phila. Dept. Pub. Health, Bur. Dist. Health Services, 1966-67; dir. Bur. Med. Policies and Standards, Office Med. Services and Facilities, Pa. Dept. Pub. Welfare, Harrisburg, 1968-69; exec. med. dir. med. assistance program N.Y.C. Dept. Health, 1969-71; dir. Dept. Ambulatory Care Services and Community Medicine, French and Polyclinic Med. Sch. and Health Ctr., N.Y.C., 1971-74; health officer, med. dir. Monroe County Health Dept., Monroe, Mich., 1975—; chief med. examiner Monroe County, 1975—; mem. environ. health adv. com. Mich. Dept. Health, 1976—; cons. numerous hosps., pvt. and civic orgns.; lectr. health planning and adminstrn. U. Mich. Sch. Pub. Health, 1976-83. bd. dirs. Mich. Assn. Local Pub. Health, 1985—, Mich. Pub. Health Physicians Forum, 1986—, Southeastern Mich. Substance Abuse Services, 1982—; mem. adv. council Area Agy. on Aging, 1985—; active numerous other civic orgns. Recipient Dr. Francis W. Shain prize Jefferson Med. Coll., 1950; Best Resident prize Albert Einstein Med. Ctr., 1956; USPHS grantee, 1965-66. Fellow Am. Pub. Health Assn. (gov. council 1978), Royal Soc. Health; mem. Am. Coll. Preventive Medicine, Southeastern Mich. Health Assn. (bd. dirs. 1975—, pres. 1983-84), Mich. Pub. Health Assn. (bd. dirs. 1984-85, 87—), Mich. Health Officers Assn. (bd. dirs. 1983—, pres. 1986—), Nat. Assn. County Health Officials, Nat. Assn. Med. Examiners, Am. Assn. Pub. Health Physicians, others. Home: 3861 N Custer Rd Monroe MI 48161 Office: 650 Stewart Rd Monroe MI 48161

LIEBERMAN, JEFFREY MARTIN, real estate executive, educator; b. Columbus, Ohio, Dec. 6, 1950; s. Richard Allen and Evelyn (Gitin) L.; m. Shelley Mona Turk, Aug. 30, 1975; children: Stacie, Ryan. BA, Ohio State U., 1973, MBA, 1974. Cert. property mgr. V.p. Rallie Co., Columbus, 1973-79; pres. Staco Assocs., Inc., Columbus, 1979—; pres. J.R. Comml. Laundries. Contbr. articles to profl. jours. Mem. Inst. for Real Estate Mgmt. (v.p.), Nat. Real Estate Tng. Inst. (pres. Columbus chpt. 1984—), Inst. for Real Estate Edn. Columbus (bd. dirs.). Avocations: photography, ham radio. Office: Staco Assocs Inc 35 E Livingston Ave Columbus OH 43215

LIEBERMAN, MICHAEL ALLEN, biochemist, researcher; b. N.Y.C., Aug. 22, 1950; s. Eugene A. and Eva (Rubin) L.; m. Deborah Linn Lipsich, Sept. 15, 1977; children: Rachel Anna, Samuel Joseph. BS, MIT, 1972; PhD, Brandeis U., 1978. Research assoc. Washington U., St. Louis, 1977-80; asst. prof. Harvard U., Boston, 1981-83; assoc. prof. U. Cin., 1983—; mem. study sect. NIH, Washington, 1986—. Contbr. articles to profl. jours. Recipient Faculty Research award Am. Cancer Soc., 1981; grantee NIH, 1983. Mem. AAAS, Am. Soc. Cell Biology, Am. Inst. Nutrition. Democrat. Jwish. Lodge: B'nai B'rith. Avocations: bowling, softball, model building. Office: U Cin 231 Bethesda Ave Cincinnati OH 45267

LIEBERTHAL, MILTON M., medical consultant, gastroenterologist; b. Jewett City, Conn., Oct. 30, 1911; s. Robert Henry and Erna (Bloomfield) L.; m. Naomi Ruth Burd, June 9, 1935; children—David Henry, Kenneth Guy, Gary Burd. A.B., Dartmouth Coll., 1932; M.D., NYU, 1935. Diplomate Am. Bd. Internal Medicine. Intern, Phila. Gen. Hosp., 1935-37, resident in internal medicine and gastroenterology, 1937-39; practice medicine, Phila., 1939-41; practice medicine specializing in gastroenterology, Bridgeport, Conn., 1946-71; dir. investigative gastroenterology Merrell-Nat. Labs., 1972-76; med. cons. Merrell Dow Pharms., Cin., 1977—; clin. prof. medicine U. Cin. Served to maj. M.C., AUS, 1942-45. Fellow ACP; mem. Am. Gastroent. Assn., Am. Soc. Gastrointestinal Endoscopy, Alpha Omega Alpha. Club: Kenwood Country (Cin.). Author: (with H.O. Conn) The Hepatic Coma Syndromes and Lactulose, 1979; The Lighter Side of Life, 1973; contbr. articles to profl. books and jours.

LIEBIG, GREGORY A., mechanical engineer; b. Michigan City, Ind., Sept. 27, 1963; s. Richard W. Liebig and J. Joyce (Bayne) McLachlan. BSME, Tri-State U., Angola, Ind., 1985. Mfg. engr. Wheel Tek, Inc., Fremont, Ind., 1984-85; staff mech. engr. Amcast Indsl. Corp., Dayton, Ohio, 1985-86; product and process devel. engr. Amcast Indsl. Corp., Cedarburg, Wis., 1986, supr., 1986-87; process engr. Western Wheel, Howell, Mich., 1987—. Named one of Outstanding Young Men of Am., 1985. Mem. ASME (assoc.), Soc. Automotive Engrs., Order of Engr. (life), Am. Nutritional Med. Assn. Office: Amcast Indsl Corp Meta-Mold Div 2440 W Highland Rd Howell MI 48843

LIEBMAN, JON CHARLES, civil engineer, educator; b. Cin., Sept. 10, 1934; s. J. Charles and Joan (Heineman) L.; m. Judith Rae Stenzel, Dec. 27, 1958; children: Christopher Brian, Rebecca Anne, Michael Jon. B.S., U. Colo., Boulder, 1956; M.S., Cornell U., Ithaca, N.Y., 1963, Ph.D., 1965. Asst. prof., then assoc. prof. Johns Hopkins U., Balt., 1965-72; prof. civil engring. U. Ill., Urbana, 1972—; assoc. head dept. U. Ill., 1976-78, head dept., 1978-84. Served from ensign to lt. USN, 1956-61. Fellow AAAS; mem. Am. Soc. Engring. Edn. (Western Electric Fund award 1969), ASCE, Assn. Environ. Engring. Profs. (dir. 1980-82), Ops. Research Soc. Am. Office: Newmark Lab 208 N Romine St Urbana IL 61801

LIEBSCHUTZ, STEVEN GERALD, travel agent; b. Evanston, Ill., Jan. 3, 1956; s. Leonard Isaac and Nancy (Portis) L. MusB cum laude, Lawrence U., Appleton, Wis., 1978. Asst. engr. Universal Recording, Chgo., 1978-79; comml. reservations agt. TV Travel, Inc., Chgo., 1982—; gen. mgr. WLFM Radio, Appleton, 1975-78. Avocations: music, photography, racquetball, travel, scuba diving, wind surfing. Home: 2124 N Sedgwick Chicago IL 60614 Office: TV Travel 75 E Wacker Dr Chicago IL 60614

LIED, MICHAEL ROBERT, lawyer; b. Offenbach, Fed. Republic Germany, Jan. 18, 1953; came to U.S., 1955; s. Wolfgang Amadeus and Inge Martha (Fuchs) L.; m. Cherlyn Sue Etchason, Dec. 25, 1975; children: Jason Alexander, Adam Blaine, Evan Christopher. BS, U. Ill., 1975, MA in Labor and Indsl. Relations, 1977; JD, U. Mich., 1983. Bar: Mich. 1983, U.S. Dist. Ct. (ea. dist.) Mich. 1983, U.S. Ct. Appeals (6th cir.) 1985, U.S. Dist. Ct. (cen. dist.) Ill. 1987, U.S. Supreme Ct. 1987. Personnel advisor Consumers Power Co., Jackson, Mich., 1977, asst. personnel dir., 1977-79; mgr. personnel H.J. Heinz Co., Holland, Mich., 1979-80; assoc. Dykema, Gossett, Spencer, Goodnow & Trigg, Detroit, 1980-87, Sutkowski & Washkuhn, Peoria, Ill., 1987—; cons. Inst. Labor and Indsl. Relations, U. Ill., Champaign/Urbana, 1976-77. Contbr. articles to profl. pubs. Mem. ABA, Assn. Trial Lawyers Am. (assoc.), Am. Immigration Lawyers Assn., Mich. Bar Assn., Detroit Bar Assn., Phi Alpha Delta (cert. appreciation 1983, cert. outstanding service 1983). Republican. Home: 6941 Dickinson Cemetery Rd Dunlap IL 61525 Office: Sutkowski & Washkuhn Jefferson Bank Bldg Suite 560 Peoria IL 61602

LIEDER, MARY ANDREA, sales and marketing consulting company executive; b. Mpls., Sept. 6, 1938; d. William H. and Anne J. (Gamradt) Berney; m. James Edward Lieder; children—Timothy, Jon, William, Kristin. A. Liberal Arts, U. Minn., 1958; B.A., Met. State U., 1976. Lic. real estate broker, Minn. Property mgr. Sage Co., Madsen Constrn. Co., Mpls., 1967-69; cons. Coult Mortgage Co., St. Paul, 1969-77; social worker Courage Ctr., Mpls., 1977-78; dir. sales and mktg. Swanson Abbott Devel. Co., Mpls., 1978-81; dir. condominium and townhouse div. Edina Realty, Mpls., 1981-83; pres., owner Lieder Corp., Mpls., 1983—; mem. examining bd. Truth in Housing, City of Mpls., 1984—; bd. dirs. Project for Pride in Living, Mpls. Mem. Minn. Multi-Housing Assn. Republican. Roman Catholic. Avocation: painting in oils and mixed media. Home: 2460 Kyle Ave N Minneapolis MN 55422 Office: Lieder Corp 3100 W Lake St Minneapolis MN 55416

LIEMANDT, PEGGY LOUISE, consultant; b. Wichita, Kans., Aug. 7, 1944; d. Frank Wellington and Margaret Elizabeth (Salser) Wichser; m. Daniel George Liemandt, Feb. 23, 1967. B.A., U. Minn., 1964. Metro Group Fashion dir. J.C. Penney Co., Chgo., 1966-69; fashion, TV dir. Donaldson's, Mpls., St. Paul, 1969-72; pres. Liemandts Tour Conv. Services, Mpls., 1972-79, Godiva Chocolates, Mpls., 1979-85; pres., chmn. bd. Truffles Chocolatier, Mpls., 1980-86; pres. Caribbean Cons., 1986—; v.p. Greenhouse Restaurants, St. Thomas, U.S. V.I., St. Martin, French West Indies and Netherland Antilles, 1986—. lectr., cons. in field. Benefit mem. Laura Baker Sch. for Retarded, 1985; vols. Minn. Soc. for Blind, 1978-79; com. mem. Minn. Sympony Orch., 1979—; benefit mem. Whitney Mus., N.Y.C., 1984; bd. dirs. Jr. Achievement, Minn., 1985—. Recipient Highest Achievement award Tobe-Coburn Sch., N.Y.C., 1984. Mem. Minn. Women's Network (exec. br.), Am. Women in Bus. Owners Assn., Sales and Mktg. Execs. of Mpls., Nat. Sales Mgmt. Assn. (dir.), Am. Fedn. Radio and TV Artists, Screen Actors Guild, Alpha Gamma Delta. Republican. Methodist. Avocations: scuba diving; snorkeling; swimming; windsurfing; water skiing. Home: 11616 Live Oak Dr Minnetonka MN 55343 Office: Truffles Group Inc 7116 Shady Oak Rd Eden Prairie MN 55344

LIEN, BRUCE HAWKINS, minerals and oil company executive; b. Waubay, S.D., Apr. 7, 1927; s. Peter Calmer and LaRece Catherine (Holm) L.; m. Deanna Jean Browning, May 4, 1978. BS in Bus., Wyo. U., 1953. Laborer, ptnr. Pete Lien & Sons, Inc., Rapid City, S.D., 1944-84, bd. chmn., 1984—. Chmn. Community Chest, Rapid City, S.D., 1956; pres., nat.

council Boys Club Am., Rapid City, S.D., N.Y.C., 1968; commr. Presdl. Scholars Commn., Washington, 1982. Served to 1st lt. U.S. Army, 1945-47, 50-53. Recipient Disting. Service award S.D. Sch. Mines, Rapid City, 1972, Disting. Service award Cosmopolitan Internat., Rapid City, 1983; named Disting. Alumnus, Wyo. U., Laramie, 1982. Mem. Internat. Lime Assn. (pres. 1973-75), Nat. Lime Assn. (pres. 1973-75, Merit award 1973, bd. dirs.), VFW. Republican. Lutheran. Club: Cosmopolitan (Rapid City, S.D.). Lodges: Masons, Elks. Home: PO Box 440 Rapid City SD 57709 Office: Pete Lien & Sons Inc 190 and Deadwood Ave PO Box 440 Rapid City SD 57709

LIEN, CHARLES HOLM, quarrying company executive; b. Waubay, S.D., Feb. 18, 1925; s. Peter Calmer and LaRece Catherine (Holm) L.; m. Barbara Jean Vidal, Sept. 27, 1953; children—Julie, LaRece, Melanie, Peter, Elizabeth, Suzanne, Sandra, Christian, Stephanie. B.S. in Engring., U. Wyo., 1950; Ph.D. (hon.), S.D. Sch. of Miners, 1982. Ptnr. Pete Lien & Sons, Rapid City, S.D., 1945-50, 1952-60, pres., owner, 1960—. Served as lt. U.S. Army, 1943-45, PTO, served to capt., 1950-52. Republican. Lutheran. Home: Box 440 Rapid City SD 57709 Office: Pete Lien & Sons Inc 190 & Deadwood Ave PO Box 440 Rapid City SD 57709 *

LIEPHART, ROGER ARTHUR, police academy administrator, educator; b. Cleve., Jan. 2, 1943; s. Arthur W. and Dorotha (Lehman) L.; m. Kathleen Ann Sorozak, June 29, 1974. Cert. in law enforcement, Case Western Res. U., 1970; cert. in security mgmt., Cuyahoga County Community Coll., 1979; cert. law enforcement instr., Ohio Dept. Edn., 1979. Lic. pvt. investigator, Ohio; cert. instr. peace officer tng., Ohio. Chief adminstr., pres. Top Security Patrol, Inc., Cleve., 1969-82; comdr., owner Top Security Police Acad., Berea, Ohio, 1977—; chief adminstr., owner County Detective Agy., Brook Park, Ohio, 1984—; spl. police officer, Parma, Ohio. Pub., author quar. newsletter relating to security bus. V.p. Parma Heights (Ohio) Rep. Club, 1975-76. Mem. Ohio Assn. Pvt. Detective Agencies. Lodge: Masons. Home: 141 Meadow Dr Berea OH 44017 Office: Top Security Police Acad 6151 Smith Rd Brook Park OH 44142-2908

LIER, NANCY JEAN, medical educator, administrator; b. Breckenridge, Mich., Sept. 21, 1942; d. Joseph and Lucinda Martha (Feltman) Smolek; m. James William Lier, June 20, 1964; 1 child, Thomas James. BS, Madonna Coll., 1964; postgrad., U. Kans., 1976-77; MS in Sci. Adminstrn., Cen. Mich. U., 1985. Supr. immunohematology St. Mary's Hosp., Saginaw, Mich., 1964-66, 67-68, supr. bacteriology, 1968-69, dir. sch. med. tech., 1967—; staff technologist Flint (Mich.) Med. Lab., 1966-67; acad. appointments include Grand Valley State Coll., Allendale, Mich., 1967—, Cen. Mich. U., Mt. Pleasant, 1967—, Saginaw Valley State Coll., University Center, Mich., 1967—, Aquinas Coll., Grand Rapids, Mich., 1967—, Lake Superior State Coll., Sault Ste. Marie, Mich., 1967—, Nazareth Coll., Kalamazoo, 1967—, Madonna Coll., Livonia, Mich., 1967—, Mich. State U., East Lansing, 1967—, Mich. Tech. U., Houghton, 1967—. Vol. Boy Scouts Am., Frankenmuth, Mich., 1972-83. Mem. Am. Soc. Clin. Pathologists (cert. med. technologist), Am. Soc. Med. Technologists. Republican. Roman Catholic. Home: 9112 E Curtis Frankenmuth MI 48734 Office: St Mary's Hosp 830 S Jefferson Saginaw MI 48601

LIETZ, JEREMY JON, school system administrator; b. Milw., Oct. 4, 1933; s. John Norman and Dorothy (Bernice) L.; m. Cora Fernandez, Feb. 24, 1983; children: Cheryl, Brian, Angela, Andrew. BS, U. Wis., Milw., 1961, MS, 1971; EdD, Marquette U., 1980. Tchr. Milw. Pub. Schs., 1961-63, diagnostic counselor, 1968-71; sch. adminstr. 1971—; Tchr. Madison (Wis.) Pub. Schs., 1964-65; research assoc. U. Wis., Madison, 1965-67; instr. Marquette U., Milw., 1980-82; lectr. HEW Conf. on Reading, Greely, Colo., 1973, Nat. Assn. Elem. Sch. Principals Conf. on Reading, St. Louis, 1974, Assn. Wis. Schs. Adminstrs. Conf., Stevens Point, Wis., 1982, also various state and nat. orgns.; bd. dirs., cons. Ednl. Leadership Inst., Shorewood, Wis., 1980—; bd. dirs. Religious Edn. Program, Cath. Elem. East, Milw., 1985-86. Author: The Elementary School Principal's Role in Special Education, 1982; contbr. articles, chpts., tests, revs. to profl. jours. Served with U.S. Army, 1954-56, ETO. Recipient Cert. of Achievement award Nat. Assn. Elem. Sch. Prins., 1974. Mem. AAAS, Assn. Wis. Sch. Adminstrs. (state planning com. 1977-79), Adminstrs. and Suprs. Council (exec. bd. dirs. 1977-79), U. Wis. (Madison) Alumni Assn., Phi Delta Kappa. Home: 2205 N Summit Ave Milwaukee WI 53202 Office: Ednl Leadership Inst PO Box 11411 Shorewood WI 53211

LIEU, JOHN, physician; b. Hankow, China, Aug. 15, 1904; s. Fan Hou and Sing Ten (Chen) L.; M.D., St. John's U., Shanghai, China, 1926; D.T.M., Liverpool (Eng.) U., 1939; m. Dorothy A. Irwin, Aug. 31, 1974; children—John, Gladys. Came to U.S., 1959, naturalized, 1964. Supt. Works & Mine Hosp., Tayeh, Hupeh, China, 1928; asst. med. officer, Shanghai Mcpl. Council, 1929-36; doctor-in-charge Mcpl. Hosp., Shanghai, 1936-45; chief surgeon Soochow (China) Hosp., 1945-46; pvt. practice, Soochow, 1946-49, Columbus, Ohio, 1962—; chief surg. dept. Mcpl. Sixth Hosp., Shanghai, 1949-57; asst. port health officer, Hongkong; dir. Emerick Hosp., Columbus State Inst., 1961-65; mem. staff Grant Hosp., Columbus. Rockerfeller scholar, 1940. Fellow Royal Soc. Health, Eng.; mem. Am., Ohio med. assns., Acad. Medicine, AAAS, Ohio Acad. Sci. Presbyn. (deacon 1968). Home: 645 Neil Ave Columbus OH 43215 Office: 370 E Town St Columbus OH 43215

LIEVONEN, EVE ELIZABETH, hospital administrator, psychotherapist, social worker; b. Calumet, Mich., July 12, 1949; d. Thomas Edwin and Elizabeth Tyne (Laakso) L. BBA, Mich. Tech. U., 1971; MSW, U. Mich., 1981. Cert. social worker, Mich. Treas., fundraiser Ozone House, Inc., Ann Arbor, Mich., 1977-79; research asst. in social work U. Mich, Ann Arbor, 1980; resident in social work VA Med. Ctr., Ann Arbor, 1980-81; chief clin. social worker White Pine Psychiat. Ctr. Saginaw (Mich.) Community Hosp., 1981-86, program adminstr., 1986—; psychotherapist Cath. Family Services, Saginaw, 1984—, Insight Internat., Saginaw, 1985. VA Med. Ctr. grantee, 1980-81. Mem. Nat. Assn. Social Workers (cert.), Mich. Soc. Psychoanalytic Psychologists (assoc.). Avocations: skiing, golf, sailing, phys. fitness, classical music. Home: 5762 Ambassador #A8 Saginaw MI 48603 Office: White Pine Psychiat Ctr Saginaw Community Hosp 3340 Hospital Rd Saginaw MI 48603

LIFFICK, THOMAS FORD, psychiatrist, educator; b. Benton Harbor, Mich., June 16, 1951; s. Howard Ivan and Nina (Moore) L.; m. Barbara Jo Nix, Aug. 7, 1971; children: Emily Christine, Meg Ellen Roxie. BA, Wabash Coll., 1973; MD, Ind. U., 1977. Diplomate Am. Bd. Psychiatry and Neurology. Internship, then residency in psychiatry Ind. U. Hosp., 1977-80; practice medicine specializing in psychiatry Evansville, Ind., 1980—; clin. asst. prof. Ind. U. Sch. Medicine, Indpls., 1980-87; cons. psychiatrist Southwestern Ind. Mental Health Ctr., Inc., Evansville, Ind., 1980-86; med. dir. Southwestern Ind. Mental Health Ctr., Inc., Evansville, 1986—; clin. assoc. prof. psychiatry Ind. U. Sch. of Medicine, Indpls., 1987—; psychiatry sect. chief Deaconess Hosp., Evansville, 1985-86; chmn. dept. of psychiatry Welborn Meml. Bapt. Hosp., 1987—. Clin. assoc. Suicide Prevention Service, Indpls., 1974-75; bd. dirs. Deaf Social Service Agy. Mem. AMA (vol. interviewer), Am. Psychiat. Assn. (vol. interviewer), Ind. State Med. Assn., Ind. Psychiat. Soc., Vanderburgh County Med. Assn. Office: Southwest Ind Mental Health Ctr 415 Mulberry St Evansville IN 47713

LIGGETT, JAMES DAVID, minister; b. Decatur, Ind., June 4, 1946; s. James David and Almeda (Buuck) L.; m. Rosemary, Aug. 21, 1971; children: Elisabeth, Mike, Kathy, Marie, Becky, Daniel. BA, Northwestern U., 1968; M of Divinity, Wis. Luth. Sem., 1972. Minister St. Matthew's Luth. Ch., Stoddard, Wis., 1972-81, St. John's Luth. Ch., Sleepy Eye, Minn., 1981—; bd. chmn. Luther High Sch., Onalaska, Wis., 1973-81; dist. sec. Minn. Dist. of WELS, 1986—; pastoral advisor D.M.L.C. Aux., New Ulm, Minn., 1985—, O.W.L.S., 1985—. Bd. dirs. Housing and Redevel. Authority, Sleepy Eye, 1986—; coach Little League Baseball Assn., Sleepy Eye, 1986—. Lodge: Lions (community rep. 1983—). Avocations: golf, racquetball. Home and Office: 217 Walnut St SE Sleepy Eye MN 54658

LIGHT, TERRY RICHARD, orthopaedic hand surgeon; b. Chgo., June 22, 1947. BA, Yale U.; MD, Chgo. Med. Sch. Asst. prof. Yale U., New Haven, 1977-80; asst. prof. Loyola U., Maywood, Ill., 1980-82, assoc. prof., 1982—; attending surgeon Hines (Ill.) VA Hosp., 1980—, Shriner's Hosp., Chgo. and Tampa, Fla., 1981—, Foster McGaw Hosp., Maywood, Ill., 1981—; hand cons., mem. med. adv. bd. DuPage Easter Seal, Villa Park, Ill., 1980—. v.p. Frank Lloyd Wright Home and Studio Found., Oak Park, Ill., 1985—. Fellow Am. Coll. Surgeons, Am. Acad. Orthopaedic Surgeons; mem. Am. Soc. for Surgery of the Hand, Chgo. Soc. for Surgery of the Hand (sec. 1985—), Twenty-First Century Orthopaedic Assn. (pres. 1979—). Avocations: collecting American arts and crafts. Office: Loyola U Med Ctr 2160 S First Ave Maywood IL 60153

LIGHTFOOT, JEAN HARVEY, university special services administrator; b. Chgo., Nov. 29, 1935; d. Will Harvey and Emma (Carroll) Allen; m. Orlando Lightfoot, Dec. 21, 1961 (div. July 1969); 1 child, Jaronda. BA, Fisk U., 1957; MA, U. Chgo., 1969; PhD, Northwestern U., 1974. Dir. spl. services U. Ill., Chgo., 1983—; assoc. prof. City Colls., Chgo., 1969-83; cons. Prescriptive Learning, Chgo., 1974-77; dir. edn. C.E.T.A., Chgo., 1979-81, dir. Summer Youth Projects Dept. Human Services, Chgo., 1979-82, dir. Career Employment Edn. Ctr. Neighborhood Inst., Chgo., 1981-82; dir. Summer Humanities Projects Ill. Inst. Tech., Chgo., 1982-83. Author: (book) Multi Ethnic Literature for Experienced English Teacher, 1975, The Family in Western Civilization, 1979. Edn. dir. Neighborhood Inst., 1982.; edn. coordinator 4th Episc. Dist. Meth. Ch., Chgo., 1980-85; bd. dirs. Joyce Found. Grant to Train Experienced Tchrs., 1985-86; mem. Study Mission of U.S. to Israel, 1985. Ford Found. grantee, 1968-69, NIMH grantee, 1975, 79; Tng. Tchrs. of Tchrs. fellow, 1972-74. Delta Sigma Theta. Avocations: soloist, singer. Home: 6901 S Oglesby Ave Chicago IL 60649 Office: U Ill Box 4348 Chicago IL 60680

LIGHTFOOT, JIM, U.S. Congressman; b. Sioux City, Iowa; m. Nancy Lightfoot; children: Terri, Jamie, Allison, James. Mem. U.S. Ho. of Reps., 5th Iowa Dist., mem. coms. Pub. Works and Transp., Govt. Ops., Select Com. on Aging, Task Force on Rural Elderly, Mil. Reform Caucus; chmn. Rural Communities task force; participant numerous world confs. to promote agr. Farm editor Sta. KMA, Shenandoah, Iowa. Vol. safety counselor FAA. Served with U.S. Army. Recipient Outstanding Service award FAA. Mem. Farm Bur., U.S. Feed Grains Council, Soybean Assn., Nat. Agr. Mktg. Assn. (Agr. Spokesman of Yr. award), Iowa Park Producers Assn., Iowa Cattleman's Assn. (Broadcasting award). Office: 1609 Longworth Washington DC 20515

LIGHTFOOT, JOE DEAN, assistant to government official; b. St. Louis, Nov. 17, 1961; s. Howard Rex and Betty Jean (Wahlers) L. BS in Recreation, N.E. Mo. State U., 1984—. REgistered investment rep. Human resources mgr. Dolgin's, Inc., St. Louis, 1984-85; ops. mgr. CDI Corp., St. Louis, 1985; staff asst. U.S. senator Thomas F. Eagleton, St. Louis, 1985-87; investment rep. Edward D. Jones and Co., St. Louis, 1987—. Named One of Outstanding Young Men Am., 1985. Mem. Nat. Recreation and Park Assn. (trustee), Mo. Parks and Recreation Assn., Mo. Parks Assn., Mo. Conservation Fedn., Landmarks Assn. St. Louis. Home: 7614 Fleta Saint Louis MO 63123 Office: Edward D Jones And Co Saint Louis MO 63043

LIGHTFOOT, JOHN DALE, physician; b. Parsons, Kans., Dec. 15, 1953; s. James Edwin and Edith Leora (Reeder) L.; m. Jo Anne Soderstrom, June 12, 1976; children: James Christopher, Jeffrey David. BA, U. Kans., 1976, MD, 1979. Diplomate Am. Bd. Med. Examiners, Am. Bd. Family Practice. Resident in family practice Luth. Gen. Hosp., Park Ridge, Ill., 1979-82; practice medicine specializing in family practice Arlington Heights, Ill., 1982—; sec. dept. family practice Northwest Community Hosp., Arlington Heights, 1987—. Mem. AMA, Ill. State Med. Soc., Chgo. Med. Soc., Am. Acad. Family Physicians. Mem. Evang. Covenant Ch. Am. Lodge: Rotary. Avocations: amateur astronomy, model RR's, collecting U.S. coins and currency. Home: 434 Willington Schaumburg IL 60194 Office: Drs Hollett Ekeberg & Lightfoot 605 W Central Arlington Heights IL 60005

LILENFIELD, IRWIN, osteopath, surgeon; b. Boston, Oct. 24, 1931; s. Harry and Fannie (Moskowitz) L.; m. Ruth Darlene Peterson, May 27, 1963; children: Dena, Amy. BS, Bklyn. Coll. Pharmacy, 1953; DO, Kirksville Coll., 1963. Diplomate Am. Osteopathic Medicine. V.p. Canton South (Ohio) Med. Ctr. Inc., 1964—; dir. Ambulatory Care Ctr. Doctors Hosp., Massillion, Ohio, 1983—; med. dir. quality rev. Doctors Hosp., 1984—; asst. prof. family medicine Ohio U., Athens, 1976—; also mem. admissions policy com. Adv. bd. Am. Cancer Soc. Stark County; Vis. Nurse Soc. Stark County; examining physician Planned Parenthood Stark County, Canton, 1969-72; Canton Boxing Commn., 1974-80. Served with U.S. Army, 1954-56. Fellow Am. Coll. Gen. Practice, Ohio State Soc. Osteopathic Gen. Practice (pres. 1977-78); mem. Am. Acad. Med. Dirs., Am. Hosp. Assn. Avocations: photography, travel. Home: 921 22d St NE Canton OH 44714

LILEY, ARTHUR, company executive; b. London, Ont., Can.; m. Betty Liley; children—Brian, Katherine. B. Indsl. Mgmt. U. Toronto; A.M.P., Harvard Bus. Sch. Vice pres., gen. mgr. Parker-Hannifin Can. Ltd., Westinghouse Air Brake Co., Fluid Power Div., Lexington, Ky.; v.p., chief operating officer Bellows Internat., Akron, Ohio; v.p., gen. mgr. Weatherhead Co., Cleve.; pres. Spicer Axel div. Dana Corp., Ft. Wayne, Ind.; chmn. bd. START, Inc.; mem. adv. council IPFW, St. Francis Coll.; bd. dirs. Sumcorp. Mem. Greater Ft. Wayne C. of C. (dir.). Address: Dana Corp Spicer Axel Div PO Box 1209 Fort Wayne IN 46801

LILL, ROBERT L., food products company executive. Pres., chief operating officer Peter Eckrich and Sons, Inc., Ft. Wayne, Ind. Office: Peter Eckrich & Sons Inc 3515 Hobson Rd Fort Wayne IN 46805 *

LILLIE, JASPER IAN, osteopathic physician; b. Kinston, N.C., Mar. 25, 1943; s. Robert Edward Atlee and Evelyn Marie (Donlon) L. BS in Metall. Engring., U. Mich., 1969, postgrad in premed, 1969-70; DO, Mich. State U., 1973. Diplomate Am. Osteo. Bd. Gen. Practice. Intern Detroit Osteo. Hosp., 1973-74; gen. practice osteo. medicine Dickinson, Mich., 1974-75, Onekama, Mich., 1977-79, Lansing, Mich., 1979—; primary care physician Regional Health Care, Inc., Manistee, Mich., 1977-79; assoc. prof. family medicine Coll. Osteo. Medicine, Mich. State U., East Lansing, 1979—; mem. staff Mich. State U. Clin. Ctr., Lansing Gen. Hosp; past dir. Potterville Family Medicine Ctr., Eaton County, Mich.; mem. steering com. med. staff Mich. State u., 1983—; mem. vol. med. staff Mich. Spl. Olympics, 1981-84. Contbr. articles to profl. jours. Mem. implementation and rev. com. No. Mich. Health Sysytems Agy., 1978-79; bd. dirs. Manistee County chpt. ARC, 1978-79; mem. health adv. com. Manistee Title IV Health and Nutrition Project, 1978-79. Served to capt. M.C. USAF, 1975-77. Mich. Dept. Corrections grantee, 1979-81. Mem. Am. Osteo. Assn., Mich. Assn. Osteo. Physicians and SUrgeons, Inc., AAAS. Club: Mich. Union (Ann Arbor). Office: Mich State U B215 W Fee Hall East Lansing MI 48824

LILLIE, RICHARD HORACE, investor, real estate developer, retired surgeon; b. Milw., Feb. 3, 1918; s. Osville Richard and Sylvia Grace (Faber) L.; BS, Haverford Coll., 1939; M.D., Harvard U., 1943; M.S. in Surgery, U. Mich., 1950; m. Jane Louise Zwicky, Sept. 24, 1949; children—Richard Horace, Diane Louise. Intern, U. Mich. Hosp., Ann Arbor, 1943-44, resident, 1946-50; chief of surgery, Milw. Hosp., 1968-80; practice medicine specializing in surgery, Milw., 1951-81; clin. prof. emeritus Med. Coll. Wis.; pres. Lillie 18-94 Corp.; trustee Northwestern Mut. Life Ins. Co., The Bradley Trusts; dir. The Lynde and Harry Bradley Found.; investor, real estate developer, 1981—. Bd. dirs. emeritus Goodwill Industries. Served with M.C. AUS, 1944-46. Mem. Am. Bd. Surgery, A.C.S., Central Surg. Assn., AMA, Wis. Surg. Soc. Episcopalian. Clubs: Univ. of Milw., Milw. Yacht, Town. Contbr. articles to surg. jours. Home: 6500 N Lake Dr Milwaukee WI 53217 Office: 811 E Wisconsin Ave Milwaukee WI 53202

LILLO, LAWRENCE EDWARD, theatre director; b. Kinuso, Alta., Can., Sept. 20, 1946; s. Marvin Victor and Ruth Lenore (Hingly) L. BA with honors, St. Francis Xavier U., Antigonish, N.S., 1967. Actor Vancouver, B.C., 1968-70; dir., founder Tamahnous Theatre, Vancouver, 1970-81; freelance theatre dir. Can. and U.S., 1981-86; dir. Grand Theatre, London, Ont., Can., 1986—; mem. arts adv. panel Can. Council, 1984—. Dir. plays including Pal Joey, Top Girls (Jessie Richardson award 1983), Streetcar Named Desire, Blood Relations (Jessie Richardson award 1984). Recipient Arts award Can. Council, 1982. Mem. Can. Actors Equity Assn., Profl. Assn. Can. Theatres, Assn. Cultural Execs. Office: Grand Theatre, 471 Richmond St, London, ON Canada N6A 3E4

LILLY, ALFRED FORREST, JR., insurance company computer executive; b. Aruba, Netherlands Antilles, Dec. 4, 1938; s. Alfred Forrest and Bertha May (Walsh) L. (parents Am. citizens); A.A., Johnson County (Kan.) Community Coll., 1974; B.A., Rockhurst Coll., 1978; m. Loree Adele Plattner, Jan. 27, 1972; children—Diana Laurene, Jennifer Ann, Robert Kyle. Asst. mgr. computer programming Kansas City (Mo.) Life Ins. Co., 1965-67; supr. computer services, 1967-73, dir. computer ops., 1973-75, dir. computer planning, 1975-83, asst. v.p. computer planning, 1984-86, asst. v.p. tech. support systems, 1986—; owner, founder Flower Software Co. Mem. Citizens Assn., Kansas City, Mo., 1962. Served with Signal Corps, AUS, 1956-59; Korea, 1958-59. Mem. Univac Users Assn., Univac Sci. Exchange (sec. Kansas City chpt. 1976-77, vice chmn. 1977-78, guide, meta), Kansas City Jr. C. of C. Methodist. Home: 7701 Westgate Dr Lenexa KS 66216 Office: PO Box 139 Kansas City MO 64141

LILLY, JAMES KENNETH, publishing executive; b. Chgo., Oct. 8, 1946; s. Charles Lewis and Carol Ellen (Rowe) L.; m. Kathleen Bradley, June 17, 1978; children: Jacob Reed, Nicholas Rodgers. BA, U. Chgo., 1968, MA, 1969, MBA, 1980. Circulation mgr. Vance Pub. Co., Chgo., 1974-82, Crain Communications, Chgo., 1982-83; circulation dir. Lake Pub. Co., Libertyville, Ill., 1983-84, Delta Communications, Chgo., 1984-86, Standard Rate and Data Services, Wilmette, Ill., 1986—; instr. U. Chgo., 1986—; mem. bus. publ. com. Audit Bur. Circulation, Schaumburg, Ill., 1986—. Avocations: conservation work, reading, home repair. Office: Standard Rate and Data Service 3004 Glenview Rd Wilmette IL 60091

LILLY, PETER BYRON, coal company executive; b. Beckley, W.Va., Sept. 26, 1948; s. Wallace Byron and Mabel Elizabeth (Dodson) L.; m. Brenda Jean Ernst, June 20, 1970; children: Lauren E., Peter E. BS in Engring., U.S. Mil. Acad., 1970; MBA, Harvard U., 1977. Commd. 1st lt. U.S. Army, 1970, advanced through grades to capt., served in Vietnam, resigned, 1975; mgmt. cons. Emory Ayers Assocs., N.Y.C., 1977-80; mgr. maintenance Kerr-McGee Coal Corp., Okla. City, 1980-81, dir. adminstrn., 1981-83; gen. mgr. Galatia Mine Kerr-McGee Coal Corp., Galatia, Ill., 1983—. Decorated Bronze Star, Purple Heart; Cross of Gallantry (South Vietnam). Mem. Nat. Mine Rescue Assn. (bd. dirs. 1984—, pres. 1986—), Ill. Coal Assn. (bd. dirs. 1983—), Ill. Mining Inst. (exec. bd. 1985—), Ill. Geol. Survey (exec. bd.). Home: 1401 Nagel Dr Marion IL 62959 Office: Kerr-McGee Coal Corp Galatia Mine PO Box 727 Harrisburg IL 62946

LILLY, SAMUEL A., human resources consultant; b. Mattoon, Ill., Aug. 4, 1940; s. Orris James and Helen C. (Davis) L.; m. Nancy Carol Van Buskirk, Mar. 4, 1962; children: Scott Eden, Eric Alan, Catherine Michelle. BS in Edn., Eastern Ill. U., 1962, MA, 1964; PhD, Miami U., Oxford, Ohio, 1972. Exec. dir. Ill. Spl. Events Com., Chgo., 1971-72, Ill. Bicentennial Com., Chgo., 1971-75; mgr. Century 21, Plainfield, Ill., 1975; pres. Lilly Assocs., Inc., Downers Grove, Ill., 1980—; dir. Learning Resources Inst., Downers Grove, Ill., 1975—. Author: Cultural History of Revolutionary Charleston, S.C., 1763-1783, 1983. Dem. precinct committeman, Bolingbrook, Ill., 1978-79, 82-83. Fellow Miami U., Oxford, 1970-71. Mem. Profl. Speakers Ill. (bd. dirs. 1986, sec. 1978-80, pres.-elect 1987—, Mem. of Yr. 1986-87), Eastern Ill. U. Alumni Assn. (bd. dirs. 1980-83), Ill. State Hist. Soc. (pres. 1976-77). Mem. Reformed Ch. of Am. Lodge: Kiwanis (pres. Downers Grove 1976-77). Avocation: reading. Home: 108 Pamela Dr Bolingbrook IL 60439 Office: Learning Resources Inst 6912 Main St #11 Downers Grove IL 60516

LIM, SHUN PING, cardiologist; b. Singapore, Jan. 12, 1947; came to U.S., 1980; Tay Boh and Si Moi (Foo) L.; m. Christine Sock Kian Ng; 1 child, Corinne Xian-li. MBBS with honors, Monash U., Clayton, Australia, 1970, PhD, 1981; M in Medicine, Nat. U. Singapore, 1975; M, Royal Australasian Coll. Physicians, 1975. Research scholar Australian Nat. Health and Med. Research Council, Canberra, 1978-79; fellow in cardiology Michael Reese Hosp., Chgo., 1980-82; chief noninvasive cardiovascular imaging Cin. V.A.M.C., 1982-86; asst. prof. U. Cin., 1982-86; cardiologist Quain and Ramstad Clinic, Bismarck, N.D., 1986—; clin. asst. prof. U. N.D., Bismarck, 1986—. Contbr. articles to profl. jours. Fellow Royal Australian Coll. Physicians; mem. AAAS, Am. Fedn. Clin. Research, Am. Heart Assn. (grantee 1984-85), Ohio Med. Assn., N.Y. Acad. Scis. (life), Sixth Dist. Med. Soc., N.D. Med. Assn. Methodist. Office: Quain & Ramstad Clinic 222 N 7th St Bismarck ND 58501

LIM, SOON-SIK, chemical engineering educator; b. Kaesung, Korea, Mar. 2, 1944; came to U.S., 1973, permanent resident, 1982; s. Bo-Young and Young-Ae (Lee) L.; m. Jae-Yeon Yoo, Apr. 21, 1973; children—Steve, Anna. B.S., Yonsei U., Seoul, Korea, 1971; M.S., Wayne State U., 1975; Ph.D., 1981. Registered profl. engr., Ohio. Research engr. Pacific Chem. Co., Seoul, Korea, 1971-73; grad. research asst. Wayne State U., 1976-81; assoc. prof. chem. and metall. engring. dept. Youngstown State U., 1981—. Contbr. articles to profl. jours. Wayne State U. scholar, 1974, grad. fellow, 1977. Mem. Am. Inst. Chem. Engrs., Am. Chem. Soc., Am. Soc. Engring. Edn., Sigma Xi, Phi Lambda Upsilon. Home: 3166 Hummingbird Hill Dr Youngstown OH 44514-2801 Office: Chem and Metall Engring Dept Youngstown OH 44555

LIMBAUGH, STEPHEN NATHANIEL, judge; b. Cape Girardeau, Mo., Nov. 17, 1927; s. Rush Hudson and Bea (Seabaugh) L.; m. DeVaughn Anne Mesplay, Dec. 27, 1950; children—Stephen Nathaniel Jr., James Pennington, Andrew Thomas. B.A., S.E. Mo. State U., Cape Girardeau, 1950; J.D., U. Mo., Columbia, 1951. Bar: Mo. Prosecuting atty. Cape Girardeau County, Mo., 1954-58; judge U.S. Dist. Ct. for Eastern and Western Dists. of Mo., St. Louis, 1983—. Served with USN, 1945-46. Recipient Citation of Merit for Outstanding Achievement and Meritorious Service in Law, U. Mo., 1982. Fellow Am. Coll. Probate Counsel, Am. Bar Found.; mem. Mo. Bar (pres. 1982-83). Republican. Methodist. Office: US Dist Ct 1114 Market St Saint Louis MO 63101

LIN, CHIN-CHU, physician, educator; b. Taichung, Republic of China, Oct. 24, 1935; came to U.S., 1969; s. Kung Yen and Nung (Chiang) L.; m. Sue S. Hsu; children: Jim, John, Juliet. BS, Nat. Taiwan U., 1956, MD, 1961. Diplomate Am. Bd. Ob-Gyn., Am. Bd. Maternal-Fetal Medicine (bd. examiner 1986—). Research fellow SUNY Downstate Med. Ctr., N.Y.C., 1969-71; resident in ob-gyn Columbia U., N.Y.C., 1972-74; fellow in maternal-fetal medicine Albert Einstein Med. Coll., 1974-76; lectr., staff Nat. Taiwan U. Hosp., Taipei, 1966-69, 1971-72; staff, asst. prof. U. Chgo., 1976-80, assoc. prof., 1980-87, prof., 1987—; maternal-child health adv. com. Dept. of Health, Chgo., 1985—. Editor-in-Chief: Taiwan Tribune Medical Issues, 1986—, author: Interauterine Growth Retardation, 1984; contbr. over 60 articles to profl. jours.; reviewer for Jour. Obstetrics and Gynecology, Jour. Perinatal Medicine. Chmn. Taiwanese United Fund, 1984-85. Disting. Scholar Lectr. award Formosa Med. Assn., 1981, Keynote Speaker award Asia-Oceania Congress Perinatology, 1986. Mem. Am. Coll. Ob-Gyn (journal reviewer 1982, Purdue Frederick award 1978), Assn. Profs. Ob-Gyn, N.Am. Taiwanese Profs. Assn., N.Am. Taiwanese Med. Assn. (chmn. ednl. com. 1984-86), Cen. Assn. Ob-Gyn., Soc. Perinatal Obstetricians, Internat. Soc. Study of Hypertension in Pregnancy. Avocations: tennis, swimming. Home: 18 S Stough Hinsdale IL 60521 Office: U Chgo Dept Ob-Gyn 5841 S Maryland Ave Chicago IL 60637

LIN, EDWARD DANIEL, anesthesiologist; b. Apr. 19, 1953; s. Henry and Ruth Lin. BS magna cum laude, SUNY, Fredonia, 1973; DO, U. Osteopathic Medicine and Health Scis., Des Moines, 1980. Intern. in gen. medicine Millard Fillmore Hosp., Buffalo, 1980-81, emergency physician, 1981-82; resident in anesthesiology Yale-New Haven Med. Ctr., 1982-84; attending anesthesiologist Doctors Hosp., Massillon, Ohio, 1984—; dep. coroner Stark County, Ohio, 1984—; asst. prof. anesthesiology Ohio U. Coll. Osteopathic Medicine, Athens, 1984—; guest lectr. on spinal opiates and pain therapy nat. profl. meetings. Inventor Urethral Catheter Preventing Ascending Urinary Tract Infections,1980; patentee in field. Fellow (Woodburn) Roswell Park Meml. Inst., Buffalo, N.Y., 1974-76. Mem. Am. Soc. Anesthesiologists, Internat. Anesthesia Research Soc., Ohio Soc. Anesthesiologists, Am. Osteopathic Assn., Ohio State Med. Assn., Ohio Ostepathic Assn., Stark County Med. Soc. Avocations: gardening, boating, classical music. Home: 556 Roxbury Ave NW Massillon OH 44646 Office: Doctors Hosp 400 Austin Ave NW Massillon OH 44646

LIN, FU-SHAN, physician; b. Taiwan, China, Oct. 15, 1941; s. Chow-Lian and Pen (Ding) L.; came to U.S., 1971, naturalized, 1977; B.M., Taipei Med. Coll., 1967; m. Chung Chiou-Jin, Nov. 17, 1968; children—Ki-Hon, Wan-In, James Anthony, Robert John. Intern, Taipei City Hosp., Taiwan, 1966-67; resident in pediatric MacKay Meml. Hosp., Taiwan, 1968-71; rotating intern Barberton (Ohio) Citizen Hosp., 1971-72; resident in pediatrics Trumbull Meml. Hosp., Warren, Ohio, 1972-73, Akron (Ohio) Children's Hosp., 1973-74; physician The Windham (Ohio) Clinic, Inc., 1974-80, Robinson Meml. Hosp., Ravenna, Ohio, 1974—; practice medicine specializing in pediatrics and family practice, Ravenna, 1980—; instr. pediatrics Northeastern Ohio Univs. Coll. Medicine, 1980—. Served with China Air Force, 1967-68. Diplomate Am. Bd. Pediatrics, Am. Bd. Family Practice. Mem. AMA, Am. Acad. Pediatrics, Am. Acad. Family Physicians, Ohio Med. Assn., Portage County Med. Soc. Office: 6693 N Chestnut St Ravenna OH 44266

LIN, JAMES C., electrical and biomedical engineer, educator; b. Seoul, Korea, Dec. 29, 1942; m. Mei Fei, Mar. 21, 1970; children—Janet, Theodore, Erik. B.S., U. Wash., 1966, M.S., 1968, Ph.D., 1971. Asst. prof. U. Wash., Seattle, 1971-74; prof. Wayne State U., Detroit, 1974-80; prof. U. Ill.-Chgo., 1980—, head dept. bioengring., 1980—, dir. robotics and automation lab., 1982—; vis. prof. in Beijing, Rome, Taiwan Univs.; cons. Battelle Meml. Inst., Columbus, Ohio, 1973-75, SRI Internat., Palo Alto, Calif., 1978-79, Arthur D. Little, Inc., Cambridge, Mass., 1980-83, Ga. Tech. Research Inst., Atlanta, 1984—. Author: Microwave Auditory Effects and Applications, 1978, Biological Effects and Health Implications of Radiofrequency Radiation, 1987; also numerous papers. Panelist NSF Presdl. Young Investigator award com., Washington, 1984, mem. NIH diagnostic radiology and spl. study sect., 1981-85. Recipient IEEE Transaction Best Paper award, 1975; Nat. Research Services award, 1982. Fellow IEEE (bd. dirs., assoc. editor transactions on biomed. engring; guest editor transactions on microwave theory and techniques); sr. mem. Biomed. Engring. Soc., Robotics Internat.; mem. Bioelectromagnetics Soc. (charter), Sigma Xi, Phi Tau Phi (v.p.). Office: Univ of Ill at Chicago Dept of Bioengineering Box 4348 Chicago IL 60680

LINCOLN, MARY LYNDA EAGLE, publisher; b. High Point, N.C., Mar. 27, 1942; d. James Harvey and Eunice (Newsom) Eagle; m. Donald Livingston, Sept. 7, 1963 (div. 1982); children: Virginia Chtistine, Mary Margaret; m. W. Bruce Lincoln, Mar. 27, 1984. Student, Wake Forest U., 1960-63; BA, Washington U., St. Louis, 1963, MA, 1965, PhD, 1971. Instr. English Washington U., 1965-66; editor No. Ill. U. Press, DeKalb, 1971-77, dir., 1980—. Contbr. articles to scholarly jours. Office: No Ill U Press DeKalb IL 60115

LIND, ALLEN EDWARD, academic administrator; b. Chgo., Apr. 29, 1949; s. Herbert Elmer and Ruth Louise (Singleton) L.; m. Rebecca Lou Shank, Jan. 30, 1970 (Dec. 1980); m. Connie Marie Hannagan, Mar. 12, 1983. BS in Engring., BA in Econs., U. Ill., 1971. Mtkg. rep. IBM, Champaign, Ill., 1971-79; assoc. dir. info. systems devel. U. Ill., Urbana, 1979-83; asst. vice chancellor info. systems Bd. Govs. State Colls. and Univs., Springfield, Ill., 1983—; cons., Springfield, 1983—. V.p. Phi Gamma Delta Corp., Champaign, 1974-84; advisor Phi Gamma Delta Bd. Chpt. Advisors. Mem. Data Processing Mgmt. Assn. (bd. dirs. 1974-79), Ednl. Computing Network (mgr.), CAUSE. Baptist. Club: Island Bay Yacht (Springfield). Avocations: golf, sailing, waterskiing. Home: 3217 Forsyth Springfield IL 62704 Office: Bd Govs State Colls & Univs 2040 Hill Meadows Dr Springfield IL 62702

LIND, DAVID CLARE, dentist; b. Indpls., Oct. 5, 1938; s. Clifford Theron and Olga Louise (Nierste) L.; m. Jane Marie Thompson, Apr. 24, 1964; children: David Clare II, John Thompson. BS, Ind. U., 1960, DDS, 1963. Gen. practice dentistry Winchester, Ind., 1964—; bd. dirs. Winchester Indsl. Devel. Corp., L.D. Pankey Found., Key Biscayne, Fla. Fellow Internat. Coll. Dentists, Am. Endodontic Soc., Acad. Gen. Dentistry, Acad. Dentistry Internat., Pierre Fauchard Acad.; mem. ADA, Am. Analgesia Soc., Acad. Operative Dentistry, Ind. Dental Assn. (vice speaker of house 1973-78, speaker 1978-82), Ind. Acad. Gen. Dentistry (pres. 1986), Winchester C. of C. (pres.). Republican. Baptist. Club: Columbia. Lodge: Elks, Rotary. Avocation: classic automobiles. Home: 605 W Franklin Winchester IN 47394 Office: 1 Lind Dr Winchester IN 47394

LIND, MARILYN MARLENE, artist, writer, genealogist; b. New Ulm, Minn., Aug. 15, 1934; d. Fred S. and Emma L. (Steinke) Thiem; student pub. schs., Aitkin, Minn.; m. Charles R. Lind, Aug. 22, 1952; children—Michael, Bonnie, Vickie. Photographic asst., Aitkin, 1951-52; bookkeeper, office mgr. Rural Electric Assn., Aitkin, 1953-54; office mgr. N.E. Minn. Edn. Assn., Cloquet, 1970-77; pres. The Linden Tree, Cloquet, 1981-87; exhibited in one-woman shows: Lake Superior Art Center, Duluth, 1972, Old Towne Gallery, Duluth, 1983; group shows include: Lutheran Brotherhood Ctr. Gallery, Mpls., 1977, Centre Internationale d'Art Contemporain de Paris, 1983. Precinct chmn. Ind. Republicans Minn., 1976-77, co-chmn. Carlton County/Senate Dist. 14, 1977-80, vice-chmn. Carlton County, 1984-85, 8th Congl. Dist. Com., 1977-80, mem. Minn. state central com., 1977-82, county, dist. and state conv. del., 1976-87. Recipient Gallery awards, Duluth, 1972, Mpls., 1977. Mem. Geneal. Soc. Carlton County (founding mem., bd. dirs. 1977-87, v.p. 1980-81, sec. 1982-84, pres. 1986-88). Lutheran. Author: Christoph and August, A Dream and a Promise, 1981; various publs. in field of genealogy research, including: Beginning Genealogy, 1984, Using Maps and Aerial Photography in your Genealogical Research, 1984, Researching and Finding YOur German Heritage, 1986; Immigration, Migration and Settlement in the United States, 1985; Printing and Publishing Your Family History, 1986; Looking Backward to Sweden and The Lind-Bure Family 1000-1986, 1986. Home and Office: 1204 W Prospect St Cloquet MN 55720

LIND, ROBERT WAYNE, physics and electrical engineering educator; b. Ishpeming, Mich., Aug. 25, 1939; s. Victor Lind and Lillian Helen (Stohl) Scheibe; m. Eugenia Sauk, Jan. 25, 1964; children: Ingrid, Erik. BS in Physics, Mich. Tech. U., 1961; PhD, U. Pitts., 1970. Engr. Ford Motor Co., Dearborn, Mich., 1963-66; research assoc. Syracuse (N.Y.) U., 1970-72; sr. research assoc. Temple U., Phila., 1972-73; research assoc. Fla. State U., Tallahassee, 1973-74; from asst. to assoc. prof. physics, chmn. W.Va. Inst. Tech., Montgomery, 1974-78; prof. physics and elec. engring. U. Wis., Platteville, 1978—; referee Am. Jour. Physics, N.Y.C., 1970—, Gen. Relativity and Gravitation, Berne, Switzerland, 1972—. Contbr. articles to profl. jours. Fulbright scholar, 1961-62. Mem. AAAS, Internat. Soc. Gen. Relativity and Gravitation, Am. Assn., Physics Tchrs. Democrat. Avocations: traveling, camping, hiking, skiing, woodworking. Home: 1010 Moundview Ct Platteville WI 53818 Office: U Wis Dept Physics Platteville WI 53818

LINDA, GERALD, marketing consultant; b. Boston, Nov. 25, 1946; s. Edward Linda and Anne Beatrice (Lipofsky) Coburn; m. Claudia W., Sept. 24, 1978; children—Jonathan Daniel Rezny, Jessica Simmone. B.S. in Bus. Adminstrn., Northeastern U., 1969, M.B.A., 1971; postgrad., U. Mich., 1971-74. Mem. faculty mktg. U. Ky., Lexington, 1975-77; assoc. research dir., ptnr. Tatham-Laird & Kudner, Chgo., 1977-80; v.p., research dir. HCM, Chgo., 1980-82, v.p., regional dir. mktg. planning and research, 1982-83, corp. sr. v.p., 1983-85; pres. Gerald Linda & Assoc., mktg. cons., 1986—. Editorial reviewer Jour. Advt., Current Issues and Research in Advt. Contbr. articles to profl. jours. Mem. Am. Mktg. Assn., Assn. for Consumer Research, Am. Soc. Tng. and Devel. Home: 2100 Fir St Glenview IL 60025 Office: Gerald Linda & Assocs 300 S Riverside Plaza Suite 660 Chicago IL 60606

LINDAHL, CAROL ANN, communications executive; b. Mpls., Oct. 30, 1947; d. Werner Leo and Wilma Ruth (Edberg) Schultz; m. Gregory John Lindahl, Jan. 20, 1973; children: Elizabeth, Allison. BA, Hamline U., 1969. Technical writer Honeywell, Mpls., 1969-72; technical editor EMR Computer, Mpls., 1972-73; publications editor Hamline U., St. Paul, 1973-81, pub. relations dir., 1981-85; adv./ sales promotion mgr. Cardiac Pacemakers, St. Paul, 1985-86, corp. communications mgr., 1986—. trustee Hamline U., St. Paul, 1971-73; bd. dirs. Eastside Neighborhood Services, Mpls., 1978-84. Mem. Internat. Assn. Bus. Communicators (Pubs. award), Women in Communications (Pubs. award), Sch. Communications Assn. (Pubs. award), Pub. Relations Soc. Am., Am. Mgmt. Assn. Methodist. Home: 2940 Merrill Roseville MN 55113 Office: Cardiac Pacemaker Inc 4100 N Hamline Saint Paul MN 55112

LINDBERG, CHARLES DAVID, lawyer; b. Moline, Ill., Sept. 11, 1928; s. Victor Samuel and Alice Christine (Johnson) L.; m. Marian J. Wagner, June 14, 1953; children: Christine, Breta, John, Eric. A.B., Augustana Coll., Rock Island, Ill., 1950; LL.B., Yale U., 1953. Bar: Ohio 1953. Since practiced in Cin.; assoc. firm Taft, Stettinius & Hollister, 1953-61, mng. ptnr., 1961—; dir. Cin. Reds Profl. Baseball Team, 1969-81, Cin. Bengals Profl. Football Team, Arga Co., Dayton-Walther Corp., Citation-Walther Corp.; corp. sec., dir. Taft Broadcasting Co.; sec. Hanna-Barbera Prodns., Inc. Bd. dirs.: Nat. Law Jour. Sec. Good Samaritan Hosp., Cin.; bd. dirs. Augustana Coll., 1978-87, sec., 1981-82, vice chmn., 1982—, chmn., 1983-86 ; pres. Cin. Bd. Edn., 1971, 74, Zion Lutheran Ch., Cin., 1966-69; chmn. policy com. Hamilton County Republican Party, 1981—; trustee Greater Cin. Center Econ. Edn., 1976—, pres. 1986— ; chmn. Better Neighborhood Sch. Com., Cin., 1975-82; chmn. law firm div. Cin. United Appeal, 1976; chmn. local govt. com. Cin. C. of C., 1977; trustee Pub. Library of Cin. and Hamilton County, 1982—. Mem. ABA, Ohio Bar Assn., Cin. Bar Assn., Greater Cin. C. of C. (trustee 1985—). Clubs: Queen City, Commonwealth, Cin. Country. Lodge: Optimists (pres. Queen City club 1987). Office: 1800 First National Bank Ctr Cincinnati OH 45202

LINDBERG, EDWIN (TED) HOWARD, clinical social worker; b. Hanover, N.H., Sept. 10, 1948; s. Edwin H. and Virginia (Aldrich) L.; m. Marilyn Jean Terrill, July 17, 1978; children: Shawn, Danielle. BA, Wesleyan U., 1970; MS in Edn., So. Ill. U., 1973; MSW, U. Mich., 1983. Cert. social worker. Clin. social worker Family and Children Services, Kalamazoo, Mich., 1983—. Mem. Nat. Assn. Social Workers. Avocations: carpentry, sports, horticulture. Office: Family and Children Services 1608 Lake St Kalamazoo MI 49001

LINDBERG, ELAYNE VERNA, art gallery administrator; b. Little Sauk, Minn., Apr. 27, 1926; d. Leslie and Velma (Breighhaupt) Averill; m. Russell H. Lindberg, July 26, 1941; children: Gary, Bonnie Lindberg Carlson. Ed. U. Minn. Cert. appraiser fine art; cert. graphoanalyst. With Dayton's Dept. Store, Mpls., 1965-71; owner, chief exec. officer Elayne Galleries, Inc., Mpls., 1969—; appraiser and restorer paintings. Author: The Power of Positive Handwriting, 1987; co-author, composer verse, sacred music, choir arrangements, including A Broken Heart I Gave, There Are Times. Mem. Am. Soc. Appraisers (cert.), World Assn. Document Examiners (charter), Internat. Soc. Appraisers, New Eng. Appraisers Assn., Cert. Antique and Art Appraisers, Fine Art Trade Guild (London), Am. Biog. Inst., West Suburban C. of C., Francis Hook Scholarship Fund. Club: Calhoun Beach. Lodge: Soroptomists (Mpls.). Pioneer in handwriting analysis of questioned documents. Home: 2950 Dean Blvd Minneapolis MN 55416 Office: 6111 Excelsior Blvd Saint Louis Park MN 55416

LINDBERG, FRANCIS LAURENCE, JR., holding company executive; b. Jacksonville, Fla., Mar. 13, 1948; s. Francis Laurence and Mildred Hortense (Parrish) L.; m. Anne Louise Stearns, Dec. 29, 1972 (div.); 1 child, Kristen Anne; m. Alexis Jean Parker, Nov. 12, 1983. Student Eckerd Coll., 1965-66; BA, Jacksonville U., 1969; MBA, U. North Fla., 1976. CPA, Ga. Actuarial asst. Gulf Life Ins. Co., Jacksonville, 1967-73; asst. actuary Am. Heritage Life, Jacksonville, 1973-77; asst. sec.-treas., prin. acctg. officer Atlantic Am. Corp., Atlanta, 1977-84; assoc. v.p. fin. Security Benefit Group, Topeka, 1985-86; exec. v.p., chief fin. officer Am. Way Group of Cos., Southfield, Mich., 1986—; bd. dirs. affiliated cos.; treas., bd. dirs., bd. advisors Good News Communications, Inc. Mem. Nat. Assn. Accts. (Membership Achievement award 1983), Am. Inst. CPA's, Ga. Soc. CPA's, Acctng. Research Assn. Republican. Episcopalian. Office: Am Way Group 19900 W Nine Mile Rd Southfield MI 48075

LINDBERG, GARY LEROY, university researcher; b. Moorhead, Minn., Sept. 15, 1955; s. Kermit Charles and Ann Marie (Schipper) L.; m. Margaret Elizabeth Olson, May 3, 1980; children: Amanda, Eric. BS, N.D. State U., 1980, MS in Animal Sci., 1983. Research asst. N.D. State U., Fargo, 1980-83; research assoc. Iowa State U., Ames, 1983—; cons. in field. Mem. Am. Dairy Sci. Assn., Am. Soc. Animal Sci., Sigma Xi, Tau Kappa Epsilon, Gamma Sigma Delta. Avocations: fishing, golfing, auto mechanics. Home: 1009 Kellogg Ave Ames IA 50010 Office: Iowa State U Nutritional Physiology Group 313 Kildee Hall Ames IA 50011

LINDBERG, MICHAEL RICHARD, mortgage banker; b. Daytona Beach, Fla., Jan. 29, 1949; s. Floyd Victor and Dorothy Lucille (Schuler) L.; m. Melody Diane Ketel, Dec. 19, 1974; children: Michael Erik, Rachel Christina. BS, Ferris State Coll., 1971. Mgr. Consolidated Apt. Corp., Mt. Pleasant, Mich., 1971-73; staff auditor Nat. Bank Detroit, 1973-76, asst. mgr. loan servicing, 1976-78; asst. treas. NBD Mortgage Co., Troy, Mich., 1978-84, mgr. adminstrn., 1984—. Treas. Pleasant Ridge (Mich.) Found., 1984, 85; mem. Founders Soc. Detroit Inst. of Arts; vol. Childerns Hosp. Mich., Detroit, 1979—. Mem. Mortgage Bankers Assn., Edison Inst. Republican. Roman Catholic. Club: Economic. Avocations: reading, computer, photography, antiques, travel. Home: 81 Oakdale Blvd Pleasant Ridge MI 48069 Office: NBD Mortgage Co 900 Tower Dr Troy MI 48098

LINDBLADE, DAVID ALAN, marketing executive; b. Davenport, Iowa, Aug. 2, 1938; s. Lester E. and Merle O. (Meyers) L.; m. Ivene L. Stoneking, Sept. 10, 1960; children: Kimberly A., Jeffery S., Christopher L. BA, Wheaton Coll., 1960; MBA, U. Iowa, 1967. Supt. prodn. Internatl. Harvester, Rock Island, Ill., 1966-68, mgr. prodn. ops., 1968-71; mgr. mfg. Internatl. Harvester, Louisville, 1971-75; mgr. purchasing Internatl. Harvester, Chgo., 1975-81, v.p., OSD, 1981-82; pres. Dalco Mktg. Services, Naperville, Ill., 1982—. Elected alderman Geneseo (Ill.) City Council, 1965. Served to capt. U.S. Army, 1960-62. Named Boss of Yr., Internat. Harvester, 1974. Mem. Soc. Automotive Engrs. (off-road motorized tech. com.), Mfrs. and Agts. Nat. Assn. Republican. Avocations: skiing, fishing, boating, sailing, hunting. Home and Office: 216 Durham Ct Naperville IL 60540

LINDBLOM, LANCE EDMUND, foundation executive, lawyer; b. Chgo., June 17, 1948; s. Edmund John and Barbara Jean (Sahlberg) L.; m. Marjorie Press, June 13, 1971; children: Derek Press, Ian Press. BA in Govt. magna cum laude, Harvard U., 1970; M of Pub. Affairs, Princeton U., 1972; JD, U. Chgo., 1978. Bar: Ill. 1978, U.S. Dist. Ct. (no. dist.) Ill. 1979, U.S. Ct. Appeals (7th cir.) 1980. Econ. and program analyst Ill. Econ. and Fiscal Commn., Ill. Gen. Assembly, 1972-73; sr. program analyst, budget examiner Ill. Bur. Budget, Exec. Office of Gov., Springfield, 1973-75, chief spl. projects unit, 1975-78; assoc, Jenner & Block, Chgo, 1978-79, 79-80; dep. dir. Mayor's Office of Budget and Mgmt., City of Chgo., 1979-80; exec. dir. J. Roderick MacArthur Found., Niles, Ill., 1980-84, pres., 1984—; sec. adv. bd. J. Roderick MacArthur Enterprises, Niles, 1981-84; bd. dirs. Donors Forum, Chgo., 1985—. Named Young Leader, Atlantik-Brucke and Am. Council on Germany, 1982. Mem. ABA (vice chmn. com. on internat. human rights of individual rights and responsibility sect., presdl. commn. inter-Am. affairs, bd. dirs. Article 19), Chgo. Council on Fgn. Relations (fgn. affairs com.). Avocations: reading; films; travel. Office: J Roderick MacArthur Found 9333 N Milwaukee Ave Niles IL 60648

LINDELL, ANDREA REGINA, college dean, registered nurse; b. Warren, Pa., Aug., 21, 1943; d. Andrew D. and Irene M. (Fabry) Lefik; m. Warner E. Lindell, May 7, 1966; children—Jennifer I., Jason M. B.S., Villa Maria Coll., 1970; M.S.N. Catholic U., 1975, D.N.Sc., 1975; diploma R.N., St. Vincent's Hosp., Erie, Pa. Instr. St. Vincent Hosp. Sch. Nursing, 1964-66; dir. Rouse Hosp., Youngsville, Pa., 1966-69; supr. Vis. Nurses Assn., Warren, Pa., 1969-70; dir. grad. program Cath. U., Washington, 1975-77; chmn., assoc. dean U. N.H., Durham, 1977-81; dean, prof. Oakland U., Rochester, Mich., 1981—; cons. Moorehead U., Ky., 1983. Editor; Jour. Profl. Nursing, 1985; contbr. articles to profl. jours. Mem. sch. bd. Strafford Sch. Dist., N.H., 1977-80; Gov.'s Blue Ribbon Commn. Direct Health Policies, Concord, N.H., 1979-81; vice chmn. New England Commn. Higher Edn. in Nursing, 1977-81; mem. Mich. Assn. Colls. Nursing, 1981—. Named Outstanding Young Woman Am., 1980. Mem. Nat. League Nursing, Am. Assn. Colls. Nursing, Sigma Theta Tau. Democrat. Roman Catholic. Avocations: water skiing; roller skating; reading; fishing; camping; Office: Oakland U 428 O Dowd Hall Rochester MI 48309

LINDEMEYER, MICHAEL ROBERT, optometrist, church musician; b. Balt., Apr. 29, 1957; s. Robert William and Alice Elizabeth (Moose) L.; m. Marilyn Ann Lueth, Aug. 25, 1984; 1 stepson, Matthew Todd. Student U. Md., 1975-78; B.S., So. Coll. Optometry, 1980, O.D., 1982. Lic. optometrist, Wis., N.Y., Mo. Optometrist, Pearle Vision Ctr., Milw., 1982-87, Drs. Roye and Assocs., 1987— . Organist, Beautiful Savior Luth. Ch., Memphis, 1980-82, Pentecost Luth. Ch., Milw., 1982—. Republican. Avocation: jogging; swimming; bowling; reading; music. Home: 10543 Beacon Hill Ct E Franklin WI 53132 Office: Drs Roy and Assocs 4850 S 74th St Greenfield WI 53220

LINDEN, DENNIS ALAN, accountant; b. Cleve., Apr. 19, 1957; s. Harold S. and Ruthe (Safier) L.; m. Karen Lavon, Aug. 12, 1979; 1 child, Amy. BSBA cum laude, Ohio State U., 1979. CPA, Ohio. Staff acct. Baden & Linden, CPA's, Cleve., 1979—, ptnr., 1985—. Treas. The Agnon Sch., Beachwood, Ohio, 1983-86, trustee, 1987—; vol. various orgns., Cleve. Mem. Am. Inst. CPA's, Ohio Soc. CPA's, Zeta Beta Tau (trustee Nu chpt. 1981—). Lodge: Masons (line officer 1983—). Avocations: sports, photography, video, family activities. Office: Baden & Linden CPA's 1430 Leader Bldg Cleveland OH 44114

LINDENBAUM, JON MICHAEL, marketing executive; b. North Muskegon, Mich., Mar. 22, 1962; s. Donald Mathias and Grace Evelyn (Wetherall) L. BA in Econs., U. Notre Dame, 1984. Dist. sales rep. Harris/Lanier, Grand Rapids, Mich., 1984-85; regional sales and mktg. mgr. Computer Aided Planning, Inc., Grand Rapids, 1985—; cons. facility mgmt. and design automation. Mem. MG Sports Car Club. Roman Catholic. Lodge: Elks. Avocations: sports car racing and restoration, skiing, sailing, theater. Home: 823 Buys Rd Muskegon MI 49445 Office: Computer Aided Planning Inc 169 Monroe Grand Rapids MI 49503

LINDER, LIONEL, newspaper editor; b. Ventura, Calif., Feb. 8, 1932; s. Dewey and Helen (Buie) L.; m. Ann L. Lum, Jan. 23, 1965; children: Lesley, Laura. BA, U. N.Mex., 1954; MS in Journalism, Northwestern U., 1960. Reporter Albuquerque Tribune, 1956-58; night editor Hollister Publs., Wilmette, Ill., 1958-59; copy editor Chgo. Daily News, 1959-61; from feature editor to news editor to asst. mng. editor Nat. Observer, Silver Spring, Md., 1961-77; asst., mng. editor Detroit News, 1977-78, mng. editor, 1978-83, exec. editor, 1981-83, editor, v.p., 1983-86, editor, 1986—; Trustee St. Clair Ambulatory Care Corps., bd. dirs. Robinwood Clinic. Served with U.S. Army, 1954-56. Mem. Am. Soc. Newspaper Editors, AP Mng. Editors. Methodist. Clubs: Grosse Pointe (Mich.) Yacht; Detroit. Home: 541 Lincoln St Grosse Pointe MI 48230 Office: The Detroit News 615 Lafayette St Detroit MI 48231

LINDGREN, RICHARD THOMAS, automation equipment company executive; b. Two Harbors, Minn., Apr. 5, 1927; s. Arvid John and Agnes (Sellman) L.; m. Lois Irene Nelson, June 17, 1950; children: Douglas John, Danna Carol. Student, Virginia (Minn.) Jr. Coll., 1947; B.B.A., U. Minn., 1949; M.B.A., Harvard U., 1951-53; LL.D., Buena Vista Coll., 1970. With Ford Motor Co., Dearborn, Mich., 1953-71; dir. mktg. ops. Ford Motor Co., 1970-71; group v.p. Allis-Chalmers Co., Milw., 1971-75; exec. v.p. Mead Corp., Dayton, Ohio, 1975; pres. Koehring Co., Milw., 1975-81; chmn. Koehring Co., 1976-81; chmn. bd. ROTEK Inc., until 1981; group v.p. Dominion Bridge Co. Ltd., Montreal, Que., Can., 1980-81, AMCA Internat. Corp., Hanover, N.H., 1980-81; pres., chief exec. officer Cross & Trecker, 1982—; dir. Outboard Marine Corp., Waukegan; vice chmn. dist. export council U.S. Dept. Commerce, 1974-75. Trustee Buena Vista Coll., 1962-70; bd. dirs. Curtis R. Froedert Meml. Hosp., Milw., Detroit br. Fed. Res. Bd., 1977-86. Served with AUS, 1945-46, ETO. Mem. Soc. Automotive Engrs., Constrn. Industry Mfrs. Assn. (dir.), Internat. Rd. Fedn. (dir. 1978-81). Lutheran. Office: PO Box 925 Bloomfield Hills MI 48013

LINDHOLM, CARL EDWARD, electronics co. exec.; b. N.Y.C., Mar. 8, 1929; s. Carl Edward and Elsie (Krone) L.; m. Louise MacDonald; children—Jeffrey, Julia, Claire. B.S., Webb Inst., N.Y.C., 1950; M.S. in Indsl. Engring, N.Y. U., 1952, M.B.A., 1954. With Motorola Inc., 1967—; v.p., dir. corp. staff, then sr. v.p., dir. corp. staff Motorola Inc., Schaumburg, Ill., 1974-75; sr. v.p., gen. mgr. automotive products div. Motorola Inc., 1975-78, sr. v.p., gen. mgr. automotive and indsl. electronics group, 1978-85, exec. v.p. internat. ops., 1985—. Served with USNR, 1955-58. Address: Motorola Inc 1303 E Algonquin Rd Schaumburg IL 60196

LINDHOLM, SARA JEAN, real estate developer; b. Montevideo, Uruguay, Feb. 15, 1941; s. James Thoburn and Mary Gray (Harris) L.; m. James Milton Lindholm, June 15, 1962 (div. Apr. 1983); children: Erika Gray, Joren Anthony. BA, Oberlin Coll., 1962; student, Univ. Chgo., 1966-70. Teaching fellow Oberlin Shansi Meml., Madurai, Ind., 1962-66; mortgage loan officer South Shore Bank, Chgo., 1977-79; pres. City Lands Corp., Chgo., 1980—. Co-author: Am. Jour. Sociology, 1977. Mem. fin. panel Housing Abondonment Task Force, Chgo., 1984—, Gov.'s Task Force State Housing Plan, 1985—, adv. bd. City Open Lands Project, 1986—; bd. dirs. Community Mental Health Council, 1986—. Fellow Leadership Greater Chgo., 1985—. Mem. Chgo. Women in Housing, Phi Beta Kappa. Office: City Land Corp 1950 East 71st St Chicago IL 60649

LINDHOLM, TENNY ALBERT, military officer; b. Ketchikan, Alaska, June 16, 1948; s. Henry Myrle and Beverly Marie (Anderson) L.; m. Lenita Kay Hauber, June 28, 1970; 1 child, Lucas. BS aero. engring., USAF Acad., 1970; MBA, So. Ill. U., 1974; MS in Ops. Research, Air Force Inst. Tech., 1982; postgrad., Ohio State U., 1985—. Commd. 2d lt. USAF, 1970, advanced through grades to lt. col.; pilot, instr. 3d Military aircraft Squadron, Dover, Del., 1971-76; comdr., tng. instr., flight examiner 56th Military Airlift Squadron, Altus, Okla., 1976-80; dir. test and evaluation aero. systems div. Wright Patterson AFB, Dayton, Ohio, 1982-85. Mem. Air Force Assn., Tau Beta Pi. Republican. Presbyterian. Avocation: jogging. Home: 915 Cascade Dr Dayton OH 45431 Office: AFIT/CI Wright Patterson AFB Dayton OH 45433

LINDHOLM, WILLIAM CHARLES, clergyman; b. Perry, Iowa, Mar. 20, 1932; s. Lester Leander and Elizabeth (Winegar) L.; m. Patricia Ann Schneider, Feb. 14, 1953; children: Jonell, Jana, William Jr. BA, Augustana Coll., 1954; MDiv, Luth. Sch. Theology, Chgo., 1958. Ordained to ministry Luth. Ch., 1958. Pastor Grace Luth. Ch., Oscoda, Mich., 1958-70, Hope Luth. Ch., East Tawas, Mich., 1958-70, Holy Cross Luth. Ch., Livonia, Mich., 1970—; chmn. Nat. Com. for Amish Religious Freedom, 1967—. Editor: Michigan Synod News, 1970—. Bd. dirs. Carthage Coll., Kenosha, Wis., 1985—. Lutheran. Home: 15343 Susanna Circle Livonia MI 48154 Office: Holy Cross Luth Ch 30650 Six Mile Rd Livonia MI 48152

LINDLEY, GENE RICHARD, truck stop executive; b. Millville, Ind., Jan. 31, 1938; s. William Nash and Edith Lucile (Waltz) L.; m. Alice Marie Smith, July 10, 1960; children: Douglas Nash, Susan Marie, Brenda Ann, Matthew Walter. BS in Agrl. Econs., Purdue U., 1960. Mgr. credit sales Standard Oil Ohio, Cleve., 1960-65; pres., gen. mgr. State Line Truck Stop, New Paris, Ohio, 1965—; bd. dirs. Preble County Banl, Eaton, Ohio. Mem. Eaton City Sch. Bd., 1981-85; precinct committeeman Eaton Reps., 1986. Served to 1st lt. U.S. Army, 1961-69. Mem. Nat. Assn. Truckstop Operators (chmn. bd. dirs. 1984-85). Presbyterian. Lodge: Rotary (fellow). Home: 101 Sunrise Circle Eaton OH 45320 Office: State Line Truck Stop Inc 6701 National Rd E New Paris OH 45347

LINDNER, CARL HENRY, financial holding company executive; b. Dayton, Ohio, Apr. 22, 1919; s. Carl Henry L. and Clara (Serrer) Linder; m. Edith Bailey, Dec. 31, 1953; children: Carl Henry III, Stephen Craig, Keith Edward. Co-founder United Dairy Farmers, 1940; pres. Am. Fin. Corp., Cin., 1959-84, chmn., 1959—, chief exec. officer, 1984—; chmn. United Brands Co., N.Y.C., 1984—, chief exec. officer, chmn. exec. com., 1984—; chmn. Penn Central Corp., Greenwich, Conn., 1983—; also dir.; dir. Mission Ins. bd. advs. Bus. Adminstrn. Coll., U. Cin. Republican. Baptist. Office: The Penn Cen Corp 500 E Putnam Ave Greenwich CT 06836 Other Address: American Financial Corp 1 E Fourth St Cincinnati OH 45202 *

LINDO-DRUSCH, NANCY JO, physician; b. St. Louis, May 19, 1954; d. Elmer Woodrow and Mary Alice (Jablonski) Lindo; m. Joseph Howard Drusch, June 4, 1977; children: Monica, Gregory. AB in Chemistry and

Psychology, Barat Coll., 1976; MD, St. Louis U., 1980. Resident in family practice St. Elizabeth Med. Ctr., Dayton, Ohio, 1980-83; commd. capt. USAF, Wurtsmith AFB, Mich., 1983, advanced through grades to maj., 1986; staff physician USAF Hosp., Wurtsmith AFB, Mich., 1983-86, Nicolet Clinic, Neenah, Wis., 1986—; pvt. practice medicine Neenah, 1986—. Fellow Am. Acad. Family Practice. Roman Catholic. Home: 524 E North St Appleton WI 54911 Office: 878 Airport Rd Menasha WI 54952

LINDQUIST, MARK DAVID, manufacturing executive; b. Alexandria, Minn., June 21, 1950; s. Vern Merle and Joan Ottelia (O'Hotto) L.; m. Kathryn Elizabeth Soergel, Sept. 12, 1981. BBS and Mech. Engring., Saint Cloud (Minn.) U., 1975; MBA, Western Mich. U., Kalamazoo, 1978; MS in Mgmt., Western Mich. U., 1981. Asst. mgr. Lindquist Equipment, Alexandria, Minn.; mgr. parts and service Skuza Equipment, Saint Cloud, 1969-75; gen. mgr. Kalamazoo Engring., Grand Rapids, 1975-81; chief exec. officer, founder LinTek Inc., Mpls., 1981-83; chief exec. officer, gen. mgr. Rapidline Mfg., Grand Rapids, 1983-87; v.p. Behler-Young Co., Grand Rapids, 1987—. Served to sgt. U.S. Army, 1970-72. Mem. Soc. Mfg. Engrs., Am. Prodn. and Internat. Control Soc., Internat. Assn. Quality Control, Air Distbn. Inst. Republican. Roman Catholic. Economics. Office: Rapid Line Mfg 4900 Clyde Park Grand Rapids MI 49509

LINDSETH, RICHARD EMIL, orthopaedic surgeon; b. Denver, Apr. 3, 1935; s. Emil Victor and Audrey Madera (Yeo) L.; m. Marilyn Martha Miller, July 7, 1959; children: Erik Lars, Ellen Sue. BA, Dartmouth Coll., 1957; MD, Harvard U., 1960. Diplomate Am. Bd. Orthopaedic Surgery. Intern, then resident in surgery SUNY, Syracuse, 1960-62; resident in orthopaedic surgery Ind. U., Indpls., 1964-67, prof. orthopaedic surgery, 1975—, acting chmn. dept. orthopaedic surgery, 1984-86; pres. Assoc. Orthopaedic Surgeons, Inc., Indpls., 1983-86. Contbr. articles to profl. jours. Fellow ACS, Am. Acad. Orthopaedic Surgeons, Am. Acad. Pediatrics, Scoliosis Research Soc.; mem. Pediatric Orthopaedic Soc. N.Am. (pres. 1986-87). Methodist. Office: Ind Sch Medicine 702 Barnhill Dr Indianapolis IN 46223

LINDSETH, VIRGINIA MACDONALD, educational psychologist; b. Ithaca, N.Y., Apr. 17, 1935; d. John Winchester and Mary Elizabeth (Browne) MacDonald; m. Jon Andrew Lindseth; children—Andrew, Steven, Karen, Peter. B.A., Cornell U., 1956; M.A., John Carroll U., 1975; Ph.D., Case Western Res. U., 1980, MBA, 1987. Cert. sch. counselor, Ohio. Dean of students Hathaway Brown Sch., Shaker Heights, Ohio, 1970-75, head Upper Sch., 1974-75; dir. studies Univ. Sch. Upper Sch., Hunting Valley, Ohio, 1975-79; asst. dir., dir. studies Lower Sch., Shaker Heights, 1979-86, ednl. cons., 1986—; dir. Ctr. for Profl. Devel. John Carroll U., University Heights, Ohio, 1986-87, adj. prof. 1984—; pres. bd. trustees Resource: Careers, Cleve., 1987—. Trustee Ursuline Coll., Pepper Pike, Ohio, 1986—. Mem. Am. Psychol. Assn. Republican. Roman Catholic.

LINDSEY, JAMES MARTIN, dentist; b. Grand Rapids, Mich., Mar. 19, 1952; s. Joe Arthur and Loralyn Lee (Anway) L.; m. Vicki Lynn Wolfcale Bugher, June 15, 1984; 1 child, Grant A. Bugher. BS in Microbiology, Ind. U., Bloomington, 1974; DDS, Ind. U., Indpls., 1979. Practice dentistry specializing in cosmetic dentistry Kokomo, Ind., 1979—. Mem. ADA, Ind. Dental Assn., Wabash Valley Dental Soc. (sec., treas. 1982—), Howard County Dental Soc. (treas. 1987—). Lodge: Elks. Avocations: travel, scuba. Home: 2516 Locust Ln Kokomo IN 46902-2954 Office: 3415 S Lafountain Suite I Kokomo IN 46902-3891

LINDSLEY, HERBERT PIPER, life insurance agent; b. Wichita, Kans., Dec. 16, 1913; s. Herbert Kitchel and Jessie McMahon (Piper) L.; A.B., U. Wichita, 1935; M.B.A., U. Pa., 1937; m. Barbara Irene Benzinger, Dec. 31, 1938; childen—Herbert Benzinger, Barbara Kitchel, Thomas Roland. Agt., Northwestern Mut. Ins. Co., N.Y.C., 1937-38; v.p., ednl. dir. Farmers & Bankers Life, Wichita, 1939-48; gen. agt. Occidental Life Calif., Wichita, 1948—; dir. Electric Furnace Co., Salem, Ohio; chmn. bd. Motel Devel. Corp., Wichita. Mem. Wichita Bd. Edn., 1951-59, pres., 1955; mem. Wichita City Commn., 1959-63, mayor, 1961-62. Republican. Congregationalist. Home and Office: 230 N Terrace Dr Wichita KS 67208

LINDSTROM, DAVID AUGUST, physician; b. Alma, Mich., June 19, 1954; s. Edward Oscar and Doris Lillian (Nelson) L.; m. Carol Ann Smith, July 23, 1977; children: Jennifer, Erik, Bret. BS in Chemistry with honors, U. mich., 1976; MD, Mich. State U., 1980. Resident Toledo and St. Vincent Hosps., 1980-82, chief resident, 1982-83; attending physician Emergency Ctr. Toledo Hosp., 1983—; clin. assoc. prof. surgery Med. Coll. Ohio, Toledo, 1984—. Fellow Am. Coll. Emergency Physicians; mem. AMA, Disaster Action Com. (bd. dirs. 1985—). Republican. Baptist. Club: Sylvania Country. Home: 5005 Cartagena Dr Toledo OH 43623 Office: Emergency Ctr Toledo Hosp 2142 N Cove Blvd Toledo OH 43623

LINE-ESKER, CATHY KAYE, training and communications coordinator; b. Peoria, Ill., July 26, 1957; d. Donald Leo and Mary Alice (Seckinger) Line; m. Daniel Richard Esker, Oct. 4, 1986. Student, Olney (Ill.) Cen. Coll., 1975-76; BA, tchrs. cert., Eastern Ill. U., 1979; postgrad., So. Ill. U., 1987—. Graphic artist, photographer Crossroads Press, Effingham, Ill., 1979-81, coordinator tng. and communications, 1981—; instr. Lakeland Coll., Mattoon, Ill., 1986—. Editor company mag. The Tear Sheet, 1981—. Unit chmn. Am. Cancer Soc., Effingham, 1984-86; adult advisor Young Dems., Effingham, 1980. Fellow NEA, Ill. Edn. Assn., Internat. Assn. Bus. Communicators, Bus. and Profl. Womens Club (Ill. Young Careerist 1985), Am. Soc. Tng. and Devel. Roman Catholic. Club: Toastmasters. Avocations: tennis, reading, painting, drawing, photograph.

LING, SUMY H.C., design engineer; b. Tainan, Taiwan, Jan. 24, 1938; d. Yuan H. Wu and Jean Y. Lee; m. Cheng C. Ling, Sept. 27, 1963; children—Katherine A., Enid A. B.S., Cheng-Kung U., Taiwan, 1960; M.S., U. Cin., 1965. Design engr. Hazelet & Erdal, Cin., 1965-73; design engr. Stacey Mfg. Co., Cin., 1973-74, mgr. design engring., 1974-77, chief engr., 1977—. Mem. Archtl. Engring. Soc. Taiwan. Buddhist. Patentee in field. Home: 7831 Shadowhill Wy Cincinnati OH 45242 Office: 259 Township Ave Cincinnati OH 45216

LINGARAJ, BANGALORE PUTTARANGASWAMY, business administrator educator; b. Bangalore, India, Jan. 29, 1940; came to U.S., 1962; d. Nagappa and Thayamma (Puttappa) Puttarangaswamy; m. Sudha Thammiah Lingaraj, Aug. 15, 1971; children: Arpana, Trupti. B Engring., U. Mysore, Bangalore, 1961; MS, Kans. State U., 1964; PhD, U. Pitts., 1973. Quality control engr. Xerox Corp., Rochester, N.Y., 1964-66; asst. prof. mgmt. Marquette U., Milw., 1970-74; prof. prodns. and ops. mgmt. Indian Inst. Mgmt., Bangalore, 1974-78; assoc. prof. mgmt. Washburn U., Topeka, 1978-81; prof. mgmt. U. Tenn., Chattanooga, 1981-83; prof. bus. Ind. U., Ft. Wayne, 1983—. Contbr. articles to profl. jours. Mem. Am. Prodn. and Inventory Control Soc., Inst. Mgmt. Scis., Decision Scis. Inst., Midwest Bus. Adminstrn. Assn. (chmn. program track 1986-87). Office: Ind U 2101 E Coliseum Blvd Fort Wayne IN 46805

LINGENFELTER, JAMES ARTHUR, commercial artist; b. Duluth, Minn., Dec. 26, 1961; s. Rodney John and Marlene Ann (Fratzke) L.; m. Catherine Maura (Srnec) L. Grad., Mpls. Art Instrn. Sch., 1980; BA in Art, Hamline U., St. Paul, 1984. Editorial cartoonist Brookings (S.D.) Daily Register, 1980-81; comml. illustrator Gold Country, Inc., Mpls., 1978—; comml. illustrator, keyliner Twin Cities Reader, Mpls., 1984-85; comml. artist Custom Screen Printing, Inc., Golden Valley, Minn., 1985-86; asst. art dir. Ling, Inc., Mpls., 1986—; editorial cartoonist The Hamline Oracle, St. Paul, 1983-84. Editorial cartoonist Hamline Vegetarian Food Service, 1984, Best Editorial Cartoon Minn. Coll. Newspapers, 1984; artist/designer collegiate sportswear "Iowa Hawkeyes Rosebowl" 1984. Roman Catholic. Club: Northwest Racquet and Swim. Avocations: basketball, cartooning, reading and movies, water skiing, golf and tennis. Home: 4301 W 110th St Bloomington MN 55439

LINGL, FRIEDRICH ALBERT, psychiatrist; b. Munich, Germany, Apr. 4, 1927; came to U.S., 1957, naturalized, 1962; s. Friedrich Hugo and Marie Luise (Lindner) L.; m. Leonore E. Trautner, Nov. 15, 1955; children—Herbert F., Angelika M. M.D., Ludwig-Maxim U., Munich, 1952. Diplomate: Am. Bd. Psychiatry and Neurology. Intern Edward W. Sparrow Hosp., 1957-58; resident internal medicine City Hosp., Augsburg, Germany, 1953-54; resident psychiatry Columbus (Ohio) State Hosp., 1958-61; supt. Hawthornden State Hosp., Northfield, Ohio, 1963-66; dir. Cleve. Psychiat. Inst., 1966-72; pvt. practice 1972—; med. dir. Windsor Hosp., 1976—; asst. clin. prof. Case Western Res. U., 1970—. Contbr. articles to med. jours. Fellow Am. Psychiat. Assn.; mem. A.M.A., Ohio Med. Assn., Ohio Psychiat. Assn., Am. Assn. Psychiat. Adminstrs., Gerontology Soc., Cleve. Psychiat. Soc. Address: 40 Farwood Dr Chagrin Falls OH 44022 Office: 6801 Mayfield Rd Cleveland OH 44124

LINK, PAUL ANTHONY, data processing executive; b. Pitts., Sept. 18, 1951; s. Roy Arthur and Delores Caroline (Heintz) L. Student, Ohio U., 1969-73. Computer operator Balt. Paint & Chem., 1975-77; programmer analyst Dutch Boy div. Balt. Paint & Chem., 1977-79; asst. ops. mgr. Dutch Boy, 1979-81; info. systems analyst Sherwin Williams Co., Cleve., 1981-84, systems analyst, 1984-85, adminstr. tech. systems, 1985—. Republican. Roman Catholic. Avocations: skiing, bicycling, bowling, tennis, golf. Home: 15410 Sprague Rd Middleburg Heights OH 44130 Office: Sherwin Williams Co 101 Prospect Ave NW Cleveland OH 44115

LINMAN, LAWRENCE L., restaurant owner; b. Chgo., Dec. 12, 1948; s. Miloe Linman and Dorothy McCastle; m. Judith Peterson, Aug. 18, 1973; children: Emilly, Carl, Karin. BS, Ill. State U., 1971, postgrad., 1972. With McDonald's Restaurants, Ill., 1966—; owner, operator McDonald's Restaurants, Kankakee, Bradley and Bourbonnais, Ill.; bd. dirs. Meadowville Bank, Kankakee; nat. operators adv. bd. McDonald's Restaurnats, 1986—. Del. Lt. Ryans Conf. on Small Bus., Springfield, Ill., 1985-86, White House Conf. on Small Bus., Washington, 1986; Indian guide YMCA, 1983—; bd. dirs. ARC, Kankakee, 1983-86. Am. Cancer Soc., Bourbonnais, 1985, Kankakee Conv. of Tourism. Recipient Archie award Hamburger U., 1973, Ronald award McDonalds, 1981, Community Service award Kankakee Jaycees, 1986. Mem. Bradley Assn. Commerce and Industry, McDonald's Operators of Chicagoland and Northwest Ind. (bd. dirs.), Kankakee C. of C., Bourbonnais C. of C. (bd. dirs.), Am. Bus. Club (pres. 1973). Lutheran. Lodge: Kiwanis. Avocations: polit. campaign pins, coin collecting, gardening, family. Office: McDonalds 575 Main St NW Bourbonnais IL 60914

LINNE, RALPH WILLIAM, construction executive; b. Covington, Ky., Nov. 16, 1951; s. William Arthur and Virginia May (Dougherty) L.; m. Deborah Faye Williams, Sept. 14, 1974; children: Sharon Marie, Aaron William. Assoc. in Applied Sci., U. Cin., 1971, BS in Constrn. Mgmt., 1975. Draftsman/designer G.F. Roth & Ptnrs., AIA, Cin., 1971-74; office engr. Kaiser Engrs., Moscow, Ohio, 1974-78; adminstrv. engr. Kaiser Engrs., North Perry, Ohio, 1978-80; operational audit engr. Kaiser Engrs., North Perry, 1980-85; supr. facilities services Illuminating Co., North Perry, 1985—. Mem. Bd. Mental Health, Lake County, Ohiom 1987—. McMaster scholar, 1969. Mem. Internat. Facility Mgmt. Assn., Nat. Inst. for the Cert. of Engring. Technicians. Republican. Baptist. Home: 8385 Findley Dr Mentor OH 44060 Office: Illuminating Co PO Box 97 Perry OH 44081

LINNENBOM, ROBERT WILLIAM, publishing executive, writer, consultant; b. St. Louis, May 22, 1934; s. Harry Joseph and Muriel Evelyn (Crump) L.; m. Rose Marie Prindle, July 18, 1952; children: Deborah, Robert, Terry Ann, Gregory, Kevin, Harry. Student, U. of Ill., Urbana, 1952-54; BS in Transp. Law, Pacific Northwestern U., 1965; cert. transp. law, U. Mo., 1974. Traffic mgr. Wagner Electric Corp., St. Louis, 1970-77; v.p. transp. Freedom Freightways, St. Louis, 1977-80; dir. transp. McQuay-Norris Co., St. Louis, 1980-81; cons., v.p. ABC Transport, St. Louis, 1981-83; pres. Logic Research Assocs., St. Louis, 1983—; pres. Midwest Sch. Traffic and Transp., St. Louis, 1970-79, bd. dirs. Author: Toto Too! 1979; Kings and Queens and the Rest of Us, 1982; (textbook) Transportation Law, 1980; (manual) Doing Business with the Peoples' Republic of China, 1986; contbr. articles on freight tariffs. Mem. Middlewest Shipper/Motor Carrier Conf. (chmn. classification, rate and tariff com. 1976-77), Soc. Packaging and Handling Engrs., Nat. Def. Exec. Res. Fed. Emergency Mgmt. Agy., St. Louis C. of C. Republican. Roman Catholic. Avocations: writing children's stories, photography, gourmet cooking. Home: 6250 Famous Ave Saint Louis MO 63139

LINSENMANN, WILLIAM MICHAEL, lawyer, former insurance company executive; b. Cleve., Mar. 25, 1919; s. Gus and Genevieve (King) L.; m. Darla Genevieve Carlson, June 11, 1942; children—Karen Kay, Darla Robin. A.B., Kent State U., 1941; J.D. magna cum laude, Cleve. Marshall Law Sch., 1950. Adjuster Liberty Mut. Ins. Co., Boston, 1940-41; adjuster Gen. Accident Ins. Co., Cleve., 1945-50; adjuster Ohio Casualty Ins. Co., Cleve., 1950-52, supr., 1950-53; claim mgr. Ohio Casualty Ins. Co., Warren, Ohio, 1953-68; claim mgr. Ohio Casualty Ins. Co., Cin., 1968-69, mgr., 1968-69; asst. v.p. Ohio Casualty Ins. Co., Hamilton, Ohio, 1969-71, v.p., 1971-80, sr. v.p., 1980-84, ret., 1984. Trustee Mercy Hosp., Hamilton. Served to 1st lt. U.S. Army, 1941-45. Mem. Ohio Bar Assn., Assn. Ins. Council, Ohio Trial Lawyers Assn., Def. Research Assn. Club: Hamilton City. Lodge: Elks. Avocations: golf, travel, reading. Home: 628 Sanders Dr Hamilton OH 45013 Office: Ohio Casualty Ins Co 3d and High Sts Hamilton OH 45011

LINSLEY, GLEN ALBERT, optometrist; b. Battle Creek, Mich., Aug. 13, 1952; s. Bernard O. and Barbara Jean (Smurr) L.; m. Donna Lee Bateman, Feb. 19, 1983; children; Chad Elston, Megan Beth. AS, Kellogg Community Coll., 1972; OD, Ohio State U., 1976. Pvt. practice optometry Mason, Mich., 1976—; optometrist State of Mich., Jackson, 1977-79; assoc. staff instr. Ferris State Coll., Jackson, 1979—; missionary optometrist, Mombasa, Kenya, 1981; dir. Lighthouse for Christ Eye Centre, Glendale, Calif., 1986—; pub. speaker. Advisor Mason Fellowship Christian Athletics, 1979-82; assoc. staff Mason Campus Life, 1982—; officer Mich. H.S. Wrestling, 1978-85; mem. exec. com. Lugham County Rep. Party. Emil H. Arnold scholar Mich. Optometric Assn., 1972; named one of Outstanding Young Men Am. 1982, 87. Mem. Am. Optometric Assn., Cen. Mich. Optometric Assn. (pres. 1985-86), Epsilon Psi Epsilon. Lodge: Kiwanis (local pres. 1980-81). Home: 604 Hall Blvd Mason MI 48854 Office: 109 E Maple St Mason MI 48854

LINSON, WILLIAM EDGAR, JR., hospital public relations executive; b. Hammond, Ind., Nov. 11, 1939; s. William E. and Dora Myrlie (Hutson) L.; children—Thaddeus Michael, Lori Melissa; m. Sue Howard Lencke, Oct. 24, 1981. B.S., Ind. State U., 1965. Sports editor Robinson (Ill.) Daily News, 1965-66; sports info. dir. Ind. State U., Terre Haute, 1966-71; asst. sports info. dir. Purdue U., West Lafayette, Ind., 1971-73; asst. commr. Mid.-Am. Athletic Conf., Columbus, Ohio, 1973-79; pub. relations dir. Grant Hosp., Columbus, 1979-83; pub. info. dir. Cox Med. Ctr., Springfield, Mo., 1983—; pub. relations cons. Health Mgmt. Services, Inc., 1980-83. Mem. Am. Soc. Hosp. Pub. Relations, Mo. Soc. Hosp. Pub. Relations, Springfield Advt. Club (1st v.p.). Methodist. Office: 1423 N Jefferson St Springfield MO 65802

LINT, LOUIS RAYMOND, lawyer; b. Grand Rapids, Mich., July 9, 1946; s. Angus R. and Maudie May (Shurlow) L.; m. Mary Jane Achterhoff, Aug. 14, 1981; 1 child, Joshua L. BS, Cen. Mich. U., 1969; JD, New Eng. Sch. Law, 1974. Bar: Mich. 1975. Sole practice Muskegon, Mich., 1975—. Mem. ABA, Mich. Bar Assn., Muskegon County Bar Assn. Republican. Clubs: Century (Muskegon); Press (Grand Rapids). Office: Muskegon Bankruptcy Clinic 1065 4th St Suite A PO Box 747 Muskegon MI 49443-0747

LINTNER, BARBARA JEAN, librarian; b. Decatur, Ill., June 1, 1942; d. Kenneth Robert and Margaret Rose (Westervelt) Bauman; m. Michael Alan Lintner, Apr. 17, 1966 (dec. 1973); children—Jeffrey Clements, Natalie Elaine. B.A., Millikin U., 1964; M.L.S., U. Ill., 1965. Extramural librarian U. Ill., Urbana, 1965-66; ref. librarian Wilmington Inst. Free Pub. Library, Del., 1966-67; children's librarian Allerton Pub. Library, Monticello, Ill., 1976-83, dir., 1984—. Pres., Piatt County Unit Am. Cancer Soc., 1976-77; leader Girl Scouts U.S.A., 1979—; troop com. mem. Boy Scouts Am., Monticello, 1980-83. Mem. ALA, Ill. Library Assn. (Davis Cup award 1981), Lincoln Trails Librarians Assn. (pres. 1981-82). Republican. Presbyterian. Club: Homemakers Extension. Home: 814 Robert Webb Monticello IL 61856 Office: Allerton Pub Library 201 N State St Monticello IL 61856

LINTON, IRMA ALBERTA, librarian, media professional, retired; b. Indpls., Sept. 13, 1914; d. Charles Henry and Ella Theresa (Griffin) Frazier; m. Charles Edward Linton, June 11, 1949; 1 son, Thomas Edward; 1 dau., Lois Ellen Stevens. B.S., Butler U., 1936, library cert., 1969; A.M., Ind. U., 1946. Elem. tchr. Indpls. Pub. Schs., 1937-51, 61-69, library services, 1961—, media profl. Montessori Sch. #55, #58, 1984-86. Leader Jr. Great Books, Montessori Sch. #91, 1986—; reviewer children's books Criterion newspaper, Sr. Advocate newspaper. Mem. Hoosier Storytelling Guild, Delta Kappa Gamma. Republican. Roman Catholic. Home: 936 N Rochester Ave Indianapolis IN 46222

LINTON, RICHARD ARTHUR, accountant; b. Eau Claire, Wis., July 2, 1958; s. George Arthur and Roscelia Kathryn (Hagen) L.; m. ChrisAnn Renee Glick, Nov. 3, 1984; 1 child, Rory Alan. BBA in Acctg., U. Wis., Eau Claire, 1980. CPA, Wis. Mgr. Hawkins, Ash, Baptie & Co., La Crosse, Wis., 1980-87; controller Midwest Bottle Gas Co., La Crosse, Wis., 1987—. Mem. Am. Inst. CPA's, Wis. Inst. CPA's, Nat. Assn. Accts. (treas., v.p. 1981-83). Republican. Lutheran. Lodge: Rotary (treas. Onalaska, Wis. chpt. 1986—). Avocations: softball, bowling. Office: Midwest Bottle Gas Co Hwy 157 La Crosse WI 54601

LINVILLE, JUDITH ANN, writer; b. Tulsa, Jan. 21, 1943; d. James A. and Frances E. (McElyea) Burch; m. Norman D. Linville, Aug. 24, 1968. BA, U. Ark., 1965, MA, 1966. Cert. secondary tchr. English, Ark. Instr. Pittsburg (Kans.) State U., 1966-70; library asst. Pub. Library Denver, 1971-73; freelance writer, St. Louis, 1973-75; features editor Jour. Newspapers, St. Louis, 1975-80; asst. editor Decor mag., St. Louis, 1980-82; sr. info. specialist U. Mo., St. Louis, 1982-85, mgr. news services, 1985-87, lectr. Cert. in Writing program, 1987—; vis. lectr., 1983-85. Author: We Have New Life To Share, 1979; contbr. feature articles to newspapers, 1974—, articles to mags., 1980—. Mem. Women in Communications, Phi Beta Kappa. Mem. Christian Ch. (Disciples of Christ), YWCA of Met. St. Louis (cert. of Leadership, 1986). Office: Univ Mo English Dept 8001 Natural Bridge Rd Saint Louis MO 63121

LINZ, ANTHONY JAMES, osteopathic physician, consultant; b. Sandusky, Ohio, June 16, 1948; s. Anthony Joseph and Margaret Jane (Ballah) Linz; m. Kathleen Ann Kovach, Aug. 18, 1973; children—Anthony Scott, Sara Elizabeth. B.S., Bowling Green State U., 1971; D.O., Des Moines Coll. Osteo. Medicine and Surgery, 1974. Diplomate Nat. Bd. Osteo. Examiners; bd. cert., diplomate Am. Osteo. Bd. Internal Medicine, Internal Medicine and Med. Diseases of Chest. Intern, Brentwood Hosp., Cleve., 1974-75, resident in internal medicine, 1975-78; subsplty. fellow in pulmonary diseases Riverside Meth. Hosp., Columbus, Ohio, 1978-80; med. dir. pulmonary services Sandusky Meml. Hosp., 1980-85; med. dir. cardio-pulmonary services, Firelands Community Hosp., 1985—; also cons. pulmonary diseases and internal medicine, active staff sect. internal medicine, chmn. dept. medicine, head div. pulmonary medicine; cons. staff dept. medicine Good Samaritan Hosp., 1982-85; also sect. internal medicine specializing pulmonary diseases; cons. pulmonary and internal medicine Providence Hosp., Sandusky, Willard Area Hosp.; clin. prof. internal medicine Ohio U. Coll. Osteo. Medicine; mem. respiratory therapy adv. bd. Firelands Campus, Bowling Green State U., 1983—; med. dir. Respiratory Therapy program., Bowling Green State U.; 39 Contbr. article on early detection lung cancer to profl. jour. Water safety instr. ARC; med. dir. Camp Superkid Asthma Camp. Recipient Sr. award in pharmacology Coll. Osteo. Medicine and Surgery, 1974; adj. assoc. prof. of applied scis., Bowling Green State U. Fellow Am. Coll. Chest Physicians; mem. Am. Osteo. Assn., Ohio Osteo. Assn. (past. pres., past v.p., past. sec.-treas. 5th dist. acad.), Am. Coll. Osteo. Internists, Am. Heart Assn., Am. Thoracic Soc., Ohio Thoracic Soc., Am. Lung Assn. (med. adv. bd. chmn., exec. bd. dirs., bd. dirs. Ohio's So. Shore sect.), Nat. Assn. Med. Dirs. Respiratory Care, Ohio Soc. Respiratory Therapy (med. adviser/dir.), Alpha Epsilon Delta, Beta Beta Beta, Atlas, Pi Kappa Alpha, Atlas Med. Fraternity. Roman Catholic.

LINZ, VINCENT ARTHUR, periodontist, television producer; b. Cin., July 20, 1953; s. Vincent Harold Linz and Virginia Zettel. BS magna cum laude, U. Cin., 1974; DDS, Ohio State U., 1977, MS, 1979. Diplomate Am. Bd. Periodontology; cert. laser surgeon, tissue integrated prosthesis surgeon. Pvt. practice periodontics Cin., 1979—; producer Big Bang Productions, Cin., 1983—; cons. Music Video Productions, Cins., 1985—, U. Cin., 1986—. Producer, dir. (video art) Sloppy Seconds, 1984 (Philo award 1984), Raw Meat, 1985 (Philo award 1985). Recipient first place award Warner/Amex Cable TV, Cin., 1985. Mem. ADA, Am. Bd. Periodontology, Am. Acad. Periodontology, Midwest Soc. Periodontology, Ohio Acad. Periodontists, Western Hills Dental Study Club. Roman Catholic. Avocations: sailing, scuba diving. Home: 5615 Wynnburne Ave Cincinnati OH 45238 Office: 4966 Glenway Cincinnati OH 45238

LIPCHIK, ELLIOT O., radiologist, radiology educator; b. Bklyn., Dec. 30, 1930; s. Samuel W. and Ida (Gutterman) L.; m. Eva Steuer, Aug. 30, 1953; children: Randolph, Brian, Andrea. BA, NYU, 1951; MD, U. Basel, Switzerland, 1958. Internship and residency Kings County Hosp., Bklyn., 1958-62; prof. radiology U. Rochester, N.Y., 1962-76; staff radiologist Mt. Sinai Hosp., Milw., 1976-85; prof. radiology, chief angiology sect. dept. radiology Med. Coll. Wis., Milw., 1985—. Contbr. articles on radiology to profl. jours. Fellow Am. Heart Assn., N.Am. Soc. Cardiovascular Radiology (chartered); mem. Am. RO Ray Soc., Assn. Univ. Radiologists, Radiol. Soc. N.Am., Milw. RO Ray Soc. (program chmn.). Home: 2641 N Lake Dr Milwaukee WI 53211 Office: Milw County Med Complex 8700 W Wisconsin Ave Milwaukee WI 53226

LIPFORD, ALBERT, savings and loan executive; b. Welch, W.Va., Oct. 10, 1943; s. Herman Leon and Lillian Beatrice (Edwards) L.; m. Clara Bell Davis, July 21, 1967; children: Teletha, Dan, Patricia, Dennis. Student, E. Tech., Cleve., 1958-61, Cuyahoga Community Coll., 1967-70. From computer ops. mgr. to systems officer Union Commerce Bank, Cleve., 1965-83; asst. v.p. Huntington Nat. Bank, Cleve., 1983-84, Cardinal Fed. Savs., Cleve., 1984—. Served with USAF, 1961-65. Baptist. Home: 1995 Ridehill Rd Cleveland OH 44121 Office: Cardinal Fed Savs 333 Euclid Ave Cleveland OH 44114

LIPIN, S. BARRY, business executive, investor; b. Chgo., Oct. 7, 1920; s. Bernard and Mary (Schrier) L.; m. Priscilla Richter, Oct. 7, 1952; m. 2d, Rachel Kucheck, Nov. 21, 1976. Student Ill. Inst. Tech., 1939-41, DePaul U. Commerce, 1943-44, DePaul Coll. Law, 1944-45. Founder/owner new and used automobile sales co., Chgo., 1945—, U.S. Auto Leasing Co., Chgo., 1954; chmn., chief exec. officer Lipin Enterprises Inc. (U.S. Auto Leasing Co., Lipin Rent-A-Car, Automobile Corp. N.Am., Rifco Auto Leasing Co., Modern Cars Inc.), Chgo., 1982—; chmn., chief exec. officer Presdl. Car Rental, Ltd. (and predecessors), Chgo., 1986—, Presdl. Limousine, Ltd., 1986—; pres., chief exec. officer Paul-Sey Investment Corp. Bd. dirs. Am. Hearing Research Found., Lipin Found., Michael Reese Hosp. Med. Research Inst. Council, Jewish Vocat. Service. Recipient State of Israel Bonds award, 1980; Automotive Industry-Leasing Div. Man of Yr. award; Spirit of Life award City of Hope, 1983, Humanitarian award Holocaust Meml. Found. Ill., 1987. Mem. Am. Automotive Leasing Assn., Automotive and Allied Industries Council (pres.), Chgo. Assn. Commerce and Industry, Ill. C. of C., Phi Kappa Tau. Clubs: Variety; Canyon Country (Palm Springs, Calif.); Covenant, Mid-America, Executive. Office: 1800 N Ashland Ave Chicago IL 60622

LIPINSKI, WILLIAM OLIVER, congressman; b. Chgo., Dec. 22, 1937; s. Oliver and Madeline (Collins) L.; m. Rose Marie Lapinski, Aug. 29, 1962; children: Laura, Dan. Student, Loras Coll., Dubuque, Iowa, 1957-58. Various positions to area supr. Chgo. Parks, 1958-75; alderman Chgo. City Council, 1975-83; mem. 98th-100th Congresses from 5th Dist. Ill., 1983—. Democratic ward committeeman, Chgo., 1975—; del. Dem. Nat. Midterm Conv., 1974, Dem. Nat. Conv., 1976, 84. Named Man of Yr. Chgo. Park Dist. 4, 1983; recipient Archer Heights Civic Assn. award, 1979, 23d Ward Businessmen and Mchts. award Chgo., 1977, Garfield Ridge Hebrew Congregation award Chgo., 1975-77. Roman Catholic. Lodges: Midway Kiwanis (past pres.); Polish Nat. Alliance. Office: US House of Reps 1032 Longworth House Office Bldg Washington DC 20515

LIPKA, JAMES B., corporate communications specialist; b. Chgo., Oct. 19, 1949; s. Bruno Joseph and Pauline Agnes (Domaszek) L.; m. Lynanne McMahon, June 27, 1982; children: Shane, David, Daniel, Melanie. BA in Theater and Communications, BA in Speech Edn., U. Ill., Chgo., 1971; MA in Theater, Trinity U., 1972. V.p. prodn. Creative Presentations Inc., Schaumburg, Ill., 1975-78; v.p. meetings div. VIP Prodns., Arlington Heights, Ill., 1978-80; freelance producer, dir. Chgo. area, 1980-81; sr. producer Motivation Media, Inc., Glenview, Ill., 1981-84; pres. Creative Mktg. Communication, Inc., Chgo., 1984—; cons. Ill. Leadership Seminar, Western Springs; seminar instr. Blue Cross & Blue Shield, Washington, 1986. Producer, dir. theatrical projects for Busch Gardens, Can. Nat. Exhbn., Blue Cross and Blue Shield, Internat. Harvester, Johnson Wax, Hyatt Hotels. Recipient Cert. of Excellence Bus. and Profl. Advt. Assn., 1983, Bronze medal Internat. Film and TV Festival N.Y., 1982, Honorable Mention Columbus Internat. Film Festival, 1985, Merit award Spectra IABC, 1987, Golden Eagle award CINE, 1987, Merit award U.S. Indsl. Film Fest. Mem. Actor's Equity Assn., Am. Fedn. TV and Radio Artists, Screen Actor's Guild. Office: Creative Mktg Communication Inc 6054 W Touhy Ave Chicago IL 60648-4506

LIPNICK, STANLEY MELVIN, lawyer; b. Washington, Nov. 14, 1934; s. Max and Cecilia (Hollins) L.; m. Judith Sara Berman, Nov. 19, 1961; children—Stuart, Laura Gail. B.A., Columbia Coll., N.Y.C., 1956; J.D. with honors, George Washington U., 1960. Bar: D.C. 1960, Colo. 1967, Ill. 1968, Fla. 1983. Law clk. U.S. Ct. Appeals, Washington, 1960-61; trial atty. FTC, Washington, 1961-66; assoc. Ireland, Stapleton, Pryor & Holmes, Denver, 1966-68; ptnr. Arnstein, Gluck, Lehr & Milligan, Chgo. and West Palm Beach, 1968—. Mem. ABA, Bar Assn. D.C., Chgo. Bar Assn. Office: Arnstein Gluck Lehr Barron & Milligan 7500 Sears Tower Chicago IL 60606

LIPNIK, MORRIS JACOB, physician; b. Detroit, Aug. 27, 1922; s. Louis and Lillian (Portney) L.; m. Lois Russine Wertheimer, Dec. 8, 1946; children—Susan, Carol. B.A., Wayne State U., 1943, M.D., 1946. Diplomate Am. Bd. Dermatology. Intern, Detroit Receiving Hosp., 1946-47; resident Johns Hopkins Hosp., Balt., 1947-48, Hosp. of U. Pa., 1949-51; practice medicine specializing in dermatology, Southfield, Mich., 1953—; mem. staff Sinai Hosp., Detroit, 1954-60, Cottage Hosp., Grosse Pointe, Mich., 1957-60, St. John Hosp. Detroit, 1954-60, Mt. Carmel Hosp., Detroit, 1966—; spl. lectr. U. Detroit Dental Sch., 1958-63; adj. clin. prof. dermatology Marygrove Coll., Detroit, 1979—. Contbr. articles to med. jours. Mem. Founders' Soc. Detroit Inst. Arts, 1962; pres. Center Theatre, Detroit, 1963; patron Detroit Symphony Orch., 1978, Mich. Opera Theatre, Detroit, 1980, Detroit Community Music Sch., 1981, 82, 83. Served to capt. AUS, 1947-49. Mem. Mich. Dermatol. Soc., AMA, Am. Acad. Dermatology, Phi Delta Epsilon. Club: Renaissance (Detroit). Office: MJ Lipnik PC 17000 W 8 Mile Rd Suite 226 Southfield MI 48075 also: 29829 Telegraph Rd Southfield MO 48034

LIPPE, EMMETT WAYNE, school system administrator; b. Aurora, Kans., Mar. 22, 1941; s. John Fred and Doris LaDonna (Woodruff) L.; m. Marjorie Joyce Frisch, June 12, 1965; children: Marc, Matthew, Justin. BS, Huntington (Ind.) Coll., 1964; MA, U. No. Colo., 1966, Mich. State U., 1967; EdS, Mich. State U., 1970; EdD, Ball State U., 1972. Tchr. bus., math. Huntington and Lakeland Schs., Ind., 1964-66; prin., supt. Tekonsha (Mich.) Community Schs., 1967-69; asst. supt. Albion (Mich.) Pub. Schs., 1969-73; chmn. dept. edn. Huntington Coll., 1973-76; supt. schs. Williamston (Mich.) Community Schs., 1976—; cons. Ohio dept. edn., Columbus, 1975-76. Mem. Inst. for Devel. Ednl. Activities, Huntington Coll. Alumni Assn. (trustee 1979—, Alumnus of Yr. 1979), Williamston C. of C. (pres. 1983), Phi Delta Kappa. Club: Exchange. Lodge: Lions. Home: 324 E Riverside Williamston MI 48895 Office: Williamston Community Schs 418 Highland St Williamston MI 48895

LIPPERT, CHRISTOPHER NELSON, dentist, consultant; b. N.Y.C., Apr. 17, 1952; s. Raymond Joseph and Shirley Ann (Nelson) L.; m. Frances Joyce Iliff, Dec. 20, 1974 (div. Apr. 1979). BS, U. Cin., 1975; DDS, Emory U., 1979. Dentist John W. Regenos DDS, Inc., Cin., 1979-87; pres., dentist Lippert & Wilkes DDS, Inc., Cin., 1987—; cons. Teret's Syndrome Found., Cin., 1983—, Health Am., Cleve., 1985—; lectr. Ohio State U., 1981—. Bd. dirs. Creekwood Condominiums, Cin., 1985-86. Mem. ADA, Am. Acad. Crown and Bridge, Ohio Dental Assn., Ohio Acad. Practice Administrn., Cin. Dental Soc. (mem. peer rev. com. 1985—), Midwest Med. Found. (bd. dirs. 1984—), Phi Eta Sigma, Sigma Alpha Epsilon, Psi Omega. Avocations: sailing, fishing, restoration of classic cars. Office: Lippert & Wilkes DDS Inc 800 Compton Rd Cincinnati OH 45231

LIPPY, STEPHEN RICHARD, real estate executive; b. Limestone, Maine, Aug. 30, 1956; s. William Henry and Joan Betty (Raab) L.; m. Karen Beth Levey, Oct. 13, 1984; 1 child, Suzanne Rosing. BA in History cum laude, Tulane U, 1978; postgrad., NYU Grad Sch. Bus., 1980-81. Cert. comml. investment mem. Asst. mgr. Mfrs. Hanover Trust, N.Y.C., 1978-81; leasing and mktg. mgr. Sunset Plaza Shopping Ctr., St. Louis, 1981-82; v.p. leasing and mktg. Love Real Estate Co., St. Louis, 1982-86; gen. mgr. Frisco Bldg./ Burnham Mgmt., St. Louis, 1986—; bd. dirs., pres. Loring Corp., Warren, Ohio, 1977—; mng. ptnr. Hawthorne Properties, Warren, 1982—, Thornlor Properties, Warren, 1984—, Southtowne Devel. Co., St. Louis, 1986—, Southview Devel. Co., St. Louis, 1986—. Bd. dirs. Jewish Fed., St. Louis, 1984, campaign chmn. Young Profls. Div. St. Louis, 1984; vice chmn; mem. young men's leadership cabinet United Jewish Appeal, N.Y.C., 1982-87. Recipient Best Vice Chmn. award Jewish Fed., St. Louis, 1984. Mem. Bldg. Owners and Mgrs. Assn., Internat. Council Shopping Ctrs. Jewish. Club: Washington U. Lunch (St. Louis). Avocations: tennis, scuba diving, ballroom dancing, family. Home: 3 Cedar Crest Saint Louis MO 63132 Office: Burnham Mgmt Co 906 Olive St #300 Saint Louis MO 63101

LIPSCHULTZ, M. RICHARD, accountant; b. Chgo., July 5, 1913; s. Morris David and Minnie (Moskowitz) L.; student Northwestern U., 1930-35; J.D., De Paul U., 1948; m. Evelyn Smolin, May 16, 1945 (dec. 1963); m. Phyllis Siegel, July 11, 1965; children—Howard Elliott, Carl Alvin, Saul Martin. Admitted to Ill. bar, 1948; auditor State of Ill., Chgo., 1938-41; conferee IRS, Chgo., 1941-49; tax acct. A.I. Grade & Co., C.P.A.s, Chgo., 1949-50; sr. ptnr. Lipschultz Bros., Levin and Gray and predecessor firms, C.P.A.s, Chgo., 1950-82; fin. v.p., dir. Miller Asso. Industries, Inc., Skokie, 1973-74; dir. Miller Builders, Inc.; dir., chmn. exec. com. Portable Electric Tools, Inc., Geneva, Ill., 1963-67; mem. exec. com. Midland Screw Corp., Chgo., 1958-66; faculty John Marshall Law Sch., 1951-64. Bd. dirs.; pres. bd. dirs. Lipschultz Bros. Family Found. Served with USAAF, 1943-46. C.P.A., Ill. Mem. Ill. Soc. C.P.A.s, Am. Inst. C.P.A.s, ABA, Fed., Chgo., Ill. bar assns., Decalogue Soc. Lawyers, Am. Legion, Nu Beta-Epsilon. Mem. B'nai B'rith. Clubs: Standard (Chgo.); Ravinia Green Country (Deerfield, Ill.). Contbr. articles to profl. jours. Home: 1671 E Mission Hills Rd Northbrook IL 60062

LIPSCHUTZ, HAROLD, radiologist; b. Phila., June 9, 1926; s. Joseph and Sarah (Stoumen) L.; m. Janice Carolyn Figge, Sept. 15, 1960; 1 child, Lewis. BS, U. Pa., 1949; MD, Jefferson U., 1954. Diplomate Am. Coll. Radiology. Intern So. div. Albert Einstein Med. Ctr., Phila., 1954-55; resident in radiology U.S. Vets. Hosp., Phila., 1955-58; practice medicine specializing in radiology Med. Corp., Chgo., 1958-72, Olympia Fields, Ill., 1972—; chmn. radiologic services Ingalls Meml. Hosp., Harvey, Ill., 1972—. Contbr. articles to profl. jours. Served with U.S. Army, 1944-46, ETO. Mem. AMA, Radiologic Soc. N.Am., Ill. Radiologic Soc., Chgo. Radiologic Soc. Jewish. Avocations: swimming, racquetball. Office: Ingalls Meml Hosp Radiology Dept One Ingalls Dr Harvey IL 60426

LIPSCOMB, DELORES, English educator; b. Lexington, Miss., Feb. 12, 1944; d. Arthur and Bobbie (Luster) Horton; m. Frank N. Lipscomb, Dec. 27, 1964 (div. Oct. 1970); 1 child, Byron N. BA, De Paul U., 1964; MA, Northeastern Ill. U., 1968; PhD, Union Grad. Sch., 1976. Tchr. English Chgo. Pub. Schs., 1964-66; instr. English Chgo. City Coll., 1969-72; asst. prof. U. Ill., Chgo., 1972-77; assoc. prof. Chgo. State U., 1977-84, prof., 1984—, dir. Tchr. Writing Ctr.; mem. exec. com. Conf. Coll. Composition and Communication, Urbana, Ill., 1980-83; cons./reader Ednl. Testing Service, Princeton, N.J., 1986—; cons. Nat. Assn. Tchr. edn. Programs, 1982—; cons. reader Coll. Composition and Communication. Author: The English Book, 1980, Composition Skills, 1981, Reading and Writing for the Mature Student, 1981, Reading and Writing Across the Curriculum, 1987, Write Away: A Guide to Teaching Composition, 1987; editor: Tapping Potential: English and Language Arts for the Black Learner, 1985; mem. editorial bd. Nat. Council Tchrs. English, Urbana, 1983-86. Mem. Nat. Council Tchrs. English, Nat. Assn. Black Lang. Arts Educators. Office: Chgo State U 95th and King Dr Chicago IL 60620

LIPSCOMB, JACK EUGENE, advertising executive; b. Springfield, Mo., Aug. 30, 1927; s. Forest W. and Elizabeth (Cotner) L.; m. Cathryn Cox, June 25, 1949; children—Cynthia Lipscomb Daniel, Lawrence W. B.A. in Bus., U. Mo., 1951. Pres. Overland Outdoor Advt., Poplar Bluff, Mo., 1960—, Pioneer Advt. Co., Springfield, 1970—, Superior Outdoor Advt., Springfield, 1970—, Modern Neon and Plastics, Springfield, 1970—, Lipscomb Bros. Co., Springfield, 1980—; v.p. Lipscomb Grain and Seed Co., Springfield, 1980—; dir. Boatmen's Nat. Bank, Springfield. Bd. dirs. Springfield Airport, 1959-66. Served to maj. USAFR, 1951-60. Mem. Nat. Outdoor Advt. Assn. Am. (vice chmn., Bd. dirs. 1958-66), Sigma Nu. Presbyterian. Club: Hickory Hills Country (Springfield). Lodges: Masons, Shriners (potentate Abou Ben Adhem 1972-73). Avocations: travel; golf. Home: 2909 Southern Hills Springfield MO 65804 Office: Pioneer Advt Co 3121 E Elm St Springfield MO 65803

LIPSKI, WAYNE EDWARD, financial analyst, accountant; b. Chgo., Dec. 21, 1956; s. Edward Anthony and Dorothy (Puzio) L.; m. Joyce Marie Kotwica, May 16, 1981. BBA cum laude, Loyola U., Chgo., 1979. CPA, Ill. Semi-sr. auditor Arthur Andersen & Co., Chgo., 1979-82; sr. mgmt. analyst Household Mfg., Inc., Prospect Heights, Ill., 1982—. Mem. Am. Inst. CPA's (Elijah Watt Sells award 1979), Ill. CPA Soc. Roman Catholic. Avocations: weightlifting, bowling, golf. Home: 1321 Horseshoe Ct Addison IL 60101 Office: Household Mfg Inc 2700 Sanders Rd Prospect Heights IL 60070

LIS, LAWRENCE FRANCIS, facsimile company executive; b. Blue Island, Ill., Jan. 27, 1941; s. Anthony C. and Ann Marion (Galazin) L.; student DeVry Inst. Tech., 1958-59; m. Barbara Jean Lisak, Oct. 19, 1963; children—Christ and Connie (twins), David S. With Telautograph Corp., Chgo., 1959-64; regional mgr. Datalog div. Litton Industries, Chgo., 1964-74; regional mgr. Rapicom Inc., Chgo., 1974-78, nat. dir. field service ops., Hillside, Ill., 1978-79, v.p. customer service div., 1979—, v.p. customer service div. Ricoh Corp. and Ricoh Corp. Ltd. subs. Ricoh Ltd., 1980—. dir. Emergency Services and Disaster Agy., Village of Chicago Ridge, 1977-82; mem. Ill. CD Council. Commander Civil Air Patrol, Ill., 1986—. Mem. Assn. Field Service Mgrs. (pres. Chgo. chpt. 1984-85), Armed Forces Communications and Electronics Assn., Suburban Amateur Radio Assn., Mendel High Sch Alumni Assn. Home: 6704 W 93d Oaklawn IL 60453 Office: 4415 W Harrison St Hillside IL 60162

LISEC, W(ARREN) MICHAEL, architect; b. Chgo., Mar. 26, 1938; s. Otto and Irene Ann (Minarik) L.; m. Katherine Ann Miller, Dec. 19, 1959; children. B.Arch., U. Ill., 1961. Registered architect, Ill., real estate broker, Ill. Designer, project architect Harry Weese & Assocs., Chgo., 1961-76, pres., 1976-77; founder, pres. Lisec & Biederman Ltd., Architects and Planners, Chgo., 1977—. Bd. dirs. Unity Temple Restoration Found., Oak Park, Ill., chmn. archtl. adv. com., 1978-85; v.p. Friends of Downtown, 1982-83, Chgo. Mem. AIA (adv. council 1985—), River Forest Bldg. Bd. Appeals, Landmark Preservation Council Ill., Nat. Trust Hist. Preservation. Contbr. articles to profl. jours. Home: 718 Bonnie Brae River Forest IL 60305 Office: 412 S Wells St Suite 900 Chicago IL 60607

LISHER, JAMES RICHARD, lawyer; b. Aug. 28, 1947; s. Leonard B. and Mary Jane (Rafferty) L.; m. Martha Gettelfinger, June 16, 1973; children—Jennifer, James Richard II. A.B., Ind. U., 1969, J.D., 1975. Bar: Ind. 1975, U.S. Dist. Ct. (so. dist.) Ind. 1975. Assoc. Rafferty & Wood, Shelbyville, Ind., 1976, Rafferty & Lisher, Shelbyville, 1976-77; dep. prosecutor Shelby County Prosecutor's Office, Shelbyville, 1976-78; ptnr. Yeager & Lisher, Shelbyville, 1977—; pros. atty. Shelby County, Shelbyville, 1983—. Speaker, faculty advisor Ind. Pros. Sch., 1986. Editor: (seminar manual) Traffic Case Defenses, 1982. Bd. dirs. Girls Club of Shelbyville, 1979-84, Bears of Blue River Festival, Shelbyville, 1982—. Recipient Citation of Merit, Young Lawyers Assn. Mem. State Bar Assn. (bd. dirs.), Ind. State Bar Assn. (bd. dirs. young lawyer sect 1979-83), Shelby County Bar Assn. (sec./treas. 1986, v.p. 1987), Ind. Pros. Attys. Assn. (bd. dirs. 1985-86, sec./ treas. 1987). Democrat. Lodges: Masons, Elks, Lions. Home: 48 W Mechanic St Shelbyville IN 46176 Office: Yeager & Lisher Law Firm 406 S Harrison St Shelbyville IN 46176

LISHER, JOHN LEONARD, lawyer; b. Indpls., Sept. 19, 1950; s. Leonard Boyd and Mary Jane (Rafferty) L.; m. Mary Katherine Sturmon, Aug. 17, 1974. B.A. with honors in History, Ind. U., 1975, J.D., 1975. Bar: Ind. 1975. Dep. atty. gen. State of Ind., Indpls., 1975-78; asst. corp. counsel City of Indpls., 1978-81; assoc. Osborn & Hiner, Indpls., 1981-86; ptnr. Osborn, Hiner & Lisher, Indpls., 1986—. Vol. Mayflower Classic, Indpls., 1981—; asst. vol. coordinator Marion County Rep. Com., Indpls., 1979-80; vol. com. to re-elect Theodore Sendak, Indpls., 1976—, Don Bogard for Atty. Gen., Indpls., 1980, Steve Goldsmith for Prosecutor, Indpls., 1979, 83, Sheila Suess for Congress, Indpls., 1980. Recipient Outstanding Young Man of Am. award Jaycees, 1979, 85, Indpls. Jaycees, 1980. Mem. ABA, Ind. Bar Assn., Indpls. Bar Assn. (membership com.), Assn. Trial Lawyers Am., Ind. U. Alumni Assn., Hoosier Alumni Assn. (charter, founder, pres.), Ind. Trial Lawyers Assn., Ind. Def. Lawyers Assn., Ind. U. Coll. Arts and Scis. (bd. dirs. 1983—, pres. 1986-87), Wabash Valley Alumni Assn. (charter), Founders Club, Presidents Club, Phi Beta Kappa, Eta Sigma Phi, Phi Eta Sigma, Delta Xi Alumni Assn. (charter, v.p., sec., Delta Xi chpt. Outstanding Alumnus award 1975, 76, 79, 83), Delta Xi Housing Corp. (pres.), Pi Kappa Alpha (midwest regional pres. 1977-86, parliamentarian nat. conv. 1982, del. convs. 1978-80, 82, 84, 86, trustee Meml. Found. 1986—). Presbyterian. Avocations: reading; golf; jogging; Roman coin collecting. Home: 7919 Buckskin Dr Indianapolis IN 46250 Office: Osborn Hiner & Lisher 8330 Woodfield Crossing Blvd Suite 380 Indianapolis IN 46240

LISLE, JOHN COLEMAN, manufacturing executive; b. Omaha, Dec. 25, 1941; s. Edwin and Julia Jean (Coleman) L.; m. Julia Lucille Livingston, June 21, 1964; children—Bonnie, Brian. Student Cornell Coll., 1960-62; B.B.A., U. Iowa, 1964. Salesman, Lisle Corp., Clarinda, Iowa, 1964-66, asst. sales mgr., 1966-70, nat. accounts sales mgr., 1970-74, mgr. tooling engring., 1974-77, pres., 1977—; dir. Citizens State Bank, Clarinda, 1983—. Dir. Clarinda Mcpl. Hosp. Republican. Methodist. Office: Lisle Corp 807 E Main Clarinda IA 51632

LISMAN, MICHAEL RAY, government administrator, clergyman; b. Richlands, Va., Feb. 3, 1952; s. Daniel and Rosevet W. Lisman. m. Diedre Lynn Payne, Sept. 15, 1972; children—Mich'El, Alexandria. B.A. in Communications, Kent State U., 1977; M.R.E., Berean Bible Coll., 1980. Ordained to ministry Apostolic Faith, 1980. Acad. dean Berean Bible Coll., Akron, Ohio, 1981-83; adj. faculty Youngstown State U., Ohio, 1982-84; retng. mgr. Alt. EEO Office and SYEP Coordinator Pvt. Ind. Council, Akron, 1982—; youth motivator Youth Motivational Task Force, Akron, 1983—; chmn. bus devel. com. 4th Ward Council, Akron, 1984—; owner, mgr. Alexandria's Books & Christian Supply, Akron, 1983—. Founding minister Maranatha Apostolic Ministries. Mem. Christian Booksellers Assn. Office: Pvt Industry Council 480 W Tuscarawas Barberton OH 44203

LISS, HERBERT MYRON, newspaper publisher, communications company executive; b. Mpls., Mar. 23, 1931; s. Joseph Milton and Libby Diane (Kramer) L.; m. Barbara Lipson, Sept. 19, 1954; children: Lori-Ellen, Kenneth Allen, Michael David. BS in Econs., U. Pa., 1952. With mktg. mgmt. Procter & Gamble Co., Cin., 1954-63, Procter & Gamble Internat., various countries, 1963-74; gen. mgr. Procter & Gamble Comml. Co., San Juan, Puerto Rico, 1974-78; v.p., mgr. internat. ops. Am. Orange Crush Co. subs. Procter & Gamble Co., Cin., 1981-84; pres. River Cities (Ohio) Communications Inc, 1985—; pub. The Downtowner Newspaper, Cin., 1985—. Bd. dirs. Charter Com., Cin., 1958-63, Promotion & Mktg. Assn. U.S., 1978-81, Jr. Achievement, Cin., 1980—, Downtown Council, Cin., 1985—. Served to 1st lt. U.S. Army, 1952-54, Korea. Clubs: Manila Yacht, Manila Polo; Equitación De Somos Aguas (Madrid). Home: 8564 Wyoming Club Dr Cincinnati OH 45215 Office: The Downtowner Newspaper 128 E 6th St Cincinnati OH 45202

LISS, JAY LAWRENCE, psychiatrist; b. St. Louis, June 14, 1941; children: Jennifer, Jessica. AB, Washington U., St. Louis, 1962, MD, 1966. Cert. Am. Bd. Psychiatry and Neurology; lic. Nat. Bd. Med. Examiners, Mo. Bd. Med. Examiners, Ill. Bd. Med. Examiners, Tex. Bd. Med. Examiners. Practice medicine specializing in psychiatry St. Louis, 1973—; attending psychiatrist Barnes Hosp. Group, St. Louis, 1973—, St. Vincent's Hosp., St. Louis, 1973—, Mo. Bapt. Hosp., St. Louis, 1974—, Jewish Hosp., St. Louis, 1974—, St. Luke's Hosp., St. Louis, 1976—; staff psychiatrist Weldon Springs Hosp., St. Charles, Mo., 1980—, Faith Hosp., St. Louis, 1981—, St. Anthony's Med. Ctr., St. Louis, 1983—; cons. enterostomal clinic, Jewish Hosp., 1973—; psychiatrist Malcolm Bliss Mental Health Ctr., St. Louis, 1973-74; med. dir. Madison County Mental Health Ctr, Ill., 1973; reviewer Am. Jour. Psychiatry. Contbr. numerous articles to profl. jours. Served to capt. U.S. Army, 1967-69, Vietnam. Decorated Bronze Star, DSM, Vietnamese Civic Action Medal; recipient Neuropsychiatry award The Roche Labs, 1972. Fellow Am. Psychiat. Assn.; mem. AMA (Physician's Recognition award for Continuing Edn., 1979, 81, 84), Mo. Med. Assn., Royal Coll. Physicians, Eastern Mo. Psychiat. Soc., St. Louis County Med. Soc. (editor jour. 1976-78, counselor 1977, 78), Am. Acad. Clin. Psychiatrists, Greater St. Louis Council for Child Psychiatry, St. Louis Met. Med. Soc. (various coms. and offices), Phi Beta Kappa, Omicron Delta Kappa, Phi Eta Sigma. Home: 24 Carrswold Clayton MO 63105 Office: 763 S New Ballas Rd Suite 350 Saint Louis MO 63141

LIST, CHARLES EDWARD, management and organization development consultant; b. Chgo., May 9, 1941; s. Kermit Paul and Johanna Emma (Staat) L.; B.A., Valparaiso U., 1963; M.A., St. Marys Coll., Winona, Minn., 1980; Ph.D. in Orgn. Devel., Union Coll., Cin., 1984; m. Susan Mary Nelson, July 20, 1968; children—Andrea Sarang, Darcy Young. Mem. personnel staff Control Data Corp., Mpls., 1965-72; mgr. human resource center Supervalu Stores, Mpls., 1973-74; dir. personnel Internat. Dairy Queen, Mpls., 1974-77; mgr. mgmt. and orgn. devel. Cardiac Pacemakers Inc., St. Paul, 1977-82; adj. faculty instr. U. Minn., Normandale Community Coll.; instr. Met. State U., St. Paul, 1972—. Served with USMC, 1963-64. Recipient Instr. Recognition award Met. State U., 1975, 80, 86. Mem. Am. Soc. Personnel Adminstrn., Am. Soc. Tng. and Devel. Episcopalian. Contbr. articles to profl. jours. Home: 4940 Winterset Dr Minnetonka MN 55343

LIST, ROBERT HANS, photographer; b. Greenfield, Mass., Nov. 14, 1953; s. Thomas Eugene and Elizabeth Catherine (Lauterback) L.; m. Ida Ann Woodling, Apr. 28, 1979; children: Alena Jeanne, Brice Robert, Claire Elizabeth. Diploma in basic portraiture, Winona Sch. Profl. Photography, 1982. Comml. printer The papers Inc., Milford, Ind., 1977-82; owner Bob List Photography, Leesburg, Ind., 1982—. Mem. Profl. Photographers Am., Wedding Photographers Internat., Michiana Profl. Photographers (Silver award 1987), Ind. Profl. Photographers, North Webster, Tippecanoe Twp. C. of C. (chmn. publicity 1984). Roman Catholic. Lodge: KC. Home and Office: Rural Rt 1 Box 246 Leesburg IN 46538

LISTER, HERBERT E., insurance company executive. Pres. Allstate Life Ins. Co., Northbrook, Ill. Office: AllState Life Ins Co Allstate Plaza Northbrook IL 60062 *

LISTIAK, RICHARD LANCE, clinical psychologist; b. Mpls., Nov. 26, 1944; s. Lancelot D. and Marquerite (Shea) L.; m. Nancy Lee Hage, June 18, 1966; children: Michael, Sarah. BA, U. Minn., Duluth, 1966; PhD, U. N.D., 1971. Lic. psychologist, Minn., Wis. Intern in psychology Nebr. Psychiat., Omaha, 1970-71; psychologist Northwestern Hosp., Thief River Falls, Minn., 1971-72; clin. psychologist Gundersen Clinic, LaCrosse, Wis., 1972—; lectr. U. Wis., LaCrosse, 1973. Contbr. articles to profl. jours. Bd. dirs. Family Service Assn., LaCrosse, 1972-77; bd. v.p. Applefest, LaCrescent, Minn., 1983-85; mem. Parent Adv. com. Jr. High., LaCrescent, 1985-86. Fellow NIMH, 1968-70. Mem. Am. Trauma Soc. (tchr. corps 1980), Am. Psychol. Assn., Soc. Personality Assessment, Midwest Psychol. Assn., Wis. Psychol. Assn., Minn. Psychol. Assn., Sigma Xi. Democrat. Roman Catholic. Lodge: KC. Avocation: flying. Office: Gundersen Clinic 1836 South Ave LaCrosse WI 54601

LISZESKI, JOSEPH MICHAL, dentist; b. Cleve., Sept. 29, 1939; s. Joseph Walter and Martha (Pizon) L.; m. Beverly Ann Svec, Aug. 31, 1963 (div. Apr. 1979); children: Joseph, Lisa, David, Lawrence, Theodore, Julie, Teresa; m. Joyce Ann Tomazin, Apr. 25, 1981; children: Jennifer, Jessica. Student, U. Dayton, 1957-60, John Carroll U., 1959; DDS, Case Western Reserve U., 1964; postgrad., U. Pitts., 1985—. Asst. records librarian Univ. Hosps., Cleve., 1961-62; med. technician St. Vincent's Charity Hosp., Cleve., 1962-64; gen. practice dentistry St. Vincent's Charity Hosp., North Ridgeville, Ohio, 1964—; dental dir. Lorain (Ohio) Free Clinic, 1986—. lay minister Catholic. Ch., N. Ridgeville, 1971-79, 85—. Fellow Acad. Gen. Dentistry; mem. ADA, Ohio Dental Assn., Lorain County Dental Soc. (treas. 1982-83, sec. 1983-84, v.p. 1984-85), Delta Pi, Psi Omega. Democrat. Club: Holy Name Soc. (v.p., 1966-68, pres. 1968-70, sec. 1971-72). Avocations: gardening, travel, bowling. Home: 2633 Elyria Ave Lorain OH 44055 Office: 8225 Avon Belden Rd Box 187 North Ridgeville OH 44039-0187

LITCHFIELD, ROBERT LOUIS, physician, cardiologist, educator; b. Bethesda, Md., Nov. 9, 1948; s. Louis Herbert and Blanche Sylvage (Johanson) L.; m. Valerie Ann Nelson, Oct. 1; children: John Louis, Michael Robert. BA, Monmouth Coll., 1971; DO, Chgo. Coll. Osteo. Medicine, 1975. Diplomate Am. Osteo. Bd. Internal Medicine, Am. Osteo. Bd. Cardiology. Intern Chgo. Coll. Osteo. Medicine, 1975-76, resident, 1976-78, asst. prof. medicine, cardiology and nuclear medicine, 1980-85, assoc. prof., 1985—, dir. intern/resident tng., 1982—; fellow U. Iowa, Iowa City, 1978-80, chief cardiology fellow, 1979-80. Trustee Calumet counil Boy Scouts Am., Calumet City, Ind., 1985—; bd. dirs. Flossmoor (Ill.) Community Chs., 1985—. Mem. Am. Heart Assn. (grantee 1985), Am. Acad. Osteo. Dirs. Med. Edn., Ill. Assn. Osteo. Physicians and Surgeons (bd. dirs. 1983—), Am. Coll. Osteo. Internists, Am. Coll. Nuclear Cardiology. Avocations: snow skiing, tennis. Home: 911 Travers Ln Flossmoor IL 60422 Office: Chgo Coll Osteo Medicine Office Postdoctoral Edn 5200 S Ellis Chicago IL 60615

LITSEY, JACQUELINE KAY, teacher; b. Lima, Ohio, Aug. 3, 1951; d. Richard Eugene and Joanne (Lowry) Crumrine; m. William Douglas, Sept. 25, 1971. BS in Edn., Ohio State U., 1973; MS in Edn., U. Dayton, 1980, U. Dayton, 1984. Elem. tchr. Wapakoneta (Ohio) City Sch., 1974—, head tchr., 1975-84; advisor social studies curriculum Wapakoneta City Schs., 1978, advisor math curriculum, 1982, advisor computer curriculum, 1983-85; consumer adv. Apollo Joint Vocat. Sch., Lima, 1980. V.p. Shawnee Twp. Auxilliary, Lima, 1976-86. Ohio Dept. Edn. grantee, 1980; Outstanding History Tchr., DAR, 1984. Mem. NEA, Ohio Edn. Assn., Western Ohio Edn. Assn., Wapakoneta Edn. Assn. (pres. 1985-87), Alpha Delta Kappa (pres. 1985-87). Avocations: aerobics instr., gardening. Home: 2772 Shagbark Dr Lima OH 45806 Office: Cridersville Elem 300 E Main Cridersville OH 41999-1159

LITTLE, DAVID EATON, osteopath; b. Kirksville, Mo., Nov. 12, 1951; s. Walter George and Joan Mary (Olive) L.; m. Sarah Hope Smith, Nov. 3, 1984; stepchildren: Bryan, David, Chad. BS, Oral Roberts U., 1973; DO, Kirksville Coll. Osteo. Medicine, 1978. Diplomate Am. Bd. Family Practice, Am. Coll. Gen. Practitioners Osteo. Medicine. Intern Doctors' Hosp., Columbus, Ohio, 1978-79; gen. practice osteo. medicine Pickerington, Ohio, 1979—; dir. osteo. medicine service Doctor's Hosp., Columbus, Ohio, 1979-80. Mem. Am. Osteo. Assn., Am. Acad. Osteopathy, Ohio Osteo. Assn., Columbus Acad. Osteo. Medicine, Am. Coll. Gen. Practioners Osteo. Medicine, Pickerington Area C. of C. (bd. dirs. 1980-81). Republican. Avocations: science fiction books and films, travel, tennis. Home: 400 Seven Pines Dr Pickerington OH 43147 Office: Tower Plaza Med Ctr 1054 Hill Rd N Pickerington OH 43147

LITTLE, DAVID RICHARD, real estate management company executive; b. Heidelberg, Fed. Republic Germany, May 25, 1957; came to U.S., 1959; s. David L. Little and Doris W. (Storz) Belcher; m. Sherri A. Volz, Mar. 14, 1981; 1 child, Eric W. Student, Des Moines Area Community Coll., 1979-

81. Installation and maintenance technician Norstan Communications, Inc., Des Moines, 1981-83; pres. and chief exec. officer Phone Systems, Ltd., Des Moines, 1982-84; telecommunications mgr. Ruan Ctr. Corp., Des Moines, 1984-85, asst. bldg. supt., 1985-86, bldg. ops. mgr., 1986—. Mem. Bldg. Owners and Mgrs. Assn. (sec., treas. 1987—). Democrat. Lutheran. Club: Engineers (Des Moines) (v.p. 1985-86, pres. 1986-87) Lodge: Masons (32 degree). Avocations: golf, fishing, traveling. Office: Ruan Ctr Corp 666 Grand Ave Lower Level 1 Des Moines IA 50309

LITTLE, JAMES R., manufacturing engineer; b. Dayton, Ohio, Jan. 11, 1960; s. Arch W. and Joanne K. (Phelan) L.; m. Robin Kindy, Aug. 9, 1985. BS MechE, U. Cin., 1983; MS in Engring. Mgmt., Stanford U., 1986. Product engr. Delco Products div. Gen. Motors Corp., Dayton, 1983-85, mfg. engr., 1986—. Recipient A.M. Kinney Design award U. Cin. Dept. Mech. Engring., 1983, Silver Design award Lincoln Arc Welding Found., Cleve., 1986. Mem. Soc. Automotive Engrs. Avocations: jogging, outdoor activities, hiking, camping. Home: 8720 Castlecreek Dr Dayton OH 45459 Office: Delco Products div GMC PO Box 1042 Dayton OH 45401

LITTLE, MAUS ELDER, psychologist, educator; b. Phila., Feb. 25, 1929; s. James Crosby and Marjorie Anne (Elder) L.; m. Shirley Mae Roffers, June 1, 1957 (div. July 1983); children: Mark Harold, Marjorie Esther. BA, N.Mex. Western U., 1954, MS, 1955; postgrad., U. Iowa, 1963-64, 68-69. Lic. psychologist, Wis. Counselor Tex. Tech., Lubbock, 1955-56; professor Northland Coll., Ashland, Wis., 1956—; pvt. practice psychologist Ashland, 1977-82. Served to sgt. U.S. Army, 1947-51, Korea. Mem. Am. Psychol. Assn., Am. Assn. Counseling and Devel., Biofeedback Soc. Am., Biofeedback Soc. Wis. (pres. 1981-82), Wis. Psychol. Assn. Republican. Episcopalian. Lodge: Elks. Avocation: reading. Home: 609 Ellis Ave Ashland WI 54806 Office: Northland Coll 1411 Ellis Ave Ashland WI 54806

LITTLE, RICHARD ALLEN, mathematics and computer science educator; b. Coshocton, Ohio, Jan. 12, 1939; s. Charles M. and Elsie Leanna (Smith) L.; m. Gail Louann Koons, June 12, 1960; children: Eric, J. Alice, Stephanie. BS in Math. cum laude, Wittenberg U., 1960; MA in Edn., Johns Hopkins U., 1961; EdM in Math., Harvard U., 1965; PhD in Math. Edn., Kent State U., 1971. Tchr. Culver Acad., Ind., 1961-65; instr., curriculum cons. Harvard U., Cambridge, Mass. and Aiyetoro, Nigeria, 1965-67; from instr. to assoc. prof. Kent State U., Canton, Ohio, 1967-75; from assoc. prof. to prof. Baldwin-Wallace Coll., Berea, Ohio, 1975—; cons. in field; vis. prof. math. Ohio State U., Columbus, 1987—; lectr. various colls. and univs.; pres. Cleve. Collaborative on Math. Edn., 1986-87. Contbr. articles to profl. jours. Bd. dirs. Canton Symphony Orch., 1973-75; Catechism tchr. St. Paul Luth. Ch., Berea, 1976-84, lector, 1980—; bd. deacons Holy Cross Luth. Ch., Canton, 1968-74, chmn., 1971-74. Mem. Nat. Council Tchrs. Math. (mem. profl. devel. and status adv. com. 1987—), Ohio Council Tchrs. Math. (pres. 1974-76, v.p. 1970-73, sec. 1982-84, dir. state math. contest, 1983—), Greater Cleve. Council Tchrs. Math. (bd. dirs. 1979-82), Greater Canton Council Tchrs. Math. (pres. 1969-70), Math. Assn. Am. (pres. Ohio sect. 1983-84, editor 1978-83). Avocations: jogging, tennis, handball. Home: 243 Kraft St Berea OH 44017 Office: Baldwin-Wallace Coll Math and Computer Sci Dept Berea OH 44017

LITTLE, ROBERT LUCAS, chemical dependency counselor; b. Columbus, Ohio, May 20, 1947; s. Robert Clifford and Mary Helen (Lucas) L.; m. Linda Darlene Hill, Nov. 16, 1968 (div. May 1985); children: Faith Elizabeth, Laura Sue; m. Barbara Lee Ruehlman, Aug. 23, 1986. AA summa cum laude, U. Cin., 1974, BS summa cum laude, 1975, postgrad., 1975-76; postgrad., Xavier U., 1980-81. Cert. alcoholism counselor, Ohio. Counselor, coordinator Cin. Council on Alcoholism, 1976-80; treatment coordinator Clermont County Council on Alcoholism, Batavia, Ohio, 1980-81; primary counselor Emerson North Hosp., Cin., 1981-84; sr. counselor Ctr. for Comprehensive Alcohol Treatment, Cin., 1984-85; outpatient coordinator Ft. Hamilton Hughes Hosp., Hamilton, Ohio, 1985-86; unit mgr. Alcohol and Drug Recovery Ctr., St. Francis/St. George Hosp., Cin., 1986—; instr. U. Cin., 1983. Served with USAF, 1968-71, Vietnam. Mem. Delta Tau Kappa. Democrat. Lutheran. Avocations: playing guitar, singing in church choir, camping, hiking. Home: 4131 Homelawn Ave Cincinnati OH 45211 Office: St Francis/St George Hospital Alcohol and Drug Recovery Ctr 5049 Crookshank Rd Cincinnati OH 45238

LITTLEFIELD, VIVIAN M., nursing educator, administrator; b. Princeton, Ky., Jan. 24, 1938; d. Willard Anson and Hester V. (Haydon) Moore; children—Darrell, Virginia. B.S. magna cum laude, Tex. Christian U., 1960; M.S., U. Colo., 1964; Ph.D., U. Denver, 1979. Staff nurse USPHS Hosp., Ft. Worth, Tex., 1960-61; instr. nursing Tex. Christian U., Ft. Worth, 1961-62; nursing supr. Colo. Gen. Hosp., Denver, 1964-65, pvt. patient practitioner, 1974-78; asst. prof. nursing U. Colo., Denver, 1965-69, asst. prof., clin. instr., 1971-74, asst. prof., 1974-76, acting asst. dean, assoc. prof. continuing edn., regional perinatal project, 1976-78; assoc. prof., chair dept. women's health care nursing U. Rochester Sch. Nursing, N.Y., 1979-84; clin. chief ob-gyn., nursing U. Rochester Strong Meml. Hosp., N.Y., 1979-84; prof., dean U. Wis. Sch. Nursing, Madison, 1984—; cons. and lectr. in field. Author: Maternity Nursing Today, 1973, 76; Health Education for Women: A guide for Nurses and Other Health Professionals, 1986. Contbr. articles to profl. jours. Bur. Health Professions Fed. trainee, 1963-64, Nat. Sci. Service award, 1976-79. Mem. Am. Nurses Assn., Health Care for Women Internat. (editorial bd. 1984—), Midwest Nursing Research Soc., Sigma Theta Tau (v.p.). Avocations: golf; tennis. Office: Univ of Wis Sch Nursing 600 Highland Ave H6/150 Madison WI 53792

LITTLER, JOHN DOUGLAS, die casting company executive; b. Portland, Ind., Feb. 1, 1951; s. Frank Perry and Julia Agnes (Younce) L.; m. Katherine Wells Countryman, July 21, 1973; children—Douglas Robert, Kathryn Ann, Mark Daniel. B.S. in Bus., Ind. U., 1972. With Littler Diecast Corp., Albany, Ind., 1972—, treas., chmn. bd., 1977—; ptnr. Priority Components, Albany, 1982—; bd. dirs. 1st State Bank Dunkirk, Ram-Z Corp. Mem. Albany Town Bd., 1976-79, Albany Planning Com., 1976-82, chmn. local St. Judes Children's Bike-A-Thon; co-founder Albany Concerned Citizens Assn., 1982; chmn. Albany Republican Town Com., 1982; cubmaster Albany Cub Scout Pack 37, 1984-86. Named Outstanding Young Man Am., Albany Jaycees, 1978. Mem. Soc. Die Castings Engrs. (pres.'s adv. com., area dir., nat. dir., tech. council, nat. sec., exec. com., nat. treas., chmn. mgmt. com., Merit award 1987), Diecasting Devel. Council (bd. dirs.), Muncie/Del. County C. of C. Methodist. Club: Ind. U. Varsity. Lodges: Elks, Lions. Home: 116 Gillcrest Dr Albany IN 47320 Office: Littler Diecast Corp 500 W Walnut St Albany IN 47320

LITTNAN, JOHN MICHAEL, sales executive; b. Milw., Dec. 22, 1942; s. Charles Carl and Zita (Pallagi) L.; m. Susan Mary Wenzel, Nov. 29, 1974; children: Ann, Monika, Nicholas. BS in Speech Therapy, U. Wis., Milw., 1967, MS in Spl. Edn., 1972. Tchr. diagnostic learning disabilities Milw. Pub. Sch. System, 1973-79; br. mgr., account exec. Dean Witter Reynolds, Milw., 1979-83; v.p. mktg. Reed & Strattford, Milw., 1984—; regional sales mgr. ISFA/INVEST, Chgo., 1986—. Contbr. articles to profl. jours. Mem. Council on Exceptional Children (chmn. constitution com., regional planning com. for standards and guidelines), Nat. Div. for Children with Learning Disabilities (rep.). Ozaukee Mental Health Assn. Home: 235 Hillside Dr Oconomowoc WI 53066 Office: ISFA/INVEST 8303 W Higgins Rd Chicago IL 60631

LITTRELL, DONALD WATTS, community development educator; b. Moberly, Mo., May 21, 1936; s. Waldo Watts and Mildred Katherine (Forrest) L.; m. Doris Sue Painter, Jan. 31, 1958; children—Charles Watts, William Painter. B.S., U. Mo.-Columbia, 1959, M.S., 1964. Mem. faculty U. Mo., Columbia, 1967—, chmn. community devel. dept., extension project leader, 1983-86 ; prof. and state extension specialist community devel. cons. U.S. Dept. Agr., 1975-76, univs. and state govts. Ark., Minn., N.D., Ga., Nebr. and Mo., 1972—; dir. nat. staff devel. project FHA, Washington, 1978-81; bd. dirs., cons. TVA, Knoxville, 1982-83; Fulbright cons., Thailand, 1986-87. Author: Theory and Practice of Community Development, 1972; also chpts. in books. Mem. Boone County Democratic Com., 1984—; mem. adv. bd. Mo. 4-H Club, 1977-80. Recipient 3 certs. of appreciation U.S. Dept. Agr., 1976-78, cert. appreciation U.S. Community Services Adminstrn., Washington, 1978; Extension fellow U. Mo., Columbia, 1984-85; scholar Farm Found., Chgo., 1984. Mem. Community Devel. Soc. (a founder, bd. dirs. 1977-78), Am. Soc. Tng. and Devel. Baptist. Avocations: fishing, hunting, reading. Home: 1309 Dawn Ridge Columbia MO 65202 Office: Univ Mo at Columbia 723 Clark Hall Columbia MO 65211

LITUCZY, VIKTOR ALLEN, architect; b. Chgo., Jan. 28, 1953; s. Boris and Nadia (Turowetz) L.; m. Linda Jean Cureton, Sept. 4, 1982. AArch, Fullerton Coll., 1973; BArch, U. Ill., 1976. Registered architect, Ill. Project architect, job capt. O'Donnell Wicklund Pigozzi, Northbrook, Ill., 1976-78; project mgr. Hansen Lind Meyer, Inc., Chgo., 1978-80, sr. designer, 1980-82, dir. design, 1982-85, prin. head research and devel. facilities, 1984—, dir. bus. devel., 1985-86, adminstrv. dir. mktg., 1985—, prin., 1986—; bd. dirs. Hansen Lind Meyer, Inc., Iowa City, Iowa. Contbr. articles to profl. jours. Mem. AIA (Grassmont Project 2000 House Design award 1968), Soc. Mktg. Profls. Services, Assn. Univ. Related Research Parks (charter), Am. Soc. Interior Design (Design award 1983). Avocations: rock climbing, volleyball, painting, photography, painting. Office: Hansen Lind Meyer Inc 350 N Clark Suite 700 Chicago IL 60610

LITVAK, RONALD, psychiatrist; b. Cleve., Aug. 11, 1938; s. Albert and Ruth (Jaffe) L.; m. Betty Ann Resnick, Aug. 14, 1960; children: Alan, Diane, Amy. BA, Case Western Res. U., 1960; MD, Ohio State U., 1964, MS, 1968. Diplomate Am. Bd. Psychiatry and Neurology, Am. Bd. Forensic Psychiatry; lic. Ohio. Intern in internal medicine Ohio State U. Hosp., Columbus, 1964-65, resident in psychiatry, 1965-68; chief resident in psychiatry Profl. Staff Ohio State U. Hosp., Columbus, 1967-68; practice medicine specializing in psychiatry Columbus, Ohio, 1964—; dir. outpatient services Harding Hosp., Worthington, Ohio, 1979-83; pres. med. staff, 1980; cons. Ohio Dept. Mental Health and Mental Retardation, 1970-78, Chillicothe VA Hosp., 1970-71, Columbus Police Dept., Worthington (Ohio) Police Dept., Indsl. Commn. of Ohio, Ohio Atty. Gen., State Med. Bd. of Ohio, Supreme Ct. of Ohio, Bd. om Commrs. and Grievances and Discipline of the Bar, Columbus City Atty., U.S. Dept. Labor, U.S. Dept. State. Contbr. articles to profl. jours. Served to maj. Med. Service Corps, U.S. Army, 1968-70. Recipient Cert. of Achievement Comdr. U.S. Walson Army Hosp., Ft. Dix, N.J., 1970, Letters of Commendation, Officers in Tng. Brigade, Ft. Dix, N.J. Fellow Am. Psychiat. Assn.; mem. AMA, Ohio State Med. Assn., Ohio Psychiat. Assn., Psychiat. Soc. Cen. ohio, Acad. Medicine of Columbus and Franklin County, Am. Acad. Psychiatry and the Law, Am. Orthopsychiat. Assn. Avocations: backpacking, weightlifting, photography, jogging, hunting. Home: 1195 Circle on the Green Worthington OH 43085 Office: 1170 Old Henderson Rd #201 Columbus OH 43220

LITVIN, MARTIN JAY, author, lecturer; b. Galesburg, Ill., Mar. 31, 1928; s. Ben and Sylvia (Gillis) L. B.S. in Social Studies, U. So. Calif., 1949. lectr. motivational seminars , creative writing and self- pub. Chgo. Pub. Library Cultural Ctr., 1986-87; vis. scholar Harvard Divinity Sch., Cambridge, Mass., 1987. Author: Sergeant Allen and Private Renick, 1971; Voices of the Prairie Land, 2 Vols., 1972; Black Angel, 1973; Hiram Revels in Illinois, 1974; Chase the Prairie Wind, 1975; The Young Mary, 1976; The Journey, 1981; A Rocking Horse Family, 1982; A Daring Young Man, 1983; Black Earth, 1984; lectr. in field. Served with U.S. Army, 1950-52. Mem. Dramatists Guild (assoc.), Alumnus of Tau Epsilon Phi. Office: care Frank A Ward PO Box 1205 Galesburg IL 61402

LITZ, STEVEN CRAIG, lawyer; b. Chgo., May 19, 1959; s. Donald and Marilyn Litz; m. Stephanie Marie Palvas, Sept. 8, 1984. BA with hons., U. Va., 1981; JD, Ind. U., 1984. Bar: Ind. 1984, U.S. Dist. Ct. (no. and so. dists.) Ind., 1984, U.S. Ct. Appeals (7th cir.) 1984. Dir., pres. Surrogate Mothers, Inc., Indpls., 1984—. Mem. ABA, Am. Trial Lawyers Assn., Nat. Assn. Criminal Def. Lawyers, Ind. Bar Assn., Ind. Assn. Criminal Def. Lawyers, Nat. Orgn. for Reform of Marijuana Laws. Avocations: skiing, tennis, camping, running, coin collecting. Office: 3601 N Pennsylvania Indianapolis IN 46205

LIU, KHANG-LEE, dentist, educator; b. China, Aug. 5, 1939; came to U.S., 1972, naturalized, 1982; s. T.P. and K.H. (Lu) L.; m. Nancy S.Y. Lee (div.); children—Christine, Helen. B.D.S., Nat. Def. Med. Ctr., Faculty of Dentistry, Taipei, 1964; M.A., U. Chgo., 1974. Asst., Nat. Def. Med. Ctr., Taipei, Taiwan, 1964-67; instr. Med. Ctr., Republic of China, 1968-72; asst. prof. U. Chgo., 1972-76; assoc. prof. Nat. Def. Med. Ctr., 1976-77; from asst. prof. to assoc. prof. dentistry Northwestern U., Chgo., 1977—; dir. McCormick Boys and Girls Dental Clin. Mem. ADA, Chgo. Dental Soc., Am. Soc. Dentistry for Children, Internat. Assn. Dental Research, Am. Acad. Pediatric Dentistry. Office: 2929 N Central St Chicago IL 60634

LIU, LEE, utility company executive; b. Hunan, China, Mar. 30, 1933; came to U.S., 1953; s. Z. Liang and Swai Chin (Chan) L.; m. Andrea Pavageau, Dec. 19, 1959; children: Monica, Christine. B.S., Iowa State U. With Iowa Electric Light & Power Co., Cedar Rapids, 1957—, jr. engr., 1957-60, relay engr., 1960-67, systems protection coordinator, 1967-70, mgr. elec. engr., 1970-74, asst. v.p., 1974-75, v.p. engring., 1975-79, sr. v.p. engring. and ops., 1979-80, exec. v.p., 1980-82, pres., 1982—, chief operating officer, 1982-83, pres., chmn. bd., chief exec. officer, 1983—, also dir.; dir. Merchants Nat. Bank, Cedar Rapids. Bd. trustees Mercy Hosp., Cedar Rapids, 1982—; mem. engring. adv. council Iowa State U., Ames, 1984—. Recipient Profl. Achievement citation Iowa State U., 1984. Mem. Edison Electric Inst., Iowa Utility Assn., Mo. Valley Electric Assn., Am. Mgmt. Assn., IEEE, Cedar Rapids C. of C. Republican. Roman Catholic. Club: Cedar Rapids Country. Lodge: Rotary Internat. Office: Iowa Electric Light & Power Co PO Box 351 Cedar Rapids IA 52406 *

LIU, PING YUAN, chemist, researcher; b. Hwai-an, China, May 12, 1931; came to U.S., 1959, naturalized, 1973; s. Soo-noon and Chee (Hang) L.; m. Lily Tehyu Chen; children—Henry Heng, Ingrid Ying. B.S., Nat. Taiwan U., 1955; M.S., Case Western Res. U., 1962, Ph.D., 1966. Research chemist Monsanto, Bloomfield, Conn., 1972-74, Amoco Chem. Corp., Naperville, Ill., 1974-77; advanced devel. chemist Gen. Electric Co., Mt. Vernon, Ind., 1977—. Translator: Chemical Plant Design with Fiber Reinforced Plastics, 1970. Numerous U.S. and fgn. patents. Sloan fellow, 1966-68. Fellow Soc. Plastics Engrs.; mem. Am. Chem. Soc., Soc. Rheology. Club: Toastmasters (Mt. Vernon) (pres. 1986-87). Avocation: bridge. Office: Gen Electric Co Hwy 69 South Mount Vernon IN 47620

LIUZZI, ROBERT C., chemical company executive; b. Boston, 1944; married. AB, Coll. of Holy Cross, 1965; LLB, U. Va., 1968. V.p., gen. counsel U.S. Fin., Inc., 1969-74; with CF Industries, Long Grove, Ill., 1975—; exec. v.p., chief fin. officer CF Industries, Lake Zurich, Ill., 1977-80, exec. v.p., operating officer, 1980-84, pres., chief exec. officer, 1985—; chmn. bd. dirs. Agri Trans Corp., Fertrade; bd. dirs. Can. Fertilizers Ltd., The Fertilizer Inst., Nat. Council Farmer Coops.; co-chmn. Petrochem. Trade Group, Washington. Office: C F Industries Inc Salem Lake Dr Long Grove IL 60047

LIVELY, JOHN K., public relations executive; b. Marshalltown, Iowa, June 11, 1933; s. Kenneth Verlou and Helen Irene (Ethington) L. AB, Cornell Coll., Mt. Vernon, Iowa, 1955; MS, Columbia U., 1956. Asst. news dir. Sta. KFJB, Marshalltown, 1958-63; night editor Sta. WHO-AM-FM TV, Des Moines, 1963-66; pub. relations counselor 3 M Co., St. Paul, 1966-73, communications mgr., 1973-78, dir. pub. relations, 1981—; mgr. Eastern pub. relations 3-M Co., N.Y.C., 1978-81. Served with U.S. Army, 1956-58. Mem. Pub. Relations Soc. Am. (accredited). Methodist. Avocations: swimming, computers. Home: 4504 Belvidere Ln Edina MN 55435 Office: 3M Co Pub Relations Dept 3M Center Saint Paul MN 55144-1000

LIVELY, PIERCE, federal judge; b. Louisville, Aug. 17, 1921; s. Henry Thad and Ruby Durrett (Keating) L.; m. Amelia Harrington, May 25, 1946; children: Susan, Katherine, Thad. A.B., Centre Coll., Ky., 1943; LL.B., U. Va., 1948. Bar: Ky. 1948. Individual practice law Danville, Ky., 1949-57; mem. firm Lively and Rodes, Danville, 1957-72; judge U.S. Ct. Appeals (6th cir.), Cin., 1972—, chief judge, 1983—; mem. Ky. Commn. on Economy and Efficiency in Govt., 1963-65, Ky. Jud. Advisory Com., 1972. Trustee Centre Coll. Served with USNR, 1943-46. Mem. Am. Bar Assn., Am. Judicature Soc., Order of Coif, Raven Soc., Phi Beta Kappa, Omicron Delta Kappa. Presbyterian. Office: Room 626 US Courthouse Cincinnati OH 45202

LIVINGSTON, DANIEL L., computer systems specialist; b. Akron, Ohio, Dec. 31, 1942; s. Daniel and Ruth Violet (Hickerson) L.; m. Sandra Ann Murgul, Apr. 26, 1969; 1 child, Matthew. BBA, U. Akron, 1976. Dir. systems and programming Premier Indsl., Cleve., 1980; asst. v.p. tech. support Cen. Nat. Bank, Cleve., 1980-81, v.p. data processing, 1981; supr. tech. support LTV Steel Co., Cleve., 1981-84, mgr. tech. support, 1984-85, mgr. data adminstrn., 1985-86; mgr. tech. support Blue Cross and Blue Shield of Ohio, Cleve., 1986—. Mem. Data Processing Mgmt. Assn. Avocations: running, gardening, golfing. Home: 35 Chadbourne Dr Hudson OH 44236 Office: Blue Cross Blue Shield of Ohio 23700 Commerce Park Dr Beachwood OH 44122

LIVINGSTON, DAVID OVERBECK, accountant; b. Oakland, Calif., Apr. 8, 1962; s. John Jacob Livingston and Sonia (Overbeck) Kraft. BBA, U. Mich., 1984. Sr. acct. Price Waterhouse, Chgo., 1984—. Mem. Am. Inst. CPA's, Ill. CPA Soc. Home: 2850 N Sheridan Rd Apt 409 Chicago IL 60601 Office: Price Waterhouse 200 E Randolph Dr Chicago IL 60601

LIVINGSTON, HOWARD MITCHELL, manufacturing company executive; b. Leatherwood, Ky., Jan. 3, 1951; s. Howard Francis and Catherine Marie (Anderson) L.; m. Rita Rene McMillan, June 21, 1969. A. Engring., Allied Inst. Tech., Chgo., 1972. Machinist, F.J. Littell Co., Chgo., 1969-71; mech. engr. Machine Products Co., Skokie, Ill., 1971-73, dir. engring., 1973-75, v.p., 1975-82; pres. Helio Precision Products, Inc., Deerfield, Ill., 1982—. Sec., Riverwoods Residents Assn., 1980, 2d v.p., 1981, 1st v.p., 1982. Indsl. Arts Commn. scholar, 1969. Mem. Soc. Auto. Engrs (assoc.), Am. Soc. Quality Control, Soc. Mfg. Engrs., Ill. Mfrs. Assn., Aircraft Owners and Pilots Assn. Republican. Lodge: Optimists. Home: 475 White Oak Ln Riverwoods IL 60015 Office: Helio Precision Products Inc 725 County Line Rd Deerfield IL 60015

LIVINGSTON, JAMES MICHAEL, air force officer, program mgr., entomologist, toxicologist; b. Philadelphia, Miss., June 26, 1944; s. Arthur L. and Carmen J. L.; m. Venita Ann Upton, June 6, 1965; children—James Robert, Suzanne Michelle. B.S., Miss. State U., 1969; M.S., U. Ark., 1971, Ph.D., 1978; Research asst. U. Ark., Fayetteville, 1971-73; commd. 1st lt. U.S. Air Force, 1973, advanced through grades to lt. col. 1979; cons. entomologist USAF Environ. Health Lab., Kelly AFB, Tex., 1973-75; environ. entomologist USAF Occupational and Environ. Health Lab., Brooks AFB, Tex., 1978-80; chief environ. quality br. Air Force Aerospace Med. Research Lab., Wright Patterson AFB, Ohio, 1980-82, staff biomed. scientist for programs, 1982-83; biotech. rep., dep. for devel. planning Aero. Systems Div., Wright Patterson AFB, 1983-85, chief integration advanced tactical fighter, 1985—; adj. prof. biology Wright State U., Dayton, Ohio; cons. toxicologist USAF Surgeon Gen., 1983. Scoutmaster Tecumseh council Boy Scouts Am. Decorated Air Force Commendation medal with oak leaf cluster, recipient Air Force Meritorious Service medal award. Mem. Entomol. Soc. Am., Soc. Environ. Toxicology and Chemistry, Sigma Xi, Alpha Zeta, Gamma Sigma Delta. Presbyterian. Contbr. articles on insect virology, ecol. and pub. health aspects of pesticides, insect population dynamics, ecol. impact of hydrocarbon fuels to profl. jours. Home: 3133 Suburban Dr Beavercreek OH 45432 Office: Advanced Tactical Fighter System Program Office Wright Patterson AFB OH 45433

LIVINGSTON, RICHARD J., chemical company manager; b. Salina, Kans., Dec. 12, 1935; s. John W. and Jeanette E. (Casper) L.; m. Lou Ann Meyer, June 10, 1961; 1 child, Alan. BS in Chem. Engring., Kans. State U., 1959, MS in Chem. Engring., 1965. Devel. engr. Phillips Petrol Co., Bartlesville, Okla., 1961-69; tech. data analyst USI Chemicals Co., N.Y.C., 1971-74, sr. data analyst, 1974-77, sr. engr. assoc., 1977-82; mgr. USI Chemicals Co., Cin., 1982—. Contbr. articles to profl. jours. Mem. Am. Inst. Chem. Engrs., Cin. Inst. Chem. Engrs. Club: Appalachian Trail. Avocations: backpacking, photography. Office: USI Chemicals Co 11500 Northlake Dr Cincinnati OH 45249

LIVINGSTON-DUNN, CONNIE LYNN, art therapist; b. Mt. Morris, Ill., Oct. 16, 1940; d. Samuel Herman and Opal Zelinda (Kretsinger) Frey; m. David William Livingston, Feb. 10, 1959 (div. 1975); children: Penni, David William, Polli; m. Mervin Keith Dunn, Mar. 3, 1978 (div. 1980). AA, Sauk Valley Coll., 1970; BA, No. Ill. U., 1978, MA, 1982. Registered art therapist. Activity therapist Dixon (Ill.) Devel. Ctr. , 1966-86; dir. art therapy clin. program Mt. Mary Coll., Milw., 1984-85, inst. instr., 1985-86. Group shows include: Rockford (Ill.) ann. juried show, Nat. Art Edn. Assn., Marriott Hotel, Chgo., 1981, Merseyside County Mus., Liverpool, Eng., 1981-83, Beloit (Wis.) Ann. Exhbn., 1983, 87, Daley Civic Ctr., Chgo., 1983, Firebird Gallery, Alexandria, Va., 1984, Ill. Art Edn. Assn., 1984—, Profl. Art Exhibit Ill. State Fair, 1987, Nat. Watercolof Okla., 1987, Rush-Presbyn. St. Lukes Med. Ctr., 1986-87; represented in permanent collection: Sauk Valley Coll., Dixon, Ill. Mem. Nat. Art Edn. Assn., Ill. Art Edn. Assn., Am. Art Therapy Assn., Ill. Art Therapy Assn. Contbr. papers to profl. confs. and publs. Home: 107 E Oregon St Polo IL 61064

LIVSEY, ROBERTA, product/business planning analyst; b. Dayton, Ohio, Dec. 9, 1955; d. L.C. and Alberta (Steele) L. B.S.B.A., Ohio State U., 1977, M.B.A., 1978. Fin. analyst Parts and Service div. Ford Motor Co., Dearborn, Mich., 1978-81, Anaconda Industries, Rolling Meadows, Ill., 1981-82; sr. acctg. analyst Oldsmobile div. Gen. Motors Corp., Lansing, Mich., 1982-84; product/bus. planning analyst, bus. planning staff, Buick-Oldsmobile-Cadillac group, 1985—. Gen. Motors scholar, 1973. Mem. Planning Execs. Inst. Home: 2190 Regency Dr East Lansing MI 48823 Office: BOC Group Gen Motors Corp 920 Townsend St Lansing MI 48921

LIZDAS, WILLIAM HENRY, bank executive; b. Kewanee, Ill., Nov. 16, 1937; s. William Victor and Rose LaVerne (DeBord) L.; m. Charlotte Emily Ellerbrock, Oct. 31, 1959; children: Penny Jo, Melissa Gail, Marta Kay. BS in Edn., Western Ill. U., 1959, MS in Edn., 1961. Asst. cashier, asst. trust officer Union Nat. Bank, Macomb, Ill., 1959-63; trust officer 1st Nat. Bank, Pekin, Ill., 1963-65; v.p., cashier State Bank of East Moline, Ill., 1965-69; pres. Colona Ave. State Bank, East Moline, 1969-72; pres. and chief exec. officer Am. Bank, Rock Island, Ill., 1972—. Mem. exec. com. Rock Island Econ. Growth Corp., 1983-84; bd. dirs. City of Rock Island Comml.-Indsl. Loan Fund, 1985—, Ill. Quad Cities Civic Ctr. Authority, 1985-86; pres. Western Ill. Univ. Found., 1981; treas. United Way of Rock Island and Scott Counties, 1971; past deacon, treas., trustee Presbyn. churches in Macomb, Pekin and Rock Island; chmn. Rock Island Community Found. 1983—. Recipient Disting. Alumni award Western Ill. U., Macomb, 1984. Mem. Bank Adminstrn. Inst. (pres. Miss. Valley chpt. 1979), Am. Inst. Banking (pres. Quad Cities chpt. 1980), Adminstrv. Mgmt. Soc. (pres. Quad Cities chpt. 1971, Merit award, Diamond Merit award), Ill. Quad Cities C. of C., Rock Island C. of C. (pres. 1983). Clubs: Contemporary, Rock Island Arsenal Golf. Lodge: Masons (32 degree). Home: 2621 36th St Rock Island IL 61201 Office: Am Bank Rock Island PO Box 1178 3730 18th Ave Rock Island IL 61204-1178

LLOYD, LEONA LORETTA, lawyer; b. Detroit, Aug. 6, 1949; d. Leon Thomas and Naomi Mattie (Chisolm) L. BS, Wayne State U., 1971, JD, 1979. Bar: Mich. 1982. Speech, English tchr. Detroit Bd. Edn., 1971-75; instr. criminal justice Wayne State U., Detroit, 1981; sr. ptnr. Lloyd and Lloyd, Detroit, 1982—. Wayne State U. scholar, 1970, 75; recipient Kizzy Image award, 1985, Nat. Coalition of 100 Black Women Achievement award, 1986, Community Service award Wayne County exec. William Lucas, 1986, cert. merit U. Detroit Black Law Students Assn., 1986, Minority Bus. of Yr. award Wayne State U. Assn. Black Bus. Students, 1986, Fred Hampton Image award, 1984; named to Black Women Hall of Fame. Mem. ABA, Wolverine Bar Assn., Mary McLeod Bethune Assn. Office: Lloyd & Lloyd 600 Renaissance Ctr Suite 1400 Detroit MI 48243

LLOYD, ROBERT WILLIAM, aluminum foundry executive; b. El Reno, Okla., July 4, 1954; s. John Henry and Dorothy (Rigg) L.; m. Carol Carter Bodine, July 10, 1976; children: Julia Carter, Jacqueline Bodine. BS in Econs., U. Pa., 1977. Asst. sales mgr. Bodine Aluminum Inc., St. Louis, 1977-79, sales mgr., 1979-83, v.p., 1983—, also bd. dirs. Bd. dirs. Ronald Beasley Sch., St. Louis, 1986—, St. Louis Rotary Club, 1985, N.W. County YMCA, St. Louis, 1984. Mem. Am. Foundry Soc., Aluminum Assn. Avocations: golf, travel. Home: #6 Black Creek Ln Saint Louis MO 63124 Office: Bodine Aluminum Inc 2100 Walton Rd Saint Louis MO 63114

LLOYD, WILLIAM LAWRENCE, manufacturing executive; b. Willow Springs, Mo., May 25, 1945; s. Jack P. and Edith M. (Bottom) L.; m. Mary Beth Balsley, June 8, 1974; children: Rachel, Adam. BS, SW Mo. State U., 1967. Gen. mgr. TRS Industries, Eminence, Mo., 1977-79, Ozark Shell Industries, West Plains, Mo., 1979-80; pres. Innovative Industries, Inc., Carthage, Mo., 1980—. Served to capt. U.S. Army, 1967-70, Vietnam. Decorated Bronze Star and Air Medal. Mem. Am. Assn. Zoos Parks and Aquariums, Carthage C. of C. (v.p. 1985-86, pres. 1987—). Lodge: Lions (Carthage Citizen of Yr. 1982). Avocations: sailing, amateur radio. Home: 1116 S Maple St Carthage MO 64836

LOBANOV-ROSTOVSKY, OLEG, arts executive; b. San Francisco, July 12, 1934; s. Andrei and Grace S. (Pope) L-R.; m. Susan Waters, Sept. 8, 1979; 1 child, Alexandra; children by previous marriage: Christopher, Nicholas. BA, U. Mich., 1956. Community concert rep. Columbia Artists Mgmt. Inc., 1958-59; mgr. Columbus (Ohio) Symphony Orch., 1959-62, Hartford (Conn.) Symphony Orch., 1962-65; Balt. Symphony, 1965-69; program officer div. humanities and arts Ford Found., 1969-75; exec. dir. Denver Symphony Orch., 1975-76; mng. dir. Nat. Symphony Orch., Washington, 1977-80; cons. Fed. Council on Arts, 1980-81; exec. dir. Del. Center for Performing Arts, 1981-82; exec. v.p., mng. dir. Detroit Symphony Orch., 1982-83, pres., 1983—; past mem. bd. dirs. Am. Symphony Orch. League; bd. dirs. Detroit Inst. of Music and Dance, Cultural Ctr., Concerned Citizens for the Arts in Mich. Mailing Address: Detroit Symphony Ford Auditorium Detroit MI 48226

LOBENHOFER, LOUIS FRED, legal educator; b. Denver, Mar. 24, 1950; s. Frederick C. and Betty Lobenhofer; m. Carol E. Clarkson, June 16, 1973; children—Kristina M., Lauren E. A.B., Coll. William and Mary, 1972; J.D., U. Colo., 1975; LL.M., U. Denver, 1979. Bar: Colo. 1975, Tax Ct. 1982. Assoc. law firm Charles H. Booth, Denver, 1975-78; asst. prof. law Ohio No. U., 1979-82, assoc. prof., 1982-85, prof., 1985—. Denver Tax Inst. scholar, 1979. Mem. ABA, Soc. Am. Law Tchrs., Phi Beta Kappa, Omicron Delta Kappa, Delta Theta Phi. Republican. Roman Catholic. Office: Ohio No U Coll Law Ada OH 45810

LOBER, PAUL HALLAM, pathology educator; b. Mpls., Sept. 25, 1919; s. Harold A. and Minnie (Toraason) L.; 1 son, Patrick B. B.S., U. Minn., 1942, M.D., 1944, Ph.D. in Pathology, 1951. Intern, resident Hennepin County Gen. Hosp., 1944-46; fellow dept. pathology U. Minn., Mpls., 1948-51; faculty Med. Sch., 1951—, prof. pathology, 1963-86, emeritus prof., 1986—; surg. pathologist Univ. Hosps., Mpls., 1951-74, Abbott-Northwestern Hosp., Mpls., 1974—. Served to capt. AUS, 1946-48. Fellow Coll. Am. Pathologists; mem. AMA, Am. Soc. Clin. Pathologists, Internat. Acad. Pathology, Am. Assn. Pathologists, Am. Soc. Cytology, N.Y. Acad. Scis., Alpha Omega Alpha. Home: 1525 W 28th St Minneapolis MN 55408 Office: Pathology Dept Abbott-Northwestern Hosp 800 E 28th St Minneapolis MN 55407

LOBERG, THOMAS JOHN, accountant; b. St. Paul, Mar. 14, 1955; s. Robert John and Rose Kathryn (Ginnaty) L.; m. Carolyn Ann Woodruff, June 30, 1979; B.S. in Acctg., U. Minn., 1976. C.P.A., Minn. Sr. auditor Arthur Andersen Co., St. Paul, 1977-79; mgr. audit Borowicz, Holmgren, Burnsville, Minn., 1980-81, audit ptnr. Borowicz, Holmgren, Loberg Co., 1981-83; ptnr., audit practice dir. Bergren, Holmgren Loberg Ltd., 1983—, now chmn., also vice chmn. bd. dirs.; dir. Metrinch Tool Co. Treas. Penny Route Charity, 1983; adviser Jr. Achievement of St. Paul, 1977-81. Named Jr. Achievement Outstanding Achiever, 1977; recipient Reader's Digest Seminar award, fall 1974. Mem. Am. Inst. CPA's, Minn. Soc. CPA's, Alpha Kappa Psi (alumni chpt. v.p., 1983-84, pres. 1984-85). Republican. Roman Catholic. Clubs: Bracketts Crossing Country (Mpls.), Mendakota Country (West St. Paul). Lodge: Elks (exalted ruler 1983-84, trustee 1984-86). Office: Bergren Holmgren & Loberg Ltd 501 E Hwy 13 Burnsville MN 55337-2877

LOCASCIO, JAMES EDWARD, dentist; b. Detroit, July 25, 1955; s. Salvatore Antonio and Mary Louise (Barduca) L.; m. Mary Agnes Hall, June 24, 1977; children: James Edward, Michael Anthony, Gina Louise. BA, Wayne State U., 1977; DDS, U. Detroit, 1981. Gen. practice dentistry Joy Road Dental Ctr., Detroit, 1981-82, W.P. Scales and Assocs., Detroit, 1982-86, Pontiac Family Dental Ctr., Waterford, Mich., 1986—. Mem. Rep. Presdl. Task Force, Washington, 1984—, Rep. Senatorial Club, Washington, 1984—, Conservative Caucus, Washington, 1982—. Mem. ADA, Mich. Dental Soc., Detroit Dist. Dental Soc., Chgo. Dental Soc. Roman Catholic. Home: 1651 Brentwood Wixom MI 48096

LOCH, JOHN ROBERT, educational administrator; b. Sharon, Pa., Aug. 25, 1940; s. Robert Addison and Mary Virginia (Beck) L.; student Waynesburg Coll., 1958; AB, Grove City Coll., 1962; postgrad Pitts. Theol. Sem., 1962; MEd, U. Pitts., 1966, PhD, 1972; cert. Harvard U., 1984. Asst. to dean men U. Pitts., 1963-64, dir. student union, 1964-70, dir. student affairs research, 1970-71, dir. suburban ednl. services Sch. Gen. Studies, 1971-75; dir. continuing edn. and pub. service Youngstown (Ohio) State U., 1975-82, dir. continuing edn./edn. outreach, 1982—, assoc. mem. grad. faculty, 1980—; research assoc. Pres's Commn. on Campus Unrest, 1970. Trustee, Mahoning Shenango Health Edn. Network, 1976—, Career Devel. Ctr. for Women, 1978-80; trustee Youngstown Area Arts Council, 1980-85, pres., 1981-83; bd. dirs. Protestant Family Services, 1981-83; trustee Mahoning County RSVP, 1983—, chmn. evaluation com., 1983-84, chmn. personnel com., 1984-85, chmn. bd. trustees, 1986-87; coordinator fund raising Nat. Unity Campaign, Mahoning County, 1980; state chmn. Young Rep. Coll. Council Pa., 1960. Mem. Adult Edn. Assn. USA, Am. Assn. Higher Edn., Nat. U. Continuing Edn. Assn., Ohio Council Higher Continuing Edn. (pres. 1979-80), Ohio Continuing Higher Edn. Assn. (co-chmn. constn. com. 1982, v.p. state univs. 1984-85, pres.-elect 1985-86, pres. 1986-87), Omicron Delta Kappa, Kappa Kappa Psi, Phi Kappa Phi (pres. 1980-81), Alpha Phi Omega, Alpha Sigma Lambda, Phi Delta Kappa. Presbyterian. Clubs: Kiwanis (dir. 1981-82), Youngstown Traffic (hon. life). Home: 242 Upland Ave Youngstown OH 44504 Office: Youngstown State U Youngstown OH 44555

LOCHER, RALPH S., justice Ohio Supreme Ct.; b. Moreni, Romania, July 24, 1915; s. Ephraim and Natalie (Voigt) L.; m. Eleanor Worthington, June 18, 1939; 1 dau., Virginia Lynn. B.A. with honors, Bluffton Coll., 1936; LL.B., Case Western Res. U., 1939. Bar: Ohio bar 1939. Former sec. to Gov. Ohio; former law dir. City of Cleve.; former mayor Cleve.; judge Ohio Ct. Common Pleas Cuyahoga County, 1969-72, Cuyahoga County Ct. Probate Div., 1973-77; justice Supreme Ct. Ohio, 1977—. Mem. Am. Bar Assn., Bar Assn. Greater Cleve., Cuyahoga County Bar Assn. Democrat. Office: State Office Tower 30 E Broad St Columbus OH 43215

LOCHIANO, STEPHEN ANTHONY, controller; b. Liberal, Kans., Mar. 2, 1949; s. Rocco LoChiano and Margie Louise (Pitts) LoChiano Wooden; m. Ellen Jane Walker, Aug. 28, 1971; children—Anthony Paul, Ryan Michael, Eric Stephen. B.S. in Bus. Adminstrn., U. Nebr., Lincoln, 1975; postgrad. U. Nebr., Omaha, 1980—. Office mgr. trainee Roberts Dairy, Omaha, 1976-78; controller Security Internat., Omaha, 1978, Jubilee Mfg. Co., Omaha, 1978-80, Omaha Box Co., 1983-85; controller Plastr Glas, Inc., Omaha, 1985—; plant acct. Weyerhaeuser Co., Omaha, 1980-83. Served as sgt. U.S. Army, 1973-75. Mem. Nat. Assn. Accts. (controllers council 1984—), Nat. Assn. Credit Mgrs., Internat. Soc. Wang Users, Toastmasters (dist. treas. 1980-81). Republican. Lutheran. Club: Park Ave. Health (Omaha). Avocations: camping, computer programming. Home: 10205 R St Omaha NE 68127 Office: Plastr Glas Inc 4200 N 30 Omaha NE 68111

LOCHRIDGE, IAN JAMES, lawyer; b. New York, N.Y., Nov. 15, 1950; s. Campbell David Lochridge and Jean Elizabeth (Brownlow) Berasaluce; 1 child, Collin James. BA, U. Ill., 1976; JD, DePaul U., 1979. Bar: Ill. 1979, U.S. Dist. Ct. (no. dist.) Ill. 1979, U.S. Ct. of Appeals (7th cir.) 1979, U.S. Supreme Ct. 1986. Law clerk to presiding justice U.S. Dist. Ct. (no. dist.), Chgo., 1979, Ill. Appellate Ct., Chgo., 1980-81; assoc. Garretson & Santora, Chgo., 1981-86, ptnr., 1986—; cons. Adoptive Parent's Guild, Cath. Charities, 1981-84, Village Mgr. Assn., Oak Park, 1982—; commr. Liquor Control Bd., Oak Park, 1986—. Bd. dirs. United Village Party, 1980-82, T.O.P. Party, 1982-86. Mem. ABA, Ill. Bar Assn., Chgo. Bar Assn., Appellate Lawyers Assn., Defense Research Inst. Avocation: white water canoeist. Office: Garretson & Santora 33 N Dearborn St Chicago IL 60602

LOCICERO, DEBBI DIANE, architect; b. Milw., June 1, 1952; d. Anthony Louis and Ilse Catherine (Grobecker) LoC. BArch, U. Wis., Milw., 1980. Registered architect, Wis. Architect U.S. Army C.E., Omaha, 1980—. Mem. Beta Sigma Phi (treas. 1985—). Avocations: running, traveling. Office: US Army CE 215 N 17th St Room 4019 Omaha NE 68102

LOCK, ROBERT JOSEPH, accountant; b. Jefferson City, Mo., June 20, 1955; s. Elmer Joseph and Clara Barbara (Luebbert) L.; m. Cheryl Lynne Garoutte, Apr. 20, 1985. BSBA in Acctg., U. Mo., 1977. CPA, Mo. Sr. Mo. State Auditor's Office, Jefferson City, 1977-82; ptnr. McBride, Lock & Assocs., Kansas City, Mo., 1982—. Mem. Am. Inst. CPA's, Mo. Soc. CPA's, Assn Govtl. Accts. Roman Catholic. Lodge: KC. Avocations: boating, golf, tennis. Home: 4009 NW73d St Kansas City MO 64151 Office: McBride Lock & Assocs 1221 Baltimore St Suite 406 Kansas City MO 64105

LOCKARD, JAMES ALLEN, educator; b. Kansas City, Mo., Mar. 10, 1945; s. Frederick Wayne and Carolyn Doris (Clayton) L.; m. Kathlynn Burkhalter, June 5, 1970; 1 child, Kathlynn Jean. BA, U. No. Iowa, 1967; MA, Northwestern U., 1968; PhD, Iowa State U., 1974. Faculty, administrator Buena Vista Coll., Storm Lake, Iowa, 1968-72, 74-80; teaching asst., instr. Iowa State U., Ames, Iowa, 1972-74; instr. continuing educator No. Ill. U., DeKalb, 1980-83, mem. faculty, 1983—. Edn. editor European Studies Jour., 1984—; editorial reviewer Innovative Higher Edn., 1975—, Media and Adult Learning, 1985—. Mem. Nat. Soc. Performance and Instruction, Assn. for Ednl. Communications and Tech., Internat. Council for Computers in Edn., Phi Kappa Phi. Avocations: computer graphics, piano, bicycling, swimming. Home: 141 Mason Ct Sycamore IL 60178 Office: No Ill U Coll of Edn Leadership and Ednl Policy DeKalb IL 60115

LOCKE, CHARLES STANLEY, manufacturing company executive, director; b. Laurel, Miss., Mar. 5, 1929; s. Richard C. and Florence (Parker) L.; m. NoraLou Fulkerson, Mar. 15, 1952; children: Cathy, Stanley, Lauren, Pamela. B.B.A., U. Miss., 1952, M.S., 1955. With Price Waterhouse & Co., C.P.A.s, New Orleans, 1955-58, Westvaco, Inc., 1958-64; controller A.E. Staley Mfg. Co., 1964-69; v.p. Brown Co., Pasadena, Calif., 1969-73; mem. exec. com.; sr. v.p. Allen Group Inc., Melville, N.Y., 1973-75; v.p. fin. Morton-Norwich Products, Inc. (name changed to Morton Thiokol 1982), Chgo., 1975-80; v.p. fin. Morton-Norwich Products, Inc. (name changed to Morton Thiokol 1982), chmn. bd., chief exec. officer, 1980-84, 1984—; chmn. bd., pres., chief exec. officer Morton Thiokol, Inc., 1982-84, chmn. bd., chief exec. officer, 1984—; dir. Avon Products, Inc., First Chgo. Corp., First Nat. Bank Chgo., NICOR, Inc., No. Ill. Gas Corp. Trustee Mus. Sci. and Industry, U. of Chgo., Rush-Presbyn.-St. Lukes Med. Ctr.; mem. Econ. Com., Mid-Am. Com., Chgo. Com., The Conf. bd.; bd. dirs. U. Chgo., The Lyric Opera. Clubs: Sky, Chicago, Commercial, Economic, Tower, Mid-America, Executives (adv. bd.), Room One Hundred; Sunset Ridge Country (Northfield, Ill.); Old Elm Country. Home: 1504 N Waukegan Rd Lake Forest IL 60045 Office: Morton Thiokol Inc 110 N Wacker Dr Chicago IL 60606

LOCKE, LINDA MARIE, marketing professional; b. Kansas City, Mo., Nov. 13, 1953; d. Robert Wallace and Mary Janet (O'Neill) L.; m. Rory Ellinger, Oct. 11, 1980; children: Margaret Ellinger-Locke, Martin Ellinger-Locke. BJ, Kans. State U., 1976; postgrad, U. Mo. Grad. research asst. U. Mo., Columbia, 1978-80; dir. devel. Mo. Assn. Social Welfare, Jefferson City, 1980-81; pres. LML Communications, Hannibal, Mo., 1982-85; dir. communications HOK Computer Service Corp., St. Louis, 1985—. Vol. Peace Corps, Souk Sebt, Morocco, 1975-77; exec. dir. Mo. ERA Campaign, St. Louis, 1981-82; mem. Melrose Ave. Neighborhood Assn., St. Louis, 1986. Recipient Ad award Progressive Architecture mag., 1985, 86, Award of Merit, Soc. Tech. Communication Architecture, 1985. Mem. Am. Mgmt. Assn., NOW (past pres. Mo. chpt.). Democrat. Home: 7340 Melrose Saint Louis MO 63130 Office: HOK Computer Service Corp 802 N First St Saint Louis MO 63102

LOCKETT, HAROLD JAMES, physician, psychiatrist; b. Wilmington, Del., July 17, 1924; s. Jesse and Annie Lessie (Colbert) L.; m. Betty Jean Griffin, June 11, 1950 (dec. Aug. 1980); 1 child, Chérie Robin. AB, Ind. U., 1948; MD, Meharry Med. Coll., 1952. Diplomate Am. Bd. Psychiatry and Neurology, Am. Bd. Child Psychiatry. Intern Los Angeles County Gen. Hosp., 1952-53; resident in psychiatry U. Mich. Med. Ctr., Ann Arbor, 1953-56; resident fellow in child psychiatry Hawthorn Ctr., Northville, Mich., 1956-58, staff psychiatrist, 1958-72, asst. dir., 1972—; clin. asst. prof. U. Mich. Med. Sch., Ann Arbor; pvt. practice in psychiatry, Ann Arbor; cons. to numerous sch. systems. Contbr. articles to profl. jours. Pres. Ann Arbor Bd. Edn., 1969-71, trustee, 1965-71; bd. dirs. Ann Arbor chpt. ACLU; pres. bd. dirs. Spaulding for Children, Chelsea, Mich., 1969-85. Fellow Am. Acad. Child Psychiatry, Am. Orthopsychiatric Assn.; mem. Am Psychiat. Assn., Nat. Med. Assn., Black Psychiatrists Am. Democrat. Avocations: tennis, art objects, paintings, African artifacts, skiing. Home: 319 Brookside Dr Ann Arbor MI 48105 Office: Hawthorn Ctr 18471 Haggerty Rd Northville MI 48167

LOCKETT, TYLER C., state supreme court justice; b. Corpus Christi, Tex., Dec. 7, 1932; s. Tyler Coleman and Evelyn (Lemond) L.; m. Sue W. Lockett, Nov. 3, 1961; children—Charles, Patrick. A.B., Washburn U., 1955, J.D., 1962. Bar: Kans. Sole practice law Wichita, 1962—; judge Ct. Common Pleas, 1971-77, Kans. Dist. Ct. 18th Dist., 1977-83; justice Supreme Court Kans., Topeka, 1983—. Office: Kans Supreme Ct Judicial Ctr 301 W 10th St Topeka KS 66612 *

LOCKHART, CHARLES FREDRICK, dentist; b. Mpls., Nov. 9, 1943; s. Walter Lawrence and Lua Jane (Bates) L.; m. Caroline Anne Kinne, Jan. 6, 1968; children: Kendra Paige, Charles Davidson. Student, U. Iowa, 1961-63, Northwestern U., 1967-68; BS in Dentistry, U. Ill., Chgo., 1971, DDS with honors, 1973. Ptnr. Northview Dental Assocs., Ltd., Northfield, Ill., 1974-85; gen. practice dentistry Chgo., 1985—; cons. Sutra, Ltd., Northbrook, Ill., 1980—. Editor Pulse Newsletter, 1974-75. Served with USN, 1964-67. Fellow Acad. Gen. Dentistry (del. 1979—, sec. 1985—), Acad. Continuing Edn. (charter); mem. ADA, Ill. State Dental Soc., Ill. Acad. Gen. Dentistry (bd. dirs. 1979—), U. Ill. Alumni Assn. (life), Psi Omega, Delta Chi, Omicron Kappa Upsilon. Methodist. Club: North Shore Country (Glenview, Ill.). Lodge: Knights of the Vine (master councillor 1982—). Avocations: wine, curling, racquetball. Home: 2067 Butternut Ln Northbrook IL 60062 Office: 4748 N Milwaukee Ave Chicago IL 60630

LOCKRIDGE, KAREN SUE, marketing executive; b. Goshen, Ind., Nov. 23, 1948; d. Leslie Eugene and Rhea Jean (Reed) L.; B.A., Purdue U., 1971. With Allen & O'Hara, Inc., mgrs. Holiday Inns, 1967-82, sales dir., asst. gen. mgr. Holiday Inn, Tampa, Fla., 1975-82; corp. dir. sales Midway Motor Lodges, Brookfield, Wis., 1982-84; v.p. sales and mktg. Midway Mgmt. Group, Inc., 1984-85; owner, operator Apricot Annie's Cafe & Bar, 1985—. Bd. dirs. Milw. Conv. and Visitors Bur. Recipient Human Relations award City of Tampa, 1980. Mem. Am. Soc. Assn. Execs., Religious Conv. Mgrs. Assn., Nat. Tour Brokers Assn., Am. Bus. Assn., Milw. Conv. and Visitors Bur., Meeting Planners Internat., Sales and Mktg. Execs. of Milw., Wis. Soc. Assn. Execs. Episcopalian. Home: 2025 E Greenwich St Milwaukee WI 53211 Office: 275 W Wisconsin Ave Milwaukee WI 53203

LOCKWOOD, DEANNA LYNNE, social welfare financial executive; b. Mpls., Sept. 14, 1947; d. Robert Paul Lockwood and Gloria Faye (Johnson) Wiles; m. Kevin David Sweeney, Sept. 16, 1972. BA, Macalester Coll., 1969; MA, U. Chgo., 1972; MBA, 1978. CPA, Ill. Indexer Am. Hosp. Assn., Chgo., 1972-74; info. analyst Blue Cross Assn., Chgo., 1974-77; acctg. mgr. Wilmette (Ill.) Park Dist., 1978-81, bus. mgr., 1981-83; acctg. mgr. Ill. Mcpl. Retirement Fund, 1983—; instr. Ill. Inst. Tech., Chgo., 1982-83. Mem. Am. Soc. Women CPA's, Chgo. Soc. Women CPA's, Am. Inst. CPA's. Office: Ill Mcpl Retirement Fund 100 S Wacker Dr Chicago IL 60606

LOCKWOOD, FRANK STEPHEN, real estate investor, venture capitalist; b. Washington, Feb. 11, 1943; s. Fred Stark and Helen (Day) L.; m. Linda Pickhardt, June 25, 1966; children: Amy Helen, Rebecca Elizabeth. BS, Ripon Coll., 1965; MBA, Emory U., 1969. Registered rep. Smith Barney, Chgo., 1969-74; v.p. Blunt, Ellis & Loewi, Barrington, Ill., 1974-78; pres. Barrington Trading, 1978-83, Thermal Services, Barrington, 1984—, FSL Enterprises Inc., Barrington, 1983—; bd. dirs. East Tenn. Bancorp, Knoxville. Served to 1st lt. U.S. Army, 1965-67. Republican. Club: Union League (Chgo.). Office: FSL Enterprises Inc PO Box 450 Barrington IL 60011-0450

LOCKWOOD, GEORGE HEPWORTH, provincial judge; b. Glasshoughton, Yorks, Eng., Apr. 18, 1923; s. George and Phoebe (Bradburn) L.; m. Lissen Karen, Jan. 27, 1962; children: Mette Norma, Michael Hepworth, Martin Bradburn. BA, Oxford U., Eng.; MA, Lincoln's Inn, London. Bus. exec., mgr. London and Kenya, 1950-53; officer Colonial Service, Kenya, 1953-57; assoc. Guy, Chapell, Guy, Wilson and Coghlin, 1958-61, Pitblado and Hoskin, Winnipeg, 1961-66; ptnr. Fillmore and Riley, Winnipeg, 1966-78; judge Ct. of Queen's Bench, Winnipeg, 1984—. Served with British RCAF, 1943-46. Office: Court of Queen's Bench, Law Courts Bldg, Winnipeg, MB Canada R3C 0V8 *

LOCKWOOD, HAROLD RAYMOND, naval officer, association executive; b. Dansville, N.Y., July 5, 1927; s. Harold DeForest and Hermina Belle (Rynders) L.; m. Marilyn Joanne Benson, Aug. 11, 1951 (dec. Sept. 1982); children: Harold B., Thomas A., Kathryn A., Nancy E. BS, U.S. Naval Acad., Annapolis, Md., 1950; student, Naval War Coll., Newport, R.I., 1960-61, George Washington U., 1964-65; MA in Polit. Sci., Marquette U., 1978. Cert. assn. exec. Commd. ensign USN, 1950, advanced through grades to capt., 1970, ret., 1975; govtl. liaison Sheet Metal Contractors Assn., Milw., 1976-78; exec. v.p. Sheet Metal Contractors Assn. of Milw., Inc., 1978—; govtl. liaison Sheet Metal Contractors Assn., Milw., 1976-86. Chpt. coordinator Wis. Environ. Balancing Bur., Milw., 1978—. Decorated Bronze Star. Mem. Navy League of U.S. (pres. Milw. council 1986), U.S. Naval Acad. Alumni Assn. (pres. Wis. chpt. 1985), U.S. Naval Inst., U.S. Strategic Inst., Am. Soc. Assn. Execs., Wis. Soc. Assn. Execs. (dir. 1986), Nat. Sheet Metal Assn. (bus. mgmt. edn. com. 1985-86, Mgr. of Yr. 1983). Republican. Club: Lac La Belle Country (Oconomowoc, Wis.). Lodge: Kiwanis. Avocations: jogging, downhill skiing, woodworking, golf. Home: 18435 Tilton Ct Brookfield WI 53005 Office: Sheet Metal and Air Conditioning Contractors Assn Milw Inc 2515 N 124th St Suite 200 Milwaukee WI 53005

LODDE, BARBARA LYNN, school system administrator; b. Milw., Aug. 17, 1949; d. John Thomas and Frances Elizabeth (Rodman) L. BA, Mt. Mary Coll., 1971; MS, U. Wis., Milw., 1981. Personnel asst. Milw. Pub. Schs., 1973-77, transp. asst., field supr., 1977—. Bookfellow Milw. Pub. Library, 1984—; mem. Milw. Symphony Women's League, 1984—; vol. bd. dirs. Wis. Conservatory of Music, 1981-83; trustee U. Wis. Sch. of Edn. Alumni Assn., 1986—. Mem. AAUW (sec. w. suburban br. 1984-85), Milw. Adminstr. and Suprs. (sec. 1981-83). Roman Catholic. Avocations: music, tennis, theater. Office: Milw Pub Schs Dept Transp 5225 W Vliet Milwaukee WI 53208

LODWICK, KATHLEEN LORRAINE, historian, educator; b. St. Louis, Feb. 7, 1944; d. Algha Claire and Kathryn Elizabeth (Worthington) L. BS with honors, Ohio U., 1964, MA, 1965; PhD, U. Ariz., 1976; postgrad. U. Hawaii, 1966-67, Nat. Taiwan Normal U., 1967-68. Asst. prof. history U. No. Colo., 1976-77; asst. prof. history Ind. State U., 1977-78; research assoc. John King Fairbank Ctr. for East Asian Research, Harvard U., 1978-79; asst. prof. history S.W. Mo. State U., Springfield, 1979-82, assoc. prof., 1982-87, prof., 1987—; dir. index/biog. guide to Chinese Recorder and Missionary Jour. project, 1977-86. Author: The Chinese Recorder Index: A Guide to Christian Missions in Asia, 1867-1941, 1986. Mem. AAUW, Am. Assn. Univ. Profs., Am. Hist. Assn., Assn. Asian Studies, Nat. Assn. Fgn. Student Affairs, UN Assn., Soc. of Friends, Phi Alpha Theta. Democrat. Home: 2934 E Southeast Circle Springfield MO 65802 Office: Southwest Mo State U History Dept Springfield MO 65802

LOEB, JEROME THOMAS, retail executive; b. St. Louis, Sept. 13, 1940; s. Harry W. and Marjorie T. Loeb; m. Carol Bodenheimer, June 15, 1963; children: Daniel W., Kelly E. BS, Tufts U., 1962; MA, Washington U., St. Louis, 1964. Asst. dir. research, dir. EDP, div. v.p., dir. mgmt. info. services Famous-Barr div. May Dept. Stores Co., St. Louis, 1964-74, v.p. mgmt. info. services/EDP parent co., 1974-77, sr. v.p., chief fin. officer Hecht's div., Washington, 1977-79; exec. v.p. devel. May Dept. Stores Co., St. Louis, 1979-81, exec. v.p., chief fin. officer, 1981—; mem. bd. dirs., 1984—, vice chmn. 1986—; bd. dirs. Centerre Trust Co. Vice chmn. bd. dirs. Jr. Achievement of Mississippi Valley, 1982—; treas., bd. dirs. Jewish Hosp. St. Louis, 1984—; treas., trustee John Burroughs Sch., 1984—; mem. Econ. Policy Council UN Assn., 1983—. Club: Westwood Country. Office: May Dept Stores Co 6th & Olive Sts Saint Louis MO 63101

LOEBACH, DAVID, labor relations specialist, military officer; b. LaSalle, Ill., June 27, 1946; s. Richard and Sophie (Stor) L.; m. Shelli Carol Denison, Oct. 2, 1976; children: Katharine, Rachel. BA, U. Ill., 1968; MA, Sangamon State U., 1975. Personnel technician Dept. Pub. Works and Bldgs., State of Ill., 1968-69; personnel analyst Dept. Trans., State of Ill., 1972-74; labor-mgmt. adminstr. Ill. Office Collective Bargaining, 1974-78; adminstrv. asst. to dir. labor State of Ill., 1978-82; ops. and tng. officer N.G. Mil. Acad., Ill., 1982-84; tng. and devel. analyst N.G. Bur. Pentagon, Washington, 1984—; asst. prof. mil. sci. No. Ill. U., DeKalb, 1985—. Served with U.S. Army, 1969-72. Mem. N.G. Assn., Reserve Officer Assn., Am. Arbitration Assn. (labor arbitrator), Fed. Mediation and Concilation Service. Avocations: photography, running, current events. Home: 859 Meadow Ln Sycamore IL 60178 Office: Northern Ill Univ PO Box 178 DeKalb IL 60115-0178

LOEBACH, MICHAEL CLAUD, otolaryngologist; b. South Bend, Ind., Jan. 2, 1946; s. Edward Raymond Loebach and Mary Jean (Brooker) Follett; m. Kathryn Jean Negles, Nov. 11, 1972; James Christopher, Christina Marie, Edward Michael. BA, St. Mary's Coll., Winona, Minn., 1968; MD, Northwestern U., 1972. Diplomate Am. Bd. Otolaryngology. Intern Rush-Presby. St. Luke's Hosp., Chgo., 1972-73; resident in otolaryngology U. Ill. Eye and Ear Infirmary, Chgo., 1975-78; staff physician Dreyer Med. Clinic, Aurora, Ill., 1978—, also treas. and bd. dirs.; pres. bd. dirs. Dreyer HMO. Chmn. cubscout pack com. Boy Scouts Am., Aurora, 1982-85. Served to lt. USN, 1973-75. Fellow ACS, Am. Acad. Otolaryngology. Republican. Roman Catholic. Avocations: downhill skiing, travel, gardening. Office: Dreyer Med Clinic 1870 W Galena Blvd Aurora IL 60506

LOEFFLER, LOWELL FREDERICK, life insurance agent; b. Grand Island, Nebr., Nov. 7, 1913; s. Frederick Frank and Eva S. (Stearns) L.; m. Wilma Aria Smith, June 16, 1940; children—Mark, Alan, Kent, Bruce. A.B., Doane Coll., 1937; M.B.A., U. Mich., 1942; C.L.U. Spl. agent Bankers Life Nebr., Lincoln, 1949-58, gen. agent, 1958-65; gen. agent Midland Nat. Life, Sioux Falls, S.D., 1965—. Chmn. bd. dirs. Child Evangelism Fellowship of Nebr., Lincoln, chmn. 1981—; nat. trustee Child Evangelism Fellowship, Inc., Warrentown, Mo., 1970—. Mem. Omaha Assn. Baptist Men (pres. 1983-85). Served as lt. (j.g.) USN, 1943-46, PTO. Republican. Baptist. Club: Golden K Kiwanis (Fremont) (pres. 1983-84). Avocations: golfing; fishing; Bible teaching; working with youth. Home: 1443 W Linden St Fremont NE 68025

LOEPPERT, HENRY VERNE, manufacturing executive; b. Chgo., Dec. 15, 1921; s. Henry Valentine and Ellen (Waterman) L.; m. Frances Kathryn Schnitzer, June 22, 1946; children: James Edwin, Peter Verne, Sue Ellen Loeppert Visscher. BSME, Northwestern U., 1944; MBA, U. Chgo., 1959. Registered profl. engr., Ill., Calif. With Boyd-Wagner Co., Chgo., 1946-61, pres., 1961-68; dir. mktg. Ingersoll Cutting Tool Co., Rockford, Ill., 1969-75; pvt. practice cons. Rockford, 1975—; pres. Stuhr Mfg. Co., Rockford, 1980—; bd. dirs. Liberty Fed. Savs. and Loan, Chgo.; pres. Ill. Engr. Council, 1961. Mem. Plan Commn., Glenview, Ill., 1957-60, chmn. 1960-66; trustee Village of Glenview, 1966-70; active Niles Twp. Bd. Edn., Skokie, Ill., 1967-70; pres. Wesley Willows Corps., Rockford, 1983-86. Served to capt. USNR, 1942-61. Fellow Inst. Prodn. Engrs. (life); mem. Soc. Mfg. Engrs. (life, pres. 1964-65), Ill. Ind. Dist. Assn. (pres. 1961-63). Clubs: Union League (Chgo.), Forest Hills Country (Rockford) (gov. 1983-86). Home: 5023 Crofton Dr Rockford IL 61111 Office: Stuhr Mfg Co PO Box 6246 Rockford IL 61125

LOEPPKE, LARRY DEAN, textbook company executive; b. Lakin, Kans., Aug. 11, 1950; s. Archie Roy and Katharine (Crowder) L.; m. Rhonda Sue Holdridge, Nov. 24, 1951; children: Teran Edward, Nyssa Adere. BA, Phillips U., 1972. From project dir. to regional dir. Inst. Cultural Affairs, Chgo., Nairobi, Kenya Africa and Lagos Nigeria, 1973-77; assoc. editor Kendall-Hunt Pub. Co., Kansas City, Mo., 1977-80, mng. editor, 1981-85, nat. field mgr., 1985—. Home: 3741 Locust St Kansas City MO 64109 Office: Kendall-Hunt Pub Co 301 E Armour Blvd Kansas City MO 64111

LOESCH, KATHARINE TAYLOR (MRS. JOHN GEORGE LOESCH), educator; b. Berkeley, Calif., Apr. 13, 1922; d. Paul Schuster and Katharine (Whiteside) Taylor; student Swarthmore Coll., 1939-41, U. Wash., 1942; B.A., Columbia U., 1944, M.A., 1949; grad. Neighborhood Playhouse Sch. of Theatre, 1946; postgrad. Ind. U., 1953; Ph.D., Northwestern U., 1961; m. John George Loesch, Aug. 28, 1948; 1 son, William Ross. Instr. speech Wellesley (Mass.) Coll., 1949-52, Loyola U., Chgo., 1956; asst. prof. English and speech Roosevelt U., Chgo., 1957, 62-65; assoc. prof. communication and theatre U. Ill. at Chgo., 1968—. Active ERA, Ill., 1975-76. Recipient Golden Anniversary Prize award Speech Assn. Am., 1969. Am. Philos. Soc. grantee, 1970; U. Ill., Chgo., grantee, 1970. Mem. Am. Soc. Aesthetics, Linguistics Soc. Am., Speech Communication Assn. (Golden Anniversary prize award 1969, chmn. interpretation div. 1979-80), MLA, Honorable Soc. Cymmrodorion, Pi Beta Phi. Episcopalian. Contbr. writings to profl. publs. Office: U Ill Dept Communication and Theatre Box 4348 Chicago IL 60680

LOEWE, LESLIE F., apparel company executive; b. St. Louis, May 4, 1921; s. Franz Joseph and Minnette (Seches) L.; m. Carol Wilson, Mar. 18, 1950. B.A. in Polit. Sci. and Econs., Washington U., St. Louis, 1942; M.B.A., Harvard Bus. Sch., 1947. Various positions Angelica Corp., St. Louis, 1947-73, exec. v.p., 1973-80, pres., chief exec. officer, 1980-84, chmn., chief exec. officer, 1984—, also bd. dirs.; dir. Medicine Shoppe Internat., Inc., St. Louis, Tipton Ctrs., Inc., Boatmen's Nat. Bank of St. Louis, Boatmen's Bancshares, Inc., St. Louis. Mem. pres.' council St. Louis U.; bd. dirs. United Way of Greater St. Louis. Served to capt. U.S. Army, 1942-46. Mem. Am. Apparel Mfrs.' Assn. Jewish. Clubs: St. Louis, Westwood Country, Harvard. Office: Angelica Corp 10176 Corporate Sq Dr Saint Louis MO 63132

LOEWENSTEIN, PAUL WILLON, plastic surgeon; b. Terre Haute, Ind., Sept. 21, 1950; s. Werner Leo and Hazel Ruth (Anderson) L.; m. Jody Hope Kaufmann, June 27, 1976; children: Andrew, Daniel. BS, Stanford U., 1972; MD, Ind. U., 1976. Diplomate Am. Bd. Surgery, Am. Bd. Plastic Surgery. Intern Ind. U. Hosp., 1976-77, resident gen. surgery, 1977-80, resident plastic surgery, 1980-82; pvt. practice Plastic Surgery Assocs., Milw., 1982—; chmn. div. plastic surgery St. Luke's Hosp., Milw., 1983; clin. asst. prof. plastic surgery Med. Coll. of Wis., Milw., 1984. Co-author: (scientific exhibit) Life Perfusion for Melanoma of the Lower Extremity (2d Place award Am. Soc. Plastic and Reconstructive Surgeons annual meeting); contbr. articles to med. jours. Bd. dirs. Brotherhood of Congregation Emanu-el, Milw., 1986. Mem. AMA, ACS, Am. Soc. Plastic and Reconstructive Surgeons, Am. Coll. Surgeons, Midwest Soc. Plastic Surgeons, Wis. Soc. Plastic Surgeons. Clubs: Ville du Parc (Mequon, Wis.). Avocations: jogging, tennis. Home: 9010 N Tennyson Bayside WI 53217 Office: Plastic Surgery Assocs 2300 N Mayfair Rd Milwaukee WI 53226

LOFGREN, MYRON JOHN, traffic accident reconstruction consultant; b. Rush City, Minn., Nov. 14, 1931; s. George Elmer and Ida Victoria (Swenson) L.; m. Bonnie Lee Payne, Oct. 23, 1954; children: Jeffrey M., Daniel K., Shelley K. Lofgren Peetz. Grad. high sch., Rush City. Sgt., reconstrn. specialist Minn. State Patrol, St. Paul, 1968-83; pvt. practice accident reconstrn. cons. Princeton, Minn., 1983—. Author: Handbook for the Accident Reconstructionist, 1978. Served as sgt. U.S. Army, 1952-54, Korea. Named Nat. Police Officer of Yr., Internat. Assn. Chiefs of Police, 1979, Police Office of Yr. Hon. Mention, Minn. Chiefs of Police Assn., 1977, Trooper of Yr., Minn. Safety Council Minn. State Patrol, 1974; recipient Service to Continuing Legal Edn. award Minn. State Bar Assn., 1973. Mem. Internat. Assn. Accident Reconstrn. Specialists (pres. 1980-86, Cert. Appreciation 1985), Nat. Com. Motor Fleet Supr. Tng., Nat. Hwy. Traffic Safety Adminstrn. Conf., Am. Legion (Law and Order award 1975), VFW. Republican. Lutheran. Lodge: Masons. Avocation: teaching. Home and Office: Rt 2 Box 330 Princeton MN 55371-9325

LOFTSGARD, LAUREL DUANE, university president; b. Hoople, N.D., Sept. 4, 1926; s. Theodore G. and Dora (Jore) L.; m. Carol June Evenson, Dec. 27, 1951; children: Bradley Trent, Cynthia Sue. B.S., N.D. State U., 1954; Ph.D., Ia. State U., 1958. With N.D. State U., 1958—, prof. agrl. econs., 1963—; dir. N.D. Water Resources Research Inst., 1965-66, v.p. acad. affairs, 1966-68, acting pres., 1968, pres., 1968—; dir. Met. Fed. Savs. and Loan Assn., Fargo. Contbr. articles to mags. and bulls. Civilian aide to sec. Army for, N.D., 1975-77. Served with inf. AUS, 1946-47; with Corps of Engrs. 1950-51. Mem. Am. Farm Econ. Assn., Western Farm Econ. Assn. (certificate of merit 1964), Neuropsychiatric Inst. (bd. dirs.), Fargo C. of C., Am. Legion, Sigma Xi, Alpha Zeta, Gamma Sigma Delta, Phi Delta Kappa, Phi Kappa Phi. Lodges: Elks, Kiwanis, Eagles. Office: ND State Univ Office of the Pres Fargo ND 58105

LOFTUS, THOMAS ADOLPH, state legislator; b. Stoughton, Wis., Apr. 24, 1945; s. Adolph Olean and Margaret Elaine (Nielson) L.; m. Barbara Carolyn Schasse, Aug. 23, 1969; children: Alec Kristian, Karl Edward. B.S., U. Wis.-Whitewater, 1970; M.A., U. Wis.-Madison, 1971. Analyst Wis. Assembly Democratic Caucus, Madison, 1974-75, adminstrv. asst. to Speaker, 1975-76; mem. Wis. State Assembly from Sun Prairie, 1977—, speaker of the Assembly, 1983—; adj. prof. polit. sci. U. Wis.-Whitewater. Served with U.S. Army, 1965-67. Democrat. Home: 1210 Columbus St Sun Prairie WI 53590 Office: Wis State Assembly 211 W State Capitol Madison WI 53702

LOGAN, BEVERLY JENNINGS, social worker; b. Topeka, Feb. 26, 1931; d. Earl Marvin and Minerva Jane (Moreland) Jennings; m. James Kenneth Logan; June 8, 1952; children: Daniel Jennings, Amy Katherine, Sarah Jane, Samuel Price. AB in Social Work, Kans. U., 1952, MSW, 1983. Lic. social worker, Kans. Presch. tchr. Assoc. Day Care, Boston, 1952-53, Harvard Presch., Cambridge, Mass., 1953-55; social worker foster care Social and Rehab. Services, Olathe, Kans., 1980-81; social worker Shawnee Mission (Kans.) Schs., 1982-83; vol. dir. Olathe Community Hosp., 1984-85, also bd. dirs., 1980—; social worker Olathe (Kans.) Pub. Schs., 1987—; bd. dirs. Olathe Hospice, 1983-84, MidAm. Health Network, Kansas City, Mo., 1984—. Dist. dir. Presl. Campaign Jimmy Carter, Johnson County, Kans., 1976. Mem. Kans. Action for Children, Johnson County Child Protection Assn. (sec. 1982-83). Democrat. Presbyterian. Clubs: Culture Class (Olathe), Holiday (Olathe). Avocations: swimming, tennis. Home: 1082 Wyckford Olathe KS 66061

LOGAN, C. RICHARD, real estate developer; b. Altoona, Pa., May 29, 1948; s. Charles Richard Sr. and Betty Jane (Conzo) L.; m. Sharon Ann McDowell, June 13, 1970; children: Kimberly Dawn, Dana Nicole. BS in Acctg., Gannon U., 1970. Leasing agt. Zamias Developers, Johnstown, Pa., 1972-81, Jacobs, Visconci & Jacobs, Cleve., 1981-82; v.p. Robert B. Aikens & Assocs. Inc., Troy, Mich., 1982—; dir. leasing Robert B. Aikens & Assocs. Inc., Troy, 1982—. Mem. Internat. Council Shopping Ctrs. (state dir.). Republican. Methodist. Lodge: Hirum 616. Avocations: fishing, golf. Home: 700 Augusta Dr Rochester Hills MI 48063 Office: Robert B Aikens & Assocs Inc 911 W Big Beaver Rd Suite 201 Troy MI 48084

LOGAN, JAMES KENNETH, judge; b. Quenemo, Kans., Aug. 21, 1929; s. John Lysle and Esther Maurine (Price) L.; m. Beverly Jo Jennings, June 8, 1952; children: Daniel Jennings, Amy Katherine, Sarah Jane, Samuel Price. A.B., U. Kans., 1952; LL.B. magna cum laude, Harvard, 1955. Bar: Kans. 1955, Calif. 1956. Law clk. U.S. Circuit Judge Huxman, 1955-56; with firm Gibson, Dunn & Crutcher, Los Angeles, 1956-57; asst. prof. law U. Kans., 1957-61; prof., dean U. Kans. (Law Sch.), 1961-68; partner Payne and Jones, Olathe, Kans., 1968-77; judge U.S. Circuit Ct., 10th Circuit, 1977—; Ezra Ripley Thayer teaching fellow Harvard Law Sch., 1961- 62; vis. prof. U. Tex. Law Sch., 1964, Stanford, 1969, U. Mich., 1976; commr. U.S. Dist. Ct., 1964-67. Author: (with W.B. Leach) Future Interests and Estate Planning, 1961, Kansas Estate Administration, 5th edit., 1986, (with A.R. Martin) Kansas Corporate Law and Practice, 2d edit., 1979; also articles. Candidate for U.S. Senate, 1968. Served with AUS, 1947-48. Rhodes scholar, 1952; recipient Disting. Service citation U. Kans., 1986. Mem. Am., Kans. bar assns., Phi Beta Kappa, Order of Coif, Beta Gamma Sigma, Omicron Delta Kappa, Pi Sigma Alpha, Alpha Kappa Psi, Phi Delta Phi. Democrat. Presbyterian. Home: 1082 Wyckford Rd Olathe KS 66061 Office: Box 790 1 Patrons Plaza Olathe KS 66061

LOGAN, SERGE EDWARD, editor, wax company executive; b. Chgo., Feb. 7, 1926; s. Carl and Alexandra (Honcharik) L.; student Superior (Wis.) State U., 1946-48; B.A. magna cum laude, U. Minn., 1950. Reporter, asst. city editor, Sunday editor Racine (Wis.) Jour.-Times, 1950-60; publs. mgr. S. C. Johnson & Son, Inc., Racine, 1960-65, community affairs mgr., editor, 1965-68, communications mgr., 1968-71, communications dir., 1971-81, asst. to vice chmn., 1981-82, dir. corporate social responsibility, 1982—, editor Johnson Mag., 1960-79. Active as scoutmaster, explorer adviser, commnr., mem. exec. bd. S.E. Wis. council Boy Scouts Am., 1951—, pres., 1966-68; sec. Johnson Wax Fund, Inc., 1965-68, trustee, 1978-81, 85—, v.p., 1982-85; public relations chmn. United Fund, 1967, 70, 72, 73. Served with USNR, 1944-46; PTO. Named Outstanding Young Man of Year, Racine Jr. C. of C., 1961; recipient Silver Beaver award Boy Scouts Am., 1963, Silver Antelope, 1973. Am. Polit. Sci. Assn. Congl. fellow on Senate staff Hubert H. Humphrey, Ho. of reps. staff James Wright, 1956-57. Mem. C. of C. (publs. com. 1967—), Meeting Planners Internat. (officer, dir. Wis. chpt.), Phi Beta Kappa. Methodist (steward). Home: 1737 Wisconsin Ave Racine WI 53403 Office: 1525 Howe St Racine WI 53403

LOGAN, STANLEY NICHOLAS, accountant; b. Gary, Ind., Nov. 29, 1954; s. Nicholas Anthony and Vassilia (Pangares) L.; m. Mercedes Izquierdo, Sept. 16. 1978; children: Mercedes, Nicole, Lauren. BA, Northwestern U., 1977. CPA, Ill. Audit mgr. Arthur Andersen and Co., Chgo., 1980—. Mem. Am. Inst. CPA's, Ill. Soc. CPA's, Ill. Psi Omega Assn. (treas., bd. dirs. 1985).

LOGLI, PAUL ALBERT, lawyer; b. Rockford, Ill., Nov. 20, 1949; s. Albert Joseph and Margaret (Salamone) L.; m. Jodean L. Miller, Oct. 26, 1985, Peter Joseph. BA cum laude, Loras Coll., 1971; JD, U. Ill., 1974. Bar: Ill. 1974, U.S. Dist. Ct. (no. dist.) Ill. 1975. Asst. state's atty. Winnebago County, Rockford, Ill., 1974-76; ptnr. North, Ohlson, Logli, Condon & Boyd, Rockford, 1976-81; assoc. judge 17th Jud. Cir., Winnebago and Boone counties, Rockford, 1981-86; state's atty. Winnebago County, 1986—; chmn. domestic relations com. Ill. Jud. Conf., 1983-84; mem. U.S. Dept. of Justice Law Enforcement Coordinating Com. (no. dist.) Ill. Bd. dirs. Rockford Symphony Orch., 1983-87, Rosecrance Meml. Homes for Children, Rockford, 1983—, Rockford Area Conv. and Visitors Bur., 1984—, Discovery Ctr. Children's Mus., 1986—; mem. adv. bd. St. Anthony Hosp. Med. Ctr., Rockford, 1983—; pres. Blackhawk Area council Boy Scouts Am., 1984-87; chmn. bldg. com. St. Peter's Cathedral. Recipient service award Northwest Ill. Chiefs of Police Assn., 1981, New Am. Theater, 1981; Disting. Service award Jaycees, 1982. Mem. Ill. State Bar Assn., Winnebago County Bar Assn., Ill. State's Attys. Assn., Nat. Dist. Attys. Assn. Republican. Roman Catholic. Lodge: Rotary (bd. dirs. 1984-85). Office: Winnebago County Courthouse 400 W State St Suite 619 Rockford IL 61101

LOGOTHETIS, DEMETRIOS GEORGE, accountant; b. Kastri, Arkadia, Greece, Oct. 1, 1956; came to U.S., 1969; s. George P. and Patra (Nikolau) L.; m. Marianna Analitis, Feb. 22, 1981; children: Effie, George. BS in Commerce, DePaul U., 1977; MBA, U. Chgo., 1978. CPA, Ill.; cert. mgmt. accountant, Ill. Staff accountant Ernst & Whinney, Chgo., 1979-80, advanced staff accountant, 1980-81, sr. accountant, 1981-83, supr., 1983-85, sr. mgr., 1985—; instr. Ill. Inst. Tech., Chgo., 1985—, DePaul U., Chgo., 1985—. Pres. Brotherhood of Karatoula, Chgo., 1983; bd. dirs. United Hellenic Am. Congress, Chgo., 1983—; mem. Chgo. Council on Fgn. Relations; sec. Holy Trinity Greek Orthodox Ch., Chgo., 1985—. Mem. Nat. Assn. Accountants, Am. Inst. CPAs, Ill. Inst. CPAs. Club: Metropolitan. Avocations: golf, soccer, Greek history. Home: 6251 W Montrose Chicago IL 60634 Office: Ernst & Whinney 150 S Wacker Dr Chicago IL 60606

LOGSDON, JOHN MARTIN, community and adult education coordinator; b. Ames, Iowa, Aug. 28, 1946; s. John Leonard and Mary Avis (Martin) L.; m. Janice Marie Smith, Jan. 20, 1965 (div. 1976); children: John Jr., Beth Anne; m. Kathy Schaefer, May 13, 1978. BS in Edn., Northwest Mo. State U., 1968; MA in Edn., Drake U., 1985. Cert. tchr., Iowa; cert. adminstr., Iowa. Instr. Atlantic (Iowa) Community Schs., 1968-70; instr. Des Moines Pub. Sch., 1970-75, coordinator community/adult edn., 1975—. Bd. dirs. Lakewood Village Assn., Lakewood-Norwalk, Iowa, 1972-75. Mem. Iowa Assn. Life-Long Learning, Iowa Community Edn. Assn., Internat. Ford Retractable Club (v.p., pres., sec. 1980-85), Early Wheels Iowa (bd. dirs. 1984—). Presbyterian. Avocations: writing, reading, traveling, collecting and restoring antique automobiles. Home: 6555 Colby Ave Des Moines IA 50311 Office: Des Moines Pub Schs 1800 Grand Ave Des Moines IA 50307

LOHMAN, JOHN FREDERICK, editor; b. Bismarck, N.D., Oct. 29, 1935; s. William Ernest and Viola (Paulson) L.; m. Dorothy Louise Stolp, July 13, 1962; children—Sheryl, Susan, Timothy, Jeffrey. B.S. in Engring., N.D. State U., 1960. Copy boy The Forum, Fargo, N.D., 1952-56, reporter, 1957-68, night editor, 1969-71, city editor, 1972-76, mng. editor, 1977-86, assoc. editor, 1987—. Mem. AP Mng. Editors Assn. Lodges: Eagles, Elks. Avocations: hunting; fishing. Home: 2316 Flickertail Dr Fargo ND 58103

LOHMANN, WILLIAM TOMBAUGH, architect; b. Burlington, Iowa, June 12, 1928; s. Carl John and Helen Rachel (Tombaugh) L.; m. Evelyn Day Ward, July 15, 1951 (dec. Dec. 1966); children: Catherine Day, Melanie Ann. Student, Burlington Jr. Coll., 1946-47; BArch Engring., Iowa State U., 1950; postgrad., Ill. Inst. Tech., 1956-58. Registered architect Ill.; cert. constrn. specifier. Draftsman Dane D. Morgan & Assocs., Burlington, 1954-56; project adminstr. Robert Babbin & Assocs., Chgo., 1958-62; specifications writer Bertrand Goldberg Assocs., Chgo., 1963-67; specifications mgr. C.F. Murphy Assocs., Chgo., 1968-82, Murphy/Jahn Inc., Chgo., 1982—; mem. Constrn. Industry Affairs Com. of Chgo., 1968-69, 70-81, co-chmn. 1981—, City of Chgo. Com. on Tests and Standards, 1973-80, City of Chgo. Adv. Com. on Bldg. Code Amendments, 1981-83. Contbg. editor tech. articles Progressive Architecture mag., 1975—; contbr. articles to profl. jours. Bd. dirs. Youth Orgs. Umbrella, Evanston, Ill., 1980-84. Served to staff sgt. USAF, 1950-54. Fellow Contrstn. Specifications Inst. (pres. Chgo. chpt. 1969-70, region award 1974); mem. AIA, ASTM. Avocations: archeology, prairie restoration.

LOHMAR, FRANK CARL, JR., educator; b. Coal City, Ill., Aug. 25, 1937; s. Frank Carl and Ann Marie (Granger) L. BS, Ill. State U., 1959; MS, Loyola U., Chgo., 1972, advanced cert. in adminstrn., 1982. Tchr. Gardner (Ill.) High Sch., 1959-62, Oak Lawn (Ill.) High Sch., 1962-68; tchr. Morris (Ill.) High Sch., 1968-70, cons. reading, 1970-82; chmn. spl. edn. Dist. 205, Dolton, Ill., 1982—; v.p. Faculty Assn., 1986—. Edn. study grantee Ill. State U., 1962. Mem. Am. Assn. Sex Educators, Counselors and Therapists (counselor 1975—, mem. nat. exec. bd. 1980-82), Assn. for Citizens with Learning Disabilities, Internat. Reading Assn., Phi Delta Kappa (treas. 1972-75, v.p. 1975-76, pres. 1976-77). Roman Catholic. Avocations: opera, the arts. Home: 300 N State St Apt 5008 Chicago IL 60610

LOHR, HAROLD RUSSELL, bishop; b. Gary, S.D., Aug. 31, 1922; s. Lester ALbert and Nora Helena (Fossum) L.; m. Theola Marie Kottke, June 21, 1947 (div. Dec. 1973); children: Philip Kyle, David Scott, Michael John; m. Edith Mary Morgan, Dec. 31, 1973. BS summa cum laude, S.D. State U., 1947; PhD, U. Calif.-Berkeley, 1950; MDiv summa cum laude, Augustana Theol. Sem., Rock Island, Ill., 1958. Ordained to ministry Augustana Luth. Ch., 1958; installed as bishop, 1980. Research chemist Argonne Nat. lab., Lemont, Ill., 1950-54; pastor Luth. Ch. of Ascension, Northfield, Ill., 1958-70; assoc. exec. Bd. Coll. Edn., N.Y.C., 1970-73; dir. research Div. Profl. Leadership, Phila., 1973-77, assoc. exec., 1977-80; synodical bishop Luth. Ch. in Am., Fargo, N.D., 1980—; mem. exec. council Luth. Ch. in Am., Fargo, 1982—; mem. commn. of peace and war, 1983-85. Contbg. author: Growth in Ministry, 1980; also articles to sci. jours. Bd. dirs. Gustavus Adolphus Coll., 1980—, Luther Northwestern Sem., St. Paul, 1980—. Served as 1st lt. inf. U.S. Army, 1943-46, ETO. Recipient Suomi award Suomi Coll., 1983. Mem. Phi Kappa Phi. Democrat. Home: South Acres 1210 49th Ave S Fargo ND 58103 Office: Luth Ch in Am 1351 Page Dr S Suite 320 Fargo ND 58103

LOHR, JOHN FREDERICK, petroleum company executive; b. Columbus, Nebr., Feb. 11, 1942; s. Elmer Harry and Loretta Helen (Saunto) L.; m. Rose Kathleen Rasmussen, Aug. 1, 1980; 1 child, John Stewart. BS in Polit. Sci., U. Utah, 1965, MS in Econs., 1967. Indsl. location cons. Upland Industries, Omaha, 1970-72; v.p. Lohr Petroleum, Columbus, Nebr., 1972-82, pres., 1982—; bd. dirs. First Nat. Bank, Columbus, Nebr., 1987—. Bd. trustees Library and Park Bds. of Columbus, Platte Community Coll.; pres. Community Concert Assn., Columbus; sec. YMCA Bd. Dirs. and Bd. Trustees; skipper C. of C. Commodores, Columbus. Served to 1st. lt. U.S. Army, 1967-70. Decorated Bronze star. Republican. Presbyterian. Lodges: Elks, Masons (master). Avocations: cactophyle, meteorology. Home: 125 E Parkway Columbus NE 68601 Office: Lohr Petroleum Co Inc 2801 13th St Columbus NE 68601

LOHR, KENNETH RAYBORNE, pharmacist, drug analyst; b. Quincy, Ill., Dec. 19, 1922; s. Rayborne Peter and Sarah Elizabeth (Houdyshell) L.; m. Eleanor Lucille Hetzler, July 23, 1943; children—Denise, Debra. B.S. in Pharmacy, U. Ill., 1950. Ptnr., mgr. Owl Drug Store, Quincy, 1951-58, Lohr's Prescription Shop, Quincy, 1958—; dir. St. Drug Analysis Service, Quincy. Served with U.S. Army, 1943-45. Recipient A.H. Robbins Bowl of Hygeia award, 1974. Fellow Am. Coll. Apothecaries; mem. Am. Inst. History of Pharmacy, Am. Pharm. Assn., Ill. Pharmacists Assn., Nat. Assn. Retail Druggists, Quincy C. of C. (dir. 1956-59). Republican. Lutheran. Contbr. articles in field to profl. jours. Home: 905 Payson Ave Quincy IL 62301 Office: 1301 Broadway St Quincy IL 62301

LOHR, RICHARD JOHN, golf course owner; b. Madison, Wis., Mar. 31, 1943; s. Lawrence G. and Elsie D. (Hagen) L.; m. Joyce E. Porath, Aug. 2, 1964; children: Eric J., Tanya E. BA, Wartburg Coll., 1965; BS, U. Wis., Stevens Point, 1968, MS in Teaching, 1978. Tchr. Wausau (Wis.) West High Sch., 1967-83; pres. Pine Valley Golf Course, Marathon, Wis., 1983—; Speaker on internat. issues, China, 1967—. Contbr. articles to Wis. Acad. Rev., 1986. Fulbright grantee, 1980. Democrat. Lutheran. Avocations: reading, golf, tennis. Home and Office: 203 136th Ave N Marathon WI 54448

LOITMAN, BERNARD S., radiologist; b. Chelsea, Mass., May 8, 1923; s. Israel and Elizabeth (Burstein) L.; m. Charlotte G. Kamberg, Dec. 25, 1949; children: Deborah Mindy Sanchez, Robert Scott, Jane Ellen, Carol Ann. AB, Harvard U., 1950; MD, Tufts U., 1953. Intern U. Calif., San Fransisco, 1953-54; resident in radiology New York Hosp., Cornell U. Med. Ctr., N.Y.C., 1954-57; radiologist Faith Hosp., St. Louis, 1957-60, VA, St. Louis, 1957-60, Jewish Hosp., St. Louis, 1960—, St. Elizabeth Hosp., Granite City, Ill., 1960—, St. Joseph Hosp., St. Charles, Mo., 1960—, St. Peters (Mo.) Hosp., 1986—, St. Joseph Hosp. W., St. Louis, 1986—; pres.-elect, chief of staff St. Elizabeth Med. Ctr., 1982—. Contbr. articles to profl. jours. Bd. dirs. Mark Twain Summer Inst., St. Louis and Clayton, Mo., 1974—, pres. St. Louis, 1982—, chmn. bd. dirs., 1986—. Served to lt. USNR, 1942-46, PTO. Fellow Am. Coll. Radiology; mem. Radiol. Soc. N.Am., AMA, Mo. Med. Assn., Mo. Radiol. Assn., St. Louis Med. Assn., Greater St. Louis Soc. Radiologist, Harvard U. Alumni Assn. (regional dir. 1981-84). Clubs: Harvard of St. Louis (pres. 1979), Polo St. Louis, Univ. (St. Louis). Avocations: squash, tuba, recorder, painting. Home: 10 Washington Terr Saint Louis MO 63112 Office: Saint Elizabeth Med Ctr Madison Ave Granite City IL 62040

LOK, SILMOND RAY, pharmaceutical executive; b. Columbus, Ohio, Dec. 14, 1948; s. Fee and Oilene (Yee) L.; m. Thresa Carlene Dale, Aug. 27, 1978. BS in Pharmacy, Ohio State U., 1973; MBA, Capital U., 1982. Registered pharmacist. Pharmacist, Federated Stores, Columbus, Ohio, 1975-82; pharm. salesman Ives Labs., Columbus, 1982, Squibb, Columbus, 1982-85; dir. pharmacy services Wendt-Bristol Co., 1985—. Mem. Grove City Civic Assn. Served to 1st lt. USAF, 1973-75. Mem. Cen. Ohio Acad. Pharmacy, Sigma Phi Epsilon, Kappa Psi (grand regent grad. chpt. 1973-75). Avocation: Kenpo karate (black belt, 1st degree). Home: 2591 McDonald Ct Grove City OH 43123

LOLLAR, ROBERT MILLER, industrial management executive; b. Lebanon, Ohio, May 17, 1915; s. Harry David and Ruby (Miller) L.; Chem E., U. Cin., 1937, M.S., 1938, Ph.D., 1940; m. Dorothy Marie Williams, Jan. 1, 1941; children—Janet Ruth (Mrs. David Schwarz), Katherine Louise (Mrs. James Punteney, Jr.). Cereal analyst Kroger Food Found., Cin., 1935-37; devel. chemist Rit Product div. Corn Products, Indpls., 1937-39, 40-41; asso. prof. U. Cin., 1941-59; tech. dir. Armour & Co., Chgo., 1959-73; mgmt. and tech. cons., pres. Lollar and Assocs., 1973—; tech. dir. Leather Industries Am., Cin., 1975-86, cons., 1986—. Dir. OSRD, 1942-45. Recipient Alsop award Am. Leather Chemists Assn., 1954, Fraser Muir Moffat medal Leather Industries Am., 1986. Mem. Am. Leather Chemists Assn. (pres., editor-in-chief), Inst. Food Technologists, Am. Chem. Soc. (nat. councillor), Am. Soc. Quality Control, World Mariculture Soc., Sigma Xi, Tau Beta Pi, Alpha Chi Sigma. Address: 5960 Donjoy Dr Cincinnati OH 45242

LOLLI, FRANK DANIEL, management information systems specialist; b. Steubenville, Ohio, Aug. 24, 1962; s. Daniel John Vincent and Dorothy Jean (Barnette) L.; m. Constance Ann Walter, May 11, 1985. A in Bus. Data Processing, COlumbus Tech. Inst., 1983. Computer operator Bank One of Columbus, Ohio, 1981-82; tech. services specialist Big Bear Stores, Inc., Columbus, 1982-84, tech. services mgr., 1984—. Office: Big Bear Stores Inc 770 W Goodale Blvd Columbus OH 43212

LOMASON, HARRY AUSTIN, II, automotive company executive; b. Detroit, Oct. 6, 1934; s. William Keithledge and Neva L.; children by previous marriage: Kimri Elizabeth Lomason Massey, Krista Anna Lomason Maxwell, William Keithledge, Peter Kevin; m. 2d Mary Alice Pushkarsky, June 26, 1971; children: Harry Austin, Heather Alice. Student, Ga. Inst. Tech., 1953-56; B.B.A., Ga. State U., 1959. With Douglas & Lomason, Farmington Hills, Mich., 1969—, asst. sec., 1966-72, v.p., sec., 1972-76, pres., chief operating officer, 1976-82, pres., chief exec. officer, 1982—, dir.; dir. Mich. Mut. Ins., Detroit. Bd. dirs., mem. exec. com. Detroit Symphony Orch., Inc., 1979—; bd. dirs. Mich. Thanksgiving Parade Found., Harper-Grace Hosp. Mem. Engring. Soc. Detroit, Soc. Automotive Engrs., Mich. Mfg. Assn. (bd. dirs.). Episcopalian. Clubs: Detroit, Detroit Athletic, Detroit Golf; Cherokee Town and Country (Atlanta); Marianna Country; Pine Lake Country (Orchard Lake, Mich.). Home: 2900 Pine Lake Rd Orchard Lake MI 48033 Office: Douglas & Lomason Co 24600 Hallwood Ct Farmington Hills MI 48018

LOMASON, WILLIAM KEITHLEDGE, automotive company executive; b. Detroit, July 12, 1910; s. Harry A. and Elizabeth (Bennett) L.; m. Neva C. Wigle, 1930 (dec. 1965); m. Ruth M. Martin, 1970. AB, U. Mich., 1932, AM, 1933. With Douglas & Lomason Co., Detroit, 1934—; treas. Douglas & Lomason Co., 1943-52, v.p., 1945-50, pres., gen. mgr., 1950-75, chmn. bd., chief exec. officer, 1976-82, chmn. bd., 1982—, also bd. dirs.; pres. Shamrock Air Lines, 1968-76. Co-author: When Management Negotiates, 1967. Bd. dirs., mem. exec. com. Nat. Right to Work Com.; bd. dirs. past chmn. and pres. Bus. Council of Ga.; dir. emeritus Mich. Mfrs. Assn. Recipient Man of Yr. award, Carrollton, Ga., 1967; named lt. col. aide de camp Gov.'s Staff, Ga., 1956. Mem. Engring. Soc. Detroit, Am. Electroplaters Soc., Alpha Chi Rho. Episcopalian. Office: 24600 Hallwood Ct Farmington Hills MI 48018

LOMAX, RICHARD EARL, land surveyor, state government official; b. Gratiot County, Mich., Jan. 25, 1936; s. Earl Bell and Lola Pearl (Sabin) L.; m. Linnie S. Sharp, Sept. 1957 (div.); children: Richard L., Rhonda L., Brian A., Robert E., John R.; m. Doye Juanita Rogers Pullano, Aug. 25, 1973. Student Chgo. Tech. Coll., 1954-55, Mich. State U., 1955-59, Lansing Community Coll., 1979-80. Registered land surveyor, Mich. Draftsman Dept. of Hwys., State of Mich., Lansing, 1954-61, plat examiner Dept. Auditor Gen., 1961-66, supr. plat sect. Dept. Treasury, 1966-70, mgr. subdiv. control Dept. Treasury, 1970-81, adminstr. subdiv. control and county zoning Dept. Commerce, 1981—; prin. Richard Lomax, Surveyor, Charlotte, Mich., 1973-76; mem. Ingham County Remonumentation and Survey Bd.,

Mich., 1977-81. Co-editor: Mich. Surveyor mag., 1983-85, editor, 1986—. Chmn. Charlotte City Planning Commn., 1976-85; sec. Tri- County Regional Planning Commn., Lansing, 1979-85, vice-chmn., 1979-86. Fellow Mich. Soc. Registered Land Surveyors (dir. 1976—, pres. 1985-86), Am. Congress on Survey and Mapping (chmn. Gt. Lakes council of affiliates 1982-84); mem. Nat. Soc. Profl. Surveyors. Republican. Home: 243 S Sheldon St Charlotte MI 48813

LOMBARD, DANIEL JOSEPH, construction engineer; b. Evergreen Park, Ill., Dec. 12, 1958; s. George Eugene and Betty (Hallstein) L. BSCE, U. Notre Dame, 1981; MBA, U. Mich., 1983. Project supr. Schal Assocs., Chgo., 1983-85; constrn. engr. Lombard Co., Alsip, Ill., 1985—. Mem. ASCE (assoc.), Am. Concrete Assn. (assoc.). Avocation: softball. Home: 12510 Navajo Dr Palos Heights IL 60463 Office: Lombard Co 4245 W 123d St Alsip IL 60463

LOMBARDO, DAVID ALBERT, writer, aviation consultant and educator; b. Chgo., Jan. 31, 1947; s. Ignace Palmeri and Diane Marion (Balducci) L. BS, U. Ill., 1974, MEd, 1977. Tchr. York Community High Sch., Elmhurst, Ill., 1974-75; instr. Coll. Edn., U. Ill., Urbana, 1975-77, asst. dir. career devel. and placement, 1977-79; with Accelerated Ground Schs., Urbana, 1978-81, dir. nat. flight inst. refresher clinics; pres. Flying Illini, Inc., Savoy, Ill., 1972-80; curriculum devel. cons. LEAP, 1975-79, CFI Programs, 1979-82; dir. program devel. Airmanship, Inc., Rockford, Ill., 1981-82; gen. aviation cons. Lombardo & Assocs., 1981-82, tech. writer, gen. aviation cons., 1982—; asst. prof. profl. aviation La. Tech. U., Ruston, 1982-85; instr. Flight Safety Internat., 1980-81; dir. tng. Frasca Internat., 1985—; chief instr. Greater St. Louis Flight Instrs. Assn., 1980-81; accident prevention counselor FAA, 1980—. Contbg. editor Pvt. Pilot Mag., 1984—. Bd. dirs. Ruston community Theater, 1983-85; founder, bd. dirs. Hill Country Arts Council, 1983-85. Served with AUS, 1966-69, Vietnam. Decorated Vietnamese Gallantry Cross; recipient Flying Col. award Delta Air Lines, 1978, Ark. Traveler award Gov. of Ark., 1978, Flight Inst. Proficiency award Phases I, II, III, IV, FAA, 1980, Plaque of Appreciation, Greater St. Louis Flight Instrs. Assn., 1981, Excellence award La. Tech. U., 1984. Recipient Teaching Excellence award La. Tech U., 1984, numerous other awards for contbns. to field. Mem. Ill. Pilots Assn. (bd. dirs. 1977-79), Univ. Aviation Assn., Alpha Eta Rho (advisor 1983-85), Chi Gamma Iota, Phi Delta Kappa. Republican. Roman Catholic. Home: PO Box 6028 Champaign IL 61821-8028 Office: Frasca Internat 606 S Neil St Champaign IL 61820

LOMBARDO, (GUY) GAETANO, venture capitalist; b. Salemi, Italy, Feb. 4, 1940; came to U.S., 1947; s. Salvatore and Anna Maria L.; Sc.B. with honors, Brown U., 1962; Ph.D. in Physics, Cornell U., 1971; m. Nancy B. Emerson, Sept. 2, 1967; children—Nicholas Emerson, Maryanne Chilton. Sr. staff Arthur D. Little Inc., Cambridge, Mass., 1967-77; v.p. logistics Morton Salt Co., Chgo., 1977-78; dir. logistics and distbn. Gould Inc., Chgo., 1978-80; corp. dir. Bendix Corp., Southfield, Mich., 1980-82; group v.p. worldwide bus. devel. Bendix Indsl. Group, 1982-84; pres., chief exec. officer Comau Productivity Systems, Troy, Mich., 1984-86; pres. Nelmar Corp., 1986—; vis. prof. ops. mgmt. Boston U., 1973. Contbr. articles on physics and bus. mgmt. to profl. jours. Home: 900 Timberlake Dr Bloomfield Hills MI 48013 Office: Nelmar Corp 2000 Town Ctr Suite 1900 Southfield MI 48075

LOMSHEK, DAVID LEE, technical vocation educator, small business owner; b. Pittsburgh, Kans., Apr. 26, 1941; s. Edward Raymond and Mavis (Clayton) L.; m. Deanna Mae Russell, Nov. 13, 1965 (div. 1985); children: Anissa, Natalia, Danika, Dominic. BS in Vocat. Tech. Edn., Pittsburg (Kans.) State U., 1982. Machinist Emerson Machine Shop, Pittsburg, 1962-66; toolmaker, machinist Helio Aircraft Co., Pittsburg, 1966-75; owner Chicopee Machine & Tool, Pittsburg, 1975—; asst. prof. Pittsburg State U., 1978—; cons. Brentwing Engring. Ic., Pittsburg, 1982—. Dem. precinct commiteeman, rural Pittsburg area, 1978-86; pres. Chicopee Rural Water Dist, Pittsburg area, 1982—. Mem. Soc. Mfg. Engrs. (cert. mfg. technologist), Am. Soc. for Metals, Am. Soc. Engring. Educators. Roman Catholic. Avocations: computer programming, reading, writing. Home: Rural Rte #2 Box 74 Pittsburg KS 66762 Office: Pittsburg State U 1701 S Broadway Pittsburg KS 66762

LONCHAR, MICHAEL JOHN, educator; b. Chgo., June 5, 1949; s. Donald Morris Jr. and Gwyneth (Lee) L.; m. Betsy Podboy, Nov. 17, 1973; 1 child, Lucas Matthew. BA, Ottawa (Kans.) U., 1971; MEd, Nat. Coll. Edn., Evanston, Ill., 1976. Cert. elem. tchr., Ill.; cert. secondary tchr., Ill. Tchr. Oakdale Sch., Waukegan, Ill., 1971-80, Andrew Cooke Magnet Sch., Waukegan, 1980—; curriculum developer Waukegan Pub. Schs., 1978-80. Mem. Am. Fedn. Tchrs. Republican. Baptist. Avocation: fishing. Office: Andrew Cooke Magnet Sch 522 Belvidere Rd Waukegan IL 60085

LONDON, ANNE ODEAN, pharmacist, author; b. Hamilton, Ind., Mar. 7, 1934; d. Harry C. and Frances E. (Kepler) Fee; m. Russell Henry Meyer, June 5, 1955 (div. Mar. 1959); 1 child, Kenton H. (dec.); m. Norman Homner Lanza, June 16, 1961 (div. Oct. 1975); 1 child, Kimberlee Anne Lanza Lee. BS, Purdue U., 1956. Cert. real estate counselor; registered pharmacist, Ill., Mich., Ind., Ohio. Pharmacist Brookhaven Drugs, Darien, Ill., 1968-72; broker McNeil Realtors, Downers Grove, Ill., 1972, Circle Real Estate, Downers Grove, 1973-78; broker/mgr. Bankman & Best, Downers Grove, 1979; realtor/broker, mgr. Dixon Gallery of Homes, Bolingbrook, Ill., 1979-85; guest speaker Eye on Classics, Cable-TV, 1985. Author (pen name A. Lee Hamilton): Prose by a Dead Poet, 1985. Mem. Realtors PAC, Notaries Assn. Ill., Will County Bd. Realtors, DuPage County Bd. Realtors. Republican. Clubs: Bridging the Arts (Downers Grove) (pres. 1984); Choralers, WRX and WCCR Radio (Purdue U.). Avocations: art, music, bridge. Office: Coldwell Banker 1105 Maple Ave Lisle IL 60532

LONE, HARRY EDWIN, waterproofing company executive, vehicle leasing company executive; b. Council Bluffs, Iowa, Oct. 20, 1923; s. Harry Edwin and Lula (Wakefield) L.; m. Wanda Lu Selindh, Mar. 16, 1946; children—Stanley Craig, Allen Eugene, Gregory Lynn, Janet Elaine Lone Davis. Student Princeton U., 1945, DePauw Coll., Greencastle, Ind., 1945-46, Purdue U., Lafayette, Ind., 1946. Motor machinist apprentice Rock Island R.R., Des Moines, 1946-47; bakery sales Continental Bakery, Des Moines, 1947-49; dairy route sales A&E Dairy, Des Moines, 1949-52; route supr. Hilan Dairy, Ames, Iowa, 1953-60; route sales mgr. Borden Co., Marshalltown, Iowa, 1960-63; ter. mgr. Gen. Foods Corp., White Plains, N.Y., 1963-78; pres., chief exec. officer Central States Waterproofing, St. Louis, 1978—; pres. Gold Key Enterprises, Maryland Heights, Mo., 1982—, Lone Advt., Maryland Heights, 1982—. Mem. nat. and state elections com. Mo. Republican Com., 1983; mem. Rep. Nat. Com., Washington, 1983; mem. Rep. Senatorial Com., Washington, 1983. Recipient Pres.' Medal of Merit, Republican Presdl. Task Force, 1982. Mem. Nat. Assn. for Remodeling Industry, Nat. Fedn. Ind. Bus., Nat. Assn. Waterproofing, Homebuilders Assn. Kansas City. Club: U.S. Senatorial. Lodges: Eagles, Toastmasters. Home: 14864 Grassmere Ct Chesterfield MO 63017 Office: Cen States Waterproofing Mo Inc 13738 Rider Trail N Earth City MO 63045

LONG, CATHERINE ELIZABETH, lawyer; b. Evanston, Ill., Mar. 1, 1956; d. John Martin Jr. and Ellenmae (Quan) L. BA, Yale U., 1978; JD, Loyola U., 1982. Bar: Ill. 1982, U.S. Dist. Ct. (no. dist.) Ill. 1982. Assoc. Keevers & Hittle, Chgo., 1983-87, supr., 1987—. Editor Blackacre, 1980-81 (Chgo. Daily Law Bulletin award 1981). Mem. ABA, Ill. Bar Assn., Chgo. Bar Assn., Women's Bar Assn. Ill. Avocations: equitation, writing, music. Office: Keevers & Hittle 230 W Monroe Chicago IL 60606

LONG, CHERYL LYNN, marketing executive; b. Chgo., May 3, 1946; d. Louis Russell and Catherine Lois (Schumann) Fritz; m. Thomas David Brown, Jan. 25, 1969 (div. Nov. 1982); m. Gregory David Long, July 3, 1985. BA, Cornell Coll., Des Moines, 1968. Advt., promotions specialist Better Homes & Gardens, Des Moines, 1974-75, mktg. specialist, 1975-77, consumer panel mgr., 1977-82, mktg. services mgr., 1982—. Mem. Advt. Fedn. Des Moines (pres. 1974-75, Advt. Woman of the Yr. 1977), Nat. Assn. Profl. Saleswomen (sec. 1984-85). Avocations: skiing, tennis, reading, archaeology. Home: 22 56th Des Moines IA 50312 Office: Meredith Corp 17th and Locust Des Moines IA 50336

LONG, DANIEL JAMES, optometrist; b. Sioux Falls, S.D., May 6, 1954; s. Palmer R. and Isabelle A. (Peterson) L.; m. Debra K. Zimbelman, June 20, 1981; 1 child, Kimberly Kay. BS, Ill. Coll. Optometry, 1977, OD, 1979. Optometrist Dakota Eyecare Assocs., P.C., Mandan, N.D., 1979—. Sunday sch. supt. Century Bapt. Ch., Bismarck, 1983—; pres. United Way, Mandan, N.D., 1984. Recipient Outstanding Young Mandanite award Mandan Jaycees, 1981. Mem. N.D. Optometric Assn. (first v.p. 1986, pres.-elect 1987), Vol. Optometric Services to Humanity (project leader 1982). Lodges: Lions (chmn. dist. sight conservation 1984—, pres. 1987), Elks. Home: 1309 1st Ave NE Mandan ND 58554 Office: Dakota Eyecare Assocs PC 104 3d Ave NW Mandan ND 58554

LONG, DAVID GORDON, marketing professional; b. Houston, July 30, 1952; s. Gordon Dewey and Velma Merle (Carter) L.; m. Patricia Anne Kelty, Dec. 27, 1974; children: David Jr., Andrew, Jennifer. Postgrad., U. Toledo; BA, Youngstown State U., 1974; MA, U. Okla., 1981. Med. service rep. Pfizer Pharm., Wichita Falls, Tex., 1977-80; acctg. mgr. Econs. Lab., Chgo., 1981-83; regional mgr. K&I Holding Co., Toledo, 1983-84; mgr. sales and mktg. Bock Laundry Machine Co., Toledo, 1984—. Served to maj. U.S. Army, 1974-77. Mem. Toledo Area Govt. Research Assn. Republican. Avocations: rowing, writing, amateur radio operator, golf, target shooting. Home: 2625 Coveview Toledo OH 43611 Office: Bock Laundry Machine Co 3600 N Summit PO Box 5127 Toledo OH 43611

LONG, DWIGHT EDWARD, audio-visual company executive; b. Cin., Sept. 23, 1936; s. Richard C. and Charlene (O'Kelly) L; m. Ethel Burroughs (div. Mar. 1981); m. Nancy Elizabeth Morris, Apr. 17, 1982; children: Connie, Lee, Cheryl, Darrell, Beth, Amy. Grad. high sch. Mgr. photo/graphics dept. Procter & Gamble Co., Cin., 1957-78; pres. Cin. Audio Visual Design, 1978-82; pres. audio/visual design div. David Douglas Corp., Cin., 1982-86; pres. Profl. Meeting Services, Cin., 1986—. Pres. Mt. Washington Pee Wee Football Assn. Mem. Assn. Multi-Image, Profl. Photographers Am., Internat. Communications Industries Assn. Avocations: photography, music, woodworking, hunting. Home and Office: 3664 Hopper Ridge Rd Cincinnati OH 45230

LONG, ERNESTINE MARTHA JOULLIAN, educator; b. St. Louis, Nov. 14, 1906; d. Ernest Cameron and Alice (Joullian) Long; A.B., U. Wis., 1927; M.S., U. Chgo., 1932; Ph.D., St. Louis U., 1976; postgrad. Washington U., St. Louis, 1932-68, Eastman Sch. Music, 1956, (NSF fellow) So. Ill. U., 1969-70. Tchr. scis. pub. schs. Normandy dist., St. Louis, 1927-66, Red Bud, Ill., 1966-70, St. Louis, 1970-75; coordinator continuing edn. U. Mo., St. Louis, 1976-79; ednl. cons. Area IV, St. Louis Pub. Schs. Recipient Community Service award St. Louis Newspaper Guild, 1978-79. Mem. AAAS, Am. Physics Tchrs. Assn., Am. Personnel and Guidance Assn. (treas. St. Louis br. 1954), Am. Chem. Soc., Central Assn. Sch. Sci. Math. Tchrs. (chmn. chemistry sect.), Am. Soc. for Microbiology, LWV, St. Louis Symphony Soc. (women's div., docent), Am. Guild Organists, NEA, Nat. Sci. Tchrs. Assn. Home: 245 N Price Rd Ladue MO 63124

LONG, GREGORY SCOTT, accountant; b. Halstead, Kans., Oct. 18, 1951; s. James E. and Lucille E. (Krueger) L.; m. Kathryn A. Fowler, June 2, 1973; children: Derek S., Leah M. BS in Bus., Ft. Hays State U., 1976; postgrad., Wichita Stae U., 1980—. CPA, Kans. Office mgr. Farmers Coop Grain, Co., Haven, Kans., 1976-77; sr. acct. Kennedy and Coe, CPA's, Hutchinson, Kans., 1977-80; asst. controller Kwik Shop, Inc. div. Dillon Cos., Inc., Hutchinson, 1980-85; mgr. Robert Spielman, CPA, Hutchinson, 1985—. Councilman City of Haven, 1982—; music dir. Haven Bapt. Ch. Mem. Am. Inst. CPA's, Hutchinson Acctg. Assn. Democrat. Lodge: Optimist. Avocations: golf, fishing. Home: 311 N Reno Haven KS 67543 Office: Robert Spielman CPA PO Box 1271 Hutchinson KS 67504-1271

LONG, JOHN CHRISTOPHER, marketing director; b. Oak Park, Ill., Apr. 14, 1928; s. John Christopher and Margaret Anne (Foley) L.; m. Lois Jeanne McCammack, Nov. 14, 1953 (div. May 1984). Student, Art Inst. Chgo., 1945, Am. Acad. Art, Chgo., 1945-47, DePaul U., 1952-53. Lic. real estate broker, Ill. Artist Schreiner Bennett, Chgo., 1945-50; supr. art buying Leo Burnett Co., Chgo., 1955-84; mktg. dir. Andre's Fotolab, Chgo., 1984—; lectr. U. Chgo. Adult Edn., 1958. Served to sgt. U.S. Army, 1950-52, Korea. Recipient Recognition award Off-the-Street Club, Chgo., 1980. Mem. Midwest Indsl. Photographers Assn. (assoc.). Roman Catholic. Avocations: violin, sailing, knife throwing. Home: 8608 Memory Trail Wonder Lake IL 60097 Office: Andre's FotoLab Inc 160 E Illinois St Chicago IL 60611

LONG, KELLY DEAN, lawyer; b. Hillsboro, Ill., Apr. 11, 1944; s. Maynard and Ruth Ann (Bateman) L.; m. Jan Long; children: Angela Sue, Adam, James. BS in Acctg., U. Ill., 1966; JD, Washington U., St. Louis, 1969. Bar: Ill. 1969, U.S. Dist. Ct. (cen. dist.) Ill. 1972, U.S. Ct. Appeals (7th cir.) 1976, U.S. Supreme Ct. 1976. Assoc. George E. Ginos, Hillsboro, 1969-70, Ralph Vandever, Hillsboro, 1972; state's atty. Montgomery County, Hillsboro, 1972-80; sole practice, Hillsboro, 1980—. Vol. fireman Hillsboro Vol. Fire Dept., 1974-83. Trustee Hillsboro Library Bd. Served to capt. U.S. Army, 1970-71. Mem. Assn. Trial Lawyers Am., Ill. Bar Assn. Ill. Trial Lawyers Assn. (matrimonial com. 1981-85), Montgomery County Bar Assn., Nat. Dist. Attorney's Assn. Home: 30 Lakewood Estates Hillsboro IL 62049 Office: PO Box 216 1 Central Park E Hillsboro IL 62049

LONG, MARGARET WICK, educational consultant; b. Guatemala City, Guatemala, Jan. 29, 1950; came to U.S., 1965; d. Stanley Arthur and Elizabeth Louise (Sanford) Wick; m. Roland Vance Long, Mar. 21, 1970; children: Diana Ruth, Nancy Elizabeth, Benjamin Roland. Student, Wheaton (Ill.) Coll., 1967-70; BS, So. Ill. U., 1971, MA, 1974, PhD, 1978. Asst. prof. English Ohio State Univ., Columbus, 1979-81; pvt. practice ednl. cons. Nashport, Ohio, 1981—; lectr. in linguistics Ohio State U., 1978-79; cons. Tri-Valley Local Sch. Dist., Dresden, Ohio, 1984—; frequent speaker in cen. Ohio, 1981—. Contbr. articles, book reviews to mags. Active Muskingum County (Ohio) Med. Auxiliary, sec., 1984-85; mem. bd. Zanesville (Ohio) Concert Assn., 1986—, Muskingum Alcoholism Ctr., Zanesville, 1986—, Cult Awareness Network Cen. Ohio, Columbus, 1986—; mem. Tri-Valley Bd. Edn., Dresden, 1983—. Mem. Ohio Sch. Bds. Assn., Speech Communication Assn., Tchrs. of English to Speakers of Other Langs. Republican. Methodist. Club: Authors (Zanesville) (program chmn. 1986-87). Avocations: reading, travel, swimming, racquetball, cooking. Home and Office: 5635 Bishop Ct Nashport OH 43830

LONG, MARK R., roofing company executive; b. Garden City, Kans., Nov. 10, 1951; s. Ronald Eugene and Clara Belle (Murphy) L.; m. Diana Kay, Aug. 20, 1973 (div. Sept. 1985); children: Brandi Diane, Nicholas Joseph, Jonathan Fredrick. AA in Edn., Dodge City Coll., 1972; student, Ft. Hays State Coll., 1972-74. Foreman Glas-flex Roofing, Dodge City, Kans., 1974-76, supt., 1976-79, salesman, estimater, 1979-80, v.p., 1980—. Mem. Leadership Dodge Program, Dodge City, 1987. Mem. Dodge City Area Homebuilders (v.p. 1983-86, bd. dirs.), Boot Hill Jaycees (pres. 1982, Jaycee of Quarter 1986), Coronado Car Club(v.p. 1975-76), Flat Land Scuba Divers (pres. 1983—). Republican. Roman Catholic. Avocations: camping, skiing, scuba diving, hunting, softball. Home: 1106 1st Dodge City KS 67801 Office: Glass-flex Roofing and Insulation Inc 304 11th St Dodge City KS 67801

LONG, NICHOLAS KINSEY, clinical psychologist; b. Akron, Ohio, May 18, 1939; s. Verl Emry and Verna Marie (Kinsey) L.; m. Devona Anderson, Aug. 27, 1966; children: Catherine Emma, Nicholas Kinsey. AB, Kenyon Coll., Gambier, Ohio, 1961; MA, U. Minn., 1963, PhD, 1968. Lic. psychologist. Clin. psychologist Dingleton Hosp., Melrose, Scotland, 1968-69; prin. investigator InterStudy, Mpls., 1969-75; gen. practice clin. psychology Nelsen & Long, P.A., Mpls., 1975—, Mpls. Clinic Psychiatry and Neurology, 1977-81; sr. clin. psychologist Prepetition Screening Program, Mpls., 1981—; cons. Andminstrn. on Aging HEW, Washington, 1975-77. Author: Information and Referral Services; Research Findings, 1977, Information and Referral Evaluation and Planning System, 1975. Vol. Walk-in Counseling Ctr., Mpls., 1971-80; chmn. religious edn. bd. Plymouth Congl. Ch., Mpls., 1980-83, bd. deacons, 1986—. Mem. Am. Psychol. Assn., Council Health Care Providers (chmn. 1976-79). Avocations: travel, computing. Office: Prepetition Screening Program 527 Park Ave S Minneapolis MN 55415

LONG, PATRICK DAVID, lawyer; b. Middletown, Ohio, Jan. 4, 1951; s. John Clarence and Marilyn (Greenfield) L.; m. Jennifer Rapp, Aug. 16, 1975; children: James, Erin. BA in Speech and English, Western Ky. U., 1973; postgrad. U. Ky., 1974-75; JD, U. Dayton, 1977. Bar: Ohio 1977. Assoc. Tracy & Tracy, Franklin, Ohio, 1977-82; ptnr. Tracy & Long, Franklin, 1982—; contact atty. Pub. Children Services Assn., 1983—. Mem. Warren County Dem. Central Com., 1976-82; pres. Franklin Area Community Services, 1983—; mayor Village of Carlisle, Ohio, 1986—. Editor Jour. Honors Bull., 1973. Mem. ACLU (cooperating atty. 1980—), ABA, Warren County Bar Assn., Ohio Bar Assn., Cin. Bar Assn., Assn. Trial Lawyers Am., Ohio Acad. Trial Lawyers, C. of C.(pres. Franklin Area chpt. 1986-87). Lodges: Lions, Rotary. Avocation: amateur radio. Office: Tracy & Long 8 E 5th St Franklin OH 45005

LONG, ROLAND JOHN, secondary school principal; b. Chgo., Nov. 15, 1921; s. John and Lillian Catherine (Sigmund) L.; m. Valerie Ann Zawila, Nov. 13, 1954; children: Ronald J., Thomas E. BS, Ill. State Normal U., 1949; MA, Northwestern U., 1951; EdD, Ill. State U., 1972. Instr. of social sci. Ball State U., Muncie, Ind., 1951; comdt. Morgan Park Mil. Acad., Chgo., 1952-54; tchr. history Hyde Park and Amundsen high schs., Chgo., 1955-62; prin. Hubbard Elementary Sch., Chgo., 1962; founder, prin. Hubbard High Sch., Chgo., 1963-85; prin. Chgo. High Sch. for Met. Studies, 1985—; mem. doctoral adv. com. of Ill. State U., 1973-75; panelist Gen. Assembly State of Ill. Sponsored Conf. Ednl. Reform. Author: Dr. Long's Old-Fashioned Basic Report Card and Parent Helper, 1977. Mem. Chgo. Police Dist. 8 steering com., 1974-77; bd. dirs. West Communities YMCA, Chgo., Greater Lawn Mental Health Ctr., Chgo.; mem. Accademia Italia, 1983. Served to 1st lt., inf., U.S. Army, ETO. Decorated Silver Star, Purple Heart, Bronze Star; Ford Found. fellow, 1973; recipient Sch. Mgmt. citation Ill. Gen. Assembly, 1972. Fellow (hon.) Harry S. Truman Library Inst.; mem. Ill. Assn. for Supervision and Curriculum Devel., Nat. Assn. of Secondary Sch. Prins., Am. Legion, Phi Delta Kappa (Educator of Yr. aw ard 1980), Pi Gamma Mu, Kappa Delta Pi. Club: Elks. Home: 6701 N Ionia Ave Chicago IL 60646 Office: 160 W Wendell St Chicago IL 60610

LONG, WRITESMAN, business educator; b. Hume, Ill., Sept. 16, 1934; s. H. Montelle and Mary Louvene (Writesman) L. B.S., Eastern Ill. U., 1956; M.S., U. Ill., 1959, advanced cert. in edn., 1965; D.Edn., No. Ill. U., 1977. Instr. bus. Blue Mound (Ill.) High Sch., 1956-64; chmn. dept. bus. edn. Kankakee (Ill.) Sr. High Sch., 1964-66; supr. bus. edn. Kankakee Eastridge and Westview High Schs., 1966-68; vis. lectr. U. Ill., Urbana, 1966, 67, 68; chmn. bus. div. Kankakee Community Coll., 1968-73, dir. instrn. and personnel, 1973-77, v.p. bus. affairs and personnel, 1977-81, instr. bus., 1981—. Mem. Am. Vocat. Assn., Nat. Bus. Edn. Assn., North Central Bus. Edn. Assn., Ill. Vocat. Assn., Ill. Bus. Edn. Assn. (disting. service award 1977), Chgo. Area Bus. Educators Assn., Delta Pi Epsilon, Phi Delta Kappa. Home: 720 Riverside Ct Kankakee IL 60901 Office: Box 888 Kankakee IL 60901

LONGAR, MARK WILLIAM, warehouse company executive; b. Eveleth, Minn., Feb. 20, 1950; s. John Anthony and Ilse (Peters) L.; m. Marie Elizabeth Gill, Aug. 5, 1972; children: John Anthony, Heidi Marie. BA, U. Notre Dame, 1972. Pres. Michiana Auto Rental, South Bend, Ind., 1972-80; transp. mgr. Steel Warehouse Co., Inc., South Bend, 1980-83, plant mgr., 1983—; mem. exec. edn. adv. bd. Ind. U. Sch. Bus., Bloomington, Ind., 1985—. Pres. Michiana High Sch. Hockey League, 1973-74, Michiana Sr. Hockey League 1982—. Roman Catholic. Lodge: Moose. Home: 5722 Bridgeton South Bend IL 46614 Office: Steel Warehouse Co Inc 2722 Tucker Dr PO Box 1377 South Bend IN 46624

LONGARDNER, CRAIG THEODOR, manufacturing executive; b. Ft. Wayne, Ind., June 2, 1955; s. Joseph Bernell and Dolores Waneta (Kiel) L.; m. Marsha Elaine Lessig, July 9, 1983. BA, Ind. U., 1977; MBA, Butler U., 1985. Cert. purchasing mgr. Divisional buyer Eaton Corp., Cleve., 1977-80; purchasing mgr. Hurco Cos., Inc., Indpls., 1980-85; materials mgr. Ransburg Corp., Indpls., 1985—; instr. bus. statistics Kellogg Community Coll., Battle Creek, Mich., 1977. Mem. Northridge Assn., Indpls., 1986, John Wayne Found. (life). Mem. Assn. MBA Execs., Nat. Assn. Purchasing Mgrs., Ind. U. Alumni Assn. (life). Republican. Presbyterian. Avocations: basketball, hunting, racquetball, camping, short stories. Home: 10404 N Delaware Indianapolis IN 46280 Office: Ransburg Corp 3939 W 56th St Indianapolis IN 46254

LONGERT, ALAN, orthopedic surgeon; b. Cleve., Feb. 5, 1937; s. Meyer Longert and Betty Miller; m. Ruth Ann Soller, May 8, 1970; 1 child, Audra Michelle. BS in Pharmacy, Ohio No. U., 1960; MD, Ohio State U., 1964. Diplomate Am. Bd. Orthopedic Surgeons. Intern Mt. Sinai Hosp., Cleve., 1964-65; resident in orthopedics Ohio State U., Columbus, 1965-69; orthopedic surgeon Columbus East Orthopedic Assocs., 1972—; chmn. dept. orthopedics Mt. Carmel East Hosp., Columbus, 1973-80, chmn. surgical adminstrn. com. 1978-83, chmn. clin. dept. council, 1983-84, chmn. planning and devel. com. 1983-87; bd. dirs. Mt. Carmel Health Found., 1985—. Served to major USAF, 1969-71. Fellow Am. Acad. Orthopedic Surgeons; mem. AMA, Clin. Orthopedic Soc., Columbus Orthopedic Soc., Mid-Am. Orthopedic Soc., Ohio State Med. Soc., Franklin County Med. Soc., Phi Delta Epsilon, U.S. Trotting Assn., Ohio Harness Horseman's Assn. Avocations: sports, Standard-bred Horses, reading, jazz music. Home: 635 Old Farm Rd Columbus OH 43213 Office: Columbus East Orthopedic Assocs 50 McNaughten Columbus OH 43213

LONGHOFER, RONALD STEPHEN, lawyer; b. Junction City, Kans., Aug. 30, 1946; s. Oscar William and Anna Mathilda (Krause) L.; m. Martha Ellen Dennis, July 9, 1981; children: Adam, Nathan, Stefanie. B.Music, U. Mich., 1968; J.D., 1975. Bar: Mich. 1975, U.S. Dist. Ct. (ea. dist.) Mich., U.S. Ct. Appeals (6th cir.), U.S. Supreme Ct. Law clk. to judge U.S. Dist. Ct. (ea. dist.) Mich., Detroit, 1975-76; ptnr. firm Honigman, Miller, Schwartz & Cohn, Detroit, 1976—. Editor Mich. Law Rev., 1974-75. Served with U.S. Army, 1968-72. Mem. ABA, Detroit Bar Assn., Fed. Bar Assn., Order of Coif, Phi Beta Kappa, Phi Kappa Phi, Pi Kappa Lambda. Clubs: Detroit Econ., U. Mich. Pres's. Home: 3901 Six Mile Rd S Lyon MI 48178 Office: Honigman Miller Schwartz & Cohn 2290 1st National Bldg Detroit MI 48226

LONGLEY, WILLIAM WARREN, physicist, computer science educator; b. Hanover, N.H., Aug. 30, 1937; s. William Warren and Anita Grace (Sallans) L.; m. Patricia Ann Sweetman, July 3, 1960; children—Elizabeth Ann, Harold William. B.A., U. Colo., 1958, M.A., 1959, Ph.D., 1963. Engr. aerospace div. Martin-Marietta Corp., Denver, 1959-63; postdoctoral fellow U. Alta., Edmonton, 1963-64; assoc. physicist Midwest Research Inst., Kansas City, Mo., 1964-68; assoc. prof. physics, computer ctr. dir. Upper Iowa U., Fayette, Iowa, 1968-81; assoc. prof. computer sci. St. Cloud State U. (Minn.), 1981-83; assoc. prof. computer sci. Peru State Coll. (Nebr.), 1983—; cons. data processing. Mem. AAAS, Am. Phys. Soc., Am. Econ. Assn., Sigma Xi. Office: Peru State Coll Peru NE 68421

LONGMEYER, JUDITH A. SHULMISTRAS, marketing executive; b. Chgo., Aug. 30, 1943; d. John A. and Ann (Jakaitis) Shulmistras; m. Joseph F. Longmeyer, Apr. 28, 1962 (div. May 1978). AA, Chgo. City Coll., 1962; BA, Roosevelt U., 1970; MBA, Northwestern U., 1975. Mem. pub. relations mktg. staff Skil Corp., Chgo., 1964-72; asst. mgr. pub. relations McGraw Edison Co., Elgin, Ill., 1973-74; ptnr. Advocates Agy., McHenry, Ill., 1975-76; mgr. mktg. services Switchgear div.,Allis Chalmers, West Allis, Wis., 1976-80; owner Intercom, Milw., 1980—; mgr. mktg. communications Micro Design div. Bell & Howell Co., Hartford, Wis., 1980-84, sales mgr. Isco, Lincoln, Nebr., 1987—; instr., Milw. Area Tech. Coll., West Allis, 1979-80. Mem. Sales and Mktg. Execs. Assn., Iota Sigma Epsilon. Club: Lincoln Track. Home: 3210 Serenity Circle #3 Lincoln NE 68516 Office: Isco Inc 4700 W Superior Lincoln NE 68504

LONGONE, DANIEL THOMAS, educator; b. Worcester, Mass., Sept. 16, 1932; s. Daniel Edward and Anne (Novick) L.; m. Janice B. Bluestein, June 13, 1954. B.S., Worcester Poly. Inst., 1954; Ph.D., Cornell U., 1958. Research fellow chemistry U. Ill., Urbana, 1958-59; mem. faculty dept. chemistry U. Mich., Ann Arbor, 1959—; asso. prof. U. Mich., 1966-71, prof., 1971—; cons. Gen. Motors Research Co., 1965-77. Am. Chem. Soc.-Petroleum Research Fund internat. fellow, 1967-68; Fulbright scholar, 1970-

71. Mem. Am. Chem. Soc., Sigma Xi, Tau Beta Pi, Phi Lambda Upsilon. Home: 1207 W Madison St Ann Arbor MI 48103 Office: U Mich 2307 Chemistry Ann Arbor MI 48109

LONGSTAFF, RICHARD DAVID, data processing executive; b. Milw., Dec. 1, 1961; s. David Allen and Eleanor (Sauer) L. BBA, U. Wis., 1984. Data systems supr. Wis. Bell., Milw., 1981-84, data communications analyst, 1984—. Asst. Spl. Olympics volleyball, Waukesha, 1982-83, track and field, Shorewood, Wis., 1985; big bro. Bethesda Home for the Mentally Retarded, Watertown, Wis., 1983-84. Mem. Data Processing Mgmt. Assn. (chmn. 1983-84, pres. 1984, scholar 1984, OUtstanding Com. Person 1984). Avocations: woodworking, lighthouses, antigue restorations, volleyball. Home: 1826 N 56th St Milwaukee WI 53208 Office: Wis Bell Inc N15W24250 Bell Dr Waukesha WI 53188

LONNEMO, KURT ROLAND, hydraulic company executive; b. Söderbärke, Sweden, Dec. 24, 1936; came to U.S., 1967; s. Karl Georg and Elna Margareta (Stalhandske) L.; m. Margareta Siv Ingrid Lilja, Sept. 9, 1958; children: Mats Roland, Hans Anders, Klas Robert. MS in Mech. Engring., Royal Inst. Tech., Stockholm, 1961. Test engr. Royal Bd. Water Power, Stockholm, 1958-59; chief engr. AB Nordisk Vickers, Stockholm, 1963-67; engring. mgr. Sperry Vickers, Troy, Mich., 1968-73, planning mgr., 1973-76, product mgr., 1976-82; application market mgr. Vickers, Inc., Troy, Mich., 1982—; cons. Swedish Water Power Assn., Stockholm, 1960-61; instr. Royal Sch. Navy, Nasby Park, Sweden, 1962; asst. prof. Royal Inst. Tech., 1964-67. Patentee in field; contbr. articles to profl. jours. Served to 2d lt. Swedish Army, 1962-63. Mem. Fluid Power Soc., Soc. Automotive Engrs. Republican. Lutheran. Avocations: woodworking, boating. Home: 1835 Lakeview Ct Bloomfield Hills MI 48013 Office: Vickers Inc 1401 Crook Rd Troy MI 48084

LONNING, ROGER DEAN, school media supervisor; b. Iowa City, Iowa, Feb. 12, 1927; s. Lennie B. and Leona Beatrice (Hanson) L.; m. Marjorie Ann Moe, Aug. 16, 1953; children—Stuart Eric, Kathy Linnea, Steven Roger. B.A., Iowa State Tchr's. Coll., 1954, M.A. in Edn., 1957; M.A.L.S., U. Minn., 1971. Librarian pub. schs., Clarion, Iowa, 1954-56; tchr. 6th grade Hawthorne Sch., Albert Lea, Minn., 1957-61; librarian Lea Coll., Albert Lea, Minn., summers 1968, 69; instr. Mankato State U. (Minn.), summers 1976, 82; media supr. High Sch. Albert Lea, 1961—; mem. adv. bd. Albert Lea Pub. Library, 1968-71. Trustee Freeborn County Hist. Soc., Albert Lea, 1966-86, pres., 1971, 72, treas., 1981-86; mem. Planning Zoning Commn., Albert Lea, 1979-83, Southeast Minn. Arts Council, 1984-87, Freeborn County Arts Com., 1986—. Served with USN, 1945-52, ETO, PTO. Mem. ALA, NEA, Minn. Edn. Assn., Albert Lea Edn. Assn., Minn. Assn. Sch. Librarians (pres. 1969-70), Minn. Edn. Media Orgn. (sec. 1976-77), Phi Delta Kappa. Republican. Office: Sr High Sch 504 W Clark Albert Lea MN 56007

LONOFF, MARC JOSHUA, economist, banker; b. N.Y.C., Feb. 14, 1952; s. Richard and Evelyn (Kushins) L.; m. Alice Lynn Sessions, July 14, 1973; 2 children. BA in Econs. with highest honors, Oberlin Coll., 1972; PhD in Econs., MIT, 1982. Teaching asst. Harvard U. and MIT, Cambridge, 1974-75; sr. assoc. Charles River Assocs., Boston, 1975-84; v.p. First Nat. Bank, Chgo., 1984; market maker Chgo. Bd. Options Exchange, 1985—. NSF grad. fellow, MIT, 1982. Mem. Am. Econs. Assn., Econometric Soc., U.S. Chess Fedn. (chessmaster; Mass. Open co-champion 1982), Phi Beta Kappa. Avocations: chess, bridge, tennis, computers. Office: First Options of Chgo 1 Financial Pl Chicago IL 60602

LOOFT, W. GENE, manufacturing company executive; b. Ottawa, Ill., Feb. 26, 1938; s. Henry Charles and Margery V. (Moss) L.; m. Beverly J. Milburn, June 7, 1959; children: Annette Susan, Steven Paul, Mark Andrew. BS in Engring., Purdue U., 1960. Registered profl. engr., Ill. Application conveyor engr. Chainbelt Co., Milw., 1960-63; app'l. bearings engr. Rex Chainbelt Co., Downers Grove, Ill., 1964-69, mgr. bearing engring., 1969-76; mgr. sales and engring. Rexnord Bearing Div., Downers Grove, 1977-81; group products mgr. Rexnord Mech. Power Div., Milw., 1982—; del. Internat. Standard Orgn. Tech. Com. 4 Rolling Bearings, 1977, 79, 81, 83; chmn. ISO sub com. TC4/SC-3 Air Frame Bearings, 1978-83, Internat. Standards Orgn. TC4/TC-20 Com. Airframe Bearings, 1984. Author: Bearing Application, 1968 (Readership award 1968). Pres. Lisle (Ill.) Baseball Leagues, 1973-74; mem., pres. Lisle Sch. Bd., 1975-81. Mem. Soc. Automotive Engrs. Home: 10411 N Greenside Ct Mequon WI 53092 Office: Rexnord-Mech Power Div 4701 W Greenfield Milwaukee WI 53201

LOOMIS, CHARLES WAYNE, psychologist; b. Madison County, Iowa, Mar. 17, 1940; s. Homer H. and Wilma L. (McNichols) L.; m. Darlene K. Bennett, June 17, 1961 (div. Jan. 1976); m. Nancy L. Goldsberry, Dec. 11, 1976; 1 child, Gwendolynn Joy. BA, Anderson Coll., 1962; MA, Kent (Ohio) State U., 1967. Vocat. rehab. counselor Ohio Bur. Vocat. Rehab., Dayton, Ohio, 1963-64; dir. rehab. services Goodwill Industries Rehab. Clinic, Canton, Ohio, 1966-69; pres. Career Devel. Ctr., Inc., Columbus, Ohio, 1969—. Served with U.S. Army, 1962-63. Mem. Nat. Rehab. Assn., Am. Psychol. Assn., Ohio Psychol. Assn., Ohio Rehab. Assn., Am. Board Vocat. Experts (diplomate), Ohio Cattlemen's Assn., Bus. and Profl. Men's Assn. Republican. Methodist. Lodge: Lions. Home: 2383 St Rt 668 S Junction City OH 43748 Office: Career Devel Ctr Inc 3556 Sullivant Ave Columbus OH 43204

LOOMIS, SALORA DALE, psychiatrist; b. Peru, Ind., Oct. 21, 1930; s. S. Dale Sr. and Rhea Pearl (Davis) L.; m. Carol Marie Davis, Jan 3, 1959; children: Stephen Dale, Patricia Marie. AB in Zoology, Ind. U., 1953, MS in Human Anatomy, 1955, MD, 1958. Diplomate Am. Bd. Psychiatry and Neurology. Intern Cook County Hosp., Chgo., 1958-59; resident in psychiatry Logansport (Ind.) State Hosp., 1959-60, Ill. State Psychiat. Inst., Chgo., 1960-62; staff psychiatrist Katharine Wright Psychiat. Clinic, Chgo., 1962-65, dir., 1965—; cons. Ill. Youth Commn. 1962-64; instr. psychiatry Northwestern U. Med. Sch., Chgo.,1962-64, assoc. 1964-67; asst. dir. Northwestern U. Psychiat. Clinics, Chgo., 1963-65; attending psychiatrist, vice chmn. dept. psychiatry St. Joseph Hosp., Chgo., 1964—; lectr. psychiatry and neurology Loyola U. Med. Sch. Chgo., 1964-65, assoc. 1965, asst. prof. 1965-73, lect. 1980—; psychiat. cons. Ill. Dept. Pub. Health, 1967—; attending psychiatrist, chmn. dept. psychiatry Ill. Masonic Med. Ctr., Chgo. 1970—; assoc. prof. psychiatry U. Ill. Coll. Medicine, Chgo., 1973—. Fellow Am. Coll. Psychiatrists, Am. Psychiat. Assn., Acad. Psychosomatic Medicine; mem. AMA, Ill. State Med. Soc. (chmn. council on mental health and addiction 1974-75, chmn. joint peer rev. com. 1975-76), Ill. Psychiat. Soc. (chmn. ethics com. 1974-75, chmn. peer rev. com. 1976-78), Chgo. Med. Socs. Office: 8 S Michigan Ave Chicago IL 60603 also: 923 W Wellington Ave Chicago IL 60657

LOOMSTEIN, ARTHUR, real estate company executive; b. St. Louis, July 27, 1939; s. Meyer and Ann (Mariam) L.; m. Kay Diane Oppenheim, Aug. 22, 1975; children: David Jay, Debi, Debra Ann. BSBA, Washington U., St. Louis, 1961, JD, 1964. Pres. Centerco Properties Inc., St. Louis, 1961—. Recipient Disting. Citizen Citation, St. Louis Regional Commerce and Growth Assn., 1973. Mem. Bldg. Owners and Mgrs. Assn. Met. St. Louis (bd. dirs. 1969-75, treas. 1971-72, pres. 1973-74), Soc. Real Property Adminstrs. (founding mem.). Jewish. Clubs: Meadowbrook Country, Town and Country Racquet (St. Louis). Avocations: swimming, golfing, thoroughbred racing. Home: 5 Somerset Downs Ladue MO 63124 Office: Centerco Properties Inc 7710 Carondelet Ave Clayton MO 63105

LOONEY, FREDERICK WILSON, data processing manager; b. Princeton, W.Va., Sept. 10, 1949; s. Irvin Wilson and Lena Viola (Phillips) L.; m. Marion Ruth Mason, May 12, 1967 (div. May 1975); children: Karen Ruth, Kristine Elizabeth; m. Gail Jeanette Frank, Nov. 22, 1975. Grad. high sch., Greensboro, N.C., 1967. Programmer, analyst Burlington Industries, Greensboro, 1967-72; systems programmer Carolina Steel Corp., Greensboro, 1972-73; data processing mgr. McGraw Edison Corp., Albion, Mich., 1973-80, Albion Industries, 1980—. Avocations: fishing, woodworking, travel. Home: 311 N Mingo St Albion MI 49224 Office: Albion Industries 800 N Clark St Albion MI 49224

LOONEY, MARY LOU, business executive, former retail company executive; b. Carroll, Iowa, July 30, 1948; d. Vincent Patrick and Edna Margaret (Schultz) Rowan; m. W.J. Pick, Jan. 7, 1967 (div. May 1975); children: Rebecca Ann, Brenda Louise; m. Ralph Bernard Looney, Oct. 1, 1977. Student U. S.D., 1969-72, Met. Tech. Community Coll., Omaha, 1980. Sec., Wall Lake Community Sch. (Iowa), 1966-67; adminstrv. asst. U. S.D., Vermillion, 1969-73; mgr., buyer Rocking Horse, Vermillion, 1973-75; bookkeeper, Nebr. Builders Product, Omaha, 1975-76; office mgr. Restaurant Mgmt., Omaha, 1976-80; controller LaGrange Equipment Co., Omaha, 1980-82, pres., 1982-84; real estate sales agt. N.P. Dodge Co., Omaha, 1984-86; pres. and chief exec. officer Preferred Bus. Referrals, Inc., Omaha, 1986—. Mem. Nat. Assn. Female Execs., Profl. Women's Assn., Greater Resources for Omaha Women. Republican. Methodist. Home: 11412 Queens Dr Omaha NE 68164

LOOSEN, SISTER ANN MARITA, nun, religious health care executive; b. Kansas City, Mo.; d. Irving R. and Mary Louise (Meaney) L. BS in Nursing, St. Mary Coll., Leavenworth, Kans., 1965; M in Health Adminstrn., U. Minn., 1967. Assoc. adminstr. St. John Hosp., Santa Monica, Calif., 1967-75; asst. dir. hosps. Sisters of Charity of Leavenworth Health Services Corp., 1975-78; adminstr. St. John Hosp., Leavenworth, 1978-80; pres. St. Francis Hosp. and Med. Ctr., Topeka, 1980—; chmn. Midwest Health Congress, Kansas City, 1986-87; bd. dirs. Cath. Health Affairs Kans., St. Joseph Hosp., Denver, St. Mary Hosp., Emporia, Kans., , Commerce Bank, Topeka. Fellow Am. Coll. Health Care Execs.; mem. Kans. Hosp. Assn. (bd. dirs. 1985—), Topeka C. of C. (bd. dirs. 1984-86). Avocations: music, cooking, walking. Office: St Francis Hosp and Med Ctr 1700 W Seventh Topeka KS 66606

LOOYENGA, ROBERT WILLIAM, chemistry educator, consultant; b. N.D., Oct. 21, 1939. BA, Hope Coll., 1961; MS, Wayne State U., 1968, PhD, 1969. Research chemist Printing Devel. Inc., Racine, Wis., 1970-72; prof. chemistry S.D. Sch. of Mines and Tech., Rapid City, 1972—; pvt. practice forensic sci., cons. Rapid City, 1974—. Fellow NSF. Mem. ACS (analytical div.), S.D. Acad. Sci., Sigma Xi. Office: SD Sch Mines and Tech 501 E Saint Joseph Rapid City SD 57701

LOPATA, MONTE LEE, accountant; b. St. Louis, Aug. 21, 1919; s. Charles and Minnie (Kligman) L.; m. Caroloyn Blumenfeld, Oct. 8, 1946; children: Lee, Loren, Heidi Ann. BSBA, Washington U., 1942; postgrad., U. Chgo., 1946. CPA, Mo. Treas. Frolic Footwear, Inc., Jonesboro, Ark., 1951-53, v.p., 1953-82, pres., 1982-87; chmn. Lopata, Lopata & Dubinsky, St. Louis, 1987—; bd. dirs. A-I Mfg. Corp., St. Louis, Guild Craftsmen, St. Louis, Arion Products, St. Louis, C&M Products, St. Louis. Served to 1st lt. USAF, 1942-46. Mem. Am. Inst. CPA, Mo. CPA's. Clubs: Westwood Country, Whittemore (St. Louis). Avocations: photographer, golfer, bridge. Home: 8021 Seminole Pl Saint Louis MO 63105 Office: Lopata Lopata & Dubinsky 7751 Carondelet Ave Suite 500 Saint Louis MO 63105

LOPEZ-BAEZ, SANDRA IVELISSE, psychologist, educator; b. Aguadilla, P.R., Sept. 8, 1952; d. Manuel G. Lopez Gonzales and Alba I. (Baez) de Lopez. BA, U. P.R., 1974; MA, Marshall U., 1975; PhD, Kent State U., 1980; cert., Gestalt Inst. Cleve., 1986. Licensed psychologist, Ohio. Dir. student support Coll. Medicine Northeast Ohio U. Coll. Medicine, Rootstown, 1979-83, adj. asst. prof., 1983—; dir. Lopez Counseling & Assocs., Louisville, Ohio, 1983—; asst. prof. Walsh Coll., Canton, Ohio, 1983—; adj. asst. prof. Northeastern Ohio U., Rootstown, 1983—; cons. Rogativa Ctr., Canton, 1984—. Named one of Outstanding Young Women in Am., 1985, 86. Mem. Ohio Psychol. Assn., Am. Psychol. Assn., Am. Assn. for Counseling and Devel., Ohio Assn. for Counseling and Devel., Ohio Assn. Multicultural Counseling and Devel. Roman Catholic. Avocations: reading, music, macrame. Home: 400 Woodmoore St Louisville OH 44641 Office: Walsh Coll 2020 Easton St NW Canton OH 44720

LOPEZ-COBOS, JESUS, conductor. Music director Cincinnati Symphony Orchestra. Office: Cin Symphony Orch 1241 Elm St Cincinnati OH 45210 *

LOPINA, LAWRENCE THOMAS, mfg. co. exec.; b. Chgo., Nov. 9, 1930; s. Thomas F. and Augustine A. (Schwantes) L.; Ph.B., U. Notre Dame, 1952; M.B.A., DePaul U., 1953; M.B.A., U. Chgo., 1963; m. Marion T. Toomey, Nov. 5, 1955; children—Joseph D., Lawrence M., Mary E., Celeste N., James P. Jr. acct. Haskins & Sells, C.P.A.s, Chgo., 1952-53; acctg. positions with Motorola, Inc., Chgo., 1953-63; div. controller then v.p. fin. fluid power group Applied Power, Inc., Milw., 1963-74; sr. v.p. fin. Broan Mfg. Co., Inc., Hartford, Wis., 1974—, former dir. Served with AUS, 1953-55. C.P.A., Wis. Mem. Nat. Assn. Accts., Fin. Execs. Inst., Wis. Inst. C.P.A.s, Beta Gamma Sigma. Club: KC. Office: 926 W State St Hartford WI 53027

LORD, JAMES GREGORY, marketing and fundraising consultant; b. Cleve., Aug. 23, 1947; s. James Nelson and Esther L.; student U. Md., Far East Campus, 1966-68, Cleve. State U., 1968-72; m. Wendy Franklin, July 10, 1977. TV news producer Far East Network, Tokyo, 1965-68; wire editor News-Herald, Willoughby, Ohio, 1968-69; pub. relations assoc. United Way, Cleve., 1969-70; free-lance pub. relations person, Cleve., 1970-72; dir. pub. relations Ketchum, Inc., Pitts., 1972-77; cons. mktg., devel. philanthropic instns., Cleve., 1977—; chief devel officer Cleve. Mus. Art, 1984-85; lectr. Served with USN, 1964-68, Japan. Author: Philanthropy and Marketing, 7th edit., 1981; The Raising of Money, 1983; Communicating with Donors, 1984; Building Your Case, 1984; The Campaign Manuals, 1985; The Development Consultant, 1985, Guide for the Professional, 2d edit, 1986, The Perfect Development Officer, 1986, others; contbr. numerous articles on philanthropy, mktg. and quality of life in Am. cities to various publs.; developed one-man photography exhbns., 15 worldwide sites, 1968-72. Home: 28050 S Woodland Rd Pepper Pike OH 44124 Office: care of Third Sector Press 2000 Euclid Ave PO Box 18044 Cleveland OH 44118

LORE, IRVING ALLAN, lawyer; b. Milw., Feb. 28, 1916; s. Michael and Jean (Dinerstein) L.; m. Clarissa Lerner, Feb. 4, 1940; children: Nancy Einhorn, Eileen Gosman. BA, U. Wis., 1935, JD, 1937. Bar: U.S. Supreme Ct., 1942. Sole practice Milw., 1937-79; of counsel Saichek & Hertel, Milw., 1979—; sec.-treas. Midwest Research Microscopy, Inc., Immunotronics, Inc. Editor: U. Wis. Law Rev., 1935-37; also articles. Bd. dirs. Milw. Sch. Engring., 1966—, United Way Greater Milw., 1971-80; mem. bd. Met. Milw. Assn. Commerce, 1962-75, Milw. Found., 1971-74, assoc., 1975—; trustee Walter Schroeder Scholarship Fund Marquette U., Milw., 1963—, Mt. Sinai Med. Ctr., Milw., 1972—; chmn. Profl. div. United Way Campaigns, 1971-72. Served to lt. (j.g.) USN, 1943-45, PTO. Recipient Humanitarian award State of Wis. Nat. Conf. Christians and Jews, 1976. Mem. ABA, Assn. Trial Lawyers Am., Wis. Bar Assn., Wis. Acad. Trial Lawyers, Milw. Bar Assn., Order of the Coif, Artus. Jewish. Clubs: Milw. Athletic, University. Lodges: Masons, Consistory, Shriners. Avocations: bowling, bridge. Home: 1610 N Prospect Ave Milwaukee WI 53202 Office: 161 W Wisconsin Ave Suite 6032 Milwaukee WI 53203

LORENZ, GARY ARNO, marketing professional; b. Oak Park, Ill., June 4, 1954; s. Herbert A. and Ann (Scaruffi) L.; m. Kathleen Maroney, May 24, 1981; 1 child, Meghan Ann. BS, Western Ill. U., 1975-78. Mktg. adminstr. Motorola Inc., Schaumburg, Ill., 1978-81, internat. mktg. adminstr., 1981-83, nat. account exec., 1983-84; dir. dealer distbn. Simon & Schuster, Deerfield, Ill., 1984-85; mgr. mktg. services Steel Tank Inst., Northbrook, Ill., 1985—. Editor: (newsletter) Tank Talk, 1986-87. Mem. Am. Mktg. Assn. Lutheran. Avocations: sailing, old home renovation. Office: Steel Tank Inst 728 Anthony Trail Northbrook IL 60062

LORENZ, ROBERT PAUL, obstetrician-gynecologist; b. Chgo., June 25, 1946; s. Paul R. and Harriet M. (Fawcett) L.; m. Christine H. Comstock, Feb. 3, 1973; children: Andrew, David. BA in Biochemistry, Princeton U., 1968; MD, U. Chgo., 1972. Diplomate Am. Bd. Ob-Gyn, Am. Bd. Spl. Expertise Maternal Fetal Medicine. Intern U. Chgo. Hosp., 1972-73; resident ob-gyn U. Mich. Hosp., 1973-76; asst. dir. dept. ob-gyn Wayne County Gen. Hosp., Eloise, Mich., 1976-77; fellow maternal-fetal medicine U. Mich., 1977-79; asst. prof. ob-gyn Pa. State U., Hershey, 1979-84, dir. obstetrics, 1980-83, chief div. maternal-fetal medicine, 1983-84; asst. prof. Wayne State U., 1984—; dir. maternal-fetal medicine, vice chief obstetrics William Beaumont Hosp., Royal Oak, Mich., 1984—; mem. Nat. Diabetes Research Interchange Adv. Com., 1982-84; bd. dirs. SHARE, Inc., Lancaster, Pa., 1982-83. Spl. editorial reviewer Obstretics and Gynecology, 1983—; editorial reviewer Am. Jour. Ob-Gyn, 1986—; contbr. articles to profl. jours. Workgroup chmn. Mich. Task Force on Infant Mortality, 1986—. Grantee March of Dimes Birth Defects Found., 1982-84, William Beaumont Hosp. Research Inst., 1986-87; research grantee Mich. Dept. Health. Fellow Am. Coll. Obstetricians and Gynecologists (adv. council Mich. sect. 1985—); mem. AMA, Soc. Perinatal Obstetricians (chmn. spl. interest group for community hosp. based perinatologists 1985), Am. Assn. Med. Systems and Informatics (ob-gyn spl. interest group), Mich. Med. Soc., Cen. Assn. Obstetricians and Gynecologists, Mich. Council Maternal and Child Health (bd. dirs. 1985—, treas. 1987), Perinatal Assn. Mich., Oakland County Med. Soc. (editorial bd.). Office: William Beaumont Hosp 3601 W 13 Mile Rd Royal Oak MI 48072

LORI, CHARLES BERNARD, physical education teacher; b. Caldwell, Ohio, Nov. 8, 1948; s. Clement Joseph and Mildred Sarah (Hill) L.; m. Norma Ruth Grover, May 30, 1980; children: Jonathan Wayne, Wendy Nicole, Sundie Kaye. BS in Edn., Kent State U., 1972; MS in Edn., Ind. U., 1977. Coach, tchr. Johnny Appleseed Middle Sch., Mansfield, Ohio, 1972-73, Penn High Sch., Mishawaka, Ind., 1973-78, Blackford High Sch., Hartford City, Ind., 1978-80, Pioneer High Sch., Ann Arbor, Mich., 1980—; coach Class AA Football State Champions, Ind., 1979, Class A Football State Champions, Mich., 1984. Coach of the Yr. United Press Internat., AP, UPI, 1980. Mem. Ind. High Sch. Football Coaches Assn. (1979 Coach of the Yr.), Pioneer Football Parents. Republican. Democrat. Club: Pioneer Booster (Ann Arbor). Avocations: travel, movies, sports. Home: 5663 New Meadow Dr Ypsilanti MI 48197 Office: Ann Arbor Pioneer High Sch 601 W Stadium Ann Arbor MI 48103

LOSCHEIDER, PAUL HENRY, academic administrator; b. Joliet, Ill., Nov. 24, 1954; s. John H. and Marian T. (Mantel) L.; m. Mary Susan Futterer, Aug. 1, 1976; children: Eric, Brian, Scott. BA in Acctg., Lewis U., Romeoville, Ill., 1976. CPA, Ill. Staff auditor Cooper & Lybrand, Aurora, Ill., 1976-78; comptroller N. Cen. Coll., Naperville, Ill., 1978-83, v.p. bus. affairs, 1983—. Mem. Nat. Assn. Coll. and Univ. Bus. Officers, Cen. Assn. Coll. and Univ. Bus. Officers, Ednl. and Instl. Ins. Adminstrs. Inc. Adv. Council. Roman Catholic. Home: 824 Magnolia Ln Naperville IL 60540 Office: North Cen Coll 30 N Brainard St Naperville IL 60566

LOSCHEN, EARL LEE, psychiatrist; b. Minden, Nebr., Jan. 10, 1944; s. Herman George and Agnes Anna (Garrelts) L.; m. Marilyn Jean Reinhardt, June 15, 1974; children: Rebecca, Elizabeth. BS, Midland Luth. Coll., 1966; MD, U. Nebr., Omaha, 1970. Diplomate Am. Bd. Psychiatry and Neurology. Asst. prof. U. Nebr., Omaha, 1973-74; asst. prof. So. Ill. U., Springfield, 1974-80, assoc. prof., asst. chmn. dept. psychiatry, 1980—; cons. Ill. Dept. Pub. Health, Springfield, 1976—, Ill. Dept. Rehab. Services, Springfield, 1977—, Aid to Retarded Citizens, Springfield, 1981—, Macoupin County Mental Health, Carlinville, Ill., 1974—. Assoc. editor (jour.) Rural Community Mental Health Newsletter, 1986; contbr. chpts. to books. Mem. com. rights of minors Ill. Commn. Children, 1974-77, com. youth and law, 1977-79; del. 1980 Ill. White House Conf. on Children, 1980, Ill. Conf. Children's Priorities of 1980's, 1981. Fellow Am. Orthopsychiat. Assn.; mem. AMA, Am. Psychiat. Assn., Nat. Assn. Rural Mental Health (bd. dirs. 1985—), Ill. State Med. Soc. (council mental health and addiction 1985-87). Avocations: photography, gardening. Office: So Ill U Sch Medicine PO Box 3926 Springfield IL 62708

LOSECCO, JOHN M., physicist, educator; b. N.Y.C., Oct. 21, 1950; s. Anthony J. and Cleonice Rose (Manzi) LoS.; m. Lynne D. Sterkin-LoSecco, Nov. 21, 1986. BS in Physics, Cooper Union U., 1972; AM in Physics, Harvard U., 1973, PhD in Physics, 1976. Research assoc. Harvard U., Cambridge, Mass., 1976-79; asst. scientist U. Mich., Ann Arbor, 1979-81; asst. prof. Calif. Inst. Tech., Pasadena, 1981-85; assoc. prof. U. Notre Dame, Ind., 1985—. Mem. Am. Phys. Soc. Office: Univ Notre Dame Physics Dept Notre Dame IN 46556

LOSEE, JOHN FREDERICK, JR., manufacturing executive; b. Milw., Apr. 27, 1951; s. John Frderick and Helen (Francis) L.; m. Jane Agnes Trawicki, Aug. 25, 1973; children: Nicole Marie, John Michael. BSME, Marquette U., 1973, MS in Indsl. Engring., 1982. Registered profl. engr., Wis.; cert. numerical control mgr., Wis. Mfg. engr. OMC-Evinrude div. Outboard Marine Corp., Milw., 1975-78, mfg. engr. supr., 1978-80, mgr. tool engring., 1980-85, mgr. process and tool engring., 1985-86, dir. mfg. engring., 1986—. Mem. Numerical Control Soc. Republican. Episcopalian. Home: W264 N6565 Hillview Dr Sussex WI 53089 Office: OMC Evinrude Div Outboard Marine Corp 6101 N 64th St PO Box 663 Milwaukee WI 53201

LOSIN, EDWARD THOMAS, research scientist; b. Racine, Wis., July 9, 1923; s. John and Sophia (Jamroz) L.; m. Laura Joy Soderstrom, June 10, 1950; children: Peter, Eric, Martha. BS, U. Ill., 1948; MA, Columbia U., 1950, PhD, 1955. Supr. high pressure lab. Columbia U., N.Y.C., 1950-54; postdoctoral fellow U. Mich., Ann Arbor, 1954-57; research chemist Union Carbide Corp., Tarrytown, N.Y., 1957-61; mgr. chemist dept. Isomet Corp., Palisades Park, N.J., 1961-63; sr. research scientist Allis-Chalmers Corp., Milw., 1963—. Contbr. articles to profl. jours. Served with USN, 1943-46, ETO. Esso postdoctoral fellow, 1954-57. Mem. Am. Chem. Soc., AAAS, N.Y. Acad. Sci., Combustion Inst., Sigma Xi, Phi Lambda Upsilon. Congregationalist. Home: 10000 N Sheridan Dr Mequon WI 53092 Office: PO Box 512 Milwaukee WI 53201

LOSS, GEORGE FRANCIS, dentist; b. Washington, Oct. 7, 1950; s. George Hugh and Marie Elizabeth (Giraffa) L.; m. Patricia Katherine Bona, July 29, 1973; children: Lauren Elizabeth, George Matthew. BA, U. Notre Dame, 1972; BS, Elmhurst Coll., 1977; DDS, Loyola U., Chgo., 1981. Gen. practice dentistry Elmhurst (Ill.) Dental Assocs., 1981—; dental assisting instr. DuPage Area Vocational Edn. Authority, Addison, Ill., 1981—; staff dentist Elmhurst Extended Care Ctr., 1981—; assoc. John K. Francis DDS, Ltd., Oakbrook, Ill., 1981—. Mem. ADA, Chgo. Dental Soc. (award of merit, 1981). Club: Elmhurst Tennis (pres. 1985—). Avocations: tennis, fishing. Home: 287 Oakland Grove Elmhurst IL 60126 Office: Elmhurst Dental Assocs 333 W 1st St Elmhurst IL 60126

LOSURE, THOMAS A., osteopathic obstetrician-gynecologist; b. South Bend, Ind., Dec. 25, 1951; s. James Allen Losure and Eleanor M. (Cripe) Bell; m. Janice Sue MacGregor, Aug. 10, 1974. BS, Ball State U., 1974; DO, Chgo. Coll. Osteo. Medicine, 1978. Intern Chgo. Coll. Osteo. Medicine, 1978-79, resident in ob-gyn, 1979-82, asst. prof., 1984—; dir. maternal-fetal medicine Rockford (Ill.) Meml. Hosp., 1986—; co-dir. Rockford Regional Perinatal Ctr., 1986—; cons. Nat. Bd. Examiners for Osteo. Physicians and Surgeons, Nat. Rural Health Care Assn.; staff perinatologist, Chgo. Osteo. Med. Ctr., Olympia Fields (Ill.) Osteo. Med. Ctr.; attending physician John F. Kennedy Meml. Hosp., 1983-84, U. Medicine & Dentistry of N.J., N.J. Sch. Osteo. Medicine, 1983-84; invited lectr. various osteo. confs., hosps., seminars. Contbr. articles, abstracts to profl. jours. Fellow Maternal-Fetal Medicine, Dept. Ob-gyn, Pa. Hosp., 1982-84. Mem. AMA, Am. Coll. Osteo. Ob-gyn., Chgo. Med. Soc., Am. Osteo. Assn., Ill. Assn. Osteo. Physicians and Surgeons, Soc. Perinatal Obstetrics, Chg. Osteo. Med. Ctr. Alumni Assn., Sigma Sigma Phi. Avocations: running, fishing, golf. Office: Rockford Meml Hosp 2400 N Rockton Rd Rockford IL 61111

LOTITO, MICHAEL JAMES, chiropractic physician; b. Chgo., Nov. 2, 1945; s. Angelo Joseph and Nadine (Mendell) L.; m. Karen Aleta Diggle, Dec. 28, 1973; children: Elizabeth Ann, David Michael. D Chiropractic, BS, Palmer Coll. Chiropractic, 1976; BA, Northeastern U., 1970, postgrad., 1970-73. Cert. basic scis., S.D. Tchr. Bellwood (Ill.) Bd. Edn., 1970-73; instr. psychology Blackhawk Coll., Moline, Ill., 1974-75; staff psychologist, asst. to dir. physiology dept., supr. x-ray dept. Palmer Coll. Chiropractic, Davenport, Iowa, 1973-76; gen. practice chiropractic, Oak Park, Ill., 1976-79; chief examining doctor Kellenburger Clinic, Elgin, Ill., 1979-80; gen. practice chiropractic, Forest Park, Ill., 1980—; clinic supr. Fullerton Clinic, Chgo., 1980-81; mem. staff patient research ctr. Nat. Coll. Chiropractic, Lombard, Ill. 1983—; mem. staff Lakeside Community Hosp., Chgo. 1987—. Mem. Am. Chiropractic Assn., Ill. Chiropractic Assn., Internat. Found. Preventive Medicine, Am. Holistic Med. Inst., Sports, N.Y. Acad. Scis., Safety and Health Care Soc., Psi Chi. Office: 7318 W Madison St Forest Park IL 60130

LOTOCKY, INNOCENT H., bishop; b. Petlykivci Stari, Buchach, Ukraine, Nov. 3, 1915; came to U.S., 1946; s. Stefan and Maria (Tytyn) L. Student at various religious insts., Ukraine, Czechoslovakia; Ph.D. in Sacred Theology, U. Vienna, Austria. Ordained priest Ukrainian Catholic Ch., consecrated bishop, 1981; cert. tchr., Mich. Superior-novice master Order St. Basil, Dawson, Pa., 1946-51; provincial superior U.S. province Order St. Basil, N.Y., 1951-53; novice master Order St. Basil, Glen Cove, N.Y., 1958-60; pastor-superior St. George Ch., N.Y.C., 1953-58; pastor St. Nicholas Ch., Chgo., 1960-62; pastor-superior Immaculate Conception Ch., Hamtramck, Mich., 1962-81, also tchr., 1962-81; bishop Diocese St. Nicholas, Chgo., 1981—; provincial counselor U.S. province Order St. Basil, 1962-80, del. to gen. chpt. Rome, 1963. Active numerous civic orgns. Mem. Nat. Council Cath. Bishops. Home and Office: Diocese St Nicholas in Chgo 2245 W Rice St Chicago IL 60622 *

LOTT, DONALD CHARLES, advertising executive; b. Phila., Nov. 12, 1937; s. Raymond Allen and Lois Marie (Pounding) L.; m. Joyce Elizabeth Block, Jan. 11, 1964 (div. May 1983); children—Kelly Elizabeth, Paul Timothy; m. Sallie Lou Rhoads, Oct. 2, 1983. A.B. in Bus. Adminstrn., Rutgers U., 1959. Asst. v.p. Fidelity Mut. Life Co., Phila., 1964-73; mgr. service engring. Am. Motors Co., Southfield, Mich., 1973-80; owner Genesus I, Inc., Southfield, 1980—. Served to lt. (j.g.) USNR, 1960-63. Mem. Mensa. Republican. Home: 1058 Wakefield Birmingham MI 48009 Office: Genesus I Inc 29600 Northwestern Hwy Southfield MI 48034

LOTT, HENRY CURTIS, mathematics teacher, basketball coach; b. Morgan City, Miss., Oct. 19, 1942; s. Guy and Colenty (Howard) L.; m. Mary Rycraw, June 9, 1975; children: Alyssa, Tammy. BS, U. Ark., 1968; MAT, Webster U., 1987. Tchr. Lake View (Ark.) High Sch., 1968-70, St. Louis Elementary Sch., 1970-71; correction officer St. Louis Dept. Correction, Clayton, Mo., 1971-72; tchr., coach Wellston (Mo.) High Sch., 1972-73, Frostfield Mid. Sch., Florissant, Mo., 1973—. Author Basic Math Life Skill, 1985. Sponsor Gentlemen Athletes, St. Louis, 1985—; pres. bd. trustees Parish Temple, St. Louis, 1976-85. Mem. NEA, Mo. Athletic Assn., Greater St. Louis Math Tchrs. Assn., St. Louis Officials, NAACP, United Black Fund. Club: Ark. Athletic. Home: 4 Bon Price Terr Olivette MO 63132 Office: McCluer High Sch 1896 S Florissant Rd Florissant MO 63131

LOTT, PATRICIA DIANE, real estate corporation executive; b. Cin., Jan. 22, 1955; d. Robert Richard and Phyllis Emily (Schlageter) Rohrkasse; m. Thomas J. Lott, June 10, 1978. BS magna cum laude, U. Cin., 1983. Adminstrn. asst. Federated Stores Realty, Inc., Cin., 1976-77, payroll and benefits adminstr., 1977-80, personnel and office adminstr., 1980-83, personnel dir., 1983-86; v.p. JMB/Federated Realty, Cin., 1986—. Mem. Am. Mgmt. Assn., Am. Soc. Personnel Adminstrn., Greater Cin. Human Resource Assn. Roman Catholic. Office: JMB/Federated Realty 7 W 7th St Cincinnati OH 45202

LOTTIER, LAWRENCE FRANCIS, JR., management professional; b. Chgo., Apr. 4, 1936; s. Lawrence F. and Elaine N. (Nacy) L.; m. Susan Marie Lavey, Apr. 4, 1981; 1 child, Erin Marie. BS in Indsl. Mgmt., U. Detroit, 1960; postgrad., Loyola U., Chgo., 1964-65. Instr. United Airlines, Chgo., 1963-65; employment rep. United Airlines, Washington, 1965-66; sr. instr. United Airlines, Chgo., 1966-70, tng. mgr., 1970-74; mgr. edn. Dana Corp., Toledo, 1974—; cons. in field, Toledo, 1977—; field mgr. Performax Systems, Toledo, 1981—. Author: Management Team, 1984. Mem. faculty Jr. Achievement of N.W. Ohio, Toledo, 1984—. Served with U.S. Army, 1960-61. Mem. Am. Soc. Tng. and Devel. (chmn. ethics com. 1985—, chmn. insts. com., editor handbook 1986, Torch award 1982), Nat. Speakers Assn., Ohio Speakers Forum (edn. com. 1985-86, 1987-88). Roman Catholic. Avocations: photography, train travel, stamp collecting, skiing, writing. Office: Dana Corp Dana U 4500 Dorr St Toledo OH 43615

LOTUACO, LUISA GO, physician; b. Gapan, Nueva Ecija, Philippines, Jan. 29, 1938; came to U.S., 1972; d. Galicano Yuzon and Alicia (Go) L.; m. George Garrett Shepherd, Aug. 7, 1976; 1 child, Lara. A.A., U. Santo Tomas, Manila, Philippines, 1951-53, D.M., 1960. Diplomate Am. Bd. Coll. Am. Pathology Pathologist, Manila Sanitarium and Hosp., Manila, Philippines, 1969-72; instr. pathology Kansas U., Kansas City, 1972, asst. prof., 1974—; pathologist St. Catherine Hosp., East Chgo., Ind., 1973-74, VA Med. Ctr., Kansas City, Mo., 1974—. Fellow Coll. Am. Pathology, Am. Assn. of Clin. Pathologists; mem. U.S. and Canadian Acad. Pathologists, Am. Soc. Microbiologists, N.Y. Acad. Sci., Am. Assn. Blood Bank, Philippe Med. Soc. of Kansas City (pres. 1981-83), Am. Med. Women's Assn., Philippine Med. Soc. Avocations: stamps; ceramics; antiques, opera, classical music. Home: 1215 W 66th Terr Kansas City MO 64113 Office: VA Med Ctr 4801 Linwood Blvd Kansas City MO 64128

LOTVEN, HOWARD LEE, lawyer; b. Springfield, Mo., Apr. 8, 1959; s. Isadore and Gytel (Tuchmeier) L. BA, Drake U., 1981; JD, U. Mo., 1984. Bar: Mo. 1984, U.S. Dist. Ct. (we. dist.) Mo. 1984. Of counsel David M. Lurie, Kansas City, Mo., 1984—, Williams & Clark, P.C., Kansas City, 1986—; sole practice Kansas City, 1984—; asst. prosecutor City of Kansas City, 1985-86. Mem. ABA, Mo. Bar Assn. (Young Lawyers' council 1986—), Kansas City Bar Assn. (mcpl. cts. com.) Assn., Delta Theta Phi. Democrat. Jewish. Avocations: music, sports. Office: 1006 Grand Suite 800 Kansas City MO 64106

LOTZ, PHILLIP MCELHINNEY, marketing training executive; b. Burlington, Iowa, June 29, 1936; s. Edwin P. and Isabelle (McElhinney) L.; m. Marjorie J. Moehn, July 26, 1958; children: Kevin, Deborah, John. BS in Bus. Adminstrn., Simpson Coll., 1959. Prin. Phil Lotz & Assocs., Burlington, Iowa, 1967-79; employment supr. J.I. Case Co., Burlington, 1959-67; mgr. mktg. tng. Mobay Corp., Kansas City, Mo., 1967-79; bd. dirs. Danville (Iowa) State Savs. Bank, 1981-85. Served to 1st lt. U.S. Army, 1959-66. Mem. Sales and Mktg. Execs. Republican. Lodge: Lions (pres. Danville 1978). Avocation: woodworking. Office: Mobay Corp PO Box 4913 Hawthorn Rd Kansas City MO 64120

LOTZER, WILLIAM JOHN, aviation company executive; b. Fond du Lac, Wis., Feb. 20, 1917; s. Jake and Margaret (Feldner) L.; student Ripon Coll., 1935-36, Marquette U., 1936-40; m. Irene B. Fleager; children by previous marriage—Margaret Reinders, John, Michael. Pres., Gran Aire, Inc., Milw., 1946-86, chmn., 1946—; former pilot examiner FAA. Bd. dirs. Youth in Aviation. Served with A.C., U.S. Navy, 1944-45. Mem. Wis. Aviation Trades Assn. (pres. 1950-53, dir. 1979-83), Wis. Hockey Hall Fame (pres. 1976-79, 86—), Nat. Aviation Trades Assn. (pres. 1958-59), Nat. Air Transp. Assn. (steering com.), Exptl. Aircraft Assn. (charter). Republican. Roman Catholic. Club: Blue Line (Fond du Lac, Wis.). Mailing Address: 8741 N 72d St #3 Milwaukee WI 53223 Office: Gran Aire Inc 9305 W Appleton Ave Milwaukee WI 53225

LOUCKY-RAMSEY, JOANNA RUTH, clergyperson; b. Syracuse, N.Y., Oct. 13, 1954; d. Lubomir George and Mildred Mary (Droppa) Loucky; m. William John Ramsey, Aug. 9, 1980. BA in English, BFA in Creative Writing, Stephens Coll., 1976; MDiv., N.Am. Bapt. Sem., 1981, MA in Religious Studies, 1983; cert. in urban ministry, Sem. Consortium Urban Pastoral Edn., 1982. Ordained to ministry Am. Bapt. Ch., 1985. Minister music and youth Emerson Ave. Bapt. Ch., Indpls., 1983—; chaplain Marion County Children's Guardian Home, Indpls., 1983-86; mem. div. ch. growth Indpls. Bapt. Assn., 1987—. Mem. Fellowship Am. Bapt. Musicians, Irvington Assn. Ministers, Am. Guild English Handbell Ringers, Irvington Music Study Club. Office: Emerson Ave Bapt Ch 308 N Emerson Ave Indianapolis IN 46219

LOUGHARY, THOMAS MICHAEL, dentist; b. Beardstown, Ill., June 13, 1959; s. Thomas Giels and Beverly Ann (Marshal) L.; m. Vicki Lynne Shaneman, May 25, 1986. Student, Knox Coll., 1977-80; DMD, So. Ill. U., Alton, 1984. Dentist Plaza Dental Ctr., Jacksonville, Ill., 1984—; gen. practice dentistry Beardstown Dental Clinic, 1985—; staff dentist Passavant Hosp., Jacksonville, Ill.; cons. Cass County Cancer Assn., Virginia, Ill., 1986—, Beardstown Board Edn., 1980—. Soloist Jacksonville Symphony Soc., 1984. Recipient monetary cert. Phi Gamma Delta Ednl. Found., 1980. Mem. ADA, Chgo. Dental Soc., G.V. Black Dental Soc., Beardstown C. of C. Republican. Lutheran. Lodges: Kiwanis, Elks. Avocations: sports, hunting, fishing, raising Irish Setters. Home: #5 Guy Dr Valevue Acres Jacksonville IL 62650 Office: Plaza Dental Ctr 72 E Central Park Plaza Jacksonville IL 62650

LOUGHEED, THOMAS ROBERT, solar energy construction company executive; b. Detroit, July 8, 1941; s. Aloysius V. and Ruth S. (Stait) L.; m. Nancy E. Godt, Mar. 28, 1970; children—Thomas S., Patrick R. Student Wayne State U., 1961, postgrad., 1969-74; student Welch Sch. Acctg., Detroit, 1962; B.S., Central Mich. U., 1964, M.B.A., 1966, M.A., 1967; postgrad., MIT, 1968. Cost auditor Fisher Body div. Gen. Motors Co., Flint, Mich., 1964; staff acct. Jim Robbins Co., Troy, Mich., 1964-66; owner Dyn-A-Systems, Flint, 1966-83; treas., sec., ptnr. Talo Enterprises, Ltd., Fenton, Mich., 1976-77; v.p., treas. Dyn Am. Land, Inc., Swartz Creek, Mich., 1972-76, pres., 1976—; officer Creative Ekistic Systems and Solar Unique Networks, Ltd., Swartz Creek, 1980—; instr. statis/research design Eastern Mich. U., Flint, 1970-71; prof. Mott Community Coll., Flint, 1966-85; instr. Mich. Dept. Treasury, Mich. State U., Flint, 1972-77. Councilman City of Swartz Creek, 1976-80, mem. Planning Commn., 1976-80. Mem. Nat. Home Builders Genesee County, Am. Solar Soc., Mich. Soc. Planning Ofcls., Assn. Govtl. Accts., Pi Sigma Alpha, Alpha Kappa Psi. Democrat. Lutheran. Avocations: music, water sports. Office: 6449 Bristol Rd Swartz Creek MI 48473

LOUGHREY, THOMAS JAMES, physical education educator; b. Cresco, Iowa, Apr. 23, 1940; s. James Lee Loughrey and Marjorie Ruth (Adams) Hughes; m. Carol Ann Busch, Aug. 2, 1969; 1 child, Jennifer Ann. BA, Luther Coll., 1962; MA, U. Iowa, 1969, PhD, 1974. Tchr., coach Iowa Grant Schs., Livingston, Wis., 1962-69; teaching asst. U. Iowa, Iowa City, 1969-71; asst. prof. Ind. State U., Terre Haute, 1971-74; assoc. prof. U. Mo., St. Louis, 1974—; vis. prof. Nat. Taiwan Normal U., Taipei, Taiwan, Republic of China, 1985; lic. ins agt. Edwin R. Cohen & Assocs., Clayton, Mo. Author: Motor Development, 1981; contbr. articles to profl. jours. Bd. dirs. St. Louis Council Camp Fire Girls, 1983-85; v.p. Chapel of the Cross Luth. Ch., St. Louis, 1984—. Named one of Outstanding Young Men Am., 1971. Mem. AAHPERD (task force on outcomes 1986—), Mo. Assn. Health, Phys. Edn., Recreation and Dance (Helen Manley award 1985, Presdl. citation 1986). Republican. Avocations: running, tennis, music, gardening, traveling. Home: 1970 Lake Clay Dr Chesterfield MO 63017 Office: U Mo 8001 Natural Bridge Saint Louis MO 63121 Office: Edwin R Cohen & Assocs 7710 Carondolet Suite 525 Clayton MO 63105

LOUIS, CANDACE MARIE, communications executive; b. Dillon, Mont., Oct. 2, 1949; d. Lyle Paul and Mary Louise (Hall) L. BA, Loretto Heights Coll., Denver, 1970; MA, U. Mo., 1973. Proofreader Columbia (Mo.) Missourian, 1973-76; info. specialist U. Mo., Columbia, 1973-76, adminstrv. asst., 1976-79, sr. info. specialist, 1979-82; pub. relations mgr. Profl. Secs. Internat., Kansas City, Mo., 1982—. Mem. Mo. Press Women (dist. v.p. 1985—), Pub. Relations Soc. Am., Internat. Assn. Bus. Communications. Roman Catholic. Avocations: reading, swimming, cats. Home: 324 NW 62d Terr Gladstone MO 64118 Office: Profl Secs Internat 301 E Armour Blvd Kansas City MO 64111-1299

LOUIS, DEAN SHERWOOD, orthopaedist, hand surgeon, educator; b. Dayton, Ohio, May 17, 1936; s. Robert and Gertrude Shaile (Taber) L.; children: Brett, Stacy, Todd, Amy. BS, U. N.H., 1958; MD, U. Vt., 1962. Cert. Am. Bd. Orthopedic Surgery. Intern Maine Med. Ctr., Portland, 1962-63; resident in orthopaedics U. Mich., Ann Arbor, 1967-70; hand fellowship Columbia-Presbyn., N.Y.C., 1970-71; from instr. to prof. orthopaedics U. Mich., Ann Arbor, 1971-85, prof. surgery, 1985—, chief orthopaedic hand surgery, 1971—; cons. VA Hosp., Ann Arbor, 1971—. Contbr. chpts. to books on orthopaedics, articles on hand surgery to various med. jours. Fellow ACS, Am. Acad. Orthopaedic Surgery (com. chmn. 1976), Am. Soc. Surgery of the Hand (com. chmn. 1973); mem. Washtenaw County Med. Soc. (mem. exec. council 1971). Avocations: skiing, camping, biking. Home: 2360 Earhart Rd Ann Arbor MI 48105 Office: U Mich Hosp 2912 THC 1500 E Med Ctr Dr Ann Arbor MI 48109-0328

LOUIS, RICHARD THOMAS TODT, electric company sales executive; b. Rolla, Mo., Jan. 11, 1958; s. William Edward and Norma Jeanne (Todt) L.; m. Tami Sue Green, Aug. 4, 1979; children: Erica Marrette, Richard Thomas Todt, Jr., Tessa Adrienne. BS, U. Mo., Rolla, 1980. Sales rep. Siemens, Atlanta, 1980-85; nat. sales mgr. Turner Electric Co. div. of Valley Forge Corp., Fairview Heights, Ill., 1985—. Republican. Roman Catholic. Avocations: golf, raquetball. Home: 2013 Mapleleaf Collinsville IL 62234

LOUNSBERRY, GARY RICHARD, human services consultant; b. Wellsville, N.Y., May 22, 1944; s. Alton Lewis and Corabelle (Buckley) L.; m. Chere Lea Thayer, June 9, 1973; children: Sarah Grace Lea, Abby Lea Edna. AB, U. Rochester, N.Y., 1966; MSW, U. Mich., 1968; MPH, U. Pitts., 1981, PhD in Social Work, 1985. Lic. specialist clin. social work, Kans. Sch. community agent Detroit Pub. Schs., 1968-70; commd. lt. (j.g.) USPHS, 1970, advanced through grades to capt., 1987; social worker Indian health USPHS, Sisseton, S.D., 1970-72, service unit dir. Indian health, 1972-74; mental health cons. Indian health USPHS, Claremore, Okla., 1974-79; career devel. trainee USPHS, Pitts., 1979-81; human services cons. Indian health services USPHS, Lawrence, Kans., 1981—; advanced through grades to comdr. USPHS; field instr. U. Okla., Norman, 1976-79, U. Kans., Lawrence, 1983—; instr. Haskell Indian Jr. Coll., Lawrence, 1982—. Fellow Am. Orthopsychiat. Assn.; mem. Commd. Officers Assn. USPHS, Am. Pub. Health Assn., Acad. Cert. Social Workers, Nat. Assn. Social Workers, Biofeedback Soc. Am. Episcopalian. Lodges: Lions (sec. Claremore chpt. 1978-79), Kiwanis (program chmn. Sisseton chpt. 1972-73). Avocations: gardening, cooking, traveling, sailing, photography. Office: USPHS Haskell Health Ctr PO Box 864 Lawrence KS 66044

LOURENCO, RUY VALENTIM, physician, educator; b. Lisbon, Portugal, Mar. 25, 1929; came to U.S., 1959, naturalized, 1966; s. Raul Valentim and Maria Amalia (Gomes-Rosa) L.; m. Susan Jane Lowenthal, Jan. 18, 1960; children: Peter Edward, Margaret Philippa. M.D., U. Lisbon, 1951. Intern Lisbon City Hosps., 1951-53, resident internal medicine, 1953-55; instr. U. Lisbon, 1955-59; fellow dept. medicine Columbia U.-Presbyn. Med. Center, N.Y.C., 1959-63; asst. prof. medicine N.J. Coll. Medicine, 1963-66, asso. prof., 1966-67; practice medicine specializing in pulmonary medicine 1967—; asso. prof. medicine and physiology U. Ill., Chgo., 1967-69; prof. U. Ill., 1969—, chmn. dept. medicine, 1977—, Foley prof. medicine, 1978—; dir. respiratory research lab. Hektoen Inst., Chgo., 1967-71; dir. pulmonary medicine Cook County Hosp., Chgo., 1969-70; attending physician U. Ill. Med. Center, Chgo., 1967—; dir. pulmonary sect. and labs U. Ill. Med. Center, 1970-77, physician-in-chief, 1977—, pres. med. staff, 1980-81; cons. task force on research in respiratory diseases NIH, 1972, mem. pathology study sect., 1972-76; mem. rev. bd. Spl. Centers of Research program, 1974; cons. career devel. program VA, 1972—; mem. nat. com. Rev. Sci. Basis of Respiratory Therapy, 1973-74. Editorial bd. Jour. Lab. and Clin. Medicine, 1975—, Am. Rev. Respiratory Diseases, 1985—; contbr. numerous articles on pulmonary diseases, respiratory physiology and biochemistry to med. jours. Bd. dirs., mem. exec. com. Chgo. Lung Assn., 1974-82; bd. dirs. Hektoen Inst. Med. Research, 1977—. Fellow AAAS, ACP, Am. Coll. Chest Physicians (pres. Ill. chpt. 1974-75, vice-chmn. com. on environ. health 1981-82, gov. 1987—); mem. Am. Fedn. Clin. Research, Am. Heart Assn., Am. Physiol. Soc., Am. Soc. Clin. Investigation, Am. Thoracic Soc. (chmn. sci. assembly 1974-75), Am. Lung Assn. (com. smoking and health 1981-83), Internat. Acad. Chest Physicians and Surgeons (chmn. nominating com. 1984—), Assn. Am. Physicians, Assn. Profs. Medicine, Central Soc. Clin Research (councillor 1973-77), Soc. Exptl. Biology and Medicine, Central Research Club, Sigma XI, Alpha Omega Alpha (faculty), Phi Kappa Phi. Home: 1000 N Lake Shore Dr Chicago IL 60611 Office: 840 S Wood St Chicago IL 60612

LOURIE, IRA STEPHEN, architect; b. N.Y.C., Mar. 25, 1950; s. Victor Joseph and Jane Muriel (Sarzin) L.; m. Patty Sue Mann, Oct. 9, 1982. BArch, U. Ky., 1974. Project architect Hellmuth, Obata, Kassabaum, Kansas City, Mo., 1987—. Prin. works include Fla. Suncoast Dome, Kansas City Marriott Plaza, Kodak remodel, Merriam, Kans., VA Med. Ctr. remodel, Kansas City, Quality Hill Redevelopment, Kansas City. Mem. AIA (assoc.). Avocations: sports, photography, travel. Home: 7309 Stearns Shawnee KS 66203 Office: Hellmuth Obata Kassabaum 323 W 8th St Suite 700 Kansas City MO 64105

LOUSBERG, PETER HERMAN, lawyer; b. Des Moines, Aug. 19, 1931; s. Peter J. and Otillia M. (Vogel) L.; m. JoAnn Beimer, Jan. 20, 1962; children: Macara Lynn, Mark, Stephen. AB, Yale U., 1953; JD cum laude, U. Notre Dame, 1956. Bar: Ill. 1956, Fla. 1972, Iowa 1985. Law clk. to presiding justice Ill. Appellate Ct., 1956-57; asst. states atty. Rock Island County, Ill., 1959-60; ptnr. Lousberg and McClean, Rock Island, Ill, 1960—; opinion commentator Sta. WHBF, 1973-74; lectr., chmn. Ill. Inst. Continuing Edn.; lectr. Ill. Trial Lawyers seminars; chmn. crime and juvenile delinquency Rock Island Model Cities Task Force, 1969; chmn. Rock Island Youth Guidance Council, 1964-69; mem. adv. bd. Ill. Dept. Corrections Juvenile Div., 1976; Ill. commr. Nat. Conf. Commrs. Uniform State Laws, 1976-78; treas. Greater Quad City Close-up Program, 1976-80. Contbr. articles to profl. jours. Bd. dirs. Rock Island Indsl.-Comml. Devel. Corp., 1977-80; bd. govs. Rock Island Community Found., 1977-82. Served to 1st lt. USMC, 1957-59. Fellow Am. Bar Found., Ill. Bar Found. (bd. dirs., 1986—, vice chmn. 1986-87, chair 1987—); mem. ABA, Ill. Bar Assn. (gov. 1969-74, chmn. spl. survey com. 1974-75, chmn. com. on mentally disabled 1979-80, chmn. spl. com. on professionalism 1986—), Chgo. Bar Assn., Rock Island Bar Assn., Rock Island C. of C. (treas. 1975, pres. 1978), Am. Trial Lawyers Assn., Ill. Trial Lawyers Assn. (bd. mgrs. 1974-78), Am. Judicature Soc., Nat. Legal Aid and Defenders Assn. (chmn. membership campaigns for Ill. 1969-71, for Midwest dist 2 1974-75), Quad Cities Council of C.'s of C. (1st chmn. 1979-80), Ill. Inst. Continuing Legal Edn. (bd. dirs. 1980-83, chmn. 1981-82), Lawyers Trust Fund Ill. (bd. dirs. 1984—), Fla. Bar Assn. (chmn. out-of-state practitioners com. 1985-86), U.S. Power Squadron. Roman Catholic. Clubs: Notre Dame, Quad Cities (Rock Island). Lodge: Rotary (bd. dirs. Quad Cities). Home: 2704 27th St Rock Island IL 61201 Office: PO Box 1088 Rock Island IL 61201

LOVE, BRUCE BLACKBURN, religious organization administrator; b. Gobles, Mich., Apr. 5, 1929; s. William W. and Myrtle May (Ramey) L.; m. Verla Nan Lindstrom, Aug. 1, 1953; children: Robert Bruce, Janice Love Speakman. AA, Moody Bible Inst., Chgo., 1952; postgrad., Ind. U., 1957-59, Kennedy Sinclaire, 1975, Calif. Coast U., Santa Anna, 1987. Ordained to ministry Evangelical Free Ch. Exec. dir. Lake County Youth For Christ, Gary, Ind., 1953-59; v.p. Youth For Christ Internat., Wheaton, Ill., 1959-70; exec. dir. Metro Chgo. Youth For Christ, Wheaton, 1970-84; assoc. pastor Wheaton Free Ch., Wheaton, 1984—; pres. Moody Alumni Assn., Chgo., 1978-80; trustee Slavic Gospel Assn., Wheaton, 1979-87; cons. Ch. Growth Services, South Bend, Ind., 1986-87. Author: International Camping, 1959, Escape From Truth, 1969; classroom curricula Management and Fund Raising, 1979-85; contbr. articles to mags. Mem. exec. bd. YMCA, Glen Ellyn, 1970; mem. Govs. Youth Council, Gary, 1969-72, Presdl. Task Force, Wheaton, 1980-87, Rep. Party Official Task Force, 1983-87. Recipient TV Special of Yr. award Johnny Cash, 1979, citation for Youth Work Pres. Reagan, 1985, citation Govs. Hatfield, Walsh, Thompson, Brown and Clemant, 1970-75; Nat. Camp Dir. of Yr., Ind., 1970;. Mem. Free Ch. Am. Republican. Avocations: gardening, sports, antiques. Home: 22 W 155 Buena Vista Glen Ellyn IL 60137 Office: Wheaton Free Ch 520 E Roosevelt Rd Wheaton IL 60187

LOVE, EVELYN MCMICHAEL, counselor, human development educator; b. Cleve., July 5, 1945; d. Marion Joseph and Lilly Bell (Cobbs) McMichael; m. Bernard Love, Mar. 18, 1978; children—Kevin, Randy. A.A., Cuyahoga Community Coll., 1968; B.A., Kent State U., 1970, M.Ed., 1971. Nat. cert. counselor; lic. profl. counselor. Youth program dir. YWCA, Cleve., 1971-72; tchr., counselor Cleve. State U., 1973-77; counselor, asst. prof. Cuyahoga Community Coll., Cleve., 1977—, counselor, workshop facilitator Career Devel. Inst., 1982-83. Recipient Teaching Excellence award, 1985. Mem. Edn. Network, Cleve., 1971-72; chmn. scholarship com. Beth-el A.M.E. Zion Ch., Cleve., 1980—. Mem. Am. Assn. Counseling and Devel., Am. Coll. Personnel Assn., Ohio Coll. Personnel Assn., Assn. for Humanistic Edn. Devel., Alpha Kappa Alpha. Democrat. Avocations: reading; singing. Office: Cuyahoga Community Coll 2900 Community College Ave Cleveland OH 44115

LOVE, JERRY BERT, accountant; b. Marion, Ind., Feb. 11, 1950; s. Clyde C. and Ruth Helene (Radabaugh) L.; m. Beverly Ann Miller, June 28, 1968; children: Suzy Ann, Jerry Bert II. BBA in Acctg. and Fin., U. Notre Dame, 1972, postgrad. CPA, 1972. Sr. supr. Ernst & Whinney, Jackson, Mich., 1972-78; exec. v.p., sec. Alfred Connable Office, Inc., Kalamazoo, Mich., 1979—; v.p., asst. sec. Lafourche Realty Co., Kalamazoo, 1979—, also bd. dirs.; v.p., sec. LRC Oil & Gas Corp., Kalamazoo, 1981—. Treas. Kalamazoo Art Ctr., 1983—; treas., bd. dirs. Childbirth Prep. Service, Jackson, 1977-82; fin. chmn., mem. adminstrv. bd. Westwood United Meth. Ch., Kalamazoo, 1982-84. Mem. Am. Inst. CPA's, Nat. Assn. Accts., Mich. Assn. CPA's, Notre Dame Alumni Assns. Roman Catholic. Clubs: Gull Lake Country and Yacht (Richmond, Mich.); West Hills Athletic (Kalamazoo). Avocations: sailing, tennis, platform tennis, running, skiing. Home: 459 Sunrise Circle Kalamazoo MI 49009 Office: Alfred Connable Office Inc 136 E Michigan Ave Suite 1201 Kalamazoo MI 49007-3936

LOVEJOY, ARLETTA E., service executive; b. Elkhart, Ind., Mar. 19, 1915; d. John George Christian and Bessie Pamillie (Shimer) Munch; m. Lowell Elsworth Carson (dec.); m. Milton Lovejoy; children: Michele Joan, Penelope Ann. Student, Ind. U., 1934-35. Sec. engring. dept. Miles Lab., Elkhart, Ind., 1936-56; repair clk. Gen. Telephone, Elkhart, 1957-59; mgr., advt. promotions Patchwork Quilt Country Inn, Middlebury, Ind., 1961—. Recipient First Place award Nat. Chicken Cooking Contest, 1971. Mem. Crystal Valley Tourist Assn. (bd. dirs. Ind. Tourist div. 1986), Ind. Innkeepers Assn., Ind. Restaurant Assn., Elkhart County Restaurant Assn. Republican. Clubs: York Extension (pres. 1965-67), Now and Then (pres. 1979) (Middlebury). Avocations: creative writing, quilting, gourmet cooking, travel. Address: Patchwork Quilt Country Inn 11748 CR #2 Middlebury IN 46540

LOVELAND, HOLLY STANDISH, information systems executive; b. Slater, S.C., Aug. 28, 1947; d. Albert C. and Lucille E. (Standish) L.; A.A., Macomb Coll., 1974; B.A. Siena Heights Coll.,1985. Applications analyst Burroughs Corp., Detroit, 1977-79; programmer analyst Ford Hosp., Detroit, 1979-80, project leader applications support, 1980; project mgr. applications support, 1980-82, mgr. systems services, 1982-84; dept. exec. VI, info. services Wayne County, Detroit, 1984-86, dir. data services City of Milw., 1986—; computer cons. Mem. Soc. for Info. Mgmt. Home: 2549 S Shore Dr Milwaukee WI 53207 Office: 809 N Broadway Rm 400 Milwaukee WI 53202

LOVELL, GERALD, manufacturing company executive. Pres. Fargo (N.D.) Glass and Paint Co. Office: Fargo Glass & Paint Co 1801 7th Ave N Fargo ND 58102 *

LOVELL, MARY ANN, educator; b. Magnolia, Ark., May 30, 1943; d. Dezzy and Priscilla (Glover) Biddle; m. Clearence Edward Lovell, June 4, 1966 (div. 1975); children—Clearesia Ann, Delia Marie, Dezzy Aquib. B.A., U. Ark., 1965; M.S., Ouachita Bapt. U., 1972. Tchr. high sch., Stutgart, Magnolia, Arkadelphia and Eudora, Ark., 1964-75, Milw., 1981—; tchr. Ethan Allen Sch., Dept. Health and Human Services State of Wis., 1986; job service specialist CETA, Wis. Dept. Industry, 1975-76; spl. project, coordinator Milwaukee County Civil Service Commn., 1976-78. Mem. Milw. Tchrs. Edn. Assn., Milw. Inner City Arts Couchil, Inc., Milw. Area Reading Council, Educators' Politically Involved Council, Am. Mgmt. Assn., State of Wis. Edn. Profls. (Local 3271). Democrat. Pentecostal. Club: Playboy (Chgo.).

LOVELL, ROBERT GIBSON, physician, educator; b. Ann Arbor, Mich., May 13, 1920; s. Alfred H. and Grace G. L.; m. Betty Sweeney, May 15, 1948; children—Robert Gibson, Christine, John, David, Cynthia. A.B., U. Mich., 1941, M.D., 1944. Intern U. Mich. Hosp., Ann Arbor, 1946-48; resident U. Mich. Hosp., 1948-50; practice medicine, specializing in internal medicine Ann Arbor, 1959—; instr. U. Mich. Med. Sch., 1950-53, asst. prof. internal medicine, 1953-57, asso. prof., 1957-73, clin. prof., 1973—, asst. dean, Med. Sch., 1957-59; allergy cons. USAF) Pres. Eisenhower's Commn. on Vets. Pensions. Author: (with Sheldon and Mathews) Manual of Clinical Allergy, 1967; Contbr. (with Sheldon and Mathews) articles to med. jours.

Served to maj., M.C. USAF, 1955-56. Fellow Am. Acad. Allergy, Am. Coll. Chest Physicians; mem. Mich. Allergy Soc. (past pres.). Episcopalian. Office: Barron Profl Bldg 4870 Clark Rd Ypsilanti MI 48197

LOVINGER, ROBERT JAY, psychologist; b. Bronx, Nov. 5, 1932; s. John and Phyllis (Schlefstein) L.; m. Sophie Lehner, June 18, 1957; children: David F., Mark A. BBA, City Coll., N.Y.C., 1953, MS, 1958; PhD, NYU, 1969. Licensed psychologist, Mich.; licensed sch. psychologist, N.Y. Psychologist NYU Testing Ctr., N.Y.C., 1959-61; psychologist Queens Coll., N.Y.C., 1961-64, lectr., 1964-67; sch. research asst. Bd. Edn., N.Y.C., 1967-70; pvt. practice psychotherapy Mt. Pleasant, Mich., 1971—; prof. Cen. Mich. U., Mt. Pleasant, 1970—. Author: Working With Religious Issues in Therapy, 1984; contbr. articles to profl. jours. Served with U.S. Army, 1954-56. Fellow Am. Othopsychiatric Assn.; mem. Am. Psychol. Assn., AAAS, Soc. for Scientific Study of Religion, Assn. for Mental Health Affiliation with Israel. Democrat. Jewish. Club: Saginaw Bay Yacht (Bay City). Avocations: sailing, photography. Office: Cen Mich U Dept Psychology Mount Pleasant MI 48859

LOVINGER, SOPHIE LEHNER, child psychologist; b. N.Y.C., Jan. 15, 1932; d. Nathaniel Harris and Anne (Rosen) Lehner; m. Robert Jay Lovinger, June 18, 1957; children: David Fredrick, Mark Andrew. BA, Bklyn. Coll., 1954; MS, City Coll., N.Y.C., 1959; PhD, NYU, 1967. Sr. clin. psychologist Bklyn. State Hosp., 1960-61; grad. fellow NYU, N.Y.C., 1961-67; psychotherapy trainee Jamaica (N.Y.) Ctr., 1964-67; asst. prof. Hofstra U., Hempstead, N.Y., 1967-70; prof. Cen. Mich. U., Mt. Pleasant, 1970—. Author: Learning Disabilities and Games, 1978; contbr. articles to profl. jours. Fellow Am. Orthopsychiatric Assn.; mem. Am. Psychol. Assn., Am. Acad. Psychotherapists, Am. Assn. Psychiatric Services for Children. Home: 714 S Main St Mount Pleasant MI 48858 Office: Cen Mich U Sloan 104 Mount Pleasant MI 48859

LOVIO, DEBRA KAYE, advertising executive; b. Detroit, Sept. 2, 1952; d. Joseph Matthew and Bernice Rita (Turkovich) L; children: Christina Anne, Debra Kaye. BJ, Wayne State U., 1974. Staff aid Detroit Free Press, 1973-74; asst. editor FTD, Southfield, Mich., 1974-76; internat. advt. specialist Burroughs Corp., Detroit, 1976-80, dir. corp. advt., 1984—; account exec. Stone & Simons Advt., Southfield, 1980-83; account supr. D'Arcy MacManus Masius, Bloomfield Hills, Mich., 1983-84. Mem. advt. bd. United Found., Detroit, 1984. Avocation: creative writing.

LOVY, ANDREW, osteopathic physician, psychiatrist; b. Budapest, Hungary, Mar. 15, 1935; came to U.S., 1939; s. Joseph and Elza (Kepecs) L.; m. Madeline Rotenberg, Aug. 16, 1959; children: Daniel, Jordan, Howard, Jonathan, Elliot, Richard, Mickey. Student Wayne State U., 1956; BS, Ill. Coll. Optometry, 1957, OD, 1958. DO, Chgo. Coll. Osteopathy, 1962. Intern, Mt. Clemens (Mich.) Hosp., 1962-63; resident VA Hosp., Augusta, Ga., 1971-74; practice medicine specializing in psychiatry, Detroit, 1982; prof. psychiatry, chmn. dept. psychiatry Chgo. Coll. Osteo. Medicine, 1981-82; dir. psychiat. tng. program Mich. Osteo. Med. Ctr., Detroit, 1982-86 ; adj. prof. psychiatry W.Va. Coll. Osteo. Medicine, 1984; clin. prof. psychiatry N.Y. Coll. Osteo. Medicine, 1984. Served with M.C., U.S. Army, 1966-68; Vietnam. Decorated Air medal, Bronze Star with oak leaf cluster, Purple Heart, Army Commendation medal. Mem. Am. Osteo. Assn., Am. Psychiat. Assn., Am. Coll. Neuropsychiatry, Assn. Acad. Psychiatrists, Assn. Clin. Hypnosis, Am. Osteo. Coll. Neuropsychiatry (pres.-elect 1982-83, pres. 1983-84), Am. Med. Joggers Assn. Author: Vietnam Diary, 1971. Office: 5435 Woodward Detroit MI 48202

LOW, ROBERT ALLEN, systems analyst; b. Terre Haute, Ind., Mar. 16, 1954; s. Eugene Allen and Clara Amelia (Willmann) L.; m. Sherry Darlene Harley, June 28, 1975; 1 child, Victoria Nicole. AAS in Data Processing, Lake Land Coll., Mattoon, Ill., 1974; BA, Eastern Ill. U., 1980, MBA, 1982. Programmer analyst First Nat. Bank, Mattoon, 1974-78; systems analyst Eastern Ill. U., Charleston, 1978-82, St. Louis County Water, 1982-83, Ill. Consol. Telephone Co., Mattoon, 1983—; asst. dir. data processing First Nat. Bank-Mattoon, 1976-78. Mem. Here 'n There Adoption Support Group, Mattoon, 1986. Mem. Data Processing Mgmt. Assn. Baptist. Home: 820 A St Charleston IL 61920 Office: Ill Consol Telephone Co 121 S 17th St Mattoon IL 61938

LOW, WALTER CHENEY, neurophysiology educator, scientist; Madera, Calif., May 11, 1950; s. George Chen and Linda Quan (Gong) L.; m. Margaret Mary Schwarz, June 4, 1983. B.S. with honors, U. Calif.-Santa Barbara, 1972; M.S., U. Mich., 1974, Ph.D., 1979. Postdoctoral fellow U. Cambridge, Eng., 1979-80, U. Vt., Burlington, 1980-83; asst. prof. neurophysiology Ind. U. Sch. Med., Indpls., 1983—; dir. grad. program in physiology and biophysics, Sch. Medicine Ind. U., 1985—. Contbr. numerous publs. to profl. jours. on brain research. Recipient Individual Nat. Research Service award Nat. Heart, Lung and Blood Inst., 1981-83, Nat. Inst. Neurol., Communicative Disorders and Stroke, 1979, Bank of Am. Lab. Scis. award, 1968; grantee NIH, 1984, 85, 87, Am. Heart Assn., 1987; Rackham U. Mich., 1976-78; internat. programs travel Ind. U., 1984; AGAN research fellow Am. Heart Assn., 1980-81; Rotary scholar, 1968-69. Mem. Soc. for Neurosci. (pres. Indpls. chpt. 1985-87), AAAS, Internat. Brain Research Orgn., Calif. Scholastic Fedn. (life), N.Y. Acad Sci., Sigma Xi. Avocations: tennis, cross-country skiing, sailing. Home: 4565 Broadway Indianapolis IN 46205 Office: Ind U Sch Medicine Dept Physiology and Biophysics Indianapolis IN 46223

LOWE, CHARLES RICHARD, public utility executive, accountant; b. Champaign, Ill., Dec. 8, 1946; s. Richard Morgan and Mary Letitia (Smith) L.; m. Martha Elizabeth Coblentz, June 17, 1967; children—Leah, Richard, Brenner. B.S., So. Ill. U., 1971. C.P.A., Ill. Sr. acct. Touche Ross & Co., St. Louis, 1971-74; ptnr. in charge Charles R. Lowe, C.P.A., St. Elmo, 1974-84; sec., treas., gen. mgr. Monarch Gas Co., 1974-83, pres. 1983-85; also chmn. bd. dirs. ; sec., treas., dir. Rainbow Farms, Inc., St. Elmo, 1983—; dir. Land No. 820, Inc., St. Elmo, 1980—; co-founder Ill. Small Utility Assn., Salem, Ill., 1980—. Mem. adminstrv. bd. St. Elmo 1st United Meth. Ch., 1978—. Recipient Outstanding Young Men of Am. award U.S. Jaycees, 1982, Loaned Exec. award St. Louis United Fund, 1972. Mem. Am. Gas Assn., Am. Inst. C.P.A.s, Ill. Inst. C.P.A.s, Ill. Gas Rate Engrs., Soc. Advancement of Mgmt. (pres. 1969-71, honor 1971), Altamont C. of C. (indsl. com. 1975-83), Jr. C. of C. Lodge: Lions (St. Elmo) (pres. 1979-81). Avocations: golfing; hunting; chess; fishing; boating. Home: 103 N Walnut St Elmo IL 62458 Office: Monarch Gas Co 408 N Main St St Elmo IL 62458

LOWE, DOROTHY JONES, educational administrator; b. Columbus, Ohio, July 14, 1923; d. Charles Herbert and Anna Gladys (Parry) Jones; m. Donald B. Lowe, Mar. 24, 1945 (div.); children—Donald Blair III, Geoffrey David, Nancy Lowe Murphy, Steven Michael. A.A., Stephens Coll., 1943; B.S., Ohio State U., 1945, B.A., 1945; M.S., No. Ill. U., 1973. Cert. tchr., curriculum and supervision, adminstr., Ill. Tchr. Batavia (Ill.) pub. schs., 1963-70, asst. prin., curriculum supr., 1970-74; prin. Alice Gustafson Sch., Batavia, 1974-87, coordinator gifted programs, 1987—; mem. faculty Nat. Coll. Edn. Bd. dirs. Tri-City Family Project, Geneva, Ill., pres., 1980-82; bd. dirs. Furnas Found., Batavia, Ill. Mem. Kane County Elem. Prins. Orgn. (pres. 1981-82), Assn. Supervision and Curriculum Devel. Congregationalist. Office: Gustafson Sch Carlisle Rd Batavia IL 60510

LOWE, GREG WILLIAM, dentist; b. Bay City, Mich., May 14, 1957; s. William David and Donna Turner L.; m. Lauralee McRoberts, June 23, 1979; 1 child, Andrew Greg. BS in Biology, Cen. Mich. U., 1979; DDS, U. Mich., 1983. Dentist Tilmann Dental Ctr, St. Helen, Mich., 1983-85; gen. practice dentistry St. Louis, Mich., 1985—. Mem. ADA, Mich. Dental Assn., Acad. Gen. Dentistry, 9th Dist. Dental Soc. Avocations: bicycling, photography, cross country skiing. Office: 622 E Washington Ave Saint Louis MI 48880

LOWE, ROBERT ALAN, dentist; b. Chgo., Sept. 15, 1955; s. Walter Donald and Anna June (Kroscher) L.; m. Jo Ann Marie Remec, Sept. 4, 1976. BS, U. Ill., Chgo., 1978; DDS, Loyola U., Maywood, Ill., 1982. Resident in gen. practice Hines (Ill.) VA Hosp., 1982-83; assoc. dentist A Dental Assocs., Glen Ellyn, Ill., 1983-84; gen. practice dentistry Woodridge, Ill., 1984—; cons. Hines VA Hosp., 1986; assoc. prof. Loyola U., 1984—. Mem. ADA, Ill. Dental Soc., Chgo. Dental Soc. (lectr. 1985—), Acad. Gen. Dentistry, Delta Sigma Delta (pres. 1981-82, Academic Achievement award 1982). Republican. Presbyterian. Office: 6825 Hobson Valley Dr #203 Woodridge IL 60517

LOWE, ROBERTO ENRIQUE, reporter; b. Rep. of Panama, Sept. 26, 1947; came to U.S., 1970; s. Oscar B. and Lethie M. (Wilson) L.; m. Roberta Dietrich, June 5, 1975 (div. Dec. 1977). AA in Behavioral Sci., Canal Zone Coll., 1970; BA in Polit. Sci., U. Wis., Oshkosh, 1972, cert. police tng., 1972, MA in History, 1975. Reporter Milw. Sentinel, 1973, The Post-Crescent, Appleton, Wis., 1974—; instr. feature writing U. Wis., Oshkosh, 1975-76; speaker various orgns. Mem. Fox Valley Lakeshore Press Club (pres. 1985-86). Unitarian. Club: Sly Fox Ski (Appleton), Pacesetters Running Club. Avocations: audio and video taping, jogging, reading, choral singing, bicycling. Home: 1221 Gunn St Apt 4 Appleton WI 54915

LOWE, ROY GOINS, lawyer; b. Lake Worth, Fla., Apr. 8, 1926; s. Roy Sereno and May (Goins) L.; A.B., U. Kans., 1948, LL.B., 1951. Admitted to Kans. bar, 1951; gen. practice, Olathe, 1951—; mem. firm Lowe, Farmer, Bacon & Roe and predecessor, 1951—. Served with USNR, 1944-46. Mem. Bar Assn. State Kans., Johnson County Bar Assn., Am. Legion, Phi Alpha Delta, Sigma Nu. Republican. Presbyn. Home: 701 W Park Olathe KS 66061 Office: Colonial Bldg Olathe KS 66061

LOWE, TERRANCE ALEXANDER, food service administrator; b. Detroit, July 28, 1951; s. Theodore Marian and Cecelia Pearl (Matel) L.; B.S., Mich. State U., 1973; M.B.A. Lake Forest Coll., 1983; m. Cathy Joyce Linville, July 27, 1974 (div. Nov. 1980); m. 2d, Nancy Eileen Leathem, Feb. 5, 1983 (div. June 1986); 1 son, Alexander Theodore. Asst. food service dir. Wishard Meml. Hosp., Indpls. 1974-77; food service dir. Altenheim Community Home, Indpls., 1977-78, Ind. Christian Retirement Park, Zionsville, 1978; food service adminstr., also project chmn. Dial-A-Dietitian, Victory Meml. Hosp., Waukegan, Ill., 1978—; founder Famous Chef's Cuisine benefit and program; lectr. Ind. U., Indpls., 1976, Purdue U., 1976; owner Stash's Egg Co., Waukegan, 1982-84; intermediate facilitator Victory Intermediate Care Ctr., 1983-84. Adv. com., vice chmn. Indpls. pub. schs. Indsl. Coop. Edn. and Training, 1975-78; corp. rep. Sch. Mgmt. Lake Forest Coll., 1983—. Recipient, Certificate of Appreciation, Purdue U. of Indpls., 1975, Indpls. Pub. Schs., 1978, Central Nine Vocational Sch. for Services, 1978; Award for outstanding contbrs. to food service industry. Mem. Am. Soc. for Hosp. Food Services Adminstrs., Internat. Food Service Execs. Assn., Kappa Sigma. Roman Catholic. Contbr. articles to profl. jours. Office: 1324 N Sheridan Rd Waukegan IL 60085

LOWE, VICTOR BROWN, former educator, school administrator; b. Ash Grove, Mo., Aug. 26, 1908; s. Charles Cletis and Susie Queen (Brown) L.; m. Esther May Allis, Nov. 26, 1937. A.A., Ozark Wesleyan U., Carthage, Mo., 1928; B.A., Baker U., Baldwin City, Kans., 1933; M.Ed., Mo. U., 1942. Cert. sch. adminstr., Mo. Prin. high sch. Highlandville Schs., Mo., 1933-38; supt. schs. Chadwick Schs., Mo., 1938-40; county supt. schs. St. Clair County, Osceola, Mo., 1940-45; supt. schs. Ash Grove Sch. Dist., Mo., 1945-62; former counselor, sch. adminstr. Springfield Schs., Mo., 1962-68; mem. Mo. legis. com. for Mo. RTA rep. Southwest Mo., 1981-86. Mem. Mo. Ret. Tchrs. Assn., Springfield Area Ret. Tchrs. (pres. 1978-80), Phi Delta Kappa. Republican. Methodist. Lodge: Masons. Avocations: traveling, reading, gardening. Home: 634 S National St Apt 206 Springfield MO 65804

LOWENSTINE, JAMES R., metal products manufacturing company executive; b. 1923; married. With Central Steel & Wire Co., Chgo., 1945—, v.p. ops., 1949-56, pres., 1956—, chmn., 1971—, also chief exec. officer, dir. Office: Central Steel & Wire Co 3000 W 51st St Chicago IL 60632 *

LOWENTHAL, HENRY, greeting card co. exec.; b. Frankfurt, Ger., Oct. 26, 1931; came to U.S., 1940, naturalized, 1945; s. Adolf and Kella (Suss) L.; m. Miriam Katzenstein, June 29, 1958; children—Sandra, Jeffry, Joan Chana, Benjamin, Avi. B.B.A. cum laude, City U. N.Y., 1952, M.B.A., 1953; J.D., N.Y. U., 1962. C.P.A. Lectr. acctg. Baruch Coll., N.Y.C., 1952-53; auditor Price Waterhouse & Co., N.Y.C., 1955-62; v.p., controller Am. Greetings Corp., Cleve., 1962-68, controller, 1966-68, sr. v.p. fin., 1977—; v.p. fin., treas. Tremco Inc., Cleve., 1968-77; mem. adv. bd. Case Western Res. U. Dept. Accountancy, 1986—. Chmn. bd. dirs. Rabbinical Coll. Telshe, 1974-77, v.p., 1977—; v.p. Hebrew Acad. Cleve., 1977—; pres. Cleve. chpt. Agudath Israel Am., 1978—; bd. dirs. Jewish Community Fedn. Cleve., 1979—; chmn. citizens rev. com. Cleveland Heights-University Heights Sch., 1972-73, mem. lay fin. com., 1974-79; mem. Cleveland Heights Citizens Adv. Com. for Community Devel., 1976-79. Served with AUS, 1953-55. Mem. Nat. Assn. Over the Counter Cos. (budget & fin. com. 1986—, bd. dirs. 1987—), Fin. Execs. Inst. (sec. N.E. Ohio chpt. 1979-80), Am. Inst. C.P.A.'s, N.Y. Soc. C.P.A.'s, Ohio Soc. C.P.A.'s, Greater Cleve. Growth Assn., Beta Gamma Sigma, Beta Alpha Psi. Home: 3394 Blanche Ave Cleveland Heights OH 44118 Office: Am Greetings Corp 10500 American Rd Cleveland OH 44144

LOWER, JOHN JOSEPH, utility company executive; b. Rushville, Ind., Nov. 24, 1921; s. John W. and Favora Francena (Goddard) L.; m. Edna D. Nixon, Nov. 26, 1942; children—Judith Elaine, Steven Joe, Mark Allen. Student Ball State U., 1939-40; cert., mgrs. internship curriculum U. Nebr., 1971; continuing edn. student Purdue U., Ohio State U., Mich. State U., Ind. U. Lineman, serviceman, power use adviser Rush County Rural Electric Coop., Rushville, Ind., 1949-59; gen. mgr. Southeastern Mich. Rural Electric Coop., Adrian, 1959-66; ins. salesman Preferred Risk Mut. Ins. Co., Huntington Woods, Mich., 1966-67; cost acct. Am. Chain & Cable Co., Adrian, 1967; mem. services dir., dept. supr. Shelby County Rural Electric Coop., Shelbyville, Ind., 1967-79; gen. mgr. Rush County Rural Electric Membership Corp., Rushville, 1979-87 (retired) ; bd. dirs. Hoosier Energy Generation and Transmission Rural Electric Coop., 1979-87, Rush County Extension Bd., 1984—, SHARES Inc., 1985—; treas. Hoosier Coop. Energy, Inc.; past pres. So. Ind. Electric Heating Inst.; area chmn. Hoosier Energy Apprenticeship Tng. Sch., 1982-83, adv. com., 1984-87. Past chmn. Shelby County Extension Bd.; bd. dirs. Shelby County Assn. Retarded Citizens, 1973-79; mem. Rush County Indsl. Devel. Com., 1985-87 . Served with U.S. Army, 1943-46; ETO, MTO. Recipient 4-H Electric Leaders cert., 1976; Joseph F. Kennedy Jr. Found. award, 1972; outstanding service award Ind. Vocat. Clubs of Am., 1976, cert. spl. services, 1977. Mem. Internat. Assn. Elec. Inspectors (dir., pres. Ind. chpt. 1976-77), IEEE (assoc.), Food and Energy Council, Ind. Farm Electrification Council, Rush County C. of C. (bd. dirs., officer 1982-85), Ind. Member Services Assn. (past pres.), Home Builders Assn. Shelby County (dir. 1977-79). Mem. Ch. of Christ. Home: 1218 N Main St Rushville IN 46173

LOWERY, DAVID BRIAN, food products executive; b. Dayton, Ohio, Sept. 25, 1956; s. Thomas James and Joan (Nickeson) L.; m. Constance Louise Graves, Nov. 17, 1984; 1 child, Lauren Elizebeth. Grad. high sch., Dayton. Asst. mgr. Lofino's, Dayton, 1973-77; owner and pres. Groceryland Inc., New Paris, Ohio, 1977—; owner Lowery Assocs., Dayton, 1981—, L & L Investments, Dayton, 1983—. Mem. Superrite, Ind. Grocers Assn., Dayton Jaycees, New Paris C. of C. Republican. Roman Catholic. Avocations: woodworking, boating, travel, home remodeling. Home: 3389 Stutsman Rd Bellbrook OH 45305 Office: Groceryland Inc 606 S Washington St New Paris OH 45347

LOWRIE, JEAN ELIZABETH, librarian, educator; b. Northville, N.Y., Oct. 11, 1918; d. A. Sydney and Edith (Roos) L. A.B., Keuka Coll., 1940, LLD (hon.), 1973; B.L.S., Western Res. U., 1941, Ph.D., 1959; M.A., Western Mich. U., 1956. Childrens librarian Toledo Pub. Library, 1941-44; librarian Elementary Sch., Oak Ridge, Tenn., 1944-51; exhange tchr.-librarian Nottingham, Eng., 1948-49; campus sch. librarian Western Mich. U., Kalamazoo, 1951-56; asso. prof. Western Mich. U. (Sch. Librarianship), 1958-61, prof., 1962-83, dir. sch., 1963-81; mem. faculty U. Ky., summer 1951, U. Calif. at Berkeley, summer 1958; Chmn. Internat. Steering Com. for Devel. Sch. Libraries; also del. World Conf. Orgns. Teaching Profession, meetings, Paris, 1964, Vancouver, 1967, Dublin, 1968, Abidjan, 1969, Sydney, 1970; pres. Internat. Assn. Sch. Librarianship, 1971-77, exec. sec., 1978—; mem. exec. bd. Internat. Fedn. Library Assns. and Instns., 1979-83. Author: Elementary School Libraries, rev, 1970, School Libraries: International Developments, 1972, also articles.; Adviser: filmstrip Using the Library, 1962. Recipient Dutton-Macrae award ALA, 1957, Profl. Achievement award Keuka Coll. Alumni, 1963. Mem. ALA (pres. 1973-74), Mich. Library Assn., Assn. Am. Library Schs., Am. Assn. Sch. Librarians (dir., past pres., 1st President's award 1978), AAUP, Delta Kappa Gamma, Beta Phi Mu. Club: Altrusa (Kalamazoo). Home: 1006 Westmoreland St Kalamazoo MI 49007

LOWRY, JAMES HAMILTON, management consultant; b. Chgo., May 28, 1939; s. William E. and Camille C. L.; B.A., Grinnel Coll., 1961; M.P.I.A., U. Pitts., 1965; P.M.D., Harvard U., 1973; 1 child, Aisha. Asso. dir. Peace Corps, Lima, Peru, 1965-67; spl. asst. to pres., project mgr. Bedford-Stuyvesant Restoration Corp., Bklyn., 1967-68; sr. asso. McKinsey & Co., Chgo., 1968-75; pres. James H. Lowry & Assos., Chgo., 1975—; mem. Small Bus. Edv. Com.; dir. Independence Bank, Johnson Products. Trustee Grinnell Coll.; bd. dirs. Chgo. United, Northwestern Hosp., Chgo. Pub. Library, Ptnrs. in Internat. Edn. John Hay Whitney fellow, 1963-65. Mem. Harvard Alumni Assn. (dir.). Clubs: Econ., Monroe, Univ. Home: 3100 Sheridan Rd Chicago IL 60657 Office: 303 E Wacker Dr Chicago IL 60601

LOWRY, JOAN MARIE DONDREA, broadcaster; b. Weirton, W.Va., June 8, 1935; d. Rudolph and Mary (Telmanik) Dondrea; m. Robert William Lowry, June 15, 1957; 1 child, Christopher Scott. B.S. in Edn., Baldwin-Wallace Coll., 1956; student Ohio Sch. Broadcasting, 1977-79. Gen. mgr., news dir. Sta. WLRO, Lorain, Ohio, 1980-82; host 35 Live, Cinemavidio TV, Elyria, Ohio, 1980-83; TV show host Continental Cable, Cleve., 1983—; pub. relations dir. Sta. WZLE, Lorain, 1982-83; broadcaster, community relations dir. Sta. WRKG, Lorain, 1983—; performer commls.; speaker in field. Appeared in motion pictures: Those Lips Those Eyes, 1982, One Trick Pony, 1982. Mem. nat. steering com. Better Hearing and Speech, 1985-86; nat. philanthropy chair Delta Zeta Sorority and Found., 1980—, trustee, 1980—; mem. Lorain Litter Control Bd., 1981-83; bd. dirs. Lorain Conty Sr. Citizens Assn., 1982-85, Lorain Consumers Council, 1980—; v.p. Bay Village PTA Council, 1973-75; active Multiple Sclerosis Soc., Am. Cancer Soc., Muscular Dystrophy Assn., others; grand marshal numerous parades. Named Woman of Achievement, Nat. YWCA and Lorain County Bus. and Industry Assn., 1983; recipient U.S. Air Force award, 1982, U.S. Navy award, 1981, Media award Am. Cancer Soc., 1982, Communication award Easter Seals Soc., 1981, Community Service award Lorain County chpt. Am. Heart Assn., 1981; ofcl. hostess for U.S. Army in Lorain County, 1980-83; Mayor's Proclamation, 1982; hon. recruiter award U.S. Army, 1981; recognition award Ohio House Reps. Mem. Lorain County Arts Council, Baldwin-Wallace Alumni Assn. (nat. pres. 1979-81), LWV (chpt. pres. 1966-67), Delta Zeta (nat. pres.) Cleve. Amateur Fencers (pres. 1965-67). Byzantine Catholic. Home: 578 Yarmouth Ln Bay Village OH 44140

LOWRY, SHELDON GAYLON, sociology educator; b. Cardston, Alta., Can., Aug. 25, 1924; s. Marcellus Anderson and Rose Belle (Wood) L.; m. Gloria Groneman, Apr. 3, 1946; children: Pamela, Martha, Kristine, Amanda Lee. BA, Brigham Young U., 1946; MA, Mich. State U., 1950, Ph.D., 1954. Cert. marriage and family counselor, 1973. Instr. Mich. State U., 1951-52; research asso. Health Info. Found., N.Y.C., 1952; asst. prof. N.C. State Coll., 1952-57; asst. prof. sociology Mich. State U., East Lansing, 1957-59; asso. prof. Mich. State U., 1959-65, prof., 1965—, asst. dean for student affairs, 1975—; del. White House Conf. on Families, 1980. Editor: Rural Sociology, 1963-65; co-author: 10-Year Cumulative Index to Rural Sociology, 1965; contbg. author: Rural Social Systems and Adult Education, Change in the Small Community, 1970 Yearbook of Agriculture; contbr. articles to profl. jours. Mem. Mich. Council on Family Relations, Rural Social Soc. (pres. 1976-77), Mich. Assn. for Marriage and Family Therapy, Am. Assn. for Marriage and Family Therapy. Mormon. Office: Mich State U Coll Social Sci East Lansing MI 48824

LOWTHIAN, PETRENA, college president; b. London, Feb. 10, 1931; d. Leslie Irton and Petrena Lowthian; m. Clyde Hennies (div.); children: David Lowthian, Geoffrey Lowthian. Student Royal Acad. Dramatic Art, 1949-52. Retail career with various orgns., London, Paris, 1949-57; founder, pres. Lowthian Coll. div. Lowthian Inc., Mpls., 1964—. Mem. adv. council Minn. State Dept. Edn., Mpls., 1974-82; mem. adv. bd. Mpls. Community Devel. Agy., Mpls., 1983—; mem. Downtown Council Mpls., 1972, chmn. retail bd., 1984—; mem. Bd. Bus. Indsl. Advisors U. Wis.-Stout, Menomonie, 1983—. Mem. Fashion Group, Inc. (regional bd. dirs. 1980). Home: 21 Turners Cross Golden Valley MN 55416 Office: Lowthian Coll 84 S 10th St Minneapolis MN 55403

LOYLAND, MARY OLSON, accounting educator; b. Madella, Minn., Oct. 27, 1942; d. Edward Lowell and Vera Catherine (Eager) Olson; m. Arthur Layland Jr., Jan. 18, 1964; children: Michael, Stacey. BA, U. N.D., 1964, MS, 1979; MS, N.D. State U., 1965; postgrad., U. Nebr., 1984—. CPA, N.D. Tchr. math. Grand Forks (N.D.) St. James Sch., 1965-69, Grand Forks Pub. Schs., 1969-70; acct. Drees, Riskey & Nordell, Grand Forks, 1979-84; prof. acctg. U. N.D., Grand Forks, 1984—. Mem. Am. Inst. CPA's, N.D. Soc. CPA's (officer 1984-86), Grand Forks Soc. CPA's. Lutheran. Avocations: skiing, farming, crafts. Home: 407 Pakenham Grand Forks ND 58201 Office: Univ ND Dept Acctg and Bus Law Grand Forks ND 58202

LOZIER, ALLAN G., manufacturing company executive; b. 1933. Student, U. Nebr. With Lozier Corp., Omaha, ltd. ptnr., 1953-57, gen. ptnr., 1957-64, pres., treas., 1964-82, chmn. bd. dirs., 1982—. Office: Lozier Corp 441 N 21st St Omaha NE 68110 *

LU, FANG-CHIH, obstetrician/gynecologist; b. Kaohsiung, Republic of China, Nov. 10, 1940; came to U.S., 1968; s. Y.C. and S. (Lin) L.; m. Margaret Kuo, June 20, 1973; children: Katherine, Jeffery, George. B of Medicine, Kashsiung Med. Coll., 1967. Diplomate Am. Bd. Ob-Gyn. Intern Little Company of Mary Hosp., Evergreen Park, Ill., 1968-69; resident obstetrician Little Company of Mary Hosp., Evergreen Park, 1969-72; mem. staff Little Co. Mary Hosp., Evergreen Park, Ill., 1972-75; practice medicine specializing in ob-gyn Bourbonnais, Ill., 1975—; mem. staff Holy Cross Hosp., Chgo., 1972-75, Ingalls Meml. Hosp., Harvey, Ill., 1975-77, St. Mary's Hosp., Kankakee, Ill., 1977—, Riverside Med. Ctr., Kankakee, 1977—. Fellow Am. Coll. Obstetricians and Gynecologists, Am. Fertility Soc.; mem. AMA, Ill. State Med. Soc., Am. Assn. Gynecologic Laparoscopists. Office: 19 Heritage Plaza Bourbonnais IL 60914

LU, SHAU-ZOU, research and development manager; b. Chi-Tran, Peoples Republic of China, Feb. 10, 1943; s. Fu-Ten and Sheng-Yuan (Wang) L.; m. Mou-ying Fu, Nov. 22, 1968; children: Linda Enn, Eva. BS, Nat. Cheng-Hung U., Tainan, Republican of China, 1966; MS, Clarkson U., 1972, PhD, 1973. Process engr. GAF Corp., Binghamton, N.Y., 1973-75, pilot plant supr., 1975-77; staff scientist, materials research and devel. Celanese Corp., Summit, N.J., 1977-81, group leader polymer devel., 1981-84; mgr. materials, phys. tech. HPD, Abbott Labs., North Chicago, Ill., 1984—; bd. dirs. E&R Enterprises, Ill. Contbr. articles to profl. jours.; patentee in field. Advisor Young's Club-North Shore, Ill., 1985-86. NSF scholar, 1967-73. Mem. Am. Inst. Chem. Engrs., Soc. Plastics Engrs., Tri-State Chinese/Am. Assn. (bd. dirs. 1982-84). Club: Tennis (officer 1984-86). Avocations: tennis, birdwatching. Home: 195 Grafton Ct Lake Bluff IL 60044 Office: Abbott Labs D-438 AP4 Abbott Park IL 60064

LUBBOCK, JAMES EDWARD, writer, photographer, publicity cons.; b. St. Louis, Sept. 12, 1924; s. Winans Fowler and Hildegard Beauregard (Whittemore) L.; B.A. in English, U. Mo., 1949; m. Charlotte Frances Ferguson, Aug. 24, 1947; children—Daniel Lawrason (dec.), Brian Wade, Kathleen Harper. Asst. editor St. Louis County Observer, 1949-51; staff writer St. Louis Globe-Democrat, 1951-53, state editor, 1954-56; mng. editor Food Merchandising mag., 1956-57; free-lance indsl. writer-photographer, cons., St. Louis, 1958—; pres. James E. Lubbock, Inc., 1981—.Served with Signal Corps, U.S. Army, 1943-46. Mem. Soc. Profl. Journalists, Sigma Delta Chi, St. Louis Press Club, ACLU, Common Cause. Democrat. Home and Office: 10734 Clearwater Dr Saint Louis MO 63123

LUBIN, HOWARD JAY, dentist; b. N.Y.C., Dec. 4, 1957; s. Irving and Thelma (Voronkov) L.; m. Svetlana Slutsky, Aug. 26, 1984; 1 child,

Adam. BS in Biochemistry magna cum laude, U. Wis., Milw., 1979; DDS, Marquette U., 1983. Assoc. Bartley V. Bell, Milw., 1983-84; sr. dentist Family Dental Ctr. at Shopko, Green Bay, Wis., 1984—. Mem. ADA, Wis. Dental Assn., Greater Milw. Dental Assn., Brown, Door,Kewaunee Dental Assn. Jewish. Avocations: fishing, jogging, gardening, reading, automobile repair. Home: 824 William Charles Ct Green Bay WI 54304 Office: Family Dental Ctr at Shopko 2401 S Oneida St Green Bay WI 54304

LUBITZ, LESTER MARC, oral and maxillofacial surgeon; b. Cleve., Jan. 29, 1948; s. Irving J. and Stella (Clossmon) L.; m. Bonnie Dodd, June 28, 1969; children: Stephanie Ellen, Rebecca Suzanne, Kathryn Michelle. BS, Ohio State U., 1969, DDS, 1973; degree in oral and maxillofacial surgery, U. Cin., 1977. Mem. Cin. Soc. Oral Maxillofacial Surgery. Home: 9100 Old Indian Hill Rd Cincinnati OH 45243 Office: 11438 Lebanon Pike Cincinnati OH 45241

LUBOTSKY, ROBERT MORRIS, architect; b. Milw., Nov. 26, 1944; s. Max M. Lubotsky and Shirley V. (Horowitz) Lerrand; m. Dale Barbara Sachnoff, Aug. 20, 1967; children: Darren, Dana. BArch, Washington U., St. Louis, 1967; MArch, Washington U., 1969. Registered architect, Ill., Fla. Assoc. Booth & Nagle Architects, Chgo., 1969-74; pres. Sisco/ Lubotsky Assoc., Chgo., 1974-84, Lubotsky, Metter, Worthington & Law, Chgo., 1984—. Pres. Preservation League of Evanston, Ill., 1985—; mem. Met. Housing and Planning Council. Recipient Design award Progressive Architecture Mag., 1982. Mem. AIA (Honor award 1976, 84, 85), Constrn. Specifications Inst.

LUBY, ELLIOT DONALD, psychiatrist; b. Detroit, Apr. 3, 1924; s. Albert A. and Ida (Zussman) L.; m. Ideane Maura Levenson, June 28, 1950; children: Arhtur, Howard, Joan. Student, U. Chgo., 1943-44; BS, U. Mo., 1945-47; MD, Wash. U., St. Louis, 1947-49. Clin. dir. Lafayette Clinic, Detroit, 1957-74; chief psychiatry Harper Hosp., Detroit, 1978—; prof. psychiatry and law Wayne State U., 1965—, pres. Comprehensive Psychiatry Services, Southfield, Mich., 1972—. Contbr. numerous articles to various publs., also several book chpts. Served to lt. USPHS, 1950-52. Recipient Gold Medal award Am. Acad. Psychosomatic Medicine, 1962. Fellow Am. Psychiat. Assn. (life), Am. Coll. Psychiatrists; mem. AMA, N.Y. Acad. Sci., Sigma Xi. Hebrew. Home: 4467 Stoney River Dr Birmingham MI 48010 Office: Harper Hosp 3990 John R Detroit MI 48201

LUCARELLI, GARY ERNEST, restaurant owner; b. Cleve., Nov. 16, 1943; s. Ernest D. and Josephine (Di Corpo) L.; m. Beatrice E. Guillard, Jan. 15, 1966; children: David G., Dennis G., Gina M. AA, Belleville (Ill.) Coll., 1963; BA, Mich. State U., 1965. Mgr. Playboy Clubs, Internat., Chgo., 1966-68, Blackhawk Restaurant, Chgo., 1968-72; dir. ops. Strang Mgmt., Cleve., 1972-80, dir. mktg., 1980-84; pres. and owner Creative Cafes, Inc., Cleve., 1984—; cons. in field. Mem. Mayor's Council on Crime Prevention, Cleve., 1984—; trustee Child Guidance Ctr. Greater Cleve., 1984—. Mem. Nat. Restaurant Assn., Ohio State Restaurant Assn., Northeast Ohio Restaurant Assn. (bd. dirs. 1986—), Greater Cleve. Growth Assn., Playhouse Sq. Bus. council (trustee 1986—). Republican. Roman Catholic. Avocations: power boating, golf, racquetball. Office: Sweetwater Cafe 1320 Huron Rd Cleveland OH 44115

LUCAS, ALEXANDER RALPH, child psychiatrist, educator; b. Vienna, Austria, July 30, 1931; came to U.S., 1940, naturalized, 1945; s. Eugene Hans and Margaret Ann (Weiss) L.; m. Margaret Alice Thompson, July 6, 1956; children: Thomas Alexander, Nancy Elizabeth, Alexander Eugene, Peter Clayton. B.S., Mich. State U., 1953; M.D., U. Mich., 1957. Diplomate: Am. Bd. Psychiatry and Neurology. Intern U. Mich. Hosp., 1957-58; resident in child psychiatry Hawthorn Center, Northville, Mich., 1958-59, 61-62; staff psychiatrist Hawthorn Center, 1963-65, sr. psychiatrist, 1965-67; resident in psychiatry Lafayette Clinic, Detroit, 1959-61; research child psychiatrist Lafayette Clinic, 1967-71, research coordinator, 1969-71; asst. prof. psychiatry Wayne State U., 1967-69, assoc. prof., 1969-71; cons. child and adolescent psychiatry Mayo Clinic, 1971—; assoc. prof. Mayo Med Sch., 1973-76, prof., 1976—; head sect. child and adolescent psychiatry Mayo Clinic, Rochester, Minn., 1971-80; cons. NIMH. Author: (with C. R. Shaw) The Psychiatric Disorders of Childhood, 1970. Fellow Am. Acad. Child Psychiatry (editorial bd. jour. 1976-82), Am. Orthopsychiat. Assn., Am. Psychiat. Assn.; mem. N.W. Pediatric Soc., Soc. Biol. Psychiatry, Soc. Profs. Child Psychiatry, Sigma Xi. Research in biol. aspects of child psychiatry, psychopharmacology, eating disorders. Office: Mayo Clinic 200 SW 1st St Rochester MN 55905

LUCAS, ALFRED WINSLOW, JR., mgmt. cons. co. exec.; b. Washington, Oct. 14, 1950; s. Alfred Winslow and Mildred Elizabeth (Lawson) L.; B.A. in Sociology, Social Welfare, St. Augustine's Coll., Raleigh, N.C., 1972; M.S.W., Syracuse U., 1974; M.P.A., Roosevelt U., Chgo., 1979; m. Debra Denise DeBerry, Aug. 20, 1977; 1 son, Michael Maurice. Planner, United Way Central N.Y., 1973-74; adminstrv. asst. to dir. community devel. People's Equal Action Community Effort Inc., Syracuse, N.Y., 1972-73; research cons. Urban Inst., Washington, 1974-75; exec. dir. New Birth Community Devel., Elgin, Ill., 1975-79; pres. Rasen Mgmt. Cons., Inc., Chgo., 1979—; asso. dir. Centers for New Horizons, Chgo., 1979-80; cons. in field. Chmn. bd. dirs. Kane County (Ill.) Community Action Agy., 1976-77; bd. dirs. Kane County Overall Econ. Devel. Com., 1977-78; trustee Mildred Lawson Lucas Meml. Found., 1981—. NIMH fellow, 1972-74. Mem. Am. Mgmt. Assn., Nat. Assn. Social Workers, Acad. Cert. Social Workers, Am. Soc. Public Adminstrs., Nat. Urban League, Am. Soc. Profl. Consultants, Kappa Alpha Psi. Roman Catholic. Author: Getting Funded, Grantsmanship and Proposal Development, 1982. Home: 9447 Bay Colony Dr 1S Des Plaines IL 60016

LUCAS, BERT A., pastor, social services administator; b. Hammond, Ind., Mar. 26, 1933; s. John William and Norma (Gladys) Graham; m. Nanci Dai Hindman, Sept. 10, 1960; children: Bradley Scott, Traci Dai. BA, Wheaton Coll., 1956; BD, No. Bapt. Theol. Sem., 1960, ThM, 1965; MSW, U. Mich., 1971; ThD, Ea. Bapt. Theol. Sem., 1978. Licensed social worker, Ohio; ordained clergyman Am. Baptist Conv. Chaplain Miami Children's Ctr., Maumee, Ohio, 1967-83; assoc. pastor First Bapt. Ch., La Porte, Ind., 1959-62; pastor Maumee Bapt. Ch., 1963-67; adminstrv. social work supr. Lucas County (Ohio) Children Services, 1967—; pastor Holland (Ohio) United Meth. Ch., 1979—; adj. prof. Bowling Green (Ohio) State U., 1972-79; family life cons. New Horizon's Acad., Holland, 1984-86, co-dir. family services 1985-86; cons. parenting, marriage enrichment, Toledo, 1986—. Rep. precinct capt., Toledo, 1984. Bert A. Lucas Day proclaimed City of Holland, 1984. Mem. Am. Assn. Counseling and Devel., Am. Assn. Marriage and Family Therapy (assoc.), Assn. for Couples in Marriage Enrichment, Hist. Preservations of Am. (Community Leader and Noteworthy Ams. award 1976-77).

LUCAS, CONSTANCE ELAINE, children's librarian; b. Dayton, Ohio, July 8, 1951; d. Kenneth Dunson and Rosa L. (Moon) Persons; m. Mitchell D. Lucas, Nov. 22, 1969 (div. Feb. 1979); children—Mitchell D., Lukinte. B.S. in Polit. Sci., Wright State U., 1980, B.S. in Edn., 1981; M.P.A., Central Mich. U., 1981. Library asst. I, Dayton and Montgomery Counties (Ohio), Dayton, 1969-73, library asst. II, 1973-80, children's librarian, 1981—; mem. adv. bd. WPTD-TV, 1984—; mem. Nat. Issue Forums, 1984—; trustee Day Break, Inc., sec., 1986-87, nominating chair, 1987. Speaker film: What's a Good Book-How to Select a Good Book, 1982. Mem. Republican Nat. Com., Washington, 1980—; mem. Shiloh Bapt. Ch.; pres. Young Reps. West, Dayton, 1981-83; 1st v.p. Ohio Rep. Council, Columbus, 1981—; del.-at-large Rep. Nat. Conv., 1984; bd. dirs. Montgomery County Rep. Central and Exec. coms., Dayton, 1977—; mem. Presdl. Task Force, 1984; del.-at-large Presdl. Library Conf., John Fitzgerald Kennedy Library for Nat. Issue Forum Conf., Boston, 1985; mem. Black Family Coalition, 1984—. Recipient Concordian cert. Nat. Rep. Com., 1980. Mem. ALA, Ohio Library Assn. (chair outreach services to ethnic communities), Dayton and Montgomery Counties Staff Assn. (spl. com., collective bargaining com.). Baptist. Lodge: Athena Chpt. #37 (corr. sec. 1980-81). Home: 2211 Ridge Creek Circle Trotwood OH 45426 Office: Madden Hills Library 2542 Germantown St Dayton OH 45408

LUCAS, HENRY FREDERICK, chemist; b. Sioux City, Iowa, May 3, 1926; s. Henry Frederick and Adeline Regina (Regner) L.; m. Patricia Dawn Williams, Oct. 3, 1953; children: Robert, Catherine, Mary, John. BS, U. Chgo., 1950. Chemist Argonne (Ill.) Nat. Lab., 1950—. Inventor Lucas cell. Served with USN, 1944-46, PTO. Mem. Radiation Research Soc., Health Physics Soc. Home: 119 Mohawk Dr Clarendon Hills IL 60514 Office: Argonne Nat Lab 9700 S Cass Argonne IL 60439

LUCAS, KATHLEEN CARMEN, auditor; b. Cin., Nov. 12, 1952; d. Melvin G. and Dorothy M. (Walsh) Gade; m. Stanley E. Lucas, Dec. 9, 1972; children: Stanley II, Benjamin. BS in Acctg., U. Cin., 1975. CPA, Ohio, Fla. Auditor U.S. Gen. Acctg. Office, Cin., 1976-78, U.S. Dept. Health and Human Services, Tallahassee, 1978-80; sr. acct. May, Zima & Co., CPA's, Tallahassee, 1980-82; sr. internal auditor City of Cin., 1982—; auditor congl. report on advanced logistics system rev., 1978; auditor-in-charge audit reports, 1983, 85; tax preparation cons., Cin., 1984—. Contbr. articles to profl. jours. Recipient Cert. of Merit, 1978. Mem. Am. Inst. CPA's, Nat. Assn. Govt. Accts. (mem. audit com. 1986—), Assn. Govt. Accts. (bd. dirs., Spl. Achievement award 1983). Roman Catholic. Avocations: reading, cycling, walking, supervising youth activities.

LUCAS, MICHAEL ALLAN, sales executive; b. Springfield, Ill., Dec. 6, 1960; s. Thomas Glenn and Mary Louis (Ruble) L.; m. Carol Jean Caleo, July 12, 1986. BSEE, Bradley U., 1983. Field sec. Phi Gamma Delta Fraternity, Lexington, Ky., 1983-85; sales mgr. Accurate Metering Systems, Elk Grove Village, Ill., 1985—. Named One of Outstanding Young Men of Am., 1985. Mem. Phi Gamma Delta (chmn. bd. advisors, Peoria chpt., 1985—). Methodist. Club: Toastmasters Internat. (Arlington Heights, Ill.). Avocations: water skiing, reading, puzzles, public speaking. Home: 2342 S Goebbert Rd #2079 Arlington Heights IL 60005 Office: Accurate Metering Systems 1731 Carmen Dr Elk Grove Village IL 60007

LUCAS, PATRICIA WHITTLINGER, small business owner; b. Madison, Wis., Mar. 17, 1925; d. Charles Edward and Jennie G. (Crowley) Whittlinger; m. Thomas Joseph Lucas, Oct. 29, 1946; children: Trisha Ruth, Kathryn Jean. Student, U. Wis., 1942-46. Asst. dept. mgr. Manchesters Dept. Store, Madison, 1946-48; library asst. LaFollette High Sch., Madison, 1969-74; co-owner Artisan Gift Shoppe, Madison, 1974—. Vol. Girl Scouts Am., Madison, 1951-62, City Health Nichols Sch., Madison, 1953, Red Cross, 1955; facilitator Anorexia/Bulimia Support Group, 1985—. Lodge: Zonta (local bd. dirs., fellowship com., attendance and reservations com.). Avocations: golf, painting, music. Home: 300 Ela Terr Madison WI 53716 Office: Artisan Gift Shoppe 4116 Monona Dr Madison WI 53716

LUCAS, STANLEY JEROME, physician; b. Cin., Mar. 23, 1929; s. Morris and Ruby (Schaen) L.; m. Judith Esther Schulzinger, May 14, 1953; children—Barbara Ellen, Daniel Nathan, Betsy Diane, Marvin Howard, Ronna Sue. B.S., U. Cin., 1948, M.D., 1951. Diplomate Am. Bd. Radiology. Intern Cin. Gen Hosp., 1951-52, resident, 1952-53, 55-57; practice medicine specializing in radiology Cin., 1957—; mem. staff William Booth Meml. Hosp., 1957-61, Speer Meml. Hosp., 1957-61, Jewish Hosp., Cin., 1961—; chmn. bd. dirs. Iona Inc.; bd. dirs. Profl. Ins. Co. Ohio. Chmn. med. div. United Appeal, 1978, Jewish Welfare Fund, 1980; bd. dirs., treas. Midwest Found. Med. Care; bd. dirs. Med. Dental Hosp. Bur.; mem. policy devel. com. Local Health Planning Agy., 1978-82. Served to capt. USAF, 1953-55. Fellow Am. Coll. Radiology; mem. Radiol. Soc. N.Am., AMA (alt. del. 1982-87, del. 1987—), Ohio State Med. Assn. (del. 1975-85, 1st dist. councilor 1985—), Cin. Acad. Medicine (pres. 1976-77), Radiol. Soc. Cin. (pres. 1967), Am. Roentgen Ray Soc., Phi Beta Kappa, Phi Eta Sigma. Club: Losantiville Country. Jewish. Home: 6760 E Beechlands St Cincinnati OH 45237 Office: 2905 Burnet St Cincinnati OH 45219

LUCAS, STEPHEN LEE, pastor; b. Muncie, Ind., Mar. 26, 1948; s. Carlos and Irene (Estep) L.; m. Barbara J. Taylor, Dec. 26, 1969; children: Candi, Jennifer, Sarah, Rachel, Tiffani, Stepheni. BA in Bible and Theology, Appalachian Bible Coll., 1977. Ordained to ministry Bible Ch., 1977. Asst. pastor Piney View (W.Va.) Bible Ch., 1974-77; pastor Mt. Hope (W.Va.) Bible Ch., 1975-79, Community Bible Ch., Paris, Ill., 1979-82, Maroa (Ill.) Bible Ch., 1982—. Served with U.S. Army, 1968-71, Korea. Mem. Ind. Fundamental Chs. of Am. Avocations: writing songs, singing, playing guitar. Home: PO Box 357 Maroa IL 61756 Office: Maroa Bible Ch 312 W Jackson Maroa IL 61756

LUCAS, THOMAS FRANCIS, dentist; b. Arlington, Mass., June 14, 1948; s. Maurice William and Mary Rita (Ewell) L. BS in Biology, Boston Coll., 1970; DDS, Case Western Reserve U., 1974. Assoc. Raymond Berlin, DMD, Olympia Fields, Ill., 1977-79; gen. practice dentistry Chgo., 1979-82; assoc. N. Suburban Dental Assoc., Skokie, Ill., 1982-86, Rita Kapmarski, DDS, Chgo., 1986—. Served to lt. USN, 1974-76. Roman Catholic. Avocations: gardening, cooking, music, opera. Home: 706 W Grace #2 Chicago IL 60613 Office: Rita Kapmarski DDS PC 6199 N Lincoln Ave Chicago IL 60659

LUCERO, KARN WILMA, personnel executive; b. Bloomington, Ind., Mar. 25, 1950; d. Schuyler Franklin and Marie Lila (Rothering) Otteson; m. Roy B. Lucero, May 10, 1975; children: Kenneth Eric, Alexander Franklin, Kara Elizabeth. BA, Ind. U., 1971, MPA, 1974. Asst. mgr. William H. Block Co., Bloomington, 1972; adminstrv. officer Govs. Office, Indpls., 1974-79; tng. dir. State Personnel Dept., Indpls., 1979—; chmn. adv. com. Affirmative Action, Indpls., 1977-78. EPA fellow, 1972. Mem. Nat. Assn. of State Tng. and Devel. Dirs., State Tng. Adv. Com., Midwest Intergovtl. Tng. Com. (sec. 1973-75), Ind. Intergovtl. Tng. Com. (pres. 1979—), Ind. U. Alumni Assn. (pres. Sch. of Pub. and Environ. Affairs Alumni Assn. 1975-76). Office: State Personnel Dept 513 State Office Bldg Indianapolis IN 46204

LUCEY, LAWRENCE HAYDN, investment counselor, lawyer; b. Henderson, Nev., Dec. 17, 1947; s. Lawrence Young and Elizabeth Ruth (Fischer) L.; m. Nancy Gina Scaramella, Nov. 6, 1981; 1 child, Clare Poole. BS, Purdue U., 1969; MBA, U. Chgo., 1975; JD, Loyola U., 1982. Bar: Ill. 1982; chartered fin. analyst, 1975. V.p. Continental Ill. Nat. Bank, Chgo., 1969-83; sr. v.p. Chgo. Corp., 1983—. Author, editor Ready Reference of Investment Sect. Ill. Ins. Code, 1984; co-author: Investment Regulations for Illinois Insurance Agents and Brokers, 1982. Fellow Fin. Analysts Fedn.; mem. Ill. State Bar Assn., Investment Analysts Soc., Chgo., Fin. Stock Assn., Inst. Chartered Fin. Analysts, Nat. Assn. Life Cos. Republican. Roman Catholic. Office: Chgo Corp 208 S LaSalle St Chicago IL 60604

LUCHTEL, KEITH EDWARD, lawyer; b. Milford, Iowa, Sept. 7, 1941; s. Leroy Phillip and Gertrude (Marley) L.; m. Patricia Ann Moss, June 4, 1966; children: Kathleen, Kristina. BS, USAF Acad., 1964; JD, Drake U., 1973. Bar: Iowa 1973, U.S. Dist. Ct. (no. and so. dists.) Iowa 1973. Commd. 2d lt. USAF, 1964, advanced through grades to capt., 1968, resigned, 1970; assoc. Nyemaster Law Firm, Des Moines, 1973-76, ptnr., 1976—; atty. City of Clive, Iowa, 1978-86. Mem. Order of Coif. Republican. Roman Catholic. Avocations: electronics, golf, tennis, reading. Home: 10521 Sunset Terr Clive IA 50322 Office: Nyemaster Goode McLaughlin et al 1900 Hub Tower Des Moines IA 50309

LUCIANO, DANIEL CHARLES, publishing company executive; b. Bradford, Pa., Feb. 17, 1942; s. John Chipreon and Anna Mae (Tingley) L.; m. Barbara Lynn Stinson, Aug. 13, 1960; children: Christine, Kent, Stephanie, Amber, Todd, Traci. Student, U. Pitts. Dist. sales mgr. Dresser Mfg., Detroit, 1972-75, Dresser Industries, Chgo., 1975-76, Gardner Pub., Princeton, N.J., 1976-79; regional sales mgr. Gardner Pub., Troy, Mich., 1979-86; assoc. pub., sales mgr. Gardner Pub., Cin., 1986—. Mem. Bus./ Profl. Advt. Assn. (pres. 1986), Jaycees (pres. Bradford, Pa. chpt. 1969). Club: tf of Detroit (pres. 1980). Avocations: boating, reading. Home: 760 Huntersknoll Cincinnati OH 45230 Office: Gardner Pub Inc 6600 Clough Pike Cincinnati OH 45244

LUCK, JAMES I., foundation director; b. Akron, Ohio, Aug. 28, 1945; s. Milton William and Gertrude (Winer) L.; children: Andrew Brewer, Edward Aldrich. BA, Ohio State U., 1967; MA, U. Ga., 1970. Dir. forensics Tex. Christian U., Ft. Worth, 1970-74; assoc. dir. Bicentennial Youth Debates, Washington, 1974-76; exec. dir. Nat. Congress Vol. and Citizenship, Washington, 1976-77; fellow Acad. Contemporary Problems, Columbus, Ohio, 1977-79; exec. dir. Battelle Meml. Inst. Fedn., Columbus, 1980-82; pres. Columbus Found., 1981—; exec. dir. Columbus Youth Found. and Edgar W. Ingram Found., Columbus, 1981—; co-chmn. Task Force on Citizen Edn., Washington, 1977; mediator Negotiated Investment Strategy, Columbus, 1979; chmn. Ohio Founds. Conf., 1985; cons. HEW, Peace Corps, U. Va. Author: Ohio-The Next 25 Years, 1978, Bicentennial Issue Analysis, 1975; editro: Proceedings of the Nat. Conf. on Argumentation, 1973; contbr. articles to profl. jours. Trustee Godman Guild Settlement House, Columbus, 1979-81, Am. Diabetes Assn., Ohio, 1984—; chmn. spl. com. on displacement Columbus City Council, 1978-80; dir. Commn. on the Future of the Professions in Soc., 1979. Mem. Council on Founds., Ohio Found. Conf., Am. Forensic Assn. Clubs: University, Execs., Columbus Met., Kit-Kat. Lodge: Rotary. Avocations: travel, reading. Home: 7183 Inverness Ct Dublin OH 43017 Office: The Columbus Found 1265 Neil Ave Columbus OH 43201

LUCKE, MARK WILLIAM, banker; b. Alexandria, Minn., Apr. 11, 1961; s. William John and Patricia Ann (Moran) L.; m. Linda Margaret Coleman, Sept. 28, 1985; 1 child, Peter Mark. BBA in Acctg., Coll. of St. Thomas, 1983. CPA, Minn. With Peat, Marwick, Mitchell & Co., Mpls., 1983-85, sr. acct., 1985-86; internal auditor First Bank System Inc., Mpls., 1986-87, credit examination officer, 1987—. Mem. Am. Inst. CPA's, Minn. Soc. CPA's, Inst. Internal Auditors. Roman Catholic. Avocations: running, biking, outdoors. Office: First Bank System Inc 1100 Soo Line Bldg Minneapolis MN 55402

LUCKENBACH, THOMAS ALEXANDER, technical and management consultant; b. Plains, Pa., Feb. 26, 1933; s. T. Thomas and Anna M. (Brinko) L.; m. Mary Anne Yagodinski, May 16, 1959; children: Thomas J., Robert J., Julie A., David P., Laura M., Caroline H. BS in Chemistry, King's Coll., 1954; PhD in Phys. Chemistry, Cath. U. of Am., 1958. Sr. chemist Harris Research Labs., Washington, 1958-61; group leader Gillette div. Toni Co., Chgo., 1961-64; research and devel. mgr. Huyck Research Ctr., Rensselaer, N.Y., 1964-74; tech. mgr., group mgr. BF Goodrich Tire Co., Akron, Ohio, 1974-82; asst. dir. of tire research BF Goodrich Tire Co., Brecksville, Ohio, 1982-85; pres. T.A. Luckenbach & Assocs., Silver Lake, Ohio, 1985—; bd. dirs., mem. adv. bd. Karis & Johnson Indsl. Communications, Independence, Ohio, 1986—; bd. dirs. Concept Devel. Inst., Hudson, Ohio, 1987—. Inventor folded fiberglas belt; contbr. 20 articles to profl. jours. Mem. Internat. Soc. Indsl. Fabric Mfrs. (v.p. 1983-85, pres. 1985), Akron Rubber Group, Am. Chem. Soc., Sigma Xi. Roman Catholic. Lodge: Rotary. Avocations: gardening, fine woodworking, photography, travel. Home and Office: 2907 Lee Rd Silver Lake Village OH 44224

LUCKER, RAYMOND ALPHONSE, bishop; b. St. Paul, Feb. 24, 1927; s. Alphonse and Josephine (Schiltgen) L. B.A., St. Paul Sem., 1948, M.A., 1952; S.T.L., U. St. Thomas, Rome, 1965, S.T.D., 1966; Ph.D., U. Minn., 1969. Ordained priest Roman Catholic Ch., 1952; asst. dir. Confrat. of Christian Doctrine, Archdiocese of St. Paul, 1952-58, dir., 1958-68; dir. dept. edn. U.S. Cath. Conf., Washington, 1969-71; consecrated bishop 1971; aux. bishop of St. Paul and Mpls., 1971-76; bishop of New Ulm, Minn., 1976—; prof. catechetics St. Paul Sem., 1957-68. Author: Aims of Religious Education, 1966, Some Presuppositions on Released Time, 1969. Home: 1400 Sixth St N New Ulm MN 56073 Office: Chancery Office 1400 Chancery Dr New Ulm MN 56073

LUDFORD, C. J., dentist, real estate investor; b. Highwood, Ill., Jan. 5, 1952; s. James Martens Ludford and Mary Dolores (Schmitt) Overton; m. Kathleen Ann Herdrich, Aug. 07, 1982; children: Aubry Lynn, Morgan Brittany. BS, Notre Dame, 1974; DDS, Loyola Dental Sch., Macomb, Ill., 1975. Founder Dental Ctr. of McHenry and Lake County, Ill., 1979—. Mem. ADA, Ill. State Dental Soc., McHenry County Dental Soc., McHenry C. of C. (bd. dirs. 1980-81). Republican. Roman Catholic. Club: McHenry Country (treas. 1984-86). Lodge: Rotary. Avocations: travel, golf. Office: 1324 N Riverside Dr McHenry IL 60050

LUDINGTON, CAROL ANN, financial consultant, accountant; b. St. Paul, Aug. 13, 1957; d. Robert S. and Betty E. Ludington. BS in Acctg. and Bus. Adminstrn. magna cum laude, Mankato (Minn.) State U., 1979. CPA, Minn. Supr. Coopers & Lybrand, Mpls., 1979-83; mgr. Peat Marwick Mitchell & Co., Mpls., 1983-85; v.p. Churchill Advisors, Inc., Mpls., 1985-87; pvt. practice fin. cons. Mpls., 1985—. Mem. Am. Inst. CPA's, Minn. Soc. CPA's (vice chairperson com. for cooperation with lawyers), Am. Arbitration Assn. (panel of arbitrators), Phi Kappa Phi. Office: International Centre PO Box 2773 Minneapolis MN 55402

LUDINGTON, JOHN SAMUEL, manufacturing company executive; b. Detroit, May 7, 1928; s. Samuel and Fredda (Holden) L.; m. Dorothy Lamson, Feb. 14, 1953; children: Thomas, Laura, Ann. B.S. in Econs, Albion (Mich.) Coll., 1951; LL.D. (hon.), Saginaw Valley State Coll.; D.B.A. (hon.), S.D. Sch. Mines and Tech.; H.H.D. (hon.), Northwood Inst. With Dow Corning Corp., Midland, Mich.; chmn., chief exec. officer Dow Corning Corp.; dir. Comerica Bank-Midland. Chmn. bd. trustees Albion Coll.; trustee Midland Community Ctr., Strosacker Found. Served with AUS. Methodist. Office: Dow Corning Corp Box 1767 Midland MI 48640 *

LUDLOW, JOHN DUER, business management educator, consultant; b. Manistique, Mich., Mar. 8, 1924; s. Archie Carlyle and Helen Maureen (Sherman) L.; m. Patricia Jane Barrett, Dec. 31, 1949; children—Lark Carlyle, John Barrett, Barrett Campbell. B.S., U.S. Mil. Acad., 1945; M.B.A., U. Chgo., 1963; Ph.D., U. Mich., 1972. Commd. 2d lt. U.S. Army Air Force, 1945, advanced through grades to lt. col., U.S. Air Force, 1963; instr. USAF Acad., 1957-61; program mgr. Strategic Air Command Airborne Command Post, Wright-Patterson AFB, Ohio, 1963-64, system program dir. B-1 Bomber Program, 1965-67, ret., 1967; research asst. U. Mich., Ann Arbor, 1967-70, research assoc., 1970-72, lectr., 1968; asst. prof. bus. mgmt. No. Mich. U., Marquette, 1972-76, assoc. prof., 1976—; cons. bus. Vol. bus. cons. SBA SCORE/ACE; vol. football coach No. Mich. U.; mem. Republican Presdl. Task Force. Decorated Air medal with oak leaf cluster, Air Force Commendation. Clubs: U. Mich. Pres.', No. Mich. U. Pres.' Lodge: Masons. Author articles, chpt. in book. Home: 405 Lakewood Ln Marquette MI 49855 Office: No Mich U Marquette MI 49855

LUDLUM, MARY ELLEN, librarian; b. Newnan, Ga., June 2, 1953; d. Ralph Arnold and Arlene Laura (Koengeter) Dobberstein; m. Daniel Spencer Ludlum, June 28, 1975; children: David Spencer (dec.), Stephen Christian. BA, Capital U., 1975; postgrad. Otterbein Coll., 1979-80; AMLS, U. Mich., 1981. Circulation asst. Capital U. Library, Columbus, Ohio, 1972-75; periodicals librarian Otterbein Coll. Library, Westerville, Ohio, 1975-76, circulation librarian, 1976-80; reference asst. U. Mich. Grad. Library, Ann Arbor, 1980-81; young adult librarian Grandview Heights Pub. Library, Columbus, 1981-83, program coordinator, 1983-85, head of programming and publicity, 1985, mgr. pub. relations, 1986—; librarian Hope Luth. Ch., Columbus, 1982-86. Bd. dirs. Friends of Grandview Heights Pub. Library. Faculty-alumni scholar U. Mich. Library Sch., Ann Arbor, 1981. Mem. ALA, AAUW, Ohio Library Assn. (asst. coordinator jr. mems. roundtable 1982-83), Franklin County Library Assn. (corr. sec. 1984-85, v.p. 1985-86), Luth. Ch. Alumni Assn. (v.p. Buckeye chpt. 1986—), Capital U. Alumnae Assn., Lutheran Ch. Library Assn, Beta Phi Mu. Lutheran. Office: Grandview Heights Pub Library 1685 W 1st Ave Columbus OH 43212

LUDOVISSIE, STEPHEN ANTHONY, real estate executive; b. LaSalle, Ill., Jan. 17, 1952; s. Anthony Wilfred and Elizabeth Ann (Gibney) L.; m. Linda Anne Saychek, June 30, 1973; children: Jeremy Stephen, Benjamin John. Student, Southwest State U., Marshall, Minn., 1970-71; BA, U. Minn., 1974; MA, Mankato (Minn.) State U., 1983. Sr. housing mgmt. officer Minn. Housing Fin. Agy., St. Paul, 1977-83; v.p. The Schuett Investment Co., Mpls., 1983-86; pres. Provesco, Inc., Plymouth, Minn., 1986—. Commr. Minnetonka Housing and Redevel. Authority, 1979-80, Plymouth Housing and Redevel. Authority, 1987—. Mem. Inst. Real Estate Mgmt. (cert. property mgr.), Nat. Apt. Assn. (cert.), Greater Mpls. Bd. Realtors (registered realtor). Avocations: tennis, racquetball. Home: 12540 54th Ave N Plymouth MN 55442

LUDWIG, JAMES CHRISTIAN OBERWETTER, architect; b. Kattowitz, Oberschlesien, Oct. 6, 1933; came to U.S. 1952, naturalized 1957; s. Georg

Karl and Margarete (Oberwetter) L.; m. Joann Painchaud Stone; children—Karen, Karl, George. Registered architect, Fla., Ind., Ill., Iowa, Mich., Ohio, Wis. With Erwin G. Fredrick, Architect, Chgo., 1958-60, Werner-Donner Architects, Chgo., 1960-62, Norman R. Werner & Assocs., Chgo., 1962-67; sole practice architecture, Chgo., 1967—; cons. Urban Planning, Inc., Arlington Hts., Ill., 1974-84; lectr. Oakton Community Coll., Des Plaines, 1979—; cons. Dean Foods/Baskin Robbins, Chgo., 1968—. Com. chmn. Boy Scouts Am., St. Tarcissus, Chgo., 1968-82; comdr. CAP, Ill. Wing, 1979-85. Served with U.S. Army, 1956-58. Mem. Nat. Council Archtl. Registration Bds., Architects Club. Lodge: Rotary. Home: 5806 N Newark Chicago IL 60631 Office: James C O Ludwig 6760 W Ardmore Chicago IL 60631

LUDWIG, JOHN ROBERT, wildlife research biologist, consultant; b. West Reading, Pa., Mar. 14, 1943; s. Robert Mandon and Grace Elaine (Nice) L.; m. Barbara Ann Ely, Aug. 28, 1965; children—Todd Alan, Kristen Sue. B.S., Pa. State U., 1965; M.A., So. Ill. U., 1967, Ph.D., 1976. Research asst., grad. fellow, teaching asst. So. Ill. U., Carbondale, 1965-69, 71-73; research asst. N.C. State U., 1969-71; camp dir. Youth Conservation Corps, So. Ill. U., Carbondale, 1971, 72; deer, elk, black bear staff biologist Ont. Ministry Natural Resources, 1973-76; white-tailed deer and wild turkey research biologist Farmland Wildlife Population and Research Group, Minn. Dept. Natural Resources, Madelia, 1976-84; regional dir. Ducks Unltd., Nev., 1984—. Pa. State scholar, 1961-65; grantee Pope and Young Club, 1981, 82, 83, Minn. Archery Assn., 1981, 82. Mem. Wildlife Soc., Nev. Wildlife Fedn., Nat. Wildlife Fedn., Ducks Unltd., Nat. Wild Turkey Fedn. (grantee 1983), Nat. Rifle Assn., Nev. Orgn. for Wildlife, Nev. Rifle and Pistol Assn., Sigma Xi. Contbr. articles to profl. jours. Home and Office: 639 Thorobred Ave Gardnerville NV 89410

LUDWIG, JOSEPH GEORGE, JR., auto company executive; b. Pitts., July 10, 1939; s. Joseph George and Dolores (Straka) L.; m. Diana Gayle Ferenc, July 31, 1970. B.S.E.E., Carnegie Mellon U., 1960; M.S.I.A., 1965. Analyst, zone mgr. Lincoln-Mercury, Ford Motor Co., Cin., 1965-67; bus. planner Ford Motor Co., Dearborn, Mich., 1967-71, mktg. mgr. Rotunda equip., Dearborn, Mich., 1971-75, strategic planner, Dearborn, Mich., 1978-80, sales planning and analysis mgr., Detroit, 1980-87, sales analysis and programming mgr., 1987— . Served to 1st lt. U.S. Army, 1961-63. Avocations: golf; travel. Home: 3885 Estates Ct Troy MI 48084 Office: Ford Motor Co 300 Renaissance Ctr PO Box 43309 Detroit MI 48243

LUDWIG, PAUL L., restaurant company executive. Pres. L-K Restaurants & Motels, Inc., Marion, Ohio. Office: L-K Restaurants & Motels Inc 1125 Ellen Kay Dr Marion OH 43302 *

LUDWIG, ROBERT CLEO, motel corporation executive; b. Grand Rapids, Ohio, June 27, 1931; s. Cleo Ralph and Dorothy (Cooper) L.; m. Marilyn Howald, July 23, 1955; children: Robert Jr., Howard, Ellen Ludwig Planicka, Donald. BBA, Bowling Green (Ohio) State U., 1955. Restaurant mgr. L-K Restaurants & Motels, Inc., Marion, Ohio, 1955-60, chain supr., 1960-62, pres., 1969-77, chmn., chief exec. officer, 1977—; v.p. Ludwig & Kibbey Enterprises, Inc., Marion, 1962-69; adv. bd. sch. bus. adminstrn. Bowling Green State U., 1976, sch. hotel and restaurant mgmt. Ashland Coll., 1977. Pres. Young Reps., Marion, 1965, Family Service Soc., Marion, 1966, United Community Services, Marion, 1968; chmn. United Way Campaign, Marion, 1967; trustee Bowling Green State U., 1978, v.p., 1981, pres., 1983, 86-87. Served as cpl. U.S. Army, 1951-53. Named Man of Yr., United Way of Marion, 1974; recipient Silver Plate award Internat. Food Service Mfr.'s Assn., 1980. Mem. N. Cen. Ohio Restaurant Assn. (pres. 1973), Internat. Gold & Silver Plate Soc. (pres. 1983), Marion Area C of C. (pres. 1984). Methodist. Lodge: Rotary (pres. Marion chpt. 1973). Avocations: golf, tennis, boating, fishing. Home: 358 Brightwood Dr Marion OH 43302 Office: L-K Restaurants & Motels Inc 1125 Ellen Kay Dr Marion OH 43302

LUDWIG, THOMAS BENTON STANHOPE, III, military officer; b. Salisbury, N.C., Feb. 25, 1952; s. Thomas B.S. Jr. and Joan (Bumgarner) L.; m. Carol Earp, June 9, 1973. BA in Psychology, U. N.C., 1974; MEd, Miss. State U., 1978. Commd. USAF, 1974, advanced through grades to capt., 1978; pilot 14 flying tng. wing USAF, Columbus AFB, Miss., 1974-75, adminstrv. officer 14 orgn. maintanence squadron, 1975-78; chief of adminstrn. 5071 air base squadron USAF, King Salmon, Alaska, 1978-79; TITAN Intercontinental Ballistic Missile dep. combat crew comdr. 1974 strategic missile squadron USAF, Little Rock AFB, 1979-82, exec. supt. officer 308 security police squadron, 1982-84; chief of pub. hdqrs. Air Force Communications Command USAF, Scott AFB, Ill., 1984—; Finan mgmt. counsellor, 1979—; resource advisor, 1980—; income tax advisor, 1974—. Pres. United Meth. Men, Jacksonville, Ark., 1982-83, Lebanon, Ill., 1985-86; v.p. Gideons North St. Clair Camp, Belleville, Ill., 1985-86; bd. dirs. Jacksonville Jaycees, 1980-82. Mem. Printing Industries Am., Air Force Assn. Lodge: Rotary (sec. Lebanon club 1986). Home: 2 Saint Joseph Dr Lebanon IL 62254-1125 Office: Hdqrs Air Force Communications Command Scott AFB IL 62225-6001

LUEBKE, MARTIN FREDERICK, retired curator; b. Concord, Wis., Oct. 2, 1917; s. Frederick John and Martha (Kretzmann) L.; m. Dorothy Lorraine Kutschinski, July 5, 1947; children—Judith, Charles. B.S., Concordia Coll., 1941; M.A., U. Mich., 1952; Ph.D., U. Ill., 1966; postdoctoral Cambridge U., 1974. Tchr. Our Savior Luth. Sch., Chgo., 1938-45; prin. Immanuel Luth. Sch., Grand Rapids, Mich., 1945-58; prof., dean. Concordia Theol. Sem., Springfield, Ill., 1958-76, Ft. Wayne, Ind., 1976-80; curator Saxon Luth. Meml., Frohna, Mo., 1980-86; asst. to pastor Chapel of the Cross-Luth., St. Louis, 1987—. Editor: Curriculum in Process, 1963; contbr. articles to profl. jours. Bd. dirs. Mich. Dist. Luth. Ch., Mo. Synod, 1957-58; mem. bd. parish edn. Luth. Ch., Mo. Synod, 1962-75; commr., sec. Perry County Tourism Commn., Perryville, Mo., 1983-86; bd. dirs. River Heritage Assn., Cape Girardeau, Mo., 1984-86. Faculty fellow Aid Assn. Luths., 1963, 73; recipient Outstanding Educators Am. award, 1972. Avocations: music; tour host. Home: 6507 Dolphin Circle Florissant MO 63033

LUECK, PAUL CURTIS, optometrist; b. Monroe, Wis., Jan. 11, 1955; s. Awal and Joan Lueck; m. Kristie Rae; 1 child, Ian. BS, Wheaton Coll., 1977; OD, Ill. Coll. Optometry, 1981. Practice optometry Darlington, Wis., 1981—. Pres. Darlington C. of C., Wis., 1984-85. Mem. Am. Optometric Assn. (pres. local chpt. 1986—). Office: 346 Main St Darlington WI 53530

LUEDTKE, ROLAND ALFRED, lawyer; b. Lincoln, Nebr., Jan. 4, 1924; s. Alfred C. and Caroline (Senne) L.; m. Helen Snyder, Dec. 1, 1951; children: Larry O., David A. B.S., U. Nebr., 1949, J.D., 1951. Bar: Nebr. 1951. Since practiced in Lincoln, 1951—; mem. Luedtke, Radcliffe & Evans (and predecessor), 1973-79; dep. sec. state State of Nebr., 1953-60; spl. legis. liaison Nebr. Dept. State, 1953-60; corps and elections counsel to sec. of state State of Nebr., 1960-65; senator Nebr. Unicameral Legislature, 1967-78, speaker, 1977-78; lt. gov. State of Nebr., 1979-83; mayor City of Lincoln, 1983-87; mem. McHenry & Watson-of-Council, Lincoln, 1987—; exec. sec. Gov. Nebr. Com. Refugee Relief, 1954-58; del., conferee nat. confs. Past pres. Lancaster County Cancer Soc.; crusade chmn. Nebr. div. Am. Cancer Soc., 1981-82; past dist. v.p., fin. chmn. Boy Scouts Am.; treas. Nebr. Young Republicans, 1953-54; jr. pres. Founders Day, Nebr. Rep. Com., 1958-59; chmn. Lancaster County Rep. Com., 1962-64; bd. dirs. Concordia Coll. Assn., Seward, Nebr., 1962-66, pres., 1965-66; bd. dirs. Lincoln Lutheran Sch. Assn., 1961-65, pres., 1964-65; bd. dirs. Immanuel Health Ctr. Omaha. Served with AUS, 1943-45, ETO. Decorated Bronze Star, Purple Heart; recipient Disting. Service award Concordia Tchrs. Coll., 1965, Disting. Alumni award Lincoln High Sch., 1983. Mem. Am. Bar Assn., Nat. Conf. State Legislators (chmn. criminal justice task force 1975-77, chmn. consumers affairs com. 1975-77, exec. com. 1977-78), Nat. Conf. Lt. Govs. (exec. com. 1981-83), U.S. Conf. Mayors (chmn. human devel. com.), Nat. Conf. Cities (bd. dirs., bd. advisor human devel. com. NLC), Nat. League Cities (bd. dirs.), Nebr. Bar Assn., Lincoln Bar Assn., Am. Legion, DAV, VFW, Lincoln C. of C., Delta Theta Phi. Lutheran. Club: Lincoln Sertoma (pres. 1962-63, chmn. bd. 1963-64). Office: 6940 O St Suite 326 Meridian Park Lincoln NE 68510

LUEPKER, ELLEN THOMPSON, social worker; b. San Mateo, Calif., Aug. 12, 1942; d. Prescott Woodford and Louise Rowell (Ingham) Thompson; m. Russell Vincent Luepker, 1966; children: Ian Russell, Carl Frederick. Student, U. Madrid, 1962-63; BA, Grinnell Coll., 1964; MSW, Smith Coll., 1966. Lic. psychologist, Minn. Psychiatric social worker adult inpatient div. U. Rochester (N.Y.) Sch. Medicine, 1966-67, instr. in psychiatry child out-patient div., 1968-69; lectr. Child Guidance Clinics of Göteborg, Sweden, 1968; psychiatric social worker San Diego Children's Hosp., 1969-70; pvt. practice psychotherapy Towson, Md., 1970-73; social work supr. Kinderschool of United Cerebral Palsy Assn. Met. Boston, South Natick, Mass., 1973-76; dir. group treatment program Mpls. Family and Children's Service, 1979-82, clin. social worker and supr., 1978-86; psychotherapist Park Pl. Clinic, Mpls., 1987—; field instr. Boston U. Sch. for Social Work, 1975-76; cons. Karolyn Carpenter, Licensed Psychologist, P.A., St. Paul, 1983-86, Scandinavian Inst. for Gestalt Therapy, Stockholm, 1986; spl. cons. Minn. Task Force on Sexual Exploitation of Clients by Psychotherapists and Counselors, St. Paul, 1984-86; lectr. in field. Contbr. articles to profl. jours., chpts. to books. Bd. dirs., past chmn. academic com. Mounds Park Acad., St. Paul; past. v.p. St. Paul Acad. Parents Assn.; past chmn. east area parent's adv. council Mpls. Pub. Schs.; past pres. Hiawatha Elementary Sch. PTA, Mpls. Bush fellow U. Minn., 1977. Mem. Minn. Soc. for Clin. Social Work (past pres.), Am. Orthopsychiatry Assn., Nat. Assn. Social Workers, Minn. Soc. for Clin. Social Work (past v.p., chmn. legisl. com.). Home: 4108 Edmund Blvd Minneapolis MN 55406

LUERSSEN, FRANK WONSON, steel company executive; b. Reading, Pa., Aug. 14, 1927; s. George V. and Mary Ann (Swoyer) L.; m. Joan M. Schlosser, June 17, 1950; children: Thomas, Mary Ellen, Catherine, Susan, Ann. B.S. in Physics, Pa., State U., 1950; M.S. in Metall. Engring, Lehigh U., 1951; LL.D. hon., Calumet Coll. Metallurgist research and devel. div. Inland Steel Co., East Chicago, Ind., 1952-54; mgr. various positions Inland Steel Co., 1954-64, mgr. research, 1964-68, v.p. research, 1968-77, v.p. steel mfg., 1977-78, pres., 1978—, chmn., 1983—; dir. Continental Ill. Corp. Author various articles on steelmaking tech. Trustee Calumet Coll., Whiting, Ind., 1972-80, Northwestern U., 1980—; v.p., bd. dirs. Munster (Ind.) Med. Research Found., 1972-84; trustee, sec., treas. Munster Sch. Bd., 1957-66. Served with USNR, 1945-47. Named disting. alumnus Pa. State U. Fellow Am. Soc. Metals, Nat. Acad. Engring.; mem. AIME (Disting. life mem., B.F. Fairless award), Am. Iron and Steel Inst. Home: 8226 Parkview Ave Munster IN 46321 Office: 30 W Monroe St Chicago IL 60603

LUETCHENS, MELVIN HARVEY, minister, religious organization administrator; b. Murdock, Nebr., July 5, 1939; s. Herold Alvin and Ruth Lydia (Schroeder) L.; m. Jolane Jeanne Bakley, June 24, 1962; children: Brenton Todd, Shawn Curtis, Lara Sue. BA, Westmar Coll., 1961; MDiv, Garrett Evang. Sem., Evanston, Ill., 1964; MA in Counseling, U. Nebr., 1971, PhD, 1981. Ordained to ministry United Meth. Ch., 1964. Pastor Mira Valley United Meth. Ch., Ord, Nebr., 1964-67; assoc. minister, dir. Cornerstone Campus Ministries, Lincoln, Nebr., 1967-71, minister, dir., 1971-82; exec. sec. Interchurch Ministries of Nebr., Lincoln, 1982—; bd. ordained ministry Nebr. Conf. United Meth. Ch., 1975—. Mem. gov.'s task force on violence against women and children State of Nebr., 1984, gov.'s health promotion coordinating council State of Nebr., 1985—, mayor's long term care com. City of Lincoln, 1985-86, elderly housing options project state of Nebr., 1985, Nebr. Pantry Network, 1986; trustee Westmar Coll., LeMars, Iowa, 1978-82; bd. dirs. Child Guidance Ctr., Lincoln, 1983—. Mem. Nat. Assn. Ecumenical Staff. Republican. Lodge: Kiwanis. Avocations: gardening, racquetball, home and car repair. Home: 6311 Adams St Lincoln NE 68507 Office: Interchurch Ministeries of Nebr 215 Centennial Mall #411 Lincoln NE 68508

LUETKEHANS, JAMES FRANCIS, clinical social worker; b. Davenport, Iowa, Jan. 22, 1930; s. Lawrence Joseph and Catherine Leona (Boeding) L.; m. Sheila Prendergast, June 16, 1955; children: Kenneth (dec.), Thomas, Daniel, Mark. PhB, St. Ambrose, Davenport, 1951; M in Social Work, St. Louis U., 1955. Social worker Bd. Childrens Guardians, St. Louis, 1955-57, Springfield (Ill.) Mental Health Ctr., 1957-61; adminstr. Aurora (Ill.) Mental Health Ctr., 1961-64, DuPage Mental Health Ctr., Wheaton, Ill., 1964-67; dir. social service Riveredge Hosp., Forest Park, Ill., 1967-74; practice family therapy Wheaton, 1974—; cons. in field. Mem. service com. DuPage Cancer Soc. Served to cpl. U.S. Army, 1951-53. Mem. Nat. Assn. Social Workers, Am. Assn. Marriage and Family Therapy, Assn. Mgmt. and Labor, Ill. Alcohol and Drug Counselors. Roman Catholic. Home and Office: 26 W 287 Tomahawk Wheaton IL 60187

LUGAR, RICHARD GREEN, U.S. senator; b. Indpls., Apr. 4, 1932; s. Marvin L. and Bertha (Green) L.; m. Charlene Smeltzer, Sept. 8, 1956; children: Mark, Robert, John, David. B.A., Denison U., 1954; B.A., M.A. (Rhodes scholar), Oxford (Eng.) U., 1956. Mayor Indpls., 1968-75; vis. prof. polit. sci. U. Indpls., 1976; mem. U.S. Senate, 1977—, chmn. com. fgn. relations, 1985-86; chmn. Nat. Rep. Senatorial Com., 1983-84; Treas. Lugar Stock Farm, Inc.; mem. Indpls. Sch. Bd., 1964-67, v.p., 1965-66; vice chmn. Adv. Commn. on Intergovtl. Relations, 1969-75; pres. Nat. League of Cities, 1970-71; mem. Nat. Commn. Standards and Goals of Criminal Justice System, 1971-73; Del., mem. resolutions com. Republican Nat. Conv., 1968, del., mem. resolutions com., Keynote speaker, 1972, del., speaker, 1980. Trustee Denison U.; trustee U. Inpls. Served to lt. (j.g.) USNR, 1957-60. Mem. Blue Key, Phi Beta Kappa, Omicron Delta Kappa, Pi Delta Epsilon, Pi Sigma Alpha, Beta Theta Pi. Methodist. Club: Rotary. Office: 306 Hart Senate Bldg Washington DC 20510

LUHMAN, WILLIAM SIMON, university administrator; b. Belvidere, Ill., May 15, 1934; s. Donald R. and H. Elizabeth (Rudberg) L. AB, Park Coll., 1956; MA, Fla. State U., 1957. City planner City of Moline, Ill., 1959-64; planning dir. Rock Island County, Ill., 1964-66; exec. dir. Bi-State Met. Planning Commn., Rock Island, 1966-71; dir. regional devel. Northeastern Ill. Planning Commn., Chgo., 1971-74, assoc. dir., 1975-76, dep. dir., 1977-79, acting exec. dir., 1979-80, asst. dir., 1980-81; v.p. Pub. Mgmt. Info. Service, Chgo., 1981; asst. dir. No. Ill. U. Ctr. Govt. Studies, DeKalb, 1981—; vis. instr. Augustana Coll., Rock Island, 1967, 69. Pres. Growth Dimensions for Belvidere and Boone County, Ill., 1982-86. Served with U.S. Army, 1957-59. Mem. Am. Soc. Pub. Adminstrn., Am. Soc. Planning Offls., Internat. City Mgmt. Assn., Ill. City Mgmt. Assn. Home: 1538 Fremont St Belvidere IL 61008 Office: No Ill U Ctr Govt Studies 148 3d St DeKalb IL 60115

LUHNOW, STEVEN KIRK, manufacturing executive; b. Kansas City, Kans., Dec. 12, 1952; s. Raymond B. and Ruth E. (Anderson) L.; m. Desiree R. Lisby, June 21, 1980; children: Zachary E., Tiffany Rose. Student, Westminster Coll., New Wilmington, Pa., 1970-73; BA, U. Kans., 1975; MBA, Wichita State U., 1987. Productivity specialist Integrate Control Systems Inc., Litchfield, Conn., 1977-80; mfg. systems and indsl. engring analyst Cessna Aircraft Corp., Wichita, Kans., 1981—. Mem. Am. Prodn. and Inventory Control Soc. Republican. Presbyterian. Avocations: restoring old houses, woodworking, stained glass. Home: 1312 N Topeka Wichita KS 67214

LUHRS, JAMES E., life insurance company executive; b. 1936. With Equitable Life Ins. Co., Des Moines, 1956—, pres., chief operating officer, from 1981, now pres., chief exec. officer. Office: Equitable Life Ins Co of Iowa 604 Locust St Des Moines IA 50306 *

LUISO, ANTHONY, international food company executive; b. Bari, Italy, Jan. 6, 1944; s. John and Antonia (Giustino) L.; m. Nancy Louise Bassett, June 26, 1976. B.B.A., Iona Coll., 1967; M.B.A., U. Chgo., 1982. Audit sr. Arthur Andersen & Co., Chgo., 1966-71; supr. auditing Beatrice Foods Co., Chgo., 1971-74, adminstr. asst. to exec. v.p., 1974-75, v.p. ops. internat. div., dairy div., 1975-77, exec. v.p. internat. div., 1977-82, prof. internat. div., 1982-83, chief operating officer internat. food group, 1984-86, pres. U.S. Food segment, 1986—. Mem. adv. council U. Chgo. Grad. Sch. of Bus. Served with USAR, 1968-74. Mem. Am. Inst. C.P.A.s. Republican. Roman Catholic. Clubs: Univ. (Chgo.), Internat. (Chgo.). Office: Beatrice Cos Inc 2 N Lasalle St Chicago IL 60602

LUKAS, LORRIE M. (LORETTA), educator; b. Hatley, Wis., Sept. 25, 1936; d. Leonard Bernard and Estelle Evelyn (Gross) Dombeck; m. Calvin H. Lukas, Sept. 14, 1957; children: Lloyd, Paul, Anne. BS, U. Wis., Milw., 1975; MS, U. Wis., Whitewater, 1978, postgrad., 1981-86. Cert. elem. tchr., Wis.; cert. tchr. emotionalyy disturbed and learning disabled. Tchr., emotionally disturbed specialist Mukwonago (Wis.) Sch. Dist., 1975-83, elem. tchr., 1983—; diagnostic cons. Mukwonago Sch. Dist., 1975-83; tchr. English UNESCO, Racine, Wis., 1983. Sec. Holy Apostles Edn. Com., New Berlin, Wis., 1978-80; bldg. rep. United Lakewood Educators, Mukwonago, 1985-86. Mem. Council Exceptional Children, Kappa Delta Pi. Roman Catholic. Avocations: genealogy, reading, writing, dancing, symphony.

LUKASIK, JEROME MICHAEL, dentist; b. Chgo., Apr. 21, 1945; s. Joseph V. and Josephine (Tyc) L.; m. Gail D. Kalina, Feb. 25, 1967; children: Christopher, Lauren. BS, John Carroll U., 1967; DDS, St. Louis U., 1970; MBA, Loyola U., Chgo., 1985. Gen. practice dentistry CHgo. and Lake Bluff, Ill., 1970-73; mgr. dental dept. HMO-Chgo. Health Assn., 1974-77; dentist Health Care Systems, Downers Grove, Ill., 1977-82; gen. practice dentistry Waukegan, Ill., 1982—; cons. Kalsik Assn., Libertyville, Ill., 1985—. Coach Libertyville Little League, 1975-77; asst. coach Greater Libertyville Soccer Assn., 1980-81; com. mem. Libertyville High Sch. Parents Assn., 1986. Served to capt. U.S. Army, 1970-73. Mem. ADA, Lake County Dental Soc., Chgo. Council on Fgn. Affairs. Roman Catholic. Avocations: jogging, golf, poetry. Home: 1111 Pine Tree Ln Libertyville IL 60048 Office: 814 Washington Waukegan IL 60085

LUKE, CHU-YEN, food educator, electrical engineer; b. Chung Leo, China, July 18, 1938; came to U.S., 1948; s. Gene Soon and Sin Hong (Chin) Look; m. Pansy Wong Luke, Aug. 17, 1963; children—Ala, Asa. E.E., Ill. Inst. Tech., Chgo., 1969. Lab. engr. Skil Corp., Chgo., 1965-69; lab. mgr. No. Electric Co., Chgo., 1969-76; food educator Oriental Food Market and Cooking Sch., Chgo., 1976—; cons. Oriental Cookbook, 1977. Served with U.S. Army, 1961. Home: 2500 N Jarvis Ave Chicago IL 60645 Office: Oriental Food Market and Cooking Sch 2801 W Howard St Chicago IL 60645

LUKEN, CHARLES, mayor. Mayor City of Cin. Office: Office of Mayor City Hall Cincinnati OH 45202 *

LUKEN, THOMAS A., congressman; b. Cin., July 9, 1925; m. Shirley Ast, 1947; 8 children. A.B., Xavier U., 1947; student, Bowling Green State U., 1943-44; LL.B., Salmon P. Chase Law Sch., 1950. Bar: Ohio 1950. Practice law Cin., from 1950; city solicitor City of Deer Park, Ohio, 1955-61; U.S. dist. atty. Dept. Justice, 1961-64; mem. Cin. City Council, 1964-67, 69-71, 73, mayor, 1971-72; mem. 93d, 95th-99th congresses from 1st Ohio Dist.; chmn. Cin. Law Observance Com. Served with USMC, 1943-45. Mem. Fed. Bar Assn. (past pres. Cin. chpt.), Am. Legion., Jaycees (life). Democrat. Lodge: K.C. Office: 2368 Rayburn House Office Bldg Washington DC 20515

LUKENS, DONALD EARL, U.S. congressman; b. Harveysburg, Ohio, Feb. 11, 1931; s. William A. and Edith (Greene) Lukens; m. Toshiko Davis, 1973. BS, Ohio State U., 1954. Acting minority counsel U.S. Ho. Reps., Washington, 1961-63; pres. Washington Young Reps. Com., 1962-63; mem. exec. com. Rep. Nat. Com., Washington, 1963-65; mem. Butler County Rep. Exec. Com., Ohio, 1966-70, 90-91st Congresses from Ohio, Washington, 1967-71, Ohio State Senate, Columbus, 1971-86, from 100th Congress from Ohio, 1987—. Candidate for nomination Ohio gubernatorial race, 1970. Served to cpt. USAF, 1954-60. Office: US House Reps Office of the House Members Washington DC 20515 *

LUKENS, ROGER LEE, veterinary technician educator; b. Alva, Okla., June 25, 1941; s. Dale G. and Marjorie (Baier) L.; m. Patricia Arlene Lukens, Dec. 26, 1963 (div. Jan. 1987); children: Natalie, Derek, Melissa, Alan. BS in Agr., Kans. State U., 1964, DVM, 1966. Lic. veterinarian, Kans. Gen. practice vet. medicine Colby (Kans.) Animal Hosp., 1966-69; dir. animal hosp. tech. Colby Community Coll., 1969-75; dir. vet. tech. Purdue U., West Lafayette, Ind., 1975—. Co-editor, technician series Burgess Pub. Co., Mpls., 1976-87. Mem. AUMA (CATAT), Assn. Vet. Technician Educators (co-editor newsletter 1985-87, pres. 1979-81), Ind. Vet. Med. Assn. (chmn., technician program planning 1980-84). Republican. Lodge: Lions. Avocations: history of Old West, fishing.

LULVES, WILLIAM JOSEPH, food scientist; b. Pitts., May 30, 1945; s. John Fenton and Carmen (Brown) L.; m. Catherine Anne Hood, Aug. 12, 1972; children: Jill, Ricardo. BS, Quincy Coll., 1968; MS, U. Mo., 1974; PhD, Iowa State U., 1981. Quality mgr. Schreiber Foods, Green Bay, Wis., 1975-78; engr. Kellogg Co., Omaha, 1981-84; sect. mgr. Kellogg Co., Battle Creek, Mich., 1984-86, project engr., 1986—. Served to 1st lt. U.S. Army, Vietnam. Decorated Bronze Star. Mem. Am. Assn. Cereal Chemists, Am. Soc. Microbiology, Inst. Food Technologists. Republican. Roman Catholic. Avocation: gardening. Home: 6129 Ormada Dr Kalamazoo MI 49004 Office: Kellogg Co 235 Porter St Battle Creek MI 49016

LUMSDEN, GEORGE JAMES, communications company executive; b. Niagara Falls, N.Y., Aug. 23, 1921; s. James and Helen Jessie (Simpson) L.; m. Marjorie G. Brouwer, Apr. 15, 1944; children—James William, Nancy Lumsden Sullivan. A.B., Hope Coll., Holland, Mich., 1944; M.A., U. Mich., 1953. Tchr., adminstr. Holland Pub. Sch., Mich., 1949-54; tng. specialist Gen. Electric Co., 1954-58; acct. exec. Lindeman Advtg., Holland, 1958-62; mem. editorial staff Jam Handy Orgn., Detroit, 1962-63; mgr. sales tng. Chrysler Corp., Detroit, 1963-80; prin. Exec. Communications, Birmingham, Mich., 1980—. Author: Tips on Talks, 1962; Impact Management, 1979; Dartnell Human Resource Development Series, 1980—; Middle Management, 1982. Trustee, First Presbyterian Ch., Birmingham, Mich., 1965-68, elder, 1975-79. Served with USN, 1942-44. Mem. Am. Legion (comdr. 1946-47), Nat. Speakers Assn., Nat. Soc. Sales Tng. Execs. (editorial honor award 1974, 78, 80). Republican. Avocations: golf; reading; travel. Home and Office: 2694 Heathfield Rd Birmingham MI 48010

LUMSDON, ROBERT WILLIAM, manufacturing executive, engineer; b. Ottumwa, Iowa, Aug. 10, 1930; s. Albert Ross and Bernice Maude (Grinstead) L.; m. Marilyn Ann Burnaugh, July 5, 1953; children: Marcia Ann, Karen Lynn, Kevin Ross, Kristen Elaine. Student, Parsons Coll. Methods engr. John Deere & Co., Ottumwa, Iowa, 1953-66; sr. process engr. Massey Ferguson Inc., Des Moines, 1966-76, corp. safety mgr., 1976-81, adminstrv. services mgr., 1981—. Served to sgt. USAF, 1949-53. Mem. Am. Welding Soc. (pres. Des Moines chpt. 1973), Iowa Mfrs. Assn. (safety com.). Democrat. Lutheran. Avocations: golf, gardening, jogging. Home: 7711 Dellwood Dr Urbandale IA 50322 Office: Massey Ferguson Inc 1901 Bell Ave Des Moines IA 50315

LUND, WILLIAM BOYCE, computer analyst, programmer; b. Indpls., Nov. 27, 1959; s. Ralph Emerson Jr. and Madge Etta (Major) L.; m. Kathleen L. Faust, May 15, 1985. BA in Math. and Computer Sci., Ind. U., 1982; postgrad., Ball State U., 1986—. Programmer, analyst RCA Consumer Services, Indpls., 1983-85; analyst, programmer Boehringer Mannheim, Indpls., 1985—. Vol. Pan Am. Games/PAX I, Indpls., 1987. Avocations: playing basketball, recreational computing, home improvement, gardening, audio visual production. Home: 221 N Oakland Ave Indianapolis IN 46201-3360 Office: Boehringer Mannheim MIS 9115 Hague Rd Indianapolis IN 46250-0100

LUNDAHL, MARGARET ANN, law librarian; b. Chgo., Nov. 26, 1948; d. John E. and Lois N. (Olausson) L.; m. Gary L. Tucker, June, 1971 (div. 1974). Student, U. Chgo., 1966-68, MBA, 1969, MA, 1976; JD, Ill. Institute Tech., 1980. Bar: Ill. 1980. Asst. bus. librarian U. Chgo. Grad. Sch. Bus., 1969-71; cataloger U. Chgo. Law Library, 1971-76; librarian Isham, Lincoln, & Beale, Chgo., 1976-83; prin. Lundahl Enterprises, Chgo., 1981—. Mem. Am. Assn. Law Libraries, ABA, Spl. Libraries Assn., Chgo. Bar Assn. Home and Office: Lundahl Enterprises 10128 Ave J Chicago IL 60617

LUNDBOHM, ERIC PAUL, automotive executive; b. Providence, R.I., Dec. 2, 1956; s. Carl Eric and Dorothy Rose (Ballestraci) L.; m. Joan Terese Franzese, May 23, 1981; children: Adrian, Kristin. BBA, U. R.I., 1983; MBA in Mktg., Ohio State U., 1985. Asst. prodn. mgr. Bradford Dyking Assn. Inc., Bradford, R.I., 1976-80; mktg. analyst IBM Corp., ISG Hdqrs., White Plains, N.Y., 1984; planning analyst TRW Automotive Worldwide, Solon, Ohio, 1985-86; mktg. mgr. TRW Aftermarket Info. Systems, Cleve.,

1986—. Univ. fellow Ohio State U., Columbus, 1984-85. Mem. Soc. Automotive Engrs., Beta Gamma Sigma. Lutheran. Avocations: travel, cooking, collecting audio and video recordings, guitar. Home: 38325 North Ln Apt 201H Willoughby OH 44094 Office: TRW Aftermarket Info Systems 8001 E Pleasant Valley Rd Cleveland OH 44131

LUNDEGARD, JOHN THOMAS, auto supply company executive; b. Mpls., June 9, 1931; s. Harold George and Gertrude (Stene) L.; m. Lucy Liggett, Aug. 8, 1953; children: Lucy Ann, David Liggett. B.B.A., U. Minn., 1953; P.M.D. in Bus. Adminstrn, Harvard U. Grad. Sch. Cert. in planning Stanford Bus. Sch. Various positions, exec. asst. to chmn. Dayton Hudson Corp., Mpls., 1956-68; various positions, pres., chief exec. officer Venture Stores, May Dept. Stores, St. Louis, 1968-79; chmn. bd., chief exec. officer Western Auto Supply Co., Kansas City, Mo., 1979—; dir. Beneficial Corp., Midland Internat., Eva Gabor Internat., Boatman's 1st Nat. Bank. Bd. dirs. United Way. Served with U.S. Army, 1953-56. Office: Western Auto Supply 2107 Grand Ave Kansas City MO 64108 *

LUNDGREN, DAVID BRIAN, accountant; b. Geneva, Ill., Jan. 24, 1956; s. Harlan Oliver and Genevieve June (Anderson) L.; m. Sandra Jo Gerencser, Sept. 18, 1982; children: Catherine Jo, Kristen Michelle. BS, Oral Roberts U., 1978; MBA, U. Chgo., 1983. CPA, Ill., Kans. Staff acct. Resinoid Engring., Chgo., 1978-79; supr. auditing Fay, Conmy & Co., CPA's, Chgo., 1979-83; controller Simon Food Holdings, Kansas City, Kans., 1983-85; pvt. practice acctg. Olathe, Kans., 1985—. Participant Leadership Olathe, 1986; treas. Kansans for Life, Olathe, 1986—; deacon First Presbyn. Ch., Olathe, 1986—; founder, pres. Beginnings, Evanston, Ill., 1978-82; mem. Bible Study Fellowship, Overland Park, Kans.; bd. dirs. Pregnancy Consol. Assistance and Relocation Efforts, Olathe, 1987—. Mem. Am. Inst. CPA's, Ill. CPA Soc., Kans. Soc. CPA's (bd. dirs. metro chpt. 1985—). Republican. Avocations: skiing, reading, running, gardening. Home: 1010 Clairborne Olathe KS 66062 Office: PO Box 1162 Olathe KS 66061

LUNDIE, LOUISE MARIE, customer service director; b. Meeme Twp., Wis., Mar. 2, 1940; d. Henry Joseph and Irene Theresa (Salm) Schwartz; A.A., Milw. Area Tech. Coll., 1978; B.S., Carroll Coll., 1982; m. Mel A. Lundie, Oct. 2, 1976; 1 dau. by previous marriage, Ann Louise Mathews. Sec. to gen. mgr. St. Regis Paper Co., Milw., 1961-65; asst. to pres. Wells Badger Corp., Milw., 1966-74; sec. to v.p. mktg. Everbrite Electric Signs, South Milwaukee, Wis., 1975, nat. sales adminstr., 1976-81, mgr. mktg. adminstrn., 1981, mgr. corp. planning, advt. and market research, 1981-84, dir. customer service, 1984-87, dir. sales services, 1987—. Pres., Adult AFS, Cudahy, Wis., 1982—. Mem. Nat. Secs. Assn. (pres. Milw. chpt. 1971-73), Adminstrv. Mgmt. Soc., Friends of Cudahy Library. Home: 5938 S Pennsylvania Ave Cudahy WI 53110 Office: Everbrite Electric Signs 315 Marion Ave S Milwaukee WI 53172

LUNDQUIST, JAMES LEE, accountant; b. Mpls., Apr. 28, 1954; s. James Oliver and Phyllis A. (Rice) L.; m. Dawn Marie Lutz, Dec. 23, 1983; 1 child, Sean Michael. BA in Acctg., St. Thomas, 1976. CPA, Minn. Audit supr. Taylor McCaskill, St. Paul, 1976-82; audit supr. Carlson, Lundquist and Co., Ltd., Mpls., 1976-82, ptnr., 1982—; fin. advisor The Beddor Cos., Mpls., 1982-87. Mem. Am. Inst. CPA's, Minn. Soc. CPA's. Republican. Lutheran. Avocations: fishing, hunting, running, racquetball, skeetshooting. Home: 22000 Tulip NW Oak Grove MN 55444 Office: Carlson Lundquist & Co Ltd 7101 Northland Circle Minneapolis MN 55428

LUNDQUIST, JULIE ANNE, lawyer; b. Chgo., Sept. 22, 1946; d. Donald Carl and Gertrude (Kelly) L. B.A., St. Olaf Coll., 1968; J.D., John Marshall Law Sch., 1978. Bar: Ill. 1978, U.S. Dist. Ct. (no. dist.) Ill. 1978. Mem. firm Lundquist & Mitchell, Zion, Ill., 1978—; instr. law and trust div. Am. Inst. Banking, Chgo., 1980—. Pres. YWCA of Lake County, Ill., 1985-87; chmn. Council of YWCAs of Ill. and St. Louis, Waukegan, Ill., 1984; treas. Com. to Elect Judge Scott, Libertyville, Ill., 1984. Mem. Ill. State Bar Assn., Chgo. Bar Assn., Lake County Bar Assn. (sec. 1984-86), Assn. Women Attys. (pres. 1981-83), Jr. Women's League. Republican. Episcopalian. Office: Lundquist & Mitchell 2610 Sheridan Rd Zion IL 60099

LUNDQUIST, KIPTON JOHN VIRGIL, plastic surgeon; b. Mpls., Dec. 10, 1948; s. Virgil John Pershing and Irma (Olson) L.; m. Martha Pauline Dugas, Sept. 3, 1971; children: Padrin, Prinna, Peter, Pharon, Perek. AB in Biology, Brown U., 1970; MD, U. Minn., 1973. Diplomate Am. Bd. Plastic Surgery. Resident in gen. surgery Hennepin County Med. Ctr., Mpls., 1974-80; fellow plastic surgery U. Mo., Kansas City, 1981-83; practice medicine specializing in plastic surgery Mpls., 1983—; plastic surgeon Fairview Southdale Meml. Hosp., Edina, Minn., 1983—. Mem. AMA, Hennepin County Med. Soc., Minn. State Med. Assn., Am. Soc. Plastic and Reconstructive Surgery, Minn. Acad. Plastic Surgeons, Minn. Acad. Medicine, Minn. Surg. Soc., Mpls. Surgical Soc. Avocations: banjo, thoroughbred horses, bass fishing, photography, canoeing. Home: 4805 Sunnyside Rd Edina MN 55424 Office: Reconstructive & Plastic Surgery 743 Medical Arts Bldg Minneapolis MN 55402

LUNDSTEDT, SVEN BERTIL, behavioral scientist, educator; b. N.Y.C., May 6, 1926; s. Sven David and Edith Maria L.; m. Jean Elizabeth Sanford, June 16, 1951; children: Margaret, Peter, Janet. AB, U. Chgo., 1952, PhD, 1955; SM, Harvard U., 1960. Lic. in psychology, N.Y., Ohio; cert. Council for Nat. Register of Health Services. Asst. dir. Found. for Research on Human Behavior, 1960-62; asst. prof. Case-Western Res. U., Cleve., 1962-64, assoc. prof., 1964-68; assoc. prof. adminstrn. sci. Ohio State U., 1968-69, prof. pub. policy and adminstrn., 1969—, Ameritech Research prof., 1987—; chmn. Battelle endowment program for tech. and human affairs, 1976-80, mem. Univ. Senate; dir. project on edn. of chief exec. officer Aspen Inst., 1978-80; advisor Task Force on Innovation, U.S. Ho. of Reps., 1983—; mem. Am. Com. on U.S. Soviet Relations, 1985—, chair trade and negotiation project; cons. E.I. duPont de Nemours & Co., B.F. Goodrich Co., Bell Telephone Labs., Battelle Meml. Inst., Nat. Fulbright Award Com. Author: Higher Education in Social Psychology, 1968; co-author: Managing Innovation, 1982; contbr. articles to profl. jours. Pres., Cleve. Mental Health Assn., 1966-68; mem. Ohio Citizen's Task Force on Corrections, 1971-72. Served with U.S. Army, 1944-46. Harvard U. fellow, 1960; grantee Bell Telephone Labs., 1964-65, NSF, 1965-67, Kettering Found., 1978-80, Atlantic Richfield Found., 1980-82. Mem. Am. Psychol. Assn., Internat. Inst. for Applied Systems Analysis (innovation task force, nat. adv. com. project internat. negotiation with Am. Acad. Arts and Scis., founder, chmn. U.S. Midwest assn. 1986—), AAAS (chmn. PIN com. on east/west trade negotiation), Am. Soc. for Pub. Adminstrn. (pres. Central Ohio chpt. 1975-77), AAUP. Unitarian. Home: 197 Riverview Park Dr Columbus OH 43214 Office: Ohio State U Sch Pub Adminstrn 1775 College Rd Columbus OH 43210

LUNDY, BARBARA JEAN, communications consultant, writer; b. Frankfurt, Germany, Aug. 1, 1953; d. Roger J. and Helen E. (Branch) L. BA in Journalism, Ohio State U., 1974. Edn. specialist Ohio Hist. Soc., Columbus, 1975-76; asst. chief communications Ohio Youth Commn., Columbus, 1976-79; pub. info. coordinator Cen. Ohio Transit Authority, Columbus, 1979-81; owner B.J. Lundy Enterprises, Columbus, 1981—; communications cons. Fedn. of Community Orgns., 1980, Driving Park Area Commn., 1980, Driving Park Civic Assn., 1980, Africa: A First Experience, 1980. Chmn. membership com. Leadership Columbus, 1980-81, mem. steering com., 1980-83, v.p. steering com., 1982-83; grad. Columbus Area Leadership Program, 1980, mem. program selection com., 1982—; mem. nominating com. Cen. Ohio Young Reps., 1981; active Met. Women's Ctr., 1980-82, mem. pub. relations com., 1981; mem. pub. relations com. Columbus Area Internat. Program, 1981. Named one of Outstanding Young Women of Am., 1981, 83. Mem. Pub. Relations Soc. Am. (pub. service com. 1980-81, chmn. speaker's bur. com. 1979-81), Columbus Area C. of C., Columbus Jaycees. Baptist. Club: Columbus Met. (nominating com. 1982-83, membership com., 1981-83).

LUNDY, PAUL ANDREW, environmental engineer; b. Sioux Falls, S.D., Aug. 30, 1944; s. Andrew Mandus and Edna Joy (Searles) L.; m. Carol Ann Barnes, Sept. 16, 1963 (div. 1967); m. Mary Ann Westergreen, Apr. 1, 1967; children—Erik Magnus Gustavus, Karl Edward. B.S. in Geol. Engring., S.D. Sch. Mines and Tech., 1967. Profl. engr., Iowa. Found. engr. Iowa Dept. Transp., Ames, 1969-71, project engr., 1971-80; environ. engr., solid and hazardous waste mgmt. Iowa Dept. Environ. Quality, Des Moines, 1980-83; water supply engr. Iowa Dept. Water, Air and Waste Mgmt., Des Moines, 1983-86; solid waste staff engr. Iowa Dept. Natural Resources, 1986—. Pres. Ames Council PTAs and PTSAs, 1977-78. Served with U.S. Army, 1967-69, USAR, 1969—. Decorated Humanitarian Service medal, 1980; recipient Pub. Service award Am. Radio Relay League, 1972, 79. Mem. Soc. Am. Mil. Engrs., Am. Indian Sci. and Engring. Soc. (regional gov. 1985—), AIME, Scabbard and Blade. Republican. Methodist. Clubs: Story County Amateur Radio, Encore Toastmasters (area gov. 1973-74). Home: 4316 Phoenix Ames IA 50010-3626 Office: 900 E Grand Des Moines IA 50319

LUNG, DAVID D(ARLING), restaurant owner; b. Kwei Chow, China, Feb. 28, 1947; came to U.S., 1973; s. Chi-Kwei and Ai-Yuan (Su) L.; m. Ingrid W. Fang, Sept. 20, 1975; children: Jannie J., Bryan T. BA in Social Work, Nat. Taiwan U., Republic of China, 1970; MA in Sociology, No. Ill. U., 1980. Cert. restaurant mgr. Mgr. Charlie Lui Restaurant, Chgo., 1976-78, Yen Ching Restaurant, Urbana, Ill., 1978-79, 79-80, Chung King Inn, St. Charles, Ill., 1979; owner China Inn Restaurant, Champaign, Ill., 1980—; pres. China Inn Enterprises, Inc., Champaign, 1982—, China Inn II, Urbana, 1985—, Creative Investment Mgmt. Corp., Champaign, 1986—; v.p. Amerasia Internat., Champaign, 1984—. Mem. Rep. Presdl. Task Force, Washington, 1980, U.S. Senatorial Club, Nat. Rep. Senatorial Com., Washington, 1982—. Recipient Award Cert. Consulate-Gen. Republic of China, 1979, Award Cert. coordination Council N.Am. Affairs, 1980, Award Cert. The Nat. Rep., 1982, Award Cert. Congl. Com., 1983-84. Mem. Am. Assn. Ind. Investors, Ill. Restaurant Assn., Cen. Ill. Better Bus. Bur., U.S. C. of C., Free Chinese Assn. (consul midwest chpt. 1975-76). Home: 1907 S Prospect Champaign IL 61821 Office: China Inn Enterprises Inc 2312 W Springfield Champaign IL 61821

LUNGREN, JOHN HOWARD, law educator, oil and gas consultant, author; b. Chgo., Feb. 11, 1925; s. Charles Howard and Edna Hughes (Edwards) L.; m. Phyllis Joan Jolidon, Dec. 12, 1953 (div.); 1 son, John Eric; m. Susan Jeanette Whitfield, Sept. 22, 1984. B.A., Beloit Coll., 1948; J.D., Marquette U., 1952; M.A., U. Wis.-Milw., 1974. Bar: Wis. 1952, Ill. 1975, Kans. 1980. Assoc. gen. counsel A. O. Smith Corp., 1964-74; gen. atty. Clark Oil & Refining Corp., 1954-64; prof. law Lewis U., Glen Ellyn, Ill., 1975-80; assoc. prof. law Washburn U. Sch. Law, Topeka, 1980-85; practice, Chgo., from 1977; with Turner & Boisseau Ltd., Wichita, Kans., 1985—; of counsel Lungren and Whitfield-Lungren, Wichita, 1987—; cons. oil and gas; Kans. rep. legal com. Interstate Oil Compact. Chmn., Milwaukee County Republican Party, 1966-70; justice of peace, Wauwatosa, Wis., 1964-68. Served with USN, 1943-46. Mem. ABA, Ill. Bar Assn., Wis. Bar Assn., Kans. Bar Assn., Wichita Bar Assn.

LUNTE, SUSAN MARIE, chemist; b. Detroit, July 17, 1958; d. Joseph Palmer and Kay Elizabeth (Dawson) Hommel; m. Craig Edward Lunte, Mar. 12, 1983. BA, Kalamazoo Coll., 1980; PhD in Chemistry, Purdue U., 1984. Analytical chemist Bioanalytical Systems, West Lafayette, Ind., 1984; analytical research chemist Procter & Gamble, Cin., 1984-87; asst. scientist Ctr. Bioanalytical Research, U. Kans., Lawrence, 1987—. Contbr. articles to profl. jours. Purdue Cancer Ctr. research grantee, 1983. Mem. Internat. Soc. for Study of Xenobiotics, Soc. for Electroanalytical Chemistry, Am. Chem. Soc., Phi Lamda Upsilon. Roman Catholic. Office: Ctr Bioanalytical Research U Kans 6059 Constant Ave Lawrence KS 66046

LUPIEN, CHARLES ALFRED, information systems executive; b. Springfield, Mass., Feb. 21, 1935; s. Arthur George and Estella Auriella (Schultz) L.; m. Marilyn Barnes, Apr. 6, 1957; children: Laura, Susan, Steven, Paula; m. Janice Gigliotti, May 22, 1981; children: Johathan, Carolyn. BSBA, Am. Internat. Coll., 1959; BSEE, Western New Eng. Coll., 1963. Cert. data processor, systems profl. Systems analyst Agway, Inc., West Springfield, Mass., 1959-63; data processing mgr. Agway, Inc., Syracuse, N.Y., 1963-66; dir. computer services Kollmorgen Corp., Holyoke, Mass., 1966-69; mgr. computer services Combustion Engr., Inc., Stamford, Conn., 1069-81; v.p. info. systems Trinova Corp (formerly Libbey-Owens-Ford Co.), Toledo, Ohio, 1981—. Author: (with others) Data Base Management Systems Requirements, 1971; contbr. articles to mags. and newspapers. Info. systems del. to Citizen Ambassador Program, People's Republic of China, 1986. Served with USN, 1952-54. Mem. Assn. Systems Mgmt., Assn. Computing Machinery, Toledo Exec. Roundtable, U. Mich. Roundtable. Club: Toledo. Avocations: tennis, running. Home: 4434 Weldwood Ln Sylvania OH 43560 Office: Trinova Corp 1705 Indian Wood Circle Maumee OH 43537

LUPKE, WALTER HERMAN, JR., financial planner; b. Ft. Wayne, Ind., Sept. 25, 1922; s. Walter Herman and Lucy Viola (Bell) L.; m. G. Frances McGahey, Aug. 11, 1944; children: Karen Ann McArdle, Hans R. BS in Chem. Engring., Purdue U., 1942. CLU, chartered property casualty underwriter. Underwriter Lupke Ins. Agy., Ft. Wayne, 1946-50, acct., 1950-51, claims mgr., 1951-52, treas., 1946-83, sales exec., 1952-83, chmn. bd., 1970-87; pvt. practice fin. planning, Ft. Wayne, 1987—. Pres. Lupke Found.; bd. dirs. Embassy Found., St. Francis Coll. Found., Kirksville Coll. Medicine Found., Luth. Hosp., Allen Wells chpt. ARC. Served with U.S. Army, 1942-46; ETO. Mem. Ind. Ins. Agts. Assn. U.S.A., Ind. Ind. Ins. Agts. Assn., Ft. Wayne Ind. Ins. Agts., Ft. Wayne C. of C. Republican. Lutheran. Lodge: Kiwanis.

LUPO, JOHN S., retail department store executive; b. 1946. BS, Miami U., 1968. With Higbee Co., Cleve., 1968—, store mgr., 1977-78, v.p., 1978-82, sr. v.p., 1982-85, pres. of merchandising, 1985—. Office: Higbee Co 100 Public Sq Cleveland OH 44113 *

LUPP, MANFRIED, construction company executive. Chmn. Fru-Con Corp., Ballwin, Mo. Office: Fru-Con Corp 1299 Clayton Rd W Ballwin MO 63011 *

LUQMANI, MUSHTAQ, marketing and international business educator, consultant; b. Karachi, Pakistan, Nov. 5, 1944; came to U.S., 1967; s. Arif A. and Badar (Beg) Lukmani; m. Zahida M. Luqmani, Mar. 15, 1973. B.S. with honors, U. Karachi, 1966; B.S. in Chem. Engring., Ind. Inst. Tech., 1969; M.B.A., Mich. State U., 1971, Ph.D. in Mktg. and Internat. Bus., 1978. Ptnr., Hotel Properties, Karachi, 1963-66; mktg. mgr. Al-Afia Resorts, Karachi, 1972-73; teaching asst. Mich. State U., East Lansing, 1973-76; assoc. prof. mktg. Western Mich. U., Kalamazoo, 1977—. Mem. Am. Mktg. Assn. (pres. West Mich. chpt. 1983-84), Acad. Mktg. Sci., Acad. Internat. Bus., West Mich. World Trade Club, Beta Gamma Sigma. Lodge: Lions (Kalamazoo). Contbr. articles to profl. jours. Home: 7600 Orchard Hill Kalamazoo MI 49002 Office: Western Mich U 230 N Hall Kalamazoo MI 49008

LURIE, JONATHAN ADAM, advertising executive; b. Willimantic, Conn., Dec. 24, 1956. BA, U. Wis., 1981. Asst. account exec. Mktg. Support, Inc., Chgo., 1981-83, account exec., 1983-85, asst. to pres., 1985—. Mem. Bus. Profl. Advt. Assn., Chgo. Advt. Club, Nat. Retail Merchants Assn. Jewish. Office: Mktg Support Inc 303 E Wacker Dr Chicago IL 60601

LURQUIN, JOHN HENRY, former educator; b. Green Bay, Wis., Mar. 15, 1924; s. Henry J. and Mary Odile (Beno) L.; m. Bernadette Margarite DeGroot, Aug. 7, 1948; children—Judith M., John J., James M., Joseph P., Jean A., Jerome T., Jane L., Jeffery A., Jennifer O., Jay M., Joyce E., Joel H., Jan C. B.S., U. Wis.-Stout, 1950, M.S., 1952; postgrad. Purdue U., 1965; Cert. Advanced Studies, U. Ill., 1971. Tchr. pub. schs., Marty, S.D., 1950-53, Pulaski, Wis., 1953-54; tchr., supr., adminstr., Evergreen Park, Ill., 1954-84; dir. vocat. edn. Evergreen Park (Ill.) High Sch. Dist. 231, 1981-83. Bd. dirs. Sch. Employees Credit Union, 1957-85, pres., 1971-75, chmn. bd., 1975-85. Served with U.S. Army, 1943-46. Decorated Bronze Star. Named Indsl. Educator of Yr., Indsl. Edn. Tchrs. of Northeast Ill. Round. Table 5, 1979; 25 Yr. Indsl. Educator, Ill. Indsl. Edn. Assn., 1981; Ill. Indsl. Arts Educator of Yr., Am. Indsl. Arts Assn., 1983. Mem. Am. Vocat. Assn., NEA, Ill. Indsl. Edn. Assn. (Indsl. Educator of Yr. 1983), Phi Delta Kappa. Roman Catholic. Lodge: K.C. Home: 5019 W 99th St Oak Lawn IL 60453

LURTON, ERNEST LEE, insurance broker; b. Santa Ana, Calif., Nov. 13, 1944; s. Charles Leland and Mary Crystal (McGannon) L.; m. Janet C. Edington, June 17, 1967; children—Matthew, Katherine. B.A., Ind. U., 1967, M.B.A., 1978. C.L.U. Pension cons. Edward B. Morris & Assocs., Inc., Indpls., 1971-74, sr. cons. group ins. and pension plans, 1974-77; pres. Risk Mgmt. Group, Indpls., 1977—, Benefit Concepts of Ind. Inc., Indpls., 1982—. Bd. dirs. Big Bros. Indpls. Served as capt. USAF, 1967-71. Mem. Nat. Assn. Securities Dealers, Nat. Assn. Life Underwriters, Am. Soc. C.L.U.s, Stanley K. Lacey Exec. Leadership Alumni Assn., Ind. U. Coll. Arts and Scis. Alumni Assn. (past pres.), Beta Theta Pi (past pres.). Republican. Mem. Christian Ch. (past chmn. bd. dirs.). Lodges: Masons, Shriners. Home: 7217 Allisonville Rd Indianapolis IN 46250 Office: One N Capitol Ave #100 A Indianapolis IN 46204

LURTON, H. WILLIAM, retail executive; b. Greenwich, Conn., Sept. 18, 1929; s. William Pearl and Elizabeth (McDow) L.; m. Susan Harvey, Oct. 26, 1980; children: Scott, Carrie, Nancy, Jennifer. B.A., Principia Coll., 1951. Sales rep. Jostens Inc., Mpls., 1955-61; yearbook sales and plant mgr. Jostens Inc., Visalia, Calif., 1961-66; gen. sales mgr. yearbook div. Jostens Inc., v.p., gen. mgr. yearbook div., 1969-70, corp. exec. v.p., 1970-71, mem. exec. com., 1970-72, pres., 1971-75, chief operating officer, 1971-72, chief exec. officer, 1972—, chmn. bd., 1975—, also dir.; dir. Deluxe Check Printers, Pentair, Inc. Bd. dirs. U.S. C. of C., Mpls. YMCA. Served with USMC, 1951-53. Mem. Mpls. C. of C. (bd. dirs.). Clubs: Wayzata (Minn.) Country, Minneapolis. Home: 3135 Jamestown Rd Long Lake MN 55356 Office: Jostens Inc 5501 Norman Center Dr Minneapolis MN 55437

LURZ, WILLIAM GLENN, dentist; b. Valentine, Nebr., Feb. 9, 1957; s. Herb L. and Eletha L. (Sharp) L. BS, U. Nebr., 1979, DDS, 1984. Assoc. South West Dental Clinic, McCook, Nebr., 1984-86; gen. practice dentistry Bassett (Nebr.) Dental Clinic, 1986—. Republican. Lodge: Lions. Avocations: music, sports. Home: 310 Park St Bassett NE 68714 Office: Bassett Dental Clinic 101 E South St Bassett NE 68714

LUSSENDEN, DONALD ALLAN, personnel executive; b. Flint, Mich., June 10, 1921; s. Charles Wesley and Bernice Marie (Booher) L.; m. Helen Jane Lipsey, Aug. 10, 1946 (div. Mar. 27, 1961); children: Kendrick, Garrett, Patricia; m. Lucille Helen Kalusniak, Jan. 20, 1962; 1 child, Debra. BA in Sociology, Wayne State U., 1949. Prodn. worker Ford Motor Co., Dearborn, Mich., 1939-41, 46-50, warranty processor, 1952-55, personnel recuriter, 1955-65, personnel coordinator, 1965-80, recruiting cons., 1983—. Served to 1st lt. U.S. Army, 1941-46, 50-52. Avocations: archaeology, history, genealogy. Home: 16413 Alpine Dr Livonia MI 48154 Office: Ford Motor Co 17000 Oakwood Blvd Allen Park MI 48121

LUSSIER, (JOSEPH) MARCEL, wholesale grocery company executive; b. Royal Oak, Mich., 1925; married. B.A., Wayne State U., 1950; student, Mich. State U. Dir. prodn. and frozen foods Allied Supermarkets, 1954-58; dir. sales merchandising Liberal Markets, 1959-64; chief operating officer Auto Servicio Noel, Valencia, Spain, 1965-67; v.p. Topco Assocs., Inc., Skokie, Ill., 1967-74; exec. v.p. Topco Assocs., Inc., 1974-78, pres., 1978—, also dir.; dir. Kingston Mktg. Co. Office: Topco Assocs Inc 7711 Gross Point Rd Skokie IL 60077 *

LUTHER, DON PRESTON, association executive; b. Flint, Mich., Dec. 8, 1920; s. Clarence Dar and Hazel Rhea (Crandall) L.; student U. Mich., 1952; B.A., Wayne State U., 1976; m. Frances Almeda Denton, June 3, 1943; children—Darleen R. Luther Hatt, Norma O. Luther Acton. Asst. ct. reporter St. Clair County, Port Huron, Mich., 1942; sec. San Diego Employers Assn., 1946-49; exec. sec. The Economic Club Detroit, 1949-64, asst. to pres., 1964-68, exec. dir., 1968—, sr. v.p., 1980—. Co-chmn. Mich. Rendezvous at EXPO 70, 1969-70; pres. Los Buenos Vecinos de Detroit, Spanish good neighbors club, 1958-59; bd. dirs. Lula Belle Stewart Center, 1976—. Served with USNR, 1942-45. Mem. Pub. Relations Soc. Am. (bd. dirs. Detroit chpt. 1983-86). Clubs: Circumnavigators (sec.-treas. Mich. chpt. 1980—), Renaissance, Detroit Press. Episcopalian. Home: 1369 Fort St # 317 Lincoln Park MI 48146 Office: 920 Free Press Bldg Detroit MI 48226

LUTHER, GEORGE AUBREY, orthopedic surgeon; b. Keokuk, Iowa, Dec. 11, 1933; s. George August and Leda (Galbraith) L.; m. Dorothy Gould Luther, Aug. 18, 1956; children: Melinda, George Bradley. AB, Cen Meth. U., 1955; MD, Vanderbilt U., 1959. Diplomate Am. Bd. Orthopaedic Surgery. Intern Vanderbilt U. Hosp., Nashville, 1959-60, resident, 1961-64, instr., 1964; resident St. Louis City Hosp., 1960-61; pres. St. Louis Orthopedic Inst., 1965—; pres. med. staff St. Joseph Hosp., St. Louis, 1982-83; trustee St. Joseph Hosp., 1981-84. Contbr. article profl. jours. Served to maj. U.S. Army, 1967-69. Fellow Am. Acad. Orthopedic Surgery, ACS (admissions com. 1982—); mem. AMA, Mo. Orthopedic Soc. (v.p. 1985-86, pres. 1986-87), St. Louis Metro. Med. Soc. (counselor 1983-85), Vanderbilt Orthopedic Soc. (pres. 1981-82), Tenn. Soc. of St. Louis. Republican. Presbyterian. Club: Bellerive Country. Avocations: music, sports. Home: 177 Ladue Oaks Ct Saint Louis MO 63141 Office: St Louis Orthopedic Inst 533 Couch Ave Saint Louis MO 63122

LUTHER, ROGER RAYMOND, engineering manager; b. Zion, Ill., Nov. 29, 1928; s. Harry Foster and Doris Elida (Casperson) L.; m. Mona Ardell Ballegooyen, mar. 23, 1951; children: Audrey, Andrew. BSMechE, Purdue U., 1952. Asst. chief engr. Anchor Coupling Co., Libertyville, Ill., 1953-64, v.p. research and devel., 1964-74, v.p. internat. ops., 1974-83; v.p. ops. Anchor Swan Corp., Worthington, Ohio, 1983-84; engring. mgr. Laserage Technology, Waukegan, Ill., 1984—. Holder 5 U.S. and 13 Fgn. patents in field. Served with U.S. Army, 1946-48. Mem. Soc. Automotive Engrs., Internat. Soc. Hybrid Microelectronics. Republican. Lodge: Masons. Avocations: photography, hunting, woodcarving. Home: 10634 W Circle Dr Zion IL 60099 Office: Laserage Technology 3021 Delandy Rd Waukegan IL 60087

LUTOCKA, PENNY CLARK, accountant; b. Tipton, Ind., June 22, 1960; d. Kenneth L. and Estelee A. (Taylor) Clark. BS, Ball State U., 1982. Acct. London, Witte & Co., Indpls., 1982—. Mem. Am. Inst. CPA's, Ind. CPA Soc. Office: London Witte & Co 901 E Tower Merchants Plaza Indianapolis IN 46204

LUTOMSKI, KARL FLORENTZ, periodontist; b. Detroit, Jan. 11, 1938; s. Michael George and Mary (Florentz) L.; m. Mary Ann Affleck, Aug. 6, 1966; children: Karen Elizabeth, Karl Florentz Jr. BS, U. Mich., 1960, DDS, 1964, MS, 1967. Asst. prof. U. Mich. Dental Sch., Ann Arbor, 1964-67; assoc. prof. U. Detroit Dental Sch., 1968-75, Mott Community Coll., Flint, Mich., 1976-79; staff periodontist St. Joseph's Hosp., Pontiac, Mich., 1980-85; practice dentistry specializing in periodontics Bloomfield, Mich., 1967—; advisor Oakland County Community Coll. Union Lake, Mich., 1968-80; cons. Delta Dental Plan, Southfield, 1985—. Bd. govs. Cranbrook Sch., Bloomfield Hills, 1976—; vol. Am. Cancer Soc. Mem. Mich. Soc. Periodontists (pres. 1970-75), Oakland County Dental Soc. (pres. 1977-79), U. Mich. Dental Sch. (past chmn., visitation com. 1969-76, past pres. bd. govs. 1979-85), ADA, Mich. Dental Assn., Multi-Lakes Cons. Assoc.. Clubs: Birmington Athletic (squash chmn. 1986); Lawrence Inst. Tech. (Southfield) (founder). Avocations: water skiing, boating, gardening, coins. Home: 445 Doningham Ln Bloomfield Hills MI 48013 Office: 1520 N Woodward Bloomfield Hills MI 48013

LUTTERS, HARRY JOHN, JR., architect, consultant; b. N.Y.C., Aug. 16, 1925; s. Harry J. and Florence (Nute) L.; m. Marion Ellen Cannon, Oct. 13, 1951; children: Susan, Kathryn, Laura, Nancy, Michael, Julie, Tracy, John, Thomas. BArch, Cornell U., 1947. Registered architect, N.Y., Calif., Minn. Prin. Lutters Architecture, Burnsville, Minn., 1974—; med. cons. Lutters Architecture/Planning/Designs, Burnsville, Minn., 1980—. Author, co-editor: Health Care Building Code Index, 1978; author, chmn.: Comparative Health Care Project Delivery Systems, 1976. Mem. Am. Inst. Architects (com. on architecture for health 1971—), Minn. Soc. Architects (com. architecture for health 1974—), Nat. Council Architectural Registration Bds. Democrat. Roman Catholic.

LUTTRELL, KARL STREET, small business owner; b. Paducah, Ky., Aug. 12, 1951; s. Eugene Melvin and Alice Jane (Street) L.; m. Charlotte Fox, July 22, 1978; 1 child, Christine Elizabeth. BA in Journalism, U. Mich., 1973, MS in Water Resource Scis., 1982. Cert. advanced emergency med. technician, Mich. Pres., gen. mgr. Sci. Diving Service, Ann Arbor, Mich.,

1981—; paramedic Huron Valley Ambulance, Ann Arbor, Mich., 1982—; tech. diving supr. Physics Dept. U. Mich., Ann Arbor, Mich., 1982—; water quality cons. Chester Engrs., Ann Arbor, Mich., 1985—; mem. emergency med. services commn. Washtenaw County, Ann Arbor, 1984-86. Contbr. photographs to U.S. News and World Report, Met. Detroit mag., others. Instr. CPR, first aid ARC, Ann Arbor, 1977—, mem. Red Alert Team, Ann Arbor, 1980-83; judge SE Mich. Sci. Fair, Ann Arbor, 1987. Recipient Vol. Service award ARC, 1982. Mem. Am. Waterworks Assn., Water Pollution Control Fedn., Undersea Med. Soc., Nat. Assn. Underwater Instrs. (cert. instr. life). Avocations: underwater photography, philately. Home: 3815 Greenbrier Blvd #283A Ann Arbor MI 48105

LUTTRELL, MICHAEL JOSEPH, pharmaceutical company executive; b. Chester, Pa., Sept. 12, 1948; s. Joseph Irving and Anna Jean (White) L.; m. Nell Louise Dewald, Nov. 17, 1973; 1 child, Margaret Louise. BS in History, Mt. St. Mary's Coll., Emmitsburg, Md., 1970; MBA in Mgmt. with highest honors, Lake Forest Coll., 1985. Lic. funeral dir. Pa. Funeral dir. G.J. White Funeral Home, Ridley Park, Pa., 1971-79; sales rep. Flint div. Baxter Healthcare Corp. (formerly Travenol Labs.), Washington, 1979-80; asst. to nat. sales mgr. Baxter Healthcare Corp. (formerly Travenol Labs.), Deerfield, Ill., 1980-82, asst. to pres., 1982, product mgr., 1982-83, mktg. specialist respiratory homecare div., 1983-84, mgr. sales devel. respiratory homecare div., 1984-85; mgr. tng. and devel. home respiratory therapy Travenol Labs., Deerfield, Ill., 1985—; bd. dirs. Baxter Travenol Employees Credit Union; editorial adv. bd. Tng. Dirs. Forum. Mem. curriculum rev. com. Lake Forest (Ill.) Grad. Sch., 1986—, Ridley Park Bicentennial Commn., 1976, Ridley Park Bus. Assn., 1971-79; chmn. Ridley Park Zoning Bd., 1977-79; mem. relief assn. Ridley Park Fire Dept., 1975-79, adv. bd. Sch. Dist. 15, Palatine, Ill. Mem. Am. Soc. Tng. and Devel., Nat. Soc. Sales Tng. Execs. Republican. Roman Catholic. Office: Baxter Healthcare Corp Respiratory Healthcare Div 1425 Lake Cook Rd Deerfield IL 60015

LUTZ, EMILY EILEEN, obstetrician, gynecologist; b. Circleville, Ohio, July 23, 1928; d. Lorin Earl Lutz and Marion Elizabeth (Rowe) Fickardt. BA, Ohio State U., 1950, MA, 1952, MD, 1959. Diplomate Am. Bd. Ob-Gyn. Intern San Francisco Gen. Hosp., 1959-60; resident U. Calif., San Francisco, 1960-64; practice medicine specializing in ob-gyn San Francisco, 1964-68, Circleville, 1968—; team physician U.S. Olympic Com., Pan Am. Games, 1983, Olympics, Los Angeles, 1984. Bd. dirs. YMCA, Circleville, 1985—. Fellow ACS, Am. Coll. Ob-Gyn, Am. Coll. Sports Medicine; mem. Am. Med. Women's Assn., Ohio State Med. Assn. (joint adv. bd. sports medicine 1975—, Spl. award sports medicine 1985), Columbus Ob-Gyn Soc. Episcopalian. Avocations: sports, refinishing old furniture, collecting stamps and pewter. Home: 360 E Main St Circleville OH 43113 Office: 135 Lewis Ave Circleville OH 43113

LUTZ, JOHN THOMAS, author; b. Dallas, Sept. 11, 1939; s. John Peter and Esther Jane (Gundelfinger) L.; m. Barbara Jean Bradley, Mar. 15, 1958; children—Steven, Jennifer, Wendy. Student Meramec Community Coll., 1965. Mem. Mystery Writers Am. (Scroll 1981, Edgar award 1986), Private-Eye Writers Am. (Shamus award 1982). Democrat. Author: The Truth of the Matter, 1971; Buyer Beware, 1976; Bonegrinder, 1977; Lazarus Man, 1979; Jericho Man, 1980; The Shadow Man, 1981; (with Steven Greene) Exiled, 1982; (with Bill Pronzini) The Eye, 1984; Nightlines, 1984; The Right to Sing the Blues, 1986; Tropical Heat, 1986; Ride the Lightning, 1987; contbr. short stories and articles to mystery and private-eye mags. Home and Office: 880 Providence Ave Webster Groves MO 63119

LUTZ, ROBERT ALLEN, mechanical engineer; b. Cedar Rapids, Iowa, Nov. 2, 1946; s. Harry William and Pauline Helen (Waite) L. BSME, Iowa State U., 1969. Registered profl. engr., Iowa. Mech. engr. Iowa Electric Light and Power Co., Cedar Rapids, 1971-75; sr. engr. Black and Veatch Cons. Engrs., Kansas City, Mo., 1975-77; mech. project engr. Rockwell-Collins, Cedar Rapids, 1977-82; engrng. con. Lutz Engrng. Corp., Cedar Rapids, 1982—; engrng cons. Honeywell Corp., Mpls.; speaker in field. Named one of Outstanding Young Men of Am., 1978. Mem. Semiconductor Equipment and Materials Inst. (chmn. flatpack standardization task force 1984-85, chmn. fine pitch leaded and leadless chip carriers task force 1986—), Experimental Aircraft Assn., Pi Tau Sigma. Avocations: water-sports, downhill skiing, nature.

LUTZ, ROBERT ANTHONY, automotive company executive; b. Zurich, Switzerland, Feb. 12, 1932; came to U.S., 1939; s. Robert H. and Marguerite (Schmid) L.; m. Betty D., Dec. 12, 1956 (div. 1979); children: Jacqueline, Carolyn, Catherine, Alexandra; m. Heide Marie Schmid, Mar. 3, 1980. B.Sc. in Prodn. Mgmt., U. Calif.-Berkeley, 1961, M.B.A. in Mktg., 1962; LL.D., Boston U., 1985. Research assoc., sr. analyst IMEDE, Lausanne, Switzerland, 1962-63; sr. analyst forward planning Gen. Motors Corp., N.Y.C., 1963-65; mgr. vehicle div. Gen. Motors Corp., Paris, 1966-69; staff asst., mng. dir. Adam Opel, Russelsheim, Fed. Republic of Germany, 1965-66, asst. domestic sales mgr., 1969, dir. sales Vorstand, 1969-70; v.p. Vorstand BMW, Munich, Fed. Republic of Germany, 1970-74; gen. mgr. Ford of Europe, Inc., Cologne, Fed. Republic of Germany, 1974-76; v.p. truck ops Ford of Europe, Inc., Brentwood, Eng., 1976-77, pres., 1977-79, chmn. bd., 1979-82, 1984-86, also dir.; exec. v.p. internat. Ford Internat., Dearborn, Mich., 1982-84; exec. v.p. Chrysler Motors Corp., Highland Park, Mich., 1986—; bd. dirs. Chrysler Corp.(parent), Highland Park, Mich.; dir. Ford Motor Co., Dearborn, Ford Motor Co. Ltd. (Britain), Brentwood. Adv. bd. U. Calif.-Berkeley Sch. Bus., 1979—. Served to capt. USMC, 1954-59, Okinawa, Japan, Korea. Named Alumnus of Yr., U. Calif.-Berkeley Sch. Bus., 1983. Kaiser Found. grantee 1962. Mem. European Adv. Council, Atlantic Inst. for Internat. Affairs, Conf. Bd., UN Assn. (econ. policy council), Soc. Automotive Engrs. Republican. Avocations: skiing; motorcycling; bicycling. Office: Chrysler Motors Corp 12000 Chrysler Dr Highland Park MI 48288-1919 *

LUUS, GEORGE AARNE, physician; b. Estonia, Apr. 23, 1937; s. Edgar and Aili (Poldmaa) L.; M.D., U. Toronto (Ont., Can.), 1962; m. Margit Jaanusson, Sept. 14, 1962 (div. 1983); children—Caroline Anna Elizabeth, Clyde Gregory Edgar, Lia Esther Isabelle; m. 2d, Donna Gervais Martell, Oct. 1, 1983. Intern Toronto East Gen. and Orthopaedic Hosp.; practice medicine specializing in family medicine, Sault Ste Marie, Ont., 1963—; mem. Algoma Dist. Med. Group, 1966—; sec. med. staff Gen. Hosp., 1972—, v.p., bd. dirs., 1973. Adv. bd. Can. Scholarship Trust Found., 1976-77. Mem. Algoma West Med. Acad., Acad. Medicine Toronto. Lodge: Rotary. Home: 42 Linstedt St, Sault Ste Marie, ON Canada P6B 3H8 Office: 240 McNabb St, Sault Ste Marie, ON Canada P6B 1Y5

LUX, DONNA MARIE, lawyer; b. Detroit, Jan. 27, 1945; d. Thomas John and Adele Rose (Mazie) Beck; m. Arthur Edward Lux, Nov. 20, 1970; children: Nicole, Kelly. BA, Cen. Mich. U., 1967; JD, Detroit Coll. Law, 1970. Bar: Mich. 1971. Assoc. Sugar, Schwartz, Silver, Schwartz & Tyler, Detroit, 1970-71; ptnr. Lux and Lux, Troy, Mich., 1971—; atty. Allied Industries, Clawson, Mich., 1983—, Saaba Corp., Troy, 1985—. Mem. State Bar Mich. Avocations: photography, art collecting.

LUX, MICHAEL LESTER, architect, consultant; b. Milw., Sept. 10, 1944; s. Lester L. and Muriel V. (Pasko) L.; m. Mabel L. Tews, Aug. 19, 1967; children: Amy L., Seth M. BArch, U. Ill., 1967. Ptnr. Mills Lux Assocs., Bloomington, 1967-80; architect State Farm Ins. Co., Bloomington, Ill., 1980—; cons. in field. Mem. Normal (Ill.) Planning Commn., 1973-74; devel. chmn. Am. Heart Assn., Springfield, Ill., 1985-87, 2d v.p., 1986—. Served with U.S. Army, 1968-70. Mem. AIA (treas. cen. Ill. chpt. 1974), Bloomington-Normal Architects Assn. (pres. 1985-86), Bloomington-Normal Jaycees (treas. 1976, Key Man 1976). Lodges: Shriners. Avocation: flying. Home: 7 Hawthorne Ridge Rural Rt 1 Downs IL 61736 Office: State Farm Ins Cos 1 State Farm Plaza Bloomington IL 61710

LUX, PHILIP GORDON, recreational vehicle and manufactured housing company executive; b. Flint, Mich., Dec. 15, 1928; s. Edward Francis and Mary Alice (McCarthy) L.; m. Donna Lee Farr, Feb. 17, 1951 (dec. 1976); children: Kimberly Ann, Sharon Kay, David Phillip; m. Judith Ann Gregory, Oct. 15, 1977. Student, Ind. U. Pres., chmn. The Lux Co., Inc., Elkhart, Ind., 1952-74; group v.p. Coachmen Industries, Inc., Middlebury, Ind., 1974-78, sr. v.p., 1978-80, exec. v.p., 1980—, vice-chmn., 1983—, dir., 1979—; dir. Stoutco Inc., Bristol, Ind. Pres. YMCA Elkhart County, 1969-70. Recipient Service to Youth award YMCA Elkhart County, 1971. Republican. Episcopalian. Club: Lions (pres. 1962-63). Office: Coachmen Industries Inc 601 E Beardsley Ave Box 3300 Elkhart IN 46514 *

LUXENBERG, MICHAEL GARY, statistician; b. Bklyn., May 29, 1949; s. Leon and Dorothy (Roth) L.; m. Joan Barbara Garfield, Aug. 17, 1980; children: Harlan Ross, Rebecca Ellen. BE, Pratt Inst., 1972; PhD, U. Minn., 1986. Electrical engr. Nat. Security Agy., Ft. Meads, Md., 1972-74; cons. in field Mpls.-St. Paul, 1981-84; pres. Profl. Data Analysts, Mpls., 1984—; instr. U. Minn., 1980. Contbr. articles to profl. jours. NIMH fellow, 1979-82. Mem. Am. Statistical Assn., Behavior Genetics Assn., Psychometric Soc. Jewish. Avocations: racquetball, reading.

LUZADRE, JOHN HINKLE, obstetrician, gynecologist; b. Logansport, Ind., Dec. 4, 1921; s. John Franklin and Mary Gladys (Hinkle) L.; B.S., U. Pitts., 1942, D.D.S., 1945; M.D., Duke U., 1951; m. Barbara Louise Cary, Sept. 24, 1949; children—John Cary, Jo Ann, Robert Allan, David James, Timothy Hart. Instr., U. Pitts. Sch. Dentistry, 1947; intern Henry Ford Hosp., Detroit, 1951-52, resident in ob-gyn, 1952-55; practice medicine specializing in ob-gyn, Grosse Pointe Farms, Mich., 1955—; mem. staffs St. John Hosp., Detroit, Cottage Hosp., Grosse Pointe Farms. Served as capt. Dental Corps, U.S. Army, 1945-47; ETO. Diplomate Am. Bd. Ob-Gyn. Fellow ACS, Am. Coll. Ob-Gyn; mem. Continental Gynecologic Soc., Alpha Omega Alpha. Republican. Presbyterian. Clubs: Country of Detroit; Hillsboro (Fla.); Tennis House (Grosse Pointe Farms). Home: 2683 S Lakeshore Rd Applegate MI 48401-9708 Office: 25599 Kelly Rd Roseville MI 48066

LUZIUS, JOSEPH WALTER, JR., pharmacist; b. St. Joseph, Minn., Apr. 17, 1953; s. Joseph Walter and Mary A. (Belgarde) L.; m. Cynthia Rae Weisman, May 14, 1981; children—Thomas, Abraham. A.A., Bemidji U., 1978; B.S. in Pharmacy, U. Minn., 1981. Lic. pharmacist, Minn. Intern, Pilot City Project, Mpls., 1979; mem. Indian Health Bd., Mpls., 1979-80; pharmacy intern VA Hosp., Mpls., 1981-82; pharmacist Walgreen's, Mpls., 1981—; pharmacy student-extern preceptor U. Minn. Coll. Pharmacy, Mpls., 1984—. Mem. Minn. Pharm. Assn., Am. Pharm. Assn., U. Minn. Alumni Assn. Avocations: tennis; fishing; hunting; racquetball; swimming. Office: 1235 E Franklin Ave Minneapolis MN 55404

LUZUM, JAMES ALOYSIUS, controller; b. Calmar, Iowa, Sept. 4, 1940; s. Bill and Leona (Schissel) L.; m. Arlene Catherine Hill, May 13, 1963; children: Michael, Julie, Steve, Kerrie. BA, Loras Coll., 1962. Auditor Ernst and Ersnt, Chgo., 1962-66; auditor, div. controller Control Data, Mpls., 1966-70; controller Weismantel Assocs., Eagan, Minn., 1970-72; controller, treas. Villaume Industries, Inc., St. Paul, 1972—. Mem. Nat. Acctg. Assn. Office: Villaume Industries Inc 2926 Lone Oak Circle Saint Paul MN 55121

LUZZO, RONALD FRANCIS, dentist; b. Chgo., Feb. 11, 1946; s. Francis P. and Ruth M. Luzzo; m. Ivelise Garcia, Mar. 6, 1971; children: Lynn, Deanna, William, Cheryl. Student, No. Ill. U., U. Miami; DDS, U. Ill., 1970; postgrad. in periodontology, U. Ky., 1970-71. Practice gen. dentistry Chgo. and Roselle, 1971—. Mem. ADA, Ill. State Dental Soc., Chgo. Dental Soc. (mems. group, various coms.). Office: 2256 W Lawrence Ave Chicago IL 60625

LYALL, KATHARINE C(ULBERT), research economist; b. Lancaster, Pa., Apr. 26, 1941; d. John D. and Eleanor G. L. B.A. in Econs., Cornell U., 1963, Ph.D. in Econs., 1969; M.B.A., NYU, 1965. Economist, Chase Manhattan Bank, N.Y.C., 1963-65; asst. prof. econs. Syracuse U., 1969-72; prof. econs. Johns Hopkins U., Balt., 1972-77; dir. grad. program in public policy Johns Hopkins U., 1979-81; dep. asst. sec. for econs. Office Econ. Affairs, HUD, Washington, 1977-79; v.p. acad. affairs U. Wis. System, Madison, 1981-85; acting pres. U. Wis. System, 1985, exec. v.p., 1986—. Author: Reforming Public Welfare, 1976, Microeconomic Issues of the 70s, 1978. Recipient award for Balt., Metro Center Policy Com., 1977. Mem. Am. Econ. Assn., Evaluation Research Soc., Phi Beta Kappa, Phi Kappa Phi. Office: Univ of Wis System Office Office of Vice Pres 1220 Linden Dr Madison WI 53706

LYBARGER, D. D., chemical company executive. Pres. Standard Oil Chem. Co., Cleve. Office: Standard Oil Chem Co Midland Bldg Cleveland OH 44115 *

LYBERG, MATTHEW LOUIS, floor covering co. exec.; b. Howell, Mich., Aug. 3, 1947; s. John King and Phyllis Jane (Long) L.; B.A., Capital U., 1969; postgrad. Evang. Luth. Theol. Sem., 1969, U. Mich., 1970; m. Mary Anne Kennedy, June 17, 1972; children—Elizabeth Jane, Sarah Anne, Basil John, Matthew Peter. Asst., Rickett Sch. for Mentally Handicapped, 1962-64; Head Start tchr. Livingston County Intermediate Sch. Dist., Howell, Mich., summers, 1962-71; tchr., dir. phys. edn. St. Joseph Sch., Howell, 1971-72; tchr., Mich. Dept. Corrections, Camp Brighton, Pinckney, 1970-75; tchr. Livingston County (Mich.) Sheriff's Dept., 1972-73; pres. Hamburg Warehouse, Inc., Hamburg, Mich., 1972—; trustee dir. Workskills Corp., Brighton, Mich., 1975—, pres., 1980—; exec. com. Livingston County Reps., 1987—; sports announcer Sta. WHMI, 1975—. Mem. fin. and stewardship bd. Zion Luth. Ch., Ann Arbor, Mich., 1979. Mem. Am. Assn. Mental Deficiency, Retail Floor Covering Inst., Jaycees, Brighton Area C. of C. (bd. dirs. 1984-86), Fellowship of Christian Athletes. Clubs: Optimist, Kiwanis. Home: 510 Aberdeen Way Howell MI 48843 Office: 10588 Hamburg Rd Hamburg MI 48139

LYDDON, JAN WENDEE, legislative researcher; b. Mason City, Iowa, Dec. 30, 1951; d. John William and Claudia A. (Smith) L.; m. Bruce E. McComb, July 3, 1974. BS, Iowa State U., 1973; MA, Mich. State U., 1982; post grad., Western Mich. U., 1982—, U. Mich., 1982—. VISTA paralegal Legal Aid Bur., Lansing, Mich., 1973-74; exec. dir. Vol. Action Ctr., Lansing, 1974-77; planning technician Dept. Social Services, Lansing, 1977-78; legis. research analyst Ho. Reps., Lansing, 1978—. Bd. dirs. Community Mental Health Bd., Lansing, 1977-84, chairwoman 1981-82. Democrat. Home: 718 Britten Ave Lansing MI 48910 Office: House Dem Research Staff 222 Seymour St PO Box 30014 Lansing MI 48909

LYDIC, FRANK AYLSWORTH, retired riverman, poet; b. Farnam, Nebr., Jan. 22, 1909; s. Robert Johnston and Lula Ethel (Aylsworth) L.; B.F.A., Kearney (Nebr.) State Coll., 1931; m. Florence Faye Meadows, July 2, 1934 (dec. 1984); children—Marcelle, Bernice Joy (dec.), Robert Norman; m. 2d, Nellie Snyder Yost, Aug. 30, 1984. Tchr. schs., Calif., 1931-56; riverman various vessels Mississippi River, from 1961; now ret.; del. Nat. Maritime Union Conv., 1966, 69, 72, 76, named union poet laureate, nat. conv., 1980. Served in U.S. Mcht. Marine, 1943-48, 56-61. Mem. Western Writers Am. (asso.), Nebr. Writers Guild, Nebr. Poets Assn. (asso.), Ill. State Poetry Soc. (pres. 1983—), Chgo. Poets and Patrons, Little Big Horn Assos. Democrat. Author: Desert Lure, 1971, 3d edit., 1984; Rhymes of a Riverman, 1973; When My Stretch on the River is Done, 1974; Nebraska! Oh Nebraska, 1975; San Francisco Revisited, 1976; At the Little Bighorn, 1976; The Far West's Race with Death, 1979; Rhymed Lines from the River, 1980; Comanche! Oh Comanche!, 1982; Custer Controversies, 1983; In Praise of Texas Jack, 1984. Home: 1505 W D St North Platte NE 69101

LYERLA, JON RANDALL, nursing home administrator; b. Highland, Ill., Nov. 4, 1952; s. James Richard and Mary Ellen (Gillespie) L.; m. Elizabeth Ann Becker, Dec. 21, 1974; 1 child, Scott Randall. BS, So. Ill. U., Edwardsville, 1976; MA, Webster U., 1987. Lic. nursing home adminstr. Office mgr. coordinator Monsanto, Creve Coeur, Mo., 1974-75; with supporting services So. Ill. U., Edwardsville, 1975-76; adminstr. Hitz Meml. Home—United Ch. Christ, Alhambra, Ill., 1976—. Named Boss Yr. Highland Bus. and Profl. Women, 1983. Mem. Am. Coll. Health Care Administrs., Am. Coll. Health Care Execs., Ill. Assn. Homes for the Aging (sec. 1987—), Am. Assn. Homes for the Aging, Gerontol. Soc. Am. Republican. Presbyterian. Lodge: Order of DeMolay (master counselor, chpt. advisor 1971-74). Avocations: bicycling, jogging, reading, yard work. Home: #19 Rushmore Dr Glen Carbon IL 62034 Office: Hitz Meml Home Belle St Alhambra IL 62001

LYKE, JAMES PATTERSON, bishop; b. Chgo., Feb. 18, 1939. A.B. in Philosophy, Quincy (Ill.) Coll., 1963; M.Div. in Theology, St. Joseph Sem., Teutopolis, Ill., 1967; Ph.D., Union Grad. Sch., Cin., 1981. Joined Order Friars Minor, Roman Cath. Ch., 1959, ordained priest, 1966, consecrated bishop, 1979; tchr. religion Padua Franciscan High Sch., Parma, Ohio, 1966-67; adminstr. Father Bertrand Elem. Sch., Memphis, 1968-69; pastor St. Thomas Ch., Memphis, 1969-77, Ch. of St. Benedict the Black; also dir. Newman Center, Grambling (La.) State U., 1977-79; aux. bishop Cleve.; also Episcopal vicar for urban region Roman Cath. Diocese Cleve., 1979—; Mem. denominational execs. Interch. Council Greater Cleve., race relations com. Greater Cleve. Roundtable. Coordinator Black Cath. Hymnal. Mem. Urban League, So. Poverty Law Center, Bread for the World, Nat. Black Evangelist Assn., Pax Christi U.S.A., NAACP Nat. Conf. Cath. Bishops (migration com., black liturgy subcom. of bishops com. on liturgy), Nat. Black Cath. Clergy Caucus (pres. 1977-79). Lodges: Knights St. Peter Claver, K.C. (4th deg.). Address: 1031 Superior Ave Cleveland OH 44114

LYMAN, ARTHUR JOSEPH, financial executive; b. Evergreen Park, Ill., May 18, 1953; s. Arthur Edward and Margaret (O'Conner) L.; m. Janet Lee Wenzel, Sept. 9, 1984; children: Christina Lee, Alissa Mary. BA, Knox Coll., 1975; M in Mgmt., Northwestern U., 1977. CPA, Ill. Audit supr. Arthur Andersen & Co., Chgo., 1977-83; fin. planning analyst Montgomery Ward & Co., Chgo., 1983-84; dir. fin. and adminstrn. cen. region Coopers & Lybrand, Chgo., 1984—. Mem. Am. Inst. CPA's, Fin. Execs. Inst., Ill. Inst. CPA's. Roman Catholic. Home: 3 Cornell Dr Lincolnshire IL 60015 Office: Coopers & Lybrand 203 N LaSalle Chicago IL 60601

LYMAN, EDWARD HARRY, otolaryngologist; b. St. Louis, Oct. 28, 1912; s. Harry Webster and Sarah Elizabeth (Long) L.; m. Caroline Hartley, Oct. 29, 1942; children: Sherman E., Ann Frances. BS in Med. Sci., MD cum laude, Washington U., St. Louis, 1937. Diplomate Am. Bd. Otolaryngology. Practice medicine specializing in otolaryngology St. Louis, 1941—; assoc. prof. Washington U., 1941—; active staff Barnes Mo. Bapt. Hosp., 1941—, Faith Hosp., St. Louis, 1941—; cons. U.S. VA Hosp., St. Louis, 1947—. Contbr. articles to profl. jours. Served to capt. U.S. Army, 1942-46. Mem. AMA, St. Louis Med. Soc., Mo. State Med. Assn., Am. Acad. otolaryngology, Triological Soc., Ear, Nose & Throat Club. St. Louis (chmn. 1963). Republican. Mem. Christian Ch. Office: 950 Francis Pl Clayton MO 63105

LYNAM, JACK, manufacturing company executive, mechanical engineer; b. Cleve., Apr. 19, 1923; s. Thomas J. and Beatrice E. (Harvey) L.; m. Dorothy E. Correll, Apr. 19, 1951; children—Patricia, Carol, Colleen, Gale, Lee. B.S., U.S. Merchant Marine Acad., 1944. Dist. mgr. Powers Regulator Co., Pitts., 1951-68; owner, pres. Advanced Tech. Sales Inc., Cleve., 1968—, Admiral Valve Inc., Cleve., 1972-85; cons. M.E., U.S. Army, Saudia Arabia, 1980, 82. Served to lt. (s.g.) USN, 1942-46, ETO and PTO. Mem. Instrument Soc. Am. (sr.), Cleve. Engrng. Soc., ASHRAE, Am. Soc. Iron and Steel Engrs. Club: Edgewater Yacht. Lodges: Rotary, Order of Alhambra. Home: 11649 Pleasant Ridge Pl Strongsville OH 44136 Office: Advanced Tech Sales Inc 3819 Ridge Rd Cleveland OH 44144

LYNCH, BEVERLY PFEIFER, librarian; b. Moorhead, Minn., Dec. 27, 1935; d. Joseph B. and Nellie K. (Bailey) Pfeifer; m. John A. Lynch, Aug. 24, 1968. B.S., N.D. State U., 1957, L.H.D. (hon.); M.S., U. Ill., 1959; Ph.D., U. Wis., 1972. Librarian Marquette U., 1959-60, 62-63; exchange librarian Plymouth (Eng.) Pub. Library, 1960-61; asst. head serials div. Yale U. Library, 1963-65, head, 1965-68; vis. lectr. U. Wis., Madison, 1970-71, U. Chgo., 1975; exec. sec. Assn. Coll. and Research Libraries, 1972-76; univ. librarian U. Ill.-Chgo., 1977—; vis. prof. U. Tex., Austin, 1978; sr. fellow UCLA Grad. Sch. Library and Info. Sci., 1982. Author: Management Strategies for Libraries, 1985, (with Thomas J. Galvin) Priorities for Academic Libraries, 1982. Named Acad. Librarian of Yr., 1981. Mem. Acad. Mgmt., ALA (pres. 1985-86), Am. Sociol. Assn., Bibliog. Soc. Am., Ctr. for Research Libraries (chmn. 1980-81, bd. dirs.), Phi Kappa Phi. Clubs: Caxton, Grolier, Arts (Chgo.). Home: 1859 N 68th St Milwaukee WI 53213 Office: U of Ill at Chicago Univ Library 801 S Morgan St PO Box 8198 Chicago IL 60680

LYNCH, BRENDA CLARK, lawyer; b. Toledo, June 10, 1954; d. Robert Ellwood and Rosalyn Jean (Meyer) Clark; m. John Edward Lynch, Jr., Nov. 16, 1984; 1 child John Edward III. B.Ed. magna cum laude, U. Toledo, 1975, J.D. cum laude, 1978; grad. Nat. Inst. Trial Advocacy, 1983. Bar: Ohio 1978, U.S. Dist. Ct. (no. dist.) Ohio 1978, U.S. Ct. Appeals (6th cir.) 1982. Summer clk. Advs. for Basic Legal Equality, Toledo, 1976; summer assoc. Shumaker, Loop & Kendrick, Toledo, 1977; assoc. Squire, Sanders & Dempsey, Cleve., 1978-84; assoc. Porter, Wright, Morris & Arthur, Cleve., 1984—. Note and comment editor U. Toledo Law Rev., 1977-78. Mem. Ohio State Bar Assn., Cleve. Bar Assn. Democrat. Office: Porter Wright Morris & Arthur 1500 Huntington Bldg Cleveland OH 44115

LYNCH, CLIFFORD JAMES, orthpaedic surgeon; b. Fargo, N.D., Nov. 12, 1931; s. John Joseph and Louise Mae (Paulson) L.; m. Margaret Kathleen Ennielo, Sept. 9, 1961; children: Mary Louise, Karen Kathleen, Susan. BA, N.D. State U., 1952; BS, U. N.D., 1954; MD, Wake Forest U., 1956. Intern Vanderbilt U. Hosp., Nashville, 1956-57; resident N.C. Bapt. Hosp., 1957-60, Newington (Conn.) Cripled Children's Hosp., 1960-61; orthpaedic surgeon Orthopaedic Ctr., Springfield, Ill., 1963—; assoc. clin. prof. So. Ill. U. Med. Sch., Springfield, 1972—; chief orthopaedic dept. St. John's Hosp., Springfield, 1979—. Served to capt. USAF, 1961-63. Fellow Am. Acad. Orthopaedic Surgeons, Arthroscopic Assn. N.Am.; mem. Cen. Ill. Orthorpaedic Assn., AMA, Med. Am. Orthopaedic Assn. Republican. Roman Catholic. Avocations: tennis, sailing, wind surfing. Home: 2518 West Lake Dr Springfield IL 62707 Office: Orthpaedic Ctr 901 West Jefferson Springfield IL 62702

LYNCH, DENNY, food products executive; b. Youngstown, Ohio, June 27, 1952; s. John James and Veronica Anne (Rogan) L.; m. Pamela Sue Arnold, Feb. 27, 1981; children: Margaret Rose, Kevin Patrick. BA in Journalism, Ohio State U., 1975. Pub. relations dir. Shelly Berman Communicators, Columbus, Ohio, 1975-79, Stockton West Burkhart, Columbus, 1979-80; dir. pub. relations, v.p. communications Wendy's Internat., Columbus, 1980—. Fundraiser Ohio State U. Cancer Research Hosp., 1986—; bd. dirs. Buckeye Boy's Ranch, Grove City, Ohio, 1985—; Cen. Ohio Jr. Achievement, Columbus, 1986—. Served with USAFR, 1971-77. Mem. Pub. Relations Soc. Am. (Communicator of Yr. Phila. chpt. 1984), Internat. Assn. Bus. Communicators (Bronze Quill award 1985). Roman Catholic. Avocation: golf. Office: Wendys Internat Inc 4288 W Dublin Granville Rd Dublin OH 43017

LYNCH, FRANCIS MICHAEL, lawyer, accountant; b. Chgo., Oct. 19, 1956; s. Frank and Mary (Burns) L. BA in Acctg. and Bus., Loras Coll., 1978; JD, John Marshall Law Sch., 1983. Bar: Ill. 1984; CPA, Ill.; lic. real estate broker, Ill. Acct. Cobitz, Vandenberg & Fennessy, Hickory Hills, Ill., 1978-82; atty. 1st Nat. Bank Lansing, Ill., 1983, Hyatt Legal Services, Homewood, Ill., 1984-85; sole practice Evergreen Park, Ill., 1985—. Mem. Ill. Bar Assn., S.W. Bar Assn., Chgo. Bar Assn., Ill. CPA Soc. Avocations: golf, racquetball, reading. Office: 3318 W 95th St Evergreen Park IL 60642

LYNCH, SHERRY KAY, counselor; b. Topeka, Kans., Nov. 20, 1957; d. Robert Emmett and Norma Lea Lynch. BA, Randolph-Macon Woman's Coll., 1979; MS, Emporia State U., 1980; PhD, Kans. State U., 1987. Vocat. rehab. counselor Rehab. Services, Topeka, 1980-81, community program cons., 1981-86. Mem. exec. com. Sexual Assault Counseling Program, Topeka, 1983-86, recruitment coordinator, 1983-86, counselor, 1981-86; area admissions rep. Randolph-Macon Woman's Coll., Lynchburg, Va., 1981-87; counseling intern, Winthrop Coll., Rock Hill, S.C., 1986-87; with Counseling Ctr., Ripon (Wis.) Coll., 1987—. Recipient Kans. 4-H Key award Extension Service of Kans. State U., 1974; named Internat. 4-H Youth Exchange Ambassador to France, 1977. Mem. Nat. Rehab. Counseling Assn. (bd. dirs. 1982—, chairperson br. devel. subcouncil 1982-87, chairperson policy and program council 1987—), Gt. Plains Rehab. Counseling Assn. (newsletter editor 1982-85, bd. dirs. 1983-87, pres. 1984-85, sec. 1986-87), Gt. Plains Rehab. Assn. (bd. dirs. 1983-85, awards chairperson 1984-85), Kans. Rehab. Counseling Assn. (bd. dirs. 1983-86, pres. 1984-85), Kans. Rehab. Assn. (bd. dirs. 1982-85, advt. chairperson 1983-85), Topeka Rehab. Assn.

(bd. dirs. 1982-85, sec. 1982-83, pres. 1983-84), Am. Assn. Counseling and Devel., Kans. Assn. Counseling and Devel., Am. Coll. Personnel Assn., Kans. Coll. Personnel Assn., Am. Rehab. Counseling Assn. Republican. Methodist. Avocation: tennis. Home: 799 Hillside Terrace #9 Ripon WI 54971 Office: Ripon Coll Counseling Ctr PO Box 248 Ripon WI 54971

LYNCH, TWINK, theater executive, consultant, trainer; b. Washington, May 8, 1934; d. Austin Francis Sr. and Gertrude Rita (MacBride) Canfield; m. John Anthony Lynch, Nov. 26, 1960; children: Mark Andrew, Christopher Michael, Nancy Maureen, Gregory Patrick. BA in English, Cath. U. Am., 1955, MA in Speech Therapy, 1961; MA in Theater, U. Kans., 1971, PhD in Community Theater, 1981. Box office asst. Olney Theatre, Md., 1956, box office mgr., 1957; clk., typist United Clay Products, Washington, 1957-58; speech therapist pub. schs., Prince George County, Md., 1959-61; instr. theater Washburn U., Topeka, 1968, pub. speaking, 1974; instr. Pa. State U. Ind. Study, University Park, 1978—; exec. dir. Assn. Kans. Theatre, Topeka, 1979-86; dir. Topeka Civic Theatre, 1971-77, 83-86, pres. 1976-77, 85-86, adminstrv. dir., 1986—, dir. Kans. Citizens for Arts, Topeka, 1985-86. Workshop leader numerous state, regional, nat. theater orgns., 1977—; cons., trainer various community theaters, 1979—. Author: (correspondence course text) Volunteer and Staff Development in Community Theatre, 1981; editor correspondence courses Pa. State U., 1981—. Officer Whitson Sch. PTA, Topeka, 1968-69; dir. Performing Arts for Children, Topeka, 1971-73, Goals for Topeka, 1972-74, Kans. Alliance Arts Edn., Topeka, 1979-83, YWCA, Topeka, 1982-83, Topeka Pub. Schs. Found., 1986—. Recipient Topeka Civic Theatre Renna Hunter award, 1968, 70; named Outstanding Community Vol., Topeka Jr. League, 1973, to Hall of Fame, Assn. Kans. Theatre, 1987. Mem. Am. Assn. Community Theatre (pres. 1984—), Am. Theatre Assn. (bd. dirs. 1984-85, Disting. Woman award 1977), Nat. Assn. Local Arts Agys. (keynoter 1985), Assn. Coll., Univ. and Community Arts Adminstrs., Theatre Trustees Am., Assn. Vol. Adminstrs. (vol.), Assn. Vol. Action Scholars. Avocations: travel, musical events. Office: 534 1/2 N Kansas Ave Topeka KS 66608

LYNE, EVERETT DENNIS, orthopaedic surgeon; b. Jersey City, Dec. 21, 1936; s. Everett and Ruth Marie (Steffans) L.; m. Dorothy Evans, June 18, 1961; children: Paisley Ann, Deirdre Elizabeth, Evans Daniel. BA, Colgate U., 1957; MD, Johns Hopkins U., 1961. Dir. multidisciplinary clinic Children's Meml. Hosp., Chgo., 1970-73, attending orthopaedic physician, 1970-74; head div. pediatric orthopaedic surgery Henry Ford Hosp., Detroit, 1974—, physician trustee, 1981-84. Contbr. numerous articles to profl. jours. Bd. dirs. Friends of the Fair Com., Detroit, 1986—. Served to comdr. USNR, 1968-70. Fellow AMA, Am. Acad. Pediatrics (sec.-treas. 1981-82, pres. orthopaedic sect. 1982-84), Am. Acad. Cerebral Palsy, Pediatric Orthopaedic Soc. (pres. study group 1980-81); mem. John's Hopkins Club. Clubs: Bloomfield Open Hunt (Mich.); Prismatic, Pithotomy. Office: Henry Ford Hosp 2799 W Grand Blvd Detroit MI 48202

LYNG, EDWARD JOSEPH, vending machine service executive; b. Chgo., Oct. 8, 1934; s. Richard Patrick and Rose Clare (Krug) L.; m. Stephanie Kroeck, Jan. 14, 1961 (dec. Oct. 1977); children: Dorsey, Jennifer, Kelley, Allison. BA, Loyola U., Chgo., 1961; MBA, U. Chgo., 1977. Sales mgr. Canteen Corp., Nutley, N.J., 1963-64; ops. mgr. Canteen Corp., St. Petersburg, Fla., 1964-65, Houston, 1966-68; gen. mgr. Canteen Corp., Phila., 1968-71; pres., chief exec. officer Lyng Canteen Service Co., Elgin, Ill., 1972—. Republican. Roman Catholic. Club: Inverness (Ill.) Golf. Lodge: Rotary. Avocations: golf, travel. Home: 1328 E Sanborn Dr Palatine IL 60067 Office: Lyng Canteen Service Co 972 N McLean Blvd Elgin IL 60120

LYNHAM, C(HARLES) RICHARD, ceramics company executive; b. Easton, Md., Feb. 24, 1942; s. John Cameron and Anna Louise (Lynch) L.; m. Sept. 19, 1964; children: Jennifer Beth, Thomas Richard. BME, Cornell U., 1965; MBA with distinction, Harvard U., 1969. Sales mgr. Nat. Carbide Die Co., McKeesport, Pa., 1969-71; v.p. sales Sinter-Met Corp., North Brunswick, N.J., 1971-72; sr. mgmt. analyst Am. Cyanamid Co., Wayne, N.J., 1972-74; gen. mgr. ceramics and additives div. Foseco Inc., Cleve., 1974-77, dir. mktg. steel mill products group, 1977-79; pres., chief exec. officer Exomet, Inc. subs. Foseco, Inc., Conneaut, Ohio, 1979-81, Fosbel Inc. subs. Foseco, Inc., Cleve., 1981-82; gen. mgr. splty. ceramics group Ferro Corp., Cleve., 1982-84, group v.p. splty. ceramics, 1984—; bd. dirs. Hi-Temp, Inc., Cleve., 1979—. Patentee teapot ladle, desulphurization of metals. Chmn. Medina (Ohio) Cable TV Commn. Served to lt. C.E., U.S. Army, 1965-67. Decorated Bronze Star with one oak leaf cluster. Mem. Am. Soc. Metals, Am. Ceramic Soc., Iron and Steel Soc., AIME, Am. Soc. Iron and Steel Engrs., Cornell U. Alumni Council, Cornell Alumni Class 1963 (past v.p., past pres.), Cornell Assn. Class Officers (pres.), Cornell Alumni Assn. (bd. dirs.). Republican. Congregationalist. Clubs: Chippewa Yacht (commodore 1982), Cornell Club of N.E. Ohio (v.p. 1985—). Avocations: sailing, genealogy. Home: 970 Hickory Grove Medina OH 44256 Office: Ferro Corp One Erieview Plaza Cleveland OH 44114

LYNN, MICHAEL EDWARD, III, professional football team executive; b. Scranton, Pa., May 18, 1936; s. Robert Norman and Gertrude (Smith) L.; m. Jorja Swaney, July 12, 1967; children: Louisa, Robert, Michael Edward IV, Lucia. Student, Pace U. Mgr. Dixiemart-Carondolet, Inc., Memphis, 1965-67; pres. Mid South Sports, Inc., Memphis, 1967-74; v.p., gen. mgr. Minn. Vikings Profl. Football Team, 1974—; founder East-West All Am. Basketball Game, 1968, Mid South Prodn. Co., 1970; chief exec. officer Memphis Am. Basketball Team, 1970. Founder Morris County Theatre League and Hightstown (N.J.) Little Theatre Group, 1961. Served with AUS, 1955-58. Roman Catholic. Office: Minnesota Vikings 9520 Viking Dr Eden Prairie MN 55344 *

LYNN, PATRICIA ANN, manufacturing company executive; b. Eau Claire, Wis., Dec. 11, 1939; d. Edward A. and Catherine J. (Jones) O'Connor; m. Jack A. Lynn, Aug. 31, 1963; children—Michael E., Cynthia C. Cert. bus. law, Upper Wabash Vocat. Coll., 1973, cert. acctg., 1974. Sec., Ind. Glass Products, Wabash, 1960-61; bookkeeper/receptionist Graycon Tools, Wabash, 1961-62, corp. sec., 1963-77, pres., 1978-81; v.p. Graycon div. Diehl Machines, Wabash, 1982—. Mem. Wabash Planning Commn., 1983—; Democrat precinct committeeperson, 1980—; mem. Wabash Community Service Orgn., 1983—; chair North Central Pvt. Industry Council, 1984. Mem. Wabash County Mgmt. Club (pres. 1982), Wabash C. of C. (treas. 1981), Am. Legion Aux. Democrat. Roman Catholic. Avocations: camping; gardening; reading. Home: 141 E Sheridan Dr Wabash IN 46992 Office: 981 S Wabash St Wabash IN 46992

LYON, JAMES CYRIL, chemical society executive; b. Eldorado, Ill., May 14, 1937; s. James S. and Helen D. (Podrasky) L.; m. Sandra K. Lasseter, June 14, 1958; children: Lori Anne, Lisa J. BS, So. Ill. U., Carbondale, 1959; MS, No. Ill. U., DeKalb, 1967. Tchr. English, coach Bremen High Sch., Midlothian, Ill., 1959-61, Maine Twp. High Sch. East, Park Ridge, Ill., 1961-64; bus. mgr., treas. Nat. Council Tchrs. of English, Urbana, Ill., 1964-71; exec. dir. Am. Oil Chemists' Soc., Champaign, Ill., 1971—; bd. dirs. Champaign-Urbana Conv. and Visitors Bur., 1984-85, past pres., bd. dirs. Champaign County Hist. Mus., 1975-81. Mem. Am. Soc. Assn. Execs., Ill. Soc. Assn. Execs., Found. for Internat. Meetings (bd. dirs. 1982), Phi Delta Kappa, Kappa Delta Pi. Republican. Club: Champaign Country. Lodge: Rotary (com. chmn. Champaign chpt. 1978—). Avocations: travel, reading, golf. Home: 2118 Robert Dr Champaign IL 61821 Office: Am Oil Chemists Soc PO Box 5037 Champaign IL 61820

LYON, PATRICIA JUNE, teacher; b. Upland, Ind., Aug. 27, 1942; s. Donald Howard Lyon and Alice Lucille (Graves) Holmes; 1 child, Jason Marshall. BS in Edn., Ball State U., 1964; MS in Edn., St. Francis Coll., 1969. Tchr. Arcola Sch, Ft. Wayne, Ind., 1964—. Active Boy Scouts Am.; bd. dirs. Arcola (Ind.) PTO, 1984—. Mem. NEA, AAUW, Delta Kappa Gamma. Avocations: reading, playing organs. Office: Arcola Sch 13119 Coldwater Rd Fort Wayne IN 46825

LYON, WAYNE BARTON, corporate executive; b. Dayton, Oct. 26, 1932; m. Maryann L., 1961; children: Karen, Craig, Blair. BChemE, U. Cin., 1955; MBA in Mktg., U. Chgo., 1969. Registered profl. engr., Mich. Tech. rep. Union Carbide, Chgo., 1955-62; product devel. mgr., v.p. bus. devel. Ill. Tool Works, Chgo., 1962-72; group v.p., exec. v.p., pres. Masco Corp., Taylor, Mich., 1972—; bd. dirs. Emco Ltd., London, Ont., Can., Mech. Tech. Inc., Latham, N.Y., 1973, Masco Industries Inc., Taylor, Mich., Mfrs. Nat. Corp.; lectr. AMA. Patentee in field. Lectr. AMA Seminars. Bd. govs., trustees Cranbrook Kingswood Schs., Bloomfield Hills, Mich., 1984—, Orchard Lake Country Club, Mich., 1985—. Served to capt. U.S. Army, 1955-63. Clubs: Fairlane (Dearborn, Mich.); Renaissance (Detroit), Detroit Athletic, Orchard Lake Country; Bloomfield Hills Country. Office: Masco Corp 21001 Van Born Rd Taylor MI 48180

LYONS, DOROTHY A., physician; b. Erie, Pa., Dec. 5, 1953; d. Richard C. and Norma L. (Wright) L.; m. Glenn W. Heffner Jr., Feb. 1, 1985. BA, Sweet Briar Coll., 1975; MD, Hahnemann Med. Coll., 1979. Diplomate Am. Acad. Neurology. Intern Cleve. Clinic, 1979-80, resident in neurology, 1980-83; mem. multispecialty group Vero Beach, Fla., 1983-84; mem. single specialty group Washington, 1984-86; pvt. practice neurology Willoughby, Ohio, 1986—. Mem. AMA, Ohio State Med. Assn., Lake County Med. Soc. Republican. Roman Catholic. Office: 36100 Euclid Ave Suite 280 Willoughby OH 44094

LYONS, J. ROLLAND, civil engr.; b. Cedar Rapids, Iowa, Apr. 27, 1909; s. Neen T. and Goldie N. (Hill) L.; B.S., U. Iowa, 1933; m. Mary Jane Doht, June 10, 1924; children—Marlene Lyons Sparks, Sharon Lyons Hutson, Lynn Lyons Panichi. Jr. hwy. engr. Works Projects Adminstrn. field engr. Dept. Transp., State Ill., Peoria, 1930-31, civil engr. I-IV Central Office, Springfield, 1934-53, civil engr. V, 1953-66, municipal sect. chief, civil engr. VI, 1966-72. Civil Def. radio officer Springfield and Sangamon County (Ill.) Civil Def. Agy., 1952—. Recipient Meritorious Service award, Am. Assn. State Hwy. Ofcls., 1968; 25 Yr. Career Service award, State Ill., 1966; Certificate Appreciation, Ill. Municipal League, 1971. Registered profl. engr., Ill.; registered land surveyor, Ill. Mem. Ill. Assn. State Hwy. Engrs., State Ill. Employees Assn., Am. Pub. Works Assn., Am. Assn. State Hwy. Ofcls., Amateur Trapshooters Assn. Clubs: K.C., Sangamon Valley Radio; Lakewood Golf and Country. Address: 3642 Lancaster Rd Springfield IL 62703

LYONS, JAMES D., reporter; b. N.Y.C., Sept. 4, 1955; s. James W. and Dorothy M. (Lang) L.; m. Julia Ann Schulten, Feb. 19, 1987. BS in Journalism, U. Colo., 1977. Reporter Sta. KAMR-TV, Amarillo, Tex., 1978-79; bur. chief Sta. KCRG-TV, Cedar Rapids, Iowa, 1979-83; investigative reporter Sta. KCRG-TV, Cedar Rapids, 1983-85; investigative producer Sta. KTUL-TV, Tulsa, 1985-86, Sta. WJW-TV, Cleve., 1986—. Producer, reporter (TV news documentary) The Policy Raiders, 1984, Investigative Reporters and Editors award; producer (TV news documentary) Tulsa's Golden Missionary, 1986, DuPont-Columbia award. Recipient Award for Young Journalists, Livingston Found., 1986, Disting. Service award Soc. Prof. Journalists, 1987. Mem. Investigative Reporters & Editors, Aircraft Owners and Pilots Assn. Avocations: sailing, flying, photography, travel. Office: WJW-TV 5800 S Marginal Rd Cleveland OH 44103

LYONS, ORVILLE RICHARD, II, insurance executive; b. Columbus, Ohio, June 4, 1942; s. Orville Richard and Virginia B. (Neff) L.; m. Gloria Jean Thompson, May 6, 1967; children: Wendy Marie, Amy Elizabeth. MS Fin. Services, The Am. Coll., 1985. CLU; chartered fin. cons. Auto underwriter Motorists Mut., Columbus, 1964-68; life underwriter Motorists Life Ins. Co., Columbus, 1968-82, v.p. life ops., 1982—. Bd. dirs. Westerville (Ohio) Parks and Recreation, 1982. Served to staff sgt. U.S. Army, 1964-70. Mem. Am. Soc. CLU's, Columbus Chpt. CLU's (trustee 1987-88), Ohio Home Office Life and Health Underwriters Assn. (pres. 1981-82). Democrat. Roman Catholic. Avocations: tennis, basketball, running. Home: 1165 Starbuck Ct Westerville OH 43081 Office: Motorists Life Ins Co 471 E Broad St Columbus OH 43215

LYONS, ROBERT HUGH, manufacturing executive; b. Evergreen Park, Ill., June 7, 1949; s. Robert Hugh and June (Walz) L.; m. Carol Lynn Jewett, Aug. 14, 1971; children: Stephanie Lynn, Andrew Hale. BSEE, Purdue U., 1971, MS in Mgmt., 1979. Mgmt. asst. Ind. Bell Telephone, Indpls., 1971-72; engr. Newport News (Va.) Shipbuilding, 1972-76; sr. engr. Booz, Allen & Hamilton, Bethesda, Md., 1976-78; assoc. strategy Hillenbrand Industries, Batesville, Ind., 1979-81, scheduling systems mgr., 1981-85; mfg. cons. Advanced Systems, Inc., Arlington Heights, Ill., 1986—. Named Hon. Hoosier Scholar State of Ind., 1967. Mem. IEEE, Soc. Mfg. Engrs., Am. Prodn. and Inventory Control Soc., Theta Tau, Beta Gamma Sigma. Methodist. Home: 15060 Clover Ln Libertyville IL 60048 Office: Advanced Systems Inc 155 E Algonquin Rd Arlington Heights IL 60005

LYONS, THOMAS FRANCIS, management educator; b. Detroit, Oct. 5, 1937; s. Edward Coleburke and Nell (Hamilton) L.; m. Ann Liu, June 22, 1963; children—Kathleen Liu, William Francis. B.B.A., U. Mich., 1959, M.B.A., 1960, M.A., 1964, Ph.D., 1967. Lic. psychologist, Ohio. Asst. prof. Iowa State U., Ames, 1967-70; research assoc. U. Mich. Sch. Medicine, Ann Arbor, 1970-72; asst. prof. Case Western Res. U., Cleve., 1972-74; sr. research assoc. Med. Sch., U. Mich., Ann Arbor, 1974-78; assoc. prof., chmn. dept. mgmt./mktg. Sch. Mgmt., U. Mich.-Dearborn, 1978-84, prof., chmn. dept. mgmt./mktg., 1984-85, prof., assoc. dean, 1985—; vis. prof., U. Hawaii, 1984-85. Served with U.S. Army, 1960-62. Mem. Am. Psychol. Assn. (James McKeen Cattell award 1968), Acad. of Mgmt., Am. Soc. Tng. and Devel., Sigma Xi. Roman Catholic. Author: Nursing Attitudes and Turnover, 1968; co-author: Method of Evaluation and Improving Ambulatory Medical Care, 1980; co-author: Evaluation and Improving Personal Medical Care Quality, 1976; contbr. articles to profl. jours. Home: 2155 Blaney St Ann Arbor MI 48103 Office: U Mich 4901 Evergreen St Dearborn MI 48128

LYONS, TIMOTHY JOHN, accountant; b. Chgo.; s. James Joseph and Josephine (Johnson) L.; m. Laura Grier Hood, Dec. 10, 1984. BS in Accountancy with highest honors, U. Ill., 1983. CPA, Ill. Mem. staff, sr. auditor Selden, Fox & Assocs., Oak Brook, Ill., 1983-85; supervising sr. acct. The Balcor Co., Skokie, Ill., 1985—. Mem. Am. Inst. CPA's (Elijah Watt Sells award 1984), Ill. CPA Soc. (Bronze medal). Home: 9244 Newcastle Morton Grove IL 60053 Office: The Balcor Co 4849 Golf Rd Skokie IL 60077

LYONS, WILLIAM DREWRY, lawyer; b. Cresco, Iowa, Oct. 10, 1927; s. Gerald Edward and Florence (Drewry) L.; m. Elizabeth K. Kane, July 18, 1953; children—Catherine L., William Drewry Jane L., Judd H., Mary C. B.S.L., U. Minn., 1950, J.D., 1952, C.P.C.U., 1962. Bar: Minn. 1952, Iowa 1952, Nebr. 1974. Sole practice, Cresco, Iowa, 1952-56; asst. supt. claims Nat. Indemnity Co., Omaha, 1956-58; br. claim mgr. Nat. Indemnity Co., St. Paul, 1958-71, v.p., claim mgr., gen. counsel, Omaha, 1971—; v.p. Nat. Fire & Marine Ins. Co., Columbia Ins. Co.; dir. Gateway Underwriters Agy., Inc., Home and Automobile Ins. Co., Nat. Indemnity Co., Nat. Fire & Marine Ins. Co., Excess and Surplus Lines Claim Assn. Served with USN, 1945-46. Mem. Nebr. Bar Assn., Omaha Bar Assn., Internat. Assn. Ins. Counsel, Central Claims Assn., Excess and Surplus Lines Assn., Nebr. Claims Assn., ABA. Democrat. Roman Catholic. Home: 6405 Country Squire Ln Omaha NE 68152 Office: 4016 Farnam St Omaha NE 68131

LYTAL, PATRICIA LOU, teacher; b. Ft. Wayne, Ind., Sept. 11, 1936; d. George F. and Geraldine (Beck) Heingartner; m. Wayne Earl Lytal; Sept. 16, 1956; children: Michael Wayne, Patrick Allen, Terry Lee, Shawn David. Tchr. oil painting Ft. Wayne Park Sch. Bd, 1980-83, Ind. U.- Purdue U. Continuing Edn., Ft. Wayne, 1986—; ind. tchr. oil painting Ft. Wayne, 1976—. Artist: (muriels) Diehm Mus. Natural History, 1981. Mem. Brown County Art Soc., Park County Art Soc. Democrat. Avocations: China painting, silverpoint drawing, fishing, swimming, traveling. Home and Office: 1625 N Glendale Dr Fort Wayne IN 46804

LYTLE, PAULA JUNE, forensic serologist; b. Detroit, June 15, 1952; d. Nathaniel and Thelma T.L. (Heard) L. BS, Detroit Inst. Tech, 1974. Registered med. technologist. Jr. med. technologist Hosp. Dept. City of Detroit, 1974-75, sr. med. technologist, 1975-77; forensic serologist Detroit Police Dept., 1977—. Mem. adult choir St. James Bapt. Ch., Bd. Christian Edn., Bible Acad. Mem. Am. Soc. Clin. Pathologists (assoc.). Democrat. Avocations: sewing, designing millinery, traveling, gardening. Home: 18603 Joann Detroit MI 48205 Office: Detroit Police Dept Crime Lab 1300 Beaubien Room 647 Detroit MI 48226

LYTLE, ROGER DWIGHT, personnel executive; b. Lincoln, Nebr., May 30, 1942; s. J. Dwight and Rowena May (Seeley) L.; m. Barbara Joan Bosse, June 30, 1965; children: Jeffrey, Douglas. BBA, U. Nebr., 1965. Mktg. rep. IBM Corp., Mpls., 1965-68; systems planning mgr. Target Stores, Mpls., 1968-71, mgr. organizational planning, 1971-73, regional personnel ops. mgr., 1973-78; dir. personnel Fabri-Ctrs. of Am., Beachwood, Ohio, 1978-84, v.p. human resources, 1984—. Bd. dirs. 70001, St. Louis, 1976-78; chmn. Personnel Planning Commn., Manchester, Mo., 1977-78. Served to 1st lt. USAR, 1966-72. Republican. Episcopalian. Avocations: piano, golf. Home: 2403 Cambridge Dr Hudson OH 44236 Office: Fabri Ctrs of Am Inc 23550 Commerce Park Rd Beachwood OH 44122

LYTTLE, BRADFORD JANES, political scientist; b. Chgo., Nov. 20, 1927; s. Charles Harold and Marcia Taft (Janes) Lyttle; m. Mary Suzuki, Dec., 1967 (div. 1969). BA in Philosophy, Earlham Coll., 1949; MA in English Lit., U. Chgo., 1951; MA in Polit. Sci., U. Ill., Chgo., 1976. Political activist, coordinator numerous peace walks, anti Vietnam war demonstrations. various locations, 1952-74. Author: You Come With Naked Hands: The Story of the San Francisco to Moscow Walk for Peace, 1962; (booklets) National Defense Through Nonviolent Resistance, 1958, Washington Action, 1969, May Ninth, 1970, The Apocalypse Equation, 1982, The Flaw in Deterrence, 1982; also numerous articles. Imprisoned for mil. draft refusal, 1954-55. Avocations: wood and metal working, bicycling, music, tennis, photography. Home: 5729 S Dorchester Ave Chicago IL 60637

MA, YU, plant molecular geneticist; b. Heng-Yang, Hu-Nan, Republic of China, Nov. 29, 1942; came to U.S., 1970; s. Tien-Ling and I-Fen (Hu) Ma; m. Yu-Heng Chu, Dec. 29, 1973; children: Grace, Alexander. BS, Nat. Taiwan U., Taipei, 1966; MS, U. Wis., 1973, PhD, 1977. Exec. sec. Biol. Research Ctr., Taipei, 1967-70; postdoctoral researcher U. Wis., 1977-81; research scientist Agrigenetics Corp., Madison, 1981-85, Agrigenetics Advanced Research Corp., Madison, 1986—. Contbr. articles to profl. jours. Mem. am. Soc. Agronomy, Genetics Soc. Am., Maize Genetics Corp., The Am. Soc. Plant Physiologists. Avocations: photography, music, stamp collecting, woodcraft. Home: 4118 Saint Clair St Madison WI 53711

MABEE, BRUCE ORLAND, organizational development management consultant; b. Chgo., Sept. 16, 1950; s. Orland Francis and Sophia (Grygiel) M. BFA, U. Ill., 1973; MS, George Williams Coll., Downers Grove, Ill., 1985. Youth devel. specialist Crisis Care Ctr., Danville, Ill., 1973; reporter, distbn. mgr. Beacon Newspapers, Bolingbrook, Ill., 1974-75, mng. editor, 1980; coordinator edn. services Village of Downers Grove, 1976-79; orgn. devel. cons. Harris Trust and Savs. Bank, Chgo., 1980-86, mgr. personal trust forums, 1986-87; cons. organizational develop., team problem solving and planning 1987—; bd. dirs./treas. Whirlwind Performance Co., Chgo. Com. vol. United Way, Chgo., 1981—, Hinsdale, Ill., 1982—, Crusade of Mercy, Chgo., 1987—. Recipient Outstanding Vol. Service award United Way Am., 1983. Office: 5138 Elmwood Pl Downers Grove IL 60515

MACADAMS, RICHARD JOSEPH, consulting and industrial process engineer; b. N.Y.C., Mar. 27, 1925; s. Robert John and Josephine Theresa (Ziegler) MacA.; m. Gerry M. Mitchell, Oct. 23, 1948; children—Monica MacAdams Smith, Michael R., Melanie R. B.S. in Mech. Engring., Lehigh U., 1946. Profl. engr., Ohio, Mich., Pa., N.Y., Okla., Fla. Plant engr. Pure Oil Co., Toledo, 1946-60; research and devel. tech. supr. Allied Chem. Plastics Div., Tonawanda, N.Y., 1960-62, project mgr., Toledo, 1962-65; div. mgr. SSOE, Inc., Toledo, 1965—, v.p., 1973-85, pres. mfg. process div., 1985—; sec. Tech. Found. Toledo, 1984—. Chmn. Bedford Twp. Plan Commn., Mich., 1978—; mem. Bedford Twp. Republican Club, 1960—. Mem. Nat. Soc. Profl. Engrs. (sec. Toledo 1968-70), Am. Inst. Chem. Engrs., Tech. Soc. Toledo (pres. 1980-81), Engr.-of-Yr. award 1985), Toledo C. of C. Republican. Roman Catholic. Club: Rotary. Home: 7066 Edinburgh Dr Lambertville MI 48144 Office: SSOE Inc 1001 Madison Ave Toledo OH 43624

MACAL, ZDENEK, conductor. Music director Milwaukee Symphony Orchestra. Office: Milw Symphony Orch 212 W Wisconsin Ave Milwaukee WI 53203 *

MACAULAY, JACQUELINE, lawyer; b. Racine, Wis., Aug. 2, 1932; d. John Robbins and Helen Converse (Huguenin) Ramsey; m. Stewart Macaulay, Mar. 27, 1954; children: Monica, John, Philip, Laura. BA, Stanford U., 1955; MS, U. Wis., 1962, PhD, 1965, JD, 1983. Researcher, lectr. U. Wis., Madison, 1964-70, 73-75; lectr. SUNY, Buffalo, 1973-74; sole practice Madison, 1983—. Active feminist issues, Madison, 1974-85. Address: 222 S Bedford Madison WI 53703

MACCANN, RICHARD DYER, film study educator; b. Wichita, Kans., Aug. 20, 1920; s. Horace Shores and Marion (Dyer) MacC.; m. Donnarae Charlotte Thompson, Oct. 12, 1957. A.B., U. Kans., 1940; M.A., Stanford U., 1942; Ph.D. in Polit. Sci., Harvard U., 1951. Staff corr. The Christian Sci. Monitor, Los Angeles, 1951-57; asst. prof. cinema U. So. Calif., 1957-62; screenwriter MGM-TV and John Houseman Prodns., Los Angeles, 1963-64; producer Subscription TV, Inc., Santa Monica, Calif., 1964; TV producer Los Angeles County Schs., 1964-65; assoc. prof. speech and journalism U. Kans., 1965-69, prof., 1969-70; vis. prof. fine arts and visual studies Harvard U., summer 1967; prof. broadcasting and film dept. communication and theater arts U. Iowa, 1970-86, vis. emeritus prof., 1987—; adviser Nat. Film Prodn. Ctr., Republic of Korea, 1963; mem. steering com., lectr. Aspen Film Conf., 1963, 64; weekly broadcaster film criticism KANU-FM, U. Kans., 1966-68; writer-producer-host The Quiet Channel, U. Iowa Cable Channel 28, Iowa City, 1983, American Silent Film, 1984. Served with AUS 1942-45. NEH sr. fellow, 1973; co-adminstr. Rockefeller Found. grantee, 1973-76; Jerome Found. grantee, 1977. Mem. Com. Constl. System, Univ. Film and Video Assn., Soc. Cinema Studies, Authors Guild, Writers Guild Am., Phi Beta Kappa. Democrat. Christian Scientist. Author: Hollywood in Transition, 1962, Film and Society, 1964, Film: A Montage of Theories, 1966, The People's Films, 1973, The New Film Index, 1975, Cinema Examined, 1982, American Movies: The First 30 Years, The First Tycoons, 1987, The First Film Makers, 1987. Editor: Cinema Jour., 1967-76; (play) Senator-at-Large, 1981; producer: Degas: Master of Motion, 1960; Murder at Best, 1981; contbr. articles to profl. jours.; contbr. poetry to Harpers Mag., Saturday Rev., Christian Science Monitor. Home: 717 Normandy Dr Iowa City IA 52240 Office: U Iowa Dept Broadcasting and Film Iowa City IA 52242

MACCARTHY, JOHN PETERS, bank executive; b. St. Louis, Apr. 6, 1933; s. John D. and Ruth (Peters) MacC.; m. Talbot Leland, June 21, 1958; children: John Leland, Talbot Peters. B.A., Princeton U., 1954; LL.B., Harvard U., 1959. Bar: Mo. 1959. Ptnr. Bryan, Cave, McPheeters & McRoberts, St. Louis, 1959-68; sec. Centerre Trust Co., St. Louis, 1969-72, exec. v.p., dir., 1972-75, pres., chief operating officer, 1975-79; chief exec. officer Centerre Trust Co., St. Louis, 1979-84; dir. Centerre Trust Co., St. Louis, 1979—; pres., chief exec. officer Centerre Bank Nat. Assn., St. Louis, 1984—; vice chmn., sec. Centerre Bancorp., St. Louis, 1975—; pres. Centerre Bancorp.; dir. Ocean Drilling & Exploration Co., New Orleans, Centerre Bank, St. Louis, Union Electric Co., St. Louis, Bank Bldg. and Equipment Corp. Pres. bd. trustees St. Louis Country Day Sch., 1977-79; pres. emeritus bd. commrs. St. Louis Art Mus., 1981—. Served to lt. USN, 1954-56. Republican. Episcopalian. Clubs: St. Louis Country (pres. 1982), Bogey (sec. 1982—); Noonday (St. Louis) (pres. 1977). Office: Centerre Bank Nat Assn 1 Centerre Plaza Saint Louis MO 63101

MACCOY, DOUGLAS MAIDLOW, veterinary surgeon; b. Washington, Aug. 15, 1947; s. Edgar Milton and Charlotte (Maidlow) MacC. B.S. in Animal Scis., Purdue U., 1969; D.V.M. magna cum laude, U. Ga., 1973. Diplomate Am. Coll. Vet. Surgeons. Intern, N.Y. State Coll. Vet. Medicine, Cornell U., Ithaca, N.Y., 1973-74, surg. resident, 1974-76, asst. prof. surgery, 1976-82; dir. avian rehab. project Coll. Vet. Medicine, U. Ill., Urbana, 1982—, asst. prof. surgery, 1982—. Mem. AVMA, Am. Animal Hosp. Assn., Assn. Avian Veterinarians, Vet. Cancer Soc., Am. Assn. Vet. Med. Records Adminstrn., Am. Assn. Vet Clinicians, Am. Motorcyclist Assn., Nat. Riflemans Assn., Raptor Research Found., Sigma Xi, Omega Tau Sigma, Phi Zeta. Home and Office: 1008 W Hazelwood Dr Urbana IL 61801

MACDONALD, CHARIE, restaurateur; b. Chgo., Sept. 9, 1935; d. George Gale and Charlotte (Dittmar) Roberson; m. James Daniel MacDonald, Apr. 8, 1961; children: Mary, David, Murphy. BA, Manhattenville Coll., 1957. Conv. sales rep. Delta Airlines, Chgo., 1957-61; mgr. Charles Martine Imports, Chgo., 1977-79; mgr., cook Foodstuffs, Glencoe, Ill., 1979-81; chef, owner Beautiful Food, Winnetka, Ill., 1982—. Leader Winnetka Girl Scout Troop 12, 1975-79. Mem. Internat. Assn. Cooking Profls., Soc. Am. Cuisine, Chgo. Culinary Guild (founding pres. 1980—). Republican. Roman Catholic. Avocations: cooking, gardening, traveling. Office: Beautiful Food 1872 Johns Dr Glenview IL 60025

MACDONALD, GERALD V., banker; b. 1938; married. B.A., U. Mich., 1960. Comml. loan officer Manufacturers Nat. Bank, Detroit, 1960—, 2d v.p., 1970-75, v.p., 1975-80, pres., chief exec. officer, 1980—, dir.; pres., chief exec. officer Manufacturers Nat. Bank, Southfield, Mich., 1980-82, pres., 1982—. Office: Mfrs Nat Bank of Detroit Mfrs Bank Tower Detroit MI 48243 *

MAC DONALD, JOHN JOSEPH, insurance company executive; b. N.Y.C., June 21, 1927; s. William C. and Kathleen M. (Howley) MacD.; m. Dolores Allen, June 26, 1954; children: Margaret Ellen, William C., Kathleen M., John. B.S. in Bus. Adminstrn, Lehigh U., 1951. With Gen. Motors Corp., 1951—, gen. asst. treas., sec. fin. com., 1973, exec. com., 1973-76; exec. v.p. Motors Ins. Corp., N.Y.C., 1976-77; pres. Motors Ins. Corp., 1977—. Mgr. Mich. Efficiency Task Force, 1976. Served with U.S. Army, 1945-46. Mem. Fin. Execs. Inst., Am. Freedom Train Found. Ind. (dir.), Phi Beta Kappa, Alpha Kappa Psi, Beta Gamma Sigma, Omicron Delta Kappa, Pi Gamma Mu. Roman Catholic. Club: Tuxedo. Office: Motors Ins Corp 3044 W Grand Blvd Detroit MI 48202 *

MACDONALD, MARY CATHERINE, data processing coordinator, systems analyst, programmer; b. Midland, Mich., Oct. 1, 1958. A.S. in Bus. Studies, Delta Coll., 1978; B.S. in Bus. Adminstrn., Central Mich. U., 1980. Student cons. physics dept. Central Mich. U., Mt. Pleasant, 1979-80; asst. registrar Mercy Coll., Detroit, 1980-82; coordinator data systems Archdiocese of Detroit, 1982—. Mem. Data Processing Mgmt. Assn. Office: Archdiocese of Detroit 1234 Washington Blvd Detroit MI 48226

MACDONALD, ROBERT RIORDAN, radiologist; b. Okmulgee, Okla., June 11, 1935; s. Robert Riordan Sr. and Ola (Anthony) MacD.; m. Mary Katherine Byrne, Sept. 22, 1962; children: Alison, Mary, Robert III, Amy. BS, St. Louis U., 1957, MD, 1961. Diplomate Nat. Bd. Med. Examiners, Am. Bd. Radiology. Intern St. Louis U. Hosps., 1961-62, resident in radiology, 1962-64; chief resident in radiology St. Louis U. Group of Hosps., 1964-65, St. Louis City Hosp., 1965-66; asst. in radiology St. Louis U. Sch. Medicine, 1965, instr. radiology, 1970, asst. clin. prof. radiology, 1982; staff radiologist St. John's Mercy Med. Ctr., St. Louis, 1968—. Mem. adv. bd. St. Louis County Dept. Community Health and Med. Care, 1983—, chmn., 1986, 87. Served to capt. USAF, 1966-68. Fellow Am. Coll. Radiology; mem. AMA (participant leadership conf. 1979-81, mem. Mo. del. to ann. meeting 1981, Mo. del. to interim session 1981, alt. del. 1983—), Greater St. Louis Soc. Radiologists (membership com. 1975), Mo. Radiol. Soc. (bd. dirs. 1985—), St. Louis Met. Med. Soc. (grievance com. 1977-82, chmn. 1982, chmn. program com. 1980, mem. Beaumont pilgrimage com. 1978-81, exec. com. 1977-81, elections com. 1979-81, chmn. 1980, mem. endowments com. 1987—, nominating com. 1982-84, chmn. 1982, mem. pub. policy and pub. relations com. 1982-83, cost effectiveness com. 1982, long range planning com. 1982, chmn. membership devel. com. 1982-84, mem. awards and honors com. 1983-85, councilor 1975, sec. 1977-79, pres.-elect 1980, pres. 1981), St. Louis Soc. Med. and Sci. Edn. (tel-med com. 1977-79, chmn. 1980, mem. endowments com. 1987—, bd. trustees 1975, 80, sec. 1976-79, chmn. bd. trustees 1981), Mo. State Med. Assn. (constitution and bylaws com. 1979, chmn. 1908-81, mem. long range planning com. 1985—, chmn. 1985—, del. to House 1976—, councilor 1981-83, v.p. 1984), St. Louis U. Alumni Council. Avocation: antique car restoration. Office: West County Radiology Group Inc 621 S N Ballas Rd Saint Louis MO 63141

MACDOUGAL, GARY EDWARD, electronic controls manufacturing executive; b. Chgo., July 3, 1936; s. Thomas William and Lorna Lee (McDougall) MacD.; m. Julianne Laurel Maxwell, June 13, 1958; children: Gary Edward, Michael Scott. B.S. in Engring., UCLA, 1958; M.B.A. with distinction, Harvard U., 1962. Cons., McKinsey & Co., Los Angeles, 1963-68; partner McKinsey & Co., 1968-69; chmn. bd., chief exec. officer Mark Controls Corp. (formerly Clayton Mark & Co.), Evanston, Ill., 1969—; also pres. Mark Controls Corp. (formerly Clayton Mark & Co.), 1971-76, 81—; dir. United Parcel Service Am., Inc., N.Y.C., Union Camp Corp., Wayne, N.J., CBI Industries, Oak Brook, Ill.; instr. UCLA, 1969. Contbr. articles to profl. jours., chpts. to books. Assoc. Northwestern U., Evanston; trustee UCLA Found., 1973-79, Russell Sage Found., N.Y.C., Annie E. Casey Found., Com. for Econ. Devel.; hon. dir. Am. Refugee com. Served to lt. USNR, 1958-61. Mem. Kappa Sigma. Episcopalian. Clubs: Harvard of N.Y; Econ. of Chgo. (bd. dirs.), Harvard Bus. Sch. (Chgo.). Home: 505 N Lake Shore Dr Apt 2711 Chicago IL 60611 Office: Mark Controls Corp 5202 Old Orchard Rd Suite 500 Skokie IL 60077

MACDOUGALL, GENEVIEVE ROCKWOOD, journalist, educator; b. Springfield, Ill., Nov. 29, 1914; d. Grover Cleveland and Flora Maurine (Fowler) Rockwood; m. Curtis D. MacDougall, June 20, 1942; children: Priscilla Ruth, Bonnie MacDougall Cottrell. BS, Northwestern U., 1936, MA, 1956, postgrad., 1963—. Reporter, Evanston (Ill.) Daily News Index, 1936-37; assoc. editor Nat. Almanac & Yearbook, Chgo., 1937-38, News Map of Week, Chgo., 1938-39; editor Springfield (Ill.) Citizens' Tribune, also area supr. Ill. Writers Project, 1940-41; reporter Chgo. City News Bur., 1942; tchr. English, social studies Skokie Jr. High Sch., Winnetka, Ill., 1956-68, coordinator TV, 1964-68; tchr. English Washburne Sch., Winnetka, 1968-81; editor Winnetka Public Schs. Staff Newsletter, 1981-87; dir. Winnetka Jr. High Archeology Field Sch., 1971-83; cons., lectr. in field. Author: Grammar Book VII, 1963, 68; (with others) 7th Grade Language Usage, 1963, rev. 1968; also articles. Winnetka Tchrs. Centennial Fund scholar, 1964, 68; named Tchr. of Year, Winnetka, 1976, Educator of Decade Northwestern U. and Found. Ill. Archeology, 1981. Mem. Winnetka Tchrs. Council (pres. 1971-72), NEA, Ill. Edn. Assn., Ill. Assn. Advancement Archeology, Women in Communications (pres. N. Shore alumni chpt. 1949-53), Pi Lambda Theta. Home: 537 Judson Ave Evanston IL 60202

MACEDA, JAIME M., chemist; b. Pagsanjan, Laguna, Philippines, Mar. 12, 1943; came to U.S., 1968; s. Vicente Fernandez and Julieta (Maceda) M.; m. Remedios Belmonte Paat, Oct. 19, 1974; 1 child, Therese Marie-Juliet. B.S. in Chemistry, Mapua Inst. Tech., Manila, 1965. Quality control supr. Mercury Drug Co., Manila, 1965-68; quality control chemist Consol. Distilled Products, Chgo., 1968-70; supr. chemistry Rosner-Hixon Lab., Chgo., 1970-78; chief chemist Rosner-Runyon Lab., Chgo., 1978-86; div. mgr. Aqualab Inc., Chgo., 1986—; judge Chgo. Pub. Schs. Sci. Fair, 1971—. Mem. Assn. Vitamin Chemists, Am. Chem. Soc. Roman Catholic. Office: Aqualab Inc 222 S Morgan St Chicago IL 60607

MACEY, EARL CHRISTOPHER, osteopathic physician and surgeon; b. Richmond, Mo., Mar. 10, 1909; s. Henry Christopher and Lucy Ann (Penny) M.; m. Dorothy Belle Gstrein, July 2, 1939; children—Martha Ann, Earl Christopher. Student Central Coll., Fayette, Mo., 1928-29; D.O., Kirksville Coll. Osteo. Medicine, Mo., 1933; postgrad. Coll. Physicians-Surgeons, Los Angeles, 1946-47, U. Mex., Mexico City, 1948, U. Nebr. Med. Sch., 1979. Intern Laughlin Hosp., Kirksville; tng. in proctology Mayo Clinic, Rochester, Minn., 1944; practice osteo. medicine and surgery, Marshall, Mo.; del. seminars, Nassau, Bahamas, 1972, Bermuda, 1974, Tokyo, 1976. Author: Poliomyelitis, 1938; Hypertension, 1940; Biblical Medicine, 1975. Mem. West-Central Mo. Assn. Osteo. Physicians and Surgeons (pres. 1941), Am. Osteo. Assn. (life), Mo. Assn. Osteo. Physicians and Surgeons (life). Democrat. Methodist. Lodges: Kiwanis (v.p. 1975), Optimist (pres. 1957). Home: 765 S Brunswick St Marshall MO 65340

MACFARLANE, JOHN CHARLES, utility company executive; b. Hallock, Minn., Nov. 8, 1939; s. Ernest Edward and Mary Bell (Yates) MacF.; m. Eunice Darlene Axvig, Apr. 13, 1963; children: Charles, James, William. BSEE, U. N.D., 1961. Staff engr. Otter Tail Power Co., Fergus Falls, Mn., 1961-64; div. engr. Otter Tail Power Co., Jamestown, N.D., 1964-71; div. mgr. Otter Tail Power Co., Langdon, N.D., 1972-78; v.p. planning and control Otter Tail Power Co., Fergus Falls, 1978-80, exec. v.p., 1981-82, pres. and chief exec. officer, 1982—, also bd. dirs.; bd. dirs. Northwest Bank, Fergus Falls, Pioneer Mut. Ins. Co. Pres. Langdon City Commn., 1974-78; chmn. Fergus Falls Port Authority, 1985-86; bd. dirs. Minn. Assn. Commerce and Industry, Minn. Safety Council; chmn. bd. dirs. U. N.D. Energy Research Adv. Council. Served with U.S. Army, 1962-64. Mem. Am. Mgmt. Assn., IEEE (chmn. Red River chpt.), U. N.D. Alumni Assn., Fergus Falls C. of C. Republican. Presbyterian. Lodges: Rotary, Masons. Office: Otter Tail Power Co 215 Cascade St S Fergus Falls MN 56537

MACGIBBON, JAMES DUNCAN, radiologist; b. Mpls., Feb. 13, 1935; s. Everett Ellsworth and Lucinda (Hedding) MacG.; m. Janice Roberta Booker, Aug. 22, 1959; children: Susan Anne, Bruce Everett, Nancy Lynn. BA, U. Minn., 1956, BS, MD, 1960. Diplomate Am. Bd. Radiology. Intern Mpls. Gen. Hosp., 1960-61; resident in radiology VA Hosp., Mpls., 1964-67; radiologist Suburban Radiologic Cons., Ltd., Edina, Minn., 1968—. Served to capt. USAF, 1962-63. Mem. AMA, Am. Coll. Radiology, Radiol. Soc. N. Am., Minn. Med. Soc., Minn. Radiol. Soc., Hennepin County Med. Soc. Republican. Roman Catholic. Club: Decathlon Athletic. Avocations: gardening, music, golf, photography. Home: 6601 Iroquois Trail Edina MN 55435 Office: Suburban Radiologic Cons Ltd 471 Southdale Med Bldg Edina MN 55435

MACGREGOR, ROBERT, psychologist; b. Canton, Ohio, Jan. 27, 1920; s. Walter and Marion (Knapp) MacG.; m. Mary Adeline Houston, Apr. 26, 1944; children—Robert, Margaret, Donald. B.A., U. Mich., 1941, M.A., 1942; Ph.D., NYU, 1954. Diplomate Am. Bd. Profl. Psychology; registered psychologist, Ill. Clin. psychologist VA, Washington, 1946-56; research dir., from instr. to asst. prof. Youth Devel. Project, U. Tex. Med. Br., Galveston, 1956-65; chief family and group therapy State of Ill. Mental Health Ctr., 1966-68; family therapy cons. Chgo. region Ill. Dept. Mental Health, 1969-75; ptnr. in family therapy Robert and Mary MacGregor, 1982—; pres. profl. staff Chgo. Read Mental Health Ctr., 1982; dir. staff tng. Henry Horner Children's Ctr., Ill. Dept. Mental Health, Chgo., 1975-84; adj. faculty Forest Inst. Profl. Psychology, Des Plaines, Ill. Served with U.S. Army, 1942-46. Fellow Am. Psychol. Assn., Am. Orthopsychiat. Assn., Am. Group Psychotherapy Assn.; mem. Southwestern Group Psychotherapy Soc. (pres. 1963-65, award 1978), Ill. Group Psychotherapy Soc. (pres. 1971, 83), Team Family Methods Assn. (hon. dir.), Am. Family Therapy Assn. (charter). Democrat. Unitarian-Universalist. Sr. author: Multiple impact Therapy with Families, 1964; contbr. articles to profl. jours. Home and Office: 19W 155 Rochdale Circle Lombard IL 60148

MACHINIS, PETER ALEXANDER, civil engineer; b. Chgo., Mar. 12, 1912; s. Alexander and Catherine (Lessares) M.; B.S., Ill. Inst. Tech., 1934; m. Fay Mezilson, Aug. 5, 1945; children—Cathy, Alexander. Civil engr. Ill. Hwy. Dept., 1935-36 engr., estimator Harvey Co., Chgo., 1937; project engr. PWA, Chgo., 1938-40; supervisory civil engr. C.E., Dept. Army, Chgo., 1941-78; asst. to exec. dir. Chgo. Urban Transp. Dist., 1978-84; sr. civil engr. Parsons Brinckerhoff, 1985—; partner MSL Engring. Consultants, Park Ridge, Ill., 1952—. Mem. Civil Def. Adv. Council Ill., 1967—. Served with USAF, also C.E., U.S. Army, 1943-45; ETO; lt. col. Res. ret. Registered profl. engr., Ill. Fellow Soc. Am. Mil. Engrs.; mem. ASCE (life), Nat. Soc. Profl. Engrs. (life), Am. Congress Surveying and Mapping, Assn. U.S. Army, Ill. Engring. Council, Mil. Order World Wars (life). Greek Orthodox (ch. trustee). Home: 10247 S Oakley Ave Chicago IL 60643

MACHISKO, DIANA S., mental health therapist; b. Ft. Thomas, Ky., Feb. 21, 1961; d. John Michael Wyatt and Diane Marie (Mitchelle) S.; m.David William. BA in Psychology, U. Cin., 1982, MEd in Counselor Edn., 1984. Dir., founder latchkey program St. Pius X Sch., Reynoldsburg, Ohio, 1985-86; sr. program dir. YMCA, Columbus, Ohio, 1986-87; mental health therapist Moundbuilders Guidance Ctr., Newark, Ohio, 1987—. Mem. Peace United Meth. Ch., Pickerington, Ohio, 1987—; coach for parks and recreation league Reynoldsburg Intermediate Girls Softball, 1985, 87; advisor Battered Women's Adv. Council, 1987—. Mem. AM. Assn. Profl. Dirs., Am. Assn. Counseling and Devel., Specialists in Groupwork (subdiv. Am. Assn. Counseling and Devel.), Kappa Kappa Gamma (advisor 1985—). Republican. Home: 385 Swallow Ct Columbus OH 43147 Office: Moundbuilders Guidance Ctr 65 Messimer Dr Newark OH 43055

MACHONGA, JOHN ANTHONY, stockbroker; b. Chgo., July 6, 1957; s. John G. and Helen F. (Pacella) M.; m. Lydia J. Rypcinski, June 4, 1983. BS in Fin., U. Ill., Chgo., 1980. Fin. counselor Talman Home, Chgo., 1981-83; stockbroker Talman Home Investments, Chgo., 1983—; bd. dirs. Southwest Sentinel Pub., Chgo., Evergreen Chronicle, Chgo., 1985—. Author: Taffy and Abendigo; author column Fin. Econs., 1984-85. Treas. Citizens for Tierney, Chgo, 1986—. Named one of Outstanding Young Men Am.. 1985. Republican. Roman Catholic. Home: 3517 N Ozanam Chicago IL 60634 Office: Talman Home Investments 4046 W 111th St Chicago IL 60953

MACHULAK, EDWARD LEON, real estate, mining and financial corporation executive; b. Milw., July 14, 1926; s. Frank and Mary (Sokolowski) M.; B.S. in Accounting, U., Wis., 1949; student spl. courses various univs.; m. Sylvia Mary Jablonski, Sept. 2, 1950; children—Edward A., John E., Lauren A., Christine M., Paul E. Chmn. bd., pres., Commerce Group Corp., Milw., 1962—, San Luis Estates, Inc., 1973—, Homespan Realty Co., Inc., 1974—, Universal Developers, Inc., 1972—, Picadilly Advt. Agy., Inc., 1974—; chmn. bd., chief exec. officer, Gen. Lumber & Supply Co., Inc., 1952—; bd. dirs., v.p., San Sebastian Gold Mines, Inc., 1969-73, chmn. bd., pres., 1973—; bd. dirs, sec., LandPak, Inc., 1985—; bd. dirs. Edjo Ltd., 1974—, sec., 1976—; ptnr., Weem Assocs., 1974—. Mem. Nat. Adv. Council U.S. SBA, 1972-74, co-chmn. 1973, 74. Recipient Recognition award U.S. SBA, 1975. Mem. Nat. Assn. Small Bus. Investment Co's (nat. chmn. legis. com. 1968-73, bd. govs. 1970-74, exec. com. 1971-74, sec. 1972-74, Disting. Service award to Am. Small Bus. 1970), Midwest Regional Assn. Small Bus. Investment Cos. (bd. dirs. 1968-74, v.p. 1970-71, pres. 1971-72, Outstanding Services award 1972), State of Wis. Council on Small Bus. Investment (chmn. 1973-74), Wis. Bd. Realtors (various coms. 1955—), Milw. Bd. Realtors (various coms. 1955—). Pres.' Council Marmion Mil. Acad., Aurora, Ill., 1966-79, lay life trustee, 1972, fin. advisor 1967-71, chmn. spl. fund raising com. 1966-67, planning com. 1972-79; chmn. adv. bd. Jesuit Retreat House, Oshkosh, Wis., 1966-68; chmn., bd. dirs. Spencerian Coll. of Bus., 1973-74; chmn. St. John Cathedral Symphony Concert Com., Milw., 1978; sustaining mem. Met. Mus. Art, 1974—. Served with AUS, 1945-46. Recognized bus. leader in Congl. Record, 1976; named Hon. Life Mem., Mid-Continental Railway, 1963. Clubs: Milw. Athletic, Tripoli Golf (Milw.); Met., Canadian (N.Y.C.). Lodge: KC (4th degree 1971—). Home: 903 W Green Tree Rd River Hills WI 53217 Office: 6001 N 91st St Milwaukee WI 53217

MACISAAC, JOHN EDWARD, forestry manufacturing executive; b. Canton, Ohio, Sept. 9, 1938; s. Harold Kenneth and Mildred Violet (Schneider) MacI.; m. Susan Marie Knipp, Sept. 16, 1961; children: Loriann, Mark, Christy, Molly. Student, Akron U., 1963-64. Design engr. Gussett Boiler, Massillon, Ohio, 1958-61; mgr. sales engring. Adamson United, Akron, 1963-70; internat. liaison Process Design, Chgo., 1971-73; pres. Sebring (Ohio) Forest, 1974—, also bd. dirs.; bd. dirs. Sourbeck, Alliance, Ohio; cons. Miller Prods., Sebring, 1974—. Active mem. com. United Fund, Alliance, 1982. Served with USAF, 1961-62. Mem. Soc. Plastic Engrs. Republican. Roman Catholic. Club: Alliance Country. Lodge: KC (chmn. Canton coms. 1979). Avocations: classic auto restoration, golf, fishing. Home: 704 Reno Dr Louisville OH 44641 Office: Sebring Forest Industries 1155 Allied Dr Sebring OH 44672

MACK, ALAN WAYNE, interior designer; b. Cleve., Oct. 30, 1947; s. Edmund B. and Florence I. (Oleska) M. BS in Interior Design, Case Western Res. U., 1969. Designer interior design dept. Halle's, Cleve., 1969, 71-73; designer Nahan Co., New Orleans, 1973-75, Hemenway's Contract Design, New Orleans, 1975-76; ptnr. Hewlett-Mack Design Assocs., New Orleans, 1976-86; dir. interior design Hansen Lind Meyer, Inc., 1986—; adv. com. interior design dept. Delgado Jr. Coll., New Orleans; mktg./merchandising adv. council St. Mary's Dominican Coll., New Orleans. Served with U.S. Army, 1969-71. Co-author audiovisual presentation Nat. Home Improvement Council Conf., 1981. Mem. ASID (profl. mem., presdl. citation, 1980, treas. La. dist. chpt. 1984), Found. for Interior Design Edn. Research (standards com., 1972-76, bd. visitors 1977-80, accreditation com., 1981). Home: 9 Parsons Ave Iowa City IA 52240

MACK, HARRY EDMUND, III, dentist; b. St. Louis, Dec. 5, 1921; s. Harry Edmund and Louella Pauline (Delvaux) M.; m. Johanna Mary Kelly, Aug. 18, 1948; childdren—Mary Catherine, Bonacorsi, Julia Anne, Eileen Johanna, Harry Edmund, Michael Patrick. A.S., U. Mo.-Columbia, 1939-42; D.D.S., St. Louis U., 1946. Pvt. practice dentistry and dental surgery, Kirkwood, Mo., 1946—. Fellow Acad. Gen. Dentistry; mem. Am. Dental Assn., Mo. Dental Assn., St. Louis Dental Soc., Phi Gamma Delta, Delta Sigma Delta. Republican. Roman Catholic. Avocations: Golf, sailing. Office: 333 S Kirkwood Rd Kirkwood MO 63122

MACK, LAWRENCE ALLEN, banker, accountant; b. Cleve., June 12, 1955; s. William Lewis and Rita Diane (Merecki) M. BS, Cornell U., 1977; M Mgmt., Northwestern U., 1981. CPA, Ohio, N.Y. Sr. acct. Peat, Marwick, Mitchell & Co., N.Y.C., 1977-79; v.p. AmeriTrust Co., Cleve., 1981—; lectr. John Carroll U., Cleve., 1984-86. Trustee Young Profls. Cleve., 1983-85. Mem. Am. Inst. CPA's, Robert Morris Assocs., Employee Stock Ownership Assn., Jr. Achievement (fund raiser 1982—), Northwestern Mgmt. Club (v.p., treas. 1984—). Avocations: swimming, ice skating, travel. Home: 3445 Colton Rd Shaker Heights OH 44122 Office: AmeriTrust Co 900 Euclid Ave Cleveland OH 44101

MACK, MARY MARGARET, educator; b. Cleve., Aug. 14, 1955; d. Edward Stephen and Bernetta Ann (Stracensky) Hudak; m. Thomas Edward Mack, July 8, 1978. B.S., Cleve. State U., 1977, M in Reading Supervision, 1986. Tchr., Lulu Diehl Jr. High Sch., Cleve., 1977-78; tchr. Charles W. Eliot Jr. High Sch., 1978—, mem. project Perform proposal writing team, 1982—. Mem. Council Exceptional Children, Assn. Supervision and Curriculum Devel. Roman Catholic. Home: 1353 E 343d St Eastlake OH 44094 Office: 15700 Lotus Dr Cleveland OH 44128

MACK, RICHARD J., industrial and mechanical engineer; b. Cleve., June 20, 1924; s. John N. and Irene N. (Pankuch) M.; m. Helen C. Dietz, July 29, 1950; children: Richard, Cathy. B in Mech. Engring., Cleve. State U., 1949. Plant engr. Stanadyne, Elyria, Ohio, 1949-60, mgr. quality control, 1971-75; plant and indsl. engr. Atlas Bolt & Screw, Cleve., 1960-64, plant mgr., 1965-71; gen. foreman ITT Harper, Morton Grove, Ill., 1964-65, mgr. mfg. services, 1980-82; mfg. mgr. Meadville (Pa.) Forging Co., 1975-77; plant and indsl. engr. Great Lakes Screw, Riverdale, Ill., 1977-80; plant supt. John Gillen Co., Cicero, Ill., 1983—; lectr. plant layout Cleve. Time Study Inst., 1968. Chmn. St. John Luth. Sch. Bd., South Euclid, Ohio, 1969-72; mem. Chgo. Heart Assn. Served to USNR, 1942-46, PTO. Mem. Soc. Mfg. Engrs., Robotics Internat., Internat. Maintenance Inst., Pi Sigma Tau. Republican. Office: John Gillen Co 2540 S 50th Ave Cicero IL 60650

MACK, WILLIAM JOSEPH, psychotherapist, rehabilitation specialist; b. Evergreen Park, Ill., Mar. 5, 1943; s. Arol Ruth (Tallut) M.; m. Margaret Crace McCullom, Jan. 8, 1966 (div. Aug. 1979); children: William, Amy. BA, U. Dayton, 1965; cert., Ind. State U., Terre Haute, 1980; MA, Ball State U., 1983. Registered social worker, Ill.; cert. addictions counselor, Ill. Mktg. rep. Texaco Inc., Lockport, Ill., 1969-73; med. rep. Merrell-Dow, Kokomo, Ind., 1973-82; program coordinator Pilsen Vocat., Chgo., 1983-85; dir. sheltered workshop Japanese Service, Chgo., 1985—; therapist Vet. Ctr., Chicago Heights, Ill., 1984-85. Instr. first aid ARC, Chgo., 1986. Served with U.S. Army, 1965-68. Mem. Nat. Assn. Social Workers, Internat. Assn. psychoSocial Profls., Mktg. Execs. for Sheltered Workshops, Am. Legion. Democrat. Roman Catholic. Avocations: flying, photography. Home: 207 Zurich Dr Lynwood IL 60411 Office: Japanese Am Service Com 4427 N Clark Chicago IL 60640

MACKE, JOHN GEORGE, manufacturers' representative company executive; b. St. Louis, Jan. 16, 1931; s. F. George and Isabella Antonette (Garlich) M.; m. Dorothy Jeanne Maher, July 13, 1957; children—John George, Daniel, Donna, James, Diane, Doris. B.S. in Elec. Engring., U. Mo.-Rolla, 1952; M.B.A., St. Louis U., 1960. Supr. motor sales Wagner Electric Corp., St. Louis, 1952-62; sales mgr. Fasco Industries, Inc., Rochester, N.Y., 1962-68; product sales mgr. Emerson Electric Motor Div., St. Louis, 1968-71; owner Whitehill Systems of South St. Louis, 1971-74; dist. mgr. John G. Twist Co., St. Louis, 1974-82; pres. John G. Macke Co., St. Louis, 1982—. Served to capt. USAF, 1952-60; Korea. Mem. Nat. Elec. Mfrs. Assn. (co. rep. 1963-68). Roman Catholic. Lodge: KC (dep. grand knight 1973-75). Avocation: flying. Home: 1508 Sugargrove Ct Saint Louis MO 63146 Office: John G Macke Co 11710 Administration Dr Saint Louis MO 63146

MACKE, KENNETH A., retail executive; b. Templeton, Iowa, Dec. 16, 1938; B.S., Drake U., 1961; m. Kathleen O'Farrell; children: Michael, Jeffrey. With Dayton Hudson Corp., and affiliates, 1961—, former chmn., chief exec. officer Target Stores, sr. v.p. corp., 1977-79, pres. corp. 1981-84, cor. chmn., chief exec. officer, chmn. exec. com., 1984—; also dir.; mem. bd. bus. and indsl. advisers U. Wis., Stout, 1978-80. Bd. dirs. Walker Art Center, Urban Coalition Mpls.; trustee Drake U.; bd. regents Augsburg Coll., Mpls., 1979-80; div. chmn. United Way Mpls., 1977, 79-80. Mem. Nat. Mass. Retailing Inst. (dir. 1977-81), Nat. Retail Mchts. Assn. (dir. 1982-83), Greater Mpls. C. of C. (dir. 1980-82). Address: Dayton-Hudson Corp 777 Nicollet Mall Minneapolis MN 55402

MACKEIGAN, JOHN MALCOLM, surgeon; b. Ottawa, Ont., Can., May 1, 1944; s. Ian Malcolm and Jean Catherine (Geddes) MacK.; m. Suzanne Marie Le Brun, June 21, 1968; children: Sara Elizabeth, Daniel John, Jeffery Paul. Student pre-medicine, Dalhousie U., Nova Scotia, Can., 1961-64, MD, 1969. Cert. Am. Bd. Colon and Rectal Surgery. Fellow in med. gastroenterology Dalhousie U., 1972, intern in gen. surgery, 1969-73; resident in colon and rectal surgery Ferguson Clinic, Grand Rapids, Mich., 1973-74, staff surgeon, 1975—; lectr. dept. surgery Dalhousie U., 1974-75; assoc. clin. prof. surgery Mich. State U., Grand Rapids, 1980—; active staff Ferguson-Droste-Ferguson, St. Mary's Hosp., Blodgett Meml. Med. Ctr., Butterworth Hosp.; chmn. infection control com. Ferguson-Droste Ferguson Hosp.; bd. dirs. Hosp. Greater Grand Rapids; pres. Hospice Greater Grand Rapids, 1986. Contbr. articles to profl. jours. Active Mich. and Kent County div. Am. Cancer Soc. Fellow ACS, Royal Coll. Physicians and Surgeons of Can., Am. Soc. Colon and Rectal Surgeons (exec. bd. dirs. 1983-85); mem. AMA, Mich. Med. Soc., Kent County Med. Soc. (program chmn. 1980, exec. com. 1982-85), Grand Rapids Surgical Soc., Bd. Mich. Soc. Colon and Rectal Surgeons (pres. 1978-79), Soc. Am. Gastrointestinal Endoscopic Surgeons (founding, instrument and procedure safety com., resident tng. com.), Am. Soc. Enteral and Parenteral Nutrition, Midwest Surgical Soc. Republican. Unitarian. Clubs: Penisular, Kent Country (Grand Rapids). Avocations: sailing, tennis, ice hockey. Home: 552 Cambridge Blvd SE Grand Rapids MI 49506 Office: Ferguson Clinic 72 Sheldon Blvd SE Grand Rapids MI 49503

MACKENTHUN, JANET RUTH, educator; b. Norwood, Minn., Oct. 6, 1939; s. Wesley James Sellnow and Edna Ida (Engelmann) Gruetzmacher; m. Arthur F. Mackenthun, Aug. 4, 1962; children: Julianne, Sharon, Alan, Brian, Eileen, Bruce. AA, Concordia Coll., 1959, BS in Edn., 1964; postgrad., Mankato State, 1965—. Tchr. grades 3, 6, 7 St. John's, Young America, Minn., 1962-66; tchr. grade 3 Chaska (Minn.) Pub. Schs., 1966-67; day care nursery sch. dir. Children's World, Waconia, Minn., 1970-71; tchr. grades 7, 8 Trinity Luth. Sch., Waconia, 1978-80; kindergarten, presch. tchr., dir. Zion Luth. Sch., Cologne, Minn., 1980-87; dir. Loving Care Learning Ctr., Norwood, Minn., 1987—. Precinct chairwoman Reps., Carver County, Minn., 1962-68; state del. ind. reps., Minn., 1986-87. Club: 4-H (Carver County) (leader 1971-87). Avocations: needlework, piano, organ, guitar. Home: 820 W Elm St Norwood MN 55368 Office: Loving Care Learning Ctr 820 West Elm Norwood MN 55368

MACKETY, CAROLYN JEAN, nurse, consultant; b. Chgo., Feb. 27, 1932; d. Gerald James and Minnette (Buis) Kruyf; m. Robert J. Martin, Oct. 3, 1952 (div. 1959); children—Daniel, David, Steven, Laura. Diploma, Hackley Hosp. Sch. Nursing, 1969; B.S., Coll. St. Francis, 1977; M.B.A., Columbia Pacific U., 1987. Nursing coordinator operating room Grant Hosp., Columbus, Ohio, 1981-84, dir. operating room services, 1984-86; pres., owner

Laser Cons., Inc., 1986—; v.p. ops. Laser Ctrs. of Am; laser nurse specialist. Mem. Assn. Operating Room Nurses, Am. Soc. Laser Medicine and Surgery (chmn.). Republican. Mem. editorial bd. Indsl. Laser Rev.; editor Laser Nursing; author: Perioperative Laser Nursing.

MACKEY, DAVID CLARK, educator, speech consultant; b. Des Moines, Aug. 4, 1955; s. Milford Irwin and Margaret Ann (Kilbourne) M.; foster children: Paul Doolan, Bill Doolan. BA in Communications, Wartburg Coll., Waverly, Iowa, 1977; MA in Adminstrn., U. No. Iowa, 1986. Cert. speech and English instr. Instr. Jefferson Schs., North Sioux City, S.D., 1977-79, Denver (Iowa) Schs., 1979—. Dist. advancement chmn. Boy Scouts Am., Cedar Falls, Iowa, 1981-83; foster parent Bromer County Social Services, Waverly, Iowa, 1981—. Recipient Bill Moss award Iowa Jaycees, 1982-83. Mem. Nat. Council Tchrs. English, Iowa Council Tchrs. of English, Jaycees (pres. 1981-82, state speech judge 1980-82, Outstanding Young Man of Am. 1984), Am. Legion (Boy's State award 1973), Wartburg Coll. Alumni Assn. (bd. dirs. 1979-83). Methodist. Clubs: Decathalon (Cedar Falls) (bd. dirs. 1984-86); Go-Dak-Wo-Teo (S.D.) (pres. 1977-78); Lodge: Lions (Lion Tamer 1986—). Avocations: team sports, bridge, cycling, swimming. Home: 1010 S Holmes Box 664 Denver IA 50622 Office: Denver High Sch Box 384 Denver IA 50622

MACKLEY, WILLIAM LEROY, counselor; b. Toledo, May 19, 1917; s. Leroy Franklin and Mabel (Monahan) M.; m. Madelyn Brighton, July 24, 1937; children: Sharon Mackley Adams, Prudence Mackley Kinsel. Communication instr. Community Family and Children's Service, Gaylord, Mich., 1976-83, counselor, 1972—; self help group instr. Alpena (Mich.) Community Coll., 1976-83. Mem. Mich. Addiction Counsellor Assn. (cert.). Democrat. Roman Catholic. Avocations: scuba diving, fishing, hunting. Home: 515 S 4th St Alpena MI 49707 Office: Community and Family Children's Services 614 Old Field St Alpena MI 49707

MACKLIN, ELIZABETH MARGARET, police officer; b. Cleve., Mar. 7, 1938; d. Lucius and Rachel (Hart) Woods; m. Moses Macklin, July 25, 1959; 1 son, Earl Allan. Student Fenn Coll., 1964-66, Case Western Res. U., 1966, Cuyahoga County Community Coll., 1969, 83. Sec., Vis. Nurse Assn., Cleve., 1957-64, Welfare Fedn., 1964-66; adminstrv. asst. Village of Woodmere (Ohio), 1967—, police officer, 1972—. Mem. declining enrollment com. Orange Schs., 1983—; mem., past officer Nat. Bapt. Conv., Ohio Bapt. State Conv. Mem. NAACP, Nat. Council Negro Women, Profl. Secs. Internat., Cuyahoga County Mayors' Secs. Assn., Woodmere Women's Civic League. Democrat. Lodges: Order Eastern Star, Dau. of Isis. Home: 3749 Brainard Rd Woodmere Village OH 44122 Office: 27899 Chagrin Blvd Woodmere Village OH 44122

MACKLIN, MARTIN RODBELL, psychiatrist; b. Raleigh, N.C., Aug. 27, 1934; s. Albert A. and Mitzi (Robdell) M.; Ruth Chimacoff; divorced; children: Meryl, Shelley; m. Anne Elizabet Warren, May 25; 1 child, Alicia. BME, Cornell U., 1957, M in Indsl. Engring., 1958; PhD in Biomed. Engring., Case Western Res. U., 1967, MD, 1977. Diplomate Am. Bd. Psychiatry and Neurology; lic. profl. engr. Investigator Am. Heart Assn., Cleve., 1969-74; vis. fellow U. Sussex, Brighton, England, 1970; assoc. prof. biomed. engring. Case Western Res. U., 1972-81, asst. prof. psychiatry, 1981—; clin. dir. Horizon Ctr. Hosp., Warrensville Township, Ohio, 1981-83; adminstrv. dir. mental health services Ashtabula County Med. Ctr., 1983; psychiat. cons. Glenbeigh Hosp., Ohio and Fla.; cons. various indsl. cos. Contbr. articles to profl. jours; patentee in field. NIH research grantee Kellogg Found., Cleve. 1967-81; Laughlinn fellow Am. Coll. Psychiatry, 1980. Mem. Am. Psychiat. Assn., Soc. Gen. Psychologists, Cleve. Acad. Medicine, Cleve. Psychiat. Soc. Avocations: woodworking, gardening. Home: 348 N Chestnut Jefferson OH 44047

MACKNIGHT, CHRISTOPHER JAMES, dentist; b. St. Louis, Mar. 3, 1957; s. Frank B. and Barbara B. (Barnett) MacK. DDS, U. Nebr., 1982. Dentist Edgewood Dental Group, Lincoln, Nebr., 1983—. V.p. cornhusker council Boy Scouts Am., 1986—; chmn. Heart Assn., Lincoln, 1985-86. Mem. ADA, Lincoln Jaycees. Democrat. Episcopalian. Home: 5140 S 56th Lincoln NE 68516 Office: Edgewood Dental Group 5504 S 56th St Suite 5 Lincoln NE 68516

MACKNIGHT, DAVID LAURENCE, dentist; b. Cin., May 24, 1947; s. Clifford Charles and Lucille W. (Nichols) M.; m. Victoria Ann MacKnight, Oct. 6, 1984; children: Andrea Steiner, Eric Thomas. BS cum laude, Ohio U., 1970; DDS summa cum laude, Ohio State U., 1974. Clin. instr. dentistry Ohio State U., 1974; resident in gen. dentistry Denver Gen. Hosp., 1974-75; gen. practice dentistry Cin., 1976—; pres. Mt. Carmel Profl. Ctr., Cin., 1986. Fellow Acad. Gen. Dentistry; mem. ADA, Cin. Dental Soc., Ohio Dental Assn., Am. Assn. Children Dentistry, Eastside Dental Study Club. Avocation: skiing, guitar, woodworking, tennis, photography. Home: 691 Bennettwood Ct Cincinnati OH 45230 Office: 473 Cininnati Batavia Pike Cincinnati OH 45244

MACKO, MICHAEL IGNATIUS, small business owner; b. East Chicago, Ind., Jan. 31, 1942; s. Michael and Margaret (Strbiak) M.; m. Valerie J. Randolph, June 6, 1964; children: Rabekah, Rachael. Gemologist cert., Bishop Noll Inst., 1961. Owner Roxana Video Stores, East Chicago, 1963—; owner, collector Macko's Antiques, LaPorte, Ind., 1980—; owner Chgo. Archtl. Antique Auction, 1982—. Contbr. articles on antiques to newspapers. Roman Catholic. Avocations: motorcycling, bass fishing.

MACKOVIC, JOHN, football coach; b. Barberton, Ohio, Oct. 1, 1943; m. Arlene Francis; children: Aimee, John. B.A. in Spanish, Wake Forest U., 1965; M.Edn. in Secondary Sch. Adminstrn., Miami U., Oxford, Ohio, 1966. Various coaching positions 1965-72; offensive backfield coach U. Ariz., Tucson, 1973-74; offensive coordinator U. Ariz., 1974-75, asst. head coach, 1976; asst. head coach, offensive coordinator Purdue U., West Lafayette, Ind., 1976-78; head football coach Wake Forest U., Winston-Salem, N.C., 1978-81; asst. football coach Dallas Cowboys, 1981-83; head football coach Kansas City Chiefs, Mo., 1983-87. Address: PO Box 935 Bermuda Run NC 27006

MAC LAREN, DAVID SERGEANT, pollution control manufacturing corporation executive; b. Cleve., Jan. 4, 1931; s. Albert Sergeant and Theadora Beidler (Potter) MacL.; children: Alison, Catherine, Carolyn. AB in Econs., Miami U., Oxford, Ohio, 1955. Chmn. bd., pres., Jet, Inc., Cleve., 1961—; founder, chmn. bd., pres. Air Injector Corp., Cleve., 1958-78; founder, pres., chmn. bd. Fluid Equipment, Inc., Cleve., 1962-72, founder, chmn. bd., pres. T&M Co., Cleve., 1963-71, founder, chmn. bd., pres. Alison Realty Co., Cleve., 1965—; chmn. bd., pres. Sergeant Realty, Inc., 1979-86; bd. dirs. Gilmore Industries, Cleve., 1975-77, MWL Systems, Los Angeles, 1979-85. Mem. tech. com. Nat. Sanitation Found., Ann Arbor, Mich., 1967—; mem. Republican State Cen. Com., 1968-72; bd. dirs. Cleve. State U. Found., 1986—. Served with arty. AUS, 1955-58. Fellow Royal Soc. Health (London); mem. Nat. Environ. Health Assn., Am. Pub. Health Assn., Nat. Water Pollution Control Fedn., Cen. Taekwondo Assn. (2d Dan), Jiu-Jitsu/Karati Black Belt Fedn. (black belt instr.), Mercedes Benz Club N.Am. (pres. 1968), H. B. Leadership Soc. (sch. headmaster soc., devel. com. 1976-78), SAR, Soc. Mayflower Descendants, Delta Kappa Epsilon (nat. dir. N.Y.C. 1974-86, dir. Kappa chpt. 1969—). Clubs: Mentor Harbor Yachting, The Country Club, Cotillion Soc. (Cleve.); Union League, Yale, Deke (N.Y.C.). Patentee in field Home: West Hill Dr Gates Mills OH 44040 Office: Jet Inc 750 Alpha Dr Cleveland OH 44143

MACLAUCHLAN, DONALD JOHN, JR., real estate company executive; b. S.I., N.Y., Mar. 2, 1935; s. Donald John and Alice Lucy (Macklin) MacL.; B.A. magna cum laude, Harvard U., 1957; m. Mary Eleanor Manor, Oct. 14, 1967; children—Douglas Laird, Phyllis Ann, Donald John III. Mortgage analyst Conn. Gen. Life Ins. Co., Hartford, 1957-60; mortgage broker James W. Rouse & Co., Balt., 1960-62; devel. mgr. Devel. & Constrn. Co., Inc., Balt., 1962-66; v.p. Nat. Homes Corp., Lafayette, Ind., 1966-75; pres., dir. The Criterion Group, Lafayette, 1975—; chmn. bd. Insight Unltd., Inc.; dir. Lafayette Parking, Inc., Sagamore Food Services, Inc. Elder, Central Presbyn. Ch., Lafayette, 1971—; mem. gen. council Presbytery of Wabash Valley, 1976-78. Mem. Lafayette Bd. Realtors (dir. 1986—), Greater Lafayette C. of C., Ind. Apt. Assn. (dir. 1980—), Tippecanoe County Apt. Assn. (dir. 1977—, pres. 1980). Republican. Clubs: Lafayette Country, Romwell Foxhounds (joint master). Office: PO Box 275 Lafayette IN 47902

MACLAUGHLIN, HARRY HUNTER, judge; b. Breckenridge, Minn., Aug. 9, 1927; s. Harry Hunter and Grace (Swank) MacL.; m. Mary Jean Shaffer, June 25, 1958; children: David, Douglas. BBA with distinction, U. Minn., 1949, JD, 1956. Bar: Minn. 1956. Law clk. to justice Minn. Supreme Ct.; ptnr. MacLaughlin & Mondale, MacLaughlin & Harstad, Mpls., 1956-72; assoc. justice Minn. Supreme Ct., 1972-77; U.S. dist. judge Dist. of Minn., Mpls., 1977—; part-time instr. William Mitchell Coll. Law, St. Paul, 1958-63; lectr. U. Minn. Law Sch., 1973—; mem. 8th Cir. Jud. Council, 1981-83. Bd. editors: Minn. Law Rev, 1954-55. Mem. Mpls. Charter Commn., 1967-72, Minn. State Coll. Bd., 1971-72, Minn. Jud. Council, 1972; mem. nat. adv. council Small Bus. Adminstrn., 1967-69. Served with USNR, 1945-46. Mem. ABA, Minn. Bar Assn., Hennepin County Bar Assn., Beta Gamma Sigma, Phi Delta Phi. Methodist. Office: 684 US Courthouse 110 S 4th St Minneapolis MN 55401

MACLEOD, JOHN GRAEME, engineering manager; b. Hastings, Eng., Feb. 20, 1930; came to U.S., 1972; s. Hugh Graeme and Hilda Norris (St. John) M.; children: Christopher, Robert, Neil; m. Margarette Cagle, Jan. 1, 1984. HNC Mech. Engring., Loughborough Coll., Eng., 1950, ONC Elec. Engring., 1951; HNC Indsl. Adminstrn., Watford Coll., Eng., 1955. Registered profl. engr., Can. Apprentice, draftsman, engr. Various Cos., Eng. and Can., 1946-67; chief engr. Rockwell Can., Montreal, 1967-72; mgr. plug valve devel. Rockwell Internat., Pitts., 1972-78; mgr. engring. Ecolaire Valve Co., Allentown, Pa., 1978-81; project mgr. new products SII McEvoy, Houston, 1981-83; mgr. research, devel. and engring. ITT Hoffman, Indpls., 1983—; chmn. pipeline valves CSA, Toronto, 1968-78; chmn. gas valves, 1968-80, chmn. oilfield valves, 1970-76; mem. adv. com. on gen. purpose valves, 1969-72. Patentee in field. Mem. Order Engrs. Que., Soc. Am. Valve Engrs., Am. Soc. for Quality Control, Soc. Mfg. Engrs., Nat. Model Railroad Assn., Mensa. Avocations: model railroading, hiking. Home: 7481 Prairie Lake Dr Indianapolis IN 46256 Office: ITT Hoffman 1700 W 10th St Indianapolis IN 46222

MAC LEOD, RICHARD ALAN, government revenue agent; b. Flint, Mich., Dec. 7, 1947; s. Archibald Charles and Georgenia Anne (Youmans) Mac L.; m. Cynthia Lou Jeziorski, Dec. 13, 1975. BA, U. Mich.-Flint, 1973; M in Taxation, DePaul U., 1979. Internal revenue agt. U.S. Treasury Dept., Chgo., 1973—. Decorated Bronze Star, Bronze Star for valor, 2 Purple Hearts, Air medal. Served to sgt. U.S. Army, 1967-69, Vietnam. Mem. Vietnam Vets. of Am., Clan Mac Leod Soc., U.S.A. Republican. Avocations: racquetball, genealogy, jogging. Home: 990 Waverly Rd Glen Ellyn IL 60137

MAC MAHON, HAROLD BERNARD, manufacturing company executive; b. Newton, Mass., Nov. 15, 1917; s. Harold A. and Alma A. (McCabe) MacM.; m. Mary M. Savage, Jan. 1, 1942; 1 child, Karen D. MacMahon Levisay. BS in Edn., Boston U., 1940. Plant mgr. Bassick div. Stewart-Warner Corp., Spring Valley, Ill., 1958-66, controller Alemite and Instrument div., Chgo., 1966-73, asst. gen. mgr., 1973-74, 86, gen. mgr. Hobbs div., Springfield, Ill., 1974-86 , v.p., 1976, gen. mgr. alemite and instruments divs.; bd. dirs. Marine Bank of Springfield. Mem. adv. council St. John's Hosp., 1978-86. Served with U.S. Army, 1943-45. Mem. Soc. Automotive Engrs., Newcomen Soc. N.Am., Greater Springfield C. of C. (bd. dirs. 1978-83), Ill. C. of C., Phi Delta Kappa. Club: Sangamo (Springfield), Carlton (Chgo.). Home: 260 E Chestnut Chicago IL 60611 Office: Stewart-Warner Corp Allemite & Instruments Div 1826 W Diversey Chicago IL 60614

MACMANUS, SUSAN ANN, political science educator, researcher; b. Tampa, Fla., Aug. 22, 1947; d. Harold Cameron and Elizabeth (Riegler) MacManus. B.A. cum laude, Fla. State U., 1968, Ph.D., 1975; M.A., U. Mich., 1969. Instr. Valencia Community Coll., Orlando, Fla., 1969-73; research asst. Fla. State U., 1973-75; asst. prof. U. Houston, 1975-79, assoc. prof., 1979-85, dir. (M.P.A.) program, 1983-85, research assoc. Ctr Pub. Policy 1982-85; prof., dir. Ph.D. program Cleve. State U., 1985—; vis. prof. U. Okla., Norman, 1981—; field research assoc. Brookings Instn., Washington, 1977-82, Columbia U., summer 1979, Princeton U., 1979—, Nat. Acad. Pub. Adminstrn., Washington, summer 1980, Cleve. State U., 1982-83, Westat, Inc., Washington, 1983—; Author: Revenue Patterns in U.S. Cities and Suburbs: A Comparative Analysis, 1978; (with others) Governing A Changing America, 1984; contbr. articles to jours., chpts. to books; writer manuals in field; editorial bds. jours. Bd. dirs. Houston Area Women's Ctr., 1977, past pres., v.p. fin., treas.; mem. LWV, Harris County (Tex.) Women's Polit. Caucus, Houston. Recipient U. Houston Coll. Social Scis. Teaching Excellence award, 1977, Herbert J. Simon Award best article in vol. 3, Internat. Jour. Pub. Adminstrn., 1981; Ford Found. fellow, 1967-68; grantee Valencia Community Coll. Faculty, 1972, U. Houston, 1976, 77, 79, 83. Mem. Am. Polit. Sci. Assn. (program com. 1983-84, chairperson sect. intergovtl. relations), So. Polit. Sci. Assn. (V.O. key award com. 1983-84), Midwest Polit. Sci. Assn., Western Polit. Sci. Assn., Southwestern Polit. Sci. Assn. (local arrangements com. 1982-83, profession com. 1977-80), Am. Soc. Pub. Adminstrn. (nominating com. Houston chpt. 1983), Policy Studies Orgn. (mem. editorial bd. jours. 1981—, exec. council 1983-85), Women's Caucus Polit. Sci. (portfolio pre-decision rev. com. 1982-83, projects and programs com. 1981, fin.-budget com. 1980-81), Acad. Polit. Sci., Mcpl. Fin. Officers Assn., Phi Beta Kappa, Phi Kappa Phi, Pi Sigma Alpha. Republican. Methodist. Home: 1417 Winchester Lakewood OH 44107 Office: Cleveland State U Coll Urban Affairs Cleveland OH 44115

MACMILLAN, PETER ALAN, lawyer; b. Mpls., Apr. 10, 1955; s. John Louis and Celeste Caroline (Eggers) MacM. B.S., Mankato State U., 1977; J.D., Hamline U., 1980; postgrad. Sch. Law, U. San Diego, 1980. Bar: Minn. 1980, U.S. Tax Ct. 1980, U.S. Dist. Ct. Minn. 1981. Sole practice, Robbinsdale, Minn., 1981-84; assoc. Rosenthal & Rondoni, Ltd., Mpls., 1984-85; shareholder Rosenthal, Rondoni & MacMillan, Ltd., 1985—. Mem. Minn. State Bar Assn., Hennepin County Bar Assn., Assn. Trial Lawyers Am., Am. Judicature Soc., ABA, Jaycees. Lutheran. Home: 8835 Lawndale Ln N Maple Grove MN 55369 Office: Rosenthal Rondoni & MacMillan Ltd 7600 Bass Lake Rd Suite 120 Minneapolis MN 55428

MACNEALY, MARK ANDREW, neurologist; b. Dayton, Ohio, Mar. 26, 1950; s. Robert Gale and Elizabeth Julia (Cowal) MacN.; m. Diana Lynn Warren, Dec. 18, 1976; children: Marcus Warren Cowal, Margeaux Nicole Lynn. BS in Pre-Med., U. Dayton, 1971; DO, Chgo. Coll. Osteo. Medicine, 1976. Diplomate Nat. Bd. Med. Examiners. Intern Grandview Hosp., Dayton, Ohio, 1976-77, staff neurologist, 1981—; resident in psychiatry U. Cin. Hosp., 1977-78; resident in neurology Martin Place Hosp., Madison Heights, Mich., 1978-81; staff neurologist Grandview Hosp. and Southview Hosp., Dayton, 1981—; clin. polysomographer Southview Hosp. and Grandview Hosp. Sleep Lab, Dayton, 1982—; vol. clin. faculty Ohio U., 1983-85. campaign mgr. primary election Farquhar for Ct. Appeals, Dayton, 1986. Mem. Soc. Noninvasive Vascular tech., Soc. Computerized Tomography and Neuro-Imaging. Republican. Roman Catholic. Avocation: amateur radio. Home: 461 Glenridge Rd Dayton OH 45429

MACON, IRENE ELIZABETH, designer, consultant; b. East St. Louis, Ill., May 11, 1935; d. David and Thelma (Eastlen) Dunn; m. Robert Teco Macon, Feb. 12, 1954; children—Leland Sean, Walter Edwin, Gary Keith, Jill Renee Macon Martin, Robin Jeffrey, Lamont. Student Forest Park Coll., Washington U., St. Louis, 1970, Bailey Tech. Coll., 1975, Lindenwood Coll., 1981. Office mgr. Cardinal Glennon Hosp., St. Louis, 1965-72; interior designer J.C. Penney Co., Jennings, Mo., 1972-73; entrepreneur Irene Designs Unltd., St. Louis, 1974—; vol. liaison Pub. Sch. System, St. Louis, 1980-82; cons. in field. Inventor venetian blinds for autos, 1981, T-blouse and diaper wrap, 1986; author 26th Word newsletter, 1986. Committeewoman Republican party, St. Louis, 1984; vice chair 4th Senatorial Dist. of Mo., 1984, vol. St. Louis Assn. Community Orgns., 1983; instr. first aid Bi-State chpt. ARC, St. Louis, 1984; block capt. Operation Brightside, St. Louis, 1984; co-chair Status and Role of Women, Union Meml. United Meth. Ch., 1986—. Named one of Top Ladies of Distinction, St. Louis, 1983. Mem. Am. Soc. Interior Designers (assoc.), NAACP, Nat. Mus. Women in the Arts (charter), Nat. Council Negro Women (1st v.p. 1984), Invention Assn. of St. Louis (subcom. head 1985), Coalition of 100 Black Women, St. Louis Assn. Fashion Designers. Methodist. Club: Presidents, (Washington). Avocations: reading; designing personal wardrobe; modeling; horseback riding; boating. Home and Office: 5469 Maple St Saint Louis MO 63112

MACQUEEN, ROBERT MITCHELL, human resources executive; b. Endicott, N.Y., Aug. 16, 1939; s. Hugh Kenneth and Helen Elizabeth (King) MacQ.; m. Nancy Louise Malowicky, June 10, 1960; children: Janet Elizabeth, Robin Louise. BA, Colgate U., 1961; postgrad., Cornell U., 1961-62. With Rexnord Inc., Milw., 1962-65, dir. human resources, 1977-85, v.p. human resources, 1985—; personnel mgr. Rexnord Inc., Warren, Pa., 1965-68; mgr. group personnel Rexnord Inc., Worcester, Mass., 1968-77; bd. dirs. New Life Inc., Barton, Vt. Mem. City Charter Commn., Westboro, Mass., 1972; bd. dirs. Milw. Council Alcoholism, 1985—. Named one of Outstanding Young Men of Am., U.S. Jaycees, 1973. Mem. Machinery and Allied Products Inst. (human resource council 1985—), Phi Beta Kappa, Pi Sigma Alpha. Republican. Avocations: reading, antiques, clocks. Home: 2324 Bonniwell Rd Mequon WI 53092 Office: Rexnord Inc 350 N Sunny Slope Brookfield WI 53005

MACRAE, DONALD ALEXANDER, emeritus business educator; b. Eldora, Iowa, Dec. 3, 1916; s. William and Mary (Stewart) MacR.; B.A., U. No. Iowa, 1943; M.A., U. Iowa, 1950, Ph.D., 1962; m. Adeline Taylor, July 8, 1943 (dec. Jan. 1963); children—Margaret Ann, Pamela, Patricia; m. 2d, Joyce M. Spooner McCrea, June 1, 1968. Prin., Solon (Iowa) High Sch., 1943-44, Riverton (Iowa) High Sch., 1944-45, 47-48; instr. U. Iowa, 1949-54; prof. bus. adminstrn. Mankato (Minn.) State U., 1954-82, prof. emeritus, 1982—. Bd. dirs. United Fund, 1971-76, Mankato Symphony Orch., 1981-84. Served with AUS, 1946-47. Mem. Am. Bus. Writing Assn., Nat. Bus. Edn. Assn., Internat. Soc. Bus. Edn., Adminstrv. Mgmt. Soc. (Merit award 1984), Clan Mac Rae Soc. N.Am., Twin Cities Scottish Club, St. Andrew's Soc. Minn., Sigma Tau Delta, Kappa Delta Pi, Pi Omega Pi, Delta Pi Epsilon, Phi Delta Kappa. Presbyterian. Home: 211 Woodshire Dr Mankato MN 56001 Office: Mankato State University Coll of Bus Mankato MN 56001

MACSAI, JOHN, architect; b. Budapest, Hungary, May 20, 1926; came to U.S., 1947, naturalized, 1954; s. Ferenc and Margit (Rosenfeld) Lusztig; m. Geraldine Marcus, May 7, 1950; children: Pamela, Aaron, Marian, Gwen. Baccalaureate summa cum laude, Kolcsey Gimnasium, Budapest, 1944; student, Atelier Art Sch., Budapest, 1941-43, Poly. U., Budapest, 1945-47; B.Arch. magna cum laude, Miami U., Oxford, Ohio, 1949. Archtl. designer Skidmore, Owings & Merrill, Chgo., Pace Assos., Chgo., Raymond Loewy Assos., Chgo., 1949-55; partner Hausner & Macsai, Chgo., 1955-71, Campbell & Macsai, Chgo., 1971-74; prin. John Macsai & Assocs. Architects, Inc., Chgo., 1975—; prof. architecture U. Ill., Chgo., 1970—. Author: High Rise Apartment Buildings—A Design Primer, 1972, Housing, 1976, Russian edit., 1980, 2d edit., 1982, Mexican edit., 1984; co-author: Designing Environments for the Aged, 1977, Housing for a Maturing Population, 1983; Works include Nat. Opinion Research Center, U. Chgo., 1967, High Energy Physics Bldg., U. Chgo., 1968, Social Services Center, U. Chgo., 1970, Harbor House, Malibu East apt. bldg., 1972, Waterford apt. bldg., 1976. Chmn. SE Council Integrated Communities, 1968-70. Recipient 13 design award citations Chgo. chpt. AIA. Fellow AIA. Jewish. Home: 1207 Judson Ave Evanston IL 60202 Office: John Macsai & Assos 168 N Michigan Ave Chicago IL 60601

MACUR, MARK JOSEPH, accountant; b. Chgo., May 18, 1957; s. Walter Michael and Anne Marie (Fusco) M.; m. Catherine Ann Bosch, May 17, 1980 (dec. Oct. 1985); 1 child, Kimberly. BS in Acctg., DePaul U., 1979. CPA, Ill. Staff acct. Bernstein & Bank, Ltd., Chgo., 1979-81; controller Croda Works Corp., Niles, Ill., 1982—. Mem. Am. Inst. CPA's, Ill. Soc. CPA's. Roman Catholic. Avocations: tennis, racquetball, jogging, reading, single parenting. Home: 4152B Cove Lane Glenview IL 60025 Office: Croda Inks Corp 7777 N Merrimac Niles IL 60648

MACWILLIAMS, MICHELE, advertising and public relations executive; b. Dearborn, Mich., May 6, 1954; d. Valentino L. and Betty Lou (Block) Asquini; m. Steven D. MacWilliams, Aug. 20, 1978. Student, Cen. Mich. U., 1972-76. Various positions with advt. dept. Grosse Pointe Foods, Detroit, 1978-80; mktg. dir. Sugar Loaf Resort, Cedar, Mich., 1980-82; account rep. R.E. Moreilliam, Detroit, 1982-83; pres. Metro Media Assocs., Inc., Bloomfield Hills, Mich., 1983—. Columnist: P.R. Potpourri, 1984—, The Reporter Newspaper, 1984—, Michigan Restaurateur, 1984; contbr. articles to jours. and mags. Mem. Mich. Hunter/Juniper Assn. Club: Aderafter of Detroit. Avocations: show thoroughbred hunter/junipers, skiing (cert. instr.), running.

MACY, JANET, educator; b. Omaha, Nov. 9, 1935; d. Val and Marie (Letovsky) Kuska; B.S., U. Nebr., 1957; M.S., Kans. State U., 1961; M.Ed., S.D. State U., 1970. With Fed. Extension Service, U.S. Dept. Agr., Washington, 1956, Kans. State U. Sta. KSAC, 1957-61, U. Nebr. Sta. KUON, 1961-62, Iowa State U. Sta. WOI-TV, 1962-67, S.D. State U. Sta. KESD-TV, 1967-71; mem. faculty U. Minn. Sta. KUOM, Mpls., 1971—, now assoc. prof. dept. family Soc. Sci.; with Meredith Pubs., Better Homes & Gardens, 1972-73; cons. U.S. Consumer Product Safety Commn., 1978-79. Recipient U. Nebr. Masters award, 1973; Minn. Edn. Assn. Sch. Bell award, 1980, 81, 82, merit award, 1983; Agrl. Communicators in Edn. Superior awards, 1966, 68, 79, 81; Am. Women in Radio and TV Communication Nutrition award, 1977. Mem. Agrl. Communicators in Edn., Am. Soc. Tng. and Devel., Minn. Intergovtl. Tng. Council, Minn. Edn. Assn., NEA, Epsilon Sigma Phi. Home: 6852 Bethany Park Dr Lincoln NE 68505

MADDEN, JOHN EDWARD, graphics company executive; b. Chgo., July 4, 1928; s. William H. and Margaret C. (Hafertep) M.; m. Carla Schommer, Apr. 17, 1951 (div. May 1978); children: Mary Jo, Julie, Martha, Peter. BSBA, Northwestern U., Evanston, Ill., 1949, MBA, 1959. V.p. Kohl & Madden Printing Ink Corp., Chgo., 1955-77; mgr. comml. ink J.M. Huber, Edison, N.J., 1978-81; exec. v.p. Graphic Color, Elk Grove Village, Ill., 1981—. Served to capt. USMC, 1951-55. Mem. Chgo. Litho Club, Printers Supplymen's Guild, Chgo. Printing Ink Mfrs. Assn. Republican. Roman Catholic. Avocations: cycling, skiing, traveling. Home: 1716 E Northfield Sq Northfield IL 60093 Office: Graphic Color Corp 750 Arthur Ave Elk Grove IL 60007

MADDEN, JOSHUA ROBERT, automotive company executive; b. Shamokin, Pa., Feb. 23, 1930; s. Joshua Elwood and Helen (Shremshock) M.; m. Jennie Buel Quirk, Dec. 5, 1953; children—Suzanne, Jill, Joshua E., Philip, Daniel. Student Muhlenberg Coll., 1947-49. Exptl. metallurgist, sr. engr. materials, devel. engr. Pontiac Motor div. Gen. Motors Co., Pontiac, Mich., 1954-77; exec. engr., chief engr. Volkswagen of Am., Troy, Mich., 1977—. Patentee in field. Bd. dirs. YMCA, Rochester, Mich., 1970-72, subcom. chmn. centennial com., 1969. Served to lt. U.S. Army, 1951-54. Recipient Nat. Industry award Soc. Plastics Industries, 1976-77. Mem. Soc. Automotive Engrs. (mem. gen. materials council), Detroit Rubber Group (tech. program organizer 1956—), Engring. Soc. Detroit. Episcopalian. Lodge: Kiwanis (pres. 1970, treas. 1971-81), Elks. Home: 772 Allston Dr Rochester MI 48063 Office: Volkswagen Am 888 W Big Beaver St Troy MI 48099

MADDEN, LAURENCE VINCENT, plant pathology educator; b. Ashland, Pa., Oct. 10, 1953; s. Lawrence Vincent and Janet Elizabeth (Wewer) M.; m. Susan Elizabeth Heady, July 7, 1984. BS, Pa. State U., 1975, MS, 1977, PhD, 1980. Research scientist Ohio State U., Wooster, 1980-82, asst. prof., 1983-86, assoc. prof., 1986—. Contbr. articles to profl. jours. U.S. Dept. Research grantee, 1984, 85, 86. Mem. Am. Phytopath. Soc. (chmn. com. 1983), Biometric Soc., Assn. Applied Biologists, Sigma Xi (chpt. pres. 1985). Avocations: photography, travel. Home: 677 Greenwood Blvd Wooster OH 44691 Office: Ohio State U OARDC Dept Plant Pathology Wooster OH 44691

MADDEX, EILEEN CALLAGHAN, retired national association director; b. Columbus, Ohio, Apr. 18, 1921; d. Cornelius James and Martha Rebecca (Durrett) Callaghan; m. Robert Leo Maddex, Jan. 26, 1946 (dec. Dec. 1977); children: Douglas E., Gregory R., Jeffrey T., Norman E., Paul M.; m. Harold Donald Miller, June 20, 1981; stepchildren: Ronald, Patricia. BS,

Ohio State U., 1944. Guidance counselor Ohio State U., Columbus, 1944-45; home economics tchr. St. Mary of the Springs Sch., Columbus, 1945-46; exec. dir. Omicron Nu, Haslett, Mich., 1966-86; exec. dir. emeritus Omicron Nu, Haslett. Pres. Haslett Woman's Club, 1965-67, 82-83; pres. Birch Lake Assn., Haslett, 1985-87. Recipient Disting. Alumni award Ohio State U., 1979. Mem. Am. Home Econs. Assn., Mich. Home Econs. Assn., Lansing Area Home Econs. In Action (scholarship chair 1981—), Ingham County Fedn. Women's Clubs (pres. 1985-87). Roman Catholic. Club: Mich. State Univ. Extension Women's (pres. 1982-83). Lodge: PEO (treas. Lansing, Mich. chpt. 1980-82, pres. 1987—). Home: 5587 Woodville Rd PO Box 153 Haslett MI 48840

MADDOX, DAVID STOKELY, pediatric dentist; b. Akron, Ohio, June 14, 1927; s. Herbert V. and Marguerite (Stokely) M.; m. Sybil Renee Harris, June 30, 1956; 1 child, David S. II. AB, Miami U., Oxford, Ohio, 1950; DDS, Case Western Reserve U., 1955. Practice dentistry specializing in pediatrics Zanesville, Ohio, 1956—; sch. dentist Zanesville City Sch. System, 1956—. Served as cpl. U.S. Army, 1946-47. Mem. ADA, Ohio Dental Assn., Ohio Soc. Dentistry for Children (pres.1960-61), Ohio Acad. Pediatric Dentistry (pres. 1979-80), Muskingum Valley Dental Soc. (pres. 1963-64), Acad. Straight Wire and Functional Orthodontics. Avocation: stained glass. Office: 2927 Bell St Zanesville OH 43701-1779

MADDOX, ODINGA LAWRENCE, minister; b. Akron, Ohio, Mar. 6, 1939; s. Stephen Henderson and Exia Pearl (Jefferies) M.; children: Sharon Lynette, Lawrence Jr., Stephen Henderson III. BS, Livingstone Coll., 1974; M in Divinity, Hood Theol. Sem., 1977; postgrad., Trinity Luth. Sem., 1986—. Minister Pleasant Ridge A.M.E. Zion Ch., Gastonia, N.C., 1971-78, St. Peter's A.M.E. Zion Ch., Cleve., 1978-85, First A.M.E. Zion Ch., Columbus, Ohio, 1985—; bd. dirs. M.J. Simms and Assocs., Inc.; educator Bd. of Edn., Cleve., 1978-85. Mem. staff, writer A.M.E. Zion Ch. Sch. Lit., 1979-83; dir. evangelism Ohio Ann. Conf., bd. evangelism, A.M.E. Zion Ch., Charlotte, N.C., 1983-85; del. A.M.E. Zion Ch. Gen. Conf., St. Louis, 1984, 88; trustee Coalition of Concern Clergy, Inc., Columbus, 1985. Mem. Ohio Council Chs., Interdenominational Ministerial Alliance (pres. 1986—), Alpha Phi Alpha. Home: 1295 E Gates St Columbus OH 43216 Office: First AEM Zion Ch 873 Bryden Rd Columbus OH 43205

MADENSKI, E. A., home products hardware executive. Chmn. Keeler Brass Co., Grand Rapids, Mich. Office: Keeler Brass Co 955 Godfrey Ave SW Grand Rapids MI 49503 *

MADEY, GREGORY RICHARD, mathematician; b. Cleve., June 30, 1947; s. Richard M. and Rose Madej; m. Wendy Ann Lawrence, Aug. 8, 1975; children—Candice, Gregory. B.S., Cleve. State U., 1974; M.S., 1975; M.S. in Ops. Research, Case Western Res. U., 1979, Ph.D., 1984. Instr math. Cuyahoga Community Coll., Cleve., 1975-79, asst. to dean instrn., 1975-77; ops. research analyst Gould Corp., Cleve. 1978-79; bus. planning analyst Goodyear Aerospace Corp., Akron, Ohio, 1979-85, mgr. bus. planning and analysis, 1985—. Author: (with others) College Mathematics, 1974; contbr. articles to IEEE Trans. Mem. Ops. Research Soc. Am., Inst. Mgmt. Sci. (sec. coll. on research and devel. 1982—, editor newsletter 1983—), Math. Assn. Am., Mil. Ops. Research Soc., Omega Rho, Pi Mu Epsilon. Office: Goodyear Aerospace Akron OH 44315

MADGETT, JOHN PATRICK, III, business executive; b. Hastings, Nebr., Dec. 12, 1940; s. John Patrick, Jr. and Marian Ellen (Dominy) M.; m. Jean Belli, June 15, 1966 (div. 1979); children—Kimberly, John Patrick, Robyn, David. B.A. in Math. and Physics, Carleton Coll., 1962; B.S.E.E., Columbia U., 1963; M.B.A., Stanford U., 1965. Case writer Harvard Bus. Sch., Cambridge, Mass., 1965; indsl. economist Stanford Research Inst., Palo Alto, Calif., 1965; fin. analyst Kaiser Aluminum & Chem. Corp., Oakland, Calif., 1965-68; pres., dir. Ajax Towing Co., Mpls., 1968-77, United Dock Service, Rochester, Ky., 1968-77, Ener-Tran, Inc., Mpls., 1975-81, United Barge Co., Mpls., 1968-77, Wellspring Energy Corp., Mpls., 1977—, Wellspring Fin. Corp., Mpls., 1980—; pres., dir. Wellspring Offshore Services Corp., New Orleans, 1980—; pres., chief exec. officer, dir. Wellspring Corp., Mpls., 1980—; chmn., dir. Wellspring Properties, 1984—; chmn. Wellspring Andrena Ltd., 1984—; dir. Trend Sci., Inc., Mpls., Minn. Ranch & Cattle Co., Mpls.; cons. German Pub. Utility Industry, Joint Engring. Council U.S.A. and Europe, N.Y.C., 1962. Co-author: World of Science and Technology, 1975. Trustee, Breck Sch., Mpls., 1978-81; active vol. mgmt. Mpls. United Way, 1968-76, fund raising Campus Crusade for Christ Internat., San Bernardino, Calif., 1978-84. Mem. Nat. Feed & Grain Dealers Assn., Water Transprt Assn., Young Pres. Orgn. (treas. 1973-80), Propellar Club. Republican. Episcopalian. Clubs: Marsh Lake, Five Fifty-Five, Minneapolis, Minikahda. Office: Wellspring Corp 4530 IDS Center 80 S 8th St Minneapolis MN 55402

MADICH, BERNADINE MARIE HOFF, savings and loan executive; b. Duluth, Minn., Mar. 4, 1934; d. Palmer and Esther (Anderson) Hoff; m. Michael Madich, May 23, 1955 (div. 1986); children: Michael R.H., Tina B. Watts, Rory G. (dec.). Student, Inst. Fin. Edn., 1972, 73, 77-78, 83-84, 86-87, cert. real estate law, 1984. Teller St. Louis County Fed. Savs. and Loan, 1972-73, sec., ins. mortgage counselor, 1973-83, loan servicing specialist, 1983-86, asst. mgr. loan servicing dept., 1986—. Pack leader Boy Scouts Am., Duluth, 1964-68; leader Girl Scouts U.S., Duluth, 1972-74; chmn. Duluth Hall of Fame, 1983-85; doscent Glensheen U. Minn. Glensheen, 1979-85; vol. St. Luke's Hosp., Duluth, 1968-72; asst. treas. Port Cities Days, Duluth, 1984-86, treas., 1987—; chairperson Duluth East High Sch. All-Sch. Reunion, 1986. Mem. Duluth Area Ins. Women (treas. 1977-79, v.p. 1979-80, pres. 1980-82), Duluth Bus. and Profl. Women (treas. 1976-78, 2d v.p., 1986, 1st v.p., 1987). Home: 4327 Gladstone St Duluth MN 55804 Office: St Louis County Fed Savs & Loan PO Box 115 Duluth MN 55801

MADIGAN, CHARLES EUGENE, marketing and sales executive; b. Lincoln, Ill., Mar. 11, 1922; s. Orville E. and Virginia M. (Moak) M.; LL.B., Am. Sch. Law, 1952; m. Jane Veach, Nov. 24, 1942; children—Janet, Virginia Ann, Barbara. Regional mgr. Alcoa Steamship Co., Inc., 1945-67; regional mgr. Bahama Ministry Tourism, Chgo., 1967-71; gen. sales mgr. Pheasant Run Lodge, St. Charles, Ill., 1971-74; dir. mktg. and sales O'Hare Inn, Des Plaines, Ill., 1974-79; v.p. Olympia Resort, Oconomowoc, Wis., 1979-82; pres. Hotel/Resorts Meeting and Conv. Cons. Served to lt. U.S. Mcht. Marines, 1944-46. Recipient Sch. award Am. Legion, 1936; plaques, VFW, 1975-76, 77, 78, 79, U.S. Army, 1979, Nat. Sheriffs Assn., 1975, Kiwanis Internat., 1979, Research Inst. Am., 1978. Republican. Lodge: Masons. Home: Rt 1 Box 2621 Hidde Springs Lake Neshkoro WI 54960 Office: 1400 E Touhy Ave Des Plaines IL 60018

MADIGAN, EDWARD R., congressman; b. Lincoln, Ill., Jan. 13, 1936; m. Evelyn M. George, 1955; children—Kimberly, Kellie, Mary Beth. Grad., Lincoln Coll., 1955, D.H.L. (hon.), 1975; D.H.L. (hon.), Millikin U., Ill. Wesleyan U. Mem. Ill. Ho. of Reps., 1967-72, 93d-99th congresses from 15th Ill. dist.; Rep. chief deputy whip 100th congress; mem. House Energy and Commerce Com.; ranking Rep. House Agr. Com. Recipient Outstanding Legislator award Ill. Assn. Sch. Supts., 1968, Outstanding Pub. Service award Lincoln Coll. Alumni Assn. Mem. Ill. Jaycees (past v.p.), Lincoln C. of C. Lodges: Elks, Kiwanis. Office: 2312 Rayburn House Office Bldg Washington DC 20515

MADIGAN, JEANNE MARIE, advertising director; b. Chgo., Mar. 18, 1958; s. John Patrick and Mary Elizabeth (Meier) M. BA, Drake U., 1976-80. Graphic designer John Bryne Co., Chgo., 1980-81; dir. art and advt. Waterloo (Iowa) Industries, 1981—. Drake U. Art scholar, 1977, 78, 79. Mem. Waterloo Mgmt. Club (v.p. 1982-83), Mktg. and Advt. Club. Avocations: water sports, triathalon, craft, travel. Home: 3656 Ravenwood Circle Apt 10 Waterloo IA 50702 Office: Waterloo Industries 300 Ansborough Ave Waterloo IA 50704

MADIGAN, MICHAEL J., state legislator; b. Chgo., Apr. 19, 1942; m. Shirley Roumagoux; children: Lisa, Tiffany, Nicole, Andrew. Ed., U. Notre Dame, Loyola U., Chgo. Mem. Ill. Ho. of Reps., 1971—, majority leader, 1977-80, minority leader, 1981-82, house speaker, 1983—; lawyer. Sec. to Alderman David W. Healey; hearing officer Ill. Commerce Commn.; del. 6th Ill. Constnl. Conv.; trustee Holy Cross Hosp.; ex officio mem. adv. com. to pres. Richard J. Daley Coll.; adv. com. Fernley Harris Sch. for Handicapped; committeeman 13th Ward Democratic Orgn. Mem. Council Fgn. Relations, City Club Chgo. Office: 316 House of Representatives State Capitol Springfield IL 62706

MADISON, THOMAS F., telephone company executive; b. Mpls., Feb. 25, 1936; s. Earl E. and Bernice E. (O'Brien) M.; m. Marilyn L. Johnson, June 22, 1956; children—Mike T., Mary A., Mark R. B.S., U. Minn., 1959. With Northwestern Bell Telephone Co., various locations, 1954—; exec. v.p. Northwestern Bell Telephone Co., Omaha, 1983-85, pres., chief exec. officer, 1985—, also dir., 1983—; bd. dirs. First Bank Systems. Bd. dirs. Creighton U., Omaha, Guthrie Theater, Mpls., Minn. Orch., Mpls., Coll. St. Thomas, Mpls. Served with USNG, 1953-54. Roman Catholic. Clubs: Omaha, Omaha Country; Minikahda, Minn. Alumni, Mpls. Athletic (Mpls.). Avocations: golfing; hunting; skiing; fishing. Home: 134 S 122d St Omaha NE 68154 Office: Northwestern Bell Telephone Co 1314 Douglas On-The-Mall Omaha NE 68102

MADSEN, CRAIG JEFFREY, dentist; b. Racine, Wis., Aug. 6, 1956; s. John Henry and Ruth Mae (Johnson) M.; m. Mary Margaret Hirsch, July 25, 1981. BS in Life Sci. cum laude, U. Wis., Kenosha, 1978; DDS, Marquette U., 1982. Gen. practice dentistry Madison, Wis., 1982-85, Madsen & Hirsch, Madison, Wis., 1985—; area dir. Quest Seminars Internat. Mem. ADA, Dane County Dental Soc., Wis. Dental Assn., Internat. Congress Oral Implantologists, AGD. Lutheran. Club: Toastmasters. Office: Madsen & Hirsch 6313 Odana Rd Madison WI 53719

MADSEN, DOROTHY LOUISE (MEG), career counseling executive; b. Rochester, N.Y.; d. Charles Robert and Louise Anna Agnes Meyer; B.A., Mundelein Coll., Chgo., 1968; m Frederick George Madsen, Feb. 17, 1945. Public relations rep. Rochester Telephone Corp., 1941-42; feature writer Rochester Democrat & Chronicle, 1939-41; exec. dir. LaPorte (Ind.) chpt. ARC, 1964; dir. adminstrv. services Bank Mktg. Assn., Chgo., 1971-74; exec. dir. Eleanor Assn., Chgo., 1974-84; founder Meg Madsen Assocs., Chgo., 1984—; women's career counselor; founder, Clearinghouse Internat. Newsletter; founder Eleanor Women's Forum, Clearinghouse Internat., Eleanor Intern Program Coll. Students and Returning Women. Served to lt. col. WAC, 1942-47, 67-70. Decorated Legion of Merit, Meritorious Service award. Mem. Res. Officers Assn., Mundelein Alumnae Assn., Central Eleanor Club, Phi Sigma Tau (charter mem. Ill. Kappa chpt.). Home and Office: 1030 N State St Chicago IL 60610

MADSEN, STEVEN D., newspaper editor and publisher; b. Mpls., Apr. 29, 1953; s. Douglas J. and Marie E. (Wandersee) M.; m. Peggy Elizabeth Lemerand, Aug. 18, 1973; children: Eric, Michael, David, Alan. BA, U. Wis., Whitewater, 1974. Staff writer Daily Jefferson County Union, Ft. Atkinson, 1972-74; advt. dir. Portage (Wis.) Daily Register, 1974-81; sales mgr. Walch Pubs., Inc., Wisconsin Dells, Wis., 1981-85; editor, pub. The Mid-County Times, Pardeeville, Wis., 1985—; v.p. Video-Tape Services, Inc., Ft. Atkinson, 1983—. Mem. Pardeeville Area Bus. Assn. (pres. 1986), Wis. Newspaper Assn., Nat. Newspaper Assn. Lutheran. Avocations: music, baseball. Home: 209 S Main St Pardeeville WI 53954-0006 Office: Mid-County Times 142 N Main St Pardeeville WI 53954-0006

MADSON, HAROLD L., electronics supply company executive. Chmn., chief exec. officer Border State Electric Supply Co., Fargo, N.D. Office: Border State Electric Supply Co 2001 1st Ave N Box 2767 Fargo ND 58108 *

MADSON, P. C., utilities company executive. Pres. Border State Electric Supply Co., Fargo, N.D. Office: Border State Electric Supply Co 2001 1st Ave N Box 2767 Fargo ND 58108 *

MADSON, ROBERT GORDON, athletic educator; b. Mpls., Mar. 8, 1959; s. James Maynard and Mary Louise (Linwood) M. Student in English writing, U. Minn., 1977-81; student, Hamline Sch. Law, 1982-83. Dir. tennis program City of St. Louis Park, Minn., 1977-79; tennis profl. Northwest Tennis Club, St. Louis Park, 1980-86; owner, dir. Bob Madson's Jr. Devel., Golden Valley, Minn., 1982—; owner, mgr. Bob Madson's Sports Psychology Enterprises, Golden Valley, 1984—; tennis dir. Golden Valley Country Club, 1980-86; dir. racquet sports Greenway Athletic Club, 1987—. Author: Overcoming the Mental Barrier, 1985. Vol. World Vision, Golden Valley, 1985-86, United Cancer Fund., St. Louis Park, and Golden Valley, 1978—; precincts vice chmn. St. Louis Park and Golden Valley Rep., 1982—, chmn., del. St. Louis Park Rep., 1980-82. Mem. U.S. Profl. Tennis Assn., Northwest Profl. Assn., U.S. Tennis Assn., Northwest Tennis Assn. (bd. dirs. 1985—). Republican. Club: Greenway Athletic. Professional tennis player ranked 38th in nation and 10th in N.W. U.S. for 1986. Avocations: team sports, music, writing, reading, skiing. Home and Office: 9143 W Olson Memorial Hwy #102 Golden Valley MN 55427

MAEDER, EDWARD CHARLES, obstetrician, gynecologist; b. Mpls., Nov. 28, 1938; s. Edward Charles and Irene (Kangas) M.; m. Phyllis Maness, Aug. 8, 1964 (div. Jan. 1986); children: Jody, Julie, Laurie, Adam. m. Joanne Eileen Giese, Feb. 5, 1986. BA, Yale U., 1958; BS, U. Minn., 1959, MD, 1963. Intern then resident U. Minn., Mpls., 1969; obstetrician, gynecologist Park Nicollet Med. Ctr., Mpls., 1969—; clin. assoc. prof. U. Minn., Mpls., 1978—. Contbr. articles to profl. jours. Served to lt. USN, 1967-69, Vietnam. Decorated Bronze Star. Fellow Am. Coll. Ob-Gyn (Minn. sect. chmn. 1986—); mem. Am. Fertility Soc., Minn. Med. Assn., Minn. Ob-Gyn Soc. (pres. 1986, bd. govs.), Hennepin County Med. Soc. Republican. Roman Catholic. Clubs: Interlachen Country, Flagship Athletic. Avocations: sports. Home: 5008 Windsor Ave Edina MN 55436 Office: Park Nicollet Med Ctr 5000 W 39th St Saint Louis Park MN 55416

MAESCHER, ALBERT THOMAS, advertising company executive; b. St. Louis, May 16, 1915; s. Albert Herbert and Florence (Schuester) M.; m. Vera Dobbs, June 23, 1942 (div. July 1948); m. Karol Ann Fahnestock, Nov. 12, 1953; 1 child, Craig Ann Cotner. Student, Washington U., 1940-41. Treas. Ridgeway Co., St. Louis, 1938-42; v.p. Oakleigh R. French and Assocs., St. Louis, 1942-52; pres. Al Maescher Advt., Inc., St. Louis, 1952—. Founder Des Peres Vol. Fire Dept., 1960; health Commr. City of Des Peres, 1966; chmn. Gridiron Dinner, St. Louis, 1946; bd. dirs. St. Louis Better Bus. Bur., 1945. Mem. Am. Mktg. Assn. (v.p. 1943), Indsl. Mktg. Assn. (v.p. 1943). Republican. Christian Scientist. Clubs: Advt. of St. Louis (past holder all offices, pres. 1944), Allied Food, Valley Mount Saddle (pres. 1960-63). Avocations: reading, painting, watching sports. Office: 11433 Olde Cobin Rd Creve Coeur MO 63141

MAGEN, JED GARY, child psychiatrist; b. Des Moines, Iowa, May 10, 1953; s. Myron Shimon and Ruth May Magen; m. Carol Ann Barrett, June 18, 1978; children: Benjamin Barrett, Zachary Barrett. BA, Oakland U., 1975; DO, Coll. Osteopathic Medicine and Surgery, Des Moines, 1978. Intern Botsford Gen. Hosp., Farmington Hills, Mich., 1978-79; with Ind. Health Service, Bowler, Wis., 1979-82; resident in psychiatry, fellow in child psychiatry U. Mich., 1982-86; clin. instr. psychiatry, research fellow Inst. Social Research U. Mich., 1986—; chief resident child psychiatry U. Mich., 1984-1985, dept. chief, 1985-86. Served with USPHS, 1979-82. mem. Am. Psychiat. Assn., Am. Osteopathic Assn. Am. Coll. Neuropsychiatry. Home: 801 Princeton Ann Arbor MI 48103 Office: Childrens Psychiat Hosp U Mich Med Ctr Ann Arbor MI 49109

MAGEN, MYRON SHIMIN, osteopathic physician, educator, university dean; b. Bklyn., Mar. 1, 1926; s. Barney and Gertrude Beatrice (Cohen) M.; m. Ruth Sherman, July 6, 1952; children—Jed, Ned, Randy. D.O., Coll. Osteo. Medicine and Surgery, 1951; Sc.D. (hon.), U. Osteo. Medicine and Health Scis., Des Moines, 1981. Rotating intern Coll. Hosp., Des Moines, 1951-52, resident in pediatrics, 1953-54; chmn. dept. pediatrics Coll. Osteo. Medicine and Surgery, Des Moines, 1958-62, Riverside Osteo. Hosp., Trenton, Mich., 1962-68, Detroit Osteo. Hosp., 1965-67; med. dir., dir. med. edn. Zieger-Botsford Hosps., Farmington, Mich., 1968-70; prof. pediatrics Mich. State Coll. Osteo. Medicine, East Lansing, 1970—, dean, 1970—; mem. spl. med. adv. group to chief med. dir. VA, 1973-77; mem. grad. med. edn. nat. div. com. HHS, Washington, 1978-80; James Watson disting. lectr. Ohio Osteo. Assn., 1974, Grad. Med. Edn. Nat. Adv. Com.,; Watson Meml. Lectr. Am. Coll. Osteo. Pediatricians, 1987. Contbr. articles to profl. jours. Served with USN, 1943-45. Recipient Disting. Service award Okla. Coll. Osteo. Medicine and Surgery, 1975; Founder's medal Tex. Coll. Osteo. Medicine, 1978;. Mem. Am. Assn. Colls. Osteo. Medicine (pres. 1977), Am. Osteo. Assn. (com. edn.; La. Burns lectr. 1977), Am. Coll. Osteo. Pediatrics (pres. 1965-66), Mich. Assn. Osteo. Physicians and Surgeons. Home: 1251 Farwood Dr East Lansing MI 48823 Office: Mich State Univ Coll Osteopathic Medicine 308 E Fee Hall East Lansing MI 48824

MAGERS, LINDA SUE, school librarian, educator; b. Marion, Ind., Oct. 23, 1955; d. Robert Eugene Eckert and Virginia Louise (Sprinkle) E.; m. Terry Lee Magers, June 10, 1978; 1 child, Timothy Allen. B.S., Ball State U., 1978, M.L.S., 1983. Tchr. English jr. high sch. and librarian, Marion, Ind., 1978-80, sch. librarian, Ind., 1980-85, tchr. writing, 1984-85. Activity coordinator, Leader Girl Scouts U.S.A.; sec. Grant County chpt. Ducks Unltd. Recipient 5 yr. pin Girl Scouts U.S.A., 1982. Mem. ALA, AIME, Ind. Library Assn., Delta Theta Tau. Clubs: Central Ind. Retriever, Michiana Retriever (Ind.), Bluegrass Retriever (Ky.). Home: 916 E 35th St Marion IN 46953

MAGGIO, ROSALIE, writer; b. Victoria, Tex., Nov. 8, 1943; d. Paul Joseph and Irene Cecelia (Nash) M.; m. David C. Koskenmaki, Dec. 28, 1968; children: Elizabeth Koskenmaki, Katherine Koskenmaki, Matthew Koskenmaki. BA, Coll. of St. Catherine, 1965; certificat, Université de Nancy, France, 1966. Editor Internat. Coll. Surgeons, Chgo., 1967-70; asst. pub. relations French Consulate Gen., Chgo., 1970-71; freelance writer, editor St. Paul, 1971—. Author: The Travels of Soc, 1985, The Nonsexist Word Finder, 1987; edited more than 60 books; contbr. more than 600 articles to mags. and ednl. publs. Recipient Northwind Story Hour Children's Writing award The Loft, Inc., Mpls., 1985. Democrat. Roman Catholic. Avocations: genealogy, peace activism, travel. Home and Office: 1297 Summit Ave Saint Paul MN 55105

MAGHAMI, MAHMOOD GHAEM, chemical engineer; b. Tehran, Iran, Sept. 5, 1960; s. Javad Ghaem and Fakhr Ghaem (Azeemi) M.; m. Anita Laleh Janooby, July 21, 1982. BS in Chem., U. Ark., 1981, MS in Chem. Engring., 1984. Contract researcher Pfizer Corp., Fayetteville, Ark., 1984-85; process engr. At&T Tech. Systems, Lee's Summit, Mo., 1985—, project leader, 1986—. Mem. Am. Chem. Soc., Am. Inst. Chem. Engrs. Home: 10926 College Ln Apt 1C Kansas City MO 64137 Office: At&T Tech Systems Dept 103110 777 N Blue Pkwy Lee's Summit MO 64063

MAGILL, FRANK JOHN, federal judge. Judge U.S. Court of Appeals Eighth Circuit, Fargo, ND, 1986—. Office: Eighth Circuit 248 US Post Office Building 657 Second Avenue Fargo ND 58102 *

MAGLINTE, DEAN D. T., radiologist; b. Siquijor, Philippines, June 24, 1941; came to U.S., 1966; s. Daniel R. and Francisca O. Maglinte; m. Eleanor Marie McGraw, Apr. 26, 1969; children: Jennifer Marie, Eleanor Danielle, Dean Joseph. AA, U. Santo Tomas, Manila, 1960, MD, 1965. Diplomate Am. Bd. Radiology. Resident in radiology Centralsygehuset, Nykobing Falster, Denmark, 1965-66; resident in radiology Phila. Gen. Hosp., 1966-70, attending radiologist, 1972-73; attending radiologist Our Lady of Lourdes Hosp., Camden, N.J., 1970-71, Northeastern Hosp., Phila., 1971-72; instr. in radiology U. Pa., Phila., 1972-73; chief gastrointestinal radiology Meth. Hosp. of Ind., Indpls., 1973—; clin. prof. radiology Ind. U. Sch. Medicine, 1987—. Assoc. editor Radiology, 1986—; reviewer Am. Jour. of Roentgenology, 1985—, Digestine Disease and Scis., 1985—; contbr. numerous articles to profl. jours. Recipient Outstanding Radiologist award Butler U.-Meth. Hosp. Radiologic Tech. Program, 1981, Third prize INd. State Med. Assn., 1981, Disting. Tchr. award Meth. Hosp. House Staff, 1981-82. Mem. Soc. Gastrointestinal Radiology, Radiologic Soc. N.Am. (Cert. of Merit, 1981), Am. Roentgen Ray Soc. (Cert. of Merit, 1981), Am. Coll. Radiology. Home: 240 Raintree Dr Zionsville IN 46077 Office: Meth Hosp Dept Radiology 7601 N Senate Blvd Indianapolis IN 46202

MAGNAN, GEORGE AUGUSTINE, systems specialist, pharmacist; b. St. Louis, Sept. 2, 1948; s. William B. and Marcella C. (Wesselny) M.; m. Nanette Marie Herye, Jan. 31, 1969; children—John William, Dawn Michelle. B.S. in Pharmacy, St. Louis Coll. Pharmacy, 1971. Registered pharmacist, Mo. Clin. pharmacist Sisters of St. Mary's Health Ctr., St. Louis, 1971-79, systems analyst, 1979-86, systems specialist, 1986—; Bd. dirs. Health Care Family (formerly START Credit Union), St. Louis, 1982—, vice chmn., 1984-85, chmn. bd. 1985—. Mem. Am. Soc. Hosp. Pharmacists, Mo. Soc. Hosp. Pharmacists, St. Louis Soc. Hosp. Pharmacists, Coll. Pharmacy Alumni Assn. (bd. dirs. 1978—, historian 1984-85, treas. 1985—), Kappa Psi (bd. dirs. 1982—). Roman Catholic. Avocations: woodworking, mechanics, water and snow skiing, hiking. Office: Sisters of St Mary's Data Ctr 7980 Clayton Rd Saint Louis MO 63117

MAGNUS, RALPH ARTHUR, social worker; b. N.Y.C., Mar. 10, 1926; s. Simon and Gertrude (Israel) M.; m. Barbara Collins, May 9, 1950; children: Julie, Bryn, Jenny. BS, Queens Coll., 1948; MSW, Columbia U., 1953. Group worker Hawthorne (N.Y.) Cedar Knolls Sch., 1953-56; supr. group work LaRue Ctr. Hosp., Indpls., 1956-58; unit supr. BelleFaire, Cleve., 1958-60; supr. milieu therapy BeechBrook, Cleve., 1960-66; exec. dir. Lad Lake, Dousman, Wis., 1966-72; pvt. practice marriage and family counseling Waukesha, Wis., 1972—; cons. Nashotah (Wis) House Sem., 1973—; instr. U. Wis., Milw., 1973—; lectr. B&R Magnus Family Cons., Delafield, Wis., 1983—; tng. coordinator Family Social and Psychotherapy Services, Milw., 1986—, bd. dirs. 1973-86. Editor: The Therapist. bd. dirs. Women's Ctr., Waukesha, v.p., 1978-84; bd. dirs., pres. Mental Health Assn., Waukesha, 1970-76, 86, Waukesha Civic Theatre, 1970-75. Served as pvt. U.S. Army, 1944-45, ETO. Mem. Nat. Assn. Social Workers (cert.), Disabled Am. Vets. Avocations: golf, reading, writing, cutting wood, hiking. Home and Office: 1115 Milwaukee St Delafield WI 53018

MAGNUSON, CURT, grocery stores company executive. Pres. Valley Markets, Inc., Grand Forks, N.D. Office: Valley Markets Inc 1925 13th Ave N Grand Forks ND 58201 *

MAGNUSON, DONALD LEE, accountant; b. Chgo., Aug. 8, 1949; s. Elmer G. and Louise (Thompson) M.; m. Barbara Chase, May 16, 1971 (div. Mar. 1984); children: Kevin, Scott. BBA, Loyola U., Chgo., 1974. CPA, Ill. Staff acct. Beatrice Foods, Chgo., 1968-70, DoAll Co., Des Plaines, Ill., 1970-72; mng. Arthur Young & Co., Chgo., 1972-82; ptnr. Laventhol & Horwath, Chgo., 1982—. Mem. fin. com. Village of Streamwood, Ill., 1975; mem. budget fin. commn. Village of Mt. Prospect, Ill., 1980-83; mem. Streeterville Orgn. Active Residents, Chgo., 1983-87; mem. budget fin. com. Chgo. Heart Assn., 1985-87, chmn. corp. involvement, mgmt. services com., 1986-87, bd. govs., 1986-87. Served with USN, 1968-74. Mem. Am. Inst. CPA's, Ill. CPA Soc. (not for profit com. 1981—, auditing procedures and acctg. and rev. services com. 1986—). Clubs: Young Execs. (v.p. communications 1985-86), Execs. (Chgo.). Home: 910 N Lake Shore Dr Chicago IL 60611 Office: Laventhol & Horwath 300 S Riverside Plaza Chicago IL 60606

MAGNUSON, JOHN CHARLES, accountant; b. Lindsborg, Kans., Dec. 16, 1946; s. Victor C. and Margaret P. (Gibson) M.; m. Darlene A. Ryding, Mar. 23, 1968; children: Charlice J., Barry R. BBA, Washburn U., 1968. CPA, Mo., Kans. Staff acct. Baird, Kurtz and Dobson, Kansas City, Mo., 1969-72, sr. acct., 1973-74; controller Tech. and Profl. Assn., Kansas City, 1972-73; pvt. practice acctg. Lindsborg, Kans., 1974-79, 82—; ptnr. Magnuson and Ahlvers, Lindsborg, 1979-82; bd. dirs. Farmers State Bank, Lindsborg; lectr. acctg. Bethany Coll., Lindsborg, 1974-78; treas. Smoky Valley Devel. Co.; mem. adv. bd. McPherson County Diversified Services. County commr. McPherson County Kans., 1982—; mem. Messiah Ch. Council; coach Babe Ruth Baseball; co-chmn. Svensk Hyllningsfest Com., 1984-85; chmn. Bethany Coll. Area Fund Drive; com. mem. Delta Sigma Pi Ednl. Found.; mem. program commn. Kans. Kiwanis Found.; dir. region VII Nat. Conf. Rep. County Ofcls., Washington, 1987—. Served with USCG, 1968-69. Mem. Kans. Soc. CPA's (mem. fed. and state taxation com., mem. state and local govt. acctg. com., mem. acctg. legis. com.), Kans. Assn. Counties (bd. dirs.), Kans. County Commrs. (chmn. taxation and fin. com.), Nat. Assn. Counties (mem. taxation and fin. com.), Smoky Valley Hist. Soc. (treas.), Lindsborg C. of C. (bd. dirs.). Lutheran. Club: Quarterback (pres.

1975-77). Lodge: Kiwanis (treas. Lindsborg 1975-81). Avocations: collecting sports memorabilia. Office: 111 N Main PO Box 110 Lindborg KS 67456

MAGNUSON, LARRY NEIL, dentist; b. Topeka, Apr. 26, 1942; s. Carl McClelland Magnuson and Rebecca Jane (Smith) Jackson; m. Mary Ann Bauer, June 29, 1969; children: Marcia Ann, Keri Lynn, Neil Eric, Ryan Carl. Student, Washburn U., 1960-63; DDS, U. Mo., Kansas City, 1967. Dentist Mo. Pub. Health Dept., 1969-70; gen. practice dentistry Iola, Kans., 1970—. Trombone player Iola Area Symphony Orch., 1973-84, Iola Mcpl. Band, 1970-82; den leader Cub Scouts Am., Iola, 1985—. Served to lt. USNR, 1967-69. Fellow Acad. Gen. Dentistry; mem. Am. Soc. Dentistry for Children, ADA, Kans. Dental Assn. (del. 1970—), Sunflower Dental Soc. (pres. 1985—), Iola C. of C. Republican. Methodist. Lodge: Optimists. Avocations: woodcarving, gardening, sailing. Home: Rural Rt 3 Iola KS 66749 Office: 202 East St Iola KS 66749

MAGNUSON, PAUL A., federal judge; b. Carthage, S.D., Feb. 9, 1937; s. Arthur and Emma Elleda (Paulson) M.; m. Sharon Schultz, Dec. 21, 1959; children—Marlene, Margaret, Kevin, Kara. B.A., Gustavus Adolphus Coll, 1959; J.D., William Mitchell Coll., 1963. Ptnr. LeVander, Gillen, MIller & Magnuson, South St. Paul, Minn., 1963-81; judge U.S. Dist. Ct., St. Paul, 1981—. Mem. Met. Health Bd., St. Paul, 1970-72; legal counsel Ind. Republican Party Minn., St. Paul, 1979-81. Recipient Disting. Alumnus award Gustavus Adolphus Coll., 1982. Mem. ABA, 1st Dist. Bar Assn. (pres. 1974-75), Dakota County Bar Assn., Am. Judicature Soc. Presbyterian. Home: 3047 Klondike Ave N Lake Elmo MN 55042 Office: US Dist Ct 316 N Robert St Saint Paul MN 55101

MAGNUSON, WARREN ROGER, church official; b. Mpls., Dec. 5, 1921; s. Edwin John and Hulda (Smith) M.; m. Margaret Linnea Johnson, June 9, 1944. A.A., Bethel Coll., 1942; B.A., U. Minn., 1946; B.D., Bethel Theol. Sem., 1946; hon. degree, Judson Coll., Elgin, Ill., 1973. Ordained to ministry Bapt. Ch., 1946. Pastor Immanuel Bapt. Ch., St. Paul, 1943-46, Washington Ave. Bapt. Ch., Ludington, Mich., 1947-50, 1st Bapt. Ch., Willmar, Minn., 1950-54, Cen. Bapt. Ch., St. Paul, 1954-69; gen. sec. Bapt. Gen. Conf., Arlington Heights, Ill., 1969—. Moderator Minn. Bapt. Conf., 1959, trustee, 1965-69; moderator Bapt. Gen. Conf., 1965, mem. bd. missions, 1965—; Mem. exec. com. Bapt. Joint Com. on Pub. Affairs, 1970—, chmn., 1970-72; mem. exec. com. Gen. Commn. on Chaplains and Armed Forces Personnel, 1969—, Bapt. World Alliance, 1970—; chmn. Bapt. World Congress, 1980—, Bapt. World Aid Div., 1982—; Bd. regents Bethel Coll.; chmn. steering com. U.S. Ch. Leaders, 1985—. Mem. Nat. Assn. Evangelicals (adminstrv. council 1970—), Am. Bible Soc. (adv. council 1969—). Home: Nordhaven Rt 1 Box 350D Aitkin MN 56431 Office: Bapt Gen Conf 2002 Arlington Heights Rd Arlington Heights IL 60005

MAGOON, DUNCAN JOHN JAMES, psychiatrist, psychoanalyat; b. Ypsilanti, Mich., Aug. 11, 1933; s. Wallace Herbert and Iris (Eppens) M.; m. Marilynn Louise Juffermans, Dec. 31, 1955; children: Duncan Neal, Cameron Shawn, Marion Molly, Jennifer Jane. MD, U. Mich., 1957. Diplomate Am. Bd. Psychiatry and Neurology. Intern Denver Gen. Hosp., 1957-58; resident Ypsilanti (Mich.) State Hosp., 1960-63; practice medicine specializing in psychoanalysis Ann Arbor, Mich., 1962—; dir. outpatient dept. Ypsilanti (Mich.) State Hosp., 1965-67; clin. instr. psychiatry U. Mich., Ann Arbor, 1965-67, Wayne State U., Detroit, 1985—; contracted psychiatrist Ypsilanti Regional Psychiat. Hosp., 1986—; bd. dirs. Children and Family Services, Ann Arbor, 1974—. Served to cpat. USAF, 1958-60. Fellow Am. Acad. Psychoanalysis; mem. AMA, Am. Psychiat. Assn., Mich. Psychait. Assn., Soc. Psychoanalytic Psychotherapy, Mich. Soc. Psychoanalytic Psychology, Detroit Psychoanalytoc Soc. (pres. 1975-77). Avocations: canoeing, sailing, skiing, fishing, hunting. Home: 2220 Washtenaw Ann Arbor MI 48104 Office: 2301 S Huron Pkwy Ann Arbor MI 48104

MAGORIAN, JAMES, author, poet; b. Palisade, Nebr., Apr. 24, 1942; s. Jack and Dorothy (Gorthey) M. B.S., U. Nebr., 1965; M.S., Ill. State U., 1969; postgrad. Oxford U., 1971, Harvard U., 1973. Author children's books: School Daze, 1978; 17%, 1978; The Magic Pretzel, 1979; Ketchup Bottles, 1979; Imaginary Radishes, 1980; Plucked Chickens, 1980; Fimperings and Torples, 1981, The Witches' Olympics, 1983, At the City Limits, 1987; author numerous books of poetry, including: Ideas for a Bridal Shower, 1980; The Edge of the Forest, 1980; Spiritual Rodeo, 1980; Tap Dancing on a Tight Rope, 1981; Training at Home to Be a Locksmith, 1981; The Emily Dickinson Jogging Book, 1984; Keeper of Fire, 1984; Weighing the Sun's Light, 1985, Summer Snow, 1985, The Magician's Handbook, 1986, Squall Line, 1986; contbr. poems to numerous publs. Hone and Office: 1225 N 46th St Lincoln NE 68503

MAGRATH, C. PETER, university president; b. N.Y.C., Apr. 23, 1933; s. Laurence Wilfrid and Guilia Maria (Dentice) M.; m. Diane Fay Skomars, Mar. 25, 1978; children: Valerie Ruth, Monette Fay. BA summa cum laude, U. N.H., 1955; PhD, Cornell U., 1962. Mem. faculty Brown U., Providence, 1961-68, prof. polit. sci., 1967-68, assoc. dean grad. sch., 1965-66; dean Coll. Arts and Scis. U. Nebr., Lincoln, 1968-69, dean faculties Coll. Arts and Scis., 1969-72, interim chancellor univ., 1971-72, prof. polit. sci., 1968-72, vice chancellor for acad. affairs, 1972; pres. SUNY, Binghamton, 1972-74, prof. polit. sci., 1972-74; pres. U. Minn., Mpls., 1974-84, U. Mo., Columbia, 1985—. Author: The Triumph of Character, 1963, Yazoo: Law and Politics in the New Republic, The Case of Fletcher v. Peck, 1966, Constitutionalism and Politics: Conflict and Consensus, 1968, Issues and Perspectives in American Government, 1971, (with others) The American Democracy, 2d edit., 1973, (with Robert L. Egbert) Strengthening Teacher Education, 1987; contbr. articles to profl. jours. Served with AUS, 1955-57. Mem. Nat. Assn. State Univs. and Land Grant Colls. (chmn. 1984-85), Assn. Am. Univs. (chmn. 1985-86), Phi Beta Kappa, Phi Kappa Phi, Pi Gamma Mu, Pi Sigma Alpha, Kappa Tau Alpha. Office: Univ Missouri Univ Hall Columbia MO 65211

MAGUIRE, JOHN CLARK, academic communications administrator; b. Macomb, Ill., July 8, 1951; s. Davis and Martha Mae (Jennings) M.; m. Deborah Ann, Aug. 28, 1971; children: Thomas Lee, Timothy Lee. BA, Western Ill U., 1973, MS, 1980. Editor, pres. Western Catalyst News, Macomb, 1969-73; reporter Macomb Daily Jour., 1973-77; asst. dir. news services Western Ill. U., 1977-82, dir. news services, 1982-87, dir. univ. relations, 1987—. Cubmaster Boy Scouts Am., Macomb, 1977—; precinct committeeman McDonough County Republican Cen. Com., Macomb, 1982-86; alderman, mem. bldg. and grounds com. City of Macomb, 1982-84; alderman, personnel chmn. City of Macomb, 1984—; chmn. McDonough County Voters Dr., Macomb, 1984. Recipient Boy Scouts Dist. Merit award, Macomb Jaycees Community Service award. Mem. Council Advancement and Support Edn. (media relations staff 1984, Bronze Medal Radio News 1985). Roman Catholic. Avocations: golf, scouting, pickleball. Home: 921 S Madison St Macomb IL 61455 Office: Western Ill U News Services 900 W Adams St Macomb IL 61455

MAGUIRE, SHIRLEY ELIZABETH, librarian; b. Montreal, Can., Apr. 19, 1948; d. Harold Stephen and Yvette (Gauthier) Edmonds; m. Andrew James Maguire, Dec. 27, 1977. BA, SUNY, Buffalo, 1970; MLS, Wayne State U., 1972. Engring. librarian Chrysler Corp., Detroit, 1973-81; librarian Chrysler Def. Inc., Detroit, 1981-82; librarian, sr. adminstrv. analyst Land Systems div. Gen. Dynamics, Troy, Mich., 1982—. Rep. precinct del. Utica, Mich., 1986, del. Rep. State Conv., 1987. Mem. Am. Soc. Metals, Standards Engring. Soc. (sec. Detroit chpt. 1983-84), Spl. Libraries Assn. Roman Catholic. Office: Gen Dynamics Land Systems Div 1902 Northwood Troy MI 48084

MAHAFFEY, GARY JOHN, architect; b. Waseca, Minn., Apr. 2, 1940; s. Jerome Charles and Margaret Minnie (Kopischke) M.; m. Marlene M. Mahaffey, Sept. 28, 1974 (div. 1987); 1 child, Shannon Lee. BArch, U. Minn., 1963; M in Environ. Design, Yale U., 1970. Registered architect, Minn. Sr. v.p. Leonard Parker Assocs., Architects, Mpls., 1964-69, 70—; staff architect Roche-Dinkeloo Assocs., Architects, New Haven, Conn., 1969-70. Served with USNG, 1964-70. Mem. Minn. Soc. AIA (sec. 1985-87). Avocations: sailing, carpentry. Home: 3844 Thomas Ave S Minneapolis MN 55410 Office: Leonard Parker Assocs 430 Oak Grove Minneapolis MN 55403

MAHAJAN, SUBHASH CHANDER, microbiologist, chemist; b. New Delhi, India, Dec. 2, 1948; Came to U.S., 1971; s. Eaquir Chand and Vidya (Wati) M.; m. Naveen Kumari, May 29, 1979. BS, Cambridge U., Eng., 1968; MS in analytica chemistry, U. Miami, 1973. Cert. quality engr. Quality assurance mgr. Dirr's Gold Seal, Miami, Fla., 1971-75; mgr. corp. quality assurance Michelin Tire, Greenville, S.C., 1975-83; project mgr. Firestone Tire and Rubber, Decatur, Ill., 1983—. Mem. Am. Soc. Quality Control. Avocation: flying. Home: 464 Bayshore Dr Decatur IL 62521 Office: Firestone Tire and Rubber 2500 N 22d St Decatur IL 62525

MAHAN, GENEVIEVE ELLIS, sociologist; b. Canton, Ohio, Aug. 1, 1909; d. William and Lillian (Ellis) Mahan; A.B., Case Western Res. U., 1931, A.M., 1941; postgrad. (Ford Found. fellow) Yale, 1952, Akademie fur Politische Bildung, Tutzing, Germany, 1963. Tchr. high schs., Canton, 1937-52; research asst. dept. sociology Yale, 1953-55; lectr. sociology Walsh Coll., Canton, 1970. Participant Instns. Atlantic and European Cooperation Seminar, Coimbra, Portugal, 1970; participant World Congress of Sociology, Evian, France, 1966. Trustee, Stark County Psychiat. Found., 1961-68. Fellow Am. Sociol. Assn.; mem. Internat. Sociol. Assn., Eastern Sociol. Soc., Am. Acad. Polit. and Social Sci., Nat., Ohio (exec. bd. 1962-69, pres. 1965) councils for social studies, AAAS, AAUW (mem. exec. bd. Canton 1966-67), Ohio Acad. Sci., Ohio Soc. N.Y. Clubs: Canton Womans, Massillon Woman's, Canton College. Research in polit. caricature, 1955—. Home: 804 5th St NW Canton OH 44703

MAHANES, W. J., transportation company executive; b. 1935. Pres. Minstar, Inc., Mpls., also bd. dirs. Office: Minstar Inc 1215 Marshall St NE Minneapolis MN 55413 *

MAHANNA, ROBERT DEAN, pharmacist; b. Hoxie, Kans., May 8, 1925; s. Raymond Wendell and Aileen P. (McCartney) M.; m. Kathleen L. McCutcheon, June 29, 1945; children: Jan, Susan, David. BS, U. Kans., 1950. Lic. pharmacist, Kans. Pres., pharmacist Mahanna Pharmacy, Inc., Hoxie, 1950—; pharmacy cons. Sheridan County Hosp.; mem. pharmacy adv. council U. Kans., 1972—, preceptor, 1974—; mem. Kans. State Bd. Pharmacy, 1976-79; mem. steering com. Kans. U. Sch. Pharmacy Centennial Com., 1985; bd. dirs. Kans. Pharmacy Service Corp., Sheridan Amusement Co. Active Boy Scouts Am.; mem. steering com. Indsl. Devel. for Hoxie, 1974-80; bd. dirs. Three County Title 5 Program, 1972-75, Malott Hall Bldg. Fund; bd. dirs. United Sch. Dist. 412, 1970-78, pres. pride program, 1973; treas. Greater N.W. Kans., Inc., 1968-76; trustee Hoxie Meth. Ch., 1978-82. Served with USN, 1943-46. Fellow Am. Coll. Apothecaries; mem. Kans. Pharmacists Assn. (pres. 1963-64, Bowl of Hygeia award 1977), Am. Pharm. Assn., Kans. Pharmacy Found. (bd. dirs.), Nat. Assn. Retail Druggists, IPA, Hoxie C. of C. (pres. 1954), ISIS Clowns (pres. 1979), Clowns of Am., Pi Kappa Alpha, Kappa Psi. Republican. Club: Gentlemen of the Creeks. Lodges: Rotary (pres. 1954, 70), Masons (past master), Order Eastern Star (past patron), Shriners, Elks (Hoxie). Avocations: clowning; antiques; furniture refinishing; gardening. Home: 1341 Sheridan Ave Hoxie KS 67740 Office: Mahanna Pharmacy 833 Main St Hoxie KS 67740

MAHER, DAVID WILLARD, lawyer; b. Chgo., Aug. 14, 1934; s. Chauncey Carter and Martha (Peppers) M.; A.B., Harvard, 1955, LL.B., 1959; m. Jill Waid Armagnac, Dec. 20, 1954; children—Philip Armagnac, Julia Armagnac. Admitted to N.Y. bar, 1960, Ill. bar, 1961; practiced in Chgo., 1961—; assoc. Kirkland & Ellis, and predecessor firm, 1960-65, ptnr., 1966-78; ptnr. Reuben & Proctor, 1978-86 , Isham, Lincoln & Beale, 1986—; Bd. dirs. Better Bus. Bur. Chgo. and No. Ill. Served to 2d lt. USAF, 1955-56. Mem. Am., Ill., Chgo. bar assns. Roman Catholic. Clubs: Bull Valley Hunt, Chicago Literary, Union League, Tavern. Home: 311 Belden Ave Chicago IL 60614 Office: 19 S LaSalle St Chicago IL 60603

MAHER, FRANK ALOYSIUS, research and development executive, psychologist; b. Jamaica, N.Y., Mar. 31, 1941; s. Frank A. and Gertrude F. (Peterson) M.; m. Barbara A. Eggers, Aug. 14, 1965 (div. 1978); children: B. Kelly, F. Scott, Erin K.; m. Karen S. Adcock, June 28, 1980. BA, U. Dayton, 1966, MS, 1971. Licensed psychologist, Ohio. Research psychologist Ritchie Inc., Dayton, Ohio, 1965-68, Bunker Ramo, Dayton, 1968-70; lectr., research assoc. Wright State U., Dayton, 1970-71; research psychologist USAF, Wright Patterson AFB, Ohio, 1971-84; dir. Perceptronics, Inc., Dayton, 1984-87; research and devel. exec. Unisys, Dayton, 1987—; counseling psychologist Eastway Mental Health Ctr., Dayton, 1974-75, Good Samaritan Mental Health Ctr., Dayton, 1979. Conbtg. author: Perceptions in Information Sciences; editor: Developmental Learning Handbook. Bd. dirs. Miami Valley Mental Health Assn., Dayton, 1974-77, Greene Mental Health Assn., Xenia, Ohio, 1977. Roman Catholic. Avocations: tennis, skiing, sailing, sports car racing. Home: 7881 Stanley Mill Centerville OH 45459 Office: Unisys 4134 Linden Ave Suite 303 Dayton OH 45432

MAHER, JOHN THOMAS, III, architect; b. Milw., Feb. 4, 1940; s. John Thomas II and Esther (Banaszek) M. BArch, U. Ill., 1963. V.p. Brust & Brust, Milw., 1968-74; pres. Maher & Assoc., Milw., 1974—. Commr. Bd. Zoning Appeals, Milw, 1974—. Mem. AIA (Best Bldg. award 1970). Club: Milw. Athletic. Avocations: tennis, sailing, golf, skiing. Home: 3036 N Marietta Ave Milwaukee WI 53211 Office: 810 N Plankinton Ave Milwaukee WI 53203

MAHER, TERRY MARINA, religious organization administrator; b. Phila., Oct. 13, 1955; d. Thomas Michael and Marion Teresa (Corbett) M. BA in History and Religious Studies, U. San Diego, 1977. Dir. religious edn. Diocese San Diego, 1977-80; dir. religious edn. Archdiocese Cin., 1982-84, assoc. dir. youth ministry, 1984—. Sec. social concerns bd. Met. Chs. United, Dayton; Justice com. Sisters of The Precious Blood; active Tour to Explore conditions in Nicaragua, New Orleans, 1983. Mem. Sanctuary, Pledge of Resistance. Democrat. Avocations: racquetball, biking, nonviolent sports. Home: 224 Squirrel Rd Dayton OH 45405 Office: Office Youth Ministry Archdiocese Cin 266 Bainbridge St Dayton OH 45402

MAHER, VERONICA MARY (CATHERINE L.), health science facility administrator; b. Detroit, Feb. 20, 1931; d. Henry Cornelius and Veronica Margaret (Kelly) M. BS in Biology summa cum laude, Marygrove Coll., 1951; MS in Biology, U. Mich., 1958; postgrad., U. Wis., 1964-68, PhD in Molecular Biology, 1968. Research assoc. dept. radiology Yale U., New Haven, 1968-69; research assoc. dept. human genetics U. Mich., Ann Arbor, 1969-70; research assoc. dept. biol. scis. John Hopskins U., Balt., 1970; research scientist dept. biology Mich. Cancer Fedn., Detroit, 1970-73, chief carcinogenesis lab. div. biol. scis., 1973-76; co-dir. carcinogenesis lab. Mich. State U., East Lansing, 1976—, prof. dept. microbiology and pub. health, dept. biochemistry, 1980—; asst. prof. dept. biology, Marygrove Coll., 1969-71; bd. trustees Marygrove Coll., 1982—; mem. adv. council Nat. Cancer Inst. Cancer Spl. Projects, 1981-85. Assoc. editor Cancer Research jour., Phila., 1978—; contbr. numerous articles to profl. jours. Recipient NSF scholarship U. Mich., 1957-58; grantee EPA, Nat. Cancer Inst., Nat. Inst. Environ. Health Scis., Dept. Energy, others. Mem. Am. Assn. Cancer Research, Am. Soc. Microbiology, Am. Soc. Biol. Chemists, Environ. Mutagen Soc. (councillor 1979-83), Genetics Soc. Am., Tissue Culture Assn. Home: 6091 Brook Haven Ln #27 East Lansing MI 48823

MAHFOOD, THOMAS JOHN, accountant, construction company executive; b. St. Louis, June 23, 1954; s. John Vincent and Matilda (Mahanna) M.; m. Mary Alice Neri, Nov. 17, 1978; 1 child, Alexandra Neri. BS, St. Louis U., 1975. CPA, Mo. Sr. auditor Ernst & Whinney, St. Louis, 1975-79; sec., treas. and bd. dirs. Profl. Builders, St. Louis, 1979—; v.p. and bd. dirs. Malo, Inc., St. Louis, 1980—; pres. and bd. dirs. G.E.T.O. Constrn. Co., Inc., St. Louis, 1982—; gen. ptnr. G.E.T. Investments, St. Louis, 1982—; bd. dirs. Escrow Mgmt., Inc., Realty Asset Mgmt. Mem. Am. Inst. CPA's, Mo. Soc. CPA's. Republican. Roman Catholic. Avocations: skeet and trap shooting, ATV riding, wine collecting. Office: GETO Constrn Co Inc PO Box 605 Chesterfield MO 63017

MAHIEU, LAWRENCE FRANK, marketing executive; b. Grosse Pointe, Mich., July 20, 1959; s. Frank A. and Emma R. (Tack) M. BS, Wayne State U., 1982. Account exec. TLW Unlimited, Southfield, Mich., 1982-83; mktg. dir. Panel Clip Co., Farmington, Mich., 1983—. Mem. Adcraft Club Detroit, Belgian Am. Assn. (bd. dirs. band St. Clair Shores, Mich. 1976), St. Charles Soc. Roman Catholic. Club: Vic Tanny Internat. (St. Clair Shores). Avocations: Grand Prix yacht racing, downhill skiing, photography, bowling. Home: 5922 Hereford Detroit MI 48224 Office: Panel Clip Co 24650 Crestview Ct Farmington MI 48024

MAHJOURI, FEREYDOON SABET, plastic/reconstructive surgeon; b. Tehran, Iran, Aug. 1, 1943; came to U.S., 1969, naturalized, 1978; s. Ali S. Mahjouri and Ghamar (Adel) M.; m. Sussan Navidi, Feb. 10, 1984; 1 child, Sormeh Sabet. MD, Tehran U., Iran, 1966. Diplomate Am. Bd. Plastic and Reconstructive Surgery; lic. physician and surgeon, Ill., Colo., Minn., Calif. Intern Tehran U. Hosps., 1966-67, research fellow Cancer Inst., 1967; surg. intern Cook County Hosp., Chgo., 1969-70, resident in gen. surgery and trauma surgery, 1970-74; resident in plastic and reconstructive surgery and surgery of hand Loyola U. Med. Ctr., Cook County Hosp., Chgo., 1974-77; practice medicine specializing in plastic surgery and hand surgery, Mpls., 1977—; mem. staff Unity Med. Ctr., Fridley, Minn., Mercy Med. Ctr., Coon Rapids, Minn., North Meml. Med. Ctr., Mpls, chmn. burn com. Served with Imperial Iranian Air Force, 1967-69. Fellow ACS, Internat. Coll. Surgeons; mem. AMA (Physicians Recognition award 1977, 80, 83), Am. Assn. for Hand Surgery, Am. Soc. Maxillofacial Surgeons, Am. Soc. for Aesthetic Plastic Surgery, Am. Assn. Plastic Surgery, Hennepin County Med. Soc., Minn. State Med. Assn., Minn. Surg. Soc., Minn. Acad. Plastic and Reconstructive Surgeons, Am. Soc. Plastic and Reconstructive Surgeons, Am. Burn Assn., Am. Soc. Abdominal Surgeons, Am. Assn. Hand Surgery, Midwestern Assn. Plastic Surgeons. Home: 16392 Ringer Rd Wayzata MN 55391 Office: Unity Profl Bldg 500 Osborne Rd Suite 110 Minneapolis MN 55432

MAHLBERG, ARDEN FRANKLIN, psychologist; b. Worthington, Minn., May 6, 1948; s. Arthur Franklin and Margaret Evelena (Swenson) M.; m. Linda Jane Sura, Sept. 22, 1976; children: Nathaniel Aaron, Nora Elizabeth. BA, St. Olaf Coll., 1970; MA, Calif. Inst. Integral Studies, 1978, PhD, 1982. Lic. psychologist, Wis. Program coordinator Klamath Mental Health Ctr., Klamath Falls, Oreg., 1982-83; psychologist Midwestern Psychol. Services, Madison, Wis., 1984—; cons. Social Security Adminstrn., Madison, 1985—. Mem. Am. Psychol. Assn., Wis. Psychol. Assn., Assn. for Transpersonal Psychology. Lutheran. Avocations: cross-country skiing, back packing, bird watching. Office: Midwestern Psychol Services 408 W Johnson St Madison WI 53703

MAHMOOD, KHALID, physician; b. Gujranwala, Pakistan, Feb. 15, 1938; came to U.S., 1971, naturalized, 1977; s. Muhammad Saied and Mumtaz Begum (Ata Mohammad) Mazharie; m. Patricia Hope Ashleman, June 15, 1975; children: Farrah Renee, Tarik Adam. F.Sc., Govt. Coll., Abbottabad, Pakistan, 1956; B.Sc., U. Punjab, 1960; MB, BS, King Edward Med. Coll., 1962. Intern Danbury (Conn.) Hosp., 1963-64, Lewis Gale Hosp., Roanoke, Va., 1964-65; resident in otolaryngology Albert Einstein Coll. Medicine, N.Y.C., 1965-69; research fellow otolaryngology U. Toronto, Ontario, Can., 1969-70; practice medicine specializing in otolaryngology Toronto, 1971, Sandusky, Ohio, 1972—; mem. cons. staff, chief otolaryngologist Good Samaritan Hosp., Sandusky, 1972-85; mem. staff, cons., chief div. otolaryngology Providence Hosp., Sandusky, 1974—; clin. asst. prof. Dept. Surgery (Otolaryngol.), Med. Coll. Ohio, Toledo, 1984—; mem. cons. staff Fireland Community Hosp., Sandusky, 1985—. Fellow ACS, Am. Acad. Otolaryngology and Head and Neck Surgery; mem. AMA, Erie County Med. Soc., Ohio State Med. Assn. Research on tritiated thymidine study of irradiated cancer larynx, 1968-69. Home: 2505 Greentree Ln Sandusky OH 44870 Office: 1221 Hayes Ave Sandusky OH 44870

MAHN, PAUL RONALD, dentist; b. Milw., Dec. 2, 1956; s. Ronald El Roy and Shirley Ann (Wahl) M. DDS, Marquette U., 1984. Gen. practice dentistry West Allis, Wis., 1984—; adj. prof. prosthodontics Marquette U., 1986. Author: (children's novel) Billy Sigfried of Wiener Street, 1978; contbr. articles to profl. jours. Mem. Am. Dental Assn., Wis. Dental Assn. (bd. editors 1986-87), Greater Milw. Dental Assn. (bd. editors 1985-87), Acad. Gen. Dentristry. Avocations: bluegrass music, writing poetry, magic, painting, tennis. Office: 10202 W Hayes Ave Milwaukee WI 53227

MAHON, PATRICK F., radiologist; b. Galway, Ireland, Apr. 15, 1935; came to U.S., 1960; Student in Premed., U. Coll., Galway, Ireland, 1954-55; MD, U. Coll., Galway, 1955-60. Diplomate Am. Bd. Radiology. Internship Ravenswood Med. Ctr., Chgo., 1960-61; gen. practice medicine Springfield, Ill., 1961-63; resident dept. radiology Mayo Clinic, Rochester, Minn., 1964-66, assoc. cons. cardiovascular sect. dept. radiology, 1967; gen. practice medicine specializing in radiology Springfield, 1967—; staff Physicians Group, Springfield, 1967—, St. John's Hosp., Springfield, 1967—; co-chmn. dept. radiology So. Ill. U. Sch. Medicine, Springfield, 1971-73, asst. chmn. dept. radiology, 1973-77, chmn. dept. radiology, 1977—, clin. prof. radiology, 1971-83, prof. radiology, 1983-; sec. dept. radiology St. John's Hosp., 1967-85, mem. exec. com., 1984-85; cons. staff Meml. Med. Ctr., Springfield, 1967—; bd. dirs. Found. Med. Care Cen. Ill., Springfield, bd. govs. 1976-79, program dir. diagnostic radiology residency, So. Ill. U. Sch. Med., 1977—, active various coms., 1977—; bd. dirs., pres. Academic Radiology, Inc., Univ. Radiologists, S.C.; pres. Springfield Radiologists, S.C., 1985—; sec., treas. Found. for Med. Care of Cen. Ill., 1972-76. Chmn. health services div. United Way of Sangamon County, 1976—, assoc. campaign chmn., 1977, campaign chmn., 1979, chmn. nominating com., 1983-84, fin. com. mem., 1981-84; chmn. Springfield Copley First Citizen Award, 1981; bd. dirs. Ill. Med. Polit. Action Com., 1974, active various offices; bd. dirs. L.P.G.A. Rail Charity Golf Classic, 1981-85. Mem. AMA, Am. Coll. Radiology (Ill. chpt.), Radiol. Soc. N.Am., Soc. Head and Neck Radiology, Soc. Chmn. Academic Radiology Depts., Soc. Univ. Radiologists, Ill. State Med. Soc. (trustee 1976-79, chmn pub. affairs com. 1986—), Sangamon County Med. Soc. (active various coms.), Ill. Radiol. Soc. (chmn. legis. adv. com. 1982—), Springfield Med. Club (sec. 1972-73, pres. 1974-75), Soc. Cardiovascular & Interventional Radiology, Springfield C. of C. (bd. dirs. 1980—, active various offices), Nat. Assn. Am. Bus. Clubs (dist. dir. region 4B 1978-80), Sons of Erin (bd. dirs. Peter F. Rossiter chpt. 1979—, pres. 1980). Clubs: Am. Bus. (pres. 1976-77), Sangamo (bd. dirs. 1983-86), Illini Country (membership com. 1981-85, chmn. 1983). Home: 1901 Illini Rd Springfield IL 62704 Office: 800 E Carpenter St Springfield IL 62769

MAHONEY, JAMES ANTHONY, JR., insurance company executive; b. Chgo., Sept. 18, 1935; s. James Anthony and Marie (Byrne) M.; m. Mary Elizabeth Rafferty, Jan. 2, 1960; children: James III, Joseph, Philip, Mary Evelyn. BBA, Marquette U., 1958. Personnel mgr. Combined Ins. Co. Am., Chgo., 1959-61, exec. sales staff, 1961-65, tng. mgr., 1965-67, asst. v.p. bldg. ops., 1968-82, v.p. adminstrv. services, 1982—. Bd. dirs. N. Suburban Mass Transit Dist., Des Plaines, Ill., 1977—, chmn. 1983-85; trustee Village of Niles, Ill., 1986. Mem. Bldg. Owners and Mgrs. Assn. Home: 8357 N Oketo Niles IL 60648 Office: Combined Ins Co Am 5050 N Broadway Chicago IL 60640

MAHONEY, MICHAEL J., criminal justice association executive; b. Chgo., Sept. 9, 1944; s. Raymond and Helen (Kennedy) M.; divorced; children: Kate, Timothy, Colleen. BA, Bellarmine Coll., 1967; MEd, Spaulding U., 1969. Asst. supt. Ill. Dept. Corrections, Joliet, 1970-71; regional dir. Nat. Council on Crime and Delinquency, Chgo., 1971-74; instr. Chgo. State U., 1977—; asst. dir. John Howard Assn., Chgo., 1975-76, exec. dir., 1977—; mem. Ill. Juvenile Justice Com., Chgo., 1985-86; bd. dirs. Nat. Commn. on Correctional Health Care, Chgo. Named Outstanding Young Citizen of Chgo., Chgo. Jaycees, 1978. Mem. Am. Correctional Assn. (pres. Ill. chpt. 1980-81). Roman Catholic. Home: 1815 N Bissell Chicago IL 60614 Office: John Howard Assn 67 E Madison St Chicago IL 60603

MAHONEY, PATRICIA ANN NORDSTROM, personal services company executive; b. Hastings, Minn., Apr. 13, 1939; d. Harold Edward and Mary Patricia (Ahern) Nordstrom; m. Edward J. Mahoney, 1962 (div. 1987); children—Patrick Sean, Erin Mary. BS cum laude, U. Minn., 1961. Tchr., head curriculum com. Hopkins (Minn.) Sr. High Sch., 1961-64; mgr. Bridal Services, Inc., Mpls., 1969-73; buyer, gen. mgr. Anderson's Wedding World Stores, Mpls., 1973-77; dir. fashion div. Nat. Bridal Service, Richmond, Va., 1975—, also dir.; mktg. and tng. specialist Minn. Dept. Edn., 1977-80; edn. cons. Mpls. Star & Tribune Newspapers, 1981-83, mgr. edn. services, 1983-

85, single copy sales mgr., 1985—. Mem. Phi Beta Kappa. Home: 5604 Colfax Ave S Minneapolis MN 55419

MAHONEY, RICHARD JOHN, manufacturing company executive; b. Springfield, Mass., Jan. 30, 1934; m. Barbara Marsden Barnett, Jan. 26, 1956; 3 children. B.S. in Chemistry, U. Mass., 1955, LL.D., 1983. Product devel. specialist Monsanto Co., 1962; market mgr. new products Monsanto Co., St. Louis, 1965-67; plastic products and resins div; market mgr. bonding products, div. sales dir. Kenilworth, N.J., 1967-71; sales dir. Agrl. div. Monsanto Co., St. Louis, 1971-74, dir. internat. ops., 1974-75, gen. mgr. overseas div., 1975; corp. v.p., mng. dir. Monsanto Agrl. Products Co., 1975-76; group v.p., mng. dir. Monsanto Plastics & Resins Co., 1976-77, exec. v.p., 1977-80, pres., 1980, chief operating officer, 1981, bd. dirs., 1979—; pres., chief exec. officer Monsanto Co., St. Louis, 1983-86; chmn., chief exec. officer Monsanto Co., 1986—; dir. Centerre Bancorp., Met. Life Ins. Co., G.D. Searle & Co., Fisher Controls Internat.; mem. U.S.-Japan Bus. Council. Bd. dirs. U.S.-USSR Trade and Econ. Council, Council Fin. Aid to Edn., trustee Washington U., St. Louis; adv. bd. St. John's Mercy Med. Ctr.; bd. mgrs. Central Inst. Deaf. Recipient Frederick S. Troy Alumni Achievement award U. Mass., Amherst, 1981; hon. fellowship Exeter Coll., Oxford, 1986. Mem. Chem. Mfrs. Assn., Soc. Chem. Industry, Bus. Council, Bus. Round Table, Conf. Bd. Clubs: Log Cabin, St. Louis, Bellerive Country. Office: Monsanto Co 800 N Lindbergh Blvd Saint Louis MO 63167

MAHONEY, THOMAS JAMES, venture capitalist; b. Lakeview, Oreg., June 24, 1951; s. Robert James and Catherine Ann (Marion) M.; m. Judith Mary Rauenhorst, Dec. 29, 1979; children: Anne, Joseph, Peter. BA, St. John's U., 1972; MBA, Coll. of St. Thomas, 1977. Acct. Control Data, Mpls., 1973-76, with internat. fin. dept., 1976-79, with mergers, acquisitions dept., 1979-83, venture capitalist, 1983—; bd. dirs. Fisher Foods, Mpls., Eastern Foods. Advisor Jr. Achievement, 1974-75; lectr. Bus. Econ. Edn. Found., 1978—, speaker Ohio Gov's Minority Bus. Conf., 1984. Mem. Leadership Mpls. (program and devel. com. 1985—), Assn. Corp. Growth (dir. 1984—, pres. 1987—), Serra Club (dir. 1984—, pres. 1987—). Republican. Roman Catholic. Avocations: instrument pilot, sports. Home: 21 Circle West Edina MN 55436

MAI, KENNETH WILLIAM, accountant; b. Cin., May 20, 1963; s. Donald C. and Irene C. (Haeberlin) M. BA, Thomas More Coll., 1984. CPA, Ohio. Acct. Kohlhepp & Assocs., Ft. Mitchell, Ky., 1984, VonLehman & Co., Cin., 1984-85; cons. Deloitte Haskins & Sells, Cin., 1985—. Named an Outstanding Am., 1986. Mem. Am. Inst. CPA's, Ky. Soc. CPA's, No. Ky. C. of C., Covington (Ky.) Jaycees (bd. dirs. 1986-87, v.p. 1987—, Dir. of Quarter 1986). Democrat. Roman Catholic. Avocations: reading, racquetball, softball. Home: 1708 Cherokee Dr Fort Wright KY 41011 Office: Deloitte Haskins & Sells 250 E 5th St Cincinnati OH 45202

MAIANU, ALEXANDRU, soil science educator, researcher; b. Moldoveni, Romania, Jan. 8, 1931; came to U.S., 1977; s. Nedelcu and Voica (Burtea) M.; B.S., U. Bucharest (Romania), 1953, M.S., 1954, Ph.D., 1962. Research soil scientist Romanian Agr. Research Inst., 1954-63; sr. research soil scientist, head Soil Reclamation Lab., Romania, 1963-77; asst. prof. soil sci. U. Bucharest, 1963-66; assoc. prof. soil sci. N.D. State U., Fargo, 1980—; nat. supr. Romanian research programs in soil reclamation, 1969-74. Pres. Emmanuel, Inc., Christian Ministry to East European countries. Recipient Ion Ionescu de la Brad award Romanian Acad. Scis., 1966, Emil Racovitza award, 1972; award Romanian Dept. Edn., 1968. Mem. Am. Soc. Agronomy, N.D. Acad. Sci., Soil Sci. Soc. Am., Internat. Soc. Soil Sci. Author: Secondary Soil Salinization, 1964; (with A. Ghidia) Improving Soil Fertility in Greenhouses, 1974; (with G. Obrejanu) Limnology of the Romanian Sector of the Danube River, 1967, Soil Study on the Experimental Stations of Romanian Agriculture, 1958. Home: PO Box 5422 Fargo ND 58105 Office: ND State U Dept Soil Sci Waldron Hall 201 H PO Box 5575 Fargo ND 58105

MAIBACH, BEN C., JR., business executive; b. Bay City, Mich., 1920. With Barton-Malow Co., Detroit, 1938—; v.p., dir.-in-charge field ops Barton-Malow Co., 1949-53, exec. v.p., 1953-60, pres., 1960-76, chmn. bd., 1976—; chmn. bd. Barton-Malow So., Inc., Sarasota, Fla., Cloverdale Equipment Co.; chmn., dir. S-C-P Leasing Corp.; dir., mem. exec. com. Amerisure Ins. Co., Amerisure Life Ins. Co., Mich. Mut. Ins. Co.; dir. Amerisure, Inc., First of Am. Bank, Detroit; chmn., dir. Hasper Equipment Co., Sunbelt Crane & Equipment, bd. chmn. Thatcher Construction Co.; chmn. Armstrong/Cloverdale Equip. Trustee Barton-Malow Found.; asst. sec., trustee Apostolic Christian Woodhaven, Detroit; bd. dirs. S.E. Mich. chpt. ARC, United Found., Rural Gospel and Med. Missions of India; trustee Lawrence Inst. Tech. Home: 14726 Fox St Detroit MI 48239 Office: Barton-Malow Co PO Box 5200 Detroit MI 48235

MAIBACH, BEN C., III, construction company executive; b. 1946. BS, Mich. State U., 1969. With Barton-Malow Corp., Oak Park, Mich., 1950—, v.p. field ops., 1951-55, exec. v.p., 1955-60, pres., 1960-76, chmn. bd. dirs., chief exec. officer, 1976—. Office: Barton-Malow Co PO Box 5200 Detroit MI 48235 *

MAIDA, ADAM J., bishop; b. East Vandergriff, Mar. 18, 1930. Student, St. Vincent Coll., Latrobe, Pa., St. Mary's U., Balt., Lateran U., Rome. Ordained priest Roman Catholic Ch., 1956, bishop, 1984. Bishop of Green Bay Wis, 1984—. Office: PO Box 66 Green Bay WI 54305 *

MAIER, HENRY W., mayor; b. Dayton, Ohio, Feb. 7, 1918; s. Charles, Jr. and Marie L. (Knisley) M.; m. Karen Lamb, May 8, 1976; children by previous marriage: Melinda Ann Maier Carlisle, Melanie Marie. B.A., U. Wis., 1940; M.A. in Polit. Sci., U. Wis.-Milw., 1964. Mem. Wis. Legislature, 1950-60, floor leader for Senate, 1953-60; mayor of Milw., 1960—. Author: Challenge to the Cities, 1966. First pres. Nat. Conf. Democratic Mayors, 1976—; past chmn. nat. adv. com. Health Care for the Homeless Program; chmn. nat. Coalition on Human Needs Budget Priorities, 1973-75; mem. Pres.'s com. on Youth Employment in the Kennedy Adminstrn.; mem. govt. adv. com. on Hwy. Beauty, U.S. Dept. Commerce in Johnson Adminstrn. Served to lt. USNR, World War II, PTO. Named one of 60 most influential men in Am. U.S. News and World Report, 1975, 76; recipient Disting. Alumni award U. Wis., 1974, disting. Urban Mayor award Nat. Urban Coalition, 1979-87, disting. Sustained Mayoral Leadership award Nat. Urban Coalition, 1987, Hubert H. Humphrey award Nat. Conf. Dem. Mayors, 1987, Michael A. diNunzio award U.S. Conf. Mayors. Mem. U.S. Conf. Mayors (pres. 1971-72, mem. exec. com., Disting. Pub. Service award 1984), Nat. League Cities (pres. 1964-65, bd. dirs.). Democrat. Longest tenure in U.S. history among mayors of cities with populations of 500,000 or more. Office: City Hall Milwaukee WI 53202

MAIER, JACK C., food products company executive. Chmn. and pres. Frisch's Restaurants, Inc., Cin. Office: Frisch's Restaurants Inc 2800 Gilbert Ave Cincinnati OH 45206 *

MAIER, THOMAS JAMES, bank executive; b. Madison, Wis., Dec. 23, 1948; s. Michael Walter and Beatrice Jane (Klein) M.; m. Barbara Merle Peet, Mar. 2, 1974; children: Nathan Peet, Brittany Peet. BA in Politics, Princeton U., 1971; MS in Acctg., NYU, 1972. With Peat, Marwick, Mitchell, & Co., Chgo., 1971-75; sr. v.p. Pioneer Bank & Trust Co., Chgo., 1976-81; v.p. fin. Lane Fin. Corp., Northbrook, Ill., 1981-83; sr. v.p., chief. fin. officer First Colonial Bankshares Corp., Chgo., 1983—. Active Grove Sch. Parents Adv. Bd., Northbrook, 1985—. Thomas J. Watson IBM Nat. Merit Scholar, Princeton U., 1967-71. Mem. Am. Inst. CPA's, Acctg. Research Assn. Club: Quadrangle (Princeton, N.J.) (social chmn. 1970-71). Avocations: skiing, golf, photography.

MAIHLE, NITA JANE, biomedical research scientist; b. Mansfield, Ohio, June 4, 1955; d. Loring J. and Maxine Landis (Weaver) M.; 1 child, Amelia Rose. BA, Miami U., Oxford, Ohio, 1976, MS, 1977; PhD, MS, Albert Einstein Coll. Medicine, 1983; postdoctoral, Cold Spring Harbor Lab, 1983-84, Case Western Reserve U., 1984-85. Postdoctoral fellow Cold Spring Harbor Labs, Long Isle, N.Y., 1983-84, Case Western Reserve U. Med. Sch., Cleve., 1984—. Ohio Bd. Regents scholar, 1973-76; named one of Outstanding Young Women Am., 1983; Muscular Dystrophy Assn. fellow, 1984, NIH fellow, 1985, American 1987—. Mem. AAAS, Am. Assn. for Cell Biology, Am. Assn. of Microbiology, Am. Assn. Univ. Women. Home: 2192 Oakdale Rd Cleveland Heights OH 44118 Office: Case Western Reserve U Sch of Medicine/Dept Molecular Biology Cleveland OH 44106

MAILE, ROBERT JOSEPH, data processing executive; b. Austin, Minn., Nov. 16, 1941. Indsl. engr. Hormel Co., Austin, 1964-68, computer analyst, 1968-77; sr. systems analyst Fisher Controls, Marshalltown, Iowa, 1977-80, project. leader, 1980-84, project mgr., 1984—86, mgr. spl. projects, 1986—. Served to sgt. USAF, 1964. Mem. Data Processing Mgmt. Assn. Roman Catholic. Lodge: Lions (bd. dirs. local club. 1984-85, 3d v.p. 1986—). Avocations: golf, fishing, canoeing, camping. Home: 1903 S 3rd Ave Marshalltown IA 50158 Office: Fisher Controls 205 South Center St Marshalltown IA 50158

MAIMAN, DENNIS JAY, neurosurgeon; b. Milw., July 26, 1953; s. Irwin and Belle Maiman; m. Donnalyn Ziger, Apr. 4, 1976; children: Nechama, Shoshana, Yehudit. BS, U. Wis., Milw., 1973; MD, Med. Coll. Wis., Milw., 1977; PhD, Marquette U., 1986. Cert. Am. Bd. Neurol. Surgery. Resident in neurosurgery Med. Coll. Wis., Milw., 1977-82, asst. prof. neurosurgery, 1982-86, assoc. prof., 1986—; chief spinal cord injury programs VA Med. Ctr., Milw., 1984—; dir. Spinal Cord Injury Ctr., Milw. Regional Med. Ctr., 1984—. Fellow ACS; mem. Am. Assn. Neurosurgeons, Am. Parapalegia Soc. (bd. dirs.), Soc. Neurosci., Cervical Spine Research Soc. Jewish. Office: Med Coll Wis Dept Neurosurgery 9200 W Wisconsin Ave Milwaukee WI 53226

MAIN, PAUL KEITH, health planner; b. Greenfield, Ind., May 22, 1931; s. Clarence B. and Ruth (Elnora) M.; m. Barbara Esther Pomeranz, Mar. 23, 1980; children—Timothy, Michal. B.A., Hanover Coll., 1953; B.D., Louisville Presbyn. Theol. Sem., 1956; postgrad. U. Edinburgh (Scotland), 1956-58; M.Community Planning, U. Cin., 1970; Ed.D., Ind. U., 1978. Pastor North Fairmount Presbyn. Ch., Cin., 1958-68; assoc. dir. Tri-State Area Health Planning Council, Evansville, Ind., 1970-76; sr. health planner Ind. State Bd. Health, Indpls., 1978—; adj. prof. Bur. Studies Adult Edn., Ind. U., 1978—. Mem. community adv. com. Multipurpose Arthritis Ctr., Ind. U. Patterson scholar, 1949-56; Patterson fellow, 1956-58; USPHS trainee, 1968-70. Mem. Am. Assn. Adult Edn., Am. Planning Assn., World Future Soc. Presbytery of the Ohio Valley. Contbr. articles to profl. jours. Home: 371 E Westfield Blvd Indianapolis IN 46220 Office: 1330 W Michigan St Indianapolis IN 46206

MAIN, ROBERT PEEBLES, hospital administrator; b. Buffalo, Nov. 13, 1943; s. Andrew and Jane (Neary) M.; m. Cleta Miller, June 13, 1964; children—Kelly Ann, Thomas. B.S. in Edn., SUNY-Buffalo, 1965; M.A. in Hosp. and Health Adminstrn., U. Iowa, 1973. Coordinator rehab. medicine services for psychiat. service and drug treatment unit VA Hosp., Iowa City, 1971-72, staff asst. to hosp. dir., 1972-74, asst. to chief staff, Oklahoma City, 1974-76; adj. asst. prof. health care adminstrn. U. Okla. Coll. Health, Oklahoma City, 1975-76; asst. hosp. dir. trainee VA Hosp., Memphis, 1976-77; assoc. hosp. dir. VA Lakeside, Chgo., 1977-79; exec. v.p. Marianjoy Rehab. Ctr., Wheaton, Ill., 1979—. Chmn. fund raising activity Ch. of Holy Spirit, Schaumburg, Ill., 1979-85; bd. dirs. Ancilla Home Health, Mended Hearts of DuPage County. Fellow Am. Coll. Healthcare Execs.; mem. Am. Hosp. Assn., Ill Hosp. Assn.(Long Term Care Panel), Chgo. Health Execs. Forum (sec., treas. 1981-82), Ill. Regents Adv. Council, DuPage Subarea Adv. Council, Health Systems Agy., Oklahoma City Met. Hosp. Council. Home: 212 Continental Ln Schaumburg IL 60194

MAINS, DOUGLAS BENJAMIN, orthopaedic surgeon; b. Aurora, Ill., July 25, 1934; s. Douglas Landis and Faith E. (Jess) M.; m. Frances Franks, June 14, 1956; children: Sheryl Elizabeth, Sheila Lynn. BS, Wheaton Coll., 1956; MD with honors, U. Ill., Chgo., 1960. Diplomate Am. Bd. Orthopaedic Surgeons. Intern USPHS Hosp., San Francisco, 1960-61; resident in orthopaedic surgery Hines VA Hosp. and Shriners Crippled Children Hosp., Chgo., 1963-67; clin. assoc. prof. Loyola U. Stritch Sch. Medicine, Maywood, Ill., 1972—; asst. prof. orthopaedics U. Iowa, Iowa City, 1973-74; Pres. Mona Kea Med. Condominium, Carol Stream, Ill., 1972-86. Patentee surgical instrument for proximal tibial osteotomy. Founder, past pres. Friends of Danada, DuPage County Forest Preserve, Glen Ellyn, Ill., 1979-81. Served with USPHS, 1960-63. Fellow ACS, Am. Acad. Orthpaedic Surgeons; mem. Alpha Omega Alpha. Presbyterian. Office: Mona Kea Orthopaedic Arthritis 515 Thornhill Dr Carol Stream IL 60188

MAIO, RONALD FRANK, emergency medicine physician; b. Chgo., Mar. 8, 1950; s. Joseph and Nora (Galli) M.; m. Jill Kristine Donovan, Dec. 6, 1975. BS, Regis Coll., 1972; DO, Mich. State U., 1976. Diplomate Am. Bd. Emergency Medicine. Intern Botsford-Zieger Hosps., Farmington Hills, Detroit, 1976-77; resident in emergency medicine Mich. State U., Univ. Affiliated Hosp., 1981-83; physician emergency medicine St. Lawrence Hosp., Lansing, Mich., 1983—; clin. instr. human medicine Mich. Stte U., East Lansing, 1981—, Coll. Osteopathic Med., East Lansing, 1981—; med. advisor Delta Fire Service, Lansing, 1983—. Served to capt. U.S. Army M.C., 1977-80. Mem. Am. Osteo. Assn., Am. Coll. Emergency Physicians, Physicians for Social Responsibility. Avocations: running, reading, traveling. Home: 1484 Sylvan Glen Okemos MI 48864 Office: St Lawrence Hosp Emergency Rm 1210 W Saginaw Lansing MI 48915

MAIOTTI, DENNIS PAUL, manufacturing company executive; b. Cleve., Oct. 14, 1950; s. Raymond Joseph and Shirley Mae (Lang) M.; m. Rebecca Mueller, Aug. 11, 1973; children: Jennifer, David. BA, Baldwin-Wallace Coll., 1972; postgrad., Ohio U., 1972-73, Northwestern U., 1974. Cert. secondary tchr. Asst. employee relations Eaton Corp., Cleve., 1973-74, mgr. prodn., 1974-76, v.p. mktg., 1976-84, exec. v.p., 1984-86; pres. Lennon Wallpaper Co., Joliet, Ill., 1986—. Editor, columnist South Life met. newspapers, Cleve., 1968-72. Mem. Wallcovering Mfgrs. Assn., Kappa Delta Pi, Delta Phi Alpha. Republican. Lutheran. Avocations: golf, tennis, boating, travel. Office: Lennon Wallpaper Co PO Box 8 807 4th Ave Joliet IL 60434

MAISEL, EUGENE FRANK, chemical company executive; b. Chgo., Sept. 3, 1925; s. Stephen and Frances (Lacki) M.; m. Marie C. Savino, June 23, 1951. BS, Roosevelt U., 1949; PhD, Ill. Inst. Tech., 1959. Plant chemist, asst. to pres. Ill. Condenser, Chgo., 1949-55; research chemist Diversey Corp., Chgo., 1955-67; v.p. research dir. Dober Chem., Chgo., 1967-72; owner, pres. Custom Chem. Co., Palatine, Ill., 1972—; cons. on aluminum and ferrous prepaint treatment, 1972—. Patentee in field. Served to U.S Army, 1943-46, CBI. Republican. Roman Catholic. Club: Anvil. Avocations: golf, tennis.

MAISELS, MICHAEL JEFFREY, pediatrician, educator; b. Johannesburg, South Africa, Oct. 18, 1937; m. Carol Yvonne Elkin, 1961; children: Lisa Jean, Gabrielle Ann, Amanda Lee, James Adam. MB, BCh, U. Witwatersrand, South Africa, 1961. Med. intern Coronation Hosp., Johannesburg, 1962; surgical intern Johannesburg Gen. Hosp., 1962; resident in pedriatrics Baragwanath Hosp., Johannesburg, 1963-65, North Shore Children's Hosp., Salem, Mass., 1966; chief resident med. outpatient dept. Children's Hosp. Med. Ctr., Boston, 1967, fellow in newborn medicine, 1967-69; research fellow Harvard Med. Sch. and Neonatal Lab., Boston Lying-in Hosp., 1967-69; chief newborn medicine M.S. Hershey (Pa.) Med. Ctr., 1972-86, assoc. prof. pediatrics, ob-gyn, 1975-80, prof., 1980-86; clin. prof. pediatrics U. Mich., Ann Arbor, 1986—; chmn. dept. pediatrics William Beaumont Hosp., Royal Oak, Mich., 1986—. Contbr. articles to profl. jours. Served to lt. col. M.C., U.S. Army, 1969-71. March of Dimes grantee, 1974-78, 1979-80. Mem. Soc. Pediatric Research, Perinatal Research Soc., N.Y. Acad. Scis., Am. Pediatric Soc. Home: 18201 Saxon Birmingham MI 48009 Office: William Beaumont Hosp 3601 W Thirteen Mile Rd Royal Oak MI 48072

MAISER, DAVID FRANCIS, communications executive; b. Shakopee, Minn., Nov. 21, 1945; s. Raymond Benedict and Cecilia Ann (Lano) M.; m. Mary Anne Whiteman, Sept. 1, 1978; children: Sarah, Megan. BA, Mankato (Minn.) State U., 1963; cert., Am. Mgmt. Assn.-Mgmt. Internship Program, Saranac Lake, N.Y., 1968. Mktg. dir. Nat. Car Rental, Mpls., 1969-73; acct. supr. Jeno F. Palucci, Mpls., 1973-75; pres., owner Trademark Communications, Inc., Minnetonka, Minn., 1975—; v.p. Lindy-Litte Joe, Inc., Brainerd, Minn., 1979—; chief exec. officer, owner Jamar Industries, Inc., Mankato, 1986—; bd. dirs. Mfrs. Walleye Council, Mpls., 1984—. Editor News mag., 1985; contbr. articles to Fishing Tackle Trade mag. Mem. Sales and Mktg. Execs., Alpha Mu Gamma. Republican. Roman Catholic. Avocations: fishing, hunting. Office: Trademark Communications Inc 15119 Minnetonka Blvd Minnetonka MN 55345-1589

MAJERS, JONATHAN JAY, dentist; b. St. Louis, June 1, 1955; s. Alfred Henry and Dolores Louise (Pfiefer) M.; m. Deborah Lynn O'Leary, May 21, 1982; 1 child, Allison Kaitlin. BA, U. Mo., 1977, DDS, 1982. Gen. practice dentistry St. Louis, 1982—. Mem. ADA, Mo. Dental Assn., Greater St. Louis Dental Soc., Synergism Investment Club, St. Louis Dental Study Club. Lodge: Rotary. Avocations: skiing, golf, tennis, traveling. Office: 11801 Manchester Rd Saint Louis MO 63131

MAJKOWSKI, KENNETH EDWIN, pharmacist; b. Chgo., July 24, 1952; s. Edwin Charles and Frances (Fryzel) M.; m. Lucinda Bronwyn Rose, Oct. 9, 1976. B in Pharmacy, Purdue U., 1975; Dr. in Pharmacy, U. Minn., 1977. Registered pharmacist, Minn. Pharmacist Scott Drug, East Gary, Ind., 1975; clin. coordinator, asst. dir. pharmacy Midway and Mounds Hosps., St. Paul, 1977-85; br. mgr. HMSS, Inc., St. Paul, 1985—; adj. asst. prof. Coll. Pharmacy U. Minn., Mpls., 1978—; cons. Deltec, St. Paul, 1984—, AVI-3M, Inc., St. Paul, 1985—; mem. speakers bur. Roche Lab., 1985—. Chmn. Midway Hosp. campaign United Way, St. Paul, 1979; block collector Am. Cancer Soc., St. Paul, 1982—; mem. edn. com. Twin Cities Diabetes Assn., Mpls., 1981-83. Mem. Am. Soc. Hosp. Pharmacists, Minn. Soc. Hosp. Pharmacists (past pres. 1986-87, pres. 1985-86, pres.-elect 1984-85, bd. dirs. 1982-87, Squibb award 1986, Pfizer award 1987), Rho Chi, Kappa Psi. Avocations: golf, biking, reading, racquetball, wines.

MAK, LEI-HOO, architect; b. Chungshan, Republic of China, Aug. 3, 1947; s. Yuen and Shunwah (Chiang) M.; m. Pui-Yee Christina Tsang, June 5, 1975; children: Karman, Karin T., William T. BS in Archtl. Engrng., Chen Kung U., Taiwan, Republic of China, 1968; MArch, Washington U., St. Louis, 1973. Registered architect, Mo. Designer and draftsman I.N. Chau & Son Architects and Engrs., Hong Kong, 1969-72; designer Jones Mayer Architects, St. Louis, 1973-77, design dir., 1977-82, prin. in charge of design, 1983—; ptnr. P.S. Chen & Ptnrs., Taipei, Republic of China, 1982-83. Mem. AIA, Nat. Council Archtl. Registration Bd., Internat. Chhinese Archtl. Soc. (pres. 1977, bd. dirs. 1983-85). Office: Jones Mayer Architecture 2190 Mason Rd Saint Louis MO 63131

MAKANOFF, LON DAVID, supermarket executive; b. Phila., Feb. 29, 1948; s. Bernard and Dorothy (Frimmel) M.; m. Rebecca Sher, Aug. 30, 1969; children—Jennifer, Eric, Amanda, Aaron. B.A. in Acctg., Phila. Coll. of Textiles and Scis., 1969; postgrad., U. Pa., 1977, NYU, 1977. Ptnr. Deloitte Haskins & Sells, Detroit, 1969-82; sr. v.p. fin., treas. Allied Supermarkets, Inc., Detroit, 1982-85, pres., chief operating officer, 1985-87, also dir.; pres., chief operating officer Meadowdale Foods, Inc., Detroit, 1987—. Audit com. Jewish Welfare Fedn., Detroit, 1982—; chmn. Gen. Foods div. United Found., Detroit, 1984; chmn. Allied Mich. Polit. Action, Detroit, 1983—; trustee Monseigneur Clement Kern Hosp. for Specialized Surgery, 1987—. Mem. Mich. Assn. C.P.A.s, Nat. Assn. Accts., Am. Inst. C.P.A.s, Fin. Execs. Inst., Detroit C. of C., Nat. Assn. Corp. Treasurers, Mich. Mchts. Council (sec., treas.). Republican. Jewish. Clubs: Detroit; Econ., Fairlane (Dearborn, Mich.). Office: Meadowdale Foods Inc 8711 Meadowdale Detroit MI 48228

MAKELY, WILLIAM ORSON, public relations executive; b. Staten Island, N.Y., Dec. 31, 1932; s. Ralph G. and Helen (Craig) M.; m. Ethel Neil Dee, Dec. 20, 1958; children: Jennifer, Katherine, Gordon. BS in English, U. Wis., 1955; MA in English, U. Chgo., 1962. Sr. editor World Book Ency., Chgo., 1969-78; dir. publ. Ill. Inst. Tech., Chgo., 1978-80; bus. devel. Sargent and Lundy Engrs., Chgo., 1980-82; free-lance writer Downers Grove, Ill., 1982-84; account exec. Bozell and Jacobs Pub. Relations, Chgo., 1984-85; dir. McKee Pub. Relations, Elk Grove Village, Ill., 1985—. Editor: City Life, 1974. Bd. dirs. Lone Tree Area council Girl Scouts USA, Oak Park, Ill., 1974-76, Friends of the Library, Downers Grove, 1977. Served with USN, 1955-57, Japan. Home: 4730 Main St Downers Grove IL 60515 Office: McKee Pub Relations 1375 Higgins Rd Elk Grove Village IL 60007

MAKENS, HUGH HARVEY, lawyer; b. Hancock, Mich., Feb. 22, 1939; s. Royal Francis and Gladys Mildred (Larsen) M.; m. Georgia Adell Hinzmann, June 27, 1965; children: Craig, Brett. BBA cum laude, Mich. Tech. U., 1961; JD, Northwestern U., 1964. Sec. electronics command contract adjustments bd. U.S. Army Electronics Command, Ft. Monmouth, N.J., 1964-66; trial atty. SEC, Detroit, 1966-72; dir. Corp. and Securities Bur., Lansing, Mich., 1972-78; ptnr. Warner, Norcross & Judd, Grand Rapids, Mich., 1978—. Contbr. articles to profl. jours. Served to capt. U.S. Army, 1964-66. Mem. ABA (chmn. state regulation of securities com. 1983-86), Mich. Bar Assn. (sect. chmn. 1984-85, council 1977—), Fed. Bar Assn. (past treas. Detroit chpt., past sec., past v.p.). Home: 7555 Aspenwood SE Grand Rapids MI 49508 Office: Warner Norcross & Judd 900 Old Kent Bldg Grand Rapids MI 49503

MAKEPEACE, TIM ROSS, retail executive; b. Watertown, S.D., Aug. 19, 1955; s. John Ross and Violet Marcella (Harvey) M.; m. Laurie Kathleen Burke, May 21, 1977 (div.); 1 child, Amy; m. Lynn Louise Cordell, Jan. 17, 1987. Cert., Gem City Coll., 1975. Mgr. Riddles Jewelry, Watertown, 1975-82; owner, operator Makepeace Jewelry, Watertown, 1982—. Mem. Am. Watchmakers Inst. (cert.). Democrat. Roman Catholic. Lodge: Elks. Avocations: bicycling, hunting. Home: 1126 N Park Watertown SD 57201 Office: Makepeace Jewelry 11 E Kemp Watertown SD 57201

MAKER, GEORGE EDWARD, obstetrician-gynecologist; b. Providence, Sept. 13, 1943; s. Francis Richard and Bessie Aletha (LaPierre) M.; m. Lynette Kay Gregory, Aug. 16, 1981. BA, Middlebury Coll., 1965; MD, U. Vt., 1976. Diplomate Am. Bd. Ob-gyn. Resident in ob-gyn U. Wis., Madison, 1976-80; mem. staff Meml. Hosp. Oconomowoc, Wis., 1980-82; mem. staff Meml. Hosp. Burlington, Wis., 1982—, chief of staff, 1986-87. Fellow Am. Coll. Ob-Gyn; mem. AMA. Home: 33200 Cardinal Trail Burlington WI 53105 Office: Burlington Clinic 190 Gardner Ave Burlington WI 53105

MAKI, WILLIAM MARTIN, engineer; b. Santa Monica, Calif., Aug. 31, 1941; s. Martin Wilbert and Gertrude Elvira (Anttila) M.; m. Katherine Sue Kauffman, June 12, 1965 (div. Oct. 1981); children: Karen, Susan; m. Peggy Lurl Worman, Apr. 10, 1982; children: Jolynn, Karen, Susan, Heather. ASME, Va. Jr. Coll., 1961; BSME, U. N.D., 1965. Design engr. Internat. Harvester, Ft. Wayne, Ind., 1965-68; test engr. Internat. Harvester, Ft. Wayne, 1968-71, project engr., 1971-81; pruduct engr. Gen. Dynamics Corp., Warren, Mich., 1982, Ford Motor Co., Dearborn, Mich., 1982, AC Spark Plug, Flint, Mich., 1983-85; resident engr. Delco Electronics, Kokomo, Ind., 1985—; cons., technician Precisioneering, Ft. Wayne, 1969-72; pres. PLM Enterprises, Inc., Ft. Wayne, 1983—. Sunday sch. supt. First Presbyn. Ch., Ft. Wayne, 1968—, deacon, 1976-80; treas. Manor Woods Community Assn., Ft. Wayne, 1981. Mem. Soc. Mfg. Engrs., Ft. Wayne Engrs. Club (treas. 1978-80). Club: Scandia (Ft. Wayne). Avocations: electronics, overhaul and repair, gardening, winemaking, hiking. Home: 9449 Crestridge Dr Fort Wayne IN 46804 Office: Delco Electronics PO Box 737 M/S 8117 Kokomo IN 46902

MAKO, WILLIAM LAWRENCE, real estate developer; b. Cleve., June 16, 1958; s. Lawrence M. and Margret E. (Borchard) M. BA in Bus., Wittenberg U., 1981. V.p. Conmak, Inc., Conneaut, Ohio, 1981-82; pres. Le Bears' Inc., Moreland Hills, Ohio, 1982-83; mgr. Wendy's Old-Fashioned Hamburgers, Bozeman, Mont., 1984; exec. v.p. Great Lakes Properties Corp., Conneaut, 1984—. Mem. Am. Resort and Residential Devel. Assn., Safari Club Internat., N. Am. Hunting Club. Republican. Roman Catholic. Avocations: hunting, fishing, outdoor sports. Home: PO Box 82 Stateline Rd Conneautville PA 16406 Office: Great Lakes Resort 6231 Weaver Rd Conneaut OH 44030

MAKOWSKI, DONNA BIRUTE, lawyer, educator; b. Chgo., Oct. 11, 1954; d. Charles J. and Jean V. (Kriauciunas) M. B.A. with honors, U. Ill.-

Chgo., 1976; J.D., John Marshall Sch. Law, 1983. Bar: Ill. 1984, U.S. Dist. Ct. (no. dist.) Ill. 1984, U.S. Ct. Appeals (7th cir.) 1984. Mgr. Jewel Food Corp., Chgo., 1972-76; tchr. fgn. lang. U. Ill.-Chgo., 1976-77, Chgo. Pub. Schs., 1976-83; course/seminar coordinator John Marshall Law Sch., Chgo., 1983-84; sole practice, Chgo., 1984—; mem. Mayor's Adv. Com. on Women's Affairs, Chgo., 1984—; of counsel John De Leon, Chgo. pro bono advocate Chgo. Vol. Legal Services. Aide Sen. Carroll Democratic Orgn., Chgo., 1981-82. Fellow Kosciusko Found., N.Y., 1983. Mem. ABA, Ill. Bar Assn., Chgo. Bar Assn. (sec. young lawyers div. 1982-83), Women's Bar Assn., Ill. Trial Lawyers Assn., Advocates Soc. Phi Kappa Phi, Phi Delta Phi. Roman Catholic. Home: 6231 N Francisco Ave Chicago IL 60659 Office: 53 W Jackson Suite 1430 Chicago IL 60604

MAKOWSKI, STEVEN MICHAEL, retail jewelery executive; b. Wausau, Wis., May 16, 1952; s. Stanley Gerald and Phyllis Aleta (Beilke) M.; m. Sheryl Diane Hyndman, Feb. 14, 1981; children: Phyllis Elizabeth, Matthew Stanislaus, Albrecht Vincent. BS in Secondary Edn., Ind. U., 1975; cert. in watch repair, Paris (Tex.) Jr. Coll., 1978. Cert. master watchmaker. Watchmaker Hopman Jewelers, Elkhart, Ind., 1978-79, 81-82, Will Jewelers, Mishawaka, Ind., 1980-81; owner, pres. Holmes Jewelry, Warren, Ind., 1982-87; owner Makowski Jewelers, Bluffton, Ind., 1987—. Mem. Warren Downtown Revitalization com., 1984—, co-chmn. Downtown Promotion com., 1983—, v.p. revitalization com. Pulse Opera House. Mem. St. Joseph Valley Watchmakers Guild (pres. 1980-81), Northeast Ind. Watchmakers Guild (pres. 1983-84), Am. Watchmakers Inst., Watchmakers Assn. of Ind. (Merit award 1982—, Disting. Service award 1984—), Warren C. of C., Nat. Antique Clock and Watch Collectors Club. Republican. Roman Catholic. Lodges: Kiwanis (v.p. 1984-85, pres. 1985-86), KC (lectr. 1982—). Home and Office: 128 W Market St Bluffton IN 46714

MAKUPSON, AMYRE PORTER, TV exec.; b. River Rouge, Mich., Sept. 30, 1947; d. Rudolph Hannibal and Amyre Ann (Porche) Porter; B.A., Fisk U., 1970; M.A., Am. U., Washington, 1972; m. Walter H. Makupson, Nov. 1, 1975; children: Rudolph Porter, Amyre Nisi. Asst. news dir. Sta. WGPR-TV, Detroit, 1975-76; public relations dir. Mich. Health Maintenance Orgn., Detroit, 1974-76, Kirwood Gen. Hosp., Detroit, 1976-77; news and pub. affairs mgr. Sta. WKBD-TV, Southfield, Mich., 1977—. Mem. adv. com. Mich. Arthritis Found., Co-Ette Club, Inc., Met. Detroit Teen Conf. Coalition; pres. bd. dirs. Detroit Wheelchair Athletic Assn.; mem. adv. com. Cystic Fibrosis Soc.; bd. dirs. Barat House, Kids In Need of Direction, Drop-out Prevention Collaborative; exec. com. March of Dimes. Recipient numerous service awards, including: Arthritis Found. Mich., Mich. Mchts. Assn., DAV, Jr. Achievement, City of Detroit, Salvation Army. Mem. Pub. Relations Soc. Am., Am. Women in Radio and TV (Outstanding Achievement award 1981), Women in Communications, Nat. Acad. TV Arts and Scis., Pub. Relations Soc. Am., Detroit Press Club, Ad-Craft. Roman Catholic. Office: 26955 W 11 Mile Rd Southfield MI 48034

MALAK, THOMAS A., sales executive; b. Cleve., Nov. 30, 1957; s. Joseph M. and Carmella (Lombardo) M.; m. Maria Stamatiades, June 10, 1986. BBA, John Carroll U., 1981; JD, Cleve. State U., 1984. Supr. Cleve. Sales Co., div. Malak Industries, Willoughby, Ohio, 1981-84; gen. mgr. Cleve. Sales Co., div. Malak Industries, Inc., Willoughby, Ohio, 1984-85, v.p., 1985-87, pres., 1987—, also bd. dirs.; pres. Port Erie Industries, Mentor, Ohio, 1985—. Named Alumni of Yr., Iota Phi Theta, 1982. Mem. Greater Cleve. Growth Assn. (vol. council small enterprises). Republican. Roman Catholic. Avocations: racquetball, golf, trivia. Home: 7283 Grant Mentor OH 44060

MALAND, ROBERT ARTHUR, management consulting company executive, consultant; b. Story City, Iowa, Oct. 2, 1940; s. Lloyd and Mildred Ardys (Nelson) M.; m. Dawn Marie Korn, Sept. 21, 1961 (div. 1972); children—Daniel, Roxanne, Rhonda, Leonard, Eric; m. Michelle Noreen Molberg, Sept. 22, 1979. A.A., U. Wis.-Barron County, 1975; B.S., U.Wis.-Whitewater, 1977. Enlisted U.S. Air Force, 1961, advanced through grades to staff sgt., 1963, served Pentagon, Washington, ret., 1969; founder, pres., chmn. bd. Maland Mgmt. Cons., Ltd., Marshfield, Wis., 1977—; adj. prof. Milton Coll. (Wis.), 1981-82; instr. Vocat. Sch., Marshfield, 1980-81. Republican Party candidate state senate 24th dist., 1980; sr. warden St. Alban's Episcopal Ch., Marshfield, 1983-87; chmn. fin. com. U. Wis. Fin. Fair, 1986-87; mem. Nat. Rep. Congl. Com., 1981-83. Served with USAFR, 1969-76. Recipient Presdl. Achievement award Republican Nat. Com., 1980. Mem. Am. Entrepreneurs Assn., Internat. Entrepreneurs Assn., Nat. Fedn. Ind. Businessmen, Am. Legion, DAV (Comdr.'s Club). Clubs: Friday Night Dance (pres. 1983-85), Toastmasters. Home: 427 Parkview Terr Marshfield WI 54449 Office: PO Box 802 Maland Mgmt Cons Ltd 110 W 2nd St Suite 1 Marshfield WI 54449

MALANY, BARBARA BUMGARDER, special education and learning disabilities educator, youth and child, consultant, businesswoman; b. Waco, Tex., Aug. 20, 1943; d. James McNabb and Helen (Welker) Bumgardner; m. LeGrand Lynn Malany, June 27, 1965; children: LeGrand Karl, Siobhan, Carlieen. BA in English with honors, U. Ill., 1965, MEd in Spl. Edn., 1972. Coordinator reading lab. Urbana High Sch., Ill., 1968-70; spl. needs tchr. Jefferson Middle Sch., Springfield, Ill., 1973-74; commr. Ill. Commn. on Children, 1974-85; instr. Lincoln Land Community Coll., Springfield, 1977-79; hearing officer Ill. State Bd. Edn., Springfield, 1980—; dir. Childrens' Edn., Cen. Bapt. Ch., Springfield, 1981-85; pres. Flowers Le Grand Ltd., Flowers and Gift Shop, Springfield, 1985—; v.p. Ill. Foster Parent Assn., Springfield, 1970-83; foster parent tng. commr. Ill. Dept. Children and Family Services, Springfield, 1978-79; mem. Ill. White House Com. on Children, 1980; dir. Rutledge Found., Springfield, 1982-86, pres., 1983-84; research asst. Inst. Research on Exceptional Children, Urbana, 1971-72. Editor quar. newspaper The Foster Parent, 1976-82. Foster parent to over 15 children, Ill., 1968—; active LWV, 1970—, Girl Scouts Am., 1981-82. Fellow U.S. Office Edn., 1971. Mem. Nat. Foster Parents Assn., Ill. Foster Parents Assn., Springfield C. of C., Women in Mgmt., Sangamon Foster Parents Assn., Council for Exceptional Children. Home: 600 S Rosehill Springfield IL 62704 Office: Flowers Le Grand The Hilton Plaza 7th and Adams Springfield IL 62701

MALANY, LE GRAND LYNN, lawyer, engineer; b. Chgo., May 14, 1941; s. LeGrand Franklin and Marion (Jaynes) M.; m. Barbara Bumgarner, June 26, 1965; children: LeGrand Karl, Siobhan, Carleen. BS in Engring. Physics, U. Ill., 1964, JD, 1970. Bar: Ill. 1970, U.S. Dist. Ct. E.D. Ill. 1970, U.S. Dist. Ct. S.C. Ill. 1974, U.S. Dist. Ct. N.D. Ill. 1981, U.S. Ct. Appeals 7th Cir. 19 72, U.Sl. Supreme Ct. 1975, U.S. Ct. Mil. Appeals 1971; registered profl. engr., Ill.; lic. real estate broker. Asst. astronomer Adler Planetarium, Chgo., 1960-63; research asst. Portland Cement Research Assn., Skokie, Ill., 1964; instr. dept. gen. engring. U. Ill., 1965-70, instr. Office Instrn. Resources, 1967-68, instr. Hwy Traffic Safety Ctr., 1968-69; lectr. Police Tng. Inst., Urbana, Ill., 1969-70; project dir. driver control program U.S. Dept. Transp., 1971-73, project dir., author driver license examiner tng. curriculum, 1973; assoc. drivers license adminstr. State of Ill., Springfield, 1973-74, asst. auditor gen., 1977-83, asst. atty. gen., dir. policy, planning and tech. State of Ill., 1983-85, chief internal auditor office of atty. gen., 1985-86, spl. asst. atty. gen., 1986—, spl. asst. auditor gen. and gen. counsel office of auditor gen., 1986—, gen. counsel state comptroller Cusas II project, 1986—; ptnr. Kabumoto, Lappe and Malany, Springfield, 1986—; pres. Microgeneral Ltd., 1983—, Mgmt. Control Systems, Inc., 1986; chmn. bd. Flowers LaGrand Ltd., 1985—; expert U.S. Fed. Energy Adminstrn., 1974; counsel juvenile div. Circuit Ct., Sangamon County, Ill., 1973-75; chief counsel Ill. Dept. Motor Vehicles, Springfield, 1974. Trustee Meret Center, Inc., 1973-75; Dem. candidate for States Atty., Sangamon County, Ill., 1980. Recipient Midwest Intergovtl. Audit Forum Recognition award, 1981. Mem. ABA, Am. Phys. Soc., Nat., Soc. Profl. Engrs., Ill. Socs. Profl. Engrs., Ill. Farm Bur., Ill. Christmas Tree Growers Assn., Ill. Foster Parents Assn. Lodge: Rotary (Springfield chpt. sec. 1983—, pres. 1986-87). Developer statewide motorcycle driver licensing program. Home: 600 S Rosehill St Springfield IL 62704 Office: 524 S 2d St Springfield IL 62706

MALCIC, LAWRENCE MICHAEL, architect, academic administrator; b. St. Louis, Sept. 22, 1955; s. Lawrence Andrew and Marie Elizabeth (Sprenger) M. BA, U. Pa., 1976, MArch, 1978. Registered architect, Mo. Asst. prof. architecture Washington U., St. Louis, 1979-82, archtl. advisor 1980-82, asst. dean bus. sch., 1982—; design prin. Gilmore Malcic & Cannon, Inc., St. Louis, 1984—; art commr. St. Louis Archdiocese, 1984—; planning cons. Parks Coll., Cahokia, Ill., 1985, U. Mo., Columbia, 1985—; art advisor Thompson Ctr., St. Louis, 1986. Author: (book) Past Shades, Future Directions, 1981; (with Michael Gessel) (art catalog) W.W. Denslow, American Illustrator, 1978. Trustee Ralph P. Ranft Scholarship Found., 1986—. Recipient first prize Hyde Park-Landmark Design Competition, Landmarks, St. Louis, Inc., 1981; named outstanding community leader under forty, St. Louis Mag., 1985. Mem. AIA (chpt. bd. dirs. 1984-86), Philomathean Soc. Roman Catholic. Club: Univ. Club of St. Louis. Avocations: travel, art, slavic and romance languages. Home: 5951 Marwinette Saint Louis MO 63116 Office: 509 Olive Saint Louis MO 63101

MALCOLM, RONALD ALAN, insurance company executive; b. Chgo., Aug. 15, 1946; s. Robert and Lula Frances (Westenberger) M.; m. Gloria Jean Burns, May 29, 1977; children—Brandi Leigh, Ali Dawn. B.J., U. Mo., 1968, postgrad., 1970-71, 77-78. Mktg. specialist Mid-Continent Aviation, North Kansas City, Mo., 1972-73; supt. mktg. communications Aetna Life & Casualty, Hartford, Conn., 1973-75; gen. mgr. Response Mktg., Kansas City, Mo., 1975-77; asst. v.p. communications services Kansas City Life, Mo., 1977—. Served with U.S. Army, 1968-70. Decorated Bronze Star, Army Commendation medal. Mem. North Central Round Table, Life Communicators Assn. (nat. exec. com. 1987—), Kansas City C. of C. (Centurion). Republican. Avocations: running; handball. Home: 43 E 52d St Kansas City MO 64112 Office: Kansas City Life Ins Co 3520 Broadway Kansas City MO 64111

MALE, MICHAEL J(OHN), veterinarian; b. DeKalb, Ill., May 3, 1952; s. Laverne P. and Betty J. (Flusch) M.; m. Barbara K. Feuerbach, Aug. 10, 1974; children—Kristine Marie, Brandon Michael. B.S., U. Ill., 1975, D.V.M., 1977. Pvt. practice vet. medicine Junction Vet. Clinic, Wilton, Iowa, 1977—. Mem. AVMA, Iowa Vet. Med. Assn., Soc. Theriogenology, Am. Assn. Swine Practitioners. Republican. Home: Box 117 RR 2 Wilton IA 52778 Office: 1015 W 5th St Wilton IA 52778

MALECKI, DAVID MICHAEL, airport manager; b. Ft. Leavenworth, Kans., Sept. 10, 1948; s. John Adam and Marylee Kathryn (Fogle) M.; m. Janice Adele Mayse, Sept. 2, 1972; children: Joshua Gerald, Madeline Elizabeth. B.S., Central Mo. State U., Warrensburg, 1973; M.P.A., U. Mo.-Kansas City, 1977. Lic. pvt. pilot FAA. Probation and parole officer Mo. Bd. Probation and Parole, Independence, 1973-76; research asst. budget and systems office City of Kansas City (Mo.), 1976-77, budget analyst, 1977-80, adminstrv. officer, asst. airport mgr. aviation dept. Richards-Gebaur Airport, 1980—. Mem. Independence Neighborhood Council, 1974-75. Served with U.S. Army, 1969-71, to sgt. Army NG, 1972—. Decorated Army Commendation Medal, Army Res. Achievement Medal with oak leaf clusters (2). Mem. N.G. Assn., Mo. N.G. Assn., Aircraft Owners and Pilots Assn., Pi Sigma Alpha. Home: 5009 Byrams Ford Rd Kansas City MO 64129 Office: Richards Gebaur Airport 15405 Maxwell St Kansas City MO 64147

MALEN, HAROLD STUART, computer systems manager; b. Chgo., Jan. 9, 1943; s. Lewis Lloyd and Carolyn (Copeland) M.; m. Mary Elizabeth Dever, Aug. 3, 1968 (div. Oct. 1971); m. Julie Ann Cohn, Oct. 27, 1973; children: Robert Douglas, Gregory Scott. BS in Commerce, DePaul U., 1965; MBA, Roosevelt U., 1978. Sr. systems staff analyst Allstate Ins. Co., Northbrook, Ill., 1966-78; project leader Unity Savs., Chgo., 1978-79; cons. CNA Ins., Chgo., 1979-81; systems mgr. Michael Reese Hosp., Chgo., 1981-84; applications program mgr. A.C. Nielsen, Deerfield, Ill., 1984—. Mem. Data Processing Mgmt. Assn. Jewish. Lodge: B'nai Brith. Avocations: golfing, basketball, baseball, bowling, gardening. Office: AC Nielsen 707 Lake Cook Rd Deerfield IL 60015

MALES, HOWARD EDWARD, management consultant, psychologist; b. N.Y.C., Aug. 18, 1954; s. Kenneth Lewis and Adele Esther (Luers) M.; m. Ruth B. Church. B.A., Drew U., 1976; M.A. U. Chgo., 1977, Ph.D., 1981. Cons. Booz, Allen and Hamilton, Inc., Chgo., 1979-80, Ernst and Whinney, Chgo., 1982-84; pres. Research Pros, Inc., Chgo., 1985—. Cons. orgnl. devel. activities univs. and hosps. Asst. chmn. DePaul U. Coll. Commerce Anniversary Com., 1982-83; chmn. grad. intern adv. bd. U. Chgo., 1983-85. Mem. Am. Psychol. Assn., Greater Chgo. Assn. Indsl./Orgnl. Psychologists. Clubs: U. Chgo. (steering com. 1981-84), Quadrangle. Home: 1642 E 56th St Chicago IL 60637

MALEWSKI, RALPH STANLEY, engineer, cable television consultant; b. Sandusky, Ohio, July 23, 1950; s. Florian and Philura E. (McCreery) M.; m. Donna Lynn Kuykendall, Apr. 23, 1980. AA, Nat. Inst. Tech., 1970. Chief engr. Monroe (Mich.) Cablevision, 1972-80; sr. tech. mgr. Westshore Cable, Westlake, Ohio, 1980-81; v.p. engring. Suburban Cable TV, Toledo, 1981-82; v.p., gen. mgr. Matrix Enterprises, Toledo, 1982-86; pres., chief exec. office Coaxial Cons. Services, Inc., Elmore, Ohio, 1974—; bd. dirs. suburban Cable TV, Toledo; cons. engr. Richmond Cable TV, Honeoye, N.Y., 1984. Contbr. various tech. articles to trade publs. Mem. Soc. Cable TV Engrs. Avocations: photography, amateur radio. Home and Office: 19200 W Portage River Rd S Elmore OH 43416

MALEY, CHARLES DAVID, lawyer; b. Highland Park, Ill., Aug. 18, 1924; s. Lyle West and Irene (Davis) M.; A.B., State U. Iowa, 1948; J.D., De Paul U., 1952; m. Mildred J. Tobin, Apr. 27, 1957; 1 dau., Annabel Irene. Bar: Ill. 1952, U.S. Supreme Ct. 1956. Assoc. firm Friedlund, Levin & Friedlund, Chgo., 1952-58; pvt. practice law, Chgo., 1958-68, Lake Bluff, Ill., 1966-72, Lake Forest, Ill., 1972-83; mem. firm Ori, Tepper, Fox & Maley, Waukegan, Ill., 1983—; pub. adminstr. Lake County, 1971-74. Asst. dist. commr. Boy Scouts Am., 1963-65; trustee Lake County Mus. Assn., 1978-79, Lake Forest-Lake Bluff Hist. Soc., 1979-81; bd. dirs. Petite Ballet, 1975-80. Mem. Lake County Republican Central Com., 1967-72, 76—, Rep. State Com., 1971-74; bd. govs. Lake County Rep. Fedn., 1980-83. Served with AUS, 1943-46, Decorated Purple Heart with oak leaf cluster, Bronze Star. Mem. ABA, Seventh Circuit, Ill., Chgo., Lake County bar assns., Am. Judicature Soc., SAR, Am. Legion (post comdr. 1967-68, 74-81, service officer 1968-69, adj. 1982-84, chaplain 1984-86), Am. Arbitration Assn. (mem. panel 1965-67), Phi Gamma Delta, Phi Alpha Delta. Republican. Presbyn. Clubs: Capitol Hill (Washington); Tower (Chgo.). Home: 241 W Washington St Lake Bluff IL 60044 Office: 301 W Washington St Suite 100 Waukegan IL 60085

MALIK, RAYMOND HOWARD, scientist, economist, corporate executive, inventor; b. Lebanon, Feb. 4, 1933; came to U.S., 1948, naturalized, 1963; s. John Z. and Clarice R. (Malik) M. B.A. in Bus. Adminstrn., Valparaiso U., 1950; B.S. in Bus. Adminstrn. and Econs., Simpson Coll., 1951; M.S. in Bus. Adminstrn., So. Ill. U., 1956, Ph. D. in Electronics and Econs., 1959. Supr. Arabian Am. Oil Co., Beirut, 1952-54; mem. grad. faculty, advisor Ill. State U., 1954-59; prof., head world trade programs Central YMCA Community Coll., Chgo., 1966-74; pres. Malik Internat. Enterprises Ltd., Chgo., 1959—; advisor U.S. Congl. Adv. Bd. Author: The Guide to Youth, Health and Longevity, 1980; inventor selectric typing elements and mechanism, 1959, pioneer developer interplanetary communications system, 1961, heater-humidifier-dehumidifier, 1963, ednl. math toy, 1965, circle of sound concept of sound propagation, 1967, introduced modular concept in color TV, 1973, Gamma ray breast cancer detector, 1976, auto-ignition instant hot water heater, 1981, water filter, purifier and softener, 1984, No Doze Warner, 1985, indoor-outdoor barbeque grill, 1985, Massager with Infra-red Heat, 1986. Deacon, mem. pastor-congl. com., youth and young adult ednl. com. St. George Orthodox Ch., Cicero, Ill.; fundraiser March of Dimes, St. Jude Hosp., Am. Cancer Soc., Am. Heart Fund, numerous others. Fulbright scholar, 1948-50; Methodist Ch. scholar, 1950-51; So. Ill. U. fellow, 1954-59. Mem. Am. Mgmt. Assn., Am. Econ. Assn., Am. Mktg. Assn., Import Clubs U.S., Internat. Bus. Council, IEEE, Internat. Platform Assn., Pres.'s Assn., AAAS, Nat. Assn. Self-Employed, Imperial Austrian Legion of Honor, Internat. Students Assn., Phi Beta Kappa, Sigma Xi, Delta Rho, Beta Gamma Sigma, Alpha Phi Omega. Mailing Address: PO Box 3194 Chicago IL 60654-0194

MALISZEWSKI, STANLEY JOHN, guidance and counseling administrator; b. Omaha, July 20, 1945; s. Stanley B. and Stella (Stafanski) M.; m. Judy Stillmock, Aug. 5, 1967; children: Karen, Ryan. BE, U. Nebr., 1968; MS in Counseling, Calif. State U., Fullerton, 1972; MS in Adminstrn., U. Nebr., 1977, PhD in Adult Edn., 1985. Secondary sch. tchr. Pomona (Calif.) Schs., 1968-72; high sch. counselor Omaha Schs., 1972-82; dir. guidance Cen. High Sch., Omaha, 1982-87; adminstr. pupil personnel services Omaha Pub. Schs., 1987—; cons. G.M. Hughes, 1983—, orgn. devel., succession planning Electronic Corp., El Segundo. Mem. Am. Assn. Counseling and Devel., Am. Sch. Counselor Assn., Am. Soc. Tng. and Devel., Assn. for Career Devel., Nebr. Sch. Counselors (pres. 1982-83), Nebr. Counselor Assn. (Outstanding Counselor of Yr. 1980). Avocations: photography, restoring old cars, sign language. Home: 11420 Grand Circle Omaha NE 68164 Office: Omaha Pub Schs 3819 Jones Omaha NE 68105

MALKASIAN, GEORGE DURAND, JR., physician, educator; b. Springfield, Mass., Oct. 26, 1927; s. George Dur and Gladys Mildred (Trombley) M.; m. Mary Ellen Koch, Oct. 16, 1954; children: Linda Jeanne, Karen Diane, Martha Ellen. A.B., Yale U., 1950; M.D., Boston U., 1954; M.S., U. Minn., 1963. Diplomate Am. Bd. Ob-Gyn. Intern Worcester (Mass.) City Hosp., 1954-55; resident in ob-gyn Mayo Grad. Sch. Hosp., Rochester, Minn., 1955-58, 60-61; mem. faculty Mayo Med. Sch., 1962—, prof. ob-gyn, 1976—, chmn. dept. ob-gyn, 1976—. Author articles in field. Served to lt. comdr. M.C., USNR, 1958-60. Named Tchr. of Year, Mayo Grad. Sch. Medicine, 1973, 77. Mem. Am. Coll. Obstetricians and Gynecologists, Am. Gynecol. and Obstetrical Soc., Am. Radium Soc., ACS, Soc. Gynecologic Oncologists, Assn. Profs. Ob-Gyn, N.Am. Ob-Gyn Soc., ACS, Central Assn. Obstetricians and Gynecologists, Minn. Soc. Obstetricians and Gynecologists. Home: 1750 11th Ave NE Rochester MN 55904 Office: Mayo Clinic 200 1st St SW Rochester MN 55905

MALKI, DEBRA BLOCK, cultural organization consultant; b. Kenosha, Wis., Feb. 12, 1951; s. Herbert Nathan and Marjorie Ellen (Zien) Block; m. Elliott Albert Malki, June 13, 1971; children: Jonathan Albert, Benjamin Adam. Student, U. Wis., 1968-71; BA in Sociology, DePaul U., 1972. Personnel staff specialist U.S. Civil Service Com., Chgo., 1972-74; ELS tchr. Pigier Rive Gauche, Paris, 1975-76; coordinator Foreigners' Community Service, Seoul, Korea, 1980-83; dir. resources Internat. Orientation Resources, Northfield, Ill., 1986—; Bd. govs. Olin-Sang-Ruby Union Inst. 1987—. Avocations: dance, travel, theater. Home: 319 Fairview Ave Winnetka IL 60093 Office: Internat Orientation Resources 540 Frontage Rd Northfield IL 60093

MALLATT, KEITH ALLEN, optometrist; b. Joplin, Mo., May 9, 1956; s. John Robinson and Evelyn Dora (Allen) M.; m. Brenda Sue Ward, July 7, 1977; children: Ryan Keith, Megan Alessa. Student, Mo. So. Coll., 1974-75, Pitts. State U., 1975-77; BS magna cum laude, U. Houston, 1979, OD summa cum laude, 1981. Lic. optometrist, Tex., Okla., Kans. Practice optometry Pittsburgh, Kans. and Galena, Kans., 1981—. Mem. Am. Optometric Assn., Kans. Optometric Assn., Okla. Optometric Assn., Am. Heart Assn., HOA Contact Lens Soc., Beta Sigma Kappa. Avocations: canoeing, hiking, skiing. Home: Park Hill Estates Galena KS 66739 Office: 2307 S Tucker Suite A Pittsburg KS 66762

MALLEN, GARY PATRICK, designer, newspaper executive; b. Kansas City, Mo., Feb. 19, 1949; s. Arthur Louis and Annebell (Putney) M.; student U. Mo., Kansas City, 1967-69; BFA, Kansas City Art Inst., 1973. Art dir. Travis/Walz/Lane Advt., Overland Park, Kans., 1973-74; v.p. Mid-Continent Advt. and Pub. Relations, Kansas City, 1975-76; pres. Gary Mallen Design Cons., Kansas City, 1975—; creative dir. Galvin/Farris/Ross Advt., Kansas City, 1976-78; mgr. creative services Kansas City Times and Star (Kansas City Star Co.), 1978-82, mktg. creative dir., 1982, promotions mgr., 1983, v.p., nat. creative dir. Am. City Bus. Jours., 1983-86, v.p. mktg., creative dir., 1986—. Bd. dirs. Bishop Hogan High Sch., 1978-79. Winner Kimberly Clark Bi-Centennial Design Competition, 1977; recipient 42 local Addy awards, 10 regional Addy awards, N.Y. Art Dirs. Club award, Dallas Soc. Visual Communications award. Mem. Kansas City Art Dirs. Club (18 awards), Ad Club of Kansas City (chmn. Addy awards com., 1981, 83, bd. dirs. 1986—). Mem. Christian Church. Clubs: Country, Kansas City. Designer books: Historic Kansas City Architecture, 1974, The Star: The First 100 Years, 1980; Folly Theatre Commemorative Book, 1981. Office: 3535 Broadway Kansas City MO 64111

MALLERDINO, ANTHONY MICHAEL, fundraising executive; b. Chgo., Apr. 8, 1959; s. Anthony Angelo and Grace Marie (Carlino) M. AB, Georgetown U., 1981; MA, U. Chgo., 1983. Campaign assoc. U. Chgo. Med. Ctr., 1982-83, coordinator records and research, 1983, asst. dir. devel., 1984-87; dir. found. and corp. relations Lake Forest (Ill.) Coll., 1987—. Roman Catholic. Office: Lake Forest Coll Devel Office Sheridan & College Rds Lake Forest IL 60045

MALLERS, GEORGE PETER, lawyer; b. Lima, Ohio, Apr. 28, 1928; s. Peter G. and Helen (Daskalakis) M.; m. Rubie Loomis, Feb. 2, 1950; children—Peter G. II, William G., Elaine. B.S., Ind. U., 1951; J.D., Valparaiso U., 1955. Bar: Ind. 1955, U.S. Dist. Ct. (so. and no. dists.) Ind., U.S. Ct. Appeals (7th cir.). Practice law Ft. Wayne, Ind., 1955—; co-mng. ptnr. Beers, Mallers, Backs, Salin & Laramore and predecessor firms, 1955—; county atty., Allen County, Ind., 1964-73; pres. Mallers Theatres, Ft. Wayne, 1949—, Holiday Theatres, Inc., Mallers Mgmt., 1964—, Mallers & Spirou Enterprises, Inc., 1971—, Georgetown Sq. Theatres I & II, 1971—, Stage Door, Inc., 1972—, M-S Amusement Corp., 1972—, Georgetown Lounge & Restaurant, Inc., 1972—, Mallers-Spirou Mgmt. Corp., 1973—, Georgetown Bowl, Inc., 1976—. Mem. Allen County Police Merit Bd., 1967-77; pres. Allen County Young Republican Club, 1956-58; asst. to Rep. county chmn. Allen County, 1958—; chmn. City-County Bd. Health, 1980—. Fellow Ind. Bar Found.; mem. ABA, Ind. Bar Assn., Allen County Bar Assn. (sec., dir. 1961-63), Am. Judicature Soc., Valparaiso U. Law Sch. Alumni Assn. (nat. pres. 1978-80), Phi Alpha Delta. Office: Ft Wayne Nat Bank Bldg Fort Wayne IN 46802

MALLETT, LYDIA GWENDOLYN, psychology cons.; b. Detroit, Aug. 22, 1954; d. Conrad Leroy and Claudia Gwendolyn (Jones) M. BA in Psychology, Mich. State U., 1976, MA in Social Psychology, 1980, M Labor and Indsl. Relations, 1981, PhD Social Psychology, 1981. Cons. Arthur Young & Co., Detroit, 1980, Action Mgmt., Flint, 1980-86; asst. prof. bus. U. Mich., Flint, 1982-83; dir. tng. Wayne County Govt., Detroit, 1983-86; sr. assoc. James H. Lowry & Assocs., Chgo., 1986—. Pres. Detroit chpt. Coalition 100 Black Women, 1981-86, nat. dir. 1986—. Mem. Am. Psychol. Assn., Am. Soc. Tng. Devel., Am. Soc. Personnel Adminstrn., Acad. Mgmt., Nat. Coalition 100 Balck Women (pres. emeritus Detroit chpt.1986-88, nat. treas.) Delta Sigma Theta. Avocation: skiing. Office: James H Lowry & Assocs 218 N Jefferson Chicago IL 60606

MALLON, JAMES HOWARD, magazine advertising executive; b. Milw., May 26, 1929; s. J. Howard and Kathryn (Carney) M.; m. Joyce Mary Russo, Sept. 22, 1956; children—James Howard III, Paul A., David C. B.S. in Bus. Adminstrn., Marquette U., 1955. Gen. sales mgr. Naegele Outdoor Advt. Co. of Wis., Milw., 1955-63, v.p., nat. sales mgr. Naegele Advt. Cos. Inc., Chgo., 1963-69; with advt. sales dept. Forbes Mag., Chgo., 1969-80, mgr. midwest sales, 1980—. Life mem. Rep. Nat. Com. Mem. Advt. Fedn. of Minn., Nat. Assn. Ry. Advt. Mgrs., Delta Sigma Pi (life mem.). Clubs: 1200 of Ill.; Chgo. Athletic, Mid Am., Agate of Chgo.; Meadow. Office: 435 Michigan Ave Suite 1312 Chicago IL 60611

MALLON, THOMAS FRANCIS, JR., foreign exchange broker; b. N.Y.C., Jan. 2, 1944; s. Thomas Francis and Rose Marie (McDonnell) M.; m. Elizabeth Ann Kiely, June 4, 1966; children: Eileen Elizabeth, Erin Cristin. BBA, Manhattan Coll., 1966; postgrad. Hofstra U., 1966-71. Acctg. clk. Exxon, N.Y.C., 1965-66; fgn. exchange clk., dealer Brown Bros., Harriman & Co., N.Y.C., 1966-69; chief fgn. exchange dealer Banca Nazionale del Lavoro, N.Y.C., 1969-70; asst. cashier, fgn. exchange dealer Security Pacific Internat. Bank, 1970-71; owner, pres. Thomas F. Mallon Assocs., N.Y.C., 1971-72; pres., bd. dirs. Kirkland Whittaker & Mallon, 1972-75; sec.-treas., bd. dirs. Mallon & Dorney Co., Ltd., 1975-81, Mallon & Dorney Co. (Can.) Ltd., 1978-79; v.p., bd. dirs. Thomas J. Roche Internat. Cons., Inc., 1979-80; sr. v.p., sec.-treas., bd. dirs. Harlow Meyer Savage Inc., N.Y.C., 1980-82, Euro-Brokers Harlow (Can.), Toronto, Ont., 1980-82; sr. v.p. Tullett & Riley, Inc., N.Y.C., Los Angeles and Toronto, 1982-83; chief exec. officer, pres., owner Thomas F. Mallon Assocs., Inc., 1982—; mem. Chgo. Merc. Exchange, 1983—; account exec. Merrill Lynch Capital Markets, N.Y.C. and Chgo., 1984-86, floor mgr. fgn. currency futures and options pits, 1985-86; v.p., mgr. Chgo. Merc. Exchange, 1986—, mem., 1983—, Internat. Monetary Market, 1985—; lectr. fgn. exchange Am. Inst. Banking, N.Y.C., 1970-72; guest speaker U. S.C., 1978. Contbg. author: The Roche Currency Survey, 1978-80. Mem. Fgn. Exchange Brokers Assn. N.Y.C. (past sec.), Forex Assn. N.Am. Roman Catholic. Club: Downtown Athletic. Home: 182 Winthrop Ln Lake Forest IL 60045 Office: 30 S Wacker Dr Chicago IL 60606

MALLORY, ARTHUR LEE, state official; b. Springfield, Mo., Dec. 26, 1932; s. Dillard A. and Ferrell (Claxton) M.; m. Joann Peters, June 6, 1954; children: Dennis Arthur (dec.), Christopher Lee, Stephanie Ann, Jennifer Lyn. B.S., S.W. Mo. State Coll., 1954; M.Ed., U. Mo., 1957, Ed.D., 1959; H.H.D., S.W. Bapt. Coll., Mo., 1972. History supr. U. Mo. Lab. Sch., Columbia, 1956-57; asst. to supt. schs. Columbia, 1957-59; asst. supt. schs. Parkway Sch. Dist., St. Louis County, Mo., 1959-64; dean evening div. U. Mo., St. Louis, 1964; pres. S.W. Mo. State Coll., Springfield, 1964-70; commr. edn. Mo. Dept. Edn., Jefferson City, 1971—; dir. Internat. House, U. Mo., Columbia, 1956-59. Vice pres. Ozarks council Boy Scouts Am., 1967, pres. Gt. Rivers council, 1972-73, mem. north central region exec. bd., 1984—; bd. dirs. Meml. Community Hosp.; Bd. dirs. Mid-Continent Regional Ednl. Lab.; chmn. bd. Mo. Council on Econ. Edn.; bd. regents Mo. State Univs.; trustee Pub. Sch. Retirement, William Jewell Coll., 1972-74; chmn. com. bds. So. Bapt. Conv., 1972-73, mem. com. or bds., 1981—; mem. exec. bd. Mo. Bapt. Conv., 1972-75, 77-80; Young Audiences, Inc. adv. com., 1986, ARC Bd., Cole County, 1986, Children's Services Commn., Chmn., 1986—, Edn. Commn. of U.S. Served with U.S. Army, 1954-56. Recipient Disting. Service award Mo. Jr. C. of C., 1966; Distinguished Service award U. Mo., 1976; Faculty/Alumni award U. Mo., 1976; Silver Beaver award Boy Scouts Am., 1983, Good Shepherd and Cross, 1986, Disting. Citizen award, 1986; hon. life mem. Mo. Congress Parents and Tchrs.; named Springfield's Outstanding Young Man of Yr., 1965; Champion of Excellence PUSH, 1978. Mem. Am. Assn. State Colls. and Univs., N. Central Assn. Colls. and Secondary Schs., Council Chief State Sch. Officers, Mo. Assn. Sch. Adminstrs., NEA, Mo. Tchrs. Assn. So. Baptist (deacon). Clubs: Masons (33 deg.), Rotary. Office: State Commr Edn Dept Elementary and Secondary Edn Jefferson City MO 65102

MALLORY, ROBERT MARK, controller, finance executive; b. Mattoon, Ill., Apr. 15, 1950; s. Robert Monroe and Betty Ann (Mudd) M.; m. Diana Marie Burde, Aug. 19, 1972; 1 child, Laura Elizabeth. BS in Accountancy, U. Ill., 1972; M Mgmt., Northwestern U., 1986. CPA, Ill. Staff acct. Price Waterhouse, Chgo., 1972-74, sr. acct., 1974-77, mgr., 1977-79; dir. internal audit Mark Controls Corp., Skokie, Ill., 1979-81; corp. controller Mark Controls Corp., Skokie, 1981-86, v.p., controller, 1986—. Mem. Am. Inst. CPA's (Elijah Watts Sells award 1972), Ill. CPA Soc., Fin. Execs. Inst., Beta Gamma Sigma. Methodist. Home: 3312 Lakewood Ct Glenview IL 60025 Office: Mark Controls Corp 5202 Old Orchard Rd Skokie IL 60077

MALLORY, THOMAS HOWARD, orthopaedic surgeon, educator; b. Ohio, Jan. 10, 1939; s. Guy Howard and Freada (Shepherd) M.; m. Kelly Lynn Smith, Dec. 31, 1964; children—Scot Thomas, Thomas Howard, Jr., Christian Smith. A.B., Miami U., Oxford, Ohio, 1961; M.D., Ohio State U., 1965. Diplomate Am. Bd. Orthopaedic Surgery. Intern, Ohio State U. Hosp., Riverside Methodist Hosp., Columbus, 1965-66; orthopaedic resident Ohio State U. Hosp., Columbus, 1966-70; fellow in hip surgery Harvard Med. Sch., Mass. Gen. Hosp., Boston, 1970-71; tchg. fellow Harvard Med. Sch., Tufts U., Boston, 1970; clin. instr. orthopaedic surgery Ohio State U., Riverside Methodist Hosp., Columbus, 1977—, Ohio State U., 1977—; mem. joint med. study groupEthicon, Richards Med. Co.; editorial adv. bd. Profl. Educ. Programs, Inc. Mem. editorial bd. Clin. Orthopaedics and Related Research. Contbr. articles to profl. jours. Served to maj. USAR, 1965-72. Mem. Am. Acad. Orthopaedic Surgeons, ACS, AMA, Assn. Bone and Joint Surgeons, Hip Soc., Knee Soc., Sir John Charnley Soc., Ohio State Med. Soc., Ohio Orthopaedic Soc., Columbus Orthopaedic Soc., Columbus Acad. Med., Mid-Am. Orthopaedic Assn., Med. Forum, Christian Med. Soc., Fellowship of Christian Athletes. Avocations: jogging, riding, polo. Office: Joint Implant Surgeons Inc 720 E Broad St Columbus OH 43215

MALLORY, TROY L., accountant; b. Sesser, Ill., July 30, 1923; s. Theodore E. and Alice (Mitchell) M.; m. Magdalene Richter, Jan. 26, 1963. Student So. Ill. U., 1941-43, Washington and Jefferson Coll., 1943-44; BS, U. Ill., 1947, MS, 1948. Staff sr., supr. Scovell, Wellington & Co., CPA's, Chgo., 1948-58; mgr. Gray Hunter Stenn, CPA's, Quincy, 1959-62, ptnr., 1962—. Mem. fin. com. United Fund, Adams County, 1961-64. Bd. dirs. Woodland Home for Orphans and Friendless, 1970—, pres., 1981-84. Served with 84th Inf. Div. AUS, 1942-45. Decorated Purple Heart, Bronze Star. Mem. Quincy C. of C. (bd. dirs. 1970-76), Am. Inst. CPA's, Ill. CPA Soc. Lodges: Rotary (bd. dirs. Quincy 1967-70, pres. 1978-79), Shriners (bd. dirs. Quincy 1982-85, v.p. 1986). Home: 51 Wilmar Dr Quincy IL 62301 Office: 200 Am Savs Bldg Quincy IL 62301

MALLOT, JERRY M., chamber of commerce executive. Pres. Wichita Area C. of C., Wichita, Kans. Office: Wichita Area C of C 350 W Douglas Ave Wichita KS 67202-2970§

MALLOY, EDWARD ALOYSIUS, priest, university administrator, educator; b. Washington, May 3, 1941; s. Edward Aloysius and Elizabeth (Clark) M. BA, U. Notre Dame, 1963, MA, 1967, ThM, 1969; PhD, Vanderbilt U., 1975. Ordained priest Roman Cath. Ch., 1970. Instr. theology Aquinas Jr. Coll., Nashville, 1972-73; teaching asst. U. Notre Dame, Ind., 1969-70, instr., 1974-75, asst. prof., 1975-81, assoc. prof., 1981—, assoc. provost, 1982-87, pres.-elect, 1987, pres., 1987—. Mem. Ind. Organ Transplantation Task Force, 1986; bd. regents U. Portland, Oreg., 1985. Mem. Cath. Theol. Soc. Am., Soc. Christian Ethics, Bus. and Higher Edn. Forum. Home: U Notre Dame 141 Sorin Hall Notre Dame IN 46556 Office: U Notre Dame Office of Pres Notre Dame IN 46556

MALLOY, JAMES B., paper goods company executive. Pres., chief operating officer Jefferson-Smurfit Corp., Alton, Ill. Office: Jefferson Smurfit Corp 401 Alton St Alton IL 62002 *

MALLOY, JAMES MATTHEW, hospital executive; b. N.Y.C., Aug. 26, 1939; s. Peter Joseph and Catherine (Cunningham) M.; m. Joan Elizabeth Wagner, Sept. 9, 1967; children—Stephen, Christopher. B.S., Manhattan Coll., 1961; M.P.H., Yale U., 1968. Asst. to dir. Yale New Haven Hosp., New Haven, Conn., 1967; assoc. adminstr. Waterbury Hosp., Conn., 1969-75; exec. dir., chief exec. officer Jersey City Med. Ctr., N.J., 1975-77; dir., chief exec. officer U. Conn. Hosp., Farmington, 1977-82, U. Ill. Hosp. and Clinics, Chgo., 1982—; cons. NIH, Bethesda, Md., 1976-84; dir. Univ. Health Consortium, Atlanta; chmn. Compass Health Plan, Chgo., 1983—; dir. Hosp. Fund, Inc., New Haven, Conprands, Inc., Chgo.; lectr. Yale U. Sch. Medicine; adj. prof. U. Ill. Coll. Medicine, Chgo.; assoc. prof. U. Ill. Sch. Pub. Health. Contbr. articles to profl. jours. Dr. Stuart Hamilton fellow Capital Area Health Consortium, 1982. Fellow Inst. Medicine Chgo., Am. Coll. Healthcare Execs.; mem. Ill. Hosp. Assn. (bd. dirs. 1984—), Met. Chgo. Healthcare Council, Yale Alumni Assn. Clubs: Yale (Chgo.); Hosp. Adminstrs. of N.Y. Avocations: sailing; tennis. Home: 666 Sheridan Rd Winnetka IL 60093 Office: Univ Ill Hosp & Clinics 1740 W Taylor St Chicago IL 60612

MALLOY, JOHNN EDWARD, radio and television educator; b. Superior, Wis., Jan. 1, 1940; s. Robert Francis and Celestine Marie (Evenson) M. BS, U. Wis., LaCrosse, 1962; MS, Winona (Minn.) State U., 1967; MS in Edn., Chgo. State U., 1970; EdS, Ea. Ill. U., 1977; ArtsD, U. No. Colo., 1982. Cert. K-14 tchr., Ill., Wis., Colo. Tchr. speech and English Merrill (Wis.) Pub. Schs., 1962-65; tchr. radio and TV Harvey (Ill.) Sch. Dist., 1965—; instr. speech and theatre Thornton Community Coll., South Holland, Ill., 1968-70, 75-77, 85; media lectr. Chgo. State U., 1970-72; supr. media lab. U. No. Colo., Greeley, 1980-82. Author: Communication in the High School: Speaking and Listening, 1972, Instructional Guides to Media Communication, 1972; producer TV mag. series Getting Around, 1981—. Active in CAP, Chgo., 1965—. Recipient degree of distinction Nat. Forensic League, Ripon, Wis., 1982, Silver Medalist Canon USA Photo Contest, 1985; Cert. of Recognition in CBS TV Worth Teaching Program, 1987. Mem. NEA, Ill. Speech and Theatre Assn., Ill. Edn. Assn., Faculty Assn. Dist. 205, Speech Communication Assn., Air Force Assn. Lutheran. Home: PO Box 487 Park Forest IL 60466 Office: Thornton Twp High Sch TV Studio 151st & Broadway Harvey IL 60426

MALLOY, MARGARET ANN PETERS, accountant; b. Lafayette, Ind., June 22, 1956; d. Robert E. and Mary Margaret (Garigan) Peters; m. Robin Paul Malloy, June 10, 1978; 1 child, Gina Elizabeth. BS, Purdue U., 1977; postgrad., U. Fla., 1979-80, Fla. Atlantic U., 1981; MAS, U. Ill., 1983. CPA, Fla., Tex. Supervisory acct. U. Fla., Gainesville, 1978-80; staff acct. Nowlen, Holt, Miner & Kisker, West Palm Beach, Fla., 1981-82; sr. acct. Briercroft Savs., Lubbock, Tex., 1983-85; controller Master Software Corp., Indpls., 1986—. Named an Outstanding Young Woman of Am. Jaycees Internat., 1982, Karl Volle Meml. scholar Purdue U., 1977. Mem. Acctg. Research Assn., Am. Acctg. Assn., Am. Inst. CPA's, Fla. Inst. CPA's, Tex. Soc. CPA's, Ind. CPA Soc., Gamma Pi Alpha, Alpha Lambda Delta.

MALMQUIST, CARL PHILLIP, psychiatrist; b. St. Paul, Mar. 10, 1933; s. Carl Phillip and Lillian Viola (Kahler) M.; m. Arlyn Virginia Bodal (dec. 1983); children: Derek, Jay. BA, U. Minn., 1954, MD, 1958, MS, 1961. Diplomate Am. Bd. Psychiatry and Neurology, Am. Bd. Child Psychiatry, Am. Bd. Adult Psychiatry; cert. forensic psychiatry. Intern U. Minn., 1962-63, Columbia Med. Ctr., N.Y.C., 1963-64; assoc. prof. dept. psychiatry U. Mich., 1965-67; assoc. prof. Inst. Child Devel. U. Minn., Mpls., 1967-70, prof., dir. child and adolescent psychiatry, 1971-72, prof. criminal justice, 1972-80, prof. dept. sociology, 1980—; cons. Hennepin County, Mpls., 1967—, Dist. Court, 1969—; mem. commn. of mentally disabled ABA, 1985. Author: Adolescent Development, 1980; bd. editors: Psychiatric Annuals, 1981; contbr. articles to profl. jours. Fellow Am. Psychiat. Assn., Am. Coll. Psychiatrists, Am. Orthopsychiat. Assn., Am. Acad. Child Psychiatry, Am. Acad. Psychiatry and Law; mem. Group for Avancement Psychiatry. Club: Edina Country. Home: 5010 Bruce Ave Minneapolis MN 55424 Office: U Minn 914 Social Science Bldg Minneapolis MN 55455

MALMQUIST, LAINE EVAN, service company executive; b. Santa Monica, Calif., Mar. 7, 1950; s. Lester A. and Mildred (Mitchell) M.; m. Steffanie Merrick, June 17, 1972; children: Robert, Kimberly. BA, Wheaton (Ill.) Coll., 1972; MBA, Mich. State U., 1973. CPA, Ill. Fin. analyst Marathon Oil Co., Findlay, Ohio, 1974-75; fin. adminstr. Service Master Corp., Downers Grove, Ill., 1975-79; budget dir. Service Master Corp., Downers Grove, 1979-83, asst. treas., 1983-84, asst. v.p., 1984, v.p., 1985—. Mem. Rep. Nat. Com., 1977—; bd. dirs., chmn. audit com. Christian Service Brigade, Wheaton, 1986; mem. anniversary com. Naperville (Ill.) Evang. Free Ch., 1976—. Mem. Am. Inst. CPA's, Ill. CPA Soc., Nat. Assn. Accts. Republican. Home: 817 Rockbridge Dr Naperville IL 60540 Office: Service Master Co 2300 Warrenville Rd Downers Grove IL 60515

MALMSTROM, FREDERICK VINCENT, research psychologist; b. Kalamazoo, Sept. 8, 1939; s. Vincent Frederick and Jean (Lebens) M.; m. Ellen Miller, June 5, 1964 (div. May 1968); m. Susan G. Gates, June 1, 1974; 1 son, Carl V. B.S., U.S. Air Force Acad., 1964; M.S., U. So. Calif., 1970; M.S., Okla. State U., 1972, Ph.D., 1978. Commd. 2d lt. U.S. Air Force, 1964, advanced through grades to capt., 1975, lt. col. Res., 1985; electronic warfare officer, 1964-71, sta. Vietnam, 1966-67, 69-70; asst. prof. behavioral sci. U.S. Air Force Acad., Colo., 1971-74, resigned, 1975; asst. prof. human factors U. So. Calif., Los Angeles, 1978-84; human factors analyst, Boeing Aerospace Co., Seattle, 1984-86; sr. research psychologist Systems Research Labs., Dayton, Ohio, 1986—; guest researcher NASA/Ames Research Ctr., Moffett Field, Calif., 1972—, Air Force Human Resources Lab., Wright-Patterson Air Force Base, Ohio, 1978-83. Contbr. articles to profl. jours. Decorated D.F.C., Air medal with 10 bronze oak leaf clusters. Mem. Psychonomic Soc., Human Factors Soc., Am. Psychol. Assn., AAAS, Sigma Xi. Office: Systems Research Labs 2800 Indian Ripple Rd Dayton OH 45440

MALMSTROM, HERBERT ALLEN, technical services director; b. Moline, Ill., Jan. 6, 1935; s. Eugene Randolf and Ester Lorella (Miller) M.; m. Joye Ann Hamm, Dec 21, 1954; children: Michael Allen, Lisa Ann, Randal Eugene. BS in Engring. Physics, St. Ambrose Coll., 1961. Test engr. Am. Air Filter, St. Louis and Rock Island, Ill., 1961-65; sr. project engr. Am. Air Filter, St. Louis, 1965-83; mgr. design engring. Engineered Air Systems, St. Louis, 1983-86, dir. tech. services, 1986—. Patentee protective shelter flow control apparatus. Mgr. Creve Coeur Baseball Assn., 1966-80; marshall Jr. Olympics, 1986. Served with USN, 1954-56. Republican. Club: Am. Air Filter Mgmt. (past pres.). Office: Engineered Air Systems 1270 N Price Rd Saint Louis MO 63132

MALONE, FRANCIS EDWARD, accountant; b. Kempton, Ill., Jan. 18, 1907; s. Frank Mark and Julia Kathern (Walgenback) M.; A.A. in Commerce, Springfield Coll. Ill., 1954; B.S.C., U. Notre Dame, 1956. Mgr., Walgenback-Walker Farm, near Kempton, 1930-42; chief statis. clk. U.S. War Dept., McCook Army Air Field, McCook, Nebr., 1945-46; bookkeeper and office mgr. Tombaugh-Turner Hybrid Corn Co., Pontiac, Ill., 1946-47; safety responsibility evaluator Ill. Div. Hwys., Springfield, 1947-49; agrl. statistician U.S. Dept. Agr. Bur. Agrl. Econs., Springfield, 1949-53; sr. accountant Raymond E. Rickbiel, C.P.A., 1955-61, Ernst & Ernst, Springfield, 1961-62; pvt. practice pub. accounting, Springfield, 1963—. Served to sgt. USAAF, 1942-45. Mem. Am. Accounting Assn., Air Force Assn., Am. Legion (adj. post 1973—), Alumni Assn. U. Notre Dame, Te Deum Internat. (sec.-treas. Ill. chpt. 1962-65), Thomist Assn. (chmn. Ill. chpt. 1957-62), K.C. Home and office: One Maple Ln Kempton IL 60946

MALONE, JEAN HAMBIDGE, educational administrator; b. South Bend, Ind., Nov. 23, 1954; d. Craig Ellis and Dorothy Jane (Piechorowski) Hambidge; 1 child, Julia Mae; B.S. in Edn., Butler U., 1976, M.S. in Edn., 1977; m. James Kevill Malone, July 8, 1978. Tchr., Indpls. Public Schs., 1977-78; dir. student center and activities Butler U., Indspl., 1978—; Eisenhower Meml. scholarship trustee, 1977-80. Bd. dirs. Heritage Place of Indpls., 1983-84, Ind. Office Campus Ministries, Intercollegiate YMCA Indpls., 1985—. Bd. dirs. Campfire of Cen. Ind. 1980-84, 86-87; Ind. Office Campus Ministries State Bd., 1985—; Recipient Outstanding Faculty award, Butler U., 1980. Mem. Ind. Assn. Women Deans, Adminstrs. and Counselors (bd. dirs. 1982-83), Ind. Assn. Coll. Personnel Admjnstrs., Ind. Assn. Women Deans, Adminstr. and Counselors (bd. dirs. 1982-83, 1986—), Nat. Assn. Women Deans, Adminstrs. and Counselors, Kappa Delta Pi, Phi Kappa Phi, Alpha Lambda Delta, Kappa Kappa Gamma. Roman Catholic. Office: 4600 Sunset Ave Indianapolis IN 46208

MALONE, PATRICK MARTIN, radiologist; b. Faribault, Minn., July 2, 1937; s. Frands Harry and Virginia Rose (Havel) M.; m. Wanda Mae Quilitz, Apr. 26, 1963; children: Daniel, Michael, Melissa, Christopher, Justin. BA, St. John's U., Collegeville, Minn., 1959; BS, MD, U. Minn., 1963. Diplomate Am. Bd. Radiology, Am. Bd. Nuclear Medicine. Resident in radiology VA Hosp. and U. Minn., Mpls., 1966-63; dir., treas. West Cen. Radiol. Assocs., Ltd., Willmar, Minn., 1970—; mem. staff, sec., treas. Rice Meml. Hosp., Willmar, 1986—, chief dept. radiology, 1987—; bd. dirs. Heritage Bank, N.A., Willmar. Bd. dirs. Prarie Woods Learning Ctr., Willmar, 1976-7. Served to capt. USAF, 1964-66. Mem. AMA, Minn. Radiol. Soc. Mid Minn. Med. Soc. (sec., treas 1972), Am. Coll. Radiology. Republican. Roman Catholic. Avocations: fiction writing, hunting, snowmobiling. Home: 1414 Grace Ave Willmar MN 56201 Office: West Cen Radiol Assocs Ltd 301 Becker Ave SW Willmar MN 56201

MALONEY, DANIEL CHARLES, professional hockey team coach; b. Barrie, Ont., Can., Sept. 24, 1950. Player Chgo. Black Hawks, NHL, 1970-73; player Los Angeles Kings, NHL, 1973-75, Detroit Red Wings, NHL, 1975-78; player Toronto Maple Leafs, NHL, 1978-82, asst. coach, 1982-84, coach, 1984-86; coach Winnipeg Jets, 1986—. Office: Winnipeg Jets, 15-1430 Maroons Rd, Winnipeg, MB Canada R3G 0L5 *

MALONEY, GARY LEE, psychologist, reality therapist; b. Casper, Wyo., Nov. 4, 1944; s. Walter Leo and Betty May (Opfer) M.; m. Sandra Ann Hawthorne, Mar. 2, 1968; children: Travis Alan, Derek Bryan. AA, Butler County Community Coll., El Dorado, Kans., 1971; BA in Psychology, Emporia State Coll., 1973, MS in Psychology, 1975. Cert. reality therapist, Kans. Master's level psychologist Sedgwick County Drug Treatment Ctr., Wichita, Kans., 1975-79; South Mental Health Ctr., 1979—; lectr., cons. reality therapy; faculty assoc., practicum supr. levels I and II, Inst. for Reality Therapy. Served to 1st lt. U.S. Army, 1966-69. Decorated Bronze Star. Lutheran. Home: 1050 North Edgemoor St Wichita KS 67208 Office: 3620 East Sunnybrook St Wichita KS 67210

MALONEY, JOHN PETER, broadcast executive; b. N.Y.C., Feb. 6, 1951; s. James Joseph and Nora Francis (Keane) M.; m. Susan Verelle Buell, May 22, 1976; children: Sean Christopher, Tara Aileen, Heather Brianne, Brendan Patrick. BA, Davidson Coll., 1973. Account exec. RKO TV, Detroit and N.Y.C, 1976-79; sales mgr. Metromedia, Inc., Detroit, 1979-82; account exec. Turner Broadcasting, Charlotte, N.C., 1974-76, Detroit, 1982-85; v.p. sales Turner Broadcasting, Chgo., 1985—. Mem. Detroit Adcraft Club, Detroit Advt. Assn., Detroit Econ. Club. Democrat. Roman Catholic. Avocations: golf, tennis, reading. Home: 704 Grand Ave Glen Ellyn IL 60137 Office: Cable News Network 303 E Wacker Dr Chicago IL 60601

MALONEY, THOMAS PATRICK, dentist; b. Evergreen Park, Ill., Feb. 17, 1954; s. Thomas Joseph and Shirley Mae (Voss) M.; m. Kimberly Marie Kresal, Apr. 23, 1983. Student, Marquette U., 1972-76; DDS, Loyola U., Maywood, Ill., 1976-80. Gen. practice dentistry Calumet City, Ill., 1980—. Chick Evans scholar Western Golf Assn., 1972, Marquette Evans scholar Four Point Club, Milw., 1974. Mem. ADA, Ill. State Dental Soc., Chgo. Dental Soc. Roman Catholic. Avocations: golf, racquetball, scuba diving, skiing, volleyball. Home: 16815 Luella South Holland IL 60473-2622 Office: 313 River Oaks Dr Calumet City IL 60409

MALOOF, JAMES ALOYSIUS, mayor, real estate company executive; b. Peoria, Ill., Oct. 18, 1919; s. Nimer and Sarah (Hamady) M.; m. Gertrude Mae Burson, June 28, 1941; children—James Michael, Mark (dec.), Nicholas, Janice. Grad. high sch., Peoria. Pres., owner Jim Maloof Realtor, Peoria, 1969—; mayor City of Peoria, 1985—. Mem. adv. bd. Peoria Civic Ctr. Commn., Jr. League Peoria, Boy's Club Peoria, Lebanon Task Force; mem. exec. mgmt. bd. St. Jude Children's Research Hosp., Memphis, chmn. bd. dirs. and co-founder midwest affiliate at Meth. Med. Ctr., chmn. first telethon, 1978, past nat. exec. v.p.; chmn. Christian edn. fund drive St. Philomena Parish, Bradley U. Athletic Fund Dr.; chmn. adv. com. Peoria Big Bros. and Big Sisters; mem. Gov.'s Build Ill. Com., Ill. Job Tng. Coordinating Council, Gov.'s Statewide Taskforce on the Homeless; mem. fundraising com. Lakeview Ctr.; bd. dirs. Econ. Devel. Council Peoria Area, Peoria Conv. and Visitors Bur., Peoria Symphony, Peoria YMCA, Meth. Med. Ctr. Found. Served with USAAF, 1943-45. Recipient Pope John award, Jefferson award, Midwest Fedn. Am-Syrian Lebanese Clubs award, Gov.'s Citation award, Cited Congl. Record, Silver Good Citizenship medal SAR, Internat. Communication and Leadership award Toastmasters Internat., County Old Settler's Assn. award, Appreciation award Zeller Clinic, Patriotism award U.S. Marine Corps, Boss of Yr. award Am. Bus. Womens Assn., Achievement award Phoenician Club, Enterprise award Observer newspaper; named Man of Yr. B'nai Brith, Tri-County Kiwanis. Mem. Peoria Area C. of C. (bd. dirs., exec. com.), Orpheus Club, Italian Am. Soc. (hon.), Peoria Fedn. Musicians (hon.), Epsilon Sigma Alpha (hon.). Republican. Roman Catholic. Club: Creve Coeur (bd. dirs.). Lodge: Kiwanis (past pres. Southwest Peoria chpt.). Established Jim Maloof Realtor scholarship, Bradley Univ. Office: City of Peoria City Hall Bldg 419 Fulton St Room 207 Peoria IL 61602

MALOOLEY, DAVID JOSEPH, electronics and computer technology educator; b. Terre Haute, Ind., Aug. 20, 1951; s. Edward Joseph and Vula (Starn) M. B.S., Ind. State U., 1975: M.S., Ind. U., 1981, doctoral candidate. Supr., Zenith Radio Corp., Paris, Ill., 1978-79; assoc. prof. electronics and computer tech. Ind. State U., Terre Haute, 1979—; cons. in field. Served to 1st lt. U.S. Army, 1975-78. Mem. Soc. Mfg. Engrs., Nat. Assn. Indsl. Tech., Am. Vocat. Assn., Instrument Soc. Am. (sr.), Phi Delta Kappa, Pi Lambda Theta, Epsilon Pi Tau. Democrat. Christian. Home: Rural Rt 52 Box 594D Terre Haute IN 47805 Office: Ind State U Terre Haute IN 47809

MALOON, JERRY LEE, physician, lawyer, medicolegal consultant; b. Union City, Ind., June 23, 1938; s. Charles Elias and Bertha Lucille (Creviston) M.; children: Jeffrey Lee, Jerry Lee II. BS, Ohio State U., 1960, MD, 1964; JD, Capital U. Law Sch., 1974. Intern Santa Monica (Calif.) Hosp., 1964-65; tng. psychiatry Cen. Ohio Psychiat. Hosp., 1969, Menninger Clinic, Topeka, 1970; clin. dir. Orient (Ohio) Devel. Ctr., 1967-69, med. dir., 1971-83; assoc. med. dir. Western Electric, Inc., Columbus, 1969-71; pvt. practice law, Columbus, 1978—; medicolegal cons., 1972—; guest lectr. law and medicine Orient Devel. Ctr. and Columbus Devel. Ctr., 1969-71; dep. coroner Franklin County (Ohio), 1978-84. Served to capt. M.C., AUS, 1965-67. Fellow Am. Coll. Legal Medicine; mem. AMA, Columbus Acad. Medicine, Franklin County Acad. Medicine, Ohio State Med. Assn., ABA, Ohio Bar Assn., Columbus Bar Assn., Am. Trial Lawyers Assn., Ohio Trial Lawyers Assn., Columbus Trial Lawyers Assn., Ohio State U. Alumni Assn., U.S. Trotting Assn., Am. Profl. Practice Assn. Club: Ohio State U. Pres.'s. Home: 501 S High St Columbus OH 43215 Office: Courthouse Sq 501 S High St Columbus OH 43215

MALOTT, ROBERT HARVEY, manufacturing company executive; b. Boston, Oct. 6, 1926; s. Deane W. and Eleanor (Thrum) M.; m. Elizabeth Harwood Hubert, June 4, 1960; children: Elizabeth Hubert, Barbara Holden, Robert Deane. A.B., U. Kans., 1948; M.B.A., Harvard U., 1950; postgrad., N.Y. U. Law Sch., 1953-55. Asst. to dean Harvard Grad. Sch. Bus. Adminstrn., 1950-52; with FMC Corp., 1952—; asst. to exec. v.p. chems. div. FMC Corp., N.Y.C., 1952-55; controller Niagara Chem. div. FMC Corp., Middleport, N.Y., 1955-59; controller organic chems. div. FMC Corp., N.Y.C., 1959-62; asst. div. mgr. FMC Corp., 1962-63, div. mgr., 1963-65, v.p., mgr. film ops. Am. Viscose div., 1966-67, exec. v.p., mem. president's office, 1967-70; mgr. machinery divs. FMC Corp., Chgo., 1970-72; pres., chief exec. officer FMC Corp., 1972—, chmn., 1973—; dir. FMC Corp., Amoco Corp., United Techs. Corp. Trustee U. Chgo.; bd. govs. Argonne Labs.; bd. overseers Hoover Instn. Served with USNR, 1944-46. Mem. Chem. Mfrs. Assn., Bus. Council, Bus. Roundtable, U.S. C. of C., Phi Beta Kappa, Beta Theta Pi, Alpha Chi Sigma. Clubs: Econ. (Chgo.), Chgo. (Chgo.), Mid-Am. (Chgo.); Links (N.Y.C.), Explorers (N.Y.C.); Indian Hill (Kenilworth, Ill.); Bohemian (San Francisco). Office: FMC Corp 200 E Randolph Dr Chicago IL 60601

MALPASS, LESLIE FREDERICK, university president; b. Hartford, Conn., May 16, 1922; s. Fred J. and Lilly (Elmslie) M.; m. Winona Helen Cassin, May 17, 1946; children: Susan Heather (Mrs. J. Poulton), Peter Gordon, Jennifer Joy (Mrs. T. Droege), Michael Andrew. B.A., Syracuse U., 1947, M.A., 1949, Ph.D., 1952. Diplomate: Am. Bd. Examiners Profl. Psychology. Psychologist Onondaga County (N.Y.) Child Guidance Center Syracuse, 1948-52; lectr. Syracuse U., also U. Buffalo, 1949-52; asst. prof. then assoc. prof. So. Ill. U., 1952-60; vis. prof. U. Fla., 1959-60; prof. psychology, chmn. div. behavioral scis. U. So. Fla., 1960-65; dean Coll. Arts and Scis., Va. Poly Inst., Blacksburg, 1965-68; v.p. acad. affairs Va. Poly Inst., 1968-74; pres. Western Ill. U., Macomb, 1974-87, pres. emeritus, 1987—; cons. in field. Dir. First Nat. Exchange Bank Va., 1965-74. Author books and articles in field. Served with M.C. AUS, 1945-46. Fellow Am. Psychol. Assn.; mem. AAAS, AAUP, Assn. Higher Edn., Sigma Xi, Psi Chi, Theta Chi Beta, Omicron Delta Kappa, Beta Gamma Sigma. Home: 3927 Swarthmore Rd Durham NC 27702 Office: Western Ill Univ Adams St Macomb IL 61455-1396

MALTZ, J. HERBERT, physician, hospital director; b. Passaic, N.J., Jan. 8, 1920; s. Michael and Esther (Rinzler) M.; m. Sybil Zun, Sept. 27, 1947; 1 child, Roger A. Student, U. Wis., 1938-41; B.A., U. Miami, 1942; M.D., Chgo. Med. Sch., 1947. Diplomate: Am. Bd. Psychiatry and Neurology. Intern Wilmington (Del.) Gen. Hosp., 1947-48; psychiat. resident Ill. Dept. Pub. Welfare, 1948-51; clin. instr. psychiatry Chgo. Med. Sch., 1951-55; practice medicine specializing in psychiatry Chgo., 1951-58; asst. to supt. Chgo. State Hosp., 1956-58, supt., 1958-66; med. dir. Ridgeway Hosp., 1966-69, Chgo. Lake Shore Hosp., 1970-85; mem. staff St. Joseph's Hosp., Chgo., Barclay Hosp., Chgo., Ill. Masonic Hosp.; former mem. faculty Northwestern U. Med. Sch., Chgo. Med. Sch. Fellow Am. Psychiat. Assn. Jewish. Home: 3260 Lake Shore Dr Chicago IL 60657 Office: 2800 N Sheridan Rd Chicago IL 60657

MALTZ, ROBERT, surgeon; b. Cin., July 21, 1935; s. William and Sarah (Goldberg) M.; m. Sylvia Moskowitz, Aug. 24, 1958; children: Mark Edward, Deborah Lynn, Steven Alan, David Stuart. BS in Zoology, U. Cin., 1958, MD, 1962. Diplomate Am. Bd. Otolaryngology, 1970. Intern Cin. Gen. Hosp., 1962-63; resident Barnes Hosp., St. Louis, 1965-69; asst. prof. surgery Stanford U. Med. Ctr., Palo Alto, Calif., 1969-71; asst. prof. otolaryngology U. Cin. Med. Ctr., 1971-75, assoc. prof. otolaryngology, 1975—; chief, div. head and neck surgery, dept. otolaryngology and maxillofacial surgery U. Cin. Med. Ctr., 1972-76; bd. dirs. Cancer Control Council, U. Cin. Med. Cntr.; cons. Bur. Crippled Children's Services, State of Ohio; mem. med. records com. Cin. Gen. Hosp., utilization rev. com., tissue com., Holmes Hosp., Med. Audit Com., Tissue Com., Cin. Gen. Hosp., med. records com. Jewish Hosp.; on staff VA Hosp., Cin., Children's Hosp. Med. Ctr., Holmes Hosp., Bethesda Hosp., Cin., Shriners Burn Inst., Cin.; del. to numerous profl. confs.; instr. short term courses in field. Contbr. articles to profl. jours. Served to capt. USAF, 1963-65, PTO. USPHS fellow, 1968-69; grantee Eli Lilly Co. grantee, 1971-76, Burroughs Wellcome Co., 1972. Fellow Am. Acad. Facial Plastic and Reconstructive Surgery (edn. com. 1972, future plans com. 1973-75, sci. program com., budget and fin. com. 1975, chmn. credentials com., no. sect., 1980-85), ACS, Royal Soc. Health, Internat. and Am. Acad. Cosmetic Surgeons, Am. Assn. Cosmetic Surgeons (sec., treas. 1976-81); mem. Cin. Acad. Medicine (chmn. pub. relations com. 1980), Acad. Medicine of Cin. (legis. com. 1985—), U. Cin. Med. Alumni Assn. (exec. council), Am. Acad. Otolaryngology and Head and Neck Surgery, Am. Council Otolaryngology, Soc. Univ. Otolaryngologists, Pan-Am. Assn. Oto-Rhino- Larnygology and Broncho-Esophagology, Ohio State Med. Assn., Cin. Acad. Medicine, Cin. Ear, Nose and Throat Soc., Omicron Delta Kappa, Sigma Sigma. Clubs: Losantiville Country, Queen City Racquet (Cin.). Avocations: tennis, golf. Home: 2601 Willowbrook Dr Cincinnati OH 45237 Office: 10496 Montgomery Rd Cincinnati OH 45242

MALZAHN, MICHAEL RICHARD, design engineer; b. Manitowoc, Wis., Dec. 17, 1957; s. Robert David and Ruth Marie (Kuester) M.; m. Mari Mandelj Sever, Apr. 26, 1986. AS, Lakeshore Tech. Inst., Cleveland, Wis., 1978; BS, U. Wis., Stout, 1984. Registered profl. engr.; cert. mfg. technologist. Drafter Haug Mfg. Co., Manitowoc, 1977-78; designer ARPS Div., New Holstien, Wis., 1978; layout designer Gould HCD, Manitowoc, 1978-80; jr. design engr. McGraw-Edison, Racine, Wis., 1984—, design engr., 1985—. Mem. Soc. Mfg. Engrs., Illumination Soc. Am., Lamplighters of Milw. Avocations: downhill and cross-country skiing, reading, outdoor sports.

MALZER, RONALD L., psychologist; b. Phila., June 17, 1951; s. Arnold and Lucy (Buslik) M.; m. Margaret Ann Dihlmann, June 30, 1985. BA, U. Pa., 1972; PhD, Northwestern U., 1980. Registered psychologist, Ill. Project dir. mastectomy counseling Northwestern U., Chgo., 1980-83; rehab. psychologist Ravenswood Hosp., Chgo., 1983—, psychol. coordinator Family Medicine Program, 1985—. Mem. Am. Psychol. Assn., Chgo. Council on Fgn. Relations, Amnesty Internat. Jewish. Avocations: Scrabble, folk guitar. Home: 4437 N Mozart St Chicago IL 60625 Office: Ravenswood Hosp PM&R 4550 N Winchester Chicago IL 60640

MAMAT, FRANK TRUSTICK, lawyer; b. Syracuse, N.Y., Sept. 4, 1949; s. Harvey Sanford and Annette (Trustick) M.; m. Kathy Lou Winters, June 23, 1975; children—Jonathan Adam, Steven Kenneth. B.A., U. Rochester, 1971; J.D., Syracuse U., 1974. Bar: D.C. 1976, Fla. 1977, Mich. 1984, U.S. Dist. Ct. (no. dist.) Ind. 1984, U.S. Dist. Ct. (ea. dist.) Mich. 1983, U.S. Ct. Appeals (D.C. cir.) 1976, U.S. Dist. Ct. (D.C. cir.) 1976, U.S. Ct. Appeals (6th cir.) 1983, U.S. Supreme Ct. 1979. Atty., NLRB, Washington, 1975-79; assoc. Proskauer, Rose, Goetz & Mendelsohn, Washington, N.Y.C., and Los Angeles, 1979-83; assoc. Fishman Group, Bloomfield Hills, Mich., 1983-85, ptnr., 1985—. Gen. counsel Rep. Com. of Oakland County, 1987—, bd. dirs. 300 Club, Mich., 1984—; Rep. Nat. Com., Nat. Rep. Senatorial Com., Presdl. Task Force; City dir. West Bloomfield, 1985-87; pres. West Bloomfield Rep. Club, 1985-87; fin. com. Rep. Com. of Oakland County, 1985—; vice. chmn. lawyers for Reagan-Bush, 1984; v.p. Fruehauf Farms, West Bloomfield, Mich., 1985—; bd. dirs. B'nai B'rith Barristers Unit, Detroit, 1983—, pres. 1985—; mem. staff Exec. Office of Pres. Of U.S. Inquiries/ Comments, Washington, 1981-83. Mem. ABA, Oakland County Bar Assn., D.C. Bar Assn., Fed. Bar Assn., Fla. Bar Assn. (Labor com. 1977—), Auburn Hills C. of C. (bd. dirs.), Founders Soc. (Detroit Inst. of Art). C-lub: Econ. of Detroit. Lodge: B'nai Brith (v.p. 1982-83, pres. 1985—). Office: Fishman Group 2050 N Woodward Ave Bloomfield Hills MI 48013

MAMER, STUART MIES, lawyer; b. East Hardin, Ill., Feb. 23, 1921; s. Louis H. and Anna (Mies) M.; m. Donna E. Jordan, Sept. 10, 1944; children: Richard A., John S., Bruce J. A.B., U. Ill., 1942, J.D., 1947. Bar: Ill. bar 1947. Assoc. Thomas & Mulliken, Champaign, 1947-55; partner firm Thomas, Mamer & Haughey, Champaign, 1955—; lectr. U. Ill. Coll. Law, Urbana, 1965-85; Mem. Atty. Registration and Disciplinary Commn. Ill., 1976-82. Chmn. fund drive Champaign County Community Chest, 1955; 1st pres. Champaign County United Fund, 1957; Pres., dir. U. Ill. McKinley Found., Champaign, 1957-69; trustee Children's Home and Aid Soc. of Ill., v.p., 1977—. Served as pilot USAAF, 1943-45. Mem. Am. Coll. Probate Counsel (bd. regents 1984—), Phi Beta Kappa, Phi Gamma Delta. Republican. Presbyterian. Home: 6 Montclair Rd Urbana IL 61801 Office: Thomas Mamer & Haughey 30 Main St 5th Floor Champaign IL 61820

MAMMEL, RUSSELL NORMAN, food distribution company executive; b. Hutchinson, Kans., Apr. 28, 1926; s. Vyvian E. and Mabel Edwina (Hursh) M.; m. Betty Crawford, Oct. 29, 1949; children: Mark, Christopher, Elizabeth, Nancy. BS, U. Kans., 1949. Sec.-treas. Mammel's Inc., Hutchinson, 1949-57, pres., 1957-59; retail gen. mgr. Kans. div. Nash Finch Co., Hutchinson, 1959-61, retail gen. mgr. Iowa div., Cedar Rapids, 1961-66, dir. store devel., Mpls., 1966-75, v.p., 1975-83, exec. v.p., 1983-85, pres., chief operating officer, 1985—, also bd. dirs. Served with AUS, 1944-46. Home: 6808 Cornelia Dr Edina MN 55435 Office: Nash Finch Co 3381 Gorham Ave Saint Louis Park MN 55426

MANASSE, HENRI RICHARD, JR., college dean, pharmacy administration educator; b. Amsterdam, Netherlands, Nov. 27, 1945; came to U.S., 1954, naturalized, 1963; s. Henri David and Janny Lynn (Borst) M.; m. Arlynn Hem, Aug. 9, 1969; children—Bryan, Sheralynn. B.S. in Pharmacy, U. Ill.-Chgo., 1968; M.A., Loyola U., Chgo., 1972; Ph.D., U. Minn., 1974. Lic. pharmacist, Ill. Research pharmacist Xttrium Labs., Chgo., 1968-69; asst. to dean Coll. Pharmacy, U. Ill.-Chgo., 1969-72, asst. prof. pharmacy adminstrn., 1974-77, assoc. dean, 1977-80, acting dean, 1980-81, dean, prof., 1981—; instr. U. Minn., Mpls., 1972-74; mem. Ill. Bd. Pharmacy, Springfield, 1982-87; pub. mem. Am. Soc. Hosp. Pharmacists Commn. on Credentialing, Bethesda, Md., 1984-86. Contbr. chpts. to books, articles to profl. jours. Pres. Downers Grove Sch. Bd. Caucus, Ill., 1984-85; bd. dirs. med service Westside Holistic Ctr., Chgo., 1979—. Recipient Lederle Faculty award Lederle Pharm. Co., 1975; named Alumnus of Yr., U. Ill. Alumni Assn., 1983. Mem. Am. Assn. Colls. Pharmacy (adminstrv. bd. 1982-86, bd. dirs. 1984-86, pres.-elect 1987—), Ill. Pharmacists Assn., Am. Pharm. Assn. Baptist. Avocations: computers; international travel. Home: 107 56th Ct Downers Grove IL 60516 Office: Univ of Ill at Chicago Coll Pharmacy Box 6998 m/c 874 Chicago IL 60680

MANATT, KATHLEEN GORDON, publishing company executive; b. Boone, Iowa, June 3, 1948; d. Richard Condon and Lewise Ryan (Gordon) M.; B.A., Coll. Wooster, 1970. Prodn. coordinator Scott, Foresman & Co., Glenview, Ill., 1970-73, editor, 1973-81, product mgr., 1981—. Mem. Assn. for Supervision and Curriculum Devel., Nat. Council Social Studies, Ill. Council Social Studies, Nat. Assn. for Bilingual Education, Am. Council Tchrs. Fgn. Langs., Common Cause, People for the Am. Way, Women Employed, So. Poverty Law Ctr., Chgo. Council Fgn. Relations, Amnesty Internat. Presbyterian. Home: 3270 N Lake Shore Dr Chicago IL 60657 Office: Scott Foresman & Co 1900 E Lake Ave Glenview IL 60025

MANBY, JOEL KINGSTON, automotive executive; b. Battle Creek, Mich., July 5, 1959; s. John Alison and Elane (Briggs) M.; m. Marki JoAnn Hobolth, July 5, 1986. BA in Econs., Albion Coll., 1981; MBA, Harvard U., 1985. Prodn. supr. GM Truck & Bus Group, Pontiac, Mich., 1982-83, asst. to mfg. mgr., 1983; mktg. mgr. GM Saturn Corp., Troy, Mich., 1985-86; dir. mktg. and strategic planning Team Mgmt. Inc., Grand Blanc, Mich., 1986—. Vol. Big Bro. and Big Sister program, Albion, Mich., 1980-81; vol. leader Youth for Christ, Pontiac, 1981-83; vol. Reagan re-election com., Harvard U., Boston, 1984; announcer Lake Orion (Mich.) High Sch. football, 1986; applicant relations com. Harvard Bus. Sch., 1985-86. GM fellow, 1983; Presdl. scholar Albion Coll., 1980, NCAA Postgrad. scholar, 1981. Republican. Club: Fellowship of Christian Athletes (pres. 1980-81), Harvard (Detroit). Avocations: piano, acting, wind surfing, tennis. Home: 5511 Parkview #302 Clarkston MI 48016 Office: Team Mgmt Inc G-6167 S Saginaw Grand Blanc MI 48439

MANCHESTER, JEAN NEESVIG, meat packing company executive; b. Baraboo, Wis., June 28, 1926; d. Henry Christan and Adeline (Keller) Kinzler; m. Burton Oswald Neesvig, May 7, 1955 (dec. Jan. 1966); children: Jonathan, Timothy, Daniel, AnnaJean; m. William B. Manchester, Aug. 17, 1968. BS in Home Econs. and Sci., U. Wis., 1948. Home economist U. Wis. Extension, Lancaster, 1948-50, Nat. Livestock & Meat Bd., Chgo., 1950-52; pres., chief exec. officer Neesvig, Inc., Madison, Wis., 1966-83, chmn., chief exec. officer, 1983—; advisor Attic Angles Bus. and Legal Bd., 1979-82; bd. visitors sch. bus. U. Wis., 1981—; bd. dirs. Affiliated Bank Jamestown, Madison Gas and Electric Co., Am. Family Mut. Ins. Co. Mem. steering com. Dane County Pub. Affairs Com., 1981-82, exec. com. U. Wis. Found., 1983—, City of Madison Zoning Bd. Appeals, Merit Award Bd., 1980-82; cabinet mem. Meth. Hosp. Corp. Bd., 1979-84, United Way Dane County, 1982-84; pres., bd. dirs. Madison Opportunity Ctr., 1974-78; bd. dirs. Greater Madison Visitor and Conv. Bd., 1976-80, pres., 1979-80. Mem. Am. Home Econs. Assn., Nat. Assn. Meat Producers (bd. dirs. 1976—), Nat. Assn. and Meat Bd. (bd. dirs. 1980—), Ill. Agrl. Assn. (bd. dirs. women's dept., Dir., dept. chmn. 1952-55), Nat. Livestock and Meat Bd. Presbyterian. Lodges: PEO, Order Eastern Star. Home: 101 Horseshoe Bend Madison WI 53705 Office: Neesvig's Inc 417 Atlas Ave Madison WI 53714

MANCZAK, JOHN EDWARD, energy business executive; b. Oak Park, Ill., Mar. 7, 1948; s. Peter Edmund and Anna Clare (Borchardt) M.; m. Susan Lois Dennis, Aug. 7, 1971; children: Brian, Melissa. BS in Engring., U. Ill., 1971; MBA, U. Chgo., 1975. Sales engr. Westinghouse Electric, Chgo., 1971-75, product mgr., 1975-78, area sales mgr., 1978-80; v.p. sales and mktg. Sheldons Mfg. Corp., Elgin, Ill., 1980-84; mktg. mgr. No. Nat. Resources, Omaha, 1984-86; v.p., gen. mgr. Energroup, Inc. subs. UtiliCorp United, Omaha, 1986—; also bd. dirs. Energroup, Inc. subs. UtiliCorp United. Loaned exec. United Way of Midlands, Omaha, 1985; vestryman St. Andrew's Episc. Ch., 1986. Mem. Am. Mktg. Assn. Republican. Avocations: golf, woodworking, church newcomer communications. Home: 8532 Hickory Omaha NE 68124 Office: Energroup Inc 1815 Capitol Ave Omaha NE 68102

MANDEL, GERALD, oil company executive; b. Elizabeth, N.J., Mar. 5, 1928; s. Irving and Sylvia (Fox) M.; m. Martha Bernstein, June 30, 1952; children: Sam Carlos, Jess. AB, Rutgers U., 1953. Asst. to pres. Deuterium Corp., N.Y.C., 1966-68; sr. v.p. Lyle B. Gumm & Assocs., Chgo., 1968-69; exec. v.p. Titan Wells, Inc., Marietta, Ohio, 1969-77; pres. Mandel Resources Corp., Lake Bluff, Ill., 1977—. Trustee The Glenkirk Assn., Northbrook, Ill., 1984—. Served as sgt. inf. U.S. Army, 1946-48, Korea. Avocations: martial arts, handguns, travel. Home: 1864 Linden Ave Highland Park IL 60035 Office: Suite V 51 Sherwood Terr Lake Bluff IL 60044

MANDEL, KARYL LYNN, accountant; b. Chgo., Dec. 14, 1935; d. Isador J. and Eve (Gellar) Karzen; m. Fredric H. Mandel, Sept. 29, 1956; children: David Scott, Douglas Jay, Jennifer Ann. Student U. Mich., 1954-56, Roosevelt U., 1956-57; AA summa cum laude, Oakton Community Coll., 1979. CPA, Ill. Pres., nat. bd. mem. Women's Am. Orgn. for Rehab. through Tng., 1961-77; pres. Excel Transp. Service Co., Elk Grove, Ill., 1958-78; tax mgr. Chunowitz, Teitelbaum & Baerson, CPA's, Northbrook, Ill., 1981-83, tax ptnr., 1984—; sec-treas. Lednam, Inc. Contbg. author: Ill. CPA's News Jour. Recipient State of Israel Solidarity award, 1976. Mem. Am. Inst. CPA's, Am. Soc. Women CPA's, Women's Am. ORT, Ill. CPA Soc. (vice chmn. estate and gift tax com. 1985-87, chmn. estate and gift tax com., 1987—, mem. legis. contact com. 1981-82, pres. North Shore chpt., award for Excellence in Acctg. Edn.), Chgo. Soc. Women CPA's, Chgo. Estate Planning Council. Office: 401 Huehl Rd Northbrook IL 60062

MANDEL, MORTON LEON, industrial corporation executive; b. Cleve., Sept. 19, 1921; s. Simon and Rose (Nusbaum) M.; m. Barbara Abrams, Feb. 27, 1949; children: Amy, Thomas, Stacy. Student, Case Western Res. U., 1940-42, Pomona Coll., 1943; LHD (hon.), Gratz Coll., 1984, Hebrew Union Coll., 1986. With Premier Indsl. Corp., Cleve., 1946—, sec.-treas., 1946-58, pres., 1958-70, chmn., 1970—, also bd. dirs. Pres. Jewish Community Ctrs. of Cleve., 1952-58, now life trustee; v.p. Jewish Community Fedn., 1971-74, pres., 1974-76, now life trustee; trustee Nat. Jewish Welfare Bd., v.p., 1964-70, pres., 1970-74, now hon. pres.; chmn. Found. Adv. Council, 1967-75; v.p. United Way Cleve., 1971-77, pres., 1977-79, chmn., 1979-81, now life trustee; v.p. Council Jewish Fedns., 1971-74, pres., 1978-81, now life trustee; pres. Bur. Careers in Jewish Service, 1967-70; mem. Commn. on Health and Social Services, City of Cleve., 1970-71; mem. ways and means com. Ops. Task Force, 1980; mem. vis. com. Sch. Applied Social Sci., Case Western Res. U., 1958-74, trustee, 1977—; trustee Mt. Sinai Hosp., Cleve., 1970-79, now trustee emeritus; trustee Cleve. Zool. Soc., 1970-73, Greater Cleve. Roundtable, 1981-83; founding pres. World Confedn. Jewish Community Centers, 1977-81, now hon. pres.; bd. govs. Jewish Agy., 1979—; trustee United Israel Appeal, 1977—, United Jewish Appeal, 1978-82; trustee Am. Jewish Joint Distbn. Com., 1975—, mem. exec. com., 1978-82; founder Cleve. Project MOVE, 1981; founder Clean-Land Ohio, 1981, trustee, 1981—; vice chmn. Cleve. Tomorrow, 1982—; founder, chmn. Mid-Town Corridor, 1982-85; trustee United Way of Am., 1985—, exec. com., 1986—; mem. Ctr. Social Policy Studies, 1983—; co-chmn. Operation Independence, 1985—. Recipient Outstanding Young Man of Yr. award Cleve. Jr. C. of C., 1956, Businessman of Yr. award Urban League of Cleve., 1973, Frank L. Weil award Nat. Jewish Welfare Bd., 1974, Charles Eisenman award Cleve. Jewish Community Fedn., 1977, Citizen of Yr. award Cleve. Area Bd. Realtors, 1973, Mgmt. Performance award Case Western Res. U., 1982, Business Statesman of Yr. award Harvard Bus. Sch. Club of Cleve., 1985, Dively award Corp. Leadership in Urban Devel., 1986, Ben-Gurion Centennial medal State of Israel Bonds, 1986; named Man of Yr. B'nai B'rith, 1980, Leader of Yr., Clean-Land Ohio, 1983. Home: 17250 Parkland Dr Shaker Heights OH 44120 Office: Premier Indsl Corp 4500 Euclid Ave Cleveland OH 44103

MANDEL, TERRY JAY, physician; b. Chgo., Aug. 7, 1953; s. Seymour L. and Beverly (Sklare) M. Student Drake Coll. Pharmacy, Des Moines, 1971-75; D.O., Chgo. Coll. Osteo. Medicine, 1979. Diplomate Am. Bd. Family Practice. Practice family medicine, Indpls., 1980—; chief family practice div. Westview Hosp., Indpls., 1983, chief infection control, 1984-85, mem. exec. com., 1984-85, mem. intern tng. com., 1984-85, chief of staff, 1985—. Mem. Am. Osteo. Assn., Am. Coll. Gen. Practitioners Osteo. Medicine, Ind. Assn. Osteo. Physicians, Rho Chi, Phi Eta Sigma, Sigma Sigma Phi. Jewish. Avocations: antiques; coin collecting; photography; political items and history. Office: 4006 N High School Rd Indianapolis IN 46254

MANDERS, KARL LEE, neurological surgeon; b. Rochester, N.Y., Jan. 21, 1927; s. David Bert and Frances Edna (Cohan) Mendelson; m. Ann Laprell, July 28, 1969; children—Karlanna, Maidena; children by previous marriage—Karl, Kerry, Kristine. Student, Cornell U., 1946; M.D., U. Buffalo, 1950. Diplomate Am. Bd. Neurol. Surgery, Am. Bd. Clin. Biofeedback. Intern U. Va. Hosp., Charlottesville, 1950-51, resident in neurol. surgery, 1951-52; resident in neurol. surgery Henry Ford Hosp., Detroit, 1954-56; practice medicine specializing in neurol. surgery Indpls., 1956—; med. dir. Community Hosp. Rehab. Ctr. for Pain, 1973—; med. dir. Head Injury and Coma Arousal Ctr., Community Hosp. North Profl. Bldg., Indpls.; chief hosp. med. and surg. neurology Community Hosp., 1983; coroner Marion County, Ind., 1977; pres. Manders-Marks, Inc., Hyperbaric Oxygen Inc. Served with USN, 1952-54, Korea. Recipient cert. achievement Dept. Army, 1969. Fellow ACS, Internat. Coll Surgeons, Am. Acad. Neurology; mem. AMA, Am. Assn. Neurol. Surgery, Congress Neurol. Surgery, Internat. Assn. Study of Pain, Am. Assn. Study of Headache, N.Y. Acad. Sci., Am. Coll. Angiology, Am. Soc. Contemporary Medicine and Surgery, Am. Holistic Med. Assn. (a founder), Undersea Med. Soc., Am. Acad. Forensic Sci., Am. Assn. Biofeedback Clinicians, Soc. Cryosurgery, Pan Pacific Surg. Assn., Biofeedback Soc. Am., Acad. Psychosomatic Medicine, Pan Am. Med. Assn., Am. Soc. Stereotaxic and Functional Neurosurgery, Soc. for Computerized Tomography and Neuroimaging, Ind. Coroners Assn. (pres. 1979), Royal Soc. Medicine, Am. Pain Soc., Midwest Pain Soc. (pres. 1988), Cen. Neurol. Soc., Interurban Neurosurg. Soc., Internat. Soc. Aquatic Medicine. Clubs: Brendonwood Country, Highland Country. Home: 5845 Highfall St Indianapolis IN 46226 Office: 5506 E 16th St Indianapolis IN 46218

MANDICH, DONALD RALPH, banker; b. 1925; married. B.B.A., U. Mich., 1946, M.B.A., 1950. With Comerica Bank-Detroit (formerly Detroit Bank & Trust Co.), Detroit, 1950—, asst. cashier, 1957-61, asst. v.p., 1961-63, v.p., 1963-69, sr. v.p., 1969-74, exec. v.p., 1974-77, pres., 1977-81, chmn., 1981—; chmn. bd., chief exec. officer Comerica Inc. (formerly Detroitbank Corp.). Office: Comerica Inc 211 W Fort St Detroit MI 48226

MANDRELL, GENE DOUGLAS, logistician; b. Clinton, Okla., Jan. 7, 1944; s. Glen Douglas and Mary Emma (Spears) M. BA, U. Okla., 1966; diploma, Indsl. Coll. Armed Forces, 1976, Armed Forces Staff Coll., 1977. Logistics specialist Hdqrs. AF Logistics Command, Wright-Patterson AFB, Ohio, 1971-79, dep. dir. command policy and current issues, 1982-87, dep. dir. concept devel. and integration, 1987—; asst. for supply policy Office Sec. AF, Washington, 1979-81; congl. fellow U.S. Ho. of Reps., Washington, 1981; vis. lectr. Air War Coll., Maxwell AFB, Ala, 1977-75. Co-author: Public Policy for the 1980's, 1981. Chmn. City Planning Commn., Huber Heights, Ohio. Served to capt. U.S. Army, 1967-70. Named one of Outstanding Young Men of Am., U.S. Jaycees, 1982. Mem. Soc. Logictics Engrs. (life, Dayton chapter vice chmn. 1977-78), Am. Def. Preparedness Assn. (life, v.p.), Air Force Assn. (life), World Future Soc. (Dayton chapter bd. dirs.), Am. Planning Assn., Internat. Inst. Forecasters, Am. Acad. Polit. and Social Scis., Am. Acad. Polit. Sci., Logistics Edn. Found., Huber Heights C. of C., Engrs. Club. Democrat. Avocations: music, photography, travel. Home: 5261 Coco Dr Huber Heights OH 45424 Office: Hdqrs AF Logistics Command Office DCS/Plans and Programs Wright-Patterson AFB OH 45433-5001

MANELLI, DONALD DEAN, writer, producer motion pictures; b. Burlington, Iowa, Oct. 20, 1936; s. Daniel Anthony and Mignon Marie M.; children by previous marriage: Daniel, Lisa. B.A., U. Notre Dame, 1959. Communications specialist Jewel Cos., 1959; script writer Coronet Films, Chgo., 1960-62; freelance writer 1962-63; creative dir. Fred A. Niles Communications Ctrs., Chgo., 1963-67; sr. writer Wild Kingdom, NBC-TV network; freelance film writer 1967-70; pres. Donald Manelli & Assocs., Inc., Chgo., 1970—. Recipient internat. film festival and TV awards. Mem. Writers Guild Am., Nat. Acad. TV Arts and Scis., Outdoor Writers Assn. Am. Office: Donald Manelli & Assocs Inc 1 E Erie St Chicago IL 60611

MANFRO, PATRICK JAMES (PATRICK JAMES HOLIDAY), radio artist; b. Kingston, N.Y., Dec. 30, 1947; s. Charles Vincent and Anna Agnes (Albany) Manfro; Asso. Sci. in Acctg., Ulster Coll., 1968; diploma Radio Electronics Inst., 1969; student St. Clair Coll., 1974—; m. Janice Lynn Truscott, July 5, 1975; children: Wesley Patrick, Whitney Dawn. Program dir., radio artist WKNY, Kingston, 1966-70; radio artist WPTR, Albany, N.Y., 1970, WPOP, Hartford, Conn., 1970, CKLW, Detroit, 1970-71, WOR-FM, N.Y.C., 1971-72; radio artist CKLW Radio, Detroit, 1972—, asst. program dir., 1978-80, program dir., 1980-83; v.p. programming CKLW/ CFXX, Detroit, 1983—; pres. Musicom Inc., audio-visual prodn. co., Detroit; pres., chief exec. officer Internat. Data Corp., Wilmington, Del.; adviser New Contemporary Sch. Announcing, Albany, 1973—; comml. announcer radio, television, 1970—. Judge, Miss Mich. Universe Pageant, 1970. Mem. N.Y. State N.G., 1968-74. Recipient 5 Year Service ribbon N.Y. State, 1973; named Runner-up Billboard Air Personality awards, 1971. Mem. AFTRA, Screen Actors Guild, Internat. Platform Assn., Smithsonian Assos., BMI Songwriters Guild. Club: Dominion Golf and Country. Home: 3466 Wildwood St, Windsor, ON Canada N8R 1X2 Office: PO Box 1142 Dearborn MI 48121

MANGELSDORF, THOMAS KELLY, mental health consultant; b. St. Louis; s. Albert Henry and Hazel (Kelly) M.; m. Helen Louise Kareth, Apr. 12, 1958 (div. Jan. 1986); children: Ellen S., Steven T., Thomas K. Jr., Laura E. BS, U. Notre Dame, 1952; MD, St. Louis U., 1956. Diplomate Am. Bd. Psychiatry and Neurology. Cons. in mental health various municipalities, 1972—. Author and editor of computerized system to interpret Minn. Multiphasic Personality Inventory profiles of patients to predict helpful psychol. and medicinal interventions. Served to capt. U.S. Army, 1960-62. Fellow Am. Psychiat. Assn.; mem. Eastern Mo. Psychiat. Assn. (sec. 1983-85). Avocation: sailing. Office: 621 S New Ballas Saint Louis MO 63141

MANGUM, RONALD SCOTT, lawyer; b. Chgo., Nov. 14, 1944; s. Roy Oliver and Marjorie Wilma (Etchason) M.; m. Kay Lynn Booton, July 14, 1973 (div. July 1983); children—Scott Arthur, Katherine Marie. B.A., Northwestern U., 1965, J.D., 1968. Bar: Ill. 1968. Asst. univ. atty. Northwestern U., 1968-73; assoc. Lord, Bissell & Brook, Chgo., 1974-76; ptnr. Liss, Mangum & Beeler, Chgo., 1976-80, Mangum, Beeler, Schad & Diamond, Chgo., 1980-82, Azar, Mangum & Jacobs, Chgo., 1982-84, Mangum, Smietanka & Johnson, Chgo., 1984—; lectr. Northwestern U., 1972-74, NYU Inst. Fed. Taxation, 1980; lectr. on health care topics to profl. groups; faculty Healthcare Fin. Mgmt. Assn. Nat. Inst., Boulder; pres. Planned Giving, Inc., 1978—, 1426 Chicago Ave. Bldg. Corp., 1975-76, Parkinson Research Corp., 1970-74. Commr. Evanston Preservation Commn., 1981-83; chmn. Am. Hearing Research Found., 1977-79, v.p., 1972-77; bd. dirs. Episcopal Charities, 1978-80; trustee Evanston Art Ctr., 1977-78; mem. health care subcom. Nat. Fire Protection Assn., 1980-82. Served to lt. col. USAR, 1969—. Recipient cert. of appreciation Ill. Inst. Continuing Legal Edn., 1972. Mem. Chgo. Bar Assn., Ill. Bar Assn., ABA, Nat. Assn. Coll. and Univ. Attys., Chgo. Estate Planning Council, Art Inst. Chgo. (life), Nat. Rifle Assn. (life), Nat. Soc. Fund Raising Execs., Res. Officers Assn. (life), Assn. U.S. Army, Psi Upsilon. Clubs: Union League (Chgo.); John Evans (bd. dirs. Evanston, Ill.). Author: (with R. M. Hendrickson) Governing Board and Adminstrator Liability, 1977; Tax Aspects of Charitable Giving, 1976. Contbr. articles to legal jours. Home: 1426 Chicago Ave Evanston IL 60201 Office: 35 E Wacker Dr Chicago IL 60601

MANGUS, DEBBIE DEE, marketing executive; b. Fort Wayne, Ind., May, 1955; d. Kenneth R. and M. Irene Miller; m. Charles D. Lewis; children—David R., Carrie A.; m. John T. Mangus, Dec., 1981; stepchildren—John T. III, April L.; stepchildren—Brandon M., Ryan E. Store activities rep. McDonald's Systems, Newport News, Va., Fort Wayne, Ind., 1978, community relations rep. Fort Wayne, Columbus, Ohio, 1979-81; regional mktg. mgr. Arby's, Inc., Columbus, 1982-83; mktg. dir. McNeill Enterprises, Inc., Chillicothe, Ohio, 1984-86; project mgr. mktg. dept. Mid-Am. Fed., Columbus, 1987—; trainer regional mktg. mgrs. Arby's, Columbus, 1982-83; mktg. cons. MEI Franchisees, Inc. Franchisees, Ohio, Ill., Ky., 1984-86 . Fund raiser Ronald McDonald House, Columbus, Indpls., 1980-81 Recipient Best Bets awards McDonald's-Indpls. region, 1980, 81. Mem. Nat. Assn. Female Execs. Methodist. Avocations: reading; softball; bicycling; crafts. Office: Mid-Am Fed 4181 Arlingate Plaza Columbus OH 43228-4115

MANI, MATHARBOOTHAM, anesthesiologist; b. Kolar Gold Field, Karnataka, India, July 29, 1945; came to U.S., 1973; s. Anna and Bala Matharbootham; m. Mildred Louise Somon, Mar. 12, 1977. BS, St. Joseph's Coll., Bangalore, India, 1965; MB, B in Surgery, Bangalore Med. Coll., 1971. Diplomate Am. Bd. Anesthesiology. Rotating houseman Combined Hosp., Bangalore, 1971, sr. houseman surgery, 1972; intern gen. surgery St. Agnes Hosp., Balt., 1973-74, resident gen. surgery, 1974-75; resident anesthesiology W.Va. U. Hosp., Morgantown, 1975-78; asst. prof. anesthesiology Med. Coll. Ga., Augusta, 1978-80, assoc. prof., 1980-83, chief cardiovascular anesthesiology, 1982-83; assoc. clin. prof. Ohio State U. Hosp., Columbus, 1983—; cardiovascular anesthesiology cons. VA Hosp., Augusta, 1978-83. Mem. Am. Soc. Anesthesiologists, Soc. Regional Anesthesia, Soc. Chest Physicians, Soc. Cardiovascular Anesthesiologists, Internat. Anesthesia Research Soc., Ohio State Soc. Anesthesiologists. Avocations: cameras, sports, stamps, outdoors, travelling. Home: 4120 Mumford Ct Columbus OH 43220 Office: Ohio State U Hosp Dept Anesthesiology Columbus OH 43210

MANIFOLD, W(ILLIAM) JOSEPH, accountant; b. Kalamazoo, Aug. 9, 1951; s. William J. and Pauline B. (Kirby) M.; m. Jane Marie Schoolmaster,

Dec. 4, 1981; children: Kelly Lynn, Kimberly Jane, Katherine Marie. BBA, Cen. Mich. U., 1973. CPA, Mich. Mgr. payroll and grant acctg. Cen. Mich. U., Mt. Pleasant, 1973-76; acct. Ernst & Whinney, Saginaw, Mich., 1976—. Treas. Saginaw County Rep. Party, 1984—, Saginaw Valley Rehab. Ctr., 1986—. Mem. Am. Inst. CPA's. Clubs: Saginaw, Saginaw Country. Home: 2386 Westbury Saginaw MI 48603 Office: Ernst & Whinney 101 N Washington Saginaw MI 48607

MANIGAULT, JUAN ALEJANDRO, human resources executive, consultant; b. Charleston, S.C., Oct. 7, 1952; s. Nathaniel Lomax and Marion Pearl (Waterman) M.; m. Kimberly Ann Kurka, July 14, 1980. A.B., U. Notre Dame, 1974; M.B.A., Ind. U.-Gary, 1984. Assoc. tennis pro Mansard Raquet Club, Griffith, Ind., 1975-77; planner Lake County Employment and Tng. Adminstrn., Crown Point, Ind., 1977-79; dir. Office Career Edn., Hobart, Ind., 1979-84; dir. devel. Kids Alive Internat., Valparaiso, Ind., 1984—; mem. State Ind. Career Edn. Adv. Com., Indpls., 1981-83; participant Leadership Calumet, Gary, Ind., 1982-83. Assoc. pub. Our Town Michiana mag. Sec. bd. dirs. Christian Haven Homes, Inc., Wheatfield, Ind.; bd. dirs. Am. Cancer Soc., Indpls.; chmn. human resource, job tng. subcom. Calumet Forum, Merrillville, Ind.; pres. Indigan Corp. Recipient Holy Cross award U. Notre Dame, 1971. Mem. U.S. Profl. Tennis Assn., Am. Soc. Pub. Adminstrn. Lodge: Rotary. Home: 700 N Waverly Rd #1317 Porter IN 46304 Office: Kids Alive Internat 2507 Cumberland Dr Valparaiso IN 46383

MANIJAK, WILLIAM, history and government educator; b. Holyoke, Mass., July 4, 1913; s. Stanley and Catherine (Padlo) M.; m. Phyllis Mae Hatch, Aug. 13, 1949; children: William Stafford, Catherine Anne. BA in English cum laude, Am. Internat. Coll., 1949; MA in Journalism, U. Wis., 1952, postgrad., 1952-59; PhD, Ball State U., 1975. Copy chief Kulzick Advt. Agy., Madison, Wis., 1952-55; continuity dir. Sta. WISC, Madison, 1956-57; pub. relations, editor Gardner Baking Co., Madison, 1957-58; editor Am. Press, Madison, 1958; asst. coordinator internat. tchr. devel. program U. Wis., Madison, 1959; dir. pub. relations, inst. history, chmn. div. social scis., sec. lay bd. trustees St. Francis Coll., Ft. Wayne, Ind., 1959-66, chmn. dept. social studies, 1960-78, v.p. coll. relations, 1966-71, prof. emeritus history and govt., 1978—, coll. athletic rep., 1966-72; book reviewer, guest columnist Ft. Wayne News-Sentinel; resource person, lectr. Negro history Sta. WANE-TV, Ft. Wayne, 1977; lectr. in field. Contbr. articles to profl jours. V.P. Community Betterment Assn., Ft. Wayne, 1966; mem. mayor's subcom. on neighborhoods, Ft. Wayne, 1970; coordinator 4th Congl. Dist. History Day, 1978. Served with USAAF, 1940-45. Recipient honors competition Am. Coll. Pub. Relations Assn., 1960; U.S. Dept. Edn. grantee, 1982. Mem. Am. Hist. Assn., Assn. Am. Historians, Ind. Hist. Soc., Ind. Acad. Social Scis., Polish-Am. Hist. Assn., Polish-Am. Mus., Kosciuszko Found., Ft. Wayne-Allen County Hist. Soc., Ft. Wayne-Allen County C. of C. (edn. and state policies coms. 1962-70), Polish Inst. Arts and Scis. Am., Sigma Delta Chi. Democrat. Roman Catholic. Lodges: KC, Elks. Home: 1719 Edenton Dr Fort Wayne IN 46804

MANION, DANIEL ANTHONY, judge; b. South Bend, Ind., Feb. 1, 1942; s. Clarence E. and Virginia (O'Brien) M.; m. Ann Murphy, June 29, 1984. BA, U. Notre Dame, 1964; JD, Ind. U., 1973. Bar: Ind., U.S. Dist. Ct. (no. and so. dists.) Ind. Dep. atty. gen. State of Ind., 1973-74; from assoc. to ptnr. Doran, Manion, Boynton, Kamm & Esmont, South Bend, 1974-86; judge U.S. Ct. Appeals (7th cir.), South Bend, 1986—. Mem. Ind. State Senate, Indpls., 1978-82. Home: 51081 Laurel Rd South Bend IN 46637 Office: US Ct Appeals (7th cir) 204 S Main St 310 Fed Bldg South Bend IN 46601 *

MANIS, MELVIN, psychologist, educator; b. N.Y.C., Feb. 18, 1931; s. Alex and Hanna (Oyle) M.; m. Jean Denby, May 28, 1954; children: Peter Eugene, David Denby. AB in Psychology, Franklin and Marshall Coll., 1951; PhD, U. Ill., 1954. Instr. psychology U. Pitts., 1956-58; research psychologist Ann Arbor VA Med. Ctr., Mich., 1958—; prof. psychology U. Mich., Ann Arbor, 1966—. Author: Cognitive Processes, 1966, An Introduction to Cognitive Psychology, 1971; editor Jour. Personality and Social Psychology, 1980-84. Served with USPHS, 1954-56. Mem. Am. Psychol. Assn., Midwestern Psychol. Assn., Soc. Exptl. Social Psychology, AAUP, Phi Beta Kappa, Sigma Xi. Democrat. Jewish. Club: Racquet (Ann Arbor). Home: 20 Harvard Pl Ann Arbor MI 48104 Office: U Mich Dept Psychology Ann Arbor MI 48109

MANLEY, DAVID THOMAS, employment benefit plan administration company executive; b. Youngstown, Ohio, Apr. 13, 1938; s. Harry T. and Margaret M. (Stein) M.; m. Virginia Borcik, Sept., 1961 (div. 1975); children—Kelly A., Scott D., Lynne M., Brian D., Leslie; m. 2d Ruth Ann Osterhage, Dec. 31, 1975; children—David Louis, Mollie O. Student Youngstown U., 1956-60. Dist. sales mgr. Res. Life, Dallas, 1960-63, Guarantee Res. Life, Hammond, Ind., 1963-64; mgr. brokerage CNA Ins. Group, Chgo., 1964-68; pres. Greater Del. Corp., Dover, 1981-85, also bd. dirs.; pres. Variable Protection Adminstrn., Cleve., 1968—, also bd. dirs.; pres. VPA Ins., Ltd., 1985—, also bd. dirs.; bd. dirs. Del. Nat. Life, Greater Del. Corp., UPI, Inc. Precinct committeeman Rep. Com., 1966-72, ward leader, 1970-72, mem. Cuyahoga County Rep. Com., 1970-72; mem. Bd. Zoning Appeals, Hinckley, Ohio Twp.; pres. Our Lady of Grace Ch. Council, 1984-87. Mem. Soc. Profl. Benefit Adminstrs., Mass Market Ins. Inst., Internat. Found. Employee Benefits, Am. Mgmt. Assn. Republican. Roman Catholic. Lodge: KC. Home: 2485 Bethany Ln Hinckley OH 44233 Office: Variable Protection Adminstrs Inc 7123 Pearl Rd Suite 300 Cleveland OH 44130

MANLEY, JOHN JOSEPH, social work administrator; b. Youngstown, Ohio, Jan. 28, 1954; s. John Joseph and Mary Lou (Rich) M.; m. Pamela A. Heydt, Mar. 3, 1984. BA cum laude in Psychology and Social Relations, Harvard U., 1976; MSW, U. Ky., 1981; postgrad., U. Cin. and Xavier Coll. Lic. social worker, Ky., Ohio; cert. Acad. Cert. Social Workers. Social worker St. Francis Hosp., Cin., 1976-77, social work supr., 1977-78; dir. social work St. Francis Hosp.-St. George Hosp., Cin., 1978—; cons. in field, 1986—. Mem. Nat. Assn. Social Workers, Soc. Hosp. Social Work Dirs., Ohio Valley Assn. Hosp. Social Work Dirs. (pres.), Ohio Soc. Hosp. Social Workers (regional dir. 1983-84, pres.-elect 1986-87, pres. 1988). Office: 3131 Queen City Ave Cincinnati OH 45238

MANLEY, JOSEPH, gynecologist/obstetrician; b. Kansas City, Kans., June 4, 1942; s. Joseph Warren and Lois Neva (Hershey) M.; m. Sue Ellen Sherrick, Apr. 8, 1964; children: Alexander, Susan. BA, U. Mo., Kansas City, 1964; MD, U. Kans., Kansas City, 1969. Diplomate Am. Bd. Ob-Gyn. Intern Menorah Med. Ctr., Kansas City, Mo., 1969-70, resident in ob-gyn, 1971-73; resident in ob-gyn St. Luke's Hosp., Kansas City, Mo., 1970-71; practice medicine specializing in ob-gyn Prairie Village, Kans., 1975—. Bd. dirs. Holy Land Christian Mission Int., Kansas City, Mo., 1982-85. Served to maj. USAF, 1973-75. Fellow ACS, Am. Coll. Ob-Gyn; mem. AMA, Kansas City (Kans.) Gynecol. Soc., Nat. Rifle Assn., MG Car Club and T Register. Avocations: water fowl hunting, classic sports cars, bird watching. Office: PO Box 8162 Prairie Village KS 66208-0162

MANLEY, PATRICK WILLIAM, architect, developer; b. Bellaire, Ohio, July 6, 1955; s. William Henry and Theresa Veronica (Slezak) M.; m. Linda Karen Cipriani, oct. 11, 1980; 1 child, Ryan Patrick. BArch, Ohio State U., 1981. Registered architect, Ohio. Designer, builder Kawecki Architects, Columbus, Ohio, 1979-83; project architect George J. Kontogiannis and Assocs., Columbus, 1983-85; pres. Patrick Manley Architects, Columbus, 1985—; cons. Jester, Jones and Feltham Architects and Planners, Columbus and Marion, Ohio, 1985—. Mem. AIA, Architects Soc. Ohio, North Columbus Jaycees, Ohio State U. Alumni Club. Avocations: golf, travel, reading, sleeping. Office: 634 N High St Columbus OH 43215

MANLOVE, ERIC DEAN, wholesale electronics manager; b. Wichita, Kans., Apr. 9, 1954; s. Merle Dean and Mary Margaret (Barnard) M.; m. Melody Yvonne Perkins, Sept. 9, 1978; children: Abraham Philip, Adam Blake. BA in Speech and Music, Harding U., 1976. Dept. mgr. RSC Electronics, Wichita, 1977—. Music dir. Cen. Ch. Christ, Wichita, 1977—; vol. ARC, Wichita, 1977-79; music tchr. Met. Christian Sch., Wichita, 1984-85. Named one of Outstanding Young Men of Am., 1981. Republican. Avocations: collecting Lincoln memorabilia, singing, playing piano and guitar. Home: 1218 Bitting Wichita KS 67203 Office: RSC Electronics 131 S Laura Wichita KS 67211

MANN, BILLY JOE, JR., computer services executive; b. Dayton, Ohio, Oct. 1, 1960; s. Billy Joe and June Elizabeth (Mossbarger) M. Student, Ohio State U., 1981-86. Data entry supr. Cole, Layer & Trumble, Dayton, 1978-79; programmer, analyst Automated Systems, Inc., Dayton, 1979-81; dir. computer services Mgmt. Foresight, Inc., Columbus, 1981—; cons. Buckeye Employee Benefits Services, Inc., Columbus, 1984-86. Mem. Am. Mgmt. Assn., Data Processing Mgmt. Assn., N. Coast Datapoint Users Group, Columbus Computer Soc. Republican. Avocations: classical music, travel. Home: 57 Laurel Dr Pataskala OH 43062 Office: Mgmt Foresight Inc 1670 Fishinger Rd Columbus OH 43221

MANN, PHILLIP LYNN, data processing company executive; b. South Charleston, W.Va., July 26, 1944; s. Clarence Edward and Virginia Charlotte (Rupe) M.; m. Edith Jane Dewell, Dec. 28, 1966 (div. 1977); 1 child, Cynthia Lynn; m. Phyllis Anita Berg, May 18, 1979; children: Stacia Lynn, Brandon Granville. BSEE, Purdue U., 1970; MBA, U. Chgo., 1975. Devel. engr. Western Electric Co., Inc., Lisle, Ill., 1970-77; v.p. Uniq Digital Techs., Inc., Batavia, Ill., 1977—. Served with USN, 1962-66. Mem. IEEE, Computer Soc. of IEEE. Avocations: radio control helicopters, fishing. Home: 428 Meadowrue Ln Batavia IL 60510 Office: Uniq Digital Techs Inc 28 S Water St Batavia IL 60510

MANN, ROBERT CHARLES, computer software engineer; b. Sterling, Mich., May 23, 1937; s. Verl Evertt and Dorothy Olga (Kussro) M.; m. Nadine Jeanne Muller, Sept. 14,1957; children: Timothy, Robert II, Michael, Valerie. BEE, Mich. State U., East Lansing, 1957. Computer operator Gen. Motors Research, Warren, Mich., 1958-60; computer programmer Chrysler Corp., Highland Park, Mich., 1960-68; systems rep. Itt Data Services, Paramus, N.J., 1968-70; sr. analyst Chevrolet Motors div. Gen. Motors Corp., Detroit, 1970-76; sr. software analyst Chevrolet Motors div. Gen. Motors Corp., Warren, 1976-85; computer software engr. Electric Data Systems, Warren, 1985—. Chmn. Bd. Evangelism Hope Luth. Ch., Warren, 1979-85. Mem. Heath Computer Users, Nat. Campers and Hikers. Avocations: woodworking, photography, camping, hunting, sailing. Home: 11260 Alger Warren MI 48093 Office: Electronic Data Systems 1410 E 14 Mile Rd Madison Heights MI 48071

MANN, ROBERT EDWARD, manufacturing company executive; b. Detroit, Aug. 3, 1954; s. Westley Edward and Josephine Antonina (Raccosta) M.; m. Shaunna Marie McDonald, Oct. 1, 1977; children: Sarah Elizabeth, Christopher Robert. BBA, Wayne State U., 1979. Auditor Coopers & Lybrand, Detroit, 1978-82; controller Automation Service Equipment Inc., Warren, Mich., 1982-84; v.p. fin. Engring. Cos.-Glynwed N.Am., Warren, 1984—. Mem. Am. Inst. CPA's, Mich. Inst. CPA's, De LaSalle Alumni Assn., Beta Alpha Psi. Roman Catholic. Club: Moravian Hills Country (Mt. Clemens, Mich.). Avocations: philosophy, floor hockey, softball, golf, snow skiing. Home: 41915 Stratton Mount Clemens MI 48044-1860 Office: Engring Cos Glynwed N Am 23220 Pinewood Warren MI 48091

MANN, ROBERT JAMES, dentist; b. Pickstown, S.D., Nov. 29, 1951; s. James Lee and Marvel Ann (Remely) M.; m. Janet LaRue Lamb, Aug. 23, 1975 (div. Apr. 1985); children: Derek Andrew, Keven Robert. BS with honors, U. Minn, 1974; DDS with high distinction, U. Minn., 1976. Gen. practice dentistry Perry, Kasper, Mann Inc. Ltd., Wabasha, Minn., 1976—. Chmn. Wabasha Kellogg Sch. Bd., 1982—; mem. health adv. com. Goodhue Wabasha Health Bd., Red Wing, Minn., 1977—; Cub Scout leader, 1984—. Mem. ADA, Minn. Dental Assn., Southeastern Dist. Dental Assn., Zumbro Valley Dental Soc. (bd. dirs.), Wabasha Jaycess, Wabasha C. of C. Club: Coffee Mill Country (bd. dirs. 1982-86). Lodges: Lions (pres. Wabasha 1978-82), Rotary. Avocations: sports, outdoors, photography, family. Office: Perry Kasper Mann Inc Ltd 115 E Main St Wabasha MN 55981

MANNING, FREDERICK JAMES, insurance company executive; b. Chgo., Oct. 20, 1947; s. Herbert and June Betty (Cohen) M.; m. Gail Hilary Phillips, Feb. 9, 1980; 1 child, Elizabeth Sarah. BS, U. Pa., 1969; JD, Harvard U., 1972. Treas. Marmon Life Ins. Co., Chgo., 1973-77; pres. Celtic Life Ins. Co., Chgo., 1978—, also chmn. bd. dirs., chief exec. officer. Trustee Michael Resse Hosp., Med. Ctr., Chgo.; bd. overseers Ill. Inst. Tech., Chgo. Mem. Am. Inst. CPA's, Young Pres. Orgn. Clubs: Standard (Chgo.), East Bank (Chgo.), Northmoor Country (Chgo.). Home: 442 W Wellington Chicago IL 60659 Office: Celtic Life Ins Co 208 S LaSalle St Chicago IL 60604

MANNING, HELEN HARTON, speech communication and theater educator; b. Albion, Mich., June 7, 1921; d. William C. and Mildred B. (Brown) Harton; m. George A. Manning, Mar. 21, 1959 (dec. May 1979); 1 child, Lora Annette. B.A., Albion Coll., 1943; M.A., Northwestern U., 1950, Ph.D., 1956. Dir. theater Hope Coll., Holland, Mich., 1950-53, chmn. speech dept., 1954-55; teaching fellow Northwestern U., Evanston, Ill., 1953-54, 55-56; faculty Albion Coll., 1956—, prof. speech communication and theater, 1966—, chmn. dept., 1970—. Editor: A Guide to Environment Theater, 1974. Founder, Albion Community Theater, 1967; mem. Sesquicentennial Com. Albion, 1982—, div. chmn., 1982-85; lay leader United Meth. Ch., Albion, 1983—; mem. adv. bd. N.Y. Arts Program, N.Y.C., 1976—. Recipient Community Service award City of Albion, 1984; Mellon research grantee Albion Coll., 1983 . Mem. Speech Communication Assn., Mich. Speech Communication Assn. (sec.-treas. 1957-61, Disting. Service award 1984), AAUW (v.p. 1970-73), Albion Coll. Alumni (bd. dirs. 1987, Disting. Alumni award 1987), Theta Alpha Phi (advisor 1956—), Delta Sigma Rho. Clubs: Emitte Lucem Tuam (v.p. 1985—), United Methodist Women (v.p. 1983-84, 85-86, pres. 1985-87, bd. dirs. 1986-87), Review (Albion). Avocations: collecting local oral history, knitting. Home: 415 Brockway Pl Albion MI 49224 Office: Albion Coll Dept Speech Communication Theater E Porter St Albion MI 49224

MANNING, HENRY EUGENE, hospital administrator; b. Moresburg, Tenn., May 19, 1935; s. Henry Barnett and Lillian Pearl (Spradling) M.; m. Hope Snider Henneke, Aug. 3, 1976; 1 child by previous marriage, Henry Eugene. B.S., L.I. U., 1960; M.S., Columbia U., 1962. Asst. adminstr. Cumberland Hosp., N.Y.C., 1962-64, adminstr., 1964-67; dep. commr. N.Y.C. Dept. Hosps., 1967-70; pres. Cuyahoga County Hosp. System, Cleve., 1970—. Office: Cuyahoga County Hosp System 3395 Scranton Rd Cleveland OH 44109

MANNING, KENNETH PAUL, chocolate company executive; b. N.Y.C., Jan. 18, 1942; s. John Joseph and Edith Helen (Hoffmann) M.; m. Maureen Lambert, Sept. 12, 1964; children—Kenneth J., John J., Elise, Paul, Caroline, Jacqueline. B.Mech.Engring., Rensselaer Poly. Inst., 1963; postgrad. in Statistics George Washington U., 1965-66; M.B.A. in Ops. Research, Am. U., 1968. With W.R. Grace & Co., N.Y.C., 1973—, v.p. European consumer div., 1975-76, pres. ednl. products div., 1976-79, pres. real estate div., 1979-81, v.p. corp. tech. group, 1981-83, pres., chief exec. officer Ambrosia Chocolate Co. div., Milw., 1983—. Mem. adv. council Marquette U.; trustee Rensselaer Newman Found., Troy, N.Y. Served as lt. USN, 1963-67, Caribbean. Decorated Nat. Def. medal, Armed Forces Res. medal. Mem. Chocolate Mfrs. Assn. (chmn. 1985-86, sec. 1986-87), Greater Milw. Com. Republican. Roman Catholic. Clubs: Union League (N.Y.C.); Univ. (Milw.). Home: 2914 E Newberry Blvd Milwaukee WI 53211 Office: Ambrosia Chocolate Co div WR Grace & Co 1133 N 5th St Milwaukee WI 53203

MANNING, SHAYNE O, structural engineer, consultant; b. Dayton, Ohio, May 14, 1954; s. Charles Arnold and Louise Irene (Palmer) M.; m. Alleen Annette Blesi, Dec. 12, 1986. BSCE magna cum laude, U. Cin., 1977, postgrad., 1977—. Registered profl. engr., Ohio, Calif., Wash. Structural engr. THP Ltd., Cin., 1977-80, ptnr., 1980—. Mem. North Avondale Neighborhood Assn., 1977—. Named Young Engr. of Yr., Tech. Soc. Council Cin., 1987. Mem. ASCE (Outstanding Service award 1982), Cin. Cons. Engrs. Assn., Am. Concrete Inst., Tau Beta Pi (pres. 1976-77), Chi Epsilon. Republican. Methodist. Avocations: swimming, cross country skiing, hiking, sports cars, motorcycles. Office: THP Ltd 100 E 8th St Suite 902 Cincinnati OH 45202

MANNING-COX, CARLA ANN, small business owner; b. St. Louis, June 1, 1951; d. James Francis and Bertha Theresa (Bohnert) Manning; m. James Harris Cox, Dec. 28, 1985. BA, U. Mo., 1973. Media asst. BHN Advt., St. Louis, 1974; media buyer GGH&M Advt., St. Louis, 1974-76; media dir. Stolz Advt., St. Louis, 1976-79; v.p. BFV&L Advt., St. Louis, 1979-86; owner, operator Carla Cox Crafts, Ladue, Mo., 1986—. Avocations: tennis, music, sewing, weaving, cooking. Office: Carla Cox Crafts 9783 Clayton Rd Ladue MO 63124

MANNIS, VALERIE SKLAR, lawyer; b. Green Bay, Wis., May 26, 1939; d. Phillip and Rose (Aaron) Sklar; m. Kent Simon Mannis, Dec. 28, 1958; children: Andrea, Marci. BS, U. Wis., 1970; JD, 1974. Bar: Wis. 1974. Staff atty. Legis. Council, Madison, Wis., 1974-75; sole practice, Madison, 1975-84; asst. to pres. Bank of Shorewood Hills (Wis.), 1984-86; bus. devel. rep. First Wis. Nat. Bank, Madison, 1986—; founding mem. Legal Assn. for Women, Madison, 1975—. Pres. Nat. Women's Polit. Caucus Dane County, Madison, 1984; bd. dirs. Madison Estate Planning Council, 1980-84, Madison Jewish Community Council, 1975-79, 82-84. Mem. ABA, Dane County Bar Assn. (chmn. property com. 1978-84), State Bar. Wis. (gov. 1980-86), Nat. Assn. Banking Women. Office: First Wis Nat Bank PO Box 7900 Madison WI 53707

MANOFF, DONALD BENJAMIN, dress company executive, accountant; b. Toledo, Apr. 20, 1937; s. Max Jack and Sylvia (Eisler) M.; m. Judith Beth Rosecrans, Dec. 27, 1970; children: Allyce, Marcy. BBA, U. Toledo, 1960. CPA, Ohio, Ill. Audit supr. Ernst & Whinney, Toledo and Chgo., 1960-70; audit mgr. Alexander Grant & Co., Chgo., 1970-76; controller Sage Foods, Des Plaines, Ill., 1976-80. Mem. Am. Inst. CPA's, Ill. Inst. CPA's, Nat. Assn. Accts. Avocation: racquetball. Home: 3826 Russett Ln Northbrook IL 60062 Office: Caron Inc 350 W Kinzie Chicago IL 60610

MANOHAR, MURLI, physician; b. Panchetia, Rajasthan, India, Jan. 1, 1935; came to U.S., 1961; s. Bhairon and Mohan (Baharat Kanwar) Singh; m. Bheeke Devi, Jan. 21, 1960; children: Chandra Prabha, Ashok Kumar. DVM, U. Rajasthan, 1960; MS, U. Minn., 1964, MPH, 1965, PhD, 1966; MD, Queen's U., Kingston, Ont., Can., 1976. Resident in internal medicine Northeastern Ohio U. Coll. Medicine and Youngstown (Ohio) Hosp. Assn., 1976-78; staff physician, hosp. epidemiologist VA Med. Ctr., Chillicothe, Ohio, 1978; sr. resident in internal medicine Hurley Med. Ctr. Mich. State U., Flint, 1979, coordinator house physicians, Coll. Human Medicine, McLaren Gen. Hosp., 1980-82; practice medicine specializing in internal medicine and infectious diseases Canton, Ohio, 1980—; dir. med. edn. Massillon (Ohio) Community Hosp., 1985—; cons. agt. orange and dermatology Vets. Out-Patient Med. Clinic, Canton, 1981—; med. dir. Manor Care Nursing Ctr., Canton, 1981-85; cons. allergy and dermatology Health Plus Health Maintenance Orgn., Toledo, 1980. Contbr. articles to profl. jours. Fellow Interam. Coll. Physicians and Surgeons; mem. AMA, ACP, AAAS, Stark County Med. Soc., Ohio State Med. Assn., World Med. Assn., Am. Soc. Internal Medicine, Am. Soc. Microbiology, Am. Pub. Health Assn., Am. Vet. Medicine Assn., Minn. Acad. Scis., Henrici Soc. Microbiologists, Can. Soc. Microbiologists, Am. Inst. Biol. Scis., Ohio Soc. Internal Medicine, U. Minn. Alumni Assn. (life), Internat. Youth Hostels Fedn. (life), Am. Med. Dirs. Assn., Am. Acad. Allergy and Clin. Immunology, Sigma Xi, Gamma Sigma Delta, Phi Zeta. Republican. Hindu. Avocations: ballroom dancing, music, reading. Office: 4942 Higbee Ave NW Suite E Canton OH 44718

MANOLIS, DEANE CHRIST, psychiatrist; b. Mpls., Sept. 10, 1936; s. Christ C. and Gertrude V. (Carlson) M.; m. Nancy B. Garrison, Mar. 11, 1961; children: Amy, James, David. BA, U. Minn., 1958, BS, MD, 1962, postgrad., 1962-66. Diplomate Am. Bd. Psychiatry and Neurology. Intern Orange County Gen. Hosp., Calif., 1962-63; resident U. Minn. Hosp., Mpls., 1963-66; psychiatrist Mpls. Clinic Psychiatry and Neurology, 1968-85, Mpls. Clinic Psychiatry, 1985—; med. dir. behavioral health services Met. Med. Ctr., Mpls., 1986—; chief psychiatry Met. Med. Ctr., 1980-81, pres. med. staff, 1983-85. Served to capt. U.S. Army, 1966-68. Fellow Am. Psychiat. Assn.; mem. Minn. Psychiat. Soc. (exec. com. council 1985—), Minn. Med. Assn. (del.), Minn. Hosp. Psychiatry Coalition (founding mem.). Methodist. Avocations: photography, travel. Office: 242A Southdale Med Bldg 6545 France Ave S Edina MN 55435

MANOOGIAN, RICHARD ALEXANDER, manufacturing company executive; b. Long Branch, N.J., July 30, 1936; s. Alex and Marie (Tatian) M.; children: James, Richard, Bridget. B.A. in Econs, Yale U., 1958. Asst. to pres. Masco Corp., Taylor, Mich., 1958-62, exec. v.p., 1962-68, pres., 1968-85, chmn., 1985—, chief exec. officer, from 1985, also dir.; chmn., dir. Masco Industries, Inc.; dir. Emco Ltd., London, Ont., Can., Nat. Bank of Detroit, Flint & Walling, Kendallville, Ind., R.P. Scherer Corp., Do It Yourself Inst. Trustee Archives Am. Art, U. Liggett Sch., Assocs. of Am. Wing, Detroit Inst. Arts, Founder's Soc., Detroit Inst. Arts, Center for Creative Studies. Mem. Young Presidents Orgn., Am. Bus. Conf. Clubs: Grosse Pointe Yacht, Grosse Pointe Hunt, Country of Detroit, Detroit Athletic. Office: Masco Corp 21001 Van Born Rd Taylor MI 48180

MANOR, DONALD IRVIN, engineering administrator; b. Eau Galle, Wis., July 27, 1941; s. Irvin Leon and Rose Ann (Berger) M.; m. Lois Marie Walter, Aug. 24, 1963; children: Christopher, Michael, Jonathan, Susan, Anne. BSME, U. Wis., 1963. Registered profl. engr., Iowa. Engr. trainee John Deere Co., Dubuque, Iowa, 1963-65, engr., supr., 1965-74, lead engr., 1974-75; staff engr. Deere & Co., Moline, Ill., 1975-79, div. mgr. tech. systems, 1979-83, div. mgr. design systems, 1983—. Bd. dirs., officer Our Savior Luth. Ch., Bettendorf, Iowa, 1977—. Recipient Jr. Engr. of Yr. Quint Cities Engr. Council, 1975, George Washington award Inst. for Advancement of Engring., 1986, Disting. Service award Los Angeles Council of Engrs. and Scientists, 1987. Mem. Soc. Automotive Engrs. (pres. local sect. 1976, mem. nat. coms. 1979-85), Soc. Mfg. Engrs. (bd. dirs. Computer & Automated Systems Assn. div. 1981—,mem. exec. com. 1982—, pres. 1986-87). Avocations: coaching softball, gardening, woodworking. Home: 3148 Middle Haven Dr Bettendorf IA 52722

MANOS, JOHN M., federal judge; b. 1922. BS, Case Inst. Tech., 1944; JD, Cleve.-Marshall Coll. Law, 1950. Bar: Ohio. Judge Ohio Ct. Common Pleas, 1963-69, Ohio Ct. Appeals, 1969-76, U.S. Dist. Ct. (no. dist.) Ohio, Cleve., 1976—. Mem. ABA, Fed. Bar Assn., Ohio Bar Assn. Office: US Dist Ct 250 US Courthouse Cleveland OH 44114 *

MANOS, PAUL WILLIAM, metal processing executive; b. Chgo., Dec. 27, 1949; s. William Paul and Margaret (Ainsworth) M.; m. Jean Constance Tapas, Oct. 15, 1983; 1 child, Dena Louisa. BS in Marine-Nuclear Engring., U.S. Mcht. Marine Acad., 1972. Engr. Gen. Electric Corp., N.Y.C., 1972-73, TAO Corp., Roslyn, N.Y., 1973-74; engr. Whiting Corp., Harvey, Ill., 1974-78, internat. sales dir., 1978-83; sales mgr. Metal Process Control, Inc., Chgo., 1984-85, v.p. sales, 1985, v.p., gen. mgr., 1986. Served with USNR, 1968-74. Mem. Iron and Steel Soc. Am., Inst. Mining, Metallurgical and Petrochem. Engrs., Assn. Iron and Steel Engrs, Am. Hellenic Ednl. Prog. Assn. Greek Orthodox. Avocations: athletic activities, automobiles. Home: 1418 Kenton Rd Deerfield IL 60015 Office: Metal Process Control Inc 332 S Michigan Ave Suite 1555 Chicago IL 60604

MANSFIELD, HARRY EDGAR, data processing executive; b. Wamego, Kans., Feb. 10, 1942; s. James and A. Irene (Hatcher) M.; m. Shirley Nadine Lamkin, July 13, 1963; children: Marsha, Denise, James, William. Student, Kans. State U., 1960-62, Abilene (Tex.) Christian U., 1964-65. Cost control mgr. O'Brien Homes, Inc., Rochester, N.Y., 1967-73; data processing mgr. Bolling Bldrs., Kansas City, Mo., 1974-76; systems mgr. Lear-Seigler Safelite, Wichita, Kans., 1976-78; data processing mgr. Pester Corp., Des Moines, 1978-80; pres. H.E. Mansfield & Assocs., Wamego, 1980-83; dir. info. services Kans. State Network, Inc., Wichita, 1983—; cons. Midwest Fire & Casualty, Wellington, Kans., 1980-82, Derby (Kans.) Police Dept., 1981-82. Mem. Wichita Area Assn. of System 34-36-38 Users (v.p. 1985), Broadcast Fin. Mgmt. (chmn. data processing standards 1985-86, bd. dirs. 1987—, chmn. MIS com. 1987—), Data Processing Mgrs. Assn., COMMON (communication hotline 1986). Office: Kans State Network Inc 905 N Main PO Box 333 Wichita KS 67201

MANSFIELD, JAMES BRUCE, neurosurgeon; b. Chgo., Nov. 21, 1945; s. Edward Elias and Esther Klara (Berkowitz) M.; m. Karen L. Mansfield, Feb. 22,1980; children: Kristin Soskich, Anthony Soskich, Robert, Jon. MB, Northwestern U., 1966, MD, 1968. Diplomate Am. Bd. Neurosurgery; lic. physician Ill., Va. Intern Presbyn.-St. Luke's Hosp., Chgo., 1968-69; resident in neurology U. Hosps. Northwestern U. Med. Sch., Chgo., 1971-72; resident in neurosurgery U. Ill., Chgo., 1971-75; pres. Neurol. and Spinal Surgery, Ltd., Elgin, Ill., 1975—; chief surgery Sherman Hosp., Elgin, 1978, Humana Hosp., Hoffman Estates, Ill., 1985—, St. Joseph Hosp., Elgin, 1986; clin. asst. prof. dept. neurosurgery and neurology U. Ill., Chgo., 1972-73, clin. instr. 1973-75, clin. assoc. 1975-85; clin. asst. prof. neurosurgery Coll. Medicine at Chgo., 1985. Contbr. articles to profl. jours. Served to lt. USN, 1969-71. Fellow ACS; mem. AMA, Kane County Med. Soc., Interurban Neurosurg. Soc., Cen. Neurosurg. Soc., Am. Assn. Neurol. Surgeons, Congress Neurol. Surgeons, Chgo. Neurol. Soc. Avocations: racquetball, travel, swimming. Office: Neurol & Spinal Surgery Ltd 901 Center St Suite 107 Elgin IL 60120

MANSFIELD, KAREN LEE, lawyer; b. Chgo., Mar. 17, 1942; d. Ralph and Hilda (Blum) Mansfield; 1 child, Nicole Rafaela. B.A. in Polit. Sci., Roosevelt U., 1963; J.D., DePaul U., 1971; student U. Chgo., 1959-60. Bar: Ill. 1972, U.S. Dist. Ct. (no. dist.) Ill. 1972. Legis. intern Ill. State Senate, Springfield, 1966-67; tchr. Chgo. Pub. Schs., 1967-70; atty. CNA Ins., Chgo., 1971-73; law clk. Ill. Apellate Ct., Chgo., 1973-75; sr. trial atty U.S. Dept. Labor, Chgo., 1975—. Contbr. articles to profl. jours. Vol. Big Sister, 1975-81; bd. dirs. Altgeld Nursery Sch., 1963-66, Hull House Jane Addams Ctr., 1977-82, Broadway Children's Ctr., 1986—; research asst. Citizens for Gov. Otto Kerner, Chgo., 1964; com. mem. Ill. Commn. on Status of Women, Chgo., 1964-70; del. Nat. Conf. on Status of Women, 1968; candidate for del. Ill. Constl. Conv., 1969. Bd. dirs. Broadway Children's Ctr., 1986—, Ill. div. United Nations Assn., 1976-72; Hull House Jane Addams. Ctr. Mem. Chgo. Council Lawyers, Women's Bar Assn. Ill., Lawyer Pilots Bar Assn., Fed. Bar Assn. Unitarian. Clubs: Friends of Gamelan (performer), 99's Internat. Orgn. Women Pilots (legis. chmn. Chgo. area chpt. 1983-86, legis. chmn.) Home: 2970 Lake Shore Dr Chicago IL 60657 Office: US Dept Labor Office of Solicitor 230 S Dearborn 8th Floor Chicago IL 60604

MANSON, BRUCE MALCOLM, construction company executive; b. Chgo., July 16, 1944; s. William Donald and Evelyn Florence (Drinnen) M.; m. Mary Jane Romans, July 30, 1966; children—Jennifer Lyn, Scott Lindsay. C.E., Bradley U., 1966. Field engr. E.W. Corrigan Constrn. Co., Chgo., 1966-68, estimator, 1968-73; project mgr. Pepper Constrn. Co., Chgo., 1973-77, v.p. div., 1977-78, v.p. engring., 1978-80, exec. v.p., 1980-85; exec. v.p., chief operating officer Inland Constrn. Co., Chgo., 1985—; cons. Carlson Reports, Mt. Prospect, 1983. Served with AUS, 1966-71. Mem. Internat. Council Shopping Ctrs. Builders Assn. Chgo., Assoc. Gen. Contractors, Barrington C. of C. Contbr. articles to profl. jours. Club: Chgo. Athletic Assn. Home: 73 Saddletree Ln North Barrington IL 60010 Office: Inland Constrn Co 640 N LaSalle St Chicago IL 60610

MANSOUR, AHDY GIRGIS, clinical social worker, social services administrator; b. Tanta, Egypt, June 23, 1933; came to U.S., 1968; s. Girgis and Helen (Guirguis) M.; m. Soad Boulos Tadros, Mar. 1, 1962; children: Manal, Bassem. B of Social Work, Cairo Sch. Social Work, 1957; MS in Social Adminstrn., Case Western Res. U., 1970. Lic. independent social worker, Ohio. Sch. social worker Ministry of Edn., Cairo, 1957-62, asst. dir. rehab. and spl. edn., 1962-68; dir. residential program Bessie Benner Metzenbaum Children's Ctr., Cleve., 1970-72; dir. child devel. ctr. Lake County Bd. Mental Retardation and Devel. Disabilities, Mentor, Ohio, 1972-78; exec. dir. Lake County Soc. Crippled Children and Adults, Mentor, 1978—; instr. Nat. Tng. Ctr. Civil Servants, 1962-68, Case Western Res. U., 1970-78, Cleve. State U., 1972-73; nat. cons. Commn. Accreditation of Rehab. Facilities, Tucson, Ariz., 1982—; adv. bd. edn. of handicappped Lakeland Community Coll., 1980—; laison to U.S. Council on Internat. Yr. Disabled Persons, 1981; bd. dirs. Council for Research on Mental Health Services to Children, 1970-72, Lake County Spl. Transp. Services for Handicapped, 1987—. Mem. Lake-Geauga Counties Vocat. Task Force, 1979—, exec. com. council agy. execs. Cleve. United Way Services, 1981—; chmn. community involvement com. Northeast Ohio Areawide Coordinating Agy., 1981—, Speakers Bur. of United Way Lake County, 1982-83, Lake County Council on Nat. Yr. Disabled Persons, 1982; gov. bd. Nat. Council Chs. of Christ in U.S.A., 1976—; bd. dirs. Greater Cleve. Child Care Assn., 1970-78, Lake-Geauga Camping Assn. for Spl. Children, 1979-83, Community Services Block Grant Adminstrn. Bd., 1983—, Lake County Pvt. Industries Council, 1983—, chmn. planning com., 1985—. Mem. Acad. Cert. Social Workers, Nat. Assn. Social Workers, Am. Assn. Mental Dificiency, Nat. Assn. Rehab. Facilities (med. com.), Ohio Assn. Rehab. Facilities (bd. dirs. 1978-85, v.p. 1980-81), Lake County Council Human Service Agy. Execs. (chmn. 1985-86). Mem. Coptic Orthodox Ch. Avocation: fishing. Home: 901 Bellwood Dr Highland Heights OH 44143 Office: Lake County Soc Crippled Children and Adults Inc 9521 Lake Shore Blvd Mentor OH 44060

MANSUR, CHARLES ISAIAH, geotechnical engineering consultant; b. Kansas City, Mo., Dec. 22, 1918; s. Isaiah and Florence (Cramer) M.; children—Richard C., Cheryl Ann; m. Betty Jo Sauer, Nov. 26, 1960. B.S. in Civil Engring., U. Mo., 1939; M.S. in San. Engring., Harvard U., 1941. Registered profl. engr., Miss., La., Kans., Mo. Chief design sect. Waterways Express Sta., Vicksburg, Miss., 1941-43, asst. chief, 1946-56; san. engr. USPHS, Washington, 1943-46; chief Lower Miss. Valley div. C.E., U.S. Army, Miss., 1957-57; v.p. then pres. Fruco & Assoc., Mo., 1959-69; sr. v.p., cons. McClelland Engrs., St. Louis, 1969-84, sr. engring. cons., 1984—. Author: (with others) Foundation Engineering, 1962. Editor: Malaria Control on Impounded Water, 1946. Mem. planning com. City of Frontenac, Mo., 1967-69, mem. com. on bldgs., 1972. Served to maj. USPHS, 1943-46. Gordon McKay fellow, 1939-41. Fellow ASCE (Thomas F. Rowland prize 1958, Thomas A. Middlebrook award 1957, J.James R. Cross medal 1959); mem. St. Louis Engrs. Club. Presbyterian. Avocations: farming, wood working. Home: 1715 N Geyer Rd Saint Louis MO 63131 Office: McClelland Engrs Inc 9921 Saint Charles Rock Rd Saint Ann MO 63074

MANTEL, THOMAS LEE, industrial engineer; b. New Castle, Pa., Mar. 5, 1939; s. Floyd Victor and Gladys Viola (Blank) Scheidemantel; m. Joanne Marie Binkley, July 2, 1966; children: Teresa Marie, Michael Lee. B in Indsl. Engring., U. Fla., 1963; M in Comml. Sci., Rollins Coll., 1969. Mfg. trainee Gen. Electric Corp., various locations, 1964-66; indsl. engr. Martin-Marietta, Orlando, Fla., 1966-70; planning analyst NCR, Dayton, Ohio, 1970-73; facilities planner Sencorp, Cin., 1973—. Mem. West Carrollton (Ohio) planning and zoning bd., 1972-73, Clermont County planning commn., Batavia, Ohio, 1974—; chmn. Stonelick Twp. Zoning Commn., Owensville, 1974-77. Mem. Bldg. Owners and Mgrs. Inst. (course instr. 1985—), Tristate Telecommunications Assn., Internat. Facilities Mgmt. Assn., World Future Assn., Cin. Bd. Realtors. Republican. Methodist. Avocations: travel, orchards. Home: 6324 Newtonville Rd Goshen OH 45122 Office: Sencorp 8485 Broadwell Rd Cincinnati OH 45244

MANTHEI, ROBIN DICKEY, research technician; b. Tucson, May 16, 1956; d. Wilbur Dunbar French and Barbara Dickey; m. Joel Robert Manthei, Sept. 4, 1976; children: Nicholas Robert, Charles Dickey. AS, Augsburg Coll., 1976; cert. med. lab. technician, Med. Inst. Minn., 1978. Med. lab. technician Lufkin Med. Lab., Mpls., 1978-82; jr. scientist U. Minn., Mpls., 1982-86; research tech. Mayo Found., Rochester, Minn., 1986—. Contbr. articles in field. Mem. Olmstead County Genealogy Soc. Episcopalian. Avocations: family genealogy, tennis. Home: 2310 2d Ave SW Rochester MN 55902

MANTOVANI, MARK PETER, lawyer; b. St. Louis, June 12, 1954; s. John F. and Marinelle (Pouyer) M.; m. Patricia Ann Hofmeister, Aug. 5, 1977; children: Regina Jonelle, Joseph Ross. BA with highest honors, Quincy (Ill.) Coll., 1976; JD, U. Mo., 1979; MBA, U. Pitts., 1980. Bar: Mo. 1979, U.S. Dist. Ct. (ea. dist.) Mo. 1985, U.S. Tax Ct. 1985. Fin. cons. Condron Assocs., Inc., Pitts., 1979-80; dir. regional office Condron Assocs., Inc., Houston, 1980-81; v.p. Condron Assocs., Inc., Mpls., 1982-83; pres. Fin. Planning Ctr., Tyler, Tex., 1984-85; sole practice law St. Louis, 1985—; pres. Mantovani Fin. Services, Inc., St. Louis, 1985—; fin. cons. Pillsbury Co., Tex. Ea. Corp., Pennzoil Co.; instr. bus. law Meramec Coll., Kirkwood, Mo., 1985—. Mem. ABA, Mo. Bar Assn. Roman Catholic. Home: 1495 Royal Springs Saint Louis MO 63122 Office: Mantovani Fin Services Inc 300 Chesterfield Ctr Chesterfield MO 63017

MANZ, CARL WALTON, surgeon, educator; b. Eau Claire, Wis., Feb. 15, 1938; s. Walton Robert and Beatrice (Hartvigh) M.; m. Diane Mary Johnson, June 28, 1958; children: James W., Barbara D., Robert C. BS, U. Wis., 1960, MD, 1963; MS, U. Minn., 1971. Diplomate Am. Bd. Gen. Surgery. Practice medicine specializing in gen. and vascular surgery Midelfort Clinic, Eau Claire, 1971—; asst. clin. prof. dept. family practice U. Wis., Madison, 1979—. Served to capt. USAR, 1964-66. Fellow ACS; mem. AMA, Wis. Med. Assn., Tri-County Med. Assn.. Avocations: biking, swimming. Home: 4442 Meadow Ln Eau Claire WI 54701 Office: Midelfort Clinic 733 Clairemont Ave Eau Claire WI 54701

MAPA, MANOLO P., physician; b. Manila, Philippines, July 20, 1943; came to U.S., 1968; s. Pedro O. and Violeta (Pangulayan) M.; m. Helouise Culanculan, Dec. 24, 1968; children: Michael, Marissa, Meilani, Manolo Jr. AA, U. St. Tomas, Manila, 1962, MD, 1967. Diplomate Am Bd. Internal Medicine. Intern Northeastern Hosp., Phila., 1968-69; resident in internal medicine L.I. Coll. Hosp., 1970-71, Queens Gen. Hosp., 1971-73; dir. Mini Care Unit Kings County Med. Cen., Bklyn., 1973-74; attending staff. East Liverpool (Ohio) City Hosp., 1974—, pres. staff; practice internal medicine 1974—. Mem. ACP, Am. Soc. Internal Medicine. Avocation: tennis. Home: 250 Boyce Dr Chester VA 26034 Office: Mapa and Mapa MD Inc 129 W 4th St East Liverpool OH 43920

MAPEL, PATRICIA JOLENE, farmer, consultant; b. Lake City, Iowa, June 24, 1933; d. John Gilbert and Blanche Evelyn (Taylor) Sharkey; m. J.R. Mapel, Sept. 1, 1952; children: Pati Jo, Mark L., Grant L., Penelope R., Kay Collene. Student, Wesley Meml. Hosp. Sch. of Nursing, 1951-52. Ptnr. farming Lake City, Iowa, 1953—; ptnr. Mapel Farms Ethanol, Inc., Lake City, Iowa, 1983—; cons. Dept. of Energy, Kansas City, 1981—; demonstrator, educator Iowa Cen. Community Coll., Ft. Dodge, Iowa. Contbr. articles to profl. jours. Bd. dirs. Cen. Sch. Preservation, Inc., Lake City, 1984—. Democrat. Mem. Ch. of Christ. Club: Entre Nou (Lake City). Lodge: Eastern Star. Avocations: sewing, leathercraft. Home and Office: R R 1 Box 147 Lake City IA 51449

MAPLE, KARL EDWARD, political science educator, consultant; b. Carbondale, Ill., Mar. 23, 1945; s. June and Vivian (Robinson) M.; married; 1 child, Mark Edward. B.S., So. Ill. U., 1967, M.S., 1968, Ph.D., 1980. Research asst. So. Ill. U., Carbondale, 1968-69; instr. Southeastern Ill. Coll., Harrisburg, 1969; instr. John Logan Coll., Carterville, Ill., 1970—, chmn. dept. social scis., 1979—; dist. asst. Congressman Paul Simon, Washington, 1981-84. Bd. dirs. Prison Family Support, Carbondale, 1970—; councilman Elkville City, Ill., 1972—. Named Outstanding Young Educator, Ill. Jaycees, 1974; disting. faculty Logan Student Body, 1982. Mem. NEA, Ill. Edn. Assn., Kappa Delta Pi, Phi Kappa Phi, Phi Delta Kappa. Democrat. Baptist. Avocations: skiing; photography. Home: 1 Maple Acres Elkville IL 62932 Office: John Logan College Carterville IL 62918

MAPLES, LARRY DEAN, financial officer; b. Sturgeon Bay, Wis.; s. Raymond R. and Phyllis L. (Buehrens) M.; m. Nancy C. Knutson, Dec. 30, 1967; children: Katherine M., Jeffrey T. BBA in Personnel, U. Wis., Madison, 1971, BBA Acctg., 1976. CPA, Wash., Wis. Sr. CPA Schenck & Assocs., Appleton, Wis., 1977-78; CPA supr. Schemck & Assocs., Appleton, Wis., 1978-80, CPA mgr., 1980-82; asst. treas., chief fin. officer Zwicker Knitting Mills, Appleton, 1982-83, treas., chief fin. officer, 1983—, also bd. dirs.; bd. dirs. Fox Valley Profl. Lawncare, Appleton, 1982—. Pres., bd. dirs. No. Wis. Planning Forum, Appleton, 1985-86. Served with U.S. Army, 1965-68. Mem. Am. Inst. CPA's, Wis. Inst. CPA's, Mfg. Soc. Am. (adv. com.). Roman Catholic. Home: 3526 W Parkridge Ave Appleton WI 54914

MAPLES, STEPHEN SEVEDUS, automation company executive; b. Tecumseh, Mich., June 18, 1950; s. Sevedus Allister and Janet Ellen (Wilcox) M.; m. Cathy Ann Beevers, Aug. 11, 1979; children—Titian Elizabeth, Kirsten Katherine. Student Eastern Mich. U., 1975-78, Ind. Vocat. Tech. U., 1978-79. Product checker Ford Motor Co., Saline, Mich., 1972-73; teaching asst. dept. chemistry Eastern Mich. U., Ypsilanti, 1975-78; application engr. Control Gaging Co., Ann Arbor, Mich., 1979-82; pres., chief engr. Acer Automation Corp., Adrian, Mich., 1982-85; chief engr. Air Hydraulics, Inc., Jackson, Mich., 1985—; metrology cons. Molden Assocs., Michigan City, Ind.; gaging cons. Lyon Machine & Tool Co., Muskegon, Mich. Served with U.S. Army, 1969-72. Mem. Phi Kappa Phi. Inventor gaging apparatus.

MAPPA, PHILIP IRWIN, real estate developer, accountant; b. Chgo., May 2, 1944; s. Samuel and Anne E. (London) M.; m. Susan Posner, Aug. 16, 1964; children—Steven Andrew, Jacqueline Suzanne. Student U. Ill., 1962-66. C.P.A., Ill. Mgr. tax Arthur Andersen & Co., Chgo., 1966-73; exec. v.p. Farnsworth, McKoane & Co., Chgo., 1973-83; pres., owner Philip I. Mappa Interests, Des Plaines, Ill., 1984—; lectr. in field. Editor: Fed. Taxes Affecting Real Estate, 1976. Contbr. articles to profl. jours. Mem. Am. Inst. C.P.A.s, Ill. C.P.A.s. Republican. Jewish. Club: Idlewild Country (Flossmoor) (bd. dirs. 1978-83). Avocations: 12" softball; tennis; racquetball; golf. Office: 1700 Higgins Rd Des Plaines IL 60018

MARAGOS, NICHOLAS ERNEST, otolaryngologist, educator, consultant; b. Waukesha, Wis., Apr. 23, 1946; s. Ernest Nicholas and Mary (Voorlas) M.; m. Constance G. Zahhos, Aug. 31, 1969; children: Anastasia, John, Mariya. BS, U. Wis., 1968, MD, 1972. Diplomate Am. Bd. Otolaryngology. Intern in surgery Mayo Grad. Sch. Medicine, Rochester, Minn., 1972-73, resident in otolaryngology, 1973-77; instr. in otolaryngology Mayo Med. Sch., Rochester, 1977—; cons. dept. otolaryngology Mayo Clinic, Rochester, 1977—. Contbr. articles to profl. jours. Served with USAR, 1974—. Fellow ACS; mem. Am. Acad. Otolaryngology, Voice Found., Minn. Soc. for Prevention of Blindness and Preservation Hearing (bd. dirs. 1979). Greek Orthodox. Avocations: musical directing, composing. Home: 3625 Lakeview Ct NE Rochester MN 55904 Office: Mayo Clinic and Found 200 1st St SW Rochester MN 55905

MARAKAS, JOHN LAMBROS, insurance company executive; b. Connellsville, Pa., July 16, 1926; s. Gust John and Elizabeth Hamilton (Cutler) M.; m. Alice Dixon, Dec. 26, 1948; children: Andy, Nancy, Donna. A.B., U. Mich., 1949. Actuarian asst. Acacia Mut., Washington, 1949-50; actuary Continental Assurance, Chgo., 1950-53; v.p., actuary, exec. v.p., pres. Res. Life Ins. Co., Dallas, 1953-70; v.p. Nationwide Corp., Columbus, Ohio, 1971-72, pres., 1972—, also dir.; pres., dir. Nationwide Life Ins. Co., Columbus, 1981—, now also gen. mgr.; pres., dir. Multi-Flex Advisers, Inc., Nat. Services, Inc., Nationwide Annuity Advisers, Inc., Nationwide Funding, Nationwide (MESCO Ins. Agy.), Nationwide (PEBSCO Inc.), Nationwide Property Mgmt., Inc., Nationwide Variable Life Ins. Co., Pacific Life Ins. Co.; dir. Farmland Ins. Co., Farmland Ins. Co., Farmland Mut. Ins. Co., Gulf Atlantic Life Ins. Co., Mich. Life Ins. Co., Nat. Casualty Co., Nat. Services, Inc., Nationwide Community Urban Redevelopment Corp., Hickey-Mitchell Ins. Agy., Inc., Nationwide Fin. Services Inc., Nationwest Ins. Services, NGA Inc., West Coast Life Ins. Co., NSC, Inc., Nationwide Cash Mgmt. Co.; trustee Nationwide Found., Nationwide Investing Found., Nationwide Multi-Flex Money Market Trust, Nationwide Separate Account Money Market Trust. Bd. dirs. Ohio affiliate Nat. Soc. to Prevent Blindness, Capital U. Served with U.S. Army, 1946-47. Mem. Am. Acad. Actuaries., Assn. Ohio Life Ins. Cos. Office: Nationwide Corp One Nationwide Plaza Columbus OH 43216 *

MARASIGAN, ANTONIO ZARCO, physician; b. Manila, Philippines, Feb. 12, 1929; came to U.S., 1964; married; children: Dominic, Antonio Jr. AA, San Beda Coll., Manila, 1950; MD, U. St. Thomas, Manila, 1955. Diplomate Am. Bd. Ob-Gyn. Resident ob-gyn Far Eastern U. Hosp., Manila, 1956-60, faculty staff ob-gyn, 1960-64; intern St. Michael Hosp., Milw., 1964, resident family practice, 1965-67; resident ob-gyn St. Mary Hosp., Milw., 1965-67, U. Wis. Hosp., Madison, 1967-69; mem. corp. staff Parkview Med. Assn., Hartford, Wis., 1971—, pres. med. staff Harford Meml. Hosp., 1978-80. Fellow Am. Coll. Ob-Gyn; mem. Wis. Ob-Gyn Soc., Milw. Gynecol. Soc., Wis. State Med. Soc. Lodge: Rotary. Office: Hartford Parkview Med Assn 1004 E Sumner Hartford WI 53027

MARASOVICH, GARY MICHAEL, chemical company specialist; b. Youngstown, Ohio, Mar. 1, 1958; s. Andrew Peter and Violette Marie (Stipanich) M. BS in Chemistrycum laude, Youngstown (Ohio) State U., 1981, BS in Engring., 1983. Chief forensic scientist Tri-State Labs., Austintown, Ohio, 1982-85; trainee tech. service, product specialist Electrochemicals, Youngstown, 1984—; mem. faculty Midwest Electronics Expn., St. Paul, 1987. Counselor Camp Millwood, North Jackson, Ohio, 1975-77; coach Ursuline High Sch., Youngstown, 1976-82, Poland (Ohio) High Sch., 1983-84, Canfield (Ohio) High Sch., 1983—. Recipient Outstanding Undergraduate in Chemistry award Am. Inst. Chemists, 1981; Diamond Shamrock scholar, 1981. Mem. Am. Electroplaters' Soc. (speaker Merrimack Valley conf. 1987), Am. Electroplating and Surface Finishing Soc. (speaker Golden West Regional conf. 1987). Home: 2762 Spitler Rd Poland OH 44514 Office: Electrochemicals 751 Elm St Youngstown OH 44502

MARCH, EDMUND SIMON, communications exec.; b. Phila., Apr. 7, 1941; s. Edmund S. and Sylvia S. (Olack) M.; B.S. in Computer Sci., Tampa Coll., 1973; m. Kay Batdorf, Nov. 1, 1978. Computer technician Honeywell, Inc., St. Petersburg, Fla., 1966-72, computer ops. analyst, Mpls., 1972-76, computer applications engr., 1976-78, telecommunications project adminstr., 1978-80, telecommunications project mgr., 1980-83, data communication services mgr., 1983—. Served with USAF, 1958-60. Mem. Assn. Data Communications Users, Honeywell Engring. Club. Republican. Roman Catholic. Home: 3112 Wilson St Saint Anthony MN 55418 Office: Honeywell Bull Inc 3800 80th St Suite 500 Bloomington MN 55431

MARCH, JACQUELINE FRONT, chemist; b. Wheeling, W.Va., July 10, 1914; d. Jacques Johann and Antoinette (Orenstein) Front; B.S., Case Western Res. U., 1937, M.A., 1939; Wyeth fellow med. research U. Chgo., 1940-42; postgrad. U. Pitts., 1945, Ohio State U., 1967, Wright State U., 1970-76; M.B.A., U. Dayton, 1979; m. Abraham W. Marcovich, Oct. 7, 1945 (dec. 1969); children—Wayne Front, Gail Ann March Cohen. Chemist, Mt. Sinai Hosp., Cleve., 1934-40; med. research chemist U. Chgo., 1940-42; research analyst Koppers Co., also info. scientist Union Carbide Corp., Mellon Inst., Pitts., 1942-45; propr. March. Med. Research Lab., etiology of diabetes, Dayton, Ohio, 1950-70; guest scientist Kettering Found., Yellow Springs, Ohio, 1953; Dayton Found. fellow Miami Valley Hosp. Research Inst., 1956. mem. chemistry faculty U. Dayton, 1959-69, info. scientist Research Inst., 1968-79; prin. investigator Air Force Wright Aero. Labs., Wright-Patterson AFB Tech. Info. Center, 1970-79; chem. info. specialist, div. tech. services Nat. Inst. Occupational Safety and Health, HHS, Cin., 1979—; propr. JFM Cons., 1980—; designer info. systems, speaker in field. Trustee Village Condominium Assn., treas., 1985-87. Recipient Recognition cert. U. Dayton, 1980. Mem. Am. Soc. Info. Sci. (treas. South Ohio 1973-75), Am. Chem. Soc. (pres. Dayton 1977, Patterson-Crane award com.; nat. councilor 1982-85), Soc. Advancement Materials and Process Engring. (pres. Midwest chpt. 1977-78), Affiliated Tech. Socs. (Outstanding Scientist and Engr. award 1978), Am. Congress Govtl. Indsl. Hygienists (rev. com. toxic chemicals 1983—), AAUP (exec. bd.), Sigma Xi (treas. Dayton 1976-79, Conrad P. Straub lectr. 1982, pres. Cin. Fed. chpt. 1986-87, rep. nat. meeting 1987—). Contbr. articles to profl. publs. Home: 154 Stillmeadow Dr Cincinnati OH 45245 Office: 4676 Columbia Pkwy Cincinnati OH 45226

MARCH, RONALD EDWARD, real estate developer; b. Chgo., Feb. 14, 1943; s. Edward Andrew and Alfreda March; m. Roberta Smith Kaiser, June 24, 1967; children: Kristen Lee, Nicole Elizabeth. BA in Journalism, Drake U., 1965, postgrad., 1965-67. Real estate analyst Shell Oil Co., Chgo., 1967-68; indsl. real estate broker Baird & Warner, Chgo., 1968-72; asst. v.p. comml. dept. Draper & Kramer, Chgo., 1972-77; pres. The Ron March Co., Schaumburg, Ill., 1977—. Mem. Internat. Council Shopping Ctrs. (N.Y.C. seminar faculty 1979, panelist San Francisco 1982, panelist Chgo. 1984), Colony Point Homeowners Assn. (pres. 1982, bd. dirs. 1983-85), Urban Land Inst. (assoc.). Republican. Clubs: Bannockburn Bath and Tennis (pres. 1979-80), The Meadows Met. Avocations: tennis, golf. Office: 1827 Walden Office Sq Suite 420 Schaumburg IL 60173

MARCICANO, GARY ROBERT, sales executive; b. Detroit, Aug. 16, 1959; s. Robert Andrew and Viola Dorothy (Ollikinen) M. Student, U. Detroit, 1981, Wayne State U., 1983. Sales biller Al Long Ford, Inc., Warren, Mich., 1981-83, exec. asst. to pres., 1983-85, bus. mgr., 1985-86, asst. sales mgr., 1986-87; sales mgr. Al Long Ford, Inc., Warren, 1987—; computer cons. Ford Motors, Inc., Detroit, 1984-85. Mem. Young Republicans. Lutheran. Avocations: golf, tennis, photography, modeling. Office: Al Long Ford Inc 13711 E 8 Mile Rd Warren MI 48089

MARCIL, WILLIAM CHRIST, publisher, broadcasting executive; b. Rolette, N.D., Mar. 9, 1936; s. Max L. and Ida (Fuerst) M.; m. Jane Black, Oct. 15, 1960; children: Debora Jane, William Christ. B.S. in Bus. Adminstrn., U. N.D., 1958. Br. mgr. Community Credit Co., Mpls., 1959-61; with Forum Pub. Co., Fargo, N.D., 1961—; pres., pub. Forum Pub. Co., 1969—; pres. Detroit Lakes Printing Co., Minn., Park Rapids Enterprises, Minn., WDAY Inc., operator WDAY-TV, WDAY radio, Fargo, WDAZ-TV, Devils Lake/Grand Forks, 1970—, KBMY-TV, Bismark, N.D., %, KMCY-TV, Minot, N.D., %, Dakota Photographics, Inc., Fargo, 1969—; dir. First Bank of N.D., Fargo. Pres. Norman Black Found.; past bd. dirs. North Central region Boy Scouts Am., Neuropsychiat. Inst.; trustee N.D. State U. Served with AUS, 1958-59. Mem. Inland Newspaper, N.D. press assns., Am. Newspaper Pubs. Assn. (past dir., chmn., pres.), Fargo and Moorhead C. of C., N.D. State C. of C. (pres.-elect), U.S. C. of C. (bd. dirs.), Sigma Delta Chi, Lambda Chi Alpha. Republican. Lodges: Masons, Shriners, Elks, Rotary. Home: 1618 S 8th St Fargo ND 58102 Office: Forum Pub Co 101 N 5th St Fargo ND 58102

MARCINIAK, DAVID BUSTER, engineer, consultant; b. Milw., July 21, 1939; s. Boleslaus Jospeh and Florence (Sydlowski); m. Mary Clair Beyer, Oct. 18, 1968; children: Michael David, Christine Renee, Joseph ANdrew. Student, U. Wis., Milw., 1957-58; BSEE, Milw. Sch. Engring., 1961. Registered profl. engr., Wis., Calif. Assoc. engr. U.S. Cold Regulation Research and Engring. Lab., Hanover, N.H., 1962-64; staff engr. Cleaver Brooks Co., Milw., 1964-66; reliability engr. Astronautics Corp. Am., Milw., 1966-68; engr. Louis Allis Co., New Berlin, Wis., 1968-75, sr. engr., cons., 1983—; reliability engr. Siemens Allis, West Allis, Wis., 1975-79, chief quality assurance engr., 1980-81; quality assurance rep. Grumman Aerospace, Bethpage, N.Y., 1979-80; mgr. reliabiltiy and product safety Allis Chalmers Corp., West Allis, 1981-83; freelance cons. engring., St. Francis, Wis., 1983—. Served with U.S. Army, 1962-64. Mem. IEEE, Soc. Reliability Engrs. (internat. rep. 1979—, v.p. Milw. chpt. 1978, pres. 1979), Inst. Environ. Scis., Am. Legion. Roman Catholic. Avocations: jogging, cross country skiing, computers. Home: 3633 E Tesch Ave Saint Francis WI 53207 Office: Louis Allis Co 16555 W Ryerson Rd New Berlin WI 53151

MARCINKOSKI, ANNETTE MARIE, educator; b. Akron, Ohio, Aug. 2, 1933; d. Frank J. and Barbara (Popielarczyk) M. BS, U. Akron, 1955; MA, U. Mich., 1959. Tchr. Flint (Mich.) Pub. Schs., 1955-63, tng. tchr. Coop. Tchr. Edn. Program, 1963-69, elem. tchr., 1969—. Active Big Sister program; sponsor Jr. Red Cross, 1959-63; tchr. Confraternity of Christian Doctrine. Mem. United Tchrs. of Flint (del. rep. assembly), Mich. Edn. Assn. (bd. dirs. 1978—, pres. Region X, 1976-77, exec. com. 1986—), NEA (regional dir. 1973-78), Elem., Kindergarten and Nursery Educators, Assn. Childhood Edn. Internat. (sec. Flint 1959-62, treas. Mich. 1970-72, pres. Mich. 1973-75), AAUW (v.p. 1967-69, area rep. in edn. 1969-72), Theta Phi Alpha (adviser Gen. Motors Inst. chpt. 1973—, chmn. bd. dirs. 1973-79, sec. Founders Found. 1978-80, nat. treas. 1980-82, chmn. nat. bd. dirs. 1986—), Cath. Bus. Women (sec. 1970-72, del. council state orgns. 1974-76), Flint Area Reading Council, Mich. Reading Assn., Flint Community Schs. Edn. Fund (bd. govs. 1984-86), Delta Kappa Gamma, Phi Delta Kappa (del. 1981-84, 86—). Home: 1911 Laurel Oak Dr Flint MI 48507 Office: 1402 W Dayton St Flint MI 48504

MARCKS, JULIE ANN, accountant; b. Green Bay, Wis., Jan. 1, 1956; d. Marvin Morris and Gertrude Augusta Dorothy (Moeller) M. BBA, U. Wis., Oshkosh, 1977, MBA, 1980. CPA, Wis. Acct., intern City of Oshkosh, 1977; acct., auditor Hawkins, Ash, Baptie & Co., Manitowoc and Marshfield, Wis., 1977-82; bus. mgr. Mid-State Tech. Inst., Wisconsin Rapids, Wis., 1982-84; sr. acct., auditor Hill, Christensen & Co., Marshfield,

1984—. Del. Wis. Assn. Sch. Books Conv., Milw., 1985, 87; bd. dirs. Wisconsin Rapids Pub. Schs., 1983—. Mem. Am. Inst. CPA's, Wis. Inst. CPA's (chmn. new member involvement 1981-83, bd. dirs. North Cen. chpt. 1984-85, long-range planning com. 1985-87). Lutheran.

MARCUCCI, NICHOLAS JOHN, architect; b. Oceanside, Calif., Nov. 18, 1956; s. Edmund Nicholas and Rosemarie (Corso) M. AA in Archtl. Engring. with highest honors, Wentworth Inst., 1977; BS in Archtl. Studies with honors, U. Ill., 1979; MArch, U. Minn., 1981. Registered architect, Minn. Jr. designer Winsor, Faricy Architects, St. Paul, 1981-86; project architect, designer Horty, Elving & Assocs., Mpls., 1986—. Participant St. Paul river front charette St. Paul Planning Dept., 1985; career advisor Minn. Soc. Architects and Boy Scouts Am., St. Paul, 1985. Mem. AIA, Minn. Soc. of AIA (profession devel. com. 1985, program convention com. 1985-86, graphics com. 1986; Citation award 1985). Roman Catholic. Home: 2207 Doswell Ave Saint Paul MN 55108 Office: Horty Elving & Assocs Inc 505 E Grant St Minneapolis MN 55404

MARCUM, BILLYE JEAN, nurse, educator; b. Lincoln, Nebr., Oct. 14, 1946; d. Glen Paul Rackley and Marly (Lucille) Waller; 1 child, Marla. Diploma in Nursing, Meth. Hosp., St. Joseph, Mo., 1967. RN, Ga., Tex., Mo. From staff to head nurse Phoebe-Putney Hosp., Albany, Ga., 1967-72; staff nurse Mo. U. Med. Ctr., Columbia, 1972; staff nurse, office nurse Bothwell Meml. Hosp., Sedalia, Mo., 1972-74; staff nurse St. Francis Hosp., Tyler, Tex., 1975-76; office nurse Lake Ozark (Mo.) Clinic, 1976-81; staff nurse, dir. edn. Lake of the Ozarks Gen. Hosp., Osage Beach, Mo., 1981—. Advisor Med. Explorer Post, Osage Beach, 1986—; chmn. steering com. community mobilization Lake Ozark Community Coll., 1986—; chmn. profl. edn. Camden County (Mo.) Cancer Soc., 1986—; chmn. Camden County Am. Heart Assn., 1986—. Mem. Mo. Assn. Healthcare Edn. (pres. 1984-85), Am. Bus. Women's Assn. (Bus. Woman of Yr. 1986). Republican. Methodist. Avocations: hiking, reading, swimming, antiques, animals. Office: Lake Ozarks Gen Hosp Box 187 C/B Osage Beach MO 65048

MARCUM, JOSEPH LARUE, ins. co. exec.; b. Hamilton, Ohio, July 2, 1923; s. Glen F. and Helen A. (Stout) M.; m. Sarah Jane Sloneker, Mar. 7, 1944; children—Catharine Ann, Joseph Timothy, Mary Christina, Sarah Jennifer, Stephen Sloneker. B.A., Antioch Coll., 1947; M.B.A. in Fin, Miami U., 1965. With Ohio Casualty Ins. Co. and affiliates, 1947—, now pres.; also dir.; dir. First Nat. Bank of Southwest Ohio. Chmn. bd. Home Fed. Savs. and Loan Assn. Served to capt., inf. U.S. Army. Mem. Soc. C.P.C.U. (nat. dir.), Am. Inst. Property and Liability Underwriters (trustee), Ohio C. of C. (vice chmn.). Presbyterian. Clubs: Queen City (Cin.), Bankers (Cin.); Canadian (N.Y.C.), Met. (N.Y.C.); El Dorado Country (Indian Wells, Calif.); Little Harbor (Mich.), Walloon Lake Country (Mich.). Home: 475 Oakwood Dr Hamilton OH 45013 Office: Ohio Casualty Corp 136 N Third St Hamilton OH 45025

MARCUS, BEN, food service company executive; b. 1912. With Marcus Corp., Milw., 1935—, chmn. bd. dirs., 1972—, chief exec. officer, 1972—, pres., 1972-80. Office: The Marcus Corp 212 W Wisconsin Ave Milwaukee WI 53203 *

MARCUS, DANIEL ROBERT, stockbroker; b. N.Y.C., June 12, 1931; s. Ralph S. and Alice R. Marcus; m. Florence R. Marzano, May 19, 1960; children—Amy B., Grant R. B.S., Northwestern U., 1955. With Bear Stearns & Co., Chgo., 1949-55, Gofen & Glossberg, Chgo., 1956-70, Freehling & Co., Chgo., 1970, Drexel Burnham Lambert, Inc., Chgo., 1971—. Vice-pres. Evanston Boys Hockey Assn., Ill., 1977-83; bd. dirs. Met. High Sch. Hockey League, Northbrook, Ill., 1980-83; mem. dist. com. Amateur Hockey Assn. Ill., 1982-85. Fellow Fin. Anlysts Fedn.; mem. Midwest Communications Assn., Security Traders Chgo., Internat. Facilty Mgrs. Assn., Chgo. Anlysts Soc. Republican. Home: 904 Michigan Evanston IL 60202 Office: Drexel Burnham Lambert One S Wacker Dr 16th Floor Chicago IL 60606

MARCUS, DAVID ALLAN, financial planner; b. Chgo., June 1, 1959; s. Seymour Harold and Ruth S. (Eiseman) M.; m. Mary Lisa Deimler, Apr. 6, 1986. BS in Gen. Bus., Ariz. State U., 1981. Agt. Pacific Mutual, Chgo., 1981—; pres. David A. Marcus and Assocs., Chgo., 1983—. Mem. Nat. Assn. Life Underwriters (Nat. Quality award 1985, Nat. Sales Achievement award 1984, 85), Nat. Assn. Health Underwriters, Chgo. Assn. Life Underwriters, Million Dollar Round Table (mem. task force 1983-86), Ariz. State Alumni Assn. (v.p. 1983). Republican. Jewish. Club: East Bank. Avocations: tennis, vacationing, coin collecting. Home: 2020 Lincoln Pkwy W 36C Chicago IL 60603 Office: 135 S LaSalle Chicago IL 60603

MARCUS, JACOB RADER, educator; b. Connellsville, Pa., Mar. 5, 1896; s. Aaron and Jennie (Rader) M.; m. Antoinette Brody, Dec. 30, 1925 (dec.); 1 dau., Merle Judith (dec.). A.B., U. Cin., 1917, LL.D., 1950; rabbi, Hebrew Union Coll., 1920; Ph.D., U. Berlin, 1925; attended, Lane Theol. Sem., 1914, U. Chgo., 1915, U. Kiel, 1923; spl. study, Paris and Jerusalem, 1925-26; LL.D., Dropsie Coll., 1955; D.H.L., Spertus Coll. Judaica, Chgo., 1977, Brandeis U., 1978, Gratz Coll., Phila., 1978. Instr. Bible, rabbinics Hebrew Union Coll., 1920, asst. prof. Jewish history, 1926-29, asso. prof., 1929-34, prof. Jewish history, 1934-59; apptd. Adolph S. Ochs prof. Jewish history 1946, Adolph S. Ochs prof. Am. Jewish history, 1959-65, Milton and Hattie Kutz Distinguished Service prof. Am. Jewish history, 1965—; dir. Am. Jewish Archives, 1947—, Am. Jewish Periodical Center, 1956—; v.p. Central Conf. Am. Rabbis, 1947, pres., 1949, hon. pres., 1978. Author: The Rise and Destiny of the German Jew, 1934, An Index to Jewish Festschriften, 1937, The Jew in the Medieval World-a Source Book, 1938, Communal Sick-Care in the German Ghetto, 1947, Early American Jewry, 2 vols., 1951-53, Memoirs of American Jews 1775-1865, 3 vols., 1955-56, American Jewry Documents Eighteenth Century, 1959, On Love, Marriage, Children . . . and Death, Too, 1966, Studies in American Jewish History, 1969, The Colonial American Jew, 3 vols., 1970, Critical Studies in American Jewish History, 3 vols., 1971, Israel Jacobson: The Founder of the Reform Movement in Judaism, 1972, The American Jewish Woman 1654-1980, The American Jewish Woman: A Documentary History, 2 vols., 1981; editor: The American Jewish Archives. Served as 2d lt., 145th Inf. U.S. Army, 1917-19. Recipient Frank L. Weil award Nat. Jewish Welfare Bd., 1955; Lee M. Friedman medal for disting. service to history, 1961. Mem. Jewish Publ. Soc. Am., Am. Jewish Hist. Soc. (hon. pres.), Am. Acad. Jewish Research, Phi Beta Kappa. Club: B'nai B'rith. Honored with publ. Essays in American Jewish History, on 10th anniversary of founding Am. Jewish Archives, 1958, A Bicentennial Festschrift for Jacob Rader Marcus, 1976, The Writings of Jacob Rader Marcus, A Bibliographic Record, 1978. Home: 401 McAlpin Ave Cincinnati OH 45220 Office: Am Jewish Archives 3101 Clifton Ave Cincinnati OH 45220

MARCUS, R(ALPH) STEVEN, manufacturing executive; b. Chapultapec, Mex., May 29, 1935; came to U.S., 1944; . S. Wesley and Floris E. (Sevigny) M.; m. Elizabeth L. Hebben, 1954 (div. 1986) m. Kasondra Dustin; children: Steven W., Gregory A., Jeffrey L. Student, Purdue U., 1954-55; MBA, Pepperdine U., 1979. Cert. mfg. engr. Pres. Powdered Products Corp., Columbus, Ohio, 1973-84; pres. Markee Corp., Columbus, 1971-84, Chmn. bd., 1984—; cons. Diamond, Inc. Santa Ana, Calif., 1983—. Contbg. author, editor Metals Handbook, 1984-85; contbr. articles to profl. jours.; patentee deburring machine. Named Exec. of Yr., Nat. Sec. Assn., 1979. Mem. Am. Powder Metallurgy Inst., Soc. Mfg. Engrs., Am. Legion, Aircraft Owners and Pilots Assn. Club: Capital (Columbus). Avocations: aircraft pilot, writing. Home: PO Box 136 Columbus OH 43216 Office: The Markee Corp 401 Dublin Ave P O Box 240 Columbus OH 43216

MARCUS, RICHARD EARL, otolaryngology educator; b. Milw., Apr. 11, 1916; s. Max and Celia (Grodin) M.; m. Fancelle Wohl, Jan. 3, 1942; children: Carlyn Marcus Ekstrom, Richard Max, Elizabeth. BS, U. Wis., 1937, MD, 1940. Dipolmate Am. Bd. Otolaryngology. Resident Milw. County Gen. Hosp., 1941-42, U. Ill. Eye and Ear Infirmary, 1946-48; asst. to F.L. Lederer, 1948-50; practice medicine specializing in otology Chgo., 1948-53, Los Angeles, 1954-55, Winnetka, Ill., 1955-60, Skokie, Ill., 1960-83; clin. prof. otolarnygology Ill. Coll. Medicine, Chgo., 1946-86, clin. prof. emeritus otolaryngology, 1986—; assoc. prof. U. Calif. Coll. Medicine, Los Angeles, 1954-55; founding mem., exec. dir. Inst. for Hearing and Speech, Winnetka, 1962—; vis. prof. U. Colo. Coll. Medicine, Denver, 1966; guest lectr. XIII Congresso Pan-Americano, 1972; faculty 1st Symposium Neurol. Surgery of the Ear, 1977. Author ELectroencephalography in the Diagnosis of Hearing Loss in the Very Young Child, 1949, Otoxic Medication in Premature Children, 1963, Vestibular Function and Additional Findings in Waardenburg's Syndrome, 1968, Reduced Incidence of Congenital and Prelingual Deafness, 1970, Cochlear abd Neural Disease: Classification and Otoaudiologic Correlations, 1974, Cochieoneural Hearing Loss Treated with Acupuncture, 1974, Innner Ear Disorders in a Family with Sickle Cell Thalassemia, 1976, Clinical Audiology: The Auditory Profile, 1977. Served to maj. USAAF, 1942-46. John and Mary R. Markle Found. scholar in med. sci., 1951. Mem. AMA, Chgo. Otolaryngol. and Otol. Soc.)pres. 1976-77), Am. Acad. Ophthalmology and Otolaryngology (award of merit 1971), Am. Laryngol. Rhinol. and Otol. Soc., Am. Neurotology Soc. (founding, sec.-treas. 1960-63, pres. 1964-65), Chgo. Hearing Soc. (bd. dirs. 1952-55), Sigma Xi. Clubs: Tavern (Chgo.), Lake Shore Country (Glencoe, Ill.).

MARCUS, STEPHEN HOWARD, hospitality and entertainment company executive; b. Mpls., May 31, 1935; s. Ben D. and Celia M.; m. Joan Glasspiegel, Nov. 3, 1962. B.B.A., U. Wis., Madison, 1957; LL.B., U. Mich., 1960. Bar: Wis. 1960. V.p. Pfister Hotel Corp., Milw., 1963-69; exec. v.p. Pfister Hotel Corp., 1969-75; pres. Marcus Hotel Corp., Milw., 1975; pres., chief operating officer, treas. Marcus Corp., Milw., 1980—; also dir. Marcus Corp.; exec. v.p. Marc Plaza Corp.; v.p. Wis. Big Boy Corp., Marcus Theatres Corp.; dir. Med. Coll. Wis., 1986—; dir. Preferred Hotels Assn., 1972—, chmn. bd., 1979; dir. Marine Corp. Pres. Milw. Conv. and Visitors Bur., 1970-71, bd. dirs., mem. exec. com., 1968—; chmn. Wis. Gov.'s Adv. Council on Tourism, 1976-81; bd. dirs. Multiple Sclerosis Soc. Milw., 1965-67, Milw. Jewish Fedn., 1968-76, Milw. Jewish Chronicle, 1973-76; asso. chmn. bus. div. United Fund Campaign, Milw., 1971; co-chmn. spl. gifts com. United Performing Arts Fund, Milw., 1972-74, bd. dirs., 1973-81, chmn. maj. gifts, 1982, co-chmn., 1983—; bd. dirs. Friends of Art, Milw., 1973-74; pres. Summerfest, 1975; bd. dirs. MECCA, Milw., 1975-82, mem. exec. com., 1977; bd. dirs. Jr. Achievement, Milw., 1976—; trustee Mt. Sinai Med. Center, 1977—, Nat. Symphony Orchestra, 1985; co-chmn. Ann. Freedom Fund Dinner, NAACP, 1980-81. Served with U.S. Army, 1960-61. Recipient Ben Nickoll award Milw. Jewish Fedn., 1969, Headliner award Milw. Press Club, 1986. Mem. Am. Hotel and Motel Assn. (dir. 1976-79, exec. com. 1978-79), Greater Milw. Hotel and Motel Assn. (pres. 1967-68), Wis. Innkeepers Assn. (pres. 1972-73), Variety Club, Milw. Assn. Commerce (bd. dirs. 1982-85), Downtown Assn., Young Pres.'s Orgn., Wis. Assn. Mfrs. and Commerce (dir. 1978-82), Greater Milw. Com. (dir. 1981). Office: The Marcus Corporation 212 W Wisconsin Ave Milwaukee WI 53203 *

MARCUSSEN, WILLIAM JAMES, manufacturing engineer; b. Oak Park, Ill., Aug. 24, 1951; s. Arthur James and Maxine (Gunn) M.; m. Marianne Burrin, Sept. 1, 1973; children: William, Thomas. BSME, Purdue U., 1973; MBA, U. Chgo., 1983. Prodn. engr. Ill. Tool Works Hi-Cone, Itasca, Ill., 1977-79, mfg. engr., 1979—. Coordinator United Way Campaign, Itasca, 1979, 85; scouting coordinator Churchill Sch., Glen Ellyn, Ill., 1985-86; elder First Presby. Ch., Glen Ellyn, 1986—. Served with USN, 1973-77, lt. comdr. Res. 1980—. Mem. Naval Res. Assn. (exec. v.p. 1985—), U.S. Naval Inst. Republican. Avocations: sailing, scuba diving, camping, photography, antiques. Home: 354 Linden Glen Ellyn IL 60137 Office: Ill Tool Works Hi-Cone 1140 Bryn Mawr Itasca IL 60143

MARCYN, EDWARD J., architect; b. Milw., Aug. 10, 1949; m. Cheryl Lynne Maheras, Sept. 27, 1975. BArch in Design, U. Ill., Chgo., 1972. Lic. architect, Ill. Draftsman Charles Luckman Assocs., Chgo., 1970-72; designer Witke & Assocs., Bellwood, Ill., 1972-73, Michael Reese Hosp., Chgo., 1973-74; architect West & Bergstrom, Hinsdale, Ill., 1974—. Mem. AIA (Northeast Ill. chpt. bd. dirs. 1980-86, chmn. office practice com. 1979-86), U. Ill. Alumni Assn. Avocations: photography, history, flying. Home: 8110 44th Ct Lyons IL 60534 Office: Phillip West Donald Bergstrom & Assocs 33 E First St Hinsdale IL 60521

MARDELL-CZUDNOWSKI, CAROL DOLORES, psychology educator; b. Chgo., Nov. 30, 1935; d. Albert and Lee (Mandel) Goldstein; m. Howard Mardell, Nov. 21, 1956 (div. Nov. 1977); children: Benjamin, Dina, Ruth; m. Moshe Marcel Czudnowski, Nov. 13, 1978. BS, U. Ill., 1956; MA, U. Chgo., 1958; PhD, Northwestern U., 1972. Tchr. various schs., Skokie and Highland Park, Ill., 1956-70; dir. research project Ill. Office Edn., Chgo., 1971-73; asst. prof. edn. Northwestern U., Evanston, Ill., 1973-74; from asst. to assoc. prof. edn. Northeastern Ill. U., Chgo., 1974-78; assoc. prof. edn. No. Ill. U., DeKalb, 1978-86, prof. edn., 1986—; visiting prof. Nat. Taiwan Normal U., Taipei, 1983-84, Université Laval, Quebec City, Can., 1984-85. Co-author: Special Education for the Early Childhood Years, 1981, 2d edition 1987, Developmental Indicators for the Assessment of Learning-Revised (DIAL-R), 1983. Mem. Am. Ednl. Reseach Assn., Am. Psychol. Assn., Council for Exceptional Children, Phi Kappa Phi, Alpha Lambda Delta, Pi Lambda Theta, Phi Delta Kappa, Kappa Delta Pi. Home: 6 Jennifer Ln DeKalb IL 60115 Office: No Ill U Dept EPSE DeKalb IL 60115

MARDER, LOUIS, educator; b. Bklyn., Sept. 26, 1915; s. Isidor and Clara (Freund) M.; m. Miriam Kugler, Aug. 31, 1940; children: Daniel Spencer, Diana Lynn. BA, Bklyn. Coll., 1941; MA, Columbia U., 1947, PhD, 1950. Indexer N.Y. Times, 1946; lectr., instr. Bklyn. Coll., 1946-53; chmn. dept English Pembroke (N.C.) State Coll., 1953-56; assoc. prof. English Kent (Ohio) State U., 1956-65; prof. English U. Ill., Chgo., 1965-80; founder, editor The Shakespeare Newsletter, Evanston, Ill., 1951—; founder, chief exec. officer The Shakespeare Data Bank, Inc., Evanston, 1984—; vis. prof. U. Toledo, 1968, U. Miami 1981, 82; lectr. Antioch Coll. Shakespeare Festival, 1953, Utah Shakespearean Festival, 1975; mem. Pres. Com. to Celebrate Shakespeare's 400th Anniversary, 1964; del. Internat. Shakespeare Com. Stratford-on-Avon, Eng., 1964, 66, 68, 72, 74, 76, 78, 80, 82, 84; cons. World Ctr. for Shakespeare Studies, London; mem. ednl. council London Globe Theatre Ctr., acad. council Shakespeare Globe Theatre Council, 1981—. Author: His Exits and His Entrances: The Story of Shakespeare's Rep., 1963; also; editor: Study Master Shakespeare Series, 1967-70, Library Shakespearean Scholarship and Criticism, 1966-70; mem. editorial bd. Shakespeare on film newsletter, 1976—; contbr. revs. to newspapers and periodicals. mem. City of Chgo. Shakespeare Festival Com., 1981-83. Served with AUS, 1943-46. Recipient Friends of Lit. citation for Shakespeare Letters; research fellow Folger Shakespeare Library, 1957; recipient Laureate medal Chgo. Cliff Dwellers, 1978. Mem. Shakespeare Soc. Am. (dir. 1968—), Shakespeare Assn. Am. (chmn. Shakespeare's fellow dramatists sect.), MLA (chmn. seminar 1969, 70-71, sect. chmn. 1972), Southeastern Renaissance Assn., Nat. Council Tchrs. English (chmn. Shakespeare sect. 1960-61, 64), Internat. Coop. Shakespeare Congress (com. 1971). Home and Office: 1217 Ashland Ave Evanston IL 60202

MARDIS, VERDENA FOX, psychologist, consultant; b. Franklin, Ohio, Oct. 10, 1914; d. Frank M. and Grace Florence (Johnson) Fox; m. Jack W. Mardis, Aug. 26, 1946; children: Kathleen Fox, Jerold Fox, Rita Jean Fox. BS in Edn., Wittenberg U., 1942; MA in Edn. Adminstrn. and Supervision, U. Dayton, 1949; MS in Sch. Psychology, Miami U., Oxford, Ohio, 1958. Cert. elementary tchr., elementary prin., sch. psychologist, supr. Tchr., elementary prin. Mad River Twp. Schs., Dayton, Ohio, 1934-57; psychologist Montgomery County Bd. Edn., Dayton, 1958-62, dir. pupil personnel, 1962-70; dir. psychology for children and youth project Children's Med. Ctr., Dayton, 1970-72; intake coordinator, psychologist Montgomery County Bd. Mental Retardation and Developmental Disabilities, Dayton, 1972-84, cons., 1984—. Named Profl. of Yr., Montgomery County Bd. Mental Retardation and Developmental Disabilities, 1980; recipient Disting. Service award Montgomery County Bd. Mental Retardation and Developmental Disabilities, 1984. Mem. Am. Assn. Retired Persons, Ohio Retired Tchrs. Assn., Montgomery County Retired Tchrs. Assn. (membership chmn. 1985—), Alpha Delta Kappa (pres., treas., historian, state sgt.-at-arms 1982-84). Democrat. Mem. United Ch. of Christ. Avocations: reading, gardening, sewing, crafts, travel. Home: 4209 White Oak Dr Dayton OH 45432-1848 Office: Montgomery County Bd MR/DD 1507 Kuntz Rd Dayton OH 45404

MARE, WILLIAM HAROLD, Bible educator, talk show host; b. Portland, Oreg., July 23, 1918; s. Scott Creighton and Sallie Gertrude (Knight) Brown, m. Clara Elizabeth Potter, Mar. 23, 1945; children—Myra Ann, Sally Elizabeth, Nancy Lee, William Harold, Jr., Judith Eileen. B.A. (hon. soc.), Wheaton Coll., 1941; B.D., Faith Theol. Sem., 1945; M.A., Wheaton Coll., 1946; Ph.D., U. Penn., 1961. Ordained to ministry Presbyterian Ch., 1945. Grad. fellow, tchr. Wheaton Coll., Ill., 1941-42; tchr. Faith Theol. Sem., Wilmington, Del., 1946-53, pastor Presbyn. Chs., Denver, Charlotte, N.C., 1953-63, prof. classics Covenant Coll. St. Louis, 1963-64; prof. N.T., Covenant Theol. Sem., St. Louis, 1963—; dir. Near East Sch. of Archaeology, Jerusalem, 1962, 64; archaeologist Jerusalem, Raddana, Heshbon, Moab, summers 1970, 72, 74, 76, 79; dir. Abila of Decapolis Excavation, No. Jordan, 1980—. Contbr. articles to profl. jours. Author: First Corinthians Expositors Bible Commentary, 1976; Mastering New Testament Greek, 1977; Archaeology of the Jerusalem Area, 1987. Treas. Mo. Roundtable, St. Louis, 1981—. Mem. Archeol. Inst. Am. (pres. St. Louis chpt. 1978-80), Nr. East Archeol. Soc. (pres. 1971—), Evang. Theol. Soc., Am. Schs. Oriental Research, Soc. Bibl. Lit. Republican. Club: Classical (St. Louis) (pres. 1977-79, 1987-89). Avocation: photography. Home: 978 Orchard Lakes Dr St Louis MO 63146 Office: Covenant Theol Sem 12330 Conway Rd St Louis MO 63141

MARGED, BARRY EDWARD, osteopath, educator; b. Phila., Jan. 20, 1947; s. Abraham Marged and Rebecca (Grant) Cohen; m. Dorothy Spector McClellan, June 21, 1968 (div. June 1972); m. Kathleen Louise Hoover, May 19, 1979; children: Gabriel Avram, Tobi Elizabeth. BS in Physics cum laude, Temple U., 1968, MA in Physics, 1972; DO, Coll. Osteo. Medicine and Surgery, Des Moines, 1977. Intern Tri County Community Hosp., Springfield, Pa., 1977-78; physicist U.S. Govt., Phila., 1968-69; tchr. Phila. Pub. Schs., 1969; instr. physics Temple U., Phila., 1969-72, Akiba Hebrew Acad., Merion, Pa., 1972-73; physician, lectr. Kent (Ohio) State U., 1980—. Author: Introductory Lab Manual for Physics, 1971, Generic Holism, 1986. Bd. dirs. ea. Ohio br. Am. Lung Assn., 1985—. Served with USPHS, 1978-80. Recipient Disting. Teaching award Kent State U., 1983. Mem. Am. Holistic Med. Soc. Avocations: cabinet making, tai chi, karate, racquetball. Office: Kent State U Health Clinic Kent OH 44242

MARGERUM, ROGER WILLIAMS, JR., architect; b. Chgo., May 14, 1930; s. Roger William Sr. and Juanita (Cloyd) M.; m. Phillis Johnson, Aug. 18, 1950 (divorced); children: Micheal B., Kim S.; m. Frances L. Esnault, July 13, 1971. BArch., U. Ill., 1956. Designer Skidmore, Owings & Merrill, Chgo., 1957-60, Perkins & Wills Assocs., Chgo., 1960-62; ptnr. Morrison & Margerum, Chgo., 1962-65; asst. to bd. chmn. Smith, Hinchman & Grylls, Detroit, 1965-73; pres. Roger Margeram Inc. Architects, Mich., 1973—. Fellow Am. Inst. Architects; mem. Am. Inst. Architects, Nat. Orgn. Minority Architects (founding dir. 1972, v.p. 1986—), Detroit Inst. Architects (sec. 1971), Mich. Soc. Architect (pres. 1983). also: 2129 Bryanston Crescent Detroit MI 48107 Office: 401 S LaSalle St Chicago IL 60605 also: 615 Griswold Detroit MI 48226

MARGOLIS, FRED SHELDON, pediatric dentist, educator; b. Lorain, Ohio, Mar. 31, 1947; s. Benjamin Barnett and Zelma (Bordo) M.; m. Susan Kreiter, Sept. 12, 1971; children—David S., Adam R. B.S., Ohio State U., 1969, D.D.S., 1973; cert. pediatric dentistry U. Ill.-Chgo., 1976. Dental intern Mount Sinai Hosp., Chgo., 1973-74; practice dentistry North Suburban Dental Assocs., Skokie, Ill., 1974-84; practice dentistry, Arlington Heights, Ill., 1979—; asst. prof. pediatric dentistry Loyola U. Dental Sch., Maywood, Ill., 1982-83, guest lectr. pediatric dentistry, 1983—; dental cons. Delta Dental Plan, Chgo., 1983—; staff dentist Glenkirk Schs., Glenview, Ill., 1984—; pres. Smile Makers Seminars, 1984—. Contbr. articles to profl. publs. Cubmaster N.E. Ill. council Boy Scouts Am., 1984, 87—, Den Leader, 1986-87. Mem. Am. Dental Assn., Am. Acad. Pediatric Dentistry, Ill. State Dental Soc., Am. Soc. Dentistry for Children, Chgo. Dental Soc. (recording sec. North Side br. 1987—), Alpha Omega. Jewish. Lodge: B'nai B'rith. Avocations: photography, golf, stained glass, piano. Office: 3419 N Arlington Heights Rd Arlington Heights IL 60004

MARGUL, STANLEY NORMAN, oral and maxillofacial surgeon; b. St. Louis, Mar. 5, 1952; s. David and Dorothy Margul; m. Jean Lynn Winston, Nov. 28, 1982. BA, Washington U., St. Louis, 1974; DDS, U. Mo., Kansas City, 1978. Diplomate Am. Bd. Oral and Maxillofacial Surgery. Resident in gen. practice Jewish Hosp., St. Louis, 1978-79; resident in oral and maxillofacial surgery Michael Reese Hosp., Chgo., 1979-82; assoc. Northwest Oral and Maxillofacial Surgery, St. Louis, 1982-84; practice dentistry specializing in oral and maxillofacial surgery Quincy, Ill., 1984—. Am. Soc. Oral and Maxillofacial Surgery fellow, 1982. Mem. ADA, Ill. Soc. Oral and Maxillofacial Surgery. Avocations: bicycle riding, gardening. Home: 11 Old Orchard Rd Quincy IL 62301 Office: 1261 Maine St Quincy IL 62301

MARGULIES, HAROLD, retired physician; b. Sioux Falls, S.D., Feb. 13, 1918; s. Samuel Saul and Nellie (Graceman) M.; m. Marjory Gutfreund, Apr. 12, 1952; children: Marc, Amy. AB, U. Minn., 1938, MS (Mayo Found.), 1948, DSc (hon.), 1974; BS, U. S.D., 1940, DSc (hon.), 1972; MD, U. Tenn., 1942. Diplomate Am. Bd. Internal Medicine. Intern Iowa Meth. Hosp., Des Moines, 1943-44; fellow in internal medicine Mayo Clinic, Rochester, Minn., 1944-45, 46-49; practice medicine specializing in internal medicine and cardiology, advisor on med. edn. World Health Orgn., Alexadria, Egypt, 1965-66; prof. medicine, party chief, mem. adv. group Ind. U. Med. Ctr., Karachi, Pakistan, 1961-64; assoc. dir. div. internat. med. edn., dir. AID contract Assn. Am. Med. Colls., Washington, 1965-67; assoc. dir. socio-econ. activities div. AMA, Washington, 1967-68, sec. council on health manpower, 1968-69; dep. asst. adminstr. program planning and evaluation Health Services and Mental Health Adminstrn., HEW, Rockville, Md., 1969-70, dir. regional med. programs, 1970-73; dep. adminstr. Health Resources Adminstrn., 1973-79; spl. asst. environ. health USPHS, 1979-81, acting dep. asst. sec. for health research, 1981-82; dir. office of health tech. assessment Nat. Ctr. for Health Services Research, USPHS, 1982-84; cons. internal medicine VA, 1949-61; dir. electrocardiographic lab. Iowa Med. Hosp., Des Moines, 1949-61, dir. edn., 1949-59, mem. teaching staff, 1949-61; adv. med. edn. WHO, Alexandria, Egypt, 1965-66; cons. for Pakistan programs White House Office Sci. and Tech., 1966-67, Nat. Adv. Commn. on Health Manpower, 1966-67. Contbr. articles to profl. jours. Trustee Des Moines Art Ctr., 1958-61. Served with USNR, 1945-46. Fellow ACP; mem. AAAS, Mayo Alumni Assn. Home: Twin Knolls W 33d Sioux Falls SD 57105

MARGULIS, FRANCINE MARJORIE, interior designer, consultant; b. N.Y.C., Jan. 17, 1926; d. Jacob S. and Dorothy (Frieder) Kopell; m. Martin Margulis, Sept. 11, 1949; children—Barbara (dec.), Barry. B.A., NYU, 1946; M.A. in Psychology, L.I.U., 1949. Pres. Mark Interior Designers, Dayton, Ohio, 1951-74; dir. interior design Elder-Beerman Corp., Dayton, 1974-81; owner, pres. Francine Margulis A.S.I.D. Interiors, Dayton, 1981—; pres. Mega Systems Research, Dayton, 1982—; instr., developer interior design program Sinclair Coll., Dayton, 1974-81; instr. U. Dayton, 1981—. Contbr. articles to profl. jours. Panelist Ohio Women's Conf., Columbus, 1982. Recipient Merit award Sinclair Coll., 1979, Achievement award U. Dayton, 1982. Mem. Am. Soc. Interior Designers (advisor), Nat. Soc. Interior Designers (founder). Jewish. Lodge: Hadassah, Miami Valley Golf. Avocation: reading. Home: 4180 Cedar Bluff Dayton OH 45415

MARGULIS, STEPHEN T., psychologist; b. N.Y.C., Sept. 24, 1935; s. Herman and Matilda (Tash) M.; B.A., CCNY, 1956; M.A., Clark U., Worcester, Mass., 1959; Ph.D., U. Minn., 1967; m. Sharon Hope Wasserman, Sept. 24, 1935; children—Pamela Ann, Daniel Robert, Lainie Shira. Asst. prof. psychology U. Fla., Gainesville, 1965-71; research psychologist Center Bldg. Tech., Nat. Bur. Standards, Washington, 1971-81; dir. research Buffalo Orgn. Social and Tech. Innovation, 1982-86, Eugene Eppinger/Bus. and Instl. Furniture Mfgr.'s Assn.; prof. Grand Valley State Coll., Allendale, Mich., 1986—; disting. lectr. La. State U., 1973; adj. assoc. prof. Pa. State U., 1980—. Mem. Gaithersburg (Md.) Citizens Adv. Com. Consumer Affairs, 1980-81. Served with U.S. Army, 1959-60, Res., 1960-65. Faculty research grantee U. Fla., 1966; recipient applied research award Progressive Architecture mag., 1985; research award Indsl. Design mag., 1985. Mem. Am. Psychol. Assn., Environ. Design Research Assn. (sec.-treas., dir. 1979-82). Jewish. Author articles in field. Office: Grand Valley State Coll Seidman Sch of Bus 257 Lake Huron Hall Allendale MI 49401

MARI, REGINALD R., JR., civil engineer, city official; b. Springfield, Ill., June 18, 1931; s. Reginald and Rose (Colantino) M. BS, U. Ill., 1955. Registered profl. engr., Ill. Foreman pipe mill Youngstown Sheet & Tube Co., Indiana Harbor, Ind., 1955-57; field supr. constrn. elevated hwys., sewers, sts., tunnels, dock walls and airport facilities City of Chgo., 1957-76, head constrn. subsect. airport programs Bur. Engring., 1976—. Mem. ASCE, Ill. Soc. Profl. Engrs., Mid Am. Commodity Exchange. Home: 5241 NE River Rd Chicago IL 60656 Office: City of Chgo Bur Engring 320 N Clark St Chicago IL 60610

MARIA, JOSEPH MARIO, metal company executive; b. Watertown, Mass., Sept. 4, 1935; s. Vincenzo and Yolanda (Cloffie) M.; m. Margjorie Jean Mercer, Jan. 22, 1934; children: Linda Jean, Laurie Anne. BS in Acctg., Econs., Northeastern U., Boston, 1958, MBA, 1963. Acctg. mgr. Cabot Corp., Boston, 1959-66; ops. mgr. plastics div. Cabot Corp., Louisville, Ken., 1966-70; asst. corp. controller Cabot Corp., Boston, 1970-75, asst. gen. mgr. chemicals div., 1975-78; gen. mgr. metals Cabot Corp., Kokomo, Ind., 1977-82; pres. Wall Culmonoy Corp., Detroit, 1982—; also bd. dirs. Wall Culmonoy Corp., Detroit, Wales (U.K.) and Toronto. Chmn. United Fund, Burlington, Mass., 1971. Served with U.S. Army Res., 1958-64. Mem. Am. Soc. Metals, Am. Mgmt. Assn. Republican. Roman Catholic. Club: Kokomo Country. Lodge: Elks. Avocations: tennis, golf, personal computers, travel. Home: 36297 Old Homestead Dr Farmington Hills MI 48018 Office: Wall Colmonoy Corp 30261 Stephenson Hwy Madison Heights MI 48071

MARICK, MICHAEL MIRON, lawyer; b. Chgo., Nov. 20, 1957; s. Miron Michael and Geraldyne Marilyn (Lid) M.; m. Lisa Amy Gelman, May 17, 1986. BA, Denison U., 1979; JD, Ill. Inst. Tech., 1982. Bar: Ill. 1982, U.S. Dist. Ct. (no. dist.) Ill. 1982, Fla. 1983. Ptnr. Hinshaw, Culbertson, Moelmann, Hoban & Fuller, Chgo., 1982-85, Phelan, Pope & John, Chgo., 1985—; instr. Ill. Inst. Tech./Chgo.-Kent Coll. Law, 1983-84, 87; comml. arbitrator Am. Arbitration Assn., Chgo., 1983—. Contbr. to Ill. Inst. Tech./Chgo.-Kent Law Rev., 1980-82; contbr. articles on ins. law and litigation to profl. jours. Treas., mem. exec. com. 42d Ward Rep. Orgn., 1984-87. Denison U. Econs. fellow, 1978, State of Ill. Gov.'s fellow, 1978. Mem. ABA (mem. exec. com., com. on legis. action young lawyers div. 1983-84), Ill. Bar Assn., Fla. Bar Assn., Chgo. Bar Assn., Omicron Delta Upsilon, Pi Sigma Alpha, Alpha Tau Omega. Republican. Presbyterian. Clubs: East Bank, Trial Lawyers. Home: 260 E Chestnut Apt 3604 Chicago IL 60611 Office: Phelan Pope & John Ltd 180 N Wacker Dr Chicago IL 60606

MARIER, DONN JOSEPH, music composer, producer; b. Chgo., July 13, 1949; s. Eward Louis and Adrianne Isola (Incerpi) M.; m. Lisa Marie Steele, July 17, 1981; 1 child, Jennifer. Degree in composition/guitar, Chog. Music Coll., 1978. Musical dir. Dick Orkin Creative, Chgo., 1974—; pres. Marier Music Corp., Chgo., 1979—; cons. Am. Soc. Composers/Pubs., N.Y.C., 1986—; exec. dir. Walnut Record Studios, Glen Ellyn, Ill., 1985—. Composer RC Cola, 1982, Capt. Zoom's Birthday, 1978 (Gold record award), Big Green Numbers, 1978 (CLEO award 1978). Active Musicians Against Drug Abuse, Los Angeles and Chgo., Citizen's Commn. on Human Rights, Chgo., 1985—. Mem. AFTRA, Screen Actors Guild, Internat. Assn. Scientologists, Broadcast Music, Inc., Am. Fedn. of Musicians. Ch. of Scientology. Avocations: lectr. tours to children against drugs. Home: 9 Walnut Rd Glen Ellyn IL 60137

MARIETTA, KARL EDWARD, electrical engineer, administrator; b. Ligonier, Pa., Nov. 10, 1949; s. Melvin Grey and Ada (Betz) M.; m. Deborah Lynn Koerner, June 7, 1975; children—Andrew Rockwell, Geoff Eckman. B.S.E.E., Carnegie-Mellon U., 1971. Registered profl. engr., Minn., Pa., Ind. Elec. engr. Hershey Elec. Co., Pa., 1971-74, operating supt., 1974-77; elec. distbn. supt. Hibbing Pub. Utilities, Minn., 1977-80, asst. gen. mgr., 1980-81, gen. mgr., 1981-85; sr. cons. Henningson, Durham & Richardson Tech. Service, Inc., 1985—, mgr. nat. program, 1986; v.p. Mktg. Dist. Energy, St. Paul, Inc.Mem. IEEE. Republican. Presbyterian. Avocations: golf, hunting, fishing, sports. Home: 10101 Johnson Ave S Bloomington MN 55437 Office: 76 W Kellogg Blvd Saint Paul MN 55102-1611

MARINKO, MONICA MARIE, psychologist; b. Cleve., Feb. 26, 1948; d. Fred Joseph and Sophia Frances (Gornik) M. BA, U. Detroit, 1970; MA, John Carroll U., 1975. Cert. sch. psychologist, Ohio. Psychologist Ashtabula (Ohio) Area City Schs., 1975—; pvt. practice sch. psychology Chesterland, Ohio, 1985—. Mem. Nat. Assn. Sch. Psychologists, Ohio Sch. Psychologists Assn., Soc. for Personality Assessment (assoc.). Avocations: tennis, classical piano. Home: 12321 Norton Dr Chesterland OH 44026 Office: Ashtabula Area City Schs 401 W 44th St Ashtabula OH 44004

MARION, KENNETH ORVIN, marketing executive; b. Paterson, N.J., Nov. 25, 1952; s. Orvin Thomas and Regina Marie (Fitzmaurice) M.; m. Barbara Ann Schard, Apr. 15, 1983; stepchildren: Christine, John. BS, St. Peter's Coll., 1974; MBA, Seton Hall U., 1979. Mkt. research analyst Hoke, Inc., Cresskill, N.J., 1977-80; sr. mktg. research analyst Mark Controls Corp., Evanston, Ill., 1980-81, product mgr., 1981-83; product mgr. Sun Electric Corp., Crystal Lake, Ill., 1983-84, dir. mktg., 1984—; cons. Evanston, 1985—; adj. faculty Oakton Community Coll., Des Plaines, Ill., 1980—. Roman Catholic. Avocations: golf, travel, music, automobiles. Home: 2305 Sherman Ave Evanston IL 60201 Office: Sun Electric Corp 1 Sun Pkwy Crystal Lake IL 60014

MARIS, CHARLES ROBERT, surgeon, otolaryngologist; b. Champaign, Ill., Nov. 24, 1948; s. Harold Franklin and Marjorie Ellen (Beermann) M.; m. Karen Lynne Richardson, Dec. 27, 1970; children: Katherine, Emily, Charles Jr. BS, Eastern Ill. U., 1971; MD, U. Ill., 1975. Diplomate Am. Bd. Surgery, Am. Bd. Otolaryngology. Resident in otolaryngology U. Nebr. Med. Ctr., Omaha, 1982; chief of surgery Sarah Bush Lincoln Health Ctr., Mattoon, Ill., 1984-85, chmn. exec. com., 1985-86, chief of staff, 1986—; bd. dirs. Eagle Bank of Charleston, Ill. Mem. Charleston Community Unit Dist. #1 Sch. Bd., 1984. Named one of Outstanding Young Men in Am., 1985. Fellow Am. Coll. Surgeons, Am. Acad. Otolaryngology-Head and Neck Surgery, Am. Acad. Facial Plastic and Reconstructive Surgery. Republican. Methodist. Office: 200 Professional Plaza Mattoon IL 61938-9250

MARITZ, WILLIAM E., communications company executive; b. St. Louis; m. Phyllis Mesker; 4 children. Grad., Princeton U., 1950. With Maritz Inc., St. Louis, now chief exec. officer. Bd. dirs. Community Sch., John Burroughs Sch., Princeton U., Sta. KETC, Mo. Bot. Garden, St. Luke's Hosp., Washington U., Brown Group, Am. Youth Found., Camping and Edn. Found., Cystic Fibrosis, others; founder, chmn. bd. Laclede's Landing Devel. Corp., St. Louis; chmn. bd. VP Fair Found. Recipient Levee Stone award Downtown St. Louis; Right Arm of St. Louis award, Regional Commerce and Growth Assn. Served with USN. Home: #10 Upper Ladue Rd Saint Louis MO 63124 Office: Maritz Inc 1375 N Highway Dr Fenton MO 63026 *

MARK, RICHARD ALLEN, accountant; b. Omaha, May 23, 1953; s. Walter Noel Mark and Frances Dorothy (Reiman) Chaffee; m. Rebecca Louise McDonald, June 26, 1977; children: Christopher Allen, Alexander James. BS, Nebraska Wesleyan U., 1975; M Mgmt., Northwestern U., 1977. Staff acct. Arthur Andersen & Co., Chgo., 1977-79, sr., 1979-81, mgr., 1981—. Treas. Sch. Community Resource Ctr., Wheaton, Ill., 1983-84; class rep. Nebr. Wesleyan U., Lincoln, 1985—; elder Hope Presbyn. Ch., Wheaton, 1987—. Mem. Am. Inst. CPA's, Ill. CPA Soc., Blue Key, Order of DeMolay, Council Young Profls., Omicron Delta Epsilon, Phi Kappa Tau (domain dir. 1984-86). Republican. Presbyterian. Club: Arrowhead Swim & Tennis (treas. Wheaton 1984—). Lodge: Masons. Home: 26 W 319 Blackhawk Wheaton IL 60187 Office: Arthur Andersen & Co 33 W Monroe Chicago IL 60603

MARK, RICHARD JOSEPH, municipal government official; b. Collinsville, Ill., July 7, 1955; s. Joseph and Cleola (Merrifield) M.; m. Melissa Adler, June 21, 1980; children: Fontez, Joseph. BS, Iowa State U., 1977. Youth service coordinator City of Collinsville, Ill., 1980-81, adminstrv. asst. to mayor, 1981-83; asst. customer service supr. Ill. Power Co., Belleville, 1983-84; dep. dir. St. Clair County Intergovtl. Grants Dept., Belleville, 1984—. Chmn. Programs/Services for Older Persons, Belleville, 1980; sec. Collinsville Humane Soc., 1984; vice chmn. Collinsville Conv. Authority. Named One of Outstanding Young Men of Am., 1981, 85; recipient Humanitarian award City of Collinsville, 1982, Collinsville Humane Soc., 1986. Mem. Ill. Assn. of Employment and Tng. Dirs. (exec. com. 1984—), Ill. Employment and Tng. Assn. (sec. 1984), Dislocated Worker Assn. Office: St Clair County Intergovtl Grants Dept 512 E Main St Belleville IL 62220

MARKAND, OMKAR NATH, neurologist, electroencephalographer; b. Chhindwara, India, Mar. 28, 1936; came to U.S., 1966; s. Mehar Chand and Shanti Markand; m. Pramila Lal, Aug. 25, 1963; children: Vaneeta, Sandhya. BS, Nagpur Med. Coll., India, 1958, MD, 1962. Diplomate Am. Bd. Psychiatry and Neurology. Asst. prof. Southwestern Med. Sch., Dallas, 1969-72; assoc. prof. Ind. U. Med. Sch., Indpls., 1972-77, prof. neurology, 1977—. Fellow Royal Coll. Physicians Can., Am. Acad. Neurology, Am. EEG Soc. Office: Ind U Sch Med Riley Hosp 702 Barnhill Dr Indianapolis IN 46223

MARKER, EVELYN LUCINDA, hospital executive; b. Westerville, Ohio, Jan. 5, 1951; d. Forrest H. and Mary Louise (Mikesell) Schar; m. Michael R. Prenzlin, Mar. 24, 1972 (div. Feb. 1981); children—Matthew Eric, Mark Andrew; m. Wayne L. Marker, Jr., Sept. 14, 1985. B.A. in English, Heidelberg Coll, 1982. Dir. devel. and pub. relations Mercy Hosp., Tiffin, Ohio, 1980—. Author: (with others) Drug Abuse Prevention for Children workbook, 1980. Bd. dirs. Sandusky Valley Substance Abuse Prevention, Tiffin, 1980-82, Northwest Ohio Health Planning Agy., Toledo, Ohio, 1978-81, United Services for Alcoholism, Tiffin, 1983-85; v.p. Community Council, Tiffin, 1984—. Mem. Nat. Assn. for Hosp. Devel. (cert.), Ohio Assn. for Hosp. Devel. (regional v.p. 1984-85), Northwest Ohio Hosp. Council, Tiffin C. of C. (bd. dirs.). Republican. Methodist. Office: Mercy Hosp 485 W Market St Tiffin OH

MARKHAM, MARION M., writer; b. Chgo., June 12, 1929; d. William Joseph and Marion (Dammann) Bork; m. Robert Bailey Markham, Dec. 30, 1955; children—Susan Markham Andersen, Jane Markham Madden. B.S. in Speech, Northwestern U., 1953. Continuity dir. Sta. WTVP, Decatur, Ill., 1953-54; TV bus. mgr. Earle Ludgin Advt. Co., Chgo., 1955-58; free-lance writer, Northbrook, Ill., 1967—. Novels include: Escape from Velos, 1981; The Halloween Candy Mystery, 1982; The Christmas Present Mystery, 1984; The Thanksgiving Day Parade Mystery, 1986; contbr. articles and short stories to mags. and jours. Bd. dirs. Northbrook Pub. Library, 1976-86, pres. bd., 1981-83. Mem. Soc. Children's Book Writers, Sci. Fiction Writers Am., Authors Guild, Mystery Writers Am. (midwest regional v.p. 1977-78, dir. 1983-87), Soc. Midland Authors (dir. Chgo. 1983-86). Home and office: 2415 Newport Rd Northbrook IL 60062

MARKHAM, MARSHALL (DANNY), newspaper editor, publisher; b. Janesville, Wis., Nov. 22, 1929; s. Dan S. and Mary J. (Earleywine) M.; m. Helen R. Gerber; children: Kim, Kurt, Colet, Collen, Kent. BS, U. Wis., 1951. Various positions, now editor Brodhead (Wis.) Ind. Register, 1952—. Coach Brodhead grade sch. basketball team, 1952-62; asst. coach. Brodhead jr. legion baseball, 1954. Mem. Wis. Newspaper Assn. (chmn. Green County Dairy Days 1984), Brodhead Jaycees (nat. dir. Wis. 1960, pres. 1961, local dir. 1985—, chmn. Brodhead Little League com. 1956, Outstanding Young Man 1957, editor Wis. J.C. mag. 1958). Methodist. Home: 601 14th St Brodhead WI 53520 Office: Brodhead Ind Register 922 W Exchange St Brodhead WI 53520

MARKIEWICZ, JAMES EDWARD, manufacturing executive; b. Chgo., Sept. 14, 1932; s. Edward James and Eugenia Elizabeth (Formanski) M.; m. Mary Lou Henneberg, June 7, 1952; 1 child, Sharon Markiewicz Schnider. Student, U. Ill., Chgo., 1950-51, Northrop Areo. Inst., 1951-52, DeVry Inst. Tech., 1952-54. Various positions Precision Extrusions Inc., Bensenville, Ill., 1950-70, v.p. mfg., 1970—. Patent quenching apparatus for extruded articles; contbr. articles to profl. jours. Served with USNR. Roman Catholic. Club: Medinah (Ill.) Country (bd. dirs. 1985-87). Home: 604 White Oak Dr Roselle IL 60172 Office: Precision Extrusions Inc 720 E Green St Bensenville IL 60106

MARKING, T(HEODORE) JOSEPH, JR., transportation and urban planner; b. Shelbyville, Ind., June 28, 1945; s. Theodore Joseph and Alvena Cecelia (Thieman) M.; B.A., So. Ill. U., 1967, M. City and Regional Planning, 1972; m. Kathy K. Hagerman, Nov. 25, 1969. Intelligence research specialist Def. Intelligence Agy., Washington, 1967-68; planner I, St. Louis City Plan Commn., 1970; transp. planner Alan M. Voorhees & Assocs., St. Louis, 1970-74, sr. transp. planner, 1974-78, assoc., 1978; sr. transp. planner Booker Assocs., Inc., St. Louis, 1978-80, chief traffic and transp. sect., 1980-85; mgr. transit planning East-West Gateway Coordinating Council, St. Louis, 1985—; planner-in-charge, Mo.; guest lectr. St. Louis Community Coll. Dist., Webster U., St. Louis U. Mem. Am. Inst. Cert. Planners (charter), Am. Planning Assn. (charter; past pres. St. Louis sect.), Inst. Transp. Engrs., Traffic Engrs. Assn. Met. St. Louis (past pres.). Office: 911 Washington Ave Saint Louis MO 63101

MARKLE, ALLAN, psychologist; b. Chgo., Feb. 4, 1941; s. Louis and Elaine (Hershman) M.; m. Marveen Ormsby, Sept. 25, 1966 (div. Oct. 1978); children: Ronald, Richard. BS, U. Ill., 1962; MA, Ga. State U., 1971, PhD, 1972. Registered psychologist, Ill. Staff psychologist Elgin State Hosp., Elgin, Ill., 1965-68; asst. prof. Lake Forest (Ill.) Coll., 1972-74; gen. practice psychology Northbrook, Ill., 1972—; coordinator behavior dysfunction clinic VA Med. Ctr., North Chicago, Ill., 1979—; coordinator outpatient Huntsville (Ala.) Mental Heath Ctr., 1974-78; adj. prof. Chgo. Med. Sch., North Chicago, Ill., 1978—; cons. Maryville Acad., Des Plaines, Ill., 1985—. Coauthor: Author's Guide to Journals in Psychology, 1976, Positive Parenting, 1977, Achievement Motivation Training, 1978; contbg. author over 25 book chapters and jour. articles. Mem. Am. Psychol. Assn., Ill. Psychol. Assn., South Ea. Psychol. Assn., Assn. for Advancement of Behavior Therapy. Jewish. Avocation: bowling. Office: VA Med Ctr North Chicago IL 60064

MARKLE, CHERI VIRGINIA CUMMINS, nurse; b. N.Y.C., Nov. 22, 1936; d. Brainard Lyle and Mildred (Schwab) Cummins; m. John Markle, Aug. 26, 1961 (dec. 1962); 1 child, Kellianne. RN, Ind. State U., 1959; BS in Rehab. Edn., Wright State U., 1975; BSN, Capital U., 1987; postgrad. in Nursing Adminstrn., Wright State U., 1987—. Coordinator Dayton (Ohio) Children's Psychiat. Hosp., 1962-75; dir. nursing Stillwater Health Ctr., Dayton, 1975-76; sr. supr. VA, Dayton, 1977-85, alcohol rehab. nurse coordinator, 1985-86; dir. nursing Odd Fellows, Springfield, Ohio, 1987—; rehab. cons., Fairborn, Ohio, 1976—. Served to 1st lt., USAF, 1959-61. Mem. Am. Nurses Assn. (cert. adminstrn. 1983, cert. gerontology 1984), Ohio Nurses Assn., Dist. 10 Nurses Assn., Nat. Assn. Female Execs., Rehab. Soc., Wright State U. Alumni Assn., Am. Legion, Alpha Sigma Alpha. Democrat. Roman Catholic. Avocations: cats, reading, music, needlework, swimming. Home: 539 South St Fairborn OH 45324 Office: Odd Fellows 404 E McCreight Ave Springfield OH 45503

MARKLE, RONALD D., manufacturing executive; b. Pitts., Aug. 12, 1932; s. Alzona A. and Elda M. (Klousner) M.; m. Geraldine F. Paul, 1954; children: James R., Jonathan F., Steven P. BE in Metall. Engring., Youngstown State U., 1971; MBA, Xavier U., 1981. Materials mgr. TRW Metals, Minerva, Ohio, 1962-73; plant mgr. Aerobraze Corp., Cin., 1973-75, v.p., plant mgr., 1975-78, v.p., gen. mgr., 1978-85, pres., chief operating officer, 1985—. Author: (with others) Ceramic-Core Removal Process-Investment Castings, 1965. Pres. Woodlawn (Ohio) Bus. Assn., 1980-82. Served to sgt. USMC, 1952-55. Mem. Am. Soc. for Metals (chmn. Cin. chpt. 1984-85), Am. Soc. Quality Control (sr.). Republican. Roman Catholic. Lodge: Kiwanis. Avocation: woodworking.

MARKLEY, JOHN MARTIN, JR., plastic and reconstructive surgeon; b. Pontiac, Mich., Feb. 12, 1941; s. John Martin and Ruth Louise (Weiler) M.; Barbara Carlson, Sept. 2, 1967. MD cum laude, U. Mich., 1966. Diplomate Am. Bd. Plastic Surgery. Resident in gen. plastic and reconstructive surgery Stanford U., Palo Alto, Calif., 1967-72; fellow in hand surgery Columbia-Roosevelt, N.Y.C., 1972-73; clin. asst. prof. U. Mich., Ann Arbor, 1974—; head dept. plastic surgery Wayne County (Mich.) Gen. Hosp., 1974-78; head sect. plastic surgery VA Hosp., Ann Arbor, 1976-78; head dept. plastic surgery St. Joseph Mercy Hosp., Ann Arbor, 1982-86; cons. hand surgery sect. plastic surgery U. Mich., 1983—. Contbr. articles to profl. jours. Mem. various neighborhood coms. Mem. Am. Soc. Surgery of the Hand, Am. Soc. Plastic and Reconstructive Surgeons, AMA, J. William Littler Soc., Mich. Acad. Plastic Surgeons, ACS, Alpha Omega Alpha, Phi Delta Epsilon. Avocations: cycling, cross-country skiing, classical guitar. Office: 3075 W Clark Rd #310 Ypsilanti MI 48104

MARKOFF, RICHARD MICHAEL, fund raiser; b. Fostoria, Ohio, Oct. 1, 1946; s. Jack Hy and Carolyn Mamie (Shiff) M.; m. Beverly Ann Schall, July 30, 1972; children: Steven Charles, Matthew Nathaniel. BS, Western Mich. U., 1968; MEd, U. Mo., 1970; PhD, U. Toledo, 1978. Dir. alumni relations Western Mich. U., Kalamazoo, 1972-74; assoc. dir. devel. Adrian (Mich.) Coll., 1977-81, assoc. to v.p. of devel., 1981-83; pres. St. Vincent Med. Ctr. Found., Toledo, 1983—; pres. Mid. Am. Conf. Alumni Devel. and Pub. Relations Officers, 1974; conf. dir. The Hows & Whys of Telephone Campaigns, 1979. Contbr. articles to profl. jours. Pres. Congregation Etz Chayim, Toledo, 1982-84; bd. trustees Darlington House Jewish Home for Aged, Toledo, 1981-82; chmn. Tenth Anniversary Security Fund Campaign, 1984; community relations com. Jewish Fedn., 1985—; mem. parents council Sylvania Schs, 1986—. Served to 1st lt. U.S. Army, 1970-72. Decorated Bronze Star; Cross of Gallantry with Palm, Vietnam, 1972; recipient Synagogue Leadership award Union of Orthodox Jewish Synagogues of Am., 1984; named One of Outstanding Young Men in Am., 1978. Mem. Ohio Hosp. Devel. Assn., Toledo Area Fundraisers (exec. com. 1985-86, chmn. 1987), VFW. Republican. Jewish. Avocations: baseball card collecting, bicycle riding. Home: 2308 Chriswood Rd Toledo OH 43617 Office: Saint Vincent Med Ctr Found 2213 Cherry Toledo OH 43623

MARKS, DANELLE MILLER, marketing executive; b. Fairfield, Calif., Oct. 5, 1958; d. Burr Van Jr. and Eleanor Amelia (Gordy) M.; m. Jerrell Kevin Marks, Aug. 31, 1985. BBA, U. Tulsa, 1980; MA in Pub. Relations, Ball State U., 1986. Dir. mktg. ATE Mgmt. and Service Co., Indpls. and Peoria, Ind. and Ill., 1980-84, CopyRite, Inc., Indpls., 1984; account exec. Pearson, Crahan, Fletcher Group, Indpls., 1984-85; mktg. dir. Medi-Span, Inc., Indpls., 1985—; cons. mass transit ATE Mgmt., Tulsa and Peoria, 1983; chmn. circlefest Indpls. Downtown Promotion Council, 1983-84. Promotional support Indpls. Civic Theatre, 1982-86, Indpls. Symphony Orch., 1985; vol. Indpls. Mus. Art Alliance, 1984-86; bd. dirs. Ind. Poison Awareness Council, Indpls., 1985-86, pres. 1987. Mem. Pub. Relations Soc. Am., Chi Omega Alumni. Republican. Lutheran. Office: Medi-Span Inc 5980 W 71st St Indianapolis IN 46268-0875

MARKS, MARTIN, podiatrist; b. Chgo., Aug. 6, 1952; s. Michael and Helen Rae (Hyman) M.; m. Sindy I. Marks, Sept. 12, 1982; children: Matthew, Samantha. BA in Psychology, Northeastern Ill. U., 1974; D Podiatric Medicine, Ill. Coll. Podiatric Medicine, 1981. Resident podiatry Am. Internat. Hosp., Zion, Ill., 1982-83, asst. dir. podiatric residency program, 1984; adj. clin. staff William School Coll. Podiatric Medicine, Chgo., 1985—; staff Valley Hi Nursing Home, Woodstock, Ill., 1985—, Regent's Park Nursing Home, Barrington, Ill., 1986—; lectr. and demonstrator surgery Am. Internat. Hosp., 1986. Contbr. articles to profl. jours. Mem. Am. Podiatric Med. Assn., Ill. Podiatric Med. Assn. Home: 219 Vintage Ln Buffalo Grove IL 60089 Office: 1311 N Green St McHenry IL 60050 also: 1410 S Barrington Rd Barrington IL 60010

MARKS, PHYLLIS R., information systems specialist; b. Cin., Dec. 1, 1959; d. Emanuel I. and Shirley R. (Hoodin) M. BSBA, Ohio State U., 1982; MBA, Xavier U., 1984. Computer cons. Batesville (Ind.) Casket Co., 1984-86; office systems analyst div. project mgmt. Battelle Meml. Inst., Columbus, Ohio, 1986—. Vol. Operation Friendship Franklin County Children Services. Mem. Nat. Assn. Female Execs. Avocation: tennis. Home: 6265 Century City N Reynoldsburg OH 43068 Office: Battelle Project Mgmt Div 505 King Ave Columbus OH 43201

MARKS, RENEE LEE, educator; b. Chgo., Nov. 20, 1936; d. Sol and Celia (Freund) Kaplan; B.J.S., Northwestern U., 1958, postgrad. (Chgo. Bd. Edn. scholar), summer 1978; B.J.S., Spertus Coll., 1972; M.A., Mundelein Coll., 1975; M.Ed. with distinction, De Paul U., 1981; postgrad. in edn1. adminstrn. Northeastern Ill. U., 1980-81; cert. in adminstrn. and supervision Nat. Coll. Edn., Evanston, Ill., 1982, postgrad., 1985—; cert. in computer sci. U. Ill.-Chgo., 1982-85; postgrad. Nat. Coll. of Edn., 1984—; m. Donald Norman Marks, June 22, 1958; children—Robin Debra Marks Dombeck, Steven Michael, Jody Ilene. Tchr. Chgo. Bd. Edn., 1976—; lectr. on Holocaust. Mem. Nat. Council for Social Studies, Chgo. Council for Social Studies, Assn. for Supervision and Curriculum Devel., Am. Ednl. Research Assn., Nat. Soc. for Study of Edn., Phi Delta Kappa. Jewish. Author, Holocaust curriculum for Chgo. Bd. Edn., 1980. Home and Office: 9036 N Menard Morton Grove IL 60053

MARKS, RONNIE FAIN, manufacturers representative, consultant; b. Detroit, May 2, 1953; s. Roger Campbell and Helen Lucille (Saunders) M.; m. Clara Helen Salisbury, June 14, 1975; children—Jennifer Marie, Ronald Austin. Student Henry Ford Coll., Dearborn, Mich., 1972-75; B.B.A., U. Detroit, 1978, M.B.A., 1981. Indsl. engr. Demco, Detroit, 1973-75, sales engr., 1975-77, asst. to v.p., 1977, mfg. mgr., 1978; account mgr. GRM Industries, Grand Rapids, Mich., 1978-83; mfrs. rep. T.S. Maentz, Inc., Troy, Mich., 1983-86; pres. Marks Mgmt. Services, Inc., Bloomfield Hills, Mich., 1985—, Challenge Sales Co., Birmingham, Mich., 1987—. Fund raiser Republican Party, Canton, Mich., 1982. Named hon. Ky. col. Fellow Am. Mktg. Assn.; mem. Assn. M.B.A. Grads., Nat. Assn. Bus. Economists, Indsl. Mktg. Group, Detroit Assn. Bus. Economists, Detroit Soc. of Clubs, Delta Sigma Pi (treas. 1976-78), Alpha Sigma Lambda. Republican. Lutheran. Clubs: Fairlane (Dearborn); Pine Lake Country (Orchard Lake, Mich.). Home: 5390 Vincennes Dr Bloomfield Hills MI 48013

MARKS, TIMOTHY LEE, publishing executive; b. Ottawa, Ill., May 8, 1959; s. Donald Lee and Helen Joyce (Smith) M.; m. Julie Anne Achord, Sept. 3, 1983. BS in Indsl. Tech. and Graphic Arts, Ill. State U., 1981. Asst. prodn. mgr. Hitchcock Pub. Co., Wheaton, Ill., 1981-83, prodn. mgr., 1983-87; tech. services rep. Blandin Paper Co., Chgo., 1987—. Named Eagle Scout Boy Scouts Am., 1973. Roman Catholic. Avocations: swimming, photography, racquetball, rapelling. Home: 1325 Morningstar Ct Naperville IL 60565 Office: Blandin Paper Co 20 N Wacker Dr Chicago IL 60606

MARKS, VIRGINIA PANCOAST, music educator; b. Phila., Feb. 9, 1940; d. Ace and Catherine (Regensberger) Pancoast; m. Edward J. Marks, 1961 (div. 1987); children: Brian Charles, Jennifer Anne. BS in Music, Temple U., 1961; USM, American U., 1965. Instr. Settlement Music Sch., Phila., 1957-62, Cornell U., Ithaca, N.Y., 1966-67, Temple U., Phila., 1968-69; prof., coordinator of keyboard studies Bowling Green (Ohio) State U., 1972—; concert pianist Recitals in major cities throughout U.S., 1964—, guest artist Spoleto Festival Spoleto, Italy. Recording Artist Educo Records. Martha Baird Rockefeller grantee; recipient Teaching award Bowling Green State U., 1980-82, 1st Prize Concert Artists Guild, N.Y.C., 1st Prize Mu Phi Epsilon Internat. Competition. Mem. Music Tchrs. Nat. Assn., Ohio Music Tchrs. Assn. (2d v.p. 1985—). Avocations: gardening, travel, finance, reading, photography. Office: Bowling Green State U Coll of Mus Arts Bowling Green OH 43403

MARKUN, PAUL RUPERT, entrepreneur, motion picture producer; b. Mpls., Sept. 4, 1944; s. John Franklin Markun and Colette Elizabeth (Loegering) Brown; m. Kay Elizabeth Weiler, Jan. 14, 1978. Dept. mgr. Douglas Film Industries, Inc., Chgo., 1970-76; v.p. The Media Works, Inc., Chgo., 1976-77; pres. Sharpe-Markun, Inc., Chgo., 1977-79, The Media Machine, Chgo., 1978-79, Skylite Communications, Inc., Chgo., 1979-85, ETEK Industries, Inc., Chgo., 1984—. Inventor Mileage Minder, 1982, AlertAlarm, 1983, Time Delay Switch, 1983. Mem. Soc. Motion Picture and TV Engrs. (sec.-treas. 1976-79, 83-85, mgr. 1979-83), Info. Film Producers Am. (sec.-treas. 1977, pres. 1978), Variety Clubs Internat. Democrat. Club: Union League (Chgo.). Avocations: golf, skiing, inventing.

MARKUS, JOEL SETH, data processing management executive; b. Kansas City, Mo., Oct. 11, 1950; s. Milton Jerome and Ethel (Ginsberg) M.; m. Glenna Rae Shinkle, Apr. 1, 1984. Student, Bradley U., 1968-71; cert. in data processing, U. Mo., 1972; A in Applied Sci., Penn Valley Community Coll., 1975. Data processing clk. United Mo. Bank Kansas City, 1973-74, programmer, 1975-76, systems programmer, 1977-81, project mgr., 1982-83, v.p. communication systems, 1982—. Scholarship chmn. Jewish Com. on Scouting, Kansas City, 1985-86, sec.-treas., 1987; active adult edn com. Beth

Shalom Congregation, Kansas City, 1987; v.p. Morningview Homes Assn., Overland Park, Kans., 1987. Recipient Shofar award Jewish Com. on Scouting, 1986; named to Eagle Scouts Boy Scouts Am., 1966. Mem. Kansas City IMS Users Group (sec. 1978-79). Democrat. Avocations: tennis, electronics. Home: 9742 Antioch Overland Park KS 66212 Office: United Mo Bank Kansas City 928 Grand Ave PO Box 226 Kansas City MO 64141

MARKWARDT, MARK, marketing communications executive; b. Sheboygan, Wis., May 18, 1951; s. Solomon Immanuel and Florence Alma (Oehldrich) M.; m. Kathleen Jo Born, Apr. 20, 1974; 1 child, Benjamin Brenton. BBA in Mktg., U. Wis., Milw., 1973. Cert. bus. communicator. Sales specifications coordinator Kohler (Wis.) Co., 1973-75; sales coordinator Hayssen Mfg. Co., Sheboygan, Wis., 1975-78; mgr. replacement parts processing Hayssen Mfg. Co., Sheboygan, 1978-81, mgr. mktg. communications, 1981—; free-lance writer and photographer, 1986—. Contbr. articles on form/fill/seal packaging machinery and applications to Snack Food, Good Packaging, Packaging mags. Mem. Internat. Exhibitors Assn., Bus./Profl. Advt. Assn. Avocation: photography. Home: 2614 N 10th St Sheboygan WI 53083 Office: Hayssen Mfg Co Hwy 42 N Sheboygan WI 53082-0571

MARLEY, ANNE HARDER, controller; b. Topeka, Jan. 22, 1959; d. Robert Clarence and Dorothy Lou (Welty) H.; m. Dennis G. Marley, May 30, 1981. BS, Baker U., 1981. CPA, Kans. Auditor Grant Thornton, Kansas City, Mo., 1981-86; controller Profl. Rehab. Mgmt., Olathe, Kans., 1986—. Youth group sponsor Valley View United Meth. Ch., Overland Park, Kans., 1981—; vol. Pets for Life, Kansas City, Mo., 1986—. Mem. Am. Inst. CPA's, Mo. Soc. CPA's, Alpha Delta Sigma, Phi Mu. Democrat. Avocations: folk art stenciling, reading, traveling. Office: Profl Rehab Mgmt 201 E Santa Fe Olathe KS 66061

MARLOW, ANDREW JOSEPH, communications executive; b. Lake City, Minn., Feb. 20, 1944; s. Robert Winfred and Eleanor May (Sirvas) M.; m. Phyllis Jean Stromberg, June 21, 1975; children: Philip Stromberg, Emily Stromberg. BA, St. Cloud State Coll., 1970. Media buyer Fischbein Advt., Mpls., 1970; instr. Rainy River Community Coll., Internat. Falls, Minn., 1970-72; producer KUOM Radio U. Minn., Mpls., 1972-78, sr. producer, 1978—. Pres. Bellgrove Improvement Assn., Hopkins, Minn., 1983; sec., v.p., pres. Men's Garden Club, Mpls., 1982-85. Mem. Minn. AP Broadcasters (pres. 1982), Assn. Minn. Pub./Ednl. Radio Stas. (rep. 1974—), Model Cities Communications Ctr. (bd. dirs. 1974-80), Migizi Communications (bd. dirs. 1978-84). Presbyterian. Avocations: gardening, computers. Home: 10700 Minnetonka Blvd Hopkins MN 55343 Office: U Minn KUOM Radio 550 Rarig Ctr 330 21st Ave S Minneapolis MN 55455

MARMON, OWEN HOLLOWAY, insurance company executive; b. Detroit, Jan. 18, 1923; s. Ira H. and Lillian H. M.; m. Marilyn J. Rowley, June 15, 1946; children: Nancy, Barbara, Rebecca. B.A., Mich. State U., 1947. With Auto-Owners Ins. Co., Lansing, Mich., 1947—; treas. Auto-Owners Ins. Co., 1971-73, v.p., treas., 1973-75, sec.-treas., 1975-81, pres., treas., 1981—, chmn., chief exec. officer, 1986—, also dir.; dir. Auto-Owners Life Ins. Co., Home-Owners Ins. Co., Owners Ins. Co., Property Owners Ins. Co., First of Am.-Central, First of Am. Bank Corp. Bd. dirs. Sparrow Hosp. Served to 1st lt. USAAF, 1942-45. Mem. Nat. Assn. Ind. Insurers (dir.). Republican. Methodist. Club: Walnut Hills Country. Office: Auto-Owners Ins Co 6101 Anacapri Blvd Lansing MI 48917

MAROHL, RUDOLPH OTTO, manufacturing executive, mechanical engineer; b. Hankinson, N.D., May 22, 1938; s. Emil W. and Lily (Henke) M.; m. Mary Beth Wipperman, Aug. 26, 1961; children—Beth Marie, Michael Anthony. B.S.M.E., U. N.D., 1962; A.S., N.D. State Sch. Sci., 1960. Mem. tech. staff Westinghouse Corp., Idaho Falls, 1962-69; v.p. Nuclear Pacific Inc., Seattle, 1970-75; pres. Central Research div. Sargent Industries, Red Wing, Minn., 1976—. Author/editor: Remote Manipulation, 1984. Bd. dirs. St. Paul's Found., Red Wing, 1984—, Red Wing Hockey Assn., 1979-81; pres. Red Wing Mfg. Assn., 1981, advisor, 1982-83. Served with U.S. Army, 1956-58; Korea. Recipient Meritorious Service award Westinghouse Corp., 1966, ASME, 1970. Mem. ASME (vice-chmn. 1969), Am. Nuclear Soc., Soc. Mfg. Engrs., Robotics Internat. (sr.), Pres. Assn. Lutheran. Lodge: Elks (Red Wing). Avocations: golf; carpentry.

MAROLD, DAVID WILLIAM, marketing executive; b. Waterloo, Iowa, July 11, 1947; s. Fredrick William Marold and Mary Elizabeth (Burrow) Sorensen; m. Karen Anne Eagle, July 24, 1971; children: Christopher, Erick, Kevin. BS, U. Iowa, 1969; MBA, No. Ill. U., 1973. Mgr. reinsurance planning Ford Motor Credit, Dearborn, Mich., 1973-78, mgr. dir. mktg., 1978-82; various positions R.L. Polk, Taylor, Mich., 1982-85, account group mgr., 1985, asst. automotive sales mgr., 1986—. Served with U.S. Army, 1970-72. Mem. Direct Mktg. Assn. Detroit (treas. 1982-83, exec. v.p. 1983-84, pres. 1984-85), Adcraft Club Detroit, Motor City Packards (pres. 1981-82). Clubs: Recess (Detroit), Packard (dir. Los Angeles chpt. 1983-87). Avocations: packard automobiles, golf. Home: 660 Potomac Northville MI 48167 Office: RL Polk 6400 Monroe Blvd Taylor MI 48180

MAROTTA, RICHARD NATHAN, engineer; b. Rockford, Ill., Sept. 1, 1941; s. Sam and Angelina (Cremi) M.; m. Linda Sue Welsby, July 24, 1968; children—Jeffery, Cynthia. Student Rockford Coll., 1962, Milw. Sch. Engring., 1964, R.C.A., 1965-68. Control engr. Ingersoll, Rockford, 1964-72; project engr. Beloit Corp., Wis., 1972-74; chief control engr. Feldmanan Inc., Rockford, 1974—; pres., owner Control Ltd., Rockford, 1974—. Patentee temperature controller, 1973, constant-speed drive, 1974. Mem. Fluid Power Soc. (pres. 1977-78). Republican, Lutheran. Avocation: electronics. Home: 1123 Prestwick Pkwy Rockford IL 61107 Office: 4902 Hydraulic Dr Rockford IL 61109

MAROUS, JAMES EDWARD, JR., banker; b. Cleve., Mar. 29, 1954; s. James Edward and Jean (Michell) M.; m. Linda Booth, July 26, 1980. B.S. in Fin. and Acctg., Miami U., Oxford, Ohio, 1976; M.B.A. in Fin., Cleve. State U., 1978; grad. Sch. Bank Mktg., Boulder, Colo., 1983. Mgmt. trainee Nat. City Bank, Cleve., 1976-79, bus. devel. officer, 1979-81; mktg. dir. Women's Fed. Savs. Bank, Cleve., 1981-84; sr. v.p. Mid-Am. Fed. Savs. and Loan, Columbus, Ohio, 1984—; dir. Fin. Instn. Marketers Ohio, Cleve., 1986—, pres., 1984-85, 85-86. Vice pres. Nat. Jr. Tennis League, Cleve., 1980-82; chmn. Mayoral Campaign, Shaker Heights, Ohio, 1983; mem. com. Arsenal Arts Ctr., Columbus, 1986—; exec. dir. Red, White and Blue Com., Columbus, 1986—. Mem. Bank Mktg. Assn., Cleve. Jaycees. Avocations: Coin collecting, cycling. Home: 1021 Cross Country Worthington OH 43085 Office: Mid-Am Fed Savs and Loan 175 S 3d St Columbus OH 43215

MAROUS, RICHARD SAYLE, tennis league administrator; b. Shaker Heights, Ohio, Mar. 13, 1922; s. James Edward and Mona (Sayle) M.; m. Janet Marie Cox, Nov. 25, 1948; children—Richard, James, Don. A.B. in Econs. and Phys. Edn., Baldwin-Wallace Coll., 1949; postgrad. Bowling Green State U., 1949-50. Tchr. pub. schs., Shaker Heights, 1950-57; dir. parks and adult edn. City of Shaker Heights, 1957-80; dir. parks, recreation and properties City of Cleve., 1980-83; exec. dir. Greater Cleve. chpt. Nat. Jr. Tennis League, 1983—; con. Exec. Caterers, Landerhaven, 1986—; cons. in field. Mem. allocation com. United Appeal; mem. Greater Cleve. council Boy Scouts Am.; mem. fine arts com. Cleve. Mus. Art; bd. dirs. YMCA. Served with USN, 1943-46. Recipient Order of Merit, Greater Cleve. council Boy Scouts Am., 1970, Pres. Citation, 1975. Mem. Nat. Recreation and Park Assn. (outstanding contbn. award 1976), Ohio Parks and Recreation Assn. (pres. 1973-74). Methodist. Club: Shaker Heights Country. Lodge: Rotary (pres. 1967-68). Contbr. articles to profl. jours. and mags. Home and office: 3295 Kenmore Rd Shaker Heights OH 44122

MAROVITZ, WILLIAM A., state senator, lawyer; b. Chgo., Sept. 29, 1944; s. Sydney Robert and Jane (Chulock) M.; B.A., U. Ill., 1966; J.D., DePaul U., 1969. Admitted to Ill. bar, 1970; tchr. Chgo. Bd. Edn., 1969-70; partner firm Marovitz, Powell, Pizer & Edelstein, Chgo., 1970-82; asst. corp. counsel City of Chgo., 1973-74; mem. Ill. State Ho. of Reps., 1975-80; mem. Ill. State Senate, 1981—. Mem. Young Men's Jewish Council; chmn. Spanish Speaking Peoples' Study Commn. in Ill., 1976—, High-Rise Fire Commn. Mem. Ill. Bar Assn., Chgo. Bar Assn., Decalogue Soc. Lawyers. Recipient Chgo. Met. Outstanding Citizen award, 1976; named Best Freshman Legislator, Ill. Young Democrats, 1975; Best Freshman Senator, 1981, Chgo. Jaycees, 1976 (Young Citizens award). Jewish. Office: 134 N LaSalle St Chicago IL 60602

MARQUARDT, THOMAS JAMES, dentist; b. Springfield, Ohio, Dec. 16, 1945; s. John William and Colette Mildred (Buchman) M.; div. Sept. 1975; children: Thomas Leo, David Thomas; m. Kerria Lou Sigler, Jan 28., 1986. DDS, Case Western Res. U., 1969. Gen. practice dentistry Sunland Tng. Ctr., Gainsville, Fla., 1971-72, Mansfield, Ohio, 1973—. Dental examiner Save-A-Child Identification Program, Mansfield, 1984-86. Served to lt. USN, 1969-71. Mem. ADA, Ohio Dental Assn., Cen. Ohio Dental Assn., Mansfield Dental Soc. (v.p. 1985, pres. elect 1986—, pres. 1986-87). Avocations: skiing, scuba diving, backpacking, photography. Home: 58 Parkwood Blvd Mansfield OH 44906 Office: 100 Vennum Ave Mansfield OH 44903

MARQUART, STEVEN LEONARD, lawyer; b. Georgetown, Minn., Feb. 2, 1954; s. Leonard Matthew and Gladys Viola (Myhre) M.; m. Cynthia Lou Smerud, June 21, 1975; children: Stephanie Lynn, Angela Marie, Andrew Steven. BA in Polit. Sci., Moorhead State U., 1976; JD with distinction, U. N.D., 1979. Bar: Minn. 1979, N.D. 1979, U.S. Dist. Ct. N.D. 1979, U.S. Dist. Ct. Minn. 1981, U.S. Ct. Appeals (8th cir.) 1981. Law Clk. U.S. Dist. Ct. N.D., Fargo, 1979-81; assoc. Cahill & Maring PA, Moorhead, Minn., 1981-85, ptnr., bd. dirs., 1985. Mem. ABA, Minn. Bar Assn., N.D. Bar Assn., Order of Coif. Roman Catholic. Home: 1913 S 23d St Fargo ND 58103 Office: Cahill & Maring PA 403 Center Ave Moorhead MN 56560

MARQUIS, ROBERT WILLIAM, psychiatrist, mental health facility administrator; b. Ft. Dodge, Iowa, Nov. 28, 1949; s. Forrest William and Geraldine Mae (Hildreth) M.; m. Susan Lynne Hosier, July 19, 1974; 1 child, Ian Andrew. BA, U. Chgo., 1972; MD, U. Iowa, 1976. Diplomate Am. Bd. Psychiatry and Neurology. Resident in psychiatry U. Chgo., 1976-79; clin. dir. Riverside Med. Ctr., Kankakee, Ill., 1979-86; med. dir. Southlake Mental Health, Merrillville, Ind., 1986—. Mem. AMA, Am. Psychiat. Assn., Ill. Psychiat. Soc., Ill. State Med. Soc., Chgo. Med. Soc. Episcopalian. Address: 20825 London Dr Olympia Fields IL 60461

MARQUIS, WILLIAM OSCAR, lawyer; b. Fort Wayne, Ind., Feb. 26, 1944; s. William Oscar Marquis and Lenor Mae (Gaffney) Marquis Jensen; m. Mary Frances Funderburk, May 11, 1976; children—Lenor, Kathryn, Timothy Patrick, Daniel, Ann. B.S., U. Wis.-Madison, 1973; J.D., South Tex. Coll. Law, 1977. Bar: Wis. 1979, U.S. Dist. Ct. (we. dist.) Wis. 1979, U.S. Dist. Ct. (ea. dist.) Wis. 1982, U.S. Tax Ct. 1983, U.S. Ct. Appeals (7th cir. 1985). With Wis. Dept. Vet. Affairs, Madison, 1977-79; corp. counsel Barron County, Wis., 1979-80; assoc. Riley, Bruns & Riley, Madison, 1980-81; assoc. Jastroch & LaBarge, S.C., Waukesha, Wis., 1981-84; ptnr. Groh, Hackbart, Marquis & Luchini, 1984—. Served to sgt. USAF, 1966-70. Mem. Assn. Trial Lawyers Am., Wis. Trial Lawyers Assn., Waukesha Bar, Milw. Bar, ABA, Wis. Bar. Office: 6525 W Bluemound Milwaukee WI 53213

MARR, PETER JACOB, automotive accessory company executive; b. La Porte, Ind., Dec. 2, 1948; s. Peter John and Evelyn Susanna (Furr) M.; m. Maureen Anne McCormick (div.); 1 child, Dennis Robert; m. Deborah Lynn Mitchell, Nov. 4, 1972; children: Melissa Anne, Aaron Peter. BS cum laude, U. Detroit, 1970; MBA, Grand Valley State U., 1975. With comml. loans dept. United Bank Denver; gen. mgr. Warm Glow Products div. Am. Seating Co., Grand Rapids, Mich., 1973-79; pres. Great Lakes Stove Co., Traverse City, Mich., 1979-81, Owens Classic, Sturgis, Mich., 1981—; adj. prof. Grand Valley State U., Allendale, Mich., 1975-80; guest lectr. internat trade seminars U.S. Dept. Commerce, 1985-86. Mem. Auto Parts Accessories Assn. (lectr. seminars Internat. Trade Com. 1985-86, com. mem. 1986-87). Avocations: triathlons, swimming, bikes, running, tennis. Office: Owens Classic Inc 1000 Progress St Sturgis MI 49091

MARRA, SAMUEL PATRICK, pharmacist, small business owner; b. Sault Ste Marie, Mich., Apr. 15, 1927; s. Leonard and Nancy (Clement); m. Jeanette L. Rohr, Sept. 2, 1949; children: Rebecca, Nancy, David, Dana, Janet. BS in Pharmacy, Ferris State Coll., 1949. bd. dirs. Chem. Bank, No. States Bancshares, Chem. Bank North. Bd. dirs. Houghton Lake Edn. Found.; pres. Houghton Lake Grenadier Band; co-chmn. Scheutte for Congress, Roscommon County, 1984, 86. Mem. Nat. Assn. Retail Druggists. Republican. Avocations: music, photography. Home: PO Box 1570 Houghton Lake MI 48629 Office: 4562 W Houghton Lake Dr Houghton Lake MI 48629

MARRERO, MICHAEL ALVIN, lawyer; b. South Bend, Ind., July 8, 1953; s. Alvin Clarence and Jean Helen (Udelhofen) M.; m. Deborah DeLong, Jan., 12, 1981; children—Amelie DeLong, Samuel Prentice. A.B., Xavier U., 1974; J.D., U. Mich., 1977. Bar: Ohio 1977. Law clk. U.S. Dist. Ct., Cin., 1977-79; assoc. Paxton & Seasongood Co. L.P.A., Cin., 1979-82; sr. staff atty. Drackett Co., Cin., 1982—. Bd. dirs., v.p. Downtown Montessori, Inc., Cin., 1984—; chmn. corp. sponsorship com. Heart mini-marathon Ohio Southwest chpt. Am. Heart Assn., 1983—; pres., trustee Family Edn. Ctr., Cin. Mem. ABA, Cin. Bar Assn., Ohio State Bar Assn., Soc. Am. Baseball Research. Democrat. Roman Catholic. Club: Clifton Track. Home: 197 Green Hills Rd Cincinnati OH 45208

MARRINAN, SUSAN FAYE, lawyer; b. Vermillion, S.D., May 29, 1948; s. H. Lyal and Ada Myrtle (Hollingsworth) Abild; children: Molly, Cara. BA, U. Minn., 1969, JD, 1973. Bar: Minn. 1973. Atty. Carlson Cos., Plymouth, Minn., 1973-74, Prudential Ins. Co., Mpls., 1974-75; v.p., gen. counsel, asst. sec. H.B. Fuller Co., St. Paul, 1977—. Fundraiser Am. Cancer Soc., St. Paul, 1984—; bd. dirs. Family Services of St. Paul, 1985, Childrens Theatre Co. Mem. Corporate Counsel Assn. (pres. 1986—), Am. Assn. Corporate Counsel (bd. dirs. Minn. chpt. 1986—). Republican. Avocations: running. Office: HB Fuller Co 2400 Energy Park Dr Saint Paul MN 55108

MARRS, DONNIE DELBERT, architect; b. Clay Center, Kans., Aug. 11, 1952; s. Wayne Wesley Marrs and Roma Lea (Haas) LeBlanc; m. Romana Ann, Dec. 24, 1973; children: Dahx, Ali Ann, Krae. BArch, Kans. State U., 1976. Registered architect, Kans. Project architect Gossen Livingston P.A., Wichita, Kans., 1977-80, Law/Kingdon Inc., Wichita, 1980; architect Salina (Kans.) Bldg. Systems, 1980-81; pres., prin. Donnie D. Marrs, AIA, Salina, 1981—. Pres. sch. bd. Sacred Heart High Sch., Salina, 1984-85. Mem. AIA, Kans. Soc. Architects. Republican. Roman Catholic. Home: 404 Seitz Dr Salina KS 67401 Office: Donnie D Marrs AIA PA 1907 S Ohio Salina KS 67401

MARSCHALL, MARLENE ELIZABETH, hospital administrator, nurse; b. St. Paul, Nov. 20, 1936; d. Bruno and Adelheid A. Mirsch; m. George Marschall, June 8, 1973. Diploma, Ancker Hosp. Sch. Nursing, 1958; B.S. cum laude in Biol. Scis./Nursing, Viterbo Coll., 1965; M.A. in Nursing Service Adminstrn., U. Iowa, 1972. With Ancker Hosp., St. Paul, 1958-60, Ancker Hosp. Sch. Nursing, St. Paul, 1960-61, St. Frances Sch. Nursing, LaCrosse, Wis., 1964-68; dir. nursing edn. St. Paul-Ramsey Med. Ctr., 1969-71, asst. dir. nursing, 1971, assoc. dir. nursing services, 1972-76, dir. nursing services, 1976-77, assoc. dir., 1977-80, sr. assoc. dir., 1980-84, hosp. dir., 1984, chief operating officer, 1984-85, exec. dir., 1985-86, pres., 1986—; preceptor, lectr., clin. faculty mem. U. Minn. Advisor, Congl. Awards Program. Recipient Air Nat. Guard recognition for Bus. and Industry Leaders in U.S., 1977. Mem. Am. Coll. Health Adminstrs., Am. Hosp. Assn., Minn. Hosp. Assn., Twin City Area Soc. Nursing Service Adminstrs., Nat. League for Nursing, Sigma Theta Tau. Roman Catholic. Contbr. articles to med. jours. Office: St Paul Ramsey Med Ctr 640 Jackson St Saint Paul MN 55101

MARSDEN, DANA S., retail company executive; b. Minot, N.D., Dec. 1, 1956; s. Lawrence David and Lila Lucille (Krause) M.; m. Marie Doll, May 17, 1980; children: Aaron, Kayla, Krystal. BA in Acctg. and Bus. Adminstrn., Mary Coll., 1979. CPA, N.D. Staff acct. Nitschke, Wolfe & Co., Bismarck, N.D., 1979-81; exec. asst. to pres. TBA Supply, Inc., Bottineau, N.D., 1981—. Pres. Retail Merchants Com., Bottineau, 1987; sec.-treas. 6th Dist. N.D. Reps., 1983-87. Mem. Am. Inst. CPA's, N.D. Soc. CPA's. Republican. Mem. Ch. Assembly of God. Lodge: Lions (local pres. 1986-87). Avocations: snow skiing, golf, bowling. Home: 715 Jay St Bottineau ND 58318 Office: TBA Supply Inc 116 E 6th St Bottineau ND 58318

MARSEE, CHARLES DEWEY, educational administrator; b. Nashville, Sept. 30, 1942; s. Dewey Marion and Essie Corina (Bolton) M.; m. Jerri Wade, Nov. 25, 1961; children: Sharon, Linda. Student, Lincoln Meml. U., 1960-62; BS, U. Tenn., 1964; MS, Fla. State U., 1968, postgrad., 1973. Tchr. sci. Dixie County High Sch., Cross City, Fla., 1964-66, Leon County High Sch., Tallahassee, 1966-68; chmn. sci. dept. Hawken Sch., Gates Mills, Ohio, 1968-80; headmaster The Andrews Sch., Willoughby, Ohio, 1980—. Trustee Willoughby Sch. Fine Arts, 1980—. Recipient Bole award Hawken Sch., 1980. Mem. Nat. Assn. Prins. Schs. for Girls, Nat. Assn. Secondary Sch. Prins., Assn. Secondary Curriculum Dirs, Ohio Assn. Secondary Sch. Adminstrs., Cleve. Regional Council Sci. Tchrs. (pres., dir.), Willoughby C. of C. (bd. dirs.). Republican. Methodist. Lodge: Rotary (pres.-elect Willoughby). Home and Office: 38588 Mentor Ave Willoughby OH 44094

MARSH, CLARE TEITGEN, school psychologist; b. Manitowoc, Wis., July 7, 1934; d. Clarence Emil and Dorothy (Napiezinski) Teitgen; m. Robert Irving Marsh, Jan. 30, 1955; children: David, Wendy Marsh Tootle, Julie, Laura Marsh Beltrame. MS in Ednl. Psychology, U. Wis., Milw., 1968. Sch. psychologist Milw. Pub. Schs., 1975-76, West Allis (Wis.)-West Milw. Pub. Schs., 1968—. NDEA fellow, 1966-68. Mem. Nat. Assn. Sch. Psychologists, Suburban Assn. Sch. Psychologists (pres. 1976-77, 86-87), Wis. Assn. Sch. Psychologists(chmn. membership com. 1980-84, sec. 85—, chmn. conv. 1987), Phi Kappa Phi, Pi Lambda Theta, Kappa Delta Pi, Sigma Tau Delta, Alpha Chi Omega. Home: 14140 W Honey Ln New Berlin WI 53151 Office: West Allis Sch System 9333 W Lincoln Ave West Allis WI 53227

MARSH, CLAYTON EDWARD, army officer; b. Worthington, Minn., Jan. 24, 1942; s. Cecil Eugene and Edna Luella (Clausen) M.; m. Carol Ruth Lundmark Franz, June 30, 1962 (div. 1979); children—Tracey Diane, Julie Doreen, Leslie Dawn, Lori Dion; m. Kyong Hui Yi, Aug. 28, 1979. B.A., St. Cloud State U., 1974; M.S., U. So. Calif., 1979. Commd. 2d lt. U.S. Army, 1967, advanced through grades to lt. col., 1985; chief Info. Systems Div., DECCO, Scott AFB, Ill., 1985—. Decorated D.F.C., Bronze Star, Army Commendation medal, Air medal. Mem. Internat. Assn. Approved Basketball Ofcls., Ill. High Sch. Assn., S.W. Athletic Ofcls. Assn. Republican. Mem. Ch. of Christ. Home: 47 Innsbruck Ln Belleville IL 62221 Office: Defense Comml Communications Office Bldg 3189 Scott AFB IL 62225

MARSH, DON E., supermarket executive; b. Muncie, Ind., Feb. 2, 1938; s. Ermal W. and Garnet (Gibson) M.; m. Marilyn Faust, Mar. 28, 1959; children—Don Ermal, Jr., Arthur Andrew, David Alan, Anne Elizabeth, Alexander Elliott. B.A., Mich. State U., 1961. With Marsh Supermarkets, Inc., Yorktown, Ind., 1961—; pres. Marsh Supermarkets, Inc., 1968—, also dir.; dir. Mchts. Nat. Bank, Muncie, Ind. Gas Co. Bd. dirs. Ball State U. Found., Hanover Coll., St. Vincent Hosp. Found. Mem. Nat. Assn. Food Chains (dir.), Am. Mgmt. Assn., Internat. Food Congress, Internat. Assn. Food Distbn. (adv. bd.), Nat. Assn. Over-the-Counter Cos. (bd. dirs.), Food Mktg. Inst. (bd. dirs.), Indpls. C. of C., Muncie C. of C., Ind. C. of C. (bd. dirs.), Ind. Retail Grocers Assn. (bd. dirs.), Ind. Retail Council (bd. dirs.), Ind. Soc. Chgo., Young Pres.'s Orgn., Newcomen Soc. N.Am., Pi Sigma Epsilon, Lambda Chi Alpha. Presbyterian. Clubs: Crooked Stick Golf (Carmel, Ind.); Columbia (Indpls.); Delaware Country; Hundred (Indpls.), Indpls. Athletic; Marco Polo (N.Y.C.); Meridian Hills Country (Indpls.), Skyline. Lodges: Masons, Elks, Rotary, Eagles. Office: Marsh Supermarkets Inc 501 Depot St Yorktown IN 47396

MARSH, FRANK I., state official; b. Norfolk, Nebr., Apr. 27, 1924; s. Frank and Delia (Andrews) M.; m. Shirley Mac McVicker, 1943; children: Sherry Ann, Corwin Frank, Stephen Alan, Mitchell Edward, Dory Michael, Melissa Lou. BS, U. Nebr., 1950. Builder, businessman, part-time instr. 1946-52, 71-75; sec. of state State of Nebr., Lincoln, 1953-70, lt. gov., 1970-74, state treas., 1975-81, 87—; state dir. Farmers Home Adminstrn., Lincoln, 1982-86. Served with AUS, 1943-46. Recipient Meritorious Service award Nat. Assn. State Treas. Mem. Nebr. Alumni Assn., Orgn. Profl. Employees of U.S. Dept. Agr. Office: State Treasurer's Office PO Box 94788 Lincoln NE 68509 *

MARSH, LEONARD C., accountant, hospital system executive; b. Goodland, Ind., Jan. 6, 1938; s. George Wilbur and Evelyn Annetta (Kittleson) M.; Janet Elaine Kuhns, Aug. 16, 1959; children: Kelly Susan, Sherry Lynn. BA, Andrews U., 1959; M in Pub. Adminstrn., U. Colo., Denver, 1984. CPA, Mich., Kans. Acct., auditor Seidman & Seidman, CPA's, Dowagiac, Mich., 1970-73, mgr., 1973; controller Shawnee Mission (Kans.) Med. Ctr., 1973-76, v.p. fin., 1976-79; v.p. fin. Adventist Health System, Shawnee Mission, 1979-86, sr. v.p. fin. no., ea. and mid. Am., 1987—, also bd. dirs., exec. com.; mem. fin. com. Adventist Health System U.S., Dallas, 1985—, also bd. dirs. Ins. Trust; cons. in field. Chmn. bd. dirs. Midland Adventist Sch., Shawnee Mission, 1976-79, Chapel Oaks Seventh-Day Adventist Ch., Kansas City, Kans.; bd. dirs. Moberly (Mo.) Regional Med. Ctr., 1977-84, Shawnee Mission Med. Ctr., 1987—. Mem. Healthcare Fin. Mgmt. Assn. (advanced, bd. dirs. Kansas City chpt.), Kans. Soc. CPA's, Am. Coll. Healthcare Execs., Seventh-Day Adventist Fin. Mgmt. Assn. (pres.). Republican. Lodges: Rotary, Lions. Avocations: boating, skiing, water skiing, collecting Matchbox toys. Home: 6814 Bell Rd Shawnee KS 66217 Office: Adventist Health System 8800 W 75th St Shawnee Mission KS 66204

MARSH, ROBERT CHARLES, writer, music critic; b. Columbus, Ohio, Aug. 5, 1924; s. Charles L. and Jane A. (Beckett) M.; m. Kathleen C. Moscrop, July 4, 1956 (div. 1985); m. Ann Noren, Feb. 25, 1987; 1 child, James McArtain. BS, Northwestern U., 1945, AM, 1946; postgrad., U. Chgo., 1948; EdD, Harvard U., 1951; postgrad., Oxford U., 1952-53, Cambridge U., 1953-56. Instr. social sci. U. Ill., 1947-49; lectr. humanities Chgo. City Jr. Coll., 1950-51; asst. prof. edn. U. Kansas City, 1951-52; vis. prof. edn. SUNY, 1953-54; humanities staff U. Chgo., 1956-58, lectr. in social thought, 1976; music critic Chgo. Sun-Times, 1956—; dir. Chgo. Opera Project, Newberry Library, 1983—. Author: Toscanini and the Art of Orchestral Performance, 1956, rev. edit., 1962, The Cleveland Orchestra, 1967, Ravinia, 1986; editor: Logic and Knowledge, 1956. Co-recipient Peabody award for ednl. broadcasting, 1976; Ford Found. fellow, 1965-66. Mem. Sigma Delta Chi. Episcopalian. Club: Arts (Chgo.). Office: Chicago Sun-Times Chicago IL 60611

MARSH, ROBERT JAMES, engineering and natural gas processing company executive; b. Los Angeles, Calif., Aug. 29, 1954; s. Stewart Hull and Elizabeth Lois (Leahy) M.; m. Jill Leone Porter, June 15, 1985. BSME, BA in Math., U. Calif., Santa Barbara, 1977. Registered profl. engr., Mich. Facilities engr. Shell Oil Co., Traverse City, Mich., 1977-82; pres. Marsh Engring., Inc., Traverse City, 1982—, Mich. Gas Processors, Traverse City, 1985—. Mem. Mich. Oil and Gas Assn., Traverse City C. of C. Office: Marsh Engring Inc 121 E Front St Suite 102 Traverse City MI 49684

MARSH, SHIRLEY MAC, state legislator; b. Benton, Ill., June 22, 1925; d. Dwight Sidney and Margaret Reese (Hager) McVicker; m. Frank Irving Marsh, Mar. 5, 1943; children: Sherry Anne Marsh Tupper, Stephen Alan, Dory Michael, Corwin Frank, Mitchell Edward, Melissa Lou. BA in Social Welfare, U. Nebr., 1972, MBA, 1978; Diploma (hon.), Lincoln (Nebr.) Sch. Commerce, 1975. Placement asst. U. Nebr., Lincoln, 1966-70; caseworker practicum Lancaster County Welfare Dept., Lincoln, 1971-72; mem. Nebr. Legislature, Lincoln, 1973—; vis. instr. Nebr. Wesleyan U., Lincoln, 1978, Doane Coll., Crete, Nebr., 1979. Mem. Lincoln Community Playhouse Guild, 1975—, panel Nat. ID Program for Advancement of Women in Higher Edn., 1983—, adv. com. Am. Coll. Ob-Gyn, Washington, 1981-86; trustee Nebr. Wesleyan U., Lincoln, 1984—, student affairs com. of bd. govs., 1983-86; bd. dirs. Nebr. Chamber Orch. Guild, Lincoln, 1985-86. Recipient Woman of Yr. award Capitol Bus. and Profl. Women's Club, 1982, Hwy. Safety award Gov. of Nebr., 1984, Ptnr. in Prevention award Nat. Soc. to Prevent Blindness, 1985. Mem. Nat. Order Women Legislators (pres. 1977-78), Nat. Rep. Legis. Assn. (exec. com. 1982-86), Nat. Fedn. Bus. and Profl. Women, AAUW (grantee 1976), Internat. Women's Orgn. (prin. exec. officer IA chpt. 1987-88), Delta Kappa Gamma. United Methodist. Avocations: reading, cooking, canoeing. Home: 2701 S 34th St Lincoln NE 68506 Office: Nebr Legislature Dist #29 State Capitol Bldg Lincoln NE 68509

MARSHALL, DAVID ALAN, accountant; b. Groton, Conn., July 14, 1958; s. Edward Thomas and Carole Jean (Turchan) M.; m. Sherry Lynn McDowell, Sept. 14, 1985. BS in Acctg., U. Akron, 1980. CPA, Ohio. Staff acct. Touche Ross & Co., Cleve., 1980-82; internal auditor Figgie Internat., Richmond, Va., 1982-84; mgr. acctg.Gastown div. EMRO Mktg., Bedford Heights, Ohio, 1984-86; supr. cash mgmt. Blue Cross/Blue Shield of Ohio, Cleve., 1986—. Mem. Am. Inst. CPA's, Ohio Soc. CPA's, Nat. Assn. Accts. Roman Catholic. Avocations: golf, basketball, reading, travel. Home: 11300 Villa Grande Dr North Royalton OH 44133 Office: Blue Cross/Blue Shield of Ohio 2060 E 9th St Cleveland OH 44115

MARSHALL, GORDON BRUCE, construction company executive; b. Hamilton, Ont., Can., Sept. 26, 1943; s. J. Gordon and Mae J. (Tucker) M.; m. Rita J. Penca, Apr. 22, 1979. BSBA, Northwestern U., 1965; MBA, U. Chgo., 1970; AAS, Coll. Lake County, 1975. CPA, Mo., Ill. Comptrollership trainee Continental Ill. Nat. Bank, Chgo., 1967-68; profit analyst Morton Salt Co., Chgo., 1968-70; sr. fin. specialist Abbott Labs., North Chicago, Ill., 1970-76; treas. Pott Industries Inc., St. Louis, 1976-81; v.p. fin., adminstrn. Pepper Constrn. Co., Chgo., 1981-84; v.p. fin., chief fin. officer The Pepper Cos. Inc., 1985—; instr. Coll. Lake County, 1975-76. Served as lt. (j.g.) USNR, 1965-67. Mem. Constrn. Fin. Mgmt. Assn. (bd. dirs., pres. 1987—), Am. Inst. CPA's, Ill. CPA Soc. Office: The Pepper Cos Inc 1000 Hart Rd Barrington IL 60010

MARSHALL, JOHN DANIEL, education educator, researcher; b. Youngstown, Ohio, Nov. 13, 1948; s. Frank George and Rita Madeline Marshall; m. Tara Lynn Fulton, Dec. 30, 1981. AA, Fullerton (Calif.) Coll., 1975; BS, Youngstown (Ohio) State U., 1976; MA, Ind. U., 1980; PhD, U. Tex., 1985. Tchr. Lilydale (Victoria, Australia) Primary Sch., 1976-79, Fitzharris Alternative Schs., Gladstone, Mich., 1980-81, Somerville (Tex.) Jr. High Sch., 1981-82; asst. instr. U. Tex., Austin, 1982-84; asst. prof. Nat. Coll. Edn., Evanston, Ill., 1985—; cons. People for the Am. Way, Austin, 1982, Tex. Edn. Agy., Austin, 1983. Contbr. articles to profl. jours. Mem. Am. Ednl. Research Assn., Assn. for Supervision and Cirriculum Devel., John Dewey Soc., World Council Curriculum and Instruction. Office: Nat Coll Edn 2840 Sheridan Rd Evanston IL 60201

MARSHALL, LINDA RAE, cosmetic company executive; b. Provo, Utah, Aug. 1, 1940; d. Arvid O. and Tola V. (Broderick) Newman; children—James, John. Student Brigham Young U., 1958-59, U. Utah, 1960-61. Buyer, Boston Store, 1961-62; sec. Milw. Gas & Light Co., 1962-64; mktg. rep. Elysee Cosmetics, Madison, Wis., 1971-75, pres., 1975—. Pres. Falk Sch. PTA, Madison. Mem. Aestheticians Internat. Assn. (adv. bd.), Cosmetic, Toiletry and Fragrance Assn. (exec. com., bd. dirs., chmn. voluntary program, chmn. small cosmetic com., membership com. task force). Club: Dental Wives. Author: Discover the Other Woman in You; monthly beauty columnist Beauty Fashion Mag.; contbg. author Cosmetic Industry Sci. and Regulatory Found., 1984. Address: Box 4084 Madison WI 53711

MARSHALL, PHILIP RICHARD, university official; b. Decatur, Ind., Nov. 13, 1926; s. E. Howard and Eurah Lucille (Ratliff) M.; m. Helen Rebecca Emmons, Aug. 19, 1951; children: Amy, Karen, Rebecca, Mary Ann. A.B., Earlham Coll., 1949; M.S., Purdue U., 1951, Ph.D., 1954. Asst. Purdue U., 1949-51, 52-53; research engr. Battelle Meml. Inst., 1951-52; instr. Albion Coll., 1953-55, asst. prof., 1955-58; asst. prof. Cornell Coll., 1958-61, assoc. prof., 1961-65; prof., dean Lycoming Coll., 1965-69; assoc. program dir. NSF, 1969; dean acad. affairs Eastern Wash. U., Cheney, 1969-70; v.p. acad. affairs Eastern Wash. U., 1970-76, exec. v.p., 1976-79; chancellor U. Wis., Stevens Point, 1979—; vis. prof. U. Iowa, summer 1962; resident faculty dir. Asso. Colls. of Midwest-Argonne Semester Program, Argonne Nat. Lab., 1964-65. Sci. editor: North American Review, 1964-65. Bd. dirs. Williamsport (Pa.) Hosp., 1965-69, Wash. State Ins. Bd., 1977-79, U. Wis. Stevens Point Found., 1979—, Central Wis. Symphony Orch., 1981—, Elderhostel, 1983—; trustee Stevens Point Area YMCA, 1982—, Sentry Found., 1984—. Mem. Sigma Xi, Phi Lambda Upsilon. Home: 21 Oakcrest Dr Stevens Point WI 54481

MARSHALL, PRENTICE H., fed. judge; b. 1926. B.S., 1949; J.D., U. Ill., 1951. Bar: Ill. bar 1951. Judge U.S. Dist. Ct. for No. Ill., 1973—; assoc. firm Johnston Thompson Raymond & Mayer, Chgo., 1953-60; ptnr. Raymond Mayer Jenner & Block, Chgo., 1961-67; spl. asst. atty. gen. State of Ill., 1964-67; hearing officer Ill. Fair Employment Practices Commn., 1967-72; faculty Am. Law Inst.; adj. prof. law Ill. Inst. Tech., Chgo.-Kent Coll. Law, 1975—; prof. law U. Ill., 1967-73. Served with USN, 1944-46. Mem. Am. Coll. Trial Lawyers, Am. Law Inst., ABA, Am. Judicature Soc., Ill., Chgo. bar assns., Bar Assn. of Seventh Cir., Phi Beta Kappa. Office: US Courthouse 219 S Dearborn St Chicago IL 60604 *

MARSHALL, ROBERT E. LEE, dentist; b. Columbia, Mo., Oct. 31, 1921; s. Robert E. Lee and Mary Essie (Tolleson) M.; m. Sally Helen Brownfield, Mar. 8, 1952; children: Robert E. Lee III, Lesa Ann. DDS, St. Louis U., 1944. Pvt. practice dentistry Lee's Summit, Mo., 1972—. Chmn. Lee's Summit Airport Commn., 1984—. Served to lt. USNR, 1942-46, capt. USPHS. Mem. ADA (life), Mo. Dental Assn., Greater Kansas City Dental Assn., Mo. Pilot's Assn., U.S. Pilot's Assn., Lee's Summit C. of C. Club: Lakewood Oaks Country. Avocations: flying, golf, fishing, foreign travel, stamp and coin collecting. Home: 618 NE Fairington Ct Lees Summit MO 64063 Office: 519 W 3d Suite A Lees Summit MO 64063

MARSHO, RICHARD STEPHEN, dataprocessing executive; b. Moline, Ill., Sept. 23, 1940; s. Marie (Hofreiter) M.; m. Linda J. Musgrove, May 2, 1964; children: Scott Major, Steven Paul. BS in Gen. Engring., U. Ill., Urbana, 1963, MBA in Fin., 1967. Mktg. rep. IBM, Springfield, Ill., 1967-69; mgr. ops. Cen. Nat. Bank, Chgo., 1969-75; systems mgr., systems auditor Cen. Ill. Light Co., Peoria, 1975—. Active allocations com. United Way, Peoria, 1978-84; mem. exec. bd. dirs. 1st Federated Ch., 1983-85, 87—. Served to 1st lt. USAF, 1963-65. Mem. Dataprocessing Mgmt. Assn. (pres. 1980), EDP Auditors Assn. (v.p. 1986). Republican. Lodge: Rotary (bd. dirs. Peoria 1986). Avocations: tennis, fishing, skiing. Home: 201 W Aspen Way Peoria IL 61614 Office: Cen Ill Light Co 300 Liberty St Peoria IL 61602

MARSO, EDWARD RAYMOND, accountant; b. Joliet, Ill., July 5, 1958; s. Raymond John and Elizabeth Ann (Vancina) M. BS in Bus., Coll. St. Francis, 1980; MBA, Lewis U., 1983. Acct. Wermer, Rogers, Doran & Ruzon, Joliet, Ill., 1984—; instr. Joliet Jr. Coll., 1986—. Mem. Am. Inst. CPAs, Ill. CPA Soc. Roman Catholic. Home: 322 Emery St Joliet IL 60432 Office: Wermer Rogers Doran & Ruzon 57 N Ottawa St Joliet IL 60431

MART, PALMER ERWIN, principal; b. Matthews, Ind., Nov. 2, 1925; s. Palmer Eri and Pauline Ada (Overmeyer) M.; m. Amarylyce Lois Schmidt, Aug. 28, 1948; children: Alyce Lynn, Patricia Jayne, Susan Kaye. BEd, Ind. U., 1949, MEd, 1953, EdD, 1977. Cert. secondary sch. principal, Ind.; cert. supt., Ind. Tchr. sci. Gary (Ind.) Pub. Schs., 1952-57; from asst. prin. to prin. Horace Mann High Sch., Gary, 1957-66; prin. Elkhart (Ind.) High Sch., 1966-69; teaching assoc. Ind. U., Bloomington, 1969-70; coordinator secondary edn. Elkhart Community Schs., 1970-72; prin. Meml. High Sch., Elkhart, 1972-84; chmn. evaluation com. State Com. for N.C.A., Bloomington, 1964-82, rev. com. North Cen. Assn. Ann. Meetings, Boulder, Colo., 1967-77. Chmn. Dist. Boy Scout Advancement, Elkhart, 1969, Joint Civic Club, Elkhart, 1980; mem. United Fund, Elkhart, 1970-72; bd. dirs. Gulfshore Home Owners Assn., Longboat Key, Fla., 1985—. Served with USN, 1943-46, PTO. Recipient Order of Arrow, Boy Scouts Am., 1941, Service award Ind. Secondary Sch. Prins. Assn., 1984; named Eagle Scout, Boy Scouts Am., 1941. Mem. Ind. Scondary Sch. Adminstrs., Nat. Assn. Secondary Sch. Prins., Ind. U. Edn. Alumni Assn., Phi Kapta Kappa, Theta Chi. Republican. Presbyterian. Lodges: Rotary, Masons. Avocations: financial planning, genealogy, outdoor recreation, reading, travelling. Home: 23456 Greenleaf Blvd Elkhart IN 46514

MARTAN, JOSEPH RUDOLF, lawyer; b. Oak Park, Ill., Mar. 28, 1949; s. Joseph John and Margarete Paulina (Rothenbock) M.; BA with honors, U. Ill., 1971; JD with honors, Ill. Inst. Tech., Chgo.-Kent Coll. Law, 1977. Admitted to Ill. bar, 1977, U.S. dist. ct. for No. dist. Ill., 1977; assoc. firm V. C. Lopez, Chgo., 1978-80; litigation counsel Goldblatt Bros., Inc., Chgo., 1980-81; br. counsel Ill. br. Am. Family Ins. Group, Schaumburg, 1981-87; atty. Judge & Knight Ltd., Park Ridge, Ill., 1987—. Mem. West Suburban Community Band, Inc., Western Springs, Ill., 1975—, pres., 1979-81. Served with U.S. Army, 1972-74, to capt. USAR, 1974-85. Decorated Army Commendation medal. Mem. Ill. State Bar Assn., Chgo. Bar Assn., Du Page County Bar Assn. (mem. civil practice com.), Bohemian Lawyer's Assn. Chgo. (sec. 1987—), Def. Research Inst., Assn. Trial Lawyers Am., Res. Officer's Assn., Assn. U.S. Army, Met. Opera Guild, Pi Sigma Alpha, Pi Sigma Alpha. Home: 4056 Gilbert Ave Western Springs IL 60558 Office: Judge & Knight 422 N Northwest Hwy Park Ridge IL 60068

MARTEL, IRA, marketing executive; b. Bronx; m. Ruth Saffati, Dec. 25, 1978; children—Josef Nissim, Eliahu Zvi, Shoshana. Student U. Mo., 1967; B.A., William Penn Coll., 1968; postgrad. U. Ariz., 1968; tchr. cert. Augustana Coll., 1970; M.S., Mont. State U., 1971; postgrad. U. S.D., 1971; Ph.D. (grad. teaching asst.), Oreg. State U., 1974. Salesman, Martel Products, Bronx, 1953-63; numis. salesman M. Geiger, Rare Coins, N.Y.C., 1959-62; sales clk. E.J. Korvette, Scarsdale, N.Y., summer 1963; pressroom asst. N.Y. Sch. Printing Pressmen, N.Y.C., 1962-64; demonstrator Tower Products Corp., Bklyn., 1965; dir. World Wide Fashions of Sioux Falls (S.D.), 1970-72; salesman Van Zee Motors, Oskaloosa, Iowa, 1966-67, Stoner Piano Co., Ottumwa, Iowa, 1967, Sears, Roebuck & Co., Sioux Falls, 1970-71; instr. Mont. State U., summer 1971; tchr. coordinator distributive edn. Sioux Falls Pub. Schs., 1968-72; research/devel. specialist Ohio State U., Columbus, 1972-73; sales/promotion specialist Vita-Mix Corp., Cleve., 1965; asst. prof. bus. and distributive edn. Emporia (Kans.) State Coll., 1974-77; assoc. prof. mktg./internat. bus. Baldwin Wallace Coll., Berea, Ohio, 1979-81; assoc. prof. mktg. and internat. bus. Lake Erie Coll., Painesville, Ohio, 1981-82; mktg. v.p. Vita-Mix Corp., Cleve., 1977—. Mem. Am. Mgmt. Assn., Assn. Home Appliance Mfrs. (internat. trade com.), Nat. Assn. Distributive Edn. Tchrs., Direct Mail Mktg. Assn., NEA, Am. Vocat. Assn., Direct Mktg. Assn., Aircraft Owners and Pilots Assn., Internat. Platform Assn. Contbr. articles to profl. jours. Home: 8710 Root Rd North Ridgeville OH 44039

MARTEL, THOMAS LEO, investment company executive; b. Flint, Mich., Mar. 5, 1959; s. Theodore L. and Lucille M. (CLevers) M.; m. Dawn Marie Thompson, Aug. 27, 1983. BS, Ferris State Coll., 1983. Programmer/analyst Hewlett-Packard Corp., Greeley, Colo., 1983-85; cons. Multiple Technologies, Southfield, Mich., 1985-86; chief exec. officer High Plains Systems, Milliken, Colo., 1985-86, Martel Internat. Network Co., Garden City, Mich., 1985—. Home: 32106 Leona Garden City MI 48135-1206

MARTEL, WILLIAM, radiologist, educator; b. N.Y.C., Oct. 1, 1927; s. Hyman and Fanny M.; m. Rhoda Kaplan, Oct. 9, 1956; children: Lisa, Pamela, Caryn, Jonathan, David. M.D., NYU, 1953. Intern, Kings County Hosp., N.Y., 1953-54; resident in radiology Mt. Sinai Hosp., N.Y.C., 1954-57; instr. radiology U. Mich., 1957-60, asst. prof., 1960-63, asso. prof., 1963-67, prof., 1967—, Fred Jenner Hodges prof., 1984—, chmn. dept. radiology, 1983—, dir. skeletal radiology, 1970-81. Contbr. articles to Radiol. Diagnoses of Arthritic Diseases. Served with USAAF, 1945-46. Recipient Amoco U. Mich. Outstanding Teaching award, 1980. Mem. Radiol. Soc. N.Am., Am. Roentgen Ray Soc., Assn. Univ. Radiologists. Home: 2972 Park Ridge St Ann Arbor MI 48103 Office: Univ Mich Hosps Dept Radiology 1500 E Med Ctr Dr Ann Arbor MI 48109

MARTELL, JOSEPH ALLEN, accountant; b. Chippewa Falls, Wis., July 3, 1958; s. Francis George and Hjordis Ilene (Kjelvik) M.; m. Barbara Jean Wienke, May 29, 1982; children: Rebecca Jean, Patricia Ann. BBA in Acctg., U. Wis., Eau Claire, 1980. CPA, Wis. Supr., acct. Hill, Christensen & Co., Marshfield, Wis., 1980-86; acctg. ops. mgr. Figi's, Inc., Marshfield, 1986—. Mem. Am. Inst. CPA's, Wis. Inst. CPA's, Marshfield Area CPA's (sec./treas. 1985). Roman Catholic. Lodge: KC. Avocations: tennis, golf, other sports. Home: 315 S Linden Ave Marshfield WI 54449 Office: Fiji's Inc Marshfield WI 54449

MARTENS, DONALD GEORGE, savings and loan executive; b. Oak Park, Ill., July 25, 1932; s. George Stanley and Leona Louise (Lange) M.; m. Karin Ruth Johnson, Nov. 12, 1983. Student, Grinnell Coll., 1950-52; BS in Commerce, U. Iowa, 1952-54; MBA, Northwestern U., 1957. CPA, Ill., Iowa. Staff acct. Price, Waterhouse & Co., Chgo., 1954-56, Peat, Marwick, Mitchell & Co., Chgo., 1958-61; various positions Evanston (Ill.) Fed. Savs. and Loan Assn., 1961-76, pres., 1976-80; chmn., pres. Marengo (Ill.) Fed. Savs. and Loan Assn., 1984—. Mem. Am. Inst. CPA's, Ill. Soc. CPA's, Evanston C. of C. (bd. dirs. 1978-79). Republican. Lutheran. Avocation: sailing. Home: 222 S Fleming Woodstock IL 60098 Office: Marengo Fed Savs & Loan Assn 200 E Grant Hwy Marengo IL 60152

MARTENS, DONALD MATHIAS, orthodontist; b. Coleman, Wis., June 25, 1925; s. Harry Alfred and Emma Genevive (Laurent) M.; m. Fern Ann Krejcarek, June 24, 1950; children: Daniel, Nance, Dean, Cathy, Cynthia, Linda, James, Jeffrey, Michele. DDS, Marquette U., 1952. Diplomate Internat. Bd. Orthodontics. Practice dentistry specializing in orthodontics Green Bay, Wis., 1952—; pres. San Luis Manor, Inc., Green Bay, 1973-86. Pres. Martens Found., Green Bay, 1982—. Served with USAAF, 1943-46. Fellow Am. Acad. Orthodontics (pres. 1971-72); mem. Brown Door Kewaunee Dental Soc. (pres. 1964), Fedn. Orthodontics Assn. (pres. 1979-81). Republican. Roman Catholic. Lodge: Optomists (pres. Green Bay club 1964). Avocations: golfing, skiing, hunting, fishing. Home: Rt 16 Tamarack Dr Green Bay WI 54303 Office: 712 Redwood Dr Green Bay WI 54304

MARTENS, ROY MICHAEL, financial analyst; b. Des Moines, Feb. 7, 1950; s. Roy Edwin and Maxine Hayworth M. BA, Luther Coll., 1972; MBA, U. Minn., 1978. Auditor Honeywell, Mpls., 1972-75; supr. Northwest SW, Mpls., 1975-78; fin. analyst Amhoist, St. Paul, 1979-81; sr. fin. analyst Farm Credit Services, St. Paul, 1981—. Mem. Twin City Cash Mgmt. Assn., Epsilon Delta Omicron. Republican. Lutheran. Club: Wayzata Yacht (measurer 1985). Avocations: skiing, sailing, running. Home: 2511 Chesnutt Ave W Minneapolis MN 55405

MARTENSON, DENNIS RAYMOND, civil engineer; b. Eau Claire, Wis., Oct. 15, 1942; s. Raymond R. and Elinor L. (Aaserude) M.; m. Catherine Marie Thompson, Sept. 15, 1962; children—Annemarie Lynn, Amy Elizabeth. B.C.E., U. Minn., 1967, M.S.C.E., 1968. Registered profl. engr., Minn. Research asst. U. Minn., Mpls., 1967; plant engr. Western Electric Co., Inc., N.Y.C., 1968-69; process control engr. Met. Sewer Bd., St. Paul, 1969-71; project engr. Pfeifer & Shultz, Inc., Mpls., 1971-72; chief san. engr. Watermation, Inc., St. Paul, 1972-75; project mgr./assoc. mem. firm Toltz, King, Duvall, Anderson & Assocs., Inc., St. Paul, 1975—. USPHS fellow, 1967; named Minn.'s Young Civil Engr. of Yr., Minn. sect. ASCE, 1975. Mem. ASCE (pres. 1976-77, Dist. 8 exec. dir. 1985—, nat. dir. 1986—), Am. Water Works Assn., Instrument Soc. Am., Nat. Assn. Corrosion Engrs., Water Pollution Control Fedn. Lutheran. Contbr. articles to profl. jours. Home: 8140 46 1/2 Ave N Minneapolis MN 55428 Office: 2500 Am Nat Bank Bldg Saint Paul MN 55101

MARTHALER, EDWARD HENRY, anesthetist; b. Melrose, Minn., Sept. 10, 1947; s. Edward John and Regina (Deuker) M.; m. Sharon Kay Christenson, Aug. 9, 1974 (div. Feb. 1985); 1 child, Kristen Kay. Grad., St. Luke's Sch. Radiol. Tech., 1968, St. Luke's Sch. Nursing, 1970, St. Luke's Sch. Anesthesia, 1972. RN; cert. RN anesthetist; registered radiol. tech. Staff anesthesist St. Luke's Hosp., Fargo, N.D., 1972-79, clin. supr., 1979-85; staff anesthesist Fargo Clinic, 1985—. Mem. Am. Nurses Assn., Am. Assn. Nurse Anesthesists, N.D. Assn. Nurse Anesthesists (pres. 1983-85). Lutheran. Avocations: sailing, reading, woodworking, photography. Home: Box 628 Fargo ND 58107 Office: Fargo Clinic Fargo ND 58102

MARTI, PAUL EDGAR, JR., architect, educator; b. Wichita, Kans., Sept. 7, 1929; s. Paul Edgar and Edna Clareen (Conley) M.; m. Audrey Lee Marti, Mar. 15, 1933; children—Dane Eric, Kara Lynn. B.Arch., Kans. State U., 1953; M.A., U. Calif.-Berkeley, 1958. Architect, Murphy-Mackey, St. Louis, 1955-57, Hellmuth-Obata-K, St. Louis, 1958-62; v.p. Smith-Entzeroth, Clayton, Mo., 1962—; juror Am. Plywood Assn. awards, Seattle, 1973; instr. archtl. tech. Washington U., St. Louis, 1979—. Contbr. articles in field to profl. jours. Chmn. Bd. Adjustment, Oakland, Mo., 1983-84. Served with USAF, 1953-55. Recipient 3d Prize, Kirkwood Civic Ctr. Competition, 1967; citation of merit Am. Plywood Assn., 1978. Mem. AIA (award of merit St. Louis 1970), Alpha Tau Omega. Club: Optimist (pres. 1968) (Clayton, Mo.). Home: 105 Minturn St Oakland MO 63122 Office: Smith-Entzeroth Architects 7701 Forsyth St Clayton MO 63105

MARTIEN, HARRY L., JR., electrical contracting company executive; b. Cleveland Heights, Ohio, Sept. 11, 1916; s. Harry L. and Iona Mary (Parsons) M.; m. Barbara Ruth Smith, Nov. 27, 1948; children—Melissa Martien Driscoll, Robert G., Katherine Martien MacMillan, Barbara, Richard. B.S.A.E./E.E., Cornell U., 1938. With Gen. Cable Corp., Cleve., Cin., N.Y.C., 1938-46; with Navy Dept. Bur. Ships, Clearfield, Utah, 1943-45; with Martien Electric Co., Cleve., 1946—, pres., 1970—. Mem. Greater Cleve. Growth Assn., United Way; pres. Cornell U. class of 1938. Mem. Nat. Elec. Contractors Assn. (past pres., dir. 1978-83), Builders Exchange (past pres., dir. 1978-83). Republican. Episcopalian. Clubs: Mayfield Country, Cleve. Skating, Hermit, Rotary, Midday. Home: 2720 Cranlyn Rd Shaker Hts OH 44122 Office: Martien Electric Co 3328 Carnegie Ave Cleveland OH 44115

MARTIN, A. JOHN, education educator; b. Grafton, N.D., Sept. 24, 1939; s. August G. and Helen Mildred (Fischer) M.; m. Marilyn Ruth Yackel, June 9, 1963 (div. Apr. 1984); children: Lisa, August. BA, Westmar Coll., 1961; MS in Edn., Moorhead State U., 1963; Specialist Edn., U. No. Iowa, 1968. Tchr. West Sioux Community Sch., Hawarden, Iowa, 1960-61; tchr. Sheldon (Iowa) Community Sch., 1961-63, prin., 1963-66; asst. prof. Buena Vista Coll., Storm Lake, Iowa, 1966-67; student teaching coordinator U. No. Iowa, Cedar Falls, 1967-69; dir. internship Drake U., Des Moines, 1969-70; chief profl. devel. Iowa Dept. Pub. Instrn., Des Moines, 1970-74, dir. instrn. and curriculum, 1974—; cons. Kettering Found., Dayton, Ohio, 1974-80. Mem. adv. com. Iowa Pub. TV Network; del. Rep. Iowa State Conv., 1976, 80, 84, 86; chair Crawford Twp. Reps., Winterset, Iowa, 1977-80. Mem. Assn. Supn. and Curriculum Devel., Am. Assn. Sch. Adminstrs., Farm Bur. Fedn., Phi Delta Kappa. Methodist. Lodge: Rotary (pres. 1979-80). Avocation: purebred sheep breeding. Office: Iowa Dept Edn Bur Instrn and Curriculum Grimes State Office Bldg Des Moines IA 50319

MARTIN, DAVID STUART, radiologist; b. Davenport, Iowa, Nov. 6, 1948; s. Mayor and Esther (Siegel) M.; m. Rickey Lynn Horwitz, May 18, 1975; children: Sheri, Craig. BS, U. Ill., 1970, MD, 1974. Cert. Am. Bd. Radiology, Nat. Bd. Med. Examiners. Resident in radiology St. Louis U., 1976-79, asst. clin. prof. radiology, 1985—; pvt. practice radiology Alexian Bros. Hosp., St. Louis, 1979—. Book reviewer Am. Jour. Roentgenology, 1979—, Radiology, 1979—; contbr. articles to profl. jours. Mem. AMA, ACR, Mo. State Med. Soc. (dist. councellor C.M.E., 1986—), Radiol. Soc. N.Am. Avocations: computer programming, racquetball. Office: Alexian Bros Hosp 3933 S Broadway Saint Louis MO 63118

MARTIN, DERACE VICTOR, information services executive; b. Kansas City, Mo., May 29, 1953; s. Warren G. and Shirley G. (Hickman) M.; m. Carol Ann West, Aug. 5, 1977; children: Andrea Rhiannon, Hayley Micnelle. BA, U. Mo., Kansas City, 1975. Dir. purchasing Milgram Food Stores, Kansas City, 1977-84; dir. adminstrn. Info. Industries, Inc., Kansas City, 1984—. Mem. Purchasing Mgmt. Assn. Avocation: long distance running. Home: 12601 E 52d St Independence MO 64055 Office: Info Industries Inc 8880 Ward Pkwy Kansas City MO 64114

MARTIN, DONALD CREAGH, surgeon; b. Port Chester, N.Y., Mar. 7, 1937; s. Donald Creagh and Margaret Eleanor (Dobson) M.; m. Jacqueline Anne Poole, Sept. 25, 1965; children—Samuel, Joseph. B.A. in Econs., Yale U., 1958; M.D., U. Pa., 1962. Diplomate Am. Bd. Surgery. Intern, Pa. Hosp., Phila., 1962-63, resident in gen. surgery and pathology, 1965-67, 70-71, 72-74, instr. anatomy, 1968-69, 71-72; practice gen. surgery, White Plains, N.Y., 1974-78, Toledo, 1978—; research asst. dept. surgery Guy's Hosp., London, 1967-68; mem. staff Toledo, Mercy, Riverside, St. Charles hosps.; clin. asst. prof. surgery Med. Coll. Ohio, Toledo, 1980—. Trustee Toledo Community Hosp. Oncology Program; bd. dirs. Lucas County chpt. Am. Cancer Soc., 1983—. Served with M.C., USNR, 1963-65. Fellow ACS, Royal Soc. Medicine, Am. Coll. Nutrition; mem. AMA, Toledo Surg. Soc., N.Y. Acad. Scis., Am. Soc. Enteral and Parenteral Nutrition, AAAS. Republican. Episcopalian. Club: Shadow Valley. Contbr. articles to med. jours. Office: 3939 Monroe Toledo OH 43606

MARTIN, EDGAR CARL, sealant manufacturing company executive; b. Cherryville, Mo., July 20, 1925; s. Carl T. and Ruth (Edgar) M.; m. Dorothea M. Coffin, Nov. 17, 1946; children: Edgar C. Jr., Donald J., Stephan L. AS, S.W. Bapt. U., 1946; postgrad., St. Louis U., 1950, Washington U., St. Louis, 1953. Mem. staff research and devel. lab. Presstite, St. Louis, 1950-60, mem. staff tech. service, 1960-64; chief chemist Plastic Sealers, St. Louis, 1964; pres., chief exec. officer BIDCO Sealants, Inc., St. Louis, 1964—. Mem. Nat. Tax Limitation Com. Mem. Nat. Fedn. Ind. Bus., Am. Foundry Soc., Adhesive and Sealant Council (bd. dirs. 1977-79). Baptist. Home: Hayden Rt Box 92 Dixon MO 65459 Office: BIDCO Sealants Inc 5939 St Louis Saint Louis MO 63120

MARTIN, GEORGE BURNIE, III, psychologist; b. Summit, N.J., Apr. 1, 1952; s. George Burnie and Patricia Ann (Johnson) M.; m. Anna Maria Maravalas, Sept. 17, 1983. B of Elective Studies, U. Minn., 1975; MA, Coll. St. Thomas, St. Paul, 1978. Lic. psychologist, Minn. Family therapist Fairview Hosp., Mpls., 1977-79; addiction therapist Pharm House Ctr., Mpls., 1979-83; family and group therapist Family Renewal Ctr., Edina, Minn., 1980-83; family therapist St. Mary's Hosp., Mpls., 1982-83; therapist Delta Pl., Hopkins, Minn., 1983-85; pvt. practice psychology Mpls., 1983—; family therapist St. Croix Valley Youth Service, Stillwater, Minn., 1985—. Avocations: scuba diving, writing and performing folk and traditional music. Home: 1318 N Avon Saint Paul MN 55117 Office: St Croix Valley Youth Service Bur 101 W Pine Stillwater MN 55082

MARTIN, JACQUES, professional hockey coach. Coach St. Louis Blues, 1986—. Office: St Louis Blues 5700 Oakland Ave Saint Louis MO 63110 *

MARTIN, JAMES EARL, marketing executive; b. Ames, Iowa, June 13, 1936; s. Albert E. and Dorothy (Sweeney) M.; m. Sharon Luette Ultsch, Aug. 3, 1960; children: Kurt, Stacey, Erin, Derek. Student, Iowa State U., 1954-55; BS, U.S. Naval Acad., 1959. Commd. ensign USN, 1959, advanced through ranks to lt., 1963, resigned, 1963; field mktg. rep. IBM Corp., Chgo., 1963-69, with mktg. staff, 1969-72; industry mktg. mgr. IBM WTC, Kuwait, 1972-73; field mktg. rep. IBM Corp., Chgo., 1973-76, sr. planner market devel., 1976—. Vol. adult leader Wabasha (Minn.) County 4-H Fedn., 1977—. Named to 100% Club, IBM Corp., 1965, 66, 67, 68, 73, 74; to Golden Circle 1967. Mem. Minn. Sheep and Wool Producers Assn., Am. Sheep Producers Council. Lutheran. Lodge: Lions (sec., treas. 1982-83). Avocations: scuba diving, custom motor vehicles, farming. Home: Rural Rt 1 Box 136A Mazeppa MN 55956

MARTIN, JAMES EDWARD, railroad executive; b. Jefferson, Ohio, Dec. 23, 1926; s. Paul Revere and Alice (Isaacson) M.; m. Margaret L. Meaney, Aug. 18, 1951; children: Craig, Ann, Kevin, Robert, Mary, Barbara. BS, Kent State U., 1951. With N.Y. Central R.R. Co., 1944-67; terminal supt. N.Y. Central R.R. Co., Toledo, 1962; transp. supt. N.Y. Central R.R. Co., Detroit, 1963; terminal supt. N.Y. Central R.R. Co., N.Y., 1963-64; div. supt. N.Y. Central R.R. Co., Detroit, 1965; dir. orgn. devel. N.Y. Central R.R. Co., N.Y.C., 1965-67; dist. transp. supt. N.Y. Central R.R. Co., Cleve., 1967; gen. supt. Lehigh Valley R.R., Bethlehem, Pa., 1967-69; vp. ops. Lehigh Valley R.R., Bethlehem, 1969-70; so. regional gen. mgr. Penn. Central Transp. Co., Indpls., 1970-74; v.p. ops. Chgo., Rock Island and Pacific R.R. Co., Chgo., 1974-76; v.p. ops. and maintenance Assoc. Am. R.R., Washington, 1976-78; sr. v.p. ops., dir. Ill. Central Gulf R.R., Chgo., 1978-83, pres., chief operating officer, dir., 1983—; Dir. Belt Ry. Co. of Chgo., Kansas City Terminal R.R., Peoria & Pekin Union R.R. Mem. Exec. Commn. Transp. Research Bd.; mem. adv. bd. Salvation Army, Chgo. Served with U.S. Army, 1945-46. Mem. Western Ry. Club (pres. 1982-83), Assn. Am. R.R.s, Terminal R.R. Assn. (dir.). Republican. Roman Catholic. Office: Ill Cen Gulf RR Co 233 N Michigan Ave Chicago IL 60601 *

MARTIN, JAMES EVERETT, religious organization adminstrator; b. Cin., Sept. 29, 1956; s. Everett Eldred and Mary Mildred (Bunch) M.; m. Kathryn Lynn Lowman, Feb. 6, 1982; 1 child, Jason Richard. AA, Sinclair Community Coll., Dayton, Ohio, 1978. Radiol. tech. asst. Kettering (Ohio) Med. Ctr., 1977-81; sales rep. Western/So. Life Ins. Co., Dayton, 1981-83, Dayton/Miami Valley Better Bus. Bur., 1983-84; dir. personnel, acct. Christ Life Ministries, Inc., Kettering, 1984—, asst youth dir., 1984-86, singles ministry dir., 1986—. V.p. men's ch. softball South Suburban YMCA, Centerville, Ohio, 1985, 86, pres., 1987. Mem. South Dayton Christian Athletic Assn. (pres. 1983-87). Avocations: racquetball, softball, weightlifting. Home: 1765 Pershing Blvd Dayton OH 45420

MARTIN, JAMES MERWYN, automotive safety administrator; b. Milton, Wis., Nov. 19, 1933; s. Merwyn Arthur and Mary Josephine (Finnane) M.; m. Elizabeth Ann Tomazewski, Aug. 27, 1960; children—Michael James, James Patrick, Mary Elizabeth. B.S., U. Wis.-Stevens Point, 1961. With Fisher Body div. Gen. Motors Corp., Janesville, Wis., 1953-61, trainee Chevrolet Motor div., 1961-62, truck prodn. foreman, 1963, safety engr. Janesville, Wis., 1964-68, safety supr. Assembly div., 1968-73, sr. adminstr. safety, Warren, Mich., 1973—; cons. in field. Served with U.S. Army, 1953-55. Mem. Am. Soc. Safety Engrs., Nat. Safety Council, Mich. Safety Council. Republican. Roman Catholic. Author manuals.

MARTIN, JERRY, III, university administrator; b. Pitts., July 26, 1942; s. Jerry and Jean (Quash) M.; m. Rita C. Lane, Feb. 28, 1964 (div. Aug. 1969); children—Danielle Renee, Trent Otis; m. Carol Moore, Mar. 27, 1972; children—Lea-Jeanne, Kara Faithe. A.A., Kennedy-King Coll., 1970; B.S., Chgo. State U., 1972; M.A., Governors State U., 1976. Salesman, Sci. Research Assocs., Chgo., 1973-80, Prescription Learning Corp., Chgo., 1980-81; tchr. Chgo. Bd. Edn., 1980-82; tchr. City Colls. of Chgo., 1980-82, admistr., 1982—. Chgo. State U. scholar, 1970; mem. 100% Club Sci. Research Assocs., 1978. Mem. Nat. Alliance Black Sch. Educators. Democrat. Presbyterian.

MARTIN, JERRY D., minister; b. Tom Bean, Tex., July 20, 1935; s. Carl Haizlip and Una B. (Pruitt) M.; m. Donna Kay Heath, June 26, 1965; children: Chad Heath, Jordan Leighann. BA, Harding Coll., 1957; BD, Crozer Theol. Sem., 1966, ThM, 1970; D of Ministry, McCormick Theol. Sem., 1981. Ordained minister, 1970. Pastor Chicago Ave. Christian Ch., Columbus, Ohio, 1968-73, Boardman Christian Ch., Youngstown, Ohio, 1973-83, Cen. Christian Ch., Danville, Ill., 1983—. Mem. Am. Assn. Pastoral Counselors. Democrat. Avocations: tennis, reading, travel. Home: 503 Dennis Dr Danville IL 61832 Office: Cen Christian Ch 1101 N Vermilion Danville IL 61832

MARTIN, JOHN BRUCE, chemical engineer; b. Auburn, Ala., Feb. 2, 1922; s. Herbert Marshall and Lannie (Steadham) M.; m. Mildred Jane Foster, Aug. 7, 1943 (dec. Nov. 1960); children—Shirlie Martin Briggs, John Bruce; m. 2d, Phyllis Barbara Rodgers, June 25, 1963; 1 child, Richard Kipp. B.S., Ala. Poly. Inst., 1943; M.Sc., Ohio State U., 1947, Ph.D., 1949. Registered profl. engr., Ohio. With Procter & Gamble Co., Cin., 1949-82, coordinator orgn. devel., research and devel., 1967-77, mgr. indsl. chem. market research, 1977-82; sr. assoc. Indumar, Inc., Cin., 1982-86, sr. v.p., 1986—; lectr. U. Cin., 1982—; adj. assoc. prof. Auburn U., 1983—. Contbr. articles to profl. jours.; patentee in field. Served with AUS, 1943-46. Decorated Air Medal, Bronze Star with oak leaf cluster; recipient Disting. Alumnus award Coll. Engring., Ohio State U., 1970, Disting. Engr. award Tech. Socs. Council Cin., 1982. Fellow Am. Inst. Chem. Engrs. (Chem. Engr. of Yr. award Ohio Valley 1971; bd. dirs. 1968-70, chmn. mktg. div. 1985); mem. Engring. Soc. Cin. (pres. 1972-73), Tech. and Sci. Socs. Cin. (pres. 1972-73), Chem. Mktg. Research Assn., Am. Soc. Engring. Edn., Am. Chem. Soc., Sigma Xi, Tau Beta Pi, Phi Kappa Phi, Phi Lambda Upsilon. Republican. Mem. Disciples of Christ Ch. Club: Clifton Track. Home: 644 Doepke Ln Cincinnati OH 45231

MARTIN, JOHN JOSEPH, communications executive; b. Evanston, Ill., May 14, 1956; s. William Aloysious and Ellen Elizabeth (Pool) M.; m. Sally Sliger, Sept. 10, 1983; children: Zachary William, Nicholas John. BS, So. Ill. U., 1979; MBA, Loyola U., Chgo., 1985. Lic. real estate broker, Ill. Account exec. Sta. WLS AM/FM Radio, Chgo., 1979-80; regional sales mgr. Sta. RKO Radio, Chgo., 1980-83; local sales mgr. Sta. WFYR Radio (subs. RKO), Chgo., 1983-84; gen. sales mgr. Sta. WUSN, Chgo., 1984-85; midwest sales mgr. CBS Radio Networks, Chgo., 1985—. Fund raiser Children's Meml. Hosp., Chgo., 1985. Ill. News Broadcasters Am. scholar, 1978. Mem. Broadcast Advt. Club, Gen. Mgrs. Club, Phi Eta Sigma. Avocations: skiing, golf, jogging, photography, music. Home: 395 Elder Ln Winnetka IL 60093 Office: CBS Radio Networks 630 N McClurg Chicago IL 60611

MARTIN, JUDITH MORAN, lawyer, tax and financial planner; b. Ann Arbor, Mich., Feb. 10, 1943; d. D. Lawrence and Donna E. (Webb) Moran; divorced; children: Laura C., Paul M., A. Lindsay; m. Daniel B. Ventres Jr., Dec. 27, 1984. BA, U. Mich., 1963; postgrad., Universite de Jean Moulin, Institut du Droit, Lyon, France, 1982; JD, U. Minn., 1982; cert., Am. Coll., 1986. Bar: Minn. 1982. Tax supr., dir. fin. planning, asst. nat. dir. Coopers & Lybrand, Mpls., 1981-84; dir. fin. planning Investors Diversified Services subs. Am. Express, Mpls. and N.Y.C., 1984-85; sr. tax mgr., dir. fin. planning KPMG Peat Marwick Main & Co. (merger KMG Main Hurdman and Peat Marwick), Mpls., 1985—; active Metro Tax Planning Group, Mpls., 1984—. Author contg. edn. materials on taxation and income and estate planning. Mem. Downtown Council Coms., Mpls., 1982-84, Mpl. Estate Planning Council, 1985—; class chmn. fundraising campaign U. Minn. Law Sch., Mpls., 1985; usher Christ Presbyn. Ch., Edina, Minn., 1983—. Mem. ABA (task force on legal fin. planning), Minn. Bar Assn., Hennepin County Bar Assn., Minn. Soc. CPA's (instr. continuing legal edn. 1983-84, continuing profl. edn. 1986—, individual trust and estate provisions 1986 tax reform act, author, instr. IRS tax reform act, impact of IRS Valuation Tables on Income and estate Tax Planning), Am. Soc. CLU's, Minn. Women Lawyers Estate, Lex Alumnae, U. Mich. Alumni Assn., U. Minn. Alumni Assn., Minn. World Trade Assn., Internat. Assn. Fin. Planners, Twin Cities Assn. Fin. Planners, Kappa Kappa Gamma. Clubs: Interlachen (Mpls.), Lafayette (Mpls.). Home: 1355 Vine Place Orono MN 55364 Office: KPMG Peat Marwick Main & Co IDS Tower Suite 1700 Minneapolis MN 55402

MARTIN, KAREN MARIE, training director; b. Dearborn, Mich., July 23, 1960; d. Chelso and Elsie (Doumanian) M. BBA, Eastern Mich. U., 1982. Mgr. Domino's Pizza Inc., Riverview, Mich., 1983-84; tng. dir. Domino's Pizza Inc., Southfield, Mich., 1984—. Mem. Nat. Orgn. Female Execs. Avocations: water sports, softball, volleyball, walleyball. Home: 4148 Crooks West Bloomfield MI 48033 Office: Domino's Pizza Inc 26011 Evergreen Suite 305 Southfield MI 48076

MARTIN, KENNETH HAROLD, textbook editor; b. Wichita, Kans., May 1, 1944; s. Harold Dean and Velma Ardis (Nelson) M.; m. Deborah Jean Rogers, July 6, 1968; children: Michael James, Geoffrey Joel. BS, Abilene Christian U., 1965, MS, 1967; postgrad., U. Okla., 1968-71. CPA, Okla. Spl. asst. to controller Montgomery Ward, Albany, N.Y., 1965; instr. gen. bus. U. Southwestern La., Lafayette, 1966-68; instr. acctg. Okla. Christian Coll., Oklahoma City, 1968-69, Oklahoma City U., 1969-72; asst. prof. acctg. Tex. A&I U., Kingsville, 1973-76; editor South-Western Pub. Co., Cin., 1977-87, sr. editor, 1987—. Editor Accounting Principals, 1978 (Best Selling Coll. Textbook 1978—). Treas. Planned Parenthood Assn. of Chaparral Country, Kingsville, 1974-76; chmn. supervising com. Tex. A&I Fed. Credit Union, Kingsville, 1975-76; pres. Sycamore Singers, 1980-82; deacon Clifton Ch. Christ, Cin., 1983-85, elder 1985—. Mem. Am. Inst. CPA's, Am. Acctg. Assn., Lambda Chi Alpha (Most Outstanding Alumnus 1975-76). Republican. Mem. Ch. Christ. Lodge: Kiwanis (treas. Kingsville 1975-76). Avocations: travel, refinishing furniture. Home: 6384 Ironwood Dr Loveland OH 45140 Office: South-Western Pub Co 5101 Madison Rd Cincinnati OH 45227

MARTIN, LAURA BELLE, real estate and farm land manager, retired teacher; b. Jackson County, Minn., Nov. 3, 1915; d. Eugene Wellington and Mary Christina (Hanson) M. BS, Mankato State U., 1968. Tchr. rural schs., Renville County, Minn., 1937-41, 45-50, Wabasso (Minn.) Pub. Sch., 1963-81; pres. Renville Farms and Feed Lots, 1982—. Sec. Hist. Renville Preservation Com., 1978-86, Town and Country Boosters, Renville, 1982-83; pub. chmn. Renville Mus., 1978—. Mem. Am. Legion Aux. Democrat. Lutheran. Avocations: antique furniture, travel, sewing. Home and Office: Box 567 Renville MN 56284

MARTIN, LEE, business executive; b. Elkhart, Ind., Feb. 7, 1920; s. Ross and Esther Lee (Schweitzer) M.; m. Geraldine Faith Fitzgarrald, July 20, 1945; children: Jennifer L., Casper, Rex, Elizabeth. B.S.M.E., MIT, 1943, M.S.M.E., 1943. With Gen. Electric Co., 1940-42; with Nibco, Inc., Elkhart, 1946—; successively v.p., gen. mgr. Nibco, Inc., 1950-56, pres, pres., 1957-76, chief exec. officer, 1976—; dir. First Nat. Bank, Elkhart. Chmn. Samaritan Inst., Denver, 1980—. Served with USN, 1943-45. Republican. Presbyterian. Clubs: Union League (Chgo.), Mid-Am. (Chgo.). Office: 500 Simpson Ave Elkhart IN 46515

MARTIN, LEE EDWIN, architect, state official; b. Lakewood, Ohio, Sept. 19, 1948; s. Ira Paige and Helen P. (Livingston) M.; m. Charlene Ann Hunt, Nov. 30, 1968; 1 child, Jeffrey Allen. Student Capital U., 1966-67; BArch, Ohio State U., 1975. Cert. energy auditor. Project architect, Holroyd & Myers, Architects, Inc., 1985-86; constrn. mgr., Busch Properties Inc., Columbus, Ohio, 1986—; state architect, 1983-85. Pres., Tribute to Vietnam Vets., Inc., Columbus, 1984-85; bd. dirs. Friends of Gov.'s Residence, Columbus, 1984; mem. Maple Grove United Meth. Ch., Columbus, Ch. in Soc. com., peace advocates. Served with USAF, 1968-72. Mem. AIA (chmn., bd. dirs., contbg. editor chpt. newsletter), VFW. Club: Governor's (Columbus). Avocations: architectural photography; scuba diving. Home: 718 E Weisheimer Rd Columbus OH 43214 Office: 4401 Indianaola Ave Columbus OH 43214

MARTIN, LORI LEE, educator; b. St. Louis, Oct. 5, 1958; d. Robert Allen and Charleen Ione (Edwards) Smith; m. Brian E. Martin, May 26, 1979. BS in Elem. Edn., Kans. State U., 1980, M of Ednl. Adminstrn., 1985. Cert. elem. tchr. and adminstr., Kans. Dir. aquatics, swim team coach, swim instr. City of Clay Center, Kans., 1981—; tchr. 5th and 6th grade Green (Kans.) Elem. Sch., 1980-84; tchr. 3d grade Lincoln Primary Ctr., Clay Center, 1984—; tchr. 5th and 6th grade Green (Kans.) Elem. Sch., 1980-84; sponsor cheerleading and pep club Clay Center High Sch., 1985—. Dir. Swim For Heart Swim-A-Thon Am. Heart Assn., Clay Center, 1981—; vol. instr. Arthritis Found., Clay Center, 1982—; founder Clay Man Triathlon, Clay Center Community Hosp., 1985. Fellow Delta Kappa Gamma; mem. Kans. Sch. Bds. Assn. (North cen. ednl. evaluation team 1983), Bus. and Profl. Women Club (sec. 1987—, North Cen. Kans. Career Woman of Yr. award 1986), Phi Kappa Phi, Beta Sigma Phi, Chi Omega. Republican. Roman Catholic. Avocations: fitness activities, gardening, vol. work. Home: Rural Rt Three Clay Center KS 67432 Office: Lincoln Primary Ctr 1020 Grant Ave Clay Center KS 67432

MARTIN, LYNN MORLEY, congresswoman; b. Evanston, Ill., Dec. 26, 1939; d. Lawrence William and Helen Catherine (Hall) Morley; children from a previous marriage: Julia Catherine, Caroline; m. Harry D. Leinenweber, Jan. 1987. B.A., U. Ill., 1960. Former tchr. pub. schs.; mem. Ill. Ho. of Reps., 1977-79, Ill. Senate, 1979-81; mem. 97th-100th Congresses from 16th Ill. Dist., 1981—. Named to Outstanding Young Women Am. U.S. Jaycees. Mem. AAUW, C. of C. of Rockford, Jr. League. Republican. Office: 1208 Longworth Office Bldg Washington DC 20515

MARTIN, MAUREEN ANN, commercial real estate executive; b. Oak Park, Ill., June 4, 1962; d. Lawrence George and Ann Florence (Hurley) M. BA magna cum laude, St. Mary's Coll., Notre Dame, Ind.; grad., Realtors Nat. Mktg. Inst. Lic. real estate agt., Ill. Mem. sales-office properties group Rubloff, Inc., Chgo., 1984—; candidate Chgo. Real Estate Bd., 1984—. Mem. Chgo. Real Estate Orgn., Kappa Gamma Pi. Roman Catholic. Avocations: sailing, traveling. Office: Rubloff Inc 111 W Washington Chicago IL 60602

MARTIN, MAURICE JOHN, psychiatrist; b. Tuscola, Ill., July 6, 1929; s. Daniel Ambrose and Mary Alta (Payne) M.; m. Ada Himma, Aug. 15, 1953; children: Daniel, Mark, Matthew, Tina, Lisa. BS, U. Ill., 1951, MD, 1954; MS, U. Minn., 1960. Diplomate Am. Bd. Internal Medicine, Am. Bd. Psychiatry and Neurology. Intern Presbyn. Hosp., Chgo., 1954-55; resident Mayo Grad. Sch. Medicine, Rochester, Minn., 1955-57, 59-62; cons. in adult psychiatry Mayo Clinic, Rochester, 1962—; head adult psychiatry Mayo Clinic, 1968-74; chmn. dept. psychiatry and psychology Mayo Clinic and Mayo Med. Sch., 1974-85, asst. prof. psychiatry and psychology, 1965-70, assoc. prof., 1970-75, prof., 1975—; pres. staff Mayo Clinic, 1981-82. Contbr. articles on psychiatry and psychosomatic medicine to profl. jours. Served to col., M.C. USAR, 1955—. Recipient H. V. Jones award Mayo Found., 1960. Fellow Am. Psychiat. Assn., Am. Coll. Psychiatrists (regent 1980-83, v.p. 1986—), Acad. Psychosomatic Medicine (pres. 1974-75, Prestigious Achievement award 1986); mem. Minn. Psychiat. Soc. (pres. 1979-81), Sigma Xi (chpt. pres. 1981-82), Alpha Omega Alpha. Home: 914 Sierra Ln Rochester MN 55904 Office: 200 First St SW Rochester MN 55905

MARTIN, PAUL JAMES, dentist; b. New Hampton, Iowa, Feb. 20, 1942; s. Paul Vincent and Gertrude Emilie (Fisher) M.; m. Ann Kirkpatrick, Aug. 21, 1965; children: David William, Rebecca Ann. BS, U. Iowa, 1964, DDS, 1969. Gen. practice dentistry Cedar Rapids, Iowa, 1973—; asst. prof. dentistry U. Iowa, 1973—. Coordinator Very Special Arts Linn County, Cedar Rapids, 1984-86; chmn. allocations panel United Way East Cen. Iowa, 1980-86; chmn. Ambroz Arts Avd. Bd., Inc., 1983—. Served to col. U.S. Army, 1969-73, col. Res. Mem. ADA, Iowa Dental Assn., Univ. Dist. Dental Soc. (peer review com. 1985—), Linn County Dental Soc. (bd. dirs. 1985—), Chgo. Dental Soc. (assoc.), Omicorn Kappa Upsilon, Psi Omega, PIerre Fauchard Acad. Roman Catholic. Avocations: jogging, swimming, travel, pottery. Home: 3640 Honey Hill Dr SE Cedar Rapids IA 52403 Office: 1030 5th Ave SE 3500 Cedar Rapids IA 52403

MARTIN, PAUL WILLIAM, JR., dentist, volunteer fire chief; b. Cleve., Aug. 13, 1934; s. Paul William and Ethel (Geren) M.; m. Susan Marie Nosker, Dec. 11, 1975; children—Mark Wallace, Lynn Roberta, Kurt William. B.A. in History, Coll. Wooster, 1956; D.D.S., Western Res. U., 1960; A.A.S. in Fire Sci. Tech., U. Akron, 1978. Lic. dentist, Ohio; cert. emergency med. technician, fire safety insp., Ohio. Gen. practice dentistry, Hudson, Ohio, 1960—; vol. firefighter Hudson Fire Dept., 1962-71, lt., 1971-75, capt., 1975-77, asst. chief, 1977-82, chief, 1982—; fire sci. advisor U. Akron, Ohio, 1979—. Mem. charter rev. com. Village of Hudson, 1971, 81. Served to capt. with USNR, 1961-82. Recipient Outstanding Young Men of Am. award, Hudson, 1970, Fireman of Yr. award Hudson Fire Dept., 1972, Community Service award Hudson Jaycees, 1982; fellow Acad. Gen. Dentistry Am. Dental Assn., 1981. Fellow Acad. Gen. Dentistry; mem. ADA, Ohio Dental Soc., Cleve. Dental Soc., Am. Soc. Dentistry for Children, Ohio Fire Chiefs Assn. (pres. 1980-81, asst. sec., treas. 1982—). Republican. Lodges: Masons, Rotary (pres. 1967-68). Avocations: photography; hiking; golfing; fishing. Home: 20 Owen Brown St Hudson OH 44236 Office: 201 N Main St Hudson OH 44236

MARTIN, RAY IVAN, family counselor, minister; b. Rock Port, Mo., Aug. 28, 1930; s. Charles Beck and Ivan Leah (Baker) M.; m. Mary Ann Wisecup, June 19, 1955; children: Craig Thomas, Cynthia Rae, Ivan Arthur, Clinton John. BA, Simpson Coll., 1955; STB, ThM, Boston U., 1957, ThD, 1968. Profl. hypnotherapist; cert. cons.; ordained to ministry United Meth. Ch. Pastor 1st Meth. Ch., North Attleboro, Mass., 1960-67; minister of counseling 1st Meth. Ch., Des Moines, 1967-72; dir., founder Des Moines Pastoral Counseling Ctr., 1972-76; owner, dir. Care & Counseling, Des Moines, 1976—; fellow, cons. New Eng. Acad. Hypnosis, Beverly, 1981—. Pres. Highland Park-Des Moines Bus. Club, 1985-86. Recipient Award of Honor, Clarindo Mental Health Clinic, Des Moines, 1969-72. Mem. Am. Acad. Family Mediators, Am. Assn. Profl. Hypnotherapists (profl.). Democrat. Avocations: smallcraft woodworking, reading, sailing, motorcycling, trailoring. Home: 2523 Sherwood Dr Des Moines IA 50310 Office: Care and Counseling 700 W Euclid Ave Des Moines IA 50313

MARTIN, RAYMOND ALBERT, theology educator; b. Mt. Carroll, Ill., Nov. 3, 1925; m. Alice Bast, May 29, 1949; children: Bill, Barbara, Mary, Tim. BA, Wartburg Coll., 1947; BD, Wartburg Theol. Sem., 1951; ThM, Princeton Theol. Sem., 1952, PhD, 1957; postdoctoral studies, Harvard Div. Sch., 1963-64. Instr. Greek Wartburg Coll., Waverly, Iowa, 1952-54; reference librarian Princeton (N.J.) Theol. Sem., 1957; missionary to India Luth. Ch., 1957-69; prof. Old Testament and N.T. Gurukul Luth. Theol. Coll., India, 1957-69; treas. Gurukul Sem., 1958-69, librarian, 1962-63; prof. bibl. and intertestmamental studies Wartburg Theol. Sem., Dubuque, 1969—; vis. prof. bibl. studies United Theol. Coll., Bangalore, India, 1981, Santal Theol. Sem. in Benagaria, Santal Parganas, Bihar, India, 1985; co-founder, sec. Soc. Bibl. Studies in India, 1965-69. Author: The Syntax of the Greek of Jeremiah, 1957, India List of Theological Periodicals, 1967, Syntactical Evidence of Semitic Sources in Greek Documents, 1974, An Introduction to New Testament Greek, 1976, James in Augsburg Commentary on the New Testament, 1982, An Introduction to Biblical Hebrew, 1987, Syntax Criticism of the Synoptic Gospels, 1987; contbr. articles and papers to profl. publs. Home: 1810 Lombard St Dubuque IA 52001 Office: Wartburg Theol Sem 333 Wartburg Pl Dubuque IA 52001

MARTIN, RAYMOND BRUCE, plumbing equipment manufacturing company executive; b. N.Y.C., Oct. 23, 1934; s. Raymond M. and Margaret (Lennon) M.; m. Suzanne Ruth Longpre, Sept. 3, 1960; 1 son, Christopher Haines. A.B., Villanova U., 1956. With Corning Glass Works (N.Y.), 1956-68, nat. plumbing sales mgr., 1966-68; v.p. mktg. Briggs Mfg. Co., Warren, Mich., 1968-69, v.p., gen. mgr. plumbing fixture div., 1969-72; pres., chief exec. officer Water Control Internat. Inc., Troy, Mich., 1972—; dir. Internat. Tech. Corp., Cash Control Products Inc. Served with AUS, 1957-58. Mem. Am. Soc. Plumbing Engrs., Plumbing Mfrs. Inst. (chmn. HUD Task Group 1981-82, chmn. communications com. 1983-86), Am. Nat. Standards Inst., Am. Soc. Sanitary Engrs., ASME (panel 19), Republican. Roman Catholic (trustee 1982-86). Clubs: Orchard Lake Country, L'Arbre Croche. Patentee in field. Office: 2820-224 W Maple Rd Troy MI 48084

MARTIN, RICHARD DALE, farmer; b. Lincoln, Ill., Aug. 19, 1937; s. Clarence S. and Leola Ferne (Theobald) M.; m. Mary Ellen Kaesebier, Mar. 1, 1959; children: Dana Ellen Martin Oltmanns, Larry Dale. Grad., Lincoln Coll., 1958. Farm owner Lincoln; treas., sec., v.p., pres. Logan County (Ill.) Extension Council, 1967-71, v.p. Logan County Exec. Council, 1970-71, rep. to Fed. Land Bank, 1985—; supr. Logan County Fair Tractor Pull, 1971-86; bd. dirs., pres. Burtonview (Ill.) Grain Co., 1971-86; treas. Logan County Farm Bur. 1984-85, v.p. 1986-87, pres. 1987—. Patentee farm machinery, 1985. Mem. New Holland (Ill.)-Middletown Sch. Adv. Council, 1967-69; leader Hollanders 4-H Club, 1973, 74; bd. dirs., pres. Growmark, 1985; active Parents chpt. Future Farmers Am., 1980; trustee Jefferson St. Christian Ch., Lincoln, 1974-84. Named Outstanding Young Farmer, Logan County Jaycees, 1972, Young Farmer of Am., U. Ill., 1973, Courier Man of Month, 1973; recipient Cert. of Achievement, Lincoln Coll., 1958, land grant, U. Ill., 1986, Tandem Corp. Computer award, 1984, plaque, U. Ill. Adv. Council, 1986, Dealer award Burrus Seed Co., 1986, Conservation Farm Family award, 1986. Mem. Prodn. Credit Assn. (pres. Lincoln council 1978,79, Disting. Service award 1983), Soil Savers of Logan County (pres., bd. dirs. 1984), Lincoln Coll. Alumni Assn. (bd. dirs. 1973), Logan County Pilots Assn. (lic. pilot, pres. 1977, 78), Prairieland Computer Club. Lodge: Elks. Avocations: flying, golf, computers. Home and Office: Rural Rte #1 Box 116 Lincoln IL 62656

MARTIN, ROBERT A., electronics company executive. Chmn., pres. NES Inc., Carpentersville, Ill. Office: NES Inc 1536 Brandy Pkwy Streamwood IL 60103 *

MARTIN, ROBERT EDWARD, architect; b. Dodge City, Kans., Mar. 17, 1928; s. Emry and Alice Jane (Boyce) M.; m. Billie Jo Lange, Aug. 16, 1952 (div. Feb. 1970); m. Kathryn M. Arvanitis, June 17, 1971; children: Lynn, Amy, Blaine. Student, McPherson Coll., 1946-48; BArch, U. Cin., 1954. Registered architect, Ohio. Architect Samborn, Steketee, Otis & Evans, Inc., Toledo, 1956-58; prin. Schauder & Martin, Toledo, 1958-72, The Collaborative, Inc., Toledo, 1972—; mem. Bd. Examiners Architects, Ohio, 1985—, Nat. Council Archtl. Registration Bds., 1986—. Artist numerous paintings. Mem. Toledo Planning Commn., 1971-74, Toledo Zoning Appeals Bd., 1973, Toledo Bd. Bldg. Standards, 1967—, Citizens Fire Adv. Commn., 1974—, Citizens Urban Area Adv. Commn., 1962, Toledo Area Council Govts., 1977-80, Spectrum Friends of Fine Arts, Inc., Toledo; chmn. bd. Toledo Area Govtl. Research Assn., 1981-85; bd. dirs. Cystic Fibrosis, Toledo, 1985. Served to capt. USAF, 1954-56. Recipient numerous watercolor awards. Mem. AIA (pres. Toledo chpt. 1966), Architects Soc. Ohio (pres. 1975), Ohio Watercolor Soc., N.W. Ohio Watercolor Soc., Toledo Fedn. Art Socs. (v.p.), Spectrum. Mem. Ch. of Brethren. Club: Tile, Toledo Artists, Sylvania Country. Lodges: Masons, Rotary. Avocation: painting. Home: 5119 Regency Dr Toledo OH 43615 Office: The Collaborative Inc 1647 S Cove Blvd PO Box 2803 Toledo OH 43606

MARTIN, ROGER BOND, landscape architect, educator; b. Virginia, Minn., Nov. 23, 1936; s. Thomas George and Audrey (Bond) M.; m. Janis Ann Kloss, Aug. 11, 1962; children: Thomas, Stephen, Jonathan. B.S., U. Minn., 1958; M. Landscape Arch., Harvard U., 1961. Asst. prof. U. Calif.-Berkeley, 1964-66; assoc. prof. U. Minn., Mpls., 1966, prof., 1968—, chmn. dept. landscape architecture, 1968-77, 83—, dir. grad. studies in landscape architecture, 1983-84; owner Roger Martin & Assoc., site planners and landscape architects, Mpls., 1966-68; prin. InterDesign, Inc., Mpls., 1968-84, Martin & Pitz Assocs., Inc., 1984—; vis. prof. U. Melbourne, 1979-80. Prin. works include: Minn. Zool. Gardens, 1978 (Am. Soc. Landscape Architects Merit award 1978), Mpls. Pkwy. Restorations, 1978 (Merit award 1978), South St. Paul Cen. Sq., 1978 (Merit award 1978), Festival Park, Chisholm, Minn., 1986. Fellow Am. Acad. in Rome, 1962-64. Fellow Am. Soc. Landscape Architects (pres. Minn. chpt. 1970-72, trustee 1980-84, nat. pres.-elect 1985, Pub. Service award 1985, Visual Image Merit award 1985); mem. Nat. Council Instrs. Landscape Architecture (pres. 1973-74). Home: 2912 45th Ave Minneapolis MN 55406 Office: Martin & Pitz Assocs Inc 1409 Willow St Minneapolis MN 55403

MARTIN, RONALD THEO, accountant; b. St. Louis, Dec. 8, 1959; s. Theo and Joan Myrtle (Kuechenmeister) M.; m. Linda Susan Rapp, Nov. 9, 1985. BS in Accountancy, U. Mo., 1982. CPA, Mo. Auditor Ernst & Whinney, St. Louis, 1982-83, cons., 1983-86; mgr. fin. planning Met. Sewer Dist., St. Louis, 1986—. Mem. Am. Inst. CPA's, Mo. Soc. CPA's, Alpha Kappa Psi. Republican. Lutheran. Avocations: golf, camping, skiing. Home: 4247 Martyridge Dr Saint Louis MO 63129 Office: Met St Louis Sewer Dist 2000 Hampton Ave Saint Louis MO 63139

MARTIN, SUSAN WORK, state revenue commissioner; b. Croswell, Mich., Oct. 24, 1950; d. Samuel McCreery and Ruth (Laramie) Work; m. James L. Winckler, May 22, 1971 (div. Dec. 1983); 1 child, Diana; m. Lawrence Wesley Martin, Jan 3, 1985; 1 son, Samuel; 1 stepson, Brian. BS in Pub. Speaking, Cen. Mich. U., 1971; MBA in Acctg., Mich. State U., 1976, postgrad. in Acctg., 1980—. CPA, Mich.; cert. mgt. acct.; CIA. Tax intern Ernst & Whinney, Lansing, Mich., 1976; asst. auditor gen. Mich. Dept. Auditing Gen., Lansing, 1976-80; grad. asst. Mich. State U. Acctng., East Lansing, 1980-81, 83-84; dep. state treas. Mich. Dept. Treasury, Lansing, 1981-84, commr. revenue, 1985—; Chmn. Mich. com. on Govtl. Acctg. and Auditing, 1983-85. Author: Basics of Fund Accounting, 1985; editor Municipal Forum, The Michigan CPA. Mich. State U. research grantee, 1982. Mem. Nat. Tax Assn. (com. 1984—), Am. Inst. CPA's (doctoral fellow 1984-85), Am. Acctg. Assn., Inst. Internal Auditors (bd. govs. Lansing chpt. 1979), Govt. Fin. Officers Assn., Assn. Govt. Accts. (Disting. Leadership award), Midwestern Assn. of State Tax Adminstrs. (sec. 1986), Mich. Assn. of CPA's Acctg. and Auditing (vice chmn. 1986), Multistate Tax Commn. (exec. com. 1986), Cen. Mich. U. Alumni Assn. (nat. bd. Dirs. 1976-77). Club: Porshe of Am. (pres. Motorstadt region 1979). Avocation: golf. Office: Mich Dept Treasury Bur of Revenue Allegan St Lansing MI 48922

MARTIN, THOMAS BROOKS, JR., computer company executive; b. Camden, N.J., Feb. 4, 1955; s. Thomas Brooks Sr. and Helen (Spicer) Martin; m. Mary Louise Kivlin, May 21, 1983; children: Catherine. AB, ScB, Brown U., 1977; MS, MIT, 1981. Engr. Westinghouse Corp., Detroit, 1977-79; sr. engagement mgr. McKinsey & Co., Chgo., 1981-86; asst. v.p. NEC Home Elecs., Wood Dale, Ill., 1986—. Mem. Phi Beta Kappa, Tau Beta Pi.

Roman Catholic. Avocations: designing high-fidelity systems, gardening, golf. Office: NEC Home Elecs 1255 Michael Dr Wood Dale IL 60191

MARTIN, TRAVIS E., psychologist, educator; b. N.Y.C., Mar. 19, 1951; s. Earl Martin and Catherine (Lavina) James; m. Cristine Beth Johnson, Aug. 10, 1975; 1 child, Robin Michael. BS, No. Mich. U., 1975; M in Human Services, Lincoln U., 1981. Cert. alcohol and drug counselor, Mich., marriage and family therpaist. Coordinator Big Bros. Phila., 1976-78; psychotherapist Eagleville Hosp., Pa., 1978-81; pvt. practice family therapy Pa., 1980-81; dir. drug and alcohol program S.E. Wis. Med. and Social Services, 1982-86; psychologist Martin Psychol. Assocs., Marquette, Mich., 1986—; dist. coordinator Big Bros. of Phila., 1976-78; psychotherapist Eagelville (Pa.) Hosp., 1978-81; dir. drug and alcohol program S.E. Wis. Med. & Social Services, 1982-86. Bd. dirs. Ctr. City Scholarship Fund, 1982-86, S.W. YMCA, 1983-86; mem. adv. com. Community Mental Health Ctr. Served with USAF, 1972-74. Mem. Am. Assn. Marriage and Family Therapy (cert.), Am. Legion. Roman Catholic. Lodge: KC. Avocations: swimming, hunting, reading, outdoor activities, spending time with son. Home: 2683 Moran Marquette MI 49855 Office: Martin Psychol Assocs 2318 US-41 South Marquette MI 49855

MARTIN, WAYNE MALLOTT, lawyer, real estate company executive; b. Chgo., Jan. 9, 1950; s. Mallott Caldwell and Helen (Honkisz) M.; m. Josephine Ann Giordano, Mar. 18, 1978; 1 child, Bradley. BA, Drake U., 1972; JD, De Paul U., 1977. Bar: Ill. 1978. Loan officer Clyde Savs. & Loan Assn., Chgo., 1972-75, Am. Nat. Bank, Chgo., 1976-77; sales dir., atty. financing Inland Real Estate Corp., Chgo., Oak Brook, then Palatine, Ill., 1977-83; pres. Inland Property Sales, Inc., Palatine, 1983-84, Oak Brook, Ill., 1984-86; Dome Investments, Inc., Northbrook, Ill., 1986—; Quest Mortgage Co., Rolling Meadows, Ill., 1986—. Mem. ABA, Ill. Bar Assn., Chgo. Bar Assn., Nat. Bd. Realtors, Ill. Bd. Realtors, Chgo. Bd. Realtors (bd. dirs. 1986—, trustee action com. 1986—, fin. com. 1986—, chmn. orientation com. 1987-88), Westside Bd. Realtors (bd. dirs. 1983-84, pres. 1984—), Interboard Real Estate Affairs Council (chmn. 1987-88). Home: 1618 RFD Picardy Ct Long Grove IL 60047 Office: 40 Quest Mortgage Co 1833 Hicks Rd Suite A Rolling Meadows IL 60008

MARTIN, WESLEY GEORGE, electrical engineer; b. Chgo., Apr. 15, 1946; s. Chester W. and Marie L. (Seifarth) M.; m. Margaret Rose Kowach, Aug. 17, 1968; children—Patrick, Christopher. B.S., Milw. Sch. Engring., 1969; cert. Alexander Hamilton Inst., N.Y.C., 1976. Registered profl. engr., Ill., Ind., Wis. Elec. engr. and estimator The Austin Co., Des Plaines, Ill., 1969-78; elec. estimator Skidmore, Owings & Merrill, Chgo., 1978-83; elec. engr. Holabird & Root, Chgo., 1983—, assoc. ptnr., 1986—; owner W.G. Martin & Assocs., cons., Palatine, Ill., 1978—. Contbr. articles to profl. jours. Democratic precinct capt., Palatine, 1979-82; cubmaster pack #91 Boy Scouts Am., 1986—. Recipient award of Merit, Chgo. Lighting Inst., 1981, 82, 83. Mem. Nat. Soc. Profl. Engrs., Ill. Soc. Profl. Engrs., Nat. Eagle Scout Assn. Roman Catholic. Home: 918 W Colfax St Palatine IL 60067 Office: Holabird & Root 300 W Adams St Chicago IL 60606

MARTIN, WILFRED SAMUEL, management consultant; b. Adamsville, Pa., June 11, 1910; s. Albert W. and Elizabeth (Porter) M.; B.S., Iowa State U., 1930; M.S., U. Cin., 1938; m. Elizabeth Myers, July 9, 1938; children—Peter, Judith (Mrs. Peter Kleinman), Nancy (Mrs. Richard Foss), Paula (Mrs. Dale Birdsell). Chem. engr. process devel. dept. Procter & Gamble Co., Cin., 1930-50, mgr. drug products mfg., 1950-51, asso. dir. chem. div., 1952-53, dir. product devel., soap products div., 1953-63, mgr. mfg. and products devel. Food Products div., 1963-71, sr. dir. research and devel., 1971-75; mgmt. cons., 1975—. Mem. Wyoming (Ohio) Bd. Edn., 1961-69, pres., 1965-68. Bd. dirs. Indsl. Research Inst., 1964-68, v.p., 1968-69, pres., 1970-71; chmn. trustee Ohio Presbyn. Homes, Columbus, Ohio, 1959-69, 73-77; vice chmn. bd. trustees Pikeville (Ky.) Coll., 1973-76, 80-86, trustee emeritus, 1986—, chmn. bd. trustees, 1976-78, 83-84, mem., 1980-84. Adv. council Clarkson Coll., Potsdam, N.Y., 1975-81. Fellow AAAS; mem. Am. Chem. Soc., Am. Inst. Chem. Engrs., Soc. Chem. Industry, Am. Oil Chemist Soc., Engring. Soc. Cin. (dir. 1972-75), N.Y. Acad. Scis., Am. Mgmt. Assn. (research devel. council 1974-81), Soc. Research Adminstrs. Club: Wyoming Golf (Cin.). Home: 504 Hickory Hill Ln Cincinnati OH 45215

MARTINAZZI, TONI, educational media specialist, consultant; b. Portland, Oreg., Apr. 27, 1936; d. Arthur Julius and Ann (Chapman) M.; m. Robert Eugene Leber, Nov. 6, 1954 (div. June 1970); children—Michael Jene, Donna Loyce, Max Arthur, Rhonda Carol; m. 2d Joseph John Kinzig, March 2, 1984. B.A. in English, Portland State U., 1969, M.A. in Teaching, 1975; postgrad. in edn. Northeastern Ill. U., 1983, DePaul U. Cert. tchr., media specialist, Ill.. Head librarian Scappoose High Sch. (Oreg.), 1969-73; head media specialist Grant High Sch., Portland, Oreg., 1975-80; librarian, High Sch. Dist. 214, Ill., 1984-85; media specialist Dist. 62, Ill., 1985—; cons. ednl. media, Chgo., 1982—; chairperson charter task force Tualatin Pub. Library (Oreg.), 1976-77, 78-79, charter chairperson adv. bd., 1977-79. Reviewer media library and ednl. jours., 1975—. Recipient commendation City of Tualatin, 1978. Mem. Gregorians, Ill. Assn. for Media in Edn., ALA, Am. Assn. Sch. Librarians (Nat. Sch. Library Program of Yr. 1987), Internat. Assn. Sch. Librarians, Nat. Trails Council, Appalachian Trail Council, Am. Hiking Soc. (transcontinental backpacker 1980-81). Republican. Roman Catholic. Club: Mazamas, Mountaineers. Home: 301 Harlem Ave Glenview IL 60025

MARTINDALE, LARRY RICHARD, computer services company consultant; b. Grove City, Ohio, Nov. 18, 1938; s. Lawrence Thomas Hoyt and Thelma Elizabeth (Strickler) M.; m. Carol Sue Woods, Dec. 22, 1959; children: Larry Richard, Lynnette Carolita, Kyle Edgar, Connie Beth, Tanya Sue. AS, Franklin U., 1972, BS, 1973. Sales analysis clk. Scoa Industries Inc., Columbus, Ohio, 1956-64, computer operator, 1964-65, computer programmer, 1965-66, systems programmer, 1966-68, programmer/analyst, 1968-73; sr. programmer/analyst Ohio State Dept. Pub. Welfare, Columbus, 1973-75; sr. analyst Cutler-Williams Inc., Dayton, Ohio, 1975-76; sr. programmer/analyst Blue Cross/Blue Shield Inc., Indpls., 1976-78; sr. staff cons. Cap Gemini Am. (formerly CGA Computers Inc. and Allen Services Corp.), Dayton, 1978—; cons. Blue Cross/Blue Shield Inc., 1975-76, Blue Cross/Blus Shield Northwest Ohio, Toledo, 1978, Federated Dept. Stores Inc., Cin., 1978-81, Dayton Newspapers, Inc., 1981, 84, Delco Electronics, Inc., Kokomo, Ind., 1981-84, Procter & Gamble, Inc., Cin., 1984—. Jr. high basketball coach Muhlenberg Twp. Sch., Darbyville, Ohio, 1956-57; youth pres. Darbyville Ch. Nazarene, 1958-60, trustee, 1968-75, treas., 1970-75, fin. sec., 1970-75; coach, bd. dirs. Derby (Ohio) Little League baseball, 1972-75, Rush County Youth basketball league, Rushville, Ind., 1978-81; fin. sec. Rushville Ch. Nazarene, 1977—, trustee, 1980—, dir. youth ministries, 1983, chmn. bd. Christian life, 1987—; coach Rush County Youth football league, Rushville, 1982-83; bd. dirs. Rushville Babe Ruth baseball league, 1981. Served with U.S. Army, 1961-63. Mem. Am. Legion. Republican. Avocations: basketball, football, softball, golf, running, bicycling. Home: Rural Rt 1 Box 95A Arlington IN 46104 Office: Cap Gemini Am 3401 Park Ctr Dr Dayton OH 45414

MARTINDALE, ROBERT MALCOLM, banking consultant; b. Springfield, Mass., Oct. 13, 1933; s. Kirby W. and Laura J. (Taylor) M.; m. Mary Cummings, Feb. 12, 1955 (div. May 1979); m. Patricia J. Richard, Aug. 4, 1979; children: David C., Gregory S., J. Thomas, Michael E., Jeffrey J. Student, Syracuse U., 1952-56; grad., N.Y. State Bankers Assn. Sch. Pub. Relations, 1957. Bus. devel. rep. Marine Midland Bank, Syracuse, N.Y., 1956-61; asst. v.p. Marine Midland Corp., Buffalo, 1961-66; v.p. mktg. Tex. Bank & Trust, Dallas, 1966-67; pres., chief exec. officer Midwest Bank Card System, Chgo., 1967-69; v.p. mktg. LaSalle Nat. Bank, Chgo., 1969-70; pres. Martindale & Assocs., Chgo., 1970—; mem. faculty Am. Inst. Banking, Chgo., 1972—; lectr. Syracuse U., Ohio State U., Columbus, U. Md., College Park, North Cen. Coll., Naperville, Ill., Thornton Community Coll., South Holland, Ill., Harper Coll., Schaumberg, Ill. Author: How to Manage Your Money. Pres. Syracuse Jaycees, 1960. Recipient Outstanding Traffic Safety Citizen award Allstate Ins. Co., Buffalo, 1965. Mem. Am. Inst. Banking, Chgo. Fin. Advertisers. Republican. Methodist. Avocations: photography, tennis. Home: 480 Greystone Ln Prospect Heights IL 60070 Office: Martindale & Assocs Inc 350 W Kensington Rd Mount Prospect IL 60056

MARTINI, MARIO, manufacturing company executive; b. Pola, Italy, Dec. 8, 1941; came to U.S., 1951; s. Atto and Romana (Bibolich) M.; m. Rosemary Troksa; children from a previous marriage: Christine, Philip, Renee, Rebecca. BSME, Purdue U., 1964; MBA, U. Chgo., 1970. Project engr. Am. Steel Foundries, Chgo., 1964-67, asst. v.p. mfg., engring., 1986—; project engr., mkt. analyst Union Tank Car Co., Chgo., 1967-71; asst. mgr. sales Evans Product, Chgo., 1971-75; v.p. mfg. Miner Enterprizes, Geneva, Ill., 1975-86. Patentee R.R. brake system. Mem. Am. Soc. Mech. Engrs. Avocations: golf, fishing. Home: 240 Beacon Pl Munster IN 46321 Office: Am Steel Foundries 3600 Prudential Plaza Chicago IL 60601

MARTINI, THOMAS PATRICK, accountant; b. Columbus, Ohio, Aug. 1, 1955; s. George Joseph and Rita J. (Waibel) M.; m. Alice Eileen Lusignolo, June 25, 1977; children: Matthew Thomas, Allison Ann. BBA in Acctg., Ohio State U., 1977. CPA, Ohio. Sr. adminstrv. specialist IBM Corp., Columbus, 1977-80; audit mgr. Coopers & Lybrand, Columbus, 1980—; audit mgr. Norman Jones & Co., Lancaster, Ohio, 1983-84. Inventor safety spoke caps. Treas., bd. dirs. South Side Learning and Devel. Ctr., Columbus, 1985—. Named one of Outstanding Young Men of Am., U.S. Jaycees, 1986. Mem. Am. Inst. CPA's, Ohio Soc. CPA's, Nat. Assn. Accts., Ohio State U. Alumni Assn. Home: 844 Caroway Blvd Gahanna OH 43230 Office: Coopers & Lybrand 100 E Broad St Columbus OH 43215

MARTINIE, STEVEN, lawyer; b. Indpls., Aug. 27, 1954. BA, George Washington U., 1976; MBA, U. Va., 1980, JD, 1983. Bar: Wis. 1983. Law clerk CIGNA, Bloomfield, Conn., 1982-83; atty. Northwestern Mut. Life Ins. Co., Milw., 1983—. Editor: (projects) U. Va. Law Rev., 1982-83. Office: Northwestern Mut Life Ins 720 E Wisconsin Ave Milwaukee WI 53202

MARTIN-SADOWSKI, SUSAN MARGARET, school psychologist; b. Detroit, Mar. 14, 1953; d. Adam and Clara (Grünfeld) Klisowski; m. Curtis Eugene Martin, Sept. 14, 1974 (div. Aug. 1985); 1 child, Jason Blair; m. Edward Thomas Sadowski, Aug. 30, 1986. BA, Ohio U., 1974, MS, 1977. Lic. school psychologist, Ohio. Sch. psychologist Charlevoix (Mich.)-Emmet Intermediate Schs., 1977-79, Vinton County Schs., McArthur, Ohio, 1979-81; coordinator assessment project S.E. Ohio Spl. Edn. Regional Resource Ctr., Athens, 1981—; pvt. practice psychology Athens, 1984—; instr. psychology Petoskey (Mich.) Coll., 1978. Co-author: Medical Diagnostic Service Directory to Southeast Ohio, 1983, 84, 85, School Psychology Directory, 1985. Mem. S.E. Ohio Spl. Edn. Regional Resource Ctr. Edn. Assn. (pres. 1983-84, treas. 1986-87, negotiator 1986), S.E. Ohio Sch. Psychology Assn. (news editor 1983-87), Ohio Assn. Spl. Edn. Regional Resource Ctrs. (treas. 1985-87), Phi Beta Phi. Democrat. Roman Catholic. Avocations: jogging, gardening, piano. Office: SE Ohio Spl Edn Regional Resource Ctr 507 Richland Ave Athens OH 45701

MARTINSEN, BLAINE LEE, deputy comptroller, administrator; b. Salt Lake City, Oct. 4, 1937; s. Henry Wilford and Aslaug Marie (Samuelsen) M.; m. Dianne Woodruff, June 4, 1966; children—Rebeccah, Matthew, Daniel, Jonathon, Steven. B.S. in Acctg., Brigham Young U., 1967; M.B.A., Syracuse U., 1984. Sr. acct. Fitzsimmons Army Med. Ctr., Aurora, Colo., 1974-76; jr. auditor Tooele Depot, Utah, 1976-78; sr. auditor Hawthorne Army Ammunition Plant, Nev., 1978-79; chief internal rev., Ft. Lewis, Wash., 1979-83; fin. mgr. Ft. Sheridan, Ill., 1984-86, deputy comptroller, 1986—. Active Boy Scouts Am., 1984-85. Served to capt. USAR, 1978—. Recipient Outstanding Performance award, Ft. Lewis, 1980, 82, Ft. Sheridan, 1985, Fitzsimmons Army Med. Ctr., 1976. Mem. Am. Soc. Mil. Comptrollers, Inst. Internal Auditors (bd. dirs. 1980-83). Republican. Mormon. Avocations: woodworking, fishing. Home: 2426 Highland Circle Lindenhurst IL 60046 Office: DCSRM 4th US Army Fort Sheridan IL 60037

MARTINY, KIM REITH, advertising agency executive; b. Neenah, Wis., Jan. 13, 1940; s. Keith C. and Marion O. (Ott) M.; m. Lynn Anne Spicer, Mar. 6, 1971; children—Lauren, Ryan. B.S. in Bus. Adminstrn., Carroll Coll., 1962. Mgr. spl. accounts Container Corp. Am., Chgo., N.Y.C., Cin., 1966-75; account exec. Baer, Kemble & Spicer, Inc., Cin., 1975-78, pres., 1978-80; pres., chief exec. officer Martiny & Co., Inc., Cin., 1981—. Mem. Mut. Advt. Agy. Network, Am. Assn. Advt. Agys. Republican. Roman Catholic. Club: Cin. Home: 6750 N Clippinger Dr Indian Hill OH 45243 Office: Martiny & Co Inc 250 W Court St Cincinnati OH 45202

MARTTILA, JOAN DOROTHY, audiologist; b. Watertown, S.D., Aug. 12, 1950; d. Vernon Hamilton Lois Geanette (Eastberg) M.; m. Richard Duncan Gast, Apr. 22, 1978; children: James, Kristen. Student, S.D. State U., 1968-71; BS, U. S.D., 1972; MA, U. Iowa, 1974. Cert. clin. competence audiology. Audiologist Mississippi Bend Area Edn. Agy. 9, Bettendorf, Iowa, 1974—; clin. assoc. U. Iowa, Iowa City, 1984-86, supr., summers 1976, 77. Chmn. edn. commn. Broadview United Meth. Ch., Bettendorf, 1983—, local lay speaker. Mem. Am. Speech-Lang.-Hearing Assn. (com. mem. 1979-81), Iowa Speech-Lang.-Hearing Assn. (v.p. standards and ethics 1983-85, 85-87), Quad Cities Speech and Hearing Assn. (pres. 1981-83). Republican. Avocations: reading, walking, swimming, tennis, family activities. Home: 4660 Lindbergh Dr Bettendorf IA 52722 Office: Truman Audiology Clinic 5506 N Pine St Davenport IA 52722

MARTY, ROGER HENRY, math educator; b. Sterling, Ohio, Oct. 16, 1942; s. Raymond Benjamin and Grace Lydia (Gasser) M.; m. Madge Dian Schroeder, Sept. 19, 1964; children: Deborah, Matthew. BS in Math., Kent State U., 1964; MA in Math, Pa. State U., 1966, PhD in Math., 1969. Math. instr. Western Mich. U., Kalamazoo, 1968-69; asst. prof. Cleve. State U., 1969-73, assoc. prof., 1973—. Contbr. articles to profl. jours. Named one of Outstanding Young Men in Am., 1979; Cleve. State U. grantee, 1977, 80; Ohio Bd. Regents grantee, 1986. Mem. Am. Math. Soc., Math. Assn. of Am., N.Y. Acad. Scis., Nat. Council Tchrs. of Math., Sigma Xi, Pi Mu Epsilon. Home: 5263 Chickadee Ln Lyndhurst OH 44124 Office: Cleve State U Euclid Ave at East 24th Cleveland OH 44115

MARTY, STEWART PARNELL, printing company executive, marketing consultant, photofinishing consultant; b. Bloomington, Ill., Sept. 21, 1950; s. Stewart Parnell and Aileen Alice (Tobiassen) M.; m. Karen Sue Hadley, Aug. 14, 1970 (div. July 1976); 1 child, Angela Marie; m. Karen Sue Hocking, Oct. 22, 1977; children—Jennifer Lynn, Elizabeth Nichole. Student Parkland Jr. Coll., Champaign, Ill., 1969, Ill. State U., Normal, 1970. Mgr. pro lab. div. Colorcraft Corp., Rockford, Ill., 1975-78; v.p., ptnr. Oaktree Advt. Agy., Bloomington, Ill., 1978-79; corp. v.p. Bruce-Green Advt. Ltd., Bloomington, 1979-83; account exec. Hagerty, Lockenvitz, Cinzkey & Assocs., Bloomington, 1983-84; pres. Kro-Mar Advt. div. Kro-Mar Industries, Normal, Ill., 1984—; pres. Wright Printing Co., Bloomington, Ill., Super-Scribe Inc., Bloomington, Ill.; mktg. and prodn. cons. for photofinishing firms. Bd. dirs. McLean County chpt. ARC, Ill., 1982-86, mem. exec. com., 1983-85, chmn. pub. relations com., 1982-86; mem. cast The Am. Passion Play, Bloomington, 1981—. Recipient Spl. Service award ARC, 1983, 85. Mem. Soc. Photofinishing Engrs., (cert.), Photo Mktg. Assn., Comedy Writers Guild. Republican. Presbyterian. Club: Bloomington Ad. Lodge: Masons. Home: 23 Delaine Dr Normal IL 61761 Office: 1106 E Bell Bloomington IL 61701

MARUSHKA, ROMAN DANIEL, stock options trader, investment consultant; b. Chgo., Nov. 18, 1956; s. Nicholas and Maria Marushka; m. Lydia Daria Kinal, June 15, 1985. BS, U. Ill., Chgo., 1978. Stock options trader, investment cons. H.A. Brandt and Assoc., Chgo., 1978-87, Geldermann Securities, Inc., Chgo., 1987—; cons. Investech, Alexandria, Va., 1985—. Pres. Chgo. Chpt. of Ukrainian Boy Scouts and Girl Scouts USA, 1985-87. Mem. Phila. Bd. of Trade, Ukrainian-Am. Justice Com., League of Ukrainian Voters. Mem. Ukrainian Catholic Ch. Clubs: Lions Sports, Wings Sports (Chgo.). Avocations: volleyball, camping, golf, traveling. Office: 327 S LaSalle Room 920 Chicago IL 60605

MARUT, EDWARD LAWRENCE, obstetrician-gynecologist; b. Passaic, N.J., July 4, 1949; s. Edward Alfred and Wanda Ann (Gawalis) M.; m. Joanne Mary Sullivan, July 18, 1970; children: Edward Ian, Kathryn Erin. BS, Boston Coll., 1970; MD, Yale U., 1974. Cert. Am. Bd. Ob-Gyn. Clin. assoc. NIH, Bethesda, Md., 1979-81; asst. prof. ob-gyn U. Ill. Coll. Med., Chgo., 1981-83; dir. family planning Michael Reese Hosp., Chgo., 1983-84, dir. IVF-ET program, 1984—, dir. reproductive endocrinology, 1986—; instr. ob-gyn uniformed services U. Healty Scis., Bethesda, 1979-81; asst. prof. ob-gyn U. Chgo., 1983—. Contbr. articles on reproductive endocrinology to profl. jours. mgr., coach, team physician Wilmette (Ill.) Soccer Teams, 1982-86, Wilmette Hockey Assn., 1982-86, Trevian Soccer Club, Winnetka, Ill., 1986—, Wilmette Baseball League, 1984—, Winnetka Hocky Club, 1986—. Served to lt. commdr. USPHS, 1979-81. Med. Research Inst. Council grantee, 1986—. Fellow Am. Coll. Ob-Gyns., Soc. Reproductive Endocrinologists; mem. Am. Fertility Soc., Endocrine Soc., Soc. for the Study of Reproduction, Assn. Prof. Ob-Gyn., Am. Soc. Primatologists. Democrat. Roman Catholic. Avocations: rock music, horror movies, video, hockey, skiing. Home: 790 Ash St Winnetka IL 60093 Office: Michael Reese Hosp and Med Ctr Lake Shore Dr at 31st St Chicago IL 60616

MARUTA, TOSHIHIKO, psychiatrist, educator; b. Suzaka, Japan, June 13, 1946; s. Shizuo and Sawa (Miyashita) M.; m. Junko Ihara, Apr. 29, 1971; children: Chica, Yuhgo. MD, Keio U., Tokyo, 1971; MS, U. Minn., 1977. Intern, then resident Mayo Grad. Sch. Med., Rochester, Minn., 1972-76; cons. Mayo Clinic, Rochester, 1977—; asst. prof. Mayo Med. Sch., Rochester, 1979-82, assoc. prof., 1982-86, prof., 1986—. Author: (book) Short-term Dynamic Psychotherapy, 1984, Workbook for Psychotherapists, 1986. Mem. Am. Psychiat. Assn., Am. Pain Soc., Internat. Assn. for Study of Pain, Japanese Psychoanalytic Assn., Midwest Pain Soc. (pres. 1985-86). Office: Mayo Clinic 200 1st St SW Rochester MN 55905

MARVIN, DAVID EDWARD SHREVE, lawyer; b. Lansing, Mich., Jan. 6, 1950; s. George Charles Marvin and Shirley Mae (Martin) Schaible; m. Mary Anne Kennedy, Sept. 16, 1972; 1 child, John. BS cum laude, Mich. State U., 1972; JD cum laude, Wayne State U., 1976. Bar: Mich. 1976, U.S. Dist. Ct. (ea. dist.) Mich. 1976, U.S. Dist. Ct. (we. dist.) Mich. 1978, U.S. Ct. Appeals (7th cir.) 1977, U.S. Ct. Appeals (6th cir.) 1979, U.S. Supreme Ct. 1979, U.S. Ct. Appeals (D.C. cir.) 1982. Asst. mgr. Alta Supply Co., Lansing, 1972-73; research asst. Wayne State U., Detroit, fall 1975; jud. intern. U.S. Dist. Ct., Detroit, summer, 1975; ptnr. Fraser Trebilcock Davis & Foster, P.C., Lansing, 1976—. Exec. editor: Wayne Law Rev., 1975-76; contbr. articles to law jours. Commr. Mich. Solar Resource Adv. Panel, Lansing, 1978-81, Mich. Commn. Profl. & Occupational Licensure, 1981-83; chmn. Ingham County Energy Commn., Mason, Mich., 1978-80 (state bar rep. assembly 1985—); treas. Lansing Lawyer Referral Service, 1981; state del. Nat. Solar Congress, Washington, 1978; hearing officer City of East Lansing, 1985; Tri-County Council of Bar Leaders (chmn. 1986—). Named Outstanding Young Man Am., 1984, The Outstanding Young Lawyer in Mich., 1985-86; Wm. D. Traitel scholar, 1975. Mem. ABA, State Bar Mich. (com. chmn., sect. council 1982—), Ingham County Bar Assn. (pres. 1985-86), Pro Bono Lawyers Service (pres. 1982-83), Lansing Regional C. of C. (v.p. 1987), Phi Alpha Delta, Phi Eta Sigma, Theta Delta Chi (pres. 1972). Republican. Clubs: Downtown Coaches (bd. dirs., pres. 1987), Mich. State U. Pres.'s. Home: 1959 Groton Way East Lansing MI 48823 Office: Fraser Trebilcock Davis & Foster PC Michigan Nat Tower 10th Floor Lansing MI 48933

MARVIN, JAMES CONWAY, librarian; b. Warroad, Minn., Aug. 3, 1927; s. William C. and Isabel (Carlquist) M.; m. Patricia Katharine Moe, Sept. 8, 1947; children: Heidi C., James Conway, Jill C., Jack C. B.A., U. Minn., 1950, M.A., 1966. City librarian Kaukauna, Wis., 1952-54; chief librarian Eau Claire, Wis., 1954-56; dir. Cedar Rapids (Iowa) Pub. Library, 1956-67, Topeka Pub. Library, 1967—; Am. Library Assn.-Rockefeller Found. vis. prof. Inst. Library Sci. U. Philippines, 1964-65; vis. lectr. dept. librarianship Emporia (Kans.) State U., 1970—; chmn. Kans. del. to White House Conf. on Libraries and Info. Services, Gov.'s Com. on Library Resources, 1980-81. Served with USNR, 1945-46. Mem. ALA, Iowa Library Assn. (past pres.), Kans. Library Assn., Philippine Library Assn. (life mem.), Mountain Plains Library Assn., Mayor's Task Force on Literacy. Club: Rotary (past pres.). Home: 40 Pepper Tree Ln Topeka KS 66611 Office: Topeka Pub Library 1515 W 10th St Topeka KS 66604

MARVIN, PHILIP, retired business administration educator; b. Troy, N.Y., May 1, 1916; s. George G. and Marjorie (Moston) M.; m. Grace E. Meerbach, Aug. 22, 1942. B.S., Rensselaer Poly. Inst., 1937; M.B.A., Ind. U., 1951, D.B.A., 1951; LL.B., LaSalle U., 1954. Research scientist Gen. Electric Co., 1937-42; dir. chem. and metall. engring. Bendix Aviation Corp. marine div., N.Y.C., 1943-44; dir. research and devel. Penn Controls, Inc., Milw., 1945-51; v.p., dir. Commonwealth Engring. Co., Dayton, Ohio, 1952-54; cons. to chmn. bd., pres. Am. Viscose Corp., 1955-56; mgr. research and devel. div. Am. Mgmt. Assn., 1956-64; pres., dir. Clark, Cooper, Field and Wohl, Inc., N.Y.C., 1964-65; dean profl. devel. U. Cin., 1965-73, prof. profl. devel. and bus. adminstrn., 1965-85, prof. emeritus, 1986—; lectr., cons. in field, 1965—. Author: Top Management and Research, 2d edit, 1953, Administrative Management, 2d edit, 1954, Planning New Products, vol. I, 1958, vol. II, 1964, Management Goals, 1968, Multiplying Management Effectiveness, 1971, Developing Decisions for Actions, 1971, Man in Motion, 1972, Product Planning Simplified, 1972, The Right Man for the Right Job at the Right Time, 1973, Fundamentals of Effective Research and Development Management, 1973, Managing Your Career, 1974, Managing Your Successful Career, 1978, Executive Time Management, 1980, also articles, TV programs. Fellow Fin. Analysts Fedn.; mem. Inst. Chartered Fin. Analysts, Newcomen Soc. N.Am., N.Y. Soc. Security Analysts, Sigma Xi, Tau Beta Pi, Beta Gamma Sigma. Patentee in field. Home: 11 Canborne Way Madison CT 06443

MARVINNEY, MICHELLE POWE, lawyer; b. Cleve., Dec. 28, 1955; d. Harold Daniel and June Dorothy (Clark) Powe; m. Craig Arthur Marvinney, May 28, 1983; 1 child, Kristen. BS, Miami U., 1978; JD, Case Western Res. U., 1984. CPA, Ohio; Bar: Ohio 1984, U.S. Dist. Ct. (no. dist.) Ohio 1984, U.S. Ct. Claims 1984, U.S. Tax Ct.1984. Supr. sr. accts. Peat, Marwick, Mitchell, Cin. and Toledo, 1978-79, 1979-81; assoc. McCarthy, Lebit, Cleve., 1984—. Office: McCarthy Lebit Crystal & Haiman 900 Illuminating Bldg Cleveland OH 44113

MARX, NANETTE JEAN, nurse; b. Kankakee, Ill., Oct. 20, 1951; d. Orville Joseph Neveau and Audrey Jean (McHie) Stewart; m. James Dale Marx, May 20, 1972; children: Sara Jean, Bridget Carol. Grad., Passavant Sch. Nursing, 1972; BS, Coll. of St. Francis, 1979; BS in Nursing, Bradley U., 1984; MS in Community Health Nursing, Northwestern Ill. U., 1987. RN, Ill. Staff nurse St. Mary's Hosp., Streator, Ill., 1972-74, 76-77, supr. evenings, 1977-83; office nurse Streator Med. Clinic, 1974-76; intensive care unit nurse St. James Hosp., Pontiac, Ill., 1983-85, cardiac rehab., health promotion nurse, 1985-87; dir. cdn. St. James Hosp., Pontiac, 1987—; presenter health programs, 1986—. Tchr., presenter: Heart Healthy, 1986-87. Instr. CPR Am. Heart Assn., Pontiac, 1986-87; mem. del. planning com. Ill. Heart Assn., Pontiac, 1986-87; pres. Livingston County Heart Assn., Pontiac, 1986-87; active clin. internship, health promotion McLean County Health Dept., Bloomington, Ill., 1987. Recipient Area Achiever award Streator Times Press, 1987. Mem. Ill. Nurses Assn., Ill. Soc. for Cardiac Health and Rehab., Cen. Ill. Health Educators, Corn Belt Health Educators, Sigma Theta Tau. Roman Catholic. Club: St. Mary's Hosp. Auxiliary. Lodge: K.C. Avocations: photography, crafts, physical fitness. Home: 1007 N Jackson Streator IL 61364 Office: St James Hosp 610 E Water Pontiac IL 61764

MARX, THOMAS GEORGE, economist; b. Trenton, N.J., Oct. 25, 1943; s. George Thomas and Ann (Szymanski) M.; m. Arlene May Varga, Aug. 23, 1969; children: Melissa Ann, Thomas Jeffrey, Jeffrey Alan. B.S. summa cum laude, Rider Coll., 1969; Ph.D., Wharton Sch., U. Pa., 1973. Fin. analyst Am. Cyanamid Co., Trenton, 1968; economist FTC, Washington, 1973; econ. cons. Foster Assocs. Inc., Washington, 1974-77; sr. economist Gen. Motors Corp., Detroit, 1977-79, mgr. indsl. econs., 1980—, dir. econs. policy studies, 1981-83; dir. corp. strategic planning group Gen. Motors Corp., 1984-86, gen. dir. market analysis and forecasting, 1986—; mem. faculty Temple U., 1972-73, U. Pa., 1972-73; adj. prof. Wayne State U., 1981—. Assoc. editor Bus. Econs., 1980—; mem. editorial bd. Akron Jour. Bus. and Econs., 1981—; author, contbr. articles to profl. jours. Served with USAF, 1961-65. Mem. Nat. Econs. Club, Am. Econ. Assn., Nat. Assn. Bus. Economists, Detroit Area Bus. Economists, Econ. Soc. Mich., So. Econ. Assn., Western Econ. Assn., Planning Forum, Assn. Pub. Policy Analysts, Pi Gamma Mu, Beta Gamma Sigma. Roman Catholic. Home: 3312 Bloomfield Park Dr West Bloomfield MI 48033 Office: Gen Motors Corp 3044 W Grand Blvd Detroit MI 48202

MARZKE, DAVID WAYNE, EDP auditor; b. Rensselaer, Ind., July 21, 1956; m. Carole Ann Mark, May 10, 1980. BS in Acctg. and Computer Sci., St. Joseph's Coll., 1978; postgrad in bus. adminstrn., Ind. U., South Bend, 1987. CPA; cert. data processor, cert. info. systems auditor. Mgr. Crowe, Chizek and Co., South Bend, 1978-87; cons. Clark Mgmt. Services Co., South Bend, 1987—. Dir. 1st United Meth. Day Care, South Bend, 1985—. Mem. Am. Inst. CPA's, Ind. CPA Soc. (chmn. small computers 1987), Mich. Assn. for Systems Mgmt. (program chmn. 1986-87), EDP, Auditors Assn. Home: 106 E Angela South Bend IN 46617

MARZOLF, STANLEY S(MITH), educator; b. Aurora, Ill., Oct. 18, 1904; s. George E. and Cora E. (Smith) M.; A.B., Wittenberg U., 1926; M.A., Ohio State U., 1930, Ph.D., 1937; m. Helen M. Gooding, Mar. 1, 1934; children—George Richard, John Edward. Tchr. chemistry Bucyrus High Sch. (Ohio), 1926-30; psychologist Ohio Dept. Pub. Welfare, Columbus, 1930-35; asst. prof. psychology Ill. State U., Normal, 1937-42, asso. prof., 1942-46, prof., 1946-68, Disting. prof., 1968-72, prof. emeritus, 1972—. Sec.-treas. Ill. Bd. Examiners in Psychology, 1958-61. Fellow Am. Psychol. Assn.; mem. Ill. Psychol. Assn. (pres. 1954), Am. Assn. Psychol. State Bds. (pres. 1962). Author: Studying the Individual, 1941; Psychological Diagnosis and Counseling in the Schools, 1956. Contbr. to profl. jours., psychol. textbooks. Home: 806 Hester Ave Normal IL 61761

MARZULLO, JOSEPH LOUIS, metals company finance executive; b. Chgo., July 8, 1951; s. Joseph Anthony and Mary M. (Tracey) M.; m. Mary ellen Laskowski, Apr. 2, 1977; children: Melissa, Meredith. BS in Acctg., No. Ill. U., 1973. CPA, Ill. Auditor Arthur Young & Co., Chgo., 1973-76; v.p. fin. Fullerton Metals Co., Northbrook, Ill., 1976—; bd. dirs. Fultean, Inc., Hammond, Ind., 1986—. Mem. Am. Inst. CPA's, Ill. Soc. CPA's, Nat. Assn. Accts. Roman Catholic. Avocations: golf, bowling, basketball, investment analysis. Home: 519 Sandy Ln Libertyville IL 60048 Office: Fullerton Metals Co 3000 Shermer Rd Northbrook IL 60065

MASAR, EDWARD JOHN, coatings laboratory executive; b. Cleve., June 26, 1943; s. Joseph C. and Elizabeth (Vicarchek) M.; m. Sherry Lynn Patterson, Oct. 17, 1964; children—Joycelyn Marie, Jacquelyn Michelle. B.S., U. Toledo, 1973, M.B.A., 1983. Group leader Inmont, Detroit, 1966-70, new product devel., 1970-72, chemist, automotive research dept., 1972-78, lab. supr., Detroit, 1978—. Served with U.S. Army, 1963-66. Mem. Nat. Paint and Coatings Assn., Assn. Finishing Processes Soc. Mfg. Engrs., Soc. Automotive Engrs. Club: Jolly Roger Sailing. Patentee in field. Office: 5935 Milford Ave Detroit MI 48210

MASCHOFF, JANET BRANDT, educational adminstr.; b. St. Louis, Aug. 24, 1937; d. Oliver William and Esther Rose (Koehler) Brandt; B.S. in Edn., Concordia Tchrs. Coll., River Forest, Ill., 1959, M.A. in Edn., 1967; Edn. Specialist, So. Ill. U., 1981; m. Karl Edgar Maschoff, June 10, 1967. Tchr., prin. Lutheran Schs., N.J. and Mo., 1959-66; with Hazelwood Sch. Dist., St. Louis County, 1967—, instructional specialist, 1971-78, prin., 1981—. Mem. Assn. Supervision and Curriculum Devel., Internat. Reading Assn., Nat. Council Tchrs. Math., Nat. Council Tchrs. English, Nat. Assn. Elem. Sch. Prins., Delta Kappa Gamma, Phi Delta Kappa, Kappa Delta Pi. Lutheran. Contbr. to ednl. materials. Home: 2280 Derhake Rd Florissant MO 63033 Office: 2324 Redman Ave Saint Louis MO 63136

MASEK, BARRY MICHAEL, accountant; b. Beatrice, Nebr., Nov. 18, 1955; s. Charles Joseph and Patricia Anne (Hynek) M.; m. Mary Ellen McNamara, Nov. 27, 1981; children: Katherine Marie, Caroline Christine. BS in Acctg., U. Nebr., 1979. CPA, Nebr., Ill. Staff asst. Arthur Andersen & Co., Chgo., 1979-81, sr. acct., 1981-84, mgr. acctg. and auditing, 1984—. Mem. Am. Inst. CPA's, Nebr. State Soc. CPA's, Ill. State Soc. CPA's. Republican. Roman Catholic. Avocations: golf, tennis, basketball, theater/plays. Home: 815 S Home Ave Park Ridge IL 60068 Office: Arthur Andersen & Co 33 W Monroe St Chicago IL 60603

MASEK, RAYMOND JOHN, lawyer; b. Cleve., Sept. 1, 1946; s. Raymond Clement and Rita Ann (Kalous) M.; m. Lynn Katherine Ramsey, May 1984. BBA, Cleve. State U., 1969, JD, 1975. Bar: Ohio 1977. Internal auditor, asst. to acctg. mgr. Procter & Gamble Co., Balt. and Cin., 1969-71; cost/fin. analyst Ford Motor Co., Toledo and Cleve., 1971-75; corp. auditor Harris Corp., Cleve., 1975-77; sr. corp. auditor Midland-Ross Corp., Cleve., 1977-78; mgr. internat. audits, corp. counsel Reliance Electric Co., Cleve., 1978—; bd. dirs. Toledo Espanola S.A. Named Outstanding Coop. Edn. Student in Sch. Bus., Cleve. State U., 1969. Mem. Cleve. State U. Bus. Alumni Assn. (dir. 1979-82), Bar Assn. of Greater Cleve., Ohio Bar Assn., Inst. Internal Auditors, ABA (internat. law sect.). Home: 8500 Lucerne Dr Chagrin Falls OH 44022-4606 Office: Reliance Electric Co 29325 Chagrin Blvd Pepper Pike OH 44122

MASIBAY, ERLINDA CABANSAG, food service director; b. Manila, May 19, 1938; came to U.S., 1973; d. Pacifico L. and Consuelo Lactaoen (Cabansag) M. BS in Home Tech., U. Philippines, Laguna, 1960. Cert. dietary mgr. Mem. program staff United Meth. Ch., Chgo., 1977-78; food service supr. Norridge (Ill.) Nursing Ctr., 1978; food service supr. Rush Presbyn. St. Luke's Med. Ctr., Chgo., 1978-81, dietetic technician, 1981-82; food service supr. St. Matthew Luth. Home, Park Ridge, Ill., 1982-83, food service dir., 1983—. Co-dir. Julia Gay United Meth. Food Pantry, Chgo., 1974-76; treas. Neighborhood Care Coalition, Chgo., 1975-77; mem. com. on aging United Meth. No. Ill. Conf., Chgo., 1984-86; mem. S.W. health com. YWCA, Chgo., 1975-76; nutritionist Lake Bluff (Ill.) Chgo. Homes for Children, 1981-82. Named Outstanding New Citizen of 1979-80, Citizenship Council of Met. Chgo., 1980. Mem. Dietary Mgrs. Assn., Am. Dietetic Assn. (registered technician), Zaragoza Assn. (sec.-treas. 1980-83), Delta Lambda. Methodist. Lodge: Order of Eastern Star. Avocations: reading, writing, photography, cooking, walking. Home: 4926 N Rockwell Chicago IL 60625 Office: St Matthew Luth Home 1601 N Western Ave Park Ridge IL 60068

MASIELLE, RICHARD, township police executive; b. Cleve., June 30, 1937; s. Michael and Rose M.; m. Karol Ann V. Jakupca, Oct. 20, 1979. Grad. Cuyahoga County (Ohio) Sheriff's Dept. Sch., 1968, Am. Inst. for Paralegal Studies, 1984. Quality control insp. TRW Inc., Cleve., 1955-65; mem. Cuyahoga County Sheriff's Dept., 1968; with Olmsted Twp. (Ohio) Police Dept., 1969—, chief of police, 1972—. Served with U.S. Army, 1960-62. Mem. Cuyahoga County Chiefs of Police Assn., Ohio Assn. Chiefs of Police, Frat. Order Police, Met. Crime Bur., Internat. Personnel Mgmt. Assn., Nat. Assn. Legal Assts. Home: 15657 Hickox Blvd Middleburg Heights OH 44130 Office: 26900 Cook Rd Olmsted Township OH 44138

MASKE, GERALD GENE, protective services official, small business owner; b. Milw., Dec. 13, 1942; s. Edward H. and Augusta T. (Kaebisch) M.; m. Marlene D. Diesner, Aug. 30, 1969; children: Eric G., Michael E. BA, U. Wis., Milw., 1963. Mgr. sales West Allis (Wis.) Auto, 1964-67; evidence technician, traffic investigator Wauwatosa (Wis.) Police Dept., 1967—; owner, pres. Jem Photog. Enterprises, Sussex, Wis., 1975—. Chmn. Sussex-Lisbon Teen Ctr., 1985—; emergency govt. dir. Village of Sussex, 1986—. Served to sgt. U.S. Army, 1963-69. Mem. Profl. Photographers Am., Wis. Indsl. Photographers Assn., Nat. Electronic Sales and Service Assn., Wis. Electronic Sales and Service Assn., Wis. and Wauwatosa Profl. Police Assn., Wis. Emergency Mgmt. Assn. Lutheran. Avocation: flying. Home: N 64 W 23607 Ivy Ave Sussex WI 53089 Office: Jem Photog Enterprises N 63 W 23951 Main St Sussex WI 53089 also: Wauwatosa Police Dept 1700 N 116th St Wauwatosa WI 53226

MASLOWSKI, WALTER CASPER, oral and maxillofacial surgeon; b. Camden, N.J., May 9, 1929; s. Casper Mayer and Cecilia May (Walinski) M.; m. Beatrice Jacquelyn Cross, June 24, 1960; children: Kassia, Trina. BS, LaSalle Coll., 1949; DDS, U. Md., 1953; MS, Ohio State U., 1960. Diplomate Am. Bd. Oral and Maxillofacial Surgery. Practice dentistry specializing in oral and maxillofacial surgery Lima, Ohio, 1965—; chief dept. oral and maxillofacial surgery St. Rita's Med. Ctr., Lima, 1965—; cons. Oakwood Forensic Ctr., Lima, 1960—; medical missionary and clinician, Poland, 1983-86. Served to capt. USAF, 1953-60, Korea. Fello Internat. Assn. Oral Surgery (founding mem.), Am. Assn. Oral and Maxillofacial Surgeons; mem. Am. Dental Soc. of Anesthesiology (del. 1965-78, adv. bd. 1987), Ohio Dental Soc. of Anesthesiology (Outstanding Service award 1978), Lima Acad. Dentistry (pres. 1977-78), Morgan Allison Soc. Oral Surgeons. Republican. Roman Catholic. Lodge: Rotary (bd. dirs. Lima chpt. 1980-83), Serra Internat. Avocations: photography, tennis, racquetball, travel, fishing. Office: 825 W Market St Lima OH 45805

MASON, CAROLYN, automobile club executive, psychotherapist, consultant; b. Buffalo, July 1, 1927; children—Gilbert D. Sylva, Nickolas A. Sylva, Christopher D. Mason. B.A., George Williams Coll., 1976, M.S.W., 1978; Ph.D., Southeastern U., 1980. Cert. clin. social worker. Pvt. practice psychotherapist, Oakbrook Terrace, Ill., 1973-79; v.p. human resources AAA/Chgo. Motor Club, Chgo., 1980-86, sr. v.p. corp. services, 1986—; cons. Chgo., Milw., 1975—. Author: Synthesis of Physiology and Psychology: Toward Wholism, 1978; artist retrospective aquatints (1st place Ill. Sesquicentennial, 1976). Co-founder All the Way House, Lombard, 1970. AAUW scholar, 1978, Hinsdale Bus. and Profl. Womens Assn. scholar, 1978; winner 1st place Oakbrook Artists Invitational, 1977. Mem. Am. Mgmt. Assn., Am. Assn. Tng. and Devel., AAUP. Democrat. Roman Catholic. Office: AAA Chicago Motor Club 999 E Touhy Ave Des Plaines IL 60018

MASON, CHARLOTTE JANE, magazine publisher, writer; b. Salem, Mo., Oct. 15, 1947; s. Everett Earnest and Effie Caroline (Bell) M. BA, Webster U., 1980, postgrad., 1983. Editor Meramec Jour., High Ridge, Mo., 1970-77; pub. info. officer Northwest Sch. Dist., House Springs, Mo., 1977-80; mktg. coordinator Webster U., St. Louis, 1980-82; pres. Mason-Totten & Assocs., High Ridge, 1983-85; pub. PRIDE Mag., High Ridge, 1985—; cons. pub. relations, 1981—. Contbr. articles to mags. Sec., v.p. Community Library Assn., Northwest Community, 1975; del. Gov.'s Conf. on Libraries, Mo., 1976; mem. exec. bd. dirs. Sheltered Workshop, Jefferson County, 1978; v.p. Commn. for Handicapped, Jefferson County, 1979-80, Outstanding Service award, 1980; juror Cir. Ct. Grand Jury, Jefferson County, 1984. Recipient Disting. Service award Boy Scouts Am., Jefferson County, 1975, Responsible Press award Community Tchrs. Assn. Northwest Sch. Dist., 1976. Mem. Nat. Assn. Female Execs., Regional Commerce and Growth Asssn., Twin City C. of C. Democrat. Avocations: photography, painting. Office: PRIDE Magazine PO Box 1487 High Ridge MO 63049

MASON, DAVID AARON, financial executive; b. Indpls., Oct. 14, 1940; s. William and Betty (Sandler) M.; m. Barbara Jo Kane, Sept. 2, 1971; children: William, Stacy. BS with high honors, U. Ill., 1963, MAS, 1965. CPA, Ill. V.p. fin. schs. div. Bell & Howell Co., Chgo., 1965-71; chief fin. officer Kennedy Bros., Chgo., 1971-72; prof. fin. and acctg. Keller Grad. Sch. Mgmt., Chgo., 1973-75; sole practice acctg. Chgo., 1972-75; sr. v.p. fin. and adminstrn., treas. Progressive Industries Corp., Dayton, Ohio, 1976—; also bd. dirs. Progressive Industries Corp.; pres. Nat. Photolabs, Inc., Dayton, 1982—; exec. v.p. Moto Photo, Inc., Dayton, 1983—; bd. dirs. FotoFair, Inc., NPL, Inc. Treas., trustee Montgomery County Devel. Corp., 1980—, pres. 1983-85; treas. mem. exec. com. Montgomery County Bus. Devel. Corp., 1981—. Mem. Am. Inst. CPA's, Ill. Soc. CPA's, Ohio SOc. CPA's, U. Ill. Alumni Assn. Home: 211 Trailwoods St Dayton OH 45415 Office: Progressive Industries 4444 Lake Center Dr Dayton OH 45426

MASON, DENNIS EVERETT, electronics executive; b. Chariton County, Mo., Aug. 19, 1936; s. Dee Wayne and Hildru Montzelle (Kuhler) M.; m. Rhea Pearl Arnold, June 24, 1961; children: Marie, Nancy. BSEE, U. Mo., Rolla, 1958; MBA, Butler U., 1965. Mgr. mktg. planning Cummins Engine Co., Columbus, Ind., 1967-71; v.p. mktg. and engring. Bowmar Instrument Corp., Ft. Wayne (Ind.) and Tucson, 1971-75; regional mgr. Exxon Corp., Oakbrook, Ill., 1975-77; dir. bus. planning Rockwell Internat. Corp., Chgo., 1977-83; dir. mktg. Zenith Electronics Corp., Glenview, Ill., 1983-85; v.p. mktg. DS Am., Rolling Meadows, Ill., 1985—; bd. dirs. Graphic Arts Mktg. Info. Service, Washington. Contbr. articles to profl. jours. Mem. bd., pres. Bd. Edn. (dist. 101), Western Springs, Ill., 1979-85. Mem. Acad. Elec. Engrs., Nat. Printing Equipment and Supply Assn. (bd. dirs. 1986—), Mensa. Republican. Unitarian. Avocation: philately. Home: 4020 Central Ave Western Springs IL 60558 Office: DS Am 5110 Tollview Dr Rolling Meadows IL 60008

MASON, EARL JAMES, JR., physician; b. Marion, Ind., Aug. 26, 1923; s. Earl James and Grace A. (Leer) M.; student Marion Coll., 1940-41; B.S. in Medicine, Ind. U., 1944, A.B. in Chemistry, 1947, M.A. in Bacteriology, 1947; Ph.D. in Microbiology, Ohio State U., 1950; M.D., Western Res. U., 1954; m. Eileen Gursansky, Dec. 2, 1967. Teaching asst. dept. bacteriology Ind. U., 1945-47; research fellow depts. ophthalmology and bacteriology Ohio State U., Columbus, 1947-48, teaching asst. dept. bacteriology, 1948-50; Crile research scholar Western Res. U., Cleve., 1951-53; Damon Runyon cancer research fellow dept. pathology Western Res. U.-Cleve. City Hosp., 1951-56; dept. chief dept. pathology USPHS Hosp., San Francisco, 1956-58; fellow pathology U. Tex. Postgrad. Sch. Medicine, M.D. Anderson Hosp. and Tumor Inst., Houston, 1958-59; asst. prof. dept. pathology Baylor U. Coll. Medicine, 1959-60; asst. pathologist Jefferson Davis Hosp., 1959-60; asst. pathologist Michael Reese Hosp. and Med. Center, Chgo., 1960-61; asso. dir. dept. pathology, dir. dept. biol. scis. Mercy Hosp., 1960-65; dir. labs. St. Mary Med. Center, Gary and Hobart, Ind., 1965—; asso. prof. pathology Chgo. Med. Sch., 1966—; clin. prof. pathology Ind. U. Med. Sch., 1976—. Diplomate Am. Bd. Pathology in anat. and clin. pathology, radioisotopic pathology and dermatopathology, Am. Bd. Nuclear Medicine. Mem. Coll. Am. Pathologists, Am. Assn. Pathologists and Bacteriologists, Am. Soc. Clin. Pathologists, Internat. Acad. Pathologists, Am. Soc. Exptl. Pathology, Am. Assn. Cancer Research, Am. Assn. Blood Banks, Am. Soc. Hematology, Am. Acad. Dermatology, Soc. Nuclear Medicine, Lake County Med. Soc., Am. Soc. Cytology, Sigma Xi. Research on cellular origin of antibodies and virus-cell interactions. Home: PO Box 485 7 Summit Rd Ogden Dunes Portage IN 46368 Office: 540 Tyler St Gary IN 46402

MASON, LINDA, softball and basketball coach; b. Indpls., Jan. 29, 1946; d. Harrison Linn and Hazel Marie (Bledsoe) Crouch; m. Robert Mason, Aug. 20, 1967; children—Cassandra, Andrew. B.S., Ind. U., 1968, M.S., 1977. Cert. phys. edn. tchr., K-12, Ind. Tchr. phys. edn. Woodview Jr. High Sch., Indpls., 1968-71; tchr. phys. edn., coach Ind. U.-Purdue U. of Indpls., 1972-76; basketball coach Butler U., Indpls., 1976-84; head softball coach, asst. basketball coach Westfield Washington High Sch., Westfield, Ind., 1985; tch. phys. edn., basketball coach Orchard Park Elementary Sch., Carmel, Ind., 1985; elem. physical edn. tchr., Carmel-Clay Schs., Carmel, 1985—; head coach Ind. Girls' High Sch. All-Stars, Indpls., 1985. Named Coach of Yr. Dist. 4, Nat. Collegiate Athletic Assn., 1983. Mem. Delta Psi Kappa.

MASON, PATRICIA ANN, chemistry educator; b. Joliet, Ill., Feb. 23, 1946; d. Victor August and Victoria Ann (Sporar) Bernickas; m. Frank Roger Mason, May 18, 1968; children: Jeffrey, Amy. AA, Joliet Jr. Coll., 1966; BS in Chemistry, Purdue U., 1968, MS in Chemistry, 1971. Analytical chemist Edwards Lab., Santa Ana, Calif., 1968-69, Gt. Lakes Chem., West LaFayette, Ind., 1969-71, St. Elizabeth Hosp., LaFayette, Ind., 1971-73; instr. Purdue U., W. LaFayette, 1977-84; chmn. Sci. Dept. Cen. Cath. High Sch. LaFayette, 1985—. Author: Selected Experiments for Gen. Chemistry, 1982, 4th edit., 1983, 84, 85. Trustee Wabash Civil Twp., West LaFayette, 1978—; sec. League of Women Voters, West LaFayette, 1974-76. Mem. Hoosier Assn. Sci. Tchrs. Inc. Republican. Roman Catholic. Avocations: travel, gardening, sewing, reading, raising cattle. Home: 1324 N 350 West LaFayette IN 47906 Office: Cen Cath High Sch 2410 S 9th St Lafayette IN 47905

MASON, PHILIP PARKER, history educator, archivist; b. Salem, Mass., Apr. 28, 1927. BA, Boston U., 1950; MA, U. Mich., 1951, PhD, 1956. Dir. archives Mich. State Archives, Lansing, 1953-58; dir. archives labor and urban affairs Reuther Library Wayne State U., Detroit, 1958—, prof. history, 1958—. Author: (book) Harper of Detroit, Jewish Archival Institute, 1975, History of the Ambassador Bridge, 1987; editor Schoolcraft's Expedition, 1958, The Literary Voyager, 1961, Great Lakes Books, Wayne State U. Press, 1986—. Served with USN, 1945-46. Fellow Soc. Am. Archivist; mem. Orgn. Am. Historians, Oral History Assn., Hist. Soc. Mich. (Merit award 1963), Mich. Labor History Soc. (sec. 1977-78), Detroit Hist. Soc. (Patriotic award 1976), Labor History (editorial bd. 1975—). Home: 8 Oxford Blvd Pleasant Ridge MI 48069 Office: Wayne State U Reuther Library Archives Labor & Urban Affairs 5402 Cass Ave Detroit MI 48202

MASON, STEVEN CHARLES, forest products company executive; b. Sarnia, Ont., Can., Feb. 22, 1936. B.S., MIT, 1957. Pres. div. Mead Corp., Dayton, Ohio, 1978-79, group v.p., 1979-81, sr. v.p. ops., 1981-82, pres., 1983—. Office: The Mead Corp Courthouse Plaza NE Dayton OH 45463

MASON, THEODORE MOYER, dentist; b. Dixon, Ill., Mar. 4, 1927; s. Theodore Remington and Fern Marie (Buzzard) M.; 1 child, Marcia Anne. Student North Central Coll., 1946-48; D.D.S., U. Ill.-Chgo., 1952. Gen. practice dentistry Dixon, Ill., 1952—; tchr. Cert. Dental Assts., Dixon, Sterling, Ill., 1957-59, also lectr. Mem. Lee County Cancer Soc., 1953-57, del., 1957-60; mem. City of Dixon Park Bd., 1969-79, pres., 1974-75; mem. Lee County Bd. Health, 1968-78, pres., 1976-78; mem. governing bd. Dixon YMCA, 1954-56. Served with USN, 1944-46. Recipient Dedication award Lee County Health Dept., Dixon, 1978. Mem. ADA, Lee-Whiteside County Dental Soc. (sec. 1960-62, pres. 1963, del. 1963), Acad. Gen. Dentistry, Am. Legion (Excellence award 1940); fellow Ill. State Dental Soc. Republican. Episcopalian. Clubs: Toastmasters (Dixon); Western Lawn Tennis Assn. (Indpls.), No. Ill. So. Wis. Tennis Assn. (Janesville, Wis.). Avocations: collecting coins, Rockwell plates; tennis; bicycling; fishing. Home and Office: 315 Crawford Ave Dixon IL 61021

MASON, THOMAS ALBERT, lawyer; b. Cleve., May 4, 1936; s. Victor Lewis and Frances (Speidel) M.; m. Elisabeth Gun Sward, Sept. 25, 1965; children—Thomas Lewis, Robert Albert. A.B., Kenyon Coll., 1958; LL.B., Case-Western Res. U., 1961. Bar: Ohio 1961. Assoc. Thompson, Hine and Flory, Cleve., 1965-73, ptnr., 1973—. Trustee Cleve. YMCA, 1975—. Served to capt. USMCR, 1962-65. Mem. Am. Coll. Real Estate Lawyers, Am. Land Title Assn. (lender's counsel group), Mortgage Bankers Assn. of Met. Cleve., ABA, Ohio Bar Assn., Cleve. Bar Assn., Am. Coll. Mortgage Attys. Republican. Episcopalian. Club: Country (Pepper Pike, Ohio). Lodge: Masons. Avocations: tennis; golf. Home: 23375 Duffield Rd Shaker Heights OH 44122 Office: Thompson Hine and Flory Nat City Bank Bldg Cleveland OH 44114

MASS, EDWARD RUDOLPH, accountant, finance executive; b. Chgo., Feb. 28, 1926; s. Rudolph and Michelena (Eiben) M.; m. Florence Urso, Sept. 4, 1948; children: MaryChris, Juli, Kurt. BS in Acctg., Northwestern U., 1950. CPA, Ill. Asst. chief acct. Signode Corp., Chgo., 1950-59; asst. treas. Stepan Chem., Northfield, Ill., 1959-67; treas. Mass Feeding Corp., Des Plaines, Ill., 1967-69; corp. controller Nuclear Chicago Corp., Des Plaines, 1969-74; v.p. fin. Cherry Corp., Waukegan, Ill., 1974—. Mem. Am. Inst. CPA's. Roman Catholic. Avocations: sports, reading, investing. Office: The Cherry Corp 3600 Sunset Ave Waukegan IL 60087

MASSARO, MICHAEL JOSEPH, manufacturing company executive; b. Newark, Ohio, Jan. 24, 1948; s. Michael and Wilma G. (Priest) M.; m. Patricia Ann Duffy, July 6, 1974; children: Andrea, Michael, Genna. BBA, Xavier U., Cin., 1971. Sales rep. Runnymede Corp., Newark, 1971-83; sales supr. Tectum, Inc., Newark, 1983-84, mktg. mgr., 1984-86, product mgr., 1986—. Mem. Ceilings and Interior Contractors Assn., Newark C. of C. Roman Catholic. Lodges: Elks, Son of Italy (trustee 1982-86). Avocations: golf, fishing, hunting. Office: Tectum Inc 105 S 6th St Newark OH 43055

MASSENGALE, MARTIN ANDREW, agronomist, university chancellor; b. Monticello, Ky., Oct. 25, 1933; s. Elbert G. and Orpha (Conn) M.; m. Ruth Audrey Klingelhofer, July 11, 1959; children: Alan Ross, Jennifer Lynn. B.S., Western Ky. U., 1952; M.S., U. Wis., 1954, Ph.D., 1956. Cert. profl. agronomist, profl. crop scientist. Research asst. agronomy U. Wis., 1952-56; asst. prof., asst. agronomist U. Ariz., 1958-62, assoc. prof., assoc. agronomist, 1962-65, prof., agronomist, 1965—, head dept., 1966-74, assoc. dean Coll. Agr. assoc. dir. Ariz. Agr. Expt. Sta., 1974-76; vice chancellor for agr. and natural resources U. Nebr., 1976-81; chancellor U. Nebr.-Lincoln, 1981—; chmn. pure seed adv. com. Ariz. Agrl. Expt. Sta.; past chmn. bd., pres. Midam. Internat. Agrl. Consortium; mem. EPA-Dept. Agr. Land Grant Univ. Coordinating Com. Environ. Quality; chmn. Agr. Registry Cert. Profls. in Agronomy, Crops and Soils.; bd. dirs. Nat. Merit Scholarship Corp., 1982—, U. Nebr. Found., Lincoln Found. Bd. dirs. Nebr. Assn. of Commerce and Idustry. Served with AUS, 1956-58. Named One of Outstanding Educators Am., 1970, Midlands Man of Yr., 1982; Faculty Recognition award Tucson Trade Bur., 1971, Ak-Sar-Ben Agrl. Achievement award 1986, Agrl. Builders Nebr. award for Outstanding Agrl. Leadership, 1986, Walter K. Briggs award, 1986. Fellow Crop Sci. Soc. Am. (past dir., pres. 1972-73), Am. Soc. Agronomy (dir., Disting. Service award 1984), AAAS (sect. chmn.); mem. Am. Grassland Council, Ariz. Crop Improvement Assn. (dir.), Am. Soc. Plant Physiology, Nat. Assn. Colls. and Tchrs. of Agr., Ariz. Acad. Sci., Nebr. Acad. Sci., Agrl. Council Am. (dir., mem. issues com.), Council Agrl. Sci. and Tech. (bd. dirs. 1982—), Sigma Xi, Phi Kappa Phi, Gamma Sigma Delta, Alpha Zeta, Phi Sigma, Gamma Alpha, Alpha Gamma Rho. Pioneer in floral initiation and photoperiodism in alfalfa, photosynthate prodn. and use in alfalfa and water-use efficiency in forage crops. Office: Univ Nebr Office of Chancellor 14th and R Sts Lincoln NE 68588

MASSEY, EDWARD LOUIS, marketing executive; b. Alton, Ill., July 15, 1959; s. Richard R. and Katherine E. (Stobbs) M. BS in Archtl. Studies with honors, U. Ill., 1983; postgrad., U. Mo., 1983, 85—. Free lance illustrator City of Alton, 1984-85; prodn. mgr. Schofield Pub., St. Louis, 1984-86; circulation mgr. Sorkin's Directories, Inc., St. Louis, 1986—; mem. focus group Nat. Council Mktg. Edn., Wentzville, Mo., 1986. Illustrator, programmer Gordon F. Moore Community Park, Alton, 1984-85. Mem. Sales and Mktg. Execs. Internat. Baptist. Home: 113 Forest Pkwy Valley Park MO 63088 Office: Sorkins Directories Inc 744 Spirit of St Louis Blvd Chesterfield MO 63017

MASSEY, JAMES D., bank holding company executive. Student, Butler U., U. Wis., Harvard U. With Mchts. Nat. Bank & Trust Co., Indpls., 1957—, mgmt. trainee, 1957-60, mgr. auto loan dept., 1960-63, br. mgr., 1963-66, v.p., 1966-70, v.p., br. adminstrn. officer, 1970-77, sr. v.p., 1977-79, exec. v.p., 1979-83, pres., chief exec. officer, 1983-86, chmn., chief exec. officer, 1986—. Office: Mchts Nat Corp 1 Mchts Plaza Indianapolis IN 46255 *

MASSEY, STEVEN JAMES, venture capitalist; b. Milw., May 1, 1959; s. Theodore Robert and Lois Lorraine (Flament) M. BS in Econs., U. Pa., 1981. CPA, Ill. Sr. auditor Arthur Young & Co., Chgo., 1981-83; v.p. Moramerica Capital Corp., Milw., 1983-85; v.p., treas. InvestAmerica Venture Group, Inc., Milw., 1985—; bd. dirs. Plastocon, Inc., Milw. Mem. Ind. Bus. Assn. of Wis. Avocations: camping, skiing, scuba diving. Office: InvestAmerica Venture Group Inc 600 E Mason St Suite 300 Milwaukee WI 53202

MASSIE, WALTER ARTHUR, psychiatrist; b. Pitts., July 21, 1922; s. Arthur Walter and Mathilda V. (Kuhns) M.; m. Anne B. Massie, Aug. 13, 1949; children: Susan, Linda, David, Carol, Nancy, Mark. Student, U. Rochester, 1944; BS, Allegheny Coll., 1948; MD, Temple U., 1948. Diplomate Am. Bd. Psychiatry and Neurology. Intern Allegheny Gen. Hosp., Pitts., 1948-49; resident in psychiatry U.S. Vets. Hosp., Coatesville, Pa., 1950-51, Norwich (Conn.) State Hosp., 1951-52, U. Pitts., 1952-53; pres. Ohio Psychiat. Clinic Dirs., 1956-59; dir. Mansfield (Ohio) Guidance Ctr., 1954-70; practice medicine specializing in psychiatry Mansfield, 1970—; chief of staff Richland Hosp., 1975—. Class agt. Allegheny Coll., 1984—. Served to lt. USN, 1950-54. Mem. AMA, Ohio Med. Assn., Richland County Med. Soc., Am. Psychiat. Assn., Ohio Psychiat. Assn. Lutheran. Avocations: flying, photography, music. Home: 1066 Bellaire Dr Mansfield OH 44907 Office: 824 Park Ave W Mansfield OH 44906

MASSOGLIA, MICHAEL DOMINIC, controller; b. Calumet, Mich., May 15, 1956; s. Dominic John and Virginia Mary (Balconi) M.; m. Tanya Susan Frazer, May 2, 1981; children: Jessica Gwen, Jason Michael. BSBA, Mich. Tech. U., 1977. CPA, Mich. Asst. controller Helen Newberry Joy, Newberry, Mich., 1977-78; asst. auditor gen. State of Mich., Lansing, 1978-81; corp. auditor Upjohn, Kalamazoo, 1981-82; dir. budgets Sisters of

Mercy, Lansing, 1982-85; group comptroller Electronic Data Systems, Troy, Mich., 1985—. Mem. Am. Inst. CPA's. Avocations: softball, cycling, investing. Home: 5579 Larkins Troy MI 48098 Office: Electronic Data Systems 3310 W Big Beaver PO Box 7019 Troy MI 48007-7019

MASSURA, EDWARD ANTHONY, accountant; b. Chgo., July 1, 1938; s. Edward Matthew and Wilma C. (Kussy) M.; m. Carol A. Barber, June 23, 1962; children: Edward J., Beth Ann, John B. BS, St. Joseph's Coll., Rensselaer, Ind., 1960; JD, DePaul U., 1963. Bar: Ill. 1963; CPA, Mich., Ill., others. Tax acct. Arthur Andersen & Co., Chgo., 1963—, ptnr., 1973—; dir. tax div. Arthur Andersen & Co., Detroit, 1974-84, dep., co-dir. internat. tax, 1983-84, ptnr.-in-charge internat. trade customs practice, 1983—. Co-author: West's Legal Forms, 2d. edit., 1984; contbr. numerous articles to bus. jours. Treas., bd. dirs. Arts Found. of Mich., Detroit, 1982—. Mem. Am. Inst. CPA's, Mich. Assn. CPA's, Detroit Internat. Tax Group (founder, co-moderator), Internat. Fiscal Assn., Licensing Exec. Soc., Mich. Dist. Export Council (chmn. 1985—), French-Am. C. of C. (councillor), World Trade Club of Detroit. Clubs: Economic (Detroit), Orchard Lake (Mich.) Country, Detroit, Renaissance (Detroit). Office: Arthur Andersen & Co 400 Renaissance Ctr Detroit MI 48243

MASSURA, EILEEN KATHLEEN, nursing educator, family therapist; b. Chgo., July 25, 1925; d. John William and Loretta (Feil) Statemeier; m. Edmund Karamanski, July 24, 1948 (dec.); children: John, Kathleen; m. Alfred Massura, Aug. 30, 1963; children: Michael, Kathryn, Mark. BS in Nursing, DePaul U., 1963; MS in Nursing, St. Xavier Coll., 1971. RN; cert. family therapist. Dir. nurses Franklin Blvd. Hosp., Chgo., 1958-62; adminstr. Mich. Ave Hosp., Chgo., 1962-64; instr. St. Xavier Coll., Chgo., 1972-74, Joliet (Ill.) Jr. Coll., 1972-81; family therapist Oak Lawn (Ill.) Family Service, 1978—; prof. nursing Govs. State U., University Park, Ill., 1981—; family therapist McCarthy & Assocs., Oak Lawn, 1982—; preceptor to grads. St. Xavier Coll., 1980—, Govs. State U., 1980—; co-leader Clin. Study Med./Surgical Nursing, Moscow, 1984; presenter Am. Nursing Rev., Ala., Fla., Va., Pa., Tex., Md., 1985-86. Leader Campfire Girls, Oak Lawn, 1964-74; mem. Marist Women's Bd., Chgo., 1978-82, Bro. Rice Women's Bd., Chgo., 1969-72. Grantee HEW, 1969-71; named Disting. Nurse Alumnae, St. Xavier Coll., 1985; named Nursing Prof. of Yr., Govs. State U., 1983. Mem. Am. Nurses Assn. (nominating com. 1982—), Ill. Nurses Assn. (program com. 1980-84), Am. Assn. Marital and Family Therapists, Sigma Theta Tau (v.p. 1971-75). Roman Catholic. Lodge: Cath. Order Foresters. Avocations: crewel, needlepoint. Office: 5660 W 95th St Oak Lawn IL 60453

MAST, ALAN G(EORGE), water conditioning company executive, consultant; b. Milw., Mar. 6, 1953; s. Glenn L. and Elizabeth A. (Hahn) M.; m. Joanne L. Lowry, Jan. 4, 1975; children—Tracy, Travis. B.S.I.E., with honors, U. Wis., 1975; M.B.A., Marquette U., 1981. Registered profl. engr., Wis.; cert. water conditioning dealer. Process engr. Falk Corp., Milw., 1976-79; engring. mgr. Watercare Corp., Manitowoc, Wis., 1979-81; v.p., mgr. Mast & Co., Inc., Cuba City, Wis., 1981—; cons. engring. Mem. Water Quality Assn., Wis. Water Quality Assn., Cuba City (Wis.) C. of C. (past v.p.), Platteville (Wis.) C. of C. (com. chmn.). Lodge: Rotary (pres.). Home: 910 Hillcrest Circle Platteville WI 53818 Office: 108 S Main St Cuba City WI 53807 Office: 250 E Main Platteville WI 53818

MAST, JOHN MARK, accountant; b. Harrisonville, Mo., June 5, 1937; s. Jonathan M. and Sarah Alma (Hershberger) M.; m. Margaret Ann Litwiller, Feb. 16, 1957; children: Jerry Dee, Kevin John, Arlin Ray. AA, Hesston (Kans.) Coll., 1957. Orderly Levering Hosp., Hanibal, Mo., 1957-59; farmer Hopedale, Ill., 1959-60; acct. Hesston Corp., Kans., 1960—; treas. Hesston Employee Activity, 1986. Mem. Kans. Mennonite Men's Chorus, 1971—; treas. Hesston Mennonite Ch., 1968-71; supervisory com. Hesston Credit Union, 1972-73. Republican. Avocations: reading, tennis, racquetball. Home: 619 Random Rd Hesston KS 67062 Office: Hesston Corp 420 W Lincoln Blvd Hesston KS 67062

MAST, MICHAEL DAVID, accountant; b. Millersburg, Ohio, Feb. 28, 1958; s. Daniel E. and Donna Mae (Giauque) M. BA in Acctg. and Bus. Adminstrn. summa cum laude, Malone Coll., 1980. CPA, Ohio. Staff acct. Bruner, Cox, Lotz, Syler & Graves, Canton, Ohio, 1980-81, tax specialist, 1981-84, tax supr., 1984-85; mgr. tax compliance The J.M. Smucker Co., Orrville, Ohio, 1985—. Mem. Am. Inst. CPA's, Ohio Soc. CPA's, Canton Jaycees (sec. 1985—). Home: 740 Manor Ave SW Canton OH 44710 Office: The JM Smucker Co Strawberry Ln Orrville OH 44667

MASTERS, CHARLES WILLIS, controller; b. Youngstown, Ohio, Jan. 19, 1952; s. George Paul and Martha Jean (Moore) M.; m. Alison Jean Deibel, May 27, 1978; children: Victor, Alexander, Charles. BS, Miami U., Oxford, Ohio, 1975. CPA, Ohio. Staff sr. acct. Ernst & Whinney, Cleve., 1976-78; supr., dir. tax ops. Touche Ross & Co., Youngstown, 1979-80; ptnr., dir. tax ops. DeNicholas, Leicht Et Al, Youngstown, 1981-82; mgr. dir. tax ops. Cohen & Co., Youngstown, 1983-84; controller Simco Mgmt. Corp., Girard, Ohio, 1984—. Coach youth sports leagues. Recipient Haskin-Sells award Haskin-Sells/Miami U., 1976. Fellow Am. Inst. CPA's (hon. mention Elijah Watts Sells award 1976), Ohio Soc. CPA's (gold medal award 1976). Club: Canfield Swim (asst. treas.). Avocation: coaching youth sports. Home: 201 S Broad St Canfield OH 44406 Office: Simco Mgmt Corp 709 Trumbull Ave Canfield OH 44420

MASTERS, JACK GERALD, mayor; b. Ft. William, Ont., Can., Sept. 27, 1931; s. John and Janet Mary (Winn) M.; m. Kathleen Jean Whatley, Sept. 4, 1953; children: Susan, Diane, Gerald, Scott. From sales mgr. to nat. sales mgr. and v.p. Sta. CKPR-CHFD-TV, Thunder Bay, Ont., 1952-77; gen. mgr., account exec. Thunder Bay Ins., 1977-80; mem. Can. Parliament, Ottawa, 1980-84; mayor City of Thunder Bay, 1985—. Mem. Liberal Party. Roman Catholic. Home: 153 Whalen St, Thunder Bay, ON Canada P7A 7H9 Office: Office of the Mayor, 500 Donald St, Thunder Bay, ON Canada P7E 5V3

MASTERS, JANICE ANN, school social worker; b. Leavenworth, Kans., Dec. 7, 1935; d. Paul Joel and Mae Valentine (Myer) Wise; m. DeArle Lee Masters, May 28, 1954; children: Gregory, Kathe Masters Owens. BS, Eastern Mich. U., 1965; MA, Mich. State U., 1970. Elem. tchr. pub. schs., Dryden, Lapeer and Haslett, Mich., 1960-69; sch. social worker Eaton County Intermediate Sch. Dist., Charlotte, Mich., 1969-71, Genesee Intermediate Sch. Dist., Flint, Mich., 1971—. Mem. NEA, Mich. Edn. Assn., Nat. Assn. Social Workers, Internat. Transactional Analysis Assn., Mich. Assn. for Emotionally Disturbed Children. Republican. Roman Catholic. Lodge: Zonta. Avocations: exhibitor and breeder of bearded collies, travel, cooking, reading. Home: PO Box 680 Lapeer WI 48446 Office: Genesee Intermediate Sch Dist Spl Services Dept 2701 Pilgrim Dr Flint MI 48507

MASTERSON, BRUCE MICHAEL, financial data company executive; b. Highland Park, Mich., May 9, 1953; s. Joseph Bernard and Eunice Elaine (Lackey) M.; m. Susan Rachel Bell, Nov. 25, 1978; children: Jason Bell-Masterson, Jessica Bell-Masterson. BA in Econs. magna cum laude, Mich. State U., 1975; MBA in Fin. and Acctg., U. Chgo., 1977. Cons. Data Resources, Inc., Chgo., 1977-79; sr. cons. Data Resources, Inc., Detroit, 1980-83; v.p. indsl. M-H/Data Resources, Inc., Chgo., 1983-85; v.p. cen. region Reuters, Chgo., 1985—. Jewish. Home: 126 Park Ave Deerfield IL 60015 Office: Reuters 1420 Board of Trade Bldg Chicago IL 60604

MASTERSON, SISTER PATRICIA JANE, psychologist, educator, consultant; b. Cleve., June 10, 1948; s. Frank W. and Rita (Jamieson) M. BA, John Carroll U., 1971; MEd, Kent State U., 1979, PhD, 1979. Lic. psychologist, Ohio. Childcare worker Parmadale Children's Village, Parma, Ohio, 1972-74; supr., therapist Child Guidance Ctr., Cleve., 1978-86; instr. Ursuline Coll., Pepper Pike, Ohio, 1985—; therapist Allerhand & Assocs., Cleveland Heights, Ohio, 1986—; cons. Glenbergh Hosps., Cleve., 1986—. Mem. Agape Peace Community, Cleve. 1982—, Sisters of Charity St. Augustine, 1966—; trustee St. Vincent Charity Hosp., Cleve. 1983-84, Woodruff Found., Cleve., 1986. Mem. Am. Psychol. Assn., Orthopsychiat. Assn. Roman Catholic. Avocations: reading, swimming, hiking, theatre, music. Home: 3122 West Blvd Cleveland OH 44111 Office: Allerhand & Assocs 2460 Fairmount Blvd Cleveland Heights OH 44106

MASUR, WOLODYMYR H., fraternal organization executive; b. Romny, Ukraine, Aug. 5, 1921; came to U.S., 1951; s. Gregory and Ewdokia (Lakyza) M.; m. Daria Buggan, Sept. 2, 1960; children: Victoria, Larissa, Markian, Melania. Student, Ukrainian Tech. Husbandry Inst., Munich, 1944-45. Adminstr. IRO Displaced Persons Camp, Munich, 1945-51; field organizer Ukrainian Nat. Aid Assn., Pitts., 1955-58, mem. exec. bd., 1958-66; pres. Ukrainian Nat. Aid Assn., Chgo., 1966—. Editor: Ukrainian Nat. Word (quarterly), 1962—, Ukrainian Nat. Tribune (weekly), 1982—; author numerous articles concerning Ukrainian issues. V.p. Ukrainian Am. Relief Com., Phila., 1966—. Mem. Fraternal Congress of Pa. and Ill., Ukrainian Congress Com. of Am. (1st v.p. 1978—, World Freedom award 1984), Org. for Def. of Four Freedoms for Ukraine (v.p. 1978—), Ukrainian Journalist Org. Am and Can. Republican. Ukrainian Orthodox. Avocation: spectator sports. Office: Ukranian Nat Aid Assn 925 N Western Ave Chicago IL 60622

MASZAK, ROBERT J., teacher; b. Joliet, Ill., Sept. 10, 1944; s. Phillip and Helen (Krol) M.; m. Sandra Durian, Dec. 23, 1967; children: Debra, Rebecca, Robert W. AA, Joliet Jr. Coll., 1964; BA in English, Ill. State U., 1966; MA in English, Ind. U., 1969; PhD in Edn., Addison State U., Toronto, Can., 1984. Cert. tchr., Ill. English tchr. Bloom High Sch., Chcago Hts., Ill., 1966—; gifted program dir. Bloom High Sch., Chicago Hts., Ill., 1970-77; instr. Homewood (Ill.) Flossmoor Parks, 1980—; cons. Game-Sim Co., Los Angeles, 1980—, cons. GIF program State of Ill.; ednl. cons. Cook County Supt. Schs., Chgo., 1982—. Author: All About Gifted Education, 1970; pub. Readings for the Gifted, 1984. Active S. Met. Assn. for Handicapped, Dalton, Ill., 1986. Named Ill. Gifted Tchr. of Yr., Ill. Gifted Program, 1975. Mem. NEA, Ill. Edn. Assn., INTERTEL, Gifted Edn. Assn. (pres. 1984-86, Outstanding Educator 1983), Gifted Ednl. Cons. (v.p. 1980-86). Roman Catholic. Clubs: Prairie State Road Runners (Joliet); Ind. Runners (Homewood) (pres. 1980—). Avocations: world class running, decathalons, philately, publishing. Home: 18758 Delta Homewood IL 60430 Office: Bloom High Sch 10th & Dixie Chicago Heights IL 60430

MATANKY, ROBERT, accountant; b. Chgo., June 16, 1935; s. John and Mae (Weber) M.; m. Alice Faye Grundwag, Dec. 24, 1958; children: Mark Alan, Bryan Keith, Lisa Lynn. BS in Accountancy, U. Ill., 1956. CPA, Ill., Fla.; cert. real estate broker, securities salesman. Pres., owner Robert Matanky & Co., P.C., Northbrook, Ill., 1976—. Pres. Northbrook Continuing Profl. Edn. Group, 1986-87. Mem. Am. Inst. CPA's, Ill. CPA Soc., Fla. Inst. CPA's. Avocations: photography, world travel. Home: 1228 North Ave Highland Park IL 60035 Office: 601 Skokie Blvd Northbrook IL 60062

MATANKY, ROBERT WILLIAM, lawyer; b. Chgo., Dec. 26, 1955; s. Eugene and Gertrude (Shiner) M.; m. Lee Mindy Frankel, Sept. 1, 1985. BS in Engring., U. Ill., 1977; JD, Ill. Inst. Tech., 1980; A in Hebrew Lit., Hebrew Theol. Coll., 1980; postdoctoral, U. Chgo., 1986—. Bar: Ill. 1980, U.S. Dist. Ct. (no. dist.) Ill. 1980, U.S. Ct. Appeals (7th cir.) 1980, U.S. Supreme Ct. 1984; lic. real estate broker, Ill., lic. ins. broker, Ill.; lic. prin. Nat. Assn. Securities Dealers. Traffic coordinator Chgo. Rock Island & Pacific R.R. Co., Chgo., 1978-79; assoc. Hollobow & Taslitz, Chgo., 1980-81; corp. counsel Matanky Realty Group, Chgo., 1981-84, asst. v.p., 1984-86, v.p., 1987—; bd. dirs. Community Bank and Trust Co. Edgewater, Chgo. Editor Decalogue Jour., 1985—. Co-chmn. lawyers div. Jewish United Fund, 1983—; bd. dirs. Hebrew Theol. Coll., Skokie, Ill., 1985—, Jewish Nat. Fund., Chgo., 1984—, Congregation Ezras Israel, Chgo., 1983—, Associated Talmud Torahs Chgo., 1982—, v.p. 1986—. Mem. ABA, Ill. Bar Assn., Chgo. Bar Assn. (real property law com.), Decalogue Soc. Lawyers (bd. mgrs. 1979—, pres. 1986-87, intra-soc. award 1985), Inst. Indsl. Engrs., Chgo. Bd. Realtors (active prin. 1985—), Real Estate Securities and Syndication Inst. (designations rev. bd.). Avocations: study of talmud, carpentry, elec. and plumbing work, golf. Office: Matanky Realty Group Inc 1901 N Halsted St Chicago IL 60614-5008

MATASOVIC, STELLA BUTKAUSKAS, metal processing equiptment executive, rancher; b. Lovington, Ill., July 19, 1916; d. C.K. and Agnes (Nickus) Butkauskas; m. John L. Matasovic, 1938 (dec. 1977); children: Linda Swiercinsky, Marilyn. B in Edn., Ill. State U., 1935. Pres. Universal Welding Supply, New Lenox, Ill., 1944—; chief exec. officer OXO Welding Supply Co., New Lenox, 1948—; pres. OXO Ranches Ridgway, Colo., 1952—. Mem. Internat. Platform Assn., Internat. Hereford Orgn., Am. Hereford Assn., Am. Hereford Aux. (pres. 1969-70), Colo. Hereford Assn., Nat. Welding Supply Assn., Am. Welding Soc., New Lenox C. of C. Club: Nat. Western (Denver).

MATCHETT, HUGH MOORE, lawyer; b. Chgo., Apr. 24, 1912; s. David Fleming and Jennie E. (Moore) M.; m. Ilo Venona Wolff, May 12, 1956. AB, Monmouth (Ill.) Coll., 1934; JD, U. Chgo., 1937. Bar: Ill. 1937. Practice, Chgo., 1937—. Served with USNR, 1942-46, MTO, PTO; lt. comdr. JAGC, USNR. Mem. Fed. Bar Assn. (chmn. mil. law com. Chgo. chpt. 1954-55, mem. com. 1960-61), ABA, Ill. Bar Assn. (mem. assembly 1980-86), Chgo. Bar Assn., Judge Advs. Assn., Tau Kappa Epsilon, Phi Alpha Delta. Republican. Presbyterian. Counsel in litigation establishing rule that charitable instns. are liable in tort to extent of their non-trust funds. Home and Office: 5834 S Stony Island Ave Chicago IL 60637

MATCHETTE, PHYLLIS LEE, editor; b. Dodge City, Kans., Dec. 24, 1921; d. James Edward and Rose Mae (McMillan) Collier; A.B. in Journalism, U. Kans., 1943; m. Robert Clarke Matchette, Dec. 4, 1943; children: Marta Susan, James Michael. Reporter, Dodge City Daily Globe, 1944; tchr. English, Dode City Jr. High Sch., 1944-45; asst. instr. Coll. Liberal Arts, U. Kans., Lawrence, 1945-47; dir. Christian edn. Southminster United Presbyn. Ch., Prairie Village, Kans., 1963-65; editor publs., dir. communications, supr. in-plant printing Village United Presbyn. Ch., Prairie Village, 1965-86 . Hon. mem. Commn. of Ecumenical Mission and Relations, hon. mem. Program Agy., United Presbyn. Ch., U.S.A.; ordained elder Village United Presbyn. Ch., 1964. Mem. Women in Communications, Kans. U. Dames (pres. 1946), Kansas City Young Matrons, Alpha Chi Omega (pres. edn. found. Phi chpt. 1951). Republican. Club: Order of Eastern Star. Home: 7405 El Monte Rd Prairie Village KS 66208 Office: 6641 Mission Rd Prairie Village KS 66208

MATEJKA, MICHAEL G., journalist; b. St. Louis, Jan. 21, 1953; s. Francis S. and Dorothy B. (Macke) M.; m. Karen M. Sandhaas, June 19, 1982; 1 child, Loretta Anne. BA, Ill. State U., 1974. Cons. Asian Cultural Forum on Devel., Bangkok, 1977-80, Agrl. Missions, N.Y.C., 1978-80; editor Union News, Bloomington, Ill., 1980—, Ill. Council on Vocat. Edn., Springfield, 1984—; chmn. Ill. Farm Worker Service Ctr. Task Force, 1982—. Editor: The Christian Rural Mission in the 80's, 1979, This Land Is Your Land, 1981. Sec. McLean County (Ill.) Dem. Cen. Com., 1984—. Mem. Internat. Labor Communications Assn., Ill. State Labor Press Assn. (pres. 1986—), Ill. State Labor History Soc. Roman Catholic. Home: 1406 W Oakland Ave Bloomington IL 61701 Office: Union News PO Box 3248 Bloomington IL 61701

MATEK, ORD, psychotherapist, educator; b. Kamenetzpadolsk, USSR, May 10, 1922; came to U.S., 1923; s. Samson and Sonia (Torgow) M.; m. Betsy Stein, July 11, 1948; children: Beth Matek Weinstein, Deborah Matek Schwartz, Joel, Michael. BS, Roosevelt U., 1949; MA, U. Chgo., 1951. Caseworker Jewish Children's Bur. of Chgo., 1951-56; adminstr. Eisenberg unit Marks Nathan Hall, Chgo., 1956-69; pvt. practice psychotherapy, Chgo., 1959—; assoc. prof. Jane Addams Coll. Social Work, U. Ill., Chgo., 1969—; cons. to social work agys., psychiat. facilities, schs.; adj. faculty Ill. Sch. Profl. Psychology. Author: The Bible Through Stamps, 1974; founding editor: Jour. Residential Group Care and Treatment; cons. editor: Jour. Social Work and Human Sexuality. Served with U.S. Army, 1943-46. Fellow Internat. Council Sex Educators and Parenthood; mem. Nat. Assn. Social Workers, Acad. Cert. Social Workers, Am. Assn. Children's Residential Ctrs., Nat. Assn. Temple Educators (Curriculum award 1965), Am. Assn. Sex Educators, Counselors and Therapists, Union Am. Hebrew Congregations, Ill. Soc. for Clin. Social Work, Ill. Group Psychotherapy Soc., Am. Art Therapy Assn. Jewish. Home: 9000 Ewing St Evanston IL 60203 Office: U Ill Box 4348 Chicago IL 60680 Other: 67 Old Orchard Skokie IL 60077

MATEN, MARK JAMES, accountant; b. Ann Arbor, Mich., Apr. 30, 1957; s. Ralph Edward and Glenda Sue (McAdam) M.; m. Deborah Leigh Gates, Oct. 23, 1982. BA, U. Mich., 1979. CPA, Mich. Staff auditor Deloitte Haskins & Sells, Detroit, 1980-83; corp. acct. Daedalus Enterprises, Ann Arbor, 1983-85; asst. controller Am. Monitor Corp., Indpls., 1985-86, v.p., 1986—. Mem. Am. Inst. CPA's.

MATERNOWSKI, JOHN ANTHONY, dentist; b. Milw., Dec. 6, 1937; s. Stanley Leo and Frances Hedwig (Kulasiewicz) M.; m. Ann Mary Moersfelder, May 30, 1961 (div. Dec. 1976); children: Greg, Cathy, Danette, Phil, Paul, Andrea, Mat; m. Judith Ann Forrett, Jan. 25, 1977 (dec. Jan 1987). DDS, Marquette U., 1962. Gen. practice dentistry Pewaukee, Wis., 1964—. V.P. Pewaukee Area Action Council, 1984—; bd. dirs. Pewaukee Sch. Bd., 1983-85. Served to lt. USNR, 1960-64. Fellow Acad. Gen. Dentistry; mem. Waukesha County Dental Soc. (mem. children's dental heath week com. 1968—, peer review com. 1985—). Republican. Roman Catholic. Lodges: Kiwanis (pres. Pewaukee 1965, sec. 1985-86), KC. Avocations: racquetball, golf, cross country skiing. Home: 301 E Wisconsin Ave Pewaukee WI 53072 Office: 250 Clark St Pewaukee WI 53072

MATHENY, THOMAS RICHARD, architect; b. Columbus, Ohio, Apr. 30, 1955; s. Richard Newton and Marilyn (Hummell) M.; m. Kathleen Mott, Sept. 6, 1980. BArch, Ohio State U., 1977, MArch, 1980. Registered architect, Ohio. Draftsman Schooley Caldwell Assocs., Columbus, 1977-78, designer, 1980-83, designer, project mgr., 1983-85, mgr. design dept., 1985—; grad. teaching assoc., Ohio State U., Columbus, 1978-80. Author: Adaptive Use of Surplus Schools, 1980; coordinator sem. series/manual, New Life for Old HOmes, 1977. Vol., mem. cons.' bur., Columbus Landmarks Found., 1977—. Galen Oman scholar, Ohio State U., 1979, Elliot Whitaker fellow, 1979; recipientfaculty prize, Dept. Architecture, Ohio State U., 1980. Mem. AIA (scholastic medal 1980), Architects Soc. Ohio, Nat. Trust for Historic Preservation, Alpha Rho Chi Alumni Assn. (pres. Ohio State U. chpt. 1981-82). Democrat. Presbyterian. Avocations: golf, tennis, hiking, guitar. Home: 277 Chatham Rd Columbus OH 43214 Office: Schooley Caldwell Assocs 969 Crupper Ave Columbus OH 43229

MATHER, ROBERT JAMES, non-profit rehabilitation facility executive, consultant; b. Manhattan, Kans., May 7, 1940; s. James Warren and Evelyn (Ezell) M.; m. Janet Hadley, June 19, 1965; children: Stacia Lynn, Kristin Ann. BS, Kent (Ohio) State U., 1965, MEd, 1968. Cert. rehab. counselor, Ohio. Grahic arts specialist Design and Devel., Independence, Ohio, 1967-68; supr., counselor Vocat. Guidance and Rehab. Services, Cleve., 1968, ednl. dir., 1968-70, assoc. exec. dir., 1970-78; pres., chief operating officer Progress Industries, Newton, Iowa, 1978—; cons. adminstrv. program Commn. on Accreditation of Rehab. Facilities, Tucson, 1967—; pres. Progress Industries Found., Newton, 1979—. Author: Projects with Industry, 1978. Served with USCG, 1959-67. Named Profl. of Yr., Iowa Assn. for Retarded Citizens, 1985. Mem. Nat. Assn. Fund Raising Execs., Iowa Assn. Rehab. and Residential Facilities, Nat. Rehab. Assn. (pres. Ohio chpt. 1978, Spl. Citation award 1985, cons. editor Jour. 1985—). Democrat. Methodist. Lodge: Rotary. Avocations: sailing, skiing, fishing. Home: 1304 W 15th St Pl S Newton IA 50208 Office: Progress Industries 1017 E 7th St N Box 366 Newton IA 50208

MATHERS, JEREMY JAMES, microbiologist, computer consultant; b. Aurora, Ill., Dec. 5, 1957; s. James Ray and Gloria Jean (Hatch) M. BS, U. Wis., Oshkosh, 1981; MS, Ill. Inst. Tech., 1985. Research scientist Kraft, Inc., Glenview, Ill., 1982—. Contbr. articles to profl. jours. Mem. Am. Acad. Microbiology (registered microbiologist), Soc. Indsl. Microbiology. Avocations: computers, reading, skiing, electronics. Home: 866 Crimson Ct Apt 307 Prospect Heights IL 60070 Office: Kraft Inc Tech Ctr 801 Waukegan Rd Glenview IL 60025

MATHERS, KRIS LEE, energy and environmental consultant, educator; b. Kankakee, Ill., Sept. 20, 1951; s. Kenneth L. and Geraldine M. (Edmondson) M. BS in Engring., U. Ill., 1974; postgrad., So. Ill. U., 1978, Colo. State U., 1980. Mem. Mathers Plantation, Momence, Ill., 1951—; advisor to dir. Ill. EPA, Springfield, 1973; pres. K.L. Mathers & Assoc., Momence, 1974—; tchr. energy and environ. Contbr. articles to profl. jours. Rep. Community Arts Council, Kankakee, 1985—. Mem. Assn. Energy Engrs. (charter sr., numerous certs. Accomplishment), The Art League, Camera Club, Kankakee Area Writers, Kankakee Are MacIntosh Users Group, The Dance Club. Clubs: Kankakee Area Singles (founder), The Dance (Kankakee) (founder).

MATHES, CARYN G., broadcast executive; b. Terre Haute, Ind., Jan. 10, 1955; d. Robert Nathaniel and Carcelia James (Rudy) M; m. Charles David Stanley, Oct. 18, 1975 (div. June 1980). BS in Print Journalism, Ind. State U., 1976. News anchor, reporter Sta. WTHI-TV, Terre Haute, 1974-78, Sta. WCKY-AM, Cin., 1978-80, Sta. WJR-AM, Detroit, 1980-82; news dir. Sta. WDET-FM, Detroit, 1982-84, gen. mgr., 1984—. Sec. bd. dirs. Mich. Pub. Theater, 1986—. Recipient Minority Achievement award Detroit YMCA, 1986. Baptist. Avocations: travel, cooking, gardening. Office: Sta WDET-FM 5057 Woodward Ave Detroit MI 48202

MATHES, RITA ROSALDA, social service counselor; b. Field, Ont., Can., Aug. 12, 1922; d. Wilfred A. Quenneville and Justine (Marie) Piquette; m. Peter Theodore Mathes, June 22, 1946; children: Linda Miltner, Barbara, Alguire Thomas, Denise Fields, Patricia Westfall, David, Suzanne Breneman, Mark, Mary, James. AA, Wayne County Community Coll., Detroit, 1972; BA in Social Work, Wayne State U., Detroit, 1974. Cert. social worker, Mich. Social worker Big Bros./Big Sisters, Southfield, Mich., 1974-81; sr. coordinator, social service counselor Older Worker's Program, Highland Park, Mich., 1983—. V.p. Women Pub. Affairs Com., Detroit, 1967—; bd. dirs. YWCA, Dearborn, Mich., 1986—; mem. Women's Conf. of Concern, Detroit, 1968—, Women's Internat. League for Peace and Freedom, Detroit, 1971—; elected council mem. Christ the King Parish, Detroit, 1970-71. Mem. Sierra Club. Democrat. Roman Catholic. Home: 15137 Penrod Detroit MI 48223

MATHESON, WILLIAM ANGUS, JR., farm machinery company executive; b. Oregon City, Oreg., Dec. 6, 1919; s. William Angus and Maude (Moore) M.; B.S. in Bus. Adminstrn., Lehigh U., 1941; m. Jeanne Elyse Manley, Feb. 14, 1942; children—Jeanne Sandra, Susan Manley, Bonnie Ann. Procurement engr. Office Chief of Ordnance, 1942-43; mgr. contract sales Eureka-Williams Corp., Bloomington, Ill., 1946-49; dist. sales mgr. Perfex Corp., Milw., 1949-51; v.p. sales Internat. Heater Co., Utica, N.Y., 1951-53; sales mgr. heating div. Heil Co., Milw., 1953-55; v.p. sales, dir. Portable Elevator Mfg. Co., Bloomington, 1955-70; exec. v.p. portable elevator div. Dynamics Corp. Am., 1971-75, pres., 1975-84; owner Matheson Enterprises, 1985—. Bd. dirs. Jr. Achievement Central Ill., 1959-71, pres. Bloomington dist., 1964. Served from pvt. to 1st lt. AUS, 1943-46. Mem. Farm Equipment Mfrs. Assn. (dir. 1961-80, pres. 1969, treas. 1970-80), Ill. C. of C. (dir. 1978-84, vice chmn. 1984), McLean County Assn. Commerce and Industry (pres. 1974), Truck Equipment and Body Distbrs. Assn. (co-founder 1963), Am. Legion, Flying Farmers, Nat. Pilots Assn., Chi Phi. Republican. Presbyterian. Clubs: Rotary, Bloomington Country, Masons, Shriners, Elks. Home: 1404 E Washington St Bloomington IL 61701 Office: 105 W Market St Bloomington IL 61701

MATHEWS, JOHN ANDREW, optometrist; b. Montmorency County, Mich., Oct. 8, 1922; s. James Wilbert and Lena Lois (McCoy) M.; m. Shirley Ruth Langton, Oct. 26, 1951; children: James, Mary, Julie, Lois, Kent, Douglas, Lori. OD, No. Ill. Coll. Optometry, 1948. Pvt. practice optometry Three Rivers, Mich., 1949—; bd. dirs. Three Rivers Savs. and Loan Assn. Mem. St. Joseph County Bd. Election Canvassers, 1966-70. Served with USAAF, 1942-46, to lt. col. USAFR, 1946-82, ret., 1982. Decorated air medals. Mem. Am. Optometric Assn., Mich. Optometric Assn., Southwestern Mich. Optometric Soc. (pres. 1968-71), Three Rivers C. of C., Am. Legion, VFW, Ret. Officers Assn. U.S., Res. Officers Assn. U.S. (life), Am. Assn. Retired Persons, Farm Bur., Nat. Rifle Assn., Mich. United Conservation Clubs. Home: 55188 Buckhorn Rd Three Rivers MI 49093 Office: 3 1/2 N Main St Three Rivers MI 49093

MATHIS, JACK DAVID, advertising executive; b. La Porte, Ind. Nov. 27, 1931; s. George Anthony and Bernice (Bennethum) M.; student U. Mo.,

1950-52; B.S., Fla. State U., 1955; m. Phyllis Dene Hoffman, Dec. 24, 1971; children—Kane Cameron, Jana Dene. With Benton & Bowles, Inc., 1955-56; owner Jack Mathis Advt., 1956—; cons. films, including That's Action!, 1977, Great Movie Stunts: Raiders of the Lost Ark, 1981, The Making of Raiders of the Lost Ark, 1981, An American Legend: The Lone Ranger, 1981; Heroes and Sidekicks: Indiana Jones and the Temple of Doom, 1984. Mem. U.S. Olympic Basketball Com. Recipient citation Mktg. Research Council N.Y. Mem. Alpha Delta Sigma. Author: Valley of the Cliffhangers. Office: Box 738 Libertyville IL 60048

MATHISEN, RHODA SHARON, communications consultant; b. Portland, Oreg., June 25, 1942; d. Daniel and Mildred Elizabeth Annette (Peterson) Hager; m. James Albert Mathisen, July 17, 1964 (div. 1977). B.A. in Edn., Music, Bible Coll., Mich., 1964. Community Relations officer Gary-Wheaton Bank, Wheaton, Ill., 1971-75; br. mgr. Stivers Temporary Personnel, Chgo., 1975-79; v.p. sales Exec. Technique, Chgo., 1980-83; prin. Mathisen Assocs., Downers Grove, Ill., 1983—; presenter seminars; lectr. various profl. orgns.; cons. Haggai Inst., Atlanta; adv. mem. Nat. Bd. Success Group, 1986. Pres. chancel choir Christ Ch. of Oak Brook, 1985-87. Mem. Bus. and Profl. Women (charter mem. Woodfield chpt.), Execs. Club Oak Brook, Women in Communications, Nat. Assn. Female Execs., Sales & Mktg. Execs. Chgo., Chgo. Council Fgn. Relations, Chgo. Assn. Commerce and Industry (named Ambassador of Month N.W. suburban chpt. 1979), Oak Brook Assn. Commerce and Industry, Women Entrepreneurs of DuPage County (membership chmn.), Art Inst. Chgo. Republican. Office: Mathisen Assocs Box 9208 Downers Grove IL 60515

MATHOG, ROBERT HENRY, otolaryngologist, educator; b. New Haven, Apr. 13, 1939; s. William and Tiby (Gans) M.; m. Deena Jane Rabinowitz, June 14, 1964; children: Tiby, Heather, Lauren, Jason. A.B., Dartmouth Coll., 1960; M.D., NYU, 1964. Intern Duke Hosp., Durham, N.C., 1964-65; resident surgery Duke Hosp., 1965-66, resident otolaryngology, 1966-69; practice medicine, specializing in otolaryngology Mpls., 1971-77, Detroit, 1977—; chief of otolaryngology Hennepin County Med. Center, Mpls., 1972-77; asst. prof. U. Minn., 1971-74, asso. prof., 1974-77; prof., chmn. dept. otolaryngology Wayne State U. Sch. Medicine, 1977—; chief otolaryngology Hennepin County Hosp., Mpls., 1972-77, Harper-Grace Hosps., Detroit, 1977—, Detroit Receiving Hosp., 1977—; cons. staff VA Hosp., Allen Park, Minn., 1977—, Children's Hosp., Detroit, 1977—, Hutzel Hosp., Detroit, 1977—. Author: Otolaryngology Clinics of North America, 1976, Textbook of Maxillofacial Trauma, 1983; editor-in-chief Videomed. Edn. Systems, 1972-75; contbr. articles to med. jours. Bd. Dirs. Bexer County Hearing Soc., 1969-71. Served to maj. USAF, 1969-71. Recipient Valentine Mott medal for proficiency in anatomy, 1961; Deafness Research Found. grantee, 1979, 80, 81; NIH grantee, 1986. Fellow ACS, Am. Acad. Otolaryngology, Head and Neck Surgery (cert. award 1976, cert. Appreciation 1978), Am. Soc. for Head and Neck Surgery, Triological Soc., Am. Otol. Soc., Am. Acad. Facial Plastic and Reconstructive Surgery (v.p. 1980), Am. Neurotology Soc.; mem. AMA, Mich. Med. Soc., Am. Head and Neck Soc., Soc. Univ. Otolaryngologists, Assn. Acad. Depts. Otolaryngology, Assn. Research in Otolaryngology (pres. 1981). Home: 27115 Wellington St Franklin MI 48025 Office: Univ Otolaryngology 27177 Lahser Rd #203 Detroit MI 48034

MATHUR, PRACHEESHWAR SWAROOP, metallurgist; b. Shahjahanpur, India, Dec. 19, 1945; came to U.S., 1967; s. Parmeshwar and Gopal Rani M.; B.Sc., Agra Coll. (India), 1962; B.Tech., Indian Inst. Tech., Kanpur, 1967; S.M., M.I.T., 1968, Sc.D., 1972; m. Meena Mathur, Dec. 27, 1976; children: Shashank, Nishant, Priyank. Metall. cons., 1969-71; research asst. M.I.T., Cambridge, 1969-72, research asso., 1968-69; mech. metalworking engr. aircraft engine group Gen. Electric Co., Lynn, Mass., 1972-78, mgr. metals processing, Cin., 1978-80, mgr. customer support, 1980—. Recipient numerous awards Gen. Electric Co. Mem. Am. Soc. Metals, AIME, ASME, Metals Soc. Eng. Contbg. author: Superalloys—Processing, 1981. Patentee in field (5).

MATHWIG, JOHN, environmental educator, consultant; b. Oshkosh, Wis., Mar. 18, 1944; s. Robert John and Ruth Dorothy (Kath) M.; m. Bonnie Lou Masik, Oct. 17, 1965; children: Jill Leslie, Jonathan Tyler. BS, U. Wis., 1966; PhD, Kans. U., 1971. Mem. faculty Coll. of Lake County, Grayslake, Ill., 1970—, prof. biology and entomology, 1976—, asst. chmn. biol. and health scis. div., 1979-83, curator insect collection, 1970—; dir. Entomology Research Lab., Lake Villa, Ill., 1982—; mosquito control cons., dir. quality control and environ. assessment Protection Unlimited, Lake Villa, 1982—; owner, mgr. WillowPoint Industries, Grayslake, 1984—; prin. investigator-mosquitos Des Plaines River Wetlands Demonstration Project, U.S. Fish and Wildlife Service Research Program, 1985—; aquatic cons., 1975—. Author: Biology Lab Manual, 1973, Environmental Biology, 1977, 3d edit., 1986, Insects and Common Pests, 1987; author, editor The Environ Newsletter, 1982—; contbr. articles in field to newspapers. Mem. Nat. Assn. Biology Tchrs., Am. Assn. Mosquito Control, Ill. Mosquito Control Assn. Presbyterian. Avocations: fishing; hunting; stamp collecting; art collecting; skiing. Home: 838 Bonniebrook Mundelein IL 60060 Office: Coll of Lake County 19351 Washington St Grayslake IL 60030

MATJASICH, CAROL ANN, marketing executive; b. Chgo., Mar. 27, 1955; d. Walter Arthur and Joan Mary (Sullivan) M. BFA in Visual Communication, No. Ill. U., 1977. Designer Design Investigation Group, Chgo., 1977-80, exec. v.p., 1980-81; owner, exec. v.p. Porter/Matjasich & Assoc., Chgo., 1981—. Mem. Nat. Assn. Women Bus. Owners, Soc. Typographical Arts, Women in Design Assn. of Profl. Design Firms, Chgo. Assn. Commerce and Industry. Office: 154 W Hubbard #404 Chicago IL 60610

MATLACK, ARDENA LAVONNE, state legislator; b. Carlton, Kans., Dec. 20, 1930; d. Walter D. and Bessie B. (Major) Williams; student Kans. Wesleyan U., 1948, Kans. State U., 1949-51, Washburn U., 1955; BA cum laude, Wichita State U., 1969; m. Don Matlack, June 10, 1951; children: Lucinda Donn, Roxanne, Terry Clyde, Rex William, Timothy Alan. Tchr., Carlton Grade Sch., 1948-49; substitute tchr. Clearwater (Kans.) Schs., 1969-74; part-time music tchr., 1960-72; mem. Kans. Ho. of Reps., 1974-84; arts council mem. Kans. Arts Commn., 1985—. Dem. precinct committeewoman, 1966-68, 1986—, mem. Dem. State Com., 1974-78; pres. Kans. State Dem. Club, 1978; chmn. Clearwater March of Dimes, 1980, Clearwater Area United Fund, 1980, 83; choir dir. United Meth. Ch., 1984-87, bell choir dir., 1987—; project leader 4-H, 1962-71. Recipient Gold Star Legis. award Assn. for legis. action by Rural Mayors, 1981. Mem. Clearwater United Methodist Women (hon. life; pres. 1972), Dist. United Meth. Women (hon. life, dist. coordinator social involvement 1975-76), Kans. Press Women's Assn. (hon.), Gold Key, Alpha Xi Delta, Mu Phi Epsilon. Clubs: Clearwater Federated Women's Study (pres. 1966-67); Kans. Fedn. Women's Dem. Clubs (Disting. Achievement award 1977, chair 4th dist. 1987—), Clearwater Bus. and Profl. Women's (pres. 1985-86), West Side Dem., South Side Dem., Sedgwick County Federated Women's Dem. (pres. 1985-87). Home and Office: 615 Elaine St Clearwater KS 67026

MATOCHA, GEORGE RICKY, architectural engineer; b. Hinsdale, Ill., Mar. 7, 1951; s. George R. and Barbara (Dehr) M.; m. Linda Kaye Huff, Dec. 28, 1974; children—George Ryan, Krystal Lynn. B.S., U. Kans., 1975. Registered architect, Ill. Draftsman, Mees Engring., Western Springs, Ill., 1975-76; asst. dir. planning and constrn. Rush Presbyn. St. Lukes Med. Ctr., Chgo., 1976-81; pres., owner Matocha Assocs., Clarendon Hills, Ill., 1981—. Prin. works include Evergreen I, Chgo. (hon. beautification award 1982), one of largest health maintenance orgn. bldg. complexes in midwest. Mem. archtl. adv. bd. City of Clarendon Hills. Mem. AIA (sec. 1986-87), Nat. Soc. Archtl. Engrs., Nat. Fire Protection Assn., Constrn. Specification Inst., Assn. Energy Engrs., Am. Soc. Hosp. Engring., Ill. Solar Energy Assn. (sec., treas., pres. 1980-85), Sigma Nu. Republican. Presbyterian. Avocations: computers; fishing; hunting. Home: 16 Mohawk Dr Clarendon Hills IL 60514 Office: 4 S Walker St Clarendon Hills IL 60514

MATOLA, LAURENCE FRANK, engineer; b. Youngstown, Ohio, Dec. 9, 1955; s. Henry Frank and Frieda Bertha (Kurtz) M.; m. Linda McClelland, May 5, 1984. BEE, Gen. Motors Inst., Flint, Mich., 1979. Assoc. engr. Gen. Motors, Warren, Ohio, 1979-81; reliability engr. Gen. Motors, Warren, 1981-85, product engr., 1985—; assoc. prof. Youngstown State U., 1981-82. Mem. Mahoning Valley Mgmt. Assn., Am. Mensa. Democrat. Lutheran. Avocations: automobile restoration, gardening, woodworking, skiing. Home: 8484 Squirrel Hill Warren OH 44484 Office: Gen Motors Warren OH 44484

MATOVINA, MARK THOMAS, retail executive; b. Hammond, Ind., Sept. 23, 1957; s. Thomas Anthony and Barbara Louise (Orr) M.; m. Patricia Ann Carney, Nov. 29, 1986. BS in Acctg., Ind. U., 1979; postgrad., Northwestern U., 1987. CPA, Ill. Auditor Alexander Grant & Co., Chgo., 1979-81; sr. auditor United Stationers Supply Co., Des Plaines, Ill., 1981-83, mgr. corp. acctg. and control, 1983-84, mgr. distbn. systems, 1984-85, mgr. bus. systems, 1986—. Mem. Am. Inst. CPA's, Ill. State Soc. CPA's. Home: 320 Dover Dr Des Plaines IL 60018 Office: United Stationers Supply Co 2200 E Golf Rd Des Plaines IL 60016

MATRANGA, LUKE FRANCIS, JR., dentist, air force officer; b. Rockford, Ill., Nov. 6, 1942; s. Luke Francis and Rena Lucy (Toti) M.; m. Cheryl Ann Fennig, Sept. 5, 1966; 1 child, Lisa Maria. DDS, Marquette U., 1966; MS, U. Tex., Houston, 1973. Commd. capt. USAF, 1966, advanced through grades to col., 1979; dental officer, Langley AFB, Va., 1966-67, Phan Rang AFB, Vietnam, 1967-68; preventive dental officer, San Vito AS, Italy, 1968-71; resident in gen. dentistry, Lackland AFB, Tex., 1971-73; chmn. dept. gen. dentistry, Scott AFB, Ill., 1973-79; base dental surgeon, Andersen AFB, Guam, 1979-81; officer-in-charge dental clinic, Bolling AFB, Washington, 1981-83; command dental surgeon Strategic Air Command, Offutt AFB, Nebr., 1983—; cons. in gen. dentistry to U.S. Air Force Surgeon Gen. Mem. editorial bd. Video denatl Corp.; editor Federalist; contbr. articles to profl. jours. Pres. Normanni Little Theater Workshop, San Vito, 1970. Decorated Bronze Star; Republic of Vietnam Gallantry Cross with Palm. Mem. ADA, Acad. Gen. Dentistry (chmn. budget and fin. com.). Republican. Roman Catholic. Lodge: K.C. Avocations: sailing; skiing; racquetball. Home: 20829 Paddock Circle Elkhorn NE 68022 Office: HQ SAC/SGD Offutt AFB NE 68113

MATSAKIS, NICHOLAS DEMETRIOU, dentist; b. Canonsburgh, Pa., Mar. 8, 1914; s. Demetrios Nicholas and Sophia Matsakis; m. Theodora Dorothy Papageorge, Dec. 2, 1945; children: Aphrodite, Demetrios, Elias. Diploma, Pancyprian Sem., Larnaca, Cyprus, 1932; DDS, Washington U., St. Louis, 1940. Gen. practice dentistry St. Louis, 1940—. Chmn. com. Justice for Cyprus, St. Louis, 1950—; hon. consul Cyprus, Ala., Ark., Kans., La., Miss., Mo., Okla., Tenn., Tex., 1970—. Served to maj. U.S. Army, 1942-46. Mem. ADA, St. Louis Dental Assn., Am. Hellenic Ednl. Prog. Assn. Home: 1410 Jamaica Ct Warson Woods MO 63122 Office: 3192 Watson Rd Saint Louis MO 63139

MATSON, NORMAN RICHARD, accountant; b. Frederic, Wis., Mar. 16, 1935; s. S.R. and Martha (Peterson) M.; m. Gayle Engedal, May 31, 1958; 1 child, Hans. BBA, U. Minn., 1957. CPA, Ill. Staff acct. Arthur Andersen & Co., Chgo., 1958-59; staff acct. Johnson Atwater & Co., Chgo., 1959-62, mng. ptnr., 1973-79; mng. ptnr. Johnson Atwater & Co., Columbus, Ohio, 1962-66, Dallas, 1966-73; sr. ptnr. Matson, Driscoll & Damico, Chgo., 1979—. Mem. Am. Inst. CPA's, Ill. CPA Soc. Lutheran. Office: Matson Driscoll & Damico 118 S Clinton St Chicago IL 60606

MATSON, VIRGINIA MAE FREEBERG (MRS. EDWARD J. MATSON), educator, author; b. Chgo., Aug. 25, 1914; d. Axel George and Mae (Dalrymple) Freeberg; m. Edward John Matson, Oct. 18, 1941; children: Karin (Mrs. Donald E. Skadden), Sara M. Drake, Edward Robert, Laurence D., David O. BA, U. Ky., 1934; MA, Northwestern U., 1941. Tchr. high schs. Chgo., 1934-42, Ridge Farm, 1944-45, Lake County (Ill.) Pub. Schs., 1956-59; founder Grove Sch., Lake Forest, Ill., 1958-87, ret., 1987; mem. Ill. Council on Exceptional Children. Author: Shadow on the Lost Rock, 1958, Saul, the King, 1968, Abba Father, 1970 (Friends Lit. Fiction award 1972), Buried Alive, 1970, A School for Peter, 1974, A Home Peter, 1983, Letters to Lauren, A History of the Methodist Campgrounds, Des Plaines. Mem. Friends of Lit. Dem. Recipient Humanitarian award Ill. Med. Soc. Aux. Home: 950 N Saint Mary's Rd Libertyville IL 60048

MATT, JANET ANN BARRY, real estate professional; b. Milw., Apr. 19, 1930; d. James Thomas and Isabelle Margaret (McCrory) Barry; m. William Aloysius Matt, Feb. 3, 1951 (dec. Feb. 1976); children: Jayne, Peg, William, Thomas, Mark, John. Student, Mt. Mary Coll., 1948-49, Marquette U., 1949-51, 62-63, 74-75. Real estate broker James T. Barry Co., Milw., 1976—. Mem. plan commn., econ. devel. com. City of Delafield, Wis., 1987. Mem. Soc. Indsl. and Office Realtors (active), Milw. Bd. Realtors. Roman Catholic. Clubs: Lake Country Racquet (Hartland, Wis.), Nagawicka Lake Yacht (Delafield). Home: 2016 Bay Point Ln Hartland WI 53029 Office: James T Barry Co Inc 1232 N Edison St Milwaukee WI 53202

MATTANO, DENIS DOMINIC, corporate credit manager; b. Milw., Dec. 14, 1942; s. Steve and Kathleen (Korta) M.; m. Karen Rebatzki, Dec. 9, 1967; 1 child Samantha Alexandra. Student, U. Wis., Milw., 1960-62, Grad. Sch. Credit and Fin. Mgmt., 1978. Supr. credit and accts. receivable George J. Meyer Mfg., Milw., 1967-70; credit dept. supr. Allen-Bradley Co., Milw., 1970-75; asst. credit mgr. The Ansul Co., Marinette, Wis., 1975-76; corp. credit mgr. Appleton (Wis.) Papers Inc., 1976—; instr. fin. statement analysis Fox Valley Tech. Inst., Appleton, 1984—. Fellow Nat. Inst. Credit. Fine Paper Mfrs. Credit Group (chmn. 1984—), Nat. Assn. Credit Mgmt. (bus. credit exec.), Credit Research Found, Nat. Rifle Assn., Acad. Model Aeronautics. Home: 1420 Fieldstone Ct Neenah WI 54956 Office: Appleton Papers Inc 823 E Wisconsin Appleton WI 54912

MATTER, MICHAEL CARL, pharmacist; b. Williamsport, Pa., Sept. 25, 1945; s. Paul H. and Mary L. (Gladewitz) M.; B.Sc. in Pharmacy, Temple U., 1968; M.B.A., Ohio U., 1984; m. Pamela Sue Gault, Feb. 9, 1974; children: Drew Michael-Paul, Graham Sang-Joon, Abby Hee-Jung, Alex Hee-Sung. Resident in hosp. pharmacy Bethesda Hosp., Zanesville, Ohio, 1968-69, spl. project pharmacist, 1969; dir. pharmacy services Med. Center Hosp., Chillicothe, Ohio, 1970-87; div. dir. support services Med. Ctr. Hosp., 1987—; evening instr. pharmacology Hocking Tech. Coll., Chillicothe, 1977-82. Mem. Am. Soc. Hosp. Pharmacists (preceptor; residency in hosp. pharmacy), Ohio Soc. Hosp. Pharmacists (treas. 1979-85), Central Ohio Soc. Hosp. Pharmacists, Nat. Order Symposiarchs (past pres. Zeta chpt.). Home: 204 Vine St Chillicothe OH 45601 Office: Med Center Hosp 272 Hospital Rd Chillicothe OH 45601

MATTERN, PERRY CHALMERS, pastor, music educator; b. Wauseon, Ohio, Feb. 20, 1950; s. Chalmers Asa and Laura Louise (Warwick) M.; m. Maureen Elise Early, June 19, 1971; children: Rachel Joanne, Sarah Renée. BA in Religion, U. Tenn., 1972; M in Div., Christian Theol. Sem., Indpls., 1976. Ordained to ministry Disciples of Christ Ch., 1976. Intern minister E. Main St. Christian Ch., Elwood, Ind., 1972-75; pastor First Christian Ch., Fostoria, Ohio, 1976-78, Dawson Springs, Ky., 1978-80; minister of youth and edn. Washington Ave. Christian Ch., Elyria, Ohio, 1980-84; assoc. pastor First Christian Ch., Salem, Ohio, 1984-85; pastor Cen. Christian Ch., Marion, Ohio, 1985—. Active Salem Peace Fellowship, 1984-85; supporter Salem Community Theatre, 1985; singer and guitarist Salem Madrigal Singers, 1984; coach Olympics of Mind; bd. dirs. Marion Employment Resource Ctr.; exec. advisor local Boy Scout troop. Mem. Christian Ch. in Ohio, Marion County Minister's Assn. (Ecumenical rep.), Disciples of Christ Hist. Soc. Democrat. Club: YMCA. Avocations: computer programming, auto mechanics, music. Office: Cen Christian Ch 421 Mount Vernon Ave Marion OH 43302

MATTERN, ROBERT LEE, dentist; b. Wabash, Ind., Apr. 6, 1934; s. Robert E. and Dorothy E. (Milliner) M.; m. Barbara A. Bonewit, June 17, 1956; children: Robert J., Diane E., Lisa S. Mattern Traver, Megan Jean. Student, Western Mich. U.; DDS, Ind. U., Indpls., 1958. Gen. practice dentsitry Wabash, 1960—. Mem. Wabash City Council, 1963-71, Wabash County United Fund Bd. Served to capt., USAF, 1968-60. Mem. ADA, Wis. Dental Assn., Wabash Valley Dental Soc. (past pres., sec.), Grant County Dental Soc., Wabash C. of C., Psi Omega. Republican. Mem. Christian Ch. Lodge: Kiwanis. (past pres., lt. gov.). Home: 174 Maple St Wabash IN 46992

MATTHAY, CAROL TOMLINSON, radiologist; b. Lodi, Wis., Oct. 16, 1917; d. Ernest Byron and Forence Vivian (Kidder) Tomlinson; m. Frank Matthay, Feb. 14, 1950 (dec. June, 1959); children: Jeannie Matthay Bergmann, Camy Matthay Hastil, Melissa. BA, U. Wis., 1939, MD, 1942. Diplomate Am. Bd. Radiology. Postdoctoral fellow Cleve. Clinic, 1943-44; resident U. Wis. Med. Sch., Madison, 1944-47; radiologist Munn-Kock Clinic, Janesville, Wis., 1947-57, Beaver Dam (Wis.) Hosps., 1948-50, Meml. Community Hosp., Edgerton, Wis., 1948-60; radiol. cons. Monroe (Wis.) Clinic, 1975-78, Mendota Clinic State Mental Hosp., Madison, Wis., 1980—; cons. Mercy Hosp., Janesville, Wis., 1973-80. Bd. dirs. Montessori Children's House, Janesville, 1962-66, YWCA, Janesville, 1970-75, Alzheimer's Family Support Group, Janesville, 1979—, Rock County Community Options Program, Janesville, 1982—. Recipient Women of Distinction award, YWCA, Janesville, 1978. Mem. AMA (Physicians award 1979, 82, 85), Wis. Radiol. Soc. (bd. dirs. 1950-53). Avocations: travel, reading, geneology, gardening. Home: 715 N Marion Ave Janesville WI 53545

MATTHES, LESA ANNE, controller; b. Ft. Sill, Okla., May 24, 1956; d. George Ray and Shirley Ann (McKinzie) Tribe; m. David William Matthes, June 14, 1974; children: Tara Anne, Amy Christine. AA in Bus., Olney (Ill.) Cen. Coll., 1987. Bookkeeper McLean Implement, Albion, 1974-81; accounts payable clk. Champion Labs., West Salem, Ill., 1981, chief fin. acct., 1981-83, div. controller, 1983-84, corp. controller, 1984—; advisor bus. dept. Olney (Ill.) Cen. Coll., 1984—. Brotherhood choir dir. West Village Christian Ch., Albion, 1978—; bd. dirs. Sandia Chico Christian Mission, Mex., 1984—. Mem. Nat. Assn. Female Execs. Republican. Avocations: reading, needlework, canoeing. Home: Rural Rte 1 Box 122 West Salem IL 62476 Office: Champion Labs 315 Northwest St West Salem IL 62476

MATTHEWS, C(HARLES) DAVID, real estate appraiser, consultant; b. Anniston, Ala., June 15, 1946; s. James Boyd and Emma Grace (McCullough) M.; m. Stephanie Ann Woods, Dec. 28, 1968; children: Alison Paige, Dylan McCullough. BS, U. Tenn., 1968. County appraiser Assessor's Office, Freeport, Ill., 1969-71; staff appraiser Ill. Dept. Highways, Springfield, 1971-72; appraiser, dir. counseling Norman Benedict Assocs., Hamden, Conn., 1972-76; mgr. appraisal dept. Citizens Realty & Ins., Evansville, Ind., 1976-80; owner, mgr. David Matthews Assocs., Evansville, 1980—; adj. real estate faculty U. Conn., 1974-76, U. Evansville, 1978—. Tympanist Chattanooga Symphony; author: (with others) Land Use Plan, Downtown Master Plan of Evansville, Indiana, 1984. Mem. Leadership Evansville, 1982, program chmn., 1983; pres. Girl's East Soccer League, Evansville, 1984; interviewer Horizons Leadership Acad., Evansville, 1984-86; arbitrator Am. Arbitration Assn., 1986—. Mem. Am. Inst. Real Estate Appraisers (nat. chmn. comprehensive exam. 1986-87, state pres. 1987), Soc. Real Estate Appraisers (local pres. 1981), Evansville Bd. Realtors (pres. 1986), Evansville C. of C. (chmn. tax assessment law task force 1982), Mensa (local sec. 1984), S. Ind. MacIntosh Users Group (charter). Methodist. Avocations: cinematographer, jazz drummer, traveling, golf. Home: 430 S Boeke Rd Evansville IN 47714 Office: 123 NW 4th St Suite 711 Evansville IN 47708

MATTHEWS, GERTRUDE ANN URCH, retired librarian, writer; b. Jackson, Mich., July 16, 1921; d. Charles P.A. and Amy (Granville) Urch; student Albion Coll., 1940-41; A.A., Jackson Jr. Coll., 1939; B.S., M.S. in Library Arts, U. Mich., 1959; m. Geoffrey Matthews, June 30, 1942 (dec.). Adult services librarian Jackson, Mich., 1959-63; asst. dir., librarian Franklin Sylvester Library, Medina, Ohio, 1963-81, now dir. older adults facility library. Pres., Hist. Soc., 1966-67; active Dollars for Scholars Com., 1966-86; mem. Bicentennial Com.; officer diocesean leval Episcopal Ch.; mem. vestry St. Paul's Ch., Medina, 1981-84. Mem. ALA, Ohio Library Assn., AAUW (dir., Community Service award 1985, Woman of Yr.), LWV (dir.). Republican. Contbr. articles to profl. and popular publs.; weekly newspaper columnist, 1958-81; bookreviewer The Nat. Librarian. Home: 750 Weymouth Medina OH 44256

MATTHEWS, JOHN L., manufacturing company executive; b. Atkins, Ark., 1914; s. John Jefferson and Naomi L. (Gipson) M.; B.S. in Banking and Fin., U. Ark., 1932; m. Mary Beth Higby, June 13, 1939; children—John Lannes, Nancy D., Jill K. Mgr., S.H. Kress Co., Oklahoma City, 1932-34; nat. sales mgr. Sears Roebuck, Chgo., 1937-40; owner Matthews Constrn. Co., Kansas City, Mo., 1945-49; pres. Van Brunt Machinery, Kansas City, 1946-49; pres. Airosol Co., Inc., Neodesha, Kans., 1949—; dir. Merc. Bank and Trust, Kansas City-St. Louis, Racon Co., Wichita, Kans. Served with U.S. Army, 1941-45; ETO. Decorated Legion of Merit, Bronze Star; Croix de Guerre with gold star. Mem. Nat. Aerosol Packers Assn. (pres. 1976-80), Chem. Spltys. Mfg. Assn. Republican. Methodist. Clubs: Kansas City, Independence, Kansas Country, Elks, Masons, Shriners. Home: 1100 N 5th St Neodesha KS 66757 Office: 525 N 11th St Neodesha KS 66757

MATTHEWS, MARGARET LONG, architect; b. Indpls., Aug. 1, 1924; d. James Arthur and Bess (Nye) Long; m. William Matthews, June 13, 1953 (div. Oct. 1973); children: William James, Charles Arthur, James Coert; m. Harold W. Osgood, Oct. 31, 1986. Architect Ch. World Service, Fed. Republic Germany, 1949; program asst. United Christian missionary Soc., Indpls., 1949-50; draftsman West & Weber, Architects, Galesburg, Ill., 1953-56; free-lance archtl. designer Galesburg, 1956-68; instr. architecture Monmouth (Ill.) Coll., 1970-75; staff architect Monarch Machine Tool Co., Sidney, Ohio, 1975-86; cons. indsl. interiors Ferris Furniture, Galesburg, 1956-68. Trustee Edison State Community Coll, Piqua, Ohio, 1980-86, chmn. bd. trustees, 1985-86. Danforth Found. Grad. Women's fellow, 1968-72. Mem. Altrusa Internat. (pres. 1984-86). Mem. Christian Ch. Avocations: timber frame construction, painting, swimming, sailing.

MATTHEWS, ROBERT WILLIAM, JR., office equipment company executive; b. Chgo., Mar. 4, 1944; s. Robert William and Kathleen Josephine (Johnson) M.; m. Linda Valory Appleby, Feb. 14, 1970 (div. 1972); 1 dau., Jennie Lin; m. Patricia Anne McKenzie, Dec. 22, 1973; children—Victoria Elizabeth, Veronica Ellen, David Andrew. B.S. in Am. Studies, Roosevelt U., 1976, M.A. in Am. Lit., 1977. Cert. Am. Records Mgmt. Assn. Mktg. rep. Xerox Corp., Mpls., 1968-70, product mktg. mgr., Ann Arbor, Mich., 1971-75; spl. account rep. Minn. Mining and Mfg. Co., Chgo., 1976-79, area mktg. specialist, 1979-81; midwest regional mgr. Canon U.S.A., Inc., Chgo., 1981—; dir. JVP Machine Co. Inc. Active Chgo. Commons Assn., Lyric Opera Guild. Served with USCGR, 1966-72. Mem. Assn. Info. and Image Mgmt., Am. Mgmt. Assn., Nat. Office Machine Dealers Assn., Mensa. Republican. Roman Catholic. Clubs: Theodore Roosevelt Assn., Safari Club Internat., Game Conservation Internat., K.C., Hemingway Soc. Author: Hemingway and the Blood Sports, 1977. Office: 100 Park Blvd Itasca IL 60143

MATTHIES, FREDERICK JOHN, architectural and engineering company executive; b. Omaha, Oct. 4, 1925; s. Fred. J. and Charlotte Leota (Metz) M.; m. Carol Mae Dean, Sept. 14, 1947; children—John Frederick, Jane Carolyn Matthies Goding. B.S. in Civil Engring., Cornell U., 1947; postgrad., U. Nebr., 1952-53. Diplomate Am. Acad. Environ. Engrs.; registered profl. engr., Iowa, Nebr., Mich., N.Y., Wash., Calif., Fla., Kans., N.C. Civil engr. Henningson, Durham & Richardson, Omaha, 1947-50, 52-54; sr. v.p. devel. Leo A. Daly Co., Omaha, 1954—; lectr. in field; mem. dist. export council U.S. Dept. Commerce, 1981-83. Contbr. articles to profl. publs. Mem. Douglas County Rep. Cen. Com., Nebr., 1968-72; bd. regents Augustana Coll., Sioux Falls., S.D., 1976—; bd. dirs. Orange County Luth. Hosp. Assn., Anaheim, Calif., 1961-62; trustee Luth. Med. Ctr., Omaha, 1978-82. Served to 1st lt. USMCR, 1943-46, 50-52, Korea. Fellow ASCE, Instn. Civil Engrs. (London); mem. Am. Water Works Assn. (life), Nat. Soc. Profl. Engrs., Air Force Assn., Am. Legion. Lutheran. Club: Happy Hollow Country (Omaha). Home: 337 S 127th St Omaha NE 68154 Office: Leo A Daly Co 8600 Indian Hills Dr Omaha NE 68114

MATTHIESEN, WALTER ROBERT, JR., computer systems specialist; b. Springfield, Ill., Apr. 10, 1961; s. Walter Robert and Mary Dianne (Donovan) M.; m. Nancy Jeanne Stewart, Apr. 26, 1980 (div. June 1986); children: Walter Robert III, Ashley Marie, Amanda Christine; m. Crystal Kay Vilcot, June 21, 1986; 1 child, Rachelle Marie. Grad. high sch., Slidell, La., 1979. Computer programmer I Ill. Dept. Pub. Aid, Springfield, 1980-81, computer programmer II, 1981-82, computer programmer III, 1982; systems analyst II Fed. Kemper Ins. Co., Decatur, Ill., 1982-83, systems analyst III, 1983-85, software specialist III, 1985-86, sr. systems software specialist, 1986—. Republican. Home: 244 Cheryl Dr Mount Zion IL 62549 Office: Fed Kemper Ins Co 2001 E Mound Rd Decatur IL 62526

MATTILA, EDWARD CHARLES, music educator; b. Duluth, Minn., Nov. 30, 1927; s. Edward H. and Ellen M. (Matson) M.; m. Nancy Ann Norton, Oct. 12, 1956; children: Amy Lara, Edward Norton. BA in Music, U. Minn., 1950, PhD in Music Theory and Composition, 1963; MMus, New Eng. Conservatory, 1956. Instr. Concordia Coll., St. Paul, 1958-62; asst. prof. Bishop Coll., Dallas, 1962-64; faculty U. Kans., Lawrence, 1964—, prof. music, 1975—, producer, host program contemporary music Sta. KANU, 1971—. Served with Signal Corps, U.S. Army, 1952-53. Grantee in field. Mem. Am. Soc. Univ. Composers, Coll. Music Soc., Am. Music Ctr. Composer: Symphony No. 1, Theme and Variations for 2 pianos; Partitions for String Orch.; 6 arrays for piano; Repercussions for Tape; Movements for Computer and Dancers, Six by Six; Seaborne for Solo Dancer & Tape. Office: U Kans Sch Fine Arts Lawrence KS 66045

MATTINGLY, ROBERT KERKER, entrepreneur; b. Zanesville, Ohio, Mar. 12, 1921; s. John Clement and Olive (Kerker) M.; m. Bette Louise Allen, Dec. 27, 1941; 1 child, Barbara Kay. Grad., High Sch., Zanesville, 1939. Pres. Mattingly Foods, Inc., Zanesville, 1945—. Bd. dirs. Goodwill Industries, Zanesville, 1970-76, Zanesville Trace, 1981—. Served to 1st lt. U.S. Army, 1942-45. Named So. Ohio Gentleman Farmer, Bob Evans, 1979, Ohio Commodore, Gov. Rhodes, 1979; recipient Pres.'s award, Syracuse China, 1978-85. Mem. Zanesville C. of C. (pres. 1976-77). Avocations: reading, swimming, traveling. Home: 3675 Frazeysburg Rd Zanesville OH 43701 Office: Mattingly Foods Inc 302 State St Zanesville OH 43701

MATTSON, GEORGE ARTHUR, interior design; b. Nov. 13, 1925; s. John and Mary Josephine Mattson; m. Carmen Kathryn Hames, Feb. 20, 1959; children: Michael, Christopher, Kathryn. Student, U. Biarritz, France, 1945-46, U. Minn., Duluth, 1946-49. Lic. faculy interior design, Minn. Designer J. Marshall Morin Interiors, Colorado Springs, Colo., 1953-61, Ericksons, Farnhams, Gabberts and Daytons, Mpls., 1962-70; design educator, head of dept. Alexandria (Minn.) Tech. Inst., 1970—. Bd. dirs. Devel. Achievement Ctr., Alexandria, Knute Nelson Meml. Home, Alexandria. Served to tech. sgt. U.S. Army and UASF, 1944-52, ETO. Mem. Found. for Interior Design Edn. Research (standards com.), Am. Soc. Interior Design (mem. corp. and edn.), Assn. Interior Design (educators' council), Alexandria C. of C. Democrat. Lutheran. Avocations: art, architecture, reading, travel, biking. Office: Alexandria Tech Inst 1601 Jefferson Alexandria MN 56308

MATTSON, LUCRETIA SUE WILSON, accountant, educator; b. Canton, Ohio, Nov. 22, 1947; d. William Raymond and Barbara Idella (Zuercher) Wilson; m. John Gaylord Mattson, May 21, 1977. BS, Muskingum Coll., 1969; M in Acctg., Utah State U., 1976; D Bus. Adminstrn. in Acctg., U. Ky., 1983. CPA, Wis. Tchr. math. Harvey High Sch., Painesville, Ohio, 1969-71, Hillsdale High Sch., Jeromesville, Ohio, 1971-73, Franklin (Ohio) Jr. High Sch., 1973-74; instr. acctg. U. Wis., Eau Claire, 1975-83, assoc. prof., 1984—; cons. Small Bus. Devel. Ctr. U. Wis., Eau Claire, 1984—; self-employed income tax preparer, Eau Claire, 1975-86; income tax preparer Bernicke Fin. Planning, Inc., Eau Claire, 1986—. Mem. Am. Inst. CPA's, Am. Acctg. Assn., Am. Taxation Assn., Am. Women's Soc. CPA's, Wis. Inst. CPA's, Beta Alpha Psi. Mennonite. Avocations: canoeing, gardening.

MATTSON, MARK ANDREW, accountant; b. Sept. 8, 1959. BSBA, Miami U., Oxford, Ohio, 1981. Acct. Price Waterhouse, Cleve., 1981-85; chief fin. officer Conrad's Tire Service, Cleve., 1985—; ptnr. Mattson & Mattson, CPA's, Westlake, Ohio, 1986—. Mem. Citizen's League Cleve., 1982—. Mem. Am. Inst. CPA's, Nat. Assn. Accts., Ohio Soc. CPA's, Delta Upsilon (trustee, treas. Miami chpt. 1982—). Home: 3121 Bay Landing Dr Westlake OH 44145 Office: Conrads Tire Service 14577 Lorain Ave Cleveland OH 44111

MATTSON, ROGER ALBERT, psychiatrist; b. Ishpeming, Mich., May 12, 1938. Student, Soumi Coll., 1956-57; BS, No. Mich. U., 1959; MD, U. Mich., 1963. Diplomate Am. Bd. Psychiatry and Neurology. Intern St. Mary's Hosp., Duluth, Minn., 1967; resident in psychiatry Mayo Clinic, Rochester, Minn., 1967-69; residency in psychiatry VA Hosp., Mpls., 1969-70; practice medicine specializing in psychiatry Duluth, Minn., 1970—; pres. Nannies Unlimited, Duluth. Served with USAF, 1964-67. Office: 1015 Med Arts Bldg Duluth MN 55802

MATTSON, VICTORIA GOUZE, dentist; b. Marshfield, Wis., June 20, 1953; d. Frank John and Naida Shilia (Milakovich) Gouze; m. Douglas Robert Mattson, Sept. 10, 1983. BS in Nursing, U. Wyo., Laramie, 1977; DDS with honors, Marquette U., Milw., 1983. RN, Colo., Wis. Nurse U. Colo. Med. Ctr. Hosp., Denver, 1977-78, Profl. Nurses, Kimberely Nurses, Milw., 1978-83; gen. practice dentistry Wausau, Wis., 1983—; instr., supervising dentist dental hygiene clinic N. Cen. Tech. Inst., Wausau, 1986-87. Organizer, mem. Am. Cancer Soc., Wausau, 1983—; dental exec. com. Wausau United Way, 1986; candidate for Marathon County coroner, Wis., 1986. Mem. ADA, Wis. Dental Assn. (alt. del. 1986-89), Cen. Wis. Dental Soc. (chmn. children's dental health 1986), Marathon County Dental Soc., Am. Nurses Assn., Women's Internat. Bowling Congress (v.p. Wausau League 1986-87, pres.-elect 1987-88), Delta Sigma Delta (scribe 1982-83), Sigma Theta Tau. Roman Catholic. Lodge: Zonta. Avocations: fly fishing, sewing. Office: PO Box 1566 Wausau WI 54401

MATULA, RICHARD ALLAN, research university president; b. Chgo., Aug. 22, 1939; s. Ludvig A. and Leone O. (Dufeck) M.; m. Brenda C. Mather, Sept. 5, 1959; children: Scott, Kristopher, Daniel, Tiffiny. BS, Purdue U., 1961, MS, 1962, PhD, 1964. Instr. Purdue U., 1963-64; asst. prof. mech. engring. U. Calif., Santa Barbara, 1964-66, U. Mich., 1966-68; assoc. prof. mech. engring. Drexel U., Phila., 1968-70; prof. Drexel U., 1970-76, chmn. thermal and fluid sci. advanced study group, 1969-72; chmn. Drexel U. (Environ. Studies Inst.), 1972-73, chmn. dept. mech. engring. and mechanics, 1973-76; dean Coll. Engring.; prof. mech. engring. La. State U., Baton Rouge, after 1976; pres. Inst. Paper Chemistry, Appleton, Wis., 1986—. Contbr. articles to profl. jours. Treas., bd. dirs. Wexford Leas Swim and Racquet Club, Inc., 1968-73; v.p. Wexford Leas Civic Assn., 1969-71. Mem. Air Pollution Control Assn., Am. Soc. Engring. Edn., ASME, AAAS, Combustion Inst., Soc. Automotive Engrs., Sigma Xi, Pi Kappa Phi, Pi Tau Sigma, Sigma Pi Sigma, Tau Beta Pi. Roman Catholic. Home: 90 N Green Bay Rd Appleton WI 54911 Office: Inst Paper Chemistry PO Box 1039 Appleton WI 54912

MATUSZEWSKI, STANLEY, clergyman; b. Morris Run, Pa., May 4, 1915; s. Andrew and Mary (Czekalski) M.; grad. St. Andrew's Prep. Sem., Rochester, N.Y.; student La Salette Coll., Hartford, Conn., Scholastic Sem., Altamont, N.Y. Ordained priest Roman Catholic Ch., 1942; disciplinarian, prof. classics, La Salette Sem., Olivet, 1942-46, dir., 1948—; superior Midwest province LaSalette Fathers; founding editor Our Lady's Digest, 1946—; exec. bd. Nat. Catholic Decency in Reading Program; faculty adv. Midwest Conf. of Internat. Relations Clubs sponsored 1944 in Chgo. by Carnegie Endowment for Internat. Peace. Trustee Nat. Shrine of Immaculate Conception, Washington. Honored by Rochester, N.Y. Centennial Com. 1934 as Monroe County (N.Y.) orator. Mem. Mariological Soc. Am. (1954 award), Missionaries of Our Lady of La Salette, Catholic Press Assn., Canon Law Soc., Catholic Broadcasters' Assn., Religious Edn. Assn., Polish-Hungarian World Fedn. (trustee). K.C. Author: Rochester Centennial Oration; Youth Marches On. Home: Box 777 Twin Lakes WI 53181

MATZ, ANNE L., psychiatric social worker; b. Freiburg, Fed. Republic Germany, Dec. 31, 1929; d. Gustav and Hilda Jabung; m. Milton Matz, June 20, 1952; children: Deborah G., David G. BA, Hunter Coll., 1952; MA, U. Chgo., 1956. Lic. independent social worker, Ohio. Child therapist Lake County Mental Health Clinic, Gary, Ind., 1956-59, St. Lukes Hosp., Cleve., 1966-70; research assoc. Jewish Children Bur., Cleve., 1970-71; gen. practice in family therapy Cleve., 1970—; co-dir. Pastoral Psychology Inst., Dept. Psychiatry Sch. Medicine Case Western Res. U.; sr. clin. instr. Dept. Psychiatry Case Western Res. U. Bd. dirs. Shaker Heights (Ohio) Youth Ctr., 1986—; chmn. Cath. social service United Way, Cleve., 1984-85; chmn. Fed. Community Planning Task Force on Services To Families and Children, 1972-73.; chmn. social services adv. bd. Cuyahoga County Welfare Dept. HEW fellowship, 1955-56; recipient Outstanding Pub. Service award Cuyahoga County Commn., 1973. Fellow Am. Orthopsychiat. Assn.; mem. Nat. Assn. Social Workers, Am. World Assn. for Social Psychiatry, Ohio Soc. Clin. Social Workers, Nat. Registry Health Care Providers in Clin. Social Work, U. Chgo. Alumni Assn. (bd. dirs. 1983—). Jewish. Avocations: hiking, cycling, travel, swimming. Office: Matz Assn 3609 Park East Beachwood OH 44122

MATZ, MILTON, clinical psychologist, management relations consultant, rabbi; b. N.Y.C., June 30, 1927; s. Joshua E. and Sonja (Kviat) Matz; m. Anne L. Jaburg, June 20, 1952; children—Deborah, David. B.A., Yeshiva U., 1947; M.H.L., rabbinic ordination, Hebrew Union Coll., 1952, D.D. (hon.), 1977; Ph.D., U. Chgo., 1966. Cert. Ohio Psychol. Assn. Bd. Examiners Psychologists, 1966; lic. Ohio Bd. Psychology, 1973. First lt. USAF, 1952-54; asst. rabbi Kehilath Anshei Maariv Temple, Chgo., 1954-57; rabbi Congregation B'nai Jehoshua, Chgo., 1957-59; dir. pastoral psychology, asso. rabbi The Temple, Cleve., 1959-66; sr. staff psychologist Fairhill Psychiat. Hosp., Cleve., 1966-69; adj. prof. Cleve. State U., 1966-70; clin. instr. Case-Western Res. Sch. Medicine, 1966-73, asst. clin. prof., 1973—, dir. Pastoral Psychology Service Inst., 1973—, clin. dir. bereavement project, 1978—; pvt. practice clin. psychology, Beachwood, Ohio, 1966—; mng. ptnr. Matz Assocs., Beachwood, 1966—; cons. dir. Erie Pastoral Psychology Inst., 1977—; mng. ptnr. Mgmt. Relations Cons. div. Matz Assocs., Beachwood, 1984—; cons. dir. pastoral tng. project Central Conf. Am. Rabbis, 1978-79; lectr. mgmt. relations, negotiation and mediation skills. Sec., v.p. Greater Cleve. Bd. Rabbis, 1964-66; bd. mem. Jewish Children's Bur. and Bellefaire Jewish Community Ctr., Cleve., 1952-64; advisory bd. Div. Child Welfare, Cuyahoga County, Ohio, 1962-66; founding mem. Cuyahoga County Community Mental Health and Retardation Bd., Cleve., 1967-71, chmn., 1972-73; chmn. Central Conf. Am. Rabbis Com. on Judaism and Health, N.Y.C., 1975-79. Diplomate Am. Assn. Pastoral Counselors; mem. Am., Ohio psychol. assns., Soc. for Indsl. and Orgnl. Psychology, Am. Assn. Pastoral Counselors, Ohio Acad. Profl. Psychology (trustee 1984—). Author numerous papers and articles on interpersonal communication, dispute resolution, treatment of marital conflict and grief, primary prevention of mental illness, psychology and religion, and pastoral tng.; recipient commendation for outstanding leadership in mental health Bd. Commrs. of Cuyahoga County, 1973. Home: 3346 Stockholm Rd Shaker Heights OH 44120 Office: 3609 Park East Beachwood OH 44122

MAUGANS, JOHN CONRAD, lawyer; b. Miami County, Ind., May 10, 1938; s. Willis William and Evelyn Jeannette (Mills) M.; A.B., Manchester Coll., 1960; LL.B. with distinction (Krannert scholar), Ind. U., 1962, J.D., 1970; m. Judith M. Gallagher, Jan. 24, 1960 (dec. June 1984); children—Lisa Denise, Stacy Erin, Kristen Cherie; m. Jo Ella Middlekauff, June 7, 1985. Admitted to Ind. bar, 1962; with firm Barnes, Hickam, Pantzer & Boyd, Indpls., 1962-63; practice in Kokomo, 1966—; ptnr. firm Bayliff, Harrigan, Cord & Maugans, P.C., 1969—; guest lectr. Coll. Bus., Manchester Coll., 1966-80. Chmn. Howard County fund dr. Manchester Coll., 1971; bd. dirs. Tribal Trails council Girl Scouts U.S.A., 1977-85, Vols. in Community Service, 1978-84, Home Health Care of Central Ind., Inc., 1983—; trustee Western Sch. Corp., 1986—. Served to capt. AUS, 1963-66. Mem. Am., Ind., Howard County bar assns., Am., Ind. trial lawyers assns., Manchester Coll. Alumni Assn. (chmn. area chpt. 1970), Manchester Coll. M. Alumni Assn. (pres. 1972), Order of Coif, Phi Delta Phi. Lutheran. Contbr. articles to legal jours. Home: 1890 S 820 W Russiaville IN 46979 Office: Box 2249 123 N Buckeye Kokomo IN 46904-2249

MAUL, GARY PIERRE, engineering educator, consultant, researcher; b. Sharon, Pa., June 27, 1947; s. David H. and Liliane M. Maul; m. Linda S. Koch, May 6, 1972; children—Hayden B., Allison R. B. Engring., Youngstown State U., 1970; M.S. in Indsl. Engring., Purdue U., 1976; Ph.D., Pa. State U., 1982. Profl. engr., Pa., Ohio. Indsl. engr. Packard Electric div. Gen. Motors, Warren, Ohio, 1972-77; asst. prof. Youngstown (Ohio) State U., 1977-79; instr. Pa. State U., University Park, 1979-82; asst. prof. indsl. engring. Ohio State U., Columbus, 1982-87, assoc. prof. 1987—; bd. dirs. MRL, Inc.; active automation research and devel.; cons. to Midwest industry. Adv. to vocat. programs Rehab. div. Ohio Indsl. Commn. Contbr. articles to profl. jours. Recipient Harrison Faculty award Ohio State U. Mem. Inst. Indsl. Engrs. (award Youngstown chpt. 1970), Alpha Pi Mu, Phi Kappa Phi. Home: 7548 Sagewood Ct Worthington OH 43085 Office: 1971 Neil Ave Columbus OH 43210

MAUPIN, STEPHANIE ZELLER, French teacher; b. St. Louis, Apr. 16, 1946; d. Robert H. and Pernelle (Santhuff) Zeller; 1 child, Britt. BEd., U. Mo., 1967; MAT in Communication Arts, Webster Coll., St. Louis, 1977, postgrad., 1979-87, St. Louis U., 1986—. Cert. tchr., Mo. Tchr. Mehlville Sch. Dist., St. Louis County, 1967—; tchr. French and English, Oakville High Sch., Mehlville Sch. Dist., 1971-84; adj. faculty Webster Coll., St. Louis, 1980, St. Louis U., 1982—. Dir. in charge exchange program St. Louis-Lyon Sister Cities Corp. NEH Fellow; Rockerfeller Found. Fgn. Language Tchrs. fellow, 1987. Mem. MLA, Nat. Council Thcrs. of English, Arts and Edn. Council, African Lit. Assn., The French Soc., Am. Assn. Tchrs. French (dir.), African Studies Assn. NEA, Assn. Supervision and Curriculum Devel., Internat. Edn. Consortium, African Studies Assn., Fgn. Language Assn. Mo. ,Webster Coll. Alumni Assn., Phi Sigma Iota. P-resentor: Mo. state Dept. Edn. Fgn. Lang. Assn. Conf., African Lit. Assn. Conf. Home: 5608 Duchesne Parque Dr Saint Louis MO 63128 Office: 5557 Milburn Rd Saint Louis MO 63129

MAURER, DAVID JOSEPH, history educator; b. Canton, Ohio, June 9, 1935; s. Harry Joseph and Elizabeth Rose (Fehn) M.; m. Ellen Joyce Swan, June 15, 1957; children: Elizabeth, William. BA, Beloit Coll., 1957; MA, Ohio State U., 1958, PhD, 1962. Prof. history Eastern Ill. U., Charleston, 1962—; vis. prof. Ohio State U., Columbus, 1971. Author: U.S. Politics and Elections, 1978; (with others) Essays in Illinois History, 1968, The Emerging University, 1974, The New Deal: State and Local, 1975. Mem. Am. Assn. for State and Local History (resident scholar 1985), Ill. State Hist. Soc. (pres. 1980-81). Episcopalian. Club: Charleston Country. Office: Eastern Ill U Dept History Charleston IL 61920

MAURER, DONALD DELBERT, medical device manufacturer; b. Lead, S.D., July 17, 1937. AAS, Milw. Sch. Engring., 1960; BS in Elec. Engring., S.D. State U., 1965; MS in Biomed. Engring., Iowa State U., 1971. With Univac Co., 1960-62; prodn. design engr. Control Data, Inc., Mpls., 1965-66; cons. engr., mgr. spl. external pacing project Medtronic, Inc., Mpls., 1966-71, research engr., 1971-74, dir. neurol. research and engring., 1974-77, co-founder neurol. rehab. div., 1974-77; research asst. Iowa State U., 1969-71; founding dir. rehab. engring. program Courage Ctr., Golden Valley, Minn., 1977-79; chmn. EMPI, Inc., Mpls., 1977-79, pres., chief exec. officer, 1979—. Contbr. articles to profl. jours. and chpts. to books; patentee in field. Mem. Health Industry Mfrs. Orgn., Am. Assn. Med. Instrumentation, IEEE, Internat. Assn. Study Pain, Am. Congress Rehab. Medicine, Neuroelectric Soc., Am. Mgmt. Assn., Am. Acad. Sci., Electrostatic Soc. Am., Eta Kappa Nu. Home: 2020 Shaw St Anoka MN 55303 Office: 1275 Grey Fox Rd Saint Paul MN 55112

MAURO, GEORGE THEODORE, corporate executive; b. N.Y.C., Mar. 7, 1938; s. Peter Terzo and Bella (Cohn) M.; m. Mary Ann Stoehr, Feb. 15, 1964; children: Mary Patricia, Christine. BA, U. N.H., 1959; MBA, U. Pa., 1972. Sr. cons. Booz, Allen & Hamilton, Inc., Phila., 1972-75, v.p., 1975-77; dir. Asset Value Analysis, U.S. Ry. Assn., Washington, 1977-79; sr. assoc. Temple Barker & Sloane, Inc., Lexington, Mass., 1979-83; dir. transp. FMC Corp., Chgo., 1984-85, dir. logistics, 1985—. Served with USAF, 1960-70. Decorated Meritorious Service medal Dept. Def., Air Force Commendation medal. Mem. Transp. Research Forum, Council Logistics Mgmt., Nat. Indsl. Transp. League, Nat. Freight Transp. Assn., Assn. for Mfg. Excellence, Beta Gamma Sigma, Tau Kappa Alpha, Psi Chi, Pi Kappa Alpha. Home: 2829 Birchwood Ave Wilmette IL 60091 Office: 200 E Randolph Dr Chicago IL 60601

MAURSTAD, DAVID INGOLF, insurance agency executive; b. North Platte, Nebr., Aug. 25, 1953; s. Ingolf Byron and Marilyn Sophia (Gimble) M.; m. Karen Sue Micek, Sept. 7, 1974; children: Ingolf, Derek, Laura. Assoc. in Fine Arts, Platte Community Coll., Columbus, Nebr., 1973; student, U. Nebr., 1976, 85-87. Asst. golf profl. Country Club of Lincoln (Nebr.), 1973-76; head golf profl. Westward Ho Country Club, Sioux Falls, S.D., 1977; ins. agt. Maurstad/Zimmerman Ins., Beatrice, Nebr., 1978-84; ins. agy. mgr. Maurstad Ins. Services, Inc., Beatrice, 1984—. Pres. Beatrice YMCA, 1982-83, Gage County United Way, Beatrice, 1985; mem. Nebr. Rep. State Cen. Com., Lincoln, 1985—; candidate Nebr. legislature, Lincoln, 1986. Named Outstanding Young Man of Am., Beatrice Jaycees, 1985. Mem. Ind. Ins. Agts. Nebr. (Young Agt. of Yr. 1985), Beatrice C. of C. (bd. dirs. 1985—). Lutheran. Lodges: Rotary, Elks, Eagles. Avocations: golfing, reading, spectator sports. Home: 1604 S 3d St Beatrice NE 68310 Office: 121 N 6th St Beatrice NE 68310

MAURUS, JEFFREY NORDIN, obstetrician, gynecologist; b. Rock Island, Ill., Aug. 26, 1947; s. Robert Leroy and Hellen Martha (Nordin) M.; m. Jo Ellen Swedberg, Aug. 30, 1969; children: Eric, Peter, Annika, Lisabet. BA, Augustana Coll., Rock Island, Ill., 1969; MD, U. Iowa, 1974. Diplomate Am. Bd. Ob-Gyn. Resident in ob-gyn W.Va. U., Morgantown, 1974-78; practice medicine specializing in ob-gyn Moline, Ill., 1978—; cons. gynecologist Augustana Coll., 1978—; cons. obstetrician-gynecologist Bethany Home, Moline, 1978—; med. dir. Family Planning Program Rock Island County Health Dept., 1979—; staff, past chmn. gynecology dept. Luth. Hosp., pres. med. staff, 1985—; courtesy staff Moline Pub. Hosp., Franciscan Hosp., Rock Island, Illini Hosp., Silvis, Ill. Past pres. Rock Island Family YMCA Swim Club; chmn. youth ministry St. John's Luth. Ch., Rock Island, 1985—. Served with USPHS, 1974-76. Fellow Am. Coll. Obstetricians and Gynecologists (chmn. Ill. sect. jr. fellows 1980-81); mem. AMA, Ill. Med. Soc. (com. maternal welfare), Mississippi Valley Soc. Obstetricians and Gynecologists (sec. 1979-85, pres. 1986—), Rock Island County Med. Soc. Club: Rock Island Arsenal Golf. Avocations: physical fitness, canoeing, swimming. Office: Med Arts Assoc Ltd 4600 3d St Moline IL 61265

MAWER, WILLIAM THOMAS, lawyer; b. Toledo, May 11, 1948; s. Clifford M. and Mary E. (Avey) M.; m. Catherine M. Greenler, Aug. 16, 1969; children—Jennifer M., Melinda J., Ryanne E. B.S., U. Toledo, 1970; J.D., Ohio No. U., 1973. Bar: Ohio 1973. Ptnr. FHM&D, L.P.A., Eaton, Ohio, 1973—; instr. Sinclair Coll., Dayton, Ohio, 1975-82; judge pro tem Eaton Municipal Ct., 1975-83. Trustee West Central Ohio council Boy Scouts Am., 1973-78; active Republican Central Com., Eaton, Ohio, 1980-84; pres. Rural Legal Aid Soc., Eaton, 1982-83; active Eaton Bd. Edn., 1984. Recipient Outstanding Jaycees award Eaton Jaycees, 1974; award of Merit, Boy Scouts Am., 1977. Mem. Ohio State Bar Assn. (taxation com.), ABA, Preble County Bar Assn. (pres. 1984-85). Lutheran. Lodges: Masons (chaplain 1974-75), Rotary. Avocations: downhill skiing; woodworking. Home: 1409 East Ave Eaton OH 45320 Office: FHM&D Co 111 S Barron St Eaton OH 45320

MAWICKE, ALBERT THOMAS, business executive; b. Chgo., July 16, 1921; s. Henry J. and Margaret (Mann) M.; student Northwestern U., 1943, U. Chgo., 1956; m. Dorothy Harris, Oct. 16, 1943 (dec. 1975); children—Jeffrey J., Paul D., Ann M. With Pontiac Graphics Corp., Chgo., 1946-50, salesman, 1950-52, sales mgr., 1952-59, sales mgr., v.p., div. mgr., 1959-63; with World Book-Childcraft Internat., 1963-68, regional mgr., 1966-68, asst. sales mgr., 1968-69, sales mgr. zone 5, 1969-70, sales mgr. zone 1, 1970-73, zone 6, 1974-75, br. mgr., 1975-79; v.p. Graphic Mgmt. Services, Elmhurst, Ill., 1979-83; pres. Mawicke & Assocs., Inc., Naperville, Ill., 1984—; faculty Bus. Inst. Coll. of DuPage, Ill.; lectr., cons. Northwestern U., 1950-62, Craftsmen Clubs, various printers, mfrs., art groups. Served from pvt. to capt. AUS, 1942-46; ETO. Decorated Bronze Star. Mem. Phi Kappa Sigma. Home and Office: 526 Grimes Ave Naperville IL 60565

MAWK, JOHN ROBERT, pediatric neurosurgeon, educator; b. San Antonio, Oct. 9, 1950; s. Charles C. and Lillian Katherine (Perry) M.; m. Kathleen Ann Carlson, Sept. 30, 1978; children: John, Jennifer, Kristin, William. BA, St. Mary's U., San Antonio, 1970; MD, U. Tex., 1974. Diplomate Am. Bd. Neurol. Surgeons. Resident in neurosurgery U. Minn., Mpls., 1980, instr. in neurosurgery, 1980-83; asst. prof. neurosurgery and pediatrics U. Ark., Little Rock, 1984-85, U. Nebr., Omaha, 1985—; chief neurosurgery, Ark. Children's Hosp., Little Rock, 1984-85; dir. pediatric neurosurgery service, U. Nebr. Med. Ctr., Omaha, 1985—. Contbr. numerous articles to profl. jours.; author books chpts. Served to lt. comdr. USNR, 1986—. Mem. AMA, Internat. Soc. Pediatric Neurosurgery, Congress Neurol. Surgeons, Am. Assn. Neurol. Surgeos, Nebr. Med. Assn., Assn. Mil. Surgeons of U.S., Alpha Omega Alpha, Lambda Chi Alpha. Republican. Lutheran. Avocations: internat. travel, photography, U.S. naval history. Home: 1429 N 131st Ave Circle Omaha NE 68154-1281 Office: U Nebr Med Ctr Neurosurgery 42d and Dewey Omaha NE 68105-1065

MAXFIELD, KENNETH WAYNE, transportation company executive; b. Leo, Ind., Oct. 26, 1924; m. Jean; 2 children. Student, Loyola U., Chgo., 1946-48; LL.B., De Paul U., 1950. Bar: Ind., Ill. bars 1950. With North Am. Van Lines Inc., 1950—; exec. v.p. corp. world hdqrs. North Am. Van Lines Inc., Fort Wayne, Ind., 1966-77; pres., chief operating officer, chmn. bd. North Am. Van Lines Inc., 1977—. Pres. bd. Jr. Achievement, Ft. Wayne, 1976-77. Served with U.S. Army, 1943-46. Mem. Ft. Wayne C. of C. (pres. 1974). Clubs: Summit (dir.); Rotary (Ft. Wayne). Office: North Am Van Lines Inc 5001 US Hwy 30 W Fort Wayne IN 46801 *

MAXTON, JULIA CURTNER, marketing manager; b. Dayton, Ohio, Feb. 8, 1940; d. Clifford Rome and Hilda Ione (Sloat) C.; m. Timothy C. Pitstick, Nov. 4, 1985; children by previous marriage—Kelly Michele, Elizabeth. B.A., Miami U., Ohio, 1961; postgrad. Sinclair Community Coll., 1980. Lic. real estate sales, Ohio, 1980. Dir. mktg. and leasing Arcade Sq., 1977-80; dir. mktg. and press Bobby Brown Racing, 1982—; dir. mktg., leasing and sales The Tipton Group, Inc., Dayton, 1982-83; account exec. Dennis Dunkelberger Adtv., 1983-84; dist. mktg. mgr. Continental Cablevision, Dayton, 1984—; cons., Halcyon Ltd., Hartford, Conn.; speaker. Bd. dirs. Good Samaritan Hosp. Named Marketeer of Yr., Dayton chpt. Am. Mgmt. Assn., 1980. Mem. Dayton Area C. of C. (adv. bd.), Am. Horse Show Assn., Tri State Horse Assn., Downtown Dayton Assn. Republican. Clubs: Sports Car of Am., Corvette Troy (Dayton). Home: 8080 Condor Ct Dayton OH 45459 Office: 90 Compark Rd Dayton OH 45459

MAXVILL, DAL, professional baseball team executive; b. Granite City, Ill., Feb. 18, 1939; m. Diana Maxvill; children: Kathy, Danny, Jeff, Tim. Profl. baseball player St. Louis Cardinals (Maj. League), 1962-72, Oakland (Calif.) Athletics, 1972, 73, 74, 75, Pitts. Pirates, 1973, 74; mem. coaching staff N.Y. Mets, 1978; coach St. Louis Cardinals, 1979-80, Atlanta Braves, 1982-85; gen. mgr. St. Louis Cardinals, 1985—. Office: St. Louis Cardinals Busch Stadium 250 Stadium Plaza Saint Louis MO 63102 *

MAXWELL, FLORENCE HINSHAW, civic worker; b. Nora, Ind., July 14, 1914; d. Asa Benton and Gertrude (Randall) Hinshaw; B.A. cum laude, Butler U., 1935; m. John Williamson Maxwell, June 5, 1936; children—Marilyn, William Douglas. Coordinator, bd. dirs. Sight Conservation and Aid to Blind, 1962-73, nat. chmn., 1969-73; active various fund drives; chmn. jamboree, hostess coms. North Central High Sch., 1959, 64; Girl Scouts U.S.A., 1937-38, 54-56; mus. chmn. Sr. Girl Scout Regional Council, 1956-57; scorekeeper Little League, 1955-57; bd. dirs. Nora Sch. Parents' Club, 1958-59, Eastwood Jr. High Sch. Triangle Club, 1959-62, Ind. State Symphony Soc. Women's Com., 1965-67, 76-79, Symphoguide chmn., 1976-79; vision screening Indpls. innercity pub. sch. kindergartens, pre-schs., 1962-69, also Headstart, 1967—; asst. Glaucoma screening clinics Gen. Hosp., Glendale Shopping Center, City County Bldg., Am. Legion Nat. Hdqrs., Ind. Health Assn. Conf., 1962-73; chmn. sight conservation and aid to blind Nat. Delta Gamma Found., Indpls., Columbus, Ohio, 1969-73; mem. telethon team Butler U. Fund, 1964; symphoguide hostess Internat. Conf. on Cities, 1971, Nat. League of Cities, 1972; mem. health adv. com. Headstart, 1976—, sec., 1980—, assessment team of compliance steering com., 1978-79, 84, 86, 87, appreciation award, 1983; founder People of Vision Aux., 1981. Recipient Cable award Delta Gamma, 1969, Outstanding Alumna award, 1973, scholarship honoree, 1981; Key to City of Indpls., 1972, those Spl. People award Women in Communication, 1980. Mem. Nat., Ind. (dir. 1962—, exec. com. 1971—, v.p. 1983-86, sec., 1971-83, Ind. del. to nat. 3-yr. program planning conf. 1985, internal analysis task force for services 1987, Sight Saving award 1974, life hon. v.p. 1983—) socs. to prevent blindness, Delta Gamma (chpt. golden anniversary celebration decade and communication chmn. 1975, treas. Alpha Tau house corp. 1975-78, nat. chmn. Parent Club Study Com. 1976-77; Service Recognition award 1977, Shield award

1981, Stellar award 1986). Republican. Address: 1502 E 80th St Indianapolis IN 46240

MAXWELL, GORDON EARL, obstetrician-gynecologist; b. Quinter, Kans., Nov. 30, 1929; s. George Earl and Mary (Hargitt) M.; m. Evelyn Mae Westhoff, May 31, 1952; children: Gregory Earl, Mary Evelyn, Cynthia Elaine, Stephanie Louise. BA, U. Kans., Lawrence, 1952; MD, U. Kans., Kansas City, 1955. Diplomate Am. Bd. Ob-Gyn. Intern Milwaukee County Gen. Hosp., Milw., 1955-56; resident in ob-gyn Confederate Meml. Med. Ctr., Shreveport, La., 1958-61; practice medicine specializing in ob-gyn Salina, Kans., 1961—; mem. staff Asbury-St. John's Hosp., Salina, 1961—; pres. staff Asbury-St. John's Hosp., 1978, Salina Clinic, 1978—; clin. cons. Salina County Health Dept., 1968—; assoc. clin. prof. U. Kans., Wichita, 1980—. Contbg. author: Medical Ethics, 1965. Trustee Kans. Wesleyan U., 1979—; bd. dirs. Land Inst., Salina, 1979. Named Outstanding Researcher of Yr.,Smoky Hill Family Practice Residency, 1981-82. Fellow Am. Coll. Obstetricians-Gynecologists; mem. AMA, Kans. Med. Assn., Salina County Med. Soc. (pres. 1983), Kans. Healing Arts Bd., Marymount Coll. Pres.' Club, N. Park Coll. Pres.' Coll. Democrat. Avocations: triathlon, travel, theology. Home: 414 Wayne Salina KS 67401 Office: The Salina Clinic 135 E Claflin Ave Salina KS 67401

MAXWELL, MARY DELENE BROWNLEE, divorce and custody consultant, marriage counselor; b. Des Moines, Aug. 29, 1910; d. Ralph Clair and Betty (Bixby) Brounlee; m. Raymond Jones Mexwell, Apr. 4, 1933 (dec. Jan. 1983): 1 child, Jo Ann Maxwell Bantin. AB, U. Ill., 1934; M, Acad. Cert. Social Workers, 1951; postgrad., U. Nev., U. Nebr., U. Calif. Counselor St. Louis Children' Ct., 1940-43; child welfare worker Douglas County Welfare, Omaha, 1943-65; dir., cons. Conciliation Ct. Dist. Cts., Omaha, 1965-81; pvt. practice divorce and custody consulting Omaha, 1981—. Bd. dirs. Legal Aid Soc., Omaha, 1966-75; chmn. scholarship com. Omaha Assn. Retarded Children, 1966-77. Mem. Am. Assn. Univ. Women, Nat. Acad. Social Workers, Am. Acad. Cert. Social Workers, Alpha Kappa Delta. Republican. Episcopalian. Avocations: travel photography, drama, music. Home and Office: 5511 Blondo Ave Omaha NE 68104

MAXWELL, PATRICIA JOY, association executive; b. Belle Plaine, Iowa, Feb. 7, 1937; d. Verne Edwin and Julia Inez (Beem) M.; student Pepperdine Coll., 1954-55; B.S., Iowa State Tchrs. Coll., 1958; M.P.A., Roosevelt U., 1982; m. Martin E. Sodetz, Jan. 21, 1984. Dir. resource devel. Boys Clubs Am., 1978-81; exec. dir. Westlake Health Services Found., 1981-84; dir. devel. and alumni affairs U. Ill. Coll. Medicine, 1984—; dir. profl. services Ency. Britannica Ednl. Corp.; cons. Prentice Hall Inc., U.S. State Dept. Mem. Am. Mktg. Assn., Chgo. Area Pub. Affairs Group, City Club of Chgo. Home: 1130 S Michigan Ave Chicago IL 60605

MAXWELL, STEVEN CHARLES, health care executive; b. Sioux City, Iowa, Sept. 23, 1940; s. Lyle Charles and Corinne Zenobia (Knudson) M.; m. Jerrilyn Lee Mammen, Dec. 30, 1961; 1 son, Timothy Allen. B.S., Drake U., Des Moines, 1962, postgrad., 1963-64. C.P.A., Iowa, Minn. Engring. planner Douglas Aircraft Co., 1962-63; staff acct. Hunzelman, Putzier & Co. (C.P.A.s), Storm Lake, Iowa, 1964-67; mem. chancellor's staff U. Ill., Chgo. Circle, 1967-69; bus. mgr. Shive-Hattery & Assos., Cedar Rapids, Iowa, 1969-74; controller Am. Coll. Testing Program, Iowa City, 1974-75; treas. Thompson Industries Ltd., Storm Lake, 1975-77; dir. Thompson Industries Ltd., 1976; treas. Gateway Foods, Mpls., 1977-82; with Tri-State Wholesale Assoc. Grocers, Inc., El Paso, 1982-85; v.p. fin. Mercy Health Ctr., Dubuque, Iowa, 1985—. Mem. Am. Inst. C.P.A.s, Minn. Soc. C.P.A.s, Iowa Soc. C.P.A.s. Presbyterian. Home: 1815 Eden Ln Dubuque IA 52001 Office: Mercy Dr Dubuque IA 52001

MAXWELL, VIRGIL ALLEN, savings and loan executive; b. Yarmouth, Iowa, Aug. 22, 1933; s. Guy Emory and Grace Marie (Keitzer) M.; m. Margaret Ann Wickard, Mar. 9, 1963; children: Pamela Sue, Todd Dwight, Scott Allen. BBA, Drake U., 1955; grad. Ind. U. Grad. Sch. Savs. and Loans, 1966-68; postgrad. U. So. Calif., 1978. Trainee Farmers Casualty Co., Des Moines, 1953-55; with Midland Fin. Savs. & Loan, and predecessor, Des Moines, 1958-76, sr. v.p., until 1976; pres., chief exec. officer Ames Savs. & Loan Assn. (Iowa), 1976—, also bd. dirs.; bd. dirs. Thrift Discount Brokerage, Inc., Pioneer Fed. Savings and Loan, Mason City; corp. sec. Fin. Info. Trust; chmn. Ames Electric Ops. Rev. and Adv. Bd. Mem. fin. com. Story County Rep. Com., 1981-82, dean's adv. council Iowa State U. Coll. Bus.; chmn. bd. trustees Congl. ch. Served with USAF, 1955-58; ret. col. Iowa Air N.G. Named Des Moines Jaycee's Boss of Yr., 1976-77. Mem. Inst. Fin. Edn. (pres. 1978-79), Fin. Info. Trust (formerly Savs. and Loan Computer Trust of Des Moines) (trustee), U.S. League Savs. Insts. (legis. com.), Iowa League Savs. Inst. (chmn.), Alpha Tau Omega. Republican. Clubs: Ames Golf and Country (fin. com.), Embassy. Lodge: Rotary. Home: 1706 Amherst Dr Ames IA 50010 Office: 424 Main St Ames IA 50010

MAY, ALAN ALFRED, lawyer; b. Detroit, Apr. 7, 1942; s. Alfred Albert and Sylvia (Sheer) M.; m. Elizabeth Miller; children—Stacy Ann, Julie Beth. B.A., U. Mich., 1963, J.D., 1966. Bar: Mich. 1967, D.C. 1976; registered nursing home adminstr., Mich. Ptnr. May and May, Detroit, 1967-79, pres. May & May, P.C., 1979—; spl. asst. atty. gen. State of Mich., 1970—; of counsel Charfoos & Christensen P.C. and predecessor firm Charfoos, Christensen & Archer, P.C., Detroit, 1970—; pres., instr. Med-Leg Seminars, Inc., 1978; lectr. Wayne State U., 1974; instr. Oakland U., 1969. Chmn. Rep. 18th Congl. Dist. Com., 1983-87, now chmn. emeritus; chmn. 19th Congl. Dist. Com., 1981-83; mem. Mich. Rep. Com., 1976-84; del. Rep. Nat. Conv., 1984; former chmn. Mich. Civil Rights Commn.; mem. Mich. Civil Service Commn.; trustee NCCJ, Mich. Cancer Found.; mem. Electoral Coll.; bd. dirs. Detroit Round Table, Charfoos Charitable Found., Temple Beth El, Birmingham, Mich. Mem. Detroit Bar Assn., Oakland County Bar Assn. Clubs: Victors, Franklin Hills Country (bd. dirs.), Presidents (trustee). Contbr. article to profl. jours. Home: 4140 Echo Rd Bloomfield Hills MI 48013 Office: May & May PC 3000 Town Ctr Suite 2600 Southfield MI 48075

MAY, ARNOLD LEE, real estate investment executive; b. Aurora, Ill., Aug. 18, 1952; s. Leroy Michael and Virginia Mae (Detilio) M.; m. Deborah Ann George, July 21, 1979; children: Erin, Michael. BA in Acctg. and Bus. Econs., Ill. Benedictine Coll., 1978; cer. CPA, Ill. Acct. Nickels Beilman Kasper and Co., Aurora, Ill., 1978-80; v.p., controller Exec. Affiliates, Big Rock, Ill., 1980-86, Aviation Systems Internat., Big Rock, 1980-86; dir. ops. Exec. Hotel Mgmt., Big Rock, 1984-86; corp. sec. Chest Mortgage Corp., Big Rock, 1984-86; pres. Clipper Mgmt. Inc., Aurora, 1986—. Fund raiser Mercy Ctr. Hosp., Aurora, 1983, 84, 85, 86. Served as sgt. U.S. Army, 1972-78. Mem. Am. Inst. CPA's, Ill. Soc. CPA's., Nat. Rifle Assn. Republican. Methodist. Lodge: Moose. Avocations: boating, trapshooting. Office: Clipper Mgmt Inc 272 Carriage Hill Dr Aurora IL 60506

MAY, AVIVA RABINOWITZ, educator, linguist, musician; b. Tel Aviv; naturalized, 1958; d. Samuel and Paula (Gordon) Rabinowitz; B.A., in Piano Pedgogy, Northeastern Ill. U., 1979; m. Stanley Lee May, children—Rochelle, Alan, Risa, Ellanna. Tchr., pianist, 1948—; tchr. adult B'nai Mitzva, 1973; tchr., music, dir. McCormick Health Ctrs., Chgo., 1978-79, Cove Sch. Perceptually Handicapped Children, Chgo., 1978-79; prof. Hebrew and Yiddish, Spertus Coll. Judaica, Chgo., 1980—; tchr. continuing edn. Northeastern Ill. U., 1978-80, also Jewish Community Ctrs.; with Office Spl. Investigations, Dept. Justice, Washington; folksinger, guitarist, 1962—; composer classical music for piano, choral work, folk songs. Recipient Magen David Adom Pub. Service award, 1973; awards from women's programs Oakton Community Coll., 1976, 78; Adults Returning to Sch. award Northeastern Ill. U.-Chgo. Ill. State grantee, 1975-79; Ill. Congressman Woody Bowman grantee, 1978-79. Mem. Music Tchrs. Nat. Assn., North Shore Music Tchrs. Assn. (a founder, charter mem., sec.), Ill. Music Tchrs. Assn., Organ and Piano Tchrs. Assn., Am. Coll. Musicians, Ill. Assn. Learning Disabilities, Sherwood Sch. Music, Friends of Holocaust Survivers, Nat. Yiddish Book Exchange, Nat. Ctr. for Jewish Films, Chgo. Jewish Hist. Soc., Oakton Community Coll. Alumni Assn., Northeastern Ill. U. Alumni Assn. Democrat. Contbr. articles to profl. jours. Address: 3600 N Lake Shore Dr Chicago IL 60613 Studio: Fine Arts Bldg 410 S Michigan Ave Chicago IL

MAY, BRADFORD LOUIS, insurance executive; b. Chgo., Jan. 23, 1952; s. Gordon S. and Beverly (Rosin) M.; m. Andrea Helene Hymen, Oct. 19, 1974; children: Aaron Geoffrey, Corri Lyn. Salesman May Wood Industries, Chgo., 1972-78; prin. Bradford L. May Assocs., Glenview, Ill., 1978—. Treas. Chgo. Club of Physically Handicapped, 1982-85; v.p. Temple Beth-El, Chgo., 1985-86. Mem. Profl. Ins. Agts. Am., Ind. Ins. Agts. Am. Republican. Jewish. Club: Highland Park (Ill.) Country (bd. dirs. 1985-87). Office: 1247 Waukegan Glenview IL 60025

MAY, C. BRANDT, railroad executive; b. Shawnee, Okla., Mar. 12, 1937; s. Barton and Celma Elois (Bowen) M.; m. Juanita Moore, Apr. 14, 1961; children: Pamela, Gregory. BSCE, Okla. State U., 1959; diploma in bus. mgmt., Columbia U., 1977. Registered profl. engr., Okla. Supt. St. Louis San Francisco Ry. Co., Tulsa, 1977-79, Amory, Miss., 1979-81; div. supt. Burlington Northern R.R. Co., Memphis, 1981; asst. gen. mgr. Burlington No. R.R. Co., Seattle, 1982-84; dir. maintenance planning Burlington No. R.R. Co., Overland Park, Kans., 1984—. Mem. devel. found. Okla. State U., Stillwater. Served with U.S. Army, 1960. Mem. ASCE, Am. Ry. Engring. Assn., Okla. State U. Alumni Assn., Chi Epsilon. Republican. Methodist. Lodge: Masons. Avocations: fishing, swimming, football. Home: 10303 Monrovia Overland Park KS 66215 Office: Burlington Northern RR Co PO Box 29136 Overland Park KS 66201-9136

MAY, DANIEL FRANCIS, airline executive; b. Rainier, Oreg., Feb. 8, 1930; s. Alfred and Frances L. (Kelly) M.; m. Radona Ashman, 1969; children: Gary, Steven, Kathleen May Rudkin. Grad., Multnomah Coll., 1951; postgrad., U. Minn., 1956-58; LLB, LaSalle Extension U., 1971. Acct. May Agy., Rainier, 1947-51, Webster Lumber Co., Mpls., 1954-56; acct. North Cen. Airlines, Inc., Mpls., 1956-62, asst. treas., 1962-63, treas., 1963-67, v.p., treas., 1967-71, v.p. fin., 1971-79; sr. v.p. fin. Republic Airlines, Inc. (formerly North Cen. Airlines, Inc.), 1979-80, exec. v.p., 1980, pres., 1980—, chief exec. officer, 1982—, chmn. bd. dirs., 1984—, pres., chief exec. officer, 1986—; bd. dirs. Republic Energy Inc., Twin City Fed. Savs. and Loan Assn., Cherne Industries, Inc., Rexnord Inc. Nat. bd. dirs. Young Life; bd. dirs. Minn. Pub. Radio; elder Presbyn. ch. Mem. Minn. Assn. Commerce and Industry (bd. dirs.). Lodge: Rotary. Office: Bd Dirs Northwest Airlines Mpls-St. Paul Internat Airport Minneapolis MN 55111 *

MAY, DAVID L., chamber of commerce executive. Pres. Independence (Mo.) C. of C. Office: Independence C of C 213 S Main PO Box 147 Independence MO 64051 *

MAY, ELIZABETH ANN, savings and loan association executive; b. Findlay, Ohio, Aug. 7, 1958; d. James DeWayne Siferd and Ruth Anne (Buchanan) Stiffler; m. Mark Matthew May, Apr. 11, 1975; children: M. Andrew, Katelyn Ann. Student, Owens Tech. Coll., Toledo, 1978-79, Inst. Fin. Edn., Chgo., 1978-86. Br. supr. Diamond Savs. and Loan Assn., Findlay, 1978-80, closing coordinator, 1981-84, mortgage underwriter, 1984-85, mortgage analyst, 1985, mortgage supr., 1985—. Choreographer and asst. dir. Belivers Music Group, Findlay, 1981-84. Democrat. Methodist. Home: 2807 N Main Findlay OH 45840 Office: Diamond Savs and Loan Assn 500 S Main Findlay OH 45840

MAY, JOHN LAWRENCE, archbishop; b. Evanston, Ill., Mar. 31, 1922; s. Peter Michael and Catherine (Allare) M. M.A., St. Mary of Lake Sem., Mundelein, Ill., 1945, S.T.L., 1947. Ordained priest Roman Catholic Ch., 1947; asst. pastor St. Gregory Ch., Chgo., 1947-56; chaplain Mercy Hosp., Chgo., 1956-59; v.p., gen. sec. Cath. Ch. Extension Soc. U.S., 1959-67, pres., from 1967; ord. titular bishop of Tagarbala and aux. bishop, Chgo., 1967-69; pastor Christ The King Parish, Chgo., 1968-69; bishop of Mobile, Ala., 1969-80, archbishop of St. Louis, 1980—. Mem. Nat. Conf. Cath. Bishops (pres. 1986—, past v.p.). Office: care Chancery Office 4445 Lindell Blvd Saint Louis MO 63108 *

MAY, MICHAEL DORAN, industrial relations specialist, consultant; b. Bloomington, Ind., Aug. 27, 1949; s. Doran William and Maryellen (Green) M.; m. Jody Scott, July 10, 1973; children: Charles Samson, Marellen Ruth, Zachary Paul. BA in Social Sci., Ind. U., 1971. Tbg. cons. Ecumenical Inst., Chgo., 1971-73; dir. internat. student programs Inst. Cultural Affairs, Chgo., 1973-79; div. mgr. Kendall & Davis Co., St. Louis, 1979—. Mem. Nat. Assn. Personnel Cons. (cert.). Republican. Roman Catholic. Avocation: bicycling. Home: 2525 Round Hill Ct Bloomington IN 47401 Office: One City Cen Suite 110 Bloomington IN 47401

MAY, PHILLIP THEODORE, JR., accounting educator; b. Milw., Mar. 2, 1935; s. Phillip Theodore and Betty Alice (Hanson) M.; m. Mary Etta Myers, June 4, 1983; children: Gardner Phillip, Douglas Phillip. BA, Lawrence U., 1957; MBA, Ind. U., 1959; PhD, U. Wis., 1967. CPA, Wis., Kans. Contract auditor Dept. Def., Washington, 1959-62; asst. prof. acctg. Washington U., St. Louis, 1966-73; assoc. prof. U. Ill., Urbana, 1973-74; prof. Wichita (Kans.) State U., 1974—. Author: Programming - Fortran IV, 1973. Pres. police/fire retirement system, Wichita, 1980-82. Served to capt. USAF, 1959-62. Recipient Regents Outstanding Prof. award Kans. Bd. Regents, 1979. Mem. Am. Inst. CPA's, Am. Acctg. Assn., Inst. Internal Auditors, Kans. Soc. CPA's (pres. 1986—). Republican. Methodist. Home: 552 N Roosevelt Wichita KS 67208 Office: Wichita State U Coll Bus Adminstrn Wichita KS 67208

MAY, PHYLLIS JEAN, businesswoman; b. Flint, Mich., May 31, 1932; d. Bert A. and Alice C. (Rushton) Irvine; grad. Dorsey Sch. Bus., 1957; cert. Internat. Corr. Schs., 1959, Nat. Tax Inst., 1978; M.B.A., Mich. U., 1970; m. John May, Apr. 24, 1971; children—Phillip, Perry, Paul. Office mgr. Comml. Constrn. Co., Flint, 1962-68; bus. mgr. new and used car dealership, Flint, 1968-70; controller 6 corps., Flint, 1970-75; fiscal dir. Rubicon Odyssey Inc., Detroit, 1976—; acad. cons. acctg. Detroit Inst. Commerce, 1980-81; pres. small bus. specializing in adminstrv. cons. and acctg., 1982—; supr. mobile service sta., upholstery and home improvement businesses; owner retail bus. Pieces and Things; notary public, 1968—; also real estate broker. Pres. PTA Westwood Heights Schs., 1972; vol. Fedn. of Blind, 1974-76, Probate Ct., 1974-76. Recipient Meritorious Service award Genesee County for Youth, 1976, Excellent Performance and High Achievement award Odyssey Inc., 1981. Mem. Am. Bus. Women's Assn. (treas. 1981, rec. sec. 1982, v.p. 1982-83, Woman of Yr. 1982), Nat. Assn. Profl. Female Execs. (bd. dirs.), Internat. Platform Assn., Pi Omicron (officer 1984-85). Baptist. Home: 12050 Barlow St Detroit MI 48205 Office: Rubicon Odyssey Inc 7441 Brush St Detroit MI 48202

MAY, R. DALE, savings and loan executive; b. Warren, Ohio, May 21, 1940; s. Ray M. and Helen (Jones) M.; m. Jean Martin, Feb. 24, 1961 (div. Sept. 1980); children: Robin R. May McNees, Linda J., Debra A.; m. Marilyn Grace DeMichael, May 2, 1981; stepchildren: Jack D. Duer, Denise M. Duer. BSBA, Youngstown (Ohio) State U., 1966. CPA, Ohio. Sr. acct. Packer, Thomas & Co., CPA's, Youngstown, 1969-72; controller Met. Savs. Bank, Youngstown, 1972-82, v.p., 1982-85, sr. v.p., 1985—. Treas. Send-A-Kid-To-Camp, Inc., Youngstown, 1976, 77, Kidney Found. of Mahoning, Trumbull, and Columbiana Countries, Youngstown, 1978, 79; advisor Jr. Achievement, Youngstown, 1978. Recipient Outstanding Chmn. award Youngstown Area Jaycees, 1973-74. Mem. Am. Inst. CPA's, Ohio Soc. CPA's, Fin. Mgrs. Soc. for Savings Insts. (pres. local chpt. 1976-77). Republican. Club: Youngstown. Avocation: fishing. Home: 1895 Lucretia Dr Girard OH 44420

MAY, RUPERT HANS, psychiatrist; b. Darmstadt, Fed. Republic Germany, Apr. 30, 1923; came to U.S., 1953; s. Johannes and Johanna (Mueller) M.; m. Evelyn Williamson, 1986; ; children from previous marriage: Jeannette, Christine, Ralph, Rupert Jr., Manfred. MD, U. Tuebingen, Fed. Rep. Germany, 1951, U. Heidelberg, Fed. Rep. Germany, 1951; MS, Ohio State U., 1955-57. Diplomate Am. Bd. Psychiatry and Neurology. Staff psychiatrist Cleve. Psychiat. Inst., 1957-62; practice psychiat. medicine Parma, Ohio, 1958—. Mem. Am. Acad. Neurology, Am. Psychiat. Assn. Home: 4597 East Sprague Rd Independence OH 44131 Office: 5500 Ridge Rd Parma OH 44129

MAYBERG, DONALD MACMILLAN, psychiatric consultant; b. Mpls., Oct. 31, 1924; s. Marc Norm and Grace Margaret (Challman) M.; m. Betty Lou Davis, Oct., 1971; children: Stephen, Susan, Marc, Nancy, Barbara. BA, U. Minn., 1948, MD, 1952. Diplomate Am. Bd. Psychiatry and Neurology. Intern Madigan Army Hosp., Tacoma, Wash., 1952-53; resident in psychiatry U. Minn., 1954-57, clin. prof. psychiatry, 1978—; dir. psychiat. edn. and tng. Abbott-Northwestern Hosp.; cons. dept. defense; FAA; bd. dir. Mpls. Psychiat. Inst. Advisor Govs. Mental Health Adv. Council Minn., 1971, 77. Served to capt. USAF, 1942-46, with M.C. 1952-54. Fellow Am. Psychiat. Assn.; mem. AMA, Minn. Psychiat. Soc. (pres. 1977-81), Assn. Academic Psychiatry, Am. Soc. Adolescent Psychiatry, Alpha Delta Phi, Nu Sigma Nu. Presbyterian. Home: 1235 Yale Place #209 Minneapolis MN 55403 Office: Mpls Psychiat Inst 2545 Chicago Ave Minneapolis MN 55404

MAYBERRY, LINDA, personnel director; b. Parma, Mo., Sept. 4, 1946; d. Orval J. and Mabel F. Hudgens; m. Leonard W. Mayberry, Oct. 7, 1967; 1 child, David Garet. Student, Ea. Cen. Coll., Union, Mo., 1972-74, S.E. Mo. State U., 1974-75, Meramec Community Coll., 1976-78 part-time, U. Mo., St. Louis, 1976-78 part-time. Personnel dir. Hoffmann Partnership, Inc., St. Louis, 1975—. Co. chmn. United Way, St. Louis, 1980—. Mem. Am. Mgmt. Assn., Human Resources Mgmt. Assn. Avocations: reading, travel. Office: The Hoffmann Partnership Inc 710 N 2d St Suite 500 S Saint Louis MO 63102

MAYER, BEATRICE CUMMINGS, civic worker; b. Montreal, P.Q., Can., Aug. 15, 1921; came to U.S., 1939, naturalized, 1944; d. Nathan and Ruth (Kellert) Cummings; B.A. in Chemistry, U. N.C., 1943; postgrad. U. Chgo., 1946; L.H.D. (hon.), Spertus Coll. Judaica, 1983, Kenyon Coll., 1987; m. Robert Bloom Mayer, Dec. 11, 1947 (dec.); children—Robert N., Mrs. Stephen P. Durchslag. Mem. vis. com. Sch. Social Service Adminstrn. U. Chgo., 1964—, dept. art, 1972; dir. women's bd., 1973—; life trustee of governing life mems. Art Inst. Chgo., 1984—; bd. dirs. Michael Reese Hosp. Corp., Chgo., 1982—, also former trustee; bd. dirs. Spole to Festival, 1980; trustee Kenyon Coll., Gambier, Ohio, 1976—, mem. adv. com. to bd. trustees, 1987—; bd. fellows Brandeis U., Waltham, Mass., 1977—; mem. womens bd. Northwestern U., 1978—; trustee Anshe Emet Synagogue, Chgo., 1974—; trustee Mus. Contemporary Art, Chgo., 1974—; mem. adv. com. N.C. Sch. of Arts U. NC., 1983—. Recipient Brandeis U. Disting. Community Service award, 1972, medallion Am. Jewish Com. Human Rights, 1976, Outstanding Achievement award in the Arts, YWCA Met. Chgo., 1979, Centennial Gold Medal for Disting. Community Service Jewish Theol. Sem., 1986, Alumni Laureate award Loyola Coll. Balt., 1984; named to Hall of Fame, Jewish Community Ctrs. Adult Services, 1987. Clubs: Tavern, Standard (Chgo.); Lake Shore Country (Glencoe, Ill.). Home: Hancock Apts 175 E Delaware Pl Apt 7403 Chicago IL 60611

MAYER, CATHERINE ANNE, psychiatrist; b. Evanston, Ill., Oct. 10, 1945; d. George Andrew and Lorna (Lindsay) M.; B.A. cum laude, Stanford U., 1967; M.D., U. Wis., 1978. Diplomate Am. Bd. Psychiatry and Neurology. Intern, C. F. Menninger Meml. Hosp., Topeka, 1978-79, resident in psychiatry, 1979-82, staff psychiatrist, 1982—. Mem. AAAS, Am. Psychiat. Assn., Alpha Omega Alpha. Office: The Menninger Found 5800 SW 6th St Topeka KS 66601

MAYER, ENDRE A., physicist, engineer; b. Ercsi, Fejer, Hungary, Feb. 17, 1929; came to U.S., 1949; s. Otto and Iren (Nilgesz) M.; m. Jean Yost; children: Susan J., Sandra J., Warren E. Student, U. Innsbruck; BS in Physics, Denison U. Registered profl. engr., Mich. Test engr. Consumers Res., Washington, N.J., 1951-54; devel. engr. Swartwout Co., Cleve., 1956-59; research physicist Bell Aerospace, Cleve., 1959; sr. devel. engr. TRW, Cleve., 1959-62; engring. mgr. Bendix Corp., Southfield, Mich., 1962-81, Schenck Pegasus Corp., Troy, Mich., 1981—. Tech. editor Fluidics Quarterly jour., 1968—; contbr. numerous articles to profl. jours.; patentee in field. Vice chair Bd. Zoning Appeals, Birmingham, Mich., 1978—. Served with U.S. Army, 1954-56. Recipient Westinghouse Corp. medallion, 1958. Mem. ASME, SAE, NSPE, AIAA, ARS. Baptist. Avocations: photography, woodworking. Home: 945 Poppleton Birmingham MI 48008 Office: Schenck Pegasus Corp 2890 John R Rd Troy MI 48099

MAYER, JAMES LAMOINE, administrative consultant, evangelist, bible educator; b. Eau Claire, Wis., Oct. 7, 1951; s. Harold L. and Eleanor C. (Williams) M. B.A., U. Wis.-Eau Claire, 1973; M.Div., Bethel Theol. Sem., 1976. Dir. communications media Bethel Theol. Sem., St. Paul, 1976-78; night chaplain coordinator Sacred Heart Hosp., Eau Claire, 1979-80, coordinator pastoral care TV ministries Sacred Heart Hosp., 1978-82; Christian edn. and liturgical cons. Shepherd of Love, Eau Claire, Wis., 1983-85; sr. pastor, rector Pilgrim Congl. Parish, Durand, Wis., 1985; adminstrnl. cons. 1986—; coordinator communications Lake St. United Meth. Ch., Eau Claire. Chmn. bd. Am. Heart Assn., 1984-86 ; pres. Eau Claire Clergy Assn., 1982; bd. dirs. Am. Cancer Soc., 1982-83. Recipient Excellence in Christian Edn. award Baptist Gen. Conf., 1976; Awana Leadership award First Baptist Ch. Awana, 1980, vol. of yr. award Am. Heart Assn., Eau Claire. Mem. Eau Claire Clergy Assn., Upper Midwest Area Gifted Assn., Christian Booksellers Assn. Democrat. Club: Triniteam. Avocations: cross country skiing; bowling; golf; photography. Office: 620 Maple St Eau Claire WI 54703

MAYER, JEROME MILTON, dentist; b. St. Louis, Aug. 29, 1947; s. Rene C. and Charlotte (Herrmann) M.; m. Pamela Eden Sheldon, Aug. 8, 1971; children: Jennifer B., Emily A. BA in English, St. Louis U., 1969; DDS, Creighton U., 1973. Dentist St. Louis, 1973—. Mem. ADA, Mo. Dental Assn., Greater St. Louis Dental Soc., Coalition for Pub. Awareness, Alpha Omega. Lodge: Elks. Office: 150 N Meramec Suite 307 Clayton MO 63105

MAYER, MICHAEL JOHN, psychologist; b. Columbia, Mo., July 7, 1941; s. Dennis Thomas and Virginia Louise (Miller) M.; m. Barbara Jo Halle, June 12, 1971. BA, Cardinal Glennon Coll., 1963; MEd, U. Mo., 1966; EdD, U. No. Colo., 1973. Licensed psychologist Ill, Mo. Counselor Quincy (Ill.) Pub. Schs., 1966-69, dir. guidance, 1970-78; psychologist Mark Twain Mental Health Ctr., Hannibal, Mo., 1978-85, Coping Resources, Inc., Columbia, 1985—; dir. psychol. services Charter Hillside Hosp., Columbia, 1985—; cons. Head Start, N.E. Mo., 1980, Still Hosp., Jefferson City, Mo., 1985, Whispering Oaks Hosp., 1985, Laughlin Pavillion, Kirksville, Mo., 1985-86. Author: How to Love, Understand, Cope with Teenagers, 1978, If Only I Had Married Myself, 1983. V.p. bd. dirs. Quincy Soc. Fine Arts, 1975; pres. bd. dirs. Family Service Assn. 1977; dir. mayor's adv. commission, Quincy, 1978. Mem. Am. Psychol. Assn., Am. Assn. Counseling and Devel., Ill. PTA (life), Phi Delta Kappa. Democrat. Roman Catholic. Home: 3812 Cedar Ln Columbia MO 65201 Office: Coping Resources PO Box 1734 Columbia MO 65205

MAYER, MICHAEL PETER, dentist; b. Cleve., Oct. 24, 1954; s. Peter and Elisabeth (Mits) M.; m. Ilse Linda Gottschick, May 23, 1981; 1 child, Michael Peter II. BS, John Carroll U., 1975; DDS, Case Western Res. U., 1979. Pvt. practice Rocky River, Ohio, 1979—; clin. instr. Case Western Res. U., 1981—. Mem. men's choir, sec. Alliance of Transylvanian Saxons, 1980-85. Recipient Disting. Service Teaching award Case Western Res. U., 1985. Mem. ADA, Ohio Dental Assn., Cleve. Dental Soc., Fedn. German-Am. Socs. (sec. 1982—, mem. exec. com. of polit. action com. 1983—), Soc. Danube Swabians. Roman Catholic. Club: Westhore Study. Avocations: choral singing, golf, bowling, folk dancing. Home: 4472 West 215 Fairview Park OH 44126 Office: 21851 Center Ridge #510 Rocky River OH 44116

MAYER, PAUL JOSEPH, microbiological company executive; b. Milw., Aug. 11, 1932; s. Arthur Anthony and Genevieve Marie (Fessler) M.; m. Patricia Lee Simpson, Feb. 16, 1952; children: Paul Jr., Theodore, Anne, Terrence, Stephen, Brian, Mary, John, William. AA, Marquette U., 1954, cert. computer sci., 1971; B in Acctg., U. Wis., 1968. Mgr. product control Louis Allis Co., Milw., 1953-60; asst. controller E. F. Schmidt Co., Milw., 1960-66; controller, sec. Milw. Faucets Inc., Wauwatosa, Wis., 1966-68; controller Charter Wire Co., Milw., 1968-69; v.p. fin. and adminstrn., sec. and treas. Chr. Hansen's Lab. Inc., Milw., 1969—; also bd. dirs. Chr. Hansen's Lab. Inc.; bd. dirs. Horan-Lally Co., Toronto, Can., Alk Am., West Hven, Conn. Chmn. Brookfield Civic Assn., 1974. Mem. Fin. Execs. Inst., Nat. Assn. Accts. (bd. dirs. 1975-76), Soc. Advancement Mgmt. (bd. dirs. 1978), Am. Acctg. Assn. Lutheran. Club: Wauwatosa YMCA. Avocations: music, reading, swimming, hiking, sailing. Home: 19555 W Gebhardt Rd

Brookfield WI 53005 Office: Chr Hansens Lab Inc 9015 W Maple St Milwaukee WI 53214

MAYER, ROBERT JAMES, financial executive; b. Cleve., Feb. 23, 1938; s. Adolph William and Charolette Mayer; m. Barbara Mae Vohnout; children: Michelle, Robert, Robyn. BS, Case Western Res. U., 1976; MBA, Cleve. State U., 1981. Controller Bartlett Snow, Cleve., 1960-72; controller Oerlikon Motch Corp., Euclid, Ohio, 1973-82, v.p., controller, 1983-84; v.p. fin., chief fin. officer Oerlikon Motch Corp., Euclid, 1985—; bd. dirs. ATI, Cleve., Upton Bradeen & James, Inc., Toronto, Can., Cone-Blanchard Machine Co., Windsor, Vt., Motch and Marryweather Machinery Co.,Cleve. Trustee Oerlikon Motch Corp. Found., Cone Automatic Found. Republican. Roman Catholic. Home: 6570 Queensway Brecksville OH 44141 Office: Oerlikon Motch Corp 1250 E 222d Euclid OH 44117

MAYER, STEPHEN EDWARD, respiratory therapist; b. St. Louis, Aug. 5, 1954; s. Marvin Edward and Viola Geraldine (Jack) M.; m. Susan Helen De Neui, Aug. 26, 1978; children—Holly, Bethany, Valerie. B.S., Iowa State U., 1977. Respiratory therapist Iowa Methodist Med. Ctr., Des Moines, 1978-80, supr. pediatric respiratory care, 1980-82, dir. respiratory care, 1982—; chmn. blood donor drive, 1984-85. Mem. adv. com. Des Moines Area Community Coll., 1982—, chmn., 1986. Mem. Iowa Soc. Respiratory Therapy (bd. dirs. 1984-85, pres.-elect, 1987). Republican. Mem. Assembly of God. Avocations: golf; hunting; fishing; outdoors; hockey. Office: Iowa Meth Med Center 1200 Pleasant St Des Moines IA 50309

MAYFIELD, LAFAYETTE (LARRY) HENRY, III, life insurance executive; b. Jackson, Mich., Dec. 28, 1944; s. L.H. and Gladys G. (Manney) M.; m. Lezlie L. Chesbrough, Aug. 15, 1967; children: Joshua, Amanda, Christian. BA, DePauw U., 1967; postgrad. in edn., Wittenberg U., 1967-68; MA in Edn., U. Guam, 1971; postgrad., Miami U., Oxford, Ohio, 1975-76. Cert. CLU. Tchr., dept. head Guam Territorial Schs., Guam Island, 1968-71; supr. secondary English Mt. Healthy Schs., Cin., 1971-77; tchr. Finneytown Pub. Schs., Cin., 1977-80; communications specialist Union Cen. Life Ins., Cin., 1980-83, asst. dir. agy. devel., 1983-86, mgr. fin. services mktg., 1986—; bd. dirs. Quijote Properties, Cin. Entertainment and travel columnist Pro-Am Golf mag., 1979-80; cons. editor Longmon Pub., Chgo., 1986. Basketball coach Gamble-Nippert YMCA, Cin., 1984-86; bd. dirs. Westwood Meth. Ch., Cin., 1976-78, 82-83. Mem. Am. Soc. Chartered Fin. Cons., Am. Soc. CLU, Chi Omicron Gamma, Tusitala Lit. Honorary. Republican. Lodge: Masons. Avocations: golf, running. Home: 3054 Feltz Ave Cincinnati OH 45211 Office: Loey and Assocs 1200 Cypress St Cincinnati OH 45206

MAYHAN, THOMAS MICHAEL, electrical engineer; b. Omaha, Dec. 25, 1958; s. Paul Matthew and Elizabeth (Ann) M. BS in Electric Engring., U. Neb., 1981. Registered profl. engr., Neb. Sr. engr. Omaha Pub. Power Dist., 1981—. Mem. IEEE. Republican. Roman Catholic. Clubs: Omaha Sports, LaSalle. Avocations: accordionist, softball, golf, volleyball, music. Home: 4702 Grover St Omaha NE 68106 Office: Omaha Pub Power Dist 4302 Leavenworth St Omaha NE 68105

MAYHUE, W. PAUL, social worker; b. Kiesar, Ark., Apr. 27, 1947; s. Frank and Pearl (McElwee) M.; m. Danneé Sue Wilson, Dec. 14, 1985; children: Darnell S. Anderson, W. Paul II. AA, Grand Rapids Jr. Coll., 1973; BA in Psychology, Grand Valley State Coll., 1976. Cert. social worker, Mich. Group worker Kent County Juvenile Ct., Grand Rapids, Mich., 1971-77; registered rep. Inventors Diversified Services, Grand Rapids, 1977-79; case worker South Kent Mental Health Clinic, Grand Rapids, 1979—; cons. Kent County Black Caucus, Grand Rapids, 1983. Active Dunham St. Block Club; del. Dem. Conv., 1980, 84, Nat. Rainbow Coalition; polit. dir. ACORN, Grand Rapids, 1981; co-chmn. Grand Rapids Voter Coalition, 1984; pres. Coalition Dems., 1985; founder Com. for Rep. Govt., Grand Rapids, 1986; Dem. nominee for State Rep. 93d dist. Mich. Recipient Carnation Community Service award , 1980. Mem. Urban League, Grand Rapids Urban League, Am. Legion. Baptist. Lodge: Elks (trustee Grand Rapids 1986—). Avocation: community organizing, politics. Office: Transitions 215 Sheldon St SE Grand Rapids MI 49503

MAYNARD, JOHN RALPH, lawyer; b. Seattle, Mar. 5, 1942; s. John R. and Frances Jane (Mitchell) Maynard Kendryk; m. Mary Ann Mascagno, May 1, 1945; children: Bryce James, Pamela Ann. BA, U. Wash., 1964; JD, Calif. Western U., San Diego, 1972; LLM, Harvard U., 1973. Bar: Calif. 1972, Wis. 1973. Assoc. firm Whyte & Hirschboeck, Milw., 1973-78, firm Minahan & Peterson, Milw., 1979—. Bd. dirs. Am. Heart Assn. of Wis., Milw., 1979-82. Served to lt. USN, 1964-69. Mem. ABA. Republican. Clubs: University (Milw.); Harvard (Wis.). Home: 6110 N Bay Ridge Ave Milwaukee WI 53217 Office: Minahan & Peterson SC 411 E Wisconsin Ave Milwaukee WI 53202

MAYNE, JACK EVERETT, food products executive; b. Petersborough, Ont., Can., Aug. 10, 1924; m. Verlin Brunner; children: Brian, Donald, Jane Mayne Cohen. BA in Chem. Engring., U. Toronto, 1946. Var. mgmt. positions Internat. Multifoods, Mpls., 1948-85, now group v.p. agri-indsl. ops., 1985—. Club: Minneapolis. Office: Internat Multifoods Corp 33 S Sixth St Minneapolis MN 55402

MAYO, WILLIAM EDWARD BARRY, orthopaedic surgeon; b. Ottawa, Ont., Can., Apr. 1, 1930; s. Reginald Sidney and Verena Mary (Haney) M.; m. Helene Puskas, June 21, 1958; children: David, Ilona, Robert, Paula. MD, U. Western Ont., 1958. Diplomate Am. Bd. Orthopaedic Surgery. Resident Latter Day Saints Hosp., Salt Lake City, 1958-60, Primary Childrens Hosp., Salt Lake City, 1960-61, Henry Ford Hosp., Detroit, 1961-64; practice medicine specializing in orthopaedic surgery, arthroscopy and arthroscopic surgery, Royal Oak, Mich., 1964—; mem. staff William Beaumont Hosp., Royal Oak; dir. Sports Medicine Clinic; bd. dirs. Mich. Nat. Bank, Farmington, 1979-85. Pres., Bloomfield Hills Mich. Stake, Latter Day Saints Ch., 1980-87; mem. exec. bd. Detroit Area council Boy Scouts Am., 1980-87, chmn. leadership tng. com., 1985-87. Recipient Silver Beaver award Boy Scouts Am. Mem. ACS, Internat. Arthroscopy Assn., Royal Soc. Medicine, Am. Acad. Orthopaedic Surgery, Arthroscopy Assn. N.Am., Sportopaedics (pres. 1985-87). Home: 4387 Barchester Dr Bloomfield Hills MI 48013 Office: 2338 N Woodward St Royal Oak MI 48013

MAYOR, RAYMOND LESLIE, obstetrician-gynecologist; b. LaCombe, Alta., Can., Apr. 22, 1929; came to U.S., 1941; s. Cecil Walter and Mary (Stoesz) M.; m. Wilma Louise, June 14, 1951; children: David Lee, Laura Lynn. BA, Andrew U., 1951; MD, Loma Linda U., 1955. Resident in ob-gyn Pontiac (Mich.) Gen. Hosp., 1958-61; pvt. practice medicine specializing in ob-gyn. Pontiac Assoc. in Ob-Gyn., 1961—. Served to capt. U.S. Army, 1956-58. Fellow Am. Coll. Ob-Gyn.; mem. AMA, OCMS. Home: 2160 Rosewood Pontiac MI 48055 Office: Pontiac Assocs in OB-Gyn 35 S Johnson Pontiac MI 48053

MAYR, JAMES JEROME, fertilizer company executive; b. Beaver Dam, Wis., Aug. 19, 1942; s. Alfred A. and Mfaxine E. (Kuehl) M.; m. Carol Ann Kaufman, Sept. 4, 1965; children: Christin and Carin (twins), Cathy, Conni. BS in Agrl. Econs., U. Wis., 1964. Mgr. trainee Oscar Mayer, Madison, Wis., 1964-65; v.p. Mayr's Seed and Feed, Beaver Dam, 1966-78; product mgr. Chem. Enterprises, Houston, 1978-80; gen. mgr. Coash, Inc., Bassett, Nebr., 1981—; cons. Beaver Dam, 1971-75; speaker fertilizer orgns., Wis. Advisor U. Wis. Coll. Agriculture; mem. com. Upper Elk Horn Natural Resources Dist., Oneill, Nebr., 1985—. Mem. Wis. Fertilizer Assn. (bd. dirs. 1970-74), Nat. Fertilizer and Solutions Assn., Nebr. Fertilizer and Chem. Assn. Republican. Roman Catholic. Lodge: KC (dep. grand knight 1978-80, 81-85). Avocations: target shooting, hunting, fishing, teaching target shooting. Home: PO Box 494 Bassett NE 68714 Office: Coash Inc PO Box 528 Bassett NE 68714

MAYSE, MICHAEL CARL, youth organization administrator; b. Detroit, May 29, 1954; s. Carl and JoAnne (Stapleton) M., m. Connie Jean Lemons; 1 child, Franklin Stuart. B.S., Central Mich. U., 1977. Dist. exec. Detroit Area council Boy Scouts Am., 1977-78, exploring exec., 1978-81, exploring exec. Bay-Lakes council, Menasha, Wis., 1981-82, exploring dir., 1982-83, fin. dir. Greater Cleve. Council, 1983-87, dir. fin. services, 1987—; nat. law enforcement conf. dir., Dallas, 1983-84. Editor Bay-Lake News, 1983-85. Res. officer Detroit Police Dept., 1978-81. Recipient Eagle Scout award Boy Scouts Am., 1970. Mem. Soc. Am. Mil. Engrs., Sigma Chi (Life Loyal Sig award 1976). Republican. Methodist. Clubs: Optimists (sec. 1982-83), Rotary. Avocations: photography; swimming; golf. Home: 13578 Cherokee Trail Middleburg Heights OH 44130 Office: Boy Scouts Am Greater Cleve Council E 22d St at Woodland Av Cleveland OH 44115-6060

MAYSTEAD, SUZANNE RAE, optometrist; b. Hillsdale, Mich., Sept. 30, 1955; d. Marvin Charles and Helen Alberta (Glendenning) Patrick; m. Ivan Karl Maystead, III, June 4, 1977. O.D., Ferris State Coll. Optometry, 1979. Research asst. to optometrist, Big Rapids, Mich., 1979-80; clin. assoc. Ferris State Coll. Optometry, Big Rapids, 1979-84; pvt. practice optometry, Portland, Mich., 1980—. Recipient Contact Lens Achievement award Bauch & Lomb, 1979. Mem. Mich. Optometric Assn., Portland C. of C. Avocations: indoor gardening, interior decorating. Club: Am. Chesapeake. Home: 7667 Peckins Rd Lyons MI 48851 Office: 1311 E Bridge St Portland MI 48875

MAZIASZ, MICHAEL M., automotive company executive; b. N.Y.C., June 21, 1941; s. Michael Joseph and Muriel Maziasz; m. Karen H. Maziasz, Aug. 15, 1964; children: Richard, Keith. BBA, Pace U., 1969; MBA with honors, N.Y. Inst. Tech., 1982. Product distributor overseas ops. Gen. Motors Corp., N.Y.C., 1959-65, analyst overseas ops., 1965-69, sr. analyst overseas ops., 1969-75; sr. staff analyst Gen. Motors Corp., Detroit, 1975-79, adminstr., 1979-83, asst. dir., 1983—. Served with N.Y.N.G. 1961-66. Mem. Delta Mu Delta. Lodge: Masons (master). Avocations: yachting, golf. Office: Gen Motors Corp W Grand Blvd Detroit MI 48202

MAZUR, JOHN BERNARD, neurological surgeon; b. Fargo, N.D., Dec. 11, 1947; s. Bernard Alexander and Gertrude Isobel (Parry) M.; m. Lynda Rose Abbink, Feb. 12, 1972. B.S. in Chemistry, U. Notre Dame, 1968; B.S. in Medicine, U.N.D., 1970; M.D., Northwestern U., 1972. Diplomate Am. Bd. Neurol. Surgery. Intern in gen. surgery Wesley Meml. Hosp., Chgo., 1972-73; physician in adult medicine Chgo. Bd. Health, 1973-74; resident in neurol. surgery U. Ill. and affiliated hosps., Chgo., 1974-78; attending staff physician Mercy Ctr. Copley Meml. Hosp., Aurora, Ill., 1978—; cons. physician Kishwaukee Community Hosp., DeKalb, Ill., 1980—, Delnor Hosp., St. Charles, Ill., 1972—, Geneva Community Hosp., Ill., 1972—; attending staff physician Cen. DuPage Hosp., 1987—; clin. asst. prof. U. Ill., Chgo., 1987. Mem. AMA, Am. Assn. Neurol. Surgeons, Congress of Neurol. Surgeons, Soc. Neurovascular Surgery, Ill. State Med. Soc. Avocations: skiing; boardsailing. Office: Fox Valley Neur Inst 1300 North Highland Aurora IL 60506

MAZUR-BAKER, DEBORAH JOAN, educator; b. Highland Park, Mich., Apr. 22, 1958; d. Frank J. and Joan A. (Cader) Mazur; m. Michael J. Baker, Sept. 20, 1986. B.S., Western Mich. U., 1981. Spl. edn. resource room tchr. Capac Community Schs., Mich., 1981-82; supr. group home Blue Water Developmental Housing, Port Huron, Mich., 1982-83; unit adminstr. group home Luth. Social Services of Mich., Detroit, 1983-85; mgr. sales Fin. Services of Am., Inc., Madison Heights, Mich., 1985-86; clinician, case mgr. Ditty, Lynch, and Assocs., Birmingham, Mich., 1986-87—; spl. edn. tchr. Pontiac Sch. Dist., 1987—. Mem. Council Exceptional Children, Mich. Head Injury-Alliance, Nat. Head Injury Alliance, Am. Behavioral Assn., Western Mich. U. Alumni Assn. (bd. dirs.).

MAZURKIEWICZ, GREGORY ALLEN, public relations executive; b. Detroit, May 26, 1950; s. Edward John and Rita (Paduchowski) M.; m. Margaret Mary Van Gorder, Dec. 21, 1973; children: Rebecca, Stephen. BA in Journalism, U. Mich., 1972; MA in Bus. Mgmt., Cen. Mich. U., 1982. Systems writer Burroughs Corp., Detroit, 1974-77; copywriter Hemsing Advt., Ferndale, Mich., 1977-79; acct. exec. Lapp Assocs., Birmingham, Mich., 1979-82; press relations specialist Gould, Inc., Troy, Mich., 1982-83; acct. exec. G. Temple Assocs., Southfield, Mich., 1983-84; v.p. Lampe Communications, Pontiac, Mich., 1984—; instr. Macomb Community Coll., Mount Clemens, Mich., 1985—. Contbg. editor Contemporary Newsmakers (quarterly pub.), 1985—. Mem. Pub. Relations Soc. Am., Kappa Tau Alpha. Democrat. Roman Catholic. Avocation: tennis. Office: Lampe Communications Inc 902 Riker Bldg Pontiac MI 48058

MAZZETTI, LINDA MARIA, learning disabilities teacher; b. Chgo., June 7, 1947; d. Paul Frank and Lillian (Cittadino) DeB.; m. James Anthony, Nov. 19, 1972; 1 child, James David. BS in Edn., No. Ill. U., 1970. Tchr. of socially maladjusted Calumet City, Ill., 1970-71; tchr. of learning disabilities Bolingbrook, Ill., 1971—; co-owner Anglers Shady Bay Resort & Campground, Hayward, Wis.; co-founder, treas. Nat. Hydrocephalus Found., Joliet, Ill., 1980—. Mem. Council for Exceptional Children. Office: Nat Hydrocephalus Found Rt1 River Rd PO Box 210A Joliet IL 60436

MAZZI, JAMES ALBERT, physician; b. Youngstown, Ohio, Jan. 17, 1931; s. Samuel P. and Marion E. (Napolitan) M.; m. Anita L. Ricci; children: Angela, Alicia. BS in Natural Sci., John Carroll U., 1953; DO, Kirksville (Mo.) Coll. Osteopathic Med., 1957. Intern Youngstown Osteopathic Hosp., 1957-58; practice osteo. medicine Struthers, Ohio, 1957—; chief dept. phys. medicine and rehab. Youngstown Osteo. Hosp., 1979—, trainer gen. practice resident program, 1983—; physician Mahoning County Jail, Youngstown, 1981—; chief staff Youngstown Osteopathic Hosp., 1983-85; med. advisor Upjohn Health Care, Youngstown, 1982—. Team physician Northeast Cath. High Sch., Youngstown, 1983—. Mem. Am. Osteo. Assn. (cert. gen. practice 1979), Coll. Gen. Practice of Am. Osteo. Assn., Ohio Osteo. Assn., 10th Dist. Acad. Osteo. Medicine. Democrat. Roman Catholic. Home: 60 Fairway Dr Youngstown OH 44505 Office: 532 Youngstown-Poland Rd Struthers OH 44471

MAZZOTTA, LAWRENCE A., financial investor; b. Kittanning, Pa., Dec. 17, 1947; s. Jack and Louise Beverly (Brochetti) M.; m. N. Katherine Babcock, June 9, 1984. BS, U. Nebr., Omaha, 1972; MPA, Syracuse U., 1974; postgrad., U. Nebr. Dir. adminstrn. Eastern Nebr. Huamn Service Agy., Omaha, 1974-75; exec. dir. Inst. for Bus., Law and Social Research Creighton U., Omaha, 1975-76; pres. Macy, Powell & Mazzotta, Omaha, 1976-81; sr. assoc. dir. U. Nebr. Hosps., Omaha, 1980-85; chmn., chief exec. officer Douglas Med. Services, Omaha, 1985—. Vice chmn. Mental Health Adv. Com., Omaha, 1982, Med. Ctr. United Way, Omaha, 1983-84; chmn bd. Eye Bank Nebr., Omaha, 1986—. Served to sgt. USAF, 1967-71. Richard King Mellon Found. fellow, 1973, U.S. Pub. Service Fellow, 1981. Mem. Gamma Theta Upsilon. Republican. Presbyterian. Club: Oak Hills Country (Omaha). Avocations: reading, golf, photography, collecting rare books. Home: 16555 Valley Circle Omaha NE 68130

MCADAMS, PETER COOPER, entertainment company excutive; b. Alton, Ill., Feb. 14, 1940; s. Henry Harold and Melba Irene (Cooper) McA.; m. Janice Marie Dennis, Nov. 22, 1972; children: Timothy, Pamela, Patricia, John. BS in Bus., Northwestern U., 1962. Bus. mgr., owner Alton (Ill.) Telegraph PTG Co., 1969-85; owner, operator P&J Enterprises, Brighton, Ill., 1980—, Brighton Orchards, 1976—; cons. newspaper industry, Brighton, 1982—; bd. dirs. Apple and Peach Mktg., Springfield, Alton Telegraph, Alton Corp. Devel. Bd. Served to capt. USAF, 1962-69. Mem. Am. Press Assn., Inland Press Assn., Ill. Press Assn., Ill. Horticulture Soc., Ill. Fruit Mktg. Bd. Lodge: Lions. Avocations: horticulture, tax planning, computer programming. Home and Office: Rt 2 Box 208 Brighton IL 62012

MCAFEE, CHARLES FRANCIS, architect; b. Los Angeles, Dec. 25, 1932; s. Arthur James and Willie Anna (Brown) McA.; m. Gloria Myrth Winston; children: Cheryl Lynn, Pamela Anita, Charyl Frena. B.Arch., U. Nebr.-Lincoln. Registered architect, Kans., Mo., Nebr., Okla., Tex., Mass., Ga., Fla. Architect, pres. Charles F. McAfee, Wichita, Kans., 1963—; mem. profl. adv. bd. architecture U. Nebr., 1979 . Archtl. works include, Wichita Eagle & Beacon Pub. Co., Chem. Lab. Vulcan Materials Co., Ulrich Mus.-McKnight Art Ctr. Pres. Wichita Urban League; pres. Phyllis Wheatly Children's Home, Wichita. Served with U.S. Army, 1953-55. Stanley O. Osborne Found. scholar, 1956; recipient Alumni Achievement award U. Nebr., 1983. Fellow AIA (mem design awards jury); mem. Nat. Orgn. Minority Architects (mem. pres. council, past pres. Onyx award), Kappa Alpha Psi. Democrat. Baptist. Club: Execlsior (Wichita). Home: 16 Crestview Lakes Wichita KS 67220 Office: Charles F McFee Architects Engrs Planners 2660 N Grove St Wichita KS 68219

MCALLISTER, JOHN DAVID, marketing executive; b. Cedar Rapids, Iowa, Nov. 7, 1950; s. Warren William and Alice B. (Carlton) McA.; m. Debra Jane Murray, Dec. 16, 1977; children: Kelly Jane, John Carlton. A in Applied Sci., Kirkwood Coll., 1971. Buyer Desmonds Dept. Store, Los Angeles, 1973-75, VanArsdels Dept. Store, St. Paul, 1975-77; sales assoc. Mac Realty, Cedar Rapids, 1978-80, Skogman Homes of Iowa, Cedar Rapids, 1980-83; dir. mktg. L.A. Laukka Devel. Co., Mpls., 1984-86, J.B. Franklin Corp., St. Paul, 1986—; Chmn. Mpls.-St. Paul selection com. for area sales person of yr. award; bd. dirs. Mpls. Parade of Homes. Served to pvt. USAR, 1971-73. Mem. Mpls. Bd. Realtors, Mpls. and St. Paul Builders Sales and Mktg. Council (v.p.), U. Iowa Club. Lutheran. Avocations: boating, hiking, camping, hunting. Home: 17090 Creekridge Trail Minnetonka MN 55345 Office: JB Franklin Corp 1781 Prior Ave N Saint Paul MN 55108

MCALLISTER, JOHN MICHAEL, restauranteur; b. Cleve., July 5, 1955; s. Roy Levi and Margaret Phyllis (Sorentino) McA.; m. Patricia May Phillip, Sept. 2, 1978; 1 child, Elizabeth Ann. Grad. high sch., Lakewood, Ohio, 1973. Chef Market St. Exchange, Cleve., 1975-79; exec. chef Cleve. Yacht Club, Rocky River, Ohio, 1979; v.p. Friends Restaurant, Lakewood, Ohio, 1979-86; exec. chef Oberlin (Ohio) Coll. Inn, 1986—; cons. L'Escargot, North Olmsted, Ohio, 1982-83. Nat. 1st Place award Helix Escargot Contest, 1982. Mem. Am. Culinary Fedn., Chaine de Rottisieur, Les Amis Du Vin (chevalier). Avocations: golf, reading. Office: Oberlin Coll Inn Oberlin OH 44074

MCALLISTER, THOMAS JAY, SR., financial planning consultant; b. Terre Haute, Ind., Nov. 15, 1937; s. Thomas Joseph and Vera Beatrice (Brown) McA.; m. Janice Kay Preusz, Sept. 17, 1955 (div. Apr. 1974); children: Deborah, Denise, Donna, Darlene, T. Jay, DeAnn; m. Mary Jane Pickard, Apr., 1978. AS in Engring., Vincennes (Ind.) U., 1957; BA in Psychology, Internat. Coll., Los Angeles, 1977. Cert. fin. planner. Mgr. Preston Chem., Columbus, Ind., 1958-62; acct. exec. Merrill Lynch, Indpls., 1962-69; v.p., mgr. R.W. Baird & Co., Indpls., 1969-75; pres. McAllister Finl. Planning, Indpls., 1975—; Mem. Registry of Fin. Planners, Atlanta, Ga., 1985—, Fin. Products Standards Bd., Denver, 1984-87. Author: Your Book for Financial Planning, 1983; contbr. articles to profl. jours. Rep. ward chmn, Indpls., 1969-72, precinct commn., Columbus, 1962-64, Indpls., 1964-68. Mem. U.S. Jaycees (McCall award 1967), Inst. Cert. Fin. Planners, Internat. Assn. Fin. Planner (state pres. 1980-81), Nat. Assn. Securities Dealers (direct participation com. 1978-81, qualifications com. 1982—, dist. com. 1984-87), Indpls. Bond Club (pres. 1977-78). Roman Catholic. Lodges: KC (Grand Knight 1962-64), Kiwanis. Avocations: racquetball, tennis, flying. Home: 7656 Bay Shore Dr Indianapolis IN 46240 Office: McAllister Fin Planning 6060 Castleway #230 Indianapolis IN 46204

MCANDREW, DENNIS PATRICK, parking management executive; b. Jefferson City, Mo., Aug. 1, 1942; s. James Francis and Marjorie (Whalen) McA.; m. Eileen Ann Wurm, Sept. 13, 1969; children: Dennis J., Michelle A., Leslie M., Jeannie T., Michael. BS, John Carroll U., Cleve., 1964. Mathematician Penn Cen. Co., Cleve., 1967-70; v.p. Apcoa, Inc., Cleve., 1971—; trustee Ohio State Parking, Cleve. 1981—. Pres. St. Felicitas PTA, 1983-84; chmn. Planning and Zoning Commn., Richmond Heights, Ohio, 1984-85; lectr., lay minister St. Felicitas Ch., Richmond Heights, 1974—. Democrat. Roman Catholic. Home: 1942 Sunset Dr Richmond Heights OH 44143 Office: Apcoa Inc 1111 Euclid Ave Cleveland OH 44115

MCANDREW, PAUL JOSEPH, JR., lawyer; b. Iowa City, Mar. 8, 1957; s. Paul Joseph and Virginia (Krowka) McA.; m. Lola Maxine Miller, Mar. 1, 1975; children: Stephanie, Susan, Rose, Paul Joseph III. BA with honors, U. Iowa, 1979, JD with high distinction, 1983. Bar: Iowa 1983, U.S. Dist. Ct. (so. dist.) Iowa 1985, U.S. Claim Ct. 1985. Law clk. presiding justice U.S. Dist. Ct. (so. dist.) Iowa, Des Moines, 1983-85; assoc. Meardon, Sueppel, Downer & Hayes, Iowa City, 1985—. Recipient 2 Am. Jurisprudence awards Lawyers Co-Operative Pub. Co., Rochester, N.Y., 1982, 83. Mem. ABA, Iowa Bar Assn.(mem. criminal law com., young lawyers sect. criminal justice com.), Am. Trial Lawyers Assn., Iowa Trial Lawyers Assn. (mem. malpractice com.), Johnson County Bar Assn., Johnson County Young Lawyers Group (co-chmn.). Democrat. Roman Catholic. Avocations: jogging, biking, traveling. Home: 2832 Brookside Iowa City IA 52240 Office: Meardon Suepel Downer & Hayes 122 S Linn Iowa City IA 52240

MCANDREWS, JAMES PATRICK, lawyer; b. Carbondale, Pa., May 11, 1929; s. James Patrick and Mary Agnes (Walsh) McA.; m. Mona Marie Steinke, Sept. 4, 1954; children: James P., George A., Catherine McAndrews Lawlor, Joseph M., Anne Marie, Michael P., Edward R., Daniel P. B.S., U. Scranton, 1949; LL.B., Fordham U., 1952; grad., Real Estate Inst., NYU, 1972. Bar: N.Y. 1953, Ohio 1974. Assoc. law firm James F. McManus, Levittown, N.Y., 1955; atty. Emigrant Savs. Bank, N.Y.C., 1955-68; counsel Tchrs. Ins. and Annuity Assn., 1968-73; assoc. Thompson, Hine & Flory, 1973-74; ptnr. Thompson, Hine & Flory, Cleve., 1974-84, Benesch, Friedlander, Coplan & Aronoff, Cleve., 1984—; mem. law faculty Am. Inst. Banking, N.Y.C., 1968-69. Served to 1st lt. USAF, 1952-54. Fellow Am. Bar Found.; mem. ABA (past chmn. real estate financing com. 1985-87), Am. Coll. Real Estate Lawyers (gov. 1983-86, treas. 1986—, chmn. membership devel. com. 1985—), Ohio Bar Assn., Bar Assn. Greater Cleve. (past chmn. council real estate sect.), Am. Land Title Assn. (chmn. lenders counsel group 1978, chmn. membership com. 1983-84), Ohio Land Title Assn. (bd. trustees 1985—, chmn. lender's counsel group 1986), Internat. Council Shopping Ctrs., Urban Land Inst., Nat. Trust Hist. Preservation, Nat. Assn. Corp. Real Estate Execs. (chmn. nomination com. Ohio 1982, v.p. Ohio chpt. 1983-84), Nat. Assn. Indsl. and Office Parks, Am. Coll. Mortgage Attys. Roman Catholic. Home: 2971 Litchfield Rd Shaker Heights OH 44120 Office: 1100 Citizens Bldg Cleveland OH 44114

MCANINCH, JACK HERBERT, small business owner; b. Indpls., May 20, 1940; s. Herbert A. and Adele Louise (Woodruff) McA.; m. Kathryn A. Luke, July 30, 1966; children: Kevin H., Daniel R., Mark S. BS, Hillsdale Coll., 1959-63; MS, St. Francis Coll., 1965-67. Office mgr. Mid Am. Electronics, Auburn, Ind., 1966-73; plant mgr. Lyall Electric, Orland, Ind., 1973; pres., owner Hermac Inc., Auburn, 1973—. Treas. U.S. Jaycees, Auburn, 1966-68. Republican. Roman Catholic. Avocations: antique car restoration, woodworking, traveling, fishing. Home: 3486 C R 427 Waterloo IN 46793 Office: Hermac Inc 540 W North St Auburn IN 46706

MCARTHUR, ROBERT BRUCE, systems analyst; b. Toledo, Sept. 14, 1938; s. James Arnold and Dorella Bertha (McAran) Mc A.; m. Elizabeth Rosar, Jan. 7, 1961 (div. June 1983); children: Lori Ann, Lynn Marie; m. Linda Lou Bartley, May 15, 1985; children: Julie Lynn, Lisa Anne. Cert. computer sci., Davis Bus. Coll., 1969. Lab. technician Owens of Ill., Inc., Toledo, 1962-67, programmer, 1969-76, systems analyst, 1976-85; systems analyst S.D. Warren Co., Muskegon, Mich., 1985—. Inventor composite can vaccum pack, 1962. Republican. Lutheran. Home: 1725 Gaylord Dr Muskegon MI 49445 Office: SD Warren Co 2400 Lakeshore Dr Muskegon MI 49441

MCARTHUR, STEVEN WARREN, financial executive; b. New Ulm, Minn., Mar. 27, 1943; s. Donald William and Elaine A. (Rockvane) McA.; m. Theresa Marie McArthur, Dec. 16, 1966; children: Erin, Sara, Shelley. BBA, U. Minn., 1967. CPA, Minn. Supr. Touche Ross, Mpls., 1972-78; mng. dir. Dayton Hudson, Mpls., 1978-81, asst. controller, 1981-82; v.p., controller B. Dalton Bookseller, Mpls., 1982-86; v.p. fin., chief fin. officer Franks Nursery and Crafts, Detroit, 1986—. Mem. Dean Search Com. U. Minn., 1981. Served to capt. USAF, 1967-72, Vietnam. Mem. Am. Inst. CPA's, Minn. Soc. CPA's, U. Minn. Sch. Bus. Alumni Assn. (chmn. 1980-81). Avocation: tennis. Office: Franks Nursery and Crafts 6501 E Navarre Detroit MI 48234

MCARTHUR, WILLIAM STUART, chemical sales and marketing executive; b. Beaumont, Tex., June 20, 1951; s. William C. and Virginia (Heidecker) McA.; m. Lauren Riendeau, May 9, 1981; children: Jonathan Stuart, Jennifer Lauren (dec.). AS, Tex. Tech. U., 1973. Sales rep. Nalco

Chem., Concord, Calif., 1974-76; sales rep. Olin Water Services, Baton Rouge, 1977-78, area mgr., 1978-79, dist. mgr., 1980-82; regional mgr. Olin Water Services, Houston, 1982-84; dir. sales Olin Water Services, Overland Park, Kans., 1985—. Republican. Avocations: reading, sport cars, golf, sailing. Home: 9629 W 116th St Overland Park KS 66210 Office: Olin Water Services 51 Corporate Woods 9393 W 110th St Overland Park KS 66210

MCATEE, JOSEPH G., law enforcement official. Police chief City of Indpls. Office: Office of the Police Chief Indianapolis IN 46204 *

MC AULIFFE, CORNELIUS (CONNIE), bookstore manager; b. Castleisland Kerry, Ireland, Nov. 24, 1932; came to U.S., Dec. 16, 1953, naturalized, 1955; s. David Joseph and Katherine (Murphy) Mc A.; m. Jane Mangan, Aug. 23, 1958; children—Mary, Ann, Kathleen, David. Student Lansing Bus. U., 1956-59. Asst. mgr., buyer McElligotta Castleisland, Ireland, 1949-53; telephone service rep. Mich. Bell Telephone Co., Lansing, 1954-59; bus. mgr. union Mich. State U., East Lansing, 1959-66, chief acct., asst. mgr. bookstore, 1966-83, mgr., 1983—. Served to sgt. U.S. Army, 1954-56. Recipient Community Service award Mich. State U. Womens Sports Booster Club, 1983. Mem. Nat. Assn. Accts., Nat. Assn. Coll. Stores, Mich. Assn. Coll. Stores (treas. 1984—), Am. Numismatic Soc., Adminstrn. and Profl. Employees Assn. (bd. dirs. 1979-82), Mich. State U. Blue Line Club (bd. dirs. 1986-89, pres. 1987-88). Democrat. Roman Catholic. Clubs: Civitan (treas. 1974-78), Lansing Skating (treas. 1976-80), Trojan Hockey (treas. 1983), University. Avocations: collecting Irish coins; golf; sports, especially hockey, football. Home: 1854 Cahill Dr East Lansing MI 48823 Office: Mich State U Bookstore East Lansing MI 48824

MC AULIFFE, MICHAEL F., bishop; b. Kansas City, Mo., Nov. 22, 1920. Student, St. Louis Prep. Sem., Cath. U. Ordained priest Roman Cath. Ch., 1945; consecrated bishop 1969; bishop diocese of Jefferson City Jefferson City, Mo., 1969—. Office: Chancery Office 605 Clark Ave PO Box 417 Jefferson City MO 65102 *

MCBAIN, ROBERT PRINCE, lawyer, accountant; b. Grand Rapids, Mich., Aug. 25, 1942; s. Robert James and Inez Marie (Prince) McB.; m. Gwendolyn Greene, Aug. 1, 1964; children—Robert Scott, James Kent. B.A., Mich. State U., 1964; J.D., U. Mich., 1966. Bar: Mich. 1968; C.P.A., Mich. Prin. Robert J. McBain & Co., P.C., Grand Rapids, Mich., 1967—; atty., cert. pub. acct., 1971—, exec. v.p., 1977—. Co-chmn. subcom. United Way of Kent County, 1974-77; treas. Goodwill Industries of Grand Rapids, 1974-79. Mem. ABA, Mich. Bar Assn., Grand Rapids Bar Assn., Am. Inst. C.P.A.s, Mich. Assn. C.P.A.s, Am. Assn. Atty.-C.P.A.s, Mich. Assn. Atty.-C.P.A.s (v.p.). Republican. Congregationalist. Lodge: Rotary.

MCBEATH, BRUCE GORDON, psychologist, consultant; b. Mpls., Apr. 1, 1940; s. Gordon Stanley and Astrid Elviria (Hjelmeir) McB.; m. Dianne Martha Aisenbrey; children: Laura, Sheila, Molly. BA, U. Minn., 1962, MSW, 1964; PhD, Saybrook Inst., San Francisco, 1986. Lic. psychologist, Minn.; cert. social worker, Minn. Asst. dir. Dept. Family and Children Services, Mpls., 1969-72; dir. Alternative Behaviors, Mpls., 1971-80; field cons. U.S. Office Edn., Mpls., 1972-73; pvt. practice psychology St. Paul, 1979—; cons. Minn. Dept. Corrections, St. Paul, 1974-85; adj. prof. psychology St. Mary's Coll., Mpls., 1985—; bd. dirs. Keewoon Clinic, Mpls., Psychosynthesis Inst. of Minn., 1979—. Contbg. author: Psychosynthesis and The Hospital Process, 1983, Reading in Psychosynthesis, 1985. Minn. Found. fellow, 1962. Mem. Acad. Cert. Social Workers, Am. Assn. Marriage and Family Therapists. Office: 1360 Energy Park Dr #330 Saint Paul MN 55108

MCBRIDE, JACK J, life and financial services executive; b. Orient, Iowa, June 24, 1936; s. Marvin Clair and Ruth (Jones) McB.; m. Mary Ann Garden, June 16, 1957; children: Jeffry J., Beth Ann, Kelley Lynn, Grant G. BA, Simpson Coll., Indianola, Iowa, 1958; postgrad. U. Conn., 1963. Spl. agt. Bankers Life Co., Des Moines, 1958-60; agy. supr. Aetna Life Annuity, Fin. Services, Inc., Hartford, Conn., 1960-65, gen. agt., Springfield, Ill., also Milw., 1972-82; agy. mgr. Equitable Life Iowa, E.I. Sales, Inc., Omaha, also Davenport, Iowa, 1965-72; supt. personal fin. security div., Aetna Life & Casualty Co., Chgo., 1982-84; instr. Life Underwriters Tng. Council, Quad Cities, 1968-69; lectr. to various univs. and colls. Contbr. articles to profl. jours. Chmn. friends bd. So. Ill. U. Med. Sch., 1975-77, bd. dirs., 1973-77; co-chmn. 1st Day Care Ctr., Springfield, Ill., 1973-77; charter chmn. stewardship St. Luke's Ch., Omaha, 1966; mem. steering com. devel. council Simpson Coll. Named Outstanding Young Man Am., 1966. Mem. Nat. Assn. Life Underwriters (past co-chmn. edn. com., chmn., dir. Iowa State com.), Springfield Gen. Agts. and Mgrs. Assn. (past pres., dir.), Sangamon Estate Planners Council (charter mem.), Adminstrv. Mgmt. Soc., Quad Cities C. of C. (speakers bar). Republican. Mem. Union Ch. Club: Merrill Hills (Waukesha, Wis.). Lodge: Masons (32 deg.), St. Andrew Soc., Rotary.

MCBRIDE, ROBERT CHARLES, manufacturing company executive; b. Wichita, Kans., Aug. 8, 1922; s. Charles Richey and Tilla Elinor (Matson) McB.; m. Mary Katherine Beebe, Oct. 19, 1951; children: Barbara Anne McBride Dalbey, Sharon Katherine McBride Hammer. Student, Park Coll., 1940, Hendrix Coll., 1943; AA, Tex. A&M U., 1943; BS, U. Kans., 1947, MBA, 1949. Controller, v.p., fin. officer W.E. Isle Co., Kansas City, Mo., 1949-52; v.p., fin. officer Knit Rite Co., Kansas City, 1952-82, ptnr., sr. v.p., chief fin. officer, 1982—; ptnr., sr. v.p., chief fin. officer Para-Med Distbrs., Kansas City, 1982—. Deacon Presbyterian ch. Served with USAAF, 1942-46, ETO, USAF, 1950-51, Korea. Mem. Systems Mgmt. Assn. (charter, Internat. Merit award 1976, Internat. Disting. Achievement award 1985), Am. Mgmt. Assn., Nat. Accts. Assn., Greater Kansas City C. of C. Republican. Lodges: Masons.

MCBRIDE, WILLIAM ALAN, architect; b. Lima, Ohio, Mar. 16, 1948; s. James Maurice and Ruth Elizabeth (Partch) McB.; m. Michele Mand McKay, May 6, 1978; children: Justine Marie, William Gamble. BA, Harvard U., 1970, MArch, 1975. Registered profl. architect, Ill. Student architect John Portman & Assocs., Atlanta, 1971-72; design architect Harry Weese & Assocs., Chgo., 1976-79; owner William McBride & Assocs., Chgo., 1980—. Patentee tubular chair, 1986; designer, architect permanent collections in Chgo. Hist. Soc., Art. Inst. Chgo. Pres. aux. bd. Chgo. Archtl. Found. Frederick Sheldon traveling fellow Harvard U., Stockholm, 1975; recipient Interior Design award Steelcase Showroom, 1987. Presbyterian. Club: Chgo. Archtl. Home: 1110 W Barry Ave Chicago IL 60657 Office: 449 N Wells Chicago IL 60610

MCBURNEY, JAMES BERNARD, consulting company executive; b. Washington, Pa., May 17, 1927; s. Bernard Reckers and Marion Laura (Perkins) McB.; m. Carolyn Martha Keathley, Apr. 1, 1973; children—Karen L., Steven B., James R. (dec.), Brenda, Susan, William, Faith. B.A., Washington and Jefferson Coll., 1948; postgrad. U. Miami Grad. Sch. Bus., 1949-51. With Sears Roebuck & Co., 1950-75, successively sales, div. mgr., personnel trainee, Miami, Fla., personnel mgr., Chattanooga, service mgr., St. Petersburg, Fla., personnel mgr., Coral Gables, Fla., asst. store mgr., Ft. Myers Fla., service staff asst., Atlanta, sales promotion mgr., nat. sales mgr. service and parts, mktg. mgr. home laundry sect., Chgo.; pres. Markoa Corp., Chgo., 1985—; affiliated with Systema Corp., 1986—. Mem. Com. for Ch. Support Chgo. Presbytery. Named Boss of Yr., Bus. Women's Assn. of Am., 1964. Mem. Internat. Council Small Bus., Am. Mktg. Assn., Soc. Personnel Adminstrs., Sales/Mktg. Execs. of Chgo., Sales/Mktg. Execs. Internat., Chgo. Sales Tng. Assn., Inst. Mgmt. Cons., Am. Soc. Personnel Adminstrn., Soc. Human Resource Profls. Greater Chgo., Chgo. Assn. Commerce and Industry, Phi Gamma Delta. Republican. Presbyterian. Avocations: music, auto and home restoration. Home: 3825 Maple Ave Northbrook IL 60062 Office: Markoa Corp PO Box 470 Deerfield IL 60015

MC CABE, ARTHUR LEE, consultant; b. Otsego, Mich., Dec. 18, 1937; s. Arthur Lee and Florence Gertrude (Mollison) McC.; student Kalamazoo Coll., 1956-58, Western Mich. U., 1958-59; m. Nancy Lee Smith, June 26, 1959; children—Janet Lee, William Arthur, Sherry Linn, Arthur Lee, Elizabeth Ann, Susan Faye. Asst. mgr. D & C Stores, Kalamazoo, 1959-60; asst. fleet supt. McNamara Motor Express Co., Kalamazoo, 1960-61; with Upjohn Co., Kalamazoo, 1961-63; chemistry technician Consumers Power Co., Kalamazoo, 1963-66, sr. chemistry technician, 1966-73, sr. radiation protection technician Palisades plant, Covert, Mich., 1973-74, chemistry supr., Palisades Nuclear Plant, 1974-78, fossil fuels specialist, Jackson, Mich., 1978-79, fuel transp. adminstr., 1979—; pres. Fuels Technology Co. Inc., 1983—. Dist. commr. Southwestern Mich. council Boy Scouts Am., 1973-74. Republican. Inventor in field. Home and office: PO Box 84 215 Hanover St Concord MI 49237

MCCABE, CHARLES KEVIN, lawyer, author; b. Springfield, Ill., Nov. 2, 1952; s. Charles Kenneth and Betty Lou (Williams) McC. B.S. in Aero. and Astronautical Engring. magna cum laude, U. Ill., 1975; J.D., U. Mich., 1978. Bar: Ill. 1978, U.S. Dist. Ct. (no. dist.) Ill. 1978, U.S. Ct. Appeals (7th cir.) 1980. Engring. co-op. student McDonnell Aircraft, St. Louis, 1972-74; chief aerodynamicist Vetter Fairing Co., Rantoul, Ill., 1974-75; assoc. Lord, Bissell, & Brook, Chgo., 1978—. Author: Qwiktran: Quick FORTRAN, 1979; FORTH Fundamentals, 1983; co-author: 32 BASIC Programs, 1981. Contbr. articles on aviation, computers to various mags., 1974—. Nat. Merit scholar U. Ill., Urbana, 1970. Mem. ABA, Ill. State Bar Assn., Chgo. Bar Assn. Office: Lord Bissell & Brook 115 S LaSalle St Chicago IL 60603

MCCABE, DONALD JAMES, educational research director; b. Flint, Mich., Oct. 4, 1932; s. Lemuel Cicero and Bernice Agnes (Webb) McCabe; m. Ann Louise Smith; children: Robert James, Linda Carol. AA, Flint Jr. Coll., 1950-52; PhB, U. Detroit, 1954, MA, 1962; PhD, Mich. State U., 1986. Tchr. L'Anse Creuse Schs., Mt. Clemens, Mich., Mt. Morris (Mich.) Bd. Edn., 1959-61; tchr. reading Flint Bd. Edn., 1962-74; research dir. AVKO Ednl. Research Found., Birch Run, Mich., 1974—, pres., 1974-76; advisor Decade of Progress com. Mich. Dept. Edn., 1980. Author: Reading Via Typing, 1980; (series) Sequential Spelling I-V, 1982; (dictionary) Word Families Plus, 1984; For Adults Only, 1986; contbr. numerous articles to profl. jours. Served as sgt. U.S. Army, 1954-57. Recipient Mary Scott award AVKO Ednl. Research Found. Inc., 1982. Mem. Internat. Reading Assn., Correctional Edn. Assn., Coalition of Literacy, Orton Dyslexia Soc. Roman Catholic. Clubs: Clio (Mich.) Golf; Flint Duplicate Bridge. Lodges: Rotary, Lions. Home: Box 83 Birch Run MI 48415 Office: AVKO Ednl Research Found Inc 3084 W Willard Rd Birch Run MI 48415

MCCABE, MICHAEL JAMES, art director; b. DeKalb, Ill., Apr. 2, 1954; s. Thomas Andrew and Mary Jean (Conlin) McC.; m. Nancy Jean McIlrath, Dec. 24, 1976; 1 child, Erin Mary. AA, Kishwaukee Community Coll., 1974; BA, Ill. State U., Normal, 1976, postgrad., 1976. Graphic designer Ad Pro, Sycamore, Ill., 1977-79; art dir. Ad Creation, DeKalb; art dir. Bader Rutter & Assocs., Brookfield, Wis., 1982-86, assoc. creative dir., 1986—; Freelance photographer Click Photography, Chgo., 1986—. Recipient numerous awards Nat. Agri-Mktg. Assn., 1980-85; Bell award Bus. Profl. Advt. Assn., Milw., 1985, 86, Cert. of Excellence award Print Mag., N.Y.C., 1986. Mem. Illustrators and Designers Club of Milw. Roman Catholic. Avocations: photography, boating, water skiing. Office: Bader Rutter & Assocs 13555 Bishops Ct Brookfield WI 53005

MCCAFFERTY, D. J., real estate sales professional; b. Detroit, Jan. 27, 1937; s. Eugene Francis and Mary Henrietta (LaChapelle) McC.; m. Marilyn Gladys Franklin, June 27, 1959; children: David Charles, Brian William. B Philosophy, U. Detroit, 1959, B in Bus. Adminstrn., 1965. CPA. Ptnr. McCafferty & Hogan CPAs, Mt. Clemens, Mich., 1964-83; registered rep. Concord Assets Securities, Detroit, 1983—; bd. dirs. First Macomb Bank, First Macomb Mortgage Co. Trustee Macomb Community Coll., Warren, Mich., 1982—, St. Joseph Hosp., Mt. Clmens, 1985—. Mem. Mich. Assn. CPAs, Am. Inst. CPAs. Republican. Roman Catholic. Lodge: Kiwanis. Avocations: reading, golf, bowling, walking. Home: 24698 Chancel Mount Clemens MI 48043 Office: Concord Assets Securities Inc 100 Renaissance Ctr Suite 2701 Detroit MI 48243

MCCAFFERTY, JOHN MARTIN, real estate executive; b. Detroit, May 28, 1956. AA, Northwestern Mich. Coll., 1976; BS with honors, No. Mich. U., 1978; BSBA with honors, U. Denver, 1982. Staff acct. Patrick J. McCafferty & Co. CPA's, Traverse City, Mich., 1978-81; investment analyst Beaumont Investment Co., Traverse City, 1982-84; v.p. Beaumont/McCafferty Devel. Group, Traverse City, 1984—; pres. McCafferty Realty Services Group, Traverse City, 1985—; v.p. McCafferty Real Estate Group, Traverse City, 1985—; pres. John Martin Homes, Ltd., Traverse City, 1987—. Bd. dirs. Traverse Hills Cooperative Assn. Inc., Traverse City, 1986—. Kenneth M. Good scholar Opportunity Found., 1982. Mem. Nat. Assn. Realtors, Community Assns. Inst., Mich. Assn. Realtors, Traverse City Bd. Realtors. Republican. Roman Catholic. Avocations: weight training, skiing, boating. Home: 650 S Airport Traverse City MI 49684 Office: PO Box 1427 Traverse City MI 49685-1427

MCCAFFERTY, OWEN EDWARD, accountant, veterinary practice consultant; b. Cleve., Sept. 5, 1952; s. Owen James and Ann Theresa (Barrett) McC.; m. Colleen Maura Mullen, Aug. 3, 1974; children: Owen Michael, Hugh Anthony, Maura Kathleen, Bridget Colleen. AB, Xavier U., 1974. CPA, Ohio. Mem. staff to sr. accountant Deloitte, Haskins, & Sells, Cleve., 1974-78; ptnr., pres. Douglas, McCafferty & Co., Inc., Rocky River, Ohio, 1978-86; pres. Owen E. McCafferty, CPA, Rocky River, 1986—; lectr. various vet. assns.; cons. in field. Editorial adv. to Vet. Econs. Mag.; contbr. articles to acctg. and veterinary jours. Recipient Meritorious Service award Ohio Vet. Med. Assn., 1986. Mem. Am. Inst. CPA's, Ohio Soc. CPA's, Vet. Hosp. Mgrs. Assn. Democrat. Roman Catholic. Office: 20545 Center Ridge Rd Rocky River OH 44145

MCCALL, JOHN THOMAS, home furnishing representative; b. Kansas City, Mo., Jan. 3, 1932; s. Jim John and Ruth Mae (Clark) McC.; m. Marilyn Marie Rigby, Feb. 14, 1958; children—Juliane Marie, Cheryl Ann, John Justin. B.B.A. in Mktg., North Tex. State Coll., 1957. With Foleys' Dept. Store div. Federated Dept. Stores, Houston, 1957-65, buyer, 1960-65; with Westwood Lighting, 1965-84, regional sales mgr. Midwest and Can., 1972-76, sr. regional sales mgr., 1976-80, nat. dir. sales shades and accessories div., 1980-81, regional sales mgr. Midwest, 1981-83, decorative accessories sales rep. for Wis. and Ill., Glen Ellyn, Ill., 1983-84, Bloomingdale, Ill., 1983-87; salesperson Baskin Hartmarx Co., in Meros Furnishings & Sportswear; ind. home furnishings rep., Wis., Ill., Mo., Minn., 1984—; salesman Baskin subs. Hartmarx Co., 1986— . Mem. nat. adv. bd. Am. Security Council; vol. Markland Children Home and Resale Shop, 1986-87; mem. Republican Nat. Com. Served with USN, 1951-54; Korea. Mem. Am. Mgmt. Assn., Internat. Entrepreneurs Assn., Mail Order Bus. Bd., Ill. Conf. Police (assoc.), Ill. Sheriffs Assn., U.S. Senatorial Club, Am. Revenue Assn., Am. Philatelic Assn. Club: Aloha Vacations. Home and Office: 259 Sutton Ct Bloomingdale IL 60108

MC CALL, JULIEN LACHICOTTE, banker; b. Florence, S.C., Apr. 1, 1921; s. Arthur M. and Julia (Lachicotte) McC.; m. Janet Jones, Sept. 30, 1950; children: Melissa, Alison Gregg, Julien Lachicotte Jr. BS, Davidson Coll., 1942, LLD (hon.), 1983; MBA, Harvard U., 1947. With First Nat. City Bank, N.Y.C., 1948-71, asst. mgr. bond dept., 1952-53, asst. cashier, 1953-55, asst. v.p., 1955-57, v.p., 1957-71; 1st v.p. Nat. City Bank, Cleve., 1971-72, pres., 1972-79, chmn., 1979-85, chief exec. officer from 1979, also bd. dirs.; chmn. Nat. City Corp., 1980-86, chief exec. officer, 1980-86, pres., 1983-86, also bd. dirs., cons.; bd. dirs. Acme Steel Co., Brush Wellman, Inc., Russell Burdsall & Ward Corp.; mem. fed. adv. council Fed. Res. Bd., 1984—. Trustee St. Luke's Hosp., United Way Services, Boy Scouts Am., Playhouse Sq. Found., Cleve. Mus. Natural History, Case Western Res. U., No. Ohio Opera Assn., Mus. Arts Assn. Served with AUS, 1942-46, Africa, ETO. Episcopalian. Clubs: Union, Pepper Pike, Chagrin Valley Hunt, Kirtland Country (Cleve.); Rolling Rock (Ligonier, Pa.). Home: Arrowhead County Line Rd Hunting Valley OH 44022 Office: 623 Euclid Ave Cleveland OH 44114

MCCALL, WILLIAM KENT, purchasing executive; b. North Kansas City, Mo., Apr. 1, 1940; s. William and Lucille Mae (Croley) McC.; married, 1964; 1 child, Sean Gaurtland. BS in Bus. Adminstrn., U. Kans., 1962, MS in Acctg., 1963. CPA, Kans. Staff acct. various firms, Kansas City, Mo., 1963-66; budget mgr. Kansas City Star Co., Kansas City, Mo., 1966-70, dir. purchasing, 1970—. Pres. Liberty (Mo.) Civic Theatre, 1973-79; bd. dirs. Theatre for Young Am., Overland Park, Kans., 1978—, Starlight Theatre, Kansas City, 1980-83; chmn. bd. dirs. St. Pius X High Sch., Kansas City, 1983-84; mem. North Kansas City Park Bd. Mem. Am. Inst. CPA's, Nat. Assn. Accts. (pres. Kansas City chpt. 1980-81), Newspaper Purchasing Mgmt. Assn. (v.p. 1987—). Republican. Episcopalian. Avocations: bridge, travel. Home: 823 E 21 Ave North Kansas City MO 64116 Office: The Kansas City Star Co 1729 Grand Kansas City MO 64108

MC CALLUM, CHARLES EDWARD, lawyer; b. Memphis, Mar. 13, 1939; s. Edward Payson and India Raimelle (Musick) McC.; m. Lois Ann Gowell Temple, Nov. 30, 1985; children—Florence Andrea, Printha Kyle, Chandler Ward Payson. B.S., MIT, 1960; J.D., Vanderbilt U., 1964. Bar: Mich. 1964. Assoc. Warner, Norcross & Judd, Grand Rapids, Mich., 1964-69, ptnr., 1969—; rep. assemblyman State Bar Mich., 1973-78; lectr. continuing legal edn. programs. Chmn. Grand Rapids Area Transit Authority, 1976-79, mem., 1972-79; regional v.p. Nat. Mcpl. League, 1978-86, mem. council, 1971-78; pres. Grand Rapids Art Mus., 1979-81, trustee, 1976-83; chmn. Butterworth Hosp., 1979—, trustee, 1977—; vice chmn. Citizens Com. for Consolidation of Govt. Services, 1981-82, chmn., 1984-86, ednl. counselor MIT, 1974—; nat. chmn. devel. com. Vanderbilt U. Law Sch., 1977-78; trustee Kent Med. Found., 1979-82; dir. Vol. Trustees of Not-for-Profit Hosps., 1983—, vice chmn., 1986—. Woodrow Wilson fellow, 1960-61; Fulbright scholar U. Manchester, Eng., 1960-61. Mem. ABA, Tenn. Bar Assn., Mich. Bar Assn. (sec., council mem., corp., fin. and bus. law sect.), Grand Rapids Bar Assn., Grand Rapids C. of C. (pres. 1975, dir. 1970-76), Order of Coif, Sigma Xi. Clubs: Kent Country, Grand Rapids Athletic, Peninsular, University. Home: 1346 Cornell Ave SE Grand Rapids MI 49506 Office: 900 Old Kent Bldg 1 Vandenberg Center Grand Rapids MI 49503

MCCALLUM, JAMES SCOTT, lieutenant governor, former state senator; b. Fond du Lac, Wis., May 2, 1950; s. George Duncan and Marilyn Joy (Libke) McC.; m. Laurie Ann Riach, June 19, 1979; children: Zachary Scott, Rory Duncan. BA, Macalester Coll., 1972; MA, Johns Hopkins U., 1974. Mem. Wis. State Senate, Madison, 1977-87; lt. gov. State of Wis., Madison, 1987—. Chmn. Fond du Lac County Reps., 1974-76; mem. resolutions com. Wis. State Rep. Conv., 1977. Named one of Outstanding Young Men Am., Jaycees, 1976; recipient Presdl. award Honor, Jaycees, 1976. Home: 165 E 6th St Fond du Lac WI 54935 Office: State of Wis 22 E State Capitol Madison WI 53715

MCCAN, TIMOTHY ALLAN, optometrist; b. Plymouth, Ind., Mar. 10, 1957; s. Larry Don and Barbara Della (Davidson) McC.; m. Janna Lynn Courtney, Feb. 11, 1984. DO, Ind. U., 1983. Gen. practice optometry Noblesville, Ind., 1983—. Mem. Am. Optometric Assn., Ind. Optometric Assn. Lodge: Kiwanis (sec. Noblesville 1985—).

MCCANSE, JAMES EDSON, manufacturing company executive; b. La Grande, Oreg., July 2, 1929; s. Edson Rodney and Lydia Bertha (Sailer) McC.; m. Lillian May Griffin, Sept. 11, 1947; children: Sandra Joanne, James Rodney, Donald Edson, Richard Lee, Bruce Dean. BS in Agrl. Engring., Oreg. State Coll., 1951, MA in Agrl. Engring, Soils and Agrl. Econs., 1963. Mgr. plant Simplot Soilbuilders, Garfield, Wash., 1954-55; mgr. fertility dept. Columbia Farm Supplies, Walla Walla, Wash., 1955-57; design engr. John Deere Indsl. Works, Moline, Ill., 1957-62; chief engr. Woods-Div. Hesston, Oregon, Ill., 1962-83, dir. safety, reliability and service, 1983-87. Patentee in field. Alderman Moline City Council, 1960-62. Mem. Am. Soc. Agrl. Engrs. (mem. safety commn., 1982—, Recognitian award 1971, 79), Soc. Automotive Engrs. (mem. safety commn. 1984—), Farm, Indsl. Equipment Inst. (chmn. mower council 1982-86), Outdoor Power Equipment Inst. (mem. tech. adv. com. 1985—), Aircraft Owners and Pilots Assn.. Republican. Mem. Reorganized Ch. Jesus Christ of Latter-day Saints. Avocations: flying, fishing, skiing, do-it-yourself projects. Home: 949 Etnyre Terrace Rd Oregon IL 61061 Office: McCanse Engring Services 949 Etnyre Terrace Rd Oregon IL 61061

MCCANTS, DAVID ARNOLD, communication educator; b. Dinwiddie County, Va., June 2, 1937; s. George Morris and Alma Louise (Skinner) McC.; m. Barbara Louise Short, Sept. 17, 1960; children: David Mark, Ellen Ashley, Matthew Reid. BA, U. Richmond, 1958; MA, Northwestern U., 1959, PhD, 1964. Instr. Amherst (Mass.) Coll., 1962-65; asst. prof. U. Ky., Lexington, 1965-68; assoc. prof. Ind. U. and Purdue U., Ft. Wayne, 1968-81, chmn. dept. of communication and theatre, 1970—, prof. communication, 1981—. Contbr. articles to profl. jours. Bd. dirs. Civic Theatre, 1980-87, pres. bd. dirs. 1985-87. Fellow Northwestern U., 1958, Danforth Found., 1958-62. Mem. Speech Communication Assn., Cen. States Speech Assn., AAUP, Religious Speech Communication Assn. (pres. 1978-79), Phi Beta Kappa, Omicron Delta Kappa, Delta Sigma Rho-Tau Kappa. Democrat. Presbyterian. Home: 5110 Exeter Dr Fort Wayne IN 46815 Office: Dept Communication and Theatre 2101 Coliseum Blvd E Fort Wayne IN 46805

MCCARROLL, CONNIE JO, osteopath, pediatrician; b. Dayton, Ohio, May 18, 1946; d. Laurence Strother and Thelma Geneva (Wysong) McC. BS, Wright State U., Dayton, 1968, MS, 1970; DO, Mich. State U., East Lansing, 1976. Intern Grandview Hosp., Dayton, Ohio, 1976-77, resident, 1981-83; chemist Monarch Marking, Dayton, 1970-73; practice medicine specializing in pediatrics Dayton, 1983—; physician advisor Headstart Program, Montgomery County, Ohio, 1984—. Contbr. articles to profl. jour. Pres. Dayton Osteopathic Polit. Action Com., 1985-86; maj. Ohio Air N.G., 1984—; served to capt. USAF, 1977-80. Named one of Outstanding Young Women Am., 1980. Mem. AAUW, Am. Osteopathic Assn., Am. Coll. Osteopathic Pediatricians, Ohio Osteopathic Assn. Republican. Episcopalian. Avocations: karate, collecting Wizard of Oz memorabilia. Office: 216 Neal Ave Dayton OH 45405

MC CARTER, JOHN WILBUR, JR., corporation executive; b. Oak Park, Ill., Mar. 2, 1938; s. John Wilbur and Ruth Rebecca McC.; m. Judith Field West, May 1, 1965; children: James Philip, Jeffrey John, Katherine Field. A.B., Princeton U., 1960; postgrad., London Sch. Econs., 1961; M.B.A., Harvard U., 1963. Cons., assoc., v.p. Booz Allen and Hamilton, Inc., Chgo., 1963-69; White House fellow Washington, 1966-67; dir. Bur. Budget and Dept. Fin., State of Ill., Springfield, 1969-73; v.p. DeKalb AgResearch, Ill., 1973-78, dir., 1975—, exec. v.p., 1978-80, pres., 1981-82; pres., chief exec. officer DeKalb-Pfizer Genetics, 1982-86, chmn., 1986; pres. DeKalb Corp., 1985-86; v.p. Booz Allen & Hamilton Inc., 1987—; dir. A.M. Castle & Co. Trustee Chgo. Public Television, 1973— , Princeton U., 1983-87 . Office: Booz Allen & Hamilton Inc 2900 Three 1st Nat Plaza Chicago IL 60602

MCCARTHY, DANIEL JOSEPH, surgeon; b. Chgo., Aug. 23, 1930; s. Daniel Joseph and Anna (Phillips) McC.; m. Bonita Brazis, Aug. 3, 1968; children: Danielle, Daniel, Declan, David, Deanna. BS, U. Ill., Chgo., 1952, MD, 1955. Diplomate Am. Bd. Abdominal Surgery. Intern U. Ill. Research and Edn. Hosp., 1955-56; resident West VA Hosp., 1960-64; surgeon Holy Cross Hosp., Chgo., 1964—, Mercy Hosp., Chgo., 1964—, Palos Hosp., Palos Heights, Ill., 1972—; asst. dir. health services U. Ill., Chgo., 1964-71; med. dir. Gen. Foods, Chgo., 1971—, Kool Air Chgo., 1971—. Contbr. articles to sport medicine ency. Served to lt. comdr., USNR. Fellow ACS; mem. AMA, Am. Coll. Sport Medicine, Ill. State Med. Assn., Chgo. Me. Services. Roman Catholic. Office: 10404 S Roberts Rd Palos Hills IL 60465

MC CARTHY, DONALD WANS, utility company executive; b. Mpls., Feb. 11, 1922; s. Donald and Carolyn (Beach) McC.; m. Anne Leslie, Jan. 2, 1947; children: Donald, Peter, Thomas, Jill. B.S., U.S. Naval Acad., 1943. Commd. ensign U.S. Navy, 1943, advanced through grades to lt.; active duty, 1943-48, 51-53; v.p., mgr. Mpls. div. No. States Power Co., Mpls., 1969-70, v.p. div. ops., 1970-72, v.p. and regional mgr., 1972-73, exec. v.p., 1973-75, pres., chief ops. officer, 1976, pres., chief exec. officer, dir., 1976-78, chmn., pres., chief exec. officer, 1978-80, 83-84, 86-87, chmn., chief exec. officer, 1980-83, 85-86, chmn., 1987—; dir. Norwest Bank, Mpls., Norwest Corp., Northwestern Nat. Life Ins. Decorated Bronze Star. Mem. Mpls. Engrs. Club. Clubs: Mpls, Woodhill Country, Minn. Address: No States Power Co (Minn) 414 Nicollet Mall Minneapolis MN 55401

MCCARTHY, GERALD DUANE, military officer, educator; b. Alton, Iowa, May 9, 1931; s. Gerald William and Edna (Kokenge) McC.; m. Mary

Ann Manley, June 15, 1957; children: Craig, Bradley, Mark. BS, U.S. Naval Acad., 1954; MS, George Washington U., 1967; grad., Naval War Coll., 1967, Nat. War Coll., 1973. Commd. ensign USN, 1954, advanced through ranks to capt.; commanding officer USS Tusk USN, New London, Conn., 1967-69; mem. staff Office of Chief of Naval Ops. USN, Washington, 1969-72; prof. naval sci. Purdue U., West Lafayette, Ind., 1975-78; ret. USN, 1978; assoc. prof. Purdue U., 1980—. Mem. U.S. Naval Acad. Alumni Assn.(liaison officer 1980—). Lodge: Rotary. Home: 443 Lourdes Ln Lafayette IN 47905 Office: Purdue U Sch Tech Knoy Hall West Lafayette IN 47907

MCCARTHY, JAMES BRYAN, management consultant; b. Evergreen Park, Ill., May 26, 1951; s. Martin Joseph and Margaret (McNeill) McC.; m. Cheryl Sleepeck McCarthy, June 3, 1978; children—James Bryan Jr., William M., Kelly Ann. B.A., U. Notre Dame, 1973; M.B.A., Keller Grad. Sch. Mgmt., Chgo., 1977; J.D., Loyola U., Chgo., 1983. Planning analyst 3M Co. Med. Products div., Hinsdale, Ill., 1973-78; asst. to pres. The Cameron Group, Addison, Ill., 1978-81; assoc. Heidrick & Struggles, Inc., Chgo., 1981-83; v.p., gen. mgr. Ferris Med. Systems, Inc., Burr Ridge, Ill., 1983-85; v.p. Paul R. Ray and Co., Inc., 1985—. Bd. dirs. United Way Hinsdale/Oak Brook, 1983—, pres., 1985-86; mem. adv. council Keller Grad. Sch. Mgmt., 1983—; mem. bd. assocs. Rush-Presbyn.-St. Luke's Med. Ctr. Mem. Assn. M.B.A. Execs., Assn. Advancement Med. Instrumentation (govt. relations com.), Chgo. Council Fgn. Relations, Chgo. High Tech. Assn. Club: Mid America (Chgo.). Home: 418 S Park Ave Hinsdale IL 60521 Office: Paul R Ray and Co Inc 200 S Wacker Dr Suite 3820 Chicago IL 60606

MC CARTHY, JEAN JEROME, physical education educator; b. St. Paul, Sept. 11, 1929; s. Joseph Justin and Florence (Quirin) McC.; m. Norma Louise Shermer, July 30, 1955; children: Patrick J., Anne L., Kevin M. BS, U. Minn., 1956, PhD, 1986; MS, Wash. State U., 1958. Teaching asst. U. Minn., 1957-59, adminstrv. asst., 1959-60; asst. prof. phys. edn. U. South Fla., 1960-62; asst. prof. phys. edn. Mankato State U., 1962-71, assoc. prof., 1971-86, prof. 1986—, baseball coach, 1962-77; cons. AAU. Mem. Minn. Gov.'s Phys. Fitness Adv. Com. Served with USAF, 1950-54. Named Region 2 Coach of Yr., NCAA, 1971, Outstanding Educators Am., 1970; U. Minn. Grad. Sch. fellow, 1959-60; Lilly Found. scholar, 1974—; Research Consortium fellow. Mem. AAHPER, Minn. Assn. Health, Phys. Edn. Recreation and Dance, Phi Delta Kappa, Phi Epsilon Kappa (scholarship award 1972). Roman Catholic.

MCCARTHY, MARY CATHERINE, surgeon; b. Oakland, Calif., Dec. 24, 1951; d. William Grover and Susan (Gans) McC.; m. Charles Bales, July 4, 1983. BS, Stanford U., 1973; MD, Ind. U., Indpls., 1977. Asst. prof. surgery Ind. U. Sch. Medicine, Indpls., 1983—; med. dir. surg. ICU Wishard Meml. U., Indpls., 1983—, coordinator surg. emergency med. service, 1983—, mem. nutritional support com., 1983—. Contbr. articles to profl. jours. Mem. AMA (Physician Recognition award 1981), ACS, Assn. Acad. Surgery, Univ. Assn. Emergency Medicine, Am. Soc. Parenteral and Enteral Nutrition, Marion County Med. Soc., Alpha Omega Alpha. Democrat. Roman Catholic. Office: Ind U Sch Medicine Dept Surgery 1001 W 10th St Indianapolis IN 46202

MCCARTHY, RAYMOND MALCOLM, finance company executive; b. Chgo., Feb. 27, 1927; s. Raymond Jerome and Margaret V. (Deady) McC.; m. Mary C. Burns, Oct. 27, 1948; children: Raymond J., John T., Sheila M., Michael J., Timothy P., Kevin P., Kathleen M., Anne T. BBA, Loyola U., Chgo., 1950; AMP, Harvard U., 1980. With Gen. Motors Acceptance Corp., N.Y.C., 1949—; exec. v.p. ops. Gen. Motors Acceptance Corp., 1980-85; pres. Gen. Motors Acceptance Corp., Detroit, 1986—, also dir. Served with USMC, 1944-46. Club: Harvard (N.Y.C.). Office: Gen Motors Acceptance Corp 3044 W Grand Blvd Detroit MI 48202

MC CARTHY, WALTER JOHN, JR., utility executive; b. N.Y.C., Apr. 20, 1925; s. Walter John and Irene (Trumbl) McC.; m. Alice Anna Ross, Sept. 3, 1947; children: Walter, David, Sharon, James, William. B.M.E., Cornell U., 1949; grad., Oak Ridge Sch. Reactor Tech., 1952; D.Eng. (hon.), Lawrence Inst. Tech., 1981; D.Sc. (hon.), Eastern Mich. U., 1983; LHD, Wayne State U., 1984; LLD, Alma (Mich.) Coll., 1985. Engr. Public Service Electric & Gas Co., Newark, 1949-56; sect. head Atomic Power Devel. Assos., Detroit, 1956-61; gen. mgr. Power Reactor Devel. Co., Detroit, 1961-68; with Detroit Edison Co., 1968—, exec. v.p. ops., 1975-77, exec. v.p. divs., 1977-79, pres., chief operating officer, 1979-81, chmn., chief exec. officer, 1981—, also dir.; dir. Perry Drug Stores Inc., Comerica, Inc., Fed. Mogul Corp. Author papers in field. Trustee Edison Inst., Cranbrook Ednl. Community, New Detroit, Harper-Grace Hosps., Interlochen Ctr. for Arts, Rackham Engring. Found.; chmn. Detroit United Fund; bd. dirs. Detroit, Econ. Alliance for Mich., Detroit Renaissance, Detroit Econ. Growth Corp., Inst. Nuclear Power Ops., Atomic Indsl. Forum; bd. dirs., chmn. Detroit Symphony Orch.; co-chmn. NCCJ. Fellow Am. Nuclear Soc., Engring. Soc. Detroit; mem. ASME, Nat. Acad. Engring. Methodist. Clubs: Detroit, Renaissance (Detroit). Office: 2000 2d Ave Detroit MI 48226

MCCARTHY, WILLIAM EDWARD, marketing professional; b. Bridgeport, Conn., Apr. 6, 1952; s. William Ralph and Ann Ellen (Shugrue) McC. BS in Acctg., Lehigh U., 1974; MBA in Mktg., U. Va., 1979. CPA. Sr. acct. Price Waterhouse & Co., N.Y.C., 1974-77; sr. bus. planner Pepsi-Cola Co., Purchase, N.Y., 1979-82; dir. corp. devel. Triangle Industries, New Brunswick, N.J., 1982-83; mgr. mktg. services McGladrey, Hendrickson & Pullen, Mpls., 1983—. Vol. Adventure Club, Mpls., 1985, New Life Homes and Family Services, Mpls., 1986. Mem. Am. Mktg. Assn. Republican. Avocations: vol. work, piano, writing. Office: McGladrey Hendrickson & Pullen 1300 Midwest Plaza E Minneapolis MN 55402

MCCARTHY, WILLIAM ROBERT, clergyman; b. Tacoma, Wash., Nov. 17, 1941; s. Denward Sylvester and Florence Elizabeth (Lohan) McC.; m. Bernice Bigler, Apr. 22, 1962; children: Brian Edward Earl, Sean David. BS, Oreg. State U., 1966; MDiv, Nashotah House, 1975. Ordained deacon Episcopal Ch., 1975, priest, 1975. Curate St. Michael's Ch., Barrington, Ill., 1975-77; vicar St. Anselm's Ch., Park Ridge, Ill., 1977-81; rector Christ Ch. Parish, Waukegan, Ill., 1981—; diocesan cursillo officer Diocese Chgo., 1977-85; spiritual dir. Ecumenical Cursillo Community, Chgo., 1977-83; mem. steering com. Happenings in Christianity, Chgo., 1978-80; chmn. Bishop's Adv. Commn. on Renewal and Evangelism, Chgo., 1983-85. Contbr. articles to profl. jours. Bd. mem. Waukegan Area Crime Stoppers, 1982-85; charter bd. dirs. Waukegan Downtown Assn., 1983—, v.p., 1986-87, pres., 1987—; founder, exec. dir. Share/Food Waukegan Area, 1985—; bd. dirs. YMCA of Lake County, 1985—. Served with USNR, 1962-65. Mem. Waukegan Downtown Ministries (coordinator 1983-85), Acad. Parish Clergy (assoc.), Assn. for Psychol. Type, Internat. Platform Assn., Phi Sigma Kappa. Club: Exchange. Lodge: Masons. Office: Christ Ch Parish 410 Grand Ave Waukegan IL 60085

MCCARTNEY, MICHAEL JERRY, lawyer; b. Antigo, Wis., Feb. 14, 1949; s. Clayton Fred and Joyce (Tesch) McC.; m. Mary Jean Exner, Oct. 3, 1969; children—Molly, Thomas, Maureen. Student U. of N.D., 1967-70; B.B.A., Troy State U., 1974; J.D., South Tex. Coll. Law., 1976. Bar: Tex. 1976, Minn. 1977, U.S. Dist. Ct. Minn. 1978. Title analyst Tenneco Oil Co., Houston, 1976-77; sole practice, Breckenridge, Minn., 1977—. Appeared in Community Theatre play The Night of January 16th, 1980. Pres., head Red United Way, Breckenridge-Wahpeton, 1981; pres. St. Mary's Ch. Council, Breckenridge, 1981-82, Richland-Wilkin Alphaen Male Chorus, Breckenridge, 1983-84; mem. adv. com. Lake Aggasiz chpt. Compasionate Friends, Breckenridge, 1983—; chmn. Wilkin County Group Home, Inc., Breckenridge, 1984-85. Served with U.S. Army, 1971-73. Mem. ABA, Am. Acad. Hosp. Attys., Minn. Soc. Hosp. Attys., Minn. Sch. Bds. Assn. Council Sch. Attys. Club: Bois de Sioux Golf (pres. 1984), Toastmaster's (pres. 1981). Lodge: Lions (pres. 1981). Home: 809 N Fifth St Circle Breckenridge MN 56520 Office: 110 N Sixth St Breckenridge MN 56520

MC CARTNEY, RALPH FARNHAM, lawyer, district judge; b. Charles City, Iowa, Dec. 11, 1924; s. Ralph C. and Helen (Farnham) McC.; J.D., U. Mich., 1950; B. Sci., Iowa State U., 1972; m. Rhoda Mae Huxsol, June 30, 1950; children—Ralph, Julia, David. Bar: Iowa 1950. Mem. firm Miller, Heuber & Miller, Des Moines, 1950-52, Frye & McCartney, Charles City, 1952-73, McCartney & Erb, Charles City, 1973-78; judge Dist. Ct. Iowa, Charles City, 1978—; mem. jud. coordinating com. Iowa Supreme Ct. Chmn., Iowa Republican Conv., 1972, 74; chmn. Supreme Ct. Adv. Com. on Adminstrn. of Clks. Offices; mem. Iowa Ho. of Reps., 1967-70, majority floor leader, 1969-70; mem. Iowa Senate, 1973-74. Bd. regents U. Iowa, Iowa State U., U. No. Iowa, Iowa Sch. for Deaf, Iowa Braille and Sight Saving Sch. Served with AUS, 1942-45. Mem. Am., Iowa bar assns., Iowa Judges Assn. Home: RFD 1 Charles City IA 50616 Office: Ct Chambers Courthouse Charles City IA 50616

MCCARTY, JOSEPH CHARLES, manufacturing company executive; b. Detroit, June 25, 1942; s. James Leo and Jean Katherine (Meyer) McC.; m. Kathleen Marie Baszuk, May 4, 1968; children: Mary Ann, Joseph Charles Jr. BS, U. Notre Dame, 1964; MBA, U. Mich., 1966. CPA, Mich.; cert. cash mgr. Auditing staff Coopers & Lybrand, Detroit, 1966-74; div. controller Acme-Cleve. Corp., Cleve., 1974-79, corp. risk mgr., 1979-82, risk and cash mgr., 1982-86, asst. treas., 1986—. Served to 1st lt. U.S. Army, 1968-71. Recipient Disting. Grad. award Ins. Inst. Am., 1982. Mem. Am. Inst. CPA's, Risk and Ins. Mgmt. Soc. (chpt. bd. dirs. 1983, chpt. sec. 1986, chpt. v.p. 1986-87, chpt. pres. 1987—, Jim Cristy award 1982), Mich. Assn. CPA's, Cleve. Treas. Club. Republican. Roman Catholic. Avocations: chess, sports, reading. Office: Acme-Cleve Corp 30195 Chagrin Blvd #300 Cleveland OH 44124

MC CARTY, THEODORE MILSON, musical instrument manufacturing company executive; b. Somerset, Ky., Oct. 10, 1909; s. Raymond Andrew and Jennie (Milson) McC.; m. Elinor H. Bauer, June 14, 1935; children: Theodore F., Susan McCarty Davis. Comml. Engr., U. Cin., 1933, post-grad., 1934-35. Asst. store mgr. Wurlitzer Co., Rochester, N.Y., 1936-38; mgr. real estate div. Cin. and Chgo. Wurlitzer Co., 1939-41; dir. procurement Wurlitzer Co., DeKalb, Ill., 1942-44; mdse. mgr. retail div. Wurlitzer Co., Chgo., 1945-48; pres., gen. mgr., dir. Gibson Inc., 1948-66; owner, pres., treas., dir. Bigsby Accessories Inc., Kalamazoo, 1966—; owner, pres., dir. Flex-Lite, Inc.; v.p., dir. Command Electronics, Kalamazoo. Patentee in music field. Bd. dirs. Glowing Embers council Girl Scouts U.S., 1968-74. Mem. Am. Music Conf. (pres., adminstr. 1961-63, 70-77, dir. 1956—, hon. life dir.), Guitar and Accessory Mfrs. Assn. (past pres., hon. life dir.), Kalamazoo Symphony Soc. (past pres.), S.A.R. (charter mem.), Alpha Kappa Psi, Alpha Tau Omega, Omicron Delta Kappa. Presbyterian. Clubs: Masons, Rotary (past pres.), Kalamazoo Country (past pres.), Park. Home: 1028 Essex Circle Bronson Woods Kalamazoo MI 49008 Winter Address: Menehune Shores 760 S Kihei Rd Apt 609 Kihei Maui HI 96753 Office: Bigsby Accessories Inc 3521 E Kilgore Rd Kalamazoo MI 49001

MCCARTY, THOMAS LEE, insurance broker; b. Vandalia, Ill., Dec. 13, 1957; s. Jimmy Lee and P. Joann (Tackett) McC.; m. Marcie Ann Schmitt, June 2, 1978. Student, Kaskaskia Coll., 1977-78. Ins. adjuster Rogers Adjustment, Vandalia, Ill., 1978-80; ins. broker Boles Ins. Agy., St. Elmo, Ill., 1979-81; ptnr., broker Boles Ins. Agy., St. Elmo, 1981-83; sec.-treas. McKellar, Robertson & McCarty Ins. Ltd., Vandalia, 1983—; co-instr. Ins. Inst. Am., Malvern, Pa., 1985. Bd. dirs. Fayette County United Fund, Vandalia, 1984-85. Mem. Independent Ins. Agts. Am., Independent Ins. Agts. Ill., Mid-Counties Agts. Assn. (sec.-treas. 1982, v.p. 1983, pres. 1984). Free Methodist. Avocations: golf, travel. Home: 1726 W St Clair St Vandalia IL 62471 Office: McKellar Robertson & McCarty Ins 106 S 5th PO Box 69 Vandalia IL 62471

MCCASKEY, EDWARD, professional sports team executive; b. Phila., Apr. 27; m. Virginia McCaskey; 11 children. Student, U. Pa., 1940. Mgr. merchandising Nat. Retail Tea an Coffee Assn., Chgo.; exec. v.p. Mchdse. Services, Inc., Chgo.; account exec. E.F. McDonald Co., Chgo.; v.p., treas. Chgo. Bears, 1967-83, chmn. bd. dirs., 1983—. Served to capt., AUS. Office: Chgo Bears 55 E Jackson (Suite 1200) Chicago IL 60604 *

MCCASKEY, MICHAEL, professional sports team executive; b. Des Plaines, Ill., Dec. 11, 1943; s. Edward B. and Virginia (Halas) McCaskey; m. Nancy McCaskey; 1 child, John. Grad., Yale U., 1965; PhD, Case Western Res. U. Tchr. UCLA, 1972-75, Harvard U. Sch. Bus., Cambridge, Mass., 1975-82; pres., chief exec. officer Chgo. Bears (NFL), 1983—. Author: The Executive Challenge: Managing Change and Ambiguity. Named Exec. of Yr. Sporting News, 1985. Office: Chgo Bears 55 E Jackson (Suite 1200) Chicago IL 60604 *

MCCASLAND, MIKE, aircraft engine company engineer; b. Big Spring, Tex., Dec. 15, 1944; s. Ardis and Fannie Douglas (Cain) McC.; m. Elise McCree, Dec. 27, 1966; 1 child, Erin Elizabeth. BS in Aerospace Engring., U. Tex., 1968; MBA, Xavier U., 1977. Component test engr. Gen. Electric Aircraft Engine Group, Cin., 1968-78, mgr. advanced tech. program, 1978-84, mgr. customer support, 1984—. Pres., bd. dirs. Afterschool Care Bd., Wyoming, Ohio, 1986-87. Served with U.S. Army, 1969-71. Republican. Methodist. Avocation: coaching youth soccer. Home: 50 Vermont Ave Wyoming OH 45215 Office: Gen Electric 111 Merchant St Rm 451 Cincinnati OH 45246

MCCASLIN, MICHAEL ERNEST, librarian; b. Lansing, Mich., Apr. 13, 1941; s. ERnest Benson and Ruth Pauline (Kennedy) McC. BA in English, Olivet Nazarene Coll., 1970; MLS, Western Mich. U., 1972. Library cons. DuPage LIbrary System, Geneva, Ill., 1972-85; dep. exec. dir. resources and tech. services div. ALA, Chgo., 1985-86; librarian Ill. State Library, Chgo., 1987—. Served with U.S. Army, 1963-65. Mem. Ill. Library Assn., Spl. Libraries Assn., Chgo. Library Club. Episcopalian. Home: 1255 W Belden Chicago IL 60614 Office: Ill State Library 100 W Randolph Chicago IL 60601

MCCASLIN, STANLEY J., computer science educator; b. Rochester, Minn., Mar. 21, 1947; s. Arol Clifton and Gale Anita (Madison) McC; m. Sharon Irene Gentry, May 20, 1972; children: Heather Lynn, Stephen Keith. BA in Physics, Macalester Coll., 1969; MS in Physics, Calif. Inst. Tech., Pasadena, 1971; MS in Computer Sci., U. Nebr., 1985. Cert. data processing, Nebr. Instr. data processing Peru State Coll., Nebr., 1971-85; dir. data processing Peru State Coll., 1971—, asst. prof. computer sci., 1985—; mem. exec. com. Peru State Coll. Faculty Assn. Treas. First Presbyn. Ch., Auburn, 1982-84, clk. of session, 1986—. NSF fellow, 1969-70. Assn. for Computing Machinery. Democrat. Presbyterian. Lodges: Elks, Kiwanis. Home: 908 5th St Peru NE 68421 Office: Peru State Coll Peru NE 68421

MCCAULEY, W. A., manufacturing company executive. Pres., chief operating officer Borror Corp., Columbus, Ohio. Office: Borror Corp 1225 Dublin Rd Columbus OH 43215 *

MCCAWLEY, JAMES DAVID, linguistics educator; b. Glasgow, Scotland, Mar. 30, 1938; s. James Quillan and Monica Maud (Bateman) McC.; m. Noriko Akatsuka, Dec. 16, 1971 (div. Aug. 1978). SM, U. Chgo., 1958; PhD, MIT, 1965. Asst. prof. linguistics U. Chgo., 1964-69, assoc. prof., 1969-70, prof., 1970—. Author: Adverbs, Vowels, and Other Objects of Wonder, 1979, Everything that Linguists have Always Wanted to Know about Logic, 1981, Thirty Million Theories of Grammar, 1983, The Eater's Guide to Chinese Characters, 1985. Mem. Linguistic Soc. Am., Soc. for Exact Philosophy, Am. Acad. Arts and Scis., Philosophy of Sci. Assn., Cognitive Sci. Assn. Libertarian. Avocations: playing piano, cooking. Home: 5329 S Dorchester Ave Chicago IL 60615 Office: Univ Chgo Dept Lenguistics 1010 E 59th St Chicago IL 60637

MCCHESNEY, KATHRYN MARIE (MRS. THOMAS DAVID MCCHESNEY), educator; b. Curwensville, Pa., Jan. 14, 1936; d. Orland William and Lillian Irene (Morrison) Spencer; B.A., U. Akron, 1962; M.L.S., Kent State U., 1965, postgrad., 1971-84; m. Thomas David McChesney, June 12, 1954; 1 son, Eric Spencer. Tchr. English, Springfield Local High Sch., Akron, Ohio, 1962-63, librarian, 1963-64, head librarian, 1965-68; asst. to dean, instr. Kent (Ohio) State U. Sch. Library Sci., 1968-69, asst. dean, 1969-77, asst. prof., 1969—. Rep. Uniontown Community Council, 1964-66. Mem. Am., Ohio (chmn. Library Edn. Roundtable 1971-72, exec. council Div. VI Library Edn. 1972-73) library assns., AAUP, Am., Ohio assns. sch. librarians, Beta Phi Mu, Phi Sigma Alpha, Phi Alpha Theta, Sigma Phi Epsilon. Club: Uniontown Jr. Womans (pres. 1965-66). Co-author: The Library in Society, 1984. Contbr. articles, book revs. to profl. periodicals. Home: 3611 Edison St NW Uniontown OH 44685 Office: Kent State U Kent OH 44242

MCCHESNEY, SAMUEL PARKER, III, real estate executive; b. Oakland, Calif., July 30, 1945; s. Samuel Parker and Edna Margaret (McCorkle) McC.; m. Vicki Storrie, June 21, 1969; children: Nathan, Amanda, Jed. BA, Washington and Lee U., 1967; JD, Case Western Res. U., 1970. Lic. real estate broker, Mo., Kans. Urban intern and multifamily housing rep. HUD, Chgo., 1970-71; project loan mgr. 1st Home Investment Corp., Overland Park, Kans., 1971-72; v.p. devel. Northland Bldg. Corp., Gladstone, Mo., 1973-74; cons. Urban Equities, Kansas City, Mo., 1975; pres., co-owner McChesney Devel. Co., Inc., Edwardsville, Kans., 1976-78; pres., owner McChesney, Inc., Kansas City, 1978—. Pres. Quivira (homeowners assn.), Inc., Lake Quivira, Kans., 1983-85; mem. planning and zoning com. Town of Lake Quivira, 1983, real estate com., 1986; mem. Johnson County Bd. Realtors; mem. patron's com. Tom Watson Golf Classic, Kansas City, 1984-85. Mem. Met. Kansas City Bd. Realtors, Kansas City C. of C. Club: Lake Quivira Country (pres. 1983-85). Avocations: golfing, travelling, reading, gardening. Home: 510 Hillcrest E Lake Quivira KS 66106 Office: 3210 Gillham Rd Kansas City MO 64109

MCCLAIN, CHARLES JAMES, university president; b. Ironton, Mo., Sept. 1, 1931; s. John F. and Hazel (Pierce) McC.; m. Norma Mae Gregory, Aug. 25, 1950; children: Anita, Melanie. B.S. in Edn, S.W. Mo. State Coll., 1954; M.Ed., U. Mo., 1957; Ed.D., U. Mo., 1961; hon. degree, Busan Nat. U. Pres. Jefferson Coll., Hillsboro, Mo., 1963-70, Northeast Mo. State U., Kirksville, 1970—. Contbr. articles to profl. jours. Mem. advisory bd. Mo. Hist. Records; trustee Blue Cross; mem. Mid-Mo. Health Consortium, NE Mo. Health and Welfare Council. Recipient Distinguished Alumnus award SW Mo. State U., 1977, Distinguished Service award U. Mo. Coll. Edn., G. Theodore Mitau award, 1985. Mem. Mo. Acad. Sci., Internat. Assn. Univ. Presidents, Phi Delta Kappa. Lodges: Mason; Rotary. Home: 706 Halliburton St Kirksville MO 63501 Office: NE Mo State Univ Office of the Pres Kirksville MO 63501-9980 *

MCCLANAHAN, BETTY COLLEEN, publishing company executive; b. Altoona, Iowa, Jan. 19, 1924; d. Ezra Guy and Minnie (Hersbergen) Plummer; m. Willard Dale McClanahan, Oct. 7, 1944; children—Bonnie Sue McClanahan Hosler, Nancy Jo McClanahan Miller, Sarah Jane McClanahan Valenti. Student Altoona, Iowa schs. With Denniston & Partridge Lumber Co., Altoona, 1942-46; farm bookkeeper, Bondurant, Iowa, 1944—; owner, mgr. Hiawatha Book Co., Bondurant, 1980—; mem. Farmers Elevator Co.; rep. Ramsey Meml. Home Guild, 1978-84; mem. steering com. Spiritual Frontiers Fellowship, Des Moines, 1978—. Adaptor psalms to music. Mem. Builders of the Adytum, Theosophical Soc., Assn. Research and Enlightenment, Huna Assoc. Mem. Ch. of the Brethren. Avocations: stamp collecting, astrology, I Ching, Tarot, esoteric philosophies, piano. Home: 420 SE Grant Ankeny IA 50021 Office: Hiawatha Book Co 7567 NE 102 Ave Bondurant IA 50035

MCCLARREN, RALPH GORDON, school principal; b. Abington, Pa., Feb. 3, 1937; s. Ralph Herbert and Marjorie Frankish (Robinson) McC.; m. Rachelle Nicholson, Jan. 5, 1963; children: Robin, Gordon Erik, Amy. BS, U.S. Naval Acad., 1960; MS in Applied Math., U. Ill., Chgo., 1973. Commd. ensign USN, 1961, advanced through grades to comdr., nuclear operator, 1961-69, ret., 1980; tchr. math. Midwestern Acad., Glenview, Ill., 1969—; prin. Immanuel Ch. Sch., Glenview, 1978—; cons. in microcomputers, Glenview, 1980—; tchr. Oakton Community Coll., Des Plaines, Ill., 1980-82. Bd. dirs. Glenview Little League. Mem. Nat. Assn. Biology Tchrs., Nat. Council Tchrs. Math. Republican. Avocations: microcomputers, photography. Home: 26 Park Dr Glenview IL 60025 Office: Midwestern Acad 74 Park Dr Glenview IL 60025

MCCLARY, STEPHEN ADAMS, accountant; b. Los Alamos, N.Mex., Sept. 30, 1960; s. John Adams and Delores Julian (O'Donnell) McC.; m. Anne Joyce Bronson, Sept. 24, 1983. BS, U. Ill., 1982. Staff auditor Touche Ross & Co., Chgo., 1982-84, sr. auditor, 1984-86, audit supr., 1986—. Mem. Am. Inst. CPA's, Ill. Inst. CPA's. Club: Exec. Breakfast of Oak Brook, Ill. Avocations: tennis, golf, backpacking, philately.

MCCLEESE, HOWARD DEAN, dentist; b. Portsmouth, Ohio, Dec. 5, 1948; s. Herman Jr. and Minnie Marie (Yeley) McC.; m. Laberta Sue Curtiss, Oct. 23, 1970; children: Howard Dean Jr., Joseph Curtis. BA, Ohio State U, 1970, DDS, 1976. Gen. practice dentistry New Boston, Ohio, 1976—. Mem. Clay Local Bd. Edn. Mem. ADA, So. Ohio Dental Soc. (pres. 1983-84, Dentist of Yr. 1986), Ohio Dental Assn., Am. Assn. Dental Examiners, Ohio State Dental Bd., Train Collectors Assn. Democrat. Baptist. Avocations: model railroading, collecting baseball cards. Home: Box 236 Rt 6 Portsmouth OH 45662 Office: 4384 Rhodes Ave New Boston OH 45662

MCCLELLAN, CHARLES ELLARD, lawyer; b. Moline, Ill., Nov. 2, 1936; s. Ellard Thomas and Vera M. (Poston) McC.; m. Jennie Cigolotti, May 6, 1961; children: Patricia, Kathleen, Thomas, Judith, Margaret. B.S. with honors, U. Ill., 1958; J.D., DePaul U., 1965. Bar: Ill. 1966; CPA, Ill. Assoc. Riordan, Malone & Schlax, Chgo., 1967-70; tax atty. Jewel Cos., Chgo., 1970-74, asst. controller taxes, 1974-77, v.p. taxes, 1977-85; prin. Larson T. McClellen, Arlington Heights, Ill., 1985-87; of counsel Martin, Craig, Chester & Sonnenschein, Chgo., 1987—; lectr. John Marshall Law Sch., Chgo., 1967-68. Editor: Merten's Law of Federal Income Tax, 1967-70. Chmn. Com. on Edn., Village of Oak Park, Ill., 1975-76; mem. Oak Park Parking and Traffic Commn., 1978-81. Mem. ABA, Am. Inst. CPA's, Ill. CPA Soc., Chgo. Bar Assn., Ill. Bar Assn., Chgo. Tax Club, Chgo. Tax Execs. Inst. (2d v.p. 1976). Office: Martin Craig Chester & Sonnenschein 55 W Monroe Suite 1200 Chicago IL 60603

MCCLELLAN, EDWARD JAY, transportation company executive; b. Chgo., Dec. 12, 1921; s. Jay C. and Clara (Moses) McC.; m. Emma Gertrude Johnson, Apr. 28, 1943; 1 child, Kenneth Wesley. BA, Gov.'s State U., 1983. With Chgo. Police Dept., 1949-66; exec. sec. local br. NAACP, Chgo., 1966-70; br. security mgr. cen. region U.S. Postal Service, Chgo., 1970-76, br. mgr. Equal Employment Opportuntiy cen. region, 1976-84; pres. Spears Trans., Inc., Chgo., 1984—. Spears Security Corp., Chgo., 1985—; cons. community relations service U.S. Justice Dept., 1967-74, Ill. Crime Commn., 1967-76. Fund raiser Easter Seal Soc., Chgo., 1984—, Nat. Negro Coll. Fund, Chgo., 1984—. Served to capt. U.S Army, 1942-48. Mem. NAACP, Ill. Notary Pub. Assn., Chgo. Police Assn. (ret.), Nat. League Postmasters (ret.). Democrat. Lutheran. Avocations: reading, golf, swimming, spectator sports. Home: 5555 S Everett Ave Chicago IL 60637 Office: Spears Transp 4552 W Patterson Chicago IL 60641

MCCLELLAN, WALTER FRITZ, facilities engineer; b. Salem, Ind., June 21, 1936; s. Lawrence Oral McClellan and Samantha Bernice (Wolfe) McClellan McKnight; m. Linda Sue Hattabaugh, Apr. 7, 1962; children: Jeffery, Jill. Student Chgo. Tech. Coll., 1960-63, Coop. Agrl. Sch., 1975-77, Ind. U. SE, 1986. With cabinet assembly dept. Willetts Cabinet Co., New Albany, Ind., 1961-62; draftsman Ferraloy, Inc., Salem, Ind., 1962-64; machine operator Bata Shoe Co., Salem, 1964; draftsman, engr. Olin Corp., Charlestown, Ind., 1964-72; engr. land mgmt. ICI Americas, Inc., Charlestown, 1972—. Served to E-3 USAF, 1955-59, to master sgt. USAFR, 1983. Republican. Baptist. Avocations: breeding, raising and showing quarter horses. Office: Ind Army Ammunition Plant Highway 62 Charlestown IN 47111

MCCLINTIC, ROBERT PARSONS, manufacturing executive; b. Hannibal, Mo., July 5, 1946; s. garnett William and Angnes Olivia (Parsons) McC.; m. Elizabeth Lee Utterback, June 17, 1967; children: Charles G., Camille E., Emily A., Benjamin A., Jonathan D., Lindsey K. Lead man, diecaster Diemakers, Inc., Monroe City, Mo., 1970-76, diecast foreman, 1976-79, sr. machine control systmes analyst, 1979-81; mfg. project engr. Black & Decker, Fayatteville, N.C., 1981-85; plant mgr. No. Diecast Corp., Harbor Springs, Mich., 1985-86; mfg. mgr. Nelson Metal Products, Grandville, Mich., 1986—; adv. indsl. electronics N.E. Mo. State Coll., Kirksville, 1979-81. Served with USNG, 1965-71. Mem. Soc. Diecast Engrs. (vice chmn.

1985), Nat. Assn. Hotchamber Magnesium Diecasters, Mich. Soc. Diecast Engrs. Democrat. Roman Catholic. Avocations: folk, country, bluegrass and gospel music, watersports. Office: Nelson Metal Products Corp 2950 Prairie St Grandville MI 49418

MCCLINTICK, OLIVER ELMER, dentist; b. New Castle, Ind., Jan. 21, 1917; s. Daniel Blaine and Ruth Edna (Allee) McC.; m. Halcie Marie Coverdale, July 3, 1937. DDS, Ind. U., 1940. Gen. practice dentistry Anderson, Ind., 1946—. Served to lt. comd. USN, 1940-46. Mem. ADA (life). Republican. Methodist. Home: 708 Central Way Anderson IN 46011 Office: 608 Anderson Bank Bldg Anderson IN 46016

MCCLOSKEY, DAVID JOSEPH, computer services specialist; b. Detroit, Sept. 26, 1948; s. Joseph Thomas and Ellen Eileen (Hill) McC.; m. Janet Susan Ross, Feb. 17, 1973; 1 child, Kathryn Eileen. BA, No. Mich. U., 1976; MBA, U. Detroit, 1984. Data base analyst Hudsons, Detroit, 1981-82; systems supr. Harper Grace Hosps., Detroit, 1982-83; mgr. systems programming Computer Communications of Am., Detroit, 1983-84; v.p. Integrated Data Techs. Corp., Dearborn, Mich., 1984—. Served with USN, 1969-72, Vietnam. Avocations: jogging, reading, fishing, hunting. Home: 5537 Devonshire Detroit MI 48224 Office: Integrated Data Techs Corp 21906 Garrison Dearborn MI 48124

MCCLOSKEY, FRANK, congressman; b. Phila., June 12, 1939; s. Frank and Helen (Warner) McC.; m. Roberta Ann Barker, Dec. 23, 1962; children: Helen-Marie, Mark. A.B. in Govt., Ind. U., 1968, J.D., 1971. Bar: Ind. 1971. Newspaperman Ind., 1963-69; mayor City of Bloomington, Ind., 1971-82; mem. 98th-100th Congresses from 8th Dist. Ind., 1983—; mem. armed services com.; chmn. postal personnel and modernization subcom. of post office and civil service com. Served with USAF, 1957-61. Democrat. Roman Catholic. Office: 127 Cannon House Office Bldg Washington DC 20515

MCCLOSKEY, JACK, professional basketball team executive; b. Mahanoy City, Pa.; m. Leslie McCloskey. BS, U. Pa., 1948, MS, 1952. Profl. basketball player Am. and Eastern Leagues and Nat. Basketball Assn.; profl. baseball player Phila. A's orgn.; basketball coach U. Pa., 1956-66, Wake Forest U., 1966-72, Portland Trailblazers, Nat. Basketball Assn., 1972-74; asst. coach Los Angeles Lakers, 1975-78, Ind. Pacers, 1979; gen. mgr. Detroit Pistons, 1980—. Office: Detroit Pistons Pontiac Silverdome 1200 Featherstone Pontiac MI 48057

MCCLOSKEY, KEITH RICHARD, physician; b. Lock Haven, Pa., Apr. 10, 1939; s. Richard K. and Gwendolyn I. (Stringfellow) McC.; m. Apr. 20, 1963; children: Patricia, Gordon. BS with highest distinction in Chemistry, U. Ill., 1960; MD, Johns Hopkins U., 1964. Diplomate Am. Bd. Pediatrics. Research assoc. life scis. dept. Martin-Marietta Corp., Balt., 1962; intern pediatrics Johns Hopkins Hosp., Balt., 1964-65, asst. resident pediatrics, 1968-69; chief resident pediatrics Sinai Hosp., Balt., 1968, Balt. City Hosps., 1969; fellow child psychiatry Johns Hopkins Hosp. and U., 1969-70; practice medicine specializing in pediatrics, Arlington Heights, Ill., 1970-73; practice medicine specializing in behavior and learning disorders in children, adolescents and adults, Arlington Heights, 1973—; psychiatry resident U. Chgo., 1976-78; vis. physician pediatric out-patient services Balt. City Hosps., 1969-70; mem. courtesy staff Northwest Community Hosp., Arlington Heights, 1970-73; attending physician Children's Meml. Hosp., Northwestern U., Chgo., 1970-73; mem. med. adv. bd. Samuel A. Kirk Devel. Tng. Ctr., Palatine, Ill., 1971-74; vis. lectr. dept. spl. edn. No. Ill. U., 1976, So. Ill. U., Carbondale, 1978; research assoc. dept. psychiatry U. Chgo., 1973—; cons. and mem. faculty minimal brain dysfunction Abbott Labs., 1975—; mem. faculty Speakers Bur., CIBA, 1976—, Nat. Coll. Juvenile Justice Inst., 1976; mem. cons. med. staff dept. pediatrics Northwest Community Hosp., 1973—; mem. adv. bd. Early Childhood Spl. Edn. Northeastern U., 1980—; mem. adv. council pre-sch. program for handicapped children Sch. Dist. 57, Mt. Prospect, Ill., 1972-74; mem. bd. govs. Northwest Suburban Council of Understanding Learning Disabilities, 1972-74. Contbr. articles to med. and psychiat. jours. Served to capt. M.C., U.S. Army, 1965-67. Fellow Am. Acad. Pediatrics, Am. Acad. Cerebral Palsy; mem. N.Y. Acad. Scis., Assn. Children with Learning Disabilities, AAAS, Johns Hopkins Med. Soc., Northwest Suburban Council on Understanding Learning Disabilities (chmn. adv. bd.), Sigma Xi, Phi Beta Kappa, Phi Alpha Mu (pres. 1959-60), Phi Eta Sigma, Phi Kappa Phi, Omega Beta Pi (pres. 1959-60).

MCCLOSKEY, THOMAS GLEN, banking executive; b. Moline, Ill., Apr. 2, 1958; s. Robert W. and Patricia (Schnarr) McC.; m. Tara E. Rickeberg, Sept. 11, 1977. BS in Acctg., U. No. Iowa, 1983. Sr. auditor Touche Ross & Co., Lincoln, Nebr., 1983-86; v.p. servicing Occidental Nebr. Fed. Savs., Omaha, 1986—. Served to sgt. USAF, 1976-80. Fellow Iowa Soc. CPA's; mem. Am. Inst. CPA's (Elijah Watts Sells award 1983), Inst. Mgmt. Accts. (Monsanto Student award 1983), Nebr. Soc. CPA's. Home: Rt 1 Box 120 Bennington NE 68007 Office: Occidental Nebr Fed Savs PO Box 14708 Omaha NE 68124

MCCLOW, THOMAS ALAN, lawyer; b. Detroit, Apr. 25, 1944; s. Kenneth Ray and Rita Beatrice (Periard) McC.; B.S., Mich. State U., 1966; J.D., Loyola U., 1969; m. Diana L. McClow, Oct. 16, 1982; children—Amy Christine, Adam Andrew. Bar: Ill. 1969, U.S. Supreme Ct. 1973. Assoc. Douglas F. Comstock, Geneva, Ill., 1970-73, John L. Nickels, Elburn, Ill., 1973-78; ptnr. Nickels & McClow, Elburn, 1978-82; ptnr. McClow & Britz, Elburn, 1982-84; prin. Law Offices of Thomas A. McClow Ltd., Geneva, Ill., 1985—; pub. conservator, guardian, adminstr. Kane County, 1975-78. Bd. dirs. Kane County Council Econ. Opportunity, 1st vice chmn., 1971-73; bd. dirs. Tri City Youth Project, 1972-73; faculty dean Parent Edn. Center, 1974-76. Mem. ABA, Ill. Bar Assn., Kane County Bar Assn. (chmn. membership and admissions com. 1979-84), Fox Valley Estate Planning Council, Mensa. Home: 919 Arbor Ave Wheaton IL 60187 Office: PO Box 721 Geneva IL 60134

MCCLOY, CARTER JAMES, investment banker; b. Cin., Feb. 3, 1931; s. Corneilus James and Mildred Pauline (Carter) McC.; student pub. schs., Batavia, Ohio; m. Martha Dean Gross, June 21, 1958. Pres., C. J. McCloy & Co., Cin., 1961-65; v.p., resident mgr. Prescott Ball & Turben, Cin., 1966-73; pres. McCloy Watterson & Co., Inc., Cin., 1974-79; v.p., mgr. Cowen & Co., Cin., 1979—, now ltd. ptnr.; dir. Med Term Co., Inc. Past pres. Ohio Municipal Adv. Council. Mem. Pub. Securities Assn., Queen City Mcpl. Bond Dealers Group (past pres.), Cin. Stock and Bond Club, Nat. Assn. Security Dealers (dist. com.). Republican. Clubs: Coldstream Country (bd. dirs.), The Bankers. Home: 440 Bishopsbridge Dr Cincinnati OH 45255 Office: 3 E 4th St Cincinnati OH 45202

MCCLOY, JOHN PATRICK, manufacturing engineer; b. Cin., Feb. 26, 1953; s. John Wilmer and Rita Helen (McQueen) McC.; m. Laurie Anne MacDonald, Nov. 26, 1977; children: Erin Leigh, Colin Patrick. BSME, U. Cin., 1980. Registered profl. engr., Mo. Supr. mfg. engring. Tex. Instruments, Dallas, 1980-81; supr. prodn. engring. Alvey Inc., St. Louis, 1981-84; supr. mfg. and systems engring. Gen. Metal Products, St. Louis, 1984-86; mgr. product devel. Nat. Industries for the Blind, St. Louis, 1986—. Patentee in field. Mem. ASME. Avocations: golf, fishing.

MCCLURE, ALVIN BRUCE, computer programmer/analyst; b. Cin., Mar. 2, 1953; s. Alphonso Bruce McClure and Jewel Lee (Smith) Yates; m. Katherine Shenkar, Nov. 7, 1979; children: Jaina, Randi. Student, U. Mich., 1971-73, 76-77, Fanshawe Coll., London, Ont., Can., 1974-75. Programmer Mfg. Data Systems, Ann Arbor, Mich., 1978-79; systems software specialist Mpls. Star and Tribune, 1979-81; systems analyst NCR COMTEN, Inc., Roseville, Minn., 1981-84; software systems support programmer INTRAN Corp., Bloomington, Minn., 1984-85; programmer/analyst Minn. Dept. Natural Resources, St. Paul, 1985—; chmn. mgmt. info. services tech. com., St. Paul, 1987—. Mem. Audio Engring Soc., Aikido Yoshinkai Assn. N.Am., Aikido Yoshinkai Assn. Minn. (lobbyist, co-chmn. 1983—). Avocations: chess, photography. Home: 3721 13th Ave Minneapolis MN 55407 Office: Minn Dept Natural Resources 500 Lafayette Rd Box 7 Saint Paul MN 55146

MCCLURE, CHARLES RICHARD, advertising agency executive; b. Dayton, Ohio, June 3, 1947; s. Richard Allison and Mary Lois McC.; m. Patricia Ann Stridsberg, Apr. 4, 1969; children: Lisa Marie, Richard Ryan. BA, Ohio State U., 1969. News reporter Sta. WBNS-TV-Radio, Columbus, Ohio, 1967-70; asst. dir. pub. relations Ohio State U., Columbus, 1970-73; communications dir. Columbus Devel. Dept., 1973-75; account exec. Paul Werth Assos., 1975-78; account exec., pub. relations mgr. Howard Swink Advt., 1978-82; v.p. Shelly Berman Communicators, 1982-87; sr. v.p. Brucken/Goettler Advt., Columbus, 1987—; mem. mktg. faculty Ohio State U., 1979—. Served to 1st lt. Army N.G., 1969-73. Mem. Am. Mktg. Assn., Pub. Relations Soc. Am., Columbus Advt. Fedn., Ohio Press Club. Episcopalian. Clubs: Athletic, Ohio State U. Faculty. Office: Brucken/Goettler 580 S High St Columbus OH 43215

MCCLURE, CHARLES STANTON, accountant; b. Loudonville, Ohio, Nov. 29, 1953; s. James E. and Phyllis A. (Long) McC.; m. Rebecca L. Mertz. BS, Ohio State U., 1976. CPA, Ohio. Mem. tax staff Arthur Andersen & Co., Cleve., 1976-81, tax mgr., 1981-87, tax ptnr., 1987—. Mem. Estate Planning Council Cleve. Mem. Am. Inst. CPA's, Ohio Soc. CPA's, Greater Cleve. Tennis Assn., Inc. (treas. 1981—). Clubs: Hermit (Cleve.); Shaker Heights (Ohio) Country. Home: 3280 Ingleside Rd Shaker Heights OH 44122 Office: Arthur Andersen & Co 1717 E 9th St Cleveland OH 44114

MCCLURE, MARY ANNE, state legislator; b. Milbank, S.D., Apr. 21, 1939; d. Charles Cornelius and Mary Lucille (Whittom) Burges; m. D.J. McClure, Nov. 17, 1963; 1 child, Kelly Joanne. BA magna cum laude, U. S.D., 1961; postgrad., U. Manchester, Eng., 1961-62; M of Pub. Adminstrn., Syracuse (N.Y.) U., 1980. Staff asst. U.S. Senator Francis Case, Washington, 1959-61; sec. to lt. gov. State of S.D., Pierre, 1963, with budget office, 1964; exec. sec. to pres. Frontier Airlines, Denver, 1963-64; tchr. Pub. High Schs., Pierre and Redfield, S.D., 1965-66, 68-70,; mem. S.D. State Senate, Pierre, 1975—, pres. pro tem, 1979-88, vice chmn. council of state govts., 1987. Vice chmn. sch. bd. Redfield Ind. Sch. Dist., 1970-74. Fulbright scholar, 1961-62, Bush Leadership fellow, 1977-80. Mem. Phi Beta Kappa. Republican. Congregationalist. Home: 910 E 2nd St Redfield SD 57469

MC CLURE, MICHAEL DESTEWART, professional baseball team marketing executive; b. Chgo., Jan. 23, 1942; s. Charles F. and Janette L. (Lawler) McC.; B.A., DePauw U., 1964; m. Brenda G. Jones, Oct. 24, 1964; children—Michael C., Matthew D. Reporter, City News Bur., Chgo., 1964-65, Chgo. Tribune, 1965-66; public relations cons. Peoples Gas Co., Chgo., 1966-69; sports dir. Sta. WLFI-TV, Lafayette, Ind., 1969-70; service bur. dir. Big Ten Conf., 1970-73; dir. public relations and mktg. Chgo. Bulls, 1973-78; v.p. public relations and mktg. Houston Oilers, 1978-81; v.p. mktg. Chgo. White Sox, 1981-87; sr. v.p. mktg. and sales Chgo. White Sox; v.p. Houston Oilers Publs., Inc., Houston Oilers Dancers, Inc.; dir. NFL Properties; founder Luv Ya Blue!, lic. program; bd. dirs. Major League Baseball Promotion Corp.; chmn. Am. League Licensing Com. Mem. Chgo. Baseball Cancer Charities Com., Major League Baseball Mktg. Adv. Com.; trustee Morgan Park Acad., 1984-85. Recipient Best in Nation awards Cosida, 1972, 73; Matrix award Houston chpt. Women in Communication, 1981; Maj. League Baseball Mktg. Excellence award, 1982; Maj. League Baseball's Top Mktg. Excellence award, 1983, 86; named One of 10 Outstanding Young Citizens, Chgo. Jaycees, 1974. Mem. Houston Advt. Fedn., Houston Sportswriters and Sportscasters Assn., DePauw U. Alumni Assn., Am. Mktg. Assn., Am. Legion, John Purdue Club, Sigma Delta Chi, Sigma Chi (significant sig 1986). Presbyterian. Editor Big Ten Records Book, 1970-73; editor Houston Oilers Pro mag., 1979. Home: 617 W Elm St Wheaton IL 60187

MC COIN, JOHN MACK, social worker; b. Sparta, N.C., Jan. 21, 1931; s. Robert Avery and Ollie (Osborne) McC.; B.S., Appalachian State Tchrs. Coll., Boone, N.C., 1957; M.S. in Social Work, Richmond (Va.) Profl. Inst., 1962; Ph.D., U. Minn., 1977. Social service worker Broughton State Hosp., Morganton, N.C., 1958-59, John Umstead State Hosp., Butner, N.C., 1960-61; clin. social worker Dorothea Dix State Hosp., Raleigh, N.C., 1962-63; child welfare case worker Wake County Welfare Dept., Raleigh, 1963-64; psychiat. social worker Toledo Mental Hygiene Clinic, 1964-66; sr. psychiat. social worker N.Y. Hosp.-Cornell U. Med. Center, 1966-68; social worker VA Hosp., Montrose, N.Y., 1968-73, also vol. mental health worker Westchester County Mental Health Assn. and Mental Health Bd., White Plains, N.Y.; seminar instr. Grad. Sch. Social Work, U. Minn., Mpls., 1973-74; social worker F.D.R. VA Health Care Facility, Montrose, 1975-77; asst. prof. social work U. Wis., Oshkosh, 1977-79, chmn. dept. community liaison com., 1978-79; asso. prof. social work Grand Valley State Colls., Allendale, Mich., 1979-81; social worker VA Med. Ctr. Battle Creek, Mich., 1981-83; supr. social worker VA Med. Ctr., Leavenworth, Kans., 1983—; cons. 44th Gen. Hosp., USAR, Menasha, Wis., 1978-79, 5540th Support Command, USAR, Grand Rapids, Mich., 1979-83; cons. in field; adj. faculty mem. social scis. dept., Kans. Community Coll., Kansas City, 1985— . Served with USMC, 1948-52; USMCR, 1957-72; lt. col. USAR, 1972—. Recipient Outstanding Performance award VA, 1971, Superior Performance award, 1982, Outstanding Performance award, 1983; grantee NIMH, 1974; cert. social worker, N.Y. Mem. Nat. Assn. Social Workers (social action com. W. Mich. br. 1980-81), Acad. Cert. Social Workers, Council Social Work Edn., Res. Officers Assn. U.S., Am. Soc. Pub. Adminstrn., Alpha Delta Mu. Democrat. Baptist. Author: Adult Foster Homes, 1983; founder (with Human Scis. Press), editor Adult Foster Care Jour., 1987. Home: 310B Kiowa St Leavenworth KS 66048

MCCOLLOUGH, PATRICK HANNA, lawyer, former state senator; b. Detroit, May 19, 1942; s. Clarence Lindsay and Lucille (Hanna) McC.; m. Sylvia Jean Chappell, Jan. 4, 1975; 1 child, Alexander Patrick. A.A., Henry Ford Community Coll., 1962; B.A., Mich. State U., 1964; M.A., U. Mich., 1967; J.D., Detroit Coll. Law, 1970. Bar: Mich. 1970, U.S. Dist. Ct. Mich. 1970. Mem. Mich. Senate, Lansing, 1971-78, 83—; dir. Region V, U.S. Def. Civil Preparedness Agy. 1979-80; dir. Region V, Fed. Emergency Mgmt. Agy. for Plans and Preparedness; sole practice Dearborn, Mich., 1970—. Named Conservation Legislator of Yr., Mich. United Conservation Club, 1973. Democrat. Presbyterian. Office: 1310 Commerce Ctr Bldg Lansing MI 48933

MCCOLLOW, THOMAS JAMES, communications company executive; b. Hartford, Wis., Mar. 29, 1925; s. Owen Conrad and Zita Ann (Gardien) McC.; m. Yvonne Parent, June 18, 1949; children: Mardi, Mark, John, Timothy. A.B., Dartmouth Coll., 1946, M.B.A., 1947. Acct. Ernst & Ernst, C.P.A.s, Milw., 1947-51; asst. office mgr. Jour. Communications, Inc., Milw., 1951-60, treas., office mgr., 1961-72, sr. v.p. fin. and corp. planning, 1973-77, pres., 1977-83, chmn. bd., 1983—; chmn. bd. Jour./Sentinel, Inc., 1983—, WTMJ, Inc., 1983—. Bd. dirs. Greater Milw. Com., Milw. Redevel. Corp., Greater Milw. United Way, Med. Coll. Wis.; trustee Marquette U. Served to lt. USNR, 1943-46. Mem. Internat. Newspaper Fin. Execs., Am. Newspaper Pubs. Assn., Phi Beta Kappa. Roman Catholic. Clubs: University, Milwaukee Country. Lodge: Rotary. Office: Jour Communications Inc PO Box 661 Milwaukee WI 53201

MCCOLLUM, ERIC EDWARD, family therapist, teacher; b. Waterloo, Iowa, Dec. 14, 1950; s. Clifford Glen and Alice Elizabeth (Erickson) McC.; m. Julia Anne Stephens, May 19, 1984. BA in Psychology, U. Iowa, 1974, MSW, 1975; PhD, Kans. State U., 1986. Lic. specialist clin. social worker, Kans. Psychiat. social worker Polk County Mental Health Ctr., Des Moines, 1975-77, The Menninger Found., Topeka, 1977—; temp. instr. Kans. State U., Manhattan, 1985. Contbr. articles to profl. jours. Mem. Am. Assn. Marriage and Family Therapy (approved supr.), Kans. Assn. Marriage and Family Therapy (bd. dirs. 1985-86, sec. 1986—). Office: The Menninger Found PO Box 829 Topeka KS 66601

MCCOMAS, JAMES DOUGLAS, university president; b. Prichard, W.Va., Dec. 23, 1928; s. Herbert and Nell (Billups) McC.; m. Francs Adele Stoltz, May 11, 1961; children: Cathleen, Patrick. B.S., W.Va. U., 1951, M.S., 1960; Ph.D., Ohio State U., 1962. High sch. tchr. 1951-54, 56-60; from asst. prof. to prof., head dept. agrl. and extension edn., prof. ednl. adminstrn. head dept. elem. and secondary edn. N.Mex. State U., 1961-67; dean Coll. Edn., Kans. State U., 1967-69; dean also prof. continuing and higher edn. U. Tenn., 1969-76; pres. Miss. State U., 1976-85, U. Toledo, 1985—; field reader U.S. Office Edn.; chmn. Southeastern Manpower Adv. Com.; mem. exec. com. Southeastern Conf.; mem. appeals bd. Nat. Council Accreditation of Tchr. Edn.; pres. Nat. Accreditation Council for Agencies Serving the Blind; mem. exec. com. Land Grant Deans Edn.; chmn. com. on equal opportunity Nat. Assn. Land Grant Colls. and State Univs.; asso. mem. Nat. Manpower Adv. Com., Gov.'s Manpower Adv. Com.; chmn. council of presidents State Univs. Miss.; pres. So. Land Grant Colls. and Univs.; chmn. Tenn. Council Deans Edn.; mem. Miss. Jr. Coll. Commn. Pres. Belmont West Community Assn., Miss. Econ. Council, East Miss. Council; bd. dirs. Toledo Symphony, Toledo Art Mus., Toledo Pub. TV Sta.; mem. Am. Council on Ednl. Community Leadership Devel. and Acad. Adminstrn.; civilian aide Sec. of Army. Served with M.C., AUS, 1954-56. Mem. Am. Sociol. Assn., Am. Higher Edn. Assn., Am. Acad. Polit. and Social Sci., Kappa Delta Pi, Gamma Sigma Delta, Alpha Zeta, Omicron Delta Kappa, Phi Kappa Phi, Beta Gamma Sigma. Home: 3425 W Bancroft Toledo OH 43606

MC COMBS, SHERWIN, oil and gas co. exec.; b. Sterling, Ill., Jan. 27, 1934; s. C. Vernon and Helen (Jennings) McC.; grad. Palmer Chiropractic Coll., 1956-60; m. Rita J. Page, Feb. 8, 1957; children—Kim, Kelly, Jeff, Terry. Owner McCombs Chiropractic Clinic, Sterling, Ill., 1960—, McCombs Petroleum Prodns., Sterling, 1966—; v.p., dir. Coyote Oil & Gas Corp., Casper Wyo., 1968-75, exec. v.p., dir., 1975—; v.p., dir. Coyote Assos., Inc., Ankeny, Iowa, 1970-72; pres., dir. Coyote Oil & Gas Programs, Inc., Ankeny, 1970-72; with McCombs-Conrad & Barrett Oil & Gas Properties, Sterling, Ill., 1972-82. Served with USNR, 1952-54. Mem. Internat., Prairie, Whiteside County chiropractic assns., Internat. Chiropractic Honor Soc. Home: 1808 Thome Dr Sterling IL 61081 Office: 507 W 3d St Sterling IL 61081

MCCONNELL, JOHN HENDERSON, metal and plastic products manufacturing executive; b. New Manchester, W.Va., May 10, 1923; s. Paul Alexander and Mary Louise (Mayhew) McC.; m. Margaret Jane Rardin, Feb. 8, 1946; children—Margaret Louise, John Porter. B.A. in Bus., Mich. State U., 1949; Dr. Law (hon.), Ohio U., 1981. Sales trainee Weirton Steel Co., W.Va., 1950-52; sales mgmt. Shenango-Steel Co., Farrell, Pa., 1952-54; founder, chief exec. officer Worthington Industries, Inc., Columbus, Ohio, 1955—; dir. Alltel Corp., Hudson, Ohio, Anchor Hocking, Lancaster, Ohio, Nat. City Corp., Cleve. Bd. dirs. Children's Hosp., Columbus; trustee Ashland Coll., Ohio. Served with USN, 1943-46. Recipient Ohio Gov.'s award Gov. State of Ohio, 1980; Horatio Alger award Horatio Alger Assn., 1983; named Outstanding Chief Exec. Officer, Fin. World Mag., 1981. Mem. Columbus Area C. of C. (chmn. 1978). Republican. Presbyterian. Clubs: Golf (New Albany, Ohio) (pres. 1983—); Brookside Country (Columbus) (pres. 1964-65). Lodge: Masons. Avocations: flying; golf. Office: Worthington Industries Inc 1205 Dearborn Dr Columbus OH 43085

MCCONNELL, JOHN THOMAS, newspaper publisher; b. Peoria, Ill., May 1, 1945; s. Golden A. and Margaret (Lyon) McC.; m. Elizabeth Jean Slane, Aug. 14, 1971; 1 son, Justin. B.A., U. Ariz., 1967. Mgr. Fast Printing Co., Peoria, 1970-71; mgmt. trainee Quad-Cities Times, Davenport, Iowa, 1972-73; asst. gen. mgr., then v.p., gen. mgr. Peoria Jour. Star, 1973-81, pub., 1981—, pres., 1987—. Bd. dirs. Peoria Downtown Devel. Council, Peoria Devel. Corp.; past trustee Methodist Hosp., Peoria. Served with USAR, 1967-69. Named Young Man of Year Peoria Jaycees, 1979. Mem. Peoria Advt. and Selling Club, Peoria C. of C. Congregationalist. Club: Peoria Country. Office: Journal Star Peoria Journal Star Inc 1 News Plaza Peoria IL 61643

MCCONNELL, MICHAEL EDWARD, lawyer; b. Columbus, Ohio, June 15, 1946; s. Edward Thomas and Jancie Onolee (Patten) McC.; m. Patricia Tille, Sept. 14, 1968; 1 child, Christine Tille. BSE, MS, Ohio State U., 1969, JD, 1976. Bar: Ohio 1976. Assoc. Fuller & Henry, Toledo, 1976-80; atty. Owens-Ill., Inc., Toledo, 1980—. Served to capt. U.S. Army, 1969-72. Mem. ABA, Ohio Bar Assn., Toledo Bar Assn. Democrat. Episcopalian. Avocations: running, tennis, skiing. Office: Owens-Ill Inc Legal Dept One Sea Gate Toledo OH 43606

MCCONNELL, SHIRLEY MAY, library consultant; b. Quincy, Ill., Aug. 29, 1947; d. Elmer Mott and Lorene (Purdy) Byrnes; m. David Michael McConnell, May 25, 1974; children: Trevor Daniel, Briana Kathleen. A in Commerce, Hannibal-LaGrange Coll., 1967; BA, Culver-Stockton Coll., 1969; MLS, U. Ill., 1971. Clk. Great River Library System, Quincy, 1967-68; library asst. Culver-Stockton Coll., Canton, Mo., 1968-69; grad. asst. U. Ill., Urbana, 1970-71; childrens library cons. Rolling Prairie Libraries, Decatur, Ill., 1971-77; adult services cons. South Cen. Library System, Madison, Wis., 1977—; v.p. Strollers Theatre, Madison, 1980; presenter workshops in field. Chmn. Personnel and Profl. Concerns Com., 1984-85, Madison Area Library Council Legis. Com., 1982-85. Mem. Wis. Library Assn. (chmn. legis. day com. 1985, sec. Pub. Library Systems sect.), Wis. Assn. Pub. Librarians (chmn. 1987, sec. 1983), Childbirth Parent Edn. Assn. Democrat. Presbyterian. Avocations: acting, photography, reading. Home: 4337 Windflower Way Madison WI 53711 Office: South Cen Library System 201 W Mifflin St Madison WI 53703

MC CONVILLE, CLARENCE JOSEPH, insurance company executive; b. LaCrosse, Wis., Aug. 22, 1925; s. Bernard J. and Mary C. (Fries) McC.; m. Gloria J. Bourbeau, May 2, 1953; children—Mary, Kathleen, Thomas, James. Student, Miami U., Oxford, Ohio, 1943-45; B.S., U. Minn., 1948, LL.B., 1950. Asst. sec. Title Ins. Co. Minn., Mpls., 1947; successively asst. v.p., sr. v.p., exec. v.p., pres. Title Ins. Co. Minn., 1971—; sr. v.p. Old Republic Internat. Corp., 1978—, also dir.; dir. Minn. Title Fin. Corp., Mississippi Valley Title Ins. Co., Founders Title Group, Norwest Bank Midland (and subs.). Mem.: Law Rev. U. Minn. Bd. dirs. Mpls. Acquatennial Assn., 1968-76; vice commodore Mpls. Acquatennial Assn., 1968; gen. festival chmn. Mpls. Acquatennial Assn., 1969. Served with USN, 1943-46. Mem. Minn. Bar Assn., Hennepin County Bar Assn., Am. Land Title Assn. (pres. 1978-79), Minn. Land Title Assn. (pres.), Nat. Title Underwriters Assn. (pres.), Mpls. Aquatennial Assn. (bd. dirs. 1968-76, vice commodore 1968, gen. festival chmn. 1969). Republican. Roman Catholic. Office: 400 2d Ave S Minneapolis MN 55401

MCCOOE, TERRY ALAN, dentist, counselor, consultant; b. New Albany, Ind., Mar. 7, 1950; s. David Louis and Dorothy Jean (Knight) McC.; m. Rebecca Ruth Staggs, Aug. 21, 1971 (div. Jan. 1986); children: Kierce Leigh, Brock Aaron. BA in Biology, Ind. U. S.E., New Albany, 1972, EdM in Counseling and Guidance, 1984; DDS, Ind. U., Indpls., 1976. Dental officer USN, Jacksonville, Fla., 1976-79; clin. instr. dentistry U. Louisville, Ky., 1979-80; assoc. dentist Drs. Harris and Coomer, Jeffersonville, Ind., 1979-80; dental officer Ind. N.G., Indpls., 1982—; dentist Drs. McCooe & Hall, Corydon, Ind., 1980—; staff cons. Res-Care, Inc., Corydon, 1980—; staff dentist and cons. Ind. Nursing Home, Corydon, 1980—, Indian Creek Nursing Home. Author poetry (Nat. Poetry award, 1968, Kennedy Library award 1964). Instr. summer swimming program New Albany-Floyd County Consol. Sch. Corp., 1970-72; recreational dir. and supr. playgrounds New Albany-Floyd County Dept. Parks and Recreation, 1970-72; softball umpire Indpls. Dept. Parks and Recreation, 1972-76; mem. New Albany-Floyd County (Ind.) Com. for the Gifted; vol. probation officer Clark County Superior Ct. #1, Jeffersonville; mem. Main St. Preservation Assn., New Albany, 1979—. Served to maj. USAR (N.G.), 1982—. Mem. Am. Assn. Counseling and Devel., Ind. Assn. Counseling and Devel., Assn. Mil. Surgeons of U.S., Assn. Specialists in Group Work, Ind. Specialists in Group Work, Harrison County C. of C., Ind. U. Alumni Assn. (life, exec. council representing Ind. U. S.E., past pres. Ind. U. S.E. assn., sec. S.E. Assn.), Am. Profl. Practice Assn., Ind. N.G. Assn. (life), Nat. Guard Assn. U.S. (life), Nat. Wildlife Fedn. (life), Nat. Audubon Soc., Wilderness Soc., Smithsonian Inst. Assocs., Ind. Assn. for the Gifted, New Albany-Floyd County Consol. Sch. Corp. Community Com. for the Gifted, Phi Beta Kappa, Kappa Delta Pi, Beta Theta Pi. Lodge: Kiwanis, DeMolay (Chevalier 1971). Avocations: sports, coin collecting, travel, theater, wildlife and environ. protection. Home: 1009 Wildwood Ln New Albany IN 47150-5428 Office: Drs McCooe & Hall 545 Country Club Dr Corydon IN 47112

MCCOOL, RICHARD BUNCH, real estate developer; b. Kokomo, Ind., Jan. 2, 1925; s. James Victor and Margaret (Bunch) M.C.; m. Victoria R. Middleton, Dec. 23, 1977; children: Kathryn, Suzanne, Rick; 1 stepchild, April. AB in Govt., Ind. U., 1950. Chmn., chief exec. officer Holida Corp., Indianapolis, 1950-70, Great Lakes Homes, Indpls., 1970-77, Am. Investment, Indpls., 1971—; bd. dirs. Am. Investment Group, Indpls., Investor Fin. Services, Indpls.; dir., gen. ptnr. Manor Group, Ind., Ky., 1977—; cons.

Wickes Corp., 1970-77. Author: Real Estate Investments, 1981; contbr. articles to mags., newspaper column on contract bridge, 1966-74. Pres., chmn. various civic orgns., 1960-77; permanent mem. Nat. Rep. Senate Com., 1984. Recipient Geisenbier award Kokomo Jaycees, 1960; named to the Hon. Order Ky. Col. Served to capt., U.S. Army, 1943-46, PTO. Mem. Am. Contract Bridge League (life master 1972), No. Ind. Bridge Assn. (pres. 1974), Pvt. Pilot Assn. (pres. 1969), Nat. Contractors Assn. (founding pres. 1970, Contractor of Yr. 1974), Apt. Assns., Cert. Mgmt. Group (pres. 1980), Ind. U. Alumni Club, Sigma Nu. Congregationalist. Clubs: Columbia, Skyline (Indpls.). Lodges: Masons, Shriners. Office: 14904 Greyhound Ct Carmel IN 46032

MCCORCLE, MARCUS DUANE, obstetrician, gynecologist; b. Bassett, Nebr., Jan. 28, 1951; s. Milton Flynn and Mary Ann (Oatman) McC.; m. Brenda Jo Fulbright, June 16, 1974; children: Christa, Matthew, Louisa, Megan. BS in Biology, Evangel Coll., 1973; MD, U. Mo., 1977. Diplomate Am. Bd. Ob-Gyn. Resident in ob-gyn St. John's Mercy Hosp., St. Louis, 1977-81; practice medicine specializing in ob-gyn Springfield, Mo., 1981—. Bd. deacons Cen. Assembly of God Ch., Springfield, 1983—. Mem. Evangel. Coll. Alumni Assn. (pres.). Republican. Avocations: bass fishing, shooting, camping, photography, computing. Office: 1000 E Primrose Springfield MO 65807

MCCORD, RONALD ROBIN, real estate company executive; b. Little Rock, July 18, 1937; s. Marks Wright and Hazel Caroline (Verg) McC.; m. Joline Iris Rahlf, June 11, 1968; children: Kimberly Joline, Jennifer Beth. BS, U. Wis., 1959. Cert. hotel adminstr. Pub. relations dir. Wis. Heart Assn., Milw., 1960-68; assoc. dir. Nat. Assn. For Mental Health, N.Y.C., 1968-71; broker, v.p. Milmark Realty, Milw., 1971—. Contbr. articles to profl. jours. Served as sgt. U.S. Army, 1959-60. Named Jaycee of Yr., Wauwatosa Jaycees, 1965, Salesman of Yr. Nationwide Motel Brokers, 1978. Mem. Am. Hotel/Motel Assn. (mem. pub. relations com. 1983—), Economy Lodging Assn. (chmn. membership com. 1986—), Wis. Innkeepers Assn. (pres. 1987), Consolidated Hotel/Motel Brokers (v.p. 1981—), Milw. Bd. Realtors (chmn. pub. relations com. 1978-85), Milw. Hotel Motel Assn. (bd. dirs. 1980-84, Meritorious Service award 1984). Presbyterian. Avocations: hunting, fishing, skiing, tennis. Home: 13145 Dunwoody Dr Elm Grove WI 53122 Office: Milmark Realty 9700 W Bluemound Rd Milwaukee WI 53226

MCCORMICK, CHARLES HAROLD, school system administrator; b. Bath, N.Y., Mar. 28, 1949; s. Harry Glenn and Evelyn Gertrude (Eaton) McC.; m. Jennifer Frances Johnson, Aug. 19, 1972; children: Shane Michael, Jeremey Isaac, Brendan Joseph, Andrew Marcus. BS, U. Rochester, 1971; MS in Edn., No. Ill. U., 1973, EdD, 1975. Lic. sch. adminstr. Psychologist DuPage County Health Dept., Wheaton, Ill., 1974-75; asst. dir., bus. mgr. Northwestern Ill. Assn., Sycamore, 1975-86; bus. mgr. DeKalb (Ill.) Community Unit Sch. Dist. #428, 1986—; cons. Ill. State Bd. Edn., Springfield, 1980-85. Co-author Conducting Educational Needs Assessment, 1984. Referee Am. Youth Soccer Orgn.; mem. Shabbona (Ill.) Bd. Edn., 1984-85. Mem. Ill. Assn. Sch. Bus. Officials, Assn. Sch. Bus. Officials Internat. (co-chmn. publs. com. 1983). Avocations: geneology, reading, golf. Office: DeKalb Community Unit Sch Dist #428 145 Fisk Ave DeKalb IL 60115

MCCORMICK, JOHN MICHAEL, sales manager; b. Louisville, Jan. 9, 1961; s. Donald Michael McCormick. Student, Concordia Coll., Milw., 1979-81, U. Wis., Milw., 1981-83. Research analyst MMT Sales, Inc., N.Y.C., 1983-84; account exec. Sta. WDSU-TV, New Orleans, 1984-85, Sta. WTMJ-TV, Milw., 1985; nat. sales mgr. Sta. WSYM-TV, Lansing, Mich., 1985-86. Office: Sta WSYM-TV 600 W St Joseph St Lansing MI 48933

MC CORMICK, MARK, justice Iowa Supreme Ct.; b. Ft. Dodge, Iowa, Apr. 13, 1933; s. Elmo Eugene and Virgilla (Lawler) McC.; m. Marla Rae McKinney, June 11, 1966; children—Marcia, Michael, Paul. A.B., Villanova U., 1955; LL.B., Georgetown U., 1960. Bar: Iowa bar 1960. Law clk. to judge U.S. Ct. Appeals, 1960-61; practice law Ft. Dodge, 1961-68; asst. county atty. Webster County, 1963-67; judge 11th and 2d jud. dists., 1968-72; justice Iowa Supreme Ct., Des Moines, 1972—. Served with USN, 1955-58. Mem. Am., Iowa bar assns., Am. Judicature Soc. Office: Capitol Bldg Des Moines IA 50319 *

MCCORMICK, WILLIAM EDWARD, business executive, consultant; b. Potters Mills, Pa., Feb. 9, 1912; s. George H. and Nellie (Mingle) McC.; m. Goldie Stover, June 6, 1935; children: John F. (dec.), Kirk W. B.S., Pa. State U., 1933, M.S., 1934. Tchr., Centre Hall (Pa.) High Sch., 1934-37; chemist Willson Products, Inc., Reading, Pa., 1937-43; indsl. hygienist Ga. Dept. Pub. Health, Atlanta, 1946; mgr. indsl. hygiene and toxicology B.F. Goodrich Co., Akron, Ohio, 1946-70; mgr. environ. control B.F. Goodrich Co., 1970-73; mng. dir. Am. Indsl. Hygiene Assn., Akron, 1973-83; exec. sec. Soc. Toxicology, 1976-83; chmn., treas. Envirotox Mgmt., Inc., 1983—; mem. exec. com. rubber sect. Nat. Safety Council, 1955-73; gen. chmn., 1971-72; mem. environ. health com. Chlorine Inst., 1968-73; mem. food, drug and cosmetic chems. com. Mfg. Chemists Assn., 1960-73, chmn., 1967-69, also mem. occupational health com., 1965-73; mem. adv. com. on heat stress U.S. Dept. Labor, 1973; mem. Nat. Adv. Com. Occupational Safety and Health, 1983-85; pres. Am. Indsl. Hygiene Found., 1984, trustee, 1982—. Contbr. articles to profl. jours. Served to capt. USPHS, 1943-46. Mem. Am. Chem. Soc., Soc. Toxicology, AAAS, Am. Indsl. Hygiene Assn. (pres. 1964), Indsl. Hygiene Roundtable, Am. Acad. Indsl. Hygiene. Republican. Episcopalian. Lodges: Masons (33 deg.) Shriner. Home: 419 Dorchester Rd Akron OH 44320 Office: 149 N Prospect St Ravenna OH 44266

MCCORMICK, WILLIAM THOMAS, JR., electric and gas company executive; b. Washington, Sept. 12, 1944; s. William Thomas and Lucy Valentine (Offutt) McC.; m. Ann Loretta du Mais, June 13, 1969; children: Christopher, Patrick. B.S., Cornell U., 1966; Ph.D., M.I.T., 1969. Mem. staff Inst. for Def. Analysis, Arlington, Va., 1969-72; mem. staff Office of Sci. and Tech., Exec. office of the Pres., Washington, 1972-73; sr. staff mem. Energy Policy Office, The White House, 1973-74; chief sci. and energy tech. br. Office Mgmt. and Budget, Exec. Office of the Pres., 1974-75; dir. commercialization U.S. Energy Research and Devel. Adminstrn., 1975-76; v.p. policy and govt. relations Am. Gas Assn., 1976-78; v.p., asst. to chmn. Am. Natural Resources Co., Detroit, 1978-80; exec. v.p. Mich. Wis. Pipeline Co., Am. Natural Resources System, Detroit, 1980-82; pres. Am. Natural Resources Co., Detroit, 1982-85; chmn., chief exec. officer Consumers Power Co., Jackson, Mich., 1985—; bd. dirs. Bancorp. Prin. author, editor: Commercialization of Synthetic Fuels in the U.S, 1975. Bd. dirs. Detroit Symphony, St. John Hosp. Alfred P. Sloan scholar, 1962-66. Mem. Econ. Club Detroit (bd. dirs.), Greater Detroit C. of C. (bd. dirs.), Econ. Alliance Mich. (bd. dirs.). Roman Catholic. Clubs: Cosmos (Washington); Detroit Athletic, Country of Detroit, Detroit. Office: Consumers Power Co 212 W Michigan Ave Jackson MI 49201

MCCOWN, FRANK J., lawyer, educator; b. Ironton, Ohio, Feb. 6, 1940; s. Henry Anderson and Adrienne (Tucker) McC.; m. 2d, Tyna L. Dilley, Mar. 3, 1979; 1 son, Brigham A. B.S. in Bus. Adminstrn., Miami U., 1962; J.D., Ohio State U., 1964. Bar: Ohio 1965. Ptnr., Crowe & McCown, Ironton, 1965—; atty. City of Ironton, 1966-82; asst. atty. gen. State of Ohio, 1971-81; instr. law Shawnee State Coll., Ohio U.-Ironton, 1971—. Author (column) It's the Law, Ironton Tribune. Mem. Democratic Exec. Com., Lawrence County, Ohio, 1965—; former Dem. candidate for Ohio Ho. of Reps.; campaign chmn. United Way of Lawrence County, 1981-82; past pres. Ironton Jaycees. Recipient Disting. Service award Ohio State U., 1967; Lawrence County Assocs. award Lawrence County Bd. Realtors, 1981; named several times Outstanding Lawyer, Lawrence County Legal Secs. Mem. Ohio State Bar Assn., Lawrence County Bar Assn. (past pres.), Ohio Land Title Assn., Phi Alpha Delta (pres. 1978-80, chmn. bd. 1980-82). Methodist. Club: Mason. Home: 1235 Shawnee Trail Ironton OH 45638 Office: Crowe and McCown 311 Park Ave Ironton OH 45638

MCCOY, EARL LEE, accountant; b. Morris, Ill., Mar. 31, 1958; s. Donald George and Pearl (Trickler) McC. BS, Ill. State U., 1979. Acct. R.R. Donnelley & Sons, Dwight, Ill., 1980—. Democrat. Roman Catholic. Lodge: KC (warden 1985-86). Home: 65 E Third St Coal City IL 60416-1031 Office: RR Donnelley & Sons Co Rural Rt 1 Box 118 Dwight IL 60420

MCCOY, GAYLE ANDERSON, association executive, audiovisual program administrator; b. Lexington, Ky., Oct. 3, 1917; s. Harry Strange and Viola Elizabeth (Hunter) McC.; m. Sara Mae Bryant, Aug. 15, 1947; children—David Anderson, Mary Elizabeth. B.A. in Advt. and Illustration, Woodbury Coll., 1949. Advt. mgr. Hymson's Tots and Teens, Lexington, 1951-54, Rothchilds Dept. Store, Rock Island, Ill., 1954-55, Hill's Dept. Store, Davenport, Iowa, 1955-58; sr. indsl. illustrator J.I. Case Co., Bettendorf, Iowa, 1958-62; audiovisual program mgr. U.S. Govt., Rock Island, 1962-80; adminstr. Deaf Missions, Council Bluffs, Iowa, 1980—; lectr. in field. Author: Effective Oral Presentation (commendation award 1969), 1969; Clearing in The Forest, 1980; also articles. Bd. dirs. George Davenport Hist. Found., Rock Island, 1979-80; active Davenport Arts Council, 1969-80; co-founder Rock Island Arsenal Hist. Found., 1970; speaker Rock Island Arsenal Speakers Bur., 1970-82. Served with U.S. Army, 1941-45. Recipient Toastmaster of Yr. award, 1974. Republican. Mem. Christian Ch. Avocations: travel; stage design. Home: Bennett & Franklin Aves Greenbriar Apt 57 Council Bluffs IA 51501 Office: Deaf Missions RR 2 Box 26 Council Bluffs IA 51501

MCCOY, JANET JO, accounting, auditing educator; b. Pittsburgh, Kans., Feb. 13, 1954; d. Joseph and Julia Matilda (Slapshak) Phillips; m. Patrick E. McCoy, Aug. 1, 1975. BE, Washburn U., 1976; MBA, Calif. State U., Hayward, 1981. CPA, Kans., N.M. Sr. acct. Peat, Marwick, Mitchell & Co., Albuquerque, 1981-85; instr. Washburn U., Topeka, 1986—. Mem. Shadywood West Homeowner's Assn., Topeka. Mem. Am. Inst. CPA's, N.Mex. Soc. CPA's, N.Mex. State Bd. Pub. Accountancy, Kans. State Bd. Pub. Accountancy, Sandia Dog Obedience Club. Republican. Roman Catholic. Avocations: golf, aerobics, dog tng. Home: 6150 SW 34th Terr Topeka KS 66610 Office: Washburn U Sch Bus Topeka KS 66621

MCCOY, JOENNE RAE, psychiatric clinic administrator; b. Detroit, Jan. 26, 1941; d. Harlan and Dorothy (Simpson) Heinmiller; children: Harlan Craig, Cathi-Jo. BA, Mich. State U., 1966; MSW, U. Mich., 1983. Tchr. Owosso and Garden City pub. schs., Mich., 1962-73; psychotherapist, group leader Wayne County Hosp., Mich., 1981-82; psychotherapist East Point, Westland, Mich., 1982-83, Midwest, Dearborn, Mich., 1982-83; owner, dir. Personal Devel. Ctrs., Inc., Plymouth, Mich., 1981—; bd. dirs. Hospice Suport Services, Inc., Livonia, Mich., 1981—; cons. Westland Convalescent Ctr., Mich., 1983—; supr. grad. students U. Mich., 1986—; cons., facilitator Women-the Emerging Entrepreneurs, Wayne State U. and Small Bus. Assn., 1985—; chmn. Substance Abuse Com., Plymouth Schs., 1982; cons. Salvation Army, Plymouth. Mem. bd. advisors (newsletter) Personal Performance, Balt., 1986—. Mem. steering com. for neighborhood programs YWCA. Soroptimist scholar, 1982. Mem. Internat. Assn. Pediatric Social Workers, Mich. Assn. Bereavement Counselors, Families in Crisis: Domestic Violence Inc., Nat. Assn. Social Workers (cert.), Nat. Assn. Female Execs., Am. Entrepreneurs Assn., Women's Network (pres.), Acad. Cert. Soc. Workers. Club: Agora. Avocation: flying. Home: 37644 N Laurel Park Dr Livonia MI 48152 Office: Personal Devel Ctrs Inc PC 37677 Profl Ctr Dr Suite 130C Livonia MI 48154-1114

MCCOY, JOHN JOSEPH, lawyer; b. Cin., Mar. 15, 1952; s. Raymond F. and Margaret T. (Hohmann) McC. BS in Math. summa cum laude, Xavier U., 1974; JD, U. Chgo., 1977. Bar: Ohio 1977, D.C. 1980. Ptnr. Taft, Stettinius & Hollister, Cin., 1977—; lectr. Greater Cin. C. of C., 1984. Pro bono rep. Jr. Achievement Greater Cin., 1978; fund raiser Dan Beard council Boy Scouts Am., 1983; fund raising team leader Cin. Regatta, Cin. Ctr. Devel. Disorders, 1983; account mgr. United Appeal, Cin., 1984. Mem. ABA, Ohio State Bar Assn., Cin. Bar Assn. (fed. cts., common pleas cts. and negligence law coms. 1984), Cin. Inn of Ct. (barrister 1984-86, sec. bd. trustees 1986—). Clubs: Cin. Athletic (sec. bd. of trustees 1986—), Fairfield Sportsmen's (Cin.). Home: 2567 Perkins Ln Cincinnati OH 45208

MCCOY, MICHAEL ROBERT, marketing executive; b. Cleve., Oct. 6, 1960; s. Robert Dale and Karen Lee (Sharrer) McC.; m. Rhonda Kay Bachus, May 31, 1986. BS, Southwest Mo. State U., 1983. Mgr. fin. services dept. Gt. So. Savs. and Loan, Springfield, Mo., 1984-85; v.p., regional mktg. dir. Mktg. One Inc., Portland, Oreg., 1985-86, v.p., dir. mktg. div., 1986-87, sr. v.p. mktg., 1987—. Travel coordinator, asst. campaign mgr. Mo. for Roy Blunt Sec. of State, 1983, 84. Named one of Outstanding Young Men Am., 1985. Mem. Springfield C. of C., Springfield Jaycees, Southwest Mo. State U. Alumni Assn., Kappa Alpha (nat. undergrad. chmn. 1982-83, Leadership and Dedication award 1983). Lodge: Sertoma. Home: 800 S Delaware Springfield MO 65802 Office: Mktg One Inc PO Box 10942 G S Springfield MO 65808

MCCOY, PAUL DWAIN, utilities company executive; b. Chgo., July 1, 1950; s. Paul A. and Agnes A. (Arlauskis) McC.; m. Diana H. Callaghan, Nov. 25, 1972; 1 child, Colleen M. BSEE, Ill. Inst. Tech., 1972. Registered profl. engr., Ill. Dist. mgr. Commonwealth Edison Co., Chgo., 1981-84, area mgr., 1984-87, commercial mgr., 1987—. Exec. v.p. Bolingbrook (Ill.) Local Devel. Corp., 1983-84. Mem. IEEE. Republican. Roman Catholic. Lodge: Rotary (treas. Oak Lawn chpt. 1985-87, dir. Calumet chpt. indsl. commn. 1987—). Avocations: cross-country skiing, bicycling. Home: 8343 Parkview Munster IN 46321 Office: Commonwealth Edison Co 7601 S Lawndale Chicago IL 60652

MCCOY, WILLIAM EARL, JR., community economic development executive; b. Grand Rapids, Mich., Nov. 19, 1953; s. William Earl and Evelyn (Duke) McC.; m. Allene Denise Garrett, Aug. 20, 1977; 1 child, Erin Nicole. BA, Alma Coll., 1975; MA in Pub. Adminstrn., Am. U., 1977. Dep. city mgr. City of Benton Harbor, Mich., 1977-79; resident fellow Acad. Contemporary Problems, Columbus, Ohio, 1979-82; country dir. Peace Corps, Maseru, Lesotho, 1982-84; spl. asst. to mgmt. Peace Corps, Washington, 1984-85; pres. The McCoy Co., Columbus, 1985—; v.p. Econ. Devel. Council, Lima, Ohio, 1986—; cons. research Joint Ctr. Polit. Studies, Washington, 1976-77, small cities Nat. League of Cities, Washington, 1978, urban affairs Ohio State U., Columbus, 1980-81, community devel. Town of Glenarden, Md., 1985; group leader, cons. City of Dayton, Ohio, 1985-87. Co-author: Managing Fiscal Retrenchment in Cities, 1980; (with others) Planning Needs of Small Cities, Black Crime: A Police View. Bd. dirs. Godman Guild, Columbus, 1980, ARC, Lima, 1987; treas., bd. dirs. Berrien County Opportunites Industrialization Ctr., Benton Harbor, 1978; mem. fin. roundtable U.S. Econ. Devel. Adminstrn., Washington, 1980; dir. city drive United Way, Benton Harbor, 1978; mem. Council on Urban Econ. Devel. Named one of Outstanding Young Men of Am., 1980. Mem. Am. Econ. Devel. Council, Am. Soc. Pub. Affairs and Adminstrn., Nat. Bus. League, Internat. Traders, Internat. Downtown Assn., Am. Entrepreneur's Assn., Nat. Main St. Network, Pi Alpha Alpha. Lodge: Rotary. Home: 6219 Polo Dr W Columbus OH 43229 Office: Lima-Allen County Econ Devel Council Bank One Tower #1205 Lima OH 45801

MCCOY, WILLIAM FRANKLIN, teacher; b. Scottsboro, Ala., July 27, 1941; s. Claude Sr. and F. Jewel (Norris) McC.; m. Barbara Ann Campbell, July 12, 1969; children: H. Melissa, Theresa L. BA in Psychology, Berea Coll., 1966; cert. teaching, DePaul U., 1971; postgrad., St. Xavier Coll., 1975. Mgr. trainee Marshall Field & Co., Chgo., 1969-71; tchr. St. Kieran Sch., Chicago Heights, Ill., 1971-72, St. Damian Sch., Oak Forest, Ill., 1972-77, Dist. #140, Tinley Park, Ill., 1977—. Dem. precinct capt., Markham, Ill., 1974—; bd. dirs. South Suburban Fed. Credit Union, Palos Heights, Ill., 1978-87, St. Gerard Sch. Bd., Markham, 1985-87; mem. Markham Civil Def. Council, 1986—, Bremen Twp. (Ill.) Youth Commn., 1977-81. Served to capt. U.S. Army, 1966-69, Vietnam. Named Teacher of Yr. award Tinley Park Jaycees, 1981. Mem. Am. Fedn. Tchrs. (sen. 1979—). Democratic. Roman Catholic. Lodge: Moose. Avocations: travel, stamps, plays, music, camping.

MCCRACKEN, GARY W., product design engineer; b. Pekin, Ill., Aug. 23, 1955; s. William Noel and Olga Mary (Nohitsch) McC.; m. Lynda Claire Howk, May 9, 1982; children: Laura Stone. BS in Graphic Arts, Ill. State U., 1978, MS in Indsl. Tech., 1983. Punch press operator Eureka Inc., Bloomington, Ill., 1977; quality control insp. Caterpillar Tractor Co., East Peoria, Ill., 1977-80; owner, operator The Sawdust Factory, Bloomington, 1983-84; safety cons. Rensis-Likert Assocs., Ann Arbor, Mich., 1984; product designer Kimball Internat. Inc., Jasper, Ind., 1984—. Mem. Soc. Plastics Engrs. Unitarian. Avocations: woodworking, home improvement, painting, golf, swimming. Office: Kimball Tech Ctr W 12th St Jasper IN 47546

MCCRACKEN-HUNT, LINDA, architect; b. Phila., Mar. 16, 1954; d. Robert John and Flora Rachel (Mazzotta) McCracken; m. Thomas Edward Hunt, July 26, 1980; children: Daniel Joseph, David Robert. BS in Environ. Design, U. Minn., 1977, BArch, 1978. Registered architect, Minn. Architect Cuningham Architects, Mpls., 1977-79, Archtl. Alliance, Mpls., 1979-82, Ankeny, Kell & Assocs., St. Paul, 1982-85; sr. architect and project mgr. U. Minn., Mpls., 1985—. Planning commr. Golden Valley (Minn.) Planning Commn., 1984—. Mem. AIA (Nat. Women in Architecture com. 1984—), Minn. Soc. Architects. Office: U Minn Phys Planning Office 503 Morrill Hall 100 Church St SE Minneapolis MN 55455

MCCRANEY, CHARLES EDWARD, fire fighter, educator; b. Pine Bluff, Ark., Oct. 31, 1946; s. Verniste and Ruby Lee (Temple) McC.; m. Marguerite Meeks, Dec. 13, 1975; children: Tabreena Vaughn, Tanneia La'Von, Timothy David. AA, Wright Coll., 1973; BA, Govs. State U., 1976; AS, Triton Coll., 1980. Ins. inspector Equifax Services, Elmhurst, Ill., 1976-77; substitute tchr. Sch. Dist. 97, Oak Park, Ill., 1976-78, Sch. Dist. 89, Maywood, Ill., 1978, Proviso Sch. Dist. 209, Maywood, Ill., 1985—; fire fighter 928th T.A.G. Fire Dept., Chgo., 1973—. Pub., editor pub. safety bulletin, Broadview, Ill., 1983—. Scout master Thatcher Woods area Boy Scouts Am., Oak Park, 1983; Maywood Emergency Service Disaster Agy., 1981. Served as sgt. USAF, 1966-70. Mem. Ill. Emergency Mgmt. Assn., O'Hare Civilian Welfare Council, 1976—. Democrat. Baptist. Avocations: music, singing. Home: 1831 S 22d Ave Maywood IL 60153

MCCRAW, SAMMY TIMOTHY, management systems surveillance specialist; b. Memphis, Jan. 23, 1946; s. Richard Clarence and Susie (Wright) McC.; m. Patricia Pompey, Oct. 30, 1982; 1 son, Jules Singer. B.A. in Econs., Memphis State U., 1972; M.S. in Ops. Mgmt., Northrop U., Los Angeles, 1975, M.B.A., 1976. Purchasing asst. Memphis State U., 1965-68; distbn. clk. Memphis Post Office, 1971-72; program adminstr. Rockwell Internat., Los Angeles, 1972-77; cost/schedule planning specialist Battelle Meml. Inst., Columbus, Ohio, 1977-85, mgmt. systems surveillance specialist, 1985—; adj. asst. prof. Cen. Wash. U.; instr. Columbia Basin Coll. Active Riverside Hills Civic Assn. Served to capt. USAR, 1968—. Decorated Bronze Star; recipient Cert. Appreciation, Project Mgmt. Inst., 1980. Mem. Project Mgmt. Inst. (pres. Cen. Ohio chpt.), Nat. Mgmt. Assn., Res. Officers Assn., Inst. Cert. Profl. Mgrs., Performance Mgmt. Assn. Democrat. Contbr. articles to profl. jours. Home: 3204 Needham Dr Dublin OH 43017 Office: 505 King Ave Columbus OH 43201

MCCRAY, BARBARA RAE, controller; b. Saginaw, Mich., Aug. 18, 1942; s. Paul H. and M. Naoma (Francis) Ellis; m. David E. McCray, Nov. 11, 1960; 1 child, Heather L. Grad. high sch., Saginaw, Mich., 1960. Exec. sec. Second Nat. Bank, Saginaw, 1958-60; office mgr. Saginaw Boat Basin, 1963; controller Brennan Marine Sales, Bay City, Mich., 1963—; also bd. dirs. Brennan Marine Sales, Bay City; v.p., bd. dirs. Print-A-Print, Inc., 1971-86; ptnr. Glass Forest, 1987—. Employer adv. bd. Mich. Employment Security Commn., 1987—; v.p., bd. dirs. Grandview Beach Assn., Indian River, Mich., 1985—. Mem. Mullet Lake Area Preservation Soc. (editor 1986—), Tri-City Stained Glass Guild (Midland, Mich.). Avocation: stained glass. Home: 1720 6th St Bay City MI 48708 Office: Brennan Marine Sales 1809 S Water St Bay City MI 48708

MCCREA, MICHAEL SHAWN, radiologist; b. Indpls., July 26, 1952; s. Fred Ronald and Mary Leota (Kincaid) McC.; m. Gay Townsend Pettebone, Dec. 3, 1977; children: Jonathan, Katherine, Carter. BA, DePauw U., 1974; MD, Ind. U., 1977. Diplomate Am. Bd. Radiology. Intern Ind. U. Med. Ctr., 1977-78; med. staff Union Hosp., Terre Haute, Ind., 1981—; resident in radiology Union Hosp., 1978-81; med. staff Vermillion County Hosp., Clinton, Ind., 1981—; vice chief of staff Clay County Hosp., Brazil, Ind., 1981—; dir. dept. radiology Clay County Hosp., 1982—, Vermillion County Hosp., Clinton, 1983—. chmn. health profl. adv. com. Wabash Valley March of Dimes, Terre Haute, 1985-86. Mem. Am. Coll. Radiology, Radiologic Soc. N.Am., Ind. Med. Assn. (pres. 5th dist. 1984-85), Terre Haute Acad. Med., Phi Beta Kappa, Phi Eta Sigma. Republican. Episcopalian. Lodge: Rotary (pres. Terre Haute 1986—). Avocations: piloting, golf. Office: 3102 Wabash Ave Terre Haute IN 47803

MCCREA, ROBERT STANLEY, obstetrician-gynecologist; b. Alliance, Ohio, Sept. 16, 1948; s. William Albert and Lois (Stanley) McC.; m. Sandra Darlyne Anderson, June 27, 1970; children: Michael James, Kelly Aileen. BS, Mt. Union Coll., Alliance, 1970; MD, U. Tex., Galveston, 1974. Diplomate Am. Bd. Ob-Gyn. Intern U. Okla., Oklahoma City, 1974-75; resident Tex. A&M U., Temple, 1975-78; staff physician Shawnee (Okla.) Med. Ctr. Clinic, 1978-82, Sandusky (Ohio) Ob-Gyn., 1982—; clinical instr. U. Okla. Coll. Medicine, Oklahoma City, 1979-82; asst. clinical prof. Med. Coll. of Ohio, Toledo, 1982—. Contbr. articles to profl. jours. Mem. Pottawatomie County Med. Soc. (pres. 1981), Am. Coll. Ob-Gyn, Ohio State Med. Soc., AMA, Am. Fertility Soc., Ohio Geneol. Soc. (spkrs. bur., 1985—). Republican. Methodist. Club: Sandusky Sailing. Avocations: boating, arabian horses. Office: Sandusky Ob-Gyn Inc 1218 Cleveland Rd Sandusky OH 44870

MCCREARY, JAY LEE, academic administrator; b. Upper Sandusky, Ohio, Oct. 4, 1951; s. Lloyd Vinton and Mary Elizabeth (Taylor) McC.; m. Robyn Lynn Keck, Dec. 21, 1973; children: Ian, Holly. BS, Ohio State U., 1973, MA, 1982. Tchr. Elgin Local Schs., Marion, Ohio, 1976-78; instr. Marion Tech. Coll., 1978-82, dir. continuing edn., 1982-85, dir. ctr. human resources devel., 1985—; cons., trainer Herman Assocs., Inc., Rittman, Ohio, 1985—. Author: Microbiology Lab Manual; editor: Using PC File III, 1985. Mem. Marion Community End. Consortium, 1983-85; active adult edn. adv. com. Tri Rivers Career Ctr., Marion, 1985-86, Indsl. Tng. Adv. Com.; Small Bus. EnterpriseCtr., 1985-86. Mem. Ohio Continuing Higher Edn. Assn., Marion Area C. of C., Upper Sandusky Area C. of C. Republican. Methodist. Avocations: sailing, fishing, music, home remodeling. Home: 16684 CH 109 R5 Upper Sandusky OH 43351 Office: Marion Tech Coll 1465 Mt Vernon Ave Marion OH 43302

MCCRYSTAL, JAMES LINCOLN, JR., lawyer; b. Sandusky, Ohio, Nov. 6, 1948; s. James Lincoln and Elizabeth (Ernst) McC.; m. Gayle Anne Newman, Oct. 5, 1985. BA, John Carroll U., 1970; JD, U. Notre Dame, 1973. Bar: Ohio 1973, U.S. Dist. Ct. (no. dist.) Ohio 1974, U.S. Ct. Appeals (6th cir.) 1977, U.S. Supreme Ct. 1979. Assoc. Weston, Hurd, Fallon, Paisley & Howley, Cleve., 1974-79, ptnr., 1980—. Chmn. Friends of Western Res. Hist. Soc. Library, Cleve., 1984-87. Mem. Erie County Bar Assn., Greater Cleve. Bar Assn., Ohio State Bar Assn. (jud. adminstrn. and legal reform com.), ABA, Def. Research Inst., Ohio Assn. Civil Trial Attys., John Carroll U. Alumni Assn. (nat. pres. 1983-85). Democrat. Roman Catholic. Avocation: sailing. Home: 2301 Chatfield Dr Cleveland Heights OH 44106

MCCUEN, JOHN FRANCIS, JR., auto parts manufacturing executive, lawyer; b. N.Y.C., Mar. 11, 1944; s. John Francis and Elizabeth Agnes (Corbett) McC.; children: Sarah, Mary, John. A.B., U. Notre Dame, 1966; J.D., U. Detroit, 1969. Bar: Mich. 1970, Fla. 1970, Ohio 1978. Legal counsel Kelsey-Hayes Co., Romulus, Mich., 1970-77; corp. counsel Sheller-Globe Corp., Toledo, 1977-79; sr. v.p., gen. counsel Sheller-Globe Corp., 1979—. Trustee Kidney Found. N.W. Ohio, 1979—, pres., 1984-86. Mem. Am. Bar Assn., Ohio Bar Assn., Fla. State Bar. Clubs: Toledo, Inverness, Catawba Island. Home: 2745 Westowne Ct Toledo OH 43615 Office: Sheller Globe Corp 1505 Jefferson Ave Toledo OH 43697

MCCUEN, JOHN JOACHIM, defense contractor executive; b. Washington, Mar. 30, 1926; s. Joseph Raymond and Josephine (Joachim) McC.; m. Gloria Joyce Seidel, June 16, 1949; children: John Joachim Jr., Les Seidel. BS, U.S. Mil. Acad., 1948; MA in Internat. Affairs, Columbia U., 1961; grad., U.S. Army War Coll., 1968. Commd. 2d. lt. U.S. Army, 1948, advanced through grades to col.; chief U.S. Def. Ln. Group, Jakarta, Indonesia, 1972-74; chief field survey office U.S. Army Tng. and Doctrine Command, Ft. Monroe, Va., 1974-76; ret. U.S. Army, 1976; mgr. tng. Chrysler Def., Center Line, Mich., 1977-82; mgr. modification ctr. Land Systems div. Gen. Dynamics, Sterling Heights, Mich., 1982-83; mgr. field ops. Land Systems div. Gen. Dynamics, Warren, Mich., 1983—; ptnr. East West Connection, Birmingham, Mich.; speaker on terrorism and counter insurgency. Author: The Art of Counter Revolutionary War-The Strategy of CounterInsurgency, 1966. Pres. Troy (Mich.) Community Concert Assn., 1985—, Mich. Oriental Art Soc., Birmingham, 1985—; mem. exec. bd. Granderview Assn. Sr. Housing and Nursing, Milford, Mich., 1984—; bd. dirs. First Ch. of Christ Scientist, Birmingham, 1986—. Mem. Soc. Logistics Engrs., Nat. Mgmt. Assn., Assn. U.S. Army. Republican. Avocation: collecting and selling oriental antiques. Home: 32863 Balmoral Birmingham MI 48009 Office: Gen Dynamics Land Systems Div PO Box 527 Warren MI 48090

MCCULLAGH, GRANT GIBSON, architect; b. Cleve., Apr. 18, 1951; s. Robert Ernest and Barbara Louise (Grant) McC.; m. Suzanne Dewar Folds, Sept. 13, 1975; 1 child, Charles Weston Folds. BArch, U. Ill., 1973; MArch, U. Pa., 1975; MBA, U. Chgo., 1979. Registered architect, Ill. Project designer Perkins & Will, Chgo., 1975-77; dir. mktg. The Austin Co., Chgo., 1977-83, asst. dist. mgr., 1983-84, dist. mgr., 1984—, v.p., 1987—. Contbr. articles to various indsl. publs. Pres. Newberry Library Soc., Chgo., 1983-86; ex officio trustee Newberry Library, Chgo., 1983—. Mem. AIA, Chgo. Architecture Found. (exec. com., trustee, v.p. 1986—), Chgo. Archtl. Found. Aux. Bd. (exec. v.p. 1983-86). Republican. Episcopalian. Clubs: Economics, Chicago, Casino, University. Home: 43 Locust Rd Winnetka IL 60093 Office: The Austin Co 401 S La Salle St Chicago IL 60605

MCCULLEY, MICHAEL TODD, architect; b. St. Louis, Oct. 30, 1949; s. Riley Jackson and Louis Jean (Todd) McC.; m. Jane Elizabeth Koski, Mar. 22, 1975. BArch, U. Ill., 1972, MArch, 1979. Registered architect, Ill., Wis. Architect Office of Delbert Smith, Urbana, Ill., 1974-75, Clark Dietz & Assocs., Urbana, 1975-77; ptnr. Mikon Design, Urbana, 1977-79; asst. prof. Bldg. Research Council U. Ill., Champaign, 1979-82; prin. investigator mech. engr. U.S. Army Constrn. Engring. Research Labs., Champaign, 1982—; adj. research asst. prof. Bldg. Research Council U. Ill., Champaign, 1981—; visiting asst. prof. sch. architecture U. Ill., Urbana, 1980-82, 85-86. Contbr. articles to profl. jours. Mem. funds appropriation com. United Way, Urbana, 1983, 84, mem. bldg. com. Wesley Ch. and Found., Urbana, 1979-85, fin. com., 1985—, chmn. fin. com., 1987—. U.S. Dept. Energy grantee, 1980-82, Ill. Dept. Energy and Natural Resources grantee, 1980-85, Carradco Windows and Doors grantee, Rantoul, Ill., 1981-83. Mem. AIA (cen. Ill. chpt. v.p. 1977, pres. elect 1985, pres. 1986, treas. 1987), Am. Soc. Heating, Refrigeration and Air Conditioning Engrs. (chmn. edn. com. student chpt. 1982-84, sec. cen. Ill. chpt. 1984, Mortar Bd. award 1983). Republican. Methodist. Lodge: Rotary. Avocations: pilot, canoeing, cycling, running, scuba. Home: 4003 Farmington Champaign IL 61821 Office: US Army Constrn Engring Research Labs 2902 Newmark Dr Champaign IL 61821

MCCULLOUGH, HENRY G(LENN) L(UTHER), quality engineer; b. Waukegan, Ill., Aug. 5, 1939; s. Fredrick Douglas and Octavia Idelphi (Anderson) McC.; m. Suman'E Duan Naro, Nov. 6, 1962; children: Barbara, Jeanine, Michelle, Charles, Edmunds, Caroline, Richard, Larry; 1 adopted child, Robert. BA in Physics, Grinnell Coll., 1961; postgrad. in Nuclear Engring., U. Ariz., 1962; postgrad. in Physics, No. Ill. U., 1972, postgrad., 1972. Registered profl. engr., Ill.; cert. quality engr. Nuclear safeguards project engr. Sargent & Lundy Engrs., Chgo., 1976-81, project mgmt. engr., 1981-84, cons. engr., 1984—. Co-author: Nuclear Glossary, 1986. Bd. dirs. Council on Energy Independence, 1979-82; mem. Immaculate Conception Parish Sch. Bd., Waukegan, Ill., 1980-81; mem. Holy Names Soc. Immaculate Conception Ch., Waukegan, 1976—; commr. Northeast Ill. Council Boy Scouts Am., 1979-83. Served to 1st lt. USAF, 1962-65. Recipient Black Achiever award Chgo. Met. YMCA, 1981; grantee NSF, 1972. Mem. Am. Nuclear Soc. (chmn. standards working group 1980-86), Am. Soc. Quality Control, Soc. Am. Mil. Engrs. Republican. Roman Catholic. Office: Sargent & Lundy Engrs 55 E Monroe Chicago IL 60603

MCCULLOUGH, JOHN JACK PATRICK, advertising and graphics executive; b. Dubuque, Iowa, Feb. 6, 1956; s. Delbert Joseph and Shirley Mae (Carr) McC.; m. Lynn Marie Conlon, Apr. 18, 1986; 1 stepson, Dylan McGuill. A in Applied Arts, Hawkeye Inst. Tech., 1976. Graphic designer Wm. C. Brown Pubs., Dubuque, Iowa, 1976-78, Carlisle Graphics, Dubuque, 1978-80, Freelance Graphic Design, Dubuque, 1980-83; owner McCullough Graphics, Inc., Dubuque, 1983—, pres., 1985—. Mem. Advertisers Dubuque (bd. dirs. 1982—), West Dubuque Jaycees. Lodge: KC. Office: 601 Fischer Bldg Dubuque IA 52001

MCCULLOUGH, MICHAEL JAMES, gas company executive; b. Des Moines, Dec. 14, 1949; s. Roger Dalton and Bernadette Ann (McPhillips) McC.; m. Janice Kay Baumert, Aug. 30, 1981; children: Christopher, Phillip. BS in Bus. and Fin., U. Nebr., Omaha, 1975, MBA, 1976. Cons. Arthur Andersen & Co., Omaha, 1977-78; project mgr. People's Natural Gas Co., Council Bluffs, Nebr., 1978-81; energy economist No. Natural Gas Co., Omaha, 1981-84, sr. gas supply analyst, 1984—. Cons. road running events, Omaha. Served with USMC, 1969-71. Avocation: computer applications. Office: No Natural Gas Co 2223 Dodge St Omaha NE 68102

MCCULLOUGH, NANCY CAMP, public relations executive; b. Honolulu, Sept. 14, 1948; d. Joseph Martin and Elizabeth Hyers (Reitz) Camp. B.F.A., Ill. Wesleyan U.-Bloomington, 1971; M.S. in Info. Scis., Ill. State U.-Normal, 1974. Mem. faculty Ill. Wesleyan U., 1971-72; cons. social rehab. Schultz & Assocs., Bloomington, Ill., 1972-74; mem. faculty Ill. State U., 1974-76; communications specialist Mennonite Health Care Assn., Bloomington, 1976-79; dir. pub. relations Ill. Agrl. Assn., Bloomington, 1979-85; founder, prin. McCullough Pub. Relations, 1985—. Chmn. pub. relations McLean County United Way, 1981; chmn. McLean County residential crusade Am. Cancer Soc., 1981-82. Recipient Pub. Relations Soc. Am. Silver Anvil award, 1986. Mem. McLean County Dance Assn. (co-founder 1976, bd. dirs. 1976-80), Agrl. Relations Council Am., Public Relations Soc. Am. (accredited mem.), Nat. Assn. Female Execs. Author: Farm In The School, 1981; contbr. articles, photog. studies to profl. publs. Home: Route 2 Box 71 Eureka IL 61530

MCCULLOUGH, RICHARD LAWRENCE, advertising agency executive; b. Chgo., Dec. 1, 1937; s. Francis John and Sadie Beatrice McC.; m. Julia Louise Kreimer, May 6, 1961; children—Steven, Jeffery, Julia. B.S., Marquette U., 1959. Account exec. Edward H. Weiss & Co., Chgo., 1960-66; account supr. Doyle Dane Bernbach, N.Y.C., 1966-68; sr. v.p. J. Walter Thompson Co., Chgo., 1969-86; pres. E.H. Brown, Chgo., 1986—. Bd. dirs. Gateway Found., Chgo., 1976—, mem. exec. com., 1976—. Served to sgt. U.S. Army, 1959-60. Mem. Country Music Assn. (dir. 1979—, pres. 1983-85). Roman Catholic. Home: 2720 Lincoln St Evanston IL 60201 Office: EH Brown Advt 20 N Wacker Dr Chicago IL 60606

MCCULLOUGH-WIGGINS, LYDIA STATORIA, pharmacist, consultant; b. Chgo., May 14, 1948; d. George Robert and Isabell (King) Boulware; m. Robert Dale McCullough, Aug. 1, 1970 (div. Oct. 1977); m. 2d, James Calvin Wiggins, Nov. 3, 1979. Student Wis. State U.-Whitewater, 1966-69; B.S. in Pharmacy, U. Ill.-Chgo., 1972; cert. UCLA, 1976-78. Registered pharmacist, Ill. Registered pharmacy apprentice Lefel Drugs, Chgo., 1971-72; pharmacy mgr. Fernwood Pharmacy, Chgo., 1972-73, Sapstein Bros. Pharmacy, Chgo., 1973-74; dir. pharmacy Martin Luther King Neighborhood Health Ctr., Chgo., 1974-80; pharmacist in charge Walgreens, Chgo., 1980—. Bd. dirs. Nia Comprehensive Ctr. Developmental Disabilities, Inc. Author: M.L.K. Drug Formulary, 1978. Recipient Cert. of Leadership, YMCA Met. Chgo., 1979; Kizzy award 1980 Black Women Hall of Fame Found., Chgo., 1981; Ann. Med. Achievement award Greater Chgo. Met. Community, 1981. Mem. Chgo. Pharmacists Assn., Am. Pharm. Assn., Ill. Pharm. Assn., Nat. Pharmacists Assn. (exec. bd.), Nat. Assn. Female Execs., U. Ill. Alumni Assn. Democrat. Baptist. Club: Christian Novice (pres. 1977-78) (Chgo.). Home: 618 S Marshall St Bellwood IL 60104

MCCULLUM, GERALD EDWIN, school administrator; b. Jeffersonville, Ind., Sept. 26, 1939; s. Gerald Edwin and Helen (Benson) McC.; m. Mary Ann Carlisle, Mar. 21, 1964; 1 child, Gerald Edwin III. BS, Ind. U., 1962, MS, 1964; cert. specialist in edn., Ball State U., 1977. Asst. prin. high sch. Garrett (Ind.)-Keyser-Butler Sch., 1966-67; prin. high sch. Argos (Ind.) Community Schs., 1967-68, Edinburg (Ind.) Community Schs., 1968-73, Mississinewa Community Schs., Gas City, Ind., 1973-78; supt. Fremont (Ind.) Community Schs., 1973-81, Scott County Sch. Dist. 2, Scottsburg, Ind., 1981—; vice chmn. Madison (Ind.) Area Spl. Services Unit, 1981—; mem. adv. bd. Prosser Vocat. Sch., New Albany, Ind., 1981—. Chmn. Local bd. 47 Selective Service, Clark, Scott and Washington Counties, Ind., 1981; exec. bd. dirs. Hoosier Falls Pvt. Industry Council, Jeffersonville, 1983; mem. Planning & Zoning Bd. Scott County, 1981. NSF fellow; Ind. Sch. Exec. fellow Lilly Endowment. Mem. Ind. Assn. Pub. Schs. Supts., Ind. Assn. Sch. Bus.. Officials, Assn. Supervision and Curriculum Devel., Am. Assn. Sch. Adminstrs., Phi Delta Kappa, Scottsburg C. of C. (bd. dirs. 1983). Methodist. Lodges: Lions (pres. Edinburg chpt., 1968-73), Kiwanis. Avocations: stamp collecting, coin collecting. Home: Rt 3 Box 219 Scottsburg IN 47170 Office: Scott County Sch Dist 2 375 E McClain Ave Scottsburg IN 47170

MCCURDY, KURT BASQUIN, real estate corporation officer; b. Portsmouth, Ohio, Dec. 24, 1952; s. Robert Kurt and Sue Ann (Basquin) McC.; m. Eileen Wirtz, May 21, 1977; children: Andrew Kurt, Patrick Robert, Meghan Eileen. Student, Ohio No. U., Ada, 1971-72; BA, Ohio State U., 1976. Sales assoc. HER Realtors, Inc., Columbus, Ohio, 1975—; appraiser Franklin County Probate Ct., Columbus, 1978—; guest lectr. Ohio State U., 1981, Franklin U., 1982-83. Contbr. articles to real estate mags. Mem. Realtors Polit. Action Com., Columbus, 1978—, Chmn.'s Club, Rep. Party, Franklin County, 1980-85; v.p., bd. dirs. Culver (Ind.) Mil. Summer Schs., 1979-84. Recipient One Million Dollar Club, Five Million Dollar Club, Ten Million Dollar Club awards Columbus Bd. Realtors, 1977, 82. Mem. Ohio Assn. Realtors (Profl. of Yr. award 1979, 83, 84, Pres's sales award 1986), HER Presidents Club, Ohio State U. Alumni Assn. Methodist. Clubs: Little Turtle Country (Westerville, Ohio), Westerville Athletic. Avocations: golf, tennis, boating, fishing, hunting. Home: 2784 Shady Ridge Dr Columbus OH 43229 Office: HER Realtors Inc 5888 Cleveland Ave Columbus OH 43229

MCCURDY, SUSAN REPLOGLE, tax and accounting practitioner; b. Marshalltown, Iowa, Feb. 12, 1949; d. Paul Gilmore and Doris Mae (Schulz) Replogle; m. John William McCurdy, Dec. 21, 1968; children—William (dec.), Kathryn, Elizabeth. A.A., Marshalltown Community Coll., 1969, B.A., U. No. Iowa, Cedar Falls, 1970; postgrad. Iowa State U., Ames, 1980—, M.A., U. No. Iowa, 1983. With McCall Monument Co., Oskaloosa, Iowa, 1968-72; sr. sec. Grace United Meth. Ch., Marshalltown, 1971-72; exec. sec. Elim Luth. Ch., Marshalltown, 1977-80; founder, ptnr. Su McCurdy Bus. Alternatives, Marshalltown 1978—; faculty Marshalltown Community Coll., 1983—. Recipient Fisher Gov. Found. scholarship, 1968-69, Lloyd V. Douglas award U. No.Iowa, 1984. Mem. Nat. Assn. Tax Practitioners; Nat. and Iowa Bus. Edn. Assns., Accts. Assn. Iowa, Marshalltown C. of C., Nat. Assn. Female Execs., Assn. Bus. Communication, Iowa Jr. Coll. Honor Soc. (permanent mem.), Honor Soc. Bus. Majors, Kappa Delta Pi, Delta Pi Epsilon (Excellence in Research award 1984). Baptist. Home: 405 E South St Marshalltown IA 50158 Office: 7 Westwood Dr Suite A Marshalltown IA 50158

MCCURLEY, F. C., insurance company executive; b. 1934; married. With Western Casualty & Surety Co., Fort Scott, Kans., 1953—, pres., chief exec. officer, dir., 1982—. Office: Western Casualty & Surety Co 14 E 1st St Fort Scott KS 66701 *

MCCURRY, MARGARET IRENE, architect; b. Chgo., Sept. 26, 1942; d. Paul D. and Irene B. (Tipler) McC.; m. Stanley Tigerman, Mar. 17, 1979. BA, Vassar Coll., 1964. Registered architect, Ill. Design coordinator Quaker Oats Co., Chgo., 1964-66; sr. interior designer Skidmore, Owings & Merrill, Chgo., 1966-77; pvt. practice Chgo., 1977-82; ptnr. Tigerman, Fugman, McCurry, Chgo., 1982—; vis. studio critic Art Inst. Chgo., 1985-86; juror internat. furniture awards Progressive Architecture Mag., N.Y.C., 1986, design grants Nat. Endowment for Arts, Washington, 1983. Exhibited at Art Inst. Chgo., 1983-86. Chmn. furniture sect. Fund Raising Auction WTTW Pub. TV, Chgo., 1975-76; mem. City of Chgo. Beautiful Com., 1968-70. Loeb fellow Harvard U., 1986-87; recipient Builders Choice Grand award Builders Mag., 1985. Mem. AIA (v.p., bd. dirs. Chgo. chpt., steering com. nat. design com., lectr. Colo. chpt. 1985, Nat. Honor award 1984, Disting. Bldg. award Chgo. chpt., 1984, 86, Disting. Interior Architecture award Chgo. chpt., 1983), Am. Soc. Interior Designers, Chgo. Archtl. Club. Episcopalian. Clubs: Arts Chgo., Womans Athletic (Chgo.). Avocations: drawing, travel, tennis, skiing, folk art. Home: 910 N Lake Shore Dr Chicago IL 60611 Office: Tigerman Fugman McCurry 444 N Wells St Chicago IL 60610

MCCUSKEY, THOMAS GEORGE, lawyer; b. Canton, Ohio, May 4, 1948; s. Richard George and Eleanor Elizabeth (Mumaw) McC.; m. Barbara June Pollack, June 22, 1970; children: Erin, David, Ian. BA, Coe Coll., 1970; JD, Drake U., 1974. Bar: Iowa 1974, Ariz. 1980. Sole practice Cedar Rapids, Iowa, 1974-75; assoc. Neiman Neiman Stone & Spellman, Des Moines, 1975-79; ptnr. Klinger Robinson & McCuskey, Cedar Rapids, 1980—. Mem. ABA, Iowa Bar Assn., Ariz. Bar Assn. Methodist. Home: 2325 Blake Blvd SE Cedar Rapids IA 52403 Office: 401 Old Marion Rd NE Cedar Rapids IA 52402

MCCUTCHEON, GARY LEE, computer information scientist; b. Arkansas City, Kans., June 22, 1945; s. Robert Lee and Lois Mildred (Young) McC.; m. Patricia Joan Morgan, Aug. 10, 1968; 1 child, Jeffrey Alan. AA, Arkansas City Jr. Coll., 1965, Kans Tech. Inst., 1968; BA summa cum laude, McPherson (Kans.) Coll., 1973; postgrad., Wichita (Kans.) State U., 1986. Systems analyst Fluid Power div. Cessna, Hutchinson, Kans., 1973-78, supr. systems and programming, 1978—. Sec.-treas. McPherson County Fire Dept., Inman, Kans., 1982—; chmn. Bd. Zoning Appeals, Inman. Served with U.S. Army, 1969-71, Vietnam. Mem. Data Processing Mgmt. Assn., Inman Jaycees (past sec., pres.). Republican. Methodist. Avocations: jogging, woodcarving, house remodeling. Home: 313 S Main St Box 323 Inman KS 67546 Office: Cessna Fluid Power Div Box 1028 Hutchinson KS 67504-1028

MCCUTCHEON, HOLLY MARIE, accountant; b. Pitts., Aug. 14, 1950. Student, Ohio Dominican Coll., 1968-69, Wittenburg U., 1979-81; BS in Acctg. and Fin. magna cum laude, Wright State U., 1983. Acct. Morris Bean & Co., Yellow Springs, Ohio, 1983-86; gen. acct. Fruehauf div. SPECO Corp., Springfield, Ohio, 1986—; cons. Glenwood Tng. Ctr., Yellow Springs, 1983-86. Coach City Recreation Youth Soccer, Springfield, 1982-85; mem. St. Raphael Adult Choir, Springfield, 1986—. Mem. Inst. Cert. Mgmt. Accts., Nat. Assn. Accts. (sec. Dayton chpt. 1985-86, sec. 1986—). Avocations: fishing, golf, tennis, cross country skiing. Office: SPECO Corp PO Box 1288 Springfield OH 45501

MCDANIEL, MICHAEL KEITH, human resource development consultant; b. Garrett, Ind., Nov. 26, 1948; s. Richard Keith and Maria Dorthy (Otterbine) McD.; m. Deborah Ann Brooks, Dec. 18, 1976; 1 child, Matthew Keith. BS, Purdue U., 1971, MS, 1973. Asst. prof. human devel. Ashland (Ohio) Coll., 1973-79; pres. McDaniel Assocs. Internat., Mansfield, Ohio, 1981—; human resource devel. cons. Ashland County Vocat. Edn., 1979—; pub. speaker, trainer; specialist in employee involvement, leadership devel., Statis. Process Control. Author various pamphlets in field. Office: McDaniel Assocs Internat 815 Marion Ave Mansfield OH 44906

MCDANIEL, ROSE LEE, educator; b. Norcross, Ga., June 26, 1929; d. Frank Lee and Mary Pearl (Bowen); m. Charles William McDaniel, Mar. 4, 1949; children—Deborah D. McDaniel Roberts, Charles F., Reginael D. Student Wilkins Sch. Cosmetology, 1947; B.Edn., Toledo U., 1964, M.Ed., 1971, Ed.S., 1975. Cosmetologist, 1947-60; tchr. elem. sch., Toledo, 1964-67, resource tchr., 1968-69, team leader Tchr. Corps, 1969-71, elem. tchr., 1971, adminstrv. intern, 1972, edn1. specialist, 1972-80; tchr. elem. sch. Fulton County (Ga.), Atlanta, 1980-81; asst. prin. Sherman Elem. Sch., Toledo, 1981-84; prin. Reynolds Elem. Sch., Toledo, 1984—. Supt. Sunday sch. Bapt. Ch., 1975-78, dir. Christian Edn., 1978-84; sec. Matrons Conv. N.W. Ohio Bapt. Assn., 1979. Recipient service cert. Family Life Edn. Ctr., 1980, Nat. Appreciation award Soc. Disting. Am. High Sch. Students, 1978. Mem. Assn. Supervision and Curriculum Devel., Internat. Reading Assn., U. Toledo Alumni Assn., Phi Delta Kappa, Alpha Chi Pi Omega (pres. 1967-69, Woman of Yr. award 1970). Democrat.

MCDERMED, RONALD DEAN, educational administrator; b. Muskegon, Mich., Aug. 12, 1951; s. Harold Walter and Frances May (Ervin) McD.; m. Irene Presnikovs, Nov. 20, 1976; children—Alina Michele, Michael Walter. B.A., Western Mich. U., 1974; M.A., Mich. State U., 1978, Ed.S., 1983, doctoral candidate, 1983—. Tchr., Portland (Mich.) Pub. Schs., 1974-79, dir. fed. programs, 1980—; prin. Mich. Elem. Schs., Fowler, 1986—; reading cons. elem., 1979-80. Trustee scholar Western Mich. U., 1971-74. Mem. NEA, Mich. Elem. and Middle Sch. Prin.'s Assn., Mich. Reading Assn., Mich. Edn. Assn., Mich. Assn. State and Fed. Program Specialists, Assn. Supervision and Curriculum Devel., Portland Community Theatre, Phi Delta Kappa. Congregationalist. Lodge: Lions.

MCDERMOTT, JOSEPH MICHAEL, civil engineer; b. Cleve., Oct. 28, 1939; s. Michael J. and Lillian Rita (Watterson) McD.; m. Kathleen Mavourneen McGrath, Sept. 24, 1966; children: Kelly, Patrick, Erin. BSCE, U. Detroit, 1962; MSCE, Northwestern U., 1963. Engring. aide Ohio Dept. Transp., Cleve., 1959-62; civil engr. Ill. Dept. Transp., Oak Park, 1963-68, asst. dir. traffic systems ctr., 1968-70, acting dir., 1970-72, dir., mgr., 1972—. Contbr. articles to profl. jours. Chmn. Addison (Ill.) Plan Commn., 1975—; pres. King's Point Homeowners Assn., 1969—; co-chmn. Addison Irishfest, 1981. Walter P. Murphy fellow Northwestern U., 1962; Caddie scholar Cleve. Dist. Golf Assn., 1957; named Engr. of Yr. Ill. Dept. Transp., 1981. Mem. ASCE (chmn. Urban Transp. div. exec. com. 1985, Frank M. Masters award 1980, Arthur M. Wellington Prize, 1981), Nat. Acad. Scis. (Transp. Research Bd. freeway ops. com. 1978-84), Inst. Transp. Engrs., Irish-Am. Heritage Ctr. Avocations: golfing, white-water rafting, traveling. Home: 523 Monarch Ln Addison IL 60101 Office: Ill Dept Transp Traffic Systems Ctr 445 Harrison St Oak Park IL 60304

MC DONALD, ALONZO LOWRY, business executive; b. Atlanta, Aug. 5, 1928; s. Alonzo Lowry and Lois (Burrell) McD.; m. Suzanne Moffitt, May 9, 1959. A.B., Emory U., 1948; M.B.A., Harvard U., 1956. Asst. to sales mgr. air conditioning div. Westinghouse Electric Corp., Staunton, Va., 1956-57; Western zone mgr. Westinghouse Electric Corp., St. Louis, 1957-60; assoc. N.Y. Office McKinsey & Co., Inc., 1960-64, prin. London Office, 1964-66, mng. prin. Zurich Office, 1966-68, mng. dir. Paris Office, 1968-73; mng. dir., chief exec. officer of firm N.Y.C., 1973-76; dir. N.Y. Office 1976-77; dep. spl. trade rep., also ambassador in charge U.S. del. Tokyo round of Multilateral Trade Negotiations, 1977-79; acting spl. trade rep. Washington, 1979; asst. to Pres. U.S., White House staff dir. 1979-81; mem. faculty Harvard U. Grad. Sch. Bus. Adminstrn., Boston, 1981; pres. The Bendix Corp., Southfield, Mich., 1981-83; chmn., chief exec. officer Avenir Group, Inc., Bloomfield Hills, Mich., 1983—. Trustee CED, 1975—; Mem. Council Fgn. Relations. Served with USMCR, 1950-52. Office: 5505 Corporate Dr Suite 400 Troy MI 48098

MCDONALD, ARLINE MARGARET, researcher, nutrition educator; b. Chuquicamata, Chile, Jan. 8, 1953; came to U.S., 1953; s. Robert Emmett and Barbara Ann (Gehres) McD. B.S., U. Ky., 1974; M.S., U. Tenn., 1976, Ph.D., 1978. Postdoctoral research fellow Northwestern U. Med. Sch., Chgo., 1978-81, asst. prof. community health and preventive medicine, 1982—; asst. prof. nutrition and med. dietetics U. Ill., Chgo. Health Scis. Center, 1981—. Mem. Chgo. Heart Assn. Recipient Chancellor's Citation, U. Tenn., 1978; Research Career Devel. award Nat. Heart, Lung and Blood Inst., NIH, 1982-87. Mem. Sigma Xi. Roman Catholic. Home: 1120 N LaSalle Dr Apt 16C Chicago IL 60610 Office: 303 E Chicago Ave Chicago IL 60611

MCDONALD, BRENDAN JOHN, university president; b. Regina, Sask., Can., May 15, 1930; married, 1954; 2 children. B.S., St. Cloud State Coll., 1954; M.A., U. Minn., 1957; Ph.D. in Higher Edn. Adminstrn., Mich. State U., 1967. Registrar, dir. admissions St. Cloud State Coll., Minn., 1956-65, v.p. adminstrn. and planning, 1972-73; researcher U. N.D., 1966; prof. edn. Mankato State Coll., Minn., 1967-72, asst. acad. v.p., 1967-72; pres. Kearney State Coll., Nebr., 1972-82, St. Cloud State U., Minn., 1982—. Trustee fellow Mich. State U., 1967. Office: St Cloud State Univ Office of the Pres Saint Cloud MN 56301

MCDONALD, CHARLES RAYMOND, manufacturing executive; b. Cleve., Oct. 2, 1927; s. Roy James and Helen (LaBarge) Gerscheski; m. Deborah Brandais, Sept. 29, 1957 (div. AUg. 1986); children: Robert, Charles, Cheryl, Robin, Scott. Student, Kent (Ohio) State U., 1947-48, Mont. Sch. Mines, 1949-50. Owner May-Ctr. Mobil, Cleve., 1952-58; v.p. Parts, Inc., Cleve., 1963-68; pres. McDonald Equipment Co., Willoughby, Ohio, 1968—; bd. dirs. Commerce Exchange Bank, Beachwood, Ohio; mem. Pres. Carter's Wage Industry Com., Washington, 1980. Chmn. Council Smaller Enterprises, Cleve., 1978-80; dir. Cleve. United Way; treas. Health Systems Agy., Region IX, Ohio, 1984-86; bd. dirs. Pvt. Industry Council, Cleve., 1983-86. Mem. Nat. Small Bus. Assn. (bd. dirs. 1984—), Nat. Fire Protecton Assn. Clubs: Shaker Heights (Ohio) Country, Cleve. Country. Lodge: Masons (32 degree). Office: McDonald Equipment Co 37200 Vine St Willoughby OH 44094

MCDONALD, EDWIN KENNETH, III, dentist; b. Chgo., Sept. 2, 1950; s. Edwin Kenneth Jr. and Frances Salata (Stokes) McD.; m. Colette McDonald, Feb. 14, 1981; children: Edwin IV, Robert MArshall. BS, U. Ill., 1971; DDS, Meharry Med. Coll., 1975. Staff dentist Chgo. Bd. Health, 1977-80; chmn. dental group Gary (Ind.) Health Care Council, 1984—. Mem. Chgo. Urban League, 1985-86. Mem. USGC Aux., 1980—. Mem. ADA, Ind. Dental Assn., Nat. Dental Assn. (souvenir program chmn. 1982), Loncoln Dental Soc. (treas. 1979-80, sec. 1980-81). Avocations: tennis, boating. Office: 3195 Broadway Gary IN 46409

MCDONALD, FRANCIS JAMES, automobile company executive; b. Saginaw, Mich., Aug. 3, 1922; s. Francis J. and Mary C. (Fordney) McD.; m. Betty Ann Dettenthaler, Dec. 27, 1944; children: Timothy Joseph, John Thomas, Marybeth McDonald Pallas. BS, Gen. Motors Inst., 1944. With Gen. Motors Corp., Detroit, 1940—; plant mgr. central foundry div. Gen. Motors Corp., 1955-56, works mgr., Detroit transmission div., 1956-63, gen. mgr. Hydra-Matic div., 1963-65, works mgr. Pontiac Motor div., 1965-68, dir. mfg. ops. Chevrolet Motor div., 1968-69, corp. v.p., gen. mgr. Pontiac Motor div., 1969-72, corp. v.p., gen. mgr. Chevrolet Motor div., 1972-74; exec. v.p. Gen. Motors Corp., Detroit, 1974-81, pres., chief operating officer, 1981-87; also chmn. exec. com., dir. Gen. Motors Corp.; dir., mem. exec. compensation and audit coms. H.J. Heinz Co.; mem.-at-large Oakland County Traffic Improvement Assn. Chmn. Research Inst., William Beaumont Hosp., Royal Oak, Mich., 1973-76, trustee, adv. bd. Troy (Mich.) br.; v.p. Boys Clubs Met. Detroit; bd. dirs. Up with People; chmn. bd. visitors Sch. Econs. and Mgmt., Oakland U., Rochester. Served to lt. (j.g.) USN, 1944-46. Mem. Soc. Automotive Engrs., Engring. Soc. Detroit, Tau Beta Pi. Club: Detroit Athletic. Office: Gen Motors Corp Gen Motors Bldg 3044 W Grand Blvd Detroit MI 48202 *

MCDONALD, JAMES EDWARD, ophthalmologist, educator; b. Ill., Nov. 9, 1922; s. Clarence T. and Honor (Cox) McD.; m. Evelyn Kosar; children: Mary Jo, Virginia, Michelle. MD, Loyola U., Chgo., 1945. Faculty U. Ill., Chgo., 1952-70; prof. and chmn. dept. ophthalmology Loyola U., Maywood, Ill., 1970—. Pres. FOCUS, Inc., Maywood, 1962—. Served to capt. AUS, 1946-48, ETO. Recipient Grand Office of Republic award Republic of Haiti, 1962; named Disting. Man, Municipality of Guatamala City, Guatamala. Mem. AMA, Am. Ophthal. Soc., Chgo. Ophthal. Soc. (pres. 1962), Am. Acad. Ophthalmology, Assn. Univ. Profs. Ophthalmology. Office: Loyola U Med Ctr Maywood IL 60153

MCDONALD, JAMES FRANCIS, electronics company executive; b. Louisville, Feb. 17, 1940; s. Matthew Joseph and Eileen Frances (Schmidt) McD.; m. Paula S. Smith; children: Jimmie L., Susan J., Ashley K. BSEE, U. Ky., 1963, MSEE, 1964. Mgr. prodn. engring. IBM Corp., Boulder, Colo., 1974-75, mgr. devel. lab., 1975-76, mgr. task force, 1976-77, mgr. bus. planning and product planning office products, 1977, systems mgr. copier products, 1977-78, lab. dir. office parts, 1978-80; gen. mgr. mfg. systems products IBM Corp., Boca Raton, Fla., 1980-84; pres., chief operating officer Gould, Inc., Rolling Meadows, Ill., 1984-86, chief operating officer, 1984, chmn., chief exec. officer, 1986—. Mem. Robot Inst. Am., (bd. dirs.), United Telecommunications, Inc. (bd. dirs. 1986—). Office: Gould Inc 10 Gould Center Rolling Meadows IL 60008

MCDONALD, PHYLLIS PARSHALL, protection services official; b. New Salem, N.Y., June 10, 1934; s. Earl LeRoy and Lena Belle (Race) P.; m. Gerald Michael McDonald, Apr. 22, 1957 (div.); children: Jennifer Suzanne, Michael Gerald, Melanie Christine. BA, SUNY, Albany, 1956, MA, 1964; EdS, George Washington U., 1966, EdD, 1972. Tchr. history Draper High Sch., Schenectady, N.Y., 1956-57; tchr. spl. edn. Christ Child Inst., Rockville, Md., 1964-66; program assoc. Council for Exceptional Children, Reston, Va., 1970-71; coordinator IRC Mark Twain Sch., Rockville, 1971-74; project dir. model inservice tng. Montgomery County (Md.) Police Dept., 1977, dir. police acad., 1978-79; dir. human resources Met. Police, Washington, 1979-81, spl. asst. to dir. of planning and research, 1981-84; dep. dir. Nat. Inst. Justice Tng. Project of URSA Inst., San Francisco and Washington, 1984-86; maj., supt. profl. standards div. Dept. of Police, Dayton, Ohio, 1986—. Dem. precinct vice chmn., 1976, chmn. Com. to rev. Youth Groups, 1978. Fellow U.S Office of Edn., 1966, State of Md., 1966-68. Mem. Police Mgmt. Assn. (bd. dirs.), Internat. Assn. Chief of Police. Democrat. Avocations: white water rafting, music, literature. Home: 37 Hess St Dayton OH 45402 Office: Dayton Police Dept 335 W 3d St Dayton OH 45402

MCDONALD, ROBERT DELOS, manufacturing company executive; b. Dubuque, Iowa, Jan. 30, 1931; s. Delos Lyon and Virginia (Kolck) McD.; m. Jane M. Locher, Jan. 16, 1960 (div. Jan. 1970); children: Jean, Patricia, Maria, Sharon, Rob; m. Marilyn I. Miller, July 4, 1978. BA in Econs., U. Iowa, 1953. Salesman A.Y. McDonald Mfg. Co., Dubuque, 1956-60, sales mgr., 1961-64, wholesale br. mgr., 1965-72, v.p., 1971-72, v.p. and corp. sec., 1972-85, sr. v.p. and corp. sec., 1983-85, pres., 1985-87, chmn. bd., pres., chief exec. officer, 1987—, also bd. dirs.; bd. dirs. Brock-McVey Co., Lexington, Ky. Bd. dirs. A.Y. McDonald Mfg. Co. Charitable Found., 1978—, pres. 1982—, Stonehill Care Ctr., Dubuque, 1984—; bd. trustees Iowa Hist. Mus. Found., Des Moines, 1984—. Served to lt. USNR, 1953-56, Korea. Mem. Am. Mgmt. Assn., Am. Supply Assn., Am. Water Works Assn., Am. Legion, Dubuque Area C. of C., Dubuque Area Indsl. Devel. Corp. (bd. dirs. 1980—), Sigma Alpha Epsilon. Roman Catholic. Republican. Clubs: Dubuque Golf & Country, Dubuque Shooting Soc. Home: 3055 Powers Ct Dubuque IA 52001 Office: A Y McDonald Mfg Co 4800 Chavenelle Rd Dubuque IA 52001

MCDONALD, R(OBERT) GRIFFITH, investment advisor; b. Ripon, Wis., Feb. 18, 1942; s. Robert E. and Gertrude (Griffith) McD.; m. Patricia Peckinpaugh, Aug. 29, 1965; children: Scott, Marti. BA, De Pauw U., Greencastle, Ind., 1964; MBA, Harvard U., 1966. Various mgmt. positions with Standard Oil of Ohio, Cleve., 1966-70; various mgmt. positions Xerox Pub. Group, Stamford, Conn., 1970-72, Xerox Univ. Microfilms, Ann Arbor, Mich., 1972-82; pres. Integrated Fin. Strategies, Ann Arbor, 1982—. Bd. dirs. Washtenaw United Way, Ann Arbor, 1980-86; chmn. Com. on Excellence in Ann Arbor Schs., 1984-85; co-convenor Ann Arbor Area 2000, 1986-87. Mem. Internat. Assn. for Fin. Planning (bd. dirs. 1986—), Ann Arbor C. of C. (bd. dirs. 1982-86, chmn. bd. 1985). Clubs: Ducks Unltd. (local chmn. 1982-85), Harvard Bus. Sch. of Detroit (v.p., bd. dirs. 1986). Avocations: bicycling, hunting, platform tennis. Office: Integrated Fin Strategies Group 2002 Hogback Rd Suite 19 Ann Arbor MI 48105

MCDONALD, STANFORD LAUREL, clinical psychologist; b. Lincoln, Nebr., Mar. 14, 1929; s. Laurel C. and Irene Virginia (Frey) McD.; m. Shirley P. Peterson, Apr. 26, 1964; children: Stacia E. V., Jeffrey J.S., Kathleen S., Patricia M. AB, Nebr. Wesleyan U., 1956; MA, U. Nebr., 1959, postgrad., 1958-60; PhD, Fielding Inst., 1974. Licensed clin. psychologist, Ill. Intern Nebr. Psychiat. Inst., Omaha, 1957-58; staff psychologist Presbyn. St. Lukes Hosp., Chgo., 1960-61; sch. psychologist Chgo. Bd. Edn., 1961-65; chief psychologist SPEED Devel. Ctr., Chicago Heights, Ill., 1965-79; pvt. practice psychology Olympia Fields, Ill., 1980—; bd. dirs. Metro Psych Group (HMO), Chgo.; mem. faculty Ill. Sch. Profl. Psychology, Chgo., 1978—; community prof. Gov's. State U., University Park, Ill., 1974—; clin. cons. alcohol treatment program Ingalls Meml. Hosp., Harvey, Ill., 1985—; active MetroPsych (PPO), Chgo., 1987—. Contbr. papers for profl. convs. Served to USMC, 1950-52, Korea. Fellow Am. Orthopsychiat. Assn.; mem. Am. Psychol. Assn., Ill. Psychol. Assn., Biofeedback Soc. Ill. (past. pres.), N.Y. Acad. Scis., Zeta Psi, Psi Chi. Lodge: Kiwanis. Avocations: personal computers, sports cars. Home: 2555 Rich Road Park Forest IL 60466 Office: 2555 W Lincoln Hwy Suite 203 Olympia Fields IL 60461

MCDONALD, STANLEIGH BUELL, training and development executive; b. St. Louis, Feb. 3, 1924; s. Buell Barger and Ruth (Pearson) McD.; m. Mary Ann Culhan, May 17, 1947; children: Kathryn, Scott, Bruce. BS, Butler U., 1948. Lectr. Gen. Motors Inst., Indpls., 1952-58; mgr. tech. tng. Allison div. Gen. Motors Corp., Indpls., 1958-62; corp. mgr. tng. Burroughs Corp., Detroit, 1962-67, J.C. Penney Co., N.Y.C., 1967-69; sr. cons. A.S. Hansen, Inc., Chgo., 1970-74; v.p. Boyden, Internat., Chgo., 1974; dir. cons. Coopers & Lybrand, Chgo., 1974-76; v.p. Schnadig Corp., Chgo., 1976-79; pres. Buell Assocs., Ltd., Chgo., 1980—. Author: Art of Conference Leadership, 1958, Ten Weeks to a Better Job, 1972 (library Jour. award 1972). Alderman City of Lake Forest, Ill., 1979-85. Served with U.S. Army, 1943-45, ETO. Mem. Employment Mgmt. Assn., Am. Compensation Assn., Am. Soc. for Tng. and Devel. Home: 434 Linden Ave Lake Forest IL 60045

MCDONALD, THOMAS JOSEPH, otolaryngologist, surgeon; b. County Down, Ireland, May 30, 1940; came to U.S., 1964; s. Francis Aloyisus and Irene (Doyle) McD.; m. Mary Margaret Brown, May 14, 1966; children: Thomas, Drew, Ryan, Darren, Robb. Student, St. Mary's Coll., Dundalk, Ireland, 1957; MD, Royal Coll. Surgeons, Dublin, Ireland, 1963; MS on Otolaryngology, U. Minn., 1974. Diplomate Am. Bd. Otolaryngology. Intern St. Mary's Hosp., Saginaw, Mich., 1964-65; resident in surgery Mayo Clinic, Rochester, Minn., 1968-69, resident on otolaryngology, 1969-72, cons. dept. otolaryngology, 1972—; mem. med. adv. bd. Hearing Industries Assn., Washington, 1980—. Mem. editorial bd. Postgrad. Medicine Jour., 1980—; contbr. 130 articles to profl. jours. Served to capt. U.S. Army, 1966-68, Vietnam. Fellow Am. Acad. Otolaryngology-Head and Neck Surgery, ACS, Am. Laryngol., Rhinol. and Otolaryngol.; mem. AMA, Minn. Med. Assn., Zumbro Valley Med. Assn., Royal Soc. Medicine, Soc. Irish and Am. Rheumatologists, Irish and Am. Pediatric Soc., Pan Am. Assn. Otorhinolaryngology, Mayo Alumni Assn. Roman Catholic. Home: 3245 Hill Court SW Rochester MN 55902 Office: Mayo Clinic 200 First St SW Rochester MN 55905

MCDONALD, W. R., employee benefits consultant, developer; b. Mt. Vernon, Ill., Nov. 1, 1929; s. Archie R. and Vernadean Pearl (Bailey) McD. BS, Ind. State U., 1953. Pres. Youth, Inc., Terre Haute, Ind., 1947; dist. mgr. New Eng. Life Ins. Co., Sacramento, 1958-62; v.p. Sutter Sq., Inc., Sacramento, 1960-62, Southland Trust Co., Tucson, 1963-65, Am. Equity Group, Inc., Indpls., 1966-68; sr. ptnr. Ins. Investors' Guidance Systems, Mt. Vernon, 1972—; pres. Interstate Investors & Growers Syndicate, Inc., Indpls., 1975—; mng. ptnr. Halia Crest Land Trust, Mt. Vernon, 1977-79; pres. Intermed. Self-Ins. Group, Mt. Vernon, 1979—; sr. gen. ptnr. Interstate Investors Golf and Garden Solar Lodges, 1980—, Investors Strategies Group, St. Louis, 1982-85, Internat. Benefits Adv. Group, St. Louis, 1984; mng. gen. ptnr. Sundowners' Retirement Resorts, 1986—; bd. dirs. Southland Trust Life Ins. Co., Phoenix, 1964; cons. So. Ill. U., Carbondale, 1973, 84—; mktg. cons. Total Health Care, Inc., Centralie, Ill., 1986—. Chmn. United Crusade, Sacramento, 1960; chmn. bd. dirs. Salvation Army, Sacramento, 1961; bd. dirs. USO, 1962. Served with USAF, 1951-57. Recipient Outstanding Flight Officer Achievement cert. USAF, 1957; named Disting. Grad., Aviation Cadets, 1952, U.S. Rookie of Year, New Eng. Life Ins. Co., 1959. Mem. Mt. Vernon C. of C. Republican. Lodge: Civitan (Sacramento Internat. chpt. pres. 1961). Office: PO Box 946 Mount Vernon IL 62864 also: 11 S Meridian Suite 810 Indianapolis IN 46204

MCDONELL, ROBERT MICHAEL, telecommunications company executive; b. Monticello, Iowa, Apr. 7, 1950; s. William Francis and Patricia Ann (Oswald) McD.; m. Mary Lynn Jacobson, Sept. 6, 1975; children: Molly, Seth. BA in Psychology, Loras Coll., 1972; MS in Psychology, Miss. State U., 1974; MBA, Nova U., 1983. Staff psychologist Famco, Inc., Dubuque, Iowa, 1974-76; juvenile probation officer Linn County Juvenile Probation, Cedar Rapids, Iowa, 1976-78; market research mgr. Norand Corp., Cedar Rapids, 1978-81, mgr. corporate communications, 1981-86; dir. corp. communications Teleconnect Co., 1986—; mem. adj. faculty Nova U., Ft. Lauderdale, Fla., 1983—. Mem. Nat. Mgmt. Assn. (Outstanding Service award 1981). Democrat. Roman Catholic. Club: Civitan. Home: 6904 Chelsea Dr NE Cedar Rapids IA 52402 Office: Teleconnect Co 500 2d Ave SE Cedar Rapids IA 52401

MCDONNELL, JOHN FINNEY, aerospace and aircraft manufacturing executive; b. Mar. 18, 1938; s. James Smith and Mary Elizabeth (Finney) McD.; m. Anne Marbury, June 16, 1961. BS in Aero. Engring., Princeton U., 1960, MS in Aero. Engring., 1962; postgrad. in bus. adminstrn. Washington U., St. Louis, 1962-66. Strength engr. McDonnell Aircraft Co. (subs. McDonnell Douglas Corp.), St. Louis, 1962, corp. analyst, 1963-65, contract coordinator, adminstr., 1965-68; asst. to v.p. fin. Douglas Aircraft Co. (subs. McDonnell Douglas Corp.), 1968; v.p. McDonnell Douglas Fin. Corp. (subs. McDonnell Douglas Corp.), 1968-71; staff v.p. fiscal McDonnell Douglas Corp., 1971-75, corp. v.p. fin. and devel., 1975-77, corp. exec. v.p., 1977-80, pres., 1980—, mem. exec. com., 1975—, also bd. dirs. Mem. Com. Decent Unbiased Campaign Tactics; bd. commrs. St. Louis Sci. Ctr.; trustee KETC, Washington U. Office: McDonnell Douglas Corp PO Box 516 Saint Louis MO 63166

MCDONNELL, SANFORD NOYES, aircraft company executive; b. Litte Rock, Oct. 12, 1922; s. William Archie and Carolyn (Cherry) McD.; m. Priscilla Robb, Sept. 3, 1946; children: Robbin McDonnell MacVittie, William Randall. BA in Econs., Princeton U., 1945; BS in Mech. Engring., U. Colo., 1948; MS in Applied Mechanics, Washington U., St. Louis, 1954. With McDonnell Douglas Corp. (formerly McDonnell Aircraft Corp.), St. Louis, 1948—, v.p., 1959-66, pres. McDonnell Aircraft div., 1966-71, corp. exec. v.p., 1971, corp. pres., 1971—, chief exec. officer, 1972—, chmn., 1980—, also bd. dirs.; bd. dirs. Centerre Bancorp., St. Louis, Squibb Corp. Active St. Louis United Way; mem. exec. bd. St. Louis and nat. councils Boy Scouts Am.; bd. dirs. Ethics Resource Ctr.; trustee, elder Presbyn. Ch. Fellow AIAA; mem. Aerospace Industries Assn. (gov.), Navy League U.S. (life), Tau Beta Pi. Office: McDonnell Douglas Corp PO Box 516 Saint Louis MO 63166

MCDONOUGH, CRAIG STEVEN, dentist; b. Cleve., Nov. 16, 1953; s. John Emerson and Carol Jean (Christen) McD.; m. Mary Margaret Adams, July 13, 1985; children: Alyson Brooke, Shaun Colin. Student, Miami U., Oxford, Ohio, 1971-74; DDS, Case Western Reserve U., 1978. Assoc. Rhodes, Rinaldi & Assoc., Inc., East Cleveland, Ohio, 1978-81; clinic dir. Ctr. Family Dentistry, Willowick, Ohio, 1981-82; gen. practice dentistry Lorain, Ohio, 1982—; clin. preceptor Cleve. Free Clinic, 1978—; faculty mem. dental sch. Case Western Reserve U., 1978—; clin. instr. Cuyahoga JVS, Brecksville, 1980—, adv. bd., 1981—; bd. dirs. Lorain County Rehab. Ctr., 1984—, 1st v.p. 1986—, pres. 1987; founding mem. Amherst (Ohio) Emergency Dental Care, 1983. Vol. United Way Campaign, Lorain County, 1982—. Mem. Acad. Reconstructive and Cosmetic Dentistry, Case Western Reserve U. Study Club, Theta Chi Alumni Assn., Psi Omega (faculty advisor 1983—). Roman Catholic. Avocations: sports, gaming, music. Home: 197 Arrowhead Dr Grafton OH 44044 Office: 1700 Cooper-Foster Park Lorain OH 44053

MCDONOUGH, GERALD CLYDE, transportation leasing company executive; b. Cleve., 1928. B.B.A., Case Western Res. U., 1953. Treas. Molded Fiberglass Co., 1964-69, Rexnord Inc., 1969-74; v.p. and treas. Reliance Electric Co., 1974-79; exec. v.p., dir. Leaseway Transp. Corp., Cleve., 1979-82, chmn. and chief exec. officer, 1982—, acting pres., chief operating officer, 1985; dir. AmeriTrust Corp., Brush Wellman Inc. Office: Leaseway Transp Corp 3700 Park East Dr Beachwood OH 44122 *

MCDONOUGH, JAMES FRANCIS, civil engineer, educator; b. Boston, June 7, 1939; s. John Joseph and Blanche Cecelia (Murphy) McD.; m. Kathryn Ann Hilvert, Mar. 9, 1985; children by previous marriage: John, James, Jennifer. BS in Civil Engring., Northeastern U., 1962, MS in Civil Engring., 1964; PhD, U. Cin., 1968, MBA, 1981. Registered profl. engr., Ohio. Project engr. Fay, Spofford & Thorndike, Boston, 1962; teaching asst. Northeastern U., 1962-64; teaching asst. U. Cin., 1965, instr. civil engring., 1965-68, asst. prof., 1968-74, assoc. prof., 1974-78, William Thoms prof. civil engring., chmn. dept. civil and environ. engring., 1978-86, assoc. dean acad. affairs, 1986—; vis. prof. faculty engring. Kabul U., Afghanistan, 1969-71; vis. prof. N.C. State U., 1971. Contbr. articles to profl. jours. Pres. Greenhills Winton Sports Assn., 1981-83, treas., 1977-81. Recipient Teaching Excellence award U. Cin., 1973-75; Dow Chem. Outstanding Young Faculty award Am. Soc. for Engring. Edn., 1975; Outstanding Engring. Educator award Am. Soc. Engring. Edn.-Western Electric, 1977; Profl. Accomplishment award Acad.-Tech. and Sci. Council Cin., 1979. Mem. Am. Soc. Engring. Edn. (v.p. 1984-86, chmn. sect. 1982-83), ASCE (zone sec. 1983, sect. pres. 1982), NSPE (chmn. Ohio state bd. registration for engrs. and surveyors 1987—), Ohio Soc. Profl. Engrs., Sigma Xi, Tau Beta Pi, Chi Epsilon, Beta Gamma Sigma. Roman Catholic. Home: 3308 Bishop St Cincinnati OH 45220 Office: U Cin Mail Location 18 Cincinnati OH 45221

MCDONOUGH, JAMES MICHAEL, plastics engineer; b. Providence, Dec. 24, 1952; s. James Michael and Nancy (Trudel) McD.; m. Gail Marie Griggs, May 4, 1986. BS in Plastics Engring., U. Lowell, 1976. Mold design engr. Tupperware Co., North Smithsfield, R.I., 1976-77; product, plastics engr. A.T. Cross Co., Lincoln, R.I., 1977-79; product engring. mgr. Bic Corp., Milford, Conn., 1979-84; devel. assoc. Dow Chem. Co., Midland, Mich., 1984—; cons. in field, Midland, Mich., 1985—. Contbr. aritcles to profl. jours. Mem. Soc. Plastics Engrs. (sr. 1975—), Am. Nat. Standards Inst. Roman Catholic. Avocations: skiing, sports cars, reading, jogging, golf. Home: 1403 Pheasant Ridge Dr Midland MI 48640 Office: Dow Chem Co 433 Bldg Midland MI 48640

MCDONOUGH, ROBERT LEROY, airline pilot; b. Chgo., June 16, 1939; s. Emmett and Eleanor Katherine (Weith) McD.; m. Judith Alexis Baker, Mar. 5, 1971; children: Alexa, Robert, Mary, Thomas. BS, USAF Acad., 1962. Registered airline transport pilot. Assoc. prof. Parsons Coll., Fairfield, Iowa, 1970-73; dir. Equine Studies Park Coll., Parkville, Mo., 1973-76; pilot Trans World Airlines, 1969—, instr., 1969—; lic. trainer McDonough Racing Stable, Kidder, Mo., 1970—, also blood stock agt. and cons. Author: Stud Manager's Handbook, 1975. Served to capt. USAF, 1962-68. Mem. Am. Pilots Assn., Am. Quarter Horse Assn., Mo. Racing Assn., Kans. Racing Assn. Avocations: sports, riding, jogging. Address: Rt 1 Kidder MO 64649

MCDOUGAL, EDWARD TURNER, film producer; b. Evanston, Ill.; s. Christopher Bouton and Winnifred (Turner) McD.; 1 adopted son, John William Wischner. BA in English, Colo. Coll., 1972. Tchr. language arts Aptakisic/Tripp Sch., Prairie View, Ill., 1972-75, Edgewood Jr. High Sch., Highland Park, Ill., 1975-76, Stanley Field Jr. High Sch., Northbrook, Ill., 1977-78; ind. film producer 1977—; bd. dirs., pres. Good News Mission, Chgo., 1985-86; mem. adv. bd. Inner City Limits, Chgo., 1986—; co-dir. World Bapt. Evang. Assn., 1986—. Writer, producer, dir., editor Sweet Medicine, 1976, Summer at Army Lake, 1978, The Shadow of His Wings, 1979, Against All Hope, 1981, Never Ashamed, 1983 (5 Crown awards including Best Film 1984, Best Youth Film 1984, Best Missionary Film 1984); writer, dir., editor The Splendors of Mission Hollow, 1978; dir., producer (TV show) The Hallelujah Club, 1977. Rep. precinct capt., Glencoe, 1985—. Recipient Spl. Recognition award Cook County Juvenile Ct. Mem. Christian Films Distbrs. Assn., World Bapt. Evangelical Assn. Avocation: chess. Home and Office: 350 Adams Ave Glencoe IL 60022

MCDOUGALL, LESLIE ANN, dentist; b. Odessa, Tex., Feb. 28, 1956; d. Clayton LeMoyne and Lorraine Elizabeth (Klank) McD. BA in Biology, U. N.C., 1978; DDS, Ohio State Coll. Dentistry, 1981. Gen. practice dentistry Marysville, Ohio, 1981. Mem. bd. Selective Service. Mem. Acad. Gen. Dentistry, Ohio Dental Assn. Republican. Presbyterian. Office: 327 E Fifth St Marysville OH 43040

MCDOWELL, ALMA SUE, financial executive; b. Bedford, Ind., Oct. 16, 1942; d. Claude Edward and Lydia Helen McD.; B.S., Ind. U., 1978, MSA, Cen. Mich. U., 1987; calculating clk., assigned risk examiner Grain Dealers Mut. Ins. Co., Indpls., 1960-62; with Keach & Grove Ins. Agy., Inc., Bedford, 1962-65; account clk., acctg. mgr. Purdue U., Indpls., 1965-71; fin. asst. to dean adminstrv. affairs Ind.-Purdue U., Indpls., 1971-75; asst. bus. mgr. Ind. U.-Purdue U., Indpls. Center Advanced Research, Inc., from 1975, controller, dir. central adminstrv. services, 1975-81; auditor U.S. Army Fin. & Acctg. Center, 1981-85, systems acct., 1985-87, chief br. other services disbursing for army, 1987—; vol. VA Hosp. Mem. Assn. Govt. Accts. (pres.), Am. Soc. Mil. Comptrollers (v.p.). Republican. Republican. Home: 5402 E 20th Pl Indianapolis IN 46218 Office: Finco-CD Indianapolis IN 46249-1326

MCDOWELL, DANIEL QUINCE, JR., airline executive; b. Bklyn., Dec. 6, 1949; s. Daniel Quince and Amelia (DeFreese) McD.; m. Lesa Belle Wurmnest, July 5, 1980. AS, Ill. Cen. U., 1977; BS, Bradley U., 1979; diploma U.S. Air Force Region Staff Coll., Colorado Springs, Colo., 1984; cert. Air Force Aux. Corp. Learning Course, Mpls., 1984. Sr. ground services rep. Overseas Nat. Airways, JFK Airport, N.Y., 1967-70; asst. carrier U.S. P.O., Roosevelt, N.Y., part-time 1969-70; sta. agt. Ozark Air Lines, Peoria, Ill., 1971-81, Mpls., 1981-85; dual aux. video bd. design cons. TriImage Tactical Systems, Sacramento, 1982—. Author: The Sign of the Eagle, 1982. Squadron comdr. CAP/U.S. Air Force Aux., Peoria, 1980-82, group staff officer, Mpls., 1983-86, Minn. wing dir. aerospace edn., 1986—. Served with USAF, 1970-71. Recipient Outstanding Achievement award Ozark Air Lines, 1985, Exceptional Service medal U.S. Air Force Aux.-CAP, 1985, Find Ribbon, 1987, Air Search and Rescue Ribbon and award, 1987; Grover Loening Aerospace, Aerospace Edn. awards, 1985. Mem. Res. Officers Assn., Am. Def. Preparedness Assn., Am. Aerospace Educators Assn., Air Force Assn. (life), Associated Photographers Internat., Am. Legion (Aviation Post 511). Avocations: creative writing, reading, freelance photography, listening to classical music, travel. Office: Ozark Airlines Twin Cities Internat Airport Saint Paul MN 55101

MCDOWELL, DENNIS JAMES, dentist; b. Waukegan, Ill., Aug. 22, 1954; s. Jack LaVerne and Lorraine Mae (Perington) McD.; children: Gary Lloyd, Kristi Lynne. BS in Chemistry with honors, Valparaiso U., 1976; DDS cum laude, Loyola U., 1980. Gen. practice dentistry Crystal Lake, Ill., 1980—. Mem. ADA, Ill. State Dental Soc., McHenry County Dental Soc. (bd. dirs. 1985—), Chgo. Dental Soc. (assoc.), Crystal Lake Jaycees. Republican. Avocations: photography, golf, fishing, skiing. Office: 4911 Rt 31 Crystal Lake IL 60014

MCDOWELL, ELLEN GUNTER, health care educator, nurse; b. Girardeau, Mo., Nov. 7, 1952; d. S.A. Martin and Audrey Dean (Withers) Gunter; m. James C. McDowell Jr., Dec. 29, 1973; 1 child, Leeann Christine. AA in Nursing, Southeast Mo. State U., 1973; BS in Nursing, U. Evansville, 1976; MS in Adminstrn., Southeast Mo. State U., 1987. Registered nurse, Mo., Ind. Staff nurse St. Francis Med. Ctr., Cape Girardeau, Mo., 1973-74, 1977-78, head nurse, 1974-75, edn. coordinator, 1978-81, dir. edn., 1978—; edn. instr. Deaconess Hosp., Evansville, Ind., 1976-77; mem. adv. council Ctr. for Health Professions, S.E. Mo. State U., Cape Girardeau, 1984—; mem. seminar faculty Mo. League for Nursing, 1986; health systems profl. delegation mem. People's Republic China, 1987. Mem. continuing edn. council, Cape Girardeau, 1979-83, adv. bd. Vocat. and Tech. Sch., Cape Girardeau, 1979—. Named Outstanding Alumnus Yr., Dept. Nursing S.E. Mo. State U., 1985. Mem. Am. Nurses Assn., Mo. Nurses Assn. (dist. chairperson continuing edn. 1979-83, bd. dirs. 1981-83), Mo. Assn. for Healthcare Edn. (dist. bd. dirs. 1983-85, pres. 1986), Bootheel Profl. Assn. for Continuing Edn. (treas. 1980-82, v.p. 1982, pres. 1983), Am. Soc. for Health Edn. and Tng., Nat. Fedn. Bus. and Profl. Women, Nat. Assn. Female Execs., Mo. Area V Health Systems Assn. (del. council 1980-83), Mo. Heart Assn., S.E. Mo. Health Educators (pres. 1982). Baptist. Avocations: oil painting, cross stitching, volleyball, choir activities. Office: St Francis Med Ctr 211 St Francis Dr Cape Girardeau MO 63701

MCDOWELL, GEORGE EDWARD, manufacturing executive; b. St. Louis, Feb. 15, 1944; s. Frank and Mary Elizabeth (Neal) McD. BA, Washington U., St. Louis, 1966; MBA, Drury Coll., 1968. CPA, Hawaii. Cost analyst Ford Motor Co., St. Louis, 1968-73; acctg. supr. ITT Grinnell Corp. subs Internat. Telephone and Telegraph Corp., Elmira, N.Y., 1973-74; acctg. mgr. Emerson Electric, St. Louis, 1974-76; data processing mgr. Ethyl Corp., St. Louis, 1976-84; v.p. Clayton Corp., St. Louis, 1984—; instr. Belleville (Ill.) Area Coll., 1982—. Contbr. articles to profl. jours. Served with U.S. Army, 1968-70. Mem. Am. Inst. CPA's, Mo. Soc. CPA's. Home: 657 Craig Woods Dr Kirkwood MO 63122 Office: Clayton Corp 4205 Forest Park Blvd Saint Louis MO 63108

MCDOWELL, MICHAEL LEE, insurance executive; b. Moline, Ill., Oct. 17, 1956; s. Jack Lee McDowell and Donna Marie (Purvis) T.; m. Janet Evelyn Pershing, Sept. 15, 1979; 1 child, Kasey Lee. BBA, U. Iowa, 1980; postgrad., Western Ill. U., 1986—. Asst. mgr. Athlete's Foot, Moline, Ill., 1979-80; field claims rep. Country Mut. Ins. Co., East Moline, Ill., 1980—. Chmn. pastor-parish com. Moline Evang. Ch., 1986. Mem. Evang. Ch. Clubs: Chgo. Track, The Athletic Congress. Home: 846 32d Ave East Moline IL 61265 Office: Country Mut Ins Co 1188 John Deere Rd East Moline IL 61244

MCDOWELL, ROBERT JOSEPH, SR., metal finishing company executive; b. Elkhart, Ind., Aug. 4, 1951; s. Robert Manson and Doris Elizabeth (Mealor) M.; m. Carol McCullough Watters, June 28, 1975; children: Robert Joseph Jr., Jacqueline Rose. AB in Polit. Sci., Ind. U., 1973. Claims rep. Crawford & Co., Atlanta, 1973-75, Crum & Forster, Knoxville, Tenn., 1975-78; real estate salesman Crossroads Real Estate, Knoxville, 1978-79; chmn., pres. chief exec. officer South Side Plating Works, Elkhart, Ind., 1979-87, Hoosier Metal Finishing, 1987—; chmn., chief exec. officer, pres., treas. McDowell Enterprises, Elkhart, 1980—. Bd. dirs. Legal Aid, Elkhart, 1981-84. HUD grantee, 1983. Mem. Am. Electroplaters Soc. (v.p. 1982-83), Nat. Assn. Metal Finishers (bd. dirs., nat. dir. 1987—), Ind. Assn. Metal Finishers (pres. 1984-87), Ind. U. Alumni Assn. (pres. 1984—, dir. exec. council), Alpha Sigma Phi (pres. 1977-78). Lodge: Elks. Avocations: photography, sailing. Office: PO Box 846 2010 Superior St Elkhart IN 46515

MC DOWELL, STEPHEN ALAN, architect; b. Kansas City, Mo., Jan. 25, 1953; s. Stephen Edgar and Elsie Vivian (Town) Mc D.; m. Mary Anne Truel Kiloh, Aug. 14, 1976. Student, U. Mo., Kansas City, 1971-72; B Environ. Design, U. Kans., 1978. Registered architect, Mo., Kans. Architect in tng. Architectural Services, Lawrence, Kans., 1978-79; architect, v.p. Patty Berkebile Nelson Immenschuh Architects, Kansas City, Mo., 1978—; profl. team leader U. Nebr., Lincoln, Kansas State U., 1985. Photographer Kansas City Guide Book, 1979. Mem., v.p. West Plaza Neighborhood Assn. Friends of Art, Kansas City, 1981-86; com. mem. Kansas City Consensus, 1985-86; assoc. div. chmn. Heart of Am. United Way, Kansas City, 1985-86. Recipient Design award Cen. State Region AIA. Mem. AIA (Honor award Cen. State Region, Kansas City chpt.), Mo. Council Architects. Club: Woodside Racquet (Westwood, Kans.). Home: 4629 Liberty Kansas City MO 64112 Office: PBNI Architects 120 W 12th St Kansas City MO 64105

MCDOWELL, THOMAS HUGH, publishing executive, brokerage house executive; b. Windber, Pa., Oct. 10, 1945; s. Charles Clifford and June Ellen (Hall) McD. Student, Kent (Ohio) State U., 1964-66. Pres. McDowell & Assoc., Akron, Ohio, 1969-80, Goldfingers, Cleve., 1980-82, Am. Trade Exchange, Euclid, Ohio, 1982—. Coach Avon Lake (Ohio) Jr. Football, 1976-82. Mem. Nat. Newspaper Assn., Nat. Assn. Trade Exchange (pres. 1984-85, bd. dirs. 1984—), Internation Reciprocal Trade Assn. Republican. Baptist. Clubs: Toastmasters (Euclid) (v.p. 1984); Rolls Royce Owners. Avocations: video games, golf, politics. Home: 5735 Noble Ct Willoughby OH 44094 Office: Am Trade Exchange 27801 Euclid Ave Euclid OH 44132

MCDUNN, WILLIAM KEVIN, accounting executive; b. Chgo., Jan. 5, 1957; s. William Dorcey and Evelyn Sylvia (Drabik) McD. BA, U. Ill., Chgo., 1979; postgrad., Loyola U., Chgo., 1985—. CPA, Ill. Asst. personnel mgr. Andy Frain, Inc., Chgo., 1979-82; acct. Stone Container Corp., Chgo., 1982-84, sr. acct., 1984-85, acctg. supr., 1985—. Mem. Am. Inst. CPA's, Ill. Soc. CPA's. Roman Catholic. Home: 5362 S Maplewood Ave Chicago IL 60632 Office: Stone Container Corp 150 N Michigan Ave Chicago IL 60601

MCEACHEN, RICHARD EDWARD, banker, lawyer; b. Omaha, Sept. 24, 1933; s. Howard D. and Ada Carolyn Helen (Baumann) McE.; m. Judith Ann Gray, June 28, 1969; children: Mark E., Neil H. BS, U. Kans., Lawrence, 1955; JD, U. Mich., 1961. Bar: Mo. 1961, Kans. 1982. Atty. Hillix, Hall, Hasburgh, Brown & Hoffhaus, Kansas City, Mo., 1961-62; sr. v.p. First Nat. Bank, Kansas City, Mo., 1962-75; exec. v.p. Commerce Bank Kansas City, 1975-85, Centerre Bank of Kansas City N.A., 1985—. Gov. Am. Royal Assn., Kansas City, Mo., 1970—, ambassador, 1980—; bd. dirs. Harry S. Truman Med. Ctr., Kansas City, 1974-86, mem. fin. com., 1975-86, treas., 1979-84, bd. govs., 1986—; trustee Clearinghouse for Midcontinent Founds., 1980—; bd. dirs. Greater Kansas City Mental Health Found., 1963-69, treas., 1964-69, v.p. 1967-69; adv. bd. Urban Services YMCA, Kansas City, 1976-83; cubmaster Kanza dist. Boy Scouts Am., 1982-83, vice chmn., 1982-83, troop com., 1983—, treas., 1986—; mem. planned gift com. William Rockhill Nelson Gallery Art; mem. adv. com. Legal Assistance Program Avila Coll., 1978-80, adv. council Future Farmers Am., 1972-82; mgr. Oppenstein Bros. Found., 1979-85, George & Dollie LaRue Found., 1981-85; trustee Village Presbyn. Ch., 1987—. Mem. Mo. Bar Assn., Kans. Bar Assn., Corp. Fiduciaries Assn. (pres. 1979-80), Estate Planning Assn. (pres. 1974-75), Estate Planning Council (bd. dirs. 1984-86); Kansas City Met. Bar Assn., Lawyers Assn. Kansas City, Mo. Bankers Assn. (trust service com. 1970-73, 78-81), Am. Inst. Banking, Delta Tau Delta Alumni (v.p. Kansas City chpt. 1978-80). Republican. Clubs: Kansas City (Mo.); Indian Hills (Mission Hills, Kans.). Home: 9100 El Monte Prairie Village KS 66207 Office: Centerre Bank Kansas City NA 1130 Walnut St PO Box 419666 Kansas City MO 64141

MCEACHERN, BARBARA ANN, speech communications educator, author, consultant; b. Bklyn., Jan. 3, 1952; d. Daniel Robert and Mary Minnie (Cunningham) McEachern; m. Morton Vogel Smith Jr., Sept. 30, 1976; children: Diambu Kibwe, Tor Yohance. BA, Ohio Wesleyan U., 1974; MA, Bowling Green State U., 1975; postgrad. Cleve. State U., 1979. Instr. speech communications Lakeland Community Coll., 1976-80, asst. prof., 1980-82, assoc. prof., 1982—. Mem. NEA, Ohio Educators Assn., Community Coll. Humanities Assn., Ohio Speech Assn., NAACP, Nat. Assn. Dramatic and Speech Arts, Black Women's Polit. Action Com., Afro-Am. Cultural and Hist. Soc. Mus., Ohio Wesleyan U. Black Alumni Network, Theta Alpha Phi. Office: Lakeland Community College Mentor OH 44060

MCELREE, JAMES MITCHELL, management consultant; b. Abilene, Tex., July 12, 1960; s. James Terry and Rhoda (Van Allen) McE.; m. Jean Marie Fellows. BS, Calvary Bible Coll., Kansas City, Mo., 1982; MBA, U. Kans., 1986. Tchr. East Bay Christian High Sch., San Pablo, Calif., 1982-83; mgmt. cons. Mackenzie and Co., Lawrence, Kans., 1986—. Republican. Avocations: athletics, reading. Home: 516 2d St Belton MO 64012 Office: Mackenzie and Co Inc 700 Massachusetts Lawrence KS 66044

MCELWEE, CARL DEAN, geophysicist; b. Braymer, Mo., Sept. 12, 1943; s. Holder Earl and Chloe Elizabeth (Roberts) McE.; m. Margery Sharon Carver, June 4, 1966; children: Pamela Dawn, Heather Ann. BA, William Jewell Coll., 1965; MA, U. Kans., 1967, PhD, 1970. Geophysicist Texaco, Inc., Houston, 1970-74, Kans. Geol. Survey, Lawrence, 1974—; adj. prof. physics and geology U. Kans., Lawrence, 1976—. Contbr. 2 chpts. to books on geohydrology; also articles to profl. jours. Active various positions First Southern Baptist Ch., Lawrence, 1974—. Grantee NSF William Jewell Coll., 1963-65, U. Kans., 1965-69; water research grantee C.E. U.S. Army, 1980-82, U.S. Geol. Survey, 1985-86. Mem. Am. Phys. Soc., Am. Geophys. Union, Soc. Exploration Geophysicists, Nat. Water Well Assn. Baptist. Avocations: woodworking, electronics, flying, gardening. Home: Rural Rt 2 Box 368 Lawrence KS 66046 Office: Kans Geol Survey 1930 Constant Ave Lawrence KS 66046

MCENIRY, ROBERT FRANCIS, associate research professor in education; b. Milw., Feb. 22, 1918; s. Frank Michael and Mary (Brown) McE. BA, St. Louis U., 1941, MA, 1944, PhL, ThLcum laude, 1953; PhD, Ohio State U., 1972. Ordained priest Roman Catholic Ch., 1951. Instr. classics St. Louis U. High Sch., 1944-47, Creighton Prep. Sch., Omaha, 1947-48; asst. prof., chmn. classics Rockhurst Coll., Kansas City, Mo., 1953-58; retreat master, counselor White House Retreat, St. Louis, 1958-68; assoc. research prof. Creighton U., Omaha, 1972—. Editor and pub. Interaction Review, 1983—; editor Scholar and Educator, 1974-76; mem. editorial bd. Counseling and Values, 1976-82; editor (book) Pastoral Counseling, 1977, Premarriage Counseling, 1978; contbr. over 180 articles to profl. jours. Mem. Bd. of Pastoral Ministry, Omaha, 1972-78. Research grantee Council for Theol. Reflection, 1975-77; recipient Research award Creighton U., 1977. Fellow Nat. Acad. Counselors and Family Therapists (editor book review 1979-82); mem. Assn. for Religion and Values in Counseling (editor newsletter 1983-86, Outstanding Service award 1985). Avocations: photography, civil war sites. Home: Creighton Univ 2500 California St Omaha NE 68178

MCEUEN, EVERETT RANDAL, safety engineer; b. Marion, Ky., June 18, 1936; s. James Everett and Lorene Agnes (Fritts) McE.; m. Sharon Lee Marshall, June 20, 1959; children—Scott, Shari, Shawn, Patrick. Laborer, warehouse supr., steel inspector/supr. U.S. Steel Co., Gary, Ind., 1955-74, safety engr., 1974-84; safety engr. P.C.L. Constrn., Denver, 1984-87; loss control engr. Near North Ins. Agy., 1987—. Pres. bd. dirs. Hobart Swin and Play Ctr., Ind., 1970, Sch. City of Hobart, 1979—; bd. dirs. Selective Service, Hobart, 1981—. Served with U.S. Army, 1958-64. Democrat. Presbyterian. Lodge: Masons. Avocation: camping. Home: 1419 1st Pl Hobart IN 46342 Office: Near North Ins Agy Inc 875 N Michigan Ave 23d Fl Chicago IL 60611

MCEWAN, JOHN THOMAS, JR., military officer, educator; b. Omaha, July 5, 1950; s. John Thomas Sr. McEwan and Margaret Louise (Headman) Trudell; children from a previous marriage: Sophia L., John T. III; m. Jean Marie Eickoff, Mar. 7, 1980; 1 child, Thomas W. AA, U. Md., 1979; BA, So. Ill. U., 1980; MA, Cen. Mich. U., 1984. Cert. instr., USAF. Enlisted U.S. Army Vietnam, 1969-71; enlisted USAF; equal opportunity non commd. officer 3902 Airbase Wing, Offutt AFB, Nebr., 1972-77, 18 Tactical Fighter Wing, Kadena AB, Japan, 1977-79, 443 Mil. Airlift Wing, Altus AFB, Okla., 1979-81; commd. 2d lt. USAF, 1980, advanced through grades to capt., 1984; equal opportunity officer USAF, Whiteman AFB, Mo., 1981-83, 91 Strategic Missile Wing, Minot AFB, N.D., 1983-84; exec. officer 91 Supply Squadron, Minot AFB, N.D., 1984—; asst. dir. Combined Fed. Campaign, Minot AFB, 1986. Nominator Outstanding Young Men/Women Am., 1984—. Named one of Outstanding Young Men in Am. U.S. Jaycees, 1983, 85. Mem. Air Force Assn., Am. Legion. Baptist. Avocations: carpentry, auto maintenance, auto racing, racquetball, fishing. Home: 141-2 Delta Dr Minot AFB ND 58704 Office: 91 SUPS/CCE Minot AFB ND 58705-5000

MCEWEN, BOB, congressman; b. Hillsboro, Ohio, Jan. 12, 1950; m. Liz McEwen, 1976. B.B.A. in Econs., U. Miami, 1972. Vice pres. Boebinger, Inc.; mem. 97th-100th Congresses from 6th Dist. Ohio. Mem. Ohio Ho. of Reps., 1974-80; elder Hillsboro Ch. of Christ. Mem. Gideons, Jaycees, Farm Bur., C. of C., Grange, Sigma Xi. Lodges: Optimist; Rotary. Office: 329 Cannon House Office Bldg Washington DC 20515

MCFADDEN, EDWARD REGIS, JR., pulmonary educator; b. Pitts., Aug. 2, 1936. BA, St. Vincent Coll., 1958; MD, U. Pitts., 1963. Assoc. prof. medicine U. Tex. Med. Br., Galveston, 1972-73; asst. prof. Harvard U., Boston, 1973-77, assoc. prof., 1977-81, 81-84; assoc. prof. MIT div. health sci., Boston, 1979-84; prof. medicine Case Western Res. U., Cleve., 1984—; dir. Airway Disease Ctr. Univ. Hosp., Cleve., 1984—, respiratory therapy, 1985—, Clin. Research Ctr., 1986—. Editor-in-chief Airway Diseases, N.Y.C., 1985—; contbr. articles to profl. jours. Recipient George W. Thorn Teaching award Peter Bent Brigham Hosp., Boston, 1980. Fellow ACP; mem. Am. Fedn. Clin. Research, Am. Thoracic Soc., So. Soc. Clin. Investigation, Am. Physiol. Soc., Am. Acad. Allergy and Immunology, Am. Soc. Clin. Investigation, Assn. Am. Physicians. Home: 2706 Landon Rd Shaker Heights OH 44122 Office: Univ Hosps Cleve 2074 Abington Rd Cleveland OH 44106

MCFADDEN, JAMES FREDERICK, JR., surgeon; b. St. Louis, Dec. 5, 1920; s. James Frederick and Olivia Genevieve (Imbs) McF.; m. Mary Cella Switzer, Sept. 15, 1956 (div. Sept. 1969); children: James Frederick, Kenneth Michael, John Switzer, Mary Cella, Joseph Robert. AB, St. Louis U., 1941, MD, 1944. Intern Boston City Hosp., 1944-45; ward surgeon neorsurg. and orthopedics McGuire Gen. Hosp., Richmond, Va., 1945; ward surgeon in internal medicine Regional Hosp., Fort Knox, Ky., 1946; ward surgeon plastic surgery Valley Forge Gen. Hosp., Phoenixville, Pa., 1946-47; intern St. Louis City Hosp., 1947-48; resident in surgery VA Hosp., St. Louis, 1948-52; clin. instr. surgery St. Louis U., 1952-62; gen. practice medicine specializing in surgery St. Louis, 1952—; mem. staff St. Mary's Hosp., 1952-77, St. John's Mercy Hosp., 1952-74, Desloge Hosp., 1952-62, Frisco RR Hosp., 1953-59, DePaul Hosp., 1954—, Christian Hosp., 1955-66, 83—. Mem. St. Louis Ambassadors, 1979-81. Served to capt. AUS, 1945-47. Named Eagle Scout Boy Scouts Am., 1935. Fellow ACS; mem. St. Louis Med Soc., Am. Soc. Clin. Hypnosis, Internat. Soc. Hypnosis, Royal Soc. Medicine (affiliate), St. Louis U. Student Conclave, Alpha Sigma Nu. Roman Catholic. Avocations: hypnosis, photography. Home: 11963 Villa Dorado Dr Saint Louis MO 63146 Office: 11500 Olive Blvd Saint Louis MO 63141

MC FADDEN, JOSEPH MICHAEL, university president; b. Joliet, Ill., Feb. 12, 1932; s. Francis Joseph and Lucille (Adler) McF.; m. Norma Cardwell, Oct. 10, 1958; children: Timothy Joseph, Mary Colleen, Jonathon Andrew. B.A., Lewis Coll., 1954; M.A., U. Chgo., 1961; Ph.D., No. Ill. U., 1968. Tchr. history Joliet Cath. High Sch., 1957-60; mem. faculty history dept. Lewis Coll., Lockport, Ill., 1960-70; assoc. prof. Lewis Coll., 1967-70, v.p. acad. affairs, 1968-70; prof. history, dean sch. Nat. and Social Sci., Kearney (Nebr.) State Coll., 1970-74; prof. history, dean Sch. Social and Behavioral Scis., Slippery Rock (Pa.) State Coll., 1974-77; pres. No. State Coll., Aberdeen, S.D., 1977-82, U. S.D., Vermillion, 1982—. Served with USNR, 1954-56. Roman Catholic. Home: Univ South Dakota Office of Pres Vermillion SD 57069

MCFADIN, ROBERT LEE, manufacturing executive; b. Milw., Dec. 16, 1921; s. Charles Lee and Madeline (Hansen) McF.; m. JoAnn Metzger, Sept. 6, 1947; children: Lindsey McFadin Spake, Barbara. BS in Mech. Engring., Mich. Tech. U., 1945. Engr. Carrier Corp., N.Y.C., 1945-48; with Marley Co., Mission, Kans., 1948—, exec. v.p. all domestic operating divs., 1968-75, pres., 1975-84, chmn., 1984—, chief exec. officer, 1975-86, also bd. dirs., also bd. dirs. subs.; bd. dirs. Nat. Gypsum Co., Dallas. Past mem. bd. dirs. Heart of Am. United Way; gen. campaign chmn. Kansas City United Way, 1977, pres., 1979, chmn., 1980; trustee Midwest Research Inst.; bd. dirs. Mid-Am. Coalition on Health Care, Civic Council Kansas City, Greater Kansas City Community Founds. and Affiliated Trusts. Served with USAAF, 1943. Mem. Atomic Indsl. Forum, Kansas City C. of C. (former bd. dirs.), NAM (past bd. dirs.), Tau Beta Pi. Clubs: Morris County Golf (Convent Station, N.J.); Kansas City Country (Kans.); River (Kansas City, Mo.). Lodge: Shriners. Home: 2700 W 69th Std Shawnee Mission KS 66208

MCFALL, DANIEL JOHN, financial planning company executive; b. Tacoma, Wash., Apr. 21, 1961; s. John Frank and Karen Ann (Horsak) McF. BS in Bus. Mgmt., U. Oregon, 1984; cert. profl. mgmt. inst. in ins. mktg. inst., Purdue U., 1987. cert. fin. planner. V.p. United Fin. Systems, Eugene, Oreg., 1984—. Mem. Eugene C. of C., West Des Moines C. of C., Oreg. State Forensic Assn. (sr. judge 1980—). Lutheran. Clubs: Shadow Hills Country, AMX Gold. Avocations: skydiving, skiing, travel, golf. Home: 411 Cherry Eugene OR 97401 Office: United Fin Systems 3636 Westown Pkwy Suite 217 West Des Moines IA 50265

MCFARLAN, DOUGLAS ROBERT, media relations executive; b. Marion, Ohio, Oct. 18, 1954; s. Robert Oliver and Bettylou (Wiener) McF.; m. Norma Jean Swierk, July 26, 1980; children: Emily Grace, Anna Louise. BA, DePauw U., 1977. Media relations mgr. Ill. Bell, Chgo., 1977-84. Chmn. Community Support Services, LaGrange, pub. relations com. Calendar Ct. Mall com., LaGrange, 1982-86; mem. adv. council LaGrange Head Start, 1983—, council St. James Luth. Ch., Western Springs, Ill., 1983-84, 86—, selection com. Gen. Motors Employee of Yr. Program, 1984. Named one of Outstanding Young Men Am., 1983, 83, 85; recipient Citizen's Commendation LaGrange Police Dept., 1982, Outstanding Community Service award LaGrange Area Head Start Program, 1982-86, Citizen of Yr. award West Suburban C. of C., 1983, 2d Place Spl. Sect. award Subruban Newspapers Am., 1984, 1st Place Community Service Suburban Newspapers Am., 1986, 1st Place Editorial Writing Suburban Newspapers Am., 1986. Democrat. Lodge: Rotary (v.p. LaGrange club 1980-86). Home: 1061 63d St La Grange IL 60253 Office: Ill Bell 225 W Randolph 30-B Chicago IL 60604

MCFARLAND, GALEN DAVID, insurance company executive; b. Norton, Kans., Dec. 18, 1951; s. Joseph Henry McFarland and Mildred June (Von Forrell) Schuette. BS in Bus., Ft. Hays State U., 1974; MBA, Kans. U., 1976. CPA, Kans. Acct. Birney and Co., CPA's, Garden City, Kans., 1977-78; auditor 1st Nat Bank, Hays, Kans., 1978-83; controller Stop 'N Shop, Inc., Hays, 1983-84, Hays State Bank, 1984-86; dist. mgr. A.L. Williams, Hays, 1986—. Mem. Am. Inst. CPA's, Kans. Soc. CPA's. Lodge: Optimist (treas. 1983-85). Avocations: hunting, basketball, softball. Home and Office: AL Williams 1503 Henry Dr Hays KS 67601

MC FARLAND, H. RICHARD, food company executive; b. Hoopeston, Ill., Aug. 19, 1930; s. Arthur Bryan and Jennie (Wilkey) McF.; m. Sarah Forney, Dec. 30, 1967. B.S., U. Ill., 1952. With Campbell Soup Co., Camden, N.J., 1957-67; mgr. purchasing Campbell Soup Co., 1961-67; dir. procurement Keebler Co., Elmhurst, Ill., 1967-69; v.p. purchasing and distbn. Ky. Fried Chicken Corp., Louisville, 1969-74; v.p. food services, sales and distbn. Ky. Fried Chicken Corp., 1974-75; pres., dir. Mid-Continent Carton Co., Louisville, 1974-75, KFC Mfg. Corp., Nashville, 1974-75; owner, pres., dir. McFarland Foods Corp., Indpls., 1975—; bd. dirs. Fountain Trust Co., Ind., Federated Foods Inc., Arlington Heights, Ill., Covington Service Corp., Ind., Spring Valley Foods, Inc., Empire, Ala., 1972-75; pres., dir. K.F.C. Advt. Inc., Ind., 1975-87; mem. K.F.C. Nat. Franchise Adv. Council, 1979-85; dir. Ky. Fried Chicken Nat. Purchasing Coop., 1981-85, chmn. ins. com., 1982-84; mem. K.F.C. Nat. Advt. Co-op, 1985—; chmn. process foods com. World's Poultry Congress, 1974; dir. KFC Nat. Advt. Council, 1985—. Life pres. U. Ill. Sr. Class of '52.; bd. dirs. Ind. Fedn. Children and Youth, 1983-84; chmn. campaign Ind. K.F.C. March of Dimes, 1978—. Served to 1st lt. USAF, 1952-54. Recipient President's award Ky. Fried Chicken Corp., 1970; hon. chief police Louisville, 1970. Mem. Ky. (dir. 1970-75), Restaurant Assn., Nat. Broiler Council (bd. dirs. 1971-74), Ind. Restaurant Assn., Am. Shorthorn Breeders Assn., Great Lakes K.F.C. Franchise Assn. (dir. 1975—, 1st v.p. 1978-79, pres. 1979-80), Delta Upsilon. Presbyn. Clubs: Main Line Ski (Phila.) (pres. 1964); Hillcrest Country. Home: 6361 Avalon Ln East Indianapolis IN 46220 Office: 6440 E 82d St Indianapolis IN 46250

MCFARLAND, JAMES DONALD, marketing company executive; b. Cleve., June 18, 1929; s. James Pernis and Frances Teresa (Koeliker) McF.; m. Constance Louise Mattern, Feb. 20, 1951 (div. May 1960); children: Karen Ilene McFarland Passmore, Christa Louise McFarland Orlaska; m. Helen Joyce Smittle, May 9, 1962; 1 child, James Andrew. Grad. high sch., Grove City, Ohio. Customer engr. IBM Corp., Columbus, Ohio, 1953-55; adjuster Nationwide Ins. Co., Columbus, 1955-65, dist. claims mgr., 1965-80; founder, pres. McFarland & Assocs., Grove City, 1973—; cons., speaker Am. Diabetes Assn., Columbus, 1986. co-chmn. Cen. Ohio Coalition for Decency, Columbus, 1986; sustaining mem. Rep. Nat. Com., Washington, 1983-86; adv. mem. Rep. Presdl. Task Force, 1985-86; chmn. bd. Heritage Bapt. Sch., Canal Winchester, Ohio, 1985-86. Served to maj. U.S. Army, 1951-73, including Korea. Named to Hon. Order Ky. Colonels, 1984. Avocations: golf, family activities. Home and Office: 1740 Borror Rd PO Box 194 Grove City OH 43123

MCFARLAND, KAY ELEANOR, state justice; b. Coffeyville, Kans., July 20, 1935; d. Kenneth W. and Margaret E. (Thrall) McF. BA magna cum laude, Washburn U., Topeka, 1957, JD, 1964. Bar: Kans. 1964. Sole practice Topeka, 1964-71; probate and juvenile judge Shawnee County, Topeka, 1971-73; dist. judge Topeka, 1973-77; justice Kans. Supreme Ct., 1977—. Mem. Kans. Bar Assn. Office: Supreme Ct Kansas State House Topeka KS 66612

MCFARLAND, ROGER WILLIAM, architect; b. Paxton, Ill., Mar. 4, 1956; s. Robert Thomas and Mildred Marie (Seegmiller) McF.; m. Carol Marie Schmidt, Oct. 4, 1981. BArch, Ill. Inst. Tech., 1979. Architect Lohan Assocs., Chgo., 1979—, project mgr., 1984-86, v.p., assoc., 1986—. Subcom. chmn. Albany Park Planning Commn., Chgo., 1986. Mem. AIA, Internat. Facilities Mgmt. Assn. Avocations: travel, photography. Office: Lohan Associates 225 N Michigan Chicago IL 60601

MCFARLANE, DORIS JEAN, educator; b. Eau Claire, Wis., July 10, 1943; d. Phillis Marie (Petrick) McFarlane May. B.S., Wis. State U., 1965; M.S., U. Wis.-LaCrosse, 1970. Tchr. pub. schs., Oconomowoc, Wis., 1965-68, dept. head, 1967-68; tchr. pub. schs., Watertown, Wis., 1969—, varsity head tennis coach, 1971—, varsity head softball coach, 1976—; tennis instr. City of Eau Claire, 1963-72. Mem. choir Our Saviors Luth. Ch., Oconomowoc, 1966—. U. Wis. fellow, 1968; winner Yard of Month award Oconomowoc Women's Club, 1983; named Coach of Yr., 1985; numerous coaching championships, 1970—. Mem. Wis. Edn. Assn., So. Wis. Edn. Assn., NEA, Wis. Fedn. Coaches, United Lakewood Educators, Delta Psi Kappa. Lutheran. Office: Riverside Jr High Sch 131 Hall St Watertown WI 53094

MCFARREN, WILLIAM PAUL, psychologist; b. Canton, Ohio, May 31, 1951; s. Paul Luther and Helen (Straub) M.; m. Peggy Ann Rice, Feb. 25, 1951; 1 child, John Paul. BA, Otterbein Coll., 1973; MS in Clin. Psychology, Eastern Mich. U., 1974; EdD in Counseling Psychology, U. No. Colo., 1978. Diplomate Am. Bd. Psychotherapy; lic. psychologist, Ohio. Psychologist Eastern Mont. Regional Mental Health Ctr., Miles City, 1975-76, Moundbuilder Guidance Ctr., Newark, Ohio, 1978-81; pvt. practice psychology Psychol. Assocs., Newark, 1981—; cons. psychologist Moundbuilders Guidance Ctr., Newark, 1981—; psychologist Licking Meml. Hosp., Newark, 1981—. Mem. Ohio Psychol. Assn. (chmn. 1986—), Am. Psychol. Assn., Nat. Register Of Health Service Providers in Psychology, Phobia Soc. Am. Republican. Methodist. Home: 178 Quentin Rd N Newark OH 43055 Office: Psychological Assocs 88 McMillen Dr Newark OH 43055

MCFATRICH, CHARLES MICHAEL, agronomist; b. Sedalia, Mo., Dec. 12, 1952; s. Charles Herbert and Dorothy Elizabeth McF.; m. Gail L. Ebey, 1983. Student, U. Tex., Arlington, 1970-71; BA, U. Mo., 1974; MS, Oreg. State U., 1977. Seed tech. researcher U. Mo., Columbia, 1977-78; soybean ops. mgr. McCurdy Seed Corp., Fremont, Iowa, 1978-81; dir. research Schettler-Diamond Brand Seed, Inc., Carroll, Iowa, 1981-85; dir. product devel. United AgriSeed, Inc., Champaign, Ill., 1985—; vis. lectr. genetics Indian Hills Coll., Ottumwa, Iowa, 1978-81. Contbr. articles on crop mgmt. to profl. jours. Mem. Am. Soc. Agronomy, Crop Sci. Soc. Am., Council for Agrl. Sci. and Tech., Nat. Audubon Soc., Whale Protection League, Smithsonian Inst. (assoc.), NOW. Home: 111 W Pennsylvania Urbana IL 61801 Office: United AgriSeed Inc PO Box 4011 Champaign IL 61820

MCFERRIN, CECIL DON, manufacturing executive; b. Sebring, Fla., Dec. 23, 1940; s. Harry Cecil and Susie (Lynn) McF.; m. Carolyn Louise Schelin, June 30, 1963 (div. Jan. 1975); children: Timothy Alan, Richard Eric, Donya Schelin. AA in Bus. Adminstrn., Coffeyville (Kans.) Jr. Coll., 1961; BBA, Kans. State Coll., 1963. V.p. Pressure Cast Products, Inc., Coffeyville, 1963-76, pres., 1976—. Served with USAF, 1963-69. Mem. Nat. Assn. Pattern Mfrs. (pres. Cleve. 1981-82). Democrat. Lodge: Rotary (pres. Coffeyville 1980-81). Home: 2704 Midland Coffeyville KS 67337 Office: Pressure Cast Products Inc 300 E 4th St PO Box 563 Coffeyville KS 67337

MCGAHA, JOHNNY EARL, criminal justice educator; b. Hobbs, N.Mex., Mar. 10, 1943; s. Desmond E. McGaha and Evelyn Lee (Wynn) Jokisch; m. Glenda S. Sharp, July 16, 1978; children: Darren, Scott, Seana. BS in Sociology, Sam Houston U., 1969, MA in Criminal Justice, 1976; PhD in Family Relations Child Devel., Okla. State U., 1986. Probation officer Kern County, Bakersfield, Calif., 1969-72; chief probation officer 64th Dist. Ct., Plainview, Tex., 1972-75; exec. dir. Cen. Ala. Youth Service, Selma, 1975-79; adminstr. Burns Internat., Tulsa, 1979-81; asst. prof. Southeast Mo. State U., Cape Girardeau, 1984—. Mem. Ala. Juvenile Justice Assn. (past pres., founder), Mo. Corrections Assn., Alpha Chi. Democrat. Episcopalian. Home: 1221 Fairlane Cape Girardeau MO 63701 Office: Southeast Mo State U Dept Criminal Justice Cape Girardeau MI 63701

MCGAHAN, JAMES EUGENE, educator; b. Wallace, Nebr., Feb. 8, 1944; s. William Conrad and Mildred Marie (Nelson) McG.; m. Martha Ida Wilhoft, Dec. 28, 1966; children: Ellen Jane, Steven John. BS, Kearney State Coll., 1966; MS, Emporia State U., 1971; Ed.D., U. No. Colo., 1978. Cert. tchr., Nebr. Tchr. Phys. sci. Central City Pub. Schs., Nebr., 1966-68; tchr. physics, chemistry Northwest High Sch., Grand Island, Nebr., 1968-75, tchr. physics, chemistry, computers, 1977—; mem. sci. cadre Ednl. Service Unit 10, 1986—; chmn. Cooper Found. Sci. Awards Com., 1986; sci. cons. Nebr. Dept. Edn., Lincoln, 1976; peer reviewer Nebr. Profl. Practices Commn., Lincoln, 1980—. Precinct capt. Hall County Democratic party, 1980-82; del. county Dem. convs., 1980, 84; del. Nebr. Dem. Conv., 1984; bd. dirs. Grand Island 2M Coordinating Council; radiol. def. officer Hall County, 1987—; commr. Profl. Rights, Relations and Responsibilities Commn., Lincoln, 1984—. Named Outstanding Young Educator, Grand Island Jr. C. of C., 1976, Disting. Educator, U. Nebr., Omaha, 1984, Outstanding Chemistry Tchr., Nebr. sect. Am. Chem. Soc., 1984. Mem. NEA, Greater Nebr. Assn. Sci. Tchrs. (bd. dirs.), Nebr. Ednl. Tech. Assn. (bd. dirs. 1987—), Nat. Sci. Tchrs. Assn., Nebr. Assn. Ednl. Data Systems (bd. dirs., Computer Tchr. of Yr. 1984), Nebr. Edn. Assn. (commr. 1984-86), Inst. Chem. Edn. (demonstrator 1986—), Northwest Edn. Assn. (polit. action chmn. 1980—), Am. Assn. Physics Tchrs. (physics tchr, resource agt. 1986—). Roman Catholic. Avocations: gardening; photography; music; computers. Home: 1205 N Howard Ave Grand Island NE 68803 Office: Northwest High Sch 2710 North Rd Grand Island NE 68803

MC GARR, FRANK J., federal judge; b. 1921. A.B., Loyola U., Chgo., 1942; J.D., Loyola U., 1950. Bar: Ill. 1950. Assoc. firm Dallstream Schiff Stern & Hardin, Chgo., 1952-54; asst. U.S. atty. No. dist. of Ill., 1954-55, first asst. U.S. atty., 1955-58; ptnr. firm McKay Solum & McGarr, Chgo., 1958-70; first asst. atty. gen. State of Ill., 1969-70; judge U.S. Dist. Ct. for No. Ill., 1970—, sr. judge, 1980-86; sr. judge 1986—; of counsel Phelan, Pope & John, Ltd., Chgo. Recipient medal of Excellence, Loyola Law Alumni Assn., 1964. Served with USN, 1942-45. Mem. Am. Coll. Trial Lawyers, 7th Cir. Bar Assn., Chgo. Bar Assn. Office: US Dist Ct Rm 1846 US Courthouse 219 S Dearborn St Chicago IL 60604 Office: Phelan Pope & John Ltd 180 N Wacker Dr Chicago IL 60606

MCGARRITY, RICHARD ALLEN, banker, accountant; b. Pitts., Jan. 19, 1948; s. George Allen and Eleanor Lucille (McGaughy) McG.; m. Noel Louise Tyson, Apr. 3, 1972; children: Ellen Elsbeth, William George. BA, Ohio Wesleyan U., 1969; MBA, Dartmouth Coll., 1975. CPA, Pa. With U.S. Steel Corp., Pitts., 1969-73; acct. Price Waterhouse, Pitts., 1975-85; sr. v.p., treas. The Kissell Co., Springfield, Ohio, 1985—. Mem. fin. com., bd. dirs. The Mental Health Services of Clark County, 1987; mem. adv. bd. bus. dept. Wittenberg U., Springfield, 1987—. Served to lt. USN, 1970-72. Mem. Am. Inst. CPA's, Pa. Inst. CPA's. Republican. Club: Springfield Country. Avocations: tennis, photography, golf, travel.

MCGARRY, DANIEL DOYLE, educational foundation administrator; b. Los Angeles, Nov. 10, 1907; s. Daniel F. and Ana (Doyle) McG.; m. Margaret M. Reddington; children: Mary Ann, Patricia Mae Harleman, Daniel J., Margaret H. BA in History, Immaculate Heart Coll., Los Angeles, 1931; MA in History, UCLA, 1938, PhD in History, 1940. Instr. of History and Philosophy Mt. St. Joseph Coll., Cin., 1940-43, The Athenaeum of Ohio, 1940-43; asst. prof. History Ind. U., Bloomington, 1946-50; assoc. prof. to prof. of History St. Louis U., 1950-76; exec. dir. Ednl. Freedom Found., St. Louis, 1976—; research dir. Thomas J. White Ednl. Found., St. Louis. Author: A History of Western Civilization, 1959, The Metalogicon of John of Salisbury: A Twelfth Century Defence of the Verbal and Logical Arts of the Trivium, 1962, Sources of Western Civilization, 1962, Historical Fiction Guide, 1963, Educational Freedom: The Case For Government Aid to Students in Independent Schools, 1966, Outline of Medieval History, 1968, Medieval History and Civilization, 1976; contbr. Encyclopedia Britannica, New Cath. Encyclopedia, Masterpieces of Cath. Lit., Latin Am. Pattern; contbr. articles to profl. jours.; editor: (jour.) Ednl. Freedom. Nat. dir., state pres. Citizens for Ednl. Freedom, Washington and St. Louis, 1965—. Fluent in Latin, French, Spanish and German. Home and Office: Ednl Freedom Found 20 Parkland Glendale MO 63122

MCGARRY, JOSEPH MICHAEL, retail executive; b. Joliet, Ill., July 12, 1957; s. John Joseph and Margaret Joann (Grabow) McG. BS, Bradley U., 1979. Supr. P.A. Bergner Co., Milw., 1979-82; store mgr. F. Mona Inc., Des Moines, Iowa, 1982-83; dist. mgr. F. Mona Inc., Naperville, Ill., 1983—. Avocation: golf. Home: 1032 F Heritage Hill Naperville IL 60540 Office: F Mona Inc 1217 E Ogden Naperville IL 60540

MCGARRY, KEVIN VINCENT, newspaper company executive; b. Bayside, N.Y., May 18, 1929; s. John James and Julia (McCarthy) McG.; m. Anne Pritchard, Sept. 15, 1956; children—Elizabeth Moore, John Manion, Kevin Vincent, Peter Thomas, Anne Julia. B.S., Fordham U., 1952; postgrad. Wharton Sch., U. Pa., 1954-55. With IBM, 1955-56, Honeywell Corp., 1956-59; advt. mgr. Wall St. Jour., Mpls., 1959-67; advt. mgr. Nat. Observer, Detroit, 1967-73; assoc. Midwest advt. mgr. Wall St. Jour., Chgo., 1973-78; Midwest advt. mgr. Wall St. Jour., Chgo., 1978—. Served to 1st lt., arty. AUS, 1952-54. Mem. Detroit Advt. Assn., Am. Mktg. Assn., Delta Sigma. Republican. Roman Catholic. Clubs: Chgo. Advertising, AdCraft, Tavern (Chgo.); Westmoreland Country (Wilmette, Ill.); University (Detroit).

MCGARRY, ROBERT GEORGE, safety engineer; b. Mpls., Jan. 4, 1917; s. Emmett Frank and Ethel Florence (Bryant) McG.; m. Janalee Judy, Sept. 22, 1986; children from previous marriage: Mary Kathleen, Nancy Margaret, Susan Elaine, Kevin Robert. BS in Indsl. Engring., U. Minn., 1939; MS in Safety Engring., Ga. Inst. Tech., 1947. Registered profl. engr., Calif.; cert. safety profl. Sr. safety engr. U.S. Fidelity & Guaranty Co., Atlanta, Mpls., 1950-63; Bechtel Corp., San Francisco, 1963-77; corp. safety engr. Burns & McDonnell Engrs., Cons., Kansas City, Mo., 1977-82; con. safety engr., Lee's Summit, Mo., 1982—; adj. instr. safety engring. Sch. Mgmt. Devel., U. Mo., Kansas City. Served with USN, 1942-46. Recipient Minn. Gov.'s Outstanding Safety Achievement award, 1969. Mem. Am. Soc. Safety Engrs. (chmn. engring. com.), Vets. of Safety Internat. (dir.-at-large), NSPE, Mo. Soc. Profl. Engrs., Profl. Engrs. in Pvt. Practice, Am. Arbitration Assn. (arbitrator). Lodges: Masons, Shriners. Home and Office: 11622 Greenwood Rd Kansas City MO 64134

MCGARVEY, WILLIAM K., otolaryngologist, surgeon; b. Marion, Ind., Aug. 3, 1937; s. Eugene J. and Rosemary (Kelley) McG.; m. Janet Lee Prentice, Feb. 27, 1975; children: Erika, Kevin. AB in Anatomy and Physiology, Ind. U., 1959, MD, 1962. Diplomate Bd. Otolaryngolgy and Head and Neck Surgery. Intern San. Francisco Gen. Hosp., 1962-63; resident in otolaryngology and head and neck surgery Ind. U. Med. Sch. and assoc. hosps., Indpls., 1963-67; practice medicine specializing in otolaryngology and head and neck surgery San Francisco, 1969-74, Indpls., 1974—; asst. prof. otolaryngology and head and neck surgery Ind. U. Sch. Medicine, 1974; asst. prof. otolaryngology and head and neck surgery, U. Calif. Med. Sch., San Francisco, 1969-74; chmn. dept. otolaryngology and head and neck surgery, Community Hosp., Indpls., 1976-78. Served with maj. U.S. Army, 1967-69, Vietnam. Fellow ACS, Am. Acad. Otolaryngology and Head and Neck Surgery, Am. Acad. Facial Plastic and Reconstructive Surgeons; mem. Am. Acad. Otolaryngic Allergy, Undersea Med. Soc. Hyperbaric Medicine. Republican. Methodist. Clubs: Meridian Hills (Indpls.) Country, Skyline (Indpls.). Lodge: Masons. Avocations: soap box derby racing, snow skiing, water skiing. Home: 1816 Wood Valley Dr Carmel IN 46032 Office: Hopkins Jones McGarvey & Biggerstaff 8402 Harcourt Rd 202 Indianapolis IN 46260

MC GARY, THOMAS HUGH, lawyer; b. Milburn, Ky., Mar. 6, 1938; s. Ollie James and Pauline Elizabeth (Tackett) McG.; A.B., Elmhurst Coll., 1961; J.D., U. Chgo., 1964; m. Madalyn Maxwell, July 4, 1968. Admitted to Ill. bar, 1964; asst. atty. gen. State of Ill., 1965-67, supr. consumer credit, 1967-71; ind. practice law, Springfield, Ill., 1971—; v.p., dir. Citizens Bank of Edinburg (Ill.), 1971—, Bank of Kenney (Ill.), 1977—, Bank of Springfield; instr. Lincolnland Coll., 1970-73; assoc. prof. med. humanities So. Ill. U. Sch. Medicine. Mem. Springfield Art Assn., Springfield Symphony Assn.; mem. Springfield Election Commn.; mem. Ill. Adv. Commn. on Group Ins.; bd. dirs. Central Ill. Youth Services Bur.; vestryman St. Paul's Cathedral. Mem. Am., Ill., Sangamon County bar assns., Am. Judicature Soc., Sangamon County Hist. Assn., Chaine de Rotisseurs. Democrat. Clubs: Sangamo (Springfield); Oakcrest Country. Home: 2018 Briarcliff Dr Springfield IL 62704 Office: 600 S 4th St Springfield IL 62703

MCGAW, DONNAMARIE ANNE, architect; b. Cleve., Jan. 13, 1957; d. John Corbly and Dorothy Theresa (Ficzner) South; m. Robert Michael McGaw, Nov. 6, 1982; 1 child, Ian Michael. BS, Kent State U., 1979, BArch with honors, 1980. Registered architect, Ohio; cert. constrn. specifier, Ohio. Draftsman Voinovich-Sgro Architects, Cleve., 1977-80, Classic Equipment Co., Tallmadge, Ohio, 1977-80; specifier writer Keeva J. Kekst Assocs., Cleve., 1980-85; prin. D.A. McGaw Assoc., Brecksville, Ohio, 1985—. Mem. AIA (profl., Women's task force 1983-84), Constrn. Specification Inst. (profl., tech. chmn. 1983-84, sec. 1987), Tau Sigma Delta. Avocations: reading, knitting, calligraphy, sewing, bicycling. Home and Office: 6804 Westwood Dr Brecksville OH 44141

MCGEE, JANE MARGARET, training specialist, management consultant; b. Milw., Sept. 30, 1955; d. James Thomas and Joan Ann (Baird) McG. BS in Home Econs. Edn., U. Nebr., 1978, MA in Adult and Continuing Edn., 1981. Home econs. tchr. Seward (Nebr.) Pub. Schs., 1977-78; extension agt.-home econs. U. Nebr., Lincoln, 1978-84; tng. and devel. adminstr. Am. Charter, Lincoln, 1984-85; tng. specialist Lincoln Electric System, 1985—. Mem. Am. Soc. Tng. and Devel. (v.p. 1987), Kappa Delta Alumni Assn. (pres. Lincoln chpt. 1986). Democrat. Roman Catholic. Club: Up Downtowners (Lincoln). Office: Lincoln Electric System 1200 N St Lincoln NE 68508

MCGEE, JOHN EDWARD, gynecologist/obstetrician; b. Granite City, Ill., Nov. 25, 1928; s. James Anthony and Anna Elizabeth (Speiser) McG.; m. Margaret Ann Grems, Oct. 17, 1953; children: Michael, Joseph, Ann, Jane, Brian, Robert, James, Maureen. BS, St. Louis U., 1949, MD, 1953. Cert. Am. Bd. Ob-Gyn. Intern Ancker Hosp., St. Paul, 1953-54; resident in internal medicine U. Minn., Mpls., 1954; resident in ob-gyn St. Louis U. Hosp., 1957-60; chief dept. ob/gyn Ft. Madison (Iowa) Hosp., 1965; chief dept. maternal child health Burlington (Iowa) Med. Ctr., 1983, chief of staff, 1986. Pres. Ft. Madison Sch. Bd., 1969; pres. S.E. Iowa Health Systems Agy., 1975. Served to lt. comdr. USNR, 1955-57. Fellow Am. Coll. Ob/Gyn; Mem. AMA, Am. Urogynecological Soc., Iowa Med. Soc. Republican. Roman Catholic. Avocations: golf, biking. Office: Burlington Ob/Gyn 610 N 4th Burlington IA 52601

MCGEE, JOHN FRANCIS, lawyer; b. Independence, Kans., Aug. 18, 1945; s. Francis J. and Bonnell Maxine (La Duke) McG. BS in Edn., U. Kans., 1968, MBA, JD, 1977. Bar: Kans. 1977, U.S. Ct. Appeals (10th cir.) 1980. Ptnr. Williamson, McGee, Griggs & DeMoss Chartered, Wichita, Kans., 1978—; bd. dirs. 1st Nat. Bank, Independence, Kans. Mem. ABA, Kans. Bar Assn., Wichita Bar Assn., Assn. Trial Lawyers Am., Kans. Trial Lawyers Assn. Republican. Methodist. Office: Williamson McGee Griggs & DeMoss Chartered 200 W Douglas 9th Floor Wichita KS 67202

MCGEE, ROBERT LEE, chemical engineer; b. Zanesville, Ohio, Nov. 11, 1958; s. Charles Virgil and Laura Bell (Dailey) McG.; m. Gail Lynne Graham, Nov. 26, 1983. BS, Muskingum Coll., New Concord, Ohio, 1981; MS, Ohio U., 1984. Research engr. Dow Chem. Co., Midland, Mich., 1983. Mem. Soc. Advancement Material and Process Engring., Sigma Xi. Republican. Presbyterian. Avocations: sports, reading. Home: 1164 S Gary Rd Midland MI 48640 Office: Dow Chem Co 1712 Bldg Door 1 Midland MI 48640

MCGEE, T(EDDY) MANFORD, otologist; b. Mayfield, Ky., Mar. 23, 1926; s. Worthy Manford and Alta Christine (Winfrey) McG.; m. Rovilla Ganote, June 13, 1950; children: Mark Manford, Matthew Manford, Timothy Manford. BS cum laude, Hope Coll., 1950; MD, John Hopkins U., 1954. Diplomate Am. Bd. Otolaryngology. Intern Henry Ford Hosp., Detroit, 1954-55, resident in otolaryngology, 1955-59, chief div. otology, dir. otologic research lab., 1960-64; clin. assoc. prof. otolaryngology Wayne State U., Detroit, 1964—; assoc. surgeon, chief dept. otology, past pres. research found. Providence (Mich.) Hosp.; mem. staff Detroit Gen. Hosp., William Beaumont Hosp., Providence Hosp., Southfield, Mich. Contbr. artilces to profl. jours. Bd. dirs. Detroit United Found., 1960-69; trustee 1st Bapt. Ch., Birmingham, Mich., 1970-79. Served to sgt. U.S. Army, 1944-46. Mem. AMA, Am. Acad. Otolaryngology and Head and Neck Surgery, Am. Laryngol., Rhinol. and Otol. Soc., Am. Otol. Soc., Am. Neurotologic Soc., Politzer Soc., Royal Soc. Medicine, Pan-Pacific Surg. Assn., Pan-Am. Med. Assn., Inc., W.Va. Med. Soc., Alaska Med. Soc., Mich. Ear, Nose and Throat Physician's Practice Assn., Mich. Otolaryn. Soc., Oakland County Med. Soc., Wayne County Med. Soc., Ear, Nose and Throat Soc. Australia, Ear, Nose and Throat Soc. New Zealand, Toynbee Soc. Australia. Republican. Club: Orchard Lake (Mich.) Country, Useppa Island (Fla.) Country, Resaissance (Detroit), Detroit Yacht. Avocations: skiing, scuba diving, golf, boating. Office: Greater Detroit Otologic Group 27555 Middlebelt Farmington Hills MI 48018

MC GEHEE, H. COLEMAN, JR., bishop; b. Richmond, Va., July 7, 1923; s. Harry Coleman and Ann Lee (Cheatwood) McG.; m. June Stewart, Feb. 1, 1946; children: Lesley, Alexander, Coleman III, Donald, Cary. BS, Va. Poly. Inst., 1944; JD, U. Richmond, 1949; MDiv, Va. Theol. Sem., 1957, DD, 1973. Bar: Va. 1949, U.S. Supreme Ct. 1949; ordained to ministry Episcopal Ch., 1958. Spl. counsel dept. hwys. State of Va., 1949-51, gen. counsel employment service, 1951, asst. atty. gen., 1951-54; rector Immanuel Ch.-on-the-Hill, Va. Sem., 1960-71; bishop Diocese of Mich., Detroit, 1973—; mem. adv. bd. Nicaraguan Network, Ctr. for Peace and Conflict Studies, Wayne State U.; bd. dirs. Mich. Religious Coalition for Abortion Rights, 1976—; trustee Va. Theol. Seminary, 1978—; pres. Episcopal Ch. Pub. Co., 1978-85. Columnist: Detroit News, 1979-85; weekly commentator: Sta. WDET-AM, Detroit, 1984—. Mem. Gov.'s Commn. on Status of Women, 1965-66, Mayor's Civic Com., Alexandria, 1967-68; sponsor Nat. Assn. for ERA, 1977—; pres. Alexandria Legal Aid Soc., 1969-71; bd. dirs. No. Va. Fairhousing Corp., 1963-67; pres. Mich. Coalition for Human Rights, 1980—; chmn. Citizens' Com. for Justice in Mich., 1983-84; sponsor Farm Labor Orgn. for Children, 1983-85. Served to 1st lt., C.E. AUS, 1943-46. Named Feminist of Yr., Detroit NOW, 1978; recipient Humanitarian award Detroit ACLU, 1984, Phillip Hart medal Mich. Women's Studies Assn., 1984. Club: Detroit Econ. (bd. dirs.). Home: 749 Henley Dr Birmingham MI 48008 Office: 4800 Woodward Ave Detroit MI 48201

MCGILL, KENNETH JAMES, JR., dentist; b. Vancouver, B.C., Can., Jan. 14, 1954; came to U.S., 1968; s. Kenneth James Sr. and Irene Thelma (Bickner) McG.; m. Jodie Lynn Webster, Mar. 21, 1982; 1 child, David James. BS in Psychology, Pacific Union Coll., 1976; MS in Marriage, Family and Child Counseling, Loma Linda (Calif.) U., 1977, DDS, 1983. Child protection placement social worker Dept. Social Services, San Bernadino, Calif., 1977-80; gen. practice dentistry Toledo, 1984-86, Lexington and Mansfield, Ohio, 1986—; vol. dentist Monument Valley (Utah) Indian Reservation, 1983; dental dir. Cordelia Martin Health Ctr., Toledo, 1984-86, cons., 1984-85. Mem. Seventh Day Adventist Ch. Avocations: waterskiing, snowskiing, golf, sailing, tennis. Home: 705 Nekik View St Huron OH 44839

MCGILLEY, SISTER MARY JANET, college president; b. Kansas City, Mo., Dec. 4, 1924; d. James P. and Peg (Ryan) McG. B.A., St. Mary Coll., 1945; M.A., Boston Coll., 1951; Ph.D., Fordham U., 1956; postgrad., U. Notre Dame, 1960, Columbia U., 1964. Social worker Kansas City, 1945-46; joined Sisters of Charity of Leavenworth, 1946; tchr. English Hayden High Sch., Topeka, 1948-50, Billings (Mont.) Central High Sch., 1951-53; faculty dept. English St. Mary Coll., Leavenworth, Kans., 1956-64; pres. St. Mary Coll., 1964—. Contbr. articles, fiction and poetry to various jours. Bd. dirs. Kans. Ind. Coll. Assn., 1964—, treas. 1982-84, v.p. 1984-85, chmn. exec. com., 1985-86; bd. dirs. Kansas City Regional Council for Higher Edn., 1968—, treas. 1984-85, v.p. 1986-87, chmn. elect 1987-88, United Way of Leavenworth, 1966-85; bd. dirs. Kans. Ind. Coll. Fund, pres., 1972-74, 77-78; mem. Mayor's Adv. Council, 1967-72; mem. com. on insts. of higher edn. North Central Assn. Colls. and Schs., 1980—, vice chair, 1985-86, chair, 1987—; mem. North Cen. Assn., chmn. commn. colls. and univs. 1986—; mem. Leavenworth Planning Council, 1977-78. Recipient Alumnae award St. Mary Coll., 1969; Disting. Service award Baker U., 1981, Leavenworth Bus. Woman of Yr. Athea award, 1986. Mem. Nat. Council Tchrs. English, Nat. Assn. Ind. Colls. and Univs. (bd. dirs. 1982-85), Am. Council Edn. (com. on women in higher edn. 1980—), Am. Assn. Higher Edn., Ind. Coll. Funds Am. (exec. com. 1974-77, trustee at large 1975-76), Leavenworth C. of C. (dir. 1964—), Assn. Am. Colls. (commn. liberal learning 1970-73, com. on curriculum and faculty devel. 1979-82), St. Mary Alumni Assn. (hon. pres. 1964—), Delta Epsilon Sigma. Democrat. Address: Saint Mary College Leavenworth KS 66048

MCGINNESS, JOYCE NOLLE, computer software company owner, consultant; b. St. Louis, Jan. 15, 1955; d. Ernest W. and Norma (Patton) Nolle; m. David S. McGinness, Nov. 24, 1977. BS, Drake U., 1976. Store mgr. Jean Nicole Stores, West Des Moines, 1977-78; programmer Computer Applications Team, Des Moines, 1978-79, payroll clk. Corn State Metal Fabrications, 1979-80, analyst, programmer F.A.C.T.S. Data Services, Inc., 1980-83; owner, system analyst McGinness Computer Consulting & Programming, Inc., 1983—. Mem. Assn. System Mgrs., Nat. Assn. Female Execs., Nat. Assn. Women Bus. Owners, (Iowa chpt. Nat. Assn. Women Bus. Owners), Metro Women's Network (chmn. 1987). Democrat. Clubs: Women's Exec. Breakfast. Avocations: sewing; jogging; camping; traveling. Home: 4118 Cottage Grove Des Moines IA 50311 Office: 1200 35th St West Des Moines IA 50265

MC GIVERIN, ARTHUR A., state justice; b. Iowa City, Iowa, Nov. 10, 1928; s. Joseph J. and Mary B. McG.; m. Mary Joan McGiverin, Apr. 20, 1951; children: Teresa, Thomas, Bruce, Nancy. B.S.C. with high honors, U. Iowa, 1951, J.D., 1956. Bar: Iowa 1956. Practice law Ottumwa, Iowa, 1956; alt. mcpl. judge Ottumwa, 1960-65; judge Iowa Dist. Ct. 8th Jud. Dist., 1965-78; asso. justice Iowa Supreme Ct., Des Moines, 1978—. Mem. Iowa Supreme Ct. Commn. on Continuing Legal Edn., 1975. Served to 1st lt. U.S. Army, 1946-48, 51-53. Mem. Iowa State Bar Assn., Am. Law Inst. Roman Catholic. Office: Supreme Ct of Iowa Capitol Bldg 10th and Grand Des Moines IA 50319 *

MCGIVNEY, JAMES, dentist; b. Queens, N.Y., July 15, 1948; s. James Bernard and Muriel (Walker) McG.; m. Joan Viola Hrin, Jan. 1, 1975; children: Veronica Mary, Melissa Ann. Student, Nassau Community Coll., 1966-67, 69-70; BS, SUNY, N.Y.C., 1972; DMD, Washington U., St. Louis, 1975. Forensic dentist Med. Examiner St. Louis, 1979—; asst. prof. Washington U., St. Louis, 1982—, St. Louis U., 1986—; practice dentistry St. Louis, 1979—; cons. Global Marine Drilling Co., Houston, 1984. Contbr. articles and papers on dentistry to profl. jours. Capt. Gravois Township Rep. Precinct. Served to lt. USN, 1976-79. Fellow am. Acad. Forensic Scis.; mem. ADA, Am. Soc. Forensic Odontology, Mo. Dental Assn., Greater St. Louis Dental Soc. Episcopalian. Lodge: Kiwanis. Avocations: tennis, golf, fishing. Home: 346 Tulip Dr Webster Groves MO 63119 Office: 66 Gasso Pl Saint Louis MO 63123

MCGONAGLE, JACK WILSON, optometrist; b. New Lexington, Ohio, Nov. 12, 1923; s. Urban S. and Hazel (Wilson) McG.; m. Rita S. Steiner, Apr. 17, 1950 (dec. 1983); children—Mike, Pat, Tim, Molly, Kathy; m. Helen L. Grieve, Nov. 25, 1983. Student, Xavier U., Cin., 1941-43, Ohio U., 1946—; O.D., Ill. Coll. Optometry, Chgo., 1949. Practice optometry, Lancaster, Ohio, 1950—. Served with AUS, 1943-46. Mem. Am. Optometric Assn., Ohio Optometric Assn., Lancaster C. of C., Am. Legion. Republican. Roman Catholic. Club: Symposiarchs, Elks. Lodge: KC. Avocations: Golf; tennis; fishing. Office: 404 E Main St Lancaster OH 43130

MCGONIGAL, PEARL, lieutenant governor Manitoba; b. Melville, Sask., Can., June 10, 1929; d. Fred and Kathryne Kuhlman; m. Marvin A. McGonigal, Nov. 3, 1948; 1 dau., Kimberly Jane. Ed. in, Melville, Sask.; LL.D. (hon.), U. Man. Formerly engaged in banking; then mdse. rep.; mem. St. James-Assiniboia (Man.) City Council, 1969-71; mem. Greater Winnipeg (Man.) City Council, 1971-81, chmn. com. on recreation and social services, 1977-79, dep. mayor and chmn. exec. policy com., 1979-81; lt. gov. Man., 1981—; mem. adv. bd. Royal Trust Co., 1987—; bd. dirs. Mediacom. Inc. Author: Frankly Feminine Cookbook, 1975; weekly columnist: Reliance Press Ltd. Newspapers, 1970-81. Bd. dirs. Winnipeg Conv. Centre, 1975-77, Red River Exhbn., 1975-81, Rainbow Stage, 1976-81, Man. Blue Cross; ex-officio mem. Man. Theatre Centre, 1977-81; mem. Winnipeg Conv. and Visitors Bur., 1973-75, Man. Environ. Concil, 1974-76, Man. Aviation Council, 1974-77; mem. selection com. Faculty Dental Hygiene, U. Man., 197-80; bd. mgmt. Winnipeg Home Improvement Program, 1979-81; chmn. adv. com. Sch. Nursing, Grace Gen. Hosp., 1972—; past chmn. St. James-Assiniboia Inter-faith Immigration Council; former mem. vestry St. Andrew's Anglican Ch.; former vol. Lions Manor, Sherbrook Day Centre; chmn. bd. mgmt. Grace Gen. Hosp., 1987—; chmn. bd. reference Catherine Booth Bible Coll., 1987. Recipient award Dist. 64 Toastmasters, 1974, award Winnipeg lodge Elks, 1975, nat. B'nai Brith Humanitarian award, 1984, Citizen of Yr. award Knights of Columbus, 1987; decorated dame Order of St. John; named hon. col. 735 Communications Regt. Mem. Beta Sigma Phi (1st Lady of Yr. 1986). Liberal. Club: Winnipeg Winter. Lodge: KC (Citizen of Yr. 1987). Home: 51 361 Westwood Dr, Winnipeg, MB Canada R3K 1G4 Office: Rm 235 Legislative Bldg, Winnipeg, MB Canada R3C 0V8

MCGOOGAN, JUDITH DIANNE, data processing executive, systems engineer; b. Stillwater, Okla., Dec. 20, 1946; d. Oran Carl and Vivian Leone (Matthews) Rose; m. John Edwin McGoogan, Aug. 31, 1968; children: Elizabeth Dianne, Julie Ann. BS in Math., U. Okla., 1968, MS in Info. and Computer Sci., 1976. Cert. in data processing. Info. systems designer Western Electric, Oklahoma City, 1968-69; cons. Oklahoma City, 1976-77; info. system staff mem. Western Electric, Oklahoma City, 1978-79, Western Electric and AT&T, Warrenville, Ill., 1979-84; dept. chief AT&T, Lisle, Ill., 1984-87; mem. tech. staff AT&T Bell Labs., Naperville, Ill., 1987; coll. recruiter AT&T, Okla. and Ill., 1978-86. Republican. Methodist. Avocations: bridge, backgammon, reading, golfing. Office: AT&T 4513 Western Ave Lisle IL 60532

MCGOVERN, EUGENIA GAYE, school superintendent; b. Boston, Oct. 21, 1943; d. Louis harry Jr. and Mary Eugenia (Coleman) Roddis; m. William Lloyd McGovern, June 29, 1963; 1 child, Elizabeth Amy. BS, U. Pitts., 1963; MA, U. Redlands, 1965; EdD, UCLA, 1970. With Beaumont (Calif.) Pub. Schs., 1964-68, Santa Maria (Calif.) Pub. Sch., 1968-70, Syracuse City Sch. Dist.chs., 1970-72, Harrisburg (Pa.) City Sch. Dist., 1972-74, Capital Area Intermediate Unit, Pa., 1974-76, Wilmington (Ohio) City Sch. Dist., 1976-79; supt. Miami (Ohio) East Sch. Dist., 1979-81, East Palestine (Ohio) City Sch. Dist., 1981—; adj. prof. edn. Wright State U., Dayton, 1978, U. Dayton, 1976-77; asst. prof. edn. Lebanon Valley Coll., 1974-75; instr. U. Calif., Santa Barbara, 1969-70, Riverside, 1966-68; cons. in field. Contbr. articles to profl. jours. Mem. adv. bd. Miami County (Ohio) Juvenile Ct., 1979-81; mem. exec. bd., planning com. Pvt. Industry Council Mahoning and Columbiana Counties, 1983—; active with People Helping People; mem. vestry and layreader St. James Episcopal Ch., 1981—; bd. dirs. Clinton County United Way, 1977-79, v.p. 1979; bd. dirs. Clinton County Human Service Assn., 1977-78. Named one of Outstanding Young Women of Yr., Wilmington Jr. C. of C., 1979. Mem. Am. Assn. Sch. Adminstrs. (del.-at-large 1982-84, com. on state assns. 1982-85, singing supts. 1979-87, small schs, com. 1987—), Buckeye Assn. Sch. Adminstrs., Columbiana County Supts. Assn. (pres. 1983-84), Phi Delta Kappa. Republican. Office: 360 W Grant St East Palestine OH 44413

MCGOVERN, MICHAEL TREVOR, hospital administrator; b. Albuquerque, Aug. 1, 1955; s. Robert Blanford and Sharlene Louise (Bowen) McG.; m. Diane Marie Nester. BA, Ohio Wesleyan U., 1980; M in Health Adminstrn., Ohio State U., 1982. Asst. exec. dir. Children's Hosp., Inc., Columbus, Ohio, 1982-86, dir. corp. devel., 1986—; exec. dir. Children's Hosp. Guidance Ctrs. div. Children's Hosp., Inc., Columbus, Ohio, 1985—; adj. instr. Ohio State U. grad. sch., Columbus, 1983—; bd. trustees Ronald McDonald House, Columbus, 1983-85, Health Banc, Columbus, 1986—. Mem. Arlington Community Team Upper Arlington, Ohio, 1985—. Served with U.S. Army, 1973-76. Recipient Internat. Study award Rotary Found., Leeds, Eng., 1982, Anne Gannett award Soc. Music Educators, 1976. Mem. Healthcare Fin. Mgmt. Assn., Am. Hosp. Assn., Am. Coll. Health Execs. (Foster G. McGaw scholar 1981), Ohio Hosp. Assns., Ohio State U. Alumni Assn. Grad. Program in Hosp. Adminstrn. Democrat. Methodist. Lodge: Kiwanis. Avocations: triathlete, golf, running, trombone. Home: 1819 Collingswood Rd Upper Arlington OH 43221 Office: Children's Hosp 700 Children's Dr Columbus OH 43205

MCGOVERN, ROBERT WILLIAM, health care company executive; b. Mpls., June 1, 1941; s. William Henry and Mary Helen (Ohnsorg) McG.; m. Dawn Marie McGovern, Apr. 7, 1967; children: Timothy, Daniel. BS in Acctg., U. Minn., 1965. CPA, Minn. Accountant Price Waterhouse, N.Y.C., 1965-73; fin. analyst Dayton-Hudson Corp., Mpls., 1973-77; controller Gold Medallion Corp., Mpls., 1977-82; treas., gen. mgr. S&M Co., Mpls., 1982-85; v.p. fin. TransHealth, Inc., Mpls., 1985—. Mem. Am. Inst. CPA's, Minn. Soc. CPA's. Republican. Roman Catholic. Avocation: golf. Home: 6519 Leesborough Ave Eden Prairie MN 55344 Office: TransHealth Inc 1301 Corporate Ctr Dr Suite 120 Eagan MN 55121

MCGOWAN, KATHLEEN ANN, physician; b. Ft. Dodge, Iowa, Apr. 13, 1955; d. Leo Patrick and Lucille Marie (Wittrock) McG. AA, Des Moines Community Coll., 1975; BS, Iowa State U., 1978; DO, Coll. Osteopathic Medicine and Surgery, Des Moines, 1981. Diplomate Nat. Bd. Examiners Osteo. Physicians and Surgeons, cert. Am. Coll. Gen. Practice. Intern Des Moines Gen. Hosp., 1981-82, resident in family practice, 1981-83, also mem. staff med. services of Southridge, 1982-83; emergency room physician Mercy Hosp. Med. Ctr., West Des Moines, 1983-85; mem. staff Mercy Valley West Mall Clinic, 1985-86, gen. practice osteo. medicine, 1985—; lectr. various colls. and hosps. Mem. AMA, Iowa Med. Soc., Polk County Med. Soc., Am. Osteo. Assn., Polk County Osteo. Assn., Iowa Soc. Osteo. Physicians and Surgeons, Am. Coll. Gen. Practitioners, Am. Med. Women's Assn., Iowa Fedn. Physicians and Dentists, Am. Coll. Energency Physicians, Inst. Food Technologists, Undergrad. Acad. Am. Osteo. Assn., Iowa Sect. Food Technologists, Coll. Osteo. Medicine and Surgery Alumni Assn., Iowa State Alumni Assn., Iowa State Food Tech. Club, Delta Omega, Alpha Lambda Delta. Roman Catholic. Avocations: sewing, cooking, tennis, baseball, dancing.

MCGOWAN, KATHLEEN JOAN, social worker; b. Berwyn, Ill., July 24, 1946; d. Robert Emmet and Joan P. (Rakas) McG.; m. Terrance P. McGuire, May 10, 1985. BA, Loyola U., Chgo., 1969; MSW, U. Ill., Chgo., 1975. Cert. social worker, Ill. Caseworker Cath. Charities, Chgo., 1969-75, supr. foster care, 1975-79, program dir. child protective services, 1979-84, dir. staff devel. and edn., 1984—; cons., lectr. Alexian Bros. Hosp., St. Louis, 1985, Alexian Bros. Med. Ctr. and Health System, Elk Grove Village, Ill., 1986; cons. Sisters of St. Joseph 3d Order of St. Francis, Bartlett, Ill., 1986. Editor: (with others) Divorce and Beyond, 1983. Mem. devel. bd. Sisters of St. Joseph, LaGrange, Ill., 1983-86, adv. bd., 1985—. Mem. Cath. Charities U.S.A. (chair membership com. 1984—), Nat. Assn. Social Workers, Acad. Cert. Social Workers, Ill. Tng. and Devel. Assn. Avocations: antique collecting, tennis. Home: 817 W Washington Blvd Oak Park IL 60302 Office: Cath Charities 126 N Desplaines Chicago IL 60606

MCGOWIN, JOSHUA SHANNON, accountant; b. Jefferson City, Mo., Nov. 21, 1957; s. Joshua Jr. and Myna Jayne (Patterson) McG.; m. Kay Caroline Casey, June 28, 1980; children: Jay Michael, Mallory Jayne. Student, U. Mo., Kansas City, 1976; BSBA in Acctg., U. Mo., 1979. CPA, Mo. Auditor Mo. Dept. Social Services, Jefferson City, 1979-82, MFA Inc., Columbia, Mo., 1982-85; pvt. practice acct. Lake Ozark, Mo., 1985—. Mem. Am. Inst. CPA's, Nat. Soc. Self-Employed, Mo. Soc. CPA's,. Republican. Lodge: Optimist. Avocations: softball, basketball, photography. Home: PO Box 387 Ulman MO 65083 Office: Rt 72 Box 75 Lake Ozark MO 65049

MCGRAIL, JEAN KATHRYN, artist, educator, poet; b. Mpls., May 1, 1947; d. Robert Vern and Mary Virginia (Kees) McGrail; m. Theodore Esser III, Sept. 28, 1985. B.S., U. Wis.-River Falls, 1970; M.F.A., Cranbrook Acad. Art, 1972; postgrad. Sch. of Art Inst. of Chgo., 1985. One woman shows include Gallery at the Commons, Chgo., 1982; group exhbns. include

Saginaw Art Mus., Mich., 1972, Met. Mus. Art, Miami, Fla., 1974, Lowe Mus. Art, Coral Gables, Fla., 1974, 76, Miller Galleries, Coconut Grove, Fla., 1978, 80, Cicchinelli Gallery, N.Y.C., 1980-82, Harper Coll., 1984; represented in permanent collections at Miami-Dade Pub. Library, U. Wis.-River Falls, MacGregor Found., others. Cranbrook Acad. Art scholar, 1971; recipient Poster Competition award Vizcaya Mus., 1974; Print award Auction WPBT, 1979. Mem. Coll. Art Assn., Chgo. Artists Coalition. Democrat. Home: 607 Columbia Ave Elgin IL 60120 Office: PO Box 1425 Elgin IL 60121

MCGRAIL, SUSAN KING, travel agency executive, accountant; b. Richmond, Va., Mar. 7, 1952; d. William Jr. and Anne Winn (Gibson) King; m. John Patrick McGrail, Jr., June 2, 1979; 1 child, Katharine Anne. BBA, Coll. William and Mary, 1974. CPA, Va. Employment counselor Avante Gard of Richmond, Inc., 1970-73; staff acct. Touche Ross & Co., Washington, 1974-75, Richmond, 1975-78; controller Continental Cablevision, Richmond, 1978-81; v.p. fin. Warner Amex Cable Communications, Cin., 1981-85; prin. Travel Agts. Internat., Cin., 1985—; sec., treas. Warner Amex Minority Loan Fund, Cin., 1981-85. Alumni career adviser Coll. William and Mary, Williamsburg, Va., 1982—, fund raiser, 1984—. Fellow Am. Inst. CPA's, Va. Soc. CPA's; mem. Am. Soc. Travel Agts., Greater Cin. C. of C. (pres.'s roundtable), Pi Beta Phi. Republican. Episcopalian. Avocations: scuba diving, snorkeling, reading. Home: 2207 Spinningwheel Ln Cincinnati OH 45244 Office: Travel Agts Internat Montgomery 10778 Montgomery Rd Cincinnati OH 45242

MCGRATH, CHARLES WILLIAM, JR., controller; b. Elmhurst, Ill., June 28, 1950; s. Charles William and Catherine Rose (Fearon) McG.; m. Antonina Gregori, July 1982; children: Gregory, William. BA, Grinnell Coll., 1972; M in Mgmt., Northwestern U., 1974. CPA, Ill. Staff acct. Price Waterhouse, Chgo., 1974-77, sr. cons., 1977-80, mgr. cons. staff, 1980-81; mgr. spl. projects Container Corp. Am., Chgo., 1981-84; dir. corp. acctg. Stone Container Corp., Chgo., 1984-86, div. controller, 1986—. Treas., bd. dirs. Catherine Bertini for Congress, Evanston, Ill., 1982; controller Porter for Congress, Evanston, 1978; Rep. precinct capt. New Trier, Kenilworth, Ill., 1984—; sec., bd. dirs. Grinnell (Iowa) Coll. Alumni Orgn., 1981-87; bd. dirs. Project Leap, Chgo., 1983-85. Mem. Am. Inst. CPA's, Ill. Soc. CPA's. Republican. Avocations: tennis, running. Home: 905 Grove Winnetka IL 60093 Office: Stone Container Corp 150 N Michigan Chicago IL 60601

MCGRATH, CRAIG JAMES, transportation executive; b. New Brunswick, N.J., May 14, 1948; s. Edward Victor and Renee Isabelle (Gorges) McG.; m. Linda Marie Williams, June 12, 1971 (div. Jan. 1986); children: Sean Patrick, Tara Allison; m. Judy K. Laffay, Feb. 14, 1987. BS in Engring., U.S. Mil. Acad., 1971; MS in Fin., Lindenwood Coll., 1984. Asst. plant mgr. V. Mueller, Ft. Lauderdale, 1976-78; v.p. western area Complete Auto Transit, Inc. div. Ryder System, Inc., Wentzville, Mo., 1978—; Recruiter U.S. Mil. Acad., St. Louis, 1984. Served to capt. U.S. Army, 1971-76. Mem. Am. Legion. Roman Catholic. Avocations: reading, jogging, racquetball, basketball, fishing. Office: Complete Auto Transit Inc 655 Parr Rd Wentzville MO 63385

MCGRATH, MICHAEL ALAN, state government officer; b. Trenton, N.J., Oct. 27, 1942; s. Lyman Levitt and Ada Frances (Hofreiter) McG.; m. Marsha Louise Palmer, Aug. 6, 1966; children: David Patrick, Stephen Gregory, Christopher Andrew. AA, Daytona Beach Jr. Coll., 1967; BA, Stetson U., 1969. Supr. 1st Trust Co., St. Paul, 1969-72; v.p. Internat. Dairy Queen, Inc., Bloomington, Minn., 1972-84; dir. ops. WISCECO, Inc., Bloomington, 1984; bus. mgr. McGraw-Hill, Inc., Edina, Minn., 1985; pres. Policy Advisors, Inc., Bloomington, 1986; treas. State of Minn., St. Paul, 1987—. Bd. dirs. Minn. State Retirement System, St. Paul, 1987—; chmn. bd. dirs. Urban Concerns Workshop, Inc., St. Paul, 1984-86; sec. League Minn. Human Rights Commn., Mpls., 1985-86; treas. 3d congl. dist. Dem. Farm Labor Party, New Hope, Minn., 1986. Served with USAF, 1962-66. Mem. Nat. Assn. State Treas.'s. Office: Office Treas State Minn 50 Sherburne St Suite 303 Saint Paul MN 55155

MCGRATH, RANDY DEE, dentist; b. Glendale, Calif., Mar. 29, 1954; d. David James and Inez Marie (Shabart) McG. BA, U. Colo., 1976; DDS, Marquette U., 1980. Assoc. dentist William Wong DDS, West Allis, Wis., 1980-85, Fred Ballerini DDS, Shorewood, Wis., 1981-86; gen. practice dentistry West Allis, 1985—; staff St. Luke's Hosp., West Allis, 1983—. Mem. Profl. Dimensions, Inc., scholarship chmn., 1986—; spl. project chmn. Skylight Music Theater, 1986—; spl. events chmn. The Next Door Found., 1986—; mem. Next Generation Theater. Mem. ADA, Wis. Dental Assn., Greater Milw. Dental Assn., Kappa Alpha Theta Alumni Club. Republican. Lutheran. Club: Milw. Athletic. Avocations: sail boarding, interior design, ballet, golf, skiing. Office: 1302 S 60 St West Allis WI 53214

MCGRATH, ROBERT EDWARD, dentist; b. Pottsville, Pa., June 27, 1947; s. Edward Joseph and Frances Virginia (Weaver) McG.; m. Cheryl Julia Scherkenbach, July 25, 1970; children: Edward Joseph, Erin Colleen, Molly Maureen. DDS, Marquette U., 1972. With Mid-Towne Dental Assn., Wisconsin Rapids, Wis., 1972-73, sec., 1973-78, pres., 1978—; mem. med. staff, surg. com. Riverview Hosp., 1972-86; cons. claims Delta Dental Ins., Stevens Point, Wis., 1978-84, Preway Inc., Wis. Rapids, 1984—; cons. advisor Blue Cross United of Wis., Milw., 1985—; regional dental dir. Wis. Dental Plan, Green Bay, 1985—. Bd. mem. Sch. Dist. Wisconsin Rapids, 1976-78, 81-86, pres. 1978-81, 86—; mem. at large Spl. Edn. Adv., Wisconsin Rapids, 1973-78. Named one of Outstanding Young Men of Am., U.S. Jaycees, 1978. Fellow Acad. Gen. Dentistry (membership com. 1985—); mem. ADA, Wis. Dental Assn. (access planning 1986—), Cen. Wis. Dental Assn., Marquette U. Alumnae Admission, U.S. Jaycees (state dir. Wisconsin Rapids chpt. 1976). Republican. Roman Catholic. Lodges: Rotary (bd. dirs. Wisconsin Rapids club 1985—), Elks. Avocations: golf, skiing, boating, children's activities. Home: 4711 Townline Rd Wisconsin Rapids WI 54494 Office: Mid Towne Dental Assocs 1730 7th St S PO Box 1178 Wisconsin Rapids WI 54494

MCGRAW, VINCENT DEPAUL, manufacturing executive; b. Kansas City, Mo., July 19, 1930; s. Edwin John and Gertrude Catherine (McKean) McG.; m. Mildred Queen, 1953 (div. 1955); m. Rose Marie Taffe, Feb. 13, 1964; children: Michele Marie, Catherine Veronica. BA, Met. State U., St. Paul, 1976. Mgr. Pinkerton's Inc., various locations, 1956-66; pres. McGraw Security Systems Inc., Mpls., 1966-70; dir. security Applebaums Food Markets Inc., St. Paul, 1969-72; pres. Acad. and Range Inc. for Maximum Safety and Security, Mpls., 1972-74; gen. mgr. Jesco Indsl. Supplies inc., New Hope, Minn., 1977—. Author: McGraw Book of Antique Inkwells, 1972; (booklet) Property Inventory, 1971; pub. (newsletter) The Stained Finger, 1981. Bd. dirs. Elderfriend's Inc., Mpls., 1975—, Cath. Ctr. Seperated and Divorced, Mpls., 1979-84, Cath. Charities Corp. Bd., Mpls., 1982-84; presentor WISE, Mpls., 1984—. Served with USN, 1947-53. Mem. Soc. Inkwell Collectors (pres., researcher 1980—), Twin Cities Purchasing Mgmt. Assn. Inc., Adminstrv. Mgmt. Soc., Am. Legion. Democrat. Lodge: KC. Avocation: collecting and researching inkwells. Home: 5136 Thomas Ave S Minneapolis MN 55410 Office: Jesco Indsl Supplies Inc 4700 Quebec Ave N New Hope MN 55428

MCGREW, LEROY ALBERT, chemistry educator; b. Galva, Ill., Nov. 1, 1938; s. Leroy Edwin and Irene Elizabeth (Youngberg) McG.; m. Carol Joyce Brown, June 2, 1963; children—Clark Edwin, Laura Ann, LeRoy Andrew. B.A., Knox Coll., 1960; M.S., U. Iowa, 1963, Ph.D., 1964. Prof. chemistry Ball State U., Muncie, Ind., 1964-77, prof. chemistry U. No. Iowa, Cedar Falls, Iowa, 1977—, head dept. chemistry, 1977—. Contbr. articles to profl. jours.; lectr. profl. mtgs. Ethyl Corp. fellow U. Iowa, 1963. Mem. Am. Chem. Soc. (div. Chem. Educ.), Iowa Acad. Sci., Sigma Xi, Phi Beta Kappa, Phi Lambda Upsilon. Lutheran. Avocations: piano, computer programming, motorcycle mechanics. Office: Dept Chemistry Univ No Iowa Cedar Falls IA 50614

MCGROARTY, BRUCE JAMES, building products manufacturing executive; b. Montreal, Que., Can., Sept. 1, 1942; came to U.S., 1980; s. Herbert Thomas and Margaret Ann (Langon) McG.; m. Bernice Dianne MacArthur, May 15, 1965; children: Shannon, Tracey, Brent, Leigh, Ryan. BBA, Ryerson U., Toronto, Ont., Can., 1968, BBM, 1975; MBA, McMaster U., Toronto, 1977. Rep. maj. accts. Abitibi-Price, Inc., Toronto, 1972-75, corp. planner, 1975-80; mgr. mktg. services Abitibi-Price Corp., Troy, Mich., 1980-83; plant mgr. Abitibi-Price Corp., Toledo, 1983-84; exec. v.p. Abitibi-Price Corp., Troy, 1984-85; pres. Abitibi-Price Corp. subs. Abitibi-Price, Inc., Troy, 1985—. Avocations: skiing, squash, hockey, boating, education. Home: 20435 Ronsdale Rd Birmingham MI 48010 Office: Abitibi-Price Corp 3250 W Big Beaver Rd Troy MI 48084

MCGUIRE, JOSEPH JAMES, architect; b. Brazil, Ind., Nov. 1, 1919; s. Michael Edward and Blanch Teresa (Sowar) McG.; m. Veronica Mary Murtaugh, June 2, 1951; children: David A., John V., Patrick J., Robert B., William T., Charles M., Jeanne M. BArch, U. Notre Dame, 1952. Registered architect Ind., N.Y. Draftsman Paul I. Cripe, Inc., Indpls., 1949; draftsman and spl. writer James Assocs., Indpls., 1955-58; head of specifications dept. Lennox, Matthews, Simmons & Ford, Inc., Indpls., 1958-74, sec., treas., 1974-83; dir., head of specifications dept. Odle/Burke Architects, Inc., Indpls., 1983—; archtl. cons. Am. Precast Assn., Indpls., 1971-76. Contbr. articles to profl. jours. Chmn. adult adv. com. Boy Scouts Am., Indpls., 1964-85, scoutmaster, 1967-75; active Commn. for Downtown, Indpls., 1983-84, Ind. U./Purdue U. Adv. Coms., 1982-84. Served with U.S. Army, 1941-45. Recipient Dist. award Merit Boy Scouts Am., 1983. Fellow Construction Specifications Inst. (pres. Indpls. chpt. 1964-65, Hunter award fellow, 1971, 76); mem. Ind. Soc. Architects (bd. dirs. 1981-86, Pierre Medal 1984), AIA (pres. Indpls. chpt. 1982-83, Pres. award 1978), Am. concrete Inst. (mem. nominations and awards com. 1983), Concrete Tech. Cert. Com. of Ind. (chmn. bd. dirs. 1973-87), Am. Legion, Disabled Am. Vets. Republican. Roman Catholic. Avocations: traveling, camping, table tennis. Home: 518 East Dr Woodruff Pl Indianapolis IN 46201 Office: Odle/Burke Architects Inc 36 S Pennsylvania St Suite 410 Indianapolis IN 46204

MCGUIRE, KATHRYN MARIE, military officer; b. Cleve., 1950; s. Nicholas John and Arlene Mae (Hadox) S.; m. James Irvin McGuire, Feb. 17, 1973; 1 child, Kelly Elizabeth. AA in Fine Arts, Prince George's Community Coll., 1972; BA in Art, St. Mary's Coll. of Md., 1979. Cert. Missile Combat Crew Commander. Commd. 2d lt. USAF, 1980, advanced through ranks to capt., 1984. Adult mem. Girls Scouts Am., Tucson, 1980-84; CPR instr. Am. Heart Assn. Mem. Air Force Assn., St. Mary's Coll. Md. Alumni Assn. Roman Catholic. Club: Whiteman AFB Officers' Open Mess.

MCGUIRE, TERRANCE PAUL, health system executive; b. Chgo., June 29, 1947; s. Vincent Bernard and Nancy (Bonoma) McG.; m. Kathleen McGowan, May 10, 1985. BA, Chgo. State U., 1974; MS in Adminstrn., U. Notre Dame, 1977; D of Edn., Internat. Grad. Sch., St. Louis, 1983. Asst. adminstr. Mendel High Sch., Chgo., 1975-77; admissions counselor St. Xavier Coll., Chgo., 1977-78; dir. human resources Cath. Charities, Chgo., 1978-83; v.p. mission effectiveness Alexian Bros. Health System, Elk Grove Village, Ill., 1983—; bd. dirs. Sisters of St. Joseph; pres. bd. dirs. Wholistic Health Ctr.; v.p. bd. dirs. Franciscan Minsitries. Mem. Am. Counseling and Human Devel. Assn., Organizational Devel. Network, Acad. Cath. Health Care Leadership. Office: Alexian Bros Health System 600 Alexian Way Elk Grove Village IL 60007

MCGUIRE, TIMOTHY J., newspaper editor, lawyer; b. Mount Pleasant, Mich., Mar. 24, 1949; s. James Edward and Anita Matilda (Starr) McG.; m. T. Jean Fannin, May 10, 1975; children—Tracy, Jason, Jeffrey. B.A., Aquinas Coll., Grand Rapids, Mich., 1971; JD cum laude, William Mitchell Coll. Law, St. Paul, 1987. Bar: Minn. 1987. Mng. editor Ypsilanti Press, Mich., 1973-75, Corpus Christi Caller, Tex., 1975-77; mng. editor Lakeland Ledger, Fla., 1977-79, Mpls. Star, 1979-82; mng. editor features and sports Mpls. Star and Tribune, 1982-84, mng. editor, 1984—. Mem. Am. Soc. Newspaper Editors, AP Mng. Editors, Minn. State Bar Assn. Roman Catholic. Avocations: sports; press law. Home: 6000 Westmore Way Golden Valley MN 55422 Office: Mpls Star and Tribune 425 Portland St Minneapolis MN 55428

MCGURR, ALOYSIUS WILLIAM, JR., civil engineer; b. Akron, Ohio, Apr. 6, 1940; s. Aloysius William and Mildred Kathryn (Gunyan) McG.; m. Lynne Arlene Baldowsky, July 15, 1972. BSCE, Purdue U., 1962. Registered profl. engr., Ill. Engr. office planning H.K. Ferguson Co., Cleve., 1966-68; city engr. City of Woodstock, Ill., 1968-70, City of Wheaton, Ill., 1970-78; pres., prin. engr. A. McGurr, Ltd., Wheaton, 1978—; cons. engr. Village of Glen Ellyn, Ill., 1978—, Village of Shorewood, Ill., 1980—. Served to 1st lt. U.S. Army, 1962-65. Mem. ASCE, NSPE, Am. Water Works Assn., Am. Pub. Works Assn., Am. Planning Assn., Ill. Soc. Profl. Engrs., Greater Wheaton C. of C. (bd. dirs. 1986-87). Roman Catholic. Lodge: Rotary (local pres. 1985-86, chmn. membership devel. 1986—, Paul Harris Fellow 1984). Avocations: model railroading, gardening, hiking, cross-country skiing. Home: 1002 N Stoddard Wheaton IL 60187 Office: 955 W Liberty Dr Wheaton IL 60187-4846

MCHAFFIE, THOMAS R., realtor; b. Indpls., Sept. 20, 1956; s. Robert E. and Mary F. (Miller) McH.; m. Amy Haerle, Dec. 26, 1982. BS in Bus., Ind. U., 1978. Mgmt. trainee Mayflower Corp., Indpls., 1978-79, agcy. instr., 1979-80, dist. mgr., 1980-81, regional mgr., 1982-83, mgr. nat. sales, 1983-85; realtor F.C. Tucker Co., Inc., Indpls., 1985—. Mem. Nat. Assn. Realtors, Ind. Assn. Realtors, Met. Indpls. Bd. Realtors, Hamilton County Bd. Realtors, Householding Bd., Delta Nu Alpha, Alpha Tau Omega. Club: Indpls. Traffic, Executive. Avocations: tennis, golf, fishing, guitar, banjo. Home: 808 Bennett Rd Carmel IN 46032

MCHARGUE, CHARLES EUGENE, accountant; b. Brazil, Ind., Mar. 26, 1952; s. Charles Albert and Norma Jane (Thompson) McH.; m. Linda Ruth Rucsh, May 29, 1977; children: Magdalena Jane, Martina Louise. BS in Acctg., Ind. State U., 1974. CPA, Ind. Staff acct. Ernst & Whinney, Terre Haute, Ind., 1974-76, sr. acct., 1976-79, mgr., 1979-80; mgr. Ernst & Whinney, Indpls., 1980-82, sr. mgr., 1982—. Treas., bd. dirs. Big Bros. Greater Indpls., Inc., 1985, 86, 87. Mem. Am. Inst. CPA's, Ind. CPA Soc. (mem. acctg. and auditing com. 1986-87). Democrat. Roman Catholic. Lodge: Kiwanis (pres. local chpt. 1985-86, Kiwanian of Yr. 1985). Avocations: computers, fishing, golf. Home: 1530 Dan Jones Rd Plainfield IN 46168 Office: Ernst & Whinney One Indiana Sq Suite 3400 Indianapolis IN 46204

MCHARRIS, WILLIAM CHARLES, chemistry and physics educator, author; b. Knoxville, Tenn., Sept. 12, 1937; s. Garrett Clifford and Margaret Alice (Zimmerman) McH.; m. Orilla Ann Spangler, Aug. 27, 1960; 1 child, Louise Alice. BA, Oberlin Coll., 1959; PhD, U. Calif., 1965. Summer trainee Oak Ridge Nat. Lab., 1957-59; research student Lawrence Berkeley Lab., Calif., 1959-65; cons. Argonne Nat. Lab., 1965—; asst. prof. Mich. State U., East Lansing, 1965-68, assoc. prof., 1968-70, prof. chemistry, physics, 1970—; vis. prof., scientist Lawrence Berkeley Lab., 1970-71, 81—. Author: Into the Atom, 1985, Aria in the Key of Death, 1987; contbr. sci. articles to profl. jours. and popular mags.; composer organ, orchestral and choral works. Alfred E. Sloan fellow, 1971-75. Mem. Am. Chem. Soc., Am. Phys. Soc., Sigma Xi (Jr. Sci. award 1972). Congregationalist. Avocation: music. Home: 512 Beech St East Lansing MI 48823 Office: Mich State Univ Dept of Chemistry East Lansing MI 48824

MCHENRY, GARL DUAINE, electronic engineer; b. Huntington, Ind., Sept. 26, 1924; s. Harley Virgil and Elsie (Hite) McH.; m. Millicent Ruth Swaidner, Aug. 25, 1946; children: Lois Kathleen McHenry Wilson, Neil Virgil. BS in Radio Engring., Ind. Tech. Coll., 1949; cert. in automation, RCA Insts., 1958; cert. in numerical control, John A. Moorhead Assoc., 1966; postgrad. in microelectronics and servos, U. Cin., 1969-75. With RCA, Gen. Electric, Indpls., 1945-51; design engr. Gen. Electric, Huntsville, Ala., 1964; quality control engr. Magnovox Co., Ft. Wayne, Ind., 1951-54; design engr. ITT Fed. Labs., Ft. Wayne, 1955-63; sr. design engr. Ledex Inc., Dayton, Ohio, 1965-73; sr. project engr. TRW Motors Inc., Dayton, 1973—; design engr., cons. Bomarc Missile, Cape Canaveral, Fla., 1958-62, land systems div. Gen. DynamicsOnt. Can., 1985; con. Boeing Aircraft, Seattle, 1963, Staco Energy Products, Dayton, 1981—. Patentee in field; author numerous papers on engring. Deacon Ch. of Christ, Markle, Ind., trustee, New Carlisle, Ohio. Served with USAF, 1943-45, ETO. Mem. IEEE (sr.). Republican. Lodge: Masons. Avocations: amateur radio, fishing, water sports. Home: 8250 E New Carlisle Rd New Carlisle OH 45344 Office: TRW Motors Inc 2275 Stanley Ave Dayton OH 45404

MC HENRY, MARTIN CHRISTOPHER, physician; b. San Francisco, Feb. 9, 1932; s. Merl and Marcella (Bricca) McH.; student U. Santa Clara (Calif.), 1950-53; M.D., U. Cin., 1957; M.S. in Medicine, U. Minn., Mpls., 1966; m. Patricia Grace Hughes, Apr. 27, 1957; children—Michael, Christopher, Timothy, Mary Ann, Jeffrey, Paul, Kevin, William, Monica, Martin Christopher. Intern, Highland Alameda County (Calif.) Hosp., Oakland, 1957-58; resident, internal medicine fellow Mayo Clinic, Rochester, Minn., 1958-61, spl. appointee in infectious diseases, 1963-64; staff physician infectious diseases Henry Ford Hosp., Detroit, 1964-67; staff physician Cleve. Clinic, 1967-72, head dept. infectious diseases, 1972—. Asst. clin. prof. Case Western Res. U., 1970-77, assoc. clin. prof. medicine, 1977—; asso. vis. physician Cleve. Met. Gen. Hosp., 1970—; cons. VA Hosp., Cleve., 1973—. Chmn. manpower com. Swine Influenza Program, Cleve., 1976. Served with USNR, 1961-63. Named Distinguished Tchr. in Medicine Cleve. Clinic, 1972; recipient 1st ann. Bruce Hubbard Stewart award Cleve. Clinic Found. for Humanities in Medicine, 1985. Diplomate Am. Bd. Internal Medicine. Fellow Infectious Diseases Soc. Am., A.C.P., Am. Coll. Chest Physicians (chmn. com. cardiopulmonary infections 1975-77, 81-83); mem. Am. Soc. Clin. Pharmacology and Therapeutics (chmn. sect. infectious diseases and antimicrobial agts., 1970-77, 80-85, dir.), Am. Thoracic Soc., Am. Soc. Clin. Pathologists, Royal Soc. Medicine of Great Britain (asso.), Am. Fedn. Clin. Research, Am. Soc. Tropical Medicine and Hygiene, Am. Soc. Microbiology, N.Y. Acad. Scis. Contbr. numerous articles to profl. jours., also chpts. to books. Home: 2779 Belgrave Rd Pepper Pike OH 44124 Office: 9500 Euclid Ave Cleveland OH 44106

MCHUGH, DONALD EMMETT, university administrator; b. Racine, Wis., Aug. 4, 1933; s. Raymond George and Anita Gertrude (Bast) McH.; m. Cynthia Ann Woodworth, June 11, 1955; children: Mark, Timothy, Kathleen, David, Lisa, Kevin. BS, Marquette U., 1955; MA, Mich. State U., 1965; PhD, Ohio State U., 1971. Mgr. human resources systems Gen. Motors Corp., Detroit, 1960-75; v.p. human resources Owens-Ill. Inc., Toledo, 1975-86; dean continuing edn. U. Toledo, 1987—; cons. Gen. Motors Corp., Detroit, 1987—, Owens-Ill. Inc., Toledo, 1987—. Served to lt. USN, 1955-60, capt. USNR. Mem. Am. Soc. Personnel Adminstrs., Am. Soc. Tng. Dirs., Nat. Univ. Continuing Edn. Assn., Naval Res. Assn. Republican. Roman Catholic. Avocations: photography, golf. Home: 3805 Brookside Rd Toledo OH 43606 Office: U Toledo Div Continuing Edn 2801 W Bancroft St Toledo OH 43606

MCHUGH, FRANK BRENDAN, market research company executive, entrepreneur; b. Phila., Dec. 29, 1935; s. Peter T. and Sarah A. (McCann) McH.; m. Carol A. Lux, Sept. 12, 1959 (div. 1975); children: Anne, Gloria, Brendan; m. Sydney L. Friel, Mar. 8, 1980. BA, La Salle Coll., Phila., 1962. Pres. The Data Group Inc., Phila., 1969-75, chmn., 1975-86; chief exec. officer Nat. Indsl. Mktg. Intelligence System, Cin., 1986—; gen. ptnr. AGB & Co., Phila., 1975—; pres. McHugh Assocs., 1986—. Served with USAF, 1953-57, Korea. Republican. Home: 8780 Spooky Hollow Rd Cincinnati OH 45242

MCINNES, DONALD GORDON, railroad executive; b. Buffalo, Nov. 6, 1940; s. Milton Gordon and Blanche Mae (Clunk) McI.; m. Betsy Campbell, Mar. 18, 1967; children—Campbell Gordon, Cody Milton. B.A., Denison U., 1963; M.S., Northwestern U., 1965; certificatein transp. Yale U., 1965. Budget mgr. operating AT&SF R.R. Co., Chgo., 1969-71, asst. trainmaster, San Bernardino, Calif., 1971-73, trainmaster, Temple, Tex., 1973-76, asst. supt., Carlsbad, N.M., 1976-77, supt. eastern div., Emporia, Kans., 1977-79, supt. Los Angeles div., San Bernardino, Calif., 1979-81, asst. to exec. v.p., Chgo., 1981-82, gen. supt. transp., 1983-87, gen. mgr. transp., 1987, gen. mgr. ea. region, 1987—. Served to 2d lt., USAF, 1965-67; capt. U.S. Army, 1967-69. Decorated Bronze Star. Republican. Episcopalian. Clubs: Tower, Topeka Country, Amarillo (Topeka). Home: 2839 SW MacVicar Topeka KS 66611 Office: 920 SE Quincy Topeka KS 66628

MC INNES, ROBERT MALCOLM, mining company executive; b. Pictou, N.S., Can., July 17, 1930; naturalized U.S. citizen, 1964; s. John Logan and Jenny MacKay (Malcolm) McI.; m. June Hughena O'Brien, Apr. 19, 1952; children: Donald, Elizabeth, Susan. B.A., Dalhousie U., Halifax, N.S., 1951, LL.B., 1953; postgrad., Harvard U. Bus. Sch., 1968. Assoc. firm Duquet, MacKay, Weldon & Tetreault, Montreal, Que., Can., 1953-57; with Pickands Mather & Co., Cleve., 1957-69, 71-87; v.p. Pickands Mather & Co., 1971-73, exec. v.p., 1973-83, pres., chief exec. officer, 1983-87; gen. counsel, treas. Diamond Shamrock Corp., 1969-71; group exec. v.p. Cleve. Cliffs Inc., 1987—; dir. MCX Inc., Brush Wellman Inc., Soc. Nat. Bank. Mem. Cleve. Bar Assn. Republican. Methodist. Clubs: Mayfield Country, Cleve. Skating, Mid-Day, Union. Home: 32300 Meadowlark Way Pepper Pike OH 44124 Office: Cleveland-Cliffs Inc 1100 Superior Ave Huntington Bldg Cleveland OH 44114 *

MCINTIRE, MURIEL ELAINE, dietitian; b. Saskatoon, Sask., Can.; d. Stafford Lenox and Nellie Susan (Whitehead) Osborne; came to U.S., 1915, naturalized, 1922; B.S., Lewis Inst. Tech., 1938; m. Claude Vernon McIntire, Nov. 23, 1941; children—Patricia Anne McIntire Maker, Susan Elaine McIntire Beranek. Intern, Walter Reed Hosp., Washington, 1940; head dietitian Sta. Hosp., Ft. Sheridan, Ill., 1939-40, Regional Hosp., Scott Field, Ill., 1940-43; therapeutic dietitian Barnes Hosp., St. Louis, 1948; head dietitian Hines (Ill.) Hosp., 1956-57; staff dietitian Ohio State U. Hosp. and Health Center, 1957-59; staff dietitian Oak Forest (Ill.) Hosp., 1960-61, exec. dietitian, 1961-69; chief dietitian Little Company of Mary Hosp., Evergreen Park, Ill., 1980. 1971-77, therapeutic dietitian, 1977-84. Served to 1st lt. USAAF, 1943-45. Named Employee of Yr., Little Company of Mary Hosp., 1980. Mem. Am. Dietetic Assn., Am. Home Econs. Assn., Soc. for Nutrition Edn., Chgo. Nutrition Assn. Co-author: Manual of Clinical Dietetics, 1975. Home: 7144 S Fair Elms Ave La Grange IL 60525

MCINTOSH, DONALD EDWARD, anesthesiologist; b. Detroit, Jan. 13, 1930; s. Charles Louis and Mary Margaret (McKenna) McI.; m. Norene Marie O'Connor, July 3, 1954; children: Bruce John, Mikail Marie, Sharon Rose. PhB, Marquette U., 1951; MD, Med. Coll. Wis., 1960. Diplomate Am. Bd. Anesthesiology. Clin. clerkship in anesthesiology Kans. U. Med. Ctr., 1962; resident in anesthesiology Kansas City Gen. Hosp., Selinas, 1964-66; fellow in pediatric anesthesiology St. Louis Sch. Medicine, 1966; pvt. practice medicine Parsons, Kans., 1961-64; practice medicine specializing in anesthesiology Research Med. Ctr., Kansas City, Mo., 1966—, chief dept. anesthesiology, 1971-78, pres. med. staff, 1982. Served to capt. U.S. Army, 1951-53, 60-61. Fellow Am. Geriatric Soc.; mem. AMA, Mo. State Med. Assn. (v.p. 1981-82), Jackson County Med. Soc. (pres. 1979, Cert. of Merit, 1983), Nat. Fedn. Cath. Physicians (v.p. 1986-87). Republican. Roman Catholic. Lodges: Elks, KC. Avocations: sailing, fishing. Home: 300 SW Green Teal Lee's Summit MO 64063 Office: Anesthesia Assocs of Kansas City Inc 6400 Prospect Ave Kansas City MO 64132

MC INTURF, FAITH MARY, engineering company executive, thoroughbred harness racing executive; b. Grand Ridge, Ill., Aug. 22, 1917; d. Lynne E. and Margaret (Garver) McInturf; grad. high sch. With The J.E. Porter Corp., Chgo., 1963-65, v.p., 1951-65, sec., 1951-65, also dir.; with Potomac Engring. Corp., 1941—, now pres., treas., bd. dirs.; dir. Chgo. Harness Racing Inc., also Balmoral Jockey Club, Inc., 1967-72, sec., dir., 1974-78; sec., treas., dir. Balmoral Park Trot, Inc., 1969-72; sec., dir. Horse Racing Promotions, Inc., 1974-77. Roman Catholic. Home: 1360 Lake Shore Dr Chicago IL 60610 Office: 919 N Michigan Ave Chicago IL 60611

MCINTYRE, DENNIS PATRICK, telecommunications specialist; b. Cin., Dec. 14, 1935; s. William F. and Mabel E. (Pegram) McI.; m. Donna Jean Johnson, Mar. 15, 1958; children: Kelly A., Terry K., Michael S., Stephen B. BA in History, Manchester Coll., 1955. Analyst Lincoln Nat. Life Ins., Fort Wayne, Ind., 1955-59; dir. communications CNA Fin. Corp., Chgo., 1959-68; mgr. communications Standard Oil Corp., Cleve., 1968-74; dir. telecommunications Conalco, St. Louis, 1974-80; v.p. voice communications A.G. Edwards & Sons, St. Louis, 1980—; Pres. Chgo. Indsl. Communications Assn., 1967-68, Mississippi Valley Telecommunications Assn., St. Louis, 1977-78; sec. Mich.-Ohio Telecommunications Assn., 1973-74. V.p. Cook County Youth Program, Chgo., 1968; youth leader Lakewood (Ohio) YMCA, 1969-74. Recipient Service to Youth award YMCA, Lakewood, 1974. Mem. Internat. Communications Assn. Methodist. Avocations:

sports, reading. Home: 12712 Cypressway Saint Louis MO 63146 Office: A G Edwards & Sons 1 N Jefferson Saint Louis MO 63103

MCINTYRE, DONALD GREGORY, dentist; b. Detroit, Mar. 23, 1933; s. Frank Daniel and Helen (McGregory) McI. DDS, U. Mich., 1957. Gen. practice dentistry Detroit, 1959—; cons. Miraj (India) Med. Ctr., 1973, St. Luke's Hosp., Vengurla, India, 1974, 75, 77, 79, Clinica Rural, El Rancho, Guatemala, 1968-71, United Mission, Katmandu, Nepal, 1979. Trustee Med. Mission Fund, Woodville, Tex., 1985—. Served to capt. dental corps USAR, 1957-59. Recipient Service to Youth award greater Detroit YMCA, 1969. Mem. ADA, F.B. Vedder Soc., Delta Sigma Delta (pres. Detroit chpt. 1972). Clubs: Circumnavigators (pres. Mich. chpt. 1985-87, bd. dirs. Found. 1975—). Home: 532 Neff Ln Grosse Pointe MI 48230 Office: 3107 Book Tower Detroit MI 48226

MCINTYRE, GARY NOEL, educator; b. Elmo, Mo., June 29, 1947; s. Bobby Noel and Marie Margaret (Davis) McI.; m. Janice Lee Thornton, June 5, 1970 (div.); 1 dau., Amy Christine. B.S. in Bus. Edn., N.W. Mo. State U., 1969; B.S. in Elem. Edn., Central Mo. State U., 1973; M.S. in Elem. Adminstrn., U. Mo.-Kansas City, 1977. Cert. tchr., elem. adminstr., Mo. Tchr. pub. schs., Adel, Iowa, 1969-71, Kansas City, Mo., 1971-78; child devel. specialist/counselor Kansas City (Mo.) pub. schs., 1978-79, sci./math. facilitator, 1979—, outdoor edn. tchr., 1979—. Mem. Am. Fedn. Tchrs., Nat. Council Tchrs. Math., Nat. Sci. Tchrs., Assn., Nat. Wildlife Assn., NAACP, Phi Delta Kappa. Democrat. Episcopalian.

MCINTYRE, WILLIAM DAVIS, JR., business executive; b. Monroe, Mich., Dec. 5, 1935; s. William D. and Prudence A. (Harrington) M.; m. Susan Lenhart, May 3, 1963; children—Michael, Molly, Frank, Ann Marie. Student U. Notre Dame, 1955-59, U. Detroit, 1954-55, participant advance mgmt. program Harvard U., 1976. With Monroe Auto Equipment Co., Monroe, 1959-80, dir. export ops., 1960-64, v.p. internat. ops., 1964-66, exec. v.p. internat. ops., 1966-80; pres. Mich. Tech. Investors Inc., Monroe, 1980—, also dir.; pres. Environ. Dynamics, Inc., Ann Arbor, Mich., 1981—; ptnr., dir., v.p. Mich. Mineral Investors Ldt., Traverse City, 1981—; dir. Monroe Bank, Trust Co., Q.E.D. Environ. Systems, Ann Arbor, Mich.; Pres. bd. dirs. Monroe County United Way, 1982-83, gen. campaign chmn. 1980, 81; gen. campaign chmn. Monroe Family YMCA Capital Funds drive, 1983; past pres. bd. dirs. Mercy-Meml. Hosp. Corp; past chmn. Monroe County chpt. ARC; past pres. St. John's Sch. Bd. Recipient Monroe Catholic Central Alumnus of Yr. award, 1982 United Way Outstanding Citizens' award, 1981 City Monroe Minuteman award, 1981, Gov. Mich. Minuteman award. Mem. Young Pres. Orgn., Soc. Automotive Engrs., Automotive Orgn. Team Inc., Monroe C. of C. (chmn. 1984, 85). Republican. Roman Catholic. Clubs: Monroe Golf, Country, Monroe Rod, Gun, Monroe, Otsego Ski (Gaylord, Mich.).

MCIVOR, TIMOTHY JAMES, electrical and industrial engineer; b. Omaha, May 13, 1949; s. James Alexander and Margaret Ann (Vantine) McI.; m. Mary Christine Quinn, Jan. 16, 1971; children: Elizabeth Christine, David Timothy, Jennifer Ann, Emily Joan. BSEE, U. Nebr., 1971, MSEE, 1973, postgrad., 1987—. Registered profl. engr., Nebr. Engr., mgr. Omaha Pub. Power Dist., 1973—. Youth counselor First Covenant Ch., Omaha, 1980-83; program chmn. Cub Scout Pack 429 Boy Scouts Am., Omaha, 1986-87. Served to 2d lt. USAFR, 1971-73. Mem. IEEE (sr., sect. bd. dirs. 1984-87), Nebraska City Jaycees (sec. 1979-80), Alpha Pi Mu. Republican. Mem. Evangelical Covenant. Avocations: electronics, remodeling projects, golf, bicycling. Home: 13412 Cedar St Omaha NE 68144 Office: Omaha Pub Power Dist 1623 Harney St Omaha NE 68102

MCKANE, TERRY JOHN, mayor; b. Lansing, Mich., July 9, 1941; s. Kenneth Bernard and Mary Ella (Hill) McK.; m. Virginia Lee Amundsen, Nov. 23, 1968; children—Heather Anne, John Thorsen, Katherine Maureen. B.A., Mich. State U., 1963, M.A., 1968. Cert. secondary tchr., Mich. Secondary tchr. Lansing Sch. Dist., Mich., 1967-82; city councilman Lansing City Council, Mich., 1971-82; mayor City of Lansing, Mich., 1982—; v.p. Mich. Mcpl. League, Ann Arbor, 1984-85; chmn. Tri-County Aging Consortium, Lansing, 1985-86; bd. dirs. Tri-County Manpower Adminstrn., Lansing, 1974—. Div. chmn. United Way Campaign, Lansing, 1982—; bd. dirs. Friends of Gov.'s Residence, Lansing, 1984-85; bd. dirs. Ingham/Eaton Emergency Food and Shelter, Lansing,; lic. lay speaker United Meth. Ch., Lansing. Recipient Outstanding Govt. Ofcl. award Mich. Rehab. Assn., 1984. Mem. Mich. Soc. Mayflower Descendants (dep. gov. 1984-86, gov. 1986—), SAR, U.S. Conf. of Mayors, Nat. League of Cities, Mich. Mcpl. League, Am. Legion. Clubs: City of Lansing, University (East Lansing). Avocation: genealogy. Home: 3300 Ginger Snap Ln Lansing MI 48911 Office: Office of Mayor City Hall 9th Floor 124 W Michigan St Lansing MI 48933

MCKAY, CARL, manufacturing corporation executive. Chmn. Devil's Lake Sioux Mfg. Corp., Ft. Totten, N.D. Office: Devils Lake Sioux Mfg Corp Fort Totten ND 58335 *

MCKAY, LARRY MICHAEL, architect; b. Hot Springs, S.D., Aug. 18, 1942; s. Lawrence George and Beulah Ioan (Petro) McK.; m. Alyce Gilman, Apr. 13, 1968; children—Heather Lynn, Larry Tyler Arthur. Student S.D. Sch. Mines and Tech., 1960-61; B.S. in Architecture, Idaho State U., 1965, postgrad., 1966-67. Cert. architect, S.D., Colo., Nebr., Wyo. Designer Ken E. Douglas & Assocs., Pocatello, Idaho, 1965-66; architect Brady Cons., Spearfish, S.D., 1966-69, Hengel Assocs., Rapid City, S.D., 1969-70, Shaver Partnership, Michigan City, Ind., 1970-72, Bell Galyardt & Wells, Rapid City, 1972-75; pvt. practice architecture, Rapid City, 1975-81; ptnr. McKay/McConnell, Rapid City, 1981—. Pres. Girls Club Rapid City, 1981-82; bd. dirs. Pennington County (S.D.) chpt. Am. Cancer Soc., 1978—, v.p., 1980-81; mem. Leadership 1982, Rapid City. Recipient Lighting Design award Illuminating Engring. Soc., 1978, Herb Martalon award Episcopal Ch., 1980. Mem. AIA (pres. elect S.D. chpt. 1987—), Black Hills Architects, Rapid City C. of C., Nat. Council Archtl. Registration Bds. Republican. Episcopalian. Club: Cosmopolitan (bd. dirs.). Lodge: Elks. Ink prints and landscapes pub. in ltd. editions, 1978-83. Home: 2215 Alamo Dr Rapid City SD 57702 Office: 2100 S 7th St Rapid City SD 57702

MC KAY, NEIL, banker; b. East Tawas, Mich., Aug. 9, 1917; s. Lloyd G. and Rose (McDonald) McK.; m. Olive D. Baird, Nov. 11, 1950; children: Julia B., Lynn B., Hunter L. A.B., U. Mich., 1939, J.D. with distinction, 1946. Bar: Mich. 1946, Ill. 1947. With firm Winston & Strawn, Chgo., 1946-63; partner Winston & Strawn, 1954-63; with First Nat. Bank of Chgo., 1963-83, from v.p. charge heavy industry lending div., gen. mgr. London br., to exec. v.p., cashier, 1970-75, vice chmn. bd., 1976-83, also dir.; exec. v.p., sec. First Chgo. Corp., 1970-75, vice chmn. bd., 1976-83; also dir.; dir. Kerr-McGee Corp., Oklahoma City, Morton-Thiokol Inc., Baird & Warner, Inc., Chgo. Mem.: U. Mich. Law Rev; assoc. editor-in-chief: U. Mich. Law Rev., 1942, sr. editor, 1946. Trustee Morton Arboretum; former trustee Kalamazoo Coll. and Ill. Inst. Tech. Served with USNR, 1942-46. Mem. ABA, Ill. Bar Assn., Chgo. Bar Assn., Order of Coif, Chgo. Hort. Assn. (dir.). Clubs: Chicago (Chgo.), Mid-Day (Chgo.); Geneva Golf.

MCKEE, CHARLES CLIFTON, conservationist; b. Telford, Tenn., Apr. 18, 1926; s. Wallace D. and Mae (Keplinger) McK.; m. Norma Jean Schurmeier, Jan. 14, 1951; children—Diane Rae, Gary Lee. Student East Tenn. State Coll., 1947-48; B.S., U. Tenn., 1950; M.S., Purdue U., 1961. Vocat. agr. tchr., Mackey, Ind., 1951-52; soil conservationist U.S. Dept. Agr.-Soil Conservation Service, Princeton, Ind., 1953-54, Petersburg, Ind., 1954-55; extension soil conservationist Coop. Extension Service, Purdue U., West Lafayette, Ind., 1955-64; exec. sec. Ind. Soil and Water Conservation Com., West Lafayette, 1964—. Served with USNR, 1944-46. Mem. Soil Conservation Soc. Am. (chpt. pres. 1960, merit award 1984), Extension Specialists Assn., Nat. Assn. State Conservation Adminstrs. (pres. 1977-78), Epsilon Sigma Phi. Republican. Methodist. Lodge: Masons. Home: 2531 State Rt 26 W West Lafayette IN 47906 Office: Purdue U Div of Soil Conservation AGAD Bldg Room 7 West Lafayette IN 47907

MC KEE, DALE, promotions, premiums and incentives co. exec.; b. Ironton, Ohio, May 24, 1938; s. Frank and Eloise McK.; B.S., U. Dayton, 1966; student Sinclair Community Coll., 1975; m. Barbara Jean Robinson, June 15, 1957; children—Dale, Jeffery Scott. Pres., McKee & Parrish Bldg. Contractors, Miamisburg, Ohio, 1968-72; pres. McKee & McKee Bldg. Contractors, Miamisburg, Ohio, 1972-79; pres., treas. World Wide Crusade, Inc., Miamisburg, 1978—; pres. Del Diablo Recording, Miamisburg, 1978-79; pres. Del Diablo Pub. Co., Miamisburg, 1978-79; asso. realtor Joe McNabb Realtor, Miamisburg, 1978-79; announcer WCXL & WQRP Radio F.M., 1978-79; v.p., dir. Bar Del, Inc., Miamisburg, 1974—; supr. Frigidaire div. Gen. Motors Corp., Dayton, 1956—. Mem. Am. Ind. Party Central Com., 1973-74; scoutmaster Sequoia council, Boy Scouts Am., 1971-73. Mem. IEEE, Dayton Area Bd. Realtors, Ohio Bd. Realtors, Internat. Platform Assn., Country Music Assn., Nashville Songwriters Assn. Internat., Am. Fedn. Musicians. Democrat. Roman Catholic. Clubs: Foremans' Club of Dayton, Moose. Composer: Ten Days I'll Be Getting Out of Prison, 1978; The Bottle Almost Empty, 1978. Home: 1232 Holly Hill Dr Miamisburg OH 45342 Office: Kettering Blvd Dayton OH 45439

MCKEE, DEBORAH SUE BOWEN, teacher; b. Plymouth, Ind., Feb. 16, 1956; d. Robert Earl and Nellie Marie (Hoke) Bowen; m. Robert Marshall McKee, Dec. 27, 1986. BS in Edn., Ind. U., 1978; MS in Edn., Butler U., 1984. 4th-6th grade tchr. St. Andrew's Sch., Indpls., 1979-84, dir. after sch. care program, 1980-83; learning disabilities tchr., emotionally handicapped tchr. Joint Ednl. Services in Spl. Edn., Knox, Ind., 1984-86; 4th grade tchr. Holy Cross Sch., South Bend, Ind., 1986—; 3d grade tchr. NorthWestern Schs., Kokomo, Ind., 1978-79; pvt. tutor. Mem. speaker's bur. Internat. Summer Spl. Olympics, South Bend, 1986; sustaining mem. Rep. Nat. Com., Washington, 1986. Mem. Spl. Edn. Tchrs. Assn. (v.p. negotiating team 1985-86). Methodist. Home: 1822 N College St South Bend IN 46628 Office: Holy Cross Sch 1020 N Wilber St South Bend IN 46628

MC KEE, GEORGE MOFFITT, JR., consulting civil engineer; b. Valparaiso, Nebr., Mar. 27, 1924; s. George Moffitt and Iva (Santrock) McK.; student Kans. State Coll. Agr. and Applied Sci., 1942-43, Bowling Green State U., 1943; B.S. in Civil Engring., U. Mich., 1947; m. Mary Lee Taylor, Aug. 11, 1945; children—Michael Craig, Thomas Lee, Mary Kathleen, Marsha Coleen, Charlotte Anne. Draftsman, Jackson Constrn. Co., Colby, Kans., 1945-46; asst. engr. Thomas County, Colby, 1946; engr. Sherman County, Goodland, Kans., 1947-51; salesman Oehlert Tractor & Equipment Co., Colby, 1951-52; owner, operator George M. McKee, Jr., cons. engrs., Colby, 1952-72; sr. v.p. engring. Contract Surety Consultants, Wichita, Kans., 1974—. Adv. rep. Kans. State U., Manhattan, 1957-62; mem. adv. com. N.W. Kans. Area Vocat. Tech. Sch., Goodland, 1967-71. Served with USMCR, 1942-45. Registered profl. civil engr., Kans., Okla., registered land Surveyor, Kans. Mem. Kans. Engring. Soc. (pres. N.W. profl. engrs. chpt. 1962-63, treas. cons. engrs. sect. 1961-63), Kansas County Engr's. Assn. (dist. v.p. 1950-51), Northwest Kans. Hwy. Ofcls. Assn. (sec. 1948-49), Nat. Soc. Profl. Engrs., Kans. State U. Alumni Assn. (pres. Thomas County 1956-57), Am. Legion (Goodland 1st vice comdr. 1948-49), Colby C. of C. (v.p. 1963-64), Goodland Jr. C. of C. (pres. 1951-52). Methodist (chmn. ofcl. bd. 1966-67). Mason (32 deg., Shriner); Order Eastern Star. Home: 34 Lakeview Circle Route 1 Towanda KS 67144 Office: 6500 W Kellogg Wichita KS 67209

MCKEE, JAMES DOUGLAS, industrial hygienist, consultant; b. Bowling Green, Ohio, Oct. 31, 1949; s. John W. and Eleanor M. (Hughes) McK.; m. Jane L. Shull, Aug. 23, 1968; 1 child, Tracy Jeanne. BLS, Bowling Green State U., 1973. Cert. safety profl., Ohio. Indsl. hygienist occupational safety health adminstrn. U.S. Dept. Labor, Toledo, 1973-81, Plaskon Products, Toledo, 1981-82; cons. Comprehensive Regulatory Mgmt., Bowling Green, 1982—, Samborn, Stekkete, Otis and Evans, Toledo, 1985—. Mem. Am. Assn. Indsl. Hygienists, Northwest Ohio Assn. Indsl. Hygienists (pres. 1986-87), Am. Conf. Gov. Indsl. Hygiene, Ohio Sideband Assn. (bd. dirs. 1983-86). Democrat. Mem. Ch. Nazarene. Lodge: Eagles. Avocations: scuba diving, photography, hunting, fishing. Home: 415 S Main St Bowling Green OH 43402

MCKEE, JANE LOUISE, librarian; b. Bowling Green, Ohio, Apr. 12, 1949; d. Donald L. and Marian A. (Wollam) Shull; m. J. Douglas McKee, Aug. 23, 1968; 1 child, Tracy Jeanne. BS in Edn., Bowling Green State U., 1971, MS, 1983. Librarian Bowling Green State U., 1971-78, Bowling Green Sr. High Sch., 1978—. Author: A Searcher's Manual, 1973. Mem. Ohio Edn. Library Media Assn. (state standards com. 1981—, northwest stering com. 1984—, northwest dir., state bd. dirs.), Met. Toledo Ednl. Purchasing Assn. (chmn. 1981-83), Ohio Sideband Assn. (treas. 1982-86), Ladies in Fellowship and Enrichment (pres. Bowling Green chpt. 1982-86), Alpha Delta Pi. Democrat. Mem. Ch. Nazarene. Lodge: Eastern Star. Avocations: scuba diving, writing. Home: 415 S Main St Bowling Green OH 43402 Office: Bowling Green Sr High Sch 530 W Poe Rd Bowling Green OH 43402

MCKEE, PAUL JOSEPH, JR., civil engineer, corporate executive; b. St. Louis, June 15, 1945; s. Paul Joseph and Leona V. (Heidel) McK.; m. Marguerite Ann Niehoff, Nov. 26, 1966; children Paul III, Christopher, Kate, Meg. BCE, Washington U., St. Louis, 1967. Registered profl. engr., Mo. Pres., chief exec. officer Paric Corp., St. Louis, 1979—, also bd. dirs. Bd. dirs. Chaminade Coll. Prep., St. Louis, Visitation, St. Louis, Christian Hosp., St. Louis. Mem. NSPE, Assn. Gen. Contractors of St. Louis, Young Pres. Orgn. Club: St. Louis (Clayton, Mo.). Avocation: hunting. Home: 12 Dunlora Huntleigh MO 63131 Office: Paric Corp 689 Craig Rd Saint Louis MO 63141

MCKEE, THOMAS FREDERICK, lawyer; b. Cleve., Oct. 27, 1948; s. Harry Wilbert and Virginia (Light) McK.; m. Linda Miller, Aug. 22, 1970. B.A. with high distinction, U. Mich., 1970; J.D., Case Western Res. U., 1975. Bar: Ohio 1975, U.S. Dist. Ct. (no. dist.) Ohio 1975, U.S. Supreme Ct. 1979. Assoc. firm Calfee, Halter & Griswold, Cleve., 1975-81, ptnr., 1982—. Contbg. editor Going Public, 1985. Mem. ABA (com. fed. regulation securities law sect.), Bar Assn. Greater Cleve., Order of Coif. Clubs: Hermit, Country (Cleve.). Home: 2947 Torrington Rd Shaker Heights OH 44122 Office: 1800 Society Bldg Cleveland OH 44114

MCKENNA, ANDREW JAMES, paper distribution company and printing company executive, baseball club executive; b. Chgo., Sept. 17, 1929; s. Andrew James and Anita (Fruin) McK.; m. Mary Joan Pickett, June 20, 1953; children: Suzanne, Karen, Andrew, William, Joan, Kathleen, Margaret. B.S., U. Notre Dame, 1951; J.D., DePaul U., 1954. Bar: Ill. Pres., chief exec. officer Schwarz Paper Co., Morton Grove, Ill., 1964—; dir. Chgo. Nat. Leauge Ball Club Inc., Chgo. Bears.; dir. Combined Internat. Corp., Dean Foods Co., Lake Shore Nat. Bank, Skyline Corp., Tribune Co. Vice chmn. bd. trustees U. Notre Dame ; trustee La Lumiere Sch.; bd. dirs. Cath. Charities of Chgo., Children's Meml. Med. Ctr. Chgo. Mem. Assn. Governing Bds. Univs. and Colls. (bd. dirs.). Clubs: Chgo, Comml, Econs, Chgo. Athletic Assn; Glen View (Golf, Ill.). Home: 60 Locust Rd Winnetka IL 60093 Office: Schwarz Paper Co 8338 N Austin Ave Morton Grove IL 60053

MCKENNA, BERNARD JAMES, financial sevices executive; b. N.Y.C., July 17, 1933; s. Bernard James and Josephine (Fitzgerald) McK.; m. Ann Jean Noe, Nov. 27, 1954; children: William C., Geralyn M., Paul G., Michael G. BBA in Fin., Hofstra U., 1962. Agt. Conn. Gen. Life Ins. Co., Garden City, N.Y., 1963-67, Granate EquipmentLeasing Co., Garden City, 1967-68; mktg. mgr. Greyhound Equipment, N.Y.C., 1968-70; sr. loan officer Ford Motor Credit Co., Dearborn, Mich., 1970-80; pres. Sawwa Bus. Credit Co., Chgo., 1980—. Vice chmn. Am. Conservatory of Music, Chgo., 1985—; pres. Chgo chpt. Cystic Fibrosis Found., 1980-81, nat. trustee, Washington. Served with U.S. Army, 1954-56. Mem. Am. Assn. Lessors Equipment (chmn. 1984—). Republican. Roman Catholic. Clubs: LaSalle, Met., Edgewood Valley. Avocations: golf, travel, reading. Home: 1621 Coachmans Rd Darien IL 60559 Office: Sawwa Bus Credit Corp 1 S Wacker Dr Chicago IL 60606

MCKENNA, JOHN JOSEPH, insurance company executive; b. Evanston, Ill., Dec. 14, 1932; s. Joseph J. and Lorraine C. (Connors) McK. BS in Commerce, Loyola U., Chgo., 1954. CLU, Chartered Fin. Cons.; cert. real estate broker, Ill. Claim adjuster Continental Casualty, Chgo., 1954; gen. mgr. Prudential Ins. and Fin. Services, Chgo., 1956—; bd. dirs. Valley Bank Services Corp., Hinckley, Ill.; mem. Chgo. Estate Planning Council, 1976—. Telethon fundraiser United Cerebral Palsy, Chgo. Served to 1st lt. inf. U.S. Army, 1954-56. Mem. Nat. Assn. Life Underwriters (chmn. elections 1984-87), Ill. Life Underwriters Assn. (pres.), Chgo. Assn. Life Underwriters (pres., Disting. Service award 1982), Gen. Agents and Mgrs. Conf. (dir. regional edn. 1984-86, Nat. Mgmt. award 1972-85), Chgo. Gen. Agents and Mgrs. Assn. (pres.), CLUs (chpt. bd. dirs. 1985-86), Loyola U. Sch. Bus. Adminstrn. Alumni Bd. Governors. Republican. Roman Catholic. Clubs: Exec. of Chgo., Snow Buddies. Avocations: golf, skiing, snowmobiling, boating, hunting. Home: 400 E Randolph Chicago IL 60601 Office: Prudential Ins & Fin Services 1901 S Meyers Rd Oakbrook Terrace IL 60148

MCKENNA, RICHARD HENRY, hospital executive; b. Covington, Ky., Dec. 19, 1927; s. Charles Joseph and Mary Florence (Wieck) McK.; B.S. in Commerce, U. Cin., 1959; M.B.A., Xavier U., 1963; m. Patricia Ann Macdonald, Jan. 6, 1979; children—Linda Ann, Theresa K., Joan Marie. Accountant, Andrew Jergens Co., Cin., 1947-55; treas., dir. Ramsey Bus. Equipment, Inc., Cin., 1955-59; asst. to pres. Oakley Die and Mfg. Co., Cin., 1959-60, Electro-Jet Tool Co., Inc., Cin., 1959-60; pvt. practice accounting, No. Ky. and Cin., 1960-62; bus. mgr. St. Joseph Hosp., Lexington, Ky., 1962-66; asst. adminstr. fin. U. Ky. Hosp., Lexington, 1966-70; v.p., chief fin. officer St. Lawrence Hosp., Lansing, Mich., 1970-87; adj. faculty Aquinas Coll., Grand Rapids, Mich., 1980—; chmn. bd. McKenna & McKenna Assocs., Inc., 1983—; chmn. bd. North Brand River Cooperative Laundry, 1986-87; v.p., chief fin. officer St. Joseph's Hosp., Inc., Savannah, Ga., 1987—, St. Joseph's Health Ctr., Inc., 1987—. Former mem. adv. com. to commr. of finance State of Ky.; chmn. cath. div. Oak Hills Bus. Com.; mem. speakers com. Oak Hill Sch. Dist. Served with U.S. Mcht. Marine, 1945-47, U.S. Army, 1948-51. C.P.A., Ohio, Ky. Mem. Healthcare Fin. Mgmt. Assn. (Follmer award, past dir. Ky. chpt.), Am. Mgmt. Assn., Am. Inst. C.P.A.s, Ky. Soc. C.P.A.s, Mich. Hosp. Assn. (former mem. com. on reimbursement), Delta Mu Delta, Alpha Sigma Lambda.

MCKENNA, SHIRLEY LEE, tile company executive; b. Chgo., Apr. 4, 1935; d. Joseph M. and Estelle N. (Blasch) Warnell; m. Robert McKenna, June 18, 1955; children: Susan, Judi, Michael. Student, U. Chgo., 1954, Art Inst. Chgo., 1955. Sec. Lisle (Ill.) High Sch., 1967-69; mgr. I.B.C. Bookstore, Lisle, 1970-78; v.p., designer McKenna Tile, Naperville, Ill., 1978—; cons. CTDI, Chgo., 1985—. Mem. NFIB, Springfield, Ill., 1987. Mem. Nat. Fedn. Ind. Bus., U.S. C. of C., Naperville Area C. of C. Roman Catholic. Office: McKenna Tile Co Inc 2385 S Washington Naperville IL 60540

MCKENNA, WILLIAM J., textile products executive; b. N.Y.C., Oct. 11, 1926; s. William T. and Florence (Valis) McK.; m. Jean T. McNulty, Aug. 27, 1949; children: Kevin, Marybeth, Peter, Dawn. B.B.A., Iona Coll., 1949; M.S. (Univ. Store Service scholar), NYU, 1950. Vice pres. Hat Corp. Am., N.Y.C., v.p. mktg., 1961-63, exec. v.p., 1963-67; pres. Manhattan Shirt Co., N.Y.C., 1967-74, Lee Co., Inc., Shawnee Mission, Kans., 1974-82, also dir.; pres., dir. Kellwood Co., St. Louis, 1982—, chief exec. officer, 1984—; dir. Genovese Drug Stores, United Mo. Bancshares, Kansas City, Mo. Trustee Maryville Coll., St. Louis U.; bd. dirs. Boys Hope. Served with USN, 1944-46, PTO. Roman Catholic. Clubs: St. Louis, Town and Country Racquet, Bellerive Country. Office: Kellwood Co PO Box 14374 Saint Louis MO 63178 *

MCKENZIE, JOHN REDMOND, JR., radiologist; b. Helena, Mont., Mar. 17, 1928; s. John Redmond Sr. and Vivian Margaret (Skinner) McK.; m. Marilyn Joyce Cartwright, Jan. 17, 1951; children: Kathleen, Linda, Matthew, Patrick, Mary, Amy, Theresa, Sheila. Pre-med degree, Carrol Coll., 1951; MD, Marquette U., 1955. Gen. practice medicine Rice Lake (Wis.) Clinic, 1956-62; resident in radiology Milw. County Hosp., 1962-65; radiologist Radiol. Assoc. fo Fox Valley, Oshkosh, Wis., 1965—. Chmn. bd. dirs. Lourdes High Sch., Oshkosh, 1968-75; bd. dirs. YMCA, Oshkosh, 1973-77. Fellow Am. Coll. Radiology; mem. AMA (alternate del. 1977-79), Radiol. Soc. N. Am., State Med. Soc. Wis. (bd. dirs. 1972-77). Roman Catholic. Avocations: reading, travel, golf, racquetball. Home: 60 Country Club Ln Oshkosh WI 54901 Office: Radiol Assoc of Fox Valley 400 Ceape Oshkosh WI 54901

MCKEON, FRANCIS JOSEPH, III, human resources director, accountant; b. St. Louis, Dec. 31, 1951; s. Francis Joseph Jr. and Marjorie (Higgins) McK.; m. Ann Catherine Blank, Oct. 24, 1980; 1 child, Colleen. BA, Boston Coll., 1974; diploma in Strategic Human Resources Mgmt., Duke U., 1986. CPA, Mo. Staff acct., audit mgr. Price Waterhouse, St. Louis, 1974-83, mgr. personnel, recruiting, 1983-85, regional dir. human resources, 1985—; bus. advisor Inroads, Inc., St. Louis, 1983-86. Bd. advisors dept. acctg. So. Ill. U., Carbondale, 1983—. Mem. Am. Inst. CPA's, Mo. Soc. CPA's (relations with educators com. 1985—), Nat. Assn. Accts., Am. Soc. Personnel Adminstrn., Am. Acctg. Assn. (Midwest steering com. 1987), Jr. Achievement (fund solicitor 1986—), Beta Alpha Psi. Republican. Roman Catholic. Club: Missouri Athletic (St. Louis). Avocations: running, golf. Office: Price Waterhouse One Centerre Plaza Saint Louis MO 63101

MC KEOWN, MARY ELIZABETH, educational administrator; d. Raymond Edmund and Alice (Fitzgerald) McNamara; B.S., U. Chgo., 1946; M.S., DePaul U., 1953; m. James Edward McKeown, Aug. 6, 1955. Supr. high sch. dept. Am. Sch., 1948-68, prin., 1968—, trustee, 1975—, v.p., 1979—. Mem. Nat. Assn. Secondary Sch. Prins., Central States Assn. Sci. and Math Tchrs. Nat. Council Tchrs. Math., Assn. for Supervision and Curriculum Devel., Adult Edn. Assn., LWV. Author study guides for algebra, geometry and calculus. Home: 1469 N Sheridan Rd Kenosha WI 53140 Office: 850 E 58th Chicago IL 60637

MCKIBBEN, CRAIG KENNETH, plant engineer; b. Defiance, Ohio, June 6, 1957; s. Kenneth Darrel and Betty Ellen (Richard) McK.; m. Robin Sue Baldwin; children: Kirk David, Kyle Andrew. BSME, Tri-State U., 1980; postgrad., Bowling Green State U., 1980—. Indsl. engr. Manville Bldg. Materials Corp., Defiance, 1980-82, gen. maintenance supr., 1982-84, plant engr., 1984-85; plant engr. Manville Sales Corp., Defiance, 1985—. Mem. council Zion's Luth. Ch., Defiance, 1982-85. Mem. Soc. Automotive Engrs. Lodges: Elks, Kiwanis. Office: Manville Sales Corp PO Box 7218 Carpenter Rd Defiance OH 43512

MCKIBBIN, ELIZABETH ANN, customer relations executive; b. Plainview, Nebr., Dec. 4, 1949; d. Lyle Dwaine and Leola Mae (Gentzler) Stingley; m. William C. Planer, June 8, 1969 (div. June 1978); m. Jerold Louis McKibbin, Nov. 24, 1984; stepchildren: Delni Jane Rasmussen, Randall L. McKibbin. Student bus. adminstrn., Lincoln Sch. Commerce, 1968-69; student, U. Nebr., 1969-70, Nebr. Western Coll., 1974-83. Exec. sec. Lincoln (Nebr.) C. of C., 1969-72; cashier Assocs. Fin. Com., Sidney, Nebr., 1972-74; prod. mgr., traffic mgr. Kolt Radio, Scottsbluff, Nebr., 1974-76; adminstrv. asst. Scottsbluff-Gering C. of C., 1976-78; pub. info. officer Nebr. Western Coll., Scottsbluff, 1978-80; customer relations dir. United Tel. System, Scottsbluff, 1980—; dir. Minatare (Nebr.) State Bank, 1985—; council mem. Nebr. Arts Council, Omaha, 1984—. Contbr. articles to profl. jours. Sec. Scottsbluff-Gering United Way, 1982-83; pres., dir. Scottsbluff-Gering United C. of C., 1987. Recipient Community Service award United Telephone Systems, 1985; named Young Career Woman of Yr. Bus. and Profl. Women, 1977, Outstanding Young woman Yr., Nebr. Jaycees, 1984, Woman of Yr. Panhandle Bus. and Profl. Women, 1986. Mem. Nebr. Broadcasters Assn., Nebr. Press Assn., Internat. Assn. Bus. Com., Pub. Relation Soc. of Am., Am. Quarter Horse Assn., Panhandle Bus. and Profl.

Women (pres. 1984-85, named Woman of Yr. 1986, named Young Career Woman of Yr. 1977). Lutheran. Club: Scottsbluff Country. Avocations: calligraphy, photography. Home: Rt 2 Box 294 Scottsbluff NE 69361 Office: United Telephone System PO Box 2128 Scottsbluff NE 69361

MCKIERNAN, SUSAN PAOLANO, university director, art educator; b. Barberton, Ohio, June 30, 1947; d. Aldo Roosevelt and Mary Josephine (Platner) Paolano; m. Brian D. McKiernan, July 29, 1967 (div. Apr. 1980); children: Sean Mathias, Kara Meaghan. BFA, U. Akron, Ohio, 1977, MS in Edn., 1987, postgrad., 1987—. Lab. asst. metals dept. U. Akron, 1977-79, instr. metals, 1979—, asst. head art dept., 1980-87, asst. dir. Sch. Art, 1987—; cons. Petrelli, Inc., Akron, 1983; instr. field trip course to manor houses, Eng., summers 1986—. Author: Walking Tour of Downtown Akron, History of Peninsula, Ohio, History of Weymouth, Ohio. Charter mem. Progress Through Preservation, Summit County, Ohio, 1983, Mus. Contemporaries, 1984; mem. Akron Art Mus., Medina County Hist. Soc.; pres. Hower House Victorians, Akron, 1984. Named one of Outstanding Young Women Am., 1982. Mem. Nat. Council Arts Adminstrs., Ohio Assn. Women Deans and Adminstrs., Ohio Assn. for Counseling and Devel., Kappa Kappa Gamma. Democrat. Episcopalian. Avocations: history, antiques, architecture, travel. Office: Univ Akron Sch of Art Akron OH 44256

MCKINLEY, CAMILLE DOMBROWSKI, psychologist; b. Buffalo, May 6, 1922; d. Eugene Anthony and Anne Victoria (Sliwinska) Dombrowski; m. Thomas Leroy Smith, Dec. 30, 1944 (div. 1977); children: Thomas Dan, Cynthia Camille, Pamela Susan; m. William Frank McKinley, Oct. 7, 1984 (dec. Mar. 1985). BA, Syracuse U., 1943; MA, Boston U., 1944; edn. specialist, Mich. State U., 1970, PhD, 1978. Acad. advisor Mich. State U., East Lansing, 1966-70, dir. Career Ctr., 1970-81, counseling psychologist Counseling Ctr., 1981—; pres. Priam Pubs., 1978—; Mem. Career Planning and Placement Council Mich. State U. Editor: Teh Mich. State Referral Directory, 1970—, The Gracious Reader, 1970-80; eidotr, publisher The CAM Report, 1978—. Founding pres. Greater Lansing chpt. Planned Parenthood, Mich., 1967; v.p. Opera Co. of Mid-Mich., 1983-85. Mem. Zeta Tau Alpha. Clubs: Presidents', Pontiac Yacht. Lodge: Zonta. Home: 611 Cowley Ave East Lansing MI 48823 Office: Mich State U 207 Student Services East Lansing MI 48824

MCKINLEY, LARRY WAYNE, public administrator; b. Logansport, Ind., Mar. 27, 1951; s. Dean L. and Judith A. (Daniels) McK.; m. Mary Ellen McNally. BS, Purdue U., 1972, MS in Edn., 1975; MBA, U. Notre Dame, 1987. Prodn. scheduler Continental Steel Corp., Kokomo, Ind., 1972-73; tchr. Kokomo Ctr. Schs., 1973-80; dir. urban devel. City of Kokomo, 1980—; bd. dirs. Kokomo Devel. Corp., Indiana Statewide Cert. Devel. Corp., Indpls.; cons. Ind. Arts Commn., Indpls., 1973-74, Ind. Classroom Tchrs. Assn., 1973-74, Howard County Democrats, Kokomo, 1979—. Home: 1631 Elmwood Ln Kokomo IN 46902 Office: City Hall Kokomo IN 46902

MCKINLEY, LAWRENCE CHARLES, technical communications executive; b. Dayton, Ohio, Dec. 5, 1937; s. Elmer Lawrence and Beulah Iris (Greer) McK.; m. Colleen Kay Shellabarger, June 10, 1960; children: Eric, Ellen, Laureen, Kirk, Reid. BS in Forestry, U. of the South, 1960; postgrad., Duke U., 1962. Research forester U.S. Forest Service, Athens, Ohio and Salem, Mo., 1957-63; lab. technician, tech. editor Monsanto Research Corp., Miamisburg, Ohio, 1963-68; tech. writer, advt. writer, project leader, sr. analyst NCR Corp., Dayton, Ohio, 1968-84; supr. tech. publications Sheffield Measurement, Dayton, 1984—; curriculum cons. Miami U., Oxford, Ohio, 1982; adj. prof. tech. editing Bowling Green U., 1982—, mem. co-op. adv. bd., 1986—; employer adv. bd. Cin. Tech. Coll., 1986—. Mem. exec. com. United Way, Greene County, 1975, Dayton Philharm. Youth Orchestra, 1980-81. Recipient Scouter Key, Boy Scouts Am., 1976, Dist. Award of Merit, 1976, 20-Yr. Vet. Pin, 1983. Mem. Soc. for Tech. Communications (spkr. 1982), Assn. for Computing Machinery (speaker 1982), Soc. for Tech. Communications (contest mgr. 1982-83), Assn. Children with Learning Disabilities (organizer, pres. Beavercreek, Ohio, 1970-72, exec. bd. Greene County, 1973). Club: Glen Helen Assn. (nature guide 1987—). Home: 1779 N Longview St Beavercreek OH 45432 Office: Sheffield Measurement Div PO Box 1127 Dayton OH 45401-1127

MCKINLEY, MICHAEL ROBERT, judge; b. Ashland, Ohio, Nov. 13, 1936; s. Robert Steele and Amy Louise (Snyder) M.; m. Norma Elizabeth Anderson, June 8, 1959; 1 child, Scott. B.A., Ohio U., 1959; J.D., Ohio State U., 1962. Bar: Ohio 1962, U.S. Supreme Ct. 1973, U.S. Dist. Ct. (no. dist.) Ohio 1975. Dir. law City of Ashland, 1964-75; sole practice, Ashland, 1963-73; ptnr. Scheaffer & McKinley, Loudonville, Ohio, 1974-80; judge probate and juvenile divs. Ct. of Common Pleas, Ashland County, 1981—; dir. instl. research Ashland Coll., 1968-73. Pres. Ashland Nat. Little League, 1965-66; chmn. bd. trustees 1st Presbyterian Ch. of Ashland, 1970. Recipient Superior Jud. Service award, Ohio Supreme Ct., 1981, 82, 83, 84, 85, Cert. of Distinction, Ohio State U., 1983. Mem. Ohio Mcpl. Attys. Assn. (pres. 1975-76), Ashland County Bar Assn. (pres. 1976-77), Ohio State Bar Assn. (chmn. local law com. 1978-80), ABA, Ohio Assn. Probate Judges (chmn. edn. com. 1983), Ohio Juvenile Judges Assn. Republican. Presbyterian. Avocations: golf; boating; swimming; traveling. Home: 404 Lake Shore Rd RFD 4 Ashland OH 44805 Office: Ashland County Courthouse W 2d St Ashland OH 44805

MCKINNEY, DAVID CHRISTIAN, land developer, urban planning consultant; b. McCook, Nebr., May 6, 1944; s. John Yokom and Doris Gladus (Petersen) McK.; m. Nancy Fuller, Jan. 21, 1967; children: Scott, Ian. BArch, IIT, 1967; MS in City and Regional Planning, Ill. Inst. Tech., 1968, PhD in City and Regional Planning, 1976. Pres. Am. Community Devel. Corp., Indpls., 1975—; cons. in field State of Ind., 1983-84, Hudson Inst., Indpls., 1985-86. Mem., sec. Met. Sch. Dist. Pike Twp., Indpls., 1984-87. Mem. Am. Inst. Cert. Planners, Am. Planning Assn. Republican. Avocations: soccer, skiing, tennis, sailing, photography. Office: Am Community Devel Corp 6025 Lafayette Rd Indianapolis IN 46254

MC KINNEY, FRANK EDWARD, JR., banker; b. Indpls., Nov. 3, 1938; s. Frank Edward and Margaret (Warner) McK.; m. Katherine Berry, Aug. 18, 1962; children: Frank Edward, III, Katherine Marie, Margaret Leonard, Madeleine Warner, Robert Warner, Heather Claire. B.S., Ind. U., 1961, M.B.A., 1962; LL.D. (hon.), Butler U., Indpls., 1975. Asst. cashier First Nat. Bank, Chgo., 1964-67; with Am. Fletcher Nat. Bank, Indpls., 1967—; exec. v.p., then pres. Am. Fletcher Nat. Bank, 1970-73, chmn. bd., 1973—; chmn. bd. Am. Fletcher Corp., 1974—, now also chief exec. officer; dir., vice chmn., mem. exec. com. Allied Bank Internat., N.Y.C.; dir., mem. exec. com. Ind. Bell Telephone Co.; dir. Am. United Life Ins. Co.; dir., mem. exec. com. Indpls. Power & Light Co., IPALCO Enterprises, Inc. Bd. dirs. Indpls. Mus. Art, Exec. Council on Fgn. Diplomats; adv. council Coll. Bus., U. Notre Dame; mem. Ind. State Olympic Com. Served to 1st. lt. AUS, 1962-64. Named to Internat. Swimming Hall Fame, 1975, Ind. U. Acad. Alumni Fellows, 1973, Ind. U. Intercollegiate Athletics Hall of Fame, 1982; recipient Disting. Service award Indpls. Jaycees, 1974. Mem. Assn. Res. City Bankers, Assn. Bank Holding Cos. (dir., vice chmn., exec. com.), Am., Ind. bankers assns., Ind. Soc. Chgo., Internat. Monetary Conf., Penrod Soc., Newcomen Soc. N.Am., Indpls. C. of C., Ind. C. of C., 500 Festival Assocs., Econ. Club Indpls. (pres. 1977), Am. Legion, Sigma Alpha Epsilon. Democrat. Roman Catholic. Clubs: Meridian Hill Country, Indpls. Athletic, Skyline, Notre Dame of Indpls. (Indpls.). Address: Am Fletcher Nat Bank 101 Monument Circle Indianapolis IN 46277

MC KINNEY, ROBERT HURLEY, lawyer, business executive; b. Indpls., Nov. 7, 1925; s. E. Kirk and Irene (Hurley) McK.; m. Arlene Frances Allsopp, Nov. 28, 1951; children: Robert, Marni, Kevin, Kent, Lisa. B.S., U.S. Naval Acad., 1946; J.D., Ind. U., 1951. Bar: Ind. 1951. Since practiced in Indpls.; sr. partner Bose McKinney & Evans, 1963—; chmn. bd. Jefferson Corp. and subsidiaries, Indpls., 1961-77, 79—; chmn. First Fed. Savs. & Loan Assn., Indpls., 1961—, Fed. Home Loan Bank Bd., 1977-79; dir. Fed. Nat. Mortgage Assn., Baker, McHenry & Welch, Inc., Jefferson Nat. Life Ins. Co.; mem. adv. com. on internat. investment Dept. State. Chmn. Urban Reinvestment Task Force, Indpls.; bd. dirs. Indpls. Legal Aid Soc., Children's Mus. Indpls.; bd. dirs., mem. exec. com. Brebeuf Prep. Sch., 1970—; trustee Indpls. Community Hosp., Marian Coll., Indpls.; del. Democratic Nat. Conv., 1968, 76, 80. Served to lt. comdr. USNR, 1946-49, 51-53. Mem. Am., Ind., Indpls. bar assns., Com. for Econ. Devel., Young Pres. Orgn. (nat. chmn. for econ. edn. 1968-69, pres. Ind. chpt. 1973-74). Club: K.M. Office: Jefferson Corp 1 Virginia Ave Indianapolis IN 46204 also: 1st Indiana Fed Savings Bank 1 N Pennsylvania St Indianapolis IN 46204

MCKINNON, ROBERT HAROLD, insurance company executive; b. Holtville, Calif., Apr. 4, 1927; s. Harold Arthur and Gladys Irene (Blanchar) McK.; m. Marian Lois Hayes, Dec. 18, 1948; children: Steven Robert, Laurie Ellen, David Martin. BS, Armstrong Coll., 1950, MBA, 1952. Regional sales mgr. Farmers Ins. Group, Austin, Tex., 1961-66, Aurora, Ill., 1966-68; dir. life sales Farmers New World Life, Los Angeles, 1968-75; v.p. mktg. Warner Ins. Group, Chgo., 1975-82; mem. Canners Exchange Dairy Adv. Com., 1977-82; sr. v.p. mktg. The Rural Cos. Scoutmaster Boy Scouts Am., 1971-72. Served with U.S. Army, 1944-45. Fellow Life Underwriters Tng. Council; mem. Am. Soc. CLU's, Soc. CPCU's, Internat. Ins. Seminars, CUP Found. (chmn. bd. dirs. 1987—). Club: Nakoma Golf (Madison, Wis.). Lodge: Rotary. Home: 402 Walnut Grove Dr Madison WI 53717 Office: 7010 Mineral Point Rd Madison WI 53705

MCKINSTRY, KEVIN LEE, insurance executive; b. Salem, Ohio, Mar. 1, 1955; s. George Thomas and Charlene Elizabeth (Davis) McK.; m. Ruby Kay Coppock, May 18, 1984; stepchildren: Leslie Brittain, Tracy Brittain. BS in Bus., Maryville Coll., 1977. CLU. Tax rep. H&R Block, Lenoir City, Tenn., 1978; ins. salesman McKinstry and Assocs., East Palestine, Ohio, 1978—. Dir. Pony Little League Baseball, 1983-84; bd. dirs. East Palestine Athletic Boosters, 1984-85; alumni rep. for Maryville Coll. Mem. Youngstown Assn. Life Underwriters (bd. dirs. 1982-84, treas. 1984-85, sec. 1985-86, 1st v.p. 1986-87, pres. 1987—), East Palestine Jaycees (pres. 1981-82, bd. dirs. 1984). Republican. Presbyterian. Avocations: volleyball and basketball officiating, basketball coaching, reading, working with children. Home: 176 E Martin St East Palestine OH 44413 Office: McKinstry and Assocs 566 Alice St PO Box 351 East Palestine OH 44413

MCKINZIE, BARBARA ANNE, accounting firm executive; b. Ada, Okla., Jan. 2, 1954; d. Leonard Terry McKinzie and Johnnie Mae (Moses) Watson. BS, East Cen. U., Ada, Okla., 1976. CPA, Ill., Okla. Supr. Touche Ross & Co., Tulsa, 1976-83; mgr. Deloitte Haskins & Sells, Chgo., 1983-85; exec. dir. Alpha Kappa Alpha, Inc., Chgo., 1985-87; mgr. Coopers & Lybrand, Chgo., 1987—; pres. BAM Assocs., Chgo., 1985—. Named one of Outstanding Young Women of Am., 1985. Mem. Am. Inst. CPA's, Am. Women's Soc. CPA's, Ill. Soc. CPA's, Am. Arbitration Assn. Baptist. Avocations: travel, racquetball. Home: 4800 Chicago Beach Dr #2702N Chicago IL 60615 Office: Coopers and Lybrand 203 N LaSalle Chicago IL 60601

MCKNIGHT, MICHAEL LANCE, marketing executive; b. Painesville, Ohio, Nov. 8, 1939; s. Clinton Blair and Marianne Virginia (Marvin) McK.; m. Deborah Sue Coggins, Jan 28, 1978; children: Ryan Michael, Drew Boynton, Courtney Blair. Student, Ohio U., 1959, Ohio State U., 1960-63; Grad. Instalment Lending Sch., Kent State U., 1975; Grad. Nat. Comml. Lending Sch., U. Okla., 1978. V.p. Ameritrust Co., Cleve., 1975-78; sales mgr. Grantham Inc., Fairport, Ohio, 1978-81, Penn Compression, Pitts., 1981-83; v.p., gen. mgr. Pvt. Safe Place, Beachwood, Ohio, 1983—; owner, operator Knight-Rydre Co., 1984—; tchr. Lake Erie Coll., Painesville, 1975-78. Loaned exec. United Way, Painesville, 1975-77; bd. dirs. Meadowlawn Homeowners Assn., Mentor, Ohio, 1984-86, Am. Cancer Soc., Painesville, 1976-78. Served with U.S. Army, 1963-66. Mem. Am. Soc. Indsl. Security, Data Processing Mgmt. Assn. (bd. dirs. 1985—), Assn. Records Mgrs. and Adminstrs., Security Practitioners Group, Assn. Contingency Planners. Republican. Lodges: Rotary, Elks. Avocations: golf, racquetball. Home: 7637 Crimson Ct Mentor OH 44060 Office: Pvt Safe Place 24025 Commerce Park Beachwood OH 44122

MCKNIGHT, ROBERT ALLEN, marketing and business consultant; b. Detroit, Apr. 24, 1943; s. L. Allen and Mildred Mary (Schwartz) McK.; m. Jacqueline Sue Estes, Nov. 23, 1966. Student Miami U., Oxford, Ohio, 1961-63; B.A., Ohio State U., 1966, M.A., 1968. Copy writer Terra Advt. Co., Columbus, Ohio, 1965; pub. info. officer Ohio Dept. Liquor Control, Columbus, 1966-68; research and pub. relations dir. Ohio Rep. Hdqrs., Columbus, 1968-71; with Columbus Air Conditioning Corp., 1971-82, pres., chmn., 1979-82; ptnr. Prime Asset Mgmt., Columbus, 1982-86 , These Are My Jewels, 1982—; owner Misc., Inc., Columbus. . Pres., Pilot Dogs, Inc., 1981-83; bd. dirs. Better Bus. Bur., 1981—; lectr. in field . Mem. Heating and Air Conditioning Assn. Ohio (pres. 1979-81), Carrier Midwest Dealer Council (chmn. 1980-82). Republican. Lutheran. Lodges: Mason (exec. sec. 1984—, 33 degree), Shriners, Rotary. Home: 4540 Tetford Rd Upper Arlington OH 43220 Office: 32 N 4th St Columbus OH 43215

MCKNIGHT, ROBERT LORNE, marketing executive, investor; b. Wichita, Kans., Feb. 23, 1947; s. Philip Charles and Margaret Catherine (McClymonds) McK.; m. Caroline King Hampton, July 29, 1972; children—Margaret Hampton, Elizabeth King. Student U. Kans., 1965-67, 68-70, Wichita State U., 1967-68. Writer Barickman Advertising, Kansas City, Mo., 1971-73; project creative dir. Rickey & Biederman, Shawnee Mission, Kans., 1973-75; pres. McKnight & Assocs., Shawnee Mission, 1975-79; mag. pub. Sosland Publishing Co., Kansas City, 1979-84; pres. Ceres Group, Overland Park, Kans., 1984—, AMERIND, Overland Park, 1985—; dir. Sugarloaf Mountain Wood Works, Hartford, Ark., 1983—; co-owner Senate Cabs, Washington, 1986, Ark. Cedar Products, 1986, Far East News Network, 1986; ptnr. Breckenridge Ventures, 1986, McClymonds Farms, 1985—. Author: Creative Services-Kansas City, 1974, Day Trips for Aviators, 1987. Captions Author: Return to Kansas, 1984. Colorado Treasures, 1987. Co-founder, pres. Park & Recreation Found. Johnson County, Overland Park, Kans., 1979—; bd. dirs. Friends of the Zoo, Kansas City, 1974-77, Planned Parenthood, Kansas City, 1975-78. Recipient various awards Kansas City Advertising Club, Art Directors Club. Life fellow Stephen Duck Soc.; mem. Grain Elevator and Processing Soc., Nat. Grain and Feed Assn., Kansas Grain and Feed Dealers, Am. Mktg. Assn., Internat. Trade Club, Am. Cons. League, Am. Soc. Agrl. Cons., Pilots Internat. Assn., Kans. Pilots Assn., Nat. Press Club. Avocations: travel; flying.

MC KNIGHT, VAL BUNDY, engineering consultant; b. Budapest, Hungary, Sept. 14, 1926; s. Valentine B. and Maria E. (Heray) Mariahegyi; came to U.S., 1966, naturalized, 1971; student Inst. Tech., Budapest; M.E.E., Tech. U. Budapest, 1954; postgrad. Bradley U., 1966-68; m. Ruby P. Fulop, Aug. 9, 1947; children—Bela, Suzy. Mgr. engring. Ministry of Constrn. Industry, Budapest, 1955-57; supervising engr. Canadian Brit. Aluminum Co., Baie Comeau, Que., 1958-66; utilities cons. Caterpillar Inc., Peoria, Ill., 1966—. Mem. Republican Nat. Com., Presdl. Task Force; radio communication advisor Civil Def. System, 1969-76; nat. adv. bd. Am. Security Council, 1975-77; deacon Westminster Presbyterian Ch. Served to lt., Budapest Mil. Acad., 1954-55. Named Innovator of Yr., 1955; knighted, Order of Knights, 1942; cert. plant engr.; registered profl. engr., Que. Mem. Am. Inst. Plant Engrs. (plant engr. of year 1976-77, 77-78, pres. chpt. 93, 1979-80, del. dir. 1981—), Nat., Ill. (govt. relations and public affairs com. 1977-80, planning resources com. 1982—) socs. profl. engrs., Corp. of Profl. Engrs. of Que., IEEE (liquid dielectric com.), Illuminating Engring. Soc., Nat. Assn. Bus. Ednl. Radio, NAM (policy com.), Engring. Inst. Can., Mfrs. Radio Frequency Adv. Council (dir. 1978—, v.p.), Assn. Energy Engrs., Nat. Machine Tool Builders Assn. (joint indsl. council), Am. Assn. Engring. Socs. (internat. affairs council), Ill. State C. of C. (energy task force). Clubs: Masons, Shriners. Home: 6831 N Michele Ln Peoria IL 61614 Office: 100 NE Adams St Peoria IL 61629

MC KONE, DON T., manufacturing company executive; b. Jackson, Mich., 1921. Grad., U. Mich., 1947. With Aerouio Corp. (subs. Trinova Corp.), Jackson, Mich., 1949-68; with Libbey-Owens-Ford Co. (name changed to Trinova Corp. in 1986) Aerouio Corp. (subs. Trinova Corp.), Toledo, Ohio, 1968—, exec. v.p., 1970-75, pres., chief operating officer, 1975-79, pres., chief exec. officer, 1979-80; Chmn. bd., dir. Trinova Corp. (formerly Libbey-Owens-Ford Co.), Maumee, Ohio, 1980—, chief exec. officer, 1980-86; chmn. bd., dir. Toledo-Lucas County Port Authority; bd. dirs. Ohio Citizens Bank, NBD Bancorp., Inc., Consumers Power Co., Ashland Oil Co., Champion Spark Plug Co. Office: Trinova Corp 1705 Indian Wood Circle Maumee OH 43537 *

MCKONE, DON T., manufacturing company executive. Chmn. Trinova Corp., Maumee, Ohio. Office: Trinova Corp 1705 Indian Wood Circle Maumee OH 43537 *

MCKOWEN, DOROTHY KEETON, librarian; b. Bonne Terre, Mo., Oct. 5, 1948; d. John Richard and Dorothy (Spoonhour) Keeton; m. Paul Edwin McKowen, Dec. 19, 1970; children: Richard James, Mark David. BS, Pacific Christian Coll., 1970; MS in Library Sci., U. So. Calif., 1973; MA in English, Purdue U., 1985. Librarian-specialist Doheny Library, U. So. Calif., Los Angeles, 1973-74; asst. librarian Pacific Christian Coll., 1974-78; serials cataloger Purdue Univ. Libraries, 1978—; ch. librarian Brady Ln. Ch. of Christ, 1986—, vice chairperson Christian Edn. Com., 1986, chairperson, 1987, pianist, 1978—; bd. dirs. Purdue Christian Campus House, 1985—, vice chairperson, 1986-87. Mem. ALA (resources and tech. services div., bd. dirs. 1986—, vice chairperson, chairperson-elect council of regional groups 1986—, conf. program com. 1986—, internat. relations com. 1986—, micropub. com., 1986-87), Ind. Library Assn. (vice chmn. tech. services div. 1983-84, chmn. 1984-85), Ohio Valley Group Tech. Services Librarians (vice chmn. 1984-85, chmn. 1985-86). Republican. Home: 7625 Summit Ln Lafayette IN 47905 Office: Purdue U Libraries W Lafayette IN 47907

MCLAIN, RON ALLEN, training company executive; b. Hatton, N.D., Jan. 9, 1952; s. Harley L. and Barbara I. (Gulbranson) McL.; m. Jane E. Homstad, Apr. 4, 1977; 1 child, Nathan R. BS, Mayville (N.D.) State Coll., 1974; MEd, U. Minn., 1976. Cert. tchr., coach, Minn. Tchr., coach Sch. Dist. 196, Rosemount, Minn., 1974-80; tng. mgr. TCF, Mpls., 1981; edn. cons. Deltak, Mpls., 1982-83, acct. exec., 1984-85, dist. mgr., 1986—. Contbg. editor Data Training mag., 1985. Bd. dirs. Christian Edn. Bd., Burnsville, Minn., 1984—. Mem. Programmers, Analysts and Computer Trainers, Assn. Info. Ctr. Profls. Republican. Avocations: tennis, windsurfing, biking, running, softball, skiing. Home: 285 Riverwoods Ln Burnsville MN 55337 Office: Deltak Tng Corp 3300 Edinborough Way Edina MN 55435

MCLATCHIE, LOIS REEDER, psychologist, educator; b. Camden, N.J., Sept. 27, 1931; d. Amos Smith and C. Inez (Landis) Reeder; m. William Richmond Locky McLatchie, June 4, 1955; children—Ruth, John, David, Elizabeth, Willa. B.A., U. Alta. (Can.), 1974; M.S., Pa. State U., 1977, Ph.D., 1981. Lic. psychologist, Ohio. Instr. psychology Pa. State U., 1976-77; psychology intern Cleve. VA Hosp., 1978-79; psychologist HMO Health-Ohio, Cleve.-West, 1984—; psychologist Western Res. Psychiat. Habilitation Ctr., Northfield, Ohio, 1979-84; adj. clin. instr. Case Western Res. U., Cleve., 1982-84; pres. Clearfield-Jefferson Mental Health Assn., 1977-78. Bd. dirs. Mental Health Assn. Pa., 1976-78. Recipient Disting. Service award Mental Health/Alta., 1973. Mem. Am. Psychol. Assn., Ohio Psychol. Assn., State Assn. Psychology, Psychol. Assn. Western Res., Republican. Baptist. Home: 1711 Lander Rd Mayfield Heights OH 44124 Office: HMO Health-Ohio Cleve West 4330 W 150th St Cleveland OH 44135

MCLAUCHLIN, LON ROYCE, telephone company official; b. Hutnsville, Tex., Dec. 9, 1934; s. Aubrey Royce and Ara Lee (Cockrell) McL.; m. Glenda Lou Porter, Sept. 6, 1955; children—Lon, Kevin, Kimberly. B.B.A., N. Tex. State U., 1957. Mgr., Southwestern Bell Telephone Co., Uvalde, Tex., 1958, Houston, 1959-68, dist. mgr., 1968-69, div. supr., Kansas City, Mo., 1969-72, div. mgr., Springfield, Mo., 1972-83, div. staff mgr., St. Louis, 1983—; dir. Centerre Bank, Springfield. Bd. dirs. Jr. Achievement, Springfield, 1972-83, Boy Scouts Am., 1974-78, St. John's Hosp., Springfield, 1975-80, Community Found., 1980-83, Better Bus. Bur., 1982-83; pres. Downtown Springfield Assn., 1982-83; pres., organizer Safety Council S.W. Mo., 1983. Named Boss of Yr., Am. Bus. Women's Assn. Springfield, 1973; recipient Caring award Springfield council Girl Scouts U.S.A., 1976. Mem. Springfield Area C. of C. (pres. 1977). Republican. Methodist. Club: Twin Oaks Country (Springfield). Lodge: Rotary (Springfield). Avocations: golf; camping. Home: 370 Greentrails Dr S Chesterfield MO 63017 Office: Southwestern Bell One Bell Center Saint Louis MO 63101

MC LAUGHLIN, HARRY ROLL, architect; b. Indpls., Nov. 29, 1922; s. William T. and Ruth E. (Roll) McL.; m. Linda Hamilton, Oct. 23, 1954; 1 child Harry Roll Jr. Student, John Herron Art Sch., Indpls., 1936, 40, 41. Registered architect, Ind., Alaska, D.C., Ohio, Ill., Md., Va., Nat. Council Registration Bds. Pres., treas. James Assocs. Inc., Indpls., 1956-81, pres. emeritus, prin. cons., 1981—; adv. bd. Pompeiiana Inc., Indpls.; specializing in restoration of historic bldgs. Restorations include Old State Bank State Meml, Vincennes, Old Opera House State Meml, New Harmony, Old Morris-Butler House, Indpls. (Merit award 1972), Market St. Restoration and Maria Creek Baptist Ch., Vincennes, Ind., Benjamin Harrison House, Old James Ball Residence, Lafayette, Ind. (1st Design award 1972), Lockerbie Sq. Master Plan and Park Sch., Indpls., Knox County Ct. House, Vincennes, 1972, J.K. Lilly House, Indpls., 1972, Waiting Station and Chapel, Crown Hill Cemetery, Indpls., 1972, Blackford-Condit several Indian houses Angel Mounds Archaeol. Site and Interpretative Center, nr. Evansville, Ind.; architect: Restorations include Glenn A. Black Mus. Archaeology, Ind. U., Bloomington; Restoration Morgan County Ct. House, Indpls. City Market, Hist. Scofield House, Madison, Ind., Ernie Pyle Birthplace, Dana, Ind., Phi Kappa Psi Nat. Hdqrs, Indpls., 1980 (Design award), East Coll. Bldg, DePauw U., Greencastle, Ind.; Contbr. articles to profl. jours.; Illustrator: Harmonist Construction. Past mem. Mayor's Progress Com., Arts and Culture Com.; past chmn. bd., past pres., now chmn. emeritus Historic Landmarks Found., Ind.; past bd. dirs. Carmel Clay Ednl. Found.; archtl. adviser, bd. advisers Historic Madison, Inc.; mem. adv. council Historic Am. Bldgs. survey Nat. Park Service, 1967-73; mem. Ind. Profl. Rev. Com. for Nat. Register Nominations, 1967-81; past adv. bd. Conner Prairie Mus., Patrick Henry Sullivan Found.; past adviser Indpls. Historic Preservation Commn.; past mem. preservation com. Ind. U.; architect mem. Meridian St. Preservation Commn., Indpls.; hon. mem. Ind. Bicentennial Commn.; bd. dirs. Park-Tudor Sch., 1972-85; past nat. bd. dirs. Preservation Action; trustee Masonic Heritage Found., Masonic Home; bd. dirs. Indpls. Pub. Library Found., 1986—, Hist. New Harmony Found., 1987—. Served with USNR, 1943-45. Recipient awards including; Ind. Gov.'s citation, 1967; Indpls. Mayor's citation for services in preservation archtl. heritage, 1972; U.S. Sec. Interior's citation, 1973; design and environment citations for work in preservation, 1975; Gov. Orr's citation, 1981. Fellow AIA (mem. nat. com. historic bldgs., chmn. historic resources com. 1970); mem. Ind. Archtl. Found., Ind. Soc. Architects (state preservation coordinator 1960—; Biennial award 1972, Design award 1978), Constrn. League Indpls. (bd. dirs. 1969-71), Nat. Trust Hist. Preservation (past trustee, bd. advisers), Soc. Archtl. Historians (past bd. dirs.), Ind. Com. for Presevation of Archtl. Records, Indpls. Mus. Art (trustee, chmn. bldgs. com., bd. govs. 1986—), Assn. Preservation Tech., Zionsville C. of C. (hon. bd. dirs.), U.S. Capitol (hon. trustee), Ind. Hist. Soc., Marion County Hist. Soc. (past v.p., bd. dirs.), Zionsville Hist. Soc., Victorian Soc. Am. (adv. bd.), Smithsonian Assos., Navy League U.S. (life), Ind. State Mus. Soc. (charter), English Speaking Union (bd. dirs. Indpls.), Milestone Car Soc. Clubs: Woodstock (Indpls.) (bd. dirs. 1982-86, pres. 1985, ex-officio 1986), Literary (Indpls.), Amateur Movie (Indpls.), Athletic (Indpls.), Packard. Lodge: Masons (33 deg.). Home: 950 W 116th St Carmel IN 46032 Office: James Assocs Inc 120 Monument Circle Indianapolis IN 46205

MCLAUGHLIN, JAMES ROBERT, savings and loan executive, controller; b. Lincoln, Nebr., Nov. 16, 1954; s. Robert Eugene and Alma H. (Niemeier) McL.; m. Jolene Kay Timblin, AUg. 18, 1978; children: Kristin, Andrew. BSBA, U. Nebr., 1977. CPA, Nebr. Asst. to supr. sr. Fox & Co., CPA's, Omaha, 1977-79; supr. sr. Fox & Co., CPA's, Nebraska City, Nebr., 1979-84; v.p., controller First Fed. Lincoln Savs. and Loan Assn., 1984—. Mem. Am. Inst. CPA's, Fin. Mgrs. Soc., Nebr. Soc. CPA's. Democrat. Lutheran. Lodge: Lions (Elmwood Nebr. bd. dirs. 1986—). Avocations: softball, volleyball, hunting. Home: Box 54 RFD #1 Unadilla NE 68454 Office: First Fed Lincoln Savs & Loan 1235 N St Lincoln NE 69508

MCLAUGHLIN, JOHN MICHAEL, JR., engineer, engineering company executive; b. Chgo., Apr. 14, 1936; s. John Michael Sr. and Helen M. (Walsh) McL.; m. Jeannine Marie Mannos, Jan. 25, 1958; children: Anne, John, Kathryn, Colleen, Michael, Erin. BS, Ill. Inst. Tech., 1958, MS, 1970. Structural engr. Austin Co., Chgo., 1962-64; ptnr. Sargent & Lundy, Chgo., 1964—. Contbr. articles to profl. jours. Pres. Home Sch. Assn., LaGrange, Ill., 1978; chmn. Bldg. Bd. Appeals, LaGrange, 1983-86. Served to 1st lt.

USAF, 1958-62. Fellow Am. Concrete Inst.; mem. ASCE, Am. Inst. Steel Constrn., Earthquake Engring. Research Inst., Bldg. Officials and Code Adminstrs. Internat., Inc., Post-Tensioning Inst., Structural Stability Research Council. Structural Engrs. Assn. Ill., Seismological Soc. Am. Office: Sargent & Lundy 55 E Monroe St Chicago IL 60603

MCLAUGHLIN, KIMBERLY KOTONIAS, accountant; b. Chisholm, Minn., Nov. 11, 1961; d. John Theoharis and Florence Katherine (Amato) Kotonias; m. Paul Joseph McLaughlin, May 24, 1986. AA in Acctg., Hibbing (Minn.) Coll., 1982; B in Acctg. magna cum laude with honors, U. Minn., Duluth, 1984. CPA, Minn. Acct. Peat Marwick Main & Co. (formerly KMG Main Hurdman), Duluth, 1984—. Am. Women's Soc. CPA's scholar, Chgo., 1983. Mem. Am. Inst. CPA's, Minn. State Soc. CPA's, Phi Kappa Phi. Roman Catholic. Club: Italian-Am. (Chisholm). Lodge: Moose. Avocations: cooking, volleyball. Office: Peat Marwick Main & Co 700 Missabe Bldg Duluth MN 55802

MC LAUGHLIN, WILLIAM GAYLORD, metal products manufacturing company executive; b. Marietta, Ohio, Sept. 28, 1936; s. William Russell and Edna Martha (Hiatt) McL.; children: Debora, Cynthia, Leslie, Teresa, Kristin, Jennifer. BS in Mech. Engring., U. Cin., 1959; MBA, Ball State U., 1967. Plant engr. Kroger Co., Marion, Ind., 1959-62; with Honeywell, Inc., Wabash, Ind., 1962-75, mgr. metal products ops., 1971-72, gen. mgr. ops., 1972-75; pres. MarkHon Industries Inc., Wabash, 1975—; mem. N. Cen. Ind. Pvt. Industry Council, 1983-84; mem. bus. adv. bd. Manchester Coll. Patentee design electronic relay rack cabinet. Pres. Wabash Assn. for Retarded Children, 1974-75; gen. chmn. United Fund Drive, 1971; mem. Wabash County Arts Council; pres. Wabash Valley Dance Theater; treas., Young Reps., Wabash, 1968-70; bd. dirs. Youth Service Bur., Sr. Citizens, Jr. Achievement; mem. ofcl. bd. Meth. ch., 1966-71; pres. Meth. men, 1975-77. Recipient Ind. Jefferson award for public service, 1981, Disting. Citizen award Wabash, 1981; named Outstanding Young Man of Year, Wabash Jr. C. of C., 1972. Mem. Indsl. C. of C. (pres. 1973-74), Wabash Area C. of C. (pres. 1976), Precision Metal Forming Assn. (chmn. Ind. dist. 1978, chmn. metal fabrication div.), Ind. Mfg. Assn. (bd. dirs.), Young Pres.'s Orgn. Club: Wabash Country (v.p. 1972-76). Lodges: Rotary (pres. Cincinnatus Soc. 1970-71, dist. youth exchange officer 1974-77, dist. gov. 1979-80), Masons. Home: 141 W Maple St Wabash IN 46992 Office: 200 Bond St Wabash IN 46992

MCLEOD, DEBRA ANN, librarian, mail order book company executive; b. St. Louis, Apr. 21, 1952; d. Frank Joseph and Virginia Veronica (Jasso) Osterloh; m. Bradley J. McLeod, June 24, 1977; children: Catherine Rose, Elizabeth Lauren. BA in History, U. Mo., St. Louis, 1974; MSLS, U. Ill., 1975. Research asst. Grad. Sch. Library Sci., U. Ill., Urbana, 1974; children's librarian St. Louis Pub. Library, 1976-77, Kent County Library System, Grand Rapids, Mich., 1977-81; children's specialist Johnson County Library, Shawnee Mission, Kans., 1981-83, coordinator children's collections, 1983—; mng. ptnr. The Book Tree, Lenexa, Kans., 1982—; library cons. Family Services of Kent County (Mich.), 1977-79. Contbg. editor Kansas City Parent, 1986—. Mem. ALA, Assn. for Library Service to Children (intellectual freedom com. 1984—, Scribner award 1980, Newbery award com. 1983), Freedom to Read Found., Shawnee Jaycee Women (pres. 1982-83). Roman Catholic. Home: 9134 Twilight Ln Lenexa KS 66219 Office: Johnson County Library System 8700 W 63d St Shawnee Mission KS 66201

MCLEOD, THOMAS CLAIBORNE, advertising agency executive; b. Saginaw, Mich., Nov. 4, 1947; s. Charles Angust and Kathleen Rose (Couch) McL.; m. Melanie Anne Hoganson, May 25, 1973; 1 child, Thomas Conor. BSBA, Ferris State Coll., 1971. Account exec. WEYI TV-25, Saginaw, 1972-80; mgr. advertising Tuffy Mufflers, Saginaw, 1980-82; owner T.C. McLeod Advertising Agy., Saginaw, 1982—. Mem. Detroit Advertising Fedn., Sales and Mktg. Execs. Flint, Mich. (Disting. Salesman award 1979), C. of C., Detroit Advertising Club. Republican. Club: Bay City (Mich) Country. Home: 2695 Granada Saginaw MI 48603 Office: TS McLeod Advertising Agy 919 S Michigan Ave Saginaw MI 48602

MCLIN, NATHANIEL, JR., educator; b. Chgo., June 19, 1928; s. Nathaniel and Anna (Polk) McL.; m. Lena Mae, July 18, 1952; children—Nathaniel Gerald, Beverly Jane. Student Wilson Jr. Coll., Chgo., 1946-50, Roosevelt U., 1950-52; M.A. Govs. State U.; postgrad. (fellow), Walden U., 1976. Technician, Michael Reese Hosp., 1951-52, U. Chgo. Goldblatt Clinic, 1952-53; bus driver Chgo. Transit Authority, 1953-64; pub. relations dir. Opera Theater of Chgo., 1959-60; mgr. McLin Opera Co., Chgo., 1960-71; salesman Watkins Products Co., 1964-65; tchr. Chgo. Com. on Urban Opportunity, 1965-71; soloist Park Dist. Opera Guild, Chgo., 1964-68; creator, developer All Souls Universalist Childrens Theatre and Opera Workshop, 1986. Active Beatrice Caffrey Found., Chgo.; dir. Trinity United Ch. Mens Chorus, Chgo., 1962-66; active fund raising campaign pub. relations YMCA, 1963-64; cultural coordinator, dir. Halsted Urban Progress ctr., Chgo., 1966-71; dir. Faces of Crime Symposium All Souls Ch., Chgo., also lay leader, 1980—. Served with U.S. Army, 1946-47. Recipient Wheelers Social Club citation for efforts in nations cultural devel., 1962. Lodge: Fraternal Order of Police (pres. lodge 83 1980-81). Author: Parole: The Ex-offender's Last Hope, 1983. Home and Office: 7630 S Hoyne St Chicago IL 60620

MCLIN, RHINE LANA, funeral director, educator; b. Dayton, Ohio, Oct. 3, 1948; d. C. Josef, Jr., and Bernice (Cottman) McL. B.A. in Sociology, Parsons Coll., 1969; M.Ed., Xavier U., Cin., 1972; postgrad. in law U. Dayton, 1974-76. Lic. funeral dir. and notary pub.; cert. tchr., Ohio. Tchr. Dayton Bd. Edn., 1970-72; divorce counselor Domestic Relations Ct., Dayton, 1972-73; law clk. Montgomery Common Pleas Ct., Dayton, 1973-74; v.p., mgr. McLin Funeral Homes, Dayton, 1972—; instr. Central State U., Wilberforce, Ohio, 1982—; speaker Dayton Pub. Schs., 1980—. Author 6-series article: Death and Dying, 1980. Adv. bd. Dayton Contemporary Dance Co., 1977, Montgomery County Welfare and Social Services, Dayton, 1983, Nat. Council on Women's Edn. Programs, 1980; mem. Democratic Voters League, Dayton, 1969; mem. Ohio Lottery Commn., 1983—; trustee Greater Dayton Sr. Citizens, 1984. Recipient Friendship award St. Mark's Masonic Lodge 165, 1980, Brotherhood award Upshaw African Meth. Episcopal Ch., 1983, Recognition award Fed. Women's Program, Dayton, 1981; One in a Million award Columbus 10-City Rally of Nat. Council Negro Women, 1984. Mem. Nat. Funeral Dirs. Assn., Ohio Funeral Dirs. Assn., Montgomery County Funeral Dirs. Assn., Women Bus. Owners Assn., NAACP (life), Nat. Council Negro Women (life), Delta Sigma Theta (recognition award 1981). Home and Office: 1130 Germantown St Dayton OH 45408

MCMAHAN, GARY LYNN, medical foundation executive; b. Kansas City, Mo., Mar. 2, 1948; s. Stanley Owen and Edith Evelena (Shannon) McM.; m. Kathy Sue Brockman, Mar. 28, 1970 (div. 1974); m. 2d, Mary Garold Hearn, Aug. 20, 1976; 1 dau., Terri Lee. B.A., U. Mo., 1970, M.P.A., 1973. Sr. program planner Bendix Corp., Kansas City, Mo., 1971-73; project adminstr. U. Mo., Kansas City, 1973-79; exec. v.p. Acad. Health Profls., 1979-80, Family Health Found. Am., 1980—. Bd. sec. AAFP-MDIS Inc., 1981—. Author: An Evaluation Profile: Summary of the Evaluation Activities of the Individual Area Health Education Centers, 1977. Mem. task force Mo. Govs. Task Force on Rural Health, Jefferson City, 1978; bd. dirs., treas. Jackson County Bd. Services for the Developmentally Disabled, Kansas City, 1981—, pres., 1985—; bd. dirs. Shepherd Ctr., Kansas City. Mem. Mid Am. Soc. Assn. Execs., Soc. Tchrs. Family Medicine, N.Am. Primary Care Research Group, Nat. Soc. Fund Raising Execs. Home: 805 Burning Tree Lee's Summit MO 64063 Office: Family Health Found Am 1740 W 92d St Kansas City MO 64114

MCMAHON, ELIZABETH ANN, marketing and communications executive; b. San Francisco; d. William Francis McMahon and Jane (Leuenberger) McMahon Kincaid. BA in Polit. Sci., Ohio Wesleyan U., 1967; MBA, NYU, 1975. Mgmt. trainee Unilever, Ltd., London, 1968-69; mgr. mktg. and products Nabisco Brands, Hanover, N.J., 1969-76; account mgr. Wells, Rich, Greene, N.Y.C., 1976-79; dir. consumer advt. Chase Manhatten Bank, N.Y.C., 1979-82; account mgr. Bozell & Jacobs, Mpls., 1982-84; mgr. mktg. communications, consumer products group 3M Co., St. Paul, 1984—; cons. HHM Assocs., Mpls., 1984—. Active Jr. League, Mpls., 1978—; bd. mgrs. N.Y.C., 1978—, bd. dirs. Mpls. Council Girl Scouts Am., 1984—; bd. dirs. Mpls. Crisis Nursery, Mpls., 1983—. Mem. Advt. Fedn., Pi Sigma Alpha, Delta Gamma. Avocations: writing, sports. Office: 3M Co 3M Ctr Bldg 223-45-01 Saint Paul MN 55144-1000

MCMAHON, JIM (JAMES ROBERT), professional football player; b. Jersey City, Aug. 21, 1959; m. Nancy McMahon; children: Ashley, Sean. Student, Brigham Young U. Profl. football player Chgo. Bears, NFL, 1982—. Mem. Chgo. Bears NFL Championship Team, 1985. Player NFL Pro Bowl, 1986. Office: Chgo Bears 55 E Jackson Blvd Suite 1200 Chicago IL 60604 *

MCMANAMAN, KENNETH CHARLES, lawyer, judge, educator, naval officer; b. Fairfield, Calif., Jan. 25, 1950; s. Charles James and Frances J. (Holys) McM.; m. Carol Ann Wilson, Apr. 15, 1972; children—Evan John, Kinsey Bridget, Kierin Rose. B.A. cum laude, S.E. Mo. State U., 1972; J.D., U. Mo.-Kansas City, 1974; grad. Naval Justice Sch., Newport, RI., 1975; M.S. in Bus. Mgmt. summa cum laude, Troy State U., Montgomery, Ala., 1978. Bar: Mo. 1975, U.S. Dist. Ct. (we. dist.) Mo. 1975, U.S. Dist. Ct. (ea. Dist.) Mo. 1978, Fla. 1976, U.S. Dist. Ct. (no., mid. dists.) Fla. 1976, U.S. Ct. Mil. Appeals 1977, U.S. Ct. Appeals (5th, 8th cirs.) 1977, U.S. Supreme Ct. 1978, Ill. 1987. Ptnr. firm O'Loughlin, O'Loughlin & McManaman, Cape Girardeau, Mo., 1978—; prof. bus. law Troy State U., Ala., 1976-78; prof. bus. law S.E. Mo. State U., Cape Girardeau, 1978-84; instr. law Mo. Dept. Pub. Safety, S.E. Mo. Regional Law Enforcement Tng. Acad., 1979—; instr. law Cape Girardeau Police Res., 1983—; mcpl. judge City of Jackson, Mo., 1980—; spl. mcpl. judge City of Cape Girardeau, 1981—. Mem. Cape Girardeau County Council on Child Abuse, 1980-81; membership dir. S.E. Mo. Scouting council Boy Scouts Am., 1980-82; mem. Cape Girardeau County Mental Health Assn., 1982—; active local and state Dem. Party, del. Nat. Dem. Conv., San Francisco, 1984, chmn. County Dem. Com., 1984-86; mem. 8th Congl. Dist. Dem. Com., 1984-86, 27th State Dem. Senatorial Com., 1984-86; bd. dirs. Areawide Task Force on Drug and Alcohol Abuse, 1984—. Served to lt. JAGC, USN, 1975, lt. commdr. USNR, 1981—. Named One of Outstanding Young Men of Am. 1981, 82, 84, 85. Mem. ABA (Mo. del. for young lawyers div. 1982-83), Mo. Bar Assn. (chmn. trial advocacy task force 1982, psychology and the law task force 1983), Mo. Bar (young lawyers sect. council, rep. dist. 13, 1980-85), Fla. Bar Assn., Kansas City Bar Assn., Assn. Trial Lawyers Am., Fed. Bar Assn., Nat. Coll. Dist. Attys., Cape Girardeau County Bar Assn. (founder, pres. young lawyers sect. 1981-82), Mo. Mcpl. and Assoc. Cir. Judges Assn., Naval Res. Assn. (v.p. Southeast Mo.-So. Ill. chpt. 1980-85), Southeast Mo. State U. Alumni Council, Sigma Chi (numerous awards), Sigma Tau Delta, Pi Delta Epsilon. Roman Catholic. Home: 1135 Shawnee Jackson MO 63755 Office: O'Loughlin O'Loughlin & McManaman 1736 N Kingshighway Cape Girardeau MO 63701

MCMANAMON, JOHN THOMAS, management consultant; b. Cleve., Dec. 14, 1938; s. John J. and Cathrine B. (Bauman) McM.; m. Donna M. Pahoresky; children: Daniel, Patricia, Mary, Timothy. BS, John Carroll Coll., 1961; postgrad. in Bus., Case Western Res. U., 1964. Mfg. co-ordinator Sherwin Williams, Cleve., 1966-68; cons. Peat, Marwick & Mitchell, Cleve., 1968-69; Datalogics, Cleve., 1969-70; dir. mgmt. info. systems Mid-continent Telephone, Hudson, Ohio, 1970-83, v.p. cons. Alltel Corp., Hudson, 1983— ; bd. dirs. Alltel Middle East, Dammam, Saudi Arabia, McKee & Assocs., Washington. Republican. Roman Catholic. Avocations: boating; traveling. Home: 148 Bayberry Dr Northfield OH 44067 Office: Alltel Corp 100 Executive Pkwy Hudson OH 44236

MCMANUS, DARCY DIANE EDGERTON, lawyer; b. Waterloo, Iowa, Mar. 27, 1951; d. Edward Keith Edgerton and Margaret Miriam (Frost) Edgerton Morton; m. Douglas Brien McManus, Aug. 12, 1972; children: Matthew Keith, Bradley David, Daniel Burton. BA, Macalester Coll., 1972; JD with honors, U. S.D., 1975. Bar: S.D. 1976, U.S. Dist. Ct. (ea. dist.) S.D. 1976, Wis. 1978. Law clk. S.D. 2d Cir. Ct., Sioux Falls, 1976-77; assoc. Morton D. Newald, S.C., Milw., 1978-84, Grady Law Office, Port Washington, 1984—. Bd. dirs., treas. Community Learning Cr., Inc., Port Washington, Wis., 1981-83; treas. First Congl. Ch., United Ch. of Christ, Port Washington, 1982-84; bd. dirs. United Way of Port Washington-Saukville, 1984—, campaign chmn., 1986-87. Nat. Merit scholar Macalester Coll., 1969; campaign chair United Way Pt. Wash., Saulkville, 1986-87. Mem. State Bar S.D., State Bar Wis., ABA, Ozaukee County Bar Assn., LWV, P.E.O. Democrat. Home: 308 E Whitefish Rd Port Washington WI 53074 Office: Grady Law Office 114 E Main Port Washington WI 53074

MC MANUS, ROBERT LEE, marketing services executive; b. Carmi, Ill., Dec. 3, 1923; s. Merle LeRoy and Laura Marie (Dissman) McM.; B.A., U. Ill., 1950; children—Laurie Ann McManus Kammerer, Katharine Sue, Bridgit Kathleen. Sales engr. James L. Lyon Co., Chgo., 1951-56; pres., R.L. McManus & Co., Peoria, Ill., 1956-65; dir. project devel. John Hackler & Co., architects, Peoria, Ill., 1966-80; corp. mktg. dir. Beling Cons. Inc., 1980—; treas. Prairie State Legal Services Corp., 1977-79, v.p., 1979-80, pres., 1980-81. Pres., Greater Peoria (Ill.) Legal Aid Soc., 1972-74, Central Ill. Agy. on Aging, 1972-75; chmn. Comprehensive Geriatric Treatment Service, 1972-75; chmn. Mayor's Commn. on Aging, 1975—; pres., Sr. Citizens Found., Inc., 1972-78. Served with USAAF, 1941-43. Fellow Constrn. Specifications Inst. (bd. dirs., region dir. 1980-83, pres. Central Ill. chpt. 1973-75, chmn. inst. tech. documents com., v.p. 1984-85, pres. 1987-88, Tech. Excellence in Specification Writing award 1973, Honor award 1978, 84); mem. U. Ill. Alumni Assn. (life). Club: Creve Coeur (Peoria, Ill.). Home: 2809 12th Ave #305 Rock Island IL 61201 Office: Beling Bldg 1001 16th St Moline IL 61265

MCMARTIN, PAULA JO, public relations manager; b. Escanaba, Mich., Aug. 21, 1955. BA in Journalism, U. Wis., Eau Claire, 1977. Reporter The Daily Chronicle, DeKalb, Ill., 1977-78; assoc. editor Sporting Goods Bus., N.Y.C., 1978; sports reporter The Beloit (Wis.) Daily News, 1978-79, The Green Bay Press-Gazette, 1979-80; editor-in-chief WIBC Mag., Greendale, Wis., 1981-86; pub. relations mgr. Women's Internat. Bowling Congress, Greendale, Wis., 1986—; photographer Woman-to-Woman Conf., Milw., 1985. Active Big Bros./Big Sisters, DeKalb, 1978; task force mem. Hales Corners (Wis.) YWCA, 1985; fundraiser Am. Heart Assn., Milw., 1985-86, frigid five mktg. com., 1986-87. Mem. Pub. Relations Soc. Am., Women in Communications (local bd. dirs.), World Bowling Writers, Nat. Women Bowling Writers, Bowling Writers Assn. Am. (bd. dirs. 1986—). Roman Catholic. Avocations: sports, cooking, reading, collecting.

MCMASTERS, BILL FRIEDRICH, dentist; b. Granite City, Ill., May 15, 1951; s. William G. and Hildgard Louise (Xander) McM.; m. Shirley Dianne Means, Sept. 7, 1972 (div. Jan. 1981); 1 child, Jennifer Dianne; m. Sandra R. Reisner, Jan. 17, 1981; 1 child, Tamara J. BS in Zoology, So. Ill. U., 1973; BS in Dentistry, U. Ill., Chgo., 1975, DDS, 1977; emergency med. technician, Scott AFB, Rantoul, Ill., 1978. Dental dir. Champaign-Urbana (Ill.) Pub. Health Dist., 1977-79; gen. practice dentistry Granite City, 1979—; cons. Colonnades Nursing Home, Granite City, 1979—. Merit badge counselor Boy Scouts Am., 1982—; Sunday sch. dir. Emmanuel Bapt. Ch., Granite City, 1984—; trustee Madison County Bapt. Assn., Granite City, 1986, mem. credential com., 1986—. Mem. ADA, Madison Dist. Dental Soc. Republican. Avocations: wood carving, gardening. Home: 2105 Lynch Ave Granite City IL 62040

MCMENAMIN, MICHAEL TERRENCE, lawyer, author; b. Akron, Ohio, Nov. 11, 1943; s. John Joseph and Maxine Ann (Lipp) McM.; m. Carol Anne Breckenridge, June 27, 1967; children—Kathleen Heather, Colleen Cara, Patrick Rankin. B.A. with honors in Polit. Sci., Western Res. U., 1965; LL.B., U. Pa., 1968. Bar: Ohio 1968, U.S. Dist. Ct. (no. dist.) Ohio 1969, U.S. Ct. Appeals (6th cir.) 1971, U.S. Supreme Ct. 1981, U.S. Ct. Appeals (3d and 4th cirs.) 1986. Assoc. Walter, Harverfield, Buescher & Chockley, Cleve., 1968-74, ptnr., 1975—. Co-author: Milking the Public: Political Scandals of the Dairy Lobby from LBJ to Jimmy Carter, 1980. Contbg. editor Inquiry Mag., 1980-84, Reason Mag., 1983—. Trustee Fairmont Montessori Assn., 1979-87 , sec., 1979-80, 81-82, treas., 1980-81, pres., 1982-85; trustee, sec. Inst. for Child Advocacy, 1977-80; active Citizens League Greater Cleve., 1968—, Council for a Competitive Economy, 1981—. Served to 1st lt. USAR, 1968-74. Mem. ABA, Ohio State Bar Assn., Greater Cleve. Bar Assn., Amnesty Internat. Home: 3386 Ingleside Rd Shaker Heights OH 44122 Office: 1215 Terminal Tower Cleveland OH 44113

MCMICHAEL, JEANE CASEY, real estate corporation executive; b. Jeffersonville, Ind., May 7, 1938; d. Emmett Ward and Carrie Evelyn (Leonard) Casey; m. Norman Kenneth Wenzler, Sept. 12, 1956 (div. 1968); m. Wilburn Arnold McMichael, June 20, 1978. Student Ind. U. Extension Ctr., Bellermine Coll., 1972-73, Ind. U. S.E., 1973—, Kentuckiana Metroversity, 1981—; Grad. Realtors Inst., Ind. U., 1982. Lic. real estate salesman, broker, Ind.; real estate broker, Ky. Owner, pres. McMichael Real Estate, Inc., Jeffersonville, 1979—; mgr., broker Bass & Weisberg Realtors, Jeffersonville, Ind., 1984—. Pres., Mr. and Mrs. class St. Mark's United Ch. of Christ; chmn. social com. Republican party Clark County (Ind.). Recipient cert. of appreciation Nat. Ctr. Citizen Involvement, 1983; award Contact Kentuckiana Teleministries, 1978. Mem. Nat. Assn. Realtors, Ind. Assn. Realtors (state dir.), Nat. Women's Council Realtors (pres. chpt., chmn. coms.; state rec. sec., 1984, state pres. 1985-86, Nat. Achievement award 1982, 83, 84; nat. gov. Ind. 1987; v.p. region III 1988, Ind. Honor Realtor award 1982, 83, 84, 85, 86), Ky. Real Estate Exchange, So. Ind. Bd. Realtors (program chmn. 1986-87, bd. dir., pres. elect. 1987, Realtor of Yr. 1985), Psi Iota Xi. Democrat. Office: Bass & Weisberg Realtors 1713 E 10th St Jeffersonville IN 47130

MCMILIN, EDWARD MULIN, facilities planner; b. Jenkintown, Pa., May 19, 1947; s. Alfred and Marjorie Ruth (McNaughton) Pfeiffer; divorced; children: Edward Jr., Maureen Ann. AA, Kansas City (Kans.) Community Jr. Coll., 1967; BArch, Kans. State U., 1971, M of Community and Regional Planning, 1973. Research asst. regional planning com. Kans. Ozarks Project Kans. State U., Manhattan, 1971-72, data analyst office univ. devel. and capital constrn., 1972-73; ednl. facilities planner dept. facilities planning and adminstrv. research Milw. Pub. Schs., 1973-82, acting dir. dept. facilities planning and adminstrv. research, 1982-83, facilities planner div. planning and long-range devel., 1983—; conf. presenter Council Ednl. Facility Planners, Milw., 1979, Orlando, Fla., 1983, San Jose, Calif., 1985, Nashville, 1986, Nat. Assn. Secondary Sch. Prins., Chgo., 1978. Author numerous ednl. specifications documents, enrollment analyses; sch. bldg. and sites plan for Milw. Pub. Schs., 1986-96; designer replacement facilities, remodeling projects numerous Milw.-area schs. Served to maj. USAR, 1972—. Mem. Internat. Facilities Mgmt. Assn. (pres. Milw. chpt. 1986), Am. Planning Assn., Internat. Council Facility Planners (chmn. metro planners group 1982—, local arrangements com. Gt. Lakes Regional Conf. 1985, pres. elect nominating com. 1985, pres. elect 1985, pres. Gt. Lakes region 1984-85, planner of yr. jury 1986), Res. Officers Assn., Kans. State U. Alumni Assn. (life). Methodist. Avocations: golf, basketball. Office: Milw Pub Schs PO Drawer 10K Milwaukee WI 53201

MCMILLAN, DRUERY WILBUR, electrical engineer, supervisor; b. St. Louis, Aug. 16, 1941; s. Alvin Taylor and Louise Genevieve (George) McM.; m. Mary Donna Collins, Nov. 21, 1965 (div. June 1978); children: Matthew Taylor, Matthias Alburt Wiley. BS in Math. and Indsl. Arts, No. Mo. State U., 1974; BEE, U. Mo., Rolla, 1976. Elec. engr. The Maytag Co., Newton, 1976-78, supr. instrumentation, 1978-81, supr. electronic engring., 1981-85, supr. elec. engring., 1985—. Designer one of first asynchronious hoist systems, 1978, one of fisrt computerized pickle machines, 1980. Clubs: Maytag Mgmt. (Newton), Maytag Speech (pres. 1984-85). Lodge: Order Golden Shillelagh. Avocations: world economics, oil painting, poetry, home computers. Home: 1315 W 8th St N Newton IA 50208 Office: The Maytag Co 403 W 4th St N Newton IA 50208

MCMILLAN, HAROLD LESLIE, food products company executive; b. Decatur, Ill., Nov. 12, 1952; s. Harold Everett and Dorothy Ellen (Lindley) McM.; m. Kathryn Ann Dressen, May 20, 1983; children: Ashley Nicole, Seth Andrew, Jacob Evan. BS, Millikin U., 1975. Quality control technician Archer Daniels Midland, Decatur, 1976-77, shift supr., 1977-81, prodn. mgr., 1981—. Mem. Am. Oil Chemists Soc., Decatur Jaycees (bd. dirs. 1979-80, Chmn. of Month 1978, Outstanding Com. Chmn. 1978-83). Democrat. Presbyterian. Avocations: detailed model assembly, racquetball, reading, bicycling. Home: 1151 N Sunnyside Rd Decatur IL 62522 Office: Archer Daniels Midland 4666 Faries Pkwy Decatur IL 62526

MCMILLAN, JAMES ALBERT, electronics engr., educator; b. Lewellen, Nebr., Feb. 6, 1926; s. William H. and Mina H. (Taylor) McM.; B.S. in Elec. Engring., U. Wash., 1951; M.S. in Mgmt., Rensselaer Poly. Inst., 1965; m. Mary Virginia Garrett, Aug. 12, 1950; children—Michael, James, Yvette, Ramelle, Robert. Commd. 2d lt. U.S. Air Force, 1950, advanced through grades to lt. col., 1970; jet fighter pilot Columbus AFB, Miss., Webb AFB, Tex., 1951-52, Nellis AFB, Nev., 1953, McChord AFB., Wash., 1953-54; electronic maintenance supr. Lowry AFB, Colo., 1954, Forbes AFB, Kans., 1954-56, also in U.K., 1956-59; electronic engr., program dir. Wright-Patterson AFB, Ohio, 1959-64; facilities dir. Air Force Aero Propulsion Lab., Wright-Patterson AFB, 1965-70, ret., 1970; instr., div. chmn. Chesterfield-Marlboro Tech. Coll., S.C., 1971-75; asst. prof., 1977, assoc. prof., chmn. indsl. programs Maysville (Ky.) Community Coll., 1976—, prof., 1986— ; cons. mgmt. and electronic maintenance, 1970—. Served with U.S. Army, 1943-45. Mem. IEEE (sr.), Soc. Mfg. Engrs. (sr.), Nat. Rifle Assn. (life), Sigma Xi (life). Republican. Presbyterian (elder). Clubs: Rotary, Masons (32 deg.), Shriners. Author: A Management Survey, 1965. Home: 6945 Scoffield Rd Ripley OH 45167

MCMILLAN, LEON, investment analyst; b. Detroit, Mar. 28, 1937; s. Lyle and Grace I. (Gardner) McM.; B.S., Wayne State U., Detroit, 1960; M.B.A., N.Y. U., 1961; m. Phyllis A. Nevitt, July 3, 1961. Trainee, Thomson & McKinnon Co., N.Y.C., 1961-63; investment analyst Nat. Bank Detroit, 1963-65, First Mich. Corp., 1965-66, Robert W. Baird Co., Milw., 1966-67; sr. investment analyst Supervised Investors Services, Chgo., 1967-71, Lincoln Nat. Investment Mgmt. Co., Chgo., 1971-81; sr. investment analyst trust dept. Continental Ill. Bank, Chgo., 1981-84; sr. investment analyst Marksmen Mgmt. & Research, North Brook, Ill., 1984—. Mem. Investment Analysts Soc. Chgo., Am. Stock Exchange Club, Old English Sheepdog Club Am. Home: 480 Lee Rd Northbrook IL 60062

MCMILLAN, MARGARET LANGSTAFF, librarian; b. Eaglegroove, Iowa; d. Harry C. and Elizabeth Louise (Tryon) McM.. BS, Cen. Mo. State U., 1921; MS, U. Mo., 1923; postgrad., U. Neuchatel, Switzerland, 1947. Dir. ibrary Columbia (Mo.) Coll., 1926-59; librarian Mo. State Hist. Soc., Columbia, 1959-60; ref. librarian Mid Continent Library Service, Independence, Mo., 1961-76; dir. library Kingswood Manor, Kansas City, Mo., 1982—; mem. faculty summer sessions Cen. Mo. State U., Warrensburg, Northwest Mo. State Coll., Maryville, U. Mo., Columbia; speaker various local groups. Recipient Pioneer Sprit award, 1985. Mem. State Hist. Soc., Pi Lambda Theta, Delta Kappa Gamma. Republican. Methodist. Club: Women's City (Kansas City). Home: 10000 Wornall Rd Apt #3101 Kansas City MO 64114

MCMILLAN, S. STERLING, economist, horse breeder; b. Cleve., June 28, 1907; s. S. Sterling McMillan and Ruth McMillan Strong; m. Elizabeth Harman Mather, Oct. 9, 1937; children: S. Sterling, Madeleine McMillan Offutt, Elizabeth, Katharine McMillan Farrand. AB, Princeton U., 1929; MBA, Harvard U., 1932; PhD, Ind. U., 1948. Security analyst No. Trust Co., Chgo., 1933-35; sec.-treas., bd. dirs., Strong, Cobb and Co., Cleve., 1935-42; regional price economist, Washington, 1942, Chgo., 1942-45; instr. Ind. U., Bloomington, 1945-47; from asst. prof. to prof. Western Res. U., Cleve. (name Case Western Res. U. 1967), 1947-69; dir. indsl. econs. div. Nat. Prodn. Authority, Washington, 1951-52; founder, chmn. bd. dirs. Predicasts, Inc., Cleve., 1960-81; farmer, horsebreeder Mountain Glen Farm, Stable, Mentor, Ohio, 1961—; chmn. Cleve. Forum Community Devel., 1964-65; mem. Ohio Crime Commn., 1967-69; cons. Nat. Planning Assn., NSF Oceanics Project, 1967-68. Author: Individual Firm Adjustments under OPA, 1949, The Growth of Civilian Atomic Energy, 1968, Case Studies of Government Cooperation in Founding New Industries, 1970; contbr. articles to profl. jours. Active Children's Aid Soc., 1953—, Ctr. Human Services, Cleve., 1970—, Welfare Fedn. Cleve. Fedn. for Community Planning, United Way, Cleve., others. Recipient Vol. of Yr. award United Torch Services, 1974. Mem. Am. Econs. Assn., Royal Econs. Soc., Am. Fin. Assn., Midwest Econs. Assn. (v.p. 1954-55), Nat. Assn. Bus. Economists, AAUP (past officer), Beta Gamma Sigma. Episcopalian. Clubs: Union, Rowfant (Cleve.); Kirtland Country (Willoughby, Ohio); Rolling Rock (Ligonier, Pa.). Home and Office: Mountain Glen Farm 10401 Griswold Rd Mentor OH 44060

MCMILLIAN, THEODORE, federal judge; b. St. Louis, Jan. 28, 1919; m. Minnie E. Foster, Dec. 8, 1941. B.S., Lincoln U., 1941, H.H.D. (hon.), 1981; LL.D., St. Louis U., 1949; H.H.D. (hon.), U. Mo., St. Louis, 1978. Mem. firm Lynch & McMillian, St. Louis, 1949-53; asst. circuit atty. City of St. Louis, 1953-56; judge U.S. Ct. Appeals (8th cir.), 1978—; judge Circuit Ct. for City St. Louis, 1956-72, Mo. Ct. Appeals eastern div., 1972-78; asso. prof. adminstrn. justice U. Mo., St. Louis, 1970—; asso. prof. Webster Coll. Grad. Program, 1977; mem. faculty Nat. Coll. Juvenile Justice, U. Nev., 1972—. Served to 1st lt. Signal Corps U.S. Army, 1942-46. Recipient Alumni Merit award St. Louis U., 1965. Mem. Lawyers Assn., Mo., Mound City bar assns., Am. Judicature Soc., Phi Beta Kappa, Alpha Sigma Nu. Office: US Courthouse 1114 Market St Room 526 Saint Louis MO 63101 and: US Court of Appeals US Ct & Customs House Saint Louis MO 63101 *

MCMINN, RONALD EMERSON, sports association executive; b. Hamilton, Ont., Can., Sept. 13, 1921; came to U.S., 1921; s. Rex Bruce and Janet (Comerford) McM.; m. Irene Audry Smith, Dec. 28, 1948. Grad. high sch., Detroit. Fireman Detroit Fire Dept., 1946-71; v.p. Detroit Amateur Baseball Fedn., 1958-66, Nat. Amateur Baseball Fedn., 1959-64; exec. dir. Nat. Amateur Baseball Fedn., Rose City, Mich., 1964—. Mem. U.S. Olympic baseball commn., 1966. Served with USNR, 1943-45, PTO. Inducted into Mich. Amateur Sports Hall Fame, 1976; recipient Derby City award Derby City Baseball Assn., Louisville, 1980, Service award, 1985 and W.P. "Dutch" Fehring award of Merit, 1987 U.S. Baseball Fedn., 1985. Mem. Detroit Firemen's Fund Assn. (trustee 1954-69, sec. 1956, 69, pres., 1960, 65). Lodges: Masons, Shriners. Home and Office: 2201 N Townline Rd Rose City MI 48654

MCMULLEN, FRANK D., JR., chamber of commerce executive. Pres. Greater Omaha C. of C., Omaha, Neb. Office: Greater Omaha C of C 1301 Harney St Omaha NE 68102 *

MCMULLEN, JAMES ROBERT, research microbiologist; b. Clinton, Ind., May 22, 1942; s. Robert LeRoy and Elsie Pauline (Buckler) McM.; m. Suetta Rae Brown, July 24, 1964; 1 son, Patrick James. B.S., Ind. State U., Terre Haute, 1964; M.S., U. Wis., 1966. Microbiologist, Comml. Solvents Corp., Terre Haute, summer 1964, research microbiologist, 1966-75; research microbiologist Internat. Minerals and Chem. Corp., Terre Haute, 1975—. Adviser, Jr. Achievement Wabash Valley, 1970; bd. dirs. v.p. Internat. Minerals and Chem. Fed. Credit Union, 1978-84. Mem. Am. Soc. Microbiology, Sigma Xi. Republican. Methodist. Club: Lost Creek Conservation. Lodges: Elks, Masons. Contbr. articles to profl. jours.; patentee process for producing zearalenone, 1972, microbiol. reduction of zearalenone, 1977. Home: 236 Van Buren Blvd Terre Haute IN 47803 Office: 1331 S 1st St Terre Haute IN 47808

MCMULLIN, JEFFREY SCOTT, manufacturing executive; b. LaCrosse, Wis., Apr. 8, 1947; s. Roger E. and Ethel S. (Van Sickle) McM; m. Cathy A. McLauchlan, Dec. 30, 1975; 1 child, Bejon. BS, U. Wis., Platteville, 1970. Dir. purchasing Alpine Enterprises, Ft. Collins, Colo., 1970-74; group leader engring. Teledyne Water Pik, Ft. Collins, 1975-78; instr. Larimer Tech., Ft. Collins, 1978-81; mgr. new ventures Robbins & Meyers, Memphis, 1981-82; v.p. engring. Metal Ware Corp., Two Rivers, Wis., 1982-83; bus. unit mgr. Streater div. Joyce, Albert Lea, Minn., 1983—. Councilman City of Loveland, Colo., 1976-80. Home: 935 Range St North Mankato MN 56001 Office: Streater div Joyce 411 S First Ave Albert Lea MN 56007

MC MURRIN, LEE RAY, educational administrator; b. Ind., June 29, 1930; s. Albert R. and Myrtle E. (Brickley) McM.; m. Frances, Aug. 19, 1956; children: Michelle, Marianne, Marshall. B.S. in Secondary Edn, Olivet Coll., Kankakee, Ill., 1952; M.Ed., U. Cin., 1955; postgrad., Miami U., Oxford, Ohio, 1955, Kent State U., 1957, Ohio State U., 1958-65; Ph.D., U. Toledo, 1971. Elem. tchr. Sharonville (Ohio) Schs., 1952-55; prin., elem. supr. Leetonia (Ohio) Schs., 1955-58; asst. supt. Dover City (Ohio) Schs., 1958-60, South-Western City Schs., Grove City, Ohio, 1960-65; asst. supt. Toledo Pub. Schs., 1965-71, dep. supt., 1971-75; supt. schs. Milw. Pub. Schs., 1975—; past pres., mem. Council Gt. City Schs.; mem. partnership coordinating com. Univ. Council on Ednl. Adminstrn.; bd. dirs. Wis. State Council Econ. Edn., Joint Council Econ. Edn. Mem. corp. bd. Milw. Children's Hosp., Milw. Symphony Orch.; bd. dirs. NCCJ, Milw., Jr. Achievement Southeastern Wis. Served with inf. U.S. Army, 1953-55. Mem. Am. Assn. Sch. Adminstrs., Wis. Assn. Sch. Dist. Adminstrs., Assn. Supervision and Curriculum Devel., Large City Supts. Group, Nat. Sch. Bds. Assn., NAACP, Phi Delta Kappa. Methodist. Clubs: Rotary (dir.), Kiwanis. Home: 3435 N Lake Dr Milwaukee WI 53211 Office: 5225 W Vliet St PO Drawer 10K Milwaukee WI 53201

MCMURRY, WILLIAM SCOTT, allied health educator; b. Poteau, Okla., Apr. 10, 1921; s. Ulysses Scott and Syntha Alice (McDonald) McM.; m. Kathryn Elizabeth Robison, Feb. 2, 1946. BS, N.E. U., Okla., 1942; DDS, U. Mo., 1950, MS, 1966; PhD, Columbia Pacific U., 1983. Commd. 2d lt., U.S. Air Force, 1941, advanced through grades to lt. col., 1963; ret., 1969; assoc. chief of staff edn. VA, Dayton, Ohio, 1973-79; asst. dean veterans affairs Wright State Med. Sch., 1975-79; ret., 1979; adj. prof. St. Petersburg (Fla.) Jr. Coll., 1967-73, Ohio State U., 1973-79; assoc. prof. allied health So. Ill. U., 1979—. Fellow Am. Assn. Oral and Maxillofacial Surgeons (ret.), Internat. Assn. Oral and Maxillofacial Surgeons; mem. Council Occupational Edn., Midwestern Oral Surgeons, Okla. State Dental Assn., Ill. Police Assn., Ret. Officers Assn., Assn. Mil. Surgeons, Assn. Ret. Fed. Employees, Air Force Assn. Republican. Lodges: Masons, Lions, Elks. Contbr. articles to profl. jours. Office: So Ill U STC Bldg Suite 118-A Carbondale IL 62901

MCNAIR, ROBERT LEE, sociology and anthropology educator; b. Norfolk, Va., June 13, 1938; s. Robert Gassaway and Iris Deane (Hart) McN.; m. Patricia Florentine Hogan, Sept. 9, 1985; children: Lisa Christine, David Lee. AS, St. Joseph (Mo.) Jr. Coll., 1958; BA, U. Mo., 1962, MA, 1970. Instr. Trenton (Mo.) Jr. Coll., 1966-67, Highlands U., Las Vegas, N.Mex., 1967-69; asst. prof. Henderson (Ky.) Community Coll., 1969-73; assoc. prof. Mt. Senario Coll., Ladysmith, Wis., 1973-82; instr. sociology and anthropology Des Moines Area Community Coll., Boone, Iowa, 1982—, chmn. dept. social scis., 1983—; contract archeologist, Boone and Ladysmith, Iowa, 1982—. Dem. vol., Las Vegas and Henderson, 1968-72; mem. Rusk County Citizen's Action Group, Ladysmith, 1976-78. Served to sgt. USNG, 1959-65, 78—. Mem. Iowa Sociologists, Anthropologists in Community Colls., Sociology Club, Social Action Club, Phi Theta Kappa. Methodist. Lodge: Rotary. Home: 416 S Greene Boone IA 50036 Office: Des Moines Area Community Coll Boone Campus Boone IA 50036

MCNAIR, RUSSELL ARTHUR, JR., lawyer; b. Detroit, Dec. 2, 1934; s. Russell Arthur and Virla (Standish) McN.; m. Rosemary M. Chesbrough, Apr. 6, 1957; children: Julie McNair Schwerin, Russell Arthur III, Douglas S. AB in Econs. cum laude, Princeton U., 1956; JD with distinction, U. Mich., 1960. Bar: Mich. 1960. Assoc. Dickinson, Wright, Moon, Van Dusen & Freeman, Detroit, 1960—, ptnr., 1968—; adj. prof. U. Detroit Sch. Law, 1968-72; speaker in field; mem. adv. bd. Fin. Transactions Inst., U. Detroit Sch. Law, 1984—. Trustee Children's Home, Detroit, 1975—, pres. 1986—. Mem. ABA, Mich. Bar Assn., Detroit Bar Assn., Am. Law Inst., Am. Coll. Real Estate Lawyers, Detroit Com. on Fgn. Relations. Republican. Presbyterian. Avocations: golf, tennis, platform tennis. Home: 308 Touraine Rd Grosse Pointe Farms MI 48236 Office: Dickinson Wright et al 800 First Nat Bldg Detroit MI 48226

MCNALLY, ANDREW, III, printer, publisher; b. Chgo., Aug. 17, 1909; s. Andrew and Eleanor (Vilas) McN.; m. Margaret Clark MacMillin, Nov. 20, 1936; children—Betty Jane, Andrew, Edward Clark. A.B., Yale U., 1931. With Chgo. factory Rand McNally & Co., 1931, N.Y. sales office v.p., dir., 1933, pres., 1948-74, chmn. bd., 1974—. Life trustee Art Inst. Chgo.; trustee Washington Crossing Found.; bd. dirs. Thousand Island Shipyard Mus.; past pres. Girl's Latin Sch., Infant Welfare Soc., Graphic Arts Tech. Found. Served as capt., C.E. Army Map Service, 1942-45. Mem. Chgo. Hist. Soc. (past pres., trustee), Geog. Soc. Chgo. (past pres.), Newberry Library Assn. (past pres.). Office: PO Box 7600 Chicago IL 60680

MCNALLY, ANDREW, IV, publishing executive; b. Chgo., Nov. 11, 1939; s. Andrew and Margaret C. (MacMillin) McN.; m. Jeanine Sanchez, July 3, 1966; children: Andrew, Carrie, Ward. B.A., U. N.C., 1963; M.B.A., U. Chgo., 1969. Bus. mgr. edn. div. Rand McNally & Co., Chgo., 1967-70; exec. v.p., sec. Rand McNally & Co., 1970-74, pres., 1974—, chief exec. officer, 1978—; bd. dirs. Harvey Hubbell Inc., First Ill. Corp., Val Pac, Inc., Graphic Arts Tech. Found. Trustee, Hill Sch., Latin Sch., Newberry Library; bd. dirs. Childrens Meml. Hosp.; mem. vis. com. of library U. Chgo. Mem. Air Force N.G., 1963-69. Mem. Young Pres. Orgn., Chgo. Map. Soc. Clubs: Chicago (Chgo.), Saddle and Cycle (Chgo.), Commonwealth (Chgo.); Glen View Golf. Home: 16 Canterbury Ct Wilmette IL 60091 Office: PO Box 7600 Chicago IL 60680

MCNALLY, EDWARD THOMAS, mfg. co. exec.; b. Pittsburg, Kans., May 28, 1914; s. Thomas Joseph and Mary Agnes (Henneberry) McN.; Ph.B. in Commerce, U. Notre Dame, 1936; postgrad. London U., 1936-37; m. Edythe Clare Williams, May 30, 1940; children: Eileen, Peggy, Thomas, Timothy, Michael, Anne. With McNally Pittsburg Mfg. Corp., 1937-43, 46—, treas., 1946-55, pres., 1955-76, chmn. bd., 1976—; dir. Commerce Bancshares Corp., Kansas City, Mo., Kansas City So. Industries Inc. (Mo.), McNally Bharat Engring. Co., Calcutta, India, Monarch Cement Co., Humboldt, Kans.; occasional lectr. bus. Pittsburg State U. Mem. adv. bd. Sch. Bus., Pittsburg State U.; trustee Mt. Carmel Hosp., Pittsburg. Served to lt. (j.g.) Supply Corps, USN, 1943-46. Named Disting. Alumni, Mo. Mil. Acad., 1969, Kans. Businessman of Year, 1974, Kansan of Year, 1975. Mem. Am. Mining Congress (pres. mfrs. div. 1960-61), Soc. Mining Engrs., Pittsburg C. of C. (pres. 1952-54). Republican. Roman Catholic. Clubs: K.C., Crestwood Country. Contbr. articles on coal to profl. publs. Office: Mc Nally Pittsburg Inc 100 N Pine St Pittsburg KS 66762

MCNALLY, REBECCA ANN, management consultant; b. Detroit, Feb. 24, 1946; d. Myron Allen and Eleanor Kathaleen (Renfroe) Wilson; m. John R. McNally, Mar. 19, 1973; 1 child, Amy Yvonne. Student, Sinclair Coll., 1975-77. With media accounts payable Marsteller, Inc., Chgo., 1967-70; office adminstr. Fairlane Assocs., Dearborn, Mich., 1970-73; real estate salesperson J.M. Kingston Realty, Dayton, Ohio, 1975-79; media coordinator Rushmore Sch., Dayton, 1979-84; comptroller Dyna-Graphics Corp., Eden Prairie, Minn., 1984-87; cons. to mgmt. Stenberg-Gruetzmacher, Mpls., 1987—; women's image cons., Mpls., 1984—; bus. systems cons., Mpls., 1985—. Writer, producer ednl. TV programs, 1981-83. Advisor 4-H Clubs of Am., Ohio and Minn., 1974—; county sec. 4-H Clubs of Am., Greene County, Ohio, 1976-79; troop leader Girl Scouts Am., Dayton, 1979-80; bd. dirs. Wright-Patterson Officers' Wives Clubs, Dayton, 1975-76. Recipient Award of Recognition 4-H Clubs of Am., 1980, Cert. of Appreciation Rushmore Sch., 1983, Community Service award Eden Prairie High Sch., 1985. Mem. Am. Mgmt. Assn. Avocations: horseback riding, golf, music, reading, needlework.

MCNAMAR, DAVID FRED, lawyer; b. Terre Haute, Ind., Mar. 26, 1940; s. Fred Leslie and Frances May (Sachs) McN.; m. Ann Brewer, June 22, 1963; children: Richard Philip, Eric Christopher, Gregory David. BS, Purdue U., 1962; JD, Ind. U., 1968. Bar: Ind. 1968, U.S. Dist. Ct. (no. and so. dists.) Ind. 1968, U.S. Tax Ct. 1968, U.S. Ct. Appeals (7th cir.) 1969, U.S. Supreme Ct. 1974. Ptnr. Steers, Sullivan, McNamar & Rogers, Indpls.; speaker health care law Ball State U., 1978—; ptnr. R & D Partnership, Indpls.; sec., bd. dirs. McCae Mgmt. Corp., Indpls. V.p., trustee Marion County Pub. Library, Indpls.; commr. criminal div. Marion Superior Ct. Served to capt. USNR, 1962-85. Mem. ABA, Nat. Health Lawyers Assn. (speaker), Ind. Bar Assn., Indpls. Bar Assn. (bd. dirs.), Ind. Health Care Assn. (speaker), Am. Health Care Assn. (speaker). Republican. Presbyterian. Clubs: Indpls. Country, Columbia (Indpls.); Long Cove, Sea Pines Golf (Hilton Head Island, S.C.). Lodges: Shriners, Masons. Home: 5555 Bay Colony Ln Indianapolis IN 46234 Office: Steers Sullivan McNamar & Rogers 251 E Ohio St Suite 500 2 Market Sq Ctr Indianapolis IN 46204

MCNAMARA, BARTLETT WILLIAM, dentist; b. Hudson, Wis., July 1, 1932; s. Raymond Paul and Margaret Ruth (McAndrew) McN.; m. Mary Katherine Michalke, July 9, 1955; children: Sheila, Tim, Kate, Pat, Molly, Michael, Dan. DDS, Marquette U., 1957. Gen. practice dentistry Edina, Minn., 1960—; cons. Edina Dental Learning, 1983—; dir. Acad. Gen. Dentistry Normandale Mastership Program, Bloomington, Minn., 1980-83. Served to lt. USN, 1953-60. Fellow Acad. Gen. Dentistry, Acad. Dentistry Internat.; mem. ADA, Am. Acad. Periodontology. Republican. Roman Catholic. Avocation: skiing. Home: 4629 Arden Ave Edina MN 55424 Office: 4934 Lincoln Dr Edina MN 55436

MCNAMARA, DAVID JOSEPH, financial and tax planning executive; b. Osceola, Iowa, Feb. 6, 1951; s. Loras Emmett and Nadine Evelyn (DeLancey) McN.; m. Ruth Ellen Hanken, Oct. 4, 1974; children—Benjamin, Shawna. B.G.S., U. Iowa, 1974. Cert. fin. planner Coll. Fin. Planning, 1985; registered investment advisor; registered prin. Nat. Assn. Securities Dealers. Bus. mgr. Cost Comparison Inc., Des Moines, 1975; exec. dir. Story County R.S.V.P., Story City, Iowa, 1975-77; communications asst. United Way Central Iowa, Des Moines, 1977, staff assoc., 1977-78, asst. campaign dir., 1979-81, assoc. exec. dir., 1982-85; pres. The Planners, 1985—; pres. Iowa Assn. RSVP Execs., Des Moines, 1975-76; cons. ACTION, Washington, 1976; cons. Story County Council on Aging, Nev., 1975-76; dir. Central Investments Ltd., Des Moines. Mem. Inst. Cert. Fin. Planners, Internat. Assn. Fin. Planners (bd. dirs. Iowa chpt. 1984-85). Republican.

MC NAMARA, LAWRENCE J., bishop; b. Chgo., Aug. 5, 1928; s. Lawrence and Margaret (Knusman) McN. B.A., St. Paul Sem., 1949; S.T.L., Catholic U. Am., 1953. Ordained priest Roman Catholic Ch., 1953; parish priest, tchr. Kansas City-St. Joseph Diocese, 1953-57; dir. diocesan Refugee Resettlement, 1957-60; chaplain Jackson County Jail, 1957-64; exec. dir. Campaign for Human Devel., 1973-77; bishop of Grand Island Nebr., 1978—. Recipient award Cath. Relief Services. Office: Chancery Office 311 W 17th St PO Box 996 Grand Island NE 68801 *

MCNAMARA, MICHAEL JOHN, accountant; b. Ottawa, Ill., Jan. 31, 1954; s. Wayne and Marie (Hollenbeck) McN.; m. Renee Terando, Aug. 9, 1985. BS in Acctg., Ill. State U., 1976, MBA, 1987. CPA, Ill. Acct. Wilcoxson & Assocs., Ltd., La Salle, Ill., 1976—. Bd. dirs. Horizon House Ill. Valley, Peru, 1981-86. Mem.Am. Inst. CPA's, Ill. CPA Soc. Home: 1315 26th St Peru IL 61354 Office: Wilcoxson & Assocs Ltd 206 Marquette La Salle IL 61301

MCNAMARA, PATRICK LEWIS, communications executive, marketing executive; b. Cleve., July 13, 1959; m. Susan Faux. Student, U. Strasbourg, France, 1978-79, U. Stuttgart, Fed. Republic Germany, 1979; BS in Mgmt., Purdue U., 1981; M in Mgmt., Northwestern U., 1986. Internal cons. Roberts Equipos, S.A., Arequipa, Peru, 1981-82; systems sales rep. bus. telephone div. RCA Corp., Chgo., 1982-83; analyst Mgmt. Analysis Ctr., Inc., Chgo., 1983-85; project cons. econ. devel. dept. City of Chgo., Tokyo, 1986; mktg. analyst bid and quote dept. Motorola, Inc., Schaumburg, Ill., 1986—; chairperson Motorola Mktg. Exchange, 1986—. Mem. Internat. Bus. Council Mid-Am., Internat. Acad. Bus.

MCNAMEE, JAMES, municipal official. Fire chief City of Cleve. Office: Cleveland Fire Dept Office of the Fire Chief 1645 Superior Avee Chief Cleveland OH 44114 *

MCNAUGHT, JANE KAY, psychologist, consultant; b. Moose Lake, Minn., June 28, 1950; d. Kenneth and Peggy (Billman) Cahoon; 1 child, Heather. BS, Bethel Coll., 1972; MS, U. Wis., 1975; PhD, U. Minn., 1982. Lic. cons. psychologist, Minn. Psychologist Anoka (Minn.) Schs., 1975-78, Washington County Mental Health Ctr., Oakdale, Minn., 1978-80, Michael Shea & Assocs., Mpls., 1979-83, Ctr. Adult and Child Therapy, Mpls., 1983—; cons. in field. Mem. Am. Psychol. Assn., Minn. State Psychologists Assn., Child Abuse and Neglect Assn. Democrat. Avocations: skiing, tennis, water sports, travel. Office: Ctr Adult and Child Therapy Box #408 Minneapolis MN 55406

MCNEAL JR., JAMES H., manufacturing company executive; b. 1927. BS, U. Del., 1951. V.p., gen. mgr. Armetal Industria Argentina de Metales, Argentina, 1961-65; pres. Budd Automotive Co., Can., 1965-72; with Budd Co., Troy, Mich., 1951—, v.p., 1972-73, group v.p. auto products, 1973-74, pres., 1974-80, now pres., chief exec. officer. Served with USN, 1945-46. Office: The Budd Co 3155 W Big Beaver Rd Box 2601 Troy MI 48084 *

MCNEE, ROSEMARIE, accountant; b. Chgo., Mar. 7, 1958; d. Raymond R. and Pamela E. (Hollingsworth) Benjamin; m. Trevor A. McNee, Aug. 19, 1982; children: Stephen, Omari, Ryan; stepchildren: Orett, Vakahria. BS in Acctg., U. Ill., Chgo., 1979. CPA, Ill. Bookkeeper Ill. Reproductive Health Ctr., Chgo., 1979-80; with acctg. dept. USG Corp., Chgo., 1980-82; mng. ptnr. McNee, Silvera & Fletcher Fin. Services, Chgo., 1982—; cons. in field. Active Big Bros./Big Sisters Am., Chgo., 1982—. Address: Werick Towers 5624 W Diversey Chicago IL 60639

MCNEELY, D. DEAN, accountant; b. Iron Mountain, Mich., June 1, 1944; s. Donald Lee and Margaret Elizabeth (Corrigan) McN.; m. Susan Kay Smith, Aug. 27, 1966; children: Shelley Jean, Scott Boyd, Shannon Meg. BA, Mich. State U., 1967. CPA, Calif., Mich., Wis. Staff acct. Hurdman & Cranstoun, San Francisco, 1969-71; acct., ptnr. Heruth, McNeely & Bohren, Martinez, Calif., 1971-78; pvt. practice acctg. D.D. McNeely Acctg. Corp., Walnut Creek, Calif., 1978-82; acct., ptnr. Roberts, Ritschke & McNeely, Ltd., Neenah, Wis., 1982—; instr. Profl. Edn. Systems, Inc., LaCross, Wis., 1986—. Contbr. articles to profl. jours. Bd. dirs. Walnut Creek Youth Athletic Assn., 1971-81, Paper Valley Youth Athletic Assn., Neenah, 1982—; pres. East Cen. Region Wis. Youth Soccer, Neenah, 1985—. Mem. Am. Inst. CPA's, Calif. Soc. CPA's, Wis. Inst. CPA's (instr. 1987—), Diablo Soc. CPA's (pres. 1976-77). Republican. Episcopalian. Lodges: Rotary (bd. dirs. 1987—), Masons. Office: Roberts Ritschke & McNeely Ltd PO Box 421 Neenah WI 54956

MCNEIL, DAVID LAVAN, medical association researcher; b. Chgo., Apr. 18, 1963; s. Clyde Jr. and Dorothy (Martin) McN.; m. Debra Ann Davis, May 18, 1985; children: Julie T., David Lavan II. Student, U. Ill., Chgo., 1981-84. Data analyst Am. Hosp. Assn., Chgo., 1982-85, research asst., 1986—; cons. Am. Hosp. Assn., 1985. Contbr. articles to profl. jours. Treas. Young Christian Adults, Chgo., 1984—. Named one of Outstanding Young Men of Am., 1985. Mem. United Black Seminarians (v.p. 1979—). Avocations: bowling, golf, singing, tennis, weight lifting. Home: 5816 S Loomis Chicago IL 60636 Office: Am Hosp Assn 840 N Lake Shore Dr Chicago IL 60611

MCNEIL, THOMAS EDWARD, military officer; b. Bay Shore, N.Y., Aug. 13, 1960; s. Peter Thomas and Geraldine (Zavoral) McN. BS in Applied Physics, Ga. Inst. Tech., 1982; postgrad. in engring. physics, USAF Inst. Tech., 1986. Commd. 2d lt. USAF, 1982, advanced through grades to capt., 1986; combat survivability engr. aeronautical systems div. USAF, Wright Patterson AFB, Ohio, 1982-85; physics instr. USAF Acad., Colorado Springs, Colo., 1986—. Recipient Mil. Excellence award Am. Legion, Atlanta, 1982. Mem. Air Force Assn., Beta Theta Pi (council rep. 1978-82). Republican. Club: Lacrosse (Wright Patterson AFB). Avocations: golf, world politics and history. Office: USAF AFIT/ENA Wright-Patterson AFB OH 45433

MCNEILL, ALESA JOSEPHFER, air force officer; b. Itazuke, Japan, Sept. 4, 1957; (father Am. citizen); d. Ernest George and Tokiko (Koyama) Engelhardt; m. Ron McNeill, Dec. 28, 1981. BA in Math. and Computer Sci. cum laude, Fla. State U., 1980. Commd. 2d lt. USAF, 1980, advanced through grades to capt., 1984; instr. pilot USAF, Columbus AFB, Miss., 1982-84, functional check flight instr., 1984-86; aircraft comdr. USAF, Minot AFB, N.D., 1986-87. Vol. People Aiding Disabled Students, 1975-76, Lowndes County Spl. Olympics, Columbus, 1985, Domestic Violence Crisis Ctr., Minot. Mem. Air Force Assn., Future Airline Pilots of Am., Women Mil. Pilots Assn. Club: Officers (Minot AFB). Avocations: downhill skiing, photography, reading, writing, jogging. Home: 705 23d Ave NW Minot ND 58701

MCNEILL, BRANDY RACHELE, state agency official; b. Washington, Aug. 16, 1956; d. Harold Aryai and Corrine Consuelo (Merritt) Siegel; m. Paul Spurgeon McNeill, Jr., Sept. 23, 1982. BS, Towson State U., 1979; MA, Adelphi U., 1981; cert. in exercise physiology, 1981; cert. in mental health, Shepard-Pratt Sch. Mental Health Studies, 1979; cert. phys. fitness specialist, YMCA, 1980. Trainer Sports Tng. Inst., N.Y.C., 1982; exercise physiologist N.Y. Nephrology, N.Y.C., 1982-83; supr. Printing House Fitness Ctr., N.Y.C., 1983; fitness dir. Fitness Ctr.-St. Bartholomew's Community Club, N.Y.C., 1984-85; dir. wellness programs State of Mo., Jefferson City, 1985—; exec. dir. Gov.'s Council on Physical Fitness, Jefferson City, 1985—; co-chmn. Show-Me State Games, Columbia, Mo., 1985—. Mem. AAUW, Am. Coll. Sports Medicine, Assn. Fitness and Bus., Y's Way to Physical Fitness (specialist), Bus. and Profl. Women. Republican. Jewish. Home: 1448 Satinwood Dr Jefferson City MO 65101 Office: Dir Wellness Programs Office of Adminstrn State of Mo Jefferson City MO 65101

MCNEILL, PAUL SPURGEON, JR., state official; b. St. Louis, July 20, 1948; s. Paul Spurgeon and Lucille Elizabeth (Werner) McN.; m. Brandy Rachele Siegel, Sept. 23, 1982. BS, U. Mo., 1970, JD, 1974, MBA, 1975; LLM, Washington U., St. Louis, 1978. Bar: Mo. 1974, U.S. Tax Ct. 1975. Asst. county counselor St. Louis County, 1975-76; commr. Mo. Tax Commn., Jefferson City, 1976-77; sr. mgr. Peat, Marwick, Mitchell, N.Y.C., 1977-85; dir. revenue State of Mo., Jefferson City, 1985—. Author: (with others) Administrative Law Handbook, 1978. Spl. asst. Mo. Gubernatorial Transition Commn., Jefferson City, 1979-80. Mem. ABA, Mo. Bar Assn., Bar Assn. Met. St. Louis, Am. Assn. CPA's, Mo. Soc. CPA's, Lambda Chi Alpha. Republican. Lutheran. Avocation: sailing. Home: 1448 Satinwood Dr Jefferson City MO 65101 Office: State of Missouri Dir Revenue PO Box 311 Jefferson City MO 65105

MCNEILL, ROBERT PATRICK, investment counselor; b. Chgo., Mar. 17, 1941; s. Donald Thomas and Katherine (Bennett) McN.; m. Martha Stephan, Sept. 12, 1964; children—Jennifer, Donald, Victoria, Stephan, Elizabeth. B.A. summa cum laude (valedictorian), U. Notre Dame, 1963; M.Letters, Oxford U., 1967. Chartered investment counselor. Assoc. Stein Roe & Farnham, Chgo., 1967-72, gen. ptnr., 1972-77, sr. ptnr., 1977-86, exec. v.p., 1986—; underwriting mem. Lloyds of London, 1980—; dir. Comml. Chgo. Corp.; vice chmn. bd. Hill Internat. Prodn. Co., Houston, 1982—; dir., adv. bd. Touche Remnant Investment Counselors, London, 1983—. Voting mem., sec Ill. Rhodes Scholarship Selection Com.; voting mem. Ill. rep. Great Lakes Dist. Rhodes Scholarship Selection Com.; bd. dirs. Kennedy Sch. for Retarded Children, Palos Park, Ill., 1972—, Winnetka United Way, Ill., 1984—, Division St. YMCA, Chgo., 1972—; assoc. Rush-Presbyterian-St. Lukes Med. Ctr., Chgo., 1975—. Rhodes scholar, 1963. Fellow Fin. Analysts Fedn.; mem. Chgo. Council on Fgn. Relations (bd. dirs., vice chmn. 1975—), Inst. European Studies (bd. govs., treas. 1981—), Investment Analysts Soc. Chgo. (chgo. com., com. on fgn. affairs, com. on internat. and domestic issues). Clubs: Sunset Ridge Country (Northfield, Ill.) (bd. dirs. 1983—); Chicago; Econ. of Chgo. Avocations: coin collecting; bridge; golf; skiing; art. Office: Stein Roe & Farnham 1 S Wacker Dr Chicago IL 60606

MC NELLY, FREDERICK WRIGHT, JR., psychologist; b. Bangor, Maine, Apr. 14, 1947; s. Frederick Wright and E. Frances (Cutter) McN.; 1 adopted son, Roger; foster children—Joseph, Ronald, Michael, Jeffrey. B.A. magna cum laude, U. Minn., 1969; M.A., U. Mich., 1971, Ph.D., 1973. Lic. foster parent, Ill. USPHS trainee, 1969-70, 72. Research coordinator NSF project U. Minn., Morris, 1968-69, lab. instructor, 1969; teaching fellow psychology U. Mich., 1970-72; ednl. examiner Ann Arbor (Mich.) Public Schs., 1971; dir. psychol. services Children Devel. Center, Rockford, Ill., 1972-82, program dir., 1982-86; lectr. Rock Valley Coll., Rockford, 1974-75; part-time pvt. practice psychology, Rockford and Belvidere, Ill., 1980-86, Beloit, Wis., 1985-86, full time 1986—; mental health cons. Rockford Head Start, 1982—; mem. health services adv. com. human resources dept., City of Rockford, 1985—; presenter state and regional workshops and confs. Active Boy Scouts Am.; chmn. spl. edn. regional advisory com. Bi-County Office of Edn., Rockford, 1976-78; mem. Nat. and Ill. Com. on Child Abuse; co-chmn. Winnebago County Child Protection Assn., 1980; elder Willow Creek United Presbyn. Ch., Rockford, 1980—; mem. stronghold renovation session com. Presbytery of Blackhawk, Oregon, Ill., 1985. Registered clin. psychologist Ill., Wis.; named U.S. Jaycees Outstanding Young Man of 1977. Mem. Am., Midwestern, Ill. No. Ill. (chmn. 1976-77) psychol. assns., Soc. Research in Child Devel., Nat., Ill. assns. retarded citizens, Am. Humane Assn. (children's div.), Nat. Register Health Service Providers in Psychology, Nat., Ill. Foster parents assns. Contbr. articles to profl. jours. Home: 11591 Beverly Ln Belvidere IL 61008 Office: Childrens Devel Center 650 N Main St Rockford IL 61103 Office: 972 N Main St Rockford IL 61103

MCNERNEY, DAWN BUTCHER, accountant; b. Lorain, Ohio, Nov. 9, 1953; d. Clark Andrew and Theresa Eve (Lukesic) Butcher; m. Ralph B. McNerney, July 17, 1976. BBA, Kent State U., 1976. CPA, Ohio; cert. fin. planner, Ohio. Tax specialist Meaden & Moore, CPAs, Cleve., 1976-84; cons. Asset Mgmt. Cons., Inc., Cleve., 1984-86; mgr. Cohen & Co. CPAs, Cleve., 1986—; guest lectr. various orgns., 1976-86. Mem. Internat. Assn. Fin. Planners, Am. Inst. CPA's, Ohio Soc. CPA's (state tax com. 1983-86, tax column editor newsletter, 1983-85), Tax Club of Cleve., Estate Planning Council, Women's City Club of Cleve. (bus. women's discussion group), Greater Akron Audubon Society. Roman Catholic. Club: Inverness Capers (Akron, Ohio). Avocations: bird watching, wildlife photography, gardening. Office: Cohen & Co Bond Ct Bldg Suite 1310 Cleveland OH 44114

MCNETT, MICHAEL MARLOWE, physician; b. Peoria, Ill., June 21, 1955; s. William Marlowe and Gloria Lee (McDonald) McN.; m. Colleen Yvonne Coyle, June 9, 1979 (div. Oct. 1986); 1 child, Michelle Anne. BA, Knox Coll., 1976; MD, So. Ill. U., 1981. Resident in family practice St. Francis Med. Ctr., Peoria, Ill., 1981-84; gen. practice medicine Eureka, Ill., 1984—; clin. assoc. U. Ill. Coll. Medicine, Peoria, 1982—; mem. pharmacy and therapeutics com. Eureka Hosp., 1984—, quality assurance com. 1986—. Mem. AMA, Am. Acad. Family Physicians. Avocations: wine appreciation, classical music. Office: McNett Clinic 109 S Major Eureka IL 61530

MCNEW, LEE MARGARET HAYES, restaurant owner; b. Detroit, June 21, 1945; d. Donald Herbert and Gloria Marshall (Allan) Hayes; m. Patrick Leon McNew, Aug. 18, 1967; children: Sarah Hayes, John Patrick. BA, U. Mich., 1967, MLS, 1973; postgrad., Detroit Coll. Law, 1974-76. Cert. tchr., Mich. Tchr. Dwight Rich Jr. High Sch., Lansing, Mich., 1967-70; tchr. and librarian John Page Jr. High Sch., Madison Heights, Mich., 1970-76; owner and v.p. Clarkston (Mich.) Cafe, Inc., 1976—. Mem. Mich. Restaurant Assn. Avocations: cooking, gardening, swimming, reading. Home: 790 Lake Angelus Shores Pontiac MI 48055 Office: Clarkston Cafe 18 S Main Clarkston MI 48016

MCNEW, PATRICK L. (PATRICK LEON MCNEW), communications executive, restaurant owner; b. Flint, Mich., May 4, 1945; s. Leon S. and Patricia J. (Murphy) McN.; m. Lee M. Hayes, Aug. 18, 1967; children: Sarah H., John Patrick. BA, Western Mich. U., 1967; MA, Mich. State U., 1969, MBA, 1970. Acct. exec. Sta. WWJ-TV, Detroit, 1970-72; salesman KATZ Communications, Detroit, 1972-74, v.p., sales mgr., 1974-84; v.p. Petry TV, Detroit, 1984—; Pres. Clarkston (Mich.) Cafe, Inc., 1976—. Mem. Mich. Assn. Broadcasters, Mich. Restaurant Assn., Mich. State U. Alumni Assn. (Outstanding Alumni award 1982). Club: Adcraft Club. Home: 790 Lake Angelus Shores Pontiac MI 48055 Office: Petry TV 3221 W Big Beaver Rd Suite 102 Troy MI 48084

MCNICHOLS, JAMES ROBERT, insurance executive; b. Chgo., July 31, 1946; s. Robert J and Anna A. (Allegretti) McN.; m. Deborah J. Locke, Sept. 21, 1968. Degree in mktg. mgmt., Elgin Community Coll., 1968; AAS, DeVry Inst. Tech., 1969. Agt. Prudential Ins. Co., Elgin, Ill., 1971—. Served with USN, 1969-71, Vietnam. Mem. McHenry chpt. Life Underwriters, Million Dollar Round Table. Roman Catholic. Avocation: golf. Home: Rt 3 Box 1750 Oliver Dr Elgin IL 60120 Office: Prudential Ins Co 1745 Grandstand Pl Elgin IL 60123

MCNICHOLS, THOMAS HENRY, JR., transportation company executive; b. Chgo., Nov. 20, 1953; s. Thomas Henry and Rosemary Adele (Hanson) McN.; m. Guadalupe Luz Rabor, Jan. 11, 1980; children: Sofronio, Dennis, Jennifer, Thomas. BS in Commerce, DePaul U., 1976. CPA, Ill. Acct. Ill. Bur. of Employment Security, Chgo., 1972-75, mgr. disbursements, 1975-77, mgr. gen. acctg., 1977-80; sr. auditor Regional Transp. Authority, Chgo., 1980-84, chief internal auditor Pace/Suburban bus div., 1984-85; head dept. fin. and adminstrn. Pace/Suburban bus div. Regional Transp. Authority, Arlington Heights, Ill., 1985—; ptnr. Thomas H. McNichols, Jr., CPA, Chgo., 1982—. Mem. Am. Inst. CPA's, Ill. CPA Soc., Ill. Govt. Fin. Office Assn., Chgo. Area Govt. Fin. Assn. Roman Catholic. Lodges: Lions, KC (grand knight 1984-86). Home: 4028 N Moody Chicago IL 60634 Office: Pace Suburban Bus Div RTA 550 W Algonquin Rd Arlington Heights IL 60005

MCNITT, MYRNA LEE, court administrator; b. Grand Rapids, Mich., Sept. 20, 1948; d. Glenn E. and Cecile K. (Schwartz) McN. BA with honors, Mich. State U., 1971; MSW, Western Mich. U., 1982. Cert. social worker, Mich. Probation officer Allegan (Mich.) County Juvenile Ct., 1971-78, asst. ct. adminstr., 1978—; cons. Adoptee Liberty Movement Assn., N.Y.C., 1981—. Officer Stop Child Abuse & Neglect, Allegan, 1980—; therapist Adult Survivors of Child Sexual Abuse, 1983—; chmn. Challenge of Children, Holland, Mich., 1980-86. Mem. Nat. Assn. Social Workers, Nat. Foster Parent Assn., Children's Charte Cts. of Mich., Mich. Foster Parent Assn. (chmn. standing program 1980—), Child Abuse and Neglect Council (Outstanding Achievement award 1985). Lutheran. Avocation: photography. Home: 340 Maple Holland MI 49423 Office: County Bldg Allegan MI 49010

MCPHAIL-KOHR, DOREEN, public relations agency executive; b. Detroit, Jan. 4, 1933; d. Harry H. and Myrtle A. (Schilke) Fante; m. Donald R. McPhail, Nov. 30, 1957 (div. 1976); children—Dean Bruce, Scott Harry. B.A., Mich. State U., 1954. Asst. dir. Detroit Town Hall, 1975-76; devel. and pub. relations dir. Grosse Pointe (Mich.) Acad., 1976-78; asst. dir. pub. relations Detroit Plaza Hotel, 1979-80; spl. events pub. relations dir. Detroit Renaissance, 1980-84, including Detroit Grand Prix, Internat. Freedom Festival, Montreux Detroit Kool Jazz Festival; account supr. Anthony M. Franco, Inc., Detroit, 1984-86; pub. relations counselor JL Communications Ltd., Detroit, 1986—; panelist U. Mich. mktg. seminar, 1982. Prodn. floor supr., personnel chmn. for art auction Sta. WTVS, 1971-75; bd. dirs. Sr. Ctr., Inc., 1960-70; bd. dirs. Grosse Pointe Human Relations Council. Mem. Pub. Relations Soc. Am. (seminar panelist 1983), Kappa Alpha Theta. Clubs: Grosse Pointe Hunt, Jr. League Detroit. Guest speaker profl. confs. Home: 925 Three Mile Dr Grosse Pointe Park MI 48230 Office: JL Communications Ltd 25801 Harper Ave Suite 2 Detroit MI 48081

MCPHERSON, EUGENE VIRGIL, broadcasting executive; b. Columbus, Ohio, Aug. 29, 1927; s. Arthur Emerson and Emma (Scott) McP.; B.A., Ohio State U., 1950; m. Nancy Marie Clark, June 13, 1953; children—Lynne, Scott. Prodn. exec. WBNS-TV, Columbus, 1952-62; exec. producer documentary unit WLWT-TV, Cin., 1962-64; dir. news and spl. projects WLWT-TV, Cin., 1964-66; v.p. news and spl. projects AVCO Broadcasting Co., Cin., 1966-69, v.p. programming, 1969-73; v.p., gen. mgr. WLWI-TV, Indpls., 1973-75; now pres. McPherson Media, Inc.; owner, operator WVLN, WSEI-FM. Served with AUS, 1946-47. Recipient creative writer producer award Alfred P. Sloan, 1966; Chris award Columbus Film Festival, 1960, 61, 62, 64, 71; Nat. Assn. TV Execs. Program award, 1968; Ohio State award, 1960, 63, 64; Freedom's Found. award, 1963, Regional Emmy, 1977; Cine Golden Eagle award, 1982; Blue Ribbon, Am. Film Festival, 1985. Mem. Broadcast Pioneers, Ill. Broadcasters Assn. (pres.). Author: (with Bleum and Cox) Television in the Public Interest, 1961. Writer, producer, dir. films The Last Prom, 1963, Death Driver, 1968, Citizen, 1962, Birth by Appointment, 1960, Diagnostic Countdown, 1962, Veil of Shadows, 1961, Rails in Crisis, 1963, Palm Trees and Ice Bergs, 1977, Tinsel Town and the Big Apple, 1979, Goodbye Carnival Girl, 1980, Atomic Legs, 1981, The Edison Adventures, 1981, The Championship, 1982, Little Arliss, 1984; Umbrella Jack, 1984; Buddies, 1985; That Funny Fat Kid, 1985; Zerk the Jerk, 1985; My First Swedish Bombshell, 1985, Charlie's Christmas Secret, 1985, Just For Kicks, 1986, Nags, 1987, My Father, the Clown, 1987, Charlie's Christmas Project, 1987. Office: 627 S Elliott St Olney IL 62450

MCPHERSON, MICHAEL JAMES, controller, corporate secretary; b. Keokuk, Iowa, Sept. 22, 1949; s. James Elmer and Lucille Ann (Biddenstadt) McP.; m. Debra Kaye Washburn, May 10, 1975; children: Scott Michael, James Dewey. AA, Keokuk Community Coll., 1970; BS, Culver-Stockton Coll., Canton, Mo., 1972. Internal auditor Gen. Growth Properties, Des Moines, 1972-74; staff acct. Crow Corp., Oskaloosa, Iowa, 1974-77; mgr. gen. acctg. Steadley Co., Inc., Carthage, Mo., 1977-81; controller, corp. sec. Steadley Co., Carthage, Mo., 1981—. Mem. Iowa Hist. Soc., Iowa City; div. leader United Way, Carthage, 1986; bd. dirs. Phelps Mus., Carthage United Way. Mem. Nat. Assn. Accts. Roman Catholic. Clubs: Broadview Country (Carthage). Home: Rt 6 Box 333 Carthage MO 64836 Office: Steadley Co 200 River St Carthage MO 64836

MCPHILLIPS, MICHAEL DONAHOE, accountant; b. Cleve., Aug. 5, 1960; s. James George and Mary Bridget (Donahoe) McP. BBA, John Carroll U., 1983; M Acctg., Case Western Reserve U., 1984. With tax dept. Hausser & Taylor CPA's, Cleve., 1984—. Mem. Am. Inst. CPA's, Ohio Soc. CPA's. Clubs: City Club Cleve., Irish-Am. Home: 12663 Harold Dr Chesterland OH 44026 Office: Hausser & Taylor CPAs 1000 Eaton Ctr Cleveland OH 44114

MCPIKE, GORDON RANDOLPH, insurance company executive; b. Indpls., Apr. 6, 1941; s. Paul Leonard and Ruth Louise (Wagner) McP.; m. Karen Deanna Royer, June 9, 1962; children: Robert Warren, Brent Gordon, Michelle Elaine, Rachelle Alaine, Craig Royer. BS, Ind. State Coll., 1963, MS, 1964. CLU; chartered fin. cons. Sales rep. Singer Sewing Machine Co., Indpls., 1962; tchr., coach Avon Community Schs., Indpls., 1964-65; computer sales and serviceman various companies, Indpls., 1965-76; ins. salesman Mutual Security Life, Indpls., 1976-83; prin., pres. McPike Ins. Agy., Inc., Indpls. and Bloomington, 1983—; pres. Tax Alternatives of Ind., Inc., Indpls., 1984—. Bd. dirs. Ch. of God, Indpls., 1975; mem. Citizens for Decency through Law, 1985-86, Indpls., Citizens Againgst Legalized Gambling, Indpls., 1986—. Mem. Am. Soc. CLU's, Am. Soc. Chartered Fin. Cons., Nat. Assn. Life Underwriters, Indpls. Assn. Life Underwriters, Million Dollar Round Table (life). Republican. Avocations: boating, fishing. Home and Office: 9420 Harbour Pointe Dr Bloomington IN 47401

MCQUADE, MICHAEL PATRICK, marketing professional; b. Columbus, Ohio, Oct. 29, 1953; s. Robert Peter and Mary Jane (Butler) McQ.; m. Jennifer Sue Skinner, Apr. 19, 1980. BBA in Mktg., Ohio U., 1976; BSEE, Ohio State U., 1984. Mktg. coordinator Thermo-Disc Inc., Mansfield, Ohio, 1984-85, mktg. mgr., 1985—. Mem. IEEE, Small Motors Mfg. Assn., Am. Mktg. Assn. Home: 3475 Possum Rd Mansfield OH 44903 Office: Therm-o-Disc Inc 1320 S Main St Mansfield OH 44907

MCQUADE, RICHARD B., JR., federal judge. Judge U.S. District Court for Northern Ohio, Toledo, 1986—. Office: 203 US Courthouse Toledo OH 43624 *

MCQUARRIE, IRVINE GRAY, neuroscientist, neurosurgeon, educator, consultant; b. Ogden, Utah, June 27, 1939; s. Irwin Bruce and Ruby Loretta (Epperson) McQ.; m. Katharine Gamble Rogers, Mar. 11, 1967 (div.); children—Michael Gray, Mollie; m. Maryann Kaminski, Aug. 14, 1980; children—Morgan Elizabeth, Gray. B.S. in Biology, U. Utah, 1961; M.D., Cornell U., 1965, Ph.D., 1977. Diplomate Am. Bd. Neurol. Surgery. Intern, asst. surgeon, surgeon N.Y. Hosp., N.Y.C., 1965-71, 72-73; research fellow dept. physiology Cornell U. Med. Coll., N.Y.C., 1971-72, 74-76, asst. prof. depts. physiology and surgery, 1976-81; vis. asst. prof. dept. anatomy Case-Western Res. U., Cleve., 1979-81, asst. prof. neurosurgery, 1981-85, assoc. prof., 1985, asst. prof. devel. genetics and anatomy, 1981-85, assoc. prof., 1985—, clin. investigator in neurol. surgery VA Med. Center, Cleve., 1981-84, med. investigator in neurol. surgery, 1984—; asst. neurosurgeon Univ. Hosps. of Cleve., 1981—. Contbr. articles to sci. jours. Served to comdr., M.C. UNSR, 1973-74. Recipient Andrew W. Mellon Tchr.-Scientist award, 1977-79; NIH fellow, 1971-72, 74-76; VA career devel. award and individual research grantee, 1981—; Paralyzed Vets. Am. grantee, 1979-82; NIH grantee, 1981—, Spinal Cord Soc. grantee, 1986—. Mem. N.Y. Acad. Scis., AAAS, Soc. for Neurosci., Am. Soc. for Cell Biology, Am. Assn. Anatomists, Congress Neurol. Surgeons, Am. Assn. Neurol. Surgeons. Democrat. Presbyterian. Research on mechanism of axonal regeneration in central nervous system; biochem. investigations on maintenance and replacement of nerve cell processes (called axons and dendrites) by complex intraneuronal transport mechanisms. Home: 13805 Shaker Blvd, Cleveland, OH 44120 Office: 2119 Abington Rd Cleveland OH 44106

MCQUAY, WILLIAM KENNETH, operations research analyst; b. Wild Wood, N.J., Oct. 14, 1945; s. Adam Hanson and Emmeline Maize (Ahl) McQ.; m. Vickie Ann Meece, May 21, 1985. BS in Maths., Towson State U., Balt., 1967; MS in Ops. Research, So. Meth. U., 1972; MS in Engring., John Hopkins U., 1977. Pvt. cons. Balt., 1975-77; ops. research analyst USAF, Dayton, Ohio, 1977—; v.p., treas. Master Craftsman Co., Xenia, Ohio, 1983—; owner Softsmith, Dayton, 1985—. Author: Computer Simulation Techniques for Military Operations Research, 1979. Served to capt. USAF, 1967-75. Mem. IEEE, Assn. Computing Machinery, Assn. Old Crows. Methodist. Avocation: horses. Home: 4544 Snypp Rd Yellow Springs OH 45387 Office: USAF Avionics Lab AFWAL/AAWA-I Wright Patterson AFB OH 45433

MCQUEEN, COY EARL, engineer, real estate developer; b. Harvard, Ill., Aug. 14, 1954; s. Melbourne D. and Lavena J. (Wille) McQ.; m. Penelope F. Bryan, Feb. 20, 1981; children: Emily Erin, Molly Malinda. Grad. high sch., Harvard, Ill. Draftsman Erect-A-Tube, Inc., Harvard, 1972-74, chief draftsman, 1974-76, engr., 1976-80, engring. mgr., 1980—. Patentee solar bi-fold door, bldg. and bi-fold door. Mem. adv. com. diversified occupation Harvard High Sch., 1986. Recipient bldg. design award Metal Bldg. Component Mfrs., 1986. Mem. Systems Builders Assn. Republican. Lodge: Moose. Office: Erect-A-Tube Inc 701 Park Harvard IL 60033

MCQUILLEN, MICHELE MARIE, personnel executive; b. Boston, May 8, 1959; d. Thomas Richard and Virginia Rita (Farrell) Bolduc; m. Daniel Paul McQuillen, July 9, 1983. BSFS, Georgetown U., 1981; MBA, Marquette U., 1987. Campaign office mgr. Valleyshore YMCA, Westbrook, Conn., 1981-82; employment specialist Marquette U., Milw., 1982-84; cons. AA and tech. recruiter, outplacement GE Med. Systems, Milw., 1984-86; placement specialist Wis. Electric Power Co., Milw., 1986—. Vol. Visiting Nurse's Assn. Milw., 1984-87; adv. com. Milw. Pub. Schs. Bus. and Office Edn., 1986—; v.p. Resident Spouse's Assn. of Med. Coll. Wis., Milw, 1987—; Wis. chmn. Georgetown Alumni Admissions Program, 1984-86. Mem. Internat. Assn. Personnel Women. Avocations: antique collecting, quilting, tennis, skiing, travel.

MC REE, EDWARD BARXDALE, hospital administrator; b. Pauls Valley, Okla., Oct. 20, 1931; s. Henry Barxdale and Mary (Shumate) McR.; B.A., Okla. City U., 1953; student U. Okla., 1953; student Central State Coll., 1954-55; m. Jan Bryant, Aug. 23, 1953; children—Scott, Kent, Chad. Adminstr. Eaton Rapids (Mich.) Community Hosp., 1957-61; pres. Ingham Med. Center, Lansing, Mich., 1961—; dir. Grad. Med. Edn., Inc., 1970—, treas., 1978-79, pres., 1979-81; pres. Mid-Mich. Emergency Services Council, 1978-81; dir. Kent Bank & Trust, Lansing, N.A., Olo Kent Bank of Lansing; bd. dirs. Blue Cross/Blue Shield of Mich. Mem. Eaton Rapids (Mich.) Bd. Edn., 1964-71, treas., 1968-71. Pres., Tri-County Emergency Med. Services Council, 1974—, also mem. bd. dirs.; bd. dirs. Blue Cross Mich., 1974-75, 1986; bd. dirs. Hosp. Purchasing Service Mich., 1973—, pres., 1976-77, chmn., 1987; bd. dirs. Mid-Mich. chpt. ARC, 1979—, treas., 1980—, chmn., 1981-83; bd. dirs. Lansing Symphony Assn., 1984—. Served with AUS, 1955-57. Mem. Mich. (v.p. 1965-68), Southwestern Mich. (pres. 1968) hosp. assns., Am. Coll. Hosp. Execs. (regent 1987—), Am. Hosp. Assn., Univ. Club Mich. State U. (bd. dirs. 1985—), Lambda Chi Alpha. Beta Beta Beta. Methodist (mem. West Mich. Conf. Bd. Finance 1972—). Lodge: Rotary (bd. dirs. Lansing club 1985—). Club: Rotary. Contbr. articles to profl. jours. Home: 123 N East St Eaton Rapids MI 48827 Office: 401 W Greenlawn Ave Lansing MI 48910

MC ROSTIE, CLAIR NEIL, economics educator; b. Owatonna, Minn., Dec. 16, 1930; s. Neil Hale and Myrtle Julia (Peterson) McR.; m. Ursula Anne Schwieger, Aug. 29, 1968. BSBA cum laude, Gustavus Adolphus Coll., 1952; MA in Mktg., Mich. State U., 1953; Ph.D. in Fin., U. Wis., 1963; postgrad., U. Minn., 1971-72, Am. Grad. Sch. Internat. Mgmt., 1980-81. Faculty Gustavus Adolphus Coll., St. Peter, Minn., 1958—; chmn. dept. econs. and bus. Gustavus Adolphus Coll., 1967-83, chmn., mem. various coms., 1971—; teaching asst. Sch. Commerce, U. Wis., 1960-62; Confer prof. entrepreneurship; lectr. European div. U. Md., 1966-67; vis. prof. Am. Grad. Sch. Internat. Mgmt., 1980-81; prof. entrepreneurship Ogden Conf.; pres. World Trade Week, Inc., 1987. Editor: Global Resources: Perspectives and Alternatives, 1978, The Future of the Market Ecomomy, 1979. Congregation pres. First Luth. Ch., St. Peter, Minn., 1972-73, chmn. pastoral call com., 1968-69, chmn. staffing com., 1975, mem. ch. council, 1968-74; chmn. Rep. council arts professions, scis., Minn., 1968-70, co-chmn. state task force on Vietnam, 1968; mem. adv. commn. Minn. Dept. Manpower Services, 1967-71; mem. North Central Regional Manpower Adv. Com.; Bd. dirs. Midwest China Resource Study Center; del. White House Conf. Aging, 1971. Served with U.S. Army, 1954-56. Recipient Leavey Found. award Freedoms Found., Valley Forge, Pa.; Research fellow Fed. Res. Bank of Chgo., 1962-63. Mem. Fin. Execs. Inst., Soc. Coll. Univ. Planning, Minn. Econs. Assn. (bd. dirs. 1974-75, 1979-80), Sierra Club (exec. com. North Star chpt., Midwest regional conservation com.; 4th officer nat. council 1972-78), Alpha Kappa Psi, Iota Delta Gamma, Sigma Epsilon. Home: Rural Route 1 Box 198 Saint Peter MN 56082 Office: Gustavus Adolphus Coll Saint Peter MN 56082

MCRUER, SCOTT DOUGLAS, accountant; b. Kansas City, Mo., June 22, 1960; s. Donald Montgomery McRuer and Dorthaleen Rebecca (Poe) McRuer Kinsler; m. Judy Lynn Simon, Oct. 18, 1986. BA, Westminster Coll., 1982. CPA, Mo. Staff auditor Price Waterhouse, Kansas City, 1982-85; auditor-in-charge Emerson Electric Co., St. Louis, 1985, sr. auditor, 1985-87; audit mgr. H & R Block, Inc., Kansas City, 1987—. Advisor Jr. Achievment, Kansas City, 1984. Mem. Am. Inst. CPA's, Mo. Soc. CPA's. Presbyterian. Avocations: photography, golf. Home: 400 NE 62d Pl Kansas City MO 64118 Office: H & R Block Inc 4410 Main St Kansas City MO 64111

MCSHEA, WILLIAM MICHAEL, accountant; b. Evergreen Park, Ill., Dec. 7, 1960; s. William J. and Virginia C. (Jurkas) McS.; m. Eileen Marie Aldrich, Apr. 26, 1986. BS in Acctg., DePaul U., 1983, MA in Acctg., 1984. CPA, Ill; cert. mgmt. acct. Mem. audit staff Arthur Andersen and Co., Chgo., 1984-87; mem. controller staff Arthur Andersen WHQ, Chgo., 1987—. Mem. Am. Inst. CPA's, Ill. CPA Soc., Beta Alpha Psi (sec. DePaul chpt. 1984). Republican. Roman Catholic. Avocations: basketball, racquetball, running, cycling, backgammon.

MCSPADEN, FRANK JAMES, real estate and investment company executive; b. Hampton, Iowa, May 8, 1932; s. James M. and Velma A. (Reed) McS.; children: Cheri L., Charles F., Jeffry J. AB in Bus., Am. Inst. Bus., 1957; BA in Econs. and Bus. Adminstrn. summa cum laude, Park Coll., 1973; MA in Valuation Sci. with distinction, Lindenwood Coll., 1981; grad., Nat. Examiners Sch. Fed. Home Loan Bank, 1985. Cert. assessment evaluator. Property tax rep. The Wickes Corp., San Diego, Calif., 1973-75; supr., mgr., staff dir. McDonalds Corp., Oakbrook, Ill., 1975-80; pres. Valuation Economics, Inc., Lombard, Ill., 1980-84; dist. appraiser Fed. Home Loan Bank, Topeka, Kans., 1984-85; v.p. appraisal div. Gem Am. Realty and Investment Corp., Dayton, Ohio, 1985—; real estate cons. McAllister Inc., Memphis, 1982-84. Editor Property Tax U.S.A., 1980-82; contbr 27 articles on property tax and appraisal to profl. jours. Capt., squad commdr. Civil Air Patrol, Cedar Rapids, Iowa, 1959-69. Served with USN, 1951-55. Mem. Am. Soc. Appraisers (sr., medal of achievement), Inst. Property Taxation (cert.), Mensa. Home: 4640 Silverwood Dr Kettering OH 45429 Office: GEM Am Realty & Investment Corp 431 Wayne Ave Dayton OH 45410

MCSWEENY, AUSTIN JOHN, psychology educator; b. Berwyn, Ill., May 2, 1946; s. Austin John and Erna Eleanor (De Sollar) McS.; m. Jane Marilee Erickson, Sept. 28, 1968; children: Andrew John, Patrick Michael. BA with honors, U. Wis., 1969; MA, No. Ill. U., 1974, PhD, 1975. Diplomate Am. Bd. Clin. Neuropsychology, Am. Bd. Profl. Psychology. Lectr., fellow Northwestern U., Evanston, Ill., 1975-78; asst. prof. W.Va. U., Morgantown, 1978-81; assoc. prof. Med. Coll. Ohio, Toledo, 1981—; cons. Kennedy Ctr., Morgantown, 1980-81, Toledo VA Med. Ctr., 1981—, Fulton County Health Ctr., Wauseon, Ohio, 1984—; adj. assoc. prof. U. Toledo, 1984—; vis. prof. U. Toledo, 1987—. Editor: (book) Practical Program Evaluation, 1982; contbr. articles to profl. jours. Bd. dirs. Presbyn. Youth Home, Clarksburg, W.Va., 1979-81, Apple Tree Nursery Sch., Toledo, 1985-86, Toledo Hearing and Speech Ctr., 1986—. Leslie Holmes fellow, 1972. Mem. N.W. Ohio Soc. Profl. Psychology (pres. 1985—), N.W. Ohio Psychol. Assn. (pres. 1986—), Ohio Acad. Neuropsychologists (pres. 1983-84), Internat. Neuropsychol. Soc. (program com.). Avocations: reading, music, flying, travel. Home: 4146 Northmoor Ottawa Hills OH 43606 Office: Med Coll Ohio Dept Psychiatry Toledo OH 43699-0008

MCTAVISH, JOAN MARIE, accountant; b. Superior, Wis., Apr. 8, 1959; d. Paul Edward and Marjorie Gertrude (Templeton) Mielke; 1 child, Katie Marie. BS magna cum laude, Bemidji State U., 1984. CPA, Minn. Cert. pub. acct. Pannell Kerr Forster, Mpls. Mem. Am. Inst. CPAs, Minn. Soc. CPAs. Avocations: music, painting, sketching, running. Home: 8307 W 31st St #111 Saint Louis Park MN 55426 Office: Pannell Kerr Forster 5353 Wayzata Blvd Suite 410 Minneapolis MN 55416

MCVEAN, DUNCAN EDWARD, pharmaceutical company executive; b. Pontiac, Mich., June 8, 1936; s. Duncan and Vernice Adelaide (Bird) McV.; m. Virginia Jean Cibor, Aug. 13, 1960; children: Cynthia Lynn, Scott Duncan. BS in Pharmacy, U. Mich., 1958, MS in Pharmacy, 1960, PhD in Pharm. Chemistry, 1963; MBA, Xavier U., Cin., 1978. Registered pharmacist Mich., Ohio. Pharm. research chemist Merrell Nat. Labs., Cin., 1965-77, dir. quality control, 1977-79; v.p. Gentek Corp., Cin., 1979-81; dir. mfg. Adria Labs., Columbus, Ohio, 1981-84; v.p. ops. Ben Venue Labs., Bedford, Ohio, 1984—; bd. dirs. Cetus/Ben Venue Therapeutics, Ben Venue Labs.; dir. pharmacy advancement program U. Mich., Ann Arbor, 1981-87. Patentee in field; author or co-author various publs. in field. Pres. Hilltop PTA, 1969-71, Civic Assn., 1982-83. Served to capt. USAF, 1963-65. Mem. Am. Pharm. Assn., Assn. Pharm. Scientists, Am. Hosp. Pharmacists Soc., Ohio Pharm. Assn., Acad. Pharm. Sci., Sigma Xi, Rho Chi. Republican. Presbyterian. Lodge: Masons. Avocations: pvt. pilot, sailing. Home: 6122 Liberty Rd Solon OH 44139 Office: Ben Venue Labs Inc 270 Northfield Rd Bedford OH 44146

MCVICKER, MARY ELLEN HARSHBARGER, museum director, art history educator; b. Mexico, Mo., May 5, 1951; d. Don Milton and Harriet Pauline (Mossholder) Harshbarger; m. Wiley Ray McVicker, June 2, 1973; children: Laura Elizabeth, Todd Michael. BA with honors, U. Mo., 1973, MA, 1975, postgrad. Adminstrv. Sec. Engring. Surveys, Columbia, Mo., 1976-77. Instr. Columbia U., Mo., 1977-78, Cen. Meth. Coll., Fayette, Mo., 1978-85, mus. dir., 1980-85; project dir. Mo. Com. for Humanities, Fayette, 1981-85, Mo. Dept. Natural Resources Office Hist. Preservation, 1978-85; owner, Memories of Mo., Inc., 1986—. Author: History Book, 1984. V.p. Friends Hist. Boonville, Mo., 1982-87; bd. dirs. Mus. Assocs. Mo. U., Columbia, 1981-83, Mo. Meth. Hist. Soc., Fayette, 1981-84; chmn. Bicentennial Celebration Methodism, Boonville, Mo., 1984. Mem. Mo. Heritage Trust (charter), AAUW (treas. 1977-79), Am. Assn. Museums, Centralia Hist. Soc. (project dir. 1978), Mus. Assocs. United Meth. Ch. (charter, bd. dir. 1981-83), Phi Beta Kappa, Mortar Bd. Democrat. Clubs: Women's (treas. 1977-79), United Meth. Women's Group (charter mem.). Avocations: collecting antiques, gardening, family farming, singing, travelling. Home: 813 Christus Dr Boonville MO 65233 Office: Memories of Mo Inc PO Box 228 Boonville MO 65233

MCVOY, PETER LEONARD, management consultant; b. Phila., Nov. 1, 1951; s. Richard Edward and Mary Fletcher (Leonard) McV.; m. Linda Marie Holtcamp, Dec. 30, 1977; children: Molly Kathleen, Katie Marie. BA, U. Notre Dame, 1973; postgrad., U. Houston, 1977; M in Pub. Adminstrn., Cleve. State U., 1979. Asst. prof. naval sci. Tex. A&M U., Galveston, 1976-77; presdl. mgmt. intern NASA Lewis Research Ctr., Cleve., 1979-81, employment devel. specialist, 1981-86; corp. mgr., tng. Blue Cross/Blue Shield, Cleve., 1986—; instr. Cuyahoga Community Coll., Cleve.,

1981-84, Lake Erie Coll., Painesville, Ohio, 1984-86; mgmt. cons. United Resource Group, Cleve., 1982-85. Served to lt. USN, 1973-77. Recipient Outstanding Achievement award Cleve. Federal Exec. Bd., 1980, Group Achievement award NASA, Cleve., 1985. Mem. Am. Soc. Tng. and Devel. Democratic. Roman Catholic. Avocations: sailing, reading, guitar. Home: 24570 Hawthorne Dr Euclid OH 44117 Office: Blue Cross Blue Shield of Ohio 2060 E Ninth St Cleveland OH 44115

MCWHORTER, JOHN FRANCIS, manufacturing engineer; b. Cleve., June 20, 1941; s. John Francis and Daisy Alice (Morrell) M. B.S. in Mgmt. Sci., Case Inst. Tech., 1963. With TRW Inc., Cleve., 1963—, process planning engr., 1963-64, tool evaluation engr., 1964-67, Jr. Achievement adv., 1965-67; computer applications engr., 1967—, prodn. engr., 1972—, mem. info. systems conf., 1982. Chmn. Cuyahoga County Youth for Goldwater, 1964; Republican precinct Committeeman, 1964-68; mem. Shaker Heights (Ohio) Rep. Club, 1964-72, sec., 1970; coordinator Ward 32 Cleve. Mayoral Campaign; 1969; mem. ARC Gallon Club, 1971. Mem. Kirley Investment Club (pres. 1982, 86), English Speaking Union (dir. Cleve. br. 1980-85), Sigma Nu. Developer more than 300 computer software applications for company. Home: 20900 Claythorne Rd Shaker Heights OH 44122 Office: TRW Valve 1455 E 185th St Cleveland OH 44110

MEAD, BEVERLEY TUPPER, physician, educator; b. New Orleans, Jan. 22, 1923; s. Harold Tupper and Helen Edith (Hunt) M.; m. Thelma Ruth Cottingham, June 8, 1947. B.S., U. S.C., 1943; M.D., Med. Coll. S.C., 1947; M.S., U. Utah, 1958. Intern Detroit Receiving Hosp., 1947-48, resident, 1948-51; asst. prof. U. Utah, 1954-61; asso. prof. U. Ky., 1961-65; prof. psychiatry and behavioral sci. Creighton U. Sch. Medicine, Omaha, 1965—; chmn. dept. Creighton U. Sch. Medicine, 1965-77, asso. dean for acad. and faculty affairs, 1980—.

MEAD, BRUCE ALLAN, printing company executive; b. Mason City, Iowa, May 18, 1942; s. Robert Nelson and Hazel Elane (Bendickson) M.; m. Donna Ellen Maloney, Sept. 3, 1984 (div.); 1 child, Allan Madison. BS, Iowa State U., 1966. Reporter Sta. WOI-TV, Ames, Iowa, 1963-66; instr. U. Okla., Norman, 1971-73; audio visual curator Okla. Sci. and Art Found., Oklahoma City, 1973-74; chief exec. officer, pres. Bruce Allan Mead Assocs., Inc. dba Quality Quick Print, Clear Lake, Iowa, 1978—. Author: (textbook/workbook) A Classroom Planetarium/Geodesics, 1977; writer producer (multi-media presentation) The Universe Within, 1974; inventor Planetarium Project Kit, 1981. Pres., founder Planetarium Theater Found., Clear Lake, 1980—; chmn. fund drive for KUNI-KHKE radio, 1986; trustee Clear Lake Hist. Soc., 1985—. Served to capt. USAF, 1966-69, Vietnam. Decorated Silver Star. Mem. Nat. Assn. Quick Printers, Printing Industries of Midwest. Lodge: Rotary (pres. Clear Lake 1986-87). Avocations: theatrical astronomy, writing, teaching, acting, blue water sailing. Home: 112 N Shore Dr Clear Lake IA 50428 Office: Bruce Allen Mead Assocs Inc I-35 and Hwy 106 Box 143 Clear Lake IA 50428

MEAD, ELIZABETH BRADLEY, house designer; b. Denver, June 13, 1921; d. Earl D. and Clara Elizabeth (Baker) Bradley; m. George Whitaker Mead, Dec. 13, 1941; children: Holly, Robert, George. Student, U. Chgo., 1939-42; BArch, U. Wis., 1975, MA in Creative Writing, 1985. Designer custom homes Elm Grove, Wis. Women's dir. United Way Fund Dr.; pres. women's soc. Elm Grove Community Meth. Ch.; pres. Women's Friends Art, Milw.; bd. dirs. Young Am. Art and Craft Fair. Mem. AIA. Avocations: swimming, skiing, painting.

MEAD, GEORGE WILSON, II, paper company executive; b. Milw., Oct. 11, 1927; s. Stanton W. and Dorothy (Williams) M.; m. Helen Patricia Anderson, Sept. 3, 1949; children: Deborah, David, Leslie. B.S., Yale U., 1950; M.S., Inst. Paper Chemistry, Wis., 1952. With Consol. Papers, Inc., Wisconsin Rapids, Wis., 1952—; v.p. ops. Consol. Papers, Inc., 1962-66, pres., chief exec. officer, 1966-71, chmn. bd., chief exec. officer, 1971—, also dir.; pres. dir. Consol. Water Power Co.; 1st Nat. Bank, Soo Line R.R., Snap-On Tools Corp. Co-chmn. bldg. fund drive Riverview Hosp., Wisconsin Rapids, 1963-64, mem. bd., 1961-77; Bd. dirs. Consol.'s Civic Found.; bd. dirs. Nat. Council for Air and Stream Improvement; trustee Lawrence U., Inst. Paper Chemistry. Mem. Am. Paper Inst. (dir. 1967-69, 80—), TAPPI (dir. 1969-72), Wis. Paper Industry Information Service (gen. chmn. 1964-65), Wis. Paper and Pulp Mfrs. Traffic Assn. (exec. com. 1963-75, dir., pres. 1973). Clubs: Elk (exalted ruler 1958), Rotarian. Office: Consol Papers Inc 231 First Ave N Wisconsin Rapids WI 54494

MEAD, WILLIAM JOHN, insurance company executive; b. Ft. Wayne, Ind., Sept. 12, 1940; s. John and Sybil (Stafford) M.; m. Susanah Mayberry, June 15, 1968; children: Katherine H., Edith T., Sybil J. BA, Cornell U., 1962. CPCU. Field rep. Stone, Satfford & Stone, Indpls., 1965-68, exec. asst., 1969-74, mng. ptnr., 1974-81; regional mgr. Comml. Union Ins. Co., Indpls., 1981—. Pres., bd. dirs. Park-Tudor Sch., Indpls., 1983-86; trustee Indpls. Mus. Art, 1978—, v.p. bd. govs. 1986—; trustee The Children's Mus., Indpls. 1980—. Served to 1st lt. U.S. Army, 1963-65. Mem. The CPCU Soc., Nat. Assn. Independent Agts., Independent Ins. Agts. of Ind., Ind. Ins. Mgr. Assn., Penrod Soc (founder 1967). Avocations: gardening, antique collecting, tennis, golf. Home: 7975 N Illinois St Indianapolis IN 46260 Office: Mead & Co 251 N Illinois St Indianapolis IN 46260

MEADER-SCHENK, DIANE MARIE, exercise physiologist; b. Hazelcrest, Ill., July 23, 1955; d. William A. and Audrey E. (Carpenter) Meader; m. Richard Allan Schenk, Oct. 15, 1983. BS, Ill. State U., 1977, MS, 1980. Tchr. Joliet (Ill.) High Schs., 1977-80; coordinator cardiac rehab. St. Mary's Hosp., Decatur, Ill., 1981—, also mem. speakers bur., 1981—; project writer State of Ill., Decatur, 1980; cons. Playmor Fitness Ctr., Decatur, 1982-86. Mem. Am. Heart Assn. Recipient Gratitude for Service award YMCA, Decatur, 1984. Mem. Am. Assn. for Cardiovascular and Pulmonary Rehab., Ill. Assn. for Cardiac Rehab. Republican. Roman Catholic. Avocations: aerobic exercise, knitting, interior decorating. Office: Saint Mary's Hosp 1800 E Lake Shore Dr Decatur IL 62525

MEADORS, JERREL E., manufacturing company executive; b. Jasper, Ind., June 11, 1934; s. Ferrel E. and Marie M. (Brittian) M.; m. Barbara Lauren Bridgewater, May 11, 1957; 1 dau., Terry Lynn. B.S., Ind. U., 1959. C.P.A., Ind. Pres., chmn. Perry Mfg. Inc., Indpls., 1968—; sec., treas. Indy Leasing & Realty, Inc., Indpls., 1976—, also dir.; owner J.E. Meadors P.A., Mgmt. Cons. to Physicians, Indpls.; ptnr. CMW Aviation, Indpls. Mem. Am. Soc. Pub. Accts., Scaffolding and Shoring Inst., Wall and Ceiling Contractors Assn. Republican. Methodist. Home: 6843 Shadow Brook Ct Indianapolis IN 46224 Office: 2535 Burton Ave Indianapolis IN 46208

MEADOWS, GLENN H., manufacturing company executive. Pres., chief exec. officer McNeil Corp., Akron, Ohio. Office: McNeil Corp Canal Sq 80 W Center St Akron OH 44308 also: McNeil (Ohio) Corp 666 W Market St Akron OH 44303 *

MEANS, RAYMOND B, library administrator; b. Des Moines, Jan. 4, 1930; s. Wilfred and Ruth (Leibfarth) Beardall; m. Rebecca Lou Chartier, Aug. 18, 1956; 1 child, Erica. B.S., U. Omaha, 1956; M.A., U. Denver, 1961. Prin. Tri-Ctr. Schs., Persia, Iowa, 1956-60; assoc. library dir. U. Nebr.-Omaha, 1960-77; library dir. Creighton U., Omaha, 1977—. Vol. Omaha Community Playhouse, 1978—; officer Dundee Presbyterian Ch., Omaha, 1964—. Mem. ALA (councilor 1972-76), Cath. Library Assn., Nebr. Library Assn. (pres. 1968, exec. sec. 1980—, Meritorious Service award 1979, Disting. Service award 1983), Internat. Council Library Assn. Execs. (sec.-treas. 1984—). Democrat. Presbyterian. Home: 678 Parkwood Ln Omaha NE 68132 Office: Creighton Univ Reinert-Alumni Meml Library California at 24th St Omaha NE 68178

MEARES, LARRY B., transportation company executive; b. Clearwater, Fla., Oct. 22, 1936; s. Bert Irvin and Hazel Evelyn (Rinker) M.; m. Regena Lea Clifton Rogers, Sept. 18, 1955 (div. 1970); children: Deborah Elizabeth, Susan Evelyn, Gregory Bert, Sandra Evelyn, Terri Ann; m. Barbara Suzanne Wojnowski, June 18, 1972; children: Ericka Helene, John Laughlin, Andrea Evelyn. BSBA, U. Fla., 1962. Cen. region mgr. Union Camp Corp., Monroe, Mich., 1964-67; corp. dir. human resources Monroe Auto Equipment Co., 1967-76; v.p. human resources Russell, Burdsall & Ward Corp., Mentor, Ohio, 1977-81; pres. LBM Assocs., Mentor, 1981—; internal cons. Leaseway Transp., Beachwood, Ohio, 1983—; cons. Mich. Tech. Investors, Monroe, 1981—, Berkman, Ruslander, Pohl, Lieber & Engel, Pitts., 1981—. Contbr. numerous articles to profl. bus. publs. Pres., chmn. United Way Monroe County, Monroe, 1965-75; mem. arbitration panel City of Monroe, 1970-74; chmn. downtown redevel., City of Monroe 1974-75. Served to sgt. USAF, 1955-59. Recipient Civic commendation Monroe C. of C., 1967, Leadership award United Way, Monroe, 1974. Mem. Am. Soc. Personnel Adminstrn. (cert.). Republican. Methodist. Club: Monroe Country (house chmn. 1968-71). Avocations: golf, reading, computers, writing, spectator sports. Home: 7712 Oakridge Dr Mentor OH 44060

MEARS, PATRICK EDWARD, lawyer; b. Flint, Mich., Oct. 3, 1951; s. Edward Patrick and Estelle Veronica (Mislik) M.; m. Geraldine O'Connor, July 18, 1981. B.A., U. Mich., 1973, J.D., 1976. Bar: N.Y. 1977, U.S. Dist. Ct. (so. and ea. dists.) N.Y. 1977, Mich. 1980, U.S. Dist. Ct. (we. and ea. dists.) Mich. 1980, U.S. Ct. Appeals (6th cir.) 1983. Assoc. firm Milbank, Tweed, Hadley & McCloy, N.Y.C., 1976-79, ptnr. Warner, Norcross & Judd, Grand Rapids, Mich., 1980—; adj. prof. Grand Valley State Coll., Allendale, Mich., 1981-84. Author: Michigan Collection Law, 1981, 2d edit., 1983, Basic Bankruptcy Law, 1986, Bankruptcy Law and Practice in Michigan, 1987, Bankruptcy Law and Practice in Michigan, 1987; also articles. Med. coordinator basketball tournament Mich. Spl. Olympics, Grand Rapids, 1983. Mem. ABA, Mich. State Bar Assn., Am. Bankruptcy Inst., Comml. Law League Am., Irish Heritage Soc. Club: Peninsular (Grand Rapids). Office: Warner Norcross and Judd 900 Old Kent Bldg Grand Rapids MI 49503

MECKELBERG, BRIAN LEE, optometrist; b. Berlin, Wis., Jan. 23, 1958; s. Weseley Edwin and Mildred Luella (Steinagle) M.; m. Joan Marie Neubauer, Oct. 20, 1984. BA, U. Wis., Eau Claire, 1980; OD, So. Coll. Optometry, Memphis, 1984. Optometrist Wautoma, Wis., 1984—. Mem. Am. Optometric Assn., Wis. Optometric Assn., Wautoma Jr. C. of C. Republican. Club: Washaia Country (Wautoma). Lodge: Rotary. Avocations: scuba diving, golf, fishing, hunting. Home: 521 W Elm St Wautoma WI 54982 Office: 118 N St Marie St Wautoma WI 54982

MECKSTROTH, JAMES ROBERT, electronics systems executive; b. Dayton, Ohio, Sept. 20, 1949; s. Harry W. and Margaret L. (Summers) M.; m. Cynthia M. Bitzer, Apr. 7, 1973; children: Jamie, Ann, Christy, Julie. BSEE, U. Cin., 1972; MS in Systems Engring., Wright State U., 1977, MBA, 1982. Engr. Technology, Inc., Dayton, 1971-74; project leader Diconix Corp., Dayton, 1974-79, mgr. product devel., 1979-82, dir. info. systems, 1982—. Patentee in field. Cubmaster Boy Scouts Am. Dayton council, 1986—. Scholar Dyna Corp., 1967. Office: Diconix Corp PO Box 3100 Dayton OH 45420

MEDARIS, FLORENCE ISABEL, osteopathic physician and surgeon; b. Kirksville, Mo.; d. Charles Edward and Nellie (Finley) Medaris; B.A., Coll. Wooster, 1932; D.O., Kirksville Coll. Osteopathy and Surgery, 1939; postgrad. U. Wis., Marquette U. Pvt. practice osteo. medicine and surgery, Milw., 1940—. Active Milwaukee County Mental Assn., Milw. Art Center, Friends of Art; mem. med. bd. dirs. Milw. Soc. Multiple Sclerosis Soc., 1973—; mem. Mayor's Beautification Com., 1968—. Dir. Zonta Manor, 1957-67, Brace Fund Bd. of Advt. Women of Milw., 1958-64, pres. bd., 1962-63, 77—; bd. mem. Bookfellows Milw.; finance com. Coll. Womens Club Found., 1971-78. Mem. Am. Osteo. Assn. (com. mental health 1964), Wis. Assn. Osteo. Physicians and Surgeons, Milw. Dist. Soc., Osteo. Physicians and Surgeons, Am. Coll. Gen. Practitioners, Applied Acad. Osteopathy, Am. Assn. U. Women, Inter-Group Council Women (pres. 1947-49, dir.), Wis. Pub. Health Assn., Council for Wis. Writers, Photog. Soc. Am., Wis. Acad. Scis., Arts and Letters, Delta Omega (nat. pres. 1952-53). Presbyn. Club: Zonta (bd. mem. Milw. 1968-69). Home: 1121 N Waverly Pl Milwaukee WI 53202 Office: 161 W Wisconsin Ave Milwaukee WI 53203

MEDEMA, CLARENCE ROBERT, JR., accountant; b. Chgo., July 29, 1954; s. Clarence Robert and Bernice (Groenewald) M.; m. Lois Ann Stehouwer, Nov. 24, 1979; children: Jennifer, Clarence III, Courtney. BS in Econs., Calvin Coll., 1975; MBA, U. Mich., 1977. CPA, Mich. Ptnr. Lettinga & Assocs., Grand Rapids, Mich., 1979-82, 86—, Byner, Medema, Grandville, Mich., 1982-85; pres. Medema Cable Co., Battle Creek, Mich., 1986—. Treas. Community Coordinated Child Care, Grand Rapids, 1979-83, Recycle Unlimited, Grand Rapids, 1985—, Council for Performing Arts and Children, Grand Rapids, 1985—. Mem. Am. Inst. CPA's, Mich. Assn. CPA's. Mem. Christian Reformed Ch. Home: 7400 Sheffield Dr Ada MI 49301 Office: Lettinga & Assocs 4246 Kalamazoo SE Grand Rapids MI 49508

MEDINA, BILL STEVENS, construction company executive; b. Lajes Field Naval Base, Azores, Portugal, Aug. 20, 1956; came to U.S., 1962; s. Abel and Renee Denise (Boniface) M.; m. Peggy Eileen Lewis, Mar. 18, 1978; children: Dustin Daniel, Dylan Michael. Student pub. schs., Salina, Kans. Motorcycle mechanic Road & Trail, Salina, Kans., 1972; landscaper Kline's Landscaping Co., Salina, 1972-73; carpenter Bradshaw Constrn. Co., Salina, 1974-76, Umphrey Builders, Salina, 1976, Abbott Constrn. Co., Salina, 1976-77; pres. Bill Medina Constrn. Co., Salina, 1977—. Mem. Salina Builders Assn. (bd. dirs.), Associated Gen. Contractors of Am. Republican. Avocations: fishing, karate. Home: 537 Aullwood Salina KS 67401 Office: Bill Medina Constrn Co PO Box 141 Salina KS 67402

MEDINI, EITAN, physician; b. Jerusalem, Feb. 28, 1941; came to U.S., 1972; s. Meir and Shulamiit (MiRahi) M.; m. Rachel Shoef, Oct. 3, 1961; children: Allen Michael, Iris. MD, Jerusalem U., 1968. Diplomate Am. Bd. Radiation Therapy. Intern U. Hosp., Tel-Aviv, Israel, 1968-72, resident radiation therapy, 1972-75; chief dept. radiation therapy VA Hosp., Mpls., 1976—; asst. prof. U. Minn., 1976—. Contbr. articles to profl. jours. Served to maj. Israeli Def. Forces, 1958-61. Mem. Am. Soc. Theraputic Radiology. Home: 6321 Sheridan Ave S Richfield MN 55423 Office: VA Hosp 54th and 48th Sts Minneapolis MN 55417

MEDINIS, DAVID MICHAEL, computer executive; b. Detroit, Oct. 4, 1957; s. Richard Eugene and Claudette (Kidd) M. BEE, Lawrence Inst. Tech., Sothfield, Mich., 1976; student, Kennedy Ctr., W.Va., 1983. Owner Environmental Services, Royal Oak, Mich., 1978-81; pres. Micro Techs., Inc., Troy, Mich., 1983—. Inventor in computer field. Recipient 1st Electronics award Ednl. Soc. Mich., 1975. Mem. Automation Soc., Computer Automation Soc. of Engring. Avocations: body building, martial arts, flying, programming. Office: Micro Techs Inc 1180 E Big Beaver Rd Troy MI 48083

MEDNICK, ROBERT, accountant; b. Chgo., Apr. 1, 1940; s. Harry and Nettie (Brenner) M.; m. Susan Lee Levinson, Oct. 28, 1962; children—Michael Jon, Julie Eden, Adam Charles. B.S. in Bus. Adminstrn., Roosevelt U., Chgo., 1962. CPA, Ill. Staff asst. Arthur Andersen & Co., Chgo., 1962-63, sr. acct., 1963-66, mgr., 1966-71, ptnr., 1971—, mng. dir. SEC policies, 1973-76, mng. dir. auditing procedures, 1976-79, vice chmn. profl. standards, 1979-82, chmn. com. profl. standards, 1982—. Contbr. articles to profl. jours. Bd. dirs. Roosevelt U., Chgo., 1980—, vice chmn., 1986—; co-chmn. adv. council Chgo. Action for Soviet Jewry, Highland Park, Ill., 1983—. Served to sgt. USAFR, 1965-69. Recipient Silver medal Ill. CPA Soc., 1962; named One of Ten Outstanding Young Men in Chgo., Chgo. Jr. C. of C., 1973-74; recipient Rolf A. Weil Disting. Service award, Roosevelt U., Chgo., 1983; Max Block award N.Y. State C.P.A. Soc., 1984; Ann. Literary award Jour. Acctg., 1986. Mem. Am. Inst. CPAs (bd. dirs., numerous coms., Elijah Watt Sells award 1962), Am. Acctg. Assn., Ill. CPA Soc. (acctg. principles com. 1973), Fin. Acctg. Standards Adv. Council. Jewish. Clubs: Mid-Day, Standard (Chgo.); Elms Swim & Tennis (Highland Park). Avocations: Tennis, collecting art.

MEEDEL, VIRGIL GENE, engineering executive; b. Columbus, Nebr., Nov. 26, 1927; s. Frederick and Ella (Blaser) M.; m. Aretta Mae Loseke, Mar. 28, 1951; children—Laurel, Marilyn, James, Tamara, Robyn. B.Sc., U. Nebr., 1958, M.Sc., 1966. Registered profl. engr., Nebr. Freight passenger agt. U.P. R.R., Nebr., 1948-58; design engr. Behlen Mfg. Co., Columbus, 1958-60, Kirkham Michael, Omaha, 1960-65; project mgr. Henningson, Durham & Richardson, Omaha, 1965-78, engring. dept. mgr., Seattle, 1978-81, dir. engring., v.p., Lubbock, Tex., 1981-82; chief bridge engr. HDR, Omaha, 1982-85; dir. ops., exec. v.p. HDR Infrastructure, Omaha, 1985—. Served with AUS, 1945-47. Mem. ASCE, Am. Ry. Engring. Assn. Republican. Presbyterian. Lodge: Rotary. Address: 8404 Indian Hills Dr Omaha NE 68117

MEEK, JOSEPH CHESTER, JR., physician, educator; b. Hiawatha, Kans., July 16, 1931; s. Joseph Chester and Florence Mildred (Eicholtz) M.; A.B., U. Kans., 1954, M.D., 1957; m. Bette Ewing, June 5, 1954; children—Thomas, Nancy, Katherine. Intern San Diego County Gen. Hosp., 1957-58; resident U. Kans. Med. Ctr., Kansas City, 1958-60; instr. medicine U. Kans., 1964-65, asst. prof., 1965-69, assoc. prof., 1969-75, prof., 1975—, vice chancellor acad. affairs, 1981-85, chmn. Dept. Internal Medicine, Wichita, 1985—. Served with USNR, 1960-62. Mem. Am. Fedn. Clin. Research, AMA, Wyandotte County Med. Assn., Kans. Med. Soc., Am. Diabetes Assn., Endocrine Soc., Central Soc. Clin. Research, Am. Thyroid Assn., Soc. Med. Coll. Dirs., Am. Heart Assn., Phi Beta Kappa, Alpha Omega Alpha. Contbr. articles to profl. jours. Home: 8825 Shadowridge Wichita KS 67226 Office: University of Kansas Sch Medicine 1010 N Kansas Ave Wichita KS 67214

MEEK, LEROY RICHARD, watchmaker, jeweler; b. Pleasant Lake, Ind., Feb. 15, 1932; s. Joseph Nathan and Beulah Naomi (Dreher) M.; m. Julia Ann Perry, Nov. 21, 1969; children—Leroy M., Sheila C. B.A. in Horology, Bradley U., 1957. Cert. master watchmaker. Watchmaker, jeweler Liechty Jewelry, Angola, Ind., 1958-62; owner, watchmaker, jeweler Meek's Jewelry, LaGrange, Ind., 1962—; guest watchmaker Watchmakers Assn. of Switzerland, Berne, 1970, Bulova Watch Co., Berne, 1970. County Vets. Service officer VA, LaGrange, 1977—. Served with USN, 1951-55, FPO, Korea. Mem. Watchmakers Assn. of Ind. (cert.), Am. Watchmakers Inst. (cert.), Northeastern Ind. Horology Guild, Ind. Jewelers Assn., VFW, Am. Legion, LaGrange C. of C. (bd. dirs. 1982—). Club: LaGrange Country (social dir. 1984). Lodges: Loyal Order of Moose (1st gov. 1976, fellowship degree 1978), Masons. Avocations: bowling; golf; fishing. Office: Meek's Jewelry 111 S Detroit St LaGrange IN 46761

MEEK, WILLIAM TAYLOR, dentist; b. Indpls., Mar. 16, 1926; s. Torrence Wendell and Gladys Cleo (Watson) M.; m. Margaret Marie Weiss, June 26, 1946; children: Leslie Ann, Claudia Lynne. DDS, Ind. U., 1953. Pvt. practice Indpls., 1953—; bd. dirs. Blue Cross-Blue Shield of Ind., Indpls., 1983—. Mem. Marion County Rep. Vets. of WWII, Hoosier Hundred of Ind. U. Found., Indpls. Zool. Soc. "500" Festival Assocs., guarantor for Starlight Musicals. Served with USN, 1944-46, PTO. Named to Sagamore of Wabash, Gov. Ind., 1983. Fellow Internat. Coll. Dentists; mem. ADA, Ind. Dental Assn., Indpls. Dist. Dental Soc., Delta Sigma Delta. Republican. Club: Columbia (Indpls.); Highland Golf and Country (Indpls.). Lodges: Masons, Shriners. Avocations: tennis. bowling, fishing. Home: 5364 Far Hill Rd Indianapolis IN 46226 Office: 5317 East 16th St Indianapolis IN 46218

MEEKER, DAVID ANTHONY, public relations executive; b. Akron, Ohio, June 1, 1939; s. Charles Anthony and Lucia Pauline (Schweikert) K.; m. Anita Marie De Jacimo, June 24, 1961; Chrisine Marie, Elizabeth Ann, Eileen Louise, David Edgerton. BS in Indsl. Journalism, Kent State U., 1961, postgrad., 1963-64. Editor Recordark Record Eastman Kodak Co., N.Y.C., 1961-62; journalist Akron (Ohio) Beacon Jour., 1962-66, St. Louis Post Dispatch, 1966-69; exec. sec. to mayor City of St. Louis, 1969-71; asst. dir. Ohio Dept. Natural Resources, Columbus, 1971-73; exec. dir. Ohio Dem. Party, Columbus, 1973-74; pres. Urbanistics, Inc., Akron, 1974-76, Meeker-Mayer Pub. Relations, Akron, 1976-84; prin. David A. Meeker and Assocs., Akron, 1984—. V.p Jr. Achievement Akron, 1985-86; trustee Keep Akron Beautiful, 1985-86, Akron Regional Devel. Bd., Ohio Ballet, St. Edward Home, Akron; pres. endowment bd. St. Vincent-St. Mary, PROhio. Alicia Patterson fellow, 1968; named Disting. Alumnus, Kent State Sch. Journalism, 1983. em. Pub. Relations Soc. Am. (accred., past pres. Akron, past chmn. nat. honors and awards com., past pres. nat. membership com., del.-at-large nat. assembly), Sigma Delta Chi (pres. Buckeye chapt. 1980, Con Kelliher award 1966). Democrat. Roman Catholic. Clubs: Cascade (Akron). Avocations: tennis, fishing, antiques. Home: 269 S Rose Blvd Akron OH 44313 Office: One Cascade Plaza 19th Floor Akron OH 44308

MEEKER, JAMES ALLEN, mechanical engineer; b. Toledo, Nov. 5, 1925; s. George Harry and Helen Charlotte (Wendt) M.; m. Jeannine Moree, July 10, 1953; children: James A. Jr., Michelle Moree. B in Mech. Engring., U. Toledo, 1953, MME, 1963, M in Engring Sci., 1966. Registered profl. engr., Ohio. Asst. to plant engr. Dura Corp., Toledo, 1953-64, plant engr., 1964-66; plant and mech. engr. Owens Ill., 1966-70; sr. mech. engr. Libbey Owens Ford Co., Toledo, 1970—. Inventor: Sheet Feeding Apparatus, 1983, Sheet Handling Apparatus, 1984. Mem. Soc. Mech. Engring. (cert. mfg. engring. robotics), U. Toledo Engring. Alumni Assn. (pres.). Lutheran. Avocations: windsurfing, volleyball, cross country skiing, photography. Home: 3212 Wendover Dr Toledo OH 43606 Office: Libbey Owens Ford Co 1701 E Broadway Toledo OH 43605

MEEKER, LORELEI, academic administrator; b. Crawfordsville, Aug. 2, 1952; d. Norman Ross and Misako (Yokoyama) M.; m. Geoffrey Mitchell Grodner, Dec. 22, 1974; 1 child, Andrew Meeker Grodner. BA, Ind. U., 1974. Paralegal Akin, Gump, Strauss, Hauer & Feld, Washington, 1976; tutor, counselor Ind. U., Bloomington, 1977-80; ops. mgr. Univ. div. Ind. U., 1981—. Mem. Workable Program Com., Bloomington, 1981; chmn. City of Bloomington Human Rights Commn., 1983; mem. com. Women's Health Issues on Women's Affairs, Bloomington, 1986-87; publicity chmn. Boy's Club Auxiliary, 1986. Mem. Ind. Mid-Am. Assn. Ednl. Opportunity (pres.-elect 1986-87, bd. dirs.). Democrat. Avocations: reading, knitting, painting, music, traveling. Home: 2710 McMillan Bloomington IN 47401 Office: Univ div Ind U Maxwell Hall 104 Bloomington IN 47401

MEEKS, CORDELL DAVID, JR., state judge; b. Kansas City, Kans., Dec. 17, 1942; s. Cordell David and Cellastine Dora (Brown) M.; m. Mary Ann Sutherland, July 15, 1967; 1 child, Cordell D. III. B.A., U. Kans., 1964, J.D., 1967; postgrad., U. Pa., 1968. Bar: Kans. 1968, U.S. Dist. Ct. Kans. 1968, U.S. Mil. Ct. Appeals 1971, U.S. Ct. Appeals (10th cir.) 1971, U.S. Supreme Ct. 1971. Staff counsel Wyandotte County Legal Aid Soc., Kansas City, Kans., 1968-70; spl. asst. atty. gen. State of Kans., Kansas City, 1975; sr. ptnr. Meeks, Sutherland, and McIntosh, Kansas City, 1972-81; judge Mcpl. Ct. Kansas City, 1976-81; dist. ct. judge 29th Judicial Dist. Kans., Kansas City, 1981—; mem. govs. com. crime prevention, Kans., 1984—; mem. Kans. adv. com. overcrowded prisons, 1983-84, Kans. Com. on Bicentennial of U.S. Constn., 1987—; pres. Wyandotte County Law Library Com., 1982-83; staff judge adv. 35th Inf. Div. Kans. N.G., 1984—. Vice pres. Jr. Achievement Greater Kansas City, 1975-76; pres. Wyandotte County chpt. ARC, 1971-73, Mental Health Assn., 1981-83, Legal Aid Soc., 1971-73, Econ. Opportunity Found., Inc., Kansas City, 1981-83; bd. dirs. Family and Childrens Service, 1983—; pres. Substance Abuse Ctr. Eastern Kans., 1985—; mem. exec. com. NCCJ, Kansas City, 1984-87. Recipient Outstanding Service award Kansas City United Way, 1979. Mem. Kans. Mcpl. Judges Assn. (pres. 1980-81), U. Kans. Law Soc. (pres. bd. govs. 1984-85), Nat. Conf. State Trial Judges (ethics and profl. responsibility com.), Am. Judicature Soc., Am. Judges Assn., ABA, Kans. Bar Assn., Am. Royal Assn. (bd. govs. 1981-87), Am. Lung Assn. (pres. elect 1987—). Democrat. Mem. A. M. E. Ch. Lodge: Optimists (bd. dirs. 1977). Avocations: jazz piano; table tennis; swimming. Home: 7915 Walker Kansas City KS 66112 Office: Wyandotte County Courthouse 701 N 7th St Kansas City KS 66101

MEEKS, CORDELL DAVID, retired state district court judge; b. Little Rock, Sept. 25, 1914; s. Charles Arthur and Mossie Ella (Green) M.; m. Cellastine Dora Brown, Dec. 22, 1940; children: Marlene, Cordell Jr., Marcena, Marquita. BA, U. Kans., 1938, JD, 1940. Bar: Kans. 1940, U.S. Supreme Ct. 1966. Asst. dist. atty. Kansas City Wyandotte County, Kans., 1947-51; mem. bd. county commrs. Wyandotte County, Kans., 1951-73; sr. ptnr. Meeks, Whyte & Meeks, Kansas City, 1958-73; chmn. bd. county commrs. Wyandotte County, Kans., 1965-73; judge State Dist. Ct., Kans., 1973-81; founder, dir. Douglass (Kans.) State Bank, 1947—, v.p. 1963—; chmn. MidAm. Council Govts., 1971-72. Author: To Heaven Through Hell,

1986. Pres. Democracy Inc., Kansas City, 1957-73; del. Dem. Nat. Conv., 1948, 64; mem. adv. com., law council Boy Scouts Am., 1964; dir. regional health and welfare council Met. Planning Commn., 1971-72. Recipient Leadership award MidAm. Council Govts., 1973, Equal Opportunity award Urban League of Greater Kansas City, 1980, Humanitarian award Nat. Black Police Officers Assn., 1980, Disting. Service to Legal Profession award Kansas City and Jackson County Bar Assns., 1981, Humanitarian award Kans. Black Legis. Caucus, 1987. Mem. Kansas City Bar Assn., Kans. Bar Assn., Wyandotte County Bar Assn. (Centennial award 1986). Methodist. Lodge: Masons.

MEEKS, HOWARD S., bishop. Bishop Episcopal Ch., Kalamazoo. Office: Episc Ch 2600 Vincent Ave Kalamazoo MI 49001 *

MEENGS, WILLIAM LLOYD, cardiologist; b. Zeeland, Mich., Dec. 23, 1942; s. Lloyd Stanley and Gertrude (Wyngarden) M.; A.B., Hope Coll., 1964; M.D., U. Mich., 1968; m. Helen Delores Van Dyke, June 10, 1964; children—Michelle Rene, William Lloyd, Lisa Ann. Intern in internal medicine Univ. Hosp., Ann Arbor, Mich., 1968-69, resident in internal medicine, 1971-73, fellow in cardiology, 1973-75; practice medicine specializing in cardiology, Petoskey, Mich., 1975—; cardiologist Burns Clinic Med. Center, Petoskey, 1975—, chmn. dept. cardiology and cardiac surgery, 1978—; cardiologist Little Traverse Hosp., Petoskey, 1975—, dir. coronary care unit, 19—; dir. cardiac catheterization lab. No. Mich. Hosps., Petoskey, 1985—, adult spl. care units, 1986—. Contbr. med. articles to profl. jours. Trustee Mich. Heart Assn., 1979-83. Served as surgeon USPHS, 1969-71. Fellow Am. Coll. Cardiology; mem. A.C.P., Am. Heart Assn., Am. Soc. Echocardiography, Alpha Omega Alpha. Home: 1052 Lindell St Petoskey MI 49770 Office: Burns Clin Med Ctr 560 W Mitchell St Petoskey MI 49770

MEERSCHAERT, JOSEPH RICHARD, physician; b. Detroit, Mar. 4, 1941; s. Hector Achiel and Marie Terese (Campbell) M.; m. Jeanette Marie Ancerewicz, Sept. 14, 1963; children—Eric, Amy, Adam. B.A., Wayne State U., 1965, M.D., 1967. Diplomate Am. Bd. Phys. Medicine and Rehab. Intern, Harper Hosp., Detroit, 1967-68; resident in phys. medicine and rehab. Wayne State U. Rehab. Inst., Detroit, 1968-71; chief div. phys. medicine Naval Hosp., Chelsea, Mass., 1971-73; attending physician William Beaumont Hosp., Royal Oak, Mich., 1973—, med. dir. rehab. unit, 1979—; pvt. practice medicine specializing in phys. medicine and rehab., Royal Oak, 1973—; mem. med. adv. bd. Nat. Wheelchair Athletic Assn., 1973—, examining physician Nat. Wheelchair Athletic Games, Marshall, Minn., 1982, U.S. team physician VII World Wheelchair Games, Stoke Mandeville, Eng.; clin. instr. Wayne State U., 1973-83, clin. asst. prof. phys. medicine and rehab., 1983—; mem. Mich. Dept. Licensing and Regulation State Bd. Phys. Therapy, 1978-81. Served with M.C., USN, 1971-73. Recipient John Hussey award Mich. Wheelchair Athletic Assn., 1981. Mem. Am. Acad. Phys. Medicine and Rehab. (reviewer, presenter), Am. Congress Rehab. Medicine, Mich. Phys. Medicine and Rehab. Soc., Am. Geriatrics Soc., Am. Assn. Electromyography and Electrodiagnosis, Mich. Rheumatism Soc., Mich. Acad. Phys. Medicine and Rehab. (chmn. program com. 1977-78, trustee 1980—, del. 1982), Oakland County Med. Soc. (alt. del. 1979-81), Met. Soc. Crippled Children and Adults (bd. dirs. 1979-82, pres. 1981-82), Alpha Omega Alpha. Roman Catholic. Contbr. articles to profl. jours. Office: 3535 W 13 Mile Rd Royal Oak MI 48072

MEERSCHAERT, LAWRENCE JOSEPH, accountant; b. Detroit, Feb. 28, 1960; s. Robert Walter and Dorothy Rose (Deneweth) M.; m. Polly Ann Lesher, May 13, 1983; children: Erik Deneweth, Mary Elizabeth. AA, Macomb County Community Coll., 1980; BBA, Eastern Mich. U., 1982; postgrad., Walsh Coll., 1986—. CPA, Mich. Agt. IRS, Detroit, 1982—. Republican. Roman Catholic. Lodge: Elks. Avocations: running, golfing, working outdoors. Home: 30022 Paul Ct Warren MI 48092 Office: IRS 477 Michigan Ave Detroit MI 48227

MEESE, ERNEST HAROLD, thoracic and cardiovascular surgeon; b. Bradford, Pa., June 23, 1929; s. Ernest D. and Blanche (Raub) M.; m. Margaret Eugenia McHenry, Oct. 4, 1952 (dec. May 1984); children: Constance Ann, Roderick Bryan, Gregory James; m. Rockell D. Dombar, Aug. 30, 1985. BA, U. Buffalo, 1950, MD, 1954. Diplomate Am. Bd. Surgery, Am. Bd. Thoracic Surgery. Resident in gen. surgery Millard Fillmore Hosp., Buffalo, 1955-59; resident in thoracic surgery U.S. Naval Hosp., St. Albans L.I., N.Y., 1961-63; group practice thoracic and cardiovascular surgery, Cin., 1965—; asst. clin. prof. surgery Cin. Med. Ctr., 1972—; head sect. thoracic and cardiovascular surgery St. Francis-St. George Hosp., Deaconess Hosp.; mem. staff Good Samaritan Hosp., Bethesda Hosp., Christ Hosp., Providence Hosp., Childrens Hosp., Epp Meml. Hosp., St. Luke Hosp., Cin. Contbr. articles to profl. jours. and textbooks. Pres. bd. dirs., chmn. service com. Cin.-Hamilton County unit Am. Cancer Soc., trustee, mem. exec. bd., chmn. Ohio div., service com.; trustee, exec. bd. Southwestern Ohio chpt. Am. Heart Assn. Served to comdr. M.C., USN, 1959-65. Fellow A.C.S., Internat. Coll. Surgeons; mem. Soc. Thoracic Surgeons, Am. Coll. Chest Physicians, Am. Coll. Angiology, Cin. Surg. Soc., Am. Coll. Cardiology; mem. Gibson Anat. Hon. Soc., AMA, Am. Thoracic Soc., Assn. Mil. Surgeons U.S., Acad. Medicine Cin., Assn. Advancement Med. Instrumentation, N.Am. Soc. Pacing and Electrophysiology, Phi Beta Kappa, Phi Chi (treas. 1952-54). Clubs: Western Hills Country, Queen City, Mediclub (pres. 1983-85) (Cin.). Lodge: Masons. Home: 174 Pedretti Rd Cincinnati OH 45238 Office: 311 Howell Ave Cincinnati OH 45220 also: 5049 Crookshank Cincinnati OH 45211

MEESE, ROBERT ALLEN, architect; b. St. Paul, Mar. 16, 1956; s. Lloyd George and Drusilla (Deis) M. BArch, U. Minn., 1981. Registered architect, Minn. Job capt., draftsman James Cooperman & Assoc., Mpls., 1979-80; assoc. architect Ellerbe Assoc., Mpls., 1981-86; project architect Boarman Assoc., Mpls., 1986-87; project mgr. Heise Vanney Reinen & Assocs. Inc., Mpls., 1987—. Prin. works include St. Paul Winter Carnival Ice Palace (Progressive Architecture award 1986), U. Minn. Hosps. Unit J. Mem. AIA (Minn. Honor award 1986). Mem. United Church of Christ. Club: Afton (Minn.) Alps Ski Patrol (advisor 1985). Home: 4521 Nokomis Ave S Minneapolis MN 55406 Office: Heise Vanney Reinen & Assocs Inc 123 N 3d St Minneapolis MN 55401

MEGLIN, LINDA MARIE, advertising executive; b. Manchester, Conn., June 4, 1952; d. Anthony Joseph and Mary Ann (Kement) M. BA, John Carroll U., 1974. Advt. mgr. Teledyne Rep., Cleve., 1975-78; dir. communications Teledyne Cen. Group, Cleve., 1979-81; pres. TRL Prodns., Cleve., 1981—. Trustee Neighborhood Montessori Sch., Cleveland Heights, Ohio, 1981—, John Carroll U., 1985—. Mem. Indsl. Marketers of Cleve., Bus. and Profl. Advt. Assn. (cert. of recognition 1979), John Carroll U. Nat. Alumni Assn. (pres. 1985—, v.p. 1983-84, chmn. jour. com. 1980-84, trustee 1978-83). Roman Catholic. Home: 21251 Beachwood Dr Rocky River OH 44116 Office: TRL Prodns 15655 Brookpark Rd Cleveland OH 44142

MEHLHOUSE, ROBERT, farmer; b. Olivia, Minn., Oct. 27, 1943; s. Lloyd William Irene Marion (Oseth) M. BBA, mankato State U., 1966. Regional sales mgr. Torjan Seed Co., Olivia, Minn., 1966-68; owner, operator Mehlhouse Farms, Olivia, 1968—; pres. Sterling Internat. Industries, Olivia, 1986—. trustee Faith Meth. Ch., Olivia; pres. Minn. Dry Bean Commodity Council, Minn. Dept. Agrl., St. Paul, 1979—; bd. dirs. Renville County Soil and Water conservation Dist.; sec., treas. Renville County Crop Improvment, 1981—. Served to capt. U.S. Army, N.G.,1967-75. Mem. Northarvest Bean Assn. (bd. dirs., v.p., pres. 1978-85), Friends of Arts. Republican. Lodge: Masons. Home and Office: Rt 1 Box 18 Olivia MN 56277

MEHTA, DEV V., polymer scientist; b. India, Dec. 28, 1938; came to U.S., 1962; BS in Chemistry, U. Bombay, 1959; MS in Chemistry, U. Gujarat, India, 1961; BS in Chem. Engring., U. Mo., Rolla, 1964, MS, 1965; PhD in Polymer Sci., U. Akron, Ohio, 1971. Postdoctoral fellow inst. polymer sci. U. Akron, 1971; sr. research scientist Ames Co. div. Miles Labs., Elkhart, Ind., 1971-76; dir. research and devel. Gelman Sci., Inc., Ann Arbor, Mich., 1976-80, dir. div. electronics, 1980-83, dir. corp. applications and tech. services, 1983—. Patentee polymer membranes, film tech. Active Big Bros. Am., 1971-76. Recipient Midwest Regional Conf. award Am. Inst. Chem. Engrs., 1964. Mem. Am. Chem. Soc., Am. Electrochem. Soc., Am. Mgmt. Assn., Japanese Electrochem. Soc., TAPPI. Home: 9747 Queens Dr Manchester MI 48158 Office: Gelman Sciences Inc 600 S Wagner Rd Ann Arbor MI 48106

MEHTA, DINESH BACHULAL, physician; b. Dar-Es-Salaam, Tanzania, Mar. 20, 1939; came to U.S., 1970; s. Bachulal and Chandrakanta Mehta; m. Shobhana Tawde, Aug. 1, 1965; children: Sujeet, Supriya. BS, B. J. Med. Sch., Poona, India, 1963; MD, Poona U., 1965. Diplomate Am. Bd. Psychiatry and Neurology. Registrar medicine Sassoon Hosps., Poona, 1962-65, Wakefield (Eng.) Hosp., 1965-69; registrar geriatrics Exeter (Eng.) Hosp., 1969-70; resident in geriatrics St. Louis State Hosp., 1960-77; staff psychiatrist Hamilton Ctr., Terre Haute, Ind., 1977—, med. dir.; clin. dir. St. Louis State Hosp., 1971-77. Contbr. articles to profl. jour. Fellow Royal Coll. Physicians, Am. Coll. Internat. Physicians; mem. Brit. Med. Assn., Am. Psychiat. Assn., Royal Coll. Physicians, Royal Coll. Psychiatrists. Jain. Avocations: philately, photography, travel. Home: 7515 Carlisle R28 Terre Haute IN 47802 Office: Hamilton Ctr 620 8th Ave Terre Haute IN 47804

MEHTA, INDER S., housewares manufacturing company executive; b. India, Jan. 28, 1939; came to U.S. 1968, naturalized, 1985; s. Harnath and Sajjan Kumari (Chajjer) M.; m. Sudha Saklecha, Feb. 6, 1965; children—Sandeep, Rajeev. M.A., U. Delhi-India, 1960; M.B.A., Marquette U., 1970. With Regal Ware, Inc., Kewaskum, Wis., 1971—, now product dir. cookware and dir. internat. sales. Mem. Cookware Mfrs. Assn. Am. (chmn. statis. com. 1977-79). Avocations: bridge; tennis. Office: Regal Ware Inc 1675 Reigle Dr Kewaskum WI 53040

MEHTA, KAYOMARSH PERVEZ, manufacturing executive, management consultant; b. Navsari, India, Oct. 7, 1947; came to U.S., 1969; s. Pervez Cowasji and Freny Pervez M.; m. Nergish Kayomarsh Bilimoria, Dec. 24, 1972; children: Roxana, Zenobia, Farhad, Rashni. BSEE, U. Baroda, India, 1969; postgrad., Ill. Inst. Tech., 1969-70; MBA in Fin. and Mktg., Northwestern U., 1973. Engr. Union Carbide Corp., Chgo., 1970-74, sr. engr., 1974-80, engring. supr., 1980-86; engring. supr. Viskase Corp., Chgo., 1986—; mgmt. cons. Faroze, Palos Hills, Ill., 1975—. V.p. Zoroastrian Assn. Met. Chgo., 1980-86, pres. 1986—. Avocations: chess, computers, sightseeing and touring. Home: 8122 Circle Dr Palos Hills IL 60465 Office: Viskase Corp 6733 W 65th St Chicago IL 60638

MEHTA, SHARDA HIMATLAL, psychologist; b. Amreli, Gujarat, India, Dec. 31, 1936; came to U.S., 1967; d. Himatlal Manilal and Nlarmada (Dave) M.; m. Leslie Comedy, Dec. 22., 1979 (div. Feb. 1981). BA, Gujarat U., India, 1960, MA, 1962; Diploma in Med. and Social Psychology, Mysore U., India, 1966. Psychologist Juvenile Home, Bombay, India, 1965-66, Tng. Sch., Petersburg, Va., 1967-72, Cen. Ohio Psychiat. Hosp., Columbus, Ohio, 1972—; Cons. in field, Columbus, 1983-86. Govt. India Edn. Dept. fellow, 1963. Mem. Gujarati Assn. Columbus Ohio (v.p. 1972). Avocations: drawing, painting, sewing, collecting antiques, traveling. Home: 207 S Huron Ave Columbus OH 43204

MEHTA, SHOBHANA D., psychiatrist; b. Poona, India, Dec. 29, 1938; d. Sitaram Ramji and Satyawati (Jadhav) Tawde; m. Dinesh B. Mehta, Aug. 1, 1965; children: Sujeet, Supriya. MBBS, B.J. Med. Coll., Poona, 1962, MD, 1965; D Psychiat. Medicine, London, 1969. Diplomate Am. Bd. Psychiatry and Neurology. Registrar in medicine Sassoon Hosp., Poona, Ind., 1962-65; registrar in psychiatry Stanley Royd Hosp., Wakefield, Eng., 1967-69, Exeter (Eng.) Vale Hosp., 1969-79; research assoc. psychiatry Mo. Inst. Psychiatry, 1970-71; clin. dir. St. Louis State Hosp., 1971-77; sr. psychiatrist Hamilton Ctr., Terre Haute, Ind., 1977-84; practice medicine specializing in psychiatry Terre Haute, 1984—; pres. med. staff Hamilton Ctr., Terre Haute, 1980. Contbr. articles to profl. jours. Bd. dirs. Terre Haute Edn. Found., 1981-83, Mental Health Assn., Terre Haute, 1986. Fellow Royal Coll. Physicians, Am. Coll. Internat. Physicians; mem. British Med. Assn., Am. Psychiat. Assn., Royal Coll. Psychiatrists. Democrat. Hindu. Avocations: reading, painting, conversation. Office: 501 E Hospital Lane Terre Haute IN 47802

MEIER, BEN, state official; b. Napoleon, N.D., Aug. 1, 1918; s. Bernhardt and Theresia (Hilzenderger) M.; m. Clara Kaczynski, Dec. 30, 1944; children: Lynn, Bernie. Student, Dakota Bus. Sch., 1943, U. Wis. Sch. Banking, 1947-48. Asst. cashier Stock Growers Bank, Napoleon, 1945-47, Gackle State Bank, N.D., 1947-49; pres. Bank of Hazelton, N.D.; pres., dir. Mandan Security Bank, N.D., 1959-70; sec. state N.D. Bismarck, 1955—. Crusade chmn. N.D. Heart Assn., 1969, N.D. Cnacer Soc., 1970. Recipient N.D. Nat. Leadership Excellency award. Mem. N.D. Bankers Assn., Nat. Assn. Secs. State (pres. 1967), Nat. Assn. State Contractors Licensing Agys. (v.p. 1969-70), Sons of Norway. Republican. Office: Office Sec State ND State Capitol Bldg 1st Floor Bismarck ND 58505 *

MEIER, DALE JOSEPH, physics educator; b. Dalles, Oreg., Apr. 21, 1922. BS, Calif. Inst. Tech., 1947, MS, 1948; PhD, UCLA, 1951. Supr. research Shell Devel. Co., Emeryville, Calif., 1951-72; prof. Mich. Molecular Inst., Midland, 1972—; cons. Lawrence Livermore (Calif.) Lab., 1972—, Dow Chem. Co., Midland, 1979—, E.I. duPont, Wilmington, Del., 1980—. Editor: Molecular Basis Transitions and Relaxations, 1978, Block Copolymers, 1983; contbr. articles to profl. jours.; patentee in field. Served to 1st lt. USMC, 1943-46. Fellow UCLA, 1949. Fellow Am. Physical Soc.; mem. Am. Chem. Soc., Soc. Rheology, Sigma Xi, Phi Lambda Upsilon. Avocations: sculpturing, photography, gardening. Home: 3320 Noeske St Midland MI 48640 Office: Mich Molecular Inst 1910 W St Andrews Rd Midland MI 48640

MEIER, GARRY EUGENE, financial executive; b. Springfield, Ill., Mar. 20, 1953; s. Fred David Sr. and Norma Jean (Tapp) M.; m. Toni Rae Ramseyer, June 4, 1983; 1 child, Justin Joseph. BBA, Kans. State U., 1975; MBA, So. Ill. U., 1985. Account mgr. IBM Corp., Kansas City, Mo., 1976-79; market support mgr. Xerox Corp., St. Louis, 1979-81; gen. ptnr. Edward D. Jones & Co., Maryland Heights, Mo., 1981—. Cons., advisor St. Peters (Mo.) Indsl. Devel. Authority, 1984—; v.p. St. Charles (Mo.) Indsl. Devel. Authority, 1986—; mem. adv. bd. sch. bus. Jefferson Coll., Hillsboro, 1983—, St. Louis U. Metro Coll., 1982—. Recipient Community Service award St. Louis U. Metro Coll., 1984. Mem. Am. Mgmt. Assn., Soc. for Advancement Mgmt., Assn. for Image and Info. Mgmt., Assn. MBA Execs. Republican. Baptist. Avocation: coaching football. Office: Edward D Jones & Co 201 Progress Pkwy Suite 103 Maryland Heights MO 63043

MEIER, GUSTAV, symphony conductor. Conductor Lansing (Mich.) Symphony. Office: Lansing Symphony 230 N Washington Suite F Lansing MI 48933 *

MEIER, HENRY GEORGE, architect; b. Indpls., July 14, 1929; s. Virgil and Elizabeth (Whiteside) M.; m. Peggy Nelson, June 28, 1953; children: Scott J., Bruce W., Paul T., Thomas A. BArch, U. Cin., 1953. Lic. architect Ind., Mich., Ky., Ill., Iowa, Fla., Ohio; lic. landscape architect Ind. Pvt. practice architecture Indpls., 1964—. Contbr. Indiana Architect mag. Bd. dirs. Am. Bapt. Chs./U.S.A., Valley Forge, Pa., 1970-77, Bd. Bldg. Appeals, Indpls., 1979-85. Served to 1st lt. USMC, 1953-55. Fellow AIA (bd. dirs. 1982-85); mem. Ind. Soc. Architects (pres. 1975, Edward D. Pierre award 1979), Constrn. Specifications Inst., Interfaith Forum on Religion Art and Architecture (v.p. 1981). Republican. Lodges: Masons, Shriners.

MEIER, KAREN LORENE, educator; b. Davenport, Iowa, Aug. 17, 1942; d. Charles Frank and Minnie Louise (Arp) Meier; B.A., U. Iowa, 1963, M.A., 1974. Tchr., librarian Plano (Ill.) High Sch., 1963-67; tchr. social studies Moline (Ill.) High Sch., 1967—, also Secondary Social Studies Coordinator. Bd. dirs. Quad-City World Affairs Council; active LWV. Recipient regional award Ill. State Hist. Soc. Mem. Nat. Council Social Studies, Ill. Council Social Studies (sec. 1973-74, v.p. 1974-75, 86—, bd. dirs. 1982-83, treas. 1984-86), Iowa Council Social Studies, NEA, Ill. Edn. Assn. (sec.-treas. regional council 1975-79, legis. chairperson 1980-81), Moline Edn. Assn. (pres. 1977-78), Am. Soc. Profl. and Exec. Women, Social Studies Suprs. Assn., Assn. Supervision and Curriculum Devel., AAUW, Women in Ednl. Adminstrn., (dir. 1985, pres. 1985-86, past pres. 1986-87, asst. pres. 1986-87, bd. dirs. 1987-88), Iowa Women in Ednl. Leadership, Alpha Delta Kappa. Home: 1855 14th St Bettendorf IA 52722 Office: 3600 23d Ave Moline IL 61265

MEIERS, DAVID EVAN, service executive; b. Hartley, Iowa, Apr. 11, 1947; s. Glen and Ruth Lenore (Olson) M.; m. Vivian Fern Nelson, Nov. 25, 1965; children: Michelle, Nicholas. BA, U. N.D., 1969, MA, 1972. Cert. assn. exec., N.D. Tchr., coach Kerkhoven (Minn.) Pub. Schs., 1969-71; prin. Wolford (N.D.) Pub. Schs., 1971-73; bus. adminstr. Three Affiliated Tribes, Newtown, N.D., 1973-76; adminstrv. dir. N.D. Srs. United, Minot, 1976-77; exec. dir. N.D. Pub. Employees Assn., Bismarck, 1977-83; exec. v.p. N.D. Hospitality Assn., Bismarck, 1983—; v.p. Assembly Govtl. Employees, Washington, 1980-82; chmn. N.D. Travel and Trade Network, Bismarck, 1984-86; mem. Gov's. Hwy. Safety Com., Bismarck, 1985-87. Candidate for N.D. Commr. of Labor, 1982. Recipient Greeter Feature award, Bismarck C. of C., 1986. Mem. Internat. Assn. Restaurant Execs. (bd. dirs. 1983-84), Internat. Assn. Hotel Execs., N.D. Jaycees (pres. Newton 1975-76, Outstanding Young Men award 1981). Democrat. Lutheran. Lodges: Kiwanis, Elks, Lions. Home: 412 Birchwood Dr Bismarck ND 58501 Office: ND Hospitality Assn 315 E Broadway Bismarck ND 58501

MEIJER, FREDERIK, retail company executive; b. 1919. married. Chmn. bd., dir. Meijer, Inc., Grand Rapids, Mich. Office: Meijer Inc 2727 Walker Ave NW Grand Rapids MI 49504 *

MEIKLE, WILLIAM MACKAY, lawyer; b. Wilkinsburg, Pa., July 13, 1933; s. William and Martha (Bohlender) M.; m. Mary Eileen Luth, Mar. 12, 1966; children—Elizabeth Ellen, Martha Pauline. B.B.A., U. Mich., 1955, J.D., 1959. Bar: Ohio 1959. Sole practice, Celina, Ohio, 1959-63; ptnr. Knapke & Meikle, Celina, 1964-76; ptnr. Meikle, Tesno & Luth, Celina, 1977-81; ptnr. Meikle, Tesno & Luth, Celina, 1982—; also asst. pros. atty. Mercer County (Ohio) 1959-74, pros. atty., 1975-76; sec., treas. Mercer County Civic Found., 1961—; pres. Mercer County Health Care Found., 1980—; sec. Western Ohio Ednl. Found., 1975—; trustee Auglaize County Family Y Inc., 1981-84. Served to capt. USAR, 1959. Mem. Ohio State Bar Assn., Ohio Assn. Civil Trial Attys. Democrat. Methodist. Home: 209 Mercer St Celina OH 45822 Office: 100 N Main St Celina OH 45822

MEINERS, ROBERT PETER, policeman; b. Chgo., Nov. 18, 1955; s. Richard Lee and Rita Marie (Guzell) M.; m. Karrie Lea Skeate, Oct. 3, 1980; 1 child, Rachel Erin. BA in Criminal Justice, Northeastern U., Chgo., 1982, MA in Polit. Sci., 1986. From police officer to detective Lincolnwood (Ill.) Police Dept., 1979—. Served with USMC, 1974-76. Recipient Outstanding Police award Chgo. Police, 1981, Dept. Commendation, Chgo. Police, 1981. Mem. Internat. Assn. Chiefs of Police. Roman Catholic. Avocations: child care, research, investigations. Office: Lincolnwood Police 6918 N Keeler Lincolnwood IL 60646

MEINERT, JOHN RAYMOND, clothing manufacturing executive; b. White Cloud, Mich., Aug. 11, 1927; m. Joyce Macdonell, Nov. 5, 1955; children: Elizabeth Joyce, Pamela Anne. Student, U. Mich., 1944-45; B.S., Northwestern U., 1949. C.P.A., Ill., 1952. Treas., dir. Posto-Photo Co., Chgo., 1948-49; with Hart Schaffner & Marx/Hartmarx Corp., Chgo., 1950—; asst. treas. Hart Schaffner & Marx, 1962-65, comptroller, 1965-69, v.p., 1966-69, sr. v.p., 1969-74, treas., 1970-72, exec. v.p., 1975-80, vice chmn., 1981-85, sr. vice chmn., 1985-86, chmn., 1987—, also bd. dirs.; dir. Amalgamated Life Ins. Co.; trustee Amalgamated Ins. Fund; instr. acctg. Northwestern U., 1949. Bd. dirs. Duncan YMCA, Chgo., 1967—; mem. Chgo. com. Council on Fgn. Relations, 1970—; mem. U. Ill. Bus. Adv. Council, 1985—; bd. dirs. Better Bus. Bureau; bus. adv. bd. Northwestern U. Served with AUS, 1945-46. Mem. Am. Inst. CPA's (v.p. 1985-86, council mem. 1971—, chmn. fin. mgmt. com. 1974-75, dir. 1975-78, audit com. 1975-78, chmn. adv. com. industry and govt. 1975-78, chmn. spl. com. bylaws 1979-81, mission commn. 1984-86, chmn. centennial industry commn. 1985-87, Gold Medal award 1985-86), Ill. CPA Soc. (hon. award, dir. 1966-68, 81-84, v.p. 1967-68, sr. v.p. 1981-82, pres. 1982-83, chmn. nominations 1983-84), Acctg. Research Assn. (trustee 1985-86), Clothing Mfrs. Assn. U.S. (pres. and dir. 1982—), Chgo. Assn. Commerce and Industry (coms on audit and fin. 1978—). Presbyterian (elder). Clubs: University (Chgo.); Rolling Green Country (Arlington Heights). Lodge: Rotary (bd. dirs.). Home: 634 Ironwood Dr Arlington Heights IL 60004 Office: 101 N Wacker Dr Chicago IL 60606

MEINHOLD, ANDREW LEE, bank executive; b. Columbus, Ohio, May 23, 1950; s. Herbert M. and Edith W. (Mould) N.; m. Allison Jean Campbell, Sept. 11, 1976; children: Jonathan C., Benjamin A. BA, Hiram Coll., 1972. Field rep. HUD, Columbus, 1972-73; planning coordinator City of East Liverpool, Ohio, 1973-75; asst. community devel. dir. City of Painesville, Ohio, 1975-77; v.p., sec. Mentor (Ohio) Savings Bank, 1977-86; sr. v.p. Peoples Savings Bank, Ashtabula, Ohio, 1986—. Mem. Painesville City Council, 1979-82. Mem. United Ch. of Christ. Club: Exchange (Mentor) (pres. 1982-83). Avocations: reading, golf. Home: 9730 Foxhill Tr Concord Twp OH 44060 Office: Peoples Savings Bank 4200 Park Ave Ashtabula OH 44004

MEINZ, MICHAEL JOHN, computer systems programmer manager; b. Mpls., Mar. 22, 1948; s. Harold John and Gladys Margaret (Pearce) M.; m. Sharon Joyce Fulks, Oct. 17, 1970. Cert. data processing, Minn. Computer programmer USN, Groton, Conn., 1967-71; computer programmer Gen. Mills, Golden Valley, Minn., 1971-73, systems programmer, 1973-77, systems programming mgr., 1977—; cons. Minn. Dept. Edn., St. Paul, 1978—. Served with USN, 1967-71. Office: Gen Mills Inc 9200 Wayzata Blvd Golden Valley MN 55440

MEIRINK, THOMAS PAUL, orthopedic surgeon; b. St. Louis, Mar. 16, 1936; s. Paul H. and Cornelia (St. Eve) M.; m. Suzanne Macdonald, Apr. 16, 1966; children—William Charles, Stephanie Regnier, Thomas Paul. BS, U. Notre Dame, 1958; MD, Loyola U., Chgo., 1962. Diplomate Am. Bd. Orthopaedic Surgeons. Intern, St. John's Hosp., St. Louis, 1962-63; resident St. Louis U., 1963-68; practice medicine specializing in orthopedic surgery, Belleville, Ill., 1968—; mem. staff St. Elizabeth's Hosp., Belleville Meml. Hosp., Firmin Desloge Hosp., St. Louis, Cardinal Glennon Hosp., St. Louis; clin. instr. St. Louis U., 1968—; clin. asst. prof. So. Ill. U. Sch. Medicine, 1983—; with Ill. Services for Crippled Children, U. Ill., Belleville, 1968—. Contbr. articles to profl. jours. Bd. dirs. Med. Utilization Review Com. for So. Ill., 1980—. Fellow ACS, Internat. Coll. Surgeons, Am. Acad. Orthopaedic Surgeons (bd. counselors 1987—); mem. AMA, Am. Trauma Soc., Am. Fracture Assn., Ill. Med. Soc. (trustee 1981-87), Ill. Orthopaedic Soc., Clin. Orthopaedic Soc., So. Ill. Med. Assn. (pres. 1981-82), St. Clair County Med. Assn. (pres. 1981), St. Louis Orthopaedic Soc., St. Louis Surg. Soc., St. Louis Rheumatism Soc., Phi Chi. Home: 41 Country Club Pl Belleville IL 62223 Office: Assoc Orthopedic Surgeons 8601 W Main St Belleville IL 62223

MEISEL, G(LEN) KURT, accountant; b. Mendota, Ill., Jan. 14, 1947; s. Glen M. and Virginia (Hohertz) M.; m. Cathy M. Hagerty, Apr. 17, 1986. BS, Bradley U., 1969. CPA, Ill. Tchr. Amboy (Ill). Sch. Dist., 1969-74; acct. Hamilton & Blaine, CPA's, Dixon, Ill., 1974-79, office mgr., 1979-85; prin. G. Kurt Meisel, CPA's, Mendota, 1985—. Pres. Amboy little league, 1979-83, mgr., 1984-85; asst. basketball coach Amboy High Sch., 1981-85. Mem. Am. Inst. CPA's, Nat. Soc. Accts. for Coops., Ill. CPA Soc. (mem. agribus. com.). Lodges: Lions, Elks. Office: 618 6th St Mendota IL 61342

MEISEL, SCOTT IRA, accountant, educator; b. Toledo, Apr. 19, 1949; s. George Ira and Gladys (Ulch) M. BSBA, Ashland (Ohio) Coll., 1972; MBA, U. Toledo, 1974. CPA, Ind. Instr. acctg. Miami U., Oxford, Ohio, 1976-78, Ind. State U., Terre Haute, Ind., 1978-81, 83-85; tax preparer H&R Block, Terre Haute, 1986; instr. acctg. Cumberland Coll., Williamsburg, Ky., 1987—; CPA exam grader, Am. Inst. CPA's, N.Y.C.; acting treas. Delta Pi Corp., Terre Haute, 1984-85, Theta Chi Frat., Terre Haute, 1980-81, 83-84; academic advisor acctg. club Ind. State U. 1978-81, 83-85, ski club, 1978-81. Mem. Am. Inst. CPA's, Am. Acctg. Assn. Lutheran. Avocations: football, softball, baseball, bowling, movies.

MEISS, RICHARD DEAN, sales professional; b. Morris, Minn., July 23, 1950; s. Harold Emil and Anna Marie (Zeltwanger) M.; m. Cheryl Lynne Fry, Nov. 26, 1977; children: Katherine, William. BA in Edn., U. Minn., Morris, 1972. Area mgr. Dale Carnegie & Assocs., St. Paul, 1972-73, Peoria,

Ill., 1973-75; nat. tng. dir. Personal Dynamics, Mpls., 1975-78; exec. v.p. Advanced Learning, Mpls., 1978-82; dir. mktg. Databar Corp., Mpls., 1982-85; v.p. sales Performax Systems, Mpls., 1985—; pub. speaker, tng. cons. Meiss & Assocs., Mpls., 1972—. Mem. bd. stewards Minnetonka Bapt. Ch., 1983, 86. Named one of Outstanding Young Men Am., 1979. Republican. Avocations: reading, boating, waterskiing, family activities. Office: Performax Systems 12755 State Hwy 55 Minneapolis MN 55441

MEISSE, GUNTHER SAGEL, radio station executive; b. Mansfield, Ohio, Nov. 28, 1942; s. Louis Albert and Barbara Marka (Sagel) M.; m. Jeanne H. Robinson, Jan. 15, 1983; children by previous marriage: Marka, Melinda, Gunther Sagel II, Robert; stepchildren: Steve, Russell. Grad. high sch., Mansfield. Salesman Service Audio Cons., 1956-61; part-time engrng. radio stas. WMAN and WCLW, Mansfield, 1956-60; one of founders Johnny Appleseed Broadcasting Co. and radio sta. WVNO, Mansfield, 1961—, gen. mgr., v.p., 1962-74, pres., 1974—; pres. GSM Media Corp. (WRGM Radio), 1976—; pres. Mid State Media Corp. (WWWY Radio), Columbus, Ind.; mem. adv. bd. Richland Trust Co., 1972—. Bd. dirs. Planned Parenthood, 1973, Renaissance Theatre, 1980-87; bd. dirs., mem. exec. com. Richland Econ. Devel. Corp. Mem. Mansfield Area C. of C. (bd. dirs. 1970-75), Advt. Club (past bd. dirs.), North Cen. Ohio Mktg. Club (past bd. dirs.), Nat. Assn. FM Broadcasters (bd. dirs. 1964-73, 75-76), FM Broadcast Pioneers (charter), Ohio Assn. Broadcasters (bd. dirs. 1980-83, v.p. 1977-78). Lodge: Rotary. Home: Bell Rd Mansfield OH 44904 Office: 2900 Park Ave W Mansfield OH 44906

MEISSNER, ANN LORING, psychologist, educator; b. Richland Center, Wis., Nov. 26, 1924; d. Frank Gilson Woodworth and Leona Bergman; m. Corbin Sherwood Kidder, Oct. 28,1979; children: Edie Meissner, John Arthur Meissner. BS, U. Mich., 1953; MS, U. Wis., 1960, PhD, 1965; MPH, U. Calif., Berkeley, 1969; diploma, Gestalt Inst., Cleve., 1983. Lic. cons. psychologist, Minn. Assoc. prof. W.Va. U., 1972-74; psychologist Alternative Behavior Assn., Mpls., 1974-79, Judson Family Ctr., Mpls., 1979-84; pvt. practice St. Paul, 1984—; dir. nursing Augsburg Coll., Mpls., 1974-76; prof. St. Mary's Coll., Mpls., 1979—; mem. staff. Gestalt Inst. Twin Citie, Mpls., 1978—; dir. Today Personnel, Mpls., 1980—; mem. State Bd. of Psychology, Mpls., 1982-86. Recipient Disting. Human Service Profl. award N. Hennipin Community Coll., Mpls., 1981. Mem. Am. Psychol. Assn., Cleve. Gestalt Inst. Alumni Assn. Episcopalian. Avocations: swimming, autoharp. Home: 442 Summit Ave #2 Saint Paul MN 55102 Office: 1360 Energy Park Dr Suite 330 Saint Paul MN 55108

MEISSNER, HAROLD C., window manufacturing company executive; b. 1917. With Andersen Corp., Bayport, Minn., 1954—, now pres., also bd. dirs. Office: Andersen Corp Foot N 5th Ave Bayport MN 55003 *

MEISSNER, LEONARD ARTHUR, JR., engineer; b. Algona, Iowa, Oct. 8, 1950; s. Leonard Arthur Sr. and Julie Eva (Vavra) M.; m. Marie Suzanne Duren, June 8, 1974; children: David Leonard, Sarah Marie. BEE, U. Wis., 1973. With data recording products div. 3M, St. Paul, 1973, various positions in tech. services, applications engrng., 1973-85; with memory techs. group lab. 3M, 1985—. Mem. Kappa Eta Kappa (pres. 1972).

MEJTA, CHERYL LEE, psychologist; b. Chgo., May 4, 1952; d. Edward and Helen (Sergel) M. BS, Bradley U., 1973, MA, 1974; PhD, Ill. Inst. Tech., 1981. Research assoc. U. Chgo., 1981-83; dir. Interventions, Chgo., 1983-85; prof. Govs. State U., University Park, Ill., 1985—; cons. Interventions, Chgo., 1985—. Contbr. articles to profl. jours. Mem. Am. Psychol. Assn., Ill. Psychol. Assn. Avocations: reading, movies. Office: Govs State Univ University Park IL 60466

MELCZER, ANDREW HENRY, health economist, administrator; b. Los Angeles, Dec. 5, 1954; s. Henry Lynn and Revlyn (Kass) M.; m. Susan Woolley, Aug. 28, 1977; children: Alissa, Micah. BS, Lewis and Clark Coll., 1976; PhD, Northwestern U., 1982. Sr. economist Ctr. for Health Services and Policy, Northwestern U., Evanston, Ill., 1980-83; healthcare cons. Evanston, 1983-84; health economist Ill. State Med. Soc., Chgo., 1984-86, dir. health policy research, 1986—; cons. Ill. Dept. Public Aid, Springfield, 1981-83, Mass. Med. Soc., Waltham, 1984-87; mem. tech. adv. group Ill. Health Care Cost Containment Council, Springfield, 1985—, Ill. Dept. Ins. Cost Containment Task Force. Treas. Beth Emet Synagogue, Evanston, 1985—. Home: 2643 Stewart Ave Evanston IL 60201 Office: Ill Med Soc 20 N Michigan Chicago IL 60602

MELE, JOANNE THERESA, dentist; b. Chgo., Dec. 5, 1943; d. Andrew and Josephine Jeanette (Calabrese) M. Diploma, St. Elizabeth's Sch. Nursing, Chgo., 1964; diploma in Dental Hygiene, Northwestern U., 1977; A.S., Triton Coll., 1979; D.D.S., Loyola U., 1983. Registered nurse, dental hygienist. Staff nurse in medicine/surgery St. Elizabeth's Hosp., Chgo., 1964-66, operating room nurse, 1966-67; head nurse operating room Cook County Hosp., Chgo., 1967-76, head nurse ICU, 1976-77; dental hygienist Mele Dental Assocs., Ltd., Oakbrook, Ill., 1977-79, practice dentistry, 1983—. Recipient Northwestern U. Dental Hygiene Clinic award, 1977; Dr. Duxler Humanitarian award scholar Loyola U., 1982. Mem. Chgo. Dental Soc., Ill. State Dental Soc., Acad. Gen. Dentistry, Am. Assn. Women Dentists, Psi Omega (Kappa chpt.). Roman Catholic. Avocations: reading; music; golfing; jogging; skiing.. Office: Mele Dental Assocs Ltd 120 Ctr Mall Suite 610 Oakbrook IL 60521

MELICK, MARGARET ANN, educational administrator; b. Oelwein, Iowa, Nov. 30, 1944; d. Floyd Henry and Anna Christina (Nielsen) Hoppes; m. Ronald James Melick, May 19, 1967; 1 child, Lisa Marie. BA, U. No. Iowa, 1966; MEd, U. Wis.-Stout, 1978. Interviewer Job Service, Burlington, Iowa, 1966-67; social studies tchr. Kempsville High Sch., Virginia Beach, Va., 1967-69; Job Corps rep. Job Service, Waterloo, Iowa, 1969-72, Ottumwa, Iowa, 1972-73; job placement specialist Job Service, Madison, Wis., 1974-76; evaluation specialist U. Wis.-Stout, Menomonie, 1978—; women's employment coach, Menomonie, 1976—; community edn. coordinator Spring Valley (Wis.) Pub. Schs., 1983-84. Vol. Girl Scouts Am., Knapp and Menomonie, Wis., 1979—. Democrat. Methodist. Home: Pine Point Rd Rt #7 Box 191 Menomonie WI 54751 Office: Univ Wis-Stout Menomonie WI 54751

MELICK, ROBERT LOUIS, health science facility administrator; b. Toledo, Dec. 8, 1931; s. Louis Lanning and Mary Alice (Swallow) M.; m. Katherine Jordan, July 11, 1964; children: Jordan Robert, Ariste Alice. AB, Princeton U., 1953; MBA, Harvard U., 1957. CPA, Mich. Sr. staff acct. Price Waterhouse, Detroit, 1957-63, mgr., 1963-84; v.p. fin. Harper-Grace Hosps., Detroit, 1984—. Served to 1st lt. U.S. Army, 1953-55. Mem. Fin. Execs. Inst., Healthcare Fin. Mgmt. Assn., Am. Inst. CPA's, Mich. Assn. CPA's. Republican. Roman Catholic. Club: Detroit Country. Home: 7 Carmel Ln Grosse Pointe Farms MI 48236 Office: Harper-Grace Hosps 3990 John R Detroit MI 48201

MELIN, ROBERT ARTHUR, lawyer; b. Milw., Sept. 13, 1940; s. Arthur John and Frances Magdalena (Lanser) M.; m. Mary Magdalen Melin, July 8, 1967; children—Arthur Walden, Robert Dismas, Nicholas O'Brien, Madalyn Mary. B.A. summa cum laude, Marquette U., 1962, J.D., 1967. Bar: Wis. 1966, U.S. Dist. Ct. (ea. dist.) Wis. 1966, U.S. Ct. Appeals (7th cir.) 1966, U.S. Ct. Mil. Appeals 1967, U.S. Supreme Ct. 1975. Law clk. U.S. Dist. Ct. Eastern Dist. Wis., 1966; instr. bus. law U. Ga., Hinesville, 1968, also lectr. bus. law U. Md., Asmara, 1970; lectr. law Haile Selassie I U. Law Faculty, Addis Ababa, Ethiopia, 1971-72; mem. firm Walther & Halling, Milw., 1973-74, Schroeder, Gedlen, Riester & Moerke, Milw., 1974-82; ptnr. Schroeder, Gedlen, Riester & Melin, Milw., 1982-84, Schroeder, Riester, Melin & Smith, 1984—. lectr. charitable solicitations and contracts Philanthropy Monthly 9th Ann. Policy Conf., N.Y.C., 1985. Chmn. Milw. Young Democrats, 1963-64. Served to capt. JAGC, AUS, 1967-70. Mem. Wis. Acad. Trial Lawyers, ABA, Wis. Bar Assn., Milw. Bar Assn., Am. Legion, Friends of Ethiopia, Delta Theta Phi, Phi Alpha Theta, Pi Gamma Mu. Roman Catholic. Author: Evidence in Ethiopia, 1972; contbg. author to Annual Survey of African Law, 1974; contbr. numerous articles to legal jours. Home: 8108 N Whitney Rd Milwaukee WI 53217 Office: 135 W Wells St Milwaukee WI 53203

MELING, DAVID LEE, dentist; b. Ottawa, Ill., Aug. 18, 1947; s. Truman LeeRoy and Betty Louise (Breitenkamp) M.; m. Judith Ann Iverson, Sept. 7, 1968; children: Anne Marie, Kristen Lee, Eric David. AA, Ill. Valley Community Coll., 1967; BS in Dentistry, U. Ill., 1969, DDS, 1971. Intern Boston Marine Hosp., 1971-72; practice dentistry Ottawa, Ill., 1974—. Served to dental surgeonUSPHS, 1971-74. Fellow Acad. Gen. Dentistry; mem. ADA, Ill. Valley Dental Soc. (pres. 1982-83). Avocations: gardening, woodcutting. Home: Rt #4 Ottawa IL 61350 Office: 720 Columbus St Ottawa IL 61350

MELLION, FRANCIS EUGENE, orthodontist; b. Akron, Ohio, Nov. 24, 1958; s. Louis Joseph and Helen (Kotti) M.; m. Laureen Bridget Fenwick, Aug. 8, 1981; children: Mark Louis, Katelyn Maureen. Student, U. Akron, 1977-79; BS, Case Western Res. U., 1981, DDS, 1983; MS, St. Louis U., 1985. Gen. dentist Offices of Dr. Richard Hodshire, Granite City, Ill., 1984-85; pvt. practice orthodontics Akron, 1985—. Recipient Dentsply Internat. Award for Proficiency in Removable Prosthodontics Dentsply Internat. Supply Co., 1983. Mem. ADA, Ohio Dental Assn., Akron Dental Soc., Stark County Dental Soc., Am. Assn. Orthodontics, Omicron Kappa Upsilon. Roman Catholic. Avocations: golf, baseball, racquetball, basketball, photography. Office: 2650 W Market St Akron OH 44313

MELLON, HOWARD JAY, accountant; b. N.Y.C., Mar. 2, 1952; s. Aaron and Judith (Gersh) M.; m. Marie C. Golda, June 11, 1978. BBA, Pace U., 1973; JD, Ohio State U., 1977. Bar: Ohio; CPA, N.Y., Ohio. Tax mgr. Arthur Andersen & Co., Columbus, Ohio, 1980-82; sole practice Columbus, 1982—; ptnr. Mellon & Mellon CPA's, Columbus, 1982—; bd. dirs., sec.-treas. First Americable Corp., Columbus, 1983—. Mem. ABA, Ohio Bar Assn., Columbus Bar Assn., Ohio Soc. CPA's, N.Y. Soc. CPA's. Home: 1149 Regency Dr Columbus OH 43220 Office: Mellon & Mellon 3300 Riverside Dr Columbus OH 43221

MELLOR, JAMES ROBB, defense company executive; b. Detroit, May 3, 1930; s. Clifford and Gladys (Robb) M.; m. Suzanne Stykos, June 8, 1953; children: James Robb, Diane Elyse, Deborah Lynn. B.S. in Elec. Engring. and Math, U. Mich., 1952, M.S., 1953. Mem. tech. staff Hughes Aircraft Co., Fullerton, Calif., 1955-58; pres. Data Systems div. Litton Industries, Van Nuys, Calif., after 1958; exec. v.p. Litton Industries, Inc., Beverly Hills, Calif.; pres., chief operating officer AM Internat., Inc., Los Angeles, to 1981; exec. v.p., dir. Gen. Dynamics Corp., 1981—; dir. Bergen Brunswig Corp., Kerr Glass Mfg. Corp. Contbr. articles to profl. publs. Bd. councilors Grad. Sch. Bus. Adminstrn. and Sch. Bus., U. So. Calif.; mem. adv. council Coll. Bus. Adminstrn., Loyola Marymount U.; bd. dirs. Hollywood Presbyterian Med. Center Found. Served to 1st lt., Signal Corps AUS, 1953-55. Mem. IEEE, Am. Mgmt. Assn., Armed Forces Communications and Electronics Assn. (dir.), Computer and Bus. Equipment Mfrs. Assn. (dir.), Sigma Xi, Tau Beta Pi, Eta Kappa Nu, Phi Kappa Phi. Clubs: Los Angeles Country, Old Warson Country, St. Louis, California. Patentee fields of storage tubes and display systems. Home: 7759 Kingsbury Blvd Saint Louis MO 63105 Office: Gen Dynamics Corp Pierre Laclede Center Saint Louis MO 63105

MELLOTT, ROBERT VERNON, radio/TV advertising executive; b. Dixon, Ill., Jan. 1, 1928; s. Edwin Vernon and Frances Rhoda (Miller) M.; m. Carolyn Frink, June 11, 1960; children—Lynn Lorraine, Susan Michelle, David Robert. B.A., DePauw U., 1950; postgrad. Ind. U., 1950-51, Law Sch., 1959-61, M.A., 1983. TV producer, dir. Jefferson Standard Broadcasting Co., Charlotte, N.C., 1951-59; asst. dist. mgr. Gen. Motors Corp., Flint, Mich., Chgo., 1961-62; TV radio comml. supr. N.W. Ayer & Son, Chgo., 1962-65; TV radio producer FCB, Chgo., 1965-67, mgr. midwest prodn., 1967-69, mgr. comml. coordination, 1969-74, v.p., mgr. comml. services, Chgo., 1974—. Mem. media adv. com. Coll. of Dupage, Glen Ellyn, Ill., 1971-82; chmn. Cub Scout com., Wheaton, Ill., 1978-79; bd. dirs. Chgo. Unltd., 1969-71. Mem. Am. Assn. Advt. Agencies (broadcast adminstrn. policy com., broadcast union relations policy com.), Phi Delta Phi, Alpha Tau Omega. Republican. Clubs: Chgo. Farmers, Chgo. Advt., Ind. U. Alumni. Home: 26 W 130 Tomahawk Dr Wheaton IL 60187 Office: FCB Ctr 101 E Erie St Chicago IL 60611-2897

MELNIKOFF, SARAH ANN, gem importer, jewelry designer; b. Chgo., Feb. 12, 1936; d. Harry E. and Marie Louise (Straub) Caylor; m. Casimir Adam Jestadt, Feb. 27, 1959 (div. Sept. 1972); 1 child, Christina Marie Jestadt-Russo; m. Sol Melnikoff, July 31, 1981. Student Gemol. Inst. Am., 1968-69, Am. Acad. Art, Chgo., 1952-56, Art Inst. Chgo., 1953, Mundelein Coll., Chgo., 1953-54. Pres., Casmira Gem, Inc., Chgo., 1963—; comml. artist, Chgo., 1957-78; U.S. del. Internat. Colored Gemstone Dealers Assn., W.Ger., 1985; lectr., cons. in field. Mem. Chgo. Salesman's Alliance, MINK Inc., Am. Gem Trade Assn. (nat. sec. 1982-86), Am. Horse Show Assn., Am. Saddlebred Horse Show Assn., Mid-Am. Horse Show Assn. (dir. 1980-83). Republican. Roman Catholic. Avocations: horses. Office: Casmira Gems 5 N Wabash Ave Suite 1100 Chicago IL 60602

MELOON, ROBERT A., newspaper publisher; b. Davenport, Iowa, July 13, 1928; s. John and Evelyn Mae (Ede) Case; children: Mark Robert, Brian Alfred. Student pub. schs., Davenport, Iowa. Reporter The Capital Times, 1957-71, assoc. editor, 1971-72, mng. editor, 1972-78, exec. editor, 1978-81, gen. mgr., 1981-83, exec. pub., 1983—. Mem. Am. Newspaper Pubs. Assn., Inland Daily Press Assn., Wis. AP Assn., Wis. Newspaper Assn. Unitarian. Home: 738 S Gammon Rd Madison WI 53719 Office: The Capital Times 1901 Fish Hatchery Rd Madison WI 53708

MELROSE, KENDRICK BASCOM, manufacturing company executive; b. Orlando, Fla., July 31, 1940; s. Henry Bascom and Dorothy (Lumleu) M.; m. Velia Russo, Apr. 1, 1967; children: Robert, Velia, Kendra. B.S. cum laude, Princeton U., 1962; M.Sc., MIT, 1965; M.B.A., U. Chgo., 1967. Mktg. mgr. Pillsbury Co., Mpls., 1967-69; dir. corp. planning Bayfield Techs., Inc., Mpls., 1969-70; with Toro Co. (mfrs. outdoor power equipment), Mpls., 1970—; exec. v.p. outdoor power equipment div. Toro Co. (mfrs. outdoor power equipment), 1980-81, pres., 1981—. Congregationalist. Office: Toro Co 8111 Lyndale Ave S Minneapolis MN 55420 *

MELSEN, GREGORY JOHN, accountant; b. Milw., Apr. 6, 1952; s. John P. and Clara S. (Pszybylski) M.; m. Barbara J. Torborg, Oct. 6, 1979; jchildren: Kristin M., John T., Michelle L. BS in Acctg., St. John's U., 1974. CPA, Minn. Mem. audit staff Touche Ross and Co., Mpls., 1974-78, audit supr., 1978-81, audit mgr., 1981-84, audit ptnr., 1984—. Chmn. allocations panel Mpls. United Way, 1986—; mem. community council Pax Christi Cath. Ch., 1985—. Mem. Am. Inst. CPA's, Minn. Soc. CPA's, Bloomington (Minn.) C. of C. (chmn. small bus. council awareness task force 1986—). Clubs: Decathlon Athletic, Edina (Minn.) Country, Northwest Racquet (Twin Cities). Avocations: tennis, golf, cross-country skiing. Home: 9649 Wyoming Terr Bloomington MN 55438 Office: Touche Ross & Co 3600 W 80th St Suite 100 Bloomington MN 55431

MELSON, JAMES B., lawyer; b. Cin., Dec. 29, 1940; s. Ferol D. and Beulah (Delph) M.; m. Patricia J. Wulle, Jan. 31, 1970; children: Keena, Lyndsay. BS, Ball State U., 1962, MA, 1966; JD, Ind. U., 1971. Tchr. Anderson (Ind.) Community Schs., 1964-72; sole practice law Anderson, 1972—; probate commr. Madison Cir. Ct., Anderson, 1983—. Served with U.S. Army, 1962-68. Mem. ABA, Ind. Bar Assn., Assn. Trial Lawyers Am. Democrat. Lodges: Elks (Esquire 1987—), Shriners. Avocations: riding, baseball, swimming, stamp collecting. Home: 1605 Daleville Ave Anderson IN 46012 Office: 932 Meridian Plaza Anderson IN 46016

MELTON, GARY BENTLEY, psychology, law educator; b. Salisbury, N.C., June 4, 1952; s. Harold Sumner Jr. and Marion Adair (Reeves) M.; m. Julia Ann Young, Aug. 25, 1973; children: Jennifer Lynn, Stephany Beth. BA, U. Va., 1973; MA, Boston U., 1975, PhD, 1978. Lic. psychologist, Nebr. Asst. prof. psychology Morehead (Ky.) State U., 1978-79, U. Va., Charlottesville, 1979-81; from asst. prof. to full prof. psychology and law U. Nebr., Lincoln, 1981—. Author: Child Advocacy: Psychological Issues and Interventions, 1983; (with others) Community Mental Health Centers and the Courts: An Evaluation of Community-Based Forensic Services, 1985, Psychological Evaluations for the Courts: A Handbook for Mental Health Professionals and Lawyers, 1987; editor numerous books. Fellow Am. Psychol. Assn. (chmn. various coms., Disting. Contribution to Psychology in the Pub. Interest award 1985, Cert. of Recognition for Psychology in the Pub. Interest 1981); mem. Am. Pub. Health Assn., Assn. Advancement Psychology (trustee 1984-85), Rural Sociol. Soc., Nebr. Bar Assn. (com. mental health). Democrat. Mem. Unitarian Ch. Office: U Nebr Dept Psychology 209 Burnett Lincoln NE 68588-0308

MELTON, JOHN LESTER, English educator; b. Walsenburg, Colo., Aug. 11, 1920; s. Harry W. and Elizabeth (Cahalan) M.; m. Virginia Anne Cadmus. B.A., U. Utah, 1948, M.A., 1949; Ph.D., Johns Hopkins U., 1955. Instr. Johns Hopkins U., Balt., 1950-55; from instr. to prof. John Carroll U., Cleve., 1955-68; assoc. prof. St. Cloud State U., Minn., 1968-69, prof. 1969-86, prof. emeritus, 1986—; cons. linguistics Western Res. U., Cleve., 1957-64. Author (TV series) Literature of the Am. Frontier, 1970. Editor: Semantic Code Dictionary, 1958. Contbr. articles to profl. jours. Mem. Home Rule Charter Commn., St. Cloud, 1970-79. Served to maj. U.S. Army, 1936-46. Mem. Internat. Arthurian Soc., Oreg. and Calif. Trails Assn., MLA, Coll. English Assn., Minn. Council Tchrs. English, Sierra Club, Phi Beta Kappa, Alpha Sigma Lambda, Lambda Iota Tau, Phi Kappa Phi. Avocations: camping, photography, travel. Home: 3040 Santa Fe Trail Saint Cloud MN 56301 Office: Saint Cloud State U Saint Cloud MN 56301

MELTON, OWEN B., JR., banking company executive; b. 1946. BS, Indiana U., 1973. Chief adminstrv. officer Fed. Home Loan Bank Bd., Washington, 1977-79; exec. v.p. Skokie (Ill.) Fed. Savs. and Loan, 1979-81; chmn. bd. dirs., pres., chief exec. officer Diamond Savs. and Loan Co., 1981-83; with First Ind. Fed. Savs. Bank, Indpls., 1972—, now pres., also bd. dirs. Served with USAF, 1967-70. Office: First Ind Fed Savs Bank 1 N Pennsylvania St Indianapolis IN 46204 *

MELVIN, BILLY ALFRED, clergyman; b. Macon, Ga., Nov. 25, 1929; s. Daniel Henry and Leola Dale (Seidell) M.; m. Marcia Darlene Eby, Oct. 26, 1952; children: Deborah Ruth, Daniel Henry II. Student, Free Will Baptist Bible Coll., Nashville, 1947-49; B.A., Taylor U., Upland, Ind., 1951; postgrad., Asbury Theol. Sem., Wilmore, Ky., 1951-53; B.D., Union Theol. Sem., Richmond, Va., 1956; D.D., Azusa (Calif.) Coll., 1968; LL.D. (hon.), Taylor U., 1984. Ordained to ministry Free Will Baptist Ch., 1951; pastor First Free Will Baptist Chs., Newport, Tenn., 1951-53, Richmond, 1953-57; pastor Bethany Ch., Norfolk, Va., 1957-69; exec. sec. Nat. Assn. Free Will Baptists, 1957-67; exec. dir. Nat. Assn. Evangelicals, 1967—. Office: Nat Assn Evangelicals PO Box 28 Wheaton IL 60189

MELVIN, JOHN LEWIS, physician, medical educator; b. Columbus, Ohio, May 26, 1935; s. John Harper and Ruth Eleanor (Wertenberger) M.; m. Harriett Elizabeth Warner, June 8, 1957; children—Megan Marie, Beth Anne, John Patrick, Mia Michelle. B.Sc., Ohio State U., 1955, M.D., 1960, M. Med.Sci., 1966. Diplomate Am. Bd. Physical Medicine and Rehab. Rotating Intern Mt. Carmel Hosp., Columbus, 1960-61; resident in phys. medicine Univ. Hosp., Columbus, 1961, 63-66; asst. prof. Ohio State U., Columbus, 1966-69, assoc. prof., 1969-73; prof., chmn. dept. Med. Coll. Wis., Milw., 1973—; cons. to numerous U.S. govtl. agys., health care insts.; lectr. in field; research assoc. Ohio State Research Found., Columbus, 1966-68; assoc. coordinator Ohio State Regional Med. Program, Columbus, 1969-71; med. dir. Curative Rehab. Ctr., Milw., 1973—. Contbr. articles to profl. jours. Bd. dirs. Vis. Nurses Assn., Milw., 1974-83; mem. com. Mental Health Planning Council, Milw., 1974-75, Wis. Council Devel. Disabilities, Madison, 1979-80; mem. planning and evaluation com. Elizabethtown Hosp. for Children and Youth, Pa., 1977; advisor Nat. Multiple Sclerosis Soc., Milw., 1979-87; mem. Wis. Nicaragua Ptnrs., 1982—; trustee Easter Seal Research Found., vice chmn., 1985, chmn. 1986—. Served to capt. M.C., U.S. Army, 1961-63. Recipient cert. of appreciation Goodwill Industries, 1972, spl. recognition award Commn. Accreditation Rehab. Facilities, 1977, Performance award Wood VA Med. Ctr., 1978; cert. of appreciation Jour. Rehab. Adminstrn., 1982; grantee Rehab. Services Adminstrn., 1979-84, 1984-87, Health Care Financing Adminstrn., 1984-85; Ford Found. fellow, 1951-53. Fellow Am. Acad. Cerebral Palsy and Devel. Medicine, Am. Acad. Phys. Medicine and Rehab.; mem. Med. Soc. Milw., Milw. Acad. Medicine, Wis. Soc. Phys. Medicine and Rehab., Wis. Med. Soc. (chmn. sect. 1978-82, spl. merit award 1979), Am. Assn. Electromyography and Electrodiagnosis (pres. 1979-80), Am. Congress Rehab. Medicine (2d v.p. 1984-85, gold medal 1971, 78), Am. Heart Assn., Am. Hosp. Assn. (chmn. 1981), AMA (cert. of appreciation 1976, 82), Am. Paraplegia Soc., Assn. Acad. Physiatrists (pres. elect 1985-87), Internat. Fedn. Phys. Medicine and Rehab. (hon. sec. 1980—), Internat. Rehab. Medicine Assn., Nat. Assn. Rehab. Facilities (pres. 1981-83, bd. dirs.), Pan Am. Med. Assn. Home: 5353 N Lake Dr Whitefish Bay WI 53217 Office: Curative Rehab Ctr 1000 N 92d St Milwaukee WI 53226

MEMMEL, ROBERT OSCAR, photography equipment manufacturing company executive; b. Wauwatosa, Wis., Feb. 8, 1925; s. Alois Sebastian and Marie (Makoutz) M.; m. Erika Backfisch, May 24, 1967; children: Heidi, Lisa. BBA, U. Wis., 1950. Account exec. K. Seitz Advt., Milw., 1950-55; advt. mgr. Am. Lace Paper, Milw., 1955-60; pres. Electro-Graphax Corp., Oconomowoc, Wis., 1960—. Painter over 100 oil paintings. Served with U.S. Army, 1945-47. Recipient numerous awards for paintings. Republican. Lodge: Oconomowoc Rotary. Avocations: sculpting, sailing, skiing. Home: W 34540 Rd Q Okauchee WI 53069

MENARD, CHARLES WALTER, JR., envelope company executive; b. Chgo., Apr. 15, 1929; s. Charles Walter and Hazel (Froehde) M.; m. Helen Bernice Ligas, May 14, 1955; children—Charles, Christopher, Juliette, C. Timothy, Jennifer. B.S. in Commerce, DePaul U., 1954. Various positions to controller St. Joseph Hosp., Chgo., 1962-64; controller, sec. Continental Envelope Corp., Chgo., 1965—. Sec. Dist. 231 Bd. Edn., Evergreen Park, Ill.; treas., bd. dirs. Evergreen Park AquaPark; treas. scholarship bd. Evergreen Park Community High Sch. Democrat. Roman Catholic. Lodge: Lions (from dir. to pres. Evergreen Park). Home: 2941 W 100th St Evergreen Park IL 60642 Office: 1301 W 35th St Chicago IL 60609

MENCER, JETTA, lawyer; b. Coshocton, Ohio, Apr. 7, 1959; d. William J. and Virginia M. (Fry) M. BS, Ohio State U., 1980, JD, 1983. Bar: Ohio, U.S. Dist. Ct. (so. dist.) Ohio. Assoc. Berry, Owens & Manning, Coshocton, 1983-86; asst. pros. atty. Coshocton County, 1983-86, Licking County, Newark, Ohio, 1986—. Treas. Coshocton County Dem. Cen. & Exec. Coms., 1984-86; chmn., 1986—; sec., bd. dirs. Heart Ohio Girl Scout Council, Inc., Zanesville, Ohio, 1985-87; fin. chmn., bd. dirs. YMCA, Coshocton, 1985—. Mem. Ohio State Bar Assn., Am. Bar Assoc., Nat. Dist. Attys. Assn. Democrat. Methodist. Office: 25 S Park Pl Newark OH 43055

MENCONI, GARY ROBERT, financial planning service executive; b. Chgo., Apr. 5, 1955; s. Benjamin H. and Dorthy P. (Lombardi) M.; m. Patricia G. Giglio, June 23, 1985. AA, Thornton Community Coll., 1975; BS in Mgmt., Calumet Coll., 1977; postgrad., Lewis U., 1983—; cert., Coll. Fin. Planning, Denver, 1984. Registered fin. planner. Sales rep. Met. Life Ins. Co., Munster, Ind., 1977-79; ins. broker J.L. Fattore and Assocs., South Holland, Ill., 1979-80; mgr. life sales Am. States Ins. Co., Wheaton, Ill., 1980-81; v.p. Instek corp., Itasca, Ill., 1981—. Mem. Internat. Assn. Fin. Planning, Inst. Cert. Fin. Planners. Republican. Roman Catholic. Avocation: all sports. Office: Instek Corp 500 Park Blvd Suite 110 Itasca IL 60143

MENDELBERG, HAVA EVA, psychologist; b. Cordoba, Argentina, Dec. 26, 1942; came to U.S., 1975; d. Israel and Celia (Rubin) Gleser; children: Tali, Gabi. BA, Hebrew U., Jerusalem, 1969; Licenciatura, U. Madrid, 1971; MS, U. Wis., 1977, PhD, 1981. Tchr. Kibbutz, Israel, 1964-66, Inst. for Leaders From Abroad, Israel, 1966-69; psychologist Family Service, Milw., 1981-82; clin. psychologist Psychoanalytic Psychology, Milw., 1981-85; pvt. practice clin. psychology Shorewood, Wis., 1985—; psychologist Municipality of Jerusalem, 1963-75, Mt. Sinai Med. Ctr., Wis., 1980-81, 81-82; prof. U. Wis., 1981-82, supr. 84-85; cons. St. Michael Hosp., Milw., 1985—, Milw. Psychiat. Hosp., 1986—; spkr. in field. Contbr. articles to profl. jours. Mem. Assn. for Mental Health (chmn. 1983—) Am. Psychol. Assn., Wis. Psychol. Assn., Psychol. Assn. Israel, Psychol. Assn. Spain, World Fedn. for Mental Health, Psychologists for Social Responsibilty. Home and Office: 1820 E Edgewood Shorewood WI 53211

MENDELSON, ANDREW DAVID, architect; b. Chgo., Oct. 24, 1955; s. Lloyd Jay and Eva (Emmanuel) M.; m. Linda Rose Hurwich, May 31, 1981. BArch, U. Ill., 1977. Registered architect Ill., Wis. Designer and draftsman Skidmore Owings & Merrill, Chgo., 1977-78; project architect J.M. Goldberg, Architect, Lake Forest, Ill., 1978-81; sr. project mgr., assoc. O'Donnell Wicklund Pigozzi, Northbrook, Ill., 1981—. Mem. AIA, Nat. Trust Hist. Preservation. Avocations: sports, art, music, reading. Office: O'Donnell Wicklund Pigozzi & Peterson 570 Lake Cook Rd Deerfield IL 60015

MENDELSON, DAVID FREY, neurology educator; b. St. Louis, Feb. 25, 1925; s. Harry and Lorine Esther (Korngold) M.; m. Mary Ann Lavis, June 21, 1956 (div. Mar. 1978); children: Lorine Ann, David Frey, Helen Elizabeth, Jonathan Joseph. BA, U. Calif., Berkeley, 1946; MD, Ind. U., Indpls., 1948. Diplomate Am. Bd. Psychiatry and Neurology. Intern Ind. U., Indpls., 1948-49; resident Barnes Hosp., St. Louis, 1950-51; fellow neurology U. Minn., Mpls., 1953-58, instr. neurology, 1956-58; practice medicine specializing in neurology St. Louis, 1958—; clin. asst. prof. St. Louis U., 1958-83, Washington U., St. Louis, 1983—. Bd. dirs. Mo. Blue Shield, St. Louis, 1964-72, trustee, 1972-85, corp. bd. 1985—. Served to capt. USAF, 1951-53. Fellow Am. Acad. Neurology; mem. Am. Med. Electroencephalography Soc., St. Louis Met. Med. Soc., St. Louis Soc. Neurol. Scis., Rocky Mountain Traumatologic Soc. Jewish. Club: St. Louis Racquet. Home: 7906 Kingsbury Clayton MO 63105 Office: 141 N Meramec Ave Saint Louis MO 63105

MENDELSON, KENNETH EARL, electrical engineer; b. Cleve., Mar. 6, 1950; s. Stuart I. Lorraine F. (Segal) M.; m. Peggy A. Ritari, Nov. 3, 1973; children: Peter A., Amy L. BS in Systems and Control, Case Western Res. U., 1972. Registered profl. engr., Ohio. Electrical engr. H.K. Ferguson Co., Cleve., 1972-81, Pickands Mather & Co., Cleve., 1981—. Mem. Internat. Assn. Elec. Inspectors (western res. div.), Inst. Elec. and Electronic Engrs., Inc., Lightning Protection Inst. (profl.). Republican. Jewish. Home: 2449 Laurelhurst Dr University Heights OH 44118 Office: Pickands Mather & Co 1100 Superior Ave Cleveland OH 44114

MENDENHALL, RICHARD MASON, JR., media artist, management consultant; b. Berkeley, Calif., May 5, 1952; s. Richard Mason and Donna June (MacMillan) M. BA, Antioch Coll., 1982; MFA, Ohio U., 1987. Mgr. equipment Antioch Coll., Yellow Springs, Ohio, 1980-82, Ohio U., Athens, 1983-85; dir. Virtual Image Studio, Athens, 1983—. Film producer Enigmatic Journey, 1985, MT Five, 1986. Avocation: personal computers. Home: 4261 Turkey Rd Hillsboro OH 45133 Office: Virtual Image Studio 84 W Carpenter St Athens OH 45701

MENDIRATTA, VEENA BHATIA, telecommunications research engineer; b. New Delhi, India, Oct. 21, 1948; came to U.S., 1976; d. Jaman Lal and Dharam (Devi) Bhatia; m. Shiv S. Mendiratta, Apr. 13, 1974; 1 son, Arjun. B.Tech., Indian Inst. Tech., 1970; M.C.P., Ohio State U., 1971, M.S. in Civil Engring., 1972; Ph.D., Northwestern U., 1981. Asst. prof. Sch. of Planning, Ahmedabad, India, 1972-74; asst. town planner State Planning Dept., Chandigarh, India, 1975-76; research engr. U. Ill.-Chgo., 1976-78; systems engr. Argonne Nat. Lab., 1981; mgr. computer modeling and simulation Ill. Central Gulf R.R., Chgo., 1981-84; mem. tech. staff AT&T Bell Labs., Naperville, Ill., 1984—; adj. prof. Elmhurst (Ill.) Coll., 1984—. Bd. dirs.: Chambord Homeowners Assn. Mem. Ops. Research Soc. Am., Inst. Mgmt. Scis. Hindu. Home: 18W758 Chateaux N Oak Brook IL 60521 Office: AT&T-Bell Labs Warrenville at Naperville Rds Naperville IL 60566

MENDOZA-RAMÍREZ, JOSE, educator; b. Santiago, Oriente, Cuba, Oct. 30, 1911; came to U.S., 1962; s. Jose Fructuoso and Josefa Ana (Ramírez) M.; m. Engracia Eusebia Toll, Nov. 26, 1944; children: Jose, Fernando. JD, U. Havana, 1940; MA, U. Iowa, 1970. Sole practice law Santiago and Havanna, 1940-62; law counsel Sec. of Treasury, Havana, 1954-57; dept. head Office of Undersec. of Treasury, Havana, 1957-58; tchr. Spanish Iowa High Schs., 1965-72. Avocations: reading, writing, music. Home: 1205 5th St #3 Coralville IA 52241

MENEFEE, FREDERICK LEWIS, advertising executive; b. Arkansas City, Kan., Oct. 22, 1932; s. Arthur LeeRoy and Vera Mae (Rather) M.; student Arkansas City Jr. Coll., 1952; B.A., U. wichita, 1958; m. Margot Leuze, Sept. 16, 1955; children—Gregory Shawn, Christina Dawn. Vice-pres., account exec. Asso. Advt. Agy., 1958-64; with McCormick-Armstrong Co., advt. agy., wichita, 1964—, agy. mgr., 1964—, account supr., 1965—, gen. mgr., 1972—; pres., chief exec. officer McCormick-Armstrong Advt. Agy., Inc., 1979—, chmn. bd., 1984—. Served with AUS, 1953-55. Named Advt. Man of Yr., Advt. Club of Wichita, 1964, Advt. Man of Yr., 9th Dist. Am. Advt. Fedn., 1965; Adm. Windwagon Smith III award Wichita Festivals Inc., 1976. Mem. Am. Advt. Fedn. (nat. bd. dirs. 1969-70, dist. gov. 1968-69, chmn. nat. council govs. 1969-70, Wichita Wagonmasters (capt. 1974-75, dir.; charter), Wichita Advt. Club (pres. 1963-64), PAWS, Inc. (pres. 1985), Alpha Delta Sigma. Home: 2235 Redbud Ln Wichita KS 67204 Office: 1501 E Douglas St Wichita KS 67201

MENEZES, ARNOLD HILDEBRAND, neurological surgeon, educator; b. Bombay, Oct. 18, 1944; s. Francis Hildebrand and Rose Menezes; m. Meenal A. Menezes; children: Francis, Maithilee. MD, Bombay U., 1966. Diplomate Am. Bd. Neurol. Surgeons. Intern Bombay U., 1966-67; resident in surgery and neurosurgery U. Iowa Hosps., Iowa City, 1968-74; asst. prof. U. Iowa Coll Medicine, Iowa City, 1975-80, assoc. prof. neurosurgery, 1981-85, prof. neurosurgery, dir. pediatric neurosurgery, 1985—. Author: (text) The Craniovertebral Junction, 1986; contbr. articles and book chpts. on neurosurgery and pediatrics. Recipient Physicians Recognition award AMA, 1976, 79, 82, 85. Fellow ACS; mem. Internat. Soc. Pediatric Neurosurgery, Am. Assn. Neurol. Surgeons, Neurosurg. Soc. Am., Congress of Neurosurgery, M.W. Neurosurg. Soc. (pres. 1981-83). Home: 1607 Ridge Rd Iowa City IA 52240 Office: Univ Hosps Div Neurosurgery Newton Rd Iowa City IA 52242

MENGEL, PAULA PADGETT, rental property administrator; b. Independence, Mo., Sept. 24, 1948; d. Darius Curtis and Rose Marie (Clemens) Padgett; m. Charles Edmund Mengel, June 5, 1978; 1 child, Michael Daniel. BA, U. Mo., Kansas City, 1970; MEd, U. Mo., Columbia, 1979. Cert. tchr., Mo. Tchr. Kansas City Pub. Schs., 1970-72; adminstrv. sec. U. Mo. Health Scis. Ctr., Columbia, 1973-78; editorial asst. Jour. Lab. and Clin. Medicine, Columbia, 1980-82; sec.-treas. Editorial Process, Inc., Columbia, 1980-82; adminstr. CPMC Apts., Moberly, Mo., 1984—. Republican. Roman Catholic. Home and Office: 733 W Rollins Moberly MO 65270-1358

MENHUSEN, MONTY JAY, physician, veterinarian, anesthesiologist, educator; b. Beloit, Kans., Nov. 15, 1948; s. Robert Snyder and Bernadette (Remus) M. BS, Kans. State U., 1970, DVM, 1972; MS, U. Ill., 1979; DO, Chgo. Coll. Osteo. Medicine and Surgery, 1979. Vet. intern Kans. State U., Manhattan, 1972-73; vet. resident in anesthesia U. Ill., Urbana, 1973-75; intern Okla. Osteo. Hosp., Tulsa, 1979-80; resident in surgery Pontiac (Mich.) Osteo. Hosp., 1980-81; resident in anesthesia U. Nebr., Omaha, 1981-83; assoc. prof. U. Kans., Wichita, 1983—; cons. Watch Air Med. Transport, Wichita, 1983—, Emergency Med. Services, Wichita, 1983—. Author clin. and research articles and book chpts. Mem. AMA, Am. Coll. Anesthesiologists, Am. Bd. Anesthesiology, Internat. Anesthesia Research Soc., Am. Soc. Anesthesiologists, Am. Coll. Vet. Anesthesiologists, Phi Zeta, Sigma Sigma Phi. Home: 2441 Winstead Circle Wichita KS 67226 Office: Anesthesia & Critical Care Services 3243 E Murdock Suite 401 Wichita KS 67208

MENNER, PAUL RAYMOND, service executive; b. St. Louis, June 27, 1957; s. Raymond H. and Mildred M. (Himstedt) M.; m. Diana Marie Javurek, June 11, 1983. Salesman Sears Roebuck Co., Crestwood, Mo., 1978-86; credit supr. Goodyear Credit Ctr., St. Louis, 1979-82; records mgr. Roosevelt Fed. Savs., Chesterfield, Mo., 1982-86, lease adminstrn. mgr., 1986—. Active Big Bros. Am., St. Louis, 1981. Avocations: home remodeling, wood refinishing, gardening. Office: Roosevelt Fed Savs 900 Roosevelt Pkwy Chesterfield MO 63017

MENSCER, DARRELL V., utility company executive; b. 1934. BS, N.C. State U., 1960. Sr. v.p. power supply Carolina Power and Light Co., 1973-80; with Pub. Service Co. of Ind., Plainfield, Ind., 1980—, now pres., chief operating officer. Served with USAF, 1952-56. Office: Pub Service Co of Ind Inc 1000 E Main St Plainfield IN 46168 *

MENTZER, JUNE ANN TOWNSEND, psychologist; b. Portsmouth, Ohio, June 15, 1920; d. Robert Presley and Edna Genevieve (Korth) Townsend; m. Robert H. Brown, Dec. 20, 1946 (div. 1963); children: Robert H. Jr., Betsy Lee, Julie Ann Brown Pridgen; m. Robert Wesley Mentzer, June 18, 1966; stepchildren: Kathryn Joyce Mentzer Tatham, Kristyn Sue. Student, Goucher Coll., 1938-40; AB, Ohio State U., 1946, MA, 1961. Lic. psychologist, Ohio. Kindergarten tchr. Newark (Ohio) City Schs., 1957-58, spl. edn. tchr., 1959-60, psychologist, 1960-63; dir. spl. edn., chief sch. psychologist Licking County Schs., Newark, 1963-79; pvt. practice psychology Newark, 1979—; psychologist and parent counselor Licking County Council for Mental Retardation, Newark, 1950-63; broadcasts on spl. edn. and psychology on stas. WHTH and WNKO, 1963-68; psychologist Licking County Headstart Program, 1969, 70, Ohio State U., Newark, 1984—. Contbr. articles on psychology, spl. edn. to Newark Advocate News, 1950—. Pres. Licking County Council for Exceptional Children, 1959. Mem. Ohio Psychologists Assn., Cen. Ohio Psychologists Assn., Licking County Mental Health Assn. (bd. dirs. 1979-82), Kappa Alpha Theta, Pi Lamda Theta, Ohio Sch. Psychologists Assn. (hon. life), Sch. Psychologists Cen. Ohio (hon. life) (pres. 1973, Huelsman award 1981, treas. polit. action com. 1985—). Republican. Presbyterian. Club: Monday Talks (Newark). Avocations: antique dealing, reading, bridge, walking. Home: 874 N Village Dr Newark OH 43055

MENTZER, MERLEEN MAE, adult education educator; b. Kingsley, Iowa, July 25, 1920; d. John David and Maggie Marie (Simonsen) Moritz; m. Lee Arnold Mentzer, June 1, 1944. Student Westman Coll., 1939, Wayne State U., Nebr., 1942, Bemidji State U., 1950, Mankato Coll., 1978, U. Minn.-St. Paul, 1979. Tchr., Kingsley, Iowa, 1938-41; owner, mgr. Mentzer's Sundries, Hackensack, Minn., 1946-76, House of Mentzers, Pine River, Minn., 1974-77; instr. Hennepin Tech., Eden Prairie, Minn., 1978—. Mem. Mpls. C. of C., Hackensack C. of C., (v.p. 1970-76), Northern Lights Federated Woman's Club (pres. 1958-59). Republican. Lutheran. Avocations: dancing; bowling; reading; theatre; seminars. Home: 6781 Tartan Curve Eden Prairie MN 55344

MENTZER, SUSAN STERNBERG, psychologist; b. N.Y.C., Mar. 22, 1949; d. Theodore and Aida Selma (Tucker) Sternberg; m. Richard Alan Mentzer, Aug. 29, 1971; children: Kimberly Lynn, Michelle Lauren. BA, Pa. State U., 1971; MA, Ohio State U., 1972, PhD, 1975. Lic. psychologist, Ohio; cert. sch. psychologist, Ohio. Intern then resident psychologist Springfield (Ohio) City Schs., 1973-74, psychologist, 1974-78; psychologist Columbus (Ohio) Pub. Schs., 1978—. Mem. Summerfield Civic Assn., Pickerington, Ohio, 1978—, Fairfield Elementary Sch. PTO, Pickerington, 1981—. Mem. NEA, Nat. Assn. Sch. Psychologists, Ohio Edn. Assn., Columbus Edn. Assn., Phi Beta Kappa, Phi Kappa Phi, Psi Chi. Avocations: swimming, aerobics. Home: 13136 Summerfield Way Pickerington OH 43147 Office: Columbus Pub Schs Sch Psychology Services 2571 Neil Ave Columbus OH 43202

MERCER, BERNARD, insurance company executive; b. 1912. Assoc. atty. N.Y.C. 1937-42; sales mgr. Sainberg and Co., N.Y.C., 1947-52; with Preferred Risk Mut. Ins. Co., Des Moines, 1952—, now chmn. bd. dirs. Served to capt. USAF, 1942-45. Office: Preferred Risk Mutual Ins Co 1111 Ashworth Rd West Des Moines IA 50265 *

MERCER, LELAND DALE, catering executive; b. Des Moines, Mar. 1, 1946; s. Kenneth Roland Mercer and Lelah Marie (Cross) Allbaugh. BS, UCLA, 1969, cert. restaurant mgmt., 1972; cert. broker, Russell Real Estate Inst., Southfield, Mich., 1975. Lic. real estate broker; cert. sanitation food and beverage mgmt. Cons. D'Massi Caterers, Blue Island, Ill., 1978-80; dir. of catering Hagerty Catering Co., Chgo., 1980-81; exec. v.p. Bax Mer, Inc., Chgo., 1985—; pres. Statewide Tax Cons. of Ill., Chgo., 1979—, Corp. Catering, Chgo., 1981—; sales cons. Drew Realty, Fennville, Mich., 1975-77. Mem. Nat. Restaurant Assn., Meeting Planners Internat., Am. Soc. Restaurant Execs., Nat. Caterers Assn. Episcopalian. Lodges: Lions, Kiwanis. Avocations: tennis, golf.

MERCER, MICHAEL WARREN, management psychologist; b. Chgo., Oct. 25, 1950; s. Philip S. and Rhea H. Mercer. BA, Am. U., 1972; MS, Ill. Inst. Tech., 1974, PhD, 1980. Cons. Sadler & Assocs., Chgo., 1977-79; mgr. human resources planning Mobil Corp., Chgo., 1979-82; dir. human resources planning and devel. Am. Hosp. Supply Corp., Evanston, Ill., 1982-86; pres. The Mercer Group, Skokie, Ill., 1985—; bd. dirs. Inst. Mgmt. Edn., Chgo. Author: How Winners Do It, 1987. Bd. dirs. Ill. Sch. Profl. Psychology, Chgo. Mem. Am. Psychol. Assn., Ill. Psychol. Assn. (pres. 1986-87, chmn. div. indsl./orgnl. psychology 1983-85). Avocations: writing, tennis, fishing, canoeing, cooking.

MERCER, ROBERT E., tire company executive; b. Elizabeth, N.J., 1924; married. Grad., Yale U., 1946. With Goodyear Tire & Rubber Co., Akron, 1947—, asst. to pres., 1973-74, pres. Kelly-Springfield Tire Co. (subs.), 1974-76, corp. exec. v.p., pres. tire div., 1976-78, corp. pres., from 1978, chief operating officer, 1980-82, vice chmn., chief exec. officer, 1982-83, chmn., chief exec. officer, 1983—, also dir. Served with USN. Office: Goodyear Tire & Rubber Co 1144 E Market St Akron OH 44316 *

MERCHANT, MARILYN WALSH, corporation executive; b. Bklyn., June 13, 1948; d. James Joseph and Wanda Josephine (Zelenski) Walsh; m. Brian Taylor Merchant, June 11, 1986; children—Therese-Marie, Elizabeth-Marie. Student U. Otaawa, 1977-79. Mem. staff purchasing dept. Simmonds Precision Co., N.Y.C., 1967-68; exec. sec. Bronson Imports, N.Y.C., 1968-75; reporter Ottawa Jour. and Emporium Echo, 1975-77; chief acct. Arcila and Assocs., N.Y.C., 1973-75; pres., gen. mgr. Mich. Etching Inc., Grand Rapids 1979-84; pres. Electroluminescent Displays Technology, Inc., 1983-85, El Diaelectrics; gen. mgr. Orr Industries, Inc., Grand Rapids, 1985; asst. to pres. ARM-S Electric, Inc., Elkhart, 1986—. Dir. Confraternity of Christian Doctrine, Okla. and Pa. Roman Catholic Ch.; mayor, Borough of Driftwood, Cameron County, Pa., 1976; adviser N.Y. State Assembly, 1974. Mem. Nat. Assn. Female Execs., Nat. Fedn. Ind. Bus., Soc. Automotive Engs. (subcom. 1979—), Soc. Mfg. Engrs., Am. Soc. Women Accts. Republican. Office: 23767 County Rd 6 Northland Ctr Elkhart IN 46514

MERCHANT, MUSHTAQ HUSSAIN, data processing executive; b. Mahuwa, India, Oct. 5, 1944; came to U.S., 1969; s. Abdul Hussain and Zehra (Alibhai) M.; m. Sandra Denise DaLama, Nov. 29. 1975; children: Jeffrey, Jennifer, Heather. BS, D.J. Coll., Karachi, Pakistan, 1968; AS, Miami Dade Jr. Coll., 1971; BS, U. West Fla., 1972; MS, U. Mo., 1973. Programmmer U.S. Gypsum, Chgo., 1973-76; software supr. Banker's Life, Chgo., 1976-79; pres. Systems Dimensions Inc., Barrington, Ill., 1979—; lectr. Copics User Group, Chgo., 1985. Author: CICDS Command Level Programming Techniques, 1986; contbr. articles to profl. jours. Avocations: photography, raquetball, tennis.

MEREDITH, EDWIN THOMAS, III, media executive; b. Chgo., Feb. 7, 1933; s. Edwin Thomas, Jr. and Anna (Kauffman) M.; m. Katherine Comfort, Sept. 4, 1953; children: Mildred K., Dianna M., Edwin Thomas. Student, U. Ariz., 1950-53. With Meredith Corp., Des Moines, 1956—, v.p., 1968-71, pres., chief exec. officer, 1971-73, chmn. bd., 1973—, also bd. dirs.; bd. dirs., mem. exec. com. Bankers Trust Co., Des Moines; bd. dirs. Mut. of Omaha. Bd. dirs. Nat. Merit Scholarship Corp., Evanston, Ill., Iowa Natural Heritage Found, Des Moines; trustee Iowa Methodist Med. Ctr., Drake U., Des Moines, Iowa 4-H Found., Ames. Served with U.S. Army, 1953-56. Clubs: Chgo; Des Moines, Wakonda (Des Moines). Office: Meredith Corp 1716 Locust St Des Moines IA 50336

MEREDITH, JAMES HARGROVE, federal judge; b. Wedderburn, Oreg., Aug. 25, 1914; s. Willis H. and Ollie (Hargrove) M.; m. Dorothy Doke, Sept. 7, 1937 (dec. Feb. 1972); 1 son, James Doke; m. Susan B. Fitzgibbon, 1977. A.B., Mo. U., 1935, LL.B., 1937. Bar: Mo. bar 1937. Pvt. practice New Madrid County, 1937-42, 46-49; spl. agt. FBI, 1942-44; ptnr. Stolar, Kuhlmann & Meredith, St. Louis, 1952-61; partner Cook, Meredith, Murphy & English, 1961-62, Stuart & Meredith, Washington, 1961-62; judge U.S. Dist. Ct., Eastern Dist. Mo., 1962—, chief judge, 1971-79; judge U.S. Fgn. Intelligence Surveillance Ct., 1979-80; chief counsel Mo. Ins. Dept., Jefferson City, 1949-52; Past dir. Bank St. Louis, Comml. Bank St. Louis County, Gen. Bancshares, Inc., Investment Securities Co., Northland Bank; v.p., gen. counsel Nat. Underwriters, Inc. Mem. Mental Health Commn. Mo., 1961-62; trustee Friends U. Mo. Library, U. Mo. Law Sch. Found. Served with USNR, 1944-46. Recipient Patriots award SR, 1974. Mem. Jud. Conf. U.S. (exec. com. 1976, subcom. on improvement judiciary 1971-81, com. to rev. circuit council conduct and disability orders, com. to celebrate Bicentennial of U.S. constn.), Mo., D.C., St. Louis, Am. bar assns., Lawyers Assn. St. Louis, Mo. Squires, VFW, Am. Legion, Order of Coif, Sigma Chi (Significant Sig award), Phi Delta Phi (Disting. Alumni award). Presbyn. Clubs: Mason (St. Louis) (Shriner), Old Warson Country (St. Louis), Mo. Athletic (St. Louis). Home: 108 Runnymede Dr Saint Louis MO 63141 Office: U S Dist Ct 1114 Market St Saint Louis MO 63101

MEREDITH, RALPH DALE, financial planning executive, tax consultant; b. Los Angeles, Aug. 26, 1940; s. Merlin Emery Meredith and Anna Marie (Hoskin) Clark; m. Marilyn Joyce Mitchell, Jan. 5, 1962; children: Brian, Devin, Erlinda, Renee. Student, Bethel Coll., 1958-59; AA, St. Clair Community Coll., 1960; BA, Mich. State U., 1962. Cost acct. Mueller Brass Co., Port Huron, Mich., 1962-66; satellite dir. H&R Block, Port Huron, 1966-77; pres. Sterling Fireplace Inc., Marysville, Mich., 1973-79, Coronado of Can., Milton, Ont., 1976-82; mgr. office supervisory jurisdiction Southmark Fin. Services, Romeo, Mich., 1983—; fin. cons. Belize Agrl. Project, 1976, Chase Manhattan Bank; instr. Internat. Assn. Grad. Engrs., 1964-65, H&R Block, 1966-77; lectr. various civic orgns. Annual speaker Mich. Extension Service, St. Clair, Macomb Counties, 1968-77. Mem. Internat. Assn. Cert. Fin. Planners, Nat. Assn. Security Dealers. Avocations: fishing, hunting, wood working. Home: 3575 W Water Port Huron MI 48060 Office: Southmark Fin Services 66691 Van Dyke Romeo MI 48065

MERENSKI, PAUL, marketing educator; b. Greenwich, Conn., Oct. 13, 1939; m. Frances M. Schaffner, Aug. 31, 1963; children—Dara, Dawn. B.S. summa cum laude in Bus. Adminstrn., Wright State U., 1971, M.B.A., 1972; Ph.D., U. Cin., 1982. Stress analyst Titan Project Office, Am. Machine and Foundry Co., Stamford, Conn., 1960-62; instr. Wright State U., Dayton, Ohio, 1972-73; account exec. No. Securities Co., Dayton, 1973-74; dist. mgr. Church's Fried Chicken Inc., Dayton, 1974-76; assoc. prof. mktg. U. Dayton, 1976—; cons. in field. Contbr. numerous articles to profl. jours. Served as officer USAF, 1962-69. Mem. Am. Mktg. Assn., Assn. Consumer Research, Am. Acad. Advt., Acad. Mktg. Sci., Inst. Mgmt. Sci., Am. Inst. Decision Scis., Mensa, Mu Kappa Tau. Address: 416 Falcon Dr New Carlisle OH 45344

MERGLER, H. KENT, investment counselor; b. Cin., July 1, 1940; s. Wilton Henry and Mildred Amelia (Pulliam) M.; BBA with honors, U. Cin., 1963, MBA, 1964; m. Judith Anne Metzger, Aug. 17, 1963; children: Stephen Kent, Timothy Alan, Kristin Lee. Portfolio mgr. Scudder, Stevens & Clark, Cin., 1964-68, v.p. investments, Chgo., 1970-73; v.p. Gibraltar Research and Mgmt., Ft. Lauderdale, Fla., 1968-70; portfolio mgr., ptnr., exec. v.p. and prin. Stein Roe & Farnham, Inc., Ft. Lauderdale, 1973-84, Chgo., 1984—, also mem. exec. com., investment policy com., chmn. account dept.; arbitrator Nat. Assn. Security Dealers, Inc., 1976-82. Chmn. adminstrv. bd. Christ United Meth. Ch., Ft. Lauderdale, 1981-83; chmn. fin. com., bd. dirs. Pine Crest Prep. Sch., 1982-84, bd. advisors, 1984-87; bd. dirs. Coral Ridge Little League, 1976-84, pres., 1980-81 . Chartered fin. analyst; chartered investment counselor. Mem. Fin. Analysts Soc. S. Fla. (pres. 1975-76, dir. 1974-78), Bond Club Ft. Lauderdale (v.p. 1980-81, dir. 1978-82), Inst. Chartered Fin. Analysts. Republican. Clubs: Coral Ridge Country (Ft. Lauderdale, Fla.); Metropolitan, Bankers (San Juan), University (Milw.); Skokie Country; Bankers (San Juan, P.R.). Home: 924 Pine Tree Ln Winnetka IL 60093 Office: 1 S Wacker Dr Chicago IL 60606

MERICKEL, MICHAEL GENE, chiropractic physician, educator; b. Wells, Minn., Apr. 9, 1952; s. Elmer Dale and Wilma Jean (Conquest) M.; m. Diane H. Steinke, June 27, 1976; children: Eric, Alexa. A in Nursing, Kettering Coll. Med. Arts, 1973; D of Chiropratic, Palmer Coll. Chiropractic, 1980. Diplomate Nat. Bd. Chiropractic Examiners; RN. RN Kettering (Ohio) Hosp., 1969-73, Walla Walla (Wash.) Hosp., 1973-75; pvt. practice chiropractic medicine Ashland, Ohio, 1981—; instr., counselor 5-Day Stop Smoking Clinic, Tri-County area, 1983—. Contbr. articles to profl. jours. tchr., research vol. Hale Farm and Village, Bath, Ohio, 1983-86; mem. Tri-County Regional Safety Council, Ashland, 1982—. Mem. Internat. Chiropractors Assn., Am. Chiropractic Assn., Ohio State Chiropractic Assn. Avocations: gardening, photography, writing, 19th century farm skills, primitive skills. Office: Ashland Chiropractic Ctr 1188 Simanton Rd Ashland OH 44805

MERIDEN, TERRY, physician; b. Damascus, Syria, Oct. 12, 1946; came to U.S., 1975; s. Izzat and Omayma (Aidi) M.; m. Lena Kahal, Nov. 17, 1975; children: Zina, Lana. BS, Sch. Sci., Damascus, 1968; MD, Sch. Medicine, Damascus, 1972, doctorate cum laude, 1973. Diplomate Am. Bd. Internal Medicine. Resident in infectious diseases Rousch Green Hosp., Romford, Eng., 1973; house officer in internal medicine and cardiology Ashford (Eng.) Group Univ. Hosps., 1973-74; sr. house officer in internal medicine and neurology Grimsby (Eng.) Group Univ. Hosps., 1974; registrar in internal medicine and rheumatology St. Annes Hosp., London, 1974-75; jr. resident in internal medicine Shadyside Hosp., Pitts., 1975-76, sr. resident in internal medicine, 1976-77; fellow in endocrinology and metabolism Shadyside Hosp. and Grad. Inst., Pitts., 1976-77; clin. asst. prof. U. Ill., Peoria, 1979; pres. Am. Diabetes Assn., Peoria, 1982-84; dir. Proctor Diabetes Unit, Peoria, 1984—, 1984—. Contbr. articles to profl. jours. Fellow ACP; mem. AMA (Recognition award 1985), ADA (chmn. profl. edn. and research 1980—, mem. editorial bd and Spanish lit bd, nat. bd. dirs. 1986—, vice chmn. nat. com. on diabetes edn. and affiliate services 1986—, Outstanding Service award 1984, Outstanding Diabetes Educator award 1986), Am. Cancer Soc. (Life Line award 1983), The Obesity Found. (Century award 1984, Recognition award 1985). Home: 410 Country Club Dr Pekin IL 61554 Office: Park Ct Med Ctr 616 S 13th St Suite E Pekin IL 61554

MERING, KENNETH DOUGLAS, sales executive; b. Des Moines, Apr. 5, 1957; s. Ray Delaplaine and Jacqueline Kline (McDonald) M.; m. Kathleen Purcell, Nov. 17, 1984. BSChemE, U. N.D., 1979. Registered profl. engr. Tool procurement engr. Johnson Controls, Milw., 1980-85; mktg. expeditor ASEA Electric, Waukesha, Wis., 1985; sales engr. Neco Hammond, Baraboo, Wis., 1986—. Vol. Spl. Olympics, Milw., 1983—. Mem. Am. Inst. Chem. Engrs. Episcopalian. Lodge: Toastmasters (adminstrv. v.p. Baraboo chpt., 1983-84), Schroeder Masters (social dir. Milw. chpt., 1981-84).

MERIWETHER, J. BRUCE, bank company executive. Pres. First Nat. Bank, Dubuque, Iowa. Office: First Nat Bank Locust at 7th Dubuque IA 52001 *

MERKELO, HENRI, physicist, educator; b. Borky, Ukraine, USSR, June 12, 1939; came to U.S., 1956; s. Alexander and Natalia (Niushko) M. Certificat d'aptitude professionnelle, Coll. Moderne et Tech., Reims, France, 1956; MS, U. Ill., 1962, PhD, 1966. Research scientist physics and thermodynamics Douglas Aircraft Co., Santa Monica, Calif., 1962; faculty U. Ill., Urbana, 1966—, dir. quantum electronics research lab., 1973—; dir. picosecond digital electronics U. Calif., Santa Barbara, 1982—; cons. Sangamo./Schlumberger, Atlanta, 1977-80, SRI, Internat., Menlo Park, Calif., 1980-82, AMP, Inc., Harrisburg, Pa., 1983—. Contbr. numerous articles to profl. jours.; patentee in field. Ford fellow, 1960-62, IMB fellow, 1963, Kodak fellow, 1964; NSF grantee, 1970—. Mem. IEEE (sr.), Am. Inst. Physics, Am. Physics Soc., Am. Optical Soc., Sigma Xi, Tau Beta Pi. Research directed to devel. of ultra high speed logic devices and circuits for high speed computing. Picosecond and femtosecond switching phenomena. Home: 7 Pine Circle Urbana IL 61801 Office: U Ill Quantum Electronics Lab 1406 W Green St Urbana IL 61801

MERKIN, WILLIAM CHARLES, wholesale floral company executive; b. Del Rio, Tex., Apr. 26, 1938; s. Charles and Ina Louise (Crenshaw) M.; m.

Peggy Jean Willis, June 16, 1957; children: Eufaula Jean, Richard Charles. BSME, U. Tex., El Paso, 1964. Mgr. elec. products div. Alcoa Conductor Products Co., Massena, N.Y., 1975-77; pres. Control Products Co. div. Alcoa, Pitts., 1977-78; gen. mgr. Alcoa Closure div. Alcoa Corp., Richmond, Ind., 1978-82; pres. Joseph H. Hill Co., Richmond, 1983—, also bd. dirs.; chmn. bd. Hill Floral Products Co., Richmond, 1986—; bd. dirs. Wayne Dairy Products, Inc., Second Nat. Corp., Second Nat. Bank Richmond; mem. adv. bd. Purdue programs at Ind. U. East, 1981—. Patentee in field. Bd. dirs. Richmond Boys Club, 1983—; pres. Bd. Aviation Commrs., Richmond, 1980—. Mem. Richmond C. of C. Republican. Lodge: Rotary. Avocations: golf, tennis, flying. Home: 3247 Latern Terr Richmond IN 47374 Office: Joseph H Hill Co 2700 Peacock Rd Richmond IN 47374

MERKLE, HELEN LOUISE, hotel executive; b. Carrington, N.D., May 23, 1950; d. Orville F. and Lillian M. (Argue) M.; B.S., N.D. State U., 1972. Asst. dir. food mgmt. Stouffer's Atlanta Inn, Atlanta, 1972-74; dir. food mgmt. Stouffer's Indpls. Inn, 1974-78; adminstrv. dir. food mgmt. Stouffer's Riverfront Towers, St. Louis, 1978-80; food mgmt. cons. Fraser Mgmt., Westlake, Ohio, 1980-83; exec. chef Marriott Hotel, Cleve., 1983—. Recipient First Place award for soups Taste of Indpls., 1976. Mem. , Am. Culinary Fedn., Cleve. Culinary Assn., Food Service Execs. Assn., Nat. Assn. Female Execs. Democrat. Lutheran. Home: 27618 B Caroline Circle Westlake OH 44145 Office: Marriott Hotel Cleve 4277 150th St Cleveland OH 44135

MERLO, NORA JEANNE, family support specialist; b. Chgo., Apr. 17, 1938; d. Fred Anton and Margaret Dolores (Moss) Hansen; m. Mark Merlo, May 26, 1962; children: Bridget Downey, Kathleen, Kevin, Sean. BA in Social Work, Lewis U., Lockport, Ill., 1976; MS in Edn. Counseling, Ill. State U., 1980. Caseworker Dept. Pub. Aid, Joliet, Ill., 1974-80; family support specialist Bur. Child Support, Joliet, Ill., 1980-86; steward Am. Fedn. State, County and Mcpl. Employees., Joliet, Ill., 1974—; pvt. practice counseling, Joliet, 1982-86. Mem. Ill. Welfare Assn. (vice chmn., chmn. membership). Roman Catholic. Avocations: duplicate bridge, needlepoint, crocheting. Office: Bur of Child Support 57 W Jefferson Joliet IL 60431

MERLOTTI, FRANK HENRY, office furniture and hardware manufacturing company executive; b. Herrin, Ill., 1926; married. With Magic Chef Co., Chgo., 1950-53; with Whirlpool Corp., Benton Harbor, Mich., 1953-57, Steelcase, Inc., Grand Rapids, Mich., 1957—; v.p. Steelcase, Inc., from 1967, now pres., chief operating officer, dir. Office: Steelcase Inc 901 44th St SE Grand Rapids MI 49508 *

MERLOTTI, MARK LOUIS, financial executive, consultant; b. St. Louis, Apr. 24, 1956; s. Louis Charles and Marie Louise (Colombo) M.; m. Cindy Lynn Sutter, May 28, 1982. BBA, U. Mo., 1978. CPA; cert. fin. planner, registered principal, Mo. Sr. acct. Peat Marwick, St. Louis, 1978-82; dir. fin. planning Mercantile Bank, St. Louis, 1982-84; v.p. Compensation Mgmt., St. Louis, 1984—. Mem. fin. devel. com. ARC, St. Louis, 1985—; fin. devel. cons. Epworth Children's Home, St. Louis, 1986. Recipient J. Mathews award Home Life Ins. Co., 1984. Mem. Am. Inst. CPA's, Internat. Assn. Fin. Planners, U. Mo. Alumni Assn. (bd. dirs. 1980—), Ducks Unlimited (co. controller 1986), Am. Athletic Assn. Republican. Roman Catholic. Club: Racquet (St. Louis) (mem. squash com. 1984—). Avocations: squash, golf, waterfowl hunting. Home: 7156 Kingsbury Saint Louis MO 63130 Office: Compensation Mgmt 100 S Brentwood Saint Louis MO 63105

MERRICK, JAMES GERARD, pediatric allergist; b. Carroll, Iowa, Sept. 17, 1949; s. Boyd Brett and Mildred Veronica (Stanek) M.; m. Roxanne Margaret LeMaster, July 26, 1975; 1 child, Anne Elizabeth. BS, U. Iowa, 1971, MD, 1975. Diplomate Am. Bd. Pediatrics, Am. Bd. Allergy and Immunology. Resident pediatrics Gunderson Clinic LaCrosse (Wis.) Luth. Hosp., 1975-76; resident pediatrics U. Iowa Hosps. and Clinics, Iowa City, 1976-78, fellow in allergy and pediatric pulmonology, 1981-83; pediatrician Med. Arts Clinic, Appleton, Wis., 1978-81, allergist, pediatric pumonologist, 1984—, also bd. dirs.; pediatrician Carle Clinic, Urbana, Ill., 1983-84; mem. pediatric spl. care com. St. Elizabeth's Hosp., Appleton, 1984—. Bd. dirs. Fox Valley Cystic Fibrosis Found., Neenah, Wis., 1986—. Home: 250 River Dr Appleton WI 54915 Office: Med Arts Clinic 401 N Oneida St Appleton WI 54911

MERRICK, PAUL FREDERICK, social worker; b. Dayton, Ohio, Mar. 5, 1940; s. Glenn Oliver and Mildred Irene (Koverman) M.; m. Edwina Catherine Cibulka, July 31, 1965; children: Brian Ferguson, Megan Aileen. BA, U. Dayton, 1962; MSW, U. Pitts., 1966. Diplomate Am. Bd. Clin. Social Work. Practitioner Cath. Social Services, Dayton, 1966-69, Family Services Assn., Dayton, 1969-72; coordinator East Dayton office Family Service Assn., Dayton, 1972-85, program coordinator, intake dept. supr. walk-in service, 1985—; coordinator office Family Service Assn., Dayton, 1984—, mem. mgmt. team, 1986—; field instr. Wright State U., Dayton, 1985—. Chmn. transp. com., Montgomery Council on Aging, Dayton, 1976-83; campaign chmn. United Way for Family Services Assn., 1986. Served with U.S. Army, 1962-64. Recipient cert. of Appreciation City of Dayton, 1970, Community Service award United Way of Dayton, 1972, Outstanding Solicitor and Co. Chairperson award United Way of Dayton, 1986. Mem. Nat. Assn. Social Workers, Acad. Cert. Social Workers, Nat. Rifle Assn. Roman Catholic. Avocation: ice skating. Home: 65 Mimosa Dr Centerville OH 45459 Office: Family Service Assn 184 Salem Ave Dayton OH 45406

MERRIFIELD, DAVID WAYNE, pharmacist, real estate developer; b. Lagrange, Ind., May 5, 1959; s. Carldean and Patsy Lou (Minnick) M.; m. Mary Kristine Mynhier, Apr. 4, 1981; children: Stacy Lynne, Kristin Leigh. BS in Pharmacy, Purdue U., 1982. Registered pharmacist, Ind., W.Va. Pharmacist Rite-Aid Corp., Montgomery, W.Va., 1982-83, Hook Drugs, Kendallville, Ind., 1983—; pres. Lagrange Community Devel. Corp., 1986—. Methodist. Home: Rural Rt #1 Box 123 Lagrange IN 46761 Office: Hook Drugs 200 W North St Kendallville IN 46755

MERRILL, DANIEL LEE, mechanical engineer; b. Kalamazoo, Sept. 16, 1958; s. Russell U. and E. Juanita (Griffin) M.; m. Lynn Marie Price, Apr. 29, 1983; children: Misty, Daniel Jr. AS in Mech. Engring., Pine Lake (Mich.) Community Coll., 1978. Chassis designer Aero Detroit, Oak Park, Mich., 1980-82; body designer Pioneer Co., Warren, Mich., 1982-83, Targa Inc., Dearborn, Mich., 1983-85; sr. body designer Tech. Engring. Cons., Ann Arbor, Mich., 1985-86, Auto Dynamics, Madison Heights, Mich., 1986, Tech Aid, Southfield, Mich., 1987—. Patentee in field. Avocation: creative financing. Home: 201 Seminole Holly MI 48442 Office: PO Box 202 Kalamazoo MI 49005

MERRILL, RICHARD THOMAS, publishing executive; b. Chgo., June 26, 1928; s. Thomas William and Mary Ann (Colvin) M.; m. Lisi Y. Snyder, June 7, 1952; children: T. William II, James R., Stephen J. B.A., U. Mo., 1950, B.J., 1951. With Commerce Clearing House, Chgo., 1953—; v.p. Commerce Clearing House, 1962-76, exec. v.p., 1976-79, pres., chief exec. officer, 1980—, also dir.; dir. CCH Australia, CCH Canadian Ltd., CCH N.J., Nat. Quotation Bur., CT Corp. System, Computax, State Capitol Info. Service, CCH Products Co., Facts on File, Blvd. Bank, Chgo., Blvd. Bancorp. Inc., Washington Service Bur., Quail Hill, Inc., Editorial Fiscal y Laboral (S.A. de C.V.). Served to capt. USAF, 1951-53. Home: 2940 Lake Placid Ln Northbrook IL 60062 Office: Commerce Clearing House Inc 2700 Lake Cook Rd Riverwoods IL 60015

MERRIMAN, DAVID RICHARD, audit supervisor; b. North Olmsted, Ohio, Sept. 28, 1961; s. Richard B. and Barbara A. (Lake) M. BBA, Eastern Mich. U., 1983. CPA, Mich. Audit intern Touche Ross & Co., Detroit, 1983; audit supr. Coopers & Lybrand, Detroit, 1984—. Named one of Outstanding Young Men in Am., 1985. Mem. Am. Inst. CPA's, Mich. Assn. CPA's, Eastern Mich. Alumni Assn. Home: 44735 N Hills Apt 102 Northville MI 48167 Office: Coopers & Lybrand 400 Renaissance Ctr Detroit MI 48243

MERRIOTT, THOMAS LEROY, real estate corporation officer, consultant; b. Estherville, Iowa, Oct. 1, 1943; s. E. LeRoy and Kathrine E. (Hollenbeck) M.; m. Georgia A. Hoffman, July 3, 1964; children: Thomas L. Jr., Samuel John. AA, Estherville Jr. Coll., 1963; BA, Mankato (Minn.) State U., 1966, postgrad., 1966-67. Cert. shopping ctr. mgr; lic. real estate broker, Colo., Ill. V.p. Village Bowl, Inc., North Mankato, Minn., 1967-70; property mgr. Gen. Growth, Muscatine, Iowa and Colo. Springs, Colo., 1970-73; v.p. Von Frellick Assocs., Denver, 1973-76; v.p. mgmt. Devel. Control Corp., Northfield, Ill., 1976-81; pres. The TLM Corp., Arlington Heights, Ill., 1981—. Mem. Buffalo Grove (Ill.) Booster Club. Mem. Internat. Council Shopping Ctrs. Republican.

MERRITT, DIANE FRANCES, obstetrician, gynecologist; b. Cleve., Jan. 14, 1949; d. Milton Paul and Wilma (Vleck) M.; m. Sándor János Kovács, Apr. 16, 1983; children: Sándor Adam, Tamás. BA, Miami U., Oxford, Ohio, 1971; MD, NYU, 1975. Diplomate Am. Bd. Ob-Gyn. Instr. Washington U., St. Louis; dir. div. pediatric and adolescent gynecology Washington U., 1981—. Fellow Am. Coll. Ob-Gyn, Am. Fertility Soc., Soc. Adolescent Medicine. Office: Dept Ob-Gyn 4911 Barnes Hosp Plaza Saint Louis MO 63110

MERRITT, HOWARD, emergency physician; b. Detroit, Aug. 26, 1953; s. Harold Robert and Charlotte (Hirschman) M. BS in Biology, Wayne State U., 1976, MD, 1981. Diplomate Nat. Bd. Med. Examiners. Intern Henry Ford Hosp., Detroit, 1981-82; staff physician dept. emergency medicine Wilkes Gen. Hosp., North Wilkesboro, N.C., 1982-85; dir. dept. emergency medicine Saline (Mich.) Community Hosp., 1985—; med. dir. occupational health services Saline Community Hosp., 1985—; physician Norfolk and So. Ry., Roanoke, Va., 1986—; flight physician Midwest Medflight, Ann Arbor, Mich., 1986—. Vol. physician Inst. for Latin Am. Concern, Omaha, 1985. Mem. So. Med. Assn., Am. Coll. Emergency Physicians, Phi Beta Kappa, Alpha Omega Alpha. Jewish. Avocations: cooking, travel, reading, ballroom dancing. Home: 3202 Gensley Ann Arbor MI 48103 Office: Saline Community Hosp 400 W Russell Saline MI 48176

MERRY, CARROLL EUGENE, communications company executive; b. Richland Center, Wis., Jan. 8, 1948; s. Elmo Carroll and Helen Evelyn (Peaslee) M.; B.S. in Journalism, U. Wis., Oshkosh, 1973; M.S. in Mgmt., Cardinal Stritch Coll., Milw., 1983; m. Amy Jo Sweet, Oct. 21, 1967; children—JaNelle Paulette, Jennifer Erin. Bur. chief Oshkosh Daily Northwestern, Berlin, Wis., 1973-74; advt. coordinator J I Case Outdoor Power Div., Winneconne, Wis., 1974-76; advt. mgr. Gehl Co., West Bend, Wis., 1976-78, mktg. communications mgr., 1978-85; Midwest regional mktg. mgr. Intertec Pub. Co., Chgo., 1985-86; mgr. advt. and sales promotion Massey-Ferguson, Inc., Des Moines, Iowa, 1986-87; sales mgr. Century Communications, Niles, Ill., 1987—. Mem. editorial adv. bd. Agri-Mktg. mag., 1983. Chmn. communications com. St. Joseph's Community Hosp., West Bend, 1980-85; v.p. Washington County 4-H Leaders Assn., 1981. Served with USAF, 1968-72. Recipient Outstanding Young Man Civic award, 1979. Mem. Nat. Agri-Mktg. Assn. (dir., sec. Badger chpt.). Office: Century Communications 6201 Howard St Niles IL 60648

MERSMANN, MARK EDWARD, accountant; b. Richmond, Kans., Mar. 19, 1941; s. Fred John and Regina (Lickteig) M.; m. Ann Pickert, June 20, 1964; children: Kenneth, Joel, Amy, Eric, Paul. BS in Acctg., Emporia State U., 1963. CPA, Mo., Kans., Colo. Ptnr. Fox & Co. CPA's, Kansas City, Mo., 1964-73, Denver, 1973-78, St. Louis, 1978-81; pres. St. John & Mersmann, Inc. CPA's, St. Louis, 1981—. Served as sgt. U.S. Army, 1963-69. Mem. Am. Inst. CPA's (peer rev. com. 1985—), Mo. Soc. CPA's. Roman Catholic. Home: 2028 Sunflower Ct Chesterfield MO 63017 Office: St John & Mersmann Inc 640 Cepi Dr Chesterfield MO 63017

MERTZ, FRED J., transportation executive; b. St. Louis, Aug. 31, 1938; s. Joseph Edward and Vita Rose (Passanante) M.; m. Rose Ann Mertz, Jan. 21, 1964; children: Michael, Michelle, Nicole. Student, St. Louis U., 1957-62. Asst. div. controller Brunswick Corp., DeLand, Fla., 1967-69; plant controller Brunswick Corp., Saint Joseph, Mo., 1969-72; plant mgr. Brunswick Corp., Saint Joseph, 1972-75; exec. v.p. Midwestern Distbn., Inc., Fort Scott, Kans., 1976-80; pres. United Services Inc., Nashville, 1980-81; exec. v.p. Prime, Inc., Springfield, Mo., 1981—; pres. Transp. Investments, Inc., Springfield, 1984—, MAM Inc., Springfield, 1984—; gen. mgr. Affordable Home Ctrs., Springfield, 1985—. Served with U.S. Army, 1962. Avocations: fishing, boating, softball, soccer. Home and Office: Box 4208 Springfield MO 65808

MERTZ, JANET S., otorhinolaryngologist; b. Kansas City, Mo., Jan. 12, 1950; d. Edgar L. and Edna M. (Walker) Schasteen; m. Jim I. Mertz, Jan. 21, 1970. MD, U. Kans., Kansas City, 1975. Diplomate Am. Bd. Otolaryngology, Am. Bd. Head and Neck Surgery. Resident in otolaryngology Mayo Clinic, Rochester, Minn., 1978-83; practice medicine specializing in otolaryngology Kansas City, 1983—; clin. assoc. prof. U. Mo., Kansas City, 1983—. Mem. AMA (Physician Recognition award 1983-89), Am. Med. Womens Assn., Am. Acad. Otolaryngology, Jackson County Med. Soc., Kansas City Otolaryngology Soc. Avocations: antiques, fine arts. Home: 6509 Belinder Shawnee Mission KS 66208 Office: 6724 Troost Suite 208 Kansas City MO 64131

MERTZ, WILLIAM HENRY, psychologist; b. Saginaw, Mich., July 15, 1948; s. Chester Jr. and Maxine June (Niven) M.; m. Susan Carol Parker, Jan. 9, 1971; children: Carolyn Michelle, Andrea Leigh. BA, U. Mich., 1970; MA, Bowling Green State U., 1973, PhD, 1975. Lic. psychologist, Ohio. Lectr. Bowling Green (Ohio) State U., 1973; psychologist Akron (Ohio) Child Guidance, 1977-82, supervising psychologist, 1982—; adj. asst. prof. Kent (Ohio) State U., 1982—. Mem. Am. Psychol. Assn., Gestalt Inst. Cleve., Psychologist for Social Responsibility. Avocations: racquetball, hiking. Office: Akron Child Guidance Ctr 344 4th St NW Barberton OH 44203

MERZ, JOHN SEVERIN, chemical company executive; b. St. Louis, Mar. 13, 1948; s. Severin and Rosina Merz; m. Susan Thieren, Nov. 24, 1973; children: John Jr., James. BSEE, U. Cin., 1971; MBA, Washington U., St. Louis, 1978. Elec. engr. Wheelabrator-Frye, Mishawaka, Ind., 1971-73; engr. Monsanto Corp., St. Louis, 1973-74, engr. supr., 1974-79; engring. mgr. Monsanto Enviro Chem. Systems, St. Louis, 1979-83, product mgr., 1983—. Served to capt. USAR, 1971-82. Mem. Air Polution Control Assn. Home: 324 Kings Ct Florissant MO 63034 Office: Monsanto Enviro Chem Systems PO Box 14547 Saint Louis MO 63178

MESCHKE, HERBERT L., state supreme court justice; b. Belfield, N.D., Mar. 18, 1928; s. G.E. and Dorothy E. Meschke; m. Shirley Ruth McNeil; children: Marie, Jean, Michael, Jill. B.A., Jamestown Coll., 1950; J.D., U. Mich., 1953. Bar: N.D. Law clk. U.S. Dist. Ct. N.D., 1953-54; practice law Minot, N.D., 1954-85; justice N.D. State Supreme Ct., 1985—; mem. N.D. Ho. of Reps., 1965-66, N.D. Senate, 1967-70. Mem. ABA, Am. Judicature Soc., N.D. Bar Assn. Office: ND Supreme Ct State Capitol Bismarck ND 58505 *

MESENHIMER, LEE ORLAND, electrical engineer; b. Lawrence, Kans., Feb. 16, 1934; s. Orland Leslie and Della Mae (Dews) M. Student, Case Western Res. U., 1952-54, 56, U. Kans., 1954-55. Registered profl. engr., Ohio. Engr. Lorain (Ohio) Products Corp., 1955-75; pres., engr. Yellow Dot Co., Avon, Ohio, 1975—; cons. engr. Mesenhimer Electronic Engr., Avon, 1984—. Patentee in field. Mem. IEEE. Lodge: Masons. Avocations: short wave radios, electronic flea markets. Office: Yellow Dot Co 2714 Jaycox Rd Avon OH 44011

MESERVE, WALTER JOSEPH, drama studies educator; b. Portland, Maine, Mar. 10, 1923; s. Walter Joseph and Bessie Adelia (Bailey) M.; m. Mollie Ann Lacey, June 18, 1981; children by previous marriage—Gayle Ellen, Peter Haynes, Jo Alison, David Bryan. Student, Portland Jr. Coll., 1941-42; A.B., Bates Coll., Lewiston, Maine, 1947; M.A., Boston U., 1948; Ph.D., U. Wash., Seattle, 1952. Instr. to prof. U. Kans., Lawrence, 1951-68; prof. dramatic lit. and theory Ind. U., Bloomington, 1968—, assoc. dean research and grad. devel., 1980-83, dir. Inst. for Am. Theatre Studies, 1983—; v.p. Feedback Services, Nashville, Ind., 1983—. Author: History of American Drama, 1965, Robert Sherwood, 1970, An Emerging Entertainment, 1977, Heralds of Promise, 1986; editor: Plays of WD Howells, 1960. Served to cpl. AC, U.S. Army, 1943-46. Fellow NEH, 1974-75, 83-84, Rockefeller Found., 1979, Guggenheim Found., 1984-85. Mem. Am. Soc. for Theatre Research (exec. com. 1980-83), Am. Studies Assn., Authors Guild, Dramatists Guild (assoc.). Club: Cosmos (Washington). Office: Ind U Dept Theatre and Drama Bloomington IN 47405

MESLOW, DOUGLAS BREDESEN, lawyer; b. San Antonio, July 25, 1959; s. Robert Bredesen and Karen Esther (Von Wald) M.; m. Jenny Moline, May 29, 1981; 1 child, Peter Bredesen. BA, St. Olaf Coll., 1981; JD, U. Minn., 1984. Bar: Minn. 1984, U.S. Dist. Ct. Minn. 1984. Assoc. Moss & Barnett, Mpls., 1984-85, Salmen & Brinkman, St. Paul, 1985—. Mem. ABA, Minn. Bar Assn., Ramsey County Bar Assn., Assn. Trial Lawyers Am. Democrat. Lutheran. Lodge: Kiwanis. Avocations: basketball, raquetball. Home: 3770 Midland White Bear Lake MN 55110 Office: Salmen & Brinkman 386 N Wabasha Suite 1250 Saint Paul MN 55102

MESSER, HENRY DAVIS, neurosurgeon; b. Madison, Fla., Sept. 22, 1927; s. Henry and Sarah (Davis) M. BS, Duke U., 1946, MD, 1950. Diplomate Am. Bd. Neurol. Surgery. Resident St. Vincent's Hosp., N.Y.C., 1957; assoc. in neurol. surgery Columbia U., N.Y.C., 1967-76; asst. prof. neurosurgery U. Mich., Ann Arbor, 1977-86; practice medicine specializing in neurosurgery Henry Ford Med. Ctr., Westland, Mich., 1982—, Peoples Community Hosp. Authority, Wayne, Mich., 1986—; Contbr. numerous articles to profl. jours. Mem. Mich. Orgn. Human Rights, Detroit, 1981-86, ACLU, 1982-84. Served to capt. USAF, 1951-53. Fellow ACS; mem. Congress Neurol. Surgeons, Am. Assn. Neurol. Surgeons. Home: 23248 Bonair Dearborn Heights MI 48127 Office: Henry Ford Med Ctr 35605 Warren Rd Westland MI 48185

MESSERSMITH, J(OHN) LEE, farmer; b. Antioch, Nebr., May 10, 1923; s. Frank E. and Luvina (Roberts) M.; m. Barbara Joan Sisley, June 14, 1952; children: Charles Lee, Jordan Scot, Douglas Drew, Terence Kim. BS, U. Nebr., 1953, MS, 1959. Instr. U. Nebr., Curtis, 1953-64; farmer Hemingford, Nebr., 1964—; tchr. Hemingford High Sch., 1965-68; instr. vocat.-agrl. Hemingfon High Sch., 1971; mgr. Price Farm Equipment, Hemingford, 1972. Chmn. bd. Hemingford Planning Commn., 1984. Mem. Nebr. Vocat.-Agrl. Assn. (pres. 1963-64, newsletter editor 1963), Alpha Zeta. Methodist. Avocations: fishing, photography, electronics, square dancing, plants, wind and solar energy, bees and honey, farm crisis, Christian counseling, singing, public speaking. Home and Office: Box 305 Hemingford NE 69348

MESSINEO, ANTHONY ONOFRIO, JR., restaurant executive; b. Lincoln, Nebr., Jan. 24, 1941; s. Anthony Onofrio and Josephine M.; B.S., U. Nebr., Lincoln, 1965; m. Carmen Monaco, Apr. 20, 1963; children—Deborah, Michael, Anthony Onofrio III. Mgr., Tony and Luigi's Restaurant, Lincoln, 1965-71, chmn. bd., 1978—, pres., 1978—; owner, chmn. bd., pres. Valentino's Pizza, Lincoln, 1971—, Valentino's of Am., Lincoln, 1978—. Mem. Young Pres. Orgn. Republican. Roman Catholic. Clubs: Sertoma, Rotary. Home: 7535 S Hampton St Lincoln NE 68506 Office: 201 N 8th St Lincoln NE 68501

MESZAROS, PAUL EUGENE, EDP internal auditor; b. Columbus, Ohio, Dec. 20, 1951; s. Alexander Joseph Meszaros Sr. and Nora Ann Slonager, Sept. 2, 1972; m. Brenda Kathleen Sarchet; children: Sean Michael, Paula Sarchet. BBA, Ohio State U., 1973; MBA, Capital U., 1980. Various positions Cott Index Co., Columbus, 1971-80; ops. analyst, hardware planner Columbus & So. Ohio Electric Co., Columbus, 1980-82; hardware planner AEP Service Corp., Columbus, 1982-85, internal EDP auditor, 1985—. Avocations: photography, bicycling, model railroading. Home: 628 Woodlake Ct Westerville OH 43081 Office: Am Electric Power Corp 1 Riverside Plaza Columbus OH 43215

METCALF, LYNNETTE CAROL, naval officer, journalist; b. Van Nuys, Calif., June 22, 1955; d. William Edward and Carol Annette (Keith) M.; m. Scott Edward Hruska, May 16, 1987. BA in Communications and Media, Our Lady of Lake, 1978; MA in Human Relations, U. Okla., 1980; MA in Mktg. Webster U., 1986. Enlisted U.S. Air Force, 1973, advanced through grades to sgt., 1975; intelligence analyst, Taiwan, Italy and Tex., 1973-76; historian, journalist, San Antonio, 1976-78; commd. officer U.S. Navy, 1978, advanced through ranks to lt., 1982; pub. relations officer, Rep. of Panama, 1979-81; mgr. system program, London, 1981-82; ops. plans/tng., McMurdo Sta., Antarctica, 1982-84; exec. officer transient personnel unit Naval Tng. Ctr., Great Lakes, Ill., 1984-86, comdg. officer transient personnel unit, 1986-87; asst. prof. naval sci. U. Notre Dame NROTC, 1987—; anchorwoman USN-TV CONTACT, 1986-87. Contbr. articles to profl. jours.; editor Naval Station Anchorline, 1979-81, WOPN Caryatides, 1985-86; author: Winter's Summer, 1983. Sec. San Vito Dei Normanni theatre group, Italy, 1975-76; coordinator Magic Box Theater, Zion, Ill., 1984-86; dir. "Too Bashful for Broadway" variety show, Naval Tng. Ctr.,1986-87. Decorated Antarctic Service medal, 1983, Sec. Navy Letter of Commendation, 1984, Expert Marksman medal, 1985. Mem. Nat. Assn. Female Execs., Women Officers' Prof. Network. (communications chair 1985-86, programs chair 1986-87). Clubs: McMurdo; Soc. of South Pole. Avocations: scuba diving, travel, reading, writing, performing.

METELKA, RONALD THOMAS, orthodontist; b. Chgo., Jan. 19, 1948; s. Charles Anton and Veronica (Cwik) M.; m. Valerie Karen Broderick, June 11, 1977; 1 child, Brenda Veronica. BS, Loyola U., Chgo., 1971; DDS, Northestern U., Chgo., 1975, MS, 1980. Assoc. dentist Northwestern U. Med. Assoc., Chgo., 1975-78; orthodontist Nat. Ctr. Dental Health, Morton Grove, Ill., 1980—; practice dentistry specializing in orthodontics Cary, Ill., 1980—; instr. Northwestern U., Chgo., 1975-78;. Mem. ADA, Am. Assn. Orthodontists, Chgo. Dental Soc., G.V. Black Soc., McHenry County Dental Soc., Cary C. of C. Republican. Roman Catholic. Avocation: tennis. Home: 1311 W Devon Ave Park Ridge IL 60068 Office: 43 E Main St Cary IL 60013

METKA, PHILLIP EDWARD, comptroller; b. Harrisburg, Pa., Dec. 30, 1938; s. Joseph Ambrose and Louise Cecile (Bokan) M.; m. Nancy Lee Cougnet. Feb. 17, 1962; children: Stacey Ann, Daniel Joseph. Student, Pa. State U., 1956-58, Northwestern U., 1967-71; BS in Acctg., No. Ill. U., 1977. CPA, Ill. Field auditor direct mktg. div. Jewel Cos., Inc., Harrisburg and Pitts., Pa., 1960-66; mgr. gen. acctg. direct mktg. div. Jewel Cos., Inc., Barrington, Ill., 1966-75; mgr. internal and tax audit direct mktg. div. Jewel Cos., Inc., Barrington, 1975-80; comptroller B.F. Shaw Printing Co., Dixon, Ill., 1980—. Bd. dirs. Dixon High Sch. Athletic Booster Club, 1985—. Mem. Am. Inst. CPA's, Internat. Newspaper Fin. Execs. Republican. Roman Catholic. Lodge: Rotary. Home: 1126 N Jefferson Ave Dixon IL 61021 Office: BF Shaw Printing Co 113 S Peoria Ave Dixon IL 61021

METOXEN, RICHARD FRANK, programming manager; b. Milw., Aug. 15, 1961; s. Edward Paul and Frances Ann (Godlib) M.; m. Janet Carol Federspiel, June 1, 1985; 1 child, Mallory Megan. Owner Design Cons., Saukville, Wis., 1981-86; programmer Centurion Computers, Brookfield, Wis., 1982-83, mgr. programming services, 1985-86; programmer Catalyst USA, Inc., Grafton, Wis., 1983-84; systems analyst Cap Gemini DASD, Brown Deer, Wis., 1984-85. Bd. dirs. Saukville (Wis.) Archtl. Control Bd., 1986, Saukville Planning Commn., 1986. Roman Catholic. Avocations: gardening, woodworking. Home: 661 N Riverside Dr Saukville WI 53080 Office: Centurion Computer Systems 15850 W Bluemound Rd Brookfield WI 53005

METRES, PHILIP JOHN, JR., psychologist; b. Bklyn., Nov. 11, 1942; s. Philip and Lily (Boulos) M.; m. Katherine Sheila Dannemann, Aug. 30, 1969; children: Philip J. III, Katherine Marie, David Michael. AB in Psychology, Coll. of Holy Cross, 1964; MA in Social Psychology, U.S. Internat. U., 1971, PhD in Profl. Psychology, 1975. Registered clin. psychologist, Ill. Instr. psychology San Diego Evening Coll., 1971-73; research psychologist Naval Health Research Ctr., San Diego, 1971-76; clin. psychologist N. Shore Ctr. for Counseling and Therapy, Northbrook, Ill., 1978—, Old Orchard Hosp., Skokie, Ill., 1978-80. Co-editor: Family Separation and Reunion: Adjustment of POW's and MIA's, 1975; contbr. articles to profl. jours. Commr. Spring Lakes Sports League, Lincolnshire, Ill., 1979-80; founding pres. Lincolnshire Citizens for Drug Awareness, 1981-82. Served to lt. USN, 1964-69, capt. Res., 1969—. Decorated Bronze Star, combat V-device. Fellow Interuniv. Seminar on Armed Forces and Soc.;

mem. Am. Psychol. Assn., Am. Assn. Marriage and Family Therapy, Naval Res. Assn. (life). Roman Catholic. Home: 49 Cambridge Ln Lincolnshire IL 60015 Office: N Shore Ctr Counseling & Therapy 655 Landwehr Rd Northbrook IL 60062

METROKOS, CAROLYN DEL ROSA, rehabilitation counselor; b. Milw., Mar. 9, 1927; d. Clarence Robert Wilburth and Marie Jo (Kroll) Roloff; m. Peter Metrokos, Dec. 22, 1944 (dec. Apr. 1985); children: Alexander, Aris; m. W.J. Zdanowski, May, 1987. BS, St. Clare's Coll., 1946; MS, Roosevelt U., 1954; PhD, Jackson U., 1975. Cert. rehab. counselor, Ill. Mem. staff dept. human services City of Chgo., 1946-52; pvt. cons. Milw., 1954—. Mem. Am. Assn. Rehab. Counselors, Am. Assn. Personnel and Guidance Counselors. Republican. Eastern Orthodox. Avocation: cross-country skiing. Home and Office: 5318 W Washington Blvd Milwaukee WI 53208 Summer Home: Pigeon Forge TN 37863

METTERS, LEONARD DAVID, auditor; b. Phila., Sept. 6, 1950; s. William John and Irene Pringle (Beren) M.; m. Alice Reith, Apr. 3, 1972; 1 child, Anne. BA, U. Va., 1972; MBA, U. Mich., 1983. CPA, cert. internal auditor. Auditor Auditor Pub. Accounts, Richmond, Va., 1977-78; sr. auditor Moore, Smith & Dale CPAs, Southfield, Mich., 1978-81, Wayne State U., Detroit, 1981-84; mgr. intenal auditing Mich. Bell Telephone, Southfield, 1984—. Mem. Am. Inst. CPAs, Inst. Internal Auditors (bd. govs. 1985-87, chmn. edn. com. 1985-86). Libertarian. Presbyterian. Avocations: tennis, reading. Home: 25401 Ravine Rd Southfield MI 48034 Office: Mich Bell Telephone 23777 Southfield Rd Southfield MI 48075

METZ, PHILIP STEVEN, surgeon; b. Omaha, May 12, 1945; s. Roman A. and Gwanetha (Hamilton) M.; m. Dianne Pearson, July 11, 1970; children: Amy Michelle, Wendy Marie, Stephanie Joy, Philip Robb. BS, Loras Coll., 1965; MD, U. Nebr., 1969. Diplomate Am. bd. Surgery and bd. Plastic Surgery. Commd. ensign USN, 1969, advanced through ranks to commdr., resigned, 1980, with res., 1980—; intern Nat. Naval Med. Ctr., Bethesda, Md., 1969-70; residentgen. surgery Oakland (Calif.) Naval Hosp., 1970-74; resident plastic and reconstructive surgery U. Utah, 1974-76; fellow hand surgery Derbyshire Royal Infirmary, Derby, Eng., 1980; dir. cleft palate team Nat. Naval Med. Ctr., Bethesda, 1977-79, chmn. plastic surgery, 1978-79; chmn. plastic surgery Bethesda Naval Hosp., Washington, 1979-80; pvt. practice Denver, 1980-82, Lincoln, Nebr., 1982—; chmn. plastic surgery Lincoln Gen. Hosp., 1986-87; cons. cleft palate team State of Nebr., 1986. Contbr. articles to profl. jours. Fellow ACS, Internat. Coll. Surgeons; mem. Am. Soc. Plastic and Reconstructive Surgery, Assn. Mil. Surgeons U.S., Assn. Mil. Plastic Surgeons, British Assn. for Surgery of the Hand, Royal Soc. Medicine, Am. Cleft Palate Assn., AMA, Am. Soc. Maxillo-Facial Surgery, Am. Assn. Hand Surgery, Lancaster County Med. Soc. Avocations: gardening, camping. Office: 801 S 48th St Lincoln NE 68510

METZENBAUM, HOWARD MORTON, U.S. senator; b. Cleve., June 4, 1917; s. Charles I. and Anna (Klafter) M.; m. Shirley Turoff, Aug. 8, 1946; children: Barbara Jo, Susan Lynn, Shelley Hope, Amy Beth. B.A., Ohio State U., 1939, LL.B., 1941. Chmn. bd. Airport Parking Co. Am., 1958-66, ITT Consumer Services Corp., 1966-68; chmn. bd. ComCorp, 1969-74, after 1975; U.S. senator from Ohio 1974, 77—; Mem. War Labor Bd., 1942-45, Ohio Bur. Code Rev., 1949-50, Cleve. Met. Housing Authority, 1968-70, Lake Erie Regional Transit Authority, 1972-73, Ohio Ho. of Reps., 1943-46, Ohio Senate, 1947-50; mem. Ohio Democratic Exec. Com., from 1966, Ohio Dem. Finance Com., from 1969. Trustee Mt. Sinai Hosp., Cleve., 1961-73, treas., 1966-73; bd. dirs. Council Human Relations, United Cerebral Palsy Assn., Nat. Council Hunger and Malnutrition, Karamu House, St. Vincent Charity Hosp., Cleve., St. Jude Research Hosp., Memphis; nat. co-chmn. Nat. Citizens' Com. Conquest Cancer; vice-chmn. fellows Brandeis U. Mem. Am., Ohio, Cuyahoga, Cleve. bar assns., Am. Assn. Trial Lawyers, Order of Coif, Phi Eta Sigma, Tau Epsilon Rho. Office: US Senate 140 Russell Senate Office Bldg Washington DC 20510 *

METZGER, DAVID DALE, architect, engineer; b. Burlington, Iowa, May 3, 1952; s. Robert Dean and Ruth Margaret (Marshall) M.; m. Inez Norma Medlang, July 12, 1976; children: Brian, Bjorn. BArch, Iowa State U., 1974; MArch, U. Ill., 1978. Intern architect Weber, Griffith & Mellican, Galesburg, Ill., 1974-76; intern architect, engr. Midland Architects, Burlington, 1978-82; pres. Metzger,& Johnson, Burlington; chmn. bd. Smith Engring. Assocs. Inc., Burlington. Bd. dirs. Low Rent Housing Agy. Burlington, 1983-85. Named one winner Residence Solar Design Competition, Ill. Com. Energy and Architecture, 1977; Passive Energy Concepts Devel. grantee, State of Iowa, 1980. Mem. AIA, Nat. Council Archtl. Registration Bds. Methodist. Lodge: Kiwanis (Burlington). Home: 1027 S Plane Burlington IA 52601 Office: Metzger Johnson & Smith Engring Assocs 1115 Summer St Burlington IA 52601

METZGER, MARVIN FRANKLIN, motel executive, realtor; b. Milw., Jan. 9, 1945; s. Marvin L. and Glenna M. (Swalheim) M.; m. Lyn Eckert, Sept. 20, 1977 (div. Oct. 1979). BBA, U. Wis., White Water, 1969. Motel broker Smith Realty Co. Inc., Milw., 1970-86; owner Glyn Holm Motel, Kenosha, Wis., 1972-78, Phoenix Inn, Milw., 1978-83, 40-Winks Motel (Oak Inn), Milw., 1978—; pres. J&M Constrn. Co., Milw., 1985—, MKM Inc., Milw., 1980—. Served with U.S. Army, 1970. Mem. Am. Hotel and Motel Assn. (com. mem.), Motel Brokers Assn. Am., Milw. Bd. Realtors, Milw. Innkeepers Assn. (bd. dirs. 1980), Milw. C. of C., Bahama Survivors Assn., Am. Legion. Presbyterian. Avocations: sailing, skiing, running, ballroom dancing, ocean cruising. Office: 40 Winks Motel (Oak Inn) 11017 E Bluemound Rd Wauwatosa WI 53226

METZL, MARILYN NEWMAN, clinical psychologist; b. N.Y.C., Apr. 12, 1938; s. George and Rose (Shanen) Newman; m. Kurt Metzl, June 25, 1961; children: Jonathan, Jordan, Jamie, Joshua. BA, Queens (N.Y.) Coll., 1959; MA, Hunter Coll., 1968; PhD, U. Kans., 1978. Cert. State Bd. Healing Arts, Mo. Dir. clin. services Psychol. Ednl. Assocs., Kansas City, Mo., 1971—; assoc. prof. Avila Coll., Kansas City, 1976-84. State of Mo. grantee, 1978, Menorah Med. Ctr. grantee, 1980. Mem. Am. Psychol. Assn., Mo. Psychol. Assn., Jackson County Med. Soc., Soc. for Research in Child Devel. Democrat. Jewish. Avocations: yoga, reading, skiing. Office: Psychol Ednl Assocs 6700 Troost Kansas City MO 64110

MEUSE, ANN TERRELL, insurance company official; b. Massillon, Ohio, Jan. 16, 1943; d. Douglass Fuqua and Jane (Chidester) Terrell; B.A. magna cum laude, Coll. White Plains (N.Y.), 1974; diploma paralegal edn. N.Y. U., 1975; m. Lewis Andrew Meuse, Apr. 16, 1960; children—Ann W., Laura A. Corp. sec., compliance dir. Gerber Life Ins. Co., White Plains, 1974-78; dir. legis. and policy research services Colonial Penn Group, Inc., Phila., 1978-82; asst. v.p., field mktg. The Signature Group, Chgo., 1982—. Mem. Chgo. Assn. Direct Marketers, Soc. Profl. Journalists, Sigma Delta Chi, Women's Direct Response Group of Chgo. Club: Toastmasters. Office: Signature Group 200 N Martingale Rd Schaumburg IL 60194

MEYER, ALBERT HENRY, manufacturing company executive; b. Grand Rapids, Mich., Oct. 19, 1935; s. Frederick Albert and Harriet (Stibbs) M.; m. Marilyn Eileen Neff, Dec. 22, 1956; children: Steven Albert, Susan Marie Meyer Wygmans. BA, U. Mich., 1957. Sales, mktg. positions Am. Seating, Grand Rapids, 1957-86, pres. archtl. products group, 1986—. Avocations: music, fishing. Home: 7478 Leyton Dr Ada MI 49301 Office: Am Seating 901 Broadway Grand Rapids MI 49504

MEYER, ALEX ALFRED, refrigeration company executive; b. Cedar Rapids, Iowa, Feb. 1, 1931; s. Leon and Elizabeth (Moffatt) M.; m. JoAnn Foerstner, Aug. 27, 1955; children: Jeffrey G., Marguerite. Student, U. Iowa, 1956. With Amana Refrigeration, Inc., Iowa, 1956—; dir. mktg. Amana Refrigeration, Inc., 1965-69, v.p. sales, 1969-74, exec. v.p., from 1974, now pres., chmn., chief exec. officer, also dir.; dir. Mchts. Nat. Bank, Cedar Rapids. Bd. dirs. Foerstner Scholarship Found., Inc.; trustee Mercy Hosp., Cedar Rapids; mem. adv. bd. Hawkeye Area council Boy Scouts Am. Served with USN, Korea. Mem. Am. Mgmt. Assn., Sigma Chi. Presbyn. Clubs: Cedar Rapids Country; Univ. Athletic (Iowa City). Office: Amana Refrigeration Inc Amana IA 52204 *

MEYER, BETTY ANNE (MRS. JOHN ROLAND BASKIN), lawyer; b. Cleve.; d. William Henry and Monica (McSherry) Meyer; student Denison U., 1941-43; A.B., Flora Stone Mather Coll., Western Res. U., 1946, LL.B., 1947; m. John Roland Baskin, May 12, 1967. Admitted to Ohio bar, 1947; asst. to dean Adelbert Coll., Western Res. U., 1948-49; asso. firm Kiefer, Waterworth, Hunter & Knecht, Cleve., 1965-74; mem. firm Knecht, Rees, Meyer, Mekedis & Shumaker, Cleve., 1974—. Mem. Alpha Phi. Home: 2679 Ashley Rd Shaker Heights OH 44122 Home: Key Largo FL 33037 Home: East Corp Martha's Vineyard MA Office: Terminal Tower Cleveland OH 44113

MEYER, BETTY JANE, former librarian; b. Indpls., July 20, 1918; d. Herbert and Gertrude (Sanders) M.; B.A., Ball State Tchrs. Coll., 1940; B.S. in L.S., Western Res. U., 1945. Student asst. Muncie Public Library (Ind.), 1936-40; library asst. Ohio State U. Library, Columbus, 1940-42, cataloger, 1945-46, asst. circulation librarian, 1946-51, acting circulation librarian, 1951-52, adminstrv. asst. to dir. libraries, 1952-57, acting asso. reference librarian, 1957-58, cataloger in charge serials, 1958-65, head serial div. catalog dept., 1965-68, head acquisition dept., 1968-71, asst. dir. libraries, tech. services, 1971-76, acting dir. libraries, 1976-77, asst. dir. libraries, tech. services, 1977-83, instr. library adminstrn., 1958-63, asst. prof., 1963-67, asso. prof., 1967-75, prof., 1975-83, prof. emeritus, 1983—; library asst. Grandview Heights Public Library, Columbus, 1942-44; student asst. Case Inst. Tech., Cleve., 1944-45; mem. Ohio Coll. Library Center Adv. Com. on Cataloging, 1971-76, mem. adv. com. on serials, 1971-76, mem. adv. com. on tech. processes, 1971-76; mem. Inter-Univ. Library Council, Tech. Services Group, 1971-83; mem. bd. trustees Columbus Area Library and Info. Council Ohio, 1980-83. Ohio State U. grantee, 1975-76. Mem. ALA, Assn. Coll. and Research Libraries, AAUP, Ohio Library Assn. (nominating com. 1978-81), Ohioana Library Assn., Ohio Valley Group Tech. Services Librarians, No. Ohio Tech. Services Librarians, Franklin County Library Assn., Acad. Library Assn. Ohio, PEO, Beta Phi Mu, Delta Kappa Gamma. Club: Ohio State U. Faculty Women's. Home: 970 High St Unit H2 Worthington OH 43085

MEYER, CHARLES GERHARD, auto company executive; b. Chgo., Dec. 1, 1938; s. Gerhard Henry and Julia Dolores (Johnson) M.; m. Nancy Elizabeth Mellor, Aug. 29, 1959; children: William Charles, Steven Kenneth, Scott Phillip, Andrew Jason. BBA, U. Wis., 1960; MBA, U. Detroit, 1963. Mktg. fin. mgr. Richier, Paris, 1972-73; fin. mgr. Tractor Europe Sales Ops., Brussels, 1973-77, Tractor Internat. Sales Ops., Troy, Mich., 1977-79; dir. bus. planning Mazda Motor, Hiroshima, Japan, 1980-84; planning assoc. Ford Corp. Strategy, Dearborn, Mich., 1984-86; fin. mgr. Ford Internat. Export Sales, Wixom, Mich., 1986—; bd. dirs. Kaanapali Royal, Lahaina, Hawaii. Com. mem. Sister City Program, Birmingham, Mich., 1986—; mem. founders group Pooh Corner-Coop Nursery, Brussels, 1974-76. Mem. U. Wis. Detroit Alumni Club (bd. dirs. 1987—), Beta Alpha Psi, Beta Gamma Sigma, Delta Sigma Pi. Republican. Lutheran. Avocations: cross country skiing, music, reading, travel, wine. Home: 22245 Orchard Way Birmingham MI 48010 Office: Ford Internat Export Sales PO Box 600 Wixom MI 48096

MEYER, CHARLES HENRY, electrical engineer; b. Cleve., Oct. 18, 1927; s. Donovan Charles and Antoinetta Alice (Hess) M.; m. Violet Irene Czeney, June 27, 1950; children: Catherine, Curt, Constance, Clifford. BSEE, Case Western Reserve U., 1950, MSEE, 1956. Registered profl. engr., Ohio, Minn. Project engr. Trane Co., LaCrosse, Wis., 1959-62; electronic controls salesman Kilroy Corp., Chagrin Falls, Ohio, 1962-64; mgr. electronics and physics Cleve. Tech. Ctr., 1964-66; electrical engr. Nordson Corp., Amherst, Ohio, 1966-69; mgr. electrical engring. McQuay-Perfex, Mpls., 1969-84; tech. mktg. mgr. Onan Corp., Mpls., 1985—; bd. dirs. King Concept Corp., Mpls. Served with USN, 1945-46, PTO. Mem. IEEE (sr.), Constrn. Specification Inst., N. Cen. Electrical Industry Engring. Soc., Nat. Fire Protection Assn. Lodges: Masons, Shriners. Avocations: camping, swimming, tennis. Office: Onan Corp 1400 73d Ave NE Minneapolis MN 55432

MEYER, CHARLES HOWARD, lawyer; b. St. Paul, Aug. 1, 1952; s. Howard Joseph and Helen Evangeline (Ericson) M.; m. Patti Jo Graf, Sept. 11, 1981; 1 child, Joseph Charles. BS in Bus. with high distinction, U. Minn., 1974; JD magna cum laude, Harvard U., 1977. Bar: Minn. 1977, U.S. Dist. Ct. Minn. 1977, U.S. Ct. Appeals (8th cir.) 1981; CPA, Minn. Staff acct. Deliotte Haskins & Sells, Mpls., 1974, 75; ptnr. Oppenheimer Law Firm, St. Paul/Mpls., 1976, 77-85; sr. tax atty. Cargill, Inc., Mpls., 1985—; lectr. continuing legal edn. seminars. Mem. ABA, Minn. State Bar Assn., Hennepin County Bar Assn., Harvard Law Sch. Assn., Am. Inst. CPA's (Elijah Watt Sells gold medal), Nat. Accts. Assn., Am. Accts. Assn., Minn. Soc. CPA's (Harold C. Utley award 1974). Lutheran. Clubs: Harvard, North Oaks Golf (Minn.). Home: 5879 Royal Oaks Dr Shoreview MN 55126 Office: Cargill Inc Law Dept North-24 Box 9300 Minneapolis MN 55440

MEYER, CHARLES RUTHERFORD, tax executive; b. Indpls., Dec. 3, 1945; s. Charles E. and Jeanette (Rutherford) M.; m. Gracia Elizabeth Johnson, July 12, 1969 (div. 1986); children: Charles J., Gracia-Jean. BS, MS in Indsl. Adminstrn., Purdue U., 1967; JD, Harvard U., 1970. CPA, Ind. With tax dept. Coopers & Lybrand, Detroit, 1970-72; with tax dept. Coopers & Lybrand, Indpls., 1972-78, tax ptnr., 1978—. Contbr. articles to profl. jours. Deacon. 2d Presbyn. Ch., 1983-85, Indpls., endowment com.; treas., bd. dirs. Washington Township Ednl. Found., Indpls., 1986-87. Mem. Am. Inst. CPA's, Ind. CPA's, Ind. Bar Assn., Ind. State C. of C. (taxation com. 1986). Club: Toastmasters (Indpls.). Lodge: Rotary. Office: Coopers & Lybrand 2900 One American Sq Indianapolis IN 46282

MEYER, CHARLES TED, psychiatrist; b. Phila., Dec. 29, 1944; s. Harry and Ruth (Donis) M.; m. Ellen W. Meyer, May 17, 1970; children: Rebeka, Eli, Joshua. BS, Albright Coll., 1966; MD, Hahnemann U., 1971. Diplomate Am. Bd. Psychiatry and Neurology. Intern Detroit Gen. Hosp., 1971-72; resident in psychiatry U. Wis., Madison, 1972-75; staff psychiatrist Mendota Mental Health Inst., Madison, 1975-78; practice medicine specializing in psychiatry Mental Health Assocs., Madison, 1978—; chmn. dept. psychiatry Meriter Hosp., Madison; cons. psychiatrist Luth. Social Services, Madison, 1979-85. Peer reviewer Champus, Madison, 1985—. Mem. AMA, Am. Psychiat. Assn., State Med. Soc. Wis., Wis. Psychiat. Assn., Dane County Med. Soc. Jewish. Office: 20 S Park St Madison WI 53715

MEYER, CLIFFORD ROBERT, machine tool manufacturing company executive; b. Cin., Sept. 25, 1923; s. Clifford Robert and Minerva (Sauer) M.; m. Maxine Annette Labermeier, Aug. 12, 1948; 1 child, Judith Ann Meyer Biggs. B.B.A., U. Cin., 1948. Vice pres., gen. mgr. Morris Machine Tool Co., Cin., 1948-56; asst. mgr. spl. machinery Cin. Milacron, Cin., 1956-60; v.p. European ops. Cin. Milacron, 1964-70, group v.p. machine tools and electronic systems, 1970-75, exec. v.p., 1975-81, pres., chief operating officer, 1981-85; mng. dir. Cin. Milacron Ltd., Birmingham, Eng., 1960-64; retired cons. Palm Harbor, Fla., 1986—; dir. Union Central Life Ins. Co., Cin., Amcast Indsl., Dayton, Sewcorp, Cin. Chmn. Hamilton County Park Levy, Ohio, 1981; bd. dirs. Cin. and Hamilton County Port Authority, 1983. Served to lt. (j.g.) USN, 1943-46, PTO. Recipient William H. Taft medal U. Cin. Alumni, 1981. Mem. Engring. Soc. Cin. Clubs: Commercial, Queen City, Hyde Park Country; East Lake Woodlands Golf; Racquet Club (Palm Harbor, Fla.). Lodges: Masons; Shriners, Rotary. Home: Buick Oldsmobile Cadillac Group 30009 Van Dyke Ave Cobbs Landing Warren MI 48090

MEYER, CYNTHIA CLAIRE, computer scientist; b. Milw., July 10, 1940; d. Frederick William and Clara Anna (Wilde) M. BA, Valparaiso U., 1962; MS, U. Colo., 1972. Systems engr. IBM Corp., Los Angeles, Calif. and Rochester, Minn., 1962-69; systems analyst Systematics Corp., Boulder, Colo., 1969-72; programmer Motorola Inc., Schaumburg, Ill., 1974-79; computer scientist Sci. Applications, Schaumburg, Ill., 1979-83, Argonne (Ill.) Nat. Lab., 1983—. Singer Elgin Choral Union, 1972-75, Colo. Chorale, Denver, 1970-72, Rochester (Minn.) Symphony Chorale, 1966-69. Mem. Assn. Computing Machinery, Assn. Computational Linguistics, Soc. Info. Display. Republican. Lutheran. Avocations: choir accompanist, organ, hiking, gardening, nature study. also: 3954 N Sherman Blvd Apt 1 Milwaukee WI 53216 Office: Argonne Nat Lab 9700 S Cass Ave Argonne IL 60439

MEYER, DAN WESLEY, accountant; b. Lafayette, Ind., Aug. 13, 1956; s. Lawrence Donald and Loretta Lou (Bush) M. BBA, U. Miss., 1977; MS in Mgmt., Purdue U., 1982; postgrad., U. Mo., 1983—. CPA, Tenn. Staff acct. Seidman and Seidman, CPA, Memphis, 1978, Moore and Gray, CPA, Corinth, Tenn., 1978-80, 83; teaching asst. Purdue U., West Lafayette, Ind., 1980-82, U. Mo., Columbia, 1983—; tax preparer Boyle Investment Co., Memphis, 1984-85; instr. Columbia Coll., Chgo., 1987. Participant March of Dimes Superwalk, various cities, 1977-79, 85-86; leader Young Life, Columbia, 1984-85; voter registrar Boone County (Mo.) Election Com., Columbia, 1986. Mem. Am. Inst. CPA's, Am. Acctg. Assn. (assoc.), Nat. Tax Assn.-Tax Inst. Am. (student), Tenn. Soc. CPA's. Mem. Evang. Free Ch. Avocations: reading, walking, volleyball. Home: 1133 Ashland #201 Columbia MO 65201 Office: U Mo 304 Gentry Hall Columbia MO 65201

MEYER, DAVID CHARLES, publisher; b. Cedar Rapids, Iowa, Nov. 30, 1943; s. Charles Edward and Margaret Elizabeth (Gump) M.; m. Patricia Ann Adams, Dec. 22, 1964. BA in Speech and Theatre, U. No. Iowa, 1965, MA in English, 1968; MA in Theol. Studies, Meadville Theol. Sch., Chgo., 1972; M in Divinity, Garrett Theol. Sem., Evanston, Ill., 1975. Instr. English U. No. Iowa, Cedar Falls, 1968-69; pastor Prairie Unitarian Soc., Madison, Wis., 1970-72; mgr. Cokesbury Bookstore, Evanston, Ill., 1974-77; asst. sales mgr. Seabury Press, N.Y.C., 1977-81; major accounts rep., spl. projects mgr. Crossroad Pub., N.Y.C., 1981-82; pres., pub., founder Meyer, Stone & Co., Inc. (formerly Meyer Pub. Enterprises), Oak Park, Ill., 1982—. Author various poems. Mem. Religious BookSellers Assn. (pres. 1986-87). Democrat. Avocations: reading, theatre, opera, music, camping. Home and Office: 714 S Humphrey Oak Park IL 60304

MEYER, DOUGLAS EDWIN, computer programmer, analyst; b. Toledo, May 14, 1957; s. Ray Warren and Elaine Joyce (Oster) M.; m. Patricia Lynn Thigpen, Mar. 4, 1978; children: Christopher Douglas, Andrew Ray. Assoc. in Data Processing, U. Toledo, 1982, BS in Bus. summa cum laude, 1984. Insp. gen. Chevrolet div. Gen. Motors Corp., Toledo, 1976-80; computer operator Automotive Warehouse Inc., Toledo, 1981; data processing mgr. Uckele Animal Health, Blissfield, Mich., 1981-82; fin. clk. Hydra-Matic div. Gen. Motors Corp., Toledo, 1982-84, programmer, analyst, 1984—. Advisor Jr. Achievement, Toledo, 1985. Mem. Phi Kappa Phi. Republican. Baptist. Avocations: watersports, racquetball, stocks, artificial intelligence programming. Home: 739 Colima Dr Toledo OH 43609 Office: Hydra Matic div GM 1455 W Alexis Rd Toledo OH 43692

MEYER, EDWARD PAUL, advertising executive; b. Chgo., May 23, 1949; s. Edward and Eleanor Kathryn (DeJong) M.; Marsha L. Tower, Aug. 10, 1974; children: Paul Edward, Sarah Linnea. BA in Econs. and Bus. Adminstrn., Wheaton (Ill.) Coll., 1967-71; MA in Communications, Weaton (Ill.) Coll., 1983. Asst. dir. Wheaton Coll. Alumni Assn., 1972-81; v.p. corp. communications Richard Ellis Co., Chgo., 1981—; cons. mktg. Service Auto Glass, Lombard, Ill., 1979—. Active with Coll. Ch. Wheaton, 1974—; pres. elect, bd. dirs. Crusader Club Wheaton Coll., 1985—; bd. dirs. Christian Service Brigade, Wheaton, 1985—. Mem. Pub. Relations Soc. Am. Republican. Home: 1303 E Harrison Wheaton IL 60187 Office: Richard Ellis Inc 200 E Randolph Dr Suite 6545 Chicago IL 60607

MEYER, FRANCES LEE, personnel consultant; b. Pitts., Oct. 19, 1947; d. Leo Francis and Eleanor Philomena (Salmon) M.; m. William Donald Heisel; 1 child, Erin Marie. BS in Psychology, Purdue U., 1969; postgrad., Bowling Green State U., 1969-72; MBA, Xavier U., Cin., 1981. Labor relations officer Ohio Dept. Corrections, Columbus, 1972-74; personnel mgr. Ohio Div. Parole and Services, Columbus, 1974-76; mgr. EEO, compensation and tng. U. Cin. Med. Ctr., 1976-78; pvt. practice personnel cons. Cin., 1978-81; mgr. employee relations Hilton-Davis Chem. Co., Cin., 1981-87; prin. Lee Meyer & Assocs., Cin., 1987—; speaker in field, Cin., 1983—. Writer Sta. WCET Pub. TV, Cin., 1983—. Sec. bd. dirs. Villages of Northgate Homeowners Assn., Cin., 1979-82; blood drive coordinator, Hilton-Davis/Hoxworth Blood Ctr., Cin., 1982-83. Mem. Greater Cin. Human Resources Assn. (bdr. dirs., treas. 1985—), Am. Soc. Personnel Adminstrn., Am. Compensation Assn., NE Personnel Assn., Greater Cin. Employers Inst., Cin. C. of C. Mem. Unitarian Universalist Ch. Club: Blue Ash YMCA. Avocations: swimming, reading, bridge, chess. Home and Office: 10893 Ponds Ln Cincinnati OH 45242

MEYER, FRED HENRY, corrosion specialist consultant; b. Cin., Oct. 15, 1926; s. Fred Henry Sr. and Barbra E. (Frankenhoff) M.; m. Marjorie Ann Frazee, Oct. 16, 1954; children: Scott Alan, Todd Anthony. BS in Chemistry, U. Cin., 1949; postgrad., Mass. Inst. Tech., 1954—, Ohio State U., 1954—, U. Mich., %. Chemist Gen. Electric Co., Cin., 1950-52; head corrosion sect. Nat. Lead Co., Cin., 1952-60; research engr. Mosler Safe Co., Hamilton, Ohio, 1960-63; materials and processing engr. Honeywell, Inc., St. Petersburg, Fla., 1963-65; research engr. United States Steel, Monroeville, Pa., 1965-66; materials cons. Air Force Wright Aero. Labs., Wright-Patterson AFB, Ohio, 1966—; bd. dirs. Meyer Cons., Dayton, Ohio; cons. Nat. Aerospace Mus. USAF, Washington, 1986; chmn. publ. Comdr. Panel Corrosion, Washington, 1979—. Editor: TriService Corrosion Conference, 1967, 74, 80, 87. V.p. Salem Bend Condominium, Trotwood, Ohio, 1986. Served with U.S. Army, 1946-47. Mem. Nat. Assn. Corrosion Engrs. Republican. Lodges: Masons, Shriners. Avocations: photography, semi-pro dancing, golf. Home: 5506 Nantucket Rd Dayton OH 45426 Office: USAF Wright Aeros Labs AFWAL MLSA Wright Patterson AFB OH 45433

MEYER, FRED MILTON, teacher; b. Quincy, Ill., July 10, 1926; s. Paul Emil and Dorothy (Simpkin) M. BA, U. Ill., 1951. Tchr. Escanaba, Mich., 1955—. Served with U.S Army, 1945-46. Democrat. Methodist. Club: Internat. Wizard of Oz (Kinderhook, Ill.) (sec. 1961—). Home: Box 95 Kinderhook IL 62345

MEYER, FRED WILLIAM, JR., memorial parks exec.; b. Fair Haven, Mich., Jan. 7, 1924; s. Fred W. and Gladys (Marshall) M.; A.B., Mich. State Coll., 1946; m. Jean Hope, Aug. 5, 1946; children—Frederick, Thomas, James, Nancy. Salesman Chapel Hill Meml. Gardens, Lansing, Mich., 1946-47; mgr. Roselawn Meml. Gardens, Saginaw, Mich., 1947-49; dist. mgr. Sunset Meml. Gardens, Evansville, Ind., 1949-53; pres., dir. Memory Gardens Mgmt. Corp., Indpls., Hamilton Meml. Gardens, Chattanooga, Covington Meml. Gardens, Ft. Wayne, Ind., Chapel Hill Meml. Gardens, Grand Rapids, Mich., Forest Lawn Memory Gardens, Indpls., Lincoln Memory Gardens, Indpls., Sherwood Meml. Gardens, Knoxville, Tenn., Chapel Hill Meml. Gardens, South Bend, Ind., Tri-Cities Meml. Gardens, Florence, Ala., White Chapel Meml. Gardens, Springfield, Mo., Nebo Meml. Park, Martinsville, Ind., Mercury Devel. Corp., Indpls., Quality Marble Imports, Indpls., Quality Printers, Indpls., Am. Bronze Craft, Inc., Judsonia, Ark. Mem. C. of C., A.I.M., Am. Cemetery Assn., Sigma Chi, Phi Kappa Delta. Elk. Clubs: Nat. Sales Executives, Athenaem Turners, Columbia, Meridian Hills Country, Woodland Country. Home: 110 E 111th St Indianapolis IN 46280 Office: 3733 N Meridian St Indianapolis IN 46208

MEYER, GLENN ARTHUR, neurosurgeon, educator; b. Baraboo, Wis., Mar. 8, 1934; m. Shirley Jean Swanson; children: Gregory Alexander, Melissa Ione, Grant Andrew. Student, U. Wis., 1951-54, U. Minn., 1954-55, U. Wis., 1955-56; BS, U. Wis., 1957, MD, 1960. Diplomate Am. Bd. Neurological Surgery; Nat. Bd. Med. Examiners. Intern Mpls. Gen. Hosp., 1960-61; resident neurological surgery U. Hosp., Madison, Wis.; instr. in neurosurgery U. Wis., Madison, 1966; asst. prof. neurosurgery U. Tex. Med. Br. Hosps., Galveston, 1969-71, assoc. prof. neurosurgery, 1971-72; assoc. prof. neurosurgery Med. Coll. Wis., Milw., 1972-83; active staff Milw. Children's Hosp., 1973—, served various coms.; prof. neurosurgery Med. Coll. Wis., Milw., 1983—; med. advisor Social Security Adminstrn., Bur. Hearings and Appeals, 1970—; cons. staff Community Meml. Hosp., Menomonee Falls, Wis., 1972—, Good Samaritan Hosp., Milw., 1973—; courtesy staff Elmbrook Meml. Hosp., Brookfield, Wis., 1972—; attending staff Columbia Hosp., Milw., 1982—; neurosurgical staff VA Hosp., Wood, Wis., 1972—; sr. attending staff Milw. County Gen. Hosp., Milw., 1972—, Froedtert Meml. Luth. Hosp., Milw., 1980—, also served various coms. Assoc. editor Clin. Neurosurgery, 1971-73; continuing edn. editor Congress Neurol. Surgery Newsletter, 1974-76. Contbr. numerous articles to profl. jours. Patentee in field. Elder Presby. Ch., 1971. Served to lt. col. U.S. Army, 1967-69. Sears Roebuck, Freida Nishan, Steenbock scholar. Fellow ACS; mem. AAAS, AMA, NIH (ad. hoc com. craniofacial anomalies), Internat. Neurosurgical Forum, Internat. Soc. Padiatric Neruosurgery, Am. Assn. Neurol. Surgeons (pediatric sect. 1985), Am. Coll. Radiology, Am. Soc.

Stereotactic and Functional Neurosurgery (com. psychosurgery), Cen. Neurosurgical Soc. (sec. 1980, pres. 1982), Congress Neurol. Surgeons (asst. chmn. program com. 1976, annual meeting editorial com. 1973-75), Found. Internat. Edn. in Neurol. Surgery, Inc., Assn. Academic Surgery, Assn. Advancement Med. Instrumentation, Interurban Neruosurgical Soc., Pediatric Oncology Group, Soc. Neruosci., So. Med. Assn., So. Neruosurgiacal Soc., Houston Neurol. Soc., State Med. Soc. Wis. (Ho. of Dels. 1976-79), Med. Soc. Milw. County (emergency med. services com. 1977-80, vice chmn. coalition med. orgns. com. 1980-82, pub. edn. com. 1982-88), Milw. Acad. Medicine (program com. 1979-81, 85, 86), Milw. Neuropsychiat. Soc. (pres. 1979), Wis. Neurosurgical Soc. (pres. 1976-77, chmn. peer rev. com. 1978-81, rep. joint com. Socioecon. Affairs 1978—), U. Wis. Med. Alumni Assn. (council 1973), Phi Chi, Phi Eta Sigma, Alpha Zeta, Phi Kappa Phi. Office: 8700 W Wisconsin Ave Milwaukee WI 53226

MEYER, GORDON WAYNE, food products executive; b. Mpls., July 4, 1954; s. Vernon Milo and Beverly Josephine (Cervenka) M.; m. Jane Carlson, July 9, 1983. Student, Iowa State U., 1972-77, 84. Asst. mgr. Granddaddy's, Ames, Iowa, 1976-77; advt. rep. Iowa State Daily, Ames, 1975-78; asst. mgr. Golden Uptown Emporium, Ames, 1978-79; mgr. Great Plains Sauce and Dough Co., Ames, 1979—. Editor Runes newsletter, 1985-87. Mem. Theta Chi. Club: Midwest Atari Group (v.p. 1986—). Avocations: reading, writing, home computing, gardening. Office: Great Plains Sauce and Dough Co 129 Main St Ames IA 50010-6388

MEYER, GRACE ALICE, interior designer; b. Thief River Falls, Minn., July 5, 1957; s. Martin Oswald and Alice Irene (Wold) Hanson; m. Kevin David Meyer, Aug. 7, 1982; children: Kelsey Alice, Kenzie Jean. Student, Trinity Coll., Bannockburn, Ill.; AA in Interior Design, Harper Coll., 1979. Designer Hufford Furniture, Chgo., 1976-77, Scandinavian Design, Northbrook, Ill., 1979-81; owner Grace A. Meyer Interior Design, Fox Lake, Ill., 1981-85, Long Lake, Ill., 1985—; instr. design Coll. Lake County, Grayslake, Ill., 1982-84; cons. Greyslake Park Dist., 1984, Evangelical Free Ch., Minn. and Ill., 1984-85. Mem. Am. Soc. Interior Designers (assoc.). Republican. Avocations: piano, tennis. Office: 2672 Bobolink Rd Long Lake MN 55356

MEYER, HAROLD LOUIS, mechanical engineer; b. Chgo., June 25, 1916; s. Norman Robert and Martha (Stoewsand) M.; m. Charlotte Alene Tilberg, June 21, 1941 (dec. 1951); 1 child, John C. Nelson. Student, Armour Inst. Tech., Chgo., 1934-42, U. Akron, 1942-44; BA in Natural Sci., Southwestern Coll., Winfield, Kans., 1951; student, Ill. Inst. Tech., 1955-73. Sales engr. Olsen & Tilgner, Chgo., 1938-39; project engr. Gen. Electric X-Ray, 1939-42, field engr., 1944-46; project engr. Goodyear Aircraft, 1942-44; chief x-ray technologist and therapist William Neton Meml. Hosp., Winfield, 1946-51; sr. design cons. Pollak and Skan, Chgo., 1952-58, cons. design specialist, 1963-68; project engr. Gaertner Scientific Co., Chgo., 1958-63; sr. design specialist Am. Steel Foundries, Chgo., 1969-74; cons. Morgen Design, Milw., 1974-76; proprietor Meyersen Engring., Addison, Ill., 1981—, also bd. dirs.; cons. dir. Miller Paint Equipment, Addison, 1976-87; design cons. R.R. Donnelley, Kraft Foods. Inventor: box sealing sta., 1939, chest X-ray equipment, 1942, G-2 airship, 1944, space program periscope, 1962, reactor test sta. periscope, 1962, beer can filling machine, 1963, atomic waste handling vehicle, 1965, ry. freight car trucks, 1974, hwy. trailer 5th wheels, 1974, motorized precision paint colorant dispensing machines, 1986. Sponsered a family of Cambodian refugees; mem. Norwood Park (Ill.) Norwegian Old Peoples Home; mem. Family Shelter Service, Glen Ellyn, Ill. Served with USNR, 1949-52. Recipient Appreciation award Lioness Club, Glendale Heights, 1985. Mem. AAAS, Chem. Engring. Product Research Panel, Ill. Inst. Tech. Alumni Assn. (new student recruiter 1985-87, Recognition award 1986, 87), Am. Registry of X-Ray Techs., Phi Kappa Sigma. Republican. Presbyterian. Lodges: Masons, Lions (dir. 1985-86). Avocations: archery, golf, semi-precious gem stones, archaeology. Office: Meyerson Engring PO Box 248 Addison IL 60101

MEYER, HENRY JOHN, appliance manufacturing executive; b. Amana, Iowa, Jan. 25, 1927; s. Fred Henry and Marie Susanna (Zimmerman) M.; m. Mildred Margaret Ackerman, Oct. 25, 1945; children: Timothy, Cynthia. Buyer Amana Refrigeration, Inc., Iowa, 1946-53, purchasing agt., 1954-64, asst. dir. purchasing, 1965-70, v.p. materials, 1971-75, sr. v.p. materials, 1975-80, exec. v.p., 1980-82, pres., chief exec. officer, 1982—; chmn. bd. dirs. Speed Queen Co., Ripon, Wis., 1982-86. Mem. Gov.'s Com. for Iowa's Future Growth, 1984; trustee Iowa Natural Heritage, 1984—. Served with U.S. Army, 1945-46. Mem. Cedar Rapids C. of C. (bd. dirs. 1984—). Republican. Mem. Amana Ch. Office: Amana Refrigeration Inc Amana IA 52204

MEYER, HENRY LEWIS, III, banker; b. Cleve., Dec. 25, 1949; s. Henry Lewis and Anne (Taylor) M.; m. Jane Kreamer, July 15, 1978; children: Patrick Harrison, Andrew Taylor. BA, Colgate U., 1972; MBA, Harvard U., Boston, 1978. Asst. v.p. Soc. Nat. Bank, Cleve., 1974-76, v.p., 1978-81, sr. v.p., 1981-83; exec. v.p. Soc. Bank, N. Am., Dayton, Ohio, 1983-85, pres., chief operating officer, 1985-87, also bd. dirs.; sr. exec. v.p. Soc. Nat. Bank, 1987—; v.p. Soc. Corp., 1987—; bd. dirs. XYOvest, Inc., Dayton, Miami Valley Capital, Dayton; trustee Dayton Found. Bd. dirs. Children's Med. Ctr., Dayton, 1986—; trustee Dayton Performing Arts Fund, 1986—, NCCJ, Dayton, 1984—, Dayton Opera Assn., 1984—. Republican. Episcopalian. Dayton Country, Dayton Racquet.

MEYER, HOWARD STUART, chemical engineer, researcher; b. Chgo., Dec. 19, 1949; s. Sam and Melaine (Seldin) M.; m. Carol Renee Lewis, Sept. 5, 1972; children—Amanda Nicole, Sarah Gabrielle, Bradley Lewis. B.S. in Chem. Engring., U. Ill., 1972; M.S. in Chem. Engring., U. Idaho, 1978. Chem. engr. Bee Chem. Co., Lansing, Ill., 1972-74; group leader Exxon Nuclear Idaho, Idaho Falls, 1974-80; mgr. Gas Research Inst., Chgo., 1980—. Mem. Am. Inst. Chem. Engrs. (Idaho sect. treas. and vice chmn. 1978-80, Chgo. sect. constn. and publicity chmn. 1982—, vice chmn. program), Am. Chem. Soc. (Glen award, fuel chemistry div. 1981). Office: Gas Research Inst 8600 W Bryn Mawr Ave Chicago IL 60631

MEYER, J. THEODORE, lawyer; b. Chgo., Apr. 13, 1936; s. Joseph Theodore and Mary Elizabeth (McHugh) M.; m. Marilu Bartholomew, Aug. 16, 1961; children—Jean, Joseph. B.S., John Carroll U., 1958; postgrad. U. Chgo.; J.D., DePaul U., 1962. Bar: Ill. 1962, U.S. Dist. Ct. (no. dist.) Ill. 1962. Ptnr. Bartholomew & Meyer, Chgo., 1963—; mem. Ill. Gen. Assembly, 1968-72, 74-82, mem. vets. affairs, personnel and pensions com., chmn. House environ. study com., 1968; chmn. energy environ. com., mem. natural resources com. Nat. Conf. State Legislators; mem. Fed. State Task Force on Energy; chmn., founder Midwest Legis. Council on Environ., 1971; chmn. Jt. House/Senate subcom. to rev. air water plans, 1978; lectr. in field. Recipient Appreciation award Ill. Wildlife Fedn., 1972; Environ. Quality award Region V, EPA, 1974; Environ. Legislator of Yr. award Ill. Gen. Assembly Ill. Environ. Council, 1978-79; Pro Bono Publico award Self-Help Action Ctr., 1975; Merit award Dept. Ill. VFW, 1977. Mem. ABA, Chgo. Bar Assn., So. Suburban Bar Assn., Nat. Rep. Legis. Assn., S.W. Bar Assn., Ill. Bar Assn., Nat. Trust Historic Perservation, Nat. Wildlife Fedn., Ill. Hist. Soc. Republican. Roman Catholic. Clubs: Beverly Tennis, Beverly Hills Univ. Office: 2355 W 111th St Chicago IL 60643

MEYER, JAMES EDWARD, computer analyst; b. St. Paul, Mar. 13, 1946; s. George Albert and Florence Elvira (Lindahl) M.; m. Beatrice June Biesanz, Oct. 24, 1969; children: April Elizabeth and Johathan Peter (twins). Student, Coll. St. Thomas, St. Paul, 1985—. Sr. database analyst Schedular Amhoist, St. Paul, 1972—; sr. data analyst Land O'Lakes Inc., Mpls., 1986—. 1st v.p. Daytons Bluff Community Council, St. Paul, 1985. Mem. Am. Production Inventory Control Soc. Roman Catholic. Home: 1436 Fremont Ave Saint Paul MN 55106 Office: Land O'Lakes Inc 4001 Lexington Ave N Arden Hills MN 55440

MEYER, LEON JACOB, wholesale company executive; b. Chgo., Nov. 12, 1923; s. Joseph and Minnie (Lebovitz) M.; student Lake Forest Coll., 1941-43; B.S., UCLA, 1948; m. Barbara Gene Bothman, Oct. 17, 1948; children—Charles Scott, John Mark, Ellen Renee. Owner, operator Christopher Distbg. Co., Santa Monica, Calif., 1951-53; pres. J. Meyer & Co., Waukegan, Ill., 1953-80, Western Candy & Tobacco Co., Carpentersville, Ill., 1970-78, Ill. Briar Pipe & Sundry Co., Waukegan, 1963-78; chmn. bd. Phillips Bros. Co., Kenosha, Wis., 1975—, Ill. Wholesale Co., 1976—. Served with U.S. Army, 1943-46; PTO. Named Sundry Man of Year, 1976, Candy Distbr. of Yr., 1976; recipient Alex Schwartz Meml. award, 1978. Mem. Nat. Assn. Tobacco Distbrs. (trustee), Ill. Assn. Candy-Tobacco Distbrs. (past chmn. bd.), Federated Merchandising Corp. (past pres.), Internat. Tobacco Wholesaler Alliance (past chmn. bd.), Nat. Automatic Merchandisers Assn., Nat. Candy Wholesalers Assn., UCLA Alumni Club, Waukegan/Lake County C. of C. Clubs: Elks, Eagles. Home: 3444 University Ave Highland Park IL 60035 Office: 4700 Industrial Dr Springfield IL 62708

MEYER, MARK EDWARD, financial analyst; b. Elgin, Ill., Mar. 5, 1960; s. Robert E. and Janet Merry (Arseneau) M. B.A., Augustana Coll., Ill., 1982; postgrad. Northwestern U., 1984—. Credit analyst Fullerton Metals Co., Northbrook, Ill., 1982-83; fin. analyst R&D div. Am. Can Co., Barrington, Ill., 1983-86. Youth adv. St. Matthew Lutheran Ch., Barrington, 1982—, chmn. youth bd., 1984. Avocations: music; electronic equipment; basketball; baseball; football. Home: 21153 N 19th St Barrington IL 60010

MEYER, NICHOLAS JOSEPH, dentist; b. Chgo., Aug. 12, 1953; s. Raymond Joseph and Frances Therese (McInerney) M.; m. Nancy Lynn Macenas, Oct. 21, 1983; children: Allison, Ashley. BA, Lewis U., 1975; DDS, Loyola U., 1979. Pvt. practice dentistry Neoga, Ill., 1979—. Contbr. articles to profl. jours. Fellow Internat. Coll. Craniomandibular Orthopaedics; mem. Am. Acad. Forensic Sci., ADA, Ill. Dental Soc. Avocations: aquatic sports, camping, reading. Home: 2503 Culpepper Effingham IL 62401 Office: 810 E 5th Neoga IL 62447

MEYER, PAUL WESLEY, orthopaedic surgeon; b. Kansas City, Mo., Aug. 31, 1914; s. Joseph Albert and Emma Marie Meyer; m. Ellen Marie Scott, Dec. 22, 1937; children: Paul W. Jr., Jo Ellen. BS, Kans. State U., 1940; MD, U. Kans., 1944. Diplomate Am. Bd. Orthopaedic Surgery. Ptnr. Dickson Diveley Orthopaedic Clinic, Kansas City, 1949—; team physician Kansas City Royals, 1969—. Bd. dirs. Cradles & Crayons. Served to capt. U.S. Army, 1945-47. Fellow ACS, Am. Acad. Orthopaedic Surgeons; mem. AMA, Am. Orthopaedic Soc. Sports Medicine, Clin. Orthopaedic Soc., Mid-Cen. States Orthopaedic Soc. (pres. 1966-67), Southwestern Surg. Congress, Kansas City Southwest Surg. Soc. (pres. 1967), Jackson County Med. Soc., Mo. Orthopaedic Soc., Kansas City Surg. Soc., Kans. Acad. Medicine (pres. 1950), Am. Acad. Cerebral Palsy, Assn. Profl. Baseball Physicians, Am. Coll. Sports Medicine, Mid-Am. Orthopaedic Assn. Republican. Methodist. Avocations: golf, fishing. Office: Dickson Diveley Orthopaedic Clinic 4320 Wornall Rd #610 Kansas City MO 64111

MEYER, RICHARD LEE, manufacturing executive, engineer; b. Ft. Wayne, Ind., Jan. 15, 1944; s. Wilbert H.F. Meyer and Dona Mae (Bruebaker) Hall; m. Sharon Ann Walters, June 15, 1985; children: Tracey Lee, Nicholas Andrew. AAS in Mech. Engring. Tech., Purdue U., 1969, BS, 1973. Engr. States Engring. Corp., Ft. Wayne, 1968-76, sales mgr., 1976-81; pres. Summit Foundry Systems, Ft. Wayne, 1981—. Mem. Am. Foundrymen Soc. (N.E. Ind. dir. 1985—), Ft. Wayne Aviation Assn. (dir. 1976). Republican. Avocations: flying, boating, bicycling. Home: 11527 Wexford Dr Fort Wayne IN 46804 Office: Summit Foundry Systems Inc 1225 E Wallace Fort Wayne IN 46803

MEYER, RICHARD TRACY, JR., allergist; b. St. Louis, Apr. 19, 1947; s. Richard Tracy and Julie Marie (Sumner) M.; m. Maureen Virginia O'Conner, Dec. 19, 1971; children: Jason Richard, Megan Tracy, Michael David. BA, St. Louis U., 1969, MD, 1973. Cert. Am. Bd. Pediatrics, Am. Bd. Allergy and Immunology. Resident Milw. Children's Hosp., 1973-76; allergy fellow Med. Coll. Va., Richmond, 1976-78; gen. practicing medicine specializing in allergy Carol Stream, Ill., 1978—. Mem. Am. Acad. Allergy and Immunology, Am. Lung Assn. DuPage-McHenry Counties (v.p. 1984, Vol. of Yr. 1984). Roman Catholic. Avocations: piano, golf, volleyball, tennis. Home: 1518 Center Wheaton IL 60187 Office: 389 Schmale Carol Stream IL 60188

MEYER, ROBERT EUGENE, financial company administration supervisor; b. Harvard, Ill., Nov. 9, 1957; s. Robert Edward and Alice Ingebor (Lundgren) M. Student, USAF Acad., 1975; BS, Bradley U., 1980. Adminstrn. supr. USA Fin. Services, Inc., Peoria, Ill., 1981—. Campaign worker Bob Michel for Congress, Peoria, 1984, 86. Mem. Phi Alpha Theta. Republican. Lutheran. Avocation: reading. Home: 6021 N Imperial Dr Apt 139 Apt J-1 Peoria IL 61614 Office: USA Fin Services Inc 4001 N War Memorial Dr Peoria IL 61614

MEYER, RONALD SHAW, professional football coach; b. Columbus, Ohio, Feb. 17, 1941; s. George S. and Mary (Harsha) M.; children from first marriage: Ron, Ralph; m. Cynthia Jane Osborne, Dec. 30, 1971; children: Elizabeth, Kathryn. BS, Purdue U., 1963, MS, 1965. Asst. football coach Purdue U., West Lafayette, Ind., 1965-70; scout Dallas Cowboys, NFL, 1971-72; head football coach U. Nev., Las Vegas, 1973-75, So. Meth. U., Dallas, 1976-81, New Eng. Patriots, NFL, Foxboro, Mass., 1982-84, Indpls. Colts, NFL, 1986—. Office: Indianapolis Colts PO Box 20000 Indianapolis IN 46220 *

MEYER, RUSSELL JOSEPH, English educator; b. Columbus, Ohio, Sept. 3, 1940; s. Kenneth Marvin and Dorothy Rose (Albert) M.; m. Helga Irene Storz, Dec. 17, 1966; children: Geoffrey Alan, Hillary Cassandra. BA, Ohio State U., 1967, MA, 1969; PhD, U. Minn., 1976. Instr. English Clarke Coll., Dubuque, Iowa, 1969-71; asst. prof. U. Mo., Columbia, 1976-82, assoc. prof., 1982—; cons. PIL Software, Columbia, 1986—. Contbr. articles to profl. jours. Served with U.S. Army, 1963-65. Mem. Spenser Soc. (sec., treas. 1981—, Isabell MacCaffrey award 1985), Porlock Soc. (editor 1977—). Avocations: computer programming, jogging, tennis. Home: 1708 Princeton Dr Columbia MO 65203 Office: U Mo Dept English Columbia MO 65201

MEYER, RUSSELL WILLIAM, JR., aircraft company executive; b. Davenport, Iowa, July 19, 1932; s. Russell William and Ellen Marie (Matthews) M.; m. Helen Scott Vaughn, Aug. 20, 1960; children: Russell William, III, Elizabeth Ellen, Jeffrey Vaughn, Christopher Matthews, Carolyn Louise. B.A., Yale U., 1954; LL.B., Harvard U., 1961. Bar: Ohio 1961. Mem. firm Arter & Hadden, Cleve., 1961-66; pres., chief exec. officer Grumman Am. Aviation Corp., Cleve., 1966-74; exec. v.p. Cessna Aircraft Co., Wichita, Kans., 1974-75; chmn. bd., chief exec. officer Cessna Aircraft Co., 1975—; dir. Gen. Dynamics Corp., 4th Nat. Bank, Wichita., Kans. Gas & Electric Co. Bd. dirs. Cleve. Yale Scholarship Com., 1962-74; chmn. bd. trustees 1st Baptist Ch., Cleve., 1972-74; bd. dirs. United Way Wichita and Sedgwick County, Wichita State U. Endowment Assn.; trustee Wesley Hosp. Endowment Assn., Wake Forest U. Served with USAF, 1955-58. Mem. Am., Ohio, Kans., Cleve. bar assns., Gen. Aviation Mfrs. Assn. (chmn. bd. 1973-74, 81-82), Wichita C. of C. (dir.). Clubs: Wichita, Wichita Country. Home: 600 Tara Ct Wichita KS 67206 Office: 5800 Pawnee Rd Wichita KS 67218

MEYER, SEYMOUR SIMON, finance portfolio manager; b. Chgo., May 20, 1928; s. Benjamin and Helen (Kimmel) M. Student, Wright Jr. Coll., Roosevelt U.; BSBA, U. Ill., 1956. Cert. substitute tchr. high sch. bus. edn., Ill. Stock market trader Chgo., 1956-86; adjudication dep. State of Ill., Chgo., 1958-62, state bank exainer, 1962; bank examiner FDIC, Chgo., 1967; substitute tchr. high sch. bus. edn., Chgo., 1968-69. Judge Chgo. Bd. Election Commrs., 1984, 86. Served with U.S. Army, 1950-52. Jewish. Avocations: rowboat racing, sightseeing, tourism.

MEYER, STEVEN MICHAEL, ophthalmologist, surgeon, lawyer, business consultant; b. Chgo., Feb. 3, 1946; s. Fred Bernard and Lucille (Hanson) M. Student Lake Forest Coll., 1964-66; MD, U. Ill.-Chgo., 1970; JD, Notre Dame U., 1982. Diplomate Nat. Bd. Med. Examiners, Am. Bd. Ophthalmology. Intern dept. surgery Case-Western Res. U., 1970-71; chief resident dept. ophthalmology U. Chgo., 1973-76; practice medicine specializing in ophthalmology, South Bend, Ind., 1976—; medico-legal cons., South Bend, 1982—; bus. cons., South Bend, 1982—; chief exec. officer Nat. Ophthalmic Mgmt., Inc., 1985-86. Author: Medical Malpractice Bases of Liability, 1985; contbr. articles to profl. jours; patentee in field. Bd. dirs. Ind. Soc. for Prevention of Blindness, Indpls., 1983—, med. adv. council, 1982—. Served with USPHS, 1971-73. Fellow Am. Acad. Opthalmology; mem. AMA, Ind. Acad. Ophthalmology, Ind. State Med. Assn., St. Joseph County Med. Soc. Avocations: video and film production, television, photography. Office: 513 N Michigan St South Bend IN 46601

MEYER, STUART LLOYD, management educator; b. N.Y.C., May 28, 1937; s. Isidore and Caroline (Brenner) M.; divorced; children: Jonathan, Eric, David. AB, Columbia U., 1957; PhD, Princeton U., 1962. Assoc. prof. physics Rutgers U., New Brunswick, N.J., 1963-66; sr. research scientist Rutherford Lab., Chilton, Eng., 1966-67; assoc. prof. physics Northwestern U., Evanston, Ill., 1967-74; program dir. NSF, Washington, 1974-75; assoc. prof. Kellogg Grad. Sch. Mgmt., Northwestern U., Evanston, 1975—; cons. in field; bd. dirs. Speedfam Televideo Cons., Evanston, Ill., Colo. Video, Boulder. Author: Data and Analysis for Scientists and Engrs., 1975 (Library Sci. selection 1976); contbr. articles to profl. jours. Office: JL Kellogg Grad Sch Mgmt 2001 Sheridan Rd Evanston IL 60201

MEYER, STUART MELVIN, orthopedic surgeon; b. Chgo., June 5, 1935; s. Martin and Sadie (Widdes) M.; m. Sandra Spak, June 17, 1956; children: Bonnie Meyer Sloan, Bruce, Stacy. BS, Roosevelt U., 1956; MD, Chgo. Med. Coll., North Chicago, Ill., 1960. Diplomate Am. Bd. Orthopedic Surgeons. Practice medicine specializing in orthopedic surgery Skokie, Ill., 1970—; assoc. prof. dept. orthopedic surgery Northwestern U.-Glenbrook and Evanston Hosps. Served with USAR, 1962-69. Home: 869 Peachtree Ln Glencoe IL 60022 Office: 9843 Gross Point Rd Skokie IL 60076

MEYER, TEARLE L., radiologist; b. Columbus, Ohio, June 25, 1935; s. Paul David and Bertha Ruth (Goodman) M.; m. Nancy Faga Weber, July 14, 1957; children: Andrew, Harlan, Paula. BA, Ohio State U., 1958, MD, 1960. Cert. Am. Bd. Radiology. Practice medicine specializing in radiology Columbus, Ohio, 1960—. Chmn. trustees Intel Health, Columbus, 1985—; trustee Am. Cancer Soc., 1985—, Franklin County Cancer Soc., 1985—, Jazz Arts Group, Columbus, 1985—. Served to lt. USN, 1962-64. Fellow Am. Coll. Radiology (bd. chancellors 1984—); mem. AMA, Ohio State Radiology Soc. (pres. 1975-76, Silver medal 1985), Cen. Ohio Radiology Soc. (pres. 1972), Franklin County Acad. Medicine. Clubs: Winding Hollow Country (pres. 1978-80), Capital (Columbus). Avocations: golfing, tennis, boating. Home: 175 S Merkle Rd Columbus OH 43209 Office: Columbus Radiology Corp 250 E Town St Columbus OH 43215

MEYER, THOMAS ARTHUR, sales executive; b. Monroe, Mich., Apr. 9, 1947; s. Arthur Theodore and Felicia Marie (Budzios) M.; m. Carol Ann Satkowski, Aug. 12, 1967; children: Dean, Darrin, Melanie, Marc. Student, Davis Jr. Coll., 1965-66, U. Detroit, 1970-72; BEE, U. Mich., 1973. Sales engr. Allen Bradley Co., Chgo., 1973-77; target market specialist Gould Modicon, Chgo., 1977-81; regional sales mgr. Gould Gettys, Chgo., 1981-82, Kollmorgen div. PMI Motors, Chgo., 1982-86; mem. mgmt. com. Kollmorgen div. PMI Motors, Syosset, N.Y., 1982-86; v.p. sales Heidenhain Corp., Elk Grove Village, Ill., 1986—. Pres. Resurrection Parish Council, Wayne, Ill., 1981-83, mem. fin. bd. 1983-86; coordinator Tri-Village Parent Support Group, Hoffman Estates, Ill., 1984-85. Served to sgt. USAF, 1966-70. Mem. IEEE, Soc. Mfg. Engrs. (sr.), Instrument Soc. Am. Roman Catholic. Lodge: Rotary, KC. Avocations: weightlifting, running, woodworking. Home: 981 Stuart Dr Bartlett IL 60103

MEYER, WILLIAM CHARLES, aeronautical company executive; b. Bronxville, N.Y., Jan. 22, 1946; s. William Charles August and Sarah MacDonald (Hanna) M.; m. Penny Edith Hudson, Dec. 27, 1969; children—William Jason August, William Ethan August. B.S. in C.E., Bucknell U., 1968; M.B.A., Cornell U., 1973. Registered profl. engr., Kans. Cost engr. Procon Inc., Pointe-Aux-Trembles, Que., Can., 1974-75; field engr. Arthur G. McKee, Nanticoke, Ont., Can., 1975; sr. field engr. R.M. Parsons Co., Sar-Cheshmeh, Iran, 1976-77, Dateland, Ariz., 1977-79; coordinator contracts Boeing Mil. Airplane Co., Wichita, Kans., 1979-84, constrn. mgr., 1984-87, mgr. contract adminstrn. and construction mgmt., 1987—. Mem. City Council Traffic Task Force, Mulvane, Kans., 1983; leader Quivira council Boy Scouts Am., 1982-85; mem. vestry St. Andrew's Episc. Ch., Derby, Kans., 1986—, Sunday sch. tchr., 1985—. Served to lt. (j.g.) USNR, 1968-71, Vietnam. Avocations: woodworking, sailing, cross-country skiing. Home: 225 Centennial Mulvane KS 67110 Office: Boeing Mil Airplane Co K78-01 Wichita KS 77730

MEYERHOFF, ARTHUR EDWARD (NED), JR., food and home care products executive; b. Milw., Apr. 21, 1930; s. Arthur Edward and Madelaine Henrietta (Goldman) M.; m. Joan Wurtzburg, Feb. 28, 1954 (div. May 1984); children: Robert Jay, Jill Robin, Jeffery David; m. Eva Tuszynska, June 14, 1984; children: Arthur Michael, Adam Kenneth, Ava Regina. Student, Harvard U., 1948-50, Northwestern U., 1950-52. Pres. Myzon Inc., Chgo., 1950-59, Gibraltar Industries, Chgo., 1952-71, Custom Promotions, Chgo., 1959-62; group product mgr. Boyle Midway div. Am. Home Products Corp., N.Y.C., 1971-76; pres. Mo. Hickory Corp., Chgo., 1976—. Republican. Roman Catholic. Avocation: music. Office: Missouri Hickory Corp 203 N Wabash Chicago IL 60601

MEYERLAND, HARRY, accountant; b. Chgo., Sept. 11, 1930; s. Max and Hilda (Retick) M.; m. Maxine Ida Rosenfeld, Nov. 10, 1968. B.S., Roosevelt U., 1956; diploma U.S. Treasury Law Enforcement Sch., 1963. C.P.A., Ill.; real estate broker, Ill. Spl. agt. IRS, No. Dist. Ill., 1963-64; ednl. dir. Bryant & Stratton Coll., Chgo., 1966-70; acctg. faculty MacCormac Jr. Coll., Chgo., 1971-72, Ill. Sch. Commerce, Chgo., 1978, 82-84, 87—. Bd. dirs. young people's div. Jewish Fedn. Met. Chgo., 1960. Served with U.S. Army, 1952-54, USAR, 1960. Mem. Am. Inst. C.P.A.s. Democrat. Jewish. Contbr. articles to profl. jours. Office: Ill Sch Commerce 3034 W Devon Chicago IL 60659

MEYERS, ANDREW JAMES, structural engineer; b. Pitts., Oct. 18, 1956; s. Andrew ConradMeyers and Mary Grace (Downes) Miller. BS, U. Pitts., 1978, MS, 1981. Registered profl. engr., Ohio. Prin. engr. Impell Corp., Melville, N.Y., 1981-84; facilities engr. Gen. Electric, Cin., 1984-86, stress analyst, 1986—. v.p. Mt. Adams Civic Assn., Cin., 1982-86. Avocations: woodworking, golf. Home: 1026 Celestial St Cincinnati OH 45202

MEYERS, CHRISTINE LAINE, publishing executive, consultant; b. Detroit, Mar. 7, 1946; d. Ernest Robert and Eva Elizabeth (Laine) M.; 1 child, Kathryn Laine. B.A., U. Mich., 1968. Editor, indsl. relations Diesel div. Gen. Motors Corp., Detroit, 1968; nat. advt. mgr. J.L. Hudson Co., Detroit, 1969-76, mgr. internal sales promotion, 1972-73, dir. pub., 1973-76; nat. advt. mgr. Pontiac Motor div., Mich., 1976-78; pres., owner Laine Meyers Assocs., Troy, Mich., 1978—; dir. Internat. Inst. Met. Detroit, Inc. Contbr. articles to profl. publs. Mem. bus. adv. council Central Mich. U., 1977—. Named Mich. Ad Woman of Yr., 1976, One of Top 10 Working Women, Glamour Mag., 1978. Mem. Women in Communications (Vanguard award 1986), Internat. Assn. Bus. Communicators, Adcraft Club, Women's Advt. Club (1st v.p. 1975), Women's Econ. Club (pres. 1976-77), Women's Forum Mich. (pres. 1986—), Detroit C. of C., Mortar Board, Quill and Scroll, Pub. Relations Com. Women for United Found., Founders Soc. Detroit Inst. Arts, Fashion Group, Pub. Relations Soc. Am., First Soc. Detroit (exec. com. 1970-71), Kappa Tau Alpha. Home: 1780 Kensington Bloomfield Hills MI 48013 Office: Laine Meyers Assocs Inc 3645 Crooks Rd Troy MI 48084

MEYERS, JAN, congresswoman; b. Lincoln, Nebr.; m. Louis Meyers; children—Valerie, Philip. A.A. in Fine Arts, William Woods Coll., 1948; B.A. in Communications (hon.), U. Nebr.-Lincoln, 1951; LittD, William Woods Coll., 1986. Mem. Overland Park City Council, Kans., 1967-72; also pres; mem. Kans. Senate, 1972-84, chmn. pub. health and welfare com., local govt. com.; mem. 99th Congress from 3d Kans. Dist., mem. com. foreign affairs, small bus. com., select com. on aging, others. 3d dist. co-chmn. Bob Dole for U.S. Senate, 1968; chmn. Johnson County Bob Bennett for Gov., 1974; mem. Johnson County Community Coll. Found.; bd. dirs. Johnson County Mental Health Assn. Recipient Outstanding Elected Ofcl. of Yr. award Assn. Community Mental Health Ctrs. Kans.; Woman of Achievement Matrix award Women in Communications; Disting. Service award Bus. and Profl. Women Kansas City; Community Service award Jr. League Kansas City 1st Disting. Legislator award Kans. Assn. Community Colls.; Outstanding Service award Kans. Library Assn., United Community Services, Kans. Pub. Health Assn.; award Gov.'s Conf. Child Abuse and Neglect; Outstanding Legislator award Kans. Action for Children; Friend award Nat.

Assn. County Park and Recreation Ofcls., 1987; numerous others. Mem. LWV (past pres. Shawnee Mission). Methodist. Office: 315 Cannon House Office Bldg Washington DC 20515

MEYERS, KAREN HOPKINS, bank personnel executive; b. N.Y.C., Oct. 23, 1948; d. Richard Anthony and Jeanne Frances (O'Brien) Hopkins; m. John Walter Wingate, June 21, 1969 (div. 1972); m. Robert Bernard Meyers, Jan. 29, 1983; 1 child, Elizabeth. BA, Mich. State U., 1970; post grad., UCLA, 1970-72; MA, Bowling Green (Ohio) State U., 1974; PhD, Bowling Green State U., 1982. Writer Allstate Ins. Co., Northbrook, Ill., 1977-79; dir. tng. Ins. Co. N. Am., Kalamazoo, 1979-81; career devel. specialist Ownes Ill., Inc., Toledo, 1981-83; personnel staff specialist First Nat. Bank, Toledo, 1983-84, dir. tng., 1984—. Citbr. articles to profl. jours. Mem. allocation com. United Way, Toledo, 1983; pres. Westmoreland Assn., 1985. Fellow Woodrow Wilson Found., 1970. Mem. Am. Soc. for Tng. and Devel., Phi Beta Kappa. Democrat. Roman Catholic. Avocations: writing children's books, needlework. Office: First Nat Bank of Toledo 606 Madison Toledo OH 43604

MEYERS, LYNN BETTY, architect; b. Chgo., Dec. 2, 1952; d. William J. and Dorothy (King) M.; m. Dana Terp, May 17, 1975; children: Sophia, Rachel. Student, Royal Acad. Architecture, Copenhagen, Denmark, 1971; BArch, Washington U., St. Louis, 1974, MArch, 1977. Registered architect, Ill. Architect Holabird & Root Architects, Chgo., 1973, 76, Hist. Pullman Found., Chgo., 1975, Jay Alpert Architects, Woodbridge, Conn., 1976, City of Chgo. Bur. Architects, 1978-80; sole practice architecture Chgo., 1980-82; prin., architect Terp Meyers Architects, Chgo., 1982—. Exhbns. include: Centre George Pompidou, Paris, 1978, Fifth Internat. Congress Union Internat. Des Femmes Architects, Seattle, 1979, Frumkin Struve Gallery, Chgo., 1981, Art. Inst. Chgo., 1983, Inst. Francais d'Architecture, Paris, 1983, Mus. Sci. and Industry, Chgo., 1985; pub. in profl. jours. including Progressive Architecture, Modo Design, Los Angeles Architect; work featured in various archtl. books; exhibited 150 Yrs. of Chgo. Architecture, Mus. Sci. and Industry, Chgo., 1985. Recipient Progressive Architecture mag. award, 1980; First Place Los Angeles AIA Real Problems Competition, 1986. Mem. AIA (task force com. for 1992 World's Fair), Union Internat. Des Femmes Architects, Chgo. Women in Architecture (v.p. 1980-81, Allied Arts award 1974), Young Chgo. Architects. Office: Terp Meyers Architects 919 N Michigan Ave Chicago IL 60611

MEYERS, MIRIAM WATKINS, language educator; b. Atlanta, Jan. 22, 1941; d. William Craton Watkins and Carolyn Grey (Franklin) Burtz; m. Chester Albert Meyers, July 29, 1967. AB with honors, Peabody Coll., 1962; MS, Georgetown U., 1968; postgrad., Yale U., U. Minn., Hamline U., Met. State U. Tchr. English, French Fairfax (Va.) County Pub. Schs., 1962-66; jr. editor, writer NASA Hdqrs., Washington, 1966-67; supr. practice teaching, instr. Yale U., New Haven, 1967-68; asst. to dir. and research coordinator Inst. for Interdisciplinary Studies, Mpls., 1969-71; exec. asst. to pres. Met. State U., St. Paul, 1971-72, asst. prof., 1971-76, assoc. prof., 1976-83, prof., 1983—; cons. Workshop Design Assocs., Mpls., 1983-84. Contbr. articles to profl. jours., chpts. to books. Vol. Minn. Civil Liberties Union, 1970-80. Recipient Algernon Sidney Sullivan award Peabody Coll., 1962, Teaching Excellence citation Met. State U., 1980, 86; named Outstanding Faculty Advisor Met. State U., 1983. Mem. NEA, Am. Dialect Soc., Nat. Council Tchrs. English, Minn. Assn. for Continuing Adult Edn. (sec. 1983-84, bd. dirs. 1983-84), Minn. Council on Teaching English, Minn. Council on Teaching Fgn. Language. Democrat. Home: 2000 W 21st St Minneapolis MN 55405 Office: Metropolitan State Univ 528 Hennepin Ave Minneapolis MN 55403-1897

MEYERS, MITCHELL SIDNEY, real estate company executive; b. Cin., July 3, 1934; s. Sidney and Claire Maxine (Baum) M.; m. Jacqueline P. Meyers, July 1, 1957; children—Pamela A. Meyers Margaritis, Barry, Eliot. B.A., Cornell U., 1956, M.B.A. with distinction, 1957. Various exec. positions Mehl Mfg. Co., Cin., 1957-63; pvt. practice real estate developer, 1963-64; v.p. East & Co., 1964-72; prin. Mitchell S. Meyers, developer and investor, 1972—. Pres., Cin. Housing for the Aged, Inc., 1979-83. Mem. Cin. Real Estate Bd., Ohio Verse Writers Guild, Greater Cin. Writers League (pres. 1982—), Phi Kappa Phi. Republican. Club: Losantiville Country. Contbr. poems to anthologies. Office: Meyers Found 105 E 4th St Suite 1114 Clopay Tower Cincinnati OH 45202

MEYLOR, COLLEEN BETH, steelmill product specialist, educator; b. Milw., Nov. 29, 1957; d. Michael Bernard and Karole Joan (Kabbeck) M. BSCE, U. Wis., Madison, 1979; MBA, Baldwin Wallace Coll., 1987. Devel. engr. Foseco, Inc., Cleve., 1980-82, product specialist, 1982-86, steelmill product specialist, 1986—; instr. Cast Metals Inst., Am. Foundry Soc., Chgo., 1984—; bd. dirs. Foseco Employees Fed. Credit Union, 1983—, treas. 1986. Mem. Profl. Engring. Soc., Am. Foundryman's Soc., Am. Women in Metal Industries, Nat. Assn. Female Execs., Iron & Steel Soc., U. Wis. Alumni Assn. Avocations: piano, sports. Home: 32747 Willowbrook Ln North Ridgeville OH 44039 Office: Foseco Inc 20200 Sheldon Rd Cleveland OH 44142

MICELI, LOUIS ANTHONY, osteopath; b. Chgo., July 20, 1948; s. Vincent and Theresa (DeGrazia) M.; m. Virginia Swanson, July 29, 1978; children: Theresa Renee, Joseph Vincent, Angela Concetta. BA cum laude, Elmhurst (Ill.) Coll., 1970; DO, Chgo. Coll. Osteo. Medicine, 1975. Diplomate Am. Bd. Osteo. Medicine and Surgery; cert. Am. Bd. Osteo. Pediatricians. Chmn. dept. pediatrics Michiana Community Hosp., South Bend, Ind., 1978-80; asst. prof. pediatrics Chgo. Coll. Osteo. Medicine, 1980—; gen. practice osteo. medicine Hammond, Ind., 1986—; attending pediatrician, chmn. dept. pediatrics South Bend Osteo. Hosp., 1978-80 ; attending pediatrician St. Joseph's Med. Ctr., South Bend, 1979-80, Chgo. Osteo. Med. Ctr., 1980—; med. advisor Elkhart (Ind.) Assn. for Children with Learning Disabilities, 1979-80, South Suburban Assn. for Children with Learning Disabilities, Olympia Fields, Ill., 1980-83, Cesarian Parents' Assn., South Bend, 1979-80; med. adv. com. Nat. March of Dimes, South Bend chpt., 1979-80; med. advisor, co-dir. prenatal edn. classes Olympia Fields Osteo. Med. Ctr., 1984—, pediatric cons., coordinator comprehensive child evaluation program, 1980-84; med. dir., pres. bd. dirs., chief pediatric cons. Trans-Allied Med.-Ednl. Services, Inc., Homewood, Ill., 1983—; chief pediatric cons. South Met. Assn. for Low-Incidence Handicapped, Homewood, 1980-84; mem. med. criteria evaluation com. Ind. II P.R.S.O., Inc., South Bend, 1979-80, perinatal study group, 1980; mem. neonatal planning services task force No. Ind. Health Services Agy., South Bend, 1980. Contbr. articles to profl. jours. Mead-Johnson Research fellow Nat. Osteo. Found., 1978; recipient Spl. Service award South Met. Assn. for Low-Incidence Handicapped, 1985. Mem. AMA, Ill. Med. Soc., Chgo. Med. Soc., Am. Osteo. Assn., Am. Coll. Osteo. Physicians (sr.), Ind. Assn. Osteo. Physicians and Surgeons. Roman Catholic. Avocations: tennis, jogging, writing. Office: 7134 Calumet Ave Hammond IN 46324

MICELI, MOLLY KLEMMA, insurance company executive; b. Norway, Oct. 14, 1950; came to U.S., 1954; d. Asle and Kari Marie (Kjetland) K.; m. Joseph Michael Miceli, Aug. 5, 1977; children: Victoria, Lisa. AAS, RN, Harper Coll., 1975; BS, Roosevelt U., 1984. RN Humana Inc., Louisville, 1980-82, facility mgr., 1982-83, dir. profl. relations, 1983-84, dir. bus. devel., 1984-85, ops. dir. group health div., 1985-86; exec. dir. Ill. group health div. Itasca, 1986—; speaker health ins.-related topics. Author health services procedural manuals; editor, contbr. Humana Hosp. Physician's Capsule, 1983-84. Recipient Cert. of Leadership YWCA, 1985, Honors Achievement award Health Ins. Assn. Am., 1986. Mem. Am. Assn. Preferred Provider Orgns. (bd. dirs. 1987—), Ill. Assn. Preferred Provider Orgns. (v.p. 1985-86, pres. 1987—, editor IAPPO Mems. Report 1986—), Ill. Hosp. Assn. (mem. pre-cert. panel task force 1987), Exec. Women (mem. program com. North Shore chpt. 1985-86), Glen Ellyn C. of C., North Suburban Assn. Commerce and Industry. Lutheran. Avocations: traveling, reading, classical music. Office: Humana Inc One Pierce Pl Itasca IL 60143

MICHAEL, FREDERICK WILLIAM, microcomputer executive; b. Columbus, Ohio, Mar. 15, 1943; s. Frederick William and Clare Marie (Sinclair) M. BS, Ohio State U., 1965. Tchr. Columbus (Ohio) Bd. Edn., 1965-71; regional mgr. Bell & Howell, San Francisco, 1971-77; product mgr. Bell & Howell, Chgo., 1977-81; dir. tng. Zenith Data Systems, Chgo., 1981-86, dir. mktg. devel., 1986—. Dir. (film) New York Film Festival, 1982 (Bronze award 1982); contbr. articles to profl. jours. Panel mem. Congl. Hearings on Info. Tech. in Edn., U.S. Ho. of Reps., 1982. Mem. Assn. Spl. Edn. Tech. (exec. bd. dirs. Chgo. 1978-80), Assn. Media Producers (exec. bd. dirs. D.C. 1980-81), Nat. Assn. Coll. Aux. Services, Assn. Tng. and Devel. Roman Catholic. Avocations: disc jockey, photographer, body bldg., reading. Home: 6230 N Kenmore #1302 Chicago IL 60660 Office: Zenith Data Systems 1000 Milwaukee Ave Glenview IL 60025

MICHAEL, JONATHAN EDWARD, insurance company executive; b. Columbus, Ohio, Mar. 19, 1954; s. James Franklin and Mary Manetta (McCloud) M.; m. Lori Jeanette Fry, Sept. 1, 1973 (div. Feb. 1985); children: Amber Nicole, Jonathan Andrew. BA, Ohio Dominican Coll., 1977. CPA, Ohio. Acct. Coopers & Lybrand, Columbus, Ohio, 1977-82; chief acct. RLI Ins. Co., Peoria, Ill., 1982-84, controller, 1984-85, v.p. fin. and chief fin. officer, 1985—, also bd. dirs.; v.p. fin., chief fin. officer RLI Corpdiv. Am. Capacity Group, Inc., Peoria, Ill., 1985—; bd. dirs. Am. Capacity Ins. Co. Mem. Am. Inst. CPA's, Ins. Acctg. and Systems Assn. Cen. Ill. (treas. 1985, sec. 1986). Roman Catholic. Club: Mt. Hawley Country (Peoria). Avocation: golf. Home: 811 Wonderview Dr Peoria IL 61525 Office: RLI Ins Corp 9025 N Lindbergh Peoria IL 61615

MICHAELIDES, CONSTANTINE EVANGELOS, architect; b. Athens, Greece, Jan. 26, 1930; came to U.S., 1955, naturalized, 1964; s. Evangelos George and Kalliopi Constantine (Kefallonitis) M.; m. Maria S. Canellakis, Sept. 3, 1955; children: Evangelos Constantine, Dimitri Canellakis. Diploma in Architecture, Nat. Tech. U., Athens, 1952; M.Arch., Harvard U., 1957. Practice architecture Athens, 1954-55, St. Louis, 1963—; asso. architect Carl Koch, Jose Luis Sert, Hideo Sasaki, Cambridge, Mass., 1957-59, Doxiadis Assos., Athens and Washington, 1959-60, Hellmuth, Obata & Kassabaum, St. Louis, 1962; instr. Grad. Sch. Design Harvard U., 1957-59, Athens Inst. Tech., 1959-60; asst. prof. architecture Washington U., St. Louis, 1960-64; asso. prof. Washington U., 1964-69, prof., 1969—; asso. dean Washington U. (Sch. Architecture), 1969-73, dean, 1973—; vis. prof. (Sch. Architecture), Ahmedabad, India, 1970; counselor Landmarks Assn. St. Louis., 1975-79. Author: Hydra: A Greek Island Town: Its Growth and Form, 1967. Mem. Municipal Commn. on Arts, Letters, University City, Mo., 1975-81. Served to lt. Greek Army Res., 1952-54. Fellow AIA (dir. St. Louis chpt. 1977-79, research award 1963-64); Mem. Tech. Chamber of Greece, Soc. Archtl. Historians, Modern Greek Studies Assn. Home: 735 Radcliffe St University City MO 63130 Office: Sch Architecture Washington U Saint Louis MO 63130

MICHAELS, ALVIN BARRY, psychiatrist; b. Detroit, Jan. 5, 1935; s. Jules Warren and Fanny (Weinberg) M.; m. Aurelia Elizabeth VerBeke, Feb. 2, 1963; children: Linda Louise, Andrew David. BS with high distinction, U. Mich., 1956, MD, 1960. Diplomate Am. Bd. Psychiatry and Neurology (examiner). Intern Wayne County Gen. Hosp., Eloise, Mich., 1960-61; resident in psychiatry U. Mich. Med. Ctr., Ann Arbor, 1961-62, 64-65, fellow in child psychiatry, 1965-67; dir. child and adolescent psychiat. services Detroit Psychiat. Inst., 1967-68; practice medicine specializing in psychiatry Birmingham, Mich., 1967—; staff William Beaumont Hosp., Royal Oak, Mich., 1967—, Kingswood Hosp., Ferndale, Mich., 1967—; mem. profl. adv. council Scoliosis Assn. Mich., 1980-84. Served to lt. USN, 1962-64. Fellow Am. Acad. Child and Adolescent Psychiatry; mem. Am. Psychiat. Assn., Am. Soc. for Adolescent Psychiatry, Am. Orthopsychiat. Assn., Mich. Psychiat. Soc. Jewish. Office: 30100 Telegraph Suite 330 Birmingham MI 48010

MICHAELS, ANTHONY BRUCE, osteopath, psychiatrist; b. N.Y.C., Mar. 3, 1948; s. Allen Lincoln and Celia Martha (Kohn) M.; m. Melodie Ann Theodore, Nov. 11, 1979; 1 child, Daniel Colin. BA cum laude, U. Mich., 1979; DO, Mich. State U., 1979. Diplomate Am. Bd. Psychiatry and Neurology. Intern Detroit Osteo. Hosp., 1975-76, psychiatrist, 1979—; resident Detroit Psychiat. Inst., 1976-79; psychiatrist Providence Hosp., Southfield, 1984—, William Beaumont Hosp., Southfield, Mich., 1985—, Mich. Osteo. Hosp., Detroit, 1979—; assoc. dir. North Point Mental Health Assocs., Farmington Hills, Mich.; practice medicine specializing in psychiatry Birmingham, Mich.; assoc. clin. prof. Mich. State U., East Lansing, 1980—. Mem. Am. Osteo. Assn., Mich. Assn. Osteo. Physicians and Surgeons, Am. Psychiat. Assn., Mich. Psychiat. Assn. Jewish. Avocations: swimming, sailing, world travel, literature. Home: 5695 Forman Rd Birmingham MI 48010 Office: 280 N Woodward Suite 405 Birmingham MI 48011

MICHAELSON, JUNE RAPPAPORT, service company executive, consultant; b. Chgo., June 8, 1931; d. Earle Samuel and Marion (Hendry) Rappaport; m. Marc Michaelson, Aug. 2, 1953; children: David, Grant. Student, Beloit Coll., 1949-51; BA, U. Ill., Chgo., 1953; MA, Northwestern U., 1957. Cert. secondary tchr. Ill. Adminstr. U.S. Job Corps, Chgo., 1968-70; mgr. youth services Sheriff's Office Cook County, Chgo., 1970-71; instr. polit. sci. and Am. history YMCA Coll., Chgo., 1971-73; mgr. travel info. ctr. Rand McNally Pub. Co., Skokie, Ill., 1977-79, editor-in-chief Mobil Travel Guide, 1977-82; pres. Hospitality Standards Ltd., Skokie, 1982—. Editor-in-chief Mobil Travel Guide. Bd. dirs. LWV, Skokie and Lincolnwood, Ill., 1958-67; pres., bd. dirs. Sharp Corner Sch. 2d Regional Ill. PTA, Skokie, 1964-68; founding mem., vice chmn. Niles Twp. Sheltered Workshop, Skokie, 1970-84; edn. chmn. Skokie Human Relations Com., 1964-67; dist. dir. Paul Simon Campaign for Gov., 1978; exec. sec. Niles (Ill.) Twp. Dem. Orgn., 1958-60; membership chmn. Bus. Execs. for Nat. Security, 1983—. Mem. Soc. Am. Travel Writers, Internat. Fedn. Travel Orgns. (assoc. Ill. chpt.). Jewish. Avocations: travelling, reading, tutoring ESL, swimming. Office: Hospitality Standards Ltd 4927 W Oakton Skokie IL 60077

MICHAK, HELEN BARBARA, educator, nurse; b. Cleve., July 31; d. Andrew and Mary (Patrick) M. Diploma Cleve. City Hosp. Sch. Nursing, 1947; BA, Miami U., Oxford, Ohio, 1951; MA, Case Western Res. U., 1960. Staff nurse Cleve. City Hosp., 1947-48; pub. health nurse Cleve. Div. Health, 1951-52; instr. Cleve. City Hosp. Sch. Nursing, 1952-56; supr. nursing Cuyahoga County Hosp., Cleve., 1956-58; pub. information dir. N.E. Ohio Am. Heart Assn., Cleve., 1960-64; dir. spl. events Higbee Co., Cleve., 1964-66; exec. dir. Cleve. Area League for Nursing, 1966-72; dir. continuing edn. nurses, adj. assoc. prof. Cleve. State U., 1972-86. Trustee N.E. Ohio Regional Med. Program, 1970-73; mem. adv. com. Dept. Nursing Cuyahoga Community Coll., 1967—; mem. long term care com. Met. Health Planning Corp., 1974-76, plan devel. com. 1977—; mem. policy bd. Ctr. Health Data N.E. Ohio, 1972-73; mem. Rep. Assembly and Health Planning and Devel. Commn., Welfare Fedn. Cleve., 1967-72; mem. Cleve. Community Health Network, 1972-73; mem. United Appeal Films and Speakers Bur., 1967-73; mem. adv. com. Ohio Fedn. Lic. Practical Nurses, 1970-73; mem. tech. adv. com. TB and Respiratory Disease Assn. Cuyahoga County, 1967-74; mem. Ohio Commn. on Nursing, 1971-74; mem. Citizens com. nursing homes Fedn. Community Planning, 1973-77; mem. com. on home health services Met. Health Planning Corp., 1973-75. Mem. Nat. League Nursing (mem. com. 1970-72), Am. Nurses Assn. (accreditation visitor 1977-78, 83-85) Ohio Nurses Assn., (com. continuing edn. 1974-79, 82-84, chmn. 1984-85), Greater Cleve. (joint practice com. 1973-74, trustee 1975-76) Nurses Assn., Cleve. Area Citizens League for Nursing (trustee 1976-79), Am. Soc. Tng. and Devel., Am. Assn. Univ. Profs., Zeta Tau Alpha. Home: 4686 Oakridge Dr North Royalton OH 44133

MICHALAK, EDWARD M., manufacturing company executive; b. Milw., Oct. 1, 1924; s. Michael and Emily S. (Bulak) M.; m. Rita Y. Glazewski, May 23, 1953; children—Barbara, Mary, Cynthia, Jean. B.S. in Gen. Engring., U.S. Mil. Acad., 1945; B.S.E.E., U. Wis.-Madison, 1952; M.B.A., U. Wis.-Milw., 1976. Registered profl. engr., Wis. Devel. engr. Cutler Hammer & Globe Union, Milw., 1952-57; solid state engr. Allen Bradley Co., Milw., 1958-67, dir. elec. engring., 1967-69, dir. product mgmt., 1969-73, corp. v.p., 1973—; engring. advisor Marquette U., Milw., 1980—; mem. engring. adv. com. Milw. Sch. Engring., 1984—. Bd. dirs. Internat. Inst. Milw., 1984—, 1st v.p., 1984-85; mem. Kosciuszko Found., N.Y.C., 1963—. Served with U.S. Army, 1945-49, PTO. Mem. IEEE, Am. Soc. Quality Control, Indsl. Research Inst. (prin. rep. 1978—, program chmn. 1984-85), Wis. Assn. Research Mgmt. (chmn. 1984-85). Avocations: swimming; skiing; photography. Home: 3414 W Poe St Milwaukee WI 53215 Office: Allen Bradley Co 1201 S 2d St Milwaukee WI 53215

MICHALIK, MATTHEW PETER, investment representative; b. Kewanee, Ill., July 23, 1960; s. Andrew F. and Donna J. (Kohler) M.; m. Mary Helen Wade, July 5, 1986. BJ, U. Mo., 1982. Investment rep. Edward D. Jones & Co., Homewood, Ill., 1984—. Mem. Homewood C. of C. Republican. Roman Catholic. Lodge: Kiwanis. Home: 943 Olive Rd #6B Homewood IL 60430 Office: Edward D Jones & Co 1757 Ridge Rd Homewood IL 60430

MICHALSKI, EDWARD CHARLES, medical products company executive; b. Chgo., July 11, 1952; s. George Charles and Rose Margaret (DiGangi) M.; m. Martha Irene Medwecky, Apr. 19, 1975; children: Kathryn Dawn, Laura Elizabeth, Mark Edward. BS in Acctg., U. Ill., 1974. CPA, Ill. Pub. acct. Peat, Marwick, Mitchell & Co., Chgo., 1974-76; sr. internal auditor Katy Industries Inc., Elgin, Ill., 1976-78; sr. fin. control analyst Travenol Labs. Inc. div. Baxter Travenol, Deerfield, Ill., 1979-80, project leader-info. systems, 1981-82, sect. mgr.-info. systems, 1983-85, mgr. info. systems, 1986—. Mem. Am. Inst. CPA's. Roman Catholic. Avocations: scuba diving, sports cars. Office: Travenol Labs Inc 1 Baxter Pkwy DF5-2W Deerfield IL 60015

MICHAM, NANCY SUE, information systems executive; b. Toledo, May 15, 1956; d. Charles Edward and Dorothy Ruth (Bittner) Linker; m. Donald Thomas Kerner, June 20, 1975 (div. June 1980); m. Ray David Micham, III, May 19, 1984. A.S. with high honors, U. Toledo, 1980; B.S.M. cum laude, Pepperdine U., 1983. Cert. systems profl., systems profl., 1986. Programmer, Owens-Ill., Toledo, 1973-80; programmer analyst Smith Tool Co., Irvine, Calif., 1980-82; systems analyst Denny's, Inc., La Mirada, Calif., 1982-83; sr. corp. systems analyst, mgr. corp. systems group Libbey-Owens-Ford Co., Toledo, 1983-86, pres. Seagate Systems Cons., 1986—. Participant ToledoScape. Mem. Nat. Mgmt. Assn., Assn. Systems Mgmt., Inst. for Cert. of Systems Profls., Nat. Assn. Female Execs. Republican. Roman Catholic. Avocations: travel, backpacking, bicycling, aerobics teaching.

MICHEL, ARTHUR GREENE, physician; b. Chgo., Feb. 25, 1941; s. David Daniel and Jane Ruth (Greene) M.; divorced; children: David, Jeffrey. BA, Amherst Coll., 1963; MD, Case Western Res. U., 1967. Diplomate Am. Bd. Surgery. Intern Michael Reese Hosp., Chgo., 1967, resident, 1968-72, attending physician, 1972—; practice medicine specializing in gen. and oncologic surgery Chgo., 1972—. Fellow ACS. Avocation: sailing. Office: 111 N Wabash Chicago IL 60602

MICHEL, PHILIP MARTIN, marketing professional; b. Bronxville, N.Y., July 11, 1939; s. Philip Harold and Margaret (Conklin) M.; m. Carina Pehrson, Apr. 11, 1970; children: Philip J., Karl P. AB, Syracuse U., 1964. Account exec. Lewis & Dobrow Advertising, Washington, 1967-68; merchandising mgr. Am. Motors Corp., Detroit, 1968-70; mgr. adv., pub. relations, sales promotion B.S.A. Co., Inc., Verona, N.J., 1970-71; dir. adv., pub. relations Sno-Jet Inc., Burlington, Vt., 1971-74; mgr. adv. and sales promotion Hilti, USA, Stamford, Conn., 1974-75; dir. mktg. communications Cessna Aircraft Co., Wichita, Kans., 1975—; v.p., bd. dirs. Warren Travel, Inc., 1985—. Mem. Bus./Profl. Adv. Assn., Adv. Club Wichita, Nat. Bus. Aircraft Assn., Gen. Aviation Mfrs. Assn., Gen. Aviation Mfrs. Assn., Audit Bur. Circulation. Republican. Presbyterian. Lodges: Elks, Rotary (v.p. West Wichita, Kans. chpt.). Avocations: music, swimming, travel. Home: 6903 Aberdeen Wichita KS 67206 Office: Cessna Aircraft Co PO Box 1521 Wichita KS 67201

MICHEL, ROBERT HENRY, congressman; b. Peoria, Ill., Mar. 2, 1923; s. Charles and Anna (Baer) M.; m. Corinne Woodruff, Dec. 26, 1948; children: Scott, Bruce, Laurie, Robin. B.S., Bradley U., 1948; L.H.D., Lincoln Coll., Bradley U. Adminstrv. asst. to Congressman Harold Velde, 1949-56; mem. 85th-100th Congresses, 18th Dist. Ill., 1957—; house minority whip 94th-96th Congresses, 1975-81; minority leader 97th and 99th Congresses, 1981—. Del. Republican Nat. Conv., 1964, 68, 72, 76, 80, 84; chmn. Nat. Rep. Congl. Com., 1973-74. Served with inf. AUS., World War II, ETO. Decorated Bronze Star (2), Purple Heart; recipient Alumnus award Bradley U., 1961. Mem. Am. Legion, V.F.W., D.A.V., Amvets, Ill. State Soc., Cosmopolitan Internat. Club: Rotarian. Office: 2112 Rayburn House Office Bldg Washington DC 20515 *

MICHELETTO, JOE RAYMOND, food products executive, controller; b. Christopher, Ill., Oct. 19, 1936; s. Steve Pete and Dena (Arro) M.; m. Marlyn Kay Thetford, Jan. 20, 1962; children: Amber, Peter, Joseph. BS in Acctg., So. Ill. U., 1962. Cost acct. Ralston Purina Co., St. Louis, 1962-63, fin. analyst, 1963-66, planning and fin. coordinator Grocery Products div., 1966-69, controller Grocery Products div., 1969-72, v.p. Grocery Products div., 1972-74, v.p., dir. adminstrn. Consumer Products div., 1974-84, corp. v.p., controller, 1985—. Served as sgt. U.S. Army, 1954-58. Mem. Fin. Execs. Inst. Roman Catholic. Office: Ralston Purina Co Checkerboard Sq Saint Louis MO 63164

MICHELS, EUGENE AUGUST, academic program director; b. Detroit, June 2, 1934; s. August Michels and Louise (St. John) LaBonte; m. Kara Lee Schales, Aug. 20, 1960 (div. Jan. 1973); m. Coanne N. Johnson, June 7, 1976; children: Cynthia, Sean. BS, Wayne State U., 1963; MSW, U. Mich., 1967. Exec. dir. Redford (Mich.) Counseling Ctr., 1969—; sch. social worker Redford Union Schs., 1965-78, coordinator adolscent unit, 1978-86, dir. day treatment, 1986—; chmn. Family Human Potential Services, Livonia, Mich., 1973-78, bd. dirs. 1973—. Served as cpl. U.S. Army, 1955-57. Mem. Nat. Assn. Social Workers (cert.). Avocation: travel. Home: 21192 Green Hill Apt 319 Farmington Hills MI 48024 Office: Redford Union Schs 18499 Beech Daly Rd Redford MI 48240

MICHELS, ROBERT MALCOLM, obstetrician, gynecologist; b. St. Johns, Mich., Dec. 27, 1923; s. Robert B. and Hazel N. (Lewis) M.; m. Beth Georgia Judd, Oct. 8, 1949; children: Susan, Malcolm, Mark, Mary Beth. BS, Mich. State U., 1945; MD, U. Mich., 1948. Cert. Am. Bd. Ob-Gyn. Practice medicine specializing in ob-gyn Flint, Mich., 1949—. Served to lt. commdr. USNR, 1944-55. Fellow Am. Coll. Ob-Gyns., ACS. Home: 1112 River Rd Flushing MI 48433 Office: 2702 Flushing Rd Flint MI 48504

MICHELSEN, JOHN ERNEST, software services company executive; b. New Brunswick, N.J., May 11, 1946; s. Ernest Arnold and Ursula (Hunter) M.; B.S., Northwestern U., 1969; M.S., Stevens Inst. Tech., 1972; M.B.A. in Fin. with honors, U. Chgo., 1978; m. Ruth Ann Flanders, June 15, 1969; children—Nancy Ellen, Rebecca Ruthann. Real-time programmer Lockheed Electronics Co., Plainfield, N.J., 1969-72; control system designer Fermi Nat. Accelerator Lab., Batavia, Ill., 1972-75; chief system designer Distributed Info. Systems Corp., Chgo., 1975-78, v.p., 1978-79; mgr. M.I.S. adminstrn. FMC Corp., Chgo., 1979-82; pres. Infopro, Inc., 1982—. Mem. Assn. Computing Machinery, Phi Eta Sigma, Tau Beta Pi, Beta Gamma Sigma. Office: 2625 Butterfield Rd Oak Brook IL 60521

MICHENER, DWIGHT WARREN, agricultural engineer, civil engineer, farmer; b. Waynesville, Ohio, June 29, 1932; s. Charles Edward and Mary Alice (Crawford) M.; m. Anita Dee Wills, Sept., 1955 (div. 1968); children—Wendy, Eric, Sara; m. 2d, Glenna Mary Witters, May 26, 1978. B.S. in Agr., Ohio State U., 1954, B.S. in Agrl. Engring., 1962. Registered profl. engr., Nev., Ohio. Agrl. engr. Soil Conservation Service, U.S. Dept. Agr., Moses Lake and Sunnyside, Wash., 1963-66, researcher Agrl. Research Service, Reno, 1966-70; sr. engr., farm devel., advisor to Toprak-su (Turkey Soil and Water Conservation Service) Engring. Cons. Inc., Denver, 1970-71; engr. Ada Devel. Project, Ethiopia, Clapp & Mayne, Inc., San Juan, P.R., 1972-74; irrigation/drainage engr. Pakistan Water and Power Devel. Authority, Harza Engring Co. Internat., Chgo., 1975-77; drainage researcher Soil Conservation Service, U.S. Dept. Agr., agrl. engring. dept. Ohio State U., Columbus, 1977-78; irrigation/drainage engr. FAO, Bagdad, Iraq, 1978; agrl. engr. Soil and Water Conservation Dists., Ohio Dept. Natural Resources, Columbus, 1979; farmer, Waynesville, Ohio, 1979—. Served to 1st lt. U.S. Army, 1955-56. Mem. ASCE, Am. Soc. Agrl. Engrs., Soil Conservation Soc., Farmer's Grange 13, Waynesville (Ohio) C. of C. Republican. Christian Scientist. Contbr. articles to profl. jours.; patentee in drainage field. Home and Office: 4980 Old State Rt 73 Waynesville OH 45068

MICK, BROOKS ALLEN, physician; b. Ashland, Ohio, June 28, 1941; s. Charles Brooks Mick and Mildred (Maycel) Skaggs; widowed; children: Laurie Ann, James Michael, Erin Colleen. BA, Ohio State U., 1963, MD, 1966. Cert. Am. Bd. Internal Medicine. Practice medicine specializing in internal medicine Findlay, Ohio, 1972—. Served to maj. USAR. Mem. AMA, Ohio State Med. Assn., Hancock County Med. Soc. Republican. Avocations: boating, scuba diving. Office: 910 N Main St Findlay OH 45840

MICKELSON, GEORGE S., governor of South Dakota; b. Mobridge, S.D., Jan. 31, 1941; s. George T. and Madge Mickelson; m. Linda McCahren; children: Mark, Amy, David. BS, U. S.D., 1963, JD, 1965. Ptnr. McCann, Martin and Mickelson, Brookings, S.D., 1968-83, Mickelson, Erickson and Helsper, Brookings, 1983-86; states atty. Brookings County, 1970-74; mem. S.D. Ho. of Reps., Pierre, 1975-80, speaker pro tempore, 1977-78, speaker of the house, 1979-80; gov. State of S.D., 1986—. Served to capt. U.S. Army, 1963-67, Vietnam. Mem. ABA, S.D. Bar Assn., Assn. Trial Lawyers Am., S.D. Trial Lawyers Assn., Am. Judicature Soc., VFW, Am. Legion. Republican. Methodist. Lodges: Masons, Shriners. Office: Office of the Governor 500 E Capitol Pierre SD 57501

MICKLE, JAMES LOWELL, private investigator and security executive; b. July 11, 1935; s. James M. and Lera V. (Ragland) M.; m. Martha L. Dennis, June 11, 1955; children—Greg, Janet, Pamela. Grad., Detroit Bus. Inst., 1961. Cert. protection profl. With Pinkerton's, Inc., Detroit and Southfield, Mich., 1960-70; with World Investigations & Security Engrs., Inc., Southfield, 1971—, pres., chief exec. officer, 1971—; speaker seminars. Served with U.S. Army, 1958-60. Mem. World Assn. Detectives (pres. 1984-85), Nat. Council Investigations and Security Services (pres. 1983-84), Mich. Assn. Pvt. Detectives and Security Agys. (pres. 1977-78). Office: World Investigations & Security Engrs Inc 17603 W Ten Mile Rd Southfield MI 48075

MICKLEWRIGHT, JERROLD JOHN, financial executive; b. Davenport, Iowa, May 6, 1934; s. Joseph Ralph and Elma (Endorf) M.; m. Mary K. Lavery, Aug. 24, 1957; children: Mollie, Mickey, Ann, Mike, Meg. BA, St. Ambrose Coll., 1960; grad., Mgt. Inst. Northwestern U., 1982. CPA, Ill., Nebr. Sr. acct. Peat, Marwick, Mitchell and Co., Cedar Rapids, Iowa, 1960-63; chief systems planning U.S. Govt., France, Germany and U.S., 1963-68; v.p. fin. W.E. O'Neil Constrn. Co., Chgo., 1969-79; v.p. fin., treas. Underwriters Salvage Co., Palatine, Ill., 1980—. Mem. St. James Sch. Bd., Highwood, Ill., 1978-80. Served with U.S. Army, 1954-56. Mem. Am. Inst. CPA's, Ill. Inst. CPA's, Nebr. Inst. CPA's. Republican. Roman Catholic. Club: Lake Barrington Shores Country. Home: 723 C Shoreline Rd Barrington IL 60010 Office: Underwriters Salvage Co 1270 W Northwest Hwy Palatine IL 60067

MIDDLETON, MARC STEPHEN, corporate insurance specialist; b. Louisville, Dec. 7, 1950; s. Joseph Scott and Virginia Marie (Schuler) M.; m. Carmen Teresa Fauscette, Feb. 22, 1969; 1 child, Marc Christopher. AA, Dalton Jr. Coll., 1970; BBA, U. Ga., 1972. Sr. risk analyst Deere and Co., Moline, Ill., 1973-78, mgr. corp. claims, 1978-79, mgr. corp. ins. dept., 1980-86; v.p. risk mgmt. services John Deere Ins. Group, Moline, 1987—; v.p. Tahoe Ins. Co., Reno, 1981-83, Sierra Gen. Life Ins. Co., Reno, 1981-83, Continental Guaranty, Ltd., Hamilton, Bermuda, 1981-83. Mem. Citizen's Adv. Council to East Moline (Ill.) Sch. Bd., 1978-80; coach YMCA Youth Basketball, Moline, 1978. Mem. Risk and Ins. Mgmt. Soc., Risk Mgmt. Council of Machinery and Allied Products Inst., Captive Ins. Cos. Assn., ESIS (Delphi panel 1985—). Roman Catholic. Avocations: tennis, hunting, fishing, woodworking. Home: 2909 55th St Ct Moline IL 61265 Office: Deere and Co John Deere Rd Moline IL 61265

MIDDLETON, RICKY LEE, lawyer; b. Flint, Mich., Apr. 27, 1949; s. LeRoy Burton and Darlene Hazel (Tennant) M. AA, Canada Coll., 1972; BA, San Jose State U., 1974; MA, Cen. Mich. U., 1977; JD, Thomas M. Cooley Sch. Law, 1982. Bar: Mich. 1985, U.S. Dist. Ct. (ea. dist.) Mich. 1986. Tchr. Planada (Calif.) Child Devel. Ctr., 1972-74; probation officer State of Mich. 90th Dist. Ct., Petoskey, 1978-80; gen. sales mgr. Orion Prodns., Lake Orion, Mich., 1981-85; pres. Champions Choice, Ltd., East Lansing, Mich., 1983—; sole practice East Lansing, 1986—; pres., bd. dirs. Mich. Basketball Adv. Council, 1981—; pres. Middleton Place North Law. Author (rulebook) Official Rulebook of 3-Player Basketball, 1983. Lectr. consequences of drunk driving. Named Disting. Sportsman Mich. Basketball Adv. Council, 1986. Mem. Am. Trial Lawyers Assn., Mich. State Bar Assn., Ingham County Bar Assn., Am. 3-Player Basketball Assn. (pres., bd. dirs. 1983—). Home: 13455 Dawn Dew Dr #5 DeWitt MI 48823 Office: PO Box 4494 East Lansing MI 48823 Office: Middleton Place North PO Box 206 DeWitt MI 48820

MIDLARSKY, ELIZABETH STECKEL, psychology educator; b. N.Y.C.; d. Abraham and Frances Lucille Rae (Wiener) Steckel; m. Manus I. Midlarsky, June 25, 1961; children: Susan Rachel, Miriam Joyce, Michael George. BA magna cum laude, CUNY, Bklyn., 1961; MA, Northwestern U., 1966, PhD, 1968. Lic. psychologist, Mich., Colo. Asst. prof. psychology U. Denver, 1968-73; dir. research and evaluation Park East Mental Health Ctr., Denver, 1973-74; assoc. prof. Met. State Coll., Denver, 1974-77; from assoc. prof. to prof. U. Detroit, 1977—, chmn. dept. psychology, 1978-81; dir. Ctr. for Study of Devel. and Aging, Detroit, 1981—; postdoctoral tng. faculty Wayne State U., Detroit, 1983-85; mem. rev. commn. NIH Human Devel.-2, Bethesda, Md., 1986—, NIMH, Rockville, Md., 1976-82; cons. NIH, Nat. Heart, Lung and Blood Inst., Bethesda, 1985—. Co-editor Humboldt Jour. Social Rehab., 1987; contbr. articles to profl. jours. and chpts. to books. Grantee Nat. Assn. Sch. Psychology, 1985-86, Nat. Inst. Aging, 1982-85, 87-89, Am. Assn. Retired Persons Andrus Found., 1982-83, 87-88. Fellow Am. Psychol. Assn.; mem. Gerontol. Soc. Am., Am. Orthopsychiat. Assn., Soc. Psychol. Study of Social Issues, Mich. Psychol. Assn. (exec. com., editor Acad. Psychol. Bull. 1982-86), Phi Beta Kappa, Sigma Xi, Psi Chi. Jewish. Avocations: writing poetry, singing, playing piano. Office: U Detroit Dept Psychology Detroit MI 48221

MIDLOCK, EUGENE JOSEPH, accountant; b. Joliet, Ill., Apr. 13, 1944; s. Louis R. and Joan (Hlavajcik) M.; m. Penelope Quayle, Sept. 14, 1978; 1 child, Stefanie. BS in Acctg., Lewis U., 1966; MBA in Acctg., DePaul U., 1968, MS in Taxation, 1977; postgrad., Harvard U. CPA, Ill. Tax acct. Ernst & Ernst, Chgo., 1968-72; supr. Ernst & Ernst, Honolulu, 1972-74; mgr. Ernst & Whinney, Brussels, Belgium, 1977-78; ptnr. in charge comml. taxation Peat, Marwick, Main & Co., Chgo., 1979—; speaker in field. Contbr. articles to profl. jours. Bd. dirs. Scholarship and Guidance Assn., Chgo.; trustee Lewis U., Romeoville, Ill. Served to 1st lt., U.S. Army N.G., 1968-74. Mem. Am. Inst. CPA's, Ill. Soc. CPA's (chmn. internat. bus. com. 1986—), Belgium Am. C. of C., Netherlands Am. C. of C. Clubs: Elmoor Country (Highland Park, Ill.); Mid Am. (Chgo.), Mid Day. Avocations: reading, chess, travel, golf. Home: 1301 Woodhill Ln Lake Forest IL 60045 Office: Peat Marwick Main & Co 303 E Wacker Dr Chicago IL 60601

MIEDEMA, SYLVIA ANN, banker; b. Chgo., June 19, 1904; m. Charles L. Klima, Jr. (dec.); children—Carol L. Martin, Charles L. III; m. Jacob A. Miedema (dec.). Student pub. schs. Dir., asst. sec. Clyde Savs. & Loan Assn., North Riverside, Ill., 1927-33, co-mgr., 1933-51, mgr., pres., 1951—, chmn., 1974—; pres., bd. dirs. Thaler Corp., N. Riverside; bd. dirs. Clyde Service Corp., Home Loan Assocs. Chgo.; chartering dir., cashier Bank for Savs. & Loan Assns., Chgo., 1968—; chartering dir. Darien Bank, Ill., 1972—; mem. Gov.'s Gannon/Proctor Commn., 1982—. Founder, pres. Burnham PTA; pres. Cicero Edn. Council, Ill.; bd. govs. Cicero Community Chest, 1970-75; bd. sponsors Evang. Hosp. Assn., Oak Brook, Ill. 1977—; mem. Berwyn-Cicero Council on Aging, 1977—; mem. adv. bd. South Suburban Home Health Service Inc., North Riverside, 1975—; chmn. North Riverside United Way drive, 1986-87. Recipient citation U.S. Treasury Dept., 1943; Women of Achievment award Dist. I, Ill. Fedn. Bus. and Profl. Women's Club, 1970; Plaque Czechoslovak Savs. & Loan League, 1978; Arnold J. Rauen Legis. Commendation award, 1984. Mem. Ill. Savs. and Loan League (chmn. adv. com. to bd. dirs. 1971-73, bd. dirs., exec. com. 1975-76, mem. polit. liaison com. legis. sect. 1976—), U.S. Savs. and Loan League (com. internat. ops. 1973, mem. mgmt. com. 1974-75), U.S. League Savs. Assns., Ill. Savs. and Loan Bd., U.S. League Savs. Assns. (mem. legis. com. 1982—), Ill. Fedn. Bus. and Profl. Women's Club.

MIELKE, WILLIAM JOHN, civil engineer; b. Waukesha, Wis., May 20, 1947; s. John Horace and Lois Margaret (Trakel) M.; m. Barbra Jean Mahnke, Dec. 28, 1968; 1 child, Anne Marie. BS in Civil Engring., U. Wis., 1971. Registered profl. engr., land surveyor, Wis. Field engr. Wis. Dept. Nat. Resources, Madison, 1968-70; civil engr. Ruekert & Mielke, Inc., Waukesha, 1971—, chief exec. officer, 1982—. Mem. Legis. Study Com. Milw. Sewerage Dist., 1985-86; mem. Southeastern Wis. Regional Planning Commn. Com., Waukesha, 1986; mem. League of Wis. Municipalities Com., Madison, 1986-87. Mem. Nat. Soc. Profl. Engrs. (chmn. profl. selection com. 1986—), Nat. Profl. Engrs. in Pvt. Practice, Wis. Soc. Profl. Engrs. (pres. Waukesha chapt. 1981-82, Young Engr. of Yr. 1982), Wis. Profl. Engrs. in Pvt. Practice (chmn. 1986-87), Wis. Assn. Cons. Engrs. (pres. elect 1987), Am. Pub. Works Assn., Am. Waterworks Assn. Republican. Episcopalian. Avocations: private pilot, scuba diving, sports. Home: 640 Glenview Oconomowoc WI 53066 Office: Ruekert & Mielke Inc 419 Frederick St Waukesha WI 53186

MIFSUD, PAUL CHARLES, real estate design and development company executive; b. Jan. 25, 1947; m. Brenda Kay Mifsud; children: Paula, Charles, Anthony. BBA, Angelo State U., San. Angelo, Tex., 1970; postgrad., Pace U., 1971-72; MBA, Case Western Res. U., 1975. Held several exec. positions Irving Trust Co., N.Y.C., 1970-72; asst. cashier Union Commerce Bank, Cleve., 1972-73, asst. v.p., 1973-77, v.p., 1977-81; exec. v.p. Voinovich Cos., Cleve., 1981-87, pres., 1987—. Asst. cubmaster Boy Scouts Am., 1981-83; co-chmn. Berea Civic Ctr. Com., 1975; mem. Greater Cleve. Growth Assn., 1973—; Citizens League Greater Cleve., 1973—; Berea Hist. Soc., 1978-84; active. Greater Cleve. Girl Scouts Devel. Com., 1981-84; trustee Woodvale Union Cemetary, 1981-83; chmn. bd., founder Maltese Am. Found., 1985—; council mem. Cuyahoga Parma Geauga Employment Consortium, 1979-80; councilman-at-large City of Berea, 1980-81; vice chmn. Cuyahoga County Rep. Exec. Com, 1978-84; fin. chmn. Whipple Mayor Com., 1983—; fundrasing coordinator Voinovich for Mayor Com. 1984-86; active Fund for Am's Future, 1985—; bd. dirs. Medina County Mental Health Bd., 1986—; fin. dir. Friends of Voinovich U.S. Senate Com., 1986—. Served with USAF, 1966-70; chmn. Bush for Pres. Com., Cuyahoga county, 1979. Name one of Outstanding Young Men. Am. U.S. Jaycees, 1978-82; recipient Disting. Pub. Service award Cleve. Area Middle East Orgn., 1981. Mem. Am. Correctional Assn., Soc. Mktg. Profl. Services, Adminstrv. Mgmt. Soc., Am. Bankers Assn. (com. on telecommunication, conf. planning coms. 1977, 80, 81, chmn. bd. 1981), Am. Inst. Banking, Bank Adminstrn. Inst., Am. Mgmt. Assn. Mem. st. Francis Xavier Ch. Avocations: philately, photography, fishing, gardening. Office: Voinovich Co 2450 Prospect Ave Cleveland OH 44115

MIGALA, LUCYNA, broadcaster, journalist, radio station executive; b. Krakow, Poland, May 22, 1944; d. Joseph and Estelle (Suwala) M.; came to U.S., 1947, naturalized, 1955; student Loyola U., Chgo., 1962-63, Chicago Conservatory of Music, 1963-70; B.S. in Journalism, Northwestern U., 1966. Radio announcer, producer sta. WOPA, Oak Park, Ill., 1963-66; writer, reporter, producer NBC news, Chgo., 1966-69, 1969-71, producer NBC local news, Washington, 1969; producer, coordinator NBC network news, Cleve., 1971-78, field producer, Chgo., 1978-79; v.p. Migala Communications Corp., 1979—; program dir., on-air personality Sta. WCEV, Cicero, Ill., 1979—; lectr. City Colls. Chgo., 1981. Columnist Free Press, Chgo., 1984—. Soloist, mgr. Lira Singers, Chgo., 1965—; mem., chmn. various cultural coms. Polish Am. Congress, 1970—; bd. dirs. Nationalities Services Center, Cleve., 1973-78; exec. com. Ill. Humanities Council, 1985-86, bd. dirs. 1983—; bd. dirs., v.p. Cicero-Berwyn Fine Arts Council, Cicero, Ill.; v.p. Chgo. chpt. Kosciuszko Found., 1983—; bd. dirs. Polish Women's Alliance Am., 1983—; gen. chmn. Midwest Chopin Piano Competition, 1984-86 ; mem. ethnic and folk arts panel Ill. Arts Council, 1984—. Washington Journalism Center fellow, spring 1969. Mem. Sigma Delta Chi. Office: Sta WCEV 5356 W Belmont Ave Chicago IL 60641

MIGDAL, SHELDON PAUL, lawyer; b. Chgo., July 3, 1936; s. Joseph David and Regina (Strasburg) M.; m. Barbara Simon, June 6, 1961; children—Pamela Anne, Andrew Alan. B.S., U. Ill., 1958; J.D., Northwestern U., 1961. Bar: Ill. 1961, C.P.A., Ill. Spl. trial atty. U.S. Dept. Justice, Washington, 1961-67; assoc. Dixon, Todhunter, Knouff & Holmes, Chgo., 1967; ptnr. Wildman, Harrold, Allen & Dixon, Chgo., 1968—. Pres., bd. dirs. Better Boys Found., Chgo., 1968—. Mem. ABA, Chgo. Bar Assn., Ill. Bar Assn., Chgo. Council of Lawyers. Home: 3552 N Pine Grove Chicago IL 60657 Office: Wildman Harrold Allen & Dixon One IBM Plaza Suite 3000 Chicago IL 60611

MIGLIORINO, ROBERT ROY, osteopathic physician, health care facility executive; b. Paterson, N.J., Mar. 8, 1941; s. Roy Charles and Albina Josephine (Litwin) M. BS, Upsala Coll., East Orange, N.J., 1963; DO, Kirksville Coll. Osteo. Medicine, 1971. Gen. practice osteo. medicine 1972-82; med. dir. Ft. Wayne State Devel. Ctr., 1982-86, No. Ind. State Devel. Ctr., 1986—. Served to 1st lt. U.S. Army, 1963-67, flight surgeon USAF Res. Mem. AMA, Am. Osteo. Assn., Ind. State Med. Assn., Ind. Assn. Osteo. Physicians and Surgeons, Aerospace Med. Assn., Soc. USAF Flight Surgeons, Mil. Osteo. Physicians Assn., Am. Radio Relay League. Roman Catholic. Lodges: Shriners, Masons. Avocations: amateur radio, cross country skiing. Office: NISDC 1234 N Notre Dame PO Box 1995 South Bend IN 46634-1995

MIHAILOVIC, BETTY LOU BONWELL, nurse educator; b. Chrisman, Ill., Nov. 17, 1937; d. Robert Bertram Bonwell and Katherine Carol (Hess) Bonwell Buchanan; m. Vladimir Mihailovic, Jan. 27, 1968 (div. May 1970); children—Jill Anne Thompson, Nena Carol. Diploma, LakeView Hosp., Danville, Ill., 1958; B., U. Ill.-Chgo., 1966; M., DePaul U., 1970. Registered nurse, Ill. Staff nurse LakeView Hosp., Danville, Ill., 1958-63; instr. nursing Danville Jr. Coll., 1963-65; tchr. nursing Chgo. Pub. Schs., 1966-68; instr. Mt. Sinai Hosp., Chgo., 1970; prof. nursing Kennedy King Coll., Chgo., 1970—, chmn. dept. nursing, 1983-86. Served to maj. USAFR. Recipient Chief Nurse award USAF, 1975, Sr. Flight Nurse award USAF, 1984. Mem. Am. Nurses Assn., Nat. League Nursing, Res. Officers Assn. (treas. 1980), U. Ill. Alumni Assn., Aerospace Med. Assn., Assn. Mil. Surgeons of U.S., Air Force Assn. Republican. Mem. Soc. of Friends. Lodge: Order Eastern Star. Avocation: golf. Home: 1 Heatherwood Ct Indian Head Park IL 60525 Office: Kennedy King Coll 6800 S Wentworth Ave Chicago IL 60621

MIHALEVICH, LAWRENCE JAMES, pharmacist; b. Kansas City, Mo., Aug. 3, 1951; s. Doctor Richard Anthony Mihalevich and Cheryl Kathryn (Dillon) Goodnight; m. Christine Louise Smith, Oct. 23, 1976; children: Jamie Leigh, Nickolas Anthony, Emily Christine. B.S. in Biology, Northeast Mo. State U., 1975; B.S. in Med. Tech., Kirksville Osteo. Hosp., 1976; B.S. in Pharmacy, U. Mo.-Kansas City, 1980. Lic. pharmacist, Iowa, Mo. Med. technologist Kirksville-Osteo. Hosp., Mo., 1976-77; pharmacist, mgr. The Medicine Store, Mt. Pleasant, Iowa, 1980-84; pharmacist, asst. mgr. K Mart Pharmacy, Burlington, Iowa, 1984-85; pharmacist mgr. Wal-Mart Pharmacy, Mt. Pleasant, Iowa, 1985—. Vice pres. Mt. Pleasant Jaycees, 1982-84, bd. dirs., 1981-82; city council mem. at large, 1986—; bd. dirs. Nat. Kidney Found. of Iowa, 1982—. Mem. Nat. Assn. Retail Druggists, Iowa Pharmacy Assn. (del. 1983, 84, legis. com. 1983, 84), Mo. Acad. Sci. Presbyterian. Avocations: track sports; travel. Home: 910 Hill Ave Mount Pleasant IA 52641 Office: Wal-Mart Pharmacy US 218 and Maple Leaf Mount Pleasant IA 52641

MIHLBAUGH, ROBERT HOLLERAN, lawyer; b. Lima, Ohio, June 17, 1932; s. Edward P. and Mary Elizabeth May (Holleran) M.; m. Barbara Lee Synck; children—Robert E. H., Michael Patrick. A.B., Notre Dame U., 1954, J.D., 1957. Bar: Ohio, 1957. Legal asst. fed. judge, South Bend, Ind., 1957-59; trial lawyer Marathon Oil Co., Findlay, Ohio, 1959-64; sole practice, Lima, Ohio, 1964—. Author: Marketing Manual, 1960; Sale Leaseback Financing, 1961. Dem. state central committeeman, Ohio, 1966-80; sec. Ohio Dem. party, 1976; mem. nat. adv. bd. SBA, Washington, 1965. Mem. ABA, Am. Arbitration Assn., Ohio State Bar Assn. (life). Roman Catholic. Avocation: lectr. Queen Elizabeth II. Home: 1471 W Market Blvd Lima OH 45805 Office: Mihlbaugh Bldg Lima OH 45802

MIHM, MICHAEL MARTIN, judge; b. Amboy, Ill., May 18, 1943; s. Martin Clarence and Frances Johannah (Morrissey) M.; m. Judith Ann Zosky, May 6, 1967; children—Molly Elizabeth, Sarah Ann, Jacob Michael, Jennifer Leah. B.A., Loras Coll., 1964; J.D., St. Louis U., 1967. Asst. prosecuting atty. St. Louis County, Clayton, Mo., 1967-68; asst. state's atty. Peoria County, Peoria, Ill., 1968-69; asst. city atty. City of Peoria, Ill., 1969-72; state's atty. Peoria County, Peoria, Ill., 1972-80; sole practice Peoria, Ill., 1980-82; U.S. dist. judge U.S. Govt., Peoria, Ill., 1982—. Past mem. adv. bd. Big Brothers-Big Sisters, Crisis Nursery, Peoria; past bd. dirs. Salvation Army, Peoria, W.D. Boyce council Boy Scouts Am., State of Ill. Treatment Alternatives to Street Crime, Gov.'s Criminal Justice Info. Council; past vice-chmn. Ill. Dangerous Drugs Adv. Council. Recipient Good Govt. award Peoria Jaycees, 1978. mem. Peoria County Bar Assn. (former bd. dirs., past chmn. entertainment com.), Ill. State Bar Assn. Roman Catholic. Clubs: St. Vincent DePaul Catholic Ch. and Men's; Mt. Hawley Country. Office: US Dist Ct 100 NE Monroe St Peoria IL 61601

MIKOLAJCZAK, JAMES ROBERT, psychiatrist; b. St. Louis, Jan. 24, 1947; s. Gustave and Gertrude (Fehlig) M.; m. Kathleen M. McDonald, Jan. 27, 1948; children: Karen, Peter. BS, St. Louis U., 1968, MD, 1972. Diplomate Nat. Bd. Med. Examiners, Am. Bd. Psychiatry and Neurology. Asst. clin. prof. psychiatry St. Louis U., 1975-86; clin. instr. psychiatry Washington U. Sch. Medicine, St. Louis, 1986—; mem. staff Jewish Hosp. St. Louis, 1986—; cons. Bur. of the Blind, St. Louis, Vocat. Rehab., St. Louis, Program on Aging Jewish Hosp., St. Louis, 1986—. Mem. Am. Psychiat. Assn., Am. Psychoanalytic Assn. Avocation: collecting rare books. Home: 414 Westrick Kirkwood MO 63122 Office: 4524 Forest Park Saint Louis MO 63108

MIKOS, DAVID EDWARD, architect; b. Chgo., Mar. 7, 1955; s. Edward J. and Anne (Latala) M.; m. Miranda M. Jevtovic, Sept. 13, 1980; 1 child, Arielle Anne. BArch with highest honors, U. Ill., 1978. Staff architect Children's Meml. Hosp., Chgo., 1977-83; sr. health designer Perkins & Will Architects, Chgo., 1983-85; pres. Anderson Mikos Architects, Chgo., 1985—; lectr. U. Ill., Chgo., 1980-81. Works include outpatient surg. facility, MRI, Cancer Ctr. Ingall's Meml. Hosp., Harvey, Ill., Children's Meml. Hosp., U. Chgo. Med. Ctr., Northwestern Meml. Hosp., Erlanger Med. Ctr., Chattanooga, Western Res. Care SYstem, Youngstown, Ohio. Contbr. articles to profl. jours. Mem. AIA (nat. com. health, Chgo. chpt. com. health), Am. Assn. Hosp. Planning, Internat. Hosp. Fedn. Office: Anderson Mikos Architects 53 W Jackson Suite 215 Chicago IL 60641

MIKRUT, JOHN JOSEPH, JR., labor arbitrator, educator; b. Erie, Pa., Mar. 23, 1944; s. John Joseph and Helen Frances (Dorobiala) M.; B.S., Edinboro Coll., 1966; postgrad. U. Mass., 1966-68; Ed.D., U. Mo., Columbia, 1976; m. Lois Ann Leonard, Aug. 26, 1968. Intern edn. dept. United Steelworkers Am., Pitts., 1967-68; instr. labor studies Pa. State U., 1968-69; labor specialist, asso. prof. labor edn. U. Mo., Columbia, 1969—; labor arbitrator Nat. Rail Adjustment Bd., Am. Can Co., Steelworkers' Union, U.S. Postal Service, Am. Postal Workers Union, Nat. Assn. Letter Carriers; mem. labor arbitration panels Fed. Mediation Conciliation Service, Nat. Mediation Bd., Am. Arbitration Assn. Chmn., City of Columbia Personnel Adv. Bd., 1976—; chmn. Columbia Mayor's Spl. Labor Negotiations Rev. Com. Mem. Nat. Acad. Arbitrators, Soc. Profls. Dispute Resolution, Iowa Pub. Employee Relations Bd., Kans. Pub. Employee Relations Bd., Ill. Edn. Employee Relations Bd., Univ. and Coll. Labor Edn. Assn., Indsl. Relations and Research Assn. Contbr. articles to profl. jours. Home: 2236 Country Ln Columbia MO 65201 Office: Univ Mo Dept Labor Edn 413 Lewis Hall Columbia MO 65211

MIKULIN, PAUL S., health care executive; b. Cleve., Nov. 2, 1950; s. George J. and Mary A. (Migalic) M.; m. Patricia A. Skotko, July 27, 1974; children: Matthew, Michael. AS, Cuyahoga Community Coll., 1974; BS, Baldwin-Wallace Coll., 1978. Respiratory therapist St. Vincent Charity Hosp., Cleve., 1969-72, dir. respiratory therapy, 1972-79; adminstr. Esther Marie Nursing Ctr., Geneva, Ohio, 1979-81; regional coordinator Van Dyke Health Care Mgmt., Inc., Peoria, Ill., 1981—; trustee Health Ventures Inc., Cleve., 1983—. Bd. dirs. Geneva Civic Ctr., 1982-84, Geneva Area Human Services, 1983. Mem. Ohio Healthcare Assn. (membership com. 1985—, team capt. area rev. 1984—, profl. devel. com. 1983), Geneva Jaycees (pres. 1984-85). Lodges: Rotary. Avocations: scuba diving, boating, hunting. Home: 4933 N Myers Rd Geneva OH 44041 Office: Van Dyke Healthcare Mgmt 162 S Broadway Geneva OH 44041

MILAM, HUGH HENRY, public relations executive, educator; b. Houston, Mar. 17, 1941; s. Hugh Henry and Rosalie Cornelia (McClamrock) M.; m. Carol Ann Marsh, Mar. 3, 1941; children—Melanie Lyn, Tod Warner. B.S., U. Houston, 1965; M.S., East Tex. State U., 1969; Ph.D., Tex. A&M U., 1975. Editor, Fort Bend Mirror, Rosenberg, Tex., 1962-65; pub. relations exec. LTV Electrosystems, Inc., Greenville & Dallas, 1967-71; dir. pub. relations Bee County Coll., Beeville, Tex., 1971-73; researcher Tex. A&M U., College Station, 1973-75; dir. pub. relations Dundalk Community Coll., Balt., 1975-76; asst. prof. journalism Ball State U., Muncie, Ind., 1976-79; assoc. dean, assoc. prof. journalism and mass communication Drake U., Des Moines, 1979—; v.p. Directions, Inc., 1980—; dir. Communications Research, LKC, Inc. Mem. Public Relations Soc. Am., Internat. Assn. Bus. Communicators, Am. Mktg. Assn. Methodist. Home: 4026 Kingman Blvd Des Moines IA 50311 Office: Dept Journalism Drake U Des Moines IA 50311

MILANO, ROBERT L., chemical company executive; b. Oak Park, Ill., July 16, 1960; s. Robert N. Milano and Saranne (Schumacher) M. BS, Purdue U., 1982; postgrad., N.D. State U., 1983. Asst. fisheries biologist Ind. Dept. Natural Resources, Indpls., 1982-83; asst. to v.p. George C. Brandt Inc., Elmhurst, Ill., 1983—. Religious educator St. John of the Cross Ch., Western Springs, Ill., 1985—. Mem. Chgo. Soc. for Coatings Tech., Chgo. Printing Ink Prodn. Assn., Wis. Paint & Coatings Assn. (program chmn. 1987—), Am. Fisheries Soc. Avocations: skiing, outdoor education, antiques. Home: 25-A Kingery Quarter Apt #102 Hinsdale IL 60521

MILBRATH, DOUGLAS E., accountant; b. Bottineau, N.D., May 15, 1953; s. Earl Morris and Pearl Marion (Robertson) M.; m. Debra Lynn Ungerathen, July 12, 1986. AA, Lake Region Jr. Coll., 1973; BBA, U. N.D., 1975. Tax acct. Keller-Raymo, Bottineau, 1975-77; farmer Milbrath Farms, Bottineau, 1977—. Treas. New Non-Partisan League, State of N.D., 1980—. Mem. Farm Bur. of N.D. Avocations: hunting, horses, photography.

MILBURN, THOMAS WALLACE, psychology educator; b. Newkirk, Okla., Jan. 29, 1923; s. Thomas McKay and Alice Beatrice (Wallace) M.; m. Joanne Nichols Fellows, Oct. 19, 1947; children: Peter Benedict, Michael Andrew, Alison Kathleen. BA in Psychology, Stanford U., 1951, MA in Psychology, 1955, PhD in Psychology, 1959. Lic. psychologist, Ohio, Calif. Counselor, research asst. Counseling Ctr. Stanford U., Palo Alto, Calif., 1954-57; head employee devel. div. U.S. Naval Ordnance Test Sta., China Lake, Calif., 1957-1967, head, behavioral sci. group, research social psychologist, 1959-62; vis. assoc. prof. Northwestern U., Evanston, Ill., 1965-68; prof. psychology DePaul U., Chgo., 1968-71; Mershon prof. psychology and pub. policy Ohio State U., Columbus, 1971—; expert cons. U.S. Navy Research and Devel. Ctr., San Diego, 1985-86; exec. participant Fed. Exec. Inst., Charlottesville, Va. Author: (with K.H. Watman) The Nature of Threat, 1976; contbr. articles to profl. jours. Resource chmn. Columbus Area Internat. Program, 1980—. Served with USN, 1943-46, PTO. Recipient Outstanding Service award Ohio State U. Council of Grad.

Students, 1984-85. Fellow AAAS, Am. Psychol. Assn.; mem. Internat. Soc. for Polit. Psychology, Internat. Studies Assn., Cen. Ohio Psychol. Assn. (pres 1986), Sigma Xi.. Democrat. Episcopalian. Club: Open Ct. (Columbus) (pres. 1986—), Copa (Columbus) (pres. 1986-87). Avocations: bicycling, rowing, racquetball, sailing, writing fiction. Home: 205 E South St Worthington OH 43085 Office: Ohio State U 1712 Neil Ave Columbus OH 43210

MILES, ALFRED LEE, educator; b. Eaton, Ohio, Aug. 4, 1913; s. James Sampson and Grace Blanche (Bittner) M.; m. Margaret Lucille Saul, Mar. 18, 1936 (div. Mar. 1949); children: Ronald Lynn, Walter Whitney; m. Virginia Null Engelman, Feb. 24, 1951; children: Victoria Ellen, Kimber Lee, Bethany Laine, Christopher, Kent; stepchildren: Dianne Fogle, Norbert Nicholas Engelman, Jr. Student Ohio State U., 1930-33, Sinclair Coll., 1945, Miami-Jacobs Coll., 1954-56. Instr. pvt. courses in real estate prins. and real estate law, Dayton, Ohio, 1949—; instr. real estate Miami Jacobs Jr. Coll. Bus., 1983—; instr. short courses Spl. Sessions Div. U. Dayton, 1971-77. Violinist, Dayton Civic Orch., 1927-29, Ohio State U. Symphony, 1930-33, Columbus Symphony, 1930-33. Named Ky. col. Mem. Internat. Platform Assn. Republican. Methodist. Club: Cincinnati. Home: 1629 Far Hills Ave Dayton OH 45419 Office: 2185 S Dixie Ave Dayton OH 45409

MILES, CHARLES HENRY, data processing training executive; b. Marshfield, Wis., June 7, 1947; s. Henry Charles and Laura Eda (Nelson) M.; m. Linda Arleen Hupe, Nov. 16, 1968; children: Richard, Roy. BS in Applied Scis., U. Wis., Parkside, 1977. Enlisted USN, Milw., 1967, advanced through ranks to petty officer 1st class, 1972, resigned, 1976; instr. bldg. automation systems tng. Johnson Controls Inc., Milw., 1977-78, supr., 1978-84, mgr. computer based tng., 1985—; lectr. Assn. Sch. Bus Officials, Atlantic City, 1984. Scoutmaster Boy Scouts Am., San Francisco, Racine, Wis., 1972—; youth advisor St. Andrew Luth. Ch., Racine, 1985—. Recipient Dist. Merit award Boy Scouts Am., 1981, Silver Beaver award Boy Scouts Am., 1983, Lamb award Luth. Ch. Am., 1986. Mem. Am. Soc. Tng. Devel. (pres. 1977, chmn. computer based tng. spl. interest group 1983-85, speaker V conf. 1986, Excellence in Tng. award 1985), Assn. Devel. Computer Based Instl. Systems. Avocation: camping. Office: Johnson Controls Inc 507 E Michigan St Milwaukee WI 53202

MILES, MICHAEL ARNOLD, food company executive; b. Chgo., June 22, 1939; s. Arnold and Alice (Morrissey) M.; m. Pamela L. Miles; children: Michael Arnold Jr., Christopher. B.S., Northwestern U., 1961. Various mgmt. positions to v.p., account supr. Leo Burnett Co., Inc., 1961-71; with Heublein, Inc., 1971-82, sr. v.p. mktg. Ky. Fried Chicken, 1971-72, v.p. gen. mgr. grocery products, 1972-75, internat., 1975-77, v.p. group exec. Internat. group, chmn. foodservice and franchise group Ky. Fried Chicken, 1977-81, sr. v.p. foods, Louisville, 1981-82; pres., chief operating officer Kraft, Inc., Glenview, Ill., 1982—; dir. Capital Holding Corp., Citizens Fidelity Corp., Dart & Kraft, Inc. Bd. dirs. Lyric Opera Chgo.; mem. adv. council J.L. Kellogg Grad. Sch. Mgmt. Northwestern U., Evanston, Ill. Office: Kraft Inc Kraft Court Glenview IL 60025 *

MILES, RANDALL JAY, agronomy educator; b. Crawfordsville, Ind., Oct. 27, 1952; s. Robert Francis and Betty Imogene (Campbell) M. BS, Purdue U., 1974, MS, 1976; PhD, Tex. A&M U., 1981. Instr. Tex. A&M U., College Station, 1976-81; asst. prof. agronomy U. Tenn., Knoxville, 1981-83, U. Mo., Columbia, 1983—; faculty advisor Farmhouse Frat., Knoxville, 1981-83, Columbia, 1986—. Contbr. articles to profl. jours. Mo. Dept. Natural Resources grantee, 1985. Mem. Am. Soc. Agronomy (div. chmn. 1986), Soil Sci. Soc. Am., Council Agrl. Sci. and Tech., AAAS, Sigma Xi (assoc.). Mem. Christian Ch. Avocations: spectator sports, gardening, woodworking, auto racing. Office: U Mo Dept Agronomy Columbia MO 65211

MILES, THOMAS TIMOTHY, communication educator; b. Terre Haute, Ind., Sept. 20, 1940; s. Victor Paul and Alberta Elizabeth (Arvin) M.; m. Sylvia Mary Palmer, Aug. 21, 1965; children: Deborah Louise, Craig Victor. BS, Ind. State U., 1963, MS, 1969, Advanced Degree in Edn., 1970; PhD, U. Iowa, 1973. Customer tng. Vertol div. Boeing, Phila., 1967-68; media cons. U. Iowa, Iowa City, 1970-72; dir., media instr. U. Akron, Ohio, 1972-84, asst. dir. library, 1984-86, assoc. prof., 1986—; bd. dirs. P.B.S. TV Station, Kent, Ohio, 1972-86. Candidate City Council, Wadsworth, Ohio, 1983, Sch. Bd., Wadsworth, 1980. Served to comdr. USN, 1964-67. Named to Ky. Col. Commonwealth of Ky., 1986. Mem. Assn. Ednl. Communications and Tech., Ohio Post-Secondary Telecommunications Council. Avocations: salt and fresh water fishing, outdoor activities. Home: 488 Cranberry Ln Wadsworth OH 44281 Office: U Akron 302 E Buchtel Ave Akron OH 44385

MILES, WENDELL A., federal judge; b. Holland, Mich., Apr. 17, 1916; s. Fred T. and Dena Del (Alverson) M.; m. Mariette Bruckert, June 8, 1946; children: Lorraine Miles Rector, Michelle Miles Kopinski, Thomas Paul. A.B., Hope Coll., 1938, LL.D. (hon.), 1980; M.A., U. Wyo., 1939; J.D., U. Mich., 1942; LL.D. (hon.), Detroit Coll. Law, 1979. Bar: Mich. Ptnr. Miles & Miles, Holland, 1948-53, Miles, Mika, Meyers, Beckett & Jones, Grand Rapids, Mich., 1961-70; pros. atty. County of Ottawa, Mich., 1949-53; U.S. dist. atty. Western Dist. Mich., Grand Rapids, 1953-60; U.S. dist. judge Western Dist. Mich., 1974—, chief judge, 1979-86, sr. chief judge, 1986—; circuit judge 20th Jud. Circuit Ct. Mich., 1970-74; instr. Hope Coll., 1948-53, Am. Inst. Banking, 1953-60; adj. prof. Am. constl. history Hope Coll., Holland, Mich., 1979—; mem. Mich. Higher Edn. Commn. Pres. Holland Bd. Edn., 1952-63. Served to capt. U.S. Army, 1942-47. Recipient Liberty Bell award, 1986. Fellow Am. Bar Found.; mem. Am., Mich., Fed., Ottawa County bar assns., Grand Rapids Bar, Am. Judicature Soc. Club: Torch. Lodges: Rotary; Masons. Office: US Dist Ct 482 Fed Bldg 110 Michigan St NW Grand Rapids MI 49503

MILEWSKI, MICHAEL GREGORY, military officer; b. Lancaster, Calif., Aug. 21, 1958; s. John Anthony and Joan Elaine (Rutledge) M.; m. Stacy Jean Snell, July 4, 1981. BA in Biology, Cen. U. Iowa, 1979; MBA, Golden Gate U., 1983. Commd. 2d lt. USAF, 1979, advanced through grades to capt., 1983; served as systems analyst 2049 Communications Group USAF, McClellan AFB, Calif., 1980-82, chief computer software 2049 Communications Group, 1982-84; mgr. info. systems implementation HQ SAC USAF, Offutt AFB, Nebr., 1984-86, chief communications Airborne Command Post, 1986—; mgr. computer tng. HQ SAC/Six, Offutt AFB, 1985-86, dir. combined fed. campaign, 1985, Air Force Aid Soc., 1984. Mem. suprvisory com. bd. dirs. SAC Fed. Credit Union, Omaha, 1986; Tchr. Sunday Sch., Omaha, 1985. Mem. Co. Grade Officers Assn. Republican. Home: 3112 Leawood Dr Omaha NE 68123 Office: 1850 ACSQ/SIK Offutt AFB NE 68113

MILIACCA, JOHN MICHAEL, architect; b. Milw., Nov. 14, 1959; d. Livio John and Beverly Rose (Tobias) M. BS in Architecture, Lawrence Inst. Tech., 1981, BArch, 1982. Sec. Cityscape Detroit, 1985—; mem. Detroit Inst. Arts. Mem. AIA (assoc., com. chairperson 1986—). Roman Catholic. Avocations: sailing, travel, photography. Home: 1141 Holcomb Apt 403 Detroit MI 48214 Office: William Kessler & Assocs 733 Saint Antoine St Detroit MI 48226

MILINICHIK, STEPHEN JOHN, drilling and production engineer; b. Allentown, Pa., Aug. 13, 1959; s. Walter and Tessie (Slavish) M.; m. Robin Colleen Garrett, Aug. 1, 1985; children: Tyler James, Jay Stephen. Student, Lehigh U., 1977-79; BS, Pa. State U., 1982. Engr. trainee Getty Oil Co., Sweetwater, Tex., 1981; staff engr. Cities Service Oil and Gas Corp., Liberal, Kans., 1982—. Mem. Am. Petroleum Inst., Soc. Petroleum Engrs., U.S. Strategic Inst., Pa. State U. Alumni Assn. Republican. Mem. Eastern Orthodox Ch. Avocations: golf, weightlifting, softball, racquetball. Home: 200 W 10th Apt C Liberal KS 67901 Office: Cities Service Oil & Gas Co 21 Plaza Dr Liberal KS 67901

MILLAN, FELIX, physician; b. Mexico City, July 27, 1928; came to U.S., 1955; s. Ruben and Irene (Espindola) M.; m. Alice Sweeney (div. Apr. 1986); children: Mark, Justin. BS, U. Mex., 1946, MD, 1953. Diplomate Am. Bd. Physical Medicine and Rehab. Rotatory intern Luth. Hosp., Cleve., 1956-57; physical medicine and rehab. resident Highland View Hosp., Cleve., 1957-59, chief resident, 1960; dir. physical medicine and rehab. Wishard Hosp., Indpls., 1960-71; asst. dir. physical medicine and rehab. Lakeside VA Hosp., Chgo., 1971-75; med. dir. Main Clinic East Chicago, Ind., 1975—; cons. physical medicine and rehab. local hosps., Lake County, Ind., 1971—. Coach Munster (Ind.) Soccer Club, 1985—. Fellow Royal Soc. Health-London; mem. Am. Coll. Legal Medicine, Am. Coll. Internat. Physicians (pres. 1982), Ind. State Med. Assn. (commn. impaired physicians 1983—), Ind. State Soccer Assn. (pres. 1982-84, referee assessor 1985—), No. Ind. Referee Assn. (sec. 1986). Democrat. Roman Catholic. Avocations: hunting, gun collecting, mil. history, stamps. Office: Main Clinic East Chicago PO Box R East Chicago IN 46312

MILLER, A. C., provincial judge. Judge Ct. of Queen's Bench, Portage la Prairie, Man., Can. Office: Court of Queen's Bench, Court House, Portage la Praire, MB Canada R1N 1M9 *

MILLER, AGNES MARIE, community services advisor; b. Blacksher, Ala., Apr. 1, 1922; s. Thomas Mobley and Ella Belle (Thomas) Walker; m. Russell W. Miller Jr., July 26, 1947; children: Dana Maurice, Ricardo Cortez, Alton Glenn. Student, Highland Park (Mich.) Coll., 1940-42, Wayne State U., 1942-43, 77-78, Loretta Heights Coll., Denver, 1973, U. Mich., Southfield, 1974. Cert. social worker. Neighborhood and consumer affairs rep. HUD, Detroit, 1978-80, community services advisor, 1980-83; vol. community services advisor, Detroit, 1983—; vol. community social worker, Detroit, 1983—; guest lectr. Wayne State U. Sch. Social Work, 1977-80. Author: (anthology) Roots: Some Students Perspectives Readings in Black History and Culture. Pres. Inter-collegiate Council, Detroit, 1940-42, Sherrill Elem. Sch. PTA, 1960-63; asst. sec. Citizens Participatory Com., Detroit, Wayne County, 1965-67; 3d v.p. Women's Pub. Affairs Com. of 1000, Inc., Detroit, 1970-75; dir. pub. affairs Women's Conf. Concerns, Detroit, 1976-83. Recipient Cert. award for Friend to Edn., Wayne County Community Coll., 1967, spl. commendation award Women's Pub. Affairs Com. of 1000, Inc., 1967, Spirit of Detroit award City Council Detroit, 1980, Key to City of Flint Mayor James W. Rutherford, 1981; named Disting. Detroit Citizen, 1983. Mem. Soc. Consumer Affairs Profls. in Bus. Democrat. Baptist. Club: Arien Activist (Detroit). Avocations: writing, lecturing, reciting poetry. Home and Office: 7121 Linsdale St Detroit MI 48204

MILLER, ANGELA PEREZ, school administrator; b. Chgo., Oct. 1, 1936; d. Jesse and Emily (Ibarra) P.; m. John F. Miller, May 6, 1961 (div.); 1 son, Dion. B.A., U. Ill., 1958; M.A., Northeastern Ill. U., 1975; M.Ed., De Paul U., 1984. Cert. elem. tchr., Ill. Tchr. Chgo. pub. schs., 1962-70; exchange tchr. Mexico City schs., 1970-71; asst. prin. Burns Elem. Sch., Chgo., 1972-77; asst. prin. Benito Juarez High Sch., Chgo., 1977-85; field adminstr. Chgo. Pub. Schs., 1985—. Mem. ELValor, Inc., De Paul U. adv. com. on Hispanic affairs. Mem. Assn. Supervision and Curriculum Devel., Am. Ednl. Research Assn., Hispanic Alliance for Career Enhancement, Ill. Adminstrs. Acad. Office: 2250 N Clifton Chicago IL 60614

MILLER, ARTHUR HAWKS, JR., librarian, consultant; b. Kalamazoo, Mar. 15, 1943; s. Arthur Hawks and Eleanor (Johnson) M.; m. Janet Carol Schroeder, June 11, 1967; children—Janelle Aileen, Andrew Hawks. A.B., Kalamazoo Coll., 1965; student U. Caen, Calvados, France, 1963-64; A.M. in English, U. Chgo., 1966, A.M. in Librarianship, 1968; Ph.D., Northwestern U., 1973. Reference librarian Newberry Library, Chgo., 1966-69, asst. librarian pub. services, 1969-72; coll. librarian Lake Forest (Ill.) Coll., 1972—; mem. Ill. Library Computer System Policy Council, Chgo., 1982—. Pres. Lake Forest/Lake Bluff Hist. 1982-85; pres. Lake County Hist. Soc., 1985—, Friends of Lake Forest Library, 1986-87; trustee Ragdale Found., 1986— . Mem. ALA (chmn. history sect. 1982-83, chmn.-elect coll. sect. 1985—, chmn. coll. sect. 1986-87), Melville Soc. Am., Ill. Library Assn., U. Chgo. Grad. Library Sch. Alumni Assn. (pres. 1983-85). Presbyterian. Club: Caxton (pres. 1978-80) (Chgo.). Home: 169 Wildwood Rd Lake Forest IL 60045 Office: Lake Forest Coll Donnelley Library Lake Forest IL 60045

MILLER, BARRY JOSEPH, lawyer, architect; b. Rochester, N.Y., July 5, 1954; s. Alfred Frank and Norene Ann (Millner) M.; m. Susan Lynn Goldberg, Aug. 6, 1978; 1 child, Jessica Nicole. B Environ. Design, Miami U., Oxford, Ohio, 1977; MArch, Kent (Ohio) State U., 1979; JD, Case Western Res. U., 1983. Bar: Ohio 1983, D.C. 1985; registered architect, Ohio. Designer R.L. Bowen & Assocs., Cleve., 1979-80; architect Tuffs & Wenzel, Cleve., 1981-82; assoc. Arter & Hadden, Cleve., 1983—. Notes editor Case Western Res. U. Law Rev., 1982-83. Mem. AIA (chmn. chpt. com.), ABA, Fed. Bar Assn., Ohio Bar Assn., Greater Cleve. Bar Assn. Avocations: drawing, writing, reading, sports, family. Office: Arter & Hadden 1100 Huntington Bldg Cleveland OH 44115

MILLER, BEN, state supreme court justice; b. Springfield, Ill., Nov. 5, 1936; s. Clifford and Mary (Luthyens) M. B.A., So. Ill. U., 1958; J.D., Vanderbilt U., 1961. Bar: Ill. 1961. Ptnr. Olsen, Cantrill & Miller, Springfield, 1961-72; prin. Ben Miller-Law Office, Springfield, 1972-76; judge 7th jud. cir. Ill. Cir. Ct., Springfield, 1976-82, presiding judge Criminal div., 1976-81, chief judge, 1981-82; justice Ill. Appellate Ct., 4th Jud. Dist., 1982-84, Ill. Supreme Ct., Springfield, 1984—; adj. prof. So. Ill. U., Springfield, 1974—; mem. Gov.'s Adv. Council on Criminal Justice Legislation, 1977-84; mem. Ad Hoc Com. on Tech. in Cts., 1985—. Mem. editorial rev. bd. Illinois Civil Practice Before Trial, Illinois Civil Trial Practice. Pres. Springfield Mental Health Assn., 1969-71; bd. govs. Aid to Retarded Citizens, 1977-80. Served to lt. USNR, 1966-69. Mem. ABA, Am. Judicature Soc., Ill. State Bar Assn., Ill. Judges Assn., Sangamon County Bar Assn., Chgo. Bar Assn., Women's Bar Assn. Ill., Cen. Ill. Women's Bar Assn. Office: Ill Supreme Ct 1 N Old State Capitol Plaza INB Center-Suite 560 Springfield IL 62701-1323

MILLER, BRADLEY EARL, principal; b. Hutchinson, Kans., May 1, 1950; s. Walter Earl and Betty (Snyder) M.; m. Marti Dale Evans, May 27, 1972; children: Jennifer Deann, Kelli Renee, Chad Earl. BA, Wichita (Kans.) State U., 1973, B Social Work, 1973, M in Sch. Adminstrn., 1980; BS, Sterling (Kans.) Coll., 1975. Cert. school adminstr. Elem. tchr. Sterling Sch. Dist., 1975-76, Maude Carpenter Children's Home, Wichita, 1976-77, Fairfield Sch. Dist., Sylvia, Kans., 1977-80; elem. prin. West Elk Sch. Dist., Howard, Kans., 1980-81, Stafford (Kans.) Sch. Dist., 1981—. Sec. bd. dirs. Stafford Hosp., 1986. Mem. Kans. Assn. Tchrs. Math. (regional coordinator 1986), Kans. Assn. Elem. Prins., Nat. Assn. Elem. Prins. Republican. Mem. Ch. Christ. Lodges: Optimists, Oddfellows. Avocations: game hunting, camping, basketball. Home: 410 E Grand Stafford KS 67578

MILLER, BURR VAN, III, investment company executive; b. Enid, Okla., Oct. 7, 1956; s. Burr Van Jr. and Eleanor Amelia (Gordy) M.; m. Michelle Kay Allaire, Feb. 11, 1984; 1 child, Patrick Glenn. AA, Riverside (Calif.) City Coll., 1976; BS, Wichita (Kans.) State U., 1983. Salesman Keebler Corp., Wichita, 1983-85; office mgr. trainee N.Y. Life Securities, Wichita, 1985-86; office mgr. N.Y. Life Securities, Fargo, N.D., 1986—. Served to sgt. Army N.G., 1980-86. Mem. Nat. Assn. Life Underwriters, Non-commd. Officers Assn. Republican. Lutheran. Avocations: flyfishing, training horses, golf. Home: 901 14th St S Fargo ND 58103 Office: NY Life Securities 1330 Page Dr Fargo ND 58103

MILLER, CALLIX EDWIN, consulting architect, engineer; b. South Bend, Ind., Mar. 27, 1924; s. Callix Edwin and Marguerite Cash (Sweeney) M.; m. Theresa Ann Pirchio, June 25, 1949; children—Madeline, Callix, John, David, Thomas. B.S. in Archtl. Engring., U. Notre Dame, 1949. Mgr. engring. Internat. Mining and Chem. Corp., Chgo., 1951-61; exec. dir. Sperry Rand Corp., N.Y.C., 1961-64; v.p. Internat. Minerals & Chem. Corp., Chgo., 1964-72; v.p. Assocs. Corp. N.Am., Dallas, 1972-78; corp. v.p. tech. resources Clark Equipment Co., Buchanan, Mich., 1978-85, consulting services covering design, planning, feasibility studies, econ. devel. Bd. dirs. Chgo. Area council Boy Scouts Am., 1967-70, Alexian Bros. Hosp., Chgo., 1966-68. Served with USNR, 1943-45. Mem. AIA, ASCE, Soc. Am. Mil. Engrs., Am. Concrete Inst. Republican. Roman Catholic. Clubs: Knollwood Country; Northbrook (Ill.) Sport; Faculty (U. Notre Dame). Lodges: Elks, K.C. Home: 16174 Baywood Ln Granger IN 46530

MILLER, CARL GEORGE, finance executive; b. Milw., Oct. 3, 1942; s. Carl Conrad and Agnes Frances (Patla) M.; m. Patricia Ann Smith, Apr. 27, 1968; children: Gregory, Brian. BS, St. Louis U., 1964. CPA, Mo. Audit mgr. Ahrens & McKeon, CPA's, St. Louis, 1967-73; supr. internal audit Gen. Dynamics Corp., St. Louis, 1973-75, mgr. fin. analysis, 1975-78, dir. fin. analysis, 1978-80; v.p., controller Quincy (Mass.) Shipbldg. div. Gen. Dynamics Corp., 1980-86; v.p. fin. Cessna Aircraft Co., Wichita, Kans., 1986—, also bd. dirs.; bd. dirs. Cessna Fin. Corp., Reims Aviation Co., Paris. Named one of Outstanding Young Men Am. Mem. Machinery and Allied Products Inst. (mem. fin. council I), Am. Inst. CPA's, Mo. Soc. CPA's, Wichita C. of C., Delta Sigma Pi (pres. 1963-64). Republican. Lutheran. Club: Crestview Country (Wichita). Avocation: sports. Office: Cessna Aircraft Co PO Box 1521 Wichita KS 67277

MILLER, CECELIA ELEANOR LOTKO (MRS. GEORGE E. CHAMBERS), retired physician; b. Chgo., Oct. 24, 1917; d. Joseph S. and Zofia H. (Baizer) Lotko; student Northwestern U., 1945-47; B.S., U. Ill., 1949, M.D., 1951; m. James R. Miller, Sept. 3, 1938 (div. 1958); 1 dau., Josephine Ann (Mrs. John E. Mitchell); m. 2d, George E. Chambers, Dec. 5, 1970; stepchildren—Ronald, Lawrence, Leon, Marilyn (Mrs. John Raglione). Intern, Cook County Hosp., Chgo., 1951-52, resident, 1952; resident Hines (Ill.) VA Hosp., 1953-54; practice medicine, specializing in anesthesiology medicine, Hammond, Ind., 1955, Chgo., 1956-77, specializing in phys. medicine, Oak Lawn, Ill., 1982-85; med. adviser Argonaut Ins. Co., Chgo., 1976-82. Mem. Field Mus. Natural History, Art Chgo., Chgo. Zool. Soc. Chgo.; mem. president's council U. Ill., 1983—. Fellow Am. Coll. Anesthesiologists (ret.); mem. AMA (ret.), Am. Med. Women's Assn., Ill., Chgo. med. socs., Am., Ill., Chgo. socs. anesthesiologists, Hines Surg. Soc., Cook County Hosp. Interns and Residents Alumni Assn., U. Ill. Alumni Assn., Dean's Club U. Ill. Coll. Medicine (charter), Alpha Epsilon Iota, Alpha Sigma Lambda. Home: 3464 Golfview Dr Hazel Crest IL 60429

MILLER, CHARLES EDWARD, dentist; b. Rochester, Ind., Jan. 16, 1940; s. Virgil Cleon and Mae (Fulton) M.; m. Marilyn Sue Swygart, Aug. 29, 1959; children: Sherri Ann, Scott Robert. AB in Zool., Ind. U., 1964; DDS, Ind. U., Indpls., 1968. Gen. practice dentistry Akron, Ind., 1968-81, 84—; ptnr. Dental Mgmt. Cons. Corp., Warsaw, Ind., 1981-84. Bd. dirs. Town of Akron, 1970-82; adv. council State of Ind., Indpls., 1973-82. Recipient Sagamore Wabash award Gov. Ind., 1982. Mem. ADA, North Cen. Dental Assn., Kosciusko County Dental Assn. (pres. 1972). Republican. Avocation: forestry. Home and Office: Box 522 Akron IN 46910

MILLER, CHARLES PETER, state senator Iowa; b. Harbor Beach, Mich., Apr. 29, 1918; s. William H. and Anna (Eppenbrock) M.; student Burlington (Iowa) Community Coll., 1947-48; grad. Palmer Coll. Chiropractic, Davenport, Iowa, 1952; m. Virginia Mae Ferrington, Aug. 3, 1946; children—Charles, David, Steven, Dennis, Evelyn, Scot. Practice chiropractic, Burlington, 1952-86 ; mem. Iowa Ho. of Reps. from Des Moines County, 1962-70, speaker pro-tem, 1965-66; mem. Iowa Senate from 30th Dist., 1970—, pres. protem, 1983-85. Mem. exec. bd. S.E. Iowa council Boy Scouts Am., 1956—. Served with USNR, 1940-46. Recipient Fellow award Palmer Acad. Chiropractic, 1966; Silver Beaver award Boy Scouts Am., 1958. Mem. Internat. Chiropractors Assn. (1st v.p. 1965; Fellowship award 1969), Chiropractic Soc. Iowa (pres. 1956-60, mem. bd. 1960-76), Am. Legion, VFW. Democrat. Lion, Eagle, Elk, K.C. Home: 801 High St Burlington IA 52601 Office: 701 Jefferson St Burlington IA 52601

MILLER, CHARLES THOMAS, transportation executive; b. Covington, Ky., Mar. 8, 1955; s. Charles Thomas and Carol Jean (Fisher) M.; m. Teresa Lynn Frohlick, May 3, 1974. AS in Aviation Adminstrn. and Tech., No. Ky. U., 1978; student, Robert Morris Coll., 1978-79, Ind. U., 1980-81. Ops. supr. St. Joseph County Airport Authority, South Bend, Ind., 1979-82; asst. to pres. Towne Air Freight Co., South Bend, 1982-84; dir. ops. Ft. Wayne (Ind.)-Allen County Airport Authority, 1984—; cons. ATE Support Services, Cin., 1984. Contbr. articles to profl. jours. Bd. dirs. Convention and Vis. Bur., South Bend, 1981-84; mem. St. Joseph County Disaster Task Force, South Bend, 1980-84, W. Covington Boosters Assn., 1975—. Mem. Am. Assn. Airport Execs. (exec. candidate 1986), Aviation Assn. Ind., South Bend C. of C., Ft. Wayne C. of C. (air service com. 1986—). Club: Old Ford Mustang. Lodges: Fraternal Order of Police, Kiwanis. Home: 5116 Fernwood Ave Fort Wayne IN 46809 Office: Ft Wayne Allen County Airport Authority Room 209 Baer Field Terminal Fort Wayne IN 46809

MILLER, CHRIS R.P., lawyer; b. Cleethorpes, Lincolnshire, Eng., Mar. 30, 1951; came to U.S., 1951; s. Richard C. and Barbara W. (Morley) M. BS, U. Kans., 1972, U. Kans., 1976; JD, U. Kans., 1983. Bar: Kans. 1984, U.S. Dist. Ct. Kans. 1984. Legal asst. Kans. Atty. Gen., Topeka, 1982-83; staff atty. Kans. Ins. Dept., Topeka, 1983-86; sole practice Lawrence, Kans., 1986—. Mem. Jaycees (pres. Lawrence chpt. 1982, v.p. Kans. chpt. 1983). Republican. Club: Flying W (pres. 1986) (Topeka). Office: PO Box 1201 Lawrence KS 66044

MILLER, CLARENCE E., Congressman; b. Lancaster, Ohio, Nov. 1, 1917; m. Helen M. Brown; children: Ronald, Jacqueline Miller Williams. D.Pub. Service (hon.), Rio Grande (Ohio) Coll. Formerly elec. engr.; mem. Lancaster City Council, 1957-63, mayor, 1963-65; mem. 90th-100th Congresses from 10th Ohio Dist., mem. appropriations com. Hon. mem. Ohio Valley Health Services Found., Ohio Mental Health Assn. Named Hon. Alumnus Ohio U., Athens. Republican. Methodist. Lodge: Elks. Address: 2208 Rayburn House Office Bldg Washington DC 20515 *

MILLER, CURTIS WAYNE, biomedical engineer; b. Vancouver, Wash., Dec. 11, 1948; s. Eldon W. and Ruth Miller; m. H. Melinda Garcia, Apr. 16, 1977; 1 son, Adrian Alan. Student Area Eleven Community Coll., Ankeny, Iowa, 1974-76. Owner, mgr. Celestial Leather, Des Moines, 1973-74; mgr. Blind Munchies Deli, Des Moines, 1973-74; dialysis technician Iowa Luth. Hosp., Des Moines, 1974-76; dir. tech. services West Suburban Kidney Ctr., Oak Park, Ill., 1977—; asst. v.p. Continental Health Care Ltd., Oak Park, 1981-86 ; lectr. in field. Mem. Nat. Assn. Nephrology Technologists (pres.), Assn. Advancement of Med. Instrumentation (mem. dialyser reuse subcom.) ESRD Network (chmn. #14 reuse task force), Nat. Assn. Patients on Hemodialysis and Transplantation (sci. adv. bd.). Contbr. articles to profl. jours.; designer in field.

MILLER, DAVID BARR, meat company executive; b. Bronxville, N.Y., Sept. 10, 1953; s. Joseph Douglas and Nancy Dickson (Rucker) M.; m. Joyce Anne Peterson, June 14, 1986. BS, U.S. Naval Acad., Annapolis, 1975; MBA, U. Mich., 1982. Commd. ensign USN, 1975; student USN Nuclear Power Sch., 1975-77; div. officer, watch officer USS Enterprise, Pacific Ocean, 1977-80; resigned USN, 1980; v.p., ptnr. Enzed Traders, Inc., Ann Arbor, Mich., 1982—. Sponsor refugee family, Bremerton, Wash., 1979-80; active Refugee Foster Care, Luth. Social Services, Mich., 1983-85; scoutmaster Boy Scouts Am., Ann Arbor, 1983-84. Mem. Nat. Buffalo Assn., Canadian Restaurant and Food Service Assn. (Assoc.), Ontario Restaurant and Food Service Assn. (Assoc.), Mich Restaurant Assn. (assoc.). Avocations: writing, harmonica, gardening. Home: 910 Patricia Ave Ann Arbor MI 48103

MILLER, DAVID PAUL, insurance company executive; b. Buffalo, July 26, 1947; s. Alfred and Edythe Clara (Nevinger) M.; m. Georgianna Losaw, June 8, 1969. A.A., Jr. Coll. Albany, 1969; B.A. in Polit. Sci., SUNY-Albany, 1971; M.S. in Spl. Edn., Rehab., U. Tenn., 1974. Cert. disability examiner; cert. systems profl. Claim adjudicator State N.Y., N.Y.C., 1971-73, trainer, supr., 1973-75; quality assurance supr., State of Wis., Madison, 1975-78; supr., systems analyst Allstate Ins. Co., Northbrook, Ill., 1978-81; systems analyst Zurich Ins., Schaumburg, Ill., 1981-83, asst. mgr., 1983-85, quality assurance cons., 1985— . Collector, Palatine Twp., 1985—; sch. trustee Palatine Twp. Sch., Palatine, Ill., 1981—; precinct capt. Palatine Twp. Republicans, Rolling Meadows, Ill., 1980—; alderman candidate Madison City Council, 1977. Named Profl. of Yr., Empire State Assn. Disability Examiners, 1974. Mem. Assn. Systems Mgmt. (treas. 1983—), Nat. Assn. Disability Examiners, Chgo. Claim Assn. (conf. sem. chmn. 1981-82). Club: Ro-Meds (Rolling Meadows)(v.p. 1981—, pres. 1985). Lodge: Masons (worshipful master 1984-85). Avocations: bowling, gardening. Home: 508 W Glencoe Rd Palatine IL 60067 Office: Zurich Ins Co 231 Martingale St Schaumburg IL 60196

MILLER, DAVID WILLIAM, marketing executive; b. Chgo., Jan. 20, 1943; s. Robert W. and Juanita (Moore) M.; m. Sandra Pollard, June 24, 1967; children: David W., Sarah Anne. BS, Bradley U., 1965, postgrad., 1965-66. Various sales and mktg. positions Gen. Electric Co., 1966-80; mgr. strategic planning Gen. Electric Co., Bridgeport, Conn., 1980-81, mgr. mktg., 1981-83; v.p. sales Nova Robotics Inc., East Hartford, Conn., 1983-84; dir. mktg. Allen Bradley Co., Highland Heights, Ohio, 1984—. Mem. Instrument Soc. Am. Avocations: golf, tennis, skiing. Home: 441 Falls Rd Chagrin Falls OH 44022

MILLER, DENIS WARREN, accountant; b. Phillipsburg, Kans., Jan. 24, 1951; s. Warren E. and Wanda M. (Keeten) M.; m. Geraldene Sue Dix, June 19, 1971; children: Heather, Michael. BBA, Ft. Hays (Kans.) State U., 1973. CPA, Kans. Staff acct. Fox & Co., Wichita, Kans., 1973-76; controller Transam. Oil Co., Hutchinson, Kans., 1976-78; office mgr. Kennedy & Coe, Smith Ctr., Kans., 1978-84; pvt. practice acctg. Phillipsburg, 1984—. Chmn. Pride, Phillipsburg, 1986. Mem. Am. Inst. CPA's, Kans. Soc. CPA's (sec.-treas. N.W. Kans. chpt. 1986-87), Smith Ctr. C. of C. (pres. 1981, 82), Phillipsburg C. of C. (pres. 1986-87), Ft. Hays State U. Alumni Assn. (bd. dirs. 1984-86). Republican. Lodges: Elks, Rotary. Avocation: farming. Office: 711 3d St Phillipsburg KS 67661

MILLER, DONALD E., rubber company executive; b. Denver, Dec. 17, 1930; s. Alex H. and Nina A. (Schlatter) M.; m. Barbara J. Rehm, June 15, 1952; children: Steven, David. Grad., Colo. Sch. Mines, 1953. With Gates Rubber Co., Denver, 1963—; field sales mgr. indsl. sales Gates Rubber Co., 1963-66, v.p. mfg., 1966-69, v.p. auto-hardware sales, 1969-73, v.p. mktg., 1973-81, group v.p. automotive, 1981-82, pres., 1982—. 1st lt. U.S. Army, 1954-56. Presbyterian. Home: 5965 E Princeton Circle Englewood CO 80111 Office: Gates Rubber Co 999 S Broadway P O Box 5887 Denver CO 80209 *

MILLER, DONNA JEAN, accountant; b. Omaha, Nov. 6, 1954; d. Kenneth William and Marian Patricia (Koldborg) M. BS in Acctg., Kans. State U., 1978. CPA, Kans. Auditor Kans. Dept. Revenue, Topeka, 1979-84; acct. Kans. Dept. Transp., Topeka, 1984—. Am. Inst. CPA's, Kans. Soc. CPA's, Topeka Assn. Govt. Accts. Avocation: gardening. Home: 1813 Moundview Dr Topeka KS 66604 Office: Kans Dept of Transp State Office Bldg 7th Floor Topeka KS 66612

MILLER, DUANE F., service executive; b. Flint, Mich., Dec. 28, 1947; s. Francis N. and Lillian A. (Snider) M.; m. Theresa Miller, Dec. 8, 1975 (div. Dec. 1978). BA, Western Mich. U., 1974. Cert. mech. contractor, Mich. Ptnr. Miller Refrigeration, Flint, 1968-74; mgr. Young Supply, Detroit, 1974-78; service engr. Kroeger Co., Livonia, Mich., 1978-84; owner N.R.G. Services, Walled Lake, Mich., 1984—. Chmn. ERA Walkathon NOW, Detroit, 1976; mgr. Walled Lake Softball League. Served with U.S. Army, 1969-70. Mem. Pontiac Oakland Refrigeration Assn. (pres. 1982-83), Walled Lake Jaycees (pres. 1979). Avocations: softball, symphony, bowling, hunting. Home and Office: 2097 Hoeft Walled Lake MI 48088

MILLER, EARL DANIEL, osteopathic physician; b. Ottumwa, Iowa, June 1, 1949; s. William Vernon and Dorothy Marie (Haven) M.; m. Phyllis Jean Wittenberger, Apr. 14, 1974; children: Patrick, Nathan, Rebecca. BS in Zoolgy, N.E. Mo. State U., 1969; DO, Kirksville Coll. Osteo. Medicine, 1973. Practice osteopatic medicine Jefferson City, Mo., 1974—; osteo. trainer Still Hosp., Jefferson City, 1974—, chief of staff, 1985—; staff physician, v.p. Patient Care, Inc., Jefferson City, 1979—. Mem. Mo. Assn. Osteo. Physicians and Surgeons (pres. 1986—), Am. Osteo. Assn. (del. 1985-86), Osage Valley Osteo. Assn. Republican. Club: Meadow Lake Acres. Avocations: hunting, fishing, beef cattle. Home: 2220 Merlin Jefferson City MO 65101 Office: 1111 Madison Jefferson City MO 65101

MILLER, EDWARD HENDERSON, orthopaedic surgeon; b. Ft. Worth, Sept. 16, 1935; s. Harry Jackson and Mary Elizabeth (Henderson) M.; m. Carol Kay Roach, Sept. 7, 1957; children: Pamela, Steven, Edward, Matthew. BSME, Purdue U., 1957; MD, U. Cin., 1961. Intern in surgery U. Calif., San Francisco, 1961-62, fellow, 1964-65, resident, 1965-68; asst. prof. surgery U. Cin., 1968-70, assoc. prof., 1971-76, prof., dir. dept. orthopaedic surgery, 1976-81; assoc. orthopaedic surgeon Orthopaedic Cons. of Cin., 1981—; assoc. dir. Bone and Joint Inst. of The Christ Hosp., Cin., 1985—; mem. attending staff Christian R. Holmes div. U. Hosp. U. Cin. Med. Ctr., The Children's Hosp. Med. Ctr., Cin., Deaconess Hosp.; cons. staff The Shriners Hosp. Cin. Burn Unit, The Good Samaritan Hosp.; mem. courtesy staff Bethesda Base Hosp., Bethesda North Hosp., Our Lady of Mercy Hosp.; various com. and adminstrv. positions with The Christ Hosp., U. Cin., Christian R. Holmes Hosp.; vis. prof. orthopaedic surgery U. Louisville, 1971, Howard U., Washington, 1971, U. Mexico City and Shriner's Crippled Children's Hosp., Mexico City, 1971; vis. prof. traumatology Munich Inst. of Tech. Med. Sch., 1972; vis. prof. Coll. Medicine and Dentistry of N.J., 1979, Orthopaedic Residents' Program, Memphis, 1982; Leroy Abbott lectr. U. Calif. San Francisco, 1980; guest faculty mem. U. Wash., 1982, Lenzerheide, Switzerland, 1983-87; presenter and speaker numerous seminars, confs., etc. to profl. orgns., hosps. and univs. Editor orthopaedic words Gould Medical Dictionary, 4th edit.; contbr. numerous articles to profl. jours. Served to capt. USAFR, 1962-64. Fellow Am. Bd. Orthopaedic Surgery (examiner 1984-86), Am. Acad. Orthopaedic Surgeons (chmn. region 6 admissions com. 1980); mem. AMA, Ohio Med. Assn., Cin. Med. Assn., Ohio Orthopaedic Soc. (sec., treas. 1986—), Cin. Orthopaedic Soc. (sec. 1974-75, pres. 1976-77), Tri-State Orthopaedic Soc., Clin. Orthopaedic Soc. (chmn. membership com. 1981-82), Am. Orthopaedic Assn., Ohio Orthopaedic Assn. (exec. com. 1973-76, sec., treas. 1986—), Am. Soc. for Surgery of Trauma, ASTME, Am. Soc. for Metals, Orthopaedic Research Soc.., LeRoy Abbott Orthopaedic Soc., Russell Hibbs Orthopaedic Soc., Societé Internationale de Chirurgie Orthopaedique et de Traumatologie. Clubs: Zanesfield Rod and Gun; Sugar Hill Gun (Cin.). Lodges: Masons, Shriners. Avocations: fishing, hunting, woodcrafts. Home: 9795 Fox Hollow Cincinnati OH 45243 Office: Orthopedic Cons of Cin Inc 111 Wellington Pl Cincinnati OH 45219

MILLER, EDWARD ROBERT, personnel executive; b. Wichita, Sept. 19, 1947; s. Robert A. and Mary H. (Fyfe) M.; m. Patricia B. George, June 21, 1969; Brent E., Alyson B. BBA, Wichita State U., 1968, MS, 1972. V.p. human resources Gates Learjet Corp., Wichita, 1981—. Active United Way of the plains, Better Bus. Bur., NCCJ. Mem. Indsl. Relations Council. Office: Gates Learjet Corp PO Box 7707 Wichita KS 67277

MILLER, ELAINE LINDA, nursing educator; b. Pitts., Apr. 2, 1950; s. James Seldon and Alice Laverne (Walls) Tilka; m. Robert V. Miller, June 2, 1973; 1 child, Benjamin. BS in Nursing, W. Va. U., 1972; M in Nursing, U. Pitts., 1975; DNS, Ind. U., 1985. Staff nurse West Penn Hosp., Pitts., 1972-74; instr. nursing Pa. State U., State Coll., 1975-77; asst. prof. nursing Edinboro (Pa.) State Coll., 1977-79; instr. nursing Slippery Rock (Pa.) State Coll., 1979-80; home care staff nurse Greenville (Pa.) Hosp., 1980-81; staff nurse Centre Community Hosp., Greencastle, Ind., 1982; instr. nursing Ind. U., Indpls., 1982-84; asst. prof. nursing U. Cin., 1984—; research asst. Ind. U., Indpls., 1981-82. U. Cin. grantee, 1985, U. Cin. grantee, 1985; Nat. Inst. Handicapped research grantee, 1986. Mem. Am. Nurses Assn. (counil of nurse researchers), Internat. Communication Assn., Midwest Nursing Research Soc., Sigma Theta Tau. Avocations: gardening, swimming, biking. Home: 4287 Fox Hollow Dr Cincinnati OH 45241 Office: U Cin Coll Nursing and Health 3110 Vine St Cincinnati OH 45221-0038

MILLER, ERIC ARNOLD, music educator; b. Knoxville, Tenn., Mar. 5, 1943; s. Arthur A. and Florence J. (Gattis) M. BS in Music Edn., N.E. Mo. State U., 1965, MA in Music, 1966. Dir. vocal music Beecher Jr. High Sch., Hazel Park, Mich., 1965-68, Wilfred Webb Jr. High Sch., Ferndale, Mich., 1968-72, Hazel Park (Mich.) High Sch., 1972-77, United Oaks and Lee O. Clark Elem. Schs., Hazel Park, 1978-85, Edison Sch., 1985—. Named Outstanding Young Educator, Hazel Park Jaycees, 1975. Mem. Assn. for Supervision and Curriculum Devel., Mich. Edn. Assn., Hazel Park Edn. Assn. (mem. exec. bd. 1979—), Mich. Music Edn. Assn., Mich. Vocal Dirs. Assn., NEA. Presbyterian. Composer: (choral) Our Time Will Come, 1975, Centennial Song, 1984. Home: 129 S LaFayette Blvd Warren MI 48091-2208 Office: 23126 Hughes St Hazel Park MI 48030

MILLER, EUGENE, financial executive; b. Chgo., Oct. 6, 1925; s. Harry and Fannie (Prosterman) M.; m. Edith Sutker, Sept. 23, 1951 (div. Sept. 1965); children: Ross, Scott, June; m. Thelma Gottlieb, Dec. 22, 1965; stepchildren: Paul Gottlieb, Alan Gottlieb. B.S., Ga. Inst. Tech., 1945; A.B. magna cum laude, Bethany Coll., 1947, L.L.D., 1969; diploma, Oxford (Eng.) U., 1947; M.S. in Journalism, Columbia U., 1948; M.B.A., NYU, 1959; postgrad., Pace U., 1973—. Reporter, then city editor Greensboro (N.C.) Daily News, 1948-52; S.W. bur. chief Bus. Week mag., Houston, 1952-54; asso. mng. editor Bus. Week mag., N.Y.C., 1954-60; dir. pub. affairs and communications McGraw-Hill, Inc., 1960-63, v.p., 1963-68; sr. v.p. pub. relations and investor relations, exec. com. N.Y. Stock Exchange, N.Y.C., 1968-73; sr. v.p. CNA Fin. Corp., Chgo., 1973-75; chmn. Eugene Miller & Assos., Glencoe, Ill., 1975-77; v.p. USG Corp., 1977-82, sr. v.p., 1982-85, mem. mgmt. com., 1982—, exec. v.p., chief fin. officer, 1985—, mem. exec. com., also bd. dirs.; adj. prof. mgmt. Grad. Sch. Bus. Adminstrn., NYU, 1963-75; prof. bus. adminstrn. Fordham U., N.Y.C., Fordham U. Grad. Sch. Bus. Adminstrn., 1969-75; chmn., prof. fin. Northeastern Ill. U., 1975—; lectr. econs., pub relations to bus. and sch. groups; dir. P.O.B. Pub. Co., Wayne, Mich., USG Corp., Chgo., U.S. Gypsum Co., Chgo., USG Industries Corp., Chgo., L&W Supply Co., Chgo., Exchange Nat. Bank, Chgo., A.P. Green Refractories Co., Mexico, Mo., Rodman & Renshaw, Inc., Coleman Cable Co., North Chicago, Ill., Masonite Corp., Merc. Systems, Inc., Chgo.; cons. to Sec. Commerce, 1961—; adv. bd. dirs. Nationwide Acceptance Corp., Chgo. Author syndicated bus. column, 1964—; author: Your Future in Securities, 1974, Barron's Guide to Graduate Business Schools, 1977, 5th edit., 1986; Contbg. editor: Pub. Relations Handbook, 1971, Boardroom Reports, 1985—. Trustee Bethany Coll., Found. for Pub. Relations Research and Edn.; pres. USG Found., 1979—; mem. alumni bd. Columbia U. Sch. Journalism; bd. overseers Ill. Inst. Tech., Chgo, Stuart Grad. Sch. Bus. Adminstrn. Served to ensign USNR, World War II; comdr. Res. Recipient Outstanding Achievement award Bethany Coll., 1963; 50th Anniversary award Columbia U. Sch. Journalism, 1963; Honors award Ohio U. Sch. Journalism, 1964; Disting. Service award in invesment edn., 1980. Mem. Am. Econs. Assn., Am. Finance Assn., Nat. Assn. Bus. Economists, Soc. Am. Bus. Writers (founder), Pub. Relations Soc. Am., Assn. Corp. Growth, Fin. Execs. Inst., Arthur Page Soc., Newcomen Soc., Sigma Delta Chi, Alpha Sigma Phi. Clubs: River, Mid-Am. (Chgo.); Green Acres Country (Northbrook, Ill.); N.Y.C.; Clubs of Inverrary (Ft. Lauderale, Fla.), Met. (Chgo.). Home: 376 Sunrise Circle Glencoe IL 60022 Office: 101 S Wacker Dr Chicago IL 60606 : 3280 Spanish Moss Terr Lauder Hill FL

MILLER, EUGENE ALBERT, banker. married. B.B.A., Detroit Inst. Tech., 1964; grad., Sch. Bank Adminstrn., Wis., 1968. With Comerica Inc. (formerly The Detroit Bank, then Detroit Bank & Trust Co.), 1955—, v.p., 1970-71, controller, 1971-74, sr. v.p., 1974-78, exec. v.p., 1978-81, pres., 1981—; with parent co. Comerica Inc. (formerly DETROITBANK Corp.), 1973—, treas., 1973-80, pres., 1981—, also bd. dirs. Office: Comerica Inc 211 W Fort St Detroit MI 48275

MILLER, EUGENE GAYLORD, insurance company executive; b. Mpls., June 11, 1944; s. Reuben and Ellen C. (Anderson) M.; m. Kathleen Susan Dally, May 27, 1983; 1 child, Scott E. CPCU. Office worker Western Nat. Mut. (formerly Mut. Creamery Ins. Co.), Mpls., 1962-64, underwriter, 1964-71, agy. field rep., 1971-75, v.p., 1975-85, sr. v.p., 1985-86, exec. v.p., 1986—. Mem. Minn. Assn. CPCU's (candidate devel. coordinator 1982-84). Republican. Lutheran. Club: Minn. 1752 (pres. 1976-77). Avocations: golf, bowling. Home: 16354 Edenwood Dr Eden Prairie MN 55344 Office: Western Nat Group 5350 W 78th St Edina MN 55435

MILLER, FRANCIS ROY, corporate executive; b. Elko, Minn., Nov. 6, 1926; s. Robert Frank and Astrid Marie (German) M.; m. JoAnn Eleanor Foss, Aug. 12, 1950; children: Nancy, Douglas, David. BA in Econs., St. Olaf Coll., 1950. Cert. adminstrv. mgr. Asst. mgr. Credit Bur., Faribault, Minn., 1950-54; ins. rep. State Farm Ins., Faribault, 1954-57; chief acct. N.W. Nat. Life Ins. Co., Mpls., 1957-62; treas. Faribault Woolen Mill Co., 1962—. Pres. Faribault Jr. Achievement, 1980-81; bd. dirs. Riverbend Ctr. for Arts, Faribault, 1986. Served with U.S. Army, 1944-45. Named Outstanding Citizen Jaycees, Faribault, 1982. Mem. Adminstrv. Mgmt. Soc. (internat. bd. dirs. 1982-84), Faribault C. of C. (pres. 1982). Republican. Club: Exchange (upper midwest) (pres. 1980-81, Outstanding Exchangite 1981). Avocations: golf, bridge. Home: 12 Green Haven Bay Faribault MN 55021 Office: Faribault Woolen Mill Co 1500 NW 2d Ave Faribault MN 55021

MILLER, FREDERICK HOWARD, podiatrist; b. Chgo., Oct. 8, 1947; s. Samuel I. and Sylvia (Ekter) M.; m. Carole Pamela Schwab, June 27, 1971; children: David, Ryan. BS, Loyola U., Chgo., 1969; DPM summa cum laude, Ill. Coll. Podiatric Medicine, 1975. Cert. Am. Bd. Podiatric Surgery and Orthopedics. Resident in podiatry Northlake (Ill.) Community Hosp., 1975-76; practice podiatry Mt. Prospect, Ill., 1976—; mem. staff Luth. Gen. Hosp., Park Ridge, Ill., 1986—, Highland Park (Ill.) Hosp., 1984—, N.W. Surgicare, Arlington Heights, Ill. Bd. dirs. Juvenile Diabetes Assn., Chgo., 1985—. Recipient award for outstanding research in foot surgery, Northlake Community Hosp., 1982. Fellow Am. Coll. Foot Surgeons. Avocation: bicycling. Office: 530 W Northwest Hwy Mount Prospect IL 60056

MILLER, FREDERICK WILLIAM, publisher, lawyer; b. Milw., Mar. 18, 1912; s. Roy W. and Kathryn (Oehlers) M.; m. Violet Jane Bagley, Mar. 31, 1939. B.A., U. Wis., 1934, J.D., 1936. Bar: Wis. 1936. Assoc. Tenney & Davis, Madison, 1935-36; atty. State of Wis., Madison, 1936-77; pub. The Capital Times Co., Madison, 1979—, also dir.; dir. Madison Newspaper, Inc., 1970—, chmn. bd., 1980—; dir. Evjue Found., Inc., Madison, 1957—. Trustee Evjue Charitable Trust, Madison, 1970—. Mem. Wis. Bar Assn. Club: Madison. Home: 2810 Arbor Dr Madison WI 53711 Office: Capital Times Co Madison Newspaper Inc 1901 Fish Hatchery Rd Madison WI 53713

MILLER, GEORGIA BLAIR, business administration educator, dean; b. Hyden, Ky., May 5, 1946; d. Rutherford Gay and Ruby Irene (Brashear) B.; m. Joseph Dean Miller, June 3, 1967; children: Joseph Blair, Deanna Blair. BS, Western Ky. U., 1967, MA, 1968; EdD, U. Ky., 1975. Cert. systems profl. Sec. Western Ky. U., Bowling Green, 1968, bus. data processing prof., 1972-76; adminstr. Shell Oil Co., Anchorage, 1969-70; high sch. bus. tchr. Greater Anchorage Area Borough, 1970-71; prof. bus. adminstrn. Ind. U. Sch. of Bus., Bloomington, 1976—; asst. dean sch. of bus. Ind. U., Indpls., 1982—; cons. in field; pres. GBM Systems, Inc., Franklin, Ind., 1984—. Contbr. articles in field. Named Ky. Col., 1980. Mem. Data Processing Mgmt. Assn. (IPA Silver award 1981, Gold award 1983, v.p. 1985-86, sec.-treas. 1987—, former region and chpt. officer), Office Systems REsearch Assn. (nat. officer 1982-84, v.p. 1984-85), Nat. Assn. Bus. Tchr. Edn. (bd. dirs. 1978-79), Adminstrv. Mgmt. Soc. (sec.-treas. 1984-85, named Bus. Educator of Yr. 1985), Ind. Exec. Adv. Bd. for Profl. Secs. Internat., 1981-85. Avocations: reading, tennis, racquetball, golfing, swimming. Home: 1713 Midland Dr Franklin IN 46131 Office: Ind U Sch Bus 801 W Michigan PO Box 647 Indianapolis IN 46223

MILLER, HUGH THOMAS, microcomputer consultant; b. Indpls., Mar. 22, 1951; s. J. Irwin and Xenia S. Miller; divorced; 1 child, Jonathan William. BA, Yale U., 1976; SM in Mgmt., MIT, 1985. Owner Hugh Miller Bookstore, New Haven, Conn., 1976-83, Hugh Miller Cons., New Haven; cons. in microcomputers Stony Creek, Conn., 1983-85; supr. decision technologies div. Electronic Data Systems, Inc., Troy, Mich., 1985-86; supr. product and mfg. engring. div. Electronic Data Systems, Inc., Bloomfield Hills, Mich., 1986—. Editor, ptnr. The Common Table, pub. firm. Mem. Am. Mktg. Assn., Mktg. Research Assn. Home: 575 Stanley St Birmingham MI 48009 Office: 1400 N Woodward Ave Bloomfield Hills MI 48013

MILLER, JAMES CLARENCE, agricultural engineer; b. Leesburg, Va., Apr. 12, 1946; s. Robert P. and Helen (Crouch) M.; m. Janis Lee Walker, Aug. 12, 1972; children: Joshua, Jason, Jeremy, Joseph. BS in Agrl. Engring., Va. Poly Inst., 1971, MS in Agrl. Engring., 1972. Foreman Todd Steel, Point of Rocks, Md., 1973; engr. John Deere Ottumwa (Iowa) Works, 1973-81; sr. engr. Deere and Co., Moline, Ill., 1981—. Served to capt. U.S. Army, 1972-81. Mem. Am. Soc. Agriculture, Quad-City Sect. Am. Soc. Agrl. Engrs. (treas. 1985-86, chmn. 1986—), Gideons (Davenport, Iowa pres. 1983—). Republican. Baptist. Avocations: fishing, gardening. Home: 2655 New Lexington Dr Bettendorf IA 52722 Office: Deere & Co John Deere Rd Moline IL 61265

MILLER, JAMES NORRIS, health science facility administrator; b. Washburn, N.D., Mar. 3, 1939; s. Leland Rupert and Mabel Pearl (Erickson) M.; m. Marvalene Jean Bauer, Apr. 17, 1960; children: Michael, Melissa. BSBA, Dickinson Coll., 1967; MS in Rehab./Hosp. Adminstrn. summa cum laude, So. Ill. U., 1971. Counselor N.D. Div. Vocat. Rehab., Bismarck, 1967-68, adminstrv. asst., 1968-70, facilities specialist, 1969-70; exec. dir. Heart of Am., Rugby, N.D., 1971-74; dir. physical medicine St. Lawrence Hosp., Lansing, Mich., 1974-79; pres. Eaton Rapids (Mich.) Community Hosp., 1979—; assoc. v.p. Ingham Med. Ctr., Lansing, 1979—. v.p. Alliance for Community Devel., Eaton Rapids, Mich., 1987—; bd. dirs. Winner's Circle, Eaton Rapids, 1986—. Served with USAF, 1957-61. Mem. Am. Coll. Health-Care Execs. Lutheran. Lodges: Masons, Lions, Rotary (v.p. Eaton Rapids club 1986—). Home: 1028 Delridge Rd East Lansing MI 48823 Office: Eaton Rapids Community Hosp 1500 S Main St Eaton Rapids MI 48827

MILLER, JAMES VERNON, sales executive; b. St. Louis, Dec. 1, 1950; s. Harold William and Helen Margaret (Bruns) M.; m. Debra Ann Rost, July 20, 1974; children: Laura Rost, Mark James. AB, Westminster Coll., 1973. Acctg. supr. Famous-Barr Co., St. Louis, 1973-75; asst. controller Crossroads Furniture Co., St. Louis, 1975-76; ins. broker Glenn and Assocs., St. Louis, 1976-77; sales mgr. Schlueter Mfg. Co., St. Louis, 1977-83, nat. sales mgr., 1983—. Mem. Jefferson City (Mo.) C. of C. Republican. Roman Catholic. Avocations: cooking, reading. Home: 932 Jason Rd Jefferson City MO 65101 Office: The Schlueter Co 209 W Main Linn MO 65051

MILLER, JAMES WARREN, management consultant; b. Cleve., Sept. 30, 1948; s. Allan John and Marjorie Hewitt (Pirtle) M.; m. Jean Louise Clark, May 23, 1970. BA in Math., Oberlin Coll., 1970. Computer operator Standard Oil of Ohio, Cleve., 1966-67, computer programmer, 1968; head systems programming dept. Oberlin (Ohio) Coll., 1970-71; mem. staff Arthur Andersen & Co., Cleve., 1971-76; mgr. Arthur Andersen & Co., Cleve. and Chgo., 1976-80; sr. mgr. Arthur Andersen & Co., Chgo., 1980—; adj. lectr. computer sci. Northwestern U., Evanston, Ill., 1986. Mem. Data Processing Mgmt. Assn., Assn. for Computing Machinery. Methodist. Club: The Monroe (Chgo.). Avocations: teaching, personal computer software devel., music. Home: 955 Mulford Evanston IL 60202 Office: Arthur Andersen & Co 33 W Monroe Chicago IL 60603

MILLER, JAVAINE CLAIR, controller; b. Independence, Iowa, Oct. 2, 1940; s. Clair C. and Esther (Walter) M.; m. Patricia L. Peirson, Sept. 25, 1964; children: Jamie C., Amy Jo. Grad., Am. Inst. Bus., Des Moines, 1964. CPA, Iowa. Ptnr. CPA firm, Denison, Iowa, 1970-73; controller CESH Corp., Denison, 1973-84, Manatts, Inc., Brooklyn, Iowa, 1984—; sec.-treas. Wendling Quarries, Wilton, Iowa, 1987—. Treas. St. Rose of Lima Ch., Denison, 1982-83; pres. Crawford County Ind. Devel. Corp., Denison, 1982-84; sec.-treas. New Brooklyn Devel., 1987—. Served with U.S. Army, 1959-62, Korea. Mem. Am. Inst. CPA's, Iowa Soc. CPA's. Republican. Roman Catholic. Avocations: indsl. devel., fishing, boating, motorcycles. Home: Rural Rt Box 3013 Brooklyn IA 52211 Office: Manatts Inc Box AJ Brooklyn IA 52211

MILLER, JAYE CLAIRE, corporate professional; b. Port Angeles, Wash., May 15, 1957; d. James William and Mary Joan (Putrow) M. BS, Fla. State U., 1978; MBA, Ohio State U., 1980. Adminstrv. asst. Escape Enterprises, Columbus, Ohio, 1980-82, tng. specialist, 1983-85, dir. tng., 1985—, dir. ops., 1986—. Vol. Grant Med. Ctr., COlumbus, 1986. Mem. Am. Soc. Tng. and Devel. Republican. Roman Catholic. Home: 170 Jackson St Columbus OH 43206 Office: Escape Enterprises 392 E Town St Columbus OH 43215

MILLER, JEFFREY CHARLES, human resources executive; b. Lafayette, Ind., Dec. 10, 1949; s. Russell Charles and Bettie June (Klinker) M.; m. Cheryl Ann Kolacz, Apr. 29, 1978; children: Matthew Charles, Kelly Elizabeth. BA in Art, Purdue U., 1972, BS in Mgmt., 1975. Sr. mdse. mgr. J.C. Penney Co., South Bend, Ind., 1975-79; asst. v.p., dir. tng. 1st Source Bank, South Bend, 1979—. Editor New Horizons newsletter, 1979—. Advisor, company contact Jr. Achievement of Mich., Inc., South Bend, 1979—. Served with USAR. Mem. Am. Soc. Tng. and Devel., Am. Soc. Personnel Adminstrn., Ind. Personnel Assn., Am. Inst. Banking, South Bend/Mishawaka C. of C. (key club mem. 1983—), Purdue Alumni Assn., Sigma Pi. Republican. Roman Catholic. Lodge: Kiwanis (past pres. South Bend). Avocations: golf, reading. Home: 11901 Buttercup Ln Granger IN 46530 Office: 1st Source Bank Human Resources Div 100 N Michigan St South Bend IN 46601

MILLER, JOHN ALBERT, university administrator, marketing consultant; b. St. Louis County, Mo., Mar. 22, 1939; s. John Adam and Emma D. (Doering) M.; m. Eunice Ann Timm, Aug. 25, 1968; children: Michael, Kristin. AA, St. Paul's Coll., 1958; BA with honors, Concordia Sr. Coll., 1960; postgrad., Wash. U., St. Louis, 1960-64; MBA, Ind. U., 1971, D.B.A. in Mktg., 1972. Proofreader, editor Concordia Pub. House, St. Louis, 1960-62, periodical sales mgr., 1964-68; asst. prof. Drake U., Des Moines, 1972-74; cons. FTC, Washington, 1974-75; vis. assoc. prof. Ind. U., Bloomington, 1975-77; assoc. prof. U. Colo., Colorado Springs, 1977-79, prof., 1977—, prof. mktg., resident dean, 1980-84; v.p. market devel. Peak Health Care Inc., Colorado Springs, 1984-85; dean, prof. mktg. Valparaiso (Ind.) U., 1986—; cons. and researcher govt. and industry; dir. health maintenance orgn.; bd. dirs. Western Health Mgmt., Colorado Springs, 1982—. Author: Labeling Research The State of the Art, 1978; contbr. articles to profl. jours. Mem. Colorado Springs Symphony Orch. Council, 1980—; cons. Citizens Goals of Colorad Springs, 1985—, Jr. League of Colorado Springs., 1981-82. Served with U.S. Army, 1962-64. U.S. Steel fellow, 1970-71. Mem. Assn. Consumer Research (membership chmn. 1978-79), Am. Mktg. Assn. (fed. govt. liaison com. 1975-76), Am. Acad. Advt., Izaak Walton League, Beta Gamma Sigma. Lutheran. Avocations: racketball, jogging. Home: 1504 Del Vista Dr Valparaiso IN 46383 Office: Valparaiso U Valparaiso IN 46383

MILLER, JOHN DUMONTHIER, JR., advertising executive; b. Detroit, Dec. 30, 1961; s. John Dumonthier Miller and Carol Ann Royal Herbert, m. Julia Lynn Davis, June 14, 1986 (div. 1987). Student, Ctr. Creative Studies, 1980-83, Oakland Community Coll., 1983-85. Asst. art dir. A & B Mktg., Royal Oak, Mich., 1980-83; art dir. Franklin Mktg., Farmington, Mich., 1983-84; owner, chief operating officer Typography, Inc., Drayton Plains, Mich., 1985—; instr. Oakland Community Coll., Auburn, Highland, Mich., 1983—. Cartoonist comicstrips Woodys World, 1981, Johnny, 1983-84; illustrator Study in Water, 1978, Mr. Johnson in Morning, 1985. Precinct del. Republican Party, Drayton Plains, 1986—, sustaining mem. Rep. Nat. Com., 1987—. Served with USNR, 1983—. Mem. Waterford Friends of Arts, Drayton Plains Jaycees, Oakland C. of C., Waterford Rep. Club. Roman Catholic. Home and Office: 4540 Dixie Hwy Suite 2 Drayton Plains MI 48020

MILLER, JOHN FRANKLIN, foundation administrator; b. Hagerstown, Md., June 4, 1940; s. Roger F. and Leola V. (Ebersole) M. B.A., St. John's Coll., Md., 1962; B.D., Yale U., 1965, M.Div., 1967; postgrad. U. Md., 1969-73. Curator/adminstr. Hampton Nat. Hist. Site, Towson, Md., 1973-79; dir. edn. Stan Hywet Hall and Gardens, Akron, Ohio, 1979-81, exec. dir., 1981—; mem. faculty Montgomery Coll., Rockville, Md., 1977-78. Editor newsletter Stan Hywet Hall Found., 1982-84; Guide to Collections, 1982. Trustee, Music from Stan Hywet, Akron, 1983—, Inter-Mus. Conservation Assn., 1981. U. Md. fellow, spring 1970. Mem. nat. Trust Hist. Preservation, Am. Assn. State and Local History, Soc. Preservation of Md. Antiquities, Washington County Hist. Soc. (life), Md. Hist. Soc., Yale U. Alumni Assn. (alumni schs. com. 1984-85), SAR (mgr. chpt. 1978). Republican. Episcopalian. Avocations: gardening; military miniatures. Home: 310 Sundale Rd Akron OH 44313 Office: 714 N Portage Path Akron OH 44303

MILLER, JOHN JERROLD-LARRAIN, magazine editor; b. Los Angeles, Aug. 25, 1951; s. Fred Thomas and Nona Mae (Bronner) M.; m. Joanne Elizabeth Edwards, Aug. 16, 1975; 1 dau., Genevieve. B.A., Albion Coll., 1973; postgrad. Western Mich. U., 1972; M.A., Adelphi U., 1974; Dramatic program dir. Albion (Mich.) Coll., 1972-75; lang. arts tchr. Maumee Valley

C.D.S., Toledo, 1975-76; mag. editor United Kennel Club, Inc., Kalamazoo, 1976—. Mem. Dog Writers Assn. Am., Theta Alpha Phi, Lutheran. Club: Park. Contbr. articles to profl. jours. Home: 154 Bulkley St Kalamazoo MI 49007 Office: United Kennel Club Inc 100 E Kilgore Rd Kalamazoo MI 49001

MILLER, JOHN RICHARD, bank executive; b. Omaha, Oct. 19, 1949; s. Richard Frank and Stella Jane (McCumber) M.; m. Pamela Marie Martinez, May 9, 1981; children: Diana Marie, Ashley Noelle. BBA, U. Nebr., Omaha, 1972, MBA, 1974. With Northwestern Nat. Bank, Omaha, 1974-80; v.p. corp. banking U.S. Nat. Bank, Omaha, 1980-82; v.p., mgr. comml. loan dept. Norwest Bank of Nebr., Omaha, 1982-86, pres., 1986—. Exec. bd. dirs. MidύAm. Council Boy Scouts Am., Omaha, 1979—, council advancement chmn., 1982—; alumni com. Leadership Omaha, 1983—; bd. dirs. Combined Health Agys. Dr. Nebr. Democrat. Methodist. Lodge: Kiwanis. Office: Norwest Bank Nebr NA 10010 Regency Circle Omaha NE 68114

MILLER, JOHN ROBERT, petroleum company executive; b. Lima, Ohio, Dec. 28, 1937; s. John O. and Mary L. (Zickafoose) M.; m. Karen A. Eier, Dec. 30, 1961; children: Robert A., Lisa A., James E. B.S.Ch.E. with honors, U. Cin., 1960, D.Comml. Sc. hon., 1983. With Standard Oil Co. (Ohio), Cleve., 1960-86, dir. fin., 1974-75, v.p. fin., 1975-78, v.p. transp., 1978-79, sr. v.p. tech. and chems., 1979-80, pres., chief operating officer, 1980-86, also bd. dirs.; bd. dirs. Eaton Corp., Fed. Reserve Bank Cleve. Mem. Tau Beta Pi. Clubs: Pepper Pike, Union. Office: 3550 Lander Rd Suite 110 Lander Ctr Pepper Pike OH 44124

MILLER, JOHN WAYNE, accountant; b. Litchfied, Ill., June 18, 1957; s. Nelson Lloyd and Carol Ann (Niemann) M. B of Acctg. with high honors, U. Ill., 1979, M of Acctg. Sci., 1980. CPA, Ill. Staff acct. Filbey, Summers, Abolt Goode & Kiddoo, Champaign, Ill., 1979-80, Peat, Marwick Mitchell, St. Louis, 1980-81; sr. mgr. Peat, Marwick, Main & Co., Chgo., 1981—. Mem. Am. Inst. CPA's, Ill. Soc. CPA's, MIT Enterprise Entrepreneurial Services Group. Republican. Lutheran. Avocations: golf, softball. Home: 1749 N Wells #1908 Chicago IL 60614 Office: Peat Marwick Main & Co 303 E Wacker Chicago IL 60601

MILLER, JOSEPH IRWIN, automotive manufacturing company executive; b. Columbus, Ind., May 26, 1909; s. Hugh Thomas and Nettie Irwin (Sweeney) M.; m. Xenia Ruth Simons, Feb. 5, 1943; children: Margaret Irwin, Catherine Gibbs, Elizabeth Ann Garr, Hugh Thomas, II, William Irwin. Grad., Taft Sch., 1927; A.B., Yale U., 1931, M.A. (hon.), 1959, L.H.D. (hon.), 1979; M.A., Oxford (Eng.) U., 1933; LL.D., Bethany Coll., 1956, Tex. Christian U., Ind. U., 1958, Oberlin Coll., Princeton, 1962, Hamilton Coll., 1964, Columbia, 1968, Mich. State U., 1968, Dartmouth, 1971, U. Notre Dame, 1972, Ball State U., 1972, Lynchburg Coll., 1985; L.H.D. (hon.), Case Inst. Tech., 1966, U. Dubuque, 1977; Hum.D., Manchester U., 1973, Moravian Coll., 1976. Asso. Cummins Engine Co., Inc., Columbus, Ind., 1934—; v.p., gen. mgr. Cummins Engine Co., Inc., 1934-42, exec. v.p., 1944-47, pres., 1947-51, chmn. bd., 1951-77, chmn. exec. and fin. com., 1977—; pres. Irwin-Union Bank & Trust Co., 1947-54, dir., 1937—, chmn., 1954-75; chmn. exec. com. Irwin Union Corp., 1976—; mem. Commn. Money and Credit, 1958-61, Pres.'s Com. Postal Reorgn., 1968, Pres.'s Com. Urban Housing, 1968; chmn. Pres.'s Com. on Trade Relations with Soviet Union and Eastern European Nations, 1965, Nat. Adv. Commn. on Health Manpower, 1966; vice chmn. UN Commn. on Multinat. Corps., 1974; adv. council U.S. Dept. Commerce, 1976; mem. Study Commn. on U.S. Policy Toward So. Africa, 1979-81. Pres. Nat. Council Chs. of Christ in U.S.A., 1960-63; chmn. bd. trustees Nat. Humanities Ctr.; mem. central and exec. coms. World Council Chs., 1961-68; trustee Ford Found., 1961-79, Yale Corp., 1959-77, Urban Inst., 1966-76, Mayo Found., 1977-82, Am. Acad. in Rome; fellow Branford Coll. Served to lt. USNR, 1942-44. Recipient Rosenberger award U. Chgo., 1977, 1st MacDowell Colony award, 1981; hon. fellow Balliol Coll., Oxford (Eng.) U.; Benjamin Franklin fellow Royal Soc. Arts. Fellow Am. Acad. Arts and Scis.; mem. Am. Philos. Soc., AIA (hon.), Ind. Acad., Bus. Council, Conf. Bd. (sr.), Phi Beta Kappa, Beta Gamma Sigma. Mem. Christian Ch. (Disciples of Christ) (elder). Clubs: Yale, Century, Links (N.Y.C.); Chicago; Indpls. Athletic, Columbia (Indpls.). Office: 301 Washington St Columbus IN 47201

MILLER, KEITH LLOYD, lawyer; b. Harvey, N.D., July 27, 1951; s. Lloyd Vernie and Marian A. (Leintz) M.; m. Linda Suzanne Nelson, Aug. 7, 1971; children—Christopher Nelson, Ann Elizabeth. B.A., Concordia Coll., Moorhead, Minn., 1972; J.D., U. N.D., 1975. Bar: Minn. 1976, U.S. Dist. Ct. Minn. 1976, U.S. Ct. Appeals (8th cir.) 1976, N.D. 1982, U.S. Dist. Ct. N.D. 1982. Assoc. Stefanson, Landberg & Alm, Moorhead, 1976-78; ptnr. Miller, Norman, Kenney, & Williams Ltd., Moorhead, 1978—; cons. Nat. Legal Services Corp., Washington, 1984—; dir. Northwestern Minn. Legal Services Corp., Moorhead, 1981-87, chmn. bd., 1983-86 . Bd. dirs. Clay County Democratic Farm Labor Party, Moorhead, 1984-86; advisor Nat. Moot Trial Competition Team Concordia Coll., 1987. Mem. Minn. Trial Lawyers Assn. (bd. govs. 1987—), Assn. Trial Lawyers Am., Minn. State Bar Assn. (state support policy bd. on legal assistance to disadvantaged), State Bar Assn. N.D. Lutheran. Office: Miller Norman Kenney & Williams Ltd 403 S 8th St PO Box 1066 Moorhead MN 56560

MILLER, KEN NORBERT, food services executive; b. Horicon, Wis., Aug. 24, 1948; s. Norbert Leo and Esther Elsie (Kuecken) M.; m. Lois Ann Chavie, May 27, 1972; children: Jeffrey, Michael, Marcy. AA in Culinary Skills, Madison (Wis.) Area Tech., 1971; student, Stout State U., 1971-72, Met. State U., 1986—. Dir. food service felt products ARA Services, Skokie, Ill., 1971-73; dir. food service Beloit (Wis.) Coll. ARA Services, 1973-76, dir. food service Rockford (Ill.) Coll., 1976-78; dist. mgr. ARA Services, Phila., 1978—; mem. adv. bd. S.W. Minn. State U., Marshall, 1980-81. Active bd. lay ministry Redeemer Luth. Ch., 1985, Loaves and Fishes program, Mpls., 1987; hockey coach Bloomington (Minn.) YMCA, 1986; little league coach Burnsville (Minn.) Youth Athletic Program, 1987. Roman Catholic. Avocations: youth sports, reading. Home: 12250 Hillsboro Ave Savage MN 55378

MILLER, KENNETH WILLIAM, II, business executive; b. Cleve., May 11, 1951; s. Kenneth William and Margaret Mary (Leonard) M.; m. Joan Ellen Pattillo, Aug. 12, 1972; children: Kenneth William III, Victoria Joan. BSEE, MIT, 1974; MS in Mgmt., MIT-Sloan, 1983. Registered investment advisor. Various Corning (N.Y.) Glass Works, 1974-81; mgr. product devel. Duracell, Tarrytown, N.Y., 1983-85; mgr. advanced tech. AT&T Fed. Systems, Burlington, N.C., 1985; v.p. ops. Frey Sci., Mansfield, 1985—; sec. and treas. Frey Holdings, Mansfield, 1985—, also bd. dirs.; bd. dirs. Mid-Am. Ventures, Mansfield, Mid-Am. Investment Mgmt., Mansfield. Mem. IEEE, AAAS, Soc. History Tech. Republican. Congregational. Lodge: Rotary. Home: 565 Brae Burn Mansfield OH 44907 Office: Frey Sci 905 Hickory Ln Mansfield OH 44905

MILLER, LARRY THOMAS, accountant; b. Omaha, Oct. 24, 1940; s. Elmer Thomas and Lucile Valentine (Hammon) M. Student U. Omaha, 1958-63. With accounting dept. Union Pacific R.R. Co., Omaha, 1959—, tax acct., 1969—. Mem. nat. adv. bd. Am. Security Council. Served with U.S. Army, M.P., 1965-67. Mem. Am. Acctg. Assn. Republican. Office: Union Pacific RR 1416 Dodge Omaha NE 68179

MILLER, MABRY BATSON, educator; b. Birmingham, Ala.; d. Ezra Orestes and Mabry Ward (Arnold) Batson; B.A., Athens (Ala.) Coll., 1937; grad. North Ala. Coll. Commerce, 1958; M.B.A., Ala. A&M U., 1974; Ph.D. (Anna M. Dice fellow), Ohio State U., 1981; m. Harry Edward Miller, Oct. 10, 1937; children—Harry Edward Jr., Mabry Miller O'Donnell. Instr. French, Athens Coll., 1938; tchr. music, high sch. choral dir., pub. schs., South Pittsburg, Tenn., 1942-43; staff asst. dept. engring., missile div. Chrysler Corp., Huntsville, Ala., 1958-61; grad. asst. Coll. Adminstrv. Sci., Ohio State U., 1977-80; asst. prof. mgmt. Drake U., 1980-86, assoc. prof., 1986—; cons., lectr., condr. workshops in field. Recipient Virginia Hammill Simms award Community Ballet Assn., Huntsville, 1971, cert. for patriotic civilian service Dept. Army, 1972; citation of merit City of Huntsville, 1972, County of Madison (Ala.), 1972. Mem. Acad. Mgmt., AAUW, Nat. Fedn. Music Clubs (life; dist. pres.), Phi Theta Kappa, Beta Gamma Sigma, Sigma Iota Epsilon, Delta Sigma Pi. Home: 4641 Woodland Ave Unit 6 West Des Moines IA 50265 Office: Drake U Aliber Hall Des Moines IA 50311

MILLER, MALCOLM HENRY, manufacturing sales executive, real estate developer; b. Elgin, Ill., Feb. 6, 1934; s. Carl Theodore and Alice Lucy (Garbisch) M. BA, U. Wis., 1957; postgrad., Am. Inst. Fgn. Trade, 1961, U. N.Mex., 1963. Lic. real estate broker, N.Mex. Sales engr. Fairbanks Morse Corp., Beloit, Wis., 1962; pvt. practice real estate Albuquerque, 1964-75; supt., v.p. Walworth Foundries, Inc., Darien, Wis., 1959-61, exec. v.p. sales, co-owner, 1975—; v.p. sales, co-owner Waukesha Specialty Co., Inc., Darien, 1975—. Loan advisor, developer Community Assn. for Sr. Housing, Albuquerque, 1967-70; Rep. candidate for state senator N.Mex., 1970; active fin. com. Bernalillo County Reps., N.Mex., 1970-80, Walworth County Reps., Wis., 1976-77. Served to 1st lt. U.S. Army, 1957-59. Mem. Am. Foundrymen's Assn., Dairy Food Industries Supply Assn., Santa Fe Opera Guild, SIgma Alpha Epsilon. Republican. Episcopalian. Clubs: Big Foot Country (Fontana, Wis.), Abbey Springs Yacht (Fontana). Lodge: Masons. Avocations: hunting, traveling, reading, opera. Home: 223 Fremont St PO Box 37 Walworth WI 53184 Office: Walworth Foundries Inc PO Box 160 Hwy 14 and Hwy 15 Interchange Darien WI 53114

MILLER, MARK KEVIN, aeronautical engineer, military officer; b. Wilmington, Del., May 7, 1948; s. John Murray and Elizabeth Jane (Bomar) M.; m. Carolyn Ann Woods, May 20, 1978 (div. Aug. 1985). BS in Aeronatical Engring., USAF Acad., 1970; MS in Aeronautical Engring., U. Dayton, 1977. Pvt. pilot license. Commd. 2d lt. USAF, 1970, advanced through ranks to maj.; procurement officer USAF, Tinker AFB, Okla., 1970-72; test dir., FT engr. USAF, Wright-Patterson AFB, Ohio, 1974-78; system safety staff engr. USAF, Andrews AFB, Md., 1978-80; resigned USAF, 1980, with res., 1980—; evaluation analysis engr. GE Aircraft Engines, Cin., 1980-81, comml. flight test engr., 1981-83, mgr. mil. field and flight test, 1984—. Mem. Soc. Flight Test Engrs., Sports Car Club Am. (bd. dirs. 1981-83). Republican. Roman Catholic. Avocations: sports car racing, skiing, soaring, racquetball. Office: GE Aircraft Engine Bus Group 1 Neumann Way MD K108 Cincinnati OH 45215

MILLER, MARK LEE, lawyer; b. Chgo., Oct. 28, 1955; s. Erwin Lee and Dorothy Jean (Gatlin) M.; m. Julia Anne Kubick, Sept. 28, 1986. AB, Loyola U., Chgo., 1975; JD, U. Ill., 1978; M in Mgmt., Northwestern U., 1986. Bar: Ill. 1978. Assoc. Rotenberg & Schwartzman, Chgo., 1978-82; sole practice Chgo., 1982—. Mem. Mayor Harold Washington's Transition Team, City of Chgo., 1983; pres. Democratic Victory Fund, Chgo., 1985. Mem. Chgo. Bar Assn. (chmn. Young Lawyer's sect., profl. responsibility com. 1981-82, young lawyer's exec. com. 1981-82). Presbyterian. Avocation: running. Office: 54 W Hubbard St Suite 400 Chicago IL 60611

MILLER, MARK RICHARD, dentist; b. Lafayette, Ind., Nov. 8, 1955; s. Richard Lloyd and Emilie Clara (Adamski) M. BS with distinction, Ohio State U., 1977, DDS, 1980. Clinical instr. Ohio State U., Columbus, 1980-81; pvt. practice dentistry Columbus, 1980—. Mem. ADA, Ohio Dental Assn., Columbus Dental Soc. Republican. Roman Catholic. Clubs: Swiss, Columbus Ski. Avocations: oil painting, skiing, golf, softball, football. Home: 1765-C Kings Ct Columbus OH 43212 Office: 1730 Schrock Rd Columbus OH 43229

MILLER, MASON FERRELL, electrical engineer; b. Rockford, Nebr., Nov. 5, 1919; s. Martin Robertson and Bertha Luella (Story) M.; B.S., U. Nebr., 1940; M.S., MIT, 1941; m. Irene Elizabeth Westerman, Sept. 25, 1942; children—Paul Martin, James Mason, Marianne. Student engr. AT&T, N.Y.C., 1941; jr. engr. U.S. Navy, Bath, Maine, 1941; with NASA, Langley AFB, Va., 1941-51, aero. research scientist, 1948-51, Cleve., 1951-55; engr. specialist AiResearch Mfg. Co., Phoenix, 1955-57; preliminary design engr. Allison div. Gen. Motors Co., Indpls., 1957-61; sr. engring. specialist, supr. N. Am. Rockwell, Columbus, Ohio, 1961-69; performance engr. Gen. Electric Co., Aircraft Engine Bus. Group, Evendale, Ohio, 1969-82, part-time, 1982—; teaching advisor Gen. Motors Inst., 1960. Mem. Washington Twp. Sch. Planning Com., Indpls., 1961; asst. scoutmaster Boy Scouts Am., Berea, Ohio, 1954-55, pack treas., Phoenix, 1956-57, cubmaster, com. chmn., Indpls., 1959-61. U. Nebr. Regent's scholar, 1936; Mass. Inst. Tech. scholar, 1940; recipient NASA Merit Service award, 1948; Cleve. City and Plain Dealer award ARC program, 1953. Mem. Am. Def. Preparedness Assn., AIAA, Internat. Platform Assn., Pi Mu Epsilon, Sigma Tau. Presbyterian (deacon). Club: Order of DeMolay. Contbr. articles in field to profl. jours. Home and Office: 6611 Franklin Street Lincoln NE 68506

MILLER, MERLYNN ALBERT, rural letter carrier, fire chief; b. Sheldon, Iowa, Aug. 31, 1927; s. Lester Ray and Florence Elizabeth (Wilson) M.; m. Mary Patricia Toal, Aug. 31, 1950; children—David, Dianne, Susan. Student pub. schs., Sheldon, Iowa. Feed driver Moorman's Feeds, Sheldon, Iowa, 1954-68; police officer City of Sheldon, 1968-80; rural letter carrier U.S. Post Office, Sheldon, 1980—; dist. coordinator Fire Assn., 1981—; fire chief City of Sheldon. Served with USN, 1945-46, PTO. Mem. Nat. Rural Letter Carriers, Internat. Assn. Arson Investigators, Iowa Rural Letter Carriers, Iowa Fire Assn., VFW (past comdr., life). Methodist. Club: Sanborn Country (Iowa). Lodge: Eagles (comdr.). Avocations: golf; bowling; fishing. Home: 1303 Kahler Ct Sheldon IA 51201

MILLER, MICHAEL GEORGE, optometrist; b. Lucas, Ohio, Nov. 3, 1955; s. Gerald Elwin and Ada Mae (Hahn) M.; m. Michelle Marie Novosel, June 8, 1985. OD, Ohio State U., 1980. Clin. instr. Ohio State U., Columbus, 1980-82; pvt. practice optometry Medina and Westlake, Ohio, 1982—. Mem. Am. Optometric Assn., Ohio Optometric Assn. (lt. gov. local zone 3, 1984-85), Medina Jaycees, Beta Sigma Kappa. Lodge: Lions (bd. dirs. Medina, 1983, lion tamer Medina, 1984). Avocations: bicycling, tennis, yard work. Home: 1133 Waterbury Dr Medina OH 44256 Office: Reserve Park I 3637 Medina Rd Suite 80 Medina OH 44256

MILLER, MICHAEL J., lawyer; b. Detroit, 1945; s. Harvey W. and Virginia (Howind) M.; married, May 19, 1979. MA in Indsl. Psychology, Wayne State U., 1970, LLB, 1976. Gen. mgr. Triangle Group, Detroit, 1968-80, sr. ptnr., 1980—. Campaign mgr. 36th Dist. Ct. candidate, Detroit, 1978, 80, 84, 86; bd. dirs. Am. Success Found., Rochester, Mich., 1985—. Served to lt. col. USAFR, 1964-84. Republican. Episcopalian. Office: The Triangle Group 19011 Woodbine Detroit MI 48219

MILLER, NINA BETH, ticket system executive; b. St. Louis, Mar. 6, 1956; d. William Max and Mary Virginia (Bray) Schatzkamer; m. Bernard Stephen Miller III, May 30, 1981. BA, Washington U., 1977. With Swensen's Restaurant, St. Louis, 1976-77, asst. mgr., 1977-78, mgr., 1978-79; asst. restaurant mgr. Famous-Barr, St. Louis, 1979-80; dir. ops. St. Louis Ticketmaster, Inc., 1980-83, gen. mgr., 1983—. Dir. children's program New Life Style Ctr., St. Louis, 1986-87. Mem. Box Office Mgmt. Internat. (membership com. 1985—, conf. speaker 1987), Gamma Phi Beta (panhellenic rep. 1975-76). Avocations: horseback riding, photography, softball, aerobics. Home: 7474 Washington Ave Saint Louis MO 63130 Office: St Louis Ticketmaster Inc 2229 Pine Saint Louis MO 63103

MILLER, PATRICIA ANN, educator; b. Charleston, W.Va., Oct. 26, 1938; d. William Jennings and Frankie Marguerite (Bragg) Nutter; m. Maurice E. Miller, July 20, 1963; children: Elizabeth, Jeffrey, Joel. BS Mus Edn., Charleston U., 1961; postgrad., Cin. Conservatory Music, 1962, 63, Miami U., Oxford, Ohio, 1965. Tchr. Ross (Ohio) High Sch., 1961-65, Hamilton (Ohio) Pub. Schs., 1973—. choir dir. Immanuel Baptist Ch., Hamilton, 1968-84, 1986—. Mem. Music Educators Nat. Conf., Ohio Music Edn. Assn., Great Miami Choral Soc. (featured soloist). Home: 707 Shultz Dr Hamilton OH 45013 Office: Hamilton High Sch 1165 Eaton Ave Hamilton OH 45013

MILLER, PATRICIA LOUISE, state senator, nurse; b. Bellefontaine, Ohio, July 4, 1936; d. Richard William and Rachel Orpha (Williams) Miller; m. Kenneth Orlan Miller, July 3, 1960; children—Tamara Sue, Matthew Ivan. R.N., Meth. Hosp. Sch. Nursing-Indpls., 1957; B.S., Ind. U., 1960. Office nurse A.D. Dennison, M.D., 1960-61; staff nurse Meth. Hosp., Indpls., 1959, Community Hosp., Indpls., 1958. Representative, State of Ind., Dist. 50, Indpls., 1982-83, senator, State of Ind., Dist. 32, Indpls., 1983—, mem. edn., health welfare and aging, labor and pension, legis. apportionment and elections coms. Mem. Bd. Edn., Met. Sch. Dist. Warren Twp., 1974-82, pres., 1979-80, 80-81; mem. Warren Twp. Citizens Screening Com. for Sch. Bd. Candidates, 1972-74, 84, Met. Zoning Bd. Appeals, Div. I, City-County Council, 1972-76; bd. dirs. Central Ind. Council on Aging, Indpls., 1977-80; mem. State Bd. of Voc. and Tech. Edn., 1978-82, sec., 1980-82; mem. Gov.'s Select Adv. Commn. for Primary and Secondary Edn., 1983; precinct committeeman Republican Party, 1968-74, ward vice chmn., 1975-78, ward chmn., 1978-85, twp. chmn., 1985—; del. Rep. State Conv., 1968, 74, 76, 1980, sgt. at arms, 1982, mem. platform com., 1984; del. Rep. Nat. Conv., 1984; active various polit. campaigns; bd. dirs. PTA, 1967-81; pres. Grassy Creek PTA, 1971-72; state del. Ind. PTA, 1978; mem. child care adv. com. Walker Career Center, 1976-80, others; bd. dirs. Ch. Fedn. Greater Indpls., 1979-82, Christian Justice Center, Inc., 1983-85, Gideon Internat. Aux., 1977—; mem. United Meth. Bd. Missions Aux. of Indpls., 1974-80, v.p., 1974-76; bd. dirs. Lucille Raines Residence, Inc., 1977-80; exec. com. S. Ind. Conf. United Meth. Women, 1977-80, lay del. S. Ind. Conf. United Meth. Ch., 1977—, fin. and adminstrn. com., 1979—, planning and research com., 1980—; sec. Indpls. S.E. Dist. Council on Ministries, 1977-78, pres., 1982; chmn. council on ministries Cumberland United Meth. Ch., 1969-76; chmn. stewardship com. Old Bethel United Meth. Ch., 1982-85, fin. com., 1982-85, adminstrv. bd., mem. council on ministries, 1981-85. Recipient Phi Lambda Theta Honor for outstanding contbr. in field of edn., 1976; Woman of the Year, Cumberland Bus. and Profl. Women, 1979; Ind. Voc. Assn. citation award, 1984, others. Mem. Indpls. Dist. Dental Soc. Women's Aux., Ind. Dental Assn. Women's Aux., Am. Dental Assn. Women's Aux., others. Clubs: Warren Twp. Rep. Franklin Rep., Lawrence Rep., Center Twp. Rep., Fall Creek Valley Rep., Marion County Council Rep. Women, Ind. Women's Rep., Indpls. Women's Rep., Ind. Fedn. Rep. Women, Nat. Fedn. Rep. Women, Beech Grove Rep., Perry Twp. Rep. Address: 1041 S Muesing Rd Indianapolis IN 46239

MILLER, PATRICIA LYNN, clinical psychologist, consultant; b. Chgo., Jan. 27, 1938; d. Joseph L. and Gertrude R. (Kontek) Lynn; m. Eric E. Miller, Feb. 27, 1960; children—Kurt, Nathan C., Peter J. Student Carleton Coll., 1955-56; A.B., U. Chgo., 1958; M.S., Ill. Inst. Tech., 1971, Ph.D., 1979. Pub. relations dir., dist. dir. Chgo. Area council Camp Fire Girls, 1958-66, asst. exec. dir., 1966-68; task force tchr. Assessment Team for 45-15 Year 'Round Sch. Plan, Valley View Sch. Dist., Romeoville, Ill., 1968-70; sch. psychologist Lockport (Ill.) Area Spl. Edn. Coop., 1971-80; pvt. practice psychology, Joliet, Ill., 1977—; instr., cons. sch. psychology program Ill. Inst. Tech., Chgo., 1975-77; field supr. Chgo. Sch. Profl. Psychology, 1981-82. Mem. Citizen's Com. for Wider Use of Schs., Mayor Daley's Youth Commn., Tribune Charities Youth Com., Chgo., 1958-68; mem. Women's Network for ERA, 1970s. State of Ill. grad. fellow, 1970. Mem. Am. Psychol. Assn., Internat. Neuropsychol. Soc., Nat. Assn. Sch. Psychologists, Ill. Sch. Psychologists Assn., Ill. Psychol. Assn., Sigma Xi. Club: Zonta. Office: 2455 Glenwood Ave Joliet IL 60435

MILLER, PATRICIA PRESTON, psychologist, real estate; b. Kansas City, Mo., Oct. 18, 1936; s. Robert M. and Essa Vivian (Bowen) P.; m. Frank D. Miller, July 25, 1957 (div. May 1971); children: Robin, Ross, Sara, Dwight. BS, U. Wyo., 1957; MA, U. Mo., Kansas City, 1971. Tchr. Job Corp. Ctr., Excelsior Springs, Mo., 1970-71; psychol. cons. Head Start, Parsons, Iowa, 1971-72; dir. counseling Crittenton Ctr., Kansas City, 1972-80; real estate broker Edward Murphy, Liberty, Mo., 1980—; psychologist Nutri-System, Gladstone, Mo., 1985—; Mem. Kansas City Real Estate. Mem. com on status of women Liberty Meth. Ch. Mem. Mo. Psychol. Assn., Phi Upsilon Omicron. Home: PO Box 41 Liberty MO 64068

MILLER, PAUL AARON, human resources developer; b. Oklahoma City, Okla., Nov. 7, 1954; s. Aaron Julius and Helen Marie (Herber) M. EdB, Bowling Green State U., 1977. Academic instr. Lorain County Vocat. Ctr., Oberlin, Ohio, 1977-80; unit mgr. CBC Industries, Columbus, Ohio, 1980-81; human resource trainer Bank One, Columbus, 1981-85; ednl. services coordinator Grady Meml. Hosp., Delaware, Ohio, 1985—. Editor: bowling Green Chess Club News; developer: (tng. program) Ya Gotta Have Heart, 1986. Mem. staff Edwards for Congress, Bowling Green, 1974. Mem. Ohio Soc. Healthcare Edn. and Tng., Ohio Hosp. Assn., Am. Soc. Tng. and Devel., Nat. Soc. Performance and Instruction. Democrat. Club: People Chess Fedn. (Bowling Green) (pres. 1974-75). Office: Grady Meml Hosp 561 W Central Ave Delaware OH 43015

MILLER, PAUL MCGRATH, JR., executive search consulting company executive; b. Bowling Green, Ky., Oct. 31, 1935; s. Paul McGrath and Lena D. (Carr) M.; m. Charlene F. Russnak, Sept. 12, 1970 (div.); children—Andrew McGrath, Christopher Paul. B. Mech. Engring., Cornell U., 1958; M.B.A., Harvard U., 1966. Foreman, Procter & Gamble, Cin., 1958-60; market analyst United Aircraft Co., Sunnyvale, Calif., 1963-64; asst. to chmn. bd. Boise Cascade Corp. (Idaho), 1966, gen. mktg. mgr. Insulite div., 1966-67, nat. sales mgr. Lumber and Plywood, 1967-68, asst. to exec. v.p. Paper Group, 1968-69; group dir. mktg. Am. Standard, Inc., N.Y.C., 1969-71; dir. corp. communications Indian Head, Inc., N.Y.C., 1971-74; v.p. mktg. Ball & Socket Mfg Co., Cheshire, Conn., 1975; v.p. mktg. Cory Coffee Service, Chgo., 1976, v.p., gen. mgr., 1977-80; v.p., ptnr. Korn/Ferry Internat., Chgo., 1980-87; ptnr. Lamalie Assocs. Inc., Chgo., 1987—. Mem. Winnetka Caucus (Ill.), 1980. Served to capt. USAF, 1960-63. Episcopalian. Clubs: Racquet Chgo., Met. (Chgo.), Harvard N.Y.C., Harvard Bus. Sch. Chgo. (dir.). Office: Lamalie Assocs Inc 120 S Riverside Plaza Chicago IL 60606

MILLER, PHILIP B., retail department store executive; b. 1938. Student, Tulane U., Johns Hopkins U. V.p. Bloomingdales, N.Y.C., 1974-76; vice chmn. bd. dirs. Lord & Taylor, N.Y.C., 1976-79; pres. Nieman-Marcus, 1979-83; chmn. bd. dirs. Marshall Fields & Co., 1983—. Office: Marshall Field & Co 111 N Washington St Chicago IL 60690 *

MILLER, R. TRAVIS, real estate executive; b. Hartford, Ill.; s. Clinton Eugene and Kathryn (Summers) M.; m. Barbara Louise French, Aug. 29, 1954; children: Kimberly R., Kelli A., Kendal L. BS, Ball State U., 1955. Sales rep. Shell Oil, Ft. Wayne, Ind., 1958-61; real estate sales rep. Sunoco Oil, Indpls., 1961-69; ind. broker Indpls., 1969-76; sr. real estate rep. McDonalds, St. Louis and Indpls., 1976-82; sr. real estate rep., mgr. Taco Bell, Indpls., Houston, and Chgo., 1982—. Served as sgt. USMC, 1952-58. Mem. Internat. Council Shopping Ctrs., Nat. Assn. Corp. Real Estate Execs. Office: Taco Bell 801 N Cass Ave Suite 202 Westmont IL 60559

MILLER, RANDAL HOWARD, health science association adminstrator; b. Fostoria, Ohio, Apr. 11, 1947; s. Richard Paul and Michaline (Tinkovicz) M.; m. Patricia June Smith, May 29, 1970 (div. Apr. 1978); 1 child, Rhett Howard; m. Angel Jo Belfiore, May 27, 1978; 1 child, Shea Michal. BS, Bowling Green (Ohio) U., 1970. Chief labs. dept. health City of Cleve., 1975-78; coordinator lab. projects St. Vincent Charity Hosp., Cleve., 1980-83; pres. Trace Elements Analysis, Inc., Richfield, Ohio, 1979—; asst. dir. clin. pathology Univ. Hosps. Cleve., 1983—; adminstr. Univ. Med. Labs., Cleve., 1984—; instr. Allied Health, Cuyahoga Community Coll., Parma, Ohio, 1976-84. Served to sgt. U.S. Army, 1970-76. Mem. Clin. La. Mgmt. Assn., Am. Soc. Clin. Pathologists, Med. Group Mgmt. Assn., Ohio Pub. Lab. Dirs., Greater Cleve. Hosp. Assn. (vice-chmn. lab. com. 1986—), Alpha Sigma Phi. Roman Catholic. Avocation: music. Mailing Address: PO Box 33022 North Royalton OH 44133 Home: 6688 Renwood Dr Independence OH 44131 Office: Univ Hosps Cleve 2074 Abington Rd Cleveland OH 44106

MILLER, RICHARD A., utility company executive; b. 1927. B.B.A., Case Western Res. U., 1950; LL.B., Harvard U., 1953. With Cleve. Electric Illuminating Co., 1960—, sr. tax acct., 1960-61, prin. tax cons., 1961-62, controller, 1962-69, v.p. fin., 1969-75, v.p. fin. and gen. counsel, 1975-77, exec. v.p., 1977-83, pres., dir., 1983-86; pres. Centerior Energy Corp., Independence, Ohio, 1986—. Served with U.S. Army, 1945-47. Office: Centerior Energy Corp 6200 Oak Tree Blvd Independence OH 44131 *

MILLER, ROBERT ARTHUR, judge; b. Aberdeen, S.D., Aug. 28, 1939; s. Edward Louis and Bertha Leone (Hitchcox) M.; m. Shirlee Ann Schlim, Sept. 5, 1964; children: Catherine Sue, Scott Edward, David Alan, Gerri Elizabeth, Robert Charles. BS in Bus. Adminstrn., U. S.D., 1961, JD, 1963. Asst. atty. gen. State of S.D., Pierre, 1963-65; sole practice Philip, S.D., 1965-71; state atty. Haakon County, Philip, 1965-71; city atty. City of Philip, 1965-71; judge State of S.D. (6th cir.), Pierre, 1971-86, presiding judge, 1975-86; supreme ct. justice State of S.D., Pierre, 1986—; trustee S.D. Retirement

System, Pierre, 1974-85, chmn. 1982-85; faculty mem. State Law Enforcement Acad., Pierre, 1976-86; mem. State Crime Comm., 1979-86. Mem. State Bar of S.D., S.D. Judges' Assn. (pres. 1974-75). Roman Catholic. Lodge: Elks. Avocations: golf, hunting. Office: South Dakota Supreme Ct 500 E Capitol Ave Pierre SD 57501

MILLER, ROBERT BRANSON, SR., ret. newspaper publisher; b. Ottawa, Kans., June 25, 1906; s. Albert Laird and Louise (Branson) M.; m. Jean Leonard, Apr. 28, 1934 (div. dec. Dec. 1976); children—Robert Branson, Allen L.; m. Olive T. Adams, Jan. 6, 1978. B.A., Williams Coll., 1929. With Battle Creek (Mich.) Enquirer, 1929-79, from reporter to pub., 1952-79; v.p., dir. Federated Publs., 1944-54, pres., 1954-64, chmn. bd., 1964-79; also exec. chmn. and dir.; sr. v.p., dir. Gannett Co. Inc., 1971-79; now chmn. Albert and Louise B. Miller Found. Mem. Chi Psi. Lodge: Rotary. Home: 300 Wah Wah Tay See Way Battle Creek MI 49015 Office:: Federated Pu Inc 155 W Van Buren St Battle Creek MI 49016

MILLER, ROBERT CARL, physicist; b. Chgo., Oct. 26, 1938; s. Carl and Violet (Nelson) M.; B.S. in Physics, Ill. Inst. Tech., 1961; M.S. in Physics, No. Ill. U., 1965, Certificate Advanced Study in Physics, 1972; m. Mary Kay Ball, Sept. 3, 1969. Researcher particle accelerator div. Argonne (Ill.) Nat. Lab., 1961-66, researcher high energy physics div., 1966—. Registered profl. engr., Ill. Mem. Am. Phys. Soc., Am. Nuclear Soc., IEEE, Nat. Soc. Profl. Engrs., Soc. Certified Data Processors, Instrument Soc. Am., Am. Inst. Aero. and Astronautics, Mensa, Internat. Soc. for Philos. Enquiry, Mega Soc. Sigma Xi, Sigma Pi Sigma. Contbr. articles to profl. jours. Home: 1105 Elizabeth Ave Naperville IL 60540 Office: High Energy Physics Div Argonne Nat Lab Bldg 362 9700 Cass Ave Argonne IL 60439

MILLER, ROBERT CLIFFORD, state agency executive; b. Clinton, Iowa, Sept. 1, 1929; s. Clifford Gebhardt and Estella Elizabeth (Ullrich) M.; m. Norma Aileen Hildebaugh, June 13, 1953; children: Blair, Brian, Lynette, James, Lea. Hwy. project inspector Iowa Dept. Transp., Sioux City, 1956-62, asst. to maintenance engr., 1962-68, area maintenance supr., 1968-70, inventory mgr., 1970-79, printing and graphics mgr., 1979—; adv. bd. Iowa Prison Industries, Anamosa, 1981-83. Pres. Epiphany Grade Sch. Parents Club, Sioux City, 1968; bd. dirs. Heelan High Sch., Sioux City, 1969. Served with USN, 1948-52. Mem. Des Moines In-Plant Printing Mgmt. Assn. (pres. 1985—, Mem. of Yr. 1985). Roman Catholic. Lodge: Elks (loyal knight 1985-86, leading knight 1986-87). Avocations: golf, boating. Home: 611 Jewel Dr Ames IA 50010 Office: Iowa Dept Transp 800 Lincolnway Ames IA 50010

MILLER, ROBERT DAVID, engineer; b. Kansas City, Mo., Aug. 2, 1958; s. Oda Charles and Winona Virginia (McCorkle) M.; m. Valerie Jean Shelton, June 13, 1981. B.S. in Engring., U. Mo., 1980. Registered profl. engr., Mo. Environ. engr. Mo. Dept. of Natural Resources, Jefferson City, 1981-83; engr. Union Electric Co., St. Louis, 1983—; mem. adv. bd. Electric Power Research Inst., Nat. Acid Precipitation Assessment Program, U.S. EPA. Mem. ASCE, Air Pollution Control Assn., Greater St. Louis Air Pollution Control Assn. (bd. dirs. 1984-86, membership chmn. 1984-85, treas. 1986-87, sec. 1987—), Chi Epsilon, Tau Beta Pi. Republican. Methodist. Office: Union Electric Co Box 149 MC 602 Saint Louis MO 63166

MILLER, ROBERT DAVID, forensic psychiatrist; b. Chapel Hill, N.C., Sept. 4, 1941; s. Augustus Taylor and Adeline Helen (Porombovics) M. BS cum laude, Davidson Coll., 1964; PhD in Biochemistry, Duke U., 1972, MD, 1973. Cert. Am. Bd. Psychiatry and Neurology, Am. Bd. Forensic Psychiatry. Resident in psychiatry Duke U., Durham, N.C., 1973-76; with psychiatry dept. Duke U., Durham, 1976-82; staff psychiatrist John Umstead Hosp., Butner, N.C., 1976-78, dir. admissions, 1978-80, resident tng. dir., 1980-82; dir. forensic tng. Mendota Mental Health Inst., Madison, 1982—. Contbr. articles to profl. jours. Fellow Am. Acad. Forensic Scis. (program chmn. 1985, sec. psychiat. sect. 1987), Am. Psychiat. Assn.; mem. Am. Acad. Psychiatry and Law (exec. council 1986, sec. Midwest chpt. 1985—, pres.-elect 1987), Internat. Acad. Law and Mental Health. Democrat. Jewish. Avocations: music, stereo and video recording. Home: 5587 Winsome Way Oregon WI 53575 Office: Mendota Mental Health Inst 301 Troy Dr Madison WI 53704

MILLER, ROBERT HASKINS, state justice; b. Columbus, Ohio, Mar. 3, 1919; s. George L. and Marian Alice (Haskins) M.; m. Audene Fausett, Mar. 14, 1943; children: Stephen F., Thomas G., David W., Stacey Ann. A.B., Kans. U., 1940, LL.B., 1942; grad., Nat. Coll. State Trial Judges, Phila., 1967. Bar: Kans. 1943. Practice in Paola, 1946-60; judge 6th Jud. Dist. Kans., Paola, 1961-69; U.S. magistrate Kans. Dist., Kansas City, 1969-75; justice Kans. Supreme Ct., 1975—; chmn. Kans. Jud. Council, 1987—. Contbg. author: Pattern (Civil Jury) Instructions for Kansas, 2d edit, 1969. Served with AUS, 1942-46. Mem. Kans. Bar Assn., Wyandotte County Bar Assn., Shawnee County Bar Assn., ABA, Am. Legion, Phi Gamma Delta, Phi Delta Phi. Presbyterian. Office: Kansas Supreme Ct Kans Jud Ctr Topeka KS 66612

MILLER, ROBERT L., JR., federal judge; b. 1950. BA, Northwestern U., 1972; JD, Ind. U., 1975. Law clk. to presiding justice U.S. Dist. Ct. (no. dist.) Ind., 1975; judge St. Joseph Superior Ct., South Bend, Ind., 1975-85, chief judge, 1981-83, judge, 1983—. Office: U S Dist Ct 325 Fed Bldg 204 S Main St South Bend IN 46601 *

MILLER, ROBERT LAWRENCE, vocational programmer, aquatics instructor; b. Chgo., July 5, 1955; s. Robert John and Lottie (Rocco) M.; m. Barbara Kay Skelton, Sept. 16, 1984; children: Michael, Alexander. BA, St. Mary's Coll., 1977. Child care supr. Clinicare Corp., Winona, Minn., 1977-79; with support staff Vols. of Am., Madison, Wis., 1980-82; adaptive aquatics instr. Madison Schs., 1980-85, East YMCA, Madison, 1979—; vocational programmer Verona (Wis.) Schs., 1984—; swimming coach Spl. Olympics, Madison, 1979—; advocate Access to Independence, Madison, 1985. Contbr. articles to profl. jour. Vol. Access to Independence, Madison, 1985, Arthritis Found., Madison, 1986, Dem. Party, Madison, 1984; mem. ARC. Mem. Wis. Edn. Assn. Roman Catholic. Avocations: sailing, swimming, camping. Home: 1910 E Main Madison WI 53704 Office: Verona Schs 300 Richards Verona WI 53593

MILLER, ROBERT LEE, engineering company executive; b. Waverly, Iowa, May 18, 1941; s. Harvey August and Marjorie (Voss) M.; m. Lanora Faye Gersema, Aug. 17, 1963; children: Greg, Dan. BSME, Iowa State U., 1964. Mgr. 600 series Deere & Co., Waterloo, Iowa, 1973-75, mgr. 700 series, 1975-81, mgr. advanced engines, 1981-84, mgr. 500 and 700 engines, 1984-85, mgr. applied engring. engines, 1985-86; dir. engring. Engines-Kohler (Wis.) Co., 1987—. Founding pres. Juvenile Diabetes Found. N.E. Iowa, Waterloo, 1981-83; chmn. bldg. and grounds Cedar Heights Presbyn. Ch., Cedar Falls, Iowa, 1982-85. Mem. Soc. Automotive Engrs. Clubs: Beaver Hills Country (Cedar Falls). Avocations: golf, downhill skiing, cross country skiing, bicycling, reading. Home: 4515 Prairie View Rd Sheboygan WI 53081 Office: Kohler Co Kohler WI 53044

MILLER, ROBERT NICHOLAS, anesthesiologist; b. St. Louis, Aug. 14, 1935; s. Louis R. and Gladys (Grotjan) M.; m. Dianne Jackson, Aug. 16, 1958; children: Deborah Miller Francois, Melanie Miller Fewell, Dawn, Brett Jackson. AB in Premed., U. Mo., 1957, MD, 1961. Diplomate Am. Bd. Anesthesiology. Resident in anesthesiology U. Mo., Columbia, 1962-64; chief of anesthesia McMillan Hosp., Barnes and Allied Hosps., St. Louis; dir. obstetrical anesthesiology St. John's Mercy Med. Ctr., St. Louis, 1975-82, chmn. dept. anesthesiology, 1982—. Editor Anesthesia &Analgesia, 1974, Laryngoscope, 1975. Mem. voting bd. Blue Cross/Blue Shield, St. Louis; mem. adv. bd. Christian Action Council, St. Louis; v.p., bd. dirs. Westminster Christian Acad., St. Louis; mem. pres. council Covenant Seminary, St. Louis. Served to capt. U.S. Army, 1964-66. Fellow Am. Coll. Obsterics and Gynecology; mem. St. Louis Soc. Anesthesiology (v.p. 1969, pres. 1970), St. Louis Gynecol. Soc., Soc. Obstet. Anesthesia and Perinatology. Office: St Johns Mercy Med Ctr 621 S New Ballas Rd Saint Louis MO 63141

MILLER, ROBERT STERLING, manufacturing executive; b. Millersburg, Ohio, Oct. 20, 1926; s. Roscoe C. and Evelyn M. Miller; m. Norma Jean Bird, June 12, 1948; children—Lee H., Sallie Jane. B.Sc. in Bus. Adminstrn., Ohio State U., 1951; M.B.A., Ohio U., 1981. Indsl. sales mgr. Miracle Adhesives Corp., New Philadelphia, Ohio, 1953-58; sales mgr. Buehler Bros. Co., Dover, Ohio, 1958-68; v.p. sales consumer div. Franklin Chem. Industries, Columbus, Ohio, 1968—. Served with USAAF, 1945. Recipient Outstanding Citizen award, Dover, 1968. Methodist. Author: Adhesives and Glues-How to Choose and Use Them, 1980; Home Construction Projects: With Adhesives and Glues, 1983, Energy Conservation with Adhesives and Sealants, 1985. Home: 4208 Greensview Dr Upper Arlington OH 43220 Office: Franklin Internat 2020 Bruck St Columbus OH 43207

MILLER, ROBERT STEVENS, JR., automobile manufacturing company executive; b. Portland, Oreg., Nov. 4, 1941; s. Robert Stevens and Barbara (Weston) M.; m. Margaret Rose Kyger, Nov. 9, 1966; children—Christopher John, Robert Stevens, Alexander Lamont. A.B. with distinction, Stanford U., 1963; LL.B., Harvard U., 1966; M.B.A., Stanford U., 1968. Bar: Calif. bar 1966. Fin. analyst Ford Motor Co., Dearborn, Mich., 1968-71; spl. studies mgr. Ford Motor Co., Mexico City, 1971-73; dir. fin. Ford Asia-Pacific, Inc., Melbourne, Australia, 1974-77, Ford Motor Co., Caracas, Venezuela, 1977-79; v.p., treas. Chrysler Corp., Detroit, 1980-81, exec. v.p. fin., 1981-85, vice chmn. bd., 1985—; dir. Moore-Oregon Lumber Co., Coos Bay, Oreg. Bd. dirs. United Found., Detroit. Mem. Calif. Bar Assn. Office: Chrysler Fin Corp PO Box 1919 Detroit MI 48288

MILLER, RODNEY EARL, music educator; b. Odessa, Tex., Mar. 24, 1952; s. Herbert Exever and Marion (Mitchel) M.; m. Josephine Ann Popolillo, Aug. 1, 1981; children: Rachael, Matthew. BM, West Tex. State U., 1974; MM, Ind. U., 1977. Solo performer "Texas" Drama, Canyon, 1970-74; asst. instr. Ind. U., Bloomington, Tex., 1974-77; instr. Taylor U., Upland, Ind., 1977-78; opera soloist Phila., 1978-80, Staatheater, Regensburg, Fed. Republic Germany, 1980-83; asst. prof. Ill. State U., Normal, 1983—. Regional finalist Met. Opera Audition, 1977; winner Nat. Verdi-Puccini Competition, 1979. Mem. Nat. Assn. Tchrs. of Singing, Alpha Chi, Pi Kappa Lambda. Presbyterian. Avocations: tennis, gourmet cooking, photography. Home: 203 Magnolia Bloomington IL 61701 Office: Ill State U Music Dept Normal IL 61761

MILLER, RONALD LEE, manufacturing and entertainment company executive; b. Columbus, Ohio, Aug. 17, 1940; s. Bruce Eugene and Opal Maxine (Boss) M.; B.S. in Mech. Engring., Ohio Tech. U., 1966; M.B.A., U. Beverly Hills, 1977, Ph.D., 1979; children—Kellie Ann, Christina Lynn, Erin Nichole, Ronald Lee II. Corp. engr. chems. div. U.S. Steel Corp., Circleville, Ohio, Pitts., 1970-72; owner Quality Mold, Grand Rapids, Mich., 1972-73; v.p. Nika Plastics, Grand Rapids, 1973-75; pres. Internat. Prototypes, Grand Rapids, 1975-79; founder, chief exec. Nat. Prototypes, Grand Rapids, 1977-79; pres. Hilco Plastics, Grand Rapids, 1977—; pres., founder Position Inc., Grand Rapids, 1980-84, RLM Prodns., Hollywood, 1980-84; pres. Hilco House, Inc., 1982-84; cons. product devel. Mem. ednl. adv. com. Grand Rapids Area Colls.; mem. U.S. Senatorial Adv. Com. Served with USMCR, 1957-58. Mem. Soc. Plastics Engrs., N.Y. Acad. Scis., Am. Mgmt. Assn. Republican. Roman Catholic. Author texts in field. Office: 4172 Danvers Ct Kentwood MI 49508

MILLER, RUSSELL DUANE, data processing manager; b. Fergus Falls, Minn., Jan. 21, 1927; s. Henry C. and Ida A. (Will) M.; m. Evelyn M. Schiermann, Jan. 28, 1948; children: Kitty L., Russell D. Jr. With Otter Tail Power Co., Fergus Falls, 1951-81, data processing mgr., 1981—; cons. Gov.'s Mgmt. Task Force, Bismark, N.D., 1982. Served with U.S. Army, 1947-48. Lutheran. Home: 1002 N Cleveland Fergus Falls MN 56537 Office: Otter Tail Power Co 215 S Cascade St Fergus Falls MN 56537

MILLER, SAMUEL DEAN, hospital laboratory director; b. Lamar, Colo., July 30, 1943; s. Daniel Long and Lida Grace (Brenneman) M.; m. Carol Diane McMurray, Dec. 2, 1983; children: Daniel Wesley, Andrew David. BA, Greenville Coll., 1966; MS in Health Systems Adminstrn., Coll. St. Francis, Joliet, Ill., 1987. Cert. clin. lab. scientist, med. tech. Med. tech. Utlaut Meml. Hosp., Greenville, Ill., 1967-69; med. tech. St. Vincent Hosp., Indpls., 1969, supr. gen. lab., 1969-74, mgr. lab. services, 1974-82, dir. lab. services, 1982—. Mem. Am Soc. Clin. Pathologists, Am. Soc. Med. Techs., Am. Hosp. Assn. Republican. Methodist. Avocations: real estate mgmt., coin collecting. Home: 6133 W Alpine Ave Indianapolis IN 46224 Office: St Vincent Hosp & Health Care Ctr 2001 W 86th St Indianapolis IN 46260

MILLER, SARABETH, educator; b. Kouts, Ind., Apr. 6, 1927; d. Clayton Everett and Eva Margaret (Noland) Reif; m. Lloyd Melvin Miller, Dec. 2, 1944; children—Virginia, Shirley, Judith, John, Nola, Steven. B.A., Valparaiso U., 1972, M.A. in L.S., 1977, postgrad., Purdue U., 1983, Ind. U., 1986. Lic. tchr., Ind. Office employee Porter County Herald, Hebron, Ind., 1954-55, Little Co. of Mary Hosp. and Home, San Pierre, Ind., 1960-65, Jasper County Co-op, Tefft, Ind., 1965-69; tchr. art DeMotte (Ind.) elem. sch., 1972-76, Kankakee Valley High Sch., Wheatfield, Ind., 1976—. Leader 4-H Club, Kouts; mem. session Kouts Presbyn. Ch. Recipient various prizes Lake Central Fair (Ind.), 1975, 80, photography award Ind. Dept. Tourism, 1976; Eli Lilly fellow, 1987. Mem. NEA, Nat. Art Edn. Assn., Ind. Tchrs. Assn., Ind. Art Edn. Assn., Kankakee Valley Tchrs. Assn. Republican. Presbyterian. Contbr. articles and photographs to various local publs. Home: 1378 S County Rd 500 E Kouts IN 46347

MILLER, SCOTT ANDREW, secondary school business educator; b. Cambridge, Ohio, Nov. 7, 1961; s. Glen Ellis and Alleen (Mount) M.; m. Mary Lou Wiggins, Aug. 7, 1982. AA, Ohio Valley Coll., Parkersburg, W.Va., 1981; B of Secondary Edn. summa cum laude, Okla. Christian Coll., 1983. Cert. tchr., Ohio. Warehouseman Carpet World Inc., Oklahoma City, 1981-83; admissions counselor Ohio Valley Coll., 1983-85; secondary tchr. Marietta (Ohio) City Schs., 1985—; Athletic coach Marietta City Schs., 1985—. Named one of Outstanding Young Men of Am., U.S. Jaycees, 1985. Mem. NEA, Ohio Edn. Assn., Nat. Bus. Tchrs. Assn., Ohio Bus. Tchrs. Assn., Ohio High Sch. Coaches Assn. Republican. Mem. Ch. of Christ. Club: Belpre Civitan. Avocations: hunting, fishing, singing. Home: 1153 Woodlawn Ave Belpre OH 45714 Office: Marietta City Schs Marietta Sr High Sch Davis Ave Marietta OH 45750

MILLER, SCOTT (SCOTTY) ROBERT, program administrator; b. Chgo., Nov. 13, 1956; s. Robert D. and Gloria (Schroeder) M.; m. Natalie Kay Bas, Aug. 17, 1985. BS, St. Cloud State U., 1978. Sr. program planner Honeywell, Edina, Minn., 1979—; tax preparer Beneficial, New Hope, Minn., 1982-83; tax cons. Thompson Tax Service, Brooklyn Park, Minn., 1984—. Republican. Clubs; Crystal Single Adults (New Hope) (large group coordinator 1983-85); One + One (New Hope) (group leader). Avocations: volleyball, softball, computers. Home: 8515 Maplebrook Parkway Brooklyn Park MN 55445

MILLER, SUSAN DALTON, marriage, family and chemical dependency counselor, program director; b. St. Louis, May 8, 1943; d. George L. and Wilma Pearl (Johnston) Davis; m. Bill J. Dalton, Apr. 19, 1962; children—Cynthia Lynn, Steven Joseph; m. 2d, John Timothy Miller, July 26, 1977; 1 dau., Christine Ryann. B.S. in Edn., U. Mo.-St. Louis, 1975, M.Ed., 1982; postgrad. Purdue U., N.E. Mo. U., Webster Coll., Ohio State U. Cert. spl. edn. tchr., social worker, chemical dependency counselor guidance counselor, teacher; counselor, coordinator career edn., handicapped behavorial problems, grant and research Ferguson-Florissant Sch. St. Louis U. laison, nat. ctr. for Research, Ohio State U., Therapy Harding Hosp., Gestalt Inst. Fla. Johnson Inst. in Individual, Family, Marital and Chemical Dependency, developed and managed chemical dependency program to schs.; commr. Occupational Status Women NVGA. Tri Counseling Ctr., Family Therapy Program, Columbus Health Dept./ Alcoholism and Drug Abuse Sect., Smoking Cessation Program, Life Extenders Inc.; mgr. Employee Assistance Programs The Ctr. for Employee Excellence, Columbus. Mem. Assn. Labor Mgmt. Cons. and Counselors on Alcoholism, E.A.S.N.A., Omicron Tau Theta. Home: 101 Forest Ridge Ct Worthington OH 43085

MILLER, SUSAN HEILMANN, newspaper publishing executive; b. Yuba City, Calif., Jan. 13, 1945; d. Paul Clay and Helen Christine (Sterud) Heilmann; m. Allen Clinton Miller III, June 24, 1967. BA, Stanford U., 1966; MS, Columbia U., 1969; PhD, Stanford U., 1976. Info. officer Montgomery County Schs., Rockville, Md., 1970-71, Palo Alto Schs., Calif., 1969-70, 71-73; news-features editor Bremerton Sun, Wash., 1976-80; night city editor Peninsula Times Tribune, Palo Alto, 1980-81; exec. editor News-Gazette, Champaign, Ill., 1981-85; dir. editorial devel. Scripps Howard Newspapers, Cin., 1985—. Contbr. articles to profl. jours. Bd. dirs. Vol. Illini Projects, U. Ill., 1983-85, Washington Journalism Ctr., 1985; mem. Pulitzer Prize Nominating Jury, 1986—, accrediting com. Accrediting Council on Journalism and Mass Communication. Mem. Am. Soc. Newspaper Editors (bd. dirs. 1985—), Assoc. Press Mng. Editors (bd. dirs.1984—), Ill. AP Mng. Editors (bd. dirs. 1984-85). Clubs: Executive (Champaign, Ill.) (bd.dirs. 1984-85); Bankers (Cin.). Office: Scripps Howard Newspapers 1100 Central Trust Tower Cincinnati OH 45202

MILLER, SYDELL LOIS, cosmetics executive, marketing professional; b. Cleve., Aug. 10, 1937; d. Jack Harvey Lubin and Evelyne (Saltzman) Brower; m. Arnold Max Miller, Oct. 19, 1958; children: Lauren Beth, Stacy Lynn. Student, U. Miami, 1955-56. Mgr. Hair Salon, Cleve., 1958-60; pres., owner Women's Retail Store, Cleve., 1960-72; exec. v.p. Ardell, Inc., Solon, Ohio, 1972-84; exec. v.p. and owner Matrix Essentials, Inc., Solon, 1980—; pres. Lauren Stacy Mktg., Inc., Solon, 1972—. Editor ednl. books and newsletter, Salons, 1981—. Mem. Mt. Sinai Hosp. Aux., Cleve., 1972—, Beachwood (Ohio) Mus., 1981—. Mem. Am. Beauty Assns. (named Woman of Yr. 1985), Beauty and Barber Supply Inst., Inc., Cosmetic, Toiletry and Fragrance Assn., Inc. Avocations: collecting art and antiques, interior design, reading. Office: Matrix Essentials Inc 30601 Carter St Solon OH 44139

MILLER, THOMAS F., graphic designer, marketing specialist; b. Milw., Apr. 19, 1941; s. Samuel Kripps and Anita Agusta (Zimmermann) M.; m. Elizabeth Helen Ganson, June 10, 1972; children: Seth Thomas, Samantha Elizabeth. BS in Edn., U. Wis., Whitewater, 1971; MFA, U. Idaho, Moscow, 1974. Instr. design U. Idaho, Moscow, 1973-74; draftsman Planning and Zoning Dept. County of Columbia, Wis., 1974-77; owner, graphic designer Thorn Studio Designers, Merrimac, Wis., 1977—; direct mgr. LPC Solar, New Richland, Minn., 1979-83; owner, ptnr. Thorn Mktg., Merrimac, Minn., 1983—; exec. dir. Wis. Vietnam Vets. Meml., 1984—. Served with USMC, 1963-66, Vietnam. Mem. Vietnam Vets Am. (v.p. Madison chpt. 1984-85, bd. dirs. 1984-86, bd. dirs. and co-founder Baraboo chpt. 1985—, mem. state council 1983—). Lutheran.

MILLER, THOMAS J., atty. gen. Iowa; b. Dubuque, Iowa, Aug. 11, 1944; s. Elmer John and Betty Maude (Kross) M.; m. Linda Cottington, Jan. 10, 1981; 1 child, Matthew. B.A., Loras Coll., Dubuque, 1966; J.D., Harvard U., 1969. Bar: Iowa bar 1969. With VISTA, 1969-70; legis. asst. to U.S. congressman, 1970-71; legal edn. dir. Balt. Legal Aid Bur., also mem. part-time faculty U. Md. Sch. Law, 1971-73; pvt. practice McGregor, Iowa, 1973-78; city atty. McGregor, 1975-78; atty. gen. of Iowa 1978—. Pres. 2d Dist. New Democratic Club, Balt., 1972. Mem. Am. Bar Assn., Iowa Bar Assn., Common Cause. Roman Catholic. Office: Attorney Generals Office Hoover Bldg 2d Floor Des Moines IA 50319

MILLER, THOMAS MILTON, banker; b. Corydon, Ind., Mar. 2, 1930; s. R. Earl and Catherine (Hudson) M.; m. Kathryn Janet Owens, Aug. 28, 1954; children: Kimberleigh Kathryn, Thomas Milton, Jennifer Allen. B.S. in Bus, Ind. U., 1952; postgrad., U. Wis. Grad. Sch. Banking, 1961. With Ind. Nat. Bank, Indpls., 1954—; head Ind. div. Ind. Nat. Bank, 1964-68, sr. v.p., head met., 1968-71, exec. v.p., head comml. banking div., 1971-76, pres., 1976—, chmn., 1979—; chmn. Ind. Nat. Corp.; dir. State Life Ins. Co., Mayflower Group, Inc., Hook Drug, Inc., London Interstate Bank, Indpls. Water Co., Boehringer Mannheim Corp., Euratlantis Maritime Bank. Trustee, mem. exec. com. Meth. Hosp.; mem. exec. com. Indpls. Conv. and Visitors Assn., chmn. bd., 1981; mem. adv. bd. Ind. U.-Purdue U., Indpls., Ind. U. Found., Served to 1st lt. AUS, 1952-54. Mem. Am. Bankers Assn. (Ind. v.p. 1967-69, regional v.p. 1969-72), Ind. C. of C. (dir., mem. exec. com.), Indpls. C. of C., Ind. U. Alumni Assn., Ind. Soc. Chgo., Sigma Chi. Republican. Methodist. Clubs: Ind. U. Varsity; Meridian Hills Country (Indpls.), Economic (Indpls.) (v.p.). Lodge: Masons. Home: 410 Somerset Dr Indianapolis IN 46260 Office: Ind Nat Corp 1 Indiana Sq Indianapolis IN 46266

MILLER, THOMAS ROY, business manager; b. Washington, Apr. 12, 1957; s. Roy Samuel and Lucille Irene (Beck) M. BA in Econs. cum laude, BS in Info and Computer Scis. cum laude, U. Calif., Irvine, 1979; MBA in Fin., U. Chgo., 1981. V.p. Samor Mgmt., Evanston, Ill., 1981-82; ops. analyst RR Donnelley, Chgo., 1982-86; bus. mgr. RR Donnelley, Lisle, Ill., 1986—; cons. 3R Group, Chgo., 1984—. Fundraiser U. Chgo. Bus. Sch., 1982—; assoc. advisor Sea Explorer Ship Privateer, Chgo., 1983—. Named Eagle Scout Boy Scouts Am., 1973. Mem. Assn. for Computing Machinery, Info. Industry Assn. (steering com. Chgo. chpt. 1984—), Phi Beta Kappa. Republican. Lutheran. Avocations: sailing, gourmet cooking, classical music. Home: 5747 N Talman Ave Chicago IL 60659 Office: RR Donnelley & Sons Co 750 Warrenville Rd Lisle IL 60532

MILLER, THOMAS W., computer company executive; b. Oakland, Calif., Nov. 6, 1934; s. Walter F. and Audrey (O'Brien) M.; m. Jacquelyn Jolley, June 15, 1957; children—Laurie, Sheri. B.S. in Chemistry, U.Calif.-Berkeley. Vice-pres. profl. services Control Data Corp., Mpls., 1976-77, v.p. U.S. mktg. ops., 1977-79, v.p. edn. div., 1979-81, v.p. bus. devel. div., 1981-83, exec. v.p. mktg., 1983-85, pres. tech. support services group, 1985-86, v.p. European ops., 1986—; dir. ETA Systems, Inc., St. Paul, The Source, McLean, Va. Bd. dirs. Assn. Computing Machinery Found., N.Y.C., 1984—. Served to 1st lt. U.S. Army, 1957-60; Germany. Mem. Computer and Bus. Equipment Mfrs. Assn. (dir. 1984—), EDUCOM. Republican. Methodist. Avocations: motorhomes; boating; photography; fishing. Office: Control Data Corp 8100 34th Ave S Minneapolis MN 55440

MILLER, TOM JOSEPH, dentist, educator; b. Chgo., Nov. 28, 1958; s. Joseph Charles and Elizabeth (Kuebler) M.; m. Karen Lynette Cedergren, July 31, 1982; 1 child, Linnea Ann. BS, Loyola U., Chgo., 1980; DDS, Loyola U., Maywood, Ill., 1984. Gen. practice dentistry Bloomingdale, Ill., 1984—; asst. prof. Loyola U., 1984—; staff dentist Cen. Dupage Hosp., Winfield, Ill., 1984—, Marklund Childrens Home, Bloomingdale, 1984—. Mem. ADA, Am. Assn. Dental Schs. (regional coor. 1983-84), Acad. Gen. Dentistry, Omicron Kappa Upsilon, Alpha Sigma Nu. Republican. Roman Catholic. Office: 245 S Gary Ave #201 Bloomingdale IL 60108

MILLER, TRUDY JOYCE, retail executive, publisher; b. Chgo.; d. Leonard John and Evelyn Grace (Winter) Clarke; m. William Robert Miller, Oct. 8, 1960; children: William, James, Brian, Catherine. Student, Marycrest Coll., 1959; student in Interior Design, Art, Prairie State Coll., 1975; student in Publishing, Northwestern U., 1983. Reporter, feature writer Hammond (Ind.) Times, 1967-73, Village Press, South Holland, Ill., 1973-75; owner The Emporium, Glenwood, Ill., 1975-76, Second Thoughts, Chicago Heights, Ill., 1976—; pres. retail outlet Second Thoughts Inc., Chicago Heights, 1984—; editor Second Thoughts Publishing, Chicago Heights, 1982—; bd. dir. Fashion Consortium, Chgo., 1984-86; speaker in field. Author: 1983 Guide to Suburban Resale and Thrift Shops, Where to Find Everything For Practically Nothing in Chicagoland, 1984. Bd. dirs. econ. devel. Thornton Coll., South Holland, 1983-85; mem. small bus. adv. bd. Prairie State Coll., Chicago Heights, 1984-85; fashion show coordinator Operation ABLE Past 50 Job Fair, Chicago Heights, 1985. Mem. Nat. Assn. Resale and Thrift Shops (founder, bd. dirs., sec. 1984-86, pres. 1986—), Internat. Assn. Independant Pubs., Chgo. Women in Pub., Nat. Assn. Women Bus. Owners, South Suburban Assn. Commerce and Industry, Women in Mgmt. S. Suburban Network (bd. dirs., editor newsletter 1984-85). Roman Catholic. Club: Toastmasters (v.p. 1984-85). Avocations: writing, collecting antique women's clothing. Office: Second Thoughts Inc 153 Halsted Chicago Heights IL 60411

MILLER, VAN GLADSTONE, medical service company executive; b. Waterloo, Iowa, July 23, 1948; s. Blaine F. and Verda R. (Bricker) M.; m. Claudia Kancius (div. Nov. 1984, remarried 1986); children: Vance J., Dax B., Christopher Paul. Student. No. Iowa U., 1968-70. Dist. mgr. Universal Hosp. Services, Des Moines, 1973-75; v.p. mktg. Royal B Supply, Des Moines, 1975-78; pres. Miller Med. Service, Waterloo, 1978-85, Van G. Miller & Assocs., Inc., Waterloo, 1985—. Served with U.S. Army, 1970-72.

Home: 6330 Kimball Ave Waterloo IA 50701 Office: Miller Med Service Inc 1051 Southtown Dr PO Box 1654 Waterloo IA 50704

MILLER, VERNON RICHARD, state senator, nursing home executive; b. Des Moines, July 27, 1939; s. Wallace Thomas and Enid Lillian (Conklin) M.; B.S., Purdue U., 1963; M.S. in Bus. Adminstrn., Ind. U., South Bend, 1973; m. Jane Kay Rothrock, Aug. 19, 1961; children—Vernon Richard, II, Pamela Sue. Dept. foreman Jomac North Ltd., Warsaw, Ind., 1959-61; lab. technician Purdue U., 1963-64; microbiologist Pabst Brewing Co., Peoria Heights, Ill., 1964-65; dept. mgr. Ocean Spray Cranberries, North Chicago, Ill., 1965-67; exec. Miller's Merry Manor, Inc., Plymouth, Ind., 1967—; mem. State of Ind. Senate, 1976—, chmn. majority caucus, 1982—, chmn. health welfare and aging com., 1980-84, chmn. appointments and claims com., 1983—; mem. fin. com., labor and pensions com., rules and regulation com. Chmn. Marshall County Ind. March of Dimes, 1973-76; blood chmn. Marshall County Red Cross, 1970-74. Mem. Am. Coll. Nursing Home Adminstrs. Republican. Methodist. Clubs: Plymouth Country, Kiwanis (pres. 1972, lt. gov. 1975), Mason, Shriner, Order Eastern Star. Office: PO Box 498 Plymouth IN 46563

MILLER, WALTER ARTHUR, educator, leasing company manager; b. Garden City, Kans., Aug. 5, 1944; s. Wiley Arthur and Elizabeth (Dague) M.; m. Virginia Meredith Hester, Aug. 2, 1969; 1 child, Hester Elizabeth. BS in Econs. and Bus. Adminstrn., McPherson Coll., 1967; MEd, Northeastern Okla. State U., 1977. Mgr. Chelsea (Okla.) Constrn., Leasing and Rental Co., 1969—; elem. tchr. Foyil (Okla.) Schs., 1972-77; elem. tchr. Unified Sch. Dist. 445, Coffeyville, Kans., 1982—, high sch. tchr., 1977-81; agt. N.Y. Life Ins., Topeka, 1981-82; mem. computer com. Unified Sch. Dist. 445, 1985—, curriculum devel. com. Longfellow Elem. Sch., Coffeyville, 1985—, screening com. spl. services, 1985—. Asst. troop leader Girl Scouts U.S.A., Coffeyville, 1985—; trustee First United Meth. Ch., Coffeyville, 1979-81; life mem. PTA. Named one of Outstanding Young Men Am., 1972. Mem. NEA, Kans. Nat. Edn. Assn. Lodge: Lions (bd. dirs. Coffeyville chpt. 1981-83, tail twister 1986). Avocations: golf, gardening, antiques, music. Home: 1208 W 5th St Coffeyville KS 67337 Office: McKinley Middle Sch 10th and Gillam Coffeyville KS 67337

MILLER, WALTER DALE, state official; b. New Underwood, S.D., Oct. 5, 1925; s. Walter A. M.; m. Mary E. Randall, June 30, 1943; children: Walter R., Nancy, Karey, Renee. Student, S.D. Sch. Mines and Tech. State rep. S.D., Pierre, 1967-87, lt. gov., 1987—. Office: Office of the Lieutenant Gov State Capitol Pierre SD 57501 *

MILLER, WAYNE CARLYLE, pharmacist; b. South Bethlehem Borough, Pa., Oct. 22, 1934; s. Fred S. and Bernice M. (Hetrick) M.; m. Marilyn J. Berkovich, July 12, 1958; children: Gwendellyn M., Ruth L., Eric S. BS in Pharmacy, U. Pitts., 1956. Pharmacist, asst. mgr. Gray Drug Drugstores, Warren, Ohio, 1956-57, Seelig Pharmacy, Columbus, Ohio, 1958-68, Gold Circle, Columbus, 1968; pharmacist Lazarus Dept. Stores, Columbus, 1968; pharmacist, pres., owner Miller Pharmacy, Columbus, 1969—; clin. instr., preceptor Pharmacy Sch. Ohio State U., Columbus, 1982—; mem., trustee Super VAL Drugs, Columbus. Mem. Big Bros./Big Sisters Assn., Columbus, 1961—, Smithsonian Assocs., Washington. Served with U.S. Army, 1957-59. Mem. Am. Pharm. Assn., Ohio State Pharm. Assn. (trustee), Acad. Pharmacy of Cen. Ohio (trustee, pres. 1979-80), Nat. Assn. Retail Druggists. Republican. Methodist. Lodge: Masons. Avocations: jogging, weightlifting, stamps, coins, antique collecting. Home: 5980 Litchfield Rd Worthington OH 43085 Office: Waymar Inc dba Miller Pharmacy 860 Oakland Park Ave Columbus OH 43224

MILLER, WILLIAM CARL, veterinarian, plant pathologist; b. St. Cloud, Minn., June 5, 1942; s. Harvey Walter and Jane I. (Stanton) M.; m. Jeanine L. Stanis, Oct. 7, 1977. BS, U. Minn., 1965, DVM, 1967. Inspector in charge Food Safety and Inspection Service USDA, Cold Spring, Minn., 1970—. Mem. AVMA, Nat. Assn. Fed. Veterinarians. Home: Rural Rt 1 Box 19 Paynesville MN 56362 Office: USDA-Food Safety Inspection Service E Hwy 23 Cold Spring MN 56320

MILLER, WILLIAM CHARLES, theological librarian, educator; b. Mpls., Oct. 26, 1947; s. Robert Charles and Cleithra Mae (Johnson) M.; m. Brenda Kathleen Barnes, July 24, 1969; children—Amy Renee, Jared Charles. B.A., Marion Coll. (Ind.), 1968; M.L.S., Kent State U. (Ohio), 1974, Ph.D., 1983. Ordained deacon Ch. of Nazarene, 1986. Library technician Kent State U., 1972-74; catalog librarian Mt. Vernon Nazarene Coll. (Ohio), 1974-76; catalog and acquisitions librarian, 1976-78; library dir., prof. theol. bibliography Nazarene Theol. Sem., Kansas City, Mo., 1978—; adj. research assoc. U. Kans., 1984-85; cons. Mid-Am. Nazarene Coll., Olathe, Kans., 1983; bd. dirs. Small Library Computing Inc. Author: Holiness Works: A Bibliography, 1986. Served with U.S. Army, 1968-72. Mem. Assn. Study of Higher Edn., ALA, Am. Theol. Library Assn. (bd. dirs. 1985—), Wesleyan Theol. Soc., Assn. Coll. and Research Libraries, Library Adminstrn. and Mgmt. Assn., Beta Phi Mu. Home: 14405 S Cottonwood Olathe KS 66062 Office: Nazarene Theol Sem 1700 E Meyer Blvd Kansas City MO 64131

MILLER, WILLIAM CHARLES, architecture educator; b. San Francisco, May 11, 1945; m. Beverly Jean McConnell, Dec. 21, 1968; children: Britt A., David A. BArch, U. Oregon, 1968; MArch, U.Ill., 1970. Registered architect Ariz., Kans. Project architect Don L. McKee, Architect, Anacortes, Wash., 1968-69, Enteleki-Architects, San Francisco, 1973-74; asst. prof. U. Ariz., Tucson, 1970-73, 74-77; assoc. prof. Kans. State U., Manhatten, 1977-86, prof., 1986—; lectr. various orgns., 1976—; guest juror at architecture schs., 1976—. Author: Alvar Aalto: An Annotated Bibliography, 1984; contbr. articles to profl. jours.; editorial bd. Jour. Archtl. Edn., 1984—. Grantee U. Ariz. 1976, NEH, 1985, Am. Scandinavian Found., 1985; fellow U. Ill., 1970. Mem. AIA, Assn. Collegiate Schs. of Architecture, Soc. Archtl. Historians, Tau Sigma Delta. Avocation: stamp collecting. Office: Kans State U Dept Architecture Manhattan KS 66506

MILLER, WILLIAM FREDERICK, controller; b. Champaign, Ill., Feb. 21, 1952; s. George Frederick and Nina Ellen (Eastman) M.; m. Teresa Jean Walker, May 23, 1981; children: Alicia, Nicholas, Justin. BS in Acctg. with honors, U. Ill., 1974. CPA, Ill. Sr. auditor Wolf & Co. CPA's, Chgo., 1974-77; internal audit mgr. computer control Beeline Fashions, Inc., Bensenville, Ill., 1977-81; controller Kaltronics Distrs. Inc., Northbrook, Ill., 1981-82; v.p. controller Network Services Co., Chgo., 1983—; Officer Network Assocs., Inc., Chgo., 1984—. Mem. Am. Inst. CPA's, Ill. Soc. CPA's, Inst. Internal Auditors. Republican. Methodist. Club: Elgin (Ill.) Coin. Lodge: Kiwanis. Avocations: coin collecting, fishing, swimming, basketball, tennis. Office: Network Services Co 180 N Wacker Dr Chicago IL 60601

MILLER, WILLIAM MARTIN, veterinarian; b. Willard, Ohio, Dec. 8, 1950; s. William Robert and Dorla Dean (Gullett) M.; m. Vicki Lynn Redden, Sept. 9, 1972; children: Martin Andrew, Steven Daniel. BS in Agr., Ohio State U., 1973, DVM, 1976. Gen. practice vet. medicine Kenton, Ohio, 1976—. Contbr. articles to profl. jours. Mem. AVMA, Ohio Vet. Med. Assn., Hardin County Vet. Med. Assn., Am. Assn. Equine Practitioners, Am. Assn. Swine Practitioners. Republican. Presbyterian. Avocations: music, photography. Home and Office: 824 W Lima St Kenton OH 43326

MILLER, WILLIAM PAUL, psychologist; b. Elyria, Ohio, Nov. 15, 1943; s. John Paul and Madalene Helen (Schultheis) M.; m. Karen Ellen Muetzel, July 17, 1971; children: Carson, Colin. BA in Psychology, Ohio State U., 1965; MEd in Sch. Psychology, Kent State U., 1971. Lic. psychologist, Ohio. Psychologist Mentor (Ohio) Schs., 1970-71; sch. psychologist Perkins Local Schs., Sandusky, Ohio, 1971—; instr. psychology Tiffin (Ohio) U., 1987—. Mem. Mental Health Bd. of Seneca, Sandusky and Wyandot Counties, Tiffin, Ohio, 1986—. Mem. Ohio Sch. Psychologists Assn., Seneca Stargazers Club. Lodges: Lions, Masons. Avocation: astronomy. Home: 405 Sycamore St Tiffin OH 44883 Office: Perkins Local Schools 1210 E Bogart Rd Sandusky OH 44870

MILLEY, NORMAN G., retail company executive. Pres. K-Mart Stores Group, Troy, Mich. Office: K Mart Corp 3100 W Big Beaver Troy MI 48084 *

MILLIGAN, EDITH, financial services executive; b. Evansville, Ind., Oct. 22, 1958; d. William West and Suzanne (Crimm) M.; m. Paul Alan Delphia, Sept. 1, 1984. B.A., Tulane U., 1980. C.L.U. Adminstrv. asst. Bryan Wagner, C.L.U., New Orleans, 1977-80; sec.-treas. Life Mktg. of La., New Orleans, 1980-81; dist. mgr. Creative Fin. Concepts, Columbus, Ohio, 1981-82; pres. Keeping Track, Inc., Columbus, 1982—. Author: Licensing Study Guide, 1982; Track Records, 1983. Field coordinator Fair and Impartial Redistricting Commn., Columbus, 1981; mem. steering com. Pres. Ford Com., New Orleans, 1976. Mem. Internat. Assn. Fin. Planning, LWV, Mensa. Republican. Home: PO Box 14453 Columbus OH 43214 Office: Keeping Track Inc PO Box 14468 Columbus OH 43214

MILLIGAN, FREDERICK JAMES, lawyer; b. Upper Sandusky, Ohio, Nov. 14, 1906; s. William G. and Grace (Kuenzli) M.; B.A., Ohio State U., 1928; LL.B., Franklin U., 1933; J.D., Capital U., 1966; m. Virginia Stone, June 30, 1934; children—Frederick James, David Timothy. Asst. nat. sec. Phi Delta Theta, 1928; asst. dean of men Ohio State U., 1929-33; admitted to Ohio bar, 1933; asst. atty. gen. State of Ohio, 1933-36; pvt. practice, Columbus, Ohio, 1937—; exec. sec. Adminstrv. La. Commn. of Ohio, 1940-42; exec. sec. to Gov. of Ohio, 1947; dir. commerce State of Ohio, 1948; sec. Louis Bromfield Malabar Farm Found., 1958-60. Pres. Central Ohio council Boy Scouts Am.; trustee Columbus Town Meeting; asst. dir. Pres.'s Commn. on Inter-govt. Relations, 1953; pres. Ohio Information Com., Inc., 1966-83; chmn. Blendon Twp. Bicentennial Commn., 1974-77. Mem. athletic council Ohio State U., 1958-64; trustee Blendon Twp., 1971-78. Served from 1st lt. to maj. USAAF, 1942-45. Decorated Legion of Merit; recipient Silver Beaver award Boy Scouts Am., 1949; Ann. History award Franklin County Hist. Soc., 1957; D.A.R. Citizenship award, 1958; Distinguished Service citation Ohioana Library Assn., 1970. Mem. Am., Ohio, Columbus bar assns., Columbus Jr. C. of C. (hon. life mem.; pres. 1934), Ohio (trustee 1952-77, pres. 1963-65, Franklin County (pres. 1954-56) hist. socs., Ohio State U. Assn. (trustee 1952-55), Amvets (state comdr. 1949). Am. Legion, S.A.R., League of Young Republican Clubs of Ohio (pres. 1941-42). Presbyn. Clubs: University (trustee 1956-58), Ohio State U. Faculty (Columbus). Home: 3785 Dempsey Rd Westerville OH 43081 Office: 3791 Dempsey Rd Westerville OH 43081

MILLIGAN, GEORGE F., bank executive; b. 1934. With Norwest Bank, Des Moines, 1963—, now pres., chief operating officer. Office: Norwest Bank Des Moines NA 7th & Walnut Sts Des Moines IA 50304 *

MILLIGAN, MICHAEL LEE, dentist; b. Kenton, Ohio, Sept. 5, 1952; s. Robert L. and Lena R. (Chiesa) M.; m. Karen S. Nice, Sept. 20, 1975; children: Kristen, Patrick, Lyndsey, Marisa. BS, U. Houston, 1975; DDM, So. Ill. U., 1978. Gen. practice dentistry Bloomington, Ill., 1978—. Mem. ADA, Ill. Dental Soc., McLean County Dental Soc. (pres. 1987—). Lodges: KC. Ill. Men's Golf Champion, 1974; Chgo. Dist. Golf Assn. Champion 1973, 74, 77. Home: 208 Grandview Dr Normal IL 61761 Office: 211 S Prospect Rd Bloomington IL 61701

MILLIGAN, ROBERT LEE, JR., computer company executive; b. Evanston, Ill., Apr. 4, 1934; s. Robert L. and Alice (Connell) M.; B.S., Northwestern U., 1958; m. Susan A. Woodrow, Mar. 23, 1957; children—William, Bonnie, Thomas, Robert III. Account rep. IBM, Chgo., 1957-66; sr. cons. L.B. Knight & Assocs., Chgo., 1966-68; v.p. mktg. Trans Union Systems Corp., Chgo., 1968-73; sr. v.p. sales mktg., sec. Systems Mgmt. Inc., Rosemont, Ill., 1973-87, dir., 1980-87; pres., chief exec. officer, owner Target Data, Inc., Northbrook, Ill., 1987—; treas. Systems Mgmt. Inc. Service Corp.; dir. Nanofast, Inc., Chgo., 1982-84. Div. mgr. N. Suburban YMCA Bldg., 1967; area chmn. Northfield Twp. Republican Party, 1965-71. Bd. dirs. United Fund, Glenview, Ill., 1967-69, Robert R. McCormick Chgo. Boys Club, 1974—; pres. bd. mgrs. Glenview Amateur Hockey Assn., 1974-79, gen. mgr. Glenbrook South High Sch. Hockey Club, 1973-78. Served with AUS, 1953-55. Mem. Data Processing Mgmt. Assn., Consumer Credit Assn. (dir., sec. 1969-70), Phi Kappa Psi. Presbyterian. Clubs: Northwestern (dir. 1973-75) (Chgo.); Glen View (Ill.). Home: 1450 Lawrence Ln Northbrook IL 60062 Office: Target Data Inc 630 Dundee Rd Suite 125 Northbrook IL 60062

MILLION, CHARLES EARLE, advertising executive; b. Hannibal, Mo., Jan. 28, 1947; s. Charles Major and Georgia Loretta (Rodefer) M. (div. 1987); 1 child, Charles Ian. B in Journalism, Ohio U., 1969. Pub. relations specialist Blue Cross of SW Ohio, Cin., 1970-72; theme park mgr. King's Island div. Fotomat Corp., Cin., 1972-73; Md. mgr. Fotomat Corp., Balt., 1973-77; v.p. LLC Corp., St. Louis, 1977-81, Direct Mail Corp. of Am., St. Louis, 1981-85, BHN Adv. and Pub. Relations, St. Louis, 1985—. Bd. dirs. Lafayette Community Assn., St. Louis, 1984—, pres. 1985—; del. State Reps. Legis. Council, St. Louis, 1986. Mem. Direct Mktg. Assn., Direct Mktg. Assn. St. Louis, Am. Assn. Adv. Agencies (Mo. del.), Ohio U. Alumni Assn. (pres. St. Louis chpt. 1984—). Home: 1686 Brandon Park Dr Apt B Manchester MO 63021 Office: BHN Advt & Pub Relations 910 N 11th Saint Louis MO 63101

MILLOY, FRANK JOSEPH, JR., physician; b. Phoenix, June 26, 1924; s. Frank Joseph and Ola (McCabe) M.; student Notre Dame U., 1942-43; M.S., Northwestern U., 1949, M.D., 1947. Intern, Cook County Hosp., Chgo., 1947-49, resident, 1953-57; practice medicine, specializing in surgery, Chgo., 1958—; asso. attending staff Presbyn.—St. Lukes Hosp.; attending staff Cook County Hosp.; mem. staff U. Ill. Research Hosp.; clin. asso. prof. surgery, U. Ill. Med. Sch.; asso. prof. surgery Rush Med. Sch. Cons. West Side Vet. Hosp. Served as apprentice seaman USNR, 1943-45; lt. M.C., USNR, 1950-52; PTO. Diplomate Am. Bd. Surgery and Thoracic Surgery. Mem. A.C.S., Chgo. Surg. Soc., Internat. Soc. Surgery, Am. Coll. Chest Physicians, Soc. Thoracic Surgeons, Phi Beta Pi. Clubs: Metropolitan, University (Chgo.). Home: 574 Jackson Ave Glencoe IL 60022 Office: 800 Westmoreland Dr Lake Forest IL 60045

MILLS, ALEXANDER CARY, communications executive; b. Dearborn, Mich., Jan. 11, 1953; s. Samual F. and Clara A. (Brewer) M.; m. Jeanette D. McFarling, Aug. 24, 1975; 1 child, Jeremy Robert. AAS, Coll. DuPage, 1979; BA, U. Ill., Chgo., 1982. Dir. media Loyola U. Med. Ctr., Maywood, Ill., 1978-81; mgr. programming Cablevision of Chgo., 1981-84; gen. mgr. DuBois Ruddy Prodns., Troy, Mich., 1984-87; mktg. dir. Mobile Images, Corp., Southfield, Mich., 1987—. Served as sgt. USAF, 1974-78. Mem. Internat. TV Assn. (Achievement award 1981), Detroit Producers Assn., Detroit Area Film Tchrs., Nat. Acad. TV Arts and Scis., Birmingham Bloomfield Art Assn. Republican. Baptist. Avocations: fishing, tennis, scuba diving, sailing, golf. Office: DuBois Ruddy Audio Visual Prodns Inc 2145 Crooks Troy MI 48084

MILLS, ARLYN ALFRED, health care administrator; b. Neillsville, Wis., Dec. 6, 1939; s. Calvin B. and Elnora L. (Uhlman) M.; m. Mary Loris, Aug. 31, 1962; children—Suzanne, David. B.S., U. Wis., 1962, M.S., 1966. Tchr., No. Ctr. for Developmentally Disabled, Chippewa Falls, Wis., 1962-64; supr. vocat. tng., 1964-66; asst. adminstr. Clark County Health Care Center, Owen, Wis., 1966-70, adminstr., 1970—; guest lectr., cons. U. Wis.-Eau Claire, 1982—, adj. instr., 1981-82; advisor, 1972—, exec. dir. Clark County Community Services, 1985— . Contbr. articles to various publs. Advisor Future Bus. Leaders Am., Owen-Withee Sr. High Sch., Owen, Wis., 1978—. Mem. Am. Coll. Health Care Adminstrn., Am. Assn. Mental Deficiency, Wis. Assn. County Homes (chmn. com.). Intercare. Roman Catholic. Office: Clark County Health Care Center Route 2 Box X Owen WI 54460

MILLS, BRUCE DENNIS, controller; b. Cleve., Oct. 9, 1951; s. Samuel and Anne (Cohen) M. BS, Case Western Res. U., 1973, MBA, 1981. CPA, Ohio. Fin. analyst Matco Tools, Stow, Ohio, 1981-82, sr. acct., 1983-84, gen. acctg. mgr., 1984-87; sr. fin. analyst Electronic Theatre Restaurants Corp., Cleve., 1982-83; controller N.Am. Systems, Inc., Bedford Heights, Ohio, 1987—. Mem. Am. Inst. CPA's, Assn. MBA Execs., Ohio Soc. CPA's. Jewish. Avocations: cycling, tennis, sailing, the arts. Home: 1079 Piermont Rd South Euclid OH 44121 Office: North Am Systems Inc 24700 Miles Rd Bedford Heights OH 44146

MILLS, DARRYL WAYNE, manufacturing executive; b. Phila., Dec. 12, 1956; s. Kelly Richard and Rebecca (Calhoun) M.; 1 child, Nadria Anne. BS in Bus. Mgmt., Wilberforce U., 1979. Mgmt. trainee Nat. Aero. & Space Adminstn., Cleve., 1976; procurement trainee Dept. of Navy, Phila., 1977; adminstrv. buyer Westinghouse Electric Co., Lima, Ohio, 1979-83; sr. purchasing analyst Hobart Corp., Troy, Ohio, 1983—. Mem. Nat. Assn. Purchasing Mgmt., Urban Bus. Assn. Democrat. Roman Catholic. Lodges: Lions (2d v.p. 1982-83), Masons. Avocations: basketball, softball, tennis, swimming, music. Home: 5976 Culzean Dr Apt 1821 Dayton OH 45426 Office: Hobart Corp World Hdqrs Blvd Troy OH 45374

MILLS, DONALD MCKENZIE, librarian; b. Virden, Man., Can., Feb. 25, 1946; s. Earl Townsend and Mable Elizabeth (Davies) M.; m. Kathrine Ann Richards, Aug. 26, 1968; children—Jennifer, Susan. B.A., U. Winnipeg, Man., Can., 1968; M.L.S., U. B.C., Vancouver, Can., 1972. Chief librarian St. Albert Pub. Library, Alta., Can., 1972-75; children's coordinator Kamloops Pub. Library, B.C., Can., 1975-78; chief librarian West Vancouver Pub. Library, B.C., Can., 1978-82, Winnipeg Pub. Library, Man., Can., 1982—. Mem. Can. Library Assn. Office: City of Winnipeg Libraries, 251 Donald St, Winnipeg, MB Canada R3C 3P5

MILLS, REBECCA ANN, advertising executive; b. Storm Lake, Iowa, May 11, 1950; d. Omer H. and Awanda Lucille (Mathison) Roth; m. Timothy Lemar Mills, Dec. 22, 1973; children: Sarah Rebecca, Abby Elizabeth. Student Northwestern U., 1968, 70; B.S. in Journalism with honors, Drake U., 1972. Editor house organ Des Moines Register & Tribune, 1972-73; coordinator Mktg. Services Corp. of Iowa Credit Union League, Des Moines, 1973-74; account exec. Prescott Co., Denver, 1974-75; co-owner, pres. Mills Agy., Storm Lake, 1975—; guest lectr. Buena Vista Coll.; featured speaker Iowa Bank Mktg. Conf., 1979, 82, Internat. Telephone Credit Union Assn. conv., Dallas, 1978. Parents adv. bd. Day Care Center; v.p. Lake Creek Ladies Bd.; mem. bd. Storm Lake High Sch. Found., 1985-86. Recipient numerous ADDY awards for excellence in advt., 1st place award in nat. bank ad news, 1984. Mem. Am. Soc. Profl. and Exec. Women, Women in Communications, Advt. Club Sioux Cities, Nat. Fedn. Ind. Bus., Des Moines Advt. Club (past chmn. edn. com.), AAUW (dir. Lake Creek 1983-86), Storm Lake C. of C. (dir., pres. 1983), Lake Creek Country (pres. 1985-86), DAR (regent Buena Vista chpt. 1981-82), Republican. Presbyterian. Clubs: Keystone (sec., pres.), Faith Hope and Charity (dir. 1982—, v.p.). Lodge: Eastern Star (past officer). Home: 131 N Emerald Dr Storm Lake IA 50588 Office: 612 Seneca St Storm Lake IA 50588

MILLS, REESE FERRIS, lawyer; b. Mansfield, Ohio, Oct. 28, 1946; s. Reese and Charlotte Gorman (Ferris) M.; m. Victoria M. Voegele, Aug. 5, 1978. B.A., Denison U., 1968; J.D., U. Mich., 1974. Bar: Ohio 1975. Tchr. pub. schs., Mansfield, 1970-73; solicitor Village of Ontario (Ohio), 1977-79; ptnr. firm Mabee, Meyers & Mills, Mansfield, 1979—; law dir. City of Mansfield, 1980—. Trustee, Mansfield YMCA, pres. bd. trustees 1977—; trustee YMCA-YWCA Bldg. Corp.; v.p. Richland County Republican Exec. Com. (Ohio). Mem. Ohio State Bar Assn., Richland County Bar Assn. Presbyterian. Clubs: Kiwanis, University (Mansfield). Home: 902 Dickson Pkwy Mansfield OH 44907 Office: Mabee Meyers Mills 24 W 3d St Suite 300 Mansfield OH 44902

MILLS, RICHARD HENRY, judge; b. Beardstown, Ill., July 19, 1929; s. Myron Epler and Helen Christine (Greve) M.; m. Rachel Ann Keagle, June 16, 1962; children: Jonathan K., Daniel Cass. BA, Ill. Coll., 1951; JD, Mercer U., 1957; LLM, U. Va., 1982. Bar: Ill. 1957, U.S. Dist. Ct. Ill. 1958, U.S. Ct. Appeals 1959, U.S. Ct. Mil. Appeals 1963, U.S. Supreme Ct. 1963. Legal advisor Ill. Youth Commn., 1958-60; state's atty. Cass County, Virginia, Ill., 1960-64; judge Ill. 8th Jud. Cir., Virginia, 1966-76, Ill. 4th Dist. Appellate Ct., Virginia, 1976-85, U.S. Dist. Ct. (cen. dist.) Ill., Springfield, 1985—; adj. prof. So. Ill. U. Sch. Medicine, 1985—; mem. adv. bd. Nat. Inst. Corrections, Washington, 1984—, Ill. Supreme Ct. Rules Com., Chgo., 1963-85. Contbr. articles to profl. jours. Pres. Abraham Lincoln council Boy Scouts Am., Springfield, 1978-80. Served to col. USAR, 1952-85, Korea, Brigadier Gen., Ill. Militia, 1986—. Recipient George Washington Honor medal Freedoms Found., 1969, 73, 75, 82, Disting. Eagle Scout Boy Scouts Am., 1985. Fellow Am. Bar Found.; mem. ABA (joint com. profl. sanctions 1984—), Ill. Bar Assn., Chgo. Bar Assn., Cass County Bar Assn. (pres. 1962-64, 75-76), 7th Cir. Bar Assn., Fed. Judges Assn. Republican. Clubs: Army & Navy (Washington); The Sangamo (Springfield). Lodge: Masons. Home: 132 Oakmont Dr Springfield IL 62704 Office: US Dist Ct 319 U S Courthouse 600 E Monroe St Springfield IL 62701

MILLS, RICHARD WARD, JR., physician; b. Chgo., Oct. 5, 1916; s. Richard Ward and Grace Dorothy (Brown) M.; m. Adrian Corder Bond, June 1946 (div. 1949); 1 child, Pamela; m. Nancy Jane Houck, Jan. 6, 1950; children: Jennifer Jane, Richard Lynn. BS, Northwestern U., 1938, B Medicine, 1941, MD, 1942. Diplomate Am. Bd. Internal Medicine. Intern U. Mich. Hosp., Ann Arbor, 1941-42, asst. resident, 1947-48, resident, 1948-49, instr., 1949-50; ptnr. F.C. Smith Clinic, Marion, Ohio, 1950-62; practice medicine specializing in internal medicine Marion, 1962—; chief staff Marion Gen. Hosp., 1976-78, chmn. dept. medicine, 1969, 72, 73; courtesy staff Ohio State U. Hosp., Columbus, 1950-58; clin. instr. Ohio State U., 1950-58; treas./sec. Compcare, Inc., Marion, 1976-79, also bd. dirs. Bd. dirs., mem. exec. com. Marion Health Found.; bd. dirs. Marion Gen. Hosp., 1976-79, Marion County Tuberculosis and Health Assn., 1957-70, pres., 1964-70. Served to lt. comdr. M.C., U.S. Navy, 1942-47, PTO. Mem. AMA, Ohio State Med. Soc., Marion County Acad. Medicine (pres.), Phi Rho Sigma (pres. 1938), Alpha Omega Alpha. Republican. Episcopalian. Lodge: Rotary. Avocations: flying, boating, photography, scuba diving. Home: 805 Chelsea Marion OH 43302 Office: 170 Fairfax Rd Marion OH 43302

MILLS, STEPHEN DUANE, data processing executive; b. Winchester, Ind., Mar. 13, 1947; s. Alva Lawrence Mills and Helen Lucille (Murrell) Franklin; m. Carolyn Sue Reas; children: Aaron Forte, Travis Andante. BS, Purdue U., 1970. Systems analyst Duncan Electric, Lafayette, Ind., 1970-77, programmer supr., 1977-79; data processing mgr. Landis & Gyr Metering, Lafayette, 1979—. Recorded album So This Is Why, 1979. Avocations: music, swimming, basketball, baseball. Home: 3909 Peters Mill Dr Lafayette IN 47905 Office: Landis & Gyr Metering PO Box 7180 Lafayette IN 47903

MILLS-NOVOA, BEVERLY ANN, psychologist; b. Indpls., Apr. 23, 1954; d. P. Gerald and Arzella (Thompson) Mills; m. Avelino Mills-Novoa, Aug. 27, 1977; children: Nicole, Megan. BA, Earlham Coll., 1976; MA, U. Minn., 1978, PhD, 1980. Lic. cons. psychologist; lic. career counselor. Cons. Control Data Corp., Mpls., 1980-83, sr. cons., 1983-87; cons. McLagan Internat., St. Paul, 1987—. Author: (play) Last Laugh, 1972. Named one of Outstanding Young Women of Am., 1978. Mem. Am. Soc. Tng. and Devel., Am. Psychol. Assn., Minn. Career Devel. Assn. (bd. dirs. 1983-86), Phi Beta Kappa. Mem. Am. Soc. Friends Ch. Avocations: cooking, running, reading, swimming. Office: McLagan Internat Rosedale Towers 1700 W Hwy 36 Suite 300 Saint Paul MN 55113

MILNARIK, RONALD MARSHALL, military career officer, endodontist; b. Chgo., Sept. 30, 1942; s. Marshall William and Florence (Galvin) M.; m. Pauline Angela Repinski, May 8, 1971; 1 child, Elizabeth Ann. BSD, U. Ill., Chgo., 1965, DDS, 1967; MA in Internat. Relations, U. Ark., 1972; MS in Oral Biology, Loyola U., Chgo., 1977. Commd. 2d lt. USAF, 1967, advanced through grades to col., 1967—, gen. dental officer, 1967-73, endodontist, 1975—; instr. endodontics Washington U. Sch. Dental Medicine, St. Louis, 1986—; dir. dental gen. practice residency USAF Hosp., Chanute AFB, Ill., 1982-84, 85-86. Mem. Rantoul (Ill.) Area Task Force on Drug and Alcohol Abuse, 1983-86; dir. Student Union Kalamazoo (Mich.) Coll., 1962-63. Mem. ADA, Am. Assn. Endodontists, Edgar D. Coolidge Endodontic Study Club, Greater St. Louis Endodontic Study Club, Air Force Assn., Sierra Club, Mid-Am. Triathletes. Republican. Lutheran. Avocations: skiing, triathlons, canoeing, caving, mountaineering. Home: 4 High Forest Dr Belleville IL 62223-4810 Office: USAF Med Ctr Scott/SGD Scott AFB IL 62225-5300

MILNE, GARTH LEROY, electronics executive; b. St. George, Utah, Sept. 26, 1942; s. Willard M. and Ruth C. (Cottan) M.; m. Kay G. Hanson, Sept. 11, 1965; children: Michelle, Jacqueline, Michael. BS, U. Utah, 1966; MBA, Harvard U., 1968. Asst. treas. internal Chrysler Corp., Highland Park, Mich., 1974-78; v.p. corp. control and devel. Chrysler Fin. Corp., Troy, Mich., 1978-79; asst. treas., dir. Motorola, Inc., Schaumburg, Ill., 1980-83, v.p., treas., 1984—. Author: (chpt.) Chief Financial Officer Handbook, 1985. Dir. Schaumburg Mormon Ch., 1980-86; commr., v.p. South Barrington Park Dist., 1987—; exec. bd. Northwest Suburban Council Boy Scouts Am., 1987—. Served with USNG, 1959-60. Mem. B.Y.U. Mgmt. Soc. Chgo. (bd. dirs. 1983-86), Phi Kappa Phi. Club: Harvard Bus. Sch. (Chgo.) (bd. dirs. 1984-86); Barrington Swim and Tennis (So. Barrington, Ill.). Avocations: church activities, sports. Home: 7 Revere Dr South Barrington IL 60010 Office: Motorola Inc 1308 E Algonquin Rd Schaumburg IL 60196

MILNE, GEORGE RICHARD ALOYSIOUS, manufacturing company official; b. Cin., Jan. 10, 1936; s. James A. and Elizabeth (Padur) M.; m. Lorraine V. Kraus, Sept. 21, 1963 (div.); children—James R., John E.; m. Mary Ruth Jenkins, Mar. 20, 1982. Student in commerce U. Cin., 1959-62, NOMA grad. fellow cert. in mgmt. adminstrv. services; B.S. in Bus. and Commerce, U. Louisville, 1963. Supr. engring. services and records Am. Radiator and Standard San. Corp., Cin., 1958-60, product liaison engr., 1960-61, ops. supr., 1961-62, buyer, Louisville, 1962-64, supr. purchases and services, 1964, purchasing agt., 1965; purchasing agt. Mascon Toy Co. div. Masco Corp., Lorain, Ohio, 1966-69, mgr. purchasing youth and recreational products div. Leisure Group, Inc. (formerly Masco Corp.), 1969-70; purchasing agt. plumbing products div. Delta Faucet Co., Taylor, Mich. and Greensburg, Ind., 1970-75, divisional purchasing agt., 1975-76, divisional purchasing mgr., Indpls., 1976-78, divisional mgr. purchasing internat., 1978—. Lectr. purchasing and economy. Bd. dirs. YMCA; active Nat. Alliance Businessmen. Served with USAF, 1955-58. Mem. Nat. Assn. Purchasing Mgmt. (Devel. Man of Yr. 1974-75, pres. 1979-82), Purchasing Mgmt. Assn. Indpls., Copper Club. Republican. Roman Catholic. Lodge: Fraternal Order of Foresters. Contbr. articles to profl. jours. Home: 9635 Greentree Dr Carmel IN 46032 Office: 55 E 111th St Indianapolis IN 46280

MILNER, HAROLD LEON, state public affairs administrator, journalist; b. Breese, Ill., Feb. 25, 1946; s. Shirley Logan and Dorena Doris (Burkett) M.; m. Cynthia Marie Young, Nov. 30, 1974; children—Leanne Marie, James Logan. B.S. in Communications, So. Ill. U., 1968; M.A. in Pub. Adminstrn., Sangamon State U., 1977; post grad. MacMurray Coll., 1971. Photo journalist Effingham Daily News, Ill., 1968; asst. dir. pub. relations MacMurray Coll., Jacksonville, Ill., 1971; dir. photo and audio-visual dept. Meml. Med. Ctr., Springfield, Ill., 1971-73; spl. asst. to U.S. Congressman George Shipley of Ill., Washington, 1974-75; speaker's press sec. Ill. Ho. of Rep., Springfield, 1975-79; spl. asst. for pub. affairs Ill. State Bd. Edn., Springfield, 1979—; pres. State Pub. Info. Officers' Roundtable, Springfield, 1981-83; chmn. Ill. State Employees Credit Union, Springfield, 1983-85, bd. dirs. Credit Union 1, Rantoul, 1985— ; mem. Gov.'s Task Force on Fin. Services, 1985-86. Mem. adv. com. Am. Heart Assn., Springfield, 1981—. Served with U.S. Army, 1968-70. Mem. Nat. Sch. Pub. Relations Assn., Nat. Assn. State Edn. Dept. Info. Officers (treas. 1985, v.p. 1986, pres. elect 1987), Jaycees. Methodist. Office: Ill State Bd Edn 100 N 1st St Springfield IL 62777

MILNER, HAROLD WILLIAM, hotel executive; b. Salt Lake City, Nov. 11, 1934; s. Kenneth W. and Olive (Schoettlin) M.; m. Susan Emmett, June 19, 1959 (div. 1976); children—John Kenneth, Mary Sue; m. Lois Friemuth, Aug. 14, 1977; 1 dau., Jennifer Rebecca. B.S., U. Utah, 1960; M.B.A., Harvard, 1962. Instr. Brigham Young U., Provo, Utah, 1962-64; v.p. Gen. Paper Corp., Mpls., 1964-65; dir. finance Amalgamated Sugar Co., Ogden, Utah, 1965-67; corp. treas. Marriott Corp., Washington, 1967-70; pres., chief exec. officer, trustee Hotel Investors, Kensington, Md., 1970-75; pres., chief exec. officer Americana Hotels Corp., Chgo., 1975-85, Kahler Corp., Rochester, Minn., 1985—. Author: A Special Report on Contract Maintenance, 1963. Served as lt. AUS, 1960. Mem. Minn. Assn. Commerce and Industry (bd. dirs. 1986—). Mem. Ch. Jesus Christ Latter-day Saints. Office: 20 2d Ave Rochester MN 55901

MILNER, IRVIN MYRON, lawyer; b. Cleve., Feb. 5, 1916; s. Nathan and Rose (Spector) M.; m. Zelda Winograd., Aug. 15, 1943. A.B. cum laude, Western Res. U. (now Case Western Res. U.), 1937, J.D., 1940, LL.M., 1970. Bar: Ohio 1940, U.S. Dist. Ct. (no. dist.) Ohio 1946. Sole practice Cleve., 1946—; exec. sec., counsel Men's Apparel Club Ohio, Cleve., 1947-48; adj. instr. Sch. Law, Case Western Res. U., 1965-66; spl. counsel Ohio Office Atty. Gen., 1963-70; legal counsel Korean Assn. Greater Cleve., 1973—. Mem. Cleve. Fgn. Consular Corps., 1970—, hon. consul Rep. of Korea for Cleve., 1970—; bd. dirs. Internat. Human Assistance Programs, Inc., 1973-79, voting corp. mem., 1980—. Served with U.S. Army, 1941-45, ETO. Decorated Order Diplomatic Service Merit-Heung-in medal (Korea); recipient Merit award Cuyahoga County Council VFW, 1958; named to Disting. Alumni Hall of Fame, Cleveland Heights High Sch., Ohio, 1983. Fellow Internat. Consular Coll. and Internat. Consular Acad., Ohio Bar Found.; mem. Greater Cleve. Bar Assn., Cuyahoga County Bar Assn. (pres. 1975-76, award of Merit 1976), Ohio State Bar Assn. (council dels. 1976-86), ABA, Greater Cleve. Vets Council (pres. 1957, Merit award 1983), Western Res. Coll. Alumni Assn. (bd. dirs. 1982—), Tau Epsilon Rho (chancellor Cleve. Grad. chpt. 1977-81, 87—), Delta Phi Alpha. Republican. Jewish. Club: Cleve. City. Lodges: Masons, Rotary. Office: Leader Bldg #711 526 Superior Rd NE Cleveland OH 44114

MIMNAUGH, ELLEN NULTY, information services executive; b. Montclair, N.J., July 31, 1940; d. John Lawrence and Catherine Josephine (Gavin) Nulty; m. J. Peter Mimnaugh, Nov. 18, 1967; children: Michael, Megan, Maureen, Patricia. BA, Rosemont Coll., 1962; MS, Columbia U., 1966. Lit. chemist Shell Chem. Co., N.Y.C., 1962-66; info. chemist Nat. Lead Co., South Amboy, N.J., 1967; mgr. user's service Douglas Aircraft Co., Long Beach, Calif., 1968-69; pres. Info. Cons. Inc., Allenhurst, N.J., 1975-78, Columbus, Ohio, 1978—. Leader Seals of Ohio Girl Scouts Am., Columbus, 1979-81; chmn. TWIG #5 Children's Hosp., Columbus, 1986. Mem. Am. Chem. Soc. (chmn. div. small chem. bus. 1987), Spl. Libraires Assn. (treas. cen. Ohio 1983-85, pres. 1987—). Roman Catholic. Avocations: bridge, gardening. Home: 2584 Coventry Rd Columbus OH 43221

MINADEO, JOSEPH NICHOLAS, treasurer; b. Cleve., May 16, 1946; s. Joseph Nicholas Minadeo and Angela Dorothy (Semeraro) Schwartz; m. Anne Carolyn Tober, April 12, 1969; children: Michelle, Joseph. Student, Carnegie Inst. Tech., 1964-66; BBA, Western Res. U., 1969. CPA, Ohio. Staff acct. Ernst & Ernst, Cleve., 1969, sr. staff acct., 1972-76; mgr. fin. accts. Prescott, Ball & Turben, Cleve., 1976-86, chief fin. officer, treas., 1986—. Served to lt. USN, 1969-72. Mem. Am. Inst. of CPA's, Ohio Soc. of CPA's, Ams. of Italian Heritage. Republican. Roman Catholic. Club: Mentor Harbor Yacht. Avocations: stained glass, boating, golf, racquetball. Office: Prescott Ball & Turben Inc 1331 Euclid Ave Cleveland OH 44115

MINARD, CRAIG, dentist; b. lakewood, Ohio, Oct. 1, 1952; s. John Richard and Shirley (Ray) M.; m. Connie Marie Cheever, Sept. 10, 1983. BS, U. Cin., 1975; DDS, Ohio State U., 1979. Gen. practice dentistry Cin. Dental Services, 1979-80, Madisonville Family, Cin., 1980-84, Cin., 1984—. Mem. Am. Dental Soc., Ohio Dental Assn., Cin. Dental Soc., Greater Cin. Dental Study Group (v.p. 1985-86, pres. 1986—). Republican. Roman Catholic. Avocation: race car driving. Home: 8056 Halyard Ct Cincinnati OH 45039 Office: 10475 Montgomery Rd 1-I Cincinnati OH 45242

MINARD, THOMAS MICHAEL, strategic planner, consultant; b. St. Charles, Ill., Dec. 31, 1944; s. Clarence Scott and Ruth L. (Larson) M. Cert., Coll. Advanced Traffic, Chgo., 1964. Gen. mgr. Iowa Terminal R.R. Co., Mason City, 1968-70; mgr. quality control C & NW Ry. Co., Chgo., 1970-73; pres. Great Plains Ry. Co., Seward, Nebr., 1973-76; mgr. railroad sales and procurement L.B. Foster Co., Des Plaines, Ill., 1976-80, project coordinator, 1981-83, transp. cons., Chgo., 1983; co-founder, v.p. Railmode, Inc., Chgo., 1984-85; transp. cons., Chgo., 1986—. Mem. Chgo. Council Fgn. Relations, Coll. Advanced Traffic Alumni Assn., Delta Nu Alpha. Address: 450 W Briar Pl Suite 13F Chicago IL 60657

MINARIK, KENNETH RONALD, optometrist; b. McKeesport, Pa., Aug. 9, 1956; s. Rudolph Andrew and Pauline (Babyak) M.; 1 child, Jennifer. BS, U. Pitts., 1976; DO, Ill. Coll. Optometry, 1980. Gen. practice optometry Chgo., 1981—; cons. Barnes-Hind, Inc., Sunnyvale, Calif., 1985—. Contbg. editor Optometric Mgmt., 1985—; contbr. articles to profl. jours. Mem. Am. Optometric Assn., Heart of Am. Contact Lens Soc., Chgo. C. of C. Republican. Roman Catholic. Home: 441 E Erie #4905 Chicago IL 60611 Office: Optical Illusion Inc 2828 N Clark St Chicago IL 60657

MINGAY, ARTHUR HAMMOND, financial executive; b. Windsor, Ont., Can., Nov. 26, 1919; s. John and Esther (Rodgers) M.; m. Florence G. Carmichael, Feb. 15, 1947; children: Cameron, Mary Jane, Margo. Student, Walkerville Collegiate, Windsor, Ont. With Can. Trust Mortgage Co., Toronto, 1938—, chmn. bd., 1978-85, also bd. dirs.; bd. dirs. Algoma Steel Corp., Inglis Ltd., Loblaw Cos. Ltd., Royal Ins. Co. Can., Sears Can. Ltd., T.I. Industries Ltd. Served as flight lt. RCAF, 1941-45. Clubs: Toronto, Granite; Rosedale Golf (Toronto).

MINK, ERNEST FREDERICK, III, manufacturing company executive; b. Oceanside, Calif., Aug. 12, 1953; s. Ernest Frederick Jr. and Carmen Marcia (Carillia) M. BME, Gen. Motors Inst., 1976; MBA, U. Va., 1981. Project engr. Fisher Body div. Gen. Motors Corp., Warren, Mich., 1976-81; sr. project engr. BOC Spl. Vehicle Activity div. Gen. Motors Corp., Warren, Mich., 1981-84; devel. engr. CPC Engring. div. Gen. Motors Corp., Warren, Mich., 1984; asst. to chief engr. Fisher Guide div. Gen. Motors Corp., Warren, Mich., 1984-85, mgr. engring. planning, 1985, mgr. bus. planning, 1986—; cons. Union Lake (Mich.) Profl. Ctr., 1986—. Mem. Am. Soc. Body Engrs., Soc. Automobile Engrs., Engring. Soc. Detroit. Avocations: off shore sailing, personal computers. Home: PO Box 117 Sterling Heights MI 48077-0117 Office: Gen Motors Corp Fisher Guide Div 6600 E 12 Mile Rd Warren MI 48090-9009

MINKALIS, CHESTER ALBERT, management consultant; b. Chgo., Jan. 29, 1949; s. Albert C. and Irene J. (Dudzik) M.; m. Linda S. McEvilly, Sept. 4, 1976; 1 child, Melissa Anne. BArch, U. Ill., Chgo., 1971; MBA, U. Chgo., 1974. Registered architect, Wis. Architect Metz Train & Youngren, Chgo., 1970-73; adminstrv. asst. Rush Presbyn. St. Luke's Med. Ctr., Chgo., 1973-75; mgmt. cons. TriBrook Group, Inc., Oak Brook, Ill., 1975-80, prin., 1980-81; v.p. Tribrook Group, Inc., Oak Brook, Ill., 1981—. Fellow Am. Assn. Health Care Cons. (chmn. 1987—, bd. dirs. 1984—); mem. AIA, Am. Coll. Healthcare Execs., U. Chgo. Health Adminstrn. Alumni Assn. (pres. 1984-85). Republican. Roman Catholic. Club: DuPage (Oak Brook). Home: 622 Balmoral Circle Naperville IL 60540 Office: TriBrook Group Inc 999 Oakmont Plaza Dr Suite 600 Westmont IL 60559

MINNESTE, VIKTOR, JR., electronic company executive; b. Haapsalu, Estonia, Jan. 15, 1932; s. Viktor and Alice (Lembra) M.; B.S. in Elec. Engring., U. Ill., 1960. Electronic engr. Bell & Howell Co., 1960-69, microstatics div. SCM Co., 1969-71, Multigraphics div. A-M Co., 1972-73; electronic engr. bus. products group Victor Comptometer Co. (merged with Walter Kidde Corp. 1977), Chgo., 1973-74, service mgr. internat. group, 1974-75, then supr. electronics design group, to 1982; project engr. Warner Electric, 1982-84; systems engr. Barrett Electronics, 1984-85; phone engr. Williams Electronics, 1986—. pub. Motteid/Thoughts, 1962-68; chmn., Estonian-Ams. Polit. Action Com., 1968-72. Served with AUS, 1952-54. Home: 3134 N Kimball Ave Chicago IL 60618 Office: 3401 N Califorina Ave Chicago IL 60618

MINNICHSOFFER, ANTHONY JOSEPH, marketing support executive; b. Osceola, Wis., Aug. 16, 1943; s. Bernard John and Stella Mary (Shimota) M.; m. Barbara Jean Moon, July 1, 1967; children: Nadine Mary, Matthew Paul. BA, U. Minn., 1967. Mng. editor Miller Pub., Mpls., 1967-68; assoc. editor The Farmer Mag., St. Paul, 1968-71; legis. asst. U.S. Senate, Washington, 1961-72; account exec. Dorn Communications, Edina, Minn., 1972-83; dir. communications Harvest States Co-op, St. Paul, 1983-85; sr. exec. Miller Meester Advt., St. Paul, 1985—. Author: Young Farmers Leadership Guide, 1982, Selling to the Top, 1986; columnist Corporate Report, 1978-83; contbg. editor: Rainbow Fin. Vol. fireman Shafer Fire Dept., 1967-71; parent council Chisago Lakes Jr. High, Lindstrom, Minn., 1982-84. Mem. Nat. Agrimktg. Assn. (Midwest judge 1982-84), Pub. Relations Soc. Roman Catholic. Lodge: KC (recorder 1983-85, adv. 1986-87, dep. grand knight 1987—). Avocations: photography, carpentry, farming. Home: 28710 Ivywood Trail Chisago City MN 55013-9634 Office: Miller Meester Adv 521 S Snelling Saint Paul MN 55116

MINNICK, CRAIG ALAN, accountant, lawyer; b. Chgo., May 1, 1951; s. Harry Harold and Betty Lou (Morrison) M.; m. Janice Agrest, May 23, 1976; children: Adam Charles, Paula Rene. BS in Acctg., U. Ill., 1973, JD, 1976. Bar: Ill. 1976, U.S. Dist. Ct. (no. dist.) Ill. 1976. Tax specialist Peat Marwick Mitchell & Co., Chgo., 1976-80; tax mgr. Ostrow Reisen Berk & Abrams Ltd., Chgo., 1980-82; mgr. in charge tax dept. B.L. Rosenberg & Co., Chgo., 1982—. Bd. dirs. Children's Heart Assn., Streamwood, Ill., 1970—. Mem. ABA, Ill. State Bar Assn., Chgo. Bar Assn., Am. Inst. CPA's, Ill. Soc. CPA's, Chgo. Estate Planning Council. Avocations: camping, photography, sports. Office: BL Rosenberg & Co 1 S Wacker Dr #1700 Chicago IL 60606

MINNOCK, EDWARD WILLIAM, JR., academic administrator, police consultant; b. Wareham, Mass., May 4, 1948; s. Edward William and Mary Gladys (Perry) M.; m. Delores Jane Alsop, Jan. 24, 1970; children: Kelly Elizabeth, Edward William III. 4S in Criminology, U. Tampa, 1974; MS in Sociology, Emporia State U., 1978; PhD, Kans. State U., 1986. Dir. criminal justice tng. Washburn U., Topeka, 1978-82, dir. continuing edn., 1983—; cons. police, 1977—, N.Mex. Criminal Justice, Santa Fe, 1979—; dir. Office Tng. Ctr., Topeka, 1985—. Contbr. articles to profl. jours. Pres. Kans. Council Community Service and Continuing Edn., 1986-87. Served with U.S. Army, 1966-70, Vietnam. Decorated Legion of Merit. Mem. Assn. Continuing Higher Edn., World Futures Soc. (v.p. 1984-85). Democrat. Roman Catholic. Avocations: scuba diving, running, soccer. Office: Washburn U Sch Applied & Continuing Edn Topeka KS 66621

MINO, YUTAKA, curator; b. Kanazawa, Japan, Oct. 23, 1941; came to U.S., 1969; s. Susumu and Satoko (Akai) M.; m. Katherine Tsiang, Aug. 5, 1975; children: Alexander Kiyoshi, Benjamin Toru. BA, Keio U., Tokyo, 1965; PhD, Harvard U., 1977. Assoc. curator Montreal (Can.) Mus. Fine Arts, 1976-77; curatorial asst. Royal Ont. (Can.) Mus., Toronto, 1969-71; curator Indpls. Mus. Art, 1977-85, Art Inst. Chgo., 1986—; vis. lectr. Musashino Art U., Tokyo, 1984-85; vis. prof. U. Mich., Ann Arbor, 1987. Author: (exhbn. catalogues) Ceramics in the Liao Dynasty, 1973, Tz'u-chou Type Wares, 1980, Beauty and Tranquility, 1983; co-author (exhbn. catalogue) Ice and Green Clouds, 1987. Met. Ctr. Far Eastern Art Studies fellowship, 1986; recipient Koyama Fujio Meml. prize, 1981. Mem. China Inst. Am. (art com. 1977). Home: 501 W Briar Pl #1E Chicago IL 60657

MINOR, CARL ALLEN, banker, insurance executive; b. DeKalb County, Mo., Feb. 17, 1917; s. Earle and Edna Alice (Heimbaugh) M.; m. Dorothy Ann Jarrett, Jan. 3, 1941; children—Allen R., Sue Ann Perkins. A.B., William Jewell Coll., 1938; M.A., U. Mo.-Kansas City, 1956. Counseling psychologist VA, Kansas City, 1945-61; with Farmers Bank of Maysville, Mo., 1961-85, pres., chief exec. officer, 1983, chmn., 1983-85, also dir.; bd. dirs. Northwest Partnership. bd. dirs. DeKalb County Indsl. Co., DeKalb County Health Services, Inc. Active Maysville Methodist Ch., 1961—; trustee Cameron Community Hosp., 1963-78, treas, 1970-78; treas. R-1 Sch. Dist., 1982—; mem. dist. com. Pony Express Boy Scouts Am., 1965; bd. dirs. Community Scholarship Fund, 1980—. Served to lt. comdr. USN, 1942-45, 50-52. Mem. Am. Assn. Individual Investors, Am. Legion (treas. 1980—), VFW. Democrat. Lodges: Rotary (pres. 1965), Masons, Shriners. Avocations: investments, farming, golf, travel, antique bicycles. Home: PO Box 86 Maysville MO 64469

MINSTER, STANLEY DEAN, laundry equipment distributor; b. Canton, Ohio, Apr. 16, 1925; s. Morris and Emma (Galpert) M.; m. Mary Ann Marks, June 8, 1947; children: Deborah, Rochelle, Robert. Purchasing agt. Gassy's Inc., Akron, Ohio, 1945-50; gen. mgr. Belenky Inc., Akron, 1950-60, v.p., 1960-70, pres., 1970—; bd. dirs. Tacata, Upper Montclair, N.J., 1982-84, 85—. Bd. dirs. United Way, Akron, 1985-86, Jewish Family Service, Akron, 1985-86; mem. arbitration com. Akron Bar Assn., 1986; pres. Akron Jewish Ctr., 1977-78. Democrat. Avocations: golf, photography. Office: Belenky Inc 1601 Frederick Blvd Akron OH 44320

MINTCHELL, GARY ALAN, machine company executive; b. Sidney, Ohio, Nov. 19, 1947; s. Jacque Eugene and Sandra Irene (Zwiebel) M.; m. Beverly Kay Moseley, June 12, 1970; children: Heather Lorelle, Derek Travis. BA, Ohio Northern U., 1969; postgrad., La. State U., 1970-71. Tchr. Delphos (Ohio) St. John Schs., 1969-70; product mgmt. Airstream div. Beatrice, Jackson Ctr., Ohio, 1971-80; quality assurance mgr. Questor Corp., Piqua, Ohio, 1980-81; mgr. product devel. GLO Internat., Dayton, Ohio, 1981-84; v.p. mktg. Cardinal Tool Corp., Engelwood, Ohio, 1984—. Mem. Sidney Sch. Bd., 1982—. Mem. Am. Mktg. Assn., The Planning Forum, Sidney Jaycees (Outstanding Community Service Award 1981). Democrat. Methodist. Lodge: Kiwanis (past pres. Sidney). Avocations: computers, photography, golf, running, coaching youth soccer. Home: 1227 Colonial Dr Sidney OH 45365 Office: Cardinal Tool Corp 100 Holiday Dr Englewood OH 45322

MINTER, STEVEN ALAN, foundation executive; b. Akron, Ohio, Oct. 23, 1938; s. Lawrence L. and Dorothy (Knox) M.; m. Dolores Kreicher, Apr. 8, 1961; children: Michele, Caroline, Robyn. EdB, Baldwin-Wallace Coll., 1960, LHD (hon.), 1974; M in Social Adminstrn., Case Western Res. U., 1963; LHD (hon.), Findlay Coll., 1984. Dir. Cuyahoga County Welfare Dept., Cleve., 1969-70; commr. Mass. Dept. Pub. Welfare, Boston, 1970-75; under sec. U.S. Dept. Edn., Washington, 1980-81; assoc. dir., program officer The Cleve. Found., 1975-80, 81-83, dir., 1984—; bd. dirs. Ohio Bell Telephone Co., Cleve., Soc. Nat. Bank, Cleve., Goodyear Tire and Rubber Co., Akron. Contbr. articles to profl. jours. Bd. dirs. Independent Sector, Washington, 1987—; trustee Coll. Wooster, 1977—. Mem. Nat. Assn. Social Workers, Assn. Black Found. Execs., NAACP (life), Am. Pub. Welfare Assn. (pres. 1977-78, bd. dirs. 1987—), Cleve. Black Profl. Assn. (Black Profl. Yr. award 1985). Democrat. Presbyterian. Avocations: golf, reading. Home: 2878 Woodbury Rd Shaker Heights OH 44120 Office: The Cleve Found 1400 Hanna Bldg Cleveland OH 44115

MINTON, J. D., insurance company executive; b. 1925; married. B.S., Creighton U., 1950. Underwriter Mut. of Omaha Ins. Co., Omaha, 1950-59; 2d v.p., asst. comptroller Mut. of Omaha Ins. Co., 1959-65, v.p., 1965-70, pres., chief operating officer, 1970—; sr. exec. v.p. United of Omaha Life Ins. Co. subs. Mut. of Omaha; also bd. dirs. Office: Mut of Omaha Ins Co Mutual of Omaha Plaza Omaha NE 68175 *

MINUTILLI, JOSEPH D., credit and insurance company executive; b. Columbus, Ohio, 1928. Grad., Ohio Wesleyan U., 1951. Chmn., pres., chief exec. officer, dir. Comml. Credit Co., Balt. Office: Comml Credit Co 300 Saint Paul Pl Baltimore MD 21202 *

MIODOVNIK, MENACHEM, obstetrician-gynecologist; b. Jerusalem, Sept. 15, 1946; s. Nachman and Ester (Elkind) M.; divorced; children: Ayal, Amir. MD, Hebrew U., Jerusalem, 1973. Diplomate Am. Bd. Ob-Gyn. Instr. dept. ob-gyn. U. Cin., 1979-81, asst. prof. dept. ob-gyn., 1981-86, asst. prof. dept. pediatrics, 1984-86, assoc. prof. dept. ob-gyn and pediatrics, 1986—; dir. perinatal treatment ctr. U. Cin. ob-gyn. dept., 1981—. Contbr. articles to profl. jours. NIH grantee, 1985-86. Fellow Am. Coll. Ob-Gyn.; mem. Soc. Gynecologic Investigation, Soc. of Perinatal Obstetricians, Am. Inst. for Ultrasound in Medicine (sr.), Israel Med. Assn. Office: U Cin Dept Ob/Gyn 231 Bethesda Ave Cincinnati OH 45267-0526

MIOTA, MARGARET ELIZABETH, psychotherapist; b. Milw., Aug. 14, 1940; s. Raymond Clarence and Elizabeth (Perusick) Frakes; m. John Matthew Miota, Sept. 1, 1962; children: Kevin Gerard, Matthew James, Nicholas John. RN, Milw. County Hosp., 1962; BSN, Alverno Coll., Milw., 1975; MSW, U. Wis., Milw., 1979. RN, Wis.; lic. psychotherapist. Head nurse Milw. County Mental Health Hosp., 1962-64; instr. Childbirth Edn. Assn., Milw., 1964-70; staff nurse West Allis (Wis.) Meml. Hosp., 1968-75; instr. Milw. County Hosp. Nursing Sch., 1975-77; clin. supr. Milw. Psychiat. Hosp., 1980—. Spl. friend Women's Crisis Line, Milw., 1982-86. Mem. Internat. Childbirth Edn. Assn., Feminst Therapy Network, Am. Assn. Marital and Family Therapists (clin.), Nat. Assn Social Workers, NOW, Nat. Museum of Women in the Arts, Delta Epsilon Sigma, Alpha Delta Mu. Avocations: yoga, biking, swimming, walking, cross country skiing. Office: Milw Psychiat Hosp 1220 Dewey Ave Wauwatosa WI 53213

MIRABILE, JASPER JOSEPH, restauranteur; b. Kansas City, Mo., July 18, 1962; s. Jasper J. Sr. and Josephine (Cropis) M. Student, U. Nev., Kans. State U. Gen. mgr. Jasper's Restaurant, Kansas City, Mo., 1980-84; owner, chef Marco Polo's, Kansas City, 1984—. Author: Jasper's Famous Dishes, 1986. Mem. Internat. Assn. Cooking Schs., Les Amis du Vin., Great Chefs Am. Democrat. Roman Catholic. Club: Prog. Waldo Mchts. (Kansas City) (pres. 1986-87). Avocations: gourmet cooking, racquetball, drafting, swimming, fishing. Office: Jasper's/Marco Polo's 405 W 75th Kansas City MO 64114

MIRANDA, CARLOS SA, food products company executive; b. Fall River, Mass., Nov. 16, 1929; s. Carlos Sa and Annette (Pratt) M.; m. Natalie Cardoso, Jan. 5, 1949; children—Carla, Lucy, John. B.S. in Mech. Engring., Marquette U., 1956. With internat. div. Kellogg Co., Battle Creek, Mich., 1964-65, gen. mgr., Brazil, 1965-80, gen. mgr. Kellogg's Spain, 1983-84, v.p. Kellogg Internat., Battle Creek, 1980—. Recipient Pero Vaz Caminha award, Brazil, 1976; conferred title Comdr. of Legion of Honor of Marshal Rondon, Brazil, 1971. Mem. ASME. Republican. Roman Catholic. Office: Kellogg Co One Kellogg Square PO Box 3599 Battle Creek MI 49016

MIRANDA, DANIEL FRANK, lawyer, real estate executive; b. Corona, Calif., June 16, 1953; s. Frank R. and Mary A. (Cintas) M.; m. Jacqueline Fry, Dec. 28, 1975; children—David Frank, Kate Elise. A.B., U. Calif.-Berkeley, 1975; J.D., (Stone scholar), Columbia U., 1979. Bar: Ill. 1979. Assoc., Sonnenschein, Carlin, Nath & Rosenthal, Chgo., 1979-81; v.p., legal and corp. sec. The Westport Co. (Conn.), 1981-84; project exec. dir. 666 Assocs., Chgo., 1981-84; pres. First Columbia Corp., Chgo. and Miami, 1984-85; dir. Dade Savs. & Loan Assn., Miami, 1984, Greater N. Michigan Ave. Assn., Chgo. Mem. ABA, Ill. State Bar Assn., Chgo. Bar Assn.

MIRICH, RODNEY LEE, obstetrician-gynecologist; b. Vancouver, Wash., Oct. 15, 1945. BS, Oreg. State U., 1967; MD, U. Oreg., 1971. Fellow Am. Coll. Ob-gyn.; mem. Am. Fertility Soc., Christian Med. Soc., Muskegon Christian Med. Soc. (pres. 1986—). Office: 1675 Leahy St #428 Muskegon MI 49441

MIRTALLO, JAY MATTHEW, pharmacist, academic educator; b. Stamford, N.Y., Oct. 29, 1953; s. Leonard and Betty Louise (Clapper) M.; m. Ginger Doll Mirtallo, May 27, 1972 (div. May 1986); children: Karissa Wesley, Taylor Jay. BS in Pharmacy cum laude, U. Toledo, 1976; MS in Hosp. Pharmacy, Ohio State U., 1978. Resident in hosp. pharmacy Ohio State U. Hosps., Columbus, 1978, clin. pharmacist, 1978—, clin. assoc. prof. coll. pharmacy, 1985—; grad. faculty coll. pharmacy Ohio State U., 1983—, adj. asst. prof. dept. surgery, 1984—; co-owner, treas. Clin. Pharmacist Cons., 1982—; cons. Travenol Labs., Deerfield, Ill., 1983-85, DataMed, Mpls., 1986—; lectr. Travenol Home Care, Deerfield, 1984-85, 86—; lectr. research, ednl. audiences. Edit. bd. Drug Intelligence and Clin. Pharmacy, 1982—, Clin. Pharmacy, 1983-86, Nutrition in Clin. Practice, 1986—; contbr. articles to profl. jours. Recipient Outstanding Young Man Am., Jaycees, 1984. Mem. Am. Soc. Parenteral and Enteral Nutrition, Am. Soc. Hosp. Pharmacists, Ohio Soc. Hosp. Pharmacists (Hosp. Pharmacist of Yr. award 1985), Cen. Ohio Soc. Hosp. Pharmacists (Outstanding Service award 1983). Roman Catholic. Office: Ohio State U Hosps Dept Pharmacy 410 W 10th Ave Columbus OH 43210

MIRUS, JUDITH ANN, arts management consultant; b. Greensboro, N.C., July 28, 1944; d. Robert Lee and Esther Clementine (Lumbrick) M. BA, DePauw U., 1966; MS in Teaching, U. Ill., 1967; postgrad., U. Minn., 1985-86. Cert. elem. and secondary tchr., Minn. Instr. U. Minn., Mpls., 1969-71; assoc. dir. Choreogram Dance Co., Mpls., 1970-72, artistic dir., 1972-78; dance dir. Mpls. Jewish Community Ctr., 1978-80; exec. dir. Minn. Ind. Choreographers Alliance, Mpls., 1980-85; ind. arts cons. Mpls., 1985—; panelist Am. Film Inst., Mpls., 1984, Colo. Dance Festival, Boulder, 1985, Minn. Arts Bd., St. Paul, 1986; site evaluator Ohio Arts Council, Columbus, 1985. Contbr. articles to jours., coordinator dance book index, St. Paul Pub.

Library, 1985-86. Chmn. internal ops. com. Mpls. Arts Commn., 1985-86; mem. sub-com. Latimer for Gov. Campaign, St. Paul, 1986. Named to Arts Leaders of 1984, City Pages newspaper, Mpls. Mem. Council of Ind. and Profl. Cons., Minn. chpt. NOW. Avocations: dance improvisation, hiking, skiing. Home and Office: 1411 Fremont Ave N Minneapolis MN 55411

MISCH, GORDON WILFRID, manufacturing company executive; b. Rocky Ridge, Ohio, Nov. 14, 1925; s. Wilfrid Adolf and Lydia Martha (Brecklen) M.; Jean Louise Sieck, Oct. 1, 1949; children: Leslie Jean, Ann Lydia, Nancy Lynn. AB, Wittenberg U., Springfield, Ohio, 1948. Controller Superior Coach Corp., Koscuisko, Miss., 1951-72; mgr. fin. services Sheller-Globe Corp., Lima, Ohio, 1973-80; v.p. fin. Superior Coaches, Lima, 1981—. Bd. dirs. Lima Family YMCA, 1984, Jr. Achievement, Lima, 1985. Mem. Nat. Assn. Accts. Republican. Lutheran. Lodges: Rotary, Elks. AAvocations: coin collecting, golf. Home: 13266 Infirmary Rd Wapakoneta OH 45895 Office: Superior Coaches 600 E Wayne St PO Box 1981 Lima OH 45802

MISCHKE, FREDERICK CHARLES, manufacturing company executive; b. Benton Harbor, Mich., Sept. 21, 1930; s. Fred William and Clara Adeline (Ruhno) M.; m. Kathleen Ann Schultz, Nov. 19, 1955 (dec. Aug. 1980); children: Stephanie, Michael, Eric; m. Lori Ann Leonard, Dec. 23, 1983. AA, Lake Mich. Coll., 1956; BBA, Western Mich. U., 1958. CPA, Ind., Mich. Staff acct. Lybrand, Ross Bros. & Montgomery, Chgo., 1958-63; supr. acctg. Lybrand, Ross Bros. & Montgomery, Niles, Mich., 1963-65; v.p., treas. Skyline Corp., Elkhart, Ind., 1965—. Pres. Jaycees, Niles, 1965, Elkhart County United Way, 1974-75, Jr. Achievement, Elkhart, 1974-75, mem. adv. bd. 1982—, Better Bus. Bur., Elkhart, 1975, bd. dirs. 1973—; mem. council Career Ctr., Elkhart, 1974-80; past sec. Sch. Bd. Parish Edn. Bd.; asst. exec. dir. Trinity Luth. Ch., 1986—. Served to sgt. USAF, 1951-55. Mem. Am. Inst. CPA's, Ind. Assn. CPA's (Civic Achievement award, 1976), Mich. Assn. CPA's, Fin. Execs. Inst. (chpt. pres. 1974-75), Nat. Assn. Accts., U.S. Power Squadron. Republican. Lutheran. Club: Elcona Country (pres. 1975). Lodge: Rotary (local pres. 1976-77). Avocations: boating, golf, bowling. Home: 23322 Greenleaf Blvd Elkhart IN 46514 Office: Skyline Corp PO Box 743 Elkhart IN 46515

MISHLER, JOHN MILTON, IV, university administrator; b. Cairo, Ill., Sept. 25, 1946; s. John Milton III and Mary Jane (Woodbury) M.; m. Mary Therese Stember, Apr. 15, 1972 (div. Nov. 1981); m. Sigrid Ruth Elizabeth Fisher, Dec. 15, 1981; 1 child, Joshua Evan. AA, Orange Coast Coll., Costa Mesa, Calif., 1966; AB, U. Calif., San Diego, 1969, ScM, 1971; DPhil, Oxford U., 1978. Cert. community coll. instr., Calif. Clin. coordinator McGaw Labs., Costa Mesa, 1972-78; research fellow Med. U., Cologne, Fed. Republic Germany, 1978-80; br. chief Nat. Heart, Lung and Blood Inst. NIH, Bethesda, Md., 1980-82; prof. U. Mo., Kansas City, 1983—, asst. vice chancellor, 1983-86, assoc. vice chancellor, 1986—. Author: Pharmacology of Hydroxyethyl Starch, 1982; contbr. 106 articles to profl. jours. Fellow Internat. Soc. Haematology; mem. Royal Coll. Pathologists, Am. Soc. Hematology, German Soc. Haematology, N.Y. Acad. Scis., Sigma Xi. Jewish. Avocations: reading, writing, music. Home: 1225 W 62d St Kansas City MO 64113 Office: U Mo Kansas City 5100 Rockhill Rd Kansas City MO 64110-2499

MISHRA, VISHWA MOHAN, educator, cons.; b. Hilsa, Patna, India, Nov. 12, 1937; s. Pandit Sheo Nath and Pandita Nitya (Rani) M.; came to U.S., 1956, naturalized, 1964; BA with honors, Patna U., 1954, MA, 1956; MA, U. Ga., 1958; PhD, U. Minn., 1968; MTS, St. John's, 1987; m. Sally Schroeder, June 18, 1977; children—Aneil Kumar, Allan Kumar, Anand Kumar, Jennifer Kumari, Andrew Kumar. Staff reporter, Hindusthan Samachar, Ltd., Patna, India, 1950-56; exec. dir. India for Christ, Inc., Mpls., 1960-64; research fellow, instr. Sch. Journalism and Mass Communication, U. Minn., 1964-68; asst. prof. U. Okla., 1968-69; asso. prof. Mich. State U., East Lansing, 1969-87, prof., 1987—; dir. market and communication research Panax Corp., East Lansing, 1975-76; adminstrv. asst., research cons. to pres. Lansing (Mich.) Community Coll., 1976—, pres. Communications Cons. Internat., Inc., 1987—. Vice chmn. Eaton-Ingham Substance Abuse Commn. Recipient NSF award, 1969; Bihar Rastrabhasha Parishad Lit. award, 1st prize, 1954. Mem. Am. Mgmt. Assn., Am. Statis. Assn., Am. Pub. Opinion Research Council, Newspaper Research Council, Radio and TV News Dirs. Assn., Assn. Edn. in Journalism, Internat. Communication Assn., Am. Platform Assn., Smithsonian Instn. Assos., Kappa Tau Alpha, Sigma Delta Chi. Clubs: East Lansing Rotary, University. Author: Communication and Modernization in Urban Slums, 1972; The Basic News Media and Techniques, 1972; Law and Disorder; co-editor Dynamics of Information Management, 1987; also monographs. Contbr. articles to scholastic jours. Home: 3911 Hemmingway Dr Okemos MI 48864

MISKIMINS, ROBERT DAVID, accountant; b. Torrington, Wyo., Feb. 15, 1953; s. Richard George and Gwendolyn Phyllis (Brown) M.; m. Janet Marie Davis, July 4, 1974; children: Harmony, Holly, Robby, Joy, Ricky. AA, Johnson County Community Coll., 1978; BS in Acctg. cum laude, Brigham Young U., 1979. CPA, Mo. Tax supr. Grant Thornton, Kansas City, Mo., 1980-87, tax mgr., 1987—; acctg. instr. St. Mary's Coll., Kansas City, Kans., 1983. Mem. Am. Inst. CPA's, Mo. Soc. CPA's (taxation com. 1985-87). Mormon. Office: Grant Thornton 1101 Walnut Suite 1600 Kansas City MO 64106

MISNER, PAUL, theology educator; b. Akron, Ohio, Feb. 14, 1936; s. Francis De Sales and Madge (Mee) M.; m. Barbara Ruybal, Aug. 19, 1972. BA, St. Charles Borromeo Sem., Phila., 1958; postgrad., Gregorian U., Rome, 1962; ThD, U. Munich, 1969. Assoc. pastor St. Basil Parish, Pitts., 1962-65; asst. prof. theol. Boston Coll., 1969-75; dir. devel. Am. Sch. Oriental Research, Cambridge, Mass., 1977-79; asst. prof. theol. Marquette U., Milw., 1979-83, assoc. prof. theol., 1983—; cons. Nat. Assn. Diocesan Ecumenical Officers, Wheeling, W.Va., 1985, 87. Author: Papacy and Development, 1976; editor N. Söderblom's Briefwechsel 1909-1931, 1981; contbr. articles to profl. jour. Fulbright fellow West German Commn., 1975-76, 1985-86. Mem. N.Am. Acad Ecumenists (bd. dirs., pres. 1984-85), Am. Acad. Religion, Coll. Theology Soc. (publs. chmn. 1982-83), Am. Cath. Hist. Assn. Democrat. Roman Catholic. Home: 3292 N 47th St Milwaukee WI 53216 Office: Theology Dept Marquette U Milwaukee WI 53233

MISSAR, RICHARD R., paint and chemical manufacturing company executive; b. Chgo., 1930, student Ill. Inst. Tech., Advanced Mgmt. Program, Harvard U., 1975. With DeSoto Inc., Des Plaines, Ill., 1950—, lab. technician chem. coatings div., 1950-55, salesman, 1955-60, product mgr., 1960-64, regional sales mgr., 1964-69, dir. mktg., 1969-71, gen. mgr., 1971-74, group v.p. chem. coatings div., 1974-75, corp. v.p. corp. mktg. adminstrn., 1975-76, exec. v.p., chief operating officer, 1976-79, pres., chief exec. officer, 1979—, now also chmn. bd., bd. dirs. Served with USMC, 1951-53. Mem. Nat. Paint and Coating Assn. Office: De Soto Inc 1700 S Mount Prospect Rd Des Plaines IL 60018

MISSI, MICHAEL GENE, sub-contract manufacturing executive; b. New Albany, Ind., Apr. 16, 1954; s. Wilfred Louis and Martha Lee (Schmidt) M.; m. Rebecca Sue Koetter, Apr. 7, 1978; children: Eric, Allison. Grad. high sch., Borden, Ind., 1972. Pres. Missi Contract Assembly, Borden, Ind., 1983—. Democrat. Roman Catholic. Avocation: woodworking. Home and Office: Rural Rte 1 Box 176 Borden IN 47106

MISTRY, SORAB PIROZSHAH, biochemistry educator; b. Bombay, India, Dec. 18, 1920; s. Pirozshah Dorabji and Jerbai Pestonji (Patel) M.; m. Margrith Gertrude Buchi, May 7, 1953; children—Dinu, Darius. B.S., U. Bombay, 1942; M.S., Indian Inst. Sci., Bangalore, 1946; Ph.D., U. Cambridge, 1951. Postdoctoral fellow U. Cambridge, 1951-52, U. Ill., 1952-54; mem. faculty U. Ill., Urbana, 1954—, assoc. prof. biochemistry, 1961-66, prof., 1966—; cons. nutrition surveys USDA, Orangeburg, S.C., 1972-75; prof. Swiss Fed. Inst. Tech., Zurich, 1979, 81, 83, 84, 85, 86, Autonoma U., Madrid, Spain, 1971, 79, 84, U. Zurich, 1957, 63, U. Amsterdam, 1956, Indian Inst. Sci., Bangalore, 1970-71. Fellow NIH, 1963-64, Med. Research Council Eng., 1951, Sethna Found. India, 1947-50. Mem. Am. Soc. Biol. Chemists, Am. Inst. Nutrition, Brit. Biochem. Soc., Swiss Chem. Soc., Sigma Xi, Phi Kappa Phi. Democrat. Zoroastrian. Home: 1011 W Green St Champaign IL 61821 Office: U Ill Dept Animal Sci Urbana IL 61801

MITAL, ANIL, engineering educator; b. Barabanki, India, Nov. 13, 1951; came to U.S., 1975; s. Virendra Nath and Malti (Gupta) M.; m. Chetna Gupta, June 12, 1981; children: Anubhav, Aashi. B.E., Allahabad U., 1974; M.S., Kans. State U., 1976; Ph.D., Tex. Tech. U., 1980. Asst. prof. indsl. engring U. Wis.-Platteville, 1979-80; asst. prof. mech. and indsl. engring, 1981-84, assoc. prof., 1984—, human factors engring grad. coordinator U. Cin., Ohio, 1981—, dir. Ergonomics Research Lab., 1981—; chmn. Internat. Found. for Indsl. Ergonomics and Safety Research, 1986—. Editor-in-chief Internat. Jour. Indls. Ergonomics, 1986—. Mem. Big Bros.-Big Sisters, Lubbock, Tex., 1977—. Nat. Inst. Occupational Safety and Health grantee, 1982-85; recipient Gold Medal for performance Allahabad U., 1974; named Young Engr. Yr. Engrs. and Scientists Cin., 1984; Jr. Morrow Research Chair, 1982-83. Mem. Am. Indsl. Hygiene Assn. (chmn. nat. ergonomics com. 1984-85), Human Factors Soc. Am. (editorial bd., chmn. indsl. ergonomics tech. group 1985-86, Outstanding Contbns. award Tri-State chpt. 1984), Human Factors Soc. Greater Cin. (pres., 1983-84), Inst. Indsl. Engrs. (treas. Cin. chpt. 1983-84, bd. dirs. ergonomics div. 1987—), Soc. Automotive Engrs. (faculty advisor 1987—, Ralph R. Teetor award 1985), Pi Tau Sigma, Alpha Pi Mu, Tau Beta Pi (faculty adviser 1981-85), Phi Kappa Phi, Omicron Delta Kappa, Delta Phi Epsilon, Sigma Xi (Disting. Research award 1984). Club: 100 Mile Joggers. Gen. editor: Trends in Ergonomics/Human Factors I, 1984, Applications of Fuzzy Set Theory in Human Factors, 1986, numerous other ergonomics jours.; contbr. numerous articles to profl. jours. Home: 937 Gawain Circle West Carrollton OH 45449 Office: Dept Mech Engring ML 72 U Cincinnati Cincinnati OH 45221

MITBY, JOHN CHESTER, lawyer; b. Antigo, Wis., Jan. 7, 1944; s. Norman Peter and Luvern T. (Jensen) M.; m. Julie Kampen, June 10, 1972; children: Tana, Jenna. B.S., U. Wis., 1966, LL.D., 1971. Bar: Wis. 1971; cert. civil trial advocate. Ptnr. Brynelson, Herrick, Bucida, Dorschel & Armstrong, Madison, Wis., 1973—; lectr. U. Wis. Law Sch. Served to capt. C.E., U.S. Army, 1966-68. Mem. ABA, Wis. Bar Assn. (past chmn. litigation sect.), Dane County Bar Assn., Civil Trial Counsel Wis. (bd. dirs.), Wis. Acad. Trial Lawyers, Assn. Trial Lawyers Am. Club: Nakoma Country (Madison). Home: 726 Oneida Pl Madison WI 53711 Office: Brynelson Herrick Bucida Dorschel & Armstrong 122 W Washington St PO Box 1767 Madison WI 53701

MITCH, PAUL STEVE, psychiatrist; b. Donora, Pa., Oct. 3, 1945; s. Steve Joseph and Rose Marie (Ferretti) M.; m. Sharon Dale Senger, June 13, 1970 (div. 1982); children—Jason, Nathan, Kristen. B.S., U. Dayton, 1967; M.D., Ohio State U., 1971. Diplomate Am. Bd. Psychiatry and Neurology, Biofeedback Cert. Inst. Am. Resident in psychiatry Med. Coll. Ohio, Toledo, 1971-74, clin. instr., 1974-76, asst. prof., 1976-77, clin. asst. prof., 1977—; med. dir. Community Mental Health Ctr.-West, Toledo, 1977-85; pvt. practice medicine specializing in psychiatry, Toledo, 1977—; psychiat. cons. N.W. Ohio Devel. Ctr., Toledo, 1978—, Sunshine Children's Home, Maumee, Ohio, 1978-85, Lott Group Home, Toledo, 1979-85. Contbr. articles to profl. jours. Recipient Sandoz award Sandoz Pharms., 1972-73. Mem. Am. Psychiat. Assn., AMA (Physicians Recognition award 1984), Biofeedback Soc. Am., Wellness Assocs., N.W. Ohio Psychiat. Assn. (pres. 1979-80). Democrat. Roman Catholic. Avocations: horticulture, music, motorcycling. Home: 12461 River Rd Grand Rapids OH 43522 Office: 3171 Republic Blvd North #101 Toledo OH 43615

MITCHELL, BERNARD JOSEPH, insurance executive; b. Chgo., Dec. 20, 1925; s. John and Stephanie Marie (Gorney) M.; m. Lorraine Marie Sinski, Feb. 22, 1946; children: Carol Ann Mitchell Johnston, Deborah Lynn Mitchell Falk, Richard Bernard. BS, DePaul U., 1950. Spl. agt. Aetna Ins. Co., Hartford, Conn., 1948-61; exec. v.p. Tower Ins. Co., Inc., Milw., 1961-72; pres. Tower Ins. Co., Inc., Pewaukee, Wis., 1972—, also chmn. bd. dirs.; pres. Fiduciaries, Inc., Pewaukee, 1972—, also bd. dirs.; bd. dirs. M.B. Victora Agy., Muscoda, Wis., Continental Bank & Trust, Milw., Strategic Data Systems, Sheboygan, Wis., Applied Quoting Systems, Hartland, Wis. Served with USAF, 1941-43. Republican. Roman Catholic. Clubs: Bluemound Country (Wauwatosa, Wis.); Wisconsin (Milw.). Office: Tower Ins Co Inc N14 W24200 Tower Pl Pewaukee WI 53072

MITCHELL, CHERYL LYNN, accountant; b. Christopher, Ill., Oct. 12, 1960; d. Robert Bernard and Betty Jean (Kish) M. BS, So. Ill. U., Carbondale, 1982. CPA, Mo. Sr. acct. Price Waterhouse, St. Louis, 1982—. Mem. Am. Inst. CPA's, Mo. Soc. CPA's, St. Louis Soc. Women CPA's. Avocations: soccer, softball, tennis. Office: Price Waterhouse One Centerre Plaza Saint Louis MO 63101

MITCHELL, DANIEL RAY, lawyer; b. Fremont, Ohio, Aug. 7, 1939; s. Daniel Ray and Ruth Esther (Murphy) M.; m. Sally Jo Meadors, June 20, 1964; children: Susan, Jill. BS, Ohio State U., 1961, JD, Harvard U., 1966. Asst. v.p. tax Brunswick Corp., Skokie, Ill., 1977-81; mgr. tax planning Amoco Corp., Chgo., 1981-86, gen. tax counsel, 1986—. Mem. ABA, Am. Inst. CPA's. Home: 1148 Oak St Winnetka IL 60093 Office: Amoco Corp 200 E Randolph Dr MC 2404A Chicago IL 60601

MITCHELL, DAVID CRERAR, orthopedist; b. Detroit, Mar. 22, 1930; s. C. Leslie and Irene (Tennant) M.; children: Peyton Leslie, David C. Jr., Timothy. MD, Duke U., 1955. Intern U. Mich., Ann Arbor, 1955-57; resident in orthopedics Mass. Gen. Hosp./Children's Hosp., Boston, 1959-63; sr. staff physician Henry Ford Hosp., Detroit, 1963—. Served to capt. U.S. Army, 1957-59. Mem. AMA, Mich. Med. Soc., Am. Acad. Orthopedic Surgeons, Clin. Orthopedic Soc., Mid-Am. Orthopedic Assn., Mich. Orthopedic Soc., Internat. Soc. Orthopedics and Traumatology, Detroit Acad. Orthopedic Surgeons. Club: Country Club of Detroit (Grosse Pointe Farms, Mich.). Avocations: photography, thoroughbred horses. Home: 271 Hillcrest Grosse Pointe Farms MI 48236 Office: Henry Ford Hosp/Lakeside 14500 Hall Rd Sterling Heights MI 48078

MITCHELL, DWAIN JESSE, county official, civil engineer, land surveyor; b. Hettick, Ill., Aug. 9, 1922; s. Marvel Jesse and Eunice Edith (Joiner) M.; m. Ruth Elaine Whittaker, July 21, 1942; children—Carolyn Jean, Roger Michael. Student So. Ill. U., 1940-42, U. Md., 1943-44. Registered land surveyor, Ill. Engr., land surveyor Christian County Hwy. Dept., Taylorville, Ill., 1946—, asst. supt. hyws., 1965—; county plat rev. officer Christian County, 1964-74; liaison mem. Christian County Hwy. Commrs., 1975—. Leader Abraham Lincoln council Boy Scouts Am., 1956-68. Served to sgt. 1st class U.S. Army, 1943-46, ETO, 50-52. Fellow Am. Congress Surveying and Mapping; mem. Ill. Registered Land Surveyors Assn. (sec.-treas. 1970-74). Democrat. American Baptist. Lodge: Order of Arrow. Avocations: photography; camping; fishing; bowling. Home: 604 Taylorville Blvd Taylorville IL 62568 Office: Christian County Hwy Dept 1000 N Cheney St Taylorville IL 62568

MITCHELL, EDWARD JAMES, III, accountant, tax consultant; b. Kansas City, Mo., Sept. 6, 1955; s. Edward James Jr. and Nancy Grace (Mast) M.; m. Martha Lucy Muraski, July 21, 1976 (div. Oct. 1985); children: Edward J., Gregory M. BBA, U. Mo., 1978, MS, 1979. CPA, Mo. Tax acct. Laventhol & Horwath, Kansas City, 1980-82, Mayer Hoffman McCann, Kansas City, 1983-86; comptroller Kings Profl. Basketball Club, Kansas City, 1983; tax acct. Mize Houser & Co., Overland Park, Kans., 1986—; bd. dirs. treas. Johnson County Mental Health Ctr., 1986; instr. undergrad. acctg. and taxation U. Mo., 1979-81. Contbr. articles to profl. jours. Mem. Am. Inst. CPA's, Mo. Soc. CPA's, Beta Alpha Psi. Republican. Roman Catholic. Avocations: bicycling, bird hunting, fishing, gardening. Home: 9010 W 168th St Stilwell KS 66085 Office: Clayton Brown & Assocs 300 W Washington Chicago IL 60606

MITCHELL, EUGENE R., insurance company executive; b. Detroit, Dec. 8, 1929; s. Max B. and Frances (Sklar) M.; m. Susan Carol, Dec. 19, 1954; children: Robert, Elizabeth, Stacey. BA, Detroit Inst. Tech., 1957. Salesman E.R. Mitchell & Assocs., Detroit, 1960-68; pres. Profl. Life Underwriters Service, Inc., Troy, Mich., 1968—; M & G Market Services, Inc., Troy; mem. adv. bd. Life of Va., Am. Agy. Life, 1982—; past mem. adv bd. Midland Mut. Life; past pres. adv. bd. Charter Nat. Life. Past chmn. Alex Karras Charities; past mem. adv. bd. Profl. Golfers Assn. Mich.; mem. tournament com. Kaline-Gehringer Golf Tournament; mem. med. credentials bd. St. Joseph Mercy Hosp., Pontiac, Mich.; mem. exec. and steering coms. Met. Detroit March of Dimes; mem. com. on bicentennial of constn. Jud. Conf. of U.S.; founding mem. U.S. Space Found. Named Agt. of Yr., Ins. Salesman Mag., 7 times, Agy. of Yr., Life of Va., 1984-85; recipient Humanitarian award March of Dimes, 1987, Pres.'s trophy Kemper Ins., 1982. Mem. Detroit Life Underwriters, Life Ins. Leaders of Mich. (life; Humanitarian award 1984), Advance Assn. Life Underwriters. Clubs: Katke-Couzens Golf, U. Mich. Pres.'s (life), Victor's (life), Oakland U. Pres.'s (life), Econs. (life). Office: Profl Life Underwriters Service Inc 3001 W Big Beaver St Suite 100 Troy MI 48084

MITCHELL, FRANK WARREN, chemical engineer; b. Shreveport, La., Nov. 19, 1954; s. James Robert and Jean Ellen (McNaught) M.; m. Anne-Marie Wilder, July 17, 1983. BSChemE, U. Ark., 1975, Clemson U., 1975; MSChemE, Ohio State U., 1979. Engr. devel. UOP Inc., Riverside, Ill., 1979-80; tech. adv. UOP Inc., Des Plaines, Ill., 1980-82, chief tech. adv., 1982-84, coordinator, 1984-87; dist. rep. UOP Inc., London, 1987—. Vol. Big Brother/Big Sister, Dupage County, Ill., 1979-80. Mem. Am. Inst. Chem. Engrs., Am. Chem. Soc., Sierra Club, Nature Conservancy, Tau Beta Pi, Theta Tau. Republican. Unitarian. Avocations: sailing, tennis. Office: care of UOP Inc 25 E Algonquin Rd Des Plaines IL 60017-5017

MITCHELL, GEORGE TRICE, physician; b. Marshall, Ill., Jan. 20, 1914; s. Roscoe Addison and Alma (Trice) M.; m. Mildred Alethia Miller, June 21, 1941; children: Linda Sue, Mary Kathryn. BS, Purdue U., 1935; MD, George Washington U., 1940. Intern Meth. Hosp., Indpls., 1940-41; gen. practice medicine Marshall, 1946—; mem. courtesy staff Union and Regional Hosps., Terre Haute, Ind.; clin. assoc. Sch. Basic Medicine U. Ill.; chmn. bd. dirs. First Nat. Bank, Marshall. Mem. adv. council premedicine Eastern Ill. U., 1965-69; alt. del. Rep. Conv., 1968, del., 1972; trustee Lakeland Jr. Coll. Served from 1st lt. to lt. col. USAAF, 1941-45. Fellow Am. Acad. Family Physicians; mem. AMA, Ill. Med. Soc. (2d v.p. 1980-81), Clark County Med. Soc. (pres.), Aesculapian Soc. of Wabash Valley (pres. 1965), Clark County Hist. Soc. (pres. 1968-70). Methodist. Lodges: Masons (32 degree), Shriners. Home: RFD 2 Marshall IL 62441 Office: 410 N 2d St Marshall IL 62441

MITCHELL, GERALD BENSON, vehicular parts supply executive; b. Goderich, Ont., Can., Aug. 29, 1927; s. Reginald and Mary Elizabeth (Sanders) M.; m. Stephanie Bennett Wood, Oct. 1, 1970; children: Fraser, Jamie, Briar, Michael, Melissa. Student, U. Western Ont. With Hayes Dana Co., Toledo, 1944-67, v.p. mfg., from 1958, pres., 1963-67; exec. v.p. Dana Corp., Toledo, 1967-73, pres., 1973-80, 84-87, chmn. bd., chief exec. officer, 1980—; exec. com. Machinery and Allied Products Inst.; dir. Anchor Hocking Corp., Mich. Nat. Bank, Mich. Nat. Corp., Direc Spicer Mexico, Hayes-Dana Can. Contbg. author: Chief Executive's Handbook, 1974. Trustee Med. Coll. Ohio at Toledo Found.; trustee Toledo Symphony Orch., Toledo Art Mus.; trustee, assoc. Hillsdale Coll.; mem. Toledo Labor-Mgmt.-Citizens Com. Mem. Western Hwy. Inst., Conf. Bd. Clubs: Inverness, Renaissance, Anglers, Ocean Reef. Office: Dana Corp PO Box 1000 4500 Dorr St Toledo OH 43697 *

MITCHELL, JAMES AUSTIN, insurance company executive; b. Cin., Dec. 16, 1941; s. James Austin and Jeannette Louise (Stiles) M.; m. Patricia Ann McNulty, Aug. 12, 1967; 1 child, J. David. A.B., Princeton U., 1963. CLU; chartered fin. cons.; FSA. Various positions Conn. Gen. Life Ins. Co., Hartford, 1963-73, v.p., controller, 1973-77; v.p., chief fin. officer Aetna Ins. Co., Hartford, 1977-82; pres. Cigna RE Corp., Hartford, 1982-84; pres., chief exec. officer IDS Life Ins. Co., Mpls., 1984—; dir. IDS Fin. Services and Affiliated Cos., Mpls. Chmn. Community Initiatives Consortium, 1984—; chmn. Vanguard Div. United Way, Mpls., 1986—. Served with U.S. Army, 1964-70. Fellow Soc. Actuaries; mem. Soc. C.L.U.s. Republican. Presbyterian. Club: Minneapolis. Avocations: tennis; skiing; reading. Home: 2685 N Shore Dr Wayzata MN 55391 Office: IDS Life Ins Co 2900 IDS Tower Minneapolis MN 55474

MITCHELL, JAMES THOMAS, missile specialist; b. Oakland, Calif., May 24, 1960; s. Hugo Bernard Mitchell and Marilyn Ruth Ehling. Ed. various naval schs., USN, 1977—; student in Polit. Sci., U. Nebr., Omaha, 1987—. Submarine qualified, cert. watch officer, USN. Enlisted USN, 1977; missile launch supr. USN, Charleston, S.C., 1979-84; strategic ops. (nuclear) Orgn. Joint Chiefs of Staff/Nat. Emergency Airborne Command Post USN, Omaha, Nebr., 1984—. Mem. North Charleston (S.C.) Citizens Adv. Council, 1983-84, Lakota Devel. Council. Mem. Amnesty Internat. Republican. Roman Catholic. Avocations: nuclear warfare studies, radiol. effects and controls studies, outdoor activities. Home: 704 Golden Gate Circle #18 Papillion NE 68046

MITCHELL, JEROME WILK, dentist; b. Pontiac, Mich., Sept. 21, 1953; s. Jas Thomas and Ruth Neil (Burton) M. Grad., U. Mich., 1976, DDS, 1980. Pub. aid dentist Martin Luther King Clinic, Chgo., 1981; dentist Headstart, Chgo., 1981; assoc. dentist Lawshae & Assoc., Chgo., 1981-84; dental dir. Correction Med. Services, Pontiac, Ill., 1982, Correctional Health Service, Pontiac, 1982-86, Correctional Med. Services, Pontiac, 1987—. Home: 104 N Orr Unit 6 Normal IL 61761

MITCHELL, JOHN FRANCIS, electronics company executive; b. Chgo., Jan. 1, 1928; s. William and Bridie (Keane) M.; B.S. in Elec. Engring., Ill. Inst. Tech., 1950; m. Margaret J. Gillis, Aug. 26, 1950; children—Catherine (Mrs. Edward Welsh III), John, Kevin. Exec. v.p., asst. chief operating officer Motorola Inc., Schaumburg, Ill., 1953-80, pres., 1980—, chief operating officer, 1986—. Served to lt. (j.g.) USNR, 1950-53. Mem. IEEE (sr.). Club: Inverness (Ill.) Country. Patentee in field. Office: Motorola Inc 1303 E Algonquin Rd Schaumburg IL 60196 *

MITCHELL, JOHN ROGER, industrial arts educator; b. Becker Twp., Minn., Oct. 20, 1935; s. Robert and Alice I. (Carson) M.; m. Donna Benay Jones, Aug. 8, 1964; children: Robert, Troy, Elizabeth. AA, U. Minn., 1959; BS, St. Cloud State Coll., 1963; MS, Bemidji State Coll., 1969. Cert. tchr., Minn. Tchr. indsl. arts, drivers edn. Upsala (Minn.) High Sch., 1965-67, Grey Eagle (Minn.) High Sch., 1963-65, Chaska (Minn.) Middle Sch., 1967—; chmn. salary com. Grey Eagle Sch., 1965. Mem. edit. com. State Resource Guide SELO's, 1970, State of the Art Study, 1980. Cubmaster Boy Scouts Am., Chanhassen, Minn, 1975-77; past bd. dirs. Excelsior (Minn.) Covenant Ch., chmn. diaconate bd., 1987—; state alt. caucus chair DFL, Chanhassen, 1982—; mem. parent com. Minn. Boys Choir, Mpls. Named Cubmaster of Yr., Boy Scouts Am., Minnetonka, 1976; recipient Scouters Key, Boy Scouts Am., Minnetonka, 1977, Nat. Pres. Leader of Distinction award, Boy Scouts Am., Minnetonka, 1975. Mem. Cen. Minn. Indsl. Arts Assn. (pres. 1964-66), Minn. Indsl. Arts Assn. (pres. 1981-82; named Indsl. Arts Tchr. of Yr., 1985; recipient Disting. Service award 1982, 84), Am. Council Indsl. Arts State Assn. Officers, Chaska Edn. Assn. (bd. rep. 1968—), NEA, Minnetonka Indsl. Arts Club, Minn. Ceramic Assn. (sec.). Lodge: Nat. Grange. Avocations: wookworking, ceramics. Home: 7605 Iroquois Chanhassen MN 55317 Office: Chaska Middle Sch Chaska MN 55318

MITCHELL, KENDALL, writer, literary critic; b. Chgo., May 25, 1923; s. John Kendall Southgate and Ann (Leichsenring) M. BA, Yale U., 1946. Instr. Am. U. of Beirut, 1946-49; pub. relations dir., dir. publs. Bldg. Owners and Mgrs. Assn. Internat., Chgo., 1951-76; cons. Bldg. Mgrs. Assn., Chgo., 1976-85; writer, reviewer Chgo. Tribune and Chgo. Sun Times, 1977—; lectr. journalism Roosevelt U., Chgo., 1981—. Author: A Chair By The Fire, 1951; translator: Lebanon, 1949. Served as pvt. USAAF, 1942-43. Mem. Nat. Book Critics Circle, Alpha Delta Phi. Episcopalian. Club: Elizabethan (New Haven). Home: 318 South Blvd Evanston IL 60202

MITCHELL, LEE MARK, communications executive, lawyer; b. Albany, N.Y., Apr. 16, 1943; s. Maurice B. and Mildred (Roth) M.; m. Barbara Lee Anderson, Aug. 27, 1966; children: Mark, Matthew. A.B., Wesleyan U., 1965; J.D., U. Chgo., 1968. Bar: Ill. 1968, D.C. 1969, U.S. Supreme Ct. 1972. Assoc. Leibman, Williams, Bennett, Baird & Minow, Chgo. and Washington, 1968-72; assoc. Sidley & Austin, Washington, 1972-74, ptnr., 1974-84, of counsel, 1984—; exec. v.p. and gen. counsel Field Enterprises, Inc., Chgo., 1981-83, pres. and chief exec. officer, 1983-84; pres., chief exec. officer Field Corp., 1984—; bd. dirs. Manistique Papers, Inc., Pioneer Press, Field Publs., Muzak, Cabot, Cabot & Forbes Co., Boston, Boulevard

Bancorp, Blvd. Bank, Chgo. Author: Openly Arrived At, 1974, With the Nation Watching, 1979; co-author: Presidential Television, 1973. Mem. LWV Presdl. Debates adv. com., Washington, 1979-80, 83; U.S. del. Brit. Legislators' Conf. on Govt. and Media, Ditchley Park, Eng., 1974; bd. visitors U. Chgo. Law Sch., 1984-86, Medill Sch. Journalism, Northwestern U., 1984—; bd. govs. Chgo. Met. Planning Council. Mem. ABA, Fed. Communications Bar Assn., Fed. Bar Assn., Inst. of Internat. Edn. (midwest regional adv. bd. 1987—). Clubs: Econ., Mid-Am., Mid-Day, Chicago (Chgo.); Nat. Press (Washington). Home: 135 Maple Hill Rd Glencoe IL 60022 Office: Field Corp 333 W Wacker Dr Chicago IL 60606

MITCHELL, NED ELSWORTH, confectionery company executive; b. Chgo., Sept. 8, 1925; s. Charles Earling and Elsie Edna (Gliot) M.; m. Artemis Diane Safrithis, June 4, 1949; children—Charles John, Mark Dennis, Peter Ned. B.S.M.E., Northwestern U., 1947; M.B.A., U. Chgo., 1957. Factory mgr. E.J. Brach & Sons, Chgo., 1957-67, v.p., 1967-74, sr. v.p., 1974-76, exec. v.p., 1976-77, pres., 1977—. Editor: (with others) Flexography, 1969. Mem. bd. zoning appeals Village of Deerfield, Ill., 1960-61; mem. sch. bd. Sch. Dist. 110, Lake County, Ill., 1965-69; mem. planning commn. Village of Riverwoods, Ill., 1964; chmn. Evang. Health Found., Oakbrook, Ill., 1983-87. Served to 2d lt. U.S. Army, 1944-53. Mem. Am. Assn. Candy Technologists, Nat. Confectioners Assn. (sec., treas. 1982-85, 86-87, v.p. 1985-86), Chocolate Mfg. Assn. (bd. dirs. 1980-84, Candy Kettle award 1984), Triangle Frat. (trustee). Clubs: Knollwood (Lake Forest); Exec. Program of U. Chgo., Economics (Chgo.). Avocations: golf, wood and metalworking, flying. Home: 505 Thornmeadow Rd Riverwoods IL 60015 Office: Jacobs Suchard/Brach Inc 4656 W Kinzie St Chicago IL 60015

MITCHELL, PAUL BLACKBURN, JR., carpet manufacturing executive; b. Bryson City, N.C., Apr. 6, 1940; s. Paul Blackburn and Mary Frances (Sawyer) M.; m. Geraldine Loretta Lombardi, May 11, 1974; children: Paul B. III, Mary Catherine, John Thomas, Julie Ann. BS in Textile Engring., N.C. State U., 1966. Devel. mgr. Rohm & Haas, Phila., 1966-70; internat. prodn. mgr. Rohm & Haas, Miami, 1970-79; asst. to pres. Schlegel, Rochester, N.Y., 1979-80; mktg. mgr. Ralston Purina, St. Louis, 1980-85; owner Carpeting Concepts, Mascoutah, Ill., 1985—; cons. PM Tex, Collinsville, Ill., 1975—. Author: Flocking, 1973, Coatings, 1974, Chemical Formulas, 1975; patentee textiles. Ill. Cub Scout chmn. Boy Scouts Am., 1981-86. Mem. Am. Assn. Textile Chemists and Colorists, Tech. Assn. of Pulp and Paper Industry, Theta Chi. Republican. Baptist. Avocations: sailing, reading. Home: 2003 Ravenwood Dr Collinsville IL 62234 Office: Carpeting Concepts PO Box 156 1510 Eisenhower St Mascoutah IL 62258

MITCHELL, ROBERT ARTHUR, university president; b. N.Y.C., Jan. 19, 1926; s. George P. and Vera A. (Duffy) M. A.B., Woodstock Coll., 1949, Ph.L., 1950; S.T.L., Facultes S.J. de Louvain, Belgium, 1957; Th.D., U. Strasbourg, France, 1965. Joined S.J., 1943, ordained priest, Roman Cath. Ch., 1956. Instr. in philosophy LeMoyne Coll., 1950-53, asst. prof. theology, 1958-59, acad. dean, 1959-63, assoc. prof. theology, acad. dean, 1965-66; pres. Loyola Coll., Shrub Oak, 1966; provincial N.Y. State Province (S.J.), 1966-72; pres. Jesuit Conf., chmn. Am. Jesuit Provincials, Washington, 1972-76; dir. Woodstock Theol. Center, 1976-79; pres. U. Detroit, 1979—; dir. Detroit Econ. Growth Corp., Detroit Econ. Growth Fund; trustee Bus./Edn. Alliance SE MIch. Bd. dirs. Georgetown U., New Detroit, Inc., Detroit Symphony Orch.; trustee Boston Coll., Loyola Marymount U., Mich. Cancer Found.; mem. adv. United Found., Detroit Sci Ctr., Met. Affairs Corp.; dir. Greater Detroit Interfaith Roundtable NCCJ. Clubs: Econ. of Detroit (dir.), Detroit Athletic, Renaissance. Office: Univ of Detroit 4001 W McNichols Rd Detroit MI 48221

MITCHELL, ROBERT JUDD, accountant, consultant; b. Imperial, Nebr., Feb. 3, 1958; s. Earl Harvey and Marilyn Ruth (Paul) M. BBA, U. Nebr., 1980, MBA, 1982. Tax cons. Touche Ross & Co., Lincoln, Nebr., 1982-85, tax supr., 1985—. Mem. Am. Inst. CPA's, Nebr. Soc. CPA's, Am. Heart Assn. (bd. dirs. 1986-87), Alpha Tau Omega (treas. 1984-85, pres., bd. dirs. 1986-87). Republican. Congregationalist. Club: Bushwood Country (Lincoln) (treas. 1983—). Avocations: athletics, fantasy sports leagues. Office: Touche Ross & Co 1040 NBC Ctr Lincoln NE 68503

MITCHELL, ROBT L., benefits specialist; b. La Salle, Ill., May 31, 1925; s. Harry Clark and Agusta Virginia (Wirtz) M.; m. L. Jean Moreau, Aug. 6, 1949; children: Risa Lynn, Bonnie Jean, Michelle Marie. BA in Indsl. Mgmt., Lake Forest Sch. Mgmt., 1965. Safety med. supr. Johnson Motors div. Outboard Marine Corp., Waukegan, Ill., 1957-70, safety and security mgr., 1965-70, benefits and tng. mgr., 1970—. Author numerous poems. Co-chmn. water safety and first aid Lake County Red Cross, Waukegan, 1961-63; precinct committeeman Waukegan Reps., 1984—; bd. dirs. Alcohol and Drug Abuse, Victory Meml. Hosp., Waukegan, 1984—. Served as sgt. USAF, 1943-46, ETO. Mem. Indsl. Safety Assn. of Lake County (pres. 1964). Roman Catholic. Lodge: KC. Avocations: golf, scuba diving. Home: 500 Leith Ave Waukegan IL 60085

MITCHELL, RODGER MALCOLM, advertising executive; b. Chgo., Mar. 25, 1935; s. Asher J. and Celia (Schumann) M.; m. Phyllis Rae Garber, June 17, 1956; children: Leslie Alison Kleinmutz, Julia Ann. BS, U. Ill., 1956; MBA, Northwestern U., 1961. Advt. mgr. Booth Fisheries, Chgo., 1956-62; acct. exec. Batten, Barton, Durstine & Osborn, Chgo., 1969-79; v.p. TRG, N.Y.C., 1979; chmn. Rodger M. Mitchell Advt. Inc., Chgo., 1980—; chmn. Murlas Commodities, Chgo., Murlas Fin., Chgo., Murlas Internat., Chgo., Windsor Agy., Chgo., Investor's Fin., Chgo., Murla's Securities, Chgo. Painter; inventor; author: How to Think, 1976. Home and Office: 921 Pontiac Wilmette IL 60091

MITCHELL, ROY EDWIN, chemical operator; b. Joliet, Ill., Apr. 26, 1956; s. Frank A. and Rosemary (Watson) M.; m. Debra J. Pesavento; 1 child, Susan Marie. Student, Joliet Jr. Coll., 1974-76. Design draftsman Durkee Foods, Joliet, 1975-77; sr. design draftsman Dynamic Engrs., Inc., Joliet, 1977-86; chem. operator Amoco Chems. Co., Joliet, 1986—. Republican. Roman Catholic. Lodge: Lions (pres. Cresthill club 1985-86, 1st. v.p. 1984-85), Elks. Home: 4417 McClintock Rd Rt 8 Joliet IL 60436 Office: Amoco Chems Co Amoco Rd Joliet IL 60434

MITCHELL, SUE JAEGER, research company executive; b. Tyler, Tex., Oct. 10, 1951; d. Richard and Norma Louise (Heim) Jaeger; m. David A. Mitchell, Nov. 4, 1983; children: Christopher J., David M., Stephanie M. BA, Ill. Benedictine Coll., 1973. Personnel asst. Trans Union Corp., Chgo., 1974, supr. employment and compensation, 1974-79; pres. S.A. Jaeger & Co., Inc., Oakbrook, Ill., 1979—. Avocations: bicycling, parenting. Home: 902 Carrol Ct Saint Charles IL 60174 Office: SA Jaeger & Co Inc 2001 Spring Rd Suite 665 Oakbrook IL 60521

MITCHELL, VERNICE VIRGINIA, nurse, poet, author; b. Scott, Miss., Mar. 11, 1921; d. Isaiah and Martha Magdalene (Edwards) Smith; m. Willis Mitchell, Aug. 17, 1940; children—Elaine, Kenneth, Liethia, John, Ransom, Paul. Diploma Princeton Continuation Coll., 1955. Lic. practical nurse. L.P.N. Cook County Sch. Nursing, Chgo., 1951-59, U. Ill. Hosp., Chgo., 1959-67, Grant Hosp., Chgo., 1967-78, Northwestern Meml. Hosp., Chgo., 1979-84, Aetna Nurse's Registry, Chgo., 1984—. Author: The Book Success Through Spiritual Truths, 1987, (poems) A Women, Chicago, The 12 Months; also numerous poetry and musical lyrics. Recipient merit cert. Am. Poetry Assn., 1982, World of Poetry, 1983, 85; Golden Poet award World of Poetry, 1985. Club: 6700 Emerald Ave. Block (pres. 1971—). Avocations: reading; writing; cooking; traveling; sewing; crocheting.

MITCHELL, WILLIAM GEORGE, communication products company executive; b. Chgo., 1931. B.A., U. Okla., 1953; J.D., Northwestern U., 1958. Chmn. bd. Beatrice Foods Co., Chgo., 1955-77; pres. Centel Corp. (formerly Central Telephone Utilities Corp.), Chgo., 1977-86, vice chmn., 1986—, also dir.; dir. No. Trust Co., Chgo., Peoples Energy Corp., Chgo., Sherwin-Williams Co. Served to lt. (j.g.) US, 1953-55. Office: Centel Corp 5725 E River Rd Chicago IL 60631

MITCHELL-MURPHY, HEATHER HOLDEN, tax consultant; b. Cleve., Dec. 19, 1957; d. Holden CHarles and Mary Ann (Honicky) M.; m. Peter Bradford Murphy. BA in Mgmt., Mich. State U., 1981; MBA, U. Mich., 1986. Asst. bank examiner Fed. Res. Bank Cleve., 1982-83; internal auditor Nat. City Bank, Cleve., 1983-84; tax cons. Arthur Young & Co., Chgo., 1986—. Named one of Outstanding Young Women of Am., 1985. Mem. Nat. Assn. for Female Execs., Kappa Kappa Gamma Alumni Assn., Mensa. Republican. Episcopalian. Home: 55 S Vail Ave #607 Arlington Heights IL 60005 Office: Arthur Young & Co 420 N Wabash Chicago IL 60611

MITCHEN, JOEL RAMON, medical technology company executive; b. Chgo., Mar. 25, 1942; s. Joseph Louis and Dorothy Lorraine (Bradshaw) M.; m. Emiko Reuther; 1 child, Michael Joseph. B.A., Carthage Coll., 1964; M.S., Purdue U., 1969, Ph.D., 1971. With Roswell Park Meml. Inst., Buffalo, 1971-73, Life Scis., Inc., St. Petersburg, Fla., 1973-77, Argonne Nat. Labs., Ill., 1977-79, Abbott Labs., North Chicago, Ill., 1979-82; owner, sci. dir. Microtech Med. Co., Inc., Waukegan, Ill., 1982—. Contbr. sci. papers to profl. lit. Patentee in field med. diagnostics. Mem. Am. Soc. Microbiologists, Sigma Xi. Roman Catholic. Avocations: electronics; photography; skiing. Office: Microtech Med Co Inc 1701 Grand Ave Waukegan IL 60085

MITNICK, MINDY FAITH, clinical psychologist, consultant; b. Miami Beach, Fla., Oct. 10, 1950; d. Myron Jackson and Stella (Fox) M.; m. Carl Marquit, Aug. 17, 1979. BA, Bryn Mawr Coll., Phila., 1972; EdM, Harvard U., 1973; MA, U. Minn., 1986. Intern Hennepin County Med. Ctr., Mpls., 1977-78; court psychologist Hennepin County Court Services, Mpls., 1978-83; psychologist Uptown Mental Health Ctr., Mpls., 1980—; bd. dirs. Minn. Com. for Prevention Child Abuse. Author: (with others) (book) Identification and Treatment of Child Incest Victims, 1983, (pamphlet) Child Sexual Abuse, 1983; also articles. Mem. Social Problems Com., United Way Priorities Com., Mpls., 1982-83. Mem. Minn. Psychol. Assn., Minn. Lic. Psychologists (bd. dirs. 1982-83, exec. bd.), Minn. Women Psychologists. Office: Uptown Mental Health Ctr 2215 Pillsbury Ave S Minneapolis MN 55404

MITROFANOV, NICHOLAS, nuclear physicist; b. Russia, Feb. 5, 1918; came to U.S., 1962, naturalized, 1970; s. Michael and Anastasia (Shirokov) M.; M.S., U. Moscow, 1940, Ph.D. in Physics, 1943; widower. Redactor jour. Columbus, Russian weekly in Austria, 1945-48; mem. faculty U. Chile, Santiago, 1950-62; research prof. U. Md., 1962-64; with Harshaw Chem. Co., Cleve., 1965—, sr. research scientist, 1962—; cons. in field. Author: Textbook of Physics, 1946; (poetry) Caravels, 1980; also articles. Patentee in field.

MITTELMAN, DAVID, pediatric ophthalmologist; b. Chgo., Apr. 18, 1945; s. Joseph and Pearl (Orlovsky) M.; m. Clarice Hollander, Sept. 8, 1968; children—Jillene, Bradley, Rebecca. B.S., U. of Ill.-Chgo. Circle, 1965, M.D., 1969. Diplomate Am. Bd. of Ophthalmology. Intern Cook County Hosp., Chgo., resident in ophthalmology U. of Ill. Chgo. Circle, 1970-73, fellow in pediatric ophthalmology, 1973-74, attending physician, 1974-78; chief pediatric ophthalmologist Cook County Hosp., Chgo., 1978-80; assoc. prof. ophthalmology, chief pediatric ophthalmologist Loyola U., Chgo., 1980—; cons. in ophthalmology Hines VA Hosp., Maywood, Ill., 1980—; cons. in vision Chgo. Bd. of Edn., 1982—. Contbr. articles to medical jours. on ophthalmology. Served to capt. USAR, 1970-76. Yarros scholar U. of Ill. Chgo. Circle, 1965. Fellow Am. Acad. Ophthalmology; mem. Am. Assn. for Pediatric Ophthalmology (membership chmn.), AMA, Ill. Med. Soc., Ill. Assn. of Ophthalmology, Chgo. Med. Soc., Chgo. Ophthalmological Soc. (mtg. chmn. 1983). Office: 1875 W Dempster St Suite 610 Park Ridge IL 60068

MITTELSTADT, N(ORBERT) GREG, adult educator; b. Beaver Dam, Wis., Mar. 28, 1949; s. Norbert Frederick and Mary Catherine (Strumberger) M.; m. Linda Jean Terhardt, July 22, 1972; children: Christian J., Mary K. BA, Lakeland Coll., 1972; MS, U. Wis., Milw., 1977; postgrad., U. Wis., 1977-80. Adult instr., program recruiter Lakeshore Tech. Inst., Cleveland, Wis., 1972—. Mem. Nat. Edn. Assn., Wis. Vocat. Assn. Lutheran. Lodge: Kiwanis (hon. Kiwanian 1967). Avocations: writing, reading, gourmet cooking, hiking, biking. Home: 4920 Evergreen Dr Sheboygan WI 53081 Office: Lakeshore Tech Inst 1290 North Cleveland WI 53081

MITTELSTAEDT, TYRONE PETER, educator, consultant; b. Detroit, Dec. 5, 1937; s. Henry Julius and Ethel Ruth (Eckhardt) M.; m. Mary Emmajean Smith; children—Amy Kathleen, Michael Damian. Student U. Detroit, 1955-57; B.S., Wayne State U., 1960, M.S., 1961, Ed.S., 1974. Cert. tchr., Mich. Tchr. educable mentally retarded Barbour Jr. High Sch., Detroit, 1961-64; tchr. educable mentally retarded workshop, Warren (Mich.) High Sch., 1964-67, developer program, 1967-68; work/study rehab. coordinator Warren Consol. Schs., 1968-71; tchr./cons. for learning disabled and emotionally impaired and vocat. rehab. services coordinator Sterling Heights (Mich.) High Sch., 1971—; instr. Wayne State U., Detroit, 1971-72; cons. spl. edn. vocat. edn. project Central Mich. U., 1971-73. Merit badge advisor Detroit Area council Boy Scouts Am., 1964-67; exec. producer, actor, Warren Consol. Schs. Player Group for Coll. Scholarships, 1965-67; mem. parent adv. com. Chippewa Valley Schs., Mt. Clemens, 1979—, fundraiser for preservation of gifted program, 1983; T-ball coach Clinton Valley Baseball Assn., Mt. Clemens, 1981; family learning team tchr. St. Michael's Catholic Community, Sterling Heights, 1980-81, minister of the word, 1982—. Recipient hon. mention Wayne State U. Art Show, 1959; Master Tchr. award Warren Consol. Schs., 1967-68. Mem. NEA, Mich. Edn. Assn., Warren Edn. Assn., State Council of Exceptional Children State Cons. (task force on mainstreaming), Nat. Honor Soc. Club: Optimist (hon. mem. Warren). Author: Curriculum Guide for Language Arts, Detroit Pub. Schs., 1962, curriculum, Warren Consol. Schs., 1971-73; co-author spl. edn. course study for Warren Consol. Schs., 1981-83. Home: 39214 Sunderland Dr Mount Clemens MI 48044 Office: 12901 15 Mile Rd Sterling Heights MI 48077

MITTLEMAN, FREDERICK STUART, psychiatrist; b. Sioux City, Iowa, Nov. 8, 1945. BS, Morningside Coll., 1967; MD, Creighton Med. Sch., 1970. Diplomate Am. Bd. Psychiatry and Neurology. Intern U. Nebr. Hosp., Omaha, 1970-71; resident in psychiatry Walter Reed Gen. Hosp., Washington, 1971-73; dir. admissions Menninger Found., Topeka, 1975-82; dir. psychiatry Menorah Med. Ct., Kanas City, Mo., 1982-85; med. dir. Research Psychiat. Ctr., Kanas City, 1985—; assoc. clin. prof. U. Mo., Kansas City, 1985—. Seved to maj. U.S. Army, 1971-75. Mem. AMA, Am. Psychiat. Assn., Am. Psychoanalytic Assn., Mo. Med. Soc., Alpha Omega Alpha. Avocations: jogging, movies, skiing, travel. Home: 4205 W 102d St Overland Park KS 66207 Office: Research Psychiat Ctr 2323 E 63d Kansas City MO 64130

MITZEL, PHILIP ALLEN, industrial engineer; b. Rugby, N.D., Aug. 21, 1955; s. Frank Micheal and Evelyn Lavern (Schlict) M.; m. Nancy Ann Houtcooper, Nov. 27, 1976; children: Jason Allen, Kristin Ann, Megan Holly. BS in Indsl. Tech., U. N.D., Grand Forks, 1981. Indsl. engr. Kohler (Wis.) Co., 1981-83, Indsl. project engr., 1983-85; sr. indsl. engr. Safeguard, Aberdeen, S.D., 1985—. Asst. den leader Boy Scouts Am., Aberdeen, S.D., 1986; mem. Ind. Tech. Adv. Bd. U. N.D., 1986-89. Epsilon Pi Tau. Republican. Methodist. Avocations: woodworking, gardening, hunting, camping. Home: 4151 W Richmond Rd Aberdeen SD 57401 Office: 2914 Industrial Ave Aberdeen SD 57401

MIXTACKI, STEVEN BERNARD, retail executive; b. Chgo., May 20, 1954; s. Bernard S. and Dorothy A. (Rodel) M.; m. Meryl L. Mitchell, Nov. 7, 1980; children: Melinda, Michael. BBA, U. Wis., 1976. CPA, Wis. Acctg. intern Oscar Mayer & Co., Madison, Wis., 1974-76; mgr. Alexander Grant & Co., Madison, 1976-80; v.p. fin., treas. Am. TV & Appliance of Madison, Inc., 1980—. Chmn. Dane County Pub. Affairs Council, Madison. Named Outstanding Jaycee Under 25, Wis. Jaycees, 1976. Mem. Nat. Assn. Accts. (v.p. Madison chpt. 1982-83), Am. Inst. CPA's, Wis. Inst. CPA's. Roman Catholic. Lodge: Rotary (trustee Madison Found. 1985—). Office: American of Madison 2404 W Beltline Hwy Madison WI 53713

MIYAMOTO, RICHARD TAKASHI, otolaryngologist; b. Zeeland, Mich., Feb. 2, 1944; s. Dave Norio and Haruko (Okano) M.; m. Cynthia VanderBurgh, June 17, 1967; children—Richard Christopher, Geoffrey Takashi. B.S. cum laude, Wheaton Coll., 1966; M.D., U. Mich., 1970; M.S. in Otology, U.So. Calif., 1978. Diplomate Am. Bd. Otolaryngology. Intern Butterworth Hosp., Grand Rapids, Mich., 1970-71, resident in surgery, 1971-72; resident in otolaryngology Ind. U. Sch. Medicine, 1972-75; fellow in otology and neurotology St. Vincent Hosp. and Otologic Med. Group, Los Angeles, 1977-78; asst. prof. Ind. U. Sch. Medicine, Indpls., 1978-83, assoc. prof., 1983—; chief Otology and Neurotology dept. Otolaryngology, Head and Neck Surgery, Ind. U., 1982—; chief Otolaryngology, Head and Neck Surgery Wishard Meml. Hosp., 1979—. Contbr. articles to profl. jours. Served to maj. USAF, 1975-77. Named Arilla DeVault Disting. investigator Ind. U., 1983. Fellow Am. Acad. Otolaryngology (gov. 1982—), ACS, Am. Otological, Rhinological, and Laryngological Soc. (Thesis Disting. for Excellence award), Am. Auditory Soc. (exec. com. 1985—), Am. Neurotology Soc. Am. Auditory Soc. (mem. exec. com. 1985—). Republican. Presbyterian. Avocation: tennis. Office: Riley Hosp 702 Barnhill Dr Suite A-56 Indianapolis IN 46223

MIYARES, BENJAMIN DAVID, editor; b. Tampa, Fla., July 23, 1940; s. Benigno and Mary Carolyn (Dominguez) M.; m. Martha Suzanne Urban, May 14, 1966; children—David, Jeffrey, Beth. B.A. in Journalism, St. Bonaventure U., Olean, N.Y., 1962. News dir. radio sta. WSET, Glens Falls, N.Y., 1962-63; with subs. Harcourt Brace Jovanovich, Inc. (Magazines for Industry), N.Y.C., 1963—; editor subs. Harcourt Brace Jovanovich, Inc. (Food and Drug Packaging mag.), 1968—, editorial dir. company, 1975—, corp. v.p., 1977-80; exec. v.p. subs. Harcourt Brace Jovanovich, Inc. (Packaging and Processing Group), 1980—, exec. editor, 1982—; publisher Candy Marketer, 1985—; cons. in field. Pres. council Nat. Packaging Week, 1975; editorial com. Am. Bus. Press, 1973-74; mem. industry adv. com. packaging sci. and engring. program Rutgers U. Mem. Dobbs Ferry Bd. Edn., pres., 1981—. Served with AUS, 1963. Mem. Packaging Inst. (v.p. 1976-78, pres. 1978-79). Office: Harcourt Brace Jovanovich 7500 Old Oak Blvd Cleveland OH 44130

MIZENKO, MARK FRANCIS, retail executive; b. Kansas City, Mo., Dec. 1, 1960; s. John Joseph and Diane (Gilley) M.; m. Helene Germaine Cournoyer, Mar. 6, 1982; 1 child, Patrick John. BA in Psychology, Muskingum Coll., 1983; MBA, Cleve. State U., 1986. Mgr. Children's Palace, Parma, Ohio, 1984-86, Mayfield Heights, Ohio, 1986—. Republican. Roman Catholic. Avocations: golf, swimming, reading, tennis, biking. Home: 7056 Pine St Chagrin Falls OH 44022 Office: Children's Palace Mayfield Rd Mayfield Heights OH 44124

MLOT, EUGENE, accountant; b. Dearborn, July 18, 1954; s. Bernard A. and Angeline (Lesinski) M.; m. Anita Marie Mihalik, Apr. 23, 1983; children: Scott Michael, Steven Anthony. BBA, Cen. Mich. U., 1977. Staff acct. Edmond J. Olejniczak, P.C., Warren, Mich., 1977-81; acct., v.p. Olejniczak and Mlot, P.C., Warren, 1981—. Mem. Am. Inst. CPA's, Mich. Assn. CPA's. Avocations: sports, reading, outdoor activities. Home: 25589 Masch Warren MI 48091

MOATS, MICHAEL EMBRY, dentist; b. Akron, Ohio, Sept. 22, 1947; s. O. Embry and Helen Louise (Whitelaw) M.; m. Gloria Jean Vanderborg, Nov. 24, 1984. BS, Davidson Coll., 1969; DDS, Loyola U., 1977. Lic. dentist, Ill. Sci. tchr. New Trier West High Sch., Northfield, Ill., 1969-73; asst. clin. prof. Loyola U. Sch. Dentist, Maywood, Ill., 1977-78; gen. practice dentistry, Buffalo Grove, Ill., 1977—. Chmn., bd. dirs. Midwest Epilepsy Ctr., Lombard, Ill., 1983—; consecrated lay minister Long Grove (Ill.) Community Ch., 1981, deacon, 1983—; bd. dirs. Am. Cancer Soc., Buffalo Grove, 1983-84; bd. dirs. Wheeling/Buffalo Grove (Ill.) United Way, 1986, OMNI Youth Services, 1986—; chmn. Family Life Conf. I and II Chgo., 1986—. Recipient Acad. Gen. Dentistry award, 1977. Paul Harris fellow, 1986; recipient Presdl. citation Rotary Internat., 1985. Mem. ADA, Ill. State Dental Soc., Chgo. Dental Soc., Soc. Occlusal Studies, Arlington Dental Study Club, Sigma Chi. Republican. Mem. Christian Ch. Lodge: Rotary (local pres. 1984-85, bd. dirs. 1985-87). Avocations: jogging, scuba diving, photography. Office: 1401 W Dundee Rd Suite 212 Buffalo Grove IL 60089

MOAYAD, CYRUS, facial plastic surgeon; b. Iran, June 27, 1928; came to U.S., 1959; s. Mir and Mahboob (Forouzan) M. BS, U. Geneva, 1952, MD, 1957. Diplomate Am. Bd. Otolaryngology, Am. Bd. Cosmetic Surgery. Intern Kingston Hosp., Ont., Can., 1958-59, Can., 1958-59; resident, fellow Cleve. Clinic Found.; asst. prof. surgery Western Res. Med. Coll., Cleve., 1960-68; practice medicine specializing in plastic surgery Valparaiso, Ind., 1968—; asst. prof. surgery Case Western Res. U., Cleve., 1968—. Contbr. articles to profl. jours. Fellow ACS, Internat. Coll. Surgeons, Am. Acad. Facial Plastic Surgery, European Acad. Facial Surgery, Joseph Soc., Am. Acad. Otolaryngology/Head, Chgo. Otolaryngology Soc., Study of Headaches Soc. Bahai. Avocations: outdoors, travel, hunting, photography. Office: 1105 E Glendale Blvd Valparaiso IN 46383

MOBERG, DAVID FORREST, journalist; b. Galesburg, Ill., Sept. 27, 1943; s. Forrest Wilbert and Ruby Tennena (Kjellander) M.; m. Deborah Jo Patton, May 23, 1981; children: Carl, Sarah. BA, Carleton Coll., Northfield, Minn., 1965; MA, U. Chgo., 1971, PhD, 1978. Reporter Newsweek mag., N.Y.C., 1965-66; lectr. various colls. and univs., Chgo., 1972-76; from assoc. editor to nat. affairs editor to sr. editor In These Times mag., Chgo., 1976—. Editor Mother, A Jour. of New Lit., 1964-65; contbr. articles and reviews to newspapers and popular mags. NIMH grantee, 1968-73. Mem. Phi Beta Kappa. Home: 5731 S Blackstone Chicago IL 60637

MOBERG, DAVID OSCAR, sociology educator; b. Montevideo, Minn., Feb. 13, 1922; s. Fred Ludwig and Anna E. (Sundberg) M.; m. Helen H. Heitzman, Mar. 16, 1946; children: David Paul, Lynette, Jonathan, Philip. AA, Bethel Jr. Coll., 1942; AB, Seattle Pacific Coll., 1947; MA, U. Wash., 1949; PhD, U. Minn., 1952. Assoc. instr. U. Wash., Seattle, 1948-49; faculty Bethel Coll., St. Paul, 1949-68; prof. sociology Bethel Coll., 1959-68, chmn. dept. social scis., 1952-68; prof. sociology Marquette U., Milw., 1968—; chmn. dept. sociology and anthropology Marquette U., 1968-77; cons. Nat. Liberty Found., 1970-71, Nat. Interfaith Coalition on Aging, 1973-75, nat. adv. bd., 1980—; guest researcher Sociology of Religion Inst., Stockholm, summer 1978; adj. prof. San Francisco Theol. Sem., 1964-73, McCormick Theol. Sem., 1975-78, 81-82; vis. prof. U. So. Calif., 1979, Princeton Theol. Sem., 1979, So. Bapt. Theol. Sem., 1982; mem. adv. bd. Ecumenical Ministry with Mature Adults, 1983—; resource scholar Christianity Today Inst., 1985—. Author: The Church as A Social Institution, 1962, 2d edit. 1984, (with Robert M. Gray) The Church and the Older Person, 1962, 2d edit., 1977, Inasmuch: Christian Social Responsibility in the 20th Century, 1965, White House Conference on Aging: Spiritual Well-Being Background and Issues, 1971, The Great Reversal: Evangelism and Social Concern, 2d edit, 1977, Wholistic Christianity: An Appeal for a Dynamic, Balanced Faith, 1985; also articles, chpts. in symposia.; editor: International Directory of Religious Information Systems, 1971, Spiritual Well-Being: Sociological Perspectives, 1979, Rev. Religious Research, 1968-72, Jour. Am. Sci. Affiliation, 1962-64, Adris Newsletter, 1971-76; co-editor Research in the Social Scientific Study of Religion, 1986—; mem. editorial bd. Christian Univ. Press, 1979-84. Fulbright lectr. U. Groningen, Netherlands, 1957-58, Fulbright lectr. Muenster U., West Germany, 1964-65. Fellow Am. Sci. Affiliation (editor jour. 1962-64, publs. com. 1984—, Social Ethics Commn. 1985—), Gerontol. Soc. Am.; mem. AAUP, Am. Sociol. Assn., Internat. Sociol. Assn. (sociology of religion research com. 1972—), Wis. Sociol. Assn. (pres. 1969-71), Midwest Sociol. Assn. (Wis. bd. dirs. 1971-73), Assn. Humanist Sociology, Assn. Devel. Religious Information Systems (coordinator ADRIS 1971—, editor ADRIS newsletter 1971-76), Religious Research Assn. (editor Rev. Religious Research 1968-72, contbg. editor 1973-77, assoc. editor 1983—, bd. dirs. 1959-61, 68-72, pres. 1981-82, H. Paul Douglass lectr. 1986), Assn. for Sociology of Religion (exec. council 1971-73, pres. 1976-77), Soc. for Sci. Study Religion (exec. council 1971-74), Evangelicals for Social Action (planning com. 1973-75), Christian Sociol. Soc. (steering com. 1973-81, newsletter lit. reviewer 1981—), Family Research Council (assoc. 1985—), Psychologists Interested in Religious Issues (profl. affiliate, 1984—). Home: 2619 E Newberry Blvd Milwaukee WI 53211 Office: Dept Social and Cultural Sci Marquette U Milwaukee WI 53233

MOBLEY, JAMES ROBERT, dentist; b. Sedalia, Mo., Oct. 25, 1944; s. Howard Holman and Esther Pauline (Webb) M.; m. Terrell Elizabeth Kirk, June 3, 1967 (div.); children: John Kirk, Joshua Scott. DDS, U. Mo.,

Kansas City, 1969. Intern U.S. Army Hosp., Honolulu, 1969-70; gen. practice dentistry Kansas City, 1972—; asst. prof. dentistry U. Mo., Kansas City, 1972-76; vol. dentist Kans. Sch. for Deaf, Olathe, 1983-86. Served to capt. USAR, 1969-72. Mem. ADA, Greater Kansas City Dental Soc. (chmn. continuing edn. com. 1975). Clubs: Carriage (Kansas City), Hockey. Avocations: tennis, golf, windsurfing. Home: 5333 Mission Rd Farway KS 66205 Office: 315 Nichols Rd Kansas City MO 64112

MOCH, MARY INEZ, librarian; b. Chgo., Aug. 13, 1943; d. Charles Michael and Mary Anna (Howanic) M. A.A., Felician Coll., 1964; B.A., Mundelein Coll., 1968; M.A., No. Ill. U., 1976. Joined Felician Sisters, Roman Catholic Ch., 1961; tchr. St. Turibius Sch., Chgo., 1964-65; tchr. St. Damian Sch. Oak Forest, Ill., 1966-67, tchr./librarian, 1975-80; tchr./librarian St. Florian Sch., Hatley, Wis., 1968-72, Christ The King Sch., Lombard, Ill., 1972-75; librarian Providence High Sch., New Lenox, Ill., 1980-82; head librarian Felician Coll., Chgo., 1982—; cons. Felician Library Service, 1976—, sec., 1979-80; Pvt. Acad. Libraries Ill. (sec./treas. 1987—). Mem. ALA, Cath. Library Assn., Ill. Online Computer Library Ctr. Users Group. Office: Felician Coll 3800 W Peterson Ave Chicago IL 60659

MOCIUK, PETER ROMAN, physician; b. Stanislaw, USSR, May 27, 1920; came to U.S., 1950; s. Nicolaus and Eugenia (Hawrysh) M.; m. Olga Barbarna, June 12, 1954; children: Andrea, Jeannette, Christina. Diploma, Stanislw Uke. Gymnasium, 1941; postgrad., U. Lviv, 1943; MD, U. Erlanger, Fed. Rep. Germany, 1949. Diplomate Am. Bd. Radiology. Internship Marien Hosp., Stuttgart, Fed. Rep. Germany, 1949-50, Unity Hosp., Bklyn., 1951; residency in radiology St. Luke's Hosp., Chgo., 1952-55; dir. radiology St. Anthony Hosp., Chgo., 1955—; clin. researcher gall bladder malfunction, 1969-74. Fellow Am. Radiol. Soc.; mem. Am. Coll. Radiology. Office: Radiology Associated 11801 Southwest Hwy Palos Heights IL 60463

MOCK, JOHN DENNIS, medical billing service executive; b. Evanston, Ill., Sept. 10, 1940; s. John T. and Esther (Harloff) M.; m. Joann G. Watt, Dec. 23, 1961; children—Susan, Blake, Eric, Troy. B.A., Franklin Coll., 1962. Mgr., Med. Bus. Bur., Inc., Evanston, Ill., 1962-74; pres. John Mock & Assocs., Inc., Chgo., 1974—; del. govt. affairs com. Ill. Med. Soc., Chgo., 1983—, com. on econs. Ill. State State Soc. Anesthesiologist, Chgo., 1983—. Pres. North Suburban YMCA, Northbrook, Ill., 1985-86; v.p. Arden Shore Home for Boys, Lake Bluff, Ill., 1983-84. Mem. Med.-Dental Hosp. Burs. Am., Inc. (Robert T. Hellrung award 1979, Stanley R. Mauck award 1979, cert. profl. bur. exec.), Ill. Collectors Assn. (pres. 1986—), Chgo. Area Med. Group Adminstrs. (pres. 1985-86). Baptist. Club: No. Suburban Aquatic (Northbrook) (pres. 1978-79). Lodge: Rotary (pres. Evanston 1983-84). Office: John Mock & Assocs Inc 4600 W Touhy Ave Lincolnwood IL 60646

MOCKENHAUPT, JEROLD DANIEL, service administrator, management consultant; b. St. Cloud, Minn., July 28, 1935; s. Hubert Engelbert and Joan Mary (Hunstiger) M.; m. Lois Ann Winkelman, July 19, 1960 (div. Oct. 1983); children: Jerel, Lisa, Julie; m. Esperanza Rodriguez, July 3, 1986; stepchildren: Aaron, Eric. Student, St. Cloud (Minn.) Cathedral, 1949-53; student in psychology, St. Cloud (Minn.) State U, 1958-60. Dept. mgr. U.C.I.T. Credit Corp., Duluth, Minn., 1961-66; loan officer Am. Nat. Bank, St. Cloud, 1966-70; adminstr. St. Cloud Med. Group, 1970-84; cons. Firemans Fund, Green Bay, Wis., 1985-86; adminstr. Cuyuna Range Clinic, Crosby, Minn., 1986—; cons. Minn. Med. Assn., Mpls., 1976, Skarns/Benton Med. Soc., St. Cloud, 1978; advisor St. Cloud Sch. Dist. 742, 1978; v.p. Cen. Minn. Clinic Mgrs., St. Cloud, 1986—. Chmn. Character Guidance, Ellsworth AFB, 1955; bd. dirs. Tri County Action Program, St. Cloud, 1981, St. Cloud Civic Orch., 1980-84. Served with USAF, 1954-57. Columbia Pacific U. scholar, 1983. Mem. Med. Group Mgmt., Mensa, Am. Soc. Allied Health Profls. Republican. Baptist. Club: Cen. Minn. Taxpayers (St. Cloud) (pres. 1970-71). Lodge: Lions. Avocation: woodworking. Home: 1560 13th Ave SE Saint Cloud MN 56301 Office: Cuyuna Range Clinic 301 1st St SE Crosby MN 56441

MODELL, ARTHUR B., professional football team executive; b. Bklyn., June 23, 1925; m. Patricia Breslin, July 25, 1969; stepchildren: John, David. Owner, pres. Cleve. Browns football team, 1961—; pres. Nat. Football League, 1967-70. Office: Cleveland Stadium Cleveland OH 44114 •

MODERSON, CHRISTOPHER PAUL, education adminstrator; b. Appleton, Wis., Apr. 12, 1959; s. Ronald George and Janice Mary (Schink) M. BS, U. Wis., Stevens Point, 1982; MS, Western Ill. U., 1984. Residence dir. Rockford (Ill.) Coll., 1984-86, dir. residential life, 1986-87, asst. dean students, 1987—. Named one of Outstanding Young Men Am., 1982. Mem. Am. Assn. Counseling and Devel., Am. Coll. Personnel Assn., Assn. Coll. and Univ. Housing Officers, Ill. Coll. Personnel Assn., Ill. Assn. Counseling and Devel., Great Lakes Assn. Coll. and Univ. Residence Halls, Nat. Assn. Coll. and Univ. Residence Halls. Clubs: Newman (Rockford), Midwest Voyageurs Canoe. Avocations: biking, skiing, cooking, music. Home: Rockford Coll Box 789 Rockford IL 61108-2393 Office: Rockford Coll Student Services Office 5050 E State St Rockford IL 61108-2393

MODERT, ELWIN LAMAR, engineer; b. Bronson, Mich., Mar. 7, 1926; s. Elwin J. and Dorothy Marie (Gunthrope) M.; m. Dorothy May Allen, Sept. 4, 1949; children: Elwin Lamar II, Timothy Donald. BS, Bryan Coll., 1950. Registered profl. engineer, Wis. Dir. personnel Bronson Reel Co., 1953-60; v.p., gen. mgr. Am. Planter Co., Bur Dak, Mich., 1960-63; mgr. quality control Bronson Specialities, 1963-65; mgr. design engr. Bostrom Div. UOP, Milw., 1965-84; project engr. Milsco Mfg. Co., Brown Deer, Wis., 1984—. Mem. ASTM, Soc. Automotive Engrs., Soc. Mfr. Engr., Standard Engrs. Soc. Presbyterian. Lodge: Kiwanis (pres. 1953-65). Home: 4141 W Hawthorne Trace Apt 201 Brown Deer WI 53209 Office: Milsco Mfg Co 9009 N 51st St Brown Deer WI 53223

MODERY, RICHARD GILLMAN, marketing and sales executive; b. Chgo., Sept. 20, 1941; s. Richard Gustave Modery and Betty Jane (Gillman) Perok; m. Kay Francis Whitby, July 31, 1966 (div. July 1977); children: Stacey Lynn, Marci Kay; m. Anne-Marie Lucette Arsenault, Feb. 27, 1979. Student, Joliet (Ill.) Jr. Coll., 1959-61, Aurora (Ill.) Coll., 1963-65, Davenport Bus. Coll., Grand Rapids, Mich., 1969-71. Mktg. products mgr. Rapistan, Inc., Grand Rapids, 1964-75; mgr. estimating, project mgmt., customer service E.W. Buschman Co., Cin., 1975-78; exec. v.p. Metzgar Conveyor Co., Grand Rapids, 1979-84; mng. dir. Transfer Technologies, Inc., Grand Rapids, 1984-87; v.p. Translogic Corp., Denver, 1987—. Patentee in field. Commr. City of East Grand Rapids, Mich. Traffic Commn., 1983-86. Served with USNG, 1963-69. Mem. Internat. Material Mgmt. Soc., Am. Mgmt. Assn. Lodge: Masons (32 degree). Avocations: photography, travel, computers.

MODIC, JAMES PAUL, retail and rental company executive; b. Cleve., Nov. 9, 1936; s. James Vincent and Pauline Mary (Tabor) M.; ed. DePaul U., 1966-70, Am. Inst. Banking, 1967-70; m. Jeanette Marie Kraus, June 14, 1958; children—John Paul, Janis Pauline Modic Hodgdon, Jennifer Paula. Methods analyst Chgo. Police Dept., 1957-58, sr. methods analyst, 1959-61, prin. methods analyst, 1961-66; supr. methods div. Continental Ill. Bank, Chgo., 1966-70, mgr. trust dept., 1970-72; owner 6 stores Gingiss Formalwear Inc., Kansas City area, 1972—; regional adv., mem. chmns. club Gingiss Internat.; owner 3 retail food stores, Kansas City area; pres. J.J. Advt., Lenexa, Kans. Dir., Kansas City Chiefs Football Club, 1976—, 1st v.p., 1977-79, treas., 1980, mem. adv. bd., 1982—, mem. coach's club, 1980—, chmn. ticket drive, 1978, 79, 81, 83. Mem. zone bd. Boy Scouts Am., Chgo., 1967-71; mem. Performing Arts Found., Botar Com., Friends of the Arts. Served with USMC, 1954-57, Res., 1957-61. Recipient award for job placement program Kansas City (Kans.) Sch. System, 1978; award of excellence Gingiss Internat., 1979; cert. Distributive Edn. Clubs Am., 1982, 83, 85. Mem. Am. Mgmt. Assn. (lectr. 1967-69), Am. Formalwear Assn. (charter), Menswear Retailers Am., Overland Park C. of C. (planning commn. 1979), Kansas City C. of C., Nat. Alliance Businessmen (v.p. Chgo. chpt., cert. of merit), 1st Marine Div. Assn. Roman Catholic. Clubs: Improved Order Red Men Lenexa Tribe No. 5, Masons (32 deg.), Shriners, Red Coat (exec. com.), Porsche of Am., Com. 101. Home: 8426 Rosehill Rd Lenexa KS 66215 Office: 5809 Johnson Dr Mission KS 66202

MOE, JOHN LARSON, electrical engineer, research and development executive; b. Mt. Clemens, Mich., Feb. 8, 1931; s. John Benjamin and Rubye Christen (Larson) M.; m. Florence Francis Wilson, Sept. 9, 1950; children: Roberta, Kathleen. BEE, Marquette U., 1952; postgrad., U. Md., Silver Spring, 1952-53. Elect. engr. U.S. Naval Ordance Lab., Silver Spring, 1952-54; elect. engr. Univac div. Remington Rand Corp., St. Paul, 1954-59; elect. engr. Started Co. div. Gen. Electronic Control Co., Mpls., 1959-62; cons. engr. St. Paul, 1962-63; v.p. engring. Waynco, Inc., Winona, Minn., 1963-76; research and devel. mgr. Watlow Winona, Inc., 1976—. Patentee in field. Mem. IEEE. Lutheran. Avocation: flying. Home: 461 Glenview Dr Winona MN 55987 Office: Watlow Winona Inc 1241 Bundy Blvd Winona MN 55987

MOE-FISHBACK, BARBARA ANN, counselor, educator; b. Grand Forks, N.D., June 24, 1955; d. Robert Alan and Ruth Ann (Wang) Moe; m. William Martin Fishback. BS in Psychology, U. N.D., 1977, MA in Counseling and Guidance, 1979, BS in Elem. Edn., 1984. Cert. elem. tchr. and counselor, S.D., N.D. Tchr. United Day Nursery, Grand Forks, 1977-78; social worker Cavalier County Social Services, Langdon, N.D., 1979-83; elem. sch. counselor Douglas Sch. System, Ellsworth AFB, S.D., 1984-87, Jacksonville (Ill.) Sch. System, 1987—. Vol. Big Sister Program, Grand Forks, 1978-84; leader Pine to Prairie Girl Scout council, Langdon, N.D., 1980-82; tchrs. asst. Head Start Program, Grand Forks, 1979. Mem. Am. Assn. Counseling and Devel., NEA, AAUW (local br. newsletter editor 1980-81, br. sec. 1981-83), S.D. Edn. Assn., Am. Sch. Counselor Assn., S.D. Assn. Counseling and Devel., S.D. Sch. Counselor Assn., West River Personnel and Guidance Assn., Kappa Alpha Theta (newsletter, magazine article editor 1976-77). Club: Jaycettes (Langdon) (dir. 1982-83). Avocations: cooking, camping, curling, ceramics, creative writing. Home: 1650 S Main St Jacksonville IL 62650 Office: Jacksonville Sch Dist Jacksonville IL 62650

MOELLER, JOHN MICHAEL, lawyer, educator; b. Omaha, Oct. 16, 1948; s. John Fallon and Constance Jean (Daboll) M.; m. Aleidine J. Kramer, July 6, 1973 (div. Dec. 1979); 1 child, John Michael II. BA, U. Nebr., Omaha, 1969, postgrad. med. sch., 1971-73, MBA, 1979; JD, Creighton U., 1971. Bar: Nebr. 1971, U.S. Dist. Ct. (D.C. dist.) 1971, U.S. Tax Ct. 1987. Assoc. Haney Law Offices, Omaha, 1973-75; ptnr. Fortune, Carter & Moeller, Omaha, 1975-79; atty., advisor hearings and appeals Social Security Adminstrn., Omaha, 1979-85; sole practice Omaha, 1985—; instr. bus. law, econs., acctg. Met. Tech. Community Coll., Omaha, 1978-80, Coll. St. Mary, Omaha, 1985—. Editor Creighton U. Law Rev., 1970-71. Served to maj. JAGC, USAR,. Mem. ABA, Nebr. Bar Assn., Res. Officer's Assn. (treas. 1984). Roman Catholic. Lodges: Kiwanis, KC. Home: 7674 Shirley St Omaha NE 68124 Office: 7389 Pacific St Suite 223 Omaha NE 68114

MOELLER, ROBERT RALPH, computer auditor, consultant; b. Mpls., Mar. 4, 1942; s. Ralph Henry and Clara Amelia (Gall) M.; m. Lois Patricia Hamblin, Sept. 9, 1969. B in Aero.Engring., U. Minn., 1968; MBA, U. Chgo., 1982. CPA, Ill. Systems analyst Sperry Corp., St. Paul, 1968-75, EDP audit mgr., 1975-78; internal audit mgr. Wickes Cos., Wheeling, Ill., 1978-81; internal audit dir. AM Internat., Chgo., 1981-82; nat. dir. computer audit, cons. info. systems Grant Thornton, Chgo., 1982—. Author: Modern Computer Audit, Security and Control, 1987; editor: FTP Auditing Computer Systems; assoc. editor Jour. Info. Systems and Computing Revs.; contbr. articles to profl. jours. Served with U.S. Army, 1965-67. Mem. Am. Inst. CPA's (computer audit subcom.), Chgo. Inst. Internal Auditors (pres., mem. internat. advanced tech. com.), Inst. for Mgmt. Acctg. (regents adv. com.), Ill. CPA Soc. (chmn. computers in auditing com.), Internat. Fedn. Info. Processing (vice chmn. computer audit and integrity working group). Club: University. Avocations: skiing; sailing. Home: 1045 Ridge Ave Evanston IL 60202 Office: Grant Thornton 600 Prudential Plaza Chicago IL 60601

MOEN, RODNEY CHARLES, state senator, communications company executive; b. Whitehall, Wis., July 26, 1937; s. Edwin O. and Tena A. (Gunderson) M.; m. Catherine Jean Wolfe, 1959; children—Scott A., Jon C., Rodd M., Catherine J., Daniel M. Student Syracuse U., 1964-65; B.A., U. So. Calif., 1972; postgrad. Ball State U., 1975-76. Contbg. editor Govt. Photography, 1970-74; gen. mgr. Western Wis. Communications Corp., Independence, Wis., 1976-83; mem. Wis. Senate, 1983—, chmn. agrl., health and human services com., 1983—. Served to lt. USN, 1955-76, Vietnam. Decorated Joint Services commendation medal. Recipient George Stoney award Nat. Fedn. Local Cable TV Programmers, 1980. Democrat. Lodge: Lions. Office: 2119 Dewey St Whitehall WI 54773

MOEN, RONALD DEAN, statistician; b. Osage, Iowa, Feb. 16, 1941; s. Lloyd Oscar and Molly Henrietta (Christiansen) M.; m. Bette Dean Davis, June 1, 1968; children—Evan Roger, Tracy Elizabeth. B.A. in Math., U. No. Iowa, 1963; M.S. in Teaching Math., U. Mo., 1966, M.A. in Stats., 1971. High sch. math. tchr., Greene, Iowa, 1963-64; teaching asst. U. Mo., Columbia, 1964-66, 69-71; math. instr. Murray State U., Ky., 1966-67, U. Wis.-Oshkosh, 1967-69; math. statistician U.S. Dept. Agr., Washington, 1971-76; dir. research applications Neotec Corp., Silver Spring, Md., 1976-82; dir. statis. methods Gen. Motors Corp., Pontiac, Mich., 1982—; instr. stats. U.S. Dept. Agr. Grad. Sch., Washington, 1973-76; instr. Deming Seminars George Washington U., Washington and Los Angeles, 1984-85. Contbg. author: (Ency. Brit. film) Road Map for Change: The Deming Approach, 1984 (Golden Eagle award 1985). Contbr. articles and papers to popular mags. and profl. publs. Active local Boy Scouts Am., 1982-84; mem. council Calvary Lutheran Ch., Clarkston, Mich., 1985—; bd. dirs. Cedar Crest Acad., Clarkston, 1984-85. NSF grantee summer insts. Rutgers U., 1967, U. Minn., 1968. Mem. Am. Soc. for Quality Control (asst. program chmn. automotive div. 1984-85), Am. Statis. Assn. (quality and productivity com. 1984-85), Am. Quality and Productivity Inst. (founding mem., awards chmn. 1983-85), Soc. Automotive Engrs. (organizer internat. congress quality and productivity session 1983-85). Avocations: tennis; swimming; skiing; hiking. Home: 7171 Deerhill Ct Clarkston MI 48016

MOENNING, KENNETH H., printing company executive; b. Quincy, Ill., May 19, 1941; s. Charles August and Freda Mary (VonderHaar) M.; m. Joann Mary Shinn, June 2, 1962; children: Michael K., Michelle J. Grad., Notre Dame High Sch., 1959. Apprentice compositor Creative Printers, Quincy, 1961-70; compositor Royal Printing Co., Quincy, 1970-75, v.p., 1975-84, pres., 1984—. Mem. Hist. Soc. Adams County, Quincy, 1984. Mem. Quincy Sales and Mktg. Club. Roman Catholic. Loges: Rotary, Optimist. Avocations: fly fishing, hunting, trap shooting. Home: 2028 S 39th Quincy IL 62301 Office: Royal Printing Co 514 Jersey Quincy IL 62301

MOGOLOV, CYNTHIA JO, telecommunications executive; b. Ida Grove, Iowa, Aug. 20, 1950; d. John F. and Marjorie I. (Asmus) Lantz; m. Larry S. Mogolov, Dec. 20, 1970; children: Robert A., David J., Daniel L. BA in Journalism, Drake U., 1972. Supr. Northwestern Bell, Des Moines, Iowa, 1972-76, planning engr., 1976-77, mgr. EEO and AAP, 1977-80, mgr. real estate, 1980-83; mgr. real estate AT&T Communications, Kansas City, Mo., 1983-85, mgr. hdqrs. material mgmt., 1985—. Leader Cub Scouts Am., Overland Park, Kans., 1986; vol. project business Jr. Achievement, Des Moines, 1982. Named Outstanding Young Person, Des Moines Jaycees, 1982. Mem. Alpha Phi (v.p. 1970-71). Republican. Jewish. Office: AT&T 1100 Walnut Kansas City MO 64141

MOHIUDDIN, MAHMOOD, biomedical engineer; b. Hyderabad, India, June 21, 1944; came to U.S., 1969; s. Ghouse and Khateeja (Begum) M.; m. Razia Khatoon, Feb. 2, 1971; children: Imran, Salman, Amaan, Hina. BSME, Osmania U., 1967; MSME, Ill. Inst. Tech., 1970; MBA, Roosevelt U., 1982. Profl. engr., Wis. Sr. devel. engr. AB Dick Co., Niles, Ill., 1970-74; designer Multigraphics Labs., Mt. Prospect, Ill., 1974-76; prin. engr. Baxter Travenol, Round Lake, Ill., 1976-80; sr. design engr. Hollister, Inc., Libertyville, Ill., 1980—. Patentee in field. Sunday sch. dir. Islamic Soc. Northwest Suburbs, Rolling Meadows, Ill., 1981—; managing dir. Muslim Students Assn., Chgo., 1984-85. Mem. Midwest Biomed. Engring. Soc. Office: Hollister Inc 2000 Hollister Dr Libertyville IL 60048

MOHLER, DELMAR RAY, institute director, accountant; b. Lafayette, Ind., Nov. 25, 1950; s. Martin T. and Donna Mae (Herrold) M.; m. Linda Ruth Mayo, May 10, 1974; children—Rachel Dawn, Elisabeth Ann, Grace Thalia, Gloria Joy. B.A., Cedarville Coll., 1979. C.P.A., Ill., Minn. Bus. mgr. New Life Media, Inc., Cedarville, Ohio, 1977-79; audit staff Benson Wells & Co., Mpls., 1979-80; audit mgr. W. Scott Wallace, C.P.A., St. Paul, 1980-84; dir. treasury ops. Moody Bible Inst., Chgo., 1984-86, mgr. investments, 1986—. Elder, Trinity Ch., Mpls., 1982-84; mem. Keeneyville Bible Ch., Ill., 1984-86, First Bapt. Ch., Arlington Heights, Ill., 1986—. Served with USN, 1971-77. Recipient Wall St. Jour. award, 1979. Mem. Minn. Soc. CPA's, Ill. Soc. CPA's, Am. Inst. CPA's (personal fin. planners div.). Republican. Avocations: golf; jogging; swimming. Home: 319 Brookwood Terr Roselle IL 60172 Office: 820 N LaSalle Dr Chicago IL 60610

MOHLER, TERENCE JOHN, psychologist; b. Toledo, July 8, 1929; s. Edward F. and Gertrude A. (Aylward) M.; m. Carol B. Kulczak, Oct. 1, 1955; children—Renee, John, Timothy. B.E., Toledo U., 1955, M.E., 1966, Ed.S. in Psychology and Counseling, 1975, postgrad., 1981-82; Ph.D., Walden U., 1979. Psychologist, Toledo Bd. Edn., 1969—; sr. partner Psychol. Assocs., Maumee, Ohio, 1970—; assoc. fellow Inst. for Advanced Study in Rational Psychotherapy, N.Y.C. Served with AUS, 1951-53; Korea. Lic. psychologist, Ohio. Mem. Am., Ohio, Northwestern Ohio, Maumee Valley psychol. assns., Soc. Behavioists, Nat. Registry Mental Health Providers, Am. Personnel and Guidance Assn., Ohio Personnel and Guidance Assn., Council for Exceptional Children, Kappa Delta Phi. Lodge: Rotary. Home: 1113 Winghaven Rd Maumee OH 43537 Office: 5757 Monclova Rd Maumee OH 43537

MOHN, CHERI ANN, artist, educator; b. Akron, Ohio, Aug. 12, 1936; d. Vachael Francis and Grace Marie (Scoville) Roberts; m. John J. Mohn, AUg. 30, 1954; 1 child, Deborah Mohn Altimus. AB, Youngstown State U., 1969. Dir., instr. Cheri Mohn Sch Art, Youngstown, Ohio, 1962-66; co-owner, dir. Village Market Pl., Columbiana, Ohio, 1972-76; dir., instr. Cheri Mohn Studio, North Lima, Ohio, 1968—; writer art column Niles (Ohio) Times, 1960's. Asst. editor, cartoonist in field. Permanent collection purchase Butler Inst. Am. Art, 1970; recipient watercolor award Mahoning Valley Watercolorists, 1984, 87, Women Artists: A Celebration, 1985. Mem. Friends Am. Art. (hon. mention 1968). Avocations: antiques, gardening. Home and Office: 12691 South Ave North Lima OH 44452

MOHNS, BENJAMIN CHARLES, JR., construction company executive; b. Milw., Sept. 11, 1951; s. Benjamin Charles Mohns and Edith Lorraine (Tutsch) Nebel; m. Nancy Ann Weinitschka, June 26, 1976; children—Bradley, Benjamin III, Heather. Pres. Mohns Inc., Waukesha, Wis., to present. Mem. Nat. Assn. Remodeling Industry (Contractor of Yr. 1983, Nat. Contractor of yr. 1985, Regional Contractor of Yr. 1985). Lutheran. Club: Nat. Corvette Owners. Avocations: car restoration; bowling; racquetball; golf. Office: Mohns Inc 110 N 121st Wauwatosa WI 53226

MOHR, JAMES LEGRAND, accountant; b. Indpls., May 20, 1950; s. George William and Joan Eillen (Goldsmith) M.; m. Aline Mary Lindquist, Dec. 29, 1973; children: Stephen, Eric, Mark. BS, Ind. U., 1972, JD, 1975. CPA, Wis. Ptnr. Peat Marwick Main & Co., Milw., 1975—. Pres. Silver Spring Neighborhood Ctr., Milw., 1985—. Mem. Am. Inst. CPA's, Wis. Inst. CPA's, Wis. Retirement Plan Profl. Ltd. (v.p. 1985—). Presbyterian. Clubs: Milw. Yacht, Ozaukee Country (Mequon, Wis.). Avocations: sailing, golf.

MOHR, WILLIAM G., utility company executive; b. Alva, Okla., Jan. 28, 1936; s. Albert Wilhelm and Kathern (Prigmore) M.; m. Sherri Haug, Dec. 28, 1976; children: Christina, Gary. BS, Northwestern U., Alva, 1962. Dir. corp. planning Kans. Gas & Electric Co., Wichita, 1962—. Bd. dirs. Wichita Urban League, 1975-78, Community Action Agy., Wichita, 1977. Served with USAF, 1956-60. Mem. Edison Electric Inst., Issues Mgmt. Assn., The Planning Forum. Republican. Lodge: Kiwanis (bd. dirs. Wichita club 1977). Avocations: hunting, fishing. Office: Kans Gas & Electric Co 120 E 1st Box 208 Wichita KS 67201

MOILANEN, THOMAS ALFRED, construction equipment distributor, funeral director; b. Hancock, Mich., Sept. 3, 1944; s. A. Edward and Elsie E. (Karkanen) M.; m. Kathleen Ann Maibach, Sept. 18, 1965; children: Todd Alan, Karl Edward. Cert., Wayne State U., 1967. Licensed funeral dir., Mich. Funeral dir. Ross B. Northorp & Son, Inc., Redford, Mich., 1967-68; sales mgr. Cloverdale Equipment Co., Oak Park, Mich., 1971; v.p., gen. mgr. Cloverdale Equipment Co., Oak Park, 1972-78, pres., chief exec. officer, bd. dirs., 1978—; pres., chief exec. officer, bd. dirs. Hasper Equipment Co., Muskegon, Mich., 1980—, SunBelt Crane & Equipment, Sarasota, Fla., 1982—, Armstrong/Cloverdale Equipment Co., Columbia, S.C., 1987—. Treas., bd. dirs. Livonia Hockey Assn., 1981-82. Mem. Associated Equipment Dealers Am. (equipment distbn. com. 1984), Mich. Constrn. Equipment Distributors Assn. (pres. 1983), Concrete Improvement Bd. (bd. dirs. 1978-79). Republican. Lodge: Kiwanis (bd. dirs. Redford 1967-69, pres. 1969-70). Avocations: hunting, golf. Home: 18332 Laraugh Northville MI 48167 Office: Cloverdale Equipment Co 13133 Cloverdale Oak Park MI 48237

MOILANEN, WILLIAM ROBERT, dentist, consultant; b. Detroit, July 29, 1950; s. Eino William and Dorothy Mae (Kemp) M.; m. Darrell Lynne Burton, Dec. 17, 1971; children: Kristin Lea, William Burton, Daniel Burton. BS, U. Mich., 1972; DDS, U. Detroit, 1976. Assoc. dentist Dr. Nils Korsnes, Plymouth, Mich., 1976-77, Dr. Joseph Smulsky, Canton, Mich., 1976-78, Dr. David Schwartz, Clawson, Mich., 1976-78; pvt. practice dentistry Fenton, Mich., 1978—; bd. dirs. Midwest Network, Inc.; cons. doctor, network dir., area dir. Quest Seminars, Reno, 1984—. State chmn. Nat. Childrens Dental Health Month, 1986. Mem. ADA, Mich. Dental Assn. (com. on dental edn.), Internat. Congress Oral Implantologists, Acad. Gen. Dentistry, Fenton Area Jaycess (pres. 1981). Lodge: Rotary. Avocations: skiing, photography. Home: 13293 Crane Ridge Dr Fenton MI 48430 Office: 14272 Fenton Rd Fenton MI 48430

MOKSNES, MARK ALAN, insurance company executive; b. Madison, Wis., Feb. 4, 1957; s. Robert Henry and Mary Martha (Vinger) M.; m. Pamela Kay Hanson, Aug. 16, 1980; children: Katie Marie, Laura Kay. BS, Augsburg Coll., Mpls., 1979. Sales rep. Delta Dental Plan, Mpls., 1979-83, dir. sales, 1983—; Chmn. Human Growth Found., 1985-86, 86-87. Mem. Mr. Basketball Com., Mpls., 1979-86. Named on of Outstanding Young Men of Am., 1985. Mem. Am. Mktg. Assn. Republican. Lutheran. Home: 7640 Heritage Rd S Eden Prairie MN 55344 Office: Delta Dental Plan Minn 7807 Creekridge Circle Minneapolis MN 55440

MOLDE, KENT DOUGLAS, radiologist; b. Montevideo, Minn., Nov. 27, 1945; s. Adolph Leonard and Eleanor Oselia (Heieren) M.; m. Julie Ann Prail, June 6, 1970; children: Ryan, Britt. BA summa cum laude, U. Minn., 1967, MD, 1970. Intern Sacramento Med. Ctr., Davis, Calif., 1970-71; resident in diagnostic radiology U. Minn., 1971-73, chief resident, 1973-74; staff radiologist Fairview Southdale Hosp., Mpls., 1976-84; chief radiology dept. Fairview Riverside Hosp., Mpls., 1984—; mem. exec. com. Fairview and Fairview Riverside Hosp., Mpls., 1984—; med. dir. NETSCAN, Mpls., 1986—; mem. NETSCAN bd. NETCARE Magnetic Resonance Imaging, Mpls., 1985—. Served to maj. USAF, 1974-76. Mem. Am. Coll. Radiology, Radiologic Soc. N.Am., Hennepin County Med. Soc., Minn. State Med. Assn., Minn. State Radiologic Soc., Phi Beta Kappa. Lutheran. Clubs: Hazeltine Natl. Golf (Chaska, Minn.); Flagship Athletic (Eden Prairie). Avocations: golfing, skiing, tennis. Office: Fairview Riverside Hosp 2312 S 6th St Minneapolis MN 55454

MOLENBEEK, ROBERT GERRIT, accountant; b. Grand Rapids, Mich., Feb. 7, 1944; s. Gerrit John and Jean (Wierenga) M.; m. Marsha Lee Rockel, Mar. 23, 1966; children: Rebecca, Tammy, Brian, Brent. AS in Bus. Adminstrn. and Acctg. with honors, Davenport Coll., 1964; BBA in Acctg. with honors, Ferris State Coll., 1966; MBA, Grand Valley State Coll., 1976. CPA, Mich. Staff acct. various firms Grand Rapids, 1969-72; staff acct., ptnr. Tuori Jacobson, CPA, Muskegon, Mich., 1972-73; sr. internal auditor Wolverine Worldwide, Rockford, Mich., 1973-75; pvt. practice acctg. Grand Rapids, 1975—; controller Sq. Real Estate, Grand Rapids, 1976-87, salesman, 1976—; pvt. practice in acctg. Grand Rapids, 1976—; cons. S & S Assocs., Grand Rapids, 1986—, Bethel Group, Inc., Grand Rapids, 1987—; bd. dirs. United Products Dist., Grand Rapids, 1977—, WKPS, Inc., Grand Rapids, 1984—. Active West Mich. R.R. Hist. Soc., Grand Rapids, 1986-

87, Muskegon R.R. Hist. Soc., 1985-87. Served with USNR, 1967-69. Mem. Am. Inst. CPA's, Mich. Assn. CPA's, Nat. Assn. Realtors, Mich. Assn. Realtors, Grand Rapids Real Estate Bd. (Multi Million Sales award 1976—, Ten Million Sales award 1980, Top Ten Sales award 1980). Avocations: railroads, hunting. Home: 4440 7 Mile Rd Belmont MI 49306 Office: Sq Real Estate Inc 169 Monroe NW Grand Rapids MI 49306

MOLENDA, MARK EDWARD, state official, accountant; b. Detroit, Oct. 10, 1941; s. Edward and Buryle Julia (Maynard) M.; m. Patricia Jean Newcomer, June 10, 1967; children: Melissa, Gregory. BA, Mich. State U., 1969, MBA, 1970. CPA, Mich. Staff auditor Arthur Young & Co., Chgo., 1970-71; auditor Auditor Gen., Lansing, Mich., 1971-72; budget dir. Mich. State Police, East Lansing, 1973-79, dir. bus. adminstrn., 1979—; officer, bd. dirs. Mark E. Molenda, CPA's, Mason, Mich. Founder Hemophilia Golf Classic, Lansing, 1978—; pres., bd. dirs. Hemophilia Found. Mich., Ann Arbor, 1980-86; bd. dirs. Nat. Hemophilia Found., N.Y.C., 1982-85; coach East Side Soccer, Mason, 1981—. Recipient Appreciation award Hemophilia Found. Mich., 1986. Mem. Am. Inst. CPA's, Mich. Assn. CPA's, State Govtl. Accts. Assn. (pres. 1976-78), Mich. Adminstrv. Officers Assn. (pres. 1986-87), Mason C. of C. Democrat. Presbyterian. Avocation: golf. Home: 848 Eaton Dr Mason MI 48854 Office: Mich State Police 714 S Harrison Rd East Lansing MI 48823

MOLENDA, MICHAEL HENRY, education professor; b. South Bend, Ind., Nov. 19, 1941; s. Henry Eugene Molenda and Helene Irene (Mendini) Beringer; m. Carolyn Sue Shockey, Aug. 17, 1968 (div. July 1984); children: James, Mark; m. Patricia Cay Albrecht, Dec. 15, 1984 (div. Jan. 1987). BA, Marquette U., 1963; MS, Syracuse U., 1965, PhD, 1971. Asst. prof. U. N.C., Greensboro, 1968-72; assoc. prof. Ind. U., Bloomington, 1972—; lectr. Tchrs. Coll., Jakarta, Indonesia, 1983; cons. Ministry Edn. Madrid, Spain, 1971, Ministry Edn. Cairo, Egypt, 1979. Co-author: Intructional Media, 1982; editor Jour. Assn. Ednl. Communications and Technology, 1982—; contbr. articles to profl. jours.; creator instructional system Diffusion Simulation Game, 1976. Alumni award Marquette U., 1964; Twente U. research fellow, 1980-81. Mem. Assn. Ednl. Communications and Technology (div. pres. 1978-79, bd. dirs. 1987—), Nat. Soc. Performance Instr. (pres. local chpt. 1985—), N.Am. Simulation and Gaming Assn. (bd. dirs., conf. pres. 1985, sec. 1986—), Communications Cons. Consortium (bd. dirs. 1986—), Phi Delta Kappa. Avocations: Mexican numismatics, aerobatic aviation, oenophile. Home: 3914 Sugar Ln E Bloomington IN 47401 Office: Ind U Edn 210 Bloomington IN 47405

MOLER, DONALD LEWIS, educator; b. Wilsey, Kans., Jan. 12, 1918; s. Ralph Lee and Bessie Myrtle (Berry) M.; B.S., Kans. State Tchrs. Coll., Emporia, 1939; M.S., U. Kans., Lawrence, 1949, Ph.D., 1951; m. Alta Margaret Ansdell, Nov. 6, 1942; 1 son, Donald Lewis Jr. Tchr., Centralia (Kans.) High Sch., 1939-42, Carthage (Mo.) High Sch., 1946-48; asst. dir. Reading Clinic, U. Kans., 1948-51; dir. reading program Eastern Ill. U., 1951-70, prof. dept. ednl. psychology and guidance, 1963—, chmn. dept., 1963-84, dean Sch. Edn., 1980; vis. scholar U. Fla., 1965. Served with Signal Corps, U.S. Army, 1942-46. Recipient C.A. Michelman award, 1974; Disting Service award Ill. Assn. Counselor Educators, 1985. Mem. Ill. Guidance and Personnel Assn. (pres. 1968-69), Ill. Counselor Educators and Suprs., Ill. Coll. Personnel Assn., Am. Personnel and Guidance Assn. (senator 1970-71), Assn. Counselor Edn. and Supervision, Assn. Humanistic Edn. and Devel., Phi Delta Kappa, Xi Phi, Pi Omega Pi, Pi Kappa Delta, Sigma Tau Gamma. Methodist. Assoc. editor Ill. Guidance and Personnel Assn. Quar., 1970-84, mng. editor, 1984—. Home: 407 W Hayes St Charleston IL 61920 Office: Eastern Illinois Univ Dept Ednl Psychology and Guidance Charleston IL 61920

MOLESKI, FREDERICK LEO, information systems administrator; b. Grand Rapids, Mich., Sept. 7, 1942; s. Leo T. and Claire (Bogdanik) M.; m. Terri Cleveland, Aug. 27, 1966 (div. Nov. 1978); children: Kristen Marie, Michele Ann. BS, Aquinas Coll., 1966; M in Natural Sci., U. S.D., 1971; PhD, U. Okla., 1976. Research assoc. Okla. Biol. Survey, Norman, 1972-76; supr. ecol. services Williams Biol. Engring. Co., Tulsa, 1976-78; mgr. environ. services Roy F. Weston, Inc., Houston, 1978-79; environ. project mgr. Office Nuclear Waste Isolation, Columbus, Ohio, 1979-84; quality assurance specialist Battelle Meml. Inst., Columbus, 1984-86, mgr. info. systems, 1986—; Mem. Gov.'s Adv. Council to Okla. Natural Heritage Program, Oklahoma City, 1976-78. Author: BPMD IDMS User's Guide, 1987. Mem. Am. Youth Hostels. Koscivszko Found. scholar, 1972; NSF grantee, 1970, 74. Mem. Assn. Systems Mgmt., Ecol. Soc. Am., Project Mgmt. Inst., Performance Mgmt. Assn., Tri Beta, Sigma Xi. Republican. Roman Catholic. Club: Battelle Meml. Inst. Model R.R. (pres. 1985—). Avocations: cycling, model R.R., backpacking, photography, dancing. Home: 894 Thomas Rd Columbus OH 43212 Office: Battelle Meml Inst Project Mgmt Div 505 King Ave Columbus OH 43201

MOLINE, SANDRA LOIS, librarian; b. San Antonio, Dec. 13, 1938; d. Udo F. and Olivia Marie (Link) Reininger; m. Jon Nelson Moline, Aug. 13, 1960; children: Kevin, Eric. BA in Chemistry, Austin Coll., 1960; postgrad., Duke U., 1962-64; MA in History of Sci., U. Wis., 1976, MLS, 1977. Tchr. chemistry and physics Durham (N.C.) High Sch., 1960-64; head physics library U. Wis., Madison, 1977—; adj. tchr. Madison Area Tech. Coll., 1965-69. Mem. Spl. Libraries Assn. (physics, astronomy, math divs.), Librarians Assembly (sec., treas. 1980, pres. 1983), Madison Acad. Staff Assn. (steering com. 1980-83, pres. 1982). Home: 17068 Hamilton Dr Lakeville MN 55044 Office: U Wis Physics Library 1150 University Ave Madison WI 53706

MOLL, EDWIN ALLAN, business executive; b. Chgo., July 16, 1934; s. Maurice and Lillian (Lederman) M.; B.S., Loyola U., 1956; Ed.M., Northwestern U., 1960, Asso. in Police Sci., 1962; m. Natalie Kepner, Mar. 11, 1962; children—Kelli Lee, Dean Allan. Vice pres. Linnea Perfumes, Inc., 1950; owner, operator three restaurants, Chgo., 1952-56; producer, moderator radio shows This is Chgo., Grant Part Concert Rev., Fort Dearborn Concert, Chgo., 1957-65; bus. mgr. Chgo. Adler Planetarium, 1958-59; adminstrv. aide to mayor Chgo., 1959-63; pres. Edwin A. Moll Pub. Relations, Chgo., from 1963; pres. Profl. Adminstrv. Services Inc., 1975-78, Profl. Service System, Inc., 1975-78; chief ranger Cook County (Ill.) Forest Preserve, 1975-76; exec. Lee Optical Co., 1976-78; chmn. bd. Profl. Med. Guidance Corp.; dir. Glenwood State Bank; chmn. bd. Am. Travel Bur., Ltd., 1979, Edwin A. Moll and Assos.; pres. Riviera 400 Club; v.p. Outer Dr. E. Comml. Devel. Corp., 1983—; mgmt. cons. to professions; lectr. pub. relations and practice mgmt. Commr., Youth Welfare, Skokie, Ill., 1963-66. Exec. bd. mem. 40th ward Democratic Orgn., Chgo., 1948-68. Bd. dirs. Ill. Vision Services Corp., Nate Gross Found., Asthmacade. Recipient citation Red Cross, 1957. Mem. Am. Soc. Assn. Execs., Soc. Optometric Assn. Execs., Optometric Council for Polit. Edn. (exec. dir. 1968-69), Ill. Optometric Assn. (exec. sec. 1963-69, Optometric Layman of Year award 1967), Ill. Pub. Health Assn., Internat., Ill., West Suburban, South Suburban, North Suburban assns. chiefs of police, Ill. Police Assn., Internat. Platform Assn., Chgo. Forum Execs., Tau Delta Phi. Clubs: Illinois Athletic (Chgo.); President's (Washington). Author: Sell Yourself Big, 1966.

MOLL, GARY DANIEL, accountant, mayor; b. St. Louis, Oct. 31, 1950; s. Othmar Herman and Elvira Charlotte (Faust) M.; m. Karen Sue Hoffmann, May 18, 1979 (div. Jan. 1986). BBA, U. Mo., 1976, MBA, 1977; postgrad., Mich. State U., 1985-86. CPA, Ill., Mo. Agent IRS, East St. Louis, Ill., 1977-81; sr. tax acct. McDonnell Douglas Corp., St. Louis, 1981—; mayor City of West Belleville, Ill., 1984—; loan officer, bd. dirs. St. Bernadette Credit Union, Lemay, Mo., 1974-79; v.p., bd. dirs. John W.C. Moll & Assocs., Arnold, Mo., 1980—; pres., bd. dirs. Moll Bros. Properties Inc., St. Louis, 1981—. Served to capt. USAFR, 1969—. Mem. Inst. Property Taxation, Tax Exec. Inst., Reserve Officers Assn., Assn. Military Surgeons of the U.S., MENSA. Republican. Club: St. Louis Track. Avocation: running, photography, flying. Home: 134 N 82d St Belleville IL 62223-2121 Office: McDonnell Douglas Corp PO Box 516 Dept H348 Saint Louis MO 63166

MOLL, JAMES EDWARD, JR., school counselor, educator; b. Detroit, Oct. 10, 1951; s. James Edward and Margaret Dorthea (Motzkus); m. Denise Lynn Therassé; children: Andrew James, Jonathan Bradley. BS, Western Mich. U., 1973; MA, Oakland U., 1980. Cert. secondary tchr., Mich. Tchr. Birmingham (Mich.) Pub. Schs., 1973-81, crisis intervention counselor, 1982—; summer sch. prin., Birmingham Pub. Schs.; counseling cons. Project Adventure, Hamilton, Mass., 1985-86. Student theatre dir. Groves High Sch., Birmingham, 1973-76. Mem. NEA, Mich. Edn. Assn. (rep. 1976-80), Birmingham Edn. Assn. (v.p. 1978-82). Democrat. Avocations: acoustic guitar, softball, hockey, tennis. Home: 26648 Greythorne Trail Farmington Hills MI 48018 Office: Wylie E Groves High Sch 20500 W 13 Mile Rd Birmingham MI 48010

MOLLET, CHRIS JOHN, lawyer; b. Bottineau, N.D., Jan. 31, 1954; s. Lyle F. and Aileen C. (Murdoch) M.; m. Lynne M. La Jone, Sept. 20, 1980. B.A. with distinction, U. Wis., 1976, J.D., 1979. Bar: Wis. 1979, Ill. 1980, U.S. Ct. Appeals (7th cir.) 1979. Staff counsel Michael Reese Hosp. and Med. Ctr., Chgo., 1980-82; assoc. Gardner, Carton & Douglas, Chgo., 1982-85; assoc. gen. counsel, asst. sec. Luth. Gen. Health Care System, Park Ridge, Ill., 1985—; asst. sec. Parkside Home Health Services Inc., 1985—, Parkside Luth. Hosp., Augustana Hosp. Health Care Ctr., Luth. Gen. Hosp., Inc., bd. dirs., v.p. Norwood Park Citizens Assn., Chgo., 1983-84. Mem. ABA, Wis. Bar Assn., Chgo. Bar Assn., Am. Acad. Hosp. Attys. Democrat. Office: Luth Gen Health Care System 1775 Dempster Ave Park Ridge IL 60068

MOLUMBY, ROBERT EUGENE, architect, city planner; b. Willow Lake, S.D., May 22, 1936; s. Joseph A. and Irma Marian (Wilkinson) M.; B.Arch., U. Notre Dame, 1959; M.A. in City and Regional Planning, U. Calif., Berkeley, 1961; m. Edith Nina Taylor, Oct. 11, 1969; children—Katherine Hall, Nina Elizabeth. Architect-planner Perkins & Will Partnership, Chgo., 1965-71; sr. planner Village of Skokie, Ill., 1971-73, acting dir. planning, 1973, dir. planning, 1973—. Assoc. mem. Evanston (Ill.) Plan Commn., 1977-78, mem., 1978-84, vice chmn., 1982-84; mem. Evanston Zoning Bd. Appeals, 1985—; sr. warden St. Mark's Episcopal Ch., Evanston, 1980-82, vestryman, 1985-86. Served as officer USN, 1961-65. Mem. Am. Planning Assn., Urban Land Inst., Chgo. Archtl. Found., Chgo. Landmarks Preservation Council. Office: 5127 Oakton St Skokie IL 60077

MON, LOURDES GAGUI, school principal; b. Bangar, Philippines, Mar. 6, 1944; came to U.S., 1967; d. Crispin Yabut and Josefa Vergara (Agas) Gagui; m. Francis Lopez Mon, July 17, 1968; children: Catherine, Joey. BS in Elem. Edn., U. of East, Manila, 1963; MEd, Loyola U., Chgo., 1976. Tchr. San Sebastian Coll., 1963-64, St. Joseph's Coll., Philippines, 1964-67, Beloit (Wis.) Pub. Schs., 1967-69, Immaculate Conception Sch., Chgo., 1969-83; prin. St. Josaphat Sch., Chgo., 1983—; ex-officio mem. St. Josaphat Sch. Bd., 1983—. Contbg. editor: Maynila mag., 1983-85; contbg. writer: T M Herald, 1983-85; assoc. editor: VIA Times mag., 1984-86, columnist, 1984—, sr. editor, 1986—. Pres. Asian Human Services, Chgo., 1986—; active Am. Profls. Civic Alliance; vol. Immigration and Naturalization Program, 1985—; mem. Filipino Am. Council Bd., 1983-85; bd. dirs. Sining Kayummanggi Theatre Group. Named Outstanding Asian of Yr., Asian Am. Coalition Chgo., 1986. Mem. Archdiocesan Prins. Assn., Nat. Cath. Edn. Assn., Filipino Am. Women's Network (chmn. Ill. chpt. 1987—). Republican. Roman Catholic. Lodge: Lions (v.p. Chgo. chpt. 1984—). Avocations: bowling, theatre. Office: St Josaphat Sch 2245 N Southport Ave Chicago IL 60614

MONAGHAN, LEO KENNETH, financial consultant, stockbroker; b. Independence, Iowa, May 14, 1952; s. Patrick Anthony and Mary Ellen (Casey) M.; m. Diane Rose Schultz, May 24, 1980; children: Anthony, Kellie. BBA, U. Notre Dame, 1974. CPA, Iowa. Vol. Peace Corps, Brazil, 1974-76; from mem. staff to ptnr. Dee Gosling & Co. CPA's, Manchester, Iowa, 1977-86; owner Monaghan Fin., Manchester, 1986—. Fin. chmn. St. Mary's Parish, Manchester, 1983—; commr. Iowa Racing Commn., 1987—. Mem. Am. Inst. CPA's, Iowa Soc. CPA's, Manchester Jaycees (treas./pres. 1978-80, Outstanding Local Pres. 1979-80, Outstanding State Dir. 1980-81). Democrat. Roman Catholic. Lodges: Lions (treas. Manchester 1983-87), KC. Avocation: racquetball. Home and Office: 117 Crescent Dr Manchester IA 52057

MONAGHAN, THOMAS STEPHEN, restaurant chain executive; b. Ann Arbor, Mich., Mar. 25, 1937; m. Marjorie Zybach, Aug. 25, 1962; children—Mary, Susan, Margaret, Barbara. Student, Ferris State Coll., U. Mich.; Ph.D. (hon.), Cleary Coll., 1982, Madonna Coll., 1983, Eastern Mich. U., 1984, So. Fla. U., 1985. Ptnr. Dominick's Pizza, Ypsilanti, Mich., 1960-65; pres., chmn. bd. founder Domino's Pizza, Inc., Ann Arbor, Mich., 1960—; dir. Nat. Bank, Detroit; speaker in field; owner Detroit Tigers, 1983—. Author: (autobiography) Pizza Tiger. Bd. dirs. Cleary Coll., Ypsilanti, Henry Ford Hosp., Detroit, Detroit Renaissance, U. Steubinville, Ohio, St. Joseph's Hosp. Devel. Bd., Ann Arbor. Served with USMC, 1956-59. Named Entrepreneur of Yr., Harvard U. Bus. Sch., 1984, Pizzaman of Yr., Nat. Assn. Pizza Owners, 1984; recipient Golden Plate award, Am. Acad. Achievement, 1984, Golden Chain award, MUFSO, 1986, Horatio Alger award, 1986, Restaurant Bus. Leadership award 1986. Mem. Young Pres. Orgn., Internat. Franchise Assn. (Entrepreneur of Yr. 1986), Nat. Restaurant Assn. (Silver Plate award 1985), Mich. Restaurant Assn., Ypsilanti C. of C., U. Mich. Pres.'s Club, Ann Arbor Pres.'s Assn., Missionary Vehicle Assn. (bd. dirs.), AIA (hon.), Mich Soc. Architects (hon.). Club: Barton Hills Country (Ann Arbor). Lodge: K.C. Avocations: collecting Frank Lloyd Wright furniture and memorabilia, classic cars. Office: Domino's Pizza Inc PO Box 997 Ann Arbor MI 48106 Home: PO Box 997 Ann Arbor MI 48106

MONAHAN, LEONARD FRANCIS, musician, singer, composer, publisher; b. Toledo, Aug. 19, 1948; s. Leonard Francis and Theresa Margaret (Geraldo) M.; m. Elaine Ann Welling, Oct. 14, 1978. B.S. in Psychology and Philosophy, U. Toledo, 1980. Musician, writer Len Monahan Prodns., Toledo, 1971-75; musician, composer, publisher World Airwave Music, Toledo, 1975—. Recipient Internat. Recognition of Christmas Music. Mem. Broadcast Music Inc., Internat. Platform Assn., Nat. Assn. Independent Recording Distbrs. Author: If You Were Big and I Were Small, 1971; The Land of Echoing Fountains, 1972, Sending You My Thoughts, 1987, Another Road, 1987; composer numerous songs. Office: 9967-US-A20 Delta OH 43515

MONARCH, JERRY DEAN, architect, educator, computer drafting consultant; b. Demopolis, Ala., Mar. 23, 1943; s. Leslie Ray and Cleo Leona (Trotter) M.; m. Constance Cloutier, Aug. 5, 1967; 1 child, Rachael Irene. BArch, Ga. Inst. Tech., 1972. Registered architect, Ga., Ohio. Apprentice architect Devel. Concepts, Atlanta, 1972-75; asst. architect Ga. Bd. Regents, Atlanta, 1975-79; architect Chas Barber & Assocs., Toledo, 1979-82, Bauer, Stark & Lashbrook, Toledo, 1982-85; instr. Owens Tech. Coll., Toledo, 1985—; cons. computers Toledo, 1985—. Columnist Depression Glass Daze, 1975—. Comr. Old West End Hist. Dist., Toledo, 1983-87. Served to sgt. USAF, 1964-68. Mem. AIA, Nat. Computer Graphics Assn., Phi Kappa Phi. Roman Catholic. Club: Glass Collectors. Avocations: collecting glass, China and Pottery. Home: 2320 Scottwood Ave Toledo OH 43620 Office: Michael J Owens Tech Coll Caller # 10000 Oregon Rd Toledo OH 43699

MONCHER, DANIEL JOSEPH, hospital executive, accountant; b. Detroit, Nov. 3, 1960; s. James Charles and Elizabeth Ann (Smilnak) M.; m. Mary Kathryn Kasten, June 2, 1984; 1 child, Nicholas Daniel. BS in Bus., Miami U., Oxford, Ohio, 1982. CPA, Ohio. Mgr. audit staff Ernst & Whinney, Toledo, 1982-86; dir. fin. Mercy Hosp., Toledo, 1986—. Mem. Am. Inst. CPA's, Ohio Soc. CPA's, Healthcare Fin. Mgmt. Assn., Evans Scholars Found. (par club, 1982—). Roman Catholic. Avocations: officiating high sch. basketball, golf, softball. Office: Mercy Hosp 2200 Jefferson Ave Toledo OH 43624

MONDABAUGH, SUSAN MAY, immunochemist; b. Glen Ridge, N.J., June 20, 1951; d. Robert Dale and Charlotte Hazel (Rowe) M.; m. David J. Uhlik, July 26, 1986. BA, Montclair State Coll., 1972; MS, NYU, 1979, PhD, 1982. Asst. scientist I Roche Diagnostics, Nutley, N.J., 1973-76, asst. scientist II, 1977-78, assoc. scientist, 1979-81, sr. scientist, 1982-83; sect. leader Ventrex Labs., Portland, Maine, 1983-84, mgr., 1985; team leader Marion Labs., Kansas City, Mo., 1985—. Inventor immunoassay method. Mem. Am. Soc. Microbiology, Am. Assn. Clin. Chemistry, N.Y. Acad. Scis. (affiliate), Sigma Xi. Democrat. Presbyterian. Avocations: tennis, bicycling, music. Office: Marion Labs PO Box 9627 Kansas City MO 64134

MONDER, STEVEN I., orchestra executive. Gen. mgr. Cin. Symphony Orchestra. Office: Cin Symphony Orchestra 1241 Elm St Cincinnati OH 45210 *

MONDRY, DAVID, retail company executive. Chmn. Highland Superstores, Inc., Taylor, Mich. Office: Highland Superstores Inc 21405 Trolley Dr Taylor MI 48180 *

MONDRY, EUGENE, retail executive. Pres. Highland Superstores, Inc., Taylor, Mich. Office: Highland Superstores Inc 21405 Trolley Dr Taylor MI 48180 *

MONDUL, DONALD DAVID, lawyer; b. Miami, Fla., Aug. 24, 1945; s. David Donald and Marian Wright (Heck) M.; m. Sharon Lynn Schramm, Apr. 25, 1971; children: Alison Marian, Ashley Megan. BS, U.S. Naval Acad., 1967; MBA, Roosevelt U., 1976; JD, John Marshall Law Sch., 1979. Bar: Ill. 1979, Fla. 1980, U.S. Patent Ct. 1980. Mktg. rep. Control Data Corp., Chgo., 1977-79; patent atty. Square D Co., Palatine, Ill., 1979-81, Ill. Tool Works, Chgo., 1981-87, Cook, Wetzel & Egan, Ltd., Chgo., 1987—; mem. adj. faculty W.R. Harper Coll., Palatine, Ill., 1979-83, Roosevelt U., Chgo., 1979-80. Served to lt. comdr. USN, 1967-77. Mem. ABA, Ill. Bar Assn., Fla. Bar, Chgo. Bar Assn., Patent Law Assn. Chgo. Presbyterian. Office: Cook Wetzel & Egan Ltd 135 S LaSalle St Suite 3300 Chicago IL 60603

MONEY, ROBERT GENE, dentist; b. Omaha, Oct. 26, 1950; s. George Clyde and Lois Jean (Mayhew) M.; m. Loraine Kay Black, June 3, 1970; children: Carol Jean, Daniel Leland. BS in Biology, U. Nebr., Omaha, 1979; DDS, U. Nebr., Lincoln/Omaha, 1983. Lic. dentist, Nebr. Dentist Franklin (Nebr.) Dental Clinic, 1983—. Deacon 1st Presbyn. Ch., Lincoln, 1981-83. Mem. ADA, Nebr. Dental Assn., Southwest Dist. Nebr. Dental Soc., Adams County Dental Soc. (sec.-treas. 1985—), Acad. Gen. Dentistry, Am. Soc. Dentistry for Children, Franklin C. of C. Republican. Lodge: Rotary (Franklin) (pres. 1986—). Avocations: reading, boating, fishing, woodworking. Home: Rural Rt 1 PO Box 305 Franklin NE 68939 Office: Franklin Dental Clinic 121 15th Ave PO Box 305 Franklin NE 68939

MONFILS, MARK JONATHAN, chemical executive; b. Madison, Wis., Oct. 13, 1949; s. Owen and Katharine Elizabeth (Westphal) M. BA, U. Minn., 1972. Sr. technician Twin City Testing Labs, St. Paul, 1976-79; tech. service rep. Rexnord Chem. Products, Mpls., 1979—. Author: (plays) 10th X-mas in South St. Paul, 1984, Santa's Workshop, 1985. artistic director various theatres, Mpls.-St. Paul, 1970—. Avocations: science fiction, collecting comic books. Office: Rexnord Chemical Products 7711 Computer Ave Minneapolis MN 55435

MONIF, GILLES R.G., physician; b. N.Y.C., May 7, 1936; s. Hassan Khan Monif and Henriette (Joseph) McQuade; m. Beatrice Laurence de la Peine, Sept. 5, 1967; children: Rex, William, Celine, Ashley. AB, Swarthmore Coll., 1957; MD cum laude, Boston U., 1961. Resident in internal medicine Bellevue Hosp., N.Y.C., 1961-63; research assoc. NIH, Bethesda, Md., 1963-65; resident in pathology NYU Sch. Medicine, 1965-68; asst. prof. ob-gyn U. Fla. Coll. of Medicine, Gainesville, 1968-71, assoc. prof. ob-gyn, 1971-84; prof. ob-gyn Creighton U. Sch. Medicine, Omaha, 1984—. Author 7 books, numerous articles on infectious diseases to profl. jours. Served with USPHS, 1963-65. Democrat. Office: Creighton U Sch Medicine Dept Ob-Gyn 601 N 30th St Omaha NE 68131

MONK, JAMES RUSSELL, lawyer, state senator; b. Sullivan, Ind., Oct. 5, 1947; s. Lyman Elihu and Charlotte May (Ellingsworth) M.; m. Sarah Jane Stewart, June 11, 1966; children—James Stewart, John Robert (dec.), Daniel Joshua. Student, Ind. State U., 1965-66; A.B., Ind. U., 1969; postgrad. U. Miami, 1974-75; J.D., U. Fla., 1977. Bar: Ind. 1978. Tchr. Plantation (Fla.) High Sch., 1969-71; tchr. South Plantation High Sch., 1971-76, dir. student activities, 1971-76; sole practice, Sullivan, 1978—; prosecutor Sullivan County, 1979-82, county atty., 1979-81; mem. Ind. State Senate, 1982—. Recipient Outstanding Freshman Legislator award Ind. Assn. Broadcasters, 1983, Legislator of Yr. award United Mine Workers Am., 1986. Mem. ABA, Ind. Bar Assn., Sullivan County Bar Assn. Democrat. Roman Catholic. Lodges: Kiwanis (past pres.), Elks, K.C. (Sullivan). Home: Rural Rt 1 Box 22 Sullivan IN 47882 Office: 110 S Main St Sullivan IN 47882 Office: 26 N 4th St Vincennes IN 47591

MONNIN, A. M., judge. Chief justice Ct. Appeal, Manitba, Can. Office: Court of Appeal, Law Courts Bldg, Winnipeg, MB Canada R3C OV8 *

MONSELL, ELIZABETH GAY, insurance company executive; b. Portland, Oreg., Oct. 19, 1955; d. Walter T. and Geraldine G. Davol; m. Craig C. Monsell, May 28, 1977. BA, Wellesley Coll., 1977; MBA, Cornell U., 1981. CPA, Ohio. Sr. acct. Price Waterhouse, San Francisco, 1981-83, Cin., 1983-85; asst. controller Union Cen. Life Ins. Co., Cin., 1985—; controller Manhattan Nat. Corp. subs. Union Cen. Life Ins. Co., Cin., 1987—. Mem. fin. com. St. Paul United Meth. Ch., Cin., 1986—. Mem. Am. Inst. CPA's, Ohio Soc. CPA's. Republican. Clubs: Wellesley, Cornell (Cin.). Office: Union Cen Life Ins Co PO Box 179 Cincinnati OH 45201

MONSON, CAROL LYNN, osteopathic physician, psychotherapist; b. Blue Island, Ill., Nov. 3, 1946; d. Marcus Edward and Margaret Bertha (Andres) M.; m. Frank E. Warden, Feb. 28, 1981. B.S., No. Ill. U., 1968, M.S., 1969; D.O., Mich State Coll. Osteo. Medicine, 1979. Lic. physician, Mich., diplomate Am. Bd. Osteo. Gen. Practitioners, Am. Bd. Osteo. Gen. Practice. Expeditor-psychotherapist H. Douglas Singer Zone Ctr., Rockford, Ill., 1969-71; psychotherapist Tri-County Mental Health, St. Johns, Mich., 1971-76; pvt. practice psychotherapy, East Lansing, Mich., 1976-80; intern Lansing Gen. Hosp., Mich., 1979-80; pvt. practice osteo. medicine, Lansing, 1980—; mem. staff Ingham Med. Hosp., Lansing Gen. Hosp.; field instr. Sch. Social Work, U. Mich., 1973-76; clin. instr. Central Mich. Dept. Psychology, 1974-75; clin. prof. Mich. State U., 1980—; mem. adv. bd. Substance Abuse Clearinghouse, Lansing, 1983-85, Kelly Health Care, Lansing, 1983-85, Americor Health Services, Lansing, 1984—. Mem. Am. Osteo Assn., Internat. Transactional Analysis Assn., Mich. Assn. Physicians and Surgeons, Ingham County Osteo. Assn., Nat. Assn. Career Women (conv. com. 1984—), Lansing Assn. Career Women. Lodge: Zonta (chmn. service com. Mid Mich. Capital Area chpt.). Avocations: gardening; orchid growing; antique collecting. Office: 3320 W Saginaw St Lansing MI 48917

MONSON, DIANNE LYNN, educator, academic administrator; b. Minot, N.D., Nov. 24, 1934; d. Albert Rachie and Iona Cordelia (Kirk) M. B.S., U. Minn., 1956, M.A., 1962, Ph.D., 1966. Tchr., Rochester Pub. Schs. (Minn.), 1966-59, U.S. Dept. Def., Schweinfurt, W.Ger., 1959-61, St. Louis Park Schs. (Minn.), 1961-62; instr. U. Minn., Mpls., 1962-66; prof. U. Wash., Seattle, 1966-82; prof. English edn. U. Minn., Mpls., 1982—, chmn. Curriculum and Instrn., 1986—. Co-author: New Horizons in the Language Arts, 1972; Children and Books, 6th edit., 1981; Experiencing Children's Literature, 1984; (monograph) Research in Children's Literature, 1976. Recipient Outstanding Educator award U. Minn. Alumni Assn., 1983. Fellow Nat. Conf. Research in English; mem. Nat. Council Tchrs. of English (exec. com. 1979-81), Internat. Reading Assn. (dir. 1980-83), ALA. Lutheran. Home: 740 River Dr Saint Paul MN 55116 Office: U Minn 145 Peik Hall Minneapolis MN 55455

MONSON, TERRY DEAN, economist, educator; b. Petoskey, Mich., Oct. 9, 1945; s. Andy Paul and Alie Marie (Heikkila) M.; m. Judith A. Sannes, Aug. 23, 1969 (dec. July 1982); m. Paula K. Jacobs, Aug. 6, 1983 (div. Feb. 1986). BA, Oakland U., 1966, MA, 1968; PhD, U. Minn., 1972. Research scientist U. Mich., Ann Arbor, 1972-75; asst. prof. Ill. State U., Normal, 1975-77; assoc. prof. Mich. Tech. U., Houghton, 1977-80, prof. econs., 1981—; cons. World Bank, Washington, 1975, 78, 81, 86, State of Mich., 1978-82. Co-editor: Trade and Employment in Developing Countries, 1981; contbr. articles to profl. jours. Mem. Am. Econ. Assn., Midwest Econ. Assn., Am. Inst. Mining Engrs., Assn. Environ. and Research Economists. Presbyterian. Home: 17 Woodland Houghton MI 49931 Office: Mich Tech U Sch Bus Houghton MI 49931

MONTAGUE, PAUL RICHARD, ophthalmology researcher; b. Santa Monica, Calif., Mar. 18, 1947; s. William Robert Montague and Vivian (Abernathy) Childers; m. Paulette Marie Saucier, Aug. 5, 1968; children: Kimberly Anne, Kelly Jo. Student, Santa Monica Coll., 1965-68, U. Iowa, 1980-81. Cert. retinal angiographer. Lab supr. Photo Art Studios, Portland, Oreg., 1969-74; ophthalmic photographer Good Samaritan Hosp., Portland, 1975-76; sr. research asst. U. Iowa, Iowa City, 1976—; dir. COMS Photo Reading Ctr., Iowa City, 1986—. Author Iowa Data Retrieval Systems, 1979. V.P. Cedar Rapids Barton, Inc., Iowa City, 1985-86. Served with U.S. Army, 1968. Mem. IEEE (computer soc.), Ophthalmic Photographers Soc. (treas. 1979-84, pres. 1984—, first place Gross Specimen award 1984), Biological Photographic Assn. Republican. Avocations: restoration of theatre pipe organs. Home: Rural Rt 1 Box 234 Swisher IA 52338 Office: U Iowa Hosps Dept Ophthalmology Iowa City IA 52242

MONTAGUE, THEODORE GILES, JR., small business owner; b. Madison, Wis., Aug. 9, 1925; s. Theodore Giles and Grace Louise (Maxcy) M.; m. Cynthia Comly, Dec. 29, 1950; children: Theodore G. III, Cynthia C. Parziale, Carrie C., Samuel C. BS in Mil. Art and Engring., U.S. Mil. Acad., West Point, N.Y., 1946. Enlisted U.S. Army, 1943, commd. 2d lt., 1946, resigned, 1949; with mgmt. Drake Bakeries, Wayne, N.J., 1951-56, v.p. sales, 1956-58, exec. v.p., 1958-60, pres., chief exec. officer, 1960-68; pres. Borden Foods div. Borden Inc., N.Y.C., 1969-72; pres. new ventures, v.p. Borden Inc., 1969-73; pres., owner Peerless Saw Co., Groveport, Ohio, 1974-85; cons. Montague Assocs., Columbus, Ohio, 1986—. Home and Office: 50 W Broad St Suite 1016 Columbus OH 43125

MONTAVON, LENORA L., medical therapy specialist; b. Portsmouth, Ohio, July 21, 1950; d. Harold George and Elsie Mae (Hodge) M. BE, Ohio U., 1973; MA, Kent (Ohio) State U., 1978. Lic. in theraputic massage, Ohio. Tchr. Newark (Ohio) Pub. Schs., 1973-83, coach volleyball, basketball, track, 1974-82, head coach varsity volleyball, 1981-82; pvt. practice med. massage therapy Columbus, Ohio, 1983—; tchr. Cen. Ohio Sch. Massage, Columbus, 1983—; athletic trainer Denison U., Granville, Ohio, 1978-82. Am. Message Therapy Assn. (2d v.p. Ohio chpt. 1985—). Avocation: tennis, volleyball, camping, jogging, karate. Home: 5696 Beechcraft Rd H Columbus OH 43229 Office: 509 S Otterbein Ave Westerville OH 43081

MONTEIRO, MANUEL JAMES, manufacturing company executive; b. New Bedford, Mass., 1926; s. Joao and Beatrice (Oliveira) M.; m. Madelyn Wilcox, Dec. 15, 1946; children: Warren James, Mark Alan, Marguerite Ann Monteiro Cavett, Marilyn Jean Monteiro Allen, John Manuel, James Robert, Robert William. BS in Acctg. and Fin., Bryant Coll. With 3M Co., 1950—, cost analyst tape lab., St. Paul, 1950-54, various internat. positions in Colombia, Brazil, 1954-65, mng. dir. 3M Brazil, 1965-71, area dir. Latin Am., 1971-73, div. v.p. Latin Am. and Africa, 1973-75, v.p. European ops., 1975-81, exec. v.p. internat. ops., 1981—; bd. dirs., St. Paul, 1986—. Served with U.S. Army, 1945-46. Recipient Disting. Alumni award Bryant Coll. Presbyterian. Office: 3M 3M Ctr Saint Paul MN 55144-1000

MONTGOMERY, BARBARA ANN BURKE, business consultant; b. Greenville, S.C., May 7, 1940; d. Rufus and Lydia Mae (Brockman) Burke; children: Charlene Cullens, Darryl Keith. AS in Bus., Wayne County Community Coll., AS in Psychology. Exec. sec. in bank, Detroit, 1967; sec., dictaphone operator Dept. Social Services, Detroit, 1967-70; supr. Sec. of State's Office, Detroit, 1970-72; social worker Wayne County Dept. Social Services, Detroit, 1972-80; bus. cons., Oak Park, Mich., 1980—; owner Barbara's Select Botique, Detroit. Author, editor poetry books: A Growing Woman, 1984, Religious Poems, 1985. Community activist, Detroit, 1975-77; mem. Com. for Barbara Rose Collins, Detroit, 1981-83; pres. Mix & Match, Oak Park, Mich., 1983—; community liaison March of Dimes, 1986, bd. dirs., 1987—. Recipient cert. Mich. Metaphys. Soc., 1978. Mem. NAACP, Black Women's Entrepreneurs, Nat. Assn. Female Execs. Democrat. Methodist. Avocations: reading, writing, travel, sports. Home: 24281 Morton Oak Park MI 48237 Office: 18946 W McNichols Detroit MI 48219

MONTGOMERY, BETTY BROYLES, social service administrator; b. Cin.; d. Homer D. Broyles; m. Donald J. Montgomery, Dec. 1942 (div. July 1950); children: Dennis, Malcolm. BA, U. Cin., 1941, MA, 1944, postgrad in devel. psychology, 1950. Lic. psychologist, Ohio. Day care cons. Ohio Dept. Pub. Welfare, Columbus, 1953-66; regional dir. Head Start Tng. Ohio U., Athens, 1966-69; dir. Head Start Tng. U. Cin., 1969-71; coordinator Sr. Citizen Telephone Network Clifton Town Meeting, Cin., 1986—; vol. psychiat. emergency services Univ. Hosp., Cin., 1986; bd. dirs. Cin. Alliance for Mentally Ill, 1986. Translator (book) Time Fourth Dimension of the Mind, 1968. Mem. Clifton Town Meeting, 1982—, Clifton Coalition on Aging, 1986—. U. Cin. scholar, 1943, 60. Mem. World Orgn. for Early Childhood Edn. (U.S. nat. com. of OMEP), Nat. Alliance for the Mentally Ill. Home: PO Box 20138 Cincinnati OH 45220

MONTGOMERY, CHARLES EDWARD, orthopaedic surgeon; b. Glenside, Pa., May 16, 1943; s. Charles Jr. and Dorothy (Elliott) M.; m. Marilyn Sue Megenhardt, June 27, 1965; children: Mindy Carol, Scott Charles. AB, Hanover Coll., 1965; MD, Ind. U., 1969. Resident in orthopaedics Luth. Hosp., Ft. Wayne, Ind., 1970-74; practice medicine specializing in orthopaedics Logansport, Ind., 1976—; bd. dirs. 1st Nat. Bank, Logansport. Served to maj. USAF, 1974-76. Fellow ACS, Am. Acad. Orthopaedic Surgeons; mem. Midwest Orthopaedic Assn., Logansport C. of C. (bd. dirs. 1980-84). Republican. Presbyterian. Lodge: Elks. Avocation: tennis. Home: 2409 Hastye Hyll Logansport IN 46947 Office: Orthopaedics of Logansport 1601 Chase Rd Logansport IN 46947

MONTGOMERY, CHARLES HOWARD, bank executive; b. Bloomington, Ill., Mar. 23, 1930; s. Dewey H. and Madeline (Wonderlin) M.; m. Diane Dickerson Cohen, Aug. 30, 1978; children: Alison, Douglas. A.B., Ill. Wesleyan U., 1951; M.S., U. Ill., 1960. C.P.A., Ill. Auditor Lybrand Ross Bros. & Montgomery, Rockford, Ill., 1955-59; with Abbott Labs., North Chicago, Ill., 1959-67; controller Abbott Labs., 1965-67; v.p. finance Anchor Coupling Co., Libertyville, 1967-69; v.p., comptroller First Nat. Bank Chgo., 1969-73, sr. v.p., 1973-75, exec. v.p., 1976—, comptroller, 1973—; comptroller 1st Chgo. Corp.; past chmn. Inter-Assn. Com. Bank Acctg. Served with AUS, 1952-53. Mem. Am. Bankers Assn. (past chmn. Task Force on Accounting), Fin. Execs. Inst., Am. Inst. C.P.A.s, Ill. Soc. C.P.A.s, Tau Kappa Epsilon, Phi Kappa Phi. Clubs: Mid-Day, University (Chgo.). Home: 5490 S Shore Dr Chicago IL 60615 Office: First Chgo Corp 1 First National Plaza Chicago IL 60670

MONTGOMERY, CHRISTOPHER, accountant; b. Hammond, Ind., Apr. 21, 1959; s. Carl Bernard and Elaine Ruth (Manuszak) M. BS in Acctg., Ind. U., 1981, postgrad., 1987—. CPA, Ind. Staff acct. Arthur Andersen, Indpls., 1980-83; sr. acct. Kimmerling, Myers & Co., Indpls., 1983-86, Blue & Co., CPA's, Indpls., 1986—. Advisor Reye's Syndrome Found., Anderson, Ind., 1981-87; participant Indpls./Scarborough Peace Games, 1984-86; liaison World Track Championships, Indpls., 1987; vol. PAXI/Pan Am. Games, Indpls., 1987; lector, coach St. Michael's Cath. Ch., Indpls., 1981-85. Mem. Am. Inst. CPA's, Ind. CPA Soc. (com. sec. 1986-87, speaker), Healthcare Fin. Mgmt. Assn. Democrat. Clubs: Indpls. Runners, Indpls. Ski. Avocations: marathon running, biathletics, coaching, small business projects. Home: 7441 Charrington Ct Indianapolis IN 46254

MONTGOMERY, DARLENE THELMA, religious organization administrator; b. Valley Falls, Kans., Oct. 27, 1929; d. Edgar and Arlouine (Collins) Moore; m. Sterling Montgomery, July 1, 1950 (dec. July 1976); children: Sterling Jr., Terri Lynne, Phillip, Michelle. BA, Washburn U., 1964; MSW, Kans. U., 1972. Lic. social worker, Kans. Social worker County Welfare Dept., Topeka, 1957-68, social work supr., 1968-73; instr. social work, dir. staff devel. State Dept. Social and Rehab. Services, Topeka, 1973-77, social services adminstr., 1977-86; adminstrv. asst. Susanna Wesley United Meth. Ch., Topeka, 1986—. Pres. County Community Resources Council, Topeka, 1983-84. Mem. Kans. Conf. Social Welfare (sec. fin. 1976-80, v.p. 1984-85), Mid Am. Congress on Aging, Delta Sigma Theta (pres. 1985-87), Kappa Mu Epsilon. Democrat. Methodist. Home: 5442 SW 12th Terr Topeka KS 66604 Office: Susanna Wesley United Meth Ch 7220 Asbury Dr Topeka KS 66614

MONTGOMERY, HENRY IRVING, financial planner; b. Decorah, Iowa, Dec. 18, 1924; s. Harry Biggs and Martha Grace (Wilkinson) M.; m. Barbara Louise Hook, Aug. 14, 1948; children—Barbara Ruth, Michael Henry, Kelly Ann, Andrew Stuart. Student U. Iowa, 1942-43, 47-48; B.B.A., Tulane U., 1952, postgrad., 1952; postgrad. U. Minn., 1976. Cert. fin. planner, Colo. Field agt. OSS, SSU, CIG, CIA, Central Europe, 1945-47; pres. Nehi Bottling Co., Decorah, Iowa, 1952-64; prin. Montgomery Assocs., Mktg. Cons., Trieste, Italy and Iowa, 1965-72; pres. Planners Fin. Services, Inc., Mpls., 1972—. Author: Race Toward Berlin, 1945. Served with U.S. Army, 1943-46; ETO. Mem. Inst. Cert. Fin. Planners (bd. dirs. 1977-82, pres. 1980-81, chmn. 1981-82, chmn. Nat. Fin. Products Standards Bd. 1984-87, Cert. Fin. Planner of Yr. 1984), Internat. Assn. Fin. Planning (internat. dir. 1976-81), Mpls. Estate Planning Council, Met. Tax Planning Group (pres. 1984-87), Twin City Fin. Planners (pres. 1976-78), Twin Cities Soc. of Inst. Cert. Fin. Planners, Am. Legion, Beta Gamma Sigma. Lodge: Elks (Decorah). Office: Planners Fin Services Inc 3500 W 80th St 670 Minneapolis MN 55431

MONTGOMERY, JACQUELINE DELORES, technical information executive; b. Selma, Ala., Aug. 31, 1944; d. Jerry David Sr. and Annie Willie (Spivey) M.; m. Claude Stanley Airall, July 29, 1967 (div. Aug. 1979). BS, Tuskegee U., 1963; MS, Purdue U., 1966; MLS, U. So. Calif., 1975; PhD, Fla. State U., Tallahassee, 1987. Biochemist Eli Lilly & Co., Indpls., 1966-69; bibliographer libraries Mich. State U., East Lansing, 1970-72; biochemist Smith, Kline, Beckman, Carlsbad, Calif., 1973-74; librarian Nat. Library Medicine, Bethesda, Md., 1975-76; groupleader Am. McGaw, Irvine, Calif., 1976-77; tech. info. mgr. Procter & Gamble, Cin., 1977—; cons. Arts Consortium, Cin., 1981. Recipient Black Achiever award YMCA Hamilton County, Cin., 1979. Mem. AAAS, Am. Cehm. Soc., Spl. Libraries Assn. (chmn. long-range planning com. 1985-86), Phi Kappa Phi. Avocations: fiber and textile arts and crafts, piano. Home: 677 Evangeline Rd Cincinnati OH 45240 Office: The Procter & Gamble Co 6300 Center Hill Rd Cincinnati OH 45224

MONTGOMERY, JAMES W., clergyman. Bishop, Episcopal Ch., Chgo. Office: Diocese of Chgo 65 E Huron St Chicago IL 60611 *

MONTGOMERY, JANICE SONDRA, school psychologist; b. Bristol, Eng.; d. James Alexander and Esme Joyce (Shattock) M.; m. Geoffrey Lathrop Bull, Oct. 22, 1977; children: David, Daniel. BS, East Tenn. State U., 1967, MA, 1969. Psychologist Bd. Edn., Wheeling, W.Va., 1969-71; psychologist, counselor Bristol (Va.) Mental Health, 1971-73; cons., educator S.W. Mental Health, Columbus, Ohio, 1973-77; sch. psychologist Scioto-Darby Schs., Hilliard, Ohio, 1978-79, Grandview Heights (Ohio) City Schs., 1979-83; dir. spl. edn. Athens (Ohio) City Schs., 1983—; pvt. practice Columbus, Ohio, 1979-83; presentor SEOVEC, Athens, 1985, Ohio Dept. Spl. Edn., Columbus, 1986; part-time tchr. East Tenn. State U., 1972-73, Harford Co. Md.; expert witness Scioto-Darby Schs., Hilliard, 1979. Author: (with Judy Beatty) The Onion Sandwich Principle, 1973. Orgn. Spl. Edn. Parent Group, Athens, 1984, Severe Behavior Handicapped Units, Athens, 1984—; mem. Gov.'s Task Force Dept. Edn., Columbus, 1985—; chmn. Athens County Task Force on Transition from Sch. to Work, 1985-87. Mem. Nat. Assn. Sch. Psychologists, Ohio Sch. Psychologist Assn. Avocations: writing poetry, composing songs, singing opera, singing. Home: 4 Lamar Dr Athens OH 45701 Office: Athens City Schs PO Box 788 Athens OH 45701

MONTGOMERY, MICHAEL BRUCE, maintenance executive, consultant; b. Frankfort, Ind., Dec. 11, 1946; s. Ralph Lee and Eileene (Johnson) M.; m. Valerie Lynn Cotner, Mar. 8, 1970; children: Erica, Kendra. Staff transp. dept. N & W Ry. Co., Roanoke, Va., 1965-73; tng. coordinator Purdue U., West Lafayette, Ind., 1973-76, foreman gen. structural, 1976-82, supt. maintenance, 1982—; cons. computer sci., West Lafayette, 1976—. Mem. facilities bd. Ind. 4-H Found., West Lafayette, 1984—; v.p. Klondike P.T.O., West Lafayette, 1986—. Served to maj. USAR, 1970—. Mem. Assn. Physical Plant Adminstrs., Lafayette Personal Computer Users Group (v.p. 1984—). Republican. Baptist. Lodge: Masons, Moose. Avocations: model railroading, prototype railroading, squash, swimming, personal computing. Home: 427 S Sharon Chapel Rd West Lafayette IN 47906 Office: Purdue U Service Bldg West Lafayette IN 47907

MONTGOMERY, ROBERT C., medical services company executive. Pres. Fargo (N.D.) Clinic, Ltd. Office: Fargo CLinic LTD 737 Broadway Fargo ND 58123 *

MONTGOMERY, THEODORE VAN TIFFLIN (TODD), JR., investment executive; b. Milw., July 4, 1943; s. Theodore Van Tifflin and Marjorie (Schwab) M.; m. Mary Lou Mock, June 19, 1965 (div. Aug. 1981); children—Elizabeth, Theodore III; m. Susan Jane Crume, Apr. 10, 1982; children—Kristin, David. A.B. in Polit. Sci., Miami U., Oxford, Ohio, 1965; M.S. in Edn., U. Wis.-Milw., 1974, Ph.D. in Urban Edn., 1984. Tchr., coach Univ. Sch. Milw., 1968-73; curriculum developer Edn. Devel. Ctr., Cambridge, Mass., 1972-73; cons. urban planning Community Devel. Agy., Milw., 1975-76; instr. urban planning U. Wis., Milw., 1976-79, adj. prof., 1983—, prof. cardinal stitch coll. investment and fin. planning, 1982—; exec. dir. Sci., Econs. and Tech. Ctr., Milw., 1978-79; v.p., officer Robert W. Baird & Co., Inc., Milw., 1979—; editor, writer, photographer Montgomery Media, Milw., 1984—. Editor, pub.; Now What Can I Do?, 1976; Now What Can I Do Now That I've Done That?, 1978. Exhibited photgraphy, Milw. and Chgo., 1970-78; photographer for Milw. Pub. Mus. internat. expdn. to Nepal, 1974. Mem. planning and allocations com. United Way Greater Milw., 1978—; mem. Friends of Mus., Milw., 1984—; mem. Internat. Inst. of Wis., mem. lakefront planning com. Milw. Civic Alliance, 1982—; bd. dirs. Wis. Olympic Ice Rink Operating Corp., Milw., 1982—, pres., 1982-84, Friends Internat. Inst. Wis. Served as lt. USNR, 1965-68, Vietnam. Mem. Nepal Studies Assn., U.S. Navy League, U. Wis.-Milw. Sch. Edn. Alumni Assn. (editorial adv. bd. Met. Edn. jour. 1985—). Club: Gyro Internat. (Milw.) (pres. 1985-86). Avocations: stamps; carpentry; gardening; photography. Office: Robert W Baird & Co Inc 777 E Wisconsin Ave Milwaukee WI 53202

MONTOYA, MARY LOUISE, accountant; b. Jefferson Barracks, Mo., Dec. 26, 1941; d. Fred E. and Viola M. (Friedrich) Larson; m. Thomas P. Montoya, Sept. 2, 1961 (div. July 1977); children: Thomas P. Jr., Teresa M.; m. Leonard H. Johnson, Dec. 31, 1983. BS, Creighton U., 1962. CPA, S.D. Ptnr. Klanderud, Montoya, Sioux Falls, S.D., 1976-85, Klanderud, Montoya, Wuebben & Feehan, P.C., Sioux Falls, 1985—. Author: (with others) Support Group Manual, 1978; editor : (with others) Young Adult Beginning Experience Manuel, 1983. Co-leader Young Adult Beginning Experience, Eastern S.D., 1986; mem. Sioux Falls Estate Planning Council, 1978—, pres., 1982. Mem. S.D. Soc. CPA's, Mensa (sec. local chpt. 1986—). Republican. Roman Catholic. Club: Sandollars Investment (treas. 1987—) (Sioux Falls). Avocations: travel, reading. Office: Klanderud Montoya Wuebben & Feehan PC 822 E 41st Sioux Falls SD 57105

MONTZ, DWIGHT HAYES, bank executive; b. Monroe, Mich., May 27, 1922; s. Charles and Mary Ethel (Plewes) M.; m. Helen Ada Cronenwett, June 12, 1947; 1 child, Kim I. Montz Diven. BA, Dartmouth Coll., 1946; MBA, U. Toledo, 1965. CPA, Mich. Credit mgr. Monroe Co-Op Oil Co., 1949-55; estimator Consolidated Paper Co., Monroe, 1955-57; acctg. supr. Union-Camp Corp., Monroe, 1957-65; ptnr. Richwine, Newton & Carlton, Monroe, 1965-69; v.p., controller Security Bank Monroe, 1969-77, sr. v.p., cashier, 1977—. Pres. adv. bd. Salvation Army, Monroe, 1977-78; fin. sec. Monroe YMCA, 1979; v.p., bd. dirs. Roselawn Meml. Park, 1980-87; pres. Monroe Council Chs., 1960. Served with USN, 1942-46. Mem. Am. Inst. CPA's, Mich. Assn. CPA's, Bank Adminstrn. Inst. (treas. 1970-71, v.p. 1971-72, pres. 1972-73). Republican. Methodist. Lodge: Kiwanis (treas. North Monroe club 1955-57, sec. Monroe club 1968-70). Home: 5811 Elmwood Dr Monroe MI 48161

MONYAK, WENDELL PETER, pharmacist; b. Chgo., Sept. 14, 1931; s. Wendell and Mary Elizabeth M.; m. Lorraine Mostek, Aug. 29, 1964. BS in Chemistry, Roosevelt U., 1957; BS in Pharmacy, St. Louis Coll. Pharmacy, 1961. Asst. chief pharmacist Little Co. of Mary Hosp., Chgo., 1961-66; chief pharmacist MacNeal Meml. Hosp., Berwyn, Ill., 1966-72; dir. pharmacy Ill. Masonic Med. Ctr., Chgo., 1972, dir. pharm. services, 1972—; teaching assoc. U. Ill., 1972-87. Author: Hospital Formulary and Therapeutic Guide for Residents and Interns, 1974, 3d edit. 1986. Pres., chmn. bd. dirs. Bohemian Home for Aged, 1986. Served with M.C., AUS, 1955-57. Mem. Am. Pharm. Assn., Am. Soc. Hosp. Pharmacists, Ill. Pharm. Assn. (Spl. Recignition award), No. Ill. Soc. Hosp. Pharmacists, Chgo. Hosp. Council. Club: Oakbrook Executive. Home: 19 W 059 Chateau N Oak Brook IL 60521 Office: 836 W Wellington St Chicago IL 60657

MONZON, CARLOS MANUEL, physician; b. Guatemala, C.A., Dec. 16, 1949; came to U.S., 1977; s. Carlos Manuel and Amparo (Letona) M.; m. Evelyn David, Sept. 26, 1975; children—Carlos Rodolfo, Juan Pablo. M.D., U. San Carlos, Guatemala, 1976. Diplomate Am. Bd. Pediatrics, Am. Bd. Pediatric Hematology and Oncology. Resident in pediatrics U. San Carlos, Guatemala, 1976-77, U. Mo.-Columbia, 1977-80; fellow in pediatric hematology and oncology Mayo Grad. Sch. Medicine, Rochester, Minn., 1980-82; instr. pediatrics U. Mo.-Columbia, 1982-83, asst. prof. child health, 1983—. Contbr. articles to med. jours. Recipient Fritz Kenny Meml. award in pediatric research, Midwest Soc. Pediatric Research, 1981. Fellow Am. Acad. Pediatrics. Home: 4038 Sonora Ct Columbia MO 65201 Office: U Mo Health Scis Ctr Dept Child Health 1 Hospital Dr Columbia MO 65201

MOODEY, JAMES R., bishop Episcopal Church; b. Bklyn., Dec. 9, 1932. BA, Hamilton Coll., Clinton, N.Y., 1954; grad., Episcopal Theol. Sch., 1957. Ordained priest Episcopal Ch., 1957. Asst. to rector Christ Ch., Cin., 1957-60; vicar Ch. of the Nativity, Newcastle, Del., 1960-65; rector St. Luke's Ch., Scranton, Pa., 1965-76, St. Paul's Ch., Phila., 1977-83; bishop coadjutor Trinity Cathedral, Cleve., 1983—. Office: Episc Ch 2230 Euclid Ave Cleveland OH 44115 *

MOODY, G. WILLIAM, aerospace manufacturing company executive; b. Cleveland Heights, Ohio, Nov. 6, 1928; s. John Walter and Anna Barbara (Keck) M.; m. Loisjean Kanouse, Sept. 17, 1955; children: Elizabeth Jean, Cynthia Ann, G. William. Student, Ohio U., 1948-49; B.S. in Civil Engring., Mich. State U., 1952; Advanced Mgmt. Program, Harvard Grad. Sch. Bus., 1982. Sales engr. Rich Mfg. Corp., Battle Creek, Mich., 1952-55; chief engr. Air Lift Co., Lansing, Mich., 1955-61; product engr. Aeroquip Corp., Jackson, Mich., 1961-62, chief engr. Barco div., 1962-68, v.p., gen. mgr., 1968-72, v.p., ops. mgr. AMB div., 1972-74, v.p., gen. mgr. aerospace div., 1974-81, group v.p. gen. products, 1981-85; pres. Aeroquip Corp., 1985—; dir. Nu-Matic Grinders Inc., Cleve., Aeroquip S.A.; sr. design engr. Clark Floor Machine Co. (Muskegon), Mich., 1962. Patentee in field. Gen. campaign chmn. Jackson County United Way, 1976, pres., 1980, bd. dirs., 1978-84; mem. Planning Commn. North Barrington, Ill., 1967-72; trustee, chmn. Foote Meml. Hosp., Jackson; chmn. Joint Com. for an Area Hosp., Barrington, 1969-72; trustee, chmn. Physicians Health Plan South Mich.; bd. dirs. United Way Mich., 1978-82. Served with U.S. Army, 1946-48. Mem. Soc. Automotive Engrs., ASME, Am. Polit. Items Coll. Soc., Am. Mgmt. Assn., Am. Philatelic Soc., Fluid Power Soc., Jackson C. of C., Psi Upsilon. Lutheran. Clubs: Town (dir.), Jackson Country, Jackson County Sportsman's. Home: 612 Bowen St Jackson MI 49203 Office: Aeroquip Corp 300 S East Ave Jackson MI 49203

MOODY, HOLMES GERALD, computer information scientist; b. La Grange, Ga., June 8, 1936; s. Holmes Glen and Irene (Johnson) M.; m. Frances Helen Roderick, July 9, 1958; Lisa Nicole Hammill, Brendan Stewart, Eric Alexander, Allison Elizabeth. BS in Indsl. Mgmt., Clemson U., 1963. Analyst U.S. Govt., Washington, 1963-69; asst. v.p. Marine Midland, Buffalo, 1969-76, Banc Ohio, Columbus, Ohio, 1976-81; cons. Battelle, Columbus, 1981—. Served with USNR. Mem. Assn. Computing Machinery (lectr. 1982—), Cen. Ohio Council for Office Automation, Cen. Ohio Fedn. of Info. Processing Socs. (pres. 1986). Home: 3118 Rock Fence Dr Columbus OH 43220 Office: Battelle 505 King Ave Columbus OH 43201

MOODY, JAMES T(YNE), federal judge; b. LaCenter, Ky., June 16, 1938; s. Harold B. and Dorothy M. (Simmons) M.; m. Kay A. Gillett, Dec. 26, 1960; children: Patrick, Jeffrey, Timothy, Kathleen. B.A., Ind. U., 1960, J.D., 1963. Bar: Ind. 1963, U.S. Dist. Ct. (no. and so. dists.) Ind. 1963, U.S. Supreme Ct. 1972. City atty. Cities of Hobart and Lake Station, Ind., 1963-73; sole practice Hobart, 1963-73; judge Lake County Superior Ct., Ind., 1973-79; magistrate U.S. Dist. for No. Dist. Ind., 1979-82; judge U.S. Dist. for No. Dist. Ind., Hammond, 1982—; mem. faculty bus. law Ind. U., 1977-80. Mem. ABA, Fed. Bar Assn., Ind. Bar Assn. Republican. Office: US Dist Ct 128 Fed Bldg 507 State St Hammond IN 46320 *

MOODY, JIM, congressman; b. Richlands, Va., Sept. 2, 1935. B.A., Haverford Coll., 1957; M.P.A., Harvard U., 1967; Ph.D. in Econs., U. Calif.-Berkeley, 1973. Served with CARE, Yugoslavia and Iran, 1958-60, Peace Corps, Bangladesh, Pakistan and Washington, 1961-64, AID, 1964-65, U.S. Dept. Transp., 1967, 69, World Bank, 1979; mem. 98th-100th Congresses from 5th Dist. Wis., 1983—. Mem. Wis. State Assembly, 1977-78; mem. Wis. State Senate, 1979-82. Democrat. Office: 1721 Longworth House Office Bldg Washington DC 20515

MOODY, ROY ALLEYNE, mechanical engineer; b. Harvey, Ill., June 15, 1926; s. Roy and Gertrude Alena (Butterfield) M.; m. Roberta Jean Ware, July 18, 1953; 1 child, Diane Linda. BSME, Rose-Hulman Inst., 1952. Registered profl. engr., Ill. Research engr. Acme Steel Corp., Riverdale, Ill., 1952-59; v.p. corp. product devel. Panduit Corp., Tinley Park, Ill., 1959—. Contbr. articles to Model Airplane News, 1971-81; patentee in field. Clubs: Chgo. Radio Car (pres. 1976, 79), Radio Operated Auto Racing (Atlanta) (pres. 1972-76). Home: 755 Ash St Flossmoor IL 60422 Office: Panduit Corp 17301 Ridgeland Ave Tinley Park IL 60477

MOON, DONG SOO, physician; b. Hamh, Rep. of Korea, Apr. 1, 1944; came to U.S., 1972; s. Suk Eun and Bok Soon (Joo) M.; m. Michelle O. Hong, Sept. 17, 1972; children: Michael, Sora, Edward. MD, Kyungbook Nat. U., 1968. Diplomate Am. Bd. Psychiatry and Neurology. Resident in psychiatry SUNY, Stonybrook, 1973-76; staff psychiatrist VA Hosp., Dayton, 1977-78, Good Samaritan Hosp., Dayton, 1979—; ptnr. Dayton Psychiat. Assocs., 1983-86; practice medine specializing in psychiatry Dayton, 1986—; asst. clin. prof. psychiatry Wright State U., Dayton, 1978—. Served to capt. Korean Army, 1968-72, Korea. Mem. Am. Psychiat. Assn., Ohio Psychiat. Assn. Office: New Perspectives Profl Counselling Ctr W 1st St Suite 1111 Dayton OH 45402

MOON, JANINE ANNETTE, telephone company executive; b. Toledo, Nov. 2, 1948; d. Menard R. and Edith E. (David) Mossing; 1 child, Lara Nicholle. B.Sc., Bowling Green State U., 1970; M.A., Ohio State U., 1977;Instr., Bishop Luers High Sch., Ft. Wayne, Ind., 1970-72; instr. Mt. Mercy Acad., Grand Rapids, Mich., 1973; instr., drama-sports dir. Forest Hills No. High Sch., Grand Rapids, 1973-76; instr. N. Central Tech. Coll., Mansfield, Ohio, 1976-79; program dir. Ohio Program in Humanities, YWCA, Mansfield, 1977-78; devel. edn. coordinator N. Central Tech. Coll., Mansfield, 1978-79; curriculum specialist United Telephone Co. of Ohio, Mansfield, 1979-81, tng. and devel. cons., 1981-84, gen. adminstrn. mgr., liaison to Pub. Utilities Commn., 1984—; seminar, workshop leader mgmt. devel. tng. communications and women's concerns cons. Bd. dirs. YWCA, Mansfield, 1976-80, pres., 1979-80; coordinator/organizer, chmn. task force for women's resource center, Mansfield, 1978-79. Mem. Am. Soc. for Tng. and Devel. (region 3 coordinator Women's Network, Profl. Devel. Leadership nat. award 1986), Am. Soc. Profl. Cons., Nat. Assn. Female Execs., AAUW, LWV, NOW, Ohio State U. Alumni Assn. Office: 665 Lexington Ave PO Box 3555 Mansfield OH 44907

MOON, ROBERT ALLEN, dentist; b. Atlantic, Iowa, May 1, 1933; s. Clarence Allen and Effie (Berry) M.;m. Janice Lilian Hahn, Sept. 5, 1954, (div. May 1972); children: Robert, Mark, David, Kevin, Jeff, Susan; m. Donna June Busse, Oct. 21, 1972. BS, Ind. U., 1955, DDS, 1958. Gen. practice dentistry, Hobart, Ind., 1961—; instr. Ind. U., 1975-80; asst. prof., dir. Ind. U. Northwest Dental Auxiliary Sch., 1986—. Bd. dirs. Lake County March of Dimes, 1971-72; mem. exec. bd. Ind. Bd. Health, 1984—. Served with USAF, 1958-61. Recipient Sagamore of Wabash award, 1981. Mem. ADA (del. 1979, 80), Am. Coll. Dentists, N.W. Dist. Dental Soc. (pres. 1968-69, editor newsletter), Ind. Dental Assn. (trustee 1970-75, dir. ann. session programs 1976, 77, 78, pres. 1980-81, Disting. Service award 1987), Internat. Coll. Dentists, Acad. Gen. Dentistry, Pierre Fauchard Acad.,

World Affairs Council N.W. Ind. (bd. dirs.), Phi Delta Kappa (pres. 1985), Delta Sigma Delta, Acacia. Methodist. Club: Rotary (pres. 1966-67). Home: 566 Harrison St Valparaiso IN 46383 Office: 904 W Ridge Rd Hobart IN 46342

MOONEY, ANDREW JAMES, business association executive; b. Evanston, Ill., Feb. 18, 1952; s. John and Anne (Meehan) M.; m. Kathleen M. Sloan, June 5, 1982. B.A. in Govt., U. Notre Dame, 1975; M.Div., U. Chgo., 1977. Dir., Office of Intergovtl. Affairs, Chgo., 1979-81; chmn., exec. dir. Chgo. Housing Authority, 1981-83; pres. Des Moines C. of C., 1983—; bd. dirs. U. Osteopathic Medicine and Health Scis. Danforth fellow. Mem. Phi Beta Kappa. Democrat. Clubs: Wakonda County, Des Moines. Avocations: flying, gardening, music. Office: Des Moines C of C 309 Court Ave Des Moines IA 50309

MOONEY, JOHN ALLEN, food company executive; b. Amery, Wis., May 17, 1918; s. Harry Edmon and Maybelle (Johnson) M.; m. Nettie O. Hayes, Aug. 29, 1940; children: John Allen, Suzann, Jean, Nancy. Student, U. Wis., River Falls. Salesman Reid Murdock & Co., Chgo., 1940-45, Consol. Foods Corp., Chgo., 1945-69; nat. sales mgr., v.p. M&R Sales Corp., Oak Park, Ill., 1969-78; pres., chief exec. officer, dir. M&R Sales Corp., 1978—; nat. sales mgr., v.p. Western Dressing, Inc., Oak Park, 1970-78; pres., chief exec. officer, dir. Western Dressing, Inc., 1978—; bd. dirs. 1st Nat. Bank LaGrange, Ill., Waunakee Alloy Casting Corp., Wis., G. Heileman Brewing Co., LaCrosse, Wis. Festmaster Oktoberfest U.S.A., LaCrosse, 1983; parade marshall Amery (Wis.) Fall Festival, 1962, River Falls (Wis.) Shrine Hosp. Benefit Football Parade, 1962; bd. govs. Shriners Hosp. Crippled Children, Mpls. and St. Paul, 1952-69, now emeritus bd. govs., Chgo., treas., 1983; chmn. Shrine Hosp. Day Shrine Hosp. Crippled Children, Chgo., 1982; assoc. bd. govs. LaGrange Meml. Hosp., 1967; trustee and pres. Gundersen Med. Found., LaCrosse, Wis.; mem. support com. Heritage Club, LaCrosse Lutheran Hosp., 1979; bd. govs. Nat. Fishing Hall of Fame, Hayward, Wis.; exec. bd. Gateway Area council, Boy Scouts Am.; mem. nat. election council Boy Scouts Am., nat. rep. LaCrosse chpt.; mem. corp. LaCrosse Luth. Hosp. Recipient Order of Arrow Boy Scouts Am., Pope John XXIII award, 1984, Community Leadership award LaCrosse Toastmasters, 1984; Named hon. mem. LaCrosse Boys Choir, 1977, Man of Yr. LaCrosse C. of C., 1983, hon. Ky. col.; Mooney Masonic Hall, Amery, established 1979. Mem. Sons of Norway, Rebild Nat. Parks Soc. (Aalborg, Denmark). Clubs: LaCrosse Plugs, LaCrosse Country, The LaCrosse Club. Lodges: Shriners (past potentate Zor Shrine Temple, Madison, Wis., hon. past potentate Medinah Temple, Chgo.), Elks, Moose. Office: 1515 N Harlem Ave Oak Park IL 60302

MOONEY, MICHAEL, food products company executive. Pres. Pizza Ventures, Inc., Wayzota, Minn. Office: Pizza Ventures Inc 900 E Wayzata Blvd Wayzata MN 55391 *

MOOR, DONALD R., office supply company executive; b. Cheyenne, Wyo., Dec. 30, 1939; s. Ross W. and Lois C. M.; m. Judy C. Chadwick, Apr. 6, 1963; children—Chad A., Kelly Jo, Jennifer L. Student Colo. State U., 1958-63. Mgr. Arabian horse farm, Rogers, Ark., 1963-64; mgr. feed mill, W.R. Grace Co., Ogallala, Nebr., 1964, rep. indsl. div., office mgr. indsl. div., adminstrv. asst. to dir. mktg. Walnut Grove Products Co., Atlantic, Iowa, 1965-69, div. mgr. for sales, St. Joseph, Mo., 1969-73; dist. mgr. Kemin Industries, Des Moines, 1973-82; pres. Midwest Office Supply, St. Jospeh, 1982—; farmer, breeder Australian shepherd dogs, Quarter horses, cattle. Recipient various sales awards Kemin Industries, 1973-82. Republican. Methodist. Avocations: rodeo; golf; fishing. Home: Route 1 Box 14 Easton MO 64443 Office: Midwest Office Supply 1501 S Belt Saint Joseph MO 64507

MOORE, BENJAMIN LUTHER, psychology, educator, consultant; b. Atlanta, Jan. 19, 1940; s. Donald L. and Carolyn C. (Carson) M.; m. Mary Evelyn Ratteree, June 8, 1963; children—Donald Todd, Kevin Carson. B.A., Emory U., 1961, M.Div., 1969; M.S., Fla. State U., 1971, Ph.D., 1973. Registered psychologist, Ill.; cert. sch. psychologist, Ill. Asst. prof. dept. psychology Ill. State U., Normal, 1973-80, assoc. prof., 1980—; clin. dir. The Baby Fold, Normal, 1976—; vis. assoc. prof. dept. psychology Ill. Wesleyan U., Bloomington, 1980; adviser Gov.'s Commn. on Children's and Adolescent's Mental Health and Devel. Disabilities, 1979-80. Served to lt. USAF, 1962-66. Decorated Air Force Commendation medal with oak leaf cluster. H.B. Trimble fellow, 1968-69; USPHS fellow, 1970-72. Mem. Am. Psychol. Assn., Ill. Psychol. Assn., Assn. Behavior Analysis, Southeastern Psychol. Assn., Omicron Delta Kappa, Theta Phi. Democrat. Methodist. Office: 108 E Willow St Normal IL 61761

MOORE, BYRON EUGENE, financial planner, securities dealer, insurance agent; b. Altamont, Mo., Aug. 14, 1940; s. William Oscar and Wanda Maree (Dean) M.; m. Lorene Ann Clark, Aug. 13, 1966; children: Devlon, Murray, Maia. BS, Kans. State U., 1962, PhD., 1973; MS, Kans. State Tchrs. Coll., Emporia, 1964; postgrad., Stanford U., 1966. Lic. securities dealer, life and health ins. agt., Kans. Tchr. physics, chemistry, math. high schs., White City, Conway Springs and McPherson, Kans., 1962-69; statis. cons. Junction City (kans.) Schs., 1970; consortium coordinator, dir. instl. research Cooperating Winfield (Kans.) Colls., 1972-79; registered rep. Waddell & Reed, Inc., Kansas City, Mo., 1980—; cons. Sterling (Kans.) Coll., 1979-80, ARCO Transp. Co., Independence, 1985. Chmn. bldg. and remodeling Ch. of the Brethren, Independence, 1982; coach Independence Soccer Club, 1983-84. Named one of Outstanding Young Men of Am., 1976; Shell Merit fellow, 1966. Mem. Internat. Assn. Fin. Planners. Democrat. Lodge: Rotary. Avocations: reading, tinkering, cards, running, basketball. Home: 315 S 5th St Independence KS 67301 Office: Waddell & Reed Fin Services 107 E Main #8 Independence KS 67301

MOORE, CAROL-LYNNE, editorial executive; b. Oklahoma City, Dec. 19, 1951; s. Robb Westbrook and Martha-Lynne (Carey) M.; m. Kaoru Yamamoto, Oct. 4, 1986. Student Stanford U., 1970-71; BFA in Dance, So. Meth. U., 1973; MC in Counseling, Ariz. State U., 1984. Cert. movement analyst, N.Y.C. Adminstr., instr. Laban Inst., N.Y.C., 1978-83; instr. Bklyn. Coll., 1978-81, Warren Lamb Assocs., London, 1981-82, Am. Dance Festival, Durham, N.C., summer 1982, U. Wash., Seattle, summer 1984, 87; editorial coordinator Kappa Delta Pi, West Lafayette, Ind., 1984—. Author: Executives in Action, 1982; Action Profiling, 1978; also book chpts. Editor: Action News, 1978-83. Founding mem. Laban Inst. Movement Studies. Ariz. State U. grad. tuition scholar, Tempe, 1983-84. Fellow Action Profilers Internat. (gen. council 1981—). Am. Assn. Laban Movement Analysts (founding mem., editor 1976-78), Am. Soc. Tng. and Devel. Democrat. Presbyterian. Office: Kappa Delta Phi PO Box A West Lafayette IN 47906

MOORE, CHARLES MONROE, psychologist, educator; b. Sparta, Wis., May 5, 1948; s. Harold J. and Charlotte (Lueck) M.; m. Mary E. Welch, Dec. 20, 1970; children: Jennifer C., Sarah M. BS, U. Wis., LaCrosse, 1970, MS, 1975; D in Psychology, Cen. Mich. U., 1982. Lic. psychologist, Wis. Psychiat. social worker Winnebago (Wis.) State Hosp., 1970-73; dir. pupil services Mauston (Wis.) sch. dist., 1975-79; asst. prof. U. Wis., LaCrosse, 1982—; cons. psychologist Sparta Clinic Ltd., 1982—, Social Security Disability Program, Madison, Wis., 1984—, LaCrosse Guidance Ctr., 1985—; cons. div. of Vocat. Rehab., LaCrosse, 1987—. Mem. Am. Psychol. Assn. (div. sch. psychology), Wis. Sch. Psychologist Assn., Nat. Assn. Sch. Psychologists. Avocations: woodworking, fishing, biking. Home: Rural Rt 5 9th Ct Sparta WI 54656 Office: U Wis Dept Psychology 341B Main Hall LaCrosse WI 54601

MOORE, CLIFFORD LEROY, pediatric psychologist; b. New Haven, June 7, 1945; s. Frederick Elvin and Helen Alberta (Morton) M. B.S., So. Conn. State Coll., 1967; M.S., U. Iowa, 1970, Ph.D., 1973; post-doctoral fellow med. ctr. div. clin. psychology U. Colo., 1974-75. Asst. prof. pediatrics and child psychiatry Albany (N.Y.) Med. Coll., 1973-74; asst. prof. dept. pediatrics, dept. child psychiatry So. Ill. U. Med. Sch., Springfield, 1975-78; vis. assoc. prof. clin. psychology Pa. State U., State College, 1979-80; dir. Pediatric Psychology and Family Psychology Ctr., Mpls., 1980—; cons. Office of Dean, Pa. State U., 1979-80. Bd. dirs. Minn. Early Learning Design, 1982—, Minn. Assn. Learning Disabilities, 1982—, Coalition of Permanence for Children, 1986—. Children's Bur. HEW fellow, 1968-70; Ford Found. dissertation fellow, 1972-73; U. Iowa scholar, 1972-73. Mem. Am. Psychol. Assn., Soc. Behavioral Medicine, Assn. Clin. Hypnosis, Minn. Psychol. Assn., Minn. Psychologists in Pvt. Practice (bd. dirs. 1982-84), Am. Assn. Mental Deficiency, Assn. Care Children in Hosps. Contbr. articles to profl. jours. Office: Pediatric and Family Psychology Ctr 309 Park Ave Med Bldg 710 E 24th St Minneapolis MN 55404 Office: 310 Unity Profl Bldg 500 NE Osborne Rd Fridley MN 55432 Office: 307 Time Med Bldg 355 Sherman St Saint Paul MN 55102

MOORE, CURTIS HARRY, college administrator; b. Faribault, Minn., Mar. 22, 1914; s. Curtis Henry and Anna (Schumacher) M.; m. Helen Grace Hines, Oct. 25, 1942; children—Julie Ann, Paul Steven, Richard Eugene. A.B., Cornell Coll., 1936; M.A., Northwestern U., 1938; Ed.D., Columbia U., 1954; D.H.L. (hon.), Rockford Coll., 1979. Coordinator men's programs, dir. adult edn., Rockford Coll., Ill., 1954-55, dean of men, 1954-59, dean evening coll. and summer sessions, 1956-79, adminstrn. liaison officer, 1979-85; mem. pre-retirement planning staff Action Ind. Maturity, Rockford, 1979—; discussion leader Retirement Planning Seminar, Rockford, 1974—. Bd. dirs. Blackhawk Area council Boy Scouts Am., 1975-84; pres. bd. Winnebago County Council on Aging, Rockford, 1980-87; chmn. Lynn Martin's Adv. Council on Aging, 1982—. Recipient Bronze Leadership award Jr. Achievement, 1980, Service award Phi Delta Kappa, 1980, Beaver award Blackhawk Area council Boy Scouts Am., 1981. Mem. Action for Ind. Maturity (cons. 1979—), Winnebago/Boone County Ret. Tchrs. Assn. (pres. bd. 1982—) Republican. Methodist. Lodge: Kiwanis (pres. 1967). Avocations: collecting owl figures; travel. Home: Wesley Willows Retirement Home 4042 Albright Ln Rockford IL 61103

MOORE, DAN TYLER, writer; b. Washington, Feb. 1, 1908; s. Dan T. and Luvean Jones (Butler) M.; m. Elizabeth Valley Oakes, Mar. 12, 1932; children: Luvean O. (Mrs. Owens), Elizabeth Oakes (Mrs. Thornton), Harriet (Mrs. Lester Ballard), Dan Tyler III. BS, Yale, 1931. Chief counter-intelligence OSS, Middle East, 1943-44; pres. Middle East Co., Cleve., 1946-48, China Co., Cleve., 1946-48; asst. to pres. Intercontinental Hotels Corp., Istanbul, Turkey, 1948-50; freelance writer Cleveland Heights, Ohio, 1950—. Author: The Terrible Game, 1957, Cloak and Cipher, 1962, Wolves, Widows and Orphans, 1966, Lecturing For Profit, 1967; contbr. articles and stories to popular mags. Pres. Greater Cleve. Muscular Dystrophy Assn., 1952-65; mem. exec. com. Cuyahoga County Dem. Party, 1951-70, mem. state exec. com., 1962-65; commr. Ohio Fed. Jury, 1961-68; trustee Cleve. Mus. Natural History, bd. dirs.; bd. dirs. Near East Coll. Assn., Karamu Theatre, Cleve. Served with AUS, 1942-44. Mem. Internat. Platform Assn. (chmn. bd., dir. gen.). Clubs: Met. (Washington, D.C.); Yale (N.Y.C.); Union, Tavern, Skating and Rowfant (Cleve.). Home: 2564 Berkshire Rd Cleveland Heights OH 44106

MOORE, DANIEL MICHAEL, electronics company executive; b. Tucson, Oct. 3, 1954; s. Daniel B. and Marilyn June (Denton) M.; m. Zella Katherine Fulton, Aug. 30, 1975 (div. Apr. 1986); children: Danielle Katherine, Daniel Zachary. AS, State Tech. Inst., 1976; BPS, Memphis State U., 1978; MS in Indsl. Engring., U. Mo., 1981. Process engr. Bendix Corp., Kansas City, Mo., 1978-80; indsl. engr. Chloride Batteries, Kansas City, Kans., 1980-81; sr. cons. Arthur Young & Co., Kansas City, Mo., 1981-83; program mgr. Northrop Wilcox, Kansas City, Mo., 1983—; instr. Met. Community Colls., Kansas City, Mo., 1983—; adj. prof. U. Mo., 1984—. Served to sgt. USMC, 1972-78. Mem. Armed Forces Communications and Electronics Assn. Republican. Mem. Christian Ch. Avocations: personal computing, motorcycling, weightlifting. Home: 14A Dundee Quarter Palatine IL 60074 Office: Northrop DSD 600 Hicks Rd Rolling Meadows IL 60008

MOORE, DAVID EUGENE, English educator; b. Bloomdale, Ohio, Jan. 4, 1938; s. Edward G. and Marie R. (Brown) M. B.S., Bowling Green State U., 1960; M.Ed., Ohio State U., 1962. Tchr., English, Risingsun (Ohio) High Sch., 1960-61, Fairmont West High Sch., Kettering, Ohio, 1964-66; instr. English, Sinclair Community Coll., Dayton, Ohio, 1963-64, 66-68; asst. prof. English/speech Monroe County Community Coll., Monroe, Mich., 1968—. Elected Instr. of Year, Monroe County Community Coll., 1971, 80; Nat. Endowment for Humanities Fund humanist S.E. Mich. Consortium on Gerontology and Humanities, 1973-75. Mem. NEA, Mich. Edn. Assn., Nat. Council Tchrs. English, Midwest MLA, Sigma Tau Delta. Methodist. Co-editor: Reflections-Collection of Monroe County Sr. Citizens, 1974-75. Home: 7578 Ida East Rd Ida MI 48140 Office: Dept English Monroe County Community Coll 1555 S Raisinville Monroe MI 48161

MOORE, DAVID JOSEPH, design engineer; b. Fostoria, Ohio, July 9, 1941; s. Paul David and Gladys Lucille (Bennett) M.; m. Jacqueline Kay Marshall, Nov. 23, 1963; children: Nicole Marie, Danielle Renee. Student, Ohio State U., 1959-61; Assoc. in Machine Design, Chgo. Tech. Coll., 1967. Designer Excello Corp., Fostoria, 1967-72; owner Sportsman Shop, Fostoria, 1972-79; process engr. United Aircraft Products, Forest, Ohio, 1979-81; design engr. Autolite div. Allied Automotive, Fostoria, 1981—. Co-inventor manufacture method of platinum tip spark plug, 1986. Bd. dirs. Fostoria Athletic Boosters, 1973-79. Mem. Soc. Mfg. Engrs., Machine Vision Internat., Fostoria Area C. of C. (dir. 1976-79). Republican. Methodist. Lodges: Lions (youth com. 1965-75), Elks (trustee 1974-79). Avocations: golf, boating, swimming, bowling. Office: Autolite div Allied Automotive 1600 N Union St Fostoria OH 44830

MOORE, DAVID MAX, internist; b. Decatur, Ill., Oct. 25, 1949; s. Max E. and Jean E. (Funk) M. BA, So. Ill. U., 1971; DO, Chgo. Coll. Osteo. Medicine, 1975. Diplomate Am. Bd. Internal Medicine. Resident in internal medicine Cook County Hosp., Chgo., 1975-78; ptnr. Assoc. Internists, Chgo., 1978-80; pvt. practice Chgo., 1980—; cons. Nat. Inst. Health Risk Project, 1985—; mem. Ill. State AIDS Adv. Council, 1985—; co-dir. AIDS Service, Ill. Masonic Med. Ctr., 1985—; clin. asst. prof. medicine U. Ill., Chgo., 1987—. Mem. Am. Coll. Physicians. Home: 2426 W Foster Ave Chicago IL 60625 Office: 1009 Wellington Ave Chicago IL 60657

MOORE, DEBRA MAY, respiratory therapy educator and curriculum developer; b. Newark, Ohio, Sept. 4, 1953; d. Walter Keith and Marian May (Stackhouse) M. BA, Ohio State U., 1978; MS, Ind. U., 1983. Cert. respiratory therapy technician, registered respiratory therapist. Mem. staff Presbyn. Hosp. Ctr., Albuquerque, 1976-77, Licking Meml. Hosp., Newark, 1972-75, 77-79; clin. coordinator Ind. Vocat. Tech. Coll., Bloomington, Ind., 1979-84, mem. adv. com., 1979-84; adv. com. Muskingham (Ohio) Area Vocat. Sch., 1977-79; grad. asst. Ind. U., 1985-86; consultation and field services specialist vocational edn. services Ind. U., 1986—. Mem. Am. Assn. Respiratory Therapy, Ind. Soc. Respiratory Therapy (bd. dirs. 1981-83, chmn. awards com. 1982-83), Am. Vocat. Assn., Ohio State Alumni Assn., Ind. Vocat. Assn., Council for Exceptional Children, Ind. U. Alumni Assn., Pi Lambda Theta, Eta Sigma Gamma. Republican. Methodist. Office: Indiana Univ VES 840 Room 111 State Rt 46 Bypass Bloomington IN 47405

MOORE, DENNIS EUGENE, educational association developer, fundraiser, and administrator; b. Detroit, Nov. 9, 1948; s. Gordon Eugene and Helen Mary (Arasin) M. BA, Albion (Mich.) Coll., 1970; MA, U. Mich., 1974, postgrad., 1974-75. Publicity officer Crucible Theatre, Sheffield, Eng., 1975-77; reporter, announcer WUPY-WQMT Radio, Marquette, Mich., 1977-78; campaign unit dir. United Found., Detroit, 1979-84; dir. devel. Greater Detroit C. of C., 1984-86; v.p. devel. Ctr. for Creative Studies Coll. Art and Design, Detroit, 1986—; program reviewer Mich. Council for the Arts, Detroit, 1986—; rep. Bus. Consortium for the Arts, Detroit, 1986—; devel. com. mem. Alliance Ind. Colls. Art, Washington, 1986—. Speaker for Bur. of United Found., Detroit, 1984—; mem. Founder's Soc., Detroit Inst. Arts, 1984—, Arts Com., New Detroit, Inc. Served with M.I. Corps, U.S. Army, 1970-72, Vietnam. Ralph A. MacMullen grantee Assn. Execs. Met. Detroit, 1985. Mem. Council for the Advancement and Support of Edn., Assn. Ind. Colls. and Univs. of Mich. (alternate 1986—), Vietnam Vets. Am., VFW. Avocations: traveling, archeology, running, meditation, Tai Chi. Home: 507 W Lincoln Royal Oak MI 48067 Office: Ctr for Creative Studies Coll of Art and Design 245 E Kirby Detroit MI 48202

MOORE, DIANA SUE, medical technologist; b. Shelbyville, Ind., Jan. 28, 1958; d. Ralph Waldo and Carmelita (Essex) M. BS in Med. Tech., Purdue U., 1980; MBA, Ind. U., 1987. Med. technologist St. Francis Hosp. Ctr., Beech Grove, Ind., 1980; med. technologist in blood bank Community Hosps. Indpls., 1980—. Mem. Am. Soc. Clin. Pathologists, Ind. State Assn. Blood Banks.

MOORE, GARY LEE, programmer, analyst; b. Rockford, Ill., Dec. 31, 1955; s. John Edward Jr. and Mary Virginia (Leary) M.; m. Karla Jean Streit, Nov. 23, 1976; children: Katie, Megan, Sean. Student, Rock Valley Coll., 1976. Payroll clk. Greenlee Tool Co., Rockford, 1977, computer operator, 1977-80, programmer, 1980-85, analyst/programmer, 1985—. Democrat. Roman Catholic. Home: 9945 Blue Bonnet Dr Machesney Park IL 61111 Office: Greenlee Tool Co 4455 Boeing Dr Rockford IL 61109

MOORE, GERALD LOUIS, chemist; b. Bay City, Mich., July 1, 1946; s. Clarence Louis and Eloise Jeanette (Manyen) M.; m. Judy Kay Jaskiewicz, July 19, 1969; children: Catherine Marie, John Matthew. BS in Chemistry, Mich. State U., 1969; MS in Polymer Chemistry, U. Mass., 1974; MA in Bus. Mgmt., Cen. Mich. U., 1981. Research chemist Monsanto Co., Springfield, Mass., 1969-72; sr. research chemist Ford Motor Co., Mt. Clemens, Mich., 1972-86; staff chemist E.I. Dupont de Nemours, Mt. Clemens, 1986-87; group mgr. research devel. The Sherwin-Williams Co., Troy, Mich., 1987—. Mem. Am. Chem. Soc. Roman Catholic. Avocations: woodworking, landscape gardening, tennis, racquetball. Home: 4698 Whispering Pines Utica MI 48087 Office: The Sherwin-Williams Co 2697 Elliott St Troy MI 48083

MOORE, GERALD THOMAS, sales executive; b. Boston, Sept. 20, 1932; s. Henry A. and Ellen M. (Murphy) M.; m. June Geraldine Stott, Apr. 23, 1955; children: Michael, Kathleen, Brian, Colleen. BS in Bus., Boston Coll., 1960. Sales mgr. Am. Cyanamid, Boston, Mass., 1956-71; v.p. Pitcher & Co., Woburn, Mass., 1971-73; br. mgr. W.R. Grace Co., Chgo., 1968-73; v.p. sales Philips Industries, Malta, Ohio, 1973—. Served to sgt. U.S. Army, 1951-53. Recipient Presidents award Constrn. Specifications Inst., 1967. Mem. Nat. Assn. Home Bldrs. Home: 2935 Coldspring Rd Zanesville OH 43701 Office: PO Box 397 Malta OH 43758

MOORE, HELEN ELIZABETH, free lance reporter; b. Rush County, Ind., Dec. 19, 1920; d. John Brackenridge and Mary Amelia (Custer) Johnson; m. John William Sheridan, July 6, 1942 (dec. Jan. 1944); m. Harry Evan Moore, May 15, 1954; 1 child, William Randolph. BS, Ind. U., 1972, MS, 1973. Ofcl. ct. reporter 37th Jud. Cir., Brookville, Ind., 1950-60; freelance reporter Rushvile, Ind., 1960—; conv. reporter various assns. Served with USMC, 1943. Recipient Sagamore of the Wabash award Gov. Ind., 1984. Mem. Women Marines Assn. (charter, nat. pres. 1966-68), Am. Legion Aux. (various offices 1950—, pres. Ind. dept. 1966-67, conv. reporter), Bus. and Profl. Women (dist. dir., various offices 1967—), Nat. Shorthand Reporters Assn., (registered profl. reporter), Ind. Shorthand Reporters Assn. (state treas., edit. Hoosier Reporter, chmn. Legal directory), Ind. German Heritage Soc. (state bd. dirs. 1984-86, recording sec.). Democrat. Methodist. Avocations: reading, genealogy, knitting, crocheting, gardening. Home and Office: PO Box 206 Rushville IN 46173

MOORE, HELEN MARIE, private school director; b. Columbus, Ohio, Nov. 1, 1934; d. William Clyde and Alice Lucille (Flesher) Soulé; m. Riley P. Moore Sr., Mar. 26, 1955 (div. 1972); children: Kathleen, Laurie, Riley, Bill. BS, Ohio State U., 1972, MS, 1980, MS in Family Relations & Human Devel., 1983. Instr. Cen. Ohio Tech. Coll., Newark, 1975; dir. Montessori Community Sch., Newark, 1972—; early childhood specialist Licking County Infant Devel. Program, Newark, 1976-80; cons. Nat. Assn. for Pub. Continuing and Adult Edn., Washington, 1976, Pike county Child Devel. Headstart Program, Piketon, Ohio, 1977-80. Mem. adv. bd. Licking County Joint Vocat. Bd., 1977-79, child care class adv. bd., 1985-87; mem. Parents Educating Parents, Newark, 1980-81; mem. citizens adv. council LWV, 1976; trustee Mental Health Assn., Newark, 1985-87; mem. Pvt. Indsutry Council. Mem. Early Childhood Educators Assn. Licking County (officer), N.Am. Montessori Tchrs. Assn., Internat. Montessori Soc., Nat. Ctr. for Montessori Edn., Nat. Assn. for Edn. Young Children, Alpha Phi. Lodge: Soroptimist. Home: 243 Denison Dr Granville OH 43023 Office: Montessori Community Sch 621 Country Club Dr Newark OH 43055

MOORE, JACK FAY, labor union official; b. Springfield, Mo., Feb. 19, 1927; s. Elba Fay and Stella (Inmon) M.; m. Betty Lou Johnston, Dec. 29, 1950; children: Thomas Joseph, Deborah Moore Mills, Marilyn Faye Moore Simpson. Student, Drury Coll., 1959. Electrician Aton-Luce Electric Co., Springfield, 1946-58; bus. mgr. Local 453 Internat. Brotherhood Elec. Workers, Springfield, 1958-76, mem. exec. council, 1966-76, internat. v.p., 1976-85, internat. sec., 1985—, sec., trustee pension benefit fund, 1985—, sec., treas. com. on polit. action com. commn., 1985—; labor mem. Mo. Bd. Mediation, 1971-75; pres. Springfield Labor Council, 1958-76; mem. exec. bd. State Com. on Polit. Edn., 1964-76; sec. EWBA, 1985—; v.p. Pension Benefit Fund, Inc., 1985—; v.p. union label and services trades dept. AFL-CIO, 1985—, trustee mortgage investment trust, 1985—; sec., treas. Nat.-Internat. Union Com., 1985—; sec., trustee NECA Pension Benefit Trust Fund, 1985—; sec., trustee NECA Retirement Plan, 1985—. Mem. Springfield Park Bd., 1962-68, Springfield Airport Bd., 1982-85, Harriman's Community Ctr. Adv. Bd. Served with USNR, 1944-46, 50-51. Mem. Mo. Elec. Workers (pres. 1960-79). Democrat. Mem. Ch. of Christ. Office: 1125 15th St NW Washington DC 20005

MOORE, JACK LESLIE, investment manager; b. Aurora, Ill., July 3, 1947; s. Fred L. and Ethel (Gamage) M.; m. Kathleen Meyer, June 17, 1978; children: Leslie Kathleen, Ryan Douglas. BBA, U. Wis., 1969. CPA, CPCU, Ill. Acct. Arthur Andersen & Co., Chgo., 1969-81; cash, risk mgr. R.R. Donnelley & Sons, Chgo., 1981-85, investment mgr., 1985—. Served with U.S. Army, 1970-72. Mem. Am. Inst. CPA's, Ill. Soc. CPA's, Assn. CPCU's. Presbyterian. Office: RR Donnelley & Sons Co 2223 S King Dr Chicago IL 60616

MOORE, JAMES CHRISTOPHER, manufacturing consultant; b. St. Louis, Oct. 9, 1948; s. Joseph Harold and Alice Louise (Schulte) M.; m. Patricia Kay Jenkins, Jan. 11, 1980; 1 child, Jennifer Louise. BSBA, MBA, U. Mo., St. Louis, 1976; MA, Webster U., 1977. With shortage control div. May Co., St. Louis, 1977-78; project planning supr. Unidynamics Inc., St. Louis, Mo., 1980-81; sr. project planner Emerson Electric, St. Louis, 1978-85; mgr., cons. Ernst & Whinney, St. Louis, 1985—. Served with USN, 1968-74. Mem. Am. Prodn. and Inventory Control Soc., Am. Def. Preparedness Assn., Inst. Cost Analysis, U. Mo. Alumni Assn. Home: 3446 Bluff View Dr Saint Charles MO 63303 Office: Ernst & Whinney 701 Market St Saint Louis MO 63101

MOORE, JAMES DOUGLASS, military officer; b. Champaign, Ill., Dec. 2, 1945; s. Cyril Edgar and Helen Elizabeth (Skinner) M.; m. Nancy Jodelle Carifa, Apr. 26, 1975; children: Micaela Krista, James Travis, Anthony Joseph, Nicholas Sands. U.S. Army, Discharged, 1970; chmn. gen. ops. Ohio Dept. Taxation, Columbus, Ohio, 1972-81; commd. 2d lt. U.S. Army, Columbus, 1966; advanced through grades to lt. col. U.S. Army, 1984; exec. officer 2d spl. forces, 11th spl. forces group, airborne U.S. Army, Columbus, 1981-85; chief inf. br. USAR Personnel Ctr., St. Louis, 1985—. Decorated two Bronze Stars, three Air medals with V device. Mem. Res. Officers Assn. Democrat. Roman Catholic. Home: 1074 Del Ebro Dr Ballwin MO 63011 Office: USAR Personnel Ctr 9700 Page Blvd Saint Louis MO 63132

MOORE, JOAN ELIZABETH, human resources executive; b. Valleyfield, Que., Can., Apr. 29, 1951. Student, U. London, 1972; BS in Social Scis., Mich. State U., 1973; JD, Case Western Res. U., 1976. Bar: Ohio. With human resources Ford Motor Co., Dearborn, Mich., 1976-80; cons. James Lash & Co., Southfield, Mich., 1980-83; pres., owner The Arbor Cons. Group, Inc., Plymouth, Mich., 1983—; owner Integrated Personnel Systems Inc., 1987—. V.p., bd. dirs. Pvt. Industry Council, Wayne County, Mich., 1985-87; grad. Leadership Detroit VII, 1986, active alumni bd.; mem. computer subcom. Mich. Tech. Council, 1986—. Mem. ABA, Ohio Bar Assn., Women Lawyers Assn. Mich., Nat. Assn. Women Bus. Owners, Am. Soc. Personnel Adminstrn., Am. Soc. for Tng. and Devel. Office: PO Box 622 711 W Ann Arbor Trail Plymouth MI 48170

MOORE, JOHN BERRYMAN, engineer; b. Phila., July 18, 1940; s. Theodore McGinnes and Elizabeth (Kurtz) M.; m. Eleanor Mae Harter, July 9,

1966; 1 child, Anne B. BSE, Princeton U., 1962; MS in Engr., Lehigh U., 1967. Devel. engr. Western Electric, Allentown, Pa., 1962-68; v.p. mktg. Surcom Systems, York, Pa., 1969-70; mgr. engring. Galt Controls, York, 1970-72; control systems engr. Bethlehem (Pa.) Steel, 1972-85; mgr. Arvin/Diamond, Lancaster, Ohio, 1986; corp. engr. Worthington Industries, Columbus, Ohio, 1986—. Mem. Township Selection Coms., Bethlehem, 1980-81; chmn. Lower Saucon Water Authority, Bethlehem, 1981-85; bd. dirs. Bethlehem Housing Opportuntiy Council, 1983-85. Republican. Presbyterian. Avocations: fishing, camping, computer. Home: 597 Deer Run Rd Westerville OH 43081

MOORE, JOHN RONALD, manufacturing executive; b. Pueblo, Colo., July 12, 1935; s. John E. and Anna (Yesberger) M.; m. Judith Russelyn Bauman, Sept. 5, 1959; children: Leland, Roni, Timothy, Elaine. BS, U. Colo., 1959; grad. advanced mgmt. program, Harvard Grad. Sch. Bus., 1981. Mgmt. trainee Montgomery Ward & Co., Denver, 1960-65; distbn. mgr. Midas Internat. Corp., Chgo., 1965-71; v.p., gen. mgr. Midas, Can., Toronto, Ont., 1972-75; pres. Auto Group Midas Internat. Corp., Chgo., 1976-82, pres., chief exec. officer, 1982—, also bd. dirs.; bd. dirs. TI Midas Ltd., London, Midas Australia Pty. Ltd., Melbourne. Served with U.S. Army, 1953-55. Mem. Ill. Mfr.'s Assn., Motor Equipment Mfrs. Assn. (pres.'s council 1982—), Internat. Franchising Assn., Econ. Club of Chgo., Comml. Club Chgo., Harvard Bus. Sch. Alumni Assn., U. Colo. Alumni Assn. Republican. Office: Midas Internat Corp 225 N Michigan Ave Chicago IL 60601

MOORE, JOHN THOMAS, psychologist; b. Middletown, Ohio, July 3, 1950; s. Earl and Mary Francis (Quitt) M.; m. Donna Carolyn Kundtz, Aug. 28, 1971; children: Sarah Elizabeth, Rebecca Anne. BA, Miami U., Oxford, Ohio, 1973; MS, Va. Poly. Inst. and State U., 1975, PhD, 1980. Psychologist Southwestern State Hosp., Marion, Va., 1979-83, Grant Blackford Mental Health Ctr., Marion, Ind., 1983-85; pvt. practice psychology Radford, Va., 1983; psychologist Richmond (Ind.) State Hosp., 1985-86, chief psychologist, 1986—; cons. clin. psychologist Aurora Chem. Dependency Unit Reid Meml. Hosp., Richmond, 1986—. Mem. Am. Psychol. Assn., Ind. Psychol. Assn., Psychologists for Social Responsibility. Mem. Soc. of Friends. Home: 820 College Ave Richmond IN 47374 Office: Richmond State Hosp Richmond IN 47374

MOORE, KENNETH CAMERON, lawyer; b. Chgo., Oct. 25, 1947; s. Kenneth Edwards and Margaret Elizabeth (Cameron) M.; m. Karen M. Nelson, June 22, 1974; children—Roger Cameron, Kenneth Nelson. B.A. summa cum laude, Hiram Coll., 1969; J.D. cum laude, Harvard U., 1973. Bar: Ohio 1973, U.S. Dist. Ct. Md. 1974, U.S. Ct. Appeals (4th cir.) 1974, D.C. 1975, U.S. Dist. Ct. (no. dist.) Ohio 1976, U.S. Ct. Appeals (6th cir.) 1977, U.S. Ct. Appeals (D.C. cir.) 1979, U.S. Supreme Ct. 1980. Law clk. to judge U.S. Ct. Appeals, 4th Circuit, Balt., 1973-74; assoc. Squire, Sanders & Dempsey, Washington, 1974-75, Cleve., 1975-82, ptnr., 1982—. Chmn. Jimmy Carter Ohio Fin. Com., 1976; del. Democratic Nat. Conv., 1976; chief legal counsel Ohio Carter-Mondale Campaign, 1976; trustee, mem. com. Cleve. Council World Affairs. Served with AUS, 1970-76. Mem. ABA, Ohio Bar Assn., Greater Cleve. Bar Assn. Club: Cleve. City. Home: 15602 Edgewater Dr Lakewood OH 44107 Office: Squire Sanders & Dempsey 1800 Huntington Bldg Cleveland OH 44115

MOORE, LARRY JOE, bank executive; b. Muncie, Ind., June 7, 1945; s. William Ithemer and Mildred Lydia (Swander) M.; m. Shirley Kay Patterson, Aug. 14, 1966; 1 child, Gregg Allen. Student, Ball State U., 1963-66. Various positions Merchants Nat. Bank, Muncie, 1967-70, mgr. accounts, 1970-85, asst. v.p., mgr. consumer loan ops., 1985—. Youth leader Union Chapel Meth. Ch., Carlos, Ind., 1981-84, cert. lay pastor, 1985—; pres. Losantville (Ind.) Town Bd., 1983-85; co-treas. Rocket Booster Club, Modoc, Ind., 1984-85. Republican. Lodge: Lions (sec., treas. Losantville chpt. 1985-86). Avocations: camping, bowling, computers. Office: Merchants Nat Bank Box 792 Muncie IN 47305

MOORE, LAWRENCE PETER, wine merchant, consultant; b. Fresno, Calif., June 21, 1944; s. Lawrence C. and Kathryn (Kalish) M.; m. Judith Light, Sept. 16, 1967; children—Jennifer Rae, Andrew Lawrence. B.A., Mich. State U., 1968, postgrad., 1968-70. Adminstrv. asst. Mich. Senate, Lansing, 1969-72; area dir. Am. Cancer Soc., Lansing, 1973-77; wine merchant, owner The Blue Goat, Traverse City, Mich., 1977—; wine instr. Northwestern Mich. Coll., Traverse City, 1978—; wine cons. to various restaurants, Traverse City, 1982—. Contbr. articles in field to mags. Ambassador, Nat. Cherry Festival, Traverse City, 1982—. Served as airman 2nd USAF, 1962-64. Ford Found. fellow, 1968-69. Mem. Soc. Wine Educators, Am. Wine Soc., Les Amis Du Vin (afiliate dir. 1978—), Delta Phi Epsilon. Republican. Episcopalian. Home: 154 Homestead Ln Traverse City MI 49684 Office: Blue Goat Inc 875 E Front St Traverse City MI 49684

MOORE, LYNN, film producer, multi media communications specialist; b. East Chicago Heights, Ill., Sept. 13, 1957; d. Clyde J. Moore and Irene S. (Dalian) Moore Kojder; student Princeton U., 1977-78, So. Ill. U., 1973-74, BSBA, Loyola U., Chgo., 1981.; pres., chief exec. officer Moore Media Internat. Corp., Chgo., 1979—, exec. producer China Films Ltd., 1979—; mktg dir. planning and product line AT&T, 1977-79; mem. Entrepreneurship Forum, Lewis U., U. Ill.; producer, host radio and TV series, MONEYMAKER$; producer, Hair '88; speaker on entrepreneurship. Author: Entrepreneurial Quotient; contbr. editor various pubs. Sponsor trade mission to Rep. of China. Recipient Women's Congl. Caucus Entrepreneurship award, Exporter of Yr. Mem. Young Pres. World Leadership Conf., 1987. Am. Women in Radio and TV, Women in Mgmt., Oak Brook Assn. Commerce and Industry. Club: Oak Brook (Ill.) Polo. Home: 3804 N Washington St Westmont IL 60559

MOORE, LYNN ELDON, operations manager; b. Long Pine, Nebr., Dec. 27, 1933; s. Shelley T. and Minnie M. (West) M.; m. Lois Jean Doty, Oct. 25, 1953; children: Betty Jean, Jerry Lynn, Myron Neil. BSEE, U. Nebr., 1960, MSEE, 1970. Registered profl. engr., Nebr. Ops. mgr. Nebr. Pub. Power Dist., York, 1960—; com. mem. Doble Engring. Co., Watertown, Mass., 1965-80; pres. Nebr. Elec. Bd., Lincoln, Nebr., 1980-85. Contbr. articles to profl. jours. Active Boy Scouts Am.; co-chmn. United Fund Raising Campaign, Lincoln, 1969; mem. Nebr. cons. com., Milford, 1975—; chmn. bd. trustees Nazarene Ch., York, 1985. Mem. NSPE, Elec. and Electronic Engrs. (sr.), Power Engring Soc., Assn. Elec. Engrs. Republican. Club: Toastmasters. Lodges: Masons, Sertoma (pres. York 1984). Avocations: hunting, fishing, camping. Home: 25 Eastridge Dr N York NE 68467 Office: Nebr Pub Power Dist PO Box 608 York NE 68467

MOORE, MARK CLIFFORD, internist; b. Devil's Lake, N.D., Jan. 26, 1948; s. Lawrence Clifford and Susan Beatrice (Teichrow) M.; m. Nancy Jean Erickson, Aug. 15, 1970; children: John, James, Eric. BA, U. N.D., 1969; MD, U. Colo., 1973. Resident U. Minn., Mpls., 1973-76; practice medicine specializing in internal medicine Fargo (N.D.) Clinic, 1978—; med. dir. Occidental Med. Dept., Fargo, 1985—. Served with USPHS, 1976-78. Mem. Am. Coll. Physicians,. Avocations: scuba diving, downhill skiing, jogging, hunting. Home: 1307 Elm Circle NE Fargo ND 58102 Office: Fargo Clinic 737 Broadway Fargo ND 58123

MOORE, MARY KAY, health science facility executive; b. Benton, Ill., Nov. 28, 1956; d. Kenneth Emerson and Josephine (Ludwig) M.; m. Thomas Mark Corpora, July 12, 1986. BS in Speech Pathology, So. Ill. U., 1978, MS in Speech Pathology, 1980, MS in Rehab. Administrn., 1981. Sr. audiology supr.Clin. Ctr. So. Ill. U., Carbondale, Ill., 1979-80; asst. administr. Ctr. for Comprehensive Services, Carbondale, Ill., 1980-82, program coordinator, 1982-85, clin. dir., exec. v.p., 1985—; guest lectr. Rehab. Inst. So. Ill., Carbondale, 1981—; cons. to ins. industry, 1982—; presenter rehab. practices with head-injured at workshops, confs., 1984—. Contbg. editor Innovations In Head Injury Rehabilitation, 1987. Fundraiser Citizens for Paul Simon U.S. Senate, Carbondale, 1984; mem. steering com. task force Ill. Dept. Rehab., Springfield, 1986—. Rehab. Services Assn. fellow, 1979-80. Mem. Nat. Rehab. Assn., Nat. Head Injury Assn., Ill. Rehab. Assn., Ill. Head Injury Assn. (v.p., bd. dirs. 1984—, conf. coordinator 1985—). Democrat. Avocations: water sports, walking, reading, traveling. Home: Rural Rt 2 Box 335 Carbondale IL 62901 Office: Ctr for Comprehensive Services PO Box 2825 Carbondale IL 62902-2825

MOORE, MCPHERSON DORSETT, lawyer; b. Pine Bluff, Ark., Mar. 1, 1947; s. Arl Van and Jesse (Dorsett) M. B.S., U. Miss., 1970; J.D., U. Ark., 1974. Bar: Ark. 1974, Mo. 1975, U.S. Patent and Trademark Office 1977, U.S. Dist. Ct. (ea. dist.) Mo. 1977, U.S. Ct. Appeals (8th, 10th and D.C. cirs.). Design engr. Tenneco, Newport News, Va., 1970-71; assoc. Rogers, Eilers & Howell, St. Louis, 1974-80; ptnr. Rogers, Howell, Moore & Haferkamp, St. Louis, 1981—. Bd. dirs. Legal Services of Eastern Mo., 1984—. Served with USAR, 1970-76. Mem. ABA, Bar Assn. Met. St. Louis (chmn. young lawyers sect. 1981-82, sec. 1984-85, v.p. 1985-86, chmn. trial sect. 1986-87, pres.-elect 1987—), Ark. Bar Assn., St. Louis County Bar Assn., Am. Intellectual Property Law Assn., Assn. Trial Lawyers Am., Phi Delta Theta Alumni (treas. St. Louis chpt. 1987—). Episcopalian. Club: University (St. Louis). Home: 49 Godwin Ln Saint Louis MO 63124 Office: Rogers Howell Moore & Haferkamp 7777 Bonhomme Ave Suite 1700 Saint Louis MO 63105

MOORE, MICHAEL LESTER, controller; b. Princeton, Ind., Jan. 25, 1946; s. Donald L. and Myrtle M (Pavey) M.; m. Theressa J. Miskell, June 1, 1963 (div. 1981); children: Tracy L., Michael T., Troy D.; m. Debra L. Dougan, Jan. 21, 1981; children: Erica L., Carrie M., Bruce N. Student, Ind. State U., Evansville, 1983-84. Enlisted USN, 1963, served in Vietnam war, resigned, 1974; staff acct. Princeton Indsl. Corp., 1978-80, mgr. corp. credit, 1980-82, sales adminstr., 1982-83; sec., treas. Amber Enterprises, Princeton, 1984-85; owner Moore and Moore Collections, Princeton, 1985-86; pvt. practice Morre Ltd. Acctg. Service, Princeton, 1966-86; controller Creative Custom Products, Inc., Princeton, 1986—. Decorated Navy Achievement medal, Nat. Def. medal, Cross of Gallantry (Vietnam), Service medal with four bronze stars (Vietnam), Campaign medal with date bar (Vietnam). Mem. Nat. Notary Assn., VFW, Am. Legion. Republican. Lodge: Moose. Avocations: fishing, camping. Office: Creative Custom Products Inc PO Box 1097 Princeton IN 47670

MOORE, M(ICHAEL) TED, radiologist; b. Chickasha, Okla., Dec. 16, 1947; s. Charles F. and Kathlyn Elaine (Jackson) M.; m. Candice Ann Davis, Nov. 18, 1972; children: Chris, Randy, Michelle, James, Michael Ted Jr. BS, Okla. State U., 1969; MD, U. Okla., 1972. Diplomate Am. Bd. Radiology. Intern St. Anthony's Hosp., Oklahoma City, 1973; resident in diagnostic radiology Bapt. Med. Ctr., Oklahoma City, 1973-76, chief resident, 1976; chief of radiology Nevada (Mo.) City Hosp., 1977—; pvt. practice specializing in radiology Nevada, Mo.; cons. Nev. State Sch. and Hosp., 1977—, Bates County Hosp., Butler, Mo., 1977—; pres. staff Nevada City Hosp., 1980-81. Mem. Nevada Bd. Adjustments, 1982—. Mem. AMA, Am. Coll. Radiology, Mo. State Radiol. Soc. (bd. dirs. 1982—), Nevada Jaycees, Community Council for Performing Arts (bd. dirs. 1980-83). Avocations: running, sailing, hunting, golf, collecting antiques. Home: 1008 N Washington Nevada MO 64772 Office: 119 W Cherry Nevada MO 64772

MOORE, NOEL EDWARD, chemical engineer, educator; b. Ft. Wayne, Ind., Dec. 23, 1934; s. Francis Harold and Nora Lehoma (Mumy) M.; m. Betty L. Bolinger, Aug. 3, 1957; children: Steven K., Todd D., Jeffrey B. BSChemE, Purdue U., 1956, PhD, 1967; SM, MIT, 1958. Registered profl. engr. Engr. Procter & Gamble, Cin., 1958; asst. prof. U. Ky., Lexington, 1964-68; prof. chem. engring., chmn. dept. chemical engring. Rose-Hulman Inst. Tech., Terre Haute, Ind., 1968—; dir. air pollution control Vigo County Health Dept., Terre Haute, 1969-72; cons.Dow Chem., Midland, Mich., 1968, Eli Lilly, Clinton, Ind., 1974-76, DuPont, Orange, Tex., 1982-83. Served to capt. U.S. Army, 1958-60. Named to Hon. Order Ky. Col., 1967; recipient Outstanding Tchr. award Inland Steel-Ryerson Found., 1982. Mem. Am. Soc. Engring. Edn., Am. Inst. Chem. Engrs., Air Pollution Control Assn. Methodist. Office: Rose-Hulman Inst Tech 5500 Wabash Ave Terre Haute IN 47803

MOORE, PHYLLIS MAE, teacher; b. Winterset, Iowa, May 29, 1946; d. Straud Alonzo and Lois Mae (Rogers) Williams; m. Richard Keith Moore, Dec. 23, 1966; children: Michael Keith, Jeffrey Scott, Joy Maria. BA in English and Speech with honors, U. No. Iowa, 1966. Cert. tchr., Iowa. English tchr. Harding Jr. High Sch., Cedar Rapids, Iowa, 1966-69, Eastwood Jr. High Sch., Syracuse, N.Y., 1969-70; tchr. English, speech, drama, gifted Roosevelt Jr. High Sch., Cedar Rapids, 1971—. Author: (poetry) Fair Oaks, 1970. Deacon, youth group leader, ch. sch. tchr. Noelridge Park Christian Ch., Cedar Rapids, 1984—; pres. Christian Student Ctr. Recipient Purple Key award. Mem. Kappa Delta Pi. Republican. Mem. Christian Ch. Home: 1605 48th St NE Cedar Rapids IA 52402 Office: Roosevelt Middle Sch 300 13th St NW Cedar Rapids IA 52405

MOORE, R. L., manufacturing company executive. Pres. Devil's Lake Sioux Mfg. Corp., Ft. Totten, N.D. Office: Devils Lake Sioux Mfg Corp Fort Totten ND 58335 *

MOORE, RALPH CORY, retired radiologist; b. Omaha, Nov. 23, 1911; s. John Clyde and Lura (Daggett) M.; B.Sc., U. Nebr., 1932, M.D., 1937; m. Dorothy Jean Keech, Apr. 13, 1946; children—Virginia, John, Barbara, David. House officer internal medicine Peter Bent Brigham Hosp., Boston, 1937-39, asst. resident radiology, 1940-41, resident, 1941-42; radiologist Nebr. Meth. Hosp., Omaha, 1946—, Childrens Meml. Hosp., Omaha, 1949—; prof. radiology U. Nebr. Coll. Medicine, 1957—. Served with AUS, 1941-46; PTO. Fellow Am. Coll. Radiology; mem. Radiol. Soc. N.Am., Am. Roentgen Ray Soc., AMA. Republican. Conglist. Contbr. articles on arteriography, decelleration trauma to profl. jours. Home: 1016 S 112 Plaza Omaha NE 68154

MOORE, RICHARD ALAN, marketing manager; b. Lebanon, Ind., Oct. 24, 1949; s. Max and Dorothy Jean Moore; B.S., Ind. U., 1977; diploma horology Bowman Tech. Sch., 1970; postgrad. Butler U.; m. Mary B. Skroch, June 14, 1980. Retail cons. Wolfe's, Terre Haute, Ind., 1972-73; retail salesman F.R. Lazarus, Indpls., 1973, 74-75, L.S. Ayres, Indpls., 1976-77; mktg. research analyst Hyster Co., Danville, Ill., 1977-79; mgr.; market devel. Stewart-Warner Co., Indpls., 1979-83; product mgr. Kysor Indsl., Byron, Ill., 1983-84; mktg. mgr. Barrett Indsl. Trucks, Marengo, Ill., 1984—. Mem. Am. Mgmt. Assn., Ind. Watchmakers Assn., Ind. U. Alumni Assn., Sigma Pi Alpha. Republican. Home: 103 Lindenwood Ct Vernon Hills IL 60061 Office: Barrett Indsl Trucks 240 N Prospect Marengo IL 60152

MOORE, RICHARD ALAN, optometrist; b. La Harpe, Ill., Jan. 6, 1948; s. Emory Royal and Betty Jane (Baldwin) M.; m. Marian Louise DeGood, Dec. 26, 1970; children: Shannon Louise, David Matthew. BA in Philosophy, Drake U., 1970; BS in Optometry, Pacific U., 1972, OD, 1974. Lic. optometrist Ill., Oreg., Calif. Pvt. practice optometry Portland, Oreg., 1974-79, Carthage, Ill., 1980—; mem. clin. faculty Pacific U., Forest Grove, Oreg., 1978-79; lectr. Ill. Paraoptometric Soc. State Seminar, 1984. Editor newsletter: Southwester (Service Above Self award 1978-79). Bd. dirs. Carthage Pk. Dist., 1982—, Hancock Cen. Sch. Dist., Carthage, 1985—; mem. Planning Commn., Carthage, 1982—. Mem. Am. Optometric Assn., Ill. Optometric Assn. (exec. council 1985-87, organizer and 1st pres. soc. pres.'s council 1987), West Cen. Ill. Optometric Soc. (pres. 1985-87), Carthage C. of C. (pres. 1983-84). Republican. Lodge: Kiwanis (Carthage pres. 1981-82). Avocations: music, travel, numismatics, genealogy, photography. Home: 229 N Marion St Carthage IL 62321 Office: Carthage Optometric Office 35 N Madison St Carthage IL 62321

MOORE, ROBERT BYRON, JR., financial analyst; b. Houston, Sept. 5, 1957; s. Robert Byron and Mary Francis (Trager) M. BBA, U. Mich., 1979; MBA, U. Ill., 1984. CPA, Ill. Experienced sr. auditor Arthur Andersen & Co., Chgo., 1979-83; research analyst U. Ill., Champaign, 1984; sr. fin. cons. Grant Thornton, Chgo., 1985—. Mem. Am. Inst. CPA's, Ill. CPA Soc., Healthcare Fin. Mgmt. Assn., Beta Alpha Psi. Avocations: golf, photography. Office: Grant Thornton Prudential Plaza 6th Floor Chicago IL 60601

MOORE, ROBERT LOUIS, psychology and religion educator; b. Little Rock, Aug. 13, 1942; s. Golden Franklin and Margaret Lucretia (DePriest) M.; m. Margaret Louise Shanahan, Aug. 2, 1986. BA, Hendrix Coll., Conway, Ark., 1964; ThM with honors, So. Meth. U., 1967, Duke U., 1968; MA, U. Chgo., 1970, PhD, 1975; postdoctoral, C.G. Jung Inst., Chgo., 1982-86, Alfred Adler Inst., Chgo., 1983. Asst. prof. philosophy Western Ill. U., Macomb, 1973-77; asst. prof. psychology and religion Chgo. Theol. Sem., 1977-79, assoc. prof. psychology, 1979-82, prof., 1982—, dir. Doctor of Ministry program, 1982-86; cons. in field. Author: John Wesley and Authority: A Psychological Perspective, 1979, (with others) The Cult Experience: Responding To The New Religious Pluralism, 1982; editor: Sources of Vitality in American Church Life, 1978, (with others) Anthropology And The Study Of Religion, 1984, (with others) Jung's Challenge To Contemporary Religion, 1986. Mem. adv. bd. Adopt-A-Sch. Project, Chgo., 1984-85; bd. dirs. C.G. Jung Inst., Chgo., 1978-82. U. Chgo. fellow, 1970-73. Fellow Ctr. Sci. Study of Religion; mem. Nat. Assn. Advancement Psychoanalysis, Am. Assn. Pastoral Counselors, Am. Acad. Religion (chmn. religion and social scis. sect. 1978-84), Soc. Sci. Study of Religion (program com. 1980-81), N. Am. Assn. Pastoral Counselors. Methodist. Avocations: running, traveling. Office: Chgo Theol Sem 5757 S University Chicago IL 60637

MOORE, ROY FLINT, III, lawyer; b. Detroit, June 13, 1950; s. Roy Flint Jr. and Doris Ellen (Murphy) M. B.A. with distinction, Wayne State U., 1975, J.D., 1979. Bar: Mich. 1979, U.S. Dist. Ct. (ea. dist.) Mich. 1979, U.S. Tax Ct. 1985. Mgmt. asst. Moore Signs, Inc., Detroit, 1968-77; freelance labor cons., Detroit, 1977-79; assoc. James A. Brescoll, P.C., Mt. Clemens, Mich., 1980-83; Wright & Goldstein, P.C., Birmingham, Mich., 1983-86, mng. ptnr., 1986—; tutor Psi Chi, Detroit, 1973; research asst. conflict resolution Wayne State U., Detroit, 1974; research asst. legal philosophy, 1977. Patron, Detroit Inst. Arts Founders Soc., 1983—. Mem. Mich. Bar Assn., ABA (comml., banking and fin. transactions litigation com. 1984—), Fed. Bar Assn., Detroit Bar Assn., Macomb Bar Assn., Phi Beta Kappa. Lutheran. Office: Wright & Goldstein PC 255 E Brown St #430 Birmingham MI 48011

MOORE, STEPHEN JAMES, accountant; b. St. Louis, Feb. 13, 1956; s. Lon Wayne and Loretta Francis (Noelker) M.; m. Jean Bante, Aug. 4, 1979; children: Michelle Marie, Colleen Garvin. BSBA, Rockhurst Coll., 1977; MA, U. Mo., 1978. CPA, Mo. Staff acct. Price Waterhouse, St. Louis, 1978-80, sr. acct., 1980-83, mgr., 1983-86, sr. mgr., 1986—; instr. U. Mo., Columbia, 1977-78, Meramec Community Coll., St. Louis, 1980. Bd. dirs., treas. Nursery Found. St. Louis, 1986-87. Gregory Found. fellow, 1977-78. Mem. Am. Inst. CPA's, Nat. Assn. Accts., Mo. Soc. CPA's, Alpha Sigma Nu. Roman Catholic. Lodge: KC. Avocations: golf, soccer. Office: Price Waterhouse 1 Centerre Plaza Saint Louis MO 63101

MOORE, THOMAS JAMES, III, data processing executive; b. Detroit, Nov. 3, 1942; s. Thomas James and Marjorie Ruth (Kaiser) M. B.S. in Acctg., Wayne State U., 1964, M.B.A. in Adminstrv. Services, 1967. Mgmt. cons. Arthur Andersen & Co., Detroit, 1966-72; project leader J.L. Hudson Co., Detroit, 1972-74; project mgr. Nat. Bank Detroit, 1974-77, mgr. data security and privacy, 1977-79; mgr. computer systems Mich. Cancer Found., Detroit, 1979-81; mgr. data processing Harper-Grace Hosps., Detroit, 1981-82, mgr. systems devel. and computer services, 1982-83, dir. mgmt. info. services, 1983-84; regional mgr. Electronic Data Systems, 1984—. Active Founders Soc. of Detroit Inst. Arts. Mem. Wayne State U. Alumni Assn., Patrons of Wayne State U. Theaters, Detroit Econ. Club, Assn. Systems Mgmt., Data Processing Mgmt. Assn., Delta Sigma Pi, Omicron Delta Kappa. Home: 555 S Woodward Ave Apt 1209 Birmingham MI 48011 Office: Electronic Data Systems 1400 N Woodward Ave Suite 201 Bloomifeld Hills MI 48013

MOORE, THOMAS P., broadcasting company executive; b. Danville, Ill., Feb. 29, 1928; s. Lester Rufus and Mabel Ellen (Jackson) M.; m. Jean LaVonne Sather, Aug. 31, 1952; children: Randyl Ellen, Patricia Kay, Gregory Sather. B.A., N. Central Coll., 1952; grad. student, Denver U., 1952-53. Newscaster Sta. KFEL-AM-FM-TV, 1952-54; account rep. Sta. KGMC, 1954-55; sales mgr. Sta. KDEN-AM-FM, 1955-62; pres., gen. mgr. Sta. WBCO AM-FM, Bucyrus, Ohio, 1962—. Lay leader, mem. program council Ohio Sandusky Conf., United Methodist Ch., 1966-69, pres. gen. laity bd. and laymen's found., 1968-72; mem. Gen Council on Ministries, 1980-84, N.W. Ohio Water Devel. Adv. Com., 1967-69, Sandusky River Basin Water Pollution Study Com., 1968-69; v.p. bd. mgrs. EUB Men, Evang. United Brethren Ch., 1958-68; pres. Rocky Mountain Conf., 1957-61; mem. gen. bd. Nat. Council Christian Chs. Am., 1968-72; charter pres. Bucyrus Bratwurst Festival, Inc., 1968; adv. bd. Bucyrus Salvation Army, 1964-68; mem. planning com. East Ohio Conf., 1972-76; mem. planning com. United Meth. Ch., chmn. commn. on minimum salaries, 1968-72, lay leader, 1972-76, vice chmn. council ministries, mem. episcopal com., 1972-76, head. del. to gen. conf., Portland, Oreg., 1976, Balt., 1984; head del. to Jurisdictional Conf., Sioux Falls, 1976, Duluth, Minn., 1984; chmn. East Ohio Conf. Council on Ministries, 1976-80; pres. United Meth. Communications, United Meth. Ch., 1972-76, mem. gen. council finance and adminstrn., 1976-80; mem. communications commn. Nat. Council Chs., 1972-76; mem. communications con. Ohio Council Chs.; mem. Episc. com., chmn. New Vision Task Group, both East Ohio Conf., North Central Jurisdiction, United Meth. Ch.; mem. exec. com. Council on Ministries, 1980-86; mem. World Meth. Council, 1986—; trustee United Theol. Sem., 1972-80; pres. Community Improvement Corp., Bucyrus; mem. Overall Econ. Devel. Com. of Crawford County; chmn. Crawford County Traffic Safety Council, 1979—. Served with USN, World War II. Named a Civic Leader of Am., 1968. Mem. Bucyrus Area C. of C. (chmn. airport study com. 1967-68, bd. dirs. 1964-67), Ohio Assn. Broadcasters (pres. 1981-84), Nat. Assn. Broadcasters (legis. liaison 1982—). Home: 1325 Home Circle W Bucyrus OH 44820 Office: 403 E Rensselaer St PO Box 789 Bucyrus OH 44820

MOORE, VERNON LEE, retired utility official; b. Kansas City, Kans., Mar. 26, 1923; s. Robert Sanford and Velma Margaret (Parker) M.; student Internat. Corr. Schs., 1963-65; m. Mary Bernice Janssens, Nov. 25, 1950; children—Russell Parker, Dana Margaret. With Kansas City Power & Light Co., Kansas City, Mo., 1948-85, tng. coordinator, 1979-85, ret., 1985, cons. tchr. Pin Oak Tng. Ctr., Kansas City, 1985—. Served with U.S. Navy, 1941-47. Presbyterian (elder). Home: 5832 W 87th Terr Overland Park KS 66207 Office: Pin Oak Tng Ctr 5700 Eugene Field Rd Kansas City MO 64120

MOORE, WALTER EMIL, JR., financial services consultant; b. Pawtucket, R.I., May 26, 1925; s. Walter Emil and Gladys (Hobson) M.; m. Alta Tarbell Wilson, Sept. 25, 1948; children—Kathy Louise, Richard Emil, John Emil. B.S., MIT, 1948; M.S., Case Inst. Tech., 1960. With Firestone Tire & Rubber Co., Akron, Ohio, 1948-86 , mgr. pvt. brand tire devel., 1958-63, mgr. truck tire engring., 1964-66, mgr. race tire devel., tech. service, 1966-68, mgr. quality assurance, 1968-83, mgr. projects, 1983-86; cons. Fin. Planning Assocs. of Bath, Ohio, Inc., 1986—. Served with USNR, 1943-45. Republican. Congregationalist. Avocations: flying; music; woodworking; personal computers. Home: 1330 Taft Ave Cuyahoga Falls OH 44223 Office: Fin Planning Assocs Bath Ohio 1050 Ghent Rd PO Box 2658 Bath OH 44210

MOORE, WILLIAM SANBORN, electronics company executive; b. Cleve., Mar. 11, 1954; s. Jerald Powers Moore and Virginia (Gilkey) Herkes. B.S. in Journalism, Bowling Green State U., 1976. Sales rep. CAM/RPC Electronics, Cleve., 1976-77; sales mgr. Target Electronics, Solon, Ohio, 1977-79; mfrs. rep. KW Electronics, Shaker Heights, Ohio, 1979—; dir. Nightcoach (dance orch.), 1979—. Bd. dirs. Valley Arts Ctr., Chagrin Falls, Ohio, 1979-80. Named Best Sales Rep. Coil. Specialty Co., 1981-85. Avocations: boating; skiing; musician. Home: 7051 Pine St Chagrin Falls OH 44022 Office: KW Electronics 3645 Warrensville Center Rd Shaker Heights OH 44122

MOORHEAD, THOMAS EDWARD, lawyer; b. Owosso, Mich., Aug. 27, 1946; s. Kenneth Edward and Lillian Jane (Becker) M.; B.A. in Communication Arts, Mich. State U., 1970; J.D., Detroit Coll. Law, 1973; m. Marjorie E. Semans, Sept. 9, 1967; children—Robert Scott, Kristine Elizabeth. Admitted to Mich. bar, 1973; legal counsel Legis. Service Bur., State of Mich., Lansing, 1973-74; ptnr. firm Des Jardins & Moorhead, P.C., Owosso, 1974-85; sole practice, Owosso, 1985—. Pres., Bentley Sch. PTO, Owosso; mem. adminstrv. bd. 1st United Meth. Ch., Owosso; bd. dirs. Shiawassee Arts Council; treas. Cub Scout Pack 67 Boy Scouts Am.; mem. Shiawassee County Republican Exec. Com. Mem. Am. Bar Assn., Shiawassee County Bar Assn. (past pres.), State Bar of Mich., Owosso Jaycees (pres.; named Outstanding Local Pres. by state assn. 1977). Republican. Home: 1265 Ada St Owosso MI 48867 Office: 217 N Washington St Suites 105-107 Owosso MI 48867

MOORHOUSE, LINDA VIRGINIA, symphony orchestra administrator; b. Lancaster, Pa., June 26, 1945; d. William James and Mary Viginia (Wild) Moorhouse. B.A., Pa. State U., 1967. Sec., San Antonio Symphony, Tex., 1970-71, adminstrv. asst., 1971-75, asst. mgr., 1975-76; gen. mgr. Canton Symphony, Ohio, 1977—. Mem. Ohio Arts Council Music Panel, 1980-82, 86-88. Mem. Met. Orch. Mgrs. Assn. (pres. 1983-85), Orgn. Ohio Orchestras (pres. 1985, 86), Am. Symphony Orch. League (bd. dirs. 1983-85). Office: Canton Symphony Orch 1001 Market Ave North Canton OH 44720

MOORMAN, ROBERT CRAIN, equipment company executive, consultant; b. Cedar Rapids, Iowa, Dec. 22, 1933; s. Edwin Forlow and Clara Louise (Crain) M.; m. Susan Carol Rook, Jan. 7, 1956 (dec. 1968); children—Michelle, Deborah, Judith; m. Tara Ann Fisher, Feb. 14, 1986. B.A. in English Lit., State U. Iowa, 1958. With Moorman Equipment Co., Cedar Rapids, Iowa, 1955—, pres., chief exec. officer, 1965—; pres., chief exec. officer Am. Phys. Qualifications Testing Corp.; chmn. young execs. Associated Equipment Distbrs., Oak Brook, Ill., 1974. Mem. Ho. of Dels., Nat. Am. Cancer Soc., N.Y.C., 1975—, bd. dirs., 1979—, chmn. legacies and planned giving com., 1982-85, mem. exec. com. bd. dirs., 1982—, vice chmn. crusade com., 1984-86, chmn. nat. crusade com., 1987—; pres. Iowa div. Am. Cancer Soc., Mason City, 1978-80, chmn. bd. dirs., 1984-87; dir. YMCA, Cedar Rapids, 1980-83, Symphony Orch. Bd., Cedar Rapids, 1982-84; bd. dirs. Community Theatre, Cedar Rapids, 1974-77, 80-83, trustee, 1980—; commr. Linn County Regional Planning Commn., Cedar Rapids, 1965-77; chmn., treas. "Keep the Airport Commn.", Cedar Rapids, 1984; mem. County Republican Central Com., Cedar Rapids, 1968-70. Recipient Annual Nat. Div. award Am. Cancer Soc., 1980. Presbyterian. Club: Cedar Rapids Country (dir. 1984—), Pickwick (Cedar Rapids) (pres. 1979-80). Lodge: Rotary (pres. 1969-70). Avocations: medicine, golf, travel, scuba diving, flying. Office: Moorman Equipment Co 5950 6th St SW Cedar Rapids IA 52404

MOORSHEAD, JOHN EARL, porcelain enamel frit manufacturer; b. Chgo., June 20, 1939; s. Robert Fletcher and Helen (Rahm) M.; m. Mary Margaret Maras (div.); children: Brett, Chad; m. Susan A. Tryner; children: Pamela, John Jr. BSChemE, Ill. Inst. Tech., 1963, MBA, 1970. Sales mgr. Chi-Vit div. Eagle-Picher Industries, Chgo., 1963-67, dist. mgr., 1967-76; dist. mgr. Chi-Vit div. Eagle-Picher Industries, Altoona, Iowa, 1976-80; sales mgr. Chi-Vit div. Eagle-Picher Industries, Oakbrook, Ill., 1980-82; v.p. sales and service Chi-Vit div. Eagle-Picher Industries, Urbana, Ohio, 1982-84, div. pres., 1984—; pres. Chgo. Vitreous Can., Ltd. div. Eagle-Picher Industries, Ingersoll, Ont., 1984—. Mem. Porcelain Enamel Inst. (bd. dirs. 1983—). Republican. Lutheran. Avocation: private piloting. Home: Box 658 Urbana OH 43078 Office: Chi-Vit Corp 720 S Edgewood Ave Urbana OH 43078

MOOSBRUGGER, STEPHEN CHARLES, accountant; b. Mpls., Mar. 3, 1956; s. Charles Albert and Nancy Catherine (Davidson) M.; m. Mary Susan Antonson, Sept. 2, 1978; 1 child, Margaret Leigh. BS cum laude, Coll. St. Thomas, St. Paul, 1978; MB in Taxation, U. Minn., 1983. CPA. Acct. Robert G. Engelhart & Co., Burnsville, Minn., 1978-81; ptnr. Deloitte, Haskins & Sells, Mpls., 1981—; assoc. prof. William Mitchell Sch. Law., St. Paul, 1985—. Program rev. chmn. United Way, Mpls., 1983. Mem. Real Estate Securities and Syndication Inst. (pres. local chpt. 1985—), Nat. Assn. Indsl. and Office Parks, Minn. Multi Housing Assn. Republican. Roman Catholic. Club: Decathlon Athletic (Bloomington) (chmn. Hobey Baker Meml. award com. 1986—). Avocations: reading, running, family, golf, hockey. Home: 1904 Sioux Ct Burnsville MN 55337 Office: Deloitte Haskins & Sells 625 Fourth Ave Suite 1000 Minneapolis MN 55415

MORALES-GALARRETA, JULIO, psychoanalyst, psychiatrist, child psychoanalyst, child psychiatrist; b. Trujillo, Peru, Dec. 1, 1936; came to U.S., 1973; s. Julio Morales-Fernandez and Lidia (Galarreta) Morales; m. Lourdes Tincopa, Dec. 3, 1967; children: Lourdes Lydia, Julio Fernando. MB, U. Trujillo, 1966; cert. psychoanalysis, St. Louis Psychoanalytic Inst., 1984, cert. child psychoanalyst, 1985. Diplomate Am. Bd. Psychiatry and Neurology; cert. psychoanalyst. Resident in psychiatry Ministry of Pub. Health, Peru, 1965-68; supr. psychiat. tng. program Ministry Pub. Health, Peru, 1970-72; physician and surgeon U. Trujillo, 1966; instr. psychaitry St. Marcos U., Peru, 1968-72; resident in psychiatry Fairfield Hills Hosp., Newtown, Conn., 1972-74; fellow in child psychiatry Washington U., St. Louis, 1974-76, instr. child psychiatry, 1976-82; dir. child devel. project St. Louis Psychonalytic Inst., 1982—, faculty psychoanalysis ans child analysis, 1984—; asst. clin. prof. psychiatry and pediatrics St. Louis U., 1983—; faculty psychoanalysis and child analysis St. Louis Psychoanalytic Inst., 1984—. Fellow Peruvian Psychiat. Assn.; mem. St. Louis Met. Med. Soc., Am. Psychiat. Assn., Am. Acad. Child Psychiatry, Am. Psychoanalytic Assn., Am. Soc. Adolescent Psychiatry. Avocations: classical music, biking. Home: 7415 Byron Pl Saint Louis MO 63105 Office: 141 N Meramec Ave Saint Louis MO 63105

MORAN, DANIEL E. (HENRY MORAN), VIII, executive arts administrator, producer, consultant; b. Dobbs Ferry, N.Y., Apr. 23, 1949; s. Daniel E. and Joan Linda (Greeff) Deschere; m. Melissa Matterson, June 29, 1974; children—Sally, Susannah; m. 2d, Madelyn Newcomer Voigts, Mar. 20, 1982; 1 dau., Sara. Student U. Tenn., 1967-69; B.F.A., Goodman Sch., Art Inst. Chgo., 1971; postgrad. in Bus. Mgmt. and Adminstrn., Wayne State U., Mich. State U., Wharton Sch.; M.B.A. with honors, Rockhurst Coll., 1986. Project dir. Ill. Arts Council, Chgo., 1971-73; asst. dir. Mich. Council for Arts, Detroit, 1973-75; exec. dir. Mid-Am. Arts Alliance, Kansas City, Mo., 1975—, bd. dirs., 1977—; mem. adv. panel Nat. Endowment Arts; cons. Am. Urban Devel. Found. Bd. dirs. Folly Theatre; mem. Kansas City Jazz Commn. Recipient certs. merit Mich. State U., Smithsonian Inst. Episcopalian. Co-producer Five TV Programs Public Broadcasting Systems; composer/lyricist two children's musicals. Home: 6641 Linden Rd Kansas City MO 64113 Office: 20 W 9th St Suite 550 Kansas City MO 64105

MORAN, EMILIO FEDERICO, professor anthropology and agriculture; b. Habana, Cuba, July 21, 1946; s. Emilio F. Sr. and Caridad B. (Corrales) M.; m. Maria del Carmen Mendez, (div. 1970); m. Millicent Fleming, Dec. 15, 1972; 1 child, Emily Victoria. BA, Springhill Coll., 1968; MA, U. Fla., 1969, PhD, 1975. Asst. prof. Ind. U., Bloomington, 1975-79, assoc. prof., 1979-84, chmn. dept. anthropology, 1980-87, prof. dept. anthropology, 1984—; vis. prof. soil sci. N.C. State U., Raleigh, 1984; adv. panelist NSF, Washington, 1987—. Author: Developing the Amazon, 1981, Human Adaptability, 1982; editor The Dilemna of Amazonian Development, 1983, The Ecosystem Concept in Anthropology, 1984; mem. editorial bd. Jour. Forest History, 1986—, Anthropology Linguistics, 1982—. Recipient A.J. Hanna Disting. Lctr. Rollins Coll., 1985; postdoctoral fellow Tinker Found., 1983-84; named Disting. Ecologist, Colo. State U., 1987. Fellow Am. Anthrop. Assn., Soc. Applied Anthropology, AAAS (nominations com. 1987—); mem. Am. Ethnologist, Latin American Studies Assn., Internat. Soil Sci. Soc. Home: 2404 Covenanter Dr Bloomington IN 47401 Office: Ind U Rawles Hall 108 Bloomington IN 47405

MORAN, JAMES BYRON, judge; b. Evanston, Ill., June 20, 1930; s. James Edward and Kathryn (Horton) M.; m. Nancy Adams; children: John, Jennifer, Sarah, Polly. AB, U. Mich., 1952; LLB magna cum laude, Harvard U., 1957. Bar: Ill. 1958. Law clk. to presiding judge U.S. Ct. of Appeals (2d cir.), 1957-58; assoc. Bell, Boyd, Lloyd, Haddad & Burns, Chgo, 1958-66, ptnr., 1966-79; judge U.S. Dist. Ct.(no. dist.) Ill., Chgo., 1979—. Dir. Com. on Ill. Govt., 1960-78, chmn., 1968-70; vice chmn., sec. Ill. Dangerous Drug Adv. Counsel, 1967-74; dir. Gateway Found., 1969—; mem. Ill. Ho. of Reps., 1965-67; mem. Evanston City Council, 1971-75. Served with AUS, 1952-54. Mem. Ill. Bar Assn., Chgo. Bar Assn., Chgo. Council Lawyers, Phi Beta Kappa. Clubs: Law, Legal. Home: 117 Kedzie St Evanston IL 60202 Office: US Courthouse 219 S Dearborn St Chicago IL 60604

MORAN, ROBERT FRANCIS, JR., library director; b. Cleve., May 3, 1938; s. Robert Francis Sr. and Jeanette (Mulholland) M.; m. Judith Mary Pacer, Dec. 28, 1968; children: Mary Jeanette, Catherine, Margaret. BA, Cath. U. Am., Washington, 1961, MLS, 1965; MBA, U. Chgo., 1976. Head librarian St. Patrick's Sem., Menlo Park, Calif., 1965-69; coordinator and reference librarian U. Chgo., 1969-72; serials librarian U. Ill., Chgo., 1972-78, acquisitions librarian, 1977-80; dir. library services Ind. U. Northwest, Gary, 1980—; v.p., sec. Northwest Ind. Area Library Services Authority, Merrillville, 1982-85. Contbr. articles to profl jours. Mem. ALA (library orgn. and mgmt. sec., library mgmt. and adminstrn. sect., com. chair 1981-86, sect. chair 1986—). Democrat. Roman Catholic. Office: Ind Univ NW Library 3400 Broadway Gary IN 46408

MORAN, THOMAS JOSEPH, justice Supreme Court Illinois; b. Waukegan, Ill., July 17, 1920; s. Cornelius Patrick and Avis Rose (Tyrrell) M.; m. Mary Jane Wasniewski, Oct. 4, 1941; children: Avis Marie, Kathleen, Mary Jane, Thomas G. B.A., Lake Forest Coll., 1947; J.D., Chgo. Kent Coll. Law, 1950; J.D. (hon.), Lake Forest Coll., 1977. Bar: Ill. Individual practice law Waukegan, Ill., 1950-56; state's atty. Lake County, Ill., 1956-58; probate ct. judge Lake County, 1958-61; judge 19th Circuit Ct., Lake and McHenry counties, Ill., 1961-64; appellate ct. judge 2d Dist., Elgin, Ill., 1964-76; justice Supreme Ct. Ill., 1976—; faculty appellate judges seminars NYU; continuing legal edn. seminars La. State U. Served with USCG, 1943-45. Mem. Inst. Jud. Adminstrn., Am. Judicature Soc., ABA, Ill., Lake County bar assns. Office: Supreme Ct Bldg Springfield IL 62756 *

MORAN, VIOLET H., nurse, nursing administrator. BS in Nursing, Mont. State U., 1959; MS in Nursing, U. Wis., 1975. RN. Staff nurse Mont. Deaconess Hosp., Bozeman, 1959; from staff nurse to head nurse VA Hosp., Madison, Wis., 1959-61; dir. staff devel. Meth. Hosp., 1961-67; coordinator staff tng. and devel. Cen. Wis. Ctr., Madison, 1967-81; assoc. dir. nursing and staff devel. U. Wis. Hosp. and Clinics, Madison, 1981—; lectr. nursing U. Wis., Madison, 1977-82, clin. asst. prof., 1986—. Editorial bd. Jour. Nursing Staff Devel., 1985—; contbr. articles to profl. jours. Mem. Am. Nurses Assn. (bd. dirs. council continuing edn. 1985—) Wis. Nurses Assn., Am. Assn. Mental Deficiency, , Madison Dist. Nurses Assn., Alpha Tau Delta, Sigma Theta Tau, Phi Kappa Phi. Office: Univ Hosps and Clinics 600 Highland Ave F6/171 Madison WI 53792

MORAND, KEVIN MARTIN, architect; b. Cin., May 13, 1952; s. John L. and Mary E. (Gross) M.; m. LeAnne W. Miller, Aug. 20, 1977; 1 child, Paige. BS in Arch., Ohio State U., 1974. Campus planner U. Cin., 1979-82; store planner May Company Dept. Stores, Cleve., 1982-84; prin. Kevin M. Morand, Architects, Cleve., 1982—. Corp. mem. AIA (chpt. dir. intern devel. program 1983—); mem. Nat. Council Archtl. Registration Bds. Roman Catholic. Avocations: golf, racquetball, swimming. Office: 1276 W 3d St Cleveland OH 44113

MORANTZ, ROBERT ALLAN, neurosurgeon; b. N.Y.C., Nov. 21, 1942; s. George and Anna (Lubarsky) M.; m. Regina Markell, June 6, 1965 (div.); children: Alison Daniela, Jessica Elana; m. Marsha Murphy, Apr. 21, 1982. AB cum laude, Columbia U., 1963; MD, N.Y. U., N.Y.C., 1967. Diplomate Am. Bd. Neurol. Surgery. Intern in surgery N.Y. U., N.Y.C., 1967-68, resident, chief resident in neurosurgery, 1968-73; asst. prof. neurosurgery U. Kans. Med. Ctr., Kansas City, 1975-78; practice medicine specializing in neurosurgery Kansas City, Mo., 1980—; cons. in neurosurgery Kansas City VA Hosp., 1975; bd. dirs. Brain Tumor Inst., Kansas City, Mo., 1985—. Contbg. author: Multidisciplinary Aspects of Brain Tumor Therapy, 1979, Comprehensive Guide to Diagnosis and Management of Neurosurgical Problems, 1979; contbr. articles to profl. jours. Served to maj. USAF, 1973-75. Mem. AMA, ACS, Am. Assn. Neurol. Surgeons, Congress Neurol. Surgery, Kans. Med. Soc., Mo. Med. Soc., Jackson County Med. Soc., Wyandotte County Med. Soc., Rocky Mountain Neurol. Soc., Soc. Neurosci., Research Soc. Neurol. Surgeons, Am. Coll. Allergists (neuro-allergy com. 1982), Southwest Oncology Group, Pediatric Oncology Group, Sigma Xi. Jewish. Home: 5335 Cherry Kansas City MO 64110 Office: 6420 Prospect Suite T411 Kansas City MO 64132

MORAVY, L. JOE, accountant; b. Mt. Pleasant, Mich., Sept. 19, 1950; s. Herbert Lee and Ida Blanche (AnKrom) M.; m. Marie Elisabeth Köhlvik, June 22, 1973; children: Leif Josef, Lars David. BSBA with honors, Mich. Tech. U., 1972; MBA, U. Mich., 1974. CPA, Ill. Staff acct. Arthur Andersen & Co., Chgo., 1974-76, sr. acct., 1976-80, mgr., 1980-87, ptnr., 1987—; lectr. bus. seminars on various acctg. topics Northwestern U., 1984—, Singapore Internat. Monetary Exchange, 1986, The World Trade Inst.; and others. Contbr. articles to profl. jours. Named one of Outstanding Young Men Am., 1986. Mem. Am. Inst. CPA's, Ill. CPA Soc., Japan Am. Soc. Chgo. Mem. Evangelical Ch. Club: University (Chgo). Home: 1007 W Frontenac Dr Arlington Heights IL 60004 Office: Arthur Andersen & Co 33 W Monroe St Chicago IL 60603

MORE, FREDERICK G., dentistry educator; b. Detroit, Mar. 22, 1942; s. Frederick and Marjorie (Smith) M.; m. Carol L. Overley, June 8, 1968; children: Jennifer Ellen, Kara Lizbeth. DDS, U. Mich., 1967, MS, 1970. Clin. instr. dentistry U. Mich. Dental Sch., Ann Arbor, 1967-70, asst. prof., 1970-77; assoc. prof. U. Mich. Dental Sch. and Hosp., Ann Arbor, 1977-86; assoc. dean U. Mich. Dental Sch., Ann Arbor, 1986—; gen. practice dentistry Ann Arbor, 1967-68, practice dentistry specializing in pediatrics, 1970—; cons. plastic surgery St. Joseph Hosp., Ann Arbor, 1974-86, Washtenaw County (Mich.) Health Dept., 1975-77. Author: Self-Instruction Manual, 1976. Pres. Early Learning Ctr., Ann Arbor, 1975-78; v.p., mem. exec. bd. King Elem. Sch., Ann Arbor, 1978-80; deacon, Presbyn. Ch., Ann Arbor, 1975—, active numerous coms. Recipient Oral Surgery award Chalmers Lyons Acad., 1967; Mott fellow, 1968. Fellow Am. Coll. Dentists; mem. ADA, Mich. Dental Assn. (del.), Washtenaw Dist. Dental Soc. (pres., sec.-treas.), Am. Acad. Pediatric Dentistry, Omicron Kappa Upsilon. Avocations: running, camping. Office: U Mich Sch Dentistry 1011 N University Ave Ann Arbor MI 48109-1078

MOREHOUSE, LAWRENCE GLEN, veterinarian, educational administrator; b. Manchester, Kans., July 21, 1925; s. Edwy O. and Ethel (Glenn) M.; m. GeorgiaAnn Lewis, Oct. 6, 1956; children: Timothy, Glenn Ellen. BS in Biol. Sci., Kans. State U., 1952, DVM, 1952; MS in Animal Pathology, Purdue U., 1956, PhD, 1960. Veterinarian County Vet. Hosp., St. Louise, 1952-53; supr. Brucellosis labs. Purdue U., Lafayette, Ind., 1953-60; staff veterinarian lab. services U.S. Dept. Agr., Washington, 1960-61; discipline leader in pathology an toxicology, animal health div. Nat. Animal Disease lab., Ames, Iowa, 1962-64; prof., chmn. dept. veterinary pathology Coll. Vet. Medicine U. Mo., Columbia, 1964-67; dir. Vet. Med. Diagnostic Lab., 1968—; cons. to U.S. Dept Agr., Surgeon Gen. U.S. Army, Am. Inst. Biol. Scis. Nat. Acad. Sci., Miss. State U., St. Louis Zoo Residency Tng. Program, Miss. Vet. Med. Assn.; adv. com. med. research and devel. U.S. Army. Co-editor: Mycotoxic Fungi, Mycotoxins, Mycotoxicoses: An Encyclopedic Handbook Handbook, 1977; contbr. numerous articles on diseases of animals to profl. jours. Served with USN, 1943-46, U.S. Army, 1952-53. Recipient Outstanding Service award U.S. Dept Agr., 1959. Fellow Royal Soc. Health, London; mem. Am. Vet. Med. Assn., Mo. Vet. Med. Assn., Nat. Assn. Vet. Lab. Diagnosticians (E.P. Pope award 1976, chmn. lab. accreditation bd. 1972—), U.S. Animal Health Assn., Am. Assn. Lab. Animal Medicine, Mo. Soc. Microbiology, Am. Assn. Avian Pathologists. Presbyterian. Home: 916 Danforth St Columbia MO 65201 Office: U Mo Vetinary Med Diagnostic Lab Columbia MO 65201

MORELAND, MICHAEL HAROLD, real estate investment company executive, consultant; b. Cin., Jan. 20, 1953; s. Harold Douglas and Juanita Andrea (Powell) M.; m. Susan Lynn Slivka, Jan. 16, 1987. B in Urban Design, U. Cin., 1976, M in City Planning, MBA, 1978. Dir. planning and devel. Lockridge & Assocs., Memphis, 1981-85; dir., v.p. Hamm Mgmt. Co., Memphis, 1982-85, Falcon Devel. Co., Orlando, Fla., 1983-85; pres. Moreland & Kruchten Constrn. Co., Memphis, 1984-86; sr. project mgr. Broadview Savs. and Loan Co., Cleve., 1986—; chmn. Moreland Cons. Inc., Memphis, 1985—. Author: Overall Economic Development Plan- Mississippi-Arkansas-Tennessee Council of Governments, 1980. Elder Presbyn. Ch., Cin., 1974-77; sec. Ind. Ry. Mus., French Lick, 1976-78; v.p. Committment Memphis, 1980-81. Republican. Home: 6979 Greenwood St Independence OH 44131 Office: Broadview Savs and Loan Co 6000 Rockside Wood Blvd Cleveland OH 44131

MORELAND, WILLIAM JOHN, real estate broker; b. Chgo., Feb. 21, 1916; s. James C. and Izora M. (McCabe) M.; A.B., U. Ill., 1938; student Northwestern U., 1937. With James C. Moreland & Son, Inc., real estate and home building, Chgo., 1938—, pres., 1952—; pres. Moreland Realty, Inc., Chgo., 1952-72. Builder, operator Howard Johnson Motor Lodge, Chgo., 1960-72. Helped develop model housing community, El Salvador, Central Am., 1960's. Presidential appointment to commerce com. for Alliance for Progress, 1962-64. Served to lt. USNR, 1941-46. Mem. Home Bldrs. Assn. Chicagoland (pres. 1961-62), Chgo. Assn. Commerce and Industry, Chgo., N.W. real estate bds., N.W. Bldrs. Assn., Nat. Assn. Home Bldrs. (hon. life dir. 1972—), Chi Psi. Republican. Roman Catholic. Office: 5717 Milwaukee Ave Chicago IL 60646

MORELLI, ANTHONY FRANK, pediatric dentist; b. Chgo., Aug. 10, 1956; s. Frank A. and Josephine M. (Cerniglia) M.; m. Tina Makris, July 24, 1982. BS, Loyola U., Chgo., 1976; DDS, Loyola U., Maywood, Ill., 1984. Cert. specialist pediatric dentistry. Pediatric dentist Infant Welfare Soc. Chgo., 1984—; chief resident Dept. Pediatric Dentistry Loyola Sch. Dentistry, Maywood, 1985-86. Mem. ADA, Chgo. Dental Soc., Am. Soc. Dentistry Children, Am. Acad. Pediatric Dentistry, Am. Bd. Pediatric Dentistry (assoc.). Home: 524 Banyon Ln LaGrange IL 60525 Office: Infant Welfare Soc Chgo 1931 N Halsted St Chicago IL 60614 also: 11125 S Kedzie Ave Chicago IL 60655 also: 2634 Grand Ave Waukegan IL 60085

MORELLI, WILLIAM ANNIBALE, SR., aerospace component manufacturing company executive; b. Cin., July 2, 1938; s. Annibale and Angiolina (DiPietro) M.; m. Velma Lois Hammond, May 12, 1962 (div. Sept. 1974); children: Paula Anne, Cathi Susan, Melissa Anne, William A., Jr.; m. Beverly Ann Bulmer, Feb. 14, 1975; stepchildren: Stacey Dawn Watson, James Keith Watson. BBA, U. Cin., 1960. Fin. analyst Federated Dept. Stores, Cin., 1961-66; mfrs. rep. Hyde Corp., Cin., 1966-75; sales mgr. Clipper Industries, Roseville, Mich., 1975-76, Bachan Aerospace Corp., Madison Heights, Mich., 1976-83; pres. Caratron Industries, Inc., Warren, Mich., 1983—. Served with Ohio N.G., 1960-66. Mem. Am. Gear Mfgs. Assn., Warren C. of C. (bd. dirs.), Italian Am. C. of C. Lodges: Masons, Shriners. Office: Caratron Industries Inc 27955 College Park Dr Warren MI 48093

MORETTI, ROBERT JAMES, behavioral science educator; b. Chgo., Aug. 28, 1949; s. James John and Elva Eve (Bonini) M.; m. Carol L. Curt, Dec. 6, 1986. B.S. in Psychology, Loyola U., Chgo., 1971, Ph.D. in Clin. Psychology, 1982; M.A. in Behavioral Sci., U. Chgo., 1976. Registered clin. psychologist, Ill.; listed Nat. Register Health Service Providers in Psychology. Research fellow Ill. State Psychiat. Inst., Chgo., 1974-76; clin. asst. prof. Loyola U. Sch. Dentistry, Chgo., 1976-81; asst. prof., chmn. behavioral scis. Northwestern U. Dental Sch., Chgo., 1981—, asst. prof. psychiatry Northwestern U. Med. Sch., 1983—; asst. prof. Grad. Sch., 1986—; staff Charter Barclay Hosp., Chgo., Old Orchard Hosp., Skokie, Ill., Northwestern Meml. Hosp. Served with Ill. Army Nat. Guard, 1971-77. Kellogg fellow Am. Fund Dental Health, 1981. Mem. Am. Psychol. Assn., Ill. Psychol. Assn., Am. Soc. Clin. Hypnosis, Am. Assn. Dental Schs., Soc. Behavioral Medicine, Inst. Advancement Health. Contbr. articles to profl. jours. Home: 3458 N Normandy Chicago IL 60634 Office: Northwestern U Dental Sch 311 Chicago Ave Chicago IL 60611

MOREY, LARRY WAYNE, nuclear training facility administrator; b. Cedar Rapids, Iowa, Apr. 22, 1949; s. Eugene Austin and LaVonne Elsie (Fritz) M.; m. Rosellen Louise Murley, Jan. 3, 1976 (div. Apr. 1980); m. Ann Marie Johnson, Oct. 16, 1982. PhD in Human Resources Devel., Pacific Western U., 1986. Prodn. scheduler Square D Mfg. Co., Cedar Rapids, Iowa, 1967-72; security cons. Vets. Pub. Safety, Cedar Rapids, 1972-77; nuclear security cons. Iowa Electric Light and Power Co., Cedar Rapids, 1977-78, security tng. instr., 1978-80, facility adminstr., 1980—; mem. Industry Edn. Council, Cedar Rapids, 1986—. Author: (book) Fire Brigade Training for DAEC, 1983, DAEC Fire Plan, 1984, ARC Disaster Plan, 1984. Chmn. first aid ARC, Cedar Rpaids, 1982, chmn. disaster, vol. cons. 1984. Served to sgt. USAF, 1969-72. Mem. Internat. Soc. Fire Service Instrs., Iowa Soc. Fire Service Instrs. Democrat. Methodist. Lodges: Masons, Order of Eastern Star, Shriners. Home: 3808 Blue Mound Dr NE Cedar Rapids IA 52402 Office: Iowa Electric Light & Power Co IE Tower Cedar Rapids IA 52401

MOREY, LLOYD WILLIAM, JR., osteopathic physician, surgeon; b. Kirksville, Mo., Mar. 30, 1930; s. Lloyd W. and Lillian B. (Green) M.; m. Ruby C. McElhanry, June 20, 1952 (div. 1966); children—Robert, Richard, Ruth, Roger; m. Barbara J. Cooper, Dec. 30, 1967 (div. 1982); children—Billy, Barbie; m. Sally K. Olson, June 18, 1982. Cert. Gen. Practice, 1973; Manipulative Osteopathy, 1978. B.S., Northeast Mo. U., 1952; D.O., Kirksville Coll. Osteo. Medicine, 1956. Intern, Milw., 1957; pres., practicing medicine specializing in osteo. medicine, Family Med. Ctr., Wauwatosa, Wis., 1963—; mem. staff St. Joseph's Northwest Gen. Hosp., Family Hosp., New Berlin Meml.; pres. Family Med. Clinics, Inc. Contbr. articles to profl. jours. Pres. Milw. Stake Sunday Sch., Ch. Jesus Christ of Latter Day Saints 1982. Fellow Am. Coll. Gen. Practitioners Osteo. Medicine and Surgery, 1967, Am. Acad. Osteo., 1971, recipient Honored Patron award Kirksville Coll. Osteo Medicine, named Wis. Gen. Practitioner of Yr., 1974. Bd. dirs. Northest Gen. Hosp.; mem. Am. Acad. Family Physicians, Am. Assn. Study Headaches, Internat. Headache Soc., Am. Osteo. Assn., Wis. Assn. Osteo. Physicians and Surgeons, Milw. Dist. Soc. Osteo. Physicians and Surgeons, Am. Coll. Gen. Practitioners Osteo. Medicine and Surgery, Milw. County Med. Soc., Wis. Med. Soc., Wis. Soc. Am. Coll. Gen. Practitioners in Osteo. Medicine and Surgery, Am. Acad. Osteopathy, Cranial Acad., Wis. Acad. Family Physicians. Republican. Avocations: photography; hunting. Home: 4047 N 92nd St Wauwatosa WI 53222 Office: Family Med Ctr Ltd 4025 N 92nd St Wauwatosa WI 53222

MORFORD, JAMES WARREN, health care executive; b. Duluth, Minn., Feb. 22, 1945; s. James Andrew and Christine (Warner) M.; m. Pamela Ann Carlson, July 20, 1974; children: James Warren II, Melissa Lyn. AA, U. Minn., 1965; BS, U. Ariz., 1969. Salesman Guest Pac Corp., Mt. Vernon, N.Y., 1970; v.p. Student Service Directory, Mt. Vernon, 1970-71; dir. mktg. Doctors Diagnostic Labs., Mpls., 1971-76, pres., 1976-78; pres., chief exec. officer Lab. Cons. Internat., Mpls., 1977-80; chief operating officer Morford Clin., Mpls., 1980—; dir. mktg. North Control Labs., St. Cloud, Minn., 1979-80; bd. dirs., co-chmn. Hennepin Counseling Ctr., Mpls., 1986—. Mem. Med. Group Mgmt. Assn., Minn. Med. Group Mgmt. Assn. Republican. Methodist. Avocations: travel, astronomy, skiing, fishing, hunting. Home: 1911 Timberline Spur Minnetonka MN 55343 Office: Morford Clinic 2545 Chicago Ave Suite 515 Minneapolis MN 55404

MORFORD, WARREN NEWTON, JR., lawyer; b. Charleston, W.Va., Aug. 24, 1954; s. Warren Newton and Vivian Diane (Jones) M.; m. Kathy S. Baker, Oct. 9, 1982. BA, Ohio State U., 1976; JD, Thomas M. Cooley Law Sch., 1979. Bar: Ohio 1980, U.S. Dist. Ct. (so. dist.) Ohio 1980. Assoc. Burd & Morford, Chesapeake, Ohio, 1979-83; sole practice, Chesapeake, 1983—; referee Lawrence County Mcpl. Ct., Chesapeake, 1981-83; atty. Union Twp. Bd. Trustees, Chesapeake, 1984—; asst. pros. atty. Lawrence County, Ohio, 1985-86 . Mem. ABA, Ohio State Bar Assn., Lawrence County Bar Assn., Assn. Trial Lawyers Am. Republican. Home: 311 Orchard Dr South Point OH 45680 Office: 406-B 2d Ave PO Box 637 Chesapeake OH 45619

MORGAN, ANNE BRUCE, health care psychologist; b. Wilmington, Ohio, Sept. 20, 1950; d. Warren Brooke and Mary Bruce (Campbell) M.; m. Saul Julian Morse, Aug. 21, 1982; 1 child, John Samuel Morse. B.A., Muskingum Coll., New Concord, Ohio, 1971; M.A., U. N.D., 1975, Ph.D., 1978. Cert. psychologist, Ill. Psychology fellow specialist, div. health care psychology U. Minn. Hosps., 1977-78; lectr. psychology, clin. supr. Sangamon State U., Springfield, Ill., 1979; instr. Lincoln Land Community Coll. Sch. Respiratory Therapy, Springfield, 1981; clin. psychologist-rehab. Meml. Med. Ctr., Springfield, 1979-82, dir. dept. health care psychology, 1982—. Mem. Am. Psychol. Assn., Midwestern Psychol. Assn., Ill. Psychol. Assn., Soc. Behavioral Medicine, Nat. Head Injury Found., LWV, Jr. League. Jewish. Contbr. articles to profl. jours. Office: 800 N Rutledge Springfield IL 62781

MORGAN, ARDYS NORD, educator; b. South Bend, Ind., Nov. 1, 1946; d. Arthur August and Janet Ardis (Eide) Nord; m. Richard William Morgan, Apr. 9, 1968; children: Elizabeth Elayne, Matthew Richard. BS in Elem. Edn., Ind. U., Bloomington, 1968; MS in Elem. Edn., Ind. U., Indpls., 1972; reading cert., Ind. U., South Bend, 1982. Tchr. South Bend, 1968-69, 73—, Indpls., 1969-70; resident lectr. Indiana/Purdue U., Indpls., 1970-73; adj. prof. Ind. U., South Bend, 1985—; cons.in computers and mainstreaming NICEL Lab, South Bend, 1986. Lilly Endowment fellow, 1987.

Mem. NEA. Home: 65480 Oak Rd North Liberty IN 46554 Office: South Bend Community School Corp 5001 S Miami South Bend IN 46614

MORGAN, ARTHUR THOMAS, steel company executive; b. Rochester, N.Y., Mar. 13, 1928; s. Joseph and Elizabeth (Perrone) Mitrano; m. Heidi Kopper, July 23, 1960; 1 child, Audrey Christina. BSMetE, Purdue U., 1951; MBA, U. Chgo. 1960. Research metallurgist Inland Steel Co., East Chicago, Ind., 1951-60, sr. metallurgist, 1961-63; chief metallurgist Borg-Warner Corp., Chicago Heights, Ill., 1964-72; works mgr. Calumet Steel Co., Chicago Heights, Ill., 1973-74, v.p, 1975-81; v.p., gen. mgr. Spencer Clark Metal Industries Inc., South Holland, Ill., 1982—, also bd. dirs.; cons. metallurgy, South Holland, 1982—; bd. dirs. FREMA, Inc., Highland, Ind. Patentee in field. Mem. ASTM, Am. Soc. for Metals, Am. Inst. Mining and Metall. Engrs. (chmn. Chgo. sect. 1978), Steel Bar Mills Assn. (chmn. 1978-79). Republican. Lutheran. Avocations: hunting, fishing, tree growing, farming. Home: 16038 Minerva Ave South Holland IL 60473 Office: Spencer Clark Metal Industries Inc 17066A S Park Ave South Holland IL 60473

MORGAN, BRUCE ALLEN, mechanical service engineer, consultant; b. Benton Harbor, Mich., Mar. 10, 1952; s. Loyd Calley and Dorothy Ellen (Pillow) M.; m. Sandra Kay Gungler, May 13, 1972; children: Kristy Marie, Karri Ann (dec.). Student, Harding Coll., 1970-71, Western Mich. U., 1971-72; apprenticeship in plumbing, U.S. Dept. Labor, 1976. Cert. master plumber, mech. contractor, test and balance specialist, Mich.; cert. in cross connection control, Mich; lic. boiler installer, Mich. Plumber, service engr. Ideal Plumbing, Benton Harbor, 1972-79; service engr., designer Flagel Plumbing, Benton Harbor, 1979-81; owner, cons. Flagel & Morgan Plumbing and Heating, Inc., Benton Harbor, 1981—. Republican. Mem. Ch. of Christ. Club: Taildraggers Flyers (Benton Harbor). Avocations: flying airplanes, golf, swimming. Home: 2594 M-140 S Watervliet MI 49098 Office: Flagel & Morgan Plumbing & Heating Inc 335 Urbandale Ave Benton Harbor MI 49022

MORGAN, BRUCE BLAKE, banker, economist; b. Kansas City, Mo., Feb. 3, 1946; s. Everett Hilger and Dorothy Aletha (Blake) M.; m. Carol Berniese Tempel, Aug. 24, 1968 (div. 1983); children: Bruce Blake, Denise Dawn. BS, Mo. Valley Coll., 1968; MS, U. Mo., Columbia, 1973; MA, U. Mo., Kansas City, 1977, PhD, 1979; diploma in banking U. Wis., 1987. Caseworker, counselor Mo. Dept. Social Services, Jefferson City, 1967-68; community devel. specialist U. Mo. Extension, Columbia, 1968-73; community devel. specialist Midwest Research Inst., Kansas City, 1973-83, also mgr. regional econs., assoc. dir., dir. econs. and social sci., sr. adv. for mgmt.; adj. grad. prof. sch. bus. and pub. adminstrn. U. Mo., Kansas City, 1975—; v.p., exec. v.p. Kansas City Bancshares, 1984-86; dir. fin. services Coopers & Lybrand, 1986—; mem. staff Mo. Girls State, 1976—. Trustee Jackson County Mental Health Levy Bd., Kansas City, 1982-83, Am. Humanics, 1982-85; chmn. bd. Kansas City CORO, 1982-83; bd. govs. Truman Med. Ctr., 1980-85, Community Mental Health Ctr. South, 1984—. Mem. Am. Inst. Cert. Planners, Community Devel. Soc. Am. (bd. dirs. 1971-81), Nat. Assn. Bus. Economists. Office: Coopers & Lybrand 1100 Main Suite 900 Kansas City MO 64105

MORGAN, CLAUDE D'VAL, III, marketing firm executive; b. Carthage, Mo., Dec. 17, 1947; s. Claude D'Val and Margaret (Speer) M.; B.S. in Bus. Adminstrn., Mo. So. State U., 1970; m. Georgia E. Cook; children—Claude D'Val IV, Thomas Michael, Amelia Morrow; stepchildren—William, Markie and Deanie Cook. News dir. KDMO-AM, Carthage, 1965-67; news dir., regional sales mgr., gen. sales mgr., asst. sta. mgr. KSNF-TV (CBS), Joplin, Mo., 1967-74; pres. Morgan & Assos., Inc., Joplin, 1974—, Avanced Mktg. Services, 1986—. Bd. dirs. Mo-kan council Boy Scouts Am., 1979—, Spiva Art Center, 1979—; mem. Jasper County Republican Com., 1968—; mem. blue ribbon adv. council U. Mo. Sch. Journalism, 1975, Mo. Council for Higher Edn., 1978. Mem. Am. Assn. Advt. Agys., Public Utility Communicators Assn., Mo. Asso. Press Broadcasters Assn., Mo. Radio/TV News Dirs. Assn., Aircraft Pilots and Owners Assn., Joplin C. of C. (dir. 1978-80). Episcopalian. Home: Loma Linda Estates Route 5 Box 1048 Joplin MO 64801 Office: 413 Virginia Ave Joplin MO 64801-1928

MORGAN, CRAIG MCDONALD, federal government agent; b. Uhrichsville, Ohio, Oct. 4, 1950; s. John Adrian and Ruth Virginia (McDonald) M.; m. Sharon Rose Levy, Aug. 7, 1977; children: Allyson Ruth, Brandon Evan. Security officer Ohio State U., Columbus, 1971-74; police investigator Ohio State U. Police, Columbus, 1974-79; criminal investigator Medicaid fraud unit Ohio Atty. Gen., Columbus, 1979-81, chief investigator, 1981-86; spl. agt. U.S. Dept. HHS Inspector Gen., Office of Investigations, Columbus, 1986—; lectr., instr. Cen. Ohio Tech. Coll., Newark, 1978; assessor Commn. on Accreditation for Law Enforcement Agencies, Inc., Fairfax, Va., 1984—; cons., ptnr. Computer Investigative Concepts, Columbus, 1985—. Mem. Fed. Law Enforcement Officers Assn., Assn. Fed. Investigators, Internat. Assn. Chiefs of Police, Fraternal Order Police, United Council on Welfare Fraud, Delta Epsilon Sigma. Presbyterian. Lodge: Masons. Avocations: reading, flying. Office: US Dept HHS Inspector General Office of Investigations 50 W Broad St Suite 1820 Columbus OH 43215

MORGAN, DENNIS RICHARD, lawyer; b. Lexington, Va., Jan. 3, 1942; s. Benjamin Richard and Gladys Belle (Brown) M. B.A., Washington and Lee U., 1964; J.D., U. Va., 1967; LL.M. in Labor Law, NYU, 1971. Bar: Ohio 1967, Va. 1967, U.S. Ct. Appeals (4th cir.) 1968, U.S. Ct. Appeals (6th cir.) 1971, U.S. Supreme Ct. 1972. Law clk. to chief judge U.S. Dist. Ct. Ea. Dist. Va., 1967-68; mem. Marshman, Snyder & Seeley (now Marshman, Snyder & Corrigan), Cleve., 1971-72; dir. labor relations Ohio Dept. Adminstrv. Services, 1972-75; asst. city atty. Columbus, Ohio, 1975-77; dir. Ohio Legis. Reference Bur., 1979-81; assoc. Clemans, Nelson & Assocs., Columbus, 1981; sole practice, Columbus, 1978—; lectr. in field; guest lectr. Central Mich. U., 1975; judge moot ct. Ohio State U. Sch. Law, 1981, 83, grad. div., 1973, 74, 76, Baldwin-Wallace Coll., 1973; legal counsel Dist. IV Communications Workers Am. Vice chmn. Franklin County Democratic Party, 1976-82, dem. com. person Ward 58, Columbus, 1973—; chmn. rules com. Ohio State Dem. Conv., 1974; co-founder, trustee Greater West Side Dem. Club; negotiator Franklin County United Way, 1977-81; regional chmn. ann. alumni fund-raising program U. Va. Sch. Law; mem. Friends of the Library, Franklin County, 1976—. Robert E. Lee Research scholar, summer, 1965; recipient Am. Jurisprudence award, 1967. Served to capt. U.S. Army, 1968-70. Mem. Indsl. Relations Research Assn., ABA, Fed. Bar Assn., Am. Judicature Soc., Pi Sigma Alpha. Roman Catholic. Clubs: Shamrock, Columbus Metroplitan (charter). Home: 1261 Woodbrook Ln #G Columbus OH 43223

MORGAN, DIX RALPH, radiation oncologist; b. Provo, Utah, Nov. 18, 1930; s. Ralph W. and Elizabeth (Fitzgerald) M.; m. Jackie Vogler, Dec. 15, 1955; children: Cynthia, Rebecca, Suzanne. BS in Chemistry, Brigham Young U., 1955; MD, U. Cin., 1960. Rotating intern Bernalillo County Hosp., Albuquerque, N.Mex., 1960-61; resident in therapeutic radiology U. Iowa, Iowa City, 1966-67, U. Ky., Lexington, 1967-70; dir. radiation Rx Fresno (Calif.) Community Hosp., 1970-79, Morgan and Prather MD's, Inc., Fresno, 1970-85, South East Mo. Cancer Ctr., Cape Girardeau, 1985—; asst. prof. radiation oncology U. Calif., San Francisco, 1979-86. Served with U.S. Army, 1950-52, Korea. Mem. AMA, Am. Soc. Therapeutic Radiology, Am. Coll. Radiology. Republican. Mormon. Home: Rt 2 Box 538B Cape Girardeau MO 63701 Office: Cape Girardeau Radiation Inc 1909 Broadway Cape Girardeau MO 63701 also: 1701 Lacey Blvd Cape Girardeau MO 63701

MORGAN, FRANK J., diversified food products company executive; b. 1925; m. Mary Morgan, May 24, 1952; children: Mark, Craig, Kevin, Susan, Karen. BS, Yale U., 1947; postgrad., Harvard U., 1967. With Chance Vought (div. United Techs.), 1947-48; with new departure div. Gen. Motors, 1948-51; with Remington Arms (subs. E.I. Dupont de Nemours), 1951-56; with ARMA (div. Am. bosch Arma Corp.), Garden City, N.Y., 1946-64, mgr. product support dept., 1956-64; with Quaker Oats Co., Chgo., 1964—, mgr. indsl. engring., 1964-68, asst. to group v.p. of mfg. and purchasing, 1968; supt. Quaker Oats Co., Cedar Rapids, Iowa, 1968; prodn. mgr. Quaker Oats Co., Chgo., 1969-70, mgr. orgn. and mgmt. devel., 1970-71, dir. orgn. and mgmt. devel., 1971; gen. mgr. Quaker Oats Co. of Can., Ltd., Peterborough, 1971, pres., chief exec. officer, from 1972; v.p. Quaker Oats Co., Chgo., 1972, v.p. grocery products ops., 1975, group v.p. U.S. grocery products, 1975-76, exec. v.p. internat. grocery products, 1976-79, mem. exec. com., bd. dirs., 1978—, exec. v.p. U.S. and Can. grocery products, 1979-83, pres., chief operating officer, 1983—; bd. dirs. Square D Co., The Molson Cos. Ltd.; guest lectr. U. Ill. Mem. Can.-Am. Com., Chgo. Com., Bd. Sponsors Good Shepherd Hosp. Barrington; chmn. Citizens Bd. of Loyola; trustee Glenwood (Ill.) Sch. for Boys. Served with USN, 1943-46. Mem. Am. Coll. Sports Medicine Found. (bd. dirs.). Club: Chgo. Sunday Evening (bd. dirs.). Office: Quaker Oats Co Quaker Tower 321 N Clark St Chicago IL 60604 *

MORGAN, G(EORGE) JOSEPH, bank executive; b. Louisville, Sept. 4, 1946; s. George A. and Marjorie (Montel) M.; m. Darlina M. Miller, July 22, 1972; children: Jason Patrick, Julie Marie. BS in Acctg., Western Ky. U., 1969; M in Banking, Rutgers U., 1975. Teller First Bank of Charlestown, Ind., 1964-69, loan officer, asst. v.p., 1969-74, loan officer, v.p., 1974-80; mgr. loan dept., sr. v.p. First Bank of Charlestown (now Ind. First Nat. Bank), 1980—, also bd. dirs.; bd. dirs. Ind. First Bankshares, Charlestown. Chmn. Charlestown Econ. Devel. Commn., 1986—, Clark County YMCA, Jeffersonville, Ind., 1983; bd. dirs. George Rogers Clark council Boy Scouts of Am., 1983-85, Multiple Sclerosis Soc., Louisville, 1984-85, North Clark Community Hosp., Charlestown, 1985—. Mem. So. Ind. Bankers (pres. 1975). Republican. Methodist. Lodges: Optimists (local pres. 1976), Shriners. Avocations: basketball, coin collecting, traveling, golf, real estate. Home: 8604 S Dogwood Charlestown IN 47111 Office: Ind First Nat Bank 890 Main St Charlestown IN 47111

MORGAN, HUGH ALLAN, publishing executive; b. Rochester, N.Y., Aug. 6, 1933; s. Hugh Sylvester Morgan and Helen Grace (Allan) Agness; m. Joyce Eleanor Nilsson, Aug. 20, 1964 (div. July 1985); children: Hugh Allan Jr., Jason Howard. BS, Yale U., 1955; MS in Mktg., Columbia U. Sch. Bus., 1958. Mkt. research analyst Shell Oil Co., N.Y.C., 1958-59; dist. mgr. McGraw Hill Pubs., Chgo., 1959-64; mgr. advt. sales Miller Pubs., Mpls., 1964-65; dist. mgr. Standard Rate and Data, Skokie, Ill., 1965-70; mgr. advt., dir. mktg. Nat. Sch. Bd., Evanston, Ill., 1970-76; pres. Publ. Mgmt, Glenview, Ill., 1976—; cons. various orgns. and assns.; adminstr. Media Comparability Council, 1979-86. Contbr. articles to profl. jours. Interviewer Yale Alumni Schs. Com., Chgo., 1975—; treas., trustee The New Ch., 1979—. Served to lt. (j.g.) USNR, 1955-58. Mem. Soc. Nat. Assn. Publs. (1st v.p. 1986-87, bd. dirs., pres. 1987-88). Rebublican. Club: Yale (Chgo. and N.Y.C.). Avocations: tennis, reading. Home: 1337 Woodview Ln Glenview IL 60025 Office: Publ Mgmt Inc 4350 DiPaolo Ctr Glenview IL 60025

MORGAN, JANE HALE, library director; b. Dines, Wyo., May 11, 1926; d. Arthur Hale and Billie (Wood) Hale; m. Joseph Charles Morgan, Aug. 12, 1955; children: Joseph Hale, Jane Frances, Ann Michele. B.A., Howard U., 1947; M.A., U. Denver, 1954. Mem. staff Detroit Pub. Library, 1954—, exec. asst. dir., 1973-75, dep. dir., 1975-78, dir., 1978—; mem. Mich. Library Consortium Bd.; exec. bd. Southeastern Mich. Regional Film Library. Trustee New Detroit, Inc., Delta Dental Plan of Mich.; v.p. United Found.; pres. Univ.-Cultural Center Assn.; bd. dirs. Rehab. Inst., YWCA, Met. Affairs Corp., United Community Services Met. Detroit; chmn. adv. council library sci. U. Mich., mem. adv. council library sci. Wayne State U.; dir. Met. Detroit Youth Found.; chmn. Mich. LSCA Adv. Council; mem. UWA Literacy Com., Lawyers' Grievance Com. Recipient Anthony Wayne award Wayne State U., 1981; named Detroit Howardite of Year, 1983. Mem. ALA, Mich. Library Assn., Women's Nat. Book Assn., Assn. Mcpl. Profl. Women, NAACP, LWV, Alpha Kappa Alpha. Democrat. Episcopalian. Club: Women's Econ. Office: Detroit Public Library 5201 Woodward Ave Detroit MI 48202

MORGAN, JOHN A., corporate director; b. Wichita, Kans., Sept. 4, 1915; s. Leo O. and Maud (Swaim) M.; m. Patricia Crowe, Mar. 31, 1946 (dec. Aug. 1975); children: Eileen, Douglas, Christine, Lisa, Gregory, Deirdre. AB, Wichita State U., 1937; MBA, Harvard U., 1939. Advt. asst. Butler Mfg. Co., Kansas City, Mo., 1939-42, various exec. positions, 1946-51, gen. mgr., exec. v.p., 1951-57, pres., 1957-67, chmn. bd., 1967-74. Chmn. bd. Midwest Research Inst., U. Kansas City, chmn. various non-candidate polit. action campaigns, Kansas City. Served to lt. USNR, 1943-46, PTO. Named Mr. Kansas City, Kansas City C. of C., 1968; recipient Chancellor's medal, U. Mo., Kansas City, 1964; named to Kansas City Bus. Leaders Hall Fame, Jr. Achievement, 1985. Avocations: hiking in the mountains. Home: 310 W 49th A-7 Kansas City MO 64112

MORGAN, LARRY GENE, accountant; b. Mo., Mar. 13, 1939; s. Glenn Eugene and Wilma Lorene Morgan; m. Bonnie Kay Barnes, Sept. 2, 1962; children: Douglas Eugene, Denise Kay. BSBA, Cen. Mo. State U., 1963, MBA, 1964. CPA, Mo. Acct., auditor, mgr. Grant Thornton, Kansas City, Mo., 1964-77; acct., auditor, owner Van Quaethem, Morgan & Co., P.C., Blue Springs, Mo., 1977—. Sec., treas. Blue Springs Econ. Devel. Commn., 1987. Served with USNG, 1960-66. Mem. Am. Inst. CPA's, Nat. Assn. Accts., Mo. Soc. CPA's, Blue Springs C. of C. (pres. 1982). Methodist. Lodges: Rotary (bd. dirs. Blue Springs 1986—), Masons. Avocations: fishing, golf. Home: 618 N 19th St Blue Springs MO 64015 Office: Van Quaethem Morgan & Co PC 600 Mock Ave Blue Springs MO 64015

MORGAN, LEONARD EUGENE, medical and commercial illustrator; b. Princeton, Ind., Dec. 12, 1948; s. Billy Gene and Ester June (Wright) M.; m. Frances Elizabeth Airdo, Jan. 31, 1970; children—Natalie Jean, Lindsay Ann. B.S. in Med. Art, U. Ill. Med. Ctr., 1974. Free-lance illustrator, serving numerous clients Naperville, Ill., 1976—; guest speaker U. Ill. Med. Ctr. Chgo., 1980—. Speaker Assn. Med. Illustrators Annual Meeting, Norfolk, Va., 1986. Contbr. articles to profl. jour. Work appeared in Illustrators 27 Annual, 1985, Am. Illustration III Annual, 1985, 1985 Print's Regional Design Annual, 1985, Studio Mag's The Creative Decade, 1976-86, Communication Arts Ann., 1987, The One Show, 1987; recipient DESI award, 1985. Mem. Assn. Med. Illustrators (1st and 2d place awards in advt. 1985), Midwest Med. Illustrators Assn. (speaker regional meeting), Artists Guild Chgo. (silver medal 1984), Graphic Artists Guild N.Y. Avocations: Fishing, travel, family activities, air brush design innovations. Home: 131 Ridgewood Ct Bolingbrook IL 60439 Office: Leonard E Morgan Inc 1163 E Ogden Ave Ste 705 Rm 130 Naperville IL 60540

MORGAN, PAUL WILLIAM, engineer, researcher; b. Highland Park, Mich., June 29, 1952; s. Kenneth Hayden and Margret Anne (Rourk) M.; m. Debra Ann Pelkey, Sept. 7, 1979 (div. Mar. 1985); children: Paul James, Thomas Edward, Anna Florence. BSEE, Wayne State U., 1975. Design engr. Marposs Gauges, Madison Heights, 1977-79; design engr. Lebow Assocs., Troy, Mich., 1979-80, quality mgr., 1980-81; project engr. Eaton-Lebow, Troy, 1981-83, sr. project engr., 1983—. Inventor and patentee in field. Home: 5976 Dwight Pontiac MI 48054 Office: Eaton Corp Lebow Products 1728 Maplelawn Troy MI 48099

MORGAN, ROBERT B., insurance company executive; b. 1934. AB, Eastern Ky. U., 1954. Tchr. Cin. Sch. System, 1954-56; underwriter Ins. Co. of N.Am., Phila., 1960-66; with Cin. Ins. Co., Inc., 1966—, asst. casualty mgr., 1966-69, asst. v.p., 1969-71, v.p., 1971-72, mgr., 1972-76, pres., 1976—; pres. Cin. Fin. Corp., 1981—. Served to capt. AUS, 1956-58. Office: Cin Fin Corp Cincinnati Financial Ctr PO Box 145496 Cincinnati OH 45214 *

MORGAN, ROBERT DALE, judge; b. Peoria, Ill., May 27, 1912; s. Harry Dale and Eleanor (Ellis) M.; m. Betty Louise Harbers, Oct. 14, 1939; children—Thomas Dale, James Robert. A.B., Bradley U., 1934; J.D., U. Chgo., 1937. Bar: Ill. bar 1937. Practice in Peoria, 1937-42, 46-67, Chgo., 1946-50; partner firm Morgan, Pendarvis & Morgan, Peoria, 1946-57, Davis, Morgan & Witherell, Peoria, 1957-67; U.S. judge So. Dist Ill. (became Central Dist. 1979), Peoria, 1967—. Contbr. articles to law revs. Mayor, Peoria, 1953-57; Bd. dirs. YMCA, Peoria, 1940-72, pres., 1947-53; Trustee Bradley U. Served from 1st lt. to maj. AUS, 1942-46. Am., Ill., Peoria County bar assns.; Am. Judicature Soc. Presbyterian. Clubs: Creve Couer (Peoria), Rotary (Peoria) (pres. 1962-63), Country (Peoria). Office: U S Dist Ct 228 Fed Bldg 100 NE Monroe Peoria IL 61602

MORGAN, ROBERT EDWARD, state justice; b. Mitchell, S.D., Aug. 13, 1924; s. Chester Lawrence and Phyllis Mae (Saterlie) M.; m. Mary Doyle, Oct. 28, 1950; children: Mary Alice, Michael Chester, Thomas Wayne, Margaret Jane; m. Mary Ann Ver Meulen, June 1, 1974; 1 child, Daniel James. Student, Creighton U., 1942, 46-47, 48; J.D., U. S.D., 1950. Bar: S.D. 1950. Mem. firm Mitchell & Chamberlain, S.D., 1950-76; justice S.D. Supreme Ct., Pierre, 1977—. Served with USAAF, 1943-45. Mem. ABA, S.D. Bar Assn. Office: U SD Sch Law Vermillion SD 57069

MORGAN, RONALD KEITH, chaplain; b. Johnstown, Pa., Apr. 27, 1934; s. Clinton E. and Vada A. (Hoffman) M.; m. Dorla Dean Kinsey, Mar. 31, 1954 (div. 1974); children: Gail Habecker, Gwen Carpenter, Glee Doody, Gay Mercer; m. Jane Lawry Malone, Sept. 24, 1983. BA, Juniata Coll., 1956; MDiv, Bethany Theol. Sem., 1960; M of Sacred Theology, United Theol. Sem., 1971. Pastor Community Ch. of the Brethren, Hutchinson, Kans., 1960-66, Mack Meml. Ch. of the Brethren, Dayton, Ohio, 1966-72; chaplain Fallsview Psychiat. Hosp., Cuyahoga Falls, Ohio, 1972-74, dir. pastoral care, 1974-80; chaplain, clin. pastoral educator Fairview Gen. Hosp., Cleve., 1980-86; dir. pastoral care Cleve. Clinic Found., 1986—; pastoral counselor St. Paul's Episcopal Ch., Akron, Ohio, 1974-76; instr. EMERGE Ashland Theol. Sem., Akron, 1976-80; clin. asst. prof. pastoral psychology Coll. Medicine N.E. Ohio U., 1978-80; cons. for chaplaincy Allen Meml. Hosp., Oberlin, Ohio, 1982-86. Mem. Clergy and Laity Concerned About Vietnam, 1967-72, coordinator 1969-70; mem. adv. bd. dirs. United Ministries in Higher Edn., Dayton, 1967-69, chmn. 1969. Rockefeller scholar, 1959-60. Fellow Am. Protestant Health Assn., Coll. Chaplains (Ohio cert. com.); mem. Assn. Clin. Pastoral Edn. (supervisory, chmn. standards com. 1986—), Audobon Soc. (pres. Akron chpt. 1974-75). Republican. Avocations: birdwatching, golf, classical music, travel, photography. Home: 3812 Circlewood Ct Fairview Park OH 44126 Office: Cleve Clinic Found Pastoral Care Dept 9500 Euclid Ave Cleveland OH 44106

MORGAN, RUTH MILDRED, medical technologist; b. Indpls., Mar. 8, 1917; d. James Franklin and Lula Floy (Heiny) M.; B.S. in Allied Health Edn., Ind. U.-Purdue U., Indpls., 1976; student Ind. U., 1954-57, 76-77, Butler U., 1958. Dental asst., med. asst. and med. technologist, Indpls., 1953—; tchr. hematology Med. Lab., 1970-79, supr. hematology, 1960-79, gen. supr., 1980—. Fin. chmn. 8th precinct 20th Ward of Indpls., 1977-79. Recipient citation Mayor Richard Lugar, 1976; registered med. technologist, lic. health facility adminstr. Mem. Am. Soc. Clin. Pathologists (affiliate), Am. Soc. Profl. and Exec. Women, Marion County Council Republican Women, Nat. Fedn. Republican Women, Am. Coll. Health Care Adminstrs. (assoc. Ind. chpt.), Brown County Art Gallery Assn., Ind. Soc. Med. Technologists. Club: Eastern Star (matron 1950). Inventor, patentee cabinets for indsl. use. Home: 3965 N Meridian Suite 6-D Indianapolis IN 46208 Office: 8801 N Meridian St Indianapolis IN 46250

MORGAN, STANLEY LEINS, pharmaceutical company executive; b. Sandyville, Ohio, Jan. 28, 1918; s. Eben T. and Nora (Leins) M.; B.S. in Chem. Engring., Case Inst. Tech., 1939; m. Eloise Morkel, Feb. 22, 1941; children—Susan, Patricia, Ann. Chem. engr. Ben Venue Labs., Inc., Bedford, Ohio, 1940-42, mgr. blood plasma lab., 1942-44, gen. mgr., chief engr., 1944-61, v.p., 1961-63, exec. v.p., 1963—, also dir.; pres. Bon Vonne Generics Co.; dir. Medmarc. Registered profl. engr., Ohio. Fellow Am. Inst. Chemists; mem. Am. Chem. Soc., Health Industries Mfrs. Assn., Am. Inst. Chem. Engrs., N.Y. Acad. Sci., Cryobiology Soc., Parental Drug Assn., Cleve. Engring. Soc., Assn. Ofcl. Racing Chemist. Methodist. Clubs: Acacia Country (Cleve.). Home: 31051 Northwood Dr Pepper Pike OH 44124 Office: 270 Northfield Rd Bedford OH 44146

MORGAN, THOMAS JAMES, manufacturing company executive; b. Allegan, Mich., Oct. 12, 1944; s. Bernith Leo and Donna Jean (Mack) M.; m. Suzanne J. Smith, may 22, 1987; children: Corri Lynn, Chad Thomas. Systems analyst McCord Corp., Wauseon, Ohio, 1972-74; systems project leader Devilbiss Co., Toledo, 1974-78, supr. tech. support, 1978-80, mgr. communications, 1980-82, mgr. mfg. and engring. systems, 1982-84; mgr. systems support Champion Spark Plug Co., Toledo, 1984—; pres. The Thornwood Group, Inc., Toledo, 1987—. Cons. Ch. of Nazarene, Sylvania, Ohio, 1974-85; pres. NYI, Sylvania, 1983. Served with USAF, 1966-70, Vietnam. Mem. Soc. Mech. Engrs. Republican. Baptist. Home: 3404 Westchester Toledo OH 43615 Office: Champion Spark Plug 900 Upton Ave Toledo OH 43661

MORGAN, TIMOTHY JOE, dentist; b. St. Charles, Mo., Aug. 10, 1953; s. Gerald Kreon and Edith Emma Francis (Knoernschild) M.; m. Jan Denise Naughton, Nov. 18, 1978; children: Rebecca Lynn, Jennifer Ann. BS in Biology, Cen. Mo. State U., 1975; DDS, U. Mo., Kansas City, 1979; Grad., U.S. Dental Inst., Chgo., 1986. Assoc. G. Neubauer and R. Prine, DDS, Blue Springs, Mo., 1979-80; gen. practice dentistry Quincy, Ill., 1980—; asst. prof. operative dentistry U. Mo., Kansas City, 1979-80; vol. Nat. Children's Dental Health Month, Quincy, 1981-86. Elder Our Redeemer Luth. Ch., Quincy, 1984-86; mem. Parent Tchrs. League, Quincy. Mem. ADA, Acad. Gen. Dentistry, Great River Dental Group, T.L. Gilmer Dental Soc.(pres. 1986—), Internat. Assn. Orthodontics. Republican. Avocations: hunting, fishing, archery, photography. Office: 2800 Broadway Quincy IL 62301

MORGAN, WILLIAM T., financial services company executive; b. 1929. With Waddell & Reed, Inc., Kansas City, Mo., 1950—, now pres., chief exec. officer. Office: Waddell & Reed Inc 2400 Pershing Rd Box 1343 Kansas City MO 64108 *

MORGEN, JOHN LEO, office furniture company executive; b. New Holstein, Wis., Dec. 1, 1932; s. Leo Henry and Rose Mary (Goebel) M.; m. Ellen Mary Shea, June 6, 1959; Kathleen, Eileen, Barbara, Jane. B.B.A., U. Wis.-Madison, 1957. Salesman, Remington Rand, Milw., 1957-61; sec., treas. M&M Office Furniture, Butler, Wis., 1961—. Mem. Wis. Rowing Assn. (bd. dirs. 1978—, Alumni Appreciation award 1984). Republican. Roman Catholic. Clubs: Eagles, Mendota, Nat. W (bd. dirs.). Avocations: golf; tennis; rowing; basketball; swimming. Home: 931 E Glenco Pl Bayside WI 53217 Office: M&M Office Furniture 12600 W Silver Spring Dr Butler WI 53007

MORGENSTERN, BARBARA, manufacturing company executive; b. Chgo., June 23, 1936; d. Henry and Phyllis Weisman; m. Sydney Morgenstern, Jan. 5, 1957; children: Jordan, Mark, Susan. BS, Roosevelt U., 1974; student, Keller Grad. Sch. Mgmt., 1976-77. V.p. NuArc Co. Inc., Chgo., 1977-80, exec. v.p., 1980—. V.p. Mt. Sinai Hosp. Service Club, Chgo., 1960-70, soc. chmn. Northwest Hosp. Womens Bd., 1969; vol. Council for Jewish Elderly, Chgo., 1973. Recipient Outstanding Support award Assn. House, Chgo., 1981, Cert. of Achievement Chgo. Graphic Arts Inst., Chgo., 1981. Mem. Midwest Indsl. Mfg. Assn., Alpha Epsilon Phi. Clubs: Bryn Mawr Country (Lincolnwood, Ill.), High Ridge Country (Lantana, Fla.). Avocations: golf, travel, theater, concerts. Office: NuArc Co Inc 6200 W Howard St Niles IL 60648

MORGENTHALER, DAVID TURNER, Investment banker; b. Chester, S.C., Aug. 5, 1919; s. Henry W. and Elizabeth (Taylor) M.; B.S. in Mech. Engring., M.S., Mass. Inst. Tech., 1941; m. Lindsay Anne Jordan, May 17, 1945; children—David T., Gary J., Todd W., Gaye Elizabeth. Sales mgr. Ervite Corp., 1945-47; mech. engr. Copes Vulcan div. Blaw-Knox Co., 1947-50; v.p., dir. sales Delavan Mfg. Co., Des Moines, 1950-57; pres. Foseco, Inc., Cleve., 1957-68; chmn. bd. Foseco Technik Ltd., Birmingham, Eng., 1964-68; chmn. bd. API Instruments Co., 1968-70, dir., 1963-70; chmn. bd. Mfg. Data Systems, Inc., Ann Arbor, Mich., 1969-81 ; chmn. exec. com., dir. LFE Corp., Waltham, Mass., 1970-85 ; sr. ptnr. Morgenthaler Assos.; mng. ptnr. Morgenthaler Ventures, 1981—; dir. Hauserman, Inc., Cleve., Tartan Labs., Inc., Pitts., Three Phoenix Co., Vitarline Pharms., Inc., Springfield Gardens, N.Y., ; cons. Brentwood Assocs.; trustee Cleve. Clinic Found.; bd. overseers Case Western Res. U. Served to capt. AUS, 1941-45. Mem. Nat. Venture Capital Assn. (past pres.), Chief Execs. Orgn., Inc. (past pres.), Young Pres. Orgn. (sr. v.p., bd. dirs.), Sigma Nu. Clubs: Westwood Country, Union, Pacific Union, Lyford Cay, Clevelander, Mid-Day. Home: 13904 Edgewater Dr Cleveland OH 44107

MORIARTY, BRIAN DAVID, bank executive; b. Holyoke, Mass., Oct. 12, 1942; s. Francis John and Paige Dawson (Smith) M.; m. Susan Elizabeth

Smith, June 29, 1968; children: Daniel Brian, Katherine Beth. BS, Miami U., Oxford, Ohio, 1964. Plant mgr., dir. employee relations Pease Co., Hamilton, Ohio, 1971-83; v.p. personnel 1st Nat. Bank Southwest Ohio, Hamilton, 1983—. Chmn. civil service commn. City of Wyoming, Ohio, 1982—. Served to capt. USMC, 1965-68, Vietnam. Mem. Ohio Bankers Assn. (vice-chmn. human resources 1986, chmn. 1987-88). Republican. Avocations: golf, World War II history. Home: 183 Compton Rd Wyoming OH 45215 Office: 1st Nat Bank Southwest Ohio Third at High St Hamilton OH 45012

MORIN, GARY MICHAEL, computer software specialist; b. Highland Park, Mich., Nov. 14, 1952; s. Ronald Nelson and Rita Josephine (Grendys) M.; m. Janice Elizabeth Johnson, July 18, 1981. BA, Oakland U., 1974, MS in Mgmt., 1980; postgrad., Purdue U., 1981-82. Statis. analyst OLHSA, Pontiac, Mich., 1978-79; assoc. bus. analyst Ex-Cell-O Corp., Troy, Mich., 1979-81, sr. systems analyst, 1982-86; sr. software specialist Digital Equipment Corp., Farmington, Mich., 1986—; bd. dirs. MTX Corp. Contbr. articles to profl. jours. Mem. AAAS, Am. Econ. Assn., Soc. Gen. Systems Research, Warren Astron. Soc. (treas. 1977-78), Great Lakes Region Astron. League (chmn. 1977-78, sec. 1985—). Democrat. Roman Catholic. Home: 1427 Sycamore Rochester MI 48063

MORIN, ROBERT JAMES, retired railroad executive; b. Superior, Wis., Mar. 15, 1927; s. Peter Emil and Violet Alma (Saterstrom) M.; m. Muriel Joan Benson, June 17, 1950; 1 son, Robert Peck. Cert., Duluth (Minn.) Bus. U., 1948; cert. jr. bus. adminstrn. U. Minn.-Duluth, 1956. Stenographer, clk. Duluth Missabe & Iron Range Ry. Co., Duluth, 1948-50, sta. clk., 1952; trainmaster's clk. Gt. No. Ry. Co., Superior, Wis., 1952-58, sec. to v.p., gen. counsel, St. Paul, 1958-65, sec. to pres., 1965-70; with Burlington No. Inc., St. Paul, 1970-84, asst. corp. sec., 1980-84, asst. corp. sec. subs. Burlington No. R.R. Co., St. Paul, 1981-84, corp. sec. subs. Burlington No. Airmotive Inc., St. Paul, 1981-83; corp. sec. BN Fin. Services, Inc., St. Paul, 1983-84, Clarkland, Inc., St. Paul, 1982-84, Clarkland Royalty, Inc., St. Paul, 1982-84, 906 Olive Corp., St. Paul, 1982-84. Served with U.S. Army, 1946-48, 50-52. Republican. Lutheran. Club: Lost Spur Country (St. Paul). Lodges: Masons, Shriners. Home: 355 Millwood Ave W Roseville MN 55113

MORIN, WILLIAM RAYMOND, restaurant executive, management consultant; b. Escanaba, Mich., Apr. 19, 1949; s. Raymond Louis and Naomi Rita (Flynn) M.; Yvonne Catherine Singleton, Aug. 7, 1971; 1 child, Timothy Raymond. AA in Bus. cum laude, Bay de Noc Community Coll., Escanaba, 1972; BS in Bus. summa cum laude, No. Mich. U., 1974; MBA, Mich. State U., 1979. Personnel analyst Kimberly-Clark Corp., Neenah, Wis., 1974-75; dir. transp. Kentwood Pub. Schs., Grand Rapids, Mich., 1975-76; office supr. State of Mich., Traverse City, 1976-79; personnel mgr. Mueller Furniture Corp., Grand Rapids, 1980-81; regional rep. franchised ops. Woodson-Holmes Enterprises, Cheyenne, Wyo., 1981-87; dir. franchising Dawn Donut Systems, Inc., Flint, 1987—; owner, mgr. Morin Mgmt., Grand Rapids, 1980-81; instr. U. Wash., 1979-80. Contbr.: (book) Principles of Modern Management, 1980. Active various civic orgns. Served as sgt. U.S. Army, 1967-70, Vietnam. Home: 2666 Randall NW Grand Rapids MI 49504 Office: Dawn Donut Systems Inc Sheraton Motel Office Complex G-4300 W Pierson Rd Flint MI 48504

MORITZ, GERALD WILLIAM, otolaryngology; b. Bklyn., June 25, 1939. BA, U. Calif., Berkeley, 1965; MD, St. Louis U., 1970. Intern St. Louis U., 1970-71, resident, 1971-72; practice medicine specializing in otolaryngology Bridgeton, Mo., 1972—. Home: 8020 Daytona Dr Saint Louis MO 63105 Office: St Louis County Otolaryngology 12255 De Paul Dr Suite 790 Bridgeton MO 63044

MORITZ, MICHAEL EVERETT, lawyer; b. Marion, Ohio, Mar. 30, 1933; s. Charles Raymond and Elisabeth Bovie (Morgan) M.; m. Lou Ann Yardley, Sept. 12, 1959; children: Ann Gibson, Jeffrey Connor, Molly Elisabeth, Catharine Morgan. BS, Ohio State U., 1958, JD summa cum laude, 1961. Bar: Ohio 1961, U.S. Tax Ct. 1970. Assoc. Dunbar, Kienzle & Murphey, Columbus, Ohio, 1961-65, ptnr., 1966-72; ptnr. Moritz, McClure, Hughes & Kerscher, Columbus, 1972-80, Baker & Hostetler, Columbus, 1980—; adj. prof. Capital U. Law Sch., Columbus, 1969-70; lectr. Ohio Legal Ctr. Inst., Columbus, 1967; bd. dirs. Cardinal Distbn., Inc., Columbus, Meret, Inc., Pickett Hotel Co. Chmn. legal div. United Appeal Franklin County, Columbus, 1964; pres. Capital City Young Rep. Club, Columbus, 1966; mem. Franklin County Rep. Exec. Com., Columbus, 1966—; trustee Kenyon Festival Theatre, 1981-86, Players Theatre of Columbus, 1986—. Served with USN, 1954-56. Recipient Disting. Service award Columbus Jaycees, 1966. Mem. ABA, Ohio Bar Assn., Columbus Bar Assn., Am. Judicature Soc., Ohio State U. Faculty Club, Order of Coif, Phi Gamma Delta, Beta Gamma Sigma. Clubs: Scioto Country, Capital, Columbus, Athletic of Columbus, Ohio State U. President's. Home: 4900 Deer Run Dr Dublin OH 43017 Office: Baker & Hostetler 65 E State St Columbus OH 43215

MORK, GORDON ROBERT, history educator; b. St. Cloud, Minn., May 6, 1938; s. Gordon Matthew and Agnes (Gibb) M.; m. Dianne Jeannette Muetzel, Aug. 11, 1963; children: Robert, Kristiana, Elizabeth. Instr. history U. Minn., Mpls., 1966; lectr., asst. prof. U. Calif., Davis, 1966-70; mem. faculty Purdue U., West Lafayette, Ind., 1970—; assoc. prof. Purdue U., West Lafayette, 1973—, dir. honors program in the humanities; resident dir. Purdue U.-Ind. U. Program, Hamburg, Fed. Republic Germany, 1975-76; research fellow in humanities U. Wis., Madison, 1969-70. Author: Modern Western Civilization: A Concise History, 2d edit., 1981. Mem. adv. bd. Teaching History, 1983—, History Teacher, 1986—. Mem. citizens task force Lafayette Sch. Corp., 1978-79; bd. dirs. Ind. Com. for the Humanities; bd. dirs., sec. Murdock-Sunnyside Bldg. Corp., 1980—. Mem. Am. Hist. Assn., Conf. Group on Cen. European History, Soc. History Edn., Leo Baeck Inst., Conf. Group on German Politics, Internat. Soc. for History Didactics, Phi Beta Kappa. Home: 1521 Cason St Lafayette IN 47904 Office: Purdue U Dept History West Lafayette IN 47907

MORK, SCOTT WILLIS, marketing professional; b. Duluth, Minn., Mar. 2, 1956; s. John Willis and Marjorie (Anderson) M.; m. Susan Lynn Cammack, Mar. 24, 1984. BBA, U. Minn., Duluth, 1979; MBA, St. Thomas Coll., St. Paul, 1987. Recruiter ABC Employment Service, Mpls., 1978-79; expeditor ITT Schadow Inc., Eden Prairie, Minn., 1979; asst. buyer ITT Schadow Inc., Eden Prairie, 1979, with customer service, 1979-81, distributor sales coordinator, 1981, mktg. analyst, 1981-84, mktg. services coordinator, 1985—. Home: 7250 Butterscotch Rd Eden Prairie MN 55344 Office: ITT Schadow Inc 8081 Wallace Rd Eden Prairie MN 55344

MORLAN, LARRY EARL, real estate development company executive; b. Brazil, Ind., Apr. 15, 1937; m. Marilyn Jean Muncie, May 20, 1956; children: Lisa Robin, Anthony Neal, Matthew Ryan. BS in Edn., Ind. State U., 1964. V.p. The Hickey Co., South Bend, Ind., 1970-74; project mgr. Johnson Constrn. Co., Colorado Springs, Colo., 1974-76; v.p. Bradbury & Stamm, Albuquerque, 1976-80, Bramalea Ltd., Houston, 1980-82; sr. v.p. Oxford Devel. Co., Indpls., 1982—. Mem. adv. bd. Distributive Edn. Clubs Am. Mem. Nat. Home Builders Assn. (bd. dirs.), Indpls. Multi-Family Council (v.p. 1985-86), Greater Cin. Home Builders Assn., Builders Assn. Greater Indpls. (bd. dirs.), Cen. Ohio Home Builders Assn. Republican. Roman Catholic. Avocations: golf, woodworking, model trains. Office: Oxford Devel Co 8606 Allisonville Rd Indianapolis IN 46250

MORLEY, GERALD KENT, neurologist and clinical neurophysiologist; b. Provo, Utah, May 12, 1939; s. Alonzo John and Eloise (Stewart) M.; m. Judith Hartman, Aug. 26, 1960; children: Brian, Bruce, Laura, Robert. BS with honors, Brigham Young U., 1960; MD, U. Utah, Salt Lake City, 1964. Diplomate Am. Bd. Neurology and Psychiatry, Am. Bd. of Qualification in Electroencephalography. Intern Phila. Gen. Hosp., 1964-65; resident neurology U. Minn., Mpls., 1967-70; staff neurologist Mpls. VA Med. Ctr., 1970—; cons. Unity Med. Ctr., Fridley, Minn., 1970—, Mt. Sinai Med. Ctr., Mpls., 1978—; Abbot Northwestern Med. Ctr., Mpls., 1984—; bd. dirs. behavioral neurology Mpls. VA Med. Ctr., 1973—, potential lab., 1982—, electromyography lab., 1970-73. Author: (chpt.) The Neurology of Pain, 1985, Aging and Dementia, 1982; contbr. numerous articles to profl. jours. Fellow Am. Acad. Neurology, Am. Acad. Electromyography and Electrodiagnosis (cert.), Am. Electroenchphalographic Soc.; mem. Internat. Soc. Neuropsychology, Behavioral Neurology Soc., Am. Soc. Neuroimaging (cert.). Avocation: developing use of computers in med. applications. Home: 8524 Hopewood Ln New Hope MN 55427 Office: Dept Neurology 5401 48th Ave Minneapolis MN 55417

MORLEY, HARRY THOMAS, JR., real estate executive; b. St. Louis, Aug. 13, 1930; s. Harry Thomas and Celeste Elizabeth (Davies) M.; m. Nelda Lee Mulholland, Sept. 3, 1960; children: Lisa, Mark, Marci. BA, U. Mo., 1955; MA, U. Denver, 1959. Dir. men's student activities Iowa State Tchrs. Coll., 1955-57; dir. student housing U. Denver, 1957-60; pvt. practice psychol. consulting St. Louis, 1960-63; dir. adminstrn. County of St. Louis, Mo., 1963-70; regional dir. HUD, Kansas City, Mo., 1970-71; asst. sec. adminstrn. HUD, 1971-73; pres. St. Louis Regional Commerce and Growth Assn., 1973-78; partner Taylor, Morley, Simon, Inc., St. Louis, 1978—; teaching cons.-lectr. Washington U., St. Louis, 1962-70. Bd. dirs., mem. exec. com. St. Louis Coll. Pharmacy; mem. exec. com. Better Bus. Bur.; chmn. Mo. Indsl. Devel. Bd.; bd. dirs. St. Luke's Hosps., Downtown St. Louis, Inc., Laclede's Landing Redevel. Corp. Served with USN, 1951-53. Mem. Am. C. of C. Execs., Nat. Assn. Homebuilders, St. Louis Homebuildres Assn. (exec. com.), St. Louis Advt. Club. Republican. Methodist. Clubs: Mo. Athletic, St. Louis, Noonday, Castle Oak Country, Round Table. Home: 14238 Forest Crest Dr Chesterfield MO 63017 Office: 1227 Fern Ridge Pkwy Saint Louis MO 63141-4451

MORLEY, JOHN C., electronic equipment company executive; b. 1931. BA, Yale U., 1954; MBA, U. Mich., 1958. Mng. dir. Esso Pappas Chem. Ae., Greece, 1969-70; pres. Esso Eastern Chems. Inc., N.Y., 1970-71; exec. v.p. Enjay Chem. Co., 1971-74; pres. Exxon Chem. Co. U.S.A., Houston, 1974-78, sr. v.p., 1978-80; pres., chief exec. officer Reliance Electric Co. Inc., Cleve., 1980—, also bd. dirs. Served to lt. (j.g.) USNR, 1954-56. Office: Reliance Electric Co Inc 29325 Chagrin Blvd Cleveland OH 44122 *

MORLING, WILLIAM HINES, computer center director; b. Chgo., May 29, 1935; s. Edgar S. and Virginia (Eastman) M.; m. Carol M. Hasselberg, Sept. 29, 1962; children: Scott E., Beth Ann. SB, Iowa State U., 1958; MBA, U. Chgo., 1966. Systems analyst UNIVAC Corp., Chgo., 1965-67; assoc. dir. computer ctr. Kent (Ohio) State U., 1967-75, budget officer, 1975-78; coordinator research and budget Ind. Commn. for Higher Edn., Indpls., 1975-78; dir. computer ctr. Kearney (Nebr.) State Coll., 1978—. Clk. of session, mem. pastor nominating com. Kearney Presbyn. Ch.; bd. dirs. Citizens Advocacy, Kearney, 1986—, pres. 1987—; program co-chair Am. Heart Assn., Buffalo County, Nebr., 1984. Mem. Coll. and U. Systems Exchange. Avocations: referee youth soccer, photography, exercise. Home: 12 Canal Heights Kearney NE 68847 Office: Kearney State Coll Kearney NE 68849

MORMAN, RONALD L(EE), manufacturing systems consultant; b. Independence, Mo., July 27, 1944; s. Virgil L. and Lola G. (Ertle) M.; m. Jane C. Bracht, Sept. 11, 1961; children: Russell, Deborah, Shawn. BS in Indsl. Mgmt. cum laude, Cen. Mo. State U., 1970. Computer operator Hallmark Cards, Kansas City, Mo., 1961-64; program supr. Thompson Hayward Chem. Co., Kansas City, Kans., 1964-66; data processing mgr. Butler Mfg. Co., Kansas City, Mo., 1966-82; pres. Morman & Assocs., Inc., Independence, 1982-86; mgr. cons. and edn. Data Systems Internat., Kansas City, Mo., 1986—. Mem. Am. Prodn. and Inventory Control Soc., Assn. Systems Mgmt. (cert. systems profl.), Independence C. of C. Democrat. Methodist. Home: 312 NE Wicklow Ct Lee's Summit MO 64064 Office: 6301 James A Reed Rd Suite 106 Kansas City MO 64133

MORREALE, ROLAND ANTHONY, corporate executive; b. N.Y.C., Mar. 19, 1934; s. Peter and Martha (Moore) M.; B.A., U. Utah, 1955; M.S., Boston U., 1958; m. Janet L. McCroskey, July 6, 1963; 1 son, Craig. Asst. dir. Menorah Med. Center, Kansas City, Mo., 1960-65; mgmt. cons. Cresap, McCormack & Paget, N.Y.C., 1965-66; owner, cons. Roland A. Morreale & Assos., Overland Park, Kans., 1966-67; corp. tng. dir. Nat. Bellas Hess Co., Kansas City, Mo., 1967-69; asst. sales mgr. Funeral Security Plans Co., Kansas City, 1969-72; asst. dir. tng. Human Resources Corp., Kansas City, 1973; corp. dir. tng. Whitaker Cable Corp., North Kansas City, Mo., 1973-74; with Met. Community Colls., Kansas City, Mo., 1974-86, placement counselor Project Outreach, Met. Inst., Community Services, 1974-75, program coordinator Pioneer Community Coll., 1975-86; co-founder, Career Crossroads for Women, 1975-81; creator Met. Computerized Vocat. Counseling Network, 1979; pres. Contemporary Services, Inc., Profl. Resources Assocs. Inc., Assessment Preparation Tng., Inc., 1980—. Founding bd. dirs. Kansas City chpt. Amigos de las Americas; co-chmn. auction com. Peter Marshall Golf Classic. Served with AUS, 1955-57. Mem. Personnel Mgmt. Assn. Greater Kansas City Mo. (Outstanding Achievement awards), Am. Soc. Tng. and Devel., Am. Soc. Personnel Adminstrn. Presbyterian. Club: Johnson County Leisure-Aires. Writer, producer Computerized Food Allergy Diet, 1983, Computerized Health Diet, Computerized Food Allergy Diet. Office: PO Box 7847 Overland Park KS 66207

MORRELL, FRANK, neurologist, educator; b. N.Y.C., June 4, 1926; s. Benjamin R. and Rose (Langson) M.; m. Lenore Korkes, Mar. 24, 1957 (div.); children: Seth, Paul, Michael, Suzanna; m. Leyla deToledo, May 25, 1978. AB, Columbia U., 1948, MD, 1951; MS, McGill U., Montreal, Can., 1955. Diplomate Am. Bd. Psychiatry and Neurology. Resident in neurology Montefiore Hosp., Bronx, N.Y., 1951-52, 53-54; fellow EEG Nat. Hosp., London, 1952-53; fellow Montreal Neurol. Inst., 1954-55; from asst. prof. to assoc. prof. neurology U. Minn., Mpls., 1955-61; prof., chmn. dept. neurology Stanford (Calif.) U., 1961-69; prof. Rush Med. Coll., Chgo., 1971—; William Lennox lectr. Western Inst. on Epilepsy, Colo., 1980; Hans Berger lectr. Med. Coll. Va., 1987; assoc. neurosci. research program MIT, Boston, 1965-76; cons. in field. Contbr. numerous articles to profl. jours. Served as cpl. USAF, 1944-45. Fellow Royal Soc. Health, Am. Acad. Neurology; mem. Am. Electro-encephalographic Soc. (pres.), Am. Epilepsy Soc., Soc. for Neurosci. Jewish. Office: Rush Presbyn-St Luke's Med Ctr 1753 W Congress Pkwy Chicago IL 60612

MORRELL, GEORGE WALTER, business executive; b. Mineola, N.Y., Apr. 27, 1946; s. George Henry and Elizabeth Gladis (Pickering) M.; m. Ruth Ann Dougherty, Apr. 24, 1982. BS, Ind. State U., 1969; MBA, Ind. U., 1976. Buyer William H. Block Co., 1970-72, divisional sales mgr., 1973-76; area mgr. Thybony Inc., 1977-84, Am. Textile Co., 1984-85; pres. G. Morrell Assocs., 1985—; mem. adv. bd. Ind. State U., Terre Haute, 1982—; admissions counselor Mo. Mil. Acad. Named to Hon. Order Ky. Cols. Mem. Am. Mktg. Assn., Profl. Ski Instrs. Am., Assn. Individual Investors, Ind. State U. Alumni Assn. (bd. dirs. 1981—, pres. 1987), Indpls. Jaycees. Club: Indpls. Athletic. Lodge: KC. Home and Office: 7010 Bloomfield Dr E Indianapolis IN 46259

MORRELL, JAMES LLOYD, controller; b. St. Paul, July 4, 1953; s. James Lawler and Mary Ellen (Kelly) M.; m. Mary Catherine Schmitz, Nov. 23, 1974; children: Michael, Matthew, Patrick, Ryan. BS in Acctg., U. Minn., 1974. CPA, Minn. Acct. Taylor McCaskill, St. Paul, 1974-78; mgr. fin. reporting Gamble Skogmo, Mpls., 1978-80; corp. controller InterRegional Fin. Group, Mpls., 1980-85; v.p., sec., controller Dain Bosworth Inc., Mpls., 1985—; bd. dirs. Insight Bond Mgmt. Co., Mpls. Mem. Am. Inst. CPA's, Minn. State Soc. CPA's. Roman Catholic. Club: Woodbury Area Hockey (Minn.) (bd. dirs., treas. 1987). Avocation: marathons. Home: 1323 Waterford Rd Woodbury MN 55125 Office: Dain Bosworth Inc 100 Dain Tower Minneapolis MN 55402

MORREO, DANIEL ANTHONY, sales esecutive; b. Boston, Mass., Oct. 28, 1959; s. Daniel Anthony and Beatrice Eleanor (Williams) M. BS, U. New Hampshire, 1981. Sales mgr. trainee Hamilton A. Stouffer Hotel, Valley Forge, Pa., 1981; sales mgr. Stouffer Greenway Plaxa Hotel, Houston, 1981-83, Stouffer St. Louis Concourse Hotel, St. Louis, Mo., 1983-85; sr. sales mgr. Stouffer Hamilton Hotel, Itasca, Ill., 1985-86; dir. sales and mktg. Stouffer Five Seasons Hotel, Ceder Rapids, Iowa, 1986—. Mem. Cedar Rapids Advt. Fedn., Hotel Sales and Mktg. Assn., Meeting Planners Internat.

MORRILL, THOMAS CLYDE, insurance company executive; b. Chgo., July 1, 1909; s. Walter and Lena Elpha (Haney) M.; m. Hazel Janet Thompson, Oct. 18, 1930; children: Dorothy Mae (Mrs. Gerald L. Kelly), Charles T. Student, Cen. Coll. Arts and Scis., Chgo., 1928-29, Northwestern U., 1929-30. With Alfred M. Best Co., Inc., 1929-45, assoc. editor, 1940-45; with N.Y. State Ins. Dept., 1945-50, dep. supt. ins., 1947-50; with State Farm Mut. Automobile Ins. Co., Bloomington, Ill., 1950-77, v.p., 1952-77; chmn. bd. State Farm Fire and Casualty Co., Bloomington, 1970-86; chmn. bd. State Farm Gen. Ins. Co., Bloomington, also dir.; bd. dirs. State Farm Life Ins. Co., State Farm Life and Accident Assurance Co. Contbr. reports to N.Y. Ins. Dept. Chmn. exec. subcom. Nat. Hwy. Safety Adv. Com., 1971-73; chmn. tech. com. on transp. White House Conf. on Aging, 1971; mem. Pres.'s Task Force on Hwy. Safety. Clubs: Union League (Chgo.); Union Hills Country, Lakes (Sun City, Ariz.). Office: One State Farm Plaza Bloomington IL 61710

MORRIS, CALVIN CURTIS, architect; b. Champaign, Ill., Mar. 5, 1955; s. Charles Calvin Morris and Audrey Jane (Carr) Dieu; m. Monica Lynn Greco, May 16, 1987. BS in Archtl. Studies, U. Ill., Champaign, 1978. Registered architect, Ill. Draftsman Archtl. Assocs. Inc., Collinsville, Ill., 1977-78, v.p., 1978—. Active Planning Commn., Collinsville, 1983-85, vice chmn., 1986. Named one of Outstanding Young Men of Am., U.S. Jaycees, 1981. Mem. AIA, Nat. Council Archtl. Registration Bds. Republican. Lutheran. Lodges: Kiwanis (treas. Collinsville chpt. 1982-83, pres. 1983-85, bd. dirs. Wyman Camp, Eureka, Mo. 1986), Masons. Office: Archtl Assocs Inc Number 1 Design Mesa Collinsville IL 62234

MORRIS, CORNELIUS JOSEPH, data processing executive, educator; b. N.Y.C., Nov. 24, 1933; s. Cornelius Joseph and Helen Theresa (Mische) M.; m. Shirley Ann Potterbaum, Dec. 26, 1960; children: David Neil, Stephen Mark, Nancy Ann. BA, Seton Hall U., 1955; postgrad., Christian Bros. Coll., 1960-61, U. Akron, 1985—. Registered bus. programmer Inst. for Cert. of Computer Profls., cert. data processor. Chief programmer Systemetrics Inc., Mountainside, N.J., 1963-65; lead systems analyst Beneficial Finance, Morristown, N.J., 1965-68; sr. programmer analyst Warner Lambert, Morris Plains, N.J., 1968-69; sr. programmer analyst Gen. Tire and Rubber Co., Akron, Ohio, 1969-74, supr. programming, 1974-77; systems mgr. DiversiTech Gen. Inc., Akron, 1977—; instr. U. Akron, 1981—, So. Ohio Coll., Akron, 1979-81, mem. adv. com., 1985—. Co-chmn. Citizens Adv. Com., Rockaway, N.J., 1968. Served to 1st lt. U.S. Army, 1955-58. Mem. Christian Missionary Alliance Ch. Club: Toastmasters (treas. 1973-78, named Able Toastmaster, 1977) (Akron). Home: 771 Penn Wood Dr Tallmadge OH 44278 Office: DiversiTech Gen Polymers Div One General St Akron OH 44329

MORRIS, DAVID LYNN, clinical psychologist; b. Frankfort, Ind., June 16, 1947; s. Gail Michael and Marilyn (Fournier) M.; m. Laurel Ruth Anderson, Aug. 4, 1984; 1 child, Janna Luiza. BA with honors, Ind. U., 1970; PhD, U. Minn., 1980. Lic. cons. psychologist, Minn. Clin. child psychologist Family Psychotherapy Assocs., Mpls., 1980—; family therapy trainer various locations Minn. and Europe, 1984—; bd. dirs. Psychotherapy Tng. Inst., St. Paul, 1984—. Contbg. author: Attachment and Intimacy, 1981. Mem. Am. Psychol. Assn., Am. Orthopsychait. Assn., Minn. Psychol. Assn., Minn. Psychologists in Pvt. Practice (bd. dirs. 1984—), Italian Soc. Family Therapy. Club: Rosemount (Minn.) Breakfast. Avocations: farming, ski marathon racing.

MORRIS, DONALD, tax specialist; b. Chgo., Oct. 13, 1945; s. Donald Charles and Cathleen (Lautner) M.; m. Linda Susan Yeager, Dec. 26, 1966 (div. June 1986); children: Keith, Sarah. BA, Calif. State U., Los Angeles, 1968; MA, De Paul U., 1972, MS in Taxation, 1987; PhD, So. Ill. U., 1978. CPA, Ill. Prof. philosophy John A. Logan Coll., Carterville, Ill., 1972-79; tax mgr. Evans-Gries & Co. CPA's, Addison, Ill., 1980-83; sr. tax advisor Alexander Grant, CPA, Chgo., 1983-84; tax mgr. Lee Evans & Co., Itasca, Ill., 1984-87; prin. Donald Morris & Assocs., CPA's, Addison, 1987—. Libertarian candidate for comptroller State of Ill., 1986. Mem. Am. Inst. CPA's, Ill. CPA Soc., Am. Philos. Assn., Chgo. Area Runners Assn. Avocations: distance running, tennis, woodworking. Home: 670 Lido Terr E Bartlett IL 60103 Office: 240 E Lake St Suite 104 Addison IL 60101

MORRIS, G. RONALD, automotive executive; b. East St. Louis, Aug. 30, 1936; s. George H. and Mildred C. M.; m. Margaret Heino, June 20, 1959; children: David, Michele, James. B.S. in Metall. Engring, U. Ill., 1959. Metall. engr. Delco-Remy div. Gen. Motors Corp., 1959-60; factory metallurgist Dubuque Tractor Works, John Deere Co., Iowa, 1960-66; with Fed.-Mogul Corp., 1966-79, v.p., group mgr. ball and roller bearing group, 1979; pres. Tenneco Automotive div. Tenneco, Inc., Deerfield, Ill., 1979-82; pres., chief exec. officer PT Components, Inc., Indpls., 1982—; chmn., pres., chief exec officer CTP Holdings Inc.; pres., chief exec. officer PT Components Inc.; bd. dirs. Ransburg Corp., Indpls., OCM Corp., Kanazawa, Japan, Mulligan & Assoc., Chgo. Trustee Indpls. Childrens Mus.; bd. dirs. Econ. Club. Indpls.; mem. adv. bd. Jr. Achievement Indpls.; mem. pres.'s council U. Ill. Mem. Am. Soc. Metals, Soc. Automotive Engrs., Engring. Soc. Detroit, Anti-Friction Bearing Mfrs. Assn. (bd. dirs., exec. com.), Indpls. C. of C. (bd. dirs., exec. com.). Republican. Presbyterian. Club: Consistory. Lodges: Elks, Masons. Office: PT Components Inc 7545 Rockville Rd Box 802 Indianapolis IN 46206 *

MORRIS, JANE ELIZABETH, home economics educator; b. Marietta, Ohio, Nov. 28, 1940; d. Harold Watson and LaRue (Graham) M. Student, U. Ky., 1960; BS, Marietta Coll., 1962; MA, Kent State U., 1970, postgrad., 1985-87; postgrad., Coll. Mt. St. Joseph, 1984-86, John Carroll U., 1986, Ashland Coll., 1987. Cert. high sch. tchr., Ohio. Tchr. home econs. Chagrin Falls (Ohio) High Sch., 1962—, sophmore class advisor, 1982-85, 87—; head cheerleading advisor, Chagrin Falls High Sch., 1970-80, freshman class advisor, 1981-82, head Fine and Practical Arts Dept., 1982-84, sophomore class advisor, 1982-85, 87. Vice chmn. The Elec. Women's Round Table, Inc., Cleve., 1968, chmn. 1969-70; treas. Trees Condominum Assn., 1981-83. Mem. NEA, Career Edn. Assn. (charter), Ohio Edn. Assn., Northeast Ohio Edn. Assn., Chagrin Falls Tchrs. Assn. (bldg. rep. 1986, 87), Alpha Xi Delta. Avocations: swimming, interior design, sewing, gourmet cooking. Office: Chagrin Falls Schs 77 E Washington St Chagrin Falls OH 44022

MORRIS, JEFFREY JOSEPH, marketing professional; b. Clearfield, Pa., Aug. 28, 1961; s. William M. and Barbara Ann (Boal) M.; m. Tama Lynn Werfel, June 2, 1984. BS in Bus., Ind. U. of Pa., 1983. Spl. account rep. Modine Mfg. Co., Racine, Wis., 1983-84, product specialist, 1984-85, product, market mgr., 1985—. Named one of Outstanding Men of Am. Republican. Lodge: Order of DeMolay (master chancelor 1980, Chevalier degree 1981). Avocations: collecting coins, skiing, racquetball, photography. Home: 724 Monroe Ave Racine WI 53405 Office: Modine Mfg Co Aftermarket Group 1500 DeKoven Ave Racine WI 53401

MORRIS, JOHN CALVIN, manufacturing company executive; b. Kansas City, Mo., Oct. 8, 1921; s. Arthur Allen and Helen (Moore) M.; m. Mary Jane Anderson, June 12, 1943; children—John M., Kenneth A., Daniel G., Kevin P. Student Rockhurst Coll., 1946-47, U. San Francisco, 1951, Northwestern U., 1964-65. Asst. sales mgr. Maurer-Neuer Meat Packers, Kansas City, Kans., 1938-49; mgr. dist. mktg. Ekco Products Inc., Chgo., 1950-68, pres., 1973—; dir. mktg. Die Supply Corp., Cleve., 1968-70; v.p. mktg. Calar Industries, Wilmette, Ill., 1968-69; v.p. Chgo. Metallic Mfg. Co., Lake Zurich, Ill., 1970-71; pres. John C. Morris & Sons, Wilmette, 1971-73; exec. v.p. A&M Coatings, Arlington Heights, Ill., 1971-73, also dir.; guest lectr. Am. Inst. Baking, 1959-68, 73—, mem. ednl. adv. com., 1973—. Served to 1st lt. USAAF, 1942-45. Decorated Air medal with 4 oak leaf clusters. Mem. Bakers Club Chgo. (bd. dirs., pres.), Am. Soc. Bakery Engrs. (adv. bd.), Chgo. Bakery Products Men's Club, Allied Trades Baking Industry (bd. dirs.). Republican. Roman Catholic. Home: 918 Pontiac Rd Wilmette IL 60091 Office: Ekco Glaco Inc 1949 N Cicero Ave Chicago IL 60639

MORRIS, JOHN DANIEL, cinematographer, audio-visual specialist, writer; b. St. Marys, Ohio, Feb. 12, 1927; s. Ferd and Georgianna (Metz) M.; m. Aida Maria Valerio, Aug. 30, 1952; children: Kathleen Marie, Barbara Ann, Sharon Ann. BFA in Radio and TV, Coll. of Music, Cin., 1955. TV producer, dir. Sta. WLWT-TV, Cin., 1949-50, Sta. WKRC-TV, Cin., 1950-53, 60-63; prodn. mgr. Sta. WCET-TV, Cin., 1953-60; audio-visual specialist, writer, cinematographer Cin. Milacron, 1964—. Served to sgt. U.S. Army, 1945-47. Roman Catholic. Avocation: playing alto saxophone and clarinet in bands. Home: 2810 Caledon Ln Cincinnati OH 45244 Office: Cin Milacron 4701 Marburg Ave Cincinnati OH 45209

MORRIS, JOSEPH J., construction company executive; b. 1928. Student, U. Tampa, Fla. State Coll., Bay City (Mich.) Jr. Coll. With Champion Home Builders Co., Dryden, Mich., 1960—, exec. v.p. adminstrn. and sales, 1972-73, pres., 1973—, chief operating officer, 1973-77, chief exec. officer, 1977—, also bd. dirs. Served with AUS, 1951-53. Office: Champion Home Builders Co 5573 North St Dryden MI 48428 *

MORRIS, KENTON, broadcast executive; b. Santa Monica, Calif. Apr. 20, 1947; s. Chester Brooks and Lili (Kenton) M.; m. Marguerite Marie Bauer, Dec. 13, 1970 (div. 1972); m. Cheryl A. Dorrier, Jan. 11, 1977. B.S., Northwestern U. Producer-dir. Sta. WGN-TV, Chgo., 1969-74; asst. programmer Sta. WGN Radio, Chgo., 1974-83, ops. mgr., 1983-85, dir. ops. and network services, 1986—Bd. dirs., past pres. Old Town Sch. Folk Music, Chgo., 1984. Avocations: travel; flying; guitar. Home: 5936 N Kenmore Chicago IL 60660 Office: WGN Radio 435 N Michigan Ave Chicago IL 60611

MORRIS, LEIGH EDWARD, hospital executive officer; b. Hartford City, Ind., Dec. 26, 1934; s. Fredus Orlando and Martha (Malott) M.; m. Marcia Renee Meredith, Oct. 7, 1967; children: Meredith Anne, Curtis Paul. BS in Commerce, Internat. Coll., 1954; BSBA, Ball State U., 1958; M in Health Adminstrn., U. Minn., 1972. Mem. labor relations staff Borg-Warner Corp., Muncie, Ind., 1961-64; various positions then personnel mgr. Internat. Harvester Co., Ft. Wayne, Ind., 1964-70; pres. Huntington (Ind.) Meml. Hosp., 1972-78, LaPorte (Ind.) Hosp., 1978—; bd. dirs. First Nat. Bank, LaPorte, Am. Hosp. Pub. Co., Hosp. Research and Edn. Trust. Chmn. LaPorte Devel. Corp., 1980-81, LaPorte chpt. ARC, 1984-86. Served with U.S. Army, 1958-60. Recipient Disting. Alumni award Ball State U., Muncie, Ind., 1968, James A. Hamilton award U. Minn., Mpls., 1972. Mem. Am. Hosp. Assn. (trustee, regional chmn. 1985—), Am. Coll. Hosp. Adminstrn., Am. Pub. Health Assn., Health Care Fin. Mgmt. Assn., Ind. Hosp. Assn. (chmn. 1980-81), LaPorte C. of C. (chmn. 1981-82), Constantian Soc. Republican. Presbyterian. Avocations: classic cars, civic affairs. Home: 1519 Indiana Ave LaPorte IN 46350 Office: LaPorte Hosp Inc PO Box 250 LaPorte IN 46350

MORRIS, LEON HERBERT, internist; b. Phila., Sept. 12, 1943; s. Benjamin and Gerry (Portney) M.; m. Barbara Anne Ames, Sept. 12, 1970; children: Lori, Michael. BA, Temple U., 1965; DO, Coll. Osteo. Medicine and Surgery, Des Moines, 1969. Diplomate Am. Bd. Internal Medicine. Intern Detroit Osteo. Hosp., 1969-70; resident in internal medicine Wayne St. U., Detroit, 1970-73; asst. prof. clin. medicine Wayne State U., Detroit, 1975—; practice osteo. medicine specializing in internal medicine Southfield, Mich., 1973—; mem. staff Harper Grace Hosp., Detroit, William Beaumont Hosp., Royal Oak, Mich., Wayne State Rehab., Detroit. Mem. ACP, Mich. Med. Soc., Wayne County Med. Soc., Detroit Med. Soc., Mich. Assn. Osteo. Medicine and Surgery. Avocations: model airplanes, raising English setters, Persian cats, Cichlid fish. Office: 17117 W 9 Mile Rd Suite 1230 Southfield MI 48075

MORRIS, LUCIEN ELLIS, anesthesiologist, educator; b. Mattoon, Ill., Nov. 30, 1914; s. James Lucien and Pearl (Ellis) M.; m. Jean Pinder, June 27, 1942; children: James Lucien, Robert Pinder, Sara Jean, Donald Charles, Laura Lee. AB, Oberlin Coll., 1936; MD, Western Res. U., 1943. Diplomate Am. Bd. Anesthesiology. Resident in anesthesia U. Wis., Madison, 1946-48, instr., 1948-49; from asst. prof. to assoc. prof. anesthesiology U. Iowa, Iowa City, 1949-54; prof., head anesthesia U. Wash., Seattle, 1954-60, clin. prof., 1961-68; prof. dept. anaesthesia, faculty of medicine U. Toronto (Ont., Can.), 1967-70; chmn. dept. anesthesia Med. Coll. Ohio, Toledo, 1970-80, prof. anesthesiology, 1970-85, emeritus prof., 1986—; vis. prof. London Hosp. Med. Coll., 1980-81; WHO travelling med. faculty to Israel and Iran, 1951; mem. com. on anesthetics NRC, 1956-61; ASA del. World Fedn. Socs. Anaesthesiology, 1960-64; dir. anesthesia research labs. Providence Hosp., Seattle, 1960-67; external examiner Coll. Medicine, U. Lagos (Nigeria), 1977. Served to capt. M.C., U.S. Army, 1944-46. Fellow Faculty Anaesthetists Royal Coll. Surgeons, Royal Soc. Medicine, Am. Coll. Clin. Pharmacology, Am. Coll. Anesthesiologists; mem. Anaesthetics Research Soc. Eng., Assn. Anaesthetists Gt. Britain and Ireland, Am. Soc. Regional Anesthesia, Assn. Univ. Anesthetists, Can. Anaesthetists Soc., Am. Soc. Anesthesiologists, Soc. for Exptl. Biology and Medicine, Internat. Anesthesia Research Soc., Am. Soc. Pharmacology, Internat. Assn. for Study of Pain, Australian Soc. Anaesthetists (hon.), Alpha Omega Alpha. Contbr. articles to profl. jours. Inventor of anaesthesia equipment, including copper kettle vaporizer. Home: 15670 Point Monroe Dr Bainbridge Island WA 98110

MORRIS, LYNN ALVIN, pharmacist; b. West Plains, Mo., Jan. 22, 1949; d. Ernest Lee and Jane (Hall) M.; m. Janet Lou Smith, Aug. 17, 1983; children: Melissa, Justin, Mandy. BS in Pharmacy, U. Mo., 1972. Registered pharmacist, life ins. rep. Pres. Family Pharmacy Inc., Ozark, Mo., 1977—, Family Pharmacy, Nixa, Strafford Republic, Kimberly City, Mo., 1977—; pharmacist cons. Northwood Hills Nursing Home, Humansville, Mo., 1985—. Mem. Nat. Assn. Retail Druggists, Mo. Pharmacy Assn., Kappa Psi. Republican. Baptist. Club: Fremont Hills Country. Lodge: Masons. Home: Rt 3 Box 73-8 Fremont Hills MO 65714 Office: Family Pharmacy 903 W Jackson Ozark MO 65721

MORRIS, MICHAEL HENRY, accountancy educator; b. Cin., Mar. 15, 1950; s. Edward William and Hilda May (Streit) M.; m. Nancy Marie Kelley, Aug. 26, 1978; children: Bradley, Jason. BS in Engring., Case Western Res. U., 1972; MBA in Fin., U. Cin., 1974, PhD in Acctg., 1980. CPA, Ohio. Project. mgr. Structural Dynamics Research Corp., Cin., 1974-75; assoc. prof. acctg. U. Notre Dame, Ind., 1979—. Contbr. articles to profl. jours. Recipient Disting. Paper award Midwest Bus. Adminstrn. Assn., 1984. Mem. Am. Inst. CPA's, Am. Acctg. Assn., Nat. Assn. Accts. Roman Catholic. Avocations: golf, tennis, woodworking. Home: 52340 Tallyho Dr N South Bend IN 46635 Office: U Notre Dame 234 Hayes-Healy Ctr Notre Dame IN 46556

MORRIS, RANDY CHARLES, lawyer, educator; b. Kansas City, Mo., Jan. 29, 1955; s. Harold Charles and Barbara Jean (Bouse) M.; m. Retha Ann Martin, July 4, 1975; children—Jason Charles, Jonathan Michael. B.A., U. Mo.-Kansas City, 1976, J.D., 1979. Bar: Mo. 1979, U.S. Dist. Ct. (we. dist.) Mo. 1979, U.S. Ct. Appeals (8th cir.) 1979, U.S. Ct. Mil. Appeals, 1981. Assoc. Donald L. Allen P.C., Lee's Summit, Mo., 1979-84; shareholder Allen & Morris, P.C., 1984—; part-time instr. Longview Community Coll., Lee's Summit, 1982—, Nat. Coll. Kansas City Extension, 1983-85, Ottawa U., Kansas City, 1985—. Sr. staff mem. The Urban Lawyer jour., 1978. Treas. Lee's Summit Bicentennial Com., 1975-77; commr. Jackson County Redevel. Authority, Mo., 1984-85 ; bd. dirs. Jackson County Bd. Services, 1986—; chmn. Citizens for Scoville, Kansas City, 1982—. Mem. Phi Kappa Phi, Pi Sigma Alpha, Phi Alpha Delta. Democrat. Methodist. Club: CCD, Inc. (Kansas City) (v.p. elections 1983—). Home: 611 SW 36th Terr Lee's Summit MO 64063 Office: 126 W 3d St Lee's Summit MO 64063

MORRIS, RAY, food company executive; b. St. Louis, July 10, 1924; m. Mary Alice Haun, Oct. 26, 1944; children: Claudia J., Janiece L., James S. Student, Hadley Tech. U.; grad. exec. program in Bus. Adminstrn., Washington U., St. Louis; student, Columbia U., Mo. With Pet Inc., St. Louis, 1946—, exec. v.p., chief operating officer, 1983-84, pres., chief operating officer, 1984-85, pres., chief exec. officer, 1985—; also bd. dirs. Pet Inc.; bd. dirs. Boatmen's Nat. Bank St. Louis. V.p. exec. bd. St. Louis area council Boy Scouts Am.; mem. exec. com., bd. dirs. United Way St. Louis; past trustee Greenbriar Hills; mem. Civic Progress, St. Louis. Served with USAF. Mem. Evaporated Milk Assn. (former pres. bd. dirs.). Clubs: Mo. Athletic, Old Warson Country (St. Louis); Atlantis Country (Fla.). Avocations: golf, hunting, fishing, travel. Home: 333 Morristown Ct Chesterfield MO 63017 Office: Pet Inc 400 S Fourth Saint Louis MO 63102

MORRIS, ROBERT CHRISTIAN, education educator; b. Anderson, Ind., Mar. 1, 1948; s. Robert Childs and Velma Jane (Vogley) M.; m. Constance E. Jones, Sept. 2, 1972 (div. Mar. 1978). AB, Duke U., 1970; MS, Ind. State U., 1971, PhD, 1977. Cert. tchr.; lic. prin., supt. Profl. football player Houston Oilers, 1970; tchr. social studies Roanoke (Va.) Schs., 1970-71, 74-76; profl. football player New Orleans Saints, 1971-73; asst. prof. edn. Auburn (Ala.) U., 1976-81; assoc. prof. edn. U. S.C., Columbia, 1981-84, No. Ill. U., DeKalb, 1984—; cons. Mt. Morris (Ill.) Pub. Schs., 1986; cons., evaluator bi-lingual programs Dixon (Ill.) Pub. Schs. Editor: Vantil on Educaton, 1978; author (pamphlet) A Field Practicum for Tchrs. of Gifted Children, 1982; contbr. 63 articles to profl. jours. sponsor Sigma Nu Auburn U., 1977-81; regional co-dir. Auburn Spl. Olympics, Auburn, 1977-81; games dir. S.C. Spl. Olympics, Columbia, 1982-84. Mem. Assn. for Supervision and Curriculum Devel., John Dewey Soc. (exec. sec.-treas. 1982—), Profs. of Curriculum, Soc. Profs. in Edn., VFW, Phi Delta Kappa (former v.p. local chpt.), Phi Kappa Sigma (sponsor/advisor local chpt.). Lodge: Civitan. Avocations: weightlifting, travel, painting. Home: 221 Pardridge Pl Apt 8 DeKalb IL 60115 Office: No Ill U Dept Curriculum Instrn and Edn DeKalb IL 60115

MORRIS, SAMUEL SOLOMON, JR., bishop; b. Norfolk, Va., Nov. 1, 1916; s. Samuel Solomon and Mayme (Lawson) M.; m. Ermine Smith, Nov. 30, 1942; children—Joyce Green, Ermine, Samuel Solomon, III. B.S., Wilberforce U., 1937; M.Div., Yale U., 1940; D.D. (Hon.), Payne Sem., 1964; LL.D., Kittrell Coll., 1963. Ordained to ministry African Meth. Episcopal Ch., 1940; pastor St. Luke A.M.E. Ch., Gallatin, Tenn. and St. John A.M.E. Ch., Springfield, Tenn., 1940-41, St. Paul A.M.E. Ch., Nashville, 1943-46, 1st A.M.E. Ch., Gary, Ind., 1949-56, Coppin A.M.E. Ch., Chgo., 1956-72; prof. Payne Sem. and Wilberforce U., 1941-43; pres. Shorter Coll., 1946-48, chmn. bd. trustees, 1972-76; bishop A.M.E. Ch., Little Rock, 1972-76, Jacksonville, Fla., 1976—; bishop A.M.E. Ch. 4th Episcopal Dist., 1984—. Author: An African Methodist Primer, 1962. Pres. Chgo. br. NAACP, 1960-62; trustee Nat. Urban League. Recipient Silver Beaver award Boy Scouts Am., 1966. Mem. Alpha Phi Alpha. Address: PO Box 53539 4448 South Michigan Ave Chicago IL 60653

MORRIS, (DONALD) WAYNE, sales executive; b. Cape Girardeau, Mo., Oct. 2, 1945; s. Donald Louis and Mary Helen (Rumfelt) M.; children: Brian Terry, Craig Allen. BBA, Washington U., St. Louis, 1967. Design dir. The Bensinger Co., St. Louis, 1967-70; mktg. dir. Color-Art, Inc., St. Louis, 1970-79; with Westinghouse Corp., Dallas, 1979-85; dist. mgr. Kimball Internat., Kansas City, Mo., 1985—; instr. Jr. Coll. Dist., St. Louis, 1978-79. Counselor Boy Scouts Am., St. Louis, 1963-66. Named Salesman of Yr., Sales and Mktg. Execs. Greater St. Louis, 1976, 79. Mem. Sales and Mktg. Execs. Internat., Inst. Bus. Designers, Nat. Orgn. Purchasing Agts. Avocations: antiques, art, music, travel. Home: 4831 Jarboe St Kansas City MO 64112 Office: Kimball Internat PO Box 22603 Kansas City MO 64113

MORRIS, WILLIS A(NTONIO), auditor; b. Detroit, Sept. 5, 1960; s. Willis L. and Jewell (Stuart) M.; m. Michelle L. Conner; children: Robert, Sondra, Kristen. BBA, Saginaw Valley State Coll., 1982. Auditor Arthur Andersen & Co., Detroit, 1982-84; EDP auditor Blue Cross/Blue Shield of Mich., Detroit, 1984—. Mem. Oak Park (Mich.) Econ. Devel. Corp., Oak Park Cable TV Adv. Commn. Named one of Outstanding Young Men of Am., 1984. Mem. NAACP, Phi Beta Sigma (state sec. 1980-81). Republican. Baptist. Avocations: reading, racquet sports, golfing. Home: 24280 Coolidge Oak Park MI 48237

MORRISON, ANNA O'DONNELL, marketing professional; b. Chgo., Feb. 16, 1959; d. John and Grace O'Donnell. BS in Mktg., U. Ill., 1980; MBA in Fin., No. Ill. U., 1983. Group product mgr. The Bradford Exchange, Niles, Ill., 1983-85; sr. mktg. mgr. The Signature Group, Schaumburg, Ill., 1985—. Named one of Outstanding Young Women Am., 1983. Mem. Women's Direct Response Group, Chgo. Assn. Direct Mktg. Republican. Roman Catholic. Home: 2023 Farnham Ct Schaumburg IL 60194 Office: The Signature Group 200 N Martingale Schaumburg IL 60194

MORRISON, GARY WILLIAM, pharmacist, farmer; b. St. Louis; s. Maxwell Boniface and Marianne (Endres) M.; m. Mary Margaret Yorg, Apr. 29, 1977; 1 child, Katherine Ann. BS Pharmacy, St. Louis Coll. Pharmacy, 1976. Lic. pharmacist. Staff pharmacist Skaggs Drug Stores, St. Charles, Mo., 1976-78; relief pharmacist 1978-80; pres. Lincoln County Pharmacy, Troy, Mo., 1980—. Mem. pharmacy subcom. State of Mo., Jefferson City, 1986. Mem. Nat. Assn. Retail Druggists, Mo. Pharm. Assn. (del. 1981—), St. Charles, Lincoln and Warren Counties Pharmacy Assn. (sec. 1979—), Clan Morrison Soc. (vice chmn. Orleans, Mass. 1986—). Roman Catholic. Avocations: hunting, fishing, beekeeping. Office: Lincoln County Pharmacy Inc #8 Lincoln Ctr Troy MO 63379

MORRISON, HARRIET BARBARA, educator; b. Boston, Feb. 23, 1934; d. Harry and Harriet (Hanrahan) M. B.S., Mass. State Coll.-Boston, 1956, M.Ed., 1958; Ed.D., Boston U., 1967. Elem. tchr. Arlington (Mass.) Pub. Schs., 1956-67, U. Mass., summer 1967; asst. prof. No. Ill. U., Dekalb, 1967-71, assoc. prof. edn., 1971-85, prof. edn., 1985—. Mem. Am. Ednl. Studies Assn., Philosophy of Edn. Soc., Midwest Philosophy Edn. Soc., Assn. Supervision and Curriculum Devel., Ill. Assn. Supervision and Curriculum Devel., Assn. Tchr. Educators, Pi Lambda Theta. Home: 314 W Sunset Pl Dekalb IL 60115 Office: Coll Edn No Ill U Dekalb IL 60115

MORRISON, JAMES HARRIS, psychologist; b. St. Louis, Oct. 29, 1918; s. Carlton Tremont and Nellie (Harris) M.; m. Mary Berthold, Jan. 6, 1942; children: Elaine, Kathleen. BS, Washington U., St. Louis, 1952; MA in Psychology, U. Mo., Kansas City, 1955. Lic. psychologist Mo., Kans., Ont. Tng. supr. Gen. Cable Co., St. Louis, 1948-50; tng. specialist Western Auto Supply Co., Kansas City, Mo., 1950-66; v.p., ptnr. Lawrence-Leiter & Co., Kansas City, 1967-85; pres. The Company, Overland Park, Kans., 1985—. Author: The Human Side of Management, 1971; (with others) Practical Transactional Analysis in Management, 1977. Bd. dirs. Kansas City chpt. ARC, 1958. Served with USN, 1944-46. Mem. Am. Psychol. Assn., Am. Soc. Tng. Dirs. (pres. local chpt. 1956). Avocations: scuba diving, backpacking, cross-country skiing. Home and Office: 9804 Hadley Overland Park KS 66212

MORRISON, PATRICIA LYNN, physician; b. Cisco, Tex., Aug. 18, 1928; d. Hugh Bivens and Frances Iantha (D'Spain) Wagoner; m. William R. Morrison, Sept. 4, 1948 (div. Apr. 1969); children: David L., Paul A., Mark E.; m. Dennis D. Schleininger, Jan. 1, 1980. BS, North Tex. State U., 1949; DO, U. Health Scis., 1954. Diplomate Am. Bd. Osteo. Medicine. Practice gen. medicine Kansas City, Mo., 1954—; instr. dept. family practice U. Health Scis., Kansas City., 1980—. Mem. Am. Osteo. Assn., Mo. Osteo. Assn., West Dist. Osteo. Assn. (sec. 1968-69, pres. 1971-74), Bus. and Profl. Womens Club (past pres. North Kansas City chpt.). Club: Pilot Internat. (North Kansas City). Avocations: scuba diving, hunting, fishing, equestrian arts. Home: 600 Wilshire Blvd Liberty MO 64068 Office: 1420 NE Vivion Rd Kansas City MO 64119

MORRISON, RAY LEON, library administrator, library science educator; b. Boise, Idaho, Sept. 17, 1952; s. Duane Alton and Wilma Lucille (Bybee) M.; m. Barbara Ann Derrenbacher, Apr. 2, 1976; children: Eric, Shawn. BJ, San Jose State U., 1974, MA in Library Sci., 1975; CAS in Library Sci., U. Ill., 1984; postgrad., U. Ark., 1985—. Reference librarian Olivet Nazarene Coll., Kankakee, Ill., 1975-80; Bibl. Inst. librarian Pittsburg (Kans.) State U., 1980-85; library dir. Mid-Am. Nazarene Coll., Olathe, Kans., 1986—. Author: Library Skills Workbook, 1981, 2d rev. edit., 1983; contbr. articles to profl. jours., book revs. to pubs. Mem. ALA, Kans. Library Assn., Christian Librarians Fellowship, Nazarene Librarians Fellowship. Republican. Mem. Ch. of Nazarene. Avocations: cross-country skiing, Olympic games, track and field, reading. Home: 1904 Parkwood Dr Olathe KS 66062 Office: Mid-Am Nazarene Coll PO Box 1776 Olathe KS 66061

MORRISON, RICKMAN JAMES, real estate broker and developer; b. Kalamazoo, Sept. 30, 1946; s. L.G. and Dorothy Jane (Strothers) M.; m. Jacqueline Ann Hallock, Oct. 11, 1969; children: Rickman J. Jr., Stephanie Lynn. BBA, Western Mich. U., 1968. Real estate salesman Chuck Jaqua Realtors, Kalamazoo, 1977-84; real estate broker Jerry Carlson Realtors, Kalamazoo, 1982—; v.p. Sun Mgmt. Co., Kalamazoo, 1984—. Commr. Kalamazoo County Bd. Commrs., 1979-84, chmn., 1982. Democrat. Avocation: sailing. Home: 1224 Hillcrest Kalamazoo MI 49008 Office: Jerry Carlson Realtors 5413 S Westnedge Ave Kalamazoo MI 49008

MORRISON, SCOTT DAVID, telecommunications company engineer; b. Duluth, Minn., May 8, 1952; s. Robert Henry and Shirley Elaine (Tester) M.; m. Jana Louise Bergeron, May 29, 1976; children—Robert Scott, Matthew John. Cert. in welding, Duluth Area Inst. Tech., 1971; student U. Wis.-Superior, 1976-77, Concordia Coll., 1986—. Cert. in quality tech., Am. Soc. Quality Control and St. Paul Tech. Vocat. Inst.; lic. vocat. instr. Assoc. in Mfg. Mgmt., North Hennepin Community Coll., 1985; cert. welder Litton Ship Systems, Pascagoula, Miss., 1971-72, Barko Hydraulics, Superior, Wis., 1972-76; welder and cert. level II non-destructive examination inspector Am. Hoist and Derrick Co., Mpls., 1978-80; quality supr. Colight Inc., Mpls., 1980, Tol-O-Matic, Inc., Mpls., 1980-82; quality assurance engr. ADC Telecommunications, Mpls., 1982-84, design assurance engr., 1985-86, product assurance engr., 1987—; engr. in devel. test procedures for telecommunications equipment Brit. Telcom Test Labs., Ipswich, West Midlands, Eng., 1986. Judge, U.S. Amateur Boxing Fedn., Mpls., 1978—. Mem. ASTM, Am. Soc. Quality Control (cert. quality engr., chmn. host and attendance subcom. 1986-87), Am. Welding Soc., Soc. Mfg. Engrs., Internat. Platform Assn. Democrat. Roman Catholic. Home: 4034 Regent Ave N Minneapolis MN 55422 Office: ADC Telecommunications 4900 W 78th St Minneapolis MN 55435

MORRISON, SHELDON ALFRED, accountant; b. Chgo., May 31, 1922; s. Sol H. and Pauline (Gerstle) M.; m. Alma Pitzele, Aug. 28, 1946 (div. Feb. 1974); m. Charlotte Felice Basil, Feb. 24, 1974; children: Gail, Robert. BS, U. Ill., 1943. CPA, Ill. Acct. Louis Samels Co., Chgo., 1946-49; pvt. practice acctg. Chgo., 1949-63; ptnr., acct. Geisman, Morrison & Wine, Chgo., 1963-78, Geisman & Morrison, Chgo., 1978-84, Klayman, Liss, Green & Schultz, Chgo., 1985—. Served as sgt. U.S. Army, 1942-45. Mem. Am. Inst. CPA's, Ill. Soc. CPA's. Home: 1975 D Tanglewood Dr Glenview IL 60025

MORRISON, STEVEN HOWARD, social service executive; b. Elgin, Ill., Aug. 8, 1945; s. John Hynie and Naomi Esther (Goldstein) M.; m. Deana Susan Peckler, June 23, 1968; children: Lisa Jay, Abby Rachel. BA, U. Ill., 1968. Program dir. B'nai B'rith, Chgo., 1968-69; asst. community services B'nai B'rith Internat., Washington, 1969-70, dir. leadership, 1970-79, dir. membership, 1979-84; exec. dir. Madison (Wis.) Jewish Community Council, 1984—; Founding pres. Vol. Illini Projects, 1964-67; mem. FEMA Allocation Com., Madison, 1985-86; mem. Martin Luther King Humanitarian Award Com., Madison, 1986; internat. pres. B'nai B'rith Youth Orgn., 1963;. Named Outstanding Young Man in Am., 1979. Mem. Conf. of Jewish Communal Service (bd. dirs. 1980-82), Am. Assn. for Counseling and Devel., Dane County Assn. Vol. Assn. Execs., Exec. Staff Assn. (pres. 1980-82). Democrat. Avocation: cooking. Office: Madison Jewish Community Council 310 N Midvale Blvd Suite 325 Madison WI 53705

MORROW, RICHARD MARTIN, oil company executive; b. Wheeling, W.Va., 1926; married. B.M.E., Ohio State U., 1948. With Amoco Corp., 1948—; v.p. Amoco Prodn. Co., 1964-66; exec. v.p. Amoco Internat. Oil Co., 1966-70; exec. v.p. Amoco Chem. Corp., 1970-74, pres., 1974-78; pres. Amoco Corp., 1978-83, chmn. chief exec. officer, 1983—; bd. dirs. First Chgo. Corp., Am. Petroleum Inst., First Nat. Bank Chgo., Westinghouse Electric Corp. Trustee U. Chgo., Rush-Presbyn.-St. Luke's Med. Ctr. Office: Amoco Corp 200 E Randolph Dr Chicago IL 60601

MORROW, THOMAS ALLEN, marketing professional; b. Elgin, Ill., Sept. 2, 1956; s. George L. and Mary (Evenburg) M.; m. Mary Patrice Bell, Jan. 10, 1981. BS, Western Mich. U., 1978; MA, U. Ill., 1980. With mktg. dept. Envirodyne Engrs., Chgo., 1980-82; mktg. specialist Wight & Co., Downers Grove, Ill., 1982-83; mgr. mktg. Groen div. Dover Corp., Elk Grove, Ill., 1983-85; sr. mktg. specialist Omron Electronics Inc., Schaumberg, Ill., 1985—. Contbr. articles to profl. jours. Mem. Instrument Soc. Am., Am. Mktg. Assn., Soc. Mktg. Profl. Services (steering com. 1980-82). Home: 200 S Kenilworth Oak Park IL 60302 Office: Omron Electronics Inc One East Commerce Dr Schaumberg IL 60173

MORSCH, ROGER GREGORY, housing authority administrator; b. Aurora, Ill., Apr. 4, 1948; s. Ronald Henry and Dorothy Marie (Cooper) M.; m. Charlyne Conger, July 24, 1971; children: Chad Gregory, Molly Danielle. BA, Western Ill. U., 1970; MS, No. Ill. U., 1978. Adminstr. Ill. Dept. Mental Health, Springfield, 1970-79; dir. planning reform project Gov.'s Office, Springfield, 1979-81; chief plan devel. Ill. Dept. Pub. Health, Springfield, 1981-84; mgr. single family programs Ill. Housing Devel. Authority, Chgo., 1984—; cons. in field. Nat. chairperson adv. council Sec. HHS, Washington, 1979-81; chmn. bd. edn. Concordia Luth. Sch., Springfield, 1981-84; chmn. bd. adult edn. Bethany Luth. ch., Naperville, Ill., 1986—; coach Little League, youth soccer, basketball Springfield and Naperville, 1977—, umpire, referee, 1979—. Named one of Outstanding Young Men Am., 1982. Mem. Homebuilders Assn. Ill. (liaison), Mortgage Bankers Assn. Ill. (liaison), Realtors Assn. Ill. (liaison), Homebuilder's Assn. Greater Chgo. (liaison, pres.'s testimonial award 1986). Lutheran. Avocations: youth sports, fishing, hunting, theater. Office: Ill Housing Devel Authority 401 N Michigan Ave Chicago IL 60611

MORSE, CARMEL LEI, film company executive, writer; b. Spokane, Wash., June 15, 1953; d. John Ola and Billie Jean (Garrett) Lindgren; m. John Christopher Keaton, Apr. 15, 1972 (div. Apr. 1977); 1 child, Theresa Jean; m. David Scott Morse, June 21, 1980. BFA, Wright State U., 1979. Freelance filmmaker, writer Dayton, Ohio, 1978-80; exec. officer Brookline Visual Arts Services, Inc. (formerly Backwoods Films), Dayton, 1980—. Author: (book) Audio-Visual Primer, 1983; (movie script) Murder Is A Negative Act, 1984. Democrat. Roman Catholic. Avocations: photography, reading. Office: Brookline Visual Arts Services PO Box 1831 Kettering OH 45429

MORSE, JAMES BINNEY, psychologist; b. Hackensack, N.J., Sept. 30, 1934; s. James King and Media Gertrude (Robertson) M.; m. Donna Dae Hamilton, June 27, 1964; children: James, Miriam. BS, Franklin and Marshall Coll., 1956; MA, Temple U., 1960, PhD, 1965. Lic. psychologist, Ohio, Pa. Assoc. prof. psychology Thiel Coll., Greenville, Pa., 1969-70; clin. psychologist Family Counseling Ctr., Kittanning, Pa., 1970-74; sr. clin. psychologist Diagnostic and Evaluation Clinic, Youngstown, Ohio, 1974-75; chief of psychol. services Jefferson County Mental Health Ctr., Steubenville, Ohio, 1975-78; dir. psychol. services Apple Creek (Ohio) Devel. Ctr., 1978-79, Youngstown Devel. Ctr., Mineral Ridge, Ohio, 1979—; cons. clin. psychologist Devel. Clinic, Howland, Ohio, 1982—. Mem. Am. Psychol. Assn. Presbyterian. Club: Canfield (Ohio) Community. Avocations: running, movies. Home: 438 Hickory Hollow Dr Canfield OH 44406 Office: Youngstown Devel Ctr 4891 E County Line Rd Mineral Ridge OH 44440

MORSE, JAMES BUCKNER, health care facility developer; b. St. Louis, July 21, 1930; s. True Delbert and Mary Louise (Hopkins) M.; m. Janet Dorothy Anderson, Dec. 26, 1952 (div. May 1983); children—True, Roger, Stuart. B.S. in Bus. Adminstrn., Washington U., St. Louis, 1952; B.S. in Civil Engring., U. Tex.-Austin, 1957. Engr. Woermann Constrn. Co., St. Louis, 1957-62; engr., mgr. Ralston Purina, St. Louis, 1962-66; mgr. Gallina Blanca Purina, Barcelona, Spain, 1966-68; v.p. Pars Parina, Tehran, Iran, 1968-69; exec. v.p. HBE Corp., St. Louis, 1969—. Chmn. Campus YMYWCA, St. Louis, 1963-66; bd. dirs. Met. YMCA, St. Louis, 1963-66; chmn. Planning Com., Webster Groves, Mo., 1963-65; mem. Mayor's Hosp. Adv. Com., St. Louis, 1980. Served to 1st lt. U.S. Army, 1952-54. Mem. Eliot Soc. of Washington U., Thurtene (hon.), Chi Epsilon, Tau Beta Pi. Republican. Club: Racquet (Ladue, Mo.). Avocations: horses; skiing; tennis. Home: 625 S Skinker Blvd Saint Louis MO 63105 Office: HBE Corp 11330 Olive St Rd Saint Louis MO 63141

MORSE, JAMES ERSKINE, dentist; b. Madison, Wis., Sept. 23, 1951; s. Erskine Vance and Lucy Ann (Howard) M.; m. Diana Sue Arvin, July 28, 1979; 1 child, Andrea Agnes. BS Indsl. Engring., Purdue U., 1973; DDS, Ind. U., 1981. Mfg. engr. Babcock & Wilcox, Akron, Ohio, 1973-76; gen. practice dentistry Crawfordsville, Ind., 1981—. Bd. dirs. Montgomery County Cancer Soc., Crawfordsville, 1984—. Mem. Ind. U. Sch. Dentistry Alumni Assn. (bd. dirs. 1985—), ADA, Ind. Dental Assn. (del. 1986—), Ben Hur Dental Assn. (sec., treas. 1983-84, pres. 1984-86). Republican. Lutheran. Lodge: Elks. Office: 1908 Indianapolis Rd PO Box 190 Crawfordsville IN 47933

MORSE, P. S., provincial judge; b. Winnipeg, Man., May 29, 1927; s. Harry Dodge and Tina (Bell) M.; m. Marjorie Jane Morse, Sept. 19, 1954 (dec.); m. Margaret Elizabeth Chown, June 30, 1987; children: David Scott, Stephen Flanders, Ruth Elizabeth. Student, Royal Can. Naval Coll., Royal Roads, B.C., 1944-46; BA, U. Man., 1948, LLB, 1952. Assoc. Aikins, MacAulay and Thorvaldson, 1952-75; judge Ct. of Queen's Bench, Winnipeg, 1975—. Office: Court of Queen's Bench, Law Courts Bldg, Winnipeg, MB Canada R3C 0V8 *

MORSE, SAM ALLEN, data processing executive; b. Mpls., Jan. 4, 1956; s. Jack Wilson and Jeannie (Cossette) M.; m. Penny Kay Freymiller, Apr. 24, 1983; children: Taylor, Allen, Morse. A in Electronic Tech., Brown Inst. Tech., 1979. Engrng. technician Johnson & Johnson, Mpls., 1978-80; research and devel. engr. Med. Graphics Corp., Shoreview, Minn., 1980-84; pres. Trumor Co. Inc., Oak Grove, Minn., 1984—. Pres. Amiga of Minn. Interest Groups, Mpls., 1986—. Columnist: Twin City Computer Mag., 1986—. Home and Office: 2745 201st Ave NW Oak Grove MN 55011

MORSE, SAUL JULIAN, lawyer; b. N.Y.C., Jan. 17, 1948; s. Leon William and Goldie (Kohn) M.; m. Anne Bruce Morgan, Aug. 21, 1982; 1 child, John Samuel Morgan. BA, U. Ill., 1969, JD, 1972. Bar: Ill. 1973, U.S. Dist. Ct. (so. dist.) Ill. 1976, U.S. Ct. Appeals (7th cir.) 1983, U.S. Supreme Ct. 1979, U.S. Tax Ct. 1982. Law clk. State of Ill. EPA, 1971-72; law clk. Ill. Commerce Commn., 1972, hearing examiner, 1972-73; trial atty. ICC, 1973-75; asst. minority legal counsel Ill. Senate, 1975, minority legal counsel, 1975-77; mem. Ill. Human Rights Commn.; gen. counsel Ill. Legis. Space Needs Commn., 1978—; sole practice, Springfield, Ill., 1977-79; ptnr. Gramlich & Morse, Springfield, Ill., 1980-85; prin. Saul J. Morse and Assocs., 1985—; gen. counsel Ill. State Med. Soc., lectr. in continuing med. edn. 1986; gen. counsel Ill. State Med. Ins. Exchange, Tele-Sav Communications, County Nursing Home Assn. Ill., Ill. Occupational Therapy Assn., Northeastern Ill. Rail Corp.; mem. faculty Ill. Inst. for Continuing Legal Edn., 3d Party Practice, 1978, also symposia; bd. dirs. Springfield Ctr. for Ind. Living, 1984—; mem. task force on transp. Republican Nat. Com., 1979-80, Springfield Jewish Community Relations Council, 1976-79, 82; mem. spl. com. on zoning and land use planning Sangamon County Bd., 1978. Named Disabled Adv. of Yr., Ill. Dept. Rehab. Services, 1985; recipient Chmn.'s Spl. award Ill. State Med. Soc., 1987. Fellow Internat. Acad. Law and Sci., Nat. Health Lawyers Assn., Am. Soc. Law and Medicine; mem. ABA (vice chmn. medicine and law com., tort and ins. practice sect., forum com. on health law), Ill. State Bar Assn. (spl. com. on reform of legis. process 1976-82, spl. com. on the disabled lawyer 1978-82, young lawyers sect. com. on role of govt. atty. 1977-80, chmn. 1982, sect. council adminstrv. law, vice chmn. 1981-82), Sangamon County Bar Assn., Phi Delta Phi. Lodge: B'nai B'rith. (bd. dirs.). Home: 2105 Noble Ave Springfield IL 62704 Office: Saul J Morse & Assocs 828 S 2d St Springfield IL 62701

MORSE, WILLIAM CHARLES, psychology educator; b. Erie, Pa., Oct. 23, 1915; s. Melvin E. Morse and Ethel Dunbar; m. Bernice G. Szafran, Mar. 5, 1937; children: Susan, James. AB, U. Mich., 1935, MA, 1939, PhD, 1947. Lic. psychologist, Mich. Dir. U. Mich. Fresh Air Camp, Ann Arbor; prof. emeritus ednl. psychology U. Mich.; cons. spl. edn. Livonia Pub. Schs., Hawthorn Ctr. Editorial reviewer Jour. Behavioral Disorders, Jour. for Exceptional Children; contbr. articles to profl. jours. Fellow Am. Orthpsychiat. Assn., Am. Psychol. Assn.; mem. Am. Ednl. Research Assn., Council for Exceptional Children, Council on Behavioral Disorders, Nat. Assn. of Sch. Psychologists, Mich. Assn. Emotionally Disturbed Children, Mich. Assn. for Emotionally Disturbed Children, Mich. Assn. Sch. Psychology, Mich. Psychol. Assn. Home: 2010 Penncraft Ct Ann Arbor MI 48103

MORTENSEN, ARVID LEGRANDE, insurance company executive, lawyer; b. Bremerton, Wash., July 11, 1941; s. George Andrew and Mary Louise (Myers) M.; m. Elaine Marie Mains, Aug. 2, 1968; children: Marie Louise, Anne Catherine, Joseph Duncan. BS in English and Psychology, Brigham Young U., 1965, MBA in Mktg. and Fin., 1967; JD cum laude, Ind. U., 1980. Bar: Ind. 1980, U.S. Supreme Ct. 1983, Mo. 1985, D.C. 1985; CLU. Agt. Conn. Mut. Life Ins. Co., Salt Lake City, 1967-68, agt. and br. mgr., Idaho Falls, Idaho, 1968-74; with Research and Rev. Service Am., Inc./Newkirk Assos., Inc., Indpls., 1974-83, sr. editor, 1975-79, mgr. advanced products and seminars, 1979-80, sr. mktg. exec., 1980-83; tax and fin. planner, Indpls., 1980-85, St. Louis and Chesterfield, Mo., 1985—. mem. sr. mgmt. com., v.p. Allied Fidelity Corp., 1983-85, Allied Fidelity Ins. Co., 1983-85, Tex. Fire and Casualty Ins. Co., 1983-85; v.p. Gen. Am. Life Ins. Co., St. Louis, 1985-86; sole practice, Indpls., 1980-85, St. Louis and Chesterfield, Mo., 1985—; active with Ch. Jesus Christ of Latter-day Saints, Idaho Falls, Idaho, Indpls., St. Louis, 1949—. Mem. Assn. Advanced Life Underwriting, ABA, Mo. Bar Assn., Bar Assn. Met. St. Louis, D.C. Bar Assn., Am. Soc. CLU's, Nat. Assn. Life Underwriters, Mo. Assn. Life Underwriters, St. Louis Assn. Life Underwriters, Internat. Assn. Fin. Planners. Author: Employee Stock Ownership Plans, 1975, Fundamentals of Corporate Qualified Retirement Plans, 1975, 78, 80; (with Norman H. Tarver) The IRA Manual, 1975-87 edits.; (with Norman H. Tarver) The Keogh Manual, 1975, 77, 78, 80 edits.; (with Norman H. Tarver) The Section 403 (b) Manual, 1975, 77, 78, 80, 84, 85, 87 edits.; (with Leo C. Hodges) The Life Insurance Trust Handbook, 1980; contbr. articles to profl. jours.; editor-in-chief various tax and fin. planning courses; bd. editors Ind. Law Rev., 1977-78. Home: 480 Hunters Hill Dr Chesterfield MO 63017 Office: 700 Market St PO Box 396 Saint Louis Mo 63166

MORTENSEN, BRUCE JAMES, construction executive; b. Oak Park, Ill., May 27, 1934; s. Earl John and Mildred Rose (Peterson) M.; Widowed, June 1982; children: Lee Charles, Barbara Ann Mortensen Bosecker. BS, Ind. U., 1957. V.p. Evansville (Ind.) Concrete Co., 1960-75; pres. Agricom Equip, Posyville, Ind., 1976-78, Castle Contracting Co., Inc., Newburgh, Ind., 1975—. V.p. Evansville Jaycees, 1972. Served to capt. USAF, 1957-59. Office: Castle Contracting Co Inc PO Box 115 Newburgh IN 47630

MORTHLAND, JOHN BOYD, lawyer; b. Hannibal, Mo., Nov. 28, 1951; s. Morrison Hibbert and Mildred Maxine (Burditt) M.; m. Corliss Christine Carr, June 9, 1973; children: Andrew Barrett, Geoffrey Carr. BBA, U. Mo., 1973; JD, Loyola U., New Orleans, 1976. Bar: Mo., U.S. Dist. Ct. (ea. dist.) Mo., U.S. Ct. Appeals (8th cir.), U.S. Supreme Ct. Assoc. Deacy & Deacy, Kansas City, Mo., 1976-77; ptnr. Wasinger, Parham & Morthland, Hannibal, Mo., 1977—. Recipient Lon O. Hocker Meml. Trial Lawyer award Mo. Bar Found., 1985. Mem. ABA. Episcopalian. Lodge: Lions. Avocations: jogging, football, fishing. Home: 2020 Hayden Park Ln Hannibal MO 63401 Office: Wasinger Parham & Morthland 2801 St Marys Ave Hannibal MO 63401

MORTIMER, JEFF SCOTT, controller; b. Springfield, Ill., Oct. 8, 1962; s. Kenneth L. and Jessie L. (McKinney) M. BS in Agrl. Econs., U. Ill., 1984. CPA, Ill. Staff acct. Clifton, Gunderson & Co., Springfield, 1984-85; controller The Norris Farm, Havana, Ill., 1986—. Mem. Am. Inst. CPA's, Ill. CPA Soc. Republican. Methodist. Avocations: water and snow skiing, biking. Home: Rural Rt 1 Box 166 Lewistown IL 61542 Office: The Norris Farm Box 486 Havana IL 62644

MORTON, CRAIG RICHARD, real estate investor; b. Mpls., Dec. 8, 1942; s. William Charles and Patricia Louise (Hare) M.; m. Kathryn Lee Jacobs, Oct. 14, 1972; children: Kelly McCall, Bradley Winslow. BA in Geography of Southeast Asia, U. Minn., 1966; postgrad., St. John's Coll., Annapolis, 1966. Vol. U.S. Peace Corps, Philippines, 1966-68; v.p. Rent Mgmt., Inc., Mpls., 1970-80; pres. Diversified Hawaiian Investments, Inc., Mpls., 1981—, Craig R. Morton & Assoc., Inc., Mpls., 1980—; founder numerous real estate limited partnerships, 1971-86. Am. Field Service scholar to Pakistan, 1960. Mem. Real Estate Securities and Syndication Inst., Nat. Assn. Realtors, Soc. Mayflower Descendants, Boy Scouts Order of the Arrow. Republican. Lutheran. Lodge: Rotary (Paul Harris fellow St. Paul 1982). Avocations: tree farming, reading, stamp collecting, woodsmanship, swimming, travel. Home: 9860 Crestwood Terr Eden Prairie MN 55344 Office: 372 St Peter St Saint Paul MN 55102

MORTON, LEO DON, pediatric dentist; b. Chgo., Mar. 30, 1951; s. Joseph and Janet (Sonnenblick) M.; m. Sheryl Kwait, June 16, 1973; children: Jeremy Seth, Amanda Leigh. BS, U. Ill., Chgo., 1972; DDS, Loyola U. of Chgo., Maywood, Ill., 1977; MS, U. Nebr., 1979. Diplomate Am. Bd. Pediatric Dentistry. Practice dentistry specializing in pediatrics Niles and Hoffman Estates, Ill., 1979—; cons. pediatric dentistry Luth. Gen. Hosp., Park Ridge, Ill., 1979—, St. Francis Hosp., Evanston, Ill., 1979—, Humana Hosp., Hoffman Estates, 1980—; assoc. prof. Loyola Dental Sch., Maywood, 1980—. Mem. ADA, Am. Acad. Pediatric Dentistry, Am. Bd. Pediatrics, Ill. Dental Assn., Chgo. Dental Assn. , Beta Epsilon Gamma. Jewish. Avocations: golf, aerobics, gourmet cooking. Home: 1215 Laurel Deerfield IL 60015 Office: Drs Shores and Morton 9101 N Greenwood Niles IL 60648 also: 2500 W Higgins Hoffman Estates IL 60195

MORTON, STEPHEN DANA, chemist; b. Madison, Wis., Sept. 7, 1932; s. Walter Albert and Rosalie (Amlie) M.; B.S., U. Wis., 1954, Ph.D., 1962. Asst. prof. chemistry Otterbein Coll., Westerville, Ohio, 1962-66; postdoctoral fellow water chemistry, pollution control U. Wis., Madison, 1966-67; water pollution research chemist WARF Inst., Madison, 1967-73; head environ. quality dept., 1973-76; mgr. quality assurance Raltech Sci. Services, 1977-82; pres. SDM Cons., 1982—. Served to 1st lt. Chem. Corps, AUS, 1954-56. Mem. Am. Chem. Soc., Am. Water Works Assn., Am. Soc. Limnology and Oceanography, Water Pollution Control Fedn., AAAS. Author: Water Pollution—Causes and Cures, 1976. Home: 1126 Sherman Ave Madison WI 53703 Office: 1202 Ann St Madison WI 53713

MORTON, SUSAN DIANE, accountant; b. North Platte, Nebr., Feb. 18, 1959; d. Lee Curtis and Alice Victoria (Nyberg) M. AA, Mid-Plains Community Coll., North Platte, 1979; BBA in Acctg., U. Nebr., 1981; MBA, Kearney (Nebr.) State Coll., 1987. CPA, Nebr. Acct. McChesney, Corkle & Waltemath, CPAs, North Platte, 1981—; tchr. acctg. Mid-Plains Community Coll., 1986. Mem. Am. Inst. CPA's, Nebr. Inst. CPA's, Mid Plains Chpt. CPA's, Bus. and Profl. Women's Club, Am. Legion Aux. Democrat. Methodist. Avocations: racquetball, bicycling, traveling, dancing. Home: 102 S Cottonwood St North Platte NE 69101

MOSAK, HAROLD H., clinical psychologist; b. Chgo., Oct. 29, 1921; s. Nathan and Lena (Lieberman) M.; m. Birdie Berman, June 27, 1948; children: Derin, Lisa, Neal. AB, U. Chgo., 1943, PhD, 1950. Diplomate Am. Bd. Profl. Psychology. Gen. practice clin. psychology Chgo., 1951—; prof. Alfred Adler Inst., Chgo., 1952—; chmn. bd. 1972—. Editor: Alfred Adler, 1973; author: A Child's Guide To Parent Rearing, 1980; co-author: A Bibliography for Adlerian Psychology, 2 vols., 1975, 1985. Served to cpl. USAAF, 1943-46. Fellow Am. Psychol. Assn.; mem. Phi Beta Kappa, Sigma Xi. Avocation: philately. Home: 3650 Crain Skokie IL 60076

MOSBY, FREDERICK ANDERSON, mechanical engineer; b. Morgantown, W.Va., Oct. 24, 1924; s. William James and Rhona Elizabeth (King) M.; m. Dorothy Mae Gaffin, Oct. 26, 1952 (dec. 1966); children: Denise, Candace, Ronald; m. Julia Irene Jones, Nov. 27, 1968; children: David, Kevin. BSME, U. Rochester, 1947. Registered profl. engr., Ohio. Design engr. Gen. Electric Co., Cleve., 1955-67, tech. leader, 1967-75, mgr. design engring., 1975-81, mgr. process engring., 1981-83, tech. mgr., 1983-85, project mgr., sr. cons., 1985—. Patentee in field. Trustee Duryee Meml., Schenectady, N.Y., 1953-55; treas., trustee St. James A.M.E. Ch., active various coms.; bd. dirs. Sussex Community Assn., 1974; pres. Shaker Dads' Club, 1977-78, active various coms. Served to ensign USN, 1944-48. Mem. Sigma Pi Phi (v.p.). Republican. Club: Elfun Soc. Avocations: bridge, golf, bowling. Office: Gen Electric Co Nela Park #3434 East Cleveland OH 44112

MOSCH, JEAN TRUDY, social worker; b. Greensburg, Pa., Nov. 20, 1957; d. John Theodore and Teresa Mosch. B in Social Work, U. Mo., 1979, MSW, 1980. Child protection social worker Kans. Dept. Social and Rehab. Services, Leavenworth, 1980-81; child protection social worker Kans. Dept. Social and Rehab. Services, Olathe, 1981-83, foster care social worker, 1983-84, supr., 1984—; adv. bd. mem. Intensive Supervision, Shawnee Mission, Kans., 1984—; mental health, mental retardation liaison Kans. Dept. Social and Rehab. Services, 1984—; mem. Network Coalition Com. on Services to Exceptional Children and Families of Johnson County, Kans., 1985—. Presbyterian. Avocations: jogging, aerobics, bowling, reading, plants. Home: 2215 E Cedar Olathe KS 66062 Office: State Kans Dept Rehab and Social Services 100 E Santa Fe Olathe KS 66061-3427

MOSCINSKI, DAVID JOSEPH, educational administrator, school psychologist; b. Stevens Point, Wis., Mar. 23, 1948; s. Edward Marcel and Helen Mary (Prondzinski) M.; m. Sharon Lynn Krueger, Aug. 14, 1971; children: Andrew, Jonathan, Matthew. BS, U. Wis., Stevens Point, 1970; MS in Edn., U. Wis.-Stout, Menomonie, 1972. Cert. sch. psychologist. Sch. psychologist Coop. Ednl. Services Agy. #8, Appleton, Wis., 1972-78; sch. psychologist Freedom (Wis.) Area Sch. Dist., 1978-86, dir. pupil services, 1986—; community prevention coordinator Project Pre-Action, Outagamie County, Wis., 1979—; cons. Wis. Dept. Pub. Instrn., Madison, 1981—. Contbg. author Wis. Sch. Psychologist Jour., 1985-86. Pres. Huntley PTA, Appleton, 1984-86; big brother Fox Valley Big Bros. Assn., coach Appleton Recreation Dept., 1982-86. Recipient Outstanding Program award Outagamie County Community Bd., 1980, Achievement award Nat. Assn. Counties, 1986. Mem. Nat. Assn. Sch. Psychologists (del. adv. bd. 1985-86), Wis. Sch. Psychologist Assn. (pres. 1985-86, Pres.' award 1986), Sch. Prevention-Intervention Network (bd. dirs. 1984—, Service award 1985), Wis. Assn. Alcohol and Other Drug Abuse (Best Program award 1983), Phi Delta Kappa (nominations com. 1984). Avocations: fishing, hunting, golf, computers. Home: 2613 N Viola St Appleton WI 54911 Office: Freedom Area Sch Dist PO Box 1008 Freedom WI 54131

MOSELEY, RICHARD HARLAN, mortgage banker; b. Kansas City, Kans., Nov. 24, 1929; s. Forrest F. and Edna B. (O'Neil) M.; m. Cathy Jean Smith, Jan. 7, 1978; children: Richard H. Jr., Jennifer L. BS, U. Pa., 1952. Pres. Res. Mortgage Corp., Kansas City, Mo., 1962—. Mem. dist. com. Boy Scouts Am., Kansas City, 1985, parade com. Am. Royal, Kansas City, 1985; pres. Big Bros./Big Sisters, Kansas City, 1974, Bishop Spencer Place, Kansas City, 1982. Recipient Outstanding Service award Big Bros./Big Sisters, 1974. Mem. Kansas City Bd. Realtors, Mortgage Bankers Assn. Republican. Episcopalian. Club: Mercury (Kansas City). Avocations: skiing, tennis, canoeing, jogging, camping. Home: 2910 W 66th Terrace Mission Hills KS 66208 Office: Reserve Mortgage Corp 800 W 47th St Kansas City MO 64112

MOSES, IRVING BYRON, architect; b. Chgo., Aug. 5, 1925; s. Morris and Dorothy (Berns) M.; m. Toby June Kornfeld, June 29, 1947; children: Barbara Moses Tarr, Jack Robert, Carol Lynn. BS in Architecture Design, U. Ill., 1950. Time, motion and material research Small Homes Council of Ill., 1947-48; archtl. designer Holsman, Holsman, Klekamp & Taylor, Chgo., 1950-51; architect, ptnr. Comm, Comm & Moses, AIA, Chgo., 1951-62; prin. I. Moses Assocs., AIA, Chgo., 1962-78, Moses Assocs., AIA, Chgo., 1978—; cons. architect Globe Engring. Co., Chgo., 1974—, Slip & Fall Litigation, 1980—; judge, arbitrator, Am. Arbitration Assn., 1976—. Author: Chicago School Architecture, 1982, Doors, 1984. Chmn. Appearance Review Commn., Highland Park, Ill., 1976-86. Served with USN, 1943-46. Mem. AIA (chmn. membership commn. 1984-86, Bldg. award, 1965, 70, 75, 85), Am. Registered Architects, Ill. Inst. Architects. Club: Cliffdwellers (Chgo.). Avocations: art, running. Home: 145 Blackhawk Rd Highland Park IL 60035 Office: Moses Assocs AIA 225 W Ohio St Chicago IL 60610

MOSESON, DARRELL D., agricultural supply company executive; b. Howard, S.D., July 27, 1926; s. Gustav Leonard and Clara Amanda (Arneson) M.; children: Nancy, Joan. B.A. in Econs. cum laude, Augustana Coll., 1950. With Cenex (Farmers Union Central Exchange), St. Paul, 1950-51; credit mgr. Cenex (Farmers Union Central Exchange), 1957-62, asst. gen. mgr., 1962-71, sr. v.p. fin., 1971-81, pres., 1981—; chmn. Central Bank for Coops, Denver. Bd. dirs. Luth. Social Service of Minn. Club: Athletic (St. Paul). Office: Farmers Union Cen Exchange Inc 5500 Cenex Dr Inver Grove Heights MN 55075 *

MOSIER, FRANK EUGENE, oil company executive; b. Kersey, Pa., July 15, 1930; s. Clarence R. and Helen I. Mosier; m. Julia M. Fife, Sept. 2, 1961; children: Terry F., Patrick E., Kathleen R. BSCE, U. Pitts., 1953. With Standard Oil Co., Cleve., 1953—, mgr. planning and devel. mktg. and refining dept., 1968-71, v.p. supply and distbn., 1972-76, v.p. supply and transp., 1976-77, sr. v.p. mktg. and refining, 1977-78, sr. v.p. supply and transp., 1978-82, sr. v.p. downstream petroleum dept., 1982-85, exec. v.p., 1985-86, pres., chief operating officer, 1986—, also bd. dirs.; sr. v.p. Downstream Petroleum, 1982-84, exec. v.p., 1985-86, also bd. dirs.; bd. dirs. Society Corp., Cleve., Centerior Energy Corp., Cleve. Trustee U. Pitts., John Carroll U., Cleve., Fairview Gen. Hosp., Cleve. Served with U.S. Army, 1953-55. Mem. Am. Inst. Chem. Engrs., Am. Petroleum Inst., Nat. Petroleum Refiners Assn. Roman Catholic. Clubs: Cleve. Yachting, Mid-Day, Pepper Pike Country, Union, Westwood Country. Office: Standard Oil Co 200 Public Sq Cleveland OH 44114

MOSIER, MARK EUGENE, dentist; b. Herington, Kans., Jan. 18, 1858; s. Richard Morrow and Gladys Elaine (Bamfield) M.; m. Kathleen McCoy, Mar. 30, 1985. BS in Biology, U. Kans., 1980; DDS, U. Mo., Kansas City, 1985. Gen. practice dentistry Herington, 1985-86, Clarinda, Iowa, 1986—; instr. U. Mo. Kansas City Dental Sch., 1984-85; mem. faculty Phillips U., Enid, Okla. 1985. Vol. Oral Cancer Screening, Health Fair, Herington, 1984, 85, Menorah Hosp. Health Fair, 1985, Dental Health Screening Herington Sch. Dist., 1985, Centre Sch. Dist. 1986. Named one of Outstanding Young Am., 1985. Mem. ADA, Kans. Dental Assn. (health and manpower com.), Christian Med. Assn., Am. Soc. Dentistry for Children, U. Mo. Kansas City Dental Alumni Assn., Pierre Fouchard Acad. (award 1985). Avocations: mountain climbing, flying, triathlons, hunting. Home: 706 W 86th Terr Kansas City MO 64114 Office: 207 N 15th Clarinda IA 51632

MOSKOFF, GEORGE RUSSELL, communications company executive; b. Bklyn., Sept. 8, 1954; s. Arthur and Miriam (Federman) M. BA in Chemistry, Skidmore Coll., 1976; MS in Biochemistry, U. Mich., 1978. Sals rep. C&R div. ICN, Irvine, Calif., 1978-80; field service NBC div. ICN, Cleve., 1980-81; mtkg. dir. Biotec, Inc., Madison, Wis., 1981; acct. mgr. Centel Business Systems, Bensenville, Ill., 1981-82; cons. Goldberg & Assoc., Geneva, Ill., 1982-83; pres. Telecom Resource Group, Ltd., Geneva, 1983—; bd. dirs. TriCity Family Services, Geneva, Ill., 1987. Contbr. articles to bus. mags. Chmn. bd. dirs. Metro-Help, Inc., Chgo., 1986. Recipient Outstanding Service award Metro-Help, Inc., 1986. Mem. Midwest Communications Assn., Midwest Telecommunications Assn., Chief Exec. Officers Club. Avocations: piano, music composition, racquetball, photography. Home: PO Box 91 Wayne IL 60184 Office: Telecom Resource Group Ltd 1035 E State St Geneva IL 60134

MOSLEY, LYNDELL GORDON, cement company executive; b. Paris, Ark., Apr. 16, 1931; s. James Woodard and Leona Mae (Scrudder) M.; m. Ruth Ann Scrudder, May 10, 1952; children: Gary, Phillip, Charles, Laura. BS, U. Tulsa, 1956; MBA, Pitts. (Kans.) State U., 1978. CPA. Bookkeeper Infantex Shoe Co., Beebe, Ark., 1949-51; auditor Arthur Andersen & Co., Kansas City, Mo., 1956-58; auditor The Monarch Cement Co., Humboldt, Kans., 1958-72, sec., treas., 1972—. Chmn. Biblesta Parade, Humboldt, 1960-61; trustee Allen County Community Coll., Iola, Kans., 1965-87. Served with USAF, 1951-53. Mem. Am. Inst. CPAs, Okla. Soc. CPAs, Southeast Kans. chpt. CPAs, Kansas C. of C. and Industry (bd. dirs. 1985-87). Republican. Baptist. Lodge: Shriner. Home: 517 N 12th Humboldt KS 66748 Office: The Monarch Cement Co Humboldt KS 66748

MOSS, HENRY SAMUEL, engineer, accountant, educator; b. N.Y.C., Oct. 11, 1926; s. Louis John and Bryna (Finegold) M.; m. Barbara Janet Lieberman, Aug. 28, 1949; children: Philip, Lawrence, David. BSME, Columbia U., 1948, MS in Indsl. Engring., 1950; MS, L.I. U., 1955. CPA, N.Y., N.J., Ill. Mgr. film and kinescope ops. RCA Corp., N.Y.C., 1953-59; mgr. systems and data processing RCA Corp., Morristown, N.J., 1959-64; mgr. mgmt. services Touche, Ross & Co., Chgo., 1964-67; ptnr., dir. mgmt. services Altschuler, Melvoin & Glasser, CPA's, Chgo., 1967-83; vis. prof. acctg. DePaul U., Chgo., 1983—. Author: Guidelines to Data Processing Management, 1966; contbr. articles to profl. jours. Mem. automation com. Jewish Fedn. Met. Chgo., 1968—; bd. dirs. Boy Scouts Am., Chgo., 1981—. Served with AUS, 1945-46. Mem. Am. Inst. CPA's (chmn. mgmt. adv. services com. 1970—). Clubs: Standard (Chgo.); Ravinia Green Country. Avocations: bridge, golf. Home: 1723 E Wildberry Dr Glenview IL 60025

MOSS, JACK JAY, diagnostic radiologist; b. Cleve., Dec. 27, 1953; s. Marvin J. and Cyrl R. Moss; m. Susan A. Moss, May 27, 1979; children: Adam M., Marla E. AB, Washington U., 1975; MD, Ohio State U., 1979. Diplomate Nat. Bd. Med. Examiners, Am. Bd. Radiology. Diagnostic radiologist Drs. Beeler and Silver Inc., Indpls., 1983—. Mem. Am. Coll. Radiology, Radiol. Soc. N.Am. Avocation: tennis. Home: 605 Holliday Ln Indianapolis IN 46260

MOSS, PAUL DEAN, toxicologist; b. Chgo., Apr. 9, 1957; s. Sheldon and Esther (Lapporte) M.; m. Patricia Anne Hartman, June 30, 1985. BS in Environ. Toxicology, U. Calif., Davis, 1980; MPH in Toxicology and Indsl. Hygiene, U. Mich., 1982. Teaching asst. dept. environ. toxicology U. Calif., Davis, 1979, lab. asst., 1978-80, research asst., 1979-80; research asst. dept. immunology Mich. Cancer Found., Detroit, 1982-83; mgr. health and safety, toxicologist Ecology and Environment, Inc., Chgo., 1984—; speaker confs. and seminars indsl. hygiene and toxicology; mem. U. Mich. Sch. Pub. Health environ. and indsl. health admissions com., 1980-82. Mem. Chancellor's Adv. Com. U. Calif., Davis, 1978-80. Mem. AAAS, Nat. Safety Mgmt. Soc., Am. Indsl. Hygiene Assn. (toxicology com. 1983—), Soc. Occupational and Environ. Health, Am. Council on Sci. and Health, Soc. Toxicology, Am. Chem. Soc., Hazardous Materials Control Research Inst., Sch. Pub. Health Student Assn. (pres.), Kappa Alpha. Democrat. Jewish. Avocations: skiing, baseball, hockey, writing poetry. Home: 1038 Pear Tree Ln Wheeling IL 60090 Office: Ecology and Environment Inc 111 W Jackson Blvd Chicago IL 60604

MOSS, ROGER L., marketing executive; b. Chgo., June 15, 1935; s. Claude and Clara M.; children from a previous marriage: Natalie L., Stephanie L.; m. Francis Lynn, 1983. BJ, Northwestern U., 1957. Pres. Joyce-Royce Inc., Birmingham, Mich., 1961-83; pres. D.M.A. Inc., Troy, Mich., 1981—, also bd. dirs.; pres. Viopharm Internat. Inc., Troy, 1986—, also bd. dirs.; pres. Elcometer Inc., Troy, 1980—, also bd. dirs.; pres. Def. Electronics, Inc., Troy, 1987—. Served to lt. U.S. Army, 1957-59. Republican. Episcopalian. Avocations: amateur radio, photography. Office: DMA Inc 1180 E Big Beaver Rd Troy MI 48083

MOSS, THEODORE JOHNSON, JR., corporate executive; b. N.Y.C., Jan. 27, 1940; s. Theodore Johnson and Lucille (Shuttleworth) M.; m. Carol Blackman, June 9, 1962 (div. June 1979); children: Lucille S., Theodore J. III.; m. Susan Sage, Aug. 25, 1980. BS, U.S. Naval Acad., Annapolis, Md., 1961; MBA, U. Pa., 1967. Commd. ensign USN, 1961, advanced through grades to lt., resigned, 1965; assoc. McKinsey & Co., Inc., N.Y.C. and London, 1967-71; v.p. Brit. Steel Corp., Inc., N.Y.C., 1971-73; cons. N.Y.C. and Detroit, 1973-83; v.p., regional mgr. Mellon Real Estate, Detroit, 1983-85; pres. River Pl. Properties, Inc., Detroit, 1985—. Republican. Episcopalian. Club: Athletic (Detroit). Office: River Pl Properties Inc 300 River Place Suite 5000 Detroit MI 48207

MOSS, WILLIE EDWARD, JR., controller; b. St. Louis, Apr. 11, 1947; s. Willie Edward Sr. and Ruth Marie (Huttrop) M.; m. Pamela Lynne Meier, Oct. 2, 1971; 1 child, Matthew Ryan. BS, Washington U., St. Louis, 1978. CPA, Mo. Controller Associated Underwriters, St. Louis, 1976-78, Klipsch Hauling, St. Louis, 1978-79, Best Beers Inc., St. Louis, 1979—. Served with U.S. Army, 1966-70, Vietnam. Mem. Am. Inst. CPA's. Presbyterian. Avocation: art glass design. Office: Best Beers Inc 5121 Manchester Ave Saint Louis MO 63110

MOTES, MARVIN EUGENE, cleaning co. exec.; b. Chillicothe, Ohio, Oct. 25, 1935; s. John Griffith and Lorraine Louise (Litter) M.; B.S. in Bus. Adminstrn., Ohio State U., 1961; m. Loretta Lee Maughmer, Feb. 2, 1957; children—Kelly Lee, Julia Ann, Lisa Joan. Office mgr. Research div. Mead Corp., Chillicothe, 1956-66; pres., gen. mgr. AA Cleaning Co., Inc., Chillicothe, 1963—, AA Cleaning Supply Co., Inc., Chillicothe, 1965—, Pickaway Indsl. Packaging Co., Inc., Circleville, Ohio, 1979—. Bd. dirs. Med. Center Hosp., Chillicothe, 1977-80, chmn. fin. com., 1979-80, treas., 1979-80;

active Small Bus. Adminstrn. Mem. Bldg. Services Contractors Assn. Democrat. Methodist. Club: Elks. Home: 1 Applewood Dr Chillicothe OH 45601 Office: 28155 River Rd Circleville OH 43113

MOTT, CHARLES HARVEY, accouting educator; b. Norwich, Conn., Nov. 29, 1930; s. Charles Harvey Mott and Mabel Ellen (Lambert) Brassil; m. Madeline Margaret Leary, Feb. 16, 1952; 1 child, Karen Elizabeth. BS in Acctg., U. Conn., 1956; MBA in Acctg., U. Hartford, 1966; PhD in Acctg., Bus. and Govt. Relations, Econs. and Mgmt., American U., 1978. CPA, Calif., Md., N.D. Facility controller chem. div. W. R. Grace & Co., Balt., 1974-76; chief acctg. officer Contee Constrn., Laurel, Md., 1976-78; assoc. prof. acctg. San Francisco State U., 1978-80, Towson (Md.) State U., 1980-86, U. N.D., Grand Forks, 1986—; prof. acctg. Univ. Balt., 1971-86; cons. Tobins Inc., Albany, N.Y., 1977-78, Lottery Inc., Balt., 1985-87, Dakota Bank, Grand Forks, 1987—. Author: Accounting Reports for Managers, 1980, Accounting and Finance for Construction, 1983. Dem. primary candidate for Congress 2d dist. Md., 1984. Served as sgt. U.S. Army, 1950-52. Research grantee Dept. Acctg. U. N.D., 1986, 87. Mem. Am. Inst. CPA's, Nat. Assn. Acctg. (scholar 1955), Calif. CPA Found., Md. Assn. CPA's, N.D. Soc. CPA's, Beta Alpha Psi. Roman Catholic. Avocations: reading, U.S. history. Home: 2233 Springbrook Ct Box #6 Grand Forks ND 58201-5248 Office: U ND Dept Acctg. and Bus. Law Box 8097 Univ Station Grand Forks ND 58202

MOTTER, MARLA JEANE, marketing executive; b. Houston, Aug. 22, 1961; d. Bruce Harold and Sheila Rita (Cohen) M. BS in Journalism, Kent State U., 1983. Mktg. devel. specialist Sunohio Co., Canton, Ohio, 1983-84, supr. market devel., 1984-85, program mgr. high voltage products, 1985-86, mktg. communications mgr., 1986—; bd. dirs. Kent State U. Alumni Assn.; cons. Hunter Environ., 1985. Mem. Canton Jaycees (project chair 1985, 86), Am. Mktg. Assn., Women in Communications. Republican. Roman Catholic. Avocations: theater, tennis.

MOTTINGER, JAN ALAN, court clerk; b. Bradford, Ohio, Jan. 8, 1938; s. William Andrew and Janis Annebel (Mohler) M.; m. Carol Ann Johnson, July 3, 1960. Cert. mgmt., Wittenbry U. cert. fire safety inspector, Ohio, fire service instr. Ohio Dept. Edn., clk. of cts., Ohio. Paper cutter operator Champion Paper, Piqua, Ohio, 1959-65; prodn. planning supr. Champion Internat., Piqua, 1965-75; CETA coordinator Dept. Transp., Sidney, Ohio, 1975-76; clk. cts. Miami County, Troy, Ohio, 1977—; bd. dirs. Miami County AAA Auto Club, Piqua and Troy. Mayor Village of Bradford, 1968-76; sec. Bradford Fire and Rescue, 1977—, tng. officer, 1977-86, fire service inspector, 1978—, asst. chief ops., 1986—; sec., trustee Bradford Community Improvement, 1982—; trustee Dettmer Hosp. Found., Troy, 1983—. Served with U.S. Army, 1956-59. Mem. Ohio Fire Service Instrs., Internat. Fire Service Instrs., Ohio Clk. of Cts. Assn. (dist. chmn. 1980, legis. com. 1980—), Ohio Mayors Assn. (1st v.p. 1975-76). Republican. Lodge: Masons, Shriners. Home: 608 N Miami Ave Bradford OH 45308 Office: Miami County Clk Cts 3d Floor Safety Bldg 201 W Main St Troy OH 45373

MOULDER, WILLIAM H., chief of police; b. Kansas City, Mo., Feb. 19, 1938; s. Roscoe B. and Charleen M. (Flye) M.; m. Louise M. Pollaro, Aug. 2, 1957; children: Deborah, Ralph, Robert. BA, U. Mo., Kansas City, 1971, MA, 1976. Cert. police officer, Mo., Iowa. From police officer to maj. Kansas City (Mo.) Police Dept., 1959-84; chief of police City of Des Moines, 1984—. Mem. Internat. Assn. Chiefs of Police, Police Exec. Research Forum, Am. Soc. Pub. Adminstrn. (sec., treas. 1986), Iowa Police Exec. Forum (tng. com. 1986). Avocations: racquetball, travel. Office: Office of the Police Chief 25 E 1st St Des Moines IA 50309

MOULTON, JOHN WESLEY, state official; b. Princeton, Ill., July 18, 1949; s. John Edward and LaWanda Rose (Miller) M.; m. Janet Lynn Drag, June 26, 1982; children: Brian Wesley, Lauren Elizabeth, Allison Nicole. BA in Mgmt., Sangamon State U., 1986. Vet. service officer Ill. Dept. Vets. Affairs, Springfield, 1975-79, exec. III, mgr. ops. and state grants, 1979—. Mem. standing com. Interagy. Com. on Handicapped Employees, 1980—; coordinator United Way Campaign, 1980—; mem. Ill. tech. adv. com. on aging; SBA Liaison to Washington, 1981-87; active Citizens for Reagan, Sangamon County Rep. Found. Served with USAF, 1967-71; to capt. USAR, 1981—. Mem. Ill. Assn. for Advancement of Archaeology, Res. Officer Assn. U.S., Amvets, VFW, Am. Legion. Lutheran (v.p. ch. council). Home: 91 Carefree Dr Chatham IL 62629 Office: 208 W Cook St Springfield IL 62705

MOULTON, ROCHELLE MARIE, employee benefits consultant; b. La Rochelle, France, July 2, 1959; d. David Morgan and Lois Ann (Gamache) M.; m. Geoffrey J. Schmidt, Apr. 9, 1986. BS in Fin., Cen. Conn. State U., 1980; MBA in Fin., Human Resources, Renssalear Poly. Inst., 1984. Analyst Aetna Life & Casualty, Hartford, Conn., 1980-81; supr. Stanadyne, Windsor, Conn., 1981-84; cons. Towers Perrin Forster & Crosby, Stamford, Conn. and Chgo., 1984—. Mem. Women in Employee Benefits (chmn. membership). Avocation: tennis. Office: Towers Perrin Forster & Crosby 200 W Madison Chicago IL 60606

MOULTRIE, JOHN WESLEY, JR., state official; b. Marion, S.C., May 23, 1904; s. John Wesley and Missouri (Crockett) M.; A.B., Allegheny Coll., Meadville, Pa., 1927; postgrad. Harvard Law Sch., 1927-28, U. Mich. Law Sch., 1929-30, U. Minn., 1935-36, 38-39; M.A., Roosevelt U., 1967; m. Alice Gibson, Oct. 1, 1939 (dec. Nov. 1962); children—John Wesley III, Stanton Randolph. Prin. rural sch., Jacksonville, Fla., 1932-33; editor-in-chief The Spotlight, Chgo., 1934-35; dir. Consumer Center, Phyllis Wheatley House, Mpls., 1941-42; interviewer, unit supr. Minn. State Employment Service, Mpls., 1942-54; interviewer, counselor Gen. Indsl. Office, Ill. State Employment Service, Chgo., 1959-65, counseling supr., 1965-69, program coordinator, 1969-81, asst. mgr. local office, 1981-85 ; real estate broker, Chgo., 1955—, ins. broker, Chgo., 1956—. Mem. Internat. Assn. Personnel in Employment Security. Methodist (pres. ch. credit union). Home: 4330 S Martin Luther King Dr Chicago IL 60653

MOUNT, HOWARD CHARLES, investment executive; b. Henry County, Ill., Aug. 11, 1928; s. Claude Charles and Myrtle Irene (Thorp) M.; m. Jeannette Marie Benson, Sept. 3, 1948; children—Scott, Kristine, Jan; m. Donna Jean Petersen, Feb. 7, 1975. B.S., Aurora Coll., 1960; M.B.A., No. Ill. U., 1968. Chartered fin. analyst. Supr. rates No. Ill. Gas, Naperville, 1960-68; group v.p. Duff and Phelps, Inc., Chgo., 1968—. Trustee Village Bd., North Aurora, Ill., 1969-82. Served with USN, 1946-48. Mem. Fin. Analysts Fedn., Chgo. Investment Analysts Soc. Republican. Presbyterian. Club: Union League (Chgo.). Avocation: gardening. Office: Duff and Phelps Inc 55 E Monroe St Chicago IL 60603

MOUSE, STANLEY GARRISON, broadcasting executive; b. Troy, Ohio, May 16, 1921; s. Frank Garrison and Nellie Marie (Elleman) M.; m. Lillian Clark Smith (dec.); children: Terri Re, Garrison Lee. BS, Kent State U., 1943; postgrad. in bus., Harvard U., 1959-60. Promotion mgr. Miami Valley Broadcasting Corp., Dayton, Ohio, 1945-57; acct. exec. Miami Valley Broadcasting Corp., Dayton, 1947-54, regional sales mgr., 1954-59, nat. sales mgr., 1959-62; group v.p. Cox Broadcasting Corp., Atlanta, 1975-77, exec. v.p., pres. broadcast div., 1977-79, exec. v.p., 1979-81, sr. v.p., 1981—; sr. v.p. Sta. WHIO-TV, Dayton, 1981—. Mem. adv. council TV Bur. Advt., pres.'s club U. Dayton; bd. dirs. A.F. Mus., Dayton. Served to capt. USAF, 1942-45, CBI. Recipient Disting. Achievement award Kent State U., 1970. Clubs: Dayton Country; Capital City, Ansley Golf (Atlanta). Home: 2700 Ridgeway Rd Dayton OH 45419 Office: WHIO-TV 1414 Wilmington Ave PO Box 1206 Dayton OH 45420

MOUSSEAU, DORIS NAOMI BARTON, elementary school principal; b. Alpena, Mich., May 6, 1934; d. Merritt Benjamin and Naomi Dora Josephine (Pieper) Barton; m. Bernard Joseph Mousseau, July 31, 1954. AA, Alpena Community Coll., 1954; BS, Wayne State U., 1959; MA, U. Mich., 1961, postgrad., 1972-75. Profl. cert. ednl. adminstr., tchr. Elem. tchr. Clarkston (Mich.) Community Schs., 1954-66; elem. sch. prin. Andersonville Sch., Clarkston, 1966—, Bailey Lake Sch., Clarkston, 1979—. Cons., research com. Youth Assistance Oakland County Ct. Services, 1968—; leader Clarkston PTA, 1967—; chairperson Clarkston Sch. Dist. United Way Campaign, 1985, 86. Recipient Outstanding Service award Davisburg Jaycees, Springfield Twp., 1977, Vol. Recognition award Oakland County (Mich.) Cts., 1984. Fellow Assn. Supervision and Curriculum Devel., MACUL (State Assn. Ednl. Computer Users); mem. NEA (del. 1964), Mich. Assn. Elem. and Middle Sch. Prins. (treas., regional del. 1982—), Mich. Edn. Assn. (pres. 1960-66, del. 1966), Clarkston Edn. Assn. (author, editor 1st directory 1963), Women's Bowling Assn., Phi Delta Kappa, Delta Kappa Gamma (pres. 1972-74, past state and nat. chmn., Woman of Distinction 1982). Republican. Club: Spring Meadows Golf. Lodge: Elks. Avocations: golf, gardening, reading, cross country skiing, clarinet. Home: 6825 Rattalee Lake Rd Clarkston MI 48016 Office: Clarkston Community Schs Bailey Lake Sch 8051 Pine Knob Rd Clarkston MI 48016

MOWERY, ANN BLAIR, data processing professional; b. St. Louis, July 14, 1956; d. Wilber Fryberger and Lane Katherine (Hughes) Twitmire; m. Donald Ray Mowery, May 28, 1983; stepchildren: Kimberly Ann, Jeffery Scott. BA in Elem. Edn., William Jewell Coll., Liberty, Mo., 1978. Tchr. grades 6-8 All Saints Consolidated Sch., Kansas City, Mo., 1978-79; computer programmer Brown Group Inc., St. Louis, 1979-80, data processing edn. mgr., 1980-82; data processing tng. coordinator Centerre Bank, NA, St. Louis, 1982-85, data processing mgmt. support, 1986—. Treas. Griffith Parent Tchrs. Group, Ferguson, Mo., 1984-85; adult coordinator North Hills Meth. Ch., 1985-86, Alanon Parent's Group, North St. Louis County. Mem. Assn. St. Louis Info. Systems Trainers (program com. 1984-86). Republican. Avocations: reading, antique collecting and refinishing, stained glass, caligraphy. Home: 855 Cernicek Ferguson MO 63135 Office: Centerre Bank NA 1 Centerre Plaza Ms 27-02 Saint Louis MO 63101

MOWRY, GREG STEPHEN, metallurgical engineer; b. Davenport, Iowa, Aug. 16, 1954; s. Greg Bernard and Angela Alice (Dierickx) M.; m. Darlene Diane Gallagher, Jul 30, 1978; children: Matthew, Stephen, Lori Lynn. BS in Metallurgy, Iowa State U., 1976, MS in Metallurgy, 1978; MSEE, Stanford U., 1982. Design engr. Hewlett-Packard, Boise, Idaho, 1978-82; scientist Magnetic Peripherals, Inc., Mpls., 1982-85, mgr. engring., 1985—. Patentee in field; contbr. articles to profl. jours. Mem. IEEE (soc. magnetic soc. Mpls. chpt. 1982-83, vice chmn. 1983-84, chmn. 1984-85). Avocations: softball, handball, radio-controlled gliders. Home: 13905 James Ave S Burnsville MN 55337 Office: Magnetic Peripherals Inc 7801 Computer Ave Minneapolis MN 55435

MOWRY, JOHN L., lawyer; b. Baxter, Iowa, Dec. 15, 1905; s. William and Grace (Conn) M.; B.A., U. Iowa, 1929, J.D., 1930; student Ohio State U., 1926-27; m. Irene E. Lounsberry, June 7, 1941; 1 dau., Madelyn E. (Mrs. Stephen R. Irvine). Admitted to Ia. bar, 1930, N.Y. bar, 1945; spl. agt. F.B.I., 1930-34; mem. staff firm Thomas E. Dewey, N.Y.C., 1935-36; with U.S. Army Air Force, 1941-45; mem. exec. dept. N.Y. State, 1946; pvt. practice law, Marshalltown, Iowa, 1936-41, 47—; owner Evans Abstract Co., also G.M.K. Inc., Marshalltown, 1950—; county atty. Marshall County (Iowa), 1939-41; mayor City of Marshalltown, 1950-55. Mem. Iowa Ho. of Reps., 1956-68, majority floor leader, 1963-65; mem. Iowa Senate 1968-72; del. Republican Nat. Conv., Miami, Fla., 1972. Mem. Soc. Former Spl. Agts. FBI (nat. pres. 1945), Marshall County, Iowa bar assns., Iowa Pioneer Lawmakers Soc., Marshall County Hist. Soc., SAR. Republican. Presbyn. Mason (Shriner), Elk. Home: 503 W Main St Marshalltown IA 50158 Office: 25 N Center St Marshalltown IA 50158

MOYER, JOHN PETER, stockbroker; b. Youngstown, Ohio, July 2, 1936; s. Sidney S. and Helen W. M.; m. Sandra Louise Meyers, Oct. 26, 1940; children—Andrew Mark, Paul Howard, Karyn Elizabeth. B.A. in History, Washington and Lee U., 1958. Sec. Moyer Mfg. Co., Youngstown, 1958-66; stockbroker Singer Deane & Scribner (now Butcher & Singer, Inc.), Youngstown, 1966—. Active Mahoning Valley council Boy Scouts Am., 1963—; chmn. Jewish Community Relations Council, 1980-83. Recipient Silver Beaver award Boy Scouts Am., 1981. Club: Rotary. Address: 5701 Sampson Dr Girard OH 44420

MOYER, NELSON PEFFLEY, III, microbiologist; b. Jacksonville, Fla., Mar. 15, 1943; s. Nelson Peffley II and Clara Marjorie (Cox) M.; m. Janis Carolyn Holland, Sept. 14, 1968; children: Trenton Eliot, Tracy Elizabeth. BS, Fla. State U., 1965; PhD, La. State U., 1974. Diplomate Am. Bd. Med. Microbiology, Am. Acad. Microbiology. Chief microbiologist Okla. State Dept. Health, Oklahoma City, 1975-82; prin. microbiologist Hygienic Lab., Iowa City, 1982—. Guest reviewer Jour. Clin. Microbiology, 1987; contbr. articles to profl. jours.and chpts. for reference and profl. books. Weblos leader Boy Scouts Am., Iowa City, 1985. Served to capt. USAF, 1966-69. Recipient Homer D. Venters award Fla. Pub. Health Assn., Jacksonville, 1970. Mem. Am. Soc. Microbiology, Iowa Pub. Health Assn., Eastern Iowa DX Assn. Methodist. Club: Iowa City Amateur Radio (sec., treas. 1983). Avocations: sailing, amateur radio, classical music, stamp collecting. Home: 28 Ealing Dr Iowa City IA 52240 Office: Hygienic Lab Oakdale Campus Iowa City IA 52242

MOYER, THOMAS J., state judge; b. Sandusky, Ohio, Apr. 18, 1939; s. Clarence and Idamae (Hessler) M.; m. Mary Francis Moyer, Dec. 15, 1984; 1 child, Drew; stepchildren: Anne, Jack, Alaine, Elizabeth. BA, Ohio State U., 1961, JD, 1964. Asst. atty. gen. State of Ohio, Columbus, 1964-66; sole practice Columbus, 1966-69; dep. asst. Office Gov. State of Ohio, Columbus, 1969-71, exec. asst., 1975-79; assoc. Crabbe, Brown, Jones, Potts & Schmidt, Columbus, 1972-75; judge U.S. Ct. Appeals (10th cir.), Columbus, 1979-86; chief justice Ohio Supreme Ct., Columbus, 1987—. Sec. bd. trustees Franklin U., Columbus, 1986-87; trustee Univ. Club, Columbus, 1986; mem. nat. council adv. com. Ohio State U. Coll. Law, Columbus. Recipient Award of Merit, Ohio Legal Ctr. Inst.; named Outstanding Young Man of Columbus, Columbus Jaycees, 1969. Mem. Ohio State Bar Assn. (exec. com., council dels.), Columbus Bar Assn. (pres. 1980-81). Republican. Clubs: Crichton, Columbus Maennerchor (Columbus). Avocations: sailing, tennis. Office: Supreme Court of Ohio 30 E Broad St Columbus OH 43266-0419

MOYLAN, STEPHEN CRAIG, architect; b. Chgo., Mar. 4, 1952; s. Martin James and Shirley Ann (Randazzo) M.; m. Cynthia Kathleen LoPresti, June 9, 1974. BArch, U. Notre Dame, 1975. Supr. engring. Roper-IBG, Wheeling, Ill., 1975-79; architect Skidmore, Owings & Merrill, Chgo., 1979-82; project mgr. Harmon Contractors, Elk Grove Village, Ill., 1982-84; architect Blumenthal & Assocs., Chgo., 1984-85, Loebl, Schlossman & Hackl, Chgo., 1985-86, Groggs & Assocs., Chgo., 1986—. Mem. AIA (chmn. young architect's com., Chgo.-intern architect com.; assoc. dir. Ill. chpt., 1983—), U.S. Judo Assn. (bronze life, 2d degree black belt). Roman Catholic. Club: Notre Dame Monogram. Home: 215 W Bradley Des Plaines IL 60016 Office: Groggs & Assocs 8 S Michigan Ave Chicago IL 60603

MRAZEK, HAZEL SCHAYES, psychiatrist; b. Healdton, Okla., Dec. 13, 1920; d. Telestore G. and Josephine (Blumont) Schayes; m. Rudolph G. Mrazek, Mar. 25,1944; children: David A., Susan J., Nancy J. BA, U. Ill., 1941, MD, 1944. Intern U. Ill., Chgo., 1944-45; resident pediatrics St. Louis Children's Hosp., 1945-46; resident in psychiatry Loyola U. Med. Ctr., Maywood, Ill., 1967-70, mem. faculty, 1967—; chief psychiatry cons. VA Hosp., Hines, Ill., 1975—. Mem. Ill. Psychiat. Soc. (treas. 1981-85, pres. 1986-87), Cen. Neuropsychiat. Assn. (sec. 1986—). Home: 172 Maplewood Rd Riverside IL 60546 Office: 2160 S 1st Ave Maywood IL 60153

MRKVICKA, EDWARD FRANCIS, JR., financial writer, publisher; b. Aurora, Ill., Oct. 17, 1944; s. Edward Francis Sr. and Ruth Caroline (Phillips) M.; m. Madelyn Helen Rimnac, July 1, 1972; children: Edward Francis III, Kelly Helen. Cert. comml. pilot, U. Ill., 1965; diploma, Dept. Def., 1967, Bank Mktg. Assn., 1972; grad. cert., Bank Mktg. Assn., 1973. Mktg. officer Downers Grove (Ill.) Nat. Bank, 1964-72; asst. v.p. and mktg. officer Bank of Westmont, Ill., 1972-73; v.p. and cashier 1st State Bank Hanover Park, Ill., 1973-76; pres. 1st Nat. Bank Marengo, Ill., 1976-81, Reliance Enterprises, Inc., Marengo, 1981—; adv. council Am. Monetary Found., Fullerton, Calif., 1987—. Pub.: (newsletter) Inside Financial; author: Battle Your Bank - And Win!, Moving Up; (with others) The Boardroom Book of Personal Finance; contbr. numerous articles to profl. jours. and newspapers. Bd. dirs. DuPage County Lung Assn., Downers Grove, Ill., 1970; mem. bd. Western Suburbs Combined Com. Appeal, Downers Grove, 1971; bd. dirs. McHenry County Easter Seals Clinic, Woodstock, Ill., 1979; v.p., treas. Marengo/Union Chamber, 1980. Served as sgt. USAF, 1965-69. Mem. Nat. Writers Union. Republican. Avocations: bowling, fishing. Office: Reliance Enterprises Inc PO Box 413 Marengo IL 60152

MROZ, JOHN MARTIN, management information consultant; b. Detroit, Dec. 21, 1957; s. Gilbert John and Florence Jean (Benner) M.; m. Lynn Marie Riddell, June 15, 1984; 1 child, Michael John. BA, Mich. State U., 1980, MBA, 1983. CPA, Mich. Auditor Arthur Andersen & Co., Detroit, 1980-81, cons., 1983—. Tech. cons. United Found., Detroit, 1985. Mem. Am. Inst. CPA's, Beta Gamma Sigma, Beta Alpha Psi. Roman Catholic.

MUCCIO, FREDRIC NOEL, physical therapist; b. Youngstown, Ohio, July 4, 1958; s. Alfred Felix and Frances Marie (Mastromatteo) M.; m. Amy Marie Bates, July 13, 1985. BS in Allied Medicine, Ohio State U., 1980. Cert. phys. therapist. Intern in phys. therapy Yale U. Med. Ctr., New Haven, Conn., 1980, Erie (Pa.) Osteo. Hosp., 1980; staff phys. therapist St. Joseph's Hosp., Warren, Ohio, 1980-82, Indsl. Commn., Columbus, Ohio, 1982-84; pvt. practice phys. therapy Columbus, 1984—; preventive health care cons., various orgns., Columbus, 1984—; bd. dirs. Bateclo Corp., Columbus. Mem. Columbus Pops Orchestra. Mem. Am. Phys. Therapy Assn. (assembly rep. Ohio, 1982-84, co-chmn. legis. com., 1985—), YMCA. Roman Catholic. Avocations: traveling, golf, jogging, skiing, reading. Home: 943 City Park Ave Columbus OH 43206 Office: 206 Northmoor Pl Columbus OH 43214

MUCCIOLI, NATHAN THOMAS, jewelry designer; b. Detroit, Apr. 25, 1951; s. Joseph Emil and Anna Maria (DiPascale) M.; m. Debra Lynn Chabot, Oct. 18, 1974; children: Keri Lynn, Blake Thomas. Student, Ctr. for Creative Studies, Detroit. Owner Muccioli Studio Gallery, Detroit, 1974—. Roman Catholic. Avocation: fishing. Office: Muccioli Studio Gallery 511 Beaubien Detroit MI 48226

MUCHLENBEIN, P. E., construction company executive; b. 1929. Student, U. Ill., 1952. With Hunt Corp., Indpls., 1956—, now pres. Served with USAF, 1953-56. Office: The Hunt Corp 2450 S Tibbs Ave Indianapolis IN 46241 •

MUDD, KIM MARIE, interior designer; b. Pekin, Ill., May 29, 1959; s. Kenneth Frank and Kathleen Marie (Buerkett) Golan; m. Rick Alan Mudd, June 12, 1982. BS in Applied Sci. and Technology, Ill. State U., 1981. Jr. designer Lincoln (Ill.) Office Supply, 1981-83; sr. designer Loth, Inc., Cin., 1984-86; design dir. Miami Bus. Interiors, Dayton, Ohio, 1986—; profl. practice trainer Loth, Inc., 1984—. Vol. mem. Dirksen Guild, Pekin, Ill. 1978-81, Lincoln Community Theatre, 1983. Mem. Ill. Home Econs. Assn., Am. Soc. Interior Designers (assoc.), Inst. Bus. Designers (affiliate), Zeta Tau Alpha. Home: 107 Fulton Ln Middletown OH 45044 Office: Miami Bus Interiors 64 Walnut St Dayton OH 45402

MUEHLBAUER, JAMES HERMAN, manufacturing company executive, mechanical engineer; b. Evansville, Ind., Nov. 13, 1940; s. Herman Joseph and Anna Louise (Overfield) M.; m. Mary Kay Koch, June 26, 1965; children: Stacey, Brad, Glen, Beth, Katy. BSME, Purdue U., 1963, MS in Indsl. Adminstrn., 1964. Registered profl. engr., Ind. Engr. George Koch Sons Inc., Evansville, 1966-67, chief estimator, 1968-72, chief engr., 1973-74, v.p., 1975-81, exec. v.p., 1982—, also bd. dirs.; v.p. Gibbs Die Casting Corp., Henderson, Ky., 1979—, also bd. dirs.; v.p., bd. dirs. Nat. Sealants and Adhesives Inc., Evansville, Ind., 1984—; bd. dirs. Citizens Realty and Ins. Co., Evansville, Union Fed. Savs. Bank, Evansville, Red Spot Paint & Varnish Co., Brake Supply Co., Evansville, Gibbs Die Casting Corp., Evansville. Author: (with others) Tool and Manufacturing Engineering Handbook, 1976; patentee in field. Past pres., past bd. dirs. Southwest Ind. Easter Seal Soc., 1970-76; bd. dirs. Evansville Indsl. Found., 1980—, past pres.; bd. dirs. U. So. Ind. Found., 1983—, Deaconess Hosp., Evansville, 1986—; mem. Met. Evansville Devel. Council, 1983—. Served to lt. U.S. Army, 1964-66, Vietnam. Recipient Tech. Achievement award Tri-State Council for Sci. and Engring., 1984. Mem. ASME, NSPE, Soc. Mfg. Engrs. (nat. chmn. finishing and coating tech. div., 1971-73), Ind. Soc. Profl. Engrs. (Engr. of Yr. Southwest Ind. chpt., 1983). Republican. Roman Catholic. Clubs: Evansville Country, Evansville Petroleum. Home: 2300 E Gum St Evansville IN 47714 Office: George Koch Sons Inc 10 S 11th Ave PO Box 358 Evansville IN 47744

MUELLER, BETTY JEAN, academic administrator; b. St. Louis, May 13, 1930; d. Dalbert Reese and Alvina Cecelia (Vezeau) Compton; m. Charles Albert Mueller, Nov. 20, 1964; children: Kurt, Beth. BA, Webster U., St. Louis, 1952, MA in Teaching, 1983. Cert. tchr. K-12, Mo. Actress Ethan Allen Players, N.Y. and Vt., 1952-54; tchr. St. Mary Magdalen Sch., Brentwood, Mo., 1961-64; theatre coordinator City of Trenton, Mich., 1975-80; asst. dir. internat. student ctr. Webster U., St. Louis, 1982-87, dir. internat. student ctr., 1987—; co-chmn. internat. groups Detroit's Furay Theatre Festival, 1980; actress, dir. Webster Theatre Guild, 1980-86; actress, model Abby Sullivan Agy., Delcia Agy., St. Louis, 1984-86. Mem. Nat. Council Tchrs. English, Nat. Assn. Fgn. Student Advisors, Higher Edn. Council. Tchrs. English as Second Lang., People to People Internat. Roman Catholic. Avocations: drama, music, art, tennis, creative stitchery. Office: Webster U 470 E Lockwood Saint Louis MO 63119

MUELLER, CHARLES FREDERICK, radiologist, educator; b. Dayton, Ohio, May 26, 1936; s. Susan Elizabeth (Wine) W.; m. Kathe Louise Lutterbei, May 28, 1966; children: Charles Jeffrey, Theodore Martin, Kathryn Suzanne. BA in English, U. Cin., 1958, MD, 1962. Diplomate Am. Bd. Radiology, Am. Bd. Nuclear Medicine. Asst. prof. radiology U. N.Mex., Albuquerque, 1968-72, assoc. prof. radiology, 1972-74; assoc. prof. radiology Ohio State U., Columbus, 1974-79, acting chmn. dept. radiology, 1975, prof. radiology, 1979—, prof. radiology, dir. post grad. program radiology, 1980—; bd. dirs. Univ. Radiologists, Inc., Columbus, v.p., 1980-86; pres., founder Ambulatory Imaging, Inc., Columbus, 1985—. Author: Emergency Radiology, 1982; contbr. articles to profl. jours. Com. chmn. Boy Scouts of Am., Columbus, 1980-84. Served to capt. USAF, 1966-68. Research grantee Ohio State U. 1975, Gen. Electric Co., 1986-88. Fellow Am. Coll. Radiologists; mem. Assn. Univ. Radiologists, Am. Roentgen Ray Soc., Radiol. Soc. N.Am., AMA, N.Mex. Soc. Radiologists (pres. 1973-74), Ohio State Radiol. Soc. (pres. 1986-87). Republican. Presbyterian. Lodges: Commandery #6, Consistory. Avocations: flying, fly fishing, hiking. Office: Ohio State Univ Hosps Dept Radiology 410 W 10th Ave Columbus OH 43210

MUELLER, DAVID B., accountant, controller; b. St. Louis, June 30, 1953; s. David H. and Laverne (Benne) M.; m. Elizabeth A. Eardley, July 21, 1979; children: Robert Brian, Caroline Ashley. BSBA, U. Mo., 1974. CPA, Mo. Sr. mgr. Arthur Andersen, St. Louis, 1974-81; corp. controller, dir. tax and data processing Apex Oil Co., St. Louis, 1981—. Mem. Am. Inst. CPA's, Mo. Soc. CPA's. Office: Apex Oil Co 8182 Maryland Clayton MO 63105

MUELLER, DAVID KEITH, entomologist; b. Evansville, Ind., Nov. 26, 1953; s. Albert F. and Etta M. (Egli) M.; m. Mary Beth Zimmer, June 18, 1977; children: Peter J., Tom Z. BS in Agr., Purdue U., 1975. Area mgr. Phostoxin Sales Inc., West Lafayette, Ind., 1976-81; pres., owner Fumigation Service & Supply, Inc., Indpls., 1981—, Insects Ltd., Inc., Indpls., 1981—. Editor Fumigants and Pheromones, 1982—; contbr. articles to profl. jours. Named Eagle Scout Boy Scouts Am. Mem. Registry Profl Entomolgists (Ohio Valley chpt. bd. dirs., pres. 1979—), Carmel (Ind.) C. of C., Ducks Unltd. (sponsor), Theta Xi. Avocations: racquetball, duck hunting, softball, family activities. Office: Insects Ltd Inc 10505 N College Ave Indianapolis IN 46280

MUELLER, DON SHERIDAN, school administrator; b. Cleve., Nov. 4, 1927; s. Don P. and Selma Christina (Ungericht) M.; B.S., Mt. Union Coll., 1948; M.A., U. Mich., 1952; Ed.S., Mich. State U., 1968; Ph.D., Clayton U., 1977; m. Vivian Jean Santrock, Aug. 27, 1947; children—Carl Frederick, Cathy Ann. Tchr., Benton-Harbor Fair Plain (Mich.) Schs., 1947-52; dir. music edn. Okemos (Mich.) Pub. Schs., 1952-64; jr-sr. high prin. Dansville (Mich.) Schs., 1964-68; prin. DeWitt (Mich.) High Sch., 1968-73; supt. Carsonville-Port Sanilac Schs., Carsonville, Mich., 1973—. Recipient Community Leader of Am. award, 1968, 72, 73-74; Acad. Am. Educators award, 1973-74. Mem. Am., Mich. assns. sch. adminstrs., Mich. Assn. Sch. Bds.,

NEA, Assn. Supervision and Curriculum Devel., Clinton Prins. Assn. (pres. 1972-73), Ingham Prins. Assn. (pres. 1967-70), Mich. Sch. Band/Orch. Assn. (sec. 1962-63, pres. dist. 5 1958-60), Okemos Edn. Assn. (pres. 1962-63), River Area Supts. Assn. (pres. 1979-80). Home: 188 S High St Box 257 Carsonville MI 48419 Office: 100 N Goetze Carsonville MI 48419

MUELLER, EDWARD JOHN, high school teacher, farmer; b. Grand Forks, N.D., May 19, 1958; s. Earl Jacob and Barbara Margaret (Reinpold) M.; m. Gloria Jean Heinz, Mar. 3, 1978 (div. July 1986); children: Andrew, Jeremy, Stacy. BS, N.D. State U., 1980. Vocat. agriculture instr. Parshall High Sch., 1980-81, Drake High Sch., 1981-84, Minot High Sch., 1984-86, Westhope High Sch., 1986—. Mem. N.D. Vocat. Agriculture Tchrs. Assn. (legis. liaison 1985—, winner state divisional Idea Exchange 1982, 84, Outstanding Young Tchr. Agriculture 1984), N.D. Edn. Assn. (chief tchr. negotiator 1983-84), Parshall Jaycees (pres. 1981). Democrat. Roman Catholic. Lodge: KC (youth activities dir. 1983, Grand Knight 1984-86). Home: Box 495 Westhope ND 58793 Office: Westhope High Sch Vocat-Agriculture Dept Westhope ND 58793

MUELLER, JAMES STEPHEN, project engineer; b. Chgo., Sept. 9, 1951; s. Frank Joseph and Lorraine Eileen (Anderson) M.; m. Virginia Hodges Rumely, Nov. 22, 1986; children: Jennifer and Scott (twins).. B.S. in Engring., U. Ill.-Chgo., 1973. Acct. Bell & Howell, Chgo., 1969-79; sr. project engr. Dynascan, Chgo., 1979—; cons. Dynaphonics, Northbrook, Ill., 1982—. Mem. Planetary Soc., U. Ill. Alumni Assn., Internat. Platform Assn. Avocations: personal computing; tennis; golf; canoeing. Home: 9350 Hamilton Ct Dr Des Plaines IL 60016 Office: Dynascan Corp Telemotive Product Group 6460 W Cortland St Chicago IL 60635

MUELLER, JOHN EDWARD, educator; b. Wishek, N.D., Nov. 5, 1939; s. Walter and Hulda F. (Buchholz) M.; m. Donna Mae Miller, Aug. 19, 1962. BS, U. N.D., 1961; MS, St. Cloud State U., 1968. Cert. tchr., Minn.; cert. data educator. Tchr. Anoka-Hennepin Dist. II, Coon Rapids, Minn., 1961-67, 68—; faculty St. Cloud State U., Minn., 1967-68; demonstrator/ developer In-Tech, Coon Rapids, 1983, 84; mem. com. software evaluation Minn. Dept. Edn., 1983-84. Instr., CAP, 1965-71. Served with U.S. Army, 1958-65. Mem. Anoka-Hennepin Edn. Assn. (mem. exec. bd. 1985—), Minn. Edn. Assn., NEA, Minn. Bus. Educators. Avocation: flying. Home: 14650 Bowers Dr Anoka MN 55303 Office: 11299 Hanson Blvd Coon Rapids MN 55433

MUELLER, JOHN HENRY, JR., psychology educator; b. Sullivan, Mo., Dec. 19, 1942; s. John Henry Sr. and Virgie Mabel (Paul) M.; m. Joyce Kay Reagan, Sept. 25, 1975 (div.); m. Theresa Marie Whitelock, May 14, 1981; children: Clark, Paul. BS, U. Mo., 1964; MA, St. Louis U., 1966, PhD, 1968. Asst. prof. psychology U. Mo., Columbia, 1968-71, assoc. prof., 1971-76, prof., 1976—. Contbr. numerous articles to profl. jours. Fellow Am. Psychol. Assn.; mem. Am. Edn. Research Assn., Brit. Psychol. Assn., Psychonomic Soc. Avocation: personal computers. Home: 2400 Lynnwood Dr Columbia MO 65203 Office: U Mo 210 McAlester Columbia MO 65211

MUELLER, JOSEPH ROBERT, utility company executive; b. Menasha, Wis., Oct. 23, 1942; s. Joseph Ernst and Josephine (Heesakker) M. BS, St. Procopivs Coll., 1964; PhD, Med. U. S.C., 1974. Mem. faculty Med. U. S.C., Charleston, 1970-75, Washington U. Sch. Medicine, St. Louis, 1975-78; mgr. EGG, Inc., Washington, 1978-81; supt. Wis. Pub. Service Corp., Green Bay, Wis., 1981—; pres., chmn. bd. and chief exec. officer Am. Triex Inc., Sobieski, Wis., 1986—; bd. dirs. Computer Research Tech., Inc., Palm Beach, Fla. Bd. dirs. United Way, Charleston, 1972-74; sr. officer U.S. Congl. wing civil air patrol, Washington, 1980—. Mem. Am. Chem. Soc., Am. Nuclear Soc., Phi Delta Chi. Republican. Roman Catholic. Avocations: flying, diving, outdoor activities. Home: 718 Schoolhouse Rd Sobieski WI 54171 Office: Wis Pub Service Corp PO Box 19002 Green Bay WI 54307

MUELLER, SHIRLEY MALONEY, neurologist; b. LaCrosse, Wis., May 7, 1942; d. Thomas Leo and Ellen (LuteKing) Maloney; 1 child, Ellen. BS, Clark Coll., 1963; MS, U. Iowa, 1967, MD, 1971. Pediatric resident U. Iowa Hosps., Iowa City, 1971-74, neurology resident, 1974-77; asst. prof. neurology Ind. U. Sch. Medicine, Indpls., 1978-83, asst. prof. physiology, 1981-83, assoc. prof. neurology, physiology, 1983-85, dir. autonomic nervous system lab, 1982-85; practice medicine specializing in neurology St. Vincent's Hosp., Indpls., 1985—; chief neurology services Wishard Meml. Hosp., Indpls., 1982-84, chief adult neurology, 1984-85; mem. Nat. Task Force on Blood Pressure in Children, 1983-84. Editor PErsonal Health Dimensions; contbr. articles to profl. jours. NIH fellow, 1977-78, Young Investigators award 1981-84. Fellow Am. Heart Assn. (state council); mem. Am. Fedn. Clin. Research, Am. Physiologic Soc., Cen. Soc. for Clin. Research, Nat. Heart, Lung & Blood Inst. (adv. com. arteriosclerosis, hypertension and lipid metabolism, 1982-85), Sigma Xi. Avocations: radio broadcasting, writing. Office: St Vincents Hosp 8402 Harcourt Rd #726 Indianapolis IN 46260

MUELLER, STEVE CARL, metallurgist; b. St. Louis, Aug. 9, 1945; s. Herbert Carl and Evelyn (Grass) M.; m. Ernestine Erline Vohs, Aug. 19, 1967; children: Karl, Julie. BS in Metall. Engring., U. Mo., Rolla, 1969, MetE, 1986. Smelter testman Phelps Dodge Corp., Morenci, Ariz., 1967-69, metallurgist, 1971-73; asst. smelter supt. Magma Copper Co., San Manuel, Ariz., 1973-76; smelter mgr. AMAX Lead Co. of Mo., Boss, 1976-85; v.p., gen. mgr. AMAX Zinc Co., Inc., Sauget, Ill., 1985—; bd. dirs. East Side Associated Industries, East St. Louis, Ill., 1985—; bd. dirs. Mining Industry Council Mo., 1978-86. Bd. dirs. Viburnum (Mo.) C-4 Sch. Bd., 1979-85; mem. fin. adv. com. to bd. dirs. St. Mary's Hosp., East St. Louis, 1986—, bd. dirs. 1987—. Mem. AIME (exec. com. St. Louis sect. 1986). Republican. Roman Catholic. Lodge: Masons, Shriners. Avocations: hunting, fishing, gardening. Home: 13344 W Watson Saint Louis MO 63127 Office: AMAX Zinc Co Inc PO Box 2347 East Saint Louis IL 62202

MUELLER, TODD ALAN, accountant; b. Sheboygan, Wis., Sept. 16, 1957; s. Donald A. and Virginia A. (Zillner) M.; m. Linda Jean Scheibl; children: Benjamin, Tanya. BBA, U. Wis., Whitewater, 1979. CPA, Wis. Staff asst. Vrakas, Blum & Co., Waukesha, Wis., 1979-82; sr. acct. Schenck & Assocs., S.C., Sheboygan, 1982-84, supr., 1984-86, mgr., 1986—. Mem. Am. Inst. CPA's, Wis. Inst. CPA's, Sheboygan County CPA's. Republican. Lutheran. Lodge: Rotary. Avocation: sports. Home: 2846 Rammer Ct Sheboygan WI 53081 Office: Schenck and Assocs SC 532 S 8th St Sheboygan WI 53081

MUELLER, VIRGINIA RUMELY, infosystems specialist; b. Detroit, May 22, 1949; d. Emmet Hoyt Scott and Mary Elizabeth (Hodges) Rumely; married; children: Jennifer Rumely, Scott Rumely. BA cum laude, DePauw U., 1971; MA in Teaching, Northwestern U., 1972; MEd, U. Ill., Chgo., 1978. Educator Chgo. Bd. Edn., 1971-82; programming trainee Zurich Ins. Co., Schaumburg, Ill., 1982-83, programmer, 1983, programmer analyst, 1983-84; systems/programming analyst Miles Labs., Inc., Elkhart, Ind., 1984-86, sr. analyst, 1986—. Author: (edn. games) Reading Funtastics: A Handbook of Games and Activities. Vol. Frank Lloyd Wright Home and Studio Found., Oak Park, Ill., 1983-84. Ford Found. scholar, 1971-72. Mem. Assn. for Systems Mgmt., Sigma Gamma (vol. 1967-68). Home: 420 Court of the Royal Arms South Bend IN 46637 Office: Miles Labs Inc 1127 Myrtle St Elkhart IN 46514

MUELLER, WILLIAM JEFFREY, lawyer; b. Omaha, Nebr., Dec. 21, 1954; s. William Paul and Martha Ann (Hatchett) M. BS, U. Nebr., 1977, JD, 1980. Bar: Nebr. 1980, U.S. Dist. Ct. Nebr. 1980, U.S. Ct. Appeals (8th cir.) 1980. Assoc. Sodoro, Daly & Sodoro, Omaha, 1981-84; assoc. Knudsen, Berkheimer, Richardson & Endacott, Lincoln, 1984-87, ptnr., 1987—; bd. dirs. Nebr. Continuing Legal Edn., Lincoln. Nat. committeeman Nebr. Young Reps., Lincoln, 1980-83, state chmn. 1981-82; mem. com. United Way of Lincoln, 1986—. Schreiber-Hunter scholar U. Nebr., 1976. Mem. ABA (chmn. membership 1983-84), Nebr. Bar Assn. (exec. council 1983-84, legis. counsel 1984—, vice chmn. judiciary com. 1985—, pres. Young Lawyers div. 1983-84), Omaha Barristers (v.p. 1982-84), Assn. Trial Attys. Am., Nebr. Assn. Trial Attys., Sons of Am. Legion, Lincoln C. of C. Club: Updowntowners (Lincoln) (pres.-elect 1987). Lodges: Lions, Elks. Home: 2917 S 20th St Lincoln NE 68502 Office: Knudsen Berkheimer et al 1327 H St 100 Capitol Park Lincoln NE 68508

MUELLER, WILLYS FRANCIS, JR., pathologist; b. Detroit, July 15, 1934; s. Willys Francis and Antoinette Frances (Stimac) M.; M.D., U. Mich., 1959; m. Dolores Mae Vella, Aug. 25, 1956; children—Renee Ann, Willys Francis, Paul E., Mark A., Maria D., Beth M., Matthew P. Intern, Providence Hosp., Detroit, 1959-60, resident, 1960-62; resident Wayne County Gen. Hosp., Eloise, Mich., 1962-64; asst. pathologist Grace Hosp., Detroit, 1964; asso. pathologist Hurley Hosp., Flint, Mich., 1964-66; asso. pathologist Hurley Med. Center, Flint, 1968—, dir. lab., 1981—; chief dep. med. examiner Genesee County, Mich., 1971—; pres. Pathology Assos. Inc.; assoc. clin. prof. Coll. Human Medicine, Mich. State U.; dir. blood services Wolverine region ARC, 1981—. Served with M.C., U.S. Army, 1966-68. Fellow Am. Soc. Clin. Pathologists, Coll. Am. Pathologists, Am. Acad. Forensic Scis.; mem. AMA (Physician's Recognition award 1974-77, 78-81, 81-84, 85-87), Genesee County, Mich. State med. socs., Mich. Soc. Pathologists (sec.-treas. 1981-83, pres. elect 1984, pres. 1985), Genesee County Med. Soc. (pres. 1987—), Nat. Assn. Med. Examiners. Republican. Roman Catholic. Club: K.C. Editor: Bull. of Genesee County Med. Soc. Home: 13335 Pomona Dr Fenton MI 48430 Office: Hurley Med Center Dept Pathology Flint MI 48502

MUELLNER, JOHN PHILLIP, librarian, educator; b. Chgo., June 20, 1936; s. John William and Catherine (McMahon) M.; div.; children—April, Phillip, Erich, Owen. A.A., Wright Jr. Coll., 1957; B.E., Chgo. State U., 1960, M.E., 1963; postgrad. Loyola U., Chgo., 1964. Cert. librarian, high sch. English tchr., elem. tchr., Ill. Tchr.-librarian Chgo. pub. schs., 1958—; librarian Schiller Park Pub. Library (Ill.), 1964—. Home: 2717 N Racine Chicago IL 60614 Office: Schiller Park Pub Library 4200 Old River Rd Schiller Park IL 60176

MUETZEL, BENJAMIN WOOD, military officer; b. San Rafael, Calif., June 8, 1958; s. Francis Wayne and Catherine Wood (Johnson) M. BS in Internat. Relations, USAF Acad., 1980; MA in Mil. History, No. Mich. U., 1985. Commd. 2d lt. USAF, 1980, advanced through grades to capt., 1984; student pilot USAF, Reese AFB, Tex., 1980-81; co-pilot upgrade USAF, Castle AFB, Calif., 1981; co-pilot KC-135A USAF, KI Sawyer AFB, Mich., 1982-85, aircraft comdr., 1985-86; ASTRA personnel officer Pentagon, Washington, 1986—. Columnist Pass in Rev., 1979-80. Mem. Air Force Assn. Republican. Roman Catholic. Club: Daedalions. Avocations: mil. history, art history. Home: 1329 S Clay Springfield MO 65807

MUGGLI, CLARA BARBARA, civic worker; b. Hebron, N.D., Nov. 10, 1927; d. Matt and Mary (Schneider) Maershbecker; student Dickinson State Coll.; m. Ewald Muggli, Sept. 27, 1948; children—Allen, Linda, Joyce, Carol, Gary, Holly. Tchr. rural schs., 1945-48; county chmn. establishment Bookmobile, 1960, bd. dirs., 1960—; bd. dirs., librarian Glen Ullin (N.D.) Public Library, 1956—; social services home health aide, 1972-76; co-owner, mgr. Rock Mus., Glen Ullin, 1970—, also instr. rocks and minerals, 1970—; sec. Glen Ullin Hist. Soc., 1978—; tchr. Sacred Heart Ch., 1969—, dir. religious edn., 1982—; weekly columnist Glen Ullin Times, 1977-84. Recipient State Homemakers award for Cultural Arts, 1975; K. C. Religious Edn. award, 1979; Best of Show award Dakota Gem and Mineral Show, 1979, 84. Mem. Morton County Hist. Soc., Central Dakota Gem and Mineral Assn., Badlands and Knife River Rock Clubs, Art Assn., Am. Legion Aux. Clubs: Homemakers. Co-author: Glen Ullin Yesteryears, 1983, A Century of Catholicism, 1984. Home: 701 Oak Ave E Glen Ullin ND 58631 Office: Sacred Heart Ch Glen Ullin ND 58631

MUHAMMAD, WALI, broadcaster; b. Chgo., Feb. 26, 1948; s. Wali and Rayya Muhammad; children: Naeemah, Hamidah. Cert. of Completion, Cen. YMCA Community Coll., Chgo., 1969; student, Cosomopolitan C. of C. Sch. Bus. Mgmt., Chgo., 1969; Cert., Midwest Sch. Broadcasting, Chgo., 1970; student, Chgo. State U., 1972-76. Personal banking officer Guaranty Bank and Trust Co., Chgo., 1972-74; pub. affairs dir. Sta. WBEE, Chgo., 1974-77, pub. affairs and music dir., news reporter, air personality, 1980; air personality Sta. WJPC, Chgo., 1977; dir. ops. Salaam Internat. Corp., Chgo., 1977-78; bd. treas., asst. mgr. Muhammed Community Enterprises, Inc., Chgo., 1978-80; mktg. cons. WDM Pub. Co., Chgo., 1980; exec. producer Projections Sta. KDIA, Oakland, Calif., 1980-81; pres. Communicator Prodns., Inc., Chgo., 1980—; acct. exec. Your Gourmet Foods, Inc., N.Y.C., 1981; radio personality Sta. WGCI-FM, Chgo., 1982—, Sta. WBMX-FM, Chgo., 1986—. Recipient Businessman's award Sta. WBMX-FM, 1975, Black Achiever's award YMCA of Am., 1976. Mem. AFTRA, Screen Actors Guild. Home: 800 S Wells St Apt 1135 Chicago IL 60607 Office: WBMX Radio 408 S Oak Park Ave Oak Park IL 60302

MUHLENBRUCH, CARL W., civil engineer; b. Decatur, Ill., Nov. 21, 1915; s. Carl William and Clara (Theobald) M.; m. Agnes M. Kringel, Nov. 22, 1939; children: Phyllis Elaine (Mrs. Richard B. Wallace), Joan Carol (Mrs. Frederick B. Wenk). B.C.E., U. Ill., 1937, C.E., 1945; M.C.E., Carnegie Inst. Tech., 1943. Research engineer Aluminum Research Labs., Pitts., 1937-39; cons. engring. 1939-50; mem. faculty Carnegie Inst. Tech., 1939-48; assoc. prof. civil engring. Northwestern U., 1948-54; pres. TEC-SEARCH, Inc. (formerly Ednl. and Tech. Consultants Inc.), 1954-67, chmn. bd., 1967—; Pres. Profl. Centers Bldg. Corp., 1961-77. Author: Experimental Mechanics and Properties of Materials; Contbr. articles engring. publs. Treas., bd. dirs. Concordia Coll. Found. Recipient Stanford E. Thompson award, 1945. Mem. Am. Econ. Devel. Council (certified indsl. developer), Am. Soc. Engring. Edn. (editor Educational Aids in Engring.), Nat. Soc. Profl. Engrs., ASCE, Sigma Xi, Tau Beta Pi, Omicron Delta Kappa. Lutheran. Club: University (Evanston). Lodge: Rotary (dist. gov. 1980-81). Home: 4071 Fairway Dr Wilmette IL 60091 Office: Tec-Search 1000 Skokie Blvd Wilmette IL 60091

MUIR, MARTHA FLORENCE, art gallery owner; b. Tulsa, Feb. 18, 1949; d. Parke Denton and Margaret Eloise (Brown) M.; m. David Lee Smith, Sept. 25, 1976. BA, U. Okla., 1971, MEd, 1972, PhD, 1977. Psychologist Child Study Ctr., Oklahoma City, 1975-77; pres. Bogart's, Inc., Milw., 1977—. Mem. Profl. Dimensions (membership dir. 1985-86), Profl. Picture Framing Assn. Republican. Methodist. Home: 2829 Lincolnshire Ct Waukesha WI 53188

MUIR, RUTH BROOKS, counselor, substance abuse service coordinator; b. Washington, Nov. 27, 1924; s. Charles and Adelaide Chenery (Masters) B.; m. Robert Mathew Muir, Nov. 26, 1947; children—Robert Brooks, Martha Louise, Heather Sue. B.A. in Art, Rollins Coll., Winter Park, Fla., 1947; M.A. in Rehab. Counseling, U. Iowa, 1979. Cert. substance abuse counselor, Iowa. Program advisor Iowa Meml. Union, Iowa City, 1959-66; counselor, coordinator Mid Eastern Council on Chem. Abuse, Iowa City, 1976-81; patient rep. Univ. Hosp., Iowa City, 1982-85; research project interviewer dept. psychiatry U. Iowa Coll. Medicine, 1985—. cons. alcohol studies dept. Psychiatry U. Iowa Coll. Medicine. Treas. bd. dirs. Crisis Ctr., Iowa City, 1975-77; sec. council elders Sr. Citizens Ctr., Iowa City, 1980-82; pres. Unitarian-Universalist Women's Fedn., Iowa City., 1985; friend of U. of I. Mus. Art.; Mem. Johnson County Arts Club U. Iowa, AAUW (cultural rep. 1986—). Home and Office: 6 Glendale Ct Iowa City IA 52240

MUIRHEAD, VINCENT URIEL, aerospace engineer; b. Dresden, Kans., Feb. 6, 1919; s. John Hadsell and Lily Irene (McKinney) M.; m. Bobby Jo Thompson, Nov. 5, 1943; children: Rosalind, Jean, Juleigh. B.S., U.S. Naval Acad., 1941; B.S. in Aero. Engring, U.S. Naval Postgrad. Sch., 1948; Aero. Engr., Calif. Inst. Tech., 1949; postgrad., U. Ariz., 1962, 64, Okla. State U., 1963. Midshipman U.S. Navy, 1937; commd. ensign 1941, advanced through grades to comdr., 1951; nav. officer U.S.S. White Plains, 1945-46; comdr. Fleet Aircraft Service Squad, 1951-52; with Bur. Aeros., Ft. Worth, 1953-54; comdr. Helicopter Utility Squadron I, Pacific Fleet, 1955-56; chief staff officer Comdr. Fleet Air, Philippines, 1956-58; exec. officer Naval Air Tng. Center, Memphis, 1958-61; ret. 1961; asst. prof. U. Kans., Lawrence, 1961-63; asso. prof. aerospace engring. U. Kans., 1964-76, prof., chmn. dept., 1976—; cons. Black & Veatch (cons. engrs.), Kansas City, Mo., 1964—. Author: Introduction to Aerospace, 1972, Thunderstorms, Tornadoes and Building Damage, 1975. Decorated Air medal. Fellow AIAA (assoc.); mem. Am. Acad. Mechanics, Am. Soc. Engring. Edn., N.Y. Acad. Scis., Sigma Gamma Tau. Mem. Ch. of Christ (elder). Research on aircraft, tornado vortices, shock tubes and waves. Home: 503 Park Hill Terr Lawrence KS 66046 Office: Dept Aerospace Engring Univ Kans Lawrence KS 66045

MUKHERJEE, KALINATH, metallurgical engineering educator, researcher; b. Calcutta, India, Feb. 19, 1932; naturalized U.S. citizen, 1966; s. Ramkrisna and Saraju Mukherjee; m. Patricia Stapleton, Aug. 20, 1959; children—Joia S., Maia S., Janam S. B.E., Calcutta U., 1956; M.S., U. Ill., Urbana, 1959, Ph.D., 1963. Metallurgist Indian Iron and Steel Co., 1956-57; research asst. U. Ill., Urbana, 1957-63, research assoc. and instr., 1963-64; asst. prof. SUNY-Stony Brook, 1964-67; assoc. prof. Poly. Inst. Bklyn., 1967-72, prof., 1972-80; dept. head metallurgy Poly. Inst. N.Y., 1974-80; prof. Mich. State U., East Lansing, 1980—, chmn. dept., 1985—. Co-editor: Lasers in Metallurgy, 1982, Laser Processing of Materials, 1985; sr. editor Met./Mat. Sci. Edn. Yearbook, 1974—; contbr. numerous articles to profl. jours. Recipient Disting. Tchr. award Poly. Inst. N.Y., 1971, Disting. Prof. award, 1979; Disting. Faculty award Mich. State U., 1986. Fellow Am. Soc. Metals, AAAS; mem. AIME, Am. Phys. Soc., Am. Soc. Engring. Edn., Sigma Xi, Alpha Sigma Mu. Democrat. Club: Metals Sci. of N.Y. Office: Mich State U Dept Metallurgy Mech & Material Sci East Lansing MI 48824

MUKHERJEE, RAMA PROSAD, plastic and reconstructive surgeon; b. Calcutta, India, Aug. 6, 1936; s. Tara Kumar and Kamala (Ganguli) M.; divorced; children: Rajorshi, Rongini. MD, Calcutta Med. Coll., 1959; FRCS, Royal Coll. Surgeons, Edinburgh, Scotland, 1965. Diplomate Am. Bd. Plastic Surgery. Intern various London Hosps., 1959-71; lectr. plastic surgery Safdarjang Hosp., New Delhi, India, 1971-72; resident in plastic surgery Christ Hosp., Cin., 1973-75; postgrad. fellow in plastic surgery NYU Med. Ctr., N.Y.C., 1977-79; dir. dept. plastic surgery Marshfield (Wis.) Clinic, 1981—. Vol. Ram Krishna Mission Seva Pratisthan, Calcutta, 1976-77. Fellow Royal Coll. Surgeons-Edinburgh; mem. Am. Cleft Palate Assn., Assn. Plastic and Reconstructive Surgery, Assn. Surgeons India. Avocations: nature study, photography, reading. Home: 1001 W Laird St Marshfield WI 54449 Office: Marshfield Clinic 1000 N Oak Ave Marshfield WI 54449

MUKOYAMA, JAMES HIDEFUMI, JR., securities executive; b. Chgo., Aug. 3, 1944; s. Hidefumi James and Miye (Maruyama) M.; m. Kyung Ja Woo, June 20, 1971; children: Sumi Martha, Jae Thomas. BA in English, U. Ill., 1965, MA in Social Studies, 1966; honor grad. U.S. Army Inf. Sch., 1966; grad. U.S. Army Command and Gen. Staff Coll., 1979, U.S. Army War Coll., 1984. Registered prin., sr. registered options prin. Nat. Assn. Securities Dealers. Asst. dept. mgr. Mitsui & Co. (USA), Inc., Chgo., 1971-74; mem. Chgo. Bd. Options Exchange, 1974-75; v.p. 1st Omaha Securities, Chgo., 1975-76, Heartland Securities, Chgo., 1976—; allied mem. N.Y. Stock Exchange; v.p. Lefta Advt., Chgo., 1976—. Mem. exec. bd. Hillside Free Meth. h., Evanston, Ill., 1982—. Served with U.S. Army, 1965-70; brigadier gen. Res., 1971—. Decorated Silver Star, Purple Heart, 3 Bronze Stars; Vietnamese Army Cross of Gallantry; Japanese Army Parachutist badge; recipient cert. of merit Korean Army, others. Mem. U. Ill. Alumni Assn. (life), Assn. U.S. Army, Mil. Order Purple Heart, Am. Legion, Res. Officers Assn., Sr. Army Res. Commdrs. Assn. Home: 4009 Tracey Ct Glenview IL 60025 Office: Heartland Securities Inc 208 S LaSalle St Chicago IL 60604

MULARZ, EDWARD JULIUS, II, aerospace engineer; b. Lakewood, Ohio, Nov. 24, 1943; s. Edward J. and Loyola M. (Leonard) M.; m. Cecilia L. Lorenger, June 17, 1967; children—Edward Julius III, Caroline M. B. Mech. Engring., U. Detroit, 1966; Ph.D., Northwestern U., 1971. Aerospace engr. propulsion lab. U.S. Army Research Tech. Lab., Cleve., 1971-81, head combustion fundamentals sect., 1981-84, chief modeling and verification br., 1984-85; chief aerothermochemistry br. 1985—. Contbr. articles to profl. jours. Fellow AIAA (assoc.); mem. ASME, Combustion Inst., Westlake Bd. Edn. (citizens adv. council), JC Internat. Sen. #31189, Train Collectors Assn. Roman Catholic. Avocations: toy trains; softball; racquetball. Home: 4066 Brewster Dr Westlake OH 44145 Office: US Army Research Activity Propulsion Directorate MS5-11 21000 Brook Park Rd Cleveland OH 44135

MULCH, ROBERT F(RANKLIN), JR., physician; b. Quincy, Ill., June 21, 1951; s. Robert Franklin and Martha Jo (Nisi) M.; m. Barbara Ann Best, Apr. 5, 1975; children: Matthew, Luke. BS, U. Ill., 1973; MD, U. Ill., Chgo., 1977. Diplomate Am. Bd. Family Practice. Intern Riverside Meth. Hosp., Columbus, Ohio, 1977-78; resident in family practice Riverside Meth. Hosp., Columbus, 1978-80; gen. practice medicine Hillsboro, Ill., 1980—; asst. clin. prof. family medicine So. Ill. U., Springfield, 1981—; chmn. utilization rev. com. Hillsboro Hosp., 1984—. Fellow Am. Acad. Family Practice; mem. Am. Heart Assn. Lutheran. Avocations: computers, boating. Office: Hillsboro Med Ctr SC 1250 E Tremont Hillsboro IL 62049

MULDARY, THOMAS WILLIAM, psychologist; b. Lackawanna, N.Y., Apr. 20, 1949; s. Charles Gallagher and Winifred Ann (Ebbitt) M.; m. Patricia Mary Spezeski, Sept. 20, 1980. BS, Eastern Mich. U., 1971, MS, 1973; PhD, U.S. Internat. U., 1979. Lic. psychologist, Mich.; lic. marriage, family and child counselor, Calif. Instr. Siena Heights Coll., Adrian, Mich., 1974-76; clin. intern USN Alcoholism Rehab. Ctr., San Diego, 1977, 78-79; adj. prof. Nat. U., San Diego, 1978-80; pvt. practice psychology Ann Arbor, Mich., 1980-82; lectr. dept. psychology Eastern Mich. U., Ypsilanti, 1980—; psychologist Warwick Assocs., Adrian, 1982—; cons. Jackson (Mich.) Police Dept., 1981—, Mich. Dept. Vocat. Rehab., Adrian, 1981-84, Bridgeway Ctr., Jackson, Mich., 1982; adj. instr. Jackson Community Coll. at Mich. State Prison, 1973-76. Author: Interpersonal Relations for Health Professionals, 1983 (Book of Yr. 1984), Burnout and Health Professionals, 1983. Mem. Am. Psychol. Assn., Mich. Psychol. Assn., Mich. Soc. Clin. Psychologists, Mich. Soc. Forensic Psychologists. Roman Catholic. Avocations: woodworking, carpentry, basketball, water skiing. Office: Warwick Assocs 805 W Maumee Adrian MI 49221

MULDER, HENRY JOHN, psychiatrist; b. Grand Rapids, Mich., June 6, 1950; s. Stanley Dean and Vivian Jeanette (Minderhout) M.; m. Anne Louise DeKorne, Dec. 29, 1970; children: Katherine Elizabeth, Julia Christine. BA, U. Mich., 1972, MD, 1977. Diplomate Am. Bd. Psychiatry and Neurology; med. lic., Mich. Staff psychiatrist Pine Rest Christian Hosp., Grand Rapids, Mich., 1981-85, chief of staff, 1984-85; med. dir. Family Service Assocs., Grand Rapids, 1981-83; dir. psychiat. services Holland (Mich.) Community Hosp., 1985—; practice medicine specializing in psychiatry Holland, 1985—; cons. Hope College, Holland, 1985-86. Mem. Am. Psychiat. Assn., Western Mich. Psychiat. Soc., Mich. State Med. Soc., Ottawa County Med. Soc., Phi Beta Kappa. Mem. Reformed Ch. Am. Avocation: music. Home: 1440 Waukazoo Dr Holland MI 49424 Office: Holland Community Hosp 602 Michigan Holland MI 49423

MULHAUSEN, WILLIAM PHILIP, educational psychologist; b. Cleve., Mar. 29, 1945; s. William Michael and Hedy (Koechle) M.; m. Kieran Ann Rechtin, June 19, 1971; children: Jeffrey W., Jason P., Tracie M. BA in Sociology, Case Western Res. U., 1967, MA in Sociology, 1969, MA in Edn., 1970; cert. in sch. psychology, John Carroll U., 1974; postgrad., Kent (Ohio) State U., 1986—. Lic. sch. psychologist, Ohio; lic. profl. counselor. Tchr. spl. edn. Cuyahoga County Bd. Mentally Retarded, Cleve., 1968-74; tchr. jr. and sr. high schs. Cleve. Pub. Schs., 1974-77, sch. psychologist, 1978—; intern sch. psychologist East Cleve. (Ohio) Pub. Schs., 1977-78; pvt. practice sch. psychology Wickliffe, 1983—; founder, exec. dir. Psycon Comprehensive Ednl. Service, Wickliffe, Ohio, 1985—; pvt. practice counseling Wickliffe, 1987—; cons. sch. psychologist Maple Heights (Ohio) Sch. System, 1983; cons. clin. hypnosis, Wickliffe, 1985—. Mem. Am. Psychol. Assn. (assoc.), Nat. Assn. Sch. Psychologists, Ohio Sch. Psychologists Assn., Ohio Psychol. Assn., Cleve. Psychol. Assn., Cleve. Assn. Sch. Psychologists, Am. Assn. for Counseling and Devel., Am. Mental Health Counselors Assn., Am. Assn. Profl. Hypnotherapists, Ohio Mental Health Counselors Assn., Cleve. Soc. Clin. Hypnosis, Alpha Kappa Delta. Avocations: musician and band leader, bowling, bocce, gardening, home remodeling. Home and Office: 28845 Hazel Ave Wickliffe OH 44092-2534

MULHOLLAN, PAIGE ELLIOTT, university president; b. Ft. Smith, Ark., Dec. 10, 1934; s. Paige Elwood and Ruth Dickinson (Berry) M.; m. Mary Bess Flack, July 8, 1956; children: Paige E. Jr., Kelly V. BBA in Mktg., U. Ark., 1956, MA in History, 1962; PhD in History, U. Tex., 1966. From asst. to assoc. prof. history U. Ark., Fayetteville, 1963-70; assoc. dean arts and scis. Kans. State U., Manhattan, 1970-73; dean arts and scis. U. Okla., Norman, 1973-78; provost, v.p. acad. affairs Ariz. State U., Tempe, 1978-81, exec. v.p., 1981-85; pres. Wright State U., Dayton, Ohio, 1985—; cons., examiner N. Cen. Assn., Chgo., 1972—. Mem. Okla. Humanities

Com., 1974-77, chmn., 1975-77; bd. dirs. Pub. Sta. WPTD-TV, Dayton Art Inst., Miami Valley Research Found., Miami Valley Joint Labor-Mgmt. Council. Served to 1st lt. U.S. Army, 1956-57. Mem. Nat Assn. State Univs. and Land Grant Colls. (commn. on arts and scis. 1973-78, chmn. 1974-76), Council of Colls. Arts and Scis. (bd. dirs. 1976-78, sec., treas. 1977-78), Dayton Area C. of C. Avocations: jogging, sailing. Home: Wright State U Rockafield House 3640 Colonel Glenn Hwy Dayton OH 45435 Office: Wright State U 3640 Colonel Glenn Hwy Dayton OH 45435

MULL, FREDERICK LLOYD, transportation executive; b. Shattuck, Okla., Sept. 2, 1948; s. Cecil Frederick and Perry Leah (Wheeler) M.; m. Nan Lynn Wiggins, Dec. 27, 1969; 1 child, Ty Justin. BS in Bus., Panhandle State U., 1970. Contractor Master Feeders, Guymon, Okla., 1966-70; agt. Farm Bur. Ins., Greeley, Colo., 1974-79; cons. Farmland Industries, Kansas City, Mo., 1977-79; pres. Mull Trucking, Inc., Sidney, Nebr., 1979—. Served with USN, 1970-74. Republican. Mem. Ch. Christ. Avocations: tennis, rodeo, fishing, reading. Home and Office: 2683 Alvarado Sidney NE 69162

MULLADY, JAMES MICHAEL, principal; b. Kankakee, Ill., May 27, 1952; s. John Louis and Pauline Ruth (Shurman) M.; m. Robin Christine Douglas, June 20, 1981; 1 child, Madison Christine. BS, Ill. State U., 1974, MS, 1975; advt. cert., U. Ill., 1983, post grad. Social studies coordinator Unit Dist. 306, Arcola, Ill., 1980-83; cooperating tchr. U. Ill., Champaign, Ill., 1982-83; dir. student services Nat. Acad. Arts, Champaign, 1983-85, prin., 1983—. Mem. Assn. Supervision and Curriculum Devel., Network for Performing and Visual Arts Schs., Ill. Prins. Assn. Club: Tuxedo (bd. mem. 1985—). Avocations: music, sports. Home: 1122 W Daniel Champaign IL 61821 Office: Nat Acad Arts 17 E University Champaign IL 61820

MULLALLY, PIERCE HARRY, steel company executive; b. Cleve., Oct. 6, 1918; s. Pierce Harry and Laura (Lynch) M.; student U. Western Ont., 1935; B.S., John Carroll U., 1939; M.D., St. Louis U., 1943; m. Mary Eileen Murphy, Feb. 22, 1943; children—Mary Kathleen, Pierce Harry. Intern, St. Vincent Charity Hosp., Cleve., 1943, resident in surgery, 1944, 47-50, staff surgeon, 1951-62, head peripheral vascular surgery, 1963-76, dir. med. edn., 1967-73, dir. dept. surgery, 1968-75, trustee, 1977-86 ; plant physician Republic Steel Corp., Cleve., 1952-68, med. dir., 1968-76, corp. dir. occupational medicine, 1976-84; cons. LTV Steel Co., 1984-86; med. dir., chmn. med. adv. bd. Ohio Health Choice Plan Inc. Vice-chmn. Cleve. Clinic-Charity Hosp. Com. Surg. Residency Tng., 1970-78; health com. Bituminous Coal Operators Assn.; trustee Wood Hudson Cancer Research Labs., Inc., 1984—; bd. dirs. Phoenix Theatre Ensemble, 1982—. Served to capt. U.S. Army, 1944-46; PTO. Diplomate Am. Bd. Surgery. Fellow ACS, Am. Coll. Angiology; mem. Am. Iron and Steel Inst. (chmn. health com. 1977-79), Am. Acad. Occupational Medicine, Am., Ohio occupational med. assns., Acad. Medicine, Cleve. (dir. 1969-72), Cleve. Surg. Soc., Western Res. Med. Dirs., Soc. Clin. Vascular Surgery. Roman Catholic. Clubs: Cleve. Skating, Cleve. Playhouse, Serra. Home: 2285 Harcourt Dr Cleveland Heights OH 44106

MULLAN, JOHN FRANCIS (SEAN), neurosurgeon, educator; b. County Derry, No. Ireland, May 17, 1925; came to U.S., 1955; s. John and Catharine Ann (Gilmartin) M.; m. Vivian Dunn, June 2, 1959; children: Joan Claire, John Charles, Brian Francis. MB, BCh, BAO, Queen's U., Belfast, No. Ireland, 1947, DSc (hon.), 1976. Diplomate Am. Bd. Neurol. Surgery. Asst. prof. to assoc. prof. neurol. surgery U. Chgo., 1955-64, prof., 1964—, chmn. dept., 1967—; dir. brain research inst. U. Chgo., 1970-84. Author: Neurosurgery for Students, 1961; contbr. over 150 articles to profl. jours.; mem. editorial bd. Jour. Neurosurgery, 1974-84, Archives of Neurology, 1976-87. Fellow ACS, Royal Coll. Surgeons; mem. Soc. Neurol. Surgeons (past pres.), World Fedn. Neurosurg. Socs. (asst. sec. 1983—), Am. Assn. Neurol. Surgeons (v.p. 1975-76), Cen. Neurosurg. Soc. (pres. 1969-70), NIH (various coms.). Roman Catholic. Avocations: walnut tree farming, gardening. Office: U Chgo Med Ctr Box 405 5841 S Maryland Chicago IL 60637

MULLANE, ROBERT E., manufacturing company executive; b. Cin., May 27, 1932; s. Robert E. and Marie M.; children: Katherine, Constance, Margaret, Sarah. Grad., Georgetown U., 1954; MBA, Harvard U., 1956. With Automatic Vending Co., 1953-73, Carousel Time, Inc., 1973-74; v.p. Bally Mfg. Corp., Chgo., 1974-79, pres., chmn. bd. dirs., chief exec. officer, 1979—; bd. dirs. Bally's Park Place, Inc. Office: Bally Mfg Corp 8700 W Bryn Mawr Chicago IL 60631 *

MULLEN, THOMAS EDGAR, real estate consultant; b. Hackensack, N.J., Feb. 10, 1936; s. Luke B. and Jean (Edgar) M.; m. Sarah Lee Huff, Aug. 17, 1984. BS in Engring., Va. Poly. Tech., 1954; grad mgmt. program, Harvard U., 1964. Cons. in field. Mgr. mktg. Eastern Airlines, N.Y.C., 1954-69; pres. Profl. Sprits Mktg., N.Y.C., 1969-72, Shelter Devel. Corp. Am., N.Y.C., 1972-79; supr. ops. Gen. Mills, Orlando Fla., 1980-86; cons., realtor A.H.M. Graves Co. Inc., Indpls., 1986—. Inventor TV Guider Holder, patent, 1971. Fund raiser Am. Cancer Soc., Miami, 1967-70, Weschester Hosp., N.Y.C., 1967-70. Mem. Met. Bd. Realtors, Na.t Assn. Realtors. Republican. Roman Catholic. Avocations: tennis, recreational pilot. Home: 6251 Behner Way Indianapolis IN 46250 Office: AHM Graves Co Inc Indianapolis IN 46256

MULLENS, DEBORAH ELAINE, hospital compensation/benefits executive; b. Huntington, W.Va., Nov. 23, 1956; d. Lester Randall and Shirley Eudora (Boggs) M.; 1 child, Eric Zachary Mullens-Steele. BS, Marshall U., 1979; postgrad., Ohio State U., 1986—. Interviewer Ohio State U., Columbus, 1982-84, compensation analyst, 1984-86; mgr. compensation and benefits Mt. Carmel East Hosp., Columbus, 1986—. Mem. Indsl. Relations Research Assn., Human Resources Assn., Am. Soc. Personnel Adminstrn., Nat. Assn. Female Execs., NAACP. Club: Singles Aware of Christ (Columbus) (pres. 1986-87). Avocations: photography, needlecrafts, reading.

MULLER, H. NICHOLAS, III, historian, educator, state historical society administrator; b. Pitts., Nov. 18, 1938; s. H.N. Jr. and Harriet (Kerschner) M.; m. Carol A. Cook, Jan. 4, 1986; children: Charles T., Brook W. BA, Dartmouth Coll., 1960; PhD, U. Rochester, N.Y., 1968. Assoc. dean U. Vt., Burlington, 1970-78, prof. history, 1974-78; pres. Colby-Sawyer Coll., New London, N.H., 1978-85; dir. State Hist. Soc. Wis., Madison, 1985—; bd. dirs. Standex Internat. Author: (with others) An Anxious Democracy, 1982; Editor: (with others) Science, Technology and Culture, 1974, In A State of Nature, 1982; sr. editor Vt. Life mag., 1975—; editor Vt. History Jour., 1977-85. Pres. Vt. Archeol. Soc., 1970-74; commr. Vt. Bicentennial Commn., Montpellier, 1972-78, commr. Wis. Commn. Bicentennial of U.S. Constitution, 1987—; chmn. Burlington Bicentennial Com., 1975-76, Vt. Council Hist. Preservation, Montpelier, 1976-78; councillor N.H. Council Humanities, 1982-85; bd. dirs. Nat. Council Pub. History, 1987—. Mem. Vt. Hist. Soc. (bd. dirs. 1969—, v.p. 1975-79, Stephen Greene Press award 1977). Club: Madison. Lodge: Rotary.

MULLIGAN, JOHN L., plastics products company executive. Chmn. Am. Western Corp., Sioux Falls, S.D. Office: Am Western Corp 1208 W Elkhorn St Sioux Falls SD 57104 *

MULLIGAN, THOMAS JAMES, accountant; b. Columbus, Ohio, July 15, 1935; s. John L. and Marie (Harcourt) M.; m. Mary Kay McCann, June 15, 1957; children: Theresa, Gerarda, Michael, Patrick, Timothy, Kathleen, Mary Beth. BS in Acctg., Ohio State U., 1957. CPA, Ohio. Sr. acct. Deloitte, Haskins & Sells, Columbus, 1961-66; pvt. practice acctg. Columbus, 1967-75; ptnr. Kirschner, Heimlich, Mulligan & Co., Columbus, 1975—. Pres. Diocesean Sch. Bd., Columbus. Served to 1st lt. Signal Corps, U.S. Army, 1957-59. Named Bd. Mem. Yr., Nat. Assn. Bds. Edn., 1983. Mem. Am. Inst. CPA's, Ohio Soc. CPA's (v.p. 1982-83, treas. 1984—, Columbus chpt. pres. 1980, bd. dirs. 1981), Phi Kappa Theta. Republican. Roman Catholic. Club: Shamrock. Lodge: KC. Home: 1273 Carbone Dr Columbus OH 43224 Office: Kirschner Heimlich Mulligan & Co 729 S Front St Columbus OH 43206

MULLIGAN, WILLIAM HENRY, JR., library administrator; b. Bklyn., Apr. 10, 1948; s. William Henry and Aileen Katherine (Colvin) M.; m. Alice Patricia Gallagher, June 14, 1969; children—William Henry III, Robert Gallagher. A.B., Assumption Coll., 1970; A.M., Clark U., 1973, Ph.D., 1982. Historian, Northborough Am. Revolution Bicentennial Commn., Mass., 1974-75; instr. history Worcester Poly. Inst., Mass., 1975-77; asst. to dir. Regional Econ. Hist. Research Ctr., Greenville, Del., 1977-82; asst. prof. history Central Mich. U., Mt. Pleasant, 1982-83, adj. prof. history, 1984—, dir. Clarke Hist. Library, 1983—; vis. lectr. Assumption Coll., Worcester, 1976; lectr. history Widener U., Chester, Pa., 1979-82. Author: Northborough during the American Revolution, 1974, Northborough: The Town and Its People, 1985; also revs. and articles. Clark U. fellow, 1970-73; Early Am. Industries Assn. grantee, 1980. Roman Catholic. Club: Rotary. Lodge: K.C. Avocation: stamp collecting. Home: 219 N Lansing St Mount Pleasant MI 48858 Office: Clarke Hist Library Central Mich U Mount Pleasant MI 48859

MULLINS, CLAUDE ANDREW, data processing executive; b. Ft. Knox, Ky., Sept. 21, 1954; s. Claudis and Kresentia (Huber) M.; m. Linda S. Kampenga, Nov. 27, 1976; children: Nicholas, Lauren. BChem, De Pauw U., 1976; MBA, Ill. Benedictine U., 1986. Mgr. Nalco Chem. Co., Naperville, Ill., 1980-84; sr. mfg. mgr. Control Data Corp., Downers Grove, Ill., 1985-86, Unisys Corp., Lombard, Ill., 1986—; bd. dirs. TTU, Naperville, 1986. Served to lt. USNR, 1976-80. Mem. Nat. Computer Graphics Assn., Soc. Mfg. Engrs. (O'Hare chpt. chmn. elect), Soc. Plastics Engrs., Am. Prodn. Inventory Control Soc. (program chair), Am. Chems. Soc., Computer Automated Systems Assn., Robitics Internat., Phi Kappa Psi. Home: 1176 Kenilworth Dr Naperville IL 60540 Office: Unisys Corp One Burroughs Ctr Lombard IL 60148

MULLINS, ELIZABETH IONE, sociology educator; b. Colemaine, Minn., Sept. 6, 1928; d. Edgar R. and Bess (Redhed) M. B.A., Miami U., Oxford, Ohio, 1950; M.A., U. Ill., 1954; Ph.D., Ind. U., 1975. Tchr., Blue Ash High Sch., Ohio, 1950-53; student personnel rep. Ind. U., Bloomington, 1954-57; coordinator activities devel. ctr. So. Ill. U., Carbondale, 1957-65; vis. lectr. Ind. U., 1972-73; asst. prof. sociology Kent State U., Ohio, 1973—. Coeditor Sociol. Focus, 1980—. Mem. ACLU, Common Cause, North Central Sociol. Assn. (exec. council 1980—), Am. Sociol. Assn. (com. 1972-75), NOW, Women Studies Assn., AAUP, Alpha Kappa Delta (v.p. 1974-78). Office: Kent State U Lowery Hall Kent OH 44242

MULLINS, JAMES LEE, library director; b. Perry, Iowa, Nov. 29, 1949; s. Kenneth Wiley and Lorene (Gift) M.; m. Kathleen Stiso, May 10, 1986; 1 stepchild, Michael Stiso. BA, U. Iowa, 1972, MA, 1973; PhD, Ind. U., 1984. Instr. Ga. So. Coll., Statesboro, 1973-74; assoc. law librarian Ind. U., Bloomington, 1974-78; dir. library Ind. U., South Bend, 1978—. Contbr. articles to profl. jours. Exec. com. South Bend Art Ctr., 1984—; mem. Mayor's Task Force Redevel., South Bend, 1986; pres. Near Westside Neighborhood Orgn., South Bend, 1986. Mem. ALA, Ind. Library Assn., Assn. Coll. and Research Libraries. Lodge: Rotary. Avocations: reading, gardening, cross-country skiing. Home: 1005 W Washington South Bend IN 46601 Office: Ind Univ Library 1700 Mishawaka Ave PO Box 7111 South Bend IN 46634

MULLINS, OBERA, microbiologist; b. Egypt, Miss., Feb. 15, 1927; d. Willie Ree and Maggie Sue (Orr) Gunn; B.S., Chgo. State U., 1974; M.S. in Health Sci. Edn., Governors State U., 1981; m. Charles Leroy Mullins, Nov. 2, 1952; children—Mary Artavia, Arthur Curtis, Charles Leroy, Charlester Teresa, William Hellman. Med. technician, microbiologist Chgo. Health Dept., Chgo., 1976—. Mem. AAUW, Am. Soc. Clin. Pathologists (cert. med. lab. technician). Roman Catholic. Home: 9325 S Marquette St Chicago IL 60617 Office: 3026 S California Ave Chicago IL 60623

MULLINS, RICHARD AUSTIN, chem. engr.; b. Seelyville, Ind., Apr. 22, 1918; s. Fred A. and Ethel (Zenor) M.; B.S. in Chem. Engring., Rose Poly. Inst., 1940; postgrad. Yale, 1942-43; m. Margaret Ann Dellacca, Nov. 27, 1946; children—Scott Alan, Mark Earl. Chemist, Ayrshire Collieries Corp., Brazil, Ind., 1940-49; chief chemist Fairview Collieries Corp., Danville, Ill., 1949-54; preparations mgr. Enos Coal Mining Co., Oakland City, Ind., 1954-72, Enoco Collieries, Inc., Bruceville, Ind., 1954-62; mining engr. Kings Station Coal Corp.; mgr. analytical procedures Old Ben Coal Corp., 1973-84; ret., 1984. Am. Mining Congress cons. to Am. Standards Assn. and Internat. Orgn. for Standards, 1960-74; mem. indsl. cons. com. Ind. Geol. Survey, 1958-72; mem. organizing com. 5th Internat. Coal Preparation Congress, Pittsburgh, 1966. Mem. exec. bd. Buffalo Trace council Boy Scouts Am., also mem. speakers bur. Bd. dirs. Princeton Boys Club. Served with AUS, 1942-46; ETO. Decorated Medaille de la France Liberee (France); recipient Eagle Scout award, Boy Scouts Am., 1935, Silver Beaver award, 1962, Wood Badge Beads award, 1960; Outstanding Community Service award Princeton Civitan Club, 1964; Engr. of Year award S.W. chpt. Ind. Soc. Profl. Engrs., 1965; Prince of Princeton award Princeton C. of C., 1981. Registered profl. engr., Ind., Ill. Mem. AIME (life mem.), ASTM (sr. mem., R.D. Glenn award 1985), Am. Chem. Soc., Nat. Soc. Profl. Engrs. (life mem.), Ind., Ill. mining insts., Ind. Coal Soc. (pres. 1958-59), Am. Mining Congress (chmn. com. coal preparation 1964-68), Am. Legion (past commn. chmn.), VFW (past co. comdr., 40 & 8 VFW), Ind. Soc. Profl. Land Surveyors, Rose Tech. Alumni Assn. (pres. 1976-77, Honor Alumnus 1980), Order of Ring, Sigma Nu. Methodist (lay speaker). Mason, Elk. Contbr. articles to profl. jours. Home: Rural Route 4 Box 159 Princeton IN 47670

MUMMERT, THOMAS ALLEN, manufacturing company executive; b. Toledo, Ohio, Dec. 24, 1946; s. James Allen and Betty Alice (Thomas) M.; student U. Toledo, 1965-66; m. Icia Linda Shearer, Dec. 17, 1966; children—Sherry Lynn, Robert Thomas, Michael Allen. Pres., Mummert Electric & Mfg. Co., Inc., Toledo, 1969-70; research engr. Am. Lincoln Corp., Bowling Green, Ohio, 1970-73; test engr. Dura div. Dura Corp., Toledo, 1973-74; research dept. head Jobst Inst., Inc., Toledo, 1975-84, mgr. med. equipment design, 1984—. Served with USN, 1968-69. Mem. AAAS, Laser Inst. Am., Biol. Engring. Soc., Ohio Acad. Sci., N.Y. Acad. Sci., Am. Soc. for Quality Control, Am. Soc. Engring. Edn., Nat. Mgmt. Assn., Assn. for Advancement of Med. Instrumentation, ASTM. Baptist. Inventor sequential dual window operating mechanism, 1974, therapeutic appliance for flexing joints, 1980, sequencing valve mechanism, 1981, electronic circuit for dynamic pressure wave pneumatic control system, 1981, artificial foot, 1981, and others; patentee in field. Home: 1448 Palmetto Ave Toledo OH 43606 Office: 653 Miami St Toledo OH 43694

MUNCY, MARTHA ELIZABETH, newspaper publisher; b. Dodge City, Kans., Nov. 5, 1919; d. Jess C. and Juliet Mildred (Pettijohn) Denious.; m. Howard E. Muncy, June 5, 1943 (div. 1969); children: Martha Juliet, Suzanne Gilbert, Howard E. Jr. Student, Lindenwood Coll. for Women, 1937-38; BA, U. Kans., 1941. Advt. mgr. Dodge City Broadcasting Co., 1942-43, copywriter, 1944-46, pres., 1973—; saleswoman Boot Hill Mus., Inc., Dodge City, 1963; pub., pres. Dodge City Daily Globe, 1973—. Mem. Kans. Cavalry, Topeka, 1976—; bd. dirs. Arrowhead West, Inc., Dodge City, 1976—, Dodge City Roundup, Inc., 1976—, Dodge City Crimestoppers, 1985—; bd. dirs., sec. Ford county Hist. R.R. Preservation and Found., Dodge City, 1984—; trustee William Allen White Found., Lawrence, Kans., 1984—. Recipient Outstanding Service award Dodge City Lions, 1981; named Kans. Outstanding Rehab. vol. Kans. Rehab. Assn., 1985. Mem. Kans. Press Women (Woman of Achievement award 1984), S.W. Kans. Press Women, S.W. Kans. Edit. Assn. (Outstanding Journalism award 1982), Dodge City Media Pros, Kans. Press. Assn., Kans. Assn. Broadcasters, Am. Assn. Univ. Women, Dodge City Women's C. of C., Dodge City C. of C., The Philomaths, DAR, Sigma Delta Chi. Republican. Presbyterian. Avocations: reading, travel. Home: 511 Annette Dodge City KS 67801 Office: Dodge City Daily Globe 705 Second Ave Dodge City KS 67801

MUNDT, ROBERT WILLIAM, orthodontist; b. Philip, S.D., Mar. 23, 1931; s. Charles Louis and Alma (MehlBrech) M.; children: Robert Jr., Barbara, Thomas, Steven, David. BS, U. Minn., 1958, DDS, 1960, MS in Dentistry, 1962. Practice dentistry specializing in orthodontics St. Paul, 1962—; cons. Cleft Lip and Palate Clinic, Children's Hosp., St. Paul, 1964—. Served with USN, 1950-54, Korea. Mem. ADA, Am. Assn. Orthodontics, St. Paul Dist. Dental Soc., Christian Med. Soc. (pres. 1973), Am. Cleft Palate Assn., Omicron Kappa Upsilon. Republican. Lodge: Rotary. Avocations: pvt. flying, skiing, watersports. Home: 1856 Gluek Ln Roseville MN 55113 Office: 312 Cen Med Bldg Saint Paul MN 55104

MUNDY, JOHN FRANCIS, lighting company executive; b. Bklyn., Jan. 23, 1946; s. Edwin Francis and Mary Elizabeth (Gillespie) M.; m. Eileen Mary Haggerty, Oct. 3, 1970; children: Elizabeth, Brian, Meghann, Kathleen. BS, Marquette U., 1969. Mktg. analyst Pa. Cen. Trans., Phila., 1969-73; mkt. mgr. food and food products Union Pacific RR, Omaha, 1973-78; v.p. Lava-Simplex Internat., Chgo., 1978-82, pres., 1982—; bd. dirs. Haggerty Enterprises, Inc. Chmn. bd. edn. Sacred Heart Ch., Winnetka, Ill., 1983-85. Served with U.S. Army, 1970-72, Vietnam. Republican. Roman Catholic. Home: 1229 Scott Ave Winnetka IL 60093 Office: Lava Simplex Internat 2321 N Keystone Ave Chicago IL 60639-3709

MUNIAK, MARK MOSES, lawyer; b. Cleve., Oct. 25, 1951; s. Joseph Michael and Lillian (Soltis) M.; m. Rose Aten; 1 child, Michael Avery. BS, U. Mich., 1973; JD, U. Toledo, 1982. Bar: Mich. 1982, U.S. Dist. Ct. (we. dist.) Mich. 1982. Assoc. Conkle & McTaggart, Boyne City, Mich., 1983-86; sole practice Charlevoix, Mich., 1986—. Bd. editors U. Toledo Rev., 1982. Recipient Am. Jurisprudence award, 1979. Mem. ABA, State Bar Mich., Emmet-Charlevoix Bar Assn. Republican. Lodge: Rotary. Avocations: cross-country skiing, distance running. Home: 04216 Poplar Ln Boyne City MI 49712 Office: 405 Bridge St Charlevoix MI 49720

MUNKACHY, LOIS DEUTSCH, educator, hypnotherapist; b. Detroit, Sept. 16, 1929; d. Louis and Ethel (Nagy) D.; B.Music Edn., Baldwin Wallace Coll., 1951; M.A., U. Mich., 1969, Ph.D., 1974; m. Ernest Frederick Munkachy, Mar. 29, 1950; 1 son, Richard Lee David. Tchr. elem. music Dearborn (Mich.) public schs., 1952-54, high sch. tchr. English and music, Westwood, Mich., 1954-68; jr. high sch. tchr. English and social studies, Woodhaven, Mich., 1968-69; tchr. elem. music Romulus (Mich.) Community Schs., 1969-72; tchr. drama, English and choir Romulus High Sch., 1972-84; hypnotherapist Universal Self-Help Center, 1981—; pres. S'unlimited and Assocs., Inc., distbrs. Success Motivation Internat., Inc., 1984—; co-dir. Mich. Hypnosis Inst. Mem. Assn. Supervision and Curriculum Devel., NEA, Mich. Edn. Assn., Nat. Writers Club, Assn. Advance Ethical Hypnosis, Nat. Soc. Hypnotherapists (pres. Mich. chpt.), Internat. Platform Assn. (profl. speaker), Phi Delta Kappa. Clubs: Huron Valley Gun Collectors. Lodge: Rosicrucians. Office: 51 E Huron River Dr Belleville MI 48111

MUNOZ, MARIO ALEJANDRO, city official; b. Havana, Cuba, Feb. 27, 1928; s. Ramón and Concepción (Bermudo) M.; came to U.S., 1961, naturalized, 1968; M.Arch., U. Havana, 1954; postgrad. City Colls. Chgo., 1974; m. Julia Josephine Garrofe, Jan. 17, 1970. Owner, Muñoz Bermudo-Construcciones, Havana, 1954-61; designer various cos., Chgo., 1961-65; designer Chgo. Transit Authority, Mdse. Mart, Chgo., 1965-69; civil engr. Dept. Water and Sewers, City of Chgo., 1969-79, supervising engr. Dept. of Sewers, 1979-85, coordinating engr., 1985—; mem. central area subway system utilities com. City of Chgo., 1974—, mem. computer graphics com., 1977-78. Mem. Am. Pub. Works Assn., Western Soc. Engrs., Chgo. Architecture Found., Chgo. Council Fgn. Relations. Roman Catholic. Clubs: Ground Hog, Execs. (speaker's table com.) (Chgo.); Oak Brook Polo. Home: 5455 N Sheridan Rd Apt 1912 Chicago IL 60640 Office: 121 N LaSalle St Chicago IL 60602

MUNRO, ROBERT ALLAN, lawyer; b. Kearney, Nebr., June 16, 1932; s. George Allan and Alta Susan (Corn) M.; m. Patricia Lee Purcell, Apr. 29, 1961; children—Michael Duncan, Diane Purcell. Student Harvard U., 1950-53; B.S., U. Nebr., 1957, J.D., 1957. Bar: Nebr. 1957, U.S. Dist. Ct. Nebr. 1957, U.S. Ct. Appeals (8th cir.) 1975, U.S. Tax Ct. 1967. Assoc. Munro & Parker, Kearney, 1957-60; county atty. Buffalo County, Kearney, 1959-63; ptnr. Munro & Munro (and predecessor firms), Kearney, 1960-75, sr. ptnr., 1975—; sec., dir. J.F. Brandt Gen. Contracting Co., Kearney; pres., dir. The RAM Co., Kearney, 1982—, Husker Hostelries, Inc., Kearney, 1983—. Sec., dir. Kearney Conv. Ctr. Inc., 1963—, pres., dir. 1983—; sec., dir. Highland Park Devel. Co., Kearney, 1964—; chmn. Buffalo County Young Reps., 1958-62; co-chmn. Gov.'s Adv. Com. on Drug and Alcohol Abuse, 1980-84; bd. dirs. Nebr. Art Collection, 1984—, mem. exec. com., 1986—. Mem. ABA, Nebr. Assn. Trial Attys., Buffalo County Bar Assn., (pres. 1964), Cen. Nebr. Bar Assn. (pres. 1970-71), Am. Judicature Soc., Nat. Trust Hist. Preservation, Smithsonian Assocs., Nebr. Bar Assn. (chmn. com. on ethics 1972-73), Am. Arbitration Assn. (panel arbitrators 1974—). Presbyterian. Club: Kearney Country. Lodges: Masons, Shriners. Home: 2915 5th Ave Kearney NE 68847 Office: 16th St at 3d Ave Munro & Munro PC PO Box 2375 Terrace Level Blackacre Pl Kearney NE 68848

MUNRO, RODERICK ANTHONY, quality engineer; b. Toronto, Ont., Can., Jan. 16, 1955; s. William George and Georgina Antoniette (Shembri) M.; came to U.S., 1956; m. Pamela Ruth Jones, Feb. 23, 1980. B.A., Adrian Coll., 1979, secondary provisional cert., 1981; M.S., Eastern Mich. U., 1984. Cert. quality engr. tchr. Lincoln Park High Sch., Mich., 1980-82; mgmt. trainee Fabricon Automotive, River Range, Mich., 1982-84; quality services coordinator ASC, Inc., Southgate, Mich., 1984-86; quality services coordinator container div. Johnson Controls, Inc., Manchester, Mich., 1987—. cons. in field, 1986—. Active Amazing Grace Evangel. Lutheran Ch., Taylor, Mich., 1980—. Served to sgt. USMCR, 1974-80. Mem. Am. Mgmt. Assn., Am. Tng. and Devel., Aircraft Owners and Pilots Assn., Am. Soc. Quality Control (cert., sr., asst. chmn. edn. Detroit chpt. 1985—), ASTM, Am. Statis. Assn., Am. Soc. Nondestructive Testing. Office: Johnson Controls Inc Plastic Container Div 912 City Rd Manchester MI 48158

MUNROE, SHIRLEY ANN, hospital association executive; b. Mpls., Mar. 31, 1924; d. Laurence John and Esther (Tuttle) M.; pre-nursing cert. La Sierra Coll., Arlington, Calif., 1943; R.N., Glendale Sanitarium and Hosp. Sch. Nursing, 1946; postgrad. UCLA Extension, 1953-55, Los Angeles City Coll., 1948-51; cert. U. Calif. at Santa Cruz extension, 1971; m. Stanley G. Fjelstrom, Dec. 26, 1954 (div. June 1957). Chief nurse, office mgr. for pvt. practice physicians, Los Angeles, 1946-51; bus. mgr. Bolander Clinic and Emergency Hosp., Van Nuys, Calif., 1951-56, Mendocino Med. Ctr., Ukiah, Calif., 1956; adminstr. Hillside Community Hosp., Ukiah, 1956-78, sec., 1956-78; dir. Ctr. for Small or Rural Hosps., Am. Hosp. Assn., Chgo., 1978-79, dir. constituency programs, 1979-83, exec. dir. constituency sects., 1984-85, v.p., 1985—; mem. adv. and eval. com. Ukiah Dist. Sch. Vocat. Nursing, 1965-78; faculty U. Calif. extension at Berkeley, Basic Adminstrn. Hosp. Adminstrs. Program, 1966-70; dir., sec. Obs. Investment Co., Ukiah, 1957-67. Asst. dir. pub. relations alumni postgrad. assembly Loma Linda U., Los Angeles, 1949-55; dir. pub. relations world meeting Aerospace Med. Assn., Los Angeles, 1953; chmn. re-edn. nursing com. Calif. Dept. Employment, 1962; cons. lectr. nurse aide edn., adult edn. Willits, Ukiah high schs., 1962; chmn. Career Project for Sr. High Sch. Girls, 1962-64; mem. Mendocino-Lake adv. com. Regional Med. Program, 1969-73; mem. vocat. edn. adv. com. Ukiah Unified Sch. Dist., 1970-73. Soloist, Presbyn. Ch., Ukiah, 1956-69, Ukiah Oratorio Soc., 1958-65; supt. children's edn. Seventh-day Adventist Ch., 1961-64, dir. pub. relations, 1967-78, chmn. fin. com., 1967-78, mem. ch. bd., 1967-78, mem. exec. com. Ill. conf., 1983—, soloist, 1958-78; mem. ch. bd. Seventh-day Adventist Ch., Elmhurst, 1979—; co-chmn. edn. com. Mendocino County br. Am. Cancer Soc., 1961-62, bd. dirs., 1961-76, pres., 1963-65; mem. steering com. Am. Heart Assn., Mendocino County br. Calif. Heart Assn.; chmn. trustees Tri-County Pre-Payment Medi-Cal Pilot Project, State of Calif., 1969-71; trustee Nor Coa Health, 1967-76, 1st v.p. 1969-71, pres., 1971-72, chmn. South Planning council, 1972-74; mem. Mendocino-Lake counties council, 1966-76; bd. dirs. Mendocino County chpt. ARC, 1968-70; bd. dirs. Blue Cross No. Calif., 1971-78, exec. bd., 1973-78, hosp. provider rep., 1970-78; leader del. People to People Internat. U.S. Citizen Ambassador Program, 1981; mem. bd. Adventist Health System/North, 1981-87, chmn. strategic planning com., 1983-87; mem. bd. Hinsdale Hosp., 1979—, mem. joint conf. com., 1980—, chmn. strategic planning com., 1983—; bd. dirs. Broadview Acad., Lafox, Ill., 1983-86. Recipient Civic Participation award, Outstanding Women in Professions award Calif. Fedn. Bus. and Profl. Women's Clubs, 1965; Outstanding Service award Mendocino-Lake br. Am. Cancer Soc., 1963, 64, 65, Notable Service award, 1968; Walker fellow, 1973. Mem. Am. Hosp. Assn. (ho. of dels. 1974-78, regional adv. bd. 1974-78, rural resource com. 1976-78, v.p.), Calif. Hosp. Assn. (membership com. 1960-61; legis. liaison 1960, panel hosp. peer rev. adminstrs. 1968-78; mem. ins. com. 1971-78), Redwood Empire Hosp. Conf. (ins. com. 1957-59, exec. com. 1968-71, 1st v.p. 1968, pres. 1969), Hosp. Council No. Calif. (bd. dirs. 1968-77, pres. 1975-76, chmn. com. on program and edn. 1968-70), Assn. Western Hosps. (edn. research found. council 1963-65), Glendale Sanitarium and Hosp. Sch. Nursing

Alumni Assn. (pres. Glendale 1947-48), Bus. and Profl. Women's Club (exec. bd. 1957-61, pres. 1959-60, 3d v.p. 1960-61, career advancement com. 1961-62, chmn. personal devel. com. 1962-64, mem. bd. 1962-65, music chmn. Redwood Empire dist. 1960-61), Republican. Club: Soroptimist (pres. Ukiah 1971-72, music chmn. 1962-63, service com. 1961-78, editor bull. 1965-66, Woman of Achievement award 1965, dir. 1970-73). Home: 233 N Garfield St Hinsdale IL 60521 Office: 840 N Lake Shore Dr Chicago IL 60611

MUNSCH, JOHN MICHAEL, engineering executive; b. Mpls., Feb. 14, 1934; s. Nicholas Thomas and Grace Margaret (Kaliher) M.; m. Jean Francis Barnett, June 25, 1960; children: John Jr., Mary, Linda, Kathleen, Carol. Cert., Dunwoody Indsl. Inst., Mpls., 1960. Sr. research shop foreman dept. phys. medicine and rehab. U. Minn., Mpls., 1967-72; program mgr. product engrng. Baxter Travenol Labs. Inc., Round Lake, Ill., 1972—; instr. evening sch. St. Paul Area Vocat. Sch., 1971-72. Patentee in field. Served as staff sgt. U.S. Army, 1954-58. Avocations: skiing, golfing. Office: Baxter Travenol Labs Inc Rt 120 and Wilson Rd PO Box 490 Round Lake IL 60073

MUNSEY, WILLIAM FISCHER, physician; b. Columbus, Ohio, Aug. 24, 1931; m. Helen R. Jarvis, Dec. 26, 1954; 3 children. Student, Capital U.; D in Podiatric Medicine, Ohio Coll. Podiatric Medicine, 1954. Podiatrist Worthington (Ohio) Podiatric Assn.; past pres. Fund for Podiatry Edn. and Research; v.p. Podiatry Ins. Co. Am. Contbr. articles to profl. jours. Deacon, elder, chmn. fin. com. Worthington Presbyn. Ch.; deacon Worthington Grace Brethern Ch. Recipient Kennison award Am. Podiatric Med. Students Assn., 1983; named one of Outstanding Young Men Yr., 1966. Fellow Am. Acad. Practice Adminstrn., Am. Coll. Foot Surgeons; mem. Am. Podiatric Med. Assn. (research del.), Ohio Podiatric Med. Assn. (W.F. Munsey Leadership award, Man of Yr.), Am. Soc. Podiatric Medicine (hon.), Ohio Coll. Podiatric Medicine Alumni. Lodges: Masons, Order of DeMolay (dist. dep.). Avocations: hunting, fishing, woodworking. Home: 8260 Greentree Dr Westerville OH 43081 Office: Worthington Podiatric Assocs 37 E Wilson Bridge Worthington OH 43085

MUNSKI, MARY-MARGARET, architect; b. Flint, Mich., Sept. 9, 1950; d. Vincent Joseph and Clara Veronica (David) M. BArch, U. Mich., 1972, MArch, 1974. Registered architect, Mich. Architect in tng. Tomblinson & Harburn Architects, Flint, 1974-75; architect Architonics, Jackson, Mich., 1975-82; project mgr. Steelcase, Grand Rapids, Mich., 1982—. Mem. AIA (treas. 1984-86, affirmative action com., women in architecture 1981-83), U. Mich. Alumni Assn. (co-pres. 1986-87). Roman Catholic. Avocations: tennis, travel, skiing, gardening, arts and crafts. Home: 2522 4 Woodlake Wyoming MI 49509 Office: Steelcase PO Box 1967 Grand Rapids MI 49501

MUNSON, NORMA FRANCES, biologist, ecologist, educator; b. Stockport, Iowa, Sept. 22, 1923; d. Glenn Edwards and Frances Emma (Wilson) M.; B.A., Concordia Coll., 1946; M.A., U. Mo., 1955; Ph.D. (NSF fellow 1957-58, Chgo. Heart Assn. fellow 1959), Pa. State U., 1962; postgrad. Ind. U., 1957, Western Mich. U., 1967, Lake Forest Coll., 1971, 72, 78; student various fgn. univs., 1964-71. Tchr., Aitkin (Minn.) High Sch., 1946-48, Detroit Lakes (Minn.) High Sch., 1948-54, Libertyville (Ill.) High Sch., 1955-79; researcher in nutrition, Libertyville, 1965—. Ruling elder First Presbyn. Ch., Libertyville, 1971-77; pres. Lake County Audubon Soc., 1975-87, Libertyville Edn. Assn., 1964-67; active Rep. Party of Ill., Citizens to Save Butler Lake, Citizens Choice, The Defenders; mem. U.S. Congl. Adv. Bd., 1985—; bd. dirs. Holy Land Christian Mission Internat. Recipient Hilda Mahling award, 1967, C. of C. award, 1971, Ill. Best Teacher's award, 1974; Best Biology of Yr. award, 1971; NSF fellow, 1970-71. Mem. Nat. Biology Tchrs. Assn. (award 1971), AAAS, Am. Inst. Biol. Sci., Am. Biog. Inst., Ill. Environ. Council, Ill. Audubon Council, Nat. Health Fedn., Internat. Platform Assn., Nat. Wildlife Fedn., N.Y. Acad. Scis., Parks and Conservation Assn., Delta Kappa Gamma. Contbr. research articles to publs. Home and Office: 206 W Maple Ave Libertyville IL 60048

MUNTER, LARRY ARLAN, sales executive; b. Duluth, Minn., Feb. 1, 1945; s. Marvin Olaus and Marion Johanna (Holten) M.; m. Linda Bernice Lilie, June 19, 1965; 1 child, Lori Lea. Student, Northwest Tech. Inst., 1965. Engr. Crown Iron Works, Mpls., 1965-68, sales engr., 1968-84; dir. sales Crown Auger Mfg., Cokato, Minn., 1984—. Trustee St. Paul's Luth. Ch., Osseo, Minn., 1985-86. Home: 10500 Sumter Ave N Brooklyn Park MN 55445 Office: Crown Auger Mfg Hwys 12 & 137 Cokato MN 55321

MUNTZ, ROBERT WILLIAM, restaurateur; b. Bklyn., May 19, 1947; s. Raymond Edward and Camilla Jane (Hargis) M.; m. Marcia Susan Reed, Dec. 29, 1979; 1 child, Andrew Robert. BS in Indsl. Mgmt., Purdue U., 1970. Dir. food and beverage ops. Hospitality Inns, Inc., Cleve., 1970-79, Harley Hotels, Inc., Cleve., 1979-80; pres. R.W. Muntz Assocs., Stow, Ohio, 1980—, Eat, Drink & Be Merry, Inc., Brecksville, Ohio, 1984—. Served with U.S. Army, 1971-72. Mem. Ohio Restaurant Assn., Nat. Restaurant Assn., Northeast Ohio Restaurant Assn., Brecksville C. of C. Republican. Avocations: swimming, cooking. Home: 3767 Vira Rd Stow OH 44224 Office: Eat Drink & Be Merry Inc 7600 Chippewa Rd Brecksville OH 44141

MUNZINGER, JUDITH MONTGOMERY, investment exececutive; b. Dayton, Ohio, June 16, 1944; s. Russell Eric and Margaret Lois (Weltzheimer) Montgomery; m. John Stephen Munzinger, May 28, 1977; children—Laurie Anne, Lisa Michelle. B.S. in Edn., Ohio State U., 1966, M.A., 1979, cert. remedial reading, 1980. Cert. tchr., Iowa. Tchr. elem. sch., Lafayette, Ind., 1966-69, Hilliard, Ohio, 1976-79; remedial reading tchr. Sioux City, Iowa, 1979-82; instr., dir. early childhood devel. Briar Cliff Coll.; talented and gifted coordinator, Sioux City, 1982-85; investment exec. Piper, Jaffray and Hopwood, Sioux City, 1985—. Treas. Siouxlanders for Talented and Gifted; mem. Coalition for Children; judge for Iowa Future Problem Solving Bowl, 1982; active Jr. League; mem. vestry, clk. St. Thomas Episcopal Ch., 1982-84; mem. Children's Hosp. support group, Columbus, Ohio, 1972-79; active Women's Assn. for Columbus Zoo, 1973-76, PTA; asst. Girl Scouts U.S.A., 1980-82. Recipient Service commendation Girl Scouts U.S.A., 1980. Mem. Iowa Reading Assn., Internat. Reading Assn., Ohio State U. Alumni Assn., Delta Zeta. Republican. Home: 4521 Country Club Blvd Sioux City IA 51104 Office: Piper Jaffray and Hopwood 421 Nebraska St Sioux City IA 51101

MURAKAMI, GLENN HIDEO, physician; b. Hilo, Sept. 14, 1946; s. Shigeo and Michie (Tatsuta) M.; m. Nancy Kay Tournell, Aug. 28, 1970; children: Ingrid, Melissa, Erin, Mark, Peter, Timothy. BA, Northwestern U., 1968, MD, 1972; cer. Diplomate Am. Bd. Intrnal Medicine, Am. Bd. Emergency Medicine. Residence in internal medicine Northwestern U. Med. Ctr., Chgo., 1972-75; emergency physician Mesa, S.C., Chgo., 1975-82, Emsco Ltd., Chgo., 1982—, Swedish Covernant Hosp., Chgo., 1975—; instr. Am. Hart Assn., Chgo., 1983-86. Mem. AMA. Democrat. Mem. Evanelical Covenant Ch. Am. Home and Office: 6566 N Hiawatha Chicago IL 60646

MURATA, TADAO, engineering and computer science educator; b. Takayama, Gifu, Japan, June 26, 1938; came to U.S., 1962; s. Yonosuke and Ryu (Aomame) M.; m. Nellie Kit-Ha Shin, 1964; children—Patricia Emi, Theresa Terumi. B.S.E.E., Tokai U., 1962; M.S.E.E., U. Ill., 1964, Ph.D. in Elec. Engring., 1966. Research asst. U. Ill., Urbana, 1962-66; asst. prof. U. Ill. at Chgo., 1966-68, assoc. prof., 1970-76, prof., 1977—; assoc. prof. Tokai U., Tokyo, Japan, 1968-70; vis. prof. U. Calif.-Berkeley, 1976-77; cons. Nat. Bur. Standards, Gaithersburg, Md., 1984-85; panel mem. Nat. Acad. Scis., Washington, 1981-82, 83-85; vis. scientist Nat. Ctr. for Sci. Research, France, 1981; guest researcher Gesellschaft für Mathematik und Datenverarbeitung, Fed. Republic of Germany, 1979. Editor IEEE Trans. on Software Engring., 1986—; contbr. articles to sci. and engring. jours. NSF grantee, 1978—, U.S.-Spain coop. research grantee, 1985-87. Fellow IEEE; mem. Assn. Computing Machinery, Info. Processing Soc. Japan, European Assn. for Theoretical Computer Sci. Avocations: golf; travel. Office: U Ill Dept Elec Engring and Computer Sci Box 4348 Chicago IL 60680

MURDOCH, BOB, professional hockey coach; b. Kirkland Lake, Ont., Can., Nov. 20, 1946. Profl. hockey player Montreal Voyageurs, Am. Hockey League, Que., Can., 1970, Montreal Canadiens, NHL, 1971-73, Los Angeles Kings, NHL, 1973-79; profl. hockey player Atlanta Flames (now Calgary Flames), NHL, 1979-82, player/coach, 1981-82, asst. coach, 1982-87; coach Chgo. Black Hawks, NHL, 1987—. Office: Chicago Black Hawks 1800 W Madison St Chicago IL 60612 *

MURDOCK, MONI (MARY MARGARET), clinical social worker; b. Mishawaka, Ind., Jan. 19, 1938; d. Joseph Weldon and Evelyn Mary (Diroll) Hennessy; m. Charles William Murdock, May 25, 1963; children: Kathleen Tracy, Michael Hennessy, Kevin Charles, Sean Joseph. BS cum laude, Marquette U., 1959; MSW, Loyola U., Chgo., 1961; postgrad., Northwestern U., Evanston, Ill., 1977-79. Caseworker Ill. Children's Home and Aid Soc., Chgo., 1961-64; clin. social worker Logan Ctr., South Bend, Ind., 1973, St. Joseph County Mental Health Ctr., South Bend, 1974-75; clin. social worker Doyle Ctr. Loyola U., Chgo., 1975-77, clin. supr., 1977—; pvt. practice psychotherapy The Family Ctr., Evanston, 1979—; mem. adv. bd. Ctr. for Family Studies Northwestern U., 1978—, pres. alumni bd., 1980-83, part time faculty mem., 1983—; chair gov. bd. Family Inst. Chgo., 1987—; mem. adj. faculty Loyola U. Sch. Social Work, 1984—; chmn. Chgo. family therapy conf. Northwestern U., 1980. Co-author: Getting to Know Us, 1983. Bd. dirs., co-founder Little Flower Montessori Sch., South Bend, 1969-74; chmn. adult edn. Little Flower Parish, South Bend, 1971-73, St. Athanasius Parish, Evanston, 1976-79; del. Nat. Assembly Cath. Laity, Notre Dame, Ind., 1981. Grantee HEW, 1959-60; stipentee VA, 1960-61. Mem. Am. Family Therapy Assn. (charter), Am. Assn. Marriage and Family Therapy (clin.), Nat. Assn. Social Workers (cert., clin.), Register Clin. Social Workers (clin. diplomat). Democrat. Invited as child and family mental health delegate to People's Republic of China, 1987; avocations: reading, bicycling, sailing, hiking, opera and classical music. Home: 2527 Marcy Ave Evanston IL 60201 Office: The Family Ctr 1830 Sherman Ave Evanston IL 60201

MURDOCK, PHELPS DUBOIS, JR., marketing and advertising agency executive; b. Kansas City, Mo., May 5, 1944; s. Phelps Dubois and Betty Jane Murdock; student U. Mo., Kansas City, 1962-66; m. Nancy Jane Winfrey, June 7, 1977; children—Susan, Kathleen, Mark, Brooks, Phelps DuBois III, Molly. Sales service mgr. Sta.-KCMO-TV, Kansas City, Mo., 1965-66; account exec. Fremerman-Papin Advt., Kansas City, Mo., 1966-71, TV prodn. mgr., 1966-70, v.p., 1970-71; mng. ptnr. New Slant Prodns., Kansas City, Mo., 1971-73; v.p., creative dir. Travis-Walz-Lane Advt., Kansas City, Mo., and Mission, Kans., 1973-76; pres., chief exec. officer Phelps Murdock Mktg. and Advt., Inc., Kansas City, Mo., 1977—; guest lectr. colls., univs. Active Heart of Am. United Way, 1966-80, mem. exec. bd., 1976, bd. dirs., 1976-80; active Help Educate Emotionally Disturbed, Inc., Kansas City, Mo., 1968-80, pres. bd. dirs. HEED Found., 1979-80; active Heart of Am. council Boy Scouts Am., 1975-85, bd. govs. Bacchus Ednl. and Cultural Found., Kansas City, Mo., 1973-76, found. chmn., 1975; mem. promotion com. Kansas City Bicentennial Commn., 1975-76; vol. coach, local youth leagues, 1975-83; cons. Com. for County Progress Campaigns, Charter Campaign, Jackson County, Mo., 1970; Kansas City Magnet Schs., 1986—. Recipient various awards including United Way Nat. Communications award, 1975; Effie citation N.Y. Mktg. Assn., 1975; 1st Place Print Ad award and 1st Place Poster award 9th Dist. Addy Awards, 1975, 1st Place Regional-Nat. TV Campaign award, 1976; Omni award, 1980-82, 86, 87; Silver award KCAD, 1981; 1st Place TV Campaign award KCAF Big One Show, 1976; Best-of-Show and Gold medal award Dallas Soc. Visual Communications, 1976; named Mic-O-Say hon. warrior, 1978. Mem. Advt. and Sales Execs. (founding), Am. Advt. Fed. Assn. Democrat. Author numerous TV, radio commls., film, TV and radio musical compositions; film and television direction; creator "Modulatin' With McCall" NBC, 1976-77. Home: #1 Chartwell Kansas City MO 64114 Office: 21 E 29th St Kansas City MO 64108

MURMAN, MICHAEL ELLIS, lawyer, prosecutor; b. Cleve., Aug. 14, 1946; s. Charles Edward and Agnes Z. (Zaytoun) M.; m. Drue Koran, Apr. 23, 1982; children: Meryl Leslie, Erin Marie. B.A., U. Dayton, 1968; J.D. magna cum laude, Cleve. State U., 1975. Bar: Ohio 1975, Fla. 1976, U.S. Supreme Ct. 1979. Tchr. Dayton Pub. Schs., Ohio, 1968-72; sole practice law, Lakewood, Ohio, 1975—; asst. pros. atty. Cuyahoga County, Cleve., 1976-79; pros. atty. City of Lakewood, 1979—. Trustee Lakewood Improvement Corp., 1978-81; pres. council St. Luke Ch., Lakewood, 1982-83. Mem. Ohio State Bar Assn., Fla. Bar Assn., Cuyahoga County Bar Assn., Cuyahoga County Law Dirs. Assn. (v.p. 1987, sec.), Cleve. Bar Assn. (exec. com. crime sect.). Republican. Roman Catholic. Office: 14701 Detroit Ave Lakewood OH 44107

MURNANE, GEORGE THOMAS, JR., insurance executive; b. El Paso, Tex., June 5, 1921; s. George Thomas Murnane Sr. and Willie (Watts) Cummings; m. Frances Ann Rusciano, Feb. 14, 1969; children: G. Thomas III, Kathleen Camille. CLU. Asst. to pres. Union Nat. Life Ins., Mpls., 1948-50; recruitment and tng. supr. Provident Mutual Ins. Co., Mpls., 1950-67; ins. broker Murnane & Assocs., Mpls., 1967—. Mem. Jesuit Retreat League, Mpls. Served to master sgt. U.S. Army, 1940-44. Mem. Nat. Assn. Life Underwriters, Am. Soc. CLU's (former pres. Mpls. chpt.), Mpls. Aquatennial Assn. (current commodore), Million Dollar Round Table (life). Republican. Roman Catholic. Club: Mpls. Athlectic, Ham 'N Eggs (current pres.). Lodge: Kiwanis. Avocations: boating, home repair, walking, biking. Home: 2812 Benton Blvd Minneapolis MN 55416

MURNIK, MARY RENGO, biology educator; b. Manistee, Mich., Aug. 30, 1942; d. John Everett and Lorraine P. (ReVolt) R.; m. James M. Murnik, July 30, 1970; 1 child, John. Student Marquette U., 1960-62; B.S., Mich. State U., 1964, Ph.D., 1969. Asst. prof. Fitchburg State Coll., Mass., 1968-70; from asst. prof. to prof. Western Ill. U., Macomb, 1970-80; prof., head biol. sci. dept. Ferris State Coll., Big Rapids, Mich., 1980—. Contbr. articles to profl. jours. Author two lab. manuals. NIH fellow HEW, Mich. State U., 1965-68; NIH grantee Western Ill. U., 1976; grantee Environ. Mutagen Soc., Edinburgh, Scotland, 1977, Western Ill. U., 1972-79. Mem. AAAS, Genetics Soc. Am., Behavior Genetics Soc., Mich. Acad. Sci., Arts and Letters, Sigma Xi. Roman Catholic. Home: 331 W Slosson St Reed City MI 49677 Office: Dept Biol Scis Ferris State Coll Big Rapids MI 49307

MURPHEY, BARBARA JEAN, school administrator; b. Adrian, Pa., Nov. 26, 1941; m. Coleman Ray Murphey, Sept. 2, 1972. BS, Ashland (Ohio) Coll., 1963; MA, Kent (Ohio) State U., 1969; EdD, U. Akron, 1987. Cert. tchr. supr., dir., supt., Ohio. Tchr. Akron (Ohio) Pub. Schs., 1963-70, tchr., coordinator, 1970-72, coordinator in curriculum, 1972-84, coordinator in bus. and fin., 1985—. Mem. Am. Vocation Ass., Ohio Vocation Assn., Am. Home Econs. Assn., Ohio Home Econs Assn. (pres. dist. B 1977-78), Am. Sch. Food Service Assn., Ohio Sch. Food Service Assn., Ohio Nutrition Council, Delta Kappa Gamma (pres. 1976-78, Annie Blanton scholar 1984), Phi Delta Kappa. Republican. Methodist. Avocations: jogging, sewing. Home: 3574 Frawood Dr Uniontown OH 44685

MURPHY, BRIAN PHILIP, human resources development consultant; b. Dayton, Ohio, Oct. 6, 1948; s. John Henry and Mary Eileen (Westrick) M.; m. Susan Beth Kamener. BS, Bowling Green (Ohio) State U., 1975, MEd, 1976. Instr. visual communication Bowling Green State U., 1976-77; curriculum specialist U. Md., College Park, 1977-79; tng. specialist Potomic Electric Power Co., Washington, 1979-81; mgr. tng. and devel. Onan Corp., Mpls., 1981-83, dir. human resource planning and devel., 1983-85; pres. The HRD Dept., Inc., St. Paul, 1985—; adv. bd. tng. and devel. U. Minn., 1985—. Contbr. articles to profl. jours. Served with USN, 1969-72. Recipient Profl. Partnership award U. Minn., 1986. Mem. Am. Soc. Tng. and Devel., Nat. Assn. Indsl. and Tech. Tchr. Educators. Office: The HRD Dept Inc 2187 Dayton Ave Saint Paul MN 55104

MURPHY, CHARLES ARNOLD, physician, surgeon; b. Detroit, Dec. 29, 1932; s. Charles L. and Hazel C. (Robinson) M.; m. Mary Lightford, Aug. 1955; m. Judith L. Dennis, Nov. 12, 1966; 1 child, Charles A. III; m. Sandra M. Walker, July 17, 1971. Student, Wayne State U., 1949-53; D.O., Coll. Osteo Medicine and Surgery, Des Moines, 1957. Diplomate Am. Osteo Bd. Gen. Practice. Intern Flint Osteo. Hosp, Mich., 1957-58; gen. practice medicine Detroit, 1958—; mem. staff Kirkwood Hosp., 1964-66, Martin Place Hosp., 1958-64, Mich. Osteo. Med. Ctr., 1959—; osteo. physician City of Detroit, 1959-63; sr. police surgeon Detroit Police Dept., 1977-79; assoc. clin. prof. family medicine Coll. Osteo. Medicine, Mich. State U.; bd. dirs., mem. exec. com. Mich. HMO Plans; mem. central peer rev. adv. com. Mich. Dept. Health; mem. council med. dirs. Health Care Network. Fellow Am. Coll. Osteo. Gen. Practitioners; mem. Am. Osteo. Assn. (ho. of dels. 1981-87), Greater Detroit Area Hosp. Council, Mich. Osteo. Assn. (ho. of dels. 1970—, trustee 1981—), NAACP (life), Wayne County Osteo. Assn. (pres. 1976, 77), Mich. Assn. Osteo. Physicians (pres. 1986-87), Mich. Assn. Gen. Practitioners in Osteo. Medicine and Surgery, Coll. Osteo. Medicine and Surgery Alumni Assn., Atlas Club, Kappa Alpha Psi, Psi Sigma Alpha. Methodist. Club: Detroit Yacht. Office: 12634 E Jefferson St Detroit MI 48215

MURPHY, CHARLES WILLIAM, management analyst; b. Kinston, N.C., Dec. 6, 1929; s. Edgar David and Blanche (Burden) M.; m. Geneva McCoy, Aug. 9, 1955; children: Charles Jr., Donald Seth, Deanna Faye, Bryan Keith. BS in Biol. Scis., N.C. A&T State U., 1954; postgrad., Butler U., 1968-69. Commd. 2d lt. U.S. Army, 1953, advanced through grades to lt. col., 1968, ret., 1974; mgmt. analyst City-County Govt., Indpls., 1974-75; mem. Minority Purchasing Council, Indpls., 1985—. Author: Southeast Asia Area Studies, Nations of the World, 1969. Mem. Indpls. Edn. Adv. Council, 1983-85, econ. devel. com. Indpls. Urban League, 1984—; chmn. Indpls. Bicentennial Com., 1976. Mem. Adminstrn. Mgmr. Soc. (personal dir. Indpls. chpt. 1977-79), Life Office Mgmt. Assn. (adminstrv. services com. 1979—), Omega Psi Phi (pres. 1979-81). Republican. Avocations: golf, music, camping. Home: 7016 Cricklewood Rd Indianapolis IN 46220 Office: Indpls Life Ins Co 2960 N Meridian PO Box 1230 Indianapolis IN 46206

MURPHY, DANIEL THOMAS, corporate professional, controller; b. Watertown, S.D., July 16, 1954; s. Andrew Louis and Genivieve Marie (Krakowski) M.; m. Teresa Marie Finley, Sept. 4, 1982; 1 child, Joseph Andrew. BS in Bus., U. S.D., 1976. CPA, Minn. Acct. Johnson West & Co., St. Paul, 1976-84; controller Blackbourn, Inc., Eden Prairie, Minn., 1984—. Mem. Am. Inst. CPA's, Minn. Soc. CPA's. Republican. Roman Catholic. Avocations: golf, softball, hunting, chess. Home: 16330 N Hillcrest Eden Prairie MN 55344 Office: Blackbourn Inc 10150 Crosstown Circle Eden Prairie MN 55344

MURPHY, DENNIS PATRICK, hotel executive; b. Buffalo, N.Y., Jan. 12, 1958; s. Dennis Charles and Dorothy E. Murphy. B in Hospitality Mgmt., Fla. Internat. U., 1980. Mgr. hotel ops. Marriott Corp., Washington, 1979-80; dir. food and beverage Mariner Corp., Houston, 1980-83; corp. dir. Innco Hospitality, Wichita, Kans., 1984-86, Clubhouse Inns of Am., 1986—; bd. dirs. Humanitech Inc., Buffalo, 1983—. Chmn. Gov.'s Youth Traffic Safety Com., N.Y., 1977-79; mem. Nat. Youth Safety Council, Washington, 1978. recipient Elsworth Statler award The Statler Found., 1978-79, Eugene Fitzsimmons award Internat. Assn. Hospitality Accts., 1980. Mem. Nat. Restaurant Assn., Soc. Wine Educators (pubs. com. 1977-79). Republican. Roman Catholic. Home: 505 N Rock Rd #206 Wichita KS 67206 Office: Innco Hospitality Inc 8080 E Central Suite 110 Wichita KS 67206

MURPHY, DIANA E., U.S. district judge; b. Faribault, Minn., Jan. 4, 1934; d. Albert W. and Adleyne (Heiker) Kuske; m. Joseph E. Murphy, Jr., July 24, 1958; children: Michael, John E. B.A. magna cum laude, U. Minn., 1954, J.D. magna cum laude, 1974; postgrad., Johannes Gutenberg U., Mainz, Germany, 1954-55, U. Minn., 1955-58. Bar: Minn. 1974. Mem. firm Lindquist & Vennum, 1974-76; mcpl. judge Hennepin County, 1976-78; Minn. dist. judge 1978-80; U.S. dist. judge Minn. Mpls., 1980—; instr. Law Sch. U. Minn., Atty. Gen.'s Advocacy Inst.;. Bd. editors: U. Minn. Law Rev. Bd. dirs. Spring Hill Conf. Ctr., 1978-84; bd. dirs. Bush Found., 1982—, chmn. bd., 1986—; bd. dirs. Amicus, 1976-80, organizer, 1st chmn. adv. council; mem. Mpls. Charter Commn., 1973-76, chmn., 1974-76; bd. dirs. Ops. De Novo, 1971-76, chmn., 1974-75; mem. Minn. Constl. Study Commn., chmn. bill of rights com., 1971-73; regent St. Johns U., 1978—, vice chmn. bd., 1985—; trustee Twin Cities Pub. TV, 1985—; bd. dirs. Mpls. United Way, 1985—. Fulbright scholar; recipient U. Minn. Outstanding Achievement award; Amicus Founders' award; YWCA Outstanding Achievement award. Fellow Am. Bar Found.; mem. Am. Bar Assn. (Ethics and Profl. Responsibility Judges Adv. Com. 1981—), Minn. Bar Assn. (bd. govs. 1977-81), Hennepin County Bar Assn. (gov. council 1976-81), Am. Law Inst., Am. Judicature Soc. (bd. dirs. 1982—, v.p. 1985—), Nat. Assn. Women Judges, Minn. Women Lawyers, U. Minn. Alumni Assn. (bd. dirs. 1975-83, pres. 1981-82), Fed. Judges Assn. (bd. dirs. 1982—, v.p. 1984—), Order of Coif, Phi Beta Kappa. Office: US District Court 670 US Courthouse 110 S 4th St Minneapolis MN 55401

MURPHY, EARL PAULUS, JR., English educator, writer, researcher; b. St. Louis, Dec. 2, 1944; s. Earl Paulus and LaVerne Roberta (Tentschert) M.; m. Janet Ellen Schey, Jan. 23, 1945 (div.); children—Heather, Vonya. B.A., Western Ky. U., 1967, M.A., 1971; Ph.D., St. Louis U., 1977; postdoctoral Columbia U., Washington U., Oxford U., Northwestern U. Tchr. English, Western Ky. U., Bowling Green, 1967-68, St. Louis U., 1973-77, Harris-Stowe State Coll., St. Louis, 1977—, dir. Humanities and Phys. Edn.; tchr. U. Md., Taipei, Taiwan, Fla. Jr. Coll. Jacksonville, Forest Park Community Coll., St. Louis. Served with USAF, 1969-72. Inst. for Internat. Edn. fellow, summer 1974; NEH grantee, 1979, 80-81, 83. Mem. MLA, Popular Culture Assn. Lutheran. Contbr. articles to profl. jours. Office: Harris-Stowe State College 3026 LaClede Ave Saint Louis MO 63103

MURPHY, ELISABETH ANNE, educator; b. Jacksonville, Ill., Dec. 23, 1950; d. Paul and Mary (Henderson) Hogan; m. Donald Edward Murphy, Nov. 29, 1975; children: Megan Elisabeth, Matthew Edward. BA, MacMurray Coll., 1973; MS, So. Ill. U., 1986. Instr. sign lang. John A. Logan Coll., Carterville, Ill., 1976-79; instr. sign lang. div. continuing edn. So. Ill. U., 1979-85; tchr. high sch. deaf students Williamson County Spl. Edn. Coop., 1973—. Cert. Council Edn. Deaf, cert. tchr., Ill. Mem. Marion Edn. Assn., Ill. Edn. Assn., NEA, Ill. Tchrs. Hearing Impaired, Ill. Assn. Deaf, Telecommunictors of Central Ill., Telecommunications ofr Deaf So. Ill. Interpretors of Deaf, Little Egypt Assn. Deaf. Roman Catholic. Home: 1104 W White St Marion IL 62959 Office: 700 E Blvd Marion IL 62959

MURPHY, GARY PETER, school psychologist; b. Eau Claire, Wis., July 2, 1948; s. Brendan Norman and Hedwig Marie (Mouschek) M.; m. Elizabeth Ann Stiefvater, Dec. 26, 1970; children: Joshua, Kate. BS, U. Wis., Stevens Point, 1972; MS in Edn., U. Wis., Eau Claire, 1975. Lic. sch. psychologist, Wis. Sch. psychologist Coop. Ednl. Service Agy. 4, Cumberland, Wis., 1975-76, Spooner (Wis.) Sch. Dist., 1976—. Served with U.S. Army, 1969-71, Vietnam. Mem. Am. Psychol. Assn. (assoc.), Wis. Sch. Psychologist Assn., Nat. Assn. Sch. Psychologists. Avocations: archery, bicycling. Office: Spooner Sch Dist 500 College St Spooner WI 54801

MURPHY, GEORGE EARL, psychiatrist, educator; b. Portland, Oreg., Oct. 17, 1922; s. George Earl and Mary Ella (Wilcox) M.; m. Amanda Daniel, Mar. 24, 1978; children: Paul Douglas, Bruce Kevin, Marc Andrew. Student, U. Wash., 1940-42, U. Portland, 1946-47; BS, Oreg. State U., 1949; MD, Washington U., St. Louis, 1952. Diplomate Am. Bd. Psychiatry and Neurology. Intern Alameda County Hosp., Oakland, Calif., 1952-53, asst. resident in medicine, 1953-54; fellow in psychosomatic medicine Washington U., St. Louis, 1954-55, asst. resident in psychiatry, 1956-57; instr. sch. of medicine Washington U., 1957-59, asst. prof. sch. of medicine, 1959-66, assoc. prof. sch. of medicine, 1966-69, prof. sch. of medicine, 1969—; asst. resident in psychiatry Mass. Gen. Hosp., Boston, 1955-56; dir. psychiatry clinic, Washington U., 1976—, psychiat. student health, 1978-83; coursemaster human sexuality Washington U., 1979—. Contbr. articles to profl. jours. Mem. University City (Mo.) Human Relations Commn., 1965-70, chmn., 1968-69; bd. dirs. Suicide Prevention, Inc., St. Louis, 1967-73. Served to 1st class petty officer USN, 1942-45. NIMH grantee, 1963-83, 85—. Fellow Am. Psychiat. Assn.; mem. Am. Psychopathological Assn., Am. Assn. Suicidology, Royal Coll. Psychiatrists, Sigma Xi. Avocation: archaelogy of the bronze age. Office: Washington U Sch Medicine Dept Psychiatry 4940 Audubon Ave Saint Louis MO 63110

MURPHY, J. J., filmmaker, educator; b. Bayonne, N.J., 1947. Assoc. prof. communication arts U. Wis., Madison; founder, dir. Orphan Films. Director: (films) Print Generation, 1974, The Night Belongs to the Police, 1981, Terminal Disorder, 1983, Frame of Mind, 1985. Office: Univ Wis Communication Arts Dept Vilas Hall Madison WI 53706

MURPHY, JANET GORMAN, college president; b. Holyoke, Mass., Jan. 10, 1937; d. Edwin Daniel and Cahterine Gertrude (Hennessey) Gorman. B.A., U. Mass., 1958, postgrad. 1960-61, Ed.D., 1974, LL.D. (hon.) 1984; M.Ed., Boston U., 1961. Tchr. English and history John J. Lynch Jr. High Sch., Holyoke, 1958-60; tchr. English, Chestnut Jr. High Sch., Springfield, Mass., 1961-63; instr. English and journalism Our Lady of Elms Coll., Chicopee, 1963-64; mem. staff Mass. State Coll., Lyndonville, Vt., 1977-83, Mo. Western State Coll., St. Joseph, 1983—. Mem. campaign staff Robert F Kennedy Presdl. Campaign, 1967. Recipient John Gunther Tchr. award NEA, 1961, award Women's Opportunity Com., Boston Fed. Exec. Bd., 1963; named one of 10 Outstanding Young Leaders of Greater Boston Area, Boston Jr. C. of C., 1973. Address: Mo Western State Coll Office of the President Saint Joseph MO 64507

MURPHY, JOHN BERNARD, electrical manufacturers agency executive; b. Geddes, S.D., July 29, 1924; s. William J. and Helen Louise (McGinnis) M.; children—Michael, Brian, Patrick. Student Sch. Bus., U. Minn., 1948. With mktg. dept. Westinghouse & Gen. Cable Corp., Mpls., 1951-63; pres., founder J.B. Murphy Assocs., Inc., Mpls., 1964—. Served with U.S. Army, World War II. Mem. North Central Elec. League, Beta Theta Pi. Democrat. Roman Catholic. Club: DeCathlon Athletic. Home: 9600 Oxborough Rd Bloomington MN 55437 Office: JB Murphy Assocs Inc 2204 W 94th St Minneapolis MN 55431

MURPHY, KATHRYN LOUISE, librarian, educator; b. Beatrice, Nebr., Apr. 19, 1932; d. Edward Philip and Bess Bertha (Weingarten) Bachle; m. Roy Edward Murphy, June 18, 1950 (dec. Jan. 1965); children—Timothy Micheal, Daniel Lee, Holly Ann Murphy Barstow. Student Hastings Coll., 1949-50; B.S. in Edn., N.W. Mo. State U., 1970; M.A., U. Mo., 1980. Bookkeeper, typist Western Tablet and Stationery, St. Joseph, Mo., 1950-55; pvt. piano tchr., St. Joseph and Maryville, Mo., 1955-64; periodicals clk., browsing room librarian Wells Learning Resources Ctr., N.W. Mo. State U., Maryville, 1965-69, cataloger, 1970-76, head cataloger, 1976-81, asst. to dir., 1983-84, asst. dir., 1984, head circulation services, 1981-83, head circulation services Owens Library, 1983-85, temp. acting dir., 1981-84, head library automated services, 1985—. Trustee, First Presbyn. Ch., Maryville, 1978-81, bd. deacons, 1971-74, 82-84, mem. session, elder, 1985—. Mem. ALA, Mo. Library Assn. Presbyterian. Home: 110 S Buchanan St Maryville MO 64468 Office: Northwest Mo State U BD Owens Library Maryville MO 64468

MURPHY, MARY KATHRYN, industrial hygienist; b. Kansas City, Mo., Apr. 16, 1941; d. Arthur Charles and Mary Agnes (Fitzgerald) Wahlstedt; m. Thomas E. Murphy Jr., Aug. 26, 1963; children: Thomas E. III, David W. BA, Avila Coll., Kansas City, 1962; MS, Cen. Mo. State U., 1975. Cert. in comprehensive practice of indsl. hygiene. Indsl. hygienist Kansas City area office Occupational Safety and Health Adminstrn., 1975-78, regional indsl. hygienist, 1979-86; dir. indsl. hygiene Chart Services, Shawnee, Kans., 1986-87; dir. indsl. hygiene activities Hall-Kimbrell Environ. Services, Lawrence, Kans., 1987—; asst. dir. safety office U. Kans. Med. Ctr., 1978-79. Summer talent fellow Kaw Valley Heart Assn., 1961. Mem. Am. Indsl. Hygiene Assn. (sec.-treas. Mid-Am. sect. 1978-79, bd. dirs. 1981, mem. auditcom.), Am. Chem. Soc., Am. Conf. Govt. Indsl. Hygienists (mem. chem. agts. threshold limit value com.), Am. Acad. Indsl. Hygiene, N.Y. Acad. Scis., AAAS, Internat. Soc. Environ. Toxicology and Cancer, Am. Coll. Toxicology, Am. Conf. on Chem. Labeling. Home: 10616 W 123rd Street Overland Park KS 66213 Office: Hall-Kimbrell Envirn Services 4840 W 15th St Lawrence KS 66044

MURPHY, MAX RAY, lawyer; b. Goshen, Ind., July 18, 1934; s. Loren A. and Lois (Mink) M.; B.A., DePauw U., 1956; J.D., Yale Law Sch., 1959; student Mich. State U., 1960; m. Ruth Leslie Henricson, June 10, 1978; children—Michael Lee, Chad Woodrow. Admitted to Mich. bar, 1960; legal asso. Glassen, Parr, Rhead & McLean, Lansing, Mich., 1960-67; instr. Lansing Bus. U., 1963-67; partner firm Dalman, Murphy, Bidol, & Bouwens, P.C., Holland, Mich., 1967—. Democratic candidate for Ingham County (Mich.) Pros. Atty., 1962, 1964; asst. pros. atty. Ottawa County, Mich., 1967-70. Mem. Ottawa County, Ingham County, Am. bar assns. Clubs: Holland Country, Michigan Jaycees. Home: 4941 Rosabelle Beach Holland MI 49424 Office: 321 Settlers Rd Holland MI 49423

MURPHY, MICHAEL D., department store executive. Chmn., chief exec. officer Lazarus Div., Columbus, Ohio. Office: Lazarus Division Town & High St Columbus OH 43215 *

MURPHY, MICHAEL EMMETT, food company executive; b. Winchester, Mass., Oct. 16, 1936; s. Michael Cornelius and Bridie (Curran) M.; m. Adele Anne Kasupski, Sept. 12, 1959; children—Leslie Maura, Glenn Stephen, Christopher McNeil. B.S. in Bus. Adminstrn, Boston Coll., 1958; M.B.A., Harvard, 1962. Financial analyst Maxwell House div. Gen. Foods Corp., White Plains, N.Y., 1962-64; cost mgr. Maxwell House div. Gen. Foods Corp., San Leandro, Calif., 1964-65; controller Maxwell House div. Gen. Foods Corp., Jacksonville, Fla., 1965-67, Hoboken, N.J., 1967-68; mgr. fin. planning and analysis Maxwell House div. Gen. Foods Corp., 1968-69; mgr. planning Hanes Corp., Winston-Salem, N.C., 1969-70; corp. controller Hanes Corp., 1970—; v.p. adminstrn. Hanes Corp. (Hanes Knitwear), 1972-74; v.p. finance Ryder System Inc., Miami, Fla., 1974-75; exec. v.p. Ryder System Inc., 1975-79; exec. v.p., dir. Sara Lee Corp., Chgo., 1979—. Jr. Achievement mgmt. adviser, 1965-66; mem. exec. com. Hudson County Tax Research Council, 1967-68; trustee Boston Coll., 1980—; chmn. Civic Fedn. Chgo., 1984-86; bd. dirs. Jobs for Youth, Chgo., 1983-86, Lyric Opera, 1986—. Served to 1st lt. AUS, 1958-60. Mem. Hoboken, Winston-Salem, Miami chambers commerce, Internat. Platform Assn., Fin. Execs. Inst., UN Assn., Ouimet Scholar Alumni Group, Beta Gamma Sigma. Roman Catholic. Home: 401 Sheridan Rd Winnetka IL 60093 Office: Sara Lee Corp 3 First Nat Plaza Chicago IL 60602

MURPHY, MYRON LEONARD, dentist; b. Cherokee, Iowa, Dec. 3, 1950; s. Leonard T. and Violet Mildred Leona (Peterson) M.; m. Mary Jane Ewoldt, Aug. 21, 1971 (div. June 1981); children: Alex Roth, Kyle Joe; m. Lori Lou Sorensen, May 25, 1982; 1 child, Lindsey Marie. Student, U. No. Iowa, 1969-72; DDS, U. Iowa, 1976. Gen. practice dentistry Holstein, Iowa, 1976—; nursing home cons. Good Samaritan Ctr., Holstein, 1976—; advisor to bd. dirs. Mid-Sioux Opportunity, Marcus, Iowa, 1986. Deacon St. Paul Luth. Ch., Holstein, 1980-83; mem. com. local Cub Scouts. Mem. ADA, Iowa Dental Assn., Northwest Dental Assn., Holstein C. of C. (pres. 1981), Holstein Jaycees. Lodges: Masons (master 1983-84), Consistory. Avocations: sailing, photography, bowling, family. Home: 404 S Main St Holstein IA 51025 Office: 101 S Main St Holstein IA 51025

MURPHY, PETER FRANCIS, accountant; b. South Bend, Ind., July 12, 1955; s. James E. and Barbara (Lill) M.; m. Donna J. Zurawski, Sept. 10, 1978. BBA, U. Notre Dame, 1977. CPA, Ill. Acct. Coopers & Lybrand, Chgo., 1977—. Mem. Am. Inst. CPA's, Ill. CPA Soc. Home: 425 Custer Ave Evanston IL 60202 Office: Coopers & Lybrand 203 N LaSalle St Chicago IL 60601

MURPHY, PETER FRANCIS, III, accountant; b. Hammond, Ind., Jan. 29, 1950; s. Peter F. and Margaret (Lane) M.; m. Judith Ann Fleck, Oct. 5, 1974; children: Brian, Kevin, Daniel. BS in Indsl. Mgmt., Purdue U., 1972; MBA, U. Evansville, 1977. CPA, Ind. Vol. VISTA, Washington, 1972-73; asst. dir. Tri-Cap Econ. Opportunity Com. Inc., Jasper, Ind., 1973-74; dir. ops. Southwest Ind. Consortium, Evansville, Ind., 1974-77; mgr. Billie Sanders, CPA, Evansville, 1977-82; comptroller Hurricane Constrn. Co., Inc., Jasper, 1982-84; prin. Peter F. Murphy CPA, Huntingburg, Ind., 1984—; bd. dirs. Havill Etc., Inc., Huntingburg. Treas. Huntingburg Sesquicentennial Com., 1987—; past pres., bd. dirs. R.E.S.C.U.E., Inc.; treas., bd. dirs. Famile Hospiz, Inc. Mem. Am. Inst. CPA's, Ind. CPA Soc., Dubois County Estate Planning Council (bd. dirs. 1987—). Lodges: Kiwanis, Civitan. Avocations: music, photography. Home: 1119 Eisenhower Ave Jasper IN 47546 Office: 502 4th St Huntingburg IN 47542

MURPHY, RICHARD CARDEN, construction company executive; b. Berwyn, Ill., June 3, 1947; s. Carden R. and Marguerite (Skocovsky) M.; m. Merriellyn Kett, Jan. 7, 1984; 1 child, Kett Clare. AB, Georgetown U., 1969; JD, U. Paris, 1973. Treas. A.C.S. Industries, Inc., Chgo., 1974-75, pres., 1975-79, chmn., 1982—; chmn. Guardian Mech. Systems, Chgo., 1979-82; bd. dirs. Janata Mgmt. Co., Chgo., Willow Automotive, Inc., Deerfield, Ill., M&M Supply Co., Berwyn, Evergreen Bldg. Corp., Chgo., Chgo. Bldg Co. Author: Long Term Planning in Eurodollar Economics, 1971, Practical Sailing in French Polynesia, 1978, Building in the Third World, 1980. Bd. dirs. Kett/Murphy Found., Chgo., 1980—. Mem. several bar assns. and constrn. trade assns. Democrat. Roman Catholic. Clubs: Chgo. Yacht, Chgo. Athletic (bd. dirs. 1980-87, pres. 1986-87); U.S. Yacht Racing Union. Office: ACS Industries Inc 1929 W Schiller St Chicago IL 60622 also: 2022 N Mohawk St Chicago IL 60614

MURPHY, ROBERT GRANT, forging company executive; b. Caracas, Venezuela, Aug. 13, 1952; s. Benton Franklin and Jane Olive (Billingsley) M.; m. Cartha Darlene DeCoster, Nov. 3, 1979; children—Angela Maria, Kristen Leigh. B.A., Ind. U., 1975; M.P.A., 1977. Coordinator Ind. U. Police Acad., Bloomington, 1972-76; investigator Inst. Research in Pub. Safety, Bloomington, 1976-77; patrolman Boulder Police Dept. (Colo.), 1977-79; v.p. Wodin Inc., Bedford Heights, Ohio, 1979-87, chief exec. officer, 1987—, also treas., chmn. bd. dirs. Bd. dirs., corr. sec. Concern for Children, Shaker Heights, Ohio, 1983-85; head usher Fairmount Presbyn. Ch., Cleveland Heights, 1982-85; trustee Hudson United Meth. Ch. Class of '88. Mem. Am. Mgmt. Assn. Presbyterian. Home: 59 Trumbull St Hudson OH 44236 Office: Wodin Inc 5441 Perkins Rd Bedford Heights OH 44146

MURPHY, SHARON FUNCHEON, lawyer; b. Lafayette, Ind., Jan. 8, 1954; s. Bernard Joseph and Helen M. (Bates) Funcheon; m. Daniel Ralph Murphy, June 14, 1980; 1 child, Megan Kathleen. BA, U. Dallas, 1976; JD, Ind. U., 1982. Bar: Ind. 1982, U.S. Dist. Ct. (no. and so. dists.) Ind. 1982. Assoc. Locke, Reynolds, Boyd & Weisell, Indpls., 1982-84, Bartlett & Robb, Lafayette, 1984-87; sole practice West Lafayette, 1987—; active moot ct. practitioner adv. bd. Ind. U. Sch. of Law, 1985—. Assoc. editor Ind. U. Law Rev., 1981-82. Diocesan adv. Roman Cath. Diocese of Lafayette, 1984—. Mem. ABA (chairperson appellate adv. com. 1986-87, tort and ins. practice sect., litigation sect., 1st place Nat. Appellate Adv. Competition, 1982), Ind. Bar Assn., Tippecanoe County Bar Assn. (treas. 1984-85). Club: Lafayette (Ind.) Duplicate Bridge (bd. dirs. 1985—). Office: PO Box 2252 350 Sagamore Pkwy W Suite 6 West Lafayette IN 47906

MURPHY, THOMAS FRANCIS, sales executive; b. New Rochelle, N.Y., May 28, 1959; s. Michael James and Mary (McLaughlin) M.; m. Therese Ann DeMars, Mar. 21, 1987. BBA, Iona Coll., 1981. Assoc. auditor Hertz Corp., N.Y.C., 1981-82, staff auditor, 1982-83, sr. auditor, 1983, budget analyst, 1983-84, budget mgr., pricing analyst, 1984-85; mgr. sales ops. FMG-Minnetonka (Minn.), Inc., 1985—. Republican. Roman Catholic. Avocations: reading, swimming, racquetball, travel. Home: 12300 Marion Ln #2307 Minnetonka MN 55343 Office: Minnetonka Inc PO Box 1A Minnetonka MN 55435

MURPHY, WALTER LILBERN, real estate investment broker; b. Kansas City, Mo., Oct. 1, 1939; s. Walter Lilbern and Helendoris (Fear) M.; m. Sheree Shiel, May 12, 1964 (div. Feb. 1985); children: Melissa, Amy, Gregory. BArch, Kans. State U., 1964. Asst. to pres. Paxton Lumber Co., Kansas City, Mo., 1964-68; salesman Jones and Co., Kansas City, 1968-76; owner, pres. Walter Murphy, Inc., Shawnee Mission, Kans., 1976—. Active City Planning Commn., Prairie Village, Kans., 1976-81; bd. dirs. pres. YMCA Downtown Chpt., Kansas City, 1980-85; scoutmaster Boy Scouts of Am., Prairie Village, 1985-87. Mem. Nat. Assn. Realtors, Kans. Assn. Realtors, Johnson County Bd. Realtors, Mo. Assn. Realtors (bd. dirs.), Apt. Owners Assn. (pres. Kansas City chpt.), Cert. Comml. Investment Mem. (cert., pres. Mo. chpt.). Republican. Avocations: wood and metal shops, blacksmithing. Office: 1900 W 75th St Suite 115 Shawnee Mission KS 66208

MURPHY, WILLIAM ALEXANDER, JR., diagnostic radiologist, educator; b. Pitts., Apr. 26, 1945; s. William Alexander and LaRue (Eshbaugh); m. Judy Marie Lang, June 18, 1977; children—Abigail Norris, William Lawrence, Joseph Ryan. B.S., U. Pitts., 1967; M.D., Pa. State U., 1971. Diplomate Am. Bd. Radiology. Medicine intern Barnes Hosp., St. Louis, 1971-72, staff radiologist, 1975—; radiology resident Washington U., St. Louis, 1972-75, prof. radiology, 1983—; sect. chief Mallinckrodt Inst. Radiology, St. Louis, 1975—; cons. Office Med. Examiner City and County St. Louis, 1977—. Contbr. numerous articles to profl. jours. and books. Fellow Am. Acad. Forensic Scis., Am. Coll. Radiology; mem. Radiol. Soc. N.Am., Am. Roentgen Ray Soc., Am. Soc. Bone and Mineral Research, Internat. Skeletal Soc., Assn. Univ. Radiologists. Methodist. Home: 60 Kingsbury Pl Saint Louis MO 63112 Office: Mallinckrodt Inst Radiology 510 S Kingshighway Blvd Saint Louis MO 63110

MURPHY-KESLING, DEBRA JEAN, secondary educator; b. Akron, Ohio, Apr. 17, 1954; d. Cecil Earl and Barbara Jean (Durden) Murphy; m. Gerald Michael Kesling, Aug. 13, 1983; 1 child, Jessica Jean. BSin Edn., U. Akron, 1976, MS in Edn., 1987. Tchr. Akron Pub. Schs., 1976—, career edn. coordinator, 1985—, computer coordinator, 1985—; speaker Kent (Ohio) State U., 1979. macrame designer Jemni Ceramics, 1981. Instr. babysitting ARC, Akron, 1984-85; chem. dependency coordinator Chem. People, Akron, 1984-85. Recipient Dist. award for community involvement East Ohio Gas Co., 1987; state winner and 3d in Ea. U.S. region Fleishmann's Yeast Community Kneads Contest, 1987. Mem. Akron Edn. Assn., PTA, Future Homemakers Am., Delta Zeta Alumni Assn. Democrat. Avocations: computers, interior design, sewing, water skiing, gardening. Home: 320 E Ido Ave Akron OH 44301 Office: Akron Pub Schs 70 N Broadway Akron OH 44301

MURRAY, ALAN EDWARD, radio broadcast engineer; b. Rice Lake, Wis., Oct. 27, 1946; s. Marcus S. and Verna M. (Gallenger) M.; m. Lois Ann Heil, Aug. 18, 1973. Student U. Wis., 1963, U. Wis.-River Falls, 1971-72, Wis. State Coll., 1964-67. FCC radio licenses 1960-62, 71, 82. Staff WJMC-FM, Rice Lake, 1962-63; dir. engring. sta. WRFW-FM, River Falls, 1971—; engr. sta. WHWC/W55AP TV, Wis. Pub. TV, 1981—. Served with radio corps USN, 1967-71. Recipient U. Wis. Outstanding Service award, 1982. Mem. Handi Ham System, Am. Radio Relay League, Soc. Broadcast Engrs. Club: Saint Croix Valley Repeaters. Office: Sta WRFW-FM Univ Wis 306 North Hall River Falls WI 54022

MURRAY, BARBARA ANN, banker; b. Mitchell, S.D., Apr. 17, 1953; d. John Richard and Shirley Ann (Larson) McNary; m. Wayne Allan Murray, Jan. 25, 1975; children—Corissa Ann, Rebecca Lea, Jeffrey Wayne, Katie Aileen. B.S. in Edn., Dakota State Coll., 1975. Substitute tchr. Sioux Falls Pub. Schs., S.D., 1975; assoc. Murray Constrn., Sioux Falls, 1975-82; telephone rep. Citibank S.D. NA, Sioux Falls, 1982-83, sr. service rep., 1983-84, unit mgr. customer service, 1984—. Mem. Nat. Assn. Female Execs. Democrat. Lutheran. Clubs: Mothers (pres. 1977-78), Christian Women's (prayer adviser 1980-82). Lodge: Order Eastern Star. Avocations: sewing; camping; hiking; sports. Home: Route 2 Box 65 Country Villa Estates Hartford SD 57033

MURRAY, CHRISTOPHER SCOTT, osteopath; b. Kansas City, Mo., Apr. 17, 1950; s. William Macon and Ileane Scott (Smith) M.; m. Jeanne Ruth LaHue, Feb. 8, 1975; children: Christine, Shane, Landon. BSBA, Rockhurst Coll., 1972; DO, Kansas City (Mo.) Coll. Osteo. Medicine, 1981. Intern Univ. Hosp., Kansas City, Mo., 1981-82; physician Blue Valley Med. Group, Kansas City, Mo., 1981; staff physician Bapt. Med. Ctr. U. Hosp., Kansas City, Mo., 1987—; med. dir. several nursing homes, Kansas City and St. Louis, 1981—. Mem. Am. Osteo. Assn., Mo. Osteo. Assn., Jackson County Osteo. Assn., Southwest Clin. Soc., Univ. Hosp. Alumni Assn. Avocations: carpentry, canoeing, model railroading, softball, family. Home: 1110 Northview Olathe KS 66061 Office: Blue Valley Med Group 7270 W 98th Terr Overland Park KS 66212

MURRAY, G(ALEN) KEITH, newspaper executive; b. Pasadena, Calif., July 1, 1950; s. Donald Graham and Mary Elizabeth (Grimm) M. BA magna cum laude, Claremont McKenna Coll., 1972; postgrad. in law, U. Calif., Davis, 1972-73. City editor Pasadena Star-News subs. Knight-Ridder, Inc., 1974-78; asst. city editor Wichita Eagle & Beacon Publ. Co., Inc. subs. Knight-Ridder, Inc., Kans., 1978-79, city editor, 1979-81, dir. info. systems, 1981-85, v.p., bus. mgr., 1986-87, v.p., gen. mgr., 1987—. bd. dirs. Big Bros. and Big Sisters of Sedgwick County, 1985—, Music Theatre of Wichita, Inc., 1986—. Mem. Soc. Profl. Journalists, Res Publica Soc., Sigma Delta Chi. Lodge: Kiwanis (chmn. pub. relations 1986—). Avocations: travel, computers, fitness. Home: 8115 Windwood Circle Wichita KS 67226 Office: Wichita Eagle-Beacon 825 E Douglas Ave Wichita KS 67202

MURRAY, GEORGE RAYMOND, accountant; b. Chgo., Dec. 28, 1935; s. Earl Edward and Georgia McDonald (Woods) M.; m. Theadora Reid, Sept. 13, 1958; children: Kathleen, Lynn, Michael, George Jr., Brian, Thomas. BS, U. Notre Dame, Ind., 1957. CPA, Ind. Ptnr. M.O. Wolfe & Co., South Bend, Ind., 1958-81, Ernst & Whinney, South Bend, 1981—; cons. Materials Handling Equipment Corp., Ft. Wayne, Ind., 1985—. Bd. dirs. Century Ctr. Bd. Mgrs., South Bend, 1977—, Michiana Pub. TV, South Bend, 1987—, South Bend Estate Planning Council, 1987—; v.p., bd. dirs. Jr. Achievement, South Bend, 1985—; advisor Ivy Tech, South Bend, 1984—. Served to sgt. U.S. Army, 1957-58. Mem. Am. Inst. CPA's, Ind. Soc. CPA's. Republican. Roman Catholic. Clubs: South Bend Country, Carlton (Chgo.). Avocations: golf, jogging. Office: Ernst & Whinney 500 1st Source Ctr South Bend IN 46601

MURRAY, JAMES EDWARD, insurance company safety executive; b. Chgo., May 9, 1929; s. Edward Henry and Elizabeth (Cotter) M.; m. Marie J. Runzo, Apr. 14, 1973; children—Betty Anne, Valerie, Marie, Rhonda, David, Paul. Student Chgo. City Jr. Coll., 1953-54; BA, Govs. State U., 1987. Lic. pilot. Mapmaker, Sanborn Map Co., Pelham, N.Y., 1954-72; casualty loss control supr. Assn. Mill & Elevator Mut. Ins. Cos., Chgo., 1972—; lectr. in field. Served as sgt. USAF, 1947-53. Mem. Am. Soc. Safety Engrs., Nat. Safety Council (exec. com.), Nat. Fire Protection Assn., Ins. Loss Control Orgn., Am. Chem. Soc. (safety and health div.), Soc. Fire Prevention Engrs. Home: 539 Walker Dr Bolingbrook IL 60439 Office: The Mill Mutuals One Pierce Pl Itasca IL 60143

MURRAY, JAMES EDWIN, teacher; b. Joliet, Ill., Dec. 20, 1946; s. Joseph Donald and Katherine Rita M.; m. Ellinder LaVerne Carothers, June 11, 1977; 1 child, Tiffany Christine. BE, Ill. State U., 1969; MA, Washington U., St. Louis, 1972; MA in Teaching, Webster U., 1985. Cert. tchr. Ill., Mo. Social studies tchr. University City (Mo.) Sch. Dist., 1969-85, dept. chmn., 1971-85, computer cen. dir., 1985—; mem. writing team Mo. Social Studies Curriculum Guide; adj. faculty Webster U., 1986—; cons. in field. Mem. NEA, University City Edn. Assn., Nat. Council for the Social Studies, Nat. Hist. Soc., Mo. Hist. Soc., Mensa. Home: 816 Aldan Dr Saint Louis MO 63132 Office: 8125 Groby Rd University City MO 63130

MURRAY, JAMES HAMILTON, chemical manufacturing executive; b. Chgo., July 27, 1928; s. Russell Christy and Marie Virginia (Duvall) M.; m. Shirley Ruth Hill, Oct. 16, 1953; children: Ellen Marie, James Hill. Student, U. Ill., Chgo., 1949-51, Roosevelt Coll., Chgo., 1952. Regional sales mgr. Glaser, Crandell Co., 1953-64; sec. Claire Mfg., Addison, Ill., 1968-83, also bd. dirs.; v.p. sales Claire Mfg. Co.), Addison, Ill., 1983—. Served with U.S. Army, 1946-48. Republican. Clubs: Ill. Athletic (Chgo.), Lincolnshire Country (Crete, Ill). Avocations: fishing, golf, gardening. Office: Claire Mfg Co 500 Vista Ave Addison IL 60101

MURRAY, JOHN L., food company executive; b. 1927. B.B.A., U. Wis., 1950. C.P.A., Wis. Accountant Touche, Ross, Bailey & Smart (C.P.A.s), prior to 1955; with Universal Foods Corp., Milw., 1955—, v.p., treas., 1966-73, v.p. fin., 1973-76, pres., 1976—, chief exec. officer, 1979—, chmn., 1984—, also dir. Office: Universal Foods Corp 433 E Michigan St Box 737 Milwaukee WI 53202 *

MURRAY, JOHN PATRICK, psychologist, educator, researcher; b. Cleve., Sept. 14, 1943; s. John Augustine and Helen Marie (Lynch) M.; m. Ann Coke Dennison, Apr. 17, 1971; children—Jonathan Coke, Ian Patrick. Ph.D., Cath. U. Am., 1970. Mem. Nat. Register of Health, D.C., Nebr., Mich. Research dir. Office U.S. Surgeon Gen., NIMH, Bethesda, Md., 1969-72; assoc. prof. psychology Macquarie U., Sydney, Australia, 1973-79, U. Mich., Ann Arbor, 1979-80; dir. youth and family policy Boys Town Ctr., Boys Town, Nebr., 1980-85; prof., head dept. human devel. and family studies Kans. State U., Manhattan, 1985—. Author: Television and Youth: 25 Years of Research and Controversy, 1980; The Future of Children's TV, 1984; (with H.T. Rubin) Status Offenders: A Sourcebook, 1983; (with E.A. Rubinstein, G.A. Comstock) Television and Social Behavior, 3 vols., 1972. Contbr. numerous articles to profl. jours. Mem. Nebr. Foster Care Rev. Bd., 1982-84 ; mem. Advocacy Office for Children and Youth, 1980-85 ; mem. Nat. Council Children and TV, 1982—. Fellow Am. Psychol. Assn.; mem. Am. Sociol. Assn., Soc. Research in Child Devel. Clubs: Royal Commonwealth Soc. (London). Home: 1731 Humboldt St Manhattan KS 66502 Office: Dept Human and Family Studies Coll Human Ecology Kans State Univ Manhattan KS 66506

MURRAY, LOIS A. HEIL, lawyer; b. Marshfield, Wis., June 3, 1953; d. Frank N. and Bertha J. (Hafenbreadl) Heil; B.A., B.S. in Acctg., U. Wis., River Falls, 1974; J.D. cum laude, U. Minn., 1978; m. Alan E. Murray, Aug. 18, 1973. Tax examiner Minn. Dept. Revenue, 1974-75; admitted to Wis. bar, 1978, Minn. bar, 1978, U.S. Dist. Ct. bar, 1978; law clk. firm Ralph Senn, River Falls, 1976; research asst. to prof. law and asso. dean Sch. Law, U. Minn., Mpls., 1976-78; law clk. Honeywell, Inc., Mpls., 1977; assoc. firm Heywood, Cari & Murray and predecessor, Hudson, Wis., 1978-80, partner, 1980—; mem. faculty Wis. Indianhead Tech. Inst., Hudson Community Edn. Bd. dirs. West Central Wis. Action Agy., 1984-85. Mem. State Bar Assn. Wis., State Bar Assn. Minn., Am. Bar Assn., St. Croix Valley Bar Assn., AAUW, LWV, Hudson Area C. of C. Roman Catholic. Home: 600 7th St Hudson WI 54016 Office: Micklesen Bldg 204 Locust St Hudson WI 54016

MURRAY, MARK ANDREW, economist; b. Lansing, Mich., July 5, 1954; s. John and Francoise G. (Martin) M.; m. Elizabeth J. Chapman, July 15, 1978; children: Hannah B., Laura E. BA, Mich. State U., 1976, M in Labor Relations specializing in Manpower Studies, 1979. Economist Mich. Dept. Social Services, Lansing, 1978-85, Mich. Dept. Commerce, Lansing, 1985—; mem. tech. steering com. Mich. Occupational Info. Coordinating Com., 1985—. Contbr. articles to profl. jours. Mem. Nat. Assn. Welfare Research and Statistics (bd. dirs. 1984-85), Nat. Assn. State Devel. Agencies (research div., bd. dirs. 1986—), Am. Pub. Welfare Assn., Omicron Delta Upsilon. Roman Catholic. Avocations: athletics, photography. Home: 1510 Boston Blvd Lansing MI 48910 Office: Mich Dept Commerce PO Box 30225 Lansing MI 48909

MURRAY, MERRILL R., college official; b. New Castle, Ind., Aug. 3, 1917; s. Arthur Gray and Mary (Dixon) M.; student Hanover Coll., 1935-36, Kent State U., 1943; B.S., Ball State U., 1949, M.S., 1951; Ed.D., Ind. U., 1960; m. Eva Jean Yergin, Mar. 30, 1940; 1 son, Michael Russell. Math. tchr. high sch., New Castle, Ind., 1949-51, 53-54; dir. USAF Dependents Schs., Burtonwood, Eng., 1952-53; prin. high sch., Ridgeville, Ind., 1954-56; research asso. Ind. U., Bloomington, 1956-58; dean of students Tri-State U., Angola, 1958-59; dean specialized edn. div. Ferris State Coll., Big Rapids, Mich., 1959-65, asst. dean Sch. Gen. Edn., 1965-69, asso. dean, 1969—, assoc. dean Coll. Optometry, 1977-82, assoc. dean emeritus, 1982—. Served with USAAF, 1943-47; col. USAF (ret.). Mem. Nat. U. Continuing Edn. Assn. (div. chmn.), Mich. Coordinating Council Continuing Higher Edn. (pres.), Am. Personnel and Guidance Assn., Am. Optometric Assn. (asso.), Mich. Optometric Assn. (asso.), Air Force Assn., Mich. Assn. Schs. and Colls., Res. Officers Assn., Am. Assn. Higher Edn., Ferris State Coll. Emeriti Assn. (pres.), Mil. Order World Wars. Phi Delta Kappa, Kappa Delta Phi, Sigma Mu Sigma. Presbyn. (elder). Lodges: Masons, Rotary (pres. 1964-65). Home: 14851 Chula Vista Dr Big Rapids MI 49307 Office: Ferris State Coll Optometry Big Rapids MI 49307

MURRAY, MICHAEL J., bank executive; b. Dubuque, Iowa, June 23, 1944; m. Christine Scribner; children: Sarah, David. BBA, U. Notre Dame, 1966; MBA, U. Wis., 1968. V.p. in charge east coast regional offices Continental Bank, Chgo., 1981-84, v.p., 1981-84, sr. v.p., 1984-85, exec. v.p., 1985—. Mem. devel. bd. subcom. export fin. Ill. Dept. Commerce and Community Affairs, Chgo., 1984; chmn. employee campaign United Way Chgo., 1986; bd. dirs. Chgo. Maternity Ctr., Northwestern Meml. Hosp.,

1987—. Roman Catholic. Clubs: Chgo., Bankers of Chgo., Econ. of Chgo.; Sky (N.Y.C.). Office: Continental Bank 231 S LaSalle St Chicago IL 60697

MURRAY, RICHARD BLAINE, lawyer; b. Coshocton, Ohio, May 19, 1936; s. Ross Wesley and Lynna Eleanor M.; m. Susan B. Wallace, Sept. 8, 1961; children—Robert B., Ross B. B.A., Ohio State U., 1959; J.D., Capital U., 1977. Bar: Ohio 1977. With indsl. mgmt. Becton Dickinson, Coshocton, Ohio, 1960-63, 63-67, asst. to gen. mgr., Brussels, 1963, plant mgr., Mt. Vernon, 1967-77; individual practice law, Mt. Vernon, Ohio, 1977—. Served with U.S. Army, 1960-63. Mem. ABA, Ohio Bar Assn., Knox County Bar Assn. Lodge: Rotary. Avocations: golf; music. Office: 110 E Gambier St Mount Vernon OH 43050

MURRAY, RICHARD WILLIAM, psychiatrist; b. Dayton, Ohio, June 21, 1924; s. Raymond William and Florence Magdalena (Knab) M.; divorced 1978; children: Mary Elizabeth, Richard William II. MD, U. Cin., 1949. Diplomate Am. Bd. Psychiatry and Neurology, Nat. Bd. Med. Examiners. Practice medicine specializing in psychiatry Oakland, Calif., 1953-76; asst. chief State Mental Hygiene Clinic, Sacramento, 1955-57; psychiatrist Adult Guidance Ctr., San Francisco, 1957-59; cons. Alameda County Mental Health, Oakland, 1959-71, Berkeley and San Francisco Mental Health, 1971-76; chief mental hygiene clinic VA Med. Ctr., Dayton, 1976-77; psychiatrist Good Samaritan Hosp., Dayton, 1977—; assoc. clin. prof. psychiatry Wright State U. Sch. Medicine, Dayton, 1977—. Served to capt. USAR, 1950—. Recipient 10 Yr. Spl. Teaching award Dept. Psychiatry, Wright State U., 1986. Fellow Am. Psychiat. Assn. (life), Ohio Psychiat. Assn. Democrat. Episcopalian. Avocations: classical music, gourmet cooking, gardening, swimming, skiing. Office: Good Samaritan Hosp 2222 Philadelphia Dr Dayton OH 45406

MURRAY, ROBB, business consultant; b. Lima, Ohio, Sept. 12, 1953; s. Emmett Jr. and Pauline (List) M. Student, Kalamazoo Coll., 1971-72, Ohio State U., 1974; BA cum laude, Bob Jones U., 1975; MA, U. Chgo., 1977; cert. advanced German, Cultural Studies Acad., 1971; cert. data processing, Sears Data Tng. Sch. Reference librarian Chgo. Pub. Library, 1977-80; computer programmer hdqtrs. Sears Roebuck & Co., Chgo., 1980-83; product cons. Davka Corp., Chgo., 1983-84; bus. systems analyst Beatrice Foods, Chgo., 1984-85; software tng. specialist Beatrice U.S. Foods, Chgo., 1985-86; bus. cons. Keyboard Cons., Chgo., 1986; conf. presenter Project Micro-Ideas, Glenview, Ill., 1982-84; pres. Classical Mosquito, Chgo., 1982-85; bus. planner Kangaroo, Inc., Chgo., 1984; industry commentator Christian Bookseller, Wheaton, Ill., 1984. Co-inventor computer adventure game, The Lion's Share, 1983; composer, producer recording, Classical Mosquito, 1982; contbr. articles to profl. jours. Counselor Metrohelp Crisis Hotline, Chgo., 1979; adult edn. instr. Lincoln Park Community Assn., Chgo., 1980; speaker, services com. mem. Second Unitarian Ch., Chgo., 1986. Mem. Soc. Tech. Communication, Ind. Computer Cons. Assn., Nat. Soc. Performance Instrn., Ill. Tng. and Devel. Assn., Chgo. Computer Soc., Chgo. Council Fgn. Relations. Democrat. Clubs: Lake Shore Ski, Broadcast Ad. Avocations: running, shopping, travel, writing, public speaking. Home: 444 St James Place #1203 Chicago IL 60614

MURRAY, ROBERT EUGENE, coal company executive; b. Martins Ferry, Ohio, Jan. 13, 1940; s. Albert Edward and Mildred Etheline (Shepherd) M.; m. Brenda Lou Moore, Aug. 26, 1962; children: Sherri Sue (dec.), Robert Edward, Jonathan Robert, Ryan Michael. B in Engring., Ohio State U., 1962; postgrad. Case Western Res. U., 1968-70, Harvard U. Grad. Sch. Bus. Advanced Mgmt. Program, U. N.D., 1982-83. Registered profl. engr., Ohio. Asst. to mgr. indsl. engring. and coal preparation N.Am. Coal Corp., 1961-63, sect. foreman, plant foreman, gen. mine foreman, Ohio div., 1963-64, asst. supt., 1964-66, supt. 1966-68, asst. to pres., Cleve., 1968-69, v.p. operations, v.p. eastern div., 1969-74, pres. Western div., 1974-83; exec. v.p. and pres. coal ops. N.Am. Coal Corp., 1985-86, pres., chief operating officer, 1986-87, pres., chief exec. officer, 1987—; pres. Coteau Properties Co., Falkirk Mining Co., Western Plains Mining Co., Mo. Valley Properties Co.; v.p., bd. dirs. Nacco Mining Co.; bd. dirs. Sabine Mining Co.; mining engring. departmental asst. Ohio State U., 1960-62; past pres., chmn. bd. N.D. Lignite Council. Exec. bd., v.p. dist. ops. Greater Cleve. council Boy Scouts Am.; past pres., bd. dirs. United Way of Bismarck; bd. regents Mary Coll.; past trustee, lay speaker, tchr., lay leader Meth. Ch., mem. adminstrv. bd. 1968-69. Mem. Mining Electro-Mech. Assn. (pres. Ohio Valley br. 1967-68), Pitts. Coal Mining Inst. Am., Soc. Mining Engrs. AIME (bd. dirs., exec. com., past chmn. coal div., exec. com. coal div., pres.-elect), Rocky Mountain Coal Mining Inst. (past pres., program chmn., chmn. adv. bd.), Nat. Coal Assn. (bd. dirs., chmn. acctg. com., low rank fuels com., chmn. ad hoc coalition on internat. electric power trade, active World Energy Conf., chmn. acctg. com.rofl. Engrs. (pres. east Ohio chpt. 1966-67), Ohio Engrs. in Industry (mem. bd. govs. 1966-67). Republican. Lodges: Masons (32d degree), Shriners. Home: 32 Cotswold Ln Moreland Hills Chagrin Falls OH 44022 Office: N Am Coal Corp 12800 Shaker Blvd Cleveland OH 44120

MURRAY, TODD EDWARD, jeweler; b. Muncie, Ind., Dec. 6, 1951; s. Donald Stevenson and Darlene Joy (Dick) M.; m. Jane Ann McNary, Sept. 2, 1972; children: Ryan Mathew, James Brooks. High sch. diploma, Muncie, 1970; cert in watchmaking, Bowman Tech., 1972. Watchmaker Murray's Jewelers, Muncie, 1972-86, Jewelry Designer, 1972—. Pres. Downtown Bus. Council, Muncie, 1984-87. Mem. E. Cen. Watchmakers Assn. Republican. Methodist. Club: Exchange. Lodge: Moose. Avocations: bowling, golf, racquetball. Home: 302 Normandy Dr Muncie IN 47304 Office: Murray's Jewelers 113 W Charles St Muncie IN 47305

MURRAY, WILLIAM JEROME, JR., architect; b. Summerville, S.C., May 15, 1954; s. William Jerome and Harriet (Reeves) M. BArch, Clemson U., 1976; MArch, U. Minn., 1978. Registered architect, Minn. Pvt. practice architecture Counterpoint Design, Mpls., 1978-80; mgr., architect Msaada, Wayzata, Minn., 1984—. Mem. AIA, Sigma Phi Epsilon (pres. 1975-76). Methodist. Avocation: semi profl. theatre. Home: PO Box 72675, Nairobi Kenya Office: Msaada First Nat Bank Bldg Suite 308 Wayzata MN 55391

MURRAY, WILLIAM MICHAEL (MIKE), lawyer; b. Ottumwa, Iowa, Dec. 28, 1947; s. William Bernard and Thelma Jean (Hart) M.; m. Ann Elizabeth Wawzonek, Oct. 11, 1973; children—Kathleen Elizabeth, Daniel Webster. B.A., U. Iowa, 1970, J.D., 1973. Bar: Iowa 1973, U.S. Dist. Ct. (so. dist.) Iowa 1976, U.S. Dist. Ct. (no. dist.) Iowa 1978, U.S. Ct. Appeals (8th cir.) 1978. Staff counsel Iowa Civil Rights Commn., Des Moines, 1973-76; assoc. Bertroche & Hagen, Des Moines, 1976-78; ptnr. Murray, Davoren & Dudley, Des Moines, 1978—. Bd. dirs. Iowa Civil Liberties Union, Des Moines, 1978-83, pres., 1982-83; bd. dirs. Polk County Legal Aid Soc., Des Moines, 1984—. Mem. Assn. Trial Lawyers Am., Assn. Trial Lawyers Iowa, ABA, Iowa State Bar Assn., Polk County Bar Assn. Democrat. Club: Des Moines Jaycees (bd. dirs. legal counsel 1980-81). Lodge: Masons. Home: 600 SW 42d St Des Moines IA 50312 Office: Murray Davoren & Dudley 5601 Hickman Rd Suites 3 & 4 Des Moines IA 50310

MURRELL, CASTELLA BURNLEY, educator, biology consultant; b. Nashville, Jan. 26, 1926; d. Stephen Alexander and Maynie (Young) Burnley; m. Irvin Maurcie Murrell (dec. 1975); children—Janis, Irvin, Bertrand, Audrey. B.S., U. Louisville, 1948; M.S., U. Ill., Urbana, 1950; postgrad. U. Chgo., summers 1960-65. Microbiologist Provident Hosp., Chgo., 1950-52; research asst. U. Ill.-Chgo., 1952-54; microbiologist U. Chgo., 1954-58; research asst. Armour Research, Chgo., 1959-60; tchr. biology Chgo. Bd. Edn., 1960—, biology cons., 1969-72. Contbr. articles to profl. jours. Recipient Sci. Fair awards Chgo. Area Sci. Tchrs. Assn., 1964, 65, 67, Ill. Outstanding Tchr. award Chgo. Bd. Edn., 1966, Fellowship Honor award, 1967, citation Chgo. Heart Assn., 1967, 68. Mem. Nat. Sci. Tchrs. Assn., Nat. Assn. Female Execs., Ill. Soc. Microbiologists, Ill. Sci. Tchrs. Assn., Chgo. Biology Roundtable, Christian Educators Assn., Alpha Kappa Alpha. Methodist. Avocations: photography; tennis. Home: 9730 S Green St Chicago IL 60643

MURRELL, MICHAEL FLEMING, publishing executive; b. Kirksville, Mo., Apr. 29, 1948; s. Charles Ernest and Anne Dorothy (Fleming) M.; m. Cynthia Marie Fern, Apr. 29, 1977 (div. July 1985); 1 stepchild, Jennifer Ellen; m. Linda Carole Daniell, Oct. 12, 1985; 1 child, James Alexander. Student, U. Mo., 1974-75; BA in Journalism, Coll. St. Thomas, St. Paul, 1969. Cert. airline transport pilot and turbojet flight engr. Advt. mgr. Kershaw Cos., Montgomery, Ala., 1975-77; mgr. pub. relations Piper Aircraft Corp., Lock Haven, Pa., 1977-78; pilot Continental Airlines, Denver, 1978-83; v.p. mktg. Rocky Mountain Piper Co., Denver, 1979-83; v.p. Miller Meester Advt., Mpls., 1983-84; pub. Johnson Hill Press, Ft. Atkinson, Wis., 1984—. Editor Sky High mag., 1984—, Cheyenne mag., 1984—; exec. editor Keep Flying mag., 1977-78, Corporate Flight mag., 1977-78. Advisor USAF Civil Air Patrol, Watertown, Wis., 1986—. Served to capt. USAF, 1969-74, Vietnam. Decorated Disting. Flying Cross, 1971, Air medal (3), 1970-71. Mem. Nat. Air Transp. Assn. Advisory Com., Airline Pilots Assn., Advt. Club Montgomery (bd. dirs. 1976-77), Sigma Delta Chi (chpt. pres. 1968-69). Avocations: running, photography, skiing. Home: 501 Thomas Rd Wales WI 53183 Office: Johnson Hill Press 1233 Janesville Ave Fort Atkinson WI 53538

MUSCHENHEIM, WILLIAM EMIL, educator; b. N.Y.C., Nov. 7, 1902; s. Frederick Augustus and Elsa (Unger) M.; m. Elizabeth Marie Bodanzky, Nov. 29, 1930; children—Carl Arthur, Anna Elizabeth Muschenheim Arms. Student, Williams Coll., 1919-21, Mass. Inst. Tech., 1921-24; M.Arch., Behrens Master Sch. Architecture, Acad. Fine Arts, Vienna, Austria, 1929. Archtl. designer Joseph Urban (architect), N.Y.C., 1929-33; prin. William Muschenheim, N.Y.C., Ann Arbor, Mich., 1934—; prof. architecture U. Mich., Ann Arbor, 1950-72; pres. Muschenheim, Hammarskjold & Arms, Inc. (architects, planners), Ann Arbor, 1968-71. Author: Elements of the Art of Architecture, 1964, Why Architecture, 1980; contbr. articles to profl. jours. Recipient gold medal Mich. Soc. Architects, 1984; Horace H. Rackham research travel grantee, 1958, 64, 72. William Muschenheim teaching fellowship established at U. Mich., 1984. Fellow AIA (edn. com. 1959-61, fgn. relations com. 1963-64); mem. Assn. Collegiate Schs. Architecture (edn. com. 1961-63, fgn. relations com. 1964-66), AAUP. Home: 1251 Heatherway Ann Arbor MI 48104

MUSE, WILLIAM VAN, university president; b. Marks, Miss., Apr. 7, 1939; s. Mose Lee and Mary Elizabeth (Hisaw) M.; m. Anna Marlene Munden, Aug. 22, 1964; children: Amy Marlene, Ellen Elizabeth, William Van. B.S. (T.H. Harris scholar), Northwestern La. State U., 1960; M.B.A. (Nat. Def. Grad. fellow), U. Ark., 1961, Ph.D. (Nat. Def. Grad. fellow), 1966. Instr. U. Ark., 1962-63; field supr. Tau Kappa Epsilon Fraternity, 1963-64; asst. prof. Ga. Inst. Tech., 1964-65; assoc. prof., chmn., dir. research Ohio U., 1965-70; dean Coll. of Bus., Appalachian State U., Boone, N.C., 1970-73, Coll. Bus. Adminstrn., U. Nebr., Omaha, 1973-79, Coll. Bus. Adminstrn., Tex. A&M U., College Station, 1979-82; vice chancellor Tex. A&M U. System, College Station, 1983-84; pres. U. Akron, Ohio, 1984—. Author: Business and Economic Problems in Appalachia, 1969, Management Practices in Fraternities, 1965; Contbr. articles to profl. jours. Found. for Econ. Edn. fellow, 1967. Mem. Blue Key, Omicron Delta Kappa, Phi Kappa Phi, Delta Sigma Pi, Beta Gamma Sigma, Pi Omega Pi, Tau Kappa Epsilon. Club: Rotarian. Office: Univ Akron Akron OH 44325

MUSGRAVE, CHARLES EDWARD, correctional facility official, music director; b. Alton, Ill., Nov. 17, 1932; s. Clay Everett and Fannie Adeline (Peek) M.; m. Barbara Jean Robertson, Aug. 11, 1952 (div. Feb. 1971); children: Michael David, Debra Ann; m. Toby Elaine Riley, Aug. 18, 1973. B in Mus. Edn., Shurtleff Coll., 1954; MS, U. Ill., 1957; postgrad., U. No. Colo., 1970. Cert. tchr., Ill., Ind. Tchr. mus. Alton (Ill.) Pub. Schs., 1953-67; v.p. Monticello Coll., Godfrey, Ill., 1967-69; asst. to v.p. U. No. Colo., Greeley, 1970; chmn. dept. mus. Duneland Sch. Corp., Chesterton, Ind., 1970-72; dir. devel. Interlochen (Mich.) Arts Acad., 1972-74; dir. mus. Ind. State Prison, Michigan City, 1974—; Sec., bd. dirs. La Porter Fed. Credit Union, Michigan City, 1975—. Author: Fussell's Individual Technique Guide, 1973. Rep. vice com. man Chesterton, 1976—, del. to state conv., Ind., 1978—; mem. Porter County (Ind.) Planning commn., 1984-85; chmn. govt. workers sect. United Way, Michigan City, 1981—; bd. dirs. Five Lakes Conservation Club, Wolcottville, Ind., 1983—, Valparaiso Community Concerts Assn., 1986. Grantee Systems Mgmt. U. W. Va., U. Chgo., 1979. Mem. Correctional Edn. Assn. (Tchr. of Yr. 1981), Ind. Soc. Chgo., Phi Delta Kappa. Methodist. Clubs: Sand Creek Golf (Chesterton), LaGrange (Ind.) Country. Lodge: Masons, Shriners. Avocations: sailing, golf, photography. Home: 750 Graham Dr Chesterton IN 46304 Office: Ind State Prison PO Box 41 Michigan City IN 46360

MUSIAL, STAN(LEY) (FRANK MUSIAL), baseball executive, hotel and restaurant executive; b. Donora, Pa., Nov. 21, 1920; s. Lukasz M.; m. Lillian Labash, 1939; children: Richard, Geraldine, Janet, Jean. Ed. high sch., Donora. Baseball player St. Louis Cardinals Farm Team, 1938-41; 1st baseman, outfielder St. Louis Cardinals, Nat. League, 1941-63; sr. v.p. St. Louis Cardinals, 1963—; pres. Stan Musial & Biggies, Inc., St. Louis. Author: Stan Musial: The Man's Own Story, 1964. Served with USNR, World War II. Voted Nat. League Rookie of Yr., 1943; named most valuable player Nat. League, 1943, 46, 48; mem. Nat. League All-Star Team, 1943-44, 46-63; voted most valuable player Baseball Writers Com., 1946; Maj. League Player of Year Sporting News, 1946, 51; Sid Mercer award N.Y. Baseball Writers, 1947; Kenesaw Mountain Landis Meml. plaque, 1948; Sports Illus. Sportsman of Yr., 1957; recipient Freedom Leadership medal, 1968; named to Baseball Hall of Fame, 1969. Holder .331 lifetime batting average. Office: Stan Musial & Biggies Inc 1017 Olive St Suite 1000A Saint Louis MO 63101

MUSICK, PAMELA A., social worker; b. Pittsburg, Kans., Nov. 20, 1946; s. James P. and Julia (Morettini) Hamilton; m. Charles Grant Heter, Dec. 7, 1970 (div. Feb. 1978); children: Jonas, Maxwell; m. Robert William Musick, Nov. 16, 1979; 1 child, Emily. BS in Edn., Pitts. State U., 1968, MS in Spl. Edn., 1981; MSW, U. Kans., 1984. Licensed social worker, Kans.; licensed spl. edn. tchr., Mo. Elem. tchr. Kansas City (Mo.) Sch. Dist., 1968-71; clin. social worker Mt. Carmel Med. Ctr., Pittsburgh, Kans., 1982-83, Crawford County Med. Health Ctr., Pittsburgh, 1983-84; alcohol drug counselor Cherokee County Mental Health Ctr., Baxter Springs, Kans., 1984-85; alcohol drug abuse spl. State of Kans. Social and Rehab. Services, Pittsburg, 1985—; cons. alcohol and drug program Highland Elem. Sch., 1985—, multi county alcohol/drug programs, 1985—; trainer continuing edn. dept. U. Kans., Chanute, 1985—; EAP coordinator Allen, Bourbon, Crawford counties. Recipient Outstanding Service award Pittsburgh Area State Dept. Social and Rehab. Services, 1985. Mem. Nat. Assn. Social Workers, Nat. Inst. Mental Health Tng. (stipend 1983), Crawford County Council on Alcoholism, Theta Alpha Phi. Home: 925 E 5th Pittsburg KS 66762 Office: Social and Rehab Services PO Box 40 20th & 69 Bypass Pittsburgh KS 66762

MUSKOPF, BARBARA JOAN, real estate associate; b. Utica, N.Y., Nov. 9, 1933; d. Leo T. and Mary (Hurd) Simmons; m. Melvin O. Muskopf, June 4, 1955; children: Walter Paul, Susan Lyn. AB, Washington U., St. Louis, 1954; CPM, Inst. Real EstateMgmt., 1984. Asst. to pres. Frank Block Assocs., St. Louis, 1954-59, Moehlenpah Engrs., St. Louis, 1959-64; asst. to comptroller Am. Optometric Assn., St. Louis, 1964-69; with pub. relations and acctg. depts. Vision Inst. Am., St. Louis, 1969-74; v.p., gen. mgr. C.A. Bianco, Inc., St. Louis, 1974-84; ptnr. Muskopf Investments, St. Louis, 1984—. Comptroller and sec. St. Philip's United Ch. Christ, St. Louis, 1983-85. Mem. Real Estate Women of St. Louis (pres. 1984), Olivette (Mo.) C. of C. (v.p., sec. 1983—), Inst. Real Estate Mgmt. (cert. property mgr.). Avocation: gourmet cooking.

MUSSATTO, CASEY, beverage company executive; b. Emporia, Kans., Mar. 29, 1961; s. Raymond Lee and Juanita Bernadine (Melenson) M.; m. Cheryl Lynn Wendt, May 28, 1983. BS in Indsl. Engring., Kans. State U., 1983. Mgr. trainee Mussatto Bros., Inc., Osage City, Kans., 1977-83, gen. mgr., 1983-84, v.p., gen. mgr., 1984-85, pres., gen. mgr., 1985—; bd. dirs. Kans. beverage industry recycling program (BIRP), 1986—; bd. dirs. Neasho Basin Devel. Co. Mem. Kans. Beer Wholesalers Assn. (nominating com. 1984—), Inst. of Indsl. Engrs. (v.p. 1982-83); Osage City C. of C. (pres. 1987). Republican. Lutheran. Home: 520 S 2d St Osage City KS 66523

MUSSEHL, ALLAN ARTHUR, program director; b. Edgerton, Wis., Aug. 12, 1942; s. Arthur John and Ruth Anna (Miller) M. BA, Milton Coll., 1965; MA, U. Wis., Madison, 1971, U. Wis., Milwaukee, 1973. Chairperson speech dept. Cumberland (Wis.) High Sch., 1965-71; asst. prof. mass communications Milton (Wis.) Coll., 1971-74; asst. prof. communications media Bemidji (Minn.) State U., 1974-79; assoc. prof. mass communications Middle Tenn. State U., Murfreesboro, 1979-85; dir. Learning Resources, assoc. prof. humanities Southeastern U., Washington, 1985-87; dir. of learning resources Nicolet Coll., Rhinelander, Wis., 1987—. Author: Man, Media and Society, 1976; also articles. Disting. Mellon fellow, Vanderbilt U., 1981. Mem. Am. Library Assn., ACLU. Democrat. Lutheran. Avocations: history and collection of original animated films. Home: Rt 2 Box 101 Comstock Lake Neshkoro WI 54960 Office: Nicolet Coll Learning Resource Ctr Rhinelander WI 54501

MUSSELMAN, KENNETH JACK, software engineering executive, consultant; b. Lansing, Mich., Sept. 15, 1947; s. Nicholas and Cornelia (Van Den Burg) M.; m. Mary Susan Tatge, June 18, 1977; children: Pamela Ann, Lea Marie. BA, Western Mich. U., 1969; MS, Purdue U., 1975, PhD, 1978. Systems engr. Pritsker and Assocs., West Lafayette, Ind., 1978-80, dir., 1980-86, v.p., 1986—. Mem. exec. bd. dirs. Purdue Luth. Ministry, West Lafayette, 1979-85. Served to lt. USN, 1970-73. Mem. Soc. Mfg. Engrs., Inst. Mgmt. Sci., Ops. Research Soc. Am., Inst. Ind. Engrs., Sigma Xi, Alpha Phi Mu, Phi Eta Sigma, Omicron Delta Kappa. Lutheran. Avocations: camping, hiking, fishing, woodworking. Home: 928 Windsor Dr West Lafayette IN 47906 Office: Pritsker and Assocs Inc PO Box 2413 West Lafayette IN 47906

MUSTION, ALAN LEE, pharmacist; b. Oklahoma City, Feb. 6, 1947; s. Granville E. and Iris E. (Graham) M.; children: Jeffrey Alan, Jennifer Chere; m. Mary Jane Bozek, Dec. 4, 1982. BS in Pharmacy, Southwestern Okla. State U., 1970. Staff pharmacist VA Med. Ctr., Oklahoma City, 1970-74, dir. pharmacy, Saginaw, Mich., 1974-76, asst. dir. pharmacy, Richmond, Va., 1976-77, dir. pharmacy, Iowa City, Iowa, 1977—; clin. instr. clin./hosp. div. U. Iowa, 1977—. Contbr. articles to profl. jours. Served to maj. USAR. Recipient VA Spl. Achievement awards, 1973, 77, 86, VA Suggestion awards, 1979, 81, 83, VA Cost Reduction award, 1983, VA Contbr. award, 1987; research grantee Travenol Labs., 1980-87, VA HSR&D grantee, 1984. Mem. Am. Soc. Hosp. Pharmacists, Iowa Soc. Hosp. Pharmacists, Assn. Mil. Surgeons of U.S., Am. Assn. Colls. Pharmacy, Res. Officers Assn., Kappa Psi. Methodist. Home: 821 Spencer Dr Iowa City IA 52240 Office: VA Med Center Hwy 6 West Iowa City IA 52240

MUTNAL, BASAVARAJ IRAPPA, internist; b. Belgaum, India, July 30, 1947; s. Irappa B. and Gangawa (Patil) M.; m. Lalitha B. Neralapur, Aug. 22, 1973; 1 child, Amar B. MBBS, Karnatar Med. Coll., 1970. Cert. Am. Bd. Internal Medicine. Ho. officer Colouth Hosp., Dundalk, Ireland, 1971-72; registrar Londonderry (Eng.) Hosp., 1973-75; resident II VA Hosp., London, Ontario, 1975-76; resident I and III St. Francis Med. Ctr., Trenton, N.J., 1976-78; staff Three Rivers (Mich.) Hosp., 1978—; gen. practice internal medicine Three Rivers. Mem. AMA, ACP, Am. Geriatric Soc., Am. Soc. Internal Medicine, Mich. State Med. Soc. Avocation: golf. Home: 52002 Kern Dr Three Rivers MI 49093 Office: Mutnal Med Ctr PO Box 348 655 Erie Three Rivers MI 49093

MUTTERPERL, ROBERT EDWARD, osteopathic internist; b. Bayonne, N.J., Feb. 16, 1947; m. Joan Mutterperl; children: Lisa, Mathew. BS, Upsala Coll., 1969; DO, Coll. Osteopathic Medicine, 1972. Diplomate Am. Bd. Internal Medicine. Intern Michael Reese Hosp., Chgo., 1973, resident, 1974-76, fellow, 1974-76, staff, 1976-81; section chief nephology Grant Hosp., Chgo., 1980-83, staff, 1976—; cons. nephrology Resurrection Hosp., Chgo., 1983—. Contbr. articles to profl. jours. Mem. AMA, Chgo. Med. Soc., Internat. Soc. Internal Medicine, Ill. Soc. Internal Medicine. Office: 4811 N Milwaukee Chicago IL 60630

MUTZ, JOHN MASSIE, lieutenant governor Ind.; b. Indpls., Nov. 5, 1935; s. John Loughery and Mary Helen (Massie) M.; m. Carolyn Hawthorne, June 21, 1958; children: Mark, Diana. B.S. in Advt. and Bus. Mgmt, Northwestern U., 1957, M.S., 1958. Copy editor Indpls. News, summer 1953, 54; dir. public relations for residential bldg. products Aluminum Co. Am., Pitts., 1958-60; dir. advt. and public relations, sec., asst. to pres. Perine Devel. Corp., Indpls., 1960-61; instr. dept. public and environ. affairs Ind. U., Indpls., 1976-79; v.p. Circle Fin. Corp., Indpls., 1962-79, Circle Leasing Corp., Indpls., 1962-79, Fast Food Mgmt. Corp., 1978-79; mem. Ind. Ho. of Reps., 1967-71, chmn. interim sch. fin. com., 1962-69, chmn. taxation sub-com. of ways and means com., 1969-70; Republican candidate state treas. Ind., 1970; mem. Ind. State Senate, 1972-80; lt. gov. State of Ind., 1981—. Mem. Sch. Property Tax Control Bd. Indpls., 1975-76; bd. govs. United Way Indpls., 1978-79; mem. bd. missions United Meth. Ch., Indpls., 1976-78; bd. dirs. Suemma Coleman Agy., 1975-79, Community Services Council Indpls., 1976-77; trustee Christian Theol. Sem., 1976-79. Mem. Nat. Restaurant Assn. (dir. 1978-79), Ind. Restaurant Assn. (dir. 1977-79), Marion County Mental Health Assn., Northwestern U. Alumni Assn., Pi Alpha Mu, Deru (pres. 1956-57), Beta Theta Pi (v.p. 1956-57). Office: Office of Lt Gov 333 State House Indianapolis IN 46204 *

MUTZ, OSCAR ULYSSES, healthcare services executive; b. Edinburg, Ind., Feb. 12, 1928; s. Harold Winterberg and Laura Belle (Sawin) M.; m. Jean Greiling, Aug. 22, 1948; children: Marcia, H. William. B.S., Ind. U., 1949. Vice pres. Peerless Corp., Indpls., 1954-63; v.p., gen. mgr. Space Conditioning, Inc., Harrisonburg, Va., 1964-66; v.p., treas. Cosco, Inc., Columbus, Ind., 1966-67; exec. v.p. 1967-69, pres., 1969-71; chmn. bd. Court Manor Corp., Columbus, 1971-73; pres. Jenn Air Corp., Indpls., 1973-75; pres., chief exec. officer Forum Group, Inc. (merger Mutz Corp. and Exception, Inc.), Indpls., 1981—; bd. dirs. Court Manor Corp., Sargent & Greenleaf, Forum Industries, Forum Group, Inc., Amli Realty Co., Capital Industries, Inc., Dictograph Security Systems, Keystone Distbn., Inc., Sovereign Group, Inc., Nat. Enterprises, Inc. Mem. dean's adv. council Ind. U. Mem. Ind. Mfrs. Assn. (chmn. 1980). Republican. Methodist. Office: Forum Group Inc 8900 Keystone Crossing Suite 1200 Indianapolis IN 46240

MUZILLA-TORMA, MARY DIANE, management executive; b. Elyria, Ohio, Aug. 13, 1956; d. Stephen Francis and Georgine (Dancisko) Muzilla; m. Gerard Joseph Torma, June 9, 1984. BA, St. Mary's Coll., 1978; MBA, Baldwin-Wallace Coll., 1980; postgrad., Case Western Res. U., 1983-85. Mgr. nursing systems Lorain (Ohio) Community Hosp., 1979-82, ops. research, 1982-85, dir. ops. research, 1985-86; dir. ops. Medisyst Inc., Lorain, 1986—; instr. Lorain Community Coll., Elyria, 1982—; cons. in field, 1983—; lectr. various orgns., 1983—; pres. Stephan Group, Lorain, 1987—. Bd. trainer Lorain United Way, 1981-83; pres. Lorain YWCA, 1983—; bd. dirs. Leadership Lorain County, 1986, Lorain Free Clinic, 1987—; coordinator County Wide Phone System Com., Lorain, 1985—. Recipient Woman of Achievement award Woman of Achievement Com., 1981, YWCA Vol. of Yr. award, 1981, Career Woman of Yr. award Bus. and Profl. Women, 1982. Mem. Nat. Hosp. Systems Soc., Hosp. Fin. Mgmt. Assn., Ops. Research Soc. Am., No. Ohio Hosp. Systems Soc. (charter, pres. 1987—), Delta Mu Delta. Democrat. Roman Catholic. Lodge: Altrusa (pres. 1983-84). Avocations: music composition, choreography, tennis, sailing, bridge. Home: 5611 Mills Creek Ln North Ridgeville OH 44039 Office: Medisyst PO Box 396 Lorain OH 44052

MUZYNSKI, BERNARD LEON, prosthodontist; b. Chgo., Aug. 4, 1948; s. Bernard L. and Evelyn (Zielinski) M.; m. Janice Jean Jankowski, Aug. 7, 1976; children: Cheryl, Lauren. BS, U. Ill., 1970; DDS, Northwestern U., 1976, MS, 1984, cert. of specialty, 1984. Lic. dentist, Ill. Gen. practice dentistry Palos Heights, Ill., 1976—; practice dentistry specializing in prosthodontics Chgo., 1984—; assoc. prof. Northwestern U. Dental Sch., Chgo., 1976-85. Served to sgt. USMCR, 1970-76. Mem. ADA, Ill. Dental Soc., Chgo. Dental Soc., Am. Prosthodontic Soc. Republican. Roman Catholic. Avocations: tennis, golf. Office: 7600 College Dr Palos Heights IL 60463

MUZZILLO, WILLIAM ALLEN, industrial engineer, automobile executive; b. Auburn, Ind., Dec. 30, 1958; s. William Joseph and Dolores T. (McGuire) M.; m. Laurie Ann Reeves, June 13, 1981; 1 child, Lance William. BS in Indsl. Engring., Purdue U., 1981, MS in Indsl. Engring., 1982. Indsl. engr. Fisher Body div. Gen. Motors Corp., Warren, Mich., 1982-84; supr. indsl. engring. Gen. Motors Corp., Kalamazoo, 1984-85, planning adminstr., 1985-86, gen. supr. labor relations B.O.C. group, 1986—; coll. recruiter Gen. Motors Corp., 1984—; adj. instr. U. Mich., Dearborn, 1984. Mem. Inst. Indsl. Engrs., Soc. Automotive Engrs., Indsl. Relations Resource Assn. Democrat. Roman Catholic. Club: Purdue U. (Kalamazoo). Avocations: golf, softball, skiing. Home: 6330 Willow Brook Dr Kalamazoo MI

49004 Office: Gen Motors Corp BOC Group 5200 E Cork St Kalamazoo MI 49001

MYER, PAUL JOSEPH, hotel company executive; b. Bad Constatt, Fed. Republic Germany, Jan. 31, 1954; came to U.S., 1954; s. Anthony Phillip and Caroline Ann (Molter) M.; m. Michelle Lynne Jacoby, Sept. 25, 1982. BS in Hotel Adminstrn. with distng., Cornell U., 1976. Mgr. Hyatt Hotels, Chgo., 1976-79; asst. and gen. mgr. Henricis Restaurants, Chgo., 1979-81; gen. mgr. Midway Hotel, Elk Grove, Ill., 1981-83; pres. Paul J. Myer & Assocs., Buffalo Grove, Ill., 1983—; v.p. Chase Waterford, Schaumburg, Ill, 1986—. Mem. Hotel Sales Mgmt. Assn., Ill. Hotel/Motel Assn. Republican. Roman Catholic. Avocations: numismatics, golf, jogging. Home and Office: 520 Burnt Ember Buffalo Grove IL 60089

MYEROWITZ, P. DAVID, cardiac surgeon; b. Balt., Jan. 18, 1947; s. Joseph Robert and Merry (Brown) M.; B.S., U. Md., 1966, M.D., 1970; M.S., U. Minn., 1977; m. Susan Karen Macks, June 18, 1967 (div.); children—Morris Brown, Elissa Suzanne, Ian Matthew. Intern in surgery U. Minn., Mpls., 1970-71, resident in surgery, 1971-72, 74-77; resident in cardiothoracic surgery U. Chgo., 1977-79; practice medicine, specializing in cardiovascular surgery, Madison, Wis., 1979—; asst. prof. thoracic and cardiovascular surgery U. Wis., Madison, 1979-85, assoc. prof., 1985, chief sect. cardiac transplantation, 1984-85, Karl P. Klassen prof., chief thoracic and cardiovascular surgeon Ohio State Univ. and Hosps., Columbus, 1985—. Served with USPHS, 1972-74. Mem. ACS, Am. Coll. Cardiology, Assn. for Acad. Surgery, Soc. Univ. Surgeons, Soc. Thoracic Surgery, Am. Coll. Chest Physicians, Am. Heart Assn., Internat. Soc. Heart Transplantation, Internat. Soc. Cardiovascular Surgery. Jewish. Contbr. articles to profl. jours. Office: Ohio State Univ Hosps Doan N-825 Columbus OH 43210

MYERS, CAROLE ANN, health transportation service executive; b. Henderson, Ky., June 14, 1938; d. James Newton and Rosalene Alberta (Eakins) Wade; m. Lawrence William Myers, Dec. 28, 1957 (dec. Feb. 1980); children: Patti Myers Crisler, Nancy Myers Allen, Sandra Myers Gurchiek, Mark William. Cert., St. Francis Hosp., 1971; student, Butler U., 1979. Cert. emergency med. tech., paramedic. Pres., chief exec. officer Myers Ambulance Service, Greenwood, Ind., 1966—. Bd. dirs. Greenwood Sr. Citizens Ctr.; mem. Rep. Sen. Inner Circle, Washington, 1984. Named Disting. Hoosier by Gov. of Ind., 1984. Mem. Ind. Ambulance Assn. (pres. 1983-85, treas. 1986—), Ind. Emergency Med. Services Commn., Am. Ambulance Assn. (sec. 1983-84, treas. 1985-86, v.p. 1987—, pres.-elect, woman of yr. 1983). Home: 150 N Madison Ave Greenwood IN 46142 Office: Myers Ambulance Service Inc 325 W Wiley St Greenwood IN 46142

MYERS, DAVID N., automobile dealership executive; b. Syracuse, N.Y., Oct. 4, 1942; s. Donald F. and Joyce R. (Richer) M.; m. Kathie Ann Denesha, Sept. 11, 1965; children—Deborah, Kimberley, Matthew. A.A.S., Auburn Community Coll., N.Y., 1962. Merchandising mgr. Gen. Motors, Cleve., 1964-78; pres. David Myers Chevrolet, Inc., North Jackson, Ohio, 1978—; v.p. Myers Marine World, Inc., 10578 Mahoning Ave., North Jackson, 1987—. Served with U.S. Army, 1962-66. Mem. Youngstown C. of C., Eastern Ohio Auto Dealers Assn. (chmn. bd. trustees 1984—). Republican. Roman Catholic. Club: Men's (Youngstown, Ohio), (pres. 1983-84). Lodge: Kiwanis (pres. 1983-84). Avocations: tennis; golf; fishing; softball. Home: 14861 Robinson Rd Newton Falls OH 44444 Office: David Myers Chevrolet 10535 Mahoning Ave N Jackson OH 44451

MYERS, DONALD ALFRED, information systems executive; b. Grand Rapids, Minn., May 9, 1944; s. Melvin and Ione Marie (Gilstead) M.; m. Nadine Carol Westad, Sept. 4, 1967; children: Amy, Margaret. BS, Bemidji (Minn.) State U., 1965; MS, U. Iowa, 1969, PhD in Math., 1971. Lectr. U. Wis., Milw., 1971-73; computer programmer J.C. Penney, Milw., 1973-76; analyst data processing systems, mgr. St. Paul Fire and Marine Ins. Co., 1976-84, mgr. actuarial info., 1984—. Mem. Minn. Hist. Soc. Mem. Data Processing Mgmt. Assn. Democratic Farm Labor. Lutheran. Office: St Paul Fire and Marine Ins Co Actuarial Dept 385 Washington St Saint Paul MN 55102

MYERS, JEFFREY ALLEN, optometrist; b. Urbana, Ohio, Apr. 19, 1959; s. Jerry Page and Nancy Jane (Miller) Myers; m. Liessen Emily Kutschbach, Sept. 4, 1982; children: James, Jennifer. BA, Otterbein Coll., 1980; BS, Ohio State U., 1982, OD, 1984. Lic. optometrist, Ohio. Pvt. practice optometry Canal Winchester, Ohio, 1984—; clin. instr. optometry Ohio State U., Columbus, 1984—; cons. VA Med. Ctr., Chillicothe, Ohio, 1986—. Scoutmaster, asst. dist. commr. Boy Scouts Am., 1977—. Recipient Dist. Award of Merit, 1987. Mem. Am. Acad. Optometry, Am. Optometric Assn., Ohio Optometric Assn. (membership com. 1984—), Cen. Ohio Optometric Assn. (trustee 1985-87, lt. gov. 1987—). Republican. Methodist. Lodges: Lions, SAR, Masons (Grand Masters' award, 1980). Office: 11925 Lithopolis Rd Canal Winchester OH 43110

MYERS, JODY ELLEN, video production executive; b. Gary, Ind., Apr. 10, 1956; d. Burton Herbert and Marilyn (Gabovich) Rosen; m. Perry D. Myers, Mar. 31, 1984; 1 child, Sean Adam. BA, Ind. U., 1978, MS in Sociology, 1979; cert., Roosevelt U., 1984. V.p. Myers Service, Chgo., 1980-85; pres. Videotek, Chgo., 1985—; film critic Facets, Chgo. 1982-84. Producer: (film) Working USA, 1985 (Frame Award 1985); author The "How To" Video Book, 1986. Mem. Videomakers (regional dir. 1985—), Videographer Soc. (bd. dirs. 1980—). Avocations: coin collecting, tennis, golf. Office: Videotek 2930 W Lunt Chicago IL 60645

MYERS, JOHN THOMAS, congressman; b. Covington, Ind., Feb. 8, 1927; m. Carol Carruthers; children: Carol Ann, Lori Jan. B.S., Ind. State U., 1951. Cashier, trust officer Fountain Trust Co.; owner operator livestock far; mem. 90th-100th congresses from 7th Ind. dist., 1967—, Appropriations Com. Served with AUS, World War II, ETO. Mem. Am. Legion, V.F.W., Wabash Valley Assn., Res. Officers Assn., C. of C., Sigma Pi. Republican. Episcopalian. Clubs: Mason, Elk, Lion. Office: US House of Representatives 2372 Rayburn House Office Bldg Washington DC 20515 *

MYERS, JULIAN SHERRY, rehabilitation counseling educator; b. Hartford, Conn., Mar. 24, 1918; s. Barney and Fanny (Sherry) M.; m. Mary Helen Scott, Aug. 12, 1960; children: Alan, Andrew, Barry, Melanie, Julie. BA, City Coll. N.Y., 1939; MA, Columbia U., 1946; PhD, NYU, 1953. Lic. psychologist, N.Y., Mass., Ohio; cert. rehabilitation counselor, N.Y., Mass., Ohio. Psychologist Inst. Phys. Medicine and Rehab., N.Y.C., 1948-51, Burke Found., White Plains, N.Y., 1951-57; assoc. prof. rehabilitation counseling Boston U., 1957-66; founder, dir. U. Cin. Rehab. Ctr., 1969-83; prof. U. Cin., 1966—; vocational cons. Social Security Adminstrn., Boston and Cin., 1957-83; cons. Rehab. Commn., Columbus, 1986. Editor: Orientation to Chronic Disease and Disability, 1965. Served to capt. Med. Specialist Corps, U.S. Army, 1942-46, USAF, 1946-57. U.S. Rehab. Services Adminstrn. fellow, 1973. Mem. Am. Psychol. Assn., Ohio Psychol. Assn., Cin. Psychol. Assn., Cin. Assn. Profl. Psychology, Ohio Assn. for Counselor Edn., Harvard Med. Alumni Assn. (assoc.). Home: 3919 Leyman Dr Cincinnati OH 45229 Office: U Cin Mail Location 2 Cincinnati OH 45221

MYERS, LANCE FLORIAN, telephone company executive; b. Goodland, Kans., Dec. 19, 1938; s. Lawrence Dave and Dorothy (Shultz) Myers Chaney; m. Rosalie Garrison; children—Sean Florian, Seth Garrison. Student in civil engring. U. Wichita, 1957-58; B.A. in Bus. Adminstrn., Bellevue Coll., 1983. Cert. data processor. Programmer, designer Cudahy Packing Co., Omaha, 1959-64; programmer/designer Northwestern Bell, Omaha, 1965-66, project mgr., 1966-68; programming dist. mgr., 1968-78, support dist. mgr., 1978—, data base adminstr., 1978—. Chmn. Republican Precinct Com., Malvern, Iowa, 1978-82. Mem. Assn. Systems Mgmt. (div. bd. dirs. 1980-81), Data Processing Mgmt. Assn. (v.p. 1973), Am. Arbitration Assn., Alpha Kappa Chi. Republican. Methodist. Avocations: genealogy, boating. Home: 106 S 37th St Suite 1 Omaha NE 68131 Office. Northwestern Bell Telephone Co 100 S 19th St Room 1170 Omaha NE 68102

MYERS, LOUIS SAMUEL, obstetrician, gynecologist; b. Detroit, June 15, 1941; s. Cecil and Bessie Myers; m. Gloria A. Garber, Mar. 19, 1972; children: Stephanie, Robert. BA in Philosophy, Wayne State U., 1962, MD, 1966. Diplomate Am. Bd. Obstetrics and Gynecology. Rotating intern Wayne State U., Detroit, 1967; ob-gyn specialist tng. U. Chgo. Lying In Hosp., 1972; attending physician Prentice Hosp., Northwestern Meml. Hosp., Chgo., 1972—, Near North Adult Med. Ctr., Chgo., 1972-77; med. dir. Albany Med. Surgery Outpatient Ctr., Chgo., 1974—; from instr. to prof. dept. ob-gyn Northwestern U., 1972—. Mem. B'nai Brith. Served to capt. M.C., USAF, 1968-70. Mem. AMA, Ill. Med. Soc., Chgo. Med. Soc., Am. Coll. Ob-Gyn, Am. Fertility Soc., Assn. Profs. in Ob-Gyn, Assn. Gynecol. Laparoscopists, Assn. Planned Parenthood Profls., Pitts. Inst. Legal Medicine. Avocations: stamp collecting, oil painting, swimming. Home: 38 Bridlewood Ln Northbrook IL 60062 Office: 845 N Michigan Ave Chicago IL 60611

MYERS, MICHAEL JOSEPH, hospital executive director; b. Sioux Falls, S.D., July 15, 1936; s. Harry Boniface and Alma Mary (Javurek) M.; m. Mary Ellen Schaefer; children: Mary Elizabeth, Helen Marie, Matthew Michael, Anne Kathryn, Nicholas Gregory, Michael Schaefer, Connor Joseph. BS, S.D. State U., 1961; JD, U. S.D., 1967, postdoctoral studies in bus., 1980-81. Bar: S.D. 1967. Newsman UPI, Mpls. and Bismarck (S.D.), 1961-62; photographer and outdoor writer Sioux Falls Argus Leader, 1962-63; photographer, feature writer, editor Sioux City (Iowa) Jour., 1963-67; assoc. Gleysteen, Nelson, Harper, Kunze & Eidsmore, Sioux City, 1967-69; asst. prof. law U. S.D., Vermillion, 1969-72; corp. counsel St. Joseph Mercy Hosp., Dubuque, Iowa, 1972-76; regional counsel Sister of Mercy Health Corp. and St. Joseph Mercy Hosp., Dubuque, 1976-77; exec. v.p. Marian Health Ctr., Sioux City, 1977-81; adminstr. St. Mary's Hosp., Rochester, Minn., 1981-85, exec. dir., chief exec. officer, 1985—; pres. Minn. Conf. Cath. Health Facilities, 1984-85; lectr. in field; bd. dirs. Norwest Bank; trustee Blue Cross/Blue Shield Minn. Assoc. chmn. United Way, Rochester, 1986, chmn., 1987; chmn. Minn. Pvt. Coll. Fund, 1986; bd. dirs. Samaritan Bethany, Inc., 1982-85. Served with USN, 1954-57. Mem. ABA, Am. Acad. Hosp. Attys., Am. Coll. Health Care Execs., Acad. Cath. Health Care Leadership, Am. Hosp. Assn. (governing council met. hosps. sect. 1986—), Minn. Hosp. Assn. (trustee 1985—), Am. Acad. Hosp. Attys., Rochester C. of C. (bd. dirs. 1983—). Roman Catholic. Lodge: Rotary. Avocations: racquetball, tennis, hunting, church, community. Office: St Marys Hosp of Rochester 1216 SW 2d St Rochester MN 55902

MYERS, PENNIE M., psychotherapist; b. Phila., Aug. 16, 1939; d. William Lee and Roberta (Appel) M.; m. William C. Cohen Jr., Jan. 2, 1959 (div. Sept. 1978); children: Susan Lee, Robert Lewis; m. Don W. Nance, Aug. 29, 1983. BA, Wichita (Kans.) State U., 1973, MA, 1975; EdD, Internat. Grad. Sch., St. Louis, 1983. Staff counseling ctr. Wichita State U., 1975-82, coordinator cons., 1982-86, marriage and family services dir., 1986—; cons. Alcoholism Family Counseling Ctr., Wichita, 1977-80, U. Kans. Med. Sch., Wichita, 1981—, Wesley Hosp. Chaplaincy, Wichita, 1985—, Coleman Co., Wichita, 1986—. Co-author: The Upset Book, 1986, Adaptive Counseling and Therapy, 1987; contbr. articles to profl. jours. Mem. Am. Assn. Marriage and Family Therapy (clin., approved supr.), Am. Psychol. Assn. Home: 14301 Brookline Ct Wichita KS 67230 Office: Wichita State U Counseling Ctr 1845 N Fairmount Wichita KS 67208

MYERS, RANDALL GAIL, infosystems executive; b. Hagerstown, Md., Nov. 29, 1957; s. Joshua John and Gaynell Rochelle (Metzer) M.; m. Gale Ann Greene, Sept. 27, 1980; 1 child, Randall Gail Jr. BA, Ashland Coll., 1979. Mgr. remote job entry Bank One Mansfield, Ohio, 1979-80; mgr. data processing Bank One Mansfield, 1980-81, data processing officer, 1981-83; mgr. data ops. United Telephone Co. Ohio, Mansfield, 1983—. Baseball player Mansfield Semi-Pro League, 1978-84, Ashland (Ohio) Ch. League Softball, 1985—. Mem. Am. Mgmt. Assn., Assn. for Computer Ops. Mgrs, COMMON Computer Users Assn. Republican. Mem. Ch. Brethren. Avocations: gardening, numismatics, hunting, guitar, geneology. Home: 419 West Liberty St Ashland OH 44805 Office: United Telephone Co Ohio 1404 Park Ave West Mansfield OH 44906

MYERS, RAYMOND IRVIN, optometrist; b. Mishawaka, Ind., Nov. 19, 1943; s. Raymond E. Myers and Adeline S. (Hiler) M.; m. Paulette K. Emerine, July 9, 1966; 1 child, Christopher Raymond. BS, U. Notre Dame, 1966, Ind. U., 1968; OD, Ind. U., 1970. Dir. edn. and manpower div. Am. Optometric Assn., St. Louis, 1970-73; mgr. internat. profl. services Bausch & Lomb, Inc., Rochester, N.Y., 1973-77; research fellow Moorfields Eye Hosp., London, 1977-78; pvt. practice optometry St. Louis, 1979—; faculty U. Mo., St. Louis, 1986—, chmn. ctr. contact lens research, 1986—. Fellow Am. Acad. Optometry; mem. Am. Optometric Assn., Assn. for Research on Vision and Ophthalmology, St. Louis Optometric Soc. (pres. 1985-86), Internat. Soc. for Contact Lens Research (co-founder, v.p. 1980—), Am. Optometric Student Assn. (co-founder, pres. 1967). Office: U Mo Sch Optometry 8001 Natural Bridge Saint Louis MO 63121

MYERS, ROBERTA FRANCES, teacher; b. Miller, Mo., May 30, 1945; d. Robert Clayton and Virginia Frances (Kabell) Duvall; m. Billy Gene Meyers, June 6, 1969; children: Tony Dale, Robert Gene. BE in Vocat. Home Econs., Southwest Mo. State U., 1967. Cert. tchr., Mo. Tchr. home econs. Hartville (Mo.) Sch., 1967-68; tchr. kindergarten Burnett Elem., Houston, 1968-69, tchr. 2d grade, 1969-71; tchr. 1st grade Fairview Elem., Carthage, Mo., 1972—. Mem. Fairview Elem. PTA, 1972—, Fall Festival Assn., Miller Youth Baseball Assn.; sec., treas. Miller Athletic Booster Club, 1985-87; tchr. sunday sch. Gray's Point Christian Ch., Miller, Mo., 1977-83. Mem. Mo. State Tchrs. Assn., Carthage Community Tchrs. Assn. (sec. 1980-83). Democrat. Home: Rural Rt 2 Box 80 Miller MO 65707 Office: Fairview Elem 1201 E Fairview Carthage MO 64836

MYERS, RODMAN JAY, financial analyst; b. Detroit, June 12, 1961; s. Rodman Nathaniel and Jeanette (Polisei) M. B in Acctg., Mich. State U., 1984. CPA, Mich. Acct. Arthur Young & Co., Detroit, 1984-87; fin. analyst Waste Mgmt., Inc., Southfield, Mich., 1987—. Recipient Rabbis' Award Temple Beth El, Bloomfield Hills, Mich., 1979, cert. appreciation IRS, Washington, 1985. Mem. Am. Assn. CPA's, Nat. Assn. Accts. (asst. sec. Detroit chpt. 1985), Mich. Assn. CPA's, Mich. State Trust for Ry. Preservation. Democrat. Jewish. Club: Oakland County Sportsman's. Avocations: tennis, golf, road racing. Home: 3833 Lakeland Ln Bloomfield Hills MI 48013

MYERS, ROGER WAYNE, agricultural products executive; b. Meade, Kans., Oct. 15, 1953; s. Archie D. and Thelma L. (McPheter) M.; m. Deanna Marie Stapleton, May 31, 1980; children: Gary Wayne, Joseph Paul. A in Bus. Mgmt., Seward County Community Coll., 1973; B in Acctg., Northwestern Okla. State U., 1976. Office mgr. Cooperative Grain & Supply, Bazine, Kans., 1976-78, gen. mgr., 1978-81; grain merchant Farmers Grain & Supply, Greensburg, Kans., 1981-84; gen mgr. Menlo-Rexford (Kans.) Cooperative, 1984—. Mem. Bazine City Council, 1981. Republican. Roman Catholic. Lodge: KC. Avocations: hunting, fishing, golf, bowling. Home: PO Box 4 Menlo KS 67746 Office: PO Box 8 Menlo KS 67746

MYERS, ROGER WAYNE, advertising executive; b. Horton, Kans., Jan. 7, 1946; s. Walter E. and Jewell K. (Dawson) M.; m. Linda B. Whichello, Sept. 11, 1971. BJ, U. Kans., 1968; MS in Journalism, Northwestern U., 1969. Creative supr. Needham, Harper & Steers, Chgo., 1975-76, Benton & Bowles, Chgo., 1976-78; pres. Myers Roach & Ptnrs., Chgo., 1978-80; exec. v.p. Burch Myers Cuttie, Inc., Chgo., 1980-85; pres. Mycomm Enterprises, Inc., Lake Forest, Ill., 1985—; juror creative competition St. Louis Ad Club, 1973; judge ADDY awards N.C. Triangle Fedn., Raleigh, 1982; bd. dirs. Think, Inc., Chicago. Contbr. articles to profl. jours. 1st. Place Fiction award Writer's Digest mag., 1974; ANDY award N.Y. Ad Club, 1975, 76, 78, 82; EFFIE award Am. Mktg. Assn., 1982-83; ADDY award Chgo. Advt. Club, 1982, 83, 84, 85; ADDY award Am. Advt. Fedn., 1980, 82, 84, 85, 86. Mem. Nat. Writer's Club, Independent Writers of Chgo., Ind. Writers Chgo.

MYERS, STEVEN DUANE, systems analyst; b. Limestone, Maine, July 3, 1960; s. James David and Judith Zoe (Hannah) M.; m. Christine Ann O'Brien, Sept. 10, 1983; 1 child, Trenton Michael. BS in Computer Sci., Cen. Mo. State U., 1982. Systems programmer Panhandle Eastern Pipeline, Kansas City, Mo., 1982-86; sr. systems analyst Marion Labs., Kansas City, 1986—. Mem. Mid-Am. Telecommunications Assn., Assn. Computing Machinery. Roman Catholic. Avocations: water skiing, snow skiing, racquetball, softball.

MYERS, THOMAS ALDEN, diversified company executive; b. Akron, Ohio, Dec. 1, 1945; s. Minor and Ruth (Libby) M.; m. Lynn Dee Ann Locke, Aug. 24, 1969; children: Emily Michlle, Timothy Alden. BBA, Ohio State U., 1968; MBA, U. Cin., 1970; postgrad. U. Akron, 1974-75. Fin. analyst Mid-Continent Telephone Corp., Hudson, Ohio, 1973-77, supr. fin. results, 1977-78; public relations account exec. Edward Howard & Co., Cleve., 1978-79; mgr. investor relations TRW Inc., Cleve., 1979-81, dir. investor relations, 1982—. Co. photographer Ohio Ballet, Akron, 1976—, trustee, 1979—; founder, dir. The Screamers & Lyric Brass Band, 1986—. Served with U.S. Army, 1970-73. Mem. Nat. Investor Relations Inst. (sec.-treas. Cleve.-Akron chpt. 1981-82, v.p. membership 1982-84), Investor Relations Assn., Ohio State U. Alumni Assn. Club: Ohio State U. Marching Band Alumni. Home: 156 N Highland Ave Akron OH 44303 Office: TRW Inc 1900 Richmond Rd Cleveland OH 44124

MYERS, THOMAS ANDREWS, college administrator; b. Latrobe, Pa., Mar. 24, 1949; s. Clarence Rolland and Mary Ruth Myers; m. Sherry K. Ransford, Dec. 11, 1982. B.A., Allegheny Coll., 1971; postgrad. Clarion State U. (Pa.), 1972. Asst. dir. Cable TV-13, Meadville, Pa., 1971-73; mgr. advt. and pub. relations Teledyne Vasco, Latrobe, 1973-83; advt. cons. Teledyne, Inc., Eastern Group, 1976-83; instr. continuing edn. St. Vincent Coll., Latrobe, 1981-83; dir. pub. relations Kalamazoo Coll. (Mich.), 1983—. Chmn. adv. com. coll. communications Seton Hill Coll., Greensburg, Pa., 1975-80; mem. exec. com. Alumni Congress Allegheny Coll., Meadville, 1978-84, 86—, chmn. communications com., 1978-82, v.p., 1982-84. Recipient Blue citation Alumni Congress Allegheny Coll., 1984. Mem. Laurel Highlands Advt. Assn. (dir. 1975-79, pres. 1978-79), Internat. Assn. Bus. Communicators. Home: 534 Pinehurst Blvd Kalamazoo MI 49007 Office: Dept Pub Relations Kalamazoo Coll Kalamazoo MI 49007

MYERS, WILLIAM GEORGE, clergyman; b. Faulkton, S.D., Aug. 29, 1938; s. William Edwin and Harriett Constance (Kuhl) M.; B.S. in Edn., No. State Coll., Aberdeen, S.D., 1956-60; M.Div. in Theology, Garrett-Evang. Theol. Sem., Evanston, Ill., 1965; M.A. in Liturgy, U. Notre Dame, 1984. Ordained elder United Methodist Ch., 1966. Asst. pastor Ingleside-Whitfield United Meth. Parish, Chgo., 1962-65; pastor-dir. Christ the Carpenter Parish and Christian Ctr., Rockford, Ill., 1965-76; chaplain, instr. St. Mary's Acad., Nauvoo, Ill., 1976—; assoc. pastor Colusa/Dallas City/Nauvoo United Meth. Chs., Ill., 1976—; dir. Radio-TV Ministry, Rockford, 1967-71; sec. Midwest Religious Broadcasting Commn., 1967-71. Advisor southside youth council NAACP, 1962-64; bd. dirs. Central Day Care Ctr., Rockford, 1969-72, Protestant Welfare Services, Rockford, 1972-74; bd. dirs., pres. Family Consultation Services, Rockford, 1974-76; pres. Nauvoo Hist. Soc., 1979-84, dir. resource and research ctr., 1984—; treas. Hancock County Theatre for Performing Arts, Ill., 1979-84; mem. United Meth. Fellowship for Worship and Other Arts. Mem. Nat. Council Tchrs. English, Ill. Council Tchrs. English, Nat. Cath. Edn. Assn., Order of Saint Luke (sub-dean), Nauvoo Ministerial Assn., Sigma Tau Delta. Democrat. Home: 290 N Page St Nauvoo IL 62354 Office: Saint Mary's Acad Nauvoo IL 62354

MYERS, WOODROW AUGUSTUS, JR., physician, state health commissioner; b. Indpls., Feb. 14, 1954; s. Woodrow Augustus Sr. and Charlotte T. (Tyler) M.; m. Debra Jackson, June 23, 1973; children: Kimberly Leilani, Zachary Augustus. BS, Stanford (Calif.) U., 1973, MBA, 1982; MD, Harvard U., 1977. Intern in internal medicine Stanford U. Med. Ctr., 1977-78, resident in internal medicine, 1978-80, fellow, critical care medicine, 1980-81; asst. prof. critical care medicine San Francisco Gen. Hosp., 1982-84; physician health advisor com. on labor and human resources U.S. Senate, Washington, 1984; commr. State Bd. of Health, Indpls., Ind., 1985—; mem. staff Wishard Meml. Hosp., Indpls., 1985—; asst. prof. medicine Ind. U. Med. Ctr., Indpls., 1985—. Robert Wood Johnson clin. scholar, Stanford U., 1980-82. Fellow ACP; mem. AMA, Nat. Med. Assn., Soc. Critical Care Medicine. Office: Ind State Bd Health 1330 W Michigan St Indianapolis IN 46206

MYERS-WALLS, JUDITH ANN, child development educator; b. Roaring Spring, Pa., Aug. 21, 1952; d. Carl Edsel and Doreen Mae (Crist) Myers; m. Richard Alvey Walls, Sept. 11, 1977; children: Amanda Leigh, Aaron Richard. BA in Psychology, Manchester Coll., 1974; MS in Child Devel., Purdue U., 1977, PhD in Child Devel., 1979. Program dir. Vernon Manor Children's Home, Wabash, Ind., 1974; houseparent Ft. Wayne (Ind.) Children's Home, 1975; materials devel. specialist Project FEATT Purdue U., West Lafayette, Ind., 1975-76; grad. asst. dept. child devel. Purdue U., West Lafayette, 1976-79, from asst. to assoc. prof., 1979—; cons. question and answer column Parents mag., N.Y.C., 1982-86. Co-author: Young Peacemakers Project Book, 1987; columnist Media and Values mag., Los Angeles, 1986—. Fellow Gen. Foods, 1978; grantee Ind. State Bd. Health, 1984, Agrl. Experiment Sta., 1982-84, Ind. Com. Humanities, 1980-81. Mem. Nat. Council Family Relations (chmn. AC program 1985-86), Ind. Council Family Relations (pres. 1983-87), Nat. Assn. Edn. Young Children, Ind. Assn. Edn. Young Children, Soc. Research Child Devel., Ind. Healthy Mothers Helath Babies Coalition (chmn. membership com. 1986-87). Democrat. Mem. Ch. of the Brethren. Avocations: family activities, camping. Home: 1010 Highland Ave Lafayette IN 47905 Office: Purdue U CDFS Bldg West Lafayette IN 47907

MYLOD, ROBERT JOSEPH, banker; b. Bklyn., Nov. 21, 1939; s. Charles Joseph and Katherine (Normile) M.; m. Monica Manieri, July 11, 1964; children: Rosemary, Robert, Kevin, Paul, Monica, Megan. B.A., St. John's U., 1961. Vice pres. Citibank (N.A.), N.Y.C., 1965-70; V.p. Citicorp., N.Y.C., 1970-73; exec. v.p. residential loan div. Advance Mortgage Corp., Detroit, 1973-75; pres. Advance Mortgage Corp., 1975-83; pres., chief operating officer, dir. Fed. Nat. Mortgage, 1983-85; chmn., pres., chief exec. officer, dir. Mich. Nat. Corp., 1985—; chmn., pres., chief exec. officer, dir. Mich. Nat. Bank, 1987—, chmn., dir., 1985—. Served to lt. (j.g.) USN, 1961-65. Office: Mich Nat Corp Wellington N 30665 Northwestern Hwy Farmington Hills MI 48018-9065

MYLONAKIS, STAMATIOS GREGORY, research and development executive; b. Athens, Greece, Aug. 18, 1937; came to U.S., 1963; s. Gregory and Vassiliki (Charalampopoulos) M.; m. Pamela H. Morton, May 15, 1965 (dec. Mar. 1978); 1 son., Gregory John. BS in Chemistry, U. Athens, 1961; MS in Phys. Organic Chemistry, Ill. Inst. Tech., 1964; PhD in Phys. Organic Chemistry, Mich. State U., 1971. Research scientist Brookhaven Nat. Lab., Upton, N.Y., 1965-68; instr. U. Calif., Berkeley, 1971-73; group leader Rohm and Haas Co., Springhouse, Pa., 1973-76; supr. DeSoto Inc., Des Plaines, Ill., 1976-79; staff scientist Borg-Warner Chems., Inc. Des Plaines, 1979-81, research and devel. mgr., 1981—. Author numerous research papers; patentee in polymer synthesis and applications fields. Mem. tech. adv. bd. Case Western Res. U., PhD thesis adv. com. Lehigh U. Served as lt., Greek Army, 1961-63. Ill. Inst. Tech. fellow, 1963-64; Mich. State U. fellow, 1968-71. Mem. Am. Chem. Soc., Sigma Xi. Office: Borg-Warner Chemicals Inc Wolf and Algonquin Rds Des Plaines IL 60018

MYRICK, YVONNE ROWENA, municipal government official; b. Gary, Ind., May 3, 1924; d. William Edward and Rowena Octavia (Fairley) Hill; m. Joseph H. Myrick, Nov. 24, 1949 (dec. Nov. 1973); children: Henry A., Yvonne R. Myrick Stokes, Timothy J. Student, Detroit Inst. Commerce, 1942; AS, Wayne County Community Coll., 1972; BS, Wayne State U., 1978. Lic. social worker, Mich. Clerical worker to acct. City of Hamtramck, Mich., 1945-67, 73—, water supr., 1986—; pres. local #666 Am. Fedn. State, County and Mcpl. Employees. Dem. precinct del., 1986; pres. Hamtramck adult br. NAACP; past leader Girl Scouts U.S.; past den mother Boy Scouts Am.; founder and past v.p. Hamtramck PTA; pub. relations Women of Ch. of God, past trustee Met. Ch. of God, founder primary ch.; mem. exec. com. 14th Congl. dist.; bd. dirs. Hamtramck Housing Corp., 1986, People's Community Service, Hamtramck, 1986. Recipient Outstanding Alumna award Wayne County Community Coll., 1973, Long and Valued Service award Community United for Action, Long and Valued Service award People's Community Service, 1984. Mem. Wayne State U. Alumni Assn., Mich. Assn. Sch. Bd. Mems., Women's Conf. Concerns, Gamma Phi Delta (youth enrichment officer 1970-72). Home: 3967 Evaline Hamtramck MI 48212

NAAS, HERMAN JAMES, bank executive; b. Oak Park, Ill., Oct. 26, 1942; s. Herman and Theresa (Holl) N.; m. Nancy Susan Butalla, May 21, 1970;

children: James, Heather, Bridget. BSME, Valparaiso (Ind.) U., 1964. Project leader Internat. Harvester Co., Broadview, Ill., 1966-74; project mgr. Abbott Labs., North Chicago, Ill., 1974-77, mgr. systems, 1979-81; mgr. systems Robert Bosch Corp., Broadview, 1978-79; v.p. fin. info. systems First Chgo. Corp., 1981—. Republican. Lutheran. Avocations: boating, golf, tennis. Home: 457 W Sheridan Pl Lake Bluff IL 60044 Office: First Chgo Corp 1 First National Plaza Chicago IL 60670

NAAS, SISTER M. JOLINDA, elementary school administrator; b. Haubstadt, Ind., May 14, 1937; d. Joseph P. and Elizabeth B. (Brenner) N. B.S., St. Benedict Coll., Ferdinand, Ind., 1967; M.A. in Elem. Edn., Ball State U., 1976, postgrad., 1978-83; Cert. elem. administrn. and supervision, Ind. Tchr. diocese Evansville, Ind., 1956-69, administr., 1972-86; tchr. Archdiocese of Los Angeles, 1969-70, adminstr., 1970-72. Participant sabbatical U. Notre Dame, 1986-87. Mem. Ind. Assn. Elem. and Middle Sch. Prins. Club: Holy Family Athletic Booster. Home: 828 Vigo St Vincennes IN 47591 Office: 800 Vigo St Vincennes IN 47591

NACHTSHEIM, EDWARD ERNEST, truck and fire engine manufacturing company executive; b. Milw., Oct. 16, 1930; s. Emil and Jennie (McCrossen) N.; m. Patricia Ann Werking, Aug. 20, 1955; children: Beth Susan, Julie Renee, Bruce Edward, Curtis Robert. B.B.A., U. Wis., 1958. Sr. accountant Price Waterhouse & Co., Milw., 1958-62; v.p. Kyle Co., Mequon, Wis., 1963-69; treas. Congoleum Corp. (formerly Bath Industries Inc.), Milw., 1969-77; pres. Holt Log Homes, Inc., Milw., 1977—, Bear Lake Reserve, Inc., Milw., 1977—; v.p. fin. FWD Corp., Clintonville, Wis., 1979-80; exec. v.p. FWD Corp., 1981—. Served with AUS, 1952-54. Mem. Am. Inst. C.P.A.s, Wis. Soc. C.P.A.s. Home: 185 Birch Tree Ct Clintonville WI 54929

NACHTWEY, PETER HAMILTON, JR., accountant, auditor; b. Rochester, N.Y., July 25, 1955; s. Peter Hamilton and Rosemary Louise (Brinkman) N.; m. Diane Brochetti, July 17, 1976. BS, Syracuse (N.Y.) U., 1978. CPA, N.Y. Auditor Touche Ross & Co., Washington, 1978-81, audit mgr., 1983—; asst. controller Frank E. Basil, Inc., Athens, Greece, 1981-83. Mem. Am. Inst. CPA's, Ohio Soc. CPA's, Constrn. Fin. Mgrs. Assn. (dir. 1987), Ohio Contractors Assn. (fin. com. 1986-87), Lomond Assn. (exec. v.p.). Roman Catholic. Lodge: Rotary (pres. 1987, treas. 1984-86). Avocations: travel, golf, skiing, running. Office: Touche Ross & Co 1801 E 9th St Cleveland OH 44122

NADAS, JOHN ADALBERT, psychiatrist; b. Innsbruck, Austria, Mar. 14, 1949; came to U.S., 1950; s. Julius Zoltan and Ibolya Erzsebet (Szöllösy) N.; m. Gabriella Ilona Ormay, Apr. 11, 1981; children: János, Miklós, István. BA, Case Western Res. U., Cleve., 1970; MD, Duke U., Durham, N.C., 1974. Diplomate Am. Bd. Psychiatry and Neurology. Resident in psychiatry U. Chgo., 1974-77; pvt. practice Munster, Ind., 1977-84; instr. psychiatry Northeastern Ohio U. Coll. Medicine, Rootstown, 1985-86; coordinator psychiat. edn. Timken Mercy Med. Ctr., Canton, Ohio, 1985—; asst. prof. Northeast Ohio U. Coll. Medicine, Rootstown, 1986—; pvt. practice Canton, 1984—; cons. Crisis Ctr., Canton, 1985—. Author: Philsophical Basis of Depth Psychotherapy, 1983. Mem. AMA, Am. Psychiat. Assn. Roman Catholic. Avocations: basketball, computer programming. Office: 1330 Timken Mercy Dr NW Suite 320 Canton OH 44708

NADEN, VERNON DEWITT, marketing executive; b. Waukegan, Ill., Feb. 5, 1947; s. Vernon D. and Beatrice (Gedvillas) N.; m. Julia Karen Lookout, Mar. 7, 1970 (div. June 1985); m. Linda Jean Edwards, June 17, 1986; children: Brian, Mike, Joseph, Annette. BS, Culver Stockton U., 1969. Dist. mgr. Johnson Outboards, Waukegan, 1970-77; nat. sales mgr. Coral Chem. Co., Waukegan, 1977-82; market mgr. Desoto, Inc., Des Plaines, Ill., 1982—. Contbr. articles to profl. jour. Mem. Nat. Coil Coaters Assn., Archtl. Assn. Mfg. Am., Metal Constrn. Assn. Constrn. Specifiers Inst., am. Spray Coaters Assn. Republican. Avocations: golf, fishing, sailing. Home: 165 W Apple Ln Gurnee IL 60031 Office: 1700 S Mt Prospect Rd Des Plaines IL 60018

NADLER, CHARLES H., lawyer, educator; b. N.Y.C., Oct. 19, 1940; s. Maurice and Florence Edith (Kahan) N.; m. Susan Lenore Gendelman, June 6, 1962 (div. Apr. 1976); m. Hanna Bergmann Weston, Aug. 14, 1982. AB, Columbia Coll., 1962; postgrad., Columbia U., 1964-69; JD, U. Iowa, 1984. Bar: Iowa 1984, U.S. Dist. Ct. (no. dist.) Iowa 1984, U.S. Dist. Ct. (so. dist.) Iowa 1985, U.S. Ct. Appeals (8th cir.) 1986. Asst. prof. Cen. Wash. U., Ellensburg, 1969-74; dir. UniServ Iowa Higher Edn. Assn., Iowa City, 1975-82; ptnr. Nadler & Weston, Cedar Rapids and Iowa City, 1984—; adj. instr. Kirkwood Community Coll., Cedar Rapids, 1984—; mediator Iowa Farmer-Creditor Mediation Service, Des Moines, 1985—. Contbr. articles to profl. jours. Pres. Iowa Civil Liberties Union, Des Moines, 1978-82, bd. dirs. 1976-78, 83—; bd. dirs. ACLU of Wash., Seattle, 1970-74. Served to lt. USN, 1962-64. Iowa Humanities Bd. grantee, 1977-79. Mem. ABA, Iowa Bar Assn., Johnson County Bar Assn., Linn County Bar Assn., Assn. Trial Lawyers Am., Fed. Bar. Assn., Nat. Lawyers Guild, Am. Arbitration Assn., Indsl. Relations Research Assn. Am. (adv. com. Iowa chpt.), ACLU. Democrat. Jewish. Avocations: amateur radio, travel, reading. Home: 715 River St Iowa City IA 52240 Office: Nadler & Weston 420 Paramount Bldg Cedar Rapids IA 52401

NAEGLER, MARY HELEN, health care company executive, accountant; b. St. Louis, May 2, 1942; d. Robert Charles and Martha Emily (Botts). BA, Bemidji (Minn.) State U., 1965, BS magna cum laude, 1982. CPA, Minn. Pvt. practice acct., tax cons. Bemidji, 1979—; acct. North Country Hosp., Bemidji, 1980-82; acct., auditor U.S. Dept. Energy, Washington, 1982-83; dir. corp. acctg. North Country Health Services, Bemidji, 1983—; cons. small bus. devel. ctr. Bemidji State U., 1984-85. Clk. Turtle Lake Twp., Minn., 1979-80; pres. St. Phillip's Parish Council, Bemidji, 1974. Served to 1st lt. USAF, 1965-69, Vietnam. Mem. Am. Inst. CPA's, Minn. Soc. CPA's, Healthcare Fin. Mgmt. Assn. Avocations: language, linguistics, fishing, gardening. Office: North Country Health Services 1100 W 38th St Bemidji MN 56601

NAESETH, GERHARD BRANDT, librarian, genealogist; b. Valley City, N.D., Apr. 14, 1913; s. Carelius Gunnarson and Emma Louise (Brandt) N.; m. Milma Delilah Petrell, Aug. 25, 1940; children: Charles Philip, Olivia Louise. BA in History magna cum laude, Luther Coll., 1934; BA in Library Sci., U. Mich., 1936, MA in Library Sci., 1939, postgrad., 1939-40; postgrad., Okla. State U., 1947-48. Cataloger Gen. Library U. Mich., Ann Arbor, 1934-37, cataloger Law Library, 1937-40; assoc. librarian Okla. State U., Stillwater, 1940-48; assoc. dir. Gen. Library U. Wis., Madison, 1948-78; dir. Vesterheim Geneal. Ctr., Madison, 1975—. Author: Naeseth-Fehn Family History, 1956, Wrolstad Family History, 1978; contbr. articles and book revs. to mags. and profl. jours. Chmn. Oslo-Madison Sister City Com., 1984-86, ch. council of Am. Luth. Ch., 1969-72; pres. Zion Luth. Ch., Stillwater, 1947-48; mem. bd. dirs. Lutherdale Bible Camp, Elkhorn, Wis., past treas.; mem. ch. council Bethel Luth. Ch., Madison, Pres. 1985-86, mem. ch. choir. Served with USN, 1943-46. Scholar Emigration Fund of 1975, Norway, 1977; recipient Knight's Cross 1st Class Royal Order of St. Olav, Norway, 1978, Award of Merit Nat. Geneal. Soc., 1984, Service medal Nordmanns-Forbundet, Norway, 1984. Mem. Am. Library Assn. (life), Wis. Library Assn., Norwegian-Am. Hist. Assn. (life), State Hist. Soc. of Wis., Norwegian-Am. Mus. Democrat. Lutheran. Home: 4909 Sherwood Rd Madison WI 53711

NAEYMI-RAD, FRANK, management information systems specialist, medical aid specialist; b. Tehran, Iran, Aug. 28, 1950; came to U.S., 1968; s. Mahmood and Talat Naeymi-Rad; m. Theresa Ivanka Kepic, Dec. 4, 1976; children: Ivana, Andrei. BS in Maths., Ill. State U., 1975; MS in Computer Sci., So. Ill. U., 1978; postgrad., Ill. Inst. Tech., 1987—. With Mid-West Digital, Lake Bluff, Ill., 1978—; programmer/analyst, tng. coordinator State Farm Ins. Co., Bloomington, Ill., 1978-81; dir. computer ctr. UHS/Chgo. Med. Sch., 1982—; instr. operating systems Coll. Lake County, Grayslake, Ill., 1986—. Home: 6235 N Legett Chicago IL 60646 Office: Chgo Med Sch 3333 Green Bay North Chicago IL 60064

NAGABHUSHAN, BELLUR LAKSHMINARAYANA, aerospace engineer; b. Tiptur, Karnataka, India, May 23, 1949; came to U.S., 1971; s. Bellur Achappa and Subbagowramma Lakshminarayana Swamy; m. Uma Rao, Apr 5, 1978. B.Tech. in Aero. Engring., Indian Inst. Tech., Madras, India, 1971; M.S. in Aerospace Engring., Va. Polytech. Inst., 1973, Ph.D. in Aerospace Engring., 1976. Researcher, instr. Va. Polytech. Inst. and State U., 1971-76; engring. specialist, project leader Goodyear Aerospace, Akron, Ohio, 1976—. Editor Jour. of Aircraft, 1985—. Contbr. articles to profl. jours. Inventor in field. Indian Inst. Tech. scholar, 1967. Fellow AIAA (mem. nat. tech. com., assoc.); mem. Aero. Soc. India. Avocations: music; traveling; sports. Home: 4526 Honeysuckle Dr North Canton OH 44720 Office: Goodyear Aerospace Corp 1210 Massillon Rd Akron OH 44315

NAGARKATTI, JAI PRAKASH, chemical company executive; b. Hyderabad, India, Feb. 18, 1947; s. Surendranath and Shakuntala (Bai) N.; m. Linda Susan Slaughter, Mar. 14, 1975; 1 child, Shanti. BS, Osmania U., 1966, MS, 1968; MS, East Tex. State U., 1972, EdD, 1976. Group leader Aldrich Chem. Co. Inc., Milw., 1977-78, supr. prodn., 1978-79, mgr. prodn., 1979-84, dir. prodn., 1985, v.p., 1985-87, pres., 1987—, also bd. dirs.; lectr. chemistry V.V. Coll., Hyderabad, 1969-70. Contbr. articles to profl. jours. Robert A. Welch fellow East Tex. State U., Commerce, 1974-76. Fellow Indian Chem. Soc.; mem. Am. Chem. Soc. (chmn. membership Milw. chpt. 1981). Avocations: philately, tennis. Office: Aldrich Chem Co Inc 940 W St Paul Ave Milwaukee WI 53201

NAGEL, JACQUELINE, communications executive; b. Detroit, Jan. 25, 1949; d. William Sidney and Clara (Tobes) Brooks; m. Irwin Leonard Nagel, June 3, 1970 (div. Dec. 1979); 1 child, Brandon William. BS, Eastern Mich. U., 1970. Pres. Plantasia, Inc., Farmington, Mich., 1974-77; account exec. Helen Grace, Inc., Phoenix, 1978-79, Sprint Communications, Southfield, Mich., 1980-82; mgr. br. Sprint Communications, Kansas City, Kans., 1982-83; mgr. div. Sprint Communications, Detroit and Cleve., 1983-86, Cleve., 1986—; bus. cons. Southfield Sch. System, 1984-85, Solon (Ohio) Sch. System, 1986—. Recipient Pres.'s Club award Southern Pacific Bell Co., 1984, GTE, 1985, U.S. Sprint. 1986. Mem. Internat. Orgn. Women Telecommunications (assoc.), Soc. Telecommunications Profls., Telecommunication Assn., Nat. Assn. Female Execs. Avocations: numismatics, golf, backgammon. Home: 34100 Ada Dr Solon OH 44139 Office: US Sprint Communications 6060 Rockside Woods Blvd Independence OH 44131

NAGEL, JAMES L., professional society administrator; b. St. Louis, Oct. 15, 1951; s. Owen Warren and Mary Jane (Queenson) N.; m. Timothea M. Ortmann, Sept. 28, 1983; children: Sarah Jane, Courtney Lynn. BS, Southeast Mo. State U., 1973; MA, Webster U., 1985. Tchr. Melville Sch. Dist., St. Louis, 1974-85; exec. dir. Mo. Assn. Homes for Aging, 1985—. Mem. Internat. Brotherhood Magicians (convention chmn. 1983—, bd. trustees 1983—), Am. Soc. Assn. Execs., Meeting Planners Internat., Nat. Speakers Assn. Lodges: Jaycees, Optimists. Avocations: magic, jogging. Office: Mo Assn Homes for Aging 6925 Hampton Ave Saint Louis MO 63109

NAGEL, MARTIN JOSEPH, electronics company executive; b. Fairmont, W.Va., Apr. 24, 1941; s. Franz Childs and Helen Marie (Soyer) N. BA in Physics, W.Va. U., 1963, MS in Physics, 1966. Prodn. engr. Gen. Electric Co., Lynn, Mass., 1966-67; design engr. Gen. Electric Co., Wilmington, Mass., 1967-70; quality control task engr. Raytheon Co., Bedford, Mass., 1971-72; cheif engr. Tenna Corp., Cleve., 1973-78, mgr. product engr., 1978-79; pres. Consumer Electronics Devel. Corp., Chagrin Falls, Ohio, 1980—. Patentee in field; contbr. articles to profl. jours. Recipient cert. merit Nat. Merit Scholarship Corp., 1959. Republican. Club: Kingswood Gun (South Russell, Ohio)(treas. 1978-81). Avocations: audiophile, guitar, flying, motorcycling.

NAGEL, THEODORE CHRISTIAN, physician; b. New Jersey City, Oct. 31, 1936; s. Harry Conrad and Anna Eliese (Von Spreckelsen) N.; m. Judith Anne Nagel, June 21, 1965 (div. 1970); children: Amanda Eliese, Kirsten Marissa; m. Judy Ann Grundstrom, Oct. 23, 1982; children: Christian Wallace, Conrad Wallace. BA, Wesleyan U., 1959; MD, Cornell U., 1963. Diplomate Am. Bd. Internal Medicine; Am. Bd. Ob-Gyn; Am. Bd. Endocrinology and Metabolism; Am. Bd. Reproductive Medicine. Asst. prof. internal medicine Northwestern U. Med. Sch., Chgo., 1973-74; assoc. prof. ob-gyn U. Minn., Mpls., 1977-78, asst. prof. ob-gyn, 1978—. Served with USNR. Mem. Am. Coll. Ob-Gyn, Am. Fertility Soc., Am. Soc. Gynecol. Laparascopists, Soc. Reproductive Endocrinologists, Soc. Reproductive Surgeons. Avocations: skiing, reading. Home: 1766 James Ave S Minneapolis MN 55403

NAGLE, DAVID R., congressman; b. Grinnell, Iowa, Apr. 15, 1943; s. William Nagle; m. Diane Lewis, July 13, 1984; 1 stepchild, Benjamin Norden. Student, U. No. Iowa, 1961-65; LLB, U. Iowa, 1968. Sole practice Waterloo and Evansdale, Iowa, 1968-73; ptnr. Ball & Nagle, P.C., Waterloo, 1973-81; sole practice Waterloo, 1981-87; mem. 100th Congress from Iowa 3rd Dist., Washington, 1987—; asst. county atty. Black Hawk County, Waterloo, 1968-70; city atty. Evansdale, 1972-73. Active B.H. County Conservation Bd., Cedar Falls, Iowa, 1975-80, pres. 1979; state chmn. Iowa Democrats., Des Moines, 1982-85. Mem. Nat. Dem. Club. Roman Catholic. Avocations: hunting, fishing, golfing.

NAGLER, WILLIAM MERLE, psychiatrist, educator, playwright; b. Detroit, May 9, 1951; s. Charles Arthur and Billie (Cugell) N. BS with honors, U. Mich., 1973, MD, 1977. Diplomate Am. Bd. Psychiatry and Neurology. Intern U. Calif. Med. Ctr., Davis, 1977-78; resident in psychiatry U. Calif., Davis, 1977-80; med. dir. Columbia Med. Ctr., Southfield, Mich., 1982—; clin. faculty Wayne State U., Detroit, 1982—; med. dir South Woodward Clinic, Birmingham, Mich., 1984—, Midwest Mental Health, Dearborn, Mich., 1985—; attending physician North Detroit Hosp., Mich., 1985—; med. dir. Ctr. Pain Therapy, Birmingham, 1986—. Author: (play) Dog Story, 1984, Turntable, 1985, No Blood, 1986 (Kernoodle Playwriting award 1986); contbr. articles to profl. jours. Harvard U. fellow, 1981. Fellow Internat. Acad. Preventive Med.; mem. AMA, Am. Acad. Forensic Sci., Huxley Inst., Dramatist Guild, Internat. Brotherhood Magicians. Clubs: Magic Circle (London). Avocations: magic, theater. Home and Office: 41620 Six Mile Rd Northville MI 48167

NAGLICH, DONALD RAY, management system specialist; b. Hammond, Ind., Feb. 13, 1951; s. Rudolph William and Irene Ann (Krawczyk) N.; m. Yi Szu Kuo, Sept. 21, 1974; children: Jason, Mai Lei. BS magna cum laude, Calumet Coll., 1983. Various positions Inland Steel, East Chicago, Ind., 1975-83, supr., 1983-85, technology engr., 1985, control supr., 1986—. Leader Cub Scouts Am., Highland, Ind., 1984-85. Roman Catholic. Avocations: automobiles, photography. Home: 3429 42d Pl Highland IN 46322 Office: Inland Steel Co 3210 Watling St East Chicago IL 46312

NAGY, DENES, consulting engineer; b. Budapest, Hungary, Oct. 19, 1929; s. Denes and Margit (Lukacs) N.; came to U.S., 1957, naturalized, 1962; student Hungarian Comml. Inst. Pest, 1950; B.A., Tech. U. Budapest, 1954, B.S. in Mech. Engring., 1954, M.S. in Mech. Engring., 1954; m. Margarita Penaherrera, Jan. 13, 1968. Design engr. Gebr. Van Swaay, Mij., engrs. and constructors, The Hague, Holland, 1956-57; project engr., design engr. Walter Scholer & Assocs., Inc., architects and engrs., Lafayette, Ind., 1957-65; project engr. Dalton-Dalton Assos., Inc., architects and engrs., Cleve., 1965-67; pres., dir., chief engr. Environ. Engring. Corp., Chgo., 1967-72; pres., dir. Martin-Nagy-Tonella Assos., Inc., cons. engrs., Chgo., 1972-76; partner, dir. MNT Internat., Quito, Ecuador, 1975—; owner, pres. Denes Nagy Assos., Ltd., Chgo. Registered profl. engr., Ind., Ill., Wash., Wis., Mass., N.Y., Calif., W.Va.; cert. energy mgr. Mem. ASME, ASHRAE, Internat. Dist. Heating Assn., Nat. Soc. Profl. Engrs., Ill. Soc. Profl. Engrs., Nat. Fire Protection Assn., Constrn. Specifications Inst., Air Pollution Control Assn., Automated Procedures for Engring. Cons. (trustee 1968-71), Soc. Am. Value Engrs., Am. Cons. Engrs. Council, Cons. Engrs. Council Ill., Ill. Architect-Engr. Council (pres. 1979, mem. exec. com.), U.S. Power Squadron, U.S. Coast Guard Aux., Internat. Visitors Center, Chgo. Council on Fgn. Relations. Office: 65 W Division St. Chicago IL 60610

NAHAT, DENNIS F., artistic director ballet company, choreographer; b. Detroit, Feb. 20, 1946; s. Fred H. and Linda M. (Haddad) N. Hon. degree, Juilliard Sch. Music, 1965. Prin. dancer Joffrey Ballet, N.Y.C., 1965-66; prin. dancer Am. Ballet Theatre, N.Y.C., 1968-76; founder, artistic dir. Cleve. Ballet, 1976—. Prin. performer Broadway show Sweet Charity, 1966-67; choreographer Two Gentlemen of Verona (Tony award 1972), 1969-70; (ballet) Celebrations and Ode (resolution award 1985), 1985; founder Sch. of Cleve. Ballet, 1972, Cleve. Ballet, 1976; founder, artistic dir. San Jose Cleve. Ballet, 1985. Grantee Nat. Endowment Arts, 1978, Andrew Mellon Found., 1985. Avocation: master chef. Office: Cleveland San Jose Ballet 1 Playhouse Sq Cleveland OH 44115

NAIDEN, JAMES, poet, literary critic, journalist; b. Sept. 24, 1943; grad. Seattle U.; postgrad. U. Iowa, U. Ark. Poet, critic lit. jour., 1968—; journalist newspapers, jours., U.S., Europe, 1968—; broadcast journalist KROS news, Clinton, Iowa, 1979-80; broadcast journalist, 1978—; author: Asphyxiations/1-40 (poetry), 1987; contbr. articles to scholarly jours.; editor The North Stone Rev., 1971—; poetry critic Mpls. Star and Tribune, 1970-85. Recipient Guillaume Apollinaire Prix, La Nuit Blanche, 1968. Mem. Twin Cities Local #13 Nat. Writers Union , Poetry Soc. Am., Dramatists Guild. Address: D Station Box 14098 Minneapolis MN 55414

NAIK, TARUN RATILAL, civil engineering educator; b. Ahmedabad, Gujarat, India, Apr. 22, 1940; came to U.S., 1962; s. Ratilal Haribhai and Gajaraben M. (Desai) N.; m. Irene de Venecia, Aug. 20, 1966; children: Eela, Nisha. BSCE, Gujarat U., Ahmedabad, 1962; MSCE, U. Wis., 1964, PhDCE, 1972. Registered profl. engr., Wis. Structural engr. Warzyn Engring., Madison, Wis., 1964-67; exec. v.p. Soils and Engring. Services, Madison, 1972-75; assoc. prof. civil engring. U. Wis., Milw., 1975—. Contbr. articles to profl. jours. Engring. program dir. Ít. Acad. Medicine and Engrs., Milw., 1983—. research grantee various co's. in Wis., Ill., Ind. Mem. Am. Concrete Inst. (past pres., founds. for equipment and machinery com., nondestructive testing of concrete com., current research com., others), ASCE, Am. Soc. Elec. Engring., ASTM, System Engring. Mgmt., Reunion Internationale des Laboratoires d'Essais et de Recherches sur les Materiaux et les Constructions, Soc. Experimental Mechanics, NSPE, Wis. Soc. Profl. Engrs. (mem. legis. cabinet, 1974-80, pres. Milw. chpt.). Avocations: photography, travel. Home: 622 N 72d St Wauwatosa WI 53213 Office: U Wis 3200 N Cramer St Milwaukee WI 53201

NAIRN, JAMES FRANCIS, packaging executive; b. Charleroi, Pa., Sept. 12, 1945; s. Francis Patrick and Gladys Romayne (Hails) N.; m. Sara Ann DeVore; 1 child, Heather Lynne. BS, West Va. U., 1975, MBA, 1980. Bus. analyst Borg Warner Chems., Parkersburg, W. Va., 1974-76; fin. analyst Borg Warner Chems., Parkersburg, W.Va., 1976-78, sales rep., 1978-80; sales mgr. PMS Consolidated, Elk Grove Village, Ill., 1980-82; v.p. Phoenix Closures, Naperville, Ill., 1982—; v.p. DEVCOM, St. Charles, Ill., 1985—; pres. Ctr. for Creative Devel., St. Charles, 1986. Served to 1st lt. U.S. Army, 1966-69, Vietnam. Decorated Bronze Star. Mem. Soc. Plastics Engrs., Packaging Inst. Am. Club: Economic (Chgo.). Avocations: chess, reading, golf. Home: 612 Marion Ave Saint Charles IL 60174 Office: Phoenix Closures 6 S 371 Rt 59 Naperville IL 60540

NAISBY, ALAN, automotive company executive; b. Sunderland, Durham, England, Feb. 15, 1956; came to U.S., 1986; s. John Robertson and Joan (Ellis) N.; m. Jane Sutton, Dec. 31, 1982. BA, Liverpool U., Eng., 1978. With product mktg. Lucas CAV, London, 1978-80; mgr. product mktg. U.S. div. Lucas CAV, Troy, Mich., 1981-82, gen. mgr. U.S. div., 1986—; gen. mgr. Korea div. Lucas CAV, Seoul, 1982-85. Mem. British Korean C. of C. (com. 1984-85). Mem. Ch. of Eng. Avocations: running, cycling, chess. Home: 2412 Somerset Blvd #104 Troy MI 48084 Office: Lucas CAV 1416 Meijer Dr Troy MI 48084

NAJAR, LEO MICHAEL, conductor, educator; b. Grand Rapids, Mich., Jan. 29, 1953; s. Ammiel George and Claire Elizabeth (Grant) N.; m. Tamara Sinkevich, Aug. 24, 1974; m. Jean Anne Van Winkle, May 10, 1986; children: John Andrew, Erik. MusB in Viola Performance, U. Mich., 1976, MusM in Viola Performance, 1977. Asst. conductor Flint (Mich.) Symphony Orch., 1975-80; dir. Flint Community Music Sch., 1976-80; music dir. Saginaw (Mich.) Symphony Orch., 1980—; guest lectr. music Wayne State U., Detroit, 1983-86, guest asst. prof. music U. Mich., Ann Arbor, 1986—. Producer and host (radio program) Preludio: The String Thing, 1978-80. Mem. Am. Symphony Orch. League (Helen M. Thompson award 1982, various coms. 1980—), Mich. Orch. Assn. (pres. 1985-87), Conductor's Guild. Club: Torch (Saginaw). Home: 2805 Overridge Ann Arbor MI 48104 Office: Saginaw Symphony Orch PO Box 415 Saginaw MI 48606

NAJARIAN, BARBARA, advertising executive, art director; b. N.Y.C., July 24, 1950; d. Edward H. and Ann (Gulbenkian) N. B.F.A., Art Ctr. Coll. Design, Los Angeles, 1971; U. Calif.-UCLA, 1972; postgrad. Royal Coll. Art, London, 1980. Freelance art dir., Los Angeles, 1973-78; art dir. Young & Rubicam-West, Los Angeles, 1978-80, Gray Advt., Inc., N.Y.C., 1980-81, J. Walter Thompson, Inc., N.Y.C., 1981-83; sr. art dir. Grey Advt., Inc., Mpls., 1983-85; creative supr. Campbell-Mithun Advt., Inc., Mpls., 1985—; creative cons. BTG Prodns., Inc., 1982-83, Janus Fin. Mktg., 1984; graphics cons. and designer. Vol., Hopkins Area Little League, Minn., 1984-86, Sloane Kettering Inst., 1980-82, Neuropsychiat. Inst., UCLA, 1974-78. Recipient Lulu award Women's Advt. Club Los Angeles, 1977; Clio award, 1982. Mem. Nat. Assn. Female Execs., Advt. Club Mpls., Copywriters and Art Dirs. Club Mpls. Office: Campbell-Mithun 222 S 9th St Minneapolis MN 55402

NALYWAJKO, EUGENE, business executive, production consultant; b. Zolotchiv, Ukraine, Aug. 8, 1926; s. John and Maria (Dudar) N.; m. Myroslawa Zalopany, May 12, 1951. B.S. in Tech., U. Mich., 1956; diploma engr. Tech. U., Regensburg, W.Ger., 1950. Plant mgr. Protexol Corp., Kenilworth, N.J., 1956-60; supr. quality control Plywood Fabricator Service, Denver, 1960-65, dir. quality control, Chgo., 1965-66; v.p. ops. Lester's of Minn., Inc., Lester, Prairie, 1966—, also dir. Mem. Forest Products Research Soc. Eastern Rights Catholic. Club: Toastmaster (Hutchinson, Minn.). Home: 230 Maple St N Lester Prairie MN 55354 Office: Lester's of Minnesota Inc Lester Prairie MN 55354

NAMDARI, BAHRAM, surgeon; b. Oct. 26, 1939; s. Rostam and Sarvar Namdari; M.D., 1966; m. Kathleen Diane Wilmore, Jan. 5, 1976; 3 children. Resident in gen. surgery St. John's Mercy Med. Ctr., St. Louis, 1969-73; fellow in cardiovascular surgery with Michael DeBakey, Baylor Coll. Medicine, Houston, 1974-75; practice medicine specializing in gen. and vascular surgery and surg. treatment of obesity, Milw., 1976—; mem. staff St. Mary's, St. Luke's, St. Michael, Good Samaritan, Trinity Meml., St. Anthony, Family, St. Francis hosps. (all Milw.). Diplomate Am. Bd. Surgery. Fellow ACS, Internat. Coll. Surgeons; mem. Med. Soc. Milwaukee County, Milw. Acad. Surgery, Wis. Med. Soc., Wis. Surg. Soc., Royal Soc Medicine Eng. (affiliate), Am. Soc. for Bariatric Surgery, AMA, World Med. Assn., Internat. Acad. Bariatric Medicine (founding mem.), Michael DeBakey Internat. Cardiovascular Soc. Contbr. articles to med. jours.; patentee med. instruments and other devices. Office: Great Lakes Med and Surg Ctr SC 2315 N Lake Dr Milwaukee WI 53211 also: 6000 S 27th St Milwaukee WI 53221

NANCE, JOEL HARRY, physician; b. N.Y.C., Oct. 10, 1942; s. Harold Claude Nance and Elizabeth (Lane) Small; m. Emily E. Kofron, July 31, 1982; children: Jared, Thomas. BS, Coll. City of N.Y., 1968; MD, Albert Einstein Coll. Medicine, 1972. Diplomate Am. Bd. Psychiatry and Neurology. Intern pediatrics Albert Einstein Coll. Medicine, N.Y.C., 1972-73; clinical instr. U. Calif., Davis, 1973-75; resident in psychiatry U. Ariz., Tucson, 1975-78; fellow in psychiatry Menninger Found., Topeka, 1978-79, staff psychiatrist, 1979—; staff psychiatrist and mem. faculty Karl Menninger Sch. of Psychiatry, Topeka, 1980—; research cons. Stanford U., Palo Alto, Calif., 1984—; teaching assoc. Topeka Inst. for Psychoanalysis, 1986—. Manealoff fellow Albert Einstein Coll. Medicine, 1969, 71. Mem. Candidates' Soc. Topeka Inst. for Psychoanalysis (pres. 1984—). Avocations: musical performance, aviation, wilderness backpacking. Home: 124 Greenwood Topeka KS 66606 Office: The Menninger Found Box 829 Topeka KS 66601

NANCE, NICKOLETTE LEOWN, automotive aftermarket company executive; b. Havana, Kans., Mar. 29, 1948; d. Earl and Sarah Alice (Harris) Thompson; m. John Robert Davis, Apr. 19, 1965 (div. May 1984); children—Joni Rene, Derrick N.; m. Thomas Levi Nance, Sept. 13, 1985. Student Independence Community Jr. Coll., 1974-76. Catalog mgr. Montgomery Wards, Independence, Kans., 1971-73; prodn. worker Automotive Controls Corp., Independence, 1974-79, purchasing clk., 1979-80, buyer, 1980—. Club: Independence Promenade (pres. 1979-81); Avocations: squaredancing; fishing; walking; gardening. Home: Rural Rt 3 Box 450 Independence KS 67301 Office: Automotive Controls Corp 1300 W Oak St Independence KS 67301

NANGLE, JOHN FRANCIS, judge; b. St. Louis, June 8, 1922; s. Sylvester Austin and Thelma (Bank) N.; 1 child, John Francis Jr. A.A., Harris Tchrs. Coll., 1941; B.S., U. Mo., 1943; J.D., Washington U., St. Louis, 1948. Bar: Mo. 1948. Practiced in Clayton, 1948-73; chief judge U.S. Dist. Ct., St. Louis, 1973—; mem. jury com. U.S. Cts. Mem. Mo. Republican Com., 1958-73; mem. St. Louis County Rep. Central Com., 1958-73, chmn., 1960-61; pres. Mo. Assn. Reps., 1961, Reps. Vets. League, 1960; mem. Rep. Nat. Com., 1972—; Bd. dirs. Masonic Home Mo. Served with AUS, 1943-46. Named Mo. Republican of Year John Marshall Club, 1970, Mo. Republican of Year Mo. Assn. Reps., 1971; recipient Most Disting. Alumnus award Harris-Stowe Coll., Most Disting. Alumnus award Washington U. Sch. Law, 1986. Mem. Am. Judicature Soc., Legion of Honor DeMolay, Am., Mo., St. Louis, St. Louis County bar assn., 8th Circuit Jud. Council, Jud. Conf. U.S. Office: US District Court US Courthouse 1114 Market St Saint Louis MO 63101

NANNE, LOUIS VINCENT, hockey club manager; b. Sault Ste. Marie, Ont., Can., June 2, 1941; s. Michael and Evelyn N.; m. Francine Yvette Potvin, Aug. 22, 1962; children: Michelle, Michael, Marc, Marty. B.S. in Mktg, U. Minn., 1963. Mem. Minn. North Stars hockey club, 1967-78, gen. mgr., 1978—, also v.p. Roman Catholic. Office: care Minn North Stars 7901 Cedar Ave S Bloomington MN 55420 *

NANOS, MARK DAVID, advertising executive; b. Corpus Christi, Tex., July 31, 1954; s. Arthur Samuel and Dorothy (Sabotka) N.; m. Vicky Ellen Dallas, Jan. 7, 1974; children: Joel M., Kyle J. Student, U. Mo., Kansas City, 1977-80. Art dir. Citizen News, San Antonio, 1973-74; ptnr. Free Lance Graphics, Kansas City, Mo.; pres. Nanos & Gray, Inc., Kansas City, 1981—, Tillmark Communications, Inc., Kansas City, 1985—. Author: The Secret To Planning Successful Brochures, 1986; inventor balloon greeting cards; designer, writer (advertisement) Tilly Balloons, 1986 (Gold Ring award Bus. Profl. Advt. Assn. 1986). Cons. pub. relations Kans. City Parks Vol. Program, 1984—. Mem. Kansas City Advt. Golf Assn. (pub. relations 1984—). Avocations: study of Judaism, ancient Greek culture, New Testament soc. ethics. Home: 804 North 41 Blue Springs MO 64015 Office: Nanos & Gray Inc 1660 Broadway Kansas City MO 64108

NANTKES, RYLAND REED, printing company executive; b. Bellwood, Nebr., Feb. 25, 1923; s. Harry Andrew and Isabel (Selzer) N.; m. Patricia Ann Andrews, Feb. 27, 1942 (div. 1961); children—Andrew Reid, Karen Ann; m. 2d, Okla Viola Sandlin, July 12, 1969. Vice pres. mfg. Epsen Lithographing Co., Omaha, 1941-60, pres., 1972—; v.p. mfg. Paramount Paper Products, Omaha, 1960-71; pres. Ralph Printing, Omaha, 1971-72; pres. Hillmer Graphics Co., chief exec. officer, also dir.; dir. HG Profl. Forms, Omaha, HG Label Works, Inc., Omaha. Republican. Presbyterian. Clubs: Omaha Country, Omaha Club. Home: 601 Martin Dr N Bellevue NE 68005 Office: Epsen Lithographing Co 2000 California St Omaha NE 68102

NAPLES, GARRY MICHAEL, U.S. postal inspector, accountant; b. Chgo., Dec. 9, 1954; s. Carmen Vincent and Loretta Jane (Sherwin) N.; m. Diana Theresa Cichon, Oct. 15, 1978; 1 child, Garry M. BS in Commerce, De Paul U., 1977, MS in Taxation, 1987. CPA, Ill. Acctg. technician FBI, Chgo., 1973-78; staff acct. Checkers, Simon & Rosner, Chgo., 1978-80, Rosenberg & Cohn, Chgo., 1980-81, Laventhol & Horwath, Chgo., 1981-82; U.S. postal inspector U.S. Postal Service, Chgo., 1982—. Lector St. Juliana Ch., Chgo. Mem. Am. Inst. CPA's, Ill. CPA Soc. Roman Catholic. Home: 7347 N Olcott Chicago IL 60648-4147 Office: Postal Inspection Service 433 W Van Buren Chicago IL 60669-2201

NAPLEY, JOHN C., banking company executive. Chmn. Pontiac (Mich.) State Bank. Office: Pontiac State Bank 28 N Saginaw St Pontiac MI 48058 *

NAPOLIELLO, DANIEL ANDREW, nurse administrator; b. Omaha, Sept. 27, 1944; Ceasare Dan and Therese Mary (Sierszynski) N.; m. Sally Ann Rodak, Jan. 7, 1967; children: John, Ann Marie, Michael. Diploma in nursing, St. Joseph Hosp., Omaha, 1965; BS in Nursing, U. S.C., 1975; MEd, Chapman Coll., 1977. Commd. U.S. Army, 1964; advanced through grades to capt. Nurse Corps U.S. Army; chief nurse 8th combat support hosp. Nurse Corps U.S. Army, Fort Ord, Calif., 1975-77, resigned, 1977; served to lt. comdr. USPHS, 1977—; dir. nursing Indian Hosp. USPHS, Rosebud, S.D., 1977-78, Winnebago, Nebr., 1984—; assoc. hosp. dir. nursing edn. USPHS, Balt., 1978-81, evening supr. nursing, coordiantor quality assurance, 1981-84; mem. USPHS Continuing End. Reb. Nursing Com., Rockville, Md., 1979-81, Indian Health Service Hosp. Nursing Profl. Splty. Group, Rockville, 1984—. Asst. dist. commr. Sioux council Boy Scouts Am., S.D., 1977-78, scoutsmaster Balt. council, Md., 1978-81, asst. dist. commr. Prairie Gold Area council, Iowa, 1982—, cubmaster, 1985—; CPR Instr. ARC, 1982—; chmn. Dist. Health and Safty Com.; Nebr. State Hist. Soc., Union Pacific R.R. Hist. Soc. Decorated Vietnam Cross of Gallantry, USPHS Achievement Medal; recipient Merit award Boy Scouts Am., 1984, Souters Key, 1985. Mem. Am. Nurses Assn., Nebr. Nurses Assn., Balt. Commd Officers Assn. Chpt. of USPHS (nurse officers rep. 1980, vice pres. 1981), Aberdeen Area Council on Nursing (pres. 1986-87), Nat. Model Railroaders Assn., Nat. Scout Collectors Soc. Democrat. Roman Catholic. Club: Camerail (Omaha). Avocations: camping, photography, model railroading, philately. Home: 1409 S Patterson St Sioux City IA 51106

NAPOLITANO, RALPH JOSEPH, electronics industry executive; b. Chgo., Nov. 14, 1942; s. Sam Anthony and Marietta Phyllis (Pastore) N.; m. Frances Marie Koller, Sept. 27, 1965; children: Sam A., Marietta A., Ralph V. BA, Nat. Coll. Edn., 1980. Allied radio corp. Merchandise Mgr., Chgo., 1965-73; corp. dir. product mgmt. Newark Electronics, Chgo., 1973-81; sales mgr. L-Tec Inc., Itasca, Ill., 1981-85; gen. mgr. Prehler Electronics, Chgo., 1985-86; pres. Kids Closet, Inc., Roselle, Ill., 1986—. Author: (manual) Product Knowledge and Its Impact on Mktg. Results, 1980. Mem. Crusade of Mercy com. Allied Radio, Chgo., 1969. Mem. Am. Radio Relay League (numerous awards 1964-73), No. Ill. DX Assn. (pres. 1968-69). Republican. Roman Catholic. Avocation: jazz music. Home: 1503 Columbia Ct Elk Grove Village IL 60007

NARA, WILLIAM OWEN, dentist; b. Ann Arbor, Mich., Nov. 23, 1958; s. Robert Owen and Ruth Lois (Kersch) N.; m. Lorraine Sue Card, Dec. 18, 1982; children: Tyler, Tiffany. BS, Mich. tech., Houghton, 1979; DDS, U. Mich., 1983. Gen. practice dentistry Houghton, 1983—; mgr. Oramedics Internat., Houghton, 1979—. Author: How to Become Dentally Self-Sufficient, 1982, Building the $100,000 Dental Practice, 1984. Mem. Phi Kappa Phi. Lodges: Rotary (bd. dirs. Houghton chpt. 1982-86), Elks. Home and Office: 200 E Montezuma Houghton MI 49931

NARDIN, TERRY, political science educator; b. N.Y.C., Jan. 19, 1942. BA, NYU, 1963; PhD, Northwestern U., 1967. Asst. prof. polit. sci. SUNY, Buffalo, 1967-73, assoc. prof., 1973-85; prof. polit. sci., dir. univ. honors program U. Wis., Milw., 1985—. Author: Law, Morality and the Relations of States, 1983; contbr. articles to profl. publs. Rockefeller Found. humanities fellow, 1978. Mem. Am. Polit. Sci. Assn., Am. Soc. for Polit. and Legal Philosophy, Conf. for Study of Polit. Thought, Internat. Studies Assn. Office: U Wis PO Box 413 Milwaukee WI 53201

NARKO, MEDARD MARTIN, lawyer; b. Chgo., Sept. 14, 1941; s. Casimer and Stephanie (Wasylik) N.; m. Mary Kathleen Hanrahan, June 8, 1963; children—Kevin, Sue. B.S., Loyola U., 1963; J.D., Northwestern U., 1966. Bar: Ill. 1966, U.S. Dist. Ct. (no. dist.) Ill. 1967, U.S. Ct. Appeals (7th cir.) 1970. Instr., John Marshall Law Sch., Chgo., 1970-71; prof. lawyers assistance program Roosevelt U., Chgo., 1975-81; ptnr. Narko & Sonenthal, Chgo., 1974-79, Medard Narko & Assocs., Oak Forest, Ill., 1979—; arbitrator Am. Arbitration Assn., Chgo.; hearing officer Ill. Pollution Control Bd., Evanston, Civil Service Commn., Evanston, Ill. Dept. Edn., State Univ. Civil Service System. City atty. City of Oak Forest, 1985—, prosecutor City of Oak Forest, 1976-85 ; atty. Oak Forest Park Dist., 1974—, Bridgeview Park Dist., Ill., 1976-80, Midlothian Park Dist., Ill., 1983—. Contbr. articles to profl. jours. Mem. Ill. Bar Assn., Chgo. Bar Assn., Ill. Trial Lawyers Assn., Assn. Trial Lawyers Am., Ill. Mcpl. League, Nat. Inst. Mcpl. Law Officers. Lodge: Rotary. Home: 5 Equestrian Way Lemont IL 60439 Office: Medard M Narko and Assocs PC 15000 S Cicero Ave Oak Forest IL 60452

NARROW, NANCY HENTIG, lawyer; b. Chgo., May 16, 1954; d. William Hector and Geneva Jeanette (Hofer) H.; m. Steven Robert Narrow, Apr. 24, 1982; children: Megan Michelle, Timothy Charles. BA, Salem Coll., 1974; JD, Washington U., St. Louis, 1981. Bar: Mo. 1981. Asst. pub. defender State Mo., Jackson, 1981-82, pub. defender, Benton, Mo., 1983-87. Bd. dirs., chmn. fundraising WISER Inc. Women's Ctr. and Safehouse, Cape Girardeau, 1982-87. Mem. ABA, Mo. Bar Assn., Mo. Assn. Criminal Def. Lawyers, Scott County Bar Assn., Cape Girardeau County Bar Assn. Phi Delta Phi. Lutheran. Club: Zonta. Home: 718 W Rodney Cape Girardeau MO 63701 Office: Public Defender Office PO Box 429 Benton MO 63736

NARSCIUS, KAZYS, physician; b. Papile, Lithuania, Apr. 3, 1924; came to U.S., 1949, naturalized 1956; s. Jonas and MaryAnn (Jaugaite) N.; m. Caezilie Matilda Sauerborn, Dec. 8, 1962. B.S., U. Detroit, 1956; M.D., U. Bonn, Fed. Republic Germany, 1961. Diplomate Am. Bd. Family Practice. Intern McNeil Meml. Hosp., Berwyn, Ill., 1963, resident in surgery, 1963; practice medicine, Bethalto, Ill.; chief of staff St. Anthonys Hosp., Alton, Ill., 1983-85. Mem. Ill. State Med. Soc., AMA, Civil Aviation Med. Assn. Home: Fairmount Addition Alton IL 62002 Office: 117 S Prairie Bethalto IL 62010

NARY, GILBERT ROY, manufacturing executive; b. Streator, Ill.; s. Bernie M. and Irene M. (Fisher) N.; m. Doris L. Howland, Feb. 6, 1948; 1 child, Linda. BEE, U. Wis., 1949. Exec. v.p. Furnas Electric Co., Batavia, Ill., 1976—; chmn. bd. Nordic Controls, Batavia, 1981—. Trustee Mercy Ctr. Healthcare, Aurora, Ill., 1980—, Furnas Found. Inc., Batavia, 1976—; bd. dirs. Aurora Found. Republican. Presbyterian. Avocations: travel, gardening, reading. Home: 327 S Rosedale Aurora IL 60506 Office: Furnas Electric Co 1000 McKee St Batavia IL 60510

NASBY, CHARLES LELAND, JR., construction supply company executive; b. Mpls., Dec. 11, 1928; s. Charles Leland and Esther (Fjeldstad) N.; m. Patricia Ann Ree, July 18, 1953; children—Gregory Charles, Timothy Arthur. B.A., St. Olaf Coll., Minn., 1951; postgrad. U. Minn., 1951-52. Cert. profl. engr., Minn. With Ceco Corp., Mpls., 1953-70, asst. mgr., 1965-70; pres., treas. dir. Charles Nasby Assocs., Inc., Mpls., 1970—, Span-Dock, Inc., Mpls., 1977—. Served with USNR, 1953-56. Vice chmn. bd. dirs. Ebenezer Soc., Mpls., 1968—; pres. Lutheran Ch. Good Shephard, 1982. Mem. Mpls. Builders Exchange (pres. 1981, bd. dirs. 1976—), ASCE, Minn. Soc. Profl. Engrs., Constrn. Specifications Inst. (sec. 1981), Comml. Constrn. Industries. Republican. Clubs: Edina Country, Torske Klubben, Rotary. Patentee in field. Home: 4624 Bruce Ave Minneapolis MN 55424 Office: 5300 Excelsior Blvd Minneapolis MN 55416

NASH, KENNETH LAVERNE, research chemist; b. Joliet, Ill., July 6, 1950; s. Ralph LeVerne and Mae Rose (Gregorash) N.; m. Robin Nash; children: Aaron, Brett. B.A., Lewis U., 1972; M.S., Fla. State U., 1975, Ph.D., 1979. Research asst. Fla. State U., Tallahassee, 1972-75, 1976-79; research chemist Dow Chem. Co., Placquemine, La., 1975-76, U.S. Geol. Survey, Denver, 1981-86; chemist Argonne (Ill.) Nat. Lab., 1979-81, 1986—; cons. in field. Contbr. numerous articles to sci. jours. Mem. Am. Chem. Soc. (co-sponsor of symposium for 1985 meeting), AAAS, Am. Nuclear Soc. Democrat. Office: Argonne Nat Lab Chemistry Div 9700 S Cass Ave Argonne IL 60439

NASH, PATRICK JAMES, real estate executive, lawyer; b. Kansas City, Mo., Apr. 21, 1941; s. Frank Casper and Thelma Jean (Carlson) N.; m. Marcia Ann Murello, Mar. 11, 1965 (div. Apr. 1982); children: David A., Daniel P.; m. Karen Jean Gottsche, May 29, 1982; stepchildren: Benjamin S. Gound, Julie Kay Gound. BS in Biology, U. Mo., Kansas City, 1963, JD, 1966. Bar: Mo. 1966, U.S. Supreme Ct. 1978. Asst. v.p., trust officer Kansas City Bank & Trust, 1966-69; mgr. comml. property J.C. Nichols Co., Kansas City, 1969-78; pres. Global Internat. Airways Corp., Kansas City, 1978-80, Windsor Internat., Inc., Kansas City, 1980-81; v.p. leasing Crown Ctr. Redevel. Corp., Kansas City, 1981—. Active United Way campaign, 1966-72; mem. petition com. Jackson County Home Rule, 1968-69, Downtown Council Spl. Events Com.; bd. dirs. Downtown Inc., 1984-86, Greater Kansas City Housing, Inc., 1974-77; trustee U. Kansas City, 1970-71. Mem. Mo. Bar Assn., Kansas City Bar Assn., Urban Land Inst. (assoc.), Kans. City Real Estate Bd., Mo. Real Estate Assn., Bldg. Owners and Mgr. Assn. (pres. 1978, 84), Nat. Assn. Corp. Real Estate Execs. (pres. 1985-87), Univ. Mo. Kansas City Nat. Alumni Assn. (bd. dirs. 1966-71, pres. 1970-71). Lodge: Rotary. Avocations: tennis, golf, swimming, astronomy. Home: 2504 W 120th Terr Leawood KS 66209 Office: Crown Center Redevel Corp 2440 Pershing Rd Kansas City MO 64108

NASH, RICHARD MARK, minister; b. Detroit, May 1, 1958; s. Richard Taylor and Joyce Elaine (Jansen) N.; m. Elizabeth Keller, June 21, 1980. BA in History cum laude, Harvard U., 1980; ThM, Dallas Theol. Seminary, 1985. Ordained minister Free Will Bapt. Ch., 1985. Instr. in lay inst. Dallas Theol. Seminary, 1983; prof. Free Will Bapt. Bible Coll., Nashville, 1985; minister of Christian edn. Cen. Free Will Bapt. Ch., Royal Oak, Mich., 1986-87; assoc. pastor for adult edn. Community Ch. of Greenwood, Ind., 1987—; curriculum writer Randall House, Nashville, 1985-86, cons., 1985; tchr. Free Will Bapt. teen summer camp, Brighton, Mich., 1986. Contbr. articles to profl. jours. Named One of Outstanding Young Men of Am., 1979, 80. Mem. Wolverine Assn. of Free Will Bapts. Avocations: shortwave radio, computers, internat. affairs, classical music, reading. Office: Community Church of Greenwood 1477 W Main St Greenwood IN 46142

NASH, STEPHEN MICHAEL, chemist, hazardous materials compliance representative; b. Spencer, Ind., Jan. 24, 1947; s. William Christian Nash and Juanita (Brown) Foley; m. Deanna Faye Wood, Mar. 29, 1983; children: Christopher Jon and Brian Michael (twins). BS in Chemistry, Ind. U., 1969; MS in Chemistry, Purdue U., Indpls., 1972. Tech. assoc. Lilly Research Labs., Indpls., 1968-69, assoc. organic chemist, 1969-73, organic chemist, 1973-78, asst. sr. organic chemist, 1978-80; hazardous materials compliance rep. Eli Lilly & Co., Indpls., 1980—; advisor Chemtrec, Washington, 1985—; bd. dirs. Hazardous Materials Adv. Council, Washington, 1986—. Contbr. articles to profl. jours.; patentee in field. Fellow Am. Inst. Chemists; mem. AAAS, Am. Chem. Soc. Avocations: skiing, golf. Office: Eli Lilly and Co Lilly Corp Ctr Indianapolis IN 46285

NASSAU, ROBERT HAMILL, manufacturing company executive; b. Plainfield, N.J., Nov. 30, 1941; s. Charles Francis and Helen (Hudson) N.; m. AnnRae Falicki, July 13, 1968; children: Aimee, Robbie, Rebecca. A.B., Dartmouth Coll., 1963, M.B.A., 1964. Fin. analyst Ford Motor World Hdqrs., Dearborn, Mich., 1964-67; with (Ford Tractor), Troy, Mich., 1967-72; mgr. market and product analysis (Ford Tractor), 1971-72; asst. controller N.Am. truck ops. Ford Motor Co., Dearborn, 1972-73; agrl. product planning mgr. Ford Tractor, Troy, 1973-76; gen. sales mgr. overseas direct markets Ford Tractor, 1976-78; gen. mgr. Ford Tractor Intercontinental Ops., 1979-80; sr. v.p. mktg. and corp. planning J.I. Case Co., Racine, Wis., 1980-82, exec. v.p. worldwide agrl. ops., 1982; pres., chief exec. officer Am. Hoist & Derrick Co., St. Paul, 1982—, also dir.; bd. dirs. Polaris Industries, Inc.; dir. First Bank Systems Met. Bd. Bd. dirs. St. Thomas Grad. Sch. Bus.; mem. Young Pres.'s Orgn. Republican. Congregationalist. Clubs: Minnesota, St. Paul Athletic, Minikahda Country. Home: 260 S Mississippi River Blvd Saint Paul MN 55105 Office: Am Hoist and Derrick Co 1800 Amhoist Tower Saint Paul MN 55102

NASSTROM, ROY RICHARD, educational administration educator; b. Oakland, Calif., Oct. 28, 1930; s. Roy Richard and Edith Dolores (Spilman) N., m. Sally Louise Shaw, Aug. 29, 1964; children—Karen, Eric. B.A., U. Calif.-Berkeley, 1956, M.A., 1964, Ph.D., 1971. Asst. to supt. Ravenswood Sch. Dist., East Palo Alto, Calif., 1964-65; acting instr. edn. U. Calif.-Berkeley, 1965-68; asst. prof. ednl. adminstrn. U. Ky., Lexington, 1969-70; asst. prof. edn. Purdue U., West Lafayette, Ind., 1971-76; asst. grad. dean Winona State U., Minn., 1976-77, prof., chmn. ednl. adminstrn. dept., 1976—; cons., speaker various orgns. and schs., 1969—. Mem. editorial bd. Ednl. Administrn. Abstracts, 1976-83, AASA Professor, 1979-82; manuscript reviewer Edn. Researcher, 1983—. Contbr. articles to profl. jours. Served as cpl. U.S. Army, 1952-54. Recipient numerous grants, 1969-86. Mem. Midwest Council Ednl. Adminstrn., Am. Ednl. Research Assn. (paper reviewer 1983—), Am. Assn. Sch. Adminstrs., Nat. Conf. Profs. of Ednl. Adminstrn., Phi Delta Kappa, Pi Sigma Alpha. Avocations: photography, bicycling. Home: 1702 Edgewood Rd Winona MN 55987 Office: Winona State U Dept Ednl Adminstrn Winona MN 55987

NASTAS, THOMAS DENNIS, corporate executive, entrepreneur; b. Detroit, June 26, 1949; s. George II and Stella (Bierut) N.; m. Vickie Lee Bolema, Aug. 14, 1982; 1 child, Danielle Ann. BA, Mich. State U., 1971, MBA, 1973. Product devel. engr. Ford Motor Co., Dearborn, Mich., 1972-73; cons. East Lansing, Mich., 1973-78; product planning mgr. Multifastener Corp., Detroit, 1978-82; pres., founder Innovative Ventures, Inc., Lansing, Mich., 1982—; chief exec. officer Mich. Product Devel. Corp., Detroit, 1986—; instr. mtkg. Mich. State U., 1978-82, Oakland U., Rochester, Mich., 1983. Mem. Bus. for Blanchard Com., Lansing, 1986. Avocations: swimming, running, bodybuilding. Office: Innovative Ventures Inc 5514 Central Circle Lansing MI 48911

NATELLO, GREGORY WILLIAM, physician; b. Darby, Pa., Mar. 30, 1954; s. Americo Vespucci and Catherine (Logan) N. AB in Biology, Gettysburg COll., 1976; DO, Phila. Coll. Osteo. Medicine, 1980. Diplomate Nat. Bd. Examiners Osteo. Physicians and Surgeons, Am. Bd. Internal Medicine. Intern Detroit Osteopathic Hosp., 1980-81; gen. practice medicine Pennsauken, N.J., 1981-82; resident in internal medicine Cleve. Clinic Found., 1982-85; fellow in geriatrics Case Western Res. U. Sch. Medicine, Cleve., 1985-86; assoc. in cardiovascular diseases U. Ala., Birmingham, 1986—; instr. physical diagnosis sch. medicine Case Western Res. U., 1984-85. Recipient award of Merit for Outstanding Achievement, Detroit Osteo. Hosp., 1981, Disting. Sr. Pres. award Cleve. Clinic Found., 1985. Mem. AMA, Am. Coll. Physicians (affiliate), Am. Coll. Chest Physicians, Phila. Coll. Osteopathic Medicine Alumni Assn. (life), Eisenhower Soc. Gettysburg, Phi Kappa Psi. Republican. Roman Catholic.

NATHANSON, SAUL DAVID, surgical oncologist, surgical investigator; b. Johannesburg, South Africa, Dec. 12, 1943; came to U.S., 1975; s. Hyman Barnett and Freda Charlotte (Weinberg) N.; m. Maxine Elaine Zacks, Nov. 29, 1966 (div. 1978); children: Laurence Cecil, Joshua Russel; m. Jerrilyn Marie Burke, Feb. 18, 1979; children: Abigail Mary, Alison Megan. MD, U. Witwatersrand, South Africa, 1966. Diplomate Am. Bd. Surgery. Intern U. Pretoria, South Africa, 1967; lectr. human anatomy U. Witwatersrand, 1968, resident in surgery, 1969-74; postdoctoral fellow in immunology UCLA, 1975-77, postdoctoral fellow in surgery, oncology, 1977-80; chief resident in surgery U. Calif.-Davis, Sacramento, 1980-82; dir. surg. research Henry Ford Hosp., Detroit, 1982—, surg. oncologist, 1982—; clin. assoc. prof. U. Mich., Herndon prof. investigative oncology, 1985—. Contbr. numerous articles to profl. jours. Ford Found. grantee, 1982, NIH grantee, 1987—. Fellow Am. Coll. Surgeons, 1987—. Mem. ACS, Am. Soc. Clin. Oncology, Am. Assn. Cancer Research, Am. Assn. Acad. Surgeons, Mich. Soc. Med. Research (bd. dirs. 1984—), Detroit Surg. Assn., AAAS, Wayne County Med. Soc., Earl F. Wolfman, Jr. Surg. Soc., South West Oncology Group, Royal Coll. Surgeons of Edinburgh, N.Y. Acad. Scis., Med. Assn. S. Africa. Republican. Jewish. Avocations: photography, classical music. Office: 2799 W Grand Blvd Detroit MI 48202

NAU, H. GENE, department store company executive. Pres., chief exec. officer Famous-Barr Co., St. Louis. Office: Famous-Barr Co 601 Olive St Saint Louis MO 63101 *

NAUERT, ROGER CHARLES, health care consultant; b. St. Louis, Jan. 6, 1943; s. Charles Henry and Vilma Amelia (Schneider) N.; B.S., Mich. State U., 1965; J.D., Northwestern U., 1969; M.B.A., U. Chgo., 1979; m. Elaine Louise Harrison, Feb. 18, 1967; children—Paul, Christina. Bar: Ill. 1969. Asst. atty. gen. State of Ill., 1969-71; chief counsel Ill. Legis. Investigating Commn., 1971-73; asst. state comptroller State of Ill., 1973-77; dir. adminstrn. and fin. Health and Hosps. Governing Commn. Cook County, Chgo., 1977-79; nat. dir. health care services Grant Thornton, Chgo., 1979—; vis. lectr. health adminstrn. Vanderbilt U.; vis. lectr. econs., fin. and health U. Chgo., 1978—; preceptor Wharton Sch., U. Pa., cons. health care mktg. Am. Mktg. Assn., 1977—. Fin. commr. Village of Bloomingdale (Ill.). Ford Found. grantee, 1968-69. Mem. Am. Hosp. Assn., Am. Public Health Assn., Am. Coll. Hosp. Adminstrs., Am. Assn. Healthcare Cons., Nat. Health Lawyers Assn., State Bar Ill., Health Care Fin. Mgmt. Assn. (faculty mem.), Alpha Phi Sigma, Phi Delta Phi, Delta Upsilon. Clubs: Plaza, LaGrange Country. Author: The Comptroller—Illinois' Chief Fiscal Control Officer, 1976; A Sociology of Health, 1977; The Demography of Illness, 1978; Proposal for a National Health Policy, 1979; Health Care Feasibility Studies, 1980; Health Care Planning Guide, 1981; Health Care Strategic Planning, 1982; Overcoming the Obstacles to Planning, 1983; Principles of Hospital Cash Management, 1984; Healthcare Networking Arrangements, 1985; Strategic Planning for Physicians, 1986; HMO's: A Once and Future Strategy, 1987. Home: 6505 Cherokee Dr Indian Head Park IL 60525 Office: 6th Floor Prudential Plaza Chicago IL 60601

NAULT, JAMES EDWARD, psychologist, educator; b. Milw., June 23, 1930; s. Howard J. and Lora L. (Rapp) N.; m. Christine Curro, June 8, 1968; children—Michael, Andrew, Matthew. B.S., U. Wis.-Milw., 1956; M.S., U. Wis.-Madison, 1958; Ph.D., Iowa State U., 1978. Lic. psychologist, Wis. Tchr. spl. edn. Milw. pub. schs., 1956-57; counselor Marquette U. Guidance Clinic, 1959-60; dir. guidance, sch. psychologist Franklin pub. schs., Milw., 1960-61; mgr. agy. and spl. services, psychologist, Milw. Area Tech. Coll., 1961—, admissions officer, 1985—, counselor, psychologist, 1986—; cons. in field; pvt. practice psychology. Active Milwaukee County council Boy Scouts Am., 1978—. Served with USAF, 1948-49, 50-51. Mem. Am. Psychol. Assn., Wis. Psychol. Assn., Amway Distbrs. Assn., Am. Legion. Club: St. Josephs Athletic. Office: 1015 N 6th St Milwaukee WI 53203

NAUMOFF, NORMAND STAN REXFORD, diagnostic imager; b. Detroit, July 4, 1931; s. Stan Lexos-Naum and Vasilka Demetra (Juguloff) N.; divorced; children: Stan, Maya. AB, U. Mich., 1953, MD, 1956. Diplomate Am. Bd. Radiology, Am. Bd. Nuclear Medicine. Commd. ensign USN, 1953, advanced through grades to; commd. 2d lt. USMC, 1957, advanced through grades to, resigned, 1966; intern Albert Einstein Meml. Hosp. Ctr., Yeshiva U., N.Y.C., 1956-57; resident in radiology U. Chgo. Clinics, 1957-59, Cook County Gen. Hosp., Chgo., 1959-60; served as chmn. radiological dept. various hosps., 1960-75; chief of radiology, nuclear medicine and sonography US VA Hosp., Iron Mountain, Mich., 1975-77; staff radiologist Christ Hosp., Oaklawn, Ill., 1977-80; chmn. diagnostic imaging Am. Internat. Hosp. and Clinics, 1980-83, vice chief of staff, 1981-82, chief of staff, 1982-83; mem. staff Lake Mich. Physicians, Inc.; cons. KRON Med. Corp., 1983—; past instr. U. Chgo., Harvard U., Wayne U. Coll. Medicine; presenter to various assns. Contbr. articles to profl. jours. Global Physicians fellow, 1966, post-doctoral fellow Northwestern U., Loyola U., MIT, Harvard U., U. Chgo., U. Calif.; recipient numerous awards and honors. Mem. AMA, Am. Coll. Radiology, Am. Soc. Nuclear Medicine, Am. Coll. Diagnostic Imaging, Radiol. Soc. N.Am., Roentgen Ray Soc., Underseas Med. Soc., Helium-Oxygne Soc., Ill. Med. Soc., Mass. Med. Soc., Mich. Med. Soc., Wayne County Med. Soc., Chgo. Med. Soc., Chelsea Med. Soc., Fellowship Global Physicians (N.Am. Council), Sigma Soc. Advancement Sci., Soc. of NMR in Medicine. Avocation: archeology of Balkans.

NAUNAS, THOMAS ASH, TV sound producer; b. Bloomsburg, Pa., Sept. 5, 1951; s. Robert Ash and Jeanne Rae (DuBois) N. BA in Religious Studies, Pa. State U., 1973; MA in South Asian Studies, U. Wis., 1975. Videographer U. Wis. Labs for Recorded Instrn., Madison, 1977-79; sound producer Sta. WHA-TV Pub. Broadcasting System, Madison, 1976—. Composer electronic music, 1973—; sound producer films Joe McCarthy: An American Ism (Columbia/DuPont Journalism award 1979), The War At Home, 1980; electronic soundtrack composer Frame of Mind, 1985, Blood Hook, 1986. Mem. World Wildlife Fund, Washington, 1985—. Recipient

Best Documentary Photography award Milw. Press Club, 1982; Nat. Endowment for Humanities fellow, 1974, 78; grantee Dane County Cultural Affairs Commn., 1984, Wis. Arts Bd. grantee 1985. Mem. ACLU, Am. Film Inst., Nat. Geographics Soc., Am. Mus. Natural History. Home: 2213 Sommers Ave Madison WI 53704

NAVIDZADEH, DOROTHY JEAN, social worker; b. Harrisville, Ohio, Mar. 26, 1928; d. Craig L. and Leona S. (Gillogly) Seebirt; m. Buick Navidzadeh, Feb. 16, 1962 (div. Feb. 1980); 1 child, Naasar Allan. BS in Social Adminstrn., Ohio State U., 1950; MSW, U. Mich., 1960. Clin. social worker Saginaw (Mich.) Valley Cons. Ctr., 1962-64; chief clin. social worker Bay Area Guidance Ctr., Bay City, Mich., 1964-68; sch. social worker Bay Area Intermediate Sch. Dist., Bay City, 1968—; assoc. clin. social worker Delta Family Clinic, Bay City, 1976-82, Bay Psychol. Assn., Bay City, 1982—; field instr. Mich. State U., East Lansing, 1970-85, U. Mich., Ann Arbor, 1965-84, Saginaw Valley State Coll., University Center, Mich., 1980—; instr. U. Mich., 1976-80, Delta Coll., University Center, 1965-70. Mem. adv. council social work program Saginaw Valley State Coll., parent adv. council Bay Area Intermediate Sch. Dist., community mental health adv. council Bay Area Community Mental Health Council, Bay-Arenac Community Mental Health Bd.; chmn. bd. dirs. Coordination Runaway Youth, Bay City. Mem. Nat. Assn. Social Workers (cert., diplomate). Avocation: cooking. Home: 2981 Lupine Dr Bay City MI 48706 Office: Bay Psychol Assocs 200 S Wenona Bay City MI 48706

NAWARA, BRUCE GERARD, accountant; b. Chgo., Jan. 15, 1957; s. Ted F. and Caroline B. (Bajzer) N.; m. Dorothea E. Antonaitis, May 14, 1983; 1 child, Stephen G. BA in Acctg., Lewis U., 1979; MS in Taxation, DePaul U., 1985. CPA, Ill. Tas supr. Coopers & Lybrand, Chgo., 1979-84; tax mgr., asst. controller W.F. Hall subs. Mobil Oil, Itasca, Ill., 1984-85; tax mgr. Comdisco, Inc., Rosemont, Ill., 1985-87, dir. tax, personnel and data processing European ops., 1987—. Mem. Am. Inst. CPA's, Ill. CPA Soc., Nat. Assn. Accts., Inst. Cert. Mgmt. Accts. Republican. Roman Catholic. Club: Chgo. Tax. Avocation: physical fitness. Home: 5844 S Melvina Ave Chicago IL 60638 Office: Comdisco Inc 6400 Shafer Ct Rosemont IL 60018

NAWROCKI, PAUL JOHN, accountant, financial executive; b. Detroit, Dec. 12, 1959; s. Alexander A. and Alvera (DiMambro) N. BBA, Western Mich. U., 1982; postgrad. in bus. adminstrn., Ind. U. CPA. Sr. mgmt., chief exec. officer Wayne County, Detroit, 1986; sr. acct. Ernst & Whinney, Detroit, 1982-85, mgr., 1986—. Supr. Vol. Income Tax Assistance, Detroit, 1984; fin. supr. Lucas for Gov. Campaign, Detroit, 1986. Western Mich. U. scholar, 1979, 81. Mem. Am. Inst. CPA's, Mich. Assn. CPA's, Health Car Fin. Mgmt. Assn., Beta Alpha Psi, Beta Gamma Sigma. Club: Western Mich. U. Fin. (Kalamazoo)(officer 1980-81). Home: 28368 Besmore Dr Warren MI 48093-2601

NAYLOR, GEORGE LEROY, lawyer, railroad executive; b. Bountiful, Utah, May 11, 1915; s. Joseph Francis and Josephine Chase (Wood) N.; student U. Utah, 1934-36; student George Washington U., 1937; J.D. (Bancroft Whitney scholar), U. San Francisco, 1953; m. Maxine Elizabeth Lewis, Jan. 18, 1941; children—Georgia Naylor Price, RoseMaree Naylor Hammer, George LeRoy II. Admitted to Calif. bar, 1954, Ill. bar, 1968; v.p., sec., legis. rep. Internat. Union of Mine, Mill & Smelter Workers, CIO, Dist. Union 2, Utah-Nevada, 1942-44; examiner So. Pacific Co., San Francisco, 1949-54, chief examiner, 1955, asst. mgr., 1956-61; carrier mem. Nat. R.R. Adjustment Bd., Chgo., 1961-77, chmn., 1970-77; atty. Village of Fox River Valley Gardens, Ill., 1974-77; practice law, legal cons., Ill. and Calif., 1977—; gen. counsel for Can-Veyor, Inc., Mountain View, Calif., 1959-64; adj. instr. dept. mgmt. U. West Fla., 1981. Served with AUS, World War II. Mem. ABA, Ill. Bar Assn., Calif. Bar Assn., Chgo. Bar Assn., San Francisco Bar Assn. Mormon. Author: Defending Carriers Before the NRAB and Public Law Boards, 1969, Choice Morsels in Tax and Property Law, 1966, Underground at Bingham Canyon, 1944; National Railroad Adjustment Board Practice Manual, 1978. Home: Rural Rt #1 Box 255 Monticello IL 61856 Office: Round Barn Station PO Box 6323 Champaign IL 61821-8323 also: 2976 Camargo Ct San Jose CA 95132

NAYLOR, ROBERT EARLE, lawyer; b. Conneaut, Ohio, Feb. 13, 1947; s. Robert Frank and Dorothy Leona (Barringer) N.; m. Christine Marie Thayer, July 11, 1970; children—Jonathan, Nancy, Tarry, Jill, Christa. B.A., Case Western Res. U., 1969, J.D., 1972. Bar: Ohio 1972, U.S. Dist. Ct. (no. dist.) Ohio 1973. Asst. pros. atty. Ashtabula County, Ohio, 1972; ptnr. Thayer & Naylor, 1972—; law dir. City of Conneaut, 1973-84; dir. Am. Turned Products; ptnr. Lake Erie Investors Co., 1976—. Fellow Ohio State Bar Found.; mem. Ohio Bar Assn., Ashtabula County Bar Assn., Sons of Legionaires, Jaycees. Democrat. Club: Exchange. Lodge: Elks. Home: 915 Lincoln Dr Conneaut OH 44030 Office: Thayer & Naylor 171 Broad St Conneaut OH 44030

NAYMIK, JAMES JOHN, process design engineer; b. Youngstown, Ohio, July 9, 1946; s. Joseph and Mary (Petrisin) N. B.S.M.T., Cleve. State U., 1974; M.B.A., Baldwin Wallace U., 1977. Project engr. Davy McKee Corp., Cleve., 1974-82; application engr. AGA Gas, Inc., Cleve., 1982-83; cons. traffic accident reconstrn., Cleve., 1983-84; sr. process design engr. Clevite Industries, Inc., 1984—. Served to cpl. USMC, 1968-70. Mem. ASME, Soc. Automotive Engrs. Eastern Orthodox. Home and Office: 6614 Crossview Rd Cleveland OH 44131

NAZARINI, ROBERT PETER, corporate professional; b. Youngstown, Ohio, July 4, 1943; s. Nicholas Stephen and Lucille (Marinelli) N.; m. Rosemary Keller, Aug. 12, 1967; children: Mark, Jill. BA, John Carroll U., 1965, MA, 1972; Mba, Case Western Reserve U., 1986. Ops. mgr. Higbees, Cleve., 1969-72; personnel mgr. V.I.P. div. Caron Internat., Reading, Pa., 1972-73; ops. mgr. O'Neils, Akron, Ohio, 1973-76; v.p. retail stores Burrows, Cleve., 1976-79; pres. Dial Industries, Cleve., 1980—. Home: 10150 Sherman Rd Chardon OH 44024 Office: Dial Industries 5040 Corbin Dr Cleveland OH 44128

NAZOS, DEMETRI ELEFTHERIOS, obstetrician, gynecologist; b. Mykonos, Greece, July 20, 1949; came to U.S., 1967, naturalized, 1983; s. Eleftherios D. and Anousso (Grypari) N.; m. Dorothea A. Lazarides, Dec. 3, 1977; children—Anna D., Elliot D. B.S., Loyola U., Chgo., 1971; M.D., U. Athens, 1976. Diplomate Am. Bd. Ob-Gyn. Intern U. Athens Hosps., 1975-76; resident Harper Grace Hosp., Wayne State U., Detroit, 1976-80; practice medicine specializing in ob-gyn., Livonia, Mich., 1980-81, Joliet, Ill., 1981—; mem. staff St. Joseph Med. Ctr., Silver Cross Hosp. Sustaining mem. Rep. Nat. Com. Presdl. Task Force. Fellow Am. Coll. Ob-Gyn., Am. Fertility Soc., mem. Royal Soc. Medicine-Eng., AMA, Greek Med. Assn., Am. Assn. Laparoscopists, Ill. Med. Assn., Southeastern Surg. Soc. Mich., Will-Grundy County Med. Soc., Nat. Rifle Assn., Ill. State Rifle Assn. Club: Senatorial. Greek Orthodox. Lodge: Rotary. Avocations: photography; hunting; gun collecting. Home: 608 E Palladium Dr Joliet IL 60435 Office: 330 N Madison St Joliet IL 60435

NEABLING, SUSAN MARIE, office and school supply company executive, bookstore administrator; b. Milw., Apr. 5, 1947; d. William J. and Eleanor C. (Schmidt) Schlapman; m. Roland L. Neabling, July 19, 1969; children—Ryan Louis, Robyn Lynn. B.A., U. Wis.-Oshkosh, 1969. Research analyst U. Wis.-Oshkosh, 1969-70, supply mgr. Univ. Bookstore, 1970-77, dir., 1977—; pres., owner Atlas Office & Sch. Supply, Inc., Neenah, Wis., 1980—; retail cons., 1980—. Chmn. parish edn. com. Grace Lutheran Ch., Winchester, Wis., 1977-80; mem. adv. bd. Luth. Campus Ministry, 1980-82; bd. dirs., exec. com. Future Neenah Devel. Corp, 1986—; pres.-elect Downtown Neenah Action Com., 1985-87, pres. 1987—. Mem. Nat. Assn. Coll. Stores (various coms.), Wis. Assn. Coll. Stores (pres. 1975-78). Republican. Office: Univ Bookstore U Wis Oshkosh WI 54901

NEAL, CHARLOTTE ANNE, ednl. adminstr.; b. Hampton, Iowa, May 8, 1937; d. Sebo and Marion Bradford (Boutin-Clock) Reysack; B.A., U. No. Iowa, 1958; M.Ed., DePaul U. (Chgo.), 1966; postgrad. No. Ill. U.; m. Paul Gordon Neal, Mar. 29, 1969; children—Rachel Elizabeth, Kory Bradford. Tchr., 4th grade, Des Moines Ind. Sch. Dist., 1958-59; tchr., 3d grade Glenview (Ill.) Pub. Schs., 1959-61, tchr. 3d grade, psychol. ednl. diagnostic Schaumburg Dist. Schs., Hoffman Estates, Ill., 1961-69; supr. learning disabilities and behavior disorders Springfield (Ill.) Pub. Schs., 1969-73; psychoednl. diagnostician Barrington (Ill.) Sch. Dist. 220, 1973-77; ednl. strategist Area Edn. Agy. 7, Cedar Falls, Iowa, 1978—; ednl. cons. Spl. Edn. Dist. Lake County, Gurnee, Ill., summer, 1968. Certified K-14 teaching and supervising in guidance, counseling, elementary supervisory K-9, elementary K-9 teaching, spl. K-12 learning disabilities. Mem. NEA, Ill. Edn. Assn. Author: Handbook for Learning Disabilities Tchrs., 1971. Home: 1102 Sunset Dr Parkersburg IA 50665 Office: 3712 Cedar Hts Dr Cedar Falls IA 50613

NEAL, JAMES THOMAS, publishing educator; b. Lebanon, Ind., Jan. 5, 1921; s. Ralph Bowman and Mary Josephine (Honan) N.; m. Georgianne Davis, June 3, 1953; children: Anne deHayden, Neal Petri, Andrea Davis Neal Schmelzer. BJ, Butler U., 1942; BS in Mil. Engring., U.S. Mil. Acad., 1945. Commd. 2d lt. U.S. Army, 1945, advanced through grades to 1st lt., 1948, resigned, 1949; editor Noblesville (Ind.) Ledger, 1949-70, pub., 1970-85; prof., chmn. dept. journalism Butler U., Indpls., 1985—. Sec. Ind. Rep. State Com., Indpls., 1957-68, chmn., 1972-73; mem. Rep. Nat. Com., Washington, 1972-73, 79-84. Recipient Disting. Service in Journalism award Ball State U., 1966. Roman Catholic. Clubs; Englewood Golf and Country (Fla.); Dramatic, Players (Indpls.). Home: 7670 E 126th St Noblesville IN 46060 Office: Butler U 4600 Sunset Ave Indianapolis IN 46208

NEAL, JUDSON SHELLY, home oxygen therapy equipment sales and marketing executive; b. Kansas City, June 5, 1947; s. John Roy and Jewell Bess (Cartland) N.; m. Stephanie Marie Neal, June 7, 1968 (div. Apr. 1978); 1 son, Scott Judson; m. Linda Kathleen Neal, Feb. 16, 1980; 1 daughter, Michelle Nicole. B.S. in Bus. Adminstrn., U. Mo., 1969; M.B.A., Rockhurst Coll., 1982. With Puritan Bennett Corp., Overland Park, Ks., 1973—, mgr. adminstrv. services, 1982-83, nat. sales mgr., 1983, group mktg. mgr., 1983-87, group mktg. and sales mgr. Mem. Bd. Edn. Holy Cross Lutheran Sch., Kansas City, 1982—. Mem. Delta Sigma Pi. Republican. Lutheran. Home: 11120 W 121st Terr Overland Park KS 66213 Office: Puritan Bennett Corp 10800 Pflumm Rd Lenexa KS 66215

NEAL, STERLING, city official; b. Cleve., Aug. 30; s. Thurman and Margaret Neal; m. Willie R. Ford, Aug. 7, 1982; children—Otis, Rickey, Cecilia, Wanda, Taunja, Youlanda. Police Tng. Course, Western Res. U., 1970; student in Comml. Law, Bus. and Ins., U. MEDC, 1976, also student in Bus. Procedure, Payroll and Taxes, 1977. Lic. Class A investigator, Ohio; FCC lic. Class C and D transmitters. Dir. security Cuyahoga Bur. Investigation Inc., Cleve., 1973-83, chief of police, 1983—; dir. nat. sales CBI Wholesalers & Distbrs., 1979-82, dir. adminstrn., 1981-83. Bd. dirs. Kinsman Opportunity Ctr., 1976, mem. adv. bd., adminstrn. dir., outreach chmn. Served with U.S. Army, 1960-62. Recipient awards Ohio Bur. Employment Services, 1979, 83. Mem. Nat. SBA, Internat. Police Congress (spl. agt. Washington). Lodge: Masons, Shriners. Home: 9203 Bessemer Ave Cleveland OH 44104 Office: 4900 Euclid Ave 206 Cleveland OH 44103

NEARMYER, LARRY EDWARD, rubber company executive, engineer; b. Nevada, Mo., Sept. 23, 1940; s. Lawrence Ivan and Ruth J. (Heilman) N.; m. Mignon Lynam, Aug. 30, 1963; children: Genevieve Louise, Chariss Anne. AA, Parsons (Kans.) Jr. Coll., 1959; BS MechE, So. Meth. U., 1963; MBA, Gannon U., 1975. Registered profl. engr., Ohio. Mfg. engr. Gen. Electric Co., Erie, Pa., 1969-76; mgr. mfg. engring. Gen. Electric Co., São Paulo, Brazil, 1976-78; mgr. quality control Gen. Electric Co., Ft. Wayne, Ind., 1978-79; mgr. mfg. engring. Johnson Controls, Milw., 1979-80; gen. mgr. ops. Sifco Custom Machine, Mpls., 1980-84; plant mgr. Hiawatha Rubber Co., Mpls., 1984—. Mem. Am. Inst. Indsl. Engrs. (sr.). Republican. Avocations: photography, woodworking, duplicate bridge. Home: 2120 Fountain Ln Plymouth MN 55447 Office: Hiawatha Rubber Co 1700 67th Ave Brooklyn Center MN 55430

NEAVOLL, GEORGE FRANKLIN, newspaper editor; b. Lebanon, Oreg., Aug. 20, 1938; s. Jesse Hunter and Mazie Maude (Meyer) N.; m. Laney Lila Hunter Hough, June 21, 1969. BS, U. Oreg., 1965. Reporter, photographer Lebanon Express, 1969-70; state editor Idaho State Jour., Pocatello, 1970-72; editorial writer The Jour.-Gazette, Ft. Wayne, Ind., 1972-75, Detroit Free Press, 1975-78; editorial page editor The Wichita (Kans.) Eagle-Beacon, 1978—. Vol. Peace Corps, India, 1967-69. Recipient Idaho Press Club Achievement award, 1972, Edward J. Meeman award Scripps-Howard Found., 1973, Honor Roll award, Izaak Walton League Am., 1974. Mem. Inter Am. Press Assn. (bd. dirs. 1985—, Jamaica Daily Gleaner award 1985), Am. Soc. Newspaper Editors, Nat. Conf. Editorial Writers, Soc. Profl. Journalists, Nat. Press Club. Episcopalian. Club: The Wichita. Home: 312 N Broadview Wichita KS 67208 Office: The Wichita Eagle-Beacon PO Box 820 Wichita KS 67201

NEBEL, RICHARD ANDREW, II., architectural engineer; b. Sturgeon Bay, Wis., Oct. 24, 1956; s. Richard Andrew Sr. and Anita Margaret (Hickey) N.; m. Carla Anne Selvick, June 2, 1984; 1 child, Richard Andrew III. BS, Milw. Sch. Engring., 1974-78. Registered profl. engr., Wis. Engr. Nebel Constrn., Sturgeon Bay, 1978-82; prin. R.A. Nebel II Engring., Sturgeon Bay, 1982—. Republican. Lodge: Elks (exalted ruler Sturgeon Bay club 1984-86). Avocations: hunting, fishing, skiing, scuba diving, flying. Office: 3625 N Duluth Ave Sturgeon Bay WI 54235

NEBENZAHL, KENNETH, rare book and map dealer; b. Far Rockaway, N.Y., Sept. 16, 1927; s. Meyer and Ethel (Levin) N.; m. Jocelyn Hart Spitz, Feb. 7, 1953; children: Kenneth (dec.), Patricia Suzanne Nebenzahl Frish, Margaret Spitz Nebenzahl Quintong, Suzanne Spitz Nebenzahl Nichol. Student, Columbia U., 1947-48; L.H.D. (hon.), Coll. William and Mary, 1983. Solicitor new bus. United Factors Corp., N.Y.C., 1947-50; sales rep. Fromm & Sichel, Inc., N.Y.C., 1950-52; v.p. Cricketeer, Inc., Chgo., 1953-58; pres. Kenneth Nebenzahl, Inc., Chgo., 1957—; dir. Imago Mundi, Ltd., London, 1976—; mem. Lloyds of London, 1978—. Author: Atlas of the American Revolution, 1974, Bibliography of Printed Battle Plans of the American Revolution, 1975, Maps of the Holy Land, 1986; Contbr. articles to profl. jours. Trustee Glencoe Public Library, 1963-69, pres., 1966-69; bd. dirs. North Suburban Library System, 1966-69, Beverly Farm Found., Godfrey, Ill., 1961-67, Nature Conservancy of Ill., 1980—; trustee Adler Planetarium, 1969—, v.p., 1974-77, chmn., 1977-81; mem. exec. com. Northwestern U. Library Council, 1973-75; sponsor Kenneth Nebenzahl, Jr. lectures history cartography Newberry Library, Chgo., 1965—, trustee, 1978—; mem. assos. council John Crerar Library, Chgo., 1972—, trustee, 1976—; mem. vis. com. to library U. Chgo., 1978—, chmn., 1987—; mem. Am. Geog. Soc. Collection adv. com. U. Wis., Milw., 1979—; bd. dirs. Evanston Hosp. Corp., 1978-85. Served with USMCR, 1945-46. Fellow Royal Geog. Soc., Am. Geog. Soc.; mem. Manuscript Soc. (dir. 1965-71), Am. Library Trustees Assn. (nat. chmn. com. intellectual freedom 1967-68), Bibliog. Soc. Am., Newberry Library Assocs. (bd. govs. 1965-78, chmn. 1976-78), Newberry Library (trustee 1978—), Antiquarian Booksellers Assn. Am. (bd. govs. 1965-67, v.p. 1975-77), Am. Antiquarian Soc., Soc. History Discoveries (dir. 1974-76), Chgo. Map Soc. (dir. 1976—), Ill. Ctr. for the Book (pres. 1986—). Clubs: Caxton (Chgo.) (bd. govs. 1961-68, 74—, pres. 1964-66), Tavern (Chgo.) (bd. govs. 1979-86), Wayfarers (Chgo.) (pres. 1979-80); Lake Shore Country (Glencoe); Century (N.Y.C.), Grolier (N.Y.C.). Home: 135 Crescent Dr Glencoe IL 60022 Office: 333 N Michigan Ave Chicago IL 60611

NEBERGALL, DONALD CHARLES, investment executive; b. Davenport, Iowa, Aug. 12, 1928; s. Ellis W. and Hilda (Bruhn) N.; m. Shirley Elaine Williams, Apr. 12, 1952; children: Robert W., Nancy L. Nebergall Bosma. BS, Iowa State U., 1951. With Poweshiek County Nat. Bank, 1958-72, sr. v.p., to 1972; founding pres. Brenton Bank and Trust Co., Cedar Rapids, Iowa, 1972-82, chmn. bd., 1982-86; v.p. Chapman Co., 1986—; bd. dirs. Telephone & Data Systems, Inc., Iowa Automated Clearing House; vice-chmn. ITS, Inc. (both subs. Iowa Bankers Assn.). V.p., bd. dirs. Iowa 4-H Found., 1972-76; div. campaign chmn. United Way; bd. dirs. ARC, Boy Scouts Am.; bd. dirs., treas., past pres. Methwick Manor Retirement Home; founding trustee Cedar Rapids Community Sch. Dist. Found. Served with AUS, 1946-48. Recipient Ptnr. in 4-H award Iowa 4-H, 1983. Mem. Cedar Rapids Greater Downtown Assn. (pres., bd. dirs.), Alpha Zeta, Gamma Sigma Delta, Delta Upsilon. Republican. Methodist. Lodge: Rotary. Office: The Chapman Co Dows Bldg 6th Fl Cedar Rapids IA 52401

NECHEMIAS, STEPHEN MURRAY, lawyer; b. St. Louis, July 27, 1944; s. Herbert Bernard and Toby Helen (Wax) N.; m. Marcia Rosentein, June 19, 1966, (div. Dec. 1981); children: Daniel Jay, Scott Michael; m. Linda Adams, Aug. 20, 1983. BS, Ohio State U., 1966; JD, U. Cin., 1969. Bar: Ohio 1969. Ptnr., Taft, Stettinius & Hollister, Cin., 1969— ; adj. prof. law No. Ky. U., Chase Coll. Law. Tax comment author: Couse's Ohio Form Book, 6th edit., 1984. Mem. Cin. Bar Assn. (chmn. taxation sect.), Legal Aid Soc. Cin. Democrat. Jewish. Home: 777 Cedar Point Dr Cincinnati OH 45230 Office: Taft Stettinius & Hollister 1800 First National Bank Center Cincinnati OH 45202

NEDRICH, JOHN LAWRENCE, transportation executive; b. Nanty-Glo, Pa., Mar. 16, 1940; s. John and Ann (Demchak) N.; B.B.A., Cleve. State U., 1970; M.B.A., Lehigh U., 1975; m. Elaine Ann Bell, Oct. 20, 1962; children—Christal Fern, Shawn Lawrence, Kelly Elaine. With, Air Products & Chems., Allentown, Pa., 1963-79, fleet mgr. AGA Burdox, Cleve., 1979-80; gen. mgr. Contract Transp. Systems subs. Sherwin Williams, Cleve., 1980-83; pres. Fleet Service Co., Cleve., 1983-85, Cloverdale Transp., Human Resource Mgmt. Co., Berea, Ohio, CKS Mgmt. Inc., 1985.; exec. dir. DI Enterprise Inc., 1986; Scoutmaster, Boy Scouts Am., 1978-79. Served with USCG, 1959-61. Mem. Pvt. Carrier Conf. (dir.), Pa. Motor Truck Assn., Contract Carrier Assn., Am. Transp. Assn. (pvt. truck council), Inst. Traffic and Transp. (chief officer bd. 1984-86), Nat. Council Phys. Distbn. Mgrs., Am. Soc. Traffic and Transp., ICC Practitioners Assn. (dist. v.p.). Roman Catholic. Office: DI Enterprises Inc PO Box 279 Berea OH 44017

NEDWEK, THOMAS WAYNE, association executive; b. Milw., Sept. 30, 1933; s. Thomas Anton and Josephine Ruth (Felski) N.; m. Charlotte A. Jager, June 16, 1956 (div. Jan. 1982); children: Thomas W. Jr., David J., Peter C., Annemarie R., Paul J. BSBA, Marquette U., 1955; postgrad. San Diego State Coll., 1958, Marquette U., 1960-61. Tchr., English Cathedral High Sch., San Diego, 1958-60; radio announcer Sta. WISN, Milw., 1960-65; instr. English Milw. Sch. Engring., 1960-62, Messmer High Sch., Milw., 1962-65; mem. pub. relations staff AC Electronics div., Gen. Motors Corp., Milw., 1965-70; sr. reporter Sta. WISN-TV, Milw., 1970-72, dir. pub. relations, 1972-76; v.p. pub. relations Milw. Sch. Engring., 1976-80; exec. dir. Milw. Bar Assn., 1980—; corp. mem. Milw. Sch. Engring., 1987—. Alderman, City of Glendale (Wis.), 1976—, plan commr., 1976-84; bd. dirs. St. Joseph's Hosp., 1980-85, World Festivals, Inc., 1978-83; v.p. Milw. Council on Alcoholism, 1980—; sec. Milw. Bar Found., 1983—; dir. Florentine Opera Club, 1986—. Served to lt. (j.g.) USN, 1955-58. Mem. Pub. Relations Soc. Am. (past pres. Wis. chpt., assembly del.), Am. Soc. Assn. Execs., Nat. Assn. Bar Execs., Wis. Soc. Assn. Execs. Roman Catholic. Club: Milw. Press (sec. 1983-85). Home: 2620 W Custer Ave Glendale WI 53209 Office: 605 E Wisconsin Ave Milwaukee WI 53202

NEE, LAWRENCE MICHAEL, marketing executive; b. South Boston, Mass.; s. Edgar Leo and Jeanne Lois (Dier) N.; m. Louise Rieksiewicz Aleksiewicz, Sept. 17, 1983; 1 child, Alexandra Marie. AAs in Biomed. Engring. Tech., Tidewater (Va.) Community Coll., 1979; BS in Engring. Tech., Norfolk (Va.) State U., 1981. Sr. QA/QL engr. Numeridex, Wheeling, Ill., 1981-82; sr. field service engr., sales and tech. support Computervision Corp., Bedford, Mass., 1982-85; v.p. Cadmonics, Inc., Schaumburg, Ill., 1985—. Served with USN, 1974-77. Mem. Assn. Field Service Mgrs. (bd. dirs. 1984-85), U.S. Golf Assn. Democrat. Roman Catholic. Avocations: golf, fishing, camping, basketball.

NEEB, WILLIAM MITCHELL, chemical company executive; b. Fremont, Ohio, Feb. 16, 1947; s. Beeker Henry and Frances Elizabeth (Leasure) N.; m. Kay Ann Guthrie, July 15, 1972. Assoc. in Electronics and Mech. Engring., Terra Tech, Fremont, 1974; BSME, U. Toledo, 1978. With prodn. div. Whirlpool Corp., Clyde, Ohio, 1970-75, facility engr., 1975-78, environ. engr., 1978-79, porcelain process engr., 1979-84; design engr. Parker Chem. Co., Madison Heights, Mich., 1984—. Commr. Boy Scouts Am., Clyde, 1980-84; mem. council Luth. Ch., Clyde, 1981-83, v.p., 1983, council Luth. Ch., Utica, Mich., 1987. Served with USN, 1966-70. Mem. Inst. Cert. Engring. Technicians, Am. Soc. Cert. Engring. Technicians (assoc.), Soc. Mech. Engrs. Lodge: Masons. Home: 1396 Royal Crescent Dr Rochester Hills MI 48064 Office: Parker Chem Co 32100 Stephenson Hwy Madison Heights MI 48071

NEEDLEMAN, SAUL B(EN), disposable medical devices company official, biochemical researcher; b. Chgo., Sept. 25, 1927; s. Jack L. and Celia (Magad) N.; m. Sondra Audrey Goldberg, June 13, 1954; children—Martin Craig, Arthur Alan, Beth Hali, Heidi Ruth. B.S. in Organic Chemistry, Ill. Inst. Tech., 1950, M.S. in Biochemistry, 1955; Ph.D. in Biochemistry and Medicine, Northwestern U., 1957. Assoc. prof. biochemistry and neurology Northwestern U., 1960-73; chief nuclear medicine VA Research Hosp., Chgo., 1965-73; chmn. dept. biochemistry Roosevelt U., Chgo., 1973-75; coordinator sci. affairs Abbott Labs., North Chicago, Ill., 1974-79; dir. clin. affairs Schering-Plough, Memphis, 1979-81; dir. med. affairs Hollister, Inc., Libertyville, Ill., 1981-85 ; cons. U.S. Naval Dental Research Program, med. expert USN Drug Program, Gt. Lakes, Ill. Mem. City of Chgo. High Sch. Sci. Fairs Council, 1960-85, Highland Park City Zoning Commn., Highland Park Sch. Bd.; precinct capt. Served with USNR, 1945-47. Recipient Presdl. award Abbott Labs., 1979; Toni Research fellow, 1954-55; Gillette Research fellow, 1953-54; recipient RESA Sci. Research award, 1960. Mem. Am. Soc. Biol. Chemistry, British Numis. Soc., Royal Soc. Numis., Am. Numis. Assn. (dist. rep.), Am. Numis. Soc., Am. Israel Numis. Assn. Author: Protein Sequence Determination, vol. 8A, 1970, 8B, 1975; Advanced Methods in Protein Sequence Determination, vol. 25, 1977, Perspectives In Numismatics, 1986; contbr. articles to tech. jours., articles on numis. history to periodicals; patentee in field. Office: PO Box 250 2000 Hollister Dr Libertyville IL 60048

NEEDLES, BELVERD EARL, JR., accounting educator; b. Lubbock, Tex., Sept. 16, 1942; s. Belverd Earl and Billie (Anderson) N.; B.B.A., Tex. Tech U., 1964, M.B.A., 1965; Ph.D., U. Ill., 1969; m. Marian Powers, May 23, 1976; children—Jennifer Helen, Jeffrey Scott, Annabelle Marian. C.P.A., Ill.; cert. mgmt. acct. Asst. prof., assoc. prof. acctg. Tex. Tech U., Lubbock, 1968-72; dean Coll. Bus. and Adminstrn., Chgo. State U., 1972-76; prof. acctg. U. Ill., Urbana, 1976-78; dir. Sch. Accountancy, DePaul U., Chgo., 1978-86, prof. acctg., 1978—. Treas., bd. dirs. C.P.A.s for Pub. Interest, 1978-86. Gen. Electric fellow, 1965-66; Deloitte Haskins and Sells fellow, 1966-68; named Disting. Alumnus Tex. Tech U., 1986; recipient Award of Merit DePaul Un., 1986. Fellow Am. Acctg. Assn. (sec. internat. sect. 1984-86, vice chmn. 1986-87, chmn. 1987-88); mem. Fedn. Schs. Accountancy (dir. 1980—, pres. 1986), Am. Inst. C.P.A.s, Acad. Internat. Bus., Ill. C.P.A. Soc., European Acctg. Assn. (exec. com. 1986—), Fin. Execs. Inst., Nat. Assn. Accts., Phi Delta Kappa, Phi Kappa Phi, Beta Alpha Psi, Beta Gamma Sigma. Club: Chgo. Athletic. Author: Accounting and Organizational Control, 1973; Modern Business, 2d edit., 1977; Principles of Accounting, 1980, 3d edit., 1987; Financial Accounting, 1982, 2d edit. 1986; The CPA Examination: A Complete Review, 7th edit., 1986; Comparative International Auditing Standards, 1985; editor Accounting Instructor's Report, 1981—, The Accounting Profession and The Middle Market, 1986.

NEEL, HARRY BRYAN, III, surgeon, scientist, educator; b. Rochester, Minn., Oct. 28, 1939; s. Harry Bryan and May Birgitta (Bjornsson) N.; m. Ingrid Helene Vaga, Aug. 29, 1964; children: Carlton Bryan, Harry Bryan IV, Roger Clifton. B.S., Cornell U., 1962; M.D., SUNY-Bklyn., 1966; Ph.D., U. Minn., 1976. Diplomate: Am. Bd. Otolaryngology. Intern Kings County Hosp., Bklyn., 1966-67; resident in gen. surgery U. Minn. Hosps., Mpls., 1967-68; resident in otolaryngology Mayo Grad. Sch. Medicine Mayo Clinic, Rochester, Minn., 1970-74, cons. in otohinolaryngology, 1974—, cons. in cell biology, 1981—, assoc. prof. otolaryngology and microbiology Med. Sch., 1979-84, prof., 1984—, also chmn. dept. otolaryngology. Author: Cryosurgery for Cancer, 1976; contbr. chpts. to books, articles to profl. jours. Vice pres. bd. dirs. Minn. Orch. in Rochester, Inc., 1982, pres., chmn., 1983-84; mem. devel. com. Minn. Orchestral Assn., 1983. Served with USPHS, 1968-70. Recipient Travel award Soc. Acad. Chmn. of Otolaryngology, 1974, Ira J. Tresley Research award Am. Acad. Facial and Reconstructive Surgery, 1982. Mem. Am. Acad. Otolaryngology, Head and Neck Surgery (prize for basic research in otolaryngology 1972), AMA, Minn. Med. Assn., Zumbro Valley Med. Soc., ACS (bd. govs. 1985—, sec.-treas. Minn. chpt. 1983-85), Am. Broncho-Esophagological Assn., Am. Rhinological and Otol. Soc. (Mosher award 1980), Am. Laryngological Assn.

(Casselberry award 1985), Assn. for Research in Otolaryngology, Assn. Acad. Depts. in Otolaryngology (sec.-treas. 1984-86, pres. elect 1986), Alumni Assn. Cornell U. (Outstanding Alumni award 1985), Am. Bd. Otolaryngology (bd. dirs. 1986—). Republican. Presbyterian. Club: Rochester Golf and Country. Home: 828 SW 8th St Rochester MN 55902 Office: Mayo Clinic 200 1st St SW Rochester MN 55905

NEEL, INGRID VAGA, pediatric allergist, educator; b. Kuressaare, Estonia, Apr. 8, 1941; d. Matthew and Margarita Vaga; m. H. Bryan Neel, Aug. 29, 1964; children: Carlton, Bryan, Roger. BA, Rutgers U., 1963; MD, SUNY, Bklyn., 1967. Diplomate Am. Bd. Pediatrics, Am. Bd. Allergy and Immunology. Resident in pediatrics found. grad. sch. Mayo Clinic, Rochester, Minn., 1971-73, fellow in allergy, 1973-75; asst. prof. pediatrics and allergy Mayo Clinic, Rochester, 1975—; staff physician Olmsted Med. Group, Rochester, 1975—, also bd. dirs.; mem. staff Olmsted Community Hosp., Rochester, 1975—; advisor Child Care Resource and Referral, Rochester, 1980—; adv. bd. Head Start, Rochester, 1984—, Olmsted Family Service Bur., 1984—; med. expert, lectr. pub. media and community edn. groups, Rochester, 1977—. Fellow Am. Acad. Pediatrics (bd. dirs. Minn. chpt. 1982-86, chmn. practice com. 1085—); mem. AMA, Am. Acad. Allergy and Immunology, Minn. Allergy Soc., Minn. Pediatric Soc., Mayo Med. Alumni Assn. Avocations: tennis, skiing, windsurfing, travel, reading. Office: Olmsted Med Group 210 SE 9th St Rochester MN 55904

NEELEY, DOUGLAS KEITH, electronics company executive; b. Marion, Ind., June 10, 1958; s. Roger Keith Neeley. BS in Mech. Tech., Purdue U., 1980; MA, Ball State U., 1983; MS, Ind. U., 1987. Process engr. Delco Electronics div. Gen. Motors, Kokomo, Ind., 1980-82, mech. designer, 1982-85; product mgr. Hughes Electronics div. Gen. Motors, Kokomo, 1985-86; product mgr. truck and bus div. Hughes Electronics div. Gen. Motors, Troy, Mich., 1987—. Home: 457 Kensington Apt 173 Rochester Hills MI 48063

NEELY, EARL FISHER, manufacturing company executive; b. Lamartine, Pa., Aug. 5, 1927; s. Lawrence Lester and Mildred Earla (Fisher) N.; m. Helen Marie Webb, June 10, 1950; children—Michael, Pamela, Bruce, Melinda. B.S., Grove City Coll., 1950. Controller Knox Glass Inc., Pa., 1950-61; v.p. finance Richards Musical Instrument Co., Elkhart, Ind., 1962-64; exec. v.p. Angelica Corp., St. Louis, 1964-84, pres., chief operating officer, dir., 1984—. Served with USMCR, 1945-46. Home: 715 Timber Trail Dr Frontenac MO 63131 Office: Angelica Corp 10176 Corporate Square Dr Saint Louis MO 63132

NEELY, JOANNE LUCINDA, school counselor; b. Pitts., July 3, 1942; d. John Miller and Gladys Elizabeth (Bartels) N. B.S., Indiana U. Pa., 1964; M.A., W.Va. U., 1967. Elem. tchr. West Jefferson Hills Sch. Dist., Clairton, Pa., 1964-67; tchr., instrnl. cons. Ritenour Sch. Dist., St. Louis, 1967—, sch. counselor, 1973—. Mem. Assn. Children with Learning Disabilities, Mo. Tchrs. Assn., Mo. Sch. Counselor Assn. Republican. Presbyterian. Lodge: Order Eastern Star (worthy matron 1977). Home: 8427 Lackland Rd Saint Louis MO 63114 Office: Ritenour Sch Dist 2420 Woodson Rd Saint Louis MO 63114

NEETZEL, RAYMOND JOHN, transportation analyst; b. St. Paul, Apr. 2, 1937; s. John R. and Alyce I. (Berge) N.; m. Laurel A. Neetzel. B.A., U. Wis.-Green Bay, 1973; cert. urban transp. planning, 1976; postgrad. St. Thomas Coll., 1978. Free-lance photographer, St. Paul, 1955-72; planning cons. City of Green Bay (Wis.), 1972-73; transit analyst Met. Transit Commn., St. Paul, 1973-76, sr. transit analyst, 1977—, mgmt. trainer, 1979—; owner Neetzel's Wood Works, Inc., 1979—; lectr., U. Aston, Birmingham, Eng., 1972, U. Wis., Green Bay, 1973; panelist Nat. Transp. Research Bd., 1977, 83. Sec. Neenah (Wis.) Planning Commn., 1967-69. Mem. Nat. Inst. Transp. Engrs., Norwegian Am. Mus. (life), Boundary Waters Conservation Alliance, Nat. Forest Recreation Assn. (nat. bd. dirs.), Nat. Assn. Alpha Phi Omega. Author: Winter Survival Techniques, 1980; also research papers in field. Office: Metropolitan Transit Commission 560 6th Ave N Minneapolis MN 55411

NEFF, BONITA DOSTAL, communication developmental facilitator; b. Grinnell, Iowa, Aug. 16, 1942; d. Lester Ernest and Mary Margaret (Hudnut) Dostal; m. Gregory Pall Neff, Apr. 27, 1974; 1 child, Kristiana. BA, U. N. Iowa, 1964, MA, 1966; PhD, U. Mich., 1973; AA cum laude, Lansing (Mich.) Community Coll., 1980. Edn. leadership fellow George Washington U., Washington, 1976-77; pub. relations, devel. specialist Mich. State U., East Lansing, 1977-80, co-investigator family and child inst. energy research team, 1980-82; asst. prof. communications Prudue U., Hammond, Ind., 1982; cons. in field. Contbr. articles to profl. jours. Chancellor's rep. Calumet (Ind.) Northwest Forum Econ. Devel., 1982-84; mem. Lake County (Ind.) Community Devel. Com., 1984—; bd. dirs. Big Bros. and Big Sisters Northwest Ind., 1984—. Recipient faculty research grant U. Mich., 1971, Consumer Product Safety Council grant, 1976-77. Mem. Internat. Communication Assn., Speech Communication Assn., Internat. Assn. Bus. Communication, Women in Communication (pres. Calumet chpt. 1985—), Inst. Ednl. Leadership, World Communication Assn., Soc. Intercultural and Ednl. Research, Nat. Computer Graphics Assn. Democrat. Roman Catholic. Avocations: ballet, tap, jazz, piano, reading. Home: 8320 Greenwood Munster IN 46321 Office: Purdue Univ Calumet Dept Communication Hammond IN 46323

NEFF, FRED LEONARD, lawyer; b. St. Paul, Nov. 1, 1948; s. Elliott and Mollie (Poboisk) N. B.S. with high distinction, U. Minn., 1970; J.D., William Mitchell Coll. Law, 1976. Bar: Minn. 1976, U.S. Dist. Ct. Minn. 1977, U.S. Ct. Appeals (8th cir.) 1985, U.S. Supreme Ct. 1985, Wis. Supreme Ct. 1986. Tchr. Hopkins (Minn.) Pub. Schs., 1970-72; instr. Inver Hills Community Coll., St. Paul, 1973-76, U. Minn., Mpls., 1974-76; sole practice, Mpls., 1976-79; asst. county atty. Sibley County, Gaylord, Minn., 1979-80; mng. atty. Hyatt Legal Services, St. Paul, 1981-83, regional ptnr., 1983-85, profl. devel. ptnr., 1985-86; owner, dir. Neff Law Firm, Edina, Mpls. and St. Paul, 1986—; counsel Am. Tool Supply Co., St. Paul, 1976-78; cons. Nat. Detective Agy., Inc., St. Paul, 1980-83. Author: Fred Neff's Self-Defense Library, 1976, Everybody's Self-Defense Book, 1978, Karate Is for Me, 1980, Running Is for Me, 1980, Lessons from the Samurai, 1986, Lessons from the Art of Kempo, 1986, Lessons from the Western Warriors, 1986. Adviser to bd. Sibley County Commrs., 1979-80; speaker before civic groups, 1976-82; mem. Hennepin County Juvenile Justice Panel, 1980-82, Hennepin County Pub. Def. Conflict Panel, 1980-82, 86—, Edina Hist. Soc.; founding sponsor Civil Justice Found., 1986—. Recipient St. Paul Citizen of Month award, Citizens Group, 1975, Student Appreciation U. Minn. award, 1978, Commendation award Sibley County Attys. Office, 1980, Leadership award Hyatt Legal Services, 1984, Mgn. Attys. Guidance award 1985, Justice award 1986, Creative Thinker award regional staff 1986, Good Neighbor award WCCO Radio, 1985, Lamp of Knowledge award Twin Cities Lawyers Guild, 1986, numerous other awards and honors. Fellow Internat. Biog. Assn., Nat. Dist. Attys. Assn.; mem. ABA, Assn. Trial Lawyers Am., Minn. Bar Assn., Hennepin County Bar Assn., Wis. Bar. Assn., Ramsey County Bar Assn., Medina C. of C., Minn. Martial Arts Assn. (pres. 1974-78 Outstanding Instr. award 1973), Nippon Kobudo Rengokai (dir. N.Central States 1972-76), Edina C. of C., Sigma Alpha Mu. Lodge: Masons, Kiwanis. Home: 4515 Andover Rd Edina MN 55435 Office: 701 4th Ave S Suite 500 Minneapolis MN 55415 also: 345 St Peter St Suite 800 Saint Paul MN 55102 also: 3407 Hazelton Rd Edina MN 55435

NEFF, JACK HILLMAN, marketing executive; b. Huntington, W. Va., Mar. 14, 1938; s. John Henry and Hilda May (Akers) N.; m. Dawn Joyce Wilson, Aug. 15, 1959; 1 child, Deborah Joyce. BSME, Carnegie-Mellon U., 1959, cert. exec. mgmt., 1978; cert. mktg. mgmt., Harvard U., 1976; cert. high tech. mktg., Stanford U., 1984. Tech. liaison cen. engring. Chrysler Corp., Highland Park, Mich., 1959-63; tech. liaison research labs. Chrysler Corp., Warren, Mich., 1963-66; v.p. sales Formsprag Co., Warren, 1966-79; v.p. mktg. Dana Corp., Toledo, 1979-81, Hobart Bros., Troy, Ohio, 1981—. Recipient Grand Mktg. award Sales and Mktg. mag., N.Y., 1981. Profl. mem. Am. Mktg. Assn., Am. Welding Soc. Republican. Presbyterian. Club: Troy Country. Avocation: sailing. Office: Hobart Bros Co 600 W Main Troy OH 45373

NEFF, RAY ALLEN, emeritus health and safety educator; b. Bristow, Va., Jan. 23, 1924; s. Charles Edward and Mary Elizabeth (Runion) N.; B.A., Bridgewater Coll., 1950; postgrad. Med. Coll. Va., 1954; M.S., Jefferson Med. Coll., 1960; Ed.D., Ball State U., 1975; m. Augusta Mae Kossman, Dec. 19, 1948; children—Charles Frederick, Robert Allen. Food cons. Commonwealth Va. Dept. Health, Richmond, 1950-54; analyst FDA, HEW, 1955; sr. analyst Smith, Kline & French Labs., Phila., 1956-58; Walter G. Karr research fellow Jefferson Med. Coll., Phila., 1958-60; health officer Cape May County (N.J.) Dept. Health, 1960-67; asst. prof. dept. health and safety Ind. State U., Terre Haute, 1967-75, assoc. prof., 1975-84, emeritus, 1984—. Vice pres., dir. research and devel. Visu-Phonics, Inc., Terre Haute, 1968-79, also dir.; dir., chmn. bd., pres. Ray A. Neff Assocs., Inc., cons., Terre Haute, 1979—; cons. Sunn Classics Prodns., Salt Lake City, 1976-78. Served with USNR, 1944-45. Fellow Soc. Mil. Historians. Am. Pub. Health Assn.; mem. Ind. Pub. Health Assn., N.J. Health Officers Assn., Royal Soc. Health (Gt. Britain). Pub., Abraham Lincoln Lithographs, 1968; Pawn of Traitors, 1969. Patentee solvent extractor, aircraft proximity device. Home: 514 N 8th St Marshall IL 62441 Office: PO Box 2507 Terre Haute IN 47802

NEFF, ROBERT CLARK, lawyer; b. St. Marys, Ohio, Feb. 11, 1921; s. Homer Armstrong and Irene (McCulloch) N.; m. Betty Baker, July 3, 1954; children—Cynthia Lee Neff Schifer, Robert Clark, Abigail Lynn (dec.); m. 2d, Helen Picking, July 24, 1975. B.A., Coll. Wooster, 1943; postgrad. U. Mich., 1946-47; LL.B., Ohio No. U., 1950. Bar: Ohio 1950, U.S. Dist. Ct. (no. dist.) Ohio 1978. Sole practice, Bucyrus, Ohio, 1950—; law dir. City of Bucyrus, 1961—. Chmn. blood program Crawford County (Ohio) unit ARC, 1955—; mem. adv. bd. Salvation Army, 1962—; clk. of session 1st Presbyterian Ch., Bucyrus, 1958—. Served with USNR, World War II; comdr. Res. ret. Mem. Ohio Bar Assn., Crawford County Bar Assn., Naval Res. Assn., Ret. Officers Assn., Nat. Inst. Mcpl. Law Officers, Am. Legion, Bucyrus Area C. of C. (bd. dirs., recipient Outstanding Citizen award, 1973), Bucyrus Citizen of Yr., 1981. Republican. Clubs: Kiwanis (past pres.), Masons. Home: 1085 Mary Ann Ln Box 406 Bucyrus OH 44820 Office: 840 S Sandusky Ave Box 406 Bucyrus OH 44820

NEGAARD, ROBERT CHARLES, wildlife artist, sculptor; b. St. Cloud, Minn., June 17, 1936. BS in Sci. and Art, St. Cloud State U., 1958. Tchr. Verndale (Minn.) High Sch., 1960-76; artist and resort operator Park Rapids, Minn., 1976—. Made and sold wildlife woodcarvings internationally, 1975—. Lutheran. Avocations: travelling, hunting, fishing. Home: Route 3 Box 138 Park Rapids MN 56470

NEHAL, SYED M., engineer, consultant; b. Ranchi, India, Dec. 8, 1933; came to U.S., 1957, naturalized, 1964; s. Syed A. and Safia B. Zafar; m. Idella E. Norman, May 13, 1960; children: Yasmin, Jeffrey, Jason, Susan. BS, Aligarh U. (India), 1955; BSEE, Ind. Inst. Tech., 1959; MS in Engring., Akron U., 1966. Registered profl. engr., Ohio, Va., W.V., Ct.; cert. energy auditor and tech. analyst, Ohio. Home study dir. Air Conditioning Tng. Sch., Youngstown, Ohio, 1961-63; dir. profl. services Rohrer & Assocs. Cons. Engrs., Akron, Ohio, 1964-71; prin., pres. Nehal & Assocs., Inc., Akron, 1971—; expert witness Expert Adv. Service, 1981; instr. seminars Ohio Dept. Energy, 1986-87; guest instr. for graduating architects Kent State U., 1987. Vol. Cuyahoga Falls Gen. Hosp., 1983. Mem. ASHRAE, ASME (local chpt. chmn. Engrs. Week, 1980), NSPE (bd. dirs. local chpt. 1969), Nat. Soc. Fire Protection Engrs., Profl. Engrs. in Pvt. Practice, Profl. Engring. Soc. (pres. 1976). Lodge: Kiwanis (bd. dirs. 1979). Avocations: gardening, painting, drawing, dogs. Home: 2343 N Revere Rd Akron OH 44313 Office: Syed M Nehal & Assocs Inc 2117 Grant Ave Cuyahoga Falls OH 44223

NEHER, LESLIE IRWIN, engineer, former air force officer; b. Marion, Ind., Sept. 15, 1906; s. Irvin Warner and Lelia Myrtle (Irwin) N.; m. Lucy Marion Price; 1 son, David Price; m. Cecelia Marguerite Hayworth, June 14, 1956; B.S. in Elec. Engring., Purdue U., 1930. Registered profl. engr., Ind., N.Mex. Engr. high voltage research, 1930-32; engr. U.S. Army, Phila., 1933-37; heating engr. gas utility, 1937-40; commd. 2d lt. U.S. Army, 1929, advanced through grades to Col., 1947; dir. tng., Tng. Command, Heavy Bombardment, Amarillo AFB, Tex., 1942-44; dir. mgmt. tng., 15th AF, Colorado Springs, Colo., 1945-46; mgr. Korea Electric Power Co., Seoul, 1946-47, ret., 1960; engr. Neher Engring. Co., Gas City, Ind., 1960—. Chmn. Midwest Indsl. Gas Council, 1969. Named Outstanding Liaison Officer, Air Force Acad., 1959; Ambassador for Peace, Republic of Korea, 1977; recipient Republic of Korea Service medal, 1977. Mem. Ind. Soc. Profl. Engrs. (Outstanding Engr. 1982, Engr. of Yr. Ind. 1986), Nat. Soc. Profl. Engrs., Midwest Indsl. Gas Assn. (chmn. 1969). Republican. Methodist. Lodge: Kiwanis (Disting. sect. 1979-85, lt. gov. 1964; Disting. Service award 1962).

NEIBEL, OLIVER JOSEPH, JR., med. services exec.; b. Kansas City, Mo., Apr. 17, 1927; s. Oliver Joseph and Eula Lee (Durham) N.; J.D., U. Va., 1952; B.S., U. Ariz., 1949; m. Patricia Helen O'Keefe, June 24, 1950 (div. 1971); children—Oliver Joseph III, Deborah Sue; m. 2d, Diane Bachus Nelson, Apr. 11, 1981. Instr., U. Washington, 1952-53; admitted to Wash. bar, 1952, Ill. bar, 1961, Nebr. bar, 1973; practiced in Seattle, 1953-57; asst. atty. gen. State of Wash., 1957-61; legislative atty. AMA, Chgo., 1961-63; exec. dir., gen. counsel Coll. Am. Pathologists, Chgo., 1963-72; v.p., gen. mgr. Physicians Lab., Omaha, 1973—. Justice of peace, Mountlake Terrace, Wash., 1955-57. Served with USNR, 1945. Mem. Am. Wash., Nebr., Ill. bar assns., Med. Group Mgmt. Assn., Phi Kappa Psi (chpt. pres. 1948-49), Delta Theta Phi, Alpha Kappa Psi, Delta Sigma Rho. Mason, Elk, Rotarian. Clubs: Wash. Athletic (Seattle); Tavern (Chgo.); Omaha Press, University (Nebr.). Home: 7918 Potter Plaza Omaha NE 68122 Office: 105 N 37th St Omaha NE 68131

NEIDHART, KENNETH DONALD, periodontist; b. Chgo., Oct. 28, 1946; s. Herman John and Alice Marie (Schurr) N.; m. Mary Lou Mancione, Oct. 13, 1973. BS, U. Ill., Chgo., 1970, DDS, 1972; MS, U. Nebr., 1976. Pvt. practice periodontology Madison, Wis., 1976—. Served to lt. USN, 1972-74. Mem. ADA, Wis. Dental Assn., Dane County Dental Soc. (pres. 1986), Am. Acad. Periodontology, Wis. Soc. Periodontists (sec. 1984-86, pres. 1986—).

NEIHEISEL, THOMAS HENRY, toy manufacturing company executive; b. Cin., Dec. 1, 1953; s. Vincent John and Mary Jane (Haverkos) N.; m. Cynthia Lynn Dirk, Aug. 5, 1977; children: Matthew Thomas and Andrew John (twins). BBA, U. Cin., 1977, MBA, 1981. Group project leader The Procter & Gamble Co., Cin., 1974-77; mgr. project services Burgoyne, Inc., Cin., 1977-81; dir. market research Kenner Products, Cin., 1982—. Alpha Kappa Psi scholar, 1977, John Burgoyne research scholar, 1976, U. Cin. Honor scholar award, 1972; recipient Eagle Scout award Boy Scouts Am., 1968. Mem. Am. Mktg. Assn., Assn. MBA Execs., Market Research Assn., Alpha Kappa Psi. Roman Catholic. Home: 10061 Cliffwood Ct Cincinnati OH 45241 Office: 1014 Vine St Cincinnati OH 45202

NEIMAN, ROBERT LEROY, management consultant; b. Chgo., Feb. 9, 1930; s. Maurice and Shirley (Albin) N.; B.S. in Communications with honors, U. Ill., 1951, M.A. in Social and Behavioral Scis., 1952; m. Marlene Kaufman (dec. Mar. 1972); m. Barbara Milkes (dec. Mar. 1983); 1 dau., Debra Bea. Asst. to pres. Utility Plastic Packaging Co., Chgo., 1953-54; from dept. mgr. to v.p. Castle and Assos., Chgo., 1954-73; v.p. Mendheim Co., Chgo., 1973-77, sr. v.p., 1977—; guest radio speaker on cancer research fund raising, 1984. Chmn. Marlene K. Neiman Meml. Found. of Am. Cancer Soc., 1972-75, chmn. Barbara J. Neiman Meml. Found. for Lung Cancer, 1983; bd. dirs. Morton Grove, Ill. unit Am. Cancer Soc. Served as 1st lt. USAF, 1951-53. Recipient Presdl. citation; Joggers award Lehmann Sports Club. Mem. Am. Personnel and Guidance Assn., Am. Inst. Indsl. Engrs., Soc. Mfg. Engrs., Am. Mgmt. Assn., Nat. Assn. Corp. and Profl. Recruiters, Air Force Assn., North Shore Assn. for Retarded, Sigma Delta Chi, Sigma Delta Pi. Club: Skokie Valley Kiwanis (program chmn.). Author articles in field. Home: 9401 Natchez Ave Morton Grove IL 60053 Office: 6055 N Lincoln Ave Chicago IL 60659 *

NEIMARK, PHILIP JOHN, financial consultant, editor; b. Chgo., Sept. 13, 1939; s. Mortimer William N. ; m. Vassa Lynn; children: Tanya Lee, Joshua Daniel. Student U. Chgo., 1956-58, Northwestern U., 1958-59; D in Bus. Mgmt. (hon.), Ricker Coll., Houlton, Maine, 1976. Mem. Chgo. Mercantile Exchange, 1968-74; owner Josephson Neimark Trading Co., Chgo., 1972-73; ptnr. Rosenthal & Co., Chgo., 1973-77; owner, prin. Philip J. Neimark Investments, Miami, Fla., 1977-79, Chgo., 1979—; pres. Neimark Fin. Pub. Co., 1985—; editor, pub. Philip J. Neimark Viewpoint, N.Y.C., 1976-85, editor Pro Trade, 1984—, Low Priced Stock Edit., 1984—; fin. editor Money Maker mag., 1979-85; mem. Internat. Monetary Market, 1971-74, N.Y. Mercantile Exchange, 1973-74, Chgo. Bd. of Options Exchange, 1973-75; editor, Low Priced Stock Edition, 1984—, Pro Trade, 1985—; mktg. dir. Callard, Madden & Assocs. Author: How to Be Lucky, 1975; contbg. editor Consumers Digest mag., 1977-85. Bd. dirs. Luth. Gen. Med. Found., Principal Vassa Internat. Mem. Fla. Exec. Planning Assn., South Fla. Fin. Planners Assn., Investment Co. Inst., Nat. Paso Fino Assn. (founder). Office: 1653 Mdse Mart Chicago IL 60654

NEINER, A. JOSEPH, financial executive, controller; b. Ft. Scott, Kans., Feb. 15,1950; s. Andrew W. and Celeste H. (Beck) N.; m. Linda M. Koenig, Aug. 16, 1969; children: Carrie L., Christine M., Joseph M., Elizabeth A. BSBA, U. Mo., St. Louis, 1972; MBA, St. Louis U., 1976. Fin. analyst Chrysler Corp., St. Louis, 1972-75; fin. mgr. Gen. Cable Corp., St. Louis, 1975-79; controller Consol. Aluminum, St. Louis, 1979-80, group controller, 1980-83, ops. controller, 1983-85, corp. controller, 1985, dir. corp. planning, 1986, v.p. fin., 1986—; condr. fin. workshop Alusuisse Ltd., Zurich, Switzerland, 1985; instr. St. Louis Jr. Coll., 1975-80, U. Mo., St. Louis, 1978. Mem. Am. Mgmt. Assn. Roman Catholic. Home: 15104 Appalachian Trail Chesterfield MO 63017 Office: Consol Aluminum 11960 Westline Industrial Dr Saint Louis MO 63146

NEINER, GLENN ALLEN, principal; b. Ft. Scott, Kans., May 2, 1941; s. Andrew William and Celeste Henrietta (Beck) N. BA, St. Mary's Coll., Winona, Minn., 1962, MEd, 1969; MA, DePaul U., 1977; PhD, U. Wis., 1978. Tchr. Cen. Catholic High Sch., Vincennes, Ind., 1962-65, Kirkwood (Mo.) High Sch., 1969-70; acad. prin. DeLaSalle Inst., Chgo., 1972-76; tchr. Bishop Gallagher High Sch., Harper Woods, Mich., 1965-69, chmn. math dept., 1970-71, adminstrv. asst., 1971-72, prin., 1978—; project asst. research and devel. Ctr. for Individualized Schooling, Madison, Wis., 1976-78; presentor conf. Individually Guided Edn. in Secondary Schs., Eau Claire, Wis., 1977, presentor 2d ann. conf., Madison, 1977. cons. ednl. publications. Chmn. 14th Dist. Acad. Nominations Com., Mich., 1981—; bd. dirs. Bd. Reconciliation and Arbitration, Chgo., 1975-76, Lewis U., Romeoville, Ill., 1975-82; trustee Bishop Gallagher Found., Harper Wods, 1986—. Mem. NEA, Nat. Assn. Secondary Sch. Principals, Mich. Assn. Secondary Sch. Prins. (Gold Cert. 1979), Am. Assn. Sch. Adminstrs., Phi Delta Kappa, Phi Kappa Phi,. Roman Catholic. Avocations: travel, racquetball, tennis, reading. Office: Bishop Gallagher High Sch 19360 Harper Harper Woods MI 48225

NEISIUS, ALEXA ANNA ESTELLA, banking administrator; b. Iron Ridge, Wis., May 28, 1918; d. Albert Herman Emil and Augusta Emilie Ottilie (Lentz) Volkmann; m. Raymond Louis Neisius, Dec. 6, 1970. Student pub. sch., Iron Ridge. Teller, bookkeeper Comml. State Bank, Iron Ridge, 1937-43, asst. cashier, 1943-49, cashier, 1949-85; br. mgr. Horicon State Bank, Iron Ridge, 1985-87. Mem. Wis. Bankers Assn. (50-Yr. Club 1987). Lutheran.

NEISLER, JAMES WENDELL HARVEY, physician, gynecologic and oncologic surgeon; b. Boulder, Colo., Mar. 30, 1933; s. Wendell Hanson and Beulah Marg (Harvey) N.; m. Diana Tamara Amberg, June 15, 1963; children: Kirsten, James R., Alexandra, Mark. BA cum laude, U. Colo., 1954, MD, 1958. Diplamate Am. Bd. Gynecol. Oncology; lic. physician, Colo., Ohio, Calif. Commd. 2d lt. USAF, 1956, advanced through grades to col., 1975; extern USAF, Ladd AFB, Fairbanks, Alaska, 1957; rotating intern Santa Clara County Hosp. USAF, San Jose, Calif., 1958-59; gen. med. officer USAF, Huntington, Eng., 1959-62, Salina, Kans., 1963; chief resident in ob/gyn., UCLA USAF, 1963-66; fellow in gen. and oncol. surgery City of Hope Nat. Med. Ctr. USAF, Duarte, Calif., 1966-67; chief ob/gyn. USAF Hosp. USAF, Wiesbaden, Fed. Republic Germany, 1968-71; fellow in gynecol. oncology U. Tex. Anderson Hosp. and Tumor Inst. USAF, Houston, 1972-75; ret. USAF, 1976; assoc. prof. ob/gyn. Med. Coll. of Ohio, Toledo, 1976—, prof., 1985—, dir. div. gynecol. oncology, div. med. edn., acting chmn. dept. ob/gyn., 1978. Contbr. articles to profl. jours. Fellow ACS, Am. Coll. Obstetricians and Gynecologists (cert.); mem. AMA, Ohio State Med. Soc., Acad. Medicine of Lucas County, Soc. Gynecol. Oncologists, Felix Rutledge Soc., Cen. Assn. Obstetricians and gynecologists, Toledo Ob/gyn. Soc., Miss. Obstetrical/Gynecol. Soc., Gulf Coast Ob/Gyn. Soc., Air ForceSoc. Clin. surgeons, Anglo-Am. Med.Soc., N.Y. Acad. Sci., Mich. Gynecol. Oncology Soc., Phi Beta Kappa, Phi Lambda Upsilon, Alpha Epsilon Delta, Alpha Omega Alpha, Phi Rho Sigma. Club: Belmont Country (Perrysburg, Ohio). Avocation: tennis. Home: 271 Riverside Dr Rossford OH 43460 Office: 2121 Hughes Ln #720 Toledo OH 43606

NEITZKE, JOHN PETER, veterinarian; b. Miami Beach, Fla., June 29, 1945; s. Cletus Peter and Marie Violet (Paulson) N.; m. Marie Frances Gleason, July 25, 1970; children: Michelle, Suzanne, Barbie Jo. BS, U. Minn., 1969, DVM, 1971; postgrad. diploma, U. Sask., Can., 1972. Resident dept. vet. pathology U. Sask., Saskatoon, 1971-73; pres. Grand Rapids (Minn.) Vet. Clinic, 1973—. Contbr. articles to profl. jours. Mem. Am. Vet. Med. Assn., Minn. Vet. Med. Assn., Arrowhead Vet. Med. Assn. Roman Catholic. Avocations: hunting, fishing, flying. Home: 4709 Sunny Beach Rd Grand Rapids MN 55744 Office: Grand Rapids Vet Clinic 1895 W Hwy #2 Grand Rapids MN 55744

NELIDOW, IRINA, editor, writer, photographer; b. N.Y.C.; d. Alexander and Dorothy Gordon (King) N. A.B. magna cum laude, Bryn Mawr Coll., 1950, M.A., 1952. Research assoc. in chemistry MIT, Harvard U., 1951-54; market editor Aviation Week, N.Y.C., 1954-56; sci. editor McGraw-Hill Book Co., St. Louis, 1965-69; asst. dir. sci. program CEMREL, St. Louis, 1969-70; sr. editor World Book Ency., Chgo., 1971-72; cons. editor U. Chgo. Press, 1973-74; pres. Nelidow Communications, Chgo., 1975—; instr. photography Field Mus. Natural History, Chgo., 1982-83, Maine-Oakton-Niles-Northfield Adult Continuing Edn. Program, 1987. Bd. dirs. Dance Concert Soc., St. Louis, 1967-71. Mem. Ind. Writers Chgo., Am. Med. Writers Assn., Chgo. Women in Pub., Common Cause, Sierra Club, Nature Conservancy, Sigma Xi. Contbr. book revs. to St. Louis Post-Dispatch.

NELL, PATRICIA ANN, allergist; b. Marshfield, Wis., Aug. 10, 1935; d. Harry William and Sarah Alice (Ingraham) N.; m. Lewis Edwards Gibson, Dec. 27, 1986. BA, State U. of Iowa, 1957, MD, 1960. Rotating intern Phila. Gen. Hosp., 1960-61; resident in pediatrics Cin. Children's Hosp., 1961-62, St. Christopher's Hosp., Phila., 1964-65; resident in allergy and immunolgy U. Wis., Madison, 1969-71; practice medicine specializing in pediatrics, allergies West Side Clinic, Green Bay, Wis., 1971-73; tng. program faculty, chief allergy St. Christopher Hosp., Temple U., Phila., 1973-78; chief pediatric allergy dept., asst. prof. pediatrics U. Ill., Chgo., 1978-86; clin. dir. pediatrics, allergy Anchor HMO, Oak Park, Ill., 1986—; Asst. prof. Rush-Presbyn. St. Luke Med. Ctr., Chgo., 1986—. Contbr. articles to profl. jours. Served to maj. USAF, 1962-68, res. 1981—, served to col. USAFR. Fellow Am. Acad. Pediatrics, Am. Thoracic Soc.; mem. Am. Med. Women Assn., Phila. Allergy Soc. (sec. 1975-78). Methodist. Club: St. Christopher (Phila.) (treas. 1974-78). Avocations: violin, cross country skiing, bicycling. Office: Anchor HMO 1049 Lake St Oak Park IL 60301

NELSON, architect; b. Milw., May 4, 1921; s. Harry Victor and Hallie M. (Rensimer) Nelson; m. Lois Wilker, Jan. 1942 (div. Jan. 1948); m. Ruth Jamar Deem, May 17, 1949 (div. Aug. 1987); children: Jamar D., Stewart D., Sigrid D. BArch, Mont. State U., 1953. Registered architect, Ariz., Mo. Prin. Nelson Architect, AIA, Flagstaff, Ariz., 1959-80; architect H.B.E., St. Louis, 1980-81, Silver Dollar City, Branson, Mo., 1981-83, Saul A. Nuccitelli, Inc., Springfield, Mo., 1983—. Served to sgt. U.S. Army, 1942-45, PTO. Mem. AIA. Presbyterian. Lodge: Masons (Grand Master Ariz. 1978-79). Home: 10 Maple Ln Kimberling City MO 65686 Office: Saul A Nuccitelli Inc 122 Park Central Sq Springfield MO 65806

NELSON, ALBERT BURLESON, dentist; b. Shipshewana, Ind., May 16, 1917; s. Joseph E. and Amanda (Mishler) N.; m. Grace Marie Murray, Nov. 28, 1940; children: Craig L., Karen Colleen Nelson Helmkamp, Roger A. Grad., Goshen Coll.; DDS, Ind. U., Indpls., 1940. Gen. practice dentistry LaGrange, Ind., 1940-43, 46—. Served to lt. cmdr. USN, 1943-46, PTO. Mem. ADA, Ind. Dental Assn., Isaac Knapp Dist. Dental Soc.

Methodist. Home: Rt 5 Woodland Hills LaGrange IN 46761 Office: 405 Union St LaGrange IN 46761

NELSON, ALBERT LEROY, teacher educator; b. Scandia, Kans., Feb. 19, 1921; s. Otto Clarence and Olive Hulda (Lundquist) N.; m. Elizabeth June Street, Aug. 20, 1947; children: James Randall, Julie Elaine. BA, Kans. Wesleyan U., 1950, LHD, 1983; MS in Edn., U. Kans., 1955, EdD, 1965. High sch. tchr. Dist. R-4, Cawker City, Kans., 1950-53; dir. audio visual services U. Kans., Lawrence, 1953-56; dir. summer sch. Kans. Wesleyan U., Salina, 1981-85, dir. tchr. edn., 1956—; manuscript editor Prentice-Hall, Inc., Englewood Cliffs, N.J., 1980—; pvt. coll. rep. Teaching Profl. Standards Bd., Kans., 1972-78. Contbr. articles to profl. jours. Pres. Salina South High Sch. PTA, 1976-77. Served to lt. (j.g.) USNR, 1942-46, PTO. Recipient Disting. Achievement award Kans. Wesleyan Alumni, 1981, Disting. Service award Kans. Wesleyan Alumni, 1979; fellow Tri-Univ. Project, 1968-69, Danforth Found. fellow, 1964. Mem. Nat. Council Social Studies, Assn. Tchr. Educators, NEA, Ret. Officers Assn., Phi Delta Kappa. Republican. Methodist. Avocations: photography, woodworking, fishing, writing. Home: 1819 Gebhart St Salina KS 67401 Office: Kans Wesleyan Coll 100 E Claflin St Salina KS 67401

NELSON, AMERICA ELIZABETH, pediatrician; b. Chgo., Apr. 9, 1932; d. Lorenzo Raymond and Blanche Juanita (Crawford) Nelson; A.B. in English, U. Mich., Ann Arbor, 1952, M.S. in Zoology, 1954; postgrad. Tenn. State U., 1952-53, U. Chgo., 1955-56; M.D., Howard U., 1961; M.P.H., U. Ill., 1973. Intern, Hahnemann Med. Sch. and Hosps., Phila., 1961-62; resident pediatrics Michael Reese Hosp., Chgo., 1962-63, U. Mich., Ann Arbor, 1964; practice medicine specializing in pediatric cardiology, Detroit, 1963; with father, practice medicine specializing in pediatrics, Baldwin, Mich., 1964-71, 75—; pediatrician Tice Clinic, U. Ill., Cook County Hosp., 1965, 66; pediatrician Mile's Sq. Health Center, Chgo., 1967; pediatrician Infant Welfare Soc., Chgo., 1968; cons. pediatrician, child devel. Kalamazoo Child Guidance Clinic, 1969-70, coordinator drug abuse program, 1969-70; med. dir. Chgo. Residential Manpower Center, 1971-72; pediatrician, child devel. Dyslexia Meml. Inst., Chgo., 1972—; founder, project dir., med. dir. Deerwood Developmental Center, Inc., Cherry Valley Twp., Lake County, Mich.; lectr. U. Ill. at Chgo. Circle, 1972-73; clin. instr. U. Ill.-Presbyn.-St. Luke's Hosp.; asst. prof. Mental Retardation Inst., N.Y. Med. Coll., 1974; cons. in field. Mem. AAAS, Pi Lambda Theta. Contbr. articles to profl. jours. Home: PO Box 760 Baldwin MI 49304

NELSON, ANITA MARIE, business educator; b. Vincennes, Ind., Feb. 20, 1946; d. Walter Joe and Rita Marie (Vieck) Primus; m. William Raymond Nelson, Dec. 6, 1975. BBA, Fontbonne Coll., 1969. Tchr. Jubilee Lodge for Girls, Brimfield, Ill., 1969-71; instr. Ill. Cen. Coll., East Peoria, 1971—. Mem. Nat. Bus. Edn. Assn., Ill. Bus. Edn. Assn., Peoria Area Bus. Edn. Assn., Ill. Vocat. Assn. Avocations: crocheting, fishing, spectator sports. Home: 3029 N Sheridan Peoria IL 61604 Office: Ill Central Coll East Peoria IL 61635

NELSON, ARDELL L., insurance executive; b. Clearlake, S.D., Aug. 26, 1943; s. Millard L. and Polly (Bjerke) N.; m. Marge J. Sivertsen, June 29, 1966; children: Chad, Stacey. BS, S.D. State U., 1966; MBA, Eastern N. Mex. U., 1968. Purchasing profl. Luth. Brotherhood Ins. Co., Mpls., 1970-72; adminstrv. mgr. Royal Ins. subs. Milbank Ins. Co., Milbank, S.D., 1972—. Pres. Am. Luth Ch. council, Milbank, 1979; mem. bd. Luth. Outdoors, Sioux Falls, S.D., 1980; chmn. Grant County Reps., Milbank, 1982-84; v.p. Milbank Chamber Council, 1986, pres., 1987—. Club: Milbank Basketball (pres. 1980—). Home: 1375 Highview Dr Milbank SD 57252 Office: Royal Ins subs Milbank Ins Co E Hwy 12 Milbank SD 57253

NELSON, BOYD EASTHAM, radiologist; b. Trenton, N.J., Dec. 31, 1941; s. Boyd Eugene and Hilda (Clegg) N.; m. Constance Ileen Lazenby, Sept. 1, 1962; children: Connie Jean, Wendy Lee, Boyd Eastham III. BS, U. Utah, 1962, MD, 1966. Diplomate Am. Bd. Radiology, Am. Bd. Nuclear Medicine. Intern USPHS Hosp., Seattle, 1966-67; resident VA Hosp., U. Calif.-Irvine, Long Beach, 1969-72; radiologist U. Calif., Irvine, 1969-73, VA Hosp., Long Beach, Calif., 1969-73, Decatur (Ill.) Meml. Hosp., 1973—; asst. clin. prof. So. Ill. U., Springfield, 1975—; clin. assoc. U. Ill., Champaign, 1975—. bd. dirs. Macon County United Way, Decatur, 1978-81, Ill. div. Am. Cancer Soc., Chgo., 1982—; pres. Macon County Cancer Soc., Decatur, 1981. Served to lt. commdr. USPHS, 1966-69. Mem. AMA, Soc. Nuclear Medicine, Am. Coll. Radiology. Home: 105 Oakridge Ct Decatur IL 62521 Office: Decatur Meml Hosp 2300 N Edward St Decatur IL 62526

NELSON, CHARLES ABBOTT, accountant; b. Sioux Falls, S.D., Aug. 17, 1961; s. Wesley Charles and Gail G. (Abbott) N.; m. Kristine Renee Christensen, June 4, 1983. BS, U. S.D., 1983. CPA, S.D. Ptnr. Nelson and Nelson, CPA's, Sioux Falls, 1984—. Treas. S.D. Family Bus. Council, Sioux Falls, 1986-87; chmn. supr. com. Air Guard Credit Union, Sioux Falls, 1983-87. Mem. Am. Inst. CPA's, Nat. Assn. Pub. Accts., S.D. Soc. CPA's, Sioux Falls Estate Planning Council, Air Force Assn. (treas. 1984—). Republican. Lutheran. Lodge: Lions (dir. 1986-87, chpt. Tailtwister 1986). Avocations: basketball, hunting, fishing, volleyball, golfing. Home: 5404 W 45th St Sioux Falls SD 57106 Office: Nelson & Nelson CPAs 1517 S Minnesota Ave Sioux Falls SD 57105

NELSON, CHARLES LESLIE, oral and maxillofacial surgeon; b. Terre Haute, Ind., Feb. 2, 1950; s. Jack Carter and Leota Myrne Nelson; m. Patti Ellen Keene, June 7, 1975; children: Matthew Carter, Erin Marie. AB, Ind. U., 1973; DDS, Ind. U., Indpls., 1976. Diplomate Am. Bd. Oral and Maxillofacial Surgeons. Asst. prof. oral and maxillofacial surgery Ind. U. Sch. Dentistry, Indpls., 1982-87, assoc. prof., 1987—; asst. dir. craniofacial anomalies team Ind. U., Indpls., 1985—. Contbr. articles to profl. jours. Served to maj. USAF, 1979-82. Mem. ADA, Ind. Dental Assn., Indpls. Dist. Dental Soc., Am. Assn. Oral and Maxillofacial Surgeons, Ind. Soc. Oral and Maxillofacial Surgeons (bd. dirs. 1985-86, v.p. 1986—, office anesthesia evaluation com.), Great Lakes Soc. Oral and Maxillofacial Surgeons, Am. Cleft Palate Assn., Am. Assn. Dental Schs., Am. Assn. Dental Research (Ind. sect.). Republican. Methodist. Lodge: Elks. Avocations: sports, woodworking. Office: Ind U Sch Dentistry 1121 W Michigan St Indianapolis IN 46202

NELSON, CRAIG MARVIN, architect; b. Mechanicsville, Iowa, June 30, 1953; s. Marvin John and Pearl Helen (Yanacheck) N.; m. Pamela Sue Utt, Sept. 7, 1974; children: Lisa Marie, Lindsay Michele. Degree in archtl. drafting, Kirkwood Community Coll., 1973; BA in Architecture, Iowa State U., 1978. Registered architect, Iowa. Staff architect Environ. Design Group, Des Moines, 1979-81; dir. plan div., project architect Bloodgood Architects, Des Moines, 1981-86; project architect Walker-Metzger Architecture, Des Moines, 1986—. Mem. Des Moines Art Ctr., 1985—; usher, mem. bldg. com. St. Ambrose Cathedral parish, Des Moines, 1985—. Mem. AIA (legis. action com. Iowa chpt.), Des Moines Architects Council (sec., treas. 1984, v.p. 1985, pres. 1986), Nat. Council Archtl. Registration Bds. Republican. Roman Catholic. Avocations: photography, landscaping, carpentry. Office: Walker Metzger Architects PC 3706 Ingersoll Ave Des Moines IA 50312

NELSON, DAVID ALDRICH, federal judge; b. Watertown, N.Y., Aug. 14, 1932; s. Carlton Low and Irene Demetria (Aldrich) N.; m. Mary Dickson, Aug. 25, 1956; children: Frederick Dickson, Claudia Baxter, Caleb Edward. A.B., Hamilton Coll., 1954; postgrad., Peterhouse, Cambridge, Eng., 1954-55; LL.B., Harvard U., 1958. Bar: Ohio 1958, N.Y. 1982. Assoc. Squire, Sanders & Dempsey, Cleve., 1958-67, ptnr., 1967-69, 72-85; circuit judge U.S. Ct. Appeals for 6th Circuit, Cin., 1985—; gen. counsel U.S. Post Office Dept., Washington, 1969-71; sr. asst. postmaster gen., gen. counsel U.S. Postal Service, Washington, 1971. Served to 1st lt. USAF, 1959-62; served to maj. USAFR, 1962-69. Fulbright scholar, 1954-55; recipient Benjamin Franklin award U.S. Post Office Dept., 1969. Fellow Am. Coll. Trial Lawyers; mem. Cleve. Bar Assn., Ohio Bar Assn., ABA, Fed. Bar Assn., Cin. Bar Assn., Phi Beta Kappa. Republican. Congregationalist. Clubs: University (Cin.); Emerson Lit. Soc. (Clinton, N.Y.). Office: 414 US Post Office and Courthouse 5th and Walnut Sts Cincinnati OH 45202

NELSON, DONALD CHARLES, diversified corporate executive; b. Akron, Ohio, Dec. 1, 1926; s. John Harry and Anna Kristina (Jones) N.; m. Jeanne Davis, Aug. 19, 1949 (div. Sept. 1979); children: Jeffrey, Debra, David, Julie, Jill, Diane, Drew; m. Patricia Ann Banks, Jan. 2, 1981. BS, U. Akron, 1950. Personnel asst. Star Drill Machine Co., Akron, 1951-52; employee relations mgr. Quaker Oats Co., Akron, 1952-58; pres., chief exec. officer P.R.G. Inc. (formerly MRC Inc.), Akron, 1958—. Pres., founder Copley (Ohio) Assn. Businessmen, 1977; bd. dirs. Goodwill Industries, Akron, 1976—. Served with USN, 1944-46. Republican. Lutheran. Lodge: Rotary (bd. dirs. Akron 1977-80). Office: PRG Inc PO Box 5445 Akron OH 44313

NELSON, ELLIOTT, food service executive; b. Indpls., Apr. 26, 1940; s. Dave and Anna (Lisker) N.; m. Estelle Calderon, June 10, 1962; children: Alan, Michelle. BS in Mktg., Ind. U., 1963. V.p. Modern Vending Co., Indpls., 1963-72, pres., 1972—; pres. Modern Food Systems Inc., Indpls., 1979—. Mem. Rep. Roundtable, Indpls. Served to staff sgt. USAF, 1962-68. Mem. Nat. Automatic Merchandising Assn. (bd. dirs. 1984—), Coffee Devel. Group (bd. dirs. 1986—), Ind. Vending Council (pres. 1984-86, bd. govs. 1984—), Nat. Restaurant Assn. Jewish. Clubs: Indpls. Athletic, Broadmoor Country (bd. dirs.). Lodge: Rotary. Avocations: golf, racquet ball. Home: 5630 N Meridian St Indianapolis IN 46208 Office: Modern Vending Inc 3910 Industrial Blvd Indianapolis IN 46254

NELSON, ELOF GUS, psychology educator; b. Mpls., Apr. 11, 1926; s. John and Ruth (Lind) N.; m. Marette J. Nelson, Sept. 25, 1947; children: Susan, Janice, Carol, Peter, Ann. BA, Gustavus Adolphus Coll., 1948; BD, Luther Northwestern Theol. Sem., 1953; MA, DMin, Andover Newton Theol. Sch., 1958-65; STD, San Francisco Theol. Sem., 1975. Sci. tchr. Hermantown High Sch., Duluth, Minn., 1949-50; parish pastor McVille (N.D.) Parish, 1953-57; dir. religion, health Fairview Hosp., Mpls., 1958-73; prof. family practice U. Minn. Med. Sch., Mpls., 1973-87; pvt. practice psychology Bloomington, Minn., 1970-87. Author: Your Life Together, 1968, Prime-Time Parents, 1971, Keeping Love Alive, 1975, (workbook) Ethics for Primary Care Physicians, 1976; also articles. Bd. dirs. Minn. Council on Families, 1962-70; bd. dirs. clin. care Minn. H.M.O.; pres. Chisago Hospice, 1982-87. Served with USN, 1943-46, PTO. Mem. Am. Assn. Marriage and Family Therapists (supr.), Am. Assn. Pastoral Therapists (charter). Lutheran. Avocations: woodworking, carving, travel, family life, music. Home: 5654 Baden Ct SW Fort Myers FL 33907 Office: U Minn Dept Family Medicine Box 381 Mayo Mineapolis MN 55455

NELSON, HOWARD CREIGHTON, publisher; b. Spokane, Wash., Jan. 3, 1939; s. Harry Nathaniel and Ruth Diener N.; m. Gloria Luz Corvalan, Oct. 17, 1965; children: Ingmar C., Ingrid M. BA in Social Sci., Journalism, Willamette U., 1960; MS in Journalism, Columbia U., 1962. Editor Signal-Am. newspaper, Weiser, Idaho, 1962-64; vol. Peace Corps, Chile, 1964-66; assoc. editor Credit Union Mag., 1968-74; owner Creative Communications, Inc., Madison, 1974—; sec., treas. Food and Energy Breakthru, Inc. Pub. Success Mktg., Success Prins. That Never Fail, Alcohol Breakthrough-Miraculous New Hope for Am. and the Free World, Success Strategy to Revitalize Am. bd. dirs. Peace Project, Madison, 1985. Avocations: polarity, reiki, reflexology, trigger-point therapy, touch for health. Home and Office: 1402 E Skyline Dr Madison WI 53705

NELSON, JAMES F., judge, religious organization administrator. BS, U. Calif., LLB, Loyola U., Los Angeles. Bar: Calif. 1954. Judge, Los Angeles Mcpl. Ct. Chmn. Baha'i Faith Nat. Spiritual Assembly Bahais of the U.S., Wilmette, Ill. *

NELSON, JAMES MITCHELL, sales executive; b. Quantico, Va., Mar. 13, 1954; s. Thomas Earl and Janet Mary (Dado) N.; m. Sheila Kay Habeck, July 24, 1976; children: Ryan, Carly, Kurt. BS in Indsl. Tech. Packaging Engrs., U. Wis., Menomonie, 1976. Terr. mgr. Internat. Paper, St. Louis, 1976-79, field sales engr., 1979-81; div. mktg. mgr. packaging group Menasha Corp., Neenah, Wis., 1981-84; sales mgr. Menasha Corp., Hartford, Wis., 1984-86, gen mgr., 1986—. Coach YMCA Youth Basketball, Milw., 1986; bd. dirs. Pvt. Industry Council S.E. Wis., 1987. Recipient Gold Addy award, 1984; named Eagle Scout Boy Scouts Am., 1969. Mem. Soc. Packaging and Handling Engrs., Sales and Mtkg. Exec., Alpha Phi Omega (leadership award 1975, pres. 1974-75). Republican. Avocations: remote control airplanes, golf, woodworking, camping. Office: Menasha Corp 621 Wacker Dr Hartford WI 53026

NELSON, JAMES RICHARD, data processing analyst; b. Phila., July 3, 1955; s. William James and Linda Marie (Ianniccari) N.; m. Aleasa Deanne Hunter, May 3, 1975; 1 child, James Anthony. Student, U. Kans., 1973-74. Collector credit dept. Ed Marlings, Topeka, 1974-75; collector credit dept. (Master Card) Am. Fletcher Nat. Bank, Indpls., 1975-76, data processor, 1976-79; sr. quality assurance analyst Am. States Ins. Co., Indpls., 1979-86; systems analyst Am. States Ins. Co., 1986—. Creator computer software Nelliecon Bowling System, 1983, Nelliecon coupon retrieval system, 1987. Served with USNR, 1973-74. Mem. Greater Indpls. Bowling Assn. (dir. 1983-87, asst. sec., treas. 1987—), Mut. Bldg. Loan League (sec., treas. 1979—).). Avocations: bowling, softball, camping, Little League coach. Home: 179 Briar Hill Dr Whiteland IN 46184 Office: Am State Ins Co 500 N Meridian St Indianapolis IN 46204

NELSON, JANIE MAE, psychologist; b. Clarks, La., Nov. 23, 1935; d. Ermon and Helen (Stewart) N.; B.Ed., Chgo. Tchrs. Coll., 1956; M.A., Roosevelt U., 1968, 77; Ph.D., Kent State U., 1981. Tchr., elem. sch., psychologist Chgo. Public Schs., 1956—. Pres., v.p. Holy Angel's Blessed Sacrament Soc., 1975-77; dir. Acad. for Counseling and Tutoring; bd. dirs. Nat. Alliance Black Feminists, 1979-81. Mem. Operation PUSH, Am. Psychol. Assn., Assn. Black Psychologists, Woman's Orgn. for Minority Affairs and Needs (co-founder, dir.), NOW, Phi Delta Kappa. Home: 7659 S Normal Blvd Chicago IL 60620 Office: 810 E 81st St Chicago IL 60619

NELSON, JAY PHILLIP, architect; b. St. Paul, Mar. 18, 1950; s. Byron and Geraldine Nelson; m. Joan Colleen Carriveau, Aug. 27, 1974. BArch, U. Minn., 1974. Registered architect, Minn., Wis. Architect Matson, Wegleitner and Abendroth Architects, Mpls., 1973-75, Perrenoud Arch.s, Mpls., 1975-81, Toltz, King, Duvall, and Anderson Architects, St. Paul, 1981-85, Arvid Elness Architects, Mpls., 1985—. Architect Water Products Bldg., Mpls., 1977, Beaver Mall, Beaver Dam, Wis., 1978, APA Optics, 1984, Dr. Martin Luther Library Addition, New Ulm, Minn., 1985—. Mem. AIA, Minn. Soc. Architects. Avocations: reading, travel, waterskiing. Home: 1735 Forestview Ln Plymouth MN 55441 Office: Arvid Elness Architects 200 Butler #510 1st Ave N Minneapolis MN 55403

NELSON, JEANNE ALLENBACH, school administrator; b. Peoria, Ill., May 9, 1931. A.A., Mt. Vernon Jr. Coll., 1951; B.F.A., Bradley U., 1953, M.A., 1968. Dir., Title I ESEA, Peoria (Ill.), Pub. Schs., 1972-81, dir. chpt. 1, ECIA and summer program, 1981—. Mem. Assn. Supervision and Curriculum Devel., Internat. Reading Assn., Jr. League Peoria, Phi Delta Kappa. Office: 3202 N Wisconsin Peoria IL 61603

NELSON, JOHN CARL, statistician, consultant; b. Sterling, Ill., Feb. 11, 1958; s. Carl Harold and Esther Mae (Stern) N. B.S. in Math., Kans State U., 1980, M.S. in Stats., 1981; M. Engring. Mgmt., Northwestern U., 1985. Statistician, Travenol Labs., Inc., Morton Grove, Ill., 1981-83; cons. ZS Assocs., Evanston, Ill., 1984-85; founder, prin. Applied Research Co., Chgo., 1985—. Co-editor: The Commodity Option Analyst, 1985. Mem. Am. Statis. Assn., Inst. Mgmt. Sci., Pi Mu Epsilon. Club: U.S. Tennis Assn. Office: Applied Research Co 53 W Jackson Suite 318 Chicago IL 60604

NELSON, JOHN CHRISTOPHER, systems analyst; b. Des Moines, Sept. 19, 1951; s. Jack Edward and Juanita Jospehine (Rock) N.; m. Jennifer Jane Wills, Aug. 10, 1974; children: Chad Douglas, Scott David. AA, Des Moines Area Community Coll., 1973, A Applied Sci., 1987. Computer programmer City of Des Moines, 1973-78; sr. systems analyst Dial Fin., Des Moines, 1978-81; systems engr. Four Phase Systems, Des Moines, 1981-83; sr. programmer/analyst, cons. Systems Devel., Des Moines, 1983-84; pres., sr. ptnr., systems analyst Dynamic Data Systems, Des Moines, 1983—. Designer computer software system, program. Mem. Nat. Eamon Users Club (pres. 1984—, founder). Home: 2701 Arnold Rd Des Moines IA 50310 Office: Dynamic Data Systems Norwest Fin 208 8th St Des Moines IA 50309

NELSON, JOHN HOWARD, university program administrator; b. Bozeman, Mont., Feb. 5, 1926; s. John Albert and Lillian Mae Nelson; m. Marilyn Joan Carlson, June 28, 1952; children—John Victor, Janet Marilyn, Marjorie Ann. B.S., Mont. State U., 1950; M.S., U. Wis., 1951, Ph.D., 1954. Successively dir. research, v.p. research and devel., v.p. corp. devel. Dairyland Food Labs., 1954-77; mgr. regulatory compliance Kraft, Inc., Glenview, Ill., 1977-78, dir. quality assurance and regulatory compliance, 1979-81, v.p. quality assurance and regulatory compliance, 1981-87; program adminstr. U. Wis., Madison, 1987—; food adv. council Wis. Dept. Agr.; mem. U.S. nat. com. Internat. Dairy Fedn. Served with USNR, 1944-46. Mem. Am. Dairy Sci. Assn. (past dir.), Am. Chem. Soc., Inst. Food Technologists, Assn. Food and Drug Ofcls., AAAS, Sigma Xi, Alpha Zeta. Contbr. articles profl. jours.; patentee in field. Office: Univ Wis Food Research Inst Madison WI 53706

NELSON, JOHN WILTON, symphonic conductor; b. San Jose, Costa Rica, Dec. 6, 1941; came to U.S., 1953; s. Wilton Mons and Thelma (Agnew) N.; m. Anita Christine Johnsen, Sept. 4, 1964; children: Kirsten, Kari. B. Music, Wheaton Coll., 1963; M.M. (Teaching fellow), Juilliard Sch., 1965, postgrad. diploma (teaching fellow), 1967. Conducting faculty Juillard Sch., N.Y.C., 1968-72; dir. Aspen Choral Inst., 1968-73. Music dir., ProArte Chorale, Ridgewood, N.J., 1965-75, condr., N.Y. Mozart Festival, 1967, Juilliard Opera Theatre, N.Y.C., 1968, music dir., Greenwich Philharmonica Orch., N.Y.C., 1966-74, condr., N.Y.C. Opera, 1973-75, Santa Fe Opera, 1973, Geneva Grand Theatre, 1974, Met. Opera, N.Y.C., 1974—, condr., music dir., Indpls. Symphony Orch., 1977—, music adviser, Nashville (Tenn.) Symphony, 1975, conducted, Chgo. Symphony, N.Y. Philharm., Boston Symphony, Phila. Orch., Indpls. Symphony Orch., Cin. Orch., London Royal Philharmonic, Suiss Romade and, others. Recipient Irving Berlin Conducting award, 1967. Office: 4600 Sunset Ave Indianapolis IN 46208 *

NELSON, JUNE KATHERINE, clinical social worker; b. Washington, Mar. 23, 1947; d. Earnest Ellsworth and Lucille Winefred (Stratman) N.; m. Donald Arthur Arms, Dec. 27, 1975. BS, U. Md., 1969; MSW, Wayne State U., 1974. Outpatient services dir. Middletown (Ohio) Area Mental Health Ctr., 1975-82; therapist Family Counseling Ctr., Middletown, 1981—; charge therapist U. Cin. Psychiat. Emergency Services, 1982-83; counselor, cons. Personal Performance Cons., Dayton, Ohio, 1982—; mental health cons. Hospice of Middletown, 1984—. Mem. Nat. Assn. Social Work, Nat. Register Clin. Social Workers, Acad. Cert. Social Workers, Ohio Soc. Clin. Social Work. Lodge: Soroptimist (corr. sec. Middletown chpt. 1984—). Home and Office: 321 S Main St Middletown OH 45044

NELSON, KATHERINE MACTAGGART, insurance company training coordinator; b. Mattoon, Ill., Aug. 27, 1953; d. Leonard John and Wandalee Mae (Clodfelder) Stabler; m. John Robert Nelson; children: Scott MacTaggart, Robert John, Matthew David. BS in Edn., Eastern Ill. U., 1973. Tchr. Owen Valley Schs., Spencer, Ind., 1974-76; acad. support coordinator Whitefish Bay Schs., Milw., 1976-80; dir. research Sullivan, Murphy Assoc., Milw., 1980-81; tng. specialist Northwestern Ins., Milw., 1981-84; tng. coordinator Cath. Knights Ins. Soc., Milw., 1984—. Mem. Milw. Zoological Soc.; founder Mgmt. Resources Exec. Sec. Roundtable, Milw., 1986. Recipient YWCA Leadership award, YWCA, 1986. Mem. Internat. Assn. Personnel Women (chmn. pub. relations 1984-85, chmn. membership and registrar, nominating com., by-laws com., vol. trainer, 1981—), Am. Soc. Tng. and Devel. (bd. dirs., chmn. pub. relations 1984, vol. trainer, 1982—), Soc. Ins. Trainers and Educators (regional conf. host 1986, vol. trainer 1982—), Law Wives Assn. (v.p. membership and soc. coms.). Republican. Presbyterian. Clubs: Milw. Athletic, Pewaukee Yacht, Fox Point Beach. Lodge: P.E.O. Sisterhood. Home: N23 W28796 Louis Ave Pewaukee WI 53072 Office: Cath Knights Ins Soc 1100 W Wells St Milwaukee WI 53233

NELSON, KATHLEEN ANN, newswriter, editor, physical education educator; b. St. Louis, Dec. 31, 1958; d. Robert James and Clara Mae (Hirsch) N.; m. David Henry Luecking, Jan. 2, 1987. BA, BJ, U. Mo., 1981. Sportswriter, editor St. Louis Post-Dispatch, 1981—. Recipient analysis award Profl. Soccer Reporters Assn., 1986, feature writing award Profl. soccer Reporters Assn., 1986. Roman Catholic. Avocations: reading, music, fitness, theatre. Home: 3449 Hereford Apt 12 Saint Louis MO 63139 Office: St Louis Post-Dispatch 900 N Tucker Saint Louis MO 63139

NELSON, KENNETH LOWELL, accounting executive; b. Fargo, N.D., Nov. 12, 1949; s. E.O. and Jewell A. (Jensen) N.; children from previous marriage: Kyle, Eric; m. Penny Jo Nelson; children: Bradley. BA, Moorhead (Minn.) State U., 1971. Supr. cost acct. Northwest Airlines, St. Paul, 1973-77; dir. customer service SES, Inc., St. Paul, 1977-80; dir. fin. & LS R.R., Wells, Mich., 1980—; pres. K.L. Nelson & Assocs., Wells, 1980—. Served with U.S. Army, 1971-73, Korea. Avocation: farming. Home: 5934 29th Ln Brampton MI 49837 Office: KL Nelson & Assocs Inc Wells MI 49894

NELSON, LARRY JAMES, insurance company executive; b. St. Cloud, Minn., Feb. 3, 1949; s. Harold Franklin and Luella A. (Dircks) N.; m. Barbara Gaye Mead, Aug. 21, 1971; children—Jacob Miles, Paul Harold. B.S. in Vocal Music Edn., St. Cloud State U., Minn., 1971. Music tchr. Pierz Pub. Sch. (Minn.), 1971-73; field rep. Horace Mann. Cos., Brainerd, Minn., 1973-76, agy. mgr., Roseville, Minn., 1977-83, asst. v.p., tng. officer Springfield, Ill., 1984-86, v.p. life and annuity bus. devel., 1987—; mem. multi-state ins. licensing program test devel. com. Ednl. Testing Service, Princeton, N.J., 1983—. Mem. Nat. Assn. Life Underwriters, Ill. Assn. Life Underwriters, Am. Soc. Chartered Life Underwriters and Chartered Fin. Cons., Gen. Agts. and Mgrs. Assn. (sec./treas. 1984-85, pres. 1986-87), Paul Bunyan Life Underwriters Assn. (sec./treas. 1974-76). Roman Catholic. Club: St. Charles Ushers (Mpls.) (sec./treas. 1983). Office: Horace Mann Cos #1 Horace Mann Plaza Springfield IL 62715

NELSON, LAURA KAY, editor; b. Larned, Kans., May 12, 1962; d. Keith Charles and Thelma Wandalee (Wright) N. A.A., Dodge City Community Coll., 1982; B.S., U. Kans., 1984. Reporter Tiller & Toiler, Larned, Kans., 1984; area reporter Tribune, Great Bend, Kans., 1984-85; assoc. editor High Plains Jour., Dodge City, Kans., 1985—. Mem. U. Kans. Alumni Assn. and Journalism Soc., Kans. Authors Club, Kans. Anthrop. Soc. Democrat. Avocations: archeology; frontier history. Home: 100 Plains Apt 15 Dodge City KS 67801 Office: High Plains Jour 1500 E Wyatt Earp Blvd Dodge City KS 67801

NELSON, LAWRENCE EVAN, manufacturing company executive; b. Chgo., Dec. 3, 1932; s. Evan Thomas and Elizabeth Marie (Stettka) N.; m. Jean H. Clayton, July 11, 1953; children: Lori Jean, Lawrence Evan. BS with honors, So. Ill. U., 1959; MBA, U. Chgo., 1969. CPA, Ill. Sr. acct. Price Waterhouse & Co., CPA's, Chgo., 1959-65; sec.-treas. Bradner Cen. Co., Chgo., 1965-73; pres. Protectoseal Co., Bensenville, Ill., 1973-84, Plan Ahead Inc., Palos Park, Ill, 1984—. Author: (book) Personal Financial Planning, 1985. Treas. City of Palos Heights, Ill., 1964-68, alderman, 1970-71; trustee Palos Heights FPD, 1977—. Served with USNR, 1952-56. Mem. Am. Inst. CPA's, Ill. Soc. CPA's. Office: Plan Ahead Inc PO Box 164 Palos Park IL 60464

NELSON, LYNN ANNE, micrographics company executive; b. Panama City, Fla., June 12, 1952; d. George Willard and Juanita Anne (Vinson) Thomas, m. Ronald Scott Nelson, Sept. 5, 1970 (div. Mar. 1978); children: Faith Nichole, Jason Jay. Student, Fullerton (Calif.) Jr. Coll., 1970-71. Microfilm technician Microfilming Services, Corona, Calif., 1970-71; microfilm technician Blue Cross/Blue Shield, Eagan, Minn., 1972-73, customer service rep., 1973-76; regional sales rep. MicroD Internat., Burnsville, Minn., 1974-83, gen. sales mgr., 1983-85, v.p., 1985—; bd. dirs. Neoteric Arts, Inc., Burnsville, 1983—. Avocations: painting, drawing, golf. Home: 1212 Hillside Dr Burnsville MN 55337 Office: MicroD Internat 15000 County Rd Five Burnsville MN 55337

NELSON, MARION, history educator, museum director; b. Fergus Falls, Minn., May 1, 1924; s. Albert Edwin and Hilda Agneta (Bergerson) N.; m.

Lila Marie Nentwick, June 17, 1957. BA, U. Minn., 1947, MA, 1950, PhD, 1960. Instr. Scandanavian art U. Minn., Mpls., 1957-59, asst. prof., 1959-63, assoc. prof., 1963-71, prof. art history, 1971—, chmn. dept. art history, 1975-78, 84-87; dir. Norwegian-Am. Mus., Decorah, Iowa, 1965—. Mem. Am. Assn. Museums, Norwegian-Am. Hist. Assn. Avocations: American arts collector. Home: 719 Fifth St SE #4 Minneapolis MN 55414 Office: U Minn Dept Art History 27 Pleasant St SE Minneapolis MN 55414

NELSON, MARSHALL SCOTT, sheriff; b. Minden, Neb., Jan. 8, 1954; s. Virgil Nick and Lois (Jensen) N.; m. Peggy K. Gardner, May 4, 1985. BS, Kearney State Coll., 1978. Dir. security Kearney (Neb.) State Coll., 1978-82; jail adminstr. City/County Jail, Minden, 1983—; sheriff Kearney County, Minden, 1983—, dir. communications, 1985—. Mem. Nat. Assn. Chief Police, Nat. Sheriff's Assn., Neb. Sheriff's Assn., Police Officer's Assn. Neb., Rep. Valley Police Officer Assn., Minden C. of C., Neb. Assn. Criminal Justice Educators, Psi Chi. Lutheran. Lodges: Optimists, Elks. Home: Rt 4 Kearney NE 68847 Office: Kearney County Sheriff's Dept PO Box 185 Minden NE 68959

NELSON, MELVIN DENNIS, utilities executive; b. Unity, Sask., Can., July 18, 1947; s. Stanley Torrey and Esther Florence (Shellrude) N.; m. Lucia K. Nelson, Oct. 11, 1969; children: Joel, Michael, David, Annemarie. BSEE, N.D. State U., 1969. Registered profl. engr., N.D. Engr. North-Western Bell Telephone, Fargo, 1968-70; project engr. Minnkota Power Cooperative, Inc., Grand Forks, N.D., 1971-74, system ops. mgr., 1974—; pres. Exec. Mgmt. Systems, Grand Forks, 1986—. Contbr. articles to tech. jours. Chmn. Faith Evang. Free Ch., Grand Forks, 1987—. Mem. IEEE. Home: 140 Rolling Hills Circle Grand Forks ND 58201 Office: Minnkota Power Cooperative 1822 State Mill Rd Grand Forks ND 58201

NELSON, MICHAEL DEAN, accountant; b. Schaller, Iowa, Sept. 15, 1956; s. Clyde Kenneth Nelson and Helen Lorraine (Johnson) Van Eman; m. Julie Ann Dummer, May 17, 1980; 1 child, Kristine. BS, U. S.D., 1979. Staff acct. Eide Helmeke & Co., CPA's, Sioux Falls, S.D., 1979-81, sr. acct., 1981-82; acctg. mgr. W. Iowa Telephone Co., Remsen, 1982—, asst. treas., 1984—. Vol. Big Bros. Am., Sioux Falls, 1981. Mem. Am. Inst. CPA's, Iowa Soc. CPA's, Northwest Iowa Soc. CPA's, Iowa Telephone Assn. (mem. comml. com.), Jaycees (dist. dir. 1984, regional dir. 1985, v.p. 1986, Clint Dunagen Meml. Nomination 1986), Remsen C. of C. (bd. dirs. 1986, v.p., sec.-treas. 1987), Delta Sigma Pi. Republican. Methodist. Avocations: bowling, golf, softball. Home: 13 N Washington Remsen IA 51050 Office: W Iowa Telephone Co 12 E 3d St Remsen IA 51050

NELSON, MICHAEL EARL, investment banking company executive; b. Ottawa, Kans., Nov. 9, 1953; s. Earl Abram and Melba Loree (Weien) N.; m. Pamela Kaye Folsom, June 2, 1973; children: Jason Michael, Brian Michael. BA in Elem. Edn., Wichita (Kans.) State U., 1976. Sch. liaison officer Wichita Police Dept., 1977-82; investment banker, v.p. R.G. Dickinson and Co., Wichita, 1982—. res. capt. Andover Police Dept., 1982—. Recipient Medal of Valor Wichita Police Dept., 1977. Mem. Aircraft Owners and Pilots Assn., Kansas Copters and Wings (pres.). Mem. Evangelical Free Ch. Avocations: flying, sailing. Office: RG Dickinson & Co 309 S Market Wichita KS 67202

NELSON, MICHAEL EDWARD, accountant; b. Chgo., June 8, 1955; s. Harry Kenneth and Charmaine Vivian (Grabowich) N.; m. Lorna Lynn Macek, Oct. 28, 1978; children: James, Kelly. BBA, Western Ill. U., 1976; MBA, DePaul U., 1982. CPA, Ill. Sr. auditor Health Care Service Corp., Chgo., 1976-79; mgr. Price Waterhouse, Chgo., 1979-84; dir. reimbursement Alexian Brothers Health System, Elk Grove Village, Ill., 1984-86; dir. fin. planning Premier Hosp. Alliance, Westchester, Ill., 1986—. Mem. Healthcare Fin. Mgmt. Assn. (advanced, bd. dirs. 1986—, Follmer award 1986). Republican. Avocations: reading, gardening, photography. Office: Premier Hosps Alliance One Westbrook Corp Ctr Westchester IL 60153

NELSON, NEIL DOUGLAS, biotechnologist; b. Yankton, S.D, Sept. 22, 1944; s. Kermit Raymond and Kathryn Joanne (Jensen) N.; m. Julie Eillen Berndt, June 27, 1981; 1 child, Chad Matthew, Green Alexa. BS in Forestry, Iowa State U., 1966; MS in Soil Sci., U. Wis., 1968, PhD in Plant Physiology, 1973. Wood scientist U.S. Forest Products Lab., Madison, Wis., 1971-77; research plant physiologist, project leader Forestry Scis. Lab., Rhinelander, Wis., 1977-82, program leader, 1983-85; pres., chief exec. officer Forgene, Inc., Rhinelander, 1986—, also bd. dirs. Contbr. articles to profl. jours. Iowa State U. scholar, 1964-66; Fulbright Postgrad. scholar Australian Nat. U., 1968-69; Fulbright Postdoctoral fellow, 1975-76; recipient Wood award Forest Products Research Soc., 1973, USDA Certs. of Merit and Appreciation, 1978, 84, 85.;. Mem. Am. Soc. Plant Physiologists, Soc. Am. Foresters, Internat. Soc. Plant Molecular Biology, Poplar Council of U.S., TAPPI, Sigma Xi, Phi Kappa Phi, Xi Sigma Pi, Gamma Sigma Delta, Fulbright Alumni Assn. Baptist. Avocations: racquetball, wine collecting, hunting, fishing. Office: Forgene Inc 7014 Firetower Rd Rhinelander WI 54501

NELSON, ROBERT BRUCE, III, insurance executive; b. Phila., Sept. 17, 1954; s. Robert Bruce and Thelma Faye (Smith) N.; m. Mary Carol Temple, June 10, 1978; 1 child, Hilary Nicole. BA in Polit. Sci. and Bus. Adminstrn., Ohio State U., 1972, postgrad., 1978. Ins. agent Aetna Life Ins. and Annuity, Columbus, Ohio, 1980-85; asst. dir. agys. Columbus Mut. Ins. Co., 1985; broker, fin. planner Kimberly Co., Columbus, 1985—; cons. Law Offices of Tenuta & Kerns, 1980, Community Christian Ch., 1985—. Recipient fund raising appreciation award St. Judes Hosp., Columbus, 1985-86. Mem. Columbus Life Underwriters. Republican. Lodge: Kiwanis (bd. dirs., pres. scholarship trust fund 1984-85). Avocations: skiing, motor cycling, skeet shooting, flying. Home: 1887 Lost Valley Rd Powell OH 43065 Office: Kimberly Co 1525 Bethel Rd Columbus OH 43220

NELSON, ROBERT EDDINGER, management and development consultant; b. Mentone, Ind., Mar. 2, 1928; s. Arthur Irven and Tural Cecile (Eddinger) N.; B.A., Northwestern U., 1949; L.H.D., Iowa Wesleyan Coll., 1969; LLD, North Cen. Coll., 1987; m. Carol J., Nov. 24, 1951; children—Janet K. Nelson Callighan, Eric P. Asst. dir. alumni relations Northwestern U., Evanston, Ill., 1950-51, 54-55; v.p. and dir. pub. relations Iowa Wesleyan Coll., Mt. Pleasant, 1955-58; vice chancellor for devel. U. Kansas City, 1959-61; v.p. instl. devel. Ill. Inst. Tech., Chgo., 1961-68; pres. Robert Johnston Corp., Oak Brook, Ill., 1968-69, Robert E. Nelson Assocs., Inc., oak Brook, Ill., 1969—; dir. Chautauqua Workshop in Fund Raising and Instl. Relations, 1970-74; dir. Continental Bank of OakBrook Terrace; nat. conf. chmn. and program dir. Am. Coll. Pub. Relations Assn., 1961; trustee, Iowa Wesleyan Coll., 1962-68; faculty mem. Ind. U. Workshops on Coll. and Univ. Devel., 1963-65, Lorretto Heights Summer Inst. for Fund Raising and Pub. Relations, 1964-68; mem. Pub. Review Panel for Grants Programs, Lilly Endowment, Inc., 1975. Served with U.S. Army, 1951-54. Mem. Council on Fin. Aid to Edn. (bd. dirs. 1957-63), Public Relations Soc. Am.; Nat. Soc. Fund Raisers, Nat. Small Bus. Assn., Chgo. Soc. Fund Raising Execs., Blue Key, Delta Tau Delta. Methodist. Clubs: Execs., Econ., Union League (Chgo.), DuPage; Masons. Author chpt in Handbook of Coll. and Univ. Adminstrn., 1970. Home: 5 Oak Brook Club Dr N101 Oak Brook IL 60521 Office: 120 Oakbrook Ctr Suite 208 Oak Brook IL 60521

NELSON, ROBERT JOHN, publisher; b. Cumberland, Wis., Apr. 5, 1926; s. Arthur N. and Alma O. (Johnson) N.; m. Constance Joan Wollan, Sept. 24, 1955 (div. 1970); children: Kevin, Pamela, Cynthia. BA cum laude, U. Minn., 1949. Section mgr. Powers Dept. Store, Mpls., 1950-51; agt. Res. Life Ins. Co., Mpls., 1951-52; rep., editor James C. Fifield Co., Mpls., 1952-67; founder, owner The Nelson Co., Hopkins, Minn., 1967—. Editor, publisher: Nelson's Law Office Directory, 1967—. Served with USAAF, 1944-45. Republican. Lutheran. Avocations: fishing, hunting, reading, traveling. Home: 5300 Vernon Ave Edina MN 55436 Office: The Nelson Co PO Box 309 Hopkins MN 55343

NELSON, S. JAMES, JR., energy company executive; b. Mpls., Apr. 11, 1942; s. Stanley J. Nelson; children: Christian, Erik, Gretchen, Scott. BS Acctg., Coll. of Holy Cross, 1964; MBA, Harvard U., 1966. Mem. staff Arthur Andersen & Co., Mpls., 1966-70, mgr., 1970-76, ptnr., 1976-80; v.p., chief fin. officer Apache Corp., Mpls., 1980-85; sr. v.p., chief fin. officer Diversified Energies, Inc., Mpls., 1985. Trustee Ucross (Wyo.) Found., 1981—. Mem. Am. Inst. CPA's, Harvard Bus. Sch. Alumni Club (bd. dirs. Minn. chpt. 1980—). Home: 708 N 1st St #212 Minneapolis MN 55401 Office: Diversified Energies Inc 201 S 7th St Minneapolis MN 55402

NELSON, SCOTT MICHAEL, lawyer, accountant; b. St. Paul, Sept. 18, 1959; s. Darhl George and Barbara Lee Mary (Greene) N.; m. Marilyn Jean Peller, Aug. 10, 1985. BS, St. John's U., 1981; JD magna cum laude, U. Minn., 1986. CPA, Minn. Staff acct. Arthur Andersen and Co., Mpls., 1981-83; lawyer Rossini and Assoc. P.A., Mpls., 1984—. Mem. ABA, Minn. State Bar Assn., Hennepin County Bar Assn., Am. Inst. CPA's, Minn. Soc. CPA's, Monday Tax Forum, Order of Coif. Democrat. Roman Catholic. Home: 1815 Aquila Ave N Golden Valley MN 55427 Office: Rossini & Assocs P A 5353 Gamble Dr Saint Louis Park MN 55416

NELSON, SCOTT RUSSELL, osteopath; b. Luverne, Minn., Jan. 28, 1954; s. John Eugene and Phyllis Adeline (Bauer) N.; m. Donna Marie McGorty, June 2, 1979; children: Jennifer Elizabeth, Melissa Rachael, Shawn Michael Thomas. BS magna cum laude, Tex. A&M U., 1978; DO, North Tex. State U., 1982. Cert. advanced cardiac/trauma life support. Intern Dallas-Ft. Worth Med. Ctr., 1983; osteo. physician, dir. Theodosia (Mo.) Med. Clinic, 1983-84; emergency osteo. physician Ozarks Med. Ctr., West Plains, Mo., 1984—, cons. osteo. physician, 1986—; dir. osteo. biomechanical evaluation and treatment service Ozarks Med. Ctr., West Plains; staff osteo. physician Baxter County Regional Hosp., Mountain Home, Ark., 1984—. Deacon Emmanuel Ch., Mountain Home, 1986. mem. Am. Osteo. Assn., So. Med. Assn., Mo. Assn. Osteo. Physicians and Surgeons, Am. Coll. Osteo. Gen. Practitioners, Beta Beta Beta, Phi Kappa Phi, Sigma Sigma Phi. Republican. Avocations: water sports, theology, jazz guitar, vocal music, computer science. Office: Ozarks Med Ctr 1103 Alaska West Plains MO 65775

NELSON, TERRY HERMAN, paper converting company executive; b. Sault St. Marie, Mich., July 18, 1946; s. Robert Franklin and Victoria Beth (Kaminsky) N.; m. Christine Ann Ney, June 6, 1969 (div. Aug. 1975); m. Linda Sue Siciliano, Nov. 10, 1978; 1 child, Donald Joseph. BSChemE, Mich. Tech. U., 1969; MBA, Keller Grad. Sch. Mgmt., 1978. Quality assurance lab mgr. Proctor and Gamble, Cheboygan, Mich., 1969-71; devel. engr. James River, Bedford Park, Ill., 1971-78, product mgr., 1978-85; v.p. mktg. Engineered Coated Products, Northbrook, Ill., 1985—. mem. Am. Soc. Quality Ctl., Hazardous Waste Mgmt. Assn. Roman Catholic. Club: Holy Name Soc. (Melrose Park, Ill.). Avocations: reading, bowling, racquetball. Home: 1522 N 17th Ave Melrose Park IL 60100 Office: Engineered Coated Products 2800 Shermer Rd Northbrook IL 60062

NELSON, TERRY LEE, accountant; b. Estherville, Iowa, Sept. 13, 1953; s. Leon Lauren and Betty Revae (Redhead) N.; m. Gail Diane Schultz, May 15, 1976; children: Bradley, Katie. BA, U. No. Iowa, 1975. Sr. acct. Mosebach Griffith, Tama, Iowa, 1975-77; mgr., supr. Ryan, Ginens & Co., Spencer, Iowa, 1977-80, Ryan, Givens & Co., Cherokee, Iowa, 1980-81; ptnr. Ringsdorf & Assocs., Estherville, Iowa, 1981—. Mem. Am. Inst. CPA's, Iowa Soc. CPA's, Mensa. Lutheran. Avocations: gardening, sports, hunting, fishing. Home: 302 N 18th St Estherville IA 51334 Office: Ringsdorf & Assocs PO Box 472 2007 Murray Rd Estherville IA 51334

NELSON, WARREN BRYANT, commodity brokerage executive; b. Manhattan, Kans., Sept. 29, 1922; s. Oscar William and Eda Caroline (Hokanson) N.; B.S. cum laude in Agrl. Econs., Kans. State U., 1942, postgrad., 1950; postgrad. Am. U., 1947; m. Betty Lou Wiley, Dec. 24, 1944; children—Barbara Ann, David William, Marcia Lynn, Robert Warren. Statistician agrl. div. Bur. Census, U.S. Dept. Commerce, Washington, 1945-48, Statis. Reporting Service, U.S. Dept. Agr., Topeka, 1948-50; price analyst Longstreet Abbott & Co., St. Louis, 1951-59, partner, 1959-69; sec. Clayton Brokerage Co., St. Louis, 1959-69, exec. v.p., 1969-72, pres., 1972-77, vice chmn. bd., 1977-86, chmn. bd. 1986—. Served to lt. USAAF, 1942-45. Decorated D.F.C. with 2 oak leaf clusters. Republican. Club: St. Louis. Home: 839 Elm Tree Ln Kirkwood MO 63122 Office: 77 W Port Plaza Suite 522 Saint Louis MO 63146

NELSON, WILLIAM E., religion official. Dir. Chgo. Bapt. Assn. Office: Chgo Baptist Assn 59 E Van Buren Suite 257 Chicago IL 60605 *

NELSON, W(ILLIAM) RICHARD, JR., TV news director; b. St. Joseph, Mo., Sept. 19, 1945; s. William R. and Gertrude (Arnhold) N. BA, Cen. Meth. Coll., 1967; MA, U. Mo., 1971. News dir. Sta. KCRG-TV, Cedar Rapids, Iowa; cons. TV Broadcasts, Ltd., Hong Kong, 1983. Served with U.S. Army, 1969-71. Mem. Soc. Profl. Journalists, Radio-TV News Dirs. Assn. Avocations: skiing, photography, computers. Home: 2407 Buckingham Dr NW #22 Cedar Rapids IA 52405 Office: KCRG-TV 501 Second Ave SE Cedar Rapids IA 52401

NEMEC, EDWARD STANLEY, radiologist; b. St. Louis, Mo., Mar. 20, 1941; s. Stanley S. and Katherine (Vidakovich) N.; m. Victoria Ann Adams, Aug. 5, 1978. Resident in radiology, St. Louis U. Med. Sch., 1975-78; BS, St. Louis U., 1969, MD, 1974. Cert. Am. Bd. Radiology. Intern in internal medicine St. Mary's Health Ctr., St. Louis, 1973-74; chief of radiology Bethesda Hosp., St. Louis, 1980—; chief exec. officer St. Louis Radiology Assocs., 1983—. Mem. AMA, Am. Coll. Radiologists, Radiol. Soc. N.Am., Mo. Med. Soc., St. Louis Soc. Radiologists, St. Louis Med. Soc. Republican. Roman Catholic. Office: St Louis Hills Med Ctr 6500 Chippewa Suite 1 Saint Louis MO 63109

NEMEC, STANLEY S., physician; b. Yugoslavia, June 16, 1911; s. Adolf and Josefina (Koblizek) N.; M.D., St. Louis U., 1936; m. Katherine M. Vidakovich Barr, June 15, 1940; children—Edward S., Mary K., Charles S., Robert S., Louise K., Dorothy K., Barbara K. Gen. med. practice, 1936-43; radiologist, St. Louis City Hosp., 1943-46; practice medicine specializing in radiology, 1946—; cons. radiologist Wabash R.R. Woodland Hosp., Moberly, Mo.; radiologist St. Charles Clinic, Marian Hosp.; asst. in radiology St. Louis U. Sch. Medicine. Diplomate Am. Bd. Radiology, Nat. Bd. Med. Examiners, Fellow Am. Coll. Radiology; mem. Radiology Soc. N.A., A.M.A., So. Med. Assn., St. Louis Med. Soc., St. Louis Soc. Neurology and Psychiatry. Author: History of the Croatian Settlement in St. Louis, 1931; Yugoslav Sokol Almanac, 1933. Editor: Sokol Magazine, 1931-34, The Koch Messenger, 1939. Contbr. articles to profl. jours. Home: Huntleigh Village 2870 S Lindbergh Blvd St Louis County MO 63131 Office: Suite 1 6500 Chippewa St Saint Louis MO 63109

NEMIROW, JOEL ALAN, small business executive, psychotherapist; b. Chgo., Sept. 18, 1951; s. Albert Louis and Betty Lillian (Hyman) N. BS, Loyola U., Chgo., 1973, MA, 1982. Registered social worker; cert. counselor. Pres. A-N Parts & Services Co. Inc., Chgo., 1974—. Pres. 5455 Edgewater Condominum Assn., Chgo., 1979-86. Mem. Am. Psychol. Assn., Am. Assn. Counseling and Devel., Am. Mental Health Counselors Assn., Ill. Psychol. Assn., Ill. Assn. for Counseling and Devel. Home: 100 E Bellevue Pl Unit 25-F Chicago IL 60611-1125 Office: A-N Parts & Service Co Inc 4023 N Broadway Chicago IL 60613-2199

NEMMERS, STEPHEN JEFFREY, military officer, clinical psychologist; b. Forest City, Iowa, Oct. 13, 1946; s. Gerald Joseph and Rosemary (Ehred) N.; m. Kristine Johnson, June 15, 1968 (div. Oct. 1986); children: Stacy Lynn, Victoria Anne. Student, Loras Coll., Dubuque, Iowa, 1964-66; BS, Iowa State U., 1968; MA, U. No. Colo., 1977; PhD, U. Iowa, 1982. Lic. psychologist, Nebr. Commd. 2d lt. USAF, 1968, advanced through grades to lt. col., 1983, navigator, 1968-73, instr. pilot, 1973-79; chief psychol. services USAF, Offutt AFB, Nebr., 1983—; cons. for mental health, hdqrs. SAC, 1984—. Decorated D.F.C. with three oak leaf clusters, Air medal with fifteen oak leaf clusters. Mem. Air Force Assn., Am. Psychol. Assn., Nebr. Psychol. Assn., Soc. Air Force Clin. Psychologists. Home: 1101 Sterling Dr Papillion NE 68128 Office: Ehrling Bergquist USAF Reg Hosp/SGHMA Offutt AFB NE 68113-5300

NEMY, A. S., brass manufacturing company executive; b. 1930. BS, Carnegie-Mellon U., 1951, MS, PhD, 1955. With Keeler Brass Co., Inc., Grand Rapids, Mich., 1982—, now chmn., pres., chief exec. officer. Office: Keeler Brass Co 955 Godfrey AveSW Grand Rapids MI 49503 *

NEPTUNE, TYLER GREGG, JR., lawyer; b. St. Paul, Dec. 22, 1948; s. Tyler Gregg and Clara Belle (Byus) N.; m. Maureen Ann Armstrong, Mar. 29, 1980; children: Kelly, Amy, Tyler III. BA in Psychology, Macalester Coll., 1971; JD, John Marshall U., 1980. Bar: Ill. 1980, U.S. Dist. Ct. (no. dist.) Ill. 1980. Employment mgr. UARCO Inc., Barrington, Ill., 1974-80; assoc. Clancy, McGuirk & Hulce, St. Charles, Ill., 1980-83; sole practice, Geneva, Ill., 1983-86; mng. ptnr. Boylan & Neptune, Geneva, 1986—; mem. oversight com. Kane County Ct., Geneva, 1982—. Served to 1st lt. U.S. Army, 1971-74. Mem. ABA, Ill. State Bar Assn., Kane County Bar Assn. (chmn. admissions com. 1984), Assn. Trial Lawyers Am. Republican. Club: Lions. Home: 2000 Normandy Ln Geneva IL 60134 Office: 115 W Campbell St PO Box 705 Geneva IL 60134

NERLINGER, JOHN WILLIAM, association executive; b. Detroit, June 22, 1920; s. John W. and Bessie Prudence (Beith) N.; m. Pearl Pauline Procup, Nov. 4, 1943; children: John Charles, Ruth Marie Nerlinger Blazevich. Student, Detroit Bus. Inst., 1938-39; B.A., Detroit Inst. Tech., 1950. Bus. mgr. Retail Gasoline Dealers Assn. Mich., Detroit, 1939-51; exec. sec. Retail Gasoline Dealers Assn. Mich., 1951-63, Nat. Congress Petroleum Retailers, Detroit, 1951-63; asst. exec. v.p. Automotive Service Industry Assn., Chgo., 1963-73; exec. v.p. Automotive Service Industry Assn., 1973-80, pres., 1981—; Vice chmn. Automotive Hall of Fame; advisor Nat. Hwy. Users Fedn. Served with AUS, 1942-45, PTO. Recipient Petroleum Man of Year award Gasoline News, 1961; Automotive Replacement Edn. award Northwood Inst., Midland, Mich., 1975; Disting. Service citation Automotive Hall of Fame, 1978; Industry Leadership award Automotive Service Industry Assn., 1978. Mem. Am. Soc. Assn. Execs. (mem. edn. com.), Chgo. Soc. Assn. Execs., Automotive Old Timers, Automotive Info. Council (dir.), Automotive Boosters Clubs Internat., Chgo. Assn. Commerce and Industry (mem. govt. relations com.), Nat. Assn. Wholesalers-Distbrs. (exec. com., dir. distbn. research and edn. found), Automotive Acad. Lutheran. Clubs: Mid-America, Inverness Golf. Lodge: Masons (32 deg.), Shriners. Home: 601 E Fairview St Arlington Heights IL 60005 Office: 444 N Michigan Ave Chicago IL 60611

NERMAN, JEROME STANLEY, truck sales executive; b. Kansas City, Mo., Feb. 26, 1920; s. Gilbert and Esther (Jacobson) N.; m. Margaret Ann Rubin, Aug. 8, 1941; 1 son, Lewis E. Pres. Arrow Truck Sales Inc., Kansas City, 1950—; dir. Central Bank Kansas City; advisor Truck Blue Book, Chgo., 1979-84; v.p. Nationwide Auctions, Inc. Chmn. fund raising Kansas City Heart Assn., 1979-81; mem. exec. com. Kehilath Israel Synagogue, Kansas City, 1984; bd. dirs. Jewish Community Ctr., Kansas City, 1984-87, v.p. exec. bd., 1985-87; treas. Friends of Shalom Plaza, 1983, bd. dirs., 1986-87; active Contemporary Art Soc., Kansas City, 1984; pres. Saddlewood Homes Assn., 1987—. Mem. Mo. Bus and Truck, Kansas City C. of C. (transp. com. 1984-87). Democrat. Clubs: Oakwood Country (Kansas City). Lodge: Shriners. Office: Arrow Truck Sales Inc 3200 Manchester Kansas City MO 64129

NERO, RAYMOND ALBERT, dentist; b. Helena, Ark., Jan. 1, 1920; s. Albert and Annie (Storm) N.; Dorothy Sylvia Phillips, June 25, 1945. BA, Lincoln U., 1942; DDS, Meharry Med. Coll., 1954. Diplomate Nat. Bd. Dental Examiners. Staff writer Mich. Chronicle, Detroit, 1943-47; gen practice dentistry Southfield, Mich., 1956—. Active Nat. Guardsmen Detroit; ex-officio mem. health subcom. Total Action Against Poverty Policy-Adv. Com., 1965—. Served to capt. (dental corps) USAF, 1955-57, Korea. Mem. ADA (life), Nat. Dental Assn., Wolverine Dental Soc. (pres. 1965-66), Mich. Dental Assn., Detroit Dist. Soc. (pres. cen. component 1985—), Am. Acad. Gen. Dentistry, Am. Endodontic Soc., Alpha Phi Alpha (life). Methodist. Avocations: travel, amateur photography, card playing. Home: 5000 Town Ctr Apt 3106 Southfield MI 48075 Office: 20905 Greenfield Suite 601 Southfield MI 48075

NESBITT, DAVID WILLIAM, semiconductor company executive; b. Syracuse, N.Y., Apr. 25, 1946; s. John Burtch and Coral (St. Denis) N.; m. Jane Pufky, July 8, 1967; children: Kara Elizabeth, Amy Kathleen. BA, U. N.H., 1967. Buyer Gen. Electric Co., Binghamton, N.Y., 1967-69; materials mgr. Gen. Electric Co., Syracuse, 1969-72; sales engr. Tex. Instruments Corp., Syracuse and Rochester, N.Y., 1972-75; dist. sales mgr. Tex. Instruments Corp., Houston, 1975-77, Arlington Heights, Ill., 1977-80; cen. area sales mgr. Siliconix Inc., Downers Grove, Ill., 1980—. Republican. Roman Catholic.

NESBITT, JOHN ARTHUR, educator; b. Detroit, Mar. 29, 1933; s. John Jackson and Anna Maye (Hartley) N.; m. Dolores Antonia Gutierrez, Apr. 8, 1961; children: John Arthur, Victoria Bowen. Student, C'ivet Coll., 1952-53; B.A., Mich. State U., 1955; M.A., Tchrs. Coll., Columbia U., 1961, Ed.D., 1968. Registered hosp. recreation dir. Program dir. Jaycees Internat., Miami, Fla., 1957-60; recreation leader Inst. Rehab. Medicine, NYU-Bellevue Med. Center, 1960-61; dir. World Commn. on Vocat. Rehab., Internat. Soc. Rehab. of Disabled, N.Y.C., 1961-63; dep. dir. gen. Internat. Recreation Assn., N.Y.C., 1964-65; asst. sec. gen. Internat. Soc. for Rehab. of Disabled, N.Y.C., 1966-68; asst. prof., coordinator rehab. services San Jose State U., 1968-69; assoc. prof., dir. Inst. Interdisciplinary Studies, 1969-72; assoc. prof., chmn. recreation edn. program U. Iowa, Iowa City, 1972-76; prof. recreation edn. program U. Iowa, 1976-85, prof., chmn. dept. leisure studies, 1986—; pres. Spl. Recreation, Inc.; dir. com. for handicapped People to People Program, 1964—; chmn. com. recreation and leisure U.S. Pres.'s Com. on Employment of Handicapped, 1972-81. Author, editor books in field; editor: Alert Mag., 1956, Jaycees Internat. World, 1957-60, Internat. Rehab. Rev, 1965-68, Therapeutic Recreation Jour, 1968-70, Jour. Iowa Parks and Recreation, 1974-76, Play, Recreation and Leisure for People Who Are Disabled, 1977, Fed. Funding for Spl. Recreation, 1978, New Concepts and New Processes in Spl. Recreation, 1978, New Horizons in Profl. Tng. in Recreation Service for Handicapped Children and Youth, 1983, Nisbet/Nesbitt Soc. Newsletter, 1983-86, Special Recreation Digest, 1984—, Spl. Recreation Compendium, 1986; sr. editor Recreation and Leisure Service for Disadvantaged, 1979; editor, compiler Spl. Recreation Compendium of 1,000 Resources for Disabled People, 1986. Bd. dirs., treas. United Cerebral Palsy Assn., San Mateo and Santa Clara County, 1970-72; bd. dirs. Harold Russell Found., 1971-73, Goodwill Industries Santa Clara County, 1969-72, rehab. counselor, master therapeutic recreation specialist. Served with USAF, 1955-57; maj. Res. Recipient numerous awards and citations for work with handicapped. Mem. Nat. Therapeutic Recreation Soc. (pres. 1970-71), Nat. Rehab. Assn., Am. Assn. Leisure and Recreation (dir.), Nat. Consortium on Phys. Edn. and Recreation for Handicapped (pres. 1976-77), Nat. Forum Comml. Recreation and Handicapped (chmn. 1979), AAHPER, Iowa Parks and Recreation Assn. (dir.), Nat. Rehab. Counseling Assn., Council Exceptional Children, Pi Sigma Epsilon. Presbyterian. Avocations: arts, gardening, travel, geneology, community service. Office: U Iowa Coll Liberal Arts Recreation Edn Program FH436 Iowa City IA 52242

NESS, DAVID JAMES, accountant; b. Escanaba, Mich., Apr. 28, 1949; s. Donald E. and Elaine E. (Ferguson) N.; m. Shirley Ann Adamski, June 17, 1972; children: Shawn, Jessica. BBA in Acctg., U. Wis., Oshkosh, 1978. CPA. Hosp. respiratory therapist Wausau and Merrill, Wis., 1970-77; sr. acct. Wipfli Ullrich, Wausau, 1978-81; supr., acct. Huberty and Assocs., Fond du Lac, Wis., 1981-84, Schenck and Assocs., Fond du Lac, 1984—. Treas. Big Bros./Big Sisters Fond du Lac County, 1986—. Mem. Am. Inst. CPA's, Wis. Soc. CPA's, Commerce Small Bus. Council (appointed). Lodge: Kiwanis (pres. Fabulous Fond du Lac club, 1986—, Kiwanian of Yr. 1984), Elks. Avocations: golf, tennis, camping, hiking. Office: Schenck and Assocs 10 Forest Ave Fond du Lac WI 54935

NESSET, MARY ANNE, psychologist; b. Detroit, Jan. 2, 1945; d. Robert Charles and Margaret (Hayes) Venners; m. Thomas E. Wojcik, Aug. 14, 1965 (div. Aug. 1984); children: Elizabeth Kelly, Katherine; m. Charles D. Nesset, Mar. 30, 1985. AA, Jackson (Mich.) Community Coll., 1964; BA, U. Mich., 1966; MA in Devel. Psychology, Oakland U., 1973; MA in Sch. Psychology, U. Detroit, 1982. Cert. sch. psychologist; lic. psychologist, Mich. Child care worker Plymouth (Mich.) State Home, 1966; elem. tchr. Sacred Heart Sch., Auburn Heights, Mich., 1966-67; sch. psychologist Utica (Mich.) Community Schs., 1974-85, Clare-Gladwin (Mich.) Ind. Sch. Dist., 1985—. Avocations: skiing, reading, knitting, aerobics, running. Home: 114 S 6th St Oscoda MI 48750 Office: Clare-Gladwin Ind Sch Dist 4041 Mannsiding Rd Clare MI 48617

NESTER, WILLIAM RAYMOND, JR., university administrator; b. Cin., Feb. 19, 1928; s. William Raymond and Evelyn (Blettner) N.; m. Mary Jane Grossman, Aug. 21, 1950; children: William Raymond, Mark Patrick, Brian Philip, Stephen Christopher. BS, U. Cin., 1950, EdM, 1953, EdD, 1965. Tchr. high sch. English and history Cin., 1950-52; dir. student union U. Cin., 1952-53, asst. dean of men, 1953-60, dean of men, 1960-67, assoc. prof. edn., 1965-70, dean of students, 1967-69, vice provost student and univ. affairs, 1969-76, prof. edn., 1970-78, assoc. sr. v.p., assoc. provost, 1976-78; v.p. student services Ohio State U., Columbus, 1978-83, prof. edn., 1978-83; pres. Kearney State Coll., Nebr., 1983—, prof. edn., 1983—. Pres. Metro-Six Athletic Conf., 1975-76, Pi Kappa Alpha Meml. Found., 1978-79. Mem. Am. Personnel and Guidance Assn., Nat. Assn. Student Personnel Adminstrs. (past regional v.p., exec. com.), AAUP, Am. Assn. Higher Edn., Ohio Assn. Student Personnel Adminstrs. (past pres.), Pi Kappa Alpha (nat. pres. 1978-80), Frat. Scholarship Officers Assn. (past pres.), Omicron Delta Kappa, Phi Delta Kappa, Phi Eta Sigma. Episcopalian. Home: 5 Northlake Dr Kearney NE 68847 Office: Kearney State Coll Office of the Pres 905 W 25th St Kearney NE 68849

NESVAN, GERALDINE ROOT, psychologist; b. Council Bluffs, Iowa, June 28, 1927; d. Fred E. and Mildred S. (Means) Root; m. Mirko Nesvan; children: Polly, Denis Ann, Debra, Jill. BA, U. Omaha, 1959; MA, U. Nebr., 1960. Lic. specialist, 1970; lic. psychologist, Nebr. Dir. psychol. services Omaha Pub. Schs., 1960-76, Children's Meml. Hosp., Omaha, 1976-84; cons. Nebr. Sch. for Deaf, 1976-82, Iowa Sch. for the Deaf, 1985-86; cons. staff Omaha Children's Clinic, 1982-84, pvt. practice, 1982—; v.p. Cats Corp., 1985—; cons. Meth. Midtown Adolescent Chem. Dependency Unit, 1978-82, 86. Pres. bd. dirs. scholarship bd. Edwards Found., bd. dirs. Nebr. Council for Children and Youths, 1986—. Fellow Am. Assn. Mental Deficiency (past state and regional pres., chmn. Region 8); mem. Am. Psychol. Assn., Nat. Assn. Sch. Psychologists (past state rep.; Founders award 1985), Nebr. Psychol. Assn., Nebr. Assn. Mental Deficiency (pres. 1978-85). Eastern Orthodox. Club: Zonta (pres. local chpt. 1986-88). Home: 7040 Rainwood Rd Omaha NE 68152 Office: 12808 Augusta Ave Omaha NE 68144

NETSCH, DAWN CLARK, state senator; b. Cin., Sept. 16, 1926; B.A. with distinction, Northwestern U., 1948, J.D. magna cum laude, 1952; m. Walter A. Netsch. Admitted to Ill. bar; individual practice law, Washington, Chgo.; law clk. U.S. Dist. Ct. Chgo.; adminstrv. and legal aide Ill. Gov. Otto Kerner, 1961-65; prof. law Northwestern U., 1965—; mem. Ill. Senate. Del. Ill. Constl. Conv.; adv. bd. Nat. Program Ednl Leadership, LWV, Mus. Contemporary Art, Ill. Welfare Assn. Democrat. Author: (with Daniel Mandelker) State and Local Government in a Federal System; contbr. articles to legal jours. Office: State Capitol Room 121C Springfield IL 62706

NETTELS, GEORGE EDWARD, JR., engineering company executive; b. Pittsburg, Kans., Oct. 20, 1927; s. George Edward and Mathilde A. (Wulke) N.; m. Mary Joanne Myers, July 19, 1952; children: Christopher Bryan, Margaret Anne, Katherine Anne, Rebecca Jane. B.S. in Civil Engring, U. Kans., Lawrence, 1950. With Black & Veatch Engrs., Kansas City, Mo., 1950-51, Spencer Chem. Co., Kansas City, Mo., 1951-55, Freeto Constrn. Co., Pittsburg, 1955-57; pres. Midwest Minerals, Inc., Pittsburg, 1957—; chmn. bd. McNally Pittsburg Mfg. Corp., 1970-76, pres., chief exec. officer, 1976—; chmn. bd. McNally Pitts. Inc., 1987—; dir. Bank IV, Pittsburgr, First Fed. Savs. & Loan Assn., Pittsburg, Kansas City Power & Light Co.; past chmn. bd. Nat. Limestone Inst.; bd. advisers Kans. U. Sch. Engring., Center Bus. and Econ. Devel. of Pittsburg State U.; bd. dirs. Pittsburg Indsl. Devel. Com. Bd. advisers Kans. U. Endowment Assn.; mem. Kans. U. Chancellor's Club, Kans., Inc.; past pres. Bd. Edn. 250, Pittsburg; past chmn. bd. trustees Mt. Carmel Hosp.; past mem. Kans. Commn. Civil Rights; chmn. Kans. Republican Com., 1966-68; Kans. del. Rep. Nat. Conv., 1968, Kans. Bus. and Industry Com. for Re-election of the President, 1972. Served with AUS, 1946-47. Recipient Disting. Service citation U. Kans., 1980, Disting. Engring. citation U. Kans., 1985; named Kansan of Yr., 1986. Mem. ASCE, Am. Mining Congress (bd. dirs., bd. govs. mfrs. div.), NAM (past dir.), Kans. C. of C. and Industry (dir., chmn. 1983-84), Kans. Right to Work (dir.), Pittsburg C. of C. (past dir.), Kans. U. Alumni Assn. (pres. 1977), Kans. Leadership Com., Tau Beta Pi, Omicron Delta Kappa, Beta Theta Pi. Presbyterian. Clubs: Crestwood Country (Pittsburg); Wolf Creek Golf (Olathe). Office: McNally Pittsburg Inc 100 N Pine St PO Box 651 Pittsburg KS 66762

NEU, NOEL DARREL, service company executive; b. Sherry, Wis., Mar. 19, 1935; s. Lee John and Katie Louise (Hayden) Neuenschwander; m. Marilyn Ann Costello, Mar. 9, 1968; children: M. Scott, D. Lance, Molly M. BA, Cornell Coll., Mt. Vernon, Iowa, 1957. Mgr. field sales, merchandiser Amoco Oil Co., Kansas City, Mo., 1957-75; econ. evaluation analyst Standard Oil, Chgo., 1966-68; gen. mgr. Iowa 80 Truckstop, Inc., Walcott, Iowa, 1975—, v.p., 1978—; bd. dirs. Iowa 80 Truckstop, Inc. and subs., Walcott, Iowa, 1978—. Served with USNR, 1952-60. Republican. Methodist. Lodges: Shriners, Masons. Avocations: classic cars, photography. Home: 3923 Fairhaven Ct Davenport IA 52807 Office: Iowa 80 Truckstop Inc PO Box 639 Walcott IA 52773

NEUENSCHWANDER, FREDERICK PHILLIP, bus. exec.; b. Akron, Ohio, Mar. 19, 1924; s. Willis Lee and Esther (Mayer) N.; student Franklin and Marshall Coll., 1942-43, U. Akron, 1946-48; m. Mary Jane Porter, Mar. 19, 1948 (dec.); children—Carol, Frederick Philip, Lynn, Dean, Richard. Chief insp. Retail Credit Co., Akron, 1948-55; exec. v.p. Wadsworth (Ohio) C. of C., 1955-62, Wadsworth Devel. Corp., 1955-62, Wooster (Ohio) C. of C., 1962-63, Wooster Expansion, Inc., 1962-63; dir. devel. dept. State of Ohio, Columbus, 1963-71; exec. v.p. James A. Rhodes & Assos., Columbus, 1971-74; prin. F.P. Neuenschwander & Assos., Worthington, Ohio, 1975—. Mem. adv. council Small Bus. Adminstrn. Exec. dir. Wadsworth United Fund, Inc., 1956-62; pres. Templed Hills, Inc.; pres. Central Ohio exec. bd. Boy Scouts Am.; vice-chmn. Ohio Water Commn., Ohio Expns. Commn.; chmn. Ohio Water and Sewer Rotary Fund Commn.; mem., past chmn. Midwest Gov.'s Adv. Council; sec. Ohio Devel. Council, Ohio Devel. Finance Commn. Adv. council Rio Grande Coll.; 1st chmn. bd. trustees Ohio Transp. Research Center; trustee Eden Theological Seminary; bd. dirs. League Against Child Abuse, United Ch. Bd. for World Ministries. Served with AUS, 1943-46. Named Outstanding Young Man of Year, Wadsworth Jr. C. of C., 1958; recipient SIR award for directing outstanding state indsl. devel. program N. Am., 1966, 68, Ohio Gov.'s award 1967. Mem. Am., Gt. Lakes indsl. devel. councils, C. of C. Execs. of Ohio, Huguenot Soc. Am., Am. Legion, Ohio Soc. N.Y. (res. v.p.). Mem. United Ch. of Christ (property mgmt. com. Ohio Conf.). Club: Worthington Hills Country. Home: 5614 Chapman Rd Delaware OH 43015-9203 Office: 7870 Olentangy River Rd Worthington OH 43085-1319

NEUGER, EDWIN, public relations agency executive; b. Cleve., July 13, 1924; s. Joseph E. and Frances (Japp) N.; m. Lorraine Wallen, June 19, 1948; children: Win, Stephen, Barbara, Debra, David. Student, U. Conn., 1943; BA, U. Minn., 1949. Pub. The Bride and Homemaker, 1949-51; pres. Applied Pub. Co., Mpls., 1951-59; founder, pres. Edwin Neuger & Assocs., Mpls., 1959—; bd. dirs. DirActions, Inc., Mpls. Lakers Basketball Co., Los Angeles Lakers Basketball Corp. V.P., bd. dirs. Goodwill Industries Mpls.; bd. dirs. West Lake YMCA. Southdale YMCA; bd. govs. Metro Mpls. YMCA. Served with USAAF, 1942-45. Recipient Silver Spur Hon. award U. Minn., 1948, Town Topper award Mpls. C. of C., 1958, Good Neighbors award WCCO Radio, 1973. Mem. Pub. Relations Soc. Am. (pres. Minn. chpt.), Advt. Fedn. Am. (bd. dirs. Minn. chpt.), Nat. Investor Relations Inst. (bd. dirs.), Soc. Advancement of Mgmt. (bd. dirs. local chpt.), Edina Basketball Assn. (bd. dirs.), Gov.'s Commn. Profl. Basketball, Kappa Sigma (bd. dirs. Minn. corp.). Lutheran. Clubs: Minn. Valley Country, Minn. Press, Daybreakers (Mpls.). Home: 6124 Hansen Rd Edina MN 55436 Office: 1221 Nicollet Mall Suite 320 Minneapolis MN 55403

NEUHAUS, WES WALLACE, advertising agency executive; b. Omaha, Apr. 27, 1951; s. Wallace George and Anna Marie (Christiansen) N.; m. Joan Parker, Oct. 20, 1984; 1 child, Kathryn Parker. B.A., U. Nebr., 1973. Account exec. Bozell, Jacobs, Kenyan & Eckhardt Inc., Omaha, 1973-78, v.p., 1978-84, Sr. v.p., 1984—; cons. Leadership Edn.-Action Devel., Lincoln, Nebr., 1982—. Profl. adv. com. U. Nebr. Sch. Journalism, 1980-81. Nebr. Regents scholar, 1969. Mem. Nat. Agri-Mktg. Assn. (pres. 1982-83, chmn. continuing edn. 1983-84), Omaha C. of C. (exec. com. agrl. council 1982); assoc. mem. Nat. Assn. Farm Broadcasters; fellow Leadership Omaha. Republican. Lutheran. Office: Bozell Jacobs Kenyon Eckhardt 10250 Regency Circle Omaha NE 68114

NEUHAUSER, DUNCAN VON BRIESEN, health services educator; b. Phila., June 20, 1939; s. Edward Blaine Duncan and Gernda (von Briesen) N.; m. Elinor Taoz, Mar. 6, 1965; children: Steven, Ann. B.A., Harvard U., 1961; M.H.A., U. Mich., 1963; M.B.A., U. Chgo., 1966, Ph.D., 1971. Research assoc. U. Chgo., 1965-70; asst. prof. Sch. Pub. Health, Harvard U., Cambridge, Mass., 1970-74, assoc. prof., 1974-79; cons. in medicine Mass. Gen. Hosp., Boston, 1975-80; prof. epidemiology and biostatistics Case Western Res. U., Cleve., 1979—; prof. medicine Case Western Res. U., Cleve., 1981—, prof. organizational behavior Sch. Mgmt., 1979—, assoc. dir. Health Systems Mgmt. Ctr., 1979-85, co-dir., 1985—; cons. in medicine Cleve. Met. Gen. Hosp., 1981—; adj. mem. med. staff Cleve. Clinic Found., 1984—. Author numerous books, sci. papers; editor: jours. Med. Care, 1983—; Health Matrix, 1982—. Vice chmn. bd. dirs. Vis. Nurse Assn. Greater Cleve., 1982-84, chmn., 1984-85; vice chmn. bd. dirs. New Eng. Grenfell Assn., Boston, 1973-85; bd. dirs. Braintree Hosp., Mass., 1975-86; trustee Internat. Grenfell Assn., St. Anthony, Nfld., Can., 1981-83, Blue Hill Maine Hosp., 1983—, Hough Norwood Health Ctr., 1983—. Keck Found. scholar, 1982—; Kellogg fellow, 1963-65; Neuhauser lectr. Soc. Pediatric Radiology, 1982; Freedlander lectr. Ohio Permanente Med. Group, 1986; recipient Trustee award Cleve. Hosp. Assn., 1987, E.F. Meyers Trustee award, 1987. Mem. Inst. Medicine Nat. Acad. Scis., Am. Pub. Health Assn., Am. Hosp. Assn., Soc. for Clin. Decision Making, Beta Gamma Sigma. Clubs: Cleve. Skating, St. Botolph (Boston), Kollege Widgwok Yacht. Home: 2655 North Park Blvd Cleveland Heights OH 44106 Office: Med Sch Case Western Reserve U 2119 Adelbert Rd Cleveland OH 44106

NEUMAN, KERMIT, lawyer, accountant, educator; b. Blumberg, Germany, July 30, 1906; came to U.S., 1911; s. Rudolph Leo and Johanna (Falk) Neumann; B.B.A., Northwestern U., 1932; J.D., Ohio No. U., 1974; m. Newell A. Hahn, Aug. 19, 1939; children—Marilyn Joanne Neuman Reid, Kermit William. Pvt. practice acctg., Chgo., 1928-50, Coldwater, Ohio, 1950—; with Avco New Idea div. Avco Corp., Coldwater, 1950-71; admitted to Fla. bar, 1974, Ohio bar, 1974; individual practice Law, Coldwater, 1974—; tchr. acctg. Ohio No. U.; solicitor Village of Coldwater, 1976-79. Pres. Rockland Fire Dept., Lake Bluff, Ill., 1949. Served as comdr. USNR, 1941-46. C.P.A., Ill., Wash., Ohio. Mem. Am. Bar Assn., Ohio Bar Assn., Mercer County Bar Assn., Am. Inst. C.P.A.'s, Ill. Soc. Cert. Pub. Accountants, U.S. Naval Inst., Navy League, Res. Officers Assn., Ret. Officers Assn. Club: Elks. Home and Office: 214 N Cedar St Coldwater OH 45828

NEUMAN, LINDA, state judge. Judge Iowa Supreme Ct., Des Moines. Office: Iowa Supreme Court State Capitol Bldg Des Moines IA 50319 *

NEUMAN, PHILLIP JEROME, lawyer; b. Augsburg, Federal Republic of Germany, Dec. 18, 1958; came to U.S., 1958; s. Donald Bernard and Barbara (Heavenrich) N. BA, U. Wis., 1980, JD, 1983. Bar: Wis. 1983, Mich. 1983, U.S. Dist. Ct. (ea. dist.) Mich. 1983. Assoc. O'Neill, Kaichen and Mills, Birmingham, Mich., 1983; ptnr. Kaichen & Neuman, Birmingham, 1984-87; assoc. Rubenstein, Isaacs, Lax & Bordman, Southfield, Mich., 1987—. Mem. ABA, Am. Trial Lawyers Assn., Oakland County Bar Assn. (young lawyers com. mem. 1985-87, vice chmn. 1987—), Mich. Bar Assn., Wis. Bar Assn. Democrat. Jewish. Lodge: B'nai Brith (advisor youth orgn. Detroit 1983-87, recording sec. Met. Detroit council 1987—). Avocations: racquetball, working with teenagers. Office: Rubenstein Issacs Lax & Bordman 17220 W 12 Mile Rd Southfield MI 48076

NEUMAN, WILLIAM LAWRENCE, JR., sociology educator, university administrator; b. Phila., Oct. 1, 1950; s. William Lawrence Sr. and Elizabeth Ruth (Mearkle) N.; m. Deanna Sue Livingstone, Aug. 21, 1970 (div. 1977); m. Diane Kathryn Mertens, June 16, 1984. AB with honors, Ind. U., 1972; MS, U. Wis., 1975, PhD, 1982. Lectr. U. Wis., Madison, 1976-82; asst. prof. sociology Whitewater, 1983—, asst. dean, 1987—; vis. asst. prof. Oberlin (Ohio) Coll., 1982. Contbr. articles to profl. jours. Grantee NSF, 1985, NEH, 1987; U. Wis. System fellow, 1986. Mem. Am. Sociol. Assn., Am. Polit. Sci. Assn., Soc. for Study of Social Problems, Midwest Sociol. Soc., PMS-Action, Inc. (chmn. bd. dirs. 1980-82), Phi Beta Kappa. Democrat. Unitarian. Avocations: jogging, sailing. Home: 4410 Yuma Dr Madison WI 53711

NEUMANN, FREDERICK LLOYD, plant breeder; b. Waterloo, Iowa, Apr. 9, 1949; s. Lloyd Frederick and Leita Evangeline (Otto) N.; m. Diane Marie Brown, Aug. 18, 1973; children: Bradley, Brian. BS, Iowa State U., 1972, MS, 1974. Research dir., plant breeder Ames Seed Farms Inc. (Iowa), producers hybrid popcorn seed, 1973-85; plant breeder Crow's Hybrid Corn Co., Milford, Ill., 1985—; mem. research com. Popcorn Inst., Chgo., 1976-85, mem. prodn. and seed research subcom., 1982-85. Treas. Laurel Tree Nursery Sch., Inc., 1981-83; bishop's com. St. Paulinus Episcopal Ch., 1986—. Mem. Am. Soc. Agronomy, Iowa Crop Improvement Assn. (com. to recommend to bd. dirs. certification requirements for hybrid corn and hybrid sorghum 1979), Crop Sci. Soc. Am., Phi Kappa Phi, Gamma Sigma Delta. Republican. Episcopalian. Home: Rural Rt 3 Box 164 Watseka IL 60970 Office: Box 306 Milford IL 60953

NEUMANN, FREDERICK LOOMIS, accounting educator, academic administrator, consultant; b. New Britain, Conn., Nov. 16, 1930; s. Carl Samuel and Rachel Louise (Clark) N.; m. Elizabeth Ann Robinson, Sept. 10, 1960; children: Bradford E., Carla C., Marshall G. A.B. magna cum laude, Dartmouth Coll., 1952, M.B.A. with highest distinction, 1953; M.B.A., U. Chgo., 1965, Ph.D., 1967. C.P.A., Ill., Conn.; cert. internal auditor. Sr. acct. Arthur Andersen & Co., N.Y.C., 1956-62; mem. faculty U. Ill., Urbana-Champaign, 1965—, asst. prof. accountancy, 1965-70, assoc. prof., 1970-75, prof., 1975—, Price Waterhouse prof. auditing, 1979—, head dept. accountancy, 1981-86; cons. in field; pres. Fedn. Schs. of Accountancy, 1987—; sec. Adminstrs. of Accountancy Programs, 1986. Author: Case Studies In Computer Control and Auditing, 1975, Questions and Problems in Auditing, 8th ed., 1985; contbr. numerous articles to profl. jours., chpts. to books. Cons. Champaign County Headstart and Child Devel. Corp., 1970—; treas. Wesley Meth. Ch., 1987—; mem. com. Champaign County Regional Blood Ctr., 1982—. Served to lt. (j.g.) USNR, 1953-56, comdr. Res. Ford Found. fellow, 1962-65, Ernst & Whinney fellow, 1972-73. Mem. Inst. Decision Scis., Am. Acctg. Assn. (chmn. auditing sect. 1976-77), Ill. CPA Soc. (bd. dirs. 1983-85), Am. Inst. CPAs, Inst. Internal Auditors (Leon Radde Outstanding Educator award 1986), EDP Auditors Assn., Acctg. Historians, Phi Beta Kappa, Beta Gamma Sigma, Beta Alpha Psi. Home: 2211 S Cottage Grove Urbana IL 61801 Office: U Ill 1206 S Sixth St Champaign IL 61820

NEUMANN, JEFFREY JAY, photographer; b. Cleve., Aug. 6, 1948; s. Fred and LaVerne (Vavra) N.; m. Charlene Rose Sparrow, Apr. 21, 1968 (dec.); children—Stephan, Corene, Lara; m. 2d, Carolyn Hannah, Nov. 4, 1972; 1 son, Jeffrey. Lithographer, camera operator Advertype, Inc., Cleve., 1972; lab. technician Vista Color Lab., Cleve., 1972-73; prodn. mgr. Mort Tucker Photography, Cleve., 1973-78; owner/photographer Photography by Jeffrey Neumann, Wadsworth, Ohio, 1978—; mem. Small Bus. Mgmt. Adv. Com., 1980-83. Mem. Internat. Platform Assn., Profl. Photographers Am. (awards), Wedding Photographers Internat. (awards), Profl. Photographers Ohio (awards), Akron Soc. Profl. Photographers, Wadsworth C. of C., Wadsworth Growth Assn. Jehovah's Witness. Home and Office: 9960 Mount Eaton Rd Wadsworth OH 44281

NEUMANN, ROY COVERT, architect; b. Columbus, Nebr., Mar. 1, 1921; s. LeRoy Franklin and Clara Louise (Covert) N.; m. Hedy Charlotte Schultz, Aug. 28, 1948; children: Tali, Scott. Student, Midland Coll., 1939-40, U. Calif.-Berkeley Armed Forces Inst., overseas, 1942-43; AB, U. Nebr., 1948, BArch, 1949; MA, Harvard U., 1952; postgrad., U. Wis., Iowa State U. Registered profl. architect, Iowa, Nebr., Kans., Minn., S.D., N.Y., N.J., Mass., Ohio, Pa., Tenn., Ky., Va., W.Va., Ga., Mich., Mo., Ill., Wis. Ptnr., architect R. Neumann Assocs., Lincoln, Nebr., 1952-55; officer mgr. Sargent, Webster, Crenshaw & Folley, Schenectady, N.Y., 1955-59; dir. architecture, ptnr. A.M. Kinney Assocs., Cin., 1959-65; officer mgr. Hunter, Campbell & Rea, Johnstown, Pa., 1965-66; dir. architecture, ptnr. Stanley Cons., Muscatine, Iowa, 1966-76; pres., chmn. bd. Neumann Monson P.C., Iowa City, 1976—; ptnr. Clinton St. Ptnrs., Iowa City, 1983—, Iris City Devel. Co. Mt. Pleasant, Iowa, 1986. Architect: Iowa City Transit Facility Bldg., 1983 , S.C. Johnson Office Bldg., Racine, Wis., addition to Davenport Cen. High Sch., 1985, V.A. Adminstrn. Office Bldg., Iowa City, 1985, Johnson County Office Bldg., Iowa City, 1986. Mem. bd. edn. Muscatine Community Sch. Dist., 1974-76. Served with USN, 1942-46, PTO. Recipient Honor award Portland Cement Assn., 1949, Proficiency award Constrn. Specifications Inst., 1983. Mem. AIA (Honor award 1975), Constrn. Specifications Inst. (pres. 1974-76, Honor award 1983, 84, 85, 86), Soc. Archtl. Historians, Archtl. Assn. London, U. Nebr. Alumni Assn., Phi Kappa Psi. Republican. Presbyterian. Clubs: Geneva Golf and Country (Muscatine); Harvard U. Lodge: Masons, Eastern Star, Elks. Avocations: golf, fishing, medieval history, big band music. Home: 2014 Burnside Dr Muscatine IA 52761 Office: Neumann Monson Architects 226 S Clinton St Iowa City IA 52240

NEUTZNER, HEINZ GEORG, information systems specialist, consultant; b. Altstadt, Czechoslavakia, Jan. 21, 1946; came to U.S., 1954; s. Josef and Karola (Balek) N.; m. Patricia Louise O'Donnell, June 17, 1967; children: Deborah Sue, Peggy Ann. BA, Bellevue Coll., 1975. Frame attendant Northwestern Bell Telephone Co., Omaha, 1966-69, electronic switchman, 1969-74, programmer, 1974-80, systems analyst, 1980-84, mgr. info. systems orgn., 1984—; pres. Advanced Microcomputer Software Cons., Omaha, 1982—. Served with USN, 1964-68. Mem. Inst. Cert. Computer Profls. (cert. data processing 1986), IBM PC User Group (v.p. 1984-85, pres. 1985-86). Republican. Avocations: chess, bridge, gardening, woodworking, personal computers. Home: 8342 N 46th St Omaha NE 68152 Office: Northwestern Bell Telephone Co 100 S 19th Omaha NE 68102

NEVALAINEN, DAVID ERIC, hematology researcher, educator; b. Moose Lake, Minn., June 30, 1944; s. Eric Nevalainen and Anna Catherine (Keyport) Chernugal; m. Jean Ellen Barrett, Oct. 26, 1986; 1 child, Eric David. Student Coll. St. Thomas, 1962-64; BS in Med. Tech. with honors, U. Minn., 1966, PhD in Hematology and Pathology, 1972. Lab. supr. Fairbanks Meml. Hosp., Alaska, 1972-73; asst. prof. Mich. Tech. U., Houghton, 1973-76, assoc. prof., 1976-79; assoc. prof. U. Wis.-Milw., 1979-81; clin. project mgr. Abbott Diagnostics div. Abbott Labs., North Chicago, Ill., 1981-83, project mgr. research and devel., 1983-84, sr. tech. mgr. Venture Tech., 1984-86, mgr. clin. affairs diagnostics div., 1986—; clin. assoc. prof. Rush Med. Coll., Chgo., 1984—. Co-author: Hematology: Laboratory Evaluation of Blood Cells, 1978. Contbr. articles to profl. jours. Mem. growth com. North Shore Congl. Ch., Fox Point, Wis., 1983-84, mem. stewardship com., 1980-83. Mem. AAAS, Am. Soc. Clin. Pathologists (cert. med. technologist,various coms. 1977—, chmn. product devel. sub-com. 1980-81, editorial adv. bd. Lab. Medicine jour. 1984—), Am. Assn. Blood Banks. Avocations: fishing, gardening, photography, canoeing, flying. Home: 1248-C Bradwell Ln Mundelein IL 60060 Office: Abbott Labs North Chicago IL 60064

NEVELS, ZEBEDEE JAMES, physician, surgeon; b. Nowata, Okla., Nov. 13, 1926; s. Zebedee James and Mary Christine (Meigs) N.; m. Virginia Nell Glass, May 5, 1951; children—Karen Leslie, James Norman. B.A., U. Kans., 1950; M.D., Howard U., 1958. Diplomate Am. Bd. Surgery. Resident in surgery Mt. Sinai Hosp., Milw., 1960-62; staff VA Hosp., Wadsworth, Kans., 1962-65; chmn. dept. surgery St. Anthony Hosp., Milw., 1973-80; practice medicine and surgery, Milw., 1980—. Served with U.S. Army, 1945-46. Mem. County Med. Soc., State Med. Soc. Wis., Nat. Med. Assn., AMA, Cream City Med. Soc. (pres. 1978-79). Democrat. Baptist. Avocations: fishing; hunting; golf; gardening. Office: 2130 W Fon du Lac Ave Milwaukee WI 53206

NEVENHEIM, ARNOLD VINCENT, hospital executive; b. Rochester, Minn., Mar. 26, 1947; s. Hervey Richard and Mary Bernadine (Haushofer) N.; m. Susan Ann Nevenheim (div.); children: Andrew John, Amy Jean; m. Jeanette Ann Boyer; children: Sheri Ann, Jeffrey Todd. Supr. Rochester Park and Recreation Dept., 1965-67; with Rochester Methodist Hosp., 1967—, asst. dir. cen. supply, 1976-81, mgr. cen. supply, 1981—; mem. adv. bd. Rochester Area Vocat. Tech. Inst. Chmn. United Way campaign at Rochester Meth. Hosp., 1981; chmn. hosp. div. United Way of Olmsted County (Minn.), 1983. Mem. Am. Soc. Hosp. Cen. Service Personnel, Internat. Soc. Hosp. Cen. Service Personnel. Lutheran. Home: 1524 Wilshire Dr NE Rochester MN 55904 Office: 201 W Center St Rochester MN 55901

NEVEU, PAMELA SUE, marketing professional; b. Urbana, Ohio, Sept. 22, 1952; d. Richard Edward and Dolores Jean (Burden) Atchison. AA with honors, Clark Tech. Coll., Springfield, Ohio, 1981. Legal sec. Bailey & Bailey, Springfield, 1975-76; sec. health dept. Clark Tech. Coll., 1976-81; adminstrv. assoc. United Way, Dayton, Ohio, 1981-82; advt. sec. NCR Corp., Dayton, 1982-83; account coordinator Reiser Williams deYong, San Francisco, 1983-86; coordinator trade shows, corp. com. Philips Industries, Inc., Dayton, Ohio, 1986-87; assoc. analyst ARINC Research Corp., Dayton, 1987—. Home: 319 W Dayton-Yellow Springs Rd Apt 240 Fairborn OH 45324

NEVID, NORBERT, insurance company executive; b. Rochester, N.Y., Jan. 8, 1934; s. Manuel E. and Betty F. N.; m. Barbara J. Landgraf, Feb. 4, 1955 (div. 1984); children: Nancy, Nathan, Nicholas. BBA, U. Wis., 1955; MBA, U. Wis., Milw., 1966. CPA, CPCU, Wis. Ins. examiner Wis. Ins. Dept., Madison, 1955-60; controller Mortgage Guaranty Ins. Co. subs. MGIC Investment Corp., Milw., 1960-65, treas., 1965-67, v.p. research, 1975—; treas. MGIC Investment Corp., Milw., 1968-75; chmn. ins. com. U.S. Swimming, Inc., Colorado Springs, Colo., 1980-82. Mem. Am. Inst. CPA's, Nat. Assn. Ind. Insurers (vice chmn. acctg. com.), Wis. Soc. CPA's, Soc. CPCU's, Greater Milw. CPCU's, Beta Alpha Psi. Home: 929 N Astor St #706 Milwaukee WI 53202 Office: MGIC MGIC Plaza 417 H 250 E Kilbourn Ave Milwaukee WI 53201

NEVILLE, GERALD RICHARD, insurance executive; b. Kansas City, Mo., Sept. 6, 1947; s. John Patrick and Dorothy Virginia (Padgett) N. BS, Southwest Mo. State U., 1972, MBA, 1982; student, CPCU program. Claims adjuster Underwriters Adjusting Co., St. Joseph, 1972-74; salesman Coachright Real Estate, St. Joseph, 1974-76; claims adjuster Crawford & Co., St. Joseph, 1976-79; claims systems adminstr. Am. Nat. Property & Casualty Co., Springfield, Mo., 1979—; instr. Southwest Mo. State U., Springfield, 1983-84. Vol. United Way, Springfield, 1983-86, Make-a-Wish Found. Mo., Springfield, 1984-86; pres. Springfield Little Theatre Stage Technicians Guild, Springfield, 1986—; bd. dirs. Springfield Little Theatre, 1986—. Baptist. Avocations: softball, golf, writing. Home: 3125 E Grand Springfield MO 65804 Office: Am Nat Property & Casualty Co 1949 E Sunshine Springfield MO 65804

NEVILLE, JOHN, actor, director; b. London, May 2, 1925; s. Reginald and Mabel L. (Fry) Neville; m. Caroline Hopper, 1948; 6 children. Ed. Royal Acad. Dramatic Art; Dr. Dramatic Arts (hon.) Lethbridge U., Alta., Can., 1979; D.F.A. (hon.) N.S. Coll. Art and Design, 1981. With Bristol Old Vic Co., London, 1953, Chichester Theatre Co., 1962; dir. Nottingham Playhouse, 1963-68, Newcastle Playhouse, 1967; hon. prof. drama, Nottingham U., 1967—; drama adviser Howard and Wyndham, Ltd.; artistic dir. Citadel Theatre, Edmonton, Alta., Can., 1973-78, Neptune Theatre, Halifax, N.S., 1978-83; artistic dir., Stratford Shakespearean Festival, Stratford, Ont., Can., 1985—; actor films: Mr. Topaz, Oscar Wilde, Billy Budd, A Study in Terror, Adventures of Gerrard. Decorated knight Order Brit. Empire. *

NEVIN, JOHN JOSEPH, tire and rubber manufacturing executive; b. Jersey City, Feb. 13, 1927; s. Edward Vincent and Anna (Burns) N.; m. Anna Filice, June 16, 1951; children: Stanley James, John Joseph, Richard Charles, Paul Edward, Gerald Patrick, Mary Anne. B.S., U. Calif., 1950; M.B.A., Harvard U., 1952. Various positions fin., product planning and mktg. Ford Motor Co., Dearborn, Mich., 1954-71; v.p. mktg. Ford Motor Co., 1969-71; pres. Zenith Radio Corp., Chgo., 1971-76; chmn. Zenith Radio Corp., 1976-79; pres. Firestone Tire & Rubber Co., Akron, Ohio, 1979-82; chief exec. officer Firestone Tire & Rubber Co., 1980—, chmn., 1981—. Gen. chmn. Summit County United Way, 1983. Served with USNR, 1945-46. Office: Firestone Tire & Rubber Co 1200 Firestone Pkwy Akron OH 44317

NEWBERG, CARL JOSEPH, service and training manager; b. Oak Park, Ill., Nov. 22, 1942; s. Carl Edward and Jane Dorothy (Davidson) N.; m. Julianne Louise Jackim, Feb. 12, 1972; children: Sam, Paul. BA in History, U. Minn., 1965; MBA, Coll. St. Thomas, 1980. Service rep. Toro Co., Mpls., 1971-73, service adminstrn. mgr., 1973-84, service and tng. mgr., 1984—. Chmn. Christian edn. bd. Mayflower Congl. Ch., Mpls., 1985-86. Served to lt. USN, 1965-70, Vietnam. Mem. U.S. Naval Inst., Nat. Assn. Service Mgrs. (bd. dirs. 1984-87). Avocations: tennis, fishing, wilderness camping, ship models. Home: 5235 12th Ave S Minneapolis MN 55417 Office: The Toro Co 8111 Lyndale Ave S Minneapolis MN 55420

NEWBERGER, SHEL, packaging executive; b. Chgo., Nov. 30, 1925; s. Oscar and Daisy N.; B.A., U. Chgo., 1944; m. Natalie Bernard, Oct. 22, 1946; children—Steven, Richard, David, Jill. Packaging salesman Cleary Box Co., Chgo., 1946-48, Chippewa Paper Products, Chgo., 1948-63, Lanzit Corrugated Box Co., Chgo., 1950-63, Consol. Packaging Corp., Chgo., 1960-63; pres., Apollo Containers, Inc., Evanston, Ill., 1963-85, prin., pres., Boyer Corp., Evanston, 1976-84. Alderman, Evanston, 1967-71; officer Evanston Recreation Bd., 1971-85; pres. Evanston Library Friends, 1986—. Served with U.S. Army, 1944-46. Mem. Chgo. Assn. Commerce and Industry, Evanston C. of C. Home: 100 Dempster St Evanston IL 60202

NEWBERRY, NICK T., insurance company executive. Chmn. Woodmen of the World Life Ins. Soc., Omaha. Office: Woodmen of the World Life Ins Soc 1700 Farnam St Omaha NE 68102 *

NEWBERRY, THOMAS BRENT, psychiatrist; b. Ogden, Utah, Aug. 11, 1943; s. John Thomas and Ethel Geraldine (Chapman) N.; m. Mary Theresa Castillo; children: Synthea, John, Brent, Jacob. AA in Medicine, Cochise Coll., 1975; BS, U. Ariz., 1976; DO, U. Health Sci., Kansas City, Mo., 1980; degree in psychiatry, Menninger Sch. Psychiatry, 1984. Psychiatry fellow Menninger Found., Topeka, Kans., 1981-84; staff psychiatrist, psychiat. cons. Kans. Correctional System, Topeka, 1984—, Colmery-O'Neil VA Hosp., Topeka, 1984—. Served with U.S. Army, 1969-71. Mem. AMA, Am. Psychiat. Assn., Am. Osteo. Assn., Am. Coll. Neuropsychiatry, Kans. Psychiat. Soc. Home: 1900 W Lyman Box 72 Topeka KS 66608 Office: Colmery-O'Neil VA Hosp 2200 Gage Blvd Topeka KS 66608

NEWBLATT, STEWART ALBERT, U.S. dist. judge; b. Detroit, Dec. 23, 1927; s. Robert Abraham and Fanny Ida (Grinberg) N.; m. Flora Irene Sandweiss, Mar. 5, 1965; children: David Jacob, Robert Abraham, Joshua Isaac. B.A. with distinction, U. Mich., 1950, J.D. with distinction, 1952. Bar: Mich. bar 1953. Partner firm White & Newblatt, Flint, Mich., 1953-62; judge 7th Jud. Circuit Mich., 1962-70; partner fir Newblatt & Grossman (and predecessor), Flint, 1970-79; U.S. dist. judge Eastern Dist. Mich., Flint, 1979—; adj. instr. U. Mich.-Flint, 1977-78, 86. Mem. Internat. Bridge Authority Mich., 1960-62. Served with AUS, 1946-47. Mem. Fed. Bar Assn., State Bar Mich., Dist. Judges Assn. 6th Circuit. Jewish. Office: Fed Bldg 600 Church St Flint MI 48503

NEWBROUGH, ARTHUR TRUETT, educational administrator; b. Connellsville, Pa., Dec. 15, 1946; s. Edgar Truett and Muriel Ethelyn (Amos) N.; m. Florence E. Ross, Jan. 27, 1968; children—Brett, Truett, Tiffany Diane. B.S. in Edn., Ill. State U., 1968, M.S. in Counseling, 1969; cert. advanced studies in ednl. adminstrn., No. Ill. U., 1980. Counselor Bloomington High Sch., Ill., 1968-70; counselor, cons., dir. Deerfield High Sch., Ill., 1970-81; ednl. cons. Ill. State Bd. Edn., Springfield, 1981-82; sch. adminstr. Highland Park High Sch., Ill., 1982-86; prin. Carl Sandburg High Sch., Orland Park, Ill., 1986—; v.p. Newbrough Resource Group, Cape Coral, Fla., 1982—. Author: Accessing the Community for Student Learning in Vocational Education, 1982; Rainbow Builders, 1983. Chief negotiator Sch. Bd. Dist. 15, McHenry, Ill., 1980-86, v.p., 1983-84, pres., 1984-86. Recipient Supt.'s Option award Twp. High Sch. Dist. 113, 1972-80. Mem. Nat. Experience Based Career Edn. Assn. (bd. dir., pres. 1983-84), Lake County Career Guidance Consortium (v.p. 1984-85, bd. dirs.). Avocations: tennis; racquetball; skiing; reading; writing. Office: Carl Sandburg High Sch 133d and La Grange Rd Orland Park IL 60462

NEWELL, ARLO FREDERIC, editor in chief; b. Stafford, Kans., Feb. 22, 1926; m. Helen Louise Jones, Aug. 1, 1947; children: Rebecca S., Samme Le, Eric F. Student, Anderson Coll., U. N.C., Duke U., Eden Theol Sem.; DD (hon.), Gulf-Coast Bible Coll. Assoc. pastor Ch. of God, Akron, Ohio; pastor Ch. of God, High Point, N.C., 1951-60, St. Louis, 1960-72, Springfield, Ohio, 1972-77; editor-in-chief Warner Press, Inc., Anderson, Ind., 1977—. Home: 1927 Mark Ln Anderson IN 46012 Office: Warner Press Inc 1200 E 5th St Anderson IN 46012

NEWEY, DEBORAH DOX, artist; b. Utica, N.Y., Aug. 17, 1958; d. James Gould and Beverly Ann (Paris) Dox; m. Arthur Tyler Newey, Oct. 4, 1980. Student, Art Inst., Chgo.; BA, North Cen. Coll., Naperville, Ill., 1980. Owner, mgr. Newey's Cordialart, Chgo., 1982—. Exhibited in fine art fairs and art galleries; designer greeting cards and acrylic paintings on canvas. Mem. Chgo. Artists Coalition. Office: Newey's Cordialart PO Box 14614 Chicago IL 60614

NEWHARD, EDMUND EUGENE, JR., data processing executive; b. Poughkeepsie, N.Y., July 17, 1952; s. Edmund Eugene Sr. and Jean Catherine (Sullivan) N.; m. Janet Ann Houseman, Nov. 24, 1976 (div. Aug. 1979); m. Susan Virginia McBride, Sept. 18, 1982; 1 child, Melissa Jean. BA in Polit. Sci., Cen. Coll., Pella, Iowa, 1974. Systems analyst Am. Valuation Cons., Des Plaines, Ill., 1977-78; programmer analyst Bandag Inc., Muscatine, Iowa, 1978-79; systems analyst Valuation Research Co., Chgo., 1979-81; mgr. fixed asset system/tax planning system tech. support UCCEL, Chgo., 1981-85; sr. devel. specialist UCCEL/Global Software, Chgo., 1985-86; specialist tech. devel. Cyborg Systems Inc., Chgo., 1986—. Active University Heights Civic Com., Naperville, Ill., 1983-86, Naperville Community Radio Watch, 1985-87. Named one of Outstanding Young Men of Am., U.S. Jaycees, 1986. Mem. Data Processing Mgmt. Assn. Republican. Avocations: golf, long distance running, gardening. Home: 1537 London Ct Naperville IL 60540

NEWILL, JAMES WAGNER, accounting executive; b. Greensburg, Pa., Dec. 22, 1934; s. James Meyers and Ruth Elizabeth (Wagner) N.; m. Helene Margaret Dolibois, Feb. 18, 1957; 1 child, J. Eric. BBA, St. Vincent Coll., Latrobe, Pa., 1962. CPA, Pa., Ohio, Fla. Staff acct. George Conti and Co., CPA, Greensburg, 1962-65; internal auditor Duquesne Light Co., Pitts., 1965-67; supr. accounts payable and gen. ledger Kennametal, Inc., Latrobe, 1967-71; asst. controller Glosser Stores, Inc., Johnstown, Pa., 1971-73; controller, asst. treas. Meriadian Plastics, Inc., Byesville, Ohio, 1973-76; regional controller Friendly Ice Cream Corp., Wilbraham, Mass., 1976-79; pres. J.W. Newill Co., Troy, Ohio, 1979—; bd. dirs. Southwest Nat. Bank, Greensburg. pres. bd. dirs. Troy-Hayner Cultural Ctr., 1982-85. Served to staff sgt. USAF, 1954-58. Mem. Am. Inst. CPA's, Pa. Inst. CPA's, Ohio Soc. CPA's, Fla. Inst. CPA's, Nat. Assn. Accts. Republican. Methodist. Lodge: Rotary (chmn. com., Paul Harris fellow), Elks. Avocations: travel, tennis, theater. Home: 1111 Hillcrest Dr Troy OH 45373 Office: 16 S Short St Troy OH 45373

NEWLIN, THOMAS CHARLES, lawyer; b. Terre Haute, Ind., June 8, 1949; s. John Terhune and Marjorie Ann (McCandless) N.; m. Laurice E. Greggs, Nov. 30, 1974; children: Thomas Charles II, Christopher Michael, Brian Andrew. BS, Ind. State U., 1971; MBA, Ind. U., Bloomington, 1973; JD cum laude, Ind. U., Indpls., 1986. Bar: Ind. 1986, U.S. Dist. Ct. (no. and so. dists.) Ind. 1986, U.S. Ct. Appeals (7th cir.) 1986. V.p. Newlin-Johnson Co. Inc., Terre Haute, 1973—; ptnr. Flescher, Flescher & Newlin, Terre Haute, 1986—; dep. prosecutor Viso County, Terre Haute, 1986; bd. dirs. Progress Bldg. Corp., 1984—. bd. dirs. Wabash Valley chpt. ARC, Terre Haute, 1978-82, Salvation Army, Terre Haute, 1978. Mem. ABA, Ind. Bar Assn., Terre Haute Bar Assn., Wabash Valley Officials Assn., Terre Haute Area C. of C. (bd. dirs. 1984). Roman Catholic. Club: Wabash Valley Roadrunners. Lodge: Elks, Rotary (bd. dirs. Terre Haute 1978). Avocations: running, downhill skiing, basketball officiating. Home: 113 Briarwood Ln Terre Haute IN 47803 Office: Fleschner Fleschner & Newlin 201 Ohio Terre Haute IN 47807

NEWLON, LARRY DEAN, computer specialist; b. Geneseo, Ill., Jan. 15, 1948; s. Walter James and Anna Louise (Rosenow) M. BS in Biology, Western Ill. U., 1970. Cert. tchr., Ill. Tchr. biology Moline (Ill.) High Sch., 1970-73; tchr. Briar Bluff Sch., Coal Valley, Ill., 1973-74; machine operator Farmall, Rock Island, Ill., 1974-75; supr. computer room Deere and Co., Moline, 1975—. Big bro. Youth Service Bur., Moline, 1980—. Lutheran. Avocations: sports, traveling. Home: 701 40th St East Moline IL 61244-1944 Office: Deere and Co 400 19th St Moline IL 61265

NEWMAN, CHARLES ROBERT, architect; b. Valparaiso, Ind., Dec. 11, 1950; s. Charles Robert Newman and Jean Lynette (Erickson) Brown. BArch, U. Ill., 1973. Registered architect, Ill., Wis. Ptnr. Benedict Sigfusson Assocs., Park Ridge, Ill., 1980-82; v.p. Constrn. Collaborative, Inc., Park Ridge, Ill., 1980-82; ptnr. Computerization, Naperville, Ill., 1984—; pres., chief exec. officer Charles Newman & Assocs., Naperville, 1985—. Mem. Warrenville (Ill.) Planning Commn., 1981-87, chmn., 1985-87; mem. Warrenville Econ. Devel. Commn., 1985-87. Co-recipient Peter Lisager award Chgo. chpt. Soc. Profl. Journalists. Mem. AIA (bd. dirs. NE Ill. chpt. 1983-85), Constrn. Specifications Inst. (pres. No. Ill. chpt. 1986—). Lodge: Lions. Office: Charles Newman and Assocs Inc 710 E Ogden Ave Suite 208 Naperville IL 60540

NEWMAN, DAVID WILLIAM, plant physiology and biochemistry educator; b. Pleasant Grove, Utah, Oct. 26, 1933; s. Frank Byrd and Edna (Holdaway) N.; m. JoAnne Marie Slighting, May 16, 1956; 1 child, Steven D. BS, U. Utah, 1955, MS, 1957, PhD, 1960; postgrad. Oak Ridge Inst. Nuclear Studies. Research fellow U. Utah, 1956-59; asst. prof. Miami U., Oxford, Ohio, 1960-66, assoc. prof., 1966-74, prof. dept. botany, 1974—. Co-author: Eco-physiology Plant Membrane L.P.A.'s; editor: Instrumental Methods of Experimental Biology, 1964; co-editor: (3 vols.) Models in Plant Physiology and Biochemistry; contbr. articles and photographs to profl. jours., mags. and textbooks. Served with U.S. Army, 1957-62. NSF grantee, indsl. research grantee; finalist nat./internat. photog. contests. Fellow Ohio Acad. Scis.; mem. AAAS, Am. Chem. Soc., Am. Soc. Plant Physiologists, Am. Oil Chemists Soc., Société Francaise de Physiologie Vegetaie, Friends of Photography, Calumet Photog. Soc. (charter), Internat. Platform Assn., Sierra Club, Phi Beta Kappa, Sigma Xi, Phi Kappa Phi, Phi Sigma. Editor: Instrumental Methods of Experimental Biology, 1964; contbr. articles to profl. jours. Home: 3713 Pamajera Dr Oxford OH 45056 Office: Botany Dept Miami U Oxford OH 45056

NEWMAN, DAVID WILLIAM, rubber company executive; b. Dayton, Ohio, Feb. 1, 1941; s. David Noah and Irene H. (Lacy) N.; m. Bonnie Louise Perry, Nov. 13, 1982; children: Corie, Betsy, David. Grad. high sch., Lebanon, Ohio. Sales rep. Gen. Films, Inc., Covington, Ohio, 1962-72; chief exec. officer Newman San. Gasket Co., Lebanon, Ohio, 1973—; mem. Gov. Council Small Bus., Columbus, Ohio, 1985—. Mem. Warren County Rep. Club,Lebanon, 1984. Served with U.S. Army, 1959-61. Mem. Southwest Ohio Rubber Mfrs. Presbyterian. Lodges: Shriners (nobel 1977—), Elks (pres. 1973-74). Avocations: fishing, traveling, gardening. Home: 398 Ridgewood Ln Lebanon OH 45036 Office: Newman San Gasket Co 964 W Main St Lebanon OH 45036

NEWMAN, FREDERICK L., research psychologist, educator; b. N.Y.C., Dec. 15, 1938; s. David A. and Helen (Gotterer) N.; m. Charlotte A. Delaney, June 15, 1964; children: Andrew David, Adam Richard. BA, Allegheney Coll., 1961; MA, Kent (Ohio) State U., 1963; PhD, U. Mass., 1966. Lic. psychologist, Pa. Asst. prof. N.Mex. State U., Los Cruces, 1966-69; assoc. prof. U. Miami, Fla., 1969-72; asst. prof. U. Pa., Phila., 1972-81; assoc. prof. Med. Coll. Pa., Phila., 1980-83, Northwestern U., Chgo., 1983-86, Sch. Pub. Health U. Ill., Chgo., 1986—; advisor to mental health dir., acting chief info. systems and evaluation Pa. Office Mental Health, Harrisburg, 1972-79; cons. Ill. Dept. Mental Health and Devel. Disabilities, Springfield, Ill. and Chgo., 1984—, Peat, Marwick, Main, Salt Lake, Utah, 1985—. Author: Integrated Clinical and Fiscal Management in MH, 1985, Client Oriented Cost Outcome Systems 2d Ed., 1980; contbr. numerous articles to profl. jours. Served to pvt. USMCR. Fellow Ctr. Advance Study Behavioral Scis., 1971-72. Fellow AAAS; mem. Am. Psychol. Assn., Psychonomics Assn., Soc. Psycholtherapy Research, Am. Pub. Health Assn., Sigma Xi. Democrat. Unitarian-Universalist. Home: 1327 Lincoln St Evanston IL 60201 Office: U Ill Sch Pub Health PO Box 6998 2035 W Taylor Chicago IL 60680

NEWMAN, GERALD, restaurant franchise company executive; b. Chgo., May 26, 1931; s. Morris and Sara (Glaser) N.; m. Bobbi F. Greenblatt, Dec. 18, 1955; children: Marc, Jeffrey. Student, Chgo. City Jr. Colls., 1949-51, U. Ill., 1949; B.S., Roosevelt U., 1957. Bookkeeper Evans Fur Co., Chgo., 1951; controller Stacy Constrn. Co., Chgo., 1951-59; co-owner, accountant Met. Roofing Co., Chgo., 1959-61; with McDonald's Corp., Oak Brook, Ill., 1961—; v.p., controller McDonald's Corp., 1969-72, exec. v.p., 1972-80, sr. exec. v.p., 1980—, also dir.; dir. Family Foods of Holland; former chmn. bd. Golden Arches of Eng., 1976—. Adv. bd. dirs. DePaul U. Sch. Acctg.; pres., chief exec. officer Ronald McDonald Children's Charities, 1984; past bd. trustees Spertus Coll. Mem. Am. Inst. Corp. Controllers. Jewish. Office: McDonalds Corp 1 McDonald Plaza Oak Brook IL 60521

NEWMAN, ISADORE, statisical researcher, psychology educator; b. N.Y.C., Dec. 3, 1942; s. Sidney and Becky (Silversmith) N.; m. Carole Spitzer; children: David, Matthew. BA in Psychology, U. Miami, 1965; MA in Psychology, New Sch. for Social Research, 1968; PhD in Ednl. Psychology, So. Ill. U., 1971. Lic. psychologist, Ohio. Prof. in dept. of Ednl. Founds. U. Akron, Ohio, 1971—, assoc. dir. Inst. Life Span Devel. and Gerontology, 1982—, coordinator Office Ednl. Research and Evaluation, 1986—; pres. Evaluation and Research Assn., Inc., Akron, 1974—; nat. cons. in research design and methodology U. Ga., U. Nev., U. Kans., Kent State U., the Rockefeller Group, U.S. Army, Ohio N.G., Ford Motor Co.; cons. Ohio Dept. Edn., Houghton Mifflin Pub. Co., various sch. systems and pub. cos.; major research and design cons. Akron Children's Hosp., Aultman Hosp., Canton, Ohio; mem. adv. com. Ctr. Family Studies, U. Akron. Pub. nine books in field; contbr. over 60 articles to profl. jours.; editor: Multiple Linear Regression Viewpoints; cons. editor: Applied Behavior Analysis, Am. Secondary Edn., Jour. Nutritional Edn.; reviewer: Am. Ednl. Research Jour. Recipient Outstanding Prof. Yr. award U. Akron, 1985. Fellow Ohio Acad. Sci. (past v.p. psychology div., psychology, social sci. div. editor); mem. Am. Psychol. Assn., Am. Ednl. Research Assn. (exec. com. spl. interest group, Outstanding Contbn. award in field of Multiple Linear Regression , 1978), Midwestern Ednl. Research Assn. (v.p. elect 1984), Western Res. Human Services (v.p., trustee). Democrat. Jewish. Home: 2995 Stanley Rd Akron OH 44313 Office: U Akron Office Ednl Research Buchtel Ave Akron OH 44325

NEWMAN, LEONARD JAY, retail jewel merchant, gemologist; b. Milw., Oct. 25, 1927; s. David and Pia Goldie (Smith) N.; m. Louise Shainberg, Jan. 14, 1951; children—Shelley, Marty, Alan, Heidi, Dee. B.S., Purdue U.; postgrad. Washington U., St. Louis. Owner, mgr. Newman's Diamond Ctr., Jasper, Ind., 1951—; tchr. The Jasper Ctr., Ind., 1970-80. Bd. dirs. VUJC Found., State Bd. Health Systems Agy., sub area Health Systems Agy.; 1st v.p. Vincennes Univ. Found.; past pres. Jasper Community Arts Commn.; pres. Friends of Arts; commnr. Boy Scouts Am.; mem. Dubois County Mental Health Assn., lay adv. bd. Convent Immaculate Conception Sisters of St. Benedict, Ferdinand, Ind., Jasper Hist. Soc., German Club, Young Abe Lincoln Soc.; bd. dirs. Dubois County Crippled Children's Soc., Bloomington (Ind.) Symphony; pres. Jasper Edn. Fund. Recipient Outstanding Citizenship award Purdue U. Alumni Assn., 1980. Mem. Nat. Assn. Jewelry Appraisers (sr.), Ind. Jewelers Orgn. Am., Retail Jewelers Am., Jasper C. of C., Jaycees (Rooster, past pres., past nat. bd. dirs., Disting. Service award 1957), Purdue Agrl. Alumni Assn. (hon.), Skull and Crescent (hon.), Hadassah, Sigma Alpha Mu, Alpha Phi Omega. Lodges: Lions, Masons, Shriners (past pres.), B'nai Brith. Home: 923 McArthur Jasper IN 47546 Office: Newman's Diamond Ctr 3D Plaza Jasper IN 47546

NEWMAN, LINNAEA ROSE, horticulturist; b. Milw., Sept. 23, 1953; d. Arthur Fred and Katherine Elnora (Cook) N. BS, U. Wis., 1977. Cert. interior horticulturist, cert. performax cons. Grower Shroeder's Flowerland, Green Bay, Wis., 1977-78; with installation Tropical Plant Rentals, Inc., Prarie View, Ill., 1978, with spl. service, 1978-84, mgr. edn. and research, 1984—; bd. govs. Nat. Council Interior Horticulture Cert., 1982-85, vice chmn., 1985-86, chmn., 1987—. Author: (with others) Retail Store Planning and Design Manual, 1986; contbr. articles to profl. jours. Named one of Outstanding Young Women Am., 1985. Mem. Entomol. Soc. Am., Internat. Soc. Arboriculture, Ohio Florists Assn. (mem. planning com. 1983—), Assoc. Landscape Contractors Am. (interior plantscape div. com., 1987—), Nat. Assn. Women in Horticulture (v.p. 1986-87). Avocations: skiing, photography, horses, travel, skydiving. Home: 1051 Midlothian Rd Mundelein IL 60060 Office: Tropical Plant Rentals Inc 15671 Aptakisic Rd Prairie View IL 60069

NEWMAN, PHILIP ROBERT, psychologist; b. Utica, N.Y., Dec. 17, 1942; s. Samuel M. and Sara Rose (Dumain) N.; A.B. with high distinction, U. Mich., 1964, Ph.D. (Woodrow Wilson fellow 1964, Univ. fellow 1964-66, Horace H. Rackham Research scholar 1969-71), 1971; m. Barbara Miller, June 12, 1966; children—Samuel Asher, Abraham Levy, Rachel Florence. Asst. prof. psychology U. Mich., Ann Arbor, 1971-72; asst. prof. psychology Union Coll., Schenectady, 1972-76; dir. human behavior curriculum project Am. Psychol. Assn., Washington, 1977-81; pvt. practice psychology, Columbus, Ohio, 1978—; cons. Agy. Instructional TV, 1979. Mem. Am. Psychol. Assn., Internat. Assn. Applied Psychology, Internat. Sociol. Assn., Soc. Psychol. Study Social Issues, Am. Sociol. Assn., Nat. Council Family Relations, Groves Conf. Marriage and Family, Eastern Psychol. Assn., Midwestern Psychol. Assn., Western Psychol. Assn., N.Y. Acad. Sci., Gerontol. Soc. Am., Am. Orthopsychiat. Assn., Phi Beta Kappa, Sigma Xi, Phi Kappa Phi. Author: (with B. Newman) Development through Life: A Psychosocial Approach, 1975, 2d edit., 1979, 3d edit., 1984, 4th edit., 1987; Infancy and Childhood Development and Its Contexts, 1978; An Introduction to the Psychology of Adolescence, 1979; Personality Development through the Life Span, 1980; Living: The Process of Adjustment, 1981; Understanding Adulthood, 1983; Principles of Psychology, 1983; Adolescent Development, 1986; editor: (with B. Newman) Development Through Life: A Case Study Approach, 1976. Home and Office: 1969 Chatfield Rd Columbus OH 43221

NEWMYER, TERRANCE ALLEN, manufacturing executive, marketing consultant; b. Paw Paw, Mich., Mar. 29, 1955; s. Clyde and Gladys (Liane) N.; m. Magaly M. Sanchez, June 1, 1975; 1 child, Jason. BS, Atlantic Union Coll., South Lancaster, Mass., 1978; MBA, Andrews U., 1984. Student labor and housing coordinator Andrews U., Berrien Springs, Mich., 1978-80, student fin. mgr., 1980-82, dir. mktg., 1982-84; v.p. mktg. Andrews Industries, Berrien Springs, 1985, pres., 1985—. Named one of Outstanding Young Men of Am., 1984. Mem. Berrien Springs C. of C. (v.p. 1986). Republican. Adventist. Lodge: Rotary. Avocations: golfing, tropical fish. Home: 3321 Ridgewood Trail Berrien Springs MI 49103

NEWNUM, RAYMOND LAVERN, internist; b. Kingman, Ind., June 18, 1925; s. Robert P. and Sylvia Grace (Alward) N.; student Purdue U., 1943-44; B.S. in Anatomy and Physiology, Ind. U., Bloomington, 1948, M.D., 1951; M.Sc., U. Minn., 1958; m. Betty Lou Coffing, Dec. 20, 1944; children—Kathleen Sue Newnum Roetzer, Janice Marie Newnum Sbrocchi, Betsy Rae, Paul Douglas, Lisa Dawn Newnum Pfleger. Rotating intern Ind. U., 1951-52; gen. practice medicine, Hagerstown, Ind., 1952-55; resident in internal medicine Mayo Found., Rochester, Minn., 1955-58; cons. in internal medicine Carle Clinic, Urbana, Ill., 1958-61; practice medicine specializing in internal medicine, Evansville, Ind., 1961-80; asst. dean, dir. Evansville Center for Med. Edn., Ind. U. Sch. Medicine; pres. staff St. Mary's Hosp., 1970-71, chief of medicine, 1965-67, clin. instr. medicine, 1973-77, cons. internal medicine, 1961-77; asst. prof. medicine Ind. U. Served with USNR, 1943-47. Diplomate Am. Bd. Internal Medicine. Fellow A.C.P. (life); mem. AMA, Ind., Vanderburgh County med. socs., Evansville, Ind. Soc. Internal Medicine (bd. dirs.), Am. Soc. Internal Medicine. Mem. Ch. Christian Fellowship. Home: 6710 Washington Ave Evansville IN 47715 Office: PO Box 3287 Evansville IN 47732

NEWPHER, JAMES ALFRED, JR., management consultant; b. New Brighton, Pa., Nov. 14, 1930; s. James Alfred and Olive Myrtle (Houlette) N.; B.S., U. Pa., 1952; M.B.A., Wharton Sch. U. Pa., 1957; m. Mildred Taylor, Aug. 23, 1953. Indsl. engr., Corning Glass Works (N.Y.), 1957-58, plant supr., 1958-60, prodn. supt., 1960-61, plant mgr., 1961-63, dept. mgr. advance products, 1963-64; asso. Booz, Allen & Hamilton, Inc., Chgo., 1964-69; v.p., mng. officer Lamalie Assocs., Chgo., 1969-73; pres., chief exec. officer Newpher & Co., Inc., Chgo., 1973—; dir. Design Tech., Inc. Served with USN, 1951-56. Decorated Purple Heart. Mem. Naval Res. Assn., Inst. Mgmt. Cons., Res. Officers Assn. Presbyn. Club: Metropolitan Chgo. Home: 1655 We-Go Trail Deerfield IL 60015 Office: 2215 York Rd Suite 202 Oakbrook IL 60521

NEWSOM, FRANCIS CARTER, physician; b. Union Point, Ga., May 14, 1918; s. Erle Thornton and Ethel (Perry) N.; m. Mary Elizabeth Varner, Mar. 20, 1943; children—Barbara Ann, Mary Carter. Student, U. Ga., 1935-37, Emory U., 1939-40; M.D., Med. Coll. Ga., 1943. Diplomate Am. Bd. Psychiatry and Neurology. Intern U.S. Naval Hosp., Portsmouth, Va., 1944; resident in psychiatry VA Hosp., Topeka, Kans., 1946-49; fellow Menninger Sch. Psychiatry, 1946-49; staff psychiatrist Topeka State Hosp., 1949-50; practice medicine specializing in psychiatry, Wichita, Kans., 1951—; clin. asst. prof. psychiatry U. Kans. Sch. Medicine, Wichita, 1974—; cons. VA Med. and Regional Office Ctr., 1951-85, Sedgwick County Dept. Mental Health, 1986—; active med. staff St. Francis Regional Med. Ctr., 1951—; pres. med. staff St. Francis Hosp., 1968. Served to lt. (j.g.) USN, 1944-46, 50-51. Fellow Am. Psychiat. Assn.; mem. Kans. Psychiat. Soc., AMA, Kans. Med. Soc., Med. Soc. Sedgwick County (bd. dirs. 1970-73). Republican. Episcopalian. Avocations: spectator sports; music; dancing; theatre. Home: 3807 E Funston St Wichita KS 67218 Office: Morrow & Newsom 3310 E Douglas St Wichita KS 67208

NEWTON, ALAN KEITH, management consultant; b. Shelbyville, Ind., Dec. 6, 1957; s. Thomas Henry and Dorothy Lee (Turner) N. BS in Physics, Ind. U., 1982. Cert. data processor; cert. systems profl. Programmer, Arthur Andersen & Co., Chgo., 1980-81; programmer/analyst SCM Corp., Marion, Ind., 1981-82; analyst State of Ind., Indpls., 1982; analyst Federated Investors, Inc., Pitts., 1982-83; cons. McGladrey Hendrickson & Pullen, Chicago, Ill., 1983-86; coordinator project control and cost, Midwest Stock Exchange, Inc., Chgo., 1986-87; systems analyst TekSyn, Inc., 1987—. Named Life Scout, Boy Scouts Am., 1970. Mem. Data Processing Mgmt. Assn., Assn. Inst. Cert. of Computer Profls. Republican. Club: Indiana University Tennis. Avocations: music, basketball, running, tennis. Home: 9422 Kungsholm Dr Indianapolis IN 46250 Office: TekSyn Inc 8650 Commerce Park Pl Indianapolis IN 46268

NEWTON, CHARLES W(HITING), JR., gynecologist obstetrictian; b. Butte, Mont., Nov. 30, 1913; s. Charles Whiting and Kate (Manwaring) N.; m. Jane Garnett, June 17, 1940 (dec.); children: Charles W., David J., William G., Mary K., Joseph B. BS, U. Wash., Seattle, 1936; MD, U. Mich., 1940. Practice medicine specializing gynecologist Ann Arbor, 1940—. Fellow Am. Coll. of Gynecologists (founder); mem. ACS, AMA, Mich. Med. Soc., Washtenaw County Ob-gyn, Cen. SOc. Ob-Gyn, Washtenaw County Med. Soc., Am. Fertility Soc., Nat. Bd. Med. Examiners. Republican. Club: Barton Hills Country (bd. dirs. 1948-57). Avocation: golf. Home: 1650 Glenwood Rd Ann Arbor MI 48104 Office: 2900 Golfside Ann Arbor MI 48104

NEWTON, JEAN S., learning disabilities specialist, consultant; b. Elgin, Ill., Mar. 30, 1952; d. Joseph Raymond and Ruth Emily (Cowan) Stage; m. Harold William Newton Jr., Sept. 2, 1972; children: Alexander William, Elizabeth Ashley. BS magna cum laude, Alverno Coll., 1975; MA, Northwestern U., 1981. Cert. learning disability tchr. Learning disability specialist Sch. Dist. 1, Racine, Wis., 1975-80, Barat Coll., Lake Forest, Ill., 1982-85; pvt. practice learning disability cons. Libertyville and Northfield, Ill., 1982—; presenter workshops on learning disabled 1985, 86. Co-coordinator Chgo. Area Cath. Engaged Encounter, 1986—; v.p. Friends Round Lake Area Library, 1987—. Mem. Profls. in Learning Disabilities, The Orton Dyslexia Soc., Council Learning Disabilities, Assn. Citizens with Learning Disabilities (mem. adv. bd. 1984—). Avocations: travel, anthropology. Home: 318 N Rosedale Ct Round Lake IL 60073 Office: 1641 N Milwaukee Ave Libertyville IL 60048

NEWTON, JEANNETTE HELENA FANTONE, retail executive; b. New Haven, Conn., Feb. 27, 1956; d. Joseph Carmine and Jeannette Katherine (Dennehy) Fantone; m. Brian Frank Newton, May 15, 1982. AA, Hartford Coll. for Women, 1976; BA in Geography, Framingham State Coll., 1978; MA in Geography, Miami U., Oxford, Ohio, 1983. Jr. analyst Federated Dept. Stores, Cin., 1979-80, analyst, 1981, sr. analyst, 1981-83, research mgr., 1983-86, dir. area research, 1986—; sr. analyst Edward J. DeBartolo, Youngstown, Ohio, 1980-81. Office: Federated Dept Stores Cincinnati OH 45066

NEWTON, MICHAEL, physician; b. Malvern, Eng., June 4, 1920; came to U.S., 1941, naturalized, 1949; s. Frank Leslie and Alice (Henderson) N.; m. Niles Polk Rumely, Mar. 27, 1943; children: Elizabeth Willoughby (Mrs. Robert M. Reed), Frances Lees (Mrs. Stephen C. Stuntz), Edward Robson, Warren Polk. B.A., Cambridge (Eng.) U., 1942, M.B., B.Ch., 1944, M.A., 1946; M.D., U. Pa., 1943. Diplomate: Am. Bd. Surgery, Am. Bd. Ob-Gyn. House surgeon in English hosps. 1944-46; tng. physiology, surgery, ob-gyn U. Pa. Med. Sch., 1946-53; prof., chmn. dept. ob-gyn U. Miss. Med. Center, Jackson, 1955-66; dir. Am. Coll. Obstetricians and Gynecologists, Chgo., 1966-74; prof. ob-gyn Pritzker Sch. Medicine, U. Chgo., 1966-77, Northwestern U. Med. Sch., 1977—; dir. Nat. Bd. Med. Examiners, 1966-69. Author articles, chpt. in books.; editor: (with E.E. Philipp and J. Barnes) Scientific Foundations of Obstetrics and Gynecology, 1970, 3d edit., 1986; editor: Jour. Reproductive Medicine; mem. editorial bd. Internat. Corr. Soc. Obstetricians and Gynecologists; mem. internat. bd. editors Excerpta Medica. Rockefeller student, 1941. Fellow Am. Gynecol. and Obstet. Soc., Am. Coll. Obstetricians and Gynecologists, A.C.S.; mem. Am. Fertility Soc., Central Assn. Obstetricians and Gynecologists (life), Assn. Profs. Gynecology and Obstetrics (hon.), Chgo. Gynecol. Soc. Home: 2440 N Lakeview Ave Chicago IL 60614 Office: 333 E Superior St Chicago IL 60611

NEWTON, THOMAS COLLINS, savings and loan executive; b. Chgo., Apr. 29, 1951; s. Donald J. and Patricia Jean (Collins) N.; m. Jeannette Ann Engquist, Apr. 5, 1974; children: Thomas Christopher, Lisa Jean. BS, U. Ill., 1973. Office mgr. Blazer Fin. Services, Homewood, Ill., 1974-78; office mgr. CIT Fin. Service, Des Plaines, Ill., 1978-80, area supr., 1980-83; v.p. Ind. Fed. Savs. and Loan Assn., Valparaiso, 1983-85, sr. v.p., 1985—. Mem. U.S. League Savs. Inst. (consumer lending com. 1986—), Nat. Marine Bankers Assn. Presbyterian. Lodge: Elks. Avocations: golf, racquetball. Office: Ind Fed Savs and Loan Assn 56 S Washington St Valparaiso IN 46383

NG, SAMUEL YUWAI, engineering consultant; b. Hong Kong, Oct. 21, 1940; s. Fook-Man and Kwok-Ching (Chui) N.; came to U.S., 1963, naturalized, 1977; B.S., Hong Kong Bapt. Coll., 1962; M.S., U. Miss., 1965; Ph.D., Okla. State U., 1970; m. Virginia Thuc-Hoa, Dec. 26, 1970; children—Randy, Debbie. Teaching asst. Hong Kong Bapt. Coll., 1961-62, instr., 1962-63; research asst. U. Miss., 1963-65, research engr., 1965; research asst. dept. civil engring. Okla. State U., 1965-70; geotech. engr., sr. project engr. Soil Exploration Co., St. Paul, 1970-79, prin. engr., dir. research and devel., 1979-85; adv. soil mechanics div. dept. civil and mineral engring. U. Minn., 1979-80; pres. Animascope Internat., 1983—, pres. Ground Engring. Tech., Inc., 1985—. Social activities chmn. Elim Youth Group T.S.T. Bapt. Ch., Hong Kong, 1960-61; deacon Chinese Christian Ch., St. Paul, 1971-77, 79-80, 84-87, elder, 1987—, chmn. bd. deacons, 1981-83, chmn. evangelism and missions com., 1977-80, adult Sunday Sch. tchr., 1978—. Christian Student scholar and distinction scholar Hong Kong Bapt. Coll., 1961, David J. Carver Jr. Meml. Fund scholar U. Richmond, 1964, U. Miss. fgn. student scholar, 1964; registered profl. engr., Minn., Iowa, Wis., Wyo., N.D., S.D. Fellow ASCE; mem. Internat. Soc. Soil Mechanics and Found. Engring., Engring. Inst. Can., Minn. Geotech. Soc., Sigma Xi, Phi Kappa Phi. Baptist.

NGUYEN, HELEN, physician; b. Hung Tem, Vietnam, Feb. 14, 1947; came to U.S., 1976; d. Lang Huu Nguyen and Phung Thi Chu. MD, U. Saigon, Vietnam, 1972. Diplomate Am. Bd. Pediatrics, Am. Bd. Allergy and Immunology. Intern then resident in pediatrics JHEP, Jacksonville, Fla., 1976-79; fellowship in allergy, clin. immunology Children's Mercy Hosp., K.U. Med. Ctr., Truman Med. Ctr., 1979-81; practice medicine specializing allergy Saint Joseph, Mo., 1981—. Fellow Am. Acad. Allergy and Immunology, Am. Coll. Allergists; mem. Mo. State Med. Assn., Bus. and Profl. Women. Club: YWCA.

NGUYEN, NGOC (JOHN) LO, small business owner, chemist; b. Tuy Hoa, Socialist Rep. Vietnam, Apr. 18, 1938; Came to U.S., 1975; s. San Ngoc and Lan Ai Thi Nguyen; m. Liz Hanh Nguyen, 1981; children: Thao, Minh Chau. MS in Chemistry and Physics, U. Saigon, Socialist Rep. Vietnam, 1967; MS in Math., U. Dalat, Socialist Rep. Vietnam, 1968; MS in ChemE, UCLA, 1978, PhD in ChemE, 1982. Process engr. Hoang Ho's Heating Co., Socialist Rep. Vietnam, 1970-75; research scientist Energy Conversion Services, Troy, Mich., 1981-86; pres. Le Cafe Francais Inc., Sterling Heights, Mich., 1984—; cons. John Engring. Cons. Co., Troy, 1986—.crw. Patentee in field. Chmn. Edn. Com., Dawson, Mich., 1984—. Mem. Electrochem. Soc., Am. Vacuum Soc. Republican. Roman Catholic. Avocations: tennis, computers. Home: 6718 Forest Park Dr Troy MI 48098 Office: Le Cafe Francais 14600 Lakeside Circle Sterling Heights MI 48078

NICE, DAVID STEWART, architect; b. La Porte, Ind., Sept. 22, 1936; s. Clyde Chamberlain and Irma (Dirks) N.; m. Ann Durbin, June 24, 1961; children: Debra Lynn, Steven Craig. BArch, U. Cin., 1960. Registered profl. architect, Ind. Head draftsman C. Wilbur Foster & Assocs., Indpls., 1960-64, Brandt & Delap, Inc., Indpls., 1964-68; prin. Brandt, Delap & Nice, Inc., Indpls., 1968-84, Pecsok, Jelliffe, Randall & Nice, Indpls., 1984—. Served with USAR, 1960-65. Mem. AIA, Ind. Soc. Architects (bd. dirs. 1962-65). Republican. Mem. United Ch. Christ. Lodge: Lions. Home: 4004 Klintilloch Ct Indianapolis IN 46237 Office: Pecsok Jelliffe Randall & Nice 1012 E 75th St Indianapolis IN 46240

NICHIPORUK, WALTER, chemist; b. Poland, Sept. 5, 1919; came to U.S., 1946, naturalized, 1952; s. Alex Andrew and Anna Josephine (Radchuk) N.; student U. Warsaw, 1938-39; U. Munich, 1946; M.S., U. Chgo., 1950; m. Elizabeth Kellner, Aug. 14, 1958; 1 son, Brian. Technologist, Enrico Fermi Inst., U. Chgo., 1950-52; chemist Calif. Inst. Tech., Pasadena, 1952-68; research asso. Ariz. State U., Tempe, 1968-74; cons. chemist, Tempe, 1974-77; chemist U.S. Dept. Energy, Argonne, Ill., 1977—; mem. translation panel Plenum Publ. Corp., N.Y.C., 1967-77; assoc. investigator NASA Apollo Returned Lunar Sample Analysis Program, 1969-71; mem. Nat. Partnership In Edn. program; local com. Chgo. Ops. Office, U.S. Dept. Energy, 1985-86; mem. Parents Com. U. Chgo., 1986—. Served with UNRRA, Germany, 1945-46. Fellow Meteoritical Soc.; mem. Am. Chem. Soc., Internat. Assn. Geochemistry and Cosmochemistry, Geochem. Soc., Sigma Xi. Asso. editor Bibliography of Meteorites, 1953; translator, reviser (V.V. Cherdyntsev) Raprostranennost' Khimicheskikh Elementov, 1961; contbr. articles to profl. jours. Home: 107 W 65th Lake Dr Westmont IL 60559 Office: US Dept Energy/New Brunswick Lab Argonne IL 60439

NICHOL, ROBERT HAMILTON, automotive executive; b. Detroit, Jan. 12, 1946; s. William B. and Martha (Wilson) N.; m. Michelle O'Brien; children: Robert Jr., Meaghan. BA, Alma (Mich.) Coll., 1968; M of Internat. Mgmt., Am. Grad. Sch., Phoenix, 1971. Supr. labor relations Chevrolet div. Gen. Motors Corp., Massena, N.Y., 1977-81; plant personnel dir. Cen. Foundry SMI div. Gen. Motors Corp., Saginaw, Mich., 1981-83, plant personnel dir. Cen. Foundry div. Grey Iron, 1983-84, coordinator labor relations Cen. Foundry div. office, 1984-85, strategic planner Cen. Foundry div., 1985-86; sr. bus. planner mech. component group Gen. Motors Corp., Detroit, 1986-87, sr. adminstr. group planning automotive component group, 1987—. Exec. com. Boy Scouts Am., Saginaw, 1980-84. Served to sgt. U.S. Army, 1968-70, Vietnam. Decorated Bronze Star with combat V, Purple Heart with bronze oak leaf cluster, Silver Star, Air medal with bronze oak leaf cluster. Mem. Indsl. Relations Research Assn. (program chmn. 1982-84), Saginaw C. of C. Republican. Methodist. Avocations: sailing, tennis. Office: Gen Motors Corp Automotive Components Group Planning 1840 Holbrook Ave Detroit MI 48212

NICHOL, WILLIAM EDISON, lieutenant governor of Nebraska; b. Windsor, Colo., Mar. 12, 1918; s. William Adam and Barbara Marie (Kraning) N.; m. Ruth Arline Ellis, Nov. 29, 1941; children—James Charles, Linda Ruth Nichol Harsch. B.S. in Edn., Nebr. Wesleyan U., 1940, B.F.A. in Music, 1940; postgrad., U. Kans., 1960. Owner, mgr. ins. agy., Scottsbluff, Nebr., 1945-60; owner credit bur., Scottsbluff, Nebr., 1960-75; mem. Unicamer Legislature, Lincoln, Nebr., 1974-86; speaker Nebr. Legislature, Lincoln, 1983-84, 85, 86; lt. gov. State of Nebr., 1986—. Mayor, City of Scottsbluff, 1958-66; Scottsbluff county commr. Republican. Methodist. Clubs: Scottsbluff Country; Nebraska, University (Lincoln). Lodge: Elks. Home: 911 Meadowlark Dr Scottsbluff NE 69361 Office: Nebr Unicameral Legislature State Capitol Lincoln NE 68509 *

NICHOLAS, LEONARD STEPHEN, electrical contractor, county official, educator; b. Tarrytown, N.Y., May 15, 1942; s. Leonard Dominic and Helen Ceclia (Pesaric) N. Student Akron U., 1963-68; cert. vocat. edn. Kent State U., 1982. Pres. D&L Electric & Heating, Akron, 1978—; tchr. Maplewood Joint Vocat. Sch., Ravenna, Ohio, 1981-83; plant engr. Cuyahoga Machine Co., Akron, 1981-83; electric insp. Summit County Dept. Bldg. Inspection, Akron, 1983—; instr. Akron U., 1983—. Author sr. electricity course, 1983. Served with USAF, 1960-62. Mem. Internat. Assn. Elec. Insps., Aircraft Owners and Pilots Assn. Republican. Club: Akron City. Avocations: motorcycle riding, restoring of cars. Home: 623 E Buchtel Ave Akron OH 44304

NICHOLAS, S. SCOTT, allergist; b. Des Moines, Dec. 23, 1936; s. Sydney S. and Dorothea (McCallom) N.; children: Mark A., Kim L., Gregory S.; m. Roslynn Robarge, June 14, 1975. BA cum laude, U. Minn., 1958, BS, 1961, MD, 1961; MS, U. Mich., 1966. Diplomate Am. Bd. Allergy and Immunology. Practice medicine specializing in allergy Mpls., 1966—; clin. assoc. prof. internal medicine U. Minn., Mpls., 1967—. Contbr. articles to profl. jours. Mem. ad hoc com. Minn. Relative Value Index, Mpls., 1971-73. Fellow Am. Coll. Allergists (mem. program com. 1986-87, mem. sci. and ednl. council 1987—), Am. Acad. Allergy, Am. Coll. Chest Physicians; mem. AMA, Minn. State Med. Assn., Mpls. Acad. Medicine (exec. council 1979—, recorder 1981-83, v.p. 1983-84, pres. 1984-85), N. Cen. Allergy Soc. (pres. 1977), Minn. Allergy Soc. (pres. 1976-77), Twin City Allergy Soc. (pres. 1970-71). Lutheran. Clubs: Mpls. Athletic, Minikahda. Avocations: skiing, golf, biking. Home: 2110 W Lake of the Isles Pkwy Minneapolis MN 55405 Office: 221 Medical Arts Bldg Minneapolis MN 55402

NICHOLLS, MERVILLE LYNN, JR., business educator; b. Decatur, Ill., Mar. 30, 1943; s. Merville L. and Agnes Louise (Larrabee) N.; m. Marea Louise Jolley, Aug. 29, 1964; children—Lynn, Layne. B.S.I.E., Millikin U., 1969; M.R.E., Grace Theol. Sem., 1972; M.Div., 1976; M.S. in Bus. Adminstrn., Saint Francis Coll., Fort Wayne, Ind., 1981, M.B.A. in Fin., 1982. Instr., bookstore mgr. Calvary Bible Coll., Kansas City., Mo., 1972-75; salesman Leiter Real Estate Co., Warsaw, Ind., 1977-79; ins. counselor Wes Miller & Assoc., Warsaw, 1980-84; vis. prof. Hong Kong Christian Coll., summer 1979; prof. Ind. Vocat. Tech. Coll., Warsaw, 1979-82; prof. bus. Fort Wayne Bible Coll., Ind., 1982-86; indsl. trainer Gen. Motors, Ft. Wayne, 1987; chmn. bus. div. Iowa Wesleyan Coll., Mt. Pleasant, 1987—. Bd. dirs. Child Evangelism Fellowship, Fort Wayne, 1982—, Liberty Hills Assn., Fort Wayne, 1983-87 ; precinct inspector nat. election, Fort Wayne, 1984. Mem. Christian Ministries Mgmt. Assn., Internat. Council on Edn. for Teaching. Republican. Mem. Missionary Ch. Lodge: Kiwanis. Avocations: genealogy; antiques; growing cacti; instrumental and vocal music; French language. Home: 5120 Tall Timber Trail Fort Wayne IN 46804

NICHOLS, JAMES JOHN, chemical company executive; b. Phila., Mar. 31, 1941; s. John Joseph and Catherine Marie (Mealy) N.; m. Elissa Jo Sheets, Sept. 7, 1968; children: Jason C., Ryan S. BS in Commerce and Engring., Drexel U., 1965. With Dow Chem. Co., various locations, 1965-83; gen. sales mgr. Dow Chem. Co., Cleve., 1983-86; zone v.p. sales Dow Chem. Corp., Cleve., 1986—. Columnist trade jour., 1968-69. Mem. allocation com. United Way, Tampa, Fla., 1982-83. Mem. Am. Mgmt. Assn., Cleve. Chem. Assn., Cleve. Paint and Coatings Assn., Producers Council Assn. (publicity chmn.), Packaging Engrs. Assn., Midwest Roofing Contractors Assn. Republican. Roman Catholic. Clubs: Sharon Country (Sharon Center, Ohio), Lakewood Country (Westlake, Ohio). Office: Dow Chem Co 14955 Sprague Rd Strongsville OH 44136

NICHOLS, JOHN D., diversified manufacturing corporation executive; b. Shanghai, China, 1930; m. Alexandra M. Curran, Dec. 4, 1971; children: Kendra E., John D. III. B.A., Harvard U., 1953, M.B.A., 1955. Various operating positions Ford Motor Corp., 1958-68; dir. fin. controls ITT Corp., 1968-69; exec. v.p., chief operating officer Aerojet-Gen. Corp., 1969-79; exec. v.p. Ill. Tool Works Inc., Chgo., 1980-81; pres. Ill. Tool Works Inc., 1981—, chief operating officer, 1981-82, chief exec. officer, dir., 1982—, chmn., 1986—; bd. dirs. IU Internat. Chmn. Jr. Achievement of Chgo; trustee U. Chgo., Argonne Nat. Lab., Chgo. Symphony Orchestra, Lyric Opera Chgo., Mus. Sci. and Industry, Lyric Opera Chgo., Mus. Sci. Industry. Served to lt. AUS, 1955-58. Clubs: Harvard (N.Y.C.); Indian Hill (Winnetka, Ill.); Olympic (San Francisco). Office: Ill Tool Works Inc 8501 Higgins Rd Chicago IL 60631

NICHOLS, MICHAEL FREDERICK, bioengineer; b. Hollywood, Calif., Oct. 10, 1948; s. Frederick Arthur and Ruby Pearl (Feightner) N.; m. Karen Lee Ivy, Nov. 20, 1976 (div. Dec. 1980); 1 child, Jennifer Michelle. BS, Calif. Poly. State U., 1970, MS, 1972; postgrad., U. Mo., 1972—. Research technician Dalton Research Ctr., Columbia, Mo., 1974-76, sr. research specialist, 1976-78, research assoc., 1978—; invited presentor NIH, 1983-86. Editor Biomedical Materials vol. 55, 1986; contbr. articles to profl. jours.; patentee in field. Mem. Am. Statis. Assn., Am. Chem. Soc., Materials Research Soc. (publ. com. 1986—, symposium chmn. 1986), Rocky Mountain Bioengring. Soc. (bd. dirs. 1986—), Sigma Xi. Avocations: white water canoeing, downhill skiing, camping. Home: 906 Colgate Columbia MO 65203 Office: Dalton Research Ctr Research Park Columbia MO 65211

NICHOLS, ROBERT GEORGE, restaurant owner; b. South Haven, Mich., Feb. 5, 1949; s. Donald F. and Elizabeth M. (Mansfield) N.; m. Renae Helen Hendrix, June 9, 1974; children: Jennifer Elizabeth, Melissa Renae, Rebecca Anne. Degree in History, West Mich. U., 1971. Owner Idler Riverboat Restaurant, South Haven, Mich., 1981—; pres. Old Harbor Village, Inc., South Haven, 1986—. Republican. Avocations: scuba diving, amateur acting. Office: Idler Riverboat Restaurant 515 Williams St South Haven MI 49090

NICHOLS, ROBERT HASTINGS, lawyer; b. Mpls., Aug. 12, 1941; s. James Hastings and Judith (Beach) N.; m. Jean Christy, Nov. 30, 1968; children—Marc O., Seth J., Ethan D., Rebecca J. A.B., Yale U., 1963; cert. in Pub. Affairs, CORO Found., 1964; J.D., U. Chgo., 1967. Bar: Ill. 1967, U.S. Dist Ct. (no. dist.) Ill. 1967, U.S. Dist. Ct. (ea. dist.) Wis. 1975; U.S. Ct. Appeals (7th cir.) 1972, U.S. Ct. Appeals (8th cir.) 1975, U.S. Ct. Appeals (D.C. cir.) 1976, U.S. Supreme Ct. 1986. Ptnr. Cotton, Watt, Jones & King, Chgo., 1967—; gen. counsel Air Line Employees Assn., Internat., Chgo., 1986—; chmn. United Airlines Pilots' System Bd. of Adjustment, Elk Grove Village, Ill., 1970—; cons. Govt. of New Zealand, Auckland, 1980; mem. Lawyers Coordinating Com., AFL-CIO. Contbr. articles to legal publs. Mem. ABA, Ill. State Bar Assn., Chgo. Council Lawyers. Democrat. Presbyterian. Club: Columbia Yacht. Home: 1030 E 49th St Chicago IL 60615 Office: Cotton Watt Jones King One IBM Plaza Chicago IL 60611

NICHOLS, ROBERT LEE, food company executive; b. Clarksburg, W.Va., Nov. 4, 1924; s. Clarence Garfield and Reatha Maude (Berry) N.; m. Vianne Hope Demaray, Oct. 21, 1973; children: Donna Beth, Michael Alan, Jeffrey Mark. Student, Bus. Coll., 1944, U. Detroit, 1959. Sales rep. Kellogg Sales Co., Battle Creek, Mich., 1944-50; dist. mgr. Kellogg Sales Co., 1950-61, asst. div. mgr., 1961-64, sales promotion dir., 1964-69, exec. v.p., gen. sales mgr., 1969-71, pres., 1976-78; pres. Fearn Internat., 1971-76, dir., 1971-82; group exec. v.p. Kellogg Co., Battle Creek, 1979-82, dir., 1977—, vice chmn., 1983—; pres., dir. Mrs. Smith's Frozen Foods Co., 1979-82, McCamly Square Corp., 1983—; dir., pres. Battle Creek Unltd., 1985; bd. dirs. Cereal Inst., 1976-79, Am. Frozen Food Inst., 1979-82, Battle Creek Gas Co., 1986—, Mich. Nat. Bank, 1986—, Cereal City Devel. Corp.; bd. govs. Acad. Food Mktg., St. Joseph U., 1976-79. Exec. v.p., bd. dirs. Jr. Achievement, Battle Creek, 1970-71'; trustee Mich. Colls. Found., 1985—, Mich. Biotechnical Inst., 1985—, Mich. Biotech. Inst., 1984—, Citizens Research Council of Mich, 1985—; mem., bd. dirs. United Way of Greater Battle Creek Area, 1984—, campaign chmn. 1985; pres. Battle Creek Unltd., 1985—; vice chmn. Battle Creek Airport Adv. Com., 1984—; mem. nat. corp. council Interlochen Ctr. for the Arts, 1986—. Mem. Battle Creek Area C. of C. Clubs: Battle Creek Country, Masons. Office: Kellogg Co One Kellogg Sq PO Box 3599 Battle Creek MI 49016-3599 *

NICHOLS, RUDY J., attorney, state senator; b. Flint, Mich., Aug. 26, 1945; s. Walter H. and Hazel G. (Marshall) N.; m. Gail Elizabeth Groh, Aug. 26, 1967; children: Jason Jay, Jodie Elizabeth. BA, Mich. State U., 1967; JD, Detroit Coll. Law, 1974. Bar: Mich., 1974. Tchr. Durand (Mich.) Area Schs., 1968-71; atty. Booth Patterson et al, Pontiac, Mich., 1974-76; dep. city atty. City of Pontiac, 1976-82; mem. Mich. Ho. Reps., Lansing, 1983, Mich. Senate, Lansing, 1984—; asst. majority whip 1984—, mem. appropriations com., 1984—; mem. judiciary com. Lansing, 1984—. Twp. dir. Oakland County Reps., Pontiac, 1980, appointments chmn., 1980-81; area chmn. 19th Congressional Dist., Pontiac, 1981; bd. dirs. Oakland County Lincoln Rep. Club. Recipient Am. Jurisprudence Excellence award, 1972; named one of Outstanding Young Men of Am., 1978, Jaycee Internat. Senator, 1980, one of Five Outstanding Young Men of Mich., 1981. Mem. Mich. Bar Assn., Oakland County Bar Assn., Jaycees (Outstanding Local Pres. award 1979). Lodges: Optimists. Avocations: reading, boating, swimming, walking, water skiing. Office: Capitol Bldg Room 127 A Lansing MI 48909

NICHOLS, THEODORE GEORGE, hosp. engr.; b. Chgo., July 27, 1927; s. Michael Feodor and Sophia (Lewandowski) N.; Student Wright Jr. Coll., 1950-53, Ill. Inst. Tech., 1956-61: m. Barbara McKillip, Mar. 14, 1975; children by previous marriage—Michael J., Julie Ann, Theodore George. Supt., Paschen Contractors, Ill. and Ind., 1947-56; dir. phys. plant Ill. Inst. Tech. Research Inst., Chgo., 1956-69; dir. engring. Rush Presbyn. St. Luke's Med. Center, Chgo., 1969—. Deacon, sec. council St. Andrews Ch., 1966-68; com. chmn., instl. rep. Chgo. Area Council Boy Scouts Am., 1967-68. Mem. Am. Hosp. Assn., Inst. Plant Maintenance, Western Soc. Engrs., Chgo. Supts. Assn. Supervised constrn. 1st indsl. nuclear reactor, 1955. Home: 111 Fernwood Dr Glenview IL 60025 Office: 1753 W Congress Pkwy Chicago IL 60612

NICHOLS, VICKI LYNN, business official; b. Cin., July 4, 1955; d. Dale Peter Nichols and Janet Josephine (Nagele) Nichols Mortimer. File clk. Dayco Corp., Cin., 1974-75, order entry processor, 1975-76, br. mgr., sec., 1976-77, sec., regional sales mgr., 1977-78, inside sales coordinator, West Chester, Ohio, 1978-80, sr. inside sales coordinator, 1980-82, office mgr., 1982-87 , indsl. hose sales, service specialist, mktg., 1987—. Author: Branch Training Manuals, 1980 (cert. of accomplishment 1982). Roman Catholic. Avocations: travel; bowling; reading; collecting Star Trek memorabilia. Home: 6924 Lakeside Dr Apt 212A West Chester OH 45069 Office: Dayco Rubber Products Corp Hdqtrs Ct 33 W First St Dayton OH 45402

NICHOLS, WILLIAM CURTIS, JR., clinical psychologist, family therapist; b. Fayette, Ala., Apr. 16, 1929; s. William Curtis and Eva Adele (Hargett) N.; m. Alice Louise Mancill, May 29, 1954; children: Alice Camille, William Mancill, David Paul. AB, U. Ala., 1953; EdD, Columbia U., 1960. Diplomate Am. Bd. Profl. Psychology. Asst. prof. sociology U. Ala., Birmingham, 1960-63; postdoctoral fellow Merrill-Palmer Inst., 1963-64, mem. psychotherapy faculty, 1965-69; prof. sociology Samford U., 1963-65; pvt. practice psychology and marriage and family therapy Grosse Pointe, Mich., 1969-73, Birmingham, Mich., 1976—; prof. home and family life, dir. marriage and family counseling Fla. State U., 1973-76; adj. clin. prof. psychology U. Detroit, 1976-83. Assoc. editor: Jour. of Divorce, 1976-83, 1985—; editor: Contemporary Family Therapy: An International Jour., 1986—, Family Therapy News, 1986—; co-author: Systematic Family Therapy, 1986 mem. editorial adv. bd.: Internat. Jour. Family Therapy, 1977-85, Sage Family Studies Abstracts, 1977—; mem. editorial bd.: Family Systems Medicine, 1982—; contbr. chpt. to Klemer's Counseling in Marital and Sexual Problems, 1977, Family and Group Therapy, 1980, Casebook of Marital Therapy, Divorce Therapy; editor chpt. in Marriage and Family Therapy, 1974; contbr. articles to profl. jours. Mem. mental health and health coms. Mayor's Commn. on Children and Youth, 1966-69; bd. dirs. Family and Children's Service, Oakland, Mich., 1977—, chmn., 1984-86. Served with C.E. U.S. Army, 1948-49. Recipient Ala. Assn. for Mental Health Service award, 1962, Spl. award for Outstanding Contbns. Fla. Assn. Marriage and Family Counselors, 1977, 82; NSF fellow U. Colo., 1963. Fellow Am. Assn. Marriage and Family Therapy (dir. 1969-72, chmn. accreditation com. 1976—, founding editor Jour. Marriage and Family Counseling 1974-76, co-chmn. Atlanta Multiregional Conf. 1975, 77, Spl. awards 1976, 78, pres.-elect 1979-80, pres. 1981-82), Am. Orthopsychiat. Assn.; mem. Am. Psychol. Assn., Mich. Inter-Profl. Assn. on Marriage, Divorce and Family (trustee 1977—, com. chmn. 1968-71, 76—), Mich. Assn. Marriage Counselors (pres. 1969-71, chmn. profl. liaison com. 1972-73), Nat. Council on Family Relations (pres. 1976-77, dir., mem. exec. com. 1969-78, editor The Family Coordinator 1970-75, assoc. editor Jour. Marriage and the Family 1976-80). Home: 31829 Sheridan Dr Birmingham MI 48009 Office: 30200 Telegraph Rd Suite 455 Birmingham MI 48010

NICHOLSON, BRENT BENTLEY, lawyer; b. Perrysburg, Ohio, Mar. 30, 1954; s. Donald Grant and Wilma Ione (Bentley) N.; m. Ann Elizabeth Loehrke, Sept. 1, 1978; children: Bradley, Lindsay. BS in Bus. Adminstrn., Bowling Green State U., 1976; JD, Ohio State U., 1979. Bar: Ohio 1979, U.S. Dist. Ct. (no. dist.) Ohio 1979, U.S. Tax Ct. 1984; CPA, Ohio. Tax atty. Arthur Young & Co., Toledo, 1979-83; assoc. Cobourn, Smith, Rohrbacher & Gibson, Toledo, 1983—; adj. asst. prof. Bowling Green State U., Ohio, 1984-85. Contbr. articles to profl. jours. Treas. N.W. Ohio chpt. March of Dimes, Toledo, 1983-85; mem. Toledo Estate Planning Council. Mem. ABA, Ohio Bar Assn., Toledo Bar Assn., Lucas County Bar Assn., Ohio Soc. CPA's, Toledo Estate Planning Council, Pi Sigma Alpha, Beta Gamma Sigma. Republican. Methodist. Avocations: reading, tennis. Home: 3750 Beechway Blvd Toledo OH 43614 Office: Cobourn Smith Rohrbacher et al 624 Adams St Toledo OH 43604

NICHOLSON, FRANK W., food company executive, consultant; b. Steubenville, Ohio, Aug. 8, 1918; s. Harry W. and Mabel Jane (Lemon) N.; m. Mary Jane Moore, Sept. 10, 1946 (div.); children: Frank W. II, Laura Jane; m. Elva Faye Leazear, Oct. 6, 1948; children: Roy R., Cathy Mae, Robert E., David R. Degree in radio engring., DeForest Engring., 1950. Lic. radiotelephone operator FCC. Machinist Wheeling Steel Corp., Steubenville, Ohio, 1936-37; snack distributor DanDee Pretz & Chip Co., Cleve., 1937-42; civilian radio inspector Signal Corps U.S. Army, Dayton, Ohio, 1942-44; sales mgr. J.T. Welsh Co., Steubenville, 1946-48; mgr. Nicholson Fine Foods, Inc., Steubenville, 1948—, also bd. dirs.; mem. adv. bd. Pochontas Foods USA, Richmond. Va., 1974-79; cons. Wiley & Assocs., Inc., Steubenville, 1980-85. Fire warden Nat. Civil Patrol, Steubenville, 1943; vestryman St. Paul's Ch., Steubenville, 1970-78. Served to sgt. U.S. Army, 1944-46; mem. Ohio Farm Bur., Columbus, 1984—. Mem. Sales and Execs. Club, Wintersville C. of C. Republican. Episcopalian. Lodge: Masons. Avocations: sailing, swimming, hiking, traveling. Office: Nicholson Fine Foods Inc 400 Williams Blvd PO Box 547 Steubenville OH 43952

NICHOLSON, LAUREL ANNE, communication consultant; b. Chgo., June 6, 1950; d. Melvin J. and Rita Helen (Goldman) Stern; m. Donald D. Nicholson, Apr. 8, 1972; children: Emily, Ellen, Benjamin. BS in Journalism, Bowling Green State U., 1972. Editor and prodn. coordinator McDonald's Corp., Oak Brook, Ill., 1972-75; owner, pres. Nicholson Communications, Elmhurst, Ill., 1975-82; mng. cons. The Wyatt Co., Chgo., 1982-85; sr. cons. Mercer-Meidinger-Hansen, Inc., Deerfield, Ill., 1985—. Author: Deadly Power, 1984, Elven Banner, 1985, Undead, 1986. Recipient Photography award of merit Soc. Publ. Designers, N.Y.C., 1975. Mem. Internat. Assn. Bus. Communicators (Gold Quill award 1985, Spectra award 1987), Chgo. Women's Network (sec., editor 1984), Women's Am. Orgn. Rehab. Through Tng. (calendar chairperson 1982), Women in Employee Benefits (sec. 1987). Club: Metropolitan (Chgo.). Office: Mercer-Meidinger-Hansen Inc 1417 Lake Cook Rd Deerfield IL 60015

NICHOLSON, LELAND R., utilities company executive; b. Carrington, N.D., Feb. 21, 1924; s. Malcom and Lena May (Kerlin) N.; m. Virginia E. Blair, Mar. 16, 1946; children: Heather Lee Nicholson Studebaker, Leland B., Holly Kay Nicholson Boles. Student, Northwestern U., 1940-41; BSEE,

U. N.D., 1949; postgrad. in utility mgmt., U. Minn., 1952. Planning and mktg. engr. Minkota Power Coop., Grand Forks, N.D., 1949-54; dir. new bus. Kans. Power & Light Co., Topeka, 1954-64, v.p. mktg., 1964-76, sr. v.p., 1976-80, exec. v.p., 1980-83, also bd. dirs.; pres. Kans. Power & Light Gas Service, Topeka, 1985—; pres. and chief operating officer The Gas Service Co., Kansas City, Mo., 1983-85; pres. Indsl. Devel. Corp., Topeka; chmn. Kans. Council on Electricity and Environment; exec. com. Kansas City Labor Mgmt. Council, 1986—; mem. Mktg. Execs. Conf.; bd. dirs. Gas Service Energy Corp., Kansas City, Merchants Nat. Bank, Topeka. Idea innovator heat pump water heater, photo cell controlled yard light, electric grill. Bd. dirs., area relations com. Kansas City (Mo.) Area Econ. Devel. Council, 1983—; bd. dirs. Kansas City Pvt. Industry Council, 1986, Kansas City Downtown Council; trustee U. Mo., Kansas City, 1984—; mktg. chmn. Kansas City Full Employment Council; past chmn., mem. Topeka-Shawnee County Planning Commn.; adult adv. com. Sea Scouts. Served to master sgt. USMC, 1942-46. Mem. Am. Gas Assn. (gas demand com. 1984—, res. investment com.), Midwest Gas Assn. (bd. dirs. 1985—), Mo. Valley Electric Assn. (chmn. 1979-81), Edison Electric Inst. (mktg. chmn. 1978-80), Assoc. Industries of Mo., Kans. Assn. Commerce and Industry, Greater Kansas City (Mo.) C. of C. (bd. dirs. 1983—). Republican. Congregationalist. Clubs: Top of First (bd. dirs. 1979-82), Shawnee Yacht (Topeka) (commodore 1972-74, 79-81). Avocations: sailing, canoeing, fishing, reading, electronics. Office: KPL Gas Service 818 Kansas Ave Topeka KS 66612

NICHOLSON, MARION CRAWFORD, mayor, manufacturers representative; b. College Park, Ga., Jan. 31, 1917; s. William Malcolm and Marion Melissa (Neely) N.; m. Catherine Vaughn Wise, Apr. 5, 1948; children: Catherine Marion, Barbara Ann. Cert. in aero. engring., Ga. inst. Tech., 1940. With Atlanta Constn. Pub. Co., 1937-40; sta. mgr. Eastern Air Lines, St. Louis, Memphis and Lake Charles, La., 1940-53; owner, operator M.C. Nicholson & Assocs., mfrs. sales rep., St. John, Mo., 1953—, Aetna Metal Products Co., St. John, 1973-86 ; Councilman, St. John, 1974, mayor, 1974-77, 83—; pres. PTA council Normandy Sch. System, 1966-67; mem. St. Louis Bd. Elec. Trade. Mem. Mayors of Small Cities St. Louis County (pres.). Presbyterian. Address: 3901 Engler Ave St Louis MO 63114

NICHOLSON, PAUL M., supermarket executive; b. Indpls., Oct. 15, 1949; s. Robert R. and Dorothy Jane (Nelis) N.; m. Rita M. Greene, June 26, 1971; children: Christopher, Bethany, Lisa. BA, Anderson Coll., 1971. CPA, Ind. Controller PayLess Supermarket Inc., Anderson, Ind., 1971-79, v.p. fin., 1979—; bd. dirs, Ultra Steak, Inc., Anderson. Mem. Am. Assn. CPA's, Ind. Assn. CPA's, Nat. Accounts Assn. Lodge: Rotary. Home: 3768 Lindberg Rd Anderson IN 46011 Office: PayLess Super Markets Inc PO Box 639 Anderson IN 46015

NICHOLSON, ROBERT ARTHUR, range management educator; b. Norton, Kans., Dec. 23, 1944; s. Olive Marie (Reh) N.; m. Sandra Marie Neely, Sept. 13, 1970; 1 child, Shaun. BS, Ft. Hays State U., 1967, MS, 1968; PhD, Colo. State U., 1972. Instr. Hutchinson (Kans.) Community Coll., 1968-70; research asst. Colo. State U., Ft. Collins, Colo., 1970-72; asst. prof. N.D. State U., Fargo, 1972-73; prof. Ft. Hays State U., Hays, Kans., 1973—; adj. prof. Kans. State U., Hays, 1986—, mus. assoc. Ft. Hays State Mus., Hays., 1986—. Contbr. articles to profl. jours. Chmn. Hays-Ellis County Planning Commn., Hays, 1981. Research grantee Woods Found., 1975, Nat. Park Service, 1978; equipment grant NSF, 1972. Mem. Soc. for Range Mgmt., Kans. Acad. Sci., Range Sci. Edn. Council (sec. 1985—), Ft. Hays State U. Alumni Assn. (Outstanding Alumnus 1977), Sigma Xi, Phi Kappa Phi. Republican. Club: Ft. Hays Range (advisor 1974—). Avocations: carpentry, hunting, fishing, bicycling, mushrooming. Home: 211 W 25th St Hays KS 67601 Office: Ft Hays State Univ 600 Park St Hays KS 67601

NICHOLSON, STUART ADAMS, lawyer, ecologist and environmental scientist; b. Albany, N.Y., May 24, 1941; s. Kenneth Gerald and Gladyce (Wenz) N.; children: Laura Ellice, Paul Michael. BS in Biology, SUNY-Albany, 1964, MS in Biology, 1965; PhD in Botany, U. Ga., 1970; JD, U. N.D., 1983. Bar: N.D. 1983, Minn. 1984. Research assoc. atomospheric sci. SUNY-Albany, 1970-71; asst. prof. biology State U. Coll., Fredonia, N.Y., 1971-75; ecologist Environment Cons. Inc., Mayville, N.Y., 1975-76; lectr. biology U. So. Pacific, Suva, Fiji, 1976-78; sr. research analyst St. Lawrence-Eastern Ont. Commn., Watertown, N.Y., 1979-80; sr. research scientist U. N.D., Grand Forks, 1980-82, assoc. dir., 1982-83, program dir., 1983-84; atty. James E. Olds Ltd., Mpls., 1984—; cons. firms, corps., 1973-79; sr. practitioner Legal Aid Assn. N.D., Grand Forks, 1982-83; mem. Voluntary Income Tax Assistance, Grand Forks, 1981; tchr. U. Ga., State U. Coll., Fredonia, U. South Pacific, Empire State Coll., 1965-67, 71-79; advisor govtl. orgns., 1972-84; ecology resource advisor N.Y. State Dept. Environ. Conservation, Albany, 1973; bd. dirs. Chautauqua County Environ. Def. Council, Jamestown, 1973-75, Grand Forks Food Coop., 1984; organizer Chautauqua Lake Biology Symposium, 1974. Contbr. articles to profl. jours.; reviewer Bull. of Torrey Bot. Club, 1974, 83. Grantee U. South Pacific, 1976-78, NSF grantee, 1974; State U. Coll. fellow, 1972-75; N.D. Pub. Service Commn. research contract 1983, Office Surface Mining research contract, 1982. Mem. ABA, Minn. State Bar Assn., State Bar Assn. N.D., Ecol. Soc. Am., Brit. Ecol. Soc., Sigma Xi, Phi Sigma, Beta Beta Beta. Home: Box 201312 Bloomington MN 55420 Office: James E Olds Ltd 10800 Lyndale Ave S Minneapolis MN 55420

NICHOLSON, THEODORE H., educational administrator; b. Chgo., July 27, 1929; B.S., Loyola U., Chgo., 1951; M.S. (State of Ill. Vets scholar), No. Ill. U., 1955; postgrad., Rockford Coll., 1955; Ph.D. (NDEA fellow, 1966-67), U. Wis.-Madison, 1967; children—Craig, Kimberlee, Christine, Rhonda, Katrina, Alexandra. Tchr., Morris Kennedy Sch., Winnebago County, Ill., 1951-53, Rockford (Ill.) Public Schs., 1953-55, evening sch., 1956-60; prin. Marsh Schs., Dist. 58, Winnebago County, 1955-59, supt., 1959-66; supt. Dearborn Twp. Sch. Dist. 8, Dearborn Heights, Mich., 1967-68, Wilmington (Ohio) City Sch., 1968-72; supr. schs., Wausau, Wis., 1972—; vis. prof. Central State U., Wilberforce, Ohio, 1969-70; teaching asst., research asst., lectr. U. Wis., summer 1976; lectr., cons. Univ. Council Ednl. Adminstrn.; mem. coordinating com. Partnership Schs.; v.p. N.C. Data Processing Ctr., 1974-81. Active Cen. Wausau Progress, 1973-82; mem. Pvt. Industry Council.; bd. dirs. Wausau Performing Art Found., 1986—. Served with USN, 1943-46. Recipient Citizenship award City of Rockford, 1960, 64; Community Leader award Sta. WXCO, Wausau, 1974. Mem. Am. Assn. Sch. Adminstrs., Wis. Assn. Sch. Dist. Adminstrs. (state bd. dirs., Adminstr. of Yr. award spl. edn. dept., 1986), Am. Assn. Supervision and Curriculum Devel., C. of C. (bd. dirs., edn com.), Phi Delta Kappa. Lodge: Elks.Contbr. articles in field to profl. publs. Office: Wausau Bd Edn 1018 S 12th Ave Wausau WI 54401

NICHOLSON, WILLIAM NOEL, clin. neuropsychologist; b. Detroit, Dec. 24, 1936; s. James Eardly and Hazel A. (Wagner) N.; A.B., Wittenberg U., 1959; M.Div., Luth. Theol. Sem., Phila., 1962; Ph.D. (HEW fellow), Mich. State U., 1972; m. Nancy Ann Marshall, June 15, 1957; children—Ann Marie, Kristin, Scott. Ordained to ministry Lutheran Ch., 1962; parish pastor Our Savior Luth. Ch., Saginaw, Mich., 1962-69; psychologist Ingham-Eaton-Clinton Mental Health Bd., 1971-72; psychologist Bay-Arenac Mental Health Bd., 1972-74; dir., psychologist Riverside Center, Bay City, Mich., 1974-75; pres. Bay Psychol. Assos., P.C., Bay City, 1975—; cons. Gov.'s Office of Drug Abuse, 1972-74. Cert., Nat. Register Health Care Providers in Psychology. Mem. Am. Psychol. Assn., Midwest Psychol. Assn., Mich. Psychol. Assn., Soc. Behavioral Medicine, Mental Health Assn. (pres. Bay-Arenac Chpt. 1981). Lutheran. Clubs: Bay City Yacht, Rotary. Author: A Guttman Facet Analysis of Attitude-Behaviors Toward Drug Users by Heroin Addicts and Mental Health Therapists, 1972; contbr. articles to profl. jours. Office: Behavioral Med Ctr 3442 E Wilder Rd Bay City MI 48706

NICKEL, CHARLES LYNN, interior designer; b. Tiffin, Ohio, July 17, 1946; s. Richard Karl and Maxine (Newby) N. BArch, Ohio State U., 1969; BS in Interior Design, U. Cin., 1976. Project designer Space Design Internat., Inc., Cin., 1976—. Served as lt. USAF, 1970-73. Mem. Alpha Rho Chi (Dwight P. Ely meml. award 1969, regional deputy 1980-83, Worthy Grand Scribe 1983—). Home: 201 St James Ave Cincinnati OH 45206 Office: Space Design Internat Inc 311 Elm St Cincinnati OH 45202

NICKEL, JEAN RENEE, nurse, school nurse; b. Ft. Dodge, Iowa, Feb. 14, 1930; d. William Wesley and Lillian Beatrice (Poduska) Eral; m. Bernard Edward Nickel, Aug. 4, 1951; children—Timothy Jerome, Theresa Ann. R.N., St. Francis Sch. Nursing, Grand Island, Nebr., 1951; B.S. in Psychology, Kearney State Coll., 1981. Office nurse Brewster Clinic, Holdrege, Nebr., 1952-58; staff nurse Valley County Hosp., Ord, Nebr., 1962-71; sch. nurse Ednl. Service Unit 10, Kearney, Nebr., 1974-76; sch. nurse Loup City Sch. Dist. (Nebr.), 1974—. Mem. Central Nebr. Sch. Nurse Assn., NEA, Am. Legion Aux. Democrat. Roman Catholic. Home: 769 R St Loup City NE 68853 Office: Loup City Middle 800 N 8th Loup City NE 68853

NICKELS, CARL EDWIN, JR., lawyer, mining company executive; b. Cleve., Jan. 22, 1931; s. Carl Edwin and Genevieve H. N.; m. Mary Eileen Keller, June 9, 1951; Richard C., Paul J., Carl E., Christopher J., Mary L., Caroline G. B.S., U. Notre Dame, 1953; J.D., Cleve. Marshall Law Sch., 1958. Bar: Ohio 1958. Staff acct. M. A. Hanna Co., Cleve., 1953-55, assoc. legal dept., 1955-65, asst. sec., 1965-74, v.p., 1974-76, sr. v.p. fin. and law, 1976-79, exec. v.p., 1979-84, pres., 1984—; bd. dirs. Allendale Mut. Ins. Co., Johnston, R.I., M.A. Hanna Co., Am. Mining Congress, Am. Iron Ore Assn. Adv. council Cleve. Playhouse. Mem. Cleve. Bar Assn., Ohio State Bar Assn. Roman Catholic. Clubs: Union, Clevelander (trustee); Westwood Country, Pepper Pike Country. Office: M A Hanna Co/Midland SW Corp 100 Erieview Plaza Cleveland OH 44114

NICKELS, ROBERT DALE, materials specialist; b. Cleve., Apr. 23, 1948; s. Burdette Elmer and Regina Mary (Zielinski) N.; m. Karen Marie Cosgrove, Oct. 17, 1980. BBA, Cleve. State U., 1978; MBA, Western Mich. U., 1987. Purchasing trainee Republic Steel Corp., Cleve., 1976; material planner, prodn. scheduler Eaton Corp., Kenosha, Wis., 1978-79; product line supr. Eaton Corp., Fletcher, N.C., 1979-83; inventory planner Stryker Corp., Kalamazoo, 1983-86; raw materials coordinator Eaton Corp., Marshall, Mich., 1987—. vol. worker Spl. Olympics, Kalamazoo, 1985, 86. Served with USN, 1968-74, Vietnam. Decorated Nat. Def. medal, Vietnam Conflict medal. Mem. Am. Prodn. and Inventory Control Soc. (bd. dirs. 1985-87, cert. CPIM 1980), Nat. Assn. Purchasing Mgmt. (cert. CPM 1985). Republican. Roman Catholic. Avocations: gardening, woodworking, hiking, walking. Home: 905 Forest St Marshall MI 49068

NICKESON, RICHARD SPROWLS, marketing executive; b. East Liverpool, Ohio, July 30, 1918; s. Floyd Henry and Lona Myrtle (Sprowls) N.; m. Virginia Helen Green, Jan. 22, 1944; children: Sandra, Holly, Linda. BA in Journalism, Westminster Coll., 1940; MA in Journalism, U. Wis., 1948. Asst. prof. journalism U. Ga., Athens, 1946-47; co-owner, mgr. Broadcast Service, Inc., Madison, Wis., 1947-50; continuity dir. sta. WKOW Radio, Madison, 1948-49; sales mgr. sta. WISC Radio, Madison, 1949-56; gen. sales mgr. sta. WISC-TV, Madison, 1956-81, exec. dir. mktg. Morgan Murphy Stns., 1981—. Moderator Lake Edge United Ch. of Christ, Madison, 1968-70; mem. Monona Grove Bd. Edn., Madison, 1968-71; vice chmn. Madison-Oslo Sister City Com., Madison, 1981—. Served to 1st lt. AC, U.S. Army, 1941-46. Mem. Broadcast Pioneers, Madison Advt. Fedn. (Silver Medal 1983), Grocery Mfrs. Reps. (bd. dirs. 1984—, Achievement award 1983). Mem. Ch. of Christ. Club: Madison Advt. (v.p. sales and mktg. 1961-62) Lodge: Optimist (pres. Madison 1955-56). Avocations: bicycle riding, writing. Home: 4402 Winnequah Rd Monona WI 53716 Office: Sta WISC-TV 7025 Raymond Rd Madison WI 53711

NICKLEN, PEGGY GENE, nurse; b. Omaha, Nebr., Aug. 27, 1952; d. Harold Edward Nicklen and Mary Elizabeth (Davis) Wiese; 1 child, Anthony Cook. B.S. in Nursing and English, Mount Marty Coll., Yankton, S.D., 1980. R.N., Nebr. Psychiat. technician Douglas County Hosp., Omaha, 1970-75; tutor Aid the Vietnamese, Yankton, S.D., 1978-80; psychiat. charge nurse St. Joseph Hosp., Omaha, 1980-82; med. charge nurse Luth. Community Hosp., Norfolk, Nebr., 1982-85; psychiat. nurse Norfolk Regional Ctr., 1985—. Editor mag. Mid Stream, 1976-80. Sec., Young Republicans, Yankton, 1979. Named Outstanding Young Woman Am., 1980. Mem. Am. Nurses Assn., Nat. Nurses Assn., Norfolk Bus. and Profl. Women. Democrat. Roman Catholic. Avocations: writing nursing articles; crocheting; reading. Home: 108 Elm St Norfolk NE 68701 Office: Norfolk Regional Ctr Norfolk NE 68701

NICKODEMUS, TIMOTHY DAVID, management consultant; b. Saginaw, Mich., Mar. 5, 1958; s. Robert Frederick and Nancy Lee (Boertman) N.; m. Jamie Lee Brown, Sept. 20, 1986. BBA, Western Mich. U., 1981, MBA, 1986. Sales engr. Du-Well Products, Bangor, Mich., 1982-84; terr. mgr. Ashworth Bros., Winchester, Va., 1984-86; pres., chief exec. officer J.R.T., Inc., Grand Rapids, Mich., 1986; exec. v.p. Brown Bros., Inc., Lansing, Mich., 1986—; mgmt. cons., Lansing, 1986—. Avocations: diving, hang gliding, swimming, sailing, skiing. Office: JRT Inc PO Box 88121 Kentwood MI 49508

NICKOLA, ROBERT MICHAEL, architecture educator; b. Chgo., Mar. 7, 1953; s. Robert A. and Helen Grace (Turner) N.; m. Peggy Ann Kucera, July 17, 1976; 1 child, Victoria Lynn. BArch, U. Ill., Chgo., 1979, MArch, 1981. Registered architect, Ill. Prin. architect, v.p. Jaeger, Nickola & Assocs., Ltd., Park Ridge, Ill., 1984—; asst. prof. architecture U. Ill., Chgo., 1982—. Served with USN, 1972-75. Recipient Juried award Chgo. Bar Assn., 1983. Mem. AIA, Assn. Collegiate Schs. Architecture (councilor, rep. 1985—), Nat. Council Archtl. Registration Bds. (cert.). Roman Catholic. Avocations: jogging, golfing, tennis. Home: 4N112 Central Bensenville IL 60106 Office: Jaeger Nickola & Assocs Ltd 104 S Main St Park Ridge IL 60068

NICOL, WILLIAM JAMES, health care management executive; b. Peoria, Ill., Sept. 2, 1943; s. William Charles and Marjorie Jean (O'Dea) N.; m. Sarah Ann Sparkman, May 16, 1970; children—William James, Darcey Meghan, John Charles. B.A., Bradley U., 1969. With Comprehensive Care Corp., Newport Beach, Calif., 1970-87, v.p. fin. and adminstrn., 1978-82, sr. v.p. fin. and adminstrn., 1982-83, exec. v.p., sec., 1983-85, vice chmn., 1985-87. also bd. dirs.; pres., chief exec. officer Rehab Care Corp., Chesterfield, Mo., 1987—, also bd. dirs.; bd. dirs. Total Phram. Care, Inc. Mem.Sheriff's Adv. Council, Orange County, Calif., 1982—. Served with U.S. Army, 1964-67. Fellow Am Acad. Med. Adminstrn.; mem. Fin. Execs. Inst. Republican. Presbyterian. Clubs: Big Canyon Country, Old Ranch Tennis. Home: 157 Herworth Dr Chesterfield MO 63017 Office: Rehab Care Corp 1795 Clarkson Rd Suite 301 Chesterfield MO 63017 also: Comprehensive Care Corp 18551 Von Karman Ave Irvine CA 92715

NICOLL, MARGARET GIBSON, marketing executive; b. Cape Girardeau, Mo., Apr. 23, 1950; d. Alexander Blair and Ruth Iva (Craig) Gibson; m. Phillip Grant Nicoll, Mar. 31, 1977; children: Meaghan Blair. BA, Duke U., 1973. Asst. editor Alumni Affairs, Duke U., Durham, N.C., 1973-76; reporter, editor Gazette Telegraph, Colorado Springs, Colo., 1977-83; asst. mktg. mgr. The Citadel/Rouse Co., Colorado Springs, 1983-84, mktg. mgr., 1984-85; group mktg. mgr. Salem Mall/Rouse Co., Dayton, Ohio, 1986—. Mem. nominating com. Jr. League of Colorado Springs, 1979-84; bd. dirs. Colorado Springs Dance Theatre, 1979-82. Mem. Internat. Council of Shopping Ctrs., Colorado Springs Press Club (bd. dirs. 1980, Honorable Mention award 1979, 80). Lutheran. Office: Salem Mall Mgmt Office 5200 Salem Ave Dayton OH 45426

NICOLL, MATTHEW NEATBY, business executive; b. Princeton, N.J., June 6, 1946; s. Frederick H. and Kate Elizabeth (Neatby) N.; m. Mary Kerr, June 16, 1973; children: William, Katherine. BA, MacMurray Coll., 1969; MBA, Denver U., 1972. Various positions Prudential Ins. Co., Denver, San Francisco, 1972-79; exec. v.p., gen. mgr. Vantage Co., Mpls., 1984-86, regional v.p., 1986—. Mem. Urban Land Inst., Nat. Assn. Indsl. Office Parks. Club: Falagship. Avocations: fishing, hunting, hockey. Home: 2443 Farview Ln Long Lake MN 55356 Office: Vantage Co 11095 Viking Dr Eden Prairie MN 55344

NIDETZ, MYRON PHILIP, medical adminstrator, health delivery systems consultant; b. Chgo., Dec. 29, 1935; s. David J. and Rose Y. (Yudell) N.; B.S., U. Ill., 1958; M.B.C., Hamilton Inst., Phila., 1972; M.P.A., Roosevelt U., 1981. Diplomate Am. Acad. Med. Adminstrs.; m. Linda Freeman, Dec. 18, 1960; children—Julia, Allison. Dir., Union Coop. Eye Care Center, Chgo., 1961-65; dir. med. adminstrv. services Michael Reese Hosp. and Med. Center, Chgo., 1966-75; asso. dir. program to improve med. care and health services in correctional instns. AMA, 1975-79; exec. dir. N. Central Dialysis Centers, Chgo., 1979—. Active Suburban Health Systems Agy., Oak Park, Ill., HCFA Network 15. Served with U.S. Army, 1959-60. Fellow Am. Public Health Assn., Royal Soc. Health; mem. Assn. Hosp. Med. Edn., Nat. Dialysis Assn. (treas.), Nat. Assn. Patients on Hemodialysis and Transplatation, Nat. Renal Adminstrs. Assn., Am. Acad. Polit. and Social Sci., Am. Geriatrics Soc., Am. Hosp. Assn., AMA, Inst. of Soc., Ethics and Life Scis., Gerontol. Soc., Assn. Univ. Programs Health Adminstrn. Home: 14800 S Minerva Ave Dolton IL 60419 Office: 55 E Washington St Chicago IL 60602

NIE, ZENON STANLEY, manufacturing company executive; b. Chgo., Nov. 19, 1950; m. Carol Ann Klockowski, Mar. 27, 1970; 1 child, Andrea Nicole. BS, U Ill., Chgo., 1971; MBA, Loyola U., Chgo., 1974. Mgr. sales stats. Zenith Electronics, Chgo., 1971-74; mktg. mgr. Hollister, Inc., Chgo., 1974-79; dir. market devel. Sealy, Inc., Chgo., 1979-81; sr. v.p. Serta, Inc., Chgo., 1981—; instr. Coll. of Lake County, Ill., 1978-81. mem. Nat. Assn. Bedding Mfrs. (chmn. stats. com. 1985—). Avocations: scuba diving, fishing, skiing, jogging. Office: Serta Inc 2800 N River Rd Des Plaines IL 60018

NIECE, RONALD LEE, biochemist; b. Lakeview, Ohio, Nov. 23, 1940; s. Melvin L. and Elizabeth Niece; children: Jeremy James, Matthew Coleman. BA, Blackburn Coll., 1962; MS, U. Wis., 1963, PhD, 1968. Research assoc. Inst. Cancer Research, Phila., 1968-69; postdoc. fellow dept. physiol. chemistry U. Wis., 1968-71, project assoc. dept. physiol., 1969, 71-82; project asst. McArdle Lab. Cancer Research, Madison, 1982-84, program coordinator, 1984-85; facility dir. U. Wis. Biotechnology Ctr., Madison, 1985—. NIH grantee, 1985, 86, NSF grantee, 1986. Mem. AAAS, Am. Chem. Soc., Genetics Soc. Am., Royal Scottish Country Dance Soc., Sigma Xi. Avocations: Scottish dancing, cross-country skiing. Home: 4337 Britha Dr 2 Madison WI 53711 Office: U Wis Biotechnology Ctr 1710 University Ave Madison WI 53705

NIEDING, SETH FRANK, health science facility administrator; b. Lorain, Ohio, Nov. 29, 1948; s. David F. and Betty E. (Poprick) N.; m. Marcia Colleen Clegg, June 20, 1970; children: Michelle, Melanie, Seth. BA in Sociology, Miami U., Oxford, Ohio, 1971; M in Social Work Adminstrn., Case Western Reserve U., 1974; postgrad., Moreno Inst., 1979, 82, Gestalt Inst. Cleve., 1983-85. Cert. social worker, alcoholism counselor, Ohio. Social worker Montgomery County Welfare Dept., Dayton, Ohio, 1971-72; intern Cleve. VA Adminstrn. Hosp., 1972-73, Fairhill Mental Health Ctr., Cleve., 1973-74; pvt. practice clin. social work Avon Lake, Ohio, 1975—; supr., planner Family Service Assn. Lorain (Ohio) County, 1975-76; alcoholism counseling coordinator Aftercare, Lorain, 1976-79; dir. Lakeland Inst., Lorain, 1979-85; clin. social worker Lakeland Guidance Ctr., Lorain, 1984-86; adminstr. depts. psychiatry, alcoholism and chemical dependency Lorain Community Hosp., 1985—; field instr., Case Western Reserve U. Sch. Applied Social Scis., 1978-80; sr. clin. instr. Case Western Reserve U. Sch. Medicine, 1985—. Mem. Nat. Assn. Social Workers, Acad. Cert. Social Workers. Avocations: family activities, boating, skiing. Home: 32689 Redwood Blvd Avon Lake OH 44012 Office: Lakeland Inst 3500 Kolbe Rd Lorain OH 44053

NIEDLING, HOPE HOTCHKISS, dietitian; b. Meriden, Ill., Feb. 14, 1922; d. Bert and Myrle Glenn (Vaughn) Hotchkiss; student North Central Coll., 1939-40; B.S., U. Ill., 1943; M.S. in Food Sci. and Nutrition, U. Wis. 1974; m. Ivan Martin Niedling, June 26, 1948. Teaching dietitian Univ. Hosp., Balt., 1944; dietitian public sch. cafeterias, Balt., 1944-48; dir. admissions Thomas Sch. Retailing, Phila., 1954-55; instr. foods U. Wis., Stevens Point, 1967-68; food service supr., instr. Mid-State, N.Central and Fox Valley Tech. Insts., Wis., 1973-75; cons. dietitian nursing homes in Wis., 1973—. Chmn., Village of Plover Cancer Fund Drive, 1977-78; bd. dirs. Stout Found., U. Wis., 1977—; sec.-treas. Joint Com. Edn. State of Wis., 1978—. Recipient Loyalty award U. Ill., 1978, award of merit U. Ill. Home Econs. Assn., 1979. Mem. Am. (ho. of dels. 1974-77), Wis. dietetic assns., No. Wis. Dietetic Assn. (pres. 1971-73), Soc. Nutrition Edn., Nutrition Today Soc., Nutritionists in Bus., Wis. Assn. Registered Parliamentarians (state corr. sec. 1978-80), Wis. Fedn. Women's Clubs (1st v.p. 1978-80), U. Ill. Home Econs. Alumni Assn. (bd. dirs. 1972-78), Colonial Dames XVII Century, Daus. Am. Colonists, Nat. Assn. Registered Parliamentarians, Wis. Public Health Assn. (mem. aging com. 1974-78), Portage County Humane Soc. (sec. 1973—), Wis. Fedn. Women's Clubs (pres. 1980-82), Gen. Fedn. Women's Clubs (sec.-treas. region 1982-84, chmn. internat. aid div. 1982-84, pres. Gt. Lakes region 1984-86, fundraiser chmn. Gt. Lakes Regional 1986-88), Colonial Dames XVII Century (1st v.p. Wis. 1981-83, pres. 1983—), DAR (Sec. 1977-80, 1st vice regent 1980-83, state regent 1983-86, chpt. regent 1972-77, chpt. registrar 1977—, pres. Wis. state officers club 1976-77, nat. bd. mgmt. 1983—), AAUW (pres. br. 1968-72, state corr. sec. 1970-72), U. Ill. Alumni Assn. (dir. 1973), NCCJ (disting. merit citation 1976; vice chmn. Wis. region 1975—; Portage County chmn. Nat. Brotherhood Week 1972—), Portage County Bicentennial of Const. of U.S., Wis. Soc. Children Am. Revolution (sr. state corr. sec. 1984-86, v.p. gen. 1987-90, sr. state 1st v.p. 1986—), Wis. Soc. Am. Revolution (state organizing sec.), DAR (nat. chmn. lineage research com. 1986-89, nat. soc. membership commn. 1986—), Wis. Fedn. Republican Women (dist. chmn. 1969-74), Gamma Sigma Delta, Epsilon Sigma Omicron. Methodist. Clubs: Order Eastern Star, Order of Amaranth, Order White Shrine of Jerusalem, Stevens Point Area Woman's (pres. 1972-74, 76-78, Stevens Point Woman's (pres. 1970-72). Address: 1008 3rd St Stevens Point WI 54481

NIEDZIELSKI, JAMES PETER, engineer; b. Bay City, Mich., Jan. 19, 1939; s. Clement John and Eleanore (Craves) N.; m. Anne Wazbinski, Sept. 3, 1960; children: Nancy, Nickalee, Aaron. Grad., Devry Tech. Inst., Chgo., 1963. Engr. Laser Systems Corp., Ann Arbor, Mich., 1963-69; prodn. mgr. Photon Sources, Inc., Livonia, Mich., 1969-75; v.p. engring. Phoenix Laser, Livonia, 1975-79; sales mgr. Rob-Con Inc., Livonia, 1979-83; chief engr. Laser Techs., South Lyon, Mich., 1983—; cons., 1980—. Mem. Soc. Mfg. Engrs. Club: Round Table (Plymouth, Mich.). Home: 8383 Rushton Rd South Lyon MI 48178 Office: Laser Techs 10131 Colonial Industry South Lyon MI 48178

NIEHAUS, JOHN THOMAS, clinical social worker; b. Cin., Feb. 2, 1937; s. William Joseph and Marie Agnes (Haggerty) N. BS in English, Xavier U., 1960; MSW, Ohio State U., 1964. Lic. ind. clin. social worker, Ohio, Ky.; cert. social worker, Ky. Social worker Cath. Charities, Cin., 1961-66; social worker, dir. Comprehensive Care Ctr. No. Ky., Covington, 1967-73; pvt. practice clin. social work Cin., 1970—; outpatient dir., social worker Mental Health Services N. Cen., Cin., 1974-80; assoc. prof. psychiatry, coordinator family therapy tng. U. Cin. Coll. Medicine, 1986—; cons. Mental Health Service N.W., Cin., 1975-76; family therapy cons. Family Services Cin., 1976-78, Hillcrest Sch., Cin., 1979-84, Cath. Charities, Cin., 1979-85. Mem. adv. bd. Cin. Recreation Com., 1968; bd. dirs. Home Health Care Service, Cin., 1972; mem. adv. bd. family service div. Salvation Army, Cin., 1975-78. Mem. Am. Assn. Marriage and Family Therapy (clin.), Am. Group Psychotherapy Assn., Nat. Assn. Social Workers, Ohio Soc. Clin. Social Work (pres. 1977-79), Acad. Cert. Social Workers. Democrat. Roman Catholic. Avocations: tennis, golf, opera, symphony, travel. Home: 570 Howell Ave Cincinnati OH 45220 Office: 106 Wellington Pl Cincinnati OH 45219

NIEHAUS, THOMAS L., manufacturing executive; b. Cin., Dec. 4, 1942; s. Roy H. and Catherine (Sheridan) N.; m. Judith Ann Thorton, July 9, 1966; children: Jeffrey Thomas, Brian Thomas, Jennifer Ann. BS in Indsl. Mfg., U. Cin., 1966. With Gen. Electric Co., various locations, 1966-72; materials mgr. Le Blond, Inc., Cin., 1972-77, Ilsco Corp., Cin., 1977-79; dir. materials OPW div. Dover Corp., Cin., 1979-83, mgr. mfg. OPW div., 1983—. Contbr. articles to profl. jours. Co. chmn. United Way, Cin., 1982; guest instr. Jr. Achievement, Cin., 1986. Mem. Am. Prodn. and Inventory Control Soc. (conf. speaker 1983-85). Republican. Roman Catholic. Avocaions: philately, photography. Home: 8720 Weller Rd Cincinnati OH 45249 Office: Dover Corp OPW Div 9393 Princeton Glendale Rd Cincinnati OH 45240-5003

NIELSEN, ARNOLD D., electronics engineer; b. Detroit, Dec. 20, 1943; s. Ejvind A. and Josephine (Reil) N.; m. Patricia Ann Szlavik, Sept. 3, 1971; 1 child, Cynthia Ann. BSEE, Wayne State U., 1968. Instrumentation engr. Chrysler Corp., Highland Park, Mich., 1970-73; instrumentation engr. Ford Motor Co., Dearborn, Mich., 1973-75, product design engr., 1975-84, electromagnetic compatibility engr., 1984—. Patentee in field. Served with USN, 1968-70. Mem. Soc. Automotive Engrs. Republican. Roman Catholic. Avocations: electronics, investing. Home: 37640 Hillcrest Wayne MI 48184 Office: Ford Motor Co 17000 Rotunda Dearborn MI 48121

NIELSEN, HARALD CHRISTIAN, chemist; b. Chgo., Apr. 18, 1930; s. Svend Aage and Seena (Hansen) N.; m. Eloise Wilma Soule, Dec. 19, 1953; children—Brenda Mae, Paul Erick, Gloria Lynn. B.A., St. Olaf Coll., 1952; Ph.D., Mich. State U., 1957. Cereal grain proteins chemist No. Regional Research Ctr., Agrl. Research Service, USDA, Peoria, Ill., 1957—. Contbr. articles to profl. jours. Pres. local 3247 Am. Fedn. Govt. Employees, AFL-CIO, 1977-86; mem. Peoria Area Combined Fed. Campaign Coordinating Com., 1980-87. Fellow AAAS; mem. Am. Chem. Soc. (sec. Peoria sect. 1977), Am. Assn. Cereal Chemists, ACLU, Sigma Xi. Democrat. Lutheran. Home: 2318 N Gale Ave Peoria IL 61604 Office: Agrl Research Service ASDA 1815 N University Ave Peoria IL 61604

NIELSEN, ROGER DENE, architect; b. Tilden, Nebr., Feb. 3, 1953; s. Howard Earl and Marion Elizabeth (Henderson) N.; m. Barbara Ann Keithley, July 9, 1982; 1 child, Rachael Louise. AA, N.E. Nebr. Coll., 1973; BArch, U. Nebr., 1977, MArch, 1979. Registered architect, Idaho, Iowa. Archtl. intern Davis, Fenton, Stange & Darling, Lincoln, Nebr., 1978; assoc. project architect Cline, Smull, Hamill & Quintieri Assocs., Boise, Idaho, 1979-85; coordinator prodn. drawings Quintieri Assocs., Boise, Idaho, 1981-85; assoc. project architect, coordinator prodn. drawings Duffy Ruble Mamura & Brygger (formerly Duffy, Beuttler, Olson & Brygger P.C.), Sioux City, Iowa, 1985—. Mem. AIA, Triangle Fraternity Alumnus Architects and Engrs. Republican. Lutheran. Office: Duffy Ruble Mamura & Brygger 314 Security Bank Sioux City IA 51101

NIELSEN, RUDOLPH R., data processing educator; b. Fenton, Iowa, Dec. 16, 1944; s. Ejlert I. and Dagney H. (Kahdal) N.; m. Sonja Larsen, Aug. 13, 1966; children: Daniel, Lynnea, Heidi. BA in Math., Concordia Coll., 1966; MS in Edn., No. Ill. U., 1972. Sci. tchr. Benton Community Schs., Van Horne, Iowa, 1972-77; computer programmer Economy Ins., Freeport, Ill., 1978-80; programmer/analyst Blue Cross/Blue Shield, Rockford, Ill., 1981-84, systems instr., 1984—; data processing instr. Highland Coll., Freeport, 1984—. V.p. Prince of Peace Ch., Freeport, 1986. Served to 1st lt. U.S. Army, 1968-71, Vietnam. Lutheran. Avocations: hiking, camping, reading. Home: 718 W Ordway St Freeport IL 61032 Office: Blue Cross Blue Shield 227 N Wyman St Rockford IL 61101

NIELSEN, STEVEN JEROME, dentist; b. Amery, Wis., Apr. 21, 1947; s. Gordon P. and Betty Lu (Olson) N.; m. Joan E. Geiser, Jan. 30, 1971; children—Stephanie Rae, Lindsay Joan. Student Gustavus Adolphus Coll., 1965-67; B.S., D.D.S., U. Minn., 1971. Intern W.Va. U., 1971-72; practice dentistry, Golden Valley, Minn., 1972—; pres. Bassett Creek Dental, Golden Valley, 1980—; cons. nursing homes. Mem. ADA, Minn. Dental Assn., Mpls. Dist. Dental Soc., Am. Acad. Dental Group Practice, W.Va. Soc. Hosp. Dentists. Republican. Lutheran. Lodge: Lions (pres. 1980-81, 100% Pres.'s award 1981). Avocations: boating; sailboarding; skiing; racquetball. Home: 3300 Carman Rd Excelsior MN 55331 Office: 5851 Duluth St Golden Valley MN 55422

NIELSEN, STUART DYBDAL, farmer; b. Dickinson, N.D., Feb. 10, 1956; s. Ernest Dybdal and Dorothy Mae (Erickson) N.; m. Kathleen Agnes Gatzke, July 20, 1978 (dec. 1980); m. Teresa Helen Dvorak, Nov. 23, 1984. AS, N.D. State U. Owner, operator Nielsen Farm, New England, N.D., 1977—. Named Outstanding Young Farmer, N.D. Jaycees, 1985. Mem. N.D. Stockmen's Assn., N.D. Wheat Producers Assn., Slope County Crop Improvement Assn. (bd. dirs., treas. 1984—). Republican. Lutheran. Lodges: Elks, Lions. Avocations: weightlifting, bowling, fishing. Home and Office: Rural Rt 3 Box 6 New England ND 58647

NIEMANN, NICHOLAS KENT, lawyer; b. Quincy, Ill., May 2, 1956; s. Ferd E. and Rita M. (Jochem) N.; m. Ann Marie Forbes, June 14, 1980; children: Katie, Becky, Christine, David. BSBA summa cum laude, Creighton U., 1978, JD magna cum laude, 1981. Bar: Nebr. 1981, U.S. Dist. Ct. Nebr. 1981, U.S. Ct. Appeals (8th cir) 1981, U.S Tax Ct. 1981, U.S. Claims Ct. 1985; CPA, Nebr. Assoc. McGill, Koley, Parsonage & Lanphier, P.C., Omaha, 1981-83; assoc. McGrath, North, O'Malley & Kratz, P.C., Omaha, 1983-85, ptnr., 1985—. Bd. dirs. West Fairacres Home. Mem. ABA, Nebr. Bar Assn., Omaha Bar Assn. (pub. service com. 1983-84), Am. Inst. CPA's (taxation sect. 1984—), Nebr. Soc. CPA's (taxation com. 1983—), Omaha C. of C. (pres. club), Alpha Sigma Nu (bd. dirs. 1986—, exec. com.), Beta Gamma Sigma, Beta Alpha Psi. Republican. Roman Catholic. Lodges: Kiwanis (membership com. Omaha club 1986—), Optimists. Avocations: golf, tennis, riding horses. Home: 236 S 123d St Omaha NE 68154 Office: McGrath North O'Malley & Kratz 1 Central Park Plaza Suite 1100 Omaha NE 68102

NIEMI, EDWIN EUGENE, psychologist; b. Ironwood, Mich., Oct. 8, 1950; s. Eugene and Mary Elizabeth (Oberlander) N.; m. Janice Marie Ferkovich, Sept. 2, 1972; children: Jason Reid, Kristin Jennifer. AA, Gogebic Community Coll., Ironwood, 1971; BS, Mich. State U., 1973; MEd, U. Wis., 1974. lic. psychologist, Minn.; cert. sch. psychologist. Group leader Woodland Hill Juvenile Treatment Ctr., Duluth, Minn., 1975-76; social worker Human Resource Ctr., Superior, Wis., 1976-78; psychologist Human Devel. Ctr., Duluth, 1978—. Chmn. Youth Devel. Council, Silver Bay and Two Harbors, Minn., 1984-85; bd. dirs. North Shore Horizon's Women Group, Two Harbors, 1985—. Mem. Minn. Lic. Psychologists, Minn. Psychol. Assn., Minn. Sch. Psychol. Assn. Democrat. Roman Catholic. Home: 824 15th Ave Two Harbors MN 55616 Office: Human Devel Ctr PO Box 269 Two Harbors MN 55616

NIEMI, JOHN ARVO, adult education educator; b. Ironwood, Mich., Dec. 6, 1932; s. Arvo John and Eva Ethel (Remes) N.; m. Muriel Winnifred Tomkins, Dec. 11, 1968. AA, Gogebic Community Coll., 1952; BA, Mich. State U., 1954; MEd, U. Alaska, 1963; EdD, UCLA, 1967; PhD (hon.), U. Helsinki, 1986. Dept. head U. Alaska, Fairbanks, 1962-64; assoc. prof. U. B.C., Vancouver, 1966-74; prof. Northern Ill. U., DeKalb, 1975—; cons. ALL Project Anchorage Community Coll., 1971-76, Tng. and Devel. Station, Prince Albert, Sask., 1973-74, Northern Inst. for Research, Tng. and Devel., Anchorage, 1978-81, U. Helsinki, 1981—; chmn. Commn. of Profs. of Adult Edn., 1985-87. Co-author Adult Education and the Disadvantaged Adult, 1970, Recruiting and Training Volunteers, 1981; editor Mass Media and Adult Edn., 1971; co-editor Technologies for Learning Outside the Classroom. Mem. Am. Assn. Adult and Continuing Edn. (chmn. various coms. 1970-85), Adult Edn. Research Conf. (exec. 1975-77), Northwest Adult Edn. Assn. (pres. 1974-76, cert. 1980). Lutheran. Avocations: travel, fishing. Home: 528 S 3d St Apt 6 DeKalb IL 60115 Office: No Ill U 101 Gabel Hall DeKalb IL 60115

NIEMOLLER, ARTHUR B., engineer; b. Wakefield, Kans., Oct. 4, 1912; s. Benjamin Henry and Minnie Christine (Carlson) N.; m. Ann Sochor, May 29, 1937 (dec. June 1982); children: Joanna Matteson, Arthur D. BSEE, Kans. State U., 1933. Registered profl. engr., N.Y., N.J., Pa., Ill., Ohio. Engr. Westinghouse, Newark, Hillside, N.J., 1937-59, Chgo., 1959-61, Pitts., 1961-65, Cin., 1965-77; pvt. practice engr. Montgomery, Ohio, 1977—. Patentee in field. Served with USN, 1933-37. Mem. IEEE, NSPE. Republican. Presbyterian. Home and Office: 7888 Mitchell Farm Ln Cincinnati OH 45242

NIERSTE, JOSEPH PAUL, software engineer; b. Marion, Ind., Feb. 20, 1952; s. Louis Lemuel and Mary Catherine (Dragstrem) N.; m. Deborah Mae Goble, Sept. 20, 1986. BA Applied Piano, Bob Jones U., 1975; MM in Musical Performance, Ball State U., 1977, MS in Computer Sci., 1984. Instr. Marion Coll., 1983-84, Ball State U., Muncie, Ind., 1983-84; software engr. Tokheim Corp., Ft. Wayne, Ind., 1984, Delco Electronics, Kokomo, Ind., 1984—. Mem. Pi Kappa Lambda. Republican. Baptist. Avocations: sports, music, computers. Home: 832 W Woodland Ave Kokomo IN 46902 Office: Delco Electronics Corp CT-40-D Kokomo IN 46902

NIES, LAWRENCE JOSEPH, data processing executive; b. De Pere, Wis., Oct. 15, 1949; s. Joseph Francis and Rosella Ann (Kabat) N.; m. Judy Ann Goldschmidt, July 31, 1971; children: Lisa Ann, Eric Jon, Heather Ann. Grad., Gale Inst. Technology; postgrad. in continuing edn., U. Wis. Data processing supr. Ariens Co., Brillion, Wis., 1976-81; pres. NSC, Inc., Brillion, 1981—. Editor Wis. Right to Life Newsletter, 1986. Contbr. articles to profl. jours. Served with U.S. Army, 1969-75. Mem. Data Processing Mgmt. Assn. (chpt. pres. 1985, Individual Performance award 1985), Brillion Athletic Assn. Republican. Roman Catholic. Avocations: motorcycling, computers, reading, fishing. Office: NSC Inc 207 S Main St Brillion WI 54110

NIES, THEODORE ALLAN, restaurant company executive; b. Manistee, Mich., Jan. 30, 1949; s. Richard and Ruth Pauline (Makinen) N.; m. Pamela Ann Bosch, Sept. 22, 1984. BS in Behaviorial Sci., Grand Valley State Coll., Allendale, Mich., 1972. Gen. mgr. Nies Enterprises, Grand Rapids, Mich., 1972-84; tng. mgr. Sbarro, Inc., Grand Rapids, 1985—. Mem. Restaurant Bus. Panel, Les Amis Du Vin.

NIESSE, JOHN EDGAR, materials engineer; b. Indpls., Nov. 30, 1927; s. John Leo and Jessie Louise (Pohlig) N.; m. Elaine Corinne Morin, Dec. 27, 1958; children: John, Ann. BS, U.S. Naval Acad., 1950; MS in Metallurgy, MIT, 1956, D in Metallurgy, 1958. Registered profl. engr., Mo. Commd. ensign USN, 1950, advanced through grades to lt., 1955, resigned, 1955; served to capt. USNR, 1980; supervising engr. Crane Co., Chgo., 1959-60; various positions Carborundum Co., Niagara Falls, N.Y., 1960-67; group leader AVCO Co. div. Space System, Lowell, Mass., 1967-72; sr. research group leader Monsanto Co., Research Triangle Park, N.C., 1972-75; prin. engrng. specialist Monsanto Co., St. Louis, 1975—. Contbr. articles to profl. jours.; patentee bond between steel surface and organic adhesives, 1976, cutting tool blank, 1976. Crane Co. fellow MIT, 1957, 58. Mem. Am. Soc. Metals, Nat. Assn. Corrosion Engrs. (chmn. various coms.), Am. Ceramics Soc., Tau Beta Pi, Sigma Xi. Home: 424 Glan Tai Dr Manchester MO 63011 Office: Monsanto Co 800 N Lindbergh BLvd Saint Louis MO 63167

NIESZ, GEORGE MELVIN, tool and die co. exec.; b. Norwood, Ohio, Aug. 6, 1926; s. George John and Anita Agnes Lucille (Chialastri) N.; student pub. schs., Norwood and Deer Park; m. Evelyn Catherine Rayburn, Oct. 18, 1946; children—Nancy L., George J., Jr. Profl. baseball player St. Louis Cardinals Orgn., 1944-45; tool and die maker Steelcraft Mfg. Co., Cin., 1946-51; supt., mgr. Abco Tool & Die Co., 1951-70; founder, pres. Niesz Tool & Die Co., Cin., 1970-85; pvt. investor, 1985—. State dir., v.p. Sycamore-Deer Park Jr. C. of C., 1956-59. Ky. Col. Mem. Am. Soc. Metals, Soc. Mfg. Engring., Cin. C. of C., Anderson Twp. C. of C. Republican. Clubs: Masons (32 deg); Shriners. Patentee portable tool attachment; chess champion. Home: 4171 Winesap Ct Cincinnati OH 45236 Office: PO Box 44147 Cincinnati OH 45236

NIETZ, CONNIE COLLINS, pharmacist; b. Toledo, Nov. 3, 1956; d. Clifford Merchant and Martha Lee (Lawrence) Collins; m. Gerald George Nietz, Oct. 4, 1980; 1 child, James Collins. B.S. in Pharmacy, Ohio Northern U., 1979. Registered pharmicist, Ohio. Pharmacy intern Collins & Parker, Inc., Oregon, Ohio, 1976-79, Mem. Med. Coll. of Ohio, Toledo, 1978-79; registered pharmacist Collins & Parker, Inc., 1979—, Aller's Pharmacy, North Baltimore, Ohio, 1980—. Del., Wood County Republican Conv., Bowling Green, Ohio, 1984. Mem. Ohio State Pharm. Assn., North Balt. Bus. Women's Club. Republican. Mem. United Brethren Ch. Club: Jr. Lit. and Lyric Circle (North Baltimore) (pres.). Avocations: music (piano and voice), needlework, calligraphy. Home: 203 Southlawn Dr North Baltimore OH 45872

NIEUWSMA, MILTON JOHN, hospital executive; b. Sioux Falls, S.D., Sept. 5, 1941; s. John and Jean (Potter) N.; B.A., Hope Coll., Holland, Mich., 1963; postgrad. Wayne State U., 1963-65; M.A., Sangamon State U., 1978; m. Marilee Gordon, Feb. 1, 1964; children—Jonathan, Gregory, Elizabeth. Public info. officer Wayne State U., Detroit, 1963-69; public relations dir. Sinai Hosp., Detroit, 1969-72; dir. div. officer services Am. Hosp. Assn., Chgo., 1972-73; asst. prof. journalism Wayne State U., Detroit, 1974; dir. public relations and devel. Meml. Med. Center, Springfield, Ill., 1975-79; v.p. for public affairs Grant Hosp., Chgo., 1979-87; v.p. devel., 1987—. governing mem. Chgo. Zool. Soc., 1981—. Bd. dirs. Springfield (Ill.) Boys Clubs, 1979-80, Sangamon County Heart Assn., 1978-80, Riverside Community Fund (Ill.), 1986; pub. relations chmn. Sangamon County Heart Fund Campaign, 1978; pres. Ford Com., 1975-76; bd. dirs. United Meth. Housing Corp., Detroit, 1968-70; chmn. Sch. Dist. 205 Caucus, 1983—; mem. exec. com. Village Riverside, 1986— . Mem. Public Relations Soc. Am., Nat. Assn., Hosp. Devel., Am. Hosp. Assn., Ill. Hosp. Assn., Lincoln Park C. of C. (bd. dirs.). Republican. Presbyterian. Contbr. articles in field to profl. jours. Home: 322 Scottswood Rd Riverside IL 60546 Office: 550 W Webster Ave Chicago IL 60614

NIGHTINGALE, EDMUND ANTHONY, transportation economist, educator; b. St. Paul, July 17, 1903; s. Edmund Alexander and Katherine Ellen (Eagan) N.; B.B.A., U. Minn., 1933, M.A., 1936, Ph.D., 1944; m. Lauretta A. Horejs, June 5, 1937; children—Edmund Joseph, Paul Lawrence. With operating dept. various railroads, 1920-33; teaching asst. econs. U. Minn., 1933-36, instr. in econs., transp., 1936-44, asst. prof., 1944-47, assoc. prof., 1947-52, prof., 1952-72, prof. emeritus, 1972—, dir. insts. in rail transp., 1948-49. Cons. to Mpls. Mayor's Citizen Adv. Com. on streetcar and bus matters, 1952-54; cons. transp. economist. Editorial statistician Minn. State Planning Bd., 1936; prin. indsl. specialist, prin. transp. economist WPB, Washington, 1942-43; cons. transp. economist to Minn. Resources Commn., Minn. Iron Range Resources and Rehab. Commn., 1941-48; cons. to dir. mil. traffic service Office Sec. Def., Washington, 1950-53; cons. Minn. Legis. Interim Com. to Study R.R. and Warehouse Commn., 1956-57; mem. Transp. Research Adv. Com., U.S. Dept. Agr., 1960-63, mem. adv. com. mktg. research and service programs, 1963-66; mem. Gov.'s Transit Authority Study Com., 1964-69; research cons. Mid-Am. Gov.'s Transp. Council, 1965-72; cons. Minn. Pub. Service Commn., 1965-72, U.S. Dept. Transp., 1969-70. Mem. Gov's Transp. Adv. Com., 1968-72. Chmn. Highlands dist. Indianhead council Boy Scouts Am., 1955-58, mem.-at-large, exec. bd., 1958-74. Recipient diploma of honor internat. prize jury VIII Pan-Am. Congress, Washington, 1953; St. George award, Cath. Com. Scouting Archdioces St. Paul, 1960. Registered practitioner ICC. Mem. Am. Soc. Traffic and Transp., Transp. Club Mpls. and St. Paul, AAUP, Am. Econ. Assn., Am. Agr. Econ. Assn., Assn. Transp. Practitioners (pres. chpt. 1957-58; regional v.p. 1961-63, chmn. com. edn. for practice 1971-73), Internat. Assn. Assessing Officers, Nat. Tax Assn. (com. on taxation pub. utility and transp. 1971—), Midwest Econs. Assn., Royal Econ. Soc., Nat. Assn. Shippers Adv. Bds. (legis. com. 1969—), N.W. Shippers Adv. Bd. (mem. legislative com. 1952-69, chmn. 1960-67), Associated Traffic Clubs Am. (v.p. edn. and research 1958-62, v.p. W. N. Central States 1962-63; Distinguished Transp. Educator, 1966), Transp. Research Forum, Beta Gamma Sigma, Beta Alpha Psi, Alpha Kappa Psi. Clubs: Transp., Campus (Mpls.). Co-author: Aviation in Minnesota, 1952; Foreign Trade via the St. Lawrence Seaway, 1965; Transportation Problems and Policies in the Trans-Missouri West, 1967. Contbr. to Freight Traffic Management at Installations of the Military Depts., Dept. of Defense, rev. edit., 1952. Contbr. articles econs., taxation, transp. jours. Home: 2120 Niles Ave Saint Paul MN 55116 Office: Curtis L Carlson Sch Mgmt U Minn Minneapolis MN 55455

NIGHTINGALE, EDMUND JOSEPH, clinical psychologist; b. St. Paul, Jan. 10, 1941; s. Edmund Anthony and Lauretta Alexandria (Horejs) N.; student Nazareth Hall Prep. Sem., 1959-61; A.B., St. Paul Sem., 1963; A.B. magna cum laude, Catholic U. of Louvain (Belgium), 1965, M.A., 1967, S.T.B. cum laude, 1967; postgrad. U. Minn., 1971; M.A., Loyola U., Chgo., 1973, Ph.D. in Clin. Psychology, 1975; m. Marie Arcara, Apr. 9, 1978; 1 son, Edmund Bernard. With Cath. Archdiocese of St. Paul and Mpls., 1967-73; intern in clin. psychology Michael Reese Hosp. and Med. Center, Chgo., 1973-74, W. Side VA Hosp., Chgo., 1974-75; staff psychologist, student counseling center, Loyola U., Chgo., 1975; staff psychologist and clin. coordinator of inpatient unit, drug dependency treatment center Hines (Ill.) VA Hosp., 1975-79, acting chief drug dependency treatment center, 1979-80; chief psychology VA Med. Ctr., Danville, Ill., 1980-86; chief psychology VA Med. Ctr. Mpls., 1986—; mem. personnel bd. Archdiocese of St. Paul and Mpls., 1968-70; lectr. psychology, Loyola U., Chgo., 1975; asst. professorial lectr. psychology, St. Xavier Coll., Chgo., 1975-78; adj. asst. prof. psychology in psychiatry, Abraham Lincoln Sch. Medicine, Med. Center U. Ill., Chgo., 1977-82; adj. prof. psychology Purdue U., 1981-87; asst. prof. psychiatry Med. Sch., U. Minn., 1987—, clin. assoc. prof. psycholgy Coll. Liberal Arts, 1986—; clin. asst. prof. U. Ill. Sch. Medicine, Urbana/Champaign, 1982-87; mem. grad. faculty in counseling psychology Ind. State U., Terre Haute, 1983-86. Bd. dirs. Inst. Postgrad. Studies, Ill. Psychol. Assn., Registered psychologist, Ill.; lic. cons. psychologist, Minn.; certified Nat. Registry of Health Service Providers in Psychology. Mem. Am. Psychol. Assn. (clin. psychology, public service, and psychotherapy divs.), Ill. Psychol. Assn. (clin. psychology and acad. sects.; sec. 1982-83, pres.-elect 1983-84, pres. 1984-85), AAAS, Assn. for Advancement of Psychology, Am. Group Psychotherapy Assn., Am. Soc. Clin. Hypnosis, Minn. Psychol. Assn., Am. Evaluation Assn., Am. Assn. Univ. Profs., Assn. VA chief Psychologists (sec.-treas. 1987—). Founding editor: Louvain Studies, 1966; editor: VA Directory of Psychology Staffing and Services, 1982, 83, 84, 85, 87. Home: 2281 Ocala Ct Mendota Heights MN 55120 Office: VA Med Center Minneapolis MN 55417

NIHAN, TAMARA ANN, accountant; b. Woodstock, Ill., Oct. 13, 1962; d. John Edward and Wilma Laura (Winkelman) N. BBA in Acctg., Augustana Coll., 1984. CPA, Ill. Staff acct. Carpenter, Mitchell, Goddard & Co., Moline, Ill., 1984-86, John E. Nihan, Acct., Woodstock, 1986; ptnr. Nihan & Nihan, Woodstock, 1987—. Mem. Am. Inst. CPA's, Ill. CPA Soc., Ind. Accts. Assn. Ill., Woodstock Profl. and Bus. Women, Woodstock C. of C. Roman Catholic. Home: 1140 Dean St Woodstock IL 60098 Office: Nihan & Nihan 203 Dean St Woodstock IL 60098

NIKKEL, VERNON LLOYD, manufacturing company executive; b. Goessel, Kans., May 26, 1928; s. Henry P. Nikkel and Martha (Dirksen) N.; m. Lennea Oetinger, June 11, 1950; children: Greta Ann, Sanford Louis. B in Mus. Edn., Bethany Coll., 1950; MS, Emporia State Coll., 1961. Mgr. Emma Creek Stock and Grain Farm, McPherson County, Kans., 1942—; tchr. music Weskan (Kans.) Pub. Schs., 1950-53, Roxbury (Kans.) Unified Pub. Schs., 1953-57; dir. music edn. Hesston (Kans.) Unified Pub. Schs., 1957-64; v.p. Hesston Indls. Relations, 1964—, dir., 1965—; pres. Hesston Devel., Inc., 1972-76. Dir. family week Rocky Mountain Mennonite Camp, 1966-70; mem. Harvey County Orch. Assn., 1971—, sec. 1973-79; bd. dirs. Hesston Performing Arts, 1982—; Sunday sch. tchr. United Meth. Ch., Hesston, 1962—, treas. bldg. com., 1969-70; dir. music West United Meth. Conf., 1975-77; mem. Wichita Ann. Conf. Council of Ministries, 1976-80; chmn. sessions planning com. United Meth. Kans. West Conf., 1977-85; del. jurisdictional conf. United Meth. Ch., 1980, 84.; Councilman City of Hesston, 1961-63; mayor City of Hesston, 1967-69; chmn. Harvey County Reps., 1984-86; mem. Tri County Memtal Health Bd., Harvey County, Kans., 1965-71; mem., chmn. bd. Kans. Blance of State Pvt. Industry Council, 1979-83; mem. CETA/Balance State Manpower Planning Council, 1979-83, chmn., 1983, pvt. Industry Council, Kans. Jobs Tng. Partnership Act, 1983—, vice-chmn., 1984—, Kans. Job Service Employer Com., 1984—, vice-chmn. 1987; chmn. bd. human resources com. Kans. Assn. Commerce and Industry, 1981-84; trustee Axtell Christian Hosp., 1985—, Bethany Coll., Lindsborg, Kans., 1985—; bd. dirs. Blue Cross/Blue Shield of Kans., 1984-86. Recipient Harvey County Community Mental Health award 1971, Citation award Kans. Dept. Employment, 1976. Mem. Am. Soc. Personnel Adminstrs. (cert.), Hesston C. of C., Newton C. of C. (bd. dirs. 1979-82, 85—), Wichita C. of C., Kans. C. of C. Lodges: Lions, Elks. Home: 230 S Weaver Hesston KS 67062 Office: Excel Inc Box 7000 Hesston KS 67062

NIKODEM, EDWARD FRANCIS, marketing executive; b. Bridgeport, Conn., Jan. 24, 1949; s. John Martin and Mary Agnes (Muszka) N.; m. Elizabeth Anne Bloom, Apr. 24, 1982; children: Deborah Alison, Rebecca Karena. BA cum laude, U. Conn., 1970; MA in English, U. Minn., 1974, MBA in Mtkg., 1976. Owner, relations analyst Parts and Service div. Ford Motor Co., Chgo., 1976-77, zone mgr., 1977-78; mktg. analyst Power Products div. Ford Motor Co., Detroit, 1978-81; mktg. specialist Credit and Diversified Fin. Ops. div. Ford Motor Co., Dearborn, Mich., 1981—; mktg. cons. Ford Fin. Services, Dearborn, 1982—. Author: (pamphlets) Employee Involvement, 1985, Career Devel., 1986. Vol. United Found., Detroit, 1984-85, cons., 1986. Served with U.S. Army, 1971-73, Vietnam. Decorated two Bronze Stars, Air Medal. Roman Catholic. Avocation: gourmet cooking. Office: Ford Motor Credit Co Box 1729 Dearborn MI 48121

NIKOLAI, JOHN LINCOLN, advertising manager; b. Rubicon, Wis., Feb. 11, 1925; s. John Leo and Theresa (Neu) N.; m. Marian Margaret Merkel, May 30, 1953; children: Anne, Stephen, Jeanne, Beth, Mary Alice, Gretchen, Zachary. BS in Biology, U. Wis., 1950. Payroll clk. Allis Chalmers, West Allis, Wis., 1950-52; fish biologist's aid Wis. Conservation Dept., Oshkosh, 1952-53; salesman Standard Oil of Ind., Richland Ctr., Wis., 1953-57, Ft. Howard Paper Co., Chippewa Falls, Wis., 1957-66; advt. mgr. Hamilton Industries, Two Rivers, Wis., 1966—. Scoutmaster Boy Scouts Am., Two Rivers, 1967-75; bd. dirs. Two Rivers Recreation Bd., 1971-74, Two Rivers Pub. Schs., 1973-79, Joseph Mann Library Bd., 1986—. Republican. Roman Catholic. Lodge: KC (grand knight 1974-75). Avocations: bicycling, travel, fishing, hunting, history. Home: 805 29th St Two Rivers WI 54241 Office: Hamilton Industries Box 137 Two Rivers WI 54241

NIKOLICH, GOJAN, public relations agency executive, writer; b. Kirchen-Hausen, W.Ger., Mar. 26, 1949; s. Srecko and Erika (Hirter) N.; m. Leslie Ann Guenveur, May 10, 1975; 1 child, Lauren Marie. BA in English, DePaul U., 1975, MA in English, 1977. Editor, Glenview (Ill.) Times, 1974-75; dir. mktg. Ill. Dept. Tourism, Chgo., 1975-81; exec. v.p. Kraus, Dunham and Nikolich Pub. Relations, Inc., Chgo., 1981—; writer, broadcaster WGN Radio, Chgo., 1978—; exec. dir. No. Ill. Tourism Council, 1982—. Newspaper travel columnist, 1976-81; chmn. editorial com. Journey Mag. Mem. adv. com. chmn. mktg. com. Chgo.-Ft. Dearborn Hist. Commn. Served with U.S. Army, 1970-73. Decorated Army Commendation medal with oak leaf cluster. Mem. Soc. Am. Travel Writers, Assn. Great Lakes Outdoor Writers. Home: 185 Walnut St Elmhurst IL 60126 Office: Kraus Dunham Nikolich 111 N Canal St Chicago IL 60606

NILLES, WILLIAM O., savings and loan association executive. Pres., dir. Metropolitan Federal Bank FSB, Fargo, N.D.; vice chmn. Met. Fin. Corp., Fargo. Office: Met Fin Corp 215 N Fifth St Fargo ND 58102 *

NILSEN, CLIFFORD THEODORE, investment company executive; b. Jamaica, N.Y., July 19, 1932; s. Carl and Sigrid (Aanensen) N.; m. Charlene A. Renninger, Sept. 12. 1956; children: Wendy, Kurt. BBA, Hofstra U., 1956. Portfolio mgr. Walston & Co., N.Y.C., 1956-62; investment officer Reliable Ins. Co., Phila., 1962-66; v.p. Savs. Bank & Trust, N.Y.C., 1966-73; sr. v.p. Eberstadt Asset Mgmt., N.Y.C., 1973-81; pres. Chem./Surveyor Funds, N.Y.C., 1979-81, Capital Investment Services of Am., Inc. (formerly Loewi Asset Mgmt. Corp.), Milw., 1981—. Mem. N.Y. Soc. Security Analysts. Methodist. Avocations: horsebreeding, reading. Office: Capital Investment Services 700 N Water St #325 Milwaukee WI 53202-4206

NILSON, CHRISTIAN, lawyer; b. Highland Park, Mich., Mar. 15, 1952; s. Robert Anton and Clara Johanna (Woupio) N. BA in Bus., Mich. State U., 1974, BS in Criminal Justice, 1975; JD, Thomas M. Cooley, Lansing, Mich., 1978; LLM in Tax, Wayne State U., 1984. Bar: Mich. 1978. Sole practice Detroit, 1975; v.p., legal officer Mfrs. Nat. Bank Detroit, 1978—. Mem. ABA, Mich. State Bar Assn. Avocation: renovating older homes. Home: 315 W Cambourne Ferndale MI 48220

NILSSON, GUNNAR PETER, savings and loan executive; b. Chgo., Aug. 27, 1945; s. Johan Petrus and Vendla Elizabeth (Lindmark) N.; m. Janet Louise Wolsko, Aug. 3, 1968; children: Kirsten, Laura, Erica. BA, Augustana U., Rock Island, Ill., 1967; MBA, Ind. U., 1971. Audit staff small bus. Arthur Andersen, Chgo., 1967-69; v.p. Nat. Homes Corp., Lafayette, Ind., 1971-74; asst. v.p. First Nat. Bank Chgo., 1974-76; sr. v.p., prin. Balcor/Am. Express, Skokie, Ill., 1976-82; dir. Lemont Savs. Assn., Northbrook, Ill., 1984—; mem. adv. bd. Bus. Forum, Chgo., 1985—. v.p. ch. council St. James Luth. Ch., Lake Forest, Ill., 1979-82; mem. one-in-mission Luth. Ch. Am., Chgo., 1985—. Served with U.S. Army, 1968-74. Mem. Union League

Chgo. Avocations: running, tennis, basketball, fishing, skiing. Office: Lemont Savs Assn 400 Skokie Blvd Suite 395 Northbrook IL 60062

NIMMO, HERBERT LEE, engineer; b. Kansas City, Kans., Oct. 8, 1934; s. Forrest Herbert and Velma Irene (Barker) N.; m. F. Elizabeth Turner, June 7, 1963; 1 child, Martha Ann. BSME, Finlay Engring. Coll., 1959. Cert. mfg. engr.; registered profl. engr., Mo. Design engr. United Mfg. & Engring. Corp., Independence, Mo., 1960-61; sr. design engr. George W. Johnson Mfg., Kansas City, Mo., 1961-62; sr. process engr. Remington Arms Co., Inc., Lake City Plant, Independence, 1962-69, area process engr., 1969-83, chief supr. quality assurance, 1983-84, chief process engr., 1984-85; mgr. mfg. engring. def. systems group Olin Corp., Independence, 1985—; co-chmn. tech. adv. bd. Cen. Mo. State U., Warrensburg, Mo., 1984—. Contbr. articles to profl. jours. Served with U.S. Army, 1954-57. Recipient Pub. Service award Am. Radio Relay League, Inc., 1977. Mem. Soc. Mfg. Engrs. (chpt. chmn. 1986-87; Achievement award 1982-83), Mo. Soc. Profl. Engrs. (chmn. profl. engrs. in industry 1982-83), Am. Soc. Metals (chmn. pub. relations 1984-85), Am. Soc. Quality Control, Soc. Am. Mil. Engrs., Am. Legion, Nat. Rifle Assn. Clubs: Independence FM Amateur Radio, Am. Radio Relay League. Avocations: amateur radio, personal computing. Home: Route 1 Box 121 Higginsville MO 64037 Office: Olin Def Systems Group Lake City Plant Independence MO 64050

NIMS, CHARLES FRANCIS, clergyman, egyptologist; b. Norwalk, Ohio, Oct. 19, 1906; s. Joel Benjamin and Grace (Wildman) N.; student U. Toledo, 1924-25; A.B., Alma Coll., 1928; B.D., McCormick Theol. Sem., 1931; Ph.D., U. Chgo., 1937; m. Myrtle Eileen Keillor, Apr. 18, 1931. Ordained to ministry Presbyn. Ch., 1931; pastor, First Ch., Eldorado, Ill., 1940-43; research asst. Oriental Inst., 1934-40; staff Sakkarah Expdn., Egypt, 1934-36; staff Epigraphic Survey, 1937-39; egyptologist Epigraphic Survey, 1946-63, field dir., 1964-72; research assoc. dept. Oriental lang. U. Chgo., 1948-67, faculty mem., 1960-61, assoc. prof., 1967-70, prof., 1970-72, emeritus, 1972—; staff mem. Chgo. Archeol. Expdn., Tolmeita, Libya, 1954, 56, 57, 58; lectr. adult edn. Field Mus. Natural History, 1976. Mem. Found. Egyptologique Reine Elizabeth, Egypt Exploration Soc., Soc. Bibl. Lit., Am. Oriental Soc., Am. Photog. Soc. Am Schs. Oriental Research, Mil. Chaplains Assn. U.S., AAUP, Am. Research Center in Egypt, L'Association Internationale pour l'Étude du Droit Pharaonique (hon. pres.); ordinary mem. Deutsches Archaologisches Instut; assoc. mem. L'Institut d' Egypte; mem. Phi Beta Kappa. Served as chaplain (capt.) U.S. Army, 1943-46. Author: (with H.H. Nelson et al) Medinet Habu IV, 1940; (with Prentice Duell) Mastaba of Mereruka, 1938; (with G.R. Hughes) Reliefs and Inscriptions in Karnak, III, 1954; Medinet Habu V-VIII (with G.R. Hughes), 1957-70; Thebes of the Pharoahs, 1965; (with E.F. Wente) The Tomb of Kheruef, 1980, The Temple of Khonsu, I, 1979; (with William Murnane) The Temple of Khonsu, II, 1981. Contbr. articles to profl. jours. Home: 5540 Blackstone Ave Chicago IL 60637 Office: Oriental Inst U Chgo Chicago IL 60637

NIMS, ROBERT WALTER, accountant; b. Jackson, Mich., Mar. 4, 1950; s. Wellington Dewitt and Doris Irene (Gramer) N.; m. Jennifer Christina King, Aug. 12, 1972; children—Robert W., Jonathan R., David D. M.B.A., Central Mich. U., 1974. C.P.A., Mich. sole practice, Mt. Pleasant, Mich., 1983—. Patentee tape reroll apparatus. Commr. Mt. Pleasant Housing Bd. Appeals, 1979-81; mem. Mt. Pleasant Planning Commn., 1981-84 chmn., 1983. Lodge: Lions. Home: 600 W Hopkins Mount Pleasant MI 48858 Office: 111 E Broadway Mount Pleasant MI 48858

NIMS, WALTER WORTHINGTON, distribution executive, accountant; b. Salem, Mass., Jan. 26, 1949; s. William Worthington and Eleanor (Edwards) N.; m. Patricia Kay McClead, Aug. 28, 1971; children: Heather Chantelle, Brittany Skye, Caira Noelle. AB, Hillsdale (Mich.) Coll., 1970; MBA, Ind. U., 1983. CPA, Ind. Mktg. rep. IBM Corp., Lima, Ohio, 1975-77; acct. Dulin, Ward & DeWald, Ft. Wayne, 1977-80; controller The Howard Co., Inc., Ft. Wayne, 1980-81, sec., treas., 1981-86, pres., treas., 1986—, also bd. dirs. Served to 1st lt. USAF, 1971-75. Mem. Am. Inst. CPA's, Ind. CPA Soc., Nat. Assn. Accts., Beta Gamma Sigma (life). Republican. Presbyterian. Lodge: Rotary. Avocations: reading, cycling, swimming. Office: The Howard Co Inc PO Box 11291 Fort Wayne IN 46857

NIMTZ, THOMAS ARTHUR, psychotherapist; b. Detroit, May 15, 1939; s. Henry C. and Alice M. (Miller) N.; m. Inge S. Schneider, Sept. 5, 1964; children: Thomas P., Kai Christopher, Maika Marie. BA, Valparaiso U., 1965; MSW, U. Denver, 1968; student, Family Inst. Chgo., 1972. Cert. social worker, Ind. With forensic unit Dr. Norman Beatty Meml. Hosp., Westville, Ind., 1968-73; dir. family treatment and studies program Dr. Norman Beatty Meml Hosp., Westville, Ind., 1983-75; clin. dir. Porter Starke Services, Inc., Valparaiso, Ind., 1975-81; pvt. practice psychotherapy Valparaiso and Muncie, 1981—; adj. prof. Valparaiso U. Bd. dirs. Greenwich House. Served with U.S. Army, 1960-63. Recipient Jean Pert Sinnot award, 1968. Mem. Am. Orthopsychiat. Assn., Nat. Assn. Social Workers, Am. Assn. for Marital Family Treatment. Home: 7550 Hohman Ave Munster IN 46321

NINKE, ARTHUR ALBERT, accountant, management consultant; b. Coloma, Mich., Aug. 20, 1909; s. Paul F. and Theresa Grace (Warskow) N.; m. Claudia Wagner, Sept. 13, 1930; children: Doris Ninke Hart, Donald, Marion, George, Arthur Albert, Thomas, Mark, Albert. Student acctg. Internat. Bus. Coll., 1928; diploma commerce Northwestern U., 1932. Auditor, Arthur Andersen & Co., C.P.A.s, Chgo., 1929-36, St. Louis, 1950-55, Midwest Stock Exchange, 1936-41, SEC, 1942-45; expense controller Butler Bros., Chgo., 1946-49; office mgr. Hargis Electronics, 1956-59; auditor HUD, Detroit, 1960-64; owner Urban Tech. Staff Assoc., cons. urban renewal projects and housing devel., Detroit, 1965-81; pres. Simplified Systems & Computer Sales, 1978—; exec. dir. Urban Mgmt. Services 1984—, Urban Computerized Services, Inc., 1984—, Computer Mgmt. Services, 1985—, Complete Bus. Service, Dallas, 1979-82, Loving Shepherd Nursing Home, Warren, Mich., 1975-83; sec. Gideons Detroit North Woodward, 1981-83, treas., 1986-87. Author: Family Bible Studies; Computer Networking; dir. TV Family Bible Hour Club, 1986—. Developer simulated machine bookkeeping system; trade mark holder Record-Checks-Systems, 1981—. Controller, Lake Superior R&D Inst., Munising, Mich., 1973-76; pres. Luth. Friendship Homes, Inc., 1975-85; lay evangelist Faith Lut. Ch., 1986—, treas., 1985-86; mng. dir. Family Evangelism Found., 1977—; controller S.E. Mich. Billy Graham Crusade, 1976-77; pres. Project Compassion Met. Detroit, Inc., 1982—; bd. dirs. Lutheran Credit Union Greater Detroit, 1982—; mem. Nat. Council on Aging. Recipient tribute Mich. State Legislature, 1982, tribute City of Warren, 1982. Mem. Nat. Soc. Pub. Accts., Nat. Assn. Housing and Redevel. Ofcls. (treas. Mich. 1973-75), Luth. Center Assn. (treas. 1975-81, dir. 1975-81), Internat. Luth. Laymen's League (treas. S.E. Mich. 1971-75, dir. 1976-81), Am. Mgmt. Assn., Fairlane Club of Dearborn. Home: 22405 Riverdale Dr Southfield MI 48034 Office: 17600 Northland Park Ct Southfield MI 48075

NISSENSON, NORMA, clinical psychologist; b. Frankfort, Ky., Nov. 18, 1917; s. Jacob and Pearl (Klass) Rosen; m. Marc Nissenson, July 6, 1940; children: Carol, Mary. BS, Northwestern U., 1983, MA, 1948. Cert. clin. psychologist, Ill. Exec. dir. Guidance Agy. Adolecents, Chgo., 1946-52; assoc prof. Roosevelt U., Chgo., 1962-70; gen. practice psychology Nissenson Assocs. Ltd., Chgo., 1962—. Bd. dirs. Moraine council Girl Scouts USA, Moraine PTA, Operation Higher Edn. Pays; pres. N. Shore Film Soc.; lectr., participant TV talk shows, Chgo., 1962—. Fellow Am. Orthopsychiat. Assn., Internat. Council Sex Edn. and Parenthood; mem. Am. Psychol. Assn., Ill. Psychol. Assn., Chgo. Psychol. Assn. (pres. 1982), Am. Assn. Counseling and Devel. (life), Am. Assn. Marriage and Family Therapist, Ill. Commn. Human Relations (state adv. council). Home: 966 Princeton Ave Highland Park IL 60035 Office: 1971 Second St Suite 700 Highland Park IL 60035

NITTERHOUSE, DENISE, business educator, consultant; b. Chambersburg, Pa., Jan. 11, 1950; d. Theodore Karper and Nellie Elizabeth (Bent) N. BA, Duke U., 1971; MBA, Harvard U., 1977, D in Bus. Adminstrn., 1981. Staff acct. Haskins & Sells, CPAS, New Haven, 1971-74; acct. Planned Parenthood League Conn., New Haven, 1974-75; instr. Kennedy Sch. Govt., Harvard U., 1976-81; asst. prof. U. Ill., Champaign, 1981-85, DePaul U., Chgo., 1985—; adj. faculty U. New Haven, 1974-75; cons. 1974—, speaker, seminar instr. 1975—. Contbr. articles to profl. jours., chapts. to books. Treas., bd. dirs. A Woman's Fund, Inc., Urbana, Ill., 1982-85. Doctoral fellow Haskins & Sells Found., 1977, Am. Acctg. Assn., 1979, thesis fellow Harvard U., 1980; named Celebration of Feminism honoree NOW, 1984. Mem. Am. Acctg. Assn. (acctg. behavior and orgns. sect.) (Midwest and regional coordinator 1985-86, working paper series coordinator 1984-85), Judgement and Decision Making Orgn. Avocation: dancing. Home: 1130 N Dearborn Apt 1811 Chicago IL 60610 Office: DePaul Univ Sch Accountancy 25 E Jackson Blvd Chicago IL 60604

NIVER, MILLARD BENJAMIN, mathematics educator; b. Bradford, Pa., Jan. 22, 1934; s. Millard Adam and Hester (Geer) N.; m. Margaret Thelma Hess, Aug. 13, 1955; children: Denise, Brett, Nanette. BS in Ed., Taylor U., 1960; MA, Purdue U., 1965; PhD, Kent State U., 1976. Math tchr. Warren (Pa.) Area Schs., 1960-67; math prof.p Malone Coll., Canton, Ohio, 1967—. Mem. Nat. Council Tchrs., Ohio Council Tchrs., Sigma Zeta (nat. recording treas. 1982—. Republican. Evangelist. Avocations: golf, bowling, woodworking, beekeeping. Home: 7940 Mose SW Navarre OH 44662 Office: Malone Coll Canton OH 44709

NIX, DENNIS WARREN, waste disposal service executive; b. St. Louis, Nov. 12, 1945; s. Frank Wilmore and Geneva Louise (Edwards) N.; m. Hee Yon (lee), Aug. 16, 1983 ; children: Shauna Lee, Robert Warren. Student, So. Ill. U., Edwardsville, 1978. Contractor various construction cos., Ill. and Mo., 1976-80; cons. toxic waste Kans. and Mo., 1980-83; founder, chmn., pres. AmerEco Environ. Services (formerly PCB Disposal Systems), Kingsville, Mo., 1983—. Inventor PCB Processing. Mem. Air Pollution Control Assn. Club: Optimist. Avocation: mil. miniatures. Office: AmerCo Environ Services Rt 1 Box 159 Kingsville MO 64061

NIX, HAROLD MANSON, accounting educator; b. Ft. Collins, Colo., June 18, 1931; s. Benjamin Manson and Eva Mae (Sampson) N.; m. Myrna Lee Miller, Dec. 15, 1969; children: Kristi Ann, John Benjamin. BA, Western State Coll., Gunnison, Colo., 1967, MA, 1969; PhD, Okla. State U., 1973. CPA, Colo., Alaska, Idaho; cert. mgmt. acct. Owner, operator Nix Lumber Co., Colorado Springs, Colo., 1949-65; assoc. prof., chmn. dept. acctg. Boise (Idaho) State U., 1973-78; prof., chmn. dept. acctg. U. Alaska, Anchorage, 1978-86; prof. acctg. Bradley U., Peoria, Ill., 1986—; cons., advisor, SBA, Anchorage, 1978-86. Contbr. articles to profl. jours. Mem. Anchorage Mcpl. Budget Adv. Commn., 1982-85. Mem. Am. Inst. CPA's, Nat. Assn. Accts., Fin. Execs. Inst. Home: Rt 1 Dunlap IL 61525 Office: Bradley U Dept Acctg Peoria IL 61625

NIX, ROBERT PATRICK, computer software analyst; b. Indpls., May 13, 1955; s. James Robert and Dorothy May (Stoner) N.; m. Susan Marie Kazmierzak, June 5, 1976; children: Christina, Eric. AAS, Purdue U., 1981. Programmer/analyst Marion Co. CDP, Indpls., 1975-77, Am. Electronics, Greenwood, Ind., 1977; software analyst Amax Data Systems, Indpls., 1977—. Roman Catholic. Lodge: KC. Avocations: fly fishing, fly tying. Home: 7728 Opelika Ct Indianapolis IN 46217 Office: Amax Data Systems 105 S Meridian St Indianapolis IN 46225

NIXON, DAVID ARTHUR, steel company product manager; b. Detroit, Feb. 21, 1942; s. Paul Edward and Irene Winifred (Welsh) N.; m. Sandra Lynn Viau, Feb. 4, 1961; children: Jeffrey, John, James. Grad. high sch., Livonia, Mich., 1960. Tool and die maker Chevrolet div. Gen Motors, Livonia, 1960-67; foreman methods engring. Gen. Electric Jet Engine Plant, Evendale, Ohio, 1967-69; process engr. Garrett Airesearch, Torrance, Calif., 1969-70; tech. service engr. LaSalle Steel Co., Hammond, Ind., 1970-80; product mgr. Quanex Corp. div. LaSalle Steel Co., Griffith, Ind., 1980—. Mem. Am. Soc. for Metals (entertainment chmn. 1978), Fluid Power Soc., Soc. Mfg. Engrs. (cert.). Methodist. Avocations: race engine building, woodworking, computers. Home: 9406 Hayes St Crown Point IN 46307 Office: Quanex-Bar Group LaSalle Steel 1045 Main St Griffith IN 46319

NIXON, JAMES FREDERICK, personnel director; b. St. Paul, Aug. 7, 1947; s. Frederick Charles and Marlys Dorothy (Coulter) N.; m. Mary Louise Sander, Nov. 25, 1972; children: JoAnna, Heather, Andrew. BA in Social Sci., St. Cloud (Minn.) State U., 1975, postgrad. in Psychology, Bus., 1975-81. Personnel dir. Benton County, Foley, Minn., 1975-79; asst. personnel dir. Anoka (Minn.) County, 1977-79; personnel dir. Gold N' Plump Poultry, St. Cloud, 1979-83; mgmt. cons. Personnel Mgmt., Mpls., 1983-84; human resource mgr. Dakotah, Inc., Webster, S.D., 1984—; Cons. St. John's U., St. Cloud, 1976-80. Mem. adv. bd. Gov.'s Crime Commn., St. Cloud, 1976-79; cons. Career Learning Ctr., Watertown, S.D., 1985—; bd. dirs. Girl Scouts Am., Huron, 1986—; bus. advisor S.D. Youth Bus. Acad. Augustana Coll., Sioux Falls, 1986. Served with USN, 1967-70, Vietnam. Mem. Am. Soc. Personnel Adminstrn., St. Cloud Area Personnel Adminstrn. Republican. Episcopalian. Home: 501 W 7th Ave Webster SD 57274 Office: Dakotah Inc N Park Ln Webster SD 57274

NIXON, RICHARD E., business executive; b. Kansas City, Mo., Sept. 5, 1939; s. Russell Erwin and Iva (Willcoxson) N.; m. Marilyn Hayde; children: Jeffrey, Douglas, Richard, John. Student, William Jewell Coll., 1959. Mgr. Liberty Loan Co., Kansas City, 1961-65; v.p. Qualified Investments Co., Kansas City, 1965-71; pres. Numart Co., Kansas City, 1971—; pres., owner Nick's R.R. Restaurant, Kansas City, Nick's Printing Co., Kansas City, Ren Fin. Services, Inc., Kansas City, Numart Garage, Independence, Mo., Country Dreams Antiques, Blue Springs, Mo. Author newsletter Flashes. Mem. Nat. Hist. Soc., Kansas City C. of C. Republican. Home: 1217 Fairway Circle Blue Springs MO 64015

NIXON, RICHARD ROY, radiologist; b. St. Louis, May 11, 1932; s. Roy Alonzo and Clara Emily (Neuman) N.; m. Inalee M. Nixon, Sept. 20, 1958 (div. Apr. 1982); m. Denise Desilit, Jan. 10, 1984; children: James, Thomas, Robert. BS, U. Notre Dame, 1953; MD, Loyola U., 1957. Intern Los Angeles County Gen. Hosp., 1957-58; resident Cook County Hosp., Chgo., 1960-63; radiologist Radiology Cons., Concordia, Kans., 1964-81, United Radiology Group, Salina, Kans., 1981—; pres. United Radiology Group, Salina, 1987—; bd. dirs. Cloud County Bank, Concordia. Served to capt. USAF, 1958-60. Mem. AMA, Am. Coll. Radiology, Radiol. Soc. N.Am., Kans. Radiol. Soc. (bd. dirs. 1987), Kans. Med. Soc. Republican. Roman Catholic. Home: 153 Channel Salina KS 67401 Office: United Radiology Group 116 S 7th St Apt A Salina KS 67401

NNAM, MICHAEL NKUZI, educator; b. Akpugo, Nigeria, Dec. 2, 1957; came to U.S., 1979; s. Nnamigwe and Adajie (Nwene) Nwonuma. BA, DePaul U., 1981, MA, 1982, PhD, 1985. Lectr. jurisprudence DePaul U., Chgo., 1985—. Author: (book) Anglo-American Jurisprudence, 1986. Mem. African Student Union (pres. 1985), Akupugo Student Union (pres. 1978), Alpha Lambda Delta. Avocations: swimming, reading. Home: 6832 N Lakewood Chicago IL 60626 Office: DePaul U 2323 N Seminary Chicago IL 60614

NOACK, LORI ANNE, accountant; b. Waterloo, Iowa, Aug. 30, 1959; d. Merlyn Edward and Emily LaVina (Lies) Hildebrand; m. Thomas Allen Noack, Aug. 1, 1981; 1 child, Bradley. BA, U. No. Iowa, 1981. CPA, Iowa, Nebr. Staff acct. Edward L. Babbitt, P.C., Omaha, 1981-84; sr. tax cons. Touche Ross & Co., Omaha, 1984-86; sr. acct. Baird, Kurtz & Dobson, Omaha, 1986—; bd. dirs. The Creche, Omaha. Mem. fund raising com. United Way of Midlands, Omaha, 1984; cons. Jr. Achievement, Omaha, 1984-85. Mem. Am. Inst. CPA's, Nebr. Soc. CPA's (mem. small bus. com. 1985). Republican. Roman Catholic. Home: 12956 Grand Ave Omaha NE 68164 Office: Baird Kurtz & Dobson 2120 S 72d St Suite 630 Omaha NE 68124

NOAH, BONNIE RUTH, day care center owner and operator; b. Licking, Mo., Aug. 16, 1931; s. Jess Clifford and Minnie Jane (Biram) Jeffries; m. Randol Harold McCuan, Feb. 14, 1954 (div. Dec. 1968); children: Richard Allen, Vance Lytton. Grad. high sch., Licking, Mo., 1950. Cert. Child Care Ctr. Dir., Mo. Owner, dir. Noah's Ark Day Care Ctrs., Fruitland, Jackson, Gordonville, Mo., 1977-86. Foster parent Cape Girardeau County Foster Parent Assn., 1980-86. Mem. Area Lic. Providers Assn. Avocations: camping, traveling.

NOBLE, DAVID JEFF, insurance holding company executive; b. Des Moines, Dec. 14, 1931; m. Barbara Lee Nelson, Feb. 28, 1954; children—Cynthia Lee, Jeff David, Jonine. Student, Drake U., 1950. Exec. v.p. Vulcan Life Ins. Co., Birmingham, Ala., 1974—; pres. Statesman Life Ins. Co., Des Moines, Iowa, 1976—; vis. adj. prof. U. Ala., Birmingham, 1980. Republican. Episcopalian. Clubs: Des Moines, Vestavia. Lodge: Zamora Shriners. Avocations: boating; fishing. Home: RR 1 PO Box 230 Cropwell AL 35054 Office: Statesman Group Inc Des Moines Bldg Des Moines IA 50309

NODDINGS, THOMAS CLAYTON, investment company executive; b. Perth Amboy, N.J., Dec. 30, 1933; s. William Clayton and Sarah Stevenson N.; B.S., Purdue U., 1955; M.B.A., Rutgers U., 1958; m. Edna Francene Christoph, Feb. 6, 1954; children—Douglas, Thomas, John. Product mgr. The Trane Co., LaCrosse, Wis., 1958-67; dir. engring. Crane Co., Chgo., 1967-71; stockbroker E. F. Hutton, Chgo., 1971-75; sr. v.p. Woolard & Co., Chgo., 1975-77; chmn., pres. Noddings & Assocs., Chgo., 1977—. Author: The Dow Jones-Irwin Guide to Convertible Securities, 1973; Listed Call Options, 1975; How the Experts Beat the Market, 1976; Advanced Investment Strategies, 1978; The Investor's Guide to Convertible Bonds, 1982; Low Risk Strategies for the High Performance Investor, 1985; SuperHedging, 1986. Office: 2001 Spring Rd Oak Brook IL 60521

NODINE, LARRY JAMES, market manager; b. Kansas City, Mo., May 26, 1955; s. Kenneth James and Kay (Lynch) N.; 1 child, Lucas. Student, Pittsburg (Kans.) State U., 1982, Tulsa U., 1984. Draftsman Peabody TecTank, Parsons, Kans., 1974-79; dir. reclamation Fuel Dynamics, Oswego, Kans., 1979-82; regional sales mgr. Peabody TecTank, Los Angeles, 1982-84; mkt. mgr. Peabody TecTank, Parsons, Kans., 1984—; advisor Internat. Cogeneration Soc., Washington, 1986—. Mem. Oswego Alumni Assn. (v.p. 1979, pres. 1980). Republican. Club: Oswego Shooting (bd. dirs. 1981). Avocations: rodeo, shooting, photography. Office: Peabody TecTank 2101 S 21st St Parsons KS 67357

NODOT, GUY ANDRÈ, architect; b. Loches, France, Nov. 6, 1945; came to U.S., 1971; s. Jean-Baptiste Roland and Madeleine Marie Louise (Schilte) N.; m. Mary Varick Seidman, Apr. 5, 1971 (div. Sept. 1977); 1 child, Jennifer Lynn; m. Jane Webb Sherman, Feb. 7, 1979; children: Syndey Webb, Erik Ashley. Diploma in architecture, Ecole Des Beaux Arts, Tours, France, 1964. Archtl. draftsman Boilles Frères, Tours, France, 1961-65, 67-69, Montenay, Tours, 1970-71; archtl. draftsman Herman Lackner & Assocs., Winnetka, Ill., 1971-79, project architect, 1979-83; ptnr. Lackner, Nodot & Assocs., Winnetka, 1983—. Served to 1st class Cypher Army, 1966-67, Nancy, France. Mem. AIA. Club: Chgo. Curling (Northbrook, Ill.). Avocations: philately, painting, skiing. Home: 926 Lee Rd Northbrook IL 60062 Office: Lackner Nodot & Assocs 778 Frontage Rd Suite 109 Northfield IL 60093

NOE, ELNORA (ELLIE), chemical company executive; b. Evansville, Ind., Aug. 23, 1928; d. Thomas Noe and Evelyn (West) Dieter; student Ind. U.-Purdue U., Indpls. Sec., Pitman Moore Co., Indpls., 1946; with Dow Chem. Co., Indpls., 1960—, public relations asst. then mgr. employee communications, 1970—, Dow Consumer Products Inc. Div., 1986—; mem. steering com. Learn About Bus. Recipient 2d place award as Businesswoman of Yr., Indpls. Bus. and Profl. Women's Assn., 1980, Indpls. Profl. Woman of Yr. award Zonta, Altrusa, Sorptomist & Pilot Service Clubs, 1985. Mem. Am. Bus. Women Assn. (Woman of Yr. award 1965; past pres.), Ind. Assn. Bus. Communicators (communicator of yr. 1977), Women in Communications (Louise Eleanor Kleinhenz award 1984), Nat. Fedn. Press Women, Women's Press Club Ind. (past v.p.). Lodge: Zonta (dist. public relations chmn. 1978-80, area dir. 1980-82, pres. Indpls. 1977-79). Office: PO Box 68511 Indianapolis IN 46268

NOE, FRANCES ELSIE (MRS. ROBERT DAVIES), physician; b. Beacon Falls, Conn., May 23, 1923; d. Alfred and Edith (Carlson) Noe; B.A., Middlebury Coll., 1944; M.N., Yale, 1947; M.D., U. Vt., 1954; m. Robert Davies, June 16, 1956; children—Kenneth Roger, Ralph Eric. Intern, Mary Hitchcock Meml. Hosp., Hanover, N.H., 1954-55; fellow cardiovascular research Mich. Heart Assn., 1955-56; resident pulmonary div. Henry Ford Hosp., Detroit, 1956-57; fellow cardiopulmonary research Wayne State U. Coll. Medicine, 1957-58, instr. anesthesia dept., 1958-61, asst. clin. prof. anesthesia dept., 1961-65, 76—; asso. staff, div. research Sinai Hosp. of Detroit, 1965-70, chief pulmonary physiology sect., div. research, 1970—. Mem. Am. Soc. Anesthesiologists, Sigma Xi. Contbr. articles in field to profl. jours. Home: 1601 Kirkway Bloomfield Hills MI 48013 Office: Sinai Hosp Detroit MI 48235

NOEL, JOHN E., accountant, real estate consultant; b. 1940. CPA, Ind. Pvt. practice acctg. Indpls., 1963—. Office: 4706 Washington Blvd Indianapolis IN 46205-1748

NOEL, ROGER ARTHUR, French language educator; b. Wanne, Belgium, Nov. 22, 1942; came to U.S., 1970; s. Adolphe and Lucie (Hemroulle) N.; m. Alice E. Gubner, Mar. 28, 1969; children: Anouk Aileen, Nadine Valerie. Li. Philosophie et Lettres, Liège, Belgium, 1965; MA in French Lit., U. Mo., 1966; PhD in French Lit., Washington U., St. Louis, 1984. Tchr. English SHAPE, Casteau, Belgium, 1967-68; lectr. English U. Liège, 1969-70; instr. French U. Mo., St. Louis, 1970-76, lectr. French, 1976-86, coordinaotr elem. courses, 1976-86; asst. prof. French Monmouth (Ill.) Coll., 1986—. Author: Joufroi de Poitiers: Traduction Critique, 1987. Served with Belgian Army, 1968-69. Mem. AAUP, Alliance Française, Fgn. Lang. Tchrs. Assn., Am. Assn. Tchrs. French, Internat. Arthurian Soc., Société Française de Saint Louis. Home: 710 E Archer Monmouth IL 61462 Office: Monmouth Coll 16 Wallace Hall Monmouth IL 61462

NOETH, CAROLYN FRANCES, speech-language pathologist; b. Cleve., July 21, 1924; d. Sam Falco and Barbara Serafina (Loparo) Armaro; A.B. magna cum laude (Univ. scholar), Western Res. U., 1963; M.Ed., U. Ill., 1972; postgrad. Nat. Coll. Edn., 1975—; m. Lawrence Andrew Noeth, June 29, 1946; children—Lawrence Andrew, Barbara Marie. Speech therapist Chgo. Public Schs., 1965; speech, lang. and hearing clinician J. Sterling Morton High Schs., Cicero-Berwyn, Ill., 1965-82, tchr. learning disabilities/behavior disorders, 1982, dist. ednl. diagnostician, 1982-84; Title I Project tchr., summers 1966-67, lang. disabilities cons., summers 1968-69, in-service tng. cons., summer 1970, dir. Title I Project, summers 1973-74, learning disabilities tchr. W. Campus of Morton, 1971-75, chmn. Educable-Mentally Handicapped-Opportunities Tchrs. Com., 1967-68, spl. edn. area and in-sch. tchrs. workshops, 1967—. Precinct elections judge, 1953-55; block capt. Mothers March of Dimes and Heart Fund, 1949-60; St. Agatha's rep. Nat. Catholic Women's League, 1952-53; collector for charities, 1967; mem. exec. bd. Morton Scholarship League, 1981-84, corr. sec., 1981-83; vol. Am. Cancer Soc., 1985—. First recipient Virda L. Stewart award for Speech, Western Res. U., 1963, recipient Outstanding Sr. award, 1963. Mem. Am. (certified), Ill. speech and hearing assns., Council Exceptional Children (div. for learning disabilities, chpt. spl. projects chmn., exec. bd. 1976-81, chpt. pres. 1979-80), Assn. Children with Learning Disabilities, Council for Learning Disabilities, Profls. in Learning Disabilities, Internat. Platform Assn., Kappa Delta Pi, Delta Kappa Gamma (chmn., co-chmn. chpt. music com. 1979—, mem. state program com. 1981-83, chpt. music rep. to state 1982—). Roman Catholic. Clubs: St. Norbert's Women's (Northbrook, Ill.), Case-Western Res. U., U. Ill. Alumni Assns., Lions (vol. Northbrook, 1966—). Chmn. in compiling and publishing Student Handbook, Cleve. Coll., 1962; contbr. lyric parodies and musical programs J. Sterling Morton High Sch. West Retirement Teas, 1972-83. Home and Office: 1849 Walnut Circle Northbrook IL 60062

NOFSINGER, WILLIAM MORRIS, engineering executive; b. Orange, N.J., Sept. 11, 1932; s. Charles William and Grace Elizabeth (Morris) N.; m. Bonnie Jean Haisler, Nov. 6, 1965; children: Barry Jean, Betsy Jayne. BS in Chem. Engring., U. Kans., 1955. Registered profl. engr. With The C.W. Nofsinger Co., Kansas City, Mo., various positions to v.p., 1959-78; pres. The C.W. Nofsinger Co., Overland Park, Kans., 1978—. Served to 1st. lt. USAFR. Fellow Am. Inst. Chem. Engrs.; mem. NSPE, Am. Chem. Soc., Mo. Soc. Profl. Engrs. Republican. Lodge: Rotary (v.p. 1983-84, pres. elect 1984-85, pres. 1985-86). Home: 6645 Brookside Rd Kansas City MO 64113

Office: The CW Nofsinger Co 4600 E 63d St Box 419173 Kansas City MO 64141-0173

NOGGLE, DENNIS ALLEN, consumer products company executive; b. Toledo, Oct. 5, 1936; s. Glenn Leslie and Lillian Mary (Buffington) N.; m. Rhea Rose Homier, July 7, 1962; children: Mara Denise, Bart Allen. Student, San Jose State U., 1956-57, U. Toledo, 1966-67. Cert. protection profl. Patrolman, instr. Ohio State Patrol, Columbus, 1959-65; supt. security Kaiser Jeep Corp., Toledo, 1965-69; dir. corp. security Sheller-Globe Corp., Toledo, 1969-76, Kimberly-Clark Corp., Neenah, Wis., 1976—; bd. dirs. Classic Paints, Inc., Dayton, Ohio. Chmn. Gov.'s Bus. Ind. Crime Prevention, Madison, Wis., 1983-84, Fox Valley Tech. Inst. Curriculum, Appleton, 1986; mem. rev. bd. Menasha (Wis.) Police Dept., 1979—. Mem. Am. Soc. Ind. Security (bd. dirs. 1979-86, v.p. internat. 1985, regional v.p. of Yr. 1978, Enrollment chmn. of yr. 1975, I.B. Hale Chpt. award 1976), Am. Soc. Ind. Security Found. (bd. dirs. 1986—), Toledo C. of C. (chmn. crime prevention 1967). Republican. Roman Catholic. Lodges: KC. Avocations: boating, water skiing, photography. Office: Kimberly-Clark Corp 401 N Lake St Neenah WI 54956

NOHA, EDWARD J., insurance company executive; b. 1926; married. BBA, Pace Coll. With Dept. Justice, 1944-52, Met. Life Ins. Co., 1952-55; exec. v.p. Allstate Ins. Co., 1955-74; chmn. bd., pres., chief exec. officer Continental Casualty Co.; chmn. bd., pres., chief exec. officer Continental Assurance Co., Chgo.; chmn. bd. Nat. Fire Ins. Co. of Hartford, Inc., Transcontinental Ins. Co. Office: Continental Casualty Co CNA Plaza Chicago IL 60685 *

NOHELTY, LORILEI MARIE, accountant; b. Marshfield, Wis., Apr. 22, 1959; d. Merlin Karl and Florence Louise (Miller) Schuette; m. Thomas Michael Nohelty, June 1, 1985; 1 child, Matthew Thomas. BBA, U. Wis., Eau Claire, 1981. CPA, Wis. Staff acct. Wipfli, Ullrich & Co., Wausau, Wis., 1981-84; sr. acct. Wipfli, Ullrich & Co., Wausau, 1984-86; acct. Cen. Wis. Bankshares, Inc., Wausau, 1986—. Mem. Am. Inst. CPA's, Wis. Inst. CPA's. Home: 8602 Callon Ave Schofield WI 54476

NOLAN, DAVID L., accountant; b. Bedford, Ind., Dec. 16, 1956; s. Donald E. and Hilda J. (Tyree) N. BS, Ind. U., New Albany, 1979. CPA, Ind. Staff acct. Welenken-Himmelfarb, Louisville, 1979-80; mgr. Deaton & Co. CPA's, Jasper, Ind., 1981-82; pvt. practice acctg. Mitchell, Ind., 1983—; tchr. Oakland City Coll., Bedford, Ind., 1984—. Author (newspaper column) Capital Ideas, 1984-85. Chmn. Mitchell Persimmon Festival, 1984; bd. dirs. Dunn Meml. Hosp. Found., Bedford, 1985-87, Lawrence County United Way, Bedford, 1987. Mem. Am. Inst. CPA's, Ind. CPA Soc., Nat. Assn. Accts., Mitchell C. of C. (pres. 1985-86). Lodge: Rotary (pres. Mitchell 1985-86). Avocations: softball, golf. Office: 112 N 7th St Mitchell IN 47446

NOLAN, HARRY JAMES, fire fighter; b. Chgo., Feb. 8, 1945; s. Victor George and Norma (Gustafson) N.; m. Margaret Mary Griffith, July 23, 1966; children: Eric James, Kimberly Anne. AS in Fine Sci., Thornton Community Coll., 1975; BA in Pub. Adminstrn., Govs. State U., 1980. Firefighter Harvey (Ill.) Fire Dept., 1967-70, lt., 1970—, dir. fire prevention, 1978—, co. officer, 1987—; life safety instr. Inspection Cert. Program, 1980-83; chmn. State Fire Marshals Inspector's Com., 1979-85. Mem. Ill. Fire Inspectors Assn. (bd. dirs. 1980-83), Ill. Firemen's Assn., Internat. Assn. Fire Fighters. Club: Lansing Country. Avocations: golf, fishing, canoeing.

NOLAN, KENNETH JOHN, insurance executive, city official; b. Chgo., Jan. 23, 1944; s. John Hubert and Catherine Marie (Witt) N.; m. Jane Ann Bauer, Feb. 13, 1971; children: Andrew Kenneth. BA, Marquette U., 1966. Claim specialist State Farm Ins. Co., Bloomington, Ill., 1967—. Treas. City of Palos Hills, Ill., 1977—. Served to staff sgt. Ill. ANG, 1967-73. Mem. Ill. Municipal League, Govt. Finance Officers Assn., Ill. Govt. Officers Assn., Chgo. Met. Finance Officers Assn., Downstate Ill. Govt. Fin. Officers Assn., Northeastern Ill. Adjusters Assn. Roman Catholic. Lodge: Elks. Avocations: golf, politics. Home: 15 Cour Montreal Palos Hills IL 60465 Office: State Farm Ins Cos 5680 S Archer Ave Chicago IL 60638

NOLAN, MICHAEL SEAN, university professor; b. Urbana, Ill., Aug. 3, 1956; s. James William and Rosemary M. (Devine) N.; m. Barbara Emma Benn, May 30, 1980. BS, Ill. State U., 1978; MS, Purdue U., 1985. Instr. Purdue U., West Lafayette, Ind., 1978-79, instr. aviation tech., 1981-85, asst. prof. aviation tech., 1985—; air traffic controller FAA, Lansing, Mich., 1979-81. Mem. Aviation Technician Educators Council (co-chmn. edn. resources com. 1985), Aviation Safety Inst., Ind. Aviation Technicians Assn. Democrat. Roman Catholic. Avocations: computers, flying, camping. Home: 924 King St Lafayette IN 47905 Office: Purdue U Aviation Technology West Lafayette IN 47906

NOLAN, RHONDA BROWN, reporter; b. Pontiac, Mich., Mar. 26, 1954; d. John Murray and Florence (Giovannitti) Brown; m. John Joseph Nolan Jr., Oct. 12, 1985. BA in Speech Communications, Teatre, French, Albion (Mich.) Coll., 1975. Cert. secondary tchr., Mich. Model, actress Detroit, 1976-78; substitute tchr. Royal Oak & Berkley, Mich., 1976-78; coach drama and activities Huntington Woods (Mich.) Sch., 1976-78; reporter, anchor, weathercaster Sta. WKZO-TV, Kalamazoo, 1978-82; reporter, weathercaster Sta. WSBT-TV, South Bend, Ind., 1983—. Active Big Bros./Big Sisters, Kalamazoo, 1982. Mem. Women in Communications, Inc. (pres. 1982, founder scholarship 1982). Avocations: sewing, cooking. Home: 3506 Hanover Ct South Bend IN 46614 Office: Sta WSBT-TV 300 W Jefferson South Bend IN 46601

NOLAND, JAMES ELLSWORTH, U.S. judge; b. LaGrange, Mo., Apr. 22, 1920; s. Otto Arthur and Elzena (Ellsworth) N.; m. Helen Warvel, Feb. 4, 1948; children: Kathleen Kimberly, James Ellsworth, Christopher Warvel. A.B., Ind. U., 1942, LL.B., 1948; M.B.A., Harvard U., 1943. Bar: Ind. 1948. Since practiced in Bloomington; partner law firm of Hickam & Noland, Indpls., 1955-66, 1st asst. city atty., 1956-57; dep. atty. gen. Ind., 1952; spl. asst. U.S. atty. gen. 1953; appointed Ind. State Election Commr., 1954; U.S. judge So. Dist. Ind., 1966—, chief judge, 1984—; Mem. com. on magistrates system Jud. Conf. U.S., 1973-81; mem. 81st (1949-51) Congress, 7th Ind., Dist.; sec. Ind. Democratic Com., 1960-66; chmn. bd. visitors Ind. Law Sch., Indpls., 1974-76. Served as capt., Transp. Corps. AUS, 1943-46. Mem. ABA (chmn. jud. adminstrn. div. 1984-85), Ind. Bar Assn., Ind. Assn. Trial Lawyers (pres. 1956), Nat. Conf. Fed. Trial Judges (chmn. 1981-82), Phi Delta Phi, Phi Kappa Psi. Mem. Moravian Ch. Office: Federal Ct Bldg Indianapolis IN 46204

NOLEN, BARBARA JEAN, social worker; b. Chgo., Jan. 8, 1955; d. Willie and Maudine (Cochran) N. BA, DePaul U., 1979, MA, 1981. Supr. Oak Community Ctr., Oak Park, Ill., 1979-80; social worker Dept. Mental Health, Chgo., 1980—, Ill. Dept. Children and Family Services, Chgo., 1980—. Avocations: racquetball, sewing, dressmaking, volleyball, jogging. Home: 1919 S 3d Ave Maywood IL 60153

NOLL, CHARLES GORDON, physicist; b. Sunbury, Pa., Dec. 2, 1948; s. J. Herman and Helen Elisabeth (Gelnett) N.; B.A., Bloomsburg (Pa.) State Coll., 1970; M.S., Ohio State U., Columbus, 1974, Ph.D., 1975; m. Alice Marie Walters, Dec. 20, 1971; children—Carlton Leigh, Benjamin Douglass, Jennifer Nicole. Lectr. physics Ohio State U., 1975-76; researcher research and devel. United McGill Corp., Columbus, 1976-78, corp. physicist, Groveport, Ohio, 1978-83, mgr. corp. research and devel., 1983—; cons. environ. problems. Mem. Am. Phys. Soc., IEEE, Electrostatics Soc. Am., Sigma Xi, Sigma Pi Sigma. Author: Ensemble Theory for Electrostatic Precipitation, 1980; Computer Aided Research Tools for Pilot Testing of Pollution Control Equipment, 1981. Home: 121 Academy Ct Gahanna OH 43230 Office: One Mission Park Groveport OH 43125

NOLL, ROBERT BLUM, psychologist, educator; b. Cleve., Dec. 13, 1947; s. Alfred Erwin and Jeanne Annette (Blum) N.; m. Hope Pierson, July 21, 1982; children: Debbie Lynn, David Glen. Lic. clin. psychologist. Assoc. prof. Mich. State U., East Lansing, 1983—. Contbr. articles to profl. jour. Served to lt. USN, 1969-74. Decorated 2 Disting. Flying Cross. Mem. Am. Psychol. Assn., Soc. Research Child Devel., Am. Orthopsychiat. Soc., Internat. Neuropsychology Assn., Soc. Behavioral Pediatrics. Avocations: bicycling, handball. Home: 306 Orchard St East Lansing MI 48823 Office: Dept Pediatrics and Human Devel B 240 Life Scis Bldg East Lansing MI 48824

NOLLAN, RICHARD CHARLES, religious printing and pub. co. exec.; b. Neenah, Wis., Oct. 29, 1935; s. Walter Theodore and Emily Anne (Vondrachek) N.; student Northwestern U., eves. 1958-62. Mgr. data processing Wine & Spirits Liquor Co., Chgo., 1957-67, Gold Seal Liquors Co., Chgo., 1967-72; dir. mgmt. info. services J.S. Paluch Co., Schiller Park, 1972-84, v.p. 1984—. Served with USMC, 1953-57; Korea. Mem. Data Processing Mgmt. Assn., Office: 3825 N Willow Rd Schiller Park IL 60176 Office: 3825 N Willow Rd Schiller Park IL 60176

NOLPH, GEORGIA BOWER, physician; b. Appleton, Minn., Jan. 26, 1938; d. Clarence Walter and Gladys Mae (Hanson) Bower; m. Karl David Nolph, July 26, 1961; children: Erika Lynn, Kristoper Karl. BA, St. Olaf Coll., 1960; MD, Woman's Med. Coll. Pa., 1964. Pvt. practice with G.H. Ferguson MD, Bala-Cynwyd, Pa., 1965-67; civil service Walter Reed Army Med. Ctr., Washington, 1967-69; instr. Community Health and Med. Practice, Columbia, 1969-70; asst. prof. U. Mo. Med. Sch., Columbia, 1970-77; assoc. prof. Family and Community Medicine, Columbia, 1977—; acting med. dir. Family Med. Care Ctr., U. Mo. Hosp. and Clinics, Columbia, 1980-87. assoc. editor. (profl. jour.) Continuing Education for the Family Physician, 1972-73. V.p. Parents for Drug Free Youth, Columbia, Mo., 1985-86, 86-87. Mem. Am. Med. Women's Assn. State Dir. 1975—, Boone County Med. Soc., Mo. State Med. Assn., Am. Bus. Women's Assn., Am. Legion. Republican. Methodist. Avocations: music, reading, travel, needlework. Home: 908 Hickory Hill Dr Columbia MO 65203 Office: U Mo Med Sch Family and Community Medicine 1 Hosp Dr Columbia MO 65212

NOLT, DOUGLAS EUGENE, campus pastor; b. Lancaster, Pa., Mar. 19, 1957; s. Donald Eugene and Lois Winona (Davis) N.; m. Judith Irene Adams, June 27, 1981; 1 child, Daniel Eugene. BA in Religion, Findlay (Ohio) Coll., 1979; M of Div., Winebrenner Theol. Sem., 1983. Ordained to ministry Ch. of God, 1983. Assoc. in ministry, campus pastor Ch. of God Gen. Conf. Findlay Coll., 1983—; pastor E. Pa. Conf. Chs. of God Gen. Conf. Mem. Nat. Assn. Coll. and Univ. Chaplains, Hancock County Ministerial Assn., Winebrenner Sem. Alumni Assn. (sec. 1984-85). Republican. Avocations: electronics, researching religious cults. Office: Findlay Coll 1000 N Main St Findlay OH 45840-3695

NOLTING, FREDERICK WILLIAM, dentist; b. Mpls., Aug. 15, 1950; s. Robert William and Lorraine Marie (Ritten) N.; m. Norma Jean Anderson, Nov. 10, 1973; children: Erick William, Andrew Frederick. BS, U. Minn., 1972, DDS, 1974, MS, 1977. Asst. prof. Sch. Dentistry U. Louisville, 1976-78; gen. practice dentistry Byron, Minn., 1978—. Contbr. articles to profl. jour. Council mem. Christ Luth. Ch., 1980—, fin. dir. 1983-86, v.p. 1985-86, pres. 1986—, Community Edn. Adv. Bd., 1981-82; mem. U.S. Taekwondo Union, U.S. Olympic Com., 1986—. Mem. ADA, Minn. Dental Assn., Zumbro Valley Dental Soc. (sec. 1982-85), Acad. Gen. Dentistry, Am. Assn. Physicists in Medicine, Upper Midwest Alpha Computer Consortium (pres. 1986—), Nat. Rifle Assn. Clubs: byron sportsman and conservation. Office: 17 Frontage Rd Byron MN 55920

NOLTING, HENRY FREDERICK, JR., management consultant, engineer; b. Indpls., Aug. 15, 1916; s. Henry F. Sr. and Selma A. (Kixmiller) N.; m. Dorothy H. Wilson, Nov. 26, 1937; children: Henry F. III, James A., Margaret L. BS in ChemE, Purdue U., 1938, MS in ChemE, 1939. Mgr. internat. lube ops. Amoco Internat., London, 1963-66; ops. mgr. Amoco Oil Corp., Chgo., 1966-69; maintenance mgr. Amoco Oil Corp., Whiting, Ind., 1969-77; pres. Nolting Assocs., Inc., Carmel, Ind., 1977—. Fellow Am. Inst. Chem. Engring. (chmn. Chgo. sect. 1956, bd. dirs. 1958-60, chmn. program com. 1956-58, pub. com. 1958-60), Alton (Ill.) Jr. C. of C. (bd. dirs. 1944-46, Man of Yr. 1945). Republican. Methodist. Home: 221 Greyhound Pass Carmel IN 46032

NONOS, MIKE GEORGE, industrial engineer; b. Gary, Ind., June 21, 1962; s. George Michael and Lorraine (Sitaras) N. BS in Indsl. Engring., Purdue U., 1984; postgrad., Ind. U., Gary. Indsl. engr. Inland Steel Co., East Chicago, Ind., 1984-85, Johnson & Johnson Co., Lemont, Ill., 1985—. Republican. Greek Orthodox. Avocations: softball, basketball, running. Office: Johnson & Johnson Products Inc I-55 & Joliet Rd Lemont IL 60439

NOON, THOMAS ROBERT, financial services company executive; b. New Lexington, Ohio, Sept. 13, 1949; s. William D. and Pauline (Stickdorn) N.; m. Jolene Kay Wymore, Jan. 18, 1970 (div. July 1978); children: Kristi Anne, Kimberly Kay; m. Kathy Josephine Youngblut, Jan. 20, 1979; children: Joshua Thomas, Matthew James. BS, Iowa State U., 1971. CPA, Iowa. Mgr. Coopers & Lybrand, Des Moines, 1971-78; v.p. fin. Ardan, Inc., Des Moines, 1978-84; chief operating officer Overland Sheepskin Co., Fairfield, Iowa, 1984; v.p. fin. Oster Communications, Inc., Cedar Falls, Iowa, 1984-87; pres. Chief Fin. Officer Services, Inc., Des Moines, 1987—; mem. adv. council Oster Communications, Inc., Cedar Falls, 1987—. Chmn. fin., mem. bldg. project com. Trinity Wesleyan Ch., Cedar Falls, 1986; zone leader, lay minster First Federated Ch., Des Moines, 1983-84. Mem. Am. Inst. CPA's, Iowa Soc. CPA's. Avocations: church, reading, sports, financial principles, teaching. Home: 2628 W 3d Cedar Falls IA 50613 Office: Chief Fin Officer Services Inc 4401 Westown Pkwy West Des Moines IA 50265

NOONAN, JAMES EDWARD, chemical executive; b. Kansas City, Mo., May 30, 1924; s. Thomas J. and Katherine Regina (Hogan) N.; m. Margaret C. Basgall, July 3, 1926; children: Margaret, Katherine, Anne, Michael, Daniel, Martin. BS in Chemistry, Rockhurst Coll., 1947; MS in Chemistry, U. Kansas, 1948. Chemist Warner-Jenkinson Co., St. Louis, 1948-58, tech. dir., 1958-65, v.p. ops., 1965-81, pres., 1981—. Mem. Inst. Food Tech., Am. Chem. Soc., Cert. Color Mfrs. Assn., (pres. bd. 1972—), Flavor and Extract Mfrs. Assn. (mem. bd. govs. 1980—). Roman Catholic. Club: Mo. Athletic (St. Louis). Avocations: scuba diving, sailing. Home: 19 Princeton Ave Saint Louis MO 63130 Office: Warner Jenkinson Co Color & Flavor Div 29 Lynnbrook Rd Saint Louis MO 63131

NOONAN, MICHAEL JOHN, accountant; b. Aurora, Ill., Sept. 5, 1947; s. Arthur Francis Noonan and Catherine (Petit) Artlip; m. Christine Dee Agnew, Jan. 24, 1973; children: Andrew Michael, Sarah Christine. BS cum laude, No. Ill. U., 1974. CPA, Ill. Mem. audit staff McGladrey, Hendrickson & Pullen, Joliet, Ill., 1074-76, tax specialist, 1976-78, tax mgr., 1978-83, tax ptnr., 1983—. Bd. dirs. Estate Planning Council Greater Joliet, 1981-82. Served as sgt. USAF, 1967-71. Mem. Ill. CPA Soc. (pres. Fox Valley chpt. 1982-83), Am. Inst. CPA's, Beta Alpha Psi. Republican. Roman Catholic. Club: Exchange (pres. 1984-85, treas. 1982-84). Home: 500 S Midland Ave Joliet IL 60436 Office: McGladrey Hendrickson & Pullem 54 N Ottawa St Joliet IL 60431

NOONAN, ROBERTA LEE, college adminstrator; child care center owner; b. Pitts., May 1, 1933; d. Harry Sidney and Nellie Catherine (Johnston) Lamneck; m. Joseph George Noonan, Oct. 23, 1955; children—James, Kathleen, Michael, Patricia, Mary, Nora, Joe. B.A., St. Xavier U., 1970, M.A., 1973; Ed.D., Nova U., 1980. Asst. buyer Boggs & Buhl, Pitts., 1949-50; pub. relations Bell Telephone, Pitts., 1951-53; service rep. pub. relations Delta Airlines, Chgo., 1953-56; columnist South Town Economist, Chgo., 1959-61; owner, dir. Bobbie Noonan's Child Care, Worth, Ill., 1964-73; child care coordinator Moraine Valley Community Coll., Palos Hills, Ill., 1973—; cons. Riley pre-sch. project, East Chicago, Ind., 1973-74, Parent-Tchr. Groups and Industry, Ill., 1983—; workshop leader pub. and pvt. pre-schs. and day care ctrs., Ill., 1980—. Author: Bold Beginning, 1973; Finger Plays for Little Folks, 1984. Mem. Pre-Sch. Owners Assn., South Suburban Assn. for Edn. Young Children (bd. dirs., sec. 1984-85), Am. Bus. Women's Assn. Republican. Roman Catholic. Avocations: nutrition counseling; music; reading; swimming. Home: 8717 W Lincoln Hwy Frankfort IL 60423-9339 Office: Moraine Valley Community Coll 10900 S 88th Ave Palos Hills IL 60465

NOONAN, SHEILA AGNES, advertising executive; b. St. Louis, Nov. 27, 1955; d. Thomas Ignatius and Jane Elizabeth (Duddy) N. Student, Webster U., 1974-76; BS in Journalism, U. Kans., 1979. Media planner D'Arcy, McManus & Masius, St. Louis, 1979-81, Fletcher, Mayo & Assocs., St. Joseph, Mo., 1981-82; project assoc. Advanswers Media and Programming, St. Louis, 1982-83; media planner Monsanto Corp., St. Louis, 1983-84; media dir. Adamson Advt., St. Louis, 1984—; lectr. Lindenwood Coll., St. Charles, Mo., 1980-83. Vol. Cardinal Glennon Children's Hosp., St. Louis, 1983—. Mem. St. Louis Bus. and Profl. Advt. Assn. Roman Catholic. Avocations: music, fitness walking, cooking, golfing, reading. Office: Adamson Advt Inc 222 S Central Ave Saint Louis MO 63105

NOONEY, GREGORY JOSEPH, retired real estate executive; b. St. Louis, Aug. 12, 1903; m. Anna M. Frein, June 24, 1930; children—Gregory J., Ann Marie, John J. B.C.S., St. Louis U., 1926. Pub. acct. Touche, Niven & Co., St. Louis, 1924-28; asst. sec.-treas. Stix, Baer & Fuller, St. Louis, 1928-33, treas., dir., 1949-50; sec.-treas., dir. Ky. Hotel Co., Louisville, 1928-33; sec.-treas., dir. Lesser Goldman Co., St. Louis, 1933-45; founder G.J. Nooney & Co., St. Louis County, Mo. and East St. Louis, Ill., 1945, chmn. bd., 1969-83, chmn. emeritus, 1983—. Former dir. Boatmen's Nat. Bank, Fed. Compress & Warehouse Co., Memphis, others. Mem. City Plan Commn. St. Louis, 1933-47, chmn., 1938-39; former mem. Mo. Mental Health Commn., St. Louis County Police Bd. Clubs: Old Warson Country (pres. 1960), Mo. Athletic (life; pres. 1948), St. Louis (pres. 1965-66); Ekwanok Country (Manchester, Vt.); Everglades (Palm Beach, Fla.); Ocean (Ocean Ridge, Fla.). Home: 900 S Hanley Rd Saint Louis MO 63105

NOPPER, RALPH JACOB, civil engr.; b. Toledo, July 5, 1916; s. Charles Joseph and Martha Elizabeth (Rippel) N.; B.Engring., U. Toledo, 1939; m. Roberta R. Newcomb, July 31, 1943; children—Linda E. (Mrs. Kenneth J. Keiser). Structural engr. A. Bentley & Sons Co., Toledo, 1937-38; constrn. engr. E.B. Badger & Sons Co., Boston, 1938-39; engr., H.C. Baker Co., Toledo, 1939-40; chief maintenance engr. Libbey-Owens-Ford Co., Toledo, 1940-81; self-employed as cons. engr., Toledo, 1940—. Registered profl. engr., Ohio. Fellow ASCE (pres. Toledo sect. 1954); mem. NSPE (life), Ohio Soc. Profl. Engrs., Toledo socs. profl. engrs (pres. 1953), Toledo Tech. Council (pres. 1952-53). Home: 3710 Harley Rd Toledo OH 43613

NORD, DOUGLAS CHARLES, political science educator, researcher, foreign affairs consultant; b. Pasadena, Calif., Aug. 17, 1952; s. Charles Seward and Kathleen Mariane (Reid) N. A.B. summa cum laude, U. Redlands, 1974; M.A. in Polit. Sci., Duke U., 1976, Ph.D., 1979. Asst. dir. Can. Studies Program, Duke U., Durham, N.C., 1976-77, lectr. polit. sci. dept., 1978-79; guest scholar Brookings Instn., Washington, 1977-78; asst. prof. polit. sci. U. Minn.-Duluth, 1979-85, assoc. prof., 1985—, dir. Internat. Studies Program. Bd. adv. Head of Lakes UN Assn.; mem. Minn. Fgn. Policy Assn. Recipient U. Minn.-Duluth Outstanding Faculty award, 1982, Internat. Faculty Devel. award, 1981. Mem. Am. Polit. Sci. Assn., Can. Polit. Sci. Assn., Internat. Studies Assn., Am. Assn. Can. Studies, Midwest Can. Studies Assn. (pres.). Contbr. writings to profl. publs.

NORDBERG, JOHN ALBERT, federal judge; b. Evanston, Ill., June 18, 1926; s. Carl Albert and Judith Ranghild (Carlson) N.; m. Jane Spaulding, June 18, 1947; children: Carol, Mary, Janet, John. B.A., Carleton Coll., 1947; J.D., U. Mich., 1950. Bar: Ill. 1950, U.S. Dist. Ct. (no. dist.) Ill. 1957, U.S. Ct. Appeals (7th cir.) 1961. Assoc. Pope & Ballard, Chgo., 1950-57; ptnr. Pope, Ballard, Shepard & Fowle, Chgo., 1957-76; judge Cir. Ct. of Cook County, Ill., 1976-82, U.S. Dist. Ct. (no. dist.) Ill., Chgo., 1983—. Editor-in-chief, bd. editors Chgo. Bar Record, 1966-74. Magistrate of Cir. Ct. and justice of peace Ill., 1957-65. Served with USN, 1944-46; PTO. Mem. ABA, Chgo. Bar Assn., Ill. State Bar Assn. (assembly rep. 1971-76), Am. Judicature Soc., Law Club Chgo., Legal Club Chgo., Order of Coif. Clubs: Union League, University (Chgo.). Office: US Dist Ct 219 S Dearborn St Chicago IL 60604 *

NORDBERG, MARY LOUISE, computer company executive; b. Mpls., Sept. 21, 1945; d. Robert Lewis Frederick Jr. and Virginia Mary (Lindberg) Hinkle; m. Steven Carl Nordberg, June 14, 1968. BA in Math., U. Minn., 1967. Programmer Control Data Corp, N.J., 1967-73; mktg. cons. Control Data Corp, Bloomington, Minn., 1973-80, dir. research & devel., 1980-83, dir. mktg., 1983-85; dir. applications ETA Systems, St. Paul, 1986—. Avocations: gardening, needlework, piano, running. Office: ETA Systems 1450 Energy Pk Dr Saint Paul MN 55108

NORDELL, MARGARET CLAIRE, gynecologist; b. Drayton, N.D., Dec. 7, 1943; s. Raymond R. and Elva M. (Young) Halcrow; m. Alan L. Nordell, June 4, 1966; 1 child, Peter. MS in Edn., Moorhead State U., 1972; BA, U. N.D., 1965, BS, MS, 1980, MD, 1982. Resident U. N.D., Loyola U. Med. Ctr., Chgo.; jr. high sch. tchr. Duluth, Minn., 1966-68; high sch. tchr. West Fargo, N.D., 1968-77, Fargo, N.D., 1972-76; obstetrician, gynecologist Valley Med. Assn., Grand Forks, N.D., 1986—. Soroptimist fellow, 1972. Republican. Episcopalian. Lodge: Eastern Star. Avocations: reading, jogging. Home: 3332 Cherry Lynn Dr Grand Forks ND 50201

NORDICK, PAMELA LYNN, sales professional; b. Gary, Ind., Aug. 29, 1957; d. William Andrew and Loretta Jane (Leath) Bartley; m. Gerard Henry Nordick, Mar. 29, 1980. Grad. high sch., Columbia Heights. Minn., 1975. Credit mgr. Pella Windows, Mpls., 1979-80; accounts payable mgr. Anchor Paper, St. Paul, 1980-82; cost acct. Heritage Communications, St. Paul, 1982-83, sales mgr., 1983-87, dir. sales and mktg., 1987—. Assoc. mem. Smithsonian Inst. Mem. Minn. Resort Assn., Minn. Restaurant Assn., Minn. Hotel Assn., Minn. Motel Assn., Minn. Assn. Campgrounds, Bloomington (Minn.) C. of C. (transp. com.). Lutheran. Avocations: theater, music, piano. Home: 4036 Hayes St NE Columbia Heights MN 55421 Office: Heritage Communications 550 Vandalia St Saint Paul MN 55114

NORDLING, BERNARD ERICK, lawyer; b. Nekoma, Kans., June 14, 1921; A.B., McPherson Coll., 1947; student George Washington U., 1941-43; LL.B., J.D., Kans. U., 1949; m. Barbara Ann Burkholder, Mar. 26, 1949. Clerical employee FBI, 1941-44; admitted to Kans. bar, 1949, U.S. Dist. Ct. Kans. 1949, U.S. Ct. Appeals (10th cir.) 1970; practiced in Hugoton, Kans., 1949—; mem. firms Kramer & Nordling, 1950-65, Kramer, Nordling, Nordling & Tate, 1966—; city atty., Hugoton, 1951-87; county atty. Stevens County (Kans.), 1957-63. exec. sec. S.W. Kans. Royalty Owners Assn., 1968—; Kans. mem. legal com. Interstate Oil Compact Commn., 1969—, mem. supply tech. adv. com. Nat. Gas Survey, FPC, 1975-77; mem. Kans. Energy Adv. Council, 1975-78, exec. com., 1976-78. Editor U. Kans. Law Rev. of Kans. Bar Jour., 1949. Mem. Hugoton Sch. Bds., 1954-68, pres. grade sch. bd., 1961-66; pres. Stevens County Library Bd., 1957-63. Trustee McPherson Coll., 1971-81, mem. exec. com., 1975-81; bd. govs. Kans. U. Law Soc., 1984—. Served with AUS, 1944-46. Mem. ABA, Kans. Bar Assn., SW Kans. Bar Assn., Am. Judicature Soc., City Attys. Assn. of Kans. (exec. com. 1975-83, pres. 1982-83), Nat. Honor Soc., Nat. Assn. Royalty Owners (bd. govs. 1980—), Order of Coif, Phi Alpha Delta. Home: 218 N Jackson St Hugoton KS 67951 Office: 209 E 6th St Hugoton KS 67951

NORDLOH, DAVID JOSEPH, English language educator; b. Cin., May 3, 1942; s. Joseph Westerman and Josephine (Fusz) N.; m. Barbara Jane Beddow, June 29, 1968; children: Geoffrey David, Jennifer Ellen. AB in English, Coll. of Holy Cross, 1964; PhD in English, Ind. U., 1969. Asst. prof. English Ind. U., Bloomington, 1969-75, assoc. prof. English, 1975-81, prof. English, 1981—; vis. assoc. prof. U. Va., Charlottesville, 1978; dir. Am. Studies Program, Ind. U., 1987—. Editor: A Selected Edition of W.D. Howells, 1974—, Twayne's United States Author's Series, 1978—; co-editor: American Literary Scholarship, 1986—; mem. editorial bd. Walter Scott Edition, 1984—, American Literary Realism 1870-1910, 1986—; contbr. to books. Pres. Bloomington Symphony Orch., 1986—. Fulbright scholar, 1982-83. Mem. Modern Lang. Assn. (chmn. div. methods of lit. research 1987), Soc. for Textual Scholarship (adv. bd. 1980—). Home: 3123 Diana Ct Bloomington IN 47401 Office: Ind U Dept English Bloomington IN 47405

NORDLUND, DONALD ELMER, business executive; b. Stromsburg, Nebr., Mar. 1, 1922; s. E.C. and Edith O. (Peterson) N.; m. Mary Jane Houston, June 5, 1948; children: Donald Craig, William Chalmers, Sarah, James. A.B., Midland Coll., 1943; J.D., U. Mich., 1948. Bar: Ill. 1949. With Stevenson, Conaghan, Hackbert, Rooks and Pitts, Chgo., 1948-55, A.E. Staley Mfg. Co., Decatur, Ill., 1956-85; v.p., dir., mem. exec. com. A.E. Staley Mfg. Co., 1958-65, pres., chief operating officer, 1965-80, dir., mem.

exec. com., 1965-85, also chmn., 1975-85; chief exec. officer Staley Continental, Inc., Rolling Meadows, Ill., 1985—, chmn., 1985—; dir. Ill. Bell Telephone Co., Amsted Industries, Inc., Sentry Ins., Sundstrand Corp., Midwest Fin. Group, Inc.; adv. council Kellogg Grad. Sch. Mgmt. Northwestern U., Evanston, Ill. Past chmn. bd. trustees Millikin U., now hon. trustee; trustee Vanderbilt U., Mus. Sci. Industry, Chgo., Rush-Presby. St. Lukes Med. Ctr.; bd. dirs. Lyric Opera Chgo.; mem. grad. dirs. council Decatur Meml. Hosp.; mem. Ill. Gov.'s Commn. on Sci. and High Tech., Nat. Commn. on Agrl. Trade and Export Policy. Served to 1st lt. AUS, 1943-46, 51-52. Mem. ABA, Chgo. Bar Assn., Decatur Bar Assn., Corn Refiners. Assn. (bd. dirs., past chmn.), Phi Alpha Delta. Club: Legal (Chgo.), Commercial (Chgo.). Office: A E Staley Mfg Co 2200 Eldorado St Decatur IL 62525

NORDSTROM, WAYNE JEROME, sales executive; b. Mpls., June 18, 1950; s. Benjamin Lawrence II and Lyla Louise (Morison) N.; m. Christina Annette Vlahovich, May 24, 1975; children: Carl Jerome, Stefanie Annette. B in Mineral Engring., U. Minn., 1974, M in Mineral Engring., 1981. Sales engr. WEMCO div. Baker Internat., Sacramento, 1974-76; metallurgist Pickands Mather Co., Hibbing (Minn.) Taconite, 1976-79, Hanna Mining Co., Nat. Steel Pellet, Keewatin, Minn., 1979-82; sales rep. ARMCO Grinding Systems, Hibbing, 1982-85; pres., gen. mgr., chmn. bd. Continental Sales and Equipment, Hibbing, 1985—. Mem. AIME (chmn. iron range subsection 1987). Methodist. Club: Algonquin (Hibbing). Avocation: fishing. Office: Continental Sales and Equipment Co PO Box 428 Hibbing MN 55746

NOREN, BRUCE ALAN, marketing executive; b. Wakefield, Mich., Oct. 23, 1957; s. Donald James and Shirley (Muniar) N.; m. Amy Lynn Seitz, May 5, 1984. BA, No. Mich. U., 1980. Mktg. mgr. Am. Bowling Congress, Greendale, Wis., 1980—. Dir. Profl. Ski Instr. Cen., 1985-86. Mem. Am. Soc. Assn. Execs. Avocations: auto restoration, snow skiing and teaching, scuba diving. Home: W181 S 9134 Parker Dr Muskego WI 53150 Office: Am Bowling Congress 5301 S 76th St Greendale WI 53129

NORGAARD, ORLAN WILLMAN, fire chief; b. Arlington, S.D., July 16, 1941; s. Willie and Elsie (Henrickson) N.; m. Gloria Jean Berg, Jan. 29, 1966; children—Brenda, Ryan. With Sioux Falls Fire Dept., S.D., 1964—, fire fighter, 1964-70, lt. II, 1970-75, capt., 1975-78, bn. chief, 1978-80, 1984—, chief, 1980-84; pres. Minnehaha County Fire Chiefs, Sioux Falls, 1984—; pres. Internat. Fire Fighters Local 814, 1970-78; state v.p. Internat. Fire Chiefs, S.D., 1981-84. Served with U.S. Army, 1960-63. Named Fire Fighter of Yr. K.C., Sioux Falls, 1978. Mem. S.D. Fire Fighters (v.p., State Fire Fighter of Yr. 1974), S.D. Fire Chiefs (v.p. 1986—), Internat. Assn. Fire Chiefs. Democrat. Lutheran. Home: 2807 S Lyndale Ave Sioux Falls SD 57105 Office: Sioux Falls Fire Dept 224 W 9th St Sioux Falls SD 57102

NORGE, WILLIAM FREDERICK, mechanical engineer; b. Chgo., Apr. 12, 1955; s. Alexander F. and Mary E. (O'Neil) N.; m. Debra L. Silinski, Aug. 16, 1980; children: Kelly, Daniel. Student, Daley City Coll., 1974-76; BSME, Ill. Inst. Tech., 1980. Draftsman, designer Walgren Labs., Bedford Park, Ill., 1976-77; machine designer Goodman Equipment, Chgo., 1977-78, Sterling Engring., Oak Brook, Ill., 1978-80; resident engr. 3-M Co., Bedford Park, 1980-83, advanced resident engr., 1983-84, supr. resident engrs., 1984—; cons. T.M. Resce & Assocs., Oaklawn, Ill., 1979—. Youth counselor Ashburn Luth. Ch., Chgo., 1979-81. Mem. Am. Soc. Mech. Engrs. (assoc.). Roman Catholic. Avocations: volleyball, basketball, sailing, carpentry, nature hikes. Office: 3-M Co 6850 S Harlem Ave Bedford Park IL 60501

NORGLE, CHARLES RONALD, United States district judge; b. Mar. 3, 1937. B.B.A., Northwestern U., 1964; J.D., John Marshall Law Sch., Chgo., 1969. Asst. state's atty. DuPage County, Ill., 1969-71, dep. pub. defender, 1971-73, assoc. judge, 1973-77, circuit judge, 1978-84; U.S. dist. judge U.S. Dist. Ct. (no. dist.) Ill., Chgo., 1984—. Mem. ABA, DuPage Bar Assn., Ill. Bar Assn., Fed. Bar Assn., DuPage Assn. Women Attys., Nat. Attys. Assn., Chgo. Legal Club. Office: Federal Courthouse 219 S Dearborn St Chicago IL 60604 *

NORMAN, JOHN WILLIAM, oil co. exec.; b. Harrisburg, Ill., Sept. 4, 1910; s. Walter Jacob and Clarissa May (Bush) N.; student pub. schs., Saline County, Ill.; m. Marcella May Souheaver, July 2, 1937. Dist. mgr. Martin Oil Co., 1936-54; with Am-Bulk Oil Co. (name changed to Norman Oil Co., 1960), Lisle, Ill., 1949—, pres., 1960—. Served with USNR, 1943-44. Mem. VFW, Am. Legion. Home: 5 S 511 Columbian St Naperville IL 60540 Office: 1018 Ogden Ave Lisle IL 60532

NORMAN, ORVAL GENE, librarian; b. Norman, Ind., Nov. 2, 1937; s. Charley Orval and Ethel Marie (Hanner) N.; m. Darlene Jeanette Meki, July 15, 1961; children: MArk Alan, David Lee, John Stephen. BA, Ind. State U., 1959; MA in Library Sci., Ind. U., 1960. Documents, asst. ref. librarian DePauw U., Greencastle, Ind., 1960-61; asst. ref. librarian Ind. State U., Terre Haute, 1961-65, acting head ref. dept., 1965-66, head ref. dept., 1966—; asst. prof. library sci. Ind. State U., 1968-69, assoc. prof. library sci., 1974. Contbr. articles to profl. jours. Mem. Am. Library Assn., Assn. Coll. and Research Libraries (chmn. membership com. 1981-83), Ind. Library Assn. (life), Am. Assn. Univ. Profs. Home: 2417 Morton St Terre Haute IN 47802 Office: Ind State U Library Terre Haute IN 47809

NORMAN, RICHARD DAVIESS, dental educator; b. Franklin, Ind., Feb. 7, 1927; s. William Byron and Edith May (Grubb) N.; m. Joan May Roler, July 15, 1951; children: Beverly Joan, Elizabeth Jane. AB, Franklin Coll., 1950; DDS, Ind. U., Indpls., 1958, MS, 1964. Analytical chemist Eli Lilly & Co., Indpls., 1950-54; research assoc. Ind. U., Indpls., 1955-58, instr., 1958-64, asst. prof., 1964-69, assoc. prof., 1969-73, prof., 1973-76; dir. dental clinic research Johnson & Johnson Dental Products Co., Heightstown, N.J., 1976-79; cons. Colts Neck, N.J., 1979-80; clin. prof. Fairleigh Dickinson U., 1979-80; prof., chmn. restorative dentistry So. Ill. U. Sch. Dental Medicine, Alton, 1980-85, dir. research, 1985—; cons. in field. Contbr. articles to profl. jours. Pres. sch. bd. Greenwood (Ind.), 1968-70. Served with AUS, 1945-47. NIH Research grantee, 1983-84, Clopper Found. Research grantee, 1983. Mem. ADA, Am. Assn. Dental Research, Internat. Assn. Dental Research (councillor St. Louis sect.), Am. Coll. Dentists, Omicron Kappa Upsilon, Sigma Phi Alpha, Sigma Xi. Republican. Presbyterian. Lodge: Masons. Home: 5 Monterey Pl Alton IL 62002 Office: 2800 College Ave Alton IL 62002

NORRIS, ALAN EUGENE, judge; b. Columbus, Ohio, Aug. 15, 1935; s. J. Russell and Dorothy A. (Shrader) N.; m. Nancy Jean Myers, Apr. 15, 1962 (dec. Jan. 1986); children: Tom Edward Jackson, Tracy Elaine. BA, Otterbein Coll., 1957; cert., U. Paris, 1956; LLB, NYU, 1960; LLM, U. Va., 1986. Bar: Ohio 1960, U.S. Dist. Ct. (so. dist) Ohio 1962, U.S. Dist. Ct. (no. dist) Ohio 1964. Law clk. to judge Ohio Supreme Ct., Columbus, 1960-61; assoc. Vorys, Sater, Seymour & Pease, Columbus, 1961-62; ptnr. Metz, Bailey, Norris & Spicer, Westerville, Ohio, 1962-80; judge Ohio Ct. Appeals (10th dist.), Columbus, 1981-86, U.S. Ct. Appeals (6th cir.), Columbus, 1986—. Contbr. articles to profl. jours. Mem. Ohio Ho. of Reps., Columbus, 1967-80. Named Outstanding Young Man, Westerville Jaycees, 1971; recipient Legislator of Yr. award Ohio Acad. Trial Lawyers, Columbus, 1972. Mem. ABA, Am. Judicature Soc., Inst. Jud. Adminstrn., Ohio Bar Assn., Columbus Bar Assn. Republican. Methodist. Lodge: Masons (master 1966-67). Office: US Ct Appeals 103 US Courthouse Columbus OH 43215

NORRIS, ANNETTE GAYE, medical social worker, educator; b. Parsons, Kans., Mar. 18, 1958; d. Leon Roy and Joan (Robinson) Cole; m. James Buker Norris, Aug. 1, 1981. BA, Washburn U. of Topeka, 1980; MSW, U. Kans., 1984. Lic. clin. social worker. Social sci. tchr. Cedar Valc (Kans.) Sch. Dist., 1980-81; med. social worker St. Francis Hosp. & Med. Ctr., Topeka, 1984—; contact person Nat. Heart Assistance & Transplant Fund, Villanova, Pa., 1985—; cons., vol. Birthright, Topeka, 1985-86. Mem. Kansans for Life Inc. Democrat. Baptist. Avocations: music, scuba diving, travel, reading. Home: 427 SW Fillmore Topeka KS 66606 Office: St Francis Hosp & Med Ctr 1700 W 7th St Topeka KS 66606

NORRIS, DALE MELVIN, entomology educator; b. Page County, Iowa, Aug. 19, 1930; s. Dale M. Sr. and Opal Loretta (Klepinger) N.; m. Eleanor Ann Brown, Sept. 7, 1951 (dec. May 1963); children: Kathleen Ann, Elizabeth Susanne; m. Mary J. Wilmar, June 12, 1965 (div.). BS, Iowa State U., 1952, MS, 1953, PhD, 1956. Asst. prof. entomology U. Fla., Gainesville, 1956-58; asst. prof. entomology U. Wis., Madison, 1958-62, assoc. prof., 1962-66, prof., 1966—; cons. numerous corps. and fgn. countries, 1956—. Editor: Perception of Behavioral Chemicals, 1981; editor Jour. Entomologia Exp. Appl., 1970—; contbr. numerous papers to scientific jours. Mem. AAAS, Am. Soc. Neurochemistry, Entomol. Soc. Am. (Founders' Meml. award, 1975), Biophysical Soc., The Protein Soc., Bioelectrochemical Soc. Club: Ky. Colonels. Avocations: painting, poetry, music, travel. Home: 101 S Rock Rd Madison WI 53705

NORRIS, JOHN HART, lawyer; b. New Bedford, Mass., Aug. 4, 1942; s. Edwin Arter and Harriet Joan (Winter) N.; m. Anne Kiley Monaghan, June 10, 1967; children—Kiley Anne, Amy O'Shea. B.A., Ind. U., 1964; J.D., U. Mich., 1967. Bar: Mich. 1968, U.S. Ct. Mil. Appeals 1969, U.S. Supreme Ct. 1974, U.S. Ct. Claims 1975, U.S. Tax Ct. 1979. Assoc., then ptnr. Monaghan, Campbell, LoPrete, McDonald and Norris, 1970-83; of counsel Dickinson, Wright, Moon, Van Dusen & Freeman, 1983-84, ptnr.1985—; bd. dirs. Holly's Hotsock, Prime Securities Corp., Ray M. Whyte Co., Ward-Williston Drilling Co., Bott Lodge Enterprises. Mem. Rep. State Fin. Com.; founder, co-chmn. Rep. majority club; bd. dirs. Boys and Girls Clubs of Southeastern Mich., 1979—, Mich. Wildlife Habitat Found., Mercy Coll., Detroit; mem. Detroit Hist. Soc., 1984—; trustee Nat. Council Salk Inst. Served with M.I., U.S. Army, 1968-70. Recipient numerous civic and non-profit assn. awards. Fellow Mich. State Bar Found.; mem. ABA (litigation and natural resources sects.), Mich. Oil and Gas Assn. (legal and legis. com.), State Bar Mich. (chmn. environ. law sect. 1982-83, probate and trust law sect., energy conservation task force, oil and gas com.), Oakland County Bar Assn., Detroit Bar Assn. (pub. adv. com.), Am. Arbitration Assn., Fin. and Estate Planning Council Detroit, Def. Orientation Conf. Assn., Detroit Zool. Soc., Blue Key Nat. Hon. Fraternity, Phi Delta Phi. Roman Catholic. Clubs: Bloomfield Hills Country; Thomas M. Cooley, Detroit Athletic, Economic (Detroit); Hundred, Prismatic, Turtle Lake, Yondotega. Contbr. articles to profl jours. Home: 1325 Buckingham St Birmingham MI 48008 Office: 525 N Woodward Ave PO Box 509 Bloomfield Hills MI 48013

NORRIS, MARTIN LAVERN, sociology educator, marriage and family therapist; b. Minden, La., Feb. 22, 1922; s. Martin Van Buren and Sarah Anne (DeLoache) N.; m. Frances Gayle Ouzts; children: Diana, Gayle. BS, La. State U., 1948, MA, 1952, PhD, 1957; BTh., Anderson U., 1949; postgrad., U. Minn., 1965-66. Vocat. counselor La. State U., Baton Rouge, 1950-51; instr. sociology La. Coll., Pineville, 1951-52; asst. prof. sociology So. Meth. U., Dallas, 1952-58; prof. Anderson (Ind.) Coll., 1958—; dir., therapist Kardatzke Marriage and Family Ctr., Anderson Coll., 1967—. Contbr. articles, pamphlets and booklets in field. Pres. Family Service Madison County, Anderson, 1963, Family Planning Madison County, Anderson, 1971-72; chmn. commn. on social concerns Ch. of God, Anderson, 1964-72; council mem. Women's Alternatives, Anderson, 1986—. Served to sgt. U.S. Army, 1943-46, PTO. Recipient Disting. Service award Anderson Coll. Alumni Assn., 1985. Mem. Am. Assn. Marriage and Family Therapy (clin.), Nat. Council Family Relations, Am. Sociol. Assn., Ind. Council Family Relations (profl., pres. 1967-69). Democrat. Mem. Ch. of God. Avocations: writing, travel, photography, woodworking. Home: 614 Maplewood Ave Anderson IN 46012 Office: Anderson U 1100 E 5th St Anderson IN 46012

NORRIS, ROBERT F., food products company executive; b. 1922; married. BS, U. Kans., 1946. With Fleming Cos., Oklahoma City, 1946-71; former exec. v.p., pres. M. Loeb Ltd., Ottawa, Can., 1971-73; chmn., pres., chief exec. officer S.M. Flickinger Co., 1973-81; v.p. sales Associated Grocers, Phoenix, 1981-83; vice chmn. Godfrey Co., Waukesha, Wis., 1983-86, chief exec. officer, 1983—, chmn., 1986—; dir. Godfrey Co., Waukesha. Served to lt. USN, 1942-46. Office: Godfrey Co 1200 W Sunset Dr Waukesha WI 53186 *

NORRIS, WILLIAM C., computer systems executive; b. Inavale, Nebr., July 14, 1911; s. William H. and Mildred A. (McCall) N.; m. Jane Malley, Sept. 15, 1943; children: W. Charles, George, Daniel, Brian, Constance, Roger, Mary N., David. B.S., U. Nebr., 1932. Sales engr. Westinghouse Electric Mfg. Co., Chgo., 1935-41; v.p., gen. mgr. Engring. Research Assocs., 1946-55, Univac (div. Sperry Rand Corp.), 1955-57; pres. Control Data Corp., Mpls., 1957-77; now past chmn. Control Data Corp., also bd. dirs.; bd. dirs. N.W. Bank Corp., N.W. Growth Fund, Tronchemics, Inc. Trustee Hill Reference Library; adv. com. White House Conf. on Balanced Nat. Growth and Econ. Devel., 1978—. Served to comdr. USNR, 1941-46. Recipient Nat. Medal Tech., 1986. Office: Control Data Corp 8100 34th Ave S Minneapolis MN 55440 *

NORTH, KENNETH EARL, lawyer; b. Chgo., Nov. 18, 1945; s. Earl and Marion (Temple) N.; m. Susan C. Gutzmer, June 6, 1970; children: Krista, Kari. AA with high honors, Coll. of DuPage, Glen Ellyn, Ill., 1970; BA with high honors, No. Ill. U., 1971; JD, Duke U., 1974. Bar: Ill. 1974, U.S. Dist. Ct. (no. dist.) Ill. 1974, Guam 1978, U.S. Tax Ct., 1975, U.S. Ct. Appeals (7th cir.), 1978, U.S. Supreme Ct., 1978, U.S. Ct. Internat. Trade 1978, U.S. Ct. Appeals (9th cir.) Ill. 1979. Div. chief DuPage County State's Attys. Office, Wheaton, 1976-78; spl. asst. U.S. atty. Terr. of Guam, Agana, 1978-79, atty. gen., 1979-80; ptnr. firm Solomon, Rosenfeld, Elliott & Stiefel Ltd., Chgo., 1982-86, Burke, Bosselman & Weaver, Chgo., 1986—; adj. prof. law John Marshall Law Sch., Chgo., 1985—, Keller Grad. Sch. Mgmt. Northwestern U.; instr. Northwestern U. Traffic Inst., 1985—; cons. Terr. of Guam, 1980-81; lectr., cons. regarding computer-aided litigation support, 1985—; counsel to various fin. instns. and domestic corps. Co-author: Criminal and Civil Tax Fraud, 1986; bd. editors Attorneys' Computer Report, 1986—; contbr. articles to legal publs. Trustee, mem. adv. bd. Ams. for Effective Law Enforcement, 1986—; v.p. Glen Ellyn Manor Civic Assn., 1981-84, pres., 1984—; police commr. Village of Glen Ellyn, 1982—. Mem. Assn. Trial Lawyers Am. (sec. criminal sect. 1986-87, 2d vice chair 1987—), ABA, Ill. Bar Assn., World Bar Assn., Chgo. Bar Assn., Chgo. Duke Bar Assn. (pres. 1986-87), Chgo. Council Fgn. Relations, Internat. Platform Assn., Mensa. Republican. Pioneer use of computer in ct. Office: Burke Bosselman & Weaver Xerox Ctr 55 W Monroe St Chicago IL 60603

NORTH, ROBERT DEAN, purchasing agent; b. Alta, Iowa, Nov. 1, 1934; s. Samuel Thurman and Evelyn Lena (Sinns) N.; m. Kay Joan Overton, June 26, 1954; children: Robert Dean Jr., Constance Lynn, Kipp Grant. Grad. high sch., Storm Lake, Iowa. Shop supr. Ranco Fertiservice, Sioux Rapids, Iowa, 1976-82, purchasing agt, asst. supr., 1982—. Mem. Lakeside city council, 1965-75, 80-82. Democrat. Methodist. Clubs: Rollin Relics Car (Strom Lake) (pres. 1984-85, 86-87; Old Iron Co. (Spencer, Iowa) (sec. 1984-85). Lodge: Moose (sgt.-at-arms 1965-68). Avocations: bowling, golf, model planes, car rebuilding. Home: 604 Lakeshore Dr Lakeside IA 50588 Office: Ranco Fertiservice HWY 71 Sioux Rapids IA 50585

NORTH, ROBERT SLATER, marketing executive; b. Chillecothe, Mo., June 11, 1938; s. James Carr and Ruth (Slater) N.; m. Linda Griggs, Dec. 27, 1958 (div. Aug. 1965); children: Margaret Lee, John Christopher, Andrew James; m. Noralou Sharpnack, July 9, 1966; children: L. Michael, J. Trent. BS, Iowa State U., 1960. Territory mgr. molasses div. Cargill Inc., Chgo., 1960-62; dist. sales mgr. salt div. Cargill Inc., N.Y.C., 1962-65; regional sales mgr. salt div. Cargill Inc., Cin., 1965-70; mktg. mgr. salt div. Cargill Inc., Mpls., 1970-72, dir. coll. recruiting, 1972-75, adv. mgr. seed div., 1975-76, regional mgr. salt div., 1976-79, exec. mktg. dir. salt div., 1979—. Instr. Project Bus., Jr. Achievement, Mpls., 1984, 85, 86; div. chmn. United Way, Mpls., 1984; race dir. July 4th Party-in-the-Park, St. Louis Pk., Minn., 1983, 84, 85, 86; choir pres. Gethsemane Ch., Hopkins, Minn., 1985; bd. dirs. Menogyn & Camp, 1987—, Minn. Choral, 1987—. Mem. Am. Mktg. Assn., Sales and Mktg. Execs Internat., Water Quality Assn. (membership chmn., mktg. com. 1983-84, pub. relations com. 1985—), Salt Inst. (water treatment com. 1984—). Republican. Lutheran. Avocations: running, biking, golf, boating, racquetball. Home: 9115 W 34th St Saint Louis Park MN 55426 Office: Cargill Inc Salt Div Box 5621 Minneapolis MN 55440

NORTHROP, DOUGLAS ANTHONY, educational administrator, educator; b. Ontario, N.Y., Apr. 12, 1935; s. Adren Henry and Anna Susanna (Hamelink) N.; m. Lynn Bradley Post, Sept. 22, 1956; children: Christopher, Jennifer, Timothy, Gregory. BA, Wesleyan U., 1956; MA, U. Chgo., 1957, PhD, 1966. Instr. Ripon (Wis.) Coll., 1960-63, asst. prof., 1963-68, assoc. prof., 1968-74, prof. English, 1974—, v.p., dean of faculty, 1977—. Contbr. articles and revs. to profl. jours. Mem., treas., v.p., pres. Ripon Sch. Bd. Edn., 1973-83; mem. exec. com. Wis. Humanites Com., Madison, 1985—. Recipient Severy award for Teaching, Ripon Coll., 1966, Uhrig award for Teaching, Ripon Coll., 1971. Mem. Modern Language Assn., Renaissance Soc. Am. Home: 528 Woodside Ave Ripon WI 54971 Office: Ripon College PO Box 248 Ripon WI 54971

NORTHROP, STUART JOHNSTON, manufacturing company executive; b. New Haven, Oct. 22, 1925; s. Filmer Stuart Cuckow and Christine (Johnston) N.; m. Cynthia Stafford Daniell, Feb. 23, 1946; children: Christine Daniell, Richard Rockwell Stafford. B.A. in Physics, Yale U., 1948. Indsl. engr. U.S. Rubber Co., Naugatuck, Conn., 1948-51; head indsl. engring. dept. Am. Cyanamid Co., Wallingford, Conn., 1951-54; mfg. mgr. Linear, Inc., Phila., 1954-57; mgr. quality control and mfg. Westinghouse Electric Co., Pitts., 1957-58; mfg. supt. SKF Industries, Phila., 1958-61; v.p. mfg. Am. Meter Co., Phila., 1961-69; founder, v.p., gen. mgr. water resources div. Singer Co., Phila.; pres., dir. Buffalo Meter Co., Four Layne Cos.; dir. Gen. Filter Co., 1969-82; chmn., chief exec. officer Huffy Corp., Dayton, Ohio, 1982—, chmn. exec. com.; dir. Lukens, Inc., Coatesville, Pa., Fischer & Porter, Phila., Union Corp., N.Y.C. County fin. chmn. George Bush Presdl. campaign, 1980; presdl. appointee Pres.'s Commn. on Ams. Outdoors, 1985—; chmn. nat. hwy. safety adv. com. Dept. Transp., 1986—. Served with USAAF, 1944-45. Named Chief Exec. Officer of Yr. for leisure industry Wall Street Transcript, 1980. Mem. Del. Valley Investors (past pres.), Interlocutors, Elihu, Am. Bus. Conf. (founding), Fin. Commn. of Fund Ams. Future, Delta Kappa Epsilon, KOA Soc. Club: Moraine Country (Dayton). Home: 226 Cheswold Ln Haverford PA 19041 Office: 1850 Kettering Tower Dayton OH 45423

NORTHUP, WILLIAM CARLTON, acct.; b. Columbia, Mo., Dec. 1, 1930; s. Lansford Lionel and Elsie Rebecca (Eaton) N.; B.S. in Statistics, U. Mo., 1953, M.B.A., 1974; m. Sharon Joan Carlson, June 27, 1970; children—Richard Carlton, Karen Frances. Research asso. Mo. Crippled Children's Service, Columbia, 1968-69, asst. supt. research and records, 1969-70, supt., 1970-76; broker London Commodity House, Inc., Chgo., 1976-77; chief accountant Nat. Congress PTA, Chgo., 1977-78; mgmt. analyst fin. systems for health and hosps. Cook County Governing Commn., Chgo., 1978-79; acct. V Cook County Hosp., 1979—; controller, dir. pub. health statistics, coordinator automatic data processing, supt. ins. Mo. Crippled Children's Service; asst. prodn. mgr., chief estimator, account exec. Am. Press; spl. advisor to Gov. Mo. on printing and pub., 1965. Mem. Columbia Fin. Study Commn., 1974, steering com. Columbia Town Meeting, 1976; bd. dirs. Camp Wannanoya, 1976; mem. steering com. Teen Auto Club, 1972; vol. probation officer Boone County Juvenile Office, 1971-72. Mem. Am. Mgmt. Assn., Am. Statis. Assn., Mo. Pub. Health Assn., Assn. M.B.A. Execs., Hosp. Fin. Mgmt. Assn., Mensa, Delta Sigma Pi. Republican. Baptist. Club: Optimists. Home: 24 Williamsburg Terr Evanston IL 60203 Office: 1825 W Harrison St Chicago IL 60612

NORTON, DALE BENTSEN, transportation equipment executive; b. Mission, Tex., Sept. 3, 1925; s. Clark Watkins and Laurel Havana (Bentsen) N.; m. Anna Jacqueline Lansdowne, Apr. 21, 1946; children: Gale Ann, Laura Lee. Student, Tex. A&M U., 1942-43, Spartan AeronauticsSch., 1946-47. Cert. airframe and powerplant mechanic. Tech. rep. Beech Aircraft, Wichita, Kans., 1952-60; service mgr. Combs Aircraft, Denver, 1960-67; customer service mgr. Gates Learjet Corp., Wichita, 1970-74, v.p. product support, 1974-81, v.p. logistics support, 1981—, pres., 1986—. Served with USAAF, 1943-46. Mem. Aircraft Mechanic Found. Republican. Methodist. Lodge: Masons. Office: Gates Learjet Corp PO Box 7707 Wichita KS 67277

NORTON, FIELDING LEWIS, JR., accountant; b. New Haven, Conn., May 25, 1938; s. Fielding Lewis and Marie Eleanor (Thompson) N.; m. Janice Kay Bannon, June 12,1960; children: Fielding L. III, James B. BS in Bus., U. Kans., 1960, MBA, 1961. CPA, Kans., Mo. Staff acct. Price Waterhouse & Co., Kansas City, Mo., 1961-64; chief acct. Natkin & Co., Kansas City, 1964-72; ptnr. Norton, Kahmann & Klayder, Olathe, Kans., 1972—; instr. Johnson County Community Coll., Overland Park, Kans., 1974—. Treas., bd. dirs. Olathe Area C. of C., 1974-75; treas. City Prairie Village, Kans., 1981—; mem. East Kans. Estate Planning Council, 1976—, pres. 1979-80. Mem. Am. Inst. CPA's, Kans. Soc. CPA's, Nat. Assn. Accts. (pres. Kansas City chpt. 1975-76), Planning Exec. Inst. (v.p. Kansas City chpt. 1969-70). Republican. Avocations: swimming, bicycling. Home: 7664 Canterbury Prairie Village KS 66208 Office: Norton Kahmann & Klayder PO Box 54 Olathe KS 66061

NORTON, JOHN JEFFREY, dentist; b. St. Paul, May 28, 1948; s. John Charles and Margret (Jeffrey) N.; m. Catherine Ann Borbas, June 14, 1974 (div. 1979); m. Concetta Marie Serafina, Jan. 30, 1981; children—Cara Elizabeth, Kelsey Ann, John Matthew. Student Coll. St. Thomas, 1966-70, Coll. Osteo. Medicine of Pacific, 1981-83; D.D.S., Creighton Dental Sch., 1974. Gen. practice dentistry, Cottage Grove, Minn., 1974—; lectr. in field; patentee in field. Advisor State Ins. Commn. and Comml. Commn., St. Paul, 1984—. Mem. Mid-Am. Orthodontic Soc. (sec. 1976—), Minn. Acad. of Orthodontics for the Gen. Practitioner (bd. dirs. 1976—). Roman Catholic. Club: St. Croix Sailing. Avocations: sail boat racing; running; skiing; cross-country skiing. Office: 7501 80th St S Cottage Grove MN 55016

NORVICH, STEVEN N., data processing executive; b. Mpls., June 13, 1943; s. Samuel G. and Ethel (Bennesovitz) N.; married, July 30, 1970 (div. 1982); m. Susan Norvich, Aug. 23, 1986. A.A., Harper Coll., 1984; M.B.A., U. Chgo., 1977; B.A., SUNY-Albany, 1985, B.S., 1985. Dir., Crane Co., Chgo., 1969-70; pres. Cyborg Internat., Chgo., 1970-77; gen. mgr. UOP Litigation Services, Des Plaines, Ill., 1977-84; v.p. G C Services, Chgo., 1984—; cons. 1983-84. Contbr. articles to profl. jours. Republican. Avocations: golf; bridge; white water rafting; landscaping. Office: G C Services 2 N Riverside #1300 Chicago IL 60606

NORWALK, THOMAS SAWYER, marketing and advertising executive; b. Cleve., Oct. 3, 1930; s. Arthur Sawyer and Isabel (Caldwell) N.; B.A., U. Miami (Fla.), 1951, postgrad., 1951-52; postgrad. U. R.I., 1953-54; m. Cynthia Ann Cantelon, Dec. 28, 1963; children—Leslie V., Laura C.P. Mgmt. trainee, then advt. coordinator Ford Motor Co., Dearborn, Mich., 1955-58; advt. mgr. internat. div. Perfect Circle Corp., Ft. Wayne, Ind., 1958-61; successively retail promotion mgr., trade advt. mgr., internat. advt. and promotion mgr. B.F. Goodrich Co., Akron, Ohio, 1961-68; advt. mgr., dir. advt., v.p., div. mgr. trading stamp systems Top Value Enterprises, Inc., Kettering, Ohio, 1968-81; pres. Miami Valley Mktg. Group, Inc., Dayton, Ohio, 1981—. Chmn. traffic safety com., Oakwood, Ohio; past trustee Miami Valley Regional Transit Authority; past mem. devel. bd. Dayton Children's Med. Ctr.; bd. dirs. Dayton Council on World Affairs, Miami Valley Internat. Trade Assn., So. Ohio Dist. Export Council (U.S. Dept. Commerce). Served to lt. comdr. USNR, 1952-55. War Meml. scholar, 1950; Livingston scholar, 1950-52. Mem. Am. Mktg. Assn., Dayton Sales and Mktg. Execs. Assn., Miami Valley Internat. Trade Assn., So. Ohio Dist. Export Council, Am. Assn. Polit. Cons., Pub. Relations Soc. Am., Direct Mktg. Assn., Internat. Advt. Assn., Dayton, Akron (past pres.) advt. clubs, Dayton Area C. of C. (past chmn. transp. com.). Republican. Episcopalian. Club: Dayton Country. Home: 1500 Devereux Dr (Oakwood) Dayton OH 45419 Office: Miami Valley Mktg Group Inc PO Box 321 Wright Brothers Branch Dayton OH 45409-0321

NORWOOD, JOY JANELL, corporate real estate executive; b. Barnes, Kans., Aug. 25, 1936; s. Howard Clayton and Gladys Melveno (Wells) Cook; divorced; 1 child, Rebecca. Student, U. Colo., 1958-63; grad., Realtors Inst. Ohio State U., 1977. Lic. real estate agt., Ohio. Registered rep. First Investors Corp., Boston, 1966-68; area supr. Wohl Shoe Co., Boston, 1968-70; residential real estate broker Coldwell Banker, Cin., 1970-78, comml. real estate broker, 1978-80; comml. real estate broker Rubloff, Cin., 1980-82; sr. real estate rep. Ky. Fried Chicken, Louisville, 1982-86; v.p. Otto Realty Corp., Cin., 1987—. Jr. high sch. tchr. Mason (Ohio) Ch.

Christ, 1986—, mem. choir., 1986—. Served with U.S. Army, 1955-58. Mem. Nat. Assn. Corp. Real Estate Execs., Internat. Council Shopping Ctrs., Cin. Bd. Realtors (polit. affairs com. 1974, Million Dollar Club award, 1972-79), Cin. Hist. Soc. Republican. Club: Flying Neutrons (Cin.). Avocations: music, flying, sailing, reading, gardening. Home: 8547 Ashwood Dr Westchester OH 45069 Office: Otto Realty Corp 2311 Grandin Rd Cincinnati OH 45208

NORWOOD, RONALD EDWARD, programmer, analyst; b. Columbus, Ohio, May 25, 1960; s. Thomas Lloyd and Marian Delores (Williams) N.; m. Sidney Carla Bengtson, Mar. 1, 1986. BBA in computer info. systems, Harding U., 1984. Programmer, analyst Guarantee Mutual Life Co., Omaha, 1984—. Republican. Avocations: jogging, softball, volleyball, basketball. Home: 818 Janesview St Apt #7 Papillion NE 68046-2074 Office: Guarantee Mutual Life Co 8801 Indian Hills Dr Omaha NE 68114

NOTHERN, ELLA LOUISE, nurse; b. Salina, Kans., Jan. 30, 1931; d. Herman Herbert and Eva Alice (Beil) Will; m. M. Roland Nothern, Nov. 22, 1950 (div. Sept. 1985); children: David Will, Matthew Roland, Nathan Jon. BA, Kans. Wesleyan U., Salina, 1973; A in Nursing, Cloud County Community Coll., Concordia, Kans., 1981. RN, Kans. Pre-sch. tchr., Glasco, Kans., 1974-75; tchr. Glasco High Sch., 1975-76; clk. bus. office Mitchell County Hosp., Beloit, Kans., 1976-77; activity dir. Nicol Home, Glasco, 1977-79; nurse psychiatric unit St. Joseph's Hosp., Concordia, 1981-84; charge nurse Good Samaritan Ctr., Minneapolis, Kans., 1984—. Mem. exec. com. Central Kans. Library System, Great Bend, 1977-84; bd. dirs. Pawnee Mental Health Ctr., Manhattan, Kans., 1982-84; mem. ambulance crew Glasco Ambulance Service, 1979-84. Mem. Lutheran Missionary Soc. (pres. 1960-61), Epsilon Sigma Alpha (pres. 1964-65). Republican. Home: Route 1 Salina KS 67401 Office: Good Samaritan Ctr Minneapolis KS 67467

NOTO, JOHN EDWARD, psychologist; b. Chgo., Dec. 4, 1947; s. John Edward and Josephine Noto; m. Linda Maria Miles, Nov. 30, 1974; children: Steven, Daniel, Laura, Jonathan. BS in Psychology and Sociology, U. Wis., 1970; MS in Counseling Psychology, Ill. State U., 1974; PhD in Clin. Psychology, The Fielding Inst., 1982. Registered social worker; registered psychologist. Staff psychologist LaSalle County Mental Health, Ottawa, Ill., 1974-76; staff therapist Tri City Mental Health, East Chicago, Ind., 1976-78; outpatient coordinator Alexian Bros. Med. Ctr., Elk Grove, Ill., 1978-82, program mgr. The Counseling Ctr., 1982-87, psychologist Mental Health and Addictions,, 1987—; clin. dir. Talkline/Kidsline, Elk Grove, 1984. Mem. Elk Grove Soccer Club, Elk Grove Youth Baseball league. Avocation: coaching youth sports activities. Home: 1081 Cypress Ln Elk Grove Village IL 60007 Office: Alexian Bros Med Ctr 800 W Biesterfield Elk Grove Village IL 60007

NOTOWIDIGDO, MUSINGGIH HARTOKO, information systems executive; b. Indonesia, Dec. 9, 1938; s. Moekarto and Martaniah (Brodjonegoro) N.; m. Sihar P. Tambunan, Oct. 1, 1966 (dec. Nov. 1976); m. Joanne S. Gutter, June 3, 1979; children: Matthew Joseph, Jonathan Paul. BME, George Washington U., 1961; MS, NYU, 1966, postgrad., 1970. Cons. Dollar Blitz & Assocs., Washington, 1962-64; ops. research analyst Am. Can Co., N.Y.C., 1966-69; prin. analyst Borden Inc., Columbus, Ohio, 1969-70, mgr. ops. research, 1970-71, mgr. ops. analysis and research, 1972-74, asst. gen. controller, officer, 1974-77, corp. dir. info. systems/econ. analysis, officer, 1977-83; v.p. info. systems Wendy's Internat., 1983—; adj. lectr. Grad. Sch. Adminstrn. Capital U. Contbr. articles to profl. jours. Mem. Fin Execs. Inst. (chmn. MIS com.), Ops. Research Soc., Inst. Mgmt. Sci., Am. Mgmt. Assn., Nat. Assn. Bus. Economists, Long Range Planning Soc., Am. Statis. Assn., AAAS, World Future Soc., Data Processing Mgmt. Assn., Soc. Info. Mgmt., N.Y. Acad. Scis. Republican. Clubs: Capital, Racquet. Home: 1965 Brandywine Dr Upper Arlington OH 43220 Office: 4288 W Dublin-Granville Rd Dublin OH 43017

NOTTKE, WILLIAM HARRY, packaging company executive; b. Kankakee, Ill., Aug. 27, 1951; s. William Harry and Adeline Mae (Brinkman) N.; m. Lora Leigh Kronsbein, Apr. 3, 1980; children—Crystal, Ashley. Student Kankakee Community Coll., 1970-72, Western Ill U., 1969-70. Customer service supr. Baker & Taylor Co., Momence, Ill., 1971-73; sales/service corr. Kankakee Container Corp. (Ill.), 1973-76; sales/service mgr. Keystone Container Corp., St. Louis, 1976-79; owner, pres. Riverdale Packaging Corp., St. Louis, 1979—, also chmn. bd. Mem. Assn. Ind. Corrugated Converters (pres. St. Louis chpt.). Methodist. Office: Riverdale Packaging Corp 11490 Warnen Rd Maryland Heights MO 63043

NOVACK, RICHARD VICTOR, diamond and gem brokerage executive; b. Mpls., Aug. 8, 1945; s. Maurice and Alice (Offerman) N.; m. Bogumila Maria-Antonia Strutynska Berlicz-Sas, June 7, 1980; children: Maurice Louis Strutynski Berlicz-Sas, André Adam Strutynski Berlicz-Sas. Degree in International Relations, U. Minn., 1967. Pres. M.L. Novack Inc., Mpls., 1967-74, Midwest Diamond Exchange, Inc., Mpls., 1975—, Diamond Exchange Assocs., Inc., 1979—, Diamond Trading Corp., Mpls., 1979—. Author: Consumers Guide to Diamond Grading, 1975. Author/inventor Computerized Diamond Trading System, 1976. Address: Midwest Diamond Exchange Box 2101 Minneapolis MN 55402

NOVAK, ART, precious metal processing engineer; b. Rockford, Ill., Apr. 12, 1952; s. Arthur S. Sr. and Juanita (Wisenant) N.; m. Linda Kay Self, Dec. 21, 1974; 1 child, Elizabeth Ashley. AA, Rock Valley Community Coll., 1972; BS, So. Ill. U., 1974. Territory mgr. Enerpac, Inc., Butler, Wis., 1974-79; regional sales mgr. Magnus, Inc., Los Gatos, Calif., 1979-82, United Refining Co., Franklin Park, Ill., 1982-84; v.p. midwest ops. Nat. Refining and Smelting, Inc., Santa Clara, Calif., 1984-87; dist. sales mgr. Sipi Metals, Inc., Chgo., 1987—. Mem. Elk Grove (Ill.) Sailors (pres. 1984—). Lutheran. Avocation: sailing on Lake Geneva, Wis. Home: 808 Galleon Elk Grove Village IL 60007-6921 Office: Sipi Metals Inc 1720 Elston Ave Chicago IL 60622

NOVAK, CHARLES ANDREW, real estate broker; b. Cleve., Jan. 8, 1936; s. Charles Frank and Anna Helen (Ondris) N.; m. Monica B. Bonsignore, Jan. 18, 1958; children: Charles A., Annette L., Louis T., Frank R., Monica M. BBA in Mktg., John Carroll U., 1957; grad., Realtors Inst., 1982. Real estate mgr. The Kroger Co., Cleve., 1957-68, Mpls., 1957-68; mgr. new stores devel. Super Value Store, Dayton, Ohio, 1968-70; dir. retail ops. Jacobs, Visconsi & Jacobs, Cleve., 1970-77; regional real estate dir. Marriott Corp., Cleve., 1977-80; salesman lic. real estate Hoty Enterprises, Cleve., 1980-81; sr. leasing rep. The Sherwin Williams Co., Cleve., 1981—; mem. adv. bd. Nat. Mall Monitor, Clearwater, Fla., 1986—. Editor: The Carroll Quarterly Literary Mag., 1957. Co. rep. United Way, Cleve., 1961-63; Umchmn. Dayton council Boy Scouts Am., 1969-70; pres. St. Ignatius Band Booster, Cleve., 1978-79. Served to capt. U.S. Army, 1958-66. Mem. Nat. Assn. Corp. Real Estate Exec. (v.p. 1985-86 No. Ohio chpt., pres. 1986-87), Internat. Council Shopping Ctrs. (pres. 1972-73), St. Ignatius Alumni Assn. (Gerald B. Garvey award 1978), John Carroll Alumni Assn. (trustee 1959-60), Alpha Kappa Psi (life). Democrat. Roman Catholic. Club: St. Vincent de Paul Soc. (v.p. 1979-84). Home: 3503 West 122d St Cleveland OH 44111 Office: The Sherwin Williams Co Real Estate Dept 101 Prospect Ave Cleveland OH 44115

NOVAK, CYNTHIA DENISE, computer technician; b. Harrisburg, Pa., May 24, 1952; d. John William Humphrey and Barbara Lucille Cooper; m. David Carl Novak, Jan. 2, 1975; 1 child, Jessica. AA in Computer Sci., Richard J. Daley Jr. Coll., Chgo., 1978. Computer technician Amoco Chemicals, Naperville, Ill., 1978. Served as pvt. U.S. Army, 1972-74. Avocation: PTO newsletter. Home: 2 S 275 Meadow Dr Batavia IL 60510 Office: Amoco Chemicals C-4 Warrenville Rd and Mill St Naperville IL 60546

NOVAK, ELIZABETH ANN, personnel executive; b. Detroit, Dec. 22, 1935; d. Ralph Bernard and Ida Margaret (Burgess) N. AAS, Westchester Community Coll., 1956; BA, Wayne State U., 1974, MBA, 1979. Sec. Dykema, Wheat, Spencer, Goodnow, Trigg, Detroit, 1966-68, Chrysler Corp., Highland, Mich., 1968-76; personnel recruiter Chrysler Def., 1976-78; instrl. devel. Gen. Dynamics Land Systems, Warren, Mich., 1978-83; supr., tech. trnr. Chrysler Def., Gen. Dynamics Land Systems, Warren, 1983—. Mem. Soc. Logistics Engrs. (chpt. officer 1979-86), Logistics Edn. Found. (sec. 1981-85), Am. Soc. Tng. and Devel. Democrat. Roman Catholic. Avocations: piano, travel. Office: Gen Dynamics Land Systems 6700 E 14 Mile Rd Warren MI 48090

NOVAK, JAMES ALAN, architect; b. Cedar Rapids, Iowa, Apr. 30, 1947; s. Elroy Henry and Arlene Jean (Dvorak) N.; m. Christina Kay Lottman, June 2, 1972; 1 child, Richard. BArch, Iowa State U., 1974, MArch, 1977. Registered architect, Iowa, Colo. Prin. project architect Olson, Popa, Novak, Architects P.C., Marion, Iowa, 1979-86; owner Novak Design Group, Cedar Rapids, Iowa, 1986—. Bd. dirs. Cedar Rapids-Marion Arts Council, ARC; trustee Brucemore Inc. Adv. bd. Iowa Prison Industries. Mem. AIA, Iowa Chpt. AIA, Cedar Rapids/Iowa City Architects Council, Tau Sigma Delta. Home: 136 Tomahawk Trail SE Cedar Rapids IA 52403 Office: Novak Design Group 411 First Ave SE Cedar Rapids IA 52401

NOVAK, JEFFREY ALLAN, manufacturing company executive; b. Milw., Aug. 24, 1954; s. Victor Anthony and Marcella Ann (Tessemer) N.; m. Karla Kimberly Nelson, Oct. 16, 1983; children: Allisyn, Maggie, Marcie. BS in Indsl. Edn. and Tech., U. Wis.-Stout, 1976, M Guidance and Counseling, 1977; postgrad. in bus. adminstrn., Cardinal Stritch Coll., 1987—. Instr. survival skills, machine shop Chippewa Falls (Wis.) High Sch., 1976-80; designer, estimator Northwoods Timber Products, Downsville, Wis., 1980-82; machine shop supr. Mason Mfg., Chippewa Falls, 1982-83, spl. project engr., 1982-85; exec. dir. PHB, Inc., Osseo, Wis., 1985-87; exec. v.p. PHB, Inc., Osseo, 1987—, also bd. dirs.; cons. in field, Chippewa Falls, 1982—. Office: PHB Inc Rt 3 Box 101 Hwy 53 Osseo WI 54758

NOVAK, MICHAEL ANDREW, ophthalmologist; b. Lorain, Ohio, Aug. 14, 1951; s. Andrew J. and Anna (Olejar) N.; m. Debra Ann Sabo, Aug. 11, 1973; children: Jennifer, Julee, Jillian, Jonathan. BA, Case Western Res. U., 1973, MD, 1977. Intern U. Hosps. Cleve., 1977-78; resident in ophthalmology Wilmer Ophthal. Inst. Johns Hopkins Hosp., Balt., 1978-81, fellow in retina and vitreous diseases and surgery, 1981-82, asst. chief service, instr., 1982-83; ptnr. Retina Assocs. of Cleve., 1983—; asst. clin. prof. Case Western Res. U., Cleve., 1983—. Contbr. articles to profl. jours. Recipient Outstanding Tchr. award Case Western Res. U. Hosps, 1985, Teaching award St. Luke's Hosp., Cleve., 1985, Teaching award, Mt. Sinai Med. Ctr., Cleve., 1986. Mem. AMA, Am. Acad. Ophthalmology, Assn. for Research in Vision and Ophthalmology, Phi Beta Kappa. Republican. Roman Catholic. Home: 5310 Fairfield Oval Solon OH 44139 Office: Retina Assocs of Cleve 26900 Cedar Rd Suite 323 Cleveland OH 44122

NOVAK, RICHARD C., mortgage company executive; b. Blue Island, Ill., Oct. 5, 1946; s. Casimir Martin and Josephine (Kaptur) Nowak; m. JoAnn Novak, Aug. 3, 1967; children: Richard, Mitchell. BS in Acctg., No. Ill. U., 1970. CPA, Ill. Sr. acct. Ernst & Whinney, Chgo., 1970-73; div. controller Am. Hosp. Supply, Evanston, Ill., 1973-76; mng. dir. Source Fin., Chgo., 1976-78; v.p. Bank of Hickory Hills, Ill., 1978-81; pres. Nova Search, Chgo., 1981-86, Republic Mortgage, Matteson, Ill., 1986—. Treas. City of Palos Heights, Ill., 1973, Arlington Heights (Ill.) Youth Athletic Assn., 1985-86; pres. Stonegate Homeowners Assn., Arlington Heights, 1981-82; commr. sr. citizens com., Arlington Heights, 1984. Served as sgt. USAF, 1964-68.

NOVAK, ROGER WAYNE, senior claims analyst; b. Uniontown, Pa., Dec. 6, 1951; s. John Lewis and Ruth (Piovarchy) N.; m. Maureen Therese Kelly, Mar. 17, 1974. BS, U. Ill., Chgo., 1973; cert. in ins., Ins. Inst. Am., 1979; Assoc. in Ins. Claims, Ins. Sch. Chgo., 1980. CPCU. Casualty supr. GAB Bus. Services, Evergreen Park, Ill., 1973-80; sr. litigation exec. Chubb Ins. Group, Chgo., 1980-84; sr. claim profl. Nat. Underwriting, Chgo., 1984-85; sr. claim analyst CNA Ins. Co., Chgo., 1985—. Mem. Soc. of CPCU's (mem. claims sect.), CPCU's of Chgo., Casualty Adjusters Chgo., Jaycees Internat. (senator 1986), Ill. Jaycees (Outstanding V.P. award 1982, 84, Outstanding Pres. award 1983), Tinley Park (Ill.) Jaycees (pres. 1982-83), Naperville (Ill.) Jaycees. Republican. Roman Catholic. Avocations: ice hockey, sports. Home: 1040 Jupiter Ct Naperville IL 60540-4973 Office: CNA Ins Cos CNA Plaza 37 South Chicago IL 60685

NOVAK, VICTOR ANTHONY, manufacturing company executive; b. Antigo, Wis., Mar. 23, 1930; s. Joseph F. and Mary C. (Jerovic) N.; m. Marcella A. Tessmer, Nov. 3, 1951; children: Deborah, Mark, Jeffrey, Lori. Cert. in Mgmt., Marquette U., 1980. Mgr. repairshop Novak's Machineshop, Antigo, 1947-52; model maker AC Spark Plug co., Oakcreek, Wis., 1952-66; supr. experimental div. Oster Corp., Glendale, Wis., 1966-72; gen. foreman toolroom Square D Co., Milw., 1972-82, mgr. tool engring., 1982—; tchr. Milw. Area Tech. Coll., 1973—. Avocations: golf, bowling, fishing, skiing. Home: 6705 Braeburn Ln Glendale WI 53209 Office: Square D Co 4041 N Richards St Milwaukee WI 53212

NOVAKOVICH, ELISABETH, hospital administrator; b. Rouen, France, Oct. 16, 1955; s. Nick John and Helena N.; m. Thomas Gerald Tinor, July 14, 1977. BA, Rosary Coll., 1977, MBA, 1982. Systems analyst Rush-Presbyn. St. Luke's Med. Ctr., Chgo., 1980-83, systems adminstr., 1983-86, asst. to the v.p., 1986—; faculty mem. Morton Coll., Cicero, Ill., 1982—, Rush-Presbyn. St. Luke's Med. Ctr., Chgo., 1986—. Mem. Women in Computing. Avocations: tennis, Egyptology. Office: Rush Presbyn St Lukes Med Ctr 1653 W Congress Pkwy Chicago IL 60612

NOVAS, PETER P., manufacturing company executive, consultant; b. Istanbul, Turkey, Apr. 5, 1929; came to U.S., 1950; s. Irakleus Konstantine and Martha Helen (Kobeli) N.; m. Thomasine Dreko, June 10, 1956; children: Jeanne B., Lorraine S. BSME, Robert Coll., Istanbul, 1949; MSME, Purdue U., 1951; BA, U. Chgo., 1967. Registered profl. engr., Ill. Mgr. ops. research Vapor Corp. (div. Singer Corp.), Chgo., 1962-67; dir. mgmt. infosystems/fin. Spector Industries, Chgo., 1967-70; dir. corp. devel. J. Schlitz Brewing Co., Milw., 1970-75; v.p. Ill. Cen. Gulf R.R. subs. Ill. Cen., IC Industries, Chgo., 1975-82; pres. Coordinated Intermodal Control, Inc., Chgo., 1982—; cons. Western Pacific Industries, San Francisco, 1973-75, Intermodal Cons. Services, Chgo., 1982—. Editor: Distribution and Transportation Handbook, 1971; contbr. articles to profl. jours.; patentee Sensors, Transducers Simulation, 1965-67. Mem. Nat. Ry. Intermodal Assn. Republican. Greek Orthodox. Avocations: painting, swimming. Home: 2405 E Kensington Arlington Heights IL 60004 Office: Coordinated Intermodal Control 875 N Michigan Ave Suite 3310 Chicago IL 60611

NOVICH, CHARLES ANTHONY, data processing executive, educator; b. Worcester, Mass., May 5, 1958; s. Anthony Albert and Joan Elizabeth (McCartney) N.; m. Carol Lynne Miles, Feb. 9, 1961. B in Computer Sci., U. Nebr., 1980. Assoc. analyst Enron, Omaha, 1980-82, sci. analyst, 1982-84, sr. system analyst, 1984—; instr. U. Nebr., Omaha, 1981—. Democrat. Avocation: computer generated designs. Home: 31 Pioneer Trail Plattsmouth NE 68048 Office: Enron Corp 2223 Dodge Omaha NE 68102

NOVICK, MARVIN, automotive supplier executive, accountant; b. N.Y.C., July 16, 1931; s. Joseph and Anna Novick; m. Margaret A. Blau, Apr. 9, 1960; children: Jeffrey, Stuart, Barry. BBA, CCNY, 1952; MBA, NYU, 1955, postgrad., 1955-58. CPA, N.Y., Mich., La., N.C. Sr. v.p. Mich. Blue Cross/Blue Shield, Detroit, 1961-70; v.p., dir. fin. Meadowbrook Ins., Southfield, Mich., 1970-72; ptnr. Touche Ross and Co., Detroit, 1972-84; vice chmn. Dura Corp., Southfield, 1984—. Chmn. Oak Park-Huntington Woods-Pleasant Ridge (Mich.) Dem. Orgn., 1970-72, 18th Dem. Congl. Dist., 1972-74; trustee Mich. Assn. for Emotional Children, 1965—, also past pres.; trustee Providence Hosp., Southfield, 1975-83, also past chmn., trustee bldg. bd., 1982—; trustee Oak Park (Mich.) Bd. Edn., 1964-71, also past pres.; trustee Temple Beth El, Birmingham, Mich., 1968—, also past pres.; trustee Union of Am. Hebrew Congregation, 1981—; chmn. fin. com. World for Prog. Judaism-Internat., 1985—; chmn. personnel com. Jewish Welfare Found., 1987—, assoc. chmn. cultural and edn. com., 1984—; bd. dirs. B'nai B'rith Centennial Lodge, 1970-79, past v.p. Recipient Honor and Service cert. Oak Park Bd. Edn., 1972, Past Pres. award Mich. Assn. Emotionally Disturbed Children, 1986; named one of Outstanding Young Men of Am., Outstanding Am. Found., 1968. Mem. Am. Inst. CPA's, Mich. Assn. CPA's, N.Y. State Assn. CPA's. Home: 12820 Burton St Oak Park MI 48237

NOVICKI, CARROLL A., electronics company executive; b. 1938. Student, U. Nebr.; MBA, Stanford U. With Dale Electronics, Inc., Columbus, Nebr., 1960—, sr. v.p., 1973-75, pres., chief exec. officer, 1975—, also bd. dirs. Office: Dale Electronics Inc 2064 12th Ave Columbus NE 68601 *

NOVOTNY, RAYMOND JOSEPH, nature center director; b. Youngstown, Ohio, Sept. 8, 1956; s. Joseph Raymond and Bernice (Borsick) N. BS, Kent (Ohio) State U., 1980. Program instr. U. N.C., Greensboro, 1981; park ranger U.S. Army Corps Engrs., Deerfield, Ohio, 1982; naturalist Morningside Nature Ctr., Gainsville, Fla., 1982-84; grants coordinator Ohio Dept. Natural Resources, Columbus, 1984-85; nature ctr. dir. Mill Creek Park, Youngstown, 1985—. Editor The Grist Mill Newsletter, 1985—. Recipient research award Gopher Tortoise Council, 1983, Grad. Student award Ohio Parks and Recreation Assn., 1985. Mem. Assn. Interpretive Naturalists, No. Ohio Assn. Herpetologists. Club: Outspokin' Wheelmen (Youngstown). Avocations: bicycling, book collecting, writing. Home: 840 Old Furnace Rd Youngstown OH 44511 Office: Mill Creek Park 816 Glenwood Ave Youngstown OH 44502

NOWACZEK, FRANK HUXLEY, cable television executive; b. Bklyn., July 6, 1930; s. Frank Huxley and Louise (Blake) N.; m. Alice Elaine Novak, May 21, 1955; children—Richard Alan, Elaine. Student St. Lawrence U., 1948-50; B.S. in Hotel Adminstrn., Cornell U., 1952; postgrad. in polit. sci. and pub. relations George Washington U., 1954-58, Am. U., 1954-57. Spl. agt. spl. ops. br. security div. Nat. Security Agy., Def. Dept., 1954-59; asst. to pres., dir. research Nat. Cable TV Assn., Washington, 1959-64; asst. to pres. TeleSystems Corp., Glenside, Pa., 1964-66; v.p., part-owner Newport Cablevision (Vt.), 1966-68; v.p. Blackburn & Co., Inc., Washington, 1968-76; v.p. Mid Atlantic region Warner Amex Cable Communications, N.Y.C., 1976-80, sr. v.p. eastern div., Ft. Washington, Pa., 1980-82, sr. v.p. nat. div., Columbus, Ohio, 1982-83; owner Cable Media Co., Worthington, Ohio, 1983-86; pres. Newcable TV Corp., 1985-86; chief operating officer Bachow & Elkin, Inc. Phila., 1986—; speaker various orgns. Served with CIC, U.S. Army, 1952-54. Mem. Soc. Relay Engrs. (Gt. Britain), Nat. Cable TV Pioneers Assn., Pa. Cable TV Assn. (pres., dir.), Pa. Cable TV Pioneers Assn., Phila. Cable TV Club (founder), Cornell Soc. Hotelmen, Am. Mgmt. Assn., Nat. Cable TV Assn. (sec. tech. standards com. 1961 chmn. membership com. 1965-66), IEEE, Cornell U. Alumni Club, (life) Cornell Soc. Hotelmen, Phi Delta Theta. Republican. Mem. Dutch Reformed Ch. Home: 283 Meditation Ln Worthington OH 43085

NOWAK, DENNIS JUDE, accountant; b. Gary, Ind., June 8, 1950; s. Edwin John and Florence Marie (Niesyto) N.; m. Michele Marie Meehan, June 16, 1973; children: Matthew Gerard, Candace Lynn. BS, Ind. U., 1975. CPA, Ind., Ill. Sr. acct. No. Ind. Pub. Service Co., Hammond, 1972-76; sr. mgr. Peat Marwick Main & Co., Chgo., 1976—. Mem. Am. Inst. CPA's, Ind. CPA Soc., Ill. CPA Soc., Ind. Soc. Chgo., N.W. Ind. Forum. Roman Catholic. Club: Briar Ridge Country (Dyer, Ind.). Avocations: golf, fishing. Home: 9518 Chestnut Ln Munster IN 46321 Office: Peat Marwick Main & co 303 E Wacker Dr Chicago IL 60601

NOWAK, MARIE SHEERAN, educator; b. St. Louis, June 24, 1920; d. Frank Thomas and Marie Regina (Connors) Sheeran; m. Joseph Nowak, 1942; children—Pauline Hayes, James. B.A., Harris Tchrs. Coll., 1942; M.A., Washington U., St. Louis, 1956. Cert. tchr., Mo. Tchr., St. Louis pub. schs., 1949—, tchr. math. and social studies Lafayette Sch., 1949-51, Carondelet Sch., 1951-56, Werner Sch., 1956-80, tchr. math. and history Long Sch., 1980-83, curriculum coordinator Stevens Sch., 1983—. Pres. St. Louis Met. Womens Polit. Caucus, 1973-74, St. Louis New Dem. Coalition, 1979-81. Mem. Mo. State Tchrs. Assn. (state exec. com., pres. St. Louis Dist. 1981-82), Am. Bus. Women's Assn., Delta Kappa Gamma. Lodge: K.C. Aux. Home: 4333 Hanover Ct Saint Louis MO 63123 Office: Stevens Middle School 1033 N Whittier Ave Saint Louis MO 63113

NOWAK, MICHAEL ROMAN, paper company executive; b. Milw., May 12, 1953; s. Joseph and Patricia (Grezsk) N.; m. Carol Ann Lands, July 2, 1977; children: Matthew, Nathan, Kevin, Koren. BA, Lawrence U., 1975; MBA, U. Chgo., 1977. Sr. fin. analyst Ford Motor Co., Dearborn, Mich., 1977-81; mgr. planning Philip Morris, N.Y.C., 1981-84; market mgr. Thilmany Pulp & Paper div. Internat. Paper Co., Kaukauna, Wis., 1984—. Mem. Planning Execs. Inst., Beta Gamma Sigma, Beta Theta Pi. Lutheran. Home: 1509 S Fidelis St Appleton WI 54915 Office: Thilmany Pulp & Paper PO Box 600 Kaukauna WI 54130

NOYCE, DONALD O., insurance executive; b. Goodland, Kans., Jan. 1, 1931; s. Alfred Dewitt and Mildred Rose (Dryden) N.; m. Darlene G. Boettcher, Oct. 13, 1958; children: Ronald, Nancy, David. BA, Kans. Wesleyan U., 1952. Underwriter Federated Ins., Owatonna, Minn., 1956-57, loss control cons., 1957-59, mktg. rep., 1959-62, account exec., 1962-69, mktg. tng. mgr., 1969—; lectr. CPA Continuing Edn. Nat. Soc. CPA's, 1980—. Author: What A CPA Should Know About Business Insurance, 1985. Dist. chmn. Boy Scouts Am., Owatonna, 1984-85, exec. bd. Boy Scouts Am., Rochester, 1984-86; rep. ward chmn., Owatonna, 1972; chmn. citizens com. Nat. Guard, Owatonna, 1981-86. Served with USN, 1952-56. Recipient Silver Beaver award Boy Scouts Am., 1981. Mem. Soc. Ins. Trainers and Educators. Lodges: Elks, Masons.

NOYES, RICHARD FRANCIS, optometrist; b. Des Moines, May 8, 1952; s. Robert F. and Mary C. N.; children—Jennifer, Bethany. B.S. in Gen. Sci., U. Iowa, 1975; B.S. in Visual Sci., Ill. Coll. Optometry, 1976, O.D., 1978. Family practice optometry, Marion, Iowa, 1978—. dir. Haiti Med. Mission, 1978—; lectr. in field. Named one of Outstanding Young Men in Am., 1986, Outstanding Young Optometrist State Iowa, 1985. Fellow Am. Coll. Optometric Physicians; mem. Iowa Optometric Assn. (legis. com. 1984, bd. dirs. 1986-87, sec.-treas. 1987—), Am. Optometric Assn., Jaycees, Beta Sigma Kappa. Republican. Lutheran. Lodge: Lions (bd. dirs. 1979—, Disting. Service award 1983), Sertoma (Outstanding Service to Mankind award 1987). Home: 1640 25th Ave Marion IA 52302 Office: 1065 East Post Rd Marion IA 52302

NUCCITELLI, SAUL ARNOLD, consulting civil engineer; b. Yonkers, N.Y., Apr. 25, 1928; s. Agostino and Antoinette (D'Amicis) N.; m. Concetta Orlandi, Dec. 23, 1969; 1 child, Saul A. BS, NYU, 1949, MCE, 1954; DCE, MIT, 1960. Registered profl. engr., N.Y., Mo., Colo., Conn., Mass.; lic. land surveyor, Mo., Colo., Conn., Mass. Asst. civil engr. Westchester County Engrs., N.Y.C., 1949-51, 53-54; project engr. H.B. Bolas Enterprises, Denver, 1954-55; asst. prof., research engr. U. Denver, 1955-58; mem. staff MIT, 1958-60; asst. prof. engring. Cooper Union Coll., N.Y.C., 1960-62; pvt. practice cons. engring., Springfield, Mo., 1962—; organizer Met. Nat. Bank, Springfield; adviser, dir. Farm & Home Savs. and Loan Assn. Contbr. articles to profl. jours. Chmn. Adv. Council on Mo. Pub. Drinking Water; bd. dirs. Community Found. Greene County, Mus. of Ozarks; past chmn. Bd. City Utilities, Springfield; past pres. Downtown Springfield Assn. Served with U.S. Army, 1951-53. Recipient Cert. of Appreciation, Mo. Mcpl. League, 1981; named Mo. Cons. Engr. of Yr., 1973. Fellow ASCE; mem. Nat. Soc. Profl. Engrs., Mo. Soc. Profl. Engrs. (past pres. Ozark chpt.), Boston Soc. Civil Engrs., Am. Concrete Inst., Am. Inst. Steel Constrn., Am. Welding Soc., ASTM, Am. Soc. Mil. Engrs., Springfield C. of C. (past v.p.). Home: 2919 Brentmoor Ave Springfield MO 65804 Office: 122 Park Central Sq Springfield MO 65806

NUDI, ALFREDO EDWARD, restaurant owner, chef; b. Pitts., July 15, 1940; s. Alfred Hugh and Mary Angela (Carbone) N. Food and beverage dir. Sheraton Gibson Hotel, Cin., 1969-71; ptnr., gen. mgr. Inn Below Rest, Tallahassee, Fla., 1971-73; asst. mgr., dir. food and beverages Holiday Inn, Longboat Key, Fla., 1973-75; food and beverage dir. Colony Beach and Tennis, Longboat Key, Fla., 1975-76; owner, chef mgr. Ristorante La Taverna, Dearborn, Mich., 1977—; pres., chief operating officer Prospect Ct. Enterprises Ltd., Dearborn, 1979—. Served with U.S. Army, 1966-68. Mem. Mich. Restaurant Assn., Mich. Chefs de Cuisine. Republican. Roman Catholic. Avocations: model railroad building, photography. Home: 18054 Prospect Ct Melvindale MI 48122 Office: Prospect Ct Enterprises PO Box 7157 Dearborn MI 48121

NUETZEL, JOHN ARLINGTON, machine tool executive; b. St. Louis, Feb. 28, 1947; s. John Arlington and Sally Lou (Bowman) N.; m. Janet Ann Schwanbeck, May 4, 1968; children: Jennifer Alice, Sarah Kistner, Dorothy Nehls. Student, St Louis U., 1965, DePauw U., 1965-68. Prin. Aviation & Indsl. Risk, St. Louis, 1968-72; pres. Midwestern Module Inc., St. Louis, 1972; corp. sec. Nuetzel Mchinery Co., St. Louis, 1972-78; regional mgr. Coherent Laser Div., Palo Alto, Calif., 1978-81; founder, v.p. Laserdyne Corp., Eden Prairie, Minn., 1981-86; founder, pres. Pulse Technologies Inc., Mpls., 1986—; editorial bd. Laser Machining Handbook, Penn Well Pub. Co., Littleton, Mass. Inventor Laser Machine System, 1984. Mem. Warson Woods (Mo.) City Council, 1971-75; chmn. bd. Incorporation Study Com., Inc., Chesterfield, Mo., 1977-79; pres. River Bend Assn., Inc., Chesterfield, 1979-80. Mem. Soc. Mfg. Engrs. (indsl. laser mfrs. adv. com. 1984—), Mensa. Club: Minnetonka Yacht (Deephaven, Minn.). Avocations: ski instr., pvt. pilot. Home: 1945 Fox Ridge Rd Long Lake MN 55356

NUGENT, DANIEL EUGENE, business executive; b. Chgo., Dec. 18, 1927; s. Daniel Edward and Pearl A. (Trieger) N.; m. Bonnie Lynn Weidman, July 1, 1950; children: Cynthia Lynn, Mark Alan, Dale Alan. BSME, Northwestern U., 1951. With U.S. Gypsum Co., Chgo., 1951-71, dir. corp. devel., to 1971; pres. Am. Louver Co., Chgo., 1971-72; v.p. ops. ITT Corp., Cleve., 1972-74, exec. v.p., St. Paul, 1974-75; pres., chief exec. officer Pentair, Inc., St. Paul, 1975-86, chmn., chief exec. officer, 1986—, also bd. dirs.; bd. dirs. Niagara of Wis. Paper Corp., Flambeau Paper Corp., Miami Paper Corp., Porter-Cable Corp., Port Huron Paper Co., Delta Internat. Machinery Corp., McNeil Ohio Corp. Vice chmn. local planning commn., 1968-72; vice chmn., trustee Harper Coll., Chgo., 1970-73; mem. exec. com. Indianhead Council Boy Scouts Am. Served with AUS, 1946-47. Mem. ASME, Am. Mgmt. Assn. Republican. Presbyterian. Club: North Oaks Golf. Office: Pentair Inc 1700 W Hwy 36 St Saint Paul MN 55113

NUNEMAKER, WESLEY, grain and livestock rancher, utility assn. exec.; b. Langdon, Kan., July 9, 1919; s. Joseph J. and Gladys Mary (Kabler) N.; student Southwestern Coll., Winfield, Kans., 1937-38, Kan. State U., 1938-39; m. Twila Virl Reece, Aug. 22, 1937; children—Marcia (Mrs. Jack Castleberry), Wayne Wesley. Farm, ranch mgr., operator, Langdon, Kans., 1940—. Dir. Ark. Valley Electric Co-op. Assn., Inc., 1955-61, 73—, chmn., 1959-61. Dist. bd. chmn. Lerado Cemetery, 1952-58; mem. Reno County Extension Council, 1949-53, chmn., 1951-53; active United Fund and Christian Rural Overseas Program drives Bell Twp., 1959-62; twp. committeeman Agrl. Stablzn. and Conservation Service, 1960-66; mem. Reno County Spl. Edn. Bd. of Control, 1973. Bd. dirs. Local High Schs., 1952-73; trustee Hutchinson Community Jr. Coll., 1959—, chmn., 1959-60, 67-68, 73-74, 78-79; bd. dirs. Central Kans. Area Vocat. Tech. Sch., 1975—, pres. 1978-79; trustee Kans. Electric Power Coop., 1976—. Recipient Kans. Master Farmer award, 1973. Mem. Kans. Farm Bur., Kans. Wheat Growers Assn., Kans. Farm. Mgmt. Assn., Top Farmers Am. Assn., Reno County Bankers Soil Conservation (mem. awards selection com. 1953), Kans. Master Farmer Assn. (pres. 1976—). Mem. Christian Ch. (elder 1971—, Sunday sch. supt. 1941-46). Home: Langdon KS 67549

NUNLEY, RICHARD RYAN, manufacturing company executive; b. Nelsonville, Ohio, Aug. 12, 1945; s. Richard Harold Armstrong and Lillian Juanita (McKee) Nunley; m. Barbara Ann Poland, Nov. 29, 1964; children: Richard Ryan Jr., Christopher Todd. BS in Indsl. Engring., Ohio U., 1967; MBA, U. Akron, 1968. V.p., gen. mgr. The Metco Corp., Canton, Ohio, 1968-74; engring. mgr. The Akro Corp., Canton, 1974-78; v.p., gen. mgr. Applied Corp. Mgmt., San Diego, 1978-84; product/project mgr. Republic Storage Systems, Canton, 1984—; engring. instr. Indsl. T.'s Inst., Akron, 1969-72; assoc. prof. mgmt. Stark Tech. Inst., North Canton, Ohio, 1975-78. Contbr. articles to profl. jours. Athletic dir. Canton Jewish Community Ctr., 1971-80. Fellow Am. Inst. Indsl Engrs., Material Handling Inst., Am. Mgmt. Assn. Lodge: Masons. Avocations: reading, racquetball, writing. Office: Republic Storage Systems Co 1038 Belden Ave NE Canton OH 44705

NUNN, PHILIP CLARK, III, management scientist; b. Cin., Apr. 4, 1933; s. Philip Clark and Frances Kay (Patton) N.; student Kenyon Coll., 1951-53; B.A., Aquinas Coll., 1969; M.S., Western Mich. U., 1983; m. Hildegarde Loretta Bauer, Jan. 17, 1953; children—Annette, Catherine, Margaret, Christopher. Cert. Project Mgmt. Profl., 1984. With Lear Siegler, Inc., Grand Rapids, Mich., 1957-70, devel. project coordinator, 1962-70; mgr. environ. systems devel. Nat. Sanitation Found., Ann Arbor, Mich., 1970-74; dir. urban and environ. studies inst. Grand Valley State Colls., Allendale, Mich., 1974-80; internat. coordinator research and devel. Amway Corp., Ada, Mich., 1980-83 ; engring. and research mgmt. cons., Comstock Park, Mich., prof. masters degree progam Project Mgmt, Devry Inst. Tech., 1986—; adj. prof. F.E. Seidman Grad. Coll. Bus. and Adminstrn., 1976-81. Health dir. Cin. area Boy Scout Camp, 1952; regular panel mem. Soundings weekly radio program WOOD-AM and FM, Grand Rapids, Mich., 1973-80; vice chmn. community health planning sect. W. Mich. Health Systems Agy., 1976-80; mem. central planning com. W. Mich. Comprehensive Health Planning Unit, 1973-76; chmn. environ. simulation sect. Summer Computer Simulation Conf., 1972; bd. dirs. Kent County Conservation League, 1964-65. Served with USAF, 1953-57. Kenyon Coll. scholar, 1951. Mem. Soc. Gen. Systems Research (chmn. orgn. and mgmt. studies 1970-74), Soc. Computer Simulation, Project Mgmt. Inst., Am. Mgmt. Assn., Alpha Delta Phi. Episcopalian. Contbr. articles to profl. jours. Home and Office: 201 Netherfield St Comstock Park MI 49321

NUSBAUM, SIDNEY LEE, wholesale distribution company executive; b. St. Louis, July 10, 1947; s. Sidney M. and Mae M. (Willis) N.; m. Jennifer L. Douglas, July 24, 1971. Student, U. Mo., St. Louis, 1965-67; BSBA, BA in Acctg., Sanford-Brown Coll., 1970. Internal auditor Wohl Shoe Co., Clayton, Mo., 1970-71; office mgr., acctg. supr. Meiners Plumbing Co., St. Louis, 1971-76; controller Climate Engring., St. Louis, 1976-78; pres., owner Arch City Supply Co., St. Louis, 1978—. Mem. Am. Numismatic Assn., Mo. Numismatic Soc. (sec. 1973-78, v.p. 1985, treas. 1987—, medal of Merit 1981), Toy Wholesalers Assn. Am., Am. Philatelic Soc. Avocation: numismatics, philately, sports. Office: Arch City Supply Co 1123 Belgrove Industrial Dr Saint Louis MO 63137

NUSS, RODNEY GEORGE, military officer; b. New Orleans, Apr. 8, 1952; s. George Leonard and Mildred Lucille (Butman) N.; m. Betty Jane Carpenter, Nov. 22, 1972 (div. Feb. 1984); m. Annette Marie Marandino, Feb. 16, 1985. BS in Math. cum laude, Tulane U., 1974; MS in Ops. Research, Air Force Inst. Tech., 1984. Commd. 2d lt. USAF, 1974, advanced through grades to maj., 1985; dep. fin. officer 29th Tng. Wing USAF, Craig AFB, Ala., 1974-77; comptroller 12th Missile Warning Group USAF, Thule Air Base, Greenland, 1977-78; missile launch officer 341st Strategic Missile Wing USAF, Malmstrom AFB, Mont., 1978-82; chief planning tech. testbed Process Analysis Br. USAF, Offutt AFB, Nebr., 1984—. Mem. Am. Assn. for Artificial Intelligence. Republican. Roman Catholic. Avocations: computers, golf, jogging. Home: 3710 Burr Oak Dr Omaha NE 68123-2217 Office: Joint Strategic Target Planning Staff JKCP Offutt AFB NE 68113-5001

NUTT, JAMES MALCOLM, osteopath; b. Muskegon, Mich., Apr. 25, 1935; s. Hiram Robert and Isabelle (Kennedy) N. BA, Albion Coll., 1957; DO, Chgo. Coll. Osteo. Medicine, 1961. Pvt. practice osteo. medicine Greenville, Mich., 1962—; med. dir. Charlotte Family Practice, 1972-80, Therma Scan, Inc., 1978—, World Health Ctr., 1981—. Named to Hon. Order of Ky. Cols., 1984. Fellow Am. Acad. Med. Preventics; mem. Internat. Acad. Preventive Medicine (co-founder), Gt. Lakes Assn. Clin. Medicine (v.p., co-founder), Mich. Assn. Osteo. Gen. Practice (bd. trustee 1973-76), The Loon Soc., Beta Beta Beta, Iota Tau Sigma, Sigma Nu. Republican. Methodist. Avocations: photography, antique cars, archtl. antiques.

NUTTER, ORLA RICHARD, dentist; b. Richland Center, Wis., Jan. 19, 1928; s. Orla Ray and Hattie Catharine (Scholl) N.; m. Barbara Ruth Becker, June 9, 1951; children—Elizabeth Nutter Greer, Thomas, Nancy, Ann Nutter Swenson. B.S., Wartburg Coll., 1950; D.D.S., Marquette U., 1957. Nat. and N.D. State Board Cert. D.D.S. Gen. practice dentistry, Rugby, N.D., 1957-59, Minot, N.D., 1959—. Pres. P.T.A., Minot, 1968. Served as tech. sgt. USAF, 1950-53. Fellow Am. Coll. Dentists, Pierre Fauchard Acad.; mem. ADA (state del. 1972—), Internat. Coll. Dentists, Christian Med. Soc., N.D. Dental Assn. (pres. 1975), Am. Legion. Republican. Lutheran. Lodges: Elks, Eagles, Masons, Shriners, K.T. Avocations: hunting; fishing; boating; lake living; cross country skiing. Home: 2 Fair Way Minot ND 58701

NUTTING, JANET GLENN, real estate consultant; b. Worthing, Sussex, Eng., Sept. 23, 1957; came to U.S., 1980; d. Philip Kennedy and Angela (Plant) N.; m. John Edward Glasgow, Dec. 26, 1981. BA with honors, Oxford (Eng.) Poly. U., 1980; MS, Northwestern U., 1982. Mktg. analyst Urban Investment and Devel. Co., Chgo., 1982-83; asst. v.p. Real Estate Research Corp., Chgo., 1984—. Contbr. articles to profl. jours. and mags. Mem. Nat. Assn. Office and Indsl. Parks, Comml. Real Estate Orgn. Mem. Ch. of Eng. Avocation: triathlon. Home: 1826 Livingston St Evanston IL 60201 Office: Real Estate Research Corp 72 W Adams Chicago IL 60603

NUZMAN, CARL EDWARD, hydrologist; b. Topeka, Aug. 5, 1930; s. Loren Manuel and Lorraine Lillian (Bowler) N.; B.S. in Agrl. Engring., Kans. State U., 1953; M.S. in Water Resources Engring., U. Kans., 1966; m. Janet Ruth Steck, Aug. 23, 1952. Engr. div. water resources Kans. Bd. Agr., Topeka, 1957-65; hydrologist Kans. Water Resources Bd., Topeka, 1965-66; hydrology supr., sales engr. Layne-Western Co., Inc., Shawnee Mission, Kans., 1967-72, mgr. hydrology div., 1972-86; v.p., chief hydrologist, Groundwater Mgmt. Inc., 1986—. Treas. local sch. bd., 1958-59. Served to 1st lt. USAF, 1953-56. Registered profl. engr., Kans., Mo. Mem. Am. Soc. Agrl. Engrs., ASCE, Am. Geophys. Union, Kans. Engring. Soc. (sec.-treas. 1965-68, Outstanding Young Engr. award Topeka chpt. 1965), Nat. Soc. Profl. Engrs., Alpha Kappa Lambda, Sigma Tau, Steel Ring. Elk. Contbr. articles to profl. jours.; author, inventor. Home: 3310-B NW Huxman Rd Silver Lake KS 66539 Office: 610 S 38th St Kansas City KS 66106

NYE, CHRISTOPHER JOHN, architect, coach; b. South Bend, Ind., Apr. 4, 1954; s. Harry A. and Bernice (Zamorski) N. BArch, U. Notre Dame, 1977. Registered architect, Ind. Draftsman John T. Leader & Assocs., South Bend, Ind., 1973-76; project mgr. John T. Leader & Assocs., South Bend, 1977-79; project architect Cole Assocs. Inc, South Bend, 1979-83, mng. architect, 1983-87, assoc., 1987—. Architect (bldg. renovation) Washington Hall, U.Notre Dame, 1985, LaFortune Hall, U. Notre Dame, 1986. Bd. dirs. Nat. Ski Patrol, Bendix Woods., 1982-85, tng. advisor, Indican, 1986; founding mem. Snite Mus., U. Notre Dame; varsity men's coach U. Notre Dame Rowing Team, 1984—. Mem. AIA, Nat. Hist. Preservation Trust, Builders Exchange (bd. dirs. 1983—, 1st v.p. 1984-86). Roman Catholic. Avocations: rowing, alpine and nordic skiing. Home: 309 LaPorte Ave South Bend IN 46616 Office: Cole Assoc Inc 2211 E Jefferson Blvd South Bend IN 46615

NYGAARD, LANCE COREY, nurse, data processing consultant; b. Casper, Wyo., June 21, 1952; s. Miles Adolph and Jenile Hansine (Mosman) N.; m. Ruth Ann Soulek, Dec. 29, 1978; 1 child, Kari Melissa. A.A. in Nursing, U. S.D., 1980; B.S. in Chemistry, 1974; M.L.S., U. Ill., 1975. Registered emergency med. technician. Library asst. Brookings Pub. Library, S.D., 1971-75, asst. dir., 1975-77; emergency med. technician Brookings Hosp., 1976-78; sr. emergency med. technician Vermillion Ambulance, S.D., 1978-80; nurse McKennan Hosp., Sioux Falls, S.D., 1980—; owner operator Data Processing Services, Sioux Falls, 1983—; applications cons. Computer Dimensions, Sioux Falls, 1984-85. Service com. Holy Cross Luth. Ch., Sioux Falls, S.D., 1986—. Republican. Lutheran. Club: Chemistry (Vermillion) (pres. 1973-74). Lodge: Sons of Norway (guard 1976-77). Avocations: World War II military history; rose gardening; photography; amateur radio. Home: 5713 Parliament Dr Sioux Falls SD 57106 Office: McKennan Hosp 800 E 21st St Sioux Falls SD 57106

NYGAARD, TERRY ROBERT, tax specialist, accountant; b. Mpls., Apr. 2, 1948; s. Robert W. and Beverly M. (Lind) N.; m. Vicki Ann Schwingler, June 20, 1970; children: Lisa, Bradley. BA, Augsburg Coll., Mpls., 1970; M in Bus. Taxation, U. Minn., 1981. CPA, Minn. Tax mgr. Deloitte Haskins & Sells, Mpls., 1969-80, Chgo., 1980-82; tax mgr. Coopers & Lybrand, Mpls., 1982-84; dir. taxes BMC Industries, Inc., St. Paul, 1984—. Mem. Am. Inst. CPA's, Minn. Soc. CPA's (com. chmn. 1975-77), Tax Execs. Inst. Home: 1309 Nursery Hill Ct Arden Hills MN 55112 Office: BMC Industries Inc 1100 Am Nat Bank Bldg Saint Paul MN 55101

NYGREN, RUNE LEN, import company executive; b. Stockholm, Nov. 30, 1919; came to U.S., 1979; s. Gustav Anders and Clara (Larsson) N.; children: Anders, Magnus. Grad., Naval Acad., Stockholm, 1944, Tech. Coll., Norrkoping, Sweden, 1948; MBA, Stockholm Bus. Sch., 1952. Export mgr. Eskilstuna (Sweden) Jernbolaget, 1952-57; pres. Näfvegvarns Bruk, Nävekvarn, Sweden, 1958-65, Nävekvarns Maskiner, Malmö, Sweden, 1965-70, Scandi-Ljungbyverken, Ljungby, Sweden, 1970-79; v.p. Interthor, Inc., Broadview, Ill., 1983—. Served to lt. Swedish Navy, 1937-45. Mem. Midamerican Swedish Trade Assn. Lutheran. Avocations: reading, skiing, boxing. Office: Interthor Inc 1817 Beach St Broadview IL 60153

NYKERK, LARRY LEE, communications educator; b. Carson City, Mich., Nov. 16, 1945; s. Glenn Donald and Dorothy Hazel (Schipper) N.; m. Judith Kay Balkema, Dec. 18,1966; children: Steven James, Jill Renee, Bryan David. Student, Taylor U., Upland, Ind., 1965; BS, Western Mich. U., Kalamazoo, 1967; MA, Mich. State U., Lansing, 1981. Tchr., coach Traverse City (Mich.) Area Schs., 1968—. Dir. (film) Artsphere, 1981, 82. Pastor parish com. Cen. United Meth. Ch., Traverse City, 1978-80; treas. Old Mission (Mich.) Sch. PTO, 1981, 82; bd. dirs. Grand Traverse YMCA, 1981-84. Nat. Humanities grantee Cen. Mich. U., Mt. Pleasant, 1986-88. Mem. NEA, Mich. Edn. Assn., Mich. Council Tchrs. English (humanities grant 1986), U.S. Tennis Assn. (dist. endorser 1984-86), Mich. Tennis Coaches Assn. (named Mich. Tennis Coach of Yr. 1984, Regional Coach of Yr., bd. dirs. 1980-86), Mich. High Sch. Tennis Coaches Assn., Mich. Orgn. Visual Instrs. and Enthusiasts (movie dir. 1976-80, conf. coordinator 1977-78, team head award 1986). Democrat. Club: Logan Raquet (dir. activities 1976-79). Avocations: cycling, cross-country skiing, windsurfing, tennis, travel. Home: 10331 E Marion Dr Traverse City MI 49684 Office: Traverse City Sr High Sch Millikon & Eastern Traverse City MI 49684

NYKIEL, ANN MARIE, dentist; b. Chgo., Jan. 23, 1958; d. Thomas and Ann (Trasko) N. BS in Biology, Loyola U., Chgo., 1980; DDS, U. Ill., Chgo., 1984. Assoc. dentist Dr. Willis Jensen, Des Plaines, Ill., 1984-85, Affiliated Dental Group, Vernon Hills, Ill., 1985—; supervising dentist Prairie State Coll., Chicago Heights, Ill., 1984-85. Recipient Mosby Scholarship award Mosby Pub. Co., 1984. Mem. ADA, Ill. State Dental Soc., Lake County Dental Assn., Chgo. Dental Soc. Roman Catholic. Home: 995 Courts of Shorewood Vernon Hills IL 60061 Office: Affiliated Dental Group 10 Phillip Rd Suite 116/117 Vernon Hills IL 60061

NYTKO, EDWARD C., printing company executive; b. Chgo., Feb. 20, 1943; s. Edward Frank and Helen Nytko; m. Deborah Harriet Nytko, Nov. 21, 1980; children: Jeffrey Daniel, Christopher Edward. BBA in Mktg., U. Tex., 1965; MBA in Fin., Loyola U., Chgo., 1969. Mgmt. trainee W.F. Hall Printing Co., Chgo., 1965-67, group v.p. Gravure, 1980-81, pres., chief operating officer, 1981, pres., chief exec. officer, 1982-85; pres., chief exec. officer Krueger Ringier Inc. (fomerly W.F. Hall Printing Co.), Itasca, Ill., 1985—; asst. to v.p. mfg. Chgo. Rotoprint, 1968-69, mgr. mfg. services, 1969-72, v.p. mfg., 1972-75, pres., 1975-81. Pres.' council Nat. Coll. Edn., Evanston, Ill., 1983—. Mem. Gravure Assn. Am. (bd. dirs. 1987—), Gravure Tech. ASsn. (bd. dirs. 1980-87). Office: Krueger Ringier Inc 1 Pierce Pl Itasca IL 60143

OAKAR, MARY ROSE, congresswoman; b. Cleve., Mar. 5, 1940; d. Joseph M. and Margaret Mary (Ellison) O. B.A. in English, Speech and Drama, Ursuline Coll., Cleve., 1962; M.A. in Fine Arts, John Carroll U., Cleve., 1966; LL.D. (hon.), Ashland (Ohio) Coll.; L.H.D. (hon.), Ursuline Coll. Instr., English and drama Lourdes Acad., Cleve., 1963-70; asst. prof. English, speech and drama Cuyahoga Community Coll., Cleve., 1968-75; mem. Cleve. City Council from 8th Ward, 1973-76, 95th-98th Congresses from 20th Dist. Ohio; mem. banking, fin. and urban affairs com., select com. on aging, post office and civil service com., com. on house adminstrn., also numerous subcoms. Founder, vol.-dir. Near West Side Civic Arts Center, Cleve., 1970; ward leader Cuyahoga County Democratic Party, 1972-76; mem. Ohio Dem. Central Com. from 20th Dist., 1974; trustee Fedn. Community Planning, Cleve., Health and Planning Commn. Cleve., Community Info. Service Cleve., Cleve. Soc. Crippled Children, Public Services Occupational Group Adv. Com., Cuyahoga Community Coll., Cleve. Ballet, Cleve. YWCA. Recipient Outstanding Service awards OEO, 1973-78, Community Service award Am. Indian Center, Cleve., 1973, Community Service award Nationalities Service Center, 1974, Community Service award Club San Lorenzo, Cleve., 1976, Cuyahoga County Dem. Woman of Yr., 1977, Ursuline Coll. Alumna of Yr. award, 1977, awards Irish Nat. Caucus, awards West Side Community Mental Health Center, awards Am. Lebanese League, awards Spanish Christian Orgn., awards Cleve. Fedn. Am.-Syrian Lebanese Clubs; cert. appreciation City of Cleve.; Woman of Yr. award Cuyahoga County Women's Polit. Caucus, 1983; decorated Knight of Order of St. Ladislaus of Hungary. Office: Room 2436 Rayburn House Office Bldg Washington DC 20515 also: 523 Federal Courthouse 215 Superior St Cleveland OH 44114

OAKES, WILLIAM WOODSIDE, dentist; b. New Albany, Ind., Aug. 26, 1947; s. Marvin V. and Myrna (Woodside) O.; m. Karen Rutherford, Nov. 27, 1982; 1 child, Tyler; 1 stepchild, Alison. BA, Hanover Coll., 1969; DDS, Ind. U., 1974. Gen. practice dentistry New Albany, 1974—; cons. Green Valley Convalescent Ctr., New Albany, 1980—; mem. staff Floyd County Meml. Hosp., 1986—. Author: The Winning Combination I, 1983, The Winning Combination II, 1985, The Winning Combination III, 1986. Fellow Am. Endodontic Soc.; mem. Floyd County Dental Soc. (pres. 1984). Office: Woodside Dental Ctr 1523 State St New Albany IN 47150

OAKLEY, HUGH THEODORE, II, principal; b. Midland, Mich., July 17, 1945; s. Hugh Theodore and Rosamond Hatie (Bowers) O.; m.Carol Ann Schultz, Aug. 4, 1967; children: Kent, Kristin, Kevin. BS, Cedarville Coll., 1967; MEd, Miami U., Ohio, 1970; PhD, Ohio State U., 1985. 5th grade tchr. Centerville (Ohio) City Schs., 1967-71; elem. sch. prin. Chillicotte (Ohio) City Schs., 1971-74; elem. sch. prin., adminstr. gifted programs Upper Arlington (Ohio) City Schs., 1974—; active in Nat. Elem. Sch. Recognition program U.S. Dept. Edn., Washington, 1986. Deacon Grace Brethren Ch., Worthington, Ohio, 1974—; mem. Glen Civic Assn., Columbus, Ohio. I/D/E/A fellow, 1977, Jenning's Adminstrv. fellow, 1982. Mem. Nat. Assn. Elem. Sch. Prins., Ohio Assn. Elem. Sch. Adminstrs. (treas. 1975), Ross County Elem. Prins. Assn. (pres. 1973-74), Assn. for Supervision and Curriculum Devel., Nat. Assn. for Gifted Children, Phi Delta Kappa. Office: Barrington Elementary School 1780 Barrington Rd Upper Arlington OH 43221

OAKLEY, ROBERT JEFFREY, metal processing executive; b. Middletown, Ohio, May 28, 1953; s. Robert Lewis and Patricia Ann (King) O.; m. Debra Lou Kaupie, Nov. 13, 1976; children: Taryn Michelle, Kristen Ann. Student in Speech and Theatre, Ariz. State U., 1971-74; student in Edn., U. Ill., 1974-75. Territory mgr. Interstate Steel, Des Plaines, Ill., 1976—. Mem. Young Exec. Forum, Steel Service Ctr. Inst. Avocations: golf, running. Home: 289 Pebble Creek Dr Barrington IL 60010 Office: Interstate Steel Co 401 E Touhy Ave Des Plaines IL 60017

OAKS, JAMES ALLAN, steel company executive; b. Ketchikan, Alaska, Nov. 16, 1928; s. Otis H. and June E. (Holmes) O.; m. Patricia L. Durenberger, Dec. 27, 1958; children: Patrick, Ann, Terese, Mary. BS, U. Wash., 1954, MBA, 1955. Sales rep. Timken Cos., Los Angeles, Denver and Billings, Mont., 1957-65; dist. mgr. Timken Cos., Los Angeles, 1965-67; advt. mgr. Timken Cos., Canton, Ohio, 1967-79; dir. communications Timken Cos., Canton, 1979-84, dir. communications and employee relations, 1984—; bd. dirs. Destiny, Inc., Cleve.; chmn. Bus. Publs. Bur. Circulation Audit, N.Y.C., 1984. Served to sgt. U.S. Army, 1950-52, including Korea. Recipient Edward Lyman Bill Meml. Citation Bus. Publs. Bur. Circulation Audit, N.Y.C., 1984, Commendation Pres.' Council Phys. Fitness and Sports, Washington, 1986. Mem. Assn. Nat. Advertisers. Roman Catholic. Club: Brookside Country (Canton) (trustee 1984—, bd. dirs.). Avocations: golf, skiing, tennis. Home: 2021 Red Coach Rd NW Canton OH 44720 Office: Timken Co 1835 Dueber Ave SW Canton OH 44706

OATES, FREDERICK BURNELL, dentist; b. Boscobel, Wis., July 1, 1945; s. Stanley LaVere and Vivian Floretta (Moran) O.; m. Linda Lee McKnight, Aug. 19, 1967; children: Eric Douglas, Brian Patrick. BS, U. Wis., 1967; DDS, Marquette U., 1971. Gen. practice dentistry Wisconsin Rapids, Wis., 1973—; mem. staff Riverview Hosp., Wisconsin Rapids, 1986—; dental cons. Delta Dental Plan, Stevens Point, Wis., 1976—. Dist. chmn. Boy Scouts Am., Wisconsin Rapids, 1985-86; div. chmn. South Wood County United Way, 1986. Served to capt. USAF, 1971-73. Fellow Acad. Gen. Dentistry; mem. ADA, Wis. Dental Assn. (ho. of dels. 1979-81, 86—), Cen. Wis. Dental Soc. (pres. 1986—), Wood County Dental Soc. (pres. 1979-80), Christian Med. Soc., Am. Legion. Lutheran. Lodge: Elks. Avocations: hunting, fishing, boating, clock building. Home: 4510 Eastwood Dr Wisconsin Rapids WI 54494 Office: Huntington Dental Assocs 1211 Huntington Box 216 Wisconsin Rapids WI 54494

OATES, JAMES ROBERT, lawyer; b. Gary, Ind., Mar. 14, 1958; s. Robert John and Maxne Margaret (McCall) Oates; m. Lisa M. Oates, May 22, 1986. BS in Mgmt. Fin., Purdue U., 1980; JD, Valparaiso U., 1983. Sole practice Merrillville, Ind., 1983—. Mem. ABA, Am. Trial Lawyers Assn, Ind. Bar Assn. Office: 7863 Broadway Suite 116 Merrillville IN 46410

OATEY, JENNIFER SUE, university administrator; b. Rochester, Minn., Aug. 30, 1949; d. Elwyn Brown and Phyllis Eileen (Quammen) Larson. BS, N. Mex. State U., 1971, MAT, 1973; PhD in Edn., U. Minn., 1981. Asst. dir. recreational sports U. Mich., Ann Arbor, 1976-77; intramural supr. Stephen Austin State U., Nacogdoches, Tex., 1975-76; campus ctr. coordinator Brainerd (Minn.) Community Coll., 1974-75; phys. edn. instr., asst. intramural dir. N.Mex. State U., Las Cruces, 1973-74; assoc. dir. recreational sports U. Minn., Mpls., 1977-85, asst. to dir. student activities, 1985-86, interim dir. Minn. Union, 1986-87, acting coordinator Minn. Union, 1987—. Bd. dirs. Univ. YWCA, 1981-83, Minn. Council on Health, 1983—; mem. Minn. Gov.'s Council in Health Promotion and Wellness, 1982-83. Mem. Nat. Intramural-Recreational Sports Assn. (dir. Minn. chpt. 1977-81, mem. editorial bd. Jour., 1981-86, asst. editor NIRSA Jour., 1986—), Assn. Coll. Unions Internat., Can. Intramural Recreation Assn., Sons of Norway, U. Minn. Alumni Assn., Phi Theta Kappa. Lutheran. Home: 333 Oak Grove Apt 308 Minneapolis MN 55403 Office: U Minn 250 CMU Minneapolis MN 55455

OBAL, MICHAEL STEVEN, corporate training director, consultant; b. Omaha, Sept. 26, 1954; s. John and Anne Elizabeth (Heck) O.; m. Cheryl Lynne Siford, May 18, 1984; 1 child: Michael Steven Jr. BA, U. Nebr., 1976. Corp. tng. dir. 1/2 Price Stores, Omaha, 1982—; lead instr. U. Nebr., Omaha, 1984-85; cons. in field, Omaha, 1983—. Served to capt. USAF, 1976-81. Mem. Am. Soc. Tng. and Devel. (bd. dirs. Nebr. chpt. 1985—, Outstanding New Mem., 1985, Air Force Assn. Home: 10524 M St Omaha NE 68127 Office: 1/2 Price Stores 12100 West Ctr Rd Omaha NE 68144

O'BANNON, FRANK LEWIS, lawyer, state senator; b. Louisville, Jan. 30, 1930; s. Robert Pressley and Rosella Faith (Dropsey) O'B.; A.B., Ind. U., 1952, J.D., 1957; m. Judith Mae Asmus, Aug. 18, 1957; children—Polly, Jennifer, Jonathan. Admitted to Ind. bar, 1957, since practiced in Corydon; partner firm Hays, O'Bannon & Funk, 1966-80, O'Bannon, Funk & Simpson, 1980—; mem. Ind. State Senate, 1970—, minority floor leader, 1979—, asst. minority floor leader, 1972-76; pres., dir. O'Bannon Pub. Co., Inc. Served with USAF, 1952-54. Mem. Ind. Dem. Editorial Assn. (pres. 1961), Am. Judicature Soc., Am. Bar Assn., Ind. Bar Assn. Democrat. Methodist. Office: 303 N Capitol St Corydon IN 47112

OBARA, ELIZABETH MARY, science educator; b. Wilkingsburg, Pa., Apr. 27, 1933; s. Marcel K. and Mia K. (Judermanns) Newman; divorced; children: John C., David J. BS, Purdue U., 1955; MS, Wright State U., 1976. Cert. secondary tchr. Tchr. sci. and phys. edn. South Bend (Ind.) Schs., 1955-56; tchr. conversational English Ursula Obershule, Hanover, Rep. Germany, 1956-57; tchr. phys. edn., sci., social studies Perly Sch., South Bend, 1957-58; tchr. sci., phys. edn. Lyons (Ill.) Schs., 1958-59; tchr. phys. edn. Centerville (Ohio) High Sch., 1959-60; tchr. sci. Newton Local

Sch., Pleasant Hill, Ohio, 1972—; mem. faculty Project Winning in Sci. Edn., Wright State U., 1986—. Contbr. articles to profl. jours. Recipient Gov.'s award, 1986-87; NSF grantee, 1985. Mem. Ohio Acad. Sci. (Acker Outstanding Tchr. award 1983-84), Nat. Sci. Tchrs. Assn., Battelle Meml. Inst. (Outstanding Sci. Dept. 1984-85), Nat. Assn. Underwater Instrs., AAUW, Wright State Scuba Diving Assn., Rock and Gem Soc., LWV. Republican. Roman Catholic. Club: Kitty Hawk Scuba Club. Lodge: Soroptomists. Avocations: scuba diving, stained glass, golf, rock hounding, goldsmithing. Home: 4714 E State Rt 571 Tipp City OH 45371 Office: Newton Local Sch Long St Pleasant Hill OH 45359

OBENBERGER, J(OSEPH) D(ENNIS), lawyer; b. Milw., May 21, 1954; s. Joseph Albert and Theresa Carol (Sottile) O.; m. Mary Ann Matejov, May 17, 1980. B.A. in Polit. Sci. and History, U. Wis., 1976, J.D., 1979; postgrad. DePaul U., 1976-77. Bar: Wis. 1979, U.S. Dist. Cts. (ea. and we. dists.) Wis. 1979, U.S. Dist. Ct. (no. dist.) Ill. 1984, U.S. Ct. Claims 1979, U.S. Ct. Mil. Appeals 1979, U.S. Ct. Appeals (7th cir.) 1979, U.S. Ct. Appeals (fed. cir.) 1984, Ill. 1983, U.S. Supreme Ct., 1985. Sole practice, Highland Park, Ill., 1983-84; assoc. Tyrrell & Flynn, Chgo., 1984—. Exec. dir. Wis. Federated Teenage Republicans, Madison, 1971; committeeman Rep. Party of Village of Fox Point, Wis., 1972; mem. city devel. com. City of Highwood, Ill., 1983, mem. city plan commn., 1984, mem. zoning bd. appeals, 1984, alderman, 1987; vice chmn., precinct 66 committeeman Deerfield Twp. Rep. Party, Ill., 1986. Served to capt. U.S. Army, 1979-83. Decorated Army Commendation medal; recipient Outstanding Achievement award Wis. Fedn. Young Reps., 1970; U.S. Army ROTC scholar, 1972. Mem. Wis. Bar Assn., Lake County Bar Assn., Chgo. Bar Assn., Nat. Inst. Trial Advocacy. Roman Catholic. Home: 322 North Ave Highwood IL 60040 Office: Tyrrell & Flynn 200 W Madison St Suite 2020 Chicago IL 60606

OBERBECK, DAVID RONALD, architect; b. Wisconsin Rapids, Wis., June 17, 1960; s. Ronald Richard and Beverly Bernice (Verjinsky) O. BArch and Environ. Design, U. Minn., 1984. Staff architect Becher-Hoppe, Wausau, Wis., 1984—. Mem. AIA (assoc.). Democrat. Lutheran. Avocations: skiing, photography, furniture design, golf, travel. Home: 111 Eldred #2 Wausau WI 54401 Office: Becher-Hoppe 330 4th St Wausau WI 54401

OBERBRECKLING, PAUL JEROME, dentist; b. Milw., Sept. 21, 1934; s. Peter Edward and Viola (Kummer) O.; m. Nancy Spangler (dec.); children: John Peter, Sara Louise, Margaret Ann, Robert James. Student, Loyola U., Los Angeles, 1953-54; DDS, Marquette U., 1960. Gen. practice dentistry Bayside, Wis., 1960-80, Mequon, Wis., 1980—; assoc. prof. fixed prosthodontics Marquette U. Sch. Dentistry, Milw., 1962-71. Author, developer: The Dental Record. Pres. Marquette U. Sch. Dentistry Alumni Bd.; bd. dirs. Dominican High Sch., Milw. Served to capt. U.S. Army, 1960-63. Mem. ADA (del.), Wis. Dental Assn. (past holder numerous offices, now sec.), Greater Milw. Dental Assn. (past bd. dirs., mem. ethics and artibration coms., del. to Wis. State Dental Assn.), Chgo. Dental Soc., Ozaukee County Dental Soc., Wis. Gnathol. Soc., Am. Acad. Orthodontics for Gen. Practitioner, Omicron Kappa Upsilon, Alpha Sigma Nu, Delta Sigma Delta. Clubs: Ozaukee (Wis.) Country, Heiliger Huegel Ski (bd. dirs. 1972-75, treas. 1975). Office: 10134 N Port Washington Rd Mequon WI 53092

OBERFRANC, CARL FRANK, trade show promotion manager; b. Oak Park, Ill., Feb. 2, 1956; s. Joseph Carl and Helen (Kaylor) O.; m. Kathleen Ann Maslanka, Aug. 4, 1984. BJ, U. Mo., 1978. Dist. sales mgr. Vance Pub. Corp., Chgo., 1978-80, 82-83, Portland, Oreg., 1980-82; promotion mgr. Vance Pub. Corp., Lincolnshire, Ill., 1983—. Office: Vance Pub Corp 400 Knightsbridge Pkwy Lincolnshire IL 60069

OBERG, LARRY REYNOLD, librarian; b. Midvale, Idaho; s. Gustav Wilhelm and Esther Marie (Watkins) O.; m. Marilyn Ann Gow, Jan. 1, 1964 (div. 1985); 1 child, Marc Aurelien. AB in Anthropology, U. Calif., Berkeley, 1977, MLS, 1978. Reference librarian Stanford (Calif.) U., 1979-80, U. Calif., Berkeley, 1981-82; dir. library Lewis-Clark State Coll., Lewiston, Idaho, 1984-86, Albion (Mich.) Coll., 1986—. Author Human Services in Postrevolutionary Cuba, 1985 (named a Choice Outstanding Acad. Book, Choice Editors 1984-85). Mem. Am. Library Assn., Mich. Library Assn., Phi Beta Kappa. Democrat. Home: 609 S Superior St Albion MI 49224 Office: Albion Coll Library Albion MI 49224

OBERLANDER, ORIN JAY, dentist; b. Chgo., Sept. 26, 1959; s. David and Evelyn (Hans) O. BA in Chem., U. Ill., 1980; BS in Dentistry, U. Ill., Chgo., 1982, DDS, 1984. Dentist Provident Hosp., chgo., 1984-85, The Dental Team, Chgo., 1984—. Mem. ADA, Chgo. Dental Soc., Ill. Dental Soc. Avocations: travel, running, music, playing violin and piano.

OBERLANDER, R. ALLAN, architect; b. Sioux Falls, S.D., July 19, 1953; s. Richard Earl and Joann L. (Helder) O.; m. Thea Helene Lubbers, Aug. 26, 1978. Student S.D. State U., 1971-73; B.A. with distinction in Architecture, Iowa State U., 1975, M.Architecture, 1978. Registered architect, Iowa. With design and drafting dept. Foss Engelstad Heil Co., Sioux City, Iowa, 1976-77; teaching asst. dept. architecture Iowa State U., Ames, 1977; designer, project architect Bussard Dikis Assocs., Des Moines, 1979-81; assoc., designer, project architect, 1981-85, assoc., designer, project architect, personnel dir., 1985-87, v.p., 1987—; com. chmn. sand castle competition for design profls., 1982, 83. Com. chmn. Community Rewards recognition pub. design contbns., Des Moines, 1981; mem. Des Moines Leadership Inst., 1983-84; bd. govs., 1984-85, 86-88; bd. govs. Des Moines Leadership Alumni, 1985-87; chmn. fundraising com. Des Moines Architecture Guide, 1986-87. Recipient Premium of Acad. Excellence award Iowa State U., 1977, 78; Leo A. Daly award Iowa State U., 1977. Mem. AIA, Des Moines Architects Council (pres. 1982, exec. bd. 1980-83), Des Moines C. of C. (exec. call program 1984—). Democrat. Roman Catholic. Clubs: Des Moines, Oakmoor. Home: 5010 Country Club Blvd Des Moines IA 50312 Office: Bussard Dikis Assocs 300 Homestead Bldg 303 Lucust St Des Moines IA 50309

OBERMAN, MOISHE DAVID, magazine publisher; b. Springfield, Ill., Mar. 3, 1914; s. Harry and Ida (Guralnik) O.; student St. Louis Coll. Pharmacy, 1931-33; m. Bobbye Friedman, Oct. 8, 1939; children—Michael Alan, Martin Jay, M.H. William, Marjorie Ann. Scrap metals broker, Springfield, 1937-41; founder Scrap Age Mag., 1944, Mill Trade Jour., 1963, Waste Age Mag., 1969, Encyclopedia of Scrap Recycling, 1976; pres., editor, pub. 3 Sons Pub. Co., Niles, Ill., 1944; pres. Emde Realty Devel. Corp., Springfield, 1957-63; exec. sec. Midwest Scrap Dealers Assn., 1941—; treas. North Shore Investments, Highland Park, Ill., 1968; exec. dir. Springfield Area Devel. and Tourist Commn., 1963-68; mem. Ill. Inst. Environ. Quality Solid Waste Task Force Com., 1971. Pres. Ill. Assn. Jewish Centers, 1934-40; editor congregation publs., treas. North Suburban Synagogue Beth El. Mem. War Production Bd., 1942-44. Recipient Meritorious Service award for outstanding contbns. to iron and steel industry St. Louis Steel Assn., 1961. Mem. Nat. Solid Waste Mgmt. Assn., Am. Pub. Works Assn. (solid waste mgmt. task force), Execs. Inc. (pres. 1963-67), Am. Soc. Assn. Execs., Internat. Platform Assn., Nat. Press Club, Springfield Jr. C. of C. (pres. 1946-47), Springfield Assn. Execs., Springfield Assn. Commerce and Industry. Jewish. Club: B'nai B'rith (sec. 1935-39, pres. 1942-45). Home: 857 Stonegate Dr Highland Park IL 60035 Office: 3605 Woodhead Dr Northbrook IL 60062

OBERMEIER, BRIAN ALAN, accountant; b. Omaha, Aug. 13, 1952; s. Clayton Godfrey and Betty (Phelps) O. BS in Acctg., Mankato (Minn.) State U., 1974. Mgr. Touche Ross & Co., St. Paul, 1974-86; v.p. fin. HMU Inc., Edina, Minn., 1986—; bd. dirs. Gallery Tower, St. Paul. Mem. Am. Soc. CPA's, Minn. Soc. CPA's. Republican. Methodist. Club: St. Paul Athletic. Avocations: handball, golf, reading. Home: 26 W 10th St #1909 Saint Paul MN 55102

OBERMEIER, KLAUS KARL, artificial intelligence scientist, researcher; b. Landshut, Fed. Republic of Germany, Feb. 5, 1954; came to U.S., 1976; s. Michael and Veronica (Pedrotti) O. Student, U. Nuernberg, Fed. Republic Germany, 1975-76; grad., U. Regensburg, Fed. Republic Germany, 1980; MA in Linguistics, Ohio State U., 1980, PhD in Linguistics, 1984. Instr. Ohio State U., Columbus, 1978-84; projects manager Battelle Meml. Inst. Columbus Labs, Columbus, 1983—. Contbr. articles to profl. jours. U. Kans. scholar, 1976-78. Mem. Am. Soc. Info. Sci., Assn. Computational Linguistics, Am. Assn. ARtificial Intelligence, Assn. Computing Machinery. Home: 179 Nottingham Rd Columbus OH 43214 Office: Battelle Meml Inst Columbus Labs 505 King Ave Columbus OH 43201

OBERMEYER, DAVID DOUGLAS, film technician; b. N.Y.C., Nov. 7, 1955; s. Ernest David and Phyllis (Horton) O. BS, Northwestern U., 1978, MFA, 1980. Film editor Treeflower Films, Chgo., 1980-81; freelance film technician Chgo., 1980-86, Chgo. Audio Works, 1984-86. Mem. Internat. Alliance Theatrical Stage Employees and Moving Picture Machine Operators of U.S. and Can. (motion picture studio mechanics div.). Democrat. Episcopalian. Office: Chicago Audio Works 1005 W Webster Chicago IL 60614

OBERRATH, KAREN LYNN, college administrator; b. Mansfield, Ohio, Mar. 10, 1954; d. Charles W. and Dorothy E. (Juergens) O. B. degree, Wittenberg U., 1976; M. degree, Ohio State U., 1979. Dir. residence hall Wittenberg U., Springfield, Ohio, 1976-77; sorority head resident Ohio State U., Columbus, 1977-78, asst. to assoc. athletic dir., 1978-79; area coordinator U. Detroit, 1979-80; asst. dir. acad. studies, Ohio State U.-Mansfield, 1980—; cons. Leadership Unltd., Mansfield C. of C., 1985-86; Discovery Sch., Mansfield, 1984, Richland County Found., Mansfield, 1983—. Contbr. articles to newsletters. Bd. dirs. YWCA, Mansfield, 1983—, grant writer, 1984—; vocat. asst. Altrusa, Mansfield, 1984-85. Mem. Nat. Assn. Women Deans (adminstr. counselors 1982-84, resolutions presenter), Ohio Assn. Women Deans (adminstr. counselors, co-chmn. program 1984-86), Am. Coll. Personnel Assn., Ohio Assn. Coll. Personnel, AAUW (program planner, legis. chmn.). Republican. Lutheran. Avocations: sports; classical piano and guitar; camping; outdoor landscaping. Home: 901 Brookfield Dr Apt 1 Mansfield OH 44907 Office: Ohio State U 680 University Dr Mansfield OH 44906

OBERSTAR, JAMES L., congressman; b. Chisholm, Minn., Sept. 10, 1934; s. Louis and Mary (Grillo) O.; m. Jo Garlick, Oct. 12, 1963; children: Thomas Edward, Katherine Noelle, Anne-Therese, Monica Rose. B.A. summa cum laude, St. Thomas Coll., 1956; postgrad. in French, Laval U., Que., Can.; M.S. in Govt. (scholar), Coll. Europe, Bruges, Belgium, 1957; postgrad. in govt, Georgetown U. Adminstrv. asst. to Congressman John A. Blatnik, 1963-74; adminstr. Pub. Works Com., U.S. Ho. of Reps., 1971-74; mem. 94th-100th Congresses from 8th Minn. Dist., 1975—. Mem. Am. Polit. Sci. Assn. Office: US House of Representatives 2351 Rayburn House Office Bldg Washington DC 20515 *

OBERT, JANE ANN, accountant; b. Lincoln, Nebr., Nov. 19, 1953; d. Clyde William and Ruth Ann (Jelinek) Whyman; m. Nils Roger Ranum, July 3, 1973 (div. 1983); m. Ivan Lee Obert, May 12, 1984; children: Kimberly Ann, Eric Lee. BS, Mo. So. State Coll., 1976. CPA, Mo. Staff acct. Cusack Mense Brown, Joplin, Mo., 1976-79, supr., 1979-81; fin. cons. Larry Ancell & Assocs., Joplin, 1981—; pvt. practice CPA Joplin, 1982—; instr. Mo. So. State Coll., 1977. Treas. Royal Heights United Meth. Ch., Joplin, 1983—, Sun. sch. tchr., choir mem. Mem. Am. Inst. CPA's, Mo. Soc. CPA's (career chmn. SW chpt. 1980-81), Nat. Assn. Accts. (bd. dirs. Joplin Tri-State chpt. 1980), Phi Theta Kappa. Republican. Club: Neo Gem and Minerals (Miami, Okla.). Avocations: camping, sewing, gems and minerals. Home and Office: 3702 College View Dr Joplin MO 64801

OBETZ, SAMUEL WENDELL, child and adolescent psychiatrist; b. Allentown, Pa., Feb. 21, 1930; s. Samuel and Hazel Elizabeth (Meckenstock) O.; m. Elizabeth Jane Winne, Aug. 22, 1958; children: Timothy, Julia, Christopher. BS, Northwestern U., 1951, MS in Physics, 1952; MS, U. Chgo., 1954; MD, U. Ill., Chgo., 1962. Diplomate Am. Bd. Psychiatry, Am. Bd. Child and Adolescent Psychiatry. Intern Detroit Receiving Hosp., 1962-63; resident in psychiatry Mayo Clinic, Rochester, Minn., 1964-68, cons. in child and adolescent psychiatry, 1968—, asst. prof. med. sch., 1975—; psychiat. cons. Gerard Schs., Austin, Minn., 1969-85, St. Olaf Coll., Northfield, Minn., 1972—. Contbr. articles to profl. jours. Served to lt. (j.g.) USNR, 1955-58. Mem. AMA, Am Psychiat. Assn., Am. Acad. Child Psychiatry. Avocations: classical music, piano. Home: 2015 Lenwood Ave SW Rochester MN 55902 Office: Mayo Clinic 200 1st St SW Rochester MN 55905

OBEY, DAVID ROSS, congressman; b. Okmulgee, Okla., Oct. 3, 1938; s. Orville John and Mary Jane (Chellis) O.; m. Joan Therese Lepinski, June 9, 1962; children: Craig David, Douglas David. B.S. in Polit. Sci, U. Wis., 1960, M.A., 1962. Mem. Wis. Gen. Assembly from Marathon County, 1963-69, asst. minority leader, 1967-69; mem. 91st-100th Congresses 7th Dist. Wis., 1969—; mem. adminstrv. com. Wis. Dem. Com., 1960-62. Named Edn. Legislator of Year rural div. N.E.A., 1968; recipient Legislative Leadership award Eagelton Inst. Politics, 1964; award of merit Nat. Council Sr. Citizens, 1976; citation for legis. statesmanship Council Exceptional Children, 1976. Office: US House of Representatives 2217 Rayburn House Office Bldg Washington DC 20515 *

OBLINGER, JOSEPHINE KNEIDL HARRINGTON (MRS. WALTER L. OBLINGER), state legislator; b. Chgo., Feb. 14, 1913; d. Thomas William and Margaret (Kneidl) Harrington; B.S., U. Ill., 1933; J.D., U. Detroit, 1968; L.H.D., Sioux Empire Coll., 1966; m. Walter L. Oblinger, Apr. 27, 1940; 1 son, Carl D. Tchr. Lanphier High Sch., Springfield, Ill., 1951-62; clk. Sangamon County, assessor Capital Twp., Springfield, 1962-69; asst. dir. Ill. Dept. Registration and Edn., Springfield, 1970—; exec. dir. Gov.'s Com. on Voluntary Action, 1970-73; asst. to pres. Lincoln Land Community Coll., 1973-77; dir. Ill. Dept. on Aging, 1977-78; mem. Ill. Ho. Reps., 1978-85; dir. Gov.'s Office Sr. Involvement, 1985—. Sec. Springfield and Sangamon County Community Action, 1965-70 pres., 1970-74; mem. finance com. Child and Family Service, Springfield, 1965-70; mem. Nat. Com. for Day Care of Children, 1960—; pres. Springfield Fedn. Tchrs. AFL-CIO, 1957-59, Ill. Fedn. Tchrs. AFL-CIO, 1959-63; mem. adv. com. to Gov.'s ACTION Office; mem. Planning Consortium for Services to Children in Ill., pres., 1978-79; chmn. mothers' march Sangamon County March of Dimes, 1980; bd. dirs., sec. Villa Vianney Retirement Ctr., officer, Republican Women's Luncheon Club, 1959, pres., 1963-67; chmn. Sangamon County Rep. com., 1965—; past pres. Ill. Fedn. Rep. Women. Del. to White House Conf. on Children, 1960; chairperson Com. Women's Affairs White House Conf. Aging, 1981. Bd. dirs., pres. Sangamon-Menard County Council on Alcoholism and Drugs, Nat. Center Vol. Action; mem. bd. Sangamon County Salvation Army, Ret. Sr. Vol. Program. Mem. Ill. Assn. County Clks. and Recorders (past pres.), Am. Bus. Women's Assn., Am., Ill., Sangamon County bar assns., Am. Assn. Vol. Services Coordinators (dir., chmn. pub. policy com.), NAACP (exec. bd.), Urban League, Am. Arbitration Assn., U. Ill. Alumni Assn., Nat. Assn. Recorders and Clks., Sangamon County Hist. Soc., Ill. Council Continuing Edn. (exec. com.), P.E.O., Kappa Delta Pi, Sigma Delta Pi, Delta Delta Delta. Clubs: Springfield Women's; Altrusa (pres. 1968-70) (Springfield). Home: RR 1 Williamsville IL 62693 Office: Governor's Office of Senior Involvement Room 1043 Stratton Bldg Springfield IL 62706

O'BRIEN, ARTHUR TERRANCE, small business owner, medical consultant; b. Kansas City, Mo., Apr. 26, 1953; s. Arthur Thomas and Iona MAe (Burton) O'B.; m. Elizabeth Ruth O'Connell, May 26, 1979; 1 child, Nina Michelle. BA, Kansas City Community Coll., 1982. Owner Big Bear Prodns., Kansas City, 1979—; cons. Drs. McCoy/Chandler, Kansas City, 1985—; ctr. dir. Alpha Plazma, Kansas City. Served with USN, 1971-79. Mem. Internat. Theatrical Agys. Assn. Republican. Roman Catholic. Lodge: Eagles. Home and Office: 2511 N 86th St Kansas City KS 66109-2066

O'BRIEN, BERNARD (BARRY) C., utility company executive; b. Pitts., May 12, 1927; s. Bernard Cornelius and Lillian (McBride) O'B.; m. Mary Lou Kelsch, Sept. 25, 1954; children: Michael, Nora. Student, MIT, 1947-48; B.S. in Commerce, Northwestern U., 1951. C.P.A. Acct. Arthur Andersen & Co., Chgo., 1951-54; acctg. supr. Ohio Valley Electric Co., Piketon, Ohio, 1954-60; with Iowa-Ill. Gas & Electric Co., Davenport, Iowa, 1960—; v.p., controller Iowa-Ill. Gas & Electric Co., 1975-82, v.p. adminstrn., 1982-84, exec. v.p., 1984, chmn., pres., 1984—; dir. Citizen's Fed. Savs. & Loan, Davenport. Pres. Jr. Achievement, Davenport, 1967-68; bd. dirs. Quad-City Devel. Group, Rock Island, Ill., 1984—. Mem. Am. Inst. C.P.A.s, Davenport C. of C. (pres. 1977-78). Clubs: Davenport (pres. 1982-83), Davenport Country (treas. 1978-79), Davenport Outing. Avocations: tennis; jogging; golf; cross-country skiing. Home: 14 Oakbrook Pl Bettendorf IA 52722 Office: Iowa-Ill Gas & Electric Co 206 E 2nd St Davenport IA 52801 *

O'BRIEN, BERNARD RAYMOND, psychiatrist; b. Lake City, Iowa, Mar. 6, 1929; s. Lawson D. and Nellie (Graham) O'B.; m. Harriet Evelyn Armstrong, nov. 4, 1948; children: Dennis J., Sheila K., Steven E., Pamela J. BA, Drake U., 1952; MA, U. Iowa, 1954. Lic. specialist clinical social worker, Kans. Supr. Dept. Social Welfare, Des Moines, Iowa, 1954-57; dir. Cath. Family Services, Sioux City, Iowa, 1957-59, Warren, Pa., 1959-64, Kansas City, Kans., 1964-78; pvt. practice psychotherapist Fairway, Kans., 1978—; cons. Buffalo (N.Y.) Pub. Housing, 1963; bd. dirs. various mental health groups; instr. grad. sch. U. Kans. Free-lance writer; also quoted in Wall Street Jour. Organizer Hotline for Youth. Served as cpl. USMC, 1946-48. Recipient award for Achievement, Family Services, 1978. Mem. Irish Am. Cultural Assn. (nat. bd dirs.). Lodge: Kiwanis (local bd. dirs.). Office: Counseling and Human Relations 4210 Johnson Dr Fairway KS 66205

O'BRIEN, CAROL JEAN, park district superintendent; b. Chgo., June 18, 1939; d. Charles August and Frances Carolyn (Reese) Boeck; m. Thomas Joseph McEvoy, Oct. 18, 1958 (div. Mar. 1982); 1 child, Corrine Marie McEvoy; John Patrick O'Brien, July 18, 1985. Grad. high sch., Maywood, Ill., 1957. Mfrs. rep. Midwest Cen., Chgo., 1969-71; supt. recreation Wood Dale (Ill.) Park Dist., 1977—. Mem. Nat. Parks and Recreation Assn., Suburban Parks and Recreation Assn. (chairperson 1983-85, sec. 1985-86, spl. projects com. 1986—), Ill. Parks and Recreation Assn. Lutheran. Avocations: racquetball, knitting, crocheting, reading, camping. Home: 21W722 Thorndale Medinah IL 60157 Office: Wood Dale Park Dist 533 N Wood Dale Rd Wood Dale IL 60191

O'BRIEN, CHARLES RICHARD, counselor, educator, student personnel administrator; b. Boston, Nov. 10, 1934; s. Charles Richard and Dorothy Margaret (DeBesse) O'B. B.A., St. John's Coll., 1956; M.S., N.D. State U., 1968; Ed.D., U. Wyo., 1972. Instr., dir. guidance Cardinal Muench Sch., Fargo, N.D., 1966-69; asst. prof. edn. N.D. State U., Fargo, 1969-73; vis. instr. Fitchburg State Coll., Mass., 1973-74; assoc. prof. counselor edn. and coll. student personnel Western Ill. U., Macomb, 1974-82, dir. Counseling Ctr., 1978—, dir. Univ. Advising Ctr., 1984—; cons. Ill. Office Edn., N.D. Office Employment Security, Newman Found. Mem. editorial bd. Counseling and Values, Wyo. Personnel and Guidance Jour. Contbr. articles to profl. jours., chpts. to books. Served with USNR, 1962-72. Recipient Cert. of Recognition, Ill. Guidance and Personnel Assn., 1976, Presdl. Merit award Western Ill. U., 1978, Disting. Service award, 1986. Mem. Am. Psychol. Assn., Am. Coll. Personnel Assn., Am. Mental Health Counselors Assn. Assn., Nat. Acad. Advising. Assn., Nat. Assn. Student Personnel Adminstrs.

O'BRIEN, DONALD EUGENE, dist. judge; b. Marcus, Iowa, Sept. 30, 1923; s. Michael John and Myrtle A. (Toomey) O'B.; m. Ruth Mahon, Apr. 15, 1950; children: Teresa, Brien, John, Shuivaun. LL.B., Creighton U., 1948. Bar: Iowa bar 1948, U.S. Supreme Ct. bar 1963. Asst. city atty. Sioux City, Iowa, 1949-53; county atty. Woodbury County, Iowa, 1955-58; mcple. judge Sioux City, Iowa, 1959-60; U.S. atty. No. Iowa, 1961-67; individual practice law Sioux City, 1967-78, U.S. Dist. judge, 1978—. Served with USAAF, 1943-45. Decorated D.F.C., air medals. Mem. Woodbury County Bar Assn., Iowa State Bar Assn. Roman Catholic. Office: US Dist Court PO Box 267 Sioux City IA 51101 *

O'BRIEN, ELMER JOHN, educator, librarian; b. Kemmerer, Wyo., Apr. 8, 1932; s. Ernest and Emily Catherine (Reinhart) O'B.; m. Betty Alice Peterson, July 2, 1966. A.B., Birmingham So. Coll., 1954; Th.M., Iliff Sch. Theology, 1957; M.A., U. Denver, 1961. Ordained to ministry Methodist Ch., 1957; pastor Meth. Ch., Pagosa Springs, Colo., 1957-60; circulation-reference librarian Boston U. Sch. Theology, Boston, 1961-65; asst. librarian Garrett-Evang. Theol. Sem., Evanston, Ill., 1965-69; librarian, prof. United Theol. Sem., Dayton, Ohio, 1969—; Abstractor Am. Bibliog. Center, 1969-73; chmn. div. exec. com. Dayton-Miami Valley Consortium Library, 1983-84. Author: Bibliography of Festschriften in Religion Published Since 1960, 1972, Religion Index Two: Festschriften, 1960-1969. Assn. Theol. Schs. in U.S. and Can. library staff devel. grantee, 1976-77, United Meth. Ch. Bd. Higher Edn. and Ministry research grantee, 1984-85. Mem. ALA, Am. Theol. Library Assn. (head bur. personnel and placement 1969-73, dir. 1973-76, v.p. 1977-78, pres. 1978-79), Delta Sigma Phi, Omicron Delta Kappa, Eta Sigma Phi, Kappa Phi Kappa. Club: Torch Internat. (v.p. Dayton club 1981-82, pres. 1982-83). Home: 7818 Lockport Blvd Centerville OH 45459

O'BRIEN, JEANNE PEW, nurse, paramedic educator; b. LeMars, Iowa, July 31, 1951; s. William George and Elaine Margaret (Holzman) P.; m. Michael Ashton O'B., May 4, 1974 (div. Jan 1980); children: Erin, Alex. Grad., St. Joseph Sch. Nursing, Omaha, 1974. RN. Head nurse intensive care unit St. Joseph Hosp., Omaha, 1976-79; paramedic tnr. coordinator Creighton U., Omaha, 1979-86; paramedic coordinator Omaha Fire Div., 1986—; lectr. Nat. Assn. Emergency Med. Technicians, Boulder, Mont., 1982—; adv. editor Aspen Pub. Co., Rockville, Md., 1985—. Author: Prehospital Trauma Life Support, 1986, Paramedic Review Manual, 1986. Mem. Nat. Assn. EMT's (instr. soc.; instr. of yr. 1983, instr.-coordinator of yr. 1984, pres.'s leadership award 1984). Democrat. Roman Catholic. Avocations: plants, photography, sports. Home: 2302 Elm St Omaha NE 68108

O'BRIEN, JOHN EDWARD, market executive; b. St. Louis, May 30, 1929; s. Edward Joseph and Norma Mary (Yaw) O'B.; m. Marilyn Jean, Aug. 15, 1953; children—Mary Pat, Cathryn Jean, Lynn Marie. A.B., N. Notre Dame, 1952. Assoc. advt. mgr. paper div. Procter & Gamble, 1954-67; v.p., dir. Campbell-Muthun Advt. Agy., Chgo., 1967-72; v.p. mktg., dir. Calgon Consumer Products, Pitts., 1972-77; pres. NoNonsense Fashions, Inc., Greensboro, N.C., 1977-82, Rexall Corp., St. Louis, 1982-84; exec. v.p. J.H. Filbert Co., Balt.; pres., owner Visu-Com, Balt. Served with USNR, 1952-54. Republican. Roman Catholic.

O'BRIEN, LAWRENCE JAMES, engineering sales company executive; b. N.Y.C., Apr. 5, 1940; memLawrence Patrick and Marion (Spellman) O'B.; m. Elizabeth Ann Lamphear, Feb. 23, 1963; children: Michael J., Kellianne, Elizabeth Ann. BEE, Manhattan Coll., 1961; MEE, Ohio State U., 1967. Registerd profl engr., Mass. Elec. engr. IBM Corp., Poughkeepsie, N.Y., 1961-62; staff engr. Raytheon Co., Lexington, Mass., 1967-72; mgmt. dir. Ohio Bd. Regents, Columbus, 1972-80; pres. M.J. Fein & Co. Mid-Am., Inc., Columbus, 1985—, also bd. dirs. Served to 1st lt. USAF, 1961-64. Mem. IEEE, Phi Alpha Kappa. Republican. Roman Catholic. Office: MJ Fein & Co MidAm Inc 2505 Coventry Rd Columbus OH 43221

O'BRIEN, PATRICK JOSEPH, utilities company executive; b. Chgo., July 15, 1941; s. Pierce Bernard and Winifred M. (Brogan) O'B.; m. Linda Louise Logston, Aug. 13, 1977; children: Heather Lin, Kathleen Anne. BS, No. Ill. U., 1963. CPA. Sr. auditor Price Waterhouse & Co., Chgo., 1963-70; v.p. Utilities, Inc., Northbrook, Ill., 1970. Commr. Village Sports League, Lincolnshire, Ill., 1986. Served as pvt. USAFR, 1964-70. Mem. Am. Inst. CPA's, Nat. Assn. Water Cos. (bd. dirs. 1986-87), Ill. Soc. CPA's. Republican. Roman Catholic. Office: Utilities Inc 2335 Sanders Rd Northbrook IL 60062

O'BRIEN, RICHARD STEPHEN, tool company executive; b. Mpls., May 9, 1936; s. Elwood John and Marie (Dunlevy) O'B.; m. Carolyn Onsrud, Aug. 23, 1959 (div. Dec. 1980); children: Shawn, Mark, Kevin, Matthew, Shannon; m. Joan Madden, May 1, 1982; i child, Brendan. BS in Econs., U. Minn., 1958; cert. Owner Pres. Mgmt. Program, Harvard U., 1986. Commd. ensign USN, 1958, advanced through grades to lt. jr. grade, 1960, resigned, 1961; account mgr. IBM Corp., Mpls., 1961-65; v.p. Sci. Computer, Mpls., 1966-70, Pemtom, Mpls., 1970-72; pres. Onsrud Cutter, Inc., Libertyville, Ill., 1973—; also bd. dirs. Onsrud Cutter, Inc., 1972—; bd. dirs. Sci. Computer, MIMA-Mgmt. Assn., Chgo., Morton Mfg. Co., Libertyville. Contbr. articles on wood and wood products to profl. jours. Mem. Am. Mktg. Assn., U. Minn. Alumni Assn.. Lake County C. of C. (bd. dirs. 1978-81). Republican. Roman Catholic. Club: Harvard Bus. of Chgo. Avocations:

skiing, hunting, fishing, racquetball. Office: Onsrud Cutter Inc 800 Liberty Dr Libertyville IL 60048

O'BRIEN, THOMAS FRANCIS, mechanical engineer, chemist; b. Chgo., Sept. 17, 1960; s. Donald Francis and Margaret Mary (Holden) O'B. BSME, BS in Chemistry, Marquette U., 1983. Process engr. Motorola Inc., Schaumburg, Ill., 1984-85, mech. engr., chemist, 1985—. Avocations: flying, tennis, dancing. Home: 1031 Emerald Dr Schaumburg IL 60273 Office: Motorola Inc 1301 E Algonquin Rd Schaumburg IL 60196

O'BRIEN, WILLIAM P., real estate consultant; b. Dallas, Dec. 20, 1946; s. Robert David O'Brien and Frances (Buster) Gould. B.Arch., U. Tex.-Arlington, 1970; M.Arch., U. Pa., 1977, M. in City Planning, 1977. Dir. devel. Good Fin. Corp., Dallas, 1971-73; real estate cons., Dallas, 1974-75; sr. project mgr. Trammel Crow Co., Chgo., 1977-81; v.p., regional mgr. Coldwell Banker, Chgo., 1981-85; pres. Rescorp Devel. Co., Chgo., 1985-86; real estate cons., Chgo., 1987—. Mem. Nat. Assn. Indsl. and Office Parks, Am. Planning Assn., Nat. Realty Com., Urban Land Inst., Alpha Rho Chi (Nat. Gold medal 1970).

O'BRYANT, MICHAEL ALFRED, building product company executive; b. Buchanan, Mich., Sept. 5, 1939; s. Alfred Phelix and Lucille Nancy (Ritter) O'B.; m. Helen Rose Harroff, Nov. 5, 1960; children: Michelle R., Timothy M. Student, Mich. State U., 1964, Purdue U., 1966. Salesman Am. United Life, Benton Harbor, Mich., 1962-68; sales mgr. Vanply Ins., Elkhart, Ind., 1968-73; nat. sales mgr. Holiday Rambler Corp., Waukesha, Ind., 1973-76; v.p. div., gen. mgr. Holiday Rambler Corp., Woodland, Calif., 1976-83; br. gen. mgr. Alumax Bldg. Products, Bristol, Ind., 1983—. Lodges: KC (bd. dirs. Elkhart chpt. 1987), Moose. Home: 51760 Winding Waters Ln Elkhart IN 46514

OBST, NORMAN PHILIP, economics educator; b. Bklyn., May 25, 1944; s. Joseph J. and Pearl L. (Newmark) O.; m. Barbara E. Brudevold, Dec. 23, 1970; children: Lindora, Jannise, Laara, Benjamin. BA, SUNY, Binghamton, 1965; MS, Purdue U., 1967, PhD, 1970. Acting asst. prof. U. Wash., Seattle, 1969-70, asst. prof., 1970-73; asst. prof. Mich. State U., East Lansing, 1973-77, assoc. prof. econs., 1977—. Contbr. articles to profl. jours. Mem. Planning Commn. Williamstown Township, Mich., 1975—, vice chmn. 1985—. Mem. Am. Econ. Assn., Midwest Econ. Soc. Avocations: chess, table tennis, fin. markets. Office: Mich State U Marshall Hall Econ Dept East Lansing MI 48824-1038

OBY, KAREN JEAN, nutritionist; b. Grafton, N.D., July 17, 1946; d. John Martin and Helen Sylvia (Gilbertson) O.; m. Thomas Jeffrey Dahle, June 27, 1981; 1 child, Aaron. BS, U. N.D., 1968; MPH, U. Calif., Berkeley, 1970. Registered dietitian; lic. to practice in N.D. Pub. health nutritionist/dietitian U. Ariz., Tucson, 1970-71; pub. health nutritionist Project HOPE, Natal, Brazil, 1972; instr. Western Mich. U., Kalamazoo, 1973-76, U. N.D., Grand Forks, 1976-79; women, infants and children nutrition coordinator N.D. State Dept. Health, Bismarck, 1979—. Health profl. advisor March of Dimes, Bismarck, 1985-87. Mem. Am. Dietetic Assn., Nat. Assn. Women, Infants and Children Dirs. (nutrition standards com. 1986-87), N.D. Dietetic Assn. (treas. 1979-80), N.D. Nutrition Council, Bismarck-MANDAN Nutrition Council (pres. 1984-85), Bismarck/MANDAN Dietetic Assn. (v.p. 1986-87), Prairie Textile Arts Guild (pres. 1986-87). Democrat. Lutheran. Avocations: needlework, reading. Home: 920 Couch St Bismarck ND 58501 Office: ND State Dept Health Capitol Bldg Jud Wing Bismarck ND 58505

OCHBERG, FRANK MARTIN, clinician-executive; b. N.Y.C., Feb. 7, 1940; s. Gerald Frank and Belle (Solomon) O.; m. Lynn Jeffie Wescott, July 1, 1962; children: Billie Jennifer, Jesse Frank, Abigail Kathryn. A.B., Harvard U., 1961; M.D., Johns Hopkins U., 1965; postgrad. in psychiatry, Stanford U., 1966-69. Diplomate: Am. Bd. Psychiatry and Neurology. Intern USPHS Hosp., San Francisco, 1965-66; resident in psychiatry Stanford U. Med. Center, 1966-69; with NIMH, 1969-79, dir. div. mental health service programs, 1973-76; dir. Mich. Dept. Mental Health, 1979-81; pres. Victimization Research and Tng. Inst., 1981—; Med. dir. St. Lawrence Mental Health Center, Lansing, 1981-84; med. dir. Dimondale Stress Reduction Ctr., 1983-85; clin. prof. psychiatry and behavioral medicine Mich. State U., East Lansing, 1979—; psychiat. adviser FBI, 1977—, U.S. Secret Service, 1978—. Co-editor: Violence and the Struggle for Existence, 1970, The Victim of Terrorism, 1982. Fellow Am. Psychiat. Assn. (past chmn. council on nat. affairs); mem. Assn. Research Nervous and Mental Diseases (past v.p.). Address: 4211 Okemos Rd Suite 6 Okemos MI 48864

OCHOA, ANNA SULTANOFF, social studies educator; b. Windsor, Ont., Can., Oct. 5, 1933; came to U.S., 1953; d. David and Vera (Makaroff) Sultanoff. BS, Wayne State U., 1955; MA, U. Mich., 1963; PhD, U. Wash., 1970. Cert. secondary social studies educator, Mich., Calif. Elem. tchr. Bendle Schs., Flint, Mich., 1955-57; secondary tchr., dept. chmn. Grand Blanc (Mich.) Schs., 1957-67; elem. tchr. Fremont (Calif.) Unified Schs., 1967-68; project asst. Tri-Univ. Project, Seattle, 1968-70; asst. prof., asst. dept. chmn. Fla. State U., Tallahassee, 1971-76; assoc. prof. social studies Ind. U., Bloomington, 1976—; cons. Global Perspectives in Edn., 1980-83, Fgn. Policy Assn., 1984—, Indpls. Children's Mus., 1984-86; chmn. adv. bd. social studies panel Nat. Assessment for Edn. Progress, 1980-83. Author: Social Studies for a Democracy, 1987; also author 4th grade text, 1978; contbr. articles to profl. jour. Grantee NSF, 1981-82, U.S. Dept. Edn., 1983-86, 85-86, Lilly Endowment, 1987—. Mem. Nat. Council for Social Studies (pres.), Ind. Council Social Studies. Democrat. Avocations: photography, theatre, reading, walking. Office: Ind U Sch Edn 3d and Jordan Bloomington IN 47405

OCHS, HERMAN, wholesale paper merchant; b. Karlsruhe, Baden, Fed. Republic of Germany, June 27, 1913; came to U.S., 1934; s. Julius and Therese (Nachmann) O.; m. Ruth A. Gershuny, Oct. 29, 1938; children: Kathy, Leslie. B, Heidelberg (Fed. Republic Germany) U., 1933. Chmn. bd. dirs. Ochs Paper Co., Inc., Indpls., 1977—. Office: Ochs Paper Co Inc 1140 Division St Indianapolis IN 46221

OCHSNER, EDWARD CONNER, diagnostic radiologist; b. Indpls., Apr. 26, 1941; s. Harold Conrad and Julia Hannah (Conner) O.; m. Soili Aulikki Poutiainan, Mar. 5, 1964; children: Mark Conrad, Erik Eiro. AB, Brown U., 1962; MD, Northwestern U., 1968. Diplomate Am. Bd. Radiology. Gen. med. officer U.S. Army, Wildflecken, Fed. Republic Germany, 1969-72; resident in radiology Meth. Hosp. Ind., Indpls., 1972-75; diagnostic radiologist, sec. Hendricks County Radiology, Inc., Danville, Ind., 1976—; chief of staff Hendricks County Hosp., Danville, 1987—; v.p. med. staff Putnam County Hosp., Greencastle, Ind., 1985. Contbr. articles (with others) to profl. jours. Served as maj. U.S. Army, 1969-72. Named Intern of Yr., Evanston Hosp., 1969. Mem. AMA, Am. Roentgen Ray Soc., Radiol. Soc. N.Am., Soc. Nuclear Medicine, Am. Inst. Ultrasound in Medicine. Avocations: fitness, tennis, automobiles, music, reading. Home: 510 E Road 200 S Danville IN 46122 Office: Hendricks County Radiology Inc PO Box 337 99 Meadow Dr Danville IN 46122

OCHSNER, OTHON HENRY, II, importer, restaurant critic; b. Chgo., May 19, 1934; s. Othon Henry and Louise Catherine (Schlichenmaier) O. A.A., Chgo. City Coll., 1961. Pub. relations staff Walgreen Co., Chgo., 1961-65; sales mgr. Porsche Car Imports, Northbrook, Ill., 1966-67; nat. sales mgr. Pirelli Tire Corp., N.Y.C., 1968-73; pres., chief exec. officer Ochsner Internat., Chgo., 1974—; also bd. dirs.; pres. Swiss-U.S.A. Racing Team, Chgo., 1976—. Author: Ochsner Pocket Guide to the Finest Restaurants in the World, 1987, Ochsner Restaurant Newsletter, 1986—. Mem. Mus. Sci. and Industry Bus. Alliance, Chgo., 1984. Served with U.S. Army, 1957-59. Mem. Am. -Swiss C. of C., Chef of Cuisine Assn. Chgo. Republican. Baptist. Avocation: visiting and reviewing world class French and Swiss restaurants worldwide. Home: 5885 N Forest Glen Ave Chicago IL 60646 Office: Ochsner Internat Inc 4341 W Peterson Chicago IL 60646

O'CONNELL, EDWARD JOSEPH, III, financial executive, accountant; b. Evergreen Park, Ill., Aug. 9, 1952; s. Edward Joseph Jr. and Mary Jane O'C.; m. Mary M. Witt, May 30, 1976; children: Kelly, Edward IV, Molly, Kevin. BBA, U. Notre Dame, 1974. CPA, Ill. Mem. audit staff Coopers and Lybrand, Chgo., 1974-78, audit mgr., 1978-81; controller Union Spl. Corp., Chgo., 1981-83, v.p., treas., 1983-85, v.p., chief fin. officer, 1985—. Mem. Am. Inst. CPA's, Ill. Soc. CPA's, Fin. Execs. Inst., Am. Apparel Mfrs. Assn. (mgmt. com.), Machinery and Allied Products Inst. (fin. council II 1983—). Roman Catholic. Club: Notre Dame of Chgo. (bd. govs. 1984-86). Avocations: rugby, running, reading, golf. Home: 10420 S Lamon Ave Oak Lawn IL 60453 Office: Union Spl Corp 400 N Franklin Chicago IL 60610

O'CONNELL, JEANNE MARIE, music educator; b. Spring Valley, Wis., Mar. 4, 1948; d. Bernard Alphonsus and Isabelle Agatha (Murphy) O'C.; m. Robert Dale Hasewinkle, Sept. 12, 1980. B Music Edn., U. Wis., Eau Claire, 1970; M Music, U. Oregon, 1976. Cert. elem. tchr., Wis., cert. in comprehensive music. Tchr. elem. and jr. high music Prescott (Wis.) Pub. Schs., 1970-73; tchr. elem. music New Richmond (Wis.) Pub. Schs., 1973-78, 79-81, Internat. Sch., Frankfurt, Fed. Republic Germany, 1979; tchr. 2d grade St. Mary's Sch., New Richmond, 1983-86. Mem. choir Minn. Chorale, Mpls., 1976-78, 81, Oratorio Soc., St. Paul, 1985—; choir dir. St. Francis Cath. Ch., Ellsworth , Wis., 1972-75; mem. steering com. Wis. Music Edn. Conf., Madison, 1974-76; program dir. New Richmond Fine Arts Ctr., 1976; mem. enrichment com. United Way, New Richmond, 1984-85. Named one of Outstanding Young Women Am., 1981; named as head of an Outstanding Elem. Music Program Wis. Music Edn. Assn., 1981. Mem. St. Croix Valley Piano Tchrs. Assn. Roman Catholic. Avocations: needlecrafts, sailing, skiing, tennis. Home and Office: 960 Fairfield Rd New Richmond WI 54017

O'CONNELL, THOMAS PHILIP, medical radiography specialist; b. Chgo., Nov. 28, 1954; s. David Walter and Gertrude Ann (Schmidt) O'C.; m. Barbara Jane Lange, Aug. 21, 1976; 1 child, Meghan Ann. AAS with high honors, Oakton Community Coll., 1974; BS, U. Health Scis./Chgo. Med. Sch., 1976; student Dale Carnegie and Assocs., Chgo., 1982. Cert. med. radiography. Chief technologist Chgo. Osteo. Hosp., 1976-79, St. Joseph Hosp., Elgin, Ill., 1979-80, Copley Hosp., Aurora, Ill. 1980; tech. specialist Pyne Corp., Itasca, Ill., 1980-84, sr. tech. specialist, edn. coord., 1984-85; imaging specialist Konica Med. Corp., Wooddale, Ill., 1985—. Republican. Roman Catholic./ Home: 946 Jefferson Square Apt H Elk Grove Village IL 60007 Office: Konica Med Corp 945-F N Edgewood Ave Wooddale IL 60193

O'CONNOR, DONNA MAE, auditor; b. Big Rapids, Mich., Nov. 1, 1951; d. Harold Orvilla and Florence Viola (Shuberg) Fredrick; m. Charles Frederick O'Connor IV, Apr. 22, 1978; children: Jennifer Joy, Charles Frederick V. BBA in Acctg. with high distinction, Ferris State Coll., 1973. CPA, Mich. Jr. acct. Hungerford & Co., P.C., Ludington, Mich., 1974-78; sr. acct. Grand Rapids, Mich., 1978-80; govtl. auditor Bur. Medicaid Fiscal Rev. div. Mich. Dept. Social Services, Grand Rapids, 1980—. Mem. fin. bd. Holy Trinity Ch., Comstock Park, Mich., 1986—, vice chmn. fin. commn., 1987—; troop leader Girl Scouts U.S., Comstock Park, 1986—. Mem. Am. Inst. CPA's, West Mich. CPA Profl. Edn., Comstock Park Jaycees. Roman Catholic. Avocations: genealogy, camping, ceramics, needle crafts. Home: 506 Netherfield Comstock Park MI 49321-9340 Office: Mich Dept Social Services 350 Ottawa NW Grand Rapids MI 49503

O'CONNOR, EARL EUGENE, U.S. district judge; b. Paola, Kans., Oct. 6, 1922; s. Nelson and Mayme (Scheetz) O'C.; m. Florence M. Landis, Nov. 3, 1951 (dec. May 1962); children: Nelson, Clayton; m. Jean A. Timmons, May 24, 1963; 1 dau., Gayle. B.S., U. Kans., 1947, LL.B., 1950. Bar: Kans. 1950. Practiced in Mission, Kans., 1950-51; asst. county atty. Johnson County, Kans., 1951-53; probate and juvenile judge 1953-55; dist. judge 10th Jud. Dist., Olathe, Kans., 1955-65; justice Kans. Supreme Ct., 1965-71; judge U.S. Dist. Ct., Dist. of Kans., Kansas City, 1971—, chief judge, 1981—. Served with AUS, World War II, ETO. Mem. Am., Kans. bar assns., Nat. Conf. Fed. Trial Judges, Nat. Conf. State Trial Judges, Phi Alpha Delta. Clubs: Mason, Rotary. Office: US Courthouse Kansas City KS 66101

O'CONNOR, JAMES JOHN, utility company executive; b. Chgo., Mar. 15, 1937; s. Fred James and Helen Elizabeth (Reilly) O'C.; m. Ellen Louise Lawlor, Nov. 24, 1960; children: Fred, John (dec.), James, Helen Elizabeth. BS, Holy Cross Coll., 1958; MBA, Harvard U., 1960; JD, Georgetown U., 1963. Bar: Ill. 1963. With Commonwealth Edison Co., Chgo., 1963—, asst. to chmn. exec. com., 1964-65, comml. mgr., 1966, asst. v.p., 1967-70, v.p., 1970-73, exec. v.p., 1973-77, pres., 1977—, chmn., 1980—, chief exec. officer, also bd. dirs.; bd. dirs. Bell & Howell Co., Corning Glass Works, Midwest Stock Exchange, Tribune Co., United Air Lines. Mem. Ill. com. United Negro Coll. Fund, Statue of Liberty-Ellis Island Centennial Commn., Christopher Columbus Quincentenary Jubilee Commn.; bd. dirs. Assocs. Harvard U. Grad. Sch. Bus. Adminstrn., Leadership Council for Met. Open Communities, Lyric Opera, Mus. Sci. and Industry, St. Xavier Coll., Reading Is Fundamental, Helen Brach Found., Leadership Greater Chgo., United Way Crusade Mercy; chmn. Citizenship Council of Met. Chgo., 1976—, Cath. Charities Chgo., 1986—, Chgo. Met. Area Savs. Bond Campaign; past chmn. Inst. Nuclear Power Ops.; trustee Adler Planetarium, Michael Reese Med. Ctr., Northwestern U., Coll. Holy Cross; bd. dirs., past chmn. Chgo. Urban League; bd. advisors Mercy Hosp. and Med. Ctr.; chmn. bd. trustees Field Mus. Natural History; mem. exec. bd. Chgo. Area Council Boy Scouts Am.; exec. v.p. The Hundred Club Cook County; mem. citizens bd. U. Chgo. Served with USAF, 1960-63; civilian aide to Sec. Army 1978-80. Mem. Am., Ill., Chgo. bar assns., Chgo. Assn. Commerce and Industry (dir.). Roman Catholic. Clubs: Comml., Econ., Chgo., Chgo. Commonwealth, Met. (Chgo.). Home: 9549 Monticello Ave Evanston IL 60203 Office: Commonwealth Edison Co PO Box 767 One First National Plaza Chicago IL 60690

O'CONNOR, JEROME ARMAND, village manager, management consultant; b. Hartford, Wis., July 14, 1934; s. George Howard and Dorothy Barbara (Lackas) O.; m. Virginia Mary Lenzner, Aug. 5, 1961 (div.); children—Edward Patrick, Kathleen Mary, Annette Marie, Michael John. M.Pub. Adminstrn., Nova U., 1978. Clk., treas., adminstr. City of Hartford (Wis.), 1968-74; dir. mgmt. services local govt. State of Wis., 1977—; owner, mgmt. cons. community research and mgmt. The Madison Group. Bd. mgrs. YMCA; mem. Washington County Econ. Devel. Com.; chmn. Washington County Mktg. Com. Served with U.S. Army, 1952-61, Res. Mem. Internat. City Mgmt. Assn., Wis. City Mgmt. Assn. (sec.-treas.), Germantown Area C. of C. Roman Catholic. Author publs. in field. Home: 21215 Oak Ln PO Box 181 Germantown WI 53022 Office: N122W7177 Fond du Lac Ave Germantown WI 53022

O'CONNOR, PETER DAVID, college administrator; b. Yonkers, N.Y., Mar. 20, 1936; s. Eugene A. and Mary C. (Donoghue) O'C.; m. Patricia T. Nichols, May 28, 1960; children—Jeanne Marie, Judith, Alison, Peter Jr., David, Séan. B.S. in Edn., Fordham U., 1958; M.A. in English, Lehigh U., 1962, Ph.D. in English, 1969. English tchr. Hicksville High Sch., N.Y., 1958-59; mem. English faculty SUNY-Oswego, 1962-77, U. P.R., Cayey, 1970-71; v.p. for acad. affairs, acad. dean Incarnate Word Coll., San Antonio, 1977-86; pres. Aquinas Coll., Grand Rapids, Mich., 1986—; facilitator, nat. inst. Council for Advancement of Small Colls., Washington, 1981, mem. task force, 1980-81; coordinator Assn. Tex. Colls. and Univs., San Antonio, 1980. Author: Major American Books, 1967; also articles. Mem. Project Equality—The Coll. Bd., 1981-86; mem. edn. com. United San Antonio, 1980-86; adv. mem. bd. trustees San Antonio Art Inst., 1979-80. Alumni Fund fellow Lehigh U., 1964. Mem. Assn. Tex. Acad. Deans and V.P.s (pres. 1985-86), Acad. Council United Colls. of San Antonio (chmn. 1983-84), Joseph Conrad Soc. (v.p. 1975-77). Democrat. Roman Catholic.

O'CONNOR, SARA ANDREWS, managing director; b. Syracuse, N.Y., Apr. 5, 1932; d. Harlan Francis and Ethel (Hoyt) Andrews; m. Boardman O'Connor, Aug. 23, 1955 (div. 1969); children: Ian, Douglas. BA with high honors, Swarthmore Coll., 1954; MA, Tufts U., 1955. Assoc. producer Theatre Co. of Boston, 1965-68, producer, 1969-71; pub. relations dir. Repertory Theatre of New Orleans, 1968-69; mng. dir. Cin. Playhouse, 1971-74, Milw. Repertory Theater, 1974—; cons. Found. for Extension and Devel. Am. Profl. Theatre, N.Y.C., 1973-83. Translator: (plays) The Workroom, 1979, At Fifty, She Discovered The Sea, 1982, Them, 1985, A Flea In Her Ear, 1986. Mem. Schlitz Audubon Ctr., Milw., 1980—, Amnesty Internat., N.Y.C., 1981—, ACLU, 1981—, Milw. Art Mus.; bd. dirs. Woodland Pattern, Milw., 1985—. Recipient Sacajawea award Profl. Dimensions, 1985. Mem. Internat. Theatre Inst. (bd. dirs. 1980—), Am. Arts Alliance (bd. dirs. 1981—), Dramatists Guild, League Resident Theatres (pres. 1984—, v.p. 1972-79), Theatre Communications Group (bd. dirs. 1978-82, pres. 1982-84), Wis. Citizens for the Arts, Theater Jocks (founder). Zen Buddhist. Avocations: swimming, hiking, cross-country skiing, reading, traveling. Office: Milw Repertory Theater 108 E Wells St Milwaukee WI 53202

O'CONNOR, THOMAS PATRICK, manufacturing company executive; b. Chgo., Sept. 6, 1945; s. Clement F. and Glory P. (McCartney) O'C.; m. Veronica Beres, Jan. 27, 1968; children: Patrick, Timothy, James. Student, So. Ill. U., 1964-66; U. Ill., Chgo., 1968-70, Ill. Benedictine Coll., 1979-83. Plant mgr. Acme Power Brake Co., Jennings, La., 1968-72; supr. EMD Gen. Motors, La Grange, Ill., 1972-84; pres. Union Rebuilt Products, Inc., Chgo., 1984—. Served with U.S. Army, 1966-68. Office: Union Rebuilt Products 3834 S Union Ave Chicago IL 60609

O'CONNOR, TIMOTHY CHARLES, computer consulting company executive; b. Detroit, Nov. 28, 1945; s. Thomas John and Anna Belle (Reardon) O'C.; m. Diane Palmer, Sept. 25, 1976 (div. Nov. 1982); m. Carolyn Jean Olson, Nov. 29, 1985; children: Colleen Ann, Karleen Marie, Kathryn Abbey. BSME, Lawrence Inst. Tech., 1971. Registered profl. engr., Mich. Engr., programmer Inatome Assocs., Oak Park, Mich., 1968-72; project engr. Giffels Assocs., Southfield, Mich., 1972-76; energy cons. Systems Tech., Ann Arbor, Mich., 1976-77; v.p. Hoyem Basso Assocs., Troy, Mich., 1977-81; pres. Automation Integrators, Birmingham, Mich., 1982—; mem. bldg. research bd. Nat. Acad. Sci., Washington, 1986-87. Author: (with others) CADD for Design Professionals, 1984; contbr. articles to profl. jours. Sponsor girls soccer Livonia Cosmos, 1985—. Mem. NSPE (cons. engr. council), Nat. Computer Graphic Assn. (founding chpt. pres. 1984-85), ASHRAE, IEEE Computer Soc., Engring. Soc. Detroit, SME Computer and Automated Systems Assn. Avocations: golf, archery, hunting, fishing. Office: Automation Integrators 30100 Telegraph #478 Birmingham MI 48010

O'CONNOR-EVANS, KATHLEEN M., epidemiologist, nurse, consultant; b. Evergreen Park, Ill., Mar. 14, 1941; d. James J. and Imelda J. (Scully) Evans; children—James P., M. Kate, J. Daniel. R.N., South Chicago Community Hosp. Sch. Nursing, 1962; B.S., St. Francis Coll., Joliet, 1976; postgrad. Roosevelt U., 1978-79, Harvard U., 1983. R.N., Ill. Staff nurse South Chicago Community Hosp., 1962-69; asst. head nurse emergency room Provident Meml. Hosp., El Paso, Tex., 1969-70; supr. R.E. Thomson Gen. Hosp., El Paso, 1970-71; dir. nursing, supr. nursing Mercy Ctr., Mercy Manor Facility, Aurora, Ill., 1971-72; charge nurse Brookwood Convalescent Ctr., Des Plaines, Ill., 1972-75; coordinator spl. projects Holy Family Hosp., Des Plaines, 1975-78, hosp. infection control coordinator, nurse epidemiologist, 1978—; tchr. Assoc. Practitioners in Infection Control, Chgo. and nationally; lectr. in field. Facilitator P.W.A. Support Group through AIDS Project. Mem. Nat. League Nursing, Nat. Assn. Practitioners Infection Control, Chgo. Assn. Practitioners Infection Control (nominating com. 1981-83, edn. com. 1985-86, Salmonella task force 1985, 86-87, chmn. cert. and recert. com. 1987—), Am. Soc. Microbiologists, Ill. Soc. Microbiologists. Roman Catholic. Author in-house publs. Home: 9370 Hamilton Ct Des Plaines IL 60016 Office: Holy Family Hosp 100 N River Rd Des Plaines IL 60016

O'CROWLEY, JAMES FRANCIS, III, marketing executive; b. Troy, N.Y., Aug. 13, 1953; s. James Francis Jr. and Mary Ruth (Faubion) O'C.; m. Susan Gail Jordan, May 11, 1985. AA, Menlo Coll., 1974; BS, U. Kans., 1976; MBA, Harvard U., 1978. Product controller Internat. Harvester, Chgo., 1978-79, asst. to pres., 1979-80, asst. to sr. v.p., 1980-82, mgr. purchasing, 1982, mgr. divestiture, 1982-83, mgr. market research, 1983-85; dir. product devel. Navistar (formerly Internat. Harvester), Chgo., 1985—; bd. dirs. Coalter Investment, Overland Park, Kans. Fund raiser Unided Way, Chgo., 1982. Clubs: Chgo. Curling; N.Y. Athletic, Harvard (N.Y.C.). Avocations: skiing, sailing, camping, golf. Home: 706 W Melrose Ave Chicago IL 60657 Office: Navistar Internat Corp 401 N Michigan Ave Chicago IL 60611

ODELL, CLARENCE BURT, geographer, editor, lecturer, consultant; b. Normal, Ill., Sept. 3, 1907; s. William Henry and Ruby F. (Conklin) O.; m. Madelyn Chellnissa Adams, June 11, 1931; 1 child, Sarah Jane. B. Ed., Ill. State U., 1930; M.A., U. Ill. 1931; Ph.D., U. Chgo., 1937. Cartographer McKnight & McKnight Pubs., 1927-30; teaching fellow U. Nebr., 1931-32; cartographer U. Chgo., 1932-37, Grad. Library Sch., 1935-36, vis. assoc. prof. geography, summer 1948, lectr. geography Univ. Coll., 1948-49, 49-50; physiography cons. Tymstone Studios, Chgo., summer 1934; instr. geography and geology Oak Park Jr. Coll., Ill., 1936-37; instr. dept. geography Memphis State U., summer 1937; assoc. prof. geography Stephen F. Austin State U., Nacogdoches, Tex., 1937-39; instr. geography U. Mo., 1939-43, asst. prof., 1943-46; div. asst. Office of Geographer, Dept. State, Washington, 1942-43; chief population sect. div. geography and cartography (later div. functional and internat. intelligence), 1943-46; chief cartography dept. Ency. Brittanica, Chgo., 1946-50; lectr. geography Univ. Coll., Northwestern U., 1947; geog. editor Denoyer-Geppert Co., Chgo., 1950-51, mng. editor, 1951-70, v.p., 1964-73; editor The Geographer, 1970-73; ret., 1973; mem. faculty Sch. Edn., Northwestern U., summers 1961, 63, 65; part-time prof. Northeastern Ill. U., 1967-73; dir. Geog. Research Inst., Wilmette, Ill., 1973—. Fellow Am. Geog. Soc., AAAS, Am. Congress Surveying and Mapping (life), Nat. Council Geog. Edn., Geog. Soc. Chgo. (pres. 1957-59, life dir. 1985); mem. Assn. Am. Geographers, Sigma Xi. Congregationalist. Club: Acacia (life mem.). Lodges: Masons (50 yr. mem.), Rotary (treas. Chgo. 1974-75, v.p. div. 1 1976-77, Chesley R. Perry award 1977, Paul Harris fellow 1982). Home: 2410 Greenwood Ave Wilmette IL 60091

O'DELL, DAVID ARTHUR, accountant; b. McPherson, Kans., Jan. 20, 1950; s. Ivan Luther and Grace Bertajean (Rife) O'D.; m. Jaymie Lynn Schmidt, Dec. 19, 1970; children: Crystal D., Rozalynn J. BS, McPherson Coll., 1972; MBA, Emporia State U., 1985. CPA, Kans. Acct. Keith Mines CPA, McPherson, 1971-82; pvt. practice acctg. McPherson, 1981—; prof. McPherson Coll., 1981—; mem. adv. bd. Christian Counseling Ctr., 1986—. Advisor bus. club McPherson Coll., 1982-84, Circle K Club, 1982-84; mem. sch. bd. Unified Sch. Dist. #418, McPherson, 1983—; bd. dirs. McPherson Nazarene Ch., 1980—, treas., 1987, del. to dist. conv., 1985-87; bd. dirs. McPherson Mus., 1984-87, Kans. Laymen's Nazarene Retreat, 1986—. Named one of Outstanding Young Men Am., 1985. Mem. Am. Inst. CPA's, Kans. Soc. CPA's, SBA (active corps of execs. 1985—), McPherson C. of C. (bd. dirs. 1986—). Republican. Lodges: Kiwanis ((treas. 1978-82, pres. 1982-83, life, recipient disting. club pres. award 1982), Gideons. Avocations: golf, reading, coin collecting, roses. Home and Office: PO Box 1032 McPherson KS 67460

O'DELL, LYNN MARIE LUEGGE (MRS. NORMAN D. O'DELL), librarian; b. Berwyn, Ill., Feb. 24, 1938; d. George Emil and Helen Marie (Pesek) Luegge; student Lyons Twp. Jr. Coll., La Grange, Ill., 1957; student No. Ill. U., Elgin Community Coll., U. Ill., Coll. of DuPage; m. Norman D. O'Dell, Dec. 14, 1957; children—Jeffrey, Jerry. Sec., Martin Co., Chgo., 1957-59; dir. Carol Stream (Ill.) Pub. Library, 1964—; chmn. automation governing com. DuPage Library System, v.p., 1982-85, pres. exec. com. adminstrv. librarians, 1985-86. Named Woman of Year, Wheaton Bus. and Profl. Woman's Club, 1968. Mem. ALA, Ill. Library Assn., Library Adminstrs. Conf. No. Ill. Lutheran (organist). Home: 182 Yuma Ln Carol Stream IL 60188 Office: 616 Hiawatha Dr Carol Stream IL 60188

O'DELL, MARGOT NUMAN, life insurance company executive; b. Green Bay, Wis., Feb. 26, 1942; d. Garno Orange and Geraldine Mae (Farrell) Numan; B.S. in Bus. Adminstrn., Franklin U., Columbus, Ohio, 1974; m. Willard Gerald Hill, II, Aug. 25, 1979; 1 child, Kathleen. Dept. mgr. Donaldson's Dept. Store, Mpls. and Rapid City, S.D., 1962-67, Lerner Shop, N.Y.C., 1967-68; buyer Hislop's Dept. Store, Auburn, N.Y., 1969-71; asst. mgr. Gentlemen's Clothing, Columbus, Ohio, 1972-74; agt. Aetna Life Ins. Co., Columbus, 1974-78; brokerage supr., 1978-80; pres. O'Dell Ins. Agy., Inc., Gahanna, Ohio, 1980—. Named Bus. Woman of Year, Columbus Profl. and Bus. Women, 1979; mem. Women's Leaders Round Table, 1976-78, Leading Producers Round Table, 1974-82, C.L.U., 1979. Mem. Nat. Assn. Health Underwriters (nat. pres. trustees Leading Producers Round Table 1980), Nat. Assn. Life Underwriters, Profl. Ins. Agts. Assn., Am. Soc.

C.L.U.s, Ohio Assn. Health Underwriters (pres. 1980, sec. 1984, 1st v.p. 1984, pres. 1985, chmn. health edn. week), Gahanna C. of C. (1st v.p. 1984). Republican. Episcopalian. Home: 5288 Wolf Run Dr Gahanna OH 43230 Office: 136 S Stygler Rd Gahanna OH 43230

ODELL, MARY JANE, state official; b. Algona, Iowa, July 28, 1923; d. Eugene and Madge (Lewis) Neville; m. John Odell, Mar. 3, 1967; children: Brad Chinn, Chris Odell. B.A., U. Iowa, 1945; hon. doctorate, Simpson Coll., 1982. Host public affairs TV programs Des Moines and Chgo., 1953-79; with Iowa Public Broadcasting Network, 1975-79, host Assignment Iowa, 1975-78, host Mary Jane Odell Program, 1975-79; sec. of state State of Iowa, 1980—; tchr. grad. classes in communications Roosevelt U., Chgo., Drake U., Des Moines. Chmn. Iowa Easter Seals campaign, 1979-83; mem. Midwest Com. Future Options; bd. dirs. Iowa Shares. Recipient Emmy award, 1972, 75; George Washington Carver award, 1978; named to Iowa Women's Hall of Fame, 1979. Republican. Address: 725 Hickman Rd Des Moines IA 50314 Office: Office Sec State State House Des Moines IA 50319

O'DELL, MICHAEL RAY, accountant, banker; b. Camden, Ohio, Sept. 27, 1951; s. Donald Lee and Donna Louise (Buell) O'D. BS in Bus., Miami U., 1977; MBA, Xavier U., 1979. CPA, Ohio. Asst. trust officer First Nat. Bank Southwestern Ohio, Hamilton, Ohio, 1977-83; acctg. officer First Nat. Bank Southwestern Ohio, Middletown, Ohio, 1983-86; comptroller First Nat. Bank Southwestern Ohio, 1986—; instr. microecons. Am. Inst. Banking, Cin., 1980-82. Bus. cons. applied econs. program Jr. Achievement, Springboro, Ohio, 1985. Served with USN, 1969-73. Mem. Am. Inst. CPA's, Ohio Soc. CPA's (com. chmn. 1985—). Club: Liberty (Ind.) Country. Avocation: golf. Home: 85-B S Lafayette Camden OH 45311 Office: First Nat Bank Southwestern Ohio 2 N Main St PO Box 220 Middletown OH 45042

ODELL, STEVEN ROY, service executive; b. Lakewood, Ohio, Apr. 12, 1950; s. Roy Lee and Bernice (Grant) O.; m. Marie A. Cavalet, Mar. 17, 1973; children: Ryan Michael, Erin Marie. Student, U. Akron, 1972. Mgr. Burger King Restaurant, Akron, Ohio, 1971-79, mgr. tng. and devel., 1979-80, dist. mgr., 1980-81, franchisee, 1981—; bd. dirs. J. JM. Inc., Akron. Active Child Life Study Group, Akron. Republican. Lodges: Rotary (asst. sgt. arms 1985—), Masons (jr. deacon 1983-85). Aovcations: golf, stamp collecting. Office: S R O Restaurant Co 4095 State Rd Cuyahoga Falls OH 44223

ODELL, STEWART IRA, obstetrician, gynecologist; b. Chgo., Dec. 14, 1938; s. Ira Stewart and Kathryn Jeanette (Scheithe) O.; m. Vivian Elizabeth Polz; Dec. 28, 1963; children: Mark, Eric, Adam, Todd, Sean. Student, Wheaton Coll., Ill., 1956-59; MD, U. Ill., Chgo., 1963. Diplomate Am. Coll. Ob-Gyn. Intern Prebyn. St. Luke's Hosp., 1963-64; obstetrician, gynecologist DuKane Obstetrics & Gynecology, Ltd., Carol Stream, Ill., 1972—; resident Presbyn. St. Luke's Hosp., 1964-67; sec., treas., v.p. Delnor Hosp., St. Charles, Ill., 1982-85, dept. chmn. 1975, 78, 81. Med. vol. refugee camp Thailand, 1980, Honduras, Dominican Republic, 1981—; bd. dirs. Wheaton (Ill.) Coll. Alumni Assn., 1976-79, Winfield (Ill.) Sch. Dist., 1979—. Served to maj., U.S. Army, 1967-71. Fellow Am. Coll. Ob-Gyn.; mem. Christian Med. Soc. Avocations: fishing, travel.

ODEN, JEAN PHIFER, special education teacher; b. Chgo., May 2, 1936; d. Dillard James and Lena (Conner) Phifer; m. James Edward Oden, Apr. 26, 1959; 1 child, Eric James. BE, Chgo. Tchrs. Coll., 1958; MEd in Learning Disabilities, Chgo. State U., 1973; postgrad., Nat. Coll. Edn., Evanston, Ill., 1986—. Tchr. elem. schs. Chgo., 1958-73, tchr. learning disabilities elem. schs., 1973-81, cons. spl. edn., ind. edn. program facilitator, 1981; learning disability specialist Phillips High Sch., Chgo., 1982-87, Englewood High Sch., Chgo., 1987—; mem. Ill. Guidelines for Learning Disabilities Devel. Com., Springfield, Ill., 1981—, Com. to Devel. State Test for Learning Disabilities Tchrs., Springfield, 1986; chair subcom. on research Ill. Dept. Rehab. Services, Chgo, 1985—. Speaker for fair housing Nat. Urban League, N.Y.C. Conf., 1980; mem. Congl. Victory Fund, Chgo., 1984, So. Christian Leadership Conf., Met. Chgo., 1979-81. U.S. Dept. Edn. grantee, 1986; recipient Citizenship award Chgo. Mayor, 1984; named State Advisor U.S. Congl. Adv. Bd., 1985. Mem. United Neighborhoods Intertwined for Total Equality (founder, exec. dir., researcher), Assn. for Citizens with Learning Disabilities, Council for Exceptional Children (liaison to state bd. Ill. div. for citizens with learning disabilities 1980), NAACP (Cert. of Merit, Southside Br. 1978), LWV, Spl. Edn. Tchrs. Assn. (1st pres., founder), Black Parents United for Edn. and Related Services (founder). Mem. M.E. Ch. Clubs: Lehigh Country (Fla.); Thousand Trails (Ottawa, Ill.). Avocations: hiking, racketball, traveling, camping.

ODER, DONALD RUDD, medical center executive, educator; b. Gibbon, Okla., Sept. 16, 1931; s. Lowell Burgess and Bessie Sarah (Rudd) O.; m. Roberta Pauline Sallee, Aug. 2, 1958; children—Joseph Rudd, Jennifer Susan, Karl Lyndon. B.S., Wichita State U., 1956; M.B.A., U. Chgo., 1980. C.P.A., Ill. Audit mgr. Arthur Andersen & Co., Chgo., 1956-66; v.p. fin. Rush-Presbyn.-St.Luke's Med. Center, Chgo., 1966-75, treas., 1970—, sr. v.p. and treas., 1975—, acting pres., 1983-84; asst. prof. health systems mgmt. Rush U. Coll. Health Scis., 1972-79, assoc. prof., 1979-85, prof., 1985—. Apptd. by gov. to Ill. Health Fin. Authority, 1979-82; bd. dirs. Better Bus. Bur., 1977—. Served with U.S. Army, 1950-53. Mem. Chgo. Assn. Commerce & Industry, Am. Coll. Hosp. Adminstrs., Am. Hosp. Assn. (regional adv. bd. 1981—), Am. Inst. C.P.A.s, Ill. C.P.A. Soc. (chmn. com. health care instns. 1975-76), Ill. Hosp. Assn. (chmn. bd. trustees 1982-83); fellow Healthcare Fin. Mgmt. Assn. (William G. Follmer award 1974, Robert H. Reeves award 1978, Alice V. Runyon award 1980), Inst. Medicine; mem. Alpha Kappa Psi. Home: 1280 Warwick Ct Deerfield IL 60015 Office: Rush-Presbyn-St Luke's Med Center 1725 W Harrison St Chicago IL 60612

O'DESKY, RICHARD NEIL, osteopathic occupational medicine physician, engineer; b. Toledo, Aug. 2, 1948; s. Louis Terril and Elizabeth Jane (Amdal) O'D.; m. Patricia Ann. B.S. in Engring., U. Toledo, 1970; D.O., U. Health Scis., Kansas City, Mo., 1978; M.S., Inst. Environ. Health, U. Cin., 1983. Engr. Richards, Bauer & Morehead, Toledo, 1972; intern Brentwood Hosp., Cleve., 1978-79; chief med. officer Indian Health Service, Chippewa Health Ctr., USPHS, Lac Du Flambeau, Wis., 1979-81, med. dir., 1979-81; resident in occupational medicine U. Cin. Med. Ctr., 1981-83; sr. assoc. Chem. Info. Services Cin., 1983-84; mem. sci. adv. com. Am. Porphyria Found, 1982—; cons. occupational health systems delivery and devel. Nat. Occupational Med. Assocs., Cin., 1983—. Served to lt. comdr. UPSHS, 1979-81; mem. Res. Mem. AMA, Am. Osteo. Assn., Am. Coll. Gen. Practitioners, Am. Occupational Med. Assn., Am. Coll. Sports Medicine, Am. Indsl. Hygiene Assn., Nat. Soc. Profl. Engrs., Sigma Sigma Phi. Office: Nat Occupational Med Assocs 15th Columbia Plaza 15th Floor 250 E 5th St Cincinnati OH 45202

O'DILLON, RICHARD HILL, physician; b. Watkinsville, Ga., Dec. 11, 1934; s. Herman Thomas and Elizabeth (Hill) O'D.; B.S., U. Ga., 1956; M.D., Med. Coll. Ga., 1960. Intern, Athens (Ga.) Gen. Hosp., 1960-61; resident Grady Meml. Hosp., Atlanta, 1963; practice medicine, specializing in clin. investigation, Rochester, N.Y., 1964—; asst. med. dir. Strasenburgh Labs., 1964-65, asso. med. dir., 1966; group dir. product devel., clin. research Merrell-Nat. Labs., Cin., 1966-75, group dir. gastrointestinal clin. research, 1975-78; dir. clin. research Duphar Labs., Inc., 1979—. Served as capt. USAF, 1961-62. Mem. AMA, So. Med. Assn., N.Y. Acad. Scis., Am. Acad. Dermatology, Ohio Med. Assn., Acad. Medicine Columbus and Franklin County, Am. Geriatrics Assn., AAAS, Gamma Sigma Epsilon, Phi Eta Sigma, Alpha Epsilon Delta, Delta Phi Alpha. Home: 728 Bluffview Dr Worthington OH 43085 Office: 200 Old Wilson Bridge Rd Worthington OH 43085

ODLAND, PAUL KENNETH, orthopedic surgeon; b. Yankton, S.D., Dec. 8, 1922; s. Ole Michael and Clara (Stensland) O.; m. Barbara Ruhl, Mar. 16, 1945; children: Judy, Paul Blair, M. Bruce. BA, Augustana Coll., Sioux Falls, S.D., 1944; BS in Medicine, U. S.D., 1945; MD, Temple U., 1946. Diplomate Am. Acad. Orthopedic Surgery. Intern U.S. Naval Hosp., 1946-47; resident orthopedic surgeon Marquette U. Medical Center, Milw., 1949-52; mem. staff Mercy Hosp., Janesville, Wis., 1952—, pres., 1957, chief of staff, 1982-83; clin. instr. U. Ill. Coll. Medicine, Rockford, 1978—; cons. Wis. Sch. for Visual Handicapped, Janesville, 1952—. Designer of total ankle replacement prosthesis, 1980; contbr. articles to profl. jours. Served to lt. (j.g.) USNR, 1946-49. Recipient Outstanding Alumni award Augustana Coll., Outstanding Alumni award U. S.D. Sch. Medicine. Mem. AMA, Am. Acad. Orthopedic Surgery, Wis. Orthopedic Soc. (pres. 1980-82). Republican. Lutheran. Club: Panam. Doctors (pres. 1978-79). Avocations: flying, sailing, skiing, TV programming. Office: Janesville Riverview Clinic 510 N Terrace St Janesville WI 53545

O'DONNELL, CLETUS FRANCIS, bishop; b. Waukun, Iowa, Aug. 22, 1917; s. Patrick E. and Isabelle A. (Duffy) O'D. M.A., St. Mary of Lake Sem., Ill., 1941; J.C.D., Catholic U. Am., 1945. Ordained priest Roman Catholic Ch., 1941; asst. pastor Our Lady of Lourdes Ch., Chgo., 1941-42; vice chancellor Archdiocese of Chgo., 1947-60, vicar, gen. counsel, 1961; apptd. titular bishop Abrittum, aux. bishop Chgo., 1960-67; consecrated bishop 1960; pastor Holy Name Cathedral, Chgo., 1966; bishop Diocese of Madison, Wis., 1967—; Chmn. Am. Bd. Cath. Missions, from 1966, Nat. Catholic Edn. Assn., from 1977. Recipient C. Albert Koob award Nat. Cath. Edn. Assn., 1978. Office: Chancery Office PO Box 111 15 E Wilson St Madison WI 53701 *

O'DONNELL, DAVID RICHARDSON, civil engr.; b. Bishop, Calif., June 2, 1937; s. Herbert Preston and Minerva Elizabeth (Richardson) O.; A.A., Am. River Community Coll., 1959; B.S., U. Idaho, 1961; children—Derek T., Irene Denise. Jr. civil engr. Calif. Dept. Water Resources, Sacramento, 1962-67; hydraulic engr. Pioneer Service & Engring. Co., Chgo., 1969-72; hydraulic structures engr. Harza Engring. Co., Chgo., 1973-75; chief engring. dept. Urban Planning Consultants, Inc., Chgo., 1975-77, Milw. Pollution Abatement Program; now sr. assoc. engr. City of Detroit. Served with U.S. Army, 1961-62. Registered profl. engr., Del., Pa., N.J., Ill., Ind., Iowa, Mich. Mem. ASCE, Am. Water Works Assn., Water Pollution Control. Fedn., Nat. Soc. Profl. Engrs. Republican. Home: 111 Cadillac Sq Apt 12 I Detroit MI 48226 Office: 735 Randolph St Detroit MI 48226

O'DONNELL, EDWARD MICHAEL, manufacturing executive; b. Johnstown, Pa., June 21, 1947; s. Edward Joseph and Kathryn (Zeunges) O'D.; m. Marianne Schutte, June 20, 1970. BS in Commerce and Engring. Sci., Drexel U., 1970; MBA, Baldwin-Wallace Coll., 1985. Auxs. gen. foreman Nat. Duquesne (Pa.) Works, U.S. Steel, Inc., 1979-81, process engr., 1981-82; asst. supt. blast furnaces Loraine (Pa.) Works, U.S. Steel, Inc. (a div. of USX), 1982-84, area mgr. steel prodn., 1984-85, process engr., 1985-86, area mgr. iron prodn., 1986—. Contbr. articles to profl. jours. Served to 1st lt. U.S. Army, 1971-73. Mem. AIME, Iron and Steel Soc. of AIME, Delta Mu Delta. Republican. Roman Catholic. Office: USS Lorain Works 1807 E 28th St MS-12 Lorain OH 44055

O'DONNELL, JOHN, real estate broker; b. Omaha, May 16, 1925; s. John Francis and Gertrude Edith (Alderman) O'Donnell. Officer Lincoln Fire Dept., Nebr., 1954-77; pres. Capitol Realty and Auction Co., Lincoln, 1972—. Served with USN, 1943-46. Republican. Roman Catholic. Lodge: VFW. Avocation: flying. Home: 1630 H St Unit B-1 Lincoln NE 68508 Office: Capitol Realty Co 2021 Garfield St Lincoln NE 68502

O'DONNELL, LAWRENCE JAMES, architect; b. Oak Park, Ill., Jan. 16, 1929; s. George Edward and Sarah (Goonrey) O'D.; m. Alice Clare Lyons, Dec. 26, 1953; children: Michael, Maureen, Kerry, Kevin. BS in Architecture, U. Ill., 1951. Registered architect, Ill. Coll. architect Lake Forest (Ill.) Coll., 1963-71; founding prin., chmn. exec. bd. O'Donnell Wicklund Pigozzi and Peterson Architects, Inc., Deerfield, Ill., 1958—, prin. for mktg., 1971—. Bd. dirs. Glenkirk Sch., Northbrook, 1982-85, mem. found. bd., 1985—. Served to cpl. U.S. Army, 1951-53. Mem. AIA, Bus. Mobilized for Loyola U. Clubs: Econ. Club, Irish Fellowship, De Paul U. Pres.'s, Loyola U. Pres.'s. Lodge: Rotary (Lake Forest). Office: 570 Lake Cook Rd Deerfield IL 60015

O'DONNELL, MABRY MILLER, speech communication and theatre arts educator; b. Huntsville, Ala., July 18, 1945. AA, Stephens Coll., 1965; BA, La. State U., 1967; MA, U. Ala., 1969; PhD, Bowling Green (Ohio) State U., 1977. Assoc. prof. speech communication Marietta (Ohio) Coll., 1969—; cons. bus. communication Bus. Resource Ctr., Marietta, 1985—. Author: Fundamentals of Speech, 1983. Mem. Speech Communication Assn., Pi Kappa Delta. Democrat. Methodist. Club: Marietta Reading. Home: 118 Meadow Ln Marietta OH 45750

O'DONNELL, MARK JOSEPH, accountant; b. St. Louis, Mar. 28, 1954; s. William E. and Jeanne M. (Collins) O'D.; m. Jane E. Wismann, Sept. 29, 1973; children: Sean, Mark Jr., Kyle. CPA, Mo. Cost acct. Hunter Engring., St. Louis, 1973-76; acct. Gen. Dynamics, St. Louis, 1976-77; acct. Lester Witte & Co., St. Louis, 1977-80, mgr., 1980-82; mng. ptnr. Bounds, Poger & O'Donnell, St. Louis, 1982—. Mem. Am. Inst. CPA's, Mo. Soc. CPA's. Roman Catholic. Avocations: nautilus, jogging, little league baseball. Office: Bounds Poger & O'Donnell 120 S Central Ave Suite 400 Saint Louis MO 63105

O'DONNELL, PHILLIP FRANCIS, improvisational actor, comedic sketch writer; b. Chgo., Feb. 21, 1952; s. Frank Phillip and Arveth Edmae (Anderson) O'D.; m. Sandra Kay Tucker, Apr. 24, 1982; 1 child, Marie Kay. BA, U. Ill., 1976; MFA, Western Ill. U., 1979. Improvisational actor, writer Sketchworks, St. Paul, 1980-81, KFAI Radio, Mpls., 1980-82, Comedy Cabaret Players, Mpls., 1981-82, Clown In The Mouth, Mpls., 1983, Comedy Gallery Improvisation, Mpls., 1984, Belly Laffs Troupe, Bloomington, Minn., 1985-86; actor New Classic Theatre, Mpls., 1986—; actor Chimera Theatre, St. Paul, 1980, Minnetonka (Minn.) Community Theatre, 1981, Jewish Community Ctr., St. Louis' Park, Minn., 1982, Theatre In The Round Players, Mpls., 1983. Author: (with others) (theatrical revues) Lunch Bag of Notre Dame, 1985, Murder on the Am. Express, 1985, Somewhere Over the Rambo, 1985-86, The Best of Belly Laffs, 1985-86. Served with U.S. Army, 1972-74. Mem. Am. Fedn. TV and Radio Artists. Avocations: reading, fishing, writing, laughing. Home: 4008 Standish Ave Minneapolis MN 55407

O'DONNELL, THOMAS PAUL, management consultant; b. Glenshaw, Pa., Jan. 20, 1926; s. James Francis and Florence Elizabeth (Holden) O'D.; m. Helen Cowden Kernaghan, Apr. 20, 1950; children: James F., William J., Mary E., Todd P. BS in Marine Engring., U.S. Merchant Marine Acad., 1946; BSME, U. Detroit, 1948. Mgr. devel. engring. corp. Owens-Illinois, Inc., Toledo, 1962-65, mgr. engring., 1965-74, gen. mgr., facilities engr. and project mgr., 1974-79, dir. sales and applications, 1979-83; pres. O'Donnell & Assoc., Whitehouse, Ohio, 1983—. Served to lt. USNR, 1943-46. Mem. ASME, Am. Soc. Energy Engrs., Am. Arbitration Assn., Am. Soc. Heating, Refrigeration and Air Conditioning Engrs., Tech. Assn. Pulp and Paper Industry. Avocations: golf, fishing, home projects. Home and Office: 10942 Springbrook Ct Whitehouse OH 43571

O'DONNELL, WILLIAM DAVID, construction firm executive; b. Brockton, Mass., Aug. 21, 1926; s. John Frank and Agnes Teresa (Flanagan) O'D.; m. Dixie Lou Anderson, Jan. 31, 1951; children—Craig Patrick, Ginger Lynn. B.S., U. N.Mex., 1953. Registered profl. engr., Ill., 1958. Engr., State of Ill., 1953-59; with Gregory-Anderson Co., Rockford, Ill., 1959—, gen. mgr., 1960-61, sec., 1961-81, pres., 1981—; dir. 1st Nat. Bank & Trust Co. of Rockford, 1st Community Bancorp, Inc., Growth Enterprise, Starvision, Inc. Dir. St. Anthony Med. Ctr., Starvision, Inc.; bd. dirs. Rockford YMCA, pres., 1984. Served with USN, 1943-47. Recipient Friend of the Boy award Optimist Club, 1966, Excalibur award for community service Rockford Register Star, 1971; named Titan of Yr., Boylan High Sch., 1974. Fellow ASCE, Nat. Soc. Profl. Engrs.; mem. No. Ill. Bldg. Contractors, Aircraft Owners and Pilots Assn., Balloon Fedn. Am., Sigma Tau, Chi Epsilon, Tau Beta Pi. Clubs: Forest Hills Country (Rockford); Adventurers (Chgo.). Lodges: Elks, Rockford Rotary (Service Above Self award 1972; v.p. 1983, pres. 1984). Home: 2004 Bradley Rd Rockford IL 61107 Office: 2525 Huffman Blvd Rockford IL 61103

O'DONOVAN, THOMAS RAPHAEL, professional association administrator; b. Detroit, Mar. 25, 1931; s. Patrick Gregory and Mary Laverne (Mitchell) O'D.; m. Gayle Marie O'Connell, Aug. 24, 1957; children: Patrick Gabriel, Lynda Mary, Julia Mary. BS in Mgmt., U. Detroit, 1954, MS, 1956; PhD in Mgmt., Corp. Fin., Mktg., Econs., Mich. State U., 1961. Tchr. mgmt. Mich. State U., East Lansing, U. Detroit, U. So. Calif., Los Angeles; adminstr., chief operating officer Mount Carmel Mercy Hosp. and Med. Ctr., Detroit, 1964-79; pres., chief exec. officer Am. Acad. Med. Adminstrs., Southfield, Mich., 1980—; adj. prof. hosp. adminstrn. Ohio State U., Columbus, U. Detroit, 1980-82; pres. Met. N.E. Detroit Hops. Inc., 1973-75; chmn. professions unit United Found. Drive, Detroit, 1976, com. emergency dept. coordination Regional Task Force on Emergency Health Care, Detroit, 1972-80, credentials com. Creater Detroit Area Hosp. Council, 1973-76, adminstrv. conf. com. Quadrangle, 1969-79; mem. ambulatory surgery panel Federal Health Services Criteria Project Dept. Health Services U. Wash., Seattle, 1975, fin. com. Eastern Mich. Regional Bd. Sisters of Mercy Health Corp., 1976-78, tech. adv. panel relative to ambulatory surgery criteria and standards Comprehensive Health Planning Council of Southeastern Mich., 1979; bd. trustees Mich. Conf. Cath. Health Care Facilities, 1979; speaker in field. Author: Ambulatory Surgical Centers: Development and Management, 1976, Executive Administration in Hospitals, 1978; co-author: Managing Health Care Organizations, 1977, Management By Objectives for Hospitals, 1982; editor Jour. Ambulatory Care Mgmt., Rockville, Md., 1979-82; mem. editorial bd. Same-Day Surgery Newsletter, Atlanta, 1979—; contbr. chpts. to books, numerous articles to profl. jours. Recipient William Newcomer award Am. Acad. Med. Adminstrs., 1971, Hon. Mention award Hosp. Adminstrn. mag., 1975; named one of Outstanding Young Men Am., 1967. Fellow Am. Acad. Med. Adminstrs. (nat. chmn. edn. council, 1972-76), Am. Coll. Hosp. Adminstrs., Royal Soc. Health; mem. Met. N.W. Detroit Hosps. Inc. (pres. 1973-75), Am. Hosp. Assn., Cath. Hosp. Assn., Am. Coll. Hosp. Adminstrs. (book of yr. com. 1971-73, chmn. 1973, mem. editorial bd. jours. 1973-82, mem. com. self assessment 1980-82), Mich. Hosp. Assn. (chmn. com. edn. 1977-80, chmn. com. in-hosp. edn. and tng. 1973-76, mem. health manpower com. 1975-77, mem. com. on shared services 1978-79, alt. del. to Am. Hosp. Assn. 1976-79, chmn. ednl. services adv. com. 1978-79), Alpha Kappa Psi. Republican. Roman Catholic. Club: Detroit Golf. Home: 19541 Wilshire Birmingham MI 48009 Office: Am Acad Med Adminstrs Congress Bldg Suite 150 30555 Southfield Rd Southfield MI 48076

OEHLER, IRA COLE, JR., manufacturing executive; b. St. Paul, Oct. 16, 1942; s. I. Cole and Betty (Scandrett) O.; m. Judith Walters, June 16, 1973; children: William Scandrett, Nicole Radford. BA, Yale U., 1964. Supt. of divisions Miss., Pacific R.R., St. Louis, 1968-78, exec. rep., 1978-83; v.p., gen. mgr. RWT Corp., Mt. Prospect, Ill., 1983-86; pres. W. Herdlein & Assocs. Inc., Tinley Park, Ill., 1987—. Bd. dirs. Downer's Grove YMCA, 1980-84, vice chmn, 1983-84. Mem. Soc. Mfg. Engrs., Assn. Integrated Mrg., Civic Arts Found. Republican. Episcopalian. Clubs: Union League, Yale (pres. 1985-87), Hinsdale Golf. Avocations: tennis, golf, skiing, sailing. Home: 127 E 7th St Hinsdale IL 60521 Office: W Herdlein & Assocs Inc 17201 Ridgeland Ave Tinley Park IL 60477

OEHRING, THOMAS SIDNEY, investment company executive, lawyer, accountant; b. Detroit, May 19, 1928; s. Louise Sidney and Marjory Ann (Cole) O.; m. Jeanne Mildred Lundberg, June 6, 1953; children: Cheryl Jeanne Bell, Karin Sue, Nanci Jane Baglien. BBA, Northwestern U., 1949; JD, U. Ill., 1956. Bar: Ill. 1957; CPA., Ill. Acct. Deloitte, Haskins & Sells, Chgo., 1949-50, sr. prin., 1956-66, tax ptnr., 1969-78; tax prin. Deloitte, Haskins & Sells, N.Y.C., 1966-69; v.p., sec. Miami Corp., Chgo., 1978—; bd. dirs. Cutler Oil and Gas Corp. Served to sgt. U.S. Army, 1950-52. Mem. ABA, Ill. Bar Assn., Chgo. Bar Assn., Am. Inst. CPA's, Ill. Soc. CPA's (chmn. tax com. 1965-66, 76-78), Ill. State C. of C. (chmn. tax com. 1976-78). Clubs: Sheridan Shores Yacht (Wilmette, Ill.); Union League (Chgo.). Avocations: sailing, fgn. travel, photography, music. Home: 18 Mayfair Ln Lincolnshire IL 60015 Office: Miami Corp 410 N Michigan Ave Chicago IL 60611

OESTERHELD, JOHN BREMMER, JR., insurance executive; b. Chgo., Dec. 23, 1941; s. John Bremmer and Louise Gertrude (Mattson) O. BA, North Park Coll., 1964; MBA, Roosevelt U., 1969; DPub. Adminstrn., Nova U., Ft. Lauderdale, Fla., 1983. Cert. reinsurance, N.Y.C., ins. producer, Ill. Pvt. practice ins. producer Arlington Heights, Ill., 1965—; acct. specialist Allstate Ins. Co., Northbrook, Ill., 1971-74; staff underwriter mgr. Am. Farm Bur., Park Ridge, Ill., 1974-79; mgr. Am. Mut. Reins. Co., Lisle, Ill., 1979-85; asst. sec. Am. Ind. Reins., Stamford, Conn., 1985-86; pvt. practice real estate sales and investments Arlington Heights, 1985-86; cons. Bryant Lloyds Brokers, London, 1986; reins. exec. Reins. Cons., Arlington Heights, 1986; prof. Harper Coll., 1969-71. Author: Reinsurance and Motor Carrier Act of 1980, 1982, Umbrella Liability Reinsurance, 1980. Treas. N. Austin Community Conv., Chgo., 1973-74, Evang. Singles Orgn., Deerfield, Ill., 1981-83; rep. Westport Unitarian Singles Group, Westport, Conn., 1985-86. Research and Devel. appointment Nat. Assn. Ind. Ins., 1980-85. Mem. Ill. Farm Bur. and Ill. Agrl. Assn., Nat. Rifle Assn., Nat. Flood Ins. Assn. (mem com. 1975-79), Ins. Service Office (farm com. 1975-79), Nat. Assn. Ind. Insurers (property com. 1975-79). Baptist. Lodge: Elks. Avocations: golf, fishing, bowling, hiking, bicycling. Home: 237 S Princeton Ave Arlington Heights IL 60005 Home (alternate): 810 E US Hwy 61 Two Harbors MN 55616

OESTMANN, MARY JANE, retired radiation specialist; b. Chgo., May 22, 1924; d. Charles Edward and Harriet Evelyn (Stoltenberg) O. BA in Math, Chemistry with honors, Denison U., 1946; MS, U. Wis., 1948, PhD, 1954; DSc., Denison U., 1975. Research chemist Inst. for Atom Energy, Oslo, 1954-55; vis. scientist AB Atom Energy, Stockholm, 1955-56; vis. prof. chem. dept. U. Iowa, Iowa City, 1957; sr. scientist Battelle Meml. Inst., Columbus, Ohio, 1957-61; assoc. chemist Argonne (Ill.) Nat. Lab, 1961-71; mgr. environ. project U.S. Nuclear Regulatory Commn., Washington, 1971-75; sr. radiation specialist U.S. Nuclear Regulatory Commn., Glen Ellyn, Ill., 1975-87. Contbr. numerous articles to scientific jours. Recipient Internat. Women's Yr. award Nuclear Regulatory Commn., 1975. Fellow Am. Inst. Chemist; mem. Am. Chem. Soc., Am. Nuclear Soc. (bd. dirs. 1983-86), Inst. Environ. Scis. (sr. mem.), Health Physics Soc. (sec.-treas. Midwest chpt. 1978, exec. com. 1983-86), Wis. Acad. Scis., Arts and Letters, Sigma Xi, Phi Beta Kappa, Sigma Delta Epsilon. Club: Browns Lake Yacht (Burlington, Wis.). Home: 2520 Cedar Dr Burlington WI 53105

OESTREICH, ALAN EMIL, pediatric radiologist, educator; b. N.Y.C., Dec. 4, 1939; s. Mitchell and Edith (Liebling) O.; m. Tamar Kahane, May 20, 1973; 1 child, Michael P. AB, Princeton U., 1961; MD, Johns Hopkins U., 1965. Cert. Am. Bd. Radiology. Intern Balt. City Hosps., 1965-66; resident in radiology Strong Meml. Hosp., Rochester, N.Y., 1966-69; pediatric radiologist U. Mo., Columbia, 1972-79, Children's Hosp., Cin., 1980—; prof. radiology and pediatrics U. Cin. Coll. Med., 1986—; vis. prof. Zurich (Switzerland) Children's Hosp., 1978. Translator Radiology of the Postoperative GI Tract, 1976; translator, editor Lumbar Myelography, 1986; author: Pediatric Radiology Med. Outline Series, 1977, 81, 84; co-author: Atlas of Pediatric Orthopedic Radiology, 1985; fgn. book rev. editor Radiology, 1984-86; editor Modern Library Collector, Cin., 1981—. Served to maj. U.S. Army, 1969-71. Fellow Am. Coll. Radiology; mem. Radiol. Soc. N.Am., Internat. Skeletal Soc., Soc. Pediatric Radiology, Nat. Med. Assn. (radiol. sect., nat. chmn. 1985-87), Italian Radiol. Soc. (hon.), Sigma Xi. Jewish. Avocations: hiking, modern library collecting. Office: Childrens Hosp X-Ray Dept Elland & Bethesda Aves Cincinnati OH 45229-2899

OESTREICH, GEORGE LOUIS, pharmacist; b. Fulton, Mo., May 19, 1947; s. Miller Crews and Lucille Agnes (McCuine) O.; m. Barbara Lee Dunavant, Aug. 27, 1967 (div. 1979); m. Jana Lynn Davis, June 21, 1980; children: Andrew Oliver, Alaina McCuine. B.S., U. Mo., 1970, M.P.A., 1982. Pres., Comprehensive Pharm. Services, Inc., Fulton, Mo., 1972—, Advanced Apothecaries, Inc., 1981—; cons. nursing homes, hosps. and govtl. agys., 1974—. Mayor, City of Fulton, Mo., 1978-86. Served with USPHS, 1970-72. Mem. Am. Pharm. Assn., Mo. Pharm. Assn., Nat. Assn. Retail Druggists, Am. Coll. Apothecaries, Am. Soc. Cons. Pharmacists, Phi Kappa Phi, Omicron Delta Kappa., Phi Alpha Alpha, Rho Chi. Democrat. Methodist. Club: Fulton Country. Home: 103 Collier Ln Fulton MO 65251 Office: Comprehensive Pharmaceutical Services Inc 600 Court St Fulton MO 65251

O'FALLON, NANCY MCCUMBER, university official; b. Jackson, Miss., Oct. 25, 1938; d. Murrell Chester and Louise Marie (Paquette) McCumber; m. John Robert O'Fallon, June 14, 1962; children—John Michael, Brian

Douglas, Deborah Lynne. B.S. in E.E., St. Louis U., 1960; M.S. in Nuclear Engring., U. Ill.-Urbana, 1961, Ph.D. in Physics, 1966. Part-time asst. prof. U. Mo., St. Louis, 1967-72, vis. asst. prof. physics, 1972-74; asst. physicist Argonne Nat. Lab., Ill., 1974-76, physicist, 1976-83, program mgr. Inst. and Control for Fossil Energy, 1978-83; asst. v.p. research U. Chgo., 1983—. Contbr. articles to profl. jours. Recipient Leadership award in edn. YWCA Met. Chgo., 1984. Nat. Merit scholar, 1956-60. Mem. Am. Phys. Soc., AAAS, Assn. Women in Sci. (nat. councilor 1980-81; treas. 1984-85), Chgo. Network. Office: Univ of Chgo at Argonne 9700 S Cass Ave Bldg 201 Argonne IL 60439

OFF, ROBERT LYNNE, fraternal organization administrator; b. Denver, May 2, 1943; s. Myron W. and Imogene O. (Taylor) O.; m. Linda K. Randall, June 1, 1968; 1 child, Karlene S. BA, Colo. State U., 1965, MA, 1967. Asst. dir. student housing S.D. State U., Brookings, 1967-68, 71-73; exec. dir. FarmHouse Internat. Frat., St. Joseph, Mo., 1973—. Pres. Mo-Kan. Regional Food Bank, St. Joseph, 1981-86; chmn., adminstrv. bd. 1st Christian Ch., St. Joseph, 1985-86. Served to capt. U.S. Army, 1968-71, Korea. Recipient Darl E. Snyder award, Colo. State U. Chpt. Farm House Frat., 1985. Mem. Frat. Execs. Assn. (pres.-elect 1986-87), Coll. Frat. Editors Assn. (pres. 1979-80), Nat. Agrl. Alumni and Devel. Assn. Democrat. Avocation: horses. Home: 1928 Francis Saint Joseph MO 64501 Office: FarmHouse Frat 2400 Frederick 110 Saint Joseph MO 64506

OFFENHISER, ANDREW BREWSTER, retail executive; b. Palo Alto, Calif., May 28, 1926; s. Paul Lloyd and Edith (Wise) O.; m. Helen Louise Forker, Nov. 1, 1952; 1 child, Nancy Louise. Student, U. Ill., 1943-44, 46-47; AB, Colby Coll., 1949; MBA, Stanford U., 1955. With passenger dept. Burlington R.R., 1950; with passenger dept. Pa. R.R., 1951, supr. service, 1951-53; div. head traffic dept. J.C. Penney Co., N.Y.C., 1956-60, asst. traffic mgr., 1960, civic affairs co-ordinator pub. relations dept., 1961-64, regional pub. relations mgr., 1973-76; with Gen. Growth Mgmt. Corp., Des Moines, 1976-81; exec. cons. Am. City Bur., Rosemont, Ill., 1981—; Mem. solicitations panel and adv. com. on solicitations Nat. Better Bus. Bur., adv. com. contbn. execs. United Community Funds and Councils Am. Mem. United Way Am. Corp. Assocs.; bd. dirs. Des Moines Symphony Assn. Served with USNR, 1944-46. Mem. Am. Retail Fedn. (state orgn. com.), SAR, Soc. Mayflower Descs., Sigma Alpha Epsilon. Republican. Roman Catholic. Home: 42 N Wise Ave Freeport IL 61032 Office: 9501 W Devon Rosemont IL 60018

OFFICE, GERALD SIMMS, JR., restaurant chain executive; b. Dayton, Ohio, Oct. 22, 1941; s. Gerald Simms and Sarah (Lieberman) O.; m. Lynn Elise Isaacson, Aug. 26, 1972; children: Jeremy Simms, Marisa Lynn. B.B.A. with distinction, U. Mich., 1963; J.D. summa cum laude, Ohio State U., 1967; LLD, Westminster Coll. Bar: Ohio 1967. Ptnr. Office & Office, Dayton, 1967-69; chmn. bd., chief exec. officer Ponderosa, Inc., Dayton, 1969—; dir. Bank One, Dayton., ChemLawn Corp., Columbus, Ohio. Trustee Dayton Devel. Council, Cin. Contemporary Art Center, Dayton Performing Arts Fund, U. Dayton, Hundred Club of Dayton; bd. overseers NYU Center for Study of Foodservice Mgmt.; mem. Bus. Com. for Arts, Inc.; hon. trustee Building Bridges Inc.; hon. mem. exec. com. Spl. Olympics Dayton and Montgomery County, Ohio.; mem. Dayton chpt. U.S. Olympic Com.; mem. adv. bd. Dayton Council on World Affairs; mem., past chmn. Area Progress Council-Dayton; trustee Dayton Free Enterprise Found., Wright State U. Found.; bd. mgrs. Air Force Mus. Found. Mem. Nat. Restaurant Assn. Address: Ponderosa Inc PO Box 578 Dayton OH 45401 *

OFFRINGA, DONALD CRAIG, accountant; b. Grand Rapids, Mich., Sept. 15, 1950; s. Albert and Margaret (Kamminga) O.; m. Jacquelyn Kay Knott, Dec. 3, 1969; children: Dennis, Melonie, Wendi. Assoc. Applied Scis., Grand Rapids Jr. Coll., 1970; BS, Ferris State Coll., 1972. CPA, Mich. Ptnr. Seidman & Seidman, Grand Rapids, 1972—; Treas. Heritage Christian Sch., Hudsonville, Mich., 1984-86, pres., 1986-87. Mem. Am. Inst. CPA's, Mich. Assn. CPA's, Econ. Club Grand Rapids, Healthcare Fin. Mgmt. Assn. (western Mich. chpt.), Jr. Achievement of Grand Rapids (bd. dirs. 1986—). Republican. Club: Sunnybrook Country (Grandville, Mich.). Avocations: golf, basketball. Home: 823 Brentwood Jenison MI 49428

OFFUTT, JOSEPH ROBERT, JR., coast guard officer, information resources executive; b. Washington, Aug. 11, 1943; s. Joseph Robert and Norma Adele (Payne) O.; m. Gayle M. Hansen, Oct. 5, 1963; children: Tina M., Wendy A. BS in Engring., U.S. Coast Guard Acad., 1965; MS in Mgmt., U.S. Navy Postgrad. Sch., 1970. Commd. ensign USCG, 1965, advanced through grades to capt., 1986; telecommunications headquarters staff USCG, Washington, 1970-75; chief telecommunications staff 17th dist. USCG, Juneau, Alaska, 1975-79; executive officer support ctr. USCG, Seattle, Wash., 1979-82; chief info. resources mgmt. div, 13th dist. USCG, Seattle, 1982-84; chief info. resources mgmt. div., 9th dist. USCG, Cleve., 1984—; faculty U. Alaska, Juneau, 1978-79, U. Puget Sound, Seattle, 1980-84. Decorated Bronze Star; recipient Administrative Excellence award Interagy. Com. Info. Resources Mgmt., 1986. Avocation: fishing. Office: USCG Dist 9 1240 E 9th St Cleveland OH 44199

OFIARA, HENRY GEORGE, JR., architect, consultant; b. Highland Park, Mich., Feb. 27, 1953; s. Henry George Sr. and Irene (Okasinski) O. Student, U. Mich., Dearborn, 1971-73; MArch, U. Mich., Ann Arbor, 1980; BArch, U. Detroit, 1976. Registered architect, Mich. Designer Profl. Cons., Livonia, Mich., 1980-81, Gunn-Levine Assoc., Detroit, 1981-83; pres. Henry Ofiara Architect, P.C., Detroit, 1984—; architect Jickling, Lyman & Powell Assoc., Birmingham, Mich., 1985—; architect cons. Chrysler Corp., Highland Park, 1983-85, Michael J. Kirk, Detroit, 1984; bd. dirs. Empicare, Inc. Organizer energy conservation seminar, Hamtramck. Mem. AIA, Empicare (adv. bd. dirs.), Founders Soc. Detroit Inst. Arts. Home: 5253 Bishop Detroit MI 48224

O'FLYNN, JAMES MAGUIRE, association executive; b. St. Louis, Mar. 4, 1933; s. John Stanley and Katherine Butler (Maguire) O'F.; m. Barbara Jeanne Wingbermuehle, Sept. 19, 1959; children: Bridget, Mary Margaret, Kathryn, James Maguire. BA, St. Louis U., 1984. V.p. Bank of St. Louis, 1966-72, exec. v.p., 1974-76; v.p. Gen. Bancshares, St. Louis, 1972-74; chmn. bd., chief exec. officer Traders Nat. Bank, Kansas City, Mo., 1976-78; pres. St. Louis Regional Commerce and Growth Assn., 1978-86, Automobile Club of Mo., St. Louis, 1986—. Bd. dirs. VP Fair, 1982—, Lindenwood Coll., 1983—, The Backstoppers, 1979—, v.p., 1980, pres., 1981, membership chmn., 1982, treas., 1983; bd. dirs. Cath. Charities, 1982—, pres., 1983-84; trustee St. Louis Coll. Pharmacy, 1981—, mem. nominating com., 1982, mem. budget com., 1983; trustee Laclede Sch. Law, 1982—; trustee, chmn. pub. relations com., mem. devel. com. St. Louis Art Mus., 1983—; mem. Mo. State 4-H Youth Adv. Council, 1981—; chmn. Port of Met. St. Louis Promotion Com., 1978—. Served with U.S. Army, 1955-57. Roman Catholic. Clubs: Mo. Athletic, St. Louis, Old Warson Country. Home: 5597 Lindell Blvd Saint Louis MO 63112 Office: Automobile Club of Mo 12901 N 40th Dr Saint Louis MO 63141 *

O'GALLAGHER, JOSEPH JAMES, physicist; b. Chgo., Oct. 23, 1939; s. James Edward and Rosalind M. (LaBreche) O'G.; m. Ellen M. Blie, Nov. 30, 1963; children: James Edward, Brian Arthur. BS, MIT, 1961; SM in Physics, U. Chgo., 1962, PhD in Physics, 1967. Research assoc. U. Chgo., 1967-69, sr. research assoc., 1977—; asst. prof. in physics U. Md., College Park, 1970-76; vis. scientist Argonne (Ill.) Nat. Lab., 1984—; sr. lectr. U. Chgo., 1988. Contbr. numerous articles to profl. jours. Alexander von Humboldt Found. fellow Max Planck Inst., 1976. Mem. Am. Phsyical Soc., Am. Solar Soc. Democrat. Roman Catholic. Avocations: music, jogging. Home: 1220 Douglas Ave Flossmoor IL 60422 Office: U Chgo 5640 S Ellis Ave Chicago IL 60637

OGBORN, BILLY LON, oral surgeon; b. Miller City, Ill., Aug. 9, 1940; s. Lon Edward and Eldora Grace (Pecord) O.; m. Rebecca Leigh Burnette, June 6, 1965; children: Rebecca Anne, William Lon. DDS, St. Louis U., 1965. Diplomate Am. Bd. Oral and Maxillofacial Surgery. Intern in oral and maxillofacial surgery La. State U. Med. Ctr., Shreveport, 1965-66, resident in oral and maxillofacial surgery, 1966-68; gen. practice in oral surgery Ogborn & Ward Oral Surgery, Cape Girardeau, Mo., 1970—; pres. B.L. Ogborn, DDS, Inc., Cape Girardeau, 1984—; pres., bd. dirs. Brokers Bonded Warehouse, Cape Girardeau, 1986—; bd. dirs. Cape Girardeau Drs. Park, 1970. Sponsor Ducks Unltd., Cape Girardeau, 1980—; mem. fin. com. Bill Emerson for Congress, Cape Girardeau, 1986; mem. fin. com., adminstrv. bd. Centiary United Meth. Ch., Cape Girardeau, 1981—; bd. dirs. Am. Cancer Soc., 1987—. Fellow Am. Assn. Oral and Maxillofacial Surgeons, Am. Coll. Oral and Maxillofacial Surgeons; mem. ADA, Mo. Dental Assn., S.E. Mo. Dental Assn., Cape Girardeau Dental Assn., Am. Acad. Implant Dentistry. Republican. Lodge: Lions. Avocations: skiing, hunting. Home: Rt 1 Cape Girardeau MO 63701 Office: #37 Doctors' Park Cape Girardeau MO 63701

OGBORN, LOREN ONIS, banker; b. Zionsville, Ind., Nov. 10, 1928; s. Loren E. and Carrie E. Ogborn; m. Dorothy L. Howard, June 11, 1949; children—Steven R., Sabrina R. Student Ind. Central Bus. Sch., 1946, La Salle Corr. Schs., 1946-48; Purdue U. Extension, 1960-63, Lake Forest Coll., 1968. With Hygrade Food Products Co., Indpls., 1949-59, asst. mgr. data processing; mgr. data processing Hammond Valve Corp. (Ind.), 1959-69; mgr. computer ops. Blue Cross-Blue Shield, Indpls., 1969-71; v.p., dir.mgmt. info. systems Gainer Bank, Gary, Ind., 1971—. Mem. Data Processing Mgmt. Assn., Assn. for Systems Mgmt. Home: 982 W 73d Ave Merrillville IN 46410 Office: Gainer Bank PO Box 209 Gary IN 46402

OGDEN, WILLIAM S., banker; b. Hackensack, N.J., 1927. B.A., Rutgers U., 1952. Former vice chmn., chief fin. officer Chase Manhattan Bank & Chase Manhattan Corp., N.Y.C.; chmn., chief exec. officer, dir. Continental Ill. Nat. Bank & Trust Co., Chgo., 1984-87; dir. Continental Ill. Corp. Served with USMC, 1946-48. Office: Continental Ill Nat Bank & Trust Co 231 S LaSalle St Chicago IL 60697

OGESEN, ROBERT BRUCE, dentist; b. Council Bluffs, Iowa, Aug. 26, 1934; s. Ever Julius and Agnes Elizabeth (Treptow) O.; m. Suzanne Jones, June 19, 1954; children: Cindy Sue, Robert B. II, Ann Elizabeth. DDS, U. Iowa, 1958. Gen. practice dentistry Iowa City, Iowa, 1961-73; with Towncrest Dental Offices, PC, Iowa City, 1973—; adj. faculty dentistry U. Iowa, 1965-85. Co-author: Hypnosis in Dentistry, 1985; contbr. articles to profl. jours. Mem. Iowa City Planning and Zoning Commn., 1971-81. Served to capt. USAF, 1958-61. Mem. ADA, Iowa Dental Assn. (council on dental care programs 1976-80), Univ. Dist. Dental Soc., Johnson County Dental Soc., Omicron Kappa Upsilon, Delta Sigma Delta. Presbyterian. Lodge: Optimist. Avocations: tennis, biking, traveling, landscaping. Home: 305 Woodridge Ave Iowa City IA 52240 Office: Towncrest Dental Offices PC 1039 Arthur St Iowa City IA 52240

OGLE, RICHARD GAYUS, oral surgeon; b. Marshall, Minn., May 10, 1940; s. Russell G. and Ethel (Geer) O.; m. Patricia Ann Reese, June 21, 1961; children—Dana K., Michelle M., Sandra L., Thomas R. B.S., U. Minn., 1962; D.D.S., 1964, M.S., 1968, M.D., 1975. Diplomate Am. Bd. Oral and Maxillofacial Surgery, Nat. Bd. Med. Examiners. Pvt. practice oral and maxillofacial surgery, Mankato, Minn., 1968-71; assoc. prof. U. Minn., Mpls., 1971-77; pvt. practice oral and maxillofacial surgery, Owatonna, Minn., 1977—. Contbr. articles to sci. jours. Basketball coach Owatonna Park and Recreation Dist., 1980-82; leader 4-H, Lakeville, Minn., 1973-75; dep. Steele County Mounted Posse, Owatonna, 1978-83. Mem. Am. Bd. Oral and Maxillofacial Surgeons (exec. adv. bd.), ADA, AMA, Internat. Coll. Surgeons, Minn. Soc. Oral and Maxillofacial Surgery (pres.), Nat. Bd. Dental Examiners (test constructor advisor com. 1976-81). Avocation: horseback riding. Office: Ogle Amundson PA 605 Hillcrest St Owatonna MN 55060

OGLESBY, PAUL LEONARD, JR., lawyer; b. Decatur, Ill., Aug. 17, 1955; s. Paul Leonard and Dorothy E. (Yeoman) O. B.A., U. Ill., 1977; J.D., So. Ill. U., 1980. Bar: Ill. 1980. Asst. state's atty. Coles County, Charleston, Ill., 1981-83; assoc. Dilsaver, Nelson & Ryan, Mattoon, Ill., 1983—. Officer USAR, 1977—. Mem. ABA, Res. Officers Assn., Ill. State Bar Assn., Coles-Cumberland Bar Assn. Republican. Methodist. Home: 1413 Lafayette Apt 4 Mattoon IL 61938 Office: Dilsaver Nelson & Ryan 1632 Broadway Mattoon IL 61938

O'HARA, JOHN PAUL, III, orthopaedic surgeon; b. Detroit, June 10, 1946; s. John P. Jr. and Genevieve Margaret (Spurgeon) O'H. BA, U. Mich., 1968, MD, 1972. Resident U. Va. Med. Ctr., Charlottesville, 1973-77; fellow Nuffield Orthopaedic Ctr., Oxford, Eng., 1977; practice medicine specializing in orthopaedic surgery Southfield, 1978—; staff Providence Hosp., Southfield, Mich., 1978—; pres. Providence Hosp. Med. Staff Research Found., 1984-85, bd. dirs., 1982—; bd. dirs. Mich. Master Health Plan, Southfield, 1982. Contbr. articles to profl. jours. Recipient Disting. Alumni award Brother Rice High Sch., 1986. Fellow Am. Acad. Orthopaedic Surgeery, Mid Am. Orthopaedic Soc.; mem. Detroit Orthopaedic Soc., Mich. Orthopaedic Soc. Roman Catholic. Clubs: Oakland Hills Country (Birmingham, Mich.), Beverly Hills (Mich.) Athletic. Avocations: earthwatch vol., travel, sports. Home: 29997 Briarbank Ct Southfield MI 48034 Office: Porretta & O'Hara Orthopaedic Surgeons PC 22250 Providence Dr #401 Southfield MI 48075

O'HARE, TERRENCE WILLIAM, systems manager; b. Bay City, Mich., Apr. 20, 1952; s. John William and Vida Flo (Roberts) O'H.; m. Sharon Marie Middleton, Aug. 4, 1973; children: Sean Michael, Blaine Patrick, Brian Daniel, Shannon Marie. AA, Delta Coll., 1972; BBA, Northwood Inst., 1974. Asst. op. technician Dow Chem. Co., Bay City, 1974-76; adjustment rep. Dow Chem. Co., Midland, Mich., 1976-79, C.F.S. systems analyst, 1979-82, C.F.S. systems mgr., 1982-85, U.S.A. treasury systems mgr., 1985—, mgr. customer fin. services and adjustment dept., 1987—. Den leader Boy Scouts Am., Bay City, 1982-83; baseball coach Bangor Township Recreation, 1985-87, soccer coach 1983-85. Episcopalian. Avocations: woodworking, working with children, golf. Home: 3952 Castle Dr Bay City MI 48706 Office: Dow Chem Co 2020 Willard H Dow Ctr Midland MI 48640

O'HEARN, MARY, educational consultant; b. Detroit, Mar. 5, 1933; d. Maurice Michael and Genevieve (Clor) O'H. BA, Sienna Heights Coll., 1960; postgrad. Mich. State U., 1961, Wayne State U., 1963, 65, 66; MA, Oakland U., 1977; JD, U. Detroit, 1986. Tchr. English, jr. high sch., Des Moines, 1952-55, Chgo., 1955-62, Warren, Mich., 1962-77; tchr. English, sr. high sch., Warren, 1977-79, lang. arts cons., 1979—; legal intern NLRB, Detroit, summer 1985; mem. Profl Staff Policy Bd., Warren, Mich. Mem. ABA, NEA, Mich. Edn. Assn., Warren Edn. Assn., Assn. Supervision and Curriculum Devel., Mich. Mensa, U. Detroit Alumni Assn., Oakland U. Alumni Assn. Club: Mich. Masters Swimmers. Home: 300 Riverfront Park Apt 5A Detroit MI 48226 Office: 31300 Anita St Warren MI 48093

O'HEARNE, JOHN JOSEPH, psychiatrist; b. Memphis, Tenn., Feb. 5, 1922; s. John Joseph and Norma Rose (Ford) O'H.; children: Patricia Ann, Marilyn Eileen, John Stephen, Brian Donal. BS, Southwestern U., Memphis, 1944; MD, U. Tenn., 1945; MS in Psychiatry, U. Colo., 1951. Diplomate Am. Bd. Psychiatry and Neurology. Intern Denver Gen. Hosp., 1945-46; fellow U. Colo., Denver, 1948-51, instr., 1949-52; instr. U. Denver, 1951; clin. dir. psychiatry Kansas City (Mo.) Gen. Hosp. and Psychiat. Receiving Ctr., 1952-56; practice medicine specializing in psychiatry Kansas City, 1956—; adj. prof. sociology U. Mo., Kansas City, 1986—; mem. staffs St. Luke's Hosp., Truman Med. Ctr., Menorah Hosp.; cons. Western Mo. Health Ctr., 1964—, Wines and Spirits Spltys., 1984—, Lifewise, Kansas City, 1984—; clin. prof. psychiatry U. Kans., 1972—, U. Mo., Kansas City, 1974—; adj. prof. sociology U. Mo., Kansas City, 1974—; pres. Transactional Analysis Inst., Kansas City, 1984—. Co-author Practical Transactional Analysis in Management, 1977; contbr. articles to profl. jours. Served to capt. AUS, 1942-45, 46-48. Recipient Bronze medal NASTAR, 1984. Fellow Am. Psychiat. Assn. (life), Am. Group Psychotherapy Assn. (dir. 1970-78, pres. 1974-78)), Internat. Assn. Group Psychotherapy (dir.), Am. Orthopsychiat. Assn. (life); mem. Am. Psychiat. Assn. (pres. Western Mo. dist. br. 1960-61, 64-65), Mo. State Med. Assn. (chmn. mental health com. 1960-62, physicians rehab. com. 1979—, chmn. 1987—), Jackson County Med. Soc. (chmn. mental health com. 1959-66), Internat. Transactional Analysis Assn. (trustee 1972-83), Internat. Wine and Food Soc. of London. Republican. Episcopalian. Club: Carriage (Kansas City). Avocations: photography, wine, travel, herb gardening. Office: 4706 Broadway Suite 103 Kansas City MO 64112

O'HERN, THOMAS MONROE, obstetrician/gynecologist; b. Hannibal, Mo., Oct. 4, 1928; s. Alfred Edward and Alma Margaret (Monroe) O'H.; m. Lorraine Rosella Brisky, Oct. 3, 1952; children: Thomas Jr., Mary K., Cynthia M., Janet L. BA, Westminster Coll., Fulton, Mo., 1949; MD, St. Louis U., 1953. Diplomate Am. Bd. Ob-Gyn. Commd. 1st lt. USAF, 1953, advanced through grades to col., 1969; intern Los Angeles County Harbor Gen. Hosp. USAF, Torrence, 1953-54; resident in ob-gyn Walter Reed Gen. Hosp. USAF, Washington, 1956-59, cons. Hdqrs., 1971-75; resigned USAF, 1975; practice medicine specializing in ob-gyn Springfield, Ill., 1975—; clin. asst. prof. ob-gyn sch. medicine So. Ill. U., 1975—. Fellow Am. Coll. Ob/Gyn; mem. AMA. Home: 1600 Park Dr Springfield IL 62704 Office: Sangamon Ob/Gyn, Ltd 1315 N 5th St Springfield IL 62702

OHL, FERRIS ELWOOD, music educator, conductor; b. Crawford County, Ohio, Sept. 10, 1914; s. George M. and Josie E. (Solze) O; m. Dorothy Doolittle, May 24, 1942; children—Vicki Ohl Braley, Laura Ohl Ross. B.M., Heidelberg Coll., 1936; M.M., Cin. Conservatory, 1946; M.S., Columbia U., 1950, diploma, 1952, Ed.D., 1955, postgrad., 1964-65. Dir. vocal and instrumental music Pioneer (Ohio) Pub. Schs., 1936-41; asst. prof. voice and chorus Heidelberg Coll., Tiffin, Ohio, 1946-47, assoc. prof., 1949-52, prof., 1953-85, chmn. dept. music, prof., 1965-85; vis. prof. Columbia Tchrs. Coll., N.Y.C., 1964-65; condr. Heidelberg Concert Choir, 1946-82, Tiffinian Male Chorus Trinity UCC Choir, 1946-66; dir. ann. Messiah; guest condr. and clinician, Ohio. Programming cons. Tiffin Arts Council. Served to maj. AUS, 1941-46. Decorated Bronze Star (2). Recipient medal U. Heidelberg (W. Ger.), 1978. Fellow Internat. Inst. Art and Letters, Internat. Sci. Info. Service, Am. Inst. Arts and Letters; mem. Nat. Assn. Tchrs. Singing (past pres.), Am. Choral Dirs. (past lt. gov.), Ohio Music Educators Assn., Ohio Music Tchrs. Assn., Internat. Platform Assn. Arranger: Ferris Ohl Choral Series, 1961-65. Lodges: Elks, Tiffin Rotary. Home: 98 Woodmere Dr Tiffin OH 44883 Office: Heidelberg Coll East Perry St Tiffin OH 44883

OHLE, LESTER C., training and development director; b. Chgo., Apr. 26, 1921; s. Ludwig Rudolph Ohle and Jennie Miller; m. Jane Armstrong, Dec. 29, 1951; children: Susan Ficklin, John Herbert. BA, Ill. Wesleyan U., 1947; postgrad., U. Chgo., 1949. Grain buyer Quaker Oats Co., Chgo., 1947-49; field rep. Calkins Mfg., Spokane, Wash., 1950-53; with sales and sales mgmt. Geigy Corp., Ardsley, N.Y., 1953-71; dir. mktg. U.S. Chem. Co., 1971-73; mgr. export/import, sales tng. mgr., sr. tng. and devel. cons. Mobay Corp., Kansas City, Mo., 1973-86; cons. in field. Served as cpl. Signal Corps U.S. Army, 1942-46, PTO. Mem. Am. Soc. Tng. and Devel., Nat. Soc. Sales Tng. Execs., Nat. Agrl. Mktg. Assn. Lodges: Masons, Optimists. Avocations: gardening, model rail roading, reading.

OHLEMACHER, JEFFREY BURTON, plant manager; b. Elyria, Ohio, Apr. 2, 1958; s. Robert Lewis and Lois Ann (Tattersall) O.; m. Cynthia Ann O'Brien, May 23, 1981; children: Michael Burton, Matthew Joseph. BSME, Ohio State U., 1981. Engr. Elyria Mfg. Corp., 1974-81, plant mgr., 1981-87, corp. sec., plant mgr. evp, plant mgr., 1987—. Active Leadership Lorain County (Ohio), 1985; bd. dirs. Arthritis Found., Amherst, Ohio, 1986—; 2d v.p. Elyria Jaycees, 1983-84, exec. v.p., 1985. Mem. ASME, Nat. Screw Machine Products Assn. (treas. Lake Erie Dist. 1983, program chmn. 1984, chmn. 1985). Republican. Clubs: Polish (Elyria), Elyria Country. Avocations: golf, running, fishing. Home: 347 Colgate Ave Elyria OH 44035 Office: Elyria Mfg Corp PO Box 479 145 Northrop St Elyria OH 44035

OHLRICH, ELIZABETH SCHOWALTER, physician, health science administrator, educator; b. Beloit, Wis., Nov. 7, 1943; d. Clarence H. and Ruth Mildred (Knoble) Schowalter; m. Warren H. Olrich, Aug. 28, 1965 (div. Jan. 1976); children: Wayne Hargen, Miles Arthur. BS with honors, U. Wis., 1965, MS, 1967, PhD, 1968, MD with honors, 1980. Research assoc. Nat. Med. Ctr. Children's Hosp., Washington, 1968-76; intern, then resident in pediatrics U. Wis. Hosp. and clinics, Madison, 1980-83; med. dir. eating disorder program U. Wis. Hosp., Madison, 1983—; research assoc. Walter Reed Army Inst. of Research, Washington, 1968-71; adj. asst. prof. Antioch Coll., Balt., 1975-76; asst. prof. dept. pediatrics U. Wis. Med. Sch., Madison, 1983-87, assoc. prof., 1987—. Contbr. articles to profl. jours. Active Med. Aid to Cen. Am., 1986. Mem. Soc. Adolescent Medicine. Democrat. Avocations: quilting, gourmet cooking, collecting wines, bird watching. Office: U Wis Hosp 600 Highland Ave Madison WI 53792

OHMAN, RICHARD MICHAEL, artist; b. Erie, Pa., May 8, 1946. BA, Mercyhurst Coll., 1972; MFA, Ohio U., 1975. Instr. Ohio U., Chillicothe, 1974-80, asst. prof. art, 1980-85; freelance artist, 1985—. Exhibited in group shows at Butler Mus., Exhbn. of Contemporary Art Palm Beach, Am. Painters in Paris, others. Recipient Wagnalls Meml. award, 1978, Yassinoff Meml. award, 1977, Internat. Photo Soc. award; Ohio Arts Council grantee. Home: PO Box 9448 Cincinnati OH 45209 Office: c/o The Loft Gallery 1117 Pendleton St Cincinnati OH 45210

OHOTNICKY, STEPHEN THADDEUS, engineering executive; b. Torrington, Conn., Dec. 22, 1943; s. Stephen Edward and Emily C. (Wilczek) O.; m. Barbara Marie Shay, June 11, 1966; children: Peter, Susan. BS, U.S. Mil. Acad., 1966; MSE, U. Mich., 1971; MBA, Eastern Mich. U., 1973. Profl. engr., Mich. Commd. 2d lt. U.S. Army, 1966, advanced through grades to capt., 1968, served in Vietnam, resigned, 1970; materials and project engr. Hydra-matic div. Gen. Motors Corp., Ypsilanti, Mich., 1971-77, supr. quality control, 1977-80, staff engr., 1980-86, supplier quality, 1986—. Chmn. Parks and Recreation Commn., Superior Township, Mich., 1976-79; scouting coordinator Washtenaw County Explorer Post 400, Ypsilanti, 1983—. NSF trainee, 1970-71. Mem. Am. Soc. for Metals, Am. Soc. for Quality Control, Engring. Soc. Detroit, West Point Soc. (sec. 1984-87). Republican. Roman Catholic. Avocations: golf, fishing, running. Home: 3135 Timberview Rd Saline MI 48176 Office: Hydra-matic div Gen Motors Corp Ecorse & Wiard Rds Ypsilanti MI 48198

OJALA, RICHARD HENRY, hotelier; b. Ann Arbor, Mich., May 1, 1950; s. Reuben Henry Ojala and Donna (Yon) Roberts; m. Cynthia Marie Cryderman, Oct. 6, 1973; children—Richard Preston, Rachel Marie, Steven Eric. B.S. in Child Devel. cum laude, Lake Superior State Coll., 1979. Ptnr. Energy Enterprises, Sault Ste. Marie, Mich., 1981-83, owner, mgr., 1983—; gen. mgr. Doral Motel, Inc., Sault Ste. Marie, 1981—; owner Doral Motel/Friendship Inn, Sault Ste. Marie, 1985—. Founder, bd. dirs. Crisis Pregnancy Ctr., 1982—, Christian Action Council, 1980; bd. dirs. Child Evangelism Fellowship, 1980—, past pres. Served with U.S. Army, 1969-71. Mem. Sault Ste. Marie C. of C., Mich. Lodging Assn. Baptist. Avocations: fishing; hunting; tennis; golf. Home: 536 E Portage St Sault Saint Marie MI 49783 Office: Doral Motel/Friendship Inn 518 E Portage St Sault Saint Marie MI 49783

O'KEEFE, FRANCIS RONALD, lawyer; b. Gt. Neck, N.Y., Oct. 7, 1950; s. Francis Joseph and Bridget Anne (Coady) O'K.; m. Pamelinda Lee, Aug. 18, 1979. A.B., Georgetown U., 1972; J.D., Cleve.-Marshall Coll., 1977. Bar: Ohio 1977, U.S. Dist. Ct. (no. dist.) Ohio 1978. sole practice, 1977-86; sec. and gen. counsel The Broadview Fin. Corp.1986—. Recipient Sindell Tort Competition prize Cleve.-Marshall Law Sch., 1977. Mem. ABA, Ohio State Bar Assn., Greater Cleve. Bar Assn., Delta Theta Phi (Article Most Useful to Practicing Attys. award 1977). Avocations: musical compositions; art. Home: 1053 Forest Cliff Dr Lakewood OH 44107 Office: Broadview Fin Corp 6000 Rockside Woods Blvd Cleveland OH 44121

O'KEEFE, GERALD FRANCIS, bishop; b. St. Paul, Mar. 30, 1918; s. Francis Patrick and Lucille Mary (McDonald) O'K. Student, St. Paul Sem., 1938-44; B.A., Coll. St. Thomas, 1945; LLD (hon.), St. Ambrose Coll., 1967, Loras Coll., 1967; LHD, Marycrest Coll., 1967. Ordained priest Roman Cath. Ch., 1944. Asst. St. Paul Cathedral, 1944, rector, 1961-67; chancellor Archdiocese of St. Paul, 1945-61, aux. bishop, 1961-67, vicar gen., 1962-67; bishop Diocese of Davenport, Iowa, 1967—; instr. St. Thomas Acad., St. Paul, 1944-45. Home: 1430 Clay St Davenport IA 52804 Office: Diocese of Davenport 2706 Gaines Davenport IA 52804

OKNER, SEYMOUR N., insurance company executive. Pres. Signature Group, Schaumburg, Ill. Office: Signature Group 200 N Martingale Rd Schaumburg IL 60194 *

OKRUTNY, JEFFREY JOSEPH, engineer; b. Pitts., July 28, 1955; s. Joseph Jr. and Joann Amelia (Bialkowski) O.; m. Teresa Jo Wynn, Aug. 20, 1977. BSCE, Ohio No. U., 1978; MS in Engring. Mgmt., U. Dayton, 1983. Design engr. Winstandley & Assocs., Kettering, Ohio, 1978; project engr. The Duriron Co., Dayton, Ohio, 1979-82; engr. computer aided design/computer aided mfg. Monarch Marking div. Pitney Bowes Inc., Miamisburg, Ohio, 1982—. Advisor Engring. and Sci. Careers Program, Dayton, 1982-86, Explorer Scouts, Miamisburg, 1986. Mem. Am. Mgmt. Assn., Dayton Engrs. Club, Order of the Engr.-Ohio No., CATIA Operators Exchange (v.p. 1985—), CADAM Users Exchange (com. chmn. 1984—), Phi Mu Delta (sec. Ada, Ohio chpt. 1976-77). Republican. Presbyterian. Avocations: 35mm photography, fgn. travel, bicycling, darkroom photography. Office: Monarch Marking PO Box 608 Dayton OH 45401

OKUNIEFF, MICHAEL, physician; b. Wilno, Poland, Apr. 24, 1923; came to U.S., 1951; s. Pinchos and Paula (Deweltow) O.; m. Beverly Sue Kailes, Apr. 21, 1956; children—Paul G., Paula E., Rise J., Rhoda Lee. M.D., U. Munich, 1949. Diplomate Am. Bd. Family Practice. Intern, Beth David Hosp., N.Y.C., 1951-52; resident in internal medicine Morrisiana City Hosp., Bronx, N.Y., 1952-53, U. Ill. Research and Ednl. Hosps., Chgo., 1953-55; practice medicine specializing in family practice, Chgo., 1956—; mem. staffs Hyde Park Community Hosp., Chgo., South Shore Hosp., Chgo. Mem. Ill. Acad. Family Practice (del. 1980-83), AMA, Ill. Med. Soc., Chgo. Med. Soc., Am. Acad. Family Practice. Home: 116 Plum Tree Ln Wilmette IL 60091 Office: 7271 S Exchange Ave Chicago IL 60649

OLAND, S. M., brewing company executive. Pres. LaBatt Brewing Co., Ltd., London, Ont., Can. Office: Labatt Brewing Co Ltd, 150 Simcoe St, London, ON Canada N6A 4M3 *

OLANDER, VALERIE VAUGHN, professional numismatist; b. Washington, Feb. 4, 1959; d. Bruce Alan Sr. and Patricia Lavon (Weiss) O.; m. Randall Mathew Gilbertson, Aug. 23, 1980 (div. Oct. 1983). Student, Waldorf Jr. Coll., 1977, U. Minn., 1978. Acctg. clk. Minn. Protective Life Ins. Co., Mpls., 1978-79; program mgr. Calstar, Inc., Mpls., 1979-85; sales rep. Undercover Wear, Inc., 1986—; ptnr. Garden of Eden Numismatic Enterprises, Mpls., 1985—. Mem. Am. Numismatic Assn. (life), Cen. States Numismatic Soc. (life), Fla. United Numismatists, Minn. Orgn. Numismatists, Nat. Assn. for Female Execs., Soc. U.S. Commemorative Coins (life, program chmn. 1986), LWV, NOW, ACLU (N.Y.C. chpt.), Ams. for Legal Reform (Washington chpt.). Lutheran. Avocations: Bavarian folk painting, ballroom dancing, crocheting. Office: Garden of Eden Numismatic Enterprises PO Box 35313 Minneapolis MN 55435

O'LAUGHLIN, JOSEPH CHRISTOPHER, gastroenterologist, educator; b. Phila., Dec. 23, 1949; s. James Clare and Sarah Catherine (Bookford) O'L.; m. Deborah Caroline Ventrone, Dec. 27, 1975; 1 child, Matthew Christopher. B.S. in Biology, U. Scranton (Pa.), 1971; D.O., Phila. Coll. Osteo. Medicine, 1975. Diplomate Am. Bd. Internal Medicine. Intern, Detroit Osteo. Hosp., 1975-76, resident in internal medicine, 1976-78; sr. postdoctoral fellow in gastroenterology U. Mo. Sch. Medicine, Columbia, 1978-80; pvt. practice medicine specializing in gastroenterology, Warren, Mich., 1980—; mem. staff BiCounty Hosp., Warren, 1980—, Mt. Clemens (Mich.) Gen. Hosp., 1980—, chmn. endoscopy com. ; clin. asst. prof. medicine Mich. State U., East Lansing, 1980—; v.p. Tri-County Gastroenterology P.C.; lectr. in field. Recipient Outstanding Contbrn. Med. Edn. award Mt. Clemens Gen. Hosp., 1982. Mem. Am. Gastroenterol. Assn., Am. Soc. Gastrointestinal Endoscopy, Detroit Gastroenterol. Soc. Contbr. chpts. to books, articles to profl. publs. Office: Tri-County Gastroenterology PC 13552 Martin St Suite A Warren MI 48093

O'LAUGHLIN, MARJORIE, state official. Treas. State of Ind., Indpls. Office: Treasurer's Office 242 State House Indianapolis IN 46204 *

OLBERG, F. FORBES, bank executive; b. 1923. Chmn. bd. dirs. Banks of Iowa, Des Moines. Office: Banks of Iowa Inc 520 Walnut Des Moines IA 50306 *

OLD, HAROLD EVANS, JR., state official; b. Mansfield, Ohio, Sept. 11, 1939; s. Harold Evans and Pearl Edna (Beaschler) O.; m. Georgia A. Bernath, June 9, 1962 (div. July 1982); children—Eric K., Philip E. B.S., Marquette U., 1961; M.A., Western Mich. U., 1970; Ph.D., Mich. State U., 1973; postgrad. Naval War Coll., 1982-83. Grad. asst. Western Mich. U., Kalamazoo, also Mich. State U., East Lansing, 1967-72; instr. U. Conn., Storrs, 1972-73; exec. mgr. Ponderosa Systems, Lansing, Mich., 1973-74; adminstr. Mich. Dept. Pub. Health, Lansing, 1974-79, Mich. Dept. Labor, Lansing, 1979—; pres. Cedar Wood Homes, Inc., Schaumburg, Ill., 1983—. Served to lt. USN, 1961-67; capt. Res. NROTC scholar, 1957. Mem. Am. Polit. Sci. Assn., Res. Officers Assn., Naval Inst., Am. Soc. Pub. Adminstrn. (pres. Lansing 1982-83), Naval Res. Assn. (pres. Lansing 1970-73, 75—), Navy League, Am. Def. Preparedness Assn., Blue Jackets Assn. Club: Mich. Comdrs.

OLDHAM, JANE KIDWELL, psychologist; b. Denver, Feb. 20, 1952; d. Robert and Betty Ann (Hooper) Kidwell; m. John William Oldham, Feb. 4, 1983; children: Sarah Jane, Rachael Anne. BA in Polit. Sci., Austin Peay State U., Clarksville, Tenn., 1974, MA in Clin. Psycology, 1977. Lic. psychologist, Ky. Dir. guidance Clarksville Acad., 1974-77; mem. staff Western State Hosp., Hopkinsville, Ky., 1977-80; clin. coordinator Massac Mental Health, Metropolis, Ill., 1980—; tchr. Shawnee Community Coll., Ullin, Ill., 1983—; cons. U.S. Dept. Labor, Golconda, 1986—. Elder United Presbyn. Ch., Metropolis, 1983—. State of Ill. grantee, 1984. Mem. Am. Psychol. Assn., Christian Assn. Psychol. Studies, Beta Sigma Phi. Republican. Lodge: Civitan (local pres. 1982-84). Home: 18 Chick St Metropolis IL 62960 Office: Massac Mental Health PO Box 901 Metropolis IL 62960

OLDS, REID HARRISON, dentist; b. Pontiac, Mich., Apr. 30, 1956; s. Jospeh Wesley and Winifred Lucille (Breithhaupt) O.; m. Tracey Rae Rust, Apr. 13, 1985. BS cum laude, Western Mich. U., 1978; DDS, U. Mich., 1982. Assoc. dentist Phillip J. Curtis DDS, Flint, Mich., 1982-83, Robert Leach DDS, Grand Blanc, Mich., 1983-85; gen. practice dentistry Mt. Morris, Mich., 1985—. Mem. ADA, Mich. Dental Assn., Genesee Dist. Dental Soc. Republican. Methodist. Avocations: golf, snow skiing, tennis, bowling, jogging. Home: 5446 Copley Square Grand Blanc MI 48439 Office: PO Box 406 Mount Morris MI 48458

OLDZIEWSKI, GEORGE ALBERT, mining company executive; b. Chgo., Sept. 27, 1918; s. Victor and Olga (Schafer) O. Student bus. adminstrn. and acctg., Bryant and Stratton, Chgo., 1946-49. Pres. OGG Mining & Investing Inc., Chgo., 1974—, bd. dirs.; with office services dept. Midas Internat. Corp., Chgo., 1976-86; pres. OGG Corp., Chgo., 1974—, also bd. dirs.; pres. OGG Resources Ltd., B.C., Can.; also bd. dirs. OGG Resources Ltd., Chgo. Served to sgt. U.S. Army, 1941-45, ETO. Roman Catholic. Avocations: golf, collecting. Home and Office: 4428 S Kilpatrick Ave Chicago IL 60632

O' LEARY, TIMOTHY MICHAEL, real estate corporation officer; b. Savanna, Ill., Mar. 24, 1946; s. John Patrick and Hazel (Shaw) O 'L.; m. Patricia Ann Woosnam, Feb. 25, 1978; children: Kevin, Kathleen, Maureen, Mary Margaret, Michael. BS, No. Ill. U., 1970, MS, 1974. Cert. comml. investment mem. Systems programmer Newel Co., Freeport, Ill., 1970-71, acting mgr. accounts receivable, 1971-73; v.p., treas. HTO Real Estate Services, Des Plaines, Ill., 1974—; chmn. profl. standards com. Chgo. Bd. Realtors, 1984—. Mem. sch. bd. St. Luke Sch., River Forest, Ill., 1985—, chmn. 1987—. Mem. Soc. Indsl. and Office Realtors (vice-chmn. regional seminar edn. 1984—, mem. exec. com. Chgo. Chpt. 1987—), Oak Park Jaycees (past pres.), Realtors Nat. Mktg. Inst. Roman Catholic. Club: Realtors 40 (Chgo.) (clk. 1985-86). Avocations: sailing, fishing. Home: 612 Ashland River Forest IL 60305 Office: HTO Real Estate Services Inc 1111 E Touhy Ave Des Plaines IL 60018

OLECKNO, WILLIAM ANTON, educator; b. St. Charles, Ill., Dec. 16, 1948; s. Adolph B. and Barbara (Walrod) O.; m. Karen Marie Guzauskas, Dec. 27, 1975. BS, Ind. U., Indpls., 1971; MPH, U. Pitts., 1973; HSD, Ind. U., 1980. Registered profl. sanitarian, Ind. Sanitarian, DuPage County Health Dept., Wheaton, Ill., 1970-71, Ill. Dept. Pub. Health, Aurora, Ill., 1972; research assoc. Consad Research Corp., Pitts., 1973; instr., coordinator environ. health scis. program Ind. U. Med. Sch., Indpls., 1973-76; asst. prof., coordinator environ. health scis., 1976-80; assoc. prof., dir. community health program No. Ill. U., DeKalb, 1980—; pub. health and safety cons. Nat. Automatic Merchandising Assn., Chgo., 1975-80; vis. lectr. Ind. U., Bloomington, 1977-78; mem. health manpower adv. council Ind. Health Careers, Inc., 1976-80; v.p. bd. dirs. Am. Heart Assn., DeKalb County, 1981-83; chmn. DeKalb County Health Planning com., 1982-83. Recipient A. Harry Bliss editorial award Jour. Environ. Health, 1984; Ill. State Merit scholar, 1967; USPHS traineeship, 1972; grantee USPHS, 1973-78, Regional Ind. Med. Program, 1975-76, HHS,1981, Ill. Environ. Health Assn., 1986. Fellow The Royal Soc. Health (London); mem. Nat. Environ. Health Assn. (chmn. individual and community water supply com. 1983-85, chmn. publs. com. 1985-87, mem. Jour. Adv. Com. 1986-87; grantee Ill. assn., 1986, presdl. citation 1984), Am. Pub. Health Assn., Ill. Environ. Health Assn. (editorial bd. jour. 1985-86, bd. dirs. 1987—), Ill. Pub. Health Assn., Eta Sigma Gamma, Phi Delta Kappa. Author: Water Quality Parameters, 1982; Alternative Methods of Centralized Wastewater Treatment, 1982; mem. editorial bd Hoosier Sanitarian, 1977-78, editor, 1978-80; contbr. articles on environ. and pub. health to profl. jours.

OLEJKO, TERRY DAVID, oral and maxillofacial surgeon; b. Lorain, Ohio, Mar. 5, 1950; s. John Joseph and Stella Marie (Berish) O.; m. Ann Morgan Fletcher, June 30, 1973; children: Daniel Fletcher, Elizabeth Morgan. BS in Chemistry, Miami U., 1972; DDS cum laude, Ohio State U., 1976; MS, U. Iowa, 1982. Diplomate Am. Bd. Oral and Maxillofacial Surgeons. Assoc. gen. dentistry Columbus, Ohio, 1976-78; intern Cuyahoga County Hosps., Cleve., 1979; resident U. Iowa Hosps. and Clinics, Iowa City, 1982; assoc. in oral and maxillofacial surgery Keen, Jordan & Claydon Ltd., Champaign and Mattoon, Ill., 1982-84; practice dentistry specializing in oral and maxillofacial surgery Delaware and Westerville, Ohio, 1984—; adj. prof. dept. oral and maxillofacial surgery Ohio State U., Columbus, 1986—; bd. dirs. Emergency Med. Service, Delaware County, Ohio. Bd. dirs. Delaware County unit Am. Cancer Soc., 1986-87. Research grantee Ross Labs. Inc., 1980; recipient Merle Hale Disting. Research award U. Iowa Hosps., 1982. Fellow Am. Assn. Oral and Maxillofacial Surgeons; mem. ADA, Ohio Dental Assn., Ohio Soc. Oral and Maxillofacial Surgeons, Ill. Soc. Oral and Maxillofacial Surgeons, Omicron Kappa Upsilon. Avocations: running, bicycling, racquetball. Home: 587 Highmeadows Village Dr Powell OH 43065 Office: 615 Copeland Mill Rd Westerville OH 43081

OLESINSKI, RICHARD WLODRZIMIERZ, metallurgical engineer; b. Cracow, Poland, Sept. 24, 1951; s. Wlodrzimierz and Zofia (Kania) O; m. Elzbieta Mayer, May 2, 1984. MS, Acad. Mining and Metallurgy, Cracow, 1974; DSc in Extractive Metallurgy, Polytechnics of Silesia, Katowice, Poland, 1978. Registered profl. engr. From postgrad. asst. to asst. prof. metallurgy Polytechnics of Silesia, 1975-79; dir. metal. progress, Eynon-Beyer chair in metallurgy Youngstown (Ohio) State U., 1980-82; research assoc. U. Fla., Gainsville, 1982-84; asst. editor Chemical Abstracts Service, Columbus, Ohio, 1985—. Contbr. articles to profl. jours. Mem. AIME (metall. soc.), Sigma Xi. Home: 2503 Abbotsford Way Dublin OH 43017

OLGAARD, MARK KERMIT, osteopath; b. Zanesville, Ohio, July 5, 1952; s. Kermit M. and Gloria M. (Anderson) O.; m. Jane E. VanDuzen, Dec. 21, 1974; children: Ericka, Kristin, Catherine. BS, Alma (Mich.) Coll., 1974; DO, Kirksville (Mo.) Coll. Osteo. Medicine, 1982. Diplomate Nat. Bd. Examiners. Intern Kirksville Osteo. Health Ctr., 1982-83; gen. practice osteo. medicine Au Gres, Mich., 1983—; mem. adv. bd. Huron Home Health, Tawas City, Mich., 1985—. Contbr. articles to profl. jours. Mem. Am. Osteo. Assn., Mich. Assn. Osteo. Physicians and Surgeons, Bay Assn. Osteo. Physicians and Surgeons (v.p. 1985-86, pres. 1987—). Office: Au Gres Family Clinic PC 302 S Main Au Gres MI 48703

OLIKER, STEPHEN LAWRENCE, advertising executive; b. Pitts., Dec. 4, 1935; s. Jerry and Madelene (Marlin) O.; m. Carol Joy Rubin, June 22, 1958; children: David Charles, Robert Jacob, Diane Lynn. BS, Syracuse U., 1957. Sr. copywriter Keller-Crescent, Evansville, Ind., 1969-75, adminstv. asst., 1980-82, assoc. creative dir., 1975-80, retail creative dir., 1982-83, creative bus. mgr., 1983—. Served with USAR. Home: 712 S Saint James Evansville IN 47714

OLIPHANT, J. J., provincial judge. Judge Ct. of Queen's Bench, Man., Can. Office: Court of Queen's Bench, Court House Box 68, Brandon, MB Canada R3C 0V8 *

OLIVA, JAYNE ELLEN, marketing professional; b. Coral Gables, Fla., Apr. 22, 1958; s. Louis Angelo and Jeannette (L'Heureux) O.; m. R. Paul Faxon, June 12, 1982. B in Communications, Boston U., 1980; MBA, Northwestern U., 1986. Asst. dir. publs. Liberty Mutual Ins. Cos., Boston, 1980-82; mgr. div. communications and mktg. The Am. Hosp. Assn., Chgo., 1982—, The Hosp. Research and Edl. Trust, Chgo., 1982—. Author Executive Writing, Speaking and Listening Skills, 1983. U. Colo. fellow; recipient award of Excellance 1983, award of Merit Soc. for Tech. Communication 1984, Cert. Achievement, 1984; named Outstanding Young Women of Am., 1984. Mem. Am. Mktg. Assn., Internat. Assn. Bus. Communicators (award of excellance, 1981, honorable mention, 1985). Avocations: sailing, travel, photography. Home: 734-3 Hinman Ave Evanston IL 60202 Office: Am Hosp Assn 840 N Lake Shore Dr Chicago IL 60611

OLIVER, ALAN MARK, osteopathic physician; b. Kansas City, Mo., Feb. 28, 1952; s. William and Freda Rose (Zackowitz) O.; m. Shirley Ann Owen, Aug. 7, 1980. D.O., U. Health Scis. Coll. Osteo. Medicine, Kansas City, Mo., 1979. Diplomate Am. Bd. Emergency Medicine. Flexible Intern Richmond Heights Gen. Hosp. (Ohio), 1979-80; resident in emergency medicine U. Ky. Med. Ctr., Lexington, 1980-82; spl. fellow critical care medicine Cleve. Clinic Found., 1981—; mem. staff St. Luke's Hosp., 1983—, chief surg. intensive care div., 1983—. NSF research grantee, 1972, 73. Mem. Soc. Critical Care Medicine, Am. Coll. Emergency Physicians, Am. Osteo. Assn., Psi Sigma Alpha. Home: 25000 S Woodland St Beachwood OH 44122 Office: St Lukes Hosp 11311 Shaker Blvd Cleveland OH 44104

OLIVER, DEBBIE A., lab technician; b. Pottsdam, Pa., July 15, 1954; d. Daniel Allen and Shirley Ann (Weidner) McWilliams; m. Richard McKinney, June 8, 1972 (div. 1977); 1 child, Alysha Rea McKinney; m. Vaughan D. Oliver, Feb. 22, 1986 (div. 1987); children: Vaughan D., John V., Lisa A. Student, U. Cin., 1972-84. Research asst. Procter & Gamble, Cin., 1978—; counselor Shelter for Battered Women and Siblings, Cin., 1982—. Republican. Presbyterian. Home: 9 Vernon Ct Fairfield OH 45014 Office: Procter & Gamble 11520 Reed Hartman Hwy Cincinnati OH 45241

OLIVER, EDWARD CARL, investment executive; b. St. Paul, May 31, 1930; s. Charles Edmund and Esther Marie (Bjugstad) O.; m. Charlotte Severson, Sept. 15, 1956; children—Charles E., Andrew T., Peter A. B.A., U. Minn., 1955. Sales rep. Armstrong Cork Co., N.Y.C., 1955; registered rep. Piper, Jaffray & Hopwood, Mpls., 1958; mgr. Mut. Funds, Inc. subs. Dayton's, Mpls., 1964; mgr. NWNL Mgmt. Corp. subs. Northwestern Nat. Life Ins. Co., Mpls., 1968-72, v.p., 1972-81, pres., dir., 1981—; v.p. Select Cash Mgmt. Fund, Inc., Select Capital Growth Fund, Inc., Select High Yield Fund, Inc., Northwestern Cash Fund, Inc. Bd. dirs. Hennepin County United Way, 1963; mem. Minn. Republican Party State Central Com., 1972-75. Served to sgt. USAF, 1951-52. Mem. Life Ins. Mktg. and Research Assn. (fin. products mktg. com.), Internat. Assn. Fin. Planners (past pres. Twin City chpt., mem. nat. governing com.), Psi Upsilon. Presbyterian (elder). Club: Mpls. Athletic. Home: 20230 Cottagewood Rd Deephaven MN 55331 Office: 20 Washington Ave S Minneapolis MN 55440

OLIVER, JERRY LEE, controller; b. Somerville, Tenn., Feb. 7, 1952; s. Aubrey Hulon and Helen Earlene (Henley) O.; m. June Marie Chapman, Aug. 21, 1982; 1 child, Peter Michael. BA in Philosophy, Rhodes Coll., 1974; MFA, U. N.C., 1978, MBA in Acctg., 1981. CPA, N.C. Staff acct. Arthur Young & Co., Washington, 1981-83; instr. U. Mo., Columbia, 1983; controller, treas. Corp. Edn. Resources, Fairfield, Iowa, 1984—. Mem. Am. Inst. CPA's, Iowa Soc. CPA's, Nat. Acctg. Assn., Phi Beta Kappa. Roman Catholic. Avocations: bus. writing, bus. book revs. Office: Corp Edn Resources Inc 116 W Burlington Fairfield IA 52556

OLIVIER, SOLANGES DESROCHES, nurse; b. Jeremie, Haiti, Feb. 18, 1933; came to U.S., 1956; d. Benoit and Aglaée (Vilvalex) Desroches; m. Oswald Olivier, June 20, 1959; children: Mildred, Ernnst, Oswald. Grad. Sch. Nursing, Port-au-Prince, 1955; student Communicable Disease Nursing, Chgo., 1957; BS in Nursing, Coll. St. Francis, Joliet, 1979; postgrad. masters program. Nurse Mother Cabrini Hosp., Chgo., 1957-61, Norwegian Am. Hosp., Chgo., 1961-65; nurse in charge Ill. State Psychiat. Inst., 1960-63; supr. Orthodox Jewish Home for Aged, Jewish Gen. Hosp., Montreal, Que., Can., 1968-69; nurse N.W. Community Hosp., Arlington Heights, Ill., 1969—; sch. nurse Ill. Deaf and Blind Sch., Glen Ellyn, Ill., 1983—. Producer craftwork, dolls for Haitian orphans. Active Our Lady of the Wayside Women's Club, Arlington Heights, 1969—; mem. altar com. Our Lady of the Wayside, 1969—; mem. St. Viator fund-raiser com., 1969—; mem. Sacred Heart of Mary Mothers Club, 1974-78, Interracial Group, Arlington Heights, 1969—. Recipient cert. Appreciation for aid to orphan children of Haiti, UNICEF, 1970-79, Good Citizen award, 1984. Mem. Haitian Nurses Assn., Can. Nurses Assn., Orthopedic Nurses Assn., R.N. Assn., Assn. St. Francis Alumnae. Roman Catholic. Home: 417 S Patton Arlington Heights IL 60005

OLLER, HARRY H., real estate appraising company executive; b. Taylorville, Ill., Feb. 4, 1935; s. Guy R. and Flossie (Morgan) O.; m. Jeanne E. Brady, Sept. 26, 1964; children: Todd, Guy, Colleen, Daniel. BA, Milliken U., 1961. Loan officer Mercantile Mortgage Co., St. Louis, 1962-65; chief appraiser Germania Federal, Alton, Ill., 1965-68; owner Oller Appraisal Co., Alton, 1969—; former instr. real estate appraising Lewis & Clark Jr. Coll., Godfrey, Ill. Author golf column One Over, Gateway Golfer mag., St. Louis. Primary candidate Madison County Bd., Godfrey, 1970; past bd. dirs. Alton-Wood River Real Estate Bd., Nat. Young Men's Assn. of Soc. of Real Estate Appraisers, Madison County Homebuilder's Assn.; past pres., bd. dirs. Metro-East Soc. Real Estate Appraisers. Served with U.S. Army, 1955-57. Mem. Am. Inst. Real Estate Appraisers (past bd. dirs. St. Louis chpt.). Republican. Roman Catholic. Avocation: golf. Office: Oller Appraisal Co 702 1st Nat Bank Bldg Alton IL 62002

OLOFSON, TOM WILLIAM, business executive; b. Oak Park, Ill., Oct. 10, 1941; s. Ragnar V. and Ingrid E. Olofson; B.B.A., U. Pitts., 1963; m. Jeanne Hamilton, Aug. 20, 1960; children—Christopher, Scott. Various mgmt. positions Bell Telephone Co. of Pa., Pitts., 1963-67; sales mgr. Xerox Corp., Detroit, 1967-68, nat. account mgr., Rochester, N.Y., 1968, mgr. govt. planning, Rochester, 1969, mgr. Kansas City (Mo.) br., 1969-74; corp. v.p. health products group Marion Labs., Inc., Kansas City, Mo., 1974-78, sr. v.p., 1978-80; exec. v.p., dir. Electronic Realty Assn., Inc., 1980-83; chmn. bd., chief exec. officer ETL Corp., 1983—, Emblem Graphic Systems, Inc., 1983—. dir. Optico Industries, Kalo Labs., Am. Stair-Glide, Marion Health and Safety, Marion Sci., Marion Internat., Bank of Kansas City, Kansas City Bank & Trust Co., ASG Corp., ICP, Inc., Calix Corp. Mem. Menninger Found.; trustee Barstow Sch.; chmn. bd. trustees Village United Presbyn. Ch.; bd. dirs. Kansas City Better Bus. Bur., Mid. Am. Immunotherapy and Surg. Research Found., Inc. Mem. Omicron Delta Kappa, Sigma Chi. Republican. Presbyterian. Club: Kansas City. Home: 4808 W 87th St Prairie Village KS 66207 Office: 501 Kansas Ave Kansas City KS 66105

OLOFSSON, DANIEL JOEL, lawyer; b. Chgo., Sept. 29, 1954; s. Joel Gustav and Patricia Marie (Casey) O.; m. Debra Lynn Dreyer, Sept. 11, 1982; 1 dau., Nicole Lynn. A.A., Thornton Community Coll., 1974; B.A., U. Ill., 1976; J.D. with honors, Chgo.-Kent Coll. Law, Ill. Inst. Tech., 1979. Bar: Ill. 1979, U.S. Dist. Ct. (no. dist.) Ill. 1979, U.S. Ct. Appeals (7th cir.) 1979, U.S. Tax Ct. 1980. Assoc. Jerry L. Lambert, Flossmoor, Ill., 1979-80, John P. Block, Chgo., 1980-82; sole practice, Dolton, Ill., 1982—. James scholar U. Ill., Champaign, 1976. Mem. Chgo. Bar Assn., South Suburban Bar Assn., Ill. State Bar Assn., ABA, Phi Theta Kappa. Democrat. Roman Catholic. Lodges: Rotary, Elks. Home: 15333 Dante Dolton IL 60419 Office: 14207 Chicago Rd Dolton IL 60419

O'LOUGHLIN, JOHN KIRBY, insurance executive; b. Bklyn., Mar. 31, 1929; s. John Francis and Anne (Kirby) O'L.; m. Janet R. Tag, July 5, 1952; children: Robert K., Steven M., Patricia A., John A. BA in Econs., St. Lawrence U., Canton, N.Y., 1951. State agt. Royal Globe Ins. Group, 1953-58; with Allstate Ins. Co., 1958—, mktg. v.p., group v.p., then exec. v.p., 1972—; pres. Allstate Life Ins. Co., 1977—; chmn. bd. Allstate Ins. Co. and Life Co. Can., 1976—, sr. exec. v.p. corp. market devel. and planning, 1980—; bd. dirs. all cos. in Allstate Ins. Group and Allstate Enterprises, Inc.; pres. Allstate Enterprises, Inc., Allstate Motor Club, Mature Outlook, Inc., Enterprises Publ. and Direct Mktg. Ctr., Inc. Trustee St. Lawrence U., U.S. Marine Staff and Command Coll. Found. Bd.; elder First United Presbyn. Ch., Lake Forest, Ill.; bd. dirs. Project Invest. Served to capt. USMCR, 1951-53. Mem. Sales and Mktg. Execs. Internat. (dir.), Alpha Tau Omega (chmn. bd. govs. found.). Clubs: Met. (Chgo.); Knollwood (Lake Forest); Lahinch (Ireland). Office: Allstate Ins Co Allstate Plaza Bldg F-8 Northbrook IL 60062

OLOYA, RICHARD OGABA, pediatrician; b. Gulu, Uganda, Dec. 4, 1945; came to U.S., 1973; s. Alipayo and Alice (Adong) O.; m. Dorothy Ipayi Vera, May 29, 1976; children: Apiyo, Alen, Okello. HSC, Cambridge (Eng.) U., 1965; MD, Bristol (Eng.) U., 1971. Diplomate Am. Bd. Pediatrics. Pediatrician-in-charge-newborns St. Joseph Hosp., Detroit, 1976-83, sr. attending pediatrician, 1985—; chief pediatrics Samaritan Hosp., Detroit, 1983-85, vice chief ob-gyn, 1983-85; c.p. Internat. Trade Exchange Corp., Detroit, 1981—; attending physician Children's Hosp. Mich., Detroit, Samaritan Hosp., Detroit; sr. attending physician St. John Hosp., Detroit. Fellow Am. Acad. Pediatrics; mem. Am. Acad. Pediatrics, Detroit Inst. Arts Founders Soc., Detroit Med. Soc., Nat. Med. Assn. Republican. Episcopalian. Avocations: gardening, inventing. Home: 1409 Buckingham Grosse Pointe Park MI 48230 Office: Internat Trade Exchange Corp 15640 E Warren Detroit MI 48224

OLROYD, JAMES LEE, podiatrist; b. Hillsboro, Ill., Feb. 3, 1947; s. Vincent Dale and Mildred Elizabeth (Jurgena) O.; m. Rebecca Young Boone, Aug. 13, 1966; children: Sarah, Pamela, Douglas, Emily. Student, St. Louis U., 1965-66; BA, So. Ill. U., Edwardsville, 1970; D in Podiatric Medicine, Ill. Coll. Podiatric Medicine, 1974. Diplomate Am. Bd. Podiatric Examiners. Resident Lindell Hosp., St. Louis, 1974-76; co-founder, dir. Lindell Hosp. Foot Clinic, St. Louis, 1975-76; pvt. practice podiatry St. Louis, 1976-78, Belleville, Ill., 1978—; mem. staff Meml. Hosp., Belleville, mem. hosp. sports medicine dept.; mem. staff St. Elizabeth's Hosp., Belleville; mem. staff Notre Dame Hills Surg. Ctr., Belleville, mem. med. adv. bd. Mem. So. Ill. U. Alumni Assn. (mem. Campaign for Excellence com., Century Club). Avocations: carpentry, water sports, bicycling, photography. Home: 209 Woodridge Dr Belleville IL 62221 Office: 7210 W Main Belleville IL 62223

OLSCAMP, PAUL JAMES, university president; b. Montreal, Que., Can., Aug. 29, 1937; s. James J. and Luella M. (Brush) O.; m. Ruth I. Pratt, Dec. 2, 1978; children by previous marriage: Rebecca Ann, Adam James. B.A., U. Western Ont., 1958, M.A., 1960; Ph.D., U. Rochester, 1962. Instr. Ohio State U., 1962, asst. prof., 1963-66, asso. prof., 1966-69, asso. dean humanities, 1969; dean faculties, prof. philosophy Roosevelt U., Chgo., 1970-71; v.p. acad. affairs Roosevelt U., 1971-72; prof. philosophy Syracuse U., 1972-75, exec. asst. to chancellor, 1972, vice chancellor student programs, 1972-75, pres. Western Wash. U., Bellingham, 1975-82, Bowling Green State U., 1982—; Grad. fellow in humanities U. Western Ont., 1959. Author: Descartes: The Discourse, Optics, Geometry and Meteorology, 1965, The Moral Philosophy of George Berkeley, 1970, An Introduction to Philosophy, 1971, Malebranche: The Search After Truth, 1980; contbr. articles to profl. jours. Mackintosh Pub. Speaking and Lecturing award U. Western Ont., 1959, 60; Grad. Studies fellow U. Rochester, 1960, 61-62; Danforth Found. asso., 1966—; Alfred J. Wright award Ohio State U., 1970. Mem. Am. Philos Assn. Office: Bowling Green State Univ Office of the Pres E Wooster St Bowling Green OH 43403 *

OLSEN, DAGNE B., state legislator; b. Dalton, Minn., Mar. 19, 1933; d. Glenn F. and Esther J. (Stortroen) Borg; m. Duane D. Olsen, June 25, 1955; children—Deanna, Douglas, Dick. B.S. in Edn., U. N.D., 1955. Cert. life secondary sch. tchr., N.D. Tchr. Gilby High Sch., 1955-57, Midway High Sch., 1960-62; mem. N.D. Ho. of Reps., 1980—, mem. edn. com., social services com. Active Manvel Community Betterment Program, 1959—; vol. chmn., past pres. United Hosp. Aux., Grand Forks; leader 4-H Club; bd. dirs. Agassiz Enterprises Tng. Ctr., Grand Forks, pres., 1982; mem. governing bd. United Hosp.; mem. N.D. Gov.'s Adv. Council on Volunteerism, 1984—; mem. exec. com. N.D. Devel. Disabilities Council, 1982—, bd. dirs. Nat. Assn. Devel. Disabilities Councils, 1985—; pres. Grand Forks County Spl. Edn. Bd.; mem. com. of 100, U. N.D., 1980; treas. council Manvel Trinity Luth. Ch.; mem. Nat. Ch. Task Force, 1979-80; mem. Eastern N.D. Dist. Ch. in Soc., 1982—; bd. dirs. Assn. Retarded Citizens N.D., 1966—; precinct committeewoman, vice chmn. dist. 19 Republican Party, 1974-80; del. N.D. Rep. Conv., 1976, 78, 80, 82, 84, mem. platform com., 1980; co-chair N.D. Legislators for Reagan-Bush, 1984. Recipient Gov.'s Statewide Leadership award for community betterment program, 1964; Outstanding Vol. Service award Office N.D. Gov., 1979; Soil Conservation award N.D. Soil Conservation Dist., 1980; Outstanding Parent award Assn. for Retarded Citizens of N.D., 1977, Mem. of Yr. award 1981; North Central Region Mem. of Yr. award Assn. Retarded Citizens U.S., 1982; named Grand Forks Woman of Yr., 1978; Outstanding Employer of Handicapped, Grand Forks Mayor's Com., 1984; Outstanding Employer of Handicapped, Gov.'s Com. on Employment of Handicapped, 1985. Mem. Nat. Order. Women Legislators, Nat. Rep. Legislators Assn., Am. Legis. Exchange Council, Farm Bur., Am. Agri-Women, N.W. Farm Mgrs. Assn., Assn. Profl. Vols., Am. Legion Aux., Gen. Fedn. Woman's Clubs (past pres. Manvel, past state chmn.), Pi Lambda Theta, Delta Phi Delta, Delta Zeta. Home: Rural Route 1 Box 37 Manvel ND 58256 Office: State Capitol Bldg Bismarck ND 58505

OLSEN, DAVID LEONARD, orthodontist; b. Green Bay, Wis., Nov. 21, 1953; s. Leonard George and Margaret Alice (Pierson) O.; m. Cynthia Louise Backes, July 29, 1977; children: Zachary, Kyle. BS, U. Wis., Green Bay, 1976; DDS, Marquette U., 1980, MS, 1983. Cert. orthodontist. Assoc. in gen. dentistry Olsen & Fuller, Green Bay, 1980-81; assoc. in orthodontics Olsen & Schmidtke, Appleton, Wis., 1983-86; practice dentistry specializing in orthodontics Appleton, 1986—. Mem. ADA, Wis. Dental Assn., Am. Assn. Orthodontists, Midwestern Soc. Orthodontists, Wis. Soc. Orthodontists, Outagamie County Dental Soc. Office: 139 W Calumet St PO Box 6005 Appleton WI 54915

OLSEN, DEE LEON, electronics company executive; b. Bingham, Utah, Sept. 29, 1931; s. Bertrum H. and Doris (Bodell) O.; m. Willadean Peterson, Jan. 26, 1951; children: Steven, Patti, Ronald, Gary, Tami. BS in Indsl. Tech., Utah State U., 1958, BS in Welding Engring., 1960. Registered profl. engr., Wis. With material joining dept. Allen Bradley, Milw., 1960-69, mgr. cabinet dept., 1969-71; v p. Eder Industries Inc., Oak Creek, Wis., 1971—. Served to sgt. USAF, 1952-56, Korea. Mem. Am. Welding Soc. (chmn. 1969-70, Meritorius award 1971). Mormon. Home: 5810 S 40th St Greenfield WI 53221 Office: Eder Industries Inc 2250 W Southbranch Blvd Oak Creek WI 53154

OLSEN, GORDON MEADE, communications executive; b. Crookston, Minn., Feb. 23, 1936; s. Alfred A. Olsen and Ruth N. Eckelberry; m. Dolores C. Gapinski, Aug. 10, 1957; 1 child, Kimberly Ann. BA, U. Minn., 1963; postgrad., San Joaquin Coll. Law, Fresno, Calif., 1973, Sangamon State U., 1985—. Pub. LaPorte City (Iowa) Progress-Rev., 1965-66; pres. Jones Press, Mpls., 1966-67; pub. Sanger (Calif.) Herald, 1968-74; communications dir. Assn. Ill. Electric Coops., Springfield, 1974—. Mem., former chmn. Springfield-Sangamon Regional Plan Commn. Mem. Am. Soc. Assn. Execs. (cert. assn. exec.), Ill. Press Assn. Republican. Roman Catholic. Office: Assn Ill Electric Coops PO Box 3787 Springfield IL 62708

OLSEN, IVAN DANIEL, dentist; b. North Platte, Nebr., Oct. 12, 1938; s. Ivan Edwin and Alice Elenor (Gustafson) O.; m. Lois Joy Blood, Sept. 22, 1961; children: John E., Christina D., Craig D. BS, Wheaton Coll., 1961; DDS, U. Nebr., 1966. Cert. Nebr. Dental Bd., Mich. Dental Bd. Intern William Beaumont Hosp., El Paso, 1966-67; gen. practice dentistry Paw Paw, Mich., 1970—. Mem. Zoning Bd. and Planning Commn., Paw Paw, 1972—. Served to capt. U.S. Army, 1966-70, Vietnam. Decorated Bronze Star. Mem. ADA, Mich. Dental Assn., Kalamazoo Valley Dental Assn. Avocations: boating, fishing, hunting.

OLSEN, KEITH RICHARD, farmer; b. Imperial, Nebr., Dec. 18, 1944; s. Anders William and Jeanette Mrytle (Boyer) O.; m. Doris Marie, Nov. 29, 1969; children; Craig, Jeffrey, Curtis. BS, U. Nebr., 1967. Farmer Venango, Nebr., 1967—; pres., bd. dirs. Perkins County Farm Bur., Grant, Nebr., 1980—. Mem. policy devel. com. Nebr. Farm Bur., Lincoln, Nebr., 1984—, Extension Adv. Com. U. Nebr., Lincoln, 1983—; treas. Perkins County Rep., Grant, 1971. Mem. Farmers Cooperative (bd. dirs. 1969-79). United Methodist. Lodge: Masons (master 1976, 80, 86). Home and Office: HCR 80 Box 37 Venango NE 69168

OLSEN, SAMUEL RICHARD, JR., printing company executive; b. Hamilton, Ohio, May 1, 1938; s. Samuel Richard and Hazel Mildred (Berg) O.; Assoc. Applied Sci., Rochester Inst. Tech., 1961; children—Kristin, Erika, Samuel Richard III; m. Roberta Apa, June 1, 1974; children—Lonnie, Erik. Vice-pres. mfg. Datagraphic N.Y., Inc., Rochester, N.Y., 1965-68; pres., chief exec. officer Form Service, Inc., Schiller Park, Ill., 1968—; pres., chief exec. officer Dealers Press, Inc., Rosemont, Ill., 1973—, also dir; v.p., dir. Form Service West, Inc., Camarillo, Calif.; founder, chief exec. officer Bus. Form Service East, Inc., Balt., 1980, Omega Mgmt. Ltd., 1983—, Computer Preferred, Inc., 1984—, CFS, Inc., Balt., 1987—. Served with USMC, 1960-63. Recipient Voight award Graphic Arts Tech. Found., 1981; named Forms Profl. Yr. N.Am. Pub., 1986. Mem. Nat. Bus. Forms Assn. (officer, dir.), Forms Mfg. Credit Interchange (chmn. 1973-74), Printing Industries Am., Internat. Bus. Forms Industries, Nat. Assn. Printers and Lithographers. Home: 772 Halbert Ln Barrington IL 60010 Office: 9500 Ainslie St Schiller Park IL 60176

OLSEN, THOMAS FOSTER, computer systems analyst; b. Oak Park, Ill., Nov. 17, 1943; s. William J. and Betty (Foster) O.; m. Marilyn Benninger, June 10, 1967; children: Alexander, Christian, Timothy. BS, Purdue U., 1965; MBA, Ind. U., 1967. Mgr. compensation Eli Lilly & Co., Indpls., 1972-75, mgr. corp. affairs, 1975-81, mgr. telecommunications and systems planning, 1981-84, mgr. systems audit, 1984—; bd. dirs. Ind. Consortium Computer and High Tech. Edn., Indpls. Scoutmaster Boy Scouts Am., Indpls., 1983—. Served with USAR, 1968-74. Named Eagle Scout, Boy Scouts Am., 1959. Mem. Sigma Pi Sigma. Methodist. Home: 7470 Noel Forest Ct Indianapolis IN 46278 Office: Eli Lilly Co Lilly Corp Ctr Dept MC371 Indianapolis IN 46285

OLSON, CARL W., construction company executive; b. Lincoln, Nebr., Nov. 16, 1905; s. Charles John and Carolina (Palm) O.; m. Charlotte Joyce Olson, Jan. 28, 1931; children: David Charles, Samuel Palm, Carolyn Joyce. BS in Archtl. Engring., U. Nebr., 1929; LLD (hon.), Midland Luth. Coll., Fremont, Nebr., 1962. V.p. Olson Constrn. Co., Lincoln, Nebr., 1929-45, pres., 1945-75, chmn., 1975—; bd. dirs., cons. dir. Provident Fed. Savs. Bank, Lincoln. Campaign chmn. Lincoln Community Chest, 1950, pres., 1951; trustee Gustavus Adolphus Coll., St. Peter, Minn., 1967-81. Recipient Disting. Service award U. Nebr. Alumni Assn., 1963, Alumni Achievement award, 1979, Builders award U. Nebr., 1983. Mem. Associated Gen. Contractors Am. (life, bd. dirs. 1947—, chmn. bldg. div. 1960); Lincoln C. of C. (bd. dirs. 1955-58). Republican. Lutheran. Clubs: Country of Lincoln (bd. dirs.), Lincoln Univ. (bd. dirs.), Nebr. (bd. dirs.). Lodges: Masons, Shriners, Royal Order of Jesters. Avocations: golf, travel, spectator sports. Home: 1301 Lincoln Mall Apt 1007 Lincoln NE 68508 Office: Olson Constrn Co 721 L St Lincoln NE 68508

OLSON, CLIFFORD LARRY, management consultant, entrepeneur; b. Karlstad, Minn., Oct. 11, 1946; s. Wallace B. and Lucille I (Pederson) O.; m. B.A. Blue Blodgett, March 18, 1967; children: Derek, Erin. B in Chemical Engrg., U. Minn., 1969, B in Physics, 1969; MBA, U. Chgo., 1972; Licence en Sciences Economiques, U. de Louvain, Brussels, 1972. CPA, Cert. mgmt. cons. Project engr. Procter & Gamble, Chgo., 1969-71; engagement mgr. McKinsey & Co., Chgo., 1972-75; ptnr., midwest regional dir. mgmt. consulting Peat, Marwick, Mitchell, St. Louis, 1976-87; prin. Olson Mgmt. Group, Inc., St. Louis, 1987—; bd. dirs. Mo. Venture Forum, St Louis. Bd. dirs.Opera Theatre of St. Louis, 1981—, Mo. State Pub. Defender Commn. Mem. Am. Inst. CPA's, Inst. Mgmt. Cons., The Planning Forum, Washington U. Elliot Soc. Episcopal. Clubs: St. Louis; Tavern Club (Chgo.); Noonday. Avocations: skiing, carpentry. Office: Olson Mgmt Group Inc 35 N Central Suite 335 Saint Louis MO 63105

OLSON, DAVID C., construction company executive; b. 1933. BS, U. Nebr., 1956. With Olson Constrn. Co., Lincoln, Nebr., 1954—, v.p., 1970-75, pres., chief exec. officer, 1975—. Served with USN, 1956-59. Office: Olson Constrn Co 721 L St Lincoln NE 68508 *

OLSON, DAVID DENNIS, district extension forester; b. Detroit, Dec. 8, 1928; s. Stanley G. and Elfrieda K. (Koll) O.; m. Emily L. Olah, July 14, 1951; children: David S., Gary S., Paul W. BS in Forestry, U. Mich., 1950; MS in Resource Devel., Mich. State U., 1970. Registered forester, Mich. Mgmt. forester U.S. Dept. Interior, Bur. Land Mgmt., Roseburg, Oreg., 1952-54, forest mgmt. div., Mich. Dept. Natural Resources, Lansing and various locations, 1954-64; forest land use agt. Mich. State U., Coop. Extension, 1964-76, dist. extension forester Upper Peninsula, Marquette, 1976—; tech. advisor Mich. Resources Inventory Program, 1979-84; apptd. state commr. Dept. Natural Resources, 1985; mem. various state planning coms. Author: (booklets) Forest Economics of Upper Peninsula, 1982, Timber Products Economy of Michigan, 1981. Pres. Gt. Lakes Forestry Expn., Mio, Mich., 1975-76; chairperson Clean Mich. Fund, 1986—. Recipient Presdl. citation Mich. 4-H Assn., 1965, Mich. County Agts. Assn., 1968, Pub. Info. award Amchem. Products, 1974, Outstanding Service award Future Farmers Am., 1976, Friend of Timberman award Mich. Assn. Timberman, 1987. Fellow Soc. Am. Foresters (Continuing Edn. award 1982, Outstanding Service award 1981); mem. Mich. Forest Assn. (pres. 1972), Mich. Soc. Am. Foresters (state chmn. 1981. Lodge: Lions (pres. Mio chpt. 1972). Home: 609 Mountain Marquette MI 49855 Office: Mich State U Upper Peninsula Extension Ctr 1030 Wright Marquette MI 49855

OLSON, DONALD EUGENE, construction executive; b. Omaha, Mar. 22, 1934; s. milton J. and Ann M. (Noonan) O.; m. Mary McCartney, 1955 (div. 1970); 1 child, Mary Ann Olson Jaworski; m. Annette Marie Slalzo, Aug. 19, 1971; children: Kevin M., David J. BS, U. Nebr., 1956. Pres. Olson Bros., Inc., Omaha, 1958—. Pres. Child Savs. Inst., Omaha, 1985-86, adm. Nebr. Navy, Omaha, 1980. Mem. Sheet Metal Nat. Contractors (bd. dirs. 1965-74, Contractor of Yr. 1973), Local Sheet Metal Contractors (past pres.), Midwest Roofing Contractors Assn. (past bd. dirs.). Republican. Roman Catholic. Lodges: Optimists (pres. Omaha 1977), Rotary, Masons. Avocations: hunting, fishing, tennis. Home: 202 S 96th St Omaha NE 68114 Office: Olson Bros Inc 2651 Saint Mary's Ave Omaha NE 68105

OLSON, DONALD GEORGE, university computer services administrator; b. Minot, N.D., May 16, 1941; s. George James and Ellen (Ranta) O.; BME, U. N.D., 1963; MME, N.D. State U., 1968; 1 son, Todd B. Analyst, programmer Bur. Reclamation, Denver, 1963-66; asst. dir. computer center N.D. State U., Fargo, 1966-69; data processing mgr. U. Calif. Sci. Lab., Los Alamos, 1969-74; dir. data processing nat. assessment ednl. progress Edn. Commn. States, Denver, 1974-77; staff mgr. Mountain Bell, Denver, 1977-80; dir. computer services Mankato (Minn.) State U., 1980-86, assoc. v.p. computer services, 1986—; cons. in field. Mem. Mankato Area Execs. Assn. Registered profl. engr., certified data processor. Mem. AAAS, Assn. Computing Machinery, YMCA, Phi Delta Theta. Republican. Presbyterian. Club: Kiwanis. Home: 1336 N 4th St Mankato MN 56001 Office: Mankato State U Computer Services Box 45 Mankato MN 56001

OLSON, EUGENE RUDOLPH, printing company executive;; b. St. Paul, Apr. 9, 1926; s. Rudolph and Martha E. (Karlson) O.; m. Leona F. Solie, June 28, 1952; children: Kathleen, Wayne, Brian. With Deluxe Check Printers Inc., St. Paul, 1944—, mgr. related products div., 1964-70, nat. dir. market research, 1970-72, v.p., 1972-76, pres., 1976—, chief exec. officer, 1977-86, chmn., 1981—, also dir.; dir. Minn. Mutual Ins. Co., 1st Trust Co., St. Paul. Bd. dirs. Bapt. Hosp. Fund; mem. World Trade Ctr. Adv. Council. Mem. Bank Stationers Assn. (dir.). Baptist. Clubs: Mpls., Midland Hills Country. Home: 2024 Evergreen Ct Saint Paul MN 55113 Office: Deluxe Check Printers Inc 1080 W County Rd F Saint Paul MN 55112

OLSON, JAMES BURTON, health care administrator; b. Fargo, N.D., Mar. 19, 1951; s. Clarence Calvin and Louise Marie (Godwin) O. B.A. in Psychology and Chemistry, St. Olaf Coll., 1973; M.A. in Health Services Adminstrn., U. Wis.-Madison, 1975. Dist. mgr. Wis. Profl. Rev. Orgn., Madison, Wis., 1975-76; asst. adminstr. St. Francis Med. Ctr., La Crosse, Wis., 1976-82; adminstr. St. Francis Home, LaCrosse, 1976-82; adminstr. Bethel Home, Viroqua, Wis., 1982—; mem. Vernon County Health Forum. Bd. dirs. Vernon County Community Options Program; pres. Viroqua Hockey Assn. Mem. Am. Coll. Hosp. Adminstrs., Health Care Fin. Mgmt. Assn., Am. Coll. Nursing Home Adminstrs., Blue Key. Republican. Lutheran. Lodge: Lions (Viroqua). Office: 614 S Rock St Viroqua WI 54665

OLSON, JANE CECILIA, residence hall administrator. Milw., Nov. 30, 1954; d. Robert Charles and Patricia Anne (Regan) O.; BA, Marquette U., 1977; MS, Shippensburg U., 1979. Residence dir. Ball State U., Muncie, Ind., 1979-81; area coordinator Appalachian State U., Boone, N.C., 1981-83, asst. dir. residence life, 1983-84; residence dir. Mich. State U., East Lansing, 1985-86, asst. to area dir., 1986—. Recipient award Southeastern Housing Officers, 1984; named one of Outstanding Young Women of Am., 1986. Mem. Am. Assn. Counseling and Devel., Am. Coll. Personnel Assn., Nat. Assn. Student Personnel Adminstrs., Assn. Coll. and Univ. Housing Officers Internat., Kappa Delta Pi. Avocations: catering, sewing, counted cross stitch, reading, travel. Home: Mich State U 1 E Wilson Hall East Lansing MI 48825 Office: Mich State U N-36 Wonders Hall East Lansing MI 48825

OLSON, LAUREL L., real estate corporation executive; b. Graceville, Minn., Mar. 14, 1931; s. Oscar and Buelah (Dodds) O.; m. Margaret Nelson, Sept. 13, 1958; children: Eric John, Karen and Kay (twins). BS in Agr., U. Minn., 1959. Investment dir., appraiser Prudential Realty Group, Downers Grove, Ill., 1964—. Mem. planning commn. City of Hutchinson, Minn., 1974-77; chmn. adminstrv. bd. Vineyard United Meth. Ch., Hutchinson, 1976-79. Served to cpl. U.S. Army, 1953-55. Mem. Am. Inst. Real Estate Appraisers, Minn. Farm Mgrs. and Appraisers Inc. (pres. 1983—). Republican. Lodge: Masons. Avocations: racquet sports, skiing, woodworking, outdoor activities. Home: 828 Biltmore Ct Naperville IL 60540 Office: Prudential Realty Group 1431 Opus Pl Suite 665 Downers Grove IL 60515

OLSON, LAWRENCE WAYNE, software company executive; b. Evanston, Ill., Nov. 23, 1945; s. Raymond G. and Arvilla N. (Bergstrom) O.; m. Dolores Ann McGovern, Feb. 19, 1966; children: Scott, Kelly, Eric. Student, Wright Coll., 1963-65, 67, Harper Jr. Coll., Palatine, Ill., 1968-70, Ill. Inst. Tech., 1970-71, Northeastern Ill. U., 1974. Cert. in data processing, computer programming. Systems programmer Walgreen Co., Deerfield, Ill., 1967-70; product mgr. Pansophic Inc., Oak Brook, Ill., 1970-73; v.p. info. services Vend-Tronics, Inc., Roselle, Ill., 1973-78; pres. Performance Programming, Schaumburg, Ill., 1978-80; chmn. bd. Performance Programming, Schaumburg, 1977-80; v.p. research devel. LPC, Inc., Lombard, Ill., 1980-83; pres. LPC, Inc., Glen Ellyn, Ill., 1983—; also bd. dirs. LPC, Inc., Glen Ellyn; bd. dirs. Inteliquest, Inc., Schaumburg; mem. Ill. Indsl. Liaison Com. Co-author numerous software products. Served with USMC, 1965-67. Mem. Assn. Data Processing Service Orgn., Ill. Inventors Council, Young Pres. Orgn., Schaumburg Athletic Assn. (coach), Mensa. Home: 826 Beacon Dr Schaumburg IL 60193 Office: LPC Inc 1200 Roosevelt Rd Glen Ellyn IL 60137

OLSON, LLOYD CLARENCE, physician, administrator; b. Spokane, Wash., Jan. 30, 1935; s. Clarence Florin and Ruth Mary (McCollum) O.; m. Irene Gertrude Frisen, Nov. 29, 1979; children: Kristen, Inger, Erik. BA, Reed Coll., 1957; MD, Harvard, 1961. Diplomate Am. Bd. Pediatrics. Intern Strong Meml. Hosp., Rochester, N.Y.; resident U. Wash., Seattle; spl. staff Rockerfeller Found., Bangkok, Thailand, 1970-73; assoc. prof. Ind. Univ., Indpls., 1973-76; prof., chmn. pediatrics Univ. Mo., Kans. City, 1976—; pediatrician-in-chief The Children's Mercy Hosp., Kans. City, 1982—; cons. U.S. Army, Washington, 1979-82, Vietnam Med. Project Saigon, 1975-76. Author: Virus Infections, 1982. Served to lt. col. U.S. Army, 1964-70. Fellow Am. Acad. Pediatrics; mem. Am. Pediatrics Soc., Infectious Diseases Soc., Soc. for Pediatrics Research, Am. Soc. for Microbiology, Phi Beta Kappa. Republican. Methodist. Home: 1320 Main St Parkville MO 64152 Office: The Children's Mercy Hosp 24th at Gillham Rd Kansas City MO 64108

OLSON, LYNNETTE GAIL, personnel executive; b. Omaha, Oct. 9, 1945; d. Norman Lester and Harriet Grace (Carlson) Skillman; m. Gary Allen Olson, Aug. 1, 1964 (div. Oct. 1972); 1 child, Michael John. BA, Augustana Coll., 1980. Legal sec. May, Johnson, Doyle & Becker PC, Sioux Falls, S.D., 1963-76; benefits mgr. Raven Industries, Inc., Sioux Falls, 1980—. Mem. Sioux Falls Personnel Assn. Republican. Avocations: music, reading, golf, bowling. Home: 1817 S Stephen Sioux Falls SD 57103 Office: Raven Industries Inc 205 E 6th St Sioux Falls SD 57117-1007

OLSON, MARGARETTE ADELINE, clinical psychologist; b. Crosby, Minn.; d. D.V. Nystrom; m. Alfred O. Olson, Jan. 1, 1942; 1 child, Mark David. BS, U. N.D., 1944, MS, 1948, PhD, 1951; postdoctoral studies Columbia U., Southwest Okla. State U., U. Minn. Lic. psychologist, S.D.; lic. nursing home adminstr.; cert. gerontologist. Bus. tchr. Mary Hardin-Baylor Coll., Belton, Tex., 1944-45; field supt. Gulf Coast Bus. Schs., Bay City, Tex., 1945-47; asst. prof., dept. chmn. U. N.D., Grand Forks, 1947-56; prof., dept. chmn. State Coll., Mayville, N.D., 1956-62; dean women, assoc. dean students Nebr. State Coll., Chadron, 1962-65; resident clin. psychology Jamestown (N.D.) and Hastings (Nebr.) State Hosps., 1965-66; prof. psychology Southwest Okla. State U., Weatherford, 1966-71; cons. clin. psychologist Okla. Gen. Hosp., Clinton, 1967-71, Concho Indian Sch. and Clinton Indian Hosp. and Indian Pub. Health, 1968-71; clin. psychologist S.D. Human Services Ctr., Yankton, 1971-85; marriage counselor. Mem. Govs. Coms. on children and youth, aging, and edn. for aging; active PTA, Handicapped Advocy Program Yankton, Yankton Area Arts Council. Mem. AAUW (grantee 1966, pres. N.D. div. 1958-60), Am. Psychol. Assn., N.D. Fedn. Women's Club, S.D. Fedn. Women's Club, Bus. and Profl. Women's Club, Nat. Assn. Women Deans, Internat. Council Psychologists (N.D. and S.D. chairperson 1980-81), S.D. Psychol. Assn. (sec.-treas. 1978-80), Nat. Assn. For Women in Careers (nat. sec. 1986—), Internat. Platform Assn., Pi Lambda Theta (nat. treas. 1958-60). Republican. Methodist. Office: Box 778 Yankton SD 57078

OLSON, MARIAN EDNA, nurse, social pschologist; b. Newman Grove, Nebr., July 20, 1923; d. Edwrd and Ethel Thelma (Hougland) Olson; diploma U. Nebr., 1944, B.S.N., 1953; M.A., State U. Iowa, 1961, M.A. in Psychlogy, 1962; Ph.D. in Psychology, UCLA, 1966. Staff nurse, supr. U. Tex. Med. Br., Galveston, 1944-49; with U. Iowa, Iowa City, 1949-59, supr. 1953-55, asst. dir. 1955-59; asst. prof. nursing UCLA, 1965-67; prof. nursing U. Hawaii, 1967-70, 78-82; dir. nursing Wilcox Hosp. and Health Center, Lihue, 1970-77; chmn. Hawaii Bd. Nursing, 1974-80; prof. nursing No. Mich. U., 1984—. Mem. Am. Nurses Assn. (mem. nat. accreditation bd. continuing edn. 1975-78), Nat. League Nursing, Am. Hosp. Assn., Am. Public Health Assn., LWV. Democrat. Roman Catholic. Home and office: 6223 County 513T Rd Rapid River MI 49878

OLSON, MARLIN LEE, educator; b. Triumph, Minn., July 29, 1927; s. Carl Leonard and Inez Viola (Johnson) O.; m. Gunvor K. Olson, Sept. 5, 1952; children: Cheryl Lynn, Deborah Lee, Jerald Leonard, Marlei Louann. BA in Bus. Adminstrn. and Edn., Seattle Pacific U.; also MEd in Adminstrn., PhD in Curriculum and Instrn., Mich. State U. Tchr. Shoreline pub. schs., Seattle, 1953-58; adminstr. Morrison Schs. Assn., San Francisco, 1958-71; dir. Christian edn. Berean Ch., Seattle, 1971-77; assoc. prof. Grace Bible Coll., Wyoming, Mich., 1977-87, prof., 1987—, acad. dean, 1985—; cons. Internat. Ctr. for Learning, Ventura, Calif. Served with U.S. Navy, 1945-48. Mem. Nat. Assn. Elem. Sch. Prins., Assn. Supervision and Curriculum Devel., Phi Delta Kappa. Republican. Participating author: Internat. Center for Learning, 1971-77. Office: 1011 Aldon SW Wyoming MI 49509

OLSON, NILS ARTHUR, osteopathic physician; b. St. Louis, Jan. 12, 1948; s. John C. and E. Hildegarde (Duever) O.; m. Shirley Rae Ledford, Oct. 15, 1977; children—Erik Arthur, Kirsten Rae. A.B., U. Mo., 1969; D.O., Kirksville Coll. Osteo. Medicine, 1973. Diplomate Am. Osteo. Bd. Gen. Practice. Gen. practice osteo. medicine, Mercer, Wis., 1974—; chmn. dept. family practice Howard Young Med. Ctr., Woodruff, Wis., 1985-87. Mem. North Lakeland Elem. Sch. Bd. Edn., Manitowish Waters, Wis., 1977—, v.p., 1977-84, pres., 1984—; v.p. Vilas County Republican party, Eagle River, Wis., 1977-79. Mem. Am. Osteo. Assn. (alt. del. Ho. of Dels. 1982-84), Wis. Assn. Osteo. Physicians and Surgeons (pres. 1981-82), Mo. Assn. Osteo. Physicians and Surgeons, Am. Coll. Gen. Practitioners in Osteo. Medicine and Surgery (Wis. Gen. Practitioner of Yr. 1982). Lodges: Lions (dep. dist. gov. 1979-80, pres. 1976-77), Masons (master 1979-80). Home: S Turtle Rd Winchester WI 54567 Office: PO Box B Mercer WI 54547

OLSON, NORMA JEAN, educator; b. Des Moines, Dec. 3, 1930; s. Floyd Robert and Faye (Spears) Brown; B.S., U. Iowa, 1952; M.A., U. Minn., 1966, Ph.D., 1978; m. Alfred Barber Olson, July 21, 1950; children—Cheri Lynne, Alan Kent. Mem. faculty North Hennepin Community Coll., Mpls., 1966-67, 70—, prof. bus., 1970—; mem. faculty Arapahoe Community Coll., 1967-69, Normandale Community Coll., 1969-70; cons. St. Benedictine Coll., Gen. Mills, U. Iowa, State of Minn. Mem. NEA, Minn. Edn. Assn., Minn. Bus. Edn., North Central Bus. Educators, AAUW, Am. Soc. Tng. Dirs., Hennepin Community Coll. Faculty Assn. (pres. 1982-83), Delta Pi Epsilon. Democrat. Methodist. Home: 6890 Utica Terr Chanhassen MN 55317 Office: 7411 85th Ave N Minneapolis MN 55445

OLSON, PAUL BUXTON, marketing educator; b. Waterloo, Iowa, Feb. 5, 1937; s. Ethan Sidney and Esther May Olson; m. Jean Elaine Rinehart, Aug. 18, 1962; children: Brent Sidney, Kimberly Jean, Julie Elaine. BA cum laude, Tarkio Coll., 1958; MEd, U. Mo., 1966; EdS, U. No. Iowa, 1975. Tchr. bus. edn. Riverton/Farragut Community Schs., 1962-68; mktg. and distributive edn. tchr. Mason City (Iowa) Community Schs., 1968—; adj. instr. mktg. No. Iowa Area Community Coll., Mason City, 1969—.Active Jr. Achievement. Served with U.S. Army, 1960-62. Named Outstanding Distributive Edn. Tchr., Iowa Distributive Edn. Tchrs. Assn., 1978, to Mktg. Edn. Hall of Fame, 1985; recipient Leadership award Jr. Achievement, 1977, Writer's award Interstate Distributive Edn. Curriculum Consortium, 1975.Mem. NEA (life), Am. Vocat. Assn. (life), Nat. Bus. Edn. Assn., Mktg. Edn. Assn. (life), Distributive Edn. Clubs Am., Iowa State Edn. Assn., Iowa Mktg. Educators (rep., sec./treas., pres.-elect 1986-87, pres. 1987—), Iowa Bus. Edn. Assn. (rep.), Iowa Vocat. Assn. (rep.), Mason City Edn. Assn. (past treas.), Assn. Supervision and Curriculum Devel., Delta Pi Epsilon (past treas.), Phi Delta Kappa (life, charter, past historian). Republican. Methodist. Lodge: Sons of Norway. Home: 2731 1st St SW Mason City IA 50401 Office: 1700 4th St SW Mason City IA 50401

OLSON, R. PAUL, psychologist; b. Gaylord, Minn., Nov. 17, 1941; s. D.C. and Lyndis A. (Iverslie) O.; m. Mary Jennifer Berg, Jan. 28, 1967; children: Andrea, Kari. BA, Carleton Coll., 1963; MDiv., Yale Div. Sch., 1966; PhD, U. Ill., 1970. Ordained to ministry United Ch. Christ, 1968; lic. cons. psychologist, Minn. Clin. psychologist The Mpls. Clinic, 1970-85, SHARE Health Care Assocs., Mpls., 1985-86; assoc. prof. dept. psychology U. Wis., Stevens Point, 1986-87; dean Ill. Sch. Profl. Psychology, Mpls., 1987—; instr. local seminars and colls., 1970—. Contbr. articles on psychology to profl. jours. V.p. Profl. Assn. treatment Homes, Mpls., 1971-75; bd. dirs. Hennepin County Mental Health Assn., 1978-79. Research grantee Mpls. Clinic Med. Found., 1981, 82, 86. Mem. Am. Psychol. Assn., Biofeedback Soc. Am., Minn. Biofeedback Soc. (pres. 1981-82), Council Nat. Register Health Service Providers in Psychology. Avocations: jogging, cross-country skiing, reading. Office: Illinois Sch Profl Psychology Mpls Campus 1313 5th St SE Minneapolis MN 55414

OLSON, RICHARD GOTTLIEB, nuclear engineer, computer analyst; b. Terre Haute, Ind., Dec. 17, 1922; s. Gottlieb William and Lucille Adella (Clifton) O.; m. Virginia Ann Abbinett, June 22, 1947; children: Stephen Philip, Mary Ann. BSEE, Rose-Hulman Inst., Terre Haute, 1947; MSE, U. Mich., 1955; postgrad., U. Mass., 1970. Control and kinetics mgr. Atomic Power Devel. Assn., Inc., Detroit, 1955-64; supr. computer facilities and tng. Power Reactor Devel. Co., Detroit, 1959-67; tech. work leader Detroit

Edison, 1965-83, sr. nuclear fuel engr., 1982—; instr. electrical engring. and math Rose Hulman Inst., Terre Haute, 1946-49, Wayne State U., Detroit, 1949-76; instr. computer devel. Cass Tech. High Sch., Detroit, 1960-70. Author: Dynamics of Fast Breeder Reactor, 1956 (Nucleonics award 1957), Instrumentation and Control, 1962 (Am. Nuclear Soc. award 1962). Mem. citizen's adv. com. Dearborn Bd. Edn., 1956-70. Served to sgt. U.S. Army, 1942-46, ETO, PTO, Korea. U. Mich. fellow, 1954, NSF fellow, 1970. Mem. IEEE (Service award 1954), Am. Nuclear Soc. (Service 1966), Assn. for Computing Machines (Service 1968), Tau Beta Pi. Home: 3501 Hipp Dearborn MI 48124 Office: Detroit Edison Co 2000 2d Ave Detroit MI 48226

OLSON, ROBERT E., business owner; b. Omaha, Sept. 24, 1924; s. William R. and Bessie A. (Pilcher) O.; m. Gloria Kuppig Olson, Sept. 4, 1948; children: Barbara, Jeanne, Jeffrey. Student, U. Nebr., Omaha, 1946-48. Owner, ptnr. Hadley-Braithwait Co., Columbus, Nebr., 1974—; bd. dirs. Equitable Savs., Columbus; bd. dirs., pres. K.O Vending Co., 1964—. Served to sgt. U.S. Army, 1943-46. Decorated Bronze Star, Purple Heart. Mem. Nebr. Tobacco Wholesalers (pres. local chpt. 1973-74), Columbus C. of C. (pres. 1969-70). Republican. Lodges: Rotary, Masons, Elks, Shriners. Home: 2773 N Park Ln Columbus NE 68601 Office: 2519-11 St Columbus NE 68601

OLSON, ROBERT GEORGE, dentist; b. Eureka, S.D., Feb. 3, 1939; s. Alfred G. and Rosella (Kollegraff) O.; m. Judy Reedy, Aug. 5, 1961; children: Jeffrey, Jennifer, Jon, Jaime, Jason, Jeremy. BS, U. Minn., 1961, DDS, 1963. Gen. practice dentistry Rapid City, S.D., 1963—; sec./treas. S.D. Bd. Dentistry, Rapid City, 1977—, Cen. Regional Dental Testing Service, Topeka, 1985—. Fellow Acad. Dentistry Internat., Internat. Coll. Dentists, Am. Coll. Dentists; mem. Am. Dental Assn., S.D. Dental Assn. (trustee 1968-77, del. 1977-86). Republican. Roman Catholic. Lodge: Elks. Avocations: skiing, flying, fishing, model trains, reading. Home: 4603 Ridgewood St Rapid City SD 57702 Office: Dental Care Ctr 2210 Jackson Blvd Rapid City SD 57702

OLSON, ROY ARTHUR, government official; b. Ashland, Wis., Dec. 8, 1938; s. Elof Herman and Beatrice Lorraine (Dolezal) O.; m. Elisabeth Rigge Behrens, June 24, 1967; children—Heather Elisabeth, Peter Roy. B.S., Northwestern U., 1960. Lic. real estate salesman, Ill. Writer, editor Chgo. Am., 1956-68; pres. Roy Olson Pub. Relations Co., Oak Park, Ill., 1968-70; asst. regional adminstr. SBA, Chgo., 1970—; dir. Am.food Industries, Chgo., Convenant Village Retirement Ctr., Northbrook, Ill., 1975-81, Brandel Care Ctr., Northbrook, 1975-81. Chmn. Northbrook Covenant Ch., 1980-81. Mem. Soc. Profl. Journalists, Art Inst. Chgo. Clubs: City (media com.), Executives, Chgo. Press, Chgo. Headline (past dir. 1964-66), Northwestern (Chgo.). Home: 2015 Prairie St Glenview IL 60025 Office: US Small Bus Adminstrn 230 S Dearborn St Chicago IL 60604

OLSON, RUE EILEEN, librarian; b. Chgo., Nov. 1, 1928; d. Paul H. and Martha M. (Fick) Meyers; student Herzl Coll., 1946-48, Northwestern U., 1948-50, Ill. State U., 1960-64; m. Richard L. Olson, July 18, 1964; children—Catherine, Karen. Accountant Ill. Farm Supply Co., Chgo., 1948-59; asst. librarian Ill. Agrl. Assn., Bloomington, 1960-66, librarian, 1966-86, dir. library services, 1986—. Mem. area Com. Nat. Library Week, 1971, area steering com., 1972; mem. steering com. Illinet/OCLC, 1985-87; mem. adv. council of librarians Grad. Sch. Library Sci. U. Ill., 1976-79; mem. Ill. State Library Adv. Com. for Interlibrary Cooperation, 1979-80; del. Ill. White House Conf. on Library and Info. Services, 1978; coordinator Vita Income Tax Assistance, Bloomington, Ill., 1986—. Mem. Am., Ill., McLean County (pres. 1970-71) library assns., Spl. Libraries Assn. (pres. Ill. 1977-78), Internat. Assn. Agrl. Librarians and Documentalists, Am. Soc. Info. Sci., Am. Mgmt. Assn. Lodge: Zonta (pres. 1987-89). Club: Bloomington. Office: Ill Agrl Assn 1701 Towanda Ave Bloomington IL 61701

OLSON, STUART W., operations research analyst; b. Wausau, Wis., Aug. 1, 1939; s. Woodrow A. and Irene V. (Burmeister) O.; m. Nancy L. Coughlin, Aug. 10, 1963; children: John S., Frederick A., Erin I. BA in Math., Augustana Coll., 1964; MS in Indsl. and Mgmt. Engring., U. Iowa, 1972; postgrad., MIT, 1984-85. Ops. research analyst armament, munitions, chem. command U.S. Army, Rock Island, Ill., 1964—. Fellow Can. Operational Research Soc.; mem. AAAS, Am. Defense Preparedness Assn., Ops. Research Soc. of Am., Assn. for Computing Machinery, U.S. Army Assn. Home: 4805 Gaines St Davenport IA 52806

OLSON, WAYNE BURTON, chemical company executive; b. Mpls., July 31, 1924; s. Reuben and Signa Carol (Soderberg) O.; m. Ardath Gerda Tangen, June 29, 1951; children: Scott, Vicky, Karen, Paul. Student, Tex. A&M U., 1943, Am. U., Shrivenham, Eng., 1945; BME, U. Minn., 1948. Registered profl. engr., Wis. Field engr. E.I. Du Pont Co., Wilmington, Del., 1951-54; sales engr. N.Am. Mogul Co., Milw., 1954-56, Perolin Chem. Co., Chgo., 1956-59; pres., chmn. bd. Wayne Cons., Inc., Waukesha, Wis., 1986—. Contbr. articles to profl. jours. Active local Rep. Orgn. Served to 1st Lt., U.S. Army, 1943-46, ETO. Mem. Am. Legion. Avocations: airplane and glider pilot, tennis, woodworking, boat bldg. Home: 1400 Hamilton Dr Brookfield WI 53005 Office: Wayne Cons Inc. N16 W22040 Jericho Dr Waukesha WI 53186

OLSON, WILBERT ORIN (BERT), sales manager; b. Baudette, Minn., Sept. 5, 1947; s. Howard John and Audrey Jean (Langton) O.; m. Jennie Lee Adams; children: Wayne James, Terry Kyle. Grad. high sch., Bozeman, Mont. Salesman Pepsi Cola Co., Bozeman, 1971-73, Clover Club Foods Co., Bozeman, 1973-74, Sweetheart Interstate Bakery, Livingston, Mont., 1974-79; div. supr. Sweetheart Interstate Bakery, Bozeman, 1979-84; gen. sales mgr. Interstate Bakeries Corp., Minot, N.D., 1984—. Coach Little League Baseball, Bozeman, 1982-84, Bozeman Soccer League, 1982-83. Served with USNG, 1965-71. Mem. AAU Wrestling Assn. Am. (lic. paremaster 1979-80). Lodge: Elks. Avocations: guitar musician, hunting, fishing, golf. Home: 2221 24th St SE Minot ND 58701

OLSON, WILLIAM HAROLD, dentist; b. Thief River Falls, Minn., Mar. 1, 1950; s. Donald L. and Sylvia M. (Borchert) O.; m. Pamela Beth Nelson, June 12, 1971; children: Erik, Katherine, Miranda. Student, U. N.D., 1969-73; BS, DDS, U. Minn., 1976. Gen. practice dentistry Grand Forks, N.D., 1977—; bd. dirs. Dental Service Corp. of N.D. Mem. ADA, N.D. Dental Assn., N.E. Dist. Dental Assn. (sec. to pres. 1978-81). Lutheran. Lodges: Rotary, Elks. Avocations: golf, fishing, hunting, high sch. hockey referee. Office: Dakota Dental Assocs PC 124 Columbia Mall Grand Forks ND 58201

OLSSON, CLIFFORD LEE, health science facility administrator; b. Seattle, Sept. 3, 1949; s. Norman Vernor and Helen F. (Hanaka) O.; m. Kyong Cha Om, Aug. 17, 1974; 1 child, Daniel. AA, San Antonio Coll., 1974; BBA in Acctg., St. Mary's U., San Antonio, 1976, MBA in Ops. Mgmt., 1981; postgrad., Trinity U. CPA, Tex. Acct. South San Antonio ISD, 1977, asst. dir. bus., purchasing agt., 1977-80; internal auditor Bexar County Hosp. Dist., San Antonio, 1980-83; program dir., internal auditor Marian Health Ctr., Sioux City, Iowa, 1983-86; dir. mktg., bus. surg. services St. Joseph Hosp., Omaha, 1986—. Served with USN, 1968-72, Vietnam. Mem. Am. Hosp. Assn., Am. Coll. Health Care Execs., Assn. Records Mgrs. and Adminstrs. (treas. 1978-79), Soc. Mgmt. and Rev. Telecommunicators (treas. 1983). Mem. Assembly of God Ch. Avocations: reading, games, travel, pocket billiards, Spanish lang. study. Home: 16218 Dorcas St Omaha NE 68130 Office: St Joseph Hosp 601 N 30th St Omaha NE 68131

OLSSON, MILTON LEE, conductor, composer; b. North Anderson, Ind., Sept. 21, 1940; s. Jonas Albin and Florence Rose (Wolf) O.; m. Trudy Kinzli, Dec. 12, 1959; children—David Carl, Stephan Bernie, Paul-Josef. B.A., Wayne State U., 1964, M.Mus., 1970; D.Mus. Arts, U. Colo., 1975. Fine arts instr. Detroit Inst. Tech., 1964-69; dir. mus. activities Detroit Parks and Recreation Dept., 1969-70; dir. talent devel. Met. Arts Complex, Detroit Model Cities Program, 1970-72; dir. choral and orchestral activities Mich. Tech. U., Houghton, 1976—, dir. arts, 1982-84, asst. head dept. humanities, 1984—; adjudicator; cons. Mich. Council Arts. Mem. Am. Choral Dirs. Assn., Am. Symphony Orch. League, Coll. Music Soc., Mich. Choral Dirs. Assn., Mich. Orch. Assn., Mich. Sch. Vocal Assn., Nat. Assn. Jazz Educators. Club: Rotary (Houghton). Composer choral works, musicals, jazz arrangements. Office: Mich Tech Coll Div of Arts and Humanities Houghton MI 49931

OLSTON, MARY KAY, school psychologist; b. Milw., Oct. 27, 1949; d. Gordon Rhodes and Mary Anne (Popp) O. BA, Carroll Coll., Waukesha, Wis., 1970; MS, U. Wis., 1971. Assoc. sch. psychologist Milw. Pub. Sch., 1971-74, sch. psychologist, 1974—; cons. U. Wis., 1973-76. Mem. Am. Psychol. Assn., Nat. Assn. Sch. Psychologists, Milw. Area Psychol. Assn. (treas. 1982-84), Alliance Française (librarian 1980-82). Home: 10541 W Woodward Ave Wauwatosa WI 53222 Office: Secondary Zone 1515 W Forest Home Milwaukee WI 53204

OLSZEWSKI, LAWRENCE J., librarian, educator; b. Bridgeport, Conn., Nov. 24, 1947; s. Jerome and Doris (Harrison) O.; m. Joyce Marie Slater, Aug. 4, 1969; 1 child, Wendi. BA, So. Conn. State U., 1969; MA, Ohio State U., 1971, PhD, 1975; MLS, Kent (Ohio) State U., 1978. Librarian PLCFC, Columbus, Ohio, 1978-85, mgr. gen. reference, 1985-86; br. mgr. Online Catalog Library Ctr., Dublin, Ohio, 1986—; adj. faculty Kent State U., 1984—; cons. So. Ohio Coll., Columbus, 1981-84. Translator: (play) In The Burning Darkness, 1969; contbr. articles to profl. jours. Mem. ALA, Am. Assn. Tchrs. Spanish and Portuguese, Ohio Library Assn., Am. Soc. for Info. Sci. Avocations: reading, swimming. Home: 1724 Moreland Dr Columbus OH 43220 Office: Online Catalog Library Ctr 6565 Frantz Rd Dublin OH 43017

OLTARZ-SCHWARTZ, SARA, lawyer; b. Ostrow, Poland, May 5, 1945; came to U.S., 1950; d. Simon and Mindy (Salzburg) Oltarz; m. Michael Alan Schwartz, Dec. 8, 1973; children: Carl, Justin. BA, NYU, 1969, JD, N.Y. Law Sch., 1972. Bar: N.Y. 1973, Mich. 1980, U.S. Dist. Ct. (so. and ea. dists.) N.Y. 1974, U.S. Ct. Appeals (2d cir.) 1975, U.S. Ct. Mil. Appeals 1976, U.S. Dist. Ct. (ea. dist.) Mich. 1982, U.S. Ct. Appeals (6th cir.) 1983, U.S. Supreme Ct. 1976. Asst. dist. atty. Kings County, Bklyn., 1972-77; adj. prof. N.Y. Law Sch., 1978-79; of counsel David F. DuMouchel, P.C., Detroit, 1983—; sole practice, Detroit, 1983—. Recipient Am. Jurisprudence award Lawyers Coop. Pub. Co., 1972. Mem. State Bar Mich., Detroit Bar Assn., Oakland County Bar Assn., Women Lawyers of Mich., Internat. Assn. Jewish Lawyers and Jurists. Office: 1930 Buhl Bldg Detroit MI 48226

OLTMAN, DWIGHT, conductor, educator; b. Imperial, Nebr., May 27, 1936; s. George L. and Lois Beryl (Wine) O.; m. Shirley Jean Studebaker, May 30, 1966; children—Michelle Leigh, Nicole Alicia. B.S., McPherson Coll., 1958; M.Mus., Wichita State U., 1963; postgrad., U. Cin., 1967-70; student, Nadia Boulager, Paris, 1960, Pierre Monteux, 1963. Asst. prof. music Manchester Coll., North Manchester, Ind., 1963-67; music dir. symphony orch. and Bach Festival Baldwin-Wallace Coll., Berea, Ohio, 1970—; music dir. Ohio Chamber Orch., Cleve., 1972—; music dir., prin. conductor Cleve. Ballet, 1976—; music dir. Cullowhee Music Festival, N.C., 1977-79; guest conductor Europe, Can., U.S.A. Mem. Am. Symphony Orch. League, Conductor's Guild, Am. Fedn. Musicians, Orgn. Ohio Orchs. (bd. dirs. 1982—). Democrat. Presbyterian. Avocations: reading; walking; theater; spectator sports. Home: 17592 Ridge Creek Strongsville OH 44136

OLTVEDT, GREGORY THOR, architect; b. Mpls., May 3, 1949; s. Thoralf Kenneth and Elaine Gertrude (Thompson) O.; m. Claudia Jean Teich, Mar. 23, 1971; children: Christopher Thor, Kirsten Marie. BArch, U. Minn., 1976. Registered architect, Minn. Architect Horty, Elving & Assocs. Inc., Mpls., 1976-84, Truman Howell Architects & Assocs. Inc., Mpls., 1984-86, Close Assocs. Inc., Mpls., 1986—. Mem. AIA (fellow in health care design 1980), Minn. Soc. AIA. Club: Calhoun Beach (Mpls.). Home: 4901 Oakland Ave S Minneapolis MN 55417 Office: Close Assocs Inc 3101 E Franklin Ave Minneapolis MN 55406

O'MAHONEY, MICHAEL TERRENCE, clinical psychologist; b. Chgo., May 7, 1943; s. James Fanahan and Mary Therese (Roche) O'M.; m. Linda Ann Bliznik, May 30, 1967; children: Jean Marie, Michael Terrence, Maura Elizabeth. BS, Ill. Inst. Tech., 1969, MS, 1970, PhD, 1972. Registered clin. psychologist, Ill. Asst. dir. psychol. services Cook County Sch. Nursing, Chgo., 1972-75; asst. prof. psychiatry Northwestern U. Med. Sch., Chgo., 1975—; dir. psychotherapy program Inst. Psychiatry Northwestern Meml. Hosp., Chgo., 1982—; asst. prof. psychiatry U. Ill. Med. Sch., Chgo., 1973-75. Contbr. articles to profl. jours. Mem. Am. Psychol. Assn., Ill. Psychol. Assn. Democrat. Roman Catholic. Home: 296 Hagans Elmhurst IL 60126 Office: Inst Psychiatry 320 E Huron Chicago IL 60611

O'MALLEY, DEBORAH SUE, accountant; b. Rushville, Ill., June 29, 1962; s. Leonard William and Karan Evonne (Ingram) Lane; m. Patrick William O'Malley, July 12, 1986. CPA, Ill. Staff acct. Doherty, Zable & Co., Chgo., 1984-85; sr. acct. Checkers, Simon & Rosner, Chgo., 1985—. Mem. Am. Inst. CPA's, Ill. CPA Soc. Avocations: travel, reading, bicycling, sports. Home: 2622 N 75th Ct Elmwood Park IL 60635 Office: Checkers Simon & Rosner One S Wacker Dr Chicago IL 60606

O'MALLEY, PATRICK WILLIAM, accountant; b. Oak Park, Ill., Apr. 16, 1961; s. Richard Lawrence and Barbara E. (Hannon) O'M.; m. Deborah Sue Lane, July 12, 1986. BA, Rosary Coll., 1984. CPA, Ill. Asst. acctg. mgr. Chemcentral, Bedford Park, Ill., 1984-85; staff acct. Coleman, Epstein, Berlin & Co., Chgo., 1985—. Mem. Am. Inst. CPA's, Ill. CPA Soc. Roman Catholic. Avocations: sports participation, travel, bicycling, reading. Home: 2622 N 75th Ct Elmwood Park IL 60635 Office: Coleman Epstein Berlin & Co 2701 W Peterson Ave Chicago IL 60659

OMDAHL, LLOYD, state official. Lt. gov. State of N.D., Bismarck, 1987—. Office: Office of the Lieutenant Governor Capitol Bldg Bismarck ND 58505 *

O'MEARA, EDWARD THOMAS, bishop; b. St. Louis, Aug. 3, 1921; s. John and Mary (Fogarty) O'M. Student, Kenrick Sem., 1943-46; S.T.D., Angelicum U., Rome, 1953. Ordained priest Roman Catholic Ch., 1946, then became monseignor, ordained bishop, 1972; asst. pastor St. Louis Cathedral, 1952-55; asst. nat. dir. Soc. for Propagation of the Faith, 1956-60; dir. Soc. for Propagation of the Faith (St. Louis area), 1960-67; nat. dir. Soc. for Propagation of the Faith (St. Louis area), N.Y.C., 1967-79; archbishop of Indpls., 1980—; apptd. titular bishop of Thisiduo and aux. bishop of St. Louis, 1972-80. Editor: World mission mag. Home: Chancery Office 1400 N Meridian St Indianapolis IN 46206 Office: Chancery Office 1350 N Pennsylvania Ave Indianapolis IN 46202 *

O'MEARA, O. TIMOTHY, mathematician, educator, university administrator; b. Cape Town, Republic of South Africa, Jan. 29, 1928; came to U.S., 1950; m. Jean T. Fadden, Sept. 12, 1953; children: Maria, Timothy, Jean, Kate, Eileen. BS, U. Cape Town, 1947, MS, 1948; PhD, Princeton (N.J.) U., 1953; LLD (hon.), U. Notre Dame, 1987. Asst. lectr. U. Natal, Republic of South Africa, 1949; lectr. U. Otago, New Zealand, 1954-56; lectr. Princeton U., 1956-57, asst. prof. math., 1958-62; prof. math. U. Notre Dame, Ind., 1962-75, chmn. dept. math., 1965-66, 68-72, Howard J. Kenna prof. math., 1976—, provost, 1978—; mem. Inst. for Advanced Study, Princeton, 1957-58, 62; vis. prof. math. Calif. Inst. Tech., 1968, U. Calif., Santa Barbara, 1976; vis. scientist U. Toronto, Can., 1978; Gauss prof. Göttingen Acad. Sci., 1978; cons. NSF, 1960—; mem. adv. council dept. math. Princeton U., 1982—. Author: Introduction to Quadratic Forms, 1963, Lectures on Linear Groups, 1974, Symplectic Groups, 1978; contbr. numerous articles to profl. jours. NSF grantee, 1963-80; Charlotte E. Proctor fellow, 1952-53, Alfred P. Sloan fellow, 1960-63. Mem. Assn. Cath. Colls. and Univs. (bd. dirs. 1986—, exec. com. bd. dirs. 1986). Office: U Notre Dame Office of Provost Notre Dame IN 46556

OMMODT, DONALD HENRY, dairy company executive; b. Flom, Minn., July 7, 1931; s. Henry and Mabel B. (Kvidt) O.; m. Evelyn Mavis Bliile, June 15, 1957; children—Linette, Kevin, Lee, Jodi. Student, Interstate Bus. Coll., Fargo, N.D. Acct. Farmers State Bank, Waubun, Minn., 1950-53; chief acct. Cass-Clay Creamery, Inc., Fargo, 1953-61, office mgr., 1961-65, gen. mgr., 1965-83, pres., 1983—; dir. Blue Cross of N.D., Fargo. Pres. Messiah Luth. Ch., Fargo, 1976-78; bd. dirs. Communicating for Agr., Fergus Falls, Minn., 1977-80. Mem. N.D. Dairy Industries Assn. (bd. dirs., past pres.), Am. Dairy Assn. (bd. dirs. N.D. 1970-80), N.D. Dairy Product Promotion Commn. (bd. dirs. 1970-80). Office: Cass-Clay Creamery Inc 1220 Main Ave Fargo ND 58108

OMORI, JOHN TAKASHI, optometrist; b. El Centro, Calif., Dec. 14, 1924; s. Juro and Towa (Ogawara) O.; m. Merry Fujihara, June 14, 1952. OD, Chgo. Coll. Optometry, 1952. Pvt. practice optometry Chgo., 1952—; cons. Kolef, Milan, Soleko, Ponte Corvo, Italy, Asia Contact Lens Lab., Madras, India, U.S. Army, Chgo. Served to staff sgt., U.S. Army, 1945-48, PTO. Mem. Am. Optometric Assn., Ill. Optometric Assn. Home: 805 Queens Ln Glenview IL 60025 Office: 3143 W Devon Ave Chicago IL 60659

ONDERCIN, DAVID GEORGE, academic administrator; b. Racine, Wis., Feb. 16, 1942; s. George Andrew and Florence (Drettwan) O.; m. Joan Maree Johnson, Aug, 21, 1964; children: Karen, John, David. BE, U. Wis., Whitewater, 1965; MS, U. Wis., Milw., 1967; PhD, U. Minn., 1973. Assoc. prof. Northwestern Coll., Roseville, Minn., 1977-81, v.p., 1981—. Mem. Am. Assn. Higher Edn., Council Ind. Colls. Republican. Evangelical. Avocation: running. Office: Northwestern Coll 3003 N Snelling Roseville MN 55113

ONDERSMA, DAVID M., bank executive. Pres., chief exec. officer First Mich. Bank Corp., Zeeland. Office: First Mich Bank Corp 101 E Main St Box 300 Zeeland MI 49464 *

O'NEIL, HERBERT EARL, metrology educator; b. Duluth, Minn., Mar. 26, 1944; s. Jack and Maxine (Brown) O'N.; m. Aino Lavarärjäavi (div.); children: Tiina, Tanya, Tara; m. Judy Elaine Coleman, Jan. 5, 1984; children: Tiia, Tyriina. BS, U. Wis., 1971, MA, 1973. Cert. tchr.; Wis., Minn. Electronics technician Litton Communication, Europe and Middle East, 1965-67; tech. engr. DeMarc Cable Corp., Elmwood, Wis., 1971-72; instr. math, sci. Marion (Wis.) Jr. High Sch., 1973-78; curriculum analyst AVCO/E Systems, Saudia Arabia, 1978-79; instr. computer hardware Cray Research, Chippewa, Wis., 1979-80; instr. metrology Hutchinson (Minn.) Vo-Tech, 1980—; chief exec. officer Alpha Omega Enterprises, Hutchinson, 1980—; adj. instr. U. Minn., St. Paul, 1981-82; asst. dir., instr. U. Wis., Green Bay, 1976-79. Pres. Hutchinson Edn. Assn., 1982-84, Hutchinson Community Video Network, 1980-82, Marion Edn. Assn., 1975-76. Served with USAF, 1962-65. Named Outstanding Vocational Educator, Minn. Dept. Edn., 1984. Mem. Instrument Soc. Am. (chmn. standards and practice com. 1986—, chmn. honors and awards com. 1985-86, chmn. edn. com. 1984-85, named Outstanding Adv., 1985), Inst. Electrical and Electronics Engrs. (sr.), Nat. Conf. Standard Labs., Metrology Soc. Avocations: chess, duplicate bridge, volyball. Home: 1201 Lewis Ave Hutchinson MN 55350 Office: Hutchinson Tech Inst 200 Century Ave Hutchinson MN 55350

O'NEIL, MICHAEL GERALD, retired business executive; b. Akron, Ohio, Jan. 29, 1922; s. William Francis and Grace (Savage) O'N.; m. Juliet P. Rudolph, Jan. 7, 1950 (div.); children: Michael, Gregory, Jeffrey, Shawn, Julie, Nancy, Susan. A.B., Coll. of Holy Cross, 1943; postgrad., Sch. Bus., Harvard, 1948; LL.D., U. Akron, 1962, Ashland, Coll., 1967. With Gencorp (formerly Gen. Tire's Rubber Co.), Akron, 1947—; staff inter-plant ops. Gencorp (formerly Gen. Tire's Rubber Co.), Venezuela, 1947-48; dir. Gencorp (formerly Gen. Tire's Rubber Co.), 1950-87, exec. asst. to pres., 1951-60, pres., 1960-83, 84-85, chmn. bd., 1981-87, chief exec. officer, 1985-87, mem. exec., finance coms.; former dir., chmn. bd. Aerojet-Gen. Corp.; dir. 1st Nat. Bank of Akron. Served as lt. USAAF, 1944-45. Clubs: Portage Country, Akron City, Detroit Athletic, Sharon Golf. Office: Gencorp Inc One General St Akron OH 44329

O'NEILL, ARTHUR J., bishop; b. East Dubuque, Ill., Dec. 14, 1917. Student, Loras Coll., Dubuque, Iowa, St. Mary's Sem., Balt. Ordained priest Roman Catholic Ch., 1943; bishop of Rockford Ill., 1968—. Office: Diocesan Chancery 1245 N Court St Rockford IL 61103

O'NEILL, EDWARD ELMER, food scientist; b. Cheyenne, Wyo., Mar. 12, 1947; s. Elmer J. and Agnes Marie (Marvel) O'N.; m. Linda K. Kraft, Aug. 7, 1970; children: Brent P., Megan M. BS, U. Nebr., Lincoln, 1969; MS, U. Minn., St. Paul, 1971. Research asst. U. Minn., St. Paul, 1969-71; food scientist Welch Foods, Inc., Westfield, N.Y., 1971-74, Fairmont Foods, Inc., Omaha, Nebr., 1974-77; dir. research Pizza Hut, Inc., Wichita, Kans., 1977—; mem. food service adv. com. AVI Pub., Westport, Conn., 1979-81. Patentee method for preparing and cooking pizza, 1983. Mem. fin. com. Calvary Meth. Ch., Wichita, 1986; coach Am. Youth Soccer Orgn., Wichita, 1986, t-ball YMCA, Wichita, 1986. Recipient scholarship Inst. Food Technologists, 1966. Mem. Inst. Food Technologists, Am. Assn. Cereal Chemists, Soc. for Advancement of Food Service Research. Clubs: Plane Apple (Wichita), Meth. Men. Avocations: reading, camping, family activities, racquetball. Office: Pizza Hut Inc 9111 E Douglas Wichita KS 67207

O'NEILL, JAMES JOHN, accountant; b. Cleve., Apr. 4, 1929; s. James John and Dorothy A. (Maher) O'N.; m. Margaret Louise OHara, Oct. 10, 1951; children: James, Raymond. BS in Bus. Adminstrn., John Carroll U., 1954. Staff mem. Hausser & Taylor, Cleve., 1951-62, ptnr., 1962—. Mem. Cleve. Com. Fgn. Relations, 1987—, Diabetes Assn. Cleve., 1987—, Greater Cleve. Growth Assn., 1987—; trustee, treas. St. Ann's Found.; trustee Cleve. Council on World Affairs. Served as sgt. USMC, 1950-51. Mem. Am. Inst. CPA's (exec. com. div. firms 1985—, mem. joint coordinating com.), Nat. Assn. Accts., Ohio Soc. CPA's. Roman Catholic. Clubs: Union, Mayfield Heights Racquet, Shaker Heights Country (Cleve.). Home: 1 Bratenahl Pl #1205 Bratenahl OH 44108 Office: Hausser & Taylor 1000 Eaton Ctr Cleveland OH 44114

O'NEILL, MICHAEL HUGH, manufacturing company executive; b. Chgo., Oct. 18, 1954; s. J.C. and Joan Marie (Fitzpatrick) O'N.; m. Linda Kay Gross, Feb. 20, 1982; children: Christopher John, Sean Michael. BS in Acctg., Regis Coll., 1976. Concert prodn. mgr. Regis Coll./Fayline Enterprises, Denver, 1973-75; expediter, buyer Fabsco Corp., Calumet Park, Ill., 1976-77; freight sales rep. AGA Trucking, Los Angeles, 1977; gen. mgr. Connecting Materials, Calumet Park, 1977-79; owner, mgr. Zodiacus Travel, Chicago Heights, Ill., 1980-83; estimator, buyer Fabsco Corp., Calumet Park, Ill., 1983-84, mgr. purchasing, 1984-87; comptroller Fabsco Corp., Calumet Park, 1987—. Advance man Adam Benjamin for Congress, Gary, Ind., 1976; active Vols. for Daley, Chgo., 1983; vol. Peter Viscloskey for Congress, Gary, 1984. Mem. Ill. Mfrs. Assn. (small mfrs. action council 1985—). Clubs: St. Patrick Bros. (Chgo.) (pres. 1978, 83). Lodge: KC. Avocations: Chicago Bears football, reading, stained glass, golf. Home: 20631 S Bensley Lynwood IL 60411 Office: Fabsco Corp 1745 W 124th St Calumet Park IL 60643

ONG, JOHN DOYLE, rubber products company executive; b. Uhrichsville, Ohio, Sept. 29, 1933; s. Louis Brosee and Mary Ellen (Liggett) O.; m. Mary Lee Schupp, July 20, 1957; children: John Francis Harlan, Richard Penn Blackburn, Mary Katherine Caine. B.A., Ohio State U., 1954, M.A., 1954; LL.B., Harvard, 1957; L.H.D., Kent State U., 1982. Bar: Ohio 1958. Asst. counsel B.F. Goodrich Co., Akron, 1961-66; group v.p. B.F. Goodrich Co., 1972-73, exec. v.p., 1973-74, vice chmn., 1974-75, pres., dir., 1975-77, pres., chief operating officer, dir., 1978-79, chmn. bd., pres., chief exec. officer, 1979-84, chmn. bd., chief exec. officer, 1984—; asst. to pres. Internat. B.F. Goodrich Co., Akron, 1966-69, v.p., 1969-70, pres., 1970-72; dir. Cooper Industries, Am. Info. Technologies Corp., The Kroger Co. Vice-pres. exploring Great Trail council Boy Scouts Am., 1974-77; bd. dirs. Nat. Alliance for Bus.; trustee Mus. Arts Assn., Cleve., Bexley Hall Sem., 1974-81, Case Western Res. U., 1980—, Kenyon Coll., 1983-85; trustee Hudson (Ohio) Library and Hist. Soc., pres., 1971-72; trustee Western Res. Acad., Hudson, 1975—, pres. bd. trustees, 1977—; nat. trustee Nat. Symphony Orch., 1975-83; mem. bus. adv. com. Transp. Center, Northwestern U., 1975-78, Carnegie-Mellon U. Grad. Sch. Indsl. Adminstrn., 1978-83; mem. adv. bd. Blossom Music Center. Served with JAGC AUS, 1957-61. Mem. Ohio Bar Assn. (bd. govs. corp. counsel sect. 1962-74, chmn. 1970), Rubber Mfrs. Assn. (dir. 1974-84), Conf. Bd., Bus. Roundtable, Phi Beta Kappa, Phi Alpha Theta. Episcopalian. Clubs: Portage Country, Akron City; Union (Cleve.); Links (N.Y.C.); Union League (N.Y.C.); Ottawa Shooting; Met.

(Washington); Rolling Rock (Ligonier, Pa.); Castalia Trout. Home: 230 Aurora St Hudson OH 44236 Office: 3925 Embassy Pkwy Akron OH 44313

ONKEN, HENRY DRALLE, plastic surgeon; b. St.Louis, Feb. 22, 1932; s. John Werner and Clara Ruth (Dralle) O.; m. Deborah Dorsett Smith, June 3, 1961; children: John D., Michael D., Katherine Minna. AB, Princeton U., 1953; MD, Harvard U., 1957. Diplomate Am. Bd. Plastic Surgery. Resident in gen. and plastic surgery Barnes Hosp., St. Louis, 1957-66; practice medicine specializing in plastic surgery St. Louis, 1966—; treas. med. staff St. Joseph Hosp., Kirkwood, Mo., 1983; sec. treas. med. staff Deaconess Hosp., St. Louis, 1986—. Bd. dirs. English Lang. Sch., 1987—; St. Louis Christmas Carolers, 1981—; co-chmn. Theater Factory of St. Louis, Webster Groves, Mo., 1984—. Served to capt. M.C. U.S. Army, 1962-64. Mem. Am. Soc. Plastic & Reconstructive Surgeons, St. Louis Area Soc. Plastic Surgeons (treas. 1984—), Mo. State Med. Assn., St. Louis Med. Soc. Democrat. Clubs: Univ. (St. Louis), Princeton (St. Louis & N.Y.C.), Aesculapian. Avocations: acting, singing, running, collecting old maps. Office: 1034 S Brentwood Suite 750 Saint Louis MO 63117

ONODA, BRIGHT YASUNORI, physician; b. Cosmopolis, Wash., July 25, 1921; s. Sanjuru and Yaeko (Shingai) O.; B.S., Hillsdale (Mich.) Coll., 1948; M.D., U. Mich., 1952; m. Teresa Peters, Aug. 13, 1976; children—Carol, Paul. Intern, Harper Hosp., Detroit, 1952-53; resident U. Chgo. Clinics, 1956-57, St. Luke's Hosp., Chgo., 1957-58; dir. dept. anesthesiology Augustana Hosp., Chgo., 1973—, med. dir. respiratory care dept., 1968—, also mem. exec. com., treas. med. staff. Bd. dirs. Augustana Hosp., 1978—. Served in U.S. Army, 1945-48. Diplomate Am. Bd. Anesthesiology. Fellow Am. Coll. Anesthesiologists; mem. AMA, Chgo. Med. Soc., Am. Soc. Anesthesiologists, Ill. Soc. Anesthesiologists, Am. Legion. Home: 9023 Tamaroa Skokie IL 60076 Office: 411 W Dickens Chicago IL 60614

OOI, BOON SENG, medical educator; b. Kuala Lumpar, Sengalore, Malaysia, Apr. 21, 1940; came to U.S., 1972; s. Keng Seng and Lily (Yue) O.; m. Yuet Mei Chong, Feb. 26, 1966; children: Joanne, James. MBBS, U. Singapore, 1964. Diplomate Bd. Internal Medicine and Nephrology. Asst. prof. medicine U. Singapore, 1969-72, U. Chgo., 1972-73; from asst. to assoc. prof. medicine U. Cin., 1973-86, prof. medicine, 1987—. Contbr. articles to profl. jours. Fellow Royal Australasian Coll. Physicians; mem. Am. Fedn. Clin. Research, Am. Soc. Nephrology, Am. Soc. Hypertension, Am. Soc. Clin. Investigation. Avocations: jogging, literature. Office: U Cin Coll Medicine Div Nephrology 231 Bethesda Ave Cincinnati OH 45267

OPACKI, NANCY JEAN, service analyst; b. Grand Rapids, Mich., 1956; d. Walter Joseph and Estelle Theresa (Stasiak) O. BS summa cum laude, Aquinas Coll., Grand Rapids, 1978; MS, U. Notre Dame, 1981. Cert. provisional secondary edn., Mich. Tchr. Assumption B.V.M., Belmont, Mich., 1978-79; analyst primary services forecasts Gen. Telephone Co. of Mich., Muskegon, 1981—; mem. switched usage access charges task force Gen. Telephone Co. of Mich., Muskegon, 1983-85. V.p. Grand Rapids area chpt. Alzheimer's Disease and Related Disorders Assn., 1982-83, pres., 1984-86, bd. dirs., 1987—. Recipient Presdl. Sports award for Bicycling, 1976, Humanitarian award Alzheimer's Disease and Related Disorders Assn. Grand Rapids Area Chpt., 1986. Mem. Assn. for Women in Math. Roman Catholic. Avocations: bicycling, photography, travel, music. Office: Gen Telephone Co of Mich 455 E Ellis Rd Muskegon MI 49441

OPDYKE, JON CHARLES, property manager; b. Lansing, Mich., Oct. 25, 1948; s. Charles Victor And Leota Maude (Tucker) O.; m. Alexa Zudurne, Mar. 13, 1970 (div. 1975); 1 child, Jon Alan Opdyke Hanson; m. Kathie Marie Hiatt; children: Austin Allen, Ryan Anthony. Grad. high sch., Lansing, Mich.; student, Lansing Community Coll., 1967-68, 70-71. Property mgr. Bank of Lansing, 1970-74, Prudential Bldg. Maintenance, Lansing, 1975-77, Villas of Woodgate, Lansing, 1977-82, Bretton Park, Flat Rock, Mich., 1982-84, Oakland Valley Apts., Auburn Hills, Mich., 1984—. Served with USNR, 1969-70, Vietnam. Jehovah's Witness. Clubs: Mich. Salmon and Sleetheaders Assn. Am., Soc. for Preservation and Continuation of Barbershop Quartet Singing in Am. Avocations: fishing, lure making, rod building, fly fishing. Home: 2792 Patrick Henry Dr Apt 712 Auburn Hills MI 48057 Office: Oakland Valley Apts I & II 2760 Patrick Henry Dr Auburn Hills MI 48057

OPELT, RILLA ANNE, small business owner; b. Duluth, Minn., Aug. 7, 1939; d. Frank Louis and Mabel Hester (Chapman) DeBot; m. Alexander Lambi Stolis, May 6, 1961 (div. 1969); children: Alexander Jr., Roxanne Kathryn, Pauline Madeline, Rilla Marie; m. Bud T. Opelt, Nov. 8, 1969; children: Buddy Jr., Theanne Lenore. BA in Socail Work, St. Scholastica, 1961, BA in Elem. Edn., 1969, postgrad. Owner, operator Mother's Helper's Inc., Duluth, 1965-79; elem. tchr. Duluth Sch. Dist., 1969-75; sec. Minn. Power, Duluth, 1978—; owner Personalized Cons., Duluth, 1983—. Cordinator Prolife Info. Network, Duluth, 1983—; dist. chmn. 7th Senate Dist. Reps., 1983—. Mem. Rep. Women. Roman Catholic. Club: Community. Avocations: dolls, miniatures, antiques collecting. Home: 302 99th Ave W Duluth MN 55808

OPENSHAW, CALVIN REYNOLDS, surgeon; b. Salt Lake City, Nov. 4, 1921; s. Clarence Roy and Elna Dehlin (Shipp) O.; m. Blanche Hiley, Dec. 11, 1948; children—Calvin Reynolds, Susan Beaver, Michael Browne; m. Evelyn Constance Miller, Dec. 19, 1973. B.S., U. Utah, 1942, M.D., 1944; M.S., U. Minn., 1953. Intern Salt Lake County Gen. Hosp., 1944-45; resident, research fellow in surgery U. Utah, Salt Lake City, 1946-47; fellow in surgery Mayo Found., 1948-51; fellow in thoracic surgery Mayo Found., 1951-53; chief thoracic surgery VA Hosp., Fort Douglas, Utah, 1955-56; practice medicine specializing in surgery Hutchinson, Kans., 1957—; mng. ptnr. GGC Enterprises, 1980-87; chief surgery dept. Hutchinson Hosp., 1977-81, 85-87; asst. clin. prof. surgery U. Utah, 1955-56; dir. Hutchinson Hosp., 1979-85. Served with USN, 1945-46, 53-55; with Res. Mem. AMA, ACS, Southwestern Surg. Congress, Am. Legion, Mensa, Priestly Soc., Prometheus Soc., Internat. Soc. Philos. Enquiry, Mayo Thoracic Soc. Republican. Congregationalist. Home: 1824 Main St Hutchinson KS 67502 Office: 2020 N Waldron Hutchinson KS 67502

OPHEIM, JANICE ELAINE, accountant; b. Mason City, Iowa, May 8, 1957; d. Earl Leslie and Shirley Maie (Surfus) O. AA, North Iowa Area Community Coll., 1977; BA, U. No. Iowa, 1979. CPA, Iowa. Asst. auditor Office of Auditor of State of Iowa, Des Moines, 1979-80, sr. auditor, 1980-83, audit supr., 1983-84, audit mgr., 1984—. Mem. Am. Inst. CPA's, Iowa Soc. CPA's (com. mem.), Assn. Govt. Accts. (program chmn. 1986-87, Chpt. Mem. of Yr. 1987). Republican. Presbyterian. Club: Mariners (Des Moines) (treas. 1985, pres. 1986—). Avocations: knitting, volleyball, golf, music, sports. Home: 7213 Wilshire Blvd Des Moines IA 50322 Office: Office of the State Auditor State Capitol Bldg Des Moines IA 50319

OPPENHEIMER, CHARLES K(ENNETH), JR., financial executive, consultant; b. Hartford, Conn., Dec. 8, 1949; s. Charles Kenneth and Marjorie (Harlow) O.; m. Bonnie Ann Toriani, Jan. 22, 1972 (div. 1977). Student Hartford Inst. Acctg., 1977-79. Pres., C & M Oppenheimer Notepaper Co., (now Park Nat. Industries), 1961—; newspaper exec. Hartford Times, 1967-75; founder, pres. Circulation Systems, Inc. (now div. Pacific Crest Communications Corp.), 1971—; exec. v.p. Gt. Northern Trust, 1974-79, also dir.; founder, pres. Plant City Corp., 1976—; newspaper exec. Jour. Pub. Co., Manchester, Conn., 1978-79; newspaper fin. mgmt. exec. Kansas City (Mo.) Star Co., 1981-83; pres., chief exec. officer Paperchase Corp. (name changed to Armcrest Corp.), 1983—, Crane & Co. Inc. subs. Amcrest Corp., 1985—; pres. Westar Nat. Inc., 1986—; exec. officer Park Nat. Corp., Plant City Corp., Transrail Corp., Pacific Crest Communications Corp., Quill & Scroll Ltd. subs. Amcrest Corp., Herald Office Equipment Co. Inc. subs. Amcrest Corp.; mgmt. and pub. cons.; condr. seminars. Mem. Internat. Circulation Mgrs. Assn., Nat. Assn. Advt. Pubs., Inst. Newspaper Controllers and Fin. Officers, Printing Industries Am., Nat. Office Machine Dealers Assn., Nat. Office Products Assn., N.Y. Fin. Execs. Assn., Rail Passenger Coalition, Ind. Merchants Assn. (bd. dirs. 1984—, pres. 1984-86). Clubs: Western Mass. Appaloosa Assn. (pres. 1975-76, dir. 1976-79), Quinniapiac River Doberman Pinscher (treas. 1975-77). Author: Expense Code Numbering System, Central Purchasing Mgrs. Manual. Address: PO Box 413036 Kansas City MO 64141 also: 300 W Maple St Independence MO 64050

OPPENHUIZEN, GREGORY JOEL, orthodontist; b. Grand Rapids, Mich., Oct. 28, 1956; s. Simon William and Alma Constance (White) O.; m. Rachelle Rae Dykstra, July 8, 1978; children: Reid Marten, Leland Joel. Student, Grand Valley State Coll., 1975; BA, Calvin Coll., 1978; DDS, U. Mich., 1982; MSD, Ind. U., 1984. Head dept. orthodontics Midwestern Orthodonic Assocs., Sterling Heights, Mich., 1984-85; assoc. Dr.s Boven and Fuder, P.C., Holland, Mich., 1985-86; ptnr. Holland Orthodontic Assocs., 1986—. Composer: Happy Day Rag, 1975 (1st Pl. Calvin Coll. Fine Arts Competition, 1975), Another Song and Dance, 1976 (1st Pl. Calvin Coll. Fine Arts Competition, 1976). Mem. Am. Assn. Orthodontists, Great Lakces Soc. Orthodontists, Mich. Soc. Orthodontists, ADA, Mich. Dental Assn., West Mich. Dental Soc., Holland-Zeeland Dental Soc. (v.p., pres. elect 1986). Mem. Ch. Am. Avocations: piano playing, piano composition, master's swimming. Home: 1237 Euna Vista Dr Holland MI 49423 Office: Holland Orthodontic Assocs 205 W 29th St Holland MI 49423

O'QUINN, MILTON LAFAYETTE, information systems executive; b. Chgo., Apr. 19, 1944; s. John William and Cleodia L. (Dawkins) O'Q.; m. Kathleen Amelia Jamerson, Oct. 3, 1981; children: Kathleen Louise, Monte Laurel, Lynn Elizabeth, Milton Lafayette, John Christopher, Lisa Donyale, Kacey Lauren. BA, Houston-Tillotson Coll., 1967; postgrad. in bus., U. Chgo., 1968-71. Sales rep. Lever Bros., 1967; account rep. Proctor & Gamble, 1968-71, Chgo., 1971-73; systems specialist Xerox Corp., Mpls., 1974-76, sales mgr., 1974-78, br. mgr. sales, 1978-80; region sales ops. mgr. Xerox Corp., Des Plaines, Ill., 1980-81, region sales program mgr., 1981-82; region sales mgr. Electronic Laser Printers, Arlington Heights, Ill., 1982-84, regional mgr. agent dealer ops., 1985-87; regional mgr. supplies Electronic Laser Printers, Bloomfield, Mich., 1987—. V.p. West Side Assn. Community Action, 1974-75; bd. dirs. Chgo. Youth Ctr., Altgeld-Roseland, 1975-77, South Shore Community Ctr., Chgo., 1975-77, Marcy Newberry Assn., 1975-77. Recipient Eagle Scout award Boy Scouts Am. Mem. Houston Tillotson Alumni Assn. (past pres.), Bloomington C. of C., Am. Legion, Kappa Alpha Psi. Lodge: Lions. Co-founder O'Quinn Royal Gladiators Drum and Bugle Corp. Home: 4822 Valleyview Dr S West Bloomfield MI 48033

ORAVECZ, MICHAEL GEORGE, physicist, researcher; b. Akron, Ohio, Jan. 31, 1956; s. John and Miriam Jane (Partsch) O. B. in Physics, U. Chgo., 1978; M. in Physics, SUNY-Stony Brook, 1979. Jr. research asst. Cloud Physics Lab. Dept. Geophysics U. Chgo., 1975-76; Yerkes Obs., Williams Bay, Wis., 1977; teaching asst. physics SUNY-Stony Brook, 1978-79, research asst. quantum electronics group Physics dept., 1979; chief scientist Sonoscan, Inc., Bensenville, Ill., 1981—. Contbr. articles to profl. jours. Sustainer Inst. for Independent Social Journalism. Mem. Am. Ceramics Soc., Am. Soc. Metals, Am. Soc. Nondestructive Testing, Internat. Soc. Hybrid Microelectronics, Am. Soc. Mech. Engrs. (mem. tech. com. on biomed. uses of acoustics, 1984—), NOW. Avocations: computers; classical music. Home: 88 W Schiller Apt #1609 Chicago IL 60610 Office: Sonoscan Inc 530 E Green St Bensenville IL 60106

ORDINACHEV, JOANN LEE, educator; b. Rogers, Ark., Mar. 17, 1936; d. Floyd Andrew and Irene Elnora Elizabeth (Johnson) Walkenbach; m. J. Dean Harter, Dec. 24, 1953 (div. 1977); m. 2d, Miles Donald Ordinachev, Mar. 11, 1978. B.S., U. Mo., 1971; M.A.T., Webster U., 1974; postgrad. St. Louis U., 1978—. Office mgr. Edwards Constrn. Co., Joplin, Mo., 1954-58; with Jasper Welfare Office, Joplin, 1958-61; tchr. St. Louis Archdiocean, 1963-68, 70-71; TV personality, tchr. Sta. KDMO Cablevision, Carthage, Mo., 1968-69; tech. reading and remedial math. specialist West County Tech. Sch., St. Louis, 1974—; owner Jody's Dyslexia Lab., Concord Village, Mo., 1982—. Mem. Am. Vocat. Assn., Mo. Vocat. Assn., Spl. Dist. Tchrs. Assn. (pres.), NEA (pres. 1980-81), Orton Dyslexia Soc., Sch. Psychologists Assn., Council Exceptional Children, Network Women Psychologist. Democrat. Eastern Orthodox.

ORDING, JEFFREY CHARLES, real estate executive; b. Chgo., Sept. 15, 1953; s. Charles Henry and Elizabeth Ann Ording; m. Connie Ording, May 7, 1983. V.p. Hemisphere Corp., Barrington, Ill., 1980-82; pres. Cable Comml. Brokerage, Inc., Northbrook, Ill., 1982-86, Royal LePage Comml. Real Estate Services, 1987—. Office: Royal LePage Comml Real Estate Services Two 1st Nat Plaza Suite 2900 Chicago IL 60603

OREAR, JEFFREY WAYNE, dentist; b. Janesville, Wis., July 17, 1956; s. Errell Thomas and Elizabeth Jean (Watt) O.; m. Barbara Joan Burger, July 24, 1982; children: Melanie Lynn, Kelly Elizabeth. BA, Ripon Coll., 1978; DDS, Northwestern U., 1982. Gen. practice dentistry Peshtigo, Wis., 1982—. Chmn. council on ministries Peshtigo United Meth. Ch., 1984—; bd. dirs. Marinette-Menominee-Peshtigo United Way, Marinette, Wis, 1986; bd. dirs. Tri-City Tennis Assn., 1986. Mem. Wis. Dental Assn., ADA, Marinette-Oconto Dental Assn. (sec., treas. 1983-84), No. Area Radio Control Soc. (v.p. 1984-85, 86-88), Peshtigo C. of C. (v.p. 1986, pres. 1987), Beta Sigma Pi. Republican. Lodge: Lions (officer bd. dirs 1986-87). Avocations: radio controlled model airplanes, tennis, skiing, fishing, photography. Home: 641 Lincoln Dr Peshtigo WI 54157 Office: 540 Oconto Ave Peshtigo WI 54157

OREFFICE, PAUL FAUSTO, chemical executive; b. Venice, Italy, Nov. 29, 1927; came to U.S., 1945, naturalized, 1951; s. Max and Elena (Friedenberg) O.; m. Franca Giuseppina Ruffini, May 26, 1956; children: Laura Emma, Andrew T. B.S. in Chem. Engring., Purdue U., 1949. With Dow Chem. Co., various internat. locations, 1953—; assigned to Switzerland, Italy, Brazil and Spain to 1969; pres. Dow Chem. Latin Am., Coral Gables, Fla., 1966-70; corporate fin. v.p. Dow Chem. Co., Midland, Mich., 1970-75, pres. Dow Chem. U.S.A., 1975-78, pres., chief exec. officer, 1978-86, chmn., pres., chief exec. officer, 1986-87, chmn., chief exec. officer, 1987—; dir. Dow Chem. Co., Dow Corning, CIGNA Corp., No. Telecom Ltd., Coca Cola Co. Trustee Am. Enterprise Inst.; mem. policy com. Bus. Roundtable. Served with AUS, 1951-53. Decorated Encomienda del Merito Civil Spain, 1966. Mem. Chem. Mfrs. Assn. (past chmn. bd., dir.), Bus. Council, Conf. Bd. Office: Dow Chem Co 2030 Willard H Dow Ctr Midland MI 48674

O'REILLY, HUGH JOSEPH, restaurant executive; b. Emporia, Kans., July 20, 1936; s. Henry Charles and Mary Esther (Rettiger) O'R.; m. Eileen Ellen Browne, Feb. 11, 1961; 1 child, Hugh Jr. Student, St. Benedicts Coll., Atchison, Kans., 1954-57, Stouffer Conservatory of Music, 1957-78. Banquet mgr. Kansas City Conservatory of Music, 1957-58, Stouffer Corp., N.Y.C., 1958-61; gen. mgr. Howard Johnsons, L.I., N.Y., 1961-65; regional mgr. Malt Village Corp., St. Louis, 1965-68; ops. cons. McDonalds Corp., Chgo., 1968-78; pres., chief exec. officer O'Reilly Mgmt. Corp., Emporia, Kans., 1978—; nat. advt. cons. McDonalds Operators Assn., Oak Brook, Ill., 1980-84. Republican. Roman Catholic. Lodge: Shriner. Avocations: golf, fishing. Office: 1202 W 6th Emporia KS 66801

OREL, HAROLD, literary critic, educator; b. Boston, Mar. 31, 1926; s. Saul and Sarah (Wicker) O.; m. Charlyn Hawkins, May 25, 1951; children—Sara Elinor, Timothy Ralston. B.A. cum laude, U. N.H., 1948; M.A., U. Mich., 1949, Ph.D., 1952; postgrad., Harvard U., 1949. Teaching fellow U. Mich., 1950-52; instr. dept. English U. Md., 1952-54, 55-56; overseas program U. Md., Germany, Austria, Eng., 1954-55; tech. editor Applied Physics Lab., Johns Hopkins U., Balt., 1953-56; flight propulsion lab. dept. Gen. Electric Co., Cin., 1957; asso. prof. U. Kans., Lawrence, 1958-63; prof. U. Kans., 1963-74, Disting. prof. English, 1974—, asst. dean faculties and research adminstrn., 1964-67; evaluator English depts. in various univs., 1970—; cons. to various univ. presses, scholarly jours., Can. Council Arts, Nat. Endowment for Humanities, Midwest Research Inst., 1958—. Author: Thomas Hardy's Epic-Drama: A Study of The Dynasts, 1963, The Development of William Butler Yeats, 1885-1900, 1968, English Romantic Poets and the Enlightenment: Nine Essays on a Literary Relationship in Studies in Voltaire and the Eighteenth Century, vol. CIII, 1973, The Final Years of Thomas Hardy, 1912-1928, 1976, Victorian Literary Critics, 1984, The Literary Achievement of Rebecca West, 1985, The Victorian Short Story: Development and Triumph of a Literary Genre, 1986, The Unknown Thomas Hardy: Less Familiar Aspects of Hardy's Life and Career, 1987; contbg. author: Thomas Hardy and the Modern World, 1974, The Genius of Thomas Hardy, 1976, Budmouth Essays on Thomas Hardy, 1976, Twilight of Dawn: Studies in English Literature in Transition, 1987; contbr. numerous articles on English lit. history and criticism to various mags.; co-editor: The Thomas Hardy Rev, 1975—; editor: The World of Victorian Humor, 1961, Six Essays in Nineteenth-Century English Literature and Thought, 1962, Thomas Hardy's Personal Writings: Prefaces, Literary Opinions, Reminiscences, 1966, British Poetry 1880-1920: Edwardian Voices, 1969, The Nineteenth-Century Writer and his Audience, 1969, Irish History and Culture, 1976, The Dynasts (Thomas Hardy), 1978, The Scottish World, 1981, Rudyard Kipling: Interviews and Recollections, 2 vols., 1983, Victorian Short Stories: An Anthology, 1987; delivered oration at ceremony commemorating 50th year since Thomas Hardy's death, Westminster Abbey, 1978. Served with USN, 1944-46. Grantee Am. Council Learned Socs., 1966; Nat. Endowment for Humanities grantee, 1975; grantee Am. Philos. Soc., 1964, 80. Fellow Royal Soc. Literature; mem. Thomas Hardy Soc. (v.p. 1968—), Am. Com. on Irish Studies (v.p. 1967-70, pres. 1970-72). Unitarian. Home: 713 Schwarz Rd Lawrence KS 66044 Office: Univ Kansas English Dept Lawrence KS 66045

ORENDORFF, JONATHAN RICHARD, underwriter; b. Moline, Ill., Apr. 21, 1960; s. Robert and Rose Marie (Giovenazzo) O.; m. Melanie Ann Hammerlund, July 23, 1983. AA, Black Hawk Coll., 1980; BS, Ill. State U., 1982. Loss control rep. Valter Inc., West Des Moines, Iowa, 1983, premium auditor, 1983-84; ins. agt. Prudential Ins. Co., Peoria, Ill., 1984-85; underwriter automobile ins. Country Cos., Bloomington, Ill., 1985-86, underwriter life ins., 1986—. Republican. Avocations: sports, reading, music. Home: 1310 N Hershey Bloomington IL 61701 Office: Country Cos Life Ins Co 1701 Towanda Ave Bloomington IL 61701

ORF, ROBERT CHRISTIAN, manufacturingn executive; b. Stillwater, Minn., May 17, 1932; s. Christian Gottlieb and Lillian Magdelen (Behm) O.; m. Shirley May Rehder, Oct. 24, 1959; children: Wayne, Cynthia, Craig. Student, U. Minn., 1961-62. Salesman Nor-Lake Sci., Inc., Hudson, Wis., 1959-72, sales mgr., 1972-82, product mgr., 1982—. Vol. St. Joseph Fire Dept., 1962-86; mem. council Trinity Luth. Ch., Hudson, 1984-86; bd. dirs. Hudson Schs., 1974-77, St. Joseph Twp., 1973-85. Republican. Avocations: woodwork, metal work, gardening, hunting, fishing. Home: Rt 2 Box 237 Hudson WI 54016 Office: Nor-Lake Sci 2d and Elm Sts Hudson WI 54016

ORHON, NECDET KADRI, physician; b. Manisa, Turkey, Aug. 13, 1928; s. MD, U. Istanbul, Turkey, 1951. Lic. to practice medicine in Ill., Iowa, Minn., Ohio, Va., Fla. Intern. U. Istanbul, Turkey, 1952-53; asst. residency in internal medicine Erlanger Hosp., Chattanooga, Tenn., 1953-54; resident in internal medicine Lloyd Noland Hosp., Birmingham-Fairfield, Ala., 1954-55; chief med. resident Good Samaritan Hosp., Lexington, Ky., 1955-56; internist Army Hosp., Turkey, 1956-58; chief resident in internal medicine, chief house doctor Glenwood Hills Hosps., Mpls., 1958-65, internist, chief house officer, 1968-69; fellow oncology Tuft U., Boston, 1966-67; internist Hillcrest Hosp., Birmingham, Ala., 1967-68; dir. emergency room. Mercy Med. Ctr., Springfield, Ohio, 1969-82; practice medicine specializing in internal medicine Springfield, Ohio, 1982—. Mem. Clark County Med. Soc., Ohio Med. Assn. Home: 2066 Northridge Dr Springfield OH 45505 Office: 411 West Handing Springfield OH 45504

ORLASKY, CINDY LEE, clinical psychologist; b. Meadville, Pa., July 27, 1951; d. Henry R. Orlasky and Jill M. (Gartner) Kearns; m. Edward G. Firth III, Sept. 21, 1974; 1 child, Jennifer Elizabeth. BA, Edinboro (Pa.) State Coll., 1972; MA, Kent State U., 1976, PhD, 1979. Lic. psychologist, Ohio, Pa. Family life educator Family and Child Services, Erie, Pa., 1976-78; counselor, trainer Pa. Coalition Against Domestic Violence, Harrisburg, 1978-79; psychologist York (Pa.) County Mental Health Clinic, 1980, Somerset (Pa.) State Hosp., 1980-83, Community Mental Health Services of Medina, Inc., Ohio, 1983—. Mem. Am. Psychol. Assn., Ohio Psychol. Assn., Am. Soc. Group Psychotherapy and Psychodrama. Democrat. Avocations: quilting, exercising, cooking, reading. Home: 6427 Wadsworth Rd Medina OH 44256 Office: Community Mental Health Services 246 Northland Dr Medina OH 44256

ORME, KIPP DWAYNE, accountant; b. Meade, Kans., Sept. 17, 1958; s. Royce Gene and Evangeline Louise (Fidler) O.; m. Susan Kathleen Caffrey, Nov. 12, 1984; children: Michelle Renee, Brian Matthew. BS in Acctg., Baker U., 1980; MBA, Kans. U., 1981. CPA, Kans. Audit sr. mgr., local office tng. mgr. Peat Marwick Main and Co., Wichita, Kans., 1981—. Office coordinator United Way, Wichita, 1987—. Mem. Am. Inst. CPA's, Inst. Cert. Mgmt. Accts., Health Care Fin. Mgmt. Assn., Kans. Soc. CPA's, Wichita C. of C. Avocations: sports, woodworking. Home: 1918 Keith Ct Wichita KS 67212 Office: Peat Marwick Main & Co 600 4th Fin Ctr Wichita KS 67202

ORMOND, ROBERT SIMMONS, radiologist; b. Detroit, Jan. 1, 1923; s. John Kelso and Charlotte Hepburn (Simmons) O.; m. Mary Louse Palmer, May 29, 1943 (dec. Aug. 1963); children: Margaret, Patricia, Robert Jr., Diana, Denise; m. Anita Sue Coulter, Aug. 8, 1964; adopted children: Linda Kay, Cheryl Lynn. AB, Princeton U., 1945; MD, U. Pa., 1947. Chief diagnosis radiology dept. Henry Ford Hosp., Detroit, 1964-70; dir. radiology dept. Hurley Med. Ctr., Flint, Mich., 1970—; clinical prof. radiology Mich. State U., East Lansing, 1973—. Contbr. articles to profl. jour. Served to lt. (j.g.) USAR. Fellow Am. Coll. Radiology; mem. Mich. Radiol. Soc. (pres. 1984-85). Avocation: tree farming. Home: 7480 E Holly Rd Holly MI 48442 Office: Hurley Med Ctr One Hurley Plaza Flint MI 48502

ORMSBY, JEANNE LOUISE, advertising executive; b. Detroit, Sept. 6, 1926; d. Irwin Duffield and Lucille Florence (Cooke) O. BA, Case Western Res. U., 1949. Account exec. Dix & Eaton, Cleve., 1969; editorial dir. Stouffer Corp., Cleve., 1969-77; pvt. practice mktg. communications Cleve., 1977-84; sr. account exec. Jaeger Advt., Berea, Ohio, 1984—. Chmn. pub. relations com. Greater Cleve. Camp Fire Girls, 1966, YWCA, Cleve., 1968; charter mem. mgmt. assistance program United Way, Cleve., 1980, bd. dirs. 1986—. Recipient Best Article of Yr. award Ohio Library Assn. Jour., 1967. Mem. Pub. Relations Soc. Am. (pres. Greater Cleve. chpt. 1969), Greater Cleve. Hosp. Assn. (founder, 1st chmn. pub. relations adv. com. 1958), Cleve. Welfare Fedn. (chmn. pub. relations workshop 1961), Bus. Profl. Advt. Assn. (bd. dirs. 1986—). Lodge: Zonta (pres. Cleve. club 1972-74). Home: 4550 Van Epps Rd Cleveland OH 44131 Office: Jaeger Advt Two Berea Commons Berea OH 44017

ORN, MICHAEL KENT, safety engineer; b. Elkhart, Ind., May 19, 1942; s. C. Russell and Esther Minerva (Wittinghill) O.; m. Judith Louise Kelly, Jan. 20, 1968; children: Todd Michael, Dean Russell II, Catherine Mary-Elizabeth. BS, Purdue U., 1965. Cert. safety profl., Ill., N.D., Wash. Safety and radiation protection officer USAMC, Savanna, Ill., 1966-68; safety officer USAMC Hdqrs., Washington, 1969-73; chief safety br. U.S. Army Safeguard Commn., Mickelson Safeguard Complex, N.D., 1973-76; exec. dir. Bd. Cert. Safety Profls., Savoy, Ill., 1976—. Contbr. articles to profl. jours. Mem. SSS Appeals Bd., Chaimpaign County, Ill., 1982—. Mem. System Safety Soc., Am. Soc. Assn Execs., Am. Soc. Safety Engrs. (chpt. pres. 1980-81). Methodist. Avocations: tennis, gardening. Office: Bd Cert Safety Profls 208 Burwash Ave Savoy IL 61874

ORNEST, HARRY, professional hockey team executive. Chmn. bd., pres., gov. St. Louis Blues, NHL. Office: St Louis Blues 5700 Oakland Ave Saint Louis MO 63110 *

O'ROURKE, EDWARD WILLIAM, bishop; b. Downs, Ill., Oct. 31, 1917; s. Martin and Mary (Hickey) O'R. Student, St. Henry's Coll., Belleville, Ill., 1935-38; B.A., St. Mary of the Lake Sem., Mundelein, Ill., 1940, M.A., 1942, S.T.L., 1944; Licentiate of Philosophy, Aquinas Inst., River Forest, Ill., 1960. Ordained priest Roman Catholic Ch., 1944, bishop, 1971; asst. chaplain Newman Found., U. Ill., 1944-59; exec. dir. Nat. Cath. Rural Life Conf., Des Moines, 1960-71; bishop of Peoria, Ill., 1971—; Dir. refugee resettlement Diocese of Peoria, 1948-59; chmn. arbitration com. Nat. Conf. Cath. Bishops, 1973-76. Author: Marriage and Family Life, 1955, Fundamentals of Philosophy, 1956, Gift of Gifts, 1977, Self Help Works, 1978, Living Like a King, 1979, Roots of Human Rights, 1981; Editor: Catholic Rural Life Mag, 1960-71. Chmn. priorities com. Peoria United Fund, 1972-73; bd. dirs. Internat. Vol. Services, 1960-71; trustee Cath. Relief Services, 1978-80; chmn. bd. Am. Coll. Louvain, 1977-80. Recipient John Henry Newman award, 1959, Nat. Cath. Rural Life Conf. Distinguished Service award, 1973. Club: K.C. (4 deg.). Office: Chancery Office 607 NE Madison Ave PO Box 1406 Peoria IL 61655 *

O'ROURKE, J. TRACY, manufacturing company executive; b. Columbia, S.C., Mar. 14, 1935; s. James Tracy and Georgia Adella (Bridges) O'R.; B.S.M.E., Auburn U., 1956; m. Lou Ann Turner, Mar. 19, 1954; 1 son, James Tracy. Teflon specialist duPont Co., Wilmington, Del., 1957-61; pres., chief exec. officer LNP Corp., Malvern, Pa., 1961-71; v.p. Carborundum, Niagara Falls, N.Y., 1971-75; exec. v.p. Chemetron, Chgo., 1975-78; sr. v.p. Allen Bradley Co. subs. Rockwell Internat. Corp., Milw., 1978-81, pres., chief operating officer, from 1981, now also chief exec. officer, dir. Served to 1st lt. USAF, 1957-59. Office: Allen-Bradley Co 1201 S 2d St Milwaukee WI 53204 *

O'ROURKE, ROBERT EUGENE, auditor; b. Granite City, Ill., June 28, 1957; s. William Robert and Helen Mae (Klueter) O'R.; m. Deborah Lynn Bladdick, Sept. 12, 1981; 1 child, Kelly Nicole. BSBA, So. Ill. U., Edwardsville, 1979. CPA, Ill. Jr./sr. acct. R.C. Fietsam & Co., CPA's, Belleville, Ill., 1979-84; staff/sr. auditor ITT Fin. Corp. subs. ITT Consumer Services Corp., St. Louis, 1984-87; fin. audit mgr. Landmark Bancshares, St. Louis, 1987—. Mem. Am. Inst. CPA's, Ill. Soc. CPA's. Avocation: sports.

ORR, DAVID IVAN, private investigator; b. N.Y.C., May 16, 1947; s. Ivan and Norma Rose (Steele) O.; m. Gayke Sandra Smith, Aug. 23, 1972 (div. Aug. 1974); 1 child, Danillie C.; m. Barbara Jean Crowder, May 16, 1985; 1 child, David, Jr. Grad., Merchant Marine Acad., 1963; degree in law enforcement, Detroit Police Acad., 1967; grad., Secret Service Sch. for Mcpl. Police, 1970; BA in Personnel Mgmt., Wayne State U., 1976. Lic. private investigator, legal asst. Police officer City of Detroit, 1967-79; gen. mgr. Profl.'s Unlimited, Inc., Detroit, 1979—. Recipient Medal of Valor City of Detroit, 1974. Mem. Detective and Police Officers Assn., Retired Police and Firefighters Assn. Office: Profls Unlimited Inc 21630 W 6 Mile Detroit MI 48219

ORR, GORDON DICKSON, JR., architect, historian; b. Meriden, Conn., May 16, 1926; s. Gordon Dickson and Eunice May (Stadtmiller) O.; m. Elayne Mercedes Soley, Sept. 20, 1952; children: Blair Dickson, Keith Gordon. BArch, Rensselaer Poly Inst., 1950; MA, U. Wis., 1971. Registered architect, Wis., R.I. Owner, prin. Office of Gordon Orr, Wallingford, Conn., 1955-60; ptnr. Tutle and Orr Architects, Winter Park, Fla., 1960-63; asst. state architect State of Wis., Madison, 1963-65; campus architect U. Wis., Madison, 1965-85; pvt. practice architecture Madison, 1985—; archival research N.W. Archtl. Archives, Mpls. Author: (book) Prairie School Review, 1980; editor Jour. of Hist. Madison, 1975-81. Mem. Urban Design Com., Madison, 1973-76, mem. chmn. Landmarks Com., Madison, 1976-82, Wis. Hist. Preservation Rev. Bd., State of Wis., 1971-83. Served with USN, 1944-46, PTO. Fellow AIA; mem. Soc. Arctl. Historians, Assn. Preservation Tech., Wis. Soc. Architects (chmn. hist. resources 1972—), Audubon Soc. Episcopalian. Clubs: Hist. Madison, Inc. (pres. 1974), St. Andrews Soc. Lodge: Madison Voyageurs. Avocations: wilderness travel by canoe, dog sledding, water colors. Home and Office: 2729 Mason St Madison WI 53705

ORR, KAY A(VONNE), governor; b. Burlington, Iowa, Jan. 2, 1939; d. Ralph Robert and Sadie Lucille (Skoglund) Stark; m. William Dayton Orr, Sept. 26, 1957; children: John William, Suzanne. Student, U. Iowa, 1956-57. Exec. asst. to Gov. Charles Thone, Lincoln, Nebr., 1979-81; treas. State of Nebr., Lincoln, 1981-86; gov. elect. 1986; governor State of Nebr., Lincoln, 1987—. Co-chmn. Thone for Gov. Com., 1977-78; del., mem. platform com. Rep. Nat. Conv., 1976, 80, 84, co-chmn. 1984; trustee Hastings (Nebr.) Coll., 1985—; appointed to USDA Users Adv. Bd. 1985, Pres.'s Adv. Com. for Arts John F. Kennedy Performing Arts Ctr., 1985. Named Outstanding Young Rep. Woman in Nebr., 1969.

ORR, ROBERT DUNKERSON, governor; b. Ann Arbor, Mich., Nov. 17, 1917; s. Samuel Lowry and Louise (Dunkerson) O.; m. Joanne Wallace, Dec. 16, 1944; children: Robert Dunkerson, Susan Orr Jones, Marjorie R. Orr Hail. A.B., Yale U., 1940; postgrad., Harvard Bus. Sch., 1940-42; hon. degrees, Ind. State U., 1973, Hanover Coll., 1974, Butler U., 1977, U. Evansville, 1985, Ind. U., %; hon., Trans State U., 1986, Purdue U., 1987. Officer, dir. Orr Iron Co., 1946-60, Sign Crafters, Inc., 1957-74, Hahn, Inc., 1957-69, Indian Industries, Inc., 1962-73; mem. Ind. Senate, 1968-72; lt. gov. Ind., 1973-80; gov. 1980—; dir. Nat. Passenger Rail Co. (Amtrack), 1981—. Leader Fgn. Ops. Adminstrn. evaluation team to, Vietnam, 1954; Pres. Buffalo Trace council Boy Scouts Am., 1957-58; v.p. Evansville's Future, Inc., 1958-62; Chmn. Vanderburgh County Republican Com., 1965-71; alternate del. Rep. Nat. Conv., 1956, 76, del. 1984; Trustee Hanover Coll., Willard Library, Evansville YMCA, 1950-70. Served to maj. AUS, 1942-46. Decorated Legion of Merit. Mem. Scroll and Key Soc., Delta Kappa Epsilon. Presbyn. (elder, trustee, deacon). Clubs: Rotary, Oak Meadow Golf, Meridian Hills, Columbia. Office: Office of Gov State Capitol Indianapolis IN 46204

ORSER, EARL HERBERT, insurance company executive; b. Toronto, Ont., Can., July 5, 1928; s. Frank Herbert and Ethel Marjorie (Cox) O.; m. Marion Queenie Ellis, Aug. 4, 1951; children: Darlene, Barbara, Beverley, Nancy. B.Comm., U. Toronto, Ont., Can., 1950, Chartered Acct., 1953. With Clarkson Gordon, 1950-61, ptnr., 1958-61; treas. Anthes Imperial Ltd., 1961-63, v.p. fin., 1963-68, also dir.; sr. v.p. Molson Industries Ltd., 1968-70, also dir.; v.p. fin. Air Can., Montreal, Que., Can., 1970-73; with T. Eaton Co. Ltd., Toronto, 1973-77, pres., chief exec. officer, 1975-77; exec. v.p., chief operating officer London Life Ins. Co., subs. Lonvest Corp., Ont., Can., 1978-80, pres., chief operating officer, 1980-81, pres., chief exec. officer, 1981—; pres. Lonvest Corp.; dep.-chmn., dir. Trilon Fin. Corp.; chmn. Toronto Coll. St. Centre Ltd.; bd. dirs. John P. Robarts Research Inst., London, Ont.; dir., deputy-chmn. SPAR Aerospace Ltd., Royal Trustco Ltd., Brascan Ltd., Interprovincial Pipe Line Ltd. Mem. Univ. Coll. com. U. Toronto, Ont., Can.; mem. exec. com. C. D. Howe Policy Analysis Com.; vice chmn. bd. govs. U. Western Ont., 1986—. Mem. Can. Life and Health Ins. Assn. (v.p. 1985—, chmn. elect.). Clubs: London Hunt, London (Ont., Can.), Granite, St. James of Montreal, Toronto. Office: London Life Ins Co 255 Dufferin Ave, London, ON Canada N6A 4K1

ORTEGA, LENETTE MARY HERTZ, bank officer; b. Joliet, Ill., Jan. 6, 1947; s. Leonard Marlyn and Julia (Zeimis) Hertz; m. Zarinelo R. Ortega, Feb. 12, 1982; children: Maximilian, Elizabeth. BS, No. Ill. U., 1969; MEd, Nat. Coll. Edn., 1978. Loan officer Fin. Resources, Chgo., 1980-81, Percy Wilson, Chgo., 1981-82, Margaretten & Co., Chgo., 1982—. Presbyterian. Office: Margaretten & Co 5519 N Cumberland #1009 Chicago IL 60656

ORTEGA-PIRON, D. JEAN, lawyer; b. Chgo., Dec. 16, 1956; d. J. Manuel and Dorothea Viola (Smith) Ortega; m. Siegfried Octaff Piron, June 16, 1984. BA cum laude, Rosary Coll., 1978; JD, Ill. Inst. Tech., 1981. Bar: Ill. 1981, U.S. Dist. Ct. (no. dist.) Ill. 1981, U.S. Ct. Appeals (7th cir.) 1982. Staff atty. Ill. Dept. Mental Health and Devel. Disabilities, Chgo., 1981-86, deputy chief counsel, 1986, chief legal counsel, 1986—. Mem. Chgo. Bar Assn. (vice chair 1984-85, chmn. mental health law com. 1985-86), Pi Gamma Mu. Office: Ill Dept Mental Health Devel Disabilities 100 W Randolph Suite 6-400 Chicago IL 60601

ORTINO, HECTOR RUBEN, chemical company executive; b. Buenos Aires, July 23, 1942; came to U.S., 1983; s. Miguel and Maria Julia (Moauro) O.; m. Beatriz Monica Mayantz, Dec. 14, 1972; children: Nicolas Martin, Gabriela Andrea. B in Acctg. and Adminstrn., Buenos Aires U., 1971. Mng. dir. Ferro Argentina, Buenos Aires, 1976-81, also bd. dirs.; mng. dir. Ferro Mexicana, Mexico City, 1982-83, also bd. dirs.; asst. to v.p. fin. Ferro Corp., Cleve., 1983-84, v.p. fin., 1984—, chief fin. officer, 1987—. Mem. Fin. Exec. Inst. Roman Catholic. Clubs: Cleve. Skating, Cleve. Athletic. Avocations: tennis, swimming, hunting. Home: 3919 Beechmont Trail Cleveland OH 44122 Office: Ferro Corp One Erieview Plaza Cleveland OH 44114

ORTINO, LEONARD JAMES, manufacturing company executive; b. Seneca Falls, N.Y., May 31, 1919; s. Michael Vito and Florence (Campeggio) O.; m. Evangeline Canellos, Apr. 1, 1945; children: Lynn Edlund, Stephanie Kittleson. BS MechE, Carnegie-Mellon U., 1945; MBA, U. Mich., 1967. Registered profl. engr., Pa. Design group leader Westinghouse Electric Co., Pitts., 1940-50; engring. mgr. IBM Corp., Poughkeepsie, N.Y., 1950-55; chief mech. engr. Beckman Instruments, Fullerton, Calif., 1955-60; chief. mech. engr. Magnavox, Ft. Wayne, Ind., 1960-66; pres. Indsl. Mgmt. Council, Morris Plains, N.J., 1966—; pres., chief exec. officer Mich. Dynamics Inc., Garden City, 1973—. Author: Optical Instruments, 1953; also articles. pres. Forest Hills (Pa.) Civic Assn., 1948-49; scoutmaster Boy Scouts Am., Seneca Falls, N.Y., 1937-40, dist. chmn., Fullerton, Calif., 1956-60. Served to 1st lt. U.S. Army, 1944-47. Mem. ASME (dist. chmn. 1952-54), Filtration Soc. (pres. 1984-86), Am. Mfg. Assn., Instrument Soc. Am. (dist. chmn. 1957-59), Mich. Mfg. Assn., Theta Kappa Phi (disting. service award 1947), Phi Kappa Phi. Republican. Roman Catholic. Lodges: Rotary, Elks. Avocations: travel, golf. Home: 9443 Hidden Lake Ct Dexter MI 48130 Office: Mich Dynamics Inc 32400 Ford Rd Garden City MI 48135

ORTIZ, N. ANTONIO, FBI agent; b. N.Y.C., Oct. 3, 1938; s. Florencio and Eugenia (Ojeda) O.; m. Hannah Laura Sax, July 30, 1960; children: Lance C., Laurence G., Cheryl Lee, Charlene R. BBA, Iona Coll., 1960. Collections mgr. Saks 34th St., N.Y.C., 1960-62; commd. USMC, 1963; advanced through grades to maj. USMC, Vietnam; resigned USMC, 1973; spl. agt. FBI, 1973—; spl. agt. recruiter FBI, Kansas City, Mo., 1984-86; field supr. FBI, Kansas City, 1986—. Mem. Midwest Coll. Placement Assn. Avocations: hist. and philos. studies. Office: FBI 811 Grand Ave Suite 300 Kansas City MO 64106

ORTMAN, WILLIAM ANDREW, SR., lawyer, business executive; b. Detroit, Mar. 22, 1934; s. Frank J. and Marcella Pauline (Gfell) O.; B.A., Wayne State U., 1958; grad. Bus. Sch. U. Mich., 1960; J.D. (regional outstanding student 1962, scholarship cert. and key, jurisprudence awards), U. Detroit, 1963; m. Lavina Mae Ladson, June 29, 1957; children—William A., Nancy Lee, Merrie Jo, Kristy Ann, Keira Therese. Bar: Mich. 1963, Ohio 1963. Radio sta. mgr., 1953-56; para-legal Law Offices Frank J. Ortman, 1956-60, real estate broker, co-partner, 1956—; indsl. relations analyst FoMoCo, 1960-62; pub. info. specialist Dept. Def., Detroit, 1962-63; sr. atty. Ortman & Ortman, Detroit, 1964—; pres. ORT-FAM Inc., 1984—; co-ptnr. The Ortman Co., 1956—; investment counselor, fin. planner, mgmt. cons.; polit. campaign specialist, 1964—; real-estate, mortgage broker, 1956—; gen. counsel, mktg. mgr. Computers Tandem Assocs., CADO of Southeast Mich., Computer Alliance Corp., 1982-83; cons. pub. relations and advt., 1962—, computer systems, 1982—; lectr. St. Joseph Comml. Coll., 1961-62; del. China-U.S. Sci. Exchange, 1984. Bd. govs., past dean Detroit Metro. Alumni Senate; councilman, Farmington Hills area, 1968-75; nominee Mich. Supreme Ct., 1972. Served with U.S. Army, 1953-56. Mem. ABA, Mich., Oakland bar assns., Delta Theta Phi (dean Hosmer Senate 1961, 62), Alpha Kappa Delta. Clubs: Detroit Athletic, German-Am. Cultural Center, Elks. Contbr., author and editor nat., state and local legal jours. Home: 28010 S Harwich Dr Farmington Hills MI 48018 Office: PO Box 42 Franklin MI 48025

ORTON, RAYMOND MERVYN, employment consultant; b. Chgo., Sept. 15, 1938; s. Raymond McClure and Blanche (Straka) O.; m. Marilynn Pearl Murphy, Oct. 17, 1959 (div. May 1975); children: Kathy Lynn Orton Kallerud, Kenneth Raymond, Kimberly Ann; m. Carol Ann Chernetzki Eiffler, June 18, 1975. AS in Computer Sci., Triton Coll., 1979; BS in Engring Tech., RCA Inst., Camden, N.J., 1968; postgrad., Roosevelt U., 1981-83. With Am. Internat., Schaumburg, Ill., 1979-81, Addressograph-Farrington, Schaumburg, Ill., 1981-83; regional service mgr. Stearns Computer, Oak Brook Terrace, Ill., 1983-84; with Network Utilities, Chgo., 1984-85; employment cons. tech. service mgmt. Gen. Employment Enterprises, Des Plaines, Ill., 1985-87; mgr. service support and tng. Video, Inc., Highland Park, Ill., 1987—; cons. in communications, Northlake, Ill., 1979—. Author: Introduction to the Oscilloscope, 1981. Served with U.S. Army, 1957-59. Mem. Am. Soc. Tng. and Devel., Assn. Field Service Mgrs. Home: 304 E Lyndale Northlake IL 60164

ORVICK, ROBERT MYRON, accountant; b. Des Moines, May 20, 1942; s. Sherman Bernard and Lucile Viola (Golackson) O.; m. Bonnie Lee Skaran, Sept. 5, 1970; children: Matthew S., Kirsten Lee. Student, Grand View Coll., 1968-69, U. Iowa, 1968-70; BA, U. No. Iowa, 1971. CPA, Ind. Employee Mario Fovinci, Modesto, Calif., 1972, Clifton Gunderson & Co., Modesto, 1972-75, Gunderson & Co., Modesto, 1975-76; mem. staff, ptnr. Kemper CPA Group, Modesto, 1977; ptnr. Kemper CPA Group, Vincennes, Ind., 1977—. Treas. Old Town Players, Inc., Vincennes, 1980-87; bd. dirs. Vincennes Civitan Club, 1982-87, pres., 1983-84; pres., bd. dirs. Wabash Valley Estate Planning Council, Vincennes, 1987. Served with USN, 1964-68, Vietnam. Named Civitan Yr. Vincennes Civitan Club, 1986. Mem. Am. Inst. CPA's, Calif. CPA Soc., Ind. CPA Soc. (treas. and bd. dirs. Terre Haute chpt. 1986-87, pres.-elect Terre Haute chpt. 1987-88), Vincennes Area C. of C. Lutheran. Lodge: Elks. Avocations: water skiing, racquetball, judo. Home: Rural Rt #1 Vincennes IN 47591 Office: Kemper CPA Group 505 N 6th St Vincennes IN 47591

ORWIN, WALTER LAWRENCE, manufacturing company executive; b. Des Moines, Aug. 26, 1927; s. Milton Lawrence and Gladys (Rosenbaum) O.; m. Elizabeth Ann Hutton, Oct. 16, 1954; children: Angela, W. Lawrence. BA, Yale U., 1950. With Kalamazoo (Mich.) Pant Co., 1951-67, pres., 1968-69; pres. Kazoo, Inc., Kalamazoo, 1970—, also bd. dirs.; bd. dirs. First Am. Bank Mich., First Am. Bank Corp., Seminole Mfg. Co. Author: An Invitation to Hard Work, 1980. Co-trustee F.W. and Elsie L. Heyl Found., 1975—; bd. dirs. Bronson Hosp. Health Found., Kalamazoo, 1986—. Served with USN, 1945-46. Clubs: Kalamazoo Country (pres. 1978-79); Yale (N.Y.C.). Lodge: Kiwanis (local pres. 1969-70). Avocations: golf, hunting, fishing.

ORWOLL, GREGG S. K., lawyer; b. Austin, Minn., Mar. 23, 1926; s. Gilbert M. and Kleonora (Kleven) O.; m. Laverne M. Flentie, Sept. 15, 1951; children—Kimball G., Kent A., Vikki A., Tristen A., Erik G. B.S., Northwestern U., 1950; J.D., U. Minn., 1953. Bar: Minn. 1953, U.S. Supreme Ct. 1973. Assoc. Dorsey, Owen, Marquart, Windhorst and West, Mpls., 1953-59; ptnr. Dorsey, Owen, Marquart, Windhorst and West, 1959-60; assoc. counsel Mayo Clinic, Rochester, Minn., 1960-63; gen. counsel Mayo Clinic, 1963-87, sr. legal counsel, 1987—; gen counsel, dir. Rochester Airport Co., 1962-84, sec., 1962-81, v.p., 1981-84; gen. counsel Mayo Med. Services, Ltd., 1972—; bd. dirs., sec., gen. counsel Mayo Med. Resources, 1984—; gen. counsel Mid-Am. Orthopedic Soc., 1982—, Minn. Orthopedic Soc., 1985—; asst. sec. Mayo Found., Rochester, 1972-76, 82-86 , sec., 1976-82, 86—; dir. Travelure Motel Corp., 1968-86, sec., 1972-83, 86, v.p., 1983-86; adj. prof. William Mitchell Coll. Law, St. Paul, 1978-84. Contbr. articles and chpts. to legal and medico-legal publs.; bd. editors HealthScan, 1984—; editorial bd. Minn. Law Rev., 1952-53. Trustee Minn. Council on Founds., 1977-82, Mayo Found., 1982-86, William Mitchell Coll. Law, 1982—; pres. Rochester Council Chs., 1968-69; mem. bd. advisers Rochester YWCA, 1966-72; bd. dirs. Rochester Med. Ctr. Ministry, Inc., 1975-81; bd. dirs. Zumbro Luth. Ch., 1962-64, 77-79, pres., 1964-65; bd. dirs. Rochester YMCA, 1966-70; trustee Courage Found., 1974-80, YMCA-YWCA Bldg. Corp., 1966-73 ; bd. visitors U. Minn. Law Sch., 1974-76, 1985—. Served with USAAF, 1944-45. Mem. Am. Acad. Hosp. Attys., Minn. Soc. Hosp. Attys. (dir. 1981-86), Minn. State Bar Assn. (chmn. legal med. com. 1977-81), ABA, Olmsted County Bar Assn. (v.p. 1977-78, pres. 1978-79), Rochester C. of C., AMA (affiliate), U. Minn. Law Alumni Assn. (bd. dirs. 1973-76, 85—), Phi Delta Theta, Phi Delta Phi. Republican. Club: Rochester University (pres. 1977). Office: Mayo Clinic 200 1st St SW Rochester MN 55905

ORYSHKEVICH, ROMAN SVIATOSLAV, physician, physiatrist, dentist, educator; b. Olesko, Ukraine, Aug. 5, 1928; came to U.S., 1955, naturalized, 1960; s. Simeon and Caroline (Deneszczuk) O.; m. Oksana Lishchynsky, June 16, 1962; children: Marta, Mark, Alexandra. D.D.S., Ruperto-Carola U., Heidelberg, Ger., 1952, M.D., 1953, Ph.D. cum laude, 1955. Cert. electromyography and electrodiagnosis. Diplomat Am. Bd. Physical Medicine & Rehab. Research fellow in cancer Esptl. Cancer Inst., Rupert-Charles U., 1953-55; rotating intern Coney Island Hosp., Bklyn., 1955-56; resident in diagnostic radiology NYU Bellevue Med. Ctr.-Univ. Hosp., 1956-57; resident, fellow in phys. medicine and rehab. Western Res. U. Highland View Hosp., Cleve., 1958-60; orthopedic surgery Met. Gen. Hosp., Cleve., 1959; asst. chief rehab. medicine service VA West Side Med. Ctr., Chgo., 1961-74, acting chief, 1974-75, chief, 1975—; dir. edn. integrated residency tng. program U. Ill. Affiliated Hosp., 1974—; clin. instr. U. Ill., 1962-65, asst. clin. prof., 1965-70, asst. prof., 1970-75, assoc. clin. prof., 1975—. Author and editor: Who and What, 1978; contbr. articles to profl jours.; splty. cons. in phys. medicine and rehab. to editorial bd. Chgo. Med. Jours., 1978—. Founder, pres. Ukrainian World Med. Mus., Chgo., 1977; founder, 1st pres. Am. Mus. Phys. Medicine and Rehab., 1980—. Fellow Am. Acad. Phys. Medicine and Rehab., Am. Congress Rehab. Medicine; mem. Assn. Acad. Physiatrists, AAUP, Am. Assn. Electromyography and Electrodiagnosis, Ill. Soc. Phys. Medicine and Rehab. (pres., dir. 1979-80), Ukrainian Med. Assn. N.Am. (dir., pres. chpt. 1977-79, fin. mgr. 17th med. conv. and congress Chgo. 1977, adminstr.and vonc. chmn. 1979), World Fedn. Ukrainian Med. Assns. (co-founder and 1st exec. sec. research and sci. 1977-79), Internat. Rehab. Medicine Assn., Rehab. Internat. U.S.A., Nat. Assn. VA Physicians, AAAS, Assn. Med. Rehab. Dirs. and Coordinators, Nat. Rehab. Assn., Nat. Assn. Disability Examiners, Am. Acad. Manipulative Medicine, AM. Med. Writers Assn., Pan Am. Med. Assn., Biofeedback Research Soc. Am., Chgo. Soc. Phys. Medicine and Rehab. (pres., founder 1978-79), Ill. Rehab. Assn., Ukrainian Acad. Med. Scis. (founder, pres. 1979-80), Gerontol. Soc., Internat. Soc. Electrophysiol. Kinesiology, Internat. Soc. Prosthetics and Orthotics, Fedn. Am. Scientists. Ukrainian Catholic. Home: 1819 N 78 Ct Elmwood Park IL 60635 Office: 820 S Damen Ave Chicago IL 60612

OSBORN, GERALD GUY, psychiatrist, educator, consultant; b. Cin., Nov. 6, 1947; s. Guy Henry and Doris Irene (Taylor) O.; m. Sue Ellen Granger, July 9, 1983; children—Erica Tyrell, Eric Gerald, Ellen Stephanie. B.A., Wilmington Coll., 1969; student Schiller U., Klein-Ingersheim, Germany, 1968-69; D.O., Kirksville Coll. Osteo. Medicine, 1973; postgrad. in psychiatry U. Sheffield (Eng.), 1973; M in Philosphy Cambridge U., 1986. Diplomate Am. Osteo. Bd. Neurology and Psychiatry (bd. examiners 1982), Am. Bd. Psychiatry and Neurology. Rotating intern Lansing (Mich.) Gen. Hosp., 1973-74; resident, postdoctoral fellow dept. psychiatry Mich. State U., East Lansing, 1974-77, chief resident in psychiatry, 1976-77, instr. in psychiatry, 1974-77, asst. prof., 1977-82, assoc. prof., 1982—, dir. residency tng. osteo. div., 1979-81, assoc. dean for acad. affairs Coll. Osteo. Medicine, 1981-83; chmn. dept. psychiatry St. Lawrence Hosp., Lansing, 1986—; assoc. adj. prof. dept. history Mich. State U., 1986—; cons. in field; psychiat. reviewer Mich. Dept. Social Services; chmn. Lansing Area Psychiatry Council, 1983. Med. dir. Catholic Social Services and Family and Child Services of Lansing; active Physicians for Social Responsibility, East Lansing. Recipient Med. Writing award Mich. Osteo. Coll. Found., 1976; teaching awards Mich. State U., 1979, 80, 82, Prof. of Yr. award, 1981; Kettering scholar, 1968. Mem. Am. Osteo. Assn. Mich. Assn. Osteo. Physicians and Surgeons, Ingham County Osteo. Soc., Am. Psychiat. Assn., Mich. Psychiat. Soc., Am. Coll. Neuropsychiatrists (sr.; bd. govs. 1982—, pres.-elect 1986—), Mich. Osteo. Neuropsychiat. Soc., Osteo. Physicians and Surgeons Calif. (assoc.), Am. Assn. Dirs. Psychiat. Residency Tng., Aircraft Owners and Pilots Assn., U.S. Internat. Sailing Assn., Sigma Sigma Phi. Democrat. Quaker. Contbr. articles to profl. publs. Home: 1313 Basswood Circle East Lansing MI 48823 Office: Mich State U Dept Psychiatry A236 E Fee Hall East Lansing MI 48824

OSBORN, GUY A., food products company executive; b. 1936. BSBA, Northwestern U., 1958. Group mktg. mgr. Pillsbury Co., Mpls., 1958-65; with Universal Foods Corp., Milw., 1971—, dir. mktg., 1971-73, v.p. spl. products, 1973-78, group v.p., 1978-82, exec. v.p., 1982-84, now chmn. bd. dirs., chief exec. officer, 1984—. Office: Universal Foods Corp 433 E Michigan Ave Milwaukee WI 53202 *

OSBORN, KENNETH LOUIS, financial exec.; b. Belleville, Ill., Jan. 9, 1946; s. William Arthur and Louise Mary (Brueggemann) O.; B.B.A., U. N.Mex., 1968; m. Roberta Marie Vodicka, Oct. 23, 1971; 1 son, David Anthony. Auditor, Ernst & Ernst, Albuquerque, 1968; budge mgr. Rockwell Internat., Chgo., 1970-74; mgr. internat. acctg. Allied Van Lines, Chgo., 1974-76; fin. mgr. Sealy, Inc., Chgo., 1976-79; sr. fin. analyst Newark Electronics, Chgo., 1979-80, internat. dir. credit, 1980-82; bus. mgr. Prime Computer, 1982; fin. cons. Sealy, Inc. Served with AUS, 1968-70. Decorated Air medal. Mem. Mensa, Soc. Am. Baseball Research. Roman Catholic. Office: 1 Oakbrook Terr Oakbrook Terrace IL 60181

OSBORN, KENT, insurance company executive; b. Stewartsville, Mo., June 10, 1940; s. Maro V. and Cleta M. O.; m. Dorcas Jean Vanderau, Apr. 10, 1960; 1 son, Bradley Craig. Acct., Cameron Mut. Ins. Co. (Mo.), 1958-61, mgr. data processing, 1961-75, acctg. mgr., 1975-77, v.p. acctg., 1977—, asst. treas., 1983-86, treas. Cameron Mut. Ins. Co., 1987—; owner Uptown Cleaners, Cameron, 1968-78. Treas., dir. Cameron Manor Nursing Home Dist., 1972-77; chmn. Cameron Chamber Indsl., 1971—; mem. Cameron Park Bd., 1969, 77; pres. Clinton County (Mo.) Indsl. Authority, 1980; deacon Baptist Ch. Named Cameron Citizen of Yr., Mcpl. League N.W. Mo., 1973. Mem. Cameron Jaycees (treas. 1960, pres. 1961, sec. 1962), Cameron C. of C. (dir.), Data Processing Mgmt. Assn. (Kansas City chpt. dir., v.p. 1976, exec. v.p. 1977, pres., 1978-79; recipient Internat. awards Bronze 1981, Silver 1981, Gold 1982), Ins. and Acctg. Statis. Assn. (v.p. property and liability Midwest chpt. 1977-78, pres. 1980-81). Office: 214 McElwain Dr Cameron MO 64429

OSBORN, MARK ELIOT, dentist; b. Buffalo, Apr. 22, 1950; s. Thomas Earl and Ruth Frances (Martin) O. BA, U. Mo., Columbia, 1972; DDS, U. Mo., Kansas City, 1977. Dir. Westport Free Health Clinic, Kansas City, Mo., 1974-76; clinician St. Louis Dept. Health, 1977-82; gen. practice dentistry Troy, Mo., 1978—. Mem. ADA, Greater St. Louis Dental Soc., Am. Soc. Dentistry for Children, St. Louis Dental Research Group, Delta Sigma Delta, Troy C. of C. Lodge: Rotary (dir. dental program, Troy, 1985—). Home: 36 Schooner Ln Lake Saint Louis MO 63367 Office: 101 W College Suite 3 Troy MO 63379

OSBORNE, HARRY ALAN, orthodontist; b. Youngstown, Ohio, Mar. 9, 1934; s. Kenneth L. and Marguerite (Filmer) O.; m. Carol June Williams, June 30, 1956; children: Elizabeth Ann, J. Scott, Linda J., Robert K. Student, Westminster Coll., New Wilmington, Pa., 1952-55; DDS, U. Pitts., 1959; MS in Dentistry, Northwestern U., 1962. Diplomate Am. Bd. Orthodontics. Intern Youngstown Hosp. Assn., 1959; practice dentistry specializing in orthodontics Canton, Ohio, 1959—. Asst. chmn. Community Bldg. YMCA, North Canton; supt. adv. com. North Canton Sch. Dist., 1960—; mem. adv. com. Soc. Bank, Canton, Ohio, 1962—; chmn. bldg. com. Faith United Meth. Ch., 1975-80. Served to capt. U.S. Army, 1961-63. Recipient Disting. Service award, Jaycees, 1968. Mem. ADA, Am. Assn. Orthodontists, Gt. Lakes Orthodontic Assn., Ohio Dental Assn., Cleve. Orthodontic Soc. (pres. 1983), Stark County Dental Soc. (pres. 1975-76). Republican. Methodist. Club: Shady Hollow Country (Massillion, Ohio) (bd. dirs. 1984-85, 87—). Avocation: golf. Home: 2441 Oakway North Canton OH 44720 Office: 1021 Schneider Rd North Canton OH 44720

OSBORNE, JAMES WALTER, orthodontist; b. McMinnville, Oreg., June 26, 1945; s. Donald C. and Miriam H. (Thornburg) O.; m. Betty Ann Osborne, Aug. 26, 1966; children: Jaime Leeann, Matthew Morgan. BS, Cen. Mo. State U., 1968; DDS, U. Mo., 1972, MS in Orthodontics, 1976. Practice dentistry specializing in orthodontics Raytown, Mo., 1976—. Pres. Lee's Summit (Mo.) Parks and Recreation Bd., 1986-87. Served to capt. U.S. Army, 1972-74. Mem. Am. Assn. Orthodontists, Mo. Soc. Orthodontists (sec./treas. 1985—), Greater Kansas City Orthodontic Soc. (pres.), ADA, Raytown C. of C. (pres.). Avocations: triathlons, biking, building. Home: 1910 W 4th Lee's Summit MO 64063 Office: 6621 Raytown Rd Raytown MO 64133

OSBORNE, JOHN HOLLAND, small business owner; b. Kingsville, Tex., June 4, 1945; s. Paul and Gladys Osborne; m. Diane Kay Meyer, Dec. 25, 1967 (div. Oct. 1980); children: Sarah, Rebekah, Kate; m. Barbara Ann Cary, June 13, 1981. BA, Wichita (Kans.) State U., 1969. V.p. ops. Superior Bldg. Maintenance, Wichita, 1972-74; acct. mgr. Uarco Bus. Forms, Wichita, 1974-76; pres. Forms Mgmt. Co., Inc., Wichita, 1976—. Served to 1st lt. U.S. Army, 1969-71, Korea. Mem. Nat. Bus. Forms Assn. (bd. dirs. 1987—), Pres.'s Assn., Am. Mgmt. Assn., VFW. Episcopalian. Clubs: Tallgrass Country, Wichita, Crestview Country. Home: 8 Via Verde Wichita KS 67230 Office: Forms Mgmt Co Inc 1330 E 1st St Wichita KS 67214

OSE, PEGGY JO, registered nurse educator; b. Wisconsin Rapids, Wis., Aug. 4, 1951; d. Donald George and Bernice Anna (Ott) Whitrock; m. Allen

Lee Ose, June 10, 1972; 1 child, Megan Elizabeth. BS in Nursing, U. Wis., Eau Claire, 1973; MS in Nursing, U. Wis., Milw., 1985. Staff nurse St. Luke's Hosp., Milw., 1973-75, instr., 1975-80, supr., 1980-83, mgr. nursing edn., 1983-84; mgr. nursing edn. St. Luke's Samaritan Health Care Inc., Milw., 1984—; advisor Milw. Area Tech. Coll., 1981-84; instr. Marquette U., Milw., 1981—; presentor numerous nursing edn. and nursing skills programs. Contbr. articles to profl. jours. Mem. Nurse Edn. Com. on Alcoholism, Am. Soc. Tng. and Devel., Am. Heart Assn., Milw. Council on Alcoholism, Nursing Inservice Educators Greater Milw. Lutheran. Avocations: decorating, cross-country skiing. Office: St Luke's Samaritan Health Care Inc 2900 W Oklahoma Ave Milwaukee WI 53215

OSELAND, DAVID FLOYD, television program director and producer; b. Chgo., Oct. 4, 1943; s. Floyd and Viola (Wahlstrom) O.; m. Joyce Levinson, Nov. 8, 1969; children: Erie, Amy. Student, DeVry Inst. Tech., Chgo., 1967-68, Elkins Inst., Chgo., 1970. Announcer, engr. Sta. WYCA-FM, Chgo., 1970-72; broadcast engr. Stas. WFMF and WLOO-FM, Chgo., 1972-73, Sta. WCIV-TV, Chgo., 1973-76; broadcast engr. Sta. WCFC-TV, Chgo., 1976-78, producer, 1978-85, program dir., 1985—; cons. in field. Producer and writer: (documentary) Sands of Time, 1979, Death and Dying, 1980 (Angel award 1981); producer and creator: (TV series) Bible Baffle, 1978 (Angel award 1979, Emmy award 1979), Saturday Night Sing, 1986 (Angel award 1987). Bd. dirs. Lydia Home Assn., Chgo., 1984-87. Mem. Nat. Acad. Arts and Scis. Home: 4926 Lunt Ave Skokie IL 60077 Office: Sta WCFC-TV 1 W Wacker Dr Chicago IL 60606

OSKIN, ERNEST THOMAS, chemical engineer, plastics company executive; b. Chgo., Dec. 29, 1927; s. Benedict Cornelias and Mary Theresa (Kozlowski) O.; m. Barbara Ann Cremers, Mar. 21, 1958; children—John Bennett, Mary Catherine. B.Chem. Engring., U. Fla., 1949; M.Engring., Princeton U., 1956. Chem. engr. Mathieson Chem., Lake Charles, La., 1949-50; plastics engr. B.F. Goodrich, Marietta, Ohio, 1952-54; sales engr. Du-Pont Co., Wilmington, Del. and Detroit, 1956-63; chmn. bd., dir. Huron Plastics Inc., St. Clair, Mich., 1963—; dir. Croswell Plastics (Mich.), Scottsburg Plastics (Ind.), Huron Products Corp., Omega Plastics, Mt. Clemens, Mich., QCP, Inc., St. Clair D&A Industries, Croswell, Mich., Harbor Plastics, St. Clair, Extrusion Techs., Mich., Huron Extruded Products, Products Mgmt. Co., Mich., Lakepoint Plastics, Port Huron, Huron Engr. Services, Huron Mold Services; pres. Huron Mgmt. Co., St. Clair. Served with U.S. Army, 1954-56. Mem. Soc. Plastics Engrs., Soc. Automotive Engrs., Soc. of Plastic Industry. Clubs: St. Clair Golf St. Clair Investment. Lodge: Rotary (pres. St. Clair chpt. 1976-77). Author: Stress Relaxation and Dynamic Properties of Ethylene Polymers, 1956; contbr. tech. articles to profl. publs. Home: 982 N Riverside Dr Saint Clair MI 48079 Office: PO Box 195 Saint Clair MI 48079

OSMOND, LYNN JOYCE, symphony orchestra manager; b. St. Catherines, Ont., Can., Mar. 31, 1957; d. George and Joyce Edith (Stanton) O. MusB with honors, Queens U., 1980; numerous courses and seminars in field, Adminstrv. asst. Assn. of Can. Orchs., Ont. Fedn. of Symphony Orchs., Toronto, 1980-81; exec. dir. Mississauga Symphony, Ont., 1981-83; youth orch. coordinator for Ont., Ont. Fedn. Symphony Orchs., Toronto, 1981-84; festival coordinator Ont. Youth Orch. Festival, 1983-85; gen. mgr. Thunder Bay Symphony Orch., Ont., 1983-85, Orch. London Ont., Can., 1985—; dir. Can. Assn. Youth Orchs., Banff, Alta.; mem. adv. bd. Performing Arts Mgmt. Confedn. Coll., Thunder Bay, 1984—; bd. dirs. Performing Arts Ctr. for Tomorrow (PACT). Arts Mgmt. Tng. grantee Can. Council, 1984. Mem. Thunder Bay Regional Arts Council (pres.), Thunder Bay Press Club, London Women's Network, Assn. Cultural Execs., Ont. Fedn. Symphony Orchs. (bd. dirs.), London C. of C., Dirs. Club of London, Am. Symphony Orch. League (bd. dirs. youth orch.), London West Progressive Conservative Small Bus. Assn. (exec. com., bd. dirs.), Queen's U. Alumni Assn. (class agt.). Conservative. Anglican. Avocations: music, sports. Home: 5-234 Central Ave, London, ON Canada N6A 1M8

OSORIO, NESTOR LAUREANO, science/engineering information specialist; b. Barranquilla, Columbia, Apr. 12, 1944; came to U.S., 1970; s. Milciades Antonio and Rosa Dolores (Monsalvo) O.; m. Mary Alfreda Budzinski, July 20, 1973; children: Gabriel Eduardo, Peter Anthony. BA in Math., Universidad Del Atlantico, Baranquilla, 1969; MA in Physics, SUNY, Geneseo, 1972, MLS, 1975. Asst. prof. physics Universidad Del Norte, Barranquilla, 1972-74; librarian Eastern Wash. U., Cheney, 1976-78; sci./engring. subject specialist Fla. Atlantic U., Boca Raton, 1978-80; sci./engring. reference librarian U. So. Fla., Tampa, 1981; sci./engring. subject specialist No. Ill. U., DeKalb, 1982—. Mem. ALA, Am. Soc. Engring. Edn. (pubs. com. 1986—), Am. Physical Soc., Am. Soc. info. Sci., Assn. Coll. and Research Libraries (sci. tech. sect. com. sci., engring. libraries 1986—), N.Y. Acad. Scis. Lodge: KC (dep. Grand Knight 1987). Office: No Ill U University Libraries DeKalb IL 60115

OSTAPOWICZ, FRANK, gynecologist, obstetrician; b. West Nanticoke, Pa., Mar. 31, 1923; s. Marian and Lottie (Wydawski) O.; m. Mary Louise Ann Lavelle, July 2, 1946 (dec. Apr. 1985); children: MaryAnn Charlene, Martin, Tamara, Sharen, David, Phillip, Christine. Student, Bucknell U., 1940-44; MD, U. Pitts., 1948. Diplomate Am. Bd. Ob-Gyn. Commd. lt. (j.g.) USN, 1948, advanced through grades to capt., 1965, retired, 1969; dir. ob-gyn St. Louis City Hosp., 1969-83, St. Mary's Hosp., St. Louis, 1983—; chmn. ob-gyn dept. St. Louis U. Sch. Medicine, 1971-73. Contbr. articles to profl. jours. Fellow Am. Coll. Ob-Gyn; mem. St. Louis Gynecol. Soc. (pres. 1983-84). Roman Catholic. Avocations: bridge, bowling, golf. Home: 3 Hillvale Dr Clayton MO 63105 Office: St Marys Health Ctr 6420 Clayton Rd Saint Louis MO 63117

OSTER, CLAUDE, osteopathic physician; b. Paris, July 9, 1936; s. Isidore and Jolana (Kreisman) Osztreicher; came to U.S., 1952; m. Terry Baren, July 3, 1958; children—Lisa, Allan, Scott. Student Wayne State U., 1954-58; D.O., Coll. Osteo. Medicine and Surgery, Des Moines, 1962. Cert. Am. Osteo. Bd. Rehab. Medicine. Intern, Detroit Osteo. Hosp., 1962-63; preceptorship in phys. medicine and rehab. Garden City (Mich.) Osteo. Hosp., 1968-71; practice osteo. medicine specializing in rehab. medicine, Detroit, 1971—; co-dir. Muscular Dystrophy Assn. Detroit Met. Clinic, 1970-77; exec. dir. Southfield (Mich.) Rehab. Hosp., 1981—; mem. staff Detroit Osteo. Hosp., Bi-County Hosp., Mich. Osteo. Med. Ctr.; prof. Mich. State U. Coll. Osteo. Medicine; mem. med. adv. com. Mutiple Sclerosis Assn. State of Mich.; mem. Workers Compensation Health Care Cost Containment Adv. Com.; Oakland County Dep. Med. Examiner; program chmn. Mich. State U. Pain Seminars, 1979-86; cons. in field. Mem. Acad. Applied Osteopathy, Am. Heart Assn. (stroke council), Am. Geriatrics Soc., Am. Osteo. Assn., Am. Osteo. Coll. Rehab. (trustee), Congress Rehab. Medicine, Am. Osteo. Coll. Rheumatology, Internat. Rehab. Medicine Assn., Internat. Assn. for Study of Pain, Am. Soc. for Study of Pain, Midwest Soc. for Study of Pain, Internat. Assn. Rehab. Facilities, Internat. Congress of Gerontology, Mich. Assn. Osteo. Physicians and Surgeons, Oakland County Assn. Osteo. Physicians and Surgeons, N.Am. Acad. Manipulative Medicine. Contbr. articles to profl. jours. Office: Southfield Rehab Hosp 22401 Foster Winter Dr Southfield MI 48075

OSTER, SUSAN MARY, educational association administrator; b. Des Moines, Oct. 2, 1953; d. Lewis H. and Mary L. (Mills) O. B.A., Purdue U., 1975; M.A., U. Iowa, 1980. Cert. counselor, 1983. Tchr., Palm Beach County Schs., West Palm Beach, Fla., 1975-77; dir. placement, instr. Coll. Lake County, Grayslake, Ill., 1980-83; central zone field services coordinator Coll. Placement Council, Inc., Bethlehem, Pa., 1983-86; nat. field services coordinator coll. Placement Council Inc., 1986—; Bd. dirs. Connections crisis line, Libertyville, Ill., 1981-82; sec. St. Gilbert Ch. Parish Council, Grayslake, Ill. Mem. Women in Mgmt. (Woman of Achievement in Edn. award Lake Suburban chpt. 1984), Midwest Coll. Placement Assn. (chmn. 1982-83), Am. Assn. Counseling and Devel., Am. Coll. Personnel Assn., New Century Town Homeowners Assn. (bd. dirs.). Club: Toastmasters (1st place award N. div. 1983). Roman Catholic. Avocations: travel, needlework, tennis, swimming, bridge. Office: Coll Placement Council PO Box 98 Libertyville IL 60048-0098

OSTERLAND, RONALD WILLIAM, electronic engineering company executive; b. Mendota, Ill., Mar. 1, 1927; s. Wilhelm Karl and Elsie Emma (Roessler) O.; widowed; 1 child, Gerry D. BA, U. Ill., 1950; BSEE, MIT, 1953; JD, U. Mo., 1956. Chief engr. A&H Radio Corp., Aurora, Ill., 1956-64; chief engr. RWO Communications, Electronics, Inc., Aurora, 1964-74, pres., chief exec. officer, 1964—. Served to lt. col. U.S. Army, 1944-46, ETO. Decorated Purple Heart, Bronze Star. Mem. Elect. Engrs. Assn., Radio Club Am. Republican. Avocations: golf, flying, parachuting, amateur radio. Home: 110 Briar Ln North Aurora IL 60542 Office: RWO Communications Electronics 715 N Elmwood Dr Aurora IL 60506

OSTMANN, BARBARA GIBBS, journalist; b. Berryville, Ark., Dec. 25, 1948; d. Rex and Virginia Dell (Oliver) Gibbs; m. Wilfred C. Ostmann, Apr. 3, 1976. AA with honors, Christian Coll., 1969; B in Journalism, U. Mo., 1971, MA, 1974; postgrad. in French studies, U. Neuchatel, Switzerland, 1973. Bilingual sec. Internat. Union for Conservation of Nature, Morges, Switzerland, 1973; tchr. journalism, English Coll. Chinese Culture, Taipei, Taiwan, 1974; food editor St. Louis Dispatch, 1975—; judge various cooking contests; mem. food editors' adv. panel Food Mktg. Inst., 1982-84; lectr. in field. Co-editor: (with Jane Baker) Food Editors' Favorites Cookbook, 1983, The St. Louis Post-Dispatch Best Recipes Cookbook, 1983, Food Editors Hometown Favorites Cookbook, 1984. Swimming instr. ARC; mem. scholarship selection com. Union High Sch., 1979. Recipient 1st Place Vesta award Am. Meat Inst., 1978, 79, 81, Cert. of Merit, 1980, 82, 1st Place Golden Carnation award Carnation Co., 1981, St. Louis YWCA Leadership award communications category, 1986; Rotary Internat. fellow, 1971-72, Mott fellow 1973-74. Mem. Women in Communications, Newspaper Food Editors and Writers Assn. Inc. (regional dir. 1981-82, pres. 1982-84, cookbook chmn., co-chmn. meeting 1981, 83), Women In Leadership Alumni Assn. (bd. dirs. 1986-87), U. Mo.-Columbia Alumni Assn., Smithsonian Inst., St. Louis Culinary Soc. (pres. 1986-87), Internat. Inst. for Dining Excellence (bd. dirs. 1987—). Office: St Louis Post Dispatch 900 N Tucker Blvd Saint Louis MO 63101

OSTREM, WALTER MARTIN, librarian, educator, consultant; b. Mpls., May 27, 1930; s. Oscar Martin and Helen Therese (Marcio) O.; m. Gertrud Franciska Tunkel, Aug. 6, 1956; children—Thomas, Paul, Francine. B.A., U. Minn., 1953, M.A., 1958; B.S., Mankato State U., 1962, M.S., 1964; postgrad. U. Mich., U. Iowa. Serials librarian Agr. Library U. Minn., 1958-59; acquisitions librarian Mankato State U., Minn., 1959-66, Eastern Mich. U., 1966-67; dir. media Iowa City Sch., 1967-69; librarian John F. Kennedy Sch., Berlin, W.Ger., 1969-73; dist. profl. librarian St. Paul Schs., 1973—; cons. in field. Served to 1st lt. U.S. Army, 1954-55. Recipient Ency. Brit. 1st place Sch. Library Media System award, 1969. Mem. Minn. Ednl. Media Orgn., Am. Fedn. Tchrs., M Club, Phi Delta Kappa. Contbr. articles in field. Home: 5536 Harriet Ave S Minneapolis MN 55419 Office: 360 Colborne St Saint Paul MN 55102

OSTRIKER, RICHARD ALAN, marketing professional; b. Chgo., Nov. 18, 1951; s. Henry Jack and Bobbette Anne (Petrando) O.; m. Jamie Kim Koelliker, June 11, 1977; 1 child, Mary Ashley. BS, Purdue U., 1973. Prodn. foreman Reynolds Metals, McCook, Ill., 1973-75; sales rep. Owens Corning Fiberglas, Dallas, 1975-79; mgr. constrn. market Owens Corning Fiberglas, Toledo, 1979-82; mgr. tubing products NL Atlas Bradford, Houston, 1982-83; mgr. mktg. devel. coated fabrics div. Uniroyal, Mishawaka, Ind., 1984—. Mem. Soc. Plastics Engrs. Republican. Roman Catholic. Lodge: Elks. Avocations: weightlifting, running, tropical fish. Office: Uniroyal 312 N Hill Mishawaka IN 46544

OSTROM, THOMAS MARSHALL, psychology educator; b. Mishawaka, Ind., Mar. 1, 1936; s. Alfred Sherman and Marion Esther (Eggleston) O.; m. Diana Forrest, Aug. 30, 1958 (div. Sept. 1977); children: Lisa Gail Webb, Steven Marshall. AB, Wabash Coll., 1958; MA, U. N.C., 1964, PhD, 1964. Prof. psychology Ohio State U., 1964—, dir. social psychology program, 1974-79, 80-85; vis. prof. U. Bergen, Norway, 1973-74, U. Manheim, Fed. Republic Germany, 1981; cir. social psychology program Ohio State U., 1974-79, 80-85; lectr. various colls. and univs. Editor: Psychological Foundations of Attitudes, 1968, Person Memory, 1980, Cognitive Responses in Persuasion, 1981; editor Jour Exptl. Social Psychology, 1980—; contbr. articles to profl. jours. Grantee NSF, 1969-75, Mershon Found., 1967-69, Office of Naval Research, 1977-84. Fellow AAAS, Am. Psychol. Assn., Soc. Psychol. Study Social Issues; mem. Soc. Exptl. Social Psychology, Psychonomic Soc. Democrat. Episcopalian. Avocations: banjo playing, Sherlock Holmes aficionado. Home: 323 Northridge Rd Columbus OH 43214 Office: Ohio State U Dept Psychology 404C W 17th Ave Columbus OH 43210

O'SULLIVAN, JOSEPH F., judge; b. Brandon, Man., Can., Feb. 25, 1927; s. Patrick and Marie Louise Poirier. BA, U. Man., 1947, LLB, 1953; MA, U. Toronto, 1949. Sole practice 1953-75; judge Ct. Appeals for Man., Winnipeg, 1975—. Pres. Man. Liberal Party, 1956-75. Office: Ct of Appeals, Law Cts Bldg, Winnipeg, MB Canada R3C 0V8 *

OSWALD, JAMES OLIVER, univ. adminstr.; b. Millersburg, Ohio, June 1, 1944; s. John A. and Ida (Lenhart) O.; B.A., Cedarville Coll., 1967; B.S., Central State U., 1967; M.A., U. Akron, 1980; m. Ruth Ann Mast, Nov. 23, 1962; children—Todd Anthony, Lori Anne. Tchr. coll. English and journalism, coach West Holmes High Sch., Millersburg, 1967-68; editor employee communications Rubbermaid, Inc., Wooster, Ohio, 1968-79; mgr. internat. communications United Telephone Co. Ohio, Mansfield, 1969-71; dir. dept. univ. publs. U. Akron, Ohio, 1971-82, asst. v.p. for instl. advancement, 1982-85. Mem. NEA, Internat. Assn. Bus. Communicators, AAUP, Am. Assn. Higher Edn., Ohio Edn. Assn., Univ. and Coll. Designers Assn., Council Advancement and Support of Edn., Pub. Relations Soc. Am., Am. Econ. Devel. Council, Mid-Am. Devel. Council, U.S. C. of C., Ohio C. of C., Orrville Area C. of C. (exec. v.p. 1986—), C. of C. Execs. of Ohio. Republican. Mem. Brethren Ch. Clubs: Akron Press. Home: 306 Washington Blvd Orrville OH 44667 Office: University of Akron 225 S Forge St Akron OH 44325

OSWALD, MARK GORDON, personnel director; b. Osage, Iowa, Jan. 5, 1951; s. Rollin Gordon and Lorraine (Jones) O.; m. Jo Santee, July 22, 1972; children: Anne, Elizabeth, Amanda. BS, Simpson Coll., 1972; MBA, U. Iowa, 1974. Fin. planner, employment rep., prodn. coordinator Collins, Cedar Rapids, Iowa, 1972-75; employee mgr. Amana (Iowa) Refigerator, 1975-77; personnel mgr. Frito-Lay, various locations, 1977-81; mgr. employement relations Frito-Lay, Dallas, 1981-85; sr. dir., personnel Pizza Hut, Inc., Wichita, Kans., 1985—. Mem. United Way, Jackson, Miss. and Plano, Tex., 1981-85, Gov.'s Task Force on Minority Bus. Suppliers, Miss., 1979-81; mem. Leadership Plano, 1984-85; chmn. Downtown Hist. Restoration com., Plano, 1984-85; bd. dirs. Info./Refferal Ctr., Plano, 1984-85. Served to capt. Med. Service Corps, U.S. Army, 1972-77. Recipient Eagle Scout award Boy Scouts Am., 1966, Industry of Yr. award Gov. of Miss., 1981; named Outstanding Young Man of Yr., U.S. Jaycees, 1979-86. Republican. Methodist. Avocations: tennis, travel. Home: 12430 Edgewood Circle Wichita KS 67206 Office: Pizza Hut Inc 9111 E Doulgas Wichita KS 67207

OSWALT, JOHN NEWELL, theology educator, religious writer; b. Mansfield, Ohio, June 21, 1940; s. Glenn Starr and Mildred LaVergne (Wachs) O.; m. Karen Suzanne Kennedy, Aug. 11, 1962; children: Elizabeth Greer, Andrew Clark, Peter Newell. AB, Taylor U., 1957-61; BDiv, Asbury Theol. Sem., 1961-64, ThM, 1965; MA, Brandeis U., 1966, PhD, 1968. Ordained to ministry, United Meth. Ch., 1978. Asst. prof. Barrington (R.I.) Coll., 1968-70; assoc. prof. Asbury Theol. Sem., Wilmore, Ky., 1970-78, prof., 1978-82; pres. Asbury Coll., Wilmore, 1983-86; prof. Trinity Evang. Div. Sch., Deerfield, Ill., 1986—. Author: Where are You, God?, 1982, Isaiah, Chapters 1-39, 1986, The Leisure Crisis, 1987. Cubmaster Wilmore Troop Boy Scouts Am., 1980-83. Nat. Def. Fgn. Lang. fellow Brandeis U., 1967-68, Univ. fellow Brandeis U., 1966-67. Mem. Soc. Biblical Lit., Wesleyan Theol. Soc., Inst. Biblical Research. Republican. Avocations: reading, gardening, scale-model trains. Home: 746 7th Ave Libertyville IL 60048 Office: Trinity Evang Div Sch 2065 Half Day Rd Deerfield IL 60015

OTIS, JAMES, JR., architect; b. Chgo., July 8, 1931; s. James and Edwina (Love) O.; m. Diane Cleveland, Apr. 9, 1955; children: James III, Julie C., David C. BArch cum laude, Princeton U., 1953; postgrad., U. Chgo., 1955-57. Registered architect, Ill. Designer Irvin A. Blietz Co., Wilmette, Ill., 1955-57; pres. Homefinders Constrn. Corp., Wilmette, 1957-59, O & F Constrn. Co., Northbrook, Ill., 1959-61; chmn. bd., chief exec. officer Otis Assocs., Inc., Northbrook, Ill., 1960—; pres. Otis Devel. Co., 1981—; bd. dirs. Northbrook Trust & Savs. Bank, Pioneer Bank, Chgo., Lane Fin. Corp., So. Minerals Corp. Prin. works include GBC Corp. Hdqrs., Plaza Towers Office Complex, Schaumburg, Ill., Combined Ins. Co. Corp. Hdqrs., Performing Arts Ctr., Northbrook Ill., All State Regional Hdqrs, Skokie, Ill. Trustee Evanston (Ill.) Hosp., Better Govt. Assn., Chgo.; governing mem. Shedd Aquarium; bd. govs. Chgo. Zool. Soc.; pres. bd. dirs. N. Suburban YMCA, Northbrook, 1971-72; mem. adv. bd. Cook County Forest Preserve Dist. Served with USNR, 1953-55. Mem. AIA, Nat. Council Archtl. Registration Bds., Northwestern U. Assocs., Chgo. Council Fgn. Relations (asso.). Republican. Episcopalian. Clubs: Princeton (pres. 1971-72), Economic, Commonwealth, Chicago, Commercial; Glenview (Ill.); Coleman Lake; Angler's. Home: 41 Bridlewood Northbrook IL 60062 Office: 400 Skokie Blvd Northbrook IL 60062

O'TOOLE, JOHN MICHAEL, playwright; b. Evanston, Ill., Nov. 23, 1948; s. John Lawrence and Elizabeth Ann (Coyne) O'T. BA, Loyola U., Chgo., 1972. Works include: Two of Mother's Friends, 1984, Armageddon, 1984, Sass, 1986, Angel Ears, 1986. Mem. Chgo. Dramatists Workshop (playwright). Home: 1008 Loyola Ave Chicago IL 60626 Office: Chgo Dramatists Workshop 3315 N Clark Chicago IL 60657

O'TOOLE, ROBERT JOSEPH, manufacturing company executive; b. Chgo., Feb. 22, 1941; s. Francis John O'Toole; children: William, Patricia, Timothy, Kathleen, John. BS in Acctg., Loyola U., Chgo., 1961. Fin. analyst A.O. Smith Corp., Milw., 1963-66, mgr. corp. fin. analysis and planning, 1966-68, sr. v.p., 1984-85, pres., 1986—; controller electric motor div. A.O. Smith Corp., Tipp City, Ohio, 1968-71, gen. plant mgr. electric motor div., 1974-79, v.p., gen. mgr., 1979-83; mng. dir. Bull Motors, Ipswich, Eng., 1971-74. Clubs: Univ., Tripoli Country (Milw.). Office: A O Smith Corp 1 Park Plaza 11270 W Park Plaza Milwaukee WI 53224-3690

O'TOOLE, ROBERT V., JR., pathologist; b. Albany, N.Y., Oct. 23, 1931; s. Robert V. Sr and Helen A. (Castello) O'T.; m. Elizabeth Samascott, Sept. 4, 1954 (div. 1965); children: John R., Michael T., Andrew J.; m. Harriet Fowler, Nov. 26, 1965; children: Rovert V. III, Cathleen C. BS in Pre Medicine, Siena Coll., 1953; MD, St. Louis U., 1957. Diplomate Am. Bd. Ob-Gyn, Am. Bd. Pathology. Commd. USAF, 1956, advanced through grades to col.; resident in obgynecolog pathology Albany Med. Ctr., 1958-62; chief ob-gyn USAF, Griffiss AFB, N.Y., 1962-64; fellow in gyn pathology Johns Hopkins U., Balt., 1964-65; chief ob-gyn pathology Wilford Hall USAF, Lockland AFB, Tex., 1965-76, resident in pathology, 1973-74; cons. to surgeon gen. USAF, 1966-76; ret. Wilford Hall USAF, Lockland AFB, Tex., 1976; assoc. prof. pathology and ob-gyn Ohio State U., 1976—, dir. cytology div. dept. pathology, 1976—; assoc. clin. prof. U. No. Tex., San Antonio, 1973-76. Co-author computer program for cytology mgmt., copyright 1983; contbr. numerous research papers and articles to prof. jours. Fellow Coll. Am. Pathologists, Am. Coll. Ob-Gyn, Air Force Soc. Clin. Surgeons (treas.), Cen. Ohio Soc. Pathologists (pres. 1984-85). Club: Quaterback (Worthington, Ohio), (v.p. 1986). Avocation: woodworking. Home: 1041 Macgregor Ave Worthington OH 43085 Office: Ohio State Univ Med Ctr N-312 Doan Hall Columbus OH 43210

OTT, KAREN LEE, owner wholesale supplier and workroom, interior decorating business; b. Cedar Rapids, Iowa, Feb. 25, 1946; d. Arthur Theodore Beorkrem and Dorathea Mae (Allen) Selby; m. William Marvin Ott, Sept. 4, 1971; children: Caroline Anne, Katherine Lee. B, U. Iowa, 1968. Cert. tchr., Iowa. Tchr. Davenport (Iowa) Community Schs., 1968-81; owner, interior decorator Interiors by Beorkrem, Davenport, 1982—; owner, operator Kalie Fabrics, Davenport, 1983—. Author (booklet) Cord Drawn Warm Window Drapery, 1987. Mem. steering com. Talented and Gifted Edn. Davenport Schs., 1985—, advisor Reading Edn. Com., 1983—; designer Festival of Trees Vis. Artists Assn., Davenport, 1986. Mem. Scott County Homebuilders Assn., Quad Cities Interior Designers (founding, steering com. 1984—). Republican. Lutheran. Home: 2841 Kelling Davenport IA 52804 Office: Interiors by Beorkrem Davenport IA 52804

OTTAWAY, LOIS MARIE, religious organization administrator; b. Wichita, Kans., Oct. 9, 1931; d. Albert Horace and Clare Marie (Russell) O. BS, Kans. State U., 1953; MA, U. Iowa, 1962; postgrad., Wheaton (Ill.) Coll., 1962-69. Deacon LaSalle St. Ch., Chgo., 1973-77, vice moderator, 1981-87; asst. dir. vol. representation Med. Assistance Programs Internat., Wheaton, 1983-84, asst. dir. ch. relations, 1984—; mgr. media relations World Relief Corp., Wheaton, 1982-83; sec.-treas. West Suburban Evang. Fellowship, Wheaton, 1984-85, v.p., 1985-86. Contbr. articles to profl. jours. Election judge DuPage County, Wheaton, 1978—. Recipient Vol. of Yr. award Programmed Activities for Correcitonal Edn., Chgo., 1972. Mem. Evangs. for Social Action (bd. dirs. 1979-80). Democrat. Club: Suburban Press of Chgo. (rec. sec. 1977-82, bd. dirs. 1982-85). Avocations: vol. service, geneal. research, growing African violets. Home: 201 N President #3A Wheaton IL 60187 Office: Med Assistance Programs Internat PO Box 50 Wheaton IL 60187

OTTAWAY, ROBERT FLINN, communications executive; b. Detroit, May 2, 1947; s. John Palmer and Roberta Florentine (Flinn) O.; m. Anne Bartley Galvin, Feb. 18, 1977; children: Robert Flinn Jr., Edward Verlinden. BA in Econs., U. Va., 1969; JD, Wayne State U., 1972. Bar: Mich. 1972. Assoc. Long, Franseth, Goodenough, Smith & May, Detroit, 1972-74; trust officer Nat. Bank Detroit, 1974-82; pres, gen. mgr. Sta. WMMQ, Lansing, Mich., 1982—. Mem. Mich. Bar Assn., Lansing Ad Club (treas. 1986—). Republican. Presbyterian. Avocations: running, tennis. Office: Sta WMMQ 913 W Holmes Rd Lansing MI 48910

OTTE, CARL, political consultant, lobbyist, retired state senator; b. Sheboygan, Wis., June 24, 1923; s. John and Magdalena (Verconteren) O.; m. Ethel Dorothy Braatz, Nov. 1, 1949; children—Allen Carl, Jane Karen, Julie Beth, Lynn Carol. Mem. Wis. State Assembly, 1967-82; mem. Wis. Senate from 9th Dist., 1983-86. Mem. Sheboygan County Bd. Suprs., 1962-68; mem. Democratic Party of Wis.; mem. VFW. Served with U.S. Army, 1943-45. Mem. Am. Fedn. Musicians. Lutheran. Lodge: Am. Legion.

OTTENWELLER, ALBERT HENRY, bishop; b. Stanford, Mont., Apr. 5, 1916; s. Charles and Mary (Hake) O. S.T.L., Cath. U. Am., 1943. Ordained priest Roman Catholic Ch., 1943, consecrated aux. bishop of Toledo, 1974; asso. pastor St. John's Parish, Delphos, Ohio, 1943-59, St. Richard's Parish, Swanton, Ohio, 1959-61; pastor St. Joseph's Parish, Blakeslee, Ohio, also mission Sacred Heart, Montpelier, Ohio, 1961-62, Our Lady of Mt. Carmel Parish, Bono, Ohio, 1962-68, St. John's Parish, Delphos, Ohio, 1968-76, St. Michael's Parish, Findlay, Ohio, 1976-77; consecrated aux. bishop of Toledo 1974, bishop of Steubenville, 1977—. Mem. Ohio Gov.'s Com. on Migrant Labor, 1955-75; mem. governing bd. Retreats Internat., 1975; chmn. laity com. Nat. Conf. Cath. Bishops, 1978. Office: Chancery Office 422 Washington St PO Box 969 Steubenville OH 43952 *

OTTERBACHER, ERIC WAYNE, chemist; b. Cheltenham, Eng., Apr. 6, 1954; came to U.S., 1954.; s. Theodore Henry and Marcia Louise (McKerlie) O.; m. Patricia Ann Smith, Aug. 23, 1975; children: Kelly, Becky, Scott. BA in Chem., Biology, Blackburn Coll., 1976; PhD in Organic Chemistry, Ind. U., 1980. Sr. research chemist Dow Chemical Co., Midland, Mich., 1980-84, project leader, 1984—. Patentee in field. chmn. fin. St. Timothy Ch., Midland, 1983-86, bd. dirs. 1985-86, pres. 1986—. Mem. Am. Chem. Soc., Internat. Union Pure and Applied Chem., Am. Inst. Chem., N.Y. Acad. Sci. Lutheran. Avocations: soccer, camping, softball. Home: 2307 Redwood Dr Midland MI 48640 Office: The Dow Chem Co 1776 Bldg Midland MI 48640

OTTING, FREDERICK PAUL, manufacturing executive; b. Milw., Mar. 4, 1916; s. Fred E. and Hilda (Felber) O.; m. Juel Papenthien, June 18, 1938; m. 2d, Margaret Steffenhagen, Sept. 2, 1978; children—Robyn M., Derf N. Student Marquette U., U. Wis.-Milw. Plant supr. Western Leather Co., Milw., 1939-48; v.p. Racine Glove Co., Rio, Wis., 1948-79; pres. Gaskets Inc., Rio, 1961—. Mem. exec. com. Nat. Safety Council. Mem. Nat. Welding Supply Assn., Am. Welding Soc., Am. Soc. Safety Engrs., Internat. Platform Assn. Republican. Presbyterian. Clubs: Marco Island Country, Marco Island Yacht; Madison; Masons, Shriners. Office: Gaskets Inc 100 Hy 16 W Rio WI 53960

OTTMAR, THOMAS CLINTON, accountant; b. Jamestown, N.D., Jan. 1, 1960; s. Clinton Raymond and Grace Bertha (Gackle) O. BSBA, U. N.D., 1982. CPA, Minn., N.D. Tax acct. Touche Ross, St. Paul, 1982—. Mem. Am. Inst. CPA's, Minn. Soc. CPA's (acctg. careers com. 1983—), N.D. Soc. CPA's, Minn. Acctg. and Fin. Council. Methodist. Club: St. Paul Athletic. Avocations: skiing, golf. Home: 2485 Woodbridge Roseville MN 55113 Office: Touche Ross 1600 Amhoist Tower Saint Paul MN 55102

OTTO, FREDRICK M., oil refinery company executive. Chmn., chief exec. officer Derby Refining Co., Wichita, Kans. Office: Derby Refining Co PO Box 1030 Wichita KS 67201 *

OTTO, WILLIAM JOHN, obstetrician, gynecologist; b. Milw., Jan. 14, 1952; s. Karl John and Caryl A. (Trettin) O.; m. Gaye G. Griffith, Nov. 6, 1976; children: Virginia, Kevin. BA cum laude, Lawrence U., 1974; MD, Baylor U., 1978. Commd. U.S. Army, 1974, advanced through grades to maj., 1984; intern Fitzsimons Army Med. Ctr., Denver, 1978-79, resident in ob-gyn, 1979-82; staff obstetrician, gynecologist U.S. Army Hosp., Wuerzberg, Fed. Republic of Germany, 1982-85; chief ob-gyn dept. U.S. Army Hosp., Ft. Leonard Wood, Mo., 1985-86; practice medicine specializing in ob-gyn Beaumont Clinic Ltd., Green Bay, Wis., 1986-87, Smith-Glynn-Callaway Clinic, Springfield, Mo., 1987—. Fellow Am. Coll. Ob-Gyn; mem. Am. Assn. Gynecol. Laparoscopists, Wis. Soc. Obstetricians and Gynecologists, Brown County Med. Soc., Wis. State Med. Soc. Home: 2937 E Alpine Springfield MO 65804 Office: Smith Glynn Callaway Clinic 3231 S National Springfield MO 65807

OTTOSON, JOSEPH WILLIAM, clergyman; b. Chgo., June 12, 1929; s. Joseph Swenson and Lillian (Bennett) Ottoson; m. Clarice I. Warme, May 26, 1956; children: David, Cynthia, Paul. BA, Northwestern U., 1952, MA, 1957, PhD, 1967; MDiv, Augustana Sem., 1956. Ordained to ministry Luth. Ch., 1958. Pastor Our Saviour's Luth. Ch., Soderville, Minn., 1958-61; campus pastor St. Cloud (Minn.) State U., 1961-83, assoc. prof., 1968-70; dir. Ministries Unltd., Brainerd, Minn., 1983—; dir. extended ministries Luth. Ch. of Cross, Nisswa, Minn., 1985—; chaplain, psychologist No. Pines Mental Health Ctr., Brainerd, 1985—; chaplain Crow Wing County Jail, Brainerd, 1984-86, St. Joseph's Med. Ctr., Brainerd, 1984—. Bd. dirs. Vol. in Probation, Brainerd, 1985—, Port, Brainerd, 1985—; pres. Am. Cancer Soc., Brainerd, 1984-86. Home: 7594 Interlachen Rd Lake Shore MN 56401

OTZMAN, GERALD FREDERICK, university administrative officer; b. Buffalo, Dec. 26, 1936; s. Harold E. and Irma L. (Odell) O.; children: Gerald (dec.), William, James, Jon; m. Helena Ann Battel, Apr. 19, 1980. BA, Albion Coll., 1958. Sports dir. Sta. WALM-Radio, Albion, Mich., 1956-59; program dir. Sta. WPON-Radio, Pontiac, Mich., 1959-64; sales mgr. Sentry Ins., Lansing, Mich., 1964-69; account exec. Allstate Ins., Lansing, 1969-70; adminstrv. officer Wayne State U., Detroit, 1970—; mem. Wayne State U. Adminstrv. Conf., Detroit, 1978—, Univ. Activities Com., 1982—, Personnel Forum, 1986—. Editor: Coll. of Nursing newsletter, 1980—. Master of Ceremonies Mich. Jr. Miss Program, Pontiac, 1965-80; area rep. United Found. Torch Dr., Detroit, 1970—. Mem. Am. Assn. of Colls. of Nursing Bus. Mgrs., Nursing Practice Corp. (treas. 1984-86). Roman Catholic. Lodge: Lions (Detroit) (pres. 1975-77). Home: 1210 Smith Ave Royal Oak MI 48073 Office: Wayne State U Coll of Nursing 5557 Cass Ave Detroit MI 48202

OUGHTON, JAMES HENRY, JR., business executive, farmer; b. Chgo., May 14, 1913; s. James H. and Barbara (Corbett) O.; student Dartmouth Coll., 1931-35; m. Jane Boyce, Jan. 23, 1940; children—Diana (dec.), Carol Oughton Biondi, Pamela Oughton Armstrong, Deborah Oughton Callahan. Pres., dir. L.E. Keeley Co., Dwight, Ill., 1936—, Nev. Corp.; past adminstr. The Keeley Inst., Dwight, 1938—; dir. 1st Nat. Bank of Dwight, Ill. Valley Investment Co.; farmer, farm mgr., livestock feeder, Ill.; sec., dir. Dwight Indsl. Assn.; past mem. Ill. Ho. of Reps. Co-chmn. 1st Indsl. Conf. on Alcoholism, 1948; chmn. Midwest Seminar on Alcoholism for Pastors, 1957, 58, 59, 60; chmn. adv. bd. Ill. Dept. Corrections; chmn. Gov.'s Task Force on Mental Health Adminstrn., 1971-72; mem. adv. bd. Ill. Dept. Mental Health; dir., mem. exec. bd. W.D. Boyce council Boy Scouts Am.; del. 31st Internat. Congress on Alcoholism and Drug Dependence, Bangkok, 1975; mem. Internat. Council on Alcohol and Addictions, Lausanne, Switzerland, 1977; mem. Ill. Trade and Investment Mission to Japan and Korea, 1985; mem. adv. council Small Bus., Fed. Reserve Bank Chgo., 1985-86. Served as lt. (j.g.) USNR, 1944-46; PTO. Republican. Episcopalian. Clubs: Univ., Union League (Chgo.). Address: 103 W South St Dwight IL 60420

OUJIRI, JOHN CHARLES, physician; b. Cedar Rapids, Iowa, July 29, 1949; s. John Anthony and Zula Maria (Cacek) O; m. Beth Ann Scholl, Sept. 21, 1974; children: Matthew, James, John, Timothy. BS in Psychology, Loras Coll., 1971; MD, U. Iowa, 1975. Diplomate Am. Bd. Family Practice. Intern, then resident Saginaw (Mich.) Coop. Hosp., 1975-78; staff physician Meml. Med. Ctr., Ashland, Wis., 1978—. Fellow Am. Acad. Family Practice. Office: Med Assocs North SC 2101 Beaser Ashland WI 54806

OULVEY, DAVID E., accountant, brokerage house executive; b. St. Louis, Jan. 9, 1958; s. William Thomas and Margaret Mary Joenella (Winkelmann) O.; m. Claret Cabrini Rullo, Aug. 23, 1986. BS, DePaul U., 1980. CPA, Ill. Acct. Philip Rootberg & Co., Chgo., 1980-82; internal auditor CFS Continental, Chgo., 1982; audit supr. Chgo. Bd. of Trade, 1982-86; mgr. corp. fin. Singer/Wenger Trading Co., Chgo., 1986—. Mem. Am. Inst. CPA's, Ill. CPA Soc. Roman Catholic. Avocation: kyokushin karate. Home: 7258 W Farwell Chicago IL 60631 Office: Singer/Wenger Trading Co Inc 141 W Jackson Suite 2120A Chicago IL 60604

OUTCALT, MERLIN BREWER, child care center administrator, consultant; b. Reedsburg, Wis., Aug. 26, 1928; s. Raymond Arthur and Ruby (Brewer) O.; m. Ruth Ann Auble, Sept. 22, 1950; children—Roger Lee, Dennis Alan, Steven Len. B.S., Ind. U., 1955, M.A. in Social Service, 1957; postgrad Ind. U. Cert. social worker. Probation officer Juvenile Court, Indpls., 1957-59; exec. dir. Travelers Aide Soc., Cin., 1959-65, Meth. Youth Service, Chgo., 1965-68; cons. United Meth. Ch., Evanston, Ill., 1968-74; exec. dir. Group Child Care Services, Chapel Hill, N.C., 1974-77, Webster-Cantrell Hall, Decatur, Ill., 1977—; Contbr. articles to profl. jours. and mags. Lay leader Decatur Dist. United Meth., Ill., 1980-87; mem. Council Community Services, Decatur, 1980-84, United Meth. Global Ministries, N.Y.C., 1984-88. Served as cpl. U.S. Army, 1950-52. Mem. Acad. Cert. Social Workers, Ill. Child Care Assn. Lodge: Rotary. Avocations: camping, traveling. Office: Webster-Cantrell Hall 1942 E Cantrell St Decatur IL 62521

OUZOUNIAN, ARMENUHI, dentist; b. Mosul, Iraq, Feb. 17, 1942; came to U.S., 1974; d. Yervant and Warda (Efram) O. DDS, U. Baghdad, Iraq, 1962, degree in anesthesiology, 1966. Cert. U.S. Bd. Dentistry; lic. dentist, Ill. Resident Fed. Teaching Hosp., Baghdad, 1963-66; anesthesiologist Maternity Hosp., Baghdad, 1966-73; gen. practice dentistry Baghdad, 1967-73; asst. various offices, Chgo., 1975-83; gen. practice dentistry Chgo., 1984-87; mem. dept. dental surgery Cabrini Hosp., Chgo., 1987—. Mem. ADA, Am. Women Dentists Assn., Ill. Dental Soc., Chgo. Dental Soc. Avocations: painting, reading, writing, research. Home: 2253 N Kildare Chicago IL 60639 Office: 3503 W 26th St Chicago IL 60623

OUZTS, DALE KEITH, broadcast executive; b. Miami, Fla., Aug. 26, 1941; s. Jacob C. and Edna P. (Sloan) O.; m. Judy Olcott, June 11, 1964 (div. Mar. 1980); children: Dale Keith Jr., Karen J.; m. Kathleen Gross, Mar. 15, 1982. BJ, U. Ga., 1965, MA, 1966; postgrad. advanced mgmt. seminar, Harvard U., 1977. Mgr. Sta. WSJK-TV, Knoxville, Tenn., 1966-69; exec. v.p., gen. mgr. Sta. KPTS-TV, Wichita, Kans., 1969-72; gen. mgr. Sta. WSSR-FM, Springfield, Ill., 1972-77; sr. v.p. Nat. Pub. Radio, Washington, 1977-79; gen. mgr. Sta. WOSU-AM-FM and Sta. WOSU-TV Ohio State U., Columbus, Ohio, 1979—, assoc. prof. communications, 1979—, assoc. prof. journalism, 1983—; adminstv. dir. Ohio State U. awards, 1979—; mem. Ohio Ednl. TV Stas., v.p., 1983-84. Recipient Disting. Service award Nat. Pub. Radio, 1986, Disting. Service award Nat. Black Program Consortium, 1985, Disting Service award PRIMA, 1977, award for fundraising and promotion Corp. Pub. Broadcasting, 1971. Mem. Nat. Assn. Ednl. Broadcasters, Ohio Assn. Broadcasters, Nat. Assn. State Univs. and Land Grant Colls. Avocations: racquetball, softball, golf, hunting, tennis. Home: 1664 Flat Rock Ct Worthington OH 43085 Office: WOSU-AM 2400 Olentangy River Rd Columbus OH 43210

OVENS, WILLIAM GEORGE, mechanical engineer, educator; b. Paterson, N.J., July 18, 1939; s. William George and Dora Jane (Mingle) O.; m. Jill J. Whiton, Aug. 24, 1963; children: Bevan Jane, Janine Elise. Student, Cornell U., 1957-59; BSME, U. Mich., 1964; MS, U. Conn., 1979, PhD, 1981. Engr. Pratt and Whitney, East Hartford, Conn., 1964-66; research asst. U. Conn., Storrs, 1966-71; lectr. Papua New Guinea U. Technology, 1972-75; asst. prof. mech. engring. Clarkson U., Potsdam, N.Y., 1975-81; from assoc. prof. to prof. mech. engring. Rose Hulman Inst. Tech., Terre Haute, Ind., 1981—; cons. Miller Brewing Co., Auburn, N.Y., 1978-80, Martin Marietta, Orlando, Fla., 1980—, IBM Corp., Boulder, Colo., 1982—, Tri-Industries, Terre Haute, Ind., 1984—. Contbr. articles to profl. jours. Recipient Andrew Kucher award U. Mich., 1964, Ralph Teetor award Soc. Automotive Engrs., 1976, Teaching Excellence award Clarkson U., 1977, 80, Blue Key award Rose-Hulman Inst. Tech., 1985. Mem. ASME (chmn. materials div. 1982-83), Am. Soc. Metals, Soc. Am. Value Engrs. (chmn. univ. liason com.). Avocations: cabinetmaker, sailing. Home: 4693 Woodshire Dr Terre Haute IN 47803 Office: Rose-Hulman Inst Tech 5500 Wabash Ave Terre Haute IN 47803

OVERBECK, JOSEPH C., heavy equipment company executive; b. 1936. BS, Millikin U., 1962. Mgr. prodn. Allis Chalmers Co., Milw., 1962-71; mgr. mfg. and planning Ford Motor Co., Dearborn, Mich., 1971-75; dir. mfg. Massey-Ferguson, Des Moines, 1975-78; with Motor Wheel Corp., Lansing, Mich., 1978—, v.p. mfg., 1980-82, pres., 1982—, also bd. dirs. Office: Motor Wheel Corp 4000 Collins Rd Lansing MI 48910 *

OVERBEEK, JAMES ALAN, lumber, restaurant and real estate executive; b. Grand Rapids, Mich., May 19, 1949; s. Robert John aand Elvera May (Wiersma) O.; m. Judith Kay Poll, July 24, 1970; children: Dawn, Brooke. B in Forestry, Mich. State U., 1971. Lumber buyer Buskirk Lumber, Grand Rapids, 1971-75; forest supr. City of Grand Rapids, 1975-79, parks dir., 1979-81, asst. city mgr., 1981-85; adminstr. The Universal Cos., Inc., Grand Rapids, 1985—. Bd. dirs. Sylvan Sch., Grand Rapids, 1985—, West Mich. Environ. Action Council; hon. bd. dirs. John Ball Park Zool. Soc., Grand Rapids. Club: Century (Grand Rapids). Office: The Universal Cos Inc 2801 E Beltline NE Grand Rapids MI 49505

OVERMIER, J(AMES) BRUCE, psychology educator; b. Queens, N.Y., Aug. 2, 1938; s. James J. Wheelwright and Emma Annette (Carlton) Jacobson; m. Judith Ann Smith, Aug. 19, 1962; 1 child, Larisa Nicole. AB in Chemistry, Kenyon Coll., 1960; MA in Psychology, Bowling Green (Ohio) U., 1962; PhD in Psychology, U. Pa., 1965. Lic. cons. psychologist, Minn. Prof. psychology, dir. Ctr. Research in Learning, Perception and Cognition U. Minn., Mpls., 1965—; mem. adv. bd. NSF, Washington, 1976-79, 86. Author: (with others) Animal Learning: Survey and Analysis, 1979; editor: Affect, Conditioning and Cognition, 1985; cons. editor Jour. Exptl. Psychology, 1971-74; editor Learning and Motivation, 1973-76; editorial bd. Behavioral Brain Research, 1979-84; contbr. chpts. to books and articles to mags. Grantee NIH, 1966—, NSF, 1966-83; Fulbright Hays scholar, 1980; Fogarty Ctr. Pub. Health Service fellow, 1984; James McKeen Cattell Found. fellow, 1985. Fellow Am. Psychol. Assn. (council 1987—); mem. Am. Assn. Univ. Profs. (local pres. 1981), Midwestern Psychol. Assn. (council 1984-87, pres. 1987), Psychonomics Soc. (sec.-treas. 1981-83, bd. govs. 1983—), Delta Kappa Epsilon. Avocations: skking, camping. Office: U Minn Dept Psychology Elliott Hall 75 E River Rd Minneapolis MN 55455

OVERMOE, ROBERT ALAN, accounting company executive; b. Mayville, N.D., Dec. 20, 1958; s. James Orland and Marian Wilma (Lee) O. BBA, U. N.D., 1981. CPA, N.D., Minn. Staff acct. Denault & Assocs., Fosston, Minn., 1981-83; pvt. practice acctg. Fosston, Minn., 1983-86; ptnr. Overmoe & Nelson, Ptnrs., Grand Forks, N.D., 1984-86; chief exec. officer Overmoe & Nelson, Ltd., Fosston and Grand Forks, 1987—; cons. Small Bus. Devel., Fosston, 1984-86; instr. acctg. Northland Community Coll., Theif River Falls, Minn., 1987. Treas. local Am. Cancer Soc. Mem. Am. Inst. CPA's, Minn. Soc. CPA's, N.D. Soc. CPA's. Republican. Pentecostal. Lodge: Rotary (sec., treas. Fosston chpt. 1984-87). Avocations: hunting, fishing, golf, motorcycling. Home: Rural Rt Fosston MN 56542 Office: Overmoe & Nelson Ltd Box 521 Fosston MN 56542

OVERSON, JEFFREY SCOTT, underwriter, insurance salesman; b. St. Paul, Aug. 13, 1959; s. Harlan H. and M. Evelyn (McNatt) O.; m. Jill A. Prestholt, Aug. 1, 1981. BA, Wartburg Coll., Waverly, Iowa, 1981. Salesman Equitable of Iowa, Iowa City, 1981-83; salesman, underwriter, disability income supr. Equitable of Iowa, Davenport, 1983—. Bd. dirs. Am. Heart Assn., Davenport, 1986—. Fellow Life Underwriters Tng. Council (Nat. Quality award 1983, 85, 86, Nat. Sales Achievement award 1985, 86); mem. Nat. Assn. Life Underwriters (Nat. Quality award 1986, Nat. Sales Achievement award 1986, bd. dirs. Davenport chpt. 1986), Davenport Jaycees, Bettendorf (Iowa) C. of C.. Lodge: Kiwanis (bd. dirs. Davenport chpt. 1986—). Avocation: racquetball. Home: 3562 N Willow Ct Bettendorf IA 52722 Office: Equitable of Iowa Davenport Bank Bldg Suite 417 Davenport IA 52801

OVERTON, GEORGE WASHINGTON, lawyer; b. Hinsdale, Ill., Jan. 25, 1918; s. George Washington and Florence Mary (Darlington) O.; m. Jane Vincent Harper, Sept. 1, 1941; children—Samuel Harper, Peter Darlington, Ann Vincent. A.B., Harvard U., 1940; J.D., U. Chgo., 1946. Bar: Ill. 1947. Counsel Wildman, Harrold, Allen & Dixon, Chgo. Bd. dirs. Open Lands Project, pres., 1978-81; bd. dirs. Upper Ill. Valley Assn., 1981—, chmn., 1981-84; mem. com. on profl. responsibility of Ill. Supreme Ct., 1986—. Mem. ABA, Ill. Bar Assn., Chgo. Bar Assn. (bd. mgrs. 1981-83), Assn. Bar City N.Y. Home: 5648 Dorchester Ave Chicago IL 60637 Office: 1 IBM Plaza Chicago IL 60611

OVERTON, ROY WILLIAM, 3D, osteopath; b. Des Moines, July 12, 1954; s. Roy William 2d and Aurora (Alanis) O.; m. Constance Nanette Hall, Nov. 10, 1979; children: Ché, Cammie, Stephanie, Alexander. BS in Chemistry, Drake U., 1976, postgrad., 1977; DO, Coll. Osteo. Medicine and Surgery, Des Moines, 1980. Intern Northwest Gen. Osteo. Hosp., Milw., 1981, emergency room physician, 1981—; pres. Diamond Family Health Clinic, Milw., 1981-85, Brookside Med. Clinic, Ltd., Milw., 1985—; mem. staff Lakeview Osteo. Hosp., Milw., Family Hosp., Milw.; sec. gen. practice dept. Northwest Gen. Osteo. Hosp., 1983-84, chief os staff, 1984—. Mem. Am. Osteo. Assn., Am. Acad. Family Physicians, Am. Coll. Gen. Practitioners Osteo. Medicine and Surgery, Wis. Osteo. Assn. Physicians and Surgeons (trustee 1985-86), Milw. Dist. Soc. Osteo. Physicians and Surgeons (v.p. 1984-85, pres. 1985-86), Southeast Wis. Individual Practice Assn. (peer review com. 1984—, bd. dirs. 1986—), Katahdin Found., Burleigh St. Better Bus. Assn. Avocations: computers, skiing, fishing, hunting, sailing. Home: 519 Madero Dr Thiensville WI 53092 Office: Brookside Med Clinic 5140 N Teutonia Ave Milwaukee WI 53209

OWEN, DAVID ALAN, controller; b. Washington, Ind., Feb. 23, 1946; s. Boyd Carlos and Gladys Sophia (Boner) O.; m. Valla Kay Inman, Apr. 19, 1969; children: Chadwick, Timothy, Todd, Abigail. BS in Acctg., Ind. U., 1968. CPA, Ind. Sr. acct. Price Waterhouse, South Bend, Ind., 1973-76; mgr. acctg. and taxes UTC-Essex Corp., Ft. Wayne, Ind., 1976-80, dir. planning and control, 1980-82, asst. controller magnet wire div., 1982-83, controller magnet wire div., 1983-85, controller wire and cable div., 1985—; bd. dirs. Taxpayers Research Assn., Ft. Wayne. Mgr. youth activities Little League and YMCA basketball, Ft. Wayne, 1979—; advisor Goodwill Industries, Ft. Wayne, 1987. Served with U.S. Army, 1968-70, Vietnam. Mem. Am. Inst. CPA's, Ind. Assn. CPA's, Delta Upsilon. Republican. Presbyterian. Club: Orchard Ridge Country (Ft. Wayne). Avocations: tennis, coaching youth sports. Home: 14620 Walnut Creek Dr Fort Wayne IN 46804 Office: UTC-Essex Wire and Cable 1710 Wall St Fort Wayne IN 46804

OWEN, FRANK WILLIAM, horticultural consultant; b. Benton Harbor, Mich., Apr. 6, 1927; s. James Phillips and Loretta (Dean) O.; m. Muriel Margaret Burnham; children: Peggy Rae Weiser, Loretta Sue Beridou, Frank William III. BS in Pomology, Mich. State U., 1950, MS in Pomology, 1952. Mechanizer Kroger Co., Cin., 1950-51; fruit specialist U. Maine, Orono, 1952-55; assoc. prof. horticulture U. Ill., Urbana, 1955-67; research dir. Hilltop Orchards and Nursery, Hartford, Mich., 1967-70; mgr. Cherry Adminstrv. Bd., Hartford, 1971-75; cons. Owen Assocs., Lawrence, Mich. and Marlton, N.J., 1975—; seminar speaker Chevron Chem. Co., San Francisco, 1982—. Author: All You'll Ever Want to know about Pruning Apple Trees, 1984. Served with USN, 1945-46. Mem. Mich. Hort. Soc., N.J. Hort. Soc., Pa. Hort. Soc., Southwestern Mich. Fieldman's Assn., Am. Soc. for Hort. Sci. Republican. Baptist. Home: 205 S Blue Creek Rd Benton Harbor MI 49022 Office: Owen Assocs 205 S Blue Creek Rd Benton Harbor MI 49022

OWEN, GARY MACK, state legislator; b. Lawrence County, Ala., Sept. 9, 1944; s. Edward Mack and Aylene (Ellenburg) O.; m. Carol Kobane, June 18, 1966 (div. Jan. 1983); 1 dau., Dawn Marie; m. DeNalda Kay Miller, Feb. 11, 1983. A.A., Washtenaw Community Coll., 1968; B.A., U. Mich., 1970, M. Urban Planning, 1972; LL.D. hon., Eastern Mich. U., 1981. Part-time faculty mem. Washtenaw Community Coll., Ann Arbor, Mich., 1971-72; mem. Mich. Ho. of Reps., 1973—; assoc. speaker pro-tem Washtenaw Community Coll., 1977; speaker Mich. Ho. of Reps., 1983—. Trustee Ypsilanti Twp., Mich., 1971-72. Served with U.S Army, 1961-63. Recipient Disting. Service Ypsilanti Jaycees, 1972; named one of five Outstanding Young Men in Mich. Mich. Jaycees, 1972. Mem. Ypsilanti C. of C. Democrat. Baptist. Office: Mich Ho of Reps Room 10 Capitol Bldg Lansing MI 48909 *

OWEN, JAMES EMMET, chemical company executive; b. Cleve., May 23, 1935; s. Walter Frederick and Catherine (Goff) O.; m. Frances Mary Rudd, June 17, 1961; children: Elizabeth, Christine, Monica, Christopher, Michael, Gabrielle, Caroline, Angela. BA, John Carroll U., 1957; PhD, Case Inst., Cleve., 1961; MBA, Case Western Res. U., 1984. Research scientist U.S. Rubber, Wayne, N.J., 1961-63; group leader Harshaw Chem., Cleve., 1963-66, dir. inorganic research, 1966-69; dir. research Harshaw/Fictrol, Cleve., 1970-85; v.p., chief operating officer Obron Corp., Painesville, Ohio, 1985—. Patentee in field; author 6 publs. Mem. Chemist Club N.Y., Coatings Soc. Roman Catholic. Home: 3002 Manchester Shaker Heights OH 44122 Office: Obron Corp 400 Obron Ln Painesville OH 44077

OWEN, JOHN EDWARD, II, musician, educator, band director; b. Sikeston, Mo., Jan. 23, 1952; s. John Edward Sr. and Helen Nadine (Duncan) O.; m. Melanie Ann Drufke, Dec. 27, 1975; children: Jonathan, Emily. MusB, Ill. Wesleyan U., Bloomington, 1974; MusM, So. Ill. U., Edwardsville, 1978; postgrad., Ohio State U., 1982—. Cert. music tchr., Ohio. Dir. of bands St. Pius X High Sch., Festus, Mo., 1974-78, Heidelberg Coll., Tiffin, Ohio, 1978—; mem. Brass Band of Columbus. Mem. Coll. Band Dir.'s Nat. Assn., Music Educator's Nat. Assn., Ohio Music Educator's Assn., Coll. Music Soc., N.Am. Brass Band Assn. Lutheran. Avocations: photography, sports. Home: 137 Hunter St Tiffin OH 44883 Office: Heidelberg Coll 243 Brenneman Hall 243 Brenneman Hall 310 E Market St Tiffin OH 44883

OWEN, LARRY MALCOLM, electric company executive; b. Lincoln, Nebr., Jan. 1, 1928; s. Leonard J. and Ruth L. (Anderson) O.; m. Marilyn Wilkens, Aug. 6, 1950; children—David L., Sue Ellen Owen Hook. B.S. in Bus. Adminstrn., U. Nebr., 1950; Dr. Bus. Adminstrn. (hon.), S.D. Sch. Mines and Tech., 1984. Mgmt. trainee J.C. Penney Co., Lincoln, 1950-52; with mgmt. Nebr. City C. of C., Nebr., 1952-55, Columbus C. of C., Nebr., 1955-57, Rapid City C. of C., Nebr., 1957-66; exec. v.p. Cedar Rapids C. of C., Iowa, 1967-70; chmn., pres., chief exec. officer Black Hills Power & Light Co., Rapid City, 1970—. Mem. exec. com. Nat. Coll., Rapid City, 1982-83; chmn. bd. trustees Rushmore Nat. Health, Rapid City, 1984-85. Served with USN, 1945-46. Mem. Edison Electric Inst. (dir. 1984-86), North Central Electric Assn. (pres. 1984), Rocky Mountain Electric League (dir. 1980—). Republican. Presbyterian. Home: 223 Berry Blvd Rapid City SD 57702 Office: Black Hills Corp 625 9th St Box 1400 Rapid City SD 57709 *

OWEN, STEVEN JAMES, engineer; b. Winnebago, Minn., Feb. 2, 1952; s. Jerry Alyn and Evelyn Marie (Foster) O.; m. Connie Jean Stelter, Feb. 10, 1973; children: Tamara Kay, John Michael, James Steven. Student, Southwest Vocat.-Tech., Jackson, Minn., 1971, Mankato (Minn.) Vocat-Tech., 1974-78, Mankato State U., 1984-85, Am. Open U./N.Y. Inst. Tech., 1985—. Pres. Pete's Electric Service, Winnebago, 1978-84; mfg. elec. engr. Electrocraft Corp., Winnebago, 1984-85; chief elec. engr., estimator, gen. foreman Vos Electric, Inc., DePere, Wis., 1985—. Vol. fire chief Winnebago Fire Dept., 1984-85; chmn. bd. edn. Our Savior's Luth. Sch., Winnebago. Served with U.S. Army, 1972-74. Mem. United Assn. Mfg. Reps., Winnebago C. of C. (pres.), Am. Legion (local chpt. vice comdr. 1984-86). Avocations: basketball, spectator sports, drag racing. Home: PO Box 537 Winnebago MN 56098 Mailing Address: PO Box 296 Rincon GA 31326

OWEN, SUZANNE, savings and loan executive; b. Lincoln, Nebr., Oct. 6, 1926; d. Arthur C. and Hazel E. (Edwards) O.; B.S. in Bus. Adminstrn., U. Nebr., Lincoln, 1948. With G.F. Lessenhop & Sons, Inc., Lincoln, 1948-57; with First Fed. Lincoln, 1963—; v.p., dir. personnel, 1975-81, 1st v.p., 1981—, sr. v.p., 1987— . Mem. Adminstrv. Mgmt. Soc. (past bd. dirs. local chpt.), Lincoln Personnel Mgmt. Assn., Phi Chi Theta. Republican. Christian Scientist. Clubs: Altrusa, Wooden Spoon, Twig Daniels Network (bd. dirs. 1987-88), Exec. Women's Breakfast Group, Pi Beta Phi Alumnae, Order of Eastern Star (Lincoln). Office: First Fed Lincoln 13th and N Sts Lincoln NE 68508

OWENS, CHARLES VINCENT, JR., diagnostic company executive and consultant; b. Kansas City, Mo., May 15, 1927; s. Charles Vincent and Helen (Barrett) O.; m. Cheryl Kreighbaum, Feb. 12, 1955; children: Melody, Kevin, Michael, John, Barbara. B.S., U. Notre Dame, 1948; M.S. (Univ. fellow), U. N.C., 1949. Public health educator Richmond County (N.C.) Health Dept., 1949-51; with Miles Labs., Inc., Elkhart, Ind., 1951-82; pres. Ames Co. div. Miles Labs., Inc., 1967-71, group v.p. profl. products group, 1971-77, exec. v.p. internat. ops., 1977-82; chmn., chief exec. officer Kyoto Diagnostics, Inc., 1983-85; dir. Elkhart Sports Group Inc., Genesis Labs., Inc., St. Jude Med. Inc.; chief exec. officer Genesis Inc., 1985—. Bd. dirs. Elkhart YWCA, 1972-76; vice chmn. Elkhart County Bd. Health, 1973-77; chmn. Child Abuse Task Force, Elkhart County, Ind., 1977-78. Served with M.C., USAAF, 1945-47. Mem. Am. Public Health Assn., Health Industry Mfg. Assn. (dir.), Pharm. Mfrs. Assn., Nat. Pharm. Council (pres. 1970-71, dir. 1965-73), Am. Mgmt. Assn., Am. Diabetes Assn., Am. Assn. Diabetes Educators, Internat. Diabetes Fedn., Am. Soc. Med. Tech. Republican. Roman Catholic.

OWENS, DONNA, city official; b. Aug. 24, 1936. Student, Stautzenberger Bus Coll. Past v.p. Lucas County Bd. Edn., Ohio; mem. Toledo City Council, 1980-84; mayor City of Toledo, 1984—. Mem. Toledo-Lucas County Council for Human Services, Internat. Inst. Greater Toledo, Lucas County Improvement Corp., Toledo Area Employment and Tng. Consortium, St. Vincent Hosp. and Med. Guild, Ohio Sch. Bd. Assn., Assn. of Two Toledos, Toledo Econ. Planning Council, Criminal Justice Coordinating Council, Toledo Mus. of Art; mem. exec. com. Toledo Met. Area Council of Govts.; bd. dirs. pub. broadcasting WGTE-TV; bd. mgrs. West Toledo YMCA; bd. dirs. YMCA, Substance Abuse Service, Inc.; adv. bd. U.S. Conf. of Mayors. Recipient Legion of Leaders award YMCA, 1976; Community Service award Post 606 VFW. Office: Office of Mayor City of Toledo One Government Center Suite 2200 Toledo OH 43604 *

OWENS, JAMES HILLIARD, management consultant; b. Conyers, Ga., Mar. 7, 1920; s. Alfred Pink and Eula Leona (McLendon) O.; m. Lavonia McInnis, May 21, 1941; children—Bonnie Faye, Virginia Carol. Grad. exec. devel. program Stanford U., 1957. With Pillsbury Co., 1938-75, various positions to corp. v.p. mktg.; pres. James H. Owens Assocs. Inc., Mpls., 1983—. Served to 2d lt. inf. U.S. Army, World War II. Mem. Inst. Mgmt. Cons. Republican. Presbyterian. Clubs: Internat. (Chgo.); Minn. Alumni (Mpls.); Minnetonka Country, Belle Aire Yacht (Excelsior, Minn.), Jefferson, Pendennis (Louisville). Home: 15220 Highland Pl Minnetonka MN 55345

OWENS, JO ANN, small business owner; b. Las Vegas, N.Mex., Mar. 15, 1937; d. Earl and Elsie Gertrude (Lander) Gibbs; m. Jay Robert Owens,

June 7, 1958 (div.); children: Judith Jo, James Earl. MBA, U. Denver, 1962. Owner Help Unique, Ltd., Deerfield, Ill., 1978—; div. mgr. Help Unique, Deerfield, 1985—; owner Creative Bus. Dynamics, Inc., 1987—; cons. tng. and devel., Northbrook, Ill., 1983—. Mem. bus. adv. council state rep. Grace Mary Stern, 1985. Mem. Nat. Assn. Temporary Services (bd. dirs. 1980—, pres. 1985), Women in Mgmt. (bd. dirs. 1980), Northbrook C. of C. and Industry (chmn. bd. dirs. 1985). Home: 2931 White Pine Dr Northbrook IL 60062 Office: Creative Bus Dynamics 130 N Waukegan Rd Deerfield IL 60015

OWENS, LEWIS FILLMORE, sports administrator, consultant, park planner; b. Lexington, Ky., Nov. 10, 1949; s. Fred Lewis and Helen Lorain (Sharpe) O.; m. Linda Sue Gress, Dec. 23, 1969; children—Forrest, Joy. B.S., Milligan Coll. (Tenn.), 1971; M.S., U. Ky., 1976. Lic. real estate agt.; lic. flight instr. Phys. dir. YMCA, Frankfort, Ky., 1971-72; tchr., coach Frankfort High Sch. (Ky.), 1972-73; coach, grad. asst. U. Ky., 1973-74; supt. E. P. Sawyer State Park, Louisville, Ky., 1974-80; nat. adminstr. AAU/U.S.A. Junior Olympic Program, 1980-85; exec. dir. AAU, 1985-86; founder, pres., chief exec. officer U.S. Sports & Fitness Assn., Indpls., 1986—; cons.; park planner; instr. for sports adminstrn. Mem. Nat. Parks and Recreation Soc., Nat. Council of Youth Sports Dirs., AAU (pres. Ky. Assn. 1980). Mem. Christian Ch. Contbr. articles to profl. jours.

OWENS, RICHARD GEORGE, mental health administrator; b. Clinton, Iowa, June 1, 1946; s. Murray Riley and Margaret McBain (Owens) O.; B.A., Hope Coll., 1968, tchr. cert., 1970; M.A., Mich. State U., 1979, postgrad., 1979; m. Susan Elizabeth Sentman, June 15, 1968; 1 son, Joshua Morgan. Designer, draftsman Stone Container Corp., Chgo., 1968-69; chmn. art dept. Covert (Mich.) public schs., 1970-73; staff writer, art cons. United Educators, Inc., Lake Bluff, Ill., 1972-74; client supr. work activity center Allegan County Com. Mental Health Services, Allegan, Mich., 1974-75, supr. sheltered workshop, 1975-76; prodn. supr. Celebration Candle, Hart, Mich., 1976-77; direct care worker Alternative Services, Inc., Livonia, Mich., 1978-79, home mgr., 1979-80, Lansing area adminstr., 1980-84, tng. dir., 1984—, chmn. ad hoc com. on staff tng. and devel., 1981—; bd. dirs. Life Ctr., Inc., 1984—, Human Potential, Inc.; instr. adult edn. Pres., Saugatuck Renaissance Guild, 1974-75. Mem. Assn. Supervision and Curriculum Devel., State Wide Care Assn., East Lansing Arts Workshop. Presbyterian. Author: Ceramics As A Career, 1973; Kohoutek and the Queen, 1974. Home: 16400 Upton Rd #246 East Lansing MI 48823 Office: 1606 Greencrest St East Lansing MI 48823

OWENS, RICHARD J., lawyer, television producer; b. Chgo.. BA, DePaul U., 1968, JD, 1971. Bar: Ill. 1971, U.S. Dist. Ct. (no. dist.) Ill. 1971, U.S. Ct. Appeals (7th cir.) 1972, U.S. Supreme Ct. 1979. Ptnr. Herbert & Owens, Chgo., 1971—, pub., 1980—; TV producer Polonia Today, Chgo., 1981—, radio producer, 1983—; v.p., gen. mgr. Ethnic TV Corp., Chgo., 1986—; producer, cons. Polit. Candidates, Chgo., 1981—; advt. cons., Chgo., 1980—. assoc. editor Polonia Today News Mag., 1980—. V.P. Copernicus Found., Chgo., 1984—, bd. dirs., gen. counsel. Recipient Am. Jurisprudence award Am. Jurisprudence Soc., 1971. Mem. ABA, Chgo. Bar Assn., Ill. State Bar Assn., Advocates Soc. (pres. 1984-85). Avocations: astronomy, sci. Office: Polonia Today/ETC 5944 N Milwaukee Ave Chicago IL 60646

OWENS, RUTH ANN, hotel clerk and auditor; b. West Frankfort, Ill., Oct. 2, 1943; d. Oscar Dean and Mary Belle (Dorris) West; m. William Kelly Owens, Sept. 4, 1964; children—William Joseph, John Dean. Office sec. Gibbs Inc. Co., Benton, Ill., 1961-64, Pekin Ins. Co., Ill., 1965-66, Valu Fair Dept. Store, Oceanside, Calif., 1969-71; auditor, hostess, desk clk. Holiday Inn, Benton, 1968-69, 71-73; desk clk. Super 8 Motel, Mt. Vernon, Ill., 1985—. Pres. Sesser Woman's Club, Ill., 1977-78, founder crime prevention program; den mother Boy Scouts Am., 1976-77, 80; former pres. Benton Woman's Club; treas. Franklin County Woman's Club, Ill.; apptd. mem. Benton Youth Bd., 1980—; mem. Rep. Nat. Com.; tchr. Sunday Sch., past pres. Women's Missionary program North Benton Bapt. Ch. Mem. Benton Garden Club (past pres.), Beta Sigma Phi (new chpt. sponsor, numerous offices, Girl of Yr. 1977, 82, 84, Sorority Sweetheart 1983). Avocations: flower gardening; baking. Home: 1201 E Anna St Benton IL 62812

OWENS, SHERRY M., advertising executive; b. Chgo., Feb. 22, 1951; d. Harry J. Owens and Mary M. (Kaskovich) Ensign. BA in Communication Arts, Loyola U., Chgo. Salesman retail advt. Chgo.-Sun Times, 1973-75, Chgo. Daily News, 1973-75; mgr. area sales, dir. credit services Dunn & Broadstreet, Chgo., 1975-76, Midwest sales mgr. credit clearing house div., 1979-80; mgr. area sales, dir. credit services Dunn & Broadstreet, Albuquerque, 1976-78, Dallas, 1978-79; account mgr. ad sales WLS-AM & FM, Chgo., 1980-82; dir. network advt. sales Music TV Networks, Chgo., 1982—. Mem. Broadcast Advt. Club of Chgo., Women in Cable. Serbian Orthodox. Avocations: pop and jazz music, travel, southwestern and modern art collector, interior design. Home: 2650 Lakeview Apt 2608 Chicago IL 60614 Office: Music TV Networks Inc 303 E Wacker Suite 428 Chicago IL 60601

OWENS, WALTER LEE, gynecologist; b. Lawrence County, Ind., Feb. 4, 1926; s. Obediah and Edna (Butler) O.; m. Charmain Thompson, June 22, 1947; children: Katherine Owens Whealton, Richard, Caroline Owens Werson, Judith. AB in Zoology, Ind. U., Bloomington, 1944; MD, Ind. U., Indpls., 1947. Diplomate Am. Bd. Ob-gyn. Chief ob-gyn Miners Meml. Hosp., Whitesburg, Ky., 1956-61; staff Dakota Clinic, Fargo, N.D., 1961-65, Bloomington Ob-Gyn Inc., 1965—. Served to capt. USAF, 1954-56. Fellow Am. Coll. Ob-Gyn.; mem. Am. Fertility Soc. Democrat. Unitarian. Avocations: woodworking, forestry. Office: Bloomington Ob-Gyn Inc 421 W 1st St Bloomington IN 47401

OWNBY, PAUL DARRELL, ceramic engineering educator; b. Salt Lake City, Nov. 9, 1935; s. Paul William and Isabel Hope (Pearson) O.; B.S., U. Utah, 1961; M.S. (Kaiser Aluminum & Chem. Co. fellow), Mo. Sch. Mines and Metallurgy, 1962; Ph.D. (Kennecott Copper fellow), Ohio State U., 1967; m. Nina Rose Mugleston, Aug. 31, 1961; children—Melissa, Heather, Kirsten, Shannon, Paul William, Evan Darrell, Martha. Research ceramist Battelle Meml. Inst., Columbus, Ohio, 1963-68; asst. prof. U. Mo., Rolla, 1968, assoc. prof., 1969-74, prof. ceramic engring., 1974—; chmn., chief exec. officer MRD Corp., 1984—; vis. scientist Max Planck Institut fur Werkstoff Wissenschaften, Stuttgart, Germany, 1974-75, 79; dir. Rinco, Inc., Rolla, Mo., 1972-77; cons. Battelle Meml. Inst., Columbus, 1968-70, Dynasil Corp. Am., 1969-74, 79-82, Eagle Picher Industries, Inc., 1968—, McDonnell Douglas Astronautics Co., 1974-76, Monsanto Co., 1979—, A.P. Green Refractories Co., 1979-80. Neighborhood commr. Central Ohio dist. Boy Scouts Am., 1966-67, instl. rep.. 1970, 73-74, troop com., 1961-62, 70-74, chmn., 1973, instl. head, 1979-83. Battelle Meml. Inst. fellow, 1973; recipient ASTM and ASM Hot Isostatic Pressing Hist. Landmark award Battelle Meml. Inst., 1985. Mem. Am. Ceramic Soc., Materials Research Soc., Ceramic Edn. Council, Keramos (outstanding Tchr. award 1985), Sigma Xi. Republican. Mem. Ch. Jesus Christ of Latter-day Saints. Inventor in field. Home: 8 Burgher Dr Rolla MO 65401 Office: U Mo Rolla MO 65401

OXLEY, MICHAEL GARVER, congressman; b. Findlay, Ohio, Feb. 11, 1944; s. George Garver and Marilyn Maxine (Wolfe) O.; m. Patricia Ann Pluguez, Nov. 27, 1971; 1 child, Michael Chadd. BA, Miami U., Oxford, Ohio, 1966; JD, Ohio State U., 1969. Former agt. FBI, 1969-71; mem. Ohio Ho. of Reps., 1973-81, 97-100th Congresses, 1981—; mem. energy and commerce com., select com. on narcotics abuse and control. Mem. ABA, Ohio Bar Assn., Findlay Bar Assn., Soc. Former Spl. Agts. FBI, Ohio Farm Bur., Sigma Chi, Omicron Delta Kappa. Lodges: Rotary, Elks. Office: 1131 Longworth House Office Bldg Washington DC 20515

OYLER, ROBERT LEON, personnel services exec.; b. Jackson, Miss., Feb. 17, 1944; s. John G. and Sara Catherine (Beckley) O.; B.A., Butler U., 1966; M.S., U. Wis., 1968; children—Kelly, Stephanie. Exec. dir. Wis. Council on Developmental Disabilities, 1969-73; pres., gen. mgr. Life Style Services, Inc., Madison, Wis., 1973—, chmn. bd. Mem. Adminstrv. Mgmt. Soc. (bd. dirs.), Am. Soc. Personnel Adminstrs., Nat. Assn. Personnel Cons., Wis. Assn. Personnel Cons., Inter-City Personnel Cons., Madison C. of C., Phi Eta Sigma, Sigma Chi. Club: Madison. Contbr. article to Am. Jour. Health. Home: W14202 Selwood Dr Rt 1 Lodi WI 53555 Office: 415 W Main Madison WI 53713

OZKAN, GUNER, physician, surgeon; b. Izmir, Turkey, Feb. 18, 1945; came to U.S., 1975; s. Ismail and Raziye (Tekin) O.; m. Gunay Karasu, Aug. 14, 1970; children—Ozgur Ismail, Zeynep Ozlem. M.D., Ege Universitesi, Izmir, 1968; specialist in physiology Ataturk U., Erzurum, Turkey, 1970. Diplomate Am. Bd. Surgery. Intern Washington Hosp. Ctr., 1975-76, resident, 1976-80; asst. prof. Ataturk U., 1968-73; staff surgeon VA Med. Ctr., Grand Island, Nebr., 1981—. Research grantee Turkish Sci. and Tech. Found., 1967-70; recipient Achievement award Upjohn Co., 1980. Islam. Avocation: swimming. Home: 1709 S Doreen St Grand Island NE 68801 Office: VA Med Ctr 2201 N Broadwell Grand Island NE 68801

PAANANEN, VICTOR NILES, English educator; b. Ashtabula, Ohio, Jan. 31, 1938; s. Niles Henry and Anni Margaret (Iloranta) P.; m. Donna Mae Jones, Aug. 15, 1964; children: Karl, Neil. AB magna cum laude, Harvard U., 1960; MA, U. Wis., 1964, PhD, 1967. Instr. English Wofford Coll., Spartanburg, S.C., 1962-63; asst. prof. Williams Coll., Williamstown, Mass., 1966-68; asst. prof. Mich. State U., East Lansing, 1968-73, assoc. prof., 1973-82, prof., 1982—, assoc. dean Grad. Sch., 1977-82, chmn. dept. English, 1986—; vis. prof. Roehampton Inst., London, 1982. Author: William Blake, 1977; contbr. articles to profl. and scholarly jours. Univ. fellow U. Wis., 1962, 63-64; Harvard Nat. scholar, 1956-60. Mem. MLA, Assn. Depts. English, Phi Beta Kappa. Episcopalian. Club: Harvard (Cen. Mich.). Home: 152 Orchard St East Lansing MI 48823 Office: Mich State Univ Dept of English Morrill Hall East Lansing MI 48824-1036

PAAU, ALAN SHIUKEE, industrial microbiologist; b. Macau, Dec. 16, 1951; came to U.S., 1971, naturalized, 1985; s. Lokfu and Ping (Li) P.; m. Florence Hau, Aug. 14, 1978. Ph.D., U. Houston, 1978. Teaching coordinator U. Houston, 1974-78; research assoc. U. Wis.-Madison, 1978-79, project scientist, 1979-81; scientist, project leader Cetus Madison Corp., Middleton, Wis., 1982-84; sr. scientist, project mgr. Agracetus Corp., Middleton, 1984—; cons. in field. Recipient Outstanding Grad. Student award, Am. Soc. Plant Physiologists, 1974. Sigma Xi grantee, 1980. Mem. Am. Soc. Microbiology, Am. Soc. Industrial Microbiology, Am. Soc. Plant Physiologists, AAAS, Sigma Xi. Roman Catholic. Contbr. articles to profl. jours. Patentee. Home: 5405 Jonquil Ct Middleton WI 53562 Office: 8520 University Green Middleton WI 53562

PACE, JOHN WALKER, academic administrator; b. Massena, Iowa, Sept. 17, 1925; s. John Harrison and Verdie Irene (Walker) P.; m. Eugenia Earle Pratt, June 22, 1947; children: Stephen John, Martha Jean, Thomas Ralph. BEd, Drake U., 1950; MA in High Edn. Adminstrn., U. Minn., 1955. Tchr. Shenandoah (Iowa) Pub. Sch., 1950-53; asst. prin. Oskaloosa (Iowa) Pub. Sch., 1953-57; asst. registrar Iowa State U., Ames, 1957-61, dir. Office of Space and Schedules, 1961—; presenter Nat. Workshop on Facilities Planning and Mgmt., Indpls., 1985, Nat. Assn. Coll. and Univ. Bus. Officers, 1983, Nat. Assn. Collegiate Registrars and Admission Officers, 1979. Pres. adv. bd. YMCA, Ames, 1983. Served with USN, 1943-46, PTO, Korea. Mem. Higher Edn. Facilities Mgmt. Assn. (participant 1961—, v.p. 1969—), Big Eight Facilities Planning and Mgmt. Assn., Soc. Coll. and Univ. Planners (charter). Democrat. Methodist. Lodge: Kiwanis (bd. dirs. Ames club 1980-83). Avocations: fishing, golfing, jogging, furniture restoration, flora culture. Office: Iowa State U Sci and Tech 207 Beardshear Ames IA 50011

PACE, PAUL JOSEPH, public health administrator; b. Milw., Feb. 2, 1927; s. Paul Roman and Rose Angeline (Robakowski) P.; m. Alma Martha Bartholomew, Aug. 30, 1950; children—Paul Bartholomew, Peter Adam. A.B., Ripon Coll., 1950; postgrad. Iowa State U., 1950-51; U. Wis., Milw., 1955, Marquette U. Med. Sch., 1956-61; M.S., Marquette U., 1963, postgrad., 1963-67. Specialist in pub. health Nat. Registry of Microbiology. Expediter, Square D Co., Milw., 1951-52; bacteriological lab. technologist Milw. Health Dept., 1952-54, bacteriologist I, 1954-58, bacteriologist II, 1958-64, bacteriologist III, asst. chief bacteriologist, 1964-67, bacteriologist V, chief bacteriologist, 1967-82, adminstr. bur. community health services, 1982—; asst. clin. prof. Dept. Preventive Medicine Med. Coll. Wis., Milw., 1986—; cons. Treas., dir. Norman B. Barr Camp, Inc., Williams Bay, Wis. Served with USNR, 1945-46; PTO. Mem. Am. Pub. Health Assn., Wis. Pub. Health Assn., AAAS, Wis. Acad. Arts Scis. and Letters, Am. Soc. for Microbiology, Wis. Assn. Milk and Food Sanitarians (Sanitarian of Yr. 1975), Internat. Assn. Mil, Food and Environ. Sanitarians (Disting. Service award 1981), Soc. Applied Bacteriology, Inst. Food Technologists, Conf. State and Territorial Pub. Health Lab. Dirs., Sigma Xi. Contbr. articles to profl. jours. Home: 5140 S 20th St Milwaukee WI 53221 Office: 841 N Broadway Milwaukee WI 53202

PACE, RICHARD YOST, architect; b. Cleve., June 11, 1956; s. Stanley Carter and Elaine (Cutchell) P. BS in Architecture, U. Mich., 1979. Registered architect, Ohio. Project architect van Dijk, Johnson & Ptnrs., Cleve., 1979—. Mem. University Circle Planning Com., 1982—. Mem. AIA, Architects Soc. Ohio, Nat. Trust Hist. Preservation, Cleve. Warehouse Dist. Devel. Corp. Club: The Country Club (Pepper Pike, Ohio). Avocations: squash, paddle tennis, golf. Home: 1727 E 116th Pl Cleveland OH 44106 Office: van Dijk Johnson & Ptnrs One Erieview Plaza Cleveland OH 44114

PACE, STANLEY CARTER, aeronautical engineer; b. Waterview, Ky., Sept. 14, 1921; s. Stanley Dan and Pearl Eagle (Carter) P.; m. Elaine Marilyn Cutchall, Aug. 21, 1945; children: Stanley Dan, Lawrence Timothy, Richard Yost. Student, U. Ky., 1939-40; B.S., U.S. Mil. Acad., 1943; M.S. in Aero. Engring., Calif. Inst. Tech., 1949. Commd. 2d lt. USAAF, 1943, advanced through grades to col., 1953; pilot, flight leader B-24 Group, 15th Air Force 1943-44; chief power plant br., procurement div. Hdqrs. Air Materiel Command Wright-Patterson AFB, Ohio, 1945-48; assignments, procurement div. Hdqrs. Air Materiel Command 1949-53, dep. chief prodn. Hdqrs. Air Materiel Command, 1952-53, resigned, 1954; with TRW, Inc., Cleve., 1954-85; successively sales mgr., asst. mgr., mgr. West Coast plant TRW, Inc.; mgr. jet div. Tapco plant, Cleve.; asst. mgr. Tapco group, 1954-58, v.p., gen. mgr., 1958-65, exec. v.p. co., 1965-77, pres., 1977-85, vice chmn., 1985, dir., 1965-85; vice chmn., dir. Gen. Dynamics Corp., St Louis, 1985; chmn., chief exec. officer Gen. Dynamics Corp., 1985—, also bd. dirs.; dir. Consol. Natural Gas Co. Head United Way drive, Cleve., 1984; former council commr., pres. Great Cleve. Council Boy Scouts Am.; former trustee Nat. Jr. Achievement, Denison U., Judson Park; trustee Washington U. Decorated Air medal with oak leaf clusters. Mem. AIAA, Soc. Automotive Engrs., Delta Tau Delta. Clubs: Union, Pepper Pike, Eldorado, Rolling Rock, Log Cabin, St. Louis, St. Louis Country. Home: 2 Chatfield Rd Saint Louis MO 63141 Office: Gen Dynamics Corp Pierre Laclede Ctr Saint Louis MO 63105

PACKARD, PETER WINCHESTER, social worker; b. Cambridge, Mass., Dec. 7, 1932; s. Frederick Clifton Jr. and Alice (Mansur) P.; m. Elizabeth Knapp, Aug. 21, 1954; children: Alexandra, Jonathan, Christopher, Lisa, Steven, Josephine. BA, Dartmouth U., 1955; MSW, Kans. U., 1965. Cert. social worker. Clin. social worker Topeka (Kans.) State Hosp., 1965-69, Colmery O'Neil VA Med. Ctr., Topeka, 1969—; cons. community youth homes, Topeka, 1970-72. Area rep. Am. Field Service, N.Y.C., 1979—; pres. bd. dirs. Internat. Ctr. of Topeka, 1985, 86. Served to capt. USAF, 1956-63. Mem. Nat. Assn. Social Workers, Kans. Soc. Clin. Social Workers (sec. 1986). Democrat. Congregationalist. Avocations: tennis, swimming, skiing. Home: 3001 Sowers Ct Topeka KS 66604 Office: Colmery O'Neil VA Med Ctr 2200 Gage Blvd Topeka KS 66622

PACTON, GREGORY WILLIAM, manufacturing executive; b. Chgo., Apr. 27, 1952; s. Gregory C. and Therese L. (Pacholski) P.; m. Kathleen A. Maciontek, Aug. 7, 1971; children: Tracy M., Christen M., Adam M. BS, DePaul U., 1978, MBA, 1980. Dir. engr. A.B. Dick Co., Chgo., 1971-84; v.p., gen. mgr. Panduit Corp., Romeoville, Ill., 1984-86; instr. DePaul U., Chgo., 1981-83. Contbr. articles to profl. jours. Mem. citizen's adv. council U46 Sch. Bd., Elgin, Ill., 1982-86. Ill. State scholar, 1970. Mem. Am. Soc. Mech. Engrs., Am. Prodn. and Inventory Control Soc., Tooling and Mfg. Assn. (vice chmn.). Avocations: photography, golf, running. Home: 1361 Hassell Dr Hoffman Estates IL 60195

PAC-URAR, IAN GEORGE, educator; b. Montreal, Quebec, Can., May 3, 1953; s. George Baitan and Sylvia (Morosan) P-U; m. Mary Lynn Streza, May 10, 1980. BA, U. Windsor, Can., 1973; BE, U. Windsor, 1974; MEd, Kent State U., 1983. Cert. tchr., Ontario, Can., Ohio; cert. prin., Ohio. Mgr. Sta. CSRW-Am Radio, Windsor, 1972-73; music specialist Essex (Ont.) County Schs., 1974-79; tchr. Richards Inst. Music Edn. and Research, Chatham, Ont., 1976-80, Canton (Ohio) Country Day Schs., 1980-84; fgn. language specialist Akron (Ohio) Pub. Schs., 1984-86; pres. PMI Systems, Canton, 1986—; cons. Richards Inst., Portola Valley, Calif., 1976-86. Contbr. articles to profl. jours. Mem. Can. Orgn. Devel. and Peace, Windsor, 1976-80; pres. Stark County Council Eastern Orthodox Chs., Canton. Ohio, 1982-83; bd. dirs. Windsor Young Artists, 1972-74, Multicultural Council Windsor, 1973-74. Mem. Assn. Supervision Curriculum Devel., Phi Delta Kappa, Kappa Delta Pi. Office: PMI Systems 1524 27th St NW Canton OH 44709

PACYNIAK, THADDEUS ADAM, architect, consultant; b. Loches, France, May 3, 1946; s. Jan and Kathy (Wowczanczyn) P.; m. Teresa Jadwiga Grygo, Apr. 24, 1971. B.Arch., U. Ill.-Chgo., 1968; student Ecole Speciale D'Architecture, Paris, 1969. Registered architect, Ill., Wis., Mo. Sr. architect Skidmore, Owings & Merrill, 1969-76; corp. architect Walgreen Drug Co., 1976-78; chief architect Anvan Corp., 1978-80; owner, operator Pacyniak & Assocs., Libertyville, Ill., 1980-85 . Mem. appearance com. Village of Libertyville., Chgo. Intercollegiate Council, 1973. Served with U.S. Army, 1975. Mem. AIA (dir. Northeast Ill. chpt.), Nat. Council Archtl. Registration Bds., Chgo. Soc. Roman Catholic.

PADBERG, HELEN SWAN, violinist; b. Shawnee, Okla., May 3, 1919; d. Frank P. and Birdie B. (Rudell) Swan; A.A., Stephens Coll., 1938; Mus.B., U. Okla., 1940; Mus.M., Northwestern U., 1941; student Jacques Gordon; m. Frank Padberg, Feb. 6, 1943; children—Frank, Kristen. Solo performances and concerts, 1932—; mem. faculty string quartet and symphony soloist Stephens Coll., 1937-38; violinist Oklahoma City Symphony Summer Concerts, 1940; soloist Northwestern U. Symphony, 1941; USO performer, 1941-44; violinist Nat. Orchestral Assn. and Am. Youth Orch., N.Y.C., 1944-46; tchr. strings Public Schs. Maywood (Ill.), 1946-47; asst. concertmaster West Suburban Symphony, Chgo., 1947-48; mem. Chgo. Women's Symphony, Chgo. Civic Orch. and chamber music groups, 1947-51; violinist Ark. String Trio, 1952-58; concertmaster Ark. Symphony and Little Rock Philharmonic, 1953-57, Marjorie Lawrence TV Series, Ark., 1953-54; pvt. tchr. violin, Little Rock, 1953-66; accompanist and performer on piano, harp. Pres., Ark. Med. Soc. Aux., 1962-63, historian, 1963—; co-founder Little Rock Chamber Music Soc., 1954; pres. bd. dirs. Vis. Nurse Assn. of Pulaski County, Ark., 1967-69. Mem. Am. Harp Soc., Chgo. Harp Soc. (sec. 1979-84), Am. Fedn. Musicians, Am. Opera Soc. of Chgo. (v.p. and program chmn. 1981-82, pres. 1984-87), Pi Kappa Lambda, Mu Phi Epsilon, Pi Beta Phi (pres. Little Rock Alumnae Club). Presbyterian. Clubs: Aesthetic (pres. Little Rock); Womens' Athletic of Chgo. Home: 175 E Delaware Pl Chicago IL 60611

PADDOCK, BRUCE G., pharmaceutical company executive; b. Duluth, Minn., Sept. 22, 1947; s. George A. and Pearl J. (Gressman) P. BS in Pharmacy, U. Minn., 1970, PharmD, 1972. Prodn. mgr. C.R. Canfield Co., Mpls., 1973-77; pres. Paddock Labs, Mpls., 1977—. Mem. Am. Pharm. Assn., Am. Soc. Cons. Pharmacists, Nat. Assn. Retail Druggists, Am. Coll. Apothecaries, Am. Soc. Hosp. Pharmacists. Office: Paddock Labs Inc 3101 N Louisana Ave Minneapolis MN 55427

PADEN, BETTY BURNS, educator; b. Evanston, Ill., July 9, 1937; d. Joseph Ferdinand and Estelle (Taggart) Burns; m. Alvin Robert Paden, Aug. 18, 1962; children—Renee Lynn, Tina Jo. A.A., Kendall Coll., 1958; B.A., Roosevelt U., 1961, M.A., 1963; Ed.D., Loyola U., Chgo., 1970; J.D., No. Ill. U., 1979. Bar: Ill. 1980. Tchr., Chgo. Pub. Schs., 1961-67; editor, writer Scott Foresman Pub. Co., Glenview, Ill., 1967-68; instr. Loyola U., Chgo., 1968-70; cons., author Addison-Wesley Pub. Co., Scott Foresman Pub. Co., Lyon and Carhahan Pub. Co., Tangley Oaks Pub. Co., Harper Row Pub. Co., 1967-82; cons. Chgo. Bd. Edn., State of Ill., Chgo. Consortium of Colls. and Univs., 1973-82; prof. elem. edn. Northeastern Ill. U., Chgo., 1970—, assoc. chairperson elem. edn. dept., 1972-77; practice law, Evanston, Ill., 1980—. Bd. dirs. Evanston Zoning Bd. Appeals, Evanston Community Devel. Corp. Named Woman of Yr., NAACP, 1983; Kalm scholar, 1957-58; Com. Organized Research, Northeastern Ill. U. grantee, 1974-75; UNI Found. fellow, 1984; UNI Kellogg fellow, 1984; UNI grantee, 1985-86. Mem. Ill. Bar Assn., Chgo. Bar Assn., Am. Bar Assn., Internat. Reading Assn., Assn. Supervision and Curriculum Devel., Assn. Tchr. Educators. Author, editor: More Power and Moving Ahead, Open Highways Series, 1968; What Are They Up To? and What Does It Take?, 1971; What a Week!, Carmen Takes a Bow, Jamila, The Young America Basic Reading Program, 1973; The Birthday Surprise, 1976; The Ruby Pin Mystery, 1976; Truth is Stranger than Fiction, 1981; What is Big? What is Small?, Ann's Surprise, Make a Clown, 1983. Office: 5500 N St Louis Ave Room 3019 Chicago IL 60625

PADEN, CAROLYN EILEEN BELKNAP, dietitian; b. Takoma Park, Md., Dec. 10, 1953; d. Donald Julius and Lydian Allyne (Plyer) Belknap; m. Raymond Louis Paden, Dec. 29, 1985. BS in Home Econs. cum laude, Southern Coll., 1977; MS in Nutrition, Loma Linda (Calif.) U., 1983. Registered dietitian. Dietitic tech. Loma Linda U. Med. Ctr., 1978-82, nutritional support dietitian, 1982-84; clin. dietitian Mercy Meml. Med. Ctr., St. Joseph, Mich., 1984-86, chief clin. dietitian, 1986—; instr. dietetics Andrews U., Berrien Springs, Mich., 1986—; researcher nutritional status of hospitalized patients Mercy Meml. Med. Ctr., St. Joseph, 1986, 87; cons. nutritional support various Berrien County hosps., 1984—. Mem. Am. Dietetic Assn., Am. Soc. Parenteral and Enteral Nutrition. Adventist. Avcoations: hiking, camping, reading, photography, crafts. Home: 8385-1 Centerfield Dr Berrien Springs MI 49103 Office: Mercy Meml Med Ctr 1234 Napier Ave Saint Joseph MI 49085

PADEN, ROBERT CHARLES, clinical psychologist; b. Colby, Kans., May 4, 1942; s. Homer Ernest and Harriet Eloise (McCafferty) P.; m. Ann H. Osborne, June 14, 1964 (div. Feb. 1971); m. Carolyn Lee Erwin, July 29, 1972; children: Matthew Lee, Lezlie Diane. BA, Wichita (Kans.) State U., 1967, MA, 1973; PhD, U. Ill., 1983. Clin. psychologist Jacksonville (Ill.) State Hosp., 1969-71; sr. staff mem. NIMH Psychosocial Rehab. Research Project, Decatur, Ill., 1971-73; program evaluator Day Probation/Edn. Program, Decatur, 1973-74; dir. profl. services Meyer Mental Health Ctr., Decatur, 1974-84; asst. prof. psychology Millikin U., Decatur, 1984, Richland Community Coll., Decatur, 1984-85; chief clin. psychologist Marshall (Mo.) Habilitation Ctr., 1985—; cons. psychometry pub. schs., Marshall, 1985—. Editorial cons. Jour. Cons./Clin. Psychology, 1985—; contbr. articles to profl. jours. Mem. Am. Psychol. Assn., Nat. Assn. Dually-Diagnosed, U. Ill. Alumni Assn. Unitarian. Home: 728 Leawood Dr Marshall MO 65340 Office: Marshall Habilitation Ctr E Slater Ave Marshall MO 65340

PADO, MICHAEL JOSEPH, architect; b. Gary, Ind., Apr. 14, 1933; s. Michael Francis and Mary Ann (Feryo) P.; m. Alice Adam, Feb. 26, 1970. BArch, Ill. Inst. Tech., 1956. Registered architect, Ill., Ind. Sr. architect Skidmore, Owings & Merrill, Chgo., 1956-57, project architect, 1960-79; facilities architect USAF, Little Rock, Ark. and Stevenville, Nfld., 1957-60; pres. Michael J. Pado, AIA, Architect, Ltd., Chgo., 1979—; cons. Officer's Club Bd., Little Rock, 1957-59. Contbr. participant: First 100 Years of Chicago Architecture, 1976; contbr. articles to profl. jours. Recipient Gold Medal, Met. Chgo. Masonry Council, 1980, Award of Excellence, Post-Tensioning Inst., 1984. Mem. AIA, Nat. Council Archtl. Registration Bds. Clubs: Arts, East Bank (Chgo.); Oak Park (Ill.) Tennis. Avocations: photography, skiing, tennis. Home: 860 N Lake Shore Dr Chicago IL 60611 Office: 161 E Erie St Chicago IL 60611

PADULA, LIBORIO JOSEPH, psychologist, educator; b. Detroit, Feb. 3, 1956; s. Felice and Catherine (Angelo) P. BA, U. Mich., Dearborn, 1978; MA, Northwestern U., 1979; postgrad., Merrill-Palmer Inst., 1979-80, U. Mich., 1981—. Psychotherapist Merrill-Palmer Inst., Detroit, 1979-80; staff psychologist U. Mich., Dearborn, 1979-83; instr. psychology Schoolcraft Coll., Livonia, Mich., 1980-85; psychologist Pheasant Ridge Ctr. Hosp., Kalamazoo, Mich., 1983—; lectr. U. Mich. Med. Sch., Ann Arbor, 1984; mem. U. Mich. Council on Sexuality and Health Care; cons. in field, Livonia, 1980—. Producer (video) A Perspective From a Gay Transvestite: A Guest Visiting a College Classroom, 1983. Instr. safety classes Am. Nat. Red Cross, Detroit. Mem. Am. Assn. Sex Educators, Counselors and Therapists (cert. sex therapist), Mich. Assn. profl. Psychologists (pub. health rep. 1985-87). U. Mich. Avocations: swimming, photography, conversation. Home: 16912 Yorkshire Dr Livonia MI 48154 Office: Pheasant Ridge Ctr Hosp 1312 Oakland Dr Kalamazoo MI 49008

PAESSLER, JOHN CLIFTON, accountant; b. Memphis, Oct. 1, 1956; s. Charles Francis and Martha Jane (Park) P.; m. Karen Dickerson, Aug. 14, 1976; children: Brian Clifford, Richard Craig. BBA, Memphis State U., 1977. CPA, Tenn. Sr. acct. Ernst & Whinney, Memphis, 1977-80; audit supr. Holiday Inns, Inc., Memphis, 1980-81; dir. audit Nat. Bank Commerce, Memphis, 1981-82; exec. v.p., chief fin. officer, sec.-treas. Commerce McGehee Mortgage, Inc., Memphis, 1982-85; chief fin. officer Catalyst Thermal Energy Corp., St. Louis, 1985—. Mem. Am. Inst. CPA's, Internat. Dist. Heating and Cooling Assn. Republican. Methodist. Avocations: bass fishing, design and constrn. of stained glass objects, tennis. Home: 431 Bluebird Ln Troy IL 62294 Office: Catalyst Thermal Energy Corp #1 Ashley Saint Louis MO 60000

PAGANO, J. ANTHONY, retail department store executive; b. Cin., Dec. 14, 1944; s. John M. and Lucy C. (Rizzo) P.; m. Mary Jane Stuntebeck, Nov. 23, 1967; children: John Christopher, Debra Lynn, Kimberly Ann. BBA in Mktg., U. Cin., 1966. Various mgr. positions Shillitos, Cin., 1966-72, store supt. Beechmont, 1972-73, store supt. Western Woods, 1973-75; asst. store mgr. Lexington (Ky.) Shillitos, 1976-83; operating v.p. selling services Shillitos, Cin., 1983-84; div. v.p. maintenance Lazarus, Cin., 1984—; bd. dirs. Shillito Rikes Credit Union. Republican. Roman Catholic. Avocations: sports. Home: 7012 Pickway Dr Cincinnati OH 45202 Office: Lazarus Dept Stores 7th and Race Sts Cincinnati OH 45202

PAGE, DAVID KEITH, lawyer, supermarket executive; b. Detroit, Aug. 23, 1933; s. Milton Walter and Hilda (Schoenfeld) P.; m. Andrea Burdick, July 6, 1954; children: Mark Daniel, Jason William, Sarah Leslie. A.B. summa cum laude, Dartmouth, 1955; LL.B. magna cum laude (editor law rev. 1958), Harvard, 1958; Fulbright scholar, London (Eng.) Sch. Econs., 1959. Bar: Mich. 1959. Ptnr. Honigman, Miller, Schwartz & Cohn, Detroit, 1959—; sec. Allied Supermarkets, Detroit, 1963-85; chmn., chief exec. officer Allied Supermarkets, 1985—, also dir. Chmn. atty's div. Detroit Allied Jewish campaign; pres., bd. dirs. Detroit Men's Ort chpt.; trustee, chmn. audit com., mem. exec. com. Children's Hosp. Mich., 1973—, chmn. bd., 1982—; Detroit Area council Boy Scouts Am., 1972—; trustee Marygrove Coll., 1977-83, Detroit Med. Ctr., 1982—; bd. govs. Detroit Jewish Welfare Fedn., 1977—, v.p., 1983—. Mem. Am., Detroit bar assns., State Bar Mich., Phi Beta Kappa. Jewish religion (trustee, pres. temple 1976-77). Clubs: Detroit, Knollwood Country. Home: 2661 Indian Mound S Birmingham MI 48010 Office: First Nat Bldg Detroit MI 48226

PAGE, DONALD ALAN, engineer, financial analyst; b. Angola, Ind., Oct. 1, 1948; s. Robert Spear and Phyllis Ray (Andrews) P.; m. Jeanette Marie Southall, Apr. 18, 1969 (div. Mar. 1975); m. Frances Therese Wilwohl, June 7, 1975; children: Gregory Phillip, Karen Suzanne. BSEE, Gannon U., 1977. Technician Digital Equipment Corp., Maynard, Mass., 1969-72; jr. engr. Elgin Electronics Co., Waterford, Pa., 1976-77; engr. Essex Group Machinery, Ft. Wayne, Ind., 1977-80; sr. engr. aerospace dept. ITT, Ft. Wayne, 1980—. Republican. Presbyterian. Lodge: Masons. Avocation: audiophile. Home: 5333 Wapiti Dr Fort Wayne IN 46804 Office: ITT Aerospace Dept 3700 E Pontiac St Fort Wayne IN 46803

PAGE, DOZZIE LYONS, educator; b. Tiptonville, Tenn., Apr. 13, 1921; d. Lessie LeRoy and Carrie (Oldham) Lyons; B.S.Ed., Chgo. Tchrs. Coll., 1968; M.S.Ed., Chgo. State U., 1976; M.A. in Bus. Edn., Govs. State U., 1979; children—Rita, Gerald. Cashier receptionist Unity Mut. Life Ins. Co., Chgo., 1939-47; sec. United Transport Service Employees Union, Chgo., 1947-51; sec. to dir. YMCA West Side, Chgo., 1951-53; sec., office mgr. Joint Council Dining Car Employees AFL CIO, Chgo., 1957-59; sr. stenographer Chgo. Police Dept., 1962-65; tchr. office practice Manpower Devel. Tng. Act, Chgo. Bd. Edn., 1965-67; tchr., coordinator distributive edn. Dunbar Vocat. High Sch., Chgo., 1968—. Mem. Office Occupations Club, Distributive Edn. Assn., Chgo. Urban League, Chgo. Bus. Edn. Assn. (exec. bd. 1983—), Ill., Am. personnel and guidance assns., Am. Vocat. Assn., Nat., Ill. bus. edn. assns., Chgo. State U. Alumni Assn., Governor's State U. Alumni Assn., Phi Delta Kappa. Home: 6127 Justine St Chicago IL 60636 Office: 3000 S King Dr Chicago IL 60616

PAGE, GARY SCOTT, oral surgeon; b. Indpls., Nov. 25, 1942; s. Burton Lawrence and Ida Jane (Atkinson) P.; m. Lynne Elaine Bugher, Apr. 26, 1981. BS in Life Scis., Ind. State U., 1966; DDS, Ind. U., Indpls., 1970; postgrad. maxillo-facial studies, U. Zurich, Switzerland, 1972-73; postdoctoral, U. Rochester, N.Y., 1974-76. Intern in oral surgery Marion County Gen. Hosp., Indpls., 1970-71, resident in oral surgery, 1971-72; practice dentistry specializing in oral surgery Indpls., 1976—. Mem. Chgo. Dental Soc., Internat. Assn. Maxillo-Facial Surgery, Internat. Congress Oral Implantologists, Am. Dental Soc. Anesthesiology, Acad. Internat. Med. Studies, Acad. Sports Dentistry, Christian Med. Soc., Amateur Athletics Union, Athletic Congress. Republican. Avocations: running, bicycling, swimming, golf, travel. Office: 1122 Shelby St Indianapolis IN 46203

PAGE, JOHN IRWIN, Bible college president; b. Ft. Scott, Kans., Oct. 2, 1930; s. John Ellis and Ava Leona (Brown) P.; m. Virginia Maxine Witt, Aug. 1, 1951; children—Brenda, Carma, Courtney, Jonathan. B.A., Kans. City Coll. and Bible Sch., 1952; M.S., Pitts. State U., 1955, Ed.S., 1969; Ph.D. Kans. State U., 1987. Pastor Ch. of God (Holiness), Stockton, Mo., 1952-58, Ft. Scott, Kans., 1959-80; prin. Ft. Scott Christian Heights Sch., 1954-80; mgr. Ironquill Estates, Ft. Scott, 1975-80; pres. Kansas City Coll. and Bible Sch., Overland Park, 1980—; v.p. Witt Engring., Inc., ElDorado Springs, Mo., 1968-80, Plainview Farms, Inc., Ft. Scott, 1974—; pres. Bourbon County Police Chaplaincy, Ft. Scott, 1965-80. Pres. Multi-County 4-C, Ft. Scott, 1970; bd. dirs. Human Relations Com., Ft. Scott, 1971; precinct worker Republican Party, Bourbon County, 1963. Named Outstanding Alumnus, Ft. Scott Community Coll., 1980, Hon. Police Col. Bourbon County Police Chaplaincy, 1965. Mem. Phi Delta Kappa (Continuous Service award 1985), Overland Park C. of C. Avocations: hunting, golf, sports. Home: 5301 W 83d St Prairie Village KS 66208 Office: Kansas City Coll and Bible Sch 7401 Metcalf St Overland Park KS 66204

PAGE, LINDA KAY, state official; b. Wadsworth, Ohio, Oct. 4, 1943; s. Frederick Meredith and Martha Irene (Vance) P. Student Franklin U., 1970-75, Sch. Banking, Ohio U., 1976-77; cert. Nat. Personnel Sch., U. Md.-Am. Bankers Assn., 1981; grad. banking program U. Wis.-Madison, 1982-84. Asst. v.p., gen. mgr. Bancohio Corp., Columbus, Ohio, 1975-78, v.p., dist. mgr., 1979-80, v.p., mgr. employee relations, 1980-81, v.p., div. mgr., 1982-83; commr. of banks State of Ohio, Columbus, 1983—; guest speaker, lectr. various banking groups. Bd. dirs. Clark County Mental Health Bd., Springfield, Ohio, 1982-83, Springfield Met. Housing, 1982-83; bd. advisers Orgn. Indsl. Standards, Springfield, 1982-83. Recipient Leadership Columbus award Sta. WTVN and Columbus Leadership Program, 1975, 82, Outstanding Service award Clark County Mental Health Bd., 1983. Mem. Nat. Assn. Bank Women (pres. 1980-81), Bus. and Profl. Women's Club, LWV, Conf. State Bank Suprs. (bd. dirs. 1984-85), dist. chmn. 1984-85), Ohio Bankers Assn. (bd. dirs. 1982-83). Democrat. Lodge: Zonta. Avocations: tennis; animal protection; matchbook collecting. Home: 1330 Erickson Ave Columbus OH 43227 Office: Dept Commerce Div of Banks 2 National Bank Pl Columbus OH 43215

PAGE, RICHARD MORTON, insurance executive; b. Waterbury, Conn., Nov. 28, 1932; s. Joseph John and Mildred (Mocciolo) P.; m. Jane F. O'Hara, Aug. 16, 1958; children: Richard, Catherine, Elizabeth, Sarah. AB, Dartmouth Coll., 1954; JD, Columbia U., 1959. Bar: Conn. Counsel Travelers Life Ins. Co., Hartford, Conn., 1959-68, 2d v.p. exec. dept., 1968-70; exec. v.p., gen. mgr. Fairfield and Ellis, Boston, 1970-74; pres., chief exec. officer Emmett and Chandler, Los Angeles, 1974-78; mng. v.p. Alexander & Alexander, N.Y.C., 1978-80, sr. v.p., regional dir., 1980-81, exec. v.p., 1981-83; chief exec. officer, chmn. bd. Alexander Howden PLC, London, 1983-84; dep. chmn., bd. dirs. Sedgwick Group PLC, London, 1985—; chmn., pres. chief exec. officer, bd. dirs. Fred S. James & Co., Inc., N.Y.C., 1985—; bd. dirs. Sedgwick Tomenson Inc., Toronto, Can. Bd. dirs. YMCA Greater N.Y., 1980-83, 85, Nat. Council Crime & Delinquency, Los Angeles, 1981-83. Served to 1st lt. U.S. Army, 1954-56. Named One of Outstanding Young Men Am., Jaycees, 1965. Mem. Dartmouth Alumni Council (Dartmouth alumni award, 1981). Republican. Roman Catholic. Clubs: Darien Country, Tokeneke (Darien), Union League (N.Y.). Avocations: mountain climbing, sailing, golf. Office: Fred James & Co Inc 230 W Monroe St Chicago IL 60606

PAGE, ROBERT EUGENE, publisher; b. Lincoln, Ill., Dec. 4, 1935; s. Garnet S. and Mildred (Congdon) P.; children—Douglas Robert, Stephen William; m. Nancy Kelly Merrill, June 7, 1984; stepchildren—Christina, Amanda. B.A., Ill. Wesleyan U., 1958, LL.D., 1986. Vice pres., gen. mgr. UPI, N.Y.C., 1960-80; gen. mgr. San Antonio Express, 1981-82; pres., pub. Boston Herald, 1982-84; pres., chief exec. officer Sun Times Co., Chgo., 1984—; pres., pub. Chgo. Sun-Times; pres. Williams Press, Chicago Heights, Ill.; dir. Peterson Outdoor Advt. Agy., Orlando, Fla. Prin. Chgo. United, Childrens Meml. Hosp.; bd. dirs. Chgo. Assn. Commerce and Industry, Chgo. Central Area Com., Lyric Opera, Chgo.; trustee Ill. Wesleyan U., Mundelein Coll. Named Outstanding Alumnus, Ill. Wesleyan U., 1979, Significant Sig, Sigma Chi, 1981. Mem. Chgo. Newspaper Pubs. Assn. (pres. 1984-85), Sigma Delta Chi. Clubs: Union League (N.Y.U.); Chgo. Home: 1501 N State Pkwy Chicago IL 60610 Office: Chgo Sun-Times 401 N Wabash Room 356 Chicago IL 60611

PAGE, ROY WILLIAM, finance executive; b. Barberton, Ohio, Feb. 6, 1947; s. Roy Ellicot and Idella Louise (Lewis) P.; m. Susan Carolyn Ulichney, June 17, 1972; 1 child, Elizabeth Susan. BS in Acctg., U. Akron, 1070; MS in Mgmt., Purdue U., 1976. Supr. gen acctg. Hewlett-Packard Co., Avondale, Pa., 1979-80; mgr. cost acctg. Grimes div. Midland Ross Corp., Urbana, Ohio, 1980-84, asst. controller Grimes div., 1984-85, dir. fin. and data processing Grimes div., 1986-87; v.p. fin. Gosiger, Inc., Urbana, 1987—; controller Janitrol div. Midland Ross Corp., Columbus, Ohio, 1985-86; instr. Wittenberg U., Springfield, Ohio, 1986—. Served to 1st lt. USAF, 1971-74. Mem. Nat. Assn. Accts. Republican. Roman Catholic. Home: 275 Ra Mar Dr Springfield OH 45502 Office: 550 Rte 55 Urbana OH 43078

PAGE, SALLY JACQUELYN, university official; b. Saginaw, Mich., July, 1943; d. William Henry and Doris Effie (Knippel) P.; B.A., U. Iowa, 1965; M.B.A., So. Ill. U., 1973. Copy editor, C.V. Mosby Co., St. Louis, 1965-69; edit. cons. Edit. Assos., Edwardsville, Ill., 1969-70; research adminstr. So. Ill. U., 1970-74, asst. to pres., affirmative action officer, 1974-77; civil rights officer U. N.D., Grand Forks, 1977—, lectr. mgmt., 1978—; polit. commentator Sta. KFJM, Nat. Public Radio affiliate, 1981—. Contbr. to profl. jours. Chairperson N.D. Equal Opportunity Affirmative Action Officers, 1987; pres., Pine to Prairie council Girl Scouts U.S.A., 1980-85 ; mem. employment com. Ill. Commn. on Status of Women, 1976-77; mem. Bicentennial Com. Edwardsville, 1976, Bikeway Task Force Edwardsville, 1975-77; mem. Civil Service Rev. Task Force, Grand Forks, 1982, civil service commr., 83, chmn., 1984, 86. Mem. AAUW (dir. Ill. 1975-77), Coll. and Univ. Personnel Assn. (research and publs. bd. 1982—) Am. Assn. Affirmative Action, Soc. Research Adminstrs., M.B.A. Assn. Republican. Presbyterian. Home: 3121 Cherry St Grand Forks ND 58201 Office: Univ ND Grand Forks ND 58202

PAGE, STEPHEN MYRL, teacher; b. Brewton, Ala.; s. Myrl Glenndon and Grace Lucille (Callon) P.; m. Ruby Ellen Cotter, July 25, 1970; 1 child, Amy Elizabeth. BS in Edn. cum laude, Southwest Mo. State U., 1969; MEd, Drury Coll., 1975. Tchr. social studies Marshfield (Mo.) Jr. High Sch., 1969—, sponser student council, 1969-74; mem. rev. com. Mo. Social Studies Curriculum Guide, 1980. Mem. Mo. State Tchrs. Assn. (social studies dept.), Marshfield Edn. Assn. (pres. 1974), Rep. Nat. Com. (sustaining). Republican. Methodist. Home: Rt 2 Box 162 A Marshfield MO 65706 Office: Marshfield Jr High Sch PO Box B Marshfield MO 65706

PAGE, THOMAS CRAMER, management educator; b. Martinsville, Ohio, Mar. 28, 1920; s. Earl S. and Elizabeth Jane (Cramer) P.; m. Jessie Morris, Sept. 11, 1944; children: Patricia Page Hugus, Thomas Morris, Susan Page. BBA, Miami U., Oxford, Ohio, 1942; MBA, Harvard U., 1947. Indsl. engr. Eastman Kodak Co., Rochester, N.Y., 1947-51; with mktg. planning, gen. mgmt. Ford Motor Co., Dearborn, Mich., 1952-69, group v.p., 1975-78; v.p. Ford Latin Am. Ford Motor Co., 1978-79, v.p. diversified products ops., 1979-81, exec. v.p., 1981-85, ret., 1985; prof. mgmt. Miami U., 1985—; bd. dirs. Firestone Tire & Rubber Co., Akron, Ohio; chmn. bd. Ford Aerospace and Communications Corp.; v.p. Ford Mktg. Corp., Dearborn, 1970-71; pres. Philco-Ford Corp., Dearborn, 1971-75. Vice chmn. Detroit United Fund, 1970-71. Served to maj. USAAF, 1943-46, USAF, 1970-71. Mem. Pres. Assn., Phila C. of C. (bd. dirs. 1972-73), Delta, Sigma Pi. Address: 5 Millrace Ct Dearborn MI 48126

PAGELS, CHARLES FREDERICK, educational administrator; b. Chgo., June 19, 1946; s. Charles F. and Anna A. (Olson) P.; m. Jacque Stallings, Feb. 12, 1975; children—Lezah, Charles. B.S., Ill. State U., 1969, M.S., 1970; Ed.D., U. Va., 1973. Cert. supt., Ill. Asst. prof. Marquette U., Milw., 1973-74; asst. prin. John Yeates High Sch., Suffolk, Va., 1974-75; asst. supt. Porta Sch. Dist., Petersburg, Ill., 1975-78; asst. supt. Indian Prairie Sch. Dist., Naperville, Ill., 1978—. Republican precinct committeeman; alderman City of Aurora, Ill. Served with USMC, 1965-71. Mem. DuPage County County Curriculum Developers (bd. dirs.), Assn. Supervision and Curriculum Devel., Ill. Assn. Supervision and Curriculum Devel. (state treas.). Contbr. articles to profl. jours. Home: 2230 W Illinois Ave Aurora IL 60506 Office: 30W026 Ogden Ave Naperville IL 60540

PAGET, GEORGE EDWARD, pharmaceutical company executive; b. Manchester, Lancashire, Eng., June 20, 1922; came to U.S., 1978; s. George Swinson and Georgina May (Hughes) P.; m. Peggy Gwendolin Lugg, Mar. 5, 1949 (div. 1984); children: Penelope Solveig, David Arthur, Peter Swinson; m. Margaret Ann Moult, Sept. 17, 1984. BS, U. Durham, Newcastle, Eng., 1944, Diploma of Child Health, 1946, MD, 1952. Toxicologist ICI, U.K., 1952-61; dir. research SK & F, U.K., 1961-67, mng. dir., 1967-72; dir. IRI, U.K., 1972-78; dir. health care Monsanto, St. Louis, 1978-86; v.p., sci. liaison G.D. Searle, Skokie, Ill., 1986—. Contbr. articles to profl. jours.; editor numerous books. Served to lt. Brit. Royal Navy, 1945-49. Mem. European Soc. Toxicology (founder), Soc. of Toxicology, Royal Soc. Medicine (hon. officer, bd. dirs.), Royal Soc. Edinburgh. Club: New Club (Edinburgh). Avocations: music, cooking. Home: 1400 Kenilwood Ln Riverwoods IL 60015 Office: GD Searle 5200 Old Orchard Rd Skokie IL 60077

PAHANISH, EDMUND, manufacturing company executive; b. Washington, Pa., Jan. 24, 1928; s. Michael and Anna Margaret (Graytok) P.; m. Delores Anita Pyle, Oct. 6, 1948; children—Richard Wayne, Brenda Faye, Deborah Kathleen. Student Kent State U., 1970. Machinist, Chester Hoist Co., Lisbon, Ohio, 1943-46; molder Eljer Co., Salem, Ohio, 1947-59; salesman Western & So. Life Ins. Co., 1959-62; welder Columbiana (Ohio) Boiler Co., 1962-65; welder-fitter Fordees Corp., Leetonia, Ohio, 1965-68; pres. Spl. Equipment Corp., Salem, 1968-78; plant mgr. JLG Industries, Bedford, Pa., 1978-82; Delta Fab Co., Salem, 1983—. Pres., Junction-Miller Rd-Inc., 1969—. Served with Signal Corps, U.S. Army, 1945-46. Named Personality of Week, Everett (Pa.) Newspaper, 1981. Mem. Am. Prodn. and Inventory Control Soc., So. Alleghenies Planning and Devel. Commn. Roman Catholic. Lodge: Rotary (Bedford, Pa.). Patentee gutter rake; inventor stenciling machine, digger, cable cutter. Home: 40090 Miller Rd Leetonia OH 44431

PAI, BIPIN KESHAV, engineering educator; b. Madras, India, Mar. 18, 1951; came to U.S., 1972; s. Keshav Narasimha and Heerabai Madhav (Shenoy) P.; m. Vrinda Shenoy, Feb. 15, 1977; children: Kavitha, Priya. B Tech, Indian Inst. Tech., Madras, 1972; MS, U. Rochester, 1973, PhD, 1978. Research asst. U. Rochester, N.Y., 1974-76, research assoc., 1978-79; asst. prof. Purdue U. Calumet, Hammond, Ind., 1979-84, assoc. prof., 1984—. Contbr. articles to profl. jours. Recipient Summer Faculty Award Purdue U., 1980; grantee Purdue U., 1981, Argonne Nat. Lab., 1985-87. Mem. ASME (faculty advisor student sect. 1981-82, 85-86, chmn. Calumet subsect. 1983-87). Hindu. Office: Purdue U Calumet 2233 171st St Hammond IN 46323

PAIDOSH, MARY CATHERINE, bank executive; b. Mpls., May 8, 1946; d. Thomas John and Josephine (Dombrowski) P. BA magna cum laude, U. Minn., 1967, MA, 1970; PhD, U. Mass., 1979; Careers in Bus. Cert., NYU, 1979. Asst. v.p. Barnett Banks Fla., Jacksonville and Tampa, 1981-84; corp. banking officer First Bank St. Paul, 1984-85; v.p., mgr. Nat. City Bank Mpls., 1985—. Fellow U. West Berlin, Fed. Republic Germany, 1968-69; Minn. Student Project for Amity Among Nations (SPAN), 1967; recipient Medallion award Robert Morris Assocs., 1984; named one of Outstanding Young Women Am., 1977. Mem. Am. Electronics Assn. (com. mem. 1987—). Republican. Roman Catholic. Avocations: golf, gardening, cooking, cross-country skiing, fgn. langs. Office: Nat City Bank Mpls 75 S 5th St Minneapolis MN 55402

PAIER, ADOLF ARTHUR, technical products and services company executive; b. Branford, Conn., Oct. 27, 1938; s. Adolf Arthur and Margaret Mary (Almond) P.; m. Geraldine Shnakis, Sept. 17, 1966; children: Nathaniel Jason, Andrew Joseph, Alena Catherine. A.A., Quinnipiac Coll., 1958; B.S. in Econs, U. Pa., 1960. Audit mgr. Touche Ross & Co., Phila., 1960-67; pres., dir. Safeguard Scientifics, Inc., King of Prussia, Pa., 1967—; dir. Morlan Internat., Inc., Phila., Novell Inc., Orem, Utah, Delta Paper, Phila., Am. Future Systems, Inc. bd. dirs. Family and Youth Programs, Norristown, Pa. Mem. Am. Inst. C.P.A.s, Young Presidents Orgn., Nat. Assn. Accountants. Office: Safeguard Powertech Systems Aberdeen Industrial Park Aberdeen SD 57401

PAIGE, LESLIE ZELDIN, school psychologist; b. Washington, Oct. 9, 1952; d. Donald and Esther (Cohen) Zeldin; m. Barry A. Paige, June 16, 1974; 1 child, Robert Harrison. BA in Psychology, U. Cin., 1974; MS in Sch. Psychology, Ft. Hays State U., 1981, postgrad., 1987—. Cert. sch. psychologist. Sch. psychologist Hays West Cen. Kans. Spl. Edn. Cooperative, 1981-85, Unified Sch. Dist. 407, Russell, Kans., 1986—. Mem. Kans. Assn. Sch. Psychologists (mem. task force on sch. psychologist evaluation, 1982-83, task force on devel. of state guidelines for behavior disorder children, 1983-85, membership chair 1984-85, certs. recognition 1984, 85), Nat. Assn. Sch. Psychologists. Avocations: skiing, backpacking, travel, gardening, reading. Home: Rural Rt 1 Box 76 Bison KS 67520 Office: Unified Sch Dist 407 802 Main Russell KS 67665

PAINE, BARBARA ANN BETZOLD, hospital food services administrator, consultant; b. Hillsboro, Ill., Dec. 4, 1954; d. Clifford Lyle and Dorothy Joan (Sorrells) Betzold; m. E. Mark Paine. Student Western Ill. U., 1973-75; B.S. cum laude in Home Econs., Kans. State U., 1977. Clin. dietitian St. Mary's Hosp., Centralia, Ill., 1977-78, dir. dietetic services, 1978—; dir. dietetic services med. cons. firm, 1982—; mem. food service adv. com. Ill. Hosp. Assn.; freelance cons.; preceptor for correspondence courses. Bd. dirs. ARC, 1979-81; mem. comml. cooking adv. com. Centralia Correctional Ctr., 1980—. Named Outstanding Working Woman of Ill., 1985. Mem. Am. Dietetic Assn., Am. Diabetes Assn., Am. Soc. Hosp. Food Service Adminstrs., Bus. and Profl. Women's Club (treas. 1983-84, Young Careerist award 1983, individual devel. award 1984, v.p. 1984-85), Dist. Bus. Profl. Womens Club (chmn. individual devel. program 1984-85), Omicron Nu (treas. 1983-87), Kappa Omicron Phi. Republican. Methodist. Developer teaching informational pamphlets for diabetic patients. Office: Saint Mary's Hosp 400 N Pleasant St Centralia IL 62801

PAINTER, DAVID LAURENCE, industrial designer, consultant; b. Monroeville, Ind., Nov. 24, 1913; s. Gurney Jasper and Grace Vida (Cribbs) P.; m. Catherine Mae Immel, Aug. 12, 1939; 1 child, David Lawrence. Diploma, Sch. of Art Inst., Chgo., 1936. V.p. Barnes & Reinecke Inc., Chgo., 1935-50; ptnr. Painter/Teague/Petertil, Indsl. Designers, Chgo., 1950-60; owner David Painter, Indsl. Designer, Chgo., 1960-72, Painter/Crabtree/Agazzi, Indsl. Designers, Glenview, 1972-80; pres. Painter/Cesaroni Design Inc., Glenview, 1980—; cons. various corps. including Tex. Instruments, White Consol. Industries, Bell & Howell, West Bend Co., Outboard Marine, Abbott Labs., Dresser Industries, 3M Co., others; various juried exhibits including Mus. Modern Art, N.Y.C., 1954, Smithsonian Instn., 1968, The Bklyn. Mus., 1969. Recipient Design award Nat. Housewares Mfg. Assn., Chgo., 1966. Mem. United Ch. Christ. Avocation: cinematic recording. Home: 718 Raleigh Rd Glenview IL 60025 Office: Painter/Cesaroni Design Inc 1865 Grove St Glenview IL 60025

PAINTER, MARK PHILIP, judge; b. Cin., Apr. 6, 1947; s. John Philip and Marjorie (West) P.; m. Sue Brunsman Painter. B.A., U. Cin., 1970; J.D., 1973. Bar: Ohio 1973, U.S. Dist. Ct. (so. dist.) Ohio 1973, U.S. Supreme Ct. 1980. Assoc. Smith & Schnacke (and predecessors firm), 1973-78; sole practice, Cin., 1978-82; judge Hamilton County Mcpl. Ct., Cin., 1982—. Contbr. articles to profl. jours. Bd. dirs. Citizens Sch. Com., Cin., 1974-76; trustee Freestore Foodbank, Cin., 1984—, Mary Jo Brueggeman Meml. Found., Cin., 1981—; mem. Republican Central Com., Cin., 1972-82. Recipient Superior Jud. Service award Ohio Supreme Ct., 1982, 84, 85. Mem. ABA, Ohio State Bar Assn., Cin. Bar Assn., Am. Judges Assn., Am. Judicature Soc. Club: Bankers (Cin.). Home: 2449 Fairview Ave Cincinnati OH 45219 Office: Hamilton County Mcpl Ct 222 E Central Pkwy Cincinnati OH 45202

PAISLEY, JOHN EDWARD, radio station executive; b. Galesburg, Ill., Dec. 24, 1949; s. Charles Bertram and Elsie A. P.; m. Lee Ann Adam, Nov. 27, 1976; childfen: Adam, Erin. BS, U. Miami, Fla., 1972. Salesman Sta. WQAD-TV, Moline, Ill., 1974-76; advt. salesman Daily Dispatch, Moline, 1976-79; realtor Tucker Swanson Realty, Galesburg, Ill., 1979-81; news and ops. dir. Sta. WAIK, Sta. WGBQ-FM, Galesburg, 1981-85, gen. mgr., 1985—. Mem. Galesburg C. of C. (tourism council). Lodge: Lions. Home: 1485 N Cherry Galesburg IL 61401 Office: WAIK Radio 235 E Main Galesburg IL 61401

PAJIC, SVETOMIR, veterinarian; b. Obrenovac, Serbia, Yugoslavia, Nov. 24, 1932; came to U.S., 1963, naturalized, 1968; s. Ljubomir and Paulina (Vukajlovic) P.; m. Gerda Martha Hanschmann, July 24, 1960; 1 child, Renata. D.V.M., Vet. Med. U., Belgrad, Yugoslavia, 1957; D.V.M., Vet. Med. U., Hannover, Fed. Republic Germany, 1964, Ph.D. in Clin. Pathology and Bacteriology 1964. Gen. practice vet. medicine specializing in large animals, Obrenovac, 1957-58; cons. Animal Health Inst., Obrenovac, 1957-58, Hemmersam & Rasmussen, Luebeck, Fed. Republic Germany, 1959-60; insp. in charge Slavonia Packing House, Osijik, Yugoslavia, 1960-62; gen. practice vet. medicine specializing in large animals, Lensahm. Fed. Republic Germany, 1962-63; vet. med. officer U.S. Dept. Agr., Elburn, Ill., 1964-68, supr. vet. med. officer, 1968—. Mem. Chgo. Council on Fgn. Relations. Mem. AVMA. Serbian Orthodox. Club: Chess (St. Charles, Ill.). Lodge: Lions. Home: 1702 Jay Ln Saint Charles IL 60174 Office: Grant St North Aurora IL 60542

PAJULA, RICHARD LEE, food company executive; b. Hurley, Wis., July 2, 1943; s. Bernard T. Pajula; m. Joan C. Bertzyk, July 20, 1968; children: Craig, Jeff. BBA, U. Wis., Superior, 1966; MS in Acctg., U. N.D., 1970. CPA, Wis., Minn. Sr. acct. Hanson, Milroy, Hanson, Superior, 1966-69; auditing mgr. Arthur Andersen & Co., Mpls., 1970-72, 75-79; v.p., controller Shelter Corp. Am., Mpls., 1972-75; v.p. ops. Jerome Foods, Inc., Barron, Wis., 1979—. Served to 1st lt. U.S. Army, 1961-62. Mem. Am. Inst. CPA's, Wis. Inst. CPA's, Minn. Inst. CPA's. Home: 1616 W Allen Rice Lake WI 54868 Office: Jerome Foods Inc 34 N 7th St Barron WI 54812

PALAZZO, FRANK ANTHONY, neurosurgeon; b. Stratford, Conn., Nov. 30, 1917; s. Lorenzo and Antonette (Baldino) P.; m. Mary Adrienne McGuire, Feb. 18, 1950; children: Francis Lorenzo, Maria Louise Palazzo Digman, Margherita Antonette Palazzo Nahrup. BS, U. Mo., 1939; MD, St. Louis U., 1943. Grad. asst. in zoology U. Mo., 1940; intern Flower and Fifth Aves. Hosp., N.Y.C., 1944, resident in radiology, 1946; fellow in neurosurgery Mayo Found., Rochester, Minn., 1947-50; practice medicine specializing in neurosurgery St. Louis, 1950—; asst. prof. neurosurgery St. Louis U., 1957; pres. staff St. Mary's Med. Ctr., St. Louis, 1980. Contbr. articles to profl. jour. Served to capt. M.C. U.S. Army, 1944-46. Fellow: ACS, Am. Assn. Neurol. Surgeons, Congress Nerol. Surgeons. Republican. Roman Catholic. Avocations: golf, fish. Office: Midwest Neurosurgeons Inc 6744 Clayton Rd Saint Louis MO 63117

PALAZZOLO, DOMINIC PAUL, pharmacist; b. Springfield, Ill., Dec. 1, 1951; s. Paul Vincent and Angeline (LaCamera) P. AA, Springfield Coll., 1971; BS, St. Louis Coll. Pharmacy, 1974. Registered pharmacist, Ill. Staff pharmacist Thrifty Drug Store, Springfield, 1974-76, mgr., 1976-83; mgr. Medicare Pharmacy, Springfield, 1983-84, Healthcare Pharmacy, Springfield, 1984-85; pharmacist Kare Pharmacy, Springfield, 1985—; exec. v.p., bd. dirs., Midwest Prodn. Group, Springfield. Producer/dir. (film) Horizons, 1982; assoc. producer (music video) Kids in the Street, 1984 (SAAM award 1985). Advisor Griffin High Sch. Key Club, Springfield, 1982—; mem. Sangamon County Rep. Found., Springfield, 1985—. Mem. Springfield Pharm. Assn., St. Louis Coll. Pharmacy Alumni Assn., Roman Cultural Soc. Roman Catholic. Lodge: Kiwanis (pres. Springfield club 1986—). Avocations: real estate, photography, stock market, golfing. Home: 2068 Faringdon Springfield IL 62702 Office: Midwest Prodn Group 312 S 4th Suite 3 Springfield IL 62702

PALEVICH, ROBERT FRANCIS, manufacturing executive; b. Chester, Pa., June 11, 1948; s. Frank Joseph and Lucille Mary (Smith) P.; m. Bonnie Lou Noyer, Aug. 7, 1971; children: Christopher, Angela, Jessica. AAS in Computer Sci., Purdue U., 1969, BS in Indsl. Supervising, 1970; MBA, Ind. U., 1975. Quality control mgr. Hardware Wholesalers, Ft. Wayne, Ind., 1970-71, asst. mgr. inventory control, 1971-72, mgr. inventory control div., 1974-78, corp. inventory control mgr., 1978—; instr. Ind. U., Ft. Wayne, 1976-78; cons. Thayer, Inc., Lafayette, Ind., 1982, Baer Farms, Lafayette, 1983, Lamar Inc., Ft. Wayne, 1984, Data Bank, Ft. Wayne, 1985, Paulausky Assocs., Ft. Wayne, 1986—. Contbr. articles to profl. jours.; designer math models, 1976. Sunday sch. tchr. Ch. Christ, Ft. Wayne; mgr. soccer, preparatory Little League, Ft. Wayne, 1985-86. Named one of Outstanding Young Men Am., 1981. Mem. Am. Prodn. and Inventory Control Soc. (treas. 1975—, v.p. research 1976-77), Nat. Assn. Bus. Econs., Purchasing Mgmt. Assn., Purdue Alumni Assn. (bd. dirs. 1977, v.p. 1980, pres. 1980-81). Republican. Club: Toastmasters (pres. 1987). Avocations: tennis, golf, swimming, racquetball. Home: 5403 Albany Ct Fort Wayne IN 46835

PALLASCH, B. MICHAEL, lawyer; b. Chgo., Mar. 30, 1933; s. Bernhard Michael and Magdalena Helena (Fixari) P.; m. Josephine Catherine O'Leary, Aug. 15, 1981. B.S.S., Georgetown U., 1954; J.D., Harvard U., 1957; postgrad., John Marshall Law Sch., 1974. Bar: Ill. 1957, U.S. Dist. Ct. (no. dist.) Ill. 1958, U.S. Tax Ct. 1961, U.S. Ct. Claims 1961. Assoc. Winston & Strawn, Chgo., 1958-66; resident mgr. br. office Winston & Strawn, Paris, 1963-65; ptnr. Winston & Strawn, Chgo., 1966-70, sr. capital ptnr., 1971—; dir., corp. sec. Tanis Inc., Houghton, Mich., 1972—, Greenbank Engring. Corp., Dover, Del., 1976—, C.B.P. Engring. Corp., Chgo., 1976—, Chgo. Cutting Services Corp., 1977—; corp. sec. Arthur Andersen Assocs. Inc., Chgo., 1976—, L'hotel de France of Ill. Inc., Chgo., 1980—; dir. Bosch Devel. Co., Longview, Tex., Lor Inc., Houghton, Mich., Rana Inc., Madison, Wis., Woodlak Co., Houghton. Bd. dirs. Martin D'Arcy Mus. Medieval and Renaissance Art, Chgo., 1975—; bd. dirs. Katherine M. Bosch Found., 1978—; asst. sec. Hundred Club of Cook County, Chgo., 1966-73, bd. dirs., sec., 1974—. Served with USAFR, 1957-63. Recipient Oustanding Woodland Mgmt. Forestry award Monroe County (Wis.) Soil and Water Conservation Dist., 1975; recipient Youth Mayor of Chgo. award, 1950. Mem. Ill. Bar Assn. (tax lectr. 1961), Advocates Soc., Field Mus. Natural History (life mem.), Max McGraw Wildlife Found. Roman Catholic. Clubs: Travellers (Paris); Saddle and Cycle (Chgo.). Home: 3000 N Sheridan Rd Chicago IL 60657 Office: Winston & Strawn One First National Plaza Suite 5000 Chicago IL 60603

PALLUCONI, DON LOUIS, retail company executive; b. Iron Mountain, Mich., July 27, 1907; s. Luigi and Carolina (Ercoli) P.; m. Louise Tramontina Schupp, June 19, 1929 (div. Mar. 1946); m. Ida Beverly Nussbaum, May 19, 1946. Cert. in horology, Ferris Inst., 1947; violin studies with Castell Sisters, Iron Mountain, Mich., 1915-21. Horologist Mason's Jewelers, Grand Rapids, Mich., 1947-48, Fox Jewelers, Grand Rapids, 1948-49, Amsterdam Jewelers, Grand Rapids, 1949-52; prin. Grand Rapids, 1952—. Served as cpl. USAF, 1943-45. Mem. Grand Rapids Fedn. Musicians (life), Iron Mountain Musicians Local (chartered, investigator), Am. Legion. Democrat. Jewish. Clubs: Edwin Leonard Post (Grand Rapids) (past comdr.), Wyoming (Mich.) Post 154. Avocations: fishing, camping, baseball, football, boxing, bass playing, orchestra leader. Home and Office: 2013 Melvin SW Wyoming MI 49509

PALM, BRUCE ARTHUR, advertising executive; b. Cleve., Jan. 13, 1932; s. Arthur C. and Eleanor Garnet (Berghoff) P.; m. Mary Anne Alexander, Apr. 25, 1983; children: T. Arthur, Scott, Susan, Linda. BA, Case Western Reserve U., 1953. Account exec. Palm & Patterson, Inc., Cleve., 1953-67, v.p., 1967-69, pres., 1969-79; sr. v.p. Bayless-Kerr & Palm, Cleve., 1979-85; pres. Palm & Patterson, Inc., Cleve., 1985—. Mem. Bus. Profl. Advt. Assn., Indsl. Marketers Cleve., Cleve. Advt. Club, Delta Kappa Epsilon. Home: 624-1 Russet Woods Ln Aurora OH 44202 Office: Palm & Patterson Inc 3690 Orange Pl Cleveland OH 44122

PALMER, BRIAN DAVID, lecture agency executive; b. Chgo., Nov. 28, 1957; s. John Peter and Karol Anne (Dragomir) P. B in Speech and Rhetorical Theory, Drake U., 1980; MBA, Lake Forest Grad. Sch. Mgmt., 1987. V.p. Nat. Speakers Bur., Lake Forest, Ill., 1980-84, 1984—; lectr. in field. Vol. Lamb's Farm, Libertyville, Ill., 1984—; arbitrator Better Bus. Bur., Chgo., 1983—. Named one of Outstanding Young Men Am., 1982. Mem. Meeting Planners Internat. (co-chmn. edn. com. 1986-87, chpt. dir.), Pi kappa Alpha, Delta Omicron Alumni Orgn. Republican. Avocations: auto racing, physical fitness, reading. Home: 1350 N Western Ave #302 Lake Forest IL 60045

PALMER, DAVID YOUMANS, retail executive; b. Cin., June 24, 1947; s. Cletus Thompson and Mary Louise (Youmans) P.; m. Kathleen Adele Wass, Sept. 6, 1969; children: Ashley Elizabeth, Zachary David. BSBA, Ohio State U., 1969; MBA, La. State U., 1971. Various mktg. and buying positions Sears Roebuck & Co., Chgo., 1971-85, mgr. fin. info., 1985—. Pres. Maplebrook Homeowners Assn., 1985. Served to 2d lt. U.S. Army, 1971. Mem. Nat. Investors Relations Inst. Home: 1205 Sandpiper Ln Naperville IL 60540 Office: Sears Roebuck & Co Sears Tower BSC 41-13 Chicago IL 60684

PALMER, EDWARD HENRY, consulting and development company executive; b. Chgo., Feb. 12, 1932; s. Brian Charles and Catherine Dorothy P.; m. Davalyn D. Nelson, June 4, 1982. B.A., Hanover Coll., 1955; S.T.M., Yale U., 1958; postgrad. Northwestern U., 1960-62. Asst. rector St. Pauls Ch., New Haven, 1958-60; with Chgo. Housing Authority, Chgo., 1960-62; with Hyde Park Kenwood Community Orgn., Chgo., 1962-64; chmn. Palmer France Assocs. Ltd., Chgo.; pres. House Group, Inc.; lectr. Ill. Inst.Tech., U. Ill.; speaker profl. orgns. Episcopalian. Clubs: Cliff Dwellers, Carlton, Quadrangle (Chgo.). Contbr. articles on housing to profl. jours. Home: 812 S Kensington LaGrange IL 60525 Office: House Group Inc 175 W Jackson Suite 915 Chicago IL 60601

PALMER, EMMA, business education instructor; b. Kilmichael, Miss., Jan. 30, 1950; d. Joe Arnold and Mattie Eiland; m. John Albert Palmer, Aug. 21, 1970; children: Ashur, John II, Joe Alvin. BSin Bus. Edn., Rust Coll., 1970; MEd in Edn., 1972. Tchr. Milw. Pub. Schs., 1970-71; lead tchr. Midwest Success Tng., Milw., 1971-72; social sci. tchr. Milw. Area Tech. Coll., 1972—. Mem. Office Tech. Assn. (v.p. 1985—), Internat. Soc. Wang Users, Soc. Office Automation Profls., Bus. and Profl. Women (v.p. 1985-86), Milw. County Zool. Soc. Democrat. Methodist. Avocations: bicycling, boating, traveling, home decorated. Home: 4740 N 19th St Milwaukee WI 53209 Office: Milw Area Tech Coll 1015 N 6th St Milwaukee WI 53203

PALMER, JAMES JOSEPH, human resources executive; b. Detroit, Sept. 28, 1943; s. James J. and Mary M. (Stockoski) P.; children from 1st marriage: Jennifer L., Julianne M.; m. Sandra R. Wahl, July 29, 1979; children: Kimberly S., Joni K., David J. MBA, U. Detroit, 1975. Various personnel positions Chrysler Corp., Detroit, 1968-81, supr. personnel adminstrn., 1985-86, mgr. human resource programs, 1986—; mgr. employee and community relations Allis-Chalmers Corp., La Porte, Ind., 1981-83; mgr. employees and communication relations Allis-Chalmers Corp., Independence, Mo., 1983-85; cons. Palmer/ Palmer and Assoc., Blue Springs, Mo., 1984-85; Palmer/ Roe & Assoc., Troy, Mich. 1985—. Asst. Sec. of State Mich., Dept. State, Lansing, 1965-68. Mem. Alpha Sigma Nu, Betta Gamma Sigma. Roman Catholic. Home: 1963 Cameo Dr Troy MI 48098-2407

PALMER, JANICE MASON, special education educator; b. Chgo., Mar. 10, 1942; d. Arthur John and Sarah Crawford (Forsyth) Blaha; m. Carl Massa, Aug. 29, 1964 (div. 1979); children—Heather Ellen, David Carl; m. Jeffrey Todd Palmer, Apr. 3, 1981. B.A., Northeastern Ill. U., 1975, M.A. in Spl. Edn., 1979. Cert. sch. adminstr., Ill. Clin. diagnostician Sch. Dist. U-46, Elgin, Ill., 1980-83; chmn. spl. edn. Clovis High Sch., Calif., 1983; sr. cons. Mason Palmer & Assocs., Schaumburg, Ill., 1984—; instr. spl. edn. Northeastern Ill. U. Grad. Coll., Chgo., 1984—, cons. Inst. Child Neurology, Arlington Heights, Ill., 1979—, various psychiat. hosps., Ill., 1984—, Nat. Dairy Council, Rosemont, Ill., 1985—. Office: Mason Palmer & Assoc 125 Mendon Ln Schaumburg IL 60193

PALMER, JERRY RICHARD, lawyer; b. Jefferson City, Mo., Aug. 22, 1940; s. Noble Edison and Harriet Jane (McCall) P.; m. Ann Leffler, Aug. 20, 1965; children—Christopher Paul, Andrea Leffler. B.A., U. Kans., 1962, J.D., 1966. Bar: Kans. 1966. Ptnr. Fisher, Patterson, Sayler & Smith, Topeka, 1966-70; assoc. Fisher & Benfer, 1971-74; sole practice, 1975-77; ptnr. Stumbo, Palmer et al., 1978-80; pres. Jerry R. Palmer P.A., 1980-85; pres. Palmer, Marquardt & Snyder P.A., 1986—. Mem. Assn. Trial Lawyers Am. (bd. govs. 1982-85), Kans. Trial Lawyers Assn. (pres. 1977), Nat. Bd. Trial Advocacy, Am. Law Inst. Democrat. Episcopalian. Avocations: skiing; sailing; photography. Home: 305 Greenwood Topeka KS 66606 Office: 112 SW 6th St Suite 102 Topeka KS 66603

PALMER, MELVIN GERALD, gemologist, consultant; b. Springfield, Ill., May 9, 1937; s. Melvin G. and Helen C. (Bleser) P.; m. Linda Lee Ball, May 16, 1964; children—Tonya Lee, Shawn Ann. LLB LaSalle U., 1969. Watch commander (lt.) Police Dept., Springfield, 1961-83 (ret.); owner, chief exec. LubeMaster 10 min. Oil Change, Springfield, 1978—, J.& L. Palmer, Inc., Springfield, 1983—; prin. Homemade Recipe Cafe. Author Palmer's Diamond Buying Guide, 1984. Served with USN, 1954-58. Fellow Am. Assn. Criminology; mem. Gemological Inst. Am. Alumni Assn., Ill. Police Assn., Policeman's Benevolent and Protective Assn. Ill. (life), Greater Springfield C. of C., Better Bus. Bur. Clubs: Abe Lincoln Gun, Shuto Kan Karate. Lodge: K.C. Avocations: shooting; karate; painting; gemology. Office: J&L Palmer Inc 1201 S 2d Springfield IL 62704

PALMER, ROBERT MEAD, orthopaedic surgeon; b. Indpls., Feb. 23, 1928; s. Walter Irving and Kathryn (Mead) P.; m. Catherine Ann Gardella, May 29, 1954; children: Christopher R., Ann Palmer McMath. AB, Ind. U., 1950, MA, 1951, MD, 1955. Diplomate Am. Bd. Orthopaedic Surgery. Resident in orthopaedic surgery Indpls. Gen. Hosp., 1957-59, Ind. U. Hosp., Indpls., 1959-60; faculty dept. orthopaedic Ind. U., Indpls., 1960-69; practice medicine specializing in orthopaedic surgery Indpls., 1969—. Contbr. articles and papers to med. jours. Fellow ACS, Am. Acad. Orthopaedic Surgeons, Am. Orthopaedic Foot and Ankle Soc.; mem. Am. Bd. Orthopaedic Surgery. Republican. Presbyterian. Lodge: Sertoma (dist. gov. Nortwest Ind. 1979-81, state dir. Ind. 1981-83, found. trustee Kansas City 1985—). Avocations: woodworking, sailing, cross-country skiing. Home: 7801 Holly Creek Ln Indianapolis IN 46240 Office: Palmer, Trainer & Clayton MD Inc 2020 W 86th St Suite 304 Indianapolis IN 46260

PALMER, ROBERT R., performing arts adminstr.; b. Chicago, Sept. 8, 1950; s. Marvin R. and Martha A. Palmer. B.A. cum laude, Augustana Coll., Rock Island, Ill., 1973; M.A. in Arts Adminstrn., U. Wis.-Madison, 1975. Mgr., U. Wis.-Madison Symphony Orchs., 1974-75, Madison Civic Music Assn., 1975—; tchr. music appreciation U. Wis. Extension, Madison Area Tech. Coll. Treas., mem. exec. com. of bd. dirs. Dane County Arts Council, 1979-80; chair Madison Com. for the Arts. Mem. Beta Gamma Sigma, Omicron Delta Kappa, Phi Mu Alpha, Alpha Phi Omega. Office: Madison Symphony 122 State St Madison WI 53703

PALMER, ROBERT TOWNE, lawyer; b. Chgo., May 25, 1947; s. Adrian Bernhardt and Gladys (Towne) P.; B.A., Colgate U., 1969; J.D., U. Notre Dame, 1974; m. Ann Therese Darin, Nov. 9, 1974; children—Justin Darin, Christian Darin. Bar: Ill. 1974, D.C. 1978, U.S. Supreme Ct. 1978. Law clk. Hon. Walter V. Schaefer, Ill. Supreme Ct., 1974-75; assoc. McDermott, Will & Emery, Chgo., 1975-81, ptnr., 1982-86; ptnr. Chadwell & Kayser, Ltd., 1987—; mem. adj. faculty Chgo. Kent Law Sch., 1975-77, Loyola U., 1976-78. Mem. ABA, Ill. State Bar Assn. (2d place Lincoln Award 1983), Chgo. Bar Assn., D.C. Bar Assn., Internat. Assn. Defense Counsel, Lambda Alpha. Republican. Episcopalian. Clubs: Chgo., Univ. Chgo., Saddle & Cycle; Dairymen's. Contbr. articles to legal jours. and textbooks. Office: Chadwell & Kayser Ltd 8500 Sears Tower Chicago IL 60606-6592

PALMER, TERRANCE LOUIS, manufacturer's representative; b. Cleve., Feb. 8, 1944; s. Joseph and Minnie (Solomon) P.; m. m. Barbara Ann Freeman, July 28, 1968; children: Stacey Alise, Jared Steven. AA, Cuyahoga Community Coll., 1966; student, Cleve. State U., 1967-68. Dir. research and devel. L.D. Kichler Co., Cleve., 1963-73; nat. sales mgr. Allegheny Steel & Prodn., Chgo., 1973-75; ptnr. Lighting Assn., Chgo., 1975-77; owner Palmer Sales Co., Chgo., 1977—, Kinder Products and Sales Co., Chgo., 1981—; mng. ptnr. Newberry Venture, Chgo., 1985—. Co-chmn. Helping Hand, Chgo., 1975-81. Avocations: football, fishing, baseball, tennis. Office: Palmer Sales 1524 S Peoria Chicago IL 60608

PALMER, WILLIAM A., food distribution company executive. Chmn. Affiliated Foods Coop., Inc., Norfolk, Nebr. Office: Affiliated Foods Coop Inc 13th St & Omaha Ave Norfolk NE 68701 *

PALMER, WILLIAM HASSELL, business executive; b. San Diego, Nov. 29, 1945; s. Walter B. and Mary I. (Hassell) P. BBA, North Tex. State U., 1969, MBA, 1976. Systems engr. Ge. Electric Co., Dallas, 1969-73; v.p. sales Lithonia Lighting, Conyers, Ga., 1973-77; broker A.G. Edwards & Sons, Dallas, 1977; v.p. mktg. Valmont Industries, Valley, Nebr., 1977-85, dir. bus. devel., 1985—. Mem. Illuminating Engring. Soc. Home: 12006 William Plaza #310 Omaha NE 68144 Office: Valmont Industires Valley NE 68064

PALMO, DUANE COULTER, marketing professional; b. Brownsville, Pa., Apr. 6, 1942; s. Powell S. and Louise (Coulter) P.; m. Madelon Marie Kosch, Nov. 25, 1967; 1 child, Alexander. BA in Graphic Design, Carnegie Inst. Tech., 1964; MA in Radio and TV, Ohio State U., 1968. Art dir. Sta. WLWC-TV, Columbus, Ohio, 1966-68; exec. v.p. Hameroff & Assocs. Advt. Agy., Columbus, 1968-76; pres. Palmo Advt., Inc., Columbus, 1976-83, The Mktg. Dept., Inc., Columbus, 1983—. Mem. Am. Mktg. Assn., Advt. Fedn. Columbus (pres. 1979-80), Columbus Area C. of C. Democrat. Roman Catholic. Club: Sales Execs. Avocations: model trains, golf, sports. Office: Mktg Dept Inc 4235 Lyon Dr Columbus OH 43220

PALOMAKI, JACOB FREDERICK, obstetrics and gynecology educator; b. Cleve., Jan. 4, 1942; s. Jacob Elmer and Ruth Helen (Eckert) P.; m. Anne Elizabeth Huxtable, May 29, 1965; children: Julie Elizabeth, Elizabeth Anne. BA, Oberlin Coll., 1963; MD, Case Western Res. U., 1967. Diplomate Am. Bd. Ob-Gyn, Nat. Bd. Med. Examiners. Asst. prof. ob-gyn Case Western Res. U., Cleve., 1974-79, asst. clin. prof., 1979-84, assoc. clin. prof., 1984—; ednl. coordinator ob-gyn Fairview Gen. Hosp., Cleve., 1975-84, chmn. dept. ob-gyn., 1984—; bd. dirs. Acad. Medicine, Cleve., Pie Mut. Ins. Co., Cleve. Trustee MD alumni assn. Case Western Res. U., 1985—; mem. med. adv. bd. Fedn. Community Planning, Cleve., 1984—. Served to maj. USAF, 1972-74. Recipient Roche award Huffman La Roche Co., 1965. Fellow ACS, Am. Coll. Ob-Gyn, Am. Fertility Soc.; mem. AMA, Cen. Assn. Ob-Gyn. Republican. Methodist. Club: Clifton. Avocations: landscaping, renovation, church music, fishing. Home: 1055 Nicholson Ave Lakewood OH 44107 Office: Fairview Gen Hosp 18101 Lorain Ave Cleveland OH 44111

PALOMBO, JOSEPH, clinical social worker; b. Cairo, July 8, 1928; came to U.S., 1949; s. Albert H. and Regina (Costi) P.; m. Dorothy D. Denton, Aug. 4, 1957 (div.). PhB, New Sch. Social Research, N.Y.C., 1954; MA in Philosophy, Yale U., 1959; MSW, U. Chgo., 1959; cert. child therapy, Inst. Psychoanalysis, 1964. Cert. social worker, ill. Pvt. practice clin. social work Chgo., 1970-78; dean Inst. Clin. Social Work, Chgo., 1981—; adminstrv. dir. child therapy program Inst. Psychoanalysis Assn., Chgo., 1970-78, faculty mem., 1970—, Barr-Harris Ctr. Inst. Psychoanalysis, Chgo., 1976-78; faculty mem. advanced cert program Smith Sch. Social Work, 1985—. Contbr. articles to prof. jour. Mem. Acad. Cert. Social Workers, Assn. Child Psychotherapists (pres. 1976), Nat. Acads. Practice in Social Work (founding), Nat. Assn. Social Workers, Ill. Soc. Clin. Social Worker, Chgo. Psychoanalythic Soc. (affiliate). Democrat. Office: Inst Clin Social Work 30 N Michigan Ave Chicago IL 60602

PALOMBO, PAUL MARTIN, university administrator, composer; b. Pitts., Sept. 10, 1937; s. Domenico and Sophia P.; m. Joyce Lee Fletcher, Aug. 21, 1965; 1 son, Paul Martin. B.S., Indiana (Pa.) State U., 1962; postgrad. Peabody Conservatory (Balt.), 1963-66, Johns Hopkins U., 1963, 65; Ph.D., Eastman Sch. Music, U. Rochester, 1969. Prof. composition, head elec. music lab, U. Cin., 1969-72, chmn. composition, theory, musicology dept., 1972-75, assoc. dean Acad. Affairs, 1975-78; dir. Sch. Music, composer-in-residence U. Wash., Seattle, 1978-82; dean. Coll. Fine Arts, U. Wis.-Stevens Point, 1982—. Pres., Central Wis. Symphony Bd.; bd. dirs. Stevens Point Arts Council, Inc. Served with USN, 1955-58. Recipient Rockefeller Selection award Balt. Symphony Orch., 1965, Howard Hanson prize Eastman Sch. Music, 1969, Composer of Yr. award Washington Music Tchrs. Assn., 1980. Mem. Broadcast Music Inc., Nat. Assn. Schs. Music, Internat. Conf. Fine Arts Deans. Roman Catholic. Lodge: Kiwanis. Works include: Proteus, Ballet in Two Acts, 1969, Ritratti Anticamente, 1974, Metatheses, 1970, Morphosis, 1970, Prisma, 1984, canto d'un' Altra Volta, 1985. Office: U Wis at Stevens Point 202A Fine Arts Center Stevens Point WI 54481

PALUTKE, WALDEMAR ALFRED, physician; b. Detroit, Aug. 19, 1937; s. Alfred Adolf and Lydia (Weiss) P.; m. Margarita Walter, Aug. 20, 1960; children: Paul, Heidi, Christina. MD, Wayne State U., 1962. Diplomate Am. Bd. Pathology. Pathologist USPHS, Detroit, 1967-69; asst. prof. Wayne State U. Med. Sch., Detroit, 1969-75, assoc. prof., 1975—; sect. chief microbiology/immunopathology Harper Hosp., Detroit, 1980—; cons. microbiology/immunopathology Citation Lab., Southfield, Mich., 1983—; vice-chief Pathology, Harper Hosp., 1987—. Contbr. articles to profl. jours. Fellow Coll. Am. Pathologists, Am. Soc. Clin. Pathologists. Avocations: music, reading, polit. and social activism, non-smoker's rights. Home: 1541 Edinborough Ann Arbor MI 48104 Office: Harper Hosp 3990 John R St Detroit MI 48201

PANCERO, JACK BLOCHER, restaurant exec.; b. Cin., Dec. 27, 1923; s. Howard and Hazel Mae (Blocher) P.; student, Ohio State U., 1941-44; m. Loraine Fielman, Aug. 4, 1944; children—Gregg Edward, Vicki Lee. Partner, Howard Pancero & Co., Cin., 1948-66; stockbroker Gradison & Co., Cin., 1966-70; real estate asso. Parchman & Oyler, Cin., 1970-72; v.p. Gregg Pancero, Inc., Kings Mills, Ohio, 1972—. Methodist. Clubs: Western Hills Country, Cincinnati, Engrs. Table, Pelican Bay. Lodges: Masons, Shriners. Home: 5730 Pinehill Ln Cincinnati OH 45238 Office: Kings Island Columbia Rd Kings Mills OH 45034

PANDEYA, NIRMALENDU KUMAR, air force officer, osteopathic plastic surgeon; b. Bihar, India, Feb. 9, 1940; came to U.S., 1958, naturalized, 1965; s. Balbhadra and Ramasawari (Tewari) P.; m. Rosadele Ruth Hahn, Dec. 1, 1961; m. Cygnet S. Schroeder, Sept. 20, 1978; children—Alok, Kiran. B.Sc., M.S. Coll., Bihar U.-Motihari, 1958; M.S., U. Nebr., 1962; postgrad. U. Minn., 1959, Ft. Hays State Coll., 1961, D.O., Coll. Osteo. Medicine and Surgery, Des Moines, 1969, Hamilton Co. Pub. Hosp.; grad. Sch. Aerospace Medicine, U.S. Air Force, 1979. Diplomate Nat. Bd. Osteo. Med. Examiners. USPHS fellow dept. ob-gyn Coll. Medicine, U. Nebr., Omaha, 1963-65; intern Doctors Hosp., Columbus, Ohio, 1969-70; resident in gen. surgery Des Moines Gen. Hosp., 1970-72, Richmond Heights Gen. Hosp. (Ohio), 1972-73; fellow in plastic surgery Umea U. Hosp. (Sweden), 1973, Karolinska Hosp., Stockholm, 1974-75; assoc. prof. clin. scis. Coll. Osteo. Medicine and Surgery, Des Moines, 1975-76, also adj. clin. prof. plastic and reconstructive surgery; practice osteo. medicine specializing in reconstructive and plastic surgery, Des Moines, 1975—; mem. staff Des Moines Gen. Hosp., Mercy Hosp. Med. Ctr., Charter Community Hosp., Davenport Osteo. Hosp., Franklin Gen. Hosp., Ringgold County Hosp., Madison County Meml. Hosp., Winterset, Iowa, Mt. Ayr Surgery Ctr. of Des Moines. Served to lt. col. M.C., USAF; flight Surgeon Iowa Air N.G. Regents fellow U. Nebr., Lincoln, 1961-62. Mem. Assn. Plastic Surgeons of India (life), Assn. Surgeons of India (life), Assn. Mil. Surgeons of U.S. (life), Assn. Mil. Plastic Surgeons, AMA, Am. Osteo. Assn., Polk County Med. Soc., Iowa Soc. Osteo. Physicians and Surgeons, Polk County Soc. Osteo. Physicians and Surgeons (pres. 1978), Soc. U.S. Air Force Clin. Surgeons, Aerospace Med. Assn., Air N.G. Alliance of Flight Surgeons, AAUP, Am. Coll. Osteo. Surgeons, Am. Acad. Osteo. Surgeons (cert.), Soc. U.S. Air Force Flight surgeons. Hindu. Club: Army Navy. Contbr. numerous articles to profl. jours. Home: 10208 SW 72nd St Cumming IA 50061 Office: Cosmetic Surgery Ctr 1000 73rd St #21 Des Moines IA 50311-1321

PANEK, LOUIS ANTHONY, rock mechanics specialist, mining educator; b. Boston, Dec. 3, 1919; m. Christine Panek, Sept. 29, 1943; children: Camilla, Amy. BS in Mining Engring. and Geology, Mich. Tech. U., 1941; MS in Mining Engring., Columbia U., 1946, PhD in Sci., 1949. Mining research engr. U.S. Bur. of Mines, Denver, 1949-84; J.S. Westwater prof. Mich. Tech. U., Houghton, 1984—. Contbr. 60 articles on applications of rock mechanics to underground mining to profl. jours. Served to capt. C.E. U.S. Army, 1941-45, CBI. Recipient Meritorious Service award U.S. Dept. Interior, 1976. Mem. AIME (R. Peele Meml. award 1957), Am. Statistical Assn., Internat. Soc. for Rock Mechanics, Sigma Xi. Avocation: photography. Office: Mich Tech Univ Mining Engineering Dept Houghton MI 49931

PANERAL, KENNETH LAWRENCE, security analyst; b. Chgo., June 18, 1935; s. Albert James and Sophia (Toppen) P.; m. Gale Rossmann, July 6, 1957; children—Kimberly Diane Deschamps, Stephen Lawrence, Robert Allen. B.S., DePaul U., 1959. Chartered fin. analyst. Sr. analyst Continental Bank, Chgo., 1962-67; v.p. A.G. Becker, Chgo., 1967-78; stockbroker William Blair & Co., Chgo., 1979; v.p. Blunt, Ellis & Loewi, Chgo., 1980-82, Rotan Mosle Inc., Chgo., 1982-85, Blunt, Ellis & Loewi, Chgo., 1985— ; pres. Transp. Soc. Chgo., 1973, dir., 1973-75. Served with U.S. Army, 1954-56. Recipient Instl. Investor All Star Recognition award Instl. Investor Mag., 1976, 78. Mem. Fin. Analysts Fedn., Chgo. Analyst Soc. Republican. Roman Catholic. Avocations: golf; coin collecting; bridge. Home: 21 Park Ln Golf IL 60029

PANG, JOSHUA KEUN-UK, trade co. exec.; b. Chinnampo, Korea, Sept. 17, 1924; s. Ne-Too and Soon-Hei (Kim) P.; came to U.S., 1951, naturalized, 1968; B.S., Roosevelt U., 1959; m. He-Young Yoon, May 30, 1963; children—Ruth, Pauline, Grace. Chemist, Realemon Co. Am., Chgo., 1957-61; chief-chemist chem. div. Bell & Gossett Co., Chgo., 1961-63, Fatty Acid Inc., div. Ziegler Chem. & Mineral Corp., Chgo., 1963-64; sr. chemist-supr. Gen. Mills Chems. Inc., Kankakee, Ill., 1964-70; pres., owner UJU Industries Inc., Broadview, Ill., 1971—, also dir. Bd. dirs. Dist. 92, Lindop Sch., Broadview, 1976—; chmn. Proviso Area Sch. Bd. Assn., Proviso Twp., Cook County, Ill., 1976-77; bd. dirs. Korean Am. Community Services, Chgo., 1979-80; mem. governing bd. Proviso Area Exceptional Children, Spl. Edn. Joint Agreement, 1981-84, 85—; alumni bd. govs. Roosevelt U., 1983—. Mem. Am. Chem. Soc., Am. Inst. Parliamentarians (region 2 treas. 1979-81, region 2 gov. 1981-82), Internat. Platform Assn., Ill. Sch. Bd. Assn., Chgo. Area Parliamentarians, Parliamentary Leaders in Action (pres. 1980-81), Nat. Speakers Assn. (dir. Ill. chpt. 1981-82, nat. parliamentarian 1982-84, 2d v.p. chpt. 1983-84). Club: Toastmasters (dist. gov. 1969-1970), DADS Assn. U. Ill. (chmn. Cook County). Home: 2532 S 9th Ave Broadview IL 60153 Office: PO Box 6351 Broadview IL 60153-6351

PANKAUSKAS, ROBERT WALTER, marketing professional; b. Chgo., July 10, 1954; s. Walter B. and Alma M. (Bayor) P.; m. Eileen McKnight, July 24, 1982; 1 child, Molly E. BS in Mktg., U. Ill., 1975; M Mgmt. in Mktg., Northwestern U., 1984. Research analyst Market Facts, Inc., Chgo., 1975-76; project dir. Sears, Roebuck & Co., Chgo., 1977-81; v.p., assoc. research dir. BBDO Chgo., 1981—. Mem. Am. Mktg. Assn. (exec., v.p. communications Chgo. chpt. 1981-82, bd. dirs. Chgo. chpt. 1982-83, Meritorious Service award 1979), Advt. Research Found. Avocations: downhill and cross-country skiing, travel. Home: 3730 N Greenview Chicago IL 60613 Office: BBDO Chgo 410 N Michigan Chicago IL 60611

PANKEY, BEVERLY ST. CLAIR, college program director; b. Martinsburg, W.Va., July 17, 1938; m. Dianne C. Pankey, 1967; children: Todd, Doug, Paige. BS, U.S. Naval Acad., 1961; BSBA, Aquinas Coll., 1978, M in Mgmt., 1979. Commd. ensign USN, 1961; advanced through grades to commdr., 1976, retired, 1980; mem. faculty dept. bus. Longwood Coll., Farmville, Va., 1980-81; dir. mktg. services Am. Seating Co., Grand Rapids, Mich., 1981-83; mktg. adminstr. John Widdicomb Co., Grand Rapids, 1983-85; dir. corp. relations Aquinas Coll., Grand Rapids, 1985—. Decorated D.S.M. Clubs: Univ., Sales and Mktg. Execs. Home: 7523 Pirates Cove SE Grand Rapids MI 49508 Office: Aquinas Coll Dir Corp Relations 1607 Robinson Rd Grand Rapids MI 49506

PANNEBECKER, KEVIN LEE, sales executive; b. Bonne Terre, Mo., Apr. 10, 1957; s. John Mark and Shirley Ruth (Sebastian) P.; m. Vicki Snow Cantrell, Oct. 4, 1980; children: Drew, Anthony. BS, U. Mo., 1979. Retail installer Hallmark Cards, Mpls., 1979-80, account mgr., 1980-82; mktg. mgr. Viking Computer, Mpls., 1982-83; account mgr. Tex. Instruments, Mpls., 1983-84; sales rep. Profl. Software, Inc., St. Louis, 1984—; owner, operator Profl. Mgmt. Assocs., St. Louis, 1986—. Named Sales Profl. of Yr., Hallmark Cards (Mpls. dist.), 1981. Pi Kappa Alpha (v.p. 1978-79). Republican. Avocations: reading, travel, photography, interested in human motivation.

PANNOZZO, ANTHONY NICHOLAS, physician; b. Campbell, Ohio, Mar. 9, 1938; s. Vincenzo C. and Vincenza C. (Campojourne) P.; m. Paulette Konya, Apr. 4, 1970; children: Pamela, Michelle, Paul. AB, Youngstown U., 1959; MD, Ohio State U., 1963. Diplomate Am. Acad. Physical Medicine and Rehab. Intern Phila. Gen. Hosp., 1963-64; resident Ohio State U. Hosp., 1964-67; med. dir. Westwood Rehab. Med. Ctr., Youngstown, Ohio, 1977—. Mem. AMA, Am. Congress Physical Medicine and Rehab., Ohio Soc. Physical Medicine and Rehab., Ohio Med. Assn., Mahoning County Med. Soc. Office: 748 Boardman-Canfield Rd Boardman OH 44512

PANZER, WESLEY JOHN, engineer, manufacturing executive; b. Burlington, WIs., Aug. 16, 1945; s. Robert Miller and Chrystal Fern (Schumaker) P.; m. Dianne Sue Cook, Aug. 7, 1965; children: Timothy, Ryan. BSME, U. Wis., Madison, 1971; MBA, U. Wis., La Crosse, 1984. Registered profl. engr., Wis.; cert. purchasing mgr. Design and devel. engr. Goodyear Tire and Rubber Co., Akron, Ohio, 1971-75; reliability engr. Trane Co., La Crosse, 1975-80, mgr. quality assurance, 1980-82, mgr. purchasing, 1982—. Co-author: Fragmentation of Polymers by the Reduced Temperature Technique, 1971. Pres., sec. Onalaska (Wis.) Police and Fire Commn., 1977—; chmn. adminstrn. bd. United Meth. Ch., Onalaska, 1979—. Served to sgt. USAF, 1964-68. Named one of Outstanding Young Men Am., U.S. Jaycees, 1979. Mem. Nat. Assn. Purchasing Mgmt., Nat. Assn. Profl. Engrs., Theta Tau. Republican. Avocations: gardening, woodworking, reading.

PAOLINO, ALBERT FRANCIS, clinical psychologist; b. Kearny, N.J., Dec. 14, 1921; s. Louis and Rose (Minelli) P.; m. Rosetta Bastulli, June 15, 1957; children—Albert Z., Renee L., Andrea R. B.S., Rutgers U., 1947; Ph.D., Western Res. U., 1956. Diplomate Am. Bd. Psychology. Chief psychologist Cleve. Boys Sch., 1950, Summit County Receiving Hosp., 1951-56, Cleve. Psychiat. Inst., 1956-63, 1973-82; research fellow surgery Western Res. U. Med. Sch., 1961-63; sr. research psychologist Brecksville VA Hosp., 1963-65; project/lab. dir. Lab. Psychosocial Research, Cleve. Psychiat. Inst., 1965-73; pvt. practice psychology, 1962—; cons. Cleve. Roman Catholic Diocese. Served with USAAF, 1942-46. Mem. Am. Psychol. Assn., Midwest Psychol. Assn., Cleve. Psychol. Assn., Cleve. Acad. Cons. Psychologists, AAAS, N.Y. Acad. Sci. Roman Catholic. Contbr. articles to profl. jours.

PAPADAKIS, CONSTANTINE NICHOLAS, engineering educator, dean; b. Athens, Greece, Feb. 2, 1946; came to U.S., 1969; s. Nicholas and Rita (Machiotti) P.; m. Eliana Apostolides, Aug. 28, 1971; 1 child, Maria. Diploma in Civil Engring., Nat. Tech. U. Athens, 1969; MS in Civil Engring., U. Cin., 1970; PhD in Civil Engring., U. Mich., 1973. Cert. profl. engr., Colo., Mich., Va., Ohio, Greece. Engring. specialist, supr. geotechnical group Bechtel, Inc., Gaithersburg, Md., 1974-78; asst. chief engr. geotechnical group Bechtel, Inc., Ann Arbor, Mich., 1978-81; v.p., bd. dirs. water resources div. STS Cons. Ltd., Ann Arbor, 1981-84; v.p. water and environ. resources dept. Tetra Tech-Honeywell, Pasadena, Calif., 1984; head dept. civil engring. Colo. State U., Ft. Collins, 1984-86; dean Sch. Engring. U. Cin., 1986—; adj. prof. civil engring. U. Mich., 1976-83; cons. Gaines & Stern Co., Cleve., 1983-84, Honeywell Europe, Maintal, Fed. Republic of Germany, 1984-85, Arthur D. Little, Boston, 1984-85. Author: Problems on Strength of Materials, 1968, Sewer Systems Design, 1969; editor: Fluid Transients and Acoustics, 1978, Pump-Turbine Schemes, 1979, Small Hydro Power Fluid Machinery, 1982; Megatrends in Hydraulics, 1987; contbr. over 40 articles to profl. jours. Council mem. St. Nicholas Ch. Parish, Ann Arbor, 1981-84; mem. City of Ft. Collins Drainage Bd., 1984-86. Recipient Horace W. King scholarship civil engring. dept. U. Mich., 1971-73, Bechtel award Merit, 1974-79, Young Engr. of Yr. award Mich. Soc. Profl. Engrs., Ann Arbor, Mich., 1982. Mem. ASCE (pres. Ann Arbor br. 1980-81, pres. elect Mich. sect. 1983-84, hydraulics div. publ. com. 1980-83), ASME (chmn. fluid transients com. 1978-80, mem. fluids engring. div. awards com. 1981-84), NSPE, Am. Soc. Engring. Edn., Order of the Engr., Internat. Assn. for Hydraulic Research, Chi Epsilon, Sigma Xi, Tau Beta Pi. Greek Orthodox. Avocations: photography, classical music, travel, swimming, racquetball. Home: 7354 Sanderson Pl Indian Hill Cincinnati OH 45243 Office: U Cin Coll Engring 651 Baldwin Hall ML18 Cincinnati OH 45221-0018

PAPARELLA, MICHAEL M., otolaryngologist; b. Detroit, Feb. 13, 1933; m. Rebecca Paparella; children: Mark, Steven, Lisa. BS, U. Mich., 1953, MD, 1957. Diplomate Am. Bd. Otolaryngology (guest examiner 1967-75, bd. dirs. 1976, mem. standards and residencies com. 1976, fgn. med. grads. com. 1978, credentials com. 1984-85, examiner 1976—); lic. physician, Mich., Mass., Ohio, Minn. Rotating intern Emanuel Hosp., Portland, Oreg., 1957-58; resident in otolaryngology Henry Ford Hosp., Detroit, 1958-61, jr. mem. staff, 1960-61; mem. geographic staff, asst. Mass. Eye and Ear Infirmary, Boston, 1963-64; instr. Harvard U. Med. Sch., Boston, 1963-64; asst. prof. otolaryngology, dir. otological research lab. Ohio State U., Columbus, 1964-67; mem. staff dept. otolaryngology Ohio State U. Hosps., 1964-67; prof., chmn. dept. otolaryngology U. Minn., Mpls., 1967-84, dir. otopathology lab., 1967—, clin. prof., 1984—; mem. staff U. Minn. Hosps., 1967-84; pres. Minn. Ear, Head and Neck Clinic, Mpls., 1984—; dir. Nat. Temporal Bone Bank Program Midwestern Ctr., Mpls., 1979—; cons. VA Hosp., Dayton, Ohio, 1964-67. Mem. editorial bd. Minn. Medicine, The Laryngoscope, Modern Medicine, Am. Jour. Clin. Research, Am. Jour. Otolaryngology, Jour. Otolaryngology, Annals Otology, Rhinology & Laryngology, Acta Oto-Laryngologica; editor: (films) Surgical Techniques and Auditory Research, Surgical Treatment for Intractable External Otitis, Tympanoplasty, parts 1 and 2, Endolymphatic Sac, Canalplasty; (books) Atlas of Ear Surgery, 1968, 2d ed., 1971, 3d ed., 1980, Biochemical Mechanisms in Hearing and Deafness, 1970, Clinical Otology: An International Symposium, 1971, Year Book of the Ear, Nose & Throat, 1972, 73, 74, 75, Otolaryngology: Basic Sciences and Related Disciplines, 1973, 2d. ed. vol. I, 1980, Otolaryngology: Ear, vol. II, 1973, 2d ed., 1980, Otolaryngology: Head and Neck, vol. III, 1973, 2d ed., 1980, Year Book of Otolaryngology, 1976, 77, 78, 79, 80, 81, 82, 83, 84, 85, 86, Boies's Fundamentals of Otolaryngology: A Textbook of Ear, Nose and Throat Diseases, 5th ed., 1978, Ear Clinics International, vols. I-III, 1982, Medicassette Otolaryngology, 1986; also contbr. numerous articles. Founder, sec., bd. dirs. Internat. Hearing Found., 1984—; mem. Pre-sch. Med. Survey Vision and Hearing. Grantee NIH, Am. Otological Soc., Deafness Research Found., Hartford Found., Guggenheim Found., Bodman Found.; recipient Kobrak Research award, 1960, Amicitiae Sacrum honor Collegium Oto-Rhino-Laryngologicum, 1976; named Brinkman lectr. U. Nijmegen, Holland, 1986, Guest of Honor 5th Asia-Oceanic Meeting, Korea, 1983. Fellow ACS, Am. Acad. Ophthalmology and Otolaryngology (assoc. sec. continuing edn., assoc. sec., chmn. undergrad. edn. subcom., chmn. otorhinolaryngology self-improvement com., chmn. subcom. on evaluation new info. and edn. of hearing and equilibrium com., head and neck surgery equilibrium subcom. 1984-86, Merit award 1975); mem. Acad. Medicine Columbus County, Acad. Medicine Franklin County, Am. Assn. for Lab. Animal Scis., AMA, Am. Neurotology Soc. (audiology study com. 1976), Am. Otological Soc. (trustee research fund, pres.), Assn. Acad. Depts. Otolaryngology (pres. pro tem, organizer 1971-72, sec.-treas. 1972-74, pres. elect 1974-76, pres. 1976-78), Barany Soc., Better Hearing Inst. (adv. bd.), Deafness Research Found. (trustee, Centurion Club), Collegium Oto-Rhino-Laryngologicum Amicitiae Sacrum, Columbus Ophthalmology and Otolaryngology Soc., Hennepin County Med. Soc., Mpls. Hearing Soc. (bd. dirs.), Minn. Acad. Medicine, Minn. Acad. Ophthalmology and Otolaryngology (council), Minn. Coll. Surgeons, New England Otolaryngological Soc., Ohio State Med. Soc., Pan Am. Med. Assn., Soc. Univ. Otolaryngologists (exec. council 1969-71), Triological Soc. (v.p. middle sect. 1976, council mem. 1976, asst. editor), Alpha Kappa Kappa, Sigma Xi. Lodge: Lions (dir. hearing ctr., adv. council hearing ctr.). Office: 701 25th Ave S Minneapolis MN 55454

PAPAROZZI, ELLEN THERESA, horticulture science educator, researcher; b. Passaic, N.J., Nov. 2, 1953; d. Frank James and Caroline Mary (France) P.; m. Walter W. Stroup, June 23, 1984. BS, Rutgers U., 1976; MS, Cornell U., 1978, PhD, 1981. Asst. prof. U. Nebr., Lincoln, 1981-87, assoc. prof., 1987—; chmn., vice-chairperson Trees for Nebr. Conf., Lincoln, 1984, 85; chairperson adv. council Coll. Agr., 1983-84. Contbr. articles to profl. jours. Mem. floristry adv. com. Southeastern Community Coll., 1985—; co-coach Nebr. Flower Judging Team, 1985; mem. Oratorio Chorus, Lincoln. Research grantee Gloeckner Found., 1982, 83, 87. Mem. Nebr. Grad. Women in Sci. (pres. 1982-85), Women in Sci. at Nebr. Acad. Scis. (session chair 1984—), Am. Soc. for Horticultural Scis. (chaiperson women in horticulture com. 1981-82, coordinator stat. colloquium 1987, chairperson Cross-commodity Research award 1987), AAAS, Nebr. Assn. of Nurserymen, Nebr. Statewide Arboretum, Internat. Soc. for Horticultural Sci., Bot. Soc. of Am. Roman Catholic. Office: U Nebr 377 Plant Sciences Lincoln NE 68586-0724

PAPE, BARBARA HARRIS, lawyer; b. Casper, Wyo., Aug. 12, 1936; d. Herbert Garfield and Leah Jean (Case) Harris; m. William Martin Pape, June 28, 1969; children: Kyri Dannan, Kirsten Tara. AA in Theatre, Stephens Coll., 1956; BJ, BA, U. Mo., 1960, MA, 1966, BS in Edn., 1968, PhD, JD, 1980. Bar: Mo. 1981, U.S. Dist. Ct. (we. dist.) Mo. 1981, U.S. Supreme Ct., 1986. Mem. faculty U. Mo., Columbia, 1966-74; daily TV show hostess Triton Prodns., Inc., Columbia, 1973-76; realtor Tara Realty, Columbia, 1977-81; sole practice, Columbia, 1981-82; ptnr. Cronan, Robinson, Lampton & Pape, Columbia, 1982-85, Barbara Harris Pape & Assocs, P.C., Columbia, 1986—. Assoc. editor Litigation mag., 1983-85; contbr. articles to mags. Bd. dirs. Columbia Resource Ctr., Inc., 1981—; pres. adv. bd. YWCA, YMCA, Columbia, 1977-78; pres. bd. trustees Coll. Arts and Scis. U. Mo., Columbia, 1986—; alumni bd. dirs. Stephens Coll., 1977-80. Recipient Roscoe Anderson award. Mem. ABA, Mo. Bar Assn., Boone County Bar Assn., Am. Assn. Trial Lawyers (vice chairperson publs. 1987—), Mo. Assn. Trial Lawyers, Mo. Criminal Def. Lawyers, Internat. Order Barristers, U. Mo. Alumni Orgn. (bd. dirs. 1986—), Kappa Tau Alpha, Delta Theta Phi. Democrat. Home: 3301 Westcreek Circle Columbia MO 65203 Office: 1200 Rogers Suite 200 Columbia MO 65201

PAPE, DUANE M., manufacturing executive; b. Marietta, Ohio, Mar. 27, 1950; s. Glen M. Freda A. (Taylor) P.; m. Cynthia L. Parent, Apr. 3, 1978; children: Kristofer D., Travis D.P. B MechE, Gen. Motors Inst., 1973. Registered profl. engr., Ohio. Layout, material handling engr. Packard Electric div. Gen. Motors Corp., Warren, Ohio, 1973-75, methods engr., 1975-76, standards engr., 1976, sr. long range planning engr., 1976-79; facilities planning mgr. Kenworth Truck Co., Seattle, 1979-83; indsl. and mfg. engring. mgr. Kenworth Truck Co., Chillicothe, Ohio, 1983—. Mem. Soc. Mfg. Engrs., Inst. Indsl. Engrs. (sr.). Club: Italian (Mercer, Pa.). Office: Kenworth Truck Co 65 Kenworth Dr Chillicothe OH 45601

PAPE, GLENN MICHAEL, lawyer, accountant, personal financial planner; b. Evergreen Park, Ill., Aug. 20, 1954; s. Gilbert Thomas Pape and Janine Elizabeth (Beheyt) Pape Riveros; m. Nancy Ann Vaske, Apr. 7, 1979; children: Katherine Jo, Courtney Johanna. BA in Classics, U. Chgo., 1978, MBA, 1981; JD, DePaul U., 1979. Bar: Ill. 1979. Cons. tax div. No. Trust Co., Chgo., 1980-81, fin. planner, 1981-82; fin. counselor Continental Ill. Nat. Bank, Chgo., 1982-84; tax mgr. Arthur Andersen & Co., Chgo., 1984—. Active Five Hosp. Homebound Elderly Program, Chgo., 1981; treas. Chamber Music Council Chgo., 1982. Mem. Chgo. Bar Assn. (fed. taxation com.), Ill. State Bar Assn., ABA, Internat. Assn. Fin. Planners, Am. Inst. CPA's, U.S. Chess Fedn., Am. Inst. CPA's. Home: 2146 University Dr Naperville IL 60565-3485 Office: Arthur Andersen & Co 33 W Monroe St Chicago IL 60603

PAPE, PATRICIA ANN, social worker, psychotherapist; b. Aurora, Ill., Aug. 2, 1940; d. Robert Frank and Helen Louise (Hanks) Grover; divorced; Scott Allen, Debra Lynn. BA, Northwestern U., 1962; MSW, George Williams Coll., 1979. Coordinator community resources DuPage Probation Dept., Wheaton, Ill., 1979-80; dir. The Abbey Alcoholism Treatment Ctr., Winfield, Ill., 1980-81; prin. Pape & Assocs., Wheaton, 1982—; dir. alcoholism counselor tng. program Coll. of DuPage, Glen Ellyn, Ill., 1982—. Mem. alcohol and drug task force Ill. Synod Luth. Ch. in Am., Chgo., 1985—. Named Woman of Yr., Entrepreneur Women in Mgmt., Oak Brook, Ill, 1986. Mem. Assn. Labor-Mgmt. Adminstrs. and Cons. Alcoholism (women's issues com. 1984-86). Home: 519 Byron Ct Wheaton IL 60187 Office: Pape & Assocs 629 S Prospect Wheaton IL 60187

PAPENDICK, MICHAEL SCOTT, dentist; b. East Lansing, Mich., Feb. 2, 1957; s. Victor Eugene and Reta Lois (Barber) P. BS, No. Ill. U., 1979; DDS, U. Ill., Chgo., 1983. Gen. practice dentistry Lincolnshire, Ill., 1983—, Joliet, Ill., 1983—, Waukegan, Ill., 1986—. Mem. ADA, U.S. Dental Inst. Home: 18547 W Geier Rd Gurnee IL 60031 Office: 430 N Milwaukee Ave #12 Lincolnshire IL 60069

PAPP, KENNETH PAUL, electrical controls company executive; b. Dearborn, Mich., Feb. 16, 1962; s. Donald Stephen and Jean Ann Papp. Student, Henry Ford Coll., 1980-82; cert., Wayne State Coll., 1982. Engring. asst. DBN Tool & Machine Co., Romulus, Mich., 1979-80; gen. mgr. SAS, Romulus, 1980-83; gen. ptnr. Alkin Controls, Farmington Hills, Mich., 1983—. Mem. Mich. chpt. Soc. Fire Protection Engrs., Nat. Fire Protection Assn. Office: Alkin Controls 20774 Orchard Lake Rd Farmington Hills MI 48024

PAPPAS, CHARLES WILLIAM, restaurateur; b. Worthington, Minn., Oct. 4, 1925; s. Michael George and Mary Dorothy (Kump) P.; m. Mary Jo Gerlicher, Nov. 22, 1949; children: Brian Stanley, Laurie Jo, Barbara Ann, Charles William II. BA, Cornell U., 1954. Co-owner Covered Wagon Restaurant, Rochester, Minn., 1946-51; co-owner Michaels Restaurant, Mankato, Minn., 1961-75, Rochester, 1951—; bd. dirs. Norwest Bank, Rochester, 1973—. Mem. Nat. Restaurant Assn., Minn. Restaurant assn., Minn. Assn. Commerce, Cornell Soc. Hotelmen, Phi Kappa Phi. Republican. Roman Catholic. Avocations: jogging, tennis, fishing. Home: 835 8th Ave SW Rochester MN 55902 Office: Michaels Restaurant 15 S Broadway Rochester MN 55904

PAPPAS, EDWARD HARVEY, lawyer; b. Midland, Mich., Nov. 24, 1947; s. Charles and Sydell (Sheinberg) P.; m. Laurie Weston, Aug. 6, 1972; children—Gregory Alan, Steven Michael. B.B.A., U. Mich., 1969, J.D., 1973. Bar: Mich. 1973, U.S. Dist. Ct. (ea. dist.) Mich. 1973, U.S. Dist. Ct. (we. dist.) Mich. 1980, U.S. Ct. Appeals (6th cir.) 1983, U.S. Supreme Ct. 1983. Ptnr. firm Dickinson, Wright, Moon, Van Dusen & Freeman, Bloomfield Hills and Detroit, Mich., 1973—; v.p., trustee Oakland-Livingston Legal Aid, 1982-85, pres., trustee, 1985—; mediator Oakland County Cir. Ct., Pontiac, Mich., 1983—; hearing panelist Mich. Atty. Discipline Bd., Detroit, 1983—. Trustee Oakland Community Coll., Mich., 1982-86 ; trustee adv. bd. Mich. Regional Anti-Defamation League of B'nai Brith, Detroit, 1983—. Mem. State Bar Mich. (co-chmn. nat. moot ct. competition com. 1974, 76, com. on atty. discipline, com. on legal aid.), Oakland County Bar Assn. (vice-chmn. continuing legal edn. com., chmn. continuing legal edn. com. 1985-86, editor Laches monthly mag.), ABA, Am. Judicature Soc., Mich. Def. Trial Lawyers, Def. Research and Trial Lawyers Assn., (com. practice and procedure), B'nai B'rith Barristers. Home: 32223 Scenic Ln Franklin MI 48025 Office: PO Box 509 Dickinson Wright Moon Van Dusen & Freeman 525 N Woodward Ave Bloomfield Hills MI 48013

PAPPAS, JOHN J., printing machines company executive. Pres. Teletype Corp., Skokie, Ill. Office: Teletype Corp 5555 Touhy Ave Skokie IL 60077 *

PAPPAS, LEONARD JOHN, lawyer; b. Cleve., Aug. 6, 1952; s. Leonard Gust and Effie (Vamis) P. B.A. cum laude, Cleve. State U., 1974; J.D., Case Western Res. U., 1983. Bar: Ohio 1984, U.S. Dist. Ct. (no. dist.) Ohio 1984. Mktg. sales exec. Bobbie Brooks, Inc., Cleve., 1975; gen. mgr. Agora Inc., Painesville, Ohio, 1977-81; bus. cons. Gatsby's Inc., Mentor, Ohio, 1983-84; sole practice, Shaker Heights, Ohio, 1984-86; assoc., Baughman & Assocs Co., L.P.A., 1986—. Mem. Assn. Trial Lawyers Am., Ohio Bar Assn., Bar Assn. Greater Cleve., Cuyahoga County Bar Assn., Am. Judicature Soc., Zeta Psi. Democrat. Greek Orthodox. Office: Baughman & Assocs Co LPA 55 Public Sq Suite 2215 Cleveland OH 44113

PAPPAS, PAUL JOSEPH, JR., restaurant owner, accountant; b. Mantorville, Minn., Feb. 11, 1947; s. Paul Joseph Pappas Sr. and Irene (Stussy) Falker; m. Suzanne Euart, Dec. 26, 1966; children: Christopher, Lisa; m. Carrie Ann Berg, Oct. 22, 1983; 1 child, Alexandra. AA, Rochester Jr. Coll., 1967; BS, Mankato State U., 1970. With Michael Restaurant, Mankato, 1967-70, owner, operator, 1976—; with Laventhol Horwath, Mpls., 1970-73; mgr. Holiday Inn, Mpls., 1973-76. Lodge: Rotary. Home: 915 Wilson St Onalaska WI 54650

PAPPAS, THEODORE GEORGE, architect; b. Detroit, Sept. 5, 1956; s. Augustus George and Helen (Fakouras) P. BArch, U. Mich., 1978, MArch, 1980. Designer, detailer O. Germany, Inc., Warren, Mich., 1978, 79; designer John Stevens & Assocs., Detroit, 1982, John Hilberry & Assocs., Detroit, 1980-83, Minoru Yamaskai & Assocs., Troy, Mich., 1984-85; pres. Theodore Pappas & Assocs., Detroit, 1983—. Detroit Civic Ambassador, Cen. Bus. Dist. Assn., 1986. Recipient Spirit of Detroit award, Detroit City Council, 1985. Mem. AIA, Detroit Chpt. Mich. Soc. Architects, Frank Lloyd Wright Home & Studio Found., Nat. Trust for Hist. Preservation, Hist. Soc. Mich., Detroit Inst. Arts Founders Soc., Detroit Symphony Sounding Bd., Cen. Bus. Dist. Assn. Downtown Detroit (named Civic Ambassador 1986). Greek Orthodox. Club: Detroit Econ. Avocations: numismatics, music, astronomy, math., archtl. history.

PAPPAS, WILLIAM JOHN, principal, educator; b. Detroit, Oct. 23, 1937; s. John Basil and Susan (Kurlas) P.; m. Susan Kay Payne, Aug. 18, 1962; 1 child Laurie Ann. BA, Western Mich. U., 1962; MA, Eastern Mich. U., 1966; cert. in edn. spl., Wayne State U., 1971. Tchr. Mt. Clemens (Mich.) High Sch., 1962-67, asst. prin., 1967-71; prin. Northview High Sch., Grand Rapids, Mich., 1971—; adj. prof. grad. sch. Cen. Mich. U., Mt. Pleasant, 1974—. Contbr. articles to profl. jours. I/D/E/A fellow 1974-76, 78-84, 86-87. Mem. Mich. Assn. Secondary Sch. Prins. (past pres., Outstanding Secondary Prin. Yr. 1985-86), Phi Delta Kappa. Episcopalian. Lodge: Lions (pres. Grand Rapids 1976). Avocaitons: reading, athletics. Home: 4636 Northview NE Grand Rapids MI 49505 Office: Northview High Sch 4451 Hunsberger NE Grand Rapids MI 49505

PARADIS, CARMEN, plastic surgeon; b. Edmont, Alta., Can., Mar. 31, 1950; came to U.S., 1978; d. Phillip Edmond and Ellen Marie (McIsaac) P. BS, U. Alta., Edmonton, 1970, MD summa cum laude, 1974. Diplomate Am. Bd. Plastic Surgery. Intern in surgery Wellesley Hosp., Toronto, Ont., Can., 1974-75; resident in gen. surgery Royal Victoria Hosp., Montréal, Que., Can., 1975-78; resident in plastic surgery Case Western Res. U., Cleve., 1978-80; Emanual B. Kaplan fellow in hand surgery Hosp. for Joint Diseases, N.Y.C., 1980-81; clin. instr. plastic surgery Case Western Res. U., Cleve., 1981-87; pvt. practice specializing in plastic surgery Euclid, Ohio, 1987—. Mem. Am. Soc. Plastic and Reconstructive Surgeons, Plastic Surgery Ednl. Found., Ohio Valley Soc. Plastic and Reconstructive Surgeons, N.E. Ohio Soc. Plastic and Reconstructive Surgeons, Ohio State Med. Soc., Acad. Medicine Cleve., Cleve. Med. Women's Soc., Cleve. Surg. Soc., Cleve. Med. Library Assn., Geauga County Med. Soc. Office: 25701 N Lakeland Blvd Suite 407 Euclid OH 44132

PARCH, GRACE DOLORES, librarian; b. Cleve.; d. Joseph Charles and Josephine Dorothy (Kumel) P. B.A., Case Western Res. U., 1946, postgrad., 1947-50; B.L.S., McGill U., 1951; M.L.S., Kent State U., 1983; postgrad., Newspaper Library Workshop, Kent State U., 1970, Cooper Sch. Art, 1971-72, API Newspaper Library Seminar, Columbia U., 1971, Coll. Librarianship, U. Wales, 1984, 85. Publicity librarian Spl. Services U.S. Army, Germany, 1951; post librarian Spl. Services U.S. Army, Italy, 1952; USAF base librarian 1953-54; br. librarian Cleveland Heights (Ohio) Pub. Library, 1954-63; asst. head reference div. Va. State Library, Richmond, 1964; dir. Twinsburg (Ohio) Pub. Library, 1965-70; dir. newspaper library Cleve. Plain Dealer, 1970—; Cons. Cath. Library Assn., 1961-64; mem. home econs. adv. com., Summit County, 1969, books/job com., 1968; mem. adv. com. Guide to Ohio Newspapers, 1793-1973, 1971-74. Contbr. articles to Plain Dealer, N. Summit Times, Twinsburg Bull., Sun Press; author: Where In the World But in the Plain Dealer Library, 1971; Editor: Directory of Newspaper Libraries in the U.S. and Canada, 1976. Mem. McGill U. Alumnae Assn. (sec. 1973), Kent State U. Alumni Assn., ALA (rep. on joint com. with Cath. Library Assn. 1967-70), John Cotton Dana award 1967, Library Pub. Relations Council award 1972), Cath. Library Assn. (co-chmn. 1960-63), Spl. Libraries Assn. (chmn. newspaper library directory com. 1974-76, chmn. pub. relations Cleve. chpt. 1973, chmn. edn. com. newspaper div. 1982-83, mem. edn. com. nominating com. 1984), Ohio Library Assn., Western Res. Hist. Soc., Am. Soc. Indexers, Cleve. Mus. Art Assn., Coll. and Research Librarians, Nat. Micrographic Assn., Women Space, Women's Nat. Book Com., Nat. Trust Hist. Preservation. Roman Catholic. Clubs: Cleve. Athletic, Cleve. Women's City. Home: 688 Jefferson St Bedford OH 44146

PARDEE, JEFFREY CLARK, county government official; b. N.Y.C., May 14, 1944; s. Jack Howard II and Florence (Brennan) P.; m. Mary Anna Weil, Dec. 23, 1966; children: Brennan James, Kennedy Clark. BBA, Eastern Mich. U., 1968; MBA in Fin., U. Detroit, 1971; postgrad., Nova U., 1975-81. Fin. analyst Sterling Axle Plant div. Ford Motor Co., Sterling Heights, Mich., 1968-73; budget dir. Genesee County, Flint, Mich., 1973-76, Oakland County, Pontiac, Mich., 1976—; treas. Flint-Genesee Corp. for Econ. Growth, 1978—; pres. Genesee County Econ. Devel. Corp., Flint, 1982—; bd. dirs. Forward Devel. Corp; chmn. bd. dirs. Communications Services Network, Inc.; adj. prof. pub. budgeting U. Mich., Flint, 1984-85. Editor Statewide News-Mich. Rental Housing Assn. Newsletter, 1985—. Merit counselor Boy Scouts Am., Grand Blanc, Mich., 1982—; councilman City of Grand Blanc, 1985—; treas. Crime Watch Assn., Gradn Blanc, 1985—, Genesee County Met. Alliance, Flint, 1986—; bd. dirs. Flint-Genesee Revolving Loan Fund, 1980—. Mem. Govt. Fin. Officers Assn. U.S. and Can. (review com. 1984—, Disting. Budget Presentation award), Am. soc. Pub. Adminstrs., G.M.I. Mgmt. and Engring. Inst. (adv. bd. 1984—). Republican. Mormon. Avocations: racquetball, auto racing. Home: 11390 Grand Oak Dr Grand Blanc MI 48439 Office: Oakland County Budget Div 1200 N Telegraph Rd Pontiac MI 48053

PARDO, ROBERT EDWARD, software marketing and development executive; b. Chgo., Apr. 26, 1951; s. Edward Edwin and Marion (Brent) P.; m. Nora Kay Okerholm, July 14, 1979; children: Kathryn Elizabeth, Christopher Robert. BA, Northwestern U., 1972. Pres. R.E. Pardo & Co., Chgo., 1978; ops. supr. Bache & Co., Chgo., 1978-79; asst. ops. mgr. Conti Commodities, Chgo., 1979-80; internat. monetary market floor ops. mgr. Salomon Bros., Chgo., 1980; pres. Pardo Corp., Evanston, Ill., 1980-87, chmn. capital mgmt., 1987—. Author, designer numerous fin. software programs; contbr. several articles to profl. mags. Mem. Assn. Data Processing Service Orgns. Republican. Avocations: running, fitness, traveling, reading, mathematics. Office: Pardo Corp 1800 Sherman Suite 609 Evanston IL 60201

PARENTEAU, JAMES EDWARD, retired military communications officer; b. Superior, Wis., Nov. 4, 1921; s. Edward Peter and Clara Mary (Malchow) P.; m. Winifred Virginia McCairns, July 2, 1942; children—Bonnie Ann Parenteau Bruck, Frank Edward. Student U. Md., 1956-58. Served to chief warrant officer U.S. Air Force, 1941-62; communications radio operator Army Air Corps, 1941-45; communications clk. Western Union Telegraph Co., Newark, 1945-46; communicaitons relay ctr. supr. U.S. Air Force, 1946-57, communications officer automatic switching ctr., 1957-62; ops. mgr. automatic digital network Air Force Communications Service, Gentile AFB, Ohio, 1962-77, ret. Recipient Outstanding Unit award Def. Communication Agy., 1969; named Outstanding Automatic Electronic Switching Ctr., Def. Communication Agy., 1976. Republican. Methodist. Clubs: Officers (Wright Patterson AFB, Ohio); Square Dance (Fairborn, Ohio) (sec., sunshine chmn.) Avocations: artistic stained glass; square dancing; volunteer medical work. Home: 1840 Bordeaux Dr Fairborn OH 45324

PARENTEAU, JEROME FRANCIS, paint and coatings manufacturing executive; b. Rochester, N.Y., Feb. 8, 1924; s. Charles Anthony and Elvera (Born) P.; student U. Mich., 1941-42, U. Minn., 1943; A.B., Syracuse U., 1948; m. Lois Scott, Nov. 29, 1946; children—Richard, Ellen. Account rep. William H. Reed, Niagara Falls, N.Y., 1948-49; mgr. advt. and communications Varcum Chem. Corp., Niagara Falls, N.Y., 1949-51; div. advt. mgr. Nat. Gypsum Co., Buffalo, 1951-54; mgr. advt. and pub. relations Seidlitz Paint & Varnish Co., Kansas City, Mo., 1954-62; v.p. advt. and pub. relations Conchemco, Inc., Kansas City, Mo., 1962-69, Seidlitz Paints Div., 1962-69, Nashua Homes Div., 1965-69, exec. v.p. Colony Paints Div., 1969-73; mgr. finance and adminstrn. coatings group Conchemco Inc. (now Valspar Corp.), Lenexa, Kans., 1973-75, v.p. finance and adminstrn. coatings group, 1975-77, v.p., gen. mgr. coatings eastern div., 1977-79, plant mgr., 1979-85, corp. risk mgr., 1985-87, corp. risk analyst, 1987—. Mem. pub. relations council Mid-Continent council Girl Scouts U.S.A., 1968-70. Served with USAAF, 1943-46. Mem. Nat. Paint, Varnish and Lacquer Assn., Pub. Relations Soc. Am. (chpt. dir. 1968-69), Am. Marketing Assn. (chpt. dir. 1966-70, chpt. v.p. 1969-70), Am. Mgmt. Assn., Risk and Ins. Mgmt. Soc., Inc., Mensa, Alpha Delta Sigma, Theta Beta Phi, Kappa Sigma. Republican. Presbyn. Mason. Contbr. articles to profl. jours. Home and Office: 12731 W 118th St Overland Park KS 66210

PARFET, RAY THEODORE, JR., pharmaceutical company executive; b. Port Huron, Mich.. Dir. Upjohn Co., Kalamazoo, 1958—, v.p., 1958-59, exec. v.p. charge research, legal, fin. and personnel activities, 1960-62, pres., gen. mgr., 1962-69, chmn. bd., chief exec. officer, 1969—, also dir.; dir. First Nat. Bank & Trust Co., Gilmore Bros. Dept. Store, Mich. Bell Telephone Co., Union Pump Co., Battle Creek, Aro Corp., Bryan, Ohio, First Am. Bank Corp, ARC. Trustee Bronson Methodist Hosp. Mem. Pharm. Mfrs. Assn. (past dir., past chmn., past dir. internat. fedn.). Address: Upjohn Co 7000 Portage Rd Kalamazoo MI 49001 *

PARHAS, STELLA A., operations executive; b. Chgo., Aug. 4, 1959; d. Arthur G. and Eugenia (Rigopoulos) P. BA, St. Xavier Coll., 1981. Dealer, service rep. Kemper Fin. Services, Chgo., 1982-84, dealer, service supr., 1984-85, tng. coordinator, 1985—, 1984—. mem. choir St. Constantine and St. Helen Chs., Palos Hills, Ill., 1984—, mem. young adult league, 1985—, officer, 1987—. Mem. Hellenic Profl. Soc. Republcan. Greek Orthodox. Home: 2816 W 98th Pl Evergreen Park IL 60642 Office: Kemper Fin Services 120 S LaSalle Chicago IL 60603

PARINS, ROBERT JAMES, lawyer, professional football executive; b. Green Bay, Wis., Aug. 23, 1918; s. Frank and Nettie (Denissen) P.; m. Elizabeth L. Carroll, Feb. 8, 1941; children—Claire, Andrée, Richard, Teresa, Lu Ann. B.A., U. Wis.-Madison, 1940, LL.B., 1942. Bar: Wis. Supreme Ct. 1942. Sole practice law, Green Bay, 1942-68, dist. atty. Brown County, Wis., 1949-50, circuit judge Brown County, 1968-82, res. judge, 1982—; pres. Green Bay Packers, Inc., 1982—. Mem. Wis. State Bar Assn. Roman Catholic. Office: Green Bay Packers PO Box 10628 Green Bay WI 54307

PARIS, PAUL NOLAN, JR., military officer; b. Dallas, Feb. 13, 1950; s. Paul Nolan and Luella Mae (Pritchett) P.; m. Edith Marilyn Palmer, Sept. 4, 1971; children: Paul III, Lauren. BA in Geography, North Tex. State U., 1972; MA in Mgmt., Webster U., 1983. Commd. 2d lt. USAF, 1972, advanced through grades to maj., 1984, B52 instr. copilot, aircraft commd., instr. pilot, wing tactics officer, emergency actions controller, B52 flight commd.; instr. geography Alpena Community Coll. Republican. Baptist. Club: Toastmasters. Avocations: sports, geneology, coin and baseball card collecting, writing. Home: 7893 W Golfview Circle Oscoda MI 48750

PARISH, PRESTON SETIER, retired pharmaceutical company executive, business consultant; b. Chgo., Nov. 10, 1919; m. Suzanne Upjohn DeLano, Apr. 17, 1948; children: Barbara Parish Gibbs, Katharine Parish Miller, Peter William, Preston Laurence, David Carter. AB, Williams Coll., 1941. Prodn. engr. The Upjohn Co., Kalamazoo, 1949-55, also bd. dirs., 1955—, v.p., 1958-60, exec. v.p., 1960-69, vice chmn. bd., chmn. exec. com., 1969-84; pres. Parish Assocs., Kalamazoo, 1985—; Bd. dirs. Kal-Aero, Inc., Kalamazoo, 1973—, VanDusen Air, Inc., Mpls., 1983-86; trustee, chmn. bd. dirs. W.E. Upjohn Unemployment Trustee Corp., Kalamazoo, 1963—. Mem. internat. adv. bd. Emory U. Family Planning Program, 1984—; mem. Canadian Warplane Heritage, Inc., Toronto, 1976—, Gov.'s Commn. on Jobs and Econ. Devel., Lansing, Mich., 1983-86; bd. dirs. Jobs for Am.'s Grads., Washington, 1981—, Jobs for Mich.'s Grads., Kalamazoo, 1981—, Kalamazoo Aviation History Museum, 1979—, Kalamazoo Coll., 1985—, Williams Coll., Williamstown, Mass., 1965—. Served to lt. maj. USMC, 1941-46. Decorated Bronze Star; recipient E. Earl Wright Community Achievement award Citizens' Com., Kalamazoo, 1984, Rogerson Cup Williams Coll. Office: Parish Assocs 415 W Michigan Ave Kalamazoo MI 49007

PARISI, HENRY EDWARD, accountant; b. Youngstown, Ohio, Nov. 2, 1953; s. Edward M. and Mary J. (Zanni) P.; m. Barbara Ann Bozdog, Sept. 5, 1981; children: Lisa, Andrea. BSBA, Youngstown State U., 1977. CPA, Ohio. Pub. acct. Goddard, Thomas & Co., Youngstown, 1974-77, Coopers & Lybrand, Cleve., 1977-78; mgr. acctg. Gen. Motors, Warren, Ohio, 1978—. Mem. Am. Inst. CPA's, Ohio Soc. CPA's, Phi Kappa Phi. Democrat. Roman Catholic. Avocations: gardening, swimming, tennis.

PARISI, JOSEPH (ANTHONY), magazine editor, writer-consultant, educator; b. Duluth, Minn., Nov. 18, 1944; s. Joseph Carl Parisi and Phyllis Susan (Quaranta) Schlecht. B.A. with honors, Coll. St. Thomas, 1966; M.A., U. Chgo., 1967, Ph.D. with honors, 1973. Asst. prof. Roosevelt U., Chgo., 1969-78; assoc. editor POETRY Mag., Chgo., 1976-83; acting editor POETRY Mag., 1983-85, editor, 1985—; vis. prof. U. Ill., Chgo., 1978—; cons., writer ALA, Chgo., 1980—; cons. NEH, 1983-87. Editor: The Poetry Anthology, 1912-1977, 1978; contbr. articles and reviews to profl. jours. Recipient Alvin Bentley award Duns Scotus Coll., 1963. Mem. Delta Epsilon Sigma. Club: Cliff Dwellers. Avocations: piano, photography, book and record collecting. Office: POETRY Mag 60 W Walton St Chicago IL 60610

PARK, DEAN ALAN, electrical engineer; b. Kansas City, Mo., July 6, 1950; s. Harry James and Lois Margaret (Corsen) P.; m. Vicki Louise Gardner, Apr. 28, 1973; children: Keri Linn, Stacy Marie. BSEE, U. Mo., Rolla, 1972. Registered profl. engr., Mo., Ill. Asst. service area engr. Ill. Power Co., Belleville, 1973-74; sr. engr. Drazen Assocs., Inc., St. Louis, 1974-80, chief engr., 1980-81; pres. Park Co., Cons. Engrs., St. Louis, 1981—; mgr. energy and rates Barnes, Henry, Meisenheimer & Gende, Inc., St. Louis, 1986—. Region coordinator Mo. JCI Senate, St. Louis, 1984-86; chmn., trustee Dorsett Village Baptist Ch., Maryland Heights, Mo., 1983—. Mem. NSPE, Mo. Soc. Profl. Engrs., Northwest Jaycees (pres. 1978-79, Internat. Senator 1982), Creve Couer C. of C. (dir. 1983—). Republican. Baptist. Home: 1958 Pepperell Dr Saint Louis MO 63146 Office: Barnes Henry Meisenheimer and Gende Inc Cons Engrs 4658 Gravois Ave Saint Louis MO 63116

PARK, JUNG IL, otolaryngologist, plastic surgeon; b. Seoul, Korea, Aug. 17, 1942; s. Jai Ki and Duk-Nam Park; m. Young-Yong Park, Jan. 10, 1972; children: Won-Sik, Min-Sik, Kyu Sik. BS, Seoul Nat. U., 1963, MD, 1967, PhD, 1972. Diplomate Korean Bd. Otolaryngology, Am. Bd. Otolaryngology. Fellow in otolaryngologic medicine U. Colo. Med. Ctr., 1977-79; resident in surgery and otolaryngology St. Louis U. Hosp., 1979-84; otolaryngologist Hammond Clinic, Munster, Ind., 1983—; asst. prof. otolaryngology Choong Ang U. Hosp., Seoul, 1975-77; mem. staff Our Lady of Mercy Hosp., Dyer, Ind. 1984; chmn. sect. otolaryngology, Munster Community Hosp., 1986, St. Margaret Hosp., Hammond, Ind., 1986. Contbr. article to profl. jour. Served to maj. R.O.K 1972-75, Korea. Fellow ACS, Am. Acad. Facial Plastic Reconstructive Surgery, Am. Acad. Cosmetic Surgeons; mem. AMA, Lake County Med. Soc., Am. Soc. Lipo Surgery. Avocations: tennis, hiking, camping, swimming. Home: 8109 Greenwood St Munster IN 46321 Office: Hammond Clinic 7905 Calumet Ave Munster IN 46321

PARK, LARRY D., systems analyst; b. Mason City, Iowa, Jan. 31, 1943; s. John and Leona Eva (Buss); m. Nancy K. Horak, Aug. 12, 1967; 1 child, Jeremy D.; 1 stepchild, Kimberly K. Younge Holsapple. BA, U. No. Iowa, 1965; MA in Teaching, Wash. State U., 1971. Tchr., coach Rockwell City (Iowa) Schs., 1965-66; sports writer Waterloo (Iowa) Courier, 1966-67; tchr., coach Marshalltown (Iowa) Schs., 1967-80; sales rep. Aid Assn. for Luths., Appleton, Wis., 1980-81; systems analyst Fisher Controls, Marshalltown, 1981—. Mem. NEA, Assn. Systems Mgmt. Lutheran. Lodge: Optimists. Avocations: bridge, sports, reading. Home: 2102 S 1st Ave Marshalltown IA 50158 Office: Fisher Controls 205 S Center Marshalltown IA 50158

PARK, QUE TE, optical industry executive; b. Pohang City, Republic of Korea, Dec. 5, 1946; came to U.S., 1981; s. In K. and K.R. (Yang) P.; m. Jung J. Kim, June 2, 1974; children: Chang S., June S., Nina S. BA, Hankuk U. Fgn. Studies, Republic of Korea, 1973, MBA, 1981; exec. program, Northwestern U. Kellogg Grad. Sch. Bus., 1984. Pres. Sambo Optical Co., Ltd., Masan, Republic of Korea, 1977-78; exec. dir. Tongkook Corp., Seoul, Republic of Korea, 1978-81; pres. Tongkook Am., Inc., Elk Grove Village, Ill., 1982-86, Samyang Optical, Inc., Elk Grove Village, 1986—. Mem. Northwest Internat. Traders Club. Mem. Assembly of God. Club: Greater O'Hare (Ill.). Avocations: reading, golf. Office: Samyang Optical Inc 1157 Pagni Dr Elk Grove Village IL 60067

PARK, YONG-JIN, metallurgical engineer, research; b. Seoul, Feb. 18, 1949; came to U.S., 1973; s. Dong-Eun and Sukim (Kim) P.; m. Soonhee Kim, May 25, 1975; children: Susie, Tracy. BS, Seoul Nat. U., 1971; MS, Carnegie Mellon U., 1974, PhD, 1977; MBA, U. Mich., 1985. Research metallurgist Assoc. Am. R.R., Chgo., 1977-79; sr. research assoc. Amax Materials Research Ctr., Ann Arbor, Mich., 1979-84, sr. research metallurgist, 1984—, staff metallurgist, 1986—. Contbr. research papers to profl. jours. Mem. AIME, Am. Soc. Metals, Am. Foundry Men's Soc. (Best Paper award 1986). Avocations: bowling, golf, traveling. Office: Amax Materials Research Ctr 1600 Huron Pkwy Ann Arobr MI 48105

PARKER, ANN ELAINE, social worker; b. Russell, Kans., Dec. 7, 1952; d. Arnold Arthur and Maxine Lucille (Smith) Mills; m. Brian Allen Parker, May 1, 1976; 1 child, Matthew Mills. BSW, U. Kans., 1975, MSW, 1981. Lic. social worker. Psychiatric social worker Larned (Kans.) State Hosp., 1975-79, 1981-83; team social worker Kans. Neurol. Inst., Topeka, 1983-85; forensic social worker Topeka State Hosp., 1985—; cons. nursing homes, Lacrosse, Kans., 1981-83. Mem. Nat. Assn. Social Workers, Alpha Chi Omega. Avocations: reading , swimming, piano, listening to music. Home: 2135 Quail Creek Dr Lawrence KS 66046 Office: Topeka State Hosp 2700 W 6th Topeka KS 66606

PARKER, DAVID GENE, professional baseball player; b. Jackson, Miss., June 9, 1951. With Pitts. Pirates, 1973-82, Cin. Reds, 1983—; Nat. League player in All-Star Game, 1977, 79, 80, 81, 85. Named Most Valuable Player Nat. League, 1978. Address: care Cin Reds 100 Riverfront Stadium Cincinnati OH 45202 *

PARKER, DORIS SIMS, association consultant; b. Marvel, Ark., Aug. 23, 1931; d. Percy L. and Earlie M. (Sims) Watson; children—Karen Stewart, Terri. B.A., Ind. Central U., 1959. Acctg. clk. U.S. Army Fin. Ctr., 1952-66; adjudicator VA Regional Office, Indpls., 1966-73; dir. recruiting, placement and regional relations Ind. Vocat. Tech. Coll., Indpls., 1973-82; exec. dir. YWCA, Indpls., 1982-85; orgn. planning and tng. cons., Indpls., 1985—; trainer/facilitator Inst. Cultural Affairs, 1985—; mem. State Adv. Council Vocat. Edn., 1978—; trainer Leadership Devel. for Pub. Service, 1968-76. Vice-chmn. human relations/human services Greater Indpls. Progress Com., 1979—; pres. Hoosier Capital council Girl Scouts U.S.A., 1979-82; mem., chmn. Nat. Com. Campaign for Human Devel., U.S. Catholic Conf., 1973-76; trustee St. Mary of the Woods Coll., Terre Haute, Ind., 1985—. Named B'nai B'rith Woman of Yr., 1968; recipient Brotherhood award NCCJ, 1975; Those Spl. People award Women in Communications, Inc., 1979. Mem. Am. Vocat. Assn., Am. Personnel and Guidance Assn., Mid-Am. Assn. Edn. Opportunity Program Personnel, Greater Indpls. Women's Polit. Caucus, Alpha Kappa Alpha. Democrat. Roman Catholic. Office: 4460 Guion Rd Indianapolis IN 46254

PARKER, EDWIN CHAMBERLIN, manufacturing company executive; b. St. Louis, Mar. 9, 1933; s. Josiah Atkins and Margaret Sinclaire (Chamberlin) P., VIII; m. Barbara Taylor, Dec. 21, 1955; children—Josiah Atkins IX, Edwin Chamberlin, Nathan Seth. B.B.A., U. Mich.-Ann Arbor, 1954, M.B.A., 1955. Lending officer Harris Bank, Chgo., 1959-65; treas. Marshall Field & Co., Chgo., 1965-71; sr. v.p., chief fin. officer Gould Inc., Rolling Meadows, Ill., 1971—; chmn., dir. Dur-o-wal, Inc., 1981—; chmn. Bridge Products Inc., Chgo., 1983—, also dir.; dir. Banco Di Roma, Chgo., Bridge Port Brass S.P.A., Bergamo, Italy. Bd. dirs. USO, Chgo., 1974, Heart Assn., Chgo., 1979. Served to lt. (j.g.) USNR, 1955-58. Clubs: Chicago, Mid-Am.; Knollwood (Lake Forest, Ill.). Office: Bridge Products Inc 2215 Sanders Rd Northbrook IL 60062

PARKER, EVELYN CAMILLE HILL KILLIAN, physician, surgeon; b. Columbus, Ohio, June 28, 1918; d. John Vincent and Myrtle (Kagy) Hill; m. E.W. Killian, Apr. 25, 1943 (dec.); children—Paul Wesley, Clyde Bernard; m. Francis W. Parker, Dec. 7, 1958. Student, U. Chgo., 1942-43; B.S., U. Ill., 1945; M.D., 1946; postgrad. in ophthalmology, Northwestern U., 1947-48. Diplomate Am. Bd. Ophthalmology. Intern Wesley Meml. Hosp., Chgo., 1946-47; resident in ophthalmology Ill. Eye and Ear Infirmary, Chgo., 1949-51; practice medicine specializing in med. and surg. ophthalmology Logansport, Ind., 1951—; sec. staff Meml. Hosp., Logansport, 1959; pres. med. staff St. Joseph Hosp., Logansport, 1965. Pres., Logansport Council for Pub. Schs., 1961,62; mem. Lake Maxinkuckee Mgmt. Com., Culver, Ind., 1981—; chmn. social concern Methodist Ch., 1963-65, ofcl. bd., 1961-65. Recipient Service award Culver Mil. Acad., 1969. Fellow Am. Acad. Ophthalmology and Otolaryngology; mem. Soc. Eye Surgeons (charter), AMA (physicians recognition award 1971, 75, 79, 82, 85), Logansport C. of C., Cass County Med. Soc. (pres. 1971), Ind. State Med. Assn., Ind. Acad. Ophthalmology and Otolaryngology (pres. 1979-80). Republican. Clubs: Altrusa (v.p. 1967-69), Culver Mothers (pres. 1968-69). Home and Office: 2500 E Broadway Logansport IN 46947

PARKER, GARY DEAN, manufacturing company executive; b. Omaha, Mar. 27, 1945; s. Norman and Dolores (Pierce) P.; m. Joanne Baker, Aug. 27, 1966; children: Jason E., Rodney R. B.S. in B.A., Nebr. Wesleyan U., B.S. in Econs. Dir. sales Lindsay Mfg. Co., Nebr., 1971-73, v.p. sales-mktg., 1973-76, sr. v.p., 1976-78, exec. v.p., 1978-83; pres. Lindsay Mfg. Co., 1983—, dir., 1977—; pres. Irrigation Assocs., Silver Springs, Md., 1981-82, dir., 1978-83; dir. Irrigation Found. & Research, Silver Springs, 1978—. Mem. Nebr. Mfg. Assn. (pres. 1982-83), Delta Omicron Epsilon. Lodge: Elks. Office: Lindsay Mfg Co PO Box 156 Lindsay NE 68644 *

PARKER, GARY HARMON, accountant; b. Salina, Kans., July 1, 1935; s. Harmon J. and Melba Eugenia (Rogers) P.; m. Luetta Yvonne Norman, Oct. 23, 1955; children: Timothy, Thomas, Lisa. AA, Garden City Community Coll., 1970; BA, Ft. Hays State U., 1972. CPA, Kans. Ptnr. Lewis, Hooper & Dick, Garden City, Kans., 1973-80, Birney & Co., Garden City, 1980—. Served to sgt. U.S. Army, 1955-58. Mem. Am. Inst. CPA's, Kans. Soc. CPA's (sec. 1984-85), Kans. Bd. Accountancy. Democrat. Presbyterian. Clubs: Southwind Country (Garden City), Broncbuster Athletic Assn. (Garden City) (pres. 1968). Avocations: golf, woodworking. Home: 2621 N 3d St Garden City KS 67846 Office: Birney & Co 1521 Fulton Terr Garden City KS 67846

PARKER, GEORGE, retired pen manufacturing company executive; b. Janesville, Wis., Nov. 9, 1929; s. Russell C. and Eleanor (Jackson) P.; m. Nancy E. Bauhan, Aug. 11, 1951; children: George Safford III, Elizabeth, Martha, Patricia. B.A., Brown U., 1951, LL.D. (hon.), 1986; M.A., U. Mich., 1952; LL.D. (hon.), Milton Coll., 1974. With Parker Pen Co., Janesville, 1952-86; beginning as asst. to gen. mgr. Gilman Engring. Co. subs. Parker Pen Co., successively asst. domestic advt. mgr., fgn. advt. mgr., dir. fgn. sales, dir. domestic sales, v.p., gen. mgr., 1958-60, exec. v.p., 1960-66, pres., 1966-77, 81-82, chief exec. officer, 1966-80, 81-82, chmn. bd., 1976-86; chmn. bd. Manpower Inc., 1976-86; pres. Caxambas Assocs. of Fla., Inc., 1986—; chmn. bd. BANCWIS Corp., 1971-84, dir. emeritus, chmn. bd. 1971-84; bd. dirs. Bank of Wis.; chmn. bd. dirs. Manpower Inc., 1976-86. Chmn. Wis. Rep. Fin. Com., 1971-73, state chmn., 1974-76; mem. Nat. Rep. Fin. Com., 1971-73; Rep. Nat. Com., 1974-76; Chmn. bd. dirs., chief exec. officer Janesville Found.; fellow Lake Forest Acad.; trustee emeritus Brown U., Beloit Coll.; chmn. bd. fellows Beloit Coll. Mem. Archeol. Assn. Am., Nat. Inst. Marine Archaeology, Psi Upsilon.

PARKER, GORDON BELL, food service executive; b. Indpls., Nov. 22, 1936; s. C. Russell and Dorothy Margaret (Bell) P.; children: Kelly Jean, Russell Scott Victor. BA in Bus. Adminstrn., Mich. State U., 1958, BA in Hotel, Restaurant, Inst. Mgmt., 1963. Cafeteria mgr. Army and Air Force Exchange Service, Chanute AFB, Ill., 1963-65; head dietitian U. Mich., Ann Arbor, 1965-66; house mgr. Elks Club, Flint, Mich., 1966-68; caterer ops. adminstr. Ford Motor Co., Dearborn, Mich., 1968—. Pres. Bklyn. Farms Homeowners Assn., Novi, Mich., 1984—; solicitor Detroit Torch Drive, 1976-82. Served as pfc. U.S. Army, 1959-61. Recipient design award Restaurants & Insts. Mag., 1986, Doctorate of Food Service Nat. Assn. Foodservice Equipment Mfrs., 1987. Mem. Soc. for Foodservice Mgmt. (pres. 1986-87), Assn. for Foodsci. Mgmt. (v.p. 1978-79), Nat. Restaurant Assn., Council on Hotel, Restaurant and Instl. Edn., Council on Indsl. Food Service. Republican. Episcopalian. Avocations: fishing, collecting antique Italian mosaic jewelry, stamp collecting, golf. Home: 34316 Thornbrook Northville MI 48018 Office: Ford Motor Co The American Rd Dearborn MI 48121

PARKER, JACQUELINE KAY, social work educator; b. Yuba City, Calif., June 3, 1934; d. LeRoy George and Veda (Kuster) P. AB, U. Calif., Berkeley, 1959, MSW, 1961, DSW, 1972. Foster care worker Santa Clara County Welfare Dept., San Jose, Calif., 1961-64; adoptions worker Alameda County Welfare Dept., Oakland, Calif., 1968-70; asst. prof. social work Va. Commonwealth U., Richmond, 1973-80, U. Oreg., Eugene, 1983-86; assoc. prof. Cleve. State U., 1986—; cons. Social Research Assocs., Inc., Midlothian, Va., 1978-80. Author biographical sketches for reference books, 1986-87, oral histories, 1973-87, also articles. Mem. Council on Social Work Edn., Friends of the Schlesinger Library; referee Radcliffe Research Scholars Program, Camgridge, Mass., 1983-84; bd. dirs. Opportunities Industrialization Ctr., Richmond, 1978-80. Mem. Nat. Assn. Social Workers. Office: Cleve State Univ Dept Social Service Euclid at E 24th St Cleveland OH 44115

PARKER, JEFFREY BERRYMAN, data processing specialist; b. Detroit, Jan. 6, 1950; s. Benjamin L. and Jean Hart (Woodard) P.; m. Charlotte J. King, May 24, 1980. B.Continuing Studies, U. Nebr.-Omaha, 1983. Cert. systems profl. Sr. programmer Foremost Ins. Co., Grand Rapids, Mich., 1978-81; project leader Mut. of Omaha, 1981-84; dept. mgr. ALR Systems & Software, Omaha, 1984—. Served with USAF, 1970-78. Fellow Life Office Mgmt. Assn.; mem. Assn. Systems Mgmt. (chpt. sec. 1983-85, spl. publs. chmn. 1985—). Republican. Mem. Christian Ch. Avocations: strategic simulations; cooking; wine making; stained glass; bookbinding. Office: ALR Systems 10334 Ellison Circle Omaha NE 68134

PARKER, JOHN OTIS, JR., healthcare company executive; b. Boston, July 26, 1944; s. John O. Sr. and Elizabeth (MacDonald) P.; m. Beverly Jane Fishow, June 12, 1971; children: Todd, Hilary. BA, Bowdoin Coll., 1966; MBA, Harvard U., 1972. Prodn. mgr. Corning (N.Y.) Glass, Big Flats, N.Y., 1975-77; dir. info services Corning (N.Y.) Glass, 1980-84; group controller Corning Ltd., Sunderland, Eng., 1977-80; v.p. info. services Travenol Labs., Inc., Deerfield, Ill., 1984-86; v.p., gen. mgr. Baxter-Travenol Labs., Inc., Deerfield, Ill., 1986—. Served to lt. USN, 1966-69, PTO. Office: Baxter-Travenol Labs Inc 1 Baxter Pkwy Deerfield IL 60015

PARKER, LEONARD SAM, architect, educator; b. Warsaw, Poland, Jan. 16, 1923; came to U.S. 1923; s. Rueben and Sarah (Kollica) Popuch; m. Betty Mae Buegen, Sept. 1, 1948 (dec. 1983); children—Bruce Aaron, Jonathan Arthur, Nancy Anne, Andrew David. B.Arch., U. Minn., 1948; M.Arch., MIT, 1950. Sr. designer Eero Saarinen Assocs., Bloomfield Hills, Mich., 1950-56; pres., dir. design The Leonard Parker Assocs., Mpls., 1957—, The Alliance Southwest, Phoenix, 1981—; prof. and asst. dir. grad. program Sch. Architecture, U. Minn., Mpls., 1959—. Author: Abandoning the Catalogs, 1979, Rivers of Modernism, 1986. Panel mem. Mpls. City Hall Restoration Com., Am. Arbitration Assn. Served with U.S. Army, 1943-46; ETO. Firm has received 56 nat. and regional awards for design excellence. Fellow AIA; mem. Minn. Soc. Architects (pres. 1981, Gold medal 1986, pres. Mpls. chpt. 1979), Tau Sigma Delta. Home: 3936 Wilmot Hill Rd Minnetonka MN 55343 Office: The Leonard Parker Assocs 430 Oak Grove Minneapolis MN 55403

PARKER, MARYLAND (MIKE), reporter, photographer; b. Oklahoma City, Feb. 5, 1926; d. Clarence N. and Minzola (Perkins) Davis; student U. Ark., Pine Bluff, 1970-71; student Marymount Coll., 1974-77; m. John Harrison Parker, Nov. 25, 1944 (dec.); children—Norma Jean Parker Brown, Janice Kay Parker Shelby, Joyce Lynn, John H. (dec.), Cherie D. Parker Hite, Patrick Scott, Charles Roger. Beautician, Maryland's Ho. of Beauty, Salina, Kans., 1964-69; youth adv. NAACP, Salina, 1970-72; newspaper reporter BACOS Newsletter, Salina, 1971-77; radio announcer Kina's BACOS Report, Salina, after 1973; reporter, photographer Kans. State Globe. Mem. Salina County Democratic Women, 1960—; part-time vol. Salvation Army, Salina, 1979—; bd. dirs. Salina Child Care Assn., Gospel Mission, 1983—. Mem. NAACP (life), Nat. Fedn. Press Women, Kans. Press Women, Internat. Platform Assn., VFW Aux., Am. Legion Aux. Mormon. Home: 920 Birch Dr PO Box 2412 Salina KS 67401

PARKER, PATRICK STREETER, manufacturing executive; b. Cleve., 1929. B.A., Williams Coll., 1951; M.B.A., Harvard U., 1953. With Parker-Hannifin Corp. and predecessor, Cleve., 1953—, sales mgr. fittings div., 1957-63, mgr. aerospace products div., 1963-65, pres. Parker Seal Co. div., 1965-67, corp. v.p., 1967-69, pres., 1969-71, pres. and chief exec. officer, 1971-77, chmn. bd. and chief exec. officer, 1977-84, chmn. bd., 1984—, pres., 1982-84, also dir.; dir. Acme-Cleve. Corp., Sherwin-Williams Co., Soc. Corp., Reliance Electric Co.; Pres. and trustee Woodruff Hosp. of Cleve. Bd. trustee Case Western Res. U.; trustee Woodruff Found. Served with USN, 1954-57. Office: Parker Hannifin Corp 17325 Euclid Ave Cleveland OH 44112

PARKER, RICHARD THOMAS, architect; b. Lakewood, Ohio, Dec. 20, 1954; s. Robert Thomas and Yoshiko (Mori) P.; m. Gwen Douglas Hendee, Sept. 21, 1981; 1 child, Eric Thomas. BArch, Kent State U., 1977. Registered architect, Ohio, N.C. Intern Todd Schmidt & Assoc., Cleve., 1977-78; design architect William Dorsky Assoc., Cleve., 1978-81; architect Dalton, VanDijk, Johnson, Cleve., 1981-83; prin. Schmidt Copeland & Assoc., Cleve., 1983—. Mem. Hist. Warehouse Dist. Devel. Corp., Cleve., 1985-86; vol. Cleve. Children's Mus., 1986. Mem. AIA (Design award, Cleve. chpt. 1985), Architects Soc. Ohio. Roman Catholic. Office: Schmidt Copeland & Assoc Inc 1220 W 6th St Cleveland OH 44113

PARKER, ROBERT RUDOLPH, podiatrist; b. Carthage, Ill., Nov. 10, 1927; s. Elmer B. and Lena Amelia (Rudolphi) P.; m. Beverly Elaine Phillipi, June 11, 1951; children: Mary Elizabeth, Robert Mitchell. DPM, Ill. Coll. Podiatric Medicine, 1951. Diplomate Am. Bd. Podiatric Surgery. Pvt. practice podiatric medicine Springfield, Ill., 1951—. Served with USN, 1945-46. Fellow Am. Coll. Foot Surgeons; mem. Am. Podiatric Med. Assn., Ill. Podiatric Med. Assn. Clubs: Sangamo, Island Bay Yacht (Springfield), Springfield Motor Boat. Lodge: Elks. Office: 1209 S 4th St Springfield IL 62703

PARKER, STEPHEN JAN, slavic language educator; b. N.Y.C., Aug. 5, 1939; s. Irving and Fan (Magarik) P.; m. Marie-Luce Monferran, June 15, 1965; children: Sandra, Richard. BA, Cornell U., 1960, MA, 1962, PhD, 1969. Asst. prof. U. Okla., Norman, 1966-67; asst. prof. U. Kans., Lawrence, 1967-73, assoc. prof., 1973-86, prof. Slavic langs. and lits., 1986—, chmn. dept. Slavic langs. and lits., 1987—. Co-author: Russia on Canvas, 1981; author: Understanding Vladimir Nabokov, 1987; co-editor The Achievements of Vladimir Nabokov, 1984; editor, publisher: The Nabokovian, 1978—. Chmn. bd. dirs. Lawrence Preservation Fund, 1979-82. NEH fellow, 1970-71. Mem. Am. Assn. for the Advancement of Slavic Studies, Am. Assn. Tchrs. of Slavic and East European Languages, MLA, Vladimir Nabokov Soc. (sec., treas. 1978—). Office: U Kans Dept Slavic Languages Lawrence KS 66045

PARKER, TERRENCE LEE, finance executive; b. Washington, Jan. 11, 1946; s. Frederick Carroll and Marthanne (Carter) P.; m. Pamela Barton, July 12, 1969 (div. July 1985); children: Kelley, Katy. BSME, U.S. Merchant Marine Acad., 1968; MCE, MBA, U. Pa., 1972. Prin. Landrum Brown/Booz Allen, Cin., 1973-80; exec. v.p., co-owner Aviation Planning Assoc., Cin., 1980—; pres. Comtrax Systems, Cin., 1984—. Served to lt. USNR. Republican. Roman Catholic. Avocations: private pilot, flight instr. Home: 198 Green Hills Rd Cincinnati OH 45208 Office: Aviation Planning Assoc 421 Arch St Cincinnati OH 45202

PARKER, TOMMIE CAROL, psychotherapist, educator; b. Birmingham, Ala.; d. Estes Carter and Anny May (Skinner) Thompson; divorced; children: Patrick, Laurie, Annette (dec.), Timothy, Gail, Daniel. BSW, U. Nebr., Omaha, 1977; MSW, U. Nebr., Lincoln, 1978. Diplomate Am. Bd. Med. Psychotherapists. Practice psychotherapy specializing in individual and family therapy Omaha, 1980; family therapist Med. Ctr. U. Nebr., Omaha, 1978—, diagnostic team leader, 1978-84, coordinator social work clin. service, 1982-86; instr., adj. faculty sch. social work U. Nebr., Omaha, 1987—; practicum instr. sch. social work U. Nebr., Omaha, 1980—. Contbr. articles to profl. jours. Chairperson planning com. state conf. Advocacy Office Children and Youth, Omaha, 1985, bd. dirs., 1984-85. Fellow Nat. Assn. Social Workers; mem. Acad. Cert. Social Workers, Am. Assn. Family Counselors and Mediators, Internat. Acad. Profl. Psychotherapy (diplomate), Mental Health Assn. of Midlands (bd. dirs.), Am. Assn. Marriage and Family Therapy (clin.). Democrat. Club: Field (Omaha). Avocations: gardening, travel, cooking, photography, decorating. Office: U Nebr Med Ctr 42d and Dewey Omaha NE 68105

PARKER, WILLIAM LAWRENCE, JR., lawyer; b. Pratt, Kans., Feb. 27, 1931; s. William Lawrence and Mabel (Atkinson) P.; m. Donna Lee Smith, Dec. 31, 1981; children—William Lawrence, III, Karen Elaine. B.A., Washburn U., 1955, J.D., 1957. Bar: Kans. 1957, U.S. Supreme Ct. 1963. Ptnr. McCullough, Parker, Wareheim & LaBunker, Topeka, Kans., 1957-71; pres. W.L. Parker, Jr., Chartered, Topeka, 1972—; mgr., house counsel Kans. Constrn. Industry Fringe Benefit Funds, Topeka, 1972—. Editor-in-chief Washburn Law Rev., 1956-57. Trustee Kans. Pub. Employees Retirement System, Topeka, 1972-76; trustee, fin. chmn. Washburn Coll., Topeka, 1973—; tech. dir. Topeka Civic Theatre, Topeka, 1972-74; tech. designer Dance Arts Topeka, 1974-83; pres. Health Care Cost Containment Task Force, Mo. and Kans., 1984—; mem. Gov.'s Task Force on Health Care, 1984—. Recipient Spl. Service award Kans. Bldg. Trades Health and Welfare Fund, 1984. Fellow Fin. Analysts Fedn.; mem. ABA (employee benefit com. 1971—, co.-chmn. subcom. 1971-86), Fringe Benefit Execs. Assn. (pres. 1974-81), Internat. Found. Employee Benefit Plans. Baptist. Lodge: Masons. Avocations: horses, farming, golf. Home: Rural Rt 1 Box 154A Parkerville KS 66872 Office: WL Parker Jr Chartered 4101 Southgate Dr PO Box 5168 Topeka KS 66605

PARKHILL, HAROLD LOYAL, artist; b. Fresno, Ohio, Feb. 16, 1928; s. Jesse Blair and Ella (Buser) P.; m. Rosalee Lavonne Croup, Aug. 5, 1950 (div. Nov. 1969); children: Lorie Cathrine, Scott Thomas, Cynthia Anne, Carrie Sue. Grad. high sch., Keene, Ohio, 1947. Farmer Fresno, 1947-52, 1964-80; bus driver Western Greyhound Lines, Calif, Ariz., N.Mex. and Tex., 1952-61; dispatcher Ea. Greyhound Lines, Cin., 1963; artist Coshocton, Ohio, 1980—. Represented in permanent collections Zanesville Art Ctr. Mem. Coshocton Art Guild; trustee Coshocton Pomerene Fine Art Ctr. Served with USNR, 1945-46, PTO. Recipient numerous best of show awards in oil and watercolor art. Mem. VFW, Am. Legion. Republican. Methodist. Lodges: Elks, Moose. Avocations: travel., gun collecting, horseback riding. Home: PO Box 85 Coshocton OH 43812

PARKHURST, JEFFREY DAY, systems analyst; b. Mpls., Feb. 10, 1959; s. Harry Day Jr. and Alma Kay (Smith) P.;m. Maggie Larsen, June 25, 1983. B in Computer Sci., U. Minn., 1982; MBA, Xavier U., Cin. Programming specialist Control Data Corp., Mpls., 1981; systems analystcustomer services div. Proctor & Gamble, Cin., 1982-84, systems analyst gen. advt. div., 1985-86, systems analyst beverage sales div., 1987—. Mgmt. Assistant Services vol. Community Chest, Cin., 1986, 87; account mgr. United Appeal, Cin., 1983, 86. Recipient Eagle Scout award Boy Scouts Am., 1975; named one of Outstanding Young Men Am., 1980. Mem. Cowan Lake (Ohio) Sailing Assn., Omicron Delta Kappa, Chi Psi (pres. 1980). Avocations: hockey, sailing, golf, investing.

PARKIN, JERRY DONALD, utility executive; b. Anamosa, Iowa, Jan. 5, 1950; s. Donald Francis and Alta Ruth (Larson) P.; m. Randall Kay Gerdeman, Nov. 30, 1974; children: Thomas, Allison. BS, Iowa State U., 1972; MA, Drake U., 1984. Adminstrv. asst. State Office for Planning, Des Moines, 1972-76; exec. dir. Pres. Ford's Campaign, Des Moines, 1976; community affairs rep. Iowa Power & Light Co., Des Moines, 1976-79, mgr. govt. affairs, 1979-86, dir. pub. affairs, 1986-87; asst. dir. state govt. affairs Deere & Co., Des Moines, 1987—. Pres. Planned Parenthood of Mid-Iowa, Des Moines, 1986. Recipient Cardinal Key award Iowa State U., 1972. Republican. Mem. United Ch. of Christ. Club: Bohemian (Des Moines); Capitol Hill (Washington). Avocations: running, collecting political campaign memorabilia. Home: 411 32d St West Des Moines IA 50265 Office: Deere & Co 310 Hubbell Bldg Des Moines IA 50309

PARKINS, GEORGE KYLE, II, orthopaedic surgeon; b. St. Louis, May 28, 1945; s. Clarence Herbert and Martha (Barclay) P.; m. Linda Gail Goldstein, Aug. 29, 1970; children: Robert, Michael. BA, Westminster Coll., 1967; MD, Columbia U., 1971. Diplomate Am. Bd. Orthopaedic Surgery. Intern Columbia Presbyn. Med. Ctr., N.Y.C., 1971-72, resident in orthopaedic surgery, 1972-73; resident in orthopaedic surgery N.Y. Orthopaedic Hosp., N.Y.C., 1975-78; practice medicine specializing in orthopaedic surgery Kansas City, Mo., 1978—; attending surgeon St. Mary's Hosp., Kansas City, 1978—; dept. chmn. St. Mary's Hosp., Kansas City, Mo., 1983-84; pres. med. staff St. Mary's Hosp., Kansas City; attending surgeon Trinity Luth., Kansas City, Mo., 1978—; chmn. dept. orthopaedic surgery Trinity Luth., Kansas City, 1985—; trustee Rehabilitation Inst. Kansas City, 1986—. Trustee Westminster Coll., Fulton, Mo., 1985—. Served to capt. USAF, 1973-75. Fellow ACS, Am. Acad. Orthopaedic Surgeons; mem. AMA, Jackson County Med. Soc., Mo. State Med. Soc. Republican. Methodist. Home: 5131 Somerset Dr Prairie Village KS 66207 Office: 2929 Baltimore Kansas City MO 64108

PARKINSON, ROBIN GENE, metallurgical engineer; b. Denver, Jan. 25, 1952; s. Robert Gene and Marie Antonette (Clifford) P.; m. Linda Cheryl Dunn, Mar. 15, 1980. BS in Metall. Engring., Colo. Sch. Mines, 1974; M in Liberal Arts, Baker U., 1984. Registered profl. engr., Mo. Asst. metallurgist Armco, Kansas City, Mo., 1974-75; assoc. metallurgist Armco-Union Wire Co., Kansas City, 1975-76; metall. engr. Armco-Union Wire Rope Co., Kansas City, 1976-81, sr. metall. engr., 1981-84, supervising metallurgist, wire rope, 1984—. Mem. Eastwood Swimming Club (pres. 1987—). Home: 7135 Sni-A-Bar Rd Kansas City MO 64129 Office: Armco-Union Wire Rope 7000 Roberts Kansas City MO 64125

PARKS, BARRY J., marketing executive; b. Chgo., July 28, 1949; s. William Henry Jr. and Beatrice Dorothea (Koscielski) P.; m. Jill Kathryn Radtke, Sept. 25, 1971; children: Janine Alison, Loren Joy, Melissa Kathryn. BA in Graphic Design, U. Ill., 1971. Prodn. dir. GKZ Inc., Chgo., 1972-75; creative dir. Perkins Bernstein, Chgo., 1975-78; v.p. mktg. Home Shopping Show, Chgo., 1978-80; dir. advt. and promotion Modern Satellite Network, N.Y.C., 1980-81; pvt. practice cons. Lansing, Ill., 1981-84; pres. Communications Mktg. & Design, Glenwood, Ill., 1984—. Contbr. articles to profl. publs. Served to sgt. Ill. N.G., 1971-77. Mem. Ind. Writers Chgo., South Suburban C. of C. Roman Catholic. Club: TOPS (Lansing). Avocations: racquetball, volleyball, computers. Office: Communications Mktg & Design Inc 305 E Glenwood/Lansing Rd Glenwood IL 60425

PARKS, HERBERT HENRY, accountant; b. Harrisburg, Ill., Apr. 19, 1939; s. Charles Henry and Genevieve (Williams) P.; m. Judith Kay O'Neal, Dec. 21, 1964; children: Christy Kay, Patrick Herbert. BS, So. Ill. U., 1964; MS, So. Ill. U., Edwardsville, 1971. Tchr. bus. Staunton (Ill.) High Sch., 1970-72; owner Parks Acctg., Staunton and Auburn, Ill., 1970—. Alderman Village of Auburn, 1976-78; ambulance vol. drive coordinator, 1979; vol. fire fighter, 1975—. Served to lt. col. USAF, 1964-70, Vietnam, Ill. Air NG, 1970—. Decorated Air medal. Mem. Ind. Accts. Assn., Nat. Assn. Tax Preparers, Nat. Guard Assn. U.S., Nat. Guard Assn. Ill., VFW, Am. Legion. Republican. Avocations: raising strawberries, navigating aircraft. Home: 1209 Commanche Rd Auburn IL 62615 Office: Parks Acctg Rt 4 at Rt 104 Auburn IL 62615

PARKS, JOHN BUNDY, controller; b. Kokomo, Ind., Aug. 25, 1941; s. John Thomas and Marjorie Ruth (Bundy) P.; m. Roberta Lynn Phillippi, June 25, 1966; children: John Carleton, Laura Lynn. BA, De Pauw U., 1963; MBA with honors, Cornell U., 1965. CPA, Ind. Fin. analyst Eli Lilly and Co., Indpls., 1965-68; ops. mgr. Eli Lilly and Co. Inc., San Juan, Puerto Rico, 1968-71; fin. adminstr. acctg. ops. and staff services Lilly Internat. Corp., Indpls., 1971; dir. adminstrn. Lilly Ind. de Espana S.A., Madrid, 1971-74; asst. treas. Eli Lilly and Co., Indpls., 1974-78, controller prodn. ops., 1978-80; dir. adminstrn. Eli Lilly Argentina S.A., Buenos Aires, 1980-83; dir. fin. planning and reporting Eli Lilly and Co., Indpls., 1983-84; controller Lilly Research Labs., Indpls., 1984-86; controller mfg. ops. Eli Lilly and Co., Indpls., 1986—. Treas., deacon Zionsville (Ind.) Fellowship Ch., 1984—. Mem. Am. Inst. CPA's, Ind. Inst. CPA's, Delta Upsilon (pres., house corp. and trustee 1983—). Republican. Avocations: reading, tennis. Office: Eli Lilly and Co Lilly Corp Ctr Indianapolis IN 46285

PARKS, STANLEY MILES, architect; b. Garden City, Kans., June 28, 1957; s. Richard Delano and Jeanette Carlton (Fry) P. BArch, Kans. State U., 1980. Registered architect, Mo. Architect Linscott, Haylett, Wimmer & Wheat, Kansas City, Mo., 1980—. Mem. AIA. Home: 4815 W 103d St Overland Park MO 66207 Office: Linscott Haylett Wimmer & Wheat 917 W 43d St Kansas City MO 64111

PARKS, STEVEN LILLARD, methods engineer; b. Iola, Kans., July 17, 1952; s. Lillard Bernard and Althea Carrie (Clinton) P.; m. Cheryl Jane Myers, Aug. 1, 1976; children: Tiffany Rose, Tara Lynn. AA, Neosho County Jr. Coll., Chanute, Kans., 1972; BBA, Pittsburg (Kans.) State U., 1974, MBA, 1975. Prodn. dept. mgr. Coleman Co., Wichita, Kans., 1976-81; methods devel. engr. Cessna Aircraft Co., Wichita, 1981-82; dir. prodn. L.S. Industries, Wichita, 1982-84; methods engr. Boeing Mil. Airplane Co., Wichita, 1984—. Chmn. fund raising Camp Wonderful, Wichita, 1984-85. Republican. Avocation: golf. Home: 313 W Waitt Rose Hill KS 67133 Office: Boeing Mil Airplane Co 3801 S Oliver Wichita KS 67277

PARKS, THOMAS ANSON, marketing professional; b. Long Beach, Calif., Nov. 14, 1940; s. Houston Thomas and Juanita (Breeden) P.; m. Sharon Rae Louis, Apr. 8, 1967; children: Thomas Anson II, Mike Louis. BAA, Hiwassee U., 1961. Instr. sales edn. NCR, Dayton, Ohio, 1982-84, sr. instr. sales edn., 1984-85, mgr. curriculum devel., 1985-86, sr. mgr. sales edn., 1986—; pres. devel. Eagle Inc., Kettering, Ohio, 1983-85; cons. sales edn., Centerville, Ohio, 1985—. Author (video series) Unix Overview, 1984. Chmn. com. Boy Scouts Am., Dayton, 1984-85. Served with USN, 1962-65. Mem. Am. Soc. Tng. and Devel. Club: NCR Country (Dayton). Lodge: Masons (master Dayton 1982-83). Office: NCR Corp 101 W Schantz Ave Dayton OH 45459

PARKYN, JOHN DUWANE, nuclear engineer; b. La Crosse, Wis., Feb. 20, 1944; s. Lionel Eric and Florence Katrina (Klum) P.; m. Betty Christine Tarnutzer, Aug. 13, 1966; children: Christine Peggy, Sarah Katherine, John Martin. Student Wis. State U., 1962-64, U. N.Mex., 1968-69; BS in Nuclear Engring. and Physics, U. Wis., 1972. Cert. assessor, Wis.; registered profl. nuclear engr., Calif.; lic. sr. reactor operator. Asst. plant engr. Ohio Med. Products Co., 1966-67; party chief U.S. Geol. Survey, Madison, Wis., 1971-72; asst. operations group Point Beach Nuclear Plant, Two Rivers, Wis., 1972-74; asst. supt. La Crosse Boiling Water Reactor, Genoa, Wis., 1974-82, supt., 1982—; mem. industry rev. bd. Inst. Nuclear Power Ops. Mem. Two Rivers City Council, 1974; mem. Vernon County Bd. Suprs., 1976—, now vice chmn. county bd., mem. fin. com., chmn. human services rev. bd., chmn. community options program; assessor Bergen Twp. (Wis.), 1976-77, Sterling Twp. (Wis.), 1977-79; chmn. Vernon County Library Com., 1976—; chmn. personnel com. Vernon County Bd. Equalized Values; chmn. Vernon County Com. for Programs of Aging; bd. dirs. Winding Rivers Library System; treas. Sch. Dist. of La Crosse; 1st v.p. Riverland council Girl Scouts U.S.A.; adv. Order of DeMolay. Served with U.S. Army, 1967-69. Mem. Am. Nuclear Soc. (chmn. Wis. sect., mem. nat. planning com.), Nat. Assn. of Former Youth Govs., Wis. Assn. RR Passengers (state pres.), Am. Legion; Wes. Assn. R.R. Passengers (state pres.). Mem. United Ch. of Christ. Lodge: Masons. Home: Pleasant Valley Stoddard WI 54658 Office: La Crosse Boiling Water Reactor Rt 1 Genoa WI 54632

PARMER, ANITA FLOY, nurse epidemiologist; b. Braymer, Mo., May 2, 1941; d. Floyd Earl and Leola Frances (Penny) Mason; m. Kenneth Dale Parmer, Sept. 6, 1964; children—Kenneth Dale, John Earl. Diploma Trinity Luth. Hosp. Sch. Nursing, Kansas City, 1962; student William Jewell Coll., Liberty, Mo., 1963; B.S. in Nursing, U. Mo., 1964. R.N., Mo., nat. cert. infection control, 1985. Staff nurse U. Mo. Med. Ctr., Columbia, 1962, Excelsior Springs (Mo.) Hosp., 1963; staff nurse Boone County Hosp. (name changed to Boone Hosp. Ctr.), Columbia, 1963, operating room staff nurse, supr., 1964-73, ednl. services instr., 1973-78, nurse epidemiologist, 1978—. Recipient Florence Nightingale award Trinity Luth. Hosp. Sch. Nursing, 1962. Mem. Am. Nurses Assn., Assn. for Practitioners in Infection Control. Republican. Methodist. Home: 35 Trails West Dr Route 5 Box 73 Columbia MO 65202 Office: Boone Hosp Ctr 1600 E Broadway Columbia MO 65201

PARMER, DAN GERALD, veterinarian; b. Wetumpka, Ala., July 3, 1926; s. James Lonnie and Virginia Gertrude (Guy) P.; student Los Angeles City Coll., 1945-46; D.V.M., Auburn U., 1950; m. Donna Louise Kesler, June 7, 1980; 1 son, Dan Gerald; 1 dau. by previous marriage, Linda Leigh. Gen. practice vet. medicine, Galveston, Tex., 1950-54, Chgo., 59—; vet. in charge Chgo. Commn. Animal Care and Control, 1974—; chmn. Ill. Impaired Vets. Com.; tchr. Highlands U., 1959. Served with USNR, 1943-45, PTO; served as staff vet. and 2d and 5th Air Force vet. chief USAF, 1954-59. Decorated 9 Battle Stars; recipient Vet. Appreciation award U. Ill., 1971, Commendation, Chgo. Commn. Animal Care and Control, 1987. Mem. Ill. Vet. Medicine Assn. (chmn. civil def. and package disaster hosps. 1968-71, Pres.' award 1986), Chgo. Vet. Medicine Assn. (bd. govs. 1969-72, 74-13, pres. 1982), South Chgo. Vet. Medicine Assn. (pres. 1965-66), Am. Animal Hosp. Assn. (dir.), AVMA (nat. com. for impaired vets.), Ill. Acad. Vet. Practice, Nat. Assn. of Professions, Am. Assn. Zoo Vets., Am. Assn. Zool. Parks and Aquariums, VFW. Democrat. Clubs: Midlothian Country, Valley Internat. Country. Lodges: Masons, Shriners, Kiwanis.Discoverer Bartonellosis in cattle in N.Am. and Western Hemisphere, 1951; co-developer bite-size high altitude in-flight feeding program USAF, 1954-56. Address: 4350 W Ford City Dr Apt 402 Chicago IL 60652

PARRAN, ANITA KATHLEEN, editor, writer, communications consultant; b. St. Louis, Oct. 21, 1951; d. George Willis and Wilma Jean (Wooten) P. AA, Stephens Coll., 1971, BA, 1973; MA in Bus. Mgmt., Webster U., 1979. Adminstrv. mgr. Murff and Assocs., Columbus, 1980-82; tech. writer Rockwell Internat., Columbus, 1982-85; communications cons. Columbus, 1985-86; publs. editor Ohio Arts Council, Columbus, 1986; free-lance writer, editor, communications cons. St. Louis, 1987—; communications cons., Columbus, 1985—. Contbr. articles to newspapers and mags. Ctr. advisor Jr. Achievement, Columbus, 1984. Mem. Nat. Assn. Female Execs., Alpha Kappa Alpha. Democrat. Methodist. Avocations: composing music, writing lyrics, creative writing, reading, ballet. Home: 244 Wooster Dr Saint Louis MO 63135 Office: 932 Drummond St Saint Louis MO 63135

PARRAULT, SARETTA LYNN, marketing communications executive; b. Chgo., Nov. 4, 1940; d. Louis Harry and Frieda Florence (Lipson) Shugall; m. Stuart E. Miller, Nov. 22, 1968 (div. Jan. 1976); children: Loren Jay, Kevin Errol; m. James Raymond Parrault, June 16, 1976; children: Scott L., Melissa Gay. AA, Oakton Community Coll., 1978; BA, Northeastern Ill. U., 1980, MA, 1987. Pres. Mktg. Strategies Unltd., Morton Grove, Ill., 1976—; cons. IBM, Greencastle, Ind., 1987, Walgreen's Inc., Deerfield, Ill., 1986—, Cambridge Human Resource Group, Inc., Northbrook, Ill., Harlem-Foster Shopping Ctr., Chgo., 1984, Plaza del Prado, Northbrook, 1983—, Oakton Community Coll., Des Plaines, Ill., 1976, Holy Family Health Care Ctr., Des Plaines, 1976, Mayer Kaplan Jewish Community Ctr., Skokie, Ill., 1976, Promotions Mgmt. Assocs., Lansing, Mich., 1977, WLS-TV, Chgo., 1980, Coll. Lake County, Highland Park, Ill., 1985, Condell Meml. Hosp., Libertyville, Ill., 1985. Editorial asst. Ruder, Finn & Rotman, Chgo., 1963-66; writer/producer/dir. (radio program) Career Insights, 1984-85; writer/producer cable TV, 1985-86. Bd. dirs. pub. relations Mayer Kaplan Jewish Community Ctr., Skokie, 1975-76; spl. events coordinator Covenant Club Ill., Chgo., 1959. Mem. Nat. Assn. Women in Careers (founder chpt., past pres.), LWV, Women's Am. Ort. Clubs: N.W. Press. (sec. 1985-86), Toastmasters (pres. Niles club 1984).

PARRIS, EILEEN KAY, English educator; b. Cin., Dec. 4, 1935; d. Henry Kennedy and Mary (Wood) P. B.S. in Edn., U. Cin., 1958, B.A. in Classics, 1958, M.A. in Classics, 1959. Cert. tchr., Ohio. Tchr., Oak Hills High Sch., Cin., 1959-62; tchr. Norwood (Ohio) High Sch., 1962—, coordinator dept. English, 1976-84, coordinator English curriculum, 1987—. Mem. NEA, Ohio Edn. Assn., Assn. Supervision and Curriculum Devel., Nat. Council Tchrs. English, Phi Beta Kappa. Home: 2145 Quatman Ave Norwood OH 45212 Office: 2020 Sherman Ave Norwood OH 45212

PARRISH, BARRY JAY, advertising executive; b. Chgo., Sept. 3, 1946; s. Hy J. and Shirley F. (Fimoff) Perelgut; B.A., Columbia Coll., 1968; M.B.A., U. Chgo., 1971; 1 son, Jeffrey Scott. Asst. advt. mgr. Libby McNeill & Libby, Chgo., 1965-67; advt. and promotion mgr. McGraw-Hill Publs. Co., Chgo., 1967-69; creative dir./account exec. Holt Communication div. Bozell & Jacobs, Chgo., 1969-72; account supr. Linder Advt. div. Dailey & Assocs., San Francisco, 1972-75; v.p./account supr. internat. Arthur E. Wilk Advt., Chgo., 1975-76; exec. v.p. Shaffer/MacGill & Assocs., Chgo., 1976-81; v.p., dir. Grey II, Grey Advt., Chgo., 1981—. TV commls. judge CLIO awards, 1978, 79, U.S. Film Festival, 1980-81, 84. Served with USMC, to 1972. Recipient awards Houston Internat. Film Festival, Nat. Employment Assn., others. Mem. Am. Mgmt. Assn., Chgo. Council on Fgn. Relations, Art Inst. Chgo., Lincoln Park Zool. Soc. Club: Chgo. Advertising. Contbr. articles to profl. jours., newspapers, mags. Home: 2800 N Orchard Chicago IL 60657 Office: Grey-Chicago Inc 2200 Merchandise Mart Plaza Chicago IL 60654

PARROTT, CARL LEONARD, JR., pathologist; b. Elizabeth City, N.C., Oct. 13, 1948; s. Carl Leonard Sr. and Nancy Elizabeth (Shelton) P.; m. Debra Lee Buirge (div.); m. Molly Ann Katz, Aug. 25, 1979; children: David, Sarah, Charles, Rebecca. BA, Yale U., 1970; MD, Emory U., 1977. Diplomate Nat. Bd. Med. Examiners; cert. Am. Bd. Pathology. Pathologist, dep. coroner Hamilton County Coroner's Office, Cin., 1981—; assoc. dir. lab. The Deaconess Hosp., Cin., 1982—. Contbr. articles to profl. jours. Mem. med. adv. com. Hoxworth Meml. Blood Ctr., Cin., 1983—. Fellow Am. Soc. Clin. Pathologists, Coll. Am. Pathologists; mem. Cin. Mediolegal Soc., Ohio Med. Assn., Acad. Medicine Cin. Avocations: sailing, gardening. Home: 327 Warren Ave Cincinnati OH 45220 Office: The Deaconess Hosp 311 Straight St Cincinnati OH 45219

PARROTT, DEAN ALLEN, minister; b. Cass City, Mich., Aug. 24, 1922; s. Earl Watts and Anna Lura (Smith) P.; m. Ione Elizabeth Kneeshaw, Apr. 18, 1942; children: Jean Parrott Dunsford, Keith, Dale. AB, Adrian (Mich.) Coll., 1953; ThB, Owosso Bible Coll., 1957; MA, Mich. State U., 1960; postgrad., Wayne State U., 1960-63, Western Mich. U., 1967-68; D Ministry, Calif. Grad. Sch. Theology, 1985. Ordained to ministry Free Meth. Ch., 1944; psychologist ltd. lic. Mich., marriage counselor, Mich. Pastor Free Meth. Ch., Sandusky, Mich., 1946-50; sr. pastor Free Meth. Ch., Adrian, Mich., 1950-53, Hillsdale, Mich., 1953-59, Lincoln Park, Mich., 1959-66, Kalamazoo, 1966-76; sr. pastor Free Meth. Ch., Westland, Mich., 1976-87, ret., 1987; del. Free Meth. Ch. N.Am. Gen. Conf., 1964, 74, 79, 85, Conf. Prophesy, Jerusalem, 1971; host daily radio Question Hour Sta. WKPR, Kalamazoo, 1966-72; counselor Christian Found. Emotional Health, Detroit, 1964-66. Contbr. articles profl. jours. Mem. Mental Health Council, Lincoln Park, 1960-66, Pastor's Adv. Bd. Planned Parenthood, Detroit, 1963-66, Kalamazoo Community Relations Bd., 1969-71, S. Mich. Conf. Bd. Adminstrs. Mem. Am. Psychol. Assn., Kalamazoo Ministerial Assn. (pres. 1971-73), Wesleyan Theol. Soc., Nat. Council Family Relations, Acad. Religion and Mental Health, Am. Inst. Family Relations, Christian Assn. Psychol. Studies. Avocations: ham radio, photography, workshop, gardening. Home: 683 Hayes Holland MI 49423

PARROTT, MICHAEL VERNE, manufacturing company executive; b. Marshall, Minn., Mar. 2, 1940; s. Robert Belgrove and Paula (Verne) P.; m. Kathryn Ann Rue, Dec. 22, 1964; children: Jennifer Rue, Deborah Corinne, Lesleigh Ann. BA, Carleton Coll., 1962; MBA, Stanford U., 1964. Mgr. dist. sales Inland Steel, Detroit, 1964-69; gen. mgr. Essex Machinery Terminals, Ft. Wayne, Ind., 1969-74; pres. Dunbar Furniture Co., Berne, Ind., 1974-75; chmn., pres., chief exec. officer ICON, Inc., Ft. Wayne, 1979—; bd. dirs. Robert B. Parrott, Inc., Kansas City, Mo., Grange Mut. Cos., Columbus, Ohio, Cogeneration Systems, Nashville, Ind. Trustee, founder The Canterbury Sch., Ft. Wayne, 1976; trustee Parkview Meml. Hosp., Ft. Wayne, 1985. Clubs: Quest (Ft. Wayne), Bus. Forum (Ft. Wayne), Ft. Wayne Country, Summit (Ft. Wayne). Home: 5529 Cider Mill Rd Fort Wayne IN 46804

PARSONS, TERRY DIANE, lawyer; b. Decorah, Iowa, July 16, 1951; d. James Henry and Dorris Mary (Moye) Hoel; m. Mark J. Parsons, Dec. 26, 1977; 1 child, Brittany Elizabeth. BA in History with honors, U. Iowa, 1973, MA, JD, 1976. Assoc. Redfern, McKinley, Olsen & Mason, Cedar Falls, Iowa, 1976-77; ptnr. Redfern, McKinley, Olsen & Mason, Cedar Falls, 1978-81, Olsen & Parsons, Cedar Falls, 1981-84, Olsen, Parsons & Ament, Cedar Falls, 1984—; lectr. U. No. Iowa, Cedar Falls, 1987. Mem. Altrusa, Cedar Falls, 1982—, pres., 1982-84; advisor Law Explorer Post, Cedar Falls, 1980-84; bd. dirs. Operation Threshold, Waterloo, Iowa, 1977-83, chmn., 1980-81; bd. dirs. Cedar Valley Econ. Devel. Corp., Black Hawk County, Iowa, 1986-87. Mem. ABA, Iowa State Bar Assn., Black Hawk County Bar Assn. (sec. 1977-78), Assn. Trial Lawyers Am., Assn. Trial Lawyers Iowa, Cedar Falls C. of C. (bd. dirs. 1983—). Avocations: hiking, camping, bicycling. Home: 2004 Washington Cedar Falls IA 50613 Office: Olsen Parsons & Ament 120 W 4th St Cedar Falls IA 50613

PARTIN, RONALD LEE, counseling educator; b. Lima, Ohio, Nov. 14, 1946; s. Troy L. and Marie (Westbrook) P.; m. Janet E. Davis, June 29, 1968; children: Matthew L., Brett M. BS, Bowling Green State U., 1968, MEd, 1970; PhD, U. Toledo, 1975. Licensed profl. counselor, Ohio. Social studies tchr. Ottawa Hills High Sch., Toledo, 1968-75; prof. Bowling Green (Ohio) State U., 1975—. Co-author P.R.I.D.E., 1980; contbr. articles to profl. jours. Mem. Ohio Assn. Counselor Educators and Suprs. (sec./treas. 1986—), Ohio Assn. for Counseling and Devel., Am. Ednl. Research Assn., Phi Delta Kappa, Phi Kappa Phi. Unitarian. Avocations: woodworking, golf, basketball, stained glass, genealogy. Home: 173 Winfield Dr Bowling Green OH 43402 Office: Bowling Green State U EDFI Bowling Green OH 43403

PARTINGTON, LARRY DALE, data processing executive; b. Lake City, Minn., July 9, 1946; s. George H. and Inez W. (Rutz) P.; m. Carol Jane Bystrom, May 7, 1966; children: Bradley James, Bret David, Rebecca Jane. Student, Winona State Coll., 1964-65, Minn. Sch. Bus., 1967. Acct. F.D. Nowlin CPA, Mpls., 1966-67; programmer Tel-E-Lect Inc., Mpls., 1967-70; tech. analyst Watkins Products, Winona, Minn., 1970-73; mgr. system & programming Peerless Chain Co., Winona, 1973—. Treas. Pickwick Mill Inc., 1983-85. Mem. Am. Prodn. and Inventory Control Soc., Internat. Tandem Users Group. Clubs: Winona Rod and Gun, Winona

Sportsmans. Avocations: hunting, fishing, golf, bowling, snowmobiling. Home: Rt 1 Box 73 B Winona MN 55987 Office: Peerless Chain Co 1416 E Sanburn Box 349 Winona MN 55987

PARTINGTON, LYNN GORDON, teacher; b. Lake City, Minn., Aug. 29, 1941; s. George H. and Inez (Rutz) P.; m. Sharon Yvonne Krueger, Sept. 7, 1963; children: Dawn, Michael. BS in Indsl. Arts, Winona State U., 1963, BS in Bus. Edn., 1985. Indsl. arts tchr. Laingsburg (Mich.) High Sch., 1963-64, St. Charles (Minn.) Sch. Dist. #857, 1964-67; indsl. arts tchr. La Crescent (Minn.) Sch. Dist. #300, 1967-84, bus. edn. tchr., 1985—; Head bus. dept. La Crescent, 1985-86; head negotiator La Crescent Sch. Dist. 300. Treas. Applefest, La Crescent, 1984; v.p. Applecore, La Crescent, 1986. Mem. NEA, Minn. Edn. Assn., Le Crescent Edn. Assn., Adminstrv. Mgmt. Soc., Jaycees (treas., Jaycee of the Yr.), Trout Unlimited, NRA, ARMA. Lutheran. Club: Gopher State Sportsmen's, Lutheran Pioneers. Avocations: camping, traveling, hunting, fishing. Home: 642 Main St La Crescent MN 55947 Office: Dist 300 Lancer Dr La Crescent MN 55947

PARTRIDGE, JON DAVID, restaurateur; b. Mpls., Jan. 22, 1962; s. Paul Wayne and Patricia Anne (Gardiner) P. BS, U. Wis., Menomonie, 1983. Owner Le Bistro Cafe, Des Moines, 1983-85, Le Bistro Banquet, Des Moines, 1983-85, Caberet Club, Des Moines, 1983-85, Weighside Cafe, Mpls., 1984-86, Caterers Unlimited, Mpls., 1984-86, Saturday Nite Cafe, Mpls., 1984—. Mem. Mpls. C. of C., Nat. Restaurant Assn. Unitarian. Avocations: sailing, skiing, swimming. Home: 1920 S 1st St 1103 Riverview Towers Minneapolis MN 55454

PARTRIDGE, PATRICIA WALSH, insurance company executive; b. Syracuse, N.Y., Apr. 4, 1951; d. William Joseph and Winifred Theresa (Eggert) Walsh; m. Stephen Kurt Partridge, July 19, 1975. Student, Syracuse U., 1969-71; BA, SUNY, Cortland, 1973. Cert. secondary edn., Minn. Office mgr. Doherty Rumble & Butler, Mpls., 1976-84; ptnr., v.p. Norbert & Partridge, Inc., Mpls., 1984-86; supr. Northwestern Nat. Life, Mpls., 1986—; instr. Dakota County Vo-Tech, Rosemont, Minn., 1984—. Peer counselor Chrysalis, Mpls., 1986. Mem. Minn. Women's Network. Democrat. Roman Catholic. Avocations: jogging, reading, theater, arts. Office: Northwestern Nat Life Ins Rt 6940 Box 20 Minneapolis MN 55420

PASANT, ATHANASE J., insurance company executive; b. Bay City, Mich., Aug. 29, 1918; s. Arthur J. and Rose M. (Novak) P.; m. Shirley K. Williston, Feb. 12, 1945; children: James, Thomas, David, Christina. B.A. in Econs., Mich. State U., 1949. Agt., brokerage mgr. Great West Life Ins. Co., Lansing, Mich., 1945-55; gen. agy. Ill. Mid-Continent Life Ins. Co., Evanston, Ill., 1955-60; pres. Apex Investments, Lansing, 1960-61; founder, pres., chmn. Jackson Nat. Life Ins. Co., Lansing, 1961—; pres., dir. Chrissy Corp., Wilmington, Del., 1981—, Jackson Nat. Life of Tex., Irving, 1981—; vice chmn. Mich. Life & Health Guarantee Assn., Lansing, 1982—. Home: 4325 MarMoor Dr Lansing MI 48917 Office: Jackson Nat Life Ins Co 5901 Executive Dr Lansing MI 48910

PASCAL, HAROLD SAUNDERS, health care exec.; b. Coffeyville, Kans., Mar. 16, 1934; s. Michael William and Jacqueline V. P.; B.S., So. Meth. U., 1956; M.B.A., Ga. So. U., 1973; m. Dinah L. Filkins, Aug. 13, 1955; children—Lee Ann, Tracey Michele. Commd. 2d lt. U.S. Army, 1957, advanced through grades to maj., 1967; served med. service dept.; asso. exec. dir. Gen. Hosp., Humana Inc., Ft. Walton Beach, Fla., 1974-75, adminstr. Sarasota (Fla.) Palms Hosp., 1975-76, exec. dir. Llano (N.Mex.) Estacado Med. Center, 1976-77; pres. Americana Hosp. Co. (Cenco Inc.), Monticello, Ill., 1977-80, Continental Health Care Ltd., 1980-87, World Health Service, Ltd., 1987—. Pres. PTA, San Antonio, 1969-70; bd. dirs. NE Sch. Dist., San Antonio, 1968-69; dir. community blood drive, San Francisco, 1964-65. Decorated Bronze Star, Air Medal, Purple Heart, Cross of Gallantry, Combat Med. Badge. Fellow Am. Acad. Med. Adminstrs. (diplomate); Am. Hosp. Assn., Am. Coll. Healthcare Execs. Adminstrs., Am. Soc. Hosp. Engrs., Ill. Hosp. Assn., Fla. Hosp. Assn., Fedn. Am. Healthsystems (dir.), Psi Chi. Presbyterian. Clubs: Hunter Riding (pres., 1972-73), Rotary, Toastmasters. Author: Plight of the Migrant Worker, 1974; Installation Supply Procedures, 1968; programmed text on Supply Procedures, 1969; Dictionary of Supply Terms, 1969. Home: 10 S 321 Jaime Ln Hinsdale IL 60521 Office: 20 N Wacker Chicago IL 60611

PASCH, KARL RICHARD, electronics executive; b. Toledo, Ohio, Dec. 25, 1939; s. Carl Herman and Edith Elaine (Dunipace) P.; m. Karen Louise Ackland, Nov. 21, 1962; children: Mark Alan, Lauri Ann, Cara Ruth, Andrew Scott. BSEE, U. Toledo, 1957-62, MSEE, 1964. Product engr. IBM Corp., Boca Raton, Fla., 1968-71; sales rep. IBM Corp., Indpls., 1971-79; mktg. planner IBM Corp., Rochester, Minn., 1979-84, mktg. planning mgr., 1984-86, project mgr., 1986—. Chmn. budget and planning panel United Way, Rochester, 1987—; v.p. bd dirs. YMCA, Rochester, 1984-85, pres. 1985—; treas. bd. Rochester area Family YMCA, 1986—; elder Trinity Presbyn., Rochester, 1984—, treas. 1985—. Served to capt. U.S. Army, 1965-68. Mem. Sigma Alpha Epsilon. Republican. Presbyterian. Avocations: softball, bowling, racquetball. Home: 1121 NE 19th St Rochester MN 55904 Office: IBM Corp Hwy 52 & NW 37th St Rochester MN 55901

PASCOE, ARTHUR WRAY, psychotherapist; b. Winnipeg, Can., Feb. 14, 1942; came to U.S., 1971; s. Arthur Raymond and Allice Pearl (Benson) P.; m. Jill L. Dickie, Sept. 10, 1975 (div. 1980); children: Michael Benson, Justin Roades. BA, U. Western Ont., London, 1965; M in Social Work, U. Manitoba, Winnipeg, 1968; PhD, Case Western Res. U., 1981. Head master Confederation Coll., Thunder Bay, Ont., Can., 1968-71; asst. prof. York U., Toronto, 1977-78; head behavioral Sci. Cons. Akron Gen. Med. Ctr., 1975-80; practice psychotherapy Akron, 1980—; adj. faculty coll. medicine NE Ohio U., 1976-80, U. Victoria, Can., 1974-85. Contbr. articles to profl. jour. Mem. Am. Assn. Family Therapy, British Assn. Family Therapists, Assn. Sex Therapists and Counselors (charter). Liberal Party Can. Congregational. Office: 77 Fir Hill Akron OH 44304

PASCOE, E(DWARD) RUDY, insurance sales executive; b. Sioux Falls, S.D., Oct. 13, 1948; s. Marvin E. Pascoe and Celesta M. (Heaton) Hymore; m. Janice A. Kistler, Sept. 2, 1967; children: Jennifer L., Matthew R. BE, U. S.D., 1972; postgrad., U. Iowa, 1972-74. Cert. life underwriter. Tchr. Jo-Daviess Area Vocat. Ctr., Elizabeth, Ill., 1972-84; pvt. practice ins. sales Elizabeth, 1974-87; personal line mgr. Herrling & Schmitt, Inc. Multi Line Ins. Agy., Freeport, Ill., 1981—. Vice coordinator Elizabeth Ambulance Corp., 1981—; fin. sec. Elizabeth United Meth. Ch., 1977—, others. Named one of Outstanding Young Men Am., Jaycees Am., 1969. Mem. Life Underwriters Assn. (sec./treas. 1976-77). Republican. Lodges: Lions (pres., v.p., sec./treas. 1973-81), Masons. Avocation: reading. Office: Herrling & Schmitt Inc PO Box 300 Freeport IL 61032

PASCUCCI, RICHARD ANTHONY, osteopath, rheumatologist, educator; b. Phila., Aug. 18, 1948; s. Robert Philip and Carmela Mary (Casale) P.; m. Patricia Comly, June 29, 1973; children: Richard Anthony Jr., Daniel, Amy Patricia, Matthew. BS in Biology, St. Joseph's U., Phila., 1970; DO, Phila. Coll. Osteopathic Medicine, 1975. Diplomate Am. Osteopathic Bd. Internal Medicine. Internship Suburban Gen. Hosp., Norristown, Pa., 1975-76, resident internal medicine, 1976-78; rheumatology fellow U. Louisville, 1978-80; attending physician Internal Medicine Assn., Norristown, 1980-84; assoc. prof. Coll. Osteopathic Medicine Mich. State U., East Lansing, Mich., 1984—. Contbr. articles to profl. jours. Mem. athletic assn. St. Thomas Aquinas Sch., East Lansing, 1985—; bd. dirs. Arthritis Found., Lansing, 1985—. Fellow Am. Rheumatism Assn.; mem. Am. Osteopathic Assn., Am. Coll. Osteopathic Internists, Pa. Osteopathic Med. Assn., Phila. Coll. Osteopathic Medicine Alumni Assn., Phila. Rheumatism Soc., Mich. Assn. Osteopathic Physicians and Surgeons, Nat. Bd. Osteopathic Examiners (cert.), Am. Osteopathic Bd. Internal Medicine and Rheumatology (cert.). Republican. Roman Catholic. Avocations: baseball, coaching basketball, piano, guitar, tennis. Office: Mich State U Coll Osteopathic Medicine B311 West Fee Hall East Lansing MI 48824

PASEK, MICHAEL ANTHONY, computer technologist; b. Duluth, Minn., Sept. 5, 1951; s. Antone William and Helene (Tunsky) P.; m. Robin Carol Solem, Nov. 1, 1986. Grad. coll. Operator, Bd. Pensions, Lutheran Ch. in Am., 1973-75; corp. mgr. Microtex Corp., Cloquet, Minn., 1975-79; v.p. internat. ops. Microtex Corp., Mpls., 1979-81, pres., 1981—; systems programmer NCR Comten, Inc., 1977-80, supr./sr. systems programmer, network software devel., 1980-83, chief software engr. switching software devel., 1984-85, lead software engr. switching software devel., 1985—; mem. Data Communications Adv. Panel. Mem. Am. Philatelic Soc. Home: 9741 Foley Blvd NW Coon Rapids MN 55433 Office: 2700 N Snelling Roseville MN 55113

PASIK, LAWRENCE IRA, allergist; b. N.Y.C., June 18, 1945; s. Saul and Selma (Elman) P.; m. Rona Dianne Weiss, June 18, 1967; children: Mindy, Aliya. BA, Harpur Coll., 1966; MD, SUNY, N.Y.C., 1970. Diplomate Am. Bd. Allergy, Am. Bd. Pediatrics, Nat. Bd. Med. Examiners. Staff physician Henry Ford Hosp., Detroit, 1976-78; pvt. practice medicine specializing in allergy West Bloomfield, Mich., 1978—; cons. to surgeon gen. USN, Washington, 1974-76; dir. allergy clinic St. Joseph Mercy Hosp., Pontiac, Mich., 1978—. Served with USN, 1974-76. N.Y. State Bd. Regents scholar, 1962-66, 66-70. Fellow Am. Acad. Pediatrics, Am. Acad. Alergy and Immunology, Mich. Allergy Soc. (treas. 1985—). Home: 2929 Bloomfield Park Dr West Bloomfield MI 48033 Office: 5640 W Maple Rd #202 West Bloomfield MI 48322

PASSMAN, RALPH S., insurance company executive; b. Cleve., Dec. 6, 1924; s. Louis and Anna (Kousin) P.; m. Shirley R. Carr, Apr. 20, 1947; children: Paul A., Suzanne R. Student U. Calif., Berkeley, 1944-45. Agy. supr. Guardian Life Ins. Co., Kansas City, Mo., 1947-53; assoc. gen. agent Washington Nat. Ins. Co., Kansas City, Mo., 1953-55; v.p. SFO, Inc., Kansas City, 1955-72; pres. Passman & Assoc., Prairie Village, Kans., 1972—; pres. Acorn Underwriters, Inc. Contbr. articles to profl. jours. Active with Boy Scouts Am., Kansas City,Mo., 1936—. Served as cpl. USMC, 1942-46. Recipient Silver Beaver award Boy Scouts Am., 1976, award of Excellence, Graphic Arts Council, 1969. Mem. Ins. Agents Assn., Gen. Agents and Mgrs. Assn., Ind. Ins. Agents Assn., Accident and Health Underwriters Assn. Greater Kansas City (pres. 1957-58), Greater Kansas City and State of Kans. Health Underwriters Assn. (bd. dirs.), Internat. Assn. Life Underwriters, Nat. Assn. Health Underwriters. Jewish. Lodge: B'nai Brith (pres. Kansas City 1968). Avocations: scouting, golf, stamp and coin collecting. Office: 4200 Somerset Dr Prairie Village KS 66208

PASTERNACK, DOUGLAS ALLAN, sales executive; b. Kansas City, Mo., Aug. 10, 1954; m. Janet Louise Reardon, May 21, 1977; children: Kathryn, Daniel. BBA, U. Mo., 1976. V.p. sales Mid West Chandelier, Kansas City, 1977—. Mem. Illuminating Engring. Soc. Club: Oakwood Country. Office: Mid West Chandelier 100 Funston Rd Kansas City KS 66115

PATAKI, ANDREW, bishop; b. Palmerton, Pa., Aug. 30, 1927. Student, St. Vincent Coll., St. Procopious Coll., Lisle, Ill., Sts. Cyril and Methodius, Byzantine Cath. Sem., Grigorian U., Rome. Ordained priest Roman Cath. Ch., 1952. Bishop Parma, Ohio, 1984—. Office: Chancery Office 1900 Carlton Rd Parma OH 44134 *

PATCH, JOE HOWARD, lube oil marketing company executive; b. East St. Louis, Ill., Mar. 4, 1929; s. Howard Frank and Kate Knight (Boswell) P.; m. Virginia Marie Sloan, June 7, 1950; children—Howard R., Joe S., Patricia E. Sanford, Dan A., Scott J., Paul A. B.A., Cornell U., 1952. Chemist, Procter & Gamble, Cin., 1952-53; refinery chemist Shell Oil Co., Houston, 1953-56, indsl. mktg., 1956-82; pres. Spec Oils Inc., Indpls., 1982—. Mem. Alpha Chi Sigma. Republican. Christian. Lodge: Elks. Home: 4241 Melbourne Road E Dr Indianapolis IN 46208

PATCHEN, JEFFREY HART, music educator; b. Syracuse, N.Y., Apr. 28, 1954; s. Hart C. and Virginia (Chase) P.; m. Cheryl Elizabeth Patchen, June 2, 1984. MusB, Ithaca Coll., 1976, MusM, 1981; MusD, Ind. U., 1986. Lifetime tchg. license, N.Y. Dir. bands East Syracuse-Minoa High Sch., 1976-82; assoc. instr. Ind. U., Bloomington, 1982-84; state music supr. Ind. Dept. Edn., Indpls., 1984—; mem. edn. panel. Ind. Arts Commn., Indpls., 1986—; bd. dirs. Very Spl. Arts, Ind., 1986—. Contbr. articles to profl. jours. Grantee Ind. U., 1985, NEA, 1987, Ind. Arts Commn., 1987. Mem. Nat. Council State Suprs. Music, Music Educators Nat. Conf., Ind. Music Educators Assn. Home: 2616 Timberly Dr 1A Indianapolis IN 46220 Office: Ind Dept Edn Rm 229 State House Indianapolis IN 46204

PATE, JENNIFER ROSE, social worker; b. Guthrie, Okla., Jan. 14, 1949; d. Diehl Leon and Jean Elizabeth (Wilson) Craven; m. James Walter Pate, Dec. 20, 1970; children: Jamie Mae, Robin Elizabeth, Brice Walter. Student, U. Okla., 1966-70; BS in Health Services Adminstrn., U. Houston, Clear Lake City, Tex., 1978. Cert. social worker, Tex., life ins. agt., Tex. Social worker Salvation Army, Freeport, Tex., 1979-81, 86—; social worker, mentally handicapped-mentally retarded liasion specialist Gulf Coast Mental Health/Mental Retardation Service, Freeport, 1982-83; clerical adminstrv. asst. Lake Jackson (Tex.) Library, 1983-84; del. Nat. Social Work Conv., San Antonio, 1979. Mem. task force on environment and air pollution Houston/Galveston (Tex.) Area Council, 1979-83; mem. panel com. Brazosport (Tex.) Community Food Pantry, 1986; adv. bd. United Way Brazoria County, Freeport, 1986—; charter mem. Gov. Clement's Com., 1982; leader, service chmn. Girl Scouts U.S., Freeport, 1972-85; active with First Freeport Meth. Ch., Cerebral Palsy Found., Rainbow Orgn. for Girls. Mem. AAUW (edn. com. 1979-85), United Meth. Women (life). Republican. Avocations: piano playing, swimming, horseback riding. Home: 1504 W 10th Freeport TX 77541 Office: Salvation Army 1618 N Ave J Freeport TX 77541

PATEL, ANANTLAL MOTIBHAI, small business owner; b. Harare, Zimbabwe, Oct. 13, 1954; came to U.S., 1973; s. Motibhai M. and Maniben Patel. BSME, Mich. Technol. U., 1976; MSME, U. Mich., 1977. Research eng. Chrysler Engring. Staff, Highland Park, Mich., 1978-80; owner, mgr. Lucille's Lounge, Canton, Mich., 1980—. Mem. Canton C. of C., Greater Detroit C. of C., Mich. Lic. Beverage Assn., Gujarat Samaj, AMSE, Soc. Mfg. Engrs. Republican. Hindu. Avocations: sports, coins, reading, travel. Office: Lucille's Lounge 43711 Michigan Ave Canton MI 48188

PATEL, JASHU PURUSHOTTAM, library educator; b. Baroda, India, July 11, 1939; came to U.S., 1970; s. Purushottam H. and Suraj (Patel) P.; m. Georgianna R. Brethauer, July 20, 1973; 1 child, Joshua. B.A., U. Baroda, 1959; M.L.S., U. Pitts., 1972, Ph.D., 1977; postgrad. Northwestern Poly. Sch. Librarianship, London, 1966. Library asst. pub. library, Slough, Bucks, Eng., 1961-63; supr. reference reading room U. London Sch. Oriental and African Studies Library, 1963-70; instr. No. Ill. U., DeKalb, 1972-73; asst. prof. Eastern Ill. U., Charleston, 1977-79; asst. prof. library sci. Chgo. State U., 1979-82, assoc. prof., 1982-87, prof., 1987—; vis. prof. Governors State U., Park Forest, Ill., summer 1980; mem. summer sch. faculty Rosary Coll. Grad. Sch. Library and Info. Sci., River Forest, Ill., 1983; panel chair, presenter papers Confs. on South Asia, U. Wis., 1981, 82, 84. Author chpt. in book; contbr. articles to library jours. Named Tchr. of Yr., Chgo. State U., 1981; grantee Chgo. State U. and Found., 1982, 83, 84, U. Ill. Pacific/Asian Am. Research Methods, 1983; recipient Faculty Excellence award, 1986, Faculty Merit award, 1981; Fulbright scholar award, 1987-88. Mem. ALA (session leader ann. conf. 1985), Assn. Library and Info. Sci. Edn. (conf. facilitator 1985), Assn. Am. Library Sch., Brit. Library Assn. Home: 65 W 146th St Riverdale IL 60627 Office: Chgo State U 95th St at King Dr Chicago IL 60628

PATEL, NALIN M., gastroenterologist; b. Karamsad, India, July 17, 1948; came to U.S., 1975; s. Maganlal L. and Santa (Patel) P.; m. Roshni Patel, Nov. 26, 1977; children: Reshma, Neel. MD, Grant Med. Sch., Bombay, India, 1974. Cert. Am. Bd. Internal Medicine. Intern Chgo. Med. Sch. VA Hosp., North Chicago, 1975-77; resident, fellow St. Joseph Hosp., Chgo., 1977-80; practice medicine specializing in gastroenterology Champaign, Ill., 1980—; gastroenterologist, cons. Burnham Hosp., Champaign, 1981—; chmn. cancer com. Burnham Hosp., 1985-86; chmn. ambulatory care Burnham Hosp., 1986—. Contbr. articles to profl. jours. Mem. Am. Soc. Internal Medicine. Avocations: painting, writing, travel. Office: 302 E Stoughton Champaign IL 61820

PATEL, NISH, health care administrator; b. Nairobi, Kenya, Feb. 9, 1953; s. Chad and Pushpa Patel; m. Kalpana Patel, Jan. 4, 1981. BA, Rutgers U., 1975; MPH, U. Pitts., 1977; postgrad., Cleve. State U., 1984-87. Jr. asst. adminstr. Martland Hosp., Newark, 1976-78; asst. adminstr. Coll. Hosp., Newark, 1978-81; assoc. adminstr. Kaiser Permanente, Cleve., 1981-87; adminstr. Cleve. Clinic, 1987—; cons. surveyor Joint Commn. Accreditation of Hosps., Chgo., 1986—. Served to lt. USNR. Mem. Am. Coll. Health Care Execs. Hindu. Lodges: Kiwanis, Masons. Avocations: tennis, classical music. Home: 3421 Burrwood Dr Richfield OH 44286 Office: Cleveland Clinic 9500 Euclid Ave Cleveland OH 44106

PATEL, RAMESH MANIBHAI, engineer; b. Umreth, Gujarat, India, Aug. 6, 1935; came to U.S., 1957; s. Manibhai Lallubhai and Kamlaben Manibhai (Kamlaben S.) P.; m. Bharati R. Bharati P. Patel, Mar. 10, 1954 (dec. 1970); children: Parul R., Mehool R.; m. Bharati Ramesh Madhuben, July 13, 1971; children: Ami R., Rahul R. BCE, M.S.U. of Baroda, Gujrat, India, 1956; MCE, U. Mich., 1958, DSc in Civil Engring., 1964; cert. fin. planner, Coll. Fin. Planning, 1982. Registered profl. engr., Mich. Sr. engr. Giffels & Rossetti Inc., Detroit, 1962-63, 64-65, job capt., 1964-65; project dir. Giffels & Rossetti Inc., Southfield, Mich., 1979—; engr. Byce & Ranney, Kalamazoo, 1963-64; fin. cons. Datachem. Inc., Indpls., 1983—; v.p. Lakshmi Investment Group Inc., West Bloomfield, Mich., 1984—. Treas. Bharatiya Family Services, Farmington Hills, Mich., 1986. Mem. ASCE (pres. southeastern Mich. br. 1977-78, Disting. Service award 1978), Am. Soc. Engrs. from India (chmn. nominating com. 1986, Disting. Service award 1986), Internat. Assn. Fin. Planners, Inst. Cert. Fin. Planners, Charotar Patidar. Republican. Club: Toastmasters (pres. 1977, area gov. 1978) (Southfield). Avocations: camping, golfing. Home: 29224 Somerset Southfield MI 48076 Office: Giffels Assocs Inc 25200 Telegraph Rd Southfield MI 48086

PATEL, YOGENDRA BHAILALBHAI, cost engineer; b. Gujaqat, India, Aug. 24, 1947; s. Bhailalbhai S. and Shushila Ben Patel; m. Amita K. Naik, June 14, 1974; children: Romil, Mitali. BEE, Bombay U., 1972; MBA in Fin. and Mgmt., Roosevelt U., Chgo., 1977. Quality control engr. Internat. Tel. & Tel. Corp., Berwyn, Ill., 1973; bus. mgr. Racine Paper Box, Chgo., 1973-75; prodn. engr. Sommer Elec. Co., Elk Grove, Ill., 1975-79; mfg. mgr. Ragex Controls, Elk Grove, Ill., 1979-81; sr. value engr. Zenith Electronics, Glenview, Ill., 1981—. Mem. Am. Soc. Cost Engrs. Avocations: sports, reading, teaching. Office: Zenith Electronics Corp 1000 Milwaukee Ave Glenview IL 60025

PATMON, HELEN LORAINE, theatre educator; b. Oklahoma City, Mar. 14, 1954; d. Bose C. and Bessie Beatrice (Reid) P. BFA, U. Okla., 1976, MFA, 1981. Spl. instr. U. Okla., Norman, 1980-81; asst. prof. speech and theatre Lincoln U., Jefferson City, Mo., 1981-87; instr. Barbizon Modeling, Oklahoma City, Mo., 1981. Mem. editorial bd. First Anthology Missouri Women, 1986. MacDowell Soc. scholar, 1975. Mem. Assn. Theatre Higher Edn., Black Theatre Network, Mo. Assn. Theatre. Avocations: refinishing furniture, camping, photography. Home: 2301 Primrose Apt. 7C Columbia MO 65202

PATOFF, MARY ELIZABETH, probation officer; b. Chgo., July 19, 1953; d. Joseph Vincient and Lottie (Hayek) Donahue; m. Michael Neil Patoff, May 5, 1978: 1 child, Michelle Lynn. BA in Social Sci. cum laude, Lewis U., 1975; M in Pub Adminstrn., Roosevelt U., 1979. Registered social worker, Ill. Probation officer juvenile div. Cook County Circuit Ct., Chgo., 1976—; pres. MB Mgmt., Inc., Des Plaines, Ill, 1980-84. Mem. Juvenile Officers Assn. Avocation: needlepoint, swimming, racquetball. Home: 9854 Robin Rd Niles IL 60648 Office: Juvenile Ct 1100 S Hamilton Chicago IL 60612

PATON, N. E., JR., marketing, public relations and broadcast counselor; b. Kansas City, Mo., Sept. 18, 1931; s. N. Emerson and Ruth L. (Britt) P.; m. Sharon Lea Davis, Aug. 12, 1967; children: Russell E., Neal E. AA, Kansas City Jr. Coll., 1951; BA, U. Mo., 1953. With news and prodn. staff Sta. KCMO-TV, Kansas City, Mo., 1953-56; owner, chief exec. officer Paton Assocs., Inc., Kansas City, 1956—. Home: 3704 W 119th Terr Leawood KS 66209 Office: Paton and Assocs Inc Box 7350 Leawood KS 66207

PATRICK, ALLEN LEE, architectural firm executive; b. Toledo, June 18, 1938; s. Raymond Albert and Dorothy Glays (Davis) P.; m. Jean Ann Dolan, Sept. 14, 1968; children: Steven J., Susan E., Meredith A. BArch, U. Cin., 1962. Lic. architect in 23 states including Ohio. Pres. Patrick & Assocs., Inc., Columbus, Ohio, 1963—. Contbg. author: Architects Handbook of Professional Practice, 1984; Encyclopedia of Architecture, 1986. Trustee Project Hope, Columbus, 1979; mem. Greater Columbus Arts Council, 1975, Mayor's Leadership Club, 1986. Mem. AIA, Am. Correctional Assn., Architect Soc. Ohio, Urban Land Inst., Columbus C. of C. Clubs: Ambassadors (Columbus), Tri-Village Breakfast, El Hajj. Lodge: Tri-Village. Office: Patrick and Assocs Inc 65 E State St Suite 500 Columbus OH 43215

PATRICK, GEORGE MILTON, dentist; b. Accoville, W.Va., Sept. 27, 1920; s. Milton Michael and Martha Mary (Mullins) P.; m. Shirley Ann Rutherford, Mar. 22, 1952 (div. June 1966); 1 child, Geoffrey Milton (dec.); m. Jane Lee Austin, Oct. 1, 1971; stepchildren: Anthony Duke Spencer, T.L.C. Hughes. BS, Capital U., 1950; DDS, Ohio State U., 1955; postgrad., U. N.C., 1972. Gen. practice dentistry Columbus, Ohio, 1956-67; dir. mktg. and research Kirkman Labs., Portland, Oreg., 1968; gen. practice dentistry specializing in orthodontics Columbus, 1968; pub. health dentist Ohio Dept. Health, Bowling Green, Ohio, 1968-80; practice dentistry specializing in pedodontics 1980-82; pvt. practice computer cons. Columbus, 1982-87. Production mgr. Vaud-Vilities, Columbus, 1979-86; singer First Community Ch., Columbus, 1972-86, opera singer Columbus Chorus, 1984-86. Served to 2d lt. U.S. Army, 1942-46, ETO. Decorated Bronze Star, Purple Heart with Oak Leaf Cluster. Mem. ADA, Ohio Dental Assn., Columbus Dental Soc. (chmn. children's dental health week), Columbus Council World Affairs, Pub. Relations Soc. (membership com. 1986). Avocations: cooking, poetry, camping, singing. Home and Office: 2511 Onandaga Dr Columbus OH 43221

PATRICK, JANE AUSTIN, association executive; b. Memphis, May 27, 1930; d. Wilfred Jack and Evelyn Eudora (Branch) Austin; m. William Thomas Spencer, Sept. 11, 1952 (div. Apr. 1970); children: Anthony Duke, Tonilee Candice Spencer Hughes; m. George Milton Patrick, Oct. 1, 1971. Student Memphis State U., 1946-47; BSBA, Ohio State U., 1979. Service rep. So. Bell Telephone and Telegraph, Memphis, 1947-52; placement dir. Mgmt. Personnel, Memphis, 1965-66; personnel asst. to exec. v.p. E & E Ins. Co., Columbus, Ohio, 1966-69; Ohio exec. dir. Nat. Soc. for Prevention of Blindness, Columbus, 1969-73; regional dir. Ohio and Ky. CARE and MEDICO, Columbus, 1979—; lectr., cons. in field. Mem. choir 1st Community Ch., Columbus, Ohio State Univ. Hosp.'s Service Bd.; bd. dirs. Columbus Council on World Affairs, 1981—, sec., 1983—. Recipient commendations Nat. Soc. Prevention Blindness and Central Ohio Lions Eye Bank, 1973, Nat. Soc. Fund-Raising Execs., 1984, 85, Plaques for Service award Upper Arlington Pub. Schs., 1986. Mem. Non-Profit Orgn. Mgmt. Inst. (pres.), Nat. Soc. Fund-Raising Execs. (cert., nat. dir.), Pub. Relations Soc. Am. (cert., membership com. chairperson), Ins. Inst. Am. (cert.), Mensa Internat., Columbus Dental Soc. Aux., Alpha Gamma Delta, Epsilon Sigma Alpha. Home: 2511 Onandaga Dr Columbus OH 43221 Office: 280 N High St Suite 1520 Columbus OH 43215

PATRICK, JOHN JOSEPH, education educator; b. East Chicago, Ind., Apr. 14, 1935; s. John W. and Elizabeth (Lazar) P.; m. Patricia Grant, Aug. 17, 1963; children—Rebecca, Barbara. A.B., Dartmouth Coll., 1957; Ed.D., Ind. U., 1969. Social studies tchr. Roosevelt High Sch., East Chicago, 1957-62; social studies tchr. Lab. High Sch., U. Chgo., 1962-65; research assoc. Sch. Edn., Ind. U., Bloomington, 1965-69, asst. prof., 1969-74, assoc. prof., 1974-77, prof. edn., 1977—, dir. social studies devel. ctr., 1986—, dir. ERIC clearinghouse for social studies, social sci. edn., 1986—; bd. dirs. Biol. Scis. Curriculum Study, 1980-83; ednl. cons. Author: Progress of the Afro-American, 1968, The Young Voter, 1974; (with L. Ehman, Howard Mehlinger) Toward Effective Instruction in Secondary Social Studies, 1974, Lessons on the Northwest Ordinance, 1987; (with R. Remy) Civics for Americans, 1980, rev. edit. 1986; (with Mehlinger) American Political Behavior, 1972, rev. edit. 1980, (with C. Keller) Lessons on The Federalist Papers, 1987; America Past and Present, 1983; (with Carol Berkin) History of the American Nation, 1984, rev. edit. 1987; Lessons on the Constitution, 1985. Bd. dirs. Law in

Am. Soc. Found., 1984—, Social Sci. Edn. Consortium, 1984—; mem. Gov.'s Task Force on Citizenship Edn., Ind., 1982-87; active Ind. Commn. on Bicentennial of U.S. Constitution. Mem. Nat. Council Social Studies, Assn. Supervision and Curriculum Devel., Social Sci. Edn. Consortium (v.p. 1985-87), Council for Basic Edn., Soc. History Edn., Phi Delta Kappa. Home: 1209 E University St Bloomington IN 47401 Office: Ind U 2805 E 10th St Bloomington IN 47405

PATRICK, ROBERT J., oil company executive, engineer; b. Clifford, Mich., May 1, 1927; s. Stanley A. and Glenadine M. (Harrison) P.; m. Rita L. Lehman, June 28, 1958; children: Christopher, Shannon. BS, U.S. Mcht. Marine Acad., 1949; BSE, U. Mich., 1951; postgrad., Johns Hopkins U., 1953-54; MBA, Washington U., 1972. Registered profl. engr., Mo., N.C., Md., Pa., W.Va., Ill., Okla., Tex., La. Asst. to sr. v.p. Md. Shipbuilding, Balt., 1951-59; sr. estimator Bethlehem Shipbuilding, Quincy, Mass., 1959-64; v.p. engring. St. Louis Shipbuilding, 1964-74, Apex Oil Co., St. Louis, 1974-84; mgr. engring. Clark Oil & Refining Co., Hartford, Ill., 1984—. Served to lt. (j.g.) USNR, 1945-57. Awarded Cert. of Appreciation, USCG, Washington, 1976. Mem. Soc. Naval Architects and Marine Engrs., Am. Bur. Shipping Western Rivers (tech. com.). Republican. Lutheran. Home: 1539 View Woods Kirkwood MO 63122

PATRICK, UEAL EUGENE, oil company executive; b. Ky., Mar. 10, 1929; s. Cleveland and Maxine (Hackworth) P.; m. Nancy Sparrow, Mar. 7, 1953 (div. 1982); children: Steve, Rick, Sherry, Mark. B.A., Mich. State U., 1955. Acct. Bond and Co., Jackson, Mich., 1955-57; controller, then exec. v.p., mgr. Midway Supply Co., Jackson, 1957-62; pres., chief exec. officer, dir. Patrick Petroleum Co., Mich., Jackson, 1969—, Patrick Petroleum Corp., Jackson, 1962—, Patrick Racing Team, Inc., 1971—; pres., chief exec. officer, sec., dir. Fayette Corp., 1966-78; pres., chief exec. officer, treas., sec. Patrick Oil and Gas Corp., 1968—, also bd. dirs.; chmn. bd. Mark Aviation, Inc., 1971-83; chmn. bd., chief exec. officer Jet Way, Inc., 1971-83; chief exec. officer, bd. dirs. K & C Corp., 1974-83; chief exec. officer, dir. Western Stamping Corp., 1972-79; pres., chief exec. officer Patrick Energy Co., 1979—; pres., chief exec. officer, dir. Patrick Trading Co. (formerly Patrick Properties, Inc.), 1980—; pres., dir. Patrick Petroleum Internat., Inc., 1972—, Patrick Petroleum Internat. Australia, Inc., 1972-80, Patrick Petroleum Internat. Indonesia, Inc., 1972-80, Patrick Petroleum U.K. Ltd., 1974-80, Patrick Petroleum Italiana, Inc. (S.P.A.), 1974-80; chmn. bd. Championship Auto Racing Teams, Inc., 1978-81, treas., 1981—; chmn. bd., chief exec. officer, dir. Belibe Coal Corp., 1978-81, Black Nugget Coal Co., Inc., 1978-79, Patrick Coal Corp., 1978-84; sec.-treas. Jackson Towing Co., 1972-84; pres., chief exec. officer, dir. Benton Petroleum Corp. (formerly Patrick Producing Co.), 1982—, Patrick Exploration and Prodn., Inc. (formerly Patrick Petroleum of Peru, Ltd.), 1981—; pres., dir. PPC Resources, Inc., 1981—, JEM Petroleum Corp., 1985—; pres., bd. dirs. Patrick Bayou Corp., 1987—; pres., treas., chief exec. officer, bd. dirs. Kinson Resources, Inc., 1987—; bd. dirs. Jackson Found., Penske Corp. Served with USAF, 1948-52. Mem. Ind. Petroleum Assn. Am. (dir. 1968-71, 79-81), Oil Investment Inst. (gov. 1970-81). Republican. Clubs: Jackson Country. Office: 301 W Michigan Ave Jackson MI 49201

PATRICK, WILLIAM BRADSHAW, lawyer, former cemetery executive; b. Indpls., Nov. 29, 1923; s. Fae William and Mary (Bradshaw) P.; m. Ursula Lantzsch, Dec. 28, 1956; children—William Bradshaw, Ursula, Nancy. A.B., The Principia, 1947; LL.B., Harvard U., 1950. Bar: Ind. sup. ct. 1950, U.S. Dist. Ct. (so. dist.) Ind. 1950, U.S. Ct. Apls. (7th cir.) 1961. Ptnr., Patrick & Patrick, Indpls., 1950-53; sole practice, Indpls., 1953—; gen. counsel Met. Planning Commn. Marion County and Indpls., 1955-66; dep. prosecutor Marion County, Ind., 1960-62; past pres., dir. The Cemetery Co., operating Meml. Park Cemetery, Indpls.; sec., dir. Rogers Typesetting Co., Indpls., 1966-85. Pres. Indpls. Legal Aid Soc., 1963. Served to lt. (j.g.) USN, 1942-46. Recipient DeMolay Legion of Honor. Mem. ABA, Ind. Bar Assn., Indpls. Bar Assn., Lawyers Assn. Indpls., Indpls. Estate Planning Council, SAR (sec. Ind. Soc. 1953-59). Clubs: Mason (33 deg.), Shriner. Address: 1000 King Cole Bldg Indianapolis IN 46204

PATRINOS, BARBARA ANN, financial counselor; b. Omaha, Nebr., Sept. 22, 1958; d. John Lewellyn and Leona Grace (Nelson) Campbell; m. Nicholas George Patrinos, Sept. 27, 1981. BSBA, U. Nebr., Omaha, 1981. Fin. counselor Comml. Fed. Savs. and Loan Assn., Omaha, 1983—. Democrat. Roman Catholic. Avocations: music, playing the harp. Home: 909 N 69th St Omaha NE 68132 Office: Comml Fed Savs and Loan 3520 N 90th St Omaha NE 68134

PATRISHKOFF, DAVID JOHN, automotive engineer; b. Canton, Ohio, Mar. 17, 1952; s. Lawrence and Veronica (Hotchkiss) P.; m. Gabriele Angelina Huth, May 8, 1979; 1 child, Geoffrey David. BA in Automotive Engring., Fachhochschule Köln, Cologne, Fed. Republic of Germany, 1978, MA in Automotive Engring., 1982. Designer Ford-Germany, Cologne, 1974-75, design engr., 1978-84; staff project engr. Gen. Motors Buick-Oldsmobile Cadillac Group, Troy, Mich., 1984—. Avocations: wine, squash, running, gourmet foods. Home: 760 Dartmouth Rochester MI 48063

PATROS, DOLORES M., educational psychologist; b. La Crosse, Wis., Feb. 15, 1938; d. Bernard F. and Alice L. (Shafto) Weiland; divorced; children: Cindy Jean Patros Baeder, Douglas M., Daniel D., Jeannette M. BS, U. Wis., 1967, MS, 1975. Cert. tchr., sch. psychologist. Tchr. North Prairie (Wis.) Sch., 1967-69, Pewaukee (Wis.) Pub. Schs., 1969-75; sch. psychologist Kenosha (Wis.) Pub. Schs., 1977-79, Cen. Elementary Sch./Area 4, La Crosse, Wis., 1979-85; prin. Arcadia (Wis.) Cath. Sch., 1985-86; psychologist Blair (Wis.) Schs., 1987—. Mem. Coulee Region Assn. of Psychologists in Schs. (pres. 1980-82).

PATRY, KENNETH FRANCIS, accountant; b. Wichita, Kans., Aug. 19, 1951; s. Francis R. and Loretta A. (Heimerman) P.; m. Jerry A. Mapes, Dec. 22, 1973; children: Tanya, Jeff, Ben. BS in Acctg., Ft. Hays Kans. State U., 1973. CPA, Nebr. Staff acct. Deloitte, Haskins and Sells, Omaha, 1973-83, ptnr., 1983—. Mem. Am. Inst. CPA's, Nebr. Soc. CPA's. Republican. Lodge: Optimists (pres. Omaha club. 1985-86). Home: 608 S 156th Ave Circle Omaha NE 68118 Office: Deloitte Haskins & Sells 1444 Woodmen Tower Omaha NE 68102

PATSTONE, ARTHUR, automotive executive; b. Quincy, Mass., July 19, 1941; s. Kenneth Hall and Mabel June (Patstone) Simonds. BSME, Northeastern U., 1964; MS in Automotive Engring., Chrysler Inst., 1966. Devel. engr. Chrysler Engring., Highland Park, Mich., 1964-68; test engr., supr. Chrysler Proving Grounds, Chelsea, Mich., 1968-83; program planner Chrysler Corp., Highland Park, 1983—. Contbr. articles to profl. jours. Exec. officer Great Lakes Wing Confederate Air Force Air Mus., Toledo, 1983-84. Mem. AOPA, Yankee Air Force Air Mus., Explt. Aircraft Assn. (pres., sec. 1978-80), Phi Kappa Phi, Tau Beta Pi, Pi Tau Sigma. Republican. Club: Internat. Aerobatic (pres. 1980-81) (Detroit). Lodge: Quiet Birdmen. Avocations: flying, sailing, autocross racing, photography, electronics. Home: 801 Center Dr Ann Arbor MI 48103 Office: Chrysler Corp 12000 Oakland Highland Park MI 48203

PATT, CAROL PRINS, consultant to non-profit organizations; b. N.Y.C., Aug. 23, 1940; d. J. Warner and Gertrude (Buttenwieser) Prins; m. Stephen L. Patt, Feb. 6, 1966; children: Jessica Eve, Audrey Elizabeth, Joseph Stephen. Student Vassar Coll., 1958-59, Barnard Coll., 1962, The Neighborhood Playhouse Sch. of Theatre, N.Y.C., 1962-64. Ptnr., Just Causes, Chgo., 1979-86; cons. in field, 1986—; cons. Music of the Baroque, Chgo., 1982-86, DePaul Conservatory of Drama, Chgo., 1983-85, Saralee Corp., Chgo. Mem. assoc. bd. United Charities Chgo. women's bd. dirs. Am. Cancer Soc., Goodman Theatre, Chgo.; costume com. Chgo. Hist. Soc.; bd. dirs. N. Dearborn Assn., bd. dirs.Chgo. Found. for Women. Mem. Nat. Soc. Fund Raising Execs. (Chgo. chpt.), Publicity Club of Chgo. Jewish. Club: Art. Avocations: gardening, travel. Home: 1405 N Dearborn Pkwy Chicago IL 60610

PATTEN, DONALD J., professional society administrator, leasing executive; b. Grand Rapids, Mich., July 22, 1922; s. Maurice Lyman and Lillian (Daily) P.; m. Donna Mae Oberlin, Oct. 13, 1943; children: Linda Patten Kidder, Donald J. Jr. Student, Grand Rapids Jr. Coll., 1946-48. Pres. Patten Monument Co., Grand Rapids, 1945-82; founder, pres. Phoenix Bronze Co., Grand Rapids, 1969-82; exec. dir. Am. Inst. Commemorative Art, Grand Rapids, 1982—; sec., treas. Classic Leasing, Grand Rapids, 1984—. Editor: (newsletter) Milestone, 1982—. Bd. dirs. Grand Rapids Bapt. Coll., 1966-85, Mich. Christian Home, Grand Rapids, 1962-79, Childrens Agy., St. Louis, Mich., 1960-77. Served as staff sgt. U.S. Army, 1943-45, ETO. Decorated Bronze Star with cluster; awarded Legion of Honor, Kiwanis, 1982; recipient Service award Am. Inst. Commemorative Art, 1982, Outstanding Merit award, 1978. Mem. Mich. Div. Monument Builders of Mich. (pres. 1953-55), Monument Builders of N.Am. (pres. N.Am. chpt. 1973-75, Outstanding Service award 1978). Republican. Lodge: Kiwanis (pres. 1957). Avocations: golf, fishing.

PATTEN, MAURINE DIANE, psychologist; b. Peoria, Ill., Aug. 30, 1940; d. Maurice H. and Esther Ann (Wilkenson) Foote; m. C. Alfred Patten, Aug. 26, 1961; children: Paul A., Bethany M. BS, Bradley U., 1961; MS, Chgo. State U., 1971; EdD, No. Ill. U., 1977. Lic. psychologist, Ill. Tchr. Elementary Schs., Skokie and Manhattan, Ill., 1961-63; dir. Southwest Coop Presch., Chgo., 1970-74; tchr. spl. edn. Dekalb County (Ill.) Spl. Edn. Assn., 1974-76, asst. dir., 1978-80; resource tchr. Sycamore (Ill.) Sch. Dist., 1976-78; asst. prof. Chgo. State U., 1980-81; psychologist Sycamore, 1981—; Cons. Arthur Andersen & Co., St. Charles, Ill., 1981—; profl. devel. workshops coordinator, 1981—. Fellow Am. Psychol. Assn., Ill. Psychol. Assn., Am. Pain Soc., Nat. Assn. Neurolinguistic Programming, Am. Registry of Lic. Psychologists and Mental Health Providers, Am. Soc. Profl. and Exec. Women. Methodist. Avocations: canoeing, reading. Home: 530 Calvin Park Blvd Rockford IL 61107 Office: 964 W State St Sycamore IL 60178

PATTERSON, ALAN BRUCE, obstetrician and gynecologist; b. Indpls., Apr. 23, 1953; s. Samuel S. and Eunice Selma (Brenner) P. BS, Tulane U., 1975; MD, Ind. U., Indpls., 1979. Diplomate Am. Bd. Ob-Gyn. Resident in ob-gyn St. Vincent Hosp., Indpls., 1979-83; mem. staff Metro Health., Indpls., 1983—; mem. staff, cons., instr. Meth. Hosp., Indpls, 1983—; cons. Indpls. Planned Parenthood, 1982-83, United Parcel Service, Indpls., 1982-83. Fellow Am. Coll. Ob-Gyn; mem. Marion County Med. Soc., Phi Beta Kappa. Jewish. Club: Indpls. Athletic. Avocations: jogging, swimming, wine collecting, photography. Home: 1643 E 77th St Indianapolis IN 46240 Office: Metro Health 2310 E 62d St Indianapolis IN 46220

PATTERSON, CARL EUGENE, farmer; b. Anthony, Kans., Oct. 2, 1915; s. James Arthur and Edna Viola (Patton) P.; m. Joan Adele Vivian Arenz, Nov. 22, 1939; children: Michael Alan and Laurel Beth (twins), Susan Evelyn. Student, Emporia State Tchrs. Coll., 1934-36. Asst. to personnel mgr. south side plant Continental Can Co., Chgo., 1940-42; farmer Anthony, Kans., 1942-46, Chesterton, Ind., 1946—. Named Outstanding Coop. Dir. Hoosier Coop. Clinic and Purdue U., West Lafayette, Ind., 1982; recipient Disting. Leadership and Faithful service award, Gt. Lakes Dist. Bd. Evang. Free Ch. Am., 1983. Mem. Ind. Farm Bur. Coop. Assn. (state dir. 1968-82, exec. com. 1976-82, dedicated leadership and service award 1982), Porter County Farm Bur. Coop., Valparaiso, Ind. (bd. dirs. 1963-75, pres. 1968-75, recognition of service award 1975), Gideons Internat. (pres. local camp 1973-76, 81-83). Republican. Avocation: bass soloist choir, ch. and related groups. Home: 231 E 1200 N Chesterton IN 46304

PATTERSON, DAVID WILLIAMS, dentist; b. El Paso, Tex., Oct. 4, 1953; s. Donald Roger and Barbara Ann (Williams) P.; m. Theresa Marie Perrin, Dec. 2, 1972; children: Heather Marie, Gregory Williams. BS, Mo. So. State Coll., 1975; DDS, U. Mo., 1979. Gen. practice dentistry Joplin, Mo., 1979—; dentist City Health Clinic, Joplin, 1979-81, 84-85. Active R-8 Sch. Dist. Math. Curriculum Rev., Joplin, 1986. Mem. ADA, Am. Soc. Dentistry for Children, Mo. Dental Assn., Southwest Mo. Dist. Dental Soc. (chmn. Children's Dental Health Month 1982). Methodist. Avocations: flying, astronomy, photography. Home: 2308 Illinois Joplin MO 64801 Office: 3302 McIntosh Joplin MO 64801

PATTERSON, DENNIS JOSEPH, management consultant; b. Honolulu, Apr. 13, 1948; s. Joseph John and Dorothy Elizabeth (Snajkowski) P.; m. Susan Tyra Pedlow, Dec. 31, 1981; 1 child, Valarie Jean. BA, Elmhurst (Ill.) Coll., 1970; MA, George Washington U., 1973. Asst. dir. Vancouver (B.C.) Gen. Hosp., 1973-76, dir., 1975-76; v.p. Shaugnessy Hosp., Vancouver, 1976-79; pres. Westcare, Vancouver, 1979-84; mgr. Ernst & Whinney, Chgo., 1984-86, sr. mgr., 1986—. Contbr. articles to profl. jours. fin. mgr. Electoral Action Movement, Vancouver, 1978. Fellow Am. Coll. Health-care Execs.; mem. Phi Gamma Mu. Republican. Anglican. Clubs: Royal Vancouver Yacht, Union League Club of Chgo. Avocation: sailboat racing. Office: Ernst & Whinney 150 S Wacker Dr Chicago IL 60606

PATTERSON, HARLAN RAY, finance educator; b. Camden, Ohio, June 27, 1931; s. Ernest Newton and Beulah Irene (Hedrick) P.; m. Carol Lee Reighard, Aug. 31, 1970; children by previous marriage: Kristan Lee, Elizabeth Jane; children: Leslie, Nolan Gene. BS, Miami U., Oxford, Ohio, 1953, MBA, 1959; PhD, Mich. State U., 1963. Asst. prof. fin. U. Ill., Champaign-Urbana, 1962-66; mem. faculty Ohio U., Athens, 1966—; prof. fin. Ohio U., 1977—; vis. prof., fellow Chgo. Merc. Exchange, 1971; fin. cons., researcher projects for industry. Contbr. articles to acad. and profl. jours. Chmn. City of Athens Adv. Bd., 1972-77; state chmn. scholarship com. for Ohio Rainbow Girls. Served as commd. officer USN, 1953-56. Won competitive appointment U.S. Naval Acad., 1950. Stonier fellow, 1961; Found. Econ. Edn. fellow, 1965, 67, 69, 71; Chgo. Bd. Trade summer intern, 1983. Mem. Phi Beta Kappa, Beta Gamma Sigma, Phi Eta Sigma, Omicron Delta Epsilon, Pi Kappa Alpha, Alpha Kappa Psi, Delta Sigma Pi. Republican. Lodges: Masons (32 deg.), Shriners, Order of Eastern Star. Home: 17 La Mar Dr Athens OH 45701

PATTERSON, JAMES ROBERT, material control analyst; b. Springfield, Ohio, Aug. 21, 1928; s. Robert Wortman and Greta (Esterline) P.; m. Virginia Dowler Lybarger, June 14, 1952 (div. Oct. 1970); children: Marjorie Esterline, Jeanne Frances, Robert Lybarger, Cornelia Elizabeth; m. Helen Ann Janoski Peltz, Apr. 8, 1972; stepchildren: Marian Peltz LaBanc, Irene Peltz Leno, Linda Sue Peltz, Jonathan Albert Peltz. Student, Coll. of Wooster, 1946-48; BS, U.S. Naval Acad., 1952; MS in Agrl. Engring., Ohio State U., 1960, postgrad., 1961-62. Commd. ensign USN, 1952, advanced through grades to lt., 1956, served on USS Iowa and USS Carpellotti, 1952-57; naval weapons instr. Ohio State U., Columbus, 1957-60; resigned USN, 1960, with res., 1962-67; secondary tchr. Chillicothe (Ohio) City Schs., 1960-62; elec. supr. Timken Co., Canton, Ohio, 1962-69, supr. maintenance, 1969-86, material control analyst, 1986—. Author: (with others) NROTC Naval Weapons Curriculum, 1958, Battle Organization, USS Independence, 1967, (with others) Merchant Marine Reserve Curriculum, 1974, Preventive Maintenance Program, 1982. Mem. Assn. Iron and Steel Engrs., Soc. Am. Mil. Engrs., U.S. Naval Inst., Naval Res. Assn., Res. Officers Assn. of the U.S. (local pres. 1975-76, 83-84, 85-86.), Am. Legion, The Ret. Officers Assn., U.S. Naval Acad. Alumni Assn., Ohio State Alumni Assn., Coll. of Wooster Alumni Assn., Culver Summer Schs. Alumni Assn., Massillon Antique Study Group (v.p. 1984—). Republican. United Presbyterian. Club: Stark Mad Miniaturist (Canton) (v.p. 1983-84). Avocations: vegetable gardening, home workshop, model railroad, history, antiques. Home: 318 4th St NE Massillon OH 44646 Office: Timken Co Maintenance Services Office Gambrinns Steel Mill Canton OH 44706

PATTERSON, LAWRENCE THOMAS, publishing executive; b. Cin., Aug. 8, 1937; s. Lawrence Thomas Sr. and Helen Adelaid (Wintering) P.; m. Diessla Stauffer, Aug. 8, 1967 (div. 1979); m. Barbara Broden, May 11, 1980; children: Blake Shannon, Kimberly Helen. BS cum laude, Miami U., Oxford, Ohio, 1957; postgrad., U. Pa., 1957; MBA, U. Mich., 1959. Sec.-treas. P-G Products Inc., Cin., 1959-61, Arrington Van Pelt Mgr., Cin., 1960-61; founder, pres. Patterson Internat. Corp., Cin., 1964-75; founder, pres., treas. Am. Youth Mktg. Corp., Cin., 1964-75; founder, pres. Patterson Fin. Services, Cin., 1975—, Swiss Fin. Services, Cin., 1982—; founder, pres. Ctr. Fin. Freedom, Cin., 1975—; founder Silver Dollar Polit. Action Com., Cin., 1982—. Author: Swiss Real Estate and How to Retire in Switzerland, 1977; pub.: Freedom Fighter Index, 1975, Conspiracy Theory Catalog, 1975; (newsletter) Monthly Lesson in Criminal Politics, 1975. Life mem. Com. to Restore the Constitution, Ft. Collins, Colo., 1975—, Commn. Monetary Research and Edn. Served to capt. USAF, 1961-62. Mem. Am. Numismatic Assn. (life), Am. Assn. State and Local History, Am. Security Council, Newsletter Assn. Am. (bd. dirs. 1976), Phi Beta Kappa, Phi Beta Sigma, Delta SIgma Pi. Lutheran. Club: Queen City (Cin.). Avocations: reading, skiing, swimming, politics. Home: 2295 Grandin Rd Cincinnati OH 45208 Office: Patterson Strategy Fin Services 105 W Fourth St Suite 633 Cincinnati OH 45202

PATTERSON, LEWIS EARL, college educator, counseling psychologist; b. Bridgewater, Pa., Oct. 10, 1934; s. Lewis Whiting and Marcella (Brubaker) P.; m. Janice Lavelle Bates, Sept. 6, 1964; 1 child, Elizabeth Anne. BSc, Pa. State U., 1956, EdM in Counseling, 1959, EdD, 1965. Cert. tchr., Ohio; lic. psychologist, Pa., Ohio. Instr. Pa. State U., Univ. Park, Pa., 1963-65; from asst. to assoc. prof. counseling Boston U., 1965-72; assoc. prof. counseling Cleve. State U., 1972-74, prof. counseling, 1974—, chmn. dept. edn. specialists, 1972-85, assoc. dean edn., 1985—; cons. to schs., agencies, career devel., mgmt., adult devel. and stress mgmt. Author: (with others) Helping Clients with Special Concerns, 1979, The Counseling Process, 3rd edit., 1982; mem. editorial bd. Career Devel. Quarterly Jour., 1984—. Trainer Am. Personnel and Guidance Assn. Workshops on Sex Equity, Ohio, 1974, Local social service agencies, workshops on mgmt., stress, 1972—; cons. JTPA Programs, Cleve. and Cuyahoga County, 1983—. Served with USAR, 1960. Recipient Career Edn. Service award Gen. Elec. Found., 1972, Nat. Alliance of Bus., 1974. Fellow Am. Orthopsychiatric Assn.; mem. Am. Assn. Counseling and Devel., Nat. Assn. Career Devel., Am. Sch. Counselors Assn. (exec. bd. Ohio chpt. 1974,), Am. Assn. Coll. for Tchr. Edn. (instl. rep., exec. bd. Ohio chpt. 1986), Ohio Assn. Counselor Edn., Greater Cleve. Adult Edn. Assn. (exec. bd. 1986), Phi Delta Kappa. Democrat. Avocations: travel, gardening. Home: 4830 Lindsey Ln Richmond Heights OH 44143 Office: Coll Edn Cleve State U Rhodes Tower Cleveland OH 44143

PATTERSON, LUCILLE JOAN, author, educator; b. Chgo.; d. William Leon and Hortense Adele (Brooks) Washington; m. Owen J. Patterson II, June 17, 1956 (div.); children: Karin Janine, Owen Jeremiah III. BA, DePaul U., 1962; MA, Northeastern Ill. U., 1973. Tchr. English, Spanish, Speech, Journalism and Afro-Am. Lit. Chgo. Pub. Schs., 1962-66, 68—, Cook County Dept. Pub. Aid, 1966-68; Upward Bound tchr. Barat Coll., Lake Forest, Ill., 1976, Loyola U., Chgo., 1977; chmn. dept. English Carver Area High Sch., 1977-82; instr. Chgo. Sun-Times Tchr. Inst., 1974-76; pres. WAPA Press; founder Young Peoples Writers Workshop. Author: (poetry) Sapphire, 1972, Windy City Rhythms, 1975, Raindrops and Mud Puddles, 1977, A Mother's Love, 1984, His Eye is on the Butterfly, 1985 (poetry, short stories) Moon in Black, 1974, (play) For My People, 1982, (poetry) A Seson of Love, 1987; producer, writer, choreographer: Touch the Sisters, 1978; author criterion reference testing program Chgo. Bd. Edn., 1980; editor Stinkin Onion Publs., The Communicator I, 1986; contbr. poetry series presented at DuSable Mus. Afro-Am. History, 1981. Recipient award for contbns. to arts and letters Nat. News Media Women, 1974, award for contbns. to journalism Loyola U. Upward Bound Program, 1977, Univ. Chgo-Blum-Kovler Ednl. award, 1978; named Disting. High Sch. Tchr., Ill. Inst. Tech., 1982. Mem. Nat. Council Tchrs. English, Ill. Assn. Tchrs. English. (minority task force 1981), Ill. Speech and Theatre Assn., Assn. Study Afro-Am. Life and History. Home: 8555 S Prairie Ave Chicago IL 60619 Office: 7740 S Ingleside Ave Chicago IL 60619

PATTERSON, MARK ROLAND, university administrator; b. LeMars, Iowa, Jan. 1, 1951; s. Frank G. and Eva Alice (Joy) P.; m. Evelyn Maxine Peterson, July 14, 1979; 1 child, Carrie Lynn. BA, Sioux Falls Coll., 1973; MEd, South Dakota State U., 1983. Social services cons. Good Samaritan Soc., Sioux Falls, 1973-76; alumni dir. Sioux Falls Coll., 1976-83, dir. career and acad. planning, 1987—; acting dir. career counseling Augustana Coll., Sioux Falls, 1983; asst. dean placement Westmar Coll., LeMars, 1983-85; dir. Career Planning Ctr., Aberdeen, S.D., 1985-87. Mem. Aberdeen Community Appeals Bd. 1985—; com. chmn. Aberdeen Small Bus. Council, 1985—; bd. dirs. Alexander Mitchell Pub. Library, Aberdeen, 1986—. Mem. Am. Assn. Counseling and Devel., S.D. Assn. Counseling and Devel., Coll. Placement Council, Midwest Coll. Placement Assn., Aberdeen Personnel Assn., Aberdeen C. of C. Republican. Baptist. Lodge: Lions (program com. 1985—). Avocations: singing, reading. Home: 3309 S West Ave Sioux Falls SD 57105 Office: Sioux Falls College CAP Ctr Sioux Falls SD 57105-1699

PATTERSON, P. J., accountant; b. Pana, Ill., June 7, 1950; d. G.G. and Doris (Stolte) Moore. Cert. tax practitioner. Acct. ADM, 1971-73, Ford Motor Co., 1973-74; asst. controller Union Iron Works, Decatur, Ill., 1974; acct. Caterpillar Co., Decatur, 1975; pvt. practice acctg., owner Patterson Acctg., Decatur, 1975—; speaker Networking Women convs., 1983-86. Bd. dirs. Boys Club, Decatur, 1985-87, Decatur Area Arts Council, 1985-87, 87—, Decatur Advantage, 1986, YWCA, Decatur, 1983-86. Mem. Ind. Accts. Assn. (treas. 1984), Nat. Assn. Income Tax Practitioners (pres. 1984—), Nat. Assn. Tax Practitioners, Nat. Assn. Income Tax Practitioners (pres. cen. Ill. chpt. 1984—), Assn. Bus. Women Am. (treas. 1982), Nat. Assn. Female Execs. (bd. dirs. 1983-86), Decatur C. of C. (Outstanding Bus. of Yr. award 1983). Republican. Baptist. Club: Decatur. Avocations: flying, boating. Home: 2437 Euel Decatur IL 62526 Office: Patterson Acctg 1212 E Pershing Decatur IL 62526

PATTERSON, RANDALL WRIGHT, accountant; b. Stamford, Conn., Mar. 6, 1954; s. Robert Muarry and Chloe Marie (Wright) P.; m. MaryEllen DePasquale, July 16, 1983. BS in Indsl. Mgmt. and Econs. with honors, Purdue U., 1976; MBA in Acctg. and Fin., U. Chgo., 1978. From asst. acct. to sr. acct. Deloitte Haskins & Sells, Hartford, Conn., 1978-84; from mgr. to sr. mgr. Deloitte Haskins & Sells, Chgo., 1985—. Mem. Am. Inst. CPA's, Conn. Soc. CPA's, Ill. CPA Soc. Clubs: Oak Brook (Ill.) Polo, Oak Brook Execs. Breakfast; Purdue of Conn. (state chpt. pres. 1983-85; Purdue of Chgo. (bd. dirs., treas. 1986-88). Lodge: Rotary. Home: 820 Red Stable Way Oak Brook IL 60521 Office: Deloitte Haskins & Sells 200 E Randolph Dr Chicago IL 60601

PATTERSON, RUSSELL, conductor, opera executive; b. Greenville, Miss., Aug. 31, 1930; s. Dudley Russell and Elizabeth (Taylor) P.; m. Teresa Gutierrez de Celis, Aug. 28, 1979; children: Richard Russell, Christopher Leonard. B.A., B.Mus., S.E. La. U., 1950; M.Mus., Kansas City Conservatory of Music, 1952; D.M.A., U. Mo. at Kansas City. prof. music Kansas City Conservatory of Music, 1960-68; mem. profl. com. Met. Opera, 1962—; condr. Kansas City Symphony, 1982-83, artistic dir., 1982-86, condr. emeritus, 1986—; cons. Ford Found. Musician with Baton Rouge Symphony, 1948-50, Brevard Music Festival, 1947-49, Kansas City Philharmonic Orch., 1951-59, Bayrische Staatsoper, Munich, Germany, 1952-53, condr., Lyric Opera of Kansas City, 1958—, Kansas City Philharmonic Orch., 1965-66, Point Lookout (Mo.) Festival, 1967—, Kansas City Ballet, 1965-66, Am. Ballet Co., European tour, 1958; gen. dir., Lyric Opera of Kansas City, 1958—, artistic dir., Missouri River Festival, 1976—. Mem. opera com. Mo. Council Arts, 1965-69; mem. music panel Nat. Endowment Arts, 1970-72; mem. Univ. Assocs. U. Mo. at Kansas City, 1970—. Recipient Alice M. Ditson condrs. award Columbia U., 1982, W.F. Yates medalion William Jewell Coll.; named Disting. Alumni Southeast La. U. Mem. Friends of Art, Opera America (v.p. 1971-73), Phi Mu Alpha Sinfonia, Pi Kappa Lambda, Mensa. Home: 4618 Warwick St Apt 1A Kansas City MO 64112 Office: Kansas City Symphony Lyric Theater 1029 Central St Kansas City MO 64105 •

PATTERSON, WANDA SUE, psychiatric counselor; b. Harrisburg, Ill.; s. James Reggie and Ruth Elvira (Adkisson) P.; m. William Martin Taylor, Mar. 27, 1980. AA, Southeastern Ill. Coll., 1965; BA, So. Ill. U., 1969; MA, Sangamon State U., Springfield, Ill., 1974. Lic. social worker. Social worker Andrew McFarland Mental Health Ctr., Springfield, 1969-74, psychologist, 1974-77; psychiat. counselor Meml. Med. Ctr., Springfield, 1977—, tng. instr. parent effectiveness, 1980—. Vol. interviewer Planned Parenthood, Springfield, 1985—. Peabody Coal Co. scholar, Harrisburg, 1963-65, Dept. Mental Health scholar, 1968-69. Mem. LWV (sec. 1985-87), AAUW, Am. Bus. Women's Assn., Depressive and Manic Depressive Assn. (founder Springfield Ill. chpt. 1986), So. Ill. U. Alumni Assn., Kappa Rho (past pres., treas, recording sec.). Avocations: cross stitch, embroidery, knitting, cooking, reading, cross country and down hill skiing. Office: Meml Med Ctr 800 N Rutledge Springfield IL 62781

PATTERSON, WILLIAM ALBERT, architect; b. Newcastle, Wyo., Oct. 31, 1953; s. William Albert and Martha Sue (Rose) P.; m. Jane Ann

Wojakowski, Sept. 8, 1979 (div. May 1986); children: Will, Ben. BArch, Kans. State U., 1977. Registered architect, Tex. Project coordinator R&B Devel., Houston, Tex., 1981, Tribble & Stephens Constrn., Houston, 1982-83; prin. W.A. Patterson, Architect, Houston, 1983-84; project architect Fullerton, Carey & Oman, Kansas City, Mo., 1984-85, project mgr., 1986—. Bd. dirs. Mcpl. Utility Dist. #175, Houston, 1982-84. Mem. AIA. Presbyterian. Home: 5800 W 69th Overland KS 66204 Office: Fullerton Carey & Oman 1100 Main Suite 2350 Kansas City MO 64105

PATTERSON-WENGER, PAMELA ANN, physical therapist; b. Clay Center, Kans., Oct. 10, 1954; d. Nolan John and Rachel Ann (Dinsmore) Patterson; m. James Donald Wenger, Dec. 8, 1979. Student, U. Kans., Lawrence, 1972-75; BS in Physical Therapy, U. Kans., Kansas City, 1976. Lic. physical therapist, Iowa, Kans., Nebr., Mo. Physical therapist dir. Profl. Physical Therapy services, Hamburg, Iowa, 1977-81; physical therapist Physical Therapy Services, Hamburg, 1981-83; dir. physical therapy Restorative Health Services, Hamburg, 1983-86, Red Oak, Iowa, 1986—; cons. Stanton (Iowa) Care Ctr., 1984—, Malvern (Iowa) Care Ctr., 1984-85, Vista Garden Care Ctr., Red Oak, 1984—, Good Samaritan Care Ctr., Red oak, 1984—, Red Oak Home Health Agy., 1985—. Active First Presby. Ch., Clay Center, 1976-83, United Trinty Ch., Hamburg, 1977—, Omaha Ballet, 1978—, Opera Omaha, 1978—, Hamburg Community Arts Council, 1985—. Mem. Am. Physical Therapy Assn., Orthopedic and Geriatric sections Am. Physical Therapy Assn., Iowa Physical Therapy Assn. Republican. Avocations: skiing, flying, tennis, golf, travel. Home: 202 N St Hamburg IA 51640 Office: Restorative Health Services 1000 Broadway Red Oak IA 51566

PATTIS, S. WILLIAM, publisher; b. Chgo., July 3, 1925; s. William Robert and Rose (Quint) P.; m. Bette Z. Levin, July 16, 1950; children: Mark Robert, Robin Quint Himovitz. B.S., U. Ill., 1949; postgrad., Northwestern U., 1949-50. Exec. v.p., pub. United Bus. Publs., 1949-59; chmn., chief exec. officer The Pattis Group, 1959—; pres. Nat. Textbook Co., Lincolnwood, Ill., 1961—; dir. Bank of Highwood, Ill., New Century Bank, Mundelein, Ill.; pres., dir. P-B Communications, Winnetka, Ill., 1978—; mem. book & library com. U.S. Info. Agy., 1986—. Author: Opportunities in Advertising, 1983, Opportunities in Magazine Publishing, 1986. Mem. Pres.'s Council Youth Opportunity, 1968-70; bd. dirs. Photography Youth Found., 1970-73; Bd. dirs. Expt. in Internat. Living, 1970, Inst. Human Creativity, 1983—. Served with C.E. U.S. Army, 1943-46. Recipient Human Relations award Am. Jewish Com., 1971. Clubs: Standard (Chgo.); Northmoor Country (Highland Park, Ill.); Tamarisk Country (Rancho Mirage, Calif.). Home: 195 Elder Ln Highland Park IL 60035 also: 70-843 Tamarisk Ln Rancho Mirage CA 92270 Office: 4761 W Touhy Ave Lincolnwood IL 60646

PATTISHALL, BEVERLY WYCKLIFFE, lawyer; b. Atlanta, May 23, 1916; s. Leon Jackson and Margaret Simkins (Woodfin) P.; children by previous marriage: Margaret Ann Arthur, Leslie Hansen, Beverly Wyckliffe, Paige Terhune Pattishall Watt, Woodfin Underwood; m. Dorothy Daniels Mashek, June 24, 1977. BS, Northwestern U., 1938; JD, U. Va., 1941. Bar: Ill. 1941, D.C. 1971. Sole practice Chgo., 1946—; ptnr. Pattishall, McAuliffe & Hofstetter and predecessor firms, Chgo., 1950—; dir. Juvenile Protective Assn. Chgo., 1946-79, pres., 1961-63, hon. dir., 1979—; dir. Vol. Interagy. Assn., 1975-78, sec., 1977-78; U.S. del. Diplomatic Confs. on Internat. Trademark Registration Treaty, Geneva, Vienna, 1970-73, Diplomatic Conf. on Revision of Paris Conv., Nairobi, 1981; mem. U.S. del. Geneva Conf. on Indsl. Property and Consumer Protection, 1978; adj. prof. trademark, trade identity and unfair trade practices law Northwestern U. Sch. Law, Evanston, Ill. Author: (with Hilliard) Trademarks, 1987, Trade Identity and Unfair Trade Practices, 1974; Unfair Competition and Unfair Trade Practices, 1985; contbr. articles to profl. jours. Served to lt. comdr. USNR, World War II, ETO, PTO; comdr. Res. ret. Fellow Am. Coll. Trial Lawyers (bd. regents 1979-83); mem. Internat. Patent and Trademark Assn. (pres. 1955-57, exec. com. 1955—), Assn. Internationale Pour La Protection De La Propriete Industrielle (mem. of hon.), ABA (chmn. sect. patent, trademark and copyright Law 1963-64), Ill. Bar Assn., Chgo. Bar Assn., D.C. Bar Assn., Chgo. Bar Found. (dir. 1977-83), U.S. Trademark Assn. (dir. 1963-65), Phi Kappa Psi. Clubs: Legal (Chgo.), Law (Chgo.) (pres. 1982-83), Econ. (Chgo.), Mid-Day, Univ. (Chgo.), Mid-America (Chgo.), Selden Soc. London (Ill. rep.), Chikaming Country (Lakeside, Mich.). Home: 2244 Lincoln Park W Chicago IL 60614 Office: Pattishall McAuliffe & Hofstetter 33 W Monroe St Chicago IL 60603

PATTON, BOBBY RAY, theatre and communication educator, actor; b. Ft. Worth, Dec. 18, 1935; s. Elton Guy and Violet Crystle (Daniel) P.; m. Bonnie Ritter, June 1, 1958 (div. Nov. 1976); m. Eleanor Nyquist, July 4, 1978. BFA, Tex. Christian U., 1958; MA, U. Kans., 1962, PhD, 1966. Instr. Hutchinson (Kans.) HIgh Sch., 1958-61; asst. prof. U. Wichita, Kans., 1961-66; assoc. prof. U. Kans., Lawrence, 1966-72, prof., chmn. div. communication and theatre, 1972—; dir. Lawrence Community Theatre, 1977-84; Green Honors prof. Tex. Christian U., Ft. Worth, 1982; vis. lectr. Kuring-Gai Coll., Sydney, Australia, 1986. Author: Decision-Making Groups, 1978, Interpersonal Communication, 1982, Responsible Public Speaking, 1984; actor freelance, 1981—, CBS Miniseries, Murder Ordained, 1987. Mem. Orgn. for Study of Communication, Language and Gender (pres. 1987-88), Speech Communication Assn., Cen. States Speech Assn. (Merit award 1984). Democrat. Unitarian-Universalist. Avocations: theatre, squash, racquetball, tennis. Home: 3017 Riverview Rd Lawrence KS 66044 Office: Div Communication and Theatre U Kans Lawrence KS 66045

PATTON, CONNIE GARCIA, educator; b. Luarca, Spain, Nov. 7, 1941; d. Antonio Garcia and Palmira Garcia (Lavin) Mendez; B.A., U. N.Mex., 1964, M.A., 1966; doctoral candidate U. Kans., 1988; m. Michael G. Patton, July 5, 1970; children—Michael Anthony, Ryan Blake. Instr., Peace Corps, 1964-66; asso. prof. fgn. lang. Emporia (Kans.) State U., 1966—; asst. chmn. fgn. lang. dept., 1984-86; court translator Lyon County Courthouse, 1974—. Bd. dirs. Sexual Offense Services, 1974-78; v.p. Big Bro.-Big Sister, 1977-79. Ford Found. grad. fellow, 1963-66; NEH grantee, 1976, 78; recipient Xi Phi Outstanding Faculty award, 1976, 77, LA&S Outstanding Tchr. award, 1986; named Outstanding Young Kansan, Jaycees, 1977. Mem. Am. Assn. Tchrs. Spanish and Portuguese, MLA, AAUP, Sigma Delta Pi. Author: Spanish Vocabulary Units, 1975; Castles in Spain, 1984. Home: 2919 Monterey Dr Emporia KS 66801 Office: 1200 Commercial St Emporia KS 66801

PATTON, DAMON LEE, software product development executive; b. Wichita, Kans., Aug. 3, 1939; s. Claude and Beryl Inez (Jones) P.; m. Erminia Luigia Fusi, Sept. 18, 1976; 1 child, Veronica. BA in Math., U. Kans., 1961. Systems engr. IBM Corp., Kansas City, Mo., 1961-69; corp. cons. CT/UCC, Dallas, 1969-72; cons. CUC, Milan, Italy, 1972-75, CRM, Milan, 1975-77; pvt. practice cons. Europe and the U.S., 1978-85; dir. software product devel. Analysts Internat., Mpls., 1986—. Co-author software product UCC 1o-IMS Data Dictionary, 1971-72. Mem. Assn. Computing Machinery. Republican. Presbyterian. Avocation: cooking. Office: Analysts Internat Corp 7615 Metro Blvd Minneapolis MN 55435

PATTON, DENISE PRETZER, chemist; b. Harlingen, Tex., Nov. 14, 1957; d. Don D. and Carolyn A. (Barndt) Pretzer; m. Thomas F. Patton, Mar. 1, 1986. BS, Kans. State U., 1981, MS, 1983, PhD, 1986. Registered pharmacist, Kans. Research asst. dept. pharm. chemistry U. Kans., Lawrence, 1981-86; scientist Upjohn Co., Kalamazoo, 1986—. Fellow Am. Found. Pharm. Edn.; mem. Am. Pharm. Assn. (U. Kans. Sr. award 1981), Am. Assn. Pharm. Scientists, Sigma Xi, Rho Chi (pres. Alpha Rho chpt. 1980-81), Phi Beta Kappa, Phi Kappa.

PATTON, GEORGE THOMAS, JR., credit agy. exec.; b. Birmingham, Ala., Sept. 22, 1929; s. George Thomas and Jewell Inez (Garner) P.; m. Hope Kirby, Dec. 20, 1953; children—Thomas Kirby, Neal Garner. B.A., Birmingham-So. Coll., 1949. With Gen. Motors Acceptance Corp., Detroit, 1949—, treas., 1970-72, v.p., 1972-78, exec. v.p., 1978—, dir., 1974—. Chmn. Municipal Planning Bd., Norwood, N.J., 1967-72; Trustee Pascack Valley Hosp., Westwood, N.J., 1975-81; chmn. planning commn. Village of Bingham Farms, Mich., 1983—. Mem. Sigma Alpha Epsilon, Omicron Delta Kappa. Presbyn. (elder). Office: Gen Motors Acceptance Corp 3044 W Grand Blvd Detroit MI 48202

PATTON, RAY BAKER, financial and urban planner, investment broker, economist; b. Enid, Okla., Jan. 24, 1932; s. Dwight Lyman Moody and Opal (Hembre) P.; B.A., U. Okla., 1955, M.R.C.P., 1960, M.A.P.A., 1969. m. Gloria Ruth Chambers, June 6, 1954; children—David Baker, Dayna Erin. Asst. dir. planning San Joaquin, Calif., 1959-61; dir. planning City of Norman (Okla.) and planning cons. U. Okla., Norman, 1961-65; dir. planning Oklahoma City, 1965-67; dir. planning St. Louis County, Mo., 1967-71; pres. Creative Environments, Inc., Clayton, Mo., 1972-74; chmn. Creative Consultants, Inc., Clayton, 1972-75; v.p. Land Dynamics, Inc., 1973-74; pres. Patton Real Estate, Inc., Success Power, Inc., St. Louis; prin. Raymond B. Patton & Assocs., Ballwin, Mo., 1975-81; dir. pub. works and planning, health commr., zoning enforcement officer City of Des Peres, Mo., 1977-79; zone mgr. Investors Diversified Services, Chesterfield, Mo., 1980-81; investment broker, fin. planner A.G. Edwards & Sons, Inc., Clayton, 1981-83; fin. planning coordinator, dir. seminars E.F. Hutton & Co., Inc., St. Louis, 1983-84; securities prin. The Patton Fin. Group, Inc., Westport Fin. Group, Inc., St. Louis, 1984-86; securities products coordinator, agy. edn. coordinator The Equitable Fin. Services, St. Louis; also motivational speaker; mem. faculty Nat. Inst. Farm and Land Brokers, 1971-76. Scoutmaster, St. Louis Area council Boy Scouts Am., 1976-80, vice chmn. adult tng., 1977-83; mem. Christian Bus. Men's Com., Chesterfield, Mo. Served with USMC, 1955-58. Named Outstanding Mcpl. Employee, State of Okla., 1963; recipient IDS Mercury award, 1980; A.G. Edwards & sons Crest award, 1982; Outstanding Exec. award E.F. Hutton, 1983, Blue Chip award, 1983; designated profl. fin. advisor 1984. Mem. Am. Inst. Cert. Planners, Am. Inst. Planners (pres. elect Mo., Kans., Okla. chpt. 1967, co-founder St. Louis Metro sect. 1969), Inst. Cert. Fin. Planners, Internat. Platform Assn., Internat. Assn. Fin. Planners, Eagle Scout Assn. (life), Fellowship Christian Fin. Advisors, Lambda Chi Alpha (pres. 1953-54). Methodist (minister of music, Ballwin 1978-83, choir dir. E. Free Ch., Ladue, Mo. 1986—). Club: Kiwanis. Contbr. articles to profl. jours. Home: 904 Chestnut Ridge Rd Saint Louis MO 63021 Office: The Centerpoint Bldg Suite 109 11885 Lackland Rd Saint Louis MO 63146

PATTON, RONALD L., minister, communication educator; b. Covington, Ky., Dec. 10, 1941; s. Charles Milton and Florence A. (De Voss), P., m. Donna Jean Avery, July 18, 1964; children: Andrew Charles, Kirk Richard. AB in Early European History, U. Cin., 1964; Min Div., MA in Edn., McCormick Theol. Sem., Chgo., 1968; D of Ministry, San Francisco Theol. Sem., San Anselmo, Calif., 1985. Ordained to ministry Presbyn. Ch., 1968. Pastor Earl Park (Ind.) Presbyn. Ch., 1968-70; assoc. pastor 1st Presbyn. Ch., Grand Haven, Mich., 1970-73; pastor Westport Presbyn. Ch., Kansas City, Mo., 1973-86; dir. Kansas City progams, instr. mass communications Mo. Valley Coll., Kansas City and Marshall, Mo., 1986-87; dir. Midwest Presby. Media Services, Kansas City, 1987—; mem. Heartland Presbytery, Kansas City, 1973—, budget com., 1981-86, racial ethnic com., 1987—. chaplain Boy Scouts Am., Kansas City, 1973-86, scoutmaster, 1985-86, cubmaster, Westwood, Kans., 1977-78; residential chmn. Am. Cancer Soc., Johnson County, Kans., 1984-85. Avocations: tennis, swimming, skiing, private pilot.

PATTON, RUFUS MERLE, accountant; b. Nokomis, Ill., Feb. 20, 1941; s. Rufus Robert and Esther Ellen (Cole) P.; m. Linda Joyce Harper, July 24, 1964; children: Robert Brian, Amy Michelle. B in Acctg., Ea. Ill. U., 1969, MBA, 1970. Acct. Peat Marwick Mitchell & Co., Chgo. and Decatur, Ill., 1970-72; comptroller Pana Hillsboro Ins., Hillsboro, Ill., 1972-73; pvt. practice acctg. Hillsboro, 1973—; pres. Montgomery County Nat. Bank, Hillsboro, 1985—, also bd. dirs. Bd. dirs. Hillsboro Sch. Dist. 3, 1981-85; mem. Ea. Ill. U. Found. Bd., Charleston, 1982—. Served as sgt. U.S. Army, 1959-62. Mem. Am. Inst. CPA's, Ill. CPA Soc. Presbyterian. Lodge: Sertoma (pres. Hillsboro Breakfest Sertoma 1976-77, dist. gov. Ill.-Wis. region 1977-78). Avocation: golf. Office: 925 S Main Hillsboro IL 62049

PATTY, R. BRUCE, architect; b. Kansas City, Mo., Jan. 25, 1935; s. Charles Everett and Sarah Louise (Pendleton) P.; m. Donna Jean Watts, June 1, 1958; children—Kristen Jennifer, Scott. B.S. in Architecture, U. Kans., 1958. Cert. Nat. Council Archtl. Registration Bds. Vice pres. Kivett & Myers (architects), Kansas City, Mo., 1959-70; prin. Patty Berkebile Nelson Immenschuh Architects Inc., Kansas City, Mo., 1970—; Mem. chancellors assos. U. Kans., 1980—; bd. dirs. Downtown, Inc., 1972—, v.p., 1978-79;. Prin. works include Kansas City Internat. Airport, 1968 (Design award Kans. chpt. AIA 1974), Truman Office Bldg, Jefferson City, Mo., 1975 (Design award State of Mo. 1976), Kansas City Police Sta, 1976 (Design award Central States AIA 1980). Recipient Disting. Alumni award U. Kans., 1983. Fellow AIA (pres. Kansas City chpt. 1974, nat. dir. 1980-82, nat. v.p. 1983, nat. pres. 1985), Royal Archtl. Inst. Can. (hon.); mem. Greater Kansas City C. of C. (chmn. aviation com. 1977-78), Fedn. Colegicos Architects, Mex. (hon.). Presbyterian. Clubs: University, Indian Hills Country. Lodge: Rotary. Home: 3840 W 56th St Fairway KS 66205 Office: 120 W 12th St Kansas City MO 64105

PAUL, JOHN JOSEPH, bishop; b. La Crosse, Wis., Aug. 17, 1918; s. Roland Philip and Louise (Gilles) P. B.A., Loras Coll., Dubuque, Iowa, 1939; S.T.B., St. Mary's Sem., Balt., 1943; M.Ed., Marquette U., 1959. Ordained priest Roman Catholic Ch., 1943; prin. Regis High Sch., Eau Claire, Wis., 1948-55; rector Holy Cross Sem., La Crosse, 1955-66, St. Joseph's Cathedral, La Crosse, 1966-77; aux. bishop Diocese of La Crosse, 1977-83, bishop, 1983—. Address: PO Box 4004 La Crosse WI 54602

PAUL, RONALD STANLEY, research institute administrator; b. Olympia, Wash., Jan. 19, 1923; s. Adolph and Olga (Klapstein) P.; m. Margery Jean Pengra, June 5, 1944; children: Kathleen Paul Crosby, Robert S., James N. Student, Linfield Coll., 1940-41, Reed Coll., 1943-44, Harvard U., 1945; BS, U. Oreg., 1947, MS, 1949, PhD, 1951. Physicist, research mgr. Gen. Electric Co., Richland, Wash., 1951-64; asso. dir. Battelle N.W. Labs., Richland, 1965-68; dir. Battelle N.W. Labs., 1971-72, Battelle Seattle Research Ctr., 1969-70; v.p. ops. Battelle Meml. Inst., Columbus, Ohio, 1973-76, sr. v.p., 1976-78, exec. v.p., 1978-81, pres., 1981—, chief exec. officer, 1984—, assoc. trustee, 1986—; lectr. modern physics Center for Grad. Studies, Richland, 1951-62; IAEA cons. to, Japan, 1962. Contbr. articles to profl. jours. Trustee Linfield Coll., 1970-73, Denison U., 1982—, Pacific Sci. Ctr., 1969-74, Oreg. Mus. Sci. and Industry, 1971-72, Columbus Ctr. Sci. and Industry, 1973—, Columbus Cancer Clinic, 1974—, Columbus Children's Hosp. Research Found., 1975—, Franklin U., 1987—; v.p. exec. bd. Cen. Ohio council Boy Scouts Am., 1976—; mem. exec. bd. of fellows Seattle-Pacific Coll., 1970-73; bd. overseers Acad. for Contemporary Problems, 1971-75; mem. nat. adv. bd. Am. U., 1982-86, Ohio State U. Found., 1985—; bd. dirs. Edward Lowe Found., 1985—. Served with USAAF, 1943-46. Recipient Silver Beaver award Boy Scouts Am., 1986. Mem. Am. Phys. Soc., Am. Nuclear Soc., Sigma Xi, Sigma Pi Sigma, Pi Mu Epsilon. Republican. Baptist. Home: 803 Lookout Point Dr Worthington OH 43085 Office: Battle Meml Inst 505 King Ave Columbus OH 43201

PAUL, SHASHI DAMAN, surgeon, pediatrician; b. New Delhi, India, July 13, 1943; s. Jaswant Singh and Shakuntla Paul; m. Promila D. Mehta, Sept. 2, 1971; children: Paresh, Sanjay, Arvin. Biomedical degree, U. Delhi Hindu Coll., New Delhi, 1961; MBBS, All India Inst. Med. Scis., New Delhi, 1965; cert., Edl. Commn. Fgn. Commn. Grads., Phila., 1965. Intern All India Inst. Med. Sci., New Delhi, 1966, Mt. Carmel Mercy Hosp., Detroit, 1967; resident in pediatrics Henry Ford Hosp., Detroit, 1968, Children's Hosp. of Mich., Detroit, 1968-71; practice medicine specializing in pediatrics Munster, Ind., 1971—; pediatrics registrar Hellington Hosp., Uxbridge, Middlesex, Eng., 1971; asst. prof. pediatrics Rush Med. Coll., Chgo., 1971—. Editor Jour. All India Inst. Med. Scis., 1964. Fellow Am. Acad. Pediatrics, Royal Coll. Physicians of Can., Am. Acad. Family Practice; mem. AMA (Physician Recognition award 1970, 73, 76, 79, 82, 85), ACP. Home: 9807 Twin Creek Blvd Munster IN 46321 Office: 8224 Calumet Rd Munster IN 46321

PAUL, THOMAS WILLIAM, healthcare center administrator; b. St. Paul, Mar. 30, 1946; s. Gilbert William and Genevieve Bell (Thomas) P.; m. Marie Kathleen Tennis, Dec. 11, 1965; children—Terra Michelle, Shantell Kathleen, Anissa Justine, Chaleece Marie. Cert. in comml. art Mpls. Vocat. Tech. Inst., 1965; diploma Chgo. Tech. Coll., 1971; credential advanced studies health service adminstrn. U. Minn., 1981; student in Health Care Adminstrn., Metro State U. Lic. nursing home adminstr., Minn. Photo lab technician Headliners of Twin Cities, Mpls., 1965-67; asst. adminstr. Birchwood Health Care Facility, Forest Lake, Minn., 1967-71, Colonial Acres Health Ctr., Golden Valley, Minn., 1971-73; exec. dir. Crest View Luth. Home, Columbia Heights, Minn., 1973—. Chmn. nursing homes div. United Way of Mpls., 1976; bd. suprs. Forest Lake Town, 1977-82, chmn., 1979-82; basketball coach Forest Lake Community Edn., 1980, softball coach, 1982; active various election campaigns, 1978-82; bd. dirs. St. Paul Camp Fire, 1979-81, United Way of Forest Lake, 1981, Forest Lake Sch. Dist., 1983—. Recipient Community Service award Anoka County Retarded Citizens Assn., 1981; Luth. Social Services grantee, 1979-80. Fellow Am. Coll. Health Care Adminstrs. (cert.); mem. Minn. Soc. Adminstrs. Nursing Care Facilities, Columbia Heights C. of C. (dir. 1982-85), Forest Lake Jaycees (life, outstanding young man 1976), U.S. Jaycee Pres.' Club. Republican. Lutheran. Contbr. articles to profl. jours. Office: Crest View Luth Home 4444 Reservoir Blvd NE Columbia Heights MN 55421

PAULSEN, DOUGLAS FRANK, biologist; b. Balt., Oct. 7, 1952; s. Douglas Frank and Janice Meriam (Benson) P.; m. Annamarie Angela Spillane, June 15, 1985. BA, Western Md. Coll., 1974; PhD, Wake Forest U., 1979. NIH postdoctoral fellow Calif. State U., Northridge, 1979-80; asst. prof. anatomy Morehouse Sch. Medicine, Atlanta, 1980-86; vis. researcher U. Iowa, Iowa City, 1986—; course dir. med. histology Morehouse Sch. Medicine, 1982-86, prin. investigator, 1982—. Contbr. articles to profl. jours. Mem. Am. Assn. Anatomists, Soc. for Developmental Biology, Tissue Culture Assn., Sigma Xi. Presbyterian. Avocations: guitar, Eastern philosophy, fishing, scuba. Home: 529 Brown St Iowa City IA 52240 Office: Univ Iowa Dept Biology Jefferson and Dubuque Sts Iowa City IA 52242

PAULSEN, JOHN QUINCY, medical administrator; b. Fargo, N.D., Oct. 24, 1928; s. Paul Marinus and Ruth (Miller) P.; m. Margaret Ann E. Brunskill, June 15, 1950; children: James Robinson, John Miller, Jean Elizabeth. BS, N.D. State U., 1950. Asst. mgr. Fargo Clinic, 1950-65, assoc. adminstr., 1965-80, exec. adminstr., 1980—; bd. dirs. Western States Life Ins. Co., First Bank-Fargo. Pres. Fargo-Moorhead YMCA, 1967-73, Fargo Bd. Edn., 1967-76, pres. bd. trustees Fargo Pub. Library, 1968-76, treas., bd. dirs. Fargo-Moorhead Symphony Orchestral Assn., 1980-85; publicity chmn. Pres. Nixon's visit to N.D. Reps., 1976. Named Fargo's Outstanding Young Man of Yr., Fargo Jaycees, 1972. Fellow Am. Coll. Med. Group Adminstrs. (pres. 1981-82); mem. N.D. Med. Group Adminstrs. (pres. 1977-78), Med. Group Mgmt. Assn. (bd. dirs. 1981-82). Republican. Presbyterian. Club: Fargo Country. Avocations: golf, tennis. Home: 1521 S 7th Fargo ND 58103 Office: Fargo Clinic Ltd 737 Broadway Fargo ND 58123

PAULSEN, KRYSTAL GAY, health services executive; b. Monroe, Mich., Jan. 27, 1952; d. John Harvey and Laura Louise (Bowman) Horton; m. Jeffrey Carter Paulsen, Aug. 25, 1973 (div. 1986);. BA, U. Mich., 1974, MA, 1977; MBA, Western Mich. U., Kalamazoo, 1981. English tchr. Grace Bible Christian Acad., Ann Arbor, Mich., 1974-76; employee relations asst. Eaton Corp., Kalamazoo, 1977-79; instr. Western Mich. U., 1978-81, adminstr., 1981-83; mgr. health services The Upjohn Co., Kalamazoo, 1983-86, also orgn. devel. cons., 1986—; cons. Eaton Corp., 1980, Nat. Waterlift, Kalamazoo, 1983; instr. Nazareth Coll., Kalamazoo, 1985. Contbr. articles to profl. publs. Pres. The Kalamazoo Network, 1983—; co-founder Profl. Women's Dialogue, Kalamazoo, 1983. Named one of Outstanding Young Women of Am., 1984. Mem. Kalamazoo County C. of C. (ambassador, co-chmn. 1982-83, outstanding leadership award 1983), Beta Gamma Sigma. Avocations: tennis, writing fiction. Home: 721 Keenway Circle Apt F Kalamazoo MI 49001 Office: The Upjohn Co 7000 Portage Rd 5025-152-1 Kalamazoo MI 49001

PAULSON, JOHN DUNDAS, oil company executive; b. Riverton, Wyo., Oct. 31, 1942; s. Alfred John and Carol Jean (Dundas) P.; m. Sharilyn Jean Lenhart, Dec. 19, 1966; children: Shanda, John, James. BS, U. Wyo., 1969. Engr. Halliburton Services, Colo., 1969-72; asst. supt. Halliburton Services, Rock Springs, Wyo., 1973-76; supt. Halliburton Services, Worland, Wyo., 1977-79; v.p. Western Prodn., Rapid City, S.D., 1979-82, pres., 1982—. Served with Army N.G., 1960-66. Mem. Soc. Petroleum Engrs. (v.p. Rock Springs sect. 1976). Republican. Presbyterian. Clubs: Arrowhead Country (Rapid City); Denver Petroleum. Lodges: Elks, Masons. Avocations: golf, skiing. Office: Western Prodn Co PO Box 2076 Rapid City SD 57709

PAULSON, LINDA FAYE, securities executive; b. Bowman, N.D., Sept. 7, 1955; d. Darrell Paulson and Joyce (Jalbert) Fossum; m. Scott Lee Van Orsdel, Aug. 13, 1977 (div. June 1983). BA in French and Bus. Adminstrn., Concordia Coll., 1977. Adminstrv. asst. Luth. Brotherhood, Mpls., 1977-79, mgr. loans and surrenders, 1979-81, mgr. loans, surrenders, and data, 1981-83, mktg. personnel asst., 1984, asst. v.p. fraternal affairs, 1985-86; asst. v.p. mutual fund services Luth. Brotherhood Securities Corp., 1986—. Mpls. city Ward Coordinator LWV, 1983-84, chair election returns, 1984-86. Named to Women in Leadership, Mpls. Jr. League, 1986. Mem. French Am. C. of C. (bd. dirs. 1985—), Bus., Econs. and Edn. Found. (bd. dirs. 1985—), Women in Founds. and Corp. Philanthropy (mem. steering com. Minn. chpt. 1985-87, chairperson Minn. 1985-86), Nat. Council on Founds., Minn. Council on Founds., Minn. Women's Fund. Lutheran. Avocations: collecting antiques, novels.

PAULSON, WILLIAM ARNOLD, JR., physician, surgeon; b. Muskegon, Mich., Oct. 26, 1927; s. William Arnold and Hildur Cecelia (Huldin) P.; m. Janice Arlene Emmons, May 24, 1952; children: Thomas M., Kelly L. BS in Pharmacy, Ferris State Coll., Big Rapids, Mich., 1953; DO, Kansas City Coll. Osteo. Medicine, 1963. Registered pharmacist Johnson Pharmacy, Muskegon, 1953-54; med. rep. S.E. Massengill Co., Bristol, Tenn., 1954-59; pvt. practice gen. medicine Muskegon, 1964—; Co-founder Planned Parenthood, Muskegon, 1965-70; pres. Brookhaven Med. Care Facility, Muskegon, 1974-75; founder, chmn. Sex Edn. Com., Muskegon, 1966-71; chmn. Gen. Practice Dept. Muskegon Gen. Hosp., 1970-76. Research asst. for first birth control pill, 1960; physician, chmn. Diabetes in an Aging Population, 1982. Bd. dirs. Muskegon, Oceana chpt. ARC, 1980-86; exec. bd. dirs. Friends of GOP, Muskegon, 1982-86. Served with USN, 1946-48. Mem. Am. Osteo. Assn., Am. Heart Assn., Am. Diabetes Assn., Osteo. Gen. Practitioners of State of Mich. (Osteo. Gen. Practitioner of Yr. 1986-87), Jaycees (pres. Muskegon chpt. 1956-57, state v.p. 1957-58), Sigma Sigma Phi (mem. exec. bd.). Republican. Presbyterian. Club: Exchange (Muskegon). Lodges: Elks (chmn. Statue of Liberty Commn.), Vikings. Avocations: skiing, boating. Office: 986 W Norton Rd Muskegon MI 49441

PAULU, BURTON, retired media educator; b. Pewaukee, Wis., June 25, 1910; s. Emanuel Marion and Sarah Marie (Murphy) P.; m. Frances Tuttle Brown, June 29, 1942; children—Sarah Leith, Nancy Jean, Thomas Scott. B.A. cum laude, U. Minn., 1931, B.S., 1932, M.A., 1934, postgrad., 1934-38; Ph.D., NYU, 1949. Mgr. Sta. KUOM, U. Minn., Mpls., 1938-57, prof., dir. radio and TV, 1957-72, prof., dir. media resources, 1972-78, ret. lectr. Sch. Journalism and Dept. of Speech, 1951-78; vis. prof. U. So. Calif., 1958, Los Angeles State Coll., 1961; assoc. dir. study of new ednl. media in Kennedy Cultural Ctr., Washington, 1949-52; Fulbright lectr. faculty of journalism Moscow State U., USSR, 1980-81, 86-87; lectr. U.S. Info. Agy., Spain and Fed. Republic Germany, 1983. Author: A Radio and Television Bibliography, 1952; Lincoln Lodge Seminar on Educational Television Proceedings, 1953; British Broadcasting: Radio and Television in the United Kingdom, 1956; British Broadcasting in Transition, 1961; Radio and Television Broadcasting on the European Continent, 1967; Radio and Television Broadcasting in Eastern Europe, 1974; Television and Radio Broadcasting in the United Kingdom, 1981. Served with U.S. Office of War Info., 1944-45. Grantee Rockefeller Found., 1942, Ford Found., 1958-59, 64-65, 70, 78, U. Minn., 1965-73; Fulbright scholar, 1953-54; recipient Citation of Radio and

TV Broadcasting on European Continent, Nat. Journalism Soc., 1967, Pioneering award Internat. Broadcasting Soc. of Netherlands, 1968, Broadcast Preceptor award San Francisco State U., 1968, 82. Mem. Minn. Fulbright Alumni Assn. (bd. dirs. 1985-87), U. Minn. Retirees Assn. (bd. dirs, pres.), AAUP, Phi Beta Kappa, Phi Kappa Phi, Phi Delta Kappa, Kappa Delta Pi, Phi Alpha Theta, Sigma Delta Chi. Democrat. Congregationalist. Avocations: photography, travel, reading, music. Home: 5005 Wentworth Ave Minneapolis MN 55419

PAULU, FRANCES BROWN, international center administrator; b. Hastings, Minn., June 22, 1920; d. Thomas Andrew and Florence Ida (Tuttle) Brown; m. Burton Paulu, June 29, 1942; children: Sarah Leith Paulu Boittin, Nancy Jean Paulu Hyde, Thomas Scott. BA magna cum laude, U. Minn., 1940, postgrad. sch. social work, 1942-44. Case worker Family Welfare Assn. Mpls., 1943-45; interviewer Community Health and Welfare Council, Mpls., 1963; sch. social worker Project Head Start, Mpls., 1966; program dir. Minn. Internat. Ctr., Mpls., 1970-72, exec. dir., 1972-84; bd. dirs. Minn. World Affairs Ctr., 1972-84, exec. dir., 1984—; mem. tourism adv. com. City of Mpls., 1976-83; mem. adv. council Minn. World Trade Ctr., 1984-86. Pres. UN Rally, 1970-72; chmn. Mpls. Charter Commn., 1972-74; bd. dirs. Urban Coalition of Mpls., 1967-70; dir. Minn. World Trade Week, 1977-81; participant Intercultural Communication Project, Japan, 1974; mem. mgmt. team Minn. Awareness Project, 1982—. DeWitt Jennings Payne scholar, 1939-40. Mem. Nat. Council for Internat. Visitors (officer and/or exec. com. mem. 1975-81, leader fact-finding team North Africa, Middle East, India 1978), Nat. Assn. for Fgn. Student Affairs, LWV (pres. Mpls. 1967-69), UN Assn. Minn. (adv. council 1979—), Mpls.-St. Paul Com. on Fgn. Relations, Phi Beta Kappa, Alpha Omicron Pi, Lambda Alpha Psi. Home: 5005 Wentworth Ave Minneapolis MN 55419 Office: Minn Internat Center 711 East River Rd Minneapolis MN 55455

PAVALON, EUGENE IRVING, lawyer; b. Chgo., Jan. 5, 1933; m. Lois M. Frenzel, Jan. 15, 1961; children—Betsy, Bruce, Lynn. B.S.L., Northwestern U., 1954, J.D., 1956. Bar: Ill. 1956. Sr. ptnr. Asher, Pavalon, Gittler and Greenfield, Ltd., Chgo., 1970—; lectr., mem. faculty various law schs. Former mem. state bd. dirs. Ind. Voters Ill. Served to capt., USAF, 1956-59. Fellow Am. Coll. Trial Lawyers, Internat. Soc. Barristers, Internat. Acad. Trial Lawyers; mem. ABA, Chgo. Bar Assn. (bd. mgrs. 1978-79), Ill. Bar Assn., Ill. Trial Lawyers Assn. (pres. 1980-81), Assn. Trial Lawyers Am. (parlimentarian 1983-84, sec. 1984-85, v.p. 1985-86, pres. elect 1986-87, pres. 1987-88), Am. Bd. of Profl. Liability Attys. (diplomat). Club: Chgo. Athletic Assn. Author: Human Rights and Health Care Law, 1980; contbr. articles to profl. jours., chpts. in books. Home: 1540 N Lake Shore Dr Chicago IL 60611 Office: 2 N LaSalle Dr Chicago IL 60602

PAVELKA, ELAINE BLANCHE, mathematics professor; b. Chgo.; d. Frank Joseph and Mildred Bohumila (Seidl) P.; B.A., M.S., Northwestern U.; Ph.D., U. Ill. With Northwestern U. Aerial Measurements Lab., Evanston, Ill.; tchr. Leyden Community High Sch., Franklin Park, Ill.; prof. math. Morton Coll., Cicero, Ill.; speaker 3d Internat. Congress Math. Edn., Karlsruhe, Germany, 1976. Recipient sci. talent award Westinghouse Elec. Co. Mem. Am. Edn. Research Assn., Am. Math. Assn. 2-Year Colls., Am. Math. Soc., Assn. Women in Math., Can. Soc. History and Philosophy of Math., Ill. Council Tchr. of Math., Ill. Math. Assn. Community Colls., Math. Assn. Am., Math. Action Group, Ga. Center Study and Teaching and Learning Math., Nat. Council Tchrs. of Math., Sch. Sci. and Math. Assn., Soc. Indsl. and Applied Math., Northwestern U. Alumni Assn., U. Ill. Alumni Assn., Am. Mensa Ltd., Intertel, Sigma Delta Epsilon, Pi Mu Epsilon. Home: PO Box 7312 Westchester IL 60153 Office: 3801 S Central Ave Cicero IL 60650

PAVEY, THOMAS GILBERT, dentist; b. Xenia, Ohio, Feb. 17, 1944; s. Paul A. and Sara (Davidson) P.; m. Anne Dickinson, June 25, 1966; children: Thomas G. II, Diane D. Student, Coll. William and Mary, 1962-64, 65-67, Ohio State U., 1965, 66-67; DMD, U. Ky., 1971. Gen. practice dentistry Dayton, Ohio, 1971—; pres. Superior Dental Care, Dayton, 1985—; dental cons. Western Ohio Health Care, Dayton, 1983-86, Dental Devel. Services, Dayton, 1986—, Allcare, Inc., Miamisbrug, Ohio, 1985—. Mem. ADA, Ohio Dental Assn.(pub. care council 1981-86, dental care council 1986—), Dayton Dental Soc. (pres. 1982-83), Soc. for Occlusal Studies. Republican. Methodist. Lodge: Rotary (sgt. of arms 1984-85). Avocations: golf, family activities. Office: 120 W 2d St Suite 1212 Hullman Bldg Dayton OH 45402

PAVIA, MICHAEL RAYMOND, JR., medicinal chemist; b. Greenwich, Conn., June 29, 1955; s. Michael Raymond and Lillian Louise (Valenta) P.; m. Julie Ann Penfil, July 27, 1986. BS in Chemistry, Lehigh U., 1977; PhD Organic Chemistry, U. Pa., 1982. Scientist Warner Lambert Co., Ann Arbor, Mich., 1982-84, sr. scientist, 1984-85, mgr. neurosci. program, 1985—. Contbr. research articles to profl. jours.; patentee in field. Mem. Am. Chem. Soc. Home: 1508 Westminster Ann Arbor MI 48104 Office: Warner Lambert Co 2800 Plymouth Rd Ann Arbor MI 48105

PAVICIC, JOSEPH NICHOLAS, securities trader; b. Virginia, Minn., Oct. 10, 1958; s. Joseph and Christine (Kaladur) P. BA in Econs., St. John's U., 1981. Lic. gen. securities trader; registered options prin. Bookkeeper Merrill Lynch Pierce Fenner & Smith, Mpls., 1981; stockbroker Midwest Securities, Mpls., 1982-83; fin. cons. Shearson Lehman Bros., Mpls., 1983-85; regional mgr. Olde & Co., Mpls., 1985—. Mem. Sierra Club (bd. trustees 1983-84). Roman Catholic. Clubs: Mpls. Athletic, Master Angler. Avocations: travel, fishing. Home: 2934 Polk St NE Minneapolis MN 55418 Office: Olde & Co 829 Marquette Ave Minneapolis MN 55402

PAVLESCAK, RIK, educational association administrator; b. Parma, Ohio, May 17, 1962; s. Thomas Edward and Kathleen Gertrude (Raufman) P. BS in Edn. summa cum laude, Kent (Ohio) State U., 1983, MEdn, 1985. Licensed social worker. Chem. dependency counselor Edwin Shaw Hosp., Akron, Ohio, 1982-83; edn. coordinator Alcohol & Drug Dependency Services, Inc., Medina, Ohio, 1983-85; student assistance program coordinator Preble County Office of Edn., Eaton, Ohio, 1985—; dir. Spl. & Worthwhile Prodn., Dayton, Ohio, 1986—; cons. Pride Can., Saskatoon, Sask., 1985-86, U. New Brunswick Orientation, Fredericton, 1986; trainer Aden Bowman Collegiate, Saskatoon, 1986;. Author: Special and Worthwhile, No Matter What, 1986, My Very Special Grandmother, 1987; co-author Creative Caring Card Set: 100 Classroom Activites, 1986. Mem. Soc. for Accelerated Learning and Teaching, Alcohol and Drug Abuse Prevention Assn. Ohio (v.p.), Pride Youth Can. (assoc.). Democrat. Mem. Unity Ch. Avocations: wellness, swimming, reading, enjoying a drug-free lifestyle. Home: 975 Harvard Blvd Dayton OH 45406 Office: Preble County Office of Edn Court House Eaton OH 45320

PAVLETIC, VICTORIA MARIE, dentist; b. Chgo., Oct. 24, 1957; d. Joseph William and Margaret Mary (Nebel) P.; m. Charles Thomas Vorderer, Apr. 19, 1986. BS, Ill. Benedictine Coll., 1979; DDS, U. Ill., Chgo., 1983. Gen. practice dentistry Palos Heights, Ill., 1983—. Avocations: nautilus, aerobics. Home: 10607 S Millard Chicago IL 60655 Office: 7600 W College Dr Palos Heights IL 60463

PAVLIC, TERENCE VICTOR, investment analyst; b. Chgo., Dec. 26, 1959; s. Robert Stephen and Mary Elizabeth (Zilg) P.; m. Shaun Anne Hyndiuk, Aug. 6, 1983; 1 child, Ashley Margret. BS in Fin., Marquette U., 1982; MBA in Fin., DePaul U., 1984. Proprietor Fault Free Tennis Supply, Elm Grove, Wis., 1979-82; staff acct. Scannel, Inc., Brookfield, Wis., 1980, Jansen & Co., Milw., 1982-83; investment counselor T.V. Pavlic & Co., Westmont, Ill., 1984-86; fin. analyst Allied Van Lines, Inc., Chgo., 1985-86; investment analyst AmeriTrust Co., Cleve., 1986—. Named one of Outstanding Young Men Am., 1985. Mem. Investment Analysts Soc. Chgo., Cleve. Soc. Investment Analysts, Cleve. Athletic Club. Republican. Roman Catholic. Avocations: sailing, golf. Home: 16010 Munn St Cleveland OH 44111 Office: AmeriTrust Co 900 Euclid Ave Cleveland OH 44101

PAVLIK, ROBERT MICHAEL, marketing executive; b. Cleve., Mar. 24, 1960; s. John Charles and Marian Agnes (O'Connor) P.; m. Barbara Jeanne Granito, Apr. 19, 1986. BSBA cum laude, Youngstown State U., 1982. Mktg. rep. ITT LIfe Ins. Corp., Cleve., 1983, John Hancock Ins. Co., Cleve., 1983-84; mktg. cons. Shaker Sq. Beverage, Cleve., 1984-85; mktg. mgr. Am. Soc. for Metals, Metals Park, Ohio, 1985—; mktg. cons. in field. Mem. N.E. Ohio Direct Mail and Mktg. Assn., Cleve. Advt. Club, Philip Morris Mktg. Team (chmn. 1981-82). Republican. Roman Catholic. Avocations: golfing, weightlifing, racquetball, swimming, automobiles. Home: 4740 Fay Dr South Euclid OH 44121 Office: Am Soc Metals Internat Rt 87 Metals Park OH 44073

PAVLO, RHODA VOTH, industrial engineer; b. Akron, Ohio, May 1, 1961; d. Howard Paul and Evelyn (Darkow) V. BS in Indsl. Engring., Purdue U., 1983; MBA, U. Akron, 1986. Sales engr. Reliance Electric, Charlotte, N.C., 1983-84; sr. estimating engr. Loral Systems Group, Akron, 1984—. Editor: Jour. of Parametrics, 1986—. Mem. com. Summit County Bd. Elections, Akron, 1986—; mem. Jr. League Akron, 1985—, Jr. Bd. Akron City Hosp., 1987—; cons. Jr. Achievement Project Bus., Akron, 1986—. Mem. Internat. Inst. Indsl. Engrs. (newsletter editor 1985-86), Internat. Soc. Parametric Analysts, Space Systems Cost Analysis Group (standardization com.). Republican. Lutheran. Avocations: running, cross country skiing, downhill skiing, aerobics, waterskiing. Home: 1189 Lisa Ann Dr Akron OH 44313 Office: Loral Systems Group 1210 Massillon Rd Akron OH 44315

PAWLAK-KANYUSIK, JAMES, legal assistant; b. Red Lake Fall, Minn., July 9, 1953; s. Stephen Edward and Doris Marie (Suprenant) Kanyusik; m. Elizabeth Nia Pawlak, July 17, 1982; 1 child, Michael. BA in Govt., St. John's U., Collegeville, Minn., 1975; BA in Mass Communications, St. Cloud State U., 1976; postgrad. in law, Calif. Western Sch. Law, 1976-77; postgrad., U. Minn., 1982-84. Dept. head Hansen, Dordell, St. Paul, 1981-86; legal asst. Kinney & Lange, P.A., Mpls., 1986—; cons. legal automation, devel. legal computer programs, Mpls.-St. Paul, 1987—. Mem. United States Chess Fedn., St. Paul Castle Chess Club. Baha'i. Home: 1346 Delaware Ave West Saint Paul MN 55118 Office: Kinney & Lange PA 625 4th Ave S Suite 1500 Minneapolis MN 55415-1659

PAWLEY, HOWARD RUSSELL, Canadian provincial minister; b. Brampton, Ont., Can., Nov. 21, 1934; s. Russell and Velma Leone (Madill) P.; m. Adele Schreyer, Nov. 26, 1960; children—Christopher Scott, Charysse. Ed. Man. Tchrs. Coll., United Coll., U. Winnipeg, Man. Law Sch. Called to bar. Mem. Man. (Ont., Can.) Legislature, 1969—; premier of Man., 1981—; minister pub. works, 1969-71, mcpl. affairs, 1969-76; atty. gen. and keeper of Gt. Seal, 1973; minister responsible for Liquor Control Act, 1976, Man. Pub. Ins. Corp. and Man. Housing and Renewal Corp.; leader Man. New Democratic Party (N.D.P.), 1979. Office: Office of Premier, Legis Bldg Room 204, Winnipeg, MB Canada R3C OV8

PAWLIAS, THEODORE JAMES, dentist; b. Rochester, Minn., June 1, 1955; s. Kenneth T. and Shirley J. (Mason) P. BA, Drake U., 1977; DDS, Loyola, Maywood, Ill., 1982. Instr. Robert Morris Coll., Carthage, Ill., 1982; gen. practice dentistry Macomb, Ill., 1982—. Asst. scoutmaster Boy Scouts Am., Macomb, 1982—, bd. dirs. Prairie council, 1987—; pres. McDonough County Cancer Soc., 1982-84, v.p. 1984-85; treas. Young Reps., Macomb, 1984—; bd. dirs. McDonough County Rehab. Ctr., Macomb, 1983—. Named Eagle Scout Boy Scouts Am. Mem. ADA, Prairie Valley Dental Soc., NRA, Ducks Unlimited, Aircraft Owners and Pilots Assn. Roman Catholic. Club: Safari Internat. (#1 Nyasaland Wildebeast 1986, #14 Heartebeast 1986). Lodges: KC (warden Macomb 1986—), Kiwanis (chmn. 1984—). Avocations: hunting, fishing, flying, travel. Home: 60 Arlington Dr Macomb IL 61455 Office: 6 Doctors Ln Macomb IL 61455

PAWLOWSKI, FRANK GEORGE, commercial banker; b. Evanston, Ill., Dec. 16, 1955; s. Frank H. and Anne M. (Fuchs) P.; m. Cynthia J. Zatarga, Apr. 12, 1980; children: Jaci Anne, Jami Lynne. BS, DePaul U., 1977, MBA, 1981. CPA, Ill. From project analyst to sr. acct. Continental Bank, Chgo., 1977-80, sr. acctg. supr., 1980-81, acctg. instr., supr., 1981-82, sr. credit analyst, 1982-84, asst. mgr., 1984-85, comml. fin. officer, 1985-86; territorial credit mgr. Merrill Lynch Bus. Fin. Services Inc., Chgo., 1986—. Ill. state scholar, 1973. Mem. Am. Inst. CPA's, Ill. CPA Soc., Delta Sigma Pi. Roman Catholic. Avocations: skiing, softball, football, photography. Home: 1370 Volkamer Trail Elk Grove Village IL 60007 Office: Merrill Lynch Bus Fin Svcs Inc 33 West Monroe St 22d Floor Chicago IL 60603

PAWLOWSKI, GREGORY GERARD, advertising executive; b. Pontiac, Mich., Nov. 18, 1953; s. Edmund Felix and Rita Anne (Machewski) P.; m. Deborah Marie Bacik, July 2, 1976; children: Lynne Marie, Michael Adam, Matthew Gregory. BS, U. Detroit, 1975. Sr. adminstr. Soc. Mfg. Engrs., Dearborn, Mich., 1979-84; mktg. mgr. Photon Sources, Livonia, Mich., 1984-86; sr. copywriter and acct. exec. Thompson Advt., Farmington Hills, Mich., 1986—. Contbr. articles to profl. jours. Pres. Briar Hill Homeowners Assn., 1984-86. Mem. Soc. Mfr. Engrs. (sr.), Adcrafters Club. Roman Catholic. Avocations: racing, fishing, skiing. Office: Thompson Advt 31690 W 12 Mile Rd Farmington Hills MI 48018

PAXTON, ALBERT ELWYN, chrome plating company executive; b. Chgo., May 19, 1902; s. Frederick H. and Harriet I. (Griffiths) P.; B.S., U. Ill., 1925; m. Edna Marjorie Rehm, July 11, 1930; children—Marilyn V., Nancy L. Editor, Mill Supplies, McGraw-Hill Publs., Chgo., 1926-34, mgr., N.Y.C., 1934-37; editorial mgr. Engring. News Record-Constrn. Methods, N.Y.C., 1938-45, pub., 1945-48; v.p. western region McGraw-Hill Pub. Co., Chgo., 1948-67; pres. Nova Chrome, Inc., Franklin Park, Ill., 1967-85; pvt. practice cons., Winnetka, Ill., 1985—. Clubs: Chgo., Univ., Westmoreland Country. Home: 667 Sheridan Rd Winnetka IL 60093

PAYDAR HAMED, NASSER, structural mechanics design educator; b. Tehran, Iran, Oct. 31, 1956; came to U.S., 1975; s. Houssain and Pouran Hamed Paydar; m. Niloofar Imami, July 28, 1979. BS, Syracuse U., 1979, MS, 1981, PhD, 1985. Instr. aerospace design Syracuse (N.Y.) U., 1981-85, researcher NSF project, 1982-85; prof. structural mechincs design Purdue U., Indpls., 1985—. Syracuse U. fellow, 1984. Mem. ASME, Sigma Xi. Avocation: tennis. Office: Purdue Univ PO Box 647 Indianapolis IN 46223

PAYNE, ARTHUR EDDIE, III, poet, singer, songwriter; b. Kansas City, Kans., Mar. 9, 1955; s. Arthur Eddie and Marion Maxine (Metcalfe) P.; 1 dau., Araina Sheree Rachelle. Student Rockhurst Coll., 1973-74, Park Coll., 1975-77, Charles Parker Music Acad., 1978-79, U. Mo.-Kansas City, 1980-82, Am. Dance Acad., 1982. Cargo serviceman Braniff Internat., Kansas City, 1978; salesman Buie and Stark Clothing, Kansas City, Mo., 1978-79; custodian Park Place Meadows, Raytown, Mo., 1979-80; transfer agt. D.S.T. Inc., Kansas City, Mo., 1980—; cons. to music bus. Recipient Cert. Appreciation Boy's Club Movement, 1980. Mem. Broadcast Music Inc. Roman Catholic. Composer over 700 songs.

PAYNE, DEMING LUTHER, plastic surgeon; b. Monticello, N.Y., Mar. 14, 1939; s. Deming Sarles Payne and Ruth (Armitage) Butts. AB, Hamilton Coll., 1961; MD, SUNY, Buffalo, 1966. Diplomate Am. Bd. Plastic Surgery. Intern Med. Coll. Va., Richmond, 1966-67, resident in gen. surgery, 1967-68, 70-73; plastic surgeon U. Rochester Strong Meml. Hosp., 1973-75; practice medicine specializing in plastic surgery Salem, Mass., 1975-77, Hinsdale, Ill., 1977—. Served to capt. USAF, 1968-70. Mem. Am. Soc. Plastic and Reconstructive Surgery, Midwest Soc. Plastic Surgery, Chgo. Plastic Surgery Soc. Republican. Avocations: fly fishing, skiing, drawing, painting. Office: 20 E Ogden Hinsdale IL 60521

PAYNE, FREDERICK LEE, municipal park administrator; b. Cin., Aug. 25, 1933; s. Fred Pollard and Ethel Mary (Fretz) P.; m. Kyleen Privette; children: Douglas Lee, Jeffrey Lyle. BS in Horticulture, Ohio State U., 1955; Cert. in Pub. Adminstrn., U. Cin., 1961. Jr. engr. Cin. Park Bd., 1956-57, landscape architect, 1957-58, supr. horticulture, 1958-66, asst. supr., 1966-72, dir. of parks, 1972—; lectr. horticulture U. Cin., 1968-72. Contbr. artilcles to profl. jours. Mem. Civic Garden Ctr., Cin., 1965—, Cin. Assn., 1972—; trustee Friends of Cin. Parks, 1975—, City Gospel Mission, 1975—. Served with USAR, 1955-63. Named to Hon. Order Ky. Cols., 1972; recipient Statesman award Cin. Assn. Execs., 1982. Mem. Am. Pub. Works Assn., Am. Hort. Soc., Am. Forestry Assn., Internat. Fedn. Park and Recreation Adminstrn., Ohio Parks and Recreation Assn. Methodist. Avocations: gerdening, hiking, geneal. research.

PAYNE, KEITH LLOYD, insurance agency executive; b. Moline, Ill., May 16, 1943; s. Francis Lee and Vivian Ruth (Stevenson) P.; m. Susan Elizabeth Johnson, June 13, 1964; children—Michelle Leigh, Frances Lynn. B.S., Western Ill. U., Macomb, 1965. Owner, Payne Ins. Agy., Orion, Ill., 1965—. Clk., Village of Orion, 1969-79, mayor, 1979-81; sec. Crime Stoppers of Henry County, Inc., 1983-85; chmn. bd. dirs. Spoon River Mental Health Ctr., Galesburg, Ill., 1985-87, trustee Methodist ch. 1984-85. Mem. Henry County Ind. Ins. Agts. (sec.-treas. 1983-84, pres. 1985-86), Ind. Ins. Agts. of Ill., Ind. Ins. Agts. of Am. (regional v.p. 1985, chmn. adminstrv. bd. 1987). Democrat. Lodges: Lions, Masons. Home: 1120 4th St Orion IL 61273 Office: Payne Ins Agy 1000 3d St Orion IL 61273

PAYNE, MARC TIMOTHY, chemical engineer; b. Pryor, Okla., July 31, 1956; s. Kenneth W. and Carol J. (Curtis) P.; m. Nancy Irene Fisher, May 17, 1974. BSChemE, U. Okla., 1978. Research engr. Monsanto Indsl. Chem., St. Louis, 1978-81, sr. research engr., 1981-83; research specialist Monsanto, St. Louis, 1983-85; MTS internat. mgr. Monsanto, Akron, Ohio, 1986; mgr. process research and devel. Monsanto Chem., Akron, Ohio, 1986—. Contbr. articles to profl. jours. Mem. AAAS, Am. Inst. Chem. Engrs., Soc. Polymer Processing, Soc. Plastics Engrs., Tau Beta Pi. Avocations: tennis, music, painting. Office: Monsanto Chem Co 260 Springside Dr Akron OH 44313

PAYNE, MEREDITH JORSTAD, physician; b. St. Louis, Feb. 7, 1927; d. Louis Helmar and Cleone Gladys (Branian) Jorstad; m. Spencer Payne, 1948 (div. 1959); m. James McGarity, 1965 (div. 1977); children: Maureen Meredith, James Louis. AB, Washington U., St. Louis, 1947, MD, 1950. Diplomate Am. Bd. Surgery, Am. Bd. Plastic Surgery. Intern gen. surgery St. Louis City Hosp., 1950-51, asst. resident surgery, 1951-54; chief surg. resident Roswell Park Meml. Hosp., Buffalo, 1954-55; chief plastic surgery resident Allentown (Pa.) Gen. Hosp., 1955-57; asst. clin. prof. surgery Washington U. Med. Sch., 1957-70; vis. surgeon Homer G. Phillips Hosp., St. Louis, 1957-70; staff St. Luke's and St. Mary's Hosp., St. Louis, 1970—; asst. prof. surgery St. Louis U. Sch. Medicine, St. Louis, 1986—; bd. dirs. Blue Cross and Blue Shield, St. Louis, 1985—; med. dir. St. Luke's Cleft Palate Clinic. Contbr. articles to profl. jours. Fellow ACS; mem. Soc. Plastic and Reconstructive Surgery, AMA, Mo. Med. Assn. (del.), St. Louis Met. Med. Soc., Am. Cleft Palate Assn., Roswell Park Surgery Assn., So. Med. Assn., Washington U. Med. Alumni Assn., Am. Geriatrics Soc., Midwestern Assn. Plastic Surgeons, Pan Am. Med. Assn., City Hosp. Alumni Assn., Soc. Head and Neck Surgeons. Club: College (bd. dirs. St. Louis 1983-85). Lodge: Order of Eastern Star, Zonta (St. Louis pres. 1968-69). Avocations: skiing, tennis, sewing, knitting, gardening. Home: 7314 Westmoreland Ave Saint Louis MO 63130 Office: 1034 S Brentwood Blvd Suite 778 Saint Louis MO 63117

PAYNE, RICHARD GREEN, aerospace company executive; b. Webster, Ky., Dec. 2, 1926; s. Chester and Flora (Osborn) P.; m. Jean Payne, Jan. 16, 1954; children—John R., Donald L., Mark. A. B.S. in Mech. Engring., Ohio State U., 1950. Supr., RCA, Indpls., 1950-52; asst. works mgr. Brown Brockmeyer, Dayton, 1952-53; mgr. Rockwell Internat., Columbus, 1953—. Mem. Salem Civic Assn., Columbus, 1980—. Served to staff sgt. U.S. Army, 1945-47. Mem. AIAA, Nat. Mgmt. Assn., Aircraft Owners and Pilots Assn., Toastmasters Internat. Republican. Lutheran. Avocations: flying; physical culture; golf. Home: 5750 Sinclair Rd Columbus OH 43229 Office: Rockwell Internat 4300 E 5th Ave Columbus OH 43216

PAYNE, STEPHANIE MCGINNIS, nurse, nursing educational administrator; b. Topeka, Dec. 30, 1945; d. Joseph Edward and Marjean Elaine (Meyer) McGinnis; m. Donald Stowe Peterson, Oct. 1, 1966 (div.); m. William A. Payne, July 14, 1986. Diploma Stormont-Vail Sch. Nursing, 1966; BS in Health Arts, Coll. St. Francis, 1982. RN, Kans., Mo. Instr. med. and surg. nursing Stormont Vail Sch. Nursing, Topeka, 1967-70; supr. surg. nursing Newman Meml. Hosp., Emporia, Kans., 1970-73; staff nurse Meml. Hosp., Topeka, 1966-67, inservice instr., 1976-77, spl. projects coordinator, 1977-78, asst. supt. nurses, 1973-75; asst. dir. edn. Spelman Meml. Hosp., Smithville, Mo., 1979, staff nurse operating room, 1984-85; nurse emergency dept. Allentown Osteo. Med. Ctr., Pa., 1985-86; nurse dept. head gen. and vascular surgery Pocono Hosp., East Stroudsburg, pa., 1986—; lectr., cons. in field. Mem. Am. Nurses Assn., Pa. Nurses Assn., Nat. League for Nursing, Am. Assn. Critical Care Nurses, Kans. State Nurses Assn., Am. Soc. Healthcare Educators and Trainers.

PAYNE, STEVE WILLIAM, dentist; b. Ft. Scott, Kans., Nov. 20, 1955; s. Clyde William and Marilyn Joan (Geer) P.; m. Susan Teresa Werbach, June 6, 1981; children: Rainie, Garett. BS, Pittsburg (Kans.) State U., 1977; DDS, U. Mo., Kansas City, 1981. Gen. practice dentistry Ft. Scott, 1981—. Mem. ADA, S.E. Dist. Dental Soc., Kans. Dental Assn. Lodge: Rotary. Avocations: golf, fishing, hunting. Office: 1115 Main Fort Scott KS 66701

PAYNE, WILLIAM J., manufacturing company executive; b. Danville, Ill., June 28, 1940; s. Joseph C. and Nina C. (Faris) P.; m. Nan Elliott Kirby, Feb. 2, 1969; children—Nina Faris, Thomas Kirby. B.S., Trinity U., San Antonio, 1962. Gen. mgr., chief exec. officer Howell Playground Equipment Co., Danville, Ill., 1971—. Chmn. bd. dirs. Danville Area Community Coll., 1974-79; mem. Ill. Community Coll. Bd., 1979—; trustee Ill. State Univs. Retirement System, 1980-83. Served to lt. comdr. USN, 1966-71. Mem. Nat. Recreation and Park Assn., Nat. Sch. Supply and Equipment Assn. (treas. 1982—). Republican. Episcopalian. Club: Danville Country. Lodges: Rotary, Elks. Home: 44 Country Club Dr Danville IL 61832 Office: 1710 E Fairchild St Danville IL 61832

PAYTON, DONALD CLIFFORD JR., dentist; b. Keytesville, Mo., July 10, 1953; s. Donald Clifford Sr. and Mary Ann (Malone) P.; m. Janet Mae Coleman, Aug. 9, 1975; children: Laura Kathleen, Thomas Coleman, Sarah Elizabeth. BS in Biology, U. Mo., Kansas City, 1975, BA in Chemistry, 1976, DDS, 1981. Gen. practice dentistry Appleton City, Mo., 1981—; cons. dentist Head Start Program, West Cen. Mo., 1981—. Bd. dirs. Appleton City Landmarks Restoration, 1985-86; sec., treas. Appleton City Indsl. Devel., 1987-88. Recipient Appreciation award Head Start Program, 1984. Mem. ADA, Am. Soc. Dentistry Children, Acad. Gen. Dentistry, Mo. Dental Assn., GGreater Kansas City Dental Assn., Delta Sigma Delta. Republican. Roman Catholic. Club: Appleton City Community (pres. 1985-86, 86-87). Lodges: Optimist, KC (council 1982—, Grand Knight 1987—). Home: 407 E Dover Appleton City MO 64724 Office: 102 W 4th St Appleton City MO 64724

PAYTON, EDGAR L., lawyer; b. Mexico, Mo., Oct. 24, 1950; s. Earl H. and Dorothy L. (Ramsey) P.; m. Judith Ann Daniel, July 18, 1981; children: Joshua Lee, Sarah Elizabeth. BS, Southwest Bapt. U., 1972; JD, U. Mo., Kansas City, 1984. Bar: Mo. 1984, U.S. Dist. Ct. (we. dist.) Mo. 1984. Communications specialist Dem. Party of Mo., Jefferson City, 1972; editor Bolivar (Mo.) Herald Free Press, 1972-74; dir. field ops. Ozarks Area Community Action, Springfield, Mo., 1974-81; law clk. to presiding justice U.S. Dist. Ct. (we. dist.) Mo., 1984-86; atty. Miller & Sanford, Springfield, 1986—. Author: Community Action Planning Manual, 1977, The Social Security Disability Program, 1986; author, editor: Guide to Community Food and Nutrition Program Planning, 1978. Chmn. Univ. Heights Bapt. Ch. Bd. Trustees, Springfield, 1986; bd. dirs. Citizens to Assure Rep. Elections, Springfield, 1985-86, Dem. Alliance, Springfield, 1985; active Citizens Adv. Rep. Assembly, Springfield, 1986, Greene County CHild Advocacy Council, Springfield, 1985-86; bd. deacons Univ. Heights Bapt. Ch., 1987. Mem. ABA, AM. Trial Lawyers Assn., Greene County Bar Assn., U. Mo.-Kansas City Law Sch. Alumni Assn. (coordinator 1984—). Home: 2536 N Marlan Springfield MO 65613 Office: Miller & Sanford 1845 S National PO Box 4288 Springfield MO 65808

PAYTON, WALTER, football player; b. Columbia, Miss., July 25, 1954; m. Connie Payton; children: Jarrett, Brittney. B.A. in Communications, Jackson State U. Running back with Chgo. Bears, 1975—; played Pro Bowl, 1976, 77, 78, 79, 80, 81, 82, 83, 84, 85; mem. NFL Championship team 1985. Named NFC Player of Year The Sporting News, 1976, 77, named to NFC All-Star Team, 1976, 77, 78; named NFL Most Valuable Player Profl. Football Writers Am., 1978, NFC Player of Yr. UPI, 1977; Most Valuable Player NFL, 1978. Office: care Chgo Bears 55 E Jackson St Suite 1200 Chicago IL 60604 *

PAZ, GEORGE, accountant; b. St. Louis, Aug. 27, 1955; s. Geronimo and Collen May (Hart) P.; m. Georgene Marie Wade, July 27, 1974; children: Stacy, Kelly, Rebecca. BSBA, U. Mo., St. Louis, 1982. CPA, Mo. Jr. acct. Gen. Am., St. Louis, 1980-82, sr. acct., 1982-83, acctg. adminstr., 1983-85, tax planning analyst, 1985-87, dir. tax planning, 1987—; bd. dirs. Gen. Am. Employees Fed. Credit Union, 1985—. Fellow Life Office Mgmt. Assn.; mem. Am. Inst. CPA's, Mo. Soc. CPA's. Lutheran. Avocations: golf, running, softball. Home: 75 Shirecreek Ct Saint Charles IL 63303 Office: Gen Am Life Ins Co 700 Market St Saint Charles MO 63101

PEACOCK, TIMOTHY HENRY, water conditioning executive; b. Marion, Ohio, Aug. 2, 1943; s. Neldon and Alice E. (Neidig) P.; m. Regina Anne Izzi, May 21, 1966; children: Tim J., Ami M., Andrew J. Student, Ohio State U., 1961-62. With credit collection dept. City Nat. Bank, Columbus, Ohio, 1968-69, Buckeye Fed. Bank, Columbus, 1970-71; v.p. Peacock Water Conditioning Co., Marion, 1971-81, pres., 1981—. Served with U.S. Army, 1965-68, Vietnam. Mem. Nat. Water Quality Assn. (cert. dealer), Nat. Fedn. Ind. Bus., Ohio Water Quality Assn., U.S. C. of C., Marion C. of C. Democrat. Roman Catholic. Home: 197 E Washington Marion OH 43302 Office: Peacock Water Conditioning Co 1800 Marion-Marysville Rd Marion OH 43302

PEAKES, LEE WALLACE, investment banker; b. Winter Haven, Fla., Dec. 28, 1945; s. Edmund W. and Roxa (Lee) P.; m. Jan Michele Schwartz, Sept. 12, 1947; children: Amanda, Adam, Ben, Matthew. BS, U. Kans., 1968, MS in Bus. Adminstrn., 1969. Asst. v.p. Commerce Bank, Kansas City, 1972-78; sr. v.p. George K. Baum and Co., Kansas City, 1978—; bd. dirs. Citizens State Bank, Paola, Kans., L.I.C.O. Inc., Kansas City, Emmons Farms Corp., Oneonta, N.Y. Councilman City of Lenexa, Kans., 1978-79; mem. Gov.'s Task Force on Capital Mkts., 1986. Served to 1st lt. U.S. Army, 1970-71. Roman Catholic. Clubs: Kansas City; Leawood (Kans.) South Country . Home: 3600 W 121st Terr Leawood KS 66209 Office: George K Baum & Co 1004 Baltimore Ave Kansas City MO 64105

PEARCE, MARVIN LEROY, JR., insurance company executive; b. Marion, Ohio, Dec. 15, 1955; s. Marvin Leroy and Dortha Jean (Evans) P.; m. Peggy Lynn Conner, May 25, 1985; 1 child, Rebecca Lynn. Grad. high sch., Clyde, Ohio, 1974. Ins. agent Pearce Ins. Agy., Fremont, Ohio, 1974—. Mem. Profl. Ins. Agents of Ohio (com. mem. 1985-87). Republican. Methodist. Avocations: hiking, landscaping, fishing, horseback riding, photography. Home: 704 County Rd 232 Fremont OH 43420 Office: 221 S Front St Fremont OH 43420

PEARCE, STEPHEN WADE, health facility administrator, psychologist; b. Peoria, Ill., Jan. 5, 1954; s. Loyal Lloyd and Yuvonia (Boggio) P.; m. Kathryn Paula Langenkamp, Aug. 12, 1977 (div. Apr. 1982). BA in Psychology, Ohio No. U., 1976; MA in Psychology, No. Ill. U., 1978; D of Psychology, Wright State U., 1983. Lic. psychologist, Ohio. Intern Miami County Mental Health Ctr., Troy, Ohio, 1983, clin. psychologist, 1984-86, clin. dir., 1986—; cons. alcohol program Wright State U. Med. Sch., Dayton, Ohio, 1982-84, cons. rehab. unit Dettmer Hosp., Troy, 1985-86, cons. crisis dept. DayMont W. Mental Health Ctr., Dayton, 1985-87. Mem. com. lay ministry peer counseling Kirkmont Presbyn. Ch., Beavercreek, Ohio, 1986. Acad. Edn. and Research in Profl. Psychology scholar, 1981. Mem. Am. Psychol. Assn., Ohio Psychol. Assn. Avocations: sports, photography, woodworking, reading. Home: 17 E Hillcrest Ave Apt 3 Dayton OH 45405 Office: Miami County Mental Health Ctr 1059 N Market St Troy OH 45373

PEARL, STEVEN LEE, dentist; b. Chgo., Dec. 18, 1943; s. Albert and Annette (Epstein) P.; m. Ellen A. Padorr, Aug. 30, 1964; children: Jeffrey, Jennifer. DDS, Northwestern U., 1968. Gen. practice dentistry Chgo., 1968—. Mem. Am. Acad. Occlusodontia, Chgo. Dental Soc., Uptown Dental Forum. Jewish. Home: 3119 Centennial Highland Park IL 60035 Office: 7104 N Western Ave Chicago IL 60645

PEARLBERG, JAY LOUIS, radiologist; b. N.Y.C., June 15, 1947; s. Benjamin and Helen (Klorman) P.; m. Deborah Baumer, Jan. 1, 1970; Children: Aliza, Benjamin, Daniel. BA, Columbia U., 1969, MA, 1970; MD, Wayne State U., 1975. Diplomate Am. Bd. Radiology. Fellow in computed Tomography St. Michael's Hosp., Toronto, Ont., 1980; sr. staff physician Henry Ford Hosp., Detroit, 1980—; cons. Chest, Park Ridge, Ill., 1984—; editorial cons. radiology, Balt., 1982—. Editorial cons. radiology jour., Balt., 1982—. Fellow Royal Coll. of Physicians; mem. Radiol. Soc. N.Am., Soc. Thoracic Radiology, Am. Med. Assn., Mich. State Med. Soc., Wayne County Med. Soc.

PEARLMAN, JERRY KENT, electronics company executive; b. Des Moines, Mar. 27, 1939; s. Leo R. Pearlman; married; children: Gregory, Neal. B.A., Princeton U., 1960; M.B.A., Harvard U., 1962. With Ford Motor Co., 1962-70; v.p. fin. dir. Behring Corp., 1970-71; controller Zenith Electronics Corp., Glenview, Ill., 1971-74, v.p., 1972-74, v.p. fin., 1974-78, sr. v.p. fin., 1978-81, sr. v.p. fin., group exec., 1981-83, pres., chief exec. officer, 1983—, chmn., 1984—, also dir.; dir. Stone Container Corp., First Chgo. Corp. Office: Zenith Electronics Corp 1000 Milwaukee Ave Glenview IL 60025 *

PEARSALL, HARRY JAMES, dentist; b. Bay City, Mich., Apr. 12, 1916; s. Roy August and Gladys Agnes (Tierney) P.; m. Betty Almina Dahlke, Oct. 5, 1946 (dec. Nov. 1982); 1 child, Paul Roy. BS, Marquette U., 1937, DDS, 1939. Gen. practice dentistry Bay City, 1939—; cons. Delta Dental Ins., Lansing, Mich., 1975-86. Mem. Bay City chpt. Revision Com., 1965-66; bd. dirs. Downtown Bay City, 1962-73. Served to maj. U.S. Army, MC, 1940-46. Mem. ADA, Am. Coll. Dentists, Internat. Coll. Dentists, Mich. Dental Assn. (pres. 1972-73), Saginaw Valley Dental Soc. (pres. 1955-56), Bay County Dental Soc. (pres. 1950-51), Am. Legion. Lodge: Elks. Home: 1820 E Worfolk Dr Apt 1 Essexville MI 48732 Office: 404 Shearer Bldg Bay City MI 48708

PEARSON, DENNIS RALPH, printing company executive; b. Hamilton, Ohio, Mar. 10, 1946; s. Ralph Leslie and Mildred Barbara (Schlenk) P.; m. Audrey Jane Swenson, Dec. 11, 1976; children—Dennis Ryan, David Lowe. B.S., Ohio U., 1968. Western dist. mgr. Harris Corp., Chgo., 1970-74; nat. sales mgr. Butler Automatic Inc., Canton, Mass., 1974-79; nat. sales and mktg. mgr. Bowers Printing Inks Coatings and Resins div. PPG Industries Inc., Chgo., 1979-85; v.p. sales and mktg. Metroweb Corp., 1985-86; v.p. nat. accounts Treasure Chest Advt. Co. Inc., Rosemont, Ill., 1987—. Deacon Northminster Presbyn. Ch., 1983-86. Mem. Printing Industry Am. Republican. Office: 9801 W Higgins Rd Suite 320 Rosemont IL 60018

PEARSON, EDNA MAE, learning disabilities educator; b. Hawley, Minn., Aug. 11, 1934; d. Thorval Alfred and Alice Ethyl (Gill) Olson; m. George Frederick Pearson, June 16, 1955; children: Timothy George, Diana Lynn, John Thorval. Assoc. in Edn., Moorhead (Minn.) State U., 1954, BS, 1957, postgrad., 1984. Cert. elem. tchr., Minn., learning disabilities tchr. Elem. tchr. Crookston (Minn.) Pub. Schs., 1954-55, West Fargo (N. D.) Pub. Schs., 1955-56; pvt. tutor Clearbrook, Minn., 1956-59; elem. tchr. Detroit Lakes (Minn.) Pub. Schs., 1959-68, learning disabilities tchr., 1969—. Fellow NEA, Minn. Edn. Assoc., Detroit Lakes Edn. Assoc.; mem. Alpha Delta Kappa (pres.). Democrat. Lutheran. Club: Happy Hillside 4-H (local key leader 1965-81). Avocations: crafts, music, camping, fishing, walking. Home: 1524 Gary Ave Detroit Lakes MN 56501 Office: Washington Ave Detroit Lakes MN 56501

PEARSON, GARY DEAN, dentist; b. Rockford, Ill., Dec. 25, 1952; s. Miles Addison and Pauline (Hammond) P.; m. Marcea Lou Schlensker, Dec. 4, 1981; 1 child, Grant Addison. BS cum laude, Rockford Coll., 1974; DDS, U. Ill., Chgo., 1978. Pvt. practice dentistry Rockton, Ill., 1978—. Recipient Gen. Assembly Scholarship, State of Ill., 1977. Mem. Am. Dental Assn., Ill. State Dental Soc., Winnebago County Dental Soc., U. Ill. Alumni Assn., Phi Theta Kappa. Lutheran. Club: Rockford Coll. Alumni. Avocation: flying, photography. Home: 295 Rockton Rd Roscoe IL 61073 Office: 213 W Main St Rockton IL 61072

PEARSON, J. D., mining company executive. Pres. Fed. Ore and Chem. Inc., Belle Fourche, S.D. Office: Fed Ore & Chem Inc 117 5th Ave Belle Fourche SD 57717 *

PEARSON, JOHN EDGAR, insurance company executive; b. Mpls., Jan. 17, 1927; s. Edgar Clarence and Viola Esther (Quist) P.; m. Sharon M. Nessler, Nov. 4, 1950; children: Cynthia Lynn, Thomas Calvin. Student, Gustavus Adolphus Coll., 1944-45, Northwestern U., 1945-46; B.B.A., U. Minn., 1948. Sales trainee Minn. Mining & Mfg. Co., St. Paul, 1948-49; group rep. Northwestern Nat. Life Ins. Co., Seattle, 1949-51; salesman Marsh & McLennan Inc., Seattle, 1951-53; with Northwestern Nat. Life Ins. Co., Mpls., 1953—, pres., 1975-76, pres., chief exec. officer, 1977-80, chmn., pres., chief exec. officer, 1981-82, chmn., chief exec. officer, 1983—, also bd. dirs.; chief exec. officer North Atlantic Life Ins. Co., 1972—, chmn. bd., 1977—, also bd. dirs.; chmn. bd. No. Life Ins. Co., 1979—, also bd. dirs.; bd. dirs. Norwest Bank, Mpls.; pres. Life and Health Ins. Med. Research Fund, 1983-85, now bd. dirs.; bd. dirs. Minn. Ins. Info. Ctr., Norwest Corp., Mpls, No. States Power, Mpls., Meth. Health Care on Minn. Bd. dirs. United Way Greater Mpls. Area, 1979—; bd. dirs. Meth. Hosp., 1979-86 , Mpls. Community Bus. Employment Alliance, 1982—, Minn. Bus. Partnership, 1977—, Minn. Project on Corp. Responsibility, 1978-84 , Mpls. Soc. Fine Arts, 1980-86 , Minn. Pvt. Coll. Fund, 1979—; chmn. Mpls. Urban Coalition, 1979-80. Served with USNR, 1944-46. Mem. Health Ins. Assn. Am. (dir. 1979-84 , chmn. 1983), Am. Council Life Ins. (dir. 1979-82, 84-86, chmn. 1986), Ins. Fedn. Minn. (dir. 1976—), Mpls. C. of C. (dir. 1979-80). Clubs: Minneapolis, Minikahda. Office: Northwestern Nat Life Ins Co 20 Washington Ave S Minneapolis MN 55440

PEARSON, LINLEY E., state attorney general; b. Long Beach, Calif., Apr. 18, 1946. B.A., The Citadel, 1966; M.B.A., Butler U., 1970; J.D., Ind. U., 1970. Bar: Ind. 1970, U.S. Dist. Ct. (so. dist.) Ind. 1970, U.S. Ct. Appeals (7th cir.) 1977. Law clk. judge Richard Givan Ind. Supreme Ct., 1969-70; pros. atty. Clinton County, 1971-81; atty. gen. State of Ind., Indpls., 1981—; ptnr. Campbell, Hardesty, Pearson & Douglas, Frankfort, Ind., 1971-81. Mem. Ind. Bar Assn., Clinton County Bar Assn. (pres. 1973). Office: Office Atty Gen 219 State House Indianapolis IN 46204 *

PEARSON, LLOYD ERIK, orthodontist; b. Mpls., Feb. 20, 1933; s. Erik Olaf and Emma Fredda (Johnson) P.; m. June Marie Olson, Sept. 14, 1957; children: Cynthia Pearson Conner, Leslie M., Bradley L. DDS, U. Minn., 1957, MS in Orthodontics, 1959. Diplomate Am. Bd. Orthodontics (bd. dirs. 1984—). Practice dentistry specializing in orthodontics Edina, Minn., 1959—. Contbr. articles to profl. jours. Mem. Am. Dental Assn., Minn. Dental Assn. (dental edn. com., del.), Mpls. Dist. Dental Soc., Am. Assn. Orthodontists, Minn. Soc. Orthodontists (past pres., chmn. edn. com.), Midwestern Orhtodontic Soc. (chmn. jud. council), Angle Orthodontic Soc. (chmn. admissions com.), Tweed Found. for Orthodontic Research, Soc. for Occlusal Studies, Omicron Kappa Upsilon. Office: 263 Southdale Med Bldg France Ave S Edina MN 55435

PEARSON, LOUISE MARY, retired manufacturing company executive; b. Inverness, Scotland, Dec. 14, 1919 (parents Am. citizens); d. Louis Houston and Jessie M. (McKenzie) Lenox; grad. high sch.; m. Nels Kenneth Pearson, June 28, 1941; children—Lorine Pearson Walters, Karla. Dir. Wauconda Tool & Engring. Co., Inc., Algonquin, Ill., 1950-86; reporter Oak Leaflet, Crystal Lake, Ill., 1944-47, Sidelights, Wilmette, Ill., 1969-72, 79-82. Active Girl Scouts U.S.A., 1955-65. Recipient award for appreciation work with Girl Scouts, 1965. Clubs: Antique Automobile of Am. (Hershey, Pa.); Veteran Motor Car (Boston); Classic Car of Am. (Madison, N.J.). Home: 125 Dole Ave Crystal Lake IL 60014

PEARSON, NELS KENNETH, retired manufacturing executive; b. Algonquin, Ill., May 2, 1918; s. Nels Pehr and Anna (Fyre) P.; student pub. schs.; m. Louise Mary Houston Lenox, June 28, 1941; children—Lorine Marie Pearson Walters, Karla Jean. Assembler, Oak Mfg. Co., Crystal Lake, Ill., 1936-38, machine operator, assembly line foreman, 1938-43, apprentice tool and die maker, 1946-50; co-founder, pres. Wauconda Tool & Engring. Co., Inc., Algonquin, 1950-86; owner, founder Kar-Lor Enterprises, 1987—; co-founder, treas. Kenmode Tool & Engring. Co., Inc., Algonquin, 1960-72. Mem. McHenry County Edn. and Tng. Com., 1961-86, treas., 1961-86. Served with AUS, 1943-46. Mem. Am. Soc. Tool and Mfg. Engrs. Clubs: Moose, Antique Auto, Classic Car, Vet. Motor Car, Horseless Carriage. Home: 125 Dole Ave Crystal Lake IL 60014 Office: Huntley Rd Algonquin IL 60102

PEARSON, NORMAN, international planning management consultant, author; b. Stanley, County Durham, Eng., Oct. 24, 1928; s. Joseph and Mary (Pearson) P.; came to Can., 1954; B.A. with honors in Town and Country Planning, U. Durham (Eng.), 1951; Ph.D. in Land Economy, Internat. Inst. Advanced Studies, 1979; M.B.A., Pacific Western U., Colo., 1980, D.B.A., 1982; PhD In Mgmt. Calif. U. for Advanced Studies, 1986—; m. Gerda Maria Josefine Riedl, July 25, 1972. Cons. to Stanley Urban Dist. Council, U.K., 1946-47; planning asst. Accrington Town Plan and Bedford County Planning Survey, U. Durham Planning Team, 1947-49; planning asst. to Allen and Mattocks, cons. planners and landscape designers, Newcastle upon Tyne, U.K., 1949-51; adminstrv. asst. Scottish Div., Nat. Coal Bd., Scotland, 1951-52; planning asst. London County Council, U.K., 1953-54; planner Central Mortgage and Housing Corp., Ottawa, Ont., Can., 1954-55; planning analyst City of Toronto Planning Bd., 1955-56; dir. of planning Hamilton Wentworth Planning Area Bd., Hamilton, Ont., Can., 1956-59; dir. planning for Burlington (Ont.) and Suburban Area Planning Bd., 1959-62, also commr. planning, 1959-62; pres. Tanfield Enterprises Ltd., London, Ont., Can., 1962—, Norman Pearson & Assocs. Ltd., Can., 1962—; cons. in planning, 1962—; life mem. U.S. Com. for Monetary Research and Edn., 1976—; spl. lectr. in planning McMaster U., Hamilton, 1956-64, Waterloo (Ont.) Luth. U., 1961-63; asst. prof. geography and planning U. Waterloo (Ont.), 1963-67; assoc. prof. geography U. Guelph (Ont.), 1967-72; prof. polit. sci. U. Western Ont., London, 1972-77; mem. Social Scis., Econ. and Legal Aspects Com. of Research Adv. Bd. Internat. Joint Commn., 1972-76; cons. to City of Waterloo, 1973-76, Province of Ont., 1969-70; adviser to Georgian Bay Regional Devel. Council, 1968-72; real estate appraiser, province of Ont., 1976—; pres., chmn. bd. govs. Pacific Western U., Canada, 1983-84. Pres. Unitarian Ch. of Hamilton, 1960-61. Served with RAF, 1951-53. Knight of Grace, Sovereign Order St. John of Jerusalem. Fellow Royal Town Planning Inst. (Bronze medal award 1957), Royal Econ. Soc.; mem. Internat. Soc. City and Regional Planners, Am., Canadian insts. planners, Canadian Polit. Sci. Assn. L'Association Internationale des Ingenieurs et des Docteurs ès Sciences Appliquées à l'Industrie. Clubs: Empire; Ontario; University (London). Author: (with others) An Inventory of Joint Programmes and Agreements Affecting Canada's Renewable Resources, 1964. Editor, co-author (with others) Regional and Resource Planning in Canada, 1963, rev. edit., 1970; editor (with others) The Pollution Reader, 1968. Contbr. numerous articles on town planning to profl. jours. and chpts. in field to books.

PEARSON, PAUL GUY, university president; b. Lake Worth, Fla., Dec. 5, 1926; s. Eric Conrad and Dora Wilma (Capen) P.; m. Winifred Clowe, June 30, 1951; children: Thomas, Jean, Andrew. Student, Palm Beach Jr. Coll., 1946-47; B.S. with honors, U. Fla., 1949, M.S., 1951, Ph.D., 1954; Litt.D. (hon.), Rutgers U., 1982; LL.D. (hon.), Juniata Coll., 1983. Asst. prof. U. Tulsa, 1954-55; asst. prof. Rutgers U., New Brunswick, N.J., 1955-60; assoc. prof. Rutgers U., 1960-64, prof., 1964-81, assoc. provost, 1972-77, exec. v.p., 1977-81, acting pres., 1978; pres., prof. Miami U., Oxford, Ohio, 1981—; dir. 2d Nat. Bank, Hamilton, Ohio, Greater Dayton (Ohio) Pub. TV, Union Cen. Life Ins., Cin. Mem. U.S. Army Sci. Bd., 1984-86. Served with USNR, 1944-46. Fellow AAAS; mem. Ecol. Soc. Am. (sec. 1961-64, v.p. 1970, treas. 1974-77), Am. Inst. Biol. Scis. (gov. 1968-79, v.p. 1977, pres. 1978). Home: Lewis Pl 310 E High St Oxford OH 45056

PEARSON, RICHARD BRUCE, school system administrator; b. Duluth, Minn., May 20, 1933; s. Arthur Bernard and Aileen (Landro) P.; m. Bertha Esther Wheeler, Aug. 19, 1961; children: Sarah Jane, Thomas Richard. BS, U. Minn., Duluth, 1955, MA, 1963. Cert elem. tchr., Minn.; cert. elem. prin., Minn.; cert supt. schs. Minn., Wis. Elem. sch. prin. Ind. Sch. Dist. 709, Duluth, 1962-66, asst. supt. schs., 1968-72, supt. schs., 1972-86; cons. Minn. Dept. Edn., St. Paul, 1966-68; supt. schs. Sch. Dist. of Superior, Wis., 1986—; Study dir. Minn. Dept. Edn., St. Paul, 1986—. Bd. dirs. Sta. WDSE-TV, Duluth, 1972-78, 87—; v.p. campaign United Way of Greater Duluth, 1977, pres. 1979-80; commr. City Planning Commn., Duluth, 1987—. Served with U.S. Army, 1956-58. Bush Found. fellow, 1979. Mem. Nat. Elem. Sch. Prin.'s Assn., Am. Assn. Sch. Adminstrs., Minn. Assn. Sch. Adminstrs., Phi Delta Kappa. Presbyterian. Lodge: Rotary (bd. dirs. Duluth chpt. 1987—). Avocations: community history and devel., reading, golf. Home: 1337 Brainerd Ave Duluth MN 55811 Office: Sch Dist Superior 3025 Tower Ave Superior WI 54880

PEARSON, RONALD DALE, retail food stores corporation executive; b. Des Moines, 1940; married. B.S. in Bus. Adminstrn., Drake U., 1962. With Hy-Vee Food Stores Inc., Chariton, Iowa, 1962—, former exec. v.p., now pres., chief operating officer; dir. Beverage Mfrs., Inc., Civic Ctr. Cts., Inc. Office: Hy-Vee Food Stores Inc 1801 Osceola Ave Chariton IA 50049 *

PEARSON, STANLEY MICHAEL, respiratory therapist; b. Bay City, Mich., Oct. 27, 1948; s. Stanley Michael and Thelma A. (Rapps) P.; m. Sheron Ann McCoy, Dec. 11, 1970; children: Michael S., Jennifer L. BS, Cen. Mich. U., 1970; grad. in respiratory therapy, U. Chgo. Hosp., 1976; MS in Edn., So. Ill. U., 1986. Registered respiratory therapist; cert. CPR technologist. Respiratory therapist Bay Med. Ctr., Bay City, Mich., 1976-77; clin. dir. respiratory therapy St. Mary's Hosp., Athens, Ga., 1977; instr. Miami (Fla.)-Dade County Coll., 1977-79; program dir. respiratory therapy G.C. Wallace Coll., Dothan, Ala., 1979-82; tech. dir. respiratory therapy Tishomingo County Hosp., Iuka, Miss., 1982-83; program coordinator respiratory therapy Sch. Tech. Careers So. Ill. U., Carbondale, 1983—. Cochmn. Cystic Fibrosis Bowl-4-Breath, Carbondale, Ill., 1986; adv. com., pres. NE Miss. Jr. Coll., Booneville, 1983; fin. advisor Respiratory Therapy Club. Mem. NBRC, Ill. Soc. Respiratory Care (bd. dirs. respiratory therapy sect. , chpt. 4 rep. 1984—), Nat. Soc. CPR Technologists, Miss. Soc. Respiratory Therapy (pres. NE chpt. 1982), Ala. Soc. for Respiratory Therapy (incorporator, bd. dirs. 1982). Avocations: piano, guitar, organ, tennis. Home: Rt 1A PO Box 44 Cobden IL 62920 Office: So Ill U Sch Tech Careers Carbondale IL 62901

PEASE, DONALD JAMES, Congressman; b. Toledo, Sept. 26, 1931; s. Russell Everett and Helen Mary (Mullen) P.; m. Jeanne Camille Wendt, Aug. 29, 1953; 1 child, Jennifer. B.S. in Journalism, Ohio U., Athens, 1953, M.A. in Govt, 1955; Fulbright scholar, Kings Coll., U. Durham, Eng., 1954-55. Mem. Ohio Senate, 1965-66, 75-76, Ohio Ho. of Reps., 1969-74, 95th to 100th Congresses from 13th Ohio Dist. Chmn. Oberlin (Ohio) Pub. Utilities Commn., 1960-61; mem. Oberlin City Council, 1961-63. Served with AUS, 1955-57. Home: 140 Elm St Oberlin OH 44074 Office: US House of Reps 1127 Longworth House Office Bldg Washington DC 20515

PEAVY, HOMER LOUIS, JR., real estate executive, accountant; b. Okmulgee, Okla., Sept. 4, 1924; s. Homer Louis and Hattie Lee (Walker) P.; children: Homer Martin, Daryl Mark. Student Kent State U., 1944-49; grad. Hammel-Actual Coll., 1962. Sales supr. Kirby Sales, Akron, Ohio, 1948-49; sales mgr. Williams-Kirby Co., Detroit, 1949-50; area distributor Peavy-Kirby Co., Phila., 1953-54; salesman James L. Peavy Realty Co., Akron, 1954-65; owner Homer Louis Peavy, Jr., Real Estate Broker, Akron, 1965—; pvt. practice acctg., Akron, 1962—; fin. aid officer Buckeye Coll., Akron, 1982. Author: Watt Watts, 1969; poet: Magic of the Muse, 1978, P.S. I Love You, 1982; contbr. poetry to Am. Poetry Anthology, 1983, New Worlds Unlimited, 1984, Treasures of the Precious Moments, 1985, Our World's Most Cherished Poems, 1985; songs: Sh...Sh, Sheree, Sheree, 1976, In Akron O, 1979; teleplay: Revenge, 1980. Bd. dirs. Internat. Elvis Gold Soc., 1978—; charter mem. Statue of Liberty-Ellis Island Found., 1984, Nat. Mus. of Women in Arts, 1986; mem. Nat. Trust for Hist. Preservation. Recipient Am. Film Inst. Cert. Recognition, 1982, Award of Merit cert. World of Poetry 10th ann. contest, 1985, Golden Poet award World of Poetry, 1985, 87. Mem. Ohioana Library Assn., Internat. Black Writers Conf., Acad. Am. Poets, Manuscript Club Akron, Kent State U. Alumni Assn. Democrat. Home and Office: 1160 Cadillac Blvd Akron OH 44320

PECA, STEPHEN PAUL, accountant, financial executive; b. Evergreen Park, Ill., Feb. 28, 1957; s. Edward A. and Adeline C. (Sarad) P. BBA, Loyola U., Chgo., 1979, postgrad., 1985—. CPA, Ill.; registered real estate broker. Devel. mgr. Urban Investment and Devel. Co., Chgo., 1979-85; corp. controller The Tucker Cos., Northbrook, Ill., 1985-86, v.p. acctg., fin., adminstrn., 1986—. Mem. Am. Inst. CPA, Nat. Assn. Accts., Am. Mgmt. Assocs., Ill. CPA Soc. Avocation: flying. Office: The Tucker Cos Inc 40 Skokie Blvd Northbrook IL 60062

PECK, ABRAHAM J., historian; b. Landsberg, Germany, May 4, 1946; s. Shalom W. and Anna (Koltun) P.; m. Jean Marcus, June 21, 1969; children: Abby, Joel. BA, Am. U., 1968, MA, 1970; PhD, U. East Anglia, Eng., 1977; postgrad., U. Hamburg, Fed. Republic Germany, 1973-74. Adminstrv. dir. Am. Jewish Archives, Cin., 1976—; lectr. in Judaic studies U. Cin., 1980—. Author: Radicals and Reactionaries, 1978; editor Jews and Christians After the Holocaust, 1982; co-editor Am. Rabbinate: A Century of Continuity and Change 1883-1983, 1985, Studies in the American Jewish Experience II, 1984; contbr. articles to profl. jours. Spl. advisor U.S. Holocaust Meml. Council, Washington, 1982-86; bd. dirs. Am. Jewish Com., Cin., 1978-84, Anti-Defamation League of Ohio, Ind. and Ken., Columbus, 1982-86, Jewish Community Relations Council, Cin., 1980-86. Fullbright Found. fellow, 1973-74; Ohio Program in the Humanities grantee, 1980, 83, 85. Mem. Am. Hist. Found., Orgn. Am. Historians, Assn. Jewish Studies, Soc. for Scholarly Pub., Soc. of Am. Archivists. Avocations: travel, raising dogs. Office: Am Jewish Archives 3101 Clifton Ave Cincinnati OH 45220

PECK, CURTISS STEVEN, management consultant; b. Kenosha, Wis., May 3, 1947; s. Curtiss Wesley and Frances Helen (Kowalkowski) P.; m. Susan Carol Kostritza, Nov. 3, 1975; children: Stephanie Jean, Curtiss Wesley II, Stacey Marie. BS, U. Wis., Milw., 1976, MS, 1980, PhD candidate, 1987. Investigator, police officer Greendale (Wis.) Police Dept., 1971-80; cons. NCTI, Milw., 1980-83; pres. Nat. Communications Tng. Inst., Milw., 1983—; instr. Cardinal Stritch Coll., Milw., 1982—; advisor Booth-Wright, Inc., Boulder, Colo., 1983—; cons. Howard & Assocs., Chgo., 1985—, Mgmt. Resources Assn., Brookfield, 1985—. Bd. dirs. Multiple Sclerosis Soc., Milw., 1983—, pres. 1985, 86; coordinator Assn. Adult Educators, Milw., 1984; advisor Goodwill Industries, Milw., 1985, 86. Served with USAF, 1966-70, USANG, 1970-80. Mem. Nat. Organizational Devel. Network, Chgo. Organizational Devel. Network, Am. Soc. for Personnel Adminstrn., Personnel and Indsl. Relations Assn., Organizational Devel. Inst. Lutheran. Avocations: golf, tennis, gardening, family traveling. Home: S68 W17924 East Dr Muskego WI 53150 Office: NCTI 15350 W National Ave New Berlin WI 53151-9990

PECK, GEORGE ROBERT, insurance agent; b. Kansas City, Kans., Aug. 25, 1936; s. George Dewey and Sue Ora (Mahan) P.; m. Elizabeth Jane Peck, June 28, 1958 (div. June 1983); 1 child, Donna Marie Cooksey; m. Mary Elizabeth Peck, Aug. 17, 1985. BA, Minn. State U., 1974. Sales rep. John Hancock Ins., Fremont, Nebr., 1959-61, Liberty Mut. Ins., Mpls., 1961-71; v.p. Gamble Alden Agy., Mpls., 1971-78; pres. Bob Peck Agy., Inc., St. Louis Park, Minn., 1978—; pres. adv. bd. Northwestern Nat. Ins. Co., Milw., 1982—. Served with USAF, 1958-61. Mem. Profl. Ins. Agents Assn. Republican. Roman Catholic. Avocations: photography, gardening, computers. Home: 12960 12th Ave N Plymouth MN 55441 Office: Bob Peck Agy Inc 1660 S Hwy 100 Suite 146 Saint Louis Park MN 55416

PECK, JOHN W., federal judge; b. Cin., June 23, 1913; s. Arthur M. and Marguerite (Comstock) P.; m. Barbara Moeser, Mar. 25, 1942 (dec. 1981); children—John Weld, James H., Charles E.; m. Janet Alcorn Wagner; 1 stepchild, Gretchen Wagner. A.B., Miami U., 1935, LL.D., 1966; J.D., U. Cin., 1938, LL.D., 1965; LL.D., Chase Law Sch., 1971. Bar: Ohio bar 1938. Partner Peck, Shaffer & Williams, Cin., 1938-61; judge Ct. Common Pleas, Hamilton County, Ohio, 1950, 54; tax commr. State of Ohio, 1951-54; judge Supreme Ct. of Ohio, 1959-60, U.S. Dist. Ct., So. Dist. Ohio, 1961-66; judge U.S. Ct. Appeals, 6th Circuit, 1966—, sr. judge, 1978—; judge Temporary Emergency Ct. Appeals, 1979—; exec. sec. gov. State of Ohio, 1949; lectr. U. Cin. Coll. Law, 1948-70, Salmon P. Chase Coll. Law, 1949-51; mem. com. on adminstrn. criminal law Jud. Conf. U.S., 1971-79. Trustee Miami U., 1959—, emeritus, 1975—; mem. Princeton City Sch. Dist. Bd. Edn., 1958-63, pres. bd., 1963-69. Served to capt. Judge Adv. Gen. Corps AUS, 1942-46. John Weld Peck Fed. Bldg. dedicated in his honor, 1984. Mem. Cincinnatus Assn., Gyro Club, Beta Theta Phi, Phi Delta Phi. Club: Cin. Literary (pres.). Home: 165 Magnolia Ave Glendale OH 45246 Office: U S Ct of Appeal PO and Courthouse Bldg 5th & Walnut Sts Cincinnati OH 45202

PECK, MARIE JOHNSTON, Latin American area studies consultant; b. New Haven, Aug. 15, 1932; d. James Howard and Marie Anna Christina (Voigt) Johnston; m. Austin Monroe Peck, July 9, 1952 (div. 1959). AS, Larson-Quinnipiac, 1952; BA, U. N. Mex., 1968, PhD, 1974. Pres. Southwestern Images, Inc., Shawnee Mission, Kans., 1978—; Visiting scholar U. N. Mex., Albuquerque, 1983; visiting instr. Wofford Coll., Spartanburg, S.C., 1984; adj. instr. Johnson County Community Coll., Overland Park, Kans., 1985-86, coordinator Brown v. Topeka Conference, 1986; cons. Brown vs. Topeka Project, Merriam, Kans., 1984—; bd. dirs. Operation SER, Colorado Springs, Co., Midcoast Radio, Inc., Kansas City. Contbr. articles to profl. jours. Fulbright scholar, 1981-82. Fellow Nat. Defense Fgn. Language, Orgn Am. States; mem. Latin Am. Studies Assn., MLA, Am. Assn. Tchrs. Spanish and Portugese, Midwest Assn. for Latin Am. Studies, Nat. Women's Studies Assn., Internat. Relations Council (speakers bur. Kansas City 1986—). Avocations: photography, outdoor activites. Home: 8226 Johnson Dr Shawnee Mission KS 66202 Office: Brown v Topeka Project 6304 Sherwood Ln Shawnee Mission KS 66203

PECK, N. JOAN, distribution company executive; b. Chgo., Sept. 7, 1936; d. Robert Lee Justice and Joy Holly (Gayler) Nutter; m. Gerald Arthur Peck, Aug. 20, 1954; children: Laura J. Peck Spratt, Jeffrey H., Russel L. Cert. prins. of banking, Am. Ins. Banking, 1967, cert. acctg., 1970; cert. govt. tax preparation, H & R Block, 1980; B in Acctg., Kirkwood Coll., 1982. Teller note and vault Security Pacific Bank, La Mirada, Calif., 1968-70; head teller City Nat. Bank, Cedar Rapids, Iowa, 1970-72, Collins Credit Union, Cedar Rapids, 1972-74; mgr. office Discovery Village, Inc., Cedar Rapids, 1982-85; acctg. mgr., v.p. Dygert-Peck Corp., Cedar Rapids, 1979—. Mem. care rev. bd. Discovery Village, Cedar Rapids, 1986—. Mem. Am. Bus. Women (Woman of Yr. 1985), Assn. Retarded Citizens, Brucemore Hist. Soc. (tour guide 1984—), Kings Sons and Daughters Internat. Mem. Disciples of Christ Ch. Avocations: sewing, quilting, flowers, gardening, piano. Home: 1110 Maplecrest Dr Marion IA 52302 Office: Dygert-Peck Co 107 35th St Marion IA 52302

PECKENPAUGH, DONALD HUGH, psychologist, educational administrator; b. East Chicago, Ind., Aug. 11, 1928; s. George Martin and Thelma Mentia (Anderson) P.; m. Mary Frances Dreesen, Sept. 2, 1950; children: Ann Dreesen, Eve Louise. PhB, U. Chgo., 1948, AM, 1954, PhD, 1968. Lic. psychologist, Ill., Ind., Minn. Pvt. practice psychology Palos Park, Ill., 1960—; adminstr. Lake Ridge Sch. System, Gary, Ind., 1984—. Author: A School System's Role in Social Renewal, 1966, A Comprehensive Concept for Vocational Educational Facilities, 1967, Partners in Education, 1967, Exemplary Programs in Multi-Cultural Education, 1974, Population and You, 1975, Moral Education, 1976, The Public School as Moral Authority, 1977, Psychoeducational Evaluation, 1984. Nat. Inst. Mental Health fellow, 1965-67. Mem. Am. Psychol. Assn., Am. Assn. Sch. Adminstrs. (life), Phi Delta Kappa. Home: 3 Brook Ln Palos Park IL 60464

PECKENPAUGH, ROBERT EARL, investment adviser; b. Potomac, Ill., July 17, 1926; s. Hilery and Zella (Stodgel) P.; m. Margaret J. Dixon, Sept. 21, 1945; children—Nancy Lynn, Carol Sue, David Robert, Daniel Mark, Jeanne Beth, Douglas John. Student, Ind. U., 1946-47; B.S., Northwestern U., 1949, M.B.A. with distinction, 1952. Chartered fin. analyst. with First Nat. Bank Chgo., 1949-52; pres. Security Suprs., Inc., Chgo., 1952-73; v.p. Chgo. Title & Trust Co., 1973-77; pres. Hotchkiss & Peckenpaugh, Inc., Chgo., 1977-84; investment mgr. Morgan Stanley Asset Mgmt. Inc., 1984-86; v.p. Morgan Stanley & Co., Inc., Chgo., 1986— . Chmn., Evang. Covenant Ch. of Hinsdale, 1981-84. Served with USNR, 1944-46. Mem. Investment Analyst Soc. Chgo. (pres. 1963-64). Clubs: Chgo., Mid-Day, Chgo. Athletic, Economic (Chgo.), Hinsdale Golf. Home: 429 S County Line Rd Hinsdale IL 60521 Office: Morgan Stanley & Co Inc 440 S LaSalle St Chicago IL 60605

PECKWAS, EDWARD ALAN, foundation administrator; b. Chgo., May 1, 1942; s. Edward Michael and Yarmilla (Herbik) P.; m. Jane Ann Bingaman, Aug. 22, 1970; children: Kimberly Marie, Dawn Marie, Amanda Jane Ann. AA in Commerce, Hannibal-LaGrange Coll., 1962; BA, No. Ill. U., 1968. Treas. Program Controled Info. Systems, 1970-71; pres. Heraldry Unlimited, Chgo., 1971-74, Kiddie Corner Corp., Chgo., 1974—; pres. Polish Geneological Soc., Chgo., 1978—, editor newsletter, 1979—; Founder Polish Geneological Soc., 1978—, editor newsletter 1979—. Contbr. articles on Polish Heraldry to profl. jours. Decorated Commenders Cross knight to the Order of Polonia Restituta. Home: 6640 W Archer Chicago IL 60638 Office: Polish Geneological Soc 984 N Milwaukee Ave Chicago IL 60622

PECORARO, VINCENT LOUIS, biomedical research scientist, educator; b. Freeport, N.Y., Aug. 31, 1956; s. Jerome Dominic and Gloria (Fragnito) P. BS, UCLA, 1977; PhD, U. Calif., Berkeley, 1981. Lab. technician UCLA, 1976-77; research asst. U. Calif.-Berkeley, 1977-81, teaching assoc., 1977-79; NIH fellow U. Wis., Madison, 1981-84; asst. prof. chemistry U. Mich., Ann Arbor, 1984—. Contbr. articles to profl. jours. Horace Rackham fellow, 1985, Eli Lilly fellow, 1986; Searle Biomed. Research scholar, 1986-89. Mem. AAAS, Am. Chem. Soc., N.Y. Acad. Scis., Am. Assn. Biol. Chemists, Am. Film Inst., Inst. Protein Structure Design, Ctr. Molecular Genetics, Sigma Xi, Phi Eta Sigma. Roman Catholic. Home: 3625 Greenbrier Ave #161C Ann Arbor MI 48105 Office: U Mich Ann Arbor MI 48109

PECSENYE, TIMOTHY, manufacturing executive; b. Toledo, June 29, 1952; s. Steven and LaDonna Mae (Brungard) P. BA, Siena Heights Coll., 1974; postgrad., U. Detroit, 1987. Cert. Payroll Profl. Accounts payable supr. Prestolite Group, Toledo, 1976-80; payroll supr. Eltra Corp., Toledo, 1980-82; payroll and taxes mgr. Allied-Signal, Morristown, N.J., 1982-84; human resources info. system staff analyst Libbey-Owens-Ford Co., Toledo, 1984-85, mgr. compensation adminstrn. and systems, 1986—. Trustee Cen. Ohio Singers Dist., Cleve., 1981-82, pres. song festival, 1987. Mem. The Assn. of Human Resources Systems Profls., German Am. Festival Soc. Inc. (asst. treas. Toledo chpt. 1978-81, 86, chmn. festival 1982-83), Greater Beneficial Union Pitts. (del. 1978, 82, alt. del. 1986), Ohio Fraternal Congress (bd. dirs. 1978-82). Republican. Lutheran. Club: Teutonia Maennerchor (Toledo) (pres. 1978-80). Avocation: participation in ethnic cultural and musical activities. Home: 4441 Woodmont Rd Toledo OH 43613 Office: Libbey-Owens-Ford Co 811 Madison Ave Toledo OH 43695

PECZKOWSKI, JAMES JOSEPH, quality assurance executive; b. South Bend, Ind., Apr. 15, 1960; s. Joseph Leonard and Angela Veronica (Kolber) P.; m. Susan Debra Thomas, Sept. 25, 1982. BS, Purdue U., 1982; postgrad., Ind. U., 1985—. Chemist City of South Bend, 1982-84, Whitehall Labs, Elkhart, Ind., 1984-86; plant chemist Ross Labs., Sturgis, Mich., 1986-87, supr. quality assurance, 1987—. Democrat. Roman Catholic. Avocations: computers, music, skiing. Home: 27627 Northland Dr Sturgis MI 49091 Office: Ross Labs 700 W Lafayette Sturgis MI 49091

PEDDADA, SHYAMAL DAS, statistical educator; b. Madras, Tamil Nadu, India, Nov. 10, 1958; came to U.S., 1980; s. Prabhakara Rao and Meenakshi Peddada. BS with honors, U. Delhi, India, 1977; MS, Indian Agrl. Research Inst., New Delhi, India, 1979; MA, U. Pitts., 1981, PhD, 1983. Asst. prof. stat. Cen. Mich. U., Mt. Pleasant, 1983—. Research fellow Indian Council Agrl. Research, 1977, Indian Agrl. Stat. Research Inst., 1977-79, teaching fellow U. Pitts., 1981-83. Mem. Am. Stats. Assn., Inst. Math. Stats. Avocations: tennis, movies, chess. Home: 1628 Sumner Lincoln NE 68502

PEDDICORD, ROLAND DALE, lawyer; b. Van Meter, Iowa, Mar. 29, 1936; s. Clifford Elwood and Juanitas Irene (Brittain) P.; children—Erin Sue, Robert Sean. B.S. in Bus. Adminstrn. with honors, Drake U., 1961, J.D. with honors, 1962. Bar: Iowa 1962. Asst. atty. gen. State of Iowa, 1962-63; assoc. Steward, Crouch & Hopkins, Des Moines, 1962-65; ptnr. Peddicord & Sutphin, Des Moines, 1965-82; lectr. in law Drake U., 1962-68; lectr. law Coll. Osteo. Medicine, Des Moines, 1965-72. Editor and chief Drake Law Rev., 1961-62. Nat. bd. dirs., mem. nat. council YMCAs of Am., sec.; bd. dirs., chmn., mem. exec. com. Med-West field com. YMCAs U.S.; bd. dirs. Greater Des Moines YMCA, 1968—, chmn. devel. com. bd. dirs., 1976-85, vice chmn. bd., 1982-86, sec. to nat. bd. Served with USMC, 1954-57. Mem. ABA, Iowa State Bar Assn., Polk County Bar Assn., Assn. Trial Lawyers Am., Iowa Trial Lawyers Assn., Iowa Acad. Trial Lawyers, Iowa Workers' Compensation Attys., Iowa Def. Counsel Assn., Def. Research Inst., Lawyer and Pilots Bar Assn., Aircraft Owners and Pilots Assn., Order of Coif, Delta Sigma Chi, Omicron Delta Kappa, Beta Gamma Sigma. Republican. Methodist. Clubs: Embassy, Hyperion, Pioneer Gun, Chaine Des Rotisseurs (vice chancelier Argentier du Bailliage De Des Moines). Office: Peddicord & Wharton 300 Fleming Bldg Des Moines IA 50309

PEDERSEN, ANN LEE, accountant; b. Galesburg, Ill., Apr. 19, 1960; d. James Joseph and Esther Suzanne (Marvel) McGovern; m. Mark David Pedersen, Aug. 31, 1985. BA in Acctg. and Bus. Adminstrn., Augustana Coll., Rock Island, Ill., 1982; MBA, No. Ill. U., 1986. CPA, Ill. Acct. Iowa-Ill. Gas & Electric Co., Davenport, Iowa, 1982-83, Commonwealth Edison Co., Chgo., 1985—. Vol. DuPage Convalescent Ctr., Wheaton, 1986—. Avocations: travel, bicycling, reading, crafts. Home: 106 S Williston St Wheaton IL 60187 Office: Commonwealth Edison Co PO Box 767 Chicago IL 60690

PEDERSEN, KENNETH NORMAN, insurance executive; b. Abilene, Tex., June 7, 1943; s. Christen J. and Eva Constance (Chaiser) P.; m. Jane Ann Pasaka, May 3, 1969; children: Brian, Beth, Christine. BBA, U. Wis., Whitewater, 1965. CPA, Ill., Wis., Tex. Sr. acct. Ernst & Ernst, Chgo., 1965-71; v.p. fin. Wrap-On Co., Inc., Chgo., 1971-82; v.p. fin., treas. EAC Industries, Chgo., 1982-83; v.p. fin. Costain Holdings, Inc., Chgo., 1983-85; v.p. fin. and adminstrn. Associated Agys., Inc., Chgo., 1985—; bd. dirs. AAI Syndicate, Chgo. Bd. dirs. Tom Russell Charitable Found., Chgo., 1975-82; trustee Barrington (Ill.) Twp. Bd., 1973-75, Luth. Ch. of Atonement, Barrington, 1977-80. Mem. Am. Inst. CPA's, Ill. CPA Soc. Republican. Clubs: Anvil (East Dundee, Ill.), Forest Grove. Home: 232 Eastern Barrington IL 60010

PEDERSEN, VAGN MOELLER, engineering company executive; b. Tommerup, Denmark, Mar. 25, 1942; came to U.S., 1971; s. Ejnar M. and Benny M. (Mortensen) P.; m. Hee Jung, Feb. 28, 1981; 1 child, Thomas. MS in Dairy Tech., U. Agr., Copenhagen, 1970. Mgr. research and devel. Charles Hansens Lab., Copenhagen, 1970-71; mgr. prodn. Charles Hansens Lab., Milw., 1971-79; sales mgr. Far East Danish Turnkey Dairies, Seoul, Korea, 1979-82; mgr. prodn. Danish Turnkey Dairies, Muscat, Oman, 1982, Plumrose, Maracaibo, Venezuela, 1982-83; from v.p. to pres. Primodan Tech., Inc., Cedarburg, Wis., 1983—. Served to sgt. Civil Def., 1964-66, Denmark. Lutheran. Avocations: hunting, outdoor activities, tennis, gardening. Home: 922 W Zedler Ln Mequon WI 53092 Office: Primodan Tech Inc PO Box 398 Cedarburg WI 53012

PEDERSON, ARNOLD S., chemical company executive. Pres. Pam Oil Inc., Sioux Falls, S.D. Office: Pam Oil Inc 1420 N Minnesota Ave Sioux Falls SD 57104 *

PEDERSON, WAYNE DOUGLAS, college administrator; b. Kennedy, Minn., May 9, 1941; s. Harvey Norwood and Dorothy Marie (Turner) P.; m. Lynette Yvonne Prosser, Sept. 1, 1962; children—Tamra, Carey, Kristin. B.S., Concordia Coll., 1963. C.P.A., Minn. Tchr. Warren Pub. Schs., Minn., 1963-66; acct. Adrian Helgeson, Mpls., 1966-69; controller Augsburg Coll., Mpls., 1969-77, v.p. fin., 1977—. Mem. Am. Inst. C.P.A.s, Minn. Soc. C.P.A.s. Avocations: hunting, running, singing. Home: 9265 Annapolis Ln Maple Grove MN 55369 Office: Augsburg Coll 731 21st Ave S Minneapolis MN 55454

PEDICINI, LOUIS JAMES, manufacturing company executive; b. Detroit, June 29, 1926; s. Louis I. and Myra Ann (Bergan) P.; m. Ellen Sylvia Mulden, June 5, 1948; 1 child, Eric Louis. B.S.E.E., Wayne U., 1955. Dept. head Gen. Motors Corp., 1948-58; exec. v.p. Lester B. Knight & Assos., Inc., Chgo., 1959-76; exec. v.p. ops. Pullman Trailmobile, Chgo., 1976-81; mng. dir. Ingersoll Engrs. Inc., Rockford, Ill., 1981—; pres. George Fischer Foundry Systems Inc., Holly, Mich., 1982—. Served with U.S. Army, 1944-46. Fellow Inst. Brit. Foundrymen; mem. Am. Foundrymen's Soc. (past dir.). Republican. Clubs: Skokie Country (Glencoe, Ill.); Plaza (Chgo.). Office: 407 Hadley St Holly MI 48442

PEDIGO, HOWARD KENNETH, engineer; b. Charleston, Ill., Aug. 5, 1931; s. Clarence and Cecil (Elliot) P.; B.S. in Civil Engring., Rose Poly. Inst., 1953; M.B.A., Ohio State U., 1963; m. Doris Dean Mullins, Mar. 21, 1954; children: Susan Kay, John Jay. Stress analyst Bendix Corp., South Bend, Ind., 1955-61; project engr. Wright Field, Dayton, Ohio, 1961-63; project mgr. TRW Corp., Cleve., 1963-64; exec. v.p. Universal Tank & Iron Co., Indpls., 1964-85; chief engr. Ind. Dept. Natural Resources, 1985—. Chmn., United Way Hendricks County (Ind.), 1973; bd. dirs. United Way Greater Indpls., 1975-77; bd. indsl. adviser Rose-Hulman Inst. Served to 1st lt. U.S. Army, 1953-55. Registered profl. engr., Ala., Ill., Ind., N.J., Ohio, Tenn., Wis. Mem. ASCE, Am. Water Works Assn. (steel tank com.), Steel Plate Fabricators Assn., Rose Tech. Alumni (class agt. 1971-73), Lambda Chi Alpha. Methodist. Lodge: Elks. Home: 633 Elm Dr Plainfield IN 46168 Office: 11221 Rockville Rd Indianapolis IN 46231

PEDOTO, GERALD JOSEPH, product acceptance specialist; b. Jersey City, Jan. 5, 1948; s. Salvatore Joseph and Rosalie (Benigno) P.; m. Karen Sue Knutty, June 28, 1975; children: Deborah Louise, Donald Lee, Timothy Scott. BS, Bowling (Ohio) Green State U., 1970; MBA, U. Akron, 1976. Cert. mgr., quality engr. Trainee indsl. engring. Timken Co., Canton, Ohio, 1970, asso. indsl. engr., 1972-73, supervisory candidate, 1973-74, foreman product inspection, 1974-75, supr. indirect labor, 1975-80, supr. heat treatment, 1980-82. Active United Way, YMCA fund drs. Served with U.S. Army, 1970-72, Korea. Nat. Mgmt. Assn., Assn. MBA Execs., Am. Soc. for Quality Control, Alpha Tau Omega, Beta Gamma Sigma, Omicron Delta Kappa. Republican. Mem. United Ch. of Christ. Home: 7765 Peachmont Ave NW North Canton OH 44720 Office: Canton Gen Offices Timken Co 1835 Dueber Ave SW Canton OH 44706

PEEBLES, MARY JOSEPHINE, psychologist; b. La Jolla, Calif., Dec. 21, 1950; d. David Coleman and Violet (Pankey) P. BA, Wellesley (Mass.) Coll., 1972; PhD, Case Western Res. U., 1977; postgrad., Topeka Inst. Psychoanalysis, 1980—. Lic. psychologist, Kans.; diplomate Am. Bd. Profl. Psychology. Intern clin. psychology Case Western Res. U. Med. Sch., Cleve., 1975-76; staff psychologist Gulf Coast Regional Mental Health Mental Retardation Community Service Ctr., Galveston, Tex., 1976-77; postdoct. fellow in child psychology Child and Adolescent Psychiatry div. U. Tex., Galveston, 1977-78; postdoct. fellow in clin. adult psychology The Menninger Found., Topeka, 1978-80, staff psychologist, faculty, supr., 1980—. Contbr. articles to profl. jours. Mem. adv. bd. Citizens for a Drug Free Community, Topeka, 1986-87. NIMH traineeship, 1972-75. Mem. Am. Psychol. Assn. (divs. psychoanalysis, psychotherapy), Kans. Psychol. Assn.(bd. govs., 1986-89), Internat. Neuro-Psychol. Soc., Soc. Clin. and Exptl. Hypnosis, Phi Beta Kappa. Avocations: classical piano, ballet, art history. Office: The Menninger Found PO Box 829 Topeka KS 66601

PEEK, CHERYL LARICE, health care administrator, psychotherapist; b. Greenville, Tenn., Aug. 23, 1949; d. Maurice Rudolph and Gloria Patricia (Manuel) Treadwell; m. Robert Peek, Nov. 24, 1979. BA, Fisk U., 1971; MA, U. Chgo., 1973. Cert. social worker. Therapist Michael Reese Hosp., Chgo., 1974-76; dir. out-patient services Gary (Ind.) Mental Health, 1976-78, asst. exec. dir., 1978-84; assoc exec dir. Easter Seal Soc., Chgo., 1984—; pvt. practice psychotherapy, Chgo., 1980—; cons. Sullivan House Child Welfare Agy., Chgo., 1984—. Mem. Acad. Cert. Social Workers, Am. Orthopsychiat. Assoc., Am. Mgmt. Assn., Nat. Assn. Social Workers, Phi Beta Kappa. Democrat. Roman Catholic. Avocations: cooking, sewing. Home: 6336 Forest Ave Hammond IN 46324 Office: Easter Seal Soc Met Chgo 220 S State Suite 1716 Chicago IL 60604

PEEK, DUANE FRANCIS, insurance company underwriting executive; b. Breese, Ill., Jan. 2, 1951; s. Henry G. and Mary Ann (Hustedde) P.; m. Charlene Thorp, Aug. 11, 1973; children: Holly, Daniel. Grad. high sch., Breese, 1969. Br. mgr. Household Fin., Cedar Rapids, 1971-75; with sales and underwriting Economy Fire and Casualty, Freeport, Ill., 1975-79; sales rep. Transamerica Ins., St. Louis, 1979-82, Fireman's Fund, Springfield, Ill., 1982-83; mgr. underwriting dept. Fireman's Fund Ins., Bettendorf, Iowa, 1983—. Republican. Roman Catholic. Avocations: golf, fishing, hunting, tennis, water sports. Home: 5467 Taylor St Davenport IA 52806 Office: Fireman's Fund Ins Corp PO Box 738 Bettendorf IA 52722

PEEK, ROLAND MANLEY, clinical psychologist, educator; b. Freeborn County, Minn., Nov. 2, 1920; s. Charles Albert and Alpha Luella (Johnson) P.; m. Mary Jane Larson, Mar. 29, 1946; children: Charles John, Anne Elizabeth, Thomas Roland. AA, Albert Lea Jr. Coll., 1940; BS, U. Minn., 1942, PhD, 1968. Lic. cons. psychologist, Minn. Chief psychologist Hastings (Minn.) State Hosp., 1951-68; chief psychol. services, coordinator research Minn. Dept. Pub. Welfare, St. Paul, 1968-73, dir. research, evaluation research mgr., 1973-78, dir. client protection office, 1978-84; clin. asst. prof. psychology U. Minn., Mpls., 1973—; pvt. practice mental health cons. St. Paul Pk., Minn., 1984—; officer Minn. Bd. Psychology, Mpls. and St. Paul, 1964-73; mem. Gov.'s Suicide Study Commn., St. Paul, 1966-69, Hosp. Rev. Bd., Anoka, Minn., 1986—. Author: (manual) A Scoring System for the Bender Gestalt Test, 1951, Organization and Structure of the MMPI, 1959; contbr. articles to profl. jours. Chmn. Town Planning Commn., Grey Cloud Twp., Minn., 1963-74, bd. suprs., 1975-84; plan com. Wash. County (Minn.) Park System, 1985-86. Served to sgt. USAF, 1942-45, PTO. Recipient Good Neighbor award, Sta. WCCO-Radio, Minn., 1982. Mem. Am. Psychol. Assn. (visiting psychologist 1969-72, council rep. 1965-67, 78-79), Minn. Psychol. Assn. (pres. 1963-68, exec. council 1961-70,citation 1982, Outstanding Service award 1986.). Democrat. Avocation: photography, hiking. Home and Office: 10559 Grey Cloud Island Dr S Saint Paul Park MN 55071

PEIRCE, PETER RAYMOND, architect; b. Toledo, Sept. 28, 1948; s. Richard H. and Elizabeth (Seeley) P.; m. Susan Oliver, June 24, 1972; m. 2d, Cherry Wright, June 23, 1979; children: Joellen Birkenkamp, Tori Kwiatkowski, Danielle Kwiatkowski. Student, U. Va., 1966-67; BS, Ohio State U., 1971; postgrad., U. Toledo Sch. Bus., 1971-74; BArch cum laude, U. Detroit, 1985; student, San Francisco Inst. Architecture and Urban Studies, 1982; student sci. exchange program, Warsaw Tech. U., Poland, 1983. Project mgr. Peirce Construction Co., Holland, Ohio, 1971-81, ptnr., 1976-82; assoc. Richard Troy and Assocs. Architects, Toledo, 1983-84; pres. PDG Architects, Inc., Toledo, 1984—; v.p. Peirce Design Group Architects, Inc., Toledo, 1986—. Mem. AIA. United Methodist. Clubs: Toledo; Catawba Island (Port Clinton, Ohio). Office: Peirce Design Group Inc 232 10th St Toledo OH 43624

PEIRCE, ROGER DALE, metal processing executive; b. Milw., Sept. 2, 1937; s. Earl Lincoln and Dale (Spangler) P.; m. Elizabeth Lane, Sept. 11, 1965; children: Christopher, Brenda. AB, Harvard U., 1959; MBA, U. Wis., 1962. Mem. acctg. staff to ptnr. Arthur Andersen & Co., Milw., 1961-85; mng. ptnr. Arthur Andersen & Co., Tucson, 1985-86; exec. v.p. Super Steel Products, Milw., 1986—. Chmn. Milw. Performing Arts Ctr., 1980-85; pres. Channel 10/36 Friends, Inc., Milw., 1984-85, Wis. Humane Soc., Milw., 1979-80, United Performing Arts Fund, MIlw., 1972-73. Served to cpl. USAR, 1962-63. Recipient Spl. Service to the Arts award Milw. Civic Alliance, 1985. Mem. Am. Inst. CPA's, Ariz. Inst. CPA's, Wis. Inst. CPA's. Club: Milw. Country, Tucson Country, Hillsboro (Fla.). Avocations: golf, tennis, bridge, travel, food. Office: Super Steel Products 7900 W Tower Ave Milwaukee WI 53223

PEIRSON, WALTER RUSSELL, oil company executive; b. Rock Island, Ill., 1926; married. Grad., U. Ill. With Standard Oil Co. (Ind.), 1955-61, Gen. Gas Corp., 1961-64, Tuloma Gas Products Co., Inc., 1964-68; v.p. mktg. Am. Oil Co., Chgo., 1968-71, exec. v.p. mktg., refining, transp. and supply, 1971-74; pres. Amoco Oil Co. (formerly Standard Oil Co. (Ind.), Chgo., 1974-78, exec. v.p., 1978—, also dir.; dir. Am. Nst. Bank, Chgo. Served with USAAF, 1943-46. Office: Amoco Corp 200 E Randolph Dr Chicago IL 60601

PEISER, IRVING JOSEPH, optometrist; b. N.Y.C., June 23, 1926; m. Natalie Diamond, Aug. 11, 1957; children: Mark, Daniel. AB, Columbia U., 1950; OD, Ill. Coll. Optometry, Chgo., 1954. Pvt. practice optometry Riverside, Ill., 1954—. Contbg. author: Vision: Its Impact on Learning, 1978. Served with USN, 1944-46, PTO. Fellow Coll. Optometrists in Vision Devel. (Service award 1975); mem. West Suburban Optometric Soc. (pres. 1970-71). Office: 2726 S Harlem Ave Riverside IL 60546

PEKOW, EUGENE, hotel company executive; b. Chgo., Aug. 11, 1930; s. Philip M. and Celia (Katz) P.; m. Esta Bette Epstein, June 29, 1952 (div. 1980); children: Charles Thomas Wayne, Penelope Susan, Cynthia Ann; m. Barbara B. Hirsch, Mar. 16, 1980. A.B. cum laude, Brown U., 1952; J.D., Northwestern U., 1955. Bar: Ill. 1955. Partner Acorn Tire & Supply Co., Chgo., 1955-65; sec.-treas., dir. Acorn Tire & Supply Co. (and subsidiaries), 1965—; v.p. Exec. House Hotels, Chgo., 1957-68; pres. Midland Hotel Co., Chgo., 1969—, Acorn Mgmt. Co., 1974—; bd. dirs., pres. Midland Bldg. Corp., Chgo.; mem. editorial bd. Chgo. Reporter, 1985—. Mem. nat. council Bus. Execs. Move for Vietnam Peace; bd. dirs. Deerfield Twp. Voters Assn., 1964-68; treas., bd. dirs. Bus. and Profl. People for Pub. Interest; bd. dirs. U. Chgo. Found. for Emotionally Disturbed Children, Community Renewal Soc., Bus. Execs. for Nat. Security; trustee Mt. Sinai Hosp. Med. Center, Schwab Rehab. Inst.; chmn. bd. dirs. Sears Roebuck YMCA, 1980-83. Mem. Am. Technion Soc. (dir. 1976-82), Greater Chgo. Hotel and Motel Assn. (bd. dirs.1979-85). Club: Standard (Chgo.). Office: The Midland Hotel 176 W Adams St Chicago IL 60603

PELIKAN, DANIEL GERARD, lawyer; b. St. Louis, Jan. 11, 1958; s. Richard R. and Mary E. (McKean) P.; m. Lisa White, Nov. 17, 1984. BJ, U. Mo., 1980; JD, St. Louis U., 1984. Bar: Mo. 1985, Ill., U.S. Dist. Ct. (ea. and we. dists.) Mo. 1985. Assoc. Thompson and Mitchell, St. Louis, 1984—; county counselor St. Charles County, Mo., 1986—. Mem. ABA, Mo. Bar Assn., Bar Assn. Met. St. Louis, St. Charles County Bar Assn. Home: 310 Jefferson Saint Charles MO 63301 Office: Thompson and Mitchell 200 N 3d St Saint Charles MO 63301

PELL, DENNIS BERNARD, real estate appraiser; b. Cleve., Oct. 9, 1948; s. Clarence B. and Rita Rose (Sheehan) P.; m. Patricia J. Strosnider, Apr. 14, 1972; children: Ann Sheehan, Brian Aubrey. BA in History, Coll. St. Thomas, 1970, MA in Edn., 1974, MBA in Finance, 1976. Staff appraiser Soc. Nat. Bank, Cleve., 1976-78; chief appraiser, asst. v.p. Ameritrust Bank, Cleve., 1978-87, v.p., 1987—. Mem. Am. Inst. Real Estate Appraisers. Democrat. Roman Catholic. Avocations: jogging, reading. Office: Ameritrust Bank Nat Assn 900 Euclid Ave Cleveland OH 44101

PELL, MARY CHASE (CHASEY), civic worker; b. Binghamton, N.Y., May 23, 1915; d. Charles Orlando and Mary (Lane) Chase; m. Wilbur F. Pell, Jr., Sept. 14, 1940; children—Wilbur F., Charles Chase. B.A., Smith Coll., 1937. Case worker Binghamton State Hosp., 1937; sociology tchr. Charles W. Wilson Meml. Hosp., Johnson City, N.Y., 1938; commentator travel and industry, sta. WSVL, Shelbyville, Ind., 1962-67. Contbr. articles to pubs. Chmn. Ind. Fund Raising Com. for Smith Coll., Indpls., 1961; bd. dirs. Nat. Mental Health Assn., 1961-79, pres. 1976-77; pres. Ind. Mental Health Meml. Found., Indpls., 1964-65, Mental Health Assn. Ind., Indpls., 1962-63; commr. Ind. Mental Health Planning Commn., Indpls., 1964-65; mem. Central Ind. Task Force on Mental Health Planning, 1965-66; mem. Ind. Com. on Nursing, Indpls., 1965-66, Central Ind. Regional Mental Health Planning Com., 1968; chmn. Manpower Conf. on Mental Health, Washington, 1969; del. Ind. Republican Conv., 1951; vice chmn. Shelbyville Rep. Com., 1951; sec. Ind. Com. for Rockefeller, 1969-70; pres. Indpls. Smith Coll. Club, 1969-70; participant Nat. Health Forum of Nat. Health Council, N.Y.C., 1971; pres. Mental Health Assn. Ill., Springfield, 1975; mem. Gov.'s Commn. for Revision of Mental Health Code Ill., 1975-76; v.p. for N.Am., World Fedn. for Mental Health, 1977-87; bd. dirs. Vis. Nurse Assn. Evanston (Ill.), 1975-87, v.p. 1981-84, pres., 1984-86; community mental health adviser Jr. League of Chgo., 1979-83; mem. Ill. Guardianship and Advocacy Commn., 1978-86, chmn., 1981; mem. adv. com. to sect. on psychiatry and the law, Rush-Presbyn.-St. Luke's Med. Ctr., Chgo., 1978-86;

gov. Task Force on Future of Mental Health in Ill., 1986-87; mem. home health adv. com. to Dept. Pub. Health, State of Ill., 1982-87; pres. Mental Health Assn. Chgo., 1983-84; pres. Smith Coll. Alumnae of Chgo., 1984-86; mem. Women's Bd. Northwestern U., Aux. of Evanston and Glenbrook Hosps., University Guild of Evanston, Jr. League Evanston, pres. Ind. Lawyers' Wives, Indpls., 1959-60; treas. Nat. Lawyers' Wives, 1961-62. Recipient Outstanding Citizen award Shelby County C. of C., 1959-60, Outstanding Vol. of Yr. award Indpls. Jr. League, 1962, Leadership award Mental Health Assn. Ind., 1971, Arts and Humanities award, Shelbyville Rotary Club, 1981; named One of Ten Most Newsworthy Women In Ind., Indpls. News, 1962, Disting. Leader in Vol. Mental Health Movement, Ill. Ho. of Reps., 1976, Miss. Col., 1976, Ala. Lt. Gov., 1980. Presbyterian. Clubs: Fortnightly (Chgo.); Garden of Evanston, Jr. League of Evanston. Home: 1427 Hinman Ave Evanston IL 60201

PELL, WILBUR FRANK, JR., senior U.S. circuit ct. judge; b. Shelbyville, Ind., Dec. 6, 1915; s. Wilbur Frank and Nelle (Dickerson) P.; m. Mary Lane Chase, Sept. 14, 1940; children: Wilbur Frank III, Charles Chase. A.B., Ind. U., 1937, LL.D. (hon.), 1981; LL.B. cum laude, Harvard U., 1940; LL.D., Yonsei U., Seoul, Korea, 1972, John Marshall Sch. Law, 1973. Bar: Ind. 1940. Practice law Shelbyville, 1940-42, 45-70; spl. agt. FBI, 1942-45; sr. ptnr. Pell & Good, 1949-56, Pell & Matchett, 1956-70; judge 7th Circuit, U.S. Ct. Appeals, 1970—, now sr. judge; dep. atty. gen., Ind., 1953-55; dir., chmn. Shelby Nat. Bank, 1947-70. Bd. dirs. Shelbyville Community Chest, 1947-49, Shelby County Fair Assn., 1951-53; dir. Shelby County Tb Assn., 1948-70, pres., 1965-66; dist. chmn. Boy Scouts Am., 1956-57; mem. pres.'s council Nat. Coll. Edn., 1972—; dir. Westminster Found., Ind. U.; hon. dir. Korean Legal Center. Fellow Am. Coll. Probate Counsel, Am. Bar Found.; mem. ABA (Judge Edward R. Finch Law Day U.S.A. Speech award 1973, ho. of dels. 1962-63), Ind. Bar Assn. (pres. 1962-63, chmn. ho. of dels. 1968-69), Fed. Bar Assn., Ill. Bar Assn., Shelby County Bar Assn. (pres. 1957-58), 7th Fed. Circuit Bar Assn., Am. Judicature Soc., Am. Coun. Assn., Shelby County C. of C. (dir. 1947-49), Nat. Conf. Bar Presidents, Riley Meml. Assn., Ind. Soc. Chgo. (pres. 1978-79), Sagamore of Wabash, Blue Key, Kappa Sigma, Alpha Phi Omega, Theta Alpha Phi, Tau Kappa Alpha, Phi Alpha Delta (hon. mem.). Republican. Presbyterian (elder, deacon). Clubs: Evanston (dist. gov. 1952-53, internat. dir. 1959-61), Union League, Legal (pres. 1976-77), Law (Chgo.) (pres. 1984-85). Office: 219 S Dearborn St Room 2760 Chicago IL 60604

PELLEGRINI, DONNA MARIE, finance executive; b. Providence, May 24, 1958; d. Vincent Domenic and Florence Mae (Bourgoin) P. BS in Econs., Vassar Coll., 1980. Credit analyst RIHT Fin. Corp., Providence, 1980-82, corp. loan officer, 1982-84; corp. loan officer BNE Corp., Hartford, Conn., 1984-85, nat. team leader, corp. loan officer, 1985-86; office mgr., v.p. Chgo. Loan Prodn. office BNE Corp., Chgo., 1986—. Mem. Nat. Assn. for Female Execs., Women in Mgmt., Inc. Club: University (Chgo.). Avocations: tennis, swimming, skiing. Home: 100 E Walton St Chicago IL 60611 Office: Bank of New Eng Corp 208 S LaSalle St Chicago IL 60604

PELLERITO, PETER MICHAEL, university administrator; b. Detroit, May 13, 1945; s. Sam Joseph and Rosalie Ann (Palazzola) P.; m. Lisa Ann Brock; children—Sam Brock, Billie Ann. B.S., Calif. State U.-Los Angeles; M.S., Mich. State U. Reporter, Los Angeles Times, 1968-69; asst. dean Northwestern Coll., Traverse City, Mich., 1970-75; broadcaster WZZM-TV, Grand Rapids, Mich., 1976-78; dir. community relations U. Mich., Ann Arbor, 1978—. Editor, writer Travel Mag., 1978-80. Pres., Am. Lung Assn. Mich., 1983-85. dirs. Washtenaw County United Way, 1987-88, Washtenaw Devel. Council, 1987-88; Plymouth City Planning Com., 1987—. Recipient Exptl. Achievement award Council Advancement and Support Higher Edn., 1981; Silver Anvil award Pub. Relations Soc. Am., 1982. Mem. Council Advancement and Support Higher Edn., Ann Arbor C. of C. (v.p. 1985, pres. elect 1987). Office: U Mich 2040 Fleming Bldg Ann Arbor MI

PELLETIER, ALCID MILTON, psychologist; b. Bridgeport, Conn., Aug. 27, 1926; s. Alcid L. and Mary Jane (Auger) P.; children: Paulette, Alcid Milton, Lionel, Debra, Jon, Jacques, Angelique. AA, Graceland Coll., 1951; BA in Psychology, U. Mo., Kansas City, 1971; MA in Psychology, Western Mich. U., 1972, EdD, 1975. Ordained to ministry, Reorganized Ch.of Jesus Christ of Latter Day Saints, 1951. Assigned to transfers, Ont., Can., Ill., Pa., Mo., Mich., 1951-72; chief forensic psychology, Kent County Jail, Grand Rapids, Mich., 1972-74; asst. to med. dir., clin. coordinator, chief psychologist, chief admissions officer, Kent Oaks Hosp., Grand Rapids, 1974-78; adminstr. Mich. Med. Weight Control Clinics, Grand Rapids, Lansing, Kalamazoo, 1978; owner, pres. Ctr. for Human Potential, P.C., Grand Rapids, 1978—; pvt. practice psychology, Grand Rapids; cons. Family Services Assn., Grand Rapids, 1972-74; instr. Calhoun County Juvenile Ct., 1974-77, Grand Valley State Colls., 1975, Western Mich. U., 1974; instr. nursing Butterworth Gen. Hosp., 1974; instr. New Clinic for Women, 1974, 77-78; condr. workshops for Mich. Supreme Ct., annually 1973-78, probate cts., Mich. Dept. Social Services, 1977, 78. Mem. sheriff's adv. com., 1976-78; mem. Human Devel. Assn., Mt. Vernon, Ill., 1959, Kent County Mental Health Assn., Mich. Soc. for Mental Health. Served with U.S. Army, 1945-46. Recipient certificate of appreciation for profl. services Western Mich. U., 1974; lic. psychologist, Mich., also certified rehab. counselor. Mem. Am., Mich. psychol. assns., Am., Mich. personnel and guidance assns., Assn. Counselor Edn. and Supervision, Am. Rehab. Counselors Assn., Mich., Am. socs. clin. hypnosis, Insts. Religion and Health. Republican. Contbr. articles to profl. jours., speeches to confs. in fields of use of hypnosis as treatment. Home: 2951 Vineland NE Grand Rapids MI 49508 Office: 2953 Vineland NE Grand Rapids MI 49508

PELLETT, THOMAS LAWRENCE, commercial banking executive; b. Mpls., Apr. 7, 1958; s. Thomas Rowand and Anne (Iffert) P.; m. Laurie Sue Lodes, May 4, 1984. BBA, So. Meth. U., 1980; postgrad. Bus. Adminstrn., So. Ill. U., 1980—. Avocations: motorsports, bicyclist, golf. Home: 525 Selma Ave Webster Groves MO 63119-4141 Office: Mfrs Hanover/The CIT Group 7733 Forsyth Blvd Suite 1280 Saint Louis MO 63105

PELLHAM, GALEN BONNIS, architect; b. Ft. Scott, Kans., June 15, 1947; s. Arley Bonnis and Clara Lorraine (Hendricks) P.; m. Marleen England, June 6, 1971; children: Amelia, Melanie, Christopher Mark. BArch, U. Ark., 1971. Assoc. Richard P. Stahl, AIA, Springfield, Mo., 1971-77; pres. Galen B. Pellham, Architect, Springfield, Mo., 1977-79, Pellham-Phillips-Hagerman Architects & Engrs., Inc. (formerly Pellham-Phillips Architects & Engrs., Inc.), Springfield, Mo., 1979—. Pres. Friends of Zoo, Springfield, 1978-80; bd. dirs. Srpingfield Little Theater, 1983-85, Chameleon Puppet Theatre, Springfield, 1986-87, Springfield Area Arts Council, 1986—. Recipient Nat. Recognition award, Prestressed Concrete Inst., 1984. Mem. AIA (sec. Springfield chpt. 1984-85, bd. dirs. 1985-86, design award 1984, 86), Mo. Council Architects (bd. dirs., sec. 1984-87). Republican. Methodist. Avocations: running, golf, tennis, raquetball, water and snow skiing. Office: Pellham-Phillips-Hagerman Architects & Engrs Inc 111 S Glenstone Springfield MO 65804

PELNAR, ROBERT ROGER, accounting company executive; b. Chgo., Sept. 27, 1943; s. Frank Ludwig and Laura Wanda (Patkowa) P.; m. Antoinette Dolores Nazarowski, Sept. 26, 1987. BS, No. Ill. U., 1969; MBA, Loyola U., Chgo., 1974. CPA, Ill. Fin. mgr. Motorola Inc., Schaumburg, Ill., 1969-76; mng. ptnr. Pelnar & Gross, CPA, Schaumburg, 1976—. Mem. N.W. Assn. Commerce and Industry, Schaumburg, 1977. Served with U.S. Army, 1966-68. Mem. Am. Inst. CPA's, Ill. Soc. CPA's. Republican. Lutheran. Lodge: Rotary (treas. Schaumburg 1978, bd. dirs. 1979). Avocations: golf, skiing. Office: Pelnar & Gross CPA 941A N Plum Grove Rd Schaumburg IL 60173

PELOQUIN, ALFRED LEO, editor; b. Bay City, Mich., Sept. 3, 1921; s. Albert Paul and Edna (LaLonde) P.; m. Eva I. Frackowiak, Nov. 16, 1957; 1 child, Albert Francis. Grad., Sacred Heart Sem. Reporter Bay City Times, Mich., 1946-59, city editor, 1959-74; met. editor Saginaw News, Mich., 1974-80, mng. editor, 1980-81; editor Flint Jour., Mich., 1981—. Bd. dirs. Flint Inst. Arts, 1983—, Internat. Inst. Flint, 1983—, Flint Urban Coalition, Flint Exec. Service Corps.; mem. citizens adv. bd., U. Mich.-Flint, 1983—. Served to 2d lt. U.S. Army, 1945-46. Mem. Am. Soc. Newspaper Editors (com. 1983—), Mich. Press Assn., Sigma Delta Chi. Roman Catholic. Clubs: University (Flint); Saginaw Valley Press (founder); Atlas Valley Country; Bay City Yacht; Detroit Press. Avocations: sailing; golf; skiing; racquetball; classical music. Office: The Flint Journal 200 E 1st St Flint MI 48502

PELTIER, GEORGE LEONARD, plastic surgeon; b. Mpls., Dec. 25, 1945; s. Leonard Frances and Marian Olive (Kani) P.; m. Kay Lorraine Christensen, Dec. 27, 1966; children: David, Eric, Sarah. BA in Chemistry, Lawrence U., Appleton, Wis., 1967; MD, U. Kans., Kansas City, 1971. Diplomate Am. Bd. Surgery, Am. Bd. Plastic Surgery. Practice medicine specializing in plastic surgery Mpls., 1980—; mem. staff Hennepin County Med. Ctr., Mpls., 1980—, chief plastic surgery, 1983—; mem. staff Met. Med. Ctr., Mpls., St. Mary's Hosp., Mpls., Fairview-Southdale Hosp., Mpls., Mt. Sinai Hosp., Mpls.; chmn. nomination com. Mpls. Med. Research Found., 1985. Contbr. articles to profl. jours. Served to maj. U.S. Army, 1973-75. Fellow ACS; mem. AMA, Minn. Med. Assn., Hennepin County Med. Soc., Am. Soc. Plastic and Reconstructive Surgeons, Minn. Acad. Plastic Surgeons, Mpls. Surgical Soc., Am. Burn Assn. Office: Hennepin County Med Ctr Surgery Dept 701 Park Ave S Minneapolis MN 55415

PELTON, RUSSELL MEREDITH, JR., lawyer; b. Chgo., May 14, 1938; s. Russell Meredith and Mildred Helen (Baumrucker) P.; m. Patty Jane Rader, Aug. 12, 1961; children—James, Thomas, Michael, Margaret. B.A., DePauw U., 1960; J.D., U. Chgo., 1963. Bar: Ill. 1963, U.S. Supreme Ct. 1979. Assoc., Peterson, Ross, Schloerb & Seidel and predecessors, Chgo., 1966-72, ptnr., 1972—; co-founder, gen. counsel Chgo. Opportunities Industrialization Ctr., 1969-83; gen. counsel Delta Dental Plan Ill., 1979—; bd. dirs. First United Life Ins. Co., 1979-82. Pres. Wilmette Jaycees, 1970; chmn. Wilmette Sch. Bd. Caucus, 1970-71; Wilmette Dist. 39 Bd. Edn., 1972-80; bd. dirs. Wilmette United Way, 1980-86, campaign chmn., 1983-85, pres., 1985-86. Served to capt. USAF, 1963-66. Mem. Chgo. Bar Assn., Ill. Bar Assn., ABA, Ill. Trial Lawyers Assn., Soc. Trial Lawyers. Home: 607 9th St Wilmette IL 60091 Office: 200 E Randolph Dr Suite 7300 Chicago IL 60601

PELVIT, LESTER, educator, principal; b. Wydmere, N.D., Apr. 6, 1923; s. Albert and Theressa (Krieser) P. Cert. in Bus., Sci. Sch., Wahpeton, N.D., 1942; BS in Edn., N.D. State Coll., 1956; MS in Ednl. Adminstrn., U. Minn., 1976. Cert. elem. tchr., secondary tchr., Minn., N.D., S.D. Tchr. Mont. Schs., Sidney, 1960-70; elem prin. Bur. Indian Affairs Sch., Twin Valley, Minn., 1970-80, Cheyenne River Reservation, N.D., 1980—; Mem. ednl. com. Sta. KFME-TV, Fargo, N.D., 1970-80. Mem. County Mus., Wahpeton, N.D., 1980—. Avocations: photography, travel. Home: Rt 1 Box 235 Wyndmere ND 58081

PELZER, CHARLES FRANCIS, geneticist, biology educator, researcher; b. Detroit, June 5, 1935; s. Francis Joseph and Edna Dorothy (Ladach) P.; m. Veronica Ann Killeen, July 7, 1972; 1 child, Mary Elizabeth. BS in Biology, U. Detroit, 1957; PhD in Human Genetics, U. Mich., 1965. Postdoctoral fellow Wabash Coll., Crawfordsville, Ind., 1965-66; instr. U. Detroit, 1966-68; asst. prof. Saginaw Valley State Coll., University Center, Mich., 1969-74, assoc. prof., 1974-79, prof., 1979—; research assoc. Mich. State U., East Lansing, 1976-77; research fellow Henry Ford Hosp., Detroit, 1982-83; v.p. Saginaw Valley Retinititis Pigmentosa Found., Mich., 1979-81; vis. scientist Am. Inst. Biol. Scis., Washington, 1975-78; grant reviewer U.S. Dept. Edn., Washington, 1984-87, Contbr. articles to profl. jours. Recipient Alumni award Saginaw Valley State Coll. Alumni Assn., 1971; grantee Ford Hosp. Found., 1983, Mich. State U., 1977, Saginaw Valley State Coll. Found., 1979-82, 83-85, 86—, Kettering Found., 1965-66, Kellogg Found., 1961, NIH, 1961-64, Monsanto Co. research grant, 1987. Fellow Human Biology Council; mem. Am. Soc. Human Genetics, Genetics Soc. Am., N.Y. Acad. Sci., Electrophorisis Soc., Nat. Assn. Biology Tchrs., others. Home: 4900 Schneider Saginaw Twp MI 48603 Office: Saginaw Valley State Coll 2250 Pierce Rd University Center MI 48710

PELZER, GERALD EDWARD, investment banking executive; b. Aurora, Ill., Sept. 11, 1938; s. George E. and Hazel L. (Brauer) P.; m. Patricia Mary Ellis, June 7, 1986; 1 child, Jennifer. BSCE, Valparaiso U., 1960; MBA, Northwestern U., 1965. CPA, Ill. Mgr. engring. NICOR, Naperville, Ill., 1960-68; cons. A.M. & G., Chgo., 1968-71; v.p. fin. Clayton Brown & Assocs. Inc., Chgo., 1971-86, pres., 1986—; also bd. dirs. Clayton Brown & Assoc. Inc.; bd. dirs. Aurora Bearing Co. Bd. dirs. Tri City Family Services, Geneva, Ill., 1985, Valparaiso U., 1985. Mem. Am. Inst. CPA's (Nat. Recognition award), Ill. Soc. CPA's (Silver medal). Lutheran. Club: St. Charles Country (pres. 1978, 79). Avocation: sport. Home: 3 N 742 Randall Saint Charles IL 60174 Office: Clayton Brown & Assoc 300 W Washington Chicago IL 60606

PEMA, PETER JAMES, osteopathic physician, educator; b. Atlantic City, Sept. 11, 1934; s. Peter and Katherine (Kendro) P.; m. Diana M. Allegrini; children—Deborah, Peter, Robert, Lisa, Jennifer. Student Temple U., 1952-55; D.O., Phila. Coll. Osteo. Medicine, 1959. Intern, Garden City-Ridgewood Hosp., Garden City, Mich., 1959-60; resident in internal medicine Detroit Osteo. Hosp., 1966-69; practice medicine specializing in internal medicine; gen. practice, Vandercook Lake, Mich., 1960-66; chief of staff Jackson (Mich.) Osteo. Hosp., 1965-66, chmn. bd. trustees, 1966; practice internal medicine, Columbus, Ohio, 1969—; chmn. dept. internal medicine Doctors Hosp., Columbus, 1975-76, vice-chmn., 1977-78; clin. assoc. prof. internal medicines Ohio U. Coll. Osteo. Medicine, Athens, 1978—; mem. City Hosp. Planning Council, Jackson, 1964-65; med. examiner Nat. osteo. Bd. Licensure, 1971—; founding mem. Med. Adv. Bd., Upper Arlington, Ohio, 1975—; hosp. insp. intern tng. Am. Osteo. Assn. Recipient Outstanding Teaching award Doctors Hosp., 1970, 71. Fellow Am. Coll. Osteo. Internists; mem. Am. Osteo. Assn., Ohio Osteo. Assn., Columbus Acad. Osteo. Medicine. Albanian Orthodox. Office: 94 W 3d Ave Columbus OH 43220

PEMBERTON, BRADLEY POWELL, lawyer; b. Ft. Scott, Kans., June 15, 1952; s. Howard Duane and Juanita Lucille (Powell) P.; m. Kathleen Frances Querrey, May 22, 1976 (div. Feb. 1984). BSBA, U. Mo., Columbia, 1974; JD, U. Mo., Kansas City, 1977. Bar: Mo. 1977, U.S. Dist. Ct. (we. dist.) Mo. 1981, U.S. Tax Ct. 1981; CPA. Tax acct. Alexander Grant & Co., Kansas City, 1977-79; assoc. Polsinelli, White, Vardeman & Shalton, Kansas City, 1979—, also bd. dirs. Active Vol. Atty. Project, Kansas City, 1984-86; bd. dirs. Synergy House Inc., Kansas City; mem. Riverfront Task Force, Kansas City. Mem. Mo. Bar Assn., Kansas City Bar Assn., Am. Inst. CPA's, Mo. Soc. CPA's, Kansas City C. of C. Democrat. Lodge: KC. Avocations: tennis, golf, water skiing, snow skiing. Home: 918 Burningtree Dr Kansas City MO 64145 Office: Polsinelli White Vardeman & Shalton 4705 Central Kansas City MO 64112

PENALUNA, JOEL PATRICK, tansportation company executive; b. Hampton, Iowa, Apr. 30, 1949; s. Kenneth Henry and Mignon Claire (Cronan) P.; m. Judith Kaye Harris, May 4, 1968; children: Darci D., Michael P. AA in Bus. Adminstrn., Ellsworth Community Coll., 1969, 83-84; cert. coach, Iowa River Valley Community Coll., 1986. Owner Penaluna Transfer, Iowa Falls, Iowa, 1975-82; pres. Penaluna Transfer, Inc., Iowa Falls, Iowa, 1982—; salesman midwest region Penn. Life Ins., Sioux City, Iowa, 1980-81; salesman Trailmobile, Inc., Des Moines, 1981-82. Counselor Crusaders Youth Group, 1986—; tech. advisor Indsl. Devel. Com., Iowa Falls, 1983-84. Mem. Iowa Falls Jaycees, Iowa Falls C. of C. Lutheran. Club: Meadow Hills Golf (Iowa Falls) (dir. 1986—). Avocations: golf, bowling, hiking, travel. Home: Rural Rt 3 Twin Hills Iowa Falls IA 50126 Office: Penaluna Transfer Inc PO Box 722 Rural Rt 3 Iowa Falls IA 50126

PENCE, JOHN THOMAS, dietitian; b. Lafayette, Ind., June 21, 1941; s. M.O. and Florence (Lindley) P.; m. Karen Sue Turner, June 19, 1976. BS, Purdue U., 1963; MS, Kans. State U., 1970. Registered dietitian. Asst. dir. residence hall food service Kans. State U., Manhattan, 1973-82, head residence hall food service, 1982-87, assoc. dir., housing head residence hall food service, 1987—, instr. hotel, restaurant, instn. mgmt. dietetics, 1987—. Author: (with others) Recipes From the Heartland '80, 1980, Recipes From the Land of Ah's, 1982. Recipient Silver Plate award Internat. Food Service Mfrs. Assn., 1987; named Kans. Employer Yr. Kans. Rehab. Assn., 1980. Mem. Am. Dietetic Assn., Am. Sch. Food Service Assn., Soc. For Advancement of Food Service Research, Nat. Assn. Coll. and Univ. Food Service (nat. treas. 1979-85, nat. pres. 1986-87, Meritorious Service award 1981, 83, 85). Republican. Methodist. Lodge: Kiwanis. Avocation: canoeing. Home: 2361 Grandview Terr Manhattan KS 66502 Office: Kans State Univ Pittman Bldg Manhattan KS 66506

PENDELL-FRANTZ, PEGGY METZKA, psychologist; b. Peoria, Ill., Aug. 4, 1947; d. Andrew and Hilda Christine (Corbett) Metzka; m. Richard Wesley Pendell, Dec. 16, 1966 (div. Sept, 1980); children: Richard Wesley II, Jessica M. Adrian E.; m. Larry Thomas Frantz, May 29, 1982; 1 child, Erik. Student, Wheaton Coll., 1966-67, Wichita State U., 1968-69; BS, Bradley U., 1971, MA, 1979; postgrad., Fielding Inst. Registered social worker, cert. psychologist, Ill.. Social worker Manteno (Ill.) State Hosp., 1971-74, research coordinator, 1974-76; psychologist Shapiro Devel. Ctr., Kankakee, Ill., 1979-80, Galesburg (Ill.) Mental Ctr., 1980; psychologist Zeller Mental Health Ctr., Peoria, 1980—, also dir. research com., 1981—; practice psychology Peoria, 1977—; cons. Parents Anonymous, Peoria, 1977-78; research advisor Naval Wapons Support Ctr., Crane, Ind., 1966. Author: Depression as an Auto-Anaesthetic Respiratory Response: Implications for Clinical Intervention, 1979. B.F. Goodrich Merit scholar, 1965. Mem. Nat. Assn. Social Workers, Ill. Assn. Masters Psychologists (legis. liaison, 1985, pres. 1985). Presbyterian. Club: Law Aux. (Peoria). Avocations: travel, needlework, swimming, writing, reading, music. Office: Zeller Mental Health Ctr 5407 N University Ave Peoria IL 61614

PENDERGRASS, KENNETH LEE, artist; b. Adrian, Mich., Mar. 4, 1952; d. Kenneth Boyd Pendergrass and Nancy Ellen (Smith) Young. Student, Ea. Mich. U., 1974-75, Siena Heights Coll., 1976-77. Goldsmith Payl J. Dangler, Tecumseh, Mich., 1977-79; goldsmith, buyer Matthew C. Hoffmann, Inc., Ann Arbor, 1979-85; pres. Pendergrass Designs, Ann Arbor, 1980—. Mem. Ann Arbor Area Bd. Realtors, 1987—. Mem. Contemporary Artists Assn. (treas. 1979-84). Roman Catholic. Avocations: glider piloting, flyfishing, tenor in choir. Home: 4218 Packard Rd #5 Ann Arbor MI 48104

PENDERGRASS, MICHAEL J., automobile company executive; b. Detroit, Oct. 6, 1957; s. Joshua and Verna (Barden) P. BS in Indsl. Mgmt., Lawrence Inst. Tech., 1985. Cert. indsl. engring. tech., Mich. Engring. technician Gt. Lakes Gas Transmission Co., Detroit, 1980-84, staff asst., 1984-85; prodn. supr. Chrysler Corp., Sterling Heights, Mich., 1986—. Youth dir. Mt. Lebanon-Strathmoor Ch., Detroit, 1980-85; recruiter Circle Y Summer Camp, Bangor, Mich., 1980—. Mem. Am Inst. Indsl. Engrs., Am. Soc. Cert. Engring. Technicians, Engring. Soc. Detroit. Democrat. Home: 16166 Gilchrist Detroit MI 48235 Office: Chrysler Corp Sterling Heights MI 48077

PENDLETON, BRIAN FRANKLIN, college dean, sociology educator; b. Kansas City, Mo., Nov. 3, 1950; s. Frank Schilling and Arline (Hendrickson) P.; m. Marcile ELaine Frank, May 27, 1979; children: Michelle Annette, Jennifer Christine. BA, U. Minn., Duluth, 1972; MA, U. N.D., 1974; PhD, Iowa State U., 1977. Postdoctoral research assoc. Iowa State U., Ames, 1977-78; asst. prof. sociology U. Akron, Ohio, 1978-82, assoc. prof., 1982—, assoc. dean grad. studies and research, 1986—; pres. Pendleton Cons., Silver Lake, Ohio, 1984—. Contbr. numerous articles to profl. jours. Recipient Outstanding Citizen cert. Ohio Senate, 1984, Appreciation placque City of Akron, 1982, Appreciation placque Cuyahoga Falls Kiwanis, 1982, Appreciation cert. Multiple Sclerosis Soc., 1982. Mem. Am. Pub. Health Assn., Am. Sociol. Assn., Internat. Rural Sociol. Assn., Midwest Sociol. Soc., Multiple Linear Regression Group, North Cen. Sociol. Assn., Population Assn. Am., Population Reference Bur., Rural Sociol. Soc., Soc. for Applied Sociology, So. Regional Demographic Group, World Population Soc., Nat. Amateur Athletic Assn. (Akron and Indpls. chpt., sport karate com., mem. bd. mgrs., chmn. laws and legis. com.), U.S. Karate Assn., U.S. Karate Fedn. (life), U.S. Judo Assn., Cen. Taekwondo Assn. Lutheran. Clubs: U. Akron Karate/Judo (faculty advisor 1978—); Ctr. for Martial Arts (Kenmore, Ohio) (bd. dirs.). Cert. 3d degree black belt. Home: 3032 Englewood Dr Silver Lake OH 44224 Office: U Akron Sociology Olin 247 Akron OH 44325

PENDLETON, JAMES HERMAN, accountant; b. Kansas City, Mo., July 3, 1933; s. Elmer Dean and Martha Lucille (Friess) P.; m. Carol Dian Frost, June 11, 1955; children: Jim Jr., Jon M., Melinda J. BBA, Cen. Mo. State U., 1955. CPA, Mo., Kans., others. Ptnr. Arthur Andersen & Co., Kansas City, 1955—. Chmn. Cen. Mo. State Found., Warrensburg, 1985—, Cystic Fibrosis Found.; bd. dirs. State Ballet of Mo., Kansas City, 1984—, ARC, Kansas City. Mem. Am. Inst. CPA;s, Mo. Soc. CPA's, Kans. Soc. CPA's, Mo. Jaycees (pres. 1968), U.S. Jaycees (nat. treas. 1969), Am. Humanics (pres. 1986), Kansas City C. of C. (aviation com.). Republican. Presbyterian. Clubs: Indian Hills Country (Mission Hills, Kans.); Kansas City; Garden of Gods (Colorado Springs); Leawood (Kans.) Country, Saddle and Sirloin. Home: 8525 Briar Ln Prairie Village KS 66207 Office: Arthur Andersen & Co 911 Main St PO Box 13406 Kansas City MO 64199

PENDLETON, THELMA BROWN, physical therapist, health service administrator; b. Rome, Ga., Jan. 30, 1911; d. John O. and Alma (Ingram) Brown; diploma Provident Hosp. Sch. Nursing, 1931; cert. Loyola U., 1942, Northwestern U., 1946; m. George W. Pendleton, Mar. 2, 1946; 1 son, George William. Pediatric nurse Rosenwald Found., Chgo., 1931-32; staff nurse Vis. Nurse Assn., Chgo., 1932-45; chief phys. therapy Provident Hosp., Chgo., 1946-55; phys. therapy cons. Parents Assn., Inc., Chgo., 1956-60; cons. United Cerebral Palsy of Greater Chgo.'s Pipers Portal Schs., 1961-63, dir., 1963-64; dir. phys. therapy services LaRabida Children's Hosp. and Research Center, Chgo., 1964-75; mem. nat. com. Joint Orthopedic Nursing Adv. Services, 1947-55; clin. supr., instr. programs in phys. therapy Northwestern U. Med. Sch., Chgo., 1947-55, 64-75; cons. United Cerebral Palsy, 1970-75; lectr. Japanese service com. on Cerebral Palsy, 1970; mem. Ill. Phys. Therapy Exam. Com., 1952-62. Recipient cert. of commendation CSC Cook County (Ill.), 1961, Citation of Merit, Wands Cerebral Palsy Unit, 1961. Mem. Am., Ill. phys. therapy assns., Provident Hosp. Nurses Alumni Assn. Democrat. Clubs: Tu-Fours Bolivia. Author: Low Budget Gourmet, 1977; (booklet) Patient Positioning, 1981; contbr. articles on phys. therapy to profl. jours.; contbr. to Am. Poetry Anthology. Address: 2631 S Indiana Ave Chicago IL 60616

PENDLEY, LARRY M., psychologist, educator; b. Dayton, Ohio, Feb. 13, 1942; s. Alfred E. and Clydia Lavelle (Lewis) P.; m. Cheri Kay Smith, Dec. 16, 1967; children: Jennifer, Megan. BS, Ohio U., 1965; MS in Edn., U. Dayton, 1971. Lic. psychologist, Ohio. Tchr. Oakwood City Schs., Dayton, 1965-71; sch. psychologist Centerville (Ohio) Schs., 1971-85; pvt. practice psychology Centerville, 1985—; bd. dirs. Social Responsibility Cons., Dayton, 1984—; founder, bd. dirs. Centerville and North Dayton tutoring services; instr. Sinclair Coll., Dayton, 1977-82. Mem. Ohio Psychol. Assn., Miami Valley Psychol. Assn., Ohio Sch. Psychologists Assn., Am. Assn. Counseling and Devel., Ohio Assn. Counseling and Devel. Republican. Lodge: Optimists (program chair 1983). Avocations: golf, tennis, sailing, hunting, fishing. Home: 5757 Hithergreen Dr Dayton OH 45429 Office: Affiliated Counseling Service 44 Marco Ln Centerville OH 45459

PENDY, MICHAEL ARTHUR, production control specialist; b. Pitts., Apr. 10, 1961. BS in Chemistry, U. Mich., 1983. Foreman mfg. Abbott Labs., Abbot Park, Ill., 1983, Rocky Mount, N.C., 1984; mfg. systems specialist Abbott Labs., Abbott Park, 1984, material control analyst, 1985, new tech. quality assurance specialist, 1985-86. Office: Abbott Labs D-82B AP8 Abbott Park IL 60064

PENGILLY, MORRIS RICHARD, clinical social worker; b. Evanston, Ill., Jan. 19, 1944; s. Parker and Isabel (Morris) P.; m. Susan Jean Griffith, Sept. 3, 1966 (div. Dec. 1983); children: Heather, Lauren; m. Joy Dawn Wyatt, May 18, 1985. BA, Hanover (Ind.) Coll., 1966; MSW, Ind. U., Indpls., 1968. Lic. Ind. Social Worker, Ohio; diplomate in clin. social work. Clin. social worker Family Services Assn., Indpls., 1968-70; social worker, supr. Ctr. Human Services, Cleve., 1970-76, program services dir., 1978-81; program dir. United Cerebral Palsy Assn., Cleve., 1976-78; pvt. practice clin. social work Cleve., 1981—. Chmn. bd. dirs. Euclid Ave. Christian Ch., Cleve., 1978, tchr., 1976-82, 85—; family life com., 1986. Named one of Outstanding Young Men Am. U.S. Jaycees, 1981. Mem. Nat. Assn. Social Workers, Ohio Soc. Clin. Social Work (legis. chmn. 1982). Democrat. Mem. Disciples of Christ Ch. Avocations: waterskiing, gardening, reading, travel.

Home: 19542 Coffinberry Blvd Fairview Pk OH 44126 Office: 3865 Rocky River Dr Suite 2 Cleveland OH 44111

PENN, DAVID JOSEPH, pastor; b. Yuba City, Calif., June 14, 1944; s. Joseph Francis and Ellen Letta (Pittenger) P.; m. Ruth Elizabeth Hetrick, Dec. 27, 1968; children: Lisa, Cristy, David II. BA, Pasadena Coll./Point Loma Nazarene Coll., 1967; MDiv., Nazarene Theol. Sem., 1971. Ordained to ministry Ch. of Nazarene, 1974. Pastor Jacobe Chapel Presbyn. Ch., Warrensburg, Mo., 1969-71; assoc. pastor Victory Hills Ch. of Nazarene, Kansas City, Mo., 1971-73; pastor Jacksonville (Ill.) Ch. of Nazarene, 1973-76, Kingwood (W.Va.) Ch. of Nazarene, 1976-82, Community Ch. of Nazarene, Racine, Wis., 1982—; sec. Ill. dist. Nazarene Youth Internat., 1974-76; chmn. Christian Life and Sunday Sch., 1985-87; mem. Wis. dist. Ministerial Credentials, 1984-87, adv. council, 1986—; mem. fin. com. Wis. Ch. of Nazarene, 1983-87. Trustee Mt. Vernon Nazarene Coll., 1981-82; exec. sec. Clyde Dupin Crusade, Kingwood, W.Va., 1979-82; chaplain Morgan County Jail, Jacksonville, 1974-76; mem. Jacksonville Welfare Bd., 1976, Jacksonville Red Cross, 1976; pres. Kingwood Ministerial Fellowship, 1980-82. Avocations: photography, fishing, people, cars. Office: Community Ch of Nazarene 8440 Hwy C Racine WI 53406

PENN, MAGGIE SCOTT, school counselor, small business owner; b. Columbia, S.C., Jan. 1, 1940; d. Walter Lee and Ruby Lee (Seawright) Scott; m. Luther Penn (dec. Oct. 1977); 1 child: Cydni Charise. BS, Eastern Mich. U., 1963, MA, 1966. Bus. tchr. Highland (Mich.) Park Bd. Edn., 1963-70, sch. counselor, 1971—; high sch. counselor, pres. Bramblewood Enterprises, Detroit, 1978—; owner Penn Hardware, Detroit. Sec. Detroit NAACP, 1978-84, bd. dirs. 1978-84; sec. Sr. Citizens of Detroit Com., 1980—, Cotillion Wives Aux., Detroit, 1979-85; mgr. state senate pol. campaign, Detroit, 1980; supervisor Peoples Community Ch. Credit Union, Detroit, 1978-84. Recipient Disting. Service award City of Detroit, 1984, Outstanding Membership award Detroit NAACP, 1970, 80-85. Mem. Am. Fedn. Tchrs, Mich. Fedn. Tchrs., Highland Park Fedn. Tchrs., Mich. Guidance Assn., Mich. Career Devel. Assn., Am. Bus. Educators, New Metro Detroit Bus. and Profl. Women (Appreciation award 1982, editor newsletter), Landlords Assn. Mich., Delta Sigma Theta, Phi Delta Kappa. Avocations: writing, speaking, organizing. Home: PO Box 21010 Coll Park Sta Detroit MI 48221 Office: Penn Hardware 7306 Puritan Detroit MI 48221

PENN, ROBERT J., steel manufacturing company executive; b. 1930. BS, U. Ill., 1955. Asst. treas. Sunbeam Corp., Pitts., 1960-68; treas. I.H.C., Inc., 1970; with Unarco Industries, Inc., Chgo., 1970—, v.p. fin., 1971-80; with UNR Industries, Inc., Chgo., 1980—, now pres., chief exec. officer. Served with AUS, 1950-54. Office: U N R Industries Inc 332 S Michigan Ave Chicago IL 60604 *

PENN, RONALD HULEN, manufacturing executive; b. Pocahontas, Ark., Dec. 31, 1951; s. Hulen and Isabell (Smith) P.; m. Janieca Ann Thielemier, May 31, 1975; children: Alicia, Candace, Dustin. BS in Mktg., Ark. State U., 1973. Office mgr. Brown Shoe Co., Houston, Mo., 1973-76; overseas technician Brown Shoe Co., South America, 1976-77; asst. plant mgr. Brown Shoe Co., Pittsfield, Ill., 1978-79, plant mgr., 1979-84, mgr. technical services, 1984—. Advisor Pikeland Community Unit Sch., Pittsfield, 1980; coach Little League Baseball, Union, Mo., 1986. Mem. Alpha Kappa Psi. Republican. Mem. Ch. of Christ. Named All Conf. and Regional Football Player Northeast Ark. Athletic Assn., 1969. Avocations: golf, fishing. Office: Brown Shoe Co 8300 Maryland Ave Saint Louis MO 63105

PENNELL, DANNY JOE, social worker; b. Jacksonville, Ill., Aug. 31, 1945; s. Donald Louis and Lela Geneva (Murray) P.; m. Janis Evelyn Reynolds, Dec. 26, 1984; children—Joel, Jason, Jaime, Chad, Colter. B.A., U. Ill., 1970, M.S.W., 1972. Social worker Dept. Child and Family Services, Danville, Ill., 1971-72, social work supr., Rockford, Ill., 1972-74; instr. Rockford Coll., 1977-78; exec. dir. Goldie B. Floberg Ctr., Rockton, Ill., 1974—; bd. dirs. Winnebago County Child Protection Assn., Rockford, 1974-76, Child Care Assn. Ill., Springfield, Ill., 1980—; cons. in field. Grantee Ill. Dept. Children and Family Services, 1970-72. Mem. Nat. Soc. Fund Raising Execs. (bd. dirs., sec. 1984-85, v.p. 1986-87), Am. Assn. Mental Deficiency, Nat. Assn. Retarded Citizens, Coordinating Council for Handicapped Children, Nat. Assn. Devel. Disabilities Mgrs. Address: 6662 Arena Roscoe IL 61073 Office: Goldie B Floberg Ctr 58 W Rockton Rd Rockton IL 61072

PENNEQUIN, ALBERT ELIE, land surveying educator; b. Tournai, Belgium, Feb. 11, 1928; came to U.S. 1970; s. Edgar and Jeanne Selly (Polak) P; m. Marie-Louise Dandov, July 30, 1952 (dec. 1971); children—Didier F.E., Roland M.; m. Marguerite Marie Trottereau, June 22, 1974. Degree in Geometre, Inst. Royal for Geometres-Experts Immobilliers, Brussels, Belgium, 1953; postgrad. U. Wis.-Whitewater, 1975—. Registered profl. land surveyor, Wis. Land surveyor Belgian govt., 1949-58; educator, land surveyor Congo govt., Coquilhatville, Mbandaka, 1958-65; French instruction supr., in-factory apprenticeship tng. supr., Caterpillar Tractor Co., Belgium, 1965-70; fgn. lang. master Lake Forest Acad., Ill., 1970-73, land surveying instr., program chmn. Gateway Tech. Inst., Elkhorn, Wis., 1973—; land surveyor, Elkhorn, 1973—; land surveyor's cons., Belgium, 1953-58, 1965-70. Contbr. articles to profl. jours. Served with Belgium Army, 1946-49. Fellow Am. Congress on Surveying and Mapping (local student chpt. advisor 1975—), mem. Wis. Soc. Land Surveyors (edn. com., land records com.). Avocations: flying; sailing; astronomy; piano playing. Office: Gateway Tech Inst Hwy H and Centralia Ave Elkhorn WI 53121

PENNIMAN, NICHOLAS GRIFFITH, IV, newspaper publisher; b. Balt., Mar. 7, 1938; s. Nicholas Griffith Penniman and Esther Cox Lony (Wight) Keeney; m. Linda Jane Simmons, Feb. 4, 1967; children: Rebecca Helmle, Nicholas G. V. AB, Princeton U., 1960. Asst. bus. mgr. Ill. State Jour. Register, Springfield, 1964-69, bus. mgr., 1969-75; asst. gen. mgr. St. Louis Post-Dispatch, 1975-84, gen. mgr., 1984-86, pub., 1986—. Vice chmn. Downtown St. Louis, Inc., 1979—; chmn. Mo. Health and Ednl. Facilities Adminstrn., St. Louis, 1982-85, Ill. State Fair Bd., Springfield, 1973-75; trustee St. Louis Country Day Sch., 1983-86; bd. dirs. St. Louis Arts and Edn. Council, St. Louis Area Council Boys Scouts Am., 1987—. Served with U.S. Army, 1962-67. Clubs: St. Louis Country, Noonday. Avocation: tennis. Home: 9043 Clayton Rd Saint Louis MO 63117 Office: St Louis Post Dispatch 900 N Tucker Blvd Saint Louis MO 63101

PENNING, RICHARD TED, chemical engineer; b. Sandusky, Ohio, Apr. 27, 1955; s. Theodore Englebry and Eunice Elizabeth (Jones) P.; m. Kimberly Ann Bleakley, Jan. 17, 1981; children: Alexander, Maxwell. BS in Engring., Case Western Res. U., 1977; MBA in Fin., U. Chgo., 1986. Devel. engr. UOP, Inc., Riverside, Ill., 1977-79, group leader, 1979-81; process coordinator UOP, Inc., Des Plaines, Ill., 1981-85; mktg. coordinator UOP, Inc., Des Plaines, 1985—. Contbr. articles to profl. jours. Mem. Am. Inst. Chem. Engrs. Republican. Presbyterian. Home: 445 W Sunset Rd Barrington IL 60010 Office: UOP Inc 25 E Algonquin Rd Des Plaines IL 60017-5017

PENNINGER, WILLIAM HOLT, JR., financial planner; b. Springfield, Mo., May 4, 1954; s. William Holt Sr. and Marjorie Marie (Emanuel) P.; m. Una Lee McLeer, Aug. 8, 1981. BS, MIT, 1976; JD, MBA, Tulane U., 1981; LLM, Tulane, 1983. Bar: La. 1981, N.Y. 1984, Mo. 1986. Customer service rep. C.I.T. Fin. Services, Inc., Springfield, Mo., 1976-77; lexis rep. Mead Data Cen., New Orleans, 1981-83; assoc. Hill, Betts & Nash, N.Y.C., 1983-85, Cole & Deitz, N.Y.C., 1985-86; fin. planner IDS Fin. Services Inc., Springfield, Mo., 1986—. Mem. ABA, La. Bar. Assn., N.Y. Bar Assn., Mo. Bar Assn., Maritime Law Assn., Assn., Internat. Assn. Fin. Planning. Republican. Presbyterian. Avocations: sailing, skin and scuba diving, quantum physics, electronic music composition, photography. Home: Route 1 Box 148 Nixa MO 65714-9623 Office: IDS Fin Services Inc John Q Hammons Bldg Suite 503 300 Hammons Pkwy Springfield MO 65806

PENNINGTON, JACK LEN, psychologist, educator; b. Greenville, Tex., Dec. 14, 1946; s. Claude G. and Pauline (Alexander) P.; m. Julia R. Carr, July 31, 1982; children: Bryan A. and Elliot C (twins). BS, East Tex. U., 1970, MS, 1971; PhD, St. Louis U., 1980. Lab. tech. Faith Hosp., St. Louis, 1972-73; prof. Forest Pk. Coll., St. Louis, 1973—; pvt. practice psychology St. Louis, 1980—; adj. faculty Stl. Louis U. Med. Ctr., 1978—; pres., bd. dirs. Life Crisis Service, St. Louis, 1980—. Home: 9708 Willow Creek Saint Louis MO 63108 Office: 4500 W Pine Saint Louis MO 63108

PENNY, TIMOTHY JOSEPH, congressman; b. Albert Lea, Minn., Nov. 19, 1951; s. Jay C. and Donna (Haukoos) P.; m. Barbara J. Christianson, Oct. 18, 1975; children: Jamison, Joseph, Molly, Marcus. B.A., Winona State U., 1974; postgrad., U. Minn., 1975. Mem. Minn. Senate from Dist. 30, 1977-82, 98th-100th Congresses from 1st Minn. Dist.; mem. agr. com., vets affairs com. Mem. Minn. State Univ. Bd., 1974-77. Recipient disting. service award U. Minn., 1982; recipient Spark Plug award Communicating for Agr., 1980. Mem. New Richland (Minn.) Jaycees, Waseca Pals, Inc., Waseca and Freeborn County Assn. for Retarded Citizens. Democrat. Lutheran. Office: US Ho of Reps Room 436 Cannon House Office Bldg Washington DC 20515

PENROD, KATHRYN MARIE, vocational education educator; b. Ft. Leonard Wood, Mo., June 6, 1953; s. Walter Jay and Mary Jenet (Elder) P. BS, Purdue U., 1975; MS, Cornell U., 1982, PhD, 1984. Staff Dept. Commerce State of Ind., Indpls., 1975; tchr. vocat. home econs. Carmel (Ind.)/Clay Schs., 1975-79; exec. dir. Mont. Council for Vocat. Edn., Helena, 1982-85; assr. prof. coop. extension Purdue U., West Lafayette, Ind., 1985—. Mem. Am. Vocat. Assn., Nat. Assn. Extension 4-H Agents, Purdue Extension Specialist Assn. Methodist. Avocations: skiing, horseback riding, reading, camping, needlecraft. Home: 321 Meridian St West Lafayette IN 47906 Office: Purdue U AGAD Bldg 4-H Dept West Lafayette IN 47906

PENROD, MICHAEL ROBERT, college administrator; b. Detroit, Jan. 23, 1942; s. Robert Francis and Marion Louise (Sutter) P. BA in Philosphy and English, Sacred Heart Sem., 1964; MA in Adminstrn. Higher Edn., Eastern Mich. U., 1971. Cert. profl. counselor, social worker, Mich. Counselor admissions and fin. aid Detroit Inst. Tech., 1969-71, dir. admissions, 1971-72; counselor spl. services unit Macomb Community Coll., Mt. Clemens, Mich., 1972—. Pres. Nat. Hist. Dist. West Village Assn., Detroit, 1979-84, v.p., 1984—; adv. council Eastern Detroit Youth Assistance Program, 1986—. Mem. Mich. Occupational Edn. Assn., Mich. Spl. Needs Assn. Roman Catholic. Avocations: cooking, gardening, travel. Home: 1057 Parker Ave Detroit MI 48214 Office: Macomb Community Coll 44575 Garfield Rd Mount Clemens MI 48044

PENSON, EDWARD MARTIN, university official; b. N.Y.C., Aug. 30, 1927; s. Michael and Cecile (Cohan) P.; m. Georgann Ellen McCune, June 25, 1975; children: Jeffery, Albert, Cynthia. B.A. cum laude, U. Fla., 1950, Ph.D., 1955; M.A., Ohio U., 1951. Prof. communication Ohio U., Athens, 1955-75, dean, 1965-68, v.p., 1969-75; pres., prof. Salem State Coll., Mass., 1975-78; prof., chancellor U. Wis.-Oshkosh, 1978—; cons. Royal-McBee, Litton Industries, Ohio Credit Union, Battelle Meml. Inst., 1963-66, U. Nev., 1980-81, Paine Art Ctr., 1985, Acad. Ednl. Devel., King Fiesal U., 1986, OshKosh B'Gosh, Inc., 1987. Contbr. numerous articles to profl. jours., chpts. to books. Bd. dirs. Assn. Retarded Citizens, Salem, Mass., 1975-78; bd. dirs. Econ. Devel. Council, North Shore, Mass., 1976-78, Ohio student loan commr., Columbus, 1971-75. Mem. Communication Assn. Am., Am. Speech Assn., Am. Assn. State and Land Grant Colls. and Univs., Am. Assn. State Colls. and Univs., Nat. Assn. Student Personnel Adminstrs., Sigma Alpha Eta, Phi Kappa Phi, Alpha Lambda Delta. Club: Rotary (Salem, Mass. and Oshkosh, Wis.). Home: 842 Algoma Blvd Oshkosh WI 54901 Office: U Wisconsin 800 Algoma Blvd Oshkosh WI 54901

PENSON, MADELINE ELAINE, social services administrator; b. Detroit, July 18, 1943; dd. Edward Myzell and Elizabeth Ernestine (Nettles) Sowell; div.; children: Starellen, Zenobia, Shanika. AA, Highland Park (Mich.) Coll., 1972; BA in Sociology, Wayne State U., 1975; MA in Edn., U. Detroit, 1982. Nurse Northville (Mich.) Hosp., 1968-71; social worker City of Highland Park, 1975-80; cook supr. V Huron Valley Men's Prison, Ysplanti, Mich., 1982-83; youth specialist IV W.F. Maxey Tng. Sch., Whitmore Lake, Mich., 1983-85; group leader VI W.F. Maxey Tng. Sch., Whitmore Lake, 1985—; vol. substitute tchr. Detroit Open Sch., 1980-82. Cons. Girl Scouts U.S., Highland Park, 1973; sponsor Campfire Girls, Highland Park, 1974; bd. dirs. Ethel Terral Nursery Sch., Highland Park, 1980. Mem. Eta Phi Beta Alpha. Democrat. Lodge: Order of Eastern Star. Avocations: skating, baseball, biking, bowling, sewing. Office: WJ Maxey Tng Sch PO Box 349 Whitmore Lake MI 48189

PENTILLA, ROY ARTHUR, loan officer, accountant; b. Waukegan, Ill., June 22, 1943; s. Arthur Jack and Verna I. (Haapala) P.; m. Joan M. Hayslip, June 6, 1964 (div. 1968); 1 child, Nicole Ann; m. Elaine Rae Brown, Apr. 24, 1971; 1 child, Charles Raymond. BA, Mich. State U., 1964; MBA, U. Mich., 1972. CPA, Calif., Mich., N.Y. Acct. Harris, Reames & Ambrose, Lansing, Mich., 1964-73, Seidman & Seidman, Buffalo, 1973-76; ptnr. Seidman & Seidman, Oakland, Calif., 1976-77; bus. mgr. Story Oldsmobile, Inc., Lansing, 1977-78; fiscal officer Job Devel. Authority State of Mich., Lansing, 1978-85, loan officer strategic fund, 1985—. Mem. Nat. Assn. Accts. (pres. Lansing), Mich. Assn. CPA's (chmn. fin. inst. com., 1984-86, Patton award), Orchard Park Jaycees (pres. 1976). Lutheran. Lodge: Elks. Avocation: skiing. Home: 2116 Quentin Lansing MI 48910 Office: Mich Strategic Fund Box 30227 Lansing MI 48909

PENWELL, MARVIN DEAN, osteopathic physician, educator; b. Decatur, Ill., May 18, 1930; s. Harry David and Mary Delema (Jackson) P.; m. Gloria Jean Liechty, June 28, 1952; children—Robert Todd, Polly Denise. B.A., Greenville Coll., 1952; D.O., Kansas City Coll. Osteopathy and Surgery, 1966. Diplomate Am. Osteo. Bd. Gen. Practice. Intern Flint Osteo. Hosp., Mich., 1966-67, mem. staff, 1967—, vice chief of staff, 1974; assoc. physician Swartz Creek Community Clinic, Mich, 1967-71; family physician Linden Med. Ctr., Mich., 1971—; cons. staff mem. Genesee Meml. Hosp., Flint; asst. clin. prof. Mich. State U., Lansing, 1978—; preceptor in edn. osteo. med. studies Phila. Coll. Osteo. Medicine, 1978-79; guest speaker Pfeizer Corp., arthritis awareness program Flint Osteo. Hosp. Mem. Am. Coll. for Advancement in Medicine, Mich. Assn. Osteo. Physicians and Surgeons, Am. Osteo. Assn., Am. Coll. Gen. Practitioners, Genesee County Osteo. Assn., Am. Guild Organists (Flint chpt.), Aircraft Owners and Pilots Assn. Republican. Lodge: Gideons. Avocations: aviation; boating; water skiing; fishing; snowmobiling. Office: Linden Med Ctr PC 319 Bridge St Linden MI 48451

PENZEL, CARL GENE, construction company executive, civil engineer; b. Jackson, Mo., Jan. 10, 1934; s. Carl Linus and Mettie Jane (Killian) P.; m. Alice Sue Meier, June 19, 1960; children—Philip Carlyle, Christopher Noel. BSCE, U. Mo.-Rolla, 1955. Registered profl. engr., Mo. Engr., Allis-Chalmers Co., West Allis, Wis., 1955; with Penzel Constrn. Co., Inc., Jackson, Mo., 1959—, v.p., 1959-80, pres., 1981—; dir. Jackson Exchange Bank. Alderman, City Council, Jackson, 1966; pres. Indsl. Devel. Co., Jackson, 1981. Served to lt. USNR, 1955-59. Named Young Engr. of Yr., Southeast Mo. sect. Mo. Soc. Profl. Engrs., 1966; Disting. Service award Jackson Jaycees, 1968. Mem. Nat. Soc. Profl. Engrs., Assn. Gen. Contractors Mo. (pres. 1980). Republican. Mem. United Ch. of Christ. Home: 1110 Jackson Trail Jackson MO 63755 Office: Penzel Constrn Co Inc Hwy 72 W Jackson MO 63755

PEOPLES, JAMES YOUNG, high school administrator; b. Snowhill, Ala., June 1, 1932; s. James and Virginia (Davis) P.; m. Dorothy Sneed, June 22, 1963; 1 son, Cedric. B.S., Ky. State U., Frankfort, 1955; M.Ed., DePaul U., 1973; EdD, Highland U., Tenn., 1984. Tchr., coach football Marshall High Sch., Chgo., 1956-68; counselor, chmn. human relations com. Sch. Dist. 147 Harvey, Ill., 1968-73; assoc. prin. for instrn., dir. continuing edn. Hillcrest High Sch., Country Club Hills, Ill., 1973—. Bd. dirs., treas. Human Resources Devel. Inst., Inc.; trustee Ky. State U. Found., Inc.; bd. dirs. vice chmn. Midway Rehab. Services Inc. Treas., ruler elder Chatham-Bethlehem Presbyn. Ch. Served with U.S. Army N.G., 1948-51. Recipient Disting. Alumni award Ky. State U., 1965, named to Athletic Hall of Fame, 1975. Mem. Assn. Supervision and Curriculum Devel., Am. Personnel and Guidance Assn., South Suburban Curriculum Assn. (pres.), Ill. Personnel and Guidance Assn., Ky. State U. Alumni Assn. (pres. 1970-74), Delta Epsilon Sigma, Kappa Alpha Psi. Democrat. Lodge: Masons. Home: 7348 S Constance Ave Chicago IL 60649 Office: Hillcrest High Sch 175th and Pulaski Rd Country Club Hills IL 60648

PEPELEA, ARTHUR MICHAEL, JR., marketing professional; b. Clinton, Ind., Nov. 27, 1949; s. Arthur M. Sr. and Pauline W. (Doolin) P.; m. Mary Jo Grubbs, Dec. 19, 1969; children: Arthur III, Amy Michelle. BS, Ball State U., 1972. Rep. Exec. Income Life, Indpls., 1974-76, regional v.p., 1976-79; nat. sales dir. Truman Nat. Life, Kansas City, Mo., 1979-84; sr. v.p., mktg. dir. Continental Benefits Corp., Anderson, Ind., 1984—, also bd. dirs.; v.p. Continental State Corp.; bd. dirs. H.L Weatherford & Assocs.; bd. dirs., officer Continental Benefits Corp. Sec./treas. Anderson Hoop Shooters, Inc.; mem. Rep. Fin. Com., Anderson, 1982; bd. dirs. St. Mary's Sch., Anderson, 1981-83. Named one of Outstanding Young Men of Am., 1985. Mem. Assn. Life Underwriters, U.S. Karate Assn. (brown belt). Roman Catholic. Club: Univ. Lodge: KC. Office: Continental Benefits Corp PO Box 759 Anderson IN 46011

PEPER, CHRISTIAN BAIRD, lawyer; b. St. Louis, Dec. 5, 1910; s. Clarence F. and Christine (Baird) P.; m. Ethel C. Kingsland, June 5, 1935; children—Catherine K. (Mrs. Kenneth B. Larson), Anne C. (Mrs. John M. Perkins), Christian B. A.B. cum laude, Harvard, 1932; LL.B., Washington U., 1935; LL.M. (Sterling fellow), Yale, 1937. Bar: Mo. bar 1934. Since practiced in St. Louis; partner Peper, Martin, Jensen, Maichel & Hetlage.; Lectr. various subjects Washington U. Law Sch., St. Louis, 1943-61; partner A.G. Edwards & Sons, 1945-67; pres. St. Charles Gas Corp., 1953-72; chmn. St. Louis Steel Casting Inc., Hydraulic Press Brick Co.; pres. Tricor Drilling Co. Editor: An Historian's Conscience: The Correspondence of Arnold J. Toynbee and Columba Cary-Elwes, 1986. Contbr. articles to profl. jours. Mem. vis. com. Harvard Div. Sch., 1964-70; trustee St. Louis Art Mus.; bd. dirs. Chatham House Found. Mem. Am., Mo., St. Louis bar assns., Order of Coif, Phi Delta Phi. Roman Catholic. Clubs: Noonday, University Harvard (St. Louis); East India (London). Home: 1454 Mason Rd Saint Louis MO 63131 Office: 720 Olive St Saint Louis MO 63101

PEPICH, BRUCE WALTER, art museum administrator; b. Elmhurst, Ill., June 5, 1952; s. Walter Thomas and Joan (Dolly) P.; m. Lisa Englander, Apr. 21, 1983. B.A. in Art History, No. Ill. U., 1974. Art dir. C.A. Wustum Mus., Racine, Wis., 1974-80, dir., 1981—; curator No. Ill. U. Student Assn., 1971-74, mem. art com. Univ. Ctr. Bd., 1972-74; juried many exhbns. in midwest, including Plaza Art Fair, Kansas City, scholastic art competitions, regional shows at Milw. Art Mus. Vice chmn. Racine United Arts Fund Drive, 1984; mem. Racine Arts Council, 1974—; bd. dirs. Racine Planning Council, 1982-84; v.p. Mayor's Discover Racine Com., 1979. Under his leadership the Wustum Mus. is now accredited by Am. Assn. Mus., Washington. Mem. Am. Assn. Museums, Am. Craft Council, Am. Film Inst. Office: Charles A Wustum Mus of Fine Arts 2519 Northwestern Ave Racine WI 53404

PEPIN, GERALD EDWARD, II, banker; b. Syracuse, N.Y., Mar. 22, 1947; s. Gerald E. and Mary (Peck) V. Pepin; m. Frances P. Pearce; 1 child, Christine VanNess. BS, Washington U., St. Louis, 1972, cert. credit mgmt.; MS, U. Mo., 1980; cert. credit mgmt., Nat. Comml. Lending Sch., Norman, Okla., 1984. Asst. v.p. Trinidad (Colo.) Nat. Bank, 1980-83; v.p. First Nat. Bank, Coffeyville, Kans., 1983-85; v.p. comml. loans First State Bank of Joplin, Mo., 1985—, mgr. retail loans and loan servicing, 1985-87, mgr. loans, 1987—. Bd. dirs. ARC, Coffeyville, 1984; v.p. Joplin Little League Softball Assn., 1986-87; coach Joplin Boy's Club Area Soccer, 1986-87, Girls Under 10 League, 1985. Mem. Coffeyville C. of C. (mem. physician recruitment com.). Republican. Episcopalian. Club: Joplin Area Bus. Lodge: Kiwanis (bd. dirs. Coffeyville chpt. 1983-85). Office: First State Bank PO Box 1373 Joplin MO 64801

PEPIN, RANDALL JOHN, livestock nutritionist, sales executive; b. Little Falls, Minn., May 1, 1953; s. Lloyd Earl and Luella Christine (Johnson) P.; m. Linda Mae Koehn, Aug. 30, 1975; children: Tricia, Kristi, Scott. BS in Animal Sci. and Agronomy, U. Minn., 1977. Dairy farm serviceman Kraft, Inc., Melrose, Minn., 1977-81; area sales mgr. Triple F Products, Des Moines, 1981-85, state sales mgr., 1985—; owner Randy's Nutrition Service, Holdingford, Minn., 1981—. Mem. Upsala (Minn.) Bus. Booster Club, 1985-86, pres., 1987; mem. council Gethsemane Luth. Ch., Upsala, 1986, vice chmn., 1987. Served with USAF, 1972-74. Mem. Am. Soc. Agronomy, Minn. Forage and Grassland Council (bd. dirs. 1987), U. Minn. Alumni Assn. Clubs: Upsala Area Archery (treas. 1985-87). Avocation: local travel, hunting, fishing, computers. Home and Office: Randy's Nutrition Service Rural Rt 1 Box 332 Holdingford MN 56340

PEPITO, WILLIAM MICHAEL, health science facility administrator; b. Manila, Philippines, Sept. 23, 1947; came to U.S., 1948; s. Tesalonico Mendoza and Amparo (Maseras) P.; m. Betty Jo Newman, Jan. 31, 1970 (dec. July 1980); children: William Michael Jr., Nicholas Alexander; m. Sharon Anita Curtis, Oct. 11, 1980; 1 child, Cara Elizabeth. Student, Pasadena City Coll., 1967; AA in Bus. Mgmt., Community Coll. N. Denver, 1977; BS in Mktg., Met. State Coll., Denver, 1980. Ins. agt. R.M.D. Assocs., Wheatridge, Colo., 1971-72; oil field servicer, dispatcher Dow Chemical Co., Commerce City, Colo., 1972-74; warehouse servicer Abbott Labs., Denver, 1974-81; supr. material control Ross Labs. div. Abbott Labs., Altavista, Va., 1981-83; mgr. mfrg. services Ross Labs. div. Abbott Labs., Sturgis, Mich., 1983—. Dist. membership chmn. Boy Scouts Am., St. Joseph and Branch Counties, Mich., 1984-85, dist. tng. chmn., 1985-86, chmn. dist. Food for Good Turn Project, 1984. Served to sgt. USAF, 1967-71. Trainer and Organizer award Boy Scouts Am., St. Joseph and Branch Counties, 1985; Carol Wagner Meml. award Jr. Achievement, Sturgis, Mich., 1984. Mem. Am. Prodn. Inventory Soc. Am., Soc. Photographic Scientists and Engrs., Nat. Council Forensic Scis. (bd. dirs. 1986), Clowns Am. Internat. Republican. Mem. Ch. Christ. Clubs: Ross Am. (pres. 1985-86). Avocations: photography, writing and producing video programs, outdoor activities, fly fishing, reading. Office: Ross Labs div Abbott Labs 700 W Lafayette Sturgis MI 49091

PEPPEL, HEIDI KAREN ROSS, interior designer; b. Watervliet, Mich., Apr. 9, 1960; d. Emil Franz and Rachel Elaine (Sonnenberg) Ross; m. Daniel Ray Peppel, Sept. 4, 1982. AA in Fine Arts, Kendall Sch. Design, 1982. Asst. mgr. Rose Johnson Inc., Grand Rapids, Mich., 1982; sales and mktg. sales space planner Doubleday Bros. & Co., Kalamazoo, 1982-83, interior designer, 1983—. Leader Lifegate Ch. Youth Group, Eau Claire, Mich., 1983-85. Mem. Am. Soc. Interior Designers (profl.). Republican. Avocations: weight training, aerobic dance. Office: Doubleday Bros & Co 1889 B South M-139 PO Box 488 Benton Harbor MI 49022

PEPPER, JAMES ARTHUR, lawyer; b. Paducah, Ky., Aug. 24, 1958; s. James Donald and Evelyn Laura (Edens) P.; m. Melanie Jane Miller, June 13, 1981; 1 child, Laura Evelyn. Ba in Polit. Sci. and German., U. Ky., 1980; JD, Ohio State U., 1983. Bar: Ohio 1983. Legal intern Office Consumers' Counsel, Columbus, Ohio, 1982-83, utility atty., 1983-85, sr. utility atty., 1985—. Mem. U. Ky. Symphony Orch., 1976-80, Upper Arlington (Ohio) Civic Orch., 1982—; pres. Lexington (Ky.) Com. Against Registration and the Draft., 1980. Mem. Nat. Audubon Soc., Columbus Audubon Soc. Democrat. Avocations: cello, basketball. Home: 3495 Torrington St Hilliard OH 43026 Office: Office of Consumers' Counsel 137 E State St Columbus OH 43215

PEPPER, JOHN ENNIS, JR., consumer products company executive; b. Pottsville, Pa., Aug. 2, 1938; s. John Ennis and Irma Elizabeth (O'Connor) P.; m. Frances Graham Garber, Sept. 9, 1967; children: John, David, Douglas, Susan. B.A., Yale U., 1960. With Procter & Gamble Co., Cin., 1963—; gen. mgr. Italian subs. Procter & Gamble Co., 1974-77; v.p., gen. mgr., packaged soap and detergent div. Proctor & Gamble Co., 1977-80, group v.p., 1980-84, exec. v.p., 1984-86, pres., 1986—, also dir. Trustee Cin. Symphony Orch., Cin. Med. Inst.; group chmn. Cin. United Appeal Campaign, 1980; bd. trustees Xavier U., 1985—. Served to lt. USN, 1960-63. Mem. Nat. Alliance Businessmen (chmn. communication com.), Soap and Detergent Assn. (bd. dirs.). Office: Procter & Gamble Co 1 Procter & Gamble Plaza Cincinnati OH 45202

PEPPER, PHYLLIS MAE, finance company executive; b. Chgo., May 14, 1936; d. Irving Pepper and Rose Sachs. BS in Math., U. Ill., 1958. Asst. mathematician Household Internat., Prospect Heights, Ill., 1958-70, now data processing mgr., 1970—. Mem. Skokie (Ill.) Civic Theater, chairperson play reading, 1961-63. Avocations: world traveler, community theater, hiking, photography, birdwatching. Office: Household Internat 2700 Sanders Rd Prospect Heights IL 60070

PEPPLER, ALICE STOLPER, publishing company marketing director; b. Saginaw, Mich., Mar. 14, 1934; d. Lothar E. and Hulda M. (Koenig) Stolper; B.S., Concordia Tchrs. Coll., River Forest, Ill., 1956; postgrad. U. Ill., 1966-67; children—Jeanne, Jon, Jan. Elem. sch. tchr., librarian, music dir. Bethany Luth. Sch., Chgo., 1956-63; editor lang. arts materials Scott, Foresman & Co., Chgo., 1963-71; sr. editor lang. arts materials Lyons & Carnahan, Chgo., 1972-74; mktg. dir. lang. arts, fgn. langs. and social studies Rand McNally & Co., Chgo., 1974-77; mktg. dir. lang. arts Scott, Foresman & Co., Chgo., 1977—; piano tchr., 1956-63. Organist, music dir. First Luth. Ch. of Trinity, 1967-76; organist, choir dir. Mt. Olive Luth. Ch., Chgo., 1976—; leader singles seminars and workshops, 1975—. Mem. Internat. Reading Assn., Nat. Council Tchrs. English, Nat., Luth. edn. assns., Evang. Luths. in Mission. Author: Bible Children I Know, 1971; God's Love for Everyone, 1971; Why Jesus Came, 1972; Divorced and Christian, 1974; Who Put the Finger on God?, 1975; Single Again—This Time with Children, 1982; also articles, poems, monograph; editor Luth. Edn. Assn. Yearbook, 1972-74. Home: 1815 Tanglewood Glenview IL 60025 Office: 1900 E Lake Ave Glenview IL 60025

PEPPLER, RAEBURN BERNICE, manufacturing company executive; b. Rhinelander, Wis., Feb. 14, 1942; d. Harold A. and Lauretta (Robinson) Carlson; m. Ronald L. Peppler, Aug. 18, 1962; children: Pamela Lynn, Kimberly Rae. Adminstrv. asst. to pres. Menasha Corp., Neenah, Wis., 1962-80, asst. sec., 1979—, office services mgr., 1980—. Pres. Neenah Police Wives' Aux., 1979-86; mem. Postal Customer Council; bd. dirs. Fox River council Girl Scouts U.S., 1981, Fox Valley Tech. Regional Adv. Bd., 1986—. Mem. Internat. Facility Mgmt. Assn., N.E. Wis. Telecommunications Assn. (sec. 1982-84, v.p. 1984-86, pres. 1987—). Republican. Roman Catholic. Avocations: cross country skiing, biking, snowmobiling. Office: Menasha Corp PO Box 367 Neenah WI 54956 Home: 1061 Hughes Ct Neenah WI 54956

PERALTA, MODESTO MANGASI, JR., cardiovascular and thoracic surgeon; b. Manila, Oct. 19, 1941; came to U.S., 1965; s. Modesto Ferrer and Jorgia (Mangasi) P.; m. Lita Racaza, May 9, 1965; children—Lorraine, Modesto III, Michelle, Nicole. B.S., Letran Coll., Manila, 1960; M.D., U. Santo Tomas, 1964. Diplomate Am. Bd. Surgery, Am. Bd. Thoracic and Cardiovascular Surgery. Instr. anatomy St. Rita Hosp., Manila, 1964-65; intern St. Joseph Hosp., Lorain, Ohio, 1965-66; resident in surgery Huron Rd. Hosp., Cleve., 1966-70; resident in thoracic surgery Hahnemann Med. Coll., Phila., 1970-72; practice medicine, specializing in thoracic and cardiovascular surgery, Cleve., 1972—; chief thoracic surgery Euclid Gen. Hosp.; chief thoracic and cardiovascular surgery Huron Rd. Hosp.; mem. staff Huron Rd. Hosp., Lake County Meml. Hosp., Hillcrest Hosp. Recipient Best Research Paper award Huron Rd. Hosp., 1969, Best Resident award, 1970; recipient Best Research paper award Ohio chpt. ACS, 1971. Mem. AMA, ACS, Am. Coll. Chest Physicians, Soc. Thoracic Surgeons, Ohio Med. Assn., Cleve. Vascular Soc., Cleve. Acad. Medicine, Cleve. Surg. Soc., Soc. Philippine Surgeons in Am., Philippine Am. Soc. Ohio (v.p. 1984-85), Assn. Philippine Physicians in Ohio (pres. 1984). Roman Catholic. Club: Mayfield Village (Ohio) Racket. Contbr. articles to med. jours. Home: 9766 Rollin Rd Waite Hill OH 44094 Office: 3070 Mayfield Rd Cleveland Heights OH 44118

PEREZ-WOODS, ROSANNE HARRIGAN, nursing educator, child development consultant; b. Miami, Fla., Feb. 24, 1945; d. John Henry and Rose (Hnatow) Harrigan; m. Helio C. Perez, May 29, 1965 (div. 1978); m. David C. Woods, Apr. 12, 1986; children: Dennis James, Michael Helio, John Henry. BS, St. Xavier Coll. Chgo., 1965; MSN, Ind. U.-Indpls., 1974; EdD, Ind. U., Bloomington, 1979. Cert. pediatric nurse practitioner Nat. Bd. Pediatric Nurse Practitioners and Assocs. Staff nurse, evening charge nurse Mercy Hosp., Chgo., 1965-66; nursing educator Chgo. State Hosp., 1966-67; pediatric nurse practitioner Marion County Health and Hosp. Corp., Indpls., 1974-75; lectr. Ind. U.-Indpls., 1974-75, asst. prof. nursing, 1975-77, project dir. prenatal nursing program, 1978-85, assoc. prof., 1980-82, prof., chmn. dept. pediatrics, family and women's health Sch. Nursing, 1982-85, adj. prof. pediatrics Sch. Medicine, 1982-85; chief nursing sect. James Whitcomb Riley Hosp. Child Devel. Program, Indpls., 1982-85; Niehoff chair and prof. maternal child health Loyola U. Marcella Niehoff Sch. Nursing, 1985—; ednl. cons. Author: Immunological Concepts Applied, 1978, Protocols for Perinatal Nursing practice, 1981; contbr. articles to profl. jours. Named Nurse of Yr., March of Dimes, 1978. Mem. Am. Nurses Assn., Ind. State Nurses Assn., Nurses Assn. of Am. Coll. Ob-Gyn. (pres. cert. corp.), Nat. Perinatal Assn. (bd. dirs.), Adult Edn. Assn. Am., Am. Nurses Found., Ind. U. Alumni Assn., AAAS, Sigma Xi, Pi Lambda Theta, Sigma Theta Tau. Republican. Roman Catholic. Lodge: Soroptomists. Office: Loyola U 6525 N Sheridan Rd DH 411 Chicago IL 60626

PERINE, MAXINE HARRIET, educator; b. Worth County, Mo., May 11, 1918; d. Robert Rozwell and Della Dale (Martin) P.; B.S. in Edn., Central Mo. State U., 1944; M.A., Columbia U., 1954, profl. diploma, 1960, Ed.D., 1977. Tchr., Worth County schs., 1935-44, Kansas City (Mo.) public schs., 1944-59; reading cons. Kansas City (Mo.) public schs., 1959-64; editor Holt, Rinehart, Winston, N.Y.C., 1964; mem. faculty U. Mich., Flint, 1964—, prof. edn. specializing in reading, 1972-86, prof. emeritus, 1986—; vis. scholar Columbia U., 1978; chair World Congress of Reading, Dublin, 1982; speaker. Mem. Internat. Reading Assn., AAUP, Kappa Delta Pi (chpt. founding counselor 1980—, internat. com. constn. and bylaws 1982-84), Delta Kappa Gamma (named Woman of Distinction 1972). Presbyterian. Author, editor in field. Office: 1321 E Court St Flint MI 48503

PERINO, NORMAN WILLIAM, auditor; b. Chgo., Apr. 14, 1958; s. Norman W. Sr. and Jacqueline (Boyle) P. BBA, U. Notre Dame, 1980; M in Acctg., DePaul U., 1983. Internal auditor Humiston-Keeling, Inc., Chgo., 1980-81; audit supr. Deloitte, Haskins & Sells, Chgo., 1983-87; sr. internat. auditor Abbott Labs., Abbott Park, Ill., 1987—. Treas. Dolton-Riverdale Intermediate Baseball League, Ill., 1978—; pres. Southeast Suburban Sr. Babe Ruth League, South Suburban Chgo., 1983—. Mem. Am. Inst. CPA's, Ill. CPA Soc., Healthcare Fin. Mgmt. Assn. Roman Catholic. Home: 1509 Hinman Evanston IL 60201 Office: Abbott Labs Abbott Park IL 60064

PERISHO, CLARENCE ROBERT, retired chemistry educator; b. Newberg, Oreg., Apr. 29, 1917; s. Floyd Warder and Ethel (Lowe) P.; m. Margaret Eunice White, June 12, 1941; children—Robert C., Ethel Ruth, June Elizabeth. B.S., William Penn Coll., Oskaloosa, Iowa, 1938; M.A., Haverford Coll., Pa., 1939; Ph.D., NYU, 1963. Mem. faculty math. and sci., Friendsville Acad., Tenn., 1939-40, Nebr. Central Coll., Central City, 1940-44, McCook Jr. Coll., Nebr., 1944-47, Nebr. Wesleyan U., 1947-54; mem. faculty chemistry Mankato State U., Minn., 1954-82, prof., 1966-82, ret., 1982. Mem. AAAS, Math. Assn. (Eng.). Quaker. Home: 804 Belgrade Ave North Mankato MN 56001

PERKINS, JAMES K., lawyer; b. Council Bluffs, Iowa, Aug. 12, 1957; s. Jack Carrol and Delores Ann (Ahrenholtz) P.; m. Jacqueline Sue King, June 19, 1976 (div. Dec. 1984); children: James Michael, Jamie Marie; m. Pamela Lynne Nerheim, Sept. 21, 1985. BA, U. Nebr., Omaha, 1981; JD, U. Iowa, 1984. Bar: Iowa 1984, Ill. 1985. Assoc. Matkov, Griffen, Parsons, Salzman & Madoff, Chgo., 1984-85; sole practice Iowa City, 1985-86; assoc. Kraschel law firm, Council Bluffs, 1986—. Democrat. Methodist. Avocations: bridge, snow skiing. Office: 403 First Federal Savings and Loan Bldg Council Bluffs IA 51501

PERKINS, JAMES PATRICK, advertising agency; b. Chgo., Dec. 6, 1939; s. John Alfred and Mary Grace (Quinlan) P.; student U. Ill., 1959-60, Western Ill. U., 1961; m. Sarah Reed Simkins, Sept. 13, 1975; children—Brian Patrick, Kevin Matthew, Quinn Cecile. Sales and mktg. exec. Glidden-Durkee, 1964-65; advt. mgr. Amvar Chem. Co., 1965-69; indsl. coatings rep. Benjamin Moore Co., 1969-71; account exec. JTC Advt., 1971-74; creative dir., pres. Laven, Fuller & Perkins Advt.-Mktg., Chgo., 1974—. Dir., Mem. adv. bd. Booth Meml. Hosp., Salvation Army, Chgo., 1978-81. Served with U.S. Army, 1961-62 Mem. Bank Mktg. Assn. Roman Catholic. Home: 1314 Scott Winnetka IL 60093 also: 233 E Ontario Chicago IL 60611

PERKINS, M. DEAN, public health administrator; b. Sullivan, Ill., Oct. 16, 1938; s. Bradford E. and Lois A. (Moore) P.; m. Louise King, Dec. 31, 1962 (div. Oct. 1973); children: Ressa Lynn, Michael Dean; m. Raynelle Ellison, Dec. 29, 1974; 1 child, Candice Denise. BS, Ill. Coll., 1960; DDS, U. Mo., Kansas City, 1976. Profl. pilot 1960-72; gen. practice dentistry Kimberling City, Mo., 1976-85; dep. chief Bur. Dental Health Mo. State Dept. Health, Jefferson City, 1985—. Mem. Am. Dental Assn., Mo. Dental Assn., Cen. Dist. Dental Soc., Mo. Pub. Health Assn. Republican. Methodist. Lodge: Rotary (Outstanding Rotarian 1978-79). Avocations: hunting, fishing, music, piloting. Home: 2420 Yorktown Dr Jefferson City MO 65101 Office: State Mo Dept Health 1730 E Elm PO Box 570 Jefferson City MO 65102

PERKINS, RICHARD CHARLES, publishing company executive; b. Moline, Ill., Oct. 11, 1948; s. Robert Donald and Marjory (DeKline) P.; m. Lynn Robey, Dec. 18, 1971; children: Abbey, Amy, Alison, Bradley. BS in Edn., No. Ill. U., 1970. Regional sales mgr. McGraw-Hill Pub. Co., Chgo., 1971, The Pattis Group, Lincolnwood, Ill., 1971-72; regional sales mgr. Boys Life mag., Chgo., 1972-75, midwest sales mgr., 1975-78; sales mgr. Miller Freeman Pub., Chgo., 1978-80; pub. Harcourt Brace Jovanovich, Chgo., 1981-85, pub. dir., 1985—. Mem. Tech. Assn. Pulp and Paper Industry, Assn. Ind. Corrugated Converters, Phi Kappa Sigma. Republican. Avocations: tennis, travel, photography. Office: Harcourt Brace Jovanovich 111 E Wacker Chicago IL 60601

PERKINS, ROBERT PETER, corporate financial executive; b. Lansing, Mich., Mar. 22, 1952; s. Leo Vernon and Eleanor Doreen (Holdosh) P.; m. Gail Ann Madar, Oct. 2, 1971; children: Erik, Melanie, Mark, Jacqueline. BBA, U. Mich., 1972. CPA, Mich. Audit mgr. Ernst & Whinney, Detroit, 1971-78; treas., chief fin. officer KMS Industries, Inc., Ann Arbor, Mich., 1978-82; exec. v.p., treas., chief fin. officer MLX Corp., Troy, Mich., 1982—. Served with U.S. Army, 1969-71. Mem. Am. Inst. CPA's, Mich. Assn. CPA's. Roman Catholic. Office: MLX Corp 100 E Big Beaver Rd Suite 804 Troy MI 48083

PERKINS, SAM G., banker; b. Olathe, Kans., July 30, 1931; s. William E. and Catherine T. (Alden) P.; m. Connie Engle, June 2, 1957. BS, U. Kans., 1953; JD, U. Mo., Kansas City, 1960. Various positions Bank IV Olathe, 1955-78, chmn., pres., 1978—. Pres. Olathe Area C. of C., 1973; treas., bd. dirs. Olathe Community Hosp., 1972-80; chmn. exec. com. Baker Univ., Baldwin, Kans., 1981—; active Friends of Art, Kansas City; bd. dirs. Olathe br. Salvation Army, 1983—; mem. citizens adv. com. 10th Judicial Dist., Johnson County, Kans., 1983—. Served to cpl. U.S. Army, 1953-55. Mem. Am. Bankers Assn., Kans. Bankers Assn., Kans. Bar Assn., Mensa, Newcomen Soc. Lodge: Rotary. Office: Bank IV Olathe PO Box 400 Olathe KS 66061

PERKINS, WILLIAM H., JR., financial company executive; b. Rushville, Ill., Aug. 4, 1921; s. William H. and Sarah Elizabeth (Logsdon) P.; m. Eileen Nelson, Jan. 14, 1949; 1 child, Gary Douglas. Ed., Ill. Coll. Pres. Howlett-Perkins Assos., Chgo.; mem. Ill. AEC, 1963-84, sec., 1970-84; mem. adv. bd. Nat. Armed Forces Mus., Smithsonian Instn., 1964-82. Sgt.-at-arms Democratic Nat. Conv., 1952, 56, del.-at-large, 1964, 68, 72; spl. asst. to chmn. Dem. Nat. Com., 1960; mem. Presdl. Inaugural Com., 1961, 65, 69, 73. Served with U.S. Army, 1944-46. Mem. Health Ins. Assn. Am., Ill. Ins. Fedn. (pres. 1965-84), Ill. C. of C. (chmn. legis. com. 1971), Chgo. Assn. Commerce and Industry (legis. com.), Internat. Platform Assn. Methodist. Clubs: Sangamo (Springfield, Ill.); Riverside Golf. Lodges: Masons, Shriners. Home: 52 N Cowley Rd Riverside IL 60546 Office: 7222 Cermak Rd Suite 701 North Riverside IL 60546

PERKINSON, DIANA AGNES ZOUZELKA, rug import company executive; b. Prostejov, Czechoslovakia, June 27, 1943; came to U.S., 1962; d. John Charles and Agnes Diana (Sincl) Zouzelka; m. David Francis Perkinson, Mar. 6, 1965; children—Dana Leissa, David. B.A., U. Lausanne (Switzerland), 1960; M.A., U. Madrid, 1961; M.B.A., Case Western Res. U., 1963; cert. internat. mktg. Oxford (Eng.) U., 1962. Assoc. Allen Hartman & Schreiber, Cleve., 1963-64; interpreter Tower Internat. Inc., Cleve., 1964-66; pres. Oriental Rug Importers Ltd., Cleve., 1979—; treas. Oriental Rug Designers, Inc., Cleve., 1980—; sec., treas. Oriental Rug Cons., Inc., Cleve., 1980—; chmn. Foxworthy's Inc. subs. Oriental Rug Importers Ft. Myers, Naples, Sanibel, Fla.; dir. Beckwith & Assocs., Inc., Cleve., Dix-Bur Investments, Ltd. Trustee, Cleve. Ballet, 1979, exec. com., 1981; mem. Cleve. Mayor's Adv. Com.; trustee Diabetes Assn. Greater Cleve.; chmn. grantsmanship Jr. League of Cleve., 1982; mem. mem. Cleve. Found.-Women in Philanthropy, 1982; trustee Diabetes Assn. Greater Cleve. Mem. Women Bus. Owners Assn., Oriental Rug Retailers Am. (dir. 1983). Republican. Roman Catholic. Clubs: Cleve. Racquet, Recreation League (Cleve.). Home: Ravencrest 14681 County Line Rd Cleveland OH 44022 also: Stratford at Pelican Bay Crayton Rd Naples FL 33940 Office: Oriental Rug Importers Ltd Inc 23533 Mercantile Rd Beachwood OH 44122

PERKOVICH, ROBERT, lawyer; b. Chgo., Dec. 15, 1951; s. John George and Dora Catherine (Cappocci) P.; m. Debra Jo Johnson, May 28, 1971 (div. 1974); m. Debra Sue Benjamin, Aug. 11, 1979. B.A., Roosevelt U., 1976; J.D., John Marshall Law Sch., 1981. Bar: Ill. 1981, U.S. Dist. Ct. (no. dist.) Ill. 1981. Tax auditor IRS, Chgo., 1976-77; field examiner Nat. Labor Relations Bd., Chgo., 1977-81, field atty., 1981-84; exec. dir. Ill. Ednl. Labor Relations Bd., Chgo. and Springfield, 1984—. Active Chgo. Council Fgn. Relations, 1982, Art Inst. Chgo., Foster Parents Plan, Warwick, R.I. Mem. ABA, Ill. State Bar Assn., Chgo. Bar Assn., ACLU, Indsl. Relations Research Assn. (treas. 1985, v.p. membership 1986), Soc. Profls. in Dispute Resolution (bd. dirs. Chgo. chpt. 1986-87), Am. Arbitration Assn. (labor arbitration panel). Roman Catholic. Office: Ill Edl Labor Relations Bd 20 N Wacker Dr Suite 1000 Chicago IL 60606 Office: 325 W Adams Springfield IL 62706

PERLE, EUGENE DANIEL, geography educator; b. Jersey City, N.J., Jan. 24, 1936; s. Harry and Helen (Bergman) P.; m. Sylvia Margaret Goetz, Dec. 26, 1963; children: Lawrence Mark, Kathryn Helena, Lisa Verenne. AB, Dartmouth Coll., 1957; MA, Syracuse U., 1959; PhD, U. Chgo., 1964. Asst. prof. Ind. U., Bloomington, 1963-65, U. Pitts., 1965-68; sr. staff scientist Ford Motor Co., Dearborn, Mich., 1968-69; assoc. prof. Wayne State U., Detroit, 1969—. Contbr. articles to profl. jours. Fullbright lectureship, 1973-74. Mem. Assn. Am. Geographers, Regional Sci. Assn., Am. Statistical Assn., Am. Collegiate Schs. of Planning. Clubs: Dartmouth Coll. of Detroit (exec. com. 1983—), Mich. Squash Racquets Assn. (v.p. 1983-85). Avocations: squash, skiing. Home: 5110 W Doherty Dr West Bloomfield MI 48033 Office: Wayne State U Dept Geography & Planning Detroit MI 48202

PERLENFEIN, WAYNE CHARLES, architect; b. Moorhead, Minn., July 7, 1951; s. Lloyd Lester and Ethel Pearl (Henningsen) P.; m. Laurie Jane Gibb, Nov. 22, 1980 (div.); 1 child, George Lloyd. BArch, N.D. State U., 1974. Arch. intern Seifert & Staszko, Fargo, N.D., 1974-77; assoc. Halvorson, Moore, Sprague & Moore, Fargo, 1977-84; prin. Rogers, Perlenfein and Assocs., Fargo, 1984—. Mem. AIA, CSI, NCARB, Tau Sigma Delta. Lodges: Lions, Elks. Avocations: skiing, swimming, golf, tennis, running. Office: Rogers Perlenfein and Assocs 123 N 15th Fargo ND 58102

PERLIK, STUART JAY, physician, neurologist; b. Chgo., Dec. 28, 1947; s. David and Thelma (Becker) P. BS summa cum laude, Loyola U., 1969, MD, 1973. Diplomate Am. Bd. Med. Examiners, Am. Bd. Neurology and Psychiatry, Ab. Bd. Qualification in Electroencephalograph; lic. physician, Ill., Calif. Intern St. Joseph's Hosp., Chgo., 1973-74, Highland Park (Ill.) Hosp., 1974-76; resident U. Ill., 1976-78, Presbyn. St. Luke's Hosp., Chgo., 1978-80; clin. assoc. prof. U. Chgo. Hosps. and Clinics; attending physician, dir. EEG lab Michael Reese Hosp. and Med. Ctr., 1982—; attending physican St. Joseph's Hosp., Chgo., 1982—; cons. Barclay Psychiat. Hosp., Chgo. Contbr. articles to profl. jours. Mem. AAAS, AMA, Ill. Med. Soc., Chgo. Med. Soc., Am. Acad. Neurology, am. Electroencephalographic Soc., Am. Epilepsy Soc., Am. Assn. Electromyography and Electrodiagnosis, N.Y. Acad. Scis. Home: 4028 Dundee Rd Northbrook IL 60062 Office: Michael Reese Hosp 29th and Ellis Ave Chicago IL 60616

PERLMAN, EDWARD, small business owner; b. Chgo., May 29, 1927; s. Nathan Hyman and Leona Perlman; m. Roberta Cohen, Mar. 10, 1951; children: David, Rachel, Daniel. BS in Mktg., U. Ill., 1950. Exec. v.p. Handy Button Machine Co., Chgo., 1950-65; stockbroker H. Hentz & Co., Chgo., 1966-71; owner, operator Mars Housewares, Evanston, Ill., 1971-81, Rachel's Stock, Chgo., 1983—. Served with USN, 1945-46, PTO. Home: 133 Timber Ln Glencoe IL 60022 Office: 934 W North Ave Chicago IL 60622

PERLMAN, KALMAN ISADORE, management consultant, pharmacist; b. Chgo., May 27, 1915; s. Morris and Mary Ada (Weiner) P.; m. Ida Faye Bauer, July 2, 1939. BS in Pharmacy, U. Ill., Chgo., 1940; BBA, Northwestern U., 1962; postgrad., Loyola U., Chgo., 1966-69. Registered pharmacist; cert. purchasing mgr. Pharmacist, mgr. various drug stores, Chgo., 1932-44; chief pharmacist various hosp. pharmacies, Chgo., 1946-70; sr. hosp. procurement specialist Health & Hosps. Governing Commn. of Cook County, Chgo., 1970-80; assoc. adminstr. Chgo. Specialty Hosp., 1981-84; instr. Northeastern Ill. U., Chgo., 1979-84; cons. mgmt. Chgo., 1984—; vol. pharmacist, purchasing agt. The Ark, Chgo., 1985—. Contbr. articles to profl. jours. Served with U.S. Army, 1944-46. Fellow AAAS; mem. AMA (affiliate), Am. Pharm. Assn., Nat. Assn. Purchasing Mgmt. Jewish. Lodges: Masons (Master 1958), El Jalla Grotto (Monarch 1967). Avocations: philately, photography, writing. Home and Office: 2726 W Catalpa Ave Chicago IL 60625

PERLMAN, LAWRENCE, business executive, lawyer; b. St. Paul, Apr. 8, 1938; s. Irving and Ruth (Mirsky) P.; m. Medora Scoll, June 18, 1961; children: David, Sara. B.A., Carleton Coll., 1960; J.D., Harvard U., 1963. Bar: Minn. 1963. Law. clk. for fed. judge 1963; partner firm Fredrikson, Byron, Colborn, Bisbee, Hansen & Perlman, Mpls., 1964-75; gen. counsel, exec. v.p. U.S. pacing ops. Medtronic, Inc., Mpls., 1975-78; sr. partner firm Oppenheimer, Wolff and Donnelly, Mpls., St. Paul, N.Y., Washington, Brussels, 1978-80; sec., gen. counsel, v.p. corp. services Control Data Corp., Mpls., 1980-83; pres., chief operating officer, dir. Comml. Credit Co., 1984-85; pres. Data Storage Products Group, 1985—, exec. v.p., 1986—; bd. dirs. Am. Hoist & Derrick Co., Control Data Corp., Bio-Medicus Corp., Inter-Regional Fin. Group, Inc., The Microelectronics and Computer Tech. Corp.; adj. prof. Law Sch., U. Minn., 1974-76, 79-80. Mem. Mpls. Bd. Estimate and Taxation, 1974-75; chmn. Mpls. Municipal Fin. Commn., 1978-79; bd. dirs. Walker Art Center, Mt. Sinai Hosp., Minn. Orchestral Assn.; trustee Carleton Coll; chmn. bd. visitors U. Minn. Law Sch., 1978-80. Mem. Phi Beta Kappa. Club: Mpls. Home: 2366 W Lake of the Isles Pkwy Minneapolis MN 55405 Office: Control Data Corp 8100 34th Ave S Minneapolis MN 55440

PERLMAN, MELVIN L., psychologist, educator; b. Chicago, May 22, 1925; s. Phillip C. and Belle I. (Letchinger) P.; m. Miriam D. Goodman, Dec. 22, 1946; 1 child, Sheri Beth. MA, U. Chgo., 1950, PhD, 1953. Registered psychologist, Ill. Coordinator tng. VA, Downey, Ill., 1953-63; asst. chief psychology Ill. State Psychol. Inst., Chgo., 1963-76, chief psychologist, 1976—. Served with USAF, 1943-46, PTO. Mem. Am. Psychol. Assn., Am. Bd. Profl. Psychologists (dir. exams. 1978-81, bd. examiners 1981—), Ill. Psychol. Assn. Home: 1301 Mulford St Evanston IL 60202 Office: Ill State Psychol Inst 1601 W Taylor St Chicago IL 60612

PERLMUTTER, ALAN JAY, real estate developer; b. St. Louis, Aug. 26, 1947; s. Lester Martin and Marion Ruth (Synes) P.; m. Konstanze Schmidt, June 8, 1969 (div. Feb. 1983); children: Danielle, Erik; Liane Sue Binowitz, Oct. 25, 1986. BA, U. Wis., 1969; MBA, Columbia U., 1970. Market researcher Mayer Co., St. Louis, 1970-71; real estate negotiator Food Fair Stores, Phila., 1971-72; v.p., ptnr. Paragan Group, St. Louis, 1972—; trustee Gateway Mall, St. Louis, 1985—; coordinator Paragon's Run for the Olympics, St. Louis, 1979-86. Recipient Centers of Excellence award Nat. Mall Monitor, 1982, BOMA Bldg. of Yr. award BOMA, 1983. Mem. Nat. Assn. Indsl. and Office Park Developers (v.p. 1985), Internat. Council Shopping Ctrs. Jewish. Clubs: Porsche, Creve Coeur Racket (St. Louis). Avocations: photography, running, auto racing, tennis. Home: 942 Somerfor Pl Saint Louis MO 63141 Office: Paragon Group 12400 Olive Blvd Saint Louis MO 63141

PERME, TONY M., retail executive; b. Chgo., Apr. 28, 1943; s. Anton Jr. and Rose (Zidar) P.; m. Sharon Perme (divorced); 1 child, Scott. BS in Econs., U. Wis., 1970. Tech. specialist U. Wis., Madison, 1968-74; owner Retail Grocery Store, Madison, 1975-84; purchasing mgr. Gilson Med. Electronics, Middleton, Wis., 1974—. Office: Gilson Med Electronics 3000 W Bertline Hwy Middleton WI 53562

PERNEY, VIOLET HELEN, psychologist; b. Cleve., Jan. 24, 1938; d. Kazimir and Balbina (Brejnak) K.; m. Lawrence Perney, July 25, 1959 (dec. 1977); children: Teresa, Christine, Lawrence, Katherine, David. BA, Case Western Reserve, 1971, MA, 1973, PhD, 1975. Lic. psychologist. Psychologist Woman's Gen. Hosp., Cleve., 1975-76; asst. prof. S.W. Mo. State U., Springfield, Mo., 1976-86; pvt. practice psychology Springfield, 1978—; dir. behavioral medicine Mo. Rehab. Ctr., Mt. Vernon, 1985—. Mem. Am. Psychol. Assn., Mo. Psychol. Assn., Ozark Area Psychol. Assn. (pres. 1984-85), S.W. Psychol. Assn., Phi Beta Kappa. Avocations: sailing, gardening. Office: Mo Rehab Ctr Mount Vernon MO 65712

PERONA, GERALD FRANK, librarian; b. Kenosha, Wis., Dec. 22, 1943; s. Frank B. and Eleanor (Angeli) P.; m. Judith Camille Domanik, Dec. 20, 1969; 1 child, Gregory Frank. BS in Secondary Edn., U. Wis., Madison, 1966; MS in Curriculum and Instruction, U. Wis., Milw., 1968, MS in Library and Infor. Sci., 1971. Tchr. Racine (Wis.) Unified Sch. Dist., 1966-70; library asst. U. Wis., Milw., 1970-71; librarian Gateway Tech. Inst., Kenosha, Wis., 1971—; chmn. library-learning resource ctrs. Gateway Tech. Inst., Kenosha, 1980—. Mem. Wis. Library Assn., Kenosha Area Library Assn. (pres. 1975-76), Wis. Vocat. Assn., Wis. Assn. Acad. Librarians. Roman Catholic. Lodge: Roma. Home: 2941 Chapel Ln Racine WI 53406 Office: Gateway Technical Institute 3520 30th Ave Kenosha WI 53142

PEROTTI, ROSE NORMA, lawyer; b. St. Louis, Aug. 10, 1930; d. Joseph and Dorothy Mary (Roleski) Perotti. B.A., Fontbonne Coll., St. Louis, 1952; J.D., St. Louis U., 1957. Bar: Mo. 1958. Trademark atty. Sutherland, Polster & Taylor, St. Louis, 1958-63, Sutherland Law Office, 1964-70; trademark atty. Monsanto Co., St. Louis, 1971-85, sr. trademark atty., 1985—. Honored with dedication of faculty office in her name, St. Louis U. Sch. Law, 1980. Mem. Mo. Bar Assn., Bar Assn. Met. St. Louis, ABA, Am. Judicature Soc., Smithsonian Assocs., Friends St. Louis Art Museum, Mo. Bot. Garden. Office: Monsanto Co 800 N Lindbergh Blvd Saint Louis MO 63167

PEROZZI, WILLIAM THOMAS, therapist, social services administrator; b. Kenosha, Wis., Mar. 23, 1943; s. Ernest and Antonia (Pascucci) P.; m. Claudia Ann, May 30, 1970; children: Christina, Daniel. BS, U. Wis., 1966; MSW, Washington U., 1970. Cert. social worker, Ill. Supr. guardianship adminstrn., case rev. adminstr. Ill. Dept. Children and Family Services, E. St. Louis, 1970—; pvt. practice family therapist Edwardsville, Ill., 1978—. Served with U.S. Army, 1966-68. Mem. Nat. Assn. Social Workers (pres. E. St. Louis chpt. 1976-77), Washington U. Alumni Assn. (pres. George Warren Brown Sch. Social Work 1981-82). Home: 44 Larkmoor Edwardsville IL 62025 Office: Ill Dept Children Family Services 10 Collinsville Ave East Saint Louis IL 62201

PERPICH, RUDY GEORGE, governor Minn.; b. Carson Lake, Minn., June 27, 1928; s. Anton and Mary (Vukelich) P.; m. Delores Helen Simic, Sept. 4, 1954; children: Ruby George, Mary Susan. A.A., Hibbing Jr. Coll., 1950; D.D.S., Marquette U., 1954. Lt. gov. State of Minn., 1971-76, gov., 1977-79, 83—; v.p., exec. cons. Control Data Worldtech, Inc., Mpls., 1979-82. Mem. Hibbing Bd. Edn., Minn., 1956-62; mem. Minn. Senate, 1962-70. Served to sgt. AUS, 1946-47. Mem. Nat. Govs. Assn. Democrat. Roman Catholic. Office: Office of Gov 130 State Capitol Saint Paul MN 55155 *

PERRET, MAURICE EDMOND, geography educator; b. La Chaux-de-Fonds, Switzerland, May 19, 1911; s. Jules Henri and Henriette Marie (Leuba) P.; Bac. es Lettres, U. Zurich (Switzerland), 1930; Licence es Lettres,

U. Neuchatel (Switzerland), 1940; M.A. (Internat. House fellow 1940-42), U. Calif. at Berkeley, 1942; Doctorat es Lettres, U. Lausanne (Switzerland), 1950. Tchr., Petropolis and Lycee Francais, Rio de Janeiro, Brazil, 1935-37; asst. consulate Switzerland, San Francisco, 1942-43; del. internat. com. Red Cross, Washington, 1943-45; del. Aid to Arab Refugees, Palestine, 1949-51; asst. Internat. Telecommunication Union, Geneva, Switzerland, 1951-52; librarian La Chaux-de-Fonds, Switzerland, 1953-54; asst. Oltremare, Rome, Italy, 1955-56; prof. Avenches, Switzerland, 1957-63; prof. geography, map librarian U. Wis., Stevens Point, 1963-81, prof. emeritus, 1981—. Curator Roman Mus., Avenches, Switzerland, 1960-63. Mem. city council Avenches, Switzerland, 1961-63. Served with Swiss Army, 1939-40. Mem. Assn. Am. Geographers, Nat. Council Geog. Edn., Am. Geog. Soc., Wis. Acad. Scis., Arts and Letters, Société vaudoise de geographie (v.p. 1960-63), Fedn. Swiss Geog. Socs. (v.p. 1961-63). Club: Travelers Century. Editorial com. Atlas Switzerland, 1960-63. Contbr. articles to profl. jours. Office: U Wis Geography Dept Stevens Point WI 54481

PERRICH, JERRY ROBERT, manufacturing company executive; b. San Bernardino, Calif., Nov. 21, 1947; s. Robert Joseph and Donaldeen Joan (Arthurs) P.; m. M. Jane Palmer, Sept. 23, 1972; children: William Joseph, Robert James, Michael Jonathan. BS in Engring., Case Inst. Tech., 1969; MS in Engring., U. Louisville, 1974, PhD in ChemE, 1976. Registered profl. engr., Ohio. Application engr. Am. Air Filter, Louisville, 1972-73; project mgr. Olin Corp., Brandenburg, Ky., 1975-77; prodn. supr. E.I. DuPont, Louisville, 1977-80; dir. engring. N.Am. Carbon, Columbus, Ohio, 1980—; cons. Louisville, 1976-80. Editor Activated Carbon, 1981; patentee in field; contbr. articles in profl. jours. Served to 1st lt. U.S. Army, 1969-72. Mem. Am. Inst. Chem. Engrs., Sigma Xi, Phi Kappa Phi, Tau Beta Pi. Home: 6250 Cherry Hill Dr Columbus OH 43213 Office: N Am Carbon 432 McCormick Blvd Columbus OH 43213

PERRY, DIANNE KAY, school guidance administrator, psychologist; b. Saginaw, Mich., Jan. 30, 1946; d. Merritt B. and Wanda Lois (Kimmel) P. BA, Alma Coll., 1968; MEd, Wayne State U., 1972; PhD in Edn., U. Mich., 1981. Cert. tchr., Mich.; lic. psychologist, Mich.; cert. hypnotherapist. Guidance adminstr. Detroit pub. schs., 1979—, cons., 1972—; assoc. prof. grad. faculty Wayne State U., 1986—; part-time instr. Wayne County Community Coll., 1971-79; counselor, ednl. cons., human relations cons.; practice psychology, Detroit, 1982—; assoc. cons. New Perspectives on Race. Named one of Outstanding Young Women Am., 1981. Mem. Mich. Personnel and Guidance Assn. (pres.-elect 1983-84), Guidance Assn. Met. Detroit (pres. 1982-83, newsletter editor 1981-82). Methodist. Author: Classroom Techniques to Improve Self-Concept, 1972, Congruencies and Incongruencies in the Expectations and Perceptions of the Role of the Elementary School Counselor in Detroit Public Schools, 1981. Home: 25051 Sherwood Circle Southfield MI 48075 Office: Costineu & Assocs 23300 Providence Dr Southfield MI 48075

PERRY, ESTON LEE, business executive; b. Martburg, Tenn., June 16, 1936; s. Eston Lee and Willimae (Heidle) P.; m. Alice Anne Schmit, Oct. 21, 1961; children—Julie Anne, Jeffrey John, Jennifer Lee. B.S., Ind. State U., 1961. With Oakley Corp., 1961—, treas., 1961-70, dir., 1965—, v.p., 1981-86, pres., 1986—; corp. officer Ind. State Bank, Terre Haute, 1975-80; pres. One Twenty Four Madison Corp., Terre Haute, 1979—, chmn. bd., 1981—. Bd. dirs. Aviation Commn., Terre Haute, pres., 1970; bd. dirs. Salvation Army, Terre Haute, 1975—, mem. exec. adv. bd., 1979—; bd. dirs. Vigo County Dept. Pub. Welfare, 1979-82, 124 Madison Corp., 1979—, Jr. Achievement Wabash Valley, 1980-86 , United Way of Wabash Valley, 1984—, United Way of Ind., 1984—, v.p., 1986; bd. dirs. Terre Haute Symphony Orch., 1984-87, Goodwill Industries of Terre Haute, 1984—, Leadership Terre Haute, 1984—, Cen. Eastside Assocs., 1984—, pres., 1984-85; bd. dirs. City of Terre Haute Hulman Links Commn., pres., 1986— mem. President's Assocs., Ind. State U., adv. bd. Ctr. Econ. Devel., 1984—; bd. overseers Sheldon Swope Art Gallery of Terre Haute, 1984-87; nat. mem. Council on Founds.; mem. adv. com. comml. air service study Ind. Dept. Commerce; bd. assocs. Rose Hulman Inst. Tech., 1986—. Served with U.S. Army, 1955-57. Mem. Jaycees Terre Haute (v.p. 1967-69), C. of C. Terre Haute (bd. dirs. 1984—), Edgewood Grove Assn. (pres. 1982), Wabash Valley Pilots Assn., Aircraft Owners and Pilots Assn., Air Safety Found., Aviation Trades Assn., Lambda Chi Alpha. Clubs: Country of Terre Haute; Sycamore Varsity (Ind. State U.). Lodges: Lions (pres. Terre Haute 1983-84), Elks. Home: 124 Madison Blvd Terre Haute IN 47803 Office: 8 S 16th St Terre Haute IN 47807

PERRY, HAROLD, radiation oncologist; b. Hamtramck, Mich., June 26, 1924; s. James Arthur and Ida Barcelona (Hill) P.; m. Agnes Marie Barnes, June 12, 1948; children: Harold Arthur, Karen Fanchon Perry, Merlien. MD, Howard U., 1948. Diplomate Am. Bd. Radiology. Asst. prof. radiology U. Cin. Coll. Medicine, 1957-63, assoc. prof. radiology, 1963-66; clin. assoc. prof. radiology Wayne State U., Detroit, 1966-68, 73-79, clin. assoc. prof. clin. oncology, 1979-82, clin. prof. radiation oncology, 1982—; assoc. mem. Southwest Oncology Group, 1976—; adj. prof. radiology Wayne State U., Detroit, 1969-73; affiliate mem. Radiation Therapy Oncology Group, 1983—. Mem. editorial bd. Internat. Jour. Bio-Med. Computers, 1969-85. Served with AUS, 1942-46. Council for Tobacco Research grantee, 1979—. Fellow Am. Coll. Radiology; mem. AAAS, AMA, Am. Cancer Soc. (bd. dirs. Hamilton County chpt. 1962-66), Nat. Med. Assn. (chmn. radiation therapy technical adv. bd. 1978—, local radiology sect. 1979), Am. Assn. for Cancer Research, Mich. State Med. Soc. (cancer com. 1971-78, legislation and socio-econs. divs. 1974), Wayne County Med. Soc. (med. resolutions com. 1974, alt. del. 1975-76), Am. Soc. Preventive Oncology, Am. Soc. Clin. Oncology, Mich. Radiol. Soc. (pres. 1977-78, alt. councilor to the Am. Coll. Radiology, 1986-87), Mich. Soc. of Therapeutic Radiologists (pres. 1982-83, chmn. bd. 1983-84), Mich. Cancer Found. (co-chmn. med. adv. com. 1980—, vice chmn. bd. trustees 1985—, bd. dirs.), Detroit Med. Soc., N.Y. Acad. Scis., Am. Radium Soc., Am. Coll. Radiology, Council of Affiliated Regional Radiation Oncology Soc. (exec. com. 1986, regional rep. 1981—), Alumni Assn. Dept. Radiation Oncology Meml. Sloan Kettering Cancer Ctr. (pres. elect 1986-87). Avocations: bowling, computer science. Home: 287 Orange Lake Dr Bloomfield Hills MI 49013 Office: Sinai Hosp Detroit 6767 W Outer Dr Detroit MI 48235

PERRY, HAROLD WALTON, JR., real estate consultant, appraiser; b. Oak Park, Ill., Nov. 21, 1946; s. Harold Walton Sr. and Jean (Bak) P.; m. Wanda Lou Gaffner, Jan. 28, 1967; children: Brett, Jennifer, Justin, Kirsten. BA in Russian Studies and Econs., U. Ill., 1972; MBA in Fin., Loyola U., 1974. Loan analyst First Mortgage Adv., Oak Brook, Ill., 1973-74; asst. v.p. James P. Foley & Assocs., Chgo., 1974-76; prin. H.W. Perry & Assocs., Chgo., 1976-79; v.p. Rubloff, Inc., Chgo., 1979-84; sr. prin. Pannell Kerr Forster, Chgo., 1984—. Served to sgt. USAF, 1967-70. Mem. Am. Inst. Real Estate Appraisers (vice chmn. admissions 1985-86), Soc. Real Estate Appraisers, Chgo. Bd. Realtors (chmn. appraisers council, fin. com.), Nat. Assn. Realtors (fin. com., subcom. legis. regulations), Nat. Assn. Corp. Real Estate Execs., Urban Land Inst. (assoc.), Lambda Alpha. Club: Univ. (Chgo.). Avocation: jogging. Home: 7N243 Longridge Rd Saint Charles IL 60174 Office: Pannell Kerr Forster 150 N Michigan Chicago IL 60174

PERRY, JOHN ARTHUR, technical writer, inventor; b. Ridgefield, Conn., Nov. 11, 1921; s. John Orrin and Sarah (McCarthy) P.; m. Inger Johanne Bye, Jan. 16, 1964; 1 child, Joan Ellen. BS, U. Rochester, 1943; MS, La. State U., 1952, PhD, 1954. Dir. instrument div. McCrone Assocs., Chgo., 1969-70; cons. Chgo., 1971-79; chemist Regis Chem. Co., Morton Grove, Ill., 1979-82, dir. research, 1982-84, v.p. research, 1984—. Author: Introduction to Analytical Gas Chromatography, 1981; patentee in field. Mem. Am. Chem. Soc., AAAS, Chgo. Gas Chromatography Discussion Group (cofounder, chmn. 1961-63, Merit award 1980). Avocations: racing one-design sailboats, reading. Office: Regis Chem Co 8210 N Austin Ave Morton Grove IL 60053

PERRY, MARK, personnel consultant; b. Cairo, Egypt, Feb. 27, 1951; came to U.S., 1980; s. Whitall Nicholson and Barbara (Ward) P.; m. Clara Ines Zapata, Jan. 22, 1979. Student in graphology, Inst. Antoine Rossier, Lausanne, Switzerland, 1975-76; student in rhythmology, Inst. Antoine Rossier, 1976-78. Tchr. English Berlitz Language Sch., Lausanne, 1971-74; pvt. practice personnel cons., handwriting analysis Switzerland, U.S., 1978—; dir. Profile Selection Co., Bloomington, Ind., 1987—; writer, translator, 1983—. Recipient Golden Poet award World of Poetry, 1986. Mem. Am. Assn. Handwriting Analysts, Internat. Graphoanalysis Soc. (cert. master graphoanalyst 1986). Republican. Avocations: basketball, volleyball. Home and Office: 3495 Inverness Farm Rd Bloomington IN 47401

PERRY, MICHAEL D., sports writer; b. Cleve., Nov. 4, 1961; s. Oscar R. and Betty S. (Madow) P. BA in Communications, U. Cin., 1984. News writer Ky. Post, Covington, 1983, Cin. Enquirer, 1984; sports writer Jour. and Courier, Lafayette, Ind., 1984—. Vol. Tippecanoe County Boy's Club, Lafayette, 1984—. Democrat. Jewish. Avocations: softball, sports, volunteering. Home: 3168 Eagles Way Dr Apt 1761 Lafayette IN 47905 Office: Jour and Courier 217 N 6th St Lafayette IN 47901

PERRY, NANCY ESTELLE, psychologist; b. Pitts., Oct. 30, 1934; d. Simon Warren and Estelle Cecelia (Zaluski) Reichard; B.S., Ohio State U., 1956, M.A. in Psychology, 1969, Ph.D. in Psychology (EPDA fellow), 1973; m. John Cleveland; children—Scott, Karen, Elaine. Nurse, various locations, 1956-63; sch. psychologist Pub. Schs. Columbus (Ohio), 1970-72; human devel. specialist Madison County (Ohio) Schs., 1972-75; pvt. practice clin. psychology, cons. psychology, Worthington, Ohio, 1975-80; tchr. U. Wis. Sch. Nursing, Milw., 1980-83, Milw. Devel. Center, 1980-83; pvt. practice Assoc. Mental Health Services, 1983—. Ohio Dept. Edn. grantee, 1973-76. Mem. Am. Nurses Assn., Wis. Nurses Assn., Am. Psychol. Assn., Ohio Psychol. Assn., Orgnl. Devel. Network, Internat. Assn. Applied Social Scientists, Am. Assn. Marriage and Family Counselors. Home: 2210 Charter Mall Mequon WI 53092 Office: 6310 N Port Washington Rd Milwaukee WI 53211

PERRY, PATRICIA KAY, social worker; b. Oak Park, Ill., Jan. 5, 1943; d. Thomas Edward and Catherine Margaret (Bradley) Skedd; m. Donald Eugene Perry, July 9, 1966; children: Sean Patrick, Kelly Kay. BA in Psychology, St. Mary of the Woods, Ind., 1964. Registered social worker, Ill. Social worker Manteno (Ill.) Mental Health Ctr., 1964-66; tchr. St. Mary's Elem. Sch., Park Forest, Ill., 1966-67; social worker Shapiro Devel. Ctr., Inc., Kankakee, Ill., 1978-79, Manteno Mental Health Ctr., 1979-85; program services counselor PACT, Inc., chgo., 1986—; grant coordinator PACT, Inc., Chgo., 1986. Roman Catholic. Avocations: stamp collecting, coaching youth projects. Home: 541 Catalpa Box 695 Beecher IL 60401 Office: PACT Inc 618 S Michigan Ave Chicago IL 60602

PERRY, RICHARD DOUGLAS, restaurateur; b. Chgo., Oct. 24, 1938; s. Ralph Marion and Nell Jane (Alexander) P. B.A., U. Ill., 1962. Expansion dir. Delta Sigma Phi, Denver, 1961-66; sales rep. McGraw Hill Book Co., N.Y.C., 1966-71; propr. Richard Perry restaurant, St. Louis, 1971—. Mem. Inst. Am. Food and Wine (charter), Master Chef's Inst. (charter), St. Louis Vintner's Forum (founding), Am. Culinary Fedn., Nat. Restaurant Assn., Mo. Restaurant Assn., Nat. Inst. for Off Premise Catering (charter), Soc. Am. Cuisine (dir., treas. 1985-86), St. Louis Culinary Soc. (dir. 1986—). Served with U.S. Army, 1961-64. Home and Office: 3265 S Jefferson Ave Saint Louis MO 63118

PERRY, ROBERT HARLAN, dentist; b. Fostoria, Ohio, Feb. 5, 1933; s. Harlan Leroy and Glenna Elizabeth (Fletcher) P.; m. Martha Katherine Green, Dec. 28, 1956; children: Katherine Jane Perry Gaunt, Kristine Elizabeth Perry Miller. DDS, Ohio State U., 1957. Pvt. practice dentistry Elyria, Ohio, 1959—; tchr. sch. of Nursing, Elyria, 1964-66. Pres. Elyria Pub. Library Bd., 1984—, Lorain County (Ohio) Hist. Soc., 1984. Served to lt. USN, 1957-59. Mem. ADA, Ohio Dental Soc., Lorain County Dental Soc., Elyria Jaycees (pres. 1964-65, Dist. Service award 1968). Republican. Congregationalist. Club: Elyria Gyro (pres. 1984); Lodge: Rotary (pres. Elyria Club 1970-71, sec. 1978—). Avocations: photography, woodworking, cooking, tool collecting. Home: 344 Vassar Ave Elyria OH 44035 Office: 673 E River St Elyria OH 44035

PERRY, ROBERT L., sociology educator; b. Toledo, Dec. 6, 1932; s. Rudolph R. and Katherine (Bogan) P.; m. Dorothy LaRouth Smith, Aug. 23, 1969; children: Baye Kito, Kai Marlene, Ravi Kumar. BA, Bowling Green (Ohio) State U., 1959, MA, 1965; PhD, Wayne State U., 1978. Asst. prof. sociology Detroit Inst. Tech., 1967-70; asst. prof. sociology Bowling Green State U., 1970-79, assoc. prof. ethnic studies and sociology, 1979—, chmn. dept. ethnic studies, 1979—; cons. Northwest Ohio Regional Council on Alcoholism, Toledo, 1984-86. Contbr. articles to profl. jours. Records reviewer Lucas County Juvenile Ct., Toledo, 1979—; mem. com. Gov.'s Council on Recovery Services, Columbus, 1985-86; bd. dirs. Ohio Hispanic Inst. of Opportunity, Inc., Toledo, 1975—; trustee Inst. for Child Advocacy, Cleve., 1979—. Served to sgt. USAF, 1953-57. Mem. Am. Sociol. Soc., N. Cen. Sociol. Assn., Nat. Assn. of Ethnic Studies, Nat. Assn. Black Studies, Am. Soc. Criminology, Kappa Alpha Psi, Sigma Delta Pi, Alpha Kappa Delta. Methodist. Avocations: running, swimming, biking. Office: Bowling Green State U Dept Ethnic Studies Bowling Green OH 43403-0216

PERRY, STEPHEN CARL, clinical therapist; b. St. Paul, Minn., May 5, 1952; s. John Robert and Leona Martha (Portz) P.; m. Veronica Ann Henderson, July 27, 1985; 1 stepchild, Mathew Henderson. MS in Edn., U. Wis., River Falls, 1979. Chem. dependency counselor Adolescent Drug Treatment, Coon Rapids, Minn., 1979-82, program dir., 1982-83; youth family counselor Youth Service Bur., St. Paul, 1984-85; clin. therapist Park Place Clinic, Mpls., 1984-85, Family Service of St. Croix Area, Stillwater, Minn., 1985—. Served to cpl. USMC, 1973-73. Mem. ALMACA, Minn. Psychol. Assn. Lutheran. Avocations: fishing, camping, softball, racquetball, gardening. Home: 317 McMenemy Circle Vadnais Heights MN 55110 Office: Family Service St Croix Area 216 W Myrtle St Stillwater MN 55082

PERRY, THOMAS KIRK, orthopaedic surgeon. BS, U. Ill., 1942, MD, 1946. Diplomate Am. Bd. Orthopaedic Surgery. Intern Los Angeles Gen. Hosp., 1946-47; resident Univ. Hosps., Madison, Wis., 1950-54; orthopedic surgeon Orthopedic Assocs., Manitowoc, Wis., 1955—. Mem. Am. Acad. Orthopedic Surgeons, AMA, Wis. Med. Soc., Wis. Orthopaedic Soc., Manitowoc County Med. Soc. Office: Orthopaedic Assocs 501 N 10th St Manitowoc WI 54220

PERRYMAN, BRUCE CLARK, academic administrator; b. Laramie, Wyo., Jan. 28, 1939; s. Homer F. and Phyllis C. (White) P.; m. Sharon Lynn Lungren, June 28, 1958; children: Kimberly Jo, Bruce Homer. BBA, BA in Mktg. Edn., U. Wyo., 1965, MS in Bus. and Edn., 1966, postgrad., 1970-71, 84—. Cert. tchr. and adminstr., Wyo.; lic. ins. agt. Dir. research unit Wyo. State Dept. Edn., Cheyenne, 1966-67, dir. of vocat. edn., 1968-71; asst. prof. bus. Adams State Coll., Alamosa, Colo., 1967-68; pres., exec. dir. Mont. Plains Edn. Ctr., Glasgow, 1971-77; field underwriter N.Y. Life Ins. Co., Worland, Wyo., 1977-79; v.p., mgr. United Savs. Bank, Worland, 1979-84; curriculum facilitator Washakie County Sch. Dist. #1, Worland, 1984-86; dir. Hibbing (Minn.) Tech. Inst., 1986—. Trustee local sch. bd., 1980-84, pres. 1982-84; council mem. Zion Luth. Ch., 1977—, pres. 1980-82; bd. dirs. City Recreation Dept., treas., 1979, Pub. Utilities Dept., 1980-84; mem. Farm Bur. Fedn.; alt. del. to Wash. Rep. Cen. Com. Served to sgt. USAF, 1958-62. Wyo. Tchrs. scholar (2); Kellog doctoral fellow Tex. Tech U., 1979. Mem. NEA (life), Am. Assn. Sch. Adminstrs., Am. Assn. Supervision and Curriculum Devel., Wyo. Assn. Supervision and Curriculum Devel., Am. Vocat. Assn., Am. Vocat. Edn. Research Assn. (charter), Phi Delta Kappa. Lodges: Elks, Masons, Rotary Internat. (past pres.). Avocations: racquetball, fishing, photography, reading, travel. Home: 766 Meadow Dr Hibbing MN 55746 Office: Hibbing Tech Inst 2900 E Beltline Hibbing MN 55746

PERSHING, DIANA KAY, financial investment executive; b. Battle Creek, Mich., Jan. 17, 1943; d. James Harry and Frances Virginia (Garrett) Prill; m. Robert George Pershing, Sept. 16, 1961; children: Carolyn Frances, Robert James Lester. Student, Kent (Ohio) State U., 1967. Real estate sec. Village Realty, Glen Ellyn, Ill., 1975-76, rep. real estate, 1976-77; real estate sales Crown Realty, Glen Ellyn, 1977-79; corp. sec. Teltend Inc., St. Charles, Ill., 1979—, also bd. dirs.; pres. DKP Prodns. Inc., Villa Park, Ill., 1985—, also bd. dirs. Mem. Nat. Assn. Female Execs. Office: DKP Prodns 739 N Harvard Villa Park IL 60181

PERSHING, ROBERT GEORGE, telecommunications company executive; b. Battle Creek, Mich., Aug. 10, 1941; s. James Arthur and Beulah Francis P.; B.S.E.E., Tri-State Coll., Angola, Inc., 1961; m. Diana Kay Prill, Sept. 16, 1961; children—Carolyn, Robert. Communications engr. Am. Elec. Power, Ind., N.Y. and Ohio, 1961-69; design supr. Wescom, Inc., Ill., 1969-74; dir. engring. Tellabs, Inc., Lisle, Ill., 1974-78; pres., chief exec. officer, chmn. bd. Teltrend, Inc., St. Charles, Ill., 1979—, also dir.; chief exec. officer DKP Prodns. Inc., St. Charles, Ill., 1986—; engring. cons. Recipient Chgo. Area Small Bus. award, 1986. Mem. IEEE. Office: 620 Stetson Saint Charles IL 60174

PERSKY, SEYMOUR HOWARD, lawyer; b. Chgo., May 22, 1922; s. Joseph E. and Bertha (Solomon) P.; A.A. magna cum laude, City Coll., Chgo., 1949; B.A., Roosevelt U., 1952; J.D., DePaul U., 1952; postgrad. Northwestern U., 1962; m. Beverly M. Lipsky, July 8, 1962; children—Jonathan E., Abby Joan. Admitted to Ill. bar, 1952, U.S. Supreme Ct. bar, 1965; resident counsel Mid-West Loan Co., Chgo., 1953-58; sr. ptnr. firm Persky, Phillips & Berzock, Chgo., 1961-63; practiced in Chgo., 1963—; pub. defender Narcotics Ct., Municipal Ct. of Chgo., 1964; lectr. Truman Jr. Coll., 1977; mem. Internat. Options Market, Internat. Monetary Market (Chgo. Merc. Exchange). Vice gen. chmn. bd. govs. Israel Bonds of Greater Chgo., 1980-87, chmn. young peoples div., 1970-72, chmn. lawyers div., 1973-74, pres. Prime Minister's Club; bd. govs. Ida Crown Jewish Acad., 1980; bd. dirs. Hillel Torah North Suburban Day Sch., Skokie, Ill. 1973, Arie Crown Day Sch., 1977, Skokie Valley Synagogue, 1977, Anti-Defamation League B'nai B'rith, 1985—, Jewish Nat. Fund, YIVO-Inst. for Jewish Research, 1984—; ptnr. DePaul U. Coll. Law; mem. endowment bd. DePaul U.; mem. Highland Park Historic Preservation Commn., Ill., 1984—. Served with USAAF, 1941-44. Recipient Resolution City Council of Chgo., 1986. Mem. ABA, Ill. Bar Assn. (chmn. subcom. unauthorized practice law com. 1962), Chgo. Bar Assn. (criminal law com., def. prisoners com.) , Ill. Acad. Criminology, Decalogue Soc., Def. Lawyers Assn., Am. Trial Lawyers Assn., Lex Legio DePaul U., Soc. Fellows DePaul U., DePaul U. Alumni Assn (mem. exec. bd., chmn. alumni class 1952), Landmarks Preservation Council Ill. Clubs: City, Execs., Cliff Dwellers, Chgo. Soc. Clubs, Carlton (Chgo.); Quadrangle (U. Chgo.). Home: 65 Prospect Ave Highland Park IL 60035 Office: 123 W Madison St Chicago IL 60602

PERSKY, STEWART ALAN, accountant; b. St. Louis, Sept. 26, 1952; s. Julius Edward Persky and Selma (Gross) Garon; m. Gail Madeliene Perry, June 23, 1974; children: Jason, Nicole, Jessica. B in Journalism, U. Mo., 1974, MBA with honors, 1977. CPA. Staff acct. Lester Witte and Co., Clayton, Mo., 1977-79; mgr. tax and healthcare Stone Carlie, Clayton, 1979-84; mgr. tax Brown, Smith and Co., Clayton, 1984-85; pvt. practice acctg. Creve Coeur and Clayton, Mo., 1985—; dir. tax and healthcare services Tiger Fireside Stone Carlie CPA's, St. Louis, 1981-84; pub. speaker on tax, fin. and healthcare planning, various orgns. Active PTA, St. Louis. Mem. Am. Inst. CPA's, Mo. Soc. CPA's, Mo. Healthcare Assn. Club: Dad and I (St. Louis) (group leader 1985). Avocations: computers, chess, bridge, racquetball, other sports. Home: 803 Somerton Ridge Saint Louis MO 63141 Office: 222 S Central Suite 902 Clayton MO 63105

PERSON, PAULA (MRS. P. BARRY PERSON), social skills organization executive, entrepreneur; b. Worcester, Mass., Feb. 19, 1935; d. Leo Joseph and Imelda Mary (Elmore) Barry; married; children: Suzanne Elizabeth Person Tapley, John Lloyd III, Christian Barry. BA in Edn. and Spanish, Marymount Coll., 1957; postgrad., Harrington Inst. Interior Design, 1974-75. Cert. elem. tchr., N.Y. Founder, tchr. Post Nursery Sch. U.S. Forces, Aschaffenbrug, Fed. Republic Germany, 1958, Post Kindergarten Sch. U.S. Forces, Aschaffenbrug, 1959-62; tchr. King Solver Sch., Ft. Knox, 1963-64, Model Sch., Louisville, 1964-66; free lance interior designer Chgo., 1974-79; pres., founder The Children's Spoon, Winnetka, Ill., 1979—; co-founder Aschaffenburg Players, 1960. Author, designer The Children's Spoon Coloring Book of Manners for Boys and Girls, 1985; creator 6 musical ditties for program and cassette tape. Active presdl. campaigns, 1972, 80; swimming instr. Red Cross, Milton, Vt., Marymount Coll. Named Showcase House Designer, Park Ridge Youth Campus Fundraiser, 1982, 84, 85. Mem. Am. Soc. Interior Design (assoc.), Nat. Assn. Female Execs., Marymount Coll. Alumnae Assn. (pres. 1977-80). Avocations: photography, travel, tennis, restaurant epicure, antiques. Office: The Children's Spoon PO Box 148 Winnetka IL 60093

PERUZZO, ALBERT LOUIS, actuary, accountant; b. Chgo., Dec. 27, 1951; s. Anthony L. and Annette (Gentile) P. BS in Math., No. Ill. U., 1973, BS in Accountancy, 1974, MBA, 1975. CPA, Ill. Auditor Deloitte, Haskins & Sells, CPA's, Chgo., 1976-79; mgr. valuation compliance CNA Ins., Chgo., 1979—. Treas., bd. dirs. Dignity/Chgo., 1982-84; dep. vol. Voter's Registrar Bd. Elections, Chgo., 1984—. Mem. Am. Acad. Actuaries, Soc. Actuaries (assoc.), Am. Inst. CPA's, Ill. CPA Soc. Democrat. Roman Catholic.

PERYAM, DAVID ROGER, psychologist; b. Encampment, Wyo., Mar. 22, 1915; s. George G. and Marguerite (Knopf) P.; m. Margaret Gail Terwilliger, Jan. 2, 1935 (dec. Apr. 1976); children: David B., Mary L., Kenneth F., Laura J.; m. Nancy Jo Peryam, June 18, 1978; children: Eugene, Christine Weidner. BA, U. Wyo., 1939; MA, Ohio State U., 1940; PhD, Ill. Inst. Tech., 1961. Lic. psychologist, Ill. Research supr. Joseph E. Seagram & Sons, Louisville, Ky., 1940-44; warehouse supt. Calvert Distilling, Relay, Md., 1947-48; chief food acceptance dept. Armed Forces Food and Container Inst., Chgo., 1949-63; tech. dir. Peryam & Kroll Research, Chgo., 1963-84, cons., 1985. Pres. Suburban Community Chest Council, Berwyn, Ill., 1958-59; bd. dirs. United Way Park Forest, Ill., 1953-86, Kich E. High Sch., Park Forest, 1957-60. Fellow ASTM (merit award 1985), Am. Psychologist Assn. (sec. div. 23 1967-70, Merit award 1985); mem. Inst. Food Technologists, Am. Mktg. Assn. Avocations: hunting, fishing, golf. Home: 113 Nashua Park Forest IL 60466 Office: Peryam & Kroll Research Corp 6323 N Avondale Chicago IL 60631

PESARESI, DANIEL JOSEPH, manufacturing company executive; b. Logansport, Ind., July 17, 1939; s. Walter and Theresa Marie (DiGilio) P.; m. Vivian Ann Montz, Aug. 26, 1961; children—Annamaria, Daniel Joseph. B.S., St. Joseph Coll., 1961. With Winamac Coil Springs, Kewanna, Ind., 1961—, pres., 1961—. Pres. Winamac Council on Aging, 1982—; pres. Winamac Econ. Devel. Corp., 1978—. Mem. Farm Equipment Mfrs. Assn. Republican. Lodges: K.C., Moose, Eagles. Home: Rural Route 4 Box 56 Winamac IN 46996 Office: Winamac Coil Springs Box 278 Kewanna IN 46939

PESCH, LEROY ALLEN, physician, educator, health and hospital consultant, business executive; b. Mt. Pleasant, Iowa, June 22, 1931; s. Herbert Lindsey and Mary Clarissa (Tyner) P.; children from previous marriage: Christopher Allen, Brian Lindsey, Daniel Ethan; m. Donna J. Stone, Dec. 28, 1975 (dec. Feb. 1985); 1 child, Tyner Ford; stepchildren: Christopher Scott Kneifel, Linda Suzanne Kneifel; m. Gerri Ann Cotton, Sept. 27, 1986. Student, State U. Iowa, 1948-49, Iowa State U., 1950-52; MD cum laude, Washington U., St. Louis, 1956. Intern Barnes Hosp., St. Louis, 1956-57; research assoc. NIH, Bethesda, Md., 1957-59; asst. resident medicine Grace-New Haven Hosp., New Haven, 1959-60; clin. fellow Yale Med. Sch., New Haven, 1960-61; instr. medicine Yale Med. Sch., 1961-62, asst. prof. medicine, 1962-63, asst. dir. liver study unit, 1961-63; assoc. physician Grace-New Haven Hosp., 1961-62; assoc. prof. medicine Rutgers U., New Brunswick, N.J., 1963-64; prof. Rutgers U., 1964-66, chmn. dept. medicine, 1965-66; assoc. dean, prof. medicine Stanford Sch. Medicine, 1966-68; mem. gen. medicine study sect. NIH, 1965-70, chmn., 1969-70; dean, dir. univ. hosps. SUNY, Buffalo, 1968-71; spl. cons. to sec. for health HEW, 1970—; prof. div. biol. scis. and medicine U. Chgo., 1972-77; prof. pathology Northwestern U., 1977-79; health and hosp. cons.; pres. Concept Group, Inc., Chgo., 1976-77, L.A. Pesch Assocs., Inc., Chgo., 1977-81; chief exec. officer Pesch and Co., 1984—; chmn., chief exec. officer Health Resources Corp. Am., 1981-84; chmn. bd. dirs. Republic Health Corp., 1985—. Contbr. articles on internal medicine to profl. jours. Bd. dirs. Buffalo Med. Found., 1969-72, Health Orgn., Western N.Y., 1968-71, Joffrey Ballet, N.Y.C., 1980—; trustee Michael Reese Hosp. and Med. Center, Chgo., 1971-76, pres., chief exec. officer, 1971-77; mem. exec. bd. Auditorium Theatre Council, Chgo.; trustee W. Clement and Jessie V. Stone Found.; mem. adv. com. Congressional Awards; pres. Pesch Family Found. Served with

USPHS, 1957-59. Mem. Am. Assn. Study of Liver Diseases, Am. Fedn. Clin. Research, Am. Soc. Biol. Chemists, AAAS, Sigma Xi, Alpha Omega Alpha. Clubs: Buffalo, Standard, Internat. Quadrangle, Mid-Am, Capitol Hill, Acapulco Yacht, Chicago Yacht. Home: 333 N Mayflower Rd Lake Forest IL 60045 Office: 207 Westminster Lake Forest IL 60045 2d Office: Republic Health Corp 14951 Dallas Pkwy Dallas TX 75240

PESCHKE, DONALD B., publisher; b. St. Louis, Aug. 1, 1947; s. Adolph E. and Grace L. (Buchmann) P. BS, Drake U., 1969. Research asst. Meredith Corp., Des Moines, 1972-77, asst. editor, 1977-78; pub., editor, chief exec. officer, chmn. Woodsmith Pub. Co., Des Moines, 1978—. Served as sgt. U.S. Army, 1970-72. Avocation: woodworking. Office: Woodsmith Pub Co 2200 Grand Ave Des Moines IA 50312

PESEK, BORIS PETER, economics educator; b. Most, Czechoslovakia, Sept. 21, 1926; came to U.S., 1950; s. Karel and Anna (Vondrakova) P.; m. Milena M. Lambertova, Oct. 28, 1948. B.A., Coe Coll., Cedar Rapids, Iowa, 1951; M.A., U. Chgo., 1953, Ph.D., 1956. Rockefeller Found. fellow Johns Hopkins U., Balt., 1956-57; prof. Mich. State U., East Lansing, 1957-67; prof. econs. U. Wis.-Milw., 1967—; vis. prof. U. Vienna, 1986; participant East European Nat. Income Project, Columbia U., 1957-63. Mem. Am. Econ. Assn. Roman Catholic. Co-author: Money, Wealth and Economic Theory, 1966; Foundations of Money and Banking, 1967. Home: 12928 N Colony Dr Mequon WI 53092 Office: U Wis-Milw Box 413 Milwaukee WI 53201

PESEK, CYRIL PAUL, JR., electronics executive; b. Mpls., Oct. 9, 1932; s. Cyril Paul and Muriel E. (Fossum) P.; m. Rae Huntington, Jan. 20, 1955; children: Kate, Julia, Elizabeth. BS in Engring., Yale U., 1954; MBA, Harvard U., 1958. Exec. v.p. Colight, Inc., Mpls., 1962-67; pres., chief exec. officer Pesek Engring. and Mfg. Co., Mpls., 1967-76; mgr. OEM div. CPT Corp., Mpls., 1977-78; pres. Western Lithoplate, St. Louis, 1979-83; chmn. bd., chief exec. officer Moniterm Corp., Mpls., 1983—. Patentee etching machine. Chmn. Wayzata Planning Commn., Minn., 1966-69; vestryman St. Martin's Ch., Wayzata, 1977-79; mem. Orono City Council, Minn., 1977-79; commr., St. Louis Mus. Sci., 1981-84; bd. dirs. United Theol. Sem., 1985—. Served to 1st lt. U.S. Army, 1954-56. Mem. Am. Electronics Assn. Republican. Episcopalian. Clubs: St. Louis Racquet (bd. dirs. 1983-84), Woodhill Country. Avocations: tennis, cross- country skiing. Home: 1235 Lyman Ave Wayzata MN 55391 Office: Moniterm Corp 5740 Green Circle DR Minnetonka MN 55343

PESEK, JAMES ROBERT, management consultant; b. Chgo., May 30, 1941; s. James F. and Elizabeth A. (Ord) P.; m. Bonnie L. Bowen, Nov. 1963; children—Becky, Shelly. B.S.M.E. with honors, U. Ill., 1964; M.B.A., U. Nebr., 1966. Cert. mgmt. cons. Adminstrv. services mgr. Cummins Engine Co., Columbus, Ind., 1966-68; cons. div. Arthur Andersen & Co., Milw., 1968-72; mgr. distbn. div. ADG, Indpls., 1972-74; mgr. Mgmt. Adv. Services Wolf & Co., Chgo., 1974-79; pres. Ind. Mgmt. Services, Hinsdale, Ill., 1979—; cons.; spkr., tchr. Mem. Am. Prodn. and Inventory Control Soc., Inst. Mgmt. Cons., Am. Arbitration Assn. Home: 6273 Fairmount Downers Grove IL 60516

PESHKIN, SAMUEL DAVID, lawyer; b. Des Moines, Oct. 6, 1925; s. Louis and Mary (Grund) P.; m. Shirley R. Isenberg, Aug. 17, 1947; children—Lawrence Allen, Linda Ann. B.A., State U. Iowa, 1948, J.D., 1951. Bar: Iowa bar 1951. Since practiced in Des Moines; partner firm Bridges & Peshkin, 1953-66, Peshkin & Robinson, 1966—; Mem. Iowa Bd. Law Examiners, 1970—. Bd. dirs. State U. Iowa Found., 1957—, Old Gold Devel. Fund, 1956—, Sch. Religion U. Iowa, 1966—. Fellow Am. Bar Found., Internat. Soc. Barristers; mem. ABA (chmn. standing com. membership 1959—, ho. of dels. 1968—, bd. govs. 1973—), Iowa Bar Assn. (bd. govs. 1958—, pres. jr. bar sect. 1958-59, award of merit 1974), Inter-Am. Bar Assn., Internat. Bar Assn., Am. Judicature Soc., State U. Iowa Alumni Assn. (dir., pres. 1957). Home: 505 36th St Apt 302 Des Moines IA 50312 Office: 1010 Fleming Bldg Des Moines IA 50309

PESKE, PATRIC O'CONNELL, criminologist, questioned document examiner; b. Akron, Ohio, Sept. 21, 1942; s. Robert Wilhelm Peske and Eileen Michele (Doherty) Bordeaux; m. Nancy L. Porosky, Nov. 25, 1967; 1 child, Arthur Aleksandor. BA, U. Akron, 1968, MA, 1972. Questioned document examiner Ohio, Pa., Mich., 1965—; dir. PMC Evaluation Services, Flint, Mich., 1981—; cons. Akron, 1972-73, Phila., 1970-72; cons., trainer, Akron, 1965-70; speaker various community service orgns., 1973-82. Contbr. articles to profl. jours. Bd. dirs. ACLU, Flint, 1979-82; advisor Sta. WFDF Radio, Flint, 1979-84. Republican. Avocations: advt. analysis, horticulture, oriental rugs, study of human truthfulness. Office: PMC Evaluation Services Drawer G-Cody Flint MI 48507

PESOLA, WILLIAM ERNEST, cable television company executive; b. Marquette, Mich., May 2, 1945; s. Ernest Ensio and Janice Mary (LeDuc) P.; m. Kathleen Mary Deschaine, July 9, 1966; children: Christie Lynn, Laurie Anne. BS, No. Mich. U., 1968, MS, 1971. Route driver Coca Cola Co., Marquette, 1963-68; tchr. Gwinn (Mich.) Schs., 1968-78; pub. Sch. News, 1969; pres. Pesola Mgmt., Marquette, 1974—; pres. Humboldt Ridge, Marquette, 1977—; treas. Elite Bar, Inc., Marquette, 1978—; v.p. Marquette Cablevision, 1981-85, also dir.; cons. cable TV, 1985—, Bresnan Communications, 1984—. Pres. Gwinn Edn. Assn., 1975-77; regional pres. Upper Peninsula Edn. Assn., 1977-78; mem. Marquette City Commn., 1977-81. Mem. NEA, Mich. Edn. Assn. Roman Catholic. Lodge: Rotary. Home: 1026 N Front St Marquette MI 49855

PESSES, PAUL D., real estate and investment management company executive; b. Davenport, Iowa, Oct. 4, 1955; s. Marvin and Elaine (Katz) P.; m. Kim Meisel, Aug. 19, 1978. BA in Econs. summa cum laude, Ohio State U., 1977; MBA, Harvard U., 1980. Bus. analyst engineered products group Cabot Corp., Boston, 1979-80; v.p., treas., dir. Metcoa, Inc., Solon, Ohio, 1980-82, Columbia Alloys Co., Twinsburg, Ohio, 1980-82; adminstrv. mgr. splty. metals and alloys Ashland Chem. Co. div. Ashland Oil, Inc., Cleve., 1983; pres. Stonestreet Capital Mgmt. Corp., Beachwood, Ohio, 1983—, also dir. Trustee Cleve. com. UNICEF; vol. Cleve. Playhouse, Kidney Found. Ohio, United Way campaign; big bro., trustee Big Bros.; treas. Pesses Charitable Found. Mem. Phi Eta Sigma, Phi Kappa Phi. Clubs: Northeast Yacht., Harvard Bus. Sch. (officer) (Cleve.), Oakwood.

PETERFISH, EVELYN JEANETTE, personnel administrator; b. Battle Creek, Mich., Aug. 4, 1934; d. George Nelson and Ruth A. (Bowers) Wriglesworth; m. Gordon James Katz, Aug. 11, 1952 (div. Jan. 1968); children: Derek E., Kevin G., Cindi R.; m. Nicholas Bratsouleas, June 28, 1968 (dec. Aug. 1968); 1 child, Nichole J.; m. Paul Peterfish, Oct. 14, 1978. Student, Mich. State U., 1965-67; cert., Argubright Bus. Coll., Battle Creek, 1969; BA, Western Mich. U., 1980, postgrad., 1984—. With City of Battle Creek, Mich., 1969-84; contract compliance officer City of Battle Creek, 1984-87; personnel adminstr. Calhoun County Community Mental Health, Battle Creek, 1987—; bd. chmn. Mcpl. Employees Retirement System, 1978, legis. chmn., 1976-77. Author training program; editor newsletter, 1969, 1971-87. Bd. dirs. Battle Creek Human Relations Bd., 1979-82, 87, Urban League, 1980-87; campaign chmn. United Way, 1978-87; coach Indoor Floor Hockey League, 1979-82; vol. S.A.F.E. Place Domestic Violence Shelter; Foster Parent, 1959-65, 1972-87; operated Foster Home for Delinquent Teen-aged Girls. Mem. Mich. Cooperative Cert. Consortium (chmn. 1986-87), Nat. Contract Compliance Assn. (newsletter staff 1986-87), Battle Creek Personnel Assn., Mich. Nat. Assn. of Human Rights Workers (vice-chmn. 1985), Mich. Indsl. Relations Research Assn., Battle Creek C. of C., Foster Parents Assn., Rental Property Owners Assn. Democrat. Home: 101 Orchard Place Battle Creek MI 49017 Office: Calhoun County Community Mental Health 190 E Michigan Ave Battle Creek MI 49017

PETERLIN, ALBERT, meteorologist; b. Carbondale, Pa., Dec. 2, 1944; s. Albert and Stella (Tokarczyk) P.; m. Barbara Catherine Lahoda, June 17, 1967; children: Jacquelyn Denise, Barbara Lee, Albert Nicholas. BS, U. Okla., 1970; MS, Purdue U., 1981. Acct. exec. Bache & Co., Orlando, Fla., 1973-74; meteorologist Nat. Weather Service, Louisville, 1974-77; agrl. meteorologist Nat. Weather Service, West Lafayette, Ind., 1978—; speaker radio interviews; chmn. bd. dirs. ERRex, Lafayette, Ind. Contbr. numerous articles to profl. jours.; developer climate model Circum Polar Vortex Area Index, 1981. Pres. Lafayette Area Cath. Athletic Assn., 1981-82; bd. dirs. Tippecanoe Soccer Assn., Lafayette, 1982-83. Served to 1st lt. USAF, 1966-73, maj. Res. Mem. Am. Meteorologist Soc., Nat. Weather Assn., Slovenian Genealogy Soc. (founder), Mini Investors Stock Club (pres.), Gamma Sigma Delta. Democrat. Avocations: genealogy, song writing, poetry, fishing, children. Home: 6625 Jeffrey Ln Lafayette IN 47905-9618 Office: Nat Weather Service Rm 220 Poultry Sci Bldg West Lafayette IN 47907

PETERMANN, RICK ALLAN, air traffic controller; b. Moorhead, Minn., Mar. 28, 1956; s. Leroy Wayne and Sharon Ann (Littlefield) P.; m. Laura Ann Bennett, Aug. 14, 1977 (div. Oct. 1982); m. Kathrine Jo McKenzie, Oct. 25, 1987. Grad. high sch., Moorhead, Minn., 1974. Cert. air traffic controller, FAA; lic. comml. pilot, FAA. Pvt. line technician AT&T Co., Kansas City, Mo., 1981-82; air traffic controller Kans. City Air Route Traffic Control Ctr., Olathe, Kans., 1982—. Served with USAF, 1976-80. Mem. Nat. Assn. Air Traffic Controllers. Avocations: golf, camping, fishing. Home: 6492 W 201st Terr Bucyrus KS 66013

PETERS, CLARENCE, electrical contractor, material handling consultant; b. Manchester, Ky., Dec. 24, 1956; s. Clark and Barbara (Mayfield) P.; m. Fanny Rusomorova, July 22, 1978; children: Cindy, Magen. Lic. elec. contractor, Indpls., Ga., Calif.; lic. material handling specialty, Calif. Mine electrician Big Creek Coal Co., Williamson, W.Va., 1975-76; machine mechanic Amtrack RR, Indpls., 1976-77; plant electrician RSR Quemetco, Indpls., 1977-78; field service Economation, Indpls., 1978-80; installation specialist, supr. and elec. engr. Pentek, Indpls., 1980-85; owner, operator P & P Machine Electric, Inc., Indpls., 1985—. Avocations: driving, shooting, travel. Home: 7245 E 35th St Indianapolis IN 46226 Office: P & P Machine Electric Inc 7245 E 35th St Indianapolis IN 46226

PETERS, DAVID LOUIS, food company executive; b. Mt. Pleasant, Pa., Oct. 12, 1945; s. William O. and Mary (Maciūpa) P.; m. Barbara J. Kelanic, Oct. 18, 1968; children: Marian, Michael. BA, California (Pa.) State U., 1971; MA, Cen. Mich. U., 1977. Area mgr. Hormel Co., Austin, Minn., 1971-76; v.p. sales Holsum Co., Waukesha, Wis., 1976-80; v.p. sales and mktg. PVO Internat., St. Louis, 1981; v.p. Doskocil Food Group, Jefferson, Wis., 1982—. Pres. Time-Out, Inc., 1983-85. Served with USMC, 1963-67. Mem. Am. Mgmt. Assn., Am. Legion. Republican. Mem. Ch. Brethren. Club: Keffle Moraine Soccer (pres. 1987—). Home: 632 Wakefield Downs Wales WI 53183 Office: 1 Rock River Rd Jefferson WI 53549

PETERS, DOROTHY MARIE, educator; b. Sutton, Nebr., Oct. 23, 1913; d. Sylvester and Anna (Olander) Peters; A.B. with high distinction, Nebr. Wesleyan U., 1941; M.A., Northwestern U., 1957; Ed.D., Ind. U., 1968. Tchr. Nebr. pub. schs., 1931-38; caseworker Douglas County Assistance Bur., Omaha, 1941; hosp. field dir., gen. field rep. ARC, 1941-50; social worker Urban League, Meth. Ch., Washington, 1951-53; asst. prin., dir. guidance, Manlius (Ill.) Community High Sch., 1953-58; dean of girls, guidance dir. Woodruff High Sch., Peoria, Ill., 1958-66; vis. prof. edn. Bradley U., Peoria, 1959-77; coordinator, dir. Title I programs Peoria Public Sch. System, 1966-68, dir. pupil services, 1968-72; dir. counseling and evaluation Title I Programs, 1972-73; vol. dir. youth service programs, vol. program cons. Central Ill. chpt. and Heart of Ill. div. ARC, Peoria, 1973-77; owner, operator Ability-Achievement Unlimited Cons. Services, Saratoga Springs, N.Y., 1978-81; spl. cons. Courage Center, Golden Valley, Minn., 1981-84; mem. sr. adv. bd. F&M Marquette Nat. Bank, 1981-85; cons. Sister Kenny Inst., Mpls., 1984-86; freelance writer, 1984—; prin. Dorothy M. Peters & Assocs., Roseville, Minn., 1986—. Bd. dirs. home service com. disaster com. Peoria chpt. ARC, 1958-73; pres., bd. dirs. Ct. Counselor Program; mem. Mayor's Human Resources Council, City of Peoria; chmn. met. adv. com. transp. for handicapped; ednl. dir., prin., bd. dirs. Catalyst High Sch., 1975-77; hon. life bd. mem. Am. Nat. Red Cross; mem. Saratoga Springs Hosp. Bldg. Rehab. Com.; founder, steering com. Open Sesame, Saratoga Springs, 1978-81; appointee N.Y. State Employment and Tng. Council, 1979-81, Saratoga County Employment and Tng. Com., 1979-81; bd. dirs. Unlimited Potential, 1979-81; mem. Metro Mobility Adv. Task Force, Mpls., 1981-85, mem. policy com., 1984—; mem. vol. action com. United Way, Mpls., 1982—; mem. Minn. State Planning Council for Developmentally Disabled, 1983—; mem. Gov.'s Task Force on Needs of Adults with Brain Impairment, 1985—; chmn. Met. Ctr. for Ind. Living, 1986—; mem. sr. ministries council United Meth. Ch., 1984—. Mem. Peoria Edn. Assn. (v.p. 1962-64), Ill. Guidance and Personnel Assn. (v.p. Area 8, 1963-64), NEA, Ill. Edn. Assn. (del. 1962-64), Am. Personnel and Guidance Assn., Am. Sch. Counselors Assn., Nat. Assn. Women Deans and Counselors (K-12 task force chmn. 1974—, editorial bd. Jour.), Ill. Vocat. Guidance Assn. (dir.), Ill. Assn. Women Deans and Counselors, Phi Kappa Phi, Psi Chi, Pi Gamma Mu, Pi Lambda Theta, Delta Kappa Gamma, Alpha Gamma Delta. Address: 2870 Aglen Ave Apt 1501 Roseville MN 55113

PETERS, ELIZABETH ANNE, educator; b. Hebron, Ill., June 9, 1940; d. Tibbets E. and Ruby Marie (Giddens) Rolls; B.S., U. Ill., 1962, M.S., 1967; postgrad. U. Ill., 1970-74, Iowa State U., 1974, Northwestern U., 1980; div. Tchr., Bremen High Sch., Midlothian, Ill., 1962-65, Waller High Sch., Chgo., 1965-67, Evanston (Ill.) High Sch., 1967-70; instr., coordinator food service adminstrn. and hotel mgmt. Coll. DuPage, Glen Ellyn, Ill., 1970-75; clin. dietitian U. Chgo. Hosps. and Clinics, 1975; asst. restaurant mgr. Hyatt Regency, Chgo., summer 1980; prof., coordinator hospitality mgmt. program Chicago City-Wide Coll., 1975-86; pres. faculty Chgo. City Wide Coll.; cons. bds. health, colls. Mem. adv. com. No. Ill. U.; judge various food contests; mem. Chgo. Council on Fgn. Relations; pres. Near North chpt. Lyric Opera; trustee Three Arts Club Chgo. Recipient Nat. Restaurant Assn. Fellowship award, 1980; Master Tchrs. Seminar Fellowship award, 1974; Nat. Leadership Devel. Fellowship award, 1975. Registered Dietitian. Mem. Nat. Restaurant Assn., Ill. Restaurant Assn., Chgo. Restaurant Assn., Am. Dietetic Assn. (dietetic tech. com.), Ill. Dietetic Assn., Chgo. Nutrition Assn., Ill Nutrition Com., Chgo. Dietetic Assn. (dir.), Soc. Nutrition Edn., Inst. Food Technologists, Restaurant Women's Club Chgo. (dir.), Council on Hotel-Restaurant Edn. Clubs: Flossmoor Country, Lake Geneva Yacht, Canyon. Home: 215 E Chestnut St Chicago IL 60611 Office: 30 E Lake St Chicago IL 60601

PETERS, HENRY AUGUSTUS, neurologist; b. Oconomowoc, Wis., Dec. 21, 1920; s. Henry Augustus and Emma N. P.; m. Jean McWilliams, 1950; children—Henry, Kurt, Eric, Mark. B.A., M.D., U. Wis. Prof. dept. neurology and rehab. medicine U. Wis. Med. Sch., Madison; mem. med. adv. bd. Muscular Dystrophy Assn. Served to lt. M.C. U.S. Navy. Fellow A.C.P.; mem. Wis. Med. Assn., Am. Acad. Neurology. Club: Rotary. Office: 600 Highland Ave Madison WI 53706

PETERS, MICHAEL THOMAS, energy corporation executive, consultant; b. West Branch, Mich., Jan. 21, 1949; s. Raymond J. and Doris I. (Carrick) P.; m. Stephanie A. Mason, Aug. 26, 1972. B.S. in Geology, Mich. State U., 1974, B.S. in Zoology, 1978. Geologist, Energy Acquisition, Okemos, Mich., 1974, Don Yohe Drilling Co., Armada, Mich., 1974-77; exploration geologist Hunt Energy Corp., Dallas, 1978-81; sr. exploration geologist Mich. Oil Co., Jackson, 1981-84; pres., cons. geologist ORION Energy Corp., Lansing, Mich., 1984—. Mem. Am. Assn. Petroleum Geologists, Soc. Exploration Geophysicists, Mich. Basin Geol. Soc. (bus. mgr. 1981-82), Mich. Oil and Gas Assn., Rocky Mountain Assn. Geologists. Avocations: scuba diving, skiing, sailing, camping, tennis. Office: ORION Energy Corp PO Box 27068 Lansing MI 48909

PETERS, MILTON EUGENE, educational psychologist; b. Anderson, Ind., July 22, 1938; s. Olen A. and Dorothy LaVerne (Lambert) P.; m. Carol Ann Dudycha, Aug. 27, 1960. BA, Wittenberg U., 1960; M in Div., Hamma Sch. Theology, 1963; MA, Bowling Green State U., 1965; PhD, U. Toledo, 1975. Lic. psychologist, Ohio. Pastor Luth. Ch. Am., 1966-69; instr. psychology Defiance (Ohio) Coll., 1969-70, Bluffton (Ohio) Coll., 1970-72; tchr., research asst. U. Toledo, 1973-75; vis. asst. prof., 1975-76; dir. instl. research, asst. prof. psychology Findlay (Ohio) Coll., 1976-85, assoc. prof. psychology, 1985—; cons., lectr. in field. Contbr. articles to profl. and religious jours. Mem. long-range planning research and evaluation com. Findlay City Schs., 1982—. Mem. Am. Psychol. Assn., Am. Ednl. Research Assn., Assn. Instl. Research, Midwestern Psychol. Assn. Clubs: Findlay Torch, Fostoria Power Squadron. Home: 614 Winterberry Dr Findlay OH 45850 Office: 1000 N Main St Findlay OH 45840

PETERS, MIRIAM L. (MIRIAM LINDBLOM PETERS), freelance writer; b. Bellefontaine, Ohio, Aug. 13, 1927; d. Martin and Miriam (Johnson) Lindblom; m. James David Peters, Apr. 5, 1952 (dec. June 1980); children: Dana M., James D. II, Benjamin J., Edward M., Joseph C. BA, Ohio Wesleyan U., 1948; postgrad., Radcliffe and Harvard Univs., 1948-49, Ohio State U., 1949-50. Lic. real estate broker, Ohio. Job analyst Nationwide Ins., Columbus, Ohio, 1950-52; real estate broker Jim Peters Agy., Bellefontaine, 1974-85; reporter Springfield (Ohio) News-Sun, 1983-86; real estate assoc. RHA Group Realty, Inc., Bellefontaine, 1987—; freelance writer, Bellefontaine, 1983—; pvt. practice bus. mgr., Bellefontaine, 1986—. Author poetry, features, short stories. Mem. Logan County Rep. Women, Bellefontaine. Mem. The Writer's Club, The Art Club, Phi Beta Kappa, Pi Delta Epsilon, Kappa Alpha Theta. Presbyterian. Lodge: Soroptimists (corr. sec. 1986-87). Avocations: reading, gardening, art, collecting cookbooks and glass cup plates. Home: PO Box 400 Bellefontaine OH 43311

PETERS, ROBERT ALLEN, drug company executive; b. Aurora, Ill., Dec. 13, 1927; s. Frank Albert and Amalia Cecelia (Harter) P.; m. Mary Jeanne Galos, June 23, 1962 (dec. May 1979); children: Robert Allen, Thomas Allen, Mary Ann. BS in Pharmacy, U. Ill., Chgo., 1951. Pharmacist Plache Drug Co., Aurora, 1951-61; co-owner, pharmacist Town & Country Drugs, Aurora, 1961-82, owner, 1982—; bd. dirs. First Am. Bank, Aurora. Bd. dirs., treas. Aurora C. of C. Served ti U.S. Army, 1946-47, Korea. Mem. Am. Pharm. Assn., Ill. Pharm. Assn., Aurora Area Pharm. Assn. Republican. Roman Catholic. Lodges: K.C., Moose. Avocations: swimming, tennis, gardening, fishing, coin collecting.

PETERS, THOMAS M., lawyer; b. Saginaw, Mich., Apr. 10, 1943; s. Donald James and Jean Eleanor (Kelly) P.; m. Jane Caryl Fetters, Jan. 6, 1968; children: Jenifer Caryl, Thomas Jr. Grad., Syracuse (N.Y.) East European Language Sch., 1966; BA, Mich. State U., 1969; JD, Wayne State U., 1973. Assoc. Vandeveer, Garzia, Tonkin, Kerr, Heaphy, Moore, Sills & Poling, Detroit, 1973-80, prin., ptnr., 1980—; mem. local and state bar coms. U.S. Dist. Ct. and U.S. Ct. Appeals. Served to staff sgt. USAF, 1965-69. Mem. ABA, Def. Research Inst., Mich. Def. Trial Counsel, Assn. Def. Trial Counsel (bd. dirs. 1978—, pres. 1985-86, award for valuable service 1986), Mediation Tribunal Assn., Am. Arbitration Assn. Clubs: Port Huron (Mich.) Golf, Otsego Ski (Gaylrod, Mich.), Beachwood Swin and Tennis (Troy, Mich.), Tournament Players (Jacksonville, Fla.). Lodge: Elks. Home: 4906 Rivers Edge Troy MI 48098 Office: Vandeveer Garzia et al 1550 N Woodward Birmingham MI 48011

PETERS, WESLEY ROBERT, marketing research executive; b. Akron, Ohio, Apr. 12, 1943; s. Wesley Hall and Phyllis Aileen (Shaver) P.; m. Cheryl Ann Losey, June 19, 1971; 1 child, Elizabeth Ann. BBA, U. Wis., 1971, MBA, 1972. Account exec. Burke Mktg. Research Co., Cin., 1973-75; v.p. Burke Mktg. Research Co., Glen Ellyn, Ill., 1975-79, Alpha Research Group, Bolingbrook, Ill., 1979-83; pres. Dimension Research, Inc., Lisle, Ill., 1983—. Coach Glen Ellyn Boys Baseball, 1977-78; mem. Cable TV Commn., Glen Ellyn, 1979-84; chmn., ch. and soc. First United Meth. Ch., Glen Ellyn, 1982-83, 86-87; v.p. Civic Betterment Party, Glen Ellyn, 1986—. Served to staff sgt. USAF, 1966-70, Vietnam. Mem. Am. Mktg. Assn., Council Am. Survey Research Orgns. Avocations: golf, sailing, baseball. Home: 322 Miller Ct Glen Ellyn IL 60137 Office: Dimension Research Inc 3080 Ogden Ave Lisle IL 60532

PETERSEN, DONALD E(UGENE), automobile company executive; b. Pipestone, Minn., Sept. 4, 1926; s. William L. and Mae (Pederson) P.; m. Jo Anne Leonard, Sept. 12, 1948; children: Leslie Carolyn, Donald Leonard. BSME, U. Wash., 1946; MBA, Stanford U., 1949; DSc (hon.), U. Detroit, 1986; LHD (hon.), Art Ctr. Coll., Pasadena, 1986. With Ford Motor Co., Dearborn, 1949—, v.p. car planning and research, 1969-71, v.p. truck ops., 1971-75, exec. v.p. diversified products ops., 1975-76, exec. v.p. internat. automotive ops., 1977-80, pres., 1980-85, chmn. bd. dirs., chief exec. officer, 1985—, also bd. dirs. Trustee Cranbrook Inst. Sci., Bloomfield, Mich., 1973—, Citizens Research Council of Mich., Safety Council for S.E. Mich., Detroit Inst. Arts, Mich. Cancer Found., Corp. Found. for Aid to Edn., TARGET; mem. adv. bd. U. Wash. Grad. Sch. Bus. Adminstrn.; bd. overseers Oreg. Health Sci. Univ.; mem. New Detroit, Inc., Detroit Renaissance, Inc.; bd. dirs. Hewlett-Packard Co., Dow Jones & Co., Inc., Detroit Strategic Planning Project, Mich. Commn. Sch. Fin. Served with USMC, 1946-47, 51-52. Recipient Disting. Alumnus award U. Wash., 1981, Arbuckle award Stanford U. Bus. Sch. Alumni Assn., 1985, 1st Am. Achievement award Brookgreen Gardens, 1986, Bus. Statesman award Harvard Bus Sch. Club Detroit, Good Neighbor award U.S. Mex. C. of C., Man of Yr. award Motor Trend Mag., 1987, Nat. Humanitarian award Nat. Jewish Ctr. Immunology and Respiratory Medicine. Mem. The Bus. Council, Bus. Roundtable (mem. policy com., mem. U.S.-Japan bus. council, mem. adv. com. for trade negotiations, mem. emergency com. for Am. trad), Bus.-Higher Edn. Forum, Soc. Automotive Engrs., Engring. Soc. Detroit, Mensa, Motor Vehicle Mfrs. Assn., Phi Beta Kappa, Sigma Xi, Tau Beta Pi. Episcopalian. Clubs: Detroit, Bloomfield Hills Country, Bloomfield Open Hunt, Ostego Ski, Detroit Economic. Office: Ford Motor Co American Rd Dearborn MI 48121

PETERSEN, GENE WILLIAM, general contractor, educator; b. Handcock, Iowa, July 14, 1946; s. Vernon William and Leona Sophie (Harmsen) P.; m. Judeen Kay Kozak, June 28, 1969; children: Heather, Benjamin. BS, Westmar Coll., Lemars, Iowa, 1968; MS, Ea. Ky. U., 1971, specialist in tech. degree, 1972. Cert. tchr. Indsl. arts instr. Lewis Ctr. Community Sch., Council Bluffs, Iowa, 1968-70; grad. asst. in indsl. tech. Ea. Ky. U., Richamond, 1971-72; instr. indsl. arts Westmar Coll., 1972-74; owner G&J Petersen Constrn., Spirit Lake, Iowa, 1974—; higher edn. cons. Iowa Indls. Arts Curriculum Guide, 1971-72. Bd. dirs. Sprit Lake Jaycees, Spirit Lake, Iowa, 1979. Presbyterian. Lodge: Lions. Home: 412 Carlton Spirit Lake IA 51360

PETERSEN, GERALD THORNTON, energy industry executive; b. Chgo., Sept. 1, 1934; s. Waldemar R. and Marion (Thornton) P.; m. Carol Krametbauer, June 22, 1957; children—Charles, James. B.S. in Chem. Engring., Northwestern U., 1957, Advanced Mgmt. cert., 1974; M.S., MIT, 1958, Ph.D., 1960. Lic. profl. engr., Wis. Various positions Gen. Electric Co., 1960-68; dir. engring. A-C Advanced Electronic Chem. Products, Greendale, Wis., 1968-70; dir. adv. tech. ctr. Allis-Chalmers Corp., Milw., 1970-76; v.p. mktg. A-C Energy & Minerals Co., Milw., 1983-84; exec. v.p., gen. mgr. A-C Coal Gas Corp., Milw., 1980-83, pres. 1985—; corp. rep. World Energy Conf., Washington, 1970-74; corp. del. Nat. Council on Synfuels Prodn., Washington, 1983—; panelist 6 internat. confs. Contbr. papers to profl. lit. Patentee coal gasification process utilizing rotary kiln. Bd. dirs. Lakes Improvement Assn., Elkhorn, Wis., Chgo. Symphony Assn. Milw.; bd. dirs. adv. council Marquette U.; active adv. council U. Wis.-Milw., 1975-80. Mem. Am. Inst. Chem. Engrs., Wis. Profl. Engrs. Soc., Am. Mining Congress (energy com. Washington 1975-80), Sigma Xi, Tau Beta Pi, Pi Mu Epsilon, Phi Mu Epsilon. Republican. Congregationalist. Club: Westmoor Country (Brookfield, Wis.). Avocations: sailing; skiing; photography. Home: Lauderdale Lakes 116 Rt 1 Box 49D Elkhorn WI 53121 Office: A-C Coal Gas Corp Box 512 Milwaukee WI 53201

PETERSEN, LINDA KAY, accountant; b. Kalamazoo, Mich., Dec. 30, 1954; d. A.J. and Donna jean (Versailles) Aartila; m. Michael G. Petersen, June 21, 1975. BA, Mich. State U., 1977; AA, Lans Community Coll., 1987. Office supr. State of Mich., Lansing, 1977-80, statistician, 1980-86, acct., 1986—. Mem. Mich. Profl. Employee's Soc. Democrat. Roman Catholic. Avocations: bowling, cross country skiing, traveling, reading crossword puzzles. Home: 3410 Cooley Lansing MI 48911 Office: Mich Dept Social Services 300 S Capitol Lansing MI 48933

PETERSEN, MARY BETH, health care and management educator; b. Durham, N.C., Dec. 8, 1948; d. Jackson B. and Dorothy H. (McGorrisk) Harper; m. Holger Petersen, Sept. 18, 1971. BS in Nursing, Marquette U., 1971, MS in Nursing, 1975. Registered nurse, Wis. Charge nurse intensive care St. Joseph's Hosp., Milw., 1972-74; lectr. continuing edn. Marquette U., Milw., 1974-76; coordinator Nursing Inservice St. Luke's Hosp., Milw.,

1976-78; dir. hosp. edn. St. Michael Hosp., Milw., 1978—; instr. Alverno Coll., Milw., U. Wis., Madison, 1986. Mem. Wis. Soc. for Healthcare Edn. and Tng. (pres. 1985-86), Wis. Heart Assn., Sigma Theta Tau. Avocations: sailing, swimming. Home: 5314 S 8th St Milwaukee WI 53221 Office: St Michael Hosp 2400 W Villard Ave Milwaukee WI 53209

PETERSEN, RAYMOND HATTON, JR., technical sales representative; b. Syracuse, N.Y., Apr. 16, 1959; s. Raymond Hatton and Theodora (McGrath) P.; m. Erika Ann O'Brien, Aug. 5, 1978; children: Jennifer Elizabeth, Erik Francis. B.A. in Econs. and History, Lake Forest Coll., 1982. Coll. agent Northwestern Mutual Life Inst. Co., Lake Forest, Ill., 1980-82; mktg. mgr. Am. Sci. Products, McGaw Park, Ill., 1982, sales rep., Mpls., 1982-83; tech. sales rep. U.S. Surgical Corp., Eau Claire, Wis., 1983-86, regional sales dir., Mpls., 1986—. Recipient U.S. Surgical Pres.'s award, 1984. Home: 111 Marquette Ave S Minneapolis MN 55401 Office: US Surgical Corp PO Box 10690 Minneapolis MN 55440

PETERSEN, ROGER AUGUST, accountant; b. Denison, Iowa, Sept. 5, 1941; s. August F. Petersen and Helen E. (Schultz) McKee; m. Maria M. Schillinger, May 25, 1968; children: Cindy M., Mark R. BBA in Acctg., U. S.D., 1963; postgrad., U. Wis., 1977. CPA, Nebr. Staff auditor Lybrand Ross Bros., Chgo., 1963; supr. Peat, Marwick, Mitchell & Co., Omaha, 1966-72; ptnr. Becker & Petersen, Bellevue, Nebr., 1972—; bd. dirs., sec., treas. Bellevue Capital Co., BSB Corp., Bowman Capital Co., Independence Fin. Corp., Southroads Capital Co., Tri-States Advt., Inc., Bus Air, Inc; bd. dirs., chief fin. officer Affiliated Midwest Bancs. Treas. Zion Luth. Sunday Sch., Omaha; pres. Aid Assn. for Lutherans, Omaha, 1985-86. Served to 1st lt. U.S. Army, 1964-65. Mem. Am. Inst. CPA's, Nebr. Soc. CPA's., German Am. Soc. Avocations: jogging, fishing, gardening, card playing, folk dancing. Home: 4867 Orchard Ave Omaha NE 68117 Office: Becker & Petersen 100 American Plaza Bellevue NE 68005

PETERSEN, RONALD LYNN, broadcasting executive; b. Goodland, Kans., Aug. 30, 1945; s. Peter Alvin and Ruth Irene (Weber) P.; m. Celia Louise Hitzman, Nov. 14, 1964; children—Ronald Lynn, Renee, Patty, Michael, Kathy. Student Central Tech. Inst., Kansas City, Mo., 1963-64. Salesman, Cutco div. Aluminum Co. Am., Kansas City, 1964-65; account exec. KDMO Radio, Carthage, Mo., 1965-68, sales mgr., 1968-73; gen. mgr. KDMO-KRGK, Carthage, 1973-83, v.p., 1983-86; mktg. mgr. Cityvision Cable TV, 1983-86; gen. sales mgr. Sta. KSYN-KQYX, Joplin, 1986—; dir. Mo. NET, Brownfield Network, 1980-86. Pres., Carthage Indsl. Devel. Authority, 1981-83, sec., 1983-87; pub. info. officer Carthage Civil Def., 1979-87 ; bd. citizens Adv. Bd. Probation and Parole, Carthage, 1981-85, pres., 1981-84. Mem. Mo. Broadcasters Assn. (dir. 1983-84, sec.-treas. 1984-85, pres. 1985-86), Carthage Area C. of C. (bd. dirs. 1985-86). Roman Catholic. Club: Rotary (bd. dirs. 1985, 86, 87). Home: 1020 S McGregor St Carthage MO 64836 Office: 2510 W 20th St Joplin MO 64801

PETERSEN, WILLIAM JOHN, writer, educator; b. Dubuque, Iowa, Jan. 30, 1901; s. Charles Lewis and Bertha Louise (Helm) P.; m. Bessie Josephine Rasmus, Sept. 25, 1937. B.A., U. Dubuque, 1926; M.A., U. Iowa, 1927, Ph.D., 1930; LL.D., Iowa Wesleyan Coll., 1958. Grad asst., fellow U. Iowa, 1926-30, instr. history, 1930-36, lectr. history, 1936—, asso. prof., 1948-69; research asso. State Hist. Soc. Iowa, 1930-47, supt., 1947-72; hist. lectr. Am. Sch. Wild Life, summers 1932, 36-40, Drake U. Tours, summers 1933, 34; prof. history Washington U., St. Louis, summers 1940, 41, 65, Iowa Wesleyan Coll., summers 1962, 63. Author: (with Edith Rule) True Tales of Iowa, 1932, Two Hundred Topics in Iowa History, 1932, Steamboating on the Upper Mississippi, 1937, rev. edit., 1968, Iowa: The Rivers of Her Valleys, 1941, A Reference Guide to Iowa History, 1942, Iowa History Reference Guide, 1952, The Story of Iowa, 2 vols, 1952, Mississippi River Panorama: Henry Lewis Great National Work, 1979, Towboating on the Mississippi, 1979; Editor: (John Plumbe, Jr.) Sketches of Iowa and Wisconsin, 1948, (Isaac Galland) Galland's Iowa Emigrant, 1950, (John B. Newhall) A Glimpse of Iowa in 1846, 1957; author-editor: (John B. Newhall) The Pageant of the Press, 1962, The Annals of Iowa-1863, Illustrated Historical Atlas of the State of Iowa in 1875, (A.T. Andreas), 1970; contbr. to profl. mags. Bd. dirs. Alvord Meml. Commn., 1940; mem. Iowa Centennial Com., 1946; chmn. Johnson County Red Cross War Fund, 1945. Recipient Iowa Library Assn. award for best contbn. to Am. lit. by an Iowan, 1937. Mem. Am. Hist. Assn., So. Hist. Assn., Miss. Valley Hist. Assn. (editorial bd. 1953-56), Soc. Am. Archivists, Am. Acad. Polit. and Social Sci., Minn., Kans. hist. socs., State Hist. Soc. Iowa, Phi Kappa Delta, Pi Gamma Mu, Zeta Sigma Pi, Delta Upsilon. Republican. Presbyn. Clubs: Mason (32 deg.), Iowa Author (pres. 1940-42); Propeller (Quad City); Westerners (Chgo.), Cliff Dwellers (Chgo.), Caxton (Chgo.); Research (Iowa City) (sec.-treas. 1944-46), Triangle (Iowa City), S.P.C.S. Rotary (Iowa City), C. of C. (Iowa City). Home: 329 Ellis Ave Iowa City IA 52240

PETERSEN, WILLIAM LAWRENCE, theology educator; b. Laredo, Tex., Jan. 19, 1950; s. Elizabeth M. Petersen. BA, U. Iowa, 1971; MDiv, Luth. Theol. Sem., Saskatoon, Can., 1975; postgrad., McGill U., 1975-77; D in Theology, Rijksuniversiteit te Utrecht, The Netherlands, 1984. Lectr. Meml. U., St. John's, Newfoundland, Can., 1977; vis. asst. prof. U. Notre Dame, Ind., 1985-86, asst. prof., 1986—. Author: The Diatessaron and Ephrem Syrus As Sources of Romanos the Melodist, 1985; contbr. articles to scholarly jours. Mem. Soc. of Biblical Lit. (mem. editorial bd. The NT in the Greek Fathers 1985—). Club: Alpine Français (Chamonix sect.). Avocations: Alpine mountaineering, skiing, music, travel. Home: 522-A University Park Ct Mishawaka IN 46545 Office: U Notre Dame Dept Theology Notre Dame IN 46556

PETERSON, ALAN JAY, accountant; b. Xenia, Ohio, Mar. 25, 1952; s. Jay L. and Hildred A. (Fenlason) P.; m. Jacqueline G. Farmer, Dec. 31, 1980. BS in Econs., Ohio State U., 1973; MBA, U. Dayton, Ohio, 1976. Staff acct. Comml. Services Co., Johnstown, Ohio, 1973-78, jr. ptnr., 1980-82, mng. ptnr., 1982—; ops. mgr. Commonwealth Commodities, Dallas, 1978-80. Area dir. Licking County United Way, Newark, Ohio, 1982, 83. Mem. Nat. Soc. Enrolled Agts. (cert.) , Nat. Assn. Tax Preparers, Ohio Soc. Enrolled Agts. (bd. dirs. 1982—, treas. Cen. Ohio chpt. 1983-84, local pres. 1983-85), U.S. C. of C., Newark Area C. of C. Avocations: darts, motorcycling. Office: 44 S Coshocton St PO Box 371 Johnstown OH 43031

PETERSON, ALICE LUCILLE, advertising executive; b. Mpls., May 5, 1938; d. Andrew and Alice (Reich) Horkey; m. Allen F. Peterson, Nov. 4, 1960 (div. May 1975); 1 child, Allen Andrew. BS, U. Minn., 1960. Mktg. communications mgr. Caloric Corp., Topton, Pa., 1975-80; advt. mgr. Raymond Corp., Greene, N.Y., 1980-81; mgr. mktg. communications Kelvinator Appliances, Pitts., 1981-85; mgr. sales promotion WCI Appliance Group, Columbus, Ohio, 1985—. Author: Caloric Combo Cook, 1976.

PETERSON, ARTHUR FERDINAND, investment management executive; b. Brainerd, Minn., Apr. 17, 1899; s. Toger and Pauline (Gulbrandsen) P.; m. Delma Drusella Coovert, Jan. 31, 1920 (dec. Dec. 1977); 1 child, Vivian Rozmund Peterson Wolter; m. Muriel Frances Herting Beisswanger, June 17, 1978. PhG, Valparaiso U., 1919, PhC, 1920; student Alexander Hamilton Inst., 1925; BS, U. Minn., 1927, postgrad. Pharmacist G.H. Sohrbeck Co., Moline, Ill., 1920-21; salesman E.R. Squibb & Sons, Chgo., 1922-24; chemist Nat. Lead Battery Co., St. Paul, 1925; profl. service rep. William S. Merrell Co., Mpls., 1926; instr. chemistry U. Minn., Mpls., 1927-29; profl. service rep. to supr. E.R. Squibb & Sons, Chgo., 1929-38; mgr. profl. service to mgr. domestic sales div. Schering Corp., Bloomfield, N.J., 1939-46; sales mgr. biologics div. Heyden Chem. Corp., N.Y.C., 1947-48; dir. mktg., mem. mgmt. com. Geigy Pharms., N.Y.C. and Ardsley, N.Y., 1949-64; pvt. practice investment mgmt., Elmhurst, Ill., 1965—. Author: Pharmaceutical Selling, Detailing and Sales Training, 1949, 2d edit., 1959; contbr. articles to profl. jours. Active Delma Coovert Meml. Endowed Scholarship, Valaparaiso U.; recipient Delma Coovert Peterson Meml. Music Faculty award, Valparaiso U., Muriel Beisswanger Peterson Library Fund, Presbyn. Ch. Found. Served with S.A.T.C., 1918. Mem. Am. Pharm. Assn., Am. Assn. Individual Investors, Midwest Pharm. Advt. Council, Am. Inst. History of Pharmacy, Am. Legion (comdr. Cedar Grove, N.J. 1953), Stockholders of Am. Inc., Tau Kappa Epsilon, Phi Delta Chi. Republican. Lutheran. Lodges: Masons, Shriners. Avocation: writing. Home and Office: 110 W Butterfield Rd #201 Elmhurst IL 60126

PETERSON, BRENDA JUNE, teacher; b. Duluth, Minn., Mar. 30, 1951; d. Alfred E. and June V. (Johnson) Bothun; m. David L. Peterson, June 22, 1985. BS, U. Minn., Duluth, 1973; MS, Mankato State U., 1981. Tchr. Washington Elem. Sch. Dist. 77, Mankato, Minn., 1973—. Mem. Minn. Edn. Assn., Delta Kappa Gamma. Avocations: sewing, crafts, sailing. Home: 488 Marvin Blvd North Mankato MN 56001 Office: Washington Elem Sch Anderson Dr Mankato MN 56001

PETERSON, BRUCE ARNOLD, shopping center development executive; b. St. Paul, Oct. 11, 1937; s. Joseph Arnold and Helen Caroline P.; m. Carol Barbara Anderson, Feb. 24, 1962; children: Dean Paul, Beth Ann. Student, Gustavus Adolphus Coll., 1955-56, U. Minn., 1956-57; cert. in acctg., Acad. of Acctg., Mpls., 1959. Adminstrv. officer, treas. Bloomberg Cos., Inc., Chanhassen, Minn., 1958-66; v.p. Western Land Corp., Mpls., 1967-68; real estate dir. Perkins Restaurants, Bloomington, Minn., 1969; v.p. real estate Fed. Dept. Stores, Detroit, 1970-71; v.p. shopping ctr. devel. Rauenhorst Corp., Mpls., 1971-74; exec. v.p. Indsl. Builders, Inc., Hastings, Minn., 1974-76; pres. Security Devel. Co., Inc., Eden Prairie, Minn., 1977—. Served with USAR, 1960-66. Mem. Internat. Council Shopping Ctrs., Nat. Assn. Corp. Real Estate Execs. Republican. Home: 1301 E 99th St Bloomington MN 55420 Office: Security Devel Co Inc 7545 Office Ridge Circle Eden Prairie MN 55344

PETERSON, CARL OSCAR, librarian, educator; b. Chgo., Oct. 20, 1921; s. Carl Oscar and Corine Marguerite (Pearson) P.; m. Marjorie Sylvia Demikis (dec. 1972); m. 2d, Shannon Mary Troy, Sept. 21, 1975; 1 son, Brian Carl. B.S. in Edn., Art Inst. Chgo., 1954, B.F.A., 1954; M.S. in Edn., Chgo. State Coll., 1970; Ed.D., Nova U., 1980. Designer, producer, purchaser printed and other forms of communications materials City of Chgo., 1955-57; with Argonne (Ill.) Nat. Lab., 1957-60; mem. staff U. Chgo., 1960-70; librarian, lectr. bus. info./communication Governors State U., Park Forest South, Ill., 1970—; vol. career counselor on careers in pub. and graphic arts in various high schs. Served with USN, 1942-46. Recipient Freedoms Found. group award, 1959. Mem. Internat. Graphic Arts Edn. Assn., Am. Vocat. Assn., Spl. Libraries Assn. Author: Business and Government Information Sources, 1972.

PETERSON, CHESTER, JR., magazine publisher; b. Salina, Kans., Mar. 24, 1937; s. Chester Sr. and Erma Ann (Reed) P.; m. Miyoko Ikegami, May 21, 1982; children: Joy, Nels, Erik, Ragnar. BS, Kans. State U., 1959, 60, MS, 1960. Assoc. editor Meredity Pub., Des Moines, 1960-64; creative contact exec. Gardner Advt., St. Louis, 1964; freelance writer and photographer Lindsborg, Kans., 1964-83; pres. Shield Pub. Co., Lindsborg, 1983—, Sunshine Travel, Inc., Lindsborg, 1983—. Dir. ops. CAP Salina (Kans.) Squadron, 1985—. Recipient cert. of Merit N.Y.C. Art Dirs. Club, 1978, BIF Ambassador award. Mem. Livestock Publs. Council (bd. dirs. 1981-84), Am. Soc. Mag. Photographers, Am. Agrl. Editor's Assn. (Editorial Photographer award 1974). Lutheran. Club: Quivera Hunting (Salina). Avocations: reading, computers, running, shooting, hunting. Home: PO Box 71 Lindsborg KS 67456 Office: Shield Pub Co Inc PO Box 511 Lindsborg KS 67456

PETERSON, DAVID ALLAN, virologist; b. Hayward, Wis., Nov. 29, 1938; s. Allen H. and Faith I. (Olsen) P.; B.S., Wis. State U., Stevens Point, 1966; M.S., Ind. U., 1970, Ph.D., 1971; m. Bonnie J. Sablovitch, May 29, 1964; children—Frank A., Ruth A. Postdoctoral research fellow dept. microbiology Rush-Presbyn.-St. Luke's Med. Ctr., Chgo., 1970-71; asst. prof. dept. microbiology Rush U. Coll. Health Scis., Chgo., 1975-81, asst. prof. dept. microbiology Rush Med. Coll., 1971-81, safety and environ. control officer dept. microbiology, 1971-81; asst. scientist med. staff Rush-Presbyn.-St. Luke's Med. Ctr., 1971-81, chief diagnostic virology lab. dept. microbiology, 1971-81; lectr. Cook Coungy Grad. Sch. Medicine, 1975-81; clin. project mgr. Abbott Labs., North Chicago, 1981-82, sr. virologist, 1982—. Served with USAF, 1957-61. Mem. Am. Soc. Microbiology, AAAS, Soc. Exptl. Biology and Medicine, Tissue Culture Assn., Ill. Soc. Microbiology. Congregationalist. Contbr. articles to profl. jours. Home: 6134 218th Ave Bristol WI 53104

PETERSON, DAVID EUGENE, dentist, hospital administrator, clinical educator; b. Holdrege, Nebr., Apr. 9, 1947; s. Elvin Eugene and Patrica Phyllis (McGimsey) P.; m. Karleen Ann Lund, Aug. 15, 1970; children—Kwen Arik, Trond Trygve. Student Dana Coll., 1965-66; D.D.S., U. Nebr., 1972. Lic. dentist, Nebr., S.D., N.D., Wis. ADA rotating intern Fla. State Hosp., Chattahoochee, 1972-73; staff dentist Royal Dental Hosp., Melbourne, Australia, 1973-75; tutor and clin. demonstrator U. Melbourne, 1974-75; dental dir. Redfield State Hosp., S.D., 1976—; clin. instr. U. Nebr., Lincoln, 1977—; missionary dentist vol. Lutheran Sudan Mission Ngaoudnere, Cameroon, 1981-82; asst. clin. prof. U. S.D., Vermillion, 1977—; lectr.-preceptor Lake Area Vo-Tech Inst., Watertown, S.D., 1977—; clin. instr. Creighton U., Omaha, 1978-81; cons. dentist N.E. S.D. Head Start, Aberdeen, 1983—. Author: (with others) Nutrition for Handicapped, 1985. Editor: (booklet) A Referral Manual, 1977, 80; co-editor: Coll. U. Nebr. Dentistry Yearbook, 1972. Contbr. articles to profl. jours. Tchr. adult Bible class Our Savior's Lutheran Ch., Redfield, S.D., 1976—, sr. hi youth group, 1976-80, congregation pres., 1984-85; council mem. World Mission Prayer League, Mpls., 1983—. Named one of Outstanding Young Men Am., 1980, Outstanding Dentist of Yr. S.D. chpt. Internat. Coll. Dentists, 1985. Mem. ADA (cert. of recognition, 1983), S.D. Dental Assn. (Gold Tooth award 1979, cert. of commendation, 1982-83, presidential award, 1983), No. Dist. Dental Soc. (del. 1979), Assn. Institutional Dentists (pres. 1983-84), Am. Cancer Soc. (outstanding Edn. Project S.D. div., 1978, Spink County bd. mem. 1976—), Wis. Dental Study Club, Uni-Hosp. Orthodontist Study Club, Uni-Hosp. Pedodontic Study Club. Avocations: jogging, bible study and teaching, reading, refinishing old furniture. Home: Rural Rt Box 1 Ashton SD 57424 Office: Redfield State Hosp Dept of Dentistry Redfield SD 57469

PETERSON, DAVID SCOTT, lawyer; b. Xenia, Ohio, June 4, 1959; s. Marshall Edwin and Marilynn L. (Siney) P.; m. Carol Ann Gallett, Apr. 13, 1985. BA, Wright State U., 1981; JD, Ohio No. U., 1984. Bar: Ohio 1984, U.S. Dist. Ct. (so. dist.) Ohio 1985. Ptnr. Peterson & Peterson, Xenia, 1984—. Mem. ABA, Ohio Bar Assn., Greene County Bar Assn., Assn. Trial Lawyers Am., Ohio Trial Lawyers Assn. Republican. Avocations: jogging, bicycling, swimming. Home: 1300 Bradfute Rd Xenia OH 45385 Office: Peterson & Peterson 670 N Detroit St Xenia OH 45385

PETERSON, DONALD ALBERT, radio and publishing executive; b. Youngstown, Ohio, Sept. 18, 1917; s. Albert and Hattie M. (Anderson) P.; m. Josephine Phelps Hoiles, July 20, 1940; children—Donald A. Jr., Jill P. McCarty. Pres. Alliance (Ohio) Brick Corp., 1965-72; pub. Alliance Rev., 1962—; pres. Sta. WFAH/WDJQ, Alliance, 1967—; chmn. bd. Alliance Fed. Savs. and Loan; dir. Valley Forge Inc., Glamorgan Park Inc. Chmn. bd. Mt. Union Coll., 1971-87. Served to lt. (j.g.) USNR, 1944-46. Recipient United Way Award of Merit, 1956; Mt. Union Coll. Alumni Service award, 1981; named Alliance Boss of Yr., 1968; nominated to Hall of Fame Ohio Found. Ind. Coll., 1987. Mem. Ohio Broadcasters Assn., Am. Newspaper Pubs. Assn., Am. Legion. Sigma Delta Chi. Republican. Methodist. Clubs: Wranglers, Filibusters, Alliance Country. Lodges: Kiwanis, Elks (Alliance). Home: 1084 Glamorgan Alliance OH 44601 Office: 40 S Linden Alliance OH 44601

PETERSON, EDWARD NOHL, physician, medical educator; b. Tulsa, Feb. 13, 1930; s. Edward Nohl and Mary Louise (Bizal) P.; m. Karen Thune Sturgeon, Sept. 12, 1953 (div. 1982); children: Elizabeth Ann, Karen Lynn, Edward Nohl III, Eric James. AA, U. Wis., 1950; BS, U. Minn., 1952, MD, 1954. Diplomate Am. Bd. Ob-Gyn. Clin. instr. ob-gyn U. Oreg. Med. Sch., Portland, 1961-65, asst. prof., 1965-68; asst. prof. U. Pitts. Sch. Medicine, 1968-73, assoc. prof., 1973-85, asst. dean., 1971-80, assoc. dean, 1980-85; adminstrv. dir. med. edn. The Toledo Hosp., 1985—; clin. prof. ob-gyn Med. Coll. Ohio, 1986—. Contbr. articles to profl. jours., chpts. in books. Served to capt. USAF, 1958-60. NIH fellow, 1966-68, grantee, 1972-75; Am. Council Edn. fellow, 1975-76. Fellow Am. Coll. Obstetricians and Gynecologists; mem. AMA, Soc. Gynecologic Investigation, Assn. Am. Med. Colls. Democrat. Presbyterian. Avocations: golf, tennis, swimming, backpacking, sailing. Home: 2447 Scottwood Ave Toledo OH 43620 Office: The Toledo Hosp 2142 N Cove Blvd Toledo OH 43606

PETERSON, GARY GLENN, communication engineer; b. Chgo., Oct. 10, 1953; s. Robert G. and Marjorie D. (Reimer) P. BA, Columbia Coll., Chgo., 1975. Film dir. Sta. WCIU-TV, Chgo., 1975-80; TV engr. Sta. WLS-TV, Chgo., 1980—; instr. Inst. Broadcast Arts, Chgo., 1979; dir. Beautiful City Players, Chgo., 1972-78. Author: (plays) Heart of Ice, 1985, The Brementown Musicians, 1983, Stone Soup, 1983, Androcles and the Lion, 1984, The Velveteen Rabbit, 1985; (musical) Tale of Two Cities, 1985; (short stories) Et Al, 1982; co-author: (play) Klondike Kalamity, 1978, Sincerely Samantha, 1984; producer and dir.: (documentary) Voice of the Ring, 1987. Mem. Nat. Acad. TV Arts and Scis. (Emmy award 1984). Avocations: astronomy, computers, movies. Office: Sta WLS-TV 190 N State Chicago IL 60601

PETERSON, GERALD LEONARD, psychology educator; b. Neenah, Wis., Aug. 22, 1945; s. Gerald F. and Mary E. (Letwon) P. BS, U. Wis., Oshkosh, 1968; MA, U. Mo., Kansas City, 1972; Ph.D., Kans. State U., 1975. Cert. psychologist, Pa. Asst prof. dept. psychology Duquesne U., Pitts., 1975-81; prof., chmn. dept. psychology Saginaw Valley State Coll., University Center, Mich., 1981—; cons. in field. Served as sgt. U.S. Army, 1968-70. Mem. Am. Psychol. Assn., Midwestern Psychol. Assn., N.Y. Acad. Scis. Roman Catholic. Contbr. articles to profl. bulls., jours. Office: Saginaw Valley State Coll 161 Brown Hall 2250 Pierce Rd University Center MI 48710

PETERSON, GREG DALE, finance executive; b. Kingman, Kans., Dec. 27, 1947; s. Dale Eric E. and Edna Lois (Beerman) P.; m. Ginger Lee Orton, June 7, 1969; children: Brent D., Marsha D., Michelle L. BS in Acctg., Emporia State U., 1969. CPA, Kans. Ptnr. Peat Marwick Mitchell and Co., Wichita, Kans., 1969-86; v.p. fin. Physician Corp. Am., Wichita, 1986—. Mem. Nat. Assn. Accountants (pres. Wichita chpt. 1981-82), Am. Inst. CPA's, Kans. Soc. CPA's, Greenleaf Home Owners Assn. (treas. 1985-86), Emporia State Alumni Assn. (bd. dirs. 1984-87). Clubs: Wichita, Tallgrass (Wichita). Avocations: hunting, fishing, golf, basketball, collecting antiques. Home: 8920 Boxthorn Wichita KS 67226 Office: Physician Corp Am 151 N Main Suite 400 Wichita KS 67202

PETERSON, GREGG LEE, radio station executive; b. Los Angeles, Feb. 28, 1943; s. Harry Roland and Hazel Irene (Gregg) P.; m. Beverly Elizabeth Wolfe; children: Gregg, Andrew, David. A.A., El Camino Coll., Torrance, Calif., 1962; B.A., U. So. Calif., 1966. Sports editor Torrance Herald, 1960-63; reporter UPI, Los Angeles, 1965-67; assignment editor Sta. KABC, Los Angeles, 1967-68; asst. news dir., then news dir. Sta. KNX, Los Angeles, 1968-82; v.p., gen. mgr. Sta. WBBM, Chgo., 1982—. Bd. dirs. Calif. Freedom of Info. Com., 1980-82. Recipient Grand award for editorializing Internat. Radio Festival N.Y., 1983, 84. Mem. Chgo. Assn. Commerce and Industry (bd. dirs. 1986—), Ill. Broadcasters Assn. (bd. dirs.), Radio Broadcasters Chgo., Radio and TV News Assn. So. Calif. (bd. dirs. 1978-82, Golden Mikes awards 1971-81), Sigma Delta Chi (bd. dirs. Los Angeles chpt. 1978-82, Disting. Service award 1982). Methodist. Avocations: swimming; tennis. Office: WBBM Radio 630 N McClurg Ct Chicago IL 60611

PETERSON, HAMLET ALBERT, pediatric orthopedic surgeon; b. Decorah, Iowa, Jan. 6, 1932; s. Hamlet Edwin and Thelma Knute (Olson) P.; children: Erik, Heidi, Nils. BA, Luther Coll., 1954; MD, U. Iowa, 1958; MS, U. Minn., 1969. Cert. Am. Bd. Orthopedic Surgery, 1968. Intern D.C. Gen. Hosp., Washington, 1958-59; resident in orthopaedics Mayo Clin., Rochester, Minn., 1962-66, cons. orthopedic surgery, 1967—; State chmn. Orthopedic Research and Edn. Found., 1984; founder Pediatric Orthopedic Study Group, 1972. Bd. dirs. Courage Ctr., Mpls., 1983-85, Am. Luth. Ch. Div. Coll. and Univ. Services, Mpls., 1982-87. Served to capt. USAF, 1959-62. Recipient Stinchfield award Hip Soc., 1974. Fellow Am. Acad. Orthopedic Surgeons (admissions com.); mem. AMA, Am. Orthopedic Assn. (Am., Brit., Can. Traveling fellowship 1971), Pediatric Orthopedic Soc., Peruvian Orthopedic Soc. (hon.), Costa Rican Orthopedic Soc. (hon.). Lutheran. Avocations: tennis, canoeing, stamp collecting. Office: Mayo Clinic 200 First St SW Rochester MN 55905

PETERSON, HAROLD OSCAR, educator, radiologist; b. Dalbo, Minn., Apr. 13, 1909; s. Adolph Oscar and Hulda (Forslund) P.; m. Margaret Dorothy Ferris, Sept. 22, 1934; children: John F., Judith Ann Peterson Lyons, Richard H., James R. BS, U. Minn., 1930, MD, 1934. Diplomate Am. Bd. Radiology (trustee 1959-65, 65-71). Intern Kansas City (Mo.) Gen. Hosp., 1933-34; resident radiology Mass. Gen. Hosp., Boston, 1935-36; from mem. faculty to prof. emeritus radiology U. Minn. Med. Sch., 1937—, chmn. dept. radiology, 1957-70; radiologist, head dept. Charles T. Miller Hosp., St. Paul, 1941-57, Children's Hosp., St. Paul, 1948-57; radiologist Bethesda Hosp., St. Paul, 1941-44, St. Joseph's Hosp., St. Paul, 1941-43, Interstate Clinic, Red Wing, Minn., 1940-57; chief staff U. Minn. Hosp., 1966—; Pancoast lectr., Phila., 1956; cons. Mpls. Gen. Hosp., 1958; Friedman lectr. U. Cin., 1959; Caldwell lectr. Am. Roentgen Ray Soc., 1961 (gold medal); Hodges lectr., Ann Arbor, Mich., 1962; Carmen lectr. St. Louis Med. Soc., 1962; ann. lectr. Canadian Assn. Radiologists, 1962; Manville lectr. La. Med. Soc., 1961; Golden lectr. N.Y. Roentgen Soc., 1964; Rigler lectr., Tel Aviv, 1965; Holmes lectr. New Eng. Roentgen Ray Soc., 1965; Kirklin Weber Meml. lectr. Mayo Clinic, 1965; Dyke lectr. Columbia, 1971; Stauffer lectr. Temple U., 1972; Rigler lectr. U. Minn., 1972; vis. prof. U. Tex. Med. Br., Galveston, 1979-80, 81, U. Tex. Health Sci. Center, San Antonio, 1980-81, 82-83, 84-85. Sr. author: Introduction to Neuroradiology, 1972; contbr. numerous articles to profl. jours. Fellow Am. Coll. Radiology (chancellor 1958-62, 65-69, v.p. 1963-64, chmn. com. tech. affairs 1965-69, gold medal St. Louis meeting 1971), Am. Coll. Chest Physicians; mem. Am. Roentgen Ray Soc. (dir. instructional courses 1957-76, exec. council 1954-57, chmn. council 1956-57, pres. 1964), Am. Soc. Neuroradiology (charter, founding mem., pres. 1967), AMA, Minn., Ramsey County Med. Socs., Minn. Radiol. Soc., Minn. Trudeau Soc., Radiol. Soc. N. Am., AAUP, Am. Trudeau Soc., AAAS, Assn. Am. Med. Colls., Minn. Soc. Neurol. Scis., Am. Soc. Pediatric Radiology (charter, founding mem.), Pan Am. Med. Assn., Minn. Acad. Medicine, Am. Acad. Neurology, Sigma Xi; hon. mem. numerous med. socs. Republican. Methodist. Club: Midland Hills Country (St. Paul). Home: 1995 W County Rd B Saint Paul MN 55113

PETERSON, JOHN DWIGHT, investment company executive; b. Indpls., July 20, 1933; s. J. Dwight and Mary Irene (Frisinger) P.; m. Nancy Jane Browning, July 16, 1955; children: Debbra Lee, John Dwight III, Penny Anne. B.S., Ind. U., 1955. With City Securities Corp., Indpls., 1955—; dir. City Securities Corp., 1966—, v.p., 1968-70, pres., 1970—, chmn., chief exec. officer, 1979—; dir. Lilly Indsl. Coatings, Inc., Farm Fans, Inc., Forum Group, Inc., Capital Industries, Duke Realty Investments. Mem. James Whitcomb Riley Meml. Assn., 1965—, Ind. Bd. Vocat. and Tech. Edn., 1973-81; mem. career edn. action com. Indpls. Pub. Schs., 1974-80; mem. Ind. U. Athletic Bd., 1971-74; pres. bd. dirs. Jr. Achievement Central Ind., 1979. Served as capt. U.S. Army, 1956. Mem. Young Pres. Orgn., Nat. Assn. Securities Dealers (dist. com. 8 1975-78), Indpls. Bond Club (pres. 1969), Sigma Chi. Presbyterian (elder). Clubs: Marion County Varsity (chmn. 1961-71); Columbia, University (Indpls.); Highland Golf and Country. Lodges: Masons, Rotary. Office: City Securities Corp 400 Circle Tower Indianapolis IN 46204 *

PETERSON, KARL LEWIS, insurance executive; b. Mojave, Calif., Oct. 27, 1943; s. Charles William and Thelma Ann (Bilski) P.; m. Nancy Marie Opalka, May 25, 1963; children—Karl Lewis, Joan Marie. B.A., Eastern Ill. U., 1963. Underwriter, Fed. Mut. Ins. Co., 1963-65, Charles L. Howard, Inc., Noblesville, Ind., 1965-66; treas. J.L. Hubbard Co., Decatur, Ill., 1966-76; ptnr., Overheul-Peterson Co., Decatur, 1980-83; pres. Creighton Jackson Co., Decatur, 1976-86; ins. trainer, risk mgr., 1986—; pub. insurance training manuals Property I, Property II, Basics of Life Insurance, 1987. mem. producer's lic. adv. com. Ill. Ins. Dept.; mem. agts. adv. bd. AI network Am. Internat. Group. Treas., Big Bros. Big Sisters, 1980-81; pres. Spring Creek Plaza low rent housing complex, 1981. Recipient Extra Spl. Person award Decatur Assn. Ins. Women, 1982. Mem. Am. Soc. C.P.C.U. (continuing profl. devel. designation), Ind. Ins. Agts. Ill. (dir. 1981-86, edn. chmn.), Jonathan Trumbul Council Ins., Profl. Ins. Agts., Am. Bus. Club. Republican. Roman Catholic. Clubs: Kaskaskia Valley Bass (sec. treas. 1970-74, bd. dirs. 1976), Decatur Chess (founder, past pres.). Contbr. articles to ins. jours. Home: 44 Barnes Dr Decatur IL 62526

PETERSON, KENNETH ALLEN, SR., superintendant of schools; b. Hammond, Ind., Jan. 20, 1939; s. Chester E. and Bertha (Hornby) P.; B.Ed. cum laude, Chgo. State U., 1963; M.S., Purdue U., 1970; NSF grantee U. Iowa, 1964-65; postgrad. U. Ill., 1977-81; m. Marilyn M. Musson, Jan. 3, 1961; children—Kimberly, Kari, Kenneth Allen. Tchr., Markham (Ill.) Sch. Dist. 144, 1961-67; prin. Brookwood Sch., Glenwood (Ill.) Sch. Dist. 1967, 1967-77, prin. Hickory Bend Sch., 1977-78, dir. spl. edn., 1978-80, asst. supt. schs., 1981-83, supt schs., 1983—; mem. No. Ill. Planning Commn. for Gifted Edn. Chmn. Steger (Ill.) Bicentennial Commn., 1976; vice chmn. Ashkum dist. Boy Scouts Am., 1981-83, lodge advisor, exec. bd. Order of Arrow Calumet council Boy Scouts Am.; program com. South Cook County council Girl Scouts U.S.A., 1971-73, 80-81, mem. fin. com., 1981—, also bd. dirs.; mem. Steger Community Devel. Commn. Recipient Order of Arrow Service award, Silver Beaver award, Dist. award of merit Boy Scouts Am. Mem. Council Exceptional Children, Assn. Supervision and Curriculum Devel., Nat. Assn. Elem. Sch. Prins., P.T.A. (life), Am. Assn. Sch. Adminstrs., Kappa Delta Pi. Republican. Lutheran. Home: 3208 Phillips Ave Steger IL 60475 Office: 201 Glenwood Dyer Rd Glenwood IL 60425

PETERSON, LARRY MICHAEL, SR., sales professional; b. Moline, Ill., Jan. 21, 1939; s. Glenn Albert Peterson and Minnette Helen (Van Paul) Wilder; m. Anna Serinis Johnson, June 13, 1957; children: Faith Ann Peterson Strop, Hope Lorraine, Larry Michael Jr. Mgr. customer service Motorola, Inc., Schaumburg, Ill., 1965-76; sales rep. Markem Corp., Keene, N.H., 1976-78, MADA Med., N.J., 1978-79; mgr. customer service Wabash/IPM, Palatine, Ill., 1979-80; product mgr. Videojet Systems, Elk Grove, Ill., 1980—. Contbg. editor: Identification Jour. Leader Boy Scouts Am., Girl Scouts USA, Schaumburg, Ill., 1973-76; project chmn. High sch. band boosters, Schaumburg, Il, 1975-77; Rep. precinct capt., Hoffman Estates, 1982; mem. bd. Elem. Sch. Dist. 13, Bloomingdale, Ill. Served with USN, 1957-62. Mem. N.W. Suburban 99 User's Group (Hoffman Estates, Ill.) (pres. 1986—). Republican. Methodist. Avocations: racquetball, computers. Home: 512 Weathersfield Way Schaumburg IL 60193 Office: Videojet Systems Internat 2200 Arthur Ave Elk Grove Village IL 60007

PETERSON, LIONEL BENJAMIN, real estate developer; b. Forest City, Ark., Sept. 12, 1933; s. James Tony and Helen Irene (Webb) P.; m. Shirley Mae Meyer, Sept. 7, 1957; children: Karen Sue, Lionel Tony, Michael Seven. Prodn. planner McDonnel-Douglas, St. Louis, 1955-76; pres. Marschel Inc., Union, Mo., 1970—, Coventry Farms Inc., Union, 1976—, Two Rivers Realty, Union, 1979—. Active East-West Gateway Task Force, St. Louis, 1977-80. Served with USN, 1951-54. Mem. Nat. Assn. Realtors, Internat. Orgn. Real Estate Appraisers (sr. appraiser 1982—), Am. Legion (treas. St. Clair, Mo. 1980-85). Lodges: Masons, Shriners, Elks. Home and Office: Rural Rt 3 Box 694 Union MO 63084

PETERSON, MARGARET SCHAWDE, public relations executive, educator, writer; b. Dodgeville, Wis., May 29, 1927; d. Herman L. and Wilma L. (Murrish) Schawde; m. Joseph F. Peterson, June 22, 1948; children—Charles J., Alan A., Richard S. B.A. in Journalism, U. Wis., 1948. Faculty asst., librarian Sch. Journalism, U. Wis., Madison, 1948-49; freelance writer, 1949—; co-owner, operator Oak Grove Cheese, Muscoda, Wis., 1953-65; office supr. M.B. Victora Agy., Muscoda, 1962-65; pub. info. coordinator, continuing edn. agt. U. Wis. Ctr. Marshfield-Wood County and Univ. Extension, Marshfield, 1965-71; pub. info. specialist Mid-State Vocat., Tech., Adult Edn. Dist., Wisconsin Rapids, Wis., 1971-76; dir. pub. affairs St. Joseph's Hosp., Marshfield, 1976—. Past pres. Marshfield United Way; chmn. bd. dirs. Wis. div. Am. Cancer Soc.; past pres. Marshfield Art Com., New Visions Gallery Inc. Recipient Mehlberg award Wis. Hosp. Pub. Relations Council, 1979; writing awards Wis. Press Women, 1971-76, Nat. Honor Citation Am. Cancer Soc., 1981. Mem. Wis. Hosp. Pub. Relations Council, Am. Soc. Hosp. Pub. Relations, Central Wis. Pub. Relations Roundtable, Central and Western Wis. Press Clubs, Delta Kappa Gamma Internat. Methodist. Clubs: P.E.O. Contbr. articles to profl. jours. Home: 500 S Lincoln Ave Marshfield WI 54449 Office: St Joseph's Hospital 611 St Joseph Ave Marshfield WI 54449

PETERSON, NANCY ANN, real estate broker; b. Fargo, N.D., Sept. 18, 1947; d. Simar Kristian and Rhoda Alice (Anderson) Nelson; m. John William Peterson, Oct. 20, 1967 (dec. Aug. 1979); 1 child, Dauvin John. BS, Moorhead State U., 1979; student Real Conservatorio, Madrid, Spain, 1981. Cert. comml. investment mgr. Owner, pres. Circle Realtors Inc., Fargo, 1971—; bd. dirs. Town & Country Realty; Honorarium prof. Classical Guitar Moorhead State U. Bd. dirs. Plains Art Mus., Moorhead, Minn., 1983—, pres., 1987—; mem. devel. council Moorhead State U., 1987; treas. O'Rourke-Plains Mus., Moorhead, 1984-85, v.p., 1986-87; v.p. O'Rourke-Plains Arts Assn., 1987—. Mem. Nat. Assn. Realtors, Fargo-Moorhead Bd. Realtors, Women's Council Realtors (pres. 1977), Fargo-Moorhead Home Builders, Linden Assoc. Lodge: Zonta. Avocations: classical guitar, fishing, scuba diving, skiing. Office: Circle Realtors Inc 1220 Main Ave Fargo ND 58103

PETERSON, RICHARD CARSON, financial management company executive, healthcare consultant; b. Wilmington, N.C., Sept. 15, 1953; s. Graham Howard and Lillie Truman (Johnson) P.; m. Karen Zurn, Feb. 14, 1982. B.A. in Econs., Duke U., 1975, M.H.A. (Equitable Assurance Soc. U.S. Scholar), 1977. Adminstrv. resident The Duke Endowment, Charlotte, N.C., 1977; adminstrv. asst. N.C. Baptist Hosps., Inc., Winston-Salem, N.C., 1977-78; mgr. mgmt. info. cons. div. Arthur Andersen & Co., Chgo., 1978—. Mem. Am. Coll. Healthcare Execs., Healthcare Fin. Mgmt. Assn., Hosp. Mgmt. System Soc., Duke U. Alumni Assn. Republican. Episcopalian. Home: 25W740 Wenona Ln Wheaton IL 60187 Office: Arthur Andersen & Co 33 W Monroe St Chgo IL 60603

PETERSON, RICHARD GUSTAF, literature educator, educational administrator; b. Chgo., Jan. 9, 1936; s. Stanley Gustaf and Mattie (DeHaan) P. B.A., U. Minn., 1956, Ph.D., 1963; M.A., Northwestern U., 1958. Instr. English, U. Minn., Mpls., 1960-62; asst. prof. English, St. Olaf Coll., Northfield, Minn., 1963-68, prof. English and classics, 1975—; exec. sec. Am. Soc. Eighteenth-Century Studies, Northfield, 1983—. Book rev. editor Eighteenth Century Studies, Davis, Calif., 1980-83. Contbr. numerous articles to profl. jours. Recipient William Riley Parker prize MLA, 1976; Am. Philos. Soc. research fellow, 1969-70. Mem. MLA, Am. Soc. for Eighteenth-Century Studies, AAUP, Classical Assn. of Midwest and South. Episcopalian. Avocations: cooking, photography, travel, woodworking. Office: St Olaf Coll Am Soc for 18th Century Studies Northfield MN 55057

PETERSON, RICHARD MICHAEL, architect; b. Akron, Ohio, June 25, 1936; s. Pat P. and Elizabeth Jane (Eoveno) P.; m. Frances Therese Vorwerk, Nov. 8, 1958; children—Richard D., Mark M., Michael D. B.S. with honors in Architecture, Kent State U., 1958. Registered architect, Ohio; cert. Nat. Council Archtl. Registration Bd. Architect in tng. Keith Haag Assocs., Cuyahoga Falls, Ohio, 1956-62, assoc., 1962-72, v.p., 1972-75; pres. Peterson/Raeder Inc., Architects, Akron, 1975—; guest design juror Kent State U. Sch. of Architecture. Served with USNR, 1954-62. Winner 2d place award Ohio Edison Illumination Design competition, 1957. Mem. AIA (pres. Akron Chpt. 1973), Architects Soc. Ohio (trustee 1973-75). Club: Optimist, Fairlawn (pres. 1981, award 1982). Republican. Roman Catholic. Home: 755 Sand Run Rd Akron OH 44313 Office: 2650 W Market St Akron OH 44313

PETERSON, ROBERT L., meat processing executive; b. Nebr., July 14, 1932; married; children: Mark R., Susan P. Ed., U. Nebr., 1951. With Wilson & Co., Jim Boyle Order Buying Co.; cattle buyer R&C Packing Co., 1956-61; cattle buyer, plant mgr., v.p. carcass prodn. IBP, 1961-69; exec. v.p. ops. Spencer Foods, 1969-71; founder, pres. Madison Foods, 1971-76; pres. Iowa Beef Processors, Inc., Dakota City, Nebr., 1976—, chmn. bd., chief exec. officer, dir., 1981—; exec. v.p., dir. Occidental Petroleum Corp., 1982—. Served with Q.M.C. U.S. Army, 1952-54. Club: Sioux City (Iowa) Country. Office: IBP Inc Box 515 Dakota City NE 68731 *

PETERSON, ROGER ANDREW, marketing educator; b. Niagara Falls, N.Y., Aug. 29, 1934; s. Walter Octave and Mary Luvance Peterson; m. Barbara L. Scott, Oct. 25, 1960 (div. Apr. 1966); m. Takako Grace Shinya, Dec. 30, 1967; children: Kristina, Reiko. BBA in Acctg. with distinction, U. Hawaii, 1972; MS in Transp., U. B.C., Can., 1974; D of Bus. Adminstrn. in Transp. and Logistics, U. Tenn., 1980. Enlisted USMC, 1952, resigned, 1956, re-enlisted, 1961, advanced through grades to staff sgt., 1966, resigned, 1968; dir. traffic and supply Channel Air Lift, Honolulu, 1967-69; gen. mgr., mgr. airline services Air Service Internat., Air Service Corp., Honolulu Internat. Airport, 1969-70; mgr. night maintenance Aero Services Inc. Honolulu Internat. Airport, 1970-71; project coordinator Hawaii environ. area rapid transit study SEAGRANT and Dept. Marine Affairs U. Hawaii, Honolulu, 1972; grad. asst. sch. travel industry mgmt. coll. bus. adminstrn. U. Hawaii, Honolulu, 1972-73; research asst. dept. transp. faculty commerce and bus. U. B.C., Vancouver, 1973-74; sr. analyst transp. and distbn. Burns Foods Ltd., Calgary, Alta., Can., 1974; dir. maintenance Day and Ross Trucking Ltd., Hartland, N.B., Can., 1974-76; asst. prof. div. adminstrn. U. N.B., Saint John, 1976-78; grad. teaching, research asst. dept. mktg. and transp. U. Tenn., Knoxville, 1978-80; prof. dept. mktg. and bus. law coll. bus. Ea. Mich. U., Ypsilanti, 1985—; pres. Peterson and Assocs. Inc., Ypsilanti, 1985—; vis. assoc. prof. transp. dept. purchasing, transp. and ops., coll. bus. Ariz. State U., Tempe, 1985; project dir. grant to further internat. edn. Ea. Mich. U. and U.S. Dept. Edn., 1985-86; following coms. all at Ea. Mich. U., chmn. com. rev. appointment, promotion and tenure procedures dept. mktg. and bus. law 1982-83, chmn. com. student skills 1981-86, chmn. screening com. disting. faculty awards Office V.p. Acad. Affairs 1984, chmn. research com. Coll. Bus. 1983-84, 85—, coordinator internat. bus. activities and programs Coll. Bus. 1982—, editor research activities newsletter Coll. Bus. 1983-84, 85—, editor research interests newsletter dept. mktg. and bus. law 1986-87, mem. adv. com. gen. aviation mgmt. program Coll. Tech. 1981—, mem. curriculum internationalization com. Coll. Bus. 1984-85, mem. dean's adv. com. space allocation Coll. Bus. 1984, mem. faculty council com. hon. degrees 1981-84, faculty council com. scholarly awards 1986-87, faculty adv. council Coll. Bus. 1981-84, chmn. sub-com. elections Coll. Bus. 1982-83, mem. personnel com. dept. mktg. and bus. law 1981-83, program rev. com. grad. programs in physics 1981-82, world bus. com. joint com. Coll. Bus. and Coll. Arts and Scis. 1984—, vis. prof. dept. fng. langs. 1981-84; cons. in field; bd. dirs. Oatencourt U.S.A., World Awareness Inc., Ypsilanti; vis. scholar dept. naval architecture and marine engring. U. Mich., Ann Arbor, 1981-82. Contbr. articles to profl. jours. Grantee Eastern Mich. U., 1981, 83. Mem. Am. Soc. Transp. and Logistics (cert.), Nat. Assn. Corp. Dirs., Royal Inst. Navigation (The Netherlands), Royal Inst. Navigation (United Kingdom), Transp. and Utilities Group of Am. Econs. Assn., The Internat. Council (exec. com. 1983—, vice chmn. 1983-85), Beta Gamma Sigma. Club: Washtenaw Sportsmans (Ypsilanti). Lodges: Masons, Shriners. Avocations: shooting, sailing, model building, travelling. Home: 1211 Whittier Rd Ypsilanti MI 48197 Office: Ea Mich U Dept Mktg Ypsilanti MI 48197

PETERSON, RONALD JOHN, obstetrician-gynecologist; b. Marshfield, Wis., Aug. 9, 1947; s. John Clemmons and Doris M. (Heden) P.; m. Kathryn Anne Rumbolz, Dec. 28, 1969; children: Amy Christine, Stephen Clifford, Laura Elizabeth. BA, Augustana Coll., 1969; MD, Northwestern U., 1973. Resident ob-gyn. U. Mich., Ann Arbor, 1973-77; practice medicine specializing in ob-gyn. John A. Hangen Assoc., Mpls., 1977—; Chmn. ob-gyn. dept. Abbott-NW Hosp., Mpls., 1982-83, treas. med. staff 1984, sec. med. staff 1985. Fellow Am. Coll. Ob-Gyn.; mem. Am. Fertility Soc., Mpls. Council Ob-Gyn. (pres. 1986). Home: 4617 Wooddale Ave S Edina MN 55424 Office: 411 Med Arts Bldg Minneapolis MN 55402

PETERSON, ROY ELSTON, healthcare executive; b. Ishpeming, Mich., Feb. 27, 1942; s. Roy E. and Marie (Fluur) P.; M. Susan M. Matthews, Aug. 15, 1964; children: Eric, Paul. BS, No. Mich. U., 1964; MA, Eastern Mich. U., 1966; PhD, Mich. State U., 1969. Radio announcer Sta. WJPD and WJAN, Ishpeming, 1958-60; announcer Sta. WLUC-TV, Marquette, Mich., 1960-64; dir. community schs. Flint (Mich.) Bd. Edn., 1964-65, dir. pub. relations, 1965-66; v.p. Mott Children's Health Ctr., Flint, 1966-85, pres., 1985—; adj. instr. U. Mich., Ann Arbor, 1980-81; cons. in field. V.p. Flushing Sch. Bd., Mich., 1983; pres. Mich. Health Council, Lansing, 1985, Mich. Council for Maternal and Child Health, Lansing, 1986; mem. Citizens' Adv. Council, U. Mich., 1986. Named one of Outstanding Young Men Am. Mem. Mich. Sch. Health Assn. (pres. 1981-82, Disting. Service award 1984) Mich. Community Coordinated Child Care Council (pres. 1974-75, Spl. Service award 1980). Lodge: Rotary. Avocations: fishing, photography, woodworking. Office: Mott Children's Health Ctr Tuuri Pl Flint MI 48503

PETERSON, SCOTT CLIFFORD, lawyer; b. Mt. Vernon, Iowa, Mar. 21, 1953; s. Clifford Warner and Sherlee (Kaplan) P.; m. Susan Kay Alexander, July 30, 1977; children: Evan S., Tobyn A. BS, U.S. Naval Acad., 1975; MA in History, U. Iowa, 1984, JD, 1984. Bar: Iowa 1986. Commd. ensign USN, 1975, advanced through ranks to lt., 1979; operational pilot USN, San Diego, 1977-80; recruiting program mgr. USN, 1980-81, resigned, 1981; capt. Iowa N.G., 1981—; asst. to ombudsman State of Iowa, Des Moines, 1985-86; asst. county atty. Linn County, Cedar Rapids, Iowa, 1986—; vol. lawyer Govt. Attys. Pro Bono, Des Moines, 1986. Organizer, pres. Iowa Equal Justice Found., Iowa City, 1983-84; mem. Dem. Cen. Com., Iowa City, 1982-84. Mem. ABA, Iowa State Bar Assn. Office: Linn County Atty's Office 3d Ave Bridge Cedar Rapids IA 52401

PETERSON, VERNON LEE, accountant; b. Chgo., May 14, 1955; s. Donald W. and Leona F. (Gierszewicz) P.; m. Lynn R. Radmann, July 27, 1979; 1 child, Andrew. BBA in Acctg., U. Wis., Milw., 1977. CPA, Wis. Staff auditor Blue Cross of Wis., Milw., 1978-79; staff auditor Nankin, Schnoll & Co., Milw., 1979-80, sr. auditor, 1980-82, audit mgr., 1982-84; dir. internal audit Green Bay (Wis.) Packaging Inc., 1984—; cons. in field, 1984—. Vol. Muscular Dystrophy Assn., Milw., 1982-83; fund raiser United Way of Brown County, Green Bay, 1985. Mem. Am. Inst. CPA's, Inst. Internal Auditors. Republican. Lutheran. Avocations: racquetball, golf, skiing, woodworking. Home: 1354 Lindale Ln Green Bay WI 54303-5652 Office: Green Bay Packaging Inc 1700 N Webster Green Bay WI 54307

PETERSON, WALLACE CARROLL, SR., economics educator; b. Omaha, Mar. 28, 1921; s. Fred Nels and Grace (Brown) P.; m. Eunice V. Peterson, Aug. 16, 1944 (dec. Nov. 24, 1985); children: Wallace Carroll Jr., Shelley Lorraine. Student, U. Omaha, 1939-40, U. Mo., 1940-42; BA in Econs. and European History, U. Nebr., 1947, MA in Econs. and European History, 1948, PhD in Econs. and European History, 1953; postgrad., Handelshochschule, St. Gallen, Switzerland, 1948-49, U. Minn., 1951, London Sch. Econs. and Polit. Sci., 1952. Reporter Lincoln (Nebr.) Jour., 1946; instr. econs. U. Nebr., Lincoln, 1951-54, asst. prof., 1954-57, assoc. prof., 1957-61, prof., 1962—, chmn. dept. econs., 1965-75, George Holmes prof. econs., 1966—, v.p. faculty senate, 1972-73, pres. faculty senate, 1973-74; S.J. Hall disting. vis. prof. U. Nev., Las Vegas, 1983-84. Author: Income, Employment and Economic Growth, 6th edit, 1986, The Welfare State in France, 1960, Elements of Economics, 1973, Our Overloaded Economy: Inflation, Unemployment, and the Crisis in American Capitalism, 1981; editor: Nebr. Jour. Econs. and Bus., 1970-80; mem. editorial bd. Jour. Post Keynesian Econs; author bi-weekly newspaper column Money in Am. (Champion Media awards); contbr. articles to profl. jours. Mem. Nebr. Dem. Cen. Com., 1968-74, vice chmn., chmn. Nebr. Polit. Accountability and Disclosure Commn., 1977-80. Served to capt. USAAF, 1942-46. Recipient Outstanding Prof. award U. Nebr. at Lincoln Buildres Orgn., 1973-74, Burlington-No. Outstanding Tchr.-Scholar award U. Nebr., 1986; faculty research fellow U. Nebr., 1954, 59, 63, Fulbright fellow, 1957-58, 64-65; Mid-Am. State Univs. honor scholar, 1982-83. Mem. Assn. for Evolutionary Econs. (pres. 1976), AAUP (pres. Nebr. 1963-64, nat. council), Am. Econs. Assn., Atlantic Midwest Econs. Assn. (pres. 1968-69), Assn. Social Econs., AAAS, Fedn. Am. Scientists, Common Cause, ACLU, UN Assn. U.S.A. (state pres.), Nebr. Council Econ. Edn. (chmn. 1976-77). Home: 4549 South St Lincoln NE 68506 Office: U Nebr Dept Econs 338 CBA Lincoln NE 68588-0489

PETERS-USDROWSKI, MARY CATHERINE, radiologist, educator; b. Denver, Aug. 23, 1940; d. John George and Alfreda Patricia (Dillon) P.; m. Lawrence Edward Usdrowski, Aug. 31, 1972; children: Kate Marie, Brian Lawrence, Mary Elizabeth. BS, St. Louis U., 1962; MD, Loyola Stritoh Sch. Med., 1966. Diplomate Am. Bd. Radiology. Intern St. Francis Hosp., Evanston, Ill., 1966-67, resident in radiology, 1967-70; asst. prof. radiology Stritch Sch. Med., Maywood, Ill., 1970—. Mem. AMA, Am. Coll. Radiology, Chgo. Radiol. Soc., Radiol. Soc. N.Am. Roman Catholic. Home: 241 Kilpatrick Wilmette IL 60091

PETITAN, DEBRA ANN BURKE, teacher, education counselor; b. Chgo., Mar. 12, 1932; d. James Marcellus and Susan Florence (Heintz) Burke; m. Kenneth Charles Petitan, Aug. 9, 1952; 1 child, Susan Florence. AA, Wilson Jr. Coll., Chgo., 1951, N.Y. Inst. Photography, 1952; BE, Chgo. State U., 1956, MS in Indsl. Edn., 1967; DSc in Applied Sci. and Tech., London Inst. Tech., 1971; postgrad., U. Wis., Bradley U., U. Calif., U. Ill. Tchr. Chgo. Bd. Edn., 1958-71, guidance counselor, 1976-84; nat. dir. edn. Nation of Islam, 1971-75; design engr. Fed. Sign and Signal Corp., Chgo., 1975-76; mem. adv. bd. Nat. Right to Work Orgn., 1976-85; cons. ednl. developer, 1978. Photographer VISTA News, 1969-70. Dir. Christian edn. Trinity United Ch. Christ, Chgo., 1978-81, family counselor, 1978-81, organizer/leader couples' ministry, 1978, organizer/leader family counseling ministry, lic. lay minister Episc. Ch. St. Edmund; chmn. Career Women for Johnson/Humphrey, Chgo., 1965. Served to capt. Civil Air Patrol, USAF, 1953-56. Named Woman of Yr. Iota Phi Lambda, 1978; recipient 250 Hr. medal Ground Observer Corps, 1952, 25 Yr. Service medallion Chgo. Bd. Edn., 1987. Mem. Epsilon Pi Tau. Republican. Clubs: Backgammon, Bridgettes (Chgo.). Avocations: computer sci., canoeing, painting, silversmith, lapidary. Office: Fort Dearborn Sch 9025 S Throop Chicago IL 60620

PETRAKOS, JAMES HARRY, architect; b. Chgo., Sept. 11, 1952; s. Harry Nicholas and Sophia (Toscas) P.; m. Constance Marie Relias, July 25, 1982; children: Harry Nicholas, Sophia Katherine. BArch, Ill. Inst. Tech., 1976. Registered architect, Ill. Project supr. Relias Bldg. Corp., Oak Brook, Ill., 1976-77; archt. designer Delta A&E, Chgo., 1977-80; asst. v.p. Banka Mango Design, Inc., Chgo., 1980-85; pres. Design Synergy, Inc., Chgo., 1985—. Mem. AIA, Inst. Bus. Designers. Greek Orthodox. Office: Design Synergy Inc 727 N Hudson Ave Chicago IL 60610

PETRAS, JEFFREY JOHN, accountant; b. Chgo., June 10, 1961; s. John Walter and Jean Frances (Angarola) P.; m. Julie Ann Speck, Nov. 23, 1984; children: Justine Jennifer, Jared Blaine. BS, Ill. State U., 1983. Credit rep. Assocs. Capital, Elk Grove, Ill., 1983-84; credit specialist Hewlett-Packard, Rolling Meadows, Ill., 1984—. Advisor Jr. Achievement, Rolling Meadows, 1985, 86. Republican. Lutheran. Avocations: softball, football, golf. Home: 5513 Chasefield Circle McHenry IL 60050 Office: Hewlett-Packard 5201 Tollview Dr Rolling Meadows IL 60008

PETRASH, GORDON PAIGE, construction product manager; b. Uniontown, Pa., Mar. 14, 1950; s. Philip and Helen Rose (Solomon) P.; m. Nancy Lea Eifinger, Dec. 18, 1970; children: Philip, Rachel, Ashley, Thaddeus. Student, Ohio State U., 1968-70; BArch, Case Western Res. U., 1972; MArch, Kent State U., 1978. Registered architect, Ohio. Designer H.K. Ferguson Inc., Cleve., 1972-74; architect Dow Chemical Corp., Cleve., 1974-76; project mgr. Dow Chemical Corp., Houston, 1978-83; research mgr. Dow Chemical Corp., Columbus, Ohio, 1983—; instr. Cuyahoga Community Coll., Cleve., 1978; bd. dirs. Insul/Crete Corp., Madison, Wis., Diamond Glow Restaurant Supply Co., Toronto, Ont., Can. Mem. AIA, Constrn. Specification Inst. Republican. Methodist. Avocations: photography, architectural history, basketball. Home: 709 Harlech Dr Newark OH 43055 Office: Dow Chem Research Ctr PO Box 515 Granville OH 43023

PETRELLI, JOSEPH LAWRENCE, actuary; b. Rochester, N.Y., May 22, 1951; s. Joseph Michael and Ann (Tranello) P.; m. Sharon Romano, Nov. 4, 1969; children: Victoria M., Joseph L. BS, Coll. Ins., 1974; MBA, Ohio State U., 1986. Actuarial trainee Ins. Services Office, N.Y., 1969-74; actuary Agway Ins., Syracuse, N.Y., 1974-78; assoc. actuary Nationwide Ins., Columbus, 1978-80; cons. actuary Demo-Tech, Columbus, 1980—; bd. dirs. Govtl. Casualty Ins. Co., Columbus, Govtl. Risk Mgrs., Ohio. Contbr. articles to profl. jours. Asst. leader Boy Scout Am. #169, Columbus, 1986; chmn. men's club St. Tim's Cath. Ch., Columbus, 1986-87. Mem. Am. Acad. Actuaries, Conf. Actuaries Pub. Practice, Casualty Actuarial Soc. Avocations: camping, racquetball. Home: 3591 Grafton Ave Columbus OH 43220-5022 Office: 5900 Sawmill Rd Suite 200 Dublin OH 43017

PETRENKO, GEORGE PETER, oil and gas company executive; b. Buenos Aires, June 1, 1952; came to U.S., 1958; s. Ivan and Milena (Wasylenko) P.; m. Branka Jovic, June 1, 1981. BA in History, Case Western Res. U., 1974; JD, Cleve. Marshall Coll. Law, 1977. Bar: Ohio 1977; CPA, Ohio. Pres., chief exec. officer Resource Exploration, Inc., Akron, Ohio, 1984—, also bd. dirs. Trustee Ohio Ballet, Akron, 1986; mem. Ohio Oil & Gas Rev. Commn., Columbus, Ohio, 1986. Mem. Ind. Oil and Gas Assn. N.Y. (trustee, v.p. 1986—), Ohio Petroleum Producers Assn. (trustee, pres. 1986—), Ind. Petroleum Assn. Am. (mem. natural gas com.). Republican. Ukrainian Orthodox. Clubs: Tanglewood Country (Chagrin Falls, Ohio). Avocations: golf, tennis, classic autos. Home: 9376 Knights Way Brecksville OH 44141 Office: Resource Exploration Inc 2876 S Arlington Rd Akron OH 44312

PETRI, THOMAS E(VERET), congressman; b. Marinette, Wis., May 28, 1940; s. Robert and Marian (Humleker) P.; m. Anne Neal, Mar. 26, 1983. BA in Govt., Harvard U., 1962, JD, 1965. Bar: Wis. 1965. Law clk. to presiding justice U.S. Dist. (we. dist.) Wis., Madison, 1965-66; vol. Peace Corps, Somalia, 1966-67; aid White House, Washington, 1969-70; dir. crime and drug studies Pres.'s Nat. Adv. Council on Exec. Orgn., 1969; pvt. practice Fond du Lac, Wis., 1970-79; mem. Wis. State Senate, Madison, 1973-79, 96th-100th Congress from 6th Dist. Wis., 1979—. Editor: National Industrial Policy: Solution or Illusion, 1984. Mem. Wis. Bar Assn. Republican. Lutheran. Avocations: reading, swimming, hiking, biking. Office: US Ho Reps 2443 Rayburn Bldg Washington DC 20515

PETRIE, JOHN RICHARD, advertising agency executive, writer; b. Astoria, Oreg., Apr. 5, 1945; s. John Richard and Margot Maxwell (Brown) P.; m. Linda Kaye Hardman, Oct. 19, 1966 (div. 1973); m. Jo Curie Joffe, Feb. 5, 1987. Student, HB Studio, 1964-65, Bowling Green U., 1966-69. Mgr. Discount Records div. CBS, Ann Arbor, Mich., 1971-73; owner King Pleasure, Ann Arbor, 1973-74; program dir. Sta. WABX-FM, Detroit, 1974-75; mgr. Midwest promotion Motown Records, Inc., Detroit, 1975, Mercury Records, Chgo., 1976; advt. mgr. Sidetracks Chgo. Daily News, 1976-77; mgr. Midwest promotion Arista Records, Inc., Chgo., 1978-79; assoc. creative dir. Leo Burnett U.S.A., Chgo., 1980-85; sr. writer HBM/Creamer-Albert J. Rosenthal, Chgo., 1986—. Contbr. articles to Playboy mag., Circus mag., other newspapers, mags. Democrat. Avocations: music, art, poetry, camping, writing. Office: HBM/Creamer-Albert J Rosenthal 400 N Michigan Ave Chicago IL 60611

PETRIE, MICHAEL FRANCIS, banker; b. Logansport, Ind., Jan. 2, 1954; s. John Francis and Helen Louise (Hirsch) P.; m. Jody Jane Jones; children: Emily JoAnn, Julia Louise. Student U. Nev., 1972-76; B.S. in Bus. Adminstrn., Ind. U., 1979; M.B.A., 1983. Loan rev. analyst Mchts. Nat. Bank, Indpls., 1979-80, real estate investment officer, 1980-82, asst. v.p., 1982-84, v.p., 1984-87, sr. v.p., 1987—; dir. Kenwood Place, Inc., Indpls., Near North Devel. Corp., Indpls.; treas. Multi-Family Property Mgmt., Inc., Indpls., 1984—. Pres. Central North Civic Assn., Indpls., 1983. Mem. Apt. Assn. Ind., Mortgage Bankers Assn., Penrod Soc., Indpls. Jaycees (v.p. 1983, v.p. chairties 1984). Republican. Roman Catholic. Club: Highland Golf and Country. Lodge: Elks. Avocations: fishing; golf; skiing; basketball. Office: Merchants Mortgage Corp 1 N Capitol Suite 1000 Indianapolis IN 46255

PETRIE, ROGER WARD, metallurgical engineer; b. Grand Rapids, Mich., May 31, 1945; s. Lynn B. and Opal A. (Hoy) P.; m. Marylee Gipner, May 1, 1971; children: Travis, Joshua, Erin. BSE in Metallurgy, U. Mich., 1968. Metall. engr. Brush Beryllium Corp., Reading, Pa., 1969-70; metallurgist Howmet Corp., Whitehall, Mich., 1970-72, Colt Industries Inc. Ind. Crucible Magnetics, Elizabethtown, Ky., 1972-78; metall. lab. supr. Dalton Foundries, Warsaw, Ind., 1978-79; mfg. engr. Hitachi Magnetics, Edmore, Mich., 1979-85; metall. engr. Thomas & Skinner, Indpls., 1985—. Webelos leader Cub Scouts, Indpls., 1986. Mem. Am. Foundry Men's soc., Am. Soc. Metals. Lodge: Lions. Avocations: photography, amature radio, computers, sports. Office: Thomas & Skinner PO Box 150B Indianapolis IN 46206

PETRIE, ROY H., obstetrician, gynecologist, educator; b. Bardwell, Ky., Nov. 9, 1940; s. Randolph Hazel and Glodine (Brown) P. BS, Western Ky. U., 1961; MD, Vanderbilt U., 1965; SCD, Columbia U., 1984. Diplomate

Am. Bd. Ob-gyn and div. Maternal/Fetal Medicine. Intern U. Rochester, 1965-66; resident Columbia-Presbyn. Med. Ctr., N.Y.C., 1966-70; fellow in perinatal biology U. S.C. Med. Ctr., Los Angeles, 1972-73; research assoc. Columbia U., N.Y.C., 1972-73; asst. prof. ob-gyn Coll. Physicians and Surgeons Columbia U., N.Y.C., 1973-79, assoc. prof. ob-gyn, dept. dir. med. edn., 1979-84; prof. ob-gyn, dir. maternal/fetal medicine Washington U., St. Louis, 1984—. Author 4 books in field; contbr. over 100 articles on pharmacology and ob-gyn to profl. jours. Served to lt. comdr., USNR, 1970-72. Recipient Purdue-Frederick award Am. Coll. of ob-gyn, 1974; named Outstanding Educator Sloane Hosp. for Women, 1979. Mem. Soc. for Gynecol. Investigation, Soc. Perinatal Obstetricians (pres. 1984-85, v.p. 1985, sec.-treas. 1981-83), N.Y. Obstetrical Soc., N.Y. Acad. Medicine (pres. ob. sect. 1980), N.Y. Perinatal Soc., St. Louis Ob-gyn Soc. Episcopalian. Office: Washington U Sch Medicine Dept Ob Gyn 4911 Barnes Hosp Plaza Saint Louis MO 63110

PETRO, PETER PAUL, JR., plastics company executive; b. Mobile, Ala., Apr. 13, 1940; s. Peter Paul and Mary P.; m. Alice Stalcup, Dec. 27, 1965; children: John, Christopher, Anne. BS in Chemistry, Spring Hill Coll., 1962; MS in Chemistry, U. Ala., 1964, PhD, 1966. Mgr., dir. product devel. Lone Star Co., Dallas, 1968-75; dir. mktg. and ops. NIPAK, Dallas, 1975-77; dir. tech. services Plexco div. Amsted Industries, Franklin Pk., Ill., 1978-81, v.p., 1981-87, exec. v.p., 1987—; cons. Analytical Labs., Dallas, 1970-72, Inst. Gas. Tech., Chgo., 1977; adv. bd. plastic com. Gas Research Inst., Chgo., 1984—. Contbr. articles to profl. jours. Served to capt. U.S. Army, 1966-68. Recipient Merit award, Am. Gas Assn., 1984. Mem. Am. Chem. Soc., Soc. Plastic Engrs., Plastic Pipe Inst. (v.p. 1984-87, pres. 1987—). Roman Catholic. Office: Plexco div Amsted Industries 3240 N Mannheim Rd Franklin Park IL 60131

PETRO, WILLIAM MICHAEL, nuclear power consultant; b. Johnstown, Pa., July 30, 1935; s. Erma Katherine (Secary) P.; m. Mary Alice Yoder, Mar. 15, 1958; children: Patricia Ann., Robert William. BSME, U.S. Naval Acad., 1957. Supr. nuclear power ops. Duquesne Light Co., Pitts., 1958-62; owner, operator Petro Coal Co., Windber, Pa., 1962-64; design engr. Bechtel Power Corp., Vernon, Calif., 1964-67; constrn. mgr., project. mgr., mktg. mgr. Westinghouse Electric Co., Pitts., 1967-74; constrn. mgr. Ariz. Nuclear Power Co., Phoenix, 1974-79; project mgr. So. Calif. Edison Co., Rosemead, 1979-80; v.p. Pub. Service of Ind., Plainfield, 1980-84; pres. Total Results Inc., Hanover, Ind., 1984—; pres. TRI Internat., Inc. Mem. Project Mgmt. Inst. (pres. 1978-79). Republican. Presbyterian. Office: Total Results Inc PO Box 47 Hanover IN 47243

PETROSKEY, DENNIS EUGENE, communications executive; b. Detroit, July 21, 1958; s. Eugene Louis and Marie Therese (Boutain) P. BJ, Mich. State U., 1980. Reporter Falmouth (Mass.) Enterprise, 1980-81; press. sec. Congressman Jim Dunn, Washington, 1981-83, Congresswoman Nancy Johnson, Washington, 1983-85; dir. communications Mich. Rep. Party, Lansing, 1985—. Mem. Rep. Communications Assn., Mayo Smith Soc. (co-founder 1983). Roman Catholic. Avocations: scriptwriting, softball, travel. Home: 1875 W Shore Dr D-1 East Lansing MI 48823 Office: Mich Rep Party 2121 E Grand River Ave Lansing MI 48912

PETRY, THOMAS EDWIN, manufacturing company executive; b. Cin., Nov. 20, 1939; s. Edwin Nicholas and Leonora Amelia (Zimpelman) P.; m. Mary Helen Gardner, Aug. 25, 1962; children: Thomas Richard, Stephen Nicholas, Daniel Gardner, Michael David. B.S., U. Cin., 1962; M.B.A., Harvard, 1964. Group v.p., treas. Eagle-Picher Industries, Inc., Cin., 1968-81; pres., chief operating officer Eagle-Picher Industries, Inc., 1981—, chief exec. officer, dir., 1982—. Republican. Clubs: Queen City, Terrace Park (Ohio) Country, Cin. Country. Office: Eagle-Picher 580 Walnut St Cincinnati OH 45202 *

PETTAPIECE, MERVYN ARTHUR (BOB), educator; b. Detroit, May 27, 1941; s. Alvy Merrill and Thelma Margaret (Mattson) P.; B.A., Mich. State U., 1963, 67; M.Ed., Wayne State U., 1971, ednl. specialist cert., 1973, Ed.D. (Univ. grad. profl. scholar), 1980; m. Sandra Marie Alber Howe, Aug. 26, 1977; 1 dau., Lori; stepchildren—Michelle Howe, Erin Howe. Tchr. math. Hutchins Jr. High Sch., Detroit, 1968-71; tchr. math. No. High Sch. Detroit, 1971-72, tchr. social studies, 1972-84; tchr. Community High Sch., Detroit, 1977—; adj. faculty mem. Coll. Edn., Wayne State U.; computing cons. Detroit Ctr. for Profl. Growth and Devel. Mem. adv. bd. Met. Detroit Youth Found., 1977-80. Mem. Nat. Assn. Core Curriculum, Mich. Council for Social Studies, Mich. Assn. Core Curriculum (sec.-treas.), Internat. Council Computers in Edn., Mich. Assn. Computer Users in Edn., Mich. Atari Computer Enthusiasts, Phi Delta Kappa. Home: 555 Brush Apt #1606 Detroit MI 48226 Office: Wayne State U 167 Old Main Detroit MI 48202

PETTERSEN, MICHAEL SCOTT, marketing executive; b. Rockford, Ill., Oct. 12, 1952; s. Frank John and Joan Elizabeth (Sells) P. BA, U. Ill., 1974. Asst. mgr. Ax In Hand, Urbana Ill., 1971-76; sales trainee Shure Bros. Inc., Evanston, Ill., 1976-77, regional sales mgr., 1978-80, mktg. mgr., 1981-84, advanced planning mgr., 1985—. Contbr. articles to profl. jour. Mem. Audio Engring. Soc., Chgo. Audio and Acoustical Group, Phi Kappa Phi. Avocations: classical guitar and arranging music, coin collecting. Home: 7215 N Hamilton Chicago IL 60645

PETTIGREW, GARY EUGENE, artist, educator; b. Boulder, Colo., Dec. 30, 1935; s. Donald Wilson and Carolyn Ruth Pettigrew; m. Judith Ann Newlon, Sept. 10, 1960; 1 son, Robert Wilson. B.F.A., U. Colo., 1958; M.F.A., Ohio U., 1963. Mem. faculty Sch. Art Ohio U., Athens, 1962—, assoc. dir., 1976-79, prof., 1982—, acting dir. Sch. of Art, 1986-87, dir., 1987—; guest artist, lectr. Western Mich. U., Kalamazoo, 1983, Cleve. Art Inst., 1982. Coll. William and Mary, Williamsburg, Va., 1980, Edinboro (Pa.) State Coll., 1973, 76; group shows include: More Than Land or Sky: Art From Appalachia, Nat. Mus. Am. Art, Smithsonian Instn., 1981-84, Accurate Depictions, Bowling Green State U., 1986; Soc. of Four Arts, Palm Beach, Fla., 1974, 79; Canton Art Inst. All-Ohio, 1979; Painting and Sculpture Biennial, Dayton Art Inst., Invitational, 1976 The Artist-Tchr. Today, SUNY-Oswego, 1968. Served with U.S. Air N.G., 1954-62; with USAF, 1961-62. Recipient Baker Fund award Ohio U., 1972, 83, research grantee, 1967; Logan award Chautauqua Art Assn., 1979; Art Assn. award, 1976; Strathmore award Butler Art Inst., Youngstown, Ohio, 1976, 75; award Dayton Art Inst., 1974, 66, Washington-Jefferson Coll., Washington, Pa., 1974; Best Painting award Springfield, (Ill.) Art Assn., 1974, Edinboro State Coll., 1972, others. Mem. Nat. Assn. Painters in Casein and Acrylic. Works represented in numerous collections. Mem. AAAL. Home: 2 Forest St Athens OH 45701

PETTINGA, CORNELIUS WESLEY, pharm. co. exec.; b. Mille Lacs, Minn., Nov. 10, 1921; s. R.C. and Adrianna (Landaal) P.; m. Yvonne Imogene Svoboda, Dec. 22, 1943; children—Julie, Steven, Mark, Tom, Jennifer. A.B., Hope Coll., 1942; postgrad., Syracuse U., 1943; Ph.D. in Chemistry, Iowa State Coll., 1949; DSc (hon.), Hope Coll., 1978. With Eli Lilly & Co., 1949—, v.p. research, devel. and control, 1964-70, v.p., asst. to pres., 1970-72, exec. v.p., 1972-86, bd. dirs., 1966-86; pres. Elizabeth Arden, Inc., 1971-72; now dir.; bd. dirs. Elanco Products Eli Lilly Internat. Corp., IVAC, Cardiac Pacemakers Inc., Physio-Control, Ind. Corp. for Sci. and Tech., Indpls, Collagen Corp., Palo Alto, Calif, Vipont Labs., Inc., Ft. Collins, Colo., SciCo., Inc., Indpls. Contbr. articles to profl. jours. Bd. overseers Sweet Briar Coll.; chmn. chancellor's adv. bd. Ind. U./Purdue U.; trustee, bd. govs., finance com., exec. com. Indpls. Mus. Art; bd. dirs. Hanover Coll.; trustee Park-Tudor Sch., Coe Coll.; mem. corp. vis. com. dept. nutrition and food sci. M.I.T.; mem. Purdue Research Found. Served with USNR, 1943-45. Fellow Nat. Cancer Inst., 1949. Mem. Am. Chem. Soc., Bus. Com. for Arts, Indpls. C. of C. (new bus. devel. com.), Sigma Xi. Clubs: Lambs (Indpls.), University (Indpls.), Woodstock (Indpls.), Meridian Hills Country (Indpls.); Piedmont (Lynchburg, Va.); John's Island (Vero Beach, Fla.). Home: 445 Somerset Dr Indianapolis IN 46260 Office: Eli Lilly Co Lilly Corporate Center 44 Winterton 1010 E 86th St Indianapolis IN 46240

PETTIT, KELLY BROOKS, metals recycling furnace manufacturing company executive; b. Wichita, Kans., Jan. 7, 1953; s. Donald Leroy and Bette Jean P.; student U. Kans., 1971-75. Aircraft salesman also commuter pilot Clopine Aircraft Co., Topeka and Lawrence Aviation (Kans.), 1970-75, part-time salesman, pilot United Corp., Topeka, 1970-75, sales mgr., 1975-78, pres., 1978—; chmn. bd., pres., chief exec. officer United Corp. Cert. airline transp. pilot. Mem. Topeka C. of C., Inst. Scrap Iron and Steel, Nat. Assn. Recycling Industries, Delta Upsilon. Republican. Episcopalian. Clubs: Topeka Country, Topeka Active 20-30's, Masons (32 deg.), Shriners. Avocations: golf, hunting, fishing, flying. Office: The United Corp 4008 NW 14th St Topeka KS 66618

PETTIT, LAWRENCE KAY, university chancellor; b. Lewistown, Mont., May 2, 1937; s. George Edwin and Dorothy Bertha (Brown) P.; m. Sharon Lee Anderson, June 21, 1961 (div. Oct. 1976); children: Jennifer Anna, Matthew Anderson, Allison Carol, Edward McLean; m. Elizabeth DuBois Medley, July 11, 1980; stepchildren: Mark Adron Medley, Lee Emmett Medley, Bryce Matthew Medley. BA cum laude, U. Mont., 1959; AM, Washington U., St. Louis, 1962; PhD, U. Wis., 1965. Legis. asst. U.S. Senate, 1959-60, 62; mem. faculty dept. polit. sci. Pa. State U., 1964-67; mem. adminstrv. staff Am. Council Edn., Washington, 1967-69; chmn. dept. polit. sci. Mont. State U., 1969-72; adminstrv. asst. to gov. State Mont., 1973; chancellor Mont. Univ. System, Helena, 1973-79; pvt. practice ednl. cons. Mont., 1979-81; dep. commr. for acad. and health affairs Tex. Coordinating Bd. for Higher Edn., 1981-83; chancellor Univ. System of South Tex., 1983-86, So. Ill. Univ., Carbondale, 1986—; mem. various nat. and regional bds. and coms. on higher edn. Author: (with H. Albinski) European Political Processes, 2d edit, 1974, (with E. Keynes) Legislative Process in the U.S. Senate, 1969, (with S. Kirkpatrick) Social Psychology of Political Life, 1972, (with J. Goetz and S. Thomas) Legislative Process in Montana, 1975. Mem. Mont. Democratic Reform Commn., 1971; bd. govs. United Way of Coastal Bend, 1985—. Served with USAR, 1955-63. U. Wis. Vilas fellow, 1965. Mem. Am. Polit. Sci. Assn., AAUP, Am. Assn. Higher Edn., Navy League of U.S., Sigma Chi. Episcopalian. Lodges: Rotary, Masons, Shriners. Office: Chancellor's Office So Ill Univ Carbondale IL 62901

PETTOFREZZO, STEVEN ANTHONY, controller, financial analyst; b. Englewood, N.J., Dec. 14, 1955; s. Anthony J. and Betty P. (Mosner) P.; m. Susan K. Stwalley, June 16, 1979. BA in Econs., Wabash Coll., Crawfordsville, Ind., 1978; MSBA, Ind. U., South Bend, 1983. Gen. mgr. Exec. Investors, Inc., South Bend, 1978-81; asst. controller Holladay Corp., South Bend, 1981-83; corp. controller Shelter Components, Inc., Elkhart, Ind., 1983—. Mem. Nat. Assn. Accountants, South Bend Jaycees (treas. 1984, pres. 1985—, named 1985 officer). Republican. Club: Tri-State Ski (Elkhart). Avocations: golf, bowling, photography. Home: 2500 Topsfield Rd #810 South Bend IN 46614 Office: Shelter Components Inc 27217 County Rd 6 Elkhart IN 46514-0026

PETTY, PETER FLOYD, environmental specialist; b. Bay City, Mich., Mar. 30, 1949; s. Clyde Elliot and Mamie E. (Morand) P.; m. Ann Marie Kanicki, Oct. 5, 1952. BS in Engring. of Meteorology and Oceanography, U. Mich., 1972. Lic. waste water treatment plant operator, Mich. Safety personnel Dow Chem. Co., Midland, Mich., 1973-75, environ. engr., 1976-81, sr. environ. specialist, 1982—. Mem. Nat. Mgmt. Assn., Mich. Sheriff's Assn., U. of Mich. Alumni Assn., Essexville Jaycees (life, Jaycee of Yr. 1982, 84, treas. 1981-85). Roman Catholic. Avocations: hunting, woodworking. Home: 908 N Sherman Bay City MI 48708 Office: Dow Chem Co 1580 T Midland MI 48674

PETTY, PRISCILLA HAYES, writer, newspaper columnist, consultant; b. Nashville, Aug. 22, 1940; d. Anderson Boyd and Margaret Louise (Lauper) Hayes; m. Gene Paul Petty, Jan. 10, 1961; children—Eric, Damon, Boyd. B.A. in English, Vanderbilt U., 1962; student Russian Inst., Dartmouth Coll., 1965. Cert. tchr., Ohio. Tchr. English, Cin. Suburban Pub. Schs., 1962-65, head dept. English, tchr., 1971-79; newspaper columnist Cin. Enquirer, 1978—, also syndicated newspaper columnist Gannett News Service, Washngton, 1982—; cons. Arthur Andersen & Co., 1981-82; writer United Western Corp., 1982. Author: History of a Boardsman (oral history), 1979, Under a Lucky Star: The Story of Frederick A. Hauck, 1986. Mem. Cin. Council World Affairs; chmn. Cin. Media-Bus. Exchange, 1983; founder, pres. bd. trustees Cin. Oral History Found., 1984—. Named Outstanding Tchr., Project Teach, Ohio Edn. Assn., 1978; recipient WICI Great Lakes Regional Communicators' award; Pulitzer Prize nominee for Harvard Bus. Rev. article. Mem. Women in Communications (Outstanding Communicator of Yr. 1985), Oral History Assn., Sigma Delta Chi. Club: Woman's City (Cin.). Home: 229 Oliver Rd Cincinnati OH 45215

PETTY, SUE WRIGHT, library director; b. Kenton, Ohio, May 17, 1953; d. Norman Wilbur and Cynthia Elizabeth (Sapp) W.; m. Raymond O. Petty, Apr. 23, 1983; children: Jeremy Michael, Joshua Matthew. BA, Ohio No. U., 1975; MLS, Ind. U., 1977. Vol., VISTA, Iowa Falls, Iowa, 1975-76; tech. services librarian Bowling Green Pub. Library, Ky., 1978-82; library dir. Mary Lou Johnson-Hardin County Dist. Library, Kenton, Ohio, 1982—. V.p. adv. council WORLDS, Lima, Ohio, 1983; mem. family ministries commn. 1st United Meth. Ch. Mem. Ohio Library Assn., ALA. Democrat. Clubs: Minerva, Newcomers (sec. 1983-84). Home: 416 N Market St Kenton OH 43326 Office: Hardin County Dist Library 325 E Columbus St Kenton OH 43326

PEW, ROBERT CUNNINGHAM, II, office equipment manufacturing company executive; b. Syracuse, N.Y., June 4, 1923; s. Robert Carroll and Bernice (Evans) P.; m. Mary Bonnell Idema, Aug. 23, 1947; children: Robert Cunningham, John Evans, Kate Bonnell. B.A., Wesleyan U., Middletown Conn.; HHD (hon.), Aquinas Coll., LLD (hon.). Labor relations exec. Doehler-Jarvis Corp., Grand Rapids, Mich., 1948-51; with Steelcase Inc., Grand Rapids, 1952—; exec. v.p. Steelcase Inc., 1964-66, pres., 1966-75, chmn. bd., pres., from 1975, now chmn. chief exec. officer; dir. Old Kent Financial Corp., Foremost Corp. Am. Bd. control Grand Valley State Coll.; bd. dirs. Econ. Devel. Corp. Grand Rapids, Mich. Strategic Fund, Nat. Orgn. on Disability; mem. Gov.'s Commn. on Jobs and Econ. Devel. Served to 1st lt. USAAF, 1942-45; to capt. USAF, 1951-52. Decorated Purple Heart, Air medal with 2 oak leaf clusters. Mem. Grand Rapids C. of C. (dir.), Grand Rapids Employers Assn. (dir.), Chi Psi. Episcopalian. Clubs: Lost Tree (North Palm Beach Fla.); Peninsular; University, Kent Country (Grand Rapids). Home: 210 Greenwich Rd NE Grand Rapids MI 49506 Office: Steelcase Inc 901 44th St Grand Rapids MI 49508

PEWS, JAMES RICHARD, accountant; b. London, Ont., Can., Apr. 6, 1961; s. Richard Garth and Suzanne Louise (Matheson) P.; m. Maureen Anne Malewitz, June 16, 1984. BS in acctg. Summa Cum Laude, No. Mich. U., 1983. CPA, Mich. Staff acct. Touche Ross & Co., Grand Rapids, Mich., 1984-86; audit supr. Dieterman, Linden, Manske, Strassburger & Co., Grand Rapids, Mich., 1986—. Mem. Am. Inst. CPA's, Mich. Assn. CPA's, Jr. Area C. of C. (chairperson). Avocations: golf, softball. Home: 1856 Adams SE Grand Rapids MI 49506 Office: Dieterman Linden Manske Strassburger & Co 140 Monroe Ctr Grand Rapids MI 49503

PEZO, MICHAEL STEPHEN, industrial engineer; b. Cleve.; s. Steve and Dolores (Meler) P.; m. Linda Marie Michalik, June 29, 1974; children: Laura, Mark, Michael. AA, Cayahoga Community Coll., 1970; BS, U. Akron, 1973. Prodn. and material planner Apex Fibre-Glass Products div. White Consol., Cleve., 1973-75; sr. mfg. engr. Gilford Instrument Labs, Oberlin, Ohio, 1975-78; indsl. engring. mgr. Keithley Instruments, Inc., Solon, Ohio, 1978—. Mem. Inst. Indst. Engrs. (pres. 1978-79, v.p. 1977-78, treas. 1976-77, 80-81), Soc. Mfg. Engring., Surface Mount Tech. Assn. Roman Catholic. Avocations: music, golf. Home: 2560 Pasadena Dr Seven Hills OH 44131 Office: Keithley Instruments Inc 28775 Aurora Rd Solon OH 44139

PFAFF, JOHN WILLIAM, architect; b. St. Louis, Nov. 23, 1942; s. William Henry and Pearl Florence (Henckler) P.; m. Mary Margaret Liebmann, Nov. 28, 1970; children—Mark John, Mandy Christina. Student Southeast Mo. State U., 1960-62; B.A., Okla. State U., 1966. Registered architect, Mo. With Gornet & Shearman, St. Louis, 1968-69, Hoffman-Saur, 1970; v.p. Kromm, Rikimaru & Johansen, Inc., 1971—. Served with U.S. Army, 1966-68. Mem. AIA, Beta Sigma Psi. Home: 1295 Lombez Dr Manchester MO 63021 Office: Kromm Rikimaru & Johansen Inc 112 S Hanley Rd Clayton MO 63105

PFALLER, MARK FRANK, II, architect; b. Milw., Apr. 23, 1948; s. Mark A. and Elizabeth Rae (Campbell) P. B.Arch., U. Notre Dame, 1973. Pvt. practice architecture, Milw., 1974-77; v.p. Mark F. Pfaller Assoc., Milw., 1977-83, exec. v.p., 1978-83 (firm merged with Herbst Jacoby & Jacoby forming Pfaller Herbst Assoc., Inc. 1980); pres., owner Mark F. Pfaller II, AIA, Architect/Constructor, 1984—; pres. Pfaller Constructors, Inc., 1985—; Bd. dirs. Pabst Theater, Milw., 1982—, Artist Series at the Pabst, 1983—. Recipient award Best Comml. Renovation Project, Builder's Choice Mag., 1982. Mem. AIA, Wis. Soc. Architects (Excellence in Architecture award 1977, 82, 83, 84, past v.p., co-chmn. pub. relations, chmn. Architecture Week Wis.), Nat. Trust for Hist. Preservation. Club: Milw. Rugby Football.

PFALZER, GERALD MARTIN, social service administrator; b. Louisville, Sept. 3, 1945; s. Clarence Carl and Catherine (Robertson) P.; m. Jacquelyn Ann Fante, Jan. 2, 1971; 1 child, Jessica Ann. BA, Bellarmine Coll., 1967; MSW, U. Windsor, 1971; post MSW cert., U. Mich., 1984; postgrad., Cen. Mich. U., 1987—. Social group worker Windsor (Ont.) Group Therapy, 1971-75; social worker Maryvale, Windsor, 1975-80; program supr. Community Care Mgmt., Detroit, 1980; program dir. Residential Care Alternatives, Detroit, 1980-87; assoc. dir. Ctr. Hosp., Detroit, 1987—. Mem. Nat. Assn. Social Workers (diplomat). Democrat. Avocations: tennis, racquetball. Home: 18160 Brentwood Dr Riverview MI 48192

PFANNKUCHE, CHRISTOPHER EDWARD KOENIG, lawyer; b. Chgo., May 1, 1955; s. Edward Louis and Barbara (Koenig) P. BA in Polit. Sci., Loyola U., Chgo., 1977, BS in Edn., 1978, JD, 1980. Bar: Ill. 1980, U.S. Dist. Ct. (no. dist.) Ill. 1980, U.S. Ct. Claims 1984, U.S. Ct. Internat. Trade 1984, U.S. Tax Ct. 1983, U.S. Ct. Mil. Appeals 1983, U.S. Ct. Appeals (7th cir.) 1983, U.S. Ct. Appeals (D.C. cir.) 1984, U.S. Supreme Ct. 1983. Asst. states atty. State's Atty.'s Office, Cook County, Skokie, Ill., 1981—, Macon County, Decatur, Ill., 1981. Author: Traffic Trial Procedure Handbook, 1981. Mem. ABA, Ill. Bar Assn., Chgo. Bar Assn., Decatur Bar Assn., N.W. Suburban Bar Assn. (membership chmn. 1982-83, law day chmn. 1982-86, bd. govs. 1985—), Nat. Dist. Attys. Assn., Assn. Trial Lawyers Am., Am. Judicature Soc., Ill. Trial Lawyers Assn., Phi Alpha Delta. Roman Catholic. Avocations: pilot, scuba diving. Home: 7220 W Greenleaf Ave Chicago IL 60631 Office: States Attys Office Cook County 5600 Old Orchard Rd Skokie IL 60077

PFAUTCH, ROY, public affairs consultant; b. St. Louis, June 24, 1936; s. Floyd and Bertha Edna (Berghoefer) P. AB, Washington U., St. Louis, 1957; BD, Princeton (N.J.) U., 1961. Asst. to pres. theol. sem. Princeton U., 1961-63; pres. Civic Service, Inc., St. Louis and Washington, 1963—; mem. adv. com. on voluntary fgn. aid, U.S. Dept. State, 1981-83, Nat. Service Council, 1982-83. Del. Rep. Nat. Conv., Dallas, 1984; co-chmn. Nat. Day Prayer, 1985, hon. co-chmn. Presdl. Inaugural, Washington, 1985; chmn. Salute to Pres. Dinner, Washington, 1986; bd. overseers Reagan scholars program Eureka (Ill.) Coll., 1982—; bd. dirs. St. Louis Pub. Library System, 1980-86. Mem. Internat. Assn. Polit. Cons., Am. Assn. Polit. Cons. (v.p., sec., pres. 1980-84) Am. Assn. Pub. Opinion Research, Mktg. Research Assn., Council Pub. Polls. Presbyterian. Clubs: St. Louis, Noonday, Racquet (St. Louis), University (Washington). Avocations: horse riding, gardening, reading. Home: 52 Portland Pl Saint Louis MO 63108 Office: Civic Services Inc 1 Mercantile Ctr Room 2612 Saint Louis MO 63101 Office: Civic Services Inc 1050 Connecticut Ave NW Suite 870 Washington DC 20036

PFEFFER, WILLIAM JUNIOR, livestock and grain farmer; b. Lebanon, Ill., Sept. 15, 1912; s. William Christian and Dora (Dougherty) P.; m. Anne Menalo, Aug. 25, 1937; children: Ruzha Pfeffer Cleaveland, Anne Pfeffer Turner, William C. II. Student, Haverford Sch., 1930-33, U. Wis., 1933-34, U. Ariz., 1934-37. Livestock and grain farmer Evergreen Farms, Lebanon, Ill.; mem. adv. council Dixon Springs Agrl. Ctr., 1976-85, U. Ill. Coll. Agriculture, 1979-85. Mem. County Edn. Survey Com., Belleville, Ill., 1937-40, Econ. Devel. Commn., 1978-81, Lebanon, 1937-41, Belleville Area Coll. Steering Com., Belleville, Human Relations Commn., Lebanon; exec. bd. dirs. Lebanon Meth. Ch., 4H extension council; county chmn. 4H; troop leader Boy Scouts Am. Recipient county and nat. Soil Conservationist award, Steer Carcass award St. Clair County Fair (numerous times); named Ill. Master Farmer, Prairie Farmer mag., 1972. Mem. Grassland and Forage Assn. (goodwill ambassador delegation to People's Republic China 1986), Southwestern Angus Assn., Ill. Cattleman's Assn., Ill. Livestock Farmers (Goodwill ambassador to South Am.), St. Clair County Farm Bur., St. Clair County Soil Conservation Dist. Republican. Methodist. Avocation: building furniture. Home and Office: Evergreen Farms Rt 2 Lebanon IL 62254

PFEIFER, EUGENE, pharmacist, nursing home consultant; b. Melrose Park, Ill., Apr. 16, 1945; s. Eugene Paul and Leota Agnus (Dreher) P.; children—Teresa Marie, Jennifer Lynn. B.S. in Zoology, No. Ill. U., 1967; B.S. in Pharmacy, U. Ill.-Chgo., 1970; M.B.A., Keller Grad. Sch. Mgmt., 1983. Registered pharmacist, Ill., Va. Dir. pharmacy Westlake Community Hosp., Melrose Park, 1970-71; staff pharmacist Northwestern Meml. Hosp., Chgo., 1975-77; pharmacist in charge Whitehall Convalescent and Nursing Home, Chgo., 1975-76; asst. dir. pharmacy/metabolic support service St. Mary of Nazareth Hosp. Ctr., Chgo., 1977-85; pharmacy mgr./cons. pharmacist Conva-Care, Inc., Glenview, Ill., 1985-87; cons. pharmacist Healthcare Pharmacy, Chgo., 1987—; off-site preceptor pharmacy residency program Rush Presbyn. St. Luke's Med. Ctr., Chgo., 1978-83. Served with USN, 1971-75. Fellow Am. Soc. Cons. Pharmacists; mem. Ill. Council Hosp. Pharmacists, Am. Soc. Hosp. Pharmacists, Am. Soc. Parenteral and Enteral Nutrition, Am. Inst. Hist. Pharmacy, Kappa Psi. Roman Catholic. Contbr. articles to profl. jours. Home: 1952 Hidden Creek Circle Palatine IL 60074 Office: Healthcare Pharmacy 2433 W 79th St Chicago IL 60652

PFEIFER, GALEN MARK, accountant; b. Hays, Kans., Oct. 10, 1959; s. Albert J. and Irene C. (Haas) P.; m. Cathy M. Michel, May 21, 1983; 1 child, Ryan. BS in Bus., Ft. Hays State U., 1981, MBA, 1982. CPA, Kans. Acct. Adams, Brown, Beran & Ball, Chartered, Hays, Kans., 1981—. Mem. Am. Inst. CPA's, Kans. Soc. CPA's. Democrat. Roman Catholic. Lodge: Kiwanis (sec. Hays 1984-86). Avocations: camping, golf. Home: 3902 Fairway Dr Hays KS 67601 Office: Adams Brown Beran & Ball PO Box 1186 718 Main Hays KS 67601

PFEIFER, KENNETH RICHARD, insurance executive, producer; b. Columbus, Ohio, Dec. 15, 1951; s. Robert Bernard and Marjorie Anne (Bast) P.; m. Gaye Ann Sinclair, June 27, 1983. BFA, Ohio State U., 1975. Agt. Nationwide Ins. Co., Columbus, 1977-84; producer Alexander & Alexander, Columbus, 1984—. Instr. leadership program USAR, Columbus, 1983—. Club: Columbus Maennerchor. Avocations: pistol marksmenship, camping, scuba diving. Home: 4675 Olentangy River Rd Columbus OH 43214 Office: Alexander & Alexander 17 S High St Columbus OH 43215

PFEIFER, M(AURICE) J(AMES), restaurant owner; b. Hays, Kans., Sept. 21, 1956; s. Albert John and Irene Cecilia (Haas) P.; m. Debra Jane Braun, Nov. 24, 1984. BS in Mktg., Fort Hays State U., 1980. Gen. mgr. Daisy Mae's, Hays, 1975-78, Brass Rail, Hays, 1978-79, Taco Shop, Inc., Hays, 1979-83; owner, operator Judge McGreevy's Suds and Snacks, Inc., Hays, 1983-85, Judge McGreevy's Food Emporium and Club, Inc., Hays, 1985—, Taco Express, Hays and Plainville, Kans., 1985—, Concertland, Inc., 1987—; franchiser for restaurants currently owned. Mem. Hays Jaycees, Hays C. of C. Democrat. Roman Catholic. Lodges: Eagles, KC. Home: 1707 Agnes Hays KS 67601 Office: Judge McGreevys Food Emporium 601 Main St Hays KS 67601

PFEIFER, RUSSEL LEE, funeral director; b. Valley City, N.D., Feb. 4, 1953; s. Joseph John and Eleanor Marie (Reid) P.; m. Mary Louise Bush, May 5, 1984. Grad., Dallas Inst. Mortuary Sci., 1980; cert. in enucleation, U. Minn., 1982. Lic. embalmer, N.D., S.D. Embalmer, funeral dir. Quam-Plaisted, Cooperstown, N.D., 1978-82, Evans-Knott, New Rockford, N.D., 1982-85, Holte Funeral Homes, Ellendale, N.D., 1985—. Mem. Ellendale Artesian Hose Co. No. 1; active Ellendale Boosters, 1985. Served with U.S. Army, 1972-74. Mem. Nat. Funeral Dirs. Assn., N.D. Funeral Dirs. Assn., Am. Legion, Nat. Rifle Assn. Lodges: Lions (charter treas.), Masons. Avocation: hunting. Office: 221 S 2d Ellendale ND 58436

PFEIFFER, DONALD JOHN, computer software engineer; b. Oshkosh, Wis., Apr. 10, 1950; s. Raymond John and Ramona Jane (Gilligan) P.; m. Mary Beth Steinke, May 7, 1983; children: Heidi Marie, Katie Anne. BSEE cum laude, Marquette U., 1972. Math. tchr., coach Lourdes Acad., Oshkosh, 1973; corrosion control engr. Wis. Pub. Service Corp., Oshkosh, 1974-76; software engr. Johnson Controls, Inc., Milw., 1977-80, software engring. supr., 1980—. Mem. IEEE, Sierra Club. Roman Catholic. Avocations: fishing, canoeing, camping, choral singing, chess. Home: 13750 W Park Ave New Berlin WI 53151 Office: Johnson Controls Inc 507 E Michigan Ave M-67 Milwaukee WI 53201

PFEIFFER, GERALD EUGENE, accountant; b. Ashton, Ill., Jan. 22, 1951; s. Vernon Louis and Helen Elizabeth (Walsh) P.; m. Marilie E. Martin, June 9, 1973; children: Ann Marie, Amy Lynn. BS, Bradley U., 1972. CPA, Ill. Staff acct. Peat, Marwick Main & Co., Peoria, Ill., 1973-77, mgr., 1977-83, ptnr., 1983—. Bd. dirs. Boys Club of Peoria, 1980-85, Peoria Civic Ballet, 1980-83, St. Thomas Sch. Bd., 1985—. Mem. Am. Inst. CPA's, Ill. Soc. CPA's. Republican. Roman Catholic. Avocations: golf, sports cars. Home: 312 Wood Ridge Dr Dunlap IL 61525-9426 Office: Peat Marwick Main & Co 1100 Commercial Bank Bldg Peoria IL 61602

PFEIFFER, KING WOODWARD, political science educator; b. Evanston, Ill., May 19, 1927; s. Rudolf Salisbury and Suzanne Mayo (Woodward) P.; m. Patricia Jeanne Taylor, Sept. 12, 1953 (dec. Aug. 1984); children: Robert Stanley, Caroline Jeanne Pfeiffer Rose. BS, U.S. Naval Acad., 1950; MA, U. So. Calif., 1967; MS, U. Notre Dame, 1977, PhD, 1983. Commd. ensign USN, 1950, advanced through grades to capt., 1970, retired, 1978; asst. prof. U. Notre Dame (Ind.), 1983—, asst. dir. sponsored programs, 1984—. Fellow Inter-Univ. Seminar; mem. Arms Control Assn., Chgo. Council on Fgn. Relations (sponsor). Episcopalian. Avocations: sailing, music. Home: 1913 Briar Way South Bend IN 46614 Office: U Notre Dame 314 Administration Bldg Notre Dame IN 46556

PFEIFFER, RONALD FREDERICK, neurologist, researcher; b. Racine, Wis., Aug. 11, 1947; s. Benjamin and Irene Alice (Ernst) P.; m. Brenda Elaine Haarberg, June 6, 1969; children: Aaron Benjamin, Gretchen Leigh. BS, U. Nebr., Lincoln, 1969; MD, U. Nebr., Omaha, 1973. Intern Walter Reed Army Med. Ctr., Washington, 1973-74, resident in neurology, 1974-77; asst. prof. neurology and pharmacology U. Nebr. Med. Ctr., Omaha, 1980-85, assoc. prof. neurology and pharmacology, 1985—, interim chmn. neurology, 1986—. Served to maj. U.S. Army, 1973-80. Mem. Am. Acad. Neurology, Cen. Soc. Neurology Research, Phi Beta Kappa. Lutheran. Office: U Nebr Med Ctr 42d & Dewey Ave Omaha NE 68105

PFENING, FREDERIC DENVER, JR., manufacturing executive; b. Columbus, Ohio, Mar. 29, 1925; s. Frederic Denver and Isadora (Wells) P.; m. Lelia R. Bucher, May 30, 1947; children: Frederic Denver, Timothy Daniel. Student, Ohio State U., 1944-48. Pres. Fred D. Pfening Co., Columbus, 1954—; pres. Pfening Properties, Pfening & Snyder, Personal Records, Indsl. Aluminum Foundry, Pfening Found.; mem. Circus World Mus., Inc., Baraboo, Wis.; vice chmn. Cen. Benefits Mutual Ins. Co. Editor Circus Hist. Soc. Jour., 1968—; author numerous works in history; contbr. articles to profl. jours. Bd. dirs. Ctr. Sci. & Industry, Friends Ohio State U. Library, 1975—; pres. Ohio Easter Seal Soc., 1978—, Columbus Mus. Art, 1982—, Columbus Tech. Inst. Found., 1982—; vice chmn. Blue Cross, Cen. Ohio, 1982—; chmn. Upper Arlington Arts Commn. Named Man of Yr., Columbus Rotary, 1982. Mem. Bakery Equipment Mfg. Assn., Am. Soc. Bakery Engrs., Newcomen Soc. Am., Chief Execs. Orgn. (sec. 1978-81), Young Pres.'s Orgn. (sec. 1962-64), Circus Hist. Soc., Indsl. Assn. Cen. Ohio, Marburn Acad. Clubs: Columbus, Scioto Country, Ohio State U. Faculty. Lodge: Rotary. Home: 2515 Dorset Rd Columbus OH 43221 Office: 1075 W 5th Ave Columbus OH 43212

PFENNINGER, JUDITH ANN, management consultant; b. Chgo., Mar. 8, 1960; d. Emil and Helen (Cybulski) P. BS with honors, Loyola U., Chgo., 1982; MBA, U. Chgo., 1984. CPA, Ill. Acct. Price Waterhouse, Chgo., 1984-85, cons., 1985-86; cons. Grant Thornton, Madison, Wis., 1986-87, sr. cons., 1987—; mem. faculty Northeastern Ill. U., Chgo., 1985, Edgewood Coll., Madison, 1986—. Bd. dirs. fin. com. Little Bros., Friends of the Elderly, Chgo., 1985-86. Mem. Am. Inst. CPA's., Ill. CPA Soc., U. CHgo. Women's Bus. Group. Home: 726 W Main St Apt 202 Madison WI 53715 Office: Grant Thornton 2 E Gilman St Madison WI 53708

PFISTER, CHARLES RUSSELL, orthodontist; b. Fairview, Ohio, Dec. 1, 1954; s. Marlene (Kalinich) P.; married Teresa Barndt. BS, Coll. Wooster, Ohio, 1977; DDS, Case Western Res. U., 1981, MS in Orthodontics, 1983. Assoc. Haddad & Fuller, Medina, Ohio, 1983-84; pvt. practice orthodontics Medina, 1984—. Mem. ADA, Am. Assn. Orthodontist, Cleve. Orthodontic Soc., Great Lakes Orthodontic Soc., Medina County Dental Soc., Medina C. of C., Jaycees. Republican. Methodist. Avocations: hunting, fishing, archery. Office: 698 E Washington Medina OH 44256

PFISTER, DEAN WILLIAM, motor manufacturing company financial executive; b. Blue Mounds, Wis., Sept. 30, 1932; s. Charles F. and Thea (Moen) P.; BA in Acctg., U. Wis., 1960; postgrad. U. Syracuse (N.Y.), 1969-70; grad. exec. mgmt. program Ind. U., Bloomington, 1979; MBA, U. Notre Dame, 1984; also spl. courses; m. Jean S. Wittwer, Aug. 31, 1957; children: David, James, Mark. Internal auditor Franklin Electric Co., Inc., Bluffton, Ind., 1971-72, plant controller, 1972-74, mgr. corp. fin., 1974-80, dir. fin., 1980, v.p. fin., sec., treas., 1980—, also dir. Franklin Electric Can., Franklin Electric Internat., Franklin Electric Fgn. Sales Corp., Oil Dynamics Inc., Tulsa, Inc. Mem. Bluffton City Council, 1981-84; pres. First United Ch. of Christ, Bluffton, 1977-80. Served with USMCR, 1953, U.S. Army, 1954-55. Mem. Fin. Execs. Inst., Bluffton C. of C., Ind. Mfrs. Assn., Nat. Assn. Over-the-Counter Cos. (bd. dirs., treas.). Republican. Clubs: Rotary, Orchard Ridge Country, Elks. Home: 411 W Washington St Bluffton IN 46714 Office: Franklin Electric Co Inc 400 E Spring St Bluffton IN 46714

PFISTER, JAMES JOSEPH, publishing company executive; b. N.Y.C., Oct. 29, 1946; s. Stanley George and Rosemary Ann (Cullen) P.; m. Kendra Elaine Nelson, Mar. 23, 1974; 1 child, Charles Joseph. BS, Northwestern U., 1970. Mktg. supr. Nat. Register Pub. Co., Wilmette, Ill., 1970-73, dist. sales mgr., 1973-76, nat. sales mgr., 1976-80, pub., 1980-85, pres., 1985—; pres. Marquis Who's Who, Wilmette, Ill., 1985—. Sec. Libertyville Home-owners Assn., Ill., 1981-83, pres., 1983-85; mem. Com. to Re-elect Ronald Reagan, 1984. Served with U.S. Army, 1967-69, Vietnam. Decorated Bronze Star with V device, Bronze Star with oak leaf cluster, Air medal, Purple Heart. Mem. Chgo. Advt. Club, Am. Assn. Mus. (cons. 1978—). Republican. Avocations: model railroad building, running, water skiing, restoring classic vehicles. Office: Nat Register Pub Co 3004 Glenview Rd Wilmette IL 60091

PFITZENMAIER, ALLAN FREDERICK, industrial engineer; b. Ann Arbor, Mich., July 3, 1945; s. Herbert Frederick and Frieda Maretta (Hirth) P.; m. Francine Mary Schweickert, Oct. 10, 1975; children: Julie Hirth, Eric Allan, Mark Frederick. BS in Indsl. Engring., U. Mich., 1967, MBA, 1973. Dist. mgr. Mich. Bell Telephone CO., Detroit, 1968-78; fin. cons. 1978-80; pres. Veco Internat., Farmington Hills, Mich., 1980—, P.H. Hunter Assoc., Southfield, Mich., 1982—, J. Allan Reynolds, Southfield, 1982—. Mem. Engring. Soc. Detroit, Inst. Environ. Sci., Inst. Indsl. Engrs. Office: Veco Internat Inc 24079 Research Dr Farmington Hills MI 48024

PFLAUM, PETER, real estate developer; b. Mpls., Dec. 17, 1942; s. Leo R. and Rosalynd C. (Cohen) P.; m. Linda Trelawny Witcher; children: Jason, Jeremy. BA, Occidental Coll., 1965; MA, U. Minn., 1971. Adminstrv. asst. to v.p. Am. Hoist, St. Paul, 1971-72; pres., chief exec. officer Lundgen Bros. Constrn. Inc., Wayzata, Minn., 1972—; bd. dirs. The Bank of Wayzata. Chmn. Plymouth (Minn.) Devel. Council, 1976-79. Club: Woodhill (Wayzata). Home: 18070 Breezy Point Rd Wayzata MN 55391

PFLUM, BARBARA ANN, pediatric allergist; b. Cin., Jan. 10, 1943; d. James Frederick and Betty Mae (Doherty) P.; m. Makram I. Gobrail, Oct. 20, 1973; children: Christina, James. BS, Coll. Mt. St. Vincent, 1967; MD, Georgetown U., 1971. Cons. Children's Med. Ctr., Dayton, Ohio, 1975—, dir. allergy clinic, 1983—. Fellow Am. Acad. Pediatrics, Am. Assn. Clin. Immunology and Allergy; mem. Am. Acad. Allergy and Immunology, Ohio Soc. Allergy and Immunology, Western Ohio Pediatric Soc. (pres. 1985-86). Roman Catholic. Home: 4502 Lytle Rd Waynesville OH 45068 Office: 229 E Stroop Rd Dayton OH 45429

PFRENDER, RICHARD EUGENE, physician, psychiatrist; b. Detroit, Sept. 3, 1936; s. Eugene and Josephine Mary (Polansky) P.; 1 child, Michael Eugene. BA, Wayne State U., 1958; MD, U. Mich., 1962, MS in Psychiatry, 1967. Diplomate Am. Bd. Psychiatry and Neurology. Intern St. Joseph Mercy Hosp., Ann Arbor, Mich., 1962-63; residentin neuropsychiatry U. Mich., Ann Arbor, 1963-67, instr., 1969-70; asst. prof. U. Washington, Seattle, 1973; pvt. practice psychiatrist Ann Arbor, Mich., 1974—; chief of staff Mercywood Hosp., Ann Arbor, 1981-82; dir. emergency room mental health St. Joseph Mercy Hosp., Ann Arbor, 1981—; trustee Catherine McAuley Health Ctr., Ann Arbor. Mem. AAAS, Am. Psychiat. Assn., Acad. Psychosomatic Medicine, N.Y. Acad. Scis., Washtenaw County Med. Soc. Avocations: tennis, fishing. Office: 5333 McAuley Dr Suite R4015 Ypsilanti MI 48197

PFUETZE, BRUCE LEONARD, medical allergist; b. S.I., Nov. 9, 1942; s. Edwin Pfuetze and Miriam Ruth (Redman) Pfuetze Arnold; m. Dana Bruff, June 22, 1969; children: Mark Stephen, Elizabeth Miriam. BS in Chemistry, U. Kans., Lawrence, 1964; MD, U. Kans., Kansas City, 1968. Pediatric resident Letterman Army Med. Ctr., San Francisco, 1971; allergy fellow Fitzsimmons Army Med. Ctr., Nat. Jewish Hosp., Colo. U. Med. ctr., Denver, 1974; chief of allergy Letterman Army Med. Ctr., San Francisco, 1975-77; allergist Kans. City Allergy and Asthma Assocs., Overland Park, Kans., 1977—. Fellow Am. Acad. Pediatrics, Am. Acad. Allergy, Am. Coll. Allergy; mem. Kans. Lung Assn. (bd. dirs. 1982-86), Greater Kansas City Allergy Soc. (pres. 1978-79). Republican. Presbyterian. Avocations: trout fishing, basketball. Home: 5347 W 100th Terrace Overland Park KS 66207 Office: Kans City Allergy and Asthma 4601 W 109th St Overland Park KS 66211

PHAN, SEM HIN, pathologist, educator; b. Jakarta, Indonesia, Sept. 15, 1949; s. Joek Sioe and Hong Tek (Hauw) P.; came to U.S., 1967; m. Katherine Assimos, June 19, 1976; children—Nicholas, Louis. B.Sc., Ind. 1971, Ph.D., 1975; M.D., U. Ind.-Indpls., 1976. Diplomate Am. Bd. Pathology. Resident U. Conn. Health Ctr., Farmington, 1976-80; practice medicine specializing in pathology, Ann Arbor, Mich., 1980—; staff Univ. Hosp., U. Mich.; asst. prof. dept. pathology Sch. Medicine, U. Mich., Ann Arbor, 1980-86, assoc. prof., 1986—; mem. pathology A study sect. NIH Pub. Health Service, Bethesda, Md., 1983-87. Contbr. articles to profl. jours. Grantee NIH, 1982—, Am. Heart Assn., 1984—; established investigatorship Am. Heart Assn., 1984—. Mem. Am. Assn. Pathologists, AAAS, Am. Thoracic Soc., N.Y. Acad. Scis., Am. Chem. Soc. Roman Catholic. Avocations: chess; philately; oenology; cooking. Office: U Mich Sch Medicine Dept Pathology M0602 Ann Arbor MI 48109

PHELAN, MARY ELIZABETH, lawyer; b. Iowa City, Sept. 18, 1958; d. William Vincent and Helen Elizabeth (Schindler) P. BA in English, St. Mary's Coll., Notre Dame, Ind., 1981; JD, Creighton U., 1984. Bar: Iowa 1984, Nebr. 1984, U.S. Dist. Ct. (no. and so. dists.) Iowa, 1984, U.S. Dist. Ct. Nebr. 1984. Assoc. Phelan, Tucker, Boyle & Mullen, Iowa City, 1984—; with local firm Chgo., 1987—. Contbr. articles to law revs. Recipient 1st place Mason Ladd Legal Writing Competition, 1985. Mem. ABA, Iowa Bar Assn., Nebr. Bar Assn., Iowa Assn. Trial Lawyers, Johnson County Bar Assn. Democrat. Roman Catholic. Office: Phelan Tucker Boyle & Mullen 321 E Market St Iowa City IA 52244

PHELAN, PHYLLIS WHITE, psychologist; b. Harrisonburg, Va., Aug. 12, 1951; d. Shirley Lewis and Jean Elwood (Driver) White; m. Kenneth Edward Phelan, May 21, 1983. BA with honors, Coll. William and Mary, 1973, MA, 1977; PhD, U. Minn., 1984. Lic. cons. psychologist. Intern Ramsey Mental Health Ctr., St. Paul, 1983-84; psychologist Mental Health Clinics of Minn. P.A., St. Paul, 1983-84, Harley Clinics, Mpls., 1983-84; psychologist, dir. eating disorders program Primary Health Care, Bloomington, Minn., 1984-87; pvt. practice psychology St. Paul, 1987—; exec. dir. Eating Disorders Inst. for Edn. and Research, St. Paul, 1987—; instr. Continuing Edn. program, U. Minn., 1983-84, clin. asst. prof. dept. psychiatry, 1986—. Contbr. articles to profl. jours. Coll. of William and Mary scholar, 1975-77; U. Minn. fellow 1981, 82-83. Mem. Am. Psychol. Assn., Minn. Psychol. Assn., Minn. Psychologists in Pvt. Practice, Minn. Women Psychologists. Avocations: travel, remodeling turn-of-the-century mansion. Home: 942 Summit Ave Saint Paul MN 55105 Office: 570 Asbury St Saint Paul MN 55105

PHELPS, BERTHA BUTTERFIELD, historian, journalist; b. Mayville, Mich., July 17, 1909; d. Eri H. and Hildah Ann (Baxter) Butterfield; m. Willard S. Phelps, Feb. 16, 1931; children—Mary Ann, Joanna, Carole. B.A., Graceland Coll., 1974; M.A., Central Mich. U., 1980. Office mgr. No. Engravers, Saginaw, Mich., 1952-55; sec. to supt. schs. Marlette Schs., Mich., 1955-58; dir., curator Mayville Mus., Mich., 1971—. Author, compiler: History of Mayville and 4 Townships, 1979; Yesteryears of Juniata, 1983. Organizer Mayville Pub. Library, 1948; active Girl Scouts Am., 1950-72, former 2d v.p. Mem. Mich. Mus. Assn., Hist. Soc. Mich., Am. Assn. State and Local History. Mem. Reorganized Ch. of Jesus Christ of Latter-day Saints. Home: 2898 Saginaw Rd Mayville MI 48744 Office: Mayville Hist Mus 22 Turner St Mayville MI 48744

PHELPS, DEAN ALAN, communications executive; b. Detroit, Sept. 19, 1940; s. Gordon Edward and Elizabeth Nina (Piriwitz) P.; Denise Cynthia Lutone, Aug. 27, 1967; children: Kathleen Marie, Dean Jr. BA, U. Cin., 1975. Gen. sales mgr. Sta. WLW, Cin., 1976-78; v.p., gen. mgr. Sta. WSKS, Hamilton, Ohio, 1978-80; gen. sales mgr. Sta. WSAI-AM-FM, Cin., 1980-81; gen. mgr. Sta. WAIT-AM/WXET-FM, Crystal Lake, Ill., 1981—. Editor: Can You Manage?, 1962. Mem. exec. bd. No. Ill. U., DeKalb, 1985-86; bd. dirs. Sch. Dist. #47, Crystal Lake, 1985-86. Mem. Nat. Assn. Broadcasters (bd. dirs. 1985-87), Radio Advt. Bur. (cert.), Broadcast Ad Club, Adcraft Club Detroit. Republican. Club: So. Explorers Pyramid. Avocations: fine arts, sailing, auctioneering. Home: 2 Joann Dr Westboro MD 01581

PHELPS, GEORGE WILLIAM, dentist, lecturer; b. Spirit Lake, Iowa, June 28, 1949; s. Paul Blake and Virginia Ann (Shadle) P.; m. Sally Jane Otis, Aug. 18, 1973; children: Jennifer, Betsy, John, Tom. BS, U. Iowa, 1972, DDS, 1975. Ptnr. Moeller & Phelps, Spencer, Iowa, 1975-85; gen. pracitce dentistry Spencer, 1985—; lectr. Profl. Dental Co., Sioux City, Iowa, 1985—. Mem. local Jaycees. Mem. ADA (del. 1982—), Iowa Dental Assn. (sec., treas. N.W. dist. 1982-85, v.p. 1985-86, pres. 1987, chmn. PR-3 state com., asst. supt. table clinics ann. state conv. 1988), Iowa Lakes Study Club, Tri County Dental Soc. Republican. Congregationalist. Club: Y's Men. Lodge: Kiwanis. Avocations: tennis, jogging, swimming, skiing, golf. Home: 1303 W 9th St Spencer IA 51301 Office: Med Arts Bldg 116 E 11th St Suite 203 Spencer IA 51301

PHELPS, RICHARD ANTHONY, computer software developer; b. Plover, Wis., Mar. 23, 1940; s. Lloyd James and Clara (Peplinski) P.; m. Patricia Kay Lundberg, Feb. 13, 1965; children: Ivy, Salem, Claire, Lloyd. Computer trainee J.C. Penney Co., Inc., Milw., 1966-67, systems analyst, 1967-73, tech. specialist, 1973-81, sr. tech. specialist, 1981—. Roman Catholic. Avocations: astronomy, music, computers. Office: J C Penney Co Inc 11800 W Burleigh Rd Milwaukee WI 53201

PHELPS, SHARON SCHMID, nurse; b. Milw., May 23, 1954; d. Merwin John and Doris Jean (Unke) Schmid; m. Roger William Phelps, Mar. 13, 1982. BAN, Coll. St. Catherines, 1976; postgrad. nursing Marquette U., 1976-79. Staff nurse Milw. Children's Hosp., 1976-77; public health nurse II, City Wauwatosa (Wis.) Health Dept., 1977-79; float staff nurse Milw. Children's Hosp., 1979-81; pub. health nurse II City Wauwatosa Health Dept., 1981—; real estate sales assoc. Schmid Realty Inc. Midwestern Ski queen U.S. Ski Assn., 1979. Mem. Nat. Assn. Sch. Nurses Republican. Roman Catholic. Clubs: Sitzmark Ski, Pewaukee Yacht, New Berlin Jr. Women's (bd. dirs.). Address: 3175 S Manor Dr New Berlin WI 53151

PHIBBS, CLIFFORD MATTHEW, surgeon, educator; b. Bemidji, Minn., Feb. 20, 1930; s. Clifford Matthew and Dorothy Jean (Wright) P.; m. Patricia Jean Palmer, June 27, 1953; children—Wayne Robert, Marc Stuart, Nancy Louise. B.S., Wash. State U., 1952; M.D., U. Wash., 1955; M.S., U. Minn., 1960. Diplomate Am. Bd. Surgery. Intern Ancker Hosp., St. Paul, 1955-56; resident in surgery U. Minn. Hosps., 1956-60; practice medicine specializing in surgery Oxboro Clinic, Mpls., 1962—, pres., 1985—; mem. staff St. Barnabas Hosp., Children's Hosp. Ctr., Northwestern-Abbott Hosp., Fairview Ridges Hosp., 1965—, chief of surgery, 1970-71, chmn. intensive care unit, 1973-76; clin. asst. prof. U. Minn., Mpls., 1975-78, clin. assoc. prof. surgery, 1978—. Contbr. articles to med. jours. Bd. dirs. Bloomington Bd. Edn., Minn., 1974—, treas., 1976, sec., 1977-78, chmn., 1981-83; mem. adv. com. jr. coll. study City of Bloomington, 1964-66, mem. community facilities com., 1966-67, advisor youth study commn., 1966-68; vice chmn. bd. Hillcrest Meth. Ch., 1970-71; mem. Bloomington Adv. and Research Council, 1969-71; bd. dirs. Bloomington Symphony Orch., 1976—, Wash. State U. Found.; dir. bd. mgmt. Minnesota Valley YMCA, 1970-75; bd. govs. Mpls. Met. YMCA, 1970—. Served to capt. M.C., U.S. Army, 1960-62. Mem. AMA (Physician's Recognition awards 1969, 73-76, 76-79, 79-82, 83-86, 87—), Assn. Surg. Edn., Royal Soc. Medicine, Minn. Med. Assn., Minn. Acad. Medicine, Minn. Surg. Soc., Mpls. Surg. Soc., Hennepin County Med. Soc., Pan-Pacific Surg. Assn., ACS, Jaycees, Bloomington C. of C. (chmn. bd. 1984, chmn. 1985-86). Home: 9613 Upton Rd S Minneapolis MN 55431 Office: 9820 Lyndale Ave S Minneapolis MN 55420

PHILIPPSEN, JOHN NEWMAN, insurance agent; b. Milw., June 6, 1952; s. John J. and Lola Mae (Johnson) P.; m. Melanie Anne Steiner, June 5, 1982; children: Jeremiah, Joel, Thomas. BBA cum laude, U. Notre Dame, 1974. CPA, Ind. Supr. Ernst & Ernst, South Bend, Ind., 1974-78; treas. Cobra Industries, Elkhart, Ind., 1978-79; supr. Ernst & Whinney, Ft. Wayne, Ind., 1979-82; v.p. fin. Markhon Industries, Inc., Wabash, Ind., 1984-87; spl. agt. Northwestern Mut. Life, Wabash, 1987—. chmn. St. Bernard's Parish Fin. Com., Wabash, 1987; adv. Wabash County Hosp. Community Adv. Forum, 1985—; pres. Wabash Chpt. Am. Cancer Soc., 1986—; treas. Boy Scouts, Wabash, 1987. Mem. Wabash C. of C. (v.p. indsl. div.), Am. Inst. CPA's, Ind. Soc. CPA's. Roman Catholic. Lodge: K.C. (Wabash). Avocations: golf, basketball, fin. planning. Office: Northwestern Mut Life 11 S Wabash St Wabash IN 46992

PHILIPS, JANET OLSON, real estate manager, curriculum specialist; b. Rockford, Ill., Jan. 9, 1929; d. Oscar Helmer and Gertrude Mildred (Huntington) Olson; m. George Edward Philips, Aug. 13, 1951 (div. Aug. 1973); children: John, Julia, Michael, Catherine, Joan. BS, U. Ill., 1950; MA, Pa. State U., 1968, PhD, 1973. Cert. Property Mgr.; lic. real estate broker, Ill. Housing mgmt. officer Ill. Housing Devel. Authority, Chgo., 1977-81; pvt. practice cons. Chgo., 1981-82; property mgr. Hispanic Housing Devel. Corp., Chgo., 1982-86; curriculum specialist Internat. Assn. Assessing Officers, Chgo., 1986—; mem. workshop faculty Inst. Real Estate Mgmt., Chgo., 1985. Co-author: Kettlestrings, 1976; contbr. articles to profl. jours. Leader Great Books Discussion group Oak Park Pub. Library, 1974—. Mem. Inst. Real Estate Mgmt. (chmn. chpt. com. 1983-85, Advanced Scholarship award 1985). Office: Internat Assn Assessing Officers 1313 E 60th St Chicago IL 60637

PHILIPS, JESSE, manufacturing company executive; b. N.Y.C., Oct. 23, 1914; s. Simon and Sara (Berkowitz) P.; m. Carol Jane Frank, Dec. 23, 1945 (div. 1971); children: Ellen Jane, Thomas Edwin; m. Caryl Ann Dombrosky, Sept. 11, 1978. A.B. magna cum laude, Oberlin Coll., 1937; M.B.A., Harvard U., 1939; D.B.A. (hon.), Hillsdale Coll., 1985; H.L.D. (hon.), U. Dayton, 1986. Pres. Philips Industries Inc., Dayton, Ohio, 1957-68, chmn. bd., chief exec. officer, 1968-86, chmn. bd. dirs.; dir. Soc. Corp., Cleve. Author: International Stabilization of Currencies, 1936, British Rationalization, 1937; contbg. author: Chief Executive Handbook. Chmn. Dayton Found. Ind. Colls., Dayton Jewish Community Devel. Council; asso. chmn. Dayton Community Chest drive.; Bd. dirs. Good Samaritan Hosp., Dayton, Dayton Jr. Achievement, Dayton Better Bus. Bur., Miami Valley council Boy Scouts Am., Dayton council Salvation Army, Jewish Community Council; trustee Oberlin Coll., U. Dayton, Ohio Found. Ind. Colls., Arthritis Found., Wright State U. Found., Sinclair Coll. Found.; mem. exec. com. President's Council on youth Exchange, Sister Cities Internat.; vis. com. Harvard U. Grad. Sch. Bus. Adminstrn. Mem. Conn. N.G., 1930-33; served with USAAF, 1942-43. Decorated comdr. Ordre Souvenain de Chypre; recipient Free Enterprise award, 1965; Disting. Service award Harvard Bus. Sch.; Exec. of Yr. award Dayton Exec. Club, 1983; Spirit of Am. Free Enterprise award Jr. Achievement and Free Enterprise Found., 1983; Big Bros. and Big Sisters award, 1983; award U. Dayton chpt. Beta Gamma Sigma; recognition award NCCJ; CEO bronze award Fin. World, 1985, 86; Nat. On Behalf of Youth award Camp Fire, 1985; Nat. Trustee of Yr. award Assn. Governing Bds. Univs. and Colls., 1986; Internat. Ambassador's award U.S. Dept. State-Sister Cities Internat., 1986; Jesse Philips Day in Dayton proclaimed Sept. 10, 1978; named Ohio gov. for a day, 1982; Andrew Wellington Cordier fellow Columbia U. Mem. Dayton C. of C. (dir.), Dayton Retail Mchts. Assn. (dir.), Nat. Retail Dry Goods Assn., Joint Distbn. Com. Clubs: Columbia Yacht (Chgo.); Meadowbrook Country (Dayton); Cavendish Bridge (N.Y.C.); St. Moritz Toboganning (Switzerland); Motor Yacht of Cote D'Azur (Cannes, France). Office: Philips Industries Inc 4801 Springfield St Dayton OH 45401

PHILLIP, BRIAN MATTHEW, architect; b. Guelph, Ont., Can., Nov. 2, 1957; s. Michael John and Germaine Joan (Victor) P.; m. Julianne McBride, Aug. 14, 1982. BS in Architecture, U. Detroit, 1979, BArch, 1980. Cert. energy auditor, Mich. Designer, draftsman Smith/Schurman Assocs., Bloomfield Hills, Mich., 1980-82, Ellis, Naeyaert Assocs., Troy, Mich., 1982-84; assoc. Alex Kohner, Southfield, Mich., 1984—; architect Mich. Bell, Detroit, 1986—; chmn. bd. Phillip, Phillip, & Assocs., Detroit, 1982—. Mem. AIA. Home: 15474 Ashton Detroit MI 48223 Office: Mich Bell Telephone Co 105 E Bethune Room 800 Detroit MI 48202

PHILLIPPI, ELMER JOSEPH, JR., data communications analyst; b. Canton, Ohio, May 31, 1944; s. Elmer Joseph and Rita M. (Tillitski) P.; m. Susan Mary Schrader, July 10, 1971. AB, Cornell U., 1966; MA, Rice U., 1970. Cert. energy auditor. Asst. prof. engring. tech. Muskingum Tech. Coll., Zanesville, Ohio, 1971-80, sec., treas. AAUP chpt; data communications analyst Chem. Abstracts Services, Columbus, Ohio, 1980-87; sr. software engr. Control Data Corp., Dayton, Ohio, 1987—; part-time instr. physics Ohio U. Editorial referee Am. Jour. Physics, 1975-85. NSF grantee, 1979. Mem. Assn. Computing Machinery (treas. Central Ohio chpt., mem. symposium com.), N.Y. Acad. Scis., Am. Mgmt. Assn., Sigma Xi. Republican. Avocations: swimming, fishing, hunting, building replica antique firearms. Home: 1099 Fergus Dr Beavercreek OH 45430

PHILLIPPI, JOHN CHARLES, regional planner; b. Canton, Ohio, July 23, 1950; s. Elmer J. and Rita M. (Tillitski) P.; m. Karen Hinton; 1 child, Diana Lynne. Student Pahlavi U., Shiraz, Iran, 1971; B.A. in Social Scis., Kent State U., 1972. Cert. planner, Ohio. Assoc. planner Stark County Regional Planning Commn., 1972-74, chief regional planner, 1974-80, chief planner community devel., 1981-86, asst. dir. 1986—; lectr. in field.; mem. Stark County Community Housing Resource Bd., 1982, Ohio Conf. Community Devel., Ohio Planning Conf. Mem. Am. Planning Assn., Am. Inst. Cert. Planners. Author numerous planning and community devel. related studies and reports. Office: Stark County Regional Planning Canton OH 44702

PHILLIPS, ANTHONY S.W. (TONY), artist, educator; b. Miami Beach, Fla., Sept. 16, 1937; s. Edgar Newton and Marion (Goodwin) P.; m. Judy Gordon, June 4, 1980; stepchildren: Leslie Gordon, Alex Gordon. BA cum laude, Trinity Coll., Hartford, Conn., 1960; BFA, Yale U., 1962, MFA, 1963. Instr. Sch. Visual Arts, N.Y.C., 1965-68; artist-in-residence U. Pa., Phila., 1968-69; from asst. prof. to prof. painting and drawing Art Inst. of Chgo., 1969—. One-man shows include: Marianne Deson Gallery, Chgo., 1982, 86; group shows include: Yale U. Stiles Coll. Gallery, 1962; NYU Gallery, 1964, Stevens Inst. Gallery, Hoboken, N.J., 1965, Inst. Contemporary Art, Phila., 1969, Wilcox Gallery Southmore Coll., Oa., 1969, Wabash Transit Gallery, Chgo., 1971, Art Inst. Chgo., 1973, 85, John Doyle Gallery, Chgo., 1976, N.A.M.E. Gallery, Chgo., 1978, 85, Indpls. Mus. Art, 1982, Mus. Contemporary Art, 1983, Aspen (Colo.) Ctr. for Visual Arts, 1983,

Hood Mus. Art, Dartmouth Coll., N.H., 1984, Lowe Art Mus., Coral Gables, Flas., 1984, Kaiser Ctr., Oakland, Cal8if., 1984, Midland (Mich.) Arts Council, 1985, Huntsville (Ala.) Mus. Art, 1985, Montgomery (Ala.) Mus. Fine Arts, 1985, Internat. Art Expo., Navy Pier, Chgo., 1983, 84, Hyde Park Art Ctr., Chgo., 1983, Mandeville Art Gallery U. Calif., San Diego, 1983, Rhona Hoffman Gallery, Chgo., 1984, Swen Parson Gallery No. Ill. U., 1984, Artist's Choice Mus., N.Y.C., 1985, Artemesia Gallery, Chgo., 1985, Paine Art Ctr., Oshkosh, Wis., 1985, Burpee Art Mus., Rockford, Ill., 1985; pub. collections include: Mus. Contemporary Art, Chgo., Art Inst. Chgo.; also creator films; contbr. articles to profl. jours., art reviews to pubs. Recipient Jacob and Bessie Levy prize Art Inst. Chgo., 1985; grantee Catherwood Found./école Américaine de Beaux-Arts, Fountainebleau, France, summer 1961, Ill. Arts Council, 1984; resident fellow U. Pa. Sch. Fine Arts, 1968-69, Djerassi Found., 1987, Va. Ctr. for the Creative Arts, 1987; artists fellow NEA, 1978, 85. Home: 807 W 16th St Chicago IL 60608 Office: Sch of Art Inst Chgo Columbus Dr and Jackson Blvd Chicago IL 60603

PHILLIPS, ARLIE EMERSON, educator; b. Moorhead, Minn., Dec. 29, 1951; s. Cecil Donald and Dorothy Maxine (Kraig) P.; m. Ryllis Marcella Pereboom. Student U. N.D., 1968-71, postgrad. in econs., 1978-79; B.S. in Elem. Edn., Valley City State Coll., 1973. Cert. elem. tchr., S.D. Elem. tchr. Bur. Indian Affairs Low Mountain Boarding Sch., Chinle, Ariz., 1974, Eagle Butte Sch. Dist., S.D., 1975; securities trader, investor, Rutland, N.D., 1976-83; elem. and jr. high. sch. math tchr. Tiospa Zina Tribal Sch., Sisseton, S.D., 1983-86; instr. bus. and chmn. fund-raising sect. Sisseton-Wahpeton Community Coll., 1986—. Mem. Nat. Soc. Fund-raising Execs., Nat. Mgmt. Assn., Nat. Council Tchrs. of Math., Internat. Council Computers in Edn. Avocations: reading, computers, stamp collecting, playing violin, golf. Home: Rural Rt 2 Box 4B Sisseton SD 57262 Office: Sisseton-Wahpeton Community Coll Agency Village CPO Box 689 Sisseton SD 57262

PHILLIPS, DAVID CLAUDE, corporate executive, accountant; b. Dayton, Ohio, Aug. 23, 1938; s. Claude G. and Elizabeth (Burkart) P.; m. Lora Liane Lucas, June 13, 1959; children: Scott, Todd, Brett. Student, Ohio U., 1956-57; BS, U. Dayton, 1962. CPA, Ohio. Staff acct. Arthur Andersen & Co., Cin., 1962-67, audit mgr., 1967-72, audit ptnr., 1972—, audit div. head, 1975-77, office mng. ptnr., 1978—. Chmn. workshops for retarded citizens, Cin., 1985-87; chmn. steering com. Museum Ctr., Cin., 1986-87. Served with U.S. Army, 1957-60. Recipient Community Service awards, Community Chest, Vol. Fundraiser of Yr., Assn. Fundraisers. Mem. Ohio Soc. CPA's, Am. Inst. CPA's. Republican. Lutheran. Clubs: Bankers, Commonwealth. Avocation: travel. Home: 689 Cedarhill Dr Cincinnati OH 45246 Office: Arthur Andersen & Co 425 Walnut St Suite 1500 Cincinnati OH 45202

PHILLIPS, DAVID HARPER, corporate welding engineer; b. Chillicothe, Ohio, Mar. 6, 1961; s. David Mallen and Helen Maxine (Harper) P. BS in Welding Engring., Ohio State U., 1984, MS, 1986. Welding engr. Wear-Ever Aluminum, Chillicothe, 1982, Goodyear Atomic Corp., Piketon, Ohio, 1983, Hughes Aircraft Corp., Carlsbad, Calif., 1984; cons. Profl. Services Inc., Columbus, Ohio, 1985; corp. welding engr. Motor Wheel Corp., Lansing, Mich., 1985—. Mem. Am. Soc. Metals, Am. Welding Soc. (tech. speaker show 1987). Office: Motor Wheel Corp 4000 Collins Rd Lansing MI 48910

PHILLIPS, DAVID LEE, data processing executive; b. Emporia, Kans., Jan. 28, 1948; s. Otis Orville and Norma Jean (Marlar) P.; m. Charlotte Patrice Setness, Feb. 2, 1972; children: Jeannine Kay, Suzanne Patrice, David Lee Jr., Sean Patrick. BS in Bus., Emporia State U., 1974. Clk. Santa Fe Railroad, Emporia, Kans., 1967-75; computer programmer Santa Fe Railroad, Topeka, 1976-82, system analyst, 1982—. Served with USAF, 1968-72, Vietnam. Named Eagle Scout Boy Scouts Am., 1965. Avocations: softball, bowling, personal computers. Home: 5607 SW 15th Topeka KS 66604 Office: Santa Fe Railroad 920 Quincy Topeka KS 66604

PHILLIPS, ELWOOD HUDSON, bookstore executive, real estate executive; b. Ludlow, Ky., May 30, 1914; s. Clarence Bell and Hallie Josephine (Hudson) P.; m. Edna Mae Johnson, May 20, 1934; children—Janet Carolyn, Martha Lee. Student U. Cin., 1933, Anderson Coll., 1952-54. Foreman, supt. sales, service mgr., packaging engr. Container Corp. Am., Cin. and Rock Island, Ill., 1932-47; owner, mgr. Phillips Book Store, Springfield, Ohio, 1947—; mgr. bookstore Anderson Coll., Ind., 1950-68; owner, mgr. Phillips Real Estate, Anderson, 1956—. Pres. Madison County (Ind.) Hist. Soc., 1985, 86, 87. Mem. Nat. Bd. Realtors, Ind. Assn. Realtors, Am. Booksellers Assn., Anderson Bd. Realtors, Christian Booksellers Assn. Democrat. Mem. Ch. of God. Avocation: geneology. Home: 807 Nursery Rd Anderson IN 46012 Office: Phillips Book Store 32 E Washington St Springfield OH 45502

PHILLIPS, FREDERICK FALLEY, architect; b. Evanston, Ill., June 18, 1946; s. David Cook and Katharine Edith (Falley) P.; m. Gay Fraker, Feb. 26, 1983. B.A., Lake Forest Coll., 1969; M.Arch., U. Pa., 1973. Registered architect, Ill., Wis. Draftsman, Harry Weese & Assocs., 1974, 75; pvt. practice architecture Frederick F. Phillips, Architect, Chgo., 1976-81; pres. Frederick Phillips and Assocs., Chgo., 1981—; bd. dirs. 3 Arts Club, 1987—; bd. dirs. Chgo. Acad. Sci., 1987— . Bd. dirs. Landmarks Preservation Council, 1981-85; mem. aux. bd. Chgo. Architecture Found., 1975—. Recipient award Townhouse for Logan Square Competition, AIA and Econ. Redevel. Corp. Logan Square, 1980; Gold medal award Willow St. Houses, Ill. Ind. Masonry Council, 1982; Disting. Bldg. award for Willow St. Houses, Chgo. chpt., AIA, 1982 for Pinewood Farm, 1983. Mem. AIA, Chgo. Archtl. Club. Clubs: Racquet (bd. govs.), Arts, Cliff Dwellers (bd. govs.)(Chgo.). Office: 53 W Jackson Blvd Suite 1752 Chicago IL 60604

PHILLIPS, I. VAN KEITH, theater educator; b. Pasadena, Calif., Sept. 19, 1943; s. Clifton Horatio and Reva Lind (Clark) P.; m. Browen Morgan, June, 1967 (div. May 1979); 1 child, Marisa Jill; m. Linda Gail Anderson, Sept. 27, 1980; 1 child, Andrew Keith. BFA, Southwestern U., 1967; MFA, U. Tex., 1969. Asst. tech. dir. Dallas Theater Ctr., 1961-63; free-lance scenic designer 1963—; prof. theater design and technology U. South Fla., Tampa, 1969-74, Purdue U., West Lafayette, Ind., 1974—; archtl. cons. Jones & Phillips Assocs., Inc., Lafayette, Ind., 1974—; scenic designer Ind. Repertory Theatre, Indpls., 1979, 80, Buffalo Opera, 1980, Cin. Ballet, 1981. Pub. dir. Tippecanoe County Rep. Party, Lafayette, 1982; bd. dirs. Lafayette Symphony, 1981-83. Named Disting. Prof. Indpls. Star, 1985. Fellow U.S. Inst. for Theatre Technology (bd. dirs.); mem. Organization de International et Theatre Design (U.S. rep. 1976), Downtown Bus. Ctr. (v.p. 1966—), United Scenic Artists. Republican. Avocations: amateur trap shooting, renovating old houses. Home: 534 S 7th St Lafayette IN 47901 Office: Jones & Phillips Assocs Inc 412 Main St Lafayette IN 47901

PHILLIPS, JAMES KENNETH, construction company executive; b. Tulsa, May 26, 1929; s. William Zachary and Sarah Edna (Roberts) P.; m. Constance Oberlander, Sept. 5, 1953; children: Wendy L. Phillips Rutland, Lori A., Vicki L. Phillips Katlin. BS, Tulsa U., 1957. Sec., treas. Phillips Construction Co. Inc., Kansas City, Kans., 1957-72, pres., 1972—; bd. dirs. Merc. Bank of Kansas City. Mem. Code Appeals Bd., Overland Pk, Kans., 1976—; bd. dirs. Johnson County (Kans.) Community Coll. Found., 1985—. Served to sgt. USAF, 1950-53. Mem. Kansas City Builders Assn.(past pres. 1985), Phi Gamma Kappa. Republican. Clubs: Milburn Country (Overland Pk.); Jesters. Lodges: Optimists (lt. gov. 1963), Shriners. Avocations: golf, hunting, fishing. Office: Phillips Construction Co 8041 W 47th St Overland Park KS 66201

PHILLIPS, JAMES RICHARD, manufacturing company administrator, labor law specialist; b. Kenosha, Wis., Sept. 4, 1925; s. Lloyd James and Segna Agnes (Ledgerwood) P.; m. Joyce Elaine Huck, Aug. 15, 1944; children—Steven James, Mary Joyce. Student U. Wis.-Racine, 1945-47, SUNY-Catskill, 1970. Adminstrv. asst.-works mgr. Simmons Co., Kenosha, Wis., 1945-58; gen. mgr. L&B Products Corp., Stottville, N.Y., 1958-72; mfg. mgr. Vega Industries, Mt. Pleasant, Iowa, 1972-77; plant mgr. Preway, Inc., Wisconsin Rapids, Wis., 1977-81; div. mfg. mgr., Colt Industries, Necedah, Wis., 1981—; pres. Universal Tax Service, Kenosha, 1951-54. Served with USN, 1942-45, PTO. Mem. Wood County Indsl. Mgmt. Club (pres. 1980-81), Wood County C. of C. (bd. dirs. 1980-81). Republican. Roman Catholic. Club: Holy Name Soc. (Stottville) (pres. 1966-67). Lodges: Lions (tail-twister 1965), Elks (exalted ruler 1971-72). Home: 4010 Wedgewood Circle Wisconsin Rapids WI 54494

PHILLIPS, JOSEPH, military officer; b. Indianola, Miss., Dec. 27, 1952; s. Eddie James Sr. and Roxie (Wise) P.; m. Alma Jean Rascoe, Nov. 19, 1977; children: Howard J., Daniel Phillips, Edward Monroe Phillips (dec.). BS in Edn., Jackson State U., 1974, MS in Edn., 1975; postgrad., U.S. Army Staff Coll., 1984, 85. Commd. U.S. Army, 1974, advanced through grades to capt., 1980; platoon leader U.S. Army, Camp Kasey, Republic of Korea, 1976-77; civil affairs officer U.S. Army, Ft. Bragg, N.C., 1977-79, logistics officer, 1979-81, company commdr., 1981-82, asst. ops. officer, 1982-83, co. commdr., 1983-84, community relations office, 1985—. Named Outstanding Young Man of Am., 1985. Mem. Phi Beta Sigma. Democrat. Lodge: Sertoma (sgt.-at-arms 1985). Avocations: racquetball, fishing, gardening, football, reading. Home: 5705 Wyckfield Way Indianapolis IN 46220-4039 Office: Pub Affairs Office Bldg 600 Fort Benjamin Harrison IN 46216-5040

PHILLIPS, LEE EDWARD, auto sales executive; b. Virginia, Minn., Nov. 14, 1950; s. Raymond Milton and Eleanor Aune (Alt) P.; m. Lynne Marie Hannula, Sept. 15, 1973; children: Kit, Ryan, Jesse. Diploma in automotive services, Eveleth (Minn.) Area Vocat. Tech. Sch., 1969. Reconditioner used cars Martin Chevrolet, Virgina, 1969-71, mgr. parts, 1971-75; mgr. parts Simonson Chevrolet-Olds, Cook, Minn., 1975-78, mgr., car sales, 1978-82, gen. mgr., 1982—. Del. Democrat Farmer Labor Dist. Conv., Virgina, 1976; constable Alango Twp., Angora, Minn. 1975—; treas., council mem. Alango Luth. Ch., Angora, 1978-81; asst. mgr. pee wee baseball, Cook II Team, 1986; radio broadcaster WKKQ Cook Community News, 1984—; head coach 2d, 3d grade soccer team Mesabi YMCA, 1987—. Mem. Soc. Sales Execs. (ring and plaque awards 1985), Parts Pacesetters (pin and plaque awards 1984-85). Avocations: traveling, racquetball, motorcycling. Home: Box 197F Angora MN 55703

PHILLIPS, MELISSA HOPE, advertising executive; b. Cleve., Mar. 4, 1957; d. Billy Hugh and Sara Alyce (Deason) P.; m. Gary Douglass Dole, Oct. 3, 1981. BA in Speech and Communications magna cum laude, Baldwin-Wallace Coll., 1979. Asst. to producer Action 3 News Sta. WKYC-TV, Cleve., 1980-81; media dir. Watts Lamb Advt., Cleve., 1981-83; advt./mktg. dir. Parmatown Mall, Cleve., 1983-84; sr. media planner Marcus Advt., Cleve., 1984-85, acct. exec., 1985—. Democrat. Avocations: writing, collecting and restoring antiques, music, films, reading. Office: Marcus Advt Inc 25700 Science Park Dr Cleveland OH 44122

PHILLIPS, MELVIN ROMINE, minister, American Baptist Churches, U.S.A.; b. Parkersburg, W.Va., July 10, 1921; s. Chester Corliss and Julia Augusta (Romine) P.; m. Carolyn Beckner, Aug. 12, 1944; children—Ann Elizabeth, Ruth Elaine, Ralph, Beth Carol. B.A., Alderson-Broaddus Coll., 1944; B.D., Colgate Rochester Div. Sch., 1946; postgrad. Marshall U., 1949-50. Ordained to ministry, Am. Bapt. Ch., 1946. Pastor, Mumford, N.Y., 1944-46, Kingwood-Masontown Bapt. Parish, W.Va., 1946-49; univ. pastor Marshall U., Huntington, W.Va., 1949-50; pastor First Bapt. Ch., Shelbyville, Ind., 1950-57; Anderson, Ind., 1957-67, Jamestown, N.Y., 1967-73; exec. minister Assoc. Chs. of Fort Wayne and Allen County, Ind., 1973—. Bd. dirs. Mental Health Assn., 1976—, Adler Inst., Samaritan Pastoral Counseling Ctr.; mem. 4th Dist. Adv. Council to Select Com. on Children, Youth and Families, U.S. Congress; bd. dirs. Ind. Council of Chs. Named Man of Year, Jaycees, 1954; recipient Ecumenical citations in Anderson and Jamestown. Mem. Ind. Council Chs. (bd. dirs., recipient Ecumenical citation 1964, pres. 1962-64), Am. Bapt. Hist. Soc., Clergy United for Action, N.Am. Acad. Ecumenists, Nat. Assn. Ecumenical Staff, Bibl. Archaeology Soc., Amnesty Internat. Club: Rotary. Home: 4616 Tacoma Ave Fort Wayne IN 46807 Office: Associated Churches 227 E Washington Blvd Fort Wayne IN 46802

PHILLIPS, MICHAEL WAYNE, nurse; b. Tucson, Dec. 22, 1957; s. Bobby Wayne and Shirley Ann (Davis) P.; m. Dianne Penelope Legg, Dec. 28, 1982. Student, La. Tech. U., 1976; AD in nursing, Northwestern State U. Sch. of Nursing, Shreveport, La., 1979; student, Southwest Mo. State U., 1982-84, U. Mo., 1986—. Registered Nurse Mo., La. Orderly Willis Knighton Med. Ctr., Shreveport, 1977-79, staff registered nurse, 1981-82; staff registered nurse Schumpert Med. Ctr., Shreveport, 1979-81, Springfield (Mo.) Gen. Hsop., 1982-84, Springfield Community Hosp., 1984, Bothwell Regional Health Ctr., Sedalia, Mo., 1985, Menorah Med. Ctr., Kansas City, Mo., 1986—, Bapt. Med. Ctr., Kansas City, Mo., 1986—. Served to 2d lt. USAR Army Nurse Corp. Mem. Am. Assn. Critical Care Nurses (item writer Critical Care Registered Nurse exam 1986). Republican. Baptist. Avocations: fishing, hunting, motorcycles, sailing. Home: 8141 Campbell Apt 201 Kansas City MO 64131

PHILLIPS, NOEL, automobile manufacturing company executive; b. 1934. Student, Rhodes U. With Burroughs Corp., S. Africa and Kenya, 1954-60; asst. mng. dir. Volkswagen of S. Africa, 1960-68, mktg. mgr., 1962, sec.treas., 1965; mng. dir. Hind Bros., Durban, S. Africa, 1968-69; exec. dir. Rennies Consol. Holdings, 1969-72; mng. dir. Volkswagen of S. Africa, 1972-78; exec. v.p. sales and mktg. Volkswagen of Am. Inc., Troy, Mich., 1978-82, pres., chief exec. officer, 1982—, also dir.; mng. dir. McCarthy Group, S. Africa. Office: Volkswagen of Am Inc 888 W Big Beaver St Troy MI 48007 *

PHILLIPS, NORMAN DAVID, photographer, lecturer; b. London, Oct. 30, 1931; came to U.S., 1980; s. Philip Schwartzberg and Edna (Rosenberg) Rose; m. Sadie Sandra Kurzfield, July 5, 1965; children—Ivan Cole, Leon Toby, Daniel Saul. Diploma in fashion design Fountayne Sch. Design, London, 1949; cert. comml. art Sir John Cass Tech. Inst., London, 1948; M.Photography, Master Photographers Assn., London, 1979. Gen. mgr. Eric Smale Studios, Kingston upon Thames, Eng., 1965-68; lectr. photography Inst. Inc. Photographers, Twickenham Coll. Tech. (Eng.), 1968-72; dir. ops. Capitol Color Labs., Ilford, Eng., 1972-73; dir. photography Wadham Artists Ltd., London, 1973-75; owner Town Square Studio, Southend on Sea, Eng., 1975-80, Norman Phillips of London, Ltd., Highland Park, Ill., 1980—; lectr. P.P.A. Affiliates, Chgo. and Wis., 1983—; cons. Russell Color Labs., London, 1969-80, Kingston upon Thames Council, 1968-72; dir., founder Health and Fitness Motivations. Contbr. articles to profl. jours.; author: Professional Photography (Merit award 1984, 85), 1983; contbr. articles on unions to profl. jours. Brit. del. World Assembly of Youth, Denmark, 1962; v.p. Nat. League Young Liberals, London, 1962; gen. sec. Homes for All Campaign, Eng., 1962-63; city councillor County Borough of West Ham, London, 1961-65; founder, pres. East London Young People's Debating Soc., 1962; bd. dirs. Children's Action Fund, Highland Park, 1986—. Served as SNR Aircraftsman Royal Air Force England, 1950-51. Recipient Handelman award, 1984, Handelman Wedding Print award 1985, Harry Hoyt Portrait award 1986. Mem. Master Photographers Assn. U.K., Master Photographers Assn. (assoc., organizer 1979, bd. dirs. 1987—), Wedding Photographers Internat., Internat. Platform Assn., Chgoland Profl. Photographers Assn. (pres. 1984-85, Man of Yr. award 1985, Sweepstakes award 1985, Merit award 1986, 87, Print of Yr. award 1986). Jewish. Club: America (Deerfield, Ill.) (tech. dir.). Avocations: physical fitness (world record holder Roman chair situps), coaching soccer. Home: 2112 St Johns Ave Apt E Highland Park IL 60035 Office: Norman Phillips of London Ltd 458 Central Ave Highland Park IL 60035

PHILLIPS, PHILIP KAY, stained glass manufacturing and retail company executive; b. Kansas City, Mo., Jan. 3, 1933; s. Ernest Lloyd and Mildred Blanche (Moser) P.; B.A., Bob Jones U., Greenville, S.C., 1958; postgrad. Central Mo. State U., 1977-78, 81-83; m. Constance Diana Lucas, June 12, 1955; children—John Allen, David Lee, Stephen Philip, Daniel Paul, Joy Christine. Ordained minister Baptist Ch., 1959; pastor Mt. Moriah Baptist Ch., Clarksburg, Mo. 1958-59; security officer Mo. Dept. Corrections, Jefferson City, Mo., 1959-64; field mgr. office Darby Corp. and Piping Contractors Inc., Kansas City, Kans., 1965-72, safety and security dir. Darby Corp. and Leavenworth Steel Inc., Kansas City, 1972-84; with Stained Glass Creations, North Kansas City, Mo., 1984—. Mem. planning com. Kans. Gov.'s Indsl. Safety and Health Conf., 1977-78, chmn. mfg. sect., 1978. Mem. Nat. Safety Mgmt. Soc., Am. Soc. Safety Engrs. (chpt. exec. com. 1980-81, treas. chpt. 1981-82, sec. chpt. 1982-83, 2d v.p. chpt. 1983-84, 1st v.p. 1984-85, chpt. pres. 1985-86), Kans. Safety Assn. (v.p., mem. exec. com. 1979-80), North Kansas City Mchts. Assn. (pres. 1986—). Home: 3205 NE 66th St Gladstone MO 64119 Office: Stained Glass Creations 316 Armour Rd North Kansas City MO 64116

PHILLIPS, PHILLIP DAVID, academic administrator; b. Chgo., Oct. 14, 1946; s. Delbert Byron and Delores Dean (Foster) P.; m. Barbara Jensen, June 8, 1968; children: Ellen Margaret, Eric George, John Michael. BA, U. Ill., 1968, BS, 1969; PhD, U. Minn., 1973. Asst. prof. U. Ky., Lexington, 1972-78; cons. WAPORA, Inc., Chgo., 1978-80; sr. cons. The Fantus Co., Chgo., 1980-82, asst. v.p., 1982-84, v.p., 1984-86; dir. corp. relations and community devel. U. Ill., Urbana, 1986—; bd. dirs. Champaign-Urbana Econ. Devel. Corp., Champaign, Ill., 1986—. Co-author: Crime: A Spatial Perspective, The American Metro System, 1980, Modern Metro Systems, 1982; numerous articles in field. Woodrow Wilson fellow, 1971-72. Mem. Am. Econ. Devel. Council, Assn. Am. Geographers, Ill. Devel. Council. Avocations: hiking, collecting antique maps. Office: U Ill Corp Relations 901 S Mathews Urbana IL 61801

PHILLIPS, SARAH VIRGINIA CYRUS, real estate executive, city official; b. Louisa, Ky.; d. W. Raymond and Isabelle Evelyn (Johnson) Cyrus; student pub. schs.; m. Donald Ray Phillips, Mar. 20, 1954; children—Donald Bruce, David Brian. Dep. circuit court clk. Lawrence County, Louisa, 1952-53; sec. Nationwide Ins. Co., Columbus, Ohio, 1953-56; jr. acountant Nationwide Mortgage Co., Columbus, 1957-63; gen. clk. Ohio State Life Ins. Co., Columbus, 1963-64; clk. council city clk., Whitehall, Ohio, 1964-71, city auditor, tax commr., 1981—; adminstrv. asst. City of Columbus, 1972-76; realtor assoc. Sparks Real Estate of Century 21, 1976-80; broker Nutrend Realty, 1980—, residential appraiser, 1976—. Publicity chmn. Whitehall Boys Baseball Assn., summers 1965-68; sec., publicity chmn. Whitehall Boys' Basketball; mem. Ohio Commn. on Status Women; pres. Downtown Women's Republican. Club, 1974-75; Whitehall Rep. Com., 1977; mem. Rep. Central Com., 1974—; mem. Whitehall City Council, 1977-81; trustee, sec.-treas. Whitehall Devel. Corp.; bd. dirs. Columbus Area Women's Polit. Caucus, 1977—, Whitehall Community Counseling Ctr., 1986—. Mem. Central Ohio Mayors and Mcpl. Officers Council (exec. sec.-treas.), Ohio Municipal Clks. Assn. (trustee, v.p. 1971), Whitehall Civic Celebrations Assn. (sec., trustee 1968-71, v.p. 1978), Govt. Fin. Officers Assn. of U.S. and Can., Assn. Govt. Accts. (pres. Columbus chpt. 1987—), Ohio Hist. Soc., LWV, Nat. Assn. Realtors, Whitehall Bus. Assn. (founding pres.), Central Ohio Fiscal Officers Network (founding chmn.). Internat. Toastmistress Club (Woman of Influence 1976, 77). Mem. Ch. of Christ (bd. dirs., treas., mem. youth com.). Home: 1010 S Yearling Rd Whitehall OH 43227 Office: 360 S Yearling Rd Whitehall OH 43213

PHILLIPS, TERRY LEMOINE, electrical engineer; b. Washington, July 27, 1938; s. Clifford LeMoin and Dorothy Louise (Schuman) P.; B.S., Purdue U., 1964, M.S., 1966; m. Lynne Ann Bruce, Aug. 12, 1962; children—Susan Rae, Stephen Kirk. Assoc. program leader, data processing Purdue U. Lab. Applications of Remote Sensing, West Lafayette, Ind., 1966-71, program leader, 1971-74, dep. dir., 1974-85; mgr. personal computer services Purdue U. Computing Ctr., 1986— ; cons. AID, Computer Scis. Corp. Scoutmaster, explorer adviser Boy Scouts Am., bd. dirs. Sagamore council; sports coordinator, youth sports, Battleground, Ind.; elder, deacon Presbyn. Ch.; bd. dirs. Tippecanoe chpt. Am. Diabetes Assn. Served with USN, 1956-59. Mem. IEEE (sr.), Assn. Computing Machinery, Data Processing Mgmt. Assn. (internat. dir., co-founder, v.p., pres. Sagamore chpt.), Tau Beta Pi, Eta Kappa Nu. Club: Rotary (dir., treas.). Home: 1522 E 600 N West Lafayette IN 47906 Office: 1291 Cumberland Ave West Lafayette IN 47906

PHILLIPS, WAYNE WOODROW, II, lawyer; b. Norwalk, Ohio, Sept. 14, 1945; s. Wayne Woodrow and Iverna Martha (Sherman) P.; B.A., Ohio No. U., 1967, J.D., 1972; m. Patricia Smith, Jan. 10, 1981; twin daughters. Bar: Ohio 1972, Ind. 1973. Acct., Edward R. Moyer, C.P.A., Bellevue, Ohio, 1967-70; tax acct. Kern, Linnemeier & Co., C.P.A.s, Ft. Wayne, Ind., 1972-74; partner Stubbins, Phillips & Co., Zanesville, Ohio, 1974—; dir. Killbuck Inc., Buckeye Water Service, Buckeye Well Surveys, Inc. Chmn. bd. dirs. Zanesville Goodwill Industries, 1976—; treas. Friends of the Library, Zanesville, 1976-77. Named Zanesville Citizen of the Month, May, 1977. Mem. Am. Bar Assn., Ohio State Bar Assn., Ind. State Bar Assn., Muskingum County Bar Assn., Ohio Soc. C.P.A.s, Am. Inst. C.P.A.s, Am. Assn. Atty-C.P.A.s, Ohio Oil and Gas Assn, Zanesville Jaycees (treas. 1975-76, pres. 1976-77), Ohio Jaycees (asst. treas. 1977-78, treas. 1978-79; senator). Republican. Episcopalian. Club: Zanesville Quarterback (treas. 1978-81). Lodges: Rotary, Masons. Home: 260 Skyline Dr Zanesville OH 43701 Office: 925 Military Rd Zanesville OH 43701

PHILLIPS, WILLIAM GEORGE, business executive; b. Cleve., Mar. 3, 1920; s. Edward George and Ina Marie (Cottle) P.; m. Laverne Anne Evenden, Aug. 7, 1943; children—Karen Anne (Mrs. David F. Berry), Connie Allynette (Mrs. Richard Tressel), Scott William. A.B., Antioch Coll., 1942. Pub. acct. Price Waterhouse & Co., Cleve., 1945-48; tax acct. Glidden Co., Cleve., 1948-52, asst. treas., 1952, treas., dir., 1953-63, adminstrv. v.p., 1963-64, pres., 1964-67, chief exec. officer, 1967; pres. Glidden-Durkee div. SCM Corp., 1967-68; pres., chief exec. officer Internat. Multifoods Corp. (formerly Internat. Milling), Mpls., 1968-70, chmn. bd., chief exec. officer, 1970-85; dep. chmn. Mpls. Fed. Res. Bank, 1979-82, chmn., 1982-86; dir. Northwestern Nat. Bank Mpls., 1969-78, Soo Line R.R. Co., 1971—, G. Heileman Brewing, 1982—, N.Am. Life and Casualty Co., 1975-82, Firestone Tire & Rubber Co., 1979—, No. States Power, 1980—. Bd. overseers U. Minn. Coll. Bus. Adminstrn.; nat. corp. adv. bd. United Negro Coll. Fund; exec. com. U.S.-Iran Joint Bus. Council; adv. bd. Nat. Alliance Businessmen; bd. dirs. Mpls. Downtown Devel. Corp., Minn. State Council on Econ. Edn.; mem. Mpls. YMCA investment com.; mem. pres.'s adv. bd. Am. Diabetes Assn.; adv. bd. Inst. Internat. Edn.; trustee Baldwin-Wallace Coll., 1960-68, Hamline U., 1978—; bd. dirs. Mpls. Found.; trustee Mpls. Soc. Fine Arts, Nat. Jewish Hosp. at Denver, Ednl. Research Council Am. Served to lt., inf. AUS, 1942-45. Mem. Conf. Bd. C. of C. of U.S. (dir., mem. U.S.-Can. com.), Ohio Soc. C.P.A.'s, Grocery Mfrs. Am. (dir.), Conf. Bd. Mem. Community Ch. Clubs: Lafayette, Minneapolis (bd. govs.), Dunes Country, Woodhill Country.

PHILLIPS, WINFRED MARSHALL, engineering educator, university administrator; b. Richmond, Va., Oct. 7, 1940; s. Claude Marshall and Gladys Marian (Barden) P.; children—Stephen, Sean. B.S.M.E., Va. Poly. Inst., 1963; M.A.E., U. Va., 1966, D.Sc., 1968. Mech. engr. U.S. Naval Weapons Lab., Dahlgren, Va., 1963; NSF trainee, teaching, research asst. dept. aerospace engring U. Va., Charlottesville, 1963-67; research scientist 1966-67; asst. prof. dept. aerospace engring. Pa. State U., University Park, 1968-74; assoc. to prof. 1974-80, assoc. dean research Coll. Engring., 1979-80; head Sch. Mech. Engring. Purdue U., West Lafayette, Ind., 1980—; vis. prof. U. Paris, 1976-77; bd. dirs. Tokheim Corp; adv. com. Raymark Corp. Sect. editor Am. Soc. Artificial Internal Organs Jour. Contbr. articles to profl. jours., chpts. to books. Bd. dirs. Central Pa. Heart Assn., 1974-80; mem. Ind. State Boiler and Pressure Vessel Code Bd., 1981—. Fellow AAAS, AIAA (assoc.), ASME, Am. Soc. Elec. Engrs.; mem. Am. Soc. Artificial Internal Organs (trustee 1982-88, sec.-treas. 1986-87), Nat. Assn. State Univs. and Land-Grant Colls. (com. quality of engring. edn., Career Research award 1974-78), Univ. Programs in Computer-Aided Engring. Design and Mfg. (bd. dirs. 1985—), Am. Phys. Soc., Am. Soc. Engring. Edn., Biomed. Engring. Soc., N.Y. Acad. Scis., Internat. Soc. Biorheology, Sigma Xi, Pi Tau Sigma, Sigma Gamma Tau, Tau Beta Pi (eminent engr.). Club: Cosmos. Lodge: Rotary (pres. local chpt. 1987-88). Home: 708 Timber Trail Lafayette IN 47905 Office: Purdue U Sch Mech Engring West Lafayette IN 47907

PHILLIPS, WYNN, psychologist, educator; b. Cleve., June 24, 1943; s. Walter Francis and Mildred Marie (Gerding) W.; divorced, July 1, 1981; children: Ian Phillips, Vann Phillips. BA, Ohio Wesleyan U., 1965; MA, Kent State U., 1972; postgrad., Feilding Inst., Santa Barbara, Calif. Lic. psychologist. Peace corps vol. U.S. Govt., Alor Star, Malaysia, 1968-70; acad. adv. Kent State U., 1970-72; dir. Geauga Drug Ctr., Burton, Ohio, 1972-74; ct. psychologist Cleve. Juvenile Ct., 1974—; adj. prof. psychology Cleve. State U., 1976—; pvt. practice Psychol. Assocs., Cleve., 1986—. Capt. Heights Coed Soccer Team, Cleveland Heights, Cleve. Heights Tennis Team; mem. Cleve. Art. Mus., Playhouse Sq. Found., Returned Peace Corps Vol. Kent. State U. fellow, 1970; Hayes Fulbright grantee U. Conn., Africa, 1976. Mem. Am. Psychol. Assn., Ohio Psychol. Assn., Cleve. Psychol. Assn., Gestalt Inst. Cleve., Mensa. Avocations: soccer, tennis, fine arts, world travel. Home: 2318 Bellfield Ave Cleveland OH 44106

PHILLIPSON, JOHN SAMUEL, retired educator; b. Rochester, N.Y., Jan. 23, 1917; s. John Samuel and Mary Agnes (Price) P. B.A., U. Rochester, 1947; M.A., U. Wis., 1949, Ph.D., 1952. Editor Rochester Daily Record, 1944-47; teaching asst. U. Wis., 1947-52; instr. English U. Wis. Extension div., 1952-53; instr. Villanova U., 1953-54, asst. prof., 1954-61; asst. prof. English U. Akron, 1961-66, assoc. prof., 1966-78, prof., 1978-86. Author: Thomas Wolfe: A Reference Guide, 1977; Critical Essays on Thomas Wolfe, 1985. Founding editor: Thomas Wolfe Rev, 1977—. Mem. Modern Humanities Research Assn. (bibliographer Annual Bibliography 1958—), Thomas Wolfe Soc. (trustee 1980—, treas. 1980-87), MLA, Am. Soc. Eighteenth Century Studies, Soc. Study So. Lit., Johnson Soc. Cen. Region, Coll. English Assn. Home: 2597 24th St Cuyahoga Falls OH 44223 Office: 302 E Buchtel Ave Akron OH 44325

PHILP, A. R., provincial judge. Judge Man. Ct. Appeals, Winnipeg. Office: Ct of Appeals, Law Cts Bldg, Winnipeg, MB Canada R3C 0V8 *

PHIPATANAKUL, CHINTANA SIRIKORANUN, allergist; b. Thailand, July 2, 1941; s. Sue Len Hee; m. Supote Phipatanakul, June 16, 1968; children: Wanda, Wesley. MD, Chula H. Med. Sch., 1965. Intern City of Memphis Hosps., Memphis, 1966-67; resident in internal medicine St. Francis Hosp., Pitts. and St. Mary's Hosp., St. Louis, 1967-70; asst. instr. in medicine St. Louis U., 1970-77, med. dir. Student Health Service, 1972-75, asst. clin. prof. internal medicine, 1977—; staff St. Louis U. Hosp., 1972—; cons. Christian Hosp., Florissant, Mo., 1975—, DePaul Hosp., St. Louis, 1978—; courtesy staff Mo. Baptist Hosp., St. Louis, 1975—. Contbr. articles to profl. jours. Leader Home & Sch. Assn. of Hillcrest Sch., St. Louis, 1986. Fellow Am. Coll. Physicians, Am. Acad. Allergy and Immunology, Am. Assn. Cert Allergists; mem. AMA (Physicians Recognition award 1970—), Mo. State Allergy Assn., Mo. State Med. Assn., St. Louis Met. Med. Soc. Seventh Day Adventist. Avocations: art, music, sports. Office: 1125 Graham Rd Florissant MO 63031

PHIPPS, EARL FREEMAN, communications company executive; b. Perrysburg, Ohio, Mar. 8, 1939; s. Freeman and Marie (Hufford) P.; m. Reva Jean Emahiser, Sept. 18, 1964; 1 child, John. BBA, U. Toledo, 1965, MBA, 1970. Mktg. mgr. Fleetwood Industries, Bowling Green, Ohio, 1975-76; regional mktg. mgr. Gulf & Western, Toledo, 1976-81; dist. sales mgr. No. Telecom, Toledo, 1981-83; mktg. mgr. Systems Designs, Perrysburg, 1983—; cons. Guardian Industries, Novi, Mich., 1986—. Served to 1st lt. U.S. Army, 1958-61, ETO. Mem. Am. Assn. for Computing Machinery, IEEE. Republican. Methodist. Avocation: photography.

PHIPPS, MICHAEL CHARLES, library administrator; b. Boone, Iowa, July 6, 1944; s. Russell Lowell and Margaret Jeanne (Lepley) P.; m. Margaret Mary Skold, Oct. 3, 1964 (div. 1980); children: Michael Anthony, Sarah Jeanne. BA in English, U. No. Iowa, Cedar Falls, 1966; MLS, U. Iowa, 1969. Tchr. English, Des Moines Tech. High Sch., 1966-67; dir. Cattermole Meml. Library, Fort Madison, Iowa, 1969-72, Waterloo Pub. Library, Iowa, 1972-83, Omaha Pub. Library, 1983—; Bd. dirs. Mississippi Valley Film Coop., Quincy, Ill., 1970-72, Films-for-Iowa Library Media Services, 1974-76; mem. Nebr. Adv. Council on Libraries, 1984; mem. Iowa Gov.'s Adv. Council on Library Services, 1976-82. Author: Reference/Information Services in Iowa Public Libraries, 1969; also articles. Cofounder Friends of Waterloo Pub. Library, 1976; mem. Black Hawk County Democratic Central Com., Waterloo, 1979-82; bd. dirs. Friends of Stas. KHKE/KUNI, Cedar Falls, Iowa, 1982-83. Recipient spl. service award Iowa Library Assn., 1975. Mem. ALA (council 1975-79), Nebr. Library Assn. (pres. pub. library sect. 1986), Mountain/Plains Library Assn., Iowa Urban Pub. Library Assn. (sec. 1978-83), ACLU, Met. Opera Guild. Office: Omaha Public Library W Dale Clark Library 215 S 15th St Omaha NE 68102-1004

PHIPPS, TERRY WAYNE, photographer, author; b. Port Huron, Mich., June 2, 1946; s. George W. and Electrica (Smith) P.; m. Becky J. Hemmingsen; 1 child, Makena Elizabeth. AA, Port Huron Jr. Coll., 1966; BS, Eastern Mich. U., 1968; MA, U. Mich., 1975; cert. in profl. photography, Famous Photographers, 1973. Profl. musician, 1963-76; cert. tchr., adminstr., Mich., Colo., Wash. Tchr. Davison (Mich.) Community Schs., 1968-85; owner, photographer The Abstraction, Davison, 1974-82; photographer, writer Traverse the Magazine; staff photographer Wheels, East Jordan, Mich., Racing News, Chesaning, Mich., Mich.; snowmoblier, East Jordan, 1985—; owner Eaglenest: Visual Design, Traverse City, Mich.; freelance photographer various publs., lectr. Eastern Mich. U., Ypsilanti, 1977, WTRX Radio, Flint, Mich., 1977, WNEM, Saginaw, Mich., 1977, Cable 8, Port Huron, Mich., 1975. Author: Meadowlarks, June Bugs and Dreams, 1976, The Queen of Almonds; photographer, writer Traverse mag. Recipient Internat. Photography and Art Show awards, Eastman Kodak, Times Herald. Mem. NEA, Mich. Edn. Assn., Sierra Club. Avocations: skiing, diving. Home: PO Box 196 Omena MI 49674

PHIUNGKEO, KHAJORN, obstetrician and gynecologist; b. Thonburi, Thailand, Aug. 22, 1937; came to U.S., 1973; s. Tum and Salee Phiungkeo; married; children: Mike, Paul, Tim. MD, U. Med. Scis., Thonburi, 1962. Diplomate Am. Bd. Ob-Gyn. Rotating intern Med. Services Dept., Bangkok, Thailand, 1962-63, 1962-63, res. in ob-gyn, 1963-64; attending staff Singhburi Hosp., Thailand, 1964-65; rotating intern St. John's Hosp., Detroit, 1965-66; resident in ob-gyn Detroit Macomb Hosp., 1966-67, Providence Hosp., Southfield, Mich., 1967-69; attending staff in ob-gyn. Vajira Hosp., Thailand, 1969-73; resident in pathology McLaren Gen. Hosp., Flint, Mich., 1973-74, emergency staff physician, 1974-75; active staff in ob-gyn Owosso (Mich.) Meml. Hosp., 1975—, chmn. ob-gyn dept., 1986—. Fellow Am. Coll. Obstetricians and Gynecologists; mem. Am. Fertility Soc., Am. Soc. Colposcopy and Cervical Pathology. Home: 1005 N Chipman Oswosso MI 48867 Office: 1457 N M-52 Owosso MI 48867

PHUNG, THANH GIA, radiologist; b. Hanoi, Vietnam; came to U.S., 1975; s. Loc Tuan Phung and Chinh Thi Le; m. Thu-cuc Thi Tran; children—Angie, Charlie, Peter, Kevin. B.S., Jean-Jacques-Rousseau Lyceum, 1965; diploma medicine, U. Saigon, Vietnam, 1973. Diplomate Am. Bd. Radiology. Resident in radiology Wayne State U., Detroit, 1977-81; radiologist Duy-Tan Mil. Hosp., Danang, Vietnam, 1973-75; X-ray technologist Riverton Hosp., Seattle, 1975-77; radiologist Plymouth Gen. Hosp., Detroit, 1977, Trail Clinics P.C., Detroit, 1977-83; fellow C.T. Oakwood Hosp., Dearborn, Mich., 1982-83; radiologist Harris-Birkhill-Wang-Songe, P.C., Dearborn, 1983—. Mem. Am. Coll. Radiology, AMA. Avocations: electronics; tennis. Office: Oakwood Hosp Dept Radiology 18101 Oakwood Blvd Dearborn MI 48124

PHYE, GARY DEAN, psychology educator, consultant, researcher, author; b. Harper, Kans., Jan. 15, 1942; s. Jesse Evans and Marion Virginia (Mayberry) P.; m. Connie Jeanne Burns, June 2, 1962; 1 dau., Julie. B.A., Wichita State U., 1964; M.A., 1965; Ph.D., U. Mo., 1970. Instr. in psychology S.W. Mo. State U., Springfield, 1965-67; asst. prof. psychology and edn. Iowa State U., Ames, 1970-74, assoc. prof., 1975—. Grantee Iowa State U., 1975-76, Iowa State Research Inst. for Studies in Edn., 1977-78, Apple Edn. Found., 1982-83. Mem. Am. Psychol. Assn., Am. Ednl. Research Assn., Midwest Psychol. Assn. Roman Catholic. Author: (with others) Educational Psychology, 1983; editor: (with Reschly) School Psychology: Perspectives and Issues, 1979; (with Andre) Cognitive Classroom Learning: Understanding, Thinking and Problem Solving, 1986. Home: 2175 Ashmore Dr Ames IA 50010 Office: Iowa State U 112 W Quadrangle Ames IA 50011

PIATT, PHIL DELBERT, civil engineer; b. Hamilton, Kans., Nov. 5, 1932; s. Phil Delbert and Ruth Elizabeth (Milliken) P.; m. Virginia Claire Best, June 15, 1957; children—Stephen, Joseph, Sharon, Linda. B.S.C.E., U. Kans., 1955, M.P.A., 1984. Registered profl. engr., Kans. Engr., Finney & Turnipseed Cons. Engrs., Topeka, 1958-66, Van Doren, Hazard, Stallings, Schnacke Cons. Engrs., 1966-69; asst. city engr. City of Topeka, 1969-76; city engr. City of Overland Park, Kans., 1976—. Contbr. to profl. publs. Served to lt. (j.g.) USN, 1956-58. Mem. Am. Pub. Works Assn. (bridges com. 1974-75, chmn. 1976-77), ASCE, Nat. Soc. Profl. Engrs., Kans. Engring. Soc. Presbyterian. Home: 10539 Reeder Overland Park KS 66214 Office: City of Overland Park 8500 Santa Fe St Overland Park KS 66212

PICARDI, GUY CARL, architect; b. St. Louis, Nov. 1, 1933; s. Guy Anthony and Elizabeth (Hall) P.; m. Mary Virginia Thompson, May 27, 1961; children—Steven Guy, Philip Vincent, Susan Dana. B.Arch., Washington U., 1955. Registered architect, Mo., Kans., Ind., N.C., Ky. Architect C.W. Lorenz, St. Louis, 1955-56; architect, v.p., exec. dir. St. Louis office Leo A. Daly Planners, Architects and Engrs., 1957—; profl. mem. St. Louis Regional Commerce and Growth Assn. Mem. fin. com. St. Richard's Parish, Creve Coeur, Mo., 1983—; mem. Hawthorn Found., St. Louis. Served to capt. U.S. Army, 1956-57, USAR, 1964. Mem. AIA, Constrn. Specifications Inst., Bldg. Ofcls. and Code Adminstrs., NCCJ, Sigma Nu. Republican. Roman Catholic. Clubs: St. Louis, Stadium (St. Louis). Avocation: jogging. Home: 11136 Bon Jour Ct Saint Louis MO 63146 Office: Leo A Daly Planners Architects Engrs 10114 Woodfield Ln Saint Louis MO 63132

PICHA, BONNIE MARIE, info systems specialist; b. Elmhurst, Ill., Feb. 2, 1951; d. Thaddeus Stanley and Anne Katherine (Sweica) Wnenkowski; m. Laddie Joseph Picha, Mar. 5, 1976; children: Bradley, Jonathan Joseph. A in Sci. with honors, Triton Coll., River Grove, Ill., 1985; student, Elmhurst Coll., 1986—. Mem. staff AT&T, Itasca, Ill., 1978-84; communications tech. AT&T, Chgo., 1984-86; info systems assoc. AT&T, Warrenville, Ill., 1986—. Pub. Horsefeathers Newspaper, Broadview, 1984—; contbr. articles relating to horse industry to profl. jours. and mags. Vol. Proviso Coordinating Com., Maywood, Ill., 1984—, Friends of the Handicapped Riders, Chgo.; precinct worker Dem. Orgn., Broadview, Ill., 1982—. Mem. Women in Technologies, Nat. Assn. Female Execs., Future Pioneers (AT&T), Chgo. Women in Pub., Phi Theta Kappa. Roman Catholic. Avocations: polo, three-day eventing, mind puzzles. Home: 2409 S 14th Ave Broadview IL 60153

PICHA, TERRY ALLAN, wholesale distribution executive; b. Denver, Aug. 30, 1941; s. Robert F. and Grace E. (Wambold) P.; m. Norma Robbins Whitt, Aug. 26, 1961 (div. Mar. 1975); 1 child, Lisa M.; m. Marcia Puhlmann, June 20, 1975; 1 child, Cassandra J. BSBA, U. Denver, 1964. CPA. Staff acct. Olesh, Bressler, Idelberg & Fischer, Denver, 1964-67, Arthur Andersen & Co., Indpls., 1967-68; various mgmt. positions Capitol Consol., Inc., Indpls., 1968-85; pres. Bunzl. Bldg. Materials Service, Inc., Indpls., 1986—, also bd. dirs.; bd. dirs. The Throop-Martin Co., Columbus, Ohio, Inland Distbn. Corp., South Bend, Ind., Bob Rans Wholesale Co., Inc., South Bend; cons. Project Bus., Indpls., 1982-84. Mem. Fin. Execs. Inst., Am. Inst. CPA's, Ind.Inst. CPA's. Republican. Presbyterian. Avocations: music, boating. Home: 405 Beechwood Dr Greenfield IN 46140 Office: Bunzl Bldg Materials Service Inc 3333 N Franklin Rd Indianapolis IN 46225

PICHELMAYER, CHARLES ANDREW, bank executive; b. Cullman, Ala., Feb. 4, 1931; s. Charles Otto and Sarah Mae (Quattlebaum) P.; m. Claudia Louise Oehlke, Apr. 16, 1966; children: Sarah Marie, Susan Louise. BS, U. Ala., 1953, MS, 1956. Asst. mgr. market research The Progressive Farmer, Birmingham, Ala., 1957-60; research acct. exec. Campbell-Ewald Advt., Detroit, 1960-61; asst. dir. mktg. and research Meldrum & Fewsmith Advt., Cleve., 1961-65; dir. research Griswold & Eshleman Advt., Cleve., 1965-72; asst. v.p. mktg. Huntington Nat. Bank, Cleve., 1972—. Served to capt. USAF, 1953-55, Korea. mem. Am. Mktg. Assn (sec., personnel placement chmn. 1962-66), Cleve. Advt. Club, Bank Mktg. Assn., Greater Cleve. Growth Assn., Theta Chi. Republican. Episcopalian. Home: 19522 Coffinberry Blvd Fairview Park OH 44126 Office: Huntington Nat Bank 917 Euclid Ave Cleveland OH 44115

PICHERT, BARBARA JEAN, airline company administrator; b. Scranton, Pa., Oct. 11, 1955; d. Walter Julius and Ruth (Cule) P. BA, Gettysburg Coll., 1977; MBA, Vanderbilt U., 1981. Field rep. A.C. Nielsen Co., Nashville, 1977-79; asst. mktg. mgr. Union Underwear, Inc., Bowling Green, Ky., 1981-83; analyst bus. systems United Airlines, Chgo., 1983-86, sr. staff auditor, 1986—. Mem. Art Inst. Chgo. Republican. Avocations: golf, scuba diving, swimming, traveling. Home: 5101 Carriage Way #203 Rolling Meadows IL 60008 Office: United Airlines-EXOAU PO Box 66100 Chicago IL 60666

PICHLER, JOSEPH ANTON, business executive, former university dean, educator; b. St. Louis, Oct. 3, 1939; s. Anton Dominick and Anita Marie (Hughes) P.; m. Susan Ellen Eyerly, Dec. 27, 1962; children: Gretchen, Christopher, Rebecca, Josh. B.B.A. (Woodrow Wilson fellow), U. Notre Dame, 1961; M.B.A., U. Chgo., 1963, Ph.D. (Ford Found. fellow); Ph.D. Standard Oil Indsl. Relations fellow), 1966. Asst. prof. bus. U. Kans., 1964-68, assoc. prof., 1968-73, prof., 1973-80; dean U. Kans. (Sch. Bus.), 1974-80; exec. v.p. Dillon Cos. Inc., 1980-82, pres., 1982-86; exec. v.p. Kroger Co., 1985-86, pres., chief operating officer, 1986—, also bd. dirs.; Spl. asst. to asst. sec. for manpower U.S. Dept. Labor, 1968-70; chmn. Kans. Manpower Services Council, 1974-78; bd. dirs. Frank Paxton Co., Johnson Co. Nat. Bank, Cities Service Corp.; indsl. cons. Author: (with Joseph McGuire) Inequality: The Poor and the Rich in America, 1969; contbg. author: Creativity and Innovation in Manpower Research and Action Programs, 1970, Contemporary Management: Issues and Viewpoints, 1973, Institutional Issues in Public Accounting, 1974, Co-Creation and Capitalism: John Paul II's Laborem Exercens, 1983; Co-editor, contbg. author: Ethics, Free Enterprise, and Public Policy, 1978; Contbr. articles to profl. jours. Bd. dirs. Kans. Charities, 1973-75, Benedictine Coll., Atchison, Kans., 1979-83; nat. bd. dirs. Boys Hope, 1983—, Tougaloo Coll., 1986—; mem. nat. bd. cons. NEH. Recipient Performance award U.S. Dept. Labor Manpower Adminstrn., 1969. Mem. Kans. Assn. Commerce and Industry. Home: 8 Downing Rd Hutchinson KS 67502

PICK, CARL ALAN, electronics executive; b. West Bend, Wis., Jan. 28, 1948; s. Robert B. and Lois P.; m. Barbara Rice, Aug. 9, 1970. BS, Yale U., 1971, MS, 1974. Pres. Gen. Robotics Corp., Hartford, Wis., 1974-84, chmn, chief exec. officer, 1984—; bd. dirs. KDG Computer Systems, London, Gen. Robotics Europe Ltd., Wales, Gen. Robotics South Pacific, Auckland. Club: Milw. Athletic. Office: Gen Robotics Corp 23 S Main St Hartford WI 53027

PICK, DOUGLAS MARTIN, pharmacist; b. Yankton, S.D., Nov. 3, 1959; s. George G. and Marilyn M. (McGeorge) P. BS in Pharmacy, Creighton U., 1983. Pharmacist Cen. Park #8, Omaha, 1983—. Fellow Nebr. Pharmacy Assn., Greater Omaha Pharmacist Assn. (Greatest Potential Retail Pharmacist 1983); mem. Rho Chi. Democrat. Roman Catholic. Avocations: golf, travel, books, tennis. Home: 6758 S 154 Omaha NE 68137 Office: Cen Park #8 13945 S Plaza Omaha NE 68137

PICKARD, WILLIAM F., plastics company executive; b. LaGrange, Ga., Jan. 28, 1941; s. William H. and Victoria (Woodward) P. AS, Mott Community Coll., 1962; BS, Western Mich. U., 1964; MSW, U. Mich., 1965; PhD, Ohio State U., 1971; PhD in Bus. Adminstrn. (hon.), Cleary Coll., 1980. Dir. employment and edn. Urban League Cleve., 1965-67; exec. dir. NAACP, Cleve., 1967-69; assoc. dir. dept. urban studies Cleve. State U., 1971-72; assoc. prof. Wayne State U., Detroit, 1972-74; owner, operator McDonald's Restaurants, Detroit, 1971—; chmn., chief exec. officer Regal Plastics, Roseville, Mich., 1985—; vis. lectr. Cleve. State U., U. Chgo., Hiram Coll., U. Toledo, U. Mich., Case Western Res. U., Ohio State U., Wayne County Community Coll., McDonald's Hamburger U.; participant mgmt. seminar Case Western Res. U., Greater Cleve. Associated Found. and Rockefeller Found., 1968; chmn. Gov.'s adv. com. on minority bus., pres. 1976; bd. dirs. First Ind. Nat. Bank. Mem. Pres.-elect Ronald Regan's transition team to SBA; chmn. econ. devel. com. Nat. Black Rep. Council, 1978, bd. dirs. com. to elect Gov. Ronald Reagan Pres., 1980, chmn. congl. liaison com., 1982; chmn. Mich. Reps. Urban Campaign to elect Gov. Reagan Pres., 1980; vice chmn. Mich. Rep. State Com., 1981; bd. control Grand Valley State Coll., Allendale, Mich.; bd. dirs. Oakwood Hosp., Kirkwood Gen. Hosp., Detroit, Detroit Black Causes, Detroit Econ. Devel. Corp., 1977, Nat. Minority Purchasing Council, Washington, Detroit Urban League, vice chmn. Named one of Ten Outstanding Young Men Cleve., Jaycees, 1969; Alice W. Gault schlor, 1962-63; Nat. Urban League fellow, 1964. Mem. Booker T. Washington Bus. Assn., NAACP, Jaycees, Alpha Phi Alpha. Home: 335 Pine Ridge Dr Bloomfield Hills MI 48013 Office: 2990 W Grand Blvd M-15 Detroit MI 48202

PICKEL, JOYCE KILEY, psychologist; b. Boston, Dec. 20, 1939; B.S. in Edn., Boston State Coll., 1961; M.Ed. (NDEA fellow 1967), R.I. Coll., 1968; M.A. (NDEA fellow 1967-68), Mich. State U., 1969; doctoral candidate No. Ill. U., 1982; m. Edward McDonald, Aug. 24, 1960 (div. Mar. 77); children—Catherine, Maureen, Edward; m. Mark Pickel, Apr. 6, 1982. Tchr. schs. in Mass. and R.I., 1962-66; guidance counselor Grand Ledge (Mich.) schs., 1966-67; diagnostician Eaton County Intermediate Sch. Dist., Charlotte, Mich., 1968-69; psychometrist, Hammond, Ind., 1969-70; coordinator programs emotionally disturbed and learning disabled, sch. psychometrist N.W. Ind. Spl. Edn. Coop., Highland 1970-72; instr. Ind. U., Northwest campus, Gary, 1970-72; program dir. Trade Winds Rehab. Center, Gary, Ind., 1972-73; supervising sch. psychologist Thornton Fractional Twp. High Sch. 215, Calumet City, Ill., 1973—; speaker on teen suicide. Vice pres. Wilbur Wright Middle Sch. PTA, Munster, Ind., 1975-76; mem. planning bd. Lake Area United Way, 1973—; 1st v.p. Greater Hammond Community Council, 1974-76. Recipient award Hammond Community Council, 1974, 75, 76, Community Service award Greater Hammond Community Council, 1975. Mem. Nat. Assn. Sch. Psychologists, Council Exceptional Children, Am. Fedn. Tchrs., Ill. Sch. Psychol. Assn. (Ted Smith Meml. award), South Met. Assn. Sch. Psychologists (pres. 1983-84, bd. dirs. 1985-86), Phi Delta Kappa. Office: 1601 Wentworth Ave Calumet City IL 60409

PICKENS, RANKIN RAY, osteopathic physician; b. Clifton, W.Va., Apr. 2, 1924; s. Ray Wanday and Mary Helena (Natross) P.; m. Mary Georgina Hackett, Dec. 28, 1970; 1 son, Ray Rankin. Student Marshall Coll.-Huntington, W.Va., 1945; B.A., U. Minn., 1948; D.O., Kirksville Coll. Osteo., 1953. Cert. gen. practice, 1978. Intern, Grandview Hosp., Dayton, Ohio, 1953-54; physician Middleport (Ohio) Fire Dept., 1955; gen. practice osteo. medicine, Middleport, 1954—; chief of staff Veterans Meml. Hosp., Pomeroy, Ohio, 1964-75, vice chief of staff, 1975-78; coroner Meigs County, Ohio, 1969—; vol. clin. instr. dept. preventive medicine Ohio State U., Columbus, 1973—; vol. clin. faculty Ohio U. Coll. Osteo. Medicine, Athens, clin. assoc. prof. family medicine, 1976—. Served to lt. USN, 1942-45; USNR, 1945-66. Mem. Am. Osteo. Assn., Ohio Osteo. Assn., Ohio State Coroners Assn. Republican. Methodist. Lodges: Rotary (pres. 1982-83), Mason, Shriners. Home: 400 Riverview Dr Pomeroy OH 45769 Office: Jones Meml Clinic 509 S 3d Ave Middleport OH 45760

PICKERING, CHARLES DENTON, auditor; b. Alamogordo, N.Mex., Aug. 2, 1950; s. Denton Wiley and Mildred Evelyn (Welch) P.; m. Deborah Anne Turner, Dec. 22, 1972 (div. Aug. 1982); m. Crenda Jo Pack, Oct. 29, 1983. BS in Acctg., Miss. State U., 1973. CPA, Ohio, Ill. Auditor U.S. Govt., 1970-80; sr. auditor Owens-Corning Fiberglas, Toledo, 1980-84; supr. internal audit Sundstrand Corp., Rockford, Ill., 1984—. Mem. Am. Inst. CPA's, Ohio Soc. CPA's, Inst. Internal Auditors. Avocation: racquetball. Home: 3560 Montlake Dr Rockford IL 61111 Office: Sundstrand Corp PO Box 7003 Rockford IL 61125-7003

PICKERING, KATHLEEN CUMINGS, association adminstrator; b. Neenah, Wis., Mar. 3, 1943; d. John Billings and Grace Ruth Anna (Wenban) Cumings; m. William Anders Pickering, Aug. 18, 1978; 1 stepchild, Pamela Faye Pickering Thompson. BA, U. Wis., Eau Claire, 1965. Mgmt. trainee Sears Roebuck & Co., Denver, 1965-66; field dir. Girl Scouts U.S., St. Paul, 1966-72, devel. dir., 1972-74; exec. dir. Girl Scouts U.S., Green Bay, Wis., 1974-77, Davenport, Iowa, 1977-78; chief exec. officer Girl Scouts U.S., Mpls., 1979—; bd. dirs. Mgmt. Assistance Project, 1987. Mem. Minn. Women's Polit. Caucus, St. Paul, 1982—; bd. dirs.-at-large Vol. Action Ctr. Mem. Assn. Girl Scout Execs., Minn. Econ. Women's Roundtable (sec. 1985, v.p. 1987), Council Agy. Execs. (v.p. 1983-84, 86, pres. 1987), Mpls. C. of C. Republican. Lutheran. Lodge: Zonta. Avocations: reading, boating, skiing. Home: 2407 Mounds Ave New Brighton MN 55112 Office: Greater Mpls Girl Scout Council 5601 Brooklyn Blvd Minneapolis MN 55429

PICKERING, ROBERT ALAN, engineer, automotive parts manufacturing company executive; b. Crawfordsville, Ind., Feb. 13, 1943; s. Robert Guy and Ada Mae (Self) P.; m. Nona Lee Mull, May 7, 1966; children: Robert Alan Jr., Daniel J. BS in Engring., U. Mich., 1966. Supt. Chevrolet div.Gen. Motors, Detroit, 1966-76; plant mgr. Volkswagen Am., Charleston, W.Va., 1976-83; v.p., gen. mgr. Tech Form Industries, Shelby, Ohio, 1983—. Mem. Am. Soc. Automotive Engrs. Republican. Episcopalian. Avocations: fishing, tennis. Home: 619 Austin Rd Mansfield OH 44903 Office: Tech Form Industries 15 E Smiley Shelby OH 44875

PICKERT, ROBERT WALTER, accountant; b. Aurora, Ill., Sept. 4, 1936; s. Conrad Bonifas and Margaret Catherine (Brummel) P.; m. Tonda Ruth Sloane, Sept. 14, 1963 (div. Nov. 1966); children: Kelly, Christopher, Katherine, Mary Ellen; m. Patricia Ann Petersen, Aug. 16, 1986. BS in Bus. Adminstrn., U. Montana, 1964. CPA, Wis. Supr. Ernst and Whinney, CPA's, Chgo., 1964-68, Milw., 1968-73; v.p. fin., ops. Republic Savings & Loan, Milw., 1973-76; prin. Robert W. Pickert, CPA, Minocqua, Wis., 1976—; bd. dirs., treas. Howard Young Med. Ctr., Inc. Woodruff, Wis.; bd. dirs. Mobile Health Services, Inc., Woodruff. Fellow Am. Inst. CPA's, Wis. Inst. CPA's. Republican. Roman Catholic. Lodge: Rotary (treas. 1978-83). Avocations: canoeing, fishing, hiking. Home: 6935 South Shore Dr Hazelhurst WI 54531 Office: 113 Front St Minocqua WI 54548-0680

PICKETT, ALBERT BERG, field quality engineer; b. Carmel, Ind., Feb. 22, 1918; s. Jasper E. and Christi Ann (Berg) P.; m. Phyllis Elaine Risinger, Aug. 1, 1941; children: Harriet Diane Pickett Stover, William Joe. Engaged in aerospace and electronics industry, 1951-71; with Indpls. Dept. Met. Devel., 1971-73; bldg. Commr., Carmel, 1973-76, mayor, 1976-82; field quality engr. FMC Ordnance Plant, San Jose, Calif., 1982—. Pres., Ind. Heartland Coordinating Commn.; vice chmn. policy com. Indpls. Regional Transp. Council. Mem. Ind. Assn. Cities and Towns (bd. dirs.), N. Cen. Mayors Roundtable Assn. Republican. Quaker. Lodges: Rotary, Masons, Shriners, Kiwanis. Home and Office: 901 S Main St Cicero IN 46034

PICKETT, NORMAN LEE, comptroller; b. Huntington, W.Va., Sept. 15, 1949; s. Norman Carl and Gloria Mae (Ronk) P.; m. Joyce Ann Watts, June 3, 1967 (div. Feb. 1986) 1 child, Norman Eric; m. Judith Anne Widdows, Mar. 1986; children: Clarissa, Suzanne, Brian. BBA, Marshall U., 1979, MBA, 1980. Enlisted U.S. Army, 1968, advanced through grades to capt.; signal instr. USASE Signal Sch., Ft. Gordon, Ga., 1967-70; supply instr. AARTS, Vietnam, 1970-72; avionic supr. 6th ACCB, Ft. Hood, Tex., 1972-74, behavioral specialist, 1974-76; communications chief W.Va. Army N.G., Charleston, 1976-77; adminstrv. asst. VA Regional Office, Huntington, W. Va., 1977-80; platoon ambulsnce leader B. Co. 24th Med. Bn., Ft. Stewart, Ga., 1980-82; med. clearing adminstr. HQ 24th Med. Bn., Hunter AAF, Ga., 1983; med. ops. HQ 24th Infantry div., Ft. Stewart, 1984; comptroller Hawley USA Hosp., Ft. Harrison, Ind., 1984-86. Cubmaster Boy Scouts Am., Burlington, Ohio, 1979, asst. cubmaster, Indpls. 1985. Mem. Am. Soc. Mil. Comptrollers. Methodist. Avocations: motorcycling, traveling. Home: 5380 Deforest Dr Columbus OH 43232

PICONE, REGINA MARIA, lawyer; b. Chgo., Mar. 27, 1959; d. Rosario August and Frances Rose (Mundo) P. BA cum laude, So. Meth. U., 1979; JD, Loyola U., Chgo., 1982. Bar: Ill. 1984, U.S. Dist. Ct. (no. dist.) Ill. 1985. Assoc. Jay A. Baier, Ltd., Chgo., 1984-86, Kasdin & Nathanson Ltd., Chgo., 1986—. Mem. ABA, Ill. Bar Assn., Chgo. Bar Assn. (tort litigation com. 1984), Assn. Trial Lawyers Am., Ill. Trial Lawyers Assn. (legis. com. 1984). Republican. Roman Catholic. Home: 1540 N State Pkwy Chicago IL 60610 Office: Kasdin & Nathanson Ltd 135 S LaSalle St Suite 1960 Chicago IL 60603

PIECEWICZ, WALTER MICHAEL, lawyer; b. Concord, Mass., Jan. 27, 1948; s. Benjamin Michael and Cecelia (Makuc) P.; A.B. magna cum laude, Colgate U., 1970; J.D., Columbia U., 1973; m. Anne T. Mikolajczyk, Oct. 28, 1978; children—Tiffany Anne, Stephanie Marie. Admitted to Ill. bar, 1973; mem. firm Levenfeld, Kanter, Baskes & Lippitz, Chgo., 1973-78, Boodell, Sears, Giambalvo & Crowley, Chgo., 1978—; dir. No. Data Systems, Inc. Mem. Am. Bar Assn., Ill. Bar Assn., Chgo. Bar Assn., Chgo. Estate Planning Council, Internat. Bus. Council Midwest, Phi Beta Kappa. Democrat. Roman Catholic. Home: 1103 N Lombard Ave Oak Park IL 60302 Office: Boodell Sears Giambalvo & Crowley 69 W Washington St Chicago IL 60602

PIELACK, LESLIE KAY, psychotherapist; b. Highland Park, Mich., Dec. 16, 1954; d. Casmere Thaddeus and Shirley Teresa (Schultz) P.; m. Lawrence Michael Oshier, June 30, 1984. BA, Oakland U., 1978, MA, 1981, postgrad., 1981-82. Registered social worker, Mich.; cert. counselor. Mem. staff direct client care Residential Systems Co., Utica, Mich., 1976-78, program coordinator, 1978-81, adminstr., area supr., 1981—; cons. psychotherapist Royal Oak, Mich., 1981—; coordinator employee conduct edn. project Residential System, Utica., 1986—; instr. Macomb Coll., Mt. Clemens, Mich., 1986—, also pilot project co-developer Mich. Dept. Mental Health, Macomb Coll. Mental Retardation Cert. Program, Mt. Clemens. Curriculum devel. and proposal Oakland U., Rochester, Mich., 1982. Mich. Competitive scholar State of Mich., 1973-78. Mem. Am. Assn. Counseling and Devel., Mich Assn. Counseling and Devel. Avocations: bonsai and rose gardening, oil painting, stained glass design, antique collection and restoration. Office: Ctr for Family Devel 524 E Fourth Royal Oak MI 48067

PIERCE, DELILA FRANCES, judge; b. St. Cloud, Minn., Jan. 21, 1934; d. Lawrence August and Alvina Elizabeth (Hechtel) Pierskalla. BS, U. Minn., 1957, JD cum laude, 1958. Bar: Minn. 1958. Assoc. Robert L. Ehlers, St. Paul, Minn., 1958-59; ptnr. Mitchell & Pierce, Mpls., 1959-65; sole practice, Mpls., 1966-73; referee Family Ct., Dist. Ct., Hennepin County, Minn., Mpls., 1973-74; judge Hennepin County Mcpl. Ct., Mpls., 1974-83, Dist. Ct. Minn. (4th jud. dist.), 1983—; mem. adv. bd. Genesis II, Mpls., 1975-76. Fellow Am. Acad. Matrimonial Lawyers; mem. Am. Judges Assn., Nat. Assn. Women Judges, ABA, Am. Judicature Soc., Minn. State Bar Assn., Hennepin County Bar Assn., Minn. Dist. Judges Assn., Minnesota County Judges Assn. (bd. dirs. 1984-87), Hennepin Hist. Soc., Mpls. Soc. Fine Arts. Office: Dist Ct Minn 4th Dist Hennepin County Govt Ctr Minneapolis MN 55487

PIERCE, EDMOND SCOTT, manufacturing company executive, real estate broker; b. Montevideo, Minn., Feb. 4, 1927; s. Lessy Nathan and Ruby Ann (Waltz) P.; m. Ardys Marjorie Halldin, July 13, 1952; children—Thomas Dean, Mary Margaret. Student Macalester Coll., 1946-48; B.B.A., U. Minn., 1954. Unit mgr. First Nat. Bank, Mpls., 1957-62; treas. Pennock Oil Co., Minn., 1962-70; pres. Nelson Internat., Willmar, Minn., 1970-76; real estate broker Pierce and Assoc., Willmar, 1976-79; pres., chief exec. officer Am. Continental Co., Willmar, 1979-86; asst. chief exec. officer BHP Electronics, Inc., Princeton, Minn., 1987—. Pres. Hwy. 12 Assoc. Minn., Willmar, 1967—; bd. dirs. Willmar Opportunities, Willmar, 19; elder Presbyn. Ch., Willmar, 1971-74. Served with USN, 1945-46, 51-52, PTO, Korea. Mem. Willmar C. of C. (pres. 1966), Am. Legion, VFW. Republican. Lodges: Elks (chmn. bd. 1976-81), Masons, Shriners. Avocations: flying, hunting, fishing, golf. Home: Country Club Terrace Willmar MN 56201 Office: BHP Electronics Inc Box 280 Willmar MN 56201

PIERCE, HENRY FLETCHER, IV, construction executive; b. Kansas City, Mo., Oct. 27, 1936; s. Henry Fletcher III and Edith Lorraine (Campbell) P.; m. Patricia Jane Isbell, June 2, 1962 (div. 1968); m. Mary Lynn Crow, July 15, 1979; children: Jane E., Carrie R., Lisa A., Henry F. V, Michelle L. BSCE, Kans. State U., 1961. Project mgr. Hunter Constrn. Co., Hays, Kans., 1961-66; pres. Pierce-Schippers Constrn. Co., Hays, 1967—. Served as pfc. USMC, 1956-58. Republican. Episcopalian. Avocations: golf, tournament bridge. Home: 1108 Amhurst Hays KS 67601

PIERCE, JO ALICE, organizational development consultant; b. Anderson, Ind., Dec. 16, 1949; d. John Edward and Alice Elizabeth (Merrick) Walker; m. William Gayle Pierce, June 24, 1971; 1 child, Jonathan W. Student, Ind. U., 1969, Ball State U., 1970, St. Mary-of-the-Woods (Ind.) Coll., 1986. Mfg. supr. Delco Remy div. Gen. Motors, Anderson, 1974-75, mfg. gen. supr., 1979-83, organizational devel. cons., 1983-86, organizational devel. cons. heavy duty bus. systems div., 1986—; ptnr. Bus. Devel. Cons. Drive chmn. United Way for Delco Remy Plant, Anderson, 1984-85, YMCA, Anderson, 1986; chmn. Midwest regional health com. Soroptimist Internat., 1986—; bd. dirs. YWCA, Anderson, 1984. Mem. Am. Soc. Tng. and Devel. Lodge: Soroptimist (pres. Anderson chpt. 1984-86). Home: PO Box 576 Anderson IN 46015 Office: Gen Motors Delco Remy Div PO Box 2439 Plant 1 Room 217 Anderson IN 46018

PIERCE, JUDY MARIE, quality standards specialist, computer programmer; b. Springfield, Mo., Jan. 9, 1957; d. Judson Lee and Patricia (Strom) P. BS in Mgmt. and Mktg., Southwest Mo. State U., 1979. Lab. analyst Kraft Inc., Springfield, 1975-80; sr. systems engr. Kraft Inc., Glenview, Ill., 1980-85, developer, instr. computer courses, 1983-84, quality standards specialist, 1985—. Deacon Presbyn. Ch., Des Plaines, Ill. Mem. Pi Omega Pi (chaplain 1978-79). Democrat. Avocations: bowling, volleyball, bicycling, candy making, collecting miniatures. Home: 9982 Holly Ln #2N Des Plaines IL 60016-1424 Office: Kraft Inc Kraft Ct Glenview IL 60025

PIERCE, MARY KATHERINE, insurance company executive; b. Detroit, Feb. 16, 1947. BBA, Western Mich. U., 1975. CPA, Mich. Pub. acct. Gerbel & Butzbach CPA's, St. Joseph, Mich., 1976-79; fin. analyst, coordinator employee devel. Clark Equipment Credit Corp., Buchanan, Mich., 1979-82, with risk mgmt. dept., 1982-85; v.p. ins. mgmt. Celfor Services Corp. subs. Clark Equipment Credit Corp., Buchanan, 1985—; chmn. supr. com. United Fed. Credit Union, Buchanan, 1981—. Mem. Am. Inst. CPA's, Mich. Soc. CPA's, Am. Women's Soc. CPA's. Exec. Profl. Women's Assn. Avocations: avid reader, motorcycles. Home: 1356 Linden Dr Saint Joseph MI 49085 Office: Celfor Services Corp Circle Dr Buchanan MI 49107

PIERCE, RALPH, consulting engineer; b. Chgo., Apr. 14, 1926; s. Charles and Fay (Reznik) P.; B.E.E., Northwestern U., 1946; m. Adrian H. Rosengard, Sept. 3, 1978; children—Marc Fredrick, Deborah Ann, Elizabeth Allison. Test engr. Am. Elec. Heater Co., Detroit, 1946-47; sr. asso. engr. Detroit Edison Co., 1947-52; sec., chief utility engr. George Wagschal Assos., Detroit, 1952-58; sr. partner Pierce, Yee & Assos., Engrs., Detroit, 1958-73; mng. partner Harley Ellington Pierce Yee & Assos., 1973-86, pres., 1986—; mem. Dept. Commerce Mission to Yugoslavia. Served to ensign USNR, 1944-46; comdr. Res. ret. Registered profl. engr., Mich., Ind., Ill., Ohio, Ky., N.Y., Washington, Mo., Fla., Can., Calif., Colo., N.Mex. Mem. Nat. Council Engring. Examiners, Nat. Soc. Profl. Engrs., Engring. Soc. Detroit, IEEE, Soc. Coll. and Univ. Planners, Illuminating Engring. Soc., Mich. Soc. Architects (assoc.). Home: 5531 Pebbleshire Rd Birmingham MI 48010 Office: 26111 Evergreen Rd Southfield MI 48076

PIERCE, SHELBY CRAWFORD, oil co. exec.; b. Port Arthur, Tex., May 26, 1932; s. William Shelby and Iris Mae (Smith) P.; B.S.E.E., Lamar State Coll. Tech., Beaumont, Tex., 1956; student M.I.T. Program for Sr. Execs., 1980; m. Marguerite Ann Grado, Apr. 2, 1954; children—Cynthia Dawn, Melissa Carol. With Amoco Oil Co., 1956—, zone supr., gen. foreman, maintenance, 1961-67, operating supt., 1967-69, coordinator results mgmt., Texas City (Tex.) refinery, 1969-72, dir. results mgmt., corp. hdqrs., Chgo., 1972-75, ops. mgr. refinery, Whiting, Ind., 1975-77, asst. refinery mgr., 1977-79, dir. crude replacement program, Chgo., 1979-81, mgr. refining and transp. engring., 1981—. Fin. chmn. Bay Area council Boy Scouts Am., 1974; dir. JETS (Jr. Engring. Tech. Soc.); chmn. bd., chmn. fin. com. Methodist Ch., 1967-72. Mem. Am. Inst. Chem. engrs. (chmn. engring. constrn. contracting com.), N.W. Ind. Bus. Roundtable (chmn. exec. com.), Sigma Tau. Republican. Home: 18840 Loomis Ave Homewood IL 60430 Office: 200 E Randolph Dr Chicago IL 60601

PIERCE, STEVEN R., photographer; b. Topeka, Aug. 12, 1958; s. Francis Elmo and Rhoda Mae (Buttel) P. BS, U. Kans., 1982. Photographer Univ. Photography, Lawrence, Kans., 1981-82, Kent Robertson & Assocs., Hocheim, West Germany, 1984-86, J. Kent Bixler Photography, Kans. City, Mo., 1986—; freelance photographer, 1982—. Club: Kans. City Track. Avocations: running marathons, languages. Home: 6300 Main #746 Kansas City MO 64113 Office: J. Kent Bixler Photography 2522 NE Vivian Kansas City MO 64118

PIERCY, NANCY STARR, technical writer; b. Niles, Ohio, June 10, 1948; d. Olin Merle and Dorotha Catherine (Strimple) Pfautz; m. Garvie Gene Piercy, Sept. 23, 1977; children: Van Alan, Wyn Arris, Michael Andrew Cherry. BS, Ind. U. Pa., 1969; postgrad. in Engring., Purdue U., 1981-84. Tchr. pub. schs. 1969-73, restaurant and retail mgr., 1973-76; sr. tech. writer Detroit Diesel Allison div. Gen. Motors, Indpls., 1977—; free-lance writer, editor, publs. cons., Indpls., 1980—. Campaign chmn. local county govt., Indiana, Pa., 1968. EEO scholar, 1966-69. Mem. League of Women Voters. Methodist. Avocations: gourmet cooking, reading, women's rights, hiking, jazz. Home: 1114 Woodpointe Dr Indianapolis IN 46234 Office: Gen Motors Detroit Diesel Allison div PO Box 894 Indianapolis IN 46206-0894

PIERCY-PONT, ANN LISA, military officer, educational technologist; b. Tacoma, Nov. 15, 1951; d. Jeff Johnston and Leatha Annabelle (Feeler) Piercy; m. Larry Thomas Moore, Feb. 5, 1970 (div. Dec. 1972); m. Steven Pont, Nov. 23, 1974. AA, Fla. State U., 1974, BA, 1976; MA, Calif. State U., Sacramento, 1981. Cert. USAF tng. instr., 1978. Commd. 2d lt. USAF, 1976, advanced through grades to maj., 1987; occupational analyst Occupational Measurement Ctr., Lackland AFB, 1976-77; instructional system devel. advisor, tng. evaluation officer 323 Flying Tng. Wing, Mather AFB, Calif., 1977-81; E-3 systems instructional system devel. tng. advisor 552 Airborne Warning and Control Wing, Tinker AFB, Okla., 1981-85; chief exportable edn. br., dep. dir. nonresident programs div. sch. systems and logistics, chief evaluation and tech. br. ops. and plans div. Air Force Inst. of Tech., Wright-Patterson AFB, Ohio, 1985—. Mem. Air Force Assn., Am. Soc. Tng. and Devel., Nat. Soc. for Performance and Instrn., Assn. for Ednl. Communications and Tech., NOW (del. 1980). Roman Catholic. Avocations: poetry, sports cars, sewing, gourmet cooking, travel. Home: 1005 Meadowlark Dr Enon OH 45323 Office: AFIT/XPX Wright-Patterson AFB OH 45433-6583

PIERSANTE, DENISE, public relations executive; b. Detroit, Jan. 9, 1954; d. Joseph Lawrence and Virginia (Grunwald) P.; m. Wilfred Lewis Was II, June 7, 1975 (div. 1981). B.A. in Communications, Mich. State U., 1978. Tchr. Northwestern Ohio Community Action Commn., Defiance, 1979-80, counselor, 1980-82, job developer, 1982-83; job developer Pvt. Industry Council, Defiance, 1983, job developer coordinator, 1983-84, dir. pub. relations and job devel., 1984-86 ; market master North Market, Columbus, Ohio, 1986-87; dir. mktg. Richard S. Zimmerman Jr., Columbus, 1987—; cons. Small Bus. Mgmt., Archbold, Ohio, 1985—; promotion dir. Miss Northwest Ohio Pageant, Defiance, 1985—; pub. relations coordinator Defiance County Social Service Agys., 1981—; author of various grants. Editor Job Tng. Partnership Act newsletter, 1984-86, (newsletter) North Market Soc., 1986-87. Defiance County Social Service Agys. newsletter, 1981-86; Value/Style Community News, 1987— . Organizer, Auglaize River Race, Defiance, 1985. Nat. Merit scholar, 1972; recipient Am. Legion Citizenship award, 1969, 72. Mem. Pub. Relations Soc. Am., Nat. Assn. Female Execs., Jaycees (Jaycee of Month 1985). Club: Bus. and Profl. Women (Defiance). Home: 2363 Meadow Village Dr Worthington OH 43085 Office: 100 S 3d St Suite 414 Columbus OH 43215

PIERSON, DANIEL WARREN, marketing executive; b. Chgo., Oct. 1, 1956; s. Daniel Webster and Octavia (Allen) P. BS, Ill. State U., 1979. Cert. data processor. Coordinator GTE, Bloomington, Ill., 1979-81; info. services adminstrn. GTE, Bloomington, 1981-82; info. planning analyst GTE Corp., Westfield, Ind., 1982-83, info. planning adminstr., 1983-85, product champion, 1985, mktg. mgr., 1985—. Producer (video documentary) The Omega Experience, 1986. Mem. Indpls. Profl. Assn. (edn. chmn. 1986—), Data Processing Mgmt. Assn (edn. co chmn. 1985—), Omega Psi Phi. Democrat. Mem. Christian Ch. Home: 6486 Miramar Ct Indianapolis IN 46250 Office: GTE Corp PO Box 407 Westfield IN 46074

PIERSON, DAVID LOWELL, orchestra manager; b. Hamilton, Ohio, Jan. 21, 1949; s. Raymond Charles and Irma Lucille (Vizedom) P.; B.Mus. Edn., Ind. U., 1972, M.A. in Arts Adminstrn., 1976; m. Deborah Pfleeger, June 11, 1977. Music tchr. Lurnea High Sch., Liverpool, N.S.W., Australia, 1972-73; asst. mgr. Dayton Philharm. Orch. Assn., Inc., 1976-77, gen. mgr., 1977—; cons. Ohio Arts Council; bd. dirs. WDPR. Adv. com. music program Career Acad., Dayton Public Schs., 1979-81; mem. Leadership Dayton, 1986; bd. dirs. Dayton Boys Choir. Ind. U. Arts Adminstrn. Program fellow, 1974-76. Mem. Orgn. Ohio Orchs. (dir. 1980, pres. 1983), Am. Symphony Orch. League, Ohio Citizens Com. for Arts, Pi Kappa Lambda. Club: Rotary. Home: 310 S Village Dr Dayton OH 45459 Office: Dayton Philharmonic Orch Montgomery Country's Mem Hall 125 E First St Dayton OH 45402

PIERSON, PAUL TIMOTHY, architect; b. Lake Charles, La., Aug. 24, 1948; s. Raymond Elvin and Martha (Shull) P.; m. Judith Ann Smith, June 10, 1972; children: Shannon Marie, Jordan Lynne. BArch, U. Cin., 1973. Registered architect, Md., Ind., Ky. Project coordinator Tartar & Kelly, Balt., 1973; architect Marks & Cooke, Towson, Md., 1973-75; assoc. Bldg. Scis., Towson, 1975-77; project architect M.C.S.T., Towson, 1977-80; sr. project architect, v.p. James Architects & Engrs., Indpls., 1980—, also bd. dirs.; mem. nat. archtl. adv. Dow Chem. Corp. Prin. works include U. Riyadh Recreational Facility, Mercantile Bank and Trust Co. Br., South Putnam Elem. Sch. Mem. Rep. Presdl. Task Force, Indpls., 1984; vol. Neighborhood Design Ctr., Balt.; trustee LockRaven United Meth. Ch., Balt., 1979-80, Epworth United Meth. Ch., Indpls., 1985—. Mem. AIA, Ind. Soc. Architects, Constrn. Specification Inst. (tech. com.), Am. Correctional Assn., Am. Jail Assn., U. Cin. Alumni Assn. Office: James Architects & Engrs Inc 2828 E 45th St Indianapolis IN 46205

PIETILA, VERNON WESLEY, auditor; b. Laurium, Mich., July 3, 1945; s. Wesley Alfred and Helen (Antilla) P.; children: Vincent, Christy, Martin. BSBA in Acctg., Mich. Tech. U., 1967; MBA in Fin., Western Mich. U., 1972; cert. in bank auditing, Rutgers U., 1985. CPA, Mich. Sr. mgr. Price Waterhouse, N.Y.C., 1976-78; sr. v.p., auditor Mfrs. Nat. Corp., Detroit, 1978—. Mem. Am. Inst. CPA's Mich. Assn. CPA's, Inst. Internat. Auditors, Banking Adminstn. Inst. Club: Economic (Detroit). Home: 945 Peach Blossom Ct Rochester Hills MI 48064 Office: 446 Lafayette Detroit MI 48226

PIETRASZEK, WAYNE EDWARD, infosystems manager; b. Chgo., June 19, 1955; s. Edward Joseph and Ann Theresa (Liptak) P. BS in Computer Sci., Ill. Inst. Tech., Chgo., 1982; postgrad., U. Chgo., 1987—. Sytems programmer Inland Steel, East Chicago, Ind., 1982-84, tech. cons., 1984-85, supr. systems software, 1985—. Mem. Inland Steel Mgmt. Assn., IEEE, Am. Assn. for Artificial Intelligence. Club: Inland Athletic Assn. Home: 6721 S Artesian St Chicago IL 60629 Office: Inland Steel Co 3210 Watling St East Chicago IN 46312

PIETROFESA, JOHN JOSEPH, teacher educator; b. N.Y.C., Sept. 12, 1940; s. Louis John and Margaret (Proietti) P.; B.E. cum laude, U. Miami, 1961, M.Ed., 1963, Ed.D., 1967; lic. psychologist; lic. social worker; m. Cathy Marks, June 22, 1985; children—John, Paul, Maria, Dolores. Counselor, Dade County (Fla.) pub. schs., 1965-67; prof. edn. Wayne State U., Detroit, 1967—, div. head theoretical and behavioral founds., 1977-83; cons. to various schs., hosps. and univs. Served to 1st lt. Mil. Police Corps, AUS, 1963-65. Mem. Am. Psychol. Assn., Am., Mich. personnel and guidance assns., Assn. Counselor Edn. and Supervision, Phi Delta Kappa. Author: The Authentic Counselor, 1971, 2d edit., 1980; School Counselor as Professional, 1971; Counseling and Guidance in the Twentieth Century, 1971; Elementary School Guidance and Counseling, 1973; Career Development, 1975; Career Education, 1976; College Student Development, 1977; Counseling: Theory Research and Practice, 1978; Guidance: An Introduction, 1980; Counseling: An Introduction, 1984; mem. editorial bd. Counseling and Values, 1972-75. Home: 481 Whippers Ln Bloomfield Hills MI 48013 Office: Wayne State U 321 Education Detroit MI 48202

PIGOTT, JOHN A., telecommunications supplies company executive; b. 1932. AB, U. Notre Dame, 1954; JD, U. Mich., 1960. Assoc. Schiff, Hartin and Waite, 1960-68; ptnr. Anixter, Bilandic and Pigott, 1968-77; with Anixter Bros., Skokie, Ill., 1977—, v.p., sec., gen. counsel, 1977-84, now pres., also bd. dirs. Served with USAF, 1955-56. Office: Anixter Bros Inc 4711 Golf Rd Skokie IL 60076 *

PIHERA, LAWRENCE JAMES, advertising agency executive, writer; b. Cleve., Jan. 9, 1933; s. Charles and Dorothy P.; student U. Hawaii, Cooper Sch. Art, Cleve. Inst. Art; m. Patricia Dunn, Aug. 22, 1955; children—Lauren, Scott. Advt. mgr. Johnson Rubber Co. and subs., 1957-58; creative dir. Mansfield Advt. (Ohio), 1958-60, G. W. Young Public Relations, Dayton, 1960-70; pres. Phiera Advt. Assos., Inc., Centerville, Ohio, 1970—; pub. relations counsel City of Trotwood, 1982—, Madison Twp., 1984—; mktg. counsel Muir Pub., 1984—, Newport/Cocke County, Tenn., 1985—; publicity dir. Indpls. 500 Racing Team; lectr. in field; cons. environ. design. Founder Trotwood Rail Mus.; bd. dirs. Centerville Fine Arts Commn. Served with USN. Recipient 1st Place Advt. Writing, 1970, 71, 74, 76, 77, 78. Mem. Soc. Bus. Cons., Art Center Dayton, Centerville C. of C. (bd. (dirs.). Author: Making of a Winner, 1972; (juvenile fiction) Wee Wams Wander, 1985; Living in Style in a Log Home, 1985, Confederation Moves Into U.S. Market, 1986, Tropical Plants in Restaurants, 1986, A Dream Come True, 1987, Will Your First Home Be Built of Logs?, 1987, Interior Plantscapes in Retirement Centers, 1987; editor: McCall Spirit, 1970, The Heritage Report, 1983—, FEG Stamping Newsletter, 1987—, Yesteryear Newsletter, Horticultural Mgmt. Report, Lincoln Log News; architecture critic Instl. Mgmt. mag.; producer, writer (film) The Log Experience, 1985; contbr. articles to profl. jours. Clubs: Dayton Advt., Am. Business (bd. dirs.), Dayton Exec.'s.

PIHLSTROM, BRUCE, periodontist, dental educator; b. Mpls., July 4, 1943; s. Earl W. and Elsie R. (Knutson) P.; m. Carol A. Minelli, July 29, 1967; children: Chris, Daniel. BS, U. Minn., 1965, DDS, 1967, MS, 1969. Diplomate Am. Bd. Periodontology. Instr. periodontics Washington U., St. Louis, 1971; clin. asst. prof. U. Minn., Mpls., 1971-72, asst. prof., 1972-78, assoc. prof., 1978-86; prof. &, &, 1986—; practice dentistry specializing in periodontics Golden Valley, Minn., 1975—; Cons. Jour. Periodontology, Chgo., 1984—, Jour. Am. Dental Assn., 1979—. Contbr. periodontal articles to profl. jours. Leader Boys Scouts Am., St. Paul, 1982-82. Served to capt. USAF, 1969-71. Research grantee NIH, 1980—. Mem. Am. Acad. Periodontology (chmn. edn. com. 1982—), ADA (cons. 1979—). Lutheran. Office: U Minn Sch Dentistry Minneapolis MN 55455

PIKE, CHARLENE HELEN, teacher; b. Detroit, Feb. 26, 1947; d. Burt A. and Lorraine J. (Dobro) Engstrom; m. David Pierce Pike, July 5, 1969. BA in Social Sci., Mich. State U., 1969; MEd, Wayne State U., 1974. Tchr. L'Anse Creuse Pub. Schs., Mt. Clemens, Mich., 1969—. Mem. Birmingham (Mich.) Power Squadron, 1975—. Mem. NEA, Nat. Middle Sch. Assn. (region trustee 1985—), Mich. Assn. Middle Sch. Educators (Outstanding Service award 1979), Mich. Council for the Social Studies (Outstanding Tchr. of Yr. award 1985), Mich. Edn. Assn., L'Anse Creuse End. Assn. (local exec. bd. 1980—). Home: 325 S Maple Royal Oak MI 48067 Office: Lanse Creuse Middle Sch S 34641 Jefferson Mount Clemens MI 48045

PIKE, JOHN BROMAN, orthodontist; b. Mpls., June 21, 1934; s. Joe Manning and Betty Wicker (Broman) P.; m. Carole May Hoffman, June 16, 1956; children: Jobeth, Julie, Janet, Jennifer. BS, U. Minn., 1958, DDS, 1959, MSD, 1961. Diplomate Am. Bd. Orthodontics. Practice dentistry specializing in orthodontics St. Cloud, Minn., 1961—. Fellow Am. Coll. Dentistry; mem. ADA, Am. Assn. Orthodontics, Minn. Dental Assn., Minn. Soc. Orthodontics (past pres.), Midwest Soc. Orthodontics (Minn. bd. dirs. 1978-84), W. Cen. Dentist Soc. (past pres.), St. Cloud Jaycees, St. Cloud C. of C., Delta Sigma Delta. Republican. Presbyterian. Lodge: Sertoma (pres. 1986-87), Elks, No. Star. Avocations: triathlete, skiing, golf. Home: 116 Dunbar Rd. Saint Cloud MN 56301 Office: 1411 St Germain Saint Cloud MN 56301

PIKE, JOHN ROBERT, foundation executive; b. Madison, Wis., June 8, 1931; s. Robert Frederick and Helen Ann (Hartmeyer) P.; B.S. with honors in Econs., U. Wis., Madison, 1953, M.S., 1957, Ph.D., 1963; postgrad. London Sch. Econs., 1959; m. Ann H. Slichter, Dec. 27, 1958; children—Susanna, Elizabeth, Kathryn. Prof. fin. U. Ill., Urbana, 1963-68; exec. dir. Wis. Investment Bd., Madison, 1968-74; dep. dir. Wis. Alumni Research Found., Madison, 1974-76, mng. dir., 1976—; dir. Menasha Woodenware, Menasha Corp., 1977-82. Chmn. bus. and fin. com., bd. dirs. Madison Art Center, 1969-76; bd. dirs. Wis. chpt. Nature Conservancy, 1971-75; mem. fin. adv. bd. Wis. Bldg. Commn., 1975-81; bd. curators Wis. Hist. Soc., 1972-81; vice chmn. bd. Madison Gen. Hosp., 1975—; bd. dirs. John A. Johnson Found., 1977—; bd. dirs. Madison Gen. Hosp., 1975-84, chmn., 1984-86, chmn. Meriter Hosp., 1987—; trustee William A. Vilas Trust Estate, 1978—. Served with AUS, 1954-56, Korea. Mem. Am. Fin. Assn. Clubs: Madison, Madison Literary. Contbr. articles to profl. jours. Home: 433 Woodward Dr Madison WI 53704 Office: Wis Alumni Research Found 614 N Walnut Madison WI 53705

PIKUNAS, JUSTIN, psychology educator; b. Lithuania, Jan. 7, 1920; came to U.S., 1950, naturalized, 1956; s. Baltrus and Anele (Radzius) P.; m. Regina Liesunaitis, Aug. 8, 1953; children: Justas, Kristina, Ramona. PhB, U. Munich, 1946, PhD, 1949. Instr. psychology U. Detroit, 1951-52, asst. prof., 1953-56, assoc. prof., 1956-61, prof., 1961-87, prof. emeritus, 1987; dir. Child Family Ctr., Detroit, 1970—; chmn. dept. psychology U. Detroit, 1974-78. Author: Fundamental Child Psychology, rev. ed., 1965, Human Development: An Emergent Science, 3d rev. ed., 1976, Pikunas Graphoscopic Scale, 3d ed. 1982. Pres. ATEITIS Fedn., 1967-73, Lithuanian Cath. Fedn. Am., 1978-80. Mem. AAAS, Am. Pschological Assn. Home: 8761 W Outer Dr Detroit MI 48219 Office: U Detroit Psychology Dept 4001 W McNichols Detroit MI 48221

PILAR, VICTOR JAMES, engineer; b. Detroit, Mich., Dec. 13, 1948; s. Charles Robert and Mary Jean (Bertolino) P.; m. Elaine Louise Dividock, June 20, 1970; children: Melanie, Melissa; m. Kathryn Mae Hile, Mar. 21, 1986; 1 child, Shawn. BS, Mich. State U., 1970. Registered profl. engr., Mich. Project engr. Orchard, Hiltz & McCliment, Livonia, Mich., 1970-73, Argonaut Realty, Detroit, 1973-74, Giffels Assocs., Southfield, Mich., 1974-84; asst. dir. civil engring. Giffels Assocs., Southfield, 1984—. Mem. ASCE, Mich. Soc. Profl. Engrs. Republican. Methodist. Avocations: golf, bowling, raquetball, baseball. Home: 17328 Lilypad Ct Northville MI 48167 Office: Giffels Assocs 25200 Telegraph Rd Southfield MI 48086

PILARCZYK, DANIEL EDWARD, archbishop; b. Dayton, Ohio, Aug. 12, 1934; s. Daniel Joseph and Frieda S. (Hilgefort) P. Student, St. Gregory Sem., Cin., 1948-53; Ph.B., Pontifical Urban U., Rome, 1955, Ph.L., 1956, S.T.B., 1958, S.T.L., 1960, S.T.D., 1961; M.A., Xavier U., 1965; Ph.D., U. Cin., 1969. Ordained priest Roman Catholic Ch., 1959; asst. chancellor Archdiocese of Cin., 1961-63; synodal judge Archdiocesan Tribunal, 1971-82; mem. faculty Athenaeum of Ohio, St. Gregory Sem., 1963-74; v.p. Athenaeum of Ohio, 1968-74, trustee, 1974—; also rector St. Gregory Sem., 1968-74; archdiocesan dir. ednl. services 1974-82, aux. bishop of Cin., 1974-82, vicar gen., 1974-82, archbishop of Cin., 1982—; Bd. dirs. Pope John Ctr., 1978-85; trustee Cath. Health Assn., 1982-85, Cath. U. Am., 1983—; trustee Pontifical Coll. Josephinum, 1983—; v.p. Nat. Conf. Cath. Bishops, 1986—. Author: Praepositini Cancellarii de Sacramentis et de Novissimis, 1964-65. Ohio Classical Conf. scholar to Athens, 1966. Mem. Am. Philol. Assn. Home: 29 E 8th St Cincinnati OH 45202 Office: 100 E 8th St Cincinnati OH 45202 *

PILLA, ANTHONY MICHAEL, bishop; b. Cleve., Nov. 12, 1932; s. George and Libera (Nista) P. Student, St. Gregory Coll. Sem., 1952-53, Borromeo Coll. Sem., 1955, St. Mary Sem., 1954, 56-59; B.A. in Philosophy, John Carroll U., Cleve., 1961, M.A. in History, 1967. Ordained priest Roman Catholic Ch., 1959; asso. St. Bartholomew Parish, Middleburg Hts., Ohio, 1959-60; prof. Borromeo Sem., Wickliffe, Ohio, 1960-72; rector-pres. Borromeo Sem., 1972-75; mem. Diocese Cleve. Liturgical Commn., 1964-69, asst. dir., 1969-72; sec. for services to clergy and religious personnel Diocese Cleve., 1975-79; titular bishop Scardona; and aux. bishop of Cleve. and vicar Eastern region Diocese of Cleve., 1979-80, apostolic adminstr., from 1980; bishop of Cleve., from 1981; trustee Borromeo Sem., 1975-79; trustee, mem. bd. overseers St. Mary Sem., 1975-79; adv. bd. permanent diaconate program Diocese of Cleve., 1975-79, mem. hospitalization and ins. bd., 1979; trustee Cath. U., from 1981; bd. dirs Cath. Communications Found, from 1981. Mem. Nat. Cath. Edn. Assn. (dir. 1972-75), U.S. Cath. Conf., Nat. Conf. Cath. Bishops, Cath. Conf. Ohio., Greater Cleve. Roundtable (trustee from 1981). Office: Chancery Office 350 Chancery Bldg Cathedral Square 1027 Superior Ave Cleveland OH 44114

PILLAERT, E(DNA) ELIZABETH, museum curator; b. Baytown, Tex., Nov. 19, 1931; d. Albert Jacob and Nettie Roseline (Kelley) P. B.A., U. St.

Thomas, 1953; M.A., U. Okla., 1963; postgrad., U. Wis., 1962-67, 70-73. Asst. curator archaeology Stovall Mus., Norman, Okla., 1959-60, ednl. liaison officer, 1960-62; research asst. U. Okla., Norman, Okla., 1962; research asst. U. Wis., Madison, 1962-65, cons. archaeol. faunal analysis, 1965—; curator osteology Zool. Mus., Madison, 1965—, chief curator, 1967—. Bd. dirs. Lysistrata Feminist Coop., Madison, 1977-81, Univ. YMCA, Madison, 1974-77. Mem. Soc. Vertebrate Paleontology, Wis. Archaeol. Soc., Okla. Anthrop. Soc., Am. Assn. Mus., NOW, Madison Audubon Soc., Stoughton Hist. Soc. Home: 216 N Prairie St Stoughton WI 53589 Office: U Wis Zool Museum 434 Noland Bldg Madison WI 53706

PILLSBURY, CEIL MORAN, accounting educator; b. Bloomington, Ill., Jan. 19, 1957; s. John Sievers and Kathleen Rose (Schwarz) Moran; m. Roger Alan Pillsbury, Mar. 3, 1984. BS, U. Mo., 1978; MS, Ill. State U., 1980; PhD, Okla. State U., 1984. CPA, Mo. Staff auditor Price Waterhouse & Co., St. Louis, 1978-79; instr. acctg. Ill. State U., Bloomington, 1980-81; research asst. Okla. State U., Stillwater, 1981-83; asst. prof. acctg. DePaul U., Chgo., 1984—; presenter at various orgns., 1985—. Contbr. articles to profl. jours. Arthur Andersen & Co. grantee, 1983, DePaul U. grantee, 1984, 86, Coopers and Lybrand grantee, 1985. Mem. Am. Inst. CPA's, Ill. CPA Soc. (met. chpt.), Am. Acctg. Assn., Beta Alpha Psi, Beta Gamma Sigma. Republican. Avocations: golf, tennis. Office: U Wis-Milw Sch of Bus 414 Bolton Hall Milwaukee WI 53201

PIMENTEL, JUAN RICARDO, engineering educator; b. La Libertad, Peru, Feb. 8, 1953; came to U.S., 1976; s. Ricardo and Consuelo Guilda (Flores) P.; m. Melissa Anne Beattie, Jan. 15, 1983. M.S. in E.E., U. Va., 1978, Ph.D., 1980. Instr. Universidad Nacional de Ingenieria, Lima, 1974-76; research asst. Nat. Radio Astronomy Obs., Charlottesville, Va., 1976-77; research asst. U. Va., Charlottesville, 1977-79; asst. prof. Gen. Motors Inst., Flint, Mich., 1979-83, assoc. prof., 1983—; cons. Indsl. Tech. Inst., Ann Arbor, Mich., Daviloti Ltd., Flint, Mich., Ship Star Assn., Teltech. Mem. IEEE (editorial bd. Network Mag.), SME, Computer Automated Systems Assn., Mfg. Automation Protocol/Tech. Office Protocol, Sigma Xi, Eta Kappa Nu, Tau Beta Pi. Roman Catholic. Office: 1700 W 3d Ave Flint MI 48502

PINCHEIRA-VALLADARES, WALDO ALBERT, otolaryngologist; b. Santiago, Chile, Jan. 2, 1931; came to U.S., 1972; s. Carlos Pincheira and Julia Ester Valladares; divorced; children: Marianne, Ricardo. BS in Biology, U. Chile, 1948, MD, 1954. Diplomate Am. Bd. Otolaryngology. Resident in surgery U. Chile, 1955-61; cancer surgery fellow Puerto Rico Oncologic Hosp., 1972-75; resident in otolaryngology/head and neck surgery U. Puerto Rico, 1977-80; practice medicine specializing in otolaryngology Ft. Dodge, Iowa, 1980—. Recipient LePetit award, 1955, Rotary Club award, both U. Chile Sch. Med., 1955, Günther award, Soc. Surgeons of Chile, 1963. Fellow Am. Coll. Surgeons, Am. Acad. Otolaryngology; mem. AMA. Avocations: Italian opera, Tae Kwon Do. Office: 3 N 17th St Fort Dodge IA 50501

PINDELSKI, JOHN ANDREW, psychologist; b. Chgo., May 31, 1950; s. Theodore T. and Julia (Kilian) P.; m. Patricia Mary Walsh, June 9, 1973; children: Joseph, Mary. BA in Psychology, Northwestern U., 1972, PhD in Psychology, 1981; MS in Psychology, Ill. Inst. Tech., 1976. Reg. psychologist; cert. substance abuse counselor. Psychologist Cermak Health, Chgo., 1981-84; pvt. practice Elmhurst, Ill., 1981—; psychologist Our Lady of Mercy Hosp., Dyer, Ind., 1986—; sr. psychologist in-depth div. Police Cons., 1987—; instr. Kendall Coll., Evanston, Ill., 1980—. Head coach Park Ridge Soccer; mem. sch. bd. Our Lady of Ransom, Niles, Ill., 1986—. Mem. Am. Psychol. Assn., Am. Rehab. Counseling Assn. Roman Catholic. Office: 240 N West Ave Elmhurst IL 60126

PINE, KATHLEEN PARAVICH, data processing executive; b. Hammond, Ind., Apr. 7, 1948; s. Franklin A. and Sally R. (Abram) Paravich; m. Robert Michael Pine, July 31, 1982. BS in Math, Marquette U., 1970; cert. info. scis., Honeywell Inst., Chgo., 1972; cert. found. banking, Am. Inst. Banking, 1979, cert. functions of banking, 1981, cert. in banking principles, 1982. Book keeper T.A. Chapman Co., Milw., 1970-72; statistician Blue Cross/Shield, Chgo., 1972; application programmer Continental Bank, Chgo., 1972-76; sr. data processing analyst ABN/Lasalle Bank, Chgo., 1976—. Mem. Pi Mu Epsilon, Phi Mu. Avocation: collecting carved items. Office: LaSalle Nat Bank 135 S LaSalle St Chicago IL 60690

PINE, WILLIAM CHARLES, JR., automotive executive; b. Lake Forest, Ill., July 17, 1950; s. William Charles and Virginia Rae (Keeley) P.; m. Mary Eileen McCarthy, June 10, 1972; children: Colin, Brian, Kirsten, Kyle, Lauren. BS, U.S. Naval Acad., 1972; MBA, George Washington U., 1977. Commd. ensign (s.c.) USN, 1972, advanced through grades to lt., 1976, resigned, 1978; with fin. staff Gen. Motors, Detroit, 1978-82, dir. forward program analysis comptrollers staff, 1982-83; fin. mgr. GM-10 div. Gen. Motors, Warren, Mich., 1983-85; fin. mgr. Saturn Corp., Troy, Mich., 1985—. Home: 45702 Purcell Dr Plymouth MI 48170 Office: Saturn Corp 1400 Stephenson Hwy Troy MI 48007

PINEAULT, JAMES JOSEPH, power company manager, consultant; b. Mpls., Nov. 22, 1932; s. Ferdinand Joseph and Regina (Lubinski) P.; m. Carol Elaine Petersen, Sept. 20, 1952; children—Susan Marie Pineault Fehr, Debra Carol Pineault Bauer, Verna Reinee Pineault Bonner. Student U. Minn., 1972-74, Mich. State U., 1968-69, Met. Coll., Mpls., 1970-73. Cert. safety profl. Operator No. States Power Co., Mpls., 1951-56; safety rep., supr. Continental Ins. Co., Mpls., 1956-74; loss control rep. CNA Ins. Co., Mpls., 1974-75; asst. dir. Occupational Safety and Health Adminstrn. State of Minn., St. Paul, 1975-79; mgr. occupational safety and health No. State Power Co., Mpls., 1979—; mem. faculty Inver Hills Community Coll.; cons. in safety field. Mem. Am. Soc. Safety Engrs. (pres. N.W. chpt. 1982-83, Safety Profl. of Yr. N.W. chpt. 1984), Edison Electric Inst. (safety, health com.), ASTM (F-18 com.). Democratic Farm Labor Party. Roman Catholic. Home: 5851 Central Ave NE Minneapolis MN 55432

PIÑERO, JORGE, dentist; b. Havana, Cuba, Nov. 10, 1956; came to U.S., 1961; s. Obdulio and Marta (Coto) P.; m. Basia Kowalik, Aug. 6, 1983. BS, Marquette U., 1980, DDS, 1983. Pvt. practice dentistry Milw., 1983—; hunting cons., Milw., 1985—. Mem. ADA, Wis. Dental Assn., Greater Milw. Dental Assn., NRA, Safari Club Internat. Republican. Roman Catholic. Avocations: hunting, fishing, taxidermy, conservation, carpentry. Home and Office: 7308 W Layton Greenfield WI 53220

PING, CHARLES JACKSON, univ. pres.; b. Phila., June 15, 1930; s. Cloudy J. and Mary M. (Marion) P.; m. Claire Oates, June 5, 1951; children—Andrew, Ann Shelton. B.A., Southwestern at Memphis, 1951; B.D., Louisville Presbyn. Theol. Sem., 1954; Ph.D., Duke, 1961. Asso. prof. philosophy Alma Coll., 1962-66; prof. philosophy Tusculum Coll., 1966-69, v.p., dean faculty, 1967-68, acting pres., 1968-69; provost Central Mich. U., Mt. Pleasant, 1969-75; pres. Ohio U., Athens, 1975—; dir. Nationwide Corp.; Adv. bd. Ind. Coll. Program Northwest Area Found., Council for Advancement Experiential Learning, Inst. Ednl. Mgmt. of Harvard U. Author: Meaningful Nonsense, 1966, also articles.; Editorial adv. bd.: Educational Record. Mem. Am. Philos. Assn., Am. Council Acad. Deans, Am. Assn. Higher Edn. Office: Ohio U Office of Pres Athens OH 45701

PINGLETON, JARED PHILIP, psychologist, minister; b. Tillamook, Oreg., Sept. 11, 1956; s. Philip Garland Pingleton and Rosemary Vincent; m. Linda Jo Rosenbaugh, Nov. 22, 1985. BS summa cum laude, Evangel Coll., Springfield, Mo., 1976; MA, U. Mo., Kansas City, 1978, Rosemead Sch. Psychology, 1981; D Psychology, Rosemead Sch. Psychology, 1984; postgrad., Assemblies of God Theol. Sem., 1976, U. Kans., 1978, Talbot Theol. Sem., 1982, Fuller Theol. Sem., 1983. Lic. psychologist; marriage, family, child counselor. Intern various facilities, 1975-83; family counselor Jackson County Juvenile Services, Kansas City, Mo., 1977-79; dir. 1st Family Ch. Counseling Ctr., Whittier, Calif., 1979-83; clin. psychology intern VA Hosp., Topeka, 1983-84; pvt. practice psychotherapy Midwest Christian Counseling Ctr., Kansas City, Mo., 1984—. Contbr. articles to profl. jours. Coll. pastor 1st Family Ch., Whittier, 1979-83. Named One of Outstanding Young Men Am., 1986. Mem. Am. Psychol. Assn., Am. Assn. Marriage and Family Therapy, Christian Assn. for Psychol. Studies (pres. Greater Kansas City chpt. 1987), Psi Chi, Pi Gamma Mu (pres. Mo. Omicron chpt. 1975-76). Mem. Assemblies of God Ch. Avocations: golf, raquetball, travel, reading, theater. Office: Midwest Christian Counseling Ctr 4620 JC Nichols Pkwy Suite 403 Kansas City MO 64112

PINION, ROBERT AYER, financial executive for manufacturing company; b. Chgo., Oct. 15, 1943; s. James Edward Pinion and Theresa Virginia (Bell) Lank; m. Irene Marcziwskyj, Jan. 15, 1970; children: Christopher, Peter. BS, Ball State U., Muncie, Ind., 1966; MBA, Loyola U., Chgo., 1975. CPA, Ill. Product planner RCA Corp., West Palm Beach, Fla., 1969-72; bus. devel. analyst Bunker Ramo Corp., Oak Brook, Ill., 1972-75; corp. controller Omron Electronics, Chgo., 1975-78; v.p. fin. Salerno Biscuit Co., Niles, Ill., 1978-82; controller, sr. fin. officer Chemplex Co., Rolling Meadows, Ill., 1982-86; v.p. fin. Babson Bros. Co., Oak Brook, Ill., 1986—. Served to lt. USN, 1966-69, Vietnam. Mem. Am. Inst. CPA's, Ill. CPA Soc. Avocation: soccer referee. Home: 2704 Millstone Ln Rolling Meadows IL 60008 Office: Babson Bros Co 2100 S York Rd Oak Brook IL 60521

PINKE, JUDITH ANN, metropolitan official; b. Ft. Snelling, Minn., Oct. 16, 1944; d. August Henry and Dorothy E. (Bartelt) Hinrichs; m. Kurt G.O. Pinke, June 29, 1974. B.A. cum laude, St. Olaf Coll., 1966; postgrad. Kennedy Sch. Govt., Harvard U., 1980. Supr., tchr. Mpls. Pub. Schs., 1966-71; writer/editor U. Minn., Mpls., 1971-72; counselor Secretarial Placement, Edina, Minn., 1972-73; asst. to commr. Minn. Dept. Labor and Industry, St. Paul, 1973-76; mgr. info. resources Minn. Dept. Adminstrn., St. Paul, 1976-77; asst. commr. for fin. and adminstrn. Minn. Dept. Transp., St. Paul, 1977-85; dir. met. systems dept. Met. Council Twin Cities Area, 1985—; reader advanced placement exams. Ednl. Testing Service, Princeton, N.J., 1968-71; curriculum planner, instr. Exec. Devel. Inst. Hamline U., 1986—; Producer televideo conf. presentation The Productive Office, 1984. Mem. Minn. Info. Policy Council 1979-85 chmn., 1982-85; mem. internal audit com. Met. Waste Control Commn.. Mem. Women in State Employment (co-founder 1976), Minn. Ctr. Women in Govt.(adv. bd., exec. com. 1985—, chmn. long range planning and evaluation com., 1985-86, chmn. alliances com., 1987—), Loft, Women's Transp. Seminar, Women Execs. in Govt. (founder Nat. Leadership Council, chair spl. membership task force), Women Execs. in State Govt., Horizon 100, LWV. Office: Met Council 300 Metro Sq Bldg Saint Paul MN 55101

PINKELMAN, FRANKLIN CHARLES, auditor; b. Toledo, May 2, 1932; s. Theodore B. and Henrietta M. (King) P.; m. Elizabeth Jean Kirwan, Apr. 30, 1960; children: Franklin, James, Nancy, Michael, Brian, Catherine. BS in Acctg., U. Detroit, 1957, MBA, 1963. Auditor Marvin Polewach, CPA, Birmingham, Mich., 1957-59, Miller Bailey & Co., CPA, Detroit, 1959-61, Nat. Bank Wyandotte, Taylor, Mich., 1961-64; asst. prof. U. Detroit, Mich., 1964-66; dep. auditor gen. Office Auditor Gen., Lansing, Mich., 1966-82; auditor gen. Office Auditor Gen., Lansing, 1982—; adj. prof. master pub. adminstrn. Program Aquinas Coll., Cen. Mich. U.; chmn. Govtl. Acctg. Standards Adv. Council. Contbr. articles to profl. jour. Bd. dirs. Northville Little League Baseball, 1977, 78; mem. Ad Hoc Com. on Code for Student Behavior; mem. adv. council Cen. Mich. U. Dean of Bus. Sch. Served to cpl. U.S. Army, 1953-55. Mem. Am. Inst. CPA's, Mich. Assn. CPA's, Nat. Assn. State Auditors, Comptrollers, and Treas. (exec. com.), Nat. State Auditors Assn. (pres. 1986), Govt. Fin. Officers Assn. Office: Office of Auditor Gen 333 S Capitol Ave Suite A Lansing MI 48913

PINKSTAFF, MARTIN LAVAUGHN, theatre company executive, educator, consultant; b. Crawford County, Ill., Dec. 2, 1926; s. Martin Conrad and Dorothy Alena (Taylor) P.; m. Mary Carolyn Mabry, Feb. 13, 1945 (dec. Jan. 1963); children: Martin Taylor, Curtis Howard, Christopher Lee; m. Evelyn Louise Kellams, Apr. 20, 1963; 1 child, Maria Louise. AA, Kaskaskia Coll., 1947; BS, U. Ill., 1949, MS, 1950; postgrad., U. Ill., Ind. U., Ind. State U., 1951-53, 61-63. Cert tchr., Ill., Ind. Tchr. Patoka (Ill.) Jr. High Sch., 1950-51, Wellington (Ill.) Jr. and Sr. High Sch., 1952-54, Kankakee (Ill.) High Sch., 1955-62; dist. mgr. Alliance Amusement, Chgo., 1963-68; ops. mgr. Midco Theatre Co., Mpls., 1969—. Editor NATO News, 1982—; co-author indsl. tng. film, 1985. Mem. legis. com. NATO Ind., Indpls., 1964; bd. dirs. Sesqui-Centennial Com., Terre Haute, 1966; chmn. Minn. Com. Action and Polit. Truth for Vets., Mpls., 1982—. Served with USN, 1944-46. Mem. Nat. Assn. Theatre Owners North Cen. States (hon.), SAR. Republican. Methodist. Club: Variey (bd. dirs. 1984-85). Avocations: reading, geneaology, marksmanship, weightlifting, gardening. Home: 415 Harrison Ave S Edina MN 55343 Office: Midco Theatre Co Foshay Tower Suite 1000 Minneapolis MN 55402

PINKUS, PAUL, accountant; b. Chgo., Jan. 12, 1952; s. Sam and Tola (Pszenica) P.; m. Karen Ann Lepp, June 17, 1973; children: Yehoshua, Binyamin, Batsheva, Shira, Ayelet, Shulamit, Rena, Shaina. BS in Acctg., U. Ill., Chgo., 1974; postgrad. in taxation, DePaul U., 1983-85. CPA, Ill. Staff acct. Altschuler, Melvoin & Glasser, Chgo., 1974-81, audit supr., 1981-82, audit mgr., 1982-84, audit ptnr., 1984—, chmn. mfr. and processors industry group, 1985—. Treas. Congregation Adas Bnai Israel, Chgo., 1987. Served with USAR, 1970-76. Mem. Am. Prodn. and Inventory Control Soc., Ill. Mfrs. Assn. Clubs: River. Avocations: Talmudic studies, sports. Home: 3500 W Granville Chicago IL 60659 Office: Altschuler Melvoin & Glasser 30 S Wacker Dr Chicago IL 60606

PINNELL, RICHARD TILDEN, music educator, guitarist; b. Whittier, Calif., Jan. 9, 1942; s. George William Lewis and Helen (Whitaker) P.; m. Maria Piedad Yarza, June 10, 1966; children: Anny Claudine, Nicole, Catherine Helen. student, U. Utah; BA, Brigham Young U., 1967, MA, 1969; CPhil, UCLA, 1973, PhD, 1976. Cert. community coll. tchr., Calif. Teaching fellow UCLA, 1970-75; instr. Santa Monica (Calif.) Coll., 1972-73, Los Angeles City Coll., 1972-77, Los Angeles Valley Coll., 1974-77, Mt. San Antonio Coll., Walnut, Calif., 1976-77; asst. prof. U. Wis., Stevens Point, 1977-84, U. Wis., La Crosse, 1984—. Performer, guest lectr., workshop participant. NDEA fellow UCLA, Fulbright Research fellow 1987—; research grantee U. Wis., Stevens Point, summers 1978, 79, 81; Univ. Scholar of the Yr., 1981. Mem. Am. Musicol. Soc., Am. Fedn. Musicians, Lute Soc. Am., Guitar Found. Am., U. Wis. Ctr. for Latin Am., Pi Kappa Lambda. Mormon. Author: Francesco Corbetta and the Baroque Guitar, 1980; contbr. articles to profl. jours. Home: 438 S 23rd St La Crosse WI 54601 Office: U Wis Dept Music La Crosse WI 54601

PINNEY, PATRICK CHAMBERS, teacher; b. Ashtabula, Ohio, Oct. 20, 1942; s. Harold Eugene and Jane Elaine (Chambers) P.; m. Carol Susanne Albrecht, Aug. 7, 1965; 1 child, Laura Megan. BS in Biology, Mount Union Coll., 1964; MS in Edn., Youngstown (Ohio) State U., 1985; postgrad., Kent (Ohio) State U., 1986—. cert. tchr., provisional supr., Ohio. Tchr. sci. Liberty High Sch., Youngstown, 1970—, sci. dept. chmn., 1975—; coordinator substance abuse program Liberty High Sch., 1984—. Speaker, vol. Hospice of Youngstown, Inc., 1981—. Served with USN, 1966-70, Vietnam. Named Jennings scholar Jenning Found.; recipient Outstanding Educator-Grand Cross of Color Internat. Order Rainbow for Girls, 1982. Mem. NEA, Ohio Edn. Assn., Liberty Edn. Assn., Nat. Assn. Core Curriculum, Phi Delta Kappa. Republican. Methodist. Lodges: Masons (steward 1975-79), Sunrise Order Eastern Star (chaplain/assoc. patron). Avocations: organ, piano, golf, contract bridge. Home: 205 Mansell Dr Youngstown OH 44505 Office: Liberty High Sch 317 Churchill Hubbard Rd Youngstown OH 44505

PINNOW, CURTIS CLARENCE, engineering executive; b. Chgo., June 11, 1942; s. Clarence Charles and LaVerne Anita (Holmes) P.; m. Marcia Lynn Proehl, Oct. 4, 1969; children: Cole Curtis, Tait Justin. BS in Mech. and Aerospace Engring., Ill. Inst. Tech., 1964; MBA, U. Minn., 1972. Mech. engr. Amphenol-Borg Corp., Cicero, Ill., 1963-65, Motorola Corp., Franklin Park, Ill., 1965-66; with tech. service engrs. 3M Co., St. Paul, 1966-69, supr. color image project, 1969-75, mgr. integral heating project, 1975-81; v.p. engring. Carter-Hoffman Corp., Mundelein, Ill., 1981—. Inventor cart door structure, 1985, universal adj. slider, 1986. Mem. Soc. Mfg. Engrs. (sr.), Assn. Prodn. and Inventory Control. Home: 1751 Cedar Glen Dr Libertyville IL 60048 Office: Carter-Hoffman Corp 1551 McCormick Ave Mundelein IL 60060

PINNOW, PAUL EDWARD, chemical company executive; b. Milw., Apr. 11, 1946; s. Roy Lee and Lila Viola (Uphoff) P.; m. Ellen Joanne Huntington, Aug. 19, 1967; children: Laura Ellen, Mark. BSChemE, Case Western Res., 1968; MBA, Xavier U., 1976. Plastics engr. Phillips Petroleum, Bartlesville, Okla., 1968-69; sales engr. Phillips Petroleum, Memphis, 1969-70; applications engr. U.S. Indsl. Chem., Tuscola, Ill., 1970-73; market devel. specialist, mgr. flame retardant sales. U.S. Indsl. Chem., Cin., 1973-76; mktg. mgr. Carstab div. Thiokol, Cin., 1976-81; founder, chief exec. officer Mark Chem. Corp., Cin., 1982—. Mem. Mfgs. Agts. Cin., Mfgs. Agts. Nat. Assn. (gov. commn. 1986—), Cin. C. of C. Republican. Presbyterian. Office: Mark Chems Corp 660 Northland Blvd Suite 14 Cincinnati OH 45240

PINSKY, STEVEN MICHAEL, radiologist, educator; b. Milw., Feb. 2, 1942; s. Leo Donald and Louise Miriam (Faldberg) P.; m. Sue Brona Rosenzweig, June 12, 1966; children—Mark Burton, Lisa Rachel. B.S., U. Wis., 1964; M.D., Loyola U., Chgo., 1967. Resident in radiology and nuclear medicine U. Chgo., 1968-70, chief resident in diagnostic radiology, 1970-71, asst., then assoc. prof. radiology and medicine, 1973-84, prof., 1984—; dir. nuclear medicine Michael Reese Med. Center, Chgo., 1973-87, vice chmn. radiology, 1984-87, chmn. radiology, 1987—, v.p. med. staff, 1986-87, trustee, 1984-86; dir. nuclear medicine tech. program Triton Coll., River Grove, Ill., 1974—. Contbr. chpts. to books, articles to med. jours. Served to maj., M.C., U.S. Army, 1971-73. Am. Cancer Soc. research fellow, 1969-70. Fellow Am. Coll. Nuclear Physicians (Ill. del., treas. 1982-84), Am. Coll. Radiology (alt. councilor 1986-87), Am. Coll of Radiology; mem. Soc. Nuclear Medicine (trustee 1979-87, pres. central chpt. 1980-81). Home: 1821 Lawrence Ln Highland Park IL 60035 Office: Michael Reese Hosp and Med Ctr Lake Shore Dr at 31st Chicago IL 60616

PINTER, WILLIAM DALE, health maintenance organization executive; b. Pinconning Mich., Feb. 18, 1943; s. Herman Gustav and Marie Emily (Fenwick) P.; m. Lynn Marie Stimac, Apr. 23, 1983; children—Bradford, Gregory, Jason. B.S. in Pharmacy, Ferris State Coll., 1965. Registered pharmacist, Ind., Mich. Pharmacist, Judd Drugs, Goshen, Ind., 1965-66; salesman Eli Lilley and Co., Detroit, 1966-67; owner, operator Nat. Pharm. Services, Inc., Detroit, 1968-84; v.p. pharmacy Independence Health Plans, Inc., Southfield, Mich., 1984—. Mem. Am. Pharm. Services, Nat. Assn. Retail Druggists, Mich. State Pharm. Assn., Health Maintenance Orgn. Pharmacists (Mich. sub-chpt.). Presbyterian. Office: Independence Health Plans 15565 Northland Dr Southfield MI 48075

PINTNER, JAMES DAVID, research chef; b. Lakewood, Ohio, Jan. 25, 1949; s. Roland Otto and Jeannette (Lane) P.; m. Linda Lee Iseli, Jan. 28, 1978 (div. July 1985); 1 child, Jessica Lee. Assoc. Applied Bus. in Hospitality Mgmt. Tech., Columbus Tech. Inst., 1981. Cert. exec. chef. Chef apprentice Sheraton Inn, Newark, Ohio, 1978-80; owner, operator Jim's Soup Co., Granville, Ohio, 1980-81; chef Granville Inn, 1980-83, Miller's Dining Room, Lakewood, 1983-84; exec. chef Light Touch Restaurant, Rocky River, Ohio, 1984-85; research chef Sandridge Gourmet Salads, Inc., Medina, Ohio, 1985—; cons. Pyramid Foods, Tucson, 1974-75, Am. Heart Assn., Columbus, Ohio, 1980; menu cons. Forrest Hills Country Club, Newark, Ohio, 1982; special chef CBS/Jack Nicklaus Muirfield Country Club, Columbus, 1982. Served with USN, 1967-71. Republican. Lutheran. Avocations: gourmet cooking, musical performance, sports. Home: 16 Dunbar Circle Medina OH 44256 Office: Sandridge Gourmet Salads Inc 130 W North St Medina OH 44256

PIOTROWSKI, JOHN EUGENE, manufacturing company executive; b. Chgo., Aug. 1, 1952; s. Eugene John and Doris E. (Janus) P.; m. Elena Maria Rinaldi, July 20, 1974; children—Joseph Eugene, Joy Maria. Assoc. B.S., Triton Coll., 1976; B.A., Northeastern Ill. U., 1981; M.B.A., Rosary Coll., 1985. Cost estimator Elcen Metal Products, Franklin Park, Ill., 1972-75; custom fabric estimator, buyer A.M. Castle Metals, Inc., 1975-77; plant mgr. Triton Industries, Chgo., 1977-84; plant mgr. Baron Blakeslee, Inc., Melrose Park, Ill., 1984—; mfg. mgr. Comfab Techs. Inc., Addison, Ill. Mem. Midwest Indsl. Mgmt. Assn. Avocations: hunting; boating; fishing; photography; piano. Home: 7225 Kelly Pl Downers Grove IL 60516 Office: Comfab Techs Inc Addison IL 60101

PIOTTER, GLEN WILLIAM, computer services professional; b. Oak Park, Ill., Nov. 5, 1932; s. George Carl and Myrtle Pauline (Zembke) P.; m. Mary Louise Jeude, July 31, 1954; children: Jeude, Thomas, Ann, David. BBA, Valparaiso U., 1954. Mgr. sales Continental Baking Co., Davenport, Iowa, 1956-64; zone mgr. sales Burroughs Corp., Davenport, 1964-76; dir. computer services Davenport Bank and Trust, 1976—; chief operating officer Tower Data Processing, Davenport, 1981—, Tower Network, Davenport, 1985—. Councilman City of LeClaire, Iowa, 1973-76, mayor, 1977; bd. dirs. LeClaire Elderly Housing Commn., 1978-82; advisor Citizens Adv. Com. for Hydroelectric Power, LeClaire, 1984—. Served to capt. USNR, 1951-84, Vietnam. Mem. Naval Res. Assn. (v.p. 1974-80), Res. Officers Assn. (pres. 1977), Data Processing Mgmt. Assn., Ill. Proprietary Network Assn. (bd. dirs. 1986—), Davenport C. of C. Republican. Lutheran.

PIPER, JOHN LEO, infosystems specialist; b. Des Moines, Nov. 16, 1939; s. Leo Leonard and Gwendolyn Jesse (Galloway) P.; m. Janice Jean Godfroy, Aug. 22, 1959; children: Anthony, David, Michael, Jeffery. AS, Grandview Coll., 1959. Systems analyst Am. Republic, Des Moines, 1959-66; systems rep. Honeywell Info., Des Moines, 1966-78; dir. info. service Nat. Beef Packaging Co., Liberal, Kans., 1978—. Author, editor: (video tapes) Introduction to Data Processing, 1968, 69, Data Processing Concepts, 1980. Mem. adv. com. Seward County Commmunity Coll., Liberal, 1978—; mem. Liberal Adv. Com., 1980—. Clubs: Evergreen Garden, Liberal Computer. Lodges: Elks, KC (Grand Knight 1983—), Lions. Home: 1030 N Carlton Liberal KS 67901 Office: Nat Beef Packaging Co Box 978 Liberal KS 67901

PIPER, ROBERTA BICKNELL, psychologist, writer; b. Chelsea, Vt., Aug. 3, 1928; d. Maurice Slack and Neva Marion (Bohonan) Bicknell; m. Henry Dan Piper, July 5, 1953; children: Andrew Dan, Jonathan Bicknell. BA, U. Vt., 1950; MA, Columbia U., 1952; MS, So. Ill. U., 1975, PhD, 1978. Psychologist Assoc. Psychotherapists, Herrin, Ill., 1978—. Author: Little Red, 1963. Mem. Am. Psychol. Assn. Avocations: tennis, ceramics, sailing, genealogy, fishing. Office: Assoc Psychotherapists 120 W Walnut Herrin IL 62948

PIPITONE, PHYLLIS LUIS, psychologist, educator, author; b. Chgo.; m. S. Joseph Pipitone, Aug. 28, 1948 (dec.); children: Guy, Daniel, Paul; m. Thomas A. Cox, Jan. 3, 1980. Student Chgo. Conservatory Music, 1941-44, Peabody Conservatory Music, 1945, Chgo. Tchrs. Coll., 1946-47, So. Meth. U., 1951-52; MA, U. Akron (Ohio), 1967; PhD, Kent (Ohio) State U., 1974. With B.S. & H. Advt. Agy., Chgo., 1941-43; instr. piano and theory Music Acad. Chgo.; psychologist, instr. U. Akron and Kent State U., 1970-79; pvt. practice psychology, Akron, 1967—; lectr. in field. Served with WAC, AUS, 1944-46. NIMH grantee, 1974, HEW Child Devel. fellow, 1974. Mem. Am. Psychol. Assn., Nat. Assn. Sch. Psychologists, Mensa, Council Exceptional Children, Am. Hypnosis Soc., Kent Psi Research Group, Am. Soc. Psychical Research. Clubs: Tuesday Musical, Weathervane Theatre Women's Bd., Akron Women's City, Wadsworth Women's. Home: 224 Pheasant Run Wadsworth OH 44281

PIPKORN, DONNA ELIZABETH, retired small business executive; b. Oshkosh, Wis., Apr. 29, 1921; d. Guy Plummer and Lillian (Marks) Grundy; m. Homer W. Pipkorn, June 20, 1952 (dec.); 1 child, Homer "Skip" W. BS in Edn., U. Wis., Oshkosh, 1943. Tchr. elem. schs. Manitowoc, Wis., 1943-46, Oshkosh, 1946-52; prin. Pipkorn Fuel & Supply Co., Oshkosh, 1957-70; sec.-treas. Pipkorn's, 1985—. Active del. Wis. Reps.; local chpt. chmn. ARC, 1984-85, bd. dirs., 1979—, vol. Mercy Hosp., also local chpt. blood bank; sec. Winnebago land chpt. United Cerebral Palsy, also pres. and sec. of vols.; docent Paine Arboreteum, 1977—; mem. Wis. Red Cross Territorial Disaster Team. Mem. Ladies Benevolent Soc. (sec.), Winnebago County Ret. Tchrs. Assn., Wis. Ret. Tchrs. Assn., Friends of Paine Art Ctr. and Arboreteum, U. Oshkosh Ret. Alumni Assn., Friends of Oshkosh Mus., Campfire Girls (treas. 1985—), Nat. Assn. Retired People (Oshkosh Friends of Srs.), Winnebago Rep. Women. Episcopalian. Clubs: Twentieth Century (hon., bd. dirs. Oshkosh chpt., parliamentarian 1978-79), Oshkosh Country, Power Boat. Home: 1255 Merritt Ave Oshkosh WI 54901

PIRONE, GIUSEPPE ANTONIO, sculptor, restaurateur; b. Boston, Nov. 29, 1936; s. Constantino Aurelio and Adelina (Cataldo) P.; divorced; 1 child, Constance. BA, Washington U., St. Louis, 1962; MFA, San Francisco Art Inst., 1970. Instr. art San Francisco Art Inst., 1970-71, Fleming Coll., Florence, Italy, 1970-73, Riverina Coll., Wagga, Australia, 1976-78; prof. art U. Sydney, Australia, 1978-83; owner, operator Bar Italia Caffé, St. Louis, 1983; artist in residence U. New Catle, Australia, 1978-80. Represented in one-man and group shows; exhibited in Europe, U.S., Australia. Served with USAF, 1954-58. Office: Bar Italia Caffé 4656 Maryland Ave Saint Louis MO 63108

PIRSCH, CAROL MCBRIDE, telephone company community relations supervisor, state senator; b. Omaha, Dec. 27, 1936; d. Lyle Erwin and Hilfrie Louise (Lebeck) McBride; student U. Miami, Oxford, Ohio, U. Nebr., Omaha; m. Allen I. Pirsch, Mar. 28, 1954; children—Pennie Elizabeth, Pamela Elaine, Patrice Eileen, Phyllis Erika, Peter Allen, Perry Andrew. Former mem. data processing staff Omaha Public Schs.; former mem. wage practices dept. Western Electric Co., Omaha; former legal sec., Omaha; former office mgr. Pirsch Food Brokerage Co., Inc., Omaha; former employment supr. Northwestern Bell Telephone Co., Omaha, now supr. community relations; mem. Nebr. Senate, 1978—. Bd. dirs. U. Nebr. at Omaha Parents Assn., Nebr. Developmental Disabilities Council; bd. dirs., past pres. Nebr. Coalition for Victims of Crime. Recipient Golden Elephant award; Outstanding Legis. Leadership award Nat. Orgn. Victim Assistance, Keystoner of the Month award, Contemporary Woman of Month award U.S. West Women. Mem. Orgn. Women Legislators, Tangier Women's Aux., Clubs: Pilot, Omaha Women's, N.W. Civic, Benson Republican Women's, Internat. Bus. and Profl. Women's Rep. Office: State Capitol Lincoln NE 68509

PISA, JOHN FRANCIS, newspaper promotion executive; b. Camden, N.J., Apr. 16, 1956; s. Peter Charles and Josephine (Altadonna) P.; m. Diane Marie Rakers, July 24, 1982; children: Jennifer Marie, Sarah Nicole. Student, Glassboro State Coll., 1974-76. Sales rep. Phila. Inquirer, 1976; office mgr. Phila. Daily News, Jenkintown, Pa., 1976-77; acct. mgr. Elizabeth (N.J.) Daily Jour. Levis Sales Inc., 1977-79; regional mgr. Phila. Bulletin, Woodbridge News Tribune Levis Sales Inc., Phila., 1979-80; regional mgr. St. Louis Post Dispatch, St. Louis Globe Dem., Denham Springs News Levis Sales Inc., St. Louis, 1980-82, v.p., 1982—; Guest speaker for Mktg. and Distributive Edn. Program, Wentzville, Mo., 1981, Scripps-Howard Newspapers Annual Meeting, Seattle, 1986. Mem. Internat. Circulation Mgrs. Assn. (assoc.). Republican. Roman Catholic. Home: 119 Whispering Oaks Dr Saint Charles MO 63303 Office: Levis Sales Inc 2019 Campus Dr Saint Charles MO 63301

PISNEY, RAYMOND FRANK, mus. dir.; b. Lime Springs, Iowa, June 2, 1940; s. Frank A. and Cora H. P. BA, Loras Coll., 1963; postgrad., Cath. U. Am., 1963; MA, U. Del., 1965. Asst. for adminstrn. and research Mt. Vernon, Va., 1965-69; historic sites adminstr. N.C. Archives and Hist. Dept., Raleigh, 1969; asst. adminstr. div. historic sites and museums N.C. Dept. Art, Culture and History, Raleigh, 1969-72; exec. dir. Woodrow Wilson Birthplace Found., Staunton, Va., 1973-78; dir. Mo. Hist. Soc., St. Louis, 1978—; pres. Va. History and Museums Fedn., 1977-78; pres. Mo. Museums Assos., 1982-84. Author: Historical Markers: A Bibliography, 1977, Historic Markers: Planning Local Programs, 1978, A Preview to Historical Marking, 1976, Old Buildings: New Resources for Work and Play, 1976; editor: Virginians Remember Woodrow Wilson, 1978, Woodrow Wilson in Retrospect, 1978, Woodrow Wilson: Idealism and Realty, 1977, Historic Preservation and Public Policy in Virginia, 1978. Hagley fellow U. Del., 1963-65; Seminar for Hist. Adminstrs. fellow, 1965. Mem. Am. Assn. Museums, Nat. Trust Historic Preservation U.S., Am. Assn. State and local History, Can. Museums Assn., Brit. Museums Assn., Internat. Council Monuments and Sites, Internat. Council Museums, Phi Alpha Theta. Roman Catholic. Office: Jefferson Meml Bldg Forest Park Saint Louis MO 63112-1099

PISSINI, DANIEL JOHN, controller; b. Warren, Ohio, Jan. 15, 1958; s. Donald Dominic and Rose Mary (Soletro) P. BSBA, Youngstown (Ohio) State U., 1980. CPA, Ohio. Staff acct. Coopers and Lybrand, Columbus, Ohio, 1980-82; controller Geo Energy, Inc., Columbus, 1983-87; v.p. fin. Charter Franchising Corp., 1987. Mem. Am. Inst. CPA's, Nat. Assn. Accts., Ohio Soc. CPA's, Ohio Oil and Gas Assn., Ohio Petroleum Accts. Soc. Democrat. Roman Catholic. Club: Agonis (Columbus), Columbus Italian. Lodge: Sons of Italy. Avocations: sports, music, youth orgns. Home: 6847 Fallen Timber Dr Dublin OH 43017 Office: Geo Energy Inc 3530 Snouffer Rd Worthington OH 43085

PITALIS, PAUL, insurance company executive, educator; b. Chgo., Nov. 11, 1934; s. Irving and Faye (Hellman) P.; m. Lois Ann Karno, Mar. 22, 1958; children—Lauren Beth, Rachael Joy. B.S., Ill. Inst. Tech., 1957. Vice pres. Ave. Ins. Service Chgo., 1960-70, Blvd. Ins. Services, Chgo., 1965-70, Instl. Ins. Co., Chgo., 1970-71; instr. Ins. Sch. Chgo., 1974—, Chgo. Bd. Underwriters, 1978-80; v.p. Merit Ins. Co., Chgo., 1971-85, exec. v.p., chief operating officer, 1985— ; founder, dir. Acad. of Ins., Skokie, Ill., 1984—. Author: Insurance Principles and Practices, 1975; Insurance Company Operations, 1978; (test material, course) Casualty Insurance Course, 1978. Chmn. Niles Twp. Com. Spl. Edn., Ill., 1978-84; mem. Village of Skokie Traffic Commn., 1981—; chmn. Niles Twp. Council Sch. Bds.; mem. spl. coms. on producer examinations Continuing Edn., Premium Fin. Cos., 1983—; pres. Sch. Bd. Skokie, Mem. Nat. Assn. Ind. Insurors (mem. spl. risks com. 1980—), C.L.U. Soc., Soc. C.P.C.U.s (treas. Chgo. chpt. 1978), Tau Epsilon Phi.. Club:Mensa, Old Orchard (Skokie) (pres. 1971). Lodges: B'nai B'rith, Masons. Home: 4516 Main St Skokie IL 60076 Office: Merit Ins Co 180 N La Salle Chicago IL 60601

PITCHER, GEORGIA ANN, psychologist, educator; b. Indpls., Feb. 22, 1927; d. Arling Edgar and Lyda Lucille (Doty) Pitcher; m. Donald Aubrey Baker, Aug. 21, 1948 (div.); children: Catherine Lucille, Martha Ann, Susan Jane, Daniel Pitcher. BS, Butler U., 1948, MS, 1951; PhD, Purdue U., 1969. Asst. prof. Butler U., Indpls., 1964-68; asst. prof. Purdue U., West Lafayette, Ind., 1969-74; dir. psychol. services St. Elizabeth Hosp., Lafayette, Ind., 1974-81; pvt. practice psychologist, Indpls., 1981—; assoc. faculty Ind. U.-Purdue U. at Indpls., 1985—. Contbr. articles to profl. jours. Bd. dirs. United Cerebral Palsy of Ind., 1971—; mem. protective services task force exec. com. State of Ind., 1976-77. Mem. Nat. Acad. Neuropsychology, Internat. Orgn. of Psychophysiology, Am. Psychol. Assn., Ind. Psychol. Assn., Am. Ednl. Research Assn., Kappa Kappa Gamma. Democrat. Home: 3725 E Thompson Rd Indianapolis IN 46237 Office: 537 Turtle Creek South Dr Suite 14 Indianapolis IN 46227

PITCHFORD, RAYMOND WESLEY, accountant; b. Richview, Ill., Nov. 7, 1934; s. Raymond Alfred and Margaret M. (Zapp) P.; m. Irma May Atteberry, Dec. 23, 1961; children: Linda M. Pitchford Younglove, Raymond Alan. BS in Acctg. and Fin., U. Ill., 1956; MBA, Washington U., St. Louis, 1963. CPA, Mo. Acct. Grove Labs., St. Louis, 1958-65; internal audit mgr. Am. Nat. Bank, St. Louis, 1966-67; acct. Vickers, Inc., St. Louis, 1967-69; mgr. adminstrn. Peabody Coal Co., St. Louis, 1969—. Mem. Am. Inst. CPA's. Avocation: travel. Home: 10942 Vargas Dr Saint Louis MO 63123 Office: Peabody Coal Co 301 N Memorial Saint Louis MO 63101

PITKIN, EDWARD MEYER, chemical wholesale distributing executive; b. Martinsville, Ind., July 22, 1949; s. William VanArsdale and Joan (Cravens) P.; m. Judith Ann Hackman, July 8, 1972; children—Brian Edward, Michelle, Nicole. B.A., Wabash Coll., 1971; Ind. Exec. Devel. Program, Ind. U., 1978. Trainee Dolly Madison Industries, Phila., 1969; trainee Ulrich Chem., Inc., Indpls., 1972, warehouse mgr., 1972-73, buyer, 1973-74, v.p. ops. and purchasing, 1974-76, exec. v.p., 1976-79, pres., 1979—. Mem. Nat. Assn. Chem. Distbrs. (region IV pres. 1983-85 , dir. 1983—), Am. Water Works Assn. (vice chmn. 1987, arrangements com. chmn. Ind. sect. 1978—), Ind. Mfrs. Assn., Purchasing Mgmt. Assn. Indpls., Indpls. C. of C., Chgo. Drug and Chem. Assn., Greater Wabash Found., Caleb Mills Soc., Stanley K. Lacy Exec. Leadership Series Alumni. Republican. Clubs: Ski, Columbia (Indpls.). Lodge: Rotary. Avocations: snow skiing; water skiing; jogging; scuba diving; wind surfing. Home: 10911 Brigantine Dr Indianapolis IN 46256 Office: Ulrich Chem Inc 3111 N Post Rd Indianapolis IN 46226

PITSCH, DONALD MARK, computer information scientist; b. Kenosha, Wis., July 28, 1950; s. Donald and Rose P.; m. Kim Halliday, Aug. 14, 1971; children: Jennifer, David. BS, Purdue U., 1972; MBA, Ill. Inst. Tech., 1983. Sr. programmer Gen. Fin., Evanston, Ill., 1972-74; sr. programmer, analyst Allstate Ins., Northbrook, Ill., 1974-75; data processing mgr. A.B. Dick Co., Chgo., 1975-83; dir. mgmt. info. systems Dart & Kraft Fin., Edina, Minn., 1983-86; mgr. IBM projects Computer Concepts & Services, Mpls., 1986-87; now with Bus. Records Corp., Mpls.; cons. Chgo. Data Systems, 1976. Tchr. Pax Christi Youth Mininstry, Eden Prairie, Minn., 1984—; mem. St. James Youth Ministry Council, Arlington Heights, Ill., 1984. Named one of Outstanding Young Men of Am., 1985. Mem. Assn. Computing Machinery (local v.p. 1983, 85, 87), Data Processing Mgmt. Assn., User IBM 38 User Group (v.p. 1986-87, pres. 1987—), World Future Soc., Sigma Iota Epsilon. Republican. Roman Catholic. Clubs: Purdue (2d v.p.1983-84), Evanston Football (coach 1975-76), Pax Christi Bridge, Pax Christi Social Justice. Avocations: swimming, bridge. Home: 10331 Englewood Dr Eden Prairie MN 55344 Office: Bus Records Corp 840 Colordao Ave S Minneapolis MN 55416

PITT, BERTRAM, cardiologist, consultant; b. Kew Gardens, N.Y., Apr. 27, 1932; s. David and Shirley (Blum) P., m. Elaine Liberstein, Aug. 10, 1962; children—Geoffrey, Jessica, Jillian. B.A., Cornell U., 1953; M.D., U. Basel, Switzerland, 1959. Diplomate Am. Bd. Internal Medicine, Am. Bd. Cardiology. Intern Beth Israel Hosp., N.Y.C., 1959-60; resident Beth Israel Hosp., Boston, 1960-63; fellow in cardiology Johns Hopkins U., Balt., 1966-67; from instr. to prof. Johns Hopkins U., 1967-77; prof. medicine, dir. div. cardiology U. Mich., Ann Arbor, 1977—; Pres. Cardiovascular Research Cons. Inc., Ann Arbor, 1980—. Author: Atlas of Cardiovascular Nuclear Medicine, 1977; editor: Cardiovascular Nuclear Medicine, 1974. Served to capt. U.S. Army, 1963-65. Mem. Am. Coll. Cardiology, Am. Soc. Clin. Investigation, Assn. Am. Physicians, Am. Physiol. Soc., Am. Heart Assn. Jewish. Home: 24 E Ridgeway Ann Arbor MI 48104 Office: Univ Hosp 1405 E Ann St Ann Arbor MI 48109

PITT, DAVID TALBERT, candy company executive; b. Memphis, Apr. 16, 1948; s. William Henry Sr. and Olivia (Talbert) P.; m. Jacqueline Ruth Miller, Apr. 3, 1971; children: Justin, Damon, Adam. BS in Edn., Carson-Newman Coll., 1970. Tchr., coach Cocoa (Fla.) High Sch., 1971-72; juvenille officer State of Fla., Titusville, 1972-77; regional sales mgr. Bradley Candy Co., Lebanon, Tenn., 1978-81; dir. candy/snack div. Stuckey's, Inc., Atlanta, 1981-83; dir. mktg. and sales Melster Candies Inc., Cambridge, Wis., 1983-85, v.p., gen. mgr., 1985—. Dir. Ft. Atkinson (Wis.) Football Club, 1983—, Wrestling Club, 1983—, Little League, 1986—. Named one of Outstanding Young Men Am., U.S. Jaycees, 1976. Mem. Nat. Confectioners Assn., Nat. Candy Wholesalers Assn. (young execs. sect.), Cambridge C. of C. Republican. Southern Baptist. Avocations: walking, sports, coaching, gardening, theater. Home: 1116 Madison Ave Fort Atkinson WI 53538 Office: Melster Candies Inc 500 Madison St Cambridge WI 53523

PITT, GAVIN ALEXANDER, management consultant; b. Berkeley, Calif., Aug. 4, 1915; s. David Alexander and Maude Elizabeth (Hanna) P.; m. Eleanore Whiting, Sept. 2, 1939; children: Gavin Alexander, Gaele Whiting, Judson Hamilton. AB, Brown U., 1938; MEd, Johns Hopkins U., 1959. Asst. dean Brown U., Providence, 1938-42; mgr. exec. tng. Macy's, N.Y.C., 1942-43; dir. personnel Hazeltine Electronics Corp., N.Y.C., 1943-45; asst. indsl. adminstr. AMF, Inc., N.Y.C., 1945-49; assoc. Booz, Allen & Hamilton, N.Y.C., 1949-55; dir. personnel services Gen. Dynamics Corp., N.Y.C., 1955-57; v.p. Johns Hopkins U. and Hosp., Balt., 1957-60; pres. Presbyn.-St. Lukes Hosp., Chgo., 1960-63; pvt. practice cons. 1963-66, 70-74; pres. St. John's Mil. Acad., Delafield, Wis., 1966-70; adminstrv. officer Antioch Coll., Yellow Springs, Ohio, 1974-79; devel. officer Wright State U., Dayton, Ohio, 1981-86; pres. Gavin Pitt Assocs., Inc., Dayton, 1986—; lectr. CUNY, 1948-57; exec. dir. Inst. Medicine of Chgo., 1963-66; bd. dirs. Balt. Life ins. Co. Author: The Twenty Minute LIfetime, 1959. Sec., bd. dirs. Am. Assn. Gifted Children, N.Y.C, 1985—, v.p. Chgo. area council Boy Scouts Am., 1961-66; trustee Latin Sch. Chgo., 1962-64; bd. corporators The Peddie Sch., Hightstown, N.J. Mem. am. mgmt. Assn. (personnel div. adv. council), Assn. Military Schs. and Colls., Nat. Council Chs. (gen. personnel com.), Brown U. Alumni Assn. (Brown Bear Disting. Alumnus 1961), Omicron Delta Kappa, Newcomen Soc. Club: Dayton Racquet, Engineers; Saddle and Cycle (Chgo.). Office: 625 N Michigan Ave Chicago IL 60611

PITT, GEORGE, lawyer; b. Chgo., July 21, 1938; s. Cornelius George and Anastasia (Geocaris) P.; m. Barbara Lynn Goodrich, Dec. 21, 1963; children: Elizabeth Nanette, Margaret Leigh. BA, Northwestern U., 1960, JD, 1963. Bar: Ill. 1963. Assoc. Chapman and Cutler, Chgo., 1963-67; ptnr. Borge and Pitt, and predecessor, 1968—. Served to 1st lt. AUS, 1964. Mem. ABA, Ill. Bar Assn., Chgo. Bar Assn., Phi Delta Phi, Phi Gamma Delta. Home: 600 N McClurg Ct Chicago IL 60611 Office: 120 S LaSalle St Chicago IL 60603 also: 2 Wall St New York NY 10005

PITTELKO, ROGER DEAN, clergyman; b. Elk Reno, Okla., Aug. 18, 1932; s. Elmer Henry and Lydia Caroline (Nieman) P.; A.A., Concordia Coll., 1952; B.A., Concordia Sem., St. Louis, 1954, M.Div., 1957, S.T.M., 1958; postgrad. Chgo. Luth. Theol. Sem., 1959-61; Th.D., Am. Div. Sch., Pineland, Fla., 1968, D.Div., 1977; D.Min., Faith Evang. Luth. Sem., Tacoma, 1983; m. Beverly A. Moellendorf, July 6, 1957; children—Dean, Susan. Ordained to ministry, Lutheran Ch.-Mo. Synod, 1958; vicar St. John Luth. Ch., S.I., N.Y., 1955-56; asst. pastor St. John Luth. Ch., New Orleans, 1958-59; pastor Concordia Luth. Ch., Berwyn, Ill., 1959-63; pastor Luth. Ch. of the Holy Spirit, Elk Grove Village, Ill., 1963—; chmn. Commn. on Worship, Luth. Ch.-Mo. Synod; asst. bishop Midwest region English dist., 1983; pres. and bishop English dist., 1987—. Mem. Luth. Acad. for Scholarship, Concordia Hist. Inst. Republican. Clubs: Maywood (Ill.) Sportsman; Itasca (Ill.) Country. Author: Guide to Introducing Lutheran Worship. Contbr. articles to jours. Home: 19405 Stamford Livonia MI 48152 Office: 23001 Grand River Ave Detroit MI 48219

PITTMAN, STEVEN ORR, accountant; b. Akron, Ohio, July 7, 1955; s. George Lee and Lottie Margaret (Orr) P.; m. Robin Valarie Haught, Sept. 3, 1977. BS in Acctg., U. Akron, Ohio, 1977. CPA, Ohio. Constrn. contract auditor Am. Elec. Power Service Corp., Canton, Ohio, 1977-78; staff acct. Bruner, Cox, Lotz, Syler & Graves, Canton, 1978-82, mgr. acctg. services, 1982-86, ptnr., 1987—; bd. dirs. Conley & Sons, Inc., Canton. Bd. dirs. Stark County Jr. Achievement, 1986. Mem. Nat. Assn. Accts., Ohio Soc. CPA's (pub. relations com. 1985-87), Beta Alpha Psi. Republican. Avocations: golf, sports car restoration. Office: Bruner Cox Lotz et al 500 Amerîtrust Canton OH 44702

PITTS, KENNETH ERNEST, psychiatrist, educator; b. St. Louis, Mar. 2, 1924; s. Ernest J. and Nancy (Hopkins) P.; m. Jacqueline M. Brookes, June 25, 1949; children: David, Daniel, Gregory. MD, Washington U., St. Louis, 1951. Cert. Am. Bd. Psychiatry and Neurology. Med. dir. Detroit Psychiat. Inst., 1963-70; clin. assoc. prof. Wayne State U. Sch. Medicine, Detroit, 1970—; med. dir. Orchard Hills Psychiat. Ctr., Farmington Hills, Mich., 1975—. Served with U.S. Army, 1942-45. Fellow Am. Psychiat. Assn. (rep. to assembly 1974—); mem. AMA, Mich. Psychiat. Soc. (pres. 1973-74). Avocations: golf, horseback riding, snow skiing, music. Home: 4610 Treasure Lake Dr Howell MI 48843 Office: Orchard Hills Psychiat Ctr Pc 23800 Orchard Lake Rd #201 Farmington Hills MI 48024

PITTS, ROBERT EARL, dentist; b. Bolivar, Mo., Mar. 2, 1943; s. Jesse Earl Vincent and Dorothy Mae (Hutcheson) P.; m. Barbara Dianne Carr, Apr. 24, 1974; children: Scott, Ryan, Elizabeth, Jeffry. DDS, U. Mo., Kansas City, 1968. Gen. practice dentistry Wichita, Kans., 1971-82; pres. Oral Health Care Services, Wichita, 1982—. Inventor Ice Ball Tray, 1978; author (booklet) Warning, 1982. Minister SOZO Ministries, Wichita, 1982—. Recipient 5-Year Service award Am. Cancer Soc., Wichita, 1976. Fellow Am. Acad. Gen. Dentistry; mem. Am. Profl. Practice Assn. Republican. Avocations: snow and water skiing, jogging. Office: Oral Health Care Services 804 S Oliver Wichita KS 67218

PITZ, JAMES PATRICK, state agency administrator; b. Aurora, Ill., Sept. 20, 1944; s. Bernard M. and Marie D. Pitz; m. Mary Constance Hodson, Sept. 7, 1968; children: James Randolph, Laura Ann, Kristen Joy, Cynthia Frances. BCE, Marquette U., 1967; MS in Engring., U. Ill., 1969. Registered profl. engr., Mich. Dist. bur. chief programming Ill. Dept. Transp., Springfield, 1975-76, bur. chief programming, 1976-78, dir. planning and programming, 1978-83; with U.S. Dept. of Treasury, Saudi Arabia, 1980; dir. Mich. Dept. Transp., Lansing, 1983—. Recipient Resident Engr.'s award Ill. Div. Hwys., 1970, Gov.'s award Gov. of Ill., 1972; named Outstanding Engr. of Yr., Mich. Soc. Profl. Engrs., 1986. Mem. Am. Soc. Civil Engrs. Roman Catholic. Avocations: golf, fishing, hunting. Office: Mich Dept Transp 425 W Ottawa St Box 30050 Lansing MI 48909

PITZEN, DANIEL FREDERICK, dairy nutrition company executive; b. Osage, Iowa, Oct. 10, 1944; s. Robert A. and Olivia G. (May) P.; m. Barbara G. Holmes, Apr. 15, 1967 (div. Aug. 1978); children: Jeffrey, Beth; m. Linda L. Meyer, Nov. 9, 1979; children: Rebecca, James, Charles, Jennifer. BS, Iowa State U., 1966, MS, 1971, PhD, 1974. Nutritionist Bayer Australia, Sydney, 1974-76; dir. field services Agri-King, Inc., Fulton, Ill., 1976-80; dir. nutrition Domain, Inc., New Richmond, Wis., 1980-84; pres. Dantzen, Inc., Clinton, Iowa, 1984-85; v.p. nutrition Maddy Nutrition Corp., Clinton, 1985—. Patentee Delay Cow Feeder. Mem. Am. Dairy Sci. Assn., Am. Soc. Animal Sci. Republican. Lutheran. Avocations: salt water aquarium, gardening. Home: 1137 10th Ave N Clinton IA 52732

PIVARNIK, ALFRED J., associate justice state supreme court; b. 1925. LL.B., Valparaiso U. Bar: Ind. 1951. Former Ind. circuit ct. judge Valparaiso; assoc. justice Ind. Supreme Ct., 1977—. Office: Ind Supreme Court Building 311 State House Indianapolis IN 46204 *

PIVARNIK, DAVID GEORGE, occupational health and safety manager; b. Cleve., Aug. 10, 1952; s. George P. and Mary (Revilak) P.; m. Marguerite Monroe, June 25, 1977; children: Josie Monroe, Kyle Masten. BS in Indsl. Edn., U. Wis., Stout, 1973, MS in Indsl. Safety, 1975. Cert. safety profl., Ohio. Safety rep. Liberty Mut. Ins. Co., Bala Cynwyd, Pa., 1975-76; safety supr. Olin Corp., Ashtabula, Ohio, 1976-77, mgr. health, safety, security and environ. affairs, 1978-79; mgr. health and safety aircraft components group, TRW, Inc., Cleve., 1978-86, mgr. occupational health and safety, TRW, Inc., Cleve., 1986—. Bd. dirs. Ashtabula County Cancer Soc., 1985-87. Mem. Am. Soc. Safety Engrs., Soc. Ohio Safety Engrs. (pres. 1987—). Republican. Methodist. Contbr. articles to profl. jours. Office: 1900 Richmond Rd Cleveland OH 44124

PIZZA, DONALD LOUIS, stockbroker; b. Chgo., June 7, 1936; s. Anthony JOhn and Virginia Marie (Long) P.; m. Elaine Marie Wachowski, June 20, 1959; children: Donald Edward, David Anthony, Donia Marie. BA, Knox Coll., 1958. Pres. AJP Food Products, Chicago Heights, Ill., 1970-77, Mktg. Counselors, Inc., Chgo., 1977-79, MNIC Investment Co., Chgo., 1979-80, 1st Suburban Bank, Olympia Fields, Ill., 1980-86, Continental Ill. Bank-S. Suburban, Olympia Fields, 1986; account exec. E.F. Hutton, Flossmoor, Ill., 1987—. Pres. Gov.'s State U. Found., University Park, Ill., 1985—; bd. dirs. South Suburban Hosp., Hazel Crest, Ill., 1979-86. Served to 1st lt. U.S. Army, 1959-61. Republican. Club: Olympia Fields. Avocations: golf, tennis, sailing, travel. Home: 2564 Oakwood Terr Olympia Fields IL 60461 Office: EF Hutton and Co 3203 Vollmer Rd Flossmoor IL 60422

PLAAS, JON RICHARD, pharmaceuticals executive; b. Grand Forks, N.Dak., Dec. 21, 1943; s. George Arthur and Frances Maude (Clark) P.; m. Joanne Lou Mahlum, June 26, 1965; children: Rachel, Joel, Elishia. BS in Engring. Sci., U.S. Mil. Acad., 1965; BS in Chem. Engring., Rose-Hulman Inst. Tech., 1969; MBA, Rockhurst Coll., 1984. Registered profl. engr., Mo. Prodn. supr. Pfizer, Inc., Terre Haute, Ind., 1965-71; dept. mgr. Pfizer, Inc., Lees Summit, Mo., 1971-74; engr. Marion Labs., Inc., Kansas City, Mo., 1974-78; dir. engring. Marion Labs., Inc., Kansas City, 1978-81, v.p. mfg., 1981—; bd. dirs. Mediflex, Inc., Overland Park, Kans. Mem. indsl. devel. com. Village of Lees Summit, 1983—; chmn. Sch. Dist. R-7 Citizens Adv. Com., Lees Summit, 1985—. Mem. Am. Inst. Chem. Engrs. Republican. Baptist. Lodge: Rotary. Avocations: golf, gardeninhg, woodworking. Home: Rural Rt 4 25301 Colbern Rd Lees Summit MO 64063 Office: Marion Labs Inc PO Box 9627 Kansas City MO 64134

PLACE, SHARON MARIE, social worker; b. Rockford, Ill., Aug. 11, 1947; d. Robert Ellis and Alice Elizabeth (Yagle) P. AS, Highland Community Coll., Freeport, Ill., 1972; BA, George Williams Coll., Downers Grove, Ill., 1973; MS, No. Ill. U., 1977. Registered social worker, Ill. Social worker King's Daus. Childrens Homes, Freeport, 1974-80, State of Ill., Rockford, 1981—; guest lectr. Highland Community Coll., Freeport, 1983—; social work cons. Walter Lawson Childrens Home, Rockford, 1985—. Bd. dirs. Stephenson County Assn. for Prevention of Child Abuse, Freeport, 1978-81. Roman Catholic. Avocations: fishing, gardening. Home: 145 Marcia Dr Freeport IL 61032 Office: Dept Children and Family Services 1003 Arthur Ave Rockford IL 61103

PLACKE, HARRY EDWARD, manufacturing executive; b. Canton, Ohio, Jan. 23, 1919; s. Russell Edward and Lillian Anita (Williams) P.; m. Norma Elaine Gray, Sept. 7, 1941; children: Karlene Kae, Brian Edward. BS in Indsl. Engring., Ohio State U., 1948. Foreman, engr. Dayton (Ohio) Mall Iron Co., 1948-51; v.p. Peerless Foundry, Cin., 1953-57; exec. v.p. Sidney (Ohio) Aluminum Foundry, 1957-66, Oberdorfer Foundry, Syracuse, N.Y., 1966-69, Hollander Mfg., Cin., 1971-74; pres. Sidney Pattern Works, Ohio, 1974—; cons., engr. A.I.T.E., Cleve., 1969-71; bd. dirs. S.P.M. Corp. Plaster Shop, Versaille, Ohio. Served to maj. USAF, 1941-46, PTO, 1951-53, Korea. Mem. Am. Foundrymen Soc. (pres. 1961-62), Sidney C. of C. (pres. 1965). Republican. Lutheran. Clubs: Shelby Oaks Golf. Lodges: Rotary, Masons. Avocations: golfer, photography, sports, bridge. Home: 819 Stratford Dr PO Box 299 Sidney OH 45365 Office: Sidney Pattern Works 736 VandeMark Rd PO Box299 Sidney OH 45365

PLACKOWSKI, THOMAS, accountant; b. Detroit, Apr. 26, 1947; s. Aloysius and Dolores (Stankey) P.; m. Shirlee Anne Johnson, June 10, 1970; children: Angela, Andrew J. AA, Northwood Inst., 1967; BS, No. Mich. U., 1970. Jr. acct. Reitz & LaFleche, Alpena, Mich., 1970-71, Lawrence Scudder & Co., Marquette, Mich., 1971-73; acct. Houghton Lake, Mich., 1973—; enrolled agt. Internal Revenue Agt., Washington, 1979—; fin. family counselor H.D. Vest Investment Securities Inc. Clk. Lake Township, Houghton Lake, Mich., 1979—. Mem. Nat. Assn. Enrolled Agts. Republican. Avocations: gardening, hunting, mushroom study. Home: 1461 N Michelson Rd PO Box 4627 Houghton Lake MI 48629 Office: Placks Acounting & Tax Service PO Box 427 Houghton Lake MI 48629

PLAHN, DIANA LYNN, dentist, pharmacist; b. Kansas City, Mo., Nov. 25, 1956; d. Edgar Deatly and Pansy Louise (Axsom) Hodges; m. Craig Jay Plahn, July 18, 1981. B.S., U. Mo.-Kansas City, 1980, D.D.S., 1984. Practice dentistry, St. Louis, 1984—; pharmacist Walgreen's, St. Louis, 1984-85, Dolgin's, Kansas City and St. Louis, 1980-85, Skaggs, Kansas City, 1981-84. Mem. ADA, Rho Chi. Republican. Lutheran. Avocations: orchids; needlework; crafts. Home: 646 Nanceen Ct Ballwin MO 63021 Office: 1617 S Brentwood Blvd Suite 255 Saint Louis MO 63144

PLANEK, CHARLES WALTER, lawyer, pilot; b. Chgo., July 20, 1956; s. Charles Peter and Joanne Marie (Murphy) P.; m. Linda Bodo, April 13, 1985. B.A. with honors in Econs., DePaul U., 1978, J.D., 1981. Bar: Ill. 1981, U.S. Dist. Ct. (no. dist.) Ill. 1981, U.S. Ct. Appeals (7th cir.) 1981. Assoc. French & Rogers, P.C., Chgo., 1980-83, Johnson Cusack & Bell Ltd., Chgo., 1983—. Mem. ABA, Chgo. Bar Assn., Ill. State Bar Assn., Pi Gamma Mu. Roman Catholic. Home: 339 S Home Ave Oak Park IL 60302 Office: Johnson Cusack & Bell 211 W Wacker Dr Chicago IL 60602

PLANK, DOUGLAS GENE, venture capital executive; b. Wisconsin Rapids, Wis., June 20, 1942; s. Harold George and Florence Ethelyn (Ingle) P.; m. Sharon Marie Skobba, Mar. 20, 1967 (div. Feb. 1976); children: Kimberly, Heather; m. Nancy Jean Baker, Sept. 24, 1977; children: Jane Kathryn, Gena Maxine. BA, Mankato (Minn.) State U., 1967. Rep. Paine Webber Jackson & Curtis, Mpls., 1972-75; indsl. sales rep. Merck & Co., Rahway, N.J., 1975-76; instl. sales rep. Dain Bosworth, Mpls., 1976-79; v.p. Piper Jaffray & Hopwood, Mpls., 1979-84; sr. v.p. Craig-Hallum, Inc., Mpls., 1984-87; pres., chmn. bd. dirs. Bluewater Holding Corp., Golden Valley, Minn., 1987—. Precinct capt. Jim Heap Com. Rep. State Legislature, Golden Valley., Minn., 1984. Served with USAR, 1964-70. Mem.

Twin City Bond Club, Mensa. Methodist. Home: 110 Jersey Ave S Golden Valley MN 55426 Office: Bluewater Holding Corp 7711 Country Club Dr Golden Valley MN 55427

PLANTENBERG, THOMAS MICHAEL, hospital administrator; b. St. Cloud, Minn., Oct. 2, 1948; s. William R. and Catherine J. (Barrus) P.; m. Barbara J. Burkard, June 19, 1971; children: Eric Thomas, Aaron William. BA in Mass Communications, U. Wis., Milw., 1976; MS in Adminstrv. Sci., U. Wis., Green Bay, 1987. Communications specialist NN Corp., Milw., 1975; feature writer, reporter Milw. Jour., 1976; asst. dir. communications and devel. St. Vincent Hosp., Green Bay, 1976-80; dir. planning and communications St. Mary's Med. Ctr., Green Bay, 1980-84, adminstrv. dir. mktg. and pub. relations, 1984; pres. Area Investment and Devel. Corp., 1983; cons. in field, Green Bay, 1980—. Author: (handbook) Public Affairs For U.S. Navy Health Care Facilities, 1982; editor, writer: Health Rev. mag., 1976-80. V.p. communications United Way Brown County, Green Bay, 1982-83; bd. dirs. Allouez Youth Hockey Assn., Green Bay, 1984-85, Loretta Wells Scholarship Found. (charter mem.), Green Bay, 1981—; v.p. Cystic Fibrosis "65 Roses" Club, Green Bay, 1986—; mem. mktg. com., bd. dirs. Brown County Civic Music Assn., Green Bay 1986—; mgr. Alloues Youth Soccer Assn., Green Bay, 1979-86. Served with USN, 1969-72; with USNR, 1976—. Recipient Chief of Naval Info. Mobilization award USN, 1986; named one of Outstanding Young Men of Am., U.S. Jaycees, 1982. Fellow Wis. Hosp. Pub. Relations Mktg. Soc. (sec. 1982-83, v.p. 1983-84, pres. 1984-85, bd. dirs. 1985-86, 2 awards of Excellence, 1974, 79); mem. Am. Soc. Healthcare Mktg., Wis. Soc Hosp. Planning Mktg. (pub. relations com. 1983-84), Am. Coll. Healthcare Mktg. (speaker nat. conf.), Wis. Hosp. Pub. Relations Assn. (bd. legis. rep. 1985). Roman Catholic. Clubs: DePere (Wis.) Sportsman's; U.S. Naval Inst. (Washington); Pittsfield Trap. Avocations: designing and building furniture, racquetball, hunting, classical music. Home: 535 Hilltop Dr Green Bay WI 54301 Office: Saint Marys Med Ctr 1726 Shawano Ave Green Bay WI 54303

PLASSMEYER, CRAIG EDWARD, accountant, auditor; b. Oak Park, Ill., Dec. 2, 1944; s. Louis Edward and Ruth Emma (Beyer) P.; m. Marge Marie Porta, Aug. 22, 1969 (dec. Mar. 1984); children: Wendy, Mark; m. Joan S. Buck, May 11, 1985; children: Becky, Molly. Student, U. Calif., Berkeley, 1963-65; BS in Chemistry and Math., U. Ill., 1967, MBA in Mktg., 1969. CPA, Ill. EDP cons. Arthur Andersen & Co., Chgo., 1969-72, Consumer Systems, Oak Brook, Ill., 1972-76; audit and data processor R.R. Donnelley & Sons, Chgo., 1976-80; v.p., audit dir. Heller Fin., Chgo., 1980-85, Sears Consumer Fin. Corp., Lincolnshire, Ill., 1985—; instr. data processing Harper Coll., Palatine, Ill., 1976. Treas. Green Trials Improvement Assn., Lisle, Ill., 1986-87. Mem. Am. Inst. CPA's, Inst. Internal Auditors (conf. speaker 1986-87). Avocations: sailing, tennis. Home: 6191 Shorewood Ct Lisle IL 60532 Office: Sears Consumer Fin Corp 455 Knightsbridge Pkwy Lincolnshire IL 60069

PLATER, WILLIAM MARMADUKE, English educator, university dean; b. East St. Louis, Ill., July 26, 1945; s. Everett Marmaduke and Marguerite (McBride) P.; m. Gail Maxwell, Oct. 16, 1971; children: Elizabeth Rachel, David Matthew. BA, U. Ill., 1967, MA in English, 1969, PhD in English, 1973. Asst. dir. Unit One, asst. to dean Coll. Liberal Arts and Scis. U. Ill., Urbana, 1971-72, acting dir. Unit One, 1972-73, asst. dean Coll. Arts and Scis., 1973-74, asst. dir. Sch. Humanities, 1974-77, assoc. coordinator interdisciplinary programs, 1977-83; prof. English, dean Sch. Liberal Arts Ind. U., Indpls., 1983-87; dean of faculties Ind. U.-Purdue U., Indpls., 1987—; cons. in field. Author: The Grim Phoenix: Reconstructing Thomas Pynchon, 1978, also articles, revs., poetry. Bd. dirs. Ind. Com. for Humanities, U. Ill. YMCA, Urbana, 1982-83. Recipient Program Innovation prize Am. Acad. Ednl. Devel., 1982. Mem. MLA, Midwest MLA, Am. Studies Assn. Home: 5719 Winthrop St Indianapolis IN 46220 Office: Ind U-Purdue U Adminstrn Bldg Indianapolis IN 46202

PLATT, GEORGE MILO, univ. adminstr.; b. Rapid City, S.D., Jan. 1, 1931; s. George Lee and Josephine M. (Paulson) P.; B.S., S.D. State U., 1953; M.A., Syracuse U., 1955, Ph.D., 1962. Asst. prof. U. S.D., 1962-65, U. Iowa, 1965-69; dir. planning and instl. research Wichita (Kans.) State U., 1969-79, asso. v.p., 1979—; Ford Found. adv. to secs. of local govt., East and West Pakistan, 1963, 65-66, 68. Served with AUS, 1955-57. Mem. Am. Soc. for Public Adminstrn., Am. Polit. Sci. Assn., Midwest Polit. Sci. Assn., Western History Assn., Soc. for Coll. and Univ. Planning. Author: (with Richard O. Niehoff) Local Government in East Pakistan, 1964; (with Alan L. Clem) A Bibliography of South Dakota Government and Politics, 1965, (with others) Administrative Problems in Pakistan, 1966. Home: 3527 E 15th St Wichita KS 67208 Office: Wichita State U Wichita KS 67208

PLATT, RICHARD THOMAS, insurance agent; b. Mitchell, S.D., June 12, 1956; s. Thomas Leonard and Myrth Annabelle (Roggee) P.; m. Laura Ann Herron, Dec. 29, 1984. BA with honors, U. S.D., 1978. Instr. Mitchell (S.D.) Pub. Schs., 1978-83; ins. agt. Boyd-Platt Fin. Services, Mitchell, 1983—. Bd. dirs. YMCA, Mitchell, 1984—; chmn. missions com. 1st United Meth. Ch., 1985-86. Named one of Outstanding Young Men in Am., 1983, 85. Fellow Nat. Assn. Life Underwriters (membership chmn. 1985); mem. Mitchell Jaycees (chaplin, 1985-86, named Outstanding Young Religious Leader 1984-85). Democrat. Avocations: running, swimming, photography.

PLATTHY, JENO, association executive; b. Dunapataj, Hungary, Aug. 13, 1920; s. Joseph K. and Maria (Dobor) P.; m. Carol Louise Abell, Sept. 25, 1976. Diploma, Peter Pazmany U., Budapest, Hungary, 1942; Ph.D., Ferencz J. U., Kolozsvar, Hungary, 1944; M.S., Cath. U., 1965; Ph.D. (hon.), Yangmingshan U., Taiwan, 1975; D.Litt. (hon.), U. Libre Asie, Philippines, 1977. Lectr. various univs. 1956-59; sec. Internat. Inst. Boston, 1959-62; adminstrv. asst. Trustees of Harvard U., Washington, 1962-85; exec. dir. Fedn. Internat. Poetry Assns., UNESCO, 1976—; pub. New Muses Quar., 1976—. Author numerous books the latest including: Winter Tunes, 1974; Ch'u Yüan, His Life and Works, 1975; Springtide, 1976; (opera) Bamboo; Collected Poems, 1981; The Poems of Jesus, 1982; Holiness in a Worldly Garment, 1984; Ut Pictures Poeta, 1984; European Odes, 1985; The Mythical Poets of Greece, 1985; Book of Dithyrambs, 1986, Asian Elegies, 1987, numerous other books, translations; editor-in-chief Monumenta Classica Perennia, 1967-84. Named poet laureate 2d World Congress of Poets, 1973; recipient Confucius award Chinese Poetry Soc., 1974. Mem. Internat. Soc. Lit., PEN, Die Literarische Union, ASCAP, Internat. Poetry Soc., Melbourne Shakespeare Soc., 3d Internat. Congress Poets (pres. 1976, poet laureate 1976). Office: Fedn Internat Poetry Assns UNESCO PO Box 579 Santa Claus IN 47579

PLAYFAIR, MARIANNE FENN, sales executive; b. Pitts., Apr. 4, 1955; d. James R. and Audrey (Kuchta) Fenn; m. Scott Robert Playfair, May 26, 1978. BS, Indiana U. of Pa., 1977; postgrad., St. Ambrose Coll., 1984-85. Mgr. restaurant Denny's, Inc., Pitts., 1977-78; clin. dietician Community Health Care, Davenport, Iowa, 1978-82; sales rep. Squibb, Inc., Davenport, 1982-85; div. mgr. Squibb, Inc., Cleve., 1985—; community health edn. cons. for local TV stas., Davenport, 1980-82. Democrat. Roman Catholic. Avocations: travel, internat. cooking and wines, interior design, reading. Home: 9155 Wilderness Passage Chagrin Falls OH 44022

PLEASANT, DEBORAH LEE, educator; b. Willard, Ohio, Feb. 25, 1951; d. Richard LeRoy and Martha Louise (Gill) Jacobs; m. James David Pleasant, Jr., May 22, 1971 (div.). Student Eastern Ky. U., 1969-70, Capital U., 1972-73; BS summa cum laude, Wright State U., 1977; MEd, U. Dayton, 1986. Social studies tchr. Hamilton (Ohio) City Schs., Taft High Sch., 1977-79; social studies tchr., cheerleader coach Beavercreek (Ohio) Local Schs., 1979—, mem. curriculum improvement com., 1980-86, v.p., 1981-82, pres., 1982-83; advisor Am. Field Service, 1980—; mem. sr. social studies test devel. com. for Ohio Tests of Scholastic Achievement, Ohio Dept. Edn., 1985. Vol. voter registrar, 1980—. Mem. NEA, Nat. Council Social Studies, Nat. Hist. Soc., Assn. Supervision and Curriculum Devel., Ohio Edn. Assn., Ohio Council Social Studies, Ohio Hist. Soc., Ohio Acad. History, Western Ohio Edn. Assn., Internat. Platform Assn., Dayton Area Council Social Studies (sec.), Ohio Assn. Supervision and Curriculum Devel., Beavercreek Classroom Tchrs. Assn., Greene County Hist. Soc., Kappa Delta Pi, Phi Alpha Theta. Democrat. Clubs: Capital U. Alumni (Dayton, Ohio); Am. Field Service (Beavercreek, Ohio). Office: Beavercreek Schs 2660 Dayton-Xenia Rd Xenia OH 45385

PLEGGENKUHLE, LAVERN ROSS, business educator; b. Sumner, Iowa, Dec. 13, 1942; s. Ross Otto and Esther Selma (Bergman) P. BA, Wartburg Coll., 1965; MS in Teaching, U. Wis., Eau Claire, 1976. Tchr. bus. edn. Lancaster (Wis.) Sch. Dist., 1965-69, Campbellsport (Wis.) Schs., 1969-70, West Allis (Wis.) West Milw. Schs., 1970—; mem. adv. com. Project TYPIST U. Wis., Whitewater, 1979-82. Mem. NEA, Wis. Bus. Edn. Assn. (treas. 1986—), Wis. Assn. Adults and Children with Learning Disabilities, Nat. Bus. Edn. Assn., Wis. Edn. Assn. Council. Lutheran. Avocations: photography, gardening. Office: Cen High Sch 8516 W Lincoln Ave West Allis WI 53227

PLESSINGER, JOHN ALLEN, plastics company executive; b. Greenville, Ohio, Oct. 25, 1940; s. Charles Walter and Lorine Bell (Hunter) P.; m. Lorrie E. Merdes, Apr. 10, 1971; children: Matthew J., Annie N. BFA, Dayton (Ohio) Art Inst., 1966, U. Dayton, 1966; MFA, Cranbrook Acad. Art., 1968. Design cons. Fiberglass of Ohio, Dayton, 1962-69; design mgr. Sperry Rand Spl. Products, Lebanon, Ohio, 1974—. Patentee in field. Gen. Motors scholar 1963-65; recipient composite award Reinforced Plastics Composites Inst., 1976. Mem. Soc. Plastics Engrs. (speaker 1983-86). Lodge: Rotary (speaker Dayton 1986). Office: Design Evolution 4 Inc 1004 W Main St PO Box 143 Lebanon OH 45036

PLINSKY, DONNELL DUANE, food sales executive; b. Salina, Kans., Feb. 14, 1950; s. Donnell Dean and Doris Lee (Kissick) P.; m. Beverly Jo Griffin, June 13, 1970; children: Megan, Meredith, Mandy. BS in English and Secondary Edn., Emporia State U., 1972. Tchr., coach U.S.D. 431, Hoisington, Kans., 1977-78; owner, operator Internat. Dairy Queen, Hoisington, 1978-84, Downs (Kans.) Cafe, 1984-85; dist. sales rep. F&A Food Sales Inc., Concordia, Kans., 1985—; bd. dirs. Kans.-Nebr. Dairy Queen, Hoisington. Charter mem. Hoisington Jaycees, 1983. Served with U.S. Army, 1972-76. Recipient Quality Purity award Internat. Dairy Queen, 1978-84, Silver Burger award Internat. Dairy Queen, 1978. Mem. Hoisington C. of C. (bd. dirs. 1982-84, v.p. 1983, pres. 1984, Presdl. Plaque 1984). Democrat. Baptist. Avocations: photography, softball, basketball. Home: 900 Beale Downs KS 67437 Office: F&A Food Sales PO Box 651 Concordia KS 66901

PLISKA, ROBERT JAMES, real estate executive, accountant; b. Detroit, Oct. 4, 1947; s. Peter and Marcella (Cousino) P.; m. Kathleen Marie Drean, Oct. 8, 1946; children—Jennifer, Christine. B.S. cum laude, U. Detroit, 1969; M.B.A., Mich. State U., 1970. C.P.A., Mich.; lic. real estate broker, ins. agt.; NASD registered rep. Mgr. Coopers & Lybrand, Detroit, 1970-80; v.p. Lambrecht Co., Detroit, 1980-85; v.p. Anthony S. Brown Devel Co., Inc., 1986—. Mem. nat. alumni bd. U. Detroit, 1980-82. Mem. Am. Inst. C.P.A.s (profl. edn. instr., speakers bur.), Mich. Assn. C.P.A.s (profl. edn. instr., mem. speakers bur., chmn. pub. service com. 1981-86), Mortgage Bankers Assn. (chmn. income property com.), Nat. Assn. Realtors, Mich. Assn. Realtors, Detroit Bd. Realtors, Adminstrv. Mgmt. Soc., Beta Alpha Psi. Roman Catholic. Clubs: Economic of Detroit; Fairlane (gov. 1979-83) (Dearborn, Mich.); Renaissance (Detroit), Toastmasters (v.p., speakers bur., pres., Competent Toastmaster award 1977). Home: 26011 Timber Trail Dearborn Heights MI 48127 Office: Anthony S Brown Devel Co Inc 280 W Maple Birmingham MI 48011

PLITT, HENRY G., theatre company executive. Chmn. Plitt Theatres, Inc., Chgo. *

PLOG, DEBORAH MOSER, state education program administrator. BS in Presch. and Elem. Edn., Mich. State U., 1976, MA in Instructional Devel., 1977, EdS in Ednl. Systems Design, 1982; M in Mgmt., Aquinas Coll., 1987. Pub. relations specialist Wausau (Wis.) C. of C., 1971-72, Wis. Dept. Agrl., Madison, 1972-73; tng. specialist Mich. State Police, Lansing, 1976-77; mgr. edn. program Mich. Supreme Ct./Mich. Jud. Inst., Lansing, 1977-83, adminstr. edn. program, 1983—; instr. Lansing Community Coll., 1985-87, cons., designer, developer to state agencies, 1977—. Mem. Nat. Soc. Tng. and Devel., Nat. Assn. Trial Ct. Adminstrs., Am. Soc. Tng. and Devel., South Cen. chpt. Am. Soc. Tng. and Devel., Am. Mgmt. Assn., Phi Kappa Phi, Omicron Nu. Avocations: antique collecting, needlepoint, reading, travelling. Office: Mich Judicial Inst 200 Washington Sq N 2d Floor Lansing MI 48909

PLOG, MICHAEL BELLAMY, education researcher; b. Port Angeles, Wash., May 30, 1944; s. Gerald Schneider and Rose Marie (Bellamy) P.; m. Barbara Ann Jones, Nov. 24, 1964 (div. June 1973); children: Valli Michelle, Michael David; m. Martha Jane Bailey, July 1, 1978; 1 child, Elizabeth Rose. Student, Rhodes Coll., 1962-64; BS, U. Tenn., Martin, 1966; MS, Memphis State U., 1968; PhD, U. Ill., 1975. Cert. secondary tchr., tchr. social studies. Intelligence research specialist Def. Intelligence Agy., Washington, 1968-69; tchr. social studies Paxton (Ill.) High Sch., 1970-72; asst. to dir. of research Decatur (Ill.) Pub. Schs., 1974-76; evaluation specialist Ill. State Bd. Edn., Springfield, 1976—; ptnr. Ctr. for Opinion Research, Springfield, 1979—. Author: The Rainbow Guide to Introductory Statistics, 1987; editor: Handbook for Evaluation of Special Education Effectiveness, 1982; contbr. articles to profl. jours., computer programs to mags. Georgetown U. and Ill. State Bd. Edn. fellow, 1980. Mem. Assn. Am. Geographers, Am. Edn. Research Assn., Evaluation Network, State Evaluation Network (founder, bd. dirs.), Tandy Users Club, Internat. Brotherhood Magicians (territorial rep. 1987), Springfield Magic Club. Unitarian-Universalist. Lodge: Rotary (sec. Springfield chpt. 1984). Avocations: magic, auctioneering. Home: 829 Evergreen Chatham IL 62629 Office: Ill State Bd Edn 100 N First Springfield IL 62777

PLOGER, ROBERT RIIS, retired military officer, engineer; b. Mackay, Idaho, Aug. 12, 1915; s. Robert and Elfrieda (Riis) P.; m. Marguerite Anne Fiehrer, June 13, 1939 (dec. Feb. 1982); children: Wayne David, Robert Riis III, Daniel Bruce, Marguerite Anne, Marianne Hill, Gregory Fiehrer; m. Jeanne Allys Pray, Nov. 20, 1982. BS, U.S. Mil. Acad., 1939; MS in Engring., Cornell U., 1947; MBA, George Washington U., 1963. Registered civil engr., D.C. Commd. 2d lt. U.S. Army, 1939; served in corps of engrs. U.S. Army, ETO, Okinawa, 1939-65; advanced through grades to maj. gen. U.S. Army, 1966; div. engr. New England div., 1965, comdg. gen. 18th engr. brigade, 1965-66, comdg. gen. engr. command, Vietnam,, 1966-67; dir. topography and mil. engring., Office Chief Engrs. U.S. Army, Washington, 1967-70; comdg. gen. Ft. Belvoir and commandant U.S. Army Engr. Sch. Va., 1970-73; ret. U.S. Army, 1973; engr. specialist Bechtel Power Corp., Ann Arbor, 1974-80, mgr. adminstrv. services, 1980-81; counselor SCORE, Ann Arbor, Mich., 1984—; lectr. Indsl. Coll. Armed Forces, 1962-65. Contbr. numerous articles on war and mil. engring. to profl. jours. Decorated Bronze Star with one oak leaf cluster, Purple Heart, DSM with bronze oak leaf cluster, Legion of Merit, Silver Star with bronze oak leaf cluster, Air medal, Legion of Merit, Korean Order Mil. Merit Chung Mu; recipient George Washington medal ICAF, 1965, Wheeler Medal Am. Soc. Mil. Engrs., 1967, Silver Beaver award Boy Scouts Am., Washington, 1973. Fellow Soc. Am. Mil. Engrs.; mem. NSPE (priveleged, pres. 1979-80), 29th Infantry Div. Assn. (Philadelphia award 1985), West Point Soc. Mich. (pres. 1981-84), Ann Arbor C. of C. (counselor service corps ret. execs.). Baptist. Avocations: tennis, skiing, sailboarding. Home: 2475 Adare Rd Ann Arbor MI 48104

PLOTTS, MATTHEW RAY, construction company comptroller; b. Findlay, Ohio, Feb. 3, 1959; s. Donald Eugene and Ann Janet (Kear) P.; m. Anne Louise Yingling, June 24, 1983. BS in Acctg., Tiffin (Ohio) U., 1981. Comptroller Vaughn Industries, Carey, Ohio, 1981—; bd. dirs. Village Bank, Wharton, Ohio. Coach baseball Carey Little League, 1981—; advisor Future Farmers Am. Carey High Sch., 1985—. Mem. Cen. Ohio Associated Bldg. Contractors (polit. action com. 1987—), Tiffin U. Alumni Club, Am. Legion, Sigma Omega Sigma, Carey Athletic Booster Club. Republican. Lodge: Eagles. Avocations: volleyball, archery, breeding German shepherds. Home: 11611 SH 103 Carey OH 43316 Office: Vaughn Industries SR 199 South Carey OH 43316

PLOUGH, CHARLES TOBIAS, JR., electronic research and development executive; b. Oakland, Calif., Sept. 7, 1926; s. Charles Tobias Sr. and Miriam Lucille (Miller) P.; m. Jean Elizabeth Rose, June 13, 1950 (div. May 1969); children: Charles III, Cathleen, Mark, Barbara; m. Janet Mary Ansell Lumley, July 5, 1969; children: Mark Ansell Lumley, Simon John Lumley. AB with honors, Amherst Coll., 1950; BSEE with honors, U. Calif., Berkeley, 1953. Mgr. tech. devel. Fairchild Semiconductor, Palo Alto, Calif., 1958-71; v.p. Multi-State Devices, Montreal, Can., 1971-78; mgr. research and devel. Dale Electronics, Norfolk, Nebr., 1978—. Patentee in field. Mem. IEEE. Lodge: Lions (sec. Norfolk 1982—). Avocations: golf, tennis. Home: 1405 Clark St Norfolk NE 68701 Office: Dale Electronics 2300 Riverside Blvd Norfolk NE 68701

PLUMMER, F(RED) TIMOTHY, management consultant, educator; b. Mpls., Jan. 19, 1933; s. Fred Randall and Ann Caroline (Moxness) P.; m. Patricia Margaret Beatty, Nov. 26, 1955; children: Roberta, Linda, Kathleen. BSME, U. Minn., 1955. Mgr. mfg. engring. Trane Co., LaCrosse, Wis., 1955-70; exec. v.p., ops. A.C. Group Borg Warner Corp, York, Pa., 1970-81, pres. York Can., 1976-81; dir. productivity improvement Borg Warner Corp, Chgo., 1981-86; v.p. Philip Crosby Assocs., Inc., Winter Park, Fla., 1986—. Trustee Village of Golf, Ill., 1985—, water commr., 1985—; bd. dirs. Jr. Achievement of York, instr. project bus. Mem. Soc. Mfg. Engrs., Midwest Mfg. Roundtable (charter), MAPI Mfg. Council. Republican. Christian Scientist. CLubs: Univ. (Chgo.), Valley-Lo Sports Assn. (Glenview, Ill.). Avocations: golf, skiing, swimming, piano. Home: 63 Park Ln Golf IL 60029 Office: Philip Crosby Assocs Inc 1751 Lake Cook Rd Deerfield IL 60015

PLUMMER, KENNETH ALEXANDER, hospital administrator; b. Chgo., Mar. 24, 1928; s. Alexander Oliver and Estella Marie (Koziol) P.; m. Marie M. Ricci, Oct. 10, 1943; children: Pamela, Diane, Kenneth, Stacy. Student North Cen. Coll., 1940-41, The Citadel, 1941-42, Far Eastern U. (Philippines), 1946-48. Commd. 2d lt. U.S. Army, 1943, advanced through grades to col., 1966, ret., 1973; dir. Ancilla Domini Health Services, Inc., Des Plaines, Ill., 1970-82; dir. Oak Park Hosp. (Ill.), 1982—; mem. Vets. Adv. Commn. City of Chgo., 1986-87; chmn. Village Oak Park Bd. Health; cons. Cambodian Refugee Program for Cath. Relief Services; moderator, instr. Air War Coll. Non-Resident Program; installed med. relief teams in Cambodian refugee camps; dir. Cable Program Network, Chgo.; spl. parade cons. Girl Scouts Chgo.; mem. govt. affairs com. Chgo. Assn. Commerce and Industry, 1976-79, Atty. Gen. Ill. Veterans Advocacy Com. Contbg. author Command Gen. Staff Rev., 1961-64; contbr. Mgmt. Rev. Decorated Bronze Star, Meritorious Service medal, Army Commendation medal; recipient Assn. of U.S. Army citation, 1961, Res. Officers Assn. award, 1964, Cath. Relief Service award, 1980, Ancilla Domini Sisters award, 1980. Mem. Mil. Order World Wars (comdr. 1962-63), Hosp. Pub. Relations Soc., Chgo. Council on Fgn. Relations, Assn. U.S. Army, Ret. Officers Assn., Am. Hosp. Assn., Cath. Hosp. Assn. Roman Catholic. Club: Oak Park. Home: 415 N Elmwood St Oak Park IL 60302 Office: Oak Park Hosp Ctr 715 Lake St Oak Park IL 60304

PLUMMER, RICHARD DUANE, city manager; b. Emporia, Kans., Aug. 8, 1930; s. Robert Fleming and Roberta (Hamlin) P.; B.S., Kans. State Tchrs. Coll., Emporia, 1955, M.S., 1963; m. Audrey Myrtle Ogden, Dec. 19, 1954; children—Terri Lynne, Richard Duane II, Ross Delevan. Auditor, Kans. Power & Light Co., 1956-64; controller Kans. Transp. Dept., Commn., Topeka, 1964-77; asst. dir. Ariz. Dept. Econ. Security, 1977; controller Kans. Supreme Ct., 1978-80; bus. mgr. Marymount Coll., Salina, Kans., 1980; city adminstr. Horton, Kans., 1981, city mgr. Larned, Kans., 1982-84 . Mem. Seaman High Sch. Dist. 345 Sch. Bd., 1971-77, pres., 1971-75. Served with USAF, 1950-53. Mem. Internat. City Mgrs. Assn. Lodge: Rotary. Office: PO Box 70 Larned KS 67550

PLUNKETT, MELBA KATHLEEN, mfg. co. exec.; b. Marietta, Ill., Mar. 20, 1929; d. Lester George and Florence Marie (Hutchins) Bonnett; student public schs.; m. James P. Plunkett, Aug. 18, 1951; children—Julie Marie Plunkett Hayden, Gregory James. Co-founder, 1961, since sec.-treas., dir. Coils, Inc., Huntley, Ill. Mem. U.S. C. of C., U.S. Mfg. Assn., Ill. C. of C., Ill. Notary Assn. Roman Catholic. Home: Route 1 Sleepy Hollow Rd West Dundee IL 60118 Office: 11716 Algonquin Rd Huntley IL 60142

PLUNKETT, PAUL EDWARD, judge; b. Boston, July 9, 1935; s. Paul M. and Mary Cecilia (Erbacher) P.; m. Martha Milan, Sept. 30, 1958; children: Paul Scott, Steven, Andrew, Kevin. B.A., Harvard U., 1957, LL.B., 1960. Asst. U.S. atty. U.S. Atty.'s Office, Chgo., 1963-66; ptnr. Plunkett Nisin et al, Chgo., 1966-78, Mayer Brown & Platt, Chgo., 1978-83; judge U.S. Dist. Ct. (no. dist.) Ill., Chgo., 1983—; adj. faculty John Marshall Law Sch., Chgo., 1964-76, 82—, Loyola U. Law Sch., Chgo., 1977-82. Mem. Fed. Bar Assn. Clubs: Legal, Law, Union League (Chgo.). Office: US Courthouse 219 S Dearborn Chicago IL 60604 *

PLUSHNIK-HEINZMAN, KAREN ELIZABETH, contract specialist; b. Detroit, July 23, 1949; d. Alfred Andrew and Esther Martell (James) Plushnik; m. Jack Roy Wagner, Feb. 9, 1973 (div. Oct. 1978); m. Howard Joseph Heinzman, Oct. 3, 1983. AA, Macomb County Community Coll., 1975; BA, U. Pitts., 1978. Contract specialist U.S. Tank Automotive Command, Warren, Mich., 1979—. Mem. Govt. Contractors Assn. (sec. 1981-86), Nat. Contract Mgmt. Assn. (sec. 1984-86). Avocations: travelling, reading, golf. Home: 28580 Aspen Dr Warren MI 48093 Office: US Tank Automotive Command Warren MI 48397-5000

PLUSQUELLIC, DONALD L., mayor; b. Akron, Ohio, July 3, 1949; m. Mary Plusquellic; children: Dave, Michelle. BS, Bowling Green State U., 1972; JD, U. Akron, 1981. Councilman Akron City Council, 1973-81, councilman-at-large, 1982-86, council pres., 1984-86; mayor City of Akron, 1987—. Home: 2785 Nesmith Lake Blvd Akron OH 44314 Office: City of Akron Office of the Mayor 200 Municipal Bldg Akron OH 44308

POCOCK, JACK ELLIOTT, marketing executive; b. Delaware, Ohio, Nov. 18, 1925; s. Ralph Hensil and Gertrude Lucile (Elliott) P.; m. Marijane Williams, Aug. 10, 1946; children—Cheryl, Frederick, Robert. B.S. in Mech. Engring., Ill. Inst. Tech., 1946. Design engr. Hughes Keenan Corp., Delaware, Ohio, 1946-50; prodn. mgr. Edmont Mfg. Co., Coshocton, Ohio, 1950-57; sales mgr. Suburban Motor Freight, Columbus, Ohio, 1957-70; v.p. mktg. Central Silica Co., Zanesville, Ohio, 1970—. Mem. bd. dirs. Grace Methodist Ch., Zanesville, 1957-85; trustee Bethesda Hosp., Zanesville, 1972-85; active ARC, Am. Cancer Soc. Served with USN, 1943-46. Republican. Club: Sales Exec. (Coshocton) (pres. 1955). Lodges: Masons, Elks, Kiwanis (Zanesville, pres. 1968). Home: 3335 Winding Way Zanesville OH 43701 Office: Cen Silica Co 806 Market St Zanesville OH 43701

POCS, EUGENE, engineering educator; b. Atašiene, Latvia, Nov. 20, 1932; s. Francis and Paulina P.; m. Mara Vilkauss, Aug. 24, 1957; children: Paul, Martin, Arnis, David. Student, Herzl Jr. Coll., 1952-53, U. Ill. Navy Pier, 1956-57; BS in Mech. Engring., U. Ill., 1959, MS, 1960; postgrad., Beloit Coll., 1961, No. Ill. U., 1967-80, Bklyn. Poly. Inst., 1971, Western Ill. U., 1971, Milw. Sch. Engring., 1980. Research engr. N. Am. Aviatiion, Downey, Calif., 1959; project engr. Ingersoll Milling Machine Co., Rockford, Ill., 1960-65; prof. engring. Rock Valley Coll., Rockford, 1966—; cons. in field, 1965—. Contbr. articles to Latvian pubs. Leader Boy Scouts Am., Rockford, 1970-75. Served as cpl. USAR, 1953-55. NSF fellow, 1971. Am. Soc. for Engring. Edn., Latvian Cath. Student Assn. (bd. dirs. 1985-86). Roman Catholic. Club: Empirical Investors (Rockford) (pres. 1964-84). Lodge: Friz-Proz-Pref (treas. 1961—). Avocations: photography, travel, reading, financial analysis, scholarly research.

POCZATEK, SHARON BONNIE, dentist; b. Chgo., Sept. 19, 1952; d. William John and Janet Bernice (Swietek) P.; m. Mark E. Klein, Dec. 28, 1977; children: Joseph Collin Poczatek, Mark Andrew Poczatek, Sharon Elizabeth Klein. BS, U. Ill., Chgo., 1975, DDS, 1977. With Chgo. Bd. Health, 1977-78; chief dental officer USPHS, Pine Ridge, S.D., 1978-80; gen. practice dentistry Mundelein, Ill., 1980-83, Chgo., 1984—; cons. U. Ill. Dental Sch., Chgo., 1977. Author (dental newsletter) Word of Mouth, 1982. Mem. Jr. Women's Club of Mundelein, 1981. Named one of Outstanding Young Women of Am., 1980. Mem. ADA (cons. 1977, 84), Am. Assn. Women Dentists. Democrat. Charismatic. Avocation: photography.

PODBOY, ALVIN MICHAEL, JR., lawyer, librarian; b. Cleve., Feb. 10, 1947; s. Alvin Michael and Josephine Esther (Nagode) P.; m. Mary Ann Gloria Esposito, Aug. 21, 1971; children: Allison Marie, Melissa Ann. AB cum laude, Ohio U., 1969; JD, Case Western Res. U., 1972, MLS, 1977. Bar: Ohio 1972, U.S. Dist. Ct. (no. dist.) Ohio 1973. Assoc. Joseph T. Svete Co. LPA, Chardon, Ohio, 1972-76; dir. pub. services Case Western Res. Sch. Law Library, Cleve., 1974-77, assoc. law librarian, 1977-78; librarian Baker & Hostetler, Cleve., 1978—. Bd. overseers Case Western Res. U., 1981—, mem. vis. com. sch. library sci., 1980-86, mem Westlaw adv. bd., 1987—; chmn. Case Western Res. Library Sch. Alumni Fund, 1979-80. Rep. precinct committeeman Cuyahoga County, Cleve., 1981-87, mem. exec. com., 1984—. Served to 1st lt. USAF, 1972. Mem. ABA, Ohio State Bar Assn., Cleve. Bar Assn., Am. Assn. Law Libraries (cert.), Ohio Regional Assn. Law Libraries (pres. 1985), Case Western Res. U. Library Sch. Alumni Assn. (pres. 1981), Arnold Air Soc., Pi Gamma Mu, Phi Alpha Theta. Roman Catholic. Club: Citizens League (Cleve.). Lodge: K.C. Avocations: alpine skiing, boating. Home: 4637 Anderson Rd South Euclid OH 44121 Office: Baker & Hostetler 3200 National City Ctr Cleveland OH 44114

PODOLIN, LEE JACOB, health care executive; b. Buffalo, Oct. 23, 1930; s. David J. and Helen J. (Feldman) P.; B.A., U. Rochester, 1952; M.P.A., Syracuse U., 1953; M.P.H., Yale U., 1959, m. Catherine McIntosh, Nov. 22, 1956; 1 son, George Philip. Statis. analyst Eastman Kodak Co., Rochester, N.Y., 1956-57; asst. dir. Montefiore Hosp., N.Y.C., 1958-63; dir. facility planning Health & Hosp. Planning Corp., N.Y.C., 1963-68; exec. dir. Met. Health Planning Corp., Cleve., 1968-76; exec. dir. Milw. Regional Med. Center, 1976-83; cons. Glunz-Strathy Assocs., Milw., 1983-84; exec. dir. Univ. Physicians Milw. Clin. Campus Practice Plan, Inc., 1984—; clin. instr. U. Wis. Med. Sch., 1984—; asst. clin. prof. Med. Coll. Wis., Milw., 1976—; adj. asst. prof. Case Western Reserve U., Cleve., 1970-76; adj. instr. Ohio State U., Columbus, 1974-76; mem. med. assistance adv. council Dept. HEW, 1970-72. Trustee Village of Fox Point, 1980-86, North Shore Library, 1980-87; bd. dirs. Fox Point Found., 1980-81. Served with U.S. Army, 1953-56. Fellow Am. Pub. Health Assn.; mem. Am. Assn. for Comprehensive Health Planning (trustee 1973-76), Am. Hosp. Assn., Am. Coll. Hosp. Adminstrs. Club: Univ. (Mil.). Home: 7415 N Lombardy Rd Fox Point WI 53217 Office: 950 N 12th St PO Box 477 Milwaukee WI 53201

POE, EARL JOHN, III, sales executive; b. St. Louis, Oct. 26, 1950; s. Earl J. and Mildred (Kennedy) P.; m. Caryn Ann Fikes, Dec. 29, 1972; children: John, Andy. BSCE, U. Mo., Rolla, 1973, MS in Engring. Mgmt., 1976. Estimator J.S. Alberici, St. Louis, 1973-77, project mgr., 1977-80; v.p. sales Crescent Planing Mill Co., St. Louis, 1980—; stp. instr. AGC of St. Louis, 1979—. Mem. Am. Soc. Engring. Mgmt. Clubs: Westborough, Town and Country (St. Louis). Lodge: Rotary (dir. 1987—). Avocations: sailing, skiing, golfing, tennis. Home: 1334 Rusticview Manchester MO 63011 Office: Crescent Planing Mill Co 3227 N 9th Saint Louis MO 63147

POE, STEVEN DEE, osteopathic physician; b. Newton, Iowa, Nov. 16, 1950; s. Donald Eugene and Doris (Berry) P. BS cum laude, Lincoln U., 1974; DO, Kirksville Coll. Osteo. Medicine, 1979. Cert. Am. Bd. Osteo. Emergency Medicine. Intern, Jacksonville (Fla.) Gen. Hosp., 1979-80; resident in emergency medicine U. Hosp. Jacksonville, 1980-82, chief resident, 1981-82; assoc. in emergency medicine Emergency Physicians, Inc., Jacksonville, 1982-83; dir. emergency medicine Normandy Osteo. Hosp., St. Louis, 1983—; dir. ambulance service Normandy Hosps.; med. dir. Normandy Fire Protection Dist.; dir. Healthcare Place N.W. Plaza, St. Louis, 1984—; assoc. prof. emergency medicine Kirksville Coll. Osteo-Medicine, 1983—, New Eng. Coll. Osteo. Medicine, 1985—; dir. emergency medicine residency program Normandy Hosp., 1986—; assoc. lectr. St. Louis Community Coll., 1983—; resident liaison Jacksonville Bd. Fire Surgeons, 1981-82. Served with USMC, 1969-71. Mem. Am. Coll. Emergency Physicians (pub. relations com., govt. affairs com. Mo. chpt.), Am. Osteo. Assn., Mo. Emergency Physicians, Mo. Osteo. Assn., Am. Coll. Osteo. Emergency Physicians, St. Louis Osteo. Assn., Beta Kappa Chi. Republican. Methodist. Avocations: flying, fishing, boating, snow skiing, hunting. Office: Normandy Osteopathic Hosp N and S 7840 Natural Bridge Saint Louis MO 63121

POEHLER, JEFFREY CHARLES, dentist; b. St. Paul, Aug. 9, 1946; s. Kenneth Merrill and Elizabeth Ann (Harmon) P.; m. Muriel Jo Wollack, Jan. 4, 1975; children: Diana Jean, Carrie Lorena. BA, U. Minn., 1969, DDS, 1971. Assoc. dentist Little Falls, Minn., 1973-74; ptr. Little Falls, 1975—. Active choir First United Ch., Little Falls, 1974—, tchr. Sunday Sch. 1981, various coms. 1975—; ministry of outreach UCC Minn. Conf., 1983-86, sec. 1984-85, chmn. 1986. Served to capt. U.S. Army, 1971-73, Vietnam. Decorated Bronze Star. Mem. ADA, Minn. Dental Assn., W. Cen. Dist. Dental Soc., Soc. for the Protection and Encouragement of Barber Shop Quartet Singing in Am. (sec. 1975-77, show chmn. 1976, program v.p. 1979). Avocations: model railroading, travel, singing, piano, weight lifting. Home: Rural Rt 1 Box 129 Royalton MN 56373 Office: Berguson & Poehler PA 74 SE 1st Ave Little Falls MN 56345

POETTER, BRUCE E., real estate executive; b. Berwyn, Ill., May 28, 1951; s. Robert K. and Nancy Marie (Classen) P.; m. Barbara Jo Nylander, Oct. 11, 1975; children: Brian E., Bradley J. BA, Hope Coll., 1974. Real estate appraiser Thorsen Realtors, Oak Brook, Ill., 1974-77, chief appraiser, 1977-81; asst. v.p. Coldwell Banker, Oak Brook, 1981-83, v.p., regional mgr., 1983—; real estate instr. Ill. Dept. Edn., Springfield, 1977—. Mem. Soc. Real Estate Appraisers (bd. dirs., chmn. Chgo. chpt. edn. com., pub. relations com. 1976-84, life mem. young adv. council 1981, sr. instr. 1979—), Am. Inst. Real Estate Appraisers (edn. com., pub. relations 1978-82), Am. Soc. Real Estate Counselors, Appraisal Inst. Republican. Presbyterian. Avocations: antique cars, boating, flying. Office: Coldwell Banker 1900 Spring Rd #400 Oak Brook IL 60521

POFAHL, ALVIN GEORGE, insurance agent; b. Jamaica, N.Y., Mar. 31, 1937; s. Alvin Frank and Ella Marie (Kelley) P.; m. Bonita Marie Farrah, Aug. 13, 1960 (div. 1985); children: Brian, Andrea, Kelley, Carolyn; m. Rosemary Palermo, Aug. 11, 1986. BS, U. Wis., 1959, Purdue U., 1962. CLU. Tchr. Cambridge (Wis.) High Sch., 1959-61, Highland Park (Ill.) High Sch., 1961-63; spl. agt. Northwestern Mutual Life, Waukegan, Ill., 1963-65; supr. Northwestern Mutual Life, Aurora, Ill., 1965-73; gen. agt. Northwestern Mutual Life, Elgin, Ill., 1973—; past pres. Aurora Area Life Underwriters. Mem. Gen. Agts. & Mgrs. Conf. (Nat. Mgmt. award), Ill. West Suburban CLU Chpt. (past. pres.), Elgin Area Life Underwriters. Republican. Roman Catholic. Lodge: Rotary (past pres. Elgin). Home: 135 Knockderry Ln Inverness IL 60067 Office: Northwestern Mutual Life 72 N Alfred St Elgin IL 60123

POFAHL, JAMES WILLARD, direct mail executive; b. Faribault, Minn., Apr. 8, 1942; s. James W. and Betty Ann (Orban) P.; m. Jean Carol Voxland, June 12, 1966 (div. July 1973); m. Mary Katherine Ryan, Apr. 5, 1974; children: Kristen Ann, Pamela Jo. BA, Luther Coll., 1964; MBA, U. Chgo., 1966; postgrad., Ohio State U., 1966-67. CPA, Minn. Staff Arthur Andersen & Co., Mpls., 1967-71; acct. The Toro Co., Bloomington, Minn., 1971-74; adminstr. Rubins, Zelle, Larson & Kaplan, Mpls., 1974-77; cons. Bouley, Heutmaker, Zibell & Co., Edina, Minn., 1977-78; controller Dimensional Displays & Design, St. Paul, 1978-79; dir. adminstrn. Nasco Internat., Ft. Atkinson, Wis., 1979—; instr. Lakewood Community Coll., White Bear, Minn., 1977, Inver Hills Community Coll., Inver Grove Heights, 1978-81, Upper Iowa U., Madison, Wis. 1986, Lakeland Coll., Madison, 1985-87; tax preparation cons., Plymouth, Minn., Ft. Atkinson, 1974—; advisor Bus. World; speaker various socs. Contbr. articles to profl. jours. Bd. dirs. Computer Uses for Edn., Mpls., 1976-78. Mem. Am. Inst. CPA's, Minn. Soc. CPA's (com. chmn. 1977-78, instr. 1978), Wis. Inst. CPA's. Lutheran. Home: 1105 Miller Ln Fort Atkinson WI 53538 Office: Nasco Internat 901 Janesville Ave Fort Atkinson WI 53538

POGUE, THOMAS FRANKLIN, economics educator, consultant; b. Roswell, N.Mex., Dec. 28, 1935; s. Talmadge Franklin and Lela (Cox) P.; m. Colette Marie LaFortune, June 3, 1961; children—Michael Frederick, Robert Franklin. B.S., N.Mex. State U., 1957; M.S., Okla. State U., 1962; Ph.D., Yale U., 1968. Asst. prof. econs. U. Iowa, Iowa City, 1965-69, assoc. prof., 1970-75, prof., 1975—, chmn. dept., 1983-84; vis. prof. Tex. Tech. U., Lubbock, 1975-76, U. Adelaide, Australia, 1985. Author: Government and Economic Choice, 1978. Contbr. articles to profl. jours. Author, researcher Gov.'s Tax Study, State of Iowa, Des Moines, 1967, Minn. Tax Study Commn., St. Paul, 1984, Iowa Econ. Devel. Policy Study, 1986-87, Iowa Econ. Devel. Plan, Des Moines, 1987. Served to capt. USAF, 1957-60. Grantee Nat. Inst. Justice, Washington, 1978-79, Consumers Research Group, Washington, 1970, HUD, 1970. Mem. Am. Econ. Assn., Nat. Tax Assn. Democrat. Presbyterian. Avocation: tennis. Home: 3 Wellesley Way Iowa City IA 52240 4ffice: U Iowa Phillips Hall Dept Econs Iowa City IA 52242

POGUE, WILLIAM ALEXANDER, diversified company executive; b. Birmingham, Ala., 1927. B.S., U.S. Mil. Acad., 1950. Various depts. engring., mfg., field constrn. Chgo. Bridge & Iron Co., 1954-57, sales engr. N.Y. Sales Office, 1957-64, sales mgr., 1964-68, mgr. Houston ops., 1968-71, v.p., mgr. So. area ops., 1971-76, sr. v.p., mgr. ops., 1976-79, exec. v.p., dir., 1979—; sr. v.p. CBI Industries Inc., Hinsdale, Ill., 1979-81, pres., 1981-82, chmn. bd., chief exec. officer, 1982—, chmn. bd., 1982—; dir. No. Trust Co., Nalco Chem. Co. Served to capt. U.S. Army, 1945-54; served with USN. Office: CBI Industries Inc 800 Jorie Blvd Oak Brook IL 60522-7001

POHL, ALAN LAWRENCE, plastic surgeon; b. Buffalo, Jan. 1, 1938; m. Carol Castleman; children: James, Andrew, Harold. Student, U. Buffalo, 1955-58, MD with honors, 1962; MS in Surgery, Tufts U., 1967. Cert. Am. Bd. Plastic Surgery, Am. Bd. Surgery, Nat. Bd. Med. Examiners. Intern Buffalo Gen. Hosp., 1962-63; resident in gen. surgery Tufts-New Eng. Med. Ctr., Boston, 19663-65, 66-68, fellow in surg. physiology, 1968; resident in plastic surgery U. Tex., Galveston, 1970-73; practice medicine specializing in plastic and reconstructive surgery Milw., 1970—. Contbr. articles to profl. jours. Served to lt. commdr. USN, 1968-70, Vietnam. Mem. ACS, AMA, Am. Soc. Plastic and Reconstructive Surgeons, Midwestern Assn. Plastic Surgeons, Wis. Soc. Plastic Surgeons, Milw. County Med. Soc., Wis. Med. Soc., Singleton Surg. Soc., Sigma Xi, Alpha Omega Alpha. Office: 10425 W North Ave Milwaukee WI 53226

POHL, KENNETH ROY, electronics company executive; b. Beloit, Wis., Nov. 11, 1941; s. Walter John and Ruth Margret (Wieck) P. Student Wis. State Coll., Whitewater, 1959-60, Milton Coll., 1963-66; A.A. in Liberal Arts. With Beloit Corp., 1960-63; mgr. trainee Faimly Fin. Corp., 1966; with Chrysler Corp., 1966-67; owner, operator bowling alley and lounge, 1967-68; with Automatic Electric Co., Genoa, Ill., 1968-69; buyer Fox Corp., Janesville, Wis., 1969-70; materials mgr. Clinton Electronic Corp., Loves Park, Ill., 1970-72, import-export mgr., supr. sales adminstrn., 1972-80, import-export mgr., corp. gen. traffic mgr., 1980—, distbn. mgr., 1981—; pres., chief exec. officer Tan Spa of Northgate Plaza Ltd., Beloit; dir. Air-Pack Enterprises Inc., Schaumburg, Ill. cons. internat. transp.; mem. Midwest Shippers Adv. Fed. Maritime Commn. Founder, exec. dir. Tri-State All Star Bowling Assn.; adv. Ladies Profl. Tournament Bowlers. Mem. Am. Prodn. and Inventory Control Soc., Nat. Maritime Council (Midwest advisors, Clipper Patriot award 1986), U.S. Trotting Assn., Ill. State C. of C. (internat. com. for trade and investments). Lutheran. Clubs: Lions, Rock River Valley Traffic (Hall of Fame); World Trade (charter mem.) (Northern, Ill.). Home: PO Box 561 Clinton WI 53525 Office: 6701 Clinton Rd Box 2277 Loves Park IL 61131

POHL, ROBERT BRYANT, psychiatrist, researcher; b. Windsor, Ont., Can., Sept. 6, 1948; s. John Bryant and Jeannette (Demers) P.; m. Linda Therese Ray; children: Steven, Kristin, Elisabeth. MD, Wayne State U., 1973. Diplomate Am. Bd. Psychiatry and Neurology. Resident in psychiatry Lafayette Clinic, Detroit, 1973-76; asst. prof. Wayne State U., Detroit, 1978-87, assoc. prof., 1987—, dir. psychiat. residency programs, 1982—; dir. outpatient dept. Lafayette Clinic, Detroit, 1979—, co-dir. anxiety research program, 1982—; Contbr. articles to profl. jours. Mem. Am. Psychiat. Assn., Soc. Biol. Psychiatry. Office: Lafayette Clinic 951 E Lafayette Detroit MI 48098

POHLAD, CARL R., professional baseball team executive, bottling company executive; b. West Des Moines, Iowa. Ed., Gonzaga U. With MEI Diversified, Inc., Mpls., 1959—, chmn. bd., 1976—; pres. Marquette Bank Mpls., N.A., pres., dir.; pres., dir. Bank Shares, Inc.; owner Minn. Twins, 1985—, also dir.; dir. Meth. Hosp. Adminstrv. Group, T.G.I. Friday's, Tex. Air Corp., Continental Air Lines, Inc. Office: MEI Diversified Inc 90 S 6th St Minneapolis MN 55402

POHLMAN, CARLYLE GEORGE, accountant; b. Lakefield, Minn., Aug. 31, 1931; s. George Reinhold and Lillian (Burmeister) P.; m. Marion Milbrath, Aug. 10, 1952; children: Scott, Laurie Sue, Lisa. BBA, U. Minn., 1953. Mem. staff Touche Ross & Co., Mpls., 1955-65, adm. ptnr., 1965-75, dir. audit ops., 1975-80, assoc. ptnr. in charge, 1980-82, ptnr. in charge, 1982—. Commodore Mpls. Aquatennial Assn., 1984; bd. dirs., v.p devel. United Arts Council, St. Paul, 1985-87. Served to 1st lt. USAF, 1953-55. Mem. Nat. Ass. Accts. (pres. Mpls. chpt. 1966-67, nat. bd. dirs. 1967-68), Minn. Soc. CPA's (bd. dirs. 1982-85). Lutheran. Clubs: Minneapolis, Mpls. Athletic; Minnesota (St. Paul); Golden Valley (Minn.) Country. Home: 6051 Laurel Ave Golden Valley MN 55416 Office: Touche Ross & Co 900 Pillsbury Ctr Minneapolis MN 55402

POHLMAN, MICHAEL JOSEPH, social worker; b. Saginaw, Mich., Sept. 6, 1947; s. Carl Henry and Burnetta Frances (Nentwig) P.; m. Susan Frances Schachtner, Oct. 17, 1969; children: Michael, Jeremy, Kara Lynn. BA, Saginaw Valley State Coll., 1969. Lic. social worker, Mich. Aftercare therapist Regional Cons. Ctr., Saginaw, 1969-70; child therapist Kalamazoo State Hosp., 1970-80; group therapy leader St. Joseph Lodge, Kalamazoo, 1974-77; dir. community placement, mem. adminstrv. staff Pheasant Ridge Ctr., Kalamazoo, 1981—; also hosp. contract mgr. for fifteen counties Pheasant Ridge Ctr., 1985—; mem. Mental Health Placement Coordinators Com., 1985—. Coordinator United Way Drive for Pheasant Ridge Ctr., 1983-86; pres. St. Monica Ch. Parish Council, Kalamazoo, 1986-88;. Republican. Roman Catholic. Lodge: Rotary (editor 1982-85, sec. 1982-84, treas. 1984-86). Avocations: bass fishing, landscaping, flower gardening. Home: 7141 Carlsbrook Portage MI 49081 Office: Pheasant Ridge Ctr 1312 Oakland Dr Kalamazoo MI 49008

POHLMAN, TIMOTHY LEE, dentist; b. Cin., Jan. 12, 1947; s. Harold C. and Irene Marie (McHugh) P.; m. Jody Ann Phillian, Aug. 10, 1974; 1 child, Gunnar Erik. Student pre-dentistry, U. Cin., 1965-68; DDS, Ohio State U., 1972. Staff dentist Cin. Health Dept., 1974-75; gen. practice dentistry Cin., 1975—. Pres. Assemblies Cin., 1982; bd. dirs. Hist. S.W. Ohio, Cin., 1986—. Served to lt. USN, 1972-74. Mem. ADA, Ohio Dental Assn. (del. 1986—), Cin. Dental Assn. (treas. 1983-85, v.p., chmn. fin. com. 1986, pres. elect 1987), T.I. Way Dental Forum (pres. 1983), Hyde Park Bus. Assn. (bd. dirs. 1977-80). Republican. Roman Catholic. Club: Wyoming (Ohio) Golf. Avocations: golf, tennis, swimming. Home: 55 Jewett Dr Wyoming OH 45215

POHLMANN, WILLIAM ALBERT, bank trust officer; b. Detroit, Sept. 9, 1939; s. William K. Pohlmann; m. Patty Lou Gooler, June 9, 1962; children: William A., Barry A. BBA in Fin., U. Wis., Milw., 1962, MBA in Fin., 1970. Asst. sec. Marine Nat. Bank, Milw., 1962-70; trust investment officer 1st Bank-Midland, Milw., 1970-72; pres. East Wis. Trustee Co., Milw., 1972-82; sr. v.p. Assoc. Manitowoc (Wis.) Bank, 1983—. Bd. dirs., treas. Manitowoc YMCA, 1976-86, Manitowoc United Way, 1980—; pres. Manitowoc Redevel. Corp., 1980—, Holy Family Hosp. Devel. Corp., Manitowoc. 1985—; exec. com. Bay Lake Council Boy Scouts Am., 1986—. Recipient Disting. Service award YMCA, 1982, Extraordinary Service award United Way, 1986. Fellow Fin. Analysts Fed.; mem. Milw. Investment Analysts Soc. Club: Y's Men (Manitowoc) (pres. 1976-77). Lodge: Rotary (pres. Manitowoc 1981-82).

POHNERT, WILLIAM HUGO, orthopaedic surgeon; b. Ann Arbor, Mich., Dec. 23, 1940; s. Harvey Hugo and Madeline (Rabbe) P.; m. Sandra N. Clark, Oct. 2, 1965; children: Tami Sue, Steven Clark, Todd David. BA, U. Mich., 1963, MD, 1967. Diplomate Am. Bd. Orthopaedic Surgery. Intern Borgess Hosp., Kalamazoo, 1967-68; resident in orthopaedics Luth. Hosp., Ft. Wayne, Ind., 1968-72; practice medicine specializing in orthopaedic surgery Kokomo (Ind.) Orthopaedic & Sports Medicine Clinic, 1975—, also sec. bd. dirs.; sports medicine clinic dir. St. Joseph Hosp., Kokomo, 1984—, chmn. physical therapy com., 1980—; chmn. physical therapy com. Howard Community Hosp., Kokomo, 1980—. Served to lt. comdr., USN, 1968-74. Fellow Am. Acad. Orthopaedic Surgeons; mem. AMA, Am. Orthopaedic Soc. Sports Medicine, Ind. Orthopaedic Soc., Ind. State Med. Soc., Howard County Med. Soc. Republican. Lodge: Masons, Shriners. Avocation: gardening, yardwork. Home: 1756 W Mulberry Kokomo IN 46901 Office: Kokomo Orthopaedic Clinic 402 S Berkly Rd Kokomo IN 46901

POINDEXTER, BARBARA KAY MULVANEY, visual art educator; b. Chgo., July 2, 1935; d. Lawrence Millard Mulvaney and Genevieve Ruth McKinley; m. Jerold David Poindexter, Aug. 29, 1959; children: Brian Neal, Todd Spencer, Amy Lynn. BFA, U. Kans., 1957, MFA, 1962; EdD, Nova U., Ft. Lauderdale, Fla., 1982. Visual artist Centron Corp., Lawrence, Kans., 1960-68; free lance artist Kansas City, Mo., 1968-70; visual art educator Longview Community Coll., Lee's Summit, Mo., 1970—; coordinator designer showcase Met. Community Colls., 1987; designer showcase Longview Farm, Lee's Summit. Designer, mural Children's Mercy Hosp., 1986; exhibitor Duck's Unltd. Invitational Art Show, St. Louis, 1986. Republican. Mem. Christian Ch. Club: Art Dir.'s (Kansas City). Avocation: landscape and portrait painting. Office: Longview Community Coll 500 Longview Rd Lee's Summit MO 64081

POINDEXTER, MARK CAREY, communications educator, researcher; b. St. Charles, Mo., Dec. 31, 1951; s. Russell L. and Jeanne Marie (Klinghammer) P.; m. Jennifer Trent, Feb. 4, 1986; 1 child, Claire Estelle. BA, Lindenwood Coll., 1973; MA, Cen. Mich. U., 1980; PhD, U. Minn., 1987. Mng. editor Lexington Advertiser-News, Mo., 1974-75; news dir. KCUR-FM, Kansas City, Mo., 1975-79; dir. broadcasting N.D. State U. KDSU-FM, Fargo, 1980-87; asst. prof. mass communication Cen. Mich. U., Mt. Pleasant, 1987—. Producer radio documentaries, including Migrant Workers (RFK Jour. award 1980). Recipient award for Best Radio Documentary N.D. AP Broadcasters Assn., 1982, 1st place awards Mo. Broadcasters Assn., 1977-80. Mem. N.D. Pub. Radio Assn. (pres. 1982-83), Nat. Pub. Radio (rep.), Speech Communication Assn. Avocation: study of linguistics and anthropology. Office: Cen Mich U Moore Hall BCA Mount Pleasant MI 48859

POINSETTE, DONALD EUGENE, business executive, value management consultant; b. Fort Wayne, Ind., Aug. 17, 1914; s. Eugene Joseph and Julia Anna (Wyss) P.; student Purdue U., 1934, Ind. U., 1935-37, 64; m. Anne Katherine Farrell, Apr. 15, 1939; children—Donald J., Eugene J., Leo J., Sharon Poinsette Smith, Irene Poinsette Snyder, Cynthia Poinsette West, Maryanne Poinsette Stohler, Philip J. With Gen. Electric Corp., RCA, Stewart Warner Corp., 1937-39; metall. research and field sales cons. P.R. Mallory Corp., 1939-49; dist. sales mgr. Derringer Metall. Corp., Chgo., 1949-50; plant engr. Cornell-Dubilier Electric Corp., Indpls., 1950-53; with Jenn-Air Corp., Indpls., 1953-74, purchasing dir., 1953-71, mgr. value engring. and quality control, 1969-74; bus. mgmt. cons. Mays and Assos., Indpls., 1974-76; Named to U.S. Finder's List, Nat. Engrs. Register, 1956. Pres., Marian Coll. Parents Club, Indpls., 1969-70; com. mem. Boy Scouts Am. Nat trustee Xavier U., 1972-73, Dad's Club, Cin. Mem. Nat. Assn. Purchasing Mgmt., Indpls. Purchasing Mgmt. Assn., Soc. Am. Value Engrs. (certified value specialist; sec.-treas. Central Ind. chpt. 1972-73), Soc. Ret. Execs. Indpls., Ind. U., Purdue U. alumni assns., Columbian (pres. 1972-73), Triad choral groups, Internat. Platform Assn., Tau Kappa Epsilon. Club: K.C. (4 deg.). Home: 5760 Susan Dr E Indianapolis IN 46250

POKORNI, ORYSIA, musician; b. Ternopil, Ukraine, USSR, Aug. 4, 1938; came to U.S., 1951; d. Gregory and Olha (Moroz) Danylkiw; m. Paul Pokorni, Jan. 25, 1958; children: Daniel, Mark. Student, Cosmopolitan Sch. Music, 1962; AA, Truman Coll., 1984. Mgr. Internat. Theatre of Chgo., 1963—; asst. office mgr. Ravenswood Hosp., Chgo., 1980-83; radio announcer WEDC, Chgo., 1965-66; choir dir. Moloda Dumka Children's Choir, Chgo., 1981-85. Accompanist various choirs and soloists, 1960—; composer songs; music arranger for children's plays. Tchr. St. Nicholas Saturday Sch., Chgo., 1966-85; active Ukrainian Women's League, Chgo., 1985. Mem. Ukrainian Congress Com. (chmn. spl. events 1984—). Home and Office: 4520 N Richmond Chicago IL 60625

POKORNOWSKI, BARBARA KAREN, small business owner, computer consultant; b. Landstuhl, Fed. Republic of Germany, Jan. 16, 1959; d. Ronald Felix and Joan Barbara (Krygier) P. BA, U. Notre Dame, 1980; MBA, Loyola U., Chgo., 1982; AAS, Coll. of DuPage, Glen Ellyn, Ill., 1983, AA, 1984. Cert. computer cons., cruise cons. Med. asst. Cen. Dupage Internists, Carol Stream, Ill., 1974-77, acct., 1973—; owner, mgr. Fun 'N Travel, Wheaton, Ill., 1978—; computer cons. BKP Enterprises, Wheaton, Ill., 1982—. Mem. Am. Soc. Travel Agts., Assn. Retail Travel Agts., Pacific Asia Travel Assn., Winfield (Ill.) Hist. Soc., U. Notre Dame Alumni Assn., Loyola U. Alumni Assn. Republican. Roman Catholic. Clubs: Dominic (Naperville, Ill.); Scuba Divers (Chgo.), Notre Dame. Avocations: skiing, boating, photography, scuba diving. Home: 26 W 260 Blair St Winfield IL 60190 Office: Fun 'N Travel 1411 E Roosevelt Rd Wheaton IL 60187

POKORNOWSKI, RONALD FELIX, internist; b. Chgo., July 8, 1933; s. Felix Florian and Isabella Helen (Mrazek) P.; m. Joan Barbara Krygier, Feb. 8, 1958; children: Barbara Karen, John Ronald. Grad. pre-med., Marquette U., 1953, MD, 1957; MD (hon.), Med. Coll. Wis., 1977. Resident internal medicine Northwestern U., Evanston and Chgo., Ill., 1961-64; gen. practice internal medicine Wheaton, Ill., 1964-72; pres. Central DuPage Internist Assocs., S.C., Carol Stream, Ill., 1972—, also bd. dirs.; v.p. Cen. DuPage Hosp. Med. Staff, 1968-69, pres. 1969-70, mem. bd. govs.; chief med. cons. Du Page Convalescent Ctr., 1980—; bd. dirs. Allmed Inc., Libertyville, Ill., Fun 'N Travel, Wheaton. Served to capt. U.S. Army, 1958-61. Recipient Spl. Appreciation award Marianjoy Rehab. Hosp., Wheaton, 1984. Mem. AMA, Ill. Med. Soc., DuPage County Med. Soc. Republican. Roman Catholic. Avocations: travel, photography. Home: 26 W 260 Blair St Winfield IL 60190 Office: Cen DuPage Internist Assocs SC 381 Main Pl Carol Stream IL 60188

POKRASS, ELLEN MARGARET, lawyer; b. Milw., Oct. 24, 1956; d. Roger Yale and Rosemary (Stein) P.; m. Michael G. McCarty, June 19, 1982. BS, Cornell U., 1979; JD summa cum laude, Syracuse Coll. Law, 1984. Bar: Wis. 1984, U.S. Dist. Ct. (ea. and we. dists.) Wis. 1984, U.S. Tax Ct. 1984. Assoc. Michael, Best & Friedrich, Milw., 1984—. Mem. ABA, Wis. Bar Assn., Milw. Bar Assn., Assn. Trial Lawyers Am., Order of Coif. Jewish. Office: Michael Best & Friedrich 250 E Wisconsin Ave Milwaukee WI 53202

POLANCIC, WILLIAM JOSEPH, accountant; b. Ottawa, Ill., Mar. 26, 1954; s. William Frank and Elizabeth Ann (Dilley) P.; m. Monica Sue Hanneken, July 26, 1980; 1 child, Allyn Elizabeth. BA in Acctg., St. Ambrose Coll., 1977; MBA in Fin., Keller Sch. Mgmt., 1984. CPA, Ill. Tax mgr. Consol. Packaging Corp., Chgo., 1978-80; asst. tax mgr. Midas Internat. Corp., Chgo., 1981-84, acctg. mgr., 1985—; v.p., cons. BPV Fin. Assocs., Chgo., 1985—. Vol. United Way, Crusade of Mercy, Chgo., 1983, Friends Shedd Aquarium, 1984. Mem. Am. Inst. CPA's, Am. Mgmt. Assn., Ill. CPA Soc. Club: Chgo. Tax. Avocations: woodworking, golf, racquetball, reading. Office: Midas Internat Corp 225 N Michigan Ave Chicago IL 60601

POLAREK, LOUISE, nurse; b. Chgo., July 19, 1927; d. Ernest William and Jonnie May (Hall) Bremer; m. Daniel Richard Hopkins, June 9, 1945 (div. 1965); children—Patricia Lynn, Daniel Mark; m. Robert Stanley Polarek, Aug. 6, 1966. Student portrait coloring, Chgo. Sch. Photography, 1946; student Selan's Beauty Sch., Chgo., 1971; diploma Chgo. Bd. Edn., 1981; diploma in Nursing, Triton Coll., 1981. Med. receptionist Rush Presbyn. St. Lukes Hosp., Chgo., 1964-66; med. sec. K.D. Kittleson, Chgo., 1971-73, Frederick J. Szymanski, Chgo., 1966-70, 1973-79; nurse MacNeal Meml. Hosp., Berwyn, Ill., 1981-82; charge nurse Pine Manor Nursing Center, Palos Hills, Ill., 1982-85; nurse West Side VA Hosp., Chgo., 1985—. Recipient Scholastic Honor award Chgo. Bd. Edn., 1981. Home: 3629 S Marshfield Ave Chicago IL 60609

POLASCIK, MARY ANN, ophthalmologist; b. Elkhorn, W.Va., Dec. 28, 1940; d. Michael and Elizabeth (Halko) Polascik; B.A., Rutgers U., 1967; M.D., Pritzker Sch. Medicine, 1971; m. Joseph Elie, Oct. 2, 1973; 1 dau.,

Laura Elizabeth Polascik. Jr. pharmacologist Ciba Pharm. Co., Summit, N.J., 1961-67; intern Billings Hosp., Chgo., 1971-72; resident in ophthalmology U. Chgo. Hosp., 1972-75; practice medicine specializing in ophthalmology, Dixon, Ill., 1975—; pres. McNichols Clinic, Ltd.; cons. ophthalmology, Dixon Devel. Ctr.; mem. staff Katherine Shaw Bethea Hosp., Dixon, Dixon Developmental Ctr. Hosp. Bd. dirs. Sinissippi Mental Health Ctr., 1977-82; bd. med. dirs. Winnebago Ctr. for Blind. Mem. AMA, Ill. Med. Soc., Ill. Assn. Ophthalmology, Am. Assn. Ophthalmology, Alpha Sigma Lambda. Roman Catholic. Clubs: Galena Territory, Dixon Country. Office: 120 S Hennepin Ave, Dixon, IL 61021

POLASKI, JAMES JOSEPH, photographer; b. Chgo., Nov. 6, 1949; s. Joseph Casmier and Isabel Elizabeth (Taller) P.; m. Anne Carol Spencer, Sept. 14, 1985. BS in Chemistry, No. Ill. U., 1972. Photo salesman Helix, Chgo., 1972-73; photo apprentice D. Krueger, Chgo., 1973-74, D. Epperson, Chgo., 1974-75; prin. Jim Polaski Photo, Chgo., 1975—; tchr.guitar, mandolin Old Town Sch. Folk Music, Chgo., 1987—. Mem. Advt. Photographers Am. (steering com. 1982-83, bd. dirs. 1983-84, 86—, 2d v.p. 1984-85, adv. bd. 1982—). Avocations: steam trains, music, computers. Office: 9 W Hubbard Chicago IL 60610

POLATSEK-VRIEND, JUNE E., social worker, consultant; b. Cleve., Mar. 20, 1946; d. Henry and Mollie (Gateman) Polatsek; children: Suzanne, Deborah. BS, Miami U., Oxford, Ohio, 1967; MA, Wayne State U., 1979, postgrad., 1986. Cert. social worker, Mich. Tchr. Sylvania (Ohio) Bd. Edn., 1972-73; med. counselor Northwood Physicians, PC, Berkley, Mich., 1979-82; therapist Huron Valley Counseling Services, Farmington, Mich., 1981-82, Personal Mastery Counseling Assn., Bloomfield Hills, Mich., 1981—; adj. faculty Wayne State U., Detroit, 1979-84; educator Common Ground, Birmingham, Mich., 1978-79, Bloomfield Hills Bd. Edn., 1981; cons. Taylor & Rubin, Attys., Southfield, Mich., 1982, Pontiac (Mich.) Gen. Hosp., 1984—, Northwood Physicians, PC, 1986—;. Author: Explorations in Human Sexuality, 1979; editor MAASECT Matters newsletter, 1980; contbr. articles to profl. jours. Bd. dirs. Gateway Montessori House, Birmingham, Mich., 1977-79. Fellow Am. Coll. Sexologists; mem. Am. Assn. Sex Educators, Counselors and Therapists (state exec. bd. 1979-83), Am. Assn. Counseling and Devel. (com. chmn. 1980, 82, 84), Soc. Sci. Study Sex, Am. Mental Health Counselor Assn. Avocations: equestrian, reading. Home and Office: Personal Mastery Counseling Assocs 2739 Berry Dr Bloomfield Hills MI 48013

POLETTE, PAUL LEROY, publishing company executive; b. Herculaneum, Mo., Jan. 15, 1928; s. Ferdinand and Fanny Marie (Justin) P.; m. Nancy Jane McCaleb, Dec. 23, 1950; children: Paula Jane, Keith Paul, Marsha Ellen. BS in Indsl. Mgmt., Washington U., St. Louis, 1969; MBA in Mgmt., St. Louis U., 1974. Supr. McDonnell-Douglas Corp., St. Louis, 1952-82; pres. Book Lures, Inc., O'Fallon, Mo., 1979—; instr. bus. St. Mary's Coll., O'Fallon, 1970-85. Photographer: Exploring Science Fiction, 1983, Supernatural, 1983, others. Mem. O'Fallon Planning Zoning Subcom., 1975, O'Fallon Bicentennial Com., 1976, St. Charles County Com. for Jr. Coll. Dist., 1984-86. Served as sgt. USAF, 1948-52. Mem. St. Charles City C. of C. Republican. Roman Catholic. Avocations: fishing, photography, travel.

POLIVKA, CAROLYN JEAN, printing company executive, accountant; b. Chgo., Apr. 4, 1953; d. Edward Paul and Jean Louise (Pelton) P. AA, Wright City Coll., Chgo., 1972; cert. in acctg. Oakton Community Coll., Des Plaines, Ill., 1982; BSBA in Finance, Roosevelt U., Chgo., 1986; postgrad., 1983-85. Head bookkeeper, supr. proof and transit First State Bank and Trust Co. of Park Ridge, Ill., 1972-76; fin. analyst-tech. Square D Co., Palatine, Ill., 1976—; treas. Advance Printing Service, Inc., Chgo., 1982—, also dir.; internat. acct. analyst, 1987—. Office: 1415 Roselle St Palatine IL 60067 Office: 5354 Northwest Hwy Chicago IL 60630

POLIVKA, CHARLES BARRY, business development executive; b. Chgo., Sept. 20, 1942; s. Charles and Mary (Krug) P.; m. Sandra Jean Kirkby, Oct. 15, 1966; 1 child, Kristin. BS in Engring, Physics, U. Ill., 1964, MS in Physics, 1966; postgrad., U. Chgo., 1970-72. Physicist Bendix Corp., Southfield, Mich., 1966-69; mgr. Zenith Radio, Niles, Ill., 1969-72; prin., v.p. mktg. Ni-Tec, Niles, 1972-83; mgr. bus. devel. Hughes Aircraft, Des Plaines, Ill., 1984—; sr. assoc. Advanced Mgmt. Cons., Washington, 1983. Editor: Relativity for Everyone, 1965; inventor elimination of ion feedback. Republican. Avocations: golfing, tennis, hunting, fishing. Office: Hughes Optical 2000 S Wolf Rd Des Plaines IL 60018

POLL, DIANE ROSE, librarian; b. Belleville, Ill., Mar. 1, 1956; d. Kenneth Edgar and Ethel Mae (Boettcher) P. BS, Ill. State U., 1978; MLS, No. Ill. U., 1982. Head children's librarian Broadview (Ill.) Pub. Library, 1979-80; librarian young people's services Barrington (Ill.) Area Library, 1980-82, head tech. services, 1982—. Mem. ALA, Ill. Library Assn. Club: Blue Water Divers (Palatine, Ill.). Office: Barrington Area Library 505 N Northwest Hwy Barrington IL 60010

POLL, HEINZ, choreographer, artistic director; b. Oberhausen, West Germany, Mar. 18, 1926; came to U.S., 1964, naturalized, 1975; s. Heinrich and Anna Margareta (Winkels) P. Co-founder, dir. The Dance Inst., U. Akron, 1967-77; founder, artistic dir., choreographer Ohio Ballet, Akron, 1968—; tchr. Chilean Instituto de Extension Musical, 1951-61, N.Y. Nat. Acad., 1965-66. Dancer with, Gottingen Mcpl. Theatre, 1946-48, Deutsches Theatre Konstanz, 1948-49, East Berlin State Opera, 1949-50, Nat. Ballet of Chile, 1951-62, Ballet de la Jeunesse Musicales de France, 1963-64, guest appearances with, Nat. Ballet Chile, 1964, Am. Dance Festival, 1965; choreographed works for, Nat. Ballet Chile, Paris Festival Ballet, Ballet de la Jeunesse Musicales de France, Nat. Ballet Can., Pa. Ballet, Ohio Ballet. Nat. Endowment for the Arts grantee, 1974-75; Recipient Ohio Dance award, 1983. Mem. NEA Dance Panel. Office: 354 E Market Akron OH 44325

POLLACK, SEYMOUR VICTOR, computer science educator; b. Bklyn., Aug. 3, 1933; s. Max and Sylvia (Harrison) P.; m. Sydell Altman, Jan. 23, 1955; children: Mark, Sherie. BChemE, Pratt Inst., 1954; MChemE, Bklyn. Poly. Inst., 1960. Lic. chem. engr., Ohio. Engr. Schwarz Labs., Mt. Vernon, N.Y., 1954-55; design engr. Curtiss-Wright, Wood-Ridge, N.J., 1955-57, Fairchild Engines, Deer Park, N.Y., 1957-59, Gen. Electric, Evendale, Ohio, 1959-62; research assoc. U. Cin., 1962-66; prof. computer sci. Washington U., St. Louis, 1966—; cons. Mo. Auto Club, St. Louis, 1969-82, United Van Lines, Fenton, Mo., 1984-86, Computer Sci. Accreditation Bd., N.Y.C., 1985—. Author: Structured Fortran, 1982, UCSD PASCAL, 1984, Studies in Computer Science, 1983, The Dos Book, 1985; cons. editor Holt Rinehart & Winston, N.Y.C., 1979-86. Bd. dirs. Hillel orgn., Washington U., 1983-84. Recipient Alumni Achievement award, Pratt Inst., 1966. Mem. Assn. for Computing Machinery, Am. Assn. for Engring. Edn. Jewish. Avocations: classical and jazz piano, jogging. Office: Washington Univ Campus Box 1045 Saint Louis MO 63130

POLLANDER, EDWARD JOSEPH, dentist; b. Youngstown, Ohio, Apr. 22, 1958; s. Edward Joseph and Mary Ann Rita (Layshock) P.; m. Pamela Jean Ladig, Oct. 19, 1985. Student, Marquette U., 1976-79; DDS, Ohio State U., 1983. Gen. practice dentistry Andover, Ohio, 1985—; Coordinator dental screeing Andover, Joseph Badger and Johnston Sch. System, 1985—. Mem. ADA, Ohio Dental Soc., Corydon-Palmer Dental Soc. Republican. Roman Catholic. Club: Trumbull Athletic (Vienna, Ohio). Avocations: tennis, scuba diving. Home: 1092 S Park Dr Brookfield OH 44403 Office: 6258 E Main St Andover OH 44003

POLLARD, CHARLES WILLIAM, health care services executive; b. Chgo., June 8, 1938; s. Charles W. and Ruth Ann (Humphrey) P.; m. Judith Ann, June 8, 1959; children: Julie Ann, Charles W., Brian, Amy. A.B., Wheaton Coll., 1960; J.D., Northwestern U., 1963. Bar: Ill. 1963. Mem. firm Wilson and McIlvaine, 1963-67, Vesceius, Perry & Pollard, Wheaton, Ill., 1968-72; prof., v.p. fin. Wheaton Coll., 1972-77; sr. v.p. Service Master Industries, Downers Grove, Ill., 1977-80; exec. v.p. Service Master Industries, 1980-81, pres., 1981-83, chief exec. officer, 1983—; dir. Gary-Wheaton Bank.; Bd. dirs. Wheaton Coll. Office: Servicemaster Industries Inc 2300 Warrenville Rd Downers Grove IL 60515 *

POLLARD, FRANCES MARGUERITE, librarian; b. Florence, Ala., Oct. 7, 1920; d. Lorenzo Marquis and Carrie (Mayfield) Pollard; Jr. Coll. diploma, Selma U., 1938; B.S., Ala. State Coll., 1941; M.S. in L.S., Western Res. U., 1949, Ph.D., 1963; postgrad. Columbia, 1952-54. Tchr. elem. sch., Waterloo, Ala., 1938-39, Marengo County Tng. Sch., Thomaston, Ala., 1941-42, Sterling High Sch., Sheffield, Ala., 1942-43; library asst. Enlisted Men's Library 2, Fort McClellan, Ala., 1943-46, Ala. State Coll., Montgomery, 1946-48; student aide children's room Sterling br. Cleve. Public Library, 1948-49; asst. librarian Ala. State Coll., 1949-61, head librarian, 1961-63; adminstrv. asst. Booth Library, Eastern Ill. U., Charleston, 1963-70, prof. library sci., head library sci. dept., 1970-79, exec. asst. for library services, 1979—; mem. Ill. State Library Adv. Com., 1967-73, subcom. LSCA Title I and Title II, 1967-77. Mem. ALA, Ill. Library Assn., Am. Acad. Polit. and Social Sci., Soc. Applied Anthropology, Am. Sociol. Assn., AAUP, AAUW, Alpha Kappa Alpha, Delta Kappa Gamma. Author: (with others) Major Problems in Education of Librarians, 1954, Illinois Literary Reflections of the Bicentennial Year, 1977. Editor: Procs. of Personnel Evaluation Inst., 1975. Home: 1330 A St Charleston IL 61920

POLLIS, MARCIA FELDMAN, social worker; b. N.Y.C., July 13, 1937; d. Murray and Eva (Taub) Feldman; m. Merle Robert Pollis, June 10, 1956; children: Gail Rachel Spiro, Andrew Stuart. BA, U. Pitts., 1973; M in Social Service Adminstrn., Case Western Res. U., 1975. Dir. social services Woodruff Hosp., Cleve., 1975-86; pvt. practice clin. social work Shaker Heights, Ohio, 1978—; supr. staff devel. St. Vincent Charity Hosp., Cleve., 1986—. Co-chmn. Peace and Social Welfare Com., Cleve., 1977-78. Fellow Acad. Cert. Social Workers; mem. Orthopsychiat. Assn., Nat. Assn. Social Workers. Avocations: writing, acting. Office: 20119 Van Aken 204 Shaker Heights OH 44122

POLLITT, GERTRUDE STEIN, psychotherapist, clinical social worker; b. Vienna, Austria, 1919; came to U.S., 1949, naturalized, 1951; d. Julius and Sidoni (Brauch) Stein; m. Erwin P. Pollitt, Jan. 13, 1951 (dec. Aug. 1977). Social Service course Brit. Council, London, 1943-44; BA, Roosevelt U., 1954; MA, U. Chgo., 1956; LHD (hon.) World U., Ariz., 1986. Cert. Chgo. Inst. Psychoanalysis, 1963, cert. clin. social worker, 1987. Resident social worker Anna Freud Residential Nursery Sch., Essex, Eng., 1944-45; dep. dir. UN, U.S. Zone, Germany, 1945-48; psychiat. social worker Jewish Children's Bur., Chgo., 1955-63; pvt. practice as psychotherapist and/or clin. social worker, Glencoe, Ill., 1961—; cons. Winnetka (Ill.) Community Nursery Sch., 1962-63, North Shore Congregation Nursery Sch., 1966-69, Oakwood Home for Aged, Highland Park (Ill.) High Sch., 1979-80; instr. profl. devel. programs Chgo. Inst. for Psychoanalysis, 1982, Sch. Social Service Adminstrn., U. Chgo.; mem. faculty profl. devel. program Sch. Social Service Adminstrn., U. Chgo.; cons. to ongoing profl. study groups on clin. issues, 1984—. Contbr. articles to profl. jours. Bd. dirs. Glencoe Youth Service, Menninger Found. Fellow Am. Orthopsychiat. Assn.; mem. Nat. Assn. Social Workers (chmn. pvt. practice com. 1965-70), Ill. Soc. Clin. Social Workers (bd. dirs.), Acad. Cert. Social Workers. Home and office: 481 Oakdale Ave Glencoe IL 60022

POLLOCK, DAVIS ALLEN, insurance company executive; b. Douds, Iowa, Aug. 31, 1942; s. David Edwin and Bertha Dorothy (Barker) P.; m. Marcia Kay Tedrow, Jan. 1, 1965; children—Eric, Kirsten. B.S., Drake U., 1964; SEP, Stanford U., 1984. Various positions Central Life Assurance Co., Des Moines, 1964-73, asst. actuary, 1973-77, v.p., 1977-79, v.p. corp. planning, 1979-82; sr. v.p. group Central Life Assurance Co., Madison, Wis., 1982-87; exec. v.p. employee benefits Central Life Assurance Co., Madison, 1987—; bd. dirs. Meriter Health Enterprises, Inc., Elderhouse, Health Care Assocs. Chmn. visioning com. Methodist Ch., Des Moines, 1978-79, pastor parish com., 1980; coach various youth sports; tutor for underprivileged children. Fellow Soc. Actuaries (edn. com. 1975-79); mem. Am. Acad. Actuaries, Des Moines Actuaries Club (pres. 1980), Phi Eta Sigma, Omicron Delta Kappa, Kappa Mu Epsilon. Republican. Lodge: Masons. Avocations: tennis; jogging. Home: 6909 Colony Dr Madison WI 53717 Office: Central Life Assurance Co 4626 Frey St Madison WI 53705

POLLOCK, E. JILL, personnel executive, software executive; b. Detroit, May 19, 1946; d. John V. and Hazel A. (King) S.; m. John Stanley Hayosh, June 30, 1967 (div. Sept. 1977); 1 child, Mark Christopher Hayosh; m. E. Owen Pollock, June 17, 1978. BA, Mich. State U., 1967; MBA, U. Detroit, 1973. Orgn. planner Ford Motor Co., Dearborn, Mich., 1977-79, mgr. personnel planning, 1979-83; treas. The Arbor Cons. Group Inc., Plymouth, Mich., 1984-87, pres., 1987—; maintable bargainer UAW contract negotiations Ford Motor Co., 1982. Author: Twentieth Century Retirement, 1985. Mem. Mich. Employment Security Adv. Council, Lansing, 1986—; co-chairperson Mich. Women's Hall Fame, Lansing, 1986—; del. White House Conf. Small Bus., 1986; bd. dirs. Eastwood Community Clinics, Detroit, 1986—, Health Care Profls. Ltd., 1986—. Mem. Internat. Council Small Bus., Internat. Assn. Personnel Women, Women's Econ. Club, Internat. Soc. Preretirement Planners, Detroit Personnel Mgmt. Assn., Small Bus. Assn. Mich. (bd. dirs. 1986—), Nat. Assn. Women Bus. Owners (treas., bd. dirs. Mich. chpt., 1984-86), Plymouth Community C. of C., Phi Mu. Episcopalian. Club: Detroit. Avocations: chorale singing, needlepoint, photography, reading. Home: 7190 Pebble Park Dr West Bloomfield MI 48033 Office: Arbor Cons Group Inc 711 W Ann Arbor Trail Plymouth MI 48170

POLOVITCH, BRUCE ELLIOT, accountant; b. Chgo., Apr. 13, 1956; s. Frank and Dorothy (Kemper) P. BS in Acctg., U. Ill., Chgo., 1980; BS in Info. Sci., Northeastern Ill. U., 1987. CPA, Ill. Sr. computer operator Rand McNally, Skokie, Ill., 1974-78; supr. Sears Roebuck & Co., Niles, Ill., 1978-81; staff acct. Ogorek & Assocs., Park Ridge, Ill., 1981-83; supr. J.C. Penneys, Niles, 1983-84; mgr. acctg. YKK (USA) Inc., Northbrook, Ill., 1984—. Mem. Am. Inst. CPA's, Ill. Inst. CPA's. Republican. Roman Catholic. Avocations: scuba diving, golf, tennis, fishing, drums.

POLSFUSS, DANIEL FRED, film maker; b. Mpls., June 11, 1954; s. Howard and Erla (Swanson) P.; m. Kae Koefod, June 14, 1986. Asst. dir., editor T. Butler Prodns., Mpls., 1977-81; editor Film Cutter, Mpls., 1981—, dir., 1983—. Film maker Shinders to Shinders, 1981, Wraith, 1983, CHINA Girl, 1985, Rain on the Lion, 1986. Recipient Best Music Video Minn. Music awards, 1984; grantee Minn. Ind. Choregraphers Alliance, 1981, Minn. State Arts Bd., 1982, Film in the Cities, 1984. Avocation: tai chi chuan. Office: Film Cutter 127 N 7th St #412 Minneapolis MN 55403

POLSINELLI, ANTHONY RENATO, manufacturing company executive; b. Canton, Ohio, Feb. 2, 1944; s. Placid John and Mary Ann (Primavera) P.; m. Joanne DeMichele, Nov. 23, 1967; 1 child, Michael. BS in Engring. Mgmt., Case Inst. Tech., 1968. Registered profl. engr., Calif. Prodn. supr. Gen Motors, Hudson, Ohio, 1967-69; mgr. indsl. engring. Bailey Meter Co., Wickliffe, Ohio, 1969-72; asst. ops. mgr. Bailey Japan Ltd., Tokyo, 1972-74; sr. engr. Anvil Industries, Brecksville, Ohio, 1975, Technicare Corp., Solon, Ohio, 1976-78; dir. corp. prodn. engring. Eaton Corp., Cleve., 1978—; indsl. adv. com. Case Inst. Tech., 1982-84. Contbr. articles to profl. mags. Mem. Soc. Mfg. Engrs. (pres. local chpt. 1982), Am. Mgmt. Assn., Inst. Indsl. Engrs. Roman Catholic. Avocations: sailing, reading, woodworking. Home: 2686 Endicott Rd Shaker Heights OH 44120 Office: Eaton Corp 32500 Chardon Rd Willoughby Hills OH 44094

POLSKY, DONALD PERRY, architect; b. Milw., Sept. 30, 1928; s. Lew and Dorothy (Geisenfeld) P.; m. Corinne Shirley Neer, Aug. 25, 1957; children: Jeffrey David, Debra Lynn. BArch, U. Nebr., Lincoln, 1951; postgrad., U. So. Calif., 1956, U. Calif., Los Angeles, 1957, U. Nebr., Omaha, 1964, U. Ill., 1965. Project architect Richard Neutra, Architect, Los Angeles, 1953-56, Daniel Dworsky, Architect, Los Angeles, 1956; prin. Polsky, AIA & Assocs., Los Angeles, 1956-62, Omaha, 1964—; dir. dept. architecture MCA, Inc., Universal City, Calif., 1962-64. Prin. works include Mills residence, 1958, apt. bldgs., 1960, Polsky residence, 1961, Milder residence, 1965. Chmn. Design Control I480 Study Mayor's Riverfront Devel., Omaha, 1969, 71; pres. Swanson Sch. Community Club, Omaha, 1972; mem. Mayor's Adv. Panel Design Services, Omaha, 1974; vice chmn. Omaha Zoning Bd. Appeals, 1976. Recipient archtl. awards Canyon Crier Newspaper, Los Angeles, 1960, House and Home Mag., Santa Barbara, Calif., 1960. Mem. AIA (award, 1968, pres. Omaha chpt. 1968), Nebr. Soc. Architects (award, 1965, pres. 1975). Republican. Jewish. Office: Donald P Polsky AIA & Assocs 8723 Oak St Omaha NE 68124

POLSON, CHERYL JEAN, education educator; b. Halstead, Kans., July 24, 1954; d. Arnold E. and Rose E. (Lindley) Keller; m. Douglas Richard Polson, Jan. 3, 1976. AA, Hutchinson Community Coll., 1974; BS, Kans. State U., 1976, MS, 1978, PhD, 1983. Grad. research asst. Kans. State U., Manhattan, 1976-78, dir. advising ctr., 1978-82, nontraditional study coordinator, 1982-85, asst. prof., 1985—; acad. advising consultant Nat. Orgn., 1983—; workshop trainer CAEL/UAW-Ford, Dearborn, MIch., 1985—; community coll. in-service Pratt (Kans.) Community Coll., 1985. Author articles to profl. jours., chpts. in books; editor: (conf. proceedings) Advising as a Form of Teaching, 1983, 84, 85; editorial bd. jour., 1983—. Recipient numerous awards. Mem. Nat. Acad. Advising Assn. (v.p. 1985-87, bd. dirs. 1981-85, nat. chairperson 1983-84), Am. Coll. Student Personnel Assn. (state chmn. 1983-85, edn. task force mem. 1985), Am. Assn. Counseling and Devel., Council for the Advancement of Exptl. Learning, Nat. Career Devel. Assn., Nat. Assn. Acad. Affairs Adminstrs., Kans. Personnel and Guidance Assn., Kans. Coll. Personnel Assn., Mo. Valley Adult Edn. Assn., Kans. Adult Edn. Assn., Am. Coll. Student Personnel (Annuit Coeptis award 1984). Avocations: weight lifting, racquetball, horseback riding, walking. Home: 11539 Goddard Overland Park KS 66210 Office: Kans State U Coll of Edn Bluemont Hall 347 Manhattan KS 66506

POLYDORIS, STEVEN NICHOLAS, communications company executive; b. Evanston, Ill., Sept. 12, 1954; s. Nicholas George and Gloria Anne (Lucas) P.; student Drake U., 1972-73; B.S.I.E., Northwestern U., 1983. With Wilder Engring. Co., 1978; pres. ENM Co., Chgo., 1979-83; pres. GN Communications, Ltd., Evanston, Ill., 1983—. Editor Chicago Film & Video News magazine, 1986—. Office: GN Communications Ltd 1723 Howard St Evanston IL 60202

POMA, KIMBERLY SMIDT, industrial engineer; b. Youngstown, Ohio, Sept. 11, 1957; d. Wesley Don and Mary Catherine (Gotshall) Smidt; m. James Paul Poma, Apr. 26, 1980; 1 child, Jonathan Paul. BS in Indsl. Engring., Youngstown State U., 1980; postgrad., Pa. State U., Harrisburg, 1983—. Process engr. Parker Hannifin Co., Ravenna, Ohio, 1980-81; indsl. engr. trainee AMP Inc., Harrisburg, 1981-83, indsl. engr. II, 1983-85; owner Frames & Flowers, Youngstown, 1986—. Guide Sci. Mus., Harrisburg, 1982-84. Mem. Inst. Indsl. Engrs., Pvt. Industry Council (local bd. dirs.). Republican. Episcopalian. Home: 180 Ewing Rd Boardman OH 44512 Office: Frames and Flowers 65 E Midlothian Blvd Youngstown OH 44507

POMA, PEDRO ALFONSO, obstetrician, gynecologist; b. Lima, Peru, Mar. 11, 1938; came to U.S., 1966; s. Cesar S. and Rosa E. (Herrera) P.; m. Lydia Maria Marca, Mar. 27, 1965; children: Ana Elizabeth, Alfonso Martin. Student, San Marcos U., Lima, 1957-59, MD, 1965. Diplomate Am. Bd. Ob-Gyn. Resident in ob-gyn Cook County Hosp., Chgo., 1968-71; resident in ob-gyn pathology Northwestern U., Chgo., 1969; practice medicine specializing in ob-gyn Melrose Park, Ill., 1972—; health advocate, 1985; mem. Met. Chgo. Healthcare Council. Host bi-weekly show Sta. WSNS-TV; mem. editorial bd. Urban Medicine, 1987—; contbr. articles to profl. jours. Recipient Community Service award, 1987; named to Hispanic Health Alliance. Fellow ACS, Am. Coll. Ob-Gyn, Am. Fertility Soc., Am. Pub. Health Assn., Cen. Assn. Ob-Gyn; mem. Ill. State Med. Soc. (trustee 1983-87, 1st v.p. 1987—), Inst. Medicine of Chgo. (gov. 1984—, v.p. 1986—), Chgo. Gynecol. Soc., Chgo. Med. Soc. (pres. 1986-87), Kennedy Inst. Ethics. Avocation: writing. Office: 675 W North Ave Suite 407 Melrose Park IL 60160

POMERANTZ, SANFORD EDWARD, psychiatrist; b. Detroit, May 26, 1941; s. Harry H. and Ruth Martha (Seskin) P.; m. Francine Martha Reed, Oct. 31, 1969; children: Jennifer, Joanna, Katherine. BA, Wayne State U., 1965, MD, 1970; B in Psychiatry, Menninger Sch. Psychiatry, 1973. Cert. Am. Bd. Psychiatry and Neurology. Pvt. practice psychiatry Topeka, 1973—; med. clin. dir. S.E. Kans. Mental Health Ctr., Humboldt, 1979—; cons. physician psychiat. Social Security Adminstrn., Topeka, 1985—; pres. Pomerantz MD Chartered, Topeka, 1980—. Mem. Am. Psychiat. Assn., Mid-Continent Psychiat. Assn., Kans. Psychiat. Soc. Avocations: astronomy, computers, robots, boating. Office: 3600 Burlingame Suite 2A Topeka KS 66614

POMERANZ, JEROME R., dermatologist; b. Newark, Dec. 29, 1930; s. Raphael and Zina (Rubinow) P.; m. Jacqueline R. Goldenberg, June 15, 1953 (div. 1973); m. Barbara P. Barna, May 5, 1978; children: Russell Carl, William Eric, Emily Suzanne. BS, George Washington U., 1952; MD, Boston U., 1956. Diplomate Am. Bd. Dermatology. Intern, then resident Johns Hopkins Hosp., Balt., 1957-58, resident in dermatology, 1960-63, fellow in allergy, 1963-65; mem. staff Johns Hopkins, Hosp.; assoc. prof. dermatology Case Western Res. U., Cleve., 1965—, assoc. prof. pathology, 1967—; mem. staff Cleve. Met. Gen. Hosp.; com. mem. Am. Bd. Dermatology, Am. Bd. Pathology, test com. for Dermatopathology1979-84, FDA Bur. Drugs, Dermatology adv. com., 1981-85. Contbr. articles to profl. jours. Served to capt. M.C., U.S. Army, 1958-60. Fellow Am. Acad. Dermatology, Am. Coll Physicians; mem. Am. Dermatol. Assn., Nat. Acad. Scis. (drug efficacy study panel 1967-69, com. to rev. use of ionizing radiation for treatment of benign diseases 1975-78), Am. Bd. Dermatology, Am. Bd. Pathology (test com. for dermatopathology 1979-84), FDA Bur. Drugs (dermatology adv. com. 1981-85), Cleve. Dermatol. Soc. (pres. 1973-75), Am. Soc. Dermatopathology, Soc. Investigative Dermatology (membership com. 1975, 76, 77, chmn. 1977), Assn. Profs. Dermatology, Am. Fedn. Clin. Research, N.Y. Acad. Scis., AAAS, Cleve. Acad. Medicine. Home: 490 Merrimac Dr Berea OH 44017 Office: Dept of Dermatology 3395 Scranton Rd Cleveland OH 44109

POMEROY, ROBERT MACLAY, II, municipal corporation executive; b. Avoca, Iowa, Sept. 1, 1920; s. Loren Maclay and Mary Ethel (Goodwin) P.; m. Jeanne Katherine Wilcox, Sept. 4, 1942; children: Elizabeth Ann, Robert Maclay III. BA, Amherst Coll., 1941. Various positions Caterpillar Inc., Peoria, Ill., 1946-62; exec. sec. Pub. Bldg. Commn. Peoria, 1962—. Served to lt. USN, 1942-46, PTO. Mem. Bldg. Owners and Mgrs. Assn. Republican. Presbyterian. Lodge: Rotary. Avocation: golf. Home: 314 Wynnwood Dr Peoria IL 61614 Office: Pub Bldg Commn Peoria Peoria County Courthouse Peoria IL 61602

POMPA, SUSAN JOY, medical products executive; b. Chgo., Oct. 14, 1951; d. Hy I. and Evelyn Cohn Kaplan; m. Roger Pompa, Nov. 18, 1976 (div. Aug. 1978); 1 child, Nicole. Student, Met. Sch. Bus., Chgo., 1970-71; degree med. records, Am. Med. Rec Assn., 1975. With med. records dept. Swedish Covenant Hosp., Chgo., 1971-74; dir. med. records Northwestern U. Med. Assocs., Chgo., 1974-75; research assoc. Am. Med. Records Assn., Chgo., 1975-76; dir. med. records HMO Rush Presbyn. St. Lukes Hosp., Chgo., 1977; pres., chief exec. officer S.J. Kaplan & Assocs., Inc., Lincolnwood, Ill., 1980—; cons. graphic arts dept. Niles West High Sch., Skokie, Ill., 1985. Patentee in field. Mem. Am. Med. Record Assn. (cert.). Avocations: cross country skiing, tennis, needlpoint. Office: SJ Kaplan & Assocs 7215 N Kildare Lincolnwood IL 60646

PONCY, PAUL DAVID, osteopath; b. Ottumwa, Iowa, Feb. 24, 1946; s. Charles Nelson and Naomi Lucille (McCrory) P.; m. Sandra Kaye Linn, Aug. 2, 1969; children: Scott, Brian. Student, William Penn Coll., 1964-65; BS, Northeast Mo. State U., 1968; DO, Kirksville Coll. Osteopathic Medicine, 1972. Rotating intern Davenport (Iowa) Osteopathic Hosp., 1972-73; practice medicine specializing in osteopathy Wilton, Iowa, 1973-75, Centerville, Iowa, 1976—; mem. adv. bd. IHCC Sch. of Nursing, Centerville,

1981—; mem. adv. com. Bd. of Health, Centerville, 1983—; mem. Appanoose County Bd. Health, Centerville, 1982—. Legis. contact physician Iowa Legis., Des Moines, 1982—. Mem. Am. Osteopathic Assn., Iowa Med. Soc., Appanoose County Med. Soc. Democrat. Lutheran. Lodge: Lions (dep. dist. gov. 1986-87, zone chmn. 1984-86, pres. Centerville club 1983-84).

POND, BYRON O., manufacturing company executive; b. 1936. BSBA, Wayne State U. With Fed. Mogul Corp., Detroit, 1958-68; with Maremont Corp., Chgo., 1968—, dir. sales exhaust systems div., 1970-74, corp. v.p., 1974-76, sr. v.p. nat. accounts, 1976-78, exec. v.p., 1978-79, pres., chief exec. officer, from 1979, now pres., chmn. bd. dirs., chief exec. officer. Office: Maremont Corp 200 E Randolph Dr Chicago IL 60601 *

POND, ROBERT EDWARD, school system administrator; b. Warren, Ind., Dec. 13, 1929; s. Ira S. and Bertha M. Pond; m. LuEllyn Irick, Apr. 23, 1950; children: David, Jane. BS, Ball State U., 1956, MS, 1964; postgrad., Bowling Green State U., 1964. Elem. tchr. Salamonie Schs., Warren, 1956-59; elem. prin. Gibsonburg (Ohio) Schs., 1959-62, supt. schs., 1962-64; supt. schs. Oysego Schs., Tontogany, Ohio, 1964-67, Salem (Ohio) Schs., 1967—. Mem. Am. Assn. Sch. Adminstrs., Buckeye Assn. Sch. Adminstrs., Nat. Sch. Pub. Relations Assn., Salem C. of C., Phi Delta Kappa, Kappa Delta Pi. Club: Saxon (Salem). Lodges: Rotary, Masons. Office: 1226 E State Salem OH 44460

PONDELL, RALPH EDWARD, microencapsulation company executive; b. Weyerhauser, Wis., Oct. 28, 1950; s. Stanley and Marie (Mikula) P.; m. Marjorie Ann Ourada, June 18, 1972; children: Angela Kay, Jill Maria. BS, U. Wis., 1974. Chemist Wis. Alumni Research Found., Madison, 1972-77; owner, chief exec. officer, engr. Coating Place, Inc., Verona, Wis., 1976—; mem. planning com. Land-O-Lakes Indsl. Pharmacy Conf., Lake Dalton, Wis., 1981-83. Contbr. articles to profl. jours. Tchr. St. Andrew's Congregation, Verona, 1983-86. Mem. Am. Pharm. Assn., Wis. Pharm. Assn., Internat. Soc. Pharm. Engrs. Roman Catholic. Avocations: woodworking, photography, bowling, whitewater canoeing. Home: 2670 Stardust Trail Verona WI 53593 Office: Coating Place Inc PO Box 248 2283 Hwy 69 Verona WI 53593

PONDER, MARIAN RUTH, educator; b. Waterloo, Iowa, July 12, 1932; d. Lee Roland and Leone Hyacinth (Holdiman) Rigdon; B.A. (Purple and Gold math. scholar), U. No. Iowa, 1952; M.S.E., Drake U., 1960; postgrad. U. Wis., 1961-62, San Diego State U., 1980-81, Carleton Coll., 1980-81, U. No. Ia., 1961-66, Drake U., 1971-75; m. Joseph Glen Ponder, June 28, 1953; children—Dwight Lee, David Glen, Dean Joseph. Tchr. math., sci. Anamosa, Iowa, 1952-53, Monroe, Iowa, 1953-56, Newton, Iowa, 1956-64, 66—, head dept. math. Newton Schs., 1978—. Ch. treas. Community Heights Alliance Ch., 1980-82, 83—, Sunday sch. secretariat, 1966-82. Maytag scholar, 1960; Maytag Corp. grantee, 1962; Delta Kappa Gamma scholar, 1960, 81. Mem. Nat. Council Tchrs. Math., NEA, Iowa Edn. Assn., Newton Community Edn. Assn. (chief negotiator 1985-87, pres. 1985-87), Iowa Council Tchrs. Math., Jasper County Hist. Soc., Jasper County Genealogical Soc., Delta Kappa Gamma (state treas. 1978—), Kappa Mu Epsilon, Kappa Delta Pi, Lambda Delta Lambda. Republican. Mem. Christian and Missionary Alliance Ch. Home: 620 E 17 St N Newton IA 50208 Office: E 4th St S Newton IA 50208

PONG, HENRY KING-FAI, dentist; b. Hong Kong, Jan. 8, 1955; Came to U.S., 1973; s. Hon-Ying and Shiu-Hoi (Chan) P.; m. Wendy Ann Brey, Nov. 24, 1979; children: Jacob Jung-Hung, Clair Wei-Si. AS, Vincennes U., 1975; BA, Oberlin Coll., 1977; DDS, Indiana U., 1981. Gen. practice dentistry Lake Station, Ind., 1981—; cons. Fountainview Nursing Home, Portage, Ind., 1981-84, Southlake Health Ctr., Merrillville, Ind., 1983—, Hobart Township Headstart, Lake Station, 1984—, Lake Park Residential Care, Lake Station, 1986; dental dir. Seebo Nursing Home, Hobart, Ind., 1984—. Cons. Lake County Assn. for the Retarded, 1985—; chmn. bd. deacons New Hope Bapt. Ch., Hobart, 1986. Mem. ADA, Ind. Dental Assn., Northwestern Dental Assn., Chgo. Dental Soc., Southlake Dental Assn., Lake Station C. of C. Lodge: Lions. Avocation: gospel singing. Home: 429 Banbury Pl Valparaiso IN 46383 Office: 3820 Central Ave Lake Station IN 46405

PONINSKI, PHIL E(DWARD), property manager; b. Chgo., Aug. 17, 1948; s. Edward Frank and Ann (Berzinski) P.; m. Mary K. Jarvis, Mar. 30, 1984. AA, Thornton Jr. Coll., 1968; BA, U. Ill., Chgo., 1971. Retail mgr. Seno Formalwear, Chgo., 1969-74; maintenance mgr. Midland Mgmt. Co., Oswego, Ill., 1974-75, resident property mgr., 1975—. Mem. Inst. Real Estate Mgmt. (accredited resident mgr. 1984). Lodge: Eagles. Avocation: motorcycling. Office: Shore Heights Village Apts 1800 Light Rd Oswego IL 60543

PONITZ, JAMES EDWARD, dentist; b. Battle Creek, Mich., Apr. 23, 1946; s. Paul Vernon and Evelyn Amelia (Schmidt) P.; m. Kathleen Grace Stewart; Children: Heather, Jeffrey. BS in lit. sci. and arts, U. Mich., 1968, DDS, 1972. Family practice dentistry Zeeland and Holland, Mich., 1962—. Mem. ADA, Holland Dental Soc. Republican. Lodge: Rotary. Avocations: running, sailing, tennis, bicycling, golf. Home: 65 Straight Ave Holland MI 49424 Office: 601 Michigan Ave Holland MI 49423

PONITZ, PAUL ROBERT, data processing executive; b. Battle Creek, Mich., Feb. 5, 1942; s. Paul Vernon and Evelyn Amelia (Schmidt) P.; m. Jane McClellan Allan, Feb. 16, 1962; children: Mark Allan, Marsha Jane, Michelle Lynn. BBA, Western Mich. U., 1964. Account clk. First Nat. Bank, Kalamazoo, Mich., 1962-64, computer programmer, 1964-66; programmer/analyst City of Kalamazoo, 1966-81, programmer mgr., 1981-82; data processing mgr. Doubleday Bros. & Co., Kalamazoo, 1982—; data processing advisor Kalamazoo Community Coll., 1985—. Mem. Data Processing Mgmt. Assn., Am. Mgmt. Assn. Republican. Mem. Reformed Ch. Am. Avocations: sailing, tennis, woodworking. Home: 1177 Marsh Rd Plainwell MI 49080 Office: Doubleday Bros & Co 1919 E Kilgore Rd Kalamazoo MI 49002

PONKA, LAWRENCE JOHN, manufacturing planning administrator; b. Detroit, Sept. 1, 1949; s. Maximillian John and Leona May (Knobloch) P. A.A., Macomb County Community Coll., 1974; B.S. in Indsl. Mgmt., Lawrence Inst. Tech., 1978; M.A. in Indsl. Mgmt., Central Mich. U., 1983. Engr.'s asst. Army Tank Automotive Command, 1967-68; with Sperry & Hutchinson Co., Southfield, Mich., 1973, Chrysler Corp., Detroit, 1973; with Gen. Motors Corp., Warren, Mich., 1973-82, engring. systems coordinator engring. staff, 1976-82, current product engring. until 1982; mfg. engr. Buick-Oldsmobile-Cadillac Group, Gen. Motors Assembly Div.-Orion Pontiac, Mich., 1982-84, sr. analyst advanced vehicle engring. Chevrolet-Pontiac-Can. group Engring. Ctr., Warren, 1985-86; mfg. planning adminstr. Detroit-Hamtramck Assembly Ctr., Cadillac Motor Car Co., Allanté, 1986—. Served with USAF, 1968-72, Vietnam. Decorated Air Force Commendation medal. Mem. Soc. Automotive Engrs., Engring. Soc. Detroit, Am. Legion, Vietnam, Japan, Okinawa DAV. Roman Catholic. Home: PO Box 872 Rochester Hills MI 48308-0872 Office: Gen Motors Corp 2500 E General Motors Blvd Detroit MI 48211-2002

PONKO, WILLIAM REUBEN, architect; b. Wausau, Wis., Apr. 4, 1948; s. Reuben Harrison and Ora Marie (Ranke) P.; m. Kathleen Ann Hilt, May 5, 1973; children—William Benjamin, Sarah Elizabeth. B.Arch. magna cum laude, U. Notre Dame, 1971. Cert. Nat. Council Archl. Registration Bds. Ptnr., architect, dir. ednl./instl. specialty LeRoy Troyer & Assocs., Mishawaka, Ind., 1971—; design instr. dept. architecture U. Notre Dame, 1976. Leonard M. Anson Meml. scholar, 1966-70. Mem. AIA (gold medal for excellence in archtl. edn. 1971), Ind. Soc. Architects (design excellence award 1978, chpt. pres. 1985). Prin. archtl. works include: St. Peter Luth. Ch., Mishawaka, Ind., 1979, 4 brs. for South Bend Pub. Library, 1983; Edward J. Funk & Sons office bldg., Kentland, Ind., 1976; Music Edn. bldg. Taylor U., Upland, Ind., 1982, Taylor U. Library, carillon tower, 1985. Office: 415 Lincolnway E Mishawaka IN 46544

PONOMARENKO, NICHOLAS, electrical engineer; b. Poltava, Russia, Feb. 19, 1949; came to U.S., 1976, naturalized, 1982; s. Michail Vasilievich and Katherina Prokhorovna (Olephirenko) P.; m. Ella Plotkin, Jan. 31, 1971; children—Vadim, Marian. M.S. in Elec. Engring., Kiev (Ukraine) Politech. Inst., 1972. Registered profl. engr., Mich. Elec. engr. Moscow Electrotech. Inst., Russia, 1972-75; designer Continental Connector Corp., N.Y.C., 1976-77; elec. engr. Treadwell Corp., N.Y.C., 1977-78, Commonwealth Corp., Jackson, Mich., 1978-79; sr. elec. engr. Bechtel Power Corp., Ann Arbor, Mich., 1979-84; staff elec. engr. Machine Vision Internat., Ann Arbor, 1983—. Mem. IEEE, Nat. Rifle Assn. Home: 3006 Lexington Dr Ann Arbor MI 48105 Office: 325 E Eisenhower Pkwy Ann Arbor MI 48104

PONSOR, KENNETH CLEDE, manufacturing executive, engineer; b. Oswego, Kans., Sept. 4, 1936; s. Kenneth O. and Laura E. (Bell) P.; m. Jean Wharton, Dec. 12, 1958 (div. Apr. 1977); m. Sharon E. Meany, Dec. 20, 1982; children: Joy, Crystal, Gayanna. BS MechE, U. Okla., 1960; MS in Adminstrn., Cornell U., 1962. Various positions with Owens-Ill., Inc., Toledo, 1961-82, v.p., gen. mgr. bus. devel., 1982—. Served to cpl. USMC, 1953-56. Republican. Roman Catholic. Office: Owens Ill Inc 1 Seagate Toledo OH 43666

PONTIKES, KENNETH NICHOLAS, computer leasing company executive; b. Chgo., 1940; m. Lynne M. Weston, June 21, 1980. B.S., So. Ill. U., 1962. With Internat. Bus. Machines, 1961-67; sales dept. OEI Sales Corp., 1967; sales rep. Officer Eletrs Inc., Chgo., 1967-68; mgr. brokerage ops. Data Power Inc., Chgo., 1968-69; pres. Comdisco, Inc., Des Plaines, Ill., 1969-76; chmn. bd., pres., chief exec. officer Comdisco, Inc., 1976—. Served with USAR, 1963-69. Office: Comdisco Inc 6400 Shafer Ct Rosemont IL 60018

PONTIUS, HAROLD THEODORE, manufacturing company owner; b. Lancaster, Ohio, Apr. 27, 1930; s. James Theodore and Esther (Mauller) P.; m. June Prince, July 26, 1952; children: Deborah Kay Pontius Vickers, Jeffrey Scott. BS in Edn., Ohio State U., 1953. With Columbus (Ohio) Coated Fabrics, 1956-58, Barnebey Cheney, Columbus, 1959-63; self-employed Columbus, 1963-65; co-founder Columbus Industries, Inc., Circleville, Ohio, 1965—; pres., bd. dirs. Columbus Industries, Inc., Ashville, Ohio, 1979—; bd. dirs. Mt. Carmel Found. Patentee expanded activated carbon, 1984. Served with USAF, 1954-56. Recipient State of Ohio Landscaping award, 1986. Mem. Nat. Assn. Mfg., Air Movement and Control Assn., Circleville C. of C. (membership chmn. 1975-80), Scioto Soc. (bd. dirs. 1982-84). Republican. Methodist. Clubs: Muirfield Golf, Country (Dublin, Ohio); Yacht and Racquet (Boca Raton, Fla.) (pres., bd. dirs. 1982-84). Lodge: Lions (bd. dirs. Amanda, Ohio 1962-65). Avocations: boating, golf. Office: Columbus Industries Inc 2938 St Rt 752 PO Box 257 Ashville OH 43103-0257

POOL, NANCY MOESSMER, communications executive, consultant; b. St. Louis County, Mo., Dec. 4, 1920; d. Oscar S. and Ruth Aline (Hutchinson) Moessmer; m. Robert J. Steuber, 1951 (div.); m. E. Rothwell Pool III, 1961 (div.); m. Victor W. Leffler, 1978 (div.). Student, William Woods Coll., 1937-38; BA in English, Washington U., 1941. V.p., gen. mgr., ptnr. Sta. KADI-FM, St. Louis, 1966-67; v.p., gen. mgr. Sta. WIL-FM, St. Louis, 1967-69, Sta. KSHE-FM, St. Louis, 1969-84, Sta. KWK/KGLD, St. Louis, 1984-85, Sta. KXOK, St. Louis, 1986—; cons. broadcasting, St. Louis, 1985—; bd. dirs. Broadcast Ctr., St. Louis. Mem. St. Louis Radio Assn. (co-founder). Avocations: jogging, tennis, music, charities. Home: 6 Edgewood Rd Ladue MO 63124 Office: Sta KXOX 7777 Bonhomme Ave Saint Louis MO 63105

POOLE, MARY ANN, educator; b. Stout, Ohio, Apr. 20, 1950; d. Wood and Lou Vivian (Skeens) Hodge.; m. Russel Ward Poole, June 14, 1975; children: Christopher Adam, Ann-Marie. BS in Edn., Ohio U., 1971; MEd, Coll. Mount St. Joseph, Ohio, 1986. Tchr. Ohio Valley Local Schs., West Union, Ohio, 1971—; sponsor cheerleading Green Local Sch., Stout, 1971-79; tchr. Head Start Program, Decatur, Ohio, 1971-72; reading recovery program tchr. Ohio Dept. Edn., Columbus, 1986. Active with Manchester (Ohio) United Meth. Ch., 1981—, co-founder of Kids for Christmas Fellowship; officer PTO Green Local Sch., Stout, 1980-84. Named Woolard Elem. Sch. Tchr. of Yr. 1986-87, Ohio Valley local Tchr. of Yr., 1986-87. Mem. NEA, Ohio Edn. Assn., Southwest Edn. Assn., Ohio Valley Local Edn. Assn. (bldg. rep. 1979-86). Democrat. Avocations: ceramics, traveling, baseball. Home: 10 Pumpkin Ridge Rd Manchester OH 45144 Office: Woolard Elem Sch 315 9th St Manchester OH 45144

POORMAN, PAUL ARTHUR, educator, media consultant; b. Lock Haven, Pa., Aug. 29, 1930; s. Wilson Paul and and Margaret (Heylmun) P.; m. Sylvia Elizabeth Powers, Nov. 22, 1952; children: Pamela (Mrs. Robert Phillips), Cynthia (Mrs. Donald Paul), Peter, Stephen, Thomas, Andrew, Robert, William. B.A., Pa. State U., 1952. Reporter State College (Pa.) Centre Daily Times, 1953-57, news editor, 1957-62; news editor Harrisburg (Pa.) Patriot, 1962-63, Phila. Bulletin, 1963-66; asst. mng. editor Detroit News, 1966-69, mng. editor, 1969-75; vis. prof. Northwestern U., Evanston, Ill., 1975-76; editor Akron (Ohio) Beacon Jour., 1976-86; prof. journalism, spl. asst. to pres. Kent (Ohio) State U., 1986—. Served with USAF 1951-53. Mem. Am. Soc. Newspaper Editors, AP Mng. Editors (regent). Office: Kent State U 2d Floor Library Kent OH 44242

POOVEY, KIRT ROBERT, energy conservation company executive; b. Wellington, Kans., Mar. 29, 1953; s. Orlo John and Louise Helena (Schultze) P.; m. Ruth Elaine Baringer, July 31, 1976; children: Jason Michael, Erin Marie. BS in Sci. Edn., Phillips U., 1975. Student intramural dir. Phillips U., Enid, Okla., 1972-75; sci. tchr. Enid Pub. Schs., 1976-77; firefighter, emergency med. technician Enid Fire Dept., 1977-80, Wellington (Kans.) Fire Dept., 1980-83, Manhattan (Kans.) Fire Dept., 1983-84; pres., owner KRIS Enterprises, Hutchinson, Kans., 1987—; pres. Enercological Mgmt. Systems, Wichita, Kans., 1985, Enercological Mgmt. Industries, Hutchinson, 1985. Pres. Christian Men's Fellowship, Wellington, 1982-83; mem. Sumner County Choral Soc., Wellington, 1982-83. Recipient Sci. Achievement award USAF, 1971, Commendation, Am. Soc. Microbiology, 1977. Mem. Nat. Assn. Realtors, Kans. Assn. Realtors, Kans. Farm Bur., Greater Hutchinson C. of C., The Planetary Soc. (charter), Nat. Arbor Day Found., Group Against Smoking Pollution, Handgun Control, Sierra Club. Republican. Mem. Christian Ch. Club: Camelot (Enid). Avocations: camping, motorcycles, reading, song writing, sports. Home: 2901 Acres Rd Hutchinson KS 67502

POPE, JOHN WARING, investments accounts administrator; b. Chgo., Jan. 9, 1913; s. Henry and Adele Freida Pope; m. Elizabeth Louise Davis, Aug. 25, 1938 (dec. Jan. 1987); children: John W. (dec.), Henry Dewitt, Elizabeth Jane (dec.), Sabina West, Roger Conant. Asst. to pres. and chmn. Bear Brand Hosiery Co., Chgo. and Kankakee, Ill., 1935-42; asst. to pres. and chmn. Paramount Textile Machinery Co., Chgo. and Kankakee, 1935-42, v.p., 1945-65; asst. to personnel dir. Quaker Oats Ordnance Corps, Grand Island, Nebr., 1942-44; prodn. planner, personnel asst. Douglas Aircraft Corp., Park Ridge, Ill., 1944-45; v.p. Pope Brace Co., Chgo. and Kankakee, 1955-65; pvt. practice investment accounts mgmt. Chgo. and Winnetka, Ill., 1948—; dir., v.p., sec. Pope Found., Inc., Chgo. and Winnetka, 1937—; owner, operator farm, Ill., 1951-60. Mem. Investment Analysts Soc. Chgo., Fin. Analysts Fedn., Inst. Chartered Fin. Analysts, Sigma Phi. Republican. Congregrationalist. Clubs: Chgo. Farmer's, Indian Hill. Home and Office: 649 Locust St Winnetka IL 60093

POPE, JON ROBERT, architect; b. Ames, Iowa, Feb. 9, 1949; s. Robert Lee and Elaine Yvonne (Ostrem) P.; m. Bonnie Jeanette Schultz, Feb. 5, 1972. BArch, U. Minn., 1973. Registered architect, Minn. Architect Anchor-Mortlock et al, Sydney, Australia, 1974-75; v.p. Pope Assocs. Inc., St. Paul, 1975-86, pres., 1986—. Mem. AIA (Minn. chpt.), Nat. Assn. of Indusl. and Office Parks. Lutheran. Office: Pope Assocs Inc 533 Saint Clair Ave Saint Paul MN 55102

POPE, ROBERT DEARBORN, manufacturing executive; b. San Francisco, Sept. 18, 1933; s. John Thomas and Valeria (Wood) P.; m. Carol Catrow, July 20, 1957; children: Jacquelyn Pope Colleran, Jill. BSBA and Prodn. Mgmt. with honors, U. Calif., Berkeley, 1956, MBA in Ops. Mgmt., 1957. Various positions Gen. Electric Co., Erie, Pa., 1957-76; various mgmt. positions Studebaker-Worthington div. McGraw-Edison Co., St. Cloud, Minn., 1976-80; pres. N.Am. region Studebaker-Worthington div. McGraw-Edison Co., Mountainside, N.J., 1980-82; pres., chief operating officer Woodward Gov. Co., Rockford, Ill., 1982—. Treas. United Way Services, Rockford, 1984—. Republican. Congregationalist. Office: Woodward Gov Co 5001 N 2d St Rockford IL 61125-7001

POPKE, LITA MASINI, lawyer; b. Chgo., May 27, 1958; d. Donald Joseph and Mary Kay (McDonough) M.; m. David Alan Popke, May 24, 1980. BA, St. Mary's Coll., 1980; JD, U. Detroit Sch. Law, 1983. Bar: Mich. 1983, U.S. Dist. Ct. (ea. dist.) Mich. 1983, U.S. Ct. Appeals (6th cir.) 1987. Atty. Harvey, Kruse, Westen & Milan, P.C., Detroit, 1983-85, Mager, Monahan, Donaldson, & Alber, Detroit, 1985—. Mem. ABA, Detroit Bar Assn. Roman Catholic. Office: Mager Monohan Donaldson & Alber 2000 First Nat Bldg Detroit MI 48226

POPKIN, MICHAEL KENNETH, psychiatrist; b. Trenton, N.J., Dec. 31, 1943; s. J. Charles and Vivian (Robinson) P.; m. Reneé B. Camhe, Dec. 19, 1971; children: Charles, Sara, Lee. AB, Princeton U., 1965; MD, U. Chgo., 1969. Diplomate Am. Bd. Psychiatry and Neurology. Intern N.Y. U. Bellevue Hosp., N.Y.C., 1969-70; resident in psychiatry Mass. Gen. Hosp., Boston, 1970-73; from assoc. prof. to prof. depts. psychiatry and medicine U. Minn. Med. Sch., Mpls., 1975—; behavioral scientist Nat. Inst. Health Diabetic Control and Complication Trial, Mpls., 1982—; bd. dirs. Minn. Ctr. Treatment for Torture Victims. Contbr. articles to profl. jours. and books. Fellow Am. Psychiat. Assn., Am. Orthopsychiat. Assn. (dir. 1985-87); mem. Acad. Psychosomatic Medicine (recipient Best Jour. Paper 1979-80, 1981-82), Am. Psychopath. Assn. (counsillor 1984-86), Alcohol Drug Abuse Mental Health Assn. (epidemiol. and services research rev. com. 1985-89), Am. Psychosomatic Soc. Jewish. Home: 901 N Tyrol Tr Golden Valley MN 55416 Office: Mayo Bldg Box 345 U Minn Hosp 420 Delaware St SE Minneapolis MN 55455

POPLAU, DAVID RICHARD, marketing professional; b. Mankato, Minn., Dec. 31, 1946; s. Ruben Charles and Cahterine (Janitschke) P.; m. Virghinia Helen Emery, Mar. 26, 1971; children: Sara, Krista, Thomas. BS in Journalism, U. Minn., 1971. Asst. advt. mgr. MAICO Hearing Inst., Mpls., 1971-74; copywriter Owatonna (Minn.) Tool Co., 1974-84; v.p. B&B Adcrafters, Mpls., 1984; mktg. communications mgr. K.O. Lee Co., Aberdeen, S.D., 1985—. Advisor Jr. Achievement, Aberdeen, 1985; media dir. Steele County Dems., Owatonna, 1981-84, Frank Bohall Campaign, Aberdeen, 1986. Mem. S.D. Ad Fedn., Photo Soc. of the Dakotas (pres. 1985—). Democrat. Roman Catholic. Lodge: Sertoma (sec. 1980-84). Home: 407 16th Ave NE Aberdeen SD 57401 Office: KO Lee Co 200 S Harrison Aberdeen SD 57402-1416

POPLAWSKI, JOSEPH WALTER, glass mfg. co. exec.; b. Chgo., July 8, 1932; s. Joseph and Catherine P.; m. Geraldine Snell, May 24, 1952; children—Joseph, Thomas, Jerald, Julianne, Scott. With Phoenix Closures Co., Chgo., 1953-81, v.p. mfg., 1978-81; v.p., plant mgr. Kerr Glass Mfg. Co., Chgo., 1981—; dir. Loring Inc. Chmn. Mohawk council Boy Scouts Am., Chgo., 1963-65. Served with U.S. Army, 1949-52. Office: 2444 W 16th St Chicago IL 60608

POPOFF, FRANK PETER, chemical company executive; b. Sofia, Bulgaria, Oct. 27, 1935; came to U.S., 1940; s. Eftim and Stoyanka (Kossoroff) P.; m. Jean Urse; children: John V., Thomas F., Steven M. B.S. in Chemistry, Ind. U., 1957, M.B.A., 1959. With Dow Chem. Co., Midland, Mich., 1959—, exec. v.p., 1985-87, pres., chief operating officer, 1987—, also bd. dirs.; exec. v.p., then pres. Dow Chem. Europe subs., Horgen, Switzerland, 1976-85; Bd. dirs. Chem. Bank & Trust Co. Midland, The Salk Inst. Office: Dow Chem Co 2030 Willard H Dow Ctr Midland MI 48674

POPPE, WASSILY, chemist; b. Riga, Latvia, Nov. 10, 1918; came to U.S., 1959, naturalized, 1965; s. Wilhelm and Barbara (Gogotoff) P.; m. Larissa Heffner, Oct. 16, 1942; 1 child, Katherine Poppe Zawadzkas. Student, Kaiser Friedrich Wilhelm U., Berlin, 1936-39; cand. chem., U. Tubingen, Fed. Republic Germany, 1947; dipl. chem., Inst. Tech. Stuttgart, Fed. Republic Germany, 1949; Ph.D., U. Pitts., 1966. Chemist Dr. Hans Kittel Chem. Lab., Germany, 1949-50; devel. chemist Karl Worwag Lack & Farbenfabrik, Germany, 1950-51; prodn. mgr. paint Pinturas Iris, Venezuela, 1951-53; lab. supr. Pinturas Tucan, Venezuela, 1953-54, tech. dir., 1954-57, plant mgr. paint prodn., 1957-59; chemist PPG Industries, Springfield, Pa., 1959-64; research asst. phys. chemistry U. Pitts., 1964-66; group leader surface chemistry Avisun Corp., Marcus-Hook, Pa., 1966-68; research assoc. Amoco Chems., Naperville, Ill., 1968-85. Fellow Am. Inst. Chemists; mem. N.Y. Acad. Sci., Am. Chem. Soc. Home and Office: 105 Main St Lombard IL 60148

POPPER, PAMELA ANNE, investment banker; b. Columbus, Ohio, Oct. 24, 1956; d. Edwin D. and Eleanor Ida P. Student Ohio State U. Assoc. dir. Conservatory of Piano, Columbus, 1974-79; v.p. The Window Man, Columbus, 1979-81; chief exec. officer The Popper Group; pres. Popper Brace Scott, Columbus, 1981—; v.p., dir. Hamilton Fin. Co., Columbus, 1983—; pres., dir. Keystone Nat. Devel. Corp.; dir. Shelter One Group Corp.; dir. Mktg. Solutions Inc, Kaiser Devel. Corp. Chmn. bd. dirs. Neoteric Dance Theatre, Columbus, 1985-87, Netcare Found., Columbus, 1985—, Columbus Contemporary Dance Theatre, 1987—; bd. dirs. Treemar Retreat, South Webster, Ohio, 1986—, Ballet Met., Columbus, 1976-79. Recipient Vol. award Netcare Corp., 1984; profl. sales awards. Mem. Columbus Life Underwriters, Columbus Area Leadership Program, Nat. Assn. Profl. Saleswomen. Republican. Home: 3346 Mansion Way Upper Arlington OH 43221 Office: Popper Group 659 F Park Meadow Westerville OH 43081

POPPLE, JOHN ARTHUR, retail executive; b. Sioux Falls, S.D., Nov. 22, 1945; s. Charles Sterling and Helen Ruth (Hinz) P.; m. Cheryl Ruth, June 27, 1970; children: Jennifer Elizabeth, Ryan Christopher. BA in Econs., U. Colo., 1968; MBA, Northwestern U., 1983. Divisional mdse. mgr. Woolco Dept. Stores, Dallas, 1968-73; mdse. mgr. Leewards Creative Crafts, Inc., Elgin, Ill., 1973-80, dir. mktg., 1980-83, v.p. mktg., 1983-85, pres., 1985—. Governing bd. United Way, Elgin, 1986. Mem. Elgin C. of C. (mem. indsl. retention task force 1986), Univ. Colo. Alumni Assn. Republican. Methodist. Clubs: U. Colo. Alumni Assn. (admission rep.). Lodge: Rotary. Avocations: skiing, running, travel. Home: 1220 Kingman Ct Elgin IL 60120 Office: Leewards Creative Crafts Inc 1200 St Charles St Elgin IL 60120

POPRICK, MARY ANN, psychologist; b. Chgo., June 25, 1939; d. Michael and Mary (Mihalcik) Poprick; B.A., De Paul U., 1960, M.A., 1964; Ph.D., Loyola U., Chgo., 1968. Intern in psychology Elgin (Ill.) State Hosp., 1961-62; staff psychologist, 1962; staff psychologist Ill. State Tng. Sch. for Girls, Geneva, 1962-63, Mt. Sinai Hosp., Chgo., 1963-64; lectr. psychology Loyola U. at Chgo., 1964-67; asst. prof. Lewis U., Lockport, 1967-70, assoc. prof., 1970-75, chmn. dept., 1968-72 (on leave 1972-73); postdoctoral intern in clin. psychology Ill. State Psychiat. Inst., Chgo., 1972-73; pvt. clin. practice David Psychiat. Clinic, Ltd., South Holland Ill., 1973-87; pvt. practice, South Holland, Ill., 1987—; assoc. sci. staff Riveredge Hosp., Forest Park, Ill., 1975-76; mem. sci. staff dept. psychiatry Christ Hosp., Oak Lawn, Ill., 1983-85 . Co-chmn. commn. on personal growth and devel. Congregation of 3d Order St. Francis of Mary Immaculate, Joliet, 1970-71; clin. resource person Cath. Archdiocese of Chgo., 1977—. Mem. Am. Psychol. Assn. (rep. from Ill. 1985—), Calif., Ill. (sec.-treas. acad. sect. 1975-77, mem. student devel. com. 1975-77, chmn. acad. sect. 1977-78, 78-79, mem. program com. 1977-78, sec. 1979-81, pres.-elect 1981-82, pres. 1982-83, past pres. 1983-84, chmn. program com. 1981-82, awards com. 1983-86), Midwestern psychol. assn., Soc. for Sci. Study Religion, AAAS, Chgo. Assn. Psychoanalytical Psychology, Kappa Gamma Pi, Psi Chi (sec. 1964-65, pres. 1965-66). Home: 547 Marquette Ave Calumet City IL 60409 Office: 16284 Prince Dr South Holland IL 60473

PORRECA, ANTHONY GABRIEL, educator; b. Providence, Apr. 8, 1941; s. Domenico Bliff and Mary Carmine (Scorpio) P. BA, Bryant Coll., 1963; MA, Boston U., 1965, EdD, 1971. Asst. prof. Bryant Coll., Smithfield, R.I., 1966-71, Boston U., 1971-72; assoc. prof. U. Tenn., Knoxville, 1973-79; prof. edn. Ohio State U., Columbus, 1979—; lectr. in field. Author, pubs. editor; contbr. articles to profl. jours. Served with R.I. N.G., 1966-72. NSF grantee, 1966. Mem. Phi Kappa Phi, Omicron Tau Theta (founder), Delta Pi

Epsilon (advisor). Home: 4088 Mountview Rd Upper Arlington OH 43220 Office: Ohio State U 121 RamseyerHall Columbus OH 43210

PORRETTA, LOUIS PAUL, educator; b. Malvern, Ohio, Sept. 24, 1926; s. Peter A. and Rosa (Tersigne) P.; B.A., Eastern Mich. U., 1950; Ed.M., Wayne State U., 1959, Ed.D., 1967; m. Elizabeth M. Murphy, Oct. 13, 1951; children—Leslie Elizabeth, Paul Louis, Jeffrey Mark. Tchr. elem. sch. Mason Consol. Sch., Erie, Mich., 1952-53, tchr., prin., 1953-54; prin. Mason Jr. High Sch., Erie, Mich., 1954-59; asst. prof. edn. Eastern Mich. U., Ypsilanti, 1959-62, asso. prof., 1962-66, prof. edn., 1967-71, prof. dept. curriculum and instruction, 1974-83, prof. emeritus, 1983—, dir. Office Internat. Projects, 1979-81; dir., owner Sylvan Learning Ctr. of Washtenaw, 1984—; chief-of-party Nat. Tchr. Edn. Center, Somalia, 1967-70; mem. edn. survey team AID, Botswana, Lesotho and Swaziland, 1970, sr. adv. U. Botswana, Lesotho and Swaziland, 1972-74; campus coordinator Swaziland Primary Curriculum Devel. Project, AID, 1978; chief-of-party projects AID, Swaziland, 1975-78, Yemen, 1981-83. Chmn. March of Dimes, Westenaw County, Mich., 1956. Mem. Assn. Tchr. Educators, Inst. Internat. Edn., AAUP, Assn. for Supervision and Curriculum Devel., Phi Delta Kappa, Pi Gamma Mu. Club: Ypsilanti Rotary. Home: 719 Cornell St Ypsilanti MI 48197 Office: Sylvan Lng Ctr Ann Arbor MI 48197

PORTER, ALLEN EDWARD, design firm executive, consultant; b. Chgo., Dec. 17, 1926; s. Morris and Betty (Friedman) P.; m. Sylvia Eve Gosen, May 19, 1963; 1 child, Marlon. Student, Chgo. Acad. Fine Arts, 1942, Art Inst. Chgo., 1943, Bradley U., 1944, Inst. Design, Chgo., 1947-49. Pres. Allen Porter Design, Los Angeles, 1951-57, Porter & Goodman Design Assocs., Los Angeles, 1958-68; chmn. Porter, Goodman & Cheatham, Los Angeles and Chgo., 1969-73; v.p. Goldsmith, Yamasaki & Specht, Chgo., 1975-76; pvt. practice cons. Chgo., 1976-81; pres. Porter/Matjasich & Assocs., Chgo., 1981—; asst. prof. design Calif. State U., Los Angeles, 1966-67; lectr. U. Ill., Chgo., 1969-73, grad. seminar leader, 1981; guest speaker Am. Mgmt. Assn., Chgo., 1972. Exhbns. include Art Dirs. Club Los Angeles, 1953-68, Am. Inst. Graphic Arts, N.Y.C., 1959-72, Am. Mgmt. Assn., N.Y.C., 1959, Type Dirs. Club N.Y.C., 1961, Japan Packaging Exhbn., Tokyo, 1967, USA Packaging Exhbn., Tokyo, 1967, U.S. State Dept. Packaging Exhbn., Vienna, 1972, Soc. Typographic Arts, Chgo., 1977-83, Chgo. Soc. Communication Arts, 1980, Art Dirs. Club N.Y., 1985; contbr. articles to profl. jours. V.p., trustee Saving and Preserving Am. Cultural Environments, Los Angeles, 1980—; founding mem. com. Simon Rodia's Towers in Watts, Los Angeles, 1958—. Served as sgt. U.S. Army, 1945-46. Recipient Honor award Nat. Set Up Paper Box Assn., 1962, Spl. award Merchandising Execs. Club Los Angeles, 1963, Spl. award Japan Package Designers Club, 1967, Silver award Paperboard Packaging Assn., 1976, Best Packaging of Yr. award Print Casebook 2, 1976, 1st award Nat. Retail Hardware Assn., 1978, 1st award Nat. Stationary and Office Equipment Assn. Mem. Soc. Typographic Arts (bd. dirs. 1974-75), Am. Inst. Graphic Arts, Package Designers Council (1st award 1957), Midwest Soc. Profl. Cons. Avocations: writing, photography. Office: Porter/Matjasich & Assocs 154 W Hubbard Chicago IL 60610

PORTER, CHARLES B., cardiologist; b. Kansas City, Mo., Dec. 22, 1951; s. Thomas Charles and Bonnie Irene (Boyd) P.; m. Susan Lee Smith, May 31, 1980; children: Monica Lee, Troy Thomas. BS in Biology, So. Meth. U., 1974; MD, U. Kans., 1977. Intern in internal medicine U. Kans., Kans. City, Kans., 1977-78, resident, 1978-80; cardiology fellow U. Tex. Health Sci. Ctr., San Antonio, 1980-83; consulting cardiologist Mid-Am. Cardiology Assn. Mid-Am. Heart Inst., Kansas City, Mo., 1983—; clin. asst. prof. medicine U. Kans., Kans. City, Kans., 1987—, clin. instr., 1983—. Contbr. articles to profl. jours. Recipient Nat. Research Service award Nat. Inst. Health, San Antonio, Tex. Fellow Am. Coll. Cardiology, Am. Coll. Chest Physicians; Am. Coll. Physicians, Met. Med. Soc. Kans. City, Mo. State Med. Assn. Episcopalian. Avocations: bicycling, tennis, photography. Home: 828 W. 56th St Kansas City MO 64113 Office: Mid-Am Cardiology Inc 4320 Wornall Rd Suite 40-II Kansas City MO 64111

PORTER, COBURN JOSEPH, pediatric cardiologist; b. Des Moines, Feb. 25, 1947; s. Doyle Wilson and Victoria Mary (Leo) P.; m. Penelope Jackson, Aug. 15, 1970; children: Blaise, Jerome, Justin. Student, Creighton U., 1965-68, MD, 1972. Diplomate Am. Bd. Pediatrics. Intern in pediatrics U. Colo., Denver, 1972-73, resident in pediatrics, 1973-75; fellow in cardiology Baylor Coll. Med., Houston, 1975-77, 80-81, asst. prof. pediatrics, 1981-84; cons. pediatrics and pediatric cardiology Mayo Clinic, Rochester, Minn., 1984—; asst. prof. pediatrics Mayo Med. Sch., Rochester, Minn., 1984—. Contbr. numerous articles, papers and presentations to med. jours., books and confs., 1976—. Served to maj. U.S. Army, 1977-80. Am. Heart Assn. grantee, 1983. Fellow Am. Acad. Pediatrics (pediatric cardiology sect.), Am. Coll. Cardiology; mem. N.Am. Soc. Pacing and Electrophysiology, Sigma Xi. Roman Catholic. Home: 2237 Telemark Ln NW Rochester MN 55901 Office: Mayo Clinic 200 SW 1st St Rochester MN 55905

PORTER, DAVID STEWART, U.S. dist. judge; b. Cin., Sept. 23, 1909; s. Charles Hamilton and Caroline (Pemberton) P.; m. Marjorie Bluett Ellis, July 26, 1956; children by previous marriage—Mary Stewart, Margaret Lee, Elizabeth Sue. A.B., U. Cin., 1932, J.D., 1934. Bar: Ohio bar 1934. Practice in Troy, 1936-49; judge Common Pleas Ct., Miami County, Ohio, 1949-66; U.S. dist. judge So. Dist., Ohio, 1966-79; sr. dist. judge So. Dist., 1979—; Active Ohio Jud. Conf.; past pres. Ohio Common Pleas Judges Assn.; faculty adviser Nat. Coll. State Trial Judges, 1964-65. Past bd. dirs. Ohio Blue Cross, Dettmer Hosp., Troy. Mem. Am., Ohio, Cin. and Miami County bar assns., Am. Judicature Soc. Presbyn. (elder). Office: 823 US Post Office and Court House Cincinnati OH 45202

PORTER, DONALD EARL, real estate agency owner; b. Beloit, Wis., Oct. 16, 1929; s. William Earl and Thelma Faire (Ewald) P.; m. Carol Mae Shoemaker, Mar. 7, 1954; children: David Earl, Pamela June. BS, U. Kans., 1953. Lic. real estate agt., Kans. Mgr. Porter Hotel, Beloit, Kans., 1958; owner, mgr. Coffee House, Beloit, 1958-63, Porter Co., Beloit, 1964—, Mitchell County Real Estate, Beloit, 1968—, Porter Farms, Beloit, 1972—; pres. Waconda Travel, Beloit, 1983—. Author: (stage play) Brown vs. Quantrill, 1986. Commr. City of Beloit, 1980—. Republican. Lutheran. Lodges: Elks, Masons. Avocations: travel, stamp collecting. Office: Mitchell County Real Estate 209 E Main Beloit KS 67420

PORTER, DONALD JAMES, judge; b. Madison, S.D., Mar. 24, 1921; s. Donald Irving and Lela Ann (Slack) P.; m. Harriet J. Whitney, Aug. 22, 1948; children: Donald A., Mary Lela, William W., Carolyn S., Elizabeth C. Student, Eastern Normal Coll., 1938-39; B.S., U. S.D., 1942, LL.B., 1943. Bar: S.D. 1943. Individual practice law Chamberlain, S.D., 1947-59; ptnr. May, Porter, Adam, Gerdes & Thompson, and (predecessor), Pierre, S.D., 1959-77; assoc. justice S.D. Supreme Ct., Pierre, 1977-79; chief judge U.S. Dist. Ct. S.D., 1979—; states atty. Brule County, S.D., 1948-52, 57-59; S.D. commr. Nat. Conf. Commrs. on Uniform State Laws, 1973-76; mem. S.D. Ho. of Reps., 1955-56. Served with U.S. Army, 1943-46, ETO. Mem. Am., S.D. bar assns., Am. Bd. Trial Advocates (charter mem. S.D. chpt.), Am. Judicature Soc. Roman Catholic. Office: US Courthouse 413 Federal Bldg Pierre SD 57501 *

PORTER, DONALD RICHARD, training specialist, teacher; b. Pitts., Aug. 31, 1944; s. Walter Thomas and Mary Rebecca (Brookes) P.; m. Patricia Helen Brown, June 8, 1968 (div. Jan. 1984); children: Jennifer Jo, Vicki Jo, Gerald Matthew; m. Mary Beth Wisniewski, Sept. 21, 1985. Student, Le Tourneau Coll., 1962-64; BEd, No. Ill. U., 1968. Cert. tchr., Ill., Fla. Tchr. Homewood (Ill.) Pub. Sch., 1968-71, St. Lucie County Schs., Ft. Pierce, Fla., 1971-72, Pasco County Schs., Port Richey, Fla., 1972-73, Crete (Ill.) Monee High Sch., 1973-74; application engr. Pullman-Standard, Chgo., 1975-81; mgr. tng. Urban Engring., Chgo., 1981—. Patentee sliding baggage door. Mem. Am. Soc. Tng. and Devel., Ill. Tng. and Devel. Assn. Republican. Roman Catholic. Avocations: golfing, bowling. Home: 1511 Ceres Dr Crown Point IN 46307 Office: Urban Engring 333 W Wacker Dr Chicago IL 60606

PORTER, GEORGE DARWIN, manufacturer's representative company executve; b. Dayton, Pa., July 25, 1937; s. Melvin Clair and Mary Gladys (Thomas) P.; diploma Robert Morris Coll., Pitts., 1957; m. Charlotte Louise Ferkan, June 8, 1963; children—George Darwin, II, Faye Ellen, Joseph Clair, David Eugene. Cert. systems profl. Mgr. data processing Magnetics, Inc., Butler, Pa., 1961-62, 63-67; computer operator Mellon Bank, Pitts., 1962-63; systems and procedures mgr. Dresser Industries Co., Bradford, Pa., 1967-68; info. systems mgr. Standard Transformer Co., Warren, Ohio, 1968-69; v.p. sales Pryor Corp., Chgo., 1969-83, pres., dir., 1983-87; pres. G.D.P. Assocs., Naperville, Ill., 1987—; instr. data processing Pa. State U. Extension, Butler, 1966; commencement speaker Dayton Area High Sch., 1985. Pres. North Rd. Elementary Sch. PTA, Warren, Ohio, 1974-75; lay pres. congregation St. Paul's Luth. Ch., Warren, 1974. Served with U.S. Army, 1958-61; ETO. Recipient numerous sales awards Pryor Corp., 1971-83, Heritage award Robert Morris Coll Alumni Assn., 1986; named to Ky. Col. State of Ky. Mem. Data Processing Mgmt. Assn., Assn. Systems Mgmt. Republican. Lutheran. Clubs: Naperville (Ill.) Country, Brookdale Racquet. Lodges: Masons, Shriners. Home and Office: 1218 Langley Circle Naperville IL 60540-2078

PORTER, H(ARRY) BOONE, Episcopal priest; b. Louisville, Jan. 10, 1923; s. Harry Boone and Charlotte (Wiseman) P.; m. Violet Monser, June 28, 1947; children: Charlotte M., H. Boone III, Michael T., Gabrielle R., Clarissa, Nicholas T. BA, Yale U., 1947; STB, Berkeley Div. Sch., 1950; STM, Gen. Theol. Sem., N.Y.C., 1952; PhD, Oxford U., 1954. Ordained to ministry Episc. Ch., 1950. From asst. to assoc. prof. Nashotah (Wis.) House, 1954-60; prof. liturgics Gen. Theol. Sem., N.Y.C., 1960-70; exec. dir. Roanridge Found., Kansas City, 1970-77; editor The Living Church, Milw., 1977—; priest in charge St. Peter's Ch., North Lake, Wis., 1980—; pres. Episcopal Lit. Fund, Inc., Milw., 1981—, New Directions Ministries, Inc., N.Y., 1980-85. Author: Ordination Prayers, 1967, Keeping the Church Year, 1977, Jeremy Taylor: Liturgist, 1979, A Song of Creation, 1986. Served to tech. sgt. U.S. Army, 1943-45, PTO. Named McMath Lectr., Diocese of Mich., 1965, Sheridan Lectr., Nashotah House, 1986. Fellow North Am. Acad. Liturgy; mem. Associated Parishes, Inc. (council, pres. 1973-75). Clubs: Yale (N.Y.C.); Pendennis (Louisville); Pequot Yacht (Southport, Conn.). Avocations: gardening, horseback riding. Office: The Living Church 816 E Juneau Ave Milwaukee WI 53202

PORTER, J. MICHAEL, association executive. President Toledo Chamber of Commerce, Toledo, OH.

PORTER, JOHN EDWARD, congressman; b. Evanston, Ill., June 1, 1935; s. Harry H. and Beatrice V. P.; m. Kathryn Cameron; 3 children. Attended, M.I.T., Northwestern U.; received B.S.B.A. degree; J.D. with distinction, U. Mich., 1961. Bar: Ill. 1961, U.S. Supreme Ct. 1968. Former honor law grad. atty., appellate div. Dept. Justice, Washington; mem. Ill. Ho. of Reps., 1973-79, 96-100th Congresses from 10th Dist., Ill.; founder, co-chmn. Congl. Human Rights Caucus; founder Congl. Coalition on Population and Devel. Past editor: Mich. Law Rev. Trustee Cove Sch. for Perceptually Handicapped Children. Recipient Best Legislator award League of Conservation Voters, 1973, Best Legislator award Ind. Voters Ill., 1974, Best Legislator award Chgo. Crime Commn., 1976. Republican. Office: 1131 Longworth House Office Bldg Washington DC 20515

PORTER, JOHN WILSON, univ. pres.; b. Ft. Wayne, Ind., Aug. 13, 1931; s. James Richard and Ola (Phillips) P.; m. Lois Helen French, May 27, 1961; children—Stephen James, Donna Agnes. B.A., Albion Coll., 1953, D.Public Adminstrn. (hon.), 1973; M.A., Mich. State U., 1957, Ph.D., 1962, LL.D. (hon.), 1977; LL.D. hon. degrees; L.H.D., Adrian Coll., 1970, U. Detroit, 1979; LL.D., Western Mich. U., 1971, Eastern Mich. U., 1975; HH.D., Kalamazoo Coll., 1973, Detroit Coll. Bus., 1975, Madonna Coll., Livonia, Mich., 1977; D.Ed., Detroit Inst. Tech., 1978; A.A., Schoolcraft Coll., Livonia, Mich., 1979. Counselor Lansing Public Schs., 1953-58; cons. Mich. Dept. Public Instrn., 1958-61; dir. Mich. Higher Edn. Assistance Authority, 1961-65; asso. supt. for higher edn. Mich. Dept. Edn., 1966-69, state supt. schs., 1969-79; pres. Eastern Mich. U., Ypsilanti, 1979—; mem. numerous profl. commns. and bds., 1959—, including; Commn. on Financing Postsecondary Edn., 1972-74, Commn. for Reform Secondary Edn., Kettering Found., 1972-75, Edn. Commn. of States, 1973-79, Nat. Commn. on Performance-Based Edn., 1974-76, Nat. Commn. on Manpower Policy, 1974-79, Mich. Employment and Tng. Services Council, 1976-79, Nat. Adv. Council on Social Security, 1977-79, Commn. on Ednl. Credit, Am. Council on Edn., 1977-80; task panel on mental health of family Commn. on Mental Health, 1977-80; mem. Nat. Council for Career Edn. (HEW), 1974-76; pres. Mich. Econ. Edn. Centers, 1980-81; bd. dirs. Chief State Sch. Officers, 1974-79; pres. Council Chief State Sch. Officers, 1977-78; dir. Mich. Bell Telephone Co.; chmn. bd. Coll. Entrance Exam. Bd., 1984-86. Mem. Mich. Commn. on Criminal Justice, 1973-79; trustee Nat. Urban League, 1973-79, Mich. Joint Council on Econ. Edn., 1977-79, Charles Stewart Mott Found., 1981—, Thomas Alva Edison Found., 1981—; bd. dirs. Mich. Internat. Council, 1977—, Nat. Sch. Vol. Program, 1978-79, Mich. Congress Parents and Tchrs.; mem. bd. overseers com. for Grad. Sch., Harvard U., 1980—; mem. edn. com. NAACP; mem. East Lansing Human Relations Commn.; chmn. Am. Assn. State Colls. and U.'s Task Force on Excellence in Edn.; mem. Mich. Council for Humanities, Mich. Martin Luther King, Jr. Holiday Commn., Nat. Commn. Coop. Edn., Gov.'s Blue Ribbon Commn. on Welfare Reform. Recipient numerous awards including Disting. Service award Mich. Congress Parents and Tchrs., 1963, Disting. Service award NAACP, Lansing, 1968; cert. of outstanding achievement Delta Kappa chpt. Phi Beta Sigma, 1970; award for disting. service Assn. Ind. Colls. and Univs. Mich., 1974; Disting. Alumni award Coll. Edn., Mich. State U., 1974; award for disting. service to edn. Mich. State U., 1974; Disting. Alumni award, 1979; award for disting. service to edn. in Mich. Mich. Assn. Secondary Sch. Prins., 1974; President's award as disting. educator Nat. Alliance Black Sch. Educators, 1977; Marcus Foster Disting. Educator award, 1979; recognition award Mich. Ednl. Research Assn., 1978; recognition award Mich. Assn. Secondary Sch. Prins., 1978; recognition award Mich. Assn. Intermediate Sch. Adminstrs., 1979; recognition award Mich. Assn. Sch. Adminstrs., 1979; Mich. Sch. Bus. Ofcls., 1979; resolution Mich. State Legislature, 1978; Anthony Wayne award Coll. Edn., Wayne State U., 1979; Educator of Decade award Mich. Assn. State and Fed. Program Specialists, 1979; Spirit of Detroit award Detroit City Council, 1981. Mem. Am. Assn. Sch. Adminstrs., Am. Assn. State Colls. and Univs. (president's council, chmn. task force on excellence in edn.), Nat. Measurement Council, NAACP (life), Mich. PTA (hon. life), Sigma Pi Phi, Phi Delta Kappa. Trustee East Lansing Edgewood United Ch. Club: Economic (Detroit) (dir. 1979—). Office: Office of Pres Eastern Mich U Ypsilanti MI 48197

PORTER, KAREN COLLINS, social service organization administrator, counselor; b. Detroit, Dec. 3, 1953; d. Cecil Allen and Mary Louise (Grzena) Collins; m. Frederick James Porter, Aug. 16, 1975; children: Suzanne Catherine, Kirstin Maureen. Student, Albion Coll., 1971-74, U. Mich., 1975; BA, U. Colo., Boulder, 1976; Ma, U. Colo., Denver, 1979. Co-dir. Loveland (Colo.) Resource Ctr., 1982-84; asst. dir. Interim House-YWCA, Detroit, 1985; program specialist First Step, Westland, Mich., 1985—; bd. dirs., sec. Loveland Childbirth Edn. Assn., 1980-82; bd. dirs., chairperson Thompson Valley Presch., Loveland, 1980-84; advocate Larimer City Sexual Assault Team, Loveland, 1982-84; bd. dirs., mem. fin. com. Samaritan Counseling Ctr., Farmington Hills, Mich., 1985—. Mem. PTO, Farmington Hills, 1984—; leader Girl Scouts Am., Farmington Hills, 1985—. Club: Farmington Community Ctr. Avocations: camping, hiking, cross-country skiing, photography. Home: 29113 Forest Hill Farmington Hills MI 48018 Office: First Step 8381 Farmington Rd Westland MI 48185

PORTER, LAURENCE MINOT, French educator, comparative literature educator; b. Ossining, N.Y., Jan. 17, 1936; s. Fairfield and Anne Elizabeth (Channing) P.; m. Elizabeth Hart, June 9, 1960 (div. Dec. 1979); children: Leon, Sarah; m. Laurel Melinda Cline, Jan. 17, 1980; 1 child, Jack. BA cum laude, Harvard U., 1957, MA, 1959, PhD, 1965. Asst. prof. French, comparative lit. Mich. State U., East Lansing, 1965-69, assoc. prof., 1969-73, prof., 1973—; Andrew W. Mellon disting. vis. prof., U. Pitts., 1980. Author: The Renaissance of the Lyric, 1978, The Literary Dream, 1979, The Interpretation of Dreams, 1987; editor: Aging in Literature, 1984, Critical Essays on Gustave Flaubert, 1986; mem. editorial bd. Degré Second, Blacksburg, Va., 1976—, Nineteenth-Century French Studies, Fredonia, N.Y., 1982—. Del. Ingham County Dem. Precinct, Lansing, Mich., 1984-85; vol. Peace Edn. Ctr., East Lansing, 1980-84, Saving Energy in East Lansing, 1985-86; treas. bd. trustees Episcopal Ministry at Mich. State U., 1970-73. Served with U.S. Army, 1957. Grantee Ford Found., 1966, Mich. State U., 1983, 87; fellow Humanities Research Ctr. Mich. State U., 1970, 74. Mem. MLA (romantic movement bibliography com. 1973-78), Mich. Soc. Psychoanalytic Psychology, Arts and Reflections Forum (steering com. 1986—), Internat. Comparative Lit. Assn., Nat. Colloquium on 19th Century French Studies (co. dir. 1977-78, program com. 1976-77, steering com. 1976-81). Avocations: road racing, folksinging. Home: 926 Sunset Ln East Lansing MI 48823 Office: Mich State U Dept Romance Langs Wells Hall East Lansing MI 48824-1027

PORTER, ROBERT COLEMAN, data processing financial executive; b. Springfield, Ill., Oct. 18, 1956; s. Harlod Lewis and Janice Christine (Weckler) P.; m. Patricia J. Gaa, May 17, 1980; 1 child, Katherine Ann. BS in Bus., Bradley U., 1979; postgrad., Sangamon State U., 1987—. CPA, Ill. From staff auditor to sr. auditor Ernst & Whinney, CPA's, Springfield, 1980-83; internal auditor Cen. Ill. Pub. Service Co, Springfield, 1983-86, auditor EDP, 1986-87, audit supr. EDP, 1987—. Recipient Recognition award Jr. Achievement. Mem. Am. Inst. CPA's, Inst. Internal Auditors (v.p. Cen. Ill. chpt. 1986-87), EDP Auditors Assn. (founding mem. Ill. chpt. 1983), Nat. Collegiate Athletic Assn. Republican. Club: Bradley U. Avocations: golf, swimming, home computer. Home: 1724 S Lincoln Springfield IL 62704 Office: Cen Ill Pub Service Co 607 E Adams Springfield IL 62701

PORTER, STUART WILLIAMS, investment company executive; b. Detroit, Jan. 11, 1937; s. Stuart Perlee and Alma Bernice (Williams) P.; m. Myrna Marlene Denham, June 27, 1964; children: Stuart, Randall. BS, U. Mich., 1960; MBA, U. Chgo., 1967, postgrad., 1967-68. Investment mgr., ptnr. Weiss Peck & Greer, 1978—. Chmn. Crusade of Mercy, 1973; chmn. investment com. Presbytery of Chgo. Served with USAF, 1961-62. Recipient Excellence in Bus. and Acctg. award Fin. Exec. Inst., 1966; Am. Acctg. Assn. fellow, 1967. Mem. Midwest Pension Conf., Investment Analysts Soc. Chgo., Fin. Analysts Fedn., Investment Tech. Symposium N.Y., Beta Gamma Sigma. Clubs: Renaissance (Detroit); Turnberry Country (Crystal Lake, Ill.); Econ., Chgo. Athletic, Tower Club. Home: 130 Wyngate Dr Barrington IL 60010 Office: 20 N Wacker Dr Suite 4120 Chicago IL 60606

PORTER, TERENCE CLIFTON, lawyer; b. St. Joseph, Mo., Dec. 13, 1934; s. Ernest Clifton and Helen Francis (Denny) P.; B.S. in Agr., J.D., U. Mo., 1958; m. Joyce Newman, June 2, 1956; children—Katherine, Michael, David, Susan. Admitted to Mo. bar, 1958; with firm Clark & Becker, Columbia, Mo., 1958-60, Becker & Porter, 1960-61, Welliver, Porter & Cleveland, 1962-70, Porter, Sprick & Powell, 1970-78, Terence C. Porter, 1979—; pres., dir. Porter Investment Co., 1982—; sec., dir. Boone County Devel. Co., Hilton Inn of Columbia. Served to lt. U.S. Army, 1958. Mem. Am., Mo. bar assns., Delf. Research Inst. Democrat. Presbyterian. Club: Kansas City. Home: 1129 Danforth Circle Columbia MO 65201 Office: 10 N Garth Columbia MO 65201

PORTER, WILLIAM FRANCIS, funeral director; b. Kansas City, June 21, 1951; s. James Francis and Frances Aileen (Hammond) P.; m. Margaret Hope Bilby; children: Patrick Wayne, Joel Ross. BS, Cen. State U., Edmond, Okla., 1973. Embalmer, funeral dir. George F. Porter & Sons, Inc., Kansas City, Kans., 1973—, v.p., 1980-83, pres., 1983-86. Mem. adv. bd. Bethany Med. Ctr., Kansas City, 1983—; pres. Cancer Action Inc., Kansas City, 1985-86; v.p. YMCA, Kansas City, 1985-86, Kansas Children's Mus., 1985-86; chmn. United Way Speakers Bur., 1986; bd. dirs. ARC, Kansas City, 1986, Leadership 2000, Kansas City, 1985-86. Mem. Kansas City C. of C., Kansas City Hosp. Assn. (bd. dirs. 1987). Methodist. Lodges: Rotary (pres. Kansas City 1985-86), Masons.

PORTHOUSE, J. DAVID, investor, small business owner; b. Ravenna, Ohio, Aug. 1, 1938; s. Cyril R. and Roberta (Diehl) P.; m. Jacqueline Spencer, June 15, 1963; children—David R., Diane D. B.S. in Chem. Engring., Purdue U., 1960; M.S. in Chem. Engring., Ohio State U., 1962, M.B.A. in Corp. Fin. and Mktg., 1963. with Monsanto Co., St. Louis, 1963-70, carboline Co, St. Louis, 1970-78; pres., 1981, chief exec. officer, 1982; prin. Champion Boats, Inc., Fred Arbogast Co, Akron; bd. dirs. Mark Twain Nat. Bank, St. Louis. Pres. Porthouse Found., Akron, Ohio, 1981—. Mem. Am. Chem. Soc. Avocations: fishing; hunting; golf.

PORTZ, PAUL EGAN, assistant controller; b. St. Paul, Mar. 18, 1947; s. Roy Henry and Patricia (Egan) P.; m. Carol Elaine Magnuson, Dec. 27, 1973; children: Michael Brandon, Jennifer Nicole. BS in Bus., U. Minn., 1969; MBA, Mankato State U., 1981. CPA, Minn. Acct. Ernst & Whinney, Mpls., 1969-73; acctg. supr. Taylor McCaskill & Co., St. Paul, 1975-79; sr. corp. auditor The Toro Co., Mpls., 1979-81; mgr. fin. reporting Burlington No. R.R., St. Paul, 1981-85; asst. controller Am. Linen Supply Co., Mpls., 1986—. Mem. Am. Inst. CPA's (continuing profl. edn. exec. com. 1978-81), Minn. Soc. CPA's (bd. dirs. 1983-86). Home: 1058 Avanti Dr Mendota Heights MN 55118 Office: Am Linen Supply Co 47 S 9th St Minneapolis MN 55402

POSATERI, JAMES JOSEPH, accountant; b. Moline, Ill., Mar. 24, 1959; s. Joseph and Gladys G. (Hensley) P. BA in Acctg. and Bus., Augustana Coll., 1981. CPA, Ill. Acct. Carpentier, Mitchell, Goddard and Co., Moline, 1983—. Mem. Ill. CPA Soc., Am. Inst. CPA's. Home: 3441-60th St Apt 4A Moline IL 61265 Office: Carpentier Mitchell Goddard & Co 1600-30th Ave Moline IL 61265

POSAWATZ, ANTHONY LEO, transportation company professional; b. Grosse Pointe, Mich., Apr. 22, 1960; s. Anthony and Katharine (Schintzler) P. BSME, Wayne State U., 1982; MBA, Dartmouth Coll., 1986. Registered profl. engr., Mich. Quality engr. truck and coach div. Gen. Motors, Pontiac, Mich., 1982, systems engr. truck and bus group, 1982-84; project mgr. truck and bus group Gen. Motors, Pontiac, 1984-86; instr. Oakland Community Coll., Auburn Hills, Mich. Grad. fellow Gen. Motors Corp., 1984-86; scholar Gen. Motors Corp., 1978-82, Wayne State U., 1978-82. Mem. Am. Soc. Quality Control (cert.), Soc. Automotive Engrs., Engring. Soc. Detroit. Roman Catholic. Club: Carpathia German. Avocations: soccer, cycling, table tennis, clarinet, saxophone. Home: 790 K Bloomfield Village Blvd Auburn Hills MI 48057 Office: Gen Motors Truck and Bus Group 660 South Blvd E 0257-01 Pontiac MI 48053

POSCH, JOHN N., orthopaedist; b. Cardiff, Wales, Feb. 18, 1946; came to U.S., 1946; BS, Boston Coll., 1968; MD, Yale U., 1972. Diplomate Am. Bd. Orthopaedic Surgery. Intern Yale New Haven Hosp., 1972-73; resident in orthopaedic surgery U. Hosp. Cleve., 1973-77; practice medicine specializing in orthopaedic surgery Cleve., 1979-80; orthopaedic surgeon Euclid Clinic Found., Cleve., 1980—. Served to lt. commdr. USNR. Fellow Am. Acad. Orthopaedic Surgeons; mem. AMA, Mid-Am. Orthopaedic Assn., Acad. Medicine Cleve., Ohio State Med. Assn., Ohio Orthopaedic Soc. Office: Euclid Clinic Found 18599 Lakeshore Blvd Cleveland OH 44121

POSEWITZ, JOHN MARTIN, advertising executive; b. Sheboygan, Wis., July 28, 1933; s. John A. and Mary H. (Yekenevicz) P.; m. Mary H. Posewitz, Apr. 8, 1961; children: Julie, John, Michael, Robert. BS, U. Wis., Menomonie, 1956. Advt. mgr. Gilson Bros. Co., Plymouth, Wis., 1960-87; mktg. services mgr. Ingersoll Equioment Co., Winneconne, Wis., 1987—. Served with U.S. Army, 1956-58, Korea. Avocations: woodcarving, furniture building, antiques, watercolors, drawings.

POSEY, JOHN ROBERT, JR., public relations executive; b. Evanston, Ill., Nov. 17, 1953; s. John Robert Sr. and Lois Alice (Ross) P.; m. Margo Jeanette Chatman, Sept. 18, 1979; 1 child, Mercedes Ariel. AB in History, Dartmouth Coll., 1975. Sales rep. Equitable Life Ins. Co., Evanston, Ill., 1976-77; mgr. pub. relations McDonald's Corp., Oakbrook, Ill., 1977-82; pres. Posey Communications, Chgo., 1982-84; dir. mktg. and neighborhood festivals Office of the Mayor, Chgo., 1984—. Mem. adv. bd. Nat. Sch. Vol. Program, Alexandria, Va., 1977-79; bd. dirs. Fort Valley (Ga.) State Coll. Bus. Sch., 1979-82; mem. Nat. Urban Affairs Council, Chgo., 1978-82. Recipient Service award Korean Sports Com. Chgo. 1982, Cert. of Excellence Communication Collaborative, 1980; named one of Outstanding Young Men of Am., 1979; named Businessman of Yr. 87th St. Bus. Assn., 1981. Mem. Jaycees. Democrat. Roman Catholic. Club: Dartmouth (Chgo.). Avocation: collecting jazz records. Home: 1311 W Farwell Chicago IL

60626 Office: Mayor's Office Spl Events 121 N LaSalle Room 703 Chicago IL 60602

POSITANO, DOMINIC FRANK, engineering executive; b. Chgo., Nov. 12, 1939; s. Nick and Helen Ann (Durante) P.; m. Sandra Kania, Sept 18, 1965; children: Vince, Jeff, Laura, Gina. BA, DePaul U., 1962; BSEE, Ill. Inst. Tech., 1962. Design engr. ITT Corp., Chgo., 1962-65; supr. GTE Automatic Electric, Northlake, Ill., 1965-75; product mgr., engring. mgr. C.P. Clare/ Gen. Industries Corp., Chgo., 1975-81; engring. mgr. Teradyne, Deerfield, Ill., 1981-85, Chgo. Laser Systems, 1985—. Mem. Internat. Soc. for Hybrid Electronics. Lodge: KC. Office: Chgo Laser Systems 4034 N Nashville Chicago IL 60634

POSNER, MARC DAVID, youth service professional; b. Wallingford, Conn., Oct. 31, 1944; s. Philip and Rose Irma (Factor) P.; m. Elizabeth Ann Wagoner, June 7, 1968; children: Matthew Tad, Jenny Sarah. BA, Bradley U., 1968. Dist. exec. Creve Coeur Council Boy Scouts Am., Peoria, Ill., 1969-72; exploring exec. Creve Coeur Council Boy Scouts Am., Peoria, 1972-75; multiple person dist. exec. W.D. Boyce Council Boy Scouts Am., Peoria, 1976-78; fin. dir. Lake Huron Area Council Boy Scouts Am., Auburn, Mich., 1978-84; scout exec. Western Res. Council Boy Scouts Am., Warren, Ohio, 1984—. Bd. dirs. fin. com. West Bluff Neighborhood Housing Service, Peoria, 1976-78; trustee Unitarian-Universalist Fellowship, Midland, Mich., 1983-84. Lodges: Elks, Kiwanis (bd. dirs. Midland, Mich. club 1981-84), Rotary (bd. dirs. Peru, Ill. club 1974-75). Avocations: American history, bicycle touring, backpacking, hiking. Home: 321 Genesee Ave NE Warren OH 44483 Office: 1662 Mahoning Ave NW Warren OH 44483

POSNER, RICHARD ALLEN, federal court judge, lecturer; b. N.Y.C., Jan. 11, 1939; s. Max and Blanche Posner; m. Charlene Ruth Horn, Aug. 13, 1962; children: Kenneth A., Eric A. A.B., Yale U., 1959; LL.B., Harvard U., 1962; LL.D. (hon.), Syracuse U., 1986. Bar: N.Y. 1963, U.S. Supreme Ct. 1966. Law clk. Justice William J. Brennan Jr. U.S. Supreme Ct., Washington, 1962-63; asst. to commr. FTC, Washington, 1963-65; asst. to solicitor gen. U.S. Dept. Justice, Washington, 1965-67; gen. counsel Pres.'s Task Force on Communications Policy, Washington, 1967-68; assoc. prof. Stanford U. Law Sch., Calif., 1968-69; prof. U. Chgo. Law Sch., 1969-78, Lee and Brena Freeman prof., 1978-81, sr. lectr., 1981—; circuit judge U.S. Ct. Appeals (7th cir.), Chgo., 1981—; research assoc. Nat. Bur. Econ. Research, Cambridge, Mass., 1971-81; pres. Lexecon Inc., Chgo., 1977-81. Author: Antitrust Law: An Economic Perspective, 1976, Economic Analysis of Law, 3d edit., 1986, The Economics of Justice, 1981, The Federal Courts: Crisis and Reform, 1985; pres.: Harvard Law Rev., 1961-62; editor: Jour. Legal Studies, 1972-81. Fellow AAAS, Am. Law Inst., British Acad.; mem. ABA, Am. Econ. Assn. Republican. Office: U S Ct of Appeals 219 S Dearborn Chicago IL 60604

POSNICK, ADOLPH, chemical company executive; b. Yellow Creek, Sask., Can., May 3, 1926; came to U.S., 1947; s. Frank and Joanne (Shimko) P.; m. Sarah Anne Briggs, May 16, 1947; children—Joann Elizabeth, Barbara Ellen. B.S. in Ceramic Engring, U. Sask., 1947. Research engr. Ferro Corp., Cleve., 1947-50; tech. dir. Ferro Enamel-Brazil, Sao Paulo, 1950-56; mng. dir. Ferro Enamel-Brazil, 1956-65; v.p. internat. ops. Ferro Corp., Cleve., 1965-74; sr. v.p. ops. Ferro Corp., 1974-75, exec. v.p., 1975-76, pres., chief exec. officer, 1976—, also dir.; dir. fgn. subsidiaries. Mem. Am., Brazilian ceramic socs., Cleve. World Trade. Clubs: Clevelander, Mid Day, Chagrin Valley Country, Union, Pepper Pike Country. Office: Ferro Corp 1 Erieview Plaza Cleveland OH 44114

POST, MARK EDWARD, architect; b. Grand Rapids, Mich., Aug. 28, 1952; s. David E. and Margaret Mary (McKay) P.; m. Helen C. Strom, June 5, 1976; children: Lindsey, Andrew. AS, Grand Rapids Jr. Coll., 1974; BArch, U. Mich., 1976, MArch, 1978. Registered architect, Mich. Architect, pres. Post Assocs., Grand Rapids, Mich., 1978—. Mem. AIA. Evangelical. Avocations: tennis, golf, skiing. Home: 3874 Baywood Dr Grand Rapids MI 49506 Office: Post Assocs Inc 201 Monroe NW Grand Rapids MI 49503

POSTEMA, RICHARD LEE, consulting chemical engineer; b. Grand Rapids, Mich., Feb. 23, 1955; s. Richard Ray and Ruth Elizabeth (Puite) P.; m. Karen Elaine Drukker, Sept. 29, 1979; children: Eric, Jennifer, Stephanie Nicole. BS, Calvin Coll., 1976; BSCE, Mich. Tech. U., 1978. Registered profl. engr., Mich. Prin. Richard Postema Assocs., Wyoming, Mich., 1978—. Mem. ASHRAE, Nat. Fire Protection Assn. Mem. Grace Ref. Ch. Home: 3251 Shoshone SW Grandville MI 49418 Office: Richard Postema Assocs 1590 44th St SW Wyoming MI 49509

POSTHUMUS, RICHARD EARL, state senator, farmer; b. Hastings, Mich., July 19, 1950; s. Earl Martin and Lola Marie (Wieland) P.; m. Pamela Ann Bartz, June 23, 1972; children—Krista, Lisa, Heather, Bryan. B.S. in Agrl. Econs. and Pub. Affairs Mgmt., Mich. State U., 1972. Exec. v.p. Farmers and Mfrs. Beet Sugar Assn., Saginaw, Mich., 1972-74, Mich. Beef Commn., Lansing, 1974-78; dir. constituent relations Republican Caucus, Mich. Ho. of Reps., 1979-82; self-employed farmer, 1974—. Third vice chmn. Mich. Republican Com., 1971-73. Mem. Alpha Gamma Rho. Home: 4102 Segwun Ave Lowell MI 49331

POSTMA, EDWARD YNZE, obstetrician/gynecologist; b. Chgo., Oct. 14, 1915; s. Richard and Gertrude (Dykstra) P.; m. Gertrude Bossenbroek, June 19, 1940 (dec. July 1972); children: Lynne, Richard, Edward, Chris, Gary; m. Norma Lou Palmbos, May 11, 1973; children: Lori, Thomas, Jon. BA, Calvin Coll., Grand Rapids, Mich., 1936; MD, U. Mich., 1940. Diplomate Am. Bd. Ob-Gyn. Intern, then resident in ob-gyn Butterworth Hosp., Grand Rapids, 1940-50, mem. ob-gyn staff, 1941—, chmn. ob-gyn dept., 1951-55; cons. Ferguson Hosp., Grand Rapids, 1951-80, PineRest Hosp., Grand Rapids, 1960-80. Contbr. articles to profl. jours. and mags. Med. missionary Christian Reformed Mission, Nigeria, 1958-59; exec. dir. Christian Reformed World Relief Com., Grand Rapids, 1962-63; pres. Grand Rapids Right to Life, 1971-73; v.p. Mich. Right to Life, Lansing, 1971-73. Served to maj. Med. Service Corps, U.S. Army, 1942-46, PTO. Fellow Am. Coll. Ob-Gyn, ACS; mem. Am. Coll. ProLife Ob-Gyn, Mich. State Med. Soc., Kent County Med. Soc. Avocations: oil painting, religious philosophy, gardening, golf. Home: 5861 Lake Harbor Rd Norton Shores MI 49441

POSTMA, SHARON, accountant; b. Sault St. Marie, Mich., May 29, 1959; d. Clifford James and Faye Elaine (Vinkemulder) P. BBA in Acct. and Econs., Lake Superior State Coll., 1981. CPA, Wis. Audit mgr. Arthur Andersen & Co., Milw., 1981—. Mem. Am. Inst. CPA's, Wis. Inst. CPA's. Avocations: golf, tennis, biking, cross country skiing. Home: 3495 N Murray Ave Milwaukee WI 53211 Office: Arthur Andersen & Co 777 E Wisconsin Ave PO Box 1215 Milwaukee WI 53201

POSTMUS, GEORGE MAYNARD, advertising executive; b. Memphis, Nov. 21, 1938; s. George M. and Ella (Brauer) P.; m. JoAnn Jarosik, Aug. 20, 1960 (div. July 1982); children: Barton J., Andrea L. BS, Western Mich. U., 1962. With Am. Seating Co., Grand Rapids, Mich., 1964-68, Steelcase Inc., Grand Rapids, 1968-72; pvt. practice advt. George Postmus Assocs., Grand Rapids, 1972—. Home: 223 Sunset NW Grand Rapids MI 49504 Office: 419 W Leonard Grand Rapids MI 49504

POTASH, JANICE SUE, accounting educator; b. Ft. Knox, Ky., Mar. 24, 1955; d. Robert S. and Madeline J. (Kirschner) Kraft; m. Steven Robert Potash, May 28, 1978; 1 child, Jamie Rebecca. BS in Bus. cum laude, Miami U., Ohio, 1977; MBA, Xavier U., 1982. CPA, Ohio. Staff acct., auditor Arthur Andersen & Co., Cin., 1977-78; acctg. supr. Children's Hosp. Med. Ctr., Cin., 1978-81; asst. prof. acctg. Miami U., Hamilton, Ohio, 1982-84, Marian Coll., Indpls., 1985—. Campaign worker jud. polit. campaigns, Cin., 1972—; mem. Women's Am. ORT, Cin., 1982-85, Indpls., 1986—; advisor Explorer post Boy Scouts Am., Kokomo, Ind., 1984. Mem. Am. Acctg. Assn., Am. Inst. CPA's, Ohio Soc. CPA's, Acctg. Research Assn., Am. Woman's Soc. CPA's, Ind. CPA Soc., Am. Soc. Women Accts. Republican. Jewish. Office: Marian Coll 3200 Cold Spring Rd Indianapolis IN 46222

POTASHNICK, MORTON DOUGLAS, construction company executive; b. Cape Girardeau, Mo., Sept. 23, 1938; s. Eugene Nathan and Vivian (Dye) P.; m. Jane Ella Yount, June 24, 1971; children: Heyde, John Douglas, Nicholas. BSBA, U. Mo., 1962. Pres. R.B. Potashnick Co., Cape Girardeau, 1974—; cons. Alaskan Pipeline, Trinidad Water, Rend Lake Inner City Water, Trans-Argentine Oil, Trailblazer, All Am. Oil, Red River Gas Pipeline projects; commr. Southeast Mo. Port Authority, 1982—; mem. rev. com. on solid waste disposal, 1986—; owner Potashnick Marine Services, Sikeston, Mo., 1983—; co-owner Great Rivers Marine Services, Cairo, Ill., 1984-86. Coach Sikeston Little League, 1984—. Served with U.S. Army, 1960-61. Mem. Pipeline Contractors Assn., Houston Pipeliners Club. Democrat. Methodist. Club: Mo. Athletic (St. Louis). Lodge: Elks. Avocations: golf, tree farming, constrn. consulting. Home: 305 Ridge Dr Sikeston MO 63801 Office: Box 190 Cape Girardeau MO 63701

POTEKIN, BARRY, restauranteur; b. Chgo., Dec. 5, 1945; s. Irv and Thelma P. Student, Wright Jr. Coll., 1964-66, Truman Coll., 1977-79, Loyola U., Chgo., 1979-82. Lic. real estate broker, nursing home adminstr., fgn. currency options trader. Co-owner Tempo Galleries, Chgo. and Nairobi, Kenya, 1965-70, Fountainebleau Manor, Chgo., 1970-76, SRG Realty, Chgo., 1976-83; v.p. mktg. Robert H. Meier and Assocs., Chgo., 1983-84; owner Gold Coast Dogs, Chgo., 1985—. C0-author: Precious Metals Delivery, 1984; contbr. articles to mags. Recipient 3-Star Fast Food Restaurant rating, Chgo. Tribune.

POTENTE, EUGENE, JR., interior designer; b. Kenosha. Wis., July 24, 1921; s. Eugene and Suzanne Marie (Schmit) P.; Ph.B., Marquette U., 1943; postgrad. Stanford U., 1943, N.Y. Sch. Interior Design, 1947; m. Joan Ciöffe, Jan. 29, 1946; children—Eugene J., Peter Michael, John Francis, Suzanne Marie. Founder, pres. Studios of Potente, Inc., Kenosha, Wis., 1949—; pres., founder Archtl. Services Assos., Kenosha, 1978—, Bus. Leasing Services of Wis. Inc., 1978—; past nat. pres. Inter-Faith Forum on Religion, Art and Architecture; vice chmn. State Capitol and Exec. Residence Bd., 1981-87. Sec., Kenosha Symphony Assn., 1968-74. Bd. dirs. Ctr. for Religion and the Arts, Wesley Theol. Sem., Washington, 1983-84. Served with AUS, 1943-46. Mem. Am. Soc. Interior Designers (treas., pres. Wis. 1985—, chmn. nat. pub. service 1986), Inst. Bus. Designers, Sigma Delta Chi. Roman Catholic. Lodge: Elks. Home: 8609 2d Ave Kenosha WI 53140 Office: 914 60th St Kenosha WI 53140

POTHAST, HENRY LYNN, school social worker; b. Marshalltown, Iowa, Apr. 2, 1952; s. Lester Raymond and Annie (Dunham) P.; student Marshalltown Community Coll., 1970-71; B.A., U. Iowa, 1974, M.S.W., 1981; postgrad. U. No. Iowa, 1977-78, Iowa State U., 1983-87; m. June Dubberke, Feb. 14, 1976; children—Emily Ann, Laura Rachael. Youth services worker Iowa Tng. Sch. for Boys, Eldora, 1974-75, youth counselor I, 1975-78, youth counselor II, 1978-79, instr. high sch. equivalency, 1975-77; social worker Area Edn. Agy. 6, Eldora, 1981—. Mem. Nat. Assn. Social Workers, Acad. Cert. Social Workers, Iowa Sch. Social Workers' Assn., Phi Beta Kappa, Phi Kappa Phi, Omicron Nu. Club: DeMolay (orator 1969-70). Home: Rt 1 Box 512 Hubbard IA 50122 Office: Area Edn Agy 6 Eldora IA 50627

POTKAY, CHARLES RAYMOND, psychologist, educator; b. Bridgeport, Conn., May 29, 1939; s. Charles Raymond and Helen Rose (Urban) P.; m. Catherine Erhard, Oct. 6, 1962; children: Sandra Louise, Susan Catherine. BA in Psychology, Loyola U., Los Angeles, 1961; MA in Clinical Psychology, Loyola U., Chgo., 1965, PhD in Clinical Psychology, 1968. Lic. psychologist, Ill. Dir. psychology clinic Western Ill. U., Macomb, 1968-72, asst. prof. psychology, assoc. prof., 1972-78, prof., 1978—; pvt. practice part time, Macomb, 1976—; psychologist, cons. County Mental Health Ctr., Beardstown, Ill., 1974-80, Fulton-McDonough Mental Health Ctr., Macomb, 1978-79, Brown County Mental Health Ctr., Sterling, Ill., 1971-74, West Cen. Ill. Spl. Edn. Coop, Macomb, 1969-70, 80, 86, Cottage Hosp., Galesburg, Ill., 1970. Author: The Rorschach Clinician, 1971; co-author Personality Theory: Research and Applications, 1986, Adjective Generation Technique, 1983; founding editor Ill. Psychol. Assn. newsletter Academically Speaking, 1977—; contbr. articles and papers to profl. jours. Chmn. Ill. Psychologists Examining Com., Springfield, 1981-83. Recipient Presdl. Merit award Western Ill. U., 1979-80, 81-83. Fellow Soc. for Personality Assessment (membership com. 1984—); mem. Am. Psychol. Assn., Midwestern Psychol. Assn., Ill. Psychol. Assn. (Outstanding Service award 1985; chmn.-elect, chmn. acad. sect.), Sigma Xi (Researcher of Yr. 1983 Western Ill. U. chpt.), Alpha Sigma Nu. Avocations: listening to music, travel. Home: 227 Kurlene Dr Macomb IL 61455 Office: Western Ill Univ Dept Psychology Macomb IL 61455

POTKIN, NATHAN NORMAN, dentist; b. Chgo., Nov. 5, 1914; s. Max and Bessie (Gross) P.; B.S., U. Ill. Sch. Pharmacy, 1933; D.D.S., U. Ill., 1944, M. Bacteriology, 1935; m. Evelyn Goldman, June 3, 1940; children—Steven, Ralph, Jeffrey, Ben. Faculty, researcher U. Ill. Coll. Dentistry, 1944-53; practice dentistry, Chgo., 1944-53, 55—; chief dental staff Northeast Hosp., Chgo.; chief staff Forkosh Hosp. Mem. Hosp., also chmn. dental com. Active Cub Scouts Am., 1955-57. Served with AUS, 1953-55. Mem. Endodontic Soc., Internat. Dental Research Assn., Ill., Chgo. dental socs. Mason (Shriner). Contbr. to profl. publs. in field. Home: 6950 N Kenneth Ave Lincolnwood IL 60646 Office: 7001 N Clark St Chicago IL 60626

POTT, MARY PATRICIA, accountant; b. Green Bay, Wis., Sept. 5, 1959; d. William S. and Patricia A. (Miswald) Collins; m. Steven M. Pott, Dec. 12, 1 981. BBA in Comprehensive Pub. Acctg., U. Wis., Eau Claire, 1981. CPA, Wis. Supr. Shinner, Hucovski & Co., Green Bay, 1981—. Mem. fin. com. YWCA, Green Bay, 1983—, Girls Couts U.S.; active Jr. Women's Club, Green Bay, 1984—; treas. Calvary Luth. Ch. Mem. Am. Inst. CPA's, WIs. Inst. CPA's, Mgmt. Women. Office: Shinners Hucovski & Co SC PO Box 819 Green Bay WI 54305-0819

POTTER, CORINNE JEAN, librarian; b. Edmonton, Alta., Can., Feb. 2, 1930; d. Vernon Harcourt and Beatrice A. (Demaray) MacNeill; m. William B. Potter, Aug. 11, 1951 (div. Jan. 1978); children—Caroline, Melanie, Theodore, William, Ellen. B.A., Augustana Coll., 1952; M.S., U. Ill., 1976. Br. librarian Rock Island (Ill.) Pub. Library, 1967-73, children's work supr., 1973-74; dir. St. Ambrose U. Library, Davenport, Iowa, 1978—; chairperson Quad City Library Dir.'s Publicity Com., 1984—. Mem. ALA, Assn. Coll. and Research Libraries (sec., v.p., pres. Iowa chpt. 1979-82), Iowa Library Assn. (com. chmn. 1983-84), Iowa Pvt. Academic Libraries Consortium (sec.-treas. 1986—). Office: St Ambrose Coll McMullen Library 518 W Locust Davenport IA 52803

POTTER, GEORGE HARRIS, banker; b. Pitts., Dec. 15, 1936; s. William Sommerville and Katharine (Rockwell) P.; A.B., Colgate U., 1959; m. Nicole Enfield Weir, May 1, 1977; children—Clara Potter Mokher, George Harris, Faris Feland, Jonathan Rockwell, Kristin Enfield Weir, David Bruce Weir, Jr., Jennifer Berkey Weir. Life underwriter Equitable Life Assurance Soc. of U.S., Pitts., 1958-59; with Pitts. Nat. Bank, 1959-64; asst. treas. First Nat. Bank of Miami (Fla.), 1964, asst. v.p., 1964, v.p., 1969-79; v.p. Central Nat. Bank of Cleve., 1979-85, Barclays Bank PLC, 1985-87, v.p., dep. mgr. Cleve. office, 1987—; dir. Nik-Pak, Inc.; mng. partner PTL Assos., 1978-86. Mem. adv. bd. Vanguard Sch., Coconut Grove, Fla., 1968-79. Mem. Nat. Assn. Corp. Dirs., Greater Cleve. Growth Assn., Phi Delta Theta. Republican. Congregationalist. Clubs: University (Pitts.); River Oaks Racquet; Hermit, Mid-Day, City of Cleve., Lakewood Country, Colgate (pres. 1982—) (Cleve.). Home: 18151 Clifton Rd Lakewood OH 44107 Office: 1111 Superior Ave Suite 700 Cleveland OH 44114

POTTER, JACK ARTHUR, optometrist; b. Peoria, Ill., Sept. 7, 1917; s. John Bernard Potter and Mary Bernadot Purcell; m. Charlotte Helen Brubaker, Apr. 5, 1941 (dec. Jan 1974); children: Jack Allen, Lynn Ann; m. Dorothy Grantz Styx, July 24, 1975. OD, Ill. Coll. Optometry, 1938; postgrad., Purdue U., 1946. Pvt. practice optometry East Peoria, Ill., 1938—; chief optometry St. Francis Hosp., Peoria, 1975-82; lectr. Bradley U., Peoria, 1949-72. Contbr. articles on reading and vision problems to profl. jours. Served with U.S. Army, 1941-45. Fellow Am. Acad. Optometry; mem. Am. Optometric Assn. (bd. trustees 1967-73, sec., treas. 1973-75), Ill. Optometric Assn. (pres. 1965-67, Optometrist of Yr. 1967, Disting. Service award 1975), Ill. Valley Optometric Soc. (pres.). Republican. Mem. Christian Ch. Lodges: Masons, Shriners. Home: 609 Hilldale Washington IL 61571 Office: Riverfront Ctr Suite 200 2400 N Main East Peoria IL 61611

POTTER, JOHN EDWARD, radio executive; b. Columbus, Ohio, Nov. 27, 1949; s. Edward John and Alverna E. (Sorg) P.; m. Kathleen Ann Heringer, Jan. 31, 1949; children: Nathan John, Sara Ann, Benjamin John. BA, Ohio State U., 1972. Announcer Sta. WCOL, Columbus, 1969-70, Sta. WMNI, Columbus, 1970-72; announcer Sta. WTVN, Columbus, 1972-75, program dir. 1975-80, account exec. 1980-84, local sales mgr., 1984—. Bd. dirs. Franklin County Heart br., 1978-80; mem. exec. com. Multiple Sclerosis Soc., 1976-80; trustee Columbus U.S.A. Assn., 1977-80; trustee Secret Santa, 1975-80; active Boy Scouts of Am., 1968—; chmn. bd. trustees Rally in the Alley, Inc., 1977-81. Recipient Ten Outstanding Young Citizens award, Columbus Jaycee's, 1978, Chuck E. Selby award, 1979; Quarter Million Dollar Club award Taft Broadcasting, 1980-81, V.I.P. Sales Club award, 1982-85 ; Disting. Sales award Sales Exec. Club, 1981; Pres's award Taft Broadcasting, 1986-87. Mem. Columbus Area C. of C., Radio Advt. Bur., Ohio Assn. Broadcasters. Roman Catholic. Clubs: Downtown Sertoma (pres.), Cath. Businessmen's Luncheon. Mem. editorial bd. WTVN, 1975-80. Office: 42 E Gay St Suite 1500 Columbus OH 43215

POTTER, JOHN W., judge; b. Toledo, Ohio, Oct. 25, 1918; s. Charles and Mary Elizabeth (Baker) P.; m. Phyllis May Bihn, Apr. 14, 1944; children: John William, Carolyn Diane, Kathryn Susan. PhB cum laude, U. Toledo, 1940; JD, U. Mich., 1946. Bar: Ohio. Assoc. Zachman, Boxell, Schroeder & Torbet, Toledo, 1946-51; ptnr. Boxell, Bebout, Torbet & Potter, Toledo, 1951-69; mayor City of Toledo, 1961-67; asst. atty. gen. State of Ohio, 1968-69; judge 6th Dist. Ct. Appeals, 1969-82, U.S. Dist. Ct., Toledo, 1982—. Sr. editor U. Mich. Law Rev., 1946; contbr. articles to profl. jours., opinions. Pres. Ohio Mcpl. League, 1965; v.p. Toledo Area C. of C., 1973-74; former assoc. pub. mem. Toledo Labor Mgmt. Commn.; past pres. U. Toledo Alumni Assn.; past pres., former bd. mem. Commn. on Relations with Toledo, Spain; former bd dirs. Toledo Zool. Soc., Cummings Sch., Toledo Opera Assn.; mem., former trustee Epworth United Meth. Ch.; former mem. bd. dirs. Conlon Ctr.; hon. chmn. Toledo Festival Arts, 1980. Served to capt. F.A., U.S. Army, 1942-46. Decorated Bronze Star; recipient Leadership award Toledo Bldg. Congress, 1965, Outstanding Alumnus award U. Toledo, 1967, award of merit Toledo Bd. Realtors, 1967, Resolution of Recognition award Ohio Ho. of Reps., 1982. Fellow Am. Bar Found., Am. Judicature Soc., 6th Jud. Cir. Dist. Judges Assn., Fed. Judges Assn.; mem. ABA, Ohio Bar Assn., Toledo Bar Assn. (exec. com. 1962-64), Lucas County Bar Assn., Nat. Trust for Hist. Preservation, Phi Kappa Phi. Club: Old Newsboys, Toledo. Lodge: Kiwanis. Home: 2418 Middlesex Dr Toledo OH 43606 Office: US Dist Ct 215 US Courthouse Toledo OH 43624

POTTER, JOSEPH DANIEL, personnel executive; b. St. Louis, Jan. 13, 1955; s. Joe Leonard and Virginia Lee (Peetz) P.; m. Lois Marie Schaper, Oct. 3, 1986 (div. Apr. 1986). Trainer, supr. Mktg. Research Conselor, St. Louis, 1978-80; mgmt. devel. specialist Church's Chicken, St. Louis, 1980-81; instrl. designer, writer Maritz Communications Co., St. Louis, 1982-86; project mgr. videodisc devel. McDonnell Douglas, St. Louis, 1986—; pvt. practice real estate cons., St. Louis, 1986—. Mem. St. Louis Ambassadors, 1986, Big Bros. Big Sisters, St. Louis, 1986, St. Vincente de Paul Soc., St. Louis, 1986. Mem. Am. Soc. for Tng. and Devel. (asst. placement dir. 1981-83, Outstanding Performance award 1983), Nat. Soc. Performance Instruction, Am. Mgmt. Assn., Nat. Assn. Realtors. Avocations: photography, cooking, running. Home: 1070 Boone St Florissant MO 63031 Office: McDonnell Douglas Health Info Systems 600 McDonnell Blvd Saint Louis MO 63042

POTTER, PAUL EDWIN, geology educator, consultant; b. Springfield, Ohio, Aug. 30, 1925; s. Edwin Forest and Mabel (Yanser) P. MS in Geology, U. Chgo., 1950, PhD in Geology, 1952; MS in Stats., U. Ill., 1959. Research assoc. Ill. Geol. Survey, Urbana, 1952-54, asst. geologist, 1954-61; assoc. prof. geology Ind. U., Bloomington, 1963-65, prof., 1965-71; prof. U. Cin., 1971—. Author: Sand and Sandstone, Paleocurrents and Basin Analysis, Introduction to Petrography of Fossils, Sedimentology of Shale. Served with U.S. Army, 1944-46. Sr. NSF fellow, 1958, Guggenheim fellow, 1961-62. Republican. Office: U Cin Dept Geology Cincinnati OH 45221

POTTER, RICHARD CLIFFORD, lawyer; b. Providence, Nov. 25, 1946; s. Peter Rex Potter and Helen Louise (McDevitt) St. Onge; m. Anne Algie, Mar. 22, 1975; children: Catherine Anne, David Henry. BA, U. N.C., 1968; JD cum laude, Ind. U., 1973. Bar: Ill. 1973, U.S. Dist. Ct. (no. dist.) Ill. 1973, U.S. Ct. Appeals (8th cir.) 1975, U.S. Ct. Appeals (3d cir.) 1978, U.S. Ct. Appeals (4th and 5th cirs.) 1979, U.S. Ct. Appeals (9th cir.) 1980, U.S. Supreme Ct. 1979. Assoc. Kirkland & Ellis, Chgo., 1973-75; atty. and ptnr. Bell, Boyd & Lloyd, Chgo., 1975—; lobbyist Boise Cascade Corp., Washington, 1981-84. Assoc. editor, exec. officer Ind. Law Jour., 1972-73; author various publs. Bd. dirs. Northbrook (Ill.) Park Dist. adv. council, 1982. Mem. ABA (co-chair litigation subcom. on FTC, vice chmn. internat. law and practice com. on internat. aspects litigation, chmn. internat. law and pracitce subcom. on settlement and ADR), Internat. Bar Assn., Legal Club Chgo., Asia-Pacific Lawyers Assn., Nat. Health Lawyers Assn. Club: University (Chgo.). Home: 2134 Butternut Ln Northbrook IL 60062 Office: Bell Boyd & Lloyd 70 W Madison Chicago IL 60602

POTTER, RITA JEAN, critical care nurse; b. Seneca, Kans., Sept. 26, 1951; d. Leo Anthony and Marie Katherine (Buessing) Mueting; m. Ronald Preston Potter, July 20, 1974. BSN, Washburn U., 1984. Staff nurse Redicare, Topeka, Kans., 1981-84; office mgr. Medassist Med. Ctr, Topeka, 1984-86; critical care nurse St. Francis Hosp., Topeka, 1980—. Vol. Am. Red Cross (3 gallon donor). Mem. Kans. State Nurses Assn. (treas. 1984-86). Republican. Roman Catholic. Avocations: crocheting, stained glass, reading. Office: St Frances Hosp 1700 W 7th Topeka KS 66614

POTTER, STEVEN EARL, aeronautical engineer; b. Wichita, Kans., Feb. 19, 1945; s. Hershel Otto and Ruth Ida (McHenry) P.; m. Lana June Strait, Apr. 6, 1968; children—Stephaine Colleen, Kent Marion. B.S. in Aero. Engring., Wichita State U., 1971, M.S. in Engring. Mechanics. Design engr. Gates Lear Jet Corp., Wichita, 1967-68; structures engr. Beech Aircraft Corp., Wichita, 1968-74; sr. specialist engr. Boeing Co., Wichita, 1974—. Patentee in field. Deacon, Baptist Ch., Conway Springs, Kans., 1982—; scoutmaster Troop 809 Boy Scouts Am. Mem. AIAA. Republican. Club: Kans. Bassmasters (Wichita) (v.p. 1977), Kans. State Bass Anglers Team. Lodge: Masons (worshipful master 1986). Home: 214 S Cranmer Conway Springs KS 67031

POTTMEYER, JOHN FRANCIS, architect; b. Pitts., Feb. 1, 1949; s. Glenn and Kathleen (Bent) P.; m. Cinda L. Geidel, Oct. 19, 1974; children: Victor I., Ian G., Amber D. BS, Kent (Ohio) State U., 1973. Registered architect, Ohio. Draftsman MKC Assocs., Inc., New Philadelphia, Ohio, 1973-80, project architect, 1980—. Mem. AIA, Constrn. Specifications Inst., Tuscarawas Philharm. Assn. (pres. 1985). Republican. Mem. United Ch. Christ. Office: MKC Assocs Inc 104 Fair Ave NE New Philadelphia OH 44663

POTTORFF, GARY NIAL, veterinarian; b. Wichita, Kans., Mar. 12, 1935; s. George Nial and Corrine Opal (McFerran) P.; m. JoAnn McCluggage, Sept. 1, 1957; children: Michael Lee, Gregory Nial. BS, DVM, Kans. State U., 1959. Veterinarian County Animal Hosp., St. Louis, 1959-61, Wichita, 1961—. Active YMCA, Wichita Bd. Edn., 1965-77, pres. 1977. Mem. AVMA, Kans. Vet. Med. Assn., Wichita Vet. Med. Assn. (pres. 1970), Am. Animal Hosp. Assn., Am. Soc. Vet. Opthalmology, Wichita C. of C. (chair legis.). Republican. Congregationalist. Lodge: Rotary. Avocations: bicycling, racing, touring. Home: 6321 E 8th Wichita KS 67208 Office: Pottorff Animal Hosp 536 S West St Wichita KS 67213

POTTORFF, JERRY LYNN, advertising executive; b. Grant City, Mo., Dec. 14, 1943; s. Ivan Stuart and Maxine (Murray) P. BS, NW Mo. State U., 1966; postgrad., U. Mo., 1967. cert. secondary tchr., Iowa. Tchr. Villisca (Iowa) Pub. Sch., 1966-68; info. specialist Blue Cross/Blue Shield, Des Moines, Iowa, 1969-73; copywriter Ad-Graphics, Des Moines, 1973-78; account exec. CMF&Z, Des Moines, 1978-84, account. supr., 1984-87, v.p., acct. supr., 1987—. mktg. taskforce United Way, Des Moines, 1976. NSF grantee, 1967. Mem. Nat. Agrl. Mktg. Assn. Democrat. Avocations: tennis, swimming, painting. Home: 3313 SW 34th Des Moines IA 50321 Office: CMF&Z Advt 600 E Court Des Moines IA 50306

POTTS, ANTHONY VINCENT, optometrist, orthokeratologist; b. Detroit, Aug. 10, 1945; s. Daniel Edward and Sophie (Dargush) P.; m. Susan Claire, July 1, 1967; children: Anthony Christian. Student, Henry Ford Community Coll., 1964-65, Eastern Mich. U., 1965-66; OD, So. Coll. Optometry, 1970. Cert. in contact lenses Nat. Eye Research Found. Practice orthokeratology and contact lenses Troy, Mich., 1975—; lectr. on orthokeratology and astigmatism numerous orgns. Served as lt. USN, 1971-73. Fellow Internat. Orthokeratology Soc. (membership chmn. 1976-83, bd. dirs. local chpt. 1976-83, chmn. Internat. Eye Research Found. sect. 1981-83, bd. dirs. nat. chpt. 1985—, adminstrv. dir. nat. chpt. 1985—); mem. Am. Optometric Assn., Mich. Optometric Assn., Met. Detroit Optometric Soc., Nat. Eye Research Found. Republican. Roman Catholic. Office: Med Square Troy 1575 West Big Beaver C-11 Troy MI 48098

POTTS, ARTHUR MOOERS, dentist; b. Waukesha, Wis., July 17, 1922; s. Arthur Frederick and Sarah (Mooers) P.; m. Elizabeth Jane Swartz, July 15, 1950; children: Christopher Arthur (dec.), Jeffery Edward, Louise helen. Student, Carroll Coll., 1940-42, U. Wis., 1943; DDS, Marquette U., 1947. Gen. practice dentistry Beloit, Wis., 1947—; guest lectr. Rock Valley Coll.; mem. dental staff Beloit Meml. Hosp. Former cubmaster Boy Scouts Am.; past dental chmn. United Givers; past. pras. Beloit Area Welfare Council,; elder 1st Presbyn. Ch.; elected mem. Beloit City Council, 1963-67; past trustee Beloit Meml. Hosp.,; past mem. Beloit Recreation Bd.; past chmn. Beloit Vicinity Art Show; past. pres. Beloit Art League; past. chmn. March of Dimes; past. pres. bd. dirs. Salvation Army; mem. Beloit Mcpl. Arts Com.; bd. dirs. Family Service Assn. Beloit. CServed to 1st lt. U.S. Army Dental Corps, 1943. Recipient Beloit Booster award; named Boss of Yr. Rock Valley Am. Bus. Womens Assn., 1975-76. Mem. ADA, Wis. Dental Soc. (exec. council), Rock County Dental Soc. (past pres.), Wis. State Dental Polit. Action Com., Beloit Jaycees (past. pres., bd. dirs.), Beta Beta Beta, Delta Sigma Delta, Tau Kappa Epsilon. Presbyterian. Lodge: Rotary (past pres.). Avocations: swimming, gardening, skiing, traveling, photography. Home: 2530 Hawthorne Dr Beloit WI 53511 Office: 400 E Grand Ave Beloit WI 53511

POTTS, BARBARA JOYCE, mayor, radiology technician; b. Los Angeles, Feb. 18, 1932; d. Theodore Thomas and Helen Mae (Kelley) Elledge; m. Donald A. Potts, Dec. 27, 1953; children—Tedd, Douglas, Dwight, Laura. A.A., Graceland Coll., 1951; grad., Radiol. Tech. Sch., 1953. Radiol. technician Independence Sanitarium and Hosp., Mo., 1953, 58-59; radiol. technician Mercy Hosp., Balt., 1954-55; city council mem.-at-large City of Independence, Mo., 1978-82, mayor, 1982—; chmn. Mid-Am. Regional Council, Kansas City, Mo., 1984-85; bd. dirs. Mo. Mcpl. League, Jefferson City, Mo., 1982—, v.p., 1986-87, pres. 1987, chmn., 1987—; chmn. Mo. Commn. on Local Govt. Cooperation, 1985—. Mem. Mo. Gov.'s Conf. on Edn., 1976, Independence Charter Rev. Bd., 1977; bd. dirs. Hope House Shelter for Abused Women, Independence, 1982—; pres. Child Placement Services, Independence, 1972—; trustee Independence Sanitarium and Hosp., 1982—, Nat. Women's Polit. Caucus, LWV. Recipient Woman of Achievement award Mid-Continent Council Girl Scouts Am., 1983, 75th Anniversary Women of Achievement award, Mid-Continent Council Girl Scouts, 1987; Jane Adams award Hope House, 1984; Community Leadership award Comprehensive Mental Health Services, Inc., 1984. Mem. Reorganized Ch. of Jesus Christ of Latter-Day Saints. Home: 18508 E 30th Terr Independence MO 64057 Office: City of Independence 111 E Maple St Independence MO 64050

POTTS, CARLA FAY, publich relations executive; b. Troy, Mo., Feb. 4, 1955; d. Joseph Guy and Mary Marguerite (Lilley) P. BA, Webster U., 1977. Dir. pub. relations and devel. NE Community Action Corp., Bowling Green, Mo., 1977—. Pres. Lincoln County Women's Dem. Club, Troy, Mo., 1985-87; vol. local polit. campaigns; bd. dirs. Legal Service, Mo. Coalition Against Domestic Violence. Mem. Nat. Soc. Fund Raising Execs., Bowling Green chpt. Bus. and Profl. Women's Assn., Mo. Assn. for Social Welfare (bd. dirs.), Mo. Assn. Community Action (bd. dirs.), LWV. Mem. Disciples of Christ Ch. Lodge: Order Eastern Star (Adah 1985-87). Home: 308 N 4th St Elsberry MO 63343 Office: 120 1/2 W Main Bowling Green MO 63334

POTTS, PORTIA ANN, home economics educator; b. Enid, Okla., Aug. 13, 1943; d. Harold Frank and Audrey (Muir) Duckett; m. William Baird Potts III, June 12, 1965. Student, Monticello Women's Coll., 1961-62, Phillips U., 1963; BS in Home Econs. Edn., Okla. State U., 1965; MS in Home Econs. Edn., Cen. Mo. State U., 1977; postgrad., Ottawa U., U. Mo., Kansas City, N.W. Mo. State U. Cert. home econs. and social studies tchr., Mo., Mass., Conn., N.J., N.Y., Pa. Home econs. instr. Chicopee (Mass.) Sch. Dist., 1967; home econs. and social studies instr. Maple Park Jr. High Sch., North Kansas City, Mo., 1970-78; home econs. instr. Maple Park Middle Sch., North Kansas City, 1981—; home service advisor, passive solar specialist Kansas City (Mo.) Power & Light Co., 1979-80; cons. in field, Kansas City, Mo., 1969—. Mem. adminstrv. council Gashland United Meth. Ch., North Kansas City, 1970—, prin.'s adv. com. Maple Park Middle Sch., 1985-86; active PTA, North Kansas City, 1981-84. Mem. NEA, North Kansas City Edn. Assn., Mortar Bd., Phi Kappa Phi. Republican. Avocations: travel, flying, tailoring, fashion design, interior design. Home: 8143 NW Twin Oaks Dr Kansas City MO 64151 Office: Maple Park Middle Sch 5300 N Bennington Kansas City MO 64151

POTTS, ROBERT PAUL, accountant; b. Alliance, Ohio, Jan. 21, 1947; s. Paul Eugene and Helen Louise (Lutz) P.; m. Jeffra Dawn Trotter, Nov. 16, 1968; 1 child, Brian. BS, Youngstown (Ohio) State U., 1971. CPA, Ohio. Cost analyst Deming Div. Crane Co., Salem, Ohio, 1969-71; sr. acct. Ernst & Whinney, Canton, Ohio, 1971-77; ptnr. Mather, Pfeifer & Mather, Alliance, Ohio, 1977-79, 83—; corp. controller Massillon (Ohio) Steel Casting, 1979-83. Mem. Am. Inst. CPA's, Ohio Soc. CPA's. Republican. Lodge: Rotary. Home: 1719 Steiner St NW North Canton OH 44720 Office: Mather Pfeifer & Mather 960 W State St Suite 120 Alliance OH 44601

POTTS-RUSK, LORETHEA, academic administrator; b. San Francisco, Apr. 7, 1947; s. Charles Robert Potts and Dorothy J. (Collette) Spence; m. Larry J. Rusk, May 31, 1986. Student, Vincennes U., 1965-66; BS, Ind. State U., 1969; postgrad., Purdue U., 1972-73. Tchr. EMR Lafayette (Ind.) Community Sch., 1969-70, tchr. TMR, 1970-73; interviewer State Employment Service, Vincennes, Ind., 1974-77; supr., claims technician State Employment Service, Indpls., 1977-83; asst. to dean of occupational edn. Vincennes U., 1983—; tng. asst., project planner Ind. Employement Security Div., Indpls., 1981-83. Vol., newsletter editor Harbor House Shelter for Battered Women, Vincennes, 1985—; mem. mktg. com. Spirit of Vincennes Rendezvous Festival, 1986. Mem. Am. Vocat. Assn., Ind. Vocat. Assn., Ind. Vocat. Adminstrs.,Internat. Assn. Peronnel in Employment Security, Ind. Assn. Personnel in Employment Security (award of Merit 1981), SW Ind. Vocat., Tng. and Employment Com. (chmn. 1986—), LWV (bd. dirs. Vincennes 1986—). Clubs: Blazer Boosters, Tennis (Vincennes). Avocations: tennis, racquetball, reading. Home: 205 Hwy 67N Apt #37 Vincennes IN 47591 Office: Vincennes U 1002 N First St Vincennes IN 47591

POTVIN, ALFRED RAOUL, engineering executive; b. Worcester, Mass., Feb. 5, 1942; s. Alfred Armand and Jacqueline (Morin) P.; m. Janet Holm, Mar. 20, 1965. B.E.E., Worcester Poly. Inst., 1964; M.E.E., Stanford U., 1965, Engr. in E.E., 1967; M.S. in Bioengring., U. Mich., 1970, M.S. in Psychology, 1970, PhD in Bioengring., 1971. Registered profl. engr., Tex. Asst. prof. elec. engring. U. Tex., Arlington, 1966-68, assoc. prof. biomed. engring. and elec. engring., 1971-76, prof., 1976-84; chmn. biomed. engring. U. Tex., 1972-84; dir. med. instrumentation systems research div. Eli Lilly & Co., Indpls., 1984—; faculty fellow, life scientist, cons. NASA, Houston and Moffett Field, 1972-76; clin. prof. biophysics U. Tex. Health Sci. Ctr., Dallas, 1967-84; mem. phys. med. device panel FDA, Washington, 1978-84; mem. adv. bd. Biomed. Engring. NSF, Washington, 1983—. Author: (with W.W. Tourtellotte) Quantitative Examination of Neurologic Functions, 1985; editorial bd. IEEE Spectrum, 1987—; co-editor spl. issue on Biosensors, IEEE Transactions on Biomed. Engring., 1986. Spl. fellow award NIH, 1968; recipient Life Scientist award NASA, 1974. Fellow IEEE (Centennial award 1984, pres. Engring. in Medicine and Biology Soc. 1983-84, gen. chmn. annual conf. 1982); mem. Am. Soc. Engring. Edn. (chmn. biomed. engring. div. 1979-80), Biomed. Engring. Soc. (sr. mem.), Alliance Engrs. in Medicine and Biology (v.p. nat. affairs 1987-89), Assn. Advancement of Med. Instrumentation. Club: Indpls. Sailing. Avocations: yachting; travel; gourmet dining; jogging.

POULOS, JAMES THOMAS, endocrinologist, educator; b. Lynn, Mass., Apr. 11, 1938; s. Thomas Dimitrios and Christine Julia (Zorzy) P.; m. Mary Margaret White, June 22, 1963; 1 son, Christopher Kreag. B.S., Tufts U., 1959, M.D., 1963. Diplomate Am. Bd. Internal Medicine, Am. Bd. Endocrinology and Metabolism. Intern, New Eng. Med. Ctr., Boston, 1963-64, resident 1964-65; resident and fellow in endocrinology U. Chgo., 1967-70; practice medicine specializing in endocrinology Arnett Clinic, Lafayette, Ind., 1970—, v.p., bd. dirs., 1979—; adj. prof. clin. pharmacology Purdue U., West Lafayette, Ind., 1976—; clin. faculty Ind. U. Sch. Medicine; bd. dirs. Lafayette Home Hosp., 1980—, pres. med. staff, 1978-79; pres. Arnett HMO, 1986—; Active Nat. Republican Senatorial Com., Natl. Rep. Congl. Com. Served with M.C., U.S. Army, 1965-67. Mem. AMA, Am. Diabetes Assn. (dir. Ind. chpt. 1980—, pres.-elect 1985, pres. 1986—), Am. Lung Assn. (pres. West Central Ind. 1982-83), Lafayette C. of C. Co-author: The Metabolic Influence of Progestins Advances in Metabolic Disorders, 1971; contbr. articles to profl. publs. Home: 1000 Windwood Ln West Lafayette IN 47906 Office: 2600 Greenbush St Lafayette IN 47904

POULOS, NICHOLAS GEORGE, account executive; b. Milw., Sept. 27, 1949; s. Nicholas George Poulos and Suzanne (Froedtert) Miles; m. Cynthia Lynn Remus, Feb. 26, 1982; children: Jason Litler, Kurtis Nicholas, Nicholas Froedtert. BA in Comparative Lit., U. Wis., Milw., 1973, MA in Comparative Lit., 1977. Nat. account mgr. Wis. Telephone, Milw., 1977-80; account exec. OPI Corp., Milw., 1980-84, Bus. Incentives, Milw., 1984—. Danforth fellow, 1975,76; U. Wis. grantee 1975. Mem. Modern Language Assn., Am. Contract Bridge League (life master), Phi Beta Kappa, Phi Kappa Phi. Avocations: reading, golf, biking, swimming, tournament bridge. Office: Bus Incentives 450 N Sunnyslope Rd Brookfield WI 53005

POULOSE, KUTTIKATT PAUL, neurologist; b. Cochin, Kerala, India, Sept. 2, 1935; s. Paul Joseph Kuttikat and Mariamkutty (Paily) Maliakal; children: Anil, Abraham, Benjamin. Interscience student, Univ. Coll., Kerala, 1951-53; MB, BS, Med. Coll., Trivandrum, Kerala, 1958, MD, 1964. Diplomate Am. Bd. Psychiatry and Neurology. Tutor in medicine Med. Coll., Kerala, 1965-66, asst. prof., 1970-72; chief of neurology VA Med. Ctr., Leavenworth, Kans., 1975, chief of medicine, 1975-80, chief of staff, 1980—; asst. prof. neurology Kans. U. Med. Ctr., Kansas City, Kans., 1975-80, assoc. prof., 1981-87, prof., 1987—; dir. continuing med. edn. VA Med. Ctr., Leavenworth, 1976-81; cons. Munson Army Hosp., Ft. Leavenworth, Kans. 1983-86. Contbr. numerous articles to profl. jours. Mem. planning com. for city recreational facility, Leavenworth, 1983. Served to maj. M.C. Indian Army, 1966-70. Recipient Superior Performance award, Administr. of Vets. Affairs, Washington, 1979. Fellow Am. Coll. Physicians, Am. Acad. Neurology, Royal Coll. Physicians, Can. Roman Catholic. Club: Officers (Ft. Leavenworth). Lodge: Lions. Avocations: reading, walking, tennis. Home: 1111 Santa Fe Leavenworth KS 66048 Office: VA Med Ctr S 4 St Leavenworth KS 66048

POULTON, DONNA LEE, accountant; b. Columbus, Ohio, Sept. 6, 1945; d. Donald Semler and Mary Lee (Johnson) P. BS, Ohio State U., 1967. CPA, Ohio. Sr. mgr. Ernst & Whinney, Columbus, 1967-84; dir. internal audit Liebert Corp., Columbus, 1984-87; fin. cons. 1987—. Treas. Quest Internat., Columbus, 1983—, Ohio Found. on the Arts, Columbus, 1985—, Zonta Internat. Found., Chgo., 1984—. Mem. Am. Inst. CPA's, Ohio Soc. CPA's, Inst. Internal Auditors. Republican. Avocations: golf, tennis. Home: 4860 Smoketalk Ln Westerville OH 43081

POUNIAN, CHARLES A., management consultant, educator; b. Chgo., Nov. 5, 1926; s. James K. and Dorothy (Garabedian) P.; m. Beatrice Koujourian, Sept. 9, 1950; children: Lynn Carol, Steven Robert. BA in Psychology, Lake Forest Coll., 1949; MS in Psychology, Ill. Inst. Tech., 1951, PhD in Psychology, 1960. Lic. psychologist, Ill. Various positions City of Chgo., 1953-60, dir. personnel, 1960-85; sr. cons. Hay Mgmt. Cons., Chgo., 1985—; prof. pub. adminstrn. Ill. Inst. Tech., Chgo., 1968—. Mem. bd. mgrs. Mid-Am. Chpt. ARC, Chgo., 1986—, McCormick Chgo. Boys and Girls Club, 1972—. Served with U.S. Army, 1944-46. Mem. Internat. Personnel Mgmt. Assn. (pres. 1986), Am. Psychol. Assn., Am. Soc. Pub. Admnstrn. (nat. council 1982-85), Orgn. Mcpl. Personnel Officers (pres. 1982). Episcopalian. Club: Midtown Tennis (Chgo.). Home: 924 Castlewood Terr Chicago IL 60640 Office: Hay Mgmt Cons 1 E Wacker Dr Chicago IL 60601

POVISH, KENNETH JOSEPH, bishop; b. Alpena, Mich., Apr. 19, 1924; s. Joseph Francis and Elizabeth (Jachcik) P. A.B., Sacred Heart Sem., Detroit, 1946; M.A., Cath. U. Am., 1950; postgrad., No. Mich. U., 1961, 63. Ordained priest Roman Catholic Ch., 1950; asst. pastorships 1950-56; pastor in Port Sanilac Mich., 1956-57, Munger, Mich., 1957-60, Bay City, Mich., 1966-70; dean St. Paul Sem., Saginaw, Mich., 1960-66; vice rector St. Paul Sem., 1962-66; bishop of Crookston Minn., 1970-75; bishop of Lansing Mich., 1975—; bd. consulators Diocese of Saginaw, 1966-70; instr. Latin and U.S. history St. Paul Sem., 1960-66. Weekly columnist Saginaw and Lansing diocesan newspapers. Bd. dirs. Cath. Charities Diocese Saginaw, 1969-70. Mem. Mich., Bay County hist. socs. Club: Kiwanis. Office: Chancery Office 300 W Ottawa Lansing MI 48933 *

POWDRILL, GARY LEO, plant engineering manager; b. Butte, Mont., Nov. 26, 1945; s. Harold Holmes and Genevieve Marie (Tansey) P.; BS, Gonzaga U., 1969; MBA, U. Detroit, 1973; MPA in Environ. Policy, Ind. U., 1984; m. Marsha A. McKeon, Oct. 6, 1979; 1 child, Amy Marie. Plant design engr. Ford Motor Co., Sterling Heights, Mich., 1969-73, div. plant engr. Chassis div., 1973-74, supr. plant engring. sect., Indpls. plant, 1974-78, mgr. plant engring., 1978-80, mgr. engring. and facilities, 1980—. Chmn. Ind. State Water Pollution Control Bd., 1986—; mem. Indpls. Mayor's Tech. Adv. Com., 1975—. Appointed chmn. Ind. State Water Pollution Control Bd., 1986—. Lic. profl. engr., Ind.; cert. plant engr. Mem. Ind. Soc. Profl. Engrs. Roman Catholic. Elk. Home: Rural Route 1 Box SC8 New Palestine IN 46163 Office: 6900 English Ave Indianapolis IN 46206

POWELEIT, MICHAEL DAVID, computer programmer, analyst; b. Covington, Ky., Nov. 27, 1954; s. Arthur August and Ida Josephine P.; m. Kathleen Susan Schutte, Oct. 27, 1984; children: Eric, Brian. AS, So. Ohio Coll., Cin., 1975. Computer programmer D.R. Frey & Co., Ft. Thomas, Ky., 1976-79; programmer, analyst Totes, Inc., Loveland, Ohio, 1979-81; sr. analyst Williamson Co., Cin., 1981—; instr. data processing So. Ohio Coll., 1983—; v.p. Williamson Fed. Credit Union, 1983—. Mem. PTA, Sharonville, Ohio, 1986—. Republican. Lutheran. Avocations: reading, bowling, teaching, coaching softball. Home: 10928 Willfleet Dr Cincinnati OH 45241 Office: Williamson Co 3500 Madison Rd Cincinnati OH 45209

POWELL, BARBARA JOAN, psychologist, educator; b. Williamsville, Ill., June 30, 1933; d. Fred Alonzo and Bertha (Hanner) P. BA in Psychology, Washington U., St. Louis, 1957, PhD, 1964; MA in Psychology, George Washington U., 1960. Diplomate Am. Bd. Profl. Psychology; lic. psychologist, Kans. Dir. psychol. services Malcolm Bliss Mental Health Ctr., St. Louis, 1969-74; staff psychologist VA Med. Ctr., Lexington, Ky., 1974-77; staff psychologist VA Med. Ctr., Kansas City, Mo., 1977—, prin. investigator alcohol research program, 1981—; acting assoc. chief of staff for research and devel. div., chief psychology VA Med. Ctr., Kansas City, 1986—; prof. Kans. U. Med. Ctr., Kansas City, 1977—; assoc. prof. med. psychology Washington U. Med Sch., St. Louis, 1973-74; assoc. prof. U. Ky. Med. Sch., Lexington, 1974-77; co-chmn. Lt. Gov.'s Task Force on Mental Health Delivery, Mo., 1974. Author: A Layman's Guide to Mental Health Problems and Treatments, 1981; co-author: Psychiatric Diagnostic Interview, 1981; contbr. 92 articles to profl. jours. Recipient awards Nat. Inst. Alcoholism and Alcohol Abuse, 1974, VA Merit Rev., 1976, 81, VA Coop. Studies, 1979, Burroughs Wellcome Co., 1984. Fellow Am. Psychol. Assn. (vis. scientist 1972); mem. Midwest Psychol. Assn., Assn. for Med. Edn. and Research in Substance Abuse, Soc. Psychologists in Addictive Behaviors, Soc. VA Psychologists. Home: 12516 W 105 Terr Overland Park KS 66215 Office: VA Med Ctr 151 4801 Linwood Blvd Kansas City MO 64128-2295

POWELL, BARRY KAY, research engineer; b. Muskegon, Mich., July 27, 1938; s. Aubrey Franklin and Christine (Reed) P.; m. Yolan Mary Horvath, Aug. 26, 1961. BS in Math., U. Mich., 1961, BS in Aero. Engring., 1961, MS in Engring. Instrumentation, 1963, Profl. Engring. diploma in info. and control, 1964. Product devel. engr. Ford Motor Co., Dearborn, Mich., 1963-64; research engr. Cadillac Gage Co., Warren, Mich., 1964-65; sr. staff mathematician Bendix Research, Southfield, Mich., 1965-73; sr. research engr. Ford Motor Co., Dearborn, 1973-76; prin. scientist, engr. Ford Sci. Lab., Dearborn, 1976—. Editor: Mathematical Models for Orbiting Space Station Control System Analysis, 1971. Patentee in field. Recipient Henry Ford Technol. award Ford Motor Co., 1984. Avocations: model railroading, tennis, music, golf. Office: Ford Motor Co Sci Research Labs 20000 Rotunda Dr Dearborn MI 48121

POWELL, CAROL CHRISTINE, restaurant owner; b. Seattle, Feb. 15, 1941; d. Benjamin Olaf and Lois Carol (Smith) Michel; m. William Fred Roth, Apr. 8, 1961 (div. Dec. 1972); children: Christine Roth, Fred Roth, Traci Roth; m. George Benjamin Powell, Dec. 22, 1972; children: Kathy Powell Morrow, George Powell Jr. Grad., Franklin High Sch., Seattle, 1959. Dishwasher Happy Chef, Cherokee, Iowa, 1978; dishwasher, waitress Randall's Cafe, Cherokee, 1978-79, mgr., 1979-82; owner, operator The Food Broker, Cherokee, 1983—. Mem. Assn. Consumer Preferred Bus., Cherokee C. of C. Democrat. Avocations: reading, exercise. Home: 320 N 6th St Cherokee IA 51012 Office: The Food Broker Hwy 59 S Cherokee IA 51012

POWELL, DAVID, manufacturing company executive. Chmn., chief exec. officer A.B. Dick Co., Chgo. Office: A B Dick Co 5700 W Touhy Ave Chicago IL 60648 *

POWELL, DYER JAMES, church and religious construction financing company executive; b. Miami, Ariz., July 4, 1938; s. James Orlando and Rachel Nadien Powell; B.S. in Bus., San Jose State Coll., 1962; m. Rita Marie, Oct. 6, 1967; children—Michael, Patrick. Vice pres. sales Miller & Schroeder, Inc., Mpls., 1968-79; chief exec. officer, chmn. Keenan & Clary, Inc., Mpls., 1979—. Bd. dirs. Elder Friends; ind. Republican del. state conv., 1982; bd. dirs. Minn. Epilepsy League. Served with U.S. Army, 1958-62. Teaching cert. securities and fin. Hennepin County Sch. Dist. Mem. Am. Mgmt. Assn. Roman Catholic. Club: Serra. Home: 5224 Richwood Dr Edina MN 55436 Office: 1200 2d Ave S Minneapolis MN 55403

POWELL, GEORGE EVERETT, JR., motor freight company executive; b. Kansas City, Mo., June 12, 1926; s. George Everett and Hilda (Brown) P.; m. Mary Catherine Kuehn, Aug. 26, 1947; children: George Everett III, Nicholas K., Richardson K., Peter E. Student, Northwestern U. With Riss & Co., Inc., Kansas City, Mo., 1947-52; treas. Riss & Co., Inc., 1950-52; with Yellow Freight System, Inc., Kansas City, Mo., 1952—; pres. Yellow Freight System, Inc., 1957-68, chmn. bd., 1968—; dir. 1st Nat. Charter Corp., Butler Mfg. Co. Trustee, mem. exec. com. Mid-West Research Inst., Kansas City, Mo., from 1961, chmn. bd. trustees, from 1968; bd. govs. Kansas City Art Inst., from 1964, chmn. bd. trustees, 1973-75. Served with USNR, 1944-46. Mem. Kansas City C. of C. (bd. dirs. 1964-68). Office: Yellow Freight System Inc of Del 10990 Roe Ave Overland Park KS 66207 *

POWELL, RICHARD ROSS, magazine publishing executive; b. Honolulu, Jan. 29, 1936; s. Charles Wilbert Beers and Ruth Powell (Bancroft) Boyer; m. Donna Mae Hein, Apr. 12, 1958; children: Bryan Scott, Charles Owen, John Wesley, Lisa Ann, Jennifer Lynn, Richard Alan. Buyer Boeing Co., Renton, Wash., 1959-61; territory mgr. James Mfg. Co., Ft. Atkinson, Wis., 1961-63; asst. sales mgr. Park Industry, Inc., Murfreesboro, Ind., 1963-66; advt. mgr. Hamlin, Inc., Lake Mills, Wis., 1966-69; div. mgr. The Pattis Group, Lincolnwood, Ill., 1969-77; v.p. pub. Lukewood Publs., Inc., Mpls., 1977-84; pres., chief executive officer North Publs. Co. formerly Machalek Publs. Co., Mpls., 1984—. Served with USAF, 1954-58. Mem. Minn. Incentive Club (pres. 1983-84), Assn. Bus. Publs., Specialty Advt. Agys. Internat. (cert.), Nat. Premium Sales Execs. (cert.). Republican. Methodist. Avocations: swimming, tennis, fishing. Home: 6312 Hillside Rd Edina MN 55436 Office: North Publ Co 15 S 9th St Minneapolis MN 55402

POWELL, ROBERT CHARLES, psychiatrist; b. Columbus, Ohio, Sept. 1, 1948; s. Robert Edwin and Thelma Pauline (Bibler) P.; m. Barbara Jean Cooper, May 1, 1983; 1 child, Adam Cooper. BA in Natural Scis., Shimer Coll., 1968; PhD in History, Duke U., 1974, MD, 1975. Cert. Am. Bd. Psychiatry and Neurology. Asst. prof. history and medicine U. Mo., Kansas City, 1975-77; asst. prof. psychiatry Northwestern U. Med. Sch., Evanston, Ill., 1979-86; pvt. practice psychiatry Schaumburg, Ill., 1979—; mem. faculty dept. social scis. Shimer Coll., Waukegan, Ill., 1979-80; lectr. history U. Wis., Milw., 1983-84. Trustee Shimer Coll., 1979—; bd. dirs. Spectrum Ednl. Ctr. Gifted and Talented Children, Palatine, Ill., 1984—; bd. reference Creative Children's Acad., Mt. Prospect., Ill., 1983—; mem. Socratic Inst., 1986. Fellow Josiah Macy Jr. Found., 1968-74. Mem. AMA, Am. Psychiat. Assn., Am. Assn. History Medicine (William Osler medal 1971). Republican. Jewish. Avocation: fgn. travel. Home: 1520 Tower Rd Winnetka IL 60093-1629 Office: 1900 E Golf Rd Suite 1150 Schaumburg IL 60173-5036

POWELL, WILLIAM HARVEY, rehabilitation center administrator; b. Kansas City, Mo., Aug. 10, 1945; s. Vincent J. and Mary E. Powell; m. Marilyn Lee McVay, Dec. 23, 1968; children: Mary E., John W. AA in Liberal Arts, Met. Jr. Coll. Kansas City, 1965; BA in Exptl. Psychology, U. Mo., Kansas City, 1968, MA in Gen. Psychology, 1976; postgrad., Midwestern Bapt. Sem., 1971; cert. mgmt. tng. program, U. Ala., Birmingham, 1978. Cert. rehab. counselor. Research assoc. VA Hosp., Kansas City, Mo., 1965-68; research asst. Kans. U. Med. Ctr., 1971-73; youth devel. specialist Argentine Youth Services, Kansas City, 1971-75; program coordinator Johnson County Mental Retardation Ctr., Overland Park, Kans., 1975-77; exec. v.p. Class Ltd., Columbus, Kans., 1977—; surveyor, cons. Commn. Accreditation Rehab. Facilities, Tucson, 1986—; instr. psychology Labette Community Coll., Parsons, Kans., 1985—; real estate broker, Columbus, 1980—. Co-author: Report on Deaf Blindness, 1985; contbr. articles to profl. jours. Pres. Columbus City Council, 1986—; pres. Kans. Assn. Rehab. Facilities; v.p. Cherokee County Ambulance Assn., 1983-85; mem. adminstrv. bd., trustee Columbus United Meth. Ch., 1981-87; v.p. Labette/Cherokee Youth Crisis Shelter, 1983-85; pres. Columbus United Fund, S.E. Kans. Regional Planning Council, 1984—; bd. dirs. Pvt. Industry Council, 1985—; mem. Columbus Econ. Devel. Steering Com., 1986—. Served to 1st lt. U.S. Army, 1968-71, Vietnam. Mem. Nat. Assn. Devel. Disabilities Mgrs. (charter), Kans. Assn. Rehab. Facilities (v.p.), Am. Assn. Mental Deficiencies, Nat. Rehab. Counselors Assn., Nat. Assn. Lic. Pvt. Residential Facilities for Mentally Retarded, Columbus C. of C. (pres. 1986). Democrat. Lodge: Lions. Avocations: racquetball, stamp collecting. Home: 110 Bennett Columbus KS 66725 Office: Class Ltd PO Box 266 Columbus KS 66725

POWELL-BROWN, ANN, educator, publicist; b. Boonville, Mo., Mar. 19, 1947; d. Edward Marsh and Ethel M. (Benton) Powell; m. Richard Lee Brown, Dec. 29, 1978. BS, Cen. Mo. State U., 1969, MSE, 1975; postgrad. U. Mo., Kansas City. Tchr. Gulfport and Biloxi (Miss.) Schs., 1969-70; mem. adj. staff Providence Coll., Taichung, Taiwan, 1971-72; mem. reading and learning disabilities staff, Kansas City (Mo.) Sch. Dist., 1973-78, mem. learning disabilities identification team, 1978-79, mem. spl. edn. placement com., 1979-83; co-owner Am. Media Enterprises, 1983—; learning disabilities cons., 1984—; v.p., bd. dirs. Nat. Tutoring Inst., 1976; adj. faculty Ottawa Coll., 1980, instr. English as 2d lang., 1976-77; adj. faculty U. Mo., Kansas City, 1981; bi-weekly columnist Kansas City Bus. Jour., 1985-86; speaker various orgns. Mem. public affairs com. Jewish Community Center, 1978; v.p. Com. for Indochinese Devel., 1977; mem. edn. council Episcopal Diocese Western Mo., 1977; mem. selection com. Paul Harris Fellowship; founder, bd. dirs. Friends of St. Mary's; mem. profl. adv. bd. Oak Park Home Health Care, 1983; mem. Kansas City Jazz Festival Com., 1983; active Kansas City Riverfront Devel. Task Force, 1987. Mem. Council Exceptional Children, Assn. Children with Learning Disabilities, Internat. Reading Assn. (state publicity com. 1983), Nat. Orgn. Women Bus. Owners, Nat. Reading Council, Quality Edn. Coalition, Doctoral Student Spl. Interest Group, Gt. Alkali Plainsmen, St. David's Welsh Soc., Eggs and Issues Breakfast, Kansas City Blues Soc., Phi Delta Kappa. Democrat. Episcopalian. Home and Office: Am Media Escorts 501 Knickerbocker Pl Kansas City MO 64111

POWER, JOSEPH EDWARD, lawyer; b. Peoria, Ill., Dec. 2, 1938; s. Joseph Edward and Margaret Elizabeth (Birkett) P.; m. Camille June Repass, Aug. 1, 1964; children—Joseph Edward, David William, James Repass. Student, Knox Coll., Galesburg, Ill., 1956-58; B.A., U. Iowa, 1960, J.D., 1964. Bar: Iowa 1964. Law clk. to judge U.S. Dist. Ct., 1964-65; mem. Bradshaw, Fowler, Proctor & Fairgrave, Des Moines, 1965—. Bd. dirs. Moingona Council Girl Scouts U.S.A., 1968-77, pres., 1971-74; mem. Des Moines CSC, 1971-73; bd. dirs. Des Moines United Way, 1976-82, v.p., 1979-81; trustee Am. Inst. Bus., 1987—; mem. Des Moines Civil War Roundtable. Served to comdr. USNR, 1965-81. Fellow Am. Coll. Probate Counsel, Am. Coll. Real Estate Lawyers; mem. ABA, Iowa Bar Assn. (chmn. probate, property and trust law com. 1983—), Polk County Bar Assn., Des Moines Estate Planners Forum (pres. 1982-83). Republican. Mem. United Ch. of Christ. Club: Des Moines. Home: 4244 Foster Dr Des Moines IA 50312 Office: Bradshaw Fowler Proctor & Fairgrave 1100 Des Moines Bldg Des Moines IA 50307

POWER, PHILIP HARWICK, publisher; b. Ann Arbor, Mich., June 3, 1938; s. Eugene Barnum and Sayde (Harwick) P.; m. Sarah Hutchins Goddard, July 5, 1971 (dec. Mar. 1987); 1 son, Nathan Eugene. BA summa cum laude, U. Mich., 1960; MA, Oxford U., Eng., 1964. Sports editor, acting city editor Fairbanks (Alaska) Daily News-Miner, 1961-62; fgn. stringer Chgo. Daily News, 1962-64; adminstrv. asst. Congressman Paul Todd, Washington, 1964-66; founder, pub. Observer Newspapers, Inc., Livonia, Mich., 1966-73; founder, chmn. bd. Suburban Communications Corp., Lavonia, 1974—; bd. dirs. Jacobson's Stores Inc., Daedalus Enterprises, Inc. Mem. Gov.'s Commn. on Future of Higher Edn., Lansing, Mich., 1983-84, Gov.'s Commn. Jobs and Econ. Devel., Lansing, 1983—, Mich. Cabinet Council on Human Investment Policy; regent U. Mich.; chmn. Mich. Job Tng. Coordinating Council, Lansing, 1983—, Mich. Found. for Arts, 1974-80; bd. dirs. Power Found., Eskimo Art Inc. Recipient First Place award Mich. Press Assn., 1969, Bus. Vol. of Yr. award Nat. Alliance of Bus., 1986; Marshall scholar, 1964. Mem. Council on Fgn. Relations. Democrat. Clubs: American (London); Century Assn. (N.Y.C.); Detroit. Home: 5075 Warren Rd Ann Arbor MI 48105 Office: Suburban Communications Corp 412 E Huron Suite 300 Ann Arbor MI 48104-1521

POWERS, ANTHONY WILLIAM, JR., data processing executive; b. Indpls., Sept. 18, 1946; s. Anthony William and Rosalie P.; BSIM, Purdue U., 1968; postgrad. U. Chgo., 1968-69; children: Timothy, Katharine. Applications analyst Control Data Corp., 1968-69; cons. staff, mgr. Arthur Andersen & Co., 1969-76; v.p. No. Trust Co., 1976-79; sr. v.p. Nat. Sharedata, Schaumburg, Ill., 1979-81; pres. Micro Book, Inc., Schaumburg, 1982-85; Am. Data Tech., 1982-85, Am. Data Tech., 1982-85; v.p. gen. mgr. MTech Midwest, 1985—. Active Boy Scouts Am. Republican. Roman Catholic. Author: Bank Calc. Home: 773 Whalom Ln Schaumburg IL 60195 Office: MTech Midwest 443 N Wabash Chicago IL 60611

POWERS, JAMES BETHEL, internal auditor, consultant; b. Tulsa, Okla., Dec. 5, 1953; s. Bethel Haid and Marguerite Lucille (Koebrich) P.; m. Vicky Kay Lano, Oct. 17, 1981; children: Vanessa Briane, Alyson Lane. BBA, Emporia State U., 1976. Internal auditor Modern Merchandising, Minnetonka, Minn., 1976-78, sr. auditor, 1978-79, sr. auditor EDP,, 1979-80, dir. internal audit, 1981-82; dir. internal audit Bermans/W.R. Grace, Brooklyn Park, Minn., 1983—. Coordinator United Way, Mpls., 1986. Mem. Inst. Internal Auditors, EDP Auditors Assn. Republican. Roman Catholic. Club: Ducks Unltd. Avocations: sports, outdoors, dog tng. Home: 2308 Indian Rd W Minnetonka MN 55343 Office: Bermans/WR Grace 7401 Boone Ave N Brooklyn Park MN 55428

POWERS, JOHN CONNER, comptroller; b. Covington, Ky., Dec. 13, 1940; s. Elmo Conner and Geneva May (Rice) P.; m. Kathy Gay Herron, June 20, 1964; children: Mark C., Laura G. BS in Commerce, U. Ky., 1963; MBA, Xavier U., 1980. CPA, Ohio. Programmer, analyst Union Cen. Life Ins., Cin., 1963-68, sr. systems analyst, 1968-76, asst. comptroller, 1976—. Fellow Life Office Mgmt. Inst.; mem. Am. Inst. CPA's, Ohio Soc. CPA's. Republican. Baptist. Home: 1269 Jeremy Ct Cincinnati OH 45240

POWERS, KATHRYN DOLORES, social services administrator; b. Chgo., Dec. 17, 1929; B.A., Colgate-Rochester U., 1951; M.S.W., Smith Coll., 1964. Child welfare worker, supr. Cook County Dept. Public Aid Children's Div., Chgo., 1953-68; dir. program Central Bapt. Children's Home/Family Services, Lake Villa, Ill., 1968-82, asst. exec. dir., 1983—;assoc. Realty World, Dale Shea & Co, 1987—; pres. bd. dirs. Community Residential Network, Inc., 1978-79; instr. field work U. Wis., 1975-76; mem. habilitation/rehab. task force Health Systems Agency, Kane, Lake and McHenry counties, Ill., 1979. Recipient Spl. Merit citation Am. Bapt. Homes and Hosps. Assn., 1979. Mem. Nat. Assn. Social Workers, Acad. Cert. Social Workers, Lake County Bd. Realtors, Am. Orthopsychiat. Assn. Home: 309 Milwaukee St Lake Villa IL 60046 Office: Box 218 Lake Villa IL 60046

POWERS, ODELL EUGENE, contractor, engineering company executive; b. Peoria, Ill., May 2, 1928; s. Clarence O. and Beulah (Fernandez) P.; m. Elizabeth Marie Johnson, Mar. 12, 1950; children: Mark Daniel, Kristin Lynne, Julianne Lynne, Elizabeth M. BS, Bradley U., 1952. Mng. dir. Caterpillar Mitsubishi, Inc., Tokyo, Japan, 1963-67; dir. internat. fin. and adminstrn. Honeywell, Inc., Mpls., 1967-69; v.p. Honeywell, Inc. (Honeywell-Europe), Brussels, 1969-71, exec. v.p., 1971-73; pres., chief exec. officer Turbodyne Corp., Mpls., 1973-76, chmn. bd., chief exec. officer, 1976-78; pres., chief operating officer McGraw-Edison Co., Rolling Meadows, Ill., 1979-81, also bd. dirs.; pres., chief operating officer S.J. Groves & Sons Co., Mpls., 1981—; bd. dirs. Internat. Multifoods, Mpls., Nicolet Instrument Corp. Trustee Bradley U. Served with AUS, 1946-47. Republican. Presbyterian. Clubs: Mpls.; Met. (N.Y.C.); Deepdale Country (N.Y.); Tucson Country, Tucson Nat.; Minikahda Country (Minn.). Office: SJ Groves & Sons Co PO Box 1267 Minneapolis MN 55440

POWERS, PAUL J(OSEPH), manufacturing executive; b. Boston, Feb. 5, 1935; s. Joseph W. and Mary T. (Sullivan) P.; m. Barbara Ross, June 3, 1961; children: Briana, Gregory, Jeffrey. BA in Econs., Merrimack Coll., 1956; MBA, George Washington U., 1962. Various mfg. and fin. positions with Chrysler Corp., Detroit and overseas, 1963-69; v.p., gen. mgr. Am. Standard, Dearborn, Mich., 1970-78; pres. Abex-Dennison, Columbus, Ohio, 1978-82; group v.p. Comml. Shearing, Inc., Youngstown, Ohio, 1982-84; pres., chief ops. officer Comml. Shearing, Inc., Youngstown, 1984-87, chmn., pres., chief exec. officer, 1987—; bd. dirs. Dollar Savs. and Trust Co. Bd. dirs. Youngstown Symphony, 1984—. Served as lt. USNR, 1957-63. Mem. Nat. Assn. Mfrs. (bd. dirs. 1986—), Nat. Fluid Power Assn. (bd. dirs. 1984—), Machinery and Allied Products Inst. Republican. Roman Catholic. Office: Comml Shearing Inc PO Box 239 1775 Logan Ave Youngstown OH 44501

POWERS, ROBERT M., food products company executive; b. 1931. BS, Emory U., 1952, MS, 1953, PhD, 1958. Research chemist A.E. Staley Mfg. Co., Decatur, Ill., 1958-61, lab. head, 1961-62, group leader, 1962-67, dir. spl. product devel. UBS div., 1968-69, dir. indsl. products research and devel. UBS div., 1969-70, dir. research and devel. UBS div., 1970-71, v.p. research and devel., 1971-75, v.p. agrl. products group, 1975-79, exec. v.p., 1979-80, pres., 1980—, also chief operating officer, bd. dirs.; bd. dirs. parent co. Staley Continental, Inc. Served with U.S. Army, 1954-55. Office: AE Staley Mfg Co 2200 Eldorado St Box 151 Decatur IL 62525 *

POWLESS, DAVID GRIFFIN, accountant; b. Marion, Ill., June 16, 1953; s. Kenneth Barnett and Emily Mary (Cygnar) P.; m. Patricia Kay Walker, Aug. 23, 1975; 1 child, Nathaniel Ryan. BS in Accountancy, U. Ill., 1975. CPA, Ill. Mgr. Gray Hunter Stenn, CPA's, Marion, 1974-81; pvt. practice acctg. Marion, 1981—. Coordinator Williamson County U. Ill. Found., Champaign, 1985—. Named Outstanding Teenager Am., 1970, one of Outstanding Young Men Am., 1985. Mem. Am. Inst. CPA's, Ill. CPA Soc., U. Ill. Alumni Assn. (bd. dirs. 1985—), Champaign Urbana Alumni Council (bd. dirs. 1983—), Phi Sigma Kappa (Outstanding Alumnus 1984, bd. dirs. and treas. 1980-87). Republican. Roman Catholic. Club: Egyptian Illini (Marion) (pres. 1981-87). Lodges: Rotary, KC.

POYNTER, WILLIAM DOUGLAS, experimental psychologist; b. Billings, Mont., Jan. 11, 1952; s. James Frederick and Nadean Sue (Minugh) P. BS, Mont. State U., 1974; postgrad., U. Wash., 1974-77; MA, Ariz. State U., 1977, PhD, 1981. Research analyst Ariz. Dept. Health Services, Phoenix, 1981-83; sr. research scientist societal analysis dept. Gen. Motors Corp. Research Labs, Warren, Mich., 1983—. Contbr. articles to profl. jours. Fellow Soc. automotive Engrs.; mem. Sigma Xi. Avocations: insect collecting, woodworking. Office: Gen Motors Corp Research Labs Societal Analysis Dept Warren MI 48090

POZA, ERNESTO JUAN, management consultant; b. Havana, Cuba, Mar. 27, 1950; came to U.S., 1961; s. Hugo Ernesto and Carmen (Valle) P.; m. Karen Elizabeth Saum, Oct. 14, 1978; 1 child, Kali Jennette. BS in Adminstrv. Sci., Yale U., 1972; MS in Mgmt., MIT, 1974. Personnel asst. Digital Equipment, Maynard, Mass., 1973-74; personnel mgr. research Sherwin Williams Co., Chgo., 1974-75; orgn. specialist Sherwin Williams Co., Cleve., 1975-77, dir. orgn. planning, 1977-79; pres., sr. mgmt. cons. E.J. Poza Assoc., Cleve., 1979—; advisor Family Firm Inst., 1986. Contbr. articles to profl. jours. Bd. dirs. Neighborhood Health Care, 1980; mem. program com. United Way, Cleve., 1985, Hispanic Leadership, 1986. Mem. Acad. Mgmt. (entrepreneurship div., 1980—, orgn. devel. network, 1975—). Avocations: cross-country skiing, golf. Office: 1384 Belmar Mews Suite 500 Cleveland OH 44121

POZORSKI, JOSEPH MICHAEL, JR., lawyer; b. Manitowoc, Wis., Aug. 10, 1957; s. Joseph A. and Alice (Lambert) F.; m. Lynn Marie Komorosky, Aug. 28, 1982; children: Joseph III, Nicole. BS, Marquette U., 1979; JD, John Marshall Law Sch., 1982. Bar: Wis. 1982, U.S. Dist. Ct. (ea. dist.) Wis. 1982. Ptnr. Kaminski & Pozorski, Manitowoc, 1982—. Bd. dirs. Marco Manor, Manitowoc, 1984-86. Lodge: Eagles (Manitowoc chpt. bd. dirs. 1986—, chmn. bd. 1984-86). Home: 3007 Barkwood Ct Manitowoc WI 54220 Office: Kaminski & Pozorski 1020 S 9th St PO Box 509 Manitowoc WI 54220-0509

POZULP, NAPOLEON CHARLES, II, psychologist; b. Chgo., Nov. 1, 1947; s. Harry Lawrence and Bernice Pozulp. Student U.S. Mcht. Marine Acad., 1965-68; BA, Ind. U., 1970; MA, No. Ill. U., 1973, PhD, 1976. Clin. therapist Rush-Presbyn.-St. Lukes Med. Ctr., Chgo., 1976-77; sr. therapist Tri-City Mental Health Ctr., East Chicago, Ind., 1977-79; dir. Assn. Cert. Psychologists, Chgo., 1979—; cons. in field. Contbr. articles to profl. jours.; editor Psychology News, 1980—. Mem. Am. Psychol. Assn., Ill. Psychol. Assn. Office: Assn Cert Psychologists 625 N Michigan Ave Suite 1740 Chicago IL 60611

PRAEGER, HERMAN ALBERT, JR., research agronomist; b. Claflin, Kans., Jan. 2, 1920; s. Herman Albert and Gertrude Edna (Grizzell) P.; B.S., Kans. State U., 1941, M.S., 1947, Ph.D., 1977; 1 dau., Gwenneth Irene. Commd. lt., U.S. Army, 1941, advanced through grades to lt. col., 1973; mem. faculty Command and Gen. Staff Coll., 1963-67; comdg. officer U.S. Army Support Group, Joint Security Area, Korea, ret., 1973; research agronomist Kans. State U., Manhattan, 1978—; adminstr. improvement of pearl millet program AID, 1978—. Decorated Legion of Merit, Bronze Star with 3 oak leaf clusters, Medal for Merit, Joint Services Commendation medal, Army Commendation medal with oak leaf cluster, Purple Heart. Mem. Assn. U.S. Army, Am. Soc. Agronomy, AAAS, Crop Sci. Soc. Am., V.F.W. Republican. Episcopalian. Club: Elks. Home: 3008 Gary Ave Manhattan KS 66502 Office: Kans State U Throckmorton Hall Manhattan KS 66506

PRAGALZ, SUSANNE MARIE, human resources executive. BA, St. Norbert Coll., 1970. Mgr. employment First Wis. Nat. Bank Madison, 1977-79, personnel officer, mgr. employee relations, 1979-83, asst. v.p., mgr. salary adminstrn., 1983-87; v.p., dir. human resources Bank of Ravenswood, Chgo., 1987—; asst. personnel dir. U. Wis. The Wisconsin Union, Madison, 1975-77. Mem. Am. Soc. Personnel Adminstrs., U. Wis. Mgmt. Inst. (council). Office: Bank of Ravenswood 1825 W Lawrence Chicago IL 60640

PRAGER, DAVID, chief justice; b. Ft. Scott, Kans., Oct. 30, 1918; s. Walter and Helen (Kishler) P.; m. Dorothy Schroeter, Sept. 8, 1945; children: Diane, David III. AB, U. Kans., 1939, LLB, 1942. Bar: Kans. 1942. Practiced in Topeka, 1946-59; dist. judge Shawnee County (Kans.) Dist. Ct., 1959-71; assoc. justice Kans. Supreme Ct., Topeka, 1971-87, chief justice, 1987—; lectr. Washburn Law Sch., 1948-68. Served to lt. USNR, 1942-46, ETO, PTO. Mem. Kans. Dist. Judges Assn. (past pres.), Order of Coif, Phi Beta Kappa, Phi Delta Theta. Lodge: Lions. Office: Supreme Ct Bldg State Capitol Topeka KS 66612

PRANGE, HENRY CARL, retail company executive; b. Sheboygan, Wis., July 22, 1927; s. H. Carl and Laura (Neuses) P.; m. Laura Vollrath, Sept. 3, 1949; children: Laura Lee, Henry Carl, William, John, Thomas. Student, Villanova Coll., 1945-46; B.B.A., U. Wis., 1949. With Mut. Buying Syndicate, Inc., N.Y.C., 1950; buyer H.C. Prange Co., Sheboygan, 1951-52; divisional mdse. mgr. H.C. Prange Co., 1953-58, gen. mdse. mgr., 1959-63, store mgr., 1964, pres., 1965-73, chmn. bd., chief exec. officer, 1973—; dir. Wis. Power & Light Co., Wigwam Mills, Frederick Atkins Inc. Bd. dirs. Wis. Taxpayers Alliance, Sheboygan Meml. Health Found., Inc. Served with USNR, 1945-46. Republican. Roman Catholic. Clubs: Sheboygan Yacht, Naples (Fla.) Bath and Tennis. Office: H C Prange Co 2314 Kohler Memorial Dr Sheboygan WI 53081 *

PRANGE, JAMES ROBERT, real estate broker; b. Hammond, Ind., Apr. 27, 1936; s. William Edwin and Mildred Loraine (Hutchinson) P.; m. Patricia Rush (div.); children: James Allen, Thomas Michael, Cynithia Sue; m. Marilyn Joyce Lavery, June 29, 1970. Grad. high sch., Crown Point, Ind., 1954. Maintenence engr. NIPSCO, Crown Point, 1954-56; pvt. practice real estate broker Merrillville, Ind., 1956—. Served with U.S. Army, 1956-59. Mem. Nat. Assn. Realtors, Nat. Assn. Ind. Fee Appraisers. Methodist. Avocations: fishing, travel. Office: ReMax Lake County Realty 1050 W 81st St Merrillville IN 46410

PRANGLEY, LESLIE NATHANIEL, III, accountant; b. Grand Rapids, Mich., Oct. 11, 1943; s. Leslie Nathaniel and Dorothy Phyllis (Sowa) P.; m. Katherine Eileen Tyler, July 25, 1965; children: Michelle Leslie, Michael Todd, Marcus Allen. BSBA, Aquinas Coll., 1968. CPA. Staff acct. James R. Rugg CPA, Grand Rapids, 1969-70, sr. acct., 1970-71, supr., 1971-73; ptnr. Rugg, Merkel & Prangley, Grand Rapids, 1973-76, Prangley & Marks, Grand Rapids, 1976-79; exec. ptnr. Prangley & Marks and Co., Grand Rapids, 1983—. Editor, author: (periodical column) Municipal Forum of the Michigan CPA, 1973-78. Bd. dirs. Am. Cancer Soc.-Kent City, Grand Rapids, 1975-80, chmn. fund drive, 1975-80. Mem. Mich. Assn. CPA's, Am. Inst. CPA's, CPA Assocs. Republican. Roman Catholic. Clubs: Blythefield Country (Belmont, Mich.) (bd. dirs. 1980-82, pres. 1981-82); Grand Rapids Optomists (bd. dirs. 1973-77, pres. 1976-77).

PRANICA, JOHN RONALD, financial executive; b. Abrams, Wis., Dec. 29, 1956; s. John Peter and Chesterine Helen (Warshall) P.; m. Rebecca Susan Weyers, Sept. 25, 1982. BBA, U. Wis., Eau Claire, 1975-79. CPA, Wis. Sr. acct. Deloitte Haskings & Sells, Appleton, WI, 1979-83; controller Firstar Bank N.A., Appleton, 1983-85; chief fin. officer Mainline Indsl. Distbrs., Appleton, 1985—. Dir., treas. Moorine Halfway House, Appleton, 1984—. Mem. Am. Inst. CPA's, Wis. Inst. CPA's, Nat. Assn. Accts. Avocations: golf, antique autos. Home: 2601 N Alexander St Appleton WI 54911

PRATER, MICHAEL EUGENE, math and science teacher; b. Iberia, Mo., Oct. 17, 1952; s. Eugene and Juanita (Atwell) P.; m. Melodie Ann Podruchny, Oct. 11, 1952; children: Eric Michael, Kari Ann, Monika Jean. BS in Edn., S.W. Mo. State U., 1974; MEd, Drury Coll., 1986. Math tchr. Crocker (Mo.) R 2 Schs., 1974-81; mgr. Ozark Wood Furnaces, Crocker, 1981-84; math, sci. tchr. Waynesville (Mo.) Schs., 1984—; pres. Crocker Community Tchrs. Assn., 1975-80, Waynesville Community Tchrs. Assn., 1984—. Mem. Nat. Assn. Math Tchrs., Mo. State Tchrs. Assn. (del. 1984—). Republican. Mem. Assembly of God Ch. Lodges: Optimists, Kiwanis. Home: Rt 2 PO Box 217A Iberia MO 65486 Office: Waynesville High Sch Business I-44 W Waynesville MO 65486

PRATHER, WILLIAM CHALMERS, lawyer, writer; b. Toledo, Ill., Feb. 20, 1921; s. Hollie Cartmill and Effie Fern (Deppen) P. B.A., U. Ill., 1942, J.D., 1947. Bar: Ill. 1947, U.S. Supreme Ct. 1978. Asst. dean U. Ill., 1942-43; atty. First Nat. Bank of Chgo., 1947-51; asst. gen. counsel U.S. Savs. and Loan League, Chgo., 1951-59; gen. counsel U.S. League of Savs. Instns., Chgo., 1959-82, gen. counsel emeritus, 1982—; sole practice, Cumberland County, Ill., 1981—. sem. lectr. in law, banking. Served to lt. Armed Forces, 1943-45. Decorated Bronze Star. Mem. ABA, Internat. Bar Assn., Fed Bar Assn., Ill. Bar. Assn., Chgo. Bar Assn., Nat. Lawyers Club Washington, Phi Delta Phi. Clubs: Cosmos, University, Mattoon Golf and Country, Exeter & County (Eng.); Phi Gamma Delta. Editor: The Legal Bulletin, 1951-81, The Federal Guide, 1954-81; author: Savings Accounts, 1981; contbr. articles to publs. Home: Applewood Farm Box 157 Toledo IL 62468 Office: US League of Savs 111 E Wacker Dr Chicago IL 60601 Office: 738 Courthouse Square Toledo IL 62468

PRATI, JOHN H., metallurgical engineer; b. El Paso, Tex., May 11, 1941; s. Silvio and Martha (Dow) P.; m. Caryl Ann Harvey, Nov. 8, 1969; children: David, Michelle, JoAnne. BS in Metall. Engring., Tex. Western Coll., 1965. Assoc. metall. engr. Westinghouse Corp., Phila., 1965-69; material and process engr. McDonnell Douglas Astronautics, Santa Monica, Calif., 1969-71; metall. engr. Teledyne CAE Turbine Engrs., Toledo, 1971-80, dept. head metall. lab., 1980-84, dept. head non-destructive evaluation Lab., 1984—. Contbr. articles to profl. jour. Mem. Am. Soc. Metals (treas. 1975-76, vice chmn. 1976-77, chmn. Toledo chpt. 1977-78), Am. Soc. Nodestructive Testing., Alpha Sigma Mu, Sigma Gamma Eplison. Phi Kappa Tau. Roman Catholic. Club: Commodore Computer (Toledo) (treas.). Avocations: computing, gardening, racquetball, fishing. Home: 7915 McLain Rd Lambertville MI 48144

PRATT, CHARLES LOUIS, psychologist; b. Shurborn, Mass., July 14, 1932; s. Louis Alfred and Evelyn (Alger) P.; divorced; children: Robert, Mark; m. Terryl Lynn Starkell, Oct. 20, 1979. BS, Boston U., 1960; postgrad., U. St. Thomas, 1961; MA in Psychology, Tex. Tech. U., 1968. Lic. clin. psychologist. Attendant Medfield (Mass.) State Hosp., 1960; vocational trainer Houston Council for Retarded, 1961-62; psychologist Okmulgee (Okla.) Guidance Ctr., 1966-70; psychologist III Rainier Sch., Buckley, Wash., 1970-71; dir. mental health Nebr. Western Coll., 1971-76; staff therapist Eastern Wyo. Ctr., Lusk, 1979-80; psychologist Profl. Services, Lemmon, S.D., 1980-83; pvt. practice psychology Rapid City, S.D., 1983—. Served with U.S. Army, 1952-55. Mem. Am. Soc. Clin. Hypnosis, Nat. Guild Hypnotists, S.D. Assn. Counseling Devel., C. of C. Avocations: reading, hiking, bicycling. Home and Office: 140 Cleveland Rapid City SD 57701

PRATT, GEORGE BYINGTON, III, pediatric radiologist; b. Goshen, Ind., Sept. 6, 1936; s. George Byington and Estelle (Hudson) P.; m. Patricia Mae Hammer, June 22, 1957 (div. 1970); children—George B. IV, Pamela; m. Susan Pettijohn, June 23, 1972; 1 child, Lisa Susan. B.A., DePauw U., 1958; M.D., Northwestern U., 1962; J.D., Ind. U., 1978. Diplomate Am. Bd. Radiology. Pediatric radiologist Radiologic Specialists of Ind., Indpls., 1968—. Contbr. articles to profl. jours. Pres. Marion City Child Abuse and Neglect Council, Indpls., 1984-86; bd. dirs. Family Support Ctr., Indpls., 1984—; v.p. Zionsville (Ind.) Park and Recreation Bd., 1978—, Zionville Little League, 1985—. Served to capt. USAF, 1963-65. Fellow Am. Coll. Legal Medicine; mem. AMA, Ind. State Med. Assn. (3d place award Med. Exhibit 1970). Lodges: Masons, Rotary. Avocations: snow and water skiing, sailing.

PRATT, JOHN EUGENE, health care management service executive; b. Grand Rapids, Mich., Apr. 13, 1950; s. John Ross and Margret Jean (Benham) P.; Patricia Agnes Pettersch, Aug. 2, 1974; children: David Ross, Ryan Michael, Shannon Elizabeth, Kyle Andrew. BS in Engring., U. Mich., 1972; MBA, Coll. Saint Thomas, St. Paul, 1980. Project dir. U. Mich., 1972-74; cons. coordinator Service Direction, Inc., Mpls., 1974-75, dir. adminstrv. services, 1976-77, area gen. mgr., 1978-80, v.p. adminstrn., 1981—. Republican. Roman Catholic. Avocations: golf, skiing. Home: 5817 Oaklawn Ave Edina MI 55424 Office: Service Direction Inc 4940 Viking Dr Minneapolis MN 55435

PRATT, PHILIP, judge; b. Pontiac, Mich., July 14, 1924; s. Peter and Helen (Stathis) P.; m. Mary C. Hill, July 26, 1952; children—Peter, Laura, Kathleen. Student (Alumni scholar), U. Mich., 1942-43, LL.B., 1950; student, U. Chgo., 1943-44. Bar: Mich. bar 1951. Title examiner Abstract & Title Co., Pontiac, 1951; asst. pros. atty. Oakland County, Mich., 1952; mem. firm Smith & Pratt, Pontiac, 1953-63; circuit judge 6th Jud. Circuit of Mich., Pontiac, 1963-70; U.S. dist. judge Eastern Dist. Mich., 1970—, chief judge, 1986—. Served with OSS AUS, 1943-46. Decorated Bronze Star medal. Mem. ABA, Oakland County Bar Assn. (pres. 1961), State Bar Mich., Am. Judicature Soc. Office: US Courthouse Detroit MI 48226

PRATT, SAMUEL MAXON, English and humanities educator; b. North Adams, Mass., May 10, 1919; s. Harry Edward and Ethel Mae (Davis) P.; widowed; 1 child, Samuel Henry. A.B., Dartmouth Col., 1941; Ph.D., Cornell U., 1951. Tchr., Greer Sch., Hope Farm, N.Y., 1941-42, Cornell U., Ithaca, N.Y., 1946-52; prof. English and humanities Ohio Wesleyan U., Delaware, 1952-84; ret., 1984; reader Ednl. Testing Service, Princeton, N.J., 1956-83. Contbr. articles to scholarly pubs. Active, Episcopal Church. Served with U.S. Army, 1942-45, ETO. Mem. AAUP (pres. local chpt. 1955-56, state chmn. 1959-60). Democrat. Avocations: golf, water skiing, maintenance of property. Home: 34 Westgate Dr Delaware OH 43015 Office: Dept English Ohio Wesleyan U Delaware OH 43015

PRAWDZIK, JOSEPH PETER, JR., accountant, financial planner; b. Chgo., Mar. 13, 1946; s. Joseph Peter Sr. and Leoan Kathryn (Kunysz) P. AA, Wright Jr. Coll., 1967; BS in Commerce, DePaul U., 1969, MBA in Mktg., 1985. CPA, Ill. Acct. Arthur Andersen & Co., Chgo., 1969-76; auditor Montgomery Ward Co., Chgo., 1976-77; mgr. auditing The Signature Group, Schaumburg, Ill., 1977-82, mgr. budgeting, 1982—. Mem. Am. Inst. CPA's, Ill. Soc. CPA's. Home: 2358 N Leavitt St Chicago IL 60647 Office: The Signature Group 200 N Martingale Rd Schaumburg IL 60194

PREHN, DONALD FREDERICK, dentist; b. Wausau, Wis., June 19, 1927; s. Delos Carl and Anita Ida (Mueller) P.; m. Patricia Lee Booth, Aug. 9, 1952; children: Ronald, Constance, Frederick, Robert. BS, U. Wis., 1949; DDS, Marquette U., 1953. Gen. practice dentistry, Wausau, 1953—; mem. dental staff Wausau Hosps., 1953—, chief dental staff, 1957-58; pres. Bear-Superior Corp., Wausau, 1981-83. Pres., mem. bd. Wausau Dist. Sch. Bd., 1966-78; pres., v.p. exec. bd. Samoset council Boy Scouts of Am., 1973—; jr. warden, vestryman St. John the Bapt. Episcopal Ch., Wausau, 1963-85; mem. exec. bd., fin. com. Episcopal Diocese Fond du Lac, Wis., 1976—; mem. Birch Trails council Girl Scouts of Am., 1972—. Served as 2d lt. inf., U.S. Army, 1946-47, PTO. Recipient Merit award Rib Mountain dist. Samoset council Boy Scouts of Am., 1977, Silver Beaver award, 1978. Mem. ADA, Wis. Dental Assn. (hosp. accreditation com. 1964-65), Cen. Wis. Dental Soc., Marathon County Dental Soc. (pres. 1958-59, cert. appreciation 1982), Marathon County Hist. Soc., Wausau Area C. of C., Am. Legion. Republican. Club: Wausau. Avocations: fishing, hunting, boating, skiing, traveling. Home: 1010 Adams St Wausau WI 54401 Office: 413 Jefferson St Wausau WI 54401

PREHN, FREDERICK CARL, dentist; b. Wausau, Wis., June 8, 1957; s. Donald Frederick and Patricia (Booth) P.; m. Linda Edwards. BS, U. Wis., 1978; DDS, Marquette U., 1982. Practice dentistry Wausau, 1982—. Mem. Wausau Sch. Bd., 1985—. Mem. ADA, Am. Assn. Hosp. Dentists, Wis. Dental Assn. Republican. Episcopalian. Avocations: skiing, hunting, fishing. Home: 1105 Highland Park Blvd Wausau WI 54401 Office: 413 Jefferson St Wausau WI 54401

PREHN, RONALD SCOTT, dentist; b. Wausau, Wis., Sept. 10, 1953; s. Donald Fredrick and Patricia Lee (Booth) P.; m. Cynthia Ann Hike, Aug. 11, 1979; children: Christyna, Tricia, Tiffany. BS in Bacteriology, U. Wis., 1976; DDS, Marquette U., 1981. Pvt. practice Sarasota, Fla., 1981-85, Wausau, Wis., 1985—; staff Sarasota Meml. Hosp., 1982-85, Wausau Hosp. Ctr., 1985—. Mem. adv. bd. Heritage Haven, Schofield, Wis., 1986.

Recipient Eagle Scout award Boy Scouts Am., Wausau, 1967. Mem. ADA, Wis. Dental Soc., Cen. Wis. Dental Assn., Marathon County Dental Soc., Am. Assn. Endodontists, L.D. Pankey Alumni Assn. Republican. Episcopalian. Lodge: Kiwanis. Office: 413 Jefferson St Wausau WI 54401

PREISSLER, SCOTT MAX, academic administrator, career planning administrator, consultant; b. Hammond, Ind., Aug. 28, 1960; s. Samuel Edgar and Wilma Jean (Hasse) P.; m. Andrea Jean Price, July 21, 1984. BA in Bus., Taylor U., 1983; EdM, Ind. U., 1985. Dir. student activities Ind. U., Richmond, 1984—; asst. dir. career devel. and placement U. Cin., 1987—; pres. Preissler & Assocs., Inc., Ind. and Ohio, 1986—. Mem. Assn. Christians in Student Devel., Nat. Assn. Student Personnel Administrators, Assn. for Counseling and Devel. Baptist. Avocations: fishing, running, travel. Home: 5421 Kenwood Rd Mail 209 Cincinnati OH 45227 Office: U Cin Mail Location 115 Cincinnati OH 45221

PREMER, DAVID JOHN, federal agency administrator; b. Chgo., Mar. 29, 1936; s. George William and Margaret Susan (Darby) P.; m. Suzanne Marie Dobbin, Sept. 19, 1958; children: Debra, Shelley, Elizabeth, Pamela. BS in Earth Scis., Southeast Mo. State U., 1958; MBA, Auburn U., 1972; grad., USAF Air Command and Staff Coll., 1972. Cert. data processing. Chief carto technologies Aerospace Ctr., U.S Def. Mapping Agy., St. Louis, 1974-76, asst. chief aerospace carto dept., 1976-79, chief geopositional and digital data div., 1979-82, chief geopositional dept., 1982-83, chief spoem tech. div., 1983-85, dep. dir. research and engring., 1985—. Pres. Green Acres homeowners Assn., St. Louis, 1982. Served with USNAR, 1953-61. Mem. IEEE, Nuclear Soc., Am. Soc. Photogrammetry and Remote Sensing, U.S. Power Squadrons (editor St. Louis. chpt., 1982-83), Nature Conservancy. Mem. Ch. of Christ. Avocations: sailing, photography. Home: 2 Elmcrest Acres Saint Louis County MO 63138 Office: Def Mapping Agy Aerospace Ctr 3200 S 2d St Saint Louis MO 63118

PRENDERGAST, JAMES T., steel company executive; b. Detroit, Feb. 10, 1921; s. Thomas Patrick and Amanda Ann (Theisen) P.; m. Doris Esther Chamberlin, May 26, 1944; children: Thomas James, Michael John, David Neal. BS, U. Detroit, 1947. Asst. controller Reichhold Chems., Ferndale, Mich., 1949-57; v.p. fin. Barsteel Corp., Detroit, 1957—. Roman Catholic. Avocations: golf, boating. Home: 20505 Vernier Harper Woods MI 48225 Office: Barsteel Corp 18695 Sherwood Detroit MI 48234

PRENTISS, ROBERT NOBLE, JR., banker; b. Evanston, Ill., Mar. 16, 1943; s. Robert N. and Jean (Keith) P.; m. Ann K. Prentiss, Dec. 16, 1968; children: Robin, Kevin. BS in Chemistry, Bowling Green State U., 1965; MBA in Fin., U. Mich., 1967. Mktg. rep. Richfield Bank, Mpls., 1971-74, trust officer, 1974-78, v.p., 1978-81, sr. v.p., 1981—; bd. dirs. Viking Engring., Mpls., bd. dirs. Richfield Bank, Lyndale, Minn. Mem. Mpls. Estate Planning Council, Met. Tax Planning (pres. 1983), Mpls. CLU's (bd. dirs. 1983-85). Republican. Club: Normandale Racquet (Mpls.). Avocations: tennis, skiing. Home: 2370 Sioux Ct New Brighton MN 55112 Office: Richfield Bank and Trust Co 6625 Lyndale Minneapolis MN 55423

PRESKA, MARGARET LOUISE ROBINSON, university president; b. Parma, N.Y., Jan. 23, 1938; d. Ralph Craven and Ellen Elvira (Niemi) Robinson; m. Daniel C. Preska, Jan. 24, 1959; children: Robert, William, Ellen. B.S. summa cum laude, SUNY, 1957; M.A., Pa. State U., 1961; Ph.D., Claremont Grad. Sch., 1969; postgrad., Manchester Coll., Oxford U., 1973. Instr. LaVerne (Calif.) Coll., 1968-75, asst. prof., 1972-75, asso. prof., 1972-75, acad. dean, 1972-75; instr. Starr King Sch. for Ministry, Berkeley, Calif., summer, 1975; v.p. acad. affairs, equal opportunity officer Mankato (Minn.) State U., 1975-79, pres., 1979—; dir. No. States Power Co., Norwest Bank, Mankato. Pres. Pomona Valley chpt. UN Assn., 1968-69, Unitarian Soc. Pomona Valley, 1968-69, PTA Lincoln Elem. Sch., Pomona, 1973-74; mem. Pomona City Charter Revision Commn., 1972; chmn. The Fielding Inst., Santa Barbara, 1983-86; bd. dirs. Elderhostel Internat., 1983—, Minn. Agrl. Interpretive Ctr. (Farmam.), 1983—; nat. pres. Campfire, Inc.; chmn. Gov.'s Council on Youth, Minn., 1983, Minn. Edn. Forum, 1984; mem. Gov.'s Commn. on Econ. Future of Minn., 1985, NCAA Pres.'s Commn., 1986—, Minn. Brainpower Compact, 1985; commr. Midwest Gov.'s Econ. Devel. Council; bd. dirs. Am. Assn. State Colls. and Univs. Carnegie Found. grantee Am. Council Edn. Deans Inst., 1974; recipient Outstanding Alumni award Pa. State, Outstanding Alumni award Claremont Grad. Sch.; named one of top 100, SUNY. Mem. AAUW, LWV, Women's Econ. Roundtable, Mpls./St. Paul Com. on Fgn. Relations., Am. Council on Edn., Am. Assn. Univ. Adminstrs. Unitarian. Clubs: Benedicts Dance, Zonta. Home: 10 Sumner Hills Mankato MN 56001 Office: Office of the Pres Box 24 Mankato State U Mankato MN 56001

PRESSE, SHARON KAY (SPINKS), teacher; b. Bedford, Ind., Mar. 18, 1944; d. Carl E. and Lorena (Lynn) S.; m. James A. Presse, Aug. 16, 1985. BS, Ind. U., 1965, MS, 1968. Cert. elem. tchr., Ind., Ill. Tchr. English Batesville (Ind.) Community Sch. Corp., 1965-67, Community Sch. Dist. 207-U, Peotone, Ill., 1967—. Mem. AAUW (life, pres. Calumet Area br. 1978-80, recording sec. 1976-78), Ind. U. Alumni Assn. (life), Ind. U. Alumni Club of N.W. Ind. (bd. dirs., treas. 1985—), Beta Sigma Phi (pres. 1976-77, named Outstanding Mem. 1977). Home: 20039 S 114th Ave Mokena IL 60448 Office: Peotone Elem Sch Conrad and Mill St Peotone IL 60468

PRESSLER, LARRY, U.S. senator; b. Humboldt, S.D., Mar. 29, 1942; s. Antone Lewis and Loretta Geneive (Claussen) P.; m. Harriet Dent, 1982. B.A., U. S.D., 1964; diploma (Rhodes scholar), Oxford U., Eng., 1965; M.A., Kennedy Sch. Govt., Harvard U., 1971; J.D., Harvard U., 1971. Mem. 94th-95th Congresses from 1st S.D. Dist.; mem. U.S. Senate from S.D., 1979—; U.S. del. Inter-Parliamentary Union for 97th Congress.; mem. commerce, sci. and transp. com., fgn. relations com., spl. com. on aging, small bus. com., chmn. subcom. of commerce and tourism. All-Am. del. 4-H agrl. fair, Cairo, 1961. Served to 1st lt. AUS, 1966-68, Vietnam. Recipient Nat. 4-H Citizenship award, 1962, Report to the Pres. 4-H award, 1962. Mem. Am. Assn. Rhodes Scholars, VFW, ABA Phi Beta Kappa. Office: 411 Russell Senate Bldg Washington DC 20510

PRESSON, ELLIS WYNN, health services executive; b. Electra, Tex., Mar. 28, 1940; s. Ellis Wilbur and Juanita M. (Morgan) P.; B.B.A., U. Tex., 1963; M.H.A., Washington U., St. Louis, 1965; m. Andrea L., July 5, 1969; children—Eric, Garett, Amber. Adminstrv. asst. Methodist Hosp. of Dallas, 1964-66; asst. adminstr. Dallas County Hosp., 1966-70; pres. Swedish Am. Hosp., Rockford, Ill., 1970-77, Research Med. Center, Kansas City, Mo., 1977-80, Research Health Services, Kansas City, 1980—. Pres., Comprehensive Mental Health and Retardation, 1972-74; treas. bd. Rockford Med. Edn. Found., 1972-75; preceptor for adminstrn. extern U. Wis., 1975-76; search com. Rockford Sch. Medicine, U. Ill., 1975-76; regional com. mem. Hosp. Adminstrv. Surveillance Program, 1973-76; bd. dirs. Ill. Hosp. and Health Service, 1972-77; mem. Health Planning NW Ill., 1973-77; licensing bd. mem. Ill. State Ambulatory Surgery Treatment Center, 1974-76. Mem. Am. Hosp. Assn., Mo. Hosp. Assn. chmn. bd., del. to Am. Hosp. Assn., mem. labor relations com.), Kansas City Area Hosp. Assn. (chmn. fin. council, dir.). Clubs: Rotary, Indian Hills Country. Home: 15613 Overbrook Ln Stanley KS 66224 Office: 6400 Prospect Kansas City MO 64132

PRESSWOOD, GAIL R., food products executive, accountant; b. St. Louis, Apr. 8, 1955; m. T. Joe Presswood, Aug. 17, 1979. BS in Bus. Adminstrn. magna cum laude, U. Mo., St. Louis, 1980. CPA, Mo. Sr. acct. Ernst & Whinney, St. Louis, 1980-82; tech. acct. Ralston Purina Co., St. Louis, 1982-85, acctg. supr., 1985-86, gen. acctg. mgr., 1986—. Mem. Am. Inst. CPA's, Mo. Soc. CPA's.

PRESTANSKI, HARRY THOMAS, public relations executive; b. Zanesville, Ohio, Aug. 31, 1947; s. Joseph Raymond and Della Theresa (Butryn) P.; m. Jeanene LaRee Versaw, Sept. 19, 1970; children: Lisa Jodene, Shari LaRee, Amy Elizabeth. BS in Journalism, Ohio U., 1972; postgrad. U. Dayton, 1973-74. Publs. editor Hobart Brothers, Troy, Ohio, 1972-75; v.p., account supr. Josephson, Cuffari & Co., Montclair, N.J., 1975-78; publicity mgr. Winnebago Industries, Forest City, Iowa, 1978-80; v.p., gen. mgr. CMF & Z Pub. Relations div. Creswell, Munsell, Fultz & Zirbel, Cedar Rapids, Iowa, 1980—. Contbr. articles to profl. jours. Served to cpl. USMC, 1966-69. Mem. Pub. Relations Soc. Am., Am. Med. Writers Assn. Republican. Roman Catholic. Home: 3419 Sue Ln NW Cedar Rapids IA 52405 Office: 4211 Signal Ridge Rd NE Cedar Rapids IA 52406

PRESTASH, RANDY JOHN, optometrist; b. Milw., Jan. 27, 1955; s. George and Anna (Stachelski) P.; m. Patricia Ann Lohman, Aug. 26, 1978. BS, Ill. Coll. Optometry, 1978, OD, 1980. Assoc. intern Ill. Coll. Optometry, Chgo., 1979-80, Chgo. Lighthouse for the Blind, 1979-80; pvt. practice optometry Oconomowoc, Wis., 1980—; clin. dir. Operation Kapawa Rotary Internat. Eye Health Mission to Phillipines, 1983, 84, 86; pres. cons. Visions of Success, Oconomowoc, 1980—; v.p. Nat. Optical Services Corp., Oconomowoc, 1980—. Named one of Outstanding Young Men Am. Jaycees, Chgo., 1979; recipient Albert H. Rodriquez Research award Ill. Coll. Optometry, 1980. Mem. Am. Optometric Assn., Wis. Optometric Assn., Kettle Moraine Optometric Assn., Vols. of Optometric Services to Humanity. Club: Fishers of Men (Oconomowoc) (v.p. 1985—). Lodge: Rotary (bd. Oconomowoc club dirs. 1985—). Avocations: sailing, windsurfing, photography, sport fishing. Home: 6028 Mary Ln Oconomowoc WI 53066 Office: 608 E Summit Ave Oconomowoc WI 53066

PRESTON, LARRY EUGENE, data processing executive, electrical engineer; b. Columbus, Ohio, Mar. 11, 1953; s. Eugene Stanley and Vianna Jane (Thompson) P.; m. Mary Amanda Paris, Nov. 23, 1985. BSEE, Gen. Motors Inst., 1977. Sr. software analyst Gen. Motors, Flint, Mich., 1977-84; owner, mgr. Bluehat Software, Flint, 1980-83; sr. software techniques analyst Gen. Electric, Cin., 1985—. Mem. IEEE. Republican. Roman Catholic. Avocations: chess, digital design software development, tennis, science fiction,renovating English Tudor houses. Home: 3662 Kendall Ave Cincinnati OH 45208 Office: Gen Electric Cincinnati OH 45208

PRETZER, DALE H., library director; b. Saginaw, Mich., Aug. 10, 1934; s. Max O. and Eleanor G. (Shay) P.; m. Marilyn Miller, Jan. 31, 1959 (div.); 1 child, Dalyce; m. Yvonne M. Le Duc, Aug. 21, 1971; children: David, Sandra, Michelle, Paul. AB, Cen. Mich. U., 1960; AMLS, U. Mich., 1963. Lab. tester Dow Corning Corp., Midland, Mich., 1956-60; asst. to dir. Mich. State U. Library, East Lansing, 1960-68; dep. state librarian State of Mich. Library, Lansing, 1968-79; owner, operator Pretzer's Spindrift, Florence, Oreg., 1979-82; dir. Hackley Pub. Library., Muskegon, Mich., 1982—. Contbr. articles to profl. jours.; host (TV show) Consider, Books of Our Time, 1984—. Mem. exec. council Mich. Library Consortium, Lansing, 1975-79, 84-86. Mem. Am. Library Assn.. Mich. Library Assn. (hon.), Mich. Assn. of Media in Edn. Presbyterian. Club: Torch (membership com.) (Muskegon). Lodges: Rotary, Elks. Home: 18586 Pawnee Dr Spring Lake MI 49456 Office: Hackley Pub Library 316 W Webster Ave Muskegon MI 49440

PREUS, DAVID WALTER, minister, bishop; b. Madison, Wis., May 28, 1922; s. Ove Jacob Hjort and Magdalene (Forde) P.; m. Ann Madsen, June 26, 1951; children: Martha, David, Stephen, Louise, Laura. BA, Luther Coll., Decorah, Iowa, 1943, DD (hon.), 1969; postgrad., U. Minn.em., 1946-47; BTh, Luther Sem., St. Paul, 1950; postgrad., Union Sem., 1951, Edinburgh U., 1951-52; LLD (hon.), Wagner Coll., 1973, Gettysburg Coll., 1976; DD (hon.), Pacific Luth. Coll., 1974, St. Olaf Coll., 1974, Dana Coll., 1979; LHD (hon.), Macalester Coll., 1976. Ordained to ministry Luth. Ch., 1950; asst. pastor First Luth. Ch., Brookings, S.D., 1950-51; pastor Trinity Luth. Ch., Vermillion, S.D., 1952-57; campus pastor U. Minn., Mpls., 1957-58; pastor Univ. Luth. Ch. of Hope, Mpls., 1958-73; v.p. Am. Luth. Ch., 1968-73, pres., presiding bishop, 1973-87; Luccock vis. pastor Yale Div. Sch., 1969; chmn. bd. youth activity Am. Luth. Ch., 1960-68; mem. exec. com. Luth. Council U.S.A.; v.p. Luth. World Fedn., 1977—; mem. central com. World Council Chs., 1973-75, 80—; Luth. del. White House Conf. on Equal Opportunity. Chmn. Greater Mpls. Fair Housing Com., Mpls. Council Chs., 1960-64; Mem. Mpls. Planning Commn., 1965-67; mem. Mpls. Sch. Bd., 1965-74, chmn., 1967-69; mem. Mpls. Bd. Estimate and Taxation, 1968-73, Mpls. Urban Coalition; sr. public adv. U.S. del. Madrid Conf. of Conf. on Security and Cooperation in Europe, 1980-81; bd. dirs. Mpls. Inst. Art, Walker Art Center, Hennepin County United Fund, Ams. for Childrens Relief, Luth. Student Found., Research Council of Gt. City Schs., Urban League, NAACP; bd. regents Augsburg Coll., Mpls. Served with Signal Corps AUS, 1943-46, PTO. Decorated comdr.'s cross Royal Norwegian Order St. Olav; recipient Regents medal Augustana Coll., Sioux Falls, S.D., 1973, Torch of Liberty award Anti-Defamation League, 1973, St. Thomas Aquinas award St. Thomas Coll. Office: 422 S 5th St Minneapolis MN 55415

PREUSS, ROGER E(MIL), artist; b. Waterville, Minn., Jan. 29, 1922; s. Emil W. and Edna (Rosenau) P.; m. MarDee Ann Germundson, Dec. 31, 1954 (dec. Mar. 1981). Student, Mankato Comml. Coll., Mpls. Sch. Art. instr. seminar Mpls. Coll. Art and Design.; former judge ann. Goodyear Nat. Conservation Awards Program. Painter of nature art; one-man shows include: St. Paul Fine Art Galleries, 1959, Albert Lea Art Center, 1963, Hist. Soc. Mont., Helena, 1964, Bicentennial exhbn., Le Sueur County Hist. Soc. Mus., Elysian, Minn., 1976, Merrill's Gallery of Fine Art, Taos, N.Mex., 1980; exhbns. include: Midwest Wildlife Conf. Exhbn., Kerr's Beverly Hills, Calif., 1947, Joslyn Meml. Mus., Omaha, 1948, Minn. Centennial, 1949, Federated Chaparral Authors, 1951, Nat. Wildlife Art, 1951, 52, N.Am. Wildlife Art, 1952, Ducks Unltd. Waterfowl exhibit, 1953, 54, St. Paul Winter Carnival, 1954, St. Paul Gallery Art Mart, 1954, Salmagundi Club, 1968, Animal Artists, Grand Cen. Art Galleries, N.Y.C., 1972, Holy Land Conservation Fund, N.Y.C., 1976, Faribault Art Ctr., 1981, Wildlife Artists of the World Exhbn., Bend, Oreg., 1984; represented in permanent collections: Demarest Meml. Mus., Hackensack, N.J., Smithsonian Instn., N.Y. Jour. Commerce, Mont. Hist. Soc., Inland Bird Banding Assn., Minn. Capitol Bldg., Mont. State U., Wildlife Am. Collection, LeSueur Hist. Soc., Voyageurs Nat. Park Interpretive Ctr., Roger Preuss Art Collection, Lucky 11 VFW Post, Mpls., Nat. Wildlife Fedn. Collection, Minn. Ceremonial House, U.S. Wildlife Service Fed. Bldg., Fort Snelling, Minn., Crater Lake Nat. Park Visitors Ctr., VA Hosp., Mpls., Luxton Collection, Banff, Alta., Can., Inst. Contemporary Arts London, Mont. Capitol Bldg., People of Century-Goldblatt Collection, Lyons, Ill., Stark Mus., Orange, Tex., others, numerous galleries and pvt. collections; designer: Fed. Duck Stamp, U.S. Dept. Interior, 1949, Commemorative Centennial Pheasant Stamp, 1981, Gold Waterfowl medallion Franklin Mint, 1983, Gold Stamp medallion Wildlife Mint, 1983; panelist: Sportsman's Roundtable, WTCN-TV, Mpls., from 1953; author: Is Wildlife Art Recognized Fine Art?, 1986; contbr.: Christmas Echos, 1955, Wing Shooting, Trap & Skeet, 1955, Along the Trout Stream, 1979; contbr. Art Impressoins mag., Can., Wildlife Art, U.S.; also illustrations and articles in Nat. Wildlife, others.; assoc. editor: Out-of-Doors mag.; compiler and artist: Outdoor Horizons, 1957, Twilight over the Wilderness, 1972, 60 limited edition prints Wildlife of America, from 1970; contbr. paintings and text Minnesota Today; creator paintings and text Preuss Wildlife Calendar; inventor: paintings and text Wildlife Am. Calendar; featured artist Art West, 1980-84, Wildlife Art; featured in film Your BFA- Care and Maintenance. Del. Nat. Wildlife Conf.; bd. dirs. Voyageurs Nat. Park Assn., Deep-Portage Conservation Found., from 1977, Wetlands for Wildlife U.S.A.; active Wildlife Am.; co-organizer, v.p., bd. dirs. Minn. Conservation Fedn., 1952-54; trustee Liberty Bell Edn. Found.; hon. life mem. Faribault Art Ctr., Waseca Arts Council. Served with USNR, World War II. Recipient Stamp Design award U.S. Fish and Wildlife Service, 1949, Minn. Outdoor award, 1956, Patron of Conservation award, 1956, award for contbns. to conservation Minn. Statehood Centennial Commn., 1958, 1st award Am. Indsl. Devel. Council, citation of merit V.F.W., Award of Merit Mil. Order Cootie, 1963, Merit award Minn. Waterfowl Assn., 1976, Silver medal Nat. S.A.R., 1978, Services to Arts and Environment award Faribault Art Ctr., 1981; named Wildlife Conservationist of Yr., Sears Found.-Nat. Wildlife Fedn. Program, 1966, Am. Bicentennial Wildlife Artist, Am. Heritage Assn., 1976; hon. mem. Ont. Chippewa Nation of Can., 1957; named Knight of Mark Twain for contbns. to Am. art Mark Twain Soc., 1978; named to Water, Woods and Wildlife Hall of Fame, named Dean of Wildfowl Artists, 1981, Hon. Ky. Col.; recipient Honor degree U.S. Vets. Venison Program, 1980. Fellow Internat. Inst. Arts (life), Soc. Animal Artists (emeritus), N.Am. Mycol. Assn.; mem. Nat. Audubon Soc., Internat. Sci. Info. Service, Nat. Wildlife Fedn. (nat. wildlife week chmn. Minn.), Minn. Ducks Unltd. (bd. dirs.), Minn. Artists Assn. (v.p., bd. dirs. 1953-59), Soc. Artists and Art Dirs., Outdoor Writers Am., Am. Artists Profl. League (emeritus), Mpls. Soc., Fine Arts, Wildlife Soc., Zool. Soc., Minn. Mycol. Soc. (pres. emeritus, hon. life mem.), Le Sueur County Hist. Soc. (hon. life mem.), Minn. Conservation Fedn. (hon. life), Wildlife Artists World (charter mem., internat. v.p. 1986—, chmn. fine arts bd.), The Prairie Chicken Soc. (patron), The Sharp-tailed Grouse Soc. (patron). Clubs: Beaverbrook (hon. life), Minn. Press (Mpls.); Explorers (N.Y.C.). Studio: 2224 Grand Ave Minneapolis MN 55405 Office: care Wildlife of America Gallery PO Box 556-A Minneapolis MN 55458

PREUSZ, GERALD CLYDE, higher education and dentistry educator; b. Loogootee, Ind., Feb. 6, 1938; s. Victor Alvin and Mildred Beatrice (Jackman) P.; m. Janet Hayes McGeorge, Sept. 12, 1959; children—Pamela, Keith (dec.), Joseph, Patricia. B.S., Ind. U., 1960, M.S., 1966, Ed.D., 1970. Cert. secondary tchr., Ind. Tchr. Lake Forest Elem. Sch., Hobart, Ind., 1960-61; high sch. tchr. George Rogers Clark Sch., Hammond, Ind., 1961-66; coordinator students Ind. U., Gary, 1966-69; asst. dean students Ind. U.-Purdue, Indpls., 1970-73, dean student affairs, 1973-77, assoc. prof. higher edn., 1978—, assoc. prof. dentistry, 1987—; cons. Ind. U. Dental Sch., Indpls., 1979—; Ind. U. Northwest, Gary, 1966-69. Contbr. articles to profl. jours. Troop chmn. Crossroads of Am. council Boy Scouts Am., Indpls., 1974-77, scoutmaster Troop 282, Indpls., 1977-79; active in Work Release Ctr. Prisoners, Indpls., 1972-75; scholarship selector Inland Container Corp., Indpls., 1975-77. Recipient Edward C. Moore teaching award Faculty Ind. U.-Purdue U., 1984, Outstanding Contbns. award Black Student Union 1975. Mem. Ind. Coll. Personnel Adminstrs. (sec., treas 1983-84), Am. Assn. Higher Edn., Nat. Assn. Student Personnel Adminstrs., Am. Coll. Personnel Adminstrs., Am. Assn. Counseling and Devel. Mem. Disciples of Christ Ch. Avocations: reading; camping; fishing; boating. Home: 121 Tulip Tree Ind U Bloomington IN 47405 Office: Ind U-Purdue U ES 3154 Bldg 902 W New York St Indianapolis IN 46223

PREVO, STEPHEN ERNEST, accountant; b. Jan. 1, 1946; s. Ralph Warren and Dorothy Irene (Ohm) P.; m. Patricia J. Fetters, Apr. 15, 1976 (div. Jan. 1985). BS, So. Ill. U., 1968. CPA, Ind. Staff acct. Price Waterhouse, St. Louis, 1968-70; sr. acct. Kemper CPA's, Robinson, Ill., 1970-71; jr. ptnr. Sackrider CPA's, Terre Haute, Ind., 1971-80; pvt. practice acctg. Terre Haute, 1980—. Mem. Am. Inst. CPA's, Ind. CPA Soc. Republican. Methodist. Avocations: golf, racquetball. Home: 376 White Oak Terre Haute IN 47804 Office: 150 Cherry St Terre Haute IN 47807

PRIBULA, SCOTT DANIEL, engineer; b. Moorhead, Minn., Apr. 15, 1960; s. Gerald Henry and Jo Ann (Brunelle) P.; m. Michelle Jane Friese, Sept. 14, 1985. BS in Constrn. Engring., N.D. State U., 1983. Estimator Nodak Constrn., Grand Forks, N.D., 1983-84; engr. Nash Finch, Mpls., 1984-85, Super Valu, Mpls., 1985—; engr./architect Studio 70, Mpls., 1985—. Mem. Nat. Assn. Wholesale Grocers. Republican. Lutheran. Avocations: tennis, skiing, baseball, woodworking. Home: 3968 Lake Curve Rd Minneapolis MN 55422

PRICE, BUDDY ALAN, podiatrist; b. Miami, Fla., Feb. 1, 1953; s. Grover Eugene and Beatrice (Shapiro) P.; student Rollins Coll., 1970-73; B.A. in Chemistry, U. South Fla., 1974; B.S. in Podiatric Medicine, Ill. Coll. Podiatric Medicine, 1979, D.P.M. cum laude, 1979. Diplomate Am. Bd. Podiatric surgery. Extern U. of Chgo. hosps., 1978; resident in podiatric medicine Northlake Community Hosp., Ill., 1979-80; rotating resident in podiatry Children's Meml. Hosp. and Shriner's Children's Meml. Hosp., both Chgo., 1979-80; practice gen. podiatry Lake Shore Foot and Ankle Ctrs., Chgo., 1980—, Munster, Ind.; adj. surg. faculty William Scholl Coll. Podiatric Medicine, Thorek Community Hosp., Chgo. Ctr. Hosp.; surg. staff Gary (Ind.) Meth. Hosp., Calumet Surg. Ctr., Munster, Broadway Community Hosp., Merrillville, Ind. Active, Big Bros. Am., Orlando, Fla., 1972-73. Cert. to CPR, Am. Heart Assn.; registered podiatrist, Ind., Ill., Fla. Mem. Ill. Podiatric Med. Assn., Am. Podiatric Med. Assn. Democrat. Jewish. Contbr. articles to profl. jours. Office: 16 W Erie St Chicago IL 60616 also: 7550 Hohman Ave Ste 300 Munster IN 46321 also: 10327 S Western Ave Chicago IL 60643 :

PRICE, CAROL ANN, computer science manager; b. Detroit, Apr. 4, 1944; d. Robert Warren and Margaret (Moody) Gaffney; m. William Robert Price, June 27, 1964; children: Derek, Ryan. BA, U. Fla., 1965; MA, Wayne State U., 1970. Math. programmer Parke Davis & Co., Detroit, 1965-69; mathematician advanced product and mfg. engring. staff Gen. Motors Corp., Warren, Mich., 1969-75, staff devel. engr., 1976-78, sr. staff project engr., 1978-81, supr., 1981-84, mgr., 1984; regional mgr. Electronic Data Systems, Warren, Mich., 1985—. Pres. Emerald Lake Homeowners, Troy, Mich., 1980-82. Mem. IEEE, Mich. Profl. Women's Network. Home: 6136 Sandshores Troy MI 48098 Office: Electronic Data Systems 3551 Hamlin Rd Auburn Hills MI 48057

PRICE, CAROL-ANN, academic administrator; b. West Orange, N.J., Apr. 10, 1936; d. Clifford Harold and Helen Anna (Hollum) Minier; m. Thomas J. Price, Sr., Apr. 17, 1955; children—Thomas J. Jr., Robert Alan. B.A. in Bus. Adminstrn., Bellevue Coll., 1975; postgrad. in bus. Creighton U., 1982-83. Cert. Nat. Assn. Coll. and Univ. Bus. Officers. Bus. mgr. Nebr. Coll. Bus., Omaha, 1975-79; controller Bellevue Coll., Nebr., 1979-80, bus. mgr., 1980-81, seminar speaker, panelist, 1982—; mgr. adminstrv. services Land Bank Nat. Data Processing Ctr., Omaha, 1981-84, dir. mgmt. services, 1984-86; bus. mgr., corp. sec. Coll. St. Mary, Omaha, 1986—. Coordinator USAF Family Services Orgn., Madrid, Spain, 1958-63; bd. dirs. Am. Kindergarten, Madrid, 1963; team leader United Way Midlands, Omaha, 1973-74, account exec. 1986; active Bellevue Coll. alumni fund raiser, 1982-85; chmn. bd. dirs. San. Improvement Dist. #5, 1985—. Mem. Adminstrv. Mgmt. Soc. Internat. (local pres. 1980-81, area asst. dir. 1982-83, internat. bd. dirs. 1983-85, internat. v.p. 1985-87. first v.p. 1987—, Merit Scroll award 1982, Diamond Merit award 1984, cert. adminstrv. mgr.). Republican. Episcopalian. Club: Bay Hills Golf (bd. dirs. 1985—) (Plattsmouth, Nebr.). Avocations: opera; symphony; theatre; travel; golf. Home: Rural Route 2 Buccaneer Bay Plattsmouth NE 68048 Office: Coll St Mary 1901 S 72 St Omaha NE 68124

PRICE, CAROLINE EDITH, illustrator; b. St. Paul, Nov. 9, 1958; s. Starling Worth and Rosemary (Dolan) P. BA in Art History, The Colo. Coll., 1980; postgrad., U. Pa., 1982, Mpls. Coll. Art & Design, 1983. Asst. to dir. mus. extension Minn. Mus. Art, St. Paul, 1980-82; free lance illustrator Mpls., 1983-86. Illustrator A Kid's Workbook on Family Violence, 1986, Bringing Out the Best, 1986, Different Like Me, 1987, Perfectionism, 1987. Mem. Walker Art Ctr. Avocations: swimming, biking, reading. Home and Office: 1783 Irving Ave S Minneapolis MN 55403

PRICE, FAYE HUGHES, mental health consultant; b. Indpls.; d. Twidell W. and Lillian Gladys (Hazlewood) Hughes; A.B. with honors (scholar 1939-43), W.Va. State Coll., 1943; postgrad. social work (scholar) Ind. U., 1943-44; M.S.W., Jane Addams Sch., U. Ill., 1951; student summer insts. U. Chgo. 1960-65; m. Frank Price, Jr., June 16, 1945; 1 dau., Faye Michele. Supr. youth activities Flanner House, Indpls., 1945-47; program dir. Parkway Community House, Chgo., 1947-56, dir., 1957-58; dir. social services mental health div. Chgo. Dept. Health, 1958-61, dir. community services, 1961-65, asso. dir. planning and devel., 1965-69, regional program dir., 1969-75, asst. dir. mental health, 1975, acting dir., 1976, asst. dir. bur. mental health, 1976-86; cons. various health, welfare and youth agencies; field instr. U. Ill., U. Chgo., Atlanta U., George Williams U.; lectr. Chgo. State U., U. Ill., other profl. workshops, seminars and confs. Active mem. Art Inst. Chgo., Bravo chpt. Chgo. Lyric Opera, Chgo. Urban League, Southside Community Art Center, Chgo., Chgo. YWCA, 9800 Parnell Ave. Block Club, Chgo., DuSable Mus., Chgo.; trustee Episc. Charities of Chgo. Recipient scholarship Mt. Zion Baptist Ch., 1938-39, Fisk U., 1943; Mother-of-Year award Chgo. State Women's Club, 1975. Mem. Nat. Assn. Social Work, Acad. Certified Social Workers, Ill. Welfare Assn., Ill. Group Psychotherapy Soc., Nat. Conf. on Social Welfare, Council on Social Work Edn., Center for Continuing Edn. of Ill. Mental Health Insts., Nat. Assn. Parliamentarians, Alpha Gamma Pi, Alpha Kappa Alpha, NAACP, U. Ill. Alumni Assn., Nat. Council Negro Women, Urban League, Municipal Employees Soc. Chgo. Episcopalian. Clubs: Jack and Jill of Am. Assos., Links, Inc. (nat. dir. trends and services) (Chgo.), Les Cameos Social, Chums. Address: 9815 S Parnell Ave Chicago IL 60628

PRICE, FRANCIS WILLIAM, JR, ophthalmologist; b. Indpls., Feb. 4, 1951; s. Francis William and Marian P.; m. Marianne O'Conner, June 8, 1974; children: Patrick, Mark, Diane. BS, U. Notre Dame, 1973; MD, Ind.

U., 1977, degree in Ophthalmology, 1981; degree corneal surgery, Tulane U., 1982. Practice opthalmology specializing in corneal surgery Indpls., 1982—. Patentee intra-ocular lens for corneal transplant surgery. Fellow Am. Acad. Ophthalmology; mem. Ind. Acad. Ophthalmology (bd. dirs. 1986—), Phi Beta Kappa, Alpha Omega Alpha. Office: 50 E 91st St Suite 103 Indianapolis IN 46240

PRICE, JACK RICHARD, obstetrician, gynecologist; b. Northville, Mich., Oct. 8, 1932; s. James Morgan and Ellen Nora (Stevens) P.; m. Beverly Belle Nunn, Aug. 21, 1954; children: Edward David, Andrew Richard, William Wayne, Julie Lynn. BA, Kalamazoo Coll., 1954; MD, Wayne State U., 1958. Diplomate Am. Bd. Ob-Gyn. Intern and resident Grace Hosp., Detroit, 1958-62; practice medicine specializing in ob-gyn Flint, Mich., 1962—; asst. clin. prof. medicine Mich. State U., East Lansing, 1970—; med. dir. Flint Community Planned Parenthood Assn., 1965—. Trustee Kalamazoo Coll., 1985—. Mem. AMA, Mich. State Med. Soc., Genesee County Med. Soc., Mich. Gynecological Soc., Flint Acad. Surgery (pres. 1984-85). Baptist. Club: Warwick Hills Golf and Country (Grand Blanc, Mich.). Avocation: philately. Home: G-9095 S Saginaw #25 Grand Blanc MI 48439 Office: 410 S Ballenger Hwy Flint MI 48504

PRICE, JACOB MYRON, history educator; b. Worcester, Mass., Nov. 8, 1925; s. Abraham Oscar and Alice (Pike) P. AB magna cum laude, Harvard U., 1947, AM, 1948, PhD, 1954; postgrad., Oxford U., Eng., 1949-50, London Sch. Econs., 1950-51. Instr. history Smith Coll., Northampton, Mass., 1954-56; from instr. to assoc. prof. history U. Mich., Ann Arbor, 1956-64, prof., 1964—, chmn. dept. history, 1979-84. Author: The Tobacco Adventure to Russia: Enterprise, Politics and Diplomacy in the Quest for a Northern Market for English Colonial Tobacco, 1676-1722, 1961, France and the Chesapeake: a History of the French Tobacco Monopoly, 1674-1791, and of Its Relationship to the British and American Tobacco Trades, 1973 (U. Mich. Press award 1974), Capital and Credit in British Overseas Trade: the View from the Chesapeake, 1700-1776, 1980; editor: (and co-author) Reading for Life: Developing the College Student's Lifetime Reading Interest, 1959, (with Val Lorwin) The Dimensions of the Past: Materials, Problems, and Opportunities for Quantitative Work in History, 1972, Joshua Johnson's Letterbook, 1771-74: Letters from a Merchant in London to his Partners in Maryland, 1979; mem. editorial com. U. Mich. Press, Ann Arbor, 1959-65, Comparative Studies in Soc. and History, 1974—; mem. Am. adv. com. Eighteenth Century Short Title Catalog, 1979—; mem. bd. editors various profl. jours. Served to sgt. USAAF, 1944-46, CBI. Recipient Gilbert Chinard award Soc. for French Hist. Studies, 1974; Fulbright scholar 1949-51; Guggenheim fellow, 1958-59, 65-66, NEH fellow, 1977-78, 84-85; Social Sci. Research Council faculty fellow, 1962-63, Am. Council Learned Socs., 1972-73; visiting fellow Newberry Library 1981, All Souls Coll., Oxford, 1984-85. Fellow Royal Hist. Soc.; mem. Am. Hist. Assn., (chmn. program com. 1976), Econ. History Assn. (pres. 1986—), Econ. History Soc. (life), Inst. Early Am. History and Culture (exec. com. assocs. 1977—), Friends of the Inst. Hist. Research, London, Midwest Conf. British Hist. Studies (com. pres. 1976-78), N.Am. Conf. on British Studies (exec. sec. 1978-83), Soc. for Comparative Study of Soc. and History (bd. dirs., sec. 1974—), Mass. Hist. Soc. (corr.), Phi Beta Kappa. Jewish. Club: Cosmos (Washington). Home: 1050 Wall St Apt 4-D Ann Arbor MI 48105 Office: U Mich Dept History Ann Arbor MI 48109-1045

PRICE, JAMES AUDIE, artist; b. St. Louis, Apr. 29, 1954; s. Arlon and Jacquelyn Romena (Smith) P. AA, St. Louis Community Coll., 1976; BA, So. Ill. U., Carbondale, 1978. Artist Milliken Pub., St. Louis, 1980-86, computer graphic artist, 1986—; artist Instructional Fair, Grand Rapids, Mich., 1984-86; free-lance design, lay-out, computer graphics artist, St. Louis. Artist (ednl. books) Numbers, 1985, Grammar, 1985; computer graphics (ednl. program) The First "R", 1986; contbr. American Poetry Anthology, 1986. Musician, entertainer VA, St. Louis, 1983. Recipient Cert. of Honor VA, 1983. Avocations: song writing, cinema, poetry, music, art. Home and Office: 436 S Clark Saint Louis MO 63135

PRICE, JANET HARTKA, data processing executive; b. Detroit, Aug. 11, 1947; s. Edward George Hartka and Vera Ida (Mallon) Ziolkowski; children: Jennifer, Erika. BA in Math, U. Mich., 1968; BS in Computer Scis., U. Wis., 1976, MBA, 1977. Programmer Ann Arbor (Mich.) Computer Co., 1969-73, systems and programming mgr., 1973-74; applications mgr. Mohr Labs, Fitchburg, Wis., 1977-78; programming mgr. Technician T&T, McFarland, Wis., 1978-80, Wis. Health and Social Services, Madison, 1980-82; dir. info. mgr. Wis. Dept. Natural Resources, Madison, 1982—. Subcom. chmn. Wis. Land Records Com., Madison, 1985—; bd. dirs. Child Devel. Inc., Madison, 1978, After Sch. Day Care Assn., Madison, 1980-82. Mem. Data Processing Dirs. Council (chmn. exec. com. 1985-86), Data Processing Dirs. Roundtable, Conservation Bus. Mgmt. Assn. (systems chmn. 1985), Soc. for Info. Mgmt. Democrat. Club: Blackhawk Ski (Middleton). Avocations: skiing, basketball, pottery, running, antiques. Office: Wis DNR PO 7921 Madison WI 53707

PRICE, JOHN MICHAEL, photographer; b. Indpls., Oct. 10, 1936; s. Chester Morris and Sarah Elizabeth (Ferguson) P.; grad. high sch.; m. Madalene Wing, May 8, 1956; children—Teresa Kay, Michael Chester. Farmer; owner, photographer Price Portrait Studio, Lizton, Ind., 1967—; owner Agri-Photo Belt Buckles. Cons., judge photography 4-H workshops, state and county fairs (Ind.), high schs., 1967—. Designer, patentee model toy barns. Supt. agrl. displays 4-H fairs, Ind., 1966—; mem. youth adv. council Hendricks County (Ind.), 1970-71; pres. band boosters New Salem (Ind.) High Sch., 1970; instr. leather craft local orgns. Recipient honors 4-H Club Continued Service, 1971, 73. Mem. profl. photographers Am., Ind. Patentee in field. Address: Box 159 Rd 900 N Lizton IN 46149

PRICE, LANIS LORETHA, social worker; b. Memphis, Dec. 26, 1953; d. Douglas L.B. and Verda Loretha (Adrock) Karnes; m. Richard Lonnell Price, Dec. 15, 1973; 1 child, Celana Lois. BA, Cen. Bible Coll., 1976. Cert. tchr., Mo.; lic. social worker, Mo.; lic. ins. broker, Mo. Tchr. Pub. Schs., Sharon, Tenn.; Hannibal, Mo., 1976-79; dir. Children's Learning Ctr., Kansas City, Kans., 1979-80; asst. dir. Suspected Child Abuse and Neglect, Russellville, Ark., 1983-85; dir. Kiddie Kollege, Jackson, Mo., 1985; adoption specialist State of Mo., Sikeston, 1986—; trainer Missionettes, Springfield, Mo., 1980-82; speaker Ladies Groups, 1976—. Asst. editor The Fellowship, 1971-76; contbr. articles to profl. jours. Counsellor, pianist The Good Life Ch., Cape Girardeau, Mo., 1985—; vol. United Way, Russellville, 1984, ARC, Russellville, 1984. Mem. AAUW, Joy Fellowship (pres. 1985—), Chi Alpha (sec. 1971-74). Republican. Club: Arthar Quademi (Springfield) (sec. 1972074). Avocation: pilot. Home: Rt 2 Box 181A Cape Girardeau MO 63701 Office: Scott County Div Family Services PO Box 130 Sikeston MO 63801

PRICE, LUCILE BRICKNER BROWN, civic worker; b. Decorah, Iowa, May 31, 1902; d. Sidney Eugene and Cora (Drake) Brickner; B.S., Iowa State U., 1925; M.A., Northwestern U., 1940; m. Maynard Wilson Brown, July 2, 1928 (dec. Apr. 1937); m. 2d, Charles Edward Price, Jan. 14, 1961 (dec. Dec. 1983). Asst. dean women Kans. State U., Manhattan, 1925-28; mem. bd. student personnel adminstrn. Northwestern U., 1937-41; personnel research Sears Roebuck & Co., Chgo., 1941-42, overseas club dir. ARC, Eng., Africa, Italy, 1942-45; dir. Child Edn. Found., N.Y.C., 1946-56. Participant 1st and 2d Iowa Humanists Summer Symposiums, 1974, 75. Del. Mid Century White House Conf. on Children and Youth, 1950; mem. com. on program and research of Children's Internat. summer villages, 1952-53; mem. bd. N.E. Iowa Mental Health Center, 1959-62, pres. bd., 1960-61; mem. Iowa State Extension Adv. Com., 1973-75; project chmn. Decorah Hist. Dist. (listed Nat. Register Historic Places); trustee Porter House Mus., Decorah, 1966-78, emeritus bd. dirs., 1982—; participant N. Central Regional Workshop Am. Assn. State and Local History, Mpls., 1975, Midwest Workshop Historic Preservation and Conservation, Iowa State U., 1976, 77; mem. Winneshiek County (Iowa) Civil Service Commn., 1978-87; rep. Class of 1940 Northwestern U. Sch. Edn., 1986—. Recipient Alumni Merit award Iowa State U., 1975. Mem. Am. Coll. Personnel Assn., (life), Am. Overseas Assn. (nat. bd.; life), AAUW (life mem., mem. bd. Decorah; recipient Named Gift award 1977), Nat. Assn. Mental Health (del. nat. conf. 1958), Norwegian-Am. Mus. (life, Vesterheim fellow), Winneshiek County Hist. Soc. (life, cert. of appreciation 1984), DAR, Pi Lambda Theta, Chi Omega. Designer, builder house for retirement living. Home: 508 W Broadway Decorah IA 52101

PRICE, MARK WALTER, lawyer; b. Portsmouth, Ohio, Apr. 3, 1956; s. Charles Walter and Martha Jeanella (Murphy) P. BS, Ohio U., Athens, 1981; JD, Capital U., Columbus, Ohio, 1984. Master commr. Ohio Supreme Ct., Columbus, 1984-87. Mem. Portsmouth City Council, 1980, vice mayor 1980. Mem. Am. Assn. Trial Lawyers. Democrat. Baptist. Avocations: reading, writing, book collecting, antique automobiles, painting. Home: 1218 Kendall Ave Portsmouth OH 45662

PRICE, MELVIN, congressman; b. East St. Louis, Ill., Jan. 1, 1905; s. Lawrence Wood and Margaret Elizabeth (Connolly) P.; m. Garaldine Freelin, July 7, 1952; 1 child, William Melvin. Ed. parochial schs., East St. Louis; grad., St. Louis U. High Sch.; student, St. Louis U., 1923-25. Sports writer East St. Louis News-Rev., 1925-27; corr. East St. Louis Jour., 1927-33, St. Louis Globe-Democrat, 1943; sec. to Congressman Edwin M. Schaefer, 1933-43; mem. 79th and 80th Congresses (1945-49) from 22d Ill. Dist.; 81st to 82d Congresses from 25th Ill. Dist., 1949-53, 83-92d Congresses from 24th Ill. Dist., 1953-73, 93d-100th Congresses from 23d Ill. Dist., 1973—; chmn. house armed service com. mem. commn. adminstrv. rev. Mem. St. Clair County Bd. Suprs., 1929-31. Served with AUS, 1943-44. Mem. Am. Legion, Amvets. Democrat. Roman Catholic. Clubs: KC, Moose, Eagle, Elk, Ancient Order of Hibernians; Nat. Press (Washington). Office: US House of Representatives Rayburn House Office Bldg Rm 2110 Washington DC 20515 *

PRICE, MICHAEL BARRY, actuary; b. Denver, Aug. 16, 1954; s. Irwin and Marlene (Zelinger) P.; m. Patricia Kay Obering, Aug. 21, 1977 (div. Feb. 1985) 1 child, Meredith Lindsay. BS, U. Nebr., 1976. Actuary Coopers and Lybrand, Chgo., 1976-78, Tillinghast & Co., St. Louis, 1978-80; sr. mgr. in charge Peat Marwick, St. Louis, 1980-85; asst. v.p., chief actuary Johnson Higgins, St. Louis, 1985-87; asst. v.p., cons. actuary Alexander & Alexander, St. Louis, 1987—; chmn. Demo Six, Inc., St. Louis, 1986—. Chmn. John DeCamp Cngl. campaign, Lincoln, 1976; trustee Leukemia Soc., St. Louis, 1987—. Mem. Am. Acad. Actuaries, Soc. Actuaries (assoc.), St. Louis Actuaries Assn., Midwest Pension Conference, Sigma Alpha Mu. Democrat. Jewish. Avocations: skiing, tennis, woodworking, bicycling. Home: 7 Laurelwood Ct Saint Louis MO 63146 Office: Alexander & Alexander 120 S Central Ave Saint Louis MO 63105

PRICE, ROBERT DIDDAMS, JR., community planner; b. Chgo., Apr. 18, 1943; s. Robert Diddams and Adelheid Marie (Haugan) P.; m. Susan Kay Mundhenk, Dec. 18, 1965; children: Jennifer, Robert III. BS in Community Planning, U. Cin., 1966, MA in Community Planning, 1968, MA in Geography, 1968. Cert. paramedic, Ohio. Sr. planner City-County Planning Commn., Rockford, Ill., 1968-70; chief research Central N.Y. Regional Planning and Devel. Bd., Syracuse, 1970-72; exec. dir. Warren County Regional Planning Commn., Lebanon, Ohio, 1972—; mem. exec. com. Ohio Ky.-Ind. Regional Council Govts., 1973—; bd. dirs., treas. Warren County Rehab., Inc., 1977—. Mem. Warren County Health Planning Com., 1978—, Warren County Litter Adv. Bd., 1985—; chmn. Warren County New Horizons Fair Housing Task Force, 1980—; bd. dirs. Cert. Devel. Corp. of Warren County, 1981—. Sec., treas. Warren County Conv. and Visitors Bur., 1980—; mem. Clearcreek Twp. Life Squad, 1975—, first lt., 1977, chief, 1978-82, Clearcreek Twp. Fire Dept., 1980—; mem. high adventure com. Dan Beard council Boy Scouts Am.; mem. Springboro Band Boosters, 1984—, pres., 1985-86, treas. 1986-87; bd. dirs. Western Ohio Emergency Med. Services Council, 1978-85, sec. 1980-84, sec.-treas., 1984-85; chmn. Warren County Emergency Med. Services Council, 1981-82; county employee coordinator Warren County United Way, 1980; mem. council St. Paul Luth. Ch., 1976-78, sec., 1976-77; merit badge counselor Boy Scouts Am., 1982—; mem. Camp Stoneybrook Bldg. Com., Girl Scouts U.S.A., 1981-82; CPR instr. ARC, 1978—; radiol. def. instr. Def. Civil Preparedness Agy., 1978—;sec. Warren County Classification and Compensation Adv. Bd., 1984-85. Recipient Community Service award Springboro-Clearcreek Twp. Jaycees, 1977; Chmn. award Ohio Jaycees, 1978 Ky. Col. award Commonwealth of Ky., 1978. Mem. Am. Planning Assn., Ohio Planning Conf. (bd. dirs. 1978—, v.p. 1979-80, pres. 1980-82), Warren County Emergency Med. Services Assn., Nat. Trust Hist. Preservation, Ohio Twp. Assn. (hon.), Ohio County Planning Dirs. Assn. (exec. com. 1982—, sec. treas. 1985—), County Commrs. Assn. Ohio (assoc.). Club: Internat. Assn. Torch, Inc. Home: 205 Pinecone Ln Springboro OH 45066 Office: 320 E Silver St Lebanon OH 45036

PRICE, ROBERT M., computer company executive; b. New Bern, N.C., Sept. 26, 1930. B.S. in Math. magna cum laude, Duke U., 1952; M.S. in Applied Math., Ga. Inst. Tech., 1958. Research engr. Gen. Dynamics div. Convair, San Diego, 1954-56; research mathematician Ga. Inst. Tech., 1956-58; mathematician Standard Oil of Calif., San Francisco, 1958-61; with Control Data Corp., Mpls., 1961—, pres. systems and services, 1973-75, pres. systems, services and mktg., 1975-77; pres. Computer Co., Control Data Corp., Mpls., 1977-80; pres., chief operating officer Control Data Corp., Mpls., 1980-86, chmn., pres., chief exec. officer, 1986—, also dir. Office: Control Data Corp 8100 34th Ave S Minneapolis MN 55440 *

PRICE, RUTH ELLEN, medical technologist, laboratory administrator; b. Chgo., May 19, 1931; d. Stanley and Kathryn Ellen (Carpenter) P.; B.A. in Biology, Willamette U., 1953; cert. in med. tech. Northwestern, 1954; M.A. in Mgmt., Central Mich. U., 1977. Med. technologist St. Catherine's Hosp., Kenosha, Wis., 1955—, clin. lab. supr., 1966—; product evaluator E. I. DuPont de Nemours, Wilmington, Del. Active Friends of the Museum, Kenosha. Mem. Am. Mgmt. Assn., Am. Soc. Clin. Pathology (assoc. mem., cert. med. technologist), Nature Conservancy, Am. Soc. Med. Tech., AAUW, Clin. Lab. Mgmt. Assn., Chi Omega. Episcopalian. Club: PEO. Home: 4510 18th St Kenosha WI 53142 Office: St Catherine's Hosp 3556 7th Ave Kenosha WI 53140

PRICE, THOMAS EMILE, export sales, investment, financial executive; b. Cin., Nov. 4, 1921; s. Edwin Charles and Lillian Elizabeth (Werk) P.; B.B.A., U. Tex., 1943; postgrad. Harvard U., 1944; m. Lois Margaret Gahr Matthews, Dec. 21, 1970; 1 dau. by previous marriage, Dorothy Elizabeth Wood Price; stepchildren—Bruce Albert, Mark Frederic, Scott Herbert, Eric William Matthews. Co-founder Price Y Cia, Inc., Cin., 1946—, sec., 1946-75, treas., 1946—, pres., 1975—, also dir.; co-founder Price Paper Products Corp., Cin., 1956, treas., 1956—, pres., 1975—, sec., 1956-75, also dir.; mem. Cin. Regional Export Expansion Com., 1961-63; dir. Central Acceptance Corp., 1954-55; founding mem. and dir. Cin. Royals Basketball Club Co., 1959-73. Referee Tri-State Tennis Championships, 1963-68, Western Tennis Championships, 1969-70, Nat. Father-Son Clay Court Championships, 1974—, Tennis Grand Masters Championships, 1975-77, 80; vol. coach Walnut Hills High Sch. Boys Team, Cin., 1970-81; chmn. and coach Greater Cin. Jr. Davis Cup, 1968-78; co-founder Tennis Patrons of Cin., Inc., 1951, trustee, 1951—, pres., 1958-63, 68; co-founder Greater Cin. Tennis Assn., 1979. Participant in fund raising drives Cin. Boys Amateur Baseball Fund; chmn. Greater Cin. YMCA World Service Fund Drive, 1962-64; trustee Cin. World Affairs Inst., 1957-60, gen. chmn., 1959. Served to 1st lt. USAAF, 1943-46; ETO. Elected to Western Hills High Sch. Sport Hall of Honor; named hon. Almaden Grand Master, 1980. Mem. Cin. World Trade Club (pres. 1959), U.S. Trotting Assn., Cin. Hist. Soc., U.S. Lawn Tennis Assn. (trustee 1959-60, 62-64, chmn. Jr. Davis Cup com. 1960-62, founder of Col. James H. Bishop award 1962), Ohio Valley (trustee 1948—, Gillespie award 1957, Dredge award 1973, pres. 1952-53), Western (trustee 1951—, mem. championships adv. com. 1969-78, pres. 1959-60, Melvin R. Bergman Disting. Service award 1979) tennis assns., Assn. Tennis Profls. (nat. championship adv. 1979—), Phi Gamma Delta. Republican. Presbyterian. Clubs: Cin. Country, Univ., Cin. Tennis (pres. 1957-58, adv. com. 1959—), Indoor Tennis, Eastern Hills Indoor Tennis. Lodge: Cin. Rotary.). Nationally ranked boys 15, 1936, jr. tennis player, 1939. History columnist Tennis Talk Greater Cin., 1978-80. Home: 504 Williamsburg Rd Cincinnati OH 45215 Office: Suite 925 Dixie Terminal Bldg Cincinnati OH 45202

PRICE, WAYNE ROGER, mental health facility executive, psychologist; b. Bklyn., May 13, 1942; s. I. Benjamin and Ann L. (Rogers) P.; m. Janice Elizabeth Gerry, Jan. 30, 1965; children: Roger, Jason, Laura. BS, Coll. William and Mary, 1964; MA, U. Ark., 1966, PhD, 1969. Cert. clin. psychologist; registered health service provider. Clin. psychologist Blue Valley Mental Health Ctr., Beatrice, Nebr., 1971-73, 1973-79, clin. dir., 1980—; clin. assoc. prof. U. Nebr., 1975—. Contbr. articles to profl. jour. Co-founder Beatrice Crisis Line; mem. Beatrice City Council, 1976-78, pres., 1978-82; dir. Gage County Indsl. Bd., Beatrice, 1976-80. Served to capt. U.S. Army, 1966-71. Recipient key to the city of Beatrice, 1982, Admiralty award Gov. Robert Kerry, State of Nebr., 1986. Fellow Nebr. Soc. Profl. Psychologists (pres. 1976-77); mem. Am. Psychol. Assn., Nebr. Psychol. Assn. (pres. 1979-80), Am. Soc. Clin. Hypnosis, Bd. Examiners of Psychologists (chmn. bd. 1983—), Am. Legion, Sigma Xi. Republican. Methodist. Lodges: Rotary (pres. Beatrice 1985-86), Elks. Avocations: bicycling, photography. Home: 711 Eighth St Beatrice NE 68310

PRICKETT, MARCUS RAY, computer software engineer; b. Modesto, Calif., Sept. 12, 1962; s. Bill Ray and Billie Jean (Riley) P. AAS in Electronics Engring. Tech., Mo. Inst. Tech., 1982, BS in Electronics Engring. Tech., 1983; postgrad., North Cen. Coll., Naperville, Ill., 1985—. Faculty asst. Mo. Inst. Tech., Kansas City, 1981-83; sr. tech. assoc. AT&T Bell Labs., Naperville, 1983—. Author: (with others) design unit and specification, 1986. Mem. DeVry Alumni Assn., Tau Alpha Pi (treas. 1983). Clubs: Clownatts, Computer Hobbiest (Naperville). Avocations: camping, hiking, bicycling, music, guitar. Office: AT&T Bell Labs 1200 E Warrenville Rd Mail Stop IX 1M-413 Naperville IL 60566-7045

PRIDDLE, HARLAND EUGENE, state secretary of agriculture; b. Hutchinson, Kans., Aug. 4, 1930; s. Edgar Horland and Sylvia (Imel) P.; m. Winifred Ann Smith, Aug. 29, 1948; children: Valorie Anne Priddle Dick, Harland G., Kevin Eugene. BS in Agr., Kans. State U., 1952; postgrad., Armed Forces Staff Coll., Norfolk, Va., 1969, Am. Inst. Banking, Hutchinson, 1978-81. Commd. 2d lt. USAF, 1952, advanced through grades to col., 1973, retired, 1974; asst. mgr. Kans. State Fair, Hutchinson, 1975-78; v.p. for mktg. Hutchinson Nat. Bank, 1978-82; sec. agr. State of Kans., Topeka, 1982—, sec. of commerce, 1987—; mem. gov.'s task force on tourism, State of Kans., 1975-78, gov.'s agr. working group, State of Kans., 1982-86. Rep. candidate for lt. gov. State of Kans., 1986; mem. Kans. Hist. Soc., Hutchinson, 1976-81. Decorated Bronze Star, Legion of Merit with bronze oak leaf cluster; named Kans. Wheat Man of Yr., Kans. Assn. Wheat Growers, 1983; recipient Disting. Service award Kans. Grange, 1983, Disting. Service award Prodn. Credit Assn., 1984, Presdl. Service award. Mem. Agr. Hall of Fame (exec. com. 1982—), Retired Officer's Assn. (pres. 1976-77), Am. Legion (comdr. 1978-79). Methodist. Lodges: Masons, Lions, Rotary (bd. dirs. Hutchinson chpt. 1976-78). Home: 3111 SE Pisces Topeka KS 66605 Office: Agriculture Bd 400 SW 8th Topeka KS 66603

PRIEST, ERIC PAUL, meteorologist; b. Ohio, Mar. 27, 1960; s. Warren Paul and Justine (Burnett) P.; m. Dawn Lynn Koraido, Dec. 4, 1982; 1 child, Erica Marie. BS in Meteorology, Pa. State U., 1982; MS in Atmospheric Scis., Creighton U., 1986. Meteorologist United Airlines, Elk Grove, Ill., 1986—. Served to capt. USAF, 1982-86. Mem. Am. Meteorol. Soc., Nat. Weather Assn. Republican. Methodist. Avocation: traveling. Home: 2122 Greenwood Ct Streamwood IL 60107

PRIJATEL, ROBERT JAMES, dentist; b. Cleve., Sept. 15, 1956; s. Edward Anthony and Emily Bernice (Svoboda) P. BS, Case Western Res. U., 1978, DDS, 1980. Gen. practice dentistry Marine Dental Services, Staten Island, N.Y., 1982-85, Highland Heights, Ohio, 1985—. Served as lt. USPHS, 1980-81. Mem. Omicron Kappa Upsilon. Roman Catholic. Avocations: racquetball, tennis, golf. Office: 5545 Wilson Mills Rd Highland Heights OH 44143

PRILL, LEO ARNOLD, veterinarian; b. Bloomer, Wis., Dec. 12, 1936; s. Arnold Leo and Dorothy Emma (Hankey) P.; m. Emma Elaine Peaslee, Aug. 31, 1963; children: James Leo, Cindy Sue, Jerry Lee. BS, Wis. State Coll., River Falls, 1957; DVM, U. Pa., 1961. Gen. practice vet. medicine New Auburn, WIs., 1961-84, Exeland, Wis., 1984—. Trustee Village of New Auburn, 1965-69, pres., 1969-84; supr. Chippewa County Bd., Chippewa Falls, Wis., 1976-84. Lutheran. Lodges: Lions (100% Pres. award 1983-84). Avocation: motorcycling. Home and Office: Rt 1 Box 185 Exeland WI 54835

PRIME, DANIEL JAMES, accountant; b. Akron, Mich., Feb. 18, 1959; s. Neil George and Luella (Weiss) P. BA, Mich. State U., 1981. Mgr. Peat, Marwick, Main & Co., Lansing, Mich., 1981. Mem. Am. Inst. CPA's, Mich. Assn. CPA's, Mich. Trucking Assn. (mem. acctg. and fin. council), Mich. State U. Alumni Assn. Lutheran. Club: Mich. State U. Pres.'s (East Lansing). Home: 1224 E Saginaw St East Lansing MI 48823 Office: Peat Marwick Main & Co 1708 Michigan National Tower Lansing MI 48933

PRIMM, TERI MARSHA, distributing company executive; b. Mpls., Aug. 18, 1960; d. Ralph Casabyanica and Fannie (Marshall) P. B.S. in Bus., U. Minn., 1982. Auditor, Touche Ross and Co., Mpls., 1981-84, mem. broker/dealer/mktg. group, 1984; spl. projects and research acct. IDS/Am. Express, Mpls., 1984-85; exec. v.p. Vanguard Distributors, Savannah, Ga., 1985—. Recipient Outstanding Achievement award Bus. Assn. of Minorities, 1982. Am. Inst. C.P.A.s scholar, 1980-81, Minn. Soc. C.P.A.s scholar, 1980-82. Mem. Nat. Assn. Black Accts. (scholarship chmn 1981-82, 83-84, vice chmn. nat. election procedures com. 1983—). Baptist.

PRIMO, MARIE NASH, shopping centers official; b. Clarksburg, W.Va., Dec. 10, 1928; d. Frank and Josephine (DiMaria) Nash; student pub. schs. Clarksburg; m. Joseph C. Primo, Sept. 27, 1953; 1 dau., Joan E. Sec., Nat. Bank Detroit, 1945-46; exec. sec. Cutting Tool Mfrs. Assn., Detroit, 1946-50; adminstrv. asst. Irwin I. Cohn atty., Detroit, 1950-84; mgr. Bloomfield Shopping Plaza, Birmingham, Mich., 1959—; North Hill Center, Avon Twp., Mich., 1957—; Drayton Plains Shopping Center (Mich.), 1958-84; South Allen Shopping Center, Allen Park, Mich., 1953-77, Huron-Tel Corner, Pontiac, Mich., 1977—; officer, dir., numerous privately held corps. Mem. steering com., treas. Univ. Liggett Antiques Show, 1971-76, advisory com., 1977-80; mem. parents' com. Wellesley Coll., 1979-1981. Mem. Founders Soc. Detroit Inst. Arts, Women's Econ. Club, Mich. Humane Soc., Detroit Sci. Center, Detroit Zool. Soc., Smithsonian Assos., Hist. Soc. Mich., Grosse Pointe War Meml. Assn., Grosse Pointe Pub. Library Assn., Mich. Opera Theatre Guild. Roman Catholic. Home: 1341 N Renaud Rd Grosse Pointe Woods MI 48236 Office: 1631 1st National Bldg Detroit MI 48226

PRIMUS, MARY JANE DAVIS, social worker, author; b. Marion, Iowa, May 31, 1924; d. Lawrence Henry and Verna Leona (Suman) Davis; B.S., Iowa State U., 1950; m. Paul C. Primus, Aug. 23, 1955; children—Kenneth Roy, Donald Karl. Asst. cashier First State Bank, Greene, Iowa, 1942-46; tchr. Oskaloosa (Iowa) pub. schs., 1950-52; extension home economist Iowa State U., Oskaloosa-Eldora, 1952-57; homemaker, dist. supr. Iowa Dept. Social Service, Webster City, 1970-77; substitute tchr. Eldora Pub. Schs., 1966-68; homemaker health aide supr. Mid-Iowa Community Action OEO, Iowa Dept. Social Service, 1968-69; ptnr. LMAJ Herbs and Spices, Unltd. Author: Through the Window, 1973; Through the Window Twice, 1974; Tracery Windows, 1975; Shuttered Windows, 1977; Wings, 1979; Wings II, 1980; area news corr., 4 newspapers; columnist Iowa Wildlife Fedn.; contbr. poems to various publs. Den mother Boy Scouts Am., Steamboat Rock, Iowa, 1966-71; leader Girl Scouts Am., Steamboat Rock, 1969-72; mem. Iowa State U. Extension Family Living Council, Hardin County, 1961-65, 82-84; outreach chmn. Iowa Family and Children Services, 1966-72; field days women's program chmn. Iowa Soil Conservation, 1968. Mem. Am. Home Econs. Assn., Nat. Council Homemaker-Home Health Aide Services, Nat. League Am. Pen Women, Nat. Soc. Lit. and the Arts, Soil Conservation Soc. Am., Am. Legion, Internat. Platform Assn., Herb Soc. Am., AAUW. Mem. Ch. of Christ (pres. 1963-65). Club: Federated Women's (Steamboat Rock). Lodges: PEO, Order Eastern Star. Office: Steamboat Rock IA 50672

PRINCE, STEVEN CHARLES, marketing professional; b. Chippewa Falls, Wis., Mar. 13, 1951; s. Keith Ambrose and Anne Marie (Bowe) P.; m. Nancy Kay Mohr, Sept. 15, 1979; children: Diana, Benjamin, Charles. AS, Dist. 1 Tech. Inst., Eau Claire, Wis., 1974. Sales surp. Pacer Industries, Chippewa Falls, Wis., 1979-80, sales mgr., 1980-82, v.p. mktg. sales, 1983—. Served with U.S. Army, 1969-71. Mem. Am. Legion. Republican. Roman

Catholic. Home: 1122 Water St Chippewa Falls WI 54729 Office: Pacer Industrie Inc 1450 First Ave Chippewa Falls WI 54729

PRINCE, THOMAS RICHARD, accounting educator; b. New Albany, Miss., Dec. 7, 1934; s. James Thompson and C. and Florence (Howell) P.; m. Eleanor Carol Polkoff, July 14, 1962; children—Thomas Andrew, John Michael, Adrienne Carol. B.S., Miss. State U., 1956, M.S., 1957; Ph.D. in Accountancy, U. Ill., 1962. C.P.A., Ill. Instr. U. Ill., 1960-62; mem. faculty Northwestern U., 1962—, prof. acctg. and info. systems, 1969—; chmn. dept. accounting and info. systems Northwestern U. (Grad. Sch. Mgmt.), 1968-75; cons. in field; dir. Applied Research Systems, Inc. Author: Extension of the Boundaries of Accounting Theory, 1962, Information Systems for Management Planning and Control, 3d edit, 1975. Served to 1st lt. AUS, 1957-60. Mem. Am. Accounting Assn., Am. Inst. C.P.A.s, Am. Econ. Assn., Inst. Mgmt. Scis., Fin. Execs. Inst., AAAS, Ill. Soc. C.P.A.s,, Nat. Assn. Accts., Alpha Tau Omega, Phi Kappa Phi, Omicron Delta Kappa, Delta Sigma Pi, Beta Alpha Psi. Congregationalist (treas. 1984). Home: 303 Richmond Rd Kenilworth IL 60043 Office: Leverone Hall Northwestern U Evanston IL 60201

PRINCE, WILLIAM COURTNEY, lawyer; b. N.Y.C., Oct. 5, 1957; s. Bruce Clark and Carol (Firchau) P. BA, U. Denver, 1980; JD, U. Mo., 1983. Bar: Mo. 1983, U.S. Dist. Ct. (we. dist.) Mo. 1983. Law clk. to presiding justice Mo. Ct. Appeals, Springfield, 1983-84; assoc. Poole, Smith & Wieland, Springfield, 1984—. Bd. dirs. Am. Heart Assn., Springfield, 1986—. Mem. ABA, Assn. Trial Lawyers Am., Greene County Bar Assn. Methodist. Avocations: running, films. Office: Poole Smith & Wieland 307 Plaza Towers Springfield MO 65804

PRINCEN, LAMBERTUS HENRICUS, agricultural science facility administrator; b. Eindhoven, The Netherlands, Aug. 31, 1930; came to U.S., 1955; s. Hermanus H.A. and Engelina C. (Verhoeckx) P.; m. Gertrudis E. Wiesen, July 14, 1955; 1 child, Norman H. BS, State U., Utrecht, The Netherlands, 1952, PhD, 1955, DSc, 1959. Research chemist Nat. Def. Research Council, Delft, The Netherlands, 1958-60; project leader No. Regional Research Ctr., Peoria, Ill., 1960-75, lab. chief, 1975-82, assoc. ctr. dir., 1982-85, ctr. dir., 1985—. Editor 5 books, 1970-81; contbr. numerous articles to profl. jours., 1955-84; patentee in field. Trustee Lakeview Mus. Arts and Scis., Peoria, 1971-78; bd. dirs., v.p. Arts and Scis. Council, Peoria, 1970-75. Fellow Ill. State Acad. Sci. (pres. 1982); mem. Am. Chem. Soc. (councilor 1973-84, chmn. organic coatings and plastics chemicals div. 1973), Am. Oil Chemists Soc. (assoc. editor jour. 1982—), Soc. Econ. Botany (councilor 1981-83), Peoria Acad. Sci. (pres. 1967-68, editor-in-chief proc. 1968-80), Peoria Orchid Soc. (pres. 1975), Peoria Audubon Soc. (pres. 1976-77), Sigma Xi. Avocations: music, cinematography, ornithology, orchid growing. Home: 677 E High Point Terr Peoria IL 61614 Office: No Regional Research Ctr ARS USDA 1815 N University St Peoria IL 61604

PRINCEVAC, SINISA MOMIR, medical facility administrator; b. Croatia, May 12, 1941; came to U.S., 1971, naturalized, 1976; s. Momir Marko and Zlata Josip (Hopental) P.; m. Spasena D. Andelkovich, July 29, 1968; children—Boby, Otmar. M.D., Med. Facility Belgrade, Yugoslavia, 1966. Diplomate Am. Bd. Family Practice. Resident in internal medicine Columbus Hosp., Chgo., 1972-74; mgr. Health Care and Assoc. Med. Services Ltd., Chgo., 1977—. Active Republican Party Task Force, 1982-83. Served to lt. Yugoslav Army, 1967-68. Mem. Chgo. Med. Soc., Ill. Med. Soc., AMA, Am. Mgmt. Assn., Internat. Assn. Physicians, Chinese Medicine Assn. Serbian Orthodox. Office: 2475 W Gunnison Chicago IL 60625 Address: Sv Ćorovića #18, 11000 Belgrade Yugoslavia

PRINDABLE, DAVID FRANCIS, real estate executive; b. Peoria, Ill., Dec. 18, 1947; s. Francis Houston and Dolores (Watson) P. BS, U. Ill., 1969; MBA, Northwestern U., 1971. Mgr. real estate Sears Roebuck & Co., Skokie, Ill., 1983-85; dir. real estate Sears Roebuck & Co., Chgo., 1985—. Br. v.p. Lakeview Council, Chgo., 1981—. Served with USAR, 1969-75. Mem. Internat. Council Shopping Ctrs. Presbyterian. Clubs: Chgo. City, Univ. of Chgo. Home: 3535 N Reta Chicago IL 60657 Office: Sears Roebuck & Co Sears Tower Chicago IL 60684

PRINDLE, LORI MAY, manufacturing company executive; b. Rockford, Ill., Aug. 20, 1952; d. William Gustav and LaVada Maxine (Kirkendall) Johnson. BS, Western Ill. U., 1975. Tchr., counsel, Bd. Edn., Rockford, Ill., 1979-80, spl. project adminstr., 1980-81; control asst. Sundstrand Corp., Rockford, 1982, supr. info. processing, 1982-84, mgr. concepts and devel., spl. events, 1984—. Mem. Am. Mgmt. Assn., Internat. Exhibitors Assn., Kappa Delta Pi, Beta Sigma Phi. Methodist. Avocations: skiing, reading. Office: Sundstrand Corp 2430 S Alpine Rd Rockford IL 61108

PRINEAS, RONALD JAMES, epidemiologist, public health educator; b. Junee, New South Wales, Australia, Sept. 19, 1937; came to U.S., 1973; s. Peter John and Nancy (MacDonald) P.; m. Julienne Swynny, Apr. 21, 1961; children—Matthew Leigh, Anna Mary, John Paul, Miranda Jane. M.B.B.S., U. Sydney, Australia, 1960; Ph.D., U. London, 1969. Med. house officer Prince Henry Hosp., Sydney, 1961; sr. med. house officer Royal Perth Hosp., Australia, 1962; registrar in medicine Royal Glasgow Infirmary, Scotland, 1963-64; research fellow London Sch. Hygiene and Tropical Medicine, 1964-67, lectr., 1967-68; asst. in medicine U. Melbourne, Australia, 1968-72; prof. epidemiology U. Minn., Mpls., 1973—, prof. medicine, 1974—; cons. WHO, Geneva, 1976—, Nat. Heart Lung and Blood Inst., 1976—; prin. investigator Nat. Health Lung and Blood Inst., 1973—. Author books, including; Blood Pressure Sounds; Their Measurement and Meaning, 1978; The Minnesota Code Manual of Electrocardiographic Findings, 1982; also numerous articles. Recipient numerous cardiovascular disease research grants and contracts. Mem. Minn. affiliate Am. Heart Assn., Mpls., 1973—, chmn. adv. groups, 1975—. Fellow Royal Coll. Physicians Edinburgh, Am. Coll. Cardiology, Am. Pub. Health Assn., Soc. Epidemiologic Research, Am. Heart Assn. Council on Epidemiology, Internat. Soc. Hypertension, Council on Human Biology, Internat. Soc. Cardiology, Soc. Controlled Clin. Trials, Am. Coll. Epidemiology, Am. Soc. Epidemiology, Internat. Soc. Human Biology; mem. Royal Coll. Physicians London. Avocations: reading; raising a family. Office: U Minnesota 611 Beacon St SE Minneapolis MN 55455

PRINS, ROBERT JACK, college administrator; b. Grand Rapids, Mich., Oct. 12, 1932; s. Jacob and Marie (Vanden Brink) P.; m. Ruth Ellen John, Oct. 10, 1950; children—Linda, Douglas, Debra, Nancy, Eric, Sarah. B.A., Hope Coll., 1954; D.B.A., Coll. Emporia, 1974. With Mich. Bell Telephone Co., Detroit area, 1954-66; dir. devel. Bethesda Hosp., Denver, 1966-68; v.p. planning and devel. Park Coll., Parkville, Mo., 1969-70; chief adminstrv. officer Coll. of Emporia, Kans., 1970-75; dir. fin. and devel. The Abbey Sch., Canon City, Colo., 1975-79; dir. devel. Kirksville Coll. Osteo. Medicine, Mo., 1979-84; v.p. devel. McKendree Coll., Lebanon, Ill., 1984-86;pres. Iowa Weslyan Coll., Mt. Pleasant, 1986—. Mem. Iowa Assn. Ind. Colls. and Univs., Council for Advancement and Support of Edn. Office: Iowa Wesleyan Coll Office of the President Mount Pleasant IA 52641

PRINTUP, SUSAN MARIE, disability claims specialist; b. St. Paul, Sept. 16, 1953; d. John Oliver and Irene Marie (Simmer) Turgeon; m. David James Printup, May 15, 1976; 1 child, Timothy James. Grad. high sch., Bloomington, Minn. Claims specialist Lincoln Nat. Life Ins. Co., Mpls., 1978-81, 86; sr. claims specialist Transamerica Life Ins. Co., Edina, Minn., 1981-85; claims specialist Wilson McShane Corp., Bloomington, 1985; sr. claims specialist Mut. Benefit Life Ins. Co., Mpls., 1986-87, United Health Care Corp., Mpls., 1987—. Republican. Roman Catholic. Avocations: piano, reading, camping, gardening, needlework. Home: 10115 Englewood Dr Eden Prairie MN 55344

PRITZ, BENJAMIN LIONEL, consumer products company executive; b. Cin., Dec. 20, 1920; s. Walter Heineman Pritz and Dorothy Stix (Lowman) Pritz Steiner; m. Louise Clarisse Aggiman, Nov. 10, 1948; children—Neil Aggiman, Alan Lowman. Vice pres. Grandpa Brands Co., Cin., 1948-80, pres., 1980—. Served with USAAF, 1942-46. Mem. Graphic Arts Soc., Asian Soc., Asian Art Soc. Jewish. Clubs: Fencers (chmn. bd. 1970-83), Pan American, Bankers, Internat. Snuff Bottle Soc. Office: Benjamin Pritz Grandpa Brands Inc 317 E 8th St Cincinnati OH 45202

PRITZKER, JAY ARTHUR, lawyer; b. Chgo., Aug. 26, 1922; s. Abraham Nicholas and Fanny (Doppelt) P.; m. Marian Friend, Aug. 31, 1947; children: Nancy (dec.), Thomas, John, Daniel, Jean. B.Sc., Northwestern U., 1941, J.D., 1947. Bar: Ill. 1947. Asst. custodian Alien Property Adminstrn., 1947; since practiced in Chgo.; partner firm Pritzker & Pritzker, 1948—; chmn. bd. Hyatt Corp., Marmon Group, Inc., Braniff, Inc.; dir. Dalfort Corp.; partner Chgo. Mill & Lumber Co., Mich.-Calif. Lumber Co. Trustee U. Chgo. Served as aviator USNR, World War II. Mem. Am., Chgo. bar assns. Clubs: Standard (Chgo.), Comml. (Chgo.), Lake Shore (Chgo.), Mid-Day (Chgo.), Arts (Chgo.), Vince (Chgo.). Office: Hyatt Corp 200 W Madison Chicago IL 60606 also: The Marmon Group Inc 39 S La Salle St Chicago IL 60603

PRITZKER, ROBERT ALAN, manufacturing executive; b. Chgo., June 30, 1926; s. Abram Nicholas and Fanny (Doppelt) P.; m. Irene Dryburgh; children: James, Linda, Karen, Matthew, Liesel. B.S. in Indsl. Engring., Ill. Inst. Tech., 1946; postgrad. in bus. adminstrn., U. Ill. Engaged in mfg. 1946—; pres., dir. Great Lakes Holdings, Inc., Union Tank Car Co., Chgo.; chief exec. officer, pres., dir. The Marmon Group, Inc., Chgo., Marmon Indsl. Corp., Chgo.; pres., dir. The Colson Group, Inc., Marmon Holdings, Inc., Marmon Industries, Inc., Chgo.; dir. Peoples Energy Corp., Hyatt Corp., Chgo., Hyatt Internat. Corp., Dalfort Corp. Vice pres., bd. dirs. Pritzker Found., Chgo.; trustee, vice chmn. Ill. Inst. Tech. Office: The Marmon Group Inc 39 S LaSalle St Chicago IL 60603

PRITZKER, THOMAS JAY, lawyer, business executive; b. Chgo., June 6, 1950; s. Jay Arthur and Marian (Friend) P.; m. Margot Lyn Barrow-Sicree, Sept. 4, 1977; children—Jason, Benjamin, David. B.A.,, Claremont Men's Coll, 1971; M.B.A., U. Chgo., 1972, J.D., 1976. Assoc. Katten, Muchin, Zavis, Pearl and Galler, Chgo., 1976-77; exec. v.p. Hyatt Corp., Chgo., 1977-80, pres., 1980—; chmn. bd. Hyatt Hotels Corp., Chgo., 1980-86; chmn. exec. com. Hyatt Hotels Corp., 1986—; ptnr. Pritzker & Pritzker, Chgo., 1976—; pres. Rosemont Shipping, Chgo., 1980-86; dir. Dalfort, Chgo. Bd Trustee, Michael Reese Hosp., Chgo. Mem. ABA, Ill. Bar Assn., Chgo. Bar Assn. Clubs: Standard (Chgo.); Lake Shore Country (Glencoe, Ill.). Office: Hyatt Corp 200 W Madison Ave Chicago IL 60606

PROBALA, ANDREW EUGENE, designer, artist; b. Cleve., Nov. 16, 1908; s. Andras and Anna (Visoky) P.; m. Ruth J. Kulish, Nov. 24, 1934; 1 child, Paul A. Student Cleve. Sch. Art, 1922-30, John Huntington Poly. Cleve., 1927-29. Draftsman, designer Rorimer-Brooks Studio, Cleve., 1927-37; designer Irvin & Gormley, Inc., Cleve., 1937-40, Fisher Air Craft, Cleve., 1941, A.E. Probala, Designer, Cleve., 1941-65, 77—, Irvin & Co., Cleve., 1965-77. Mem. Cleve. Soc. Artists (pres. 1969-72). Republican. Avocations: designing; painting; building. Address: Andrew E Probala Designer 630 Osborn Bldg Cleveland OH 44115

PROBASCO, JACK FRANCIS, facilities planner; b. Somerset, Ohio, Apr. 11, 1941; s. John Henry and Dolores M. (Miller) P.; m. Irene Marie Adamusko, May 18, 1968; children: Amy, Matthew, Donna. BS, Ohio State U., 1963; grad. cert., Am. U., Washington, 1968; MA, Cen. Mich. U., 1973. Statistician U.S. Bureau of Census, Suitland, Md., 1964-70; sr. systems analyst Ohio Dept. Fin., Columbus, 1970-72; facilities planner Ohio Bd. Regents, Columbus, 1972-79, Ohio State U., Columbus, 1979—; cons. various orgns., 1979—. Contbr. numerous articles to profl. jours.; author various space planning guidelines. Mem. Whitehall (Ohio) City Council, 1973-77, Mid Ohio Regional Planning Com., Columbus, 1975-76, Whitehall Planning Com., 1971-72, Columbus Energy Task Force, 1980-82. Served with U.S. Army N.G., 1964-70. Mem. Council Edn. Facility Planners, Internat. (chmn. higher edn. com. 1981-86, bd. dirs. 1986—, pres. Great Lakes region 1986-87, editor jour. issue, 1985, Disting. Service award, Columbus, 1983, 86). Roman Catholic. Avocations: gardening, traveling. Home: 5569 Farms Dr Columbus OH 43213 Office: Ohio State U 8 Bricker Hall Columbus OH 43210

PROCHNOW, HERBERT VICTOR, former government official, banker, author; b. Wilton, Wis., May 19, 1897; s. Adolph and Alvina (Liefke) P.; m. Laura Virginia Stinson, June 12, 1928 (dec. Aug. 1977); 1 son, Herbert Victor. B.A., U. Wis., 1921, M.A., 1922, LL.D., 1956; Ph.D., Northwestern U., 1947, LL.D., 1963; LL.D. hon. Litt. D, Millikin U., 1952; LL.D., Ripon Coll., Wis., 1950, Lake Forest Coll., 1964, Monmouth Coll., 1965, U. N.D., 1966; D.H.L., Thiel Coll., 1965. Prin. Kendall (Wis.) High Sch.; asst. prof. bus. adminstrn. Ind. U.; advt. mgr. Union Trust Co., Chgo.; officer First Nat. Bank of Chgo., pres., 1962-68, dir., 1960-68, hon. dir., 1968-73; former dir. Carter H. Golembe Assos., Inc., 1972-76; dir. Banco di Roma, Chgo., 1973-87; columnist Chgo. Tribune, 1968-70; sec. Fed. adv. council Fed. Res. System, 1945—; apptd. spl. asst. to sec. of state, 1955, dep. under sec. of state for econ. affairs, 1955-56; alt. gov. for U.S. Internat. Bank and Internat. Monetary Fund., 1955-56; pres. Internat. Monetary Conf., 1968, now cons., hon. mem. Co-author: The Next Century Is America's, 1938, Practical Bank Credit, 1963, (with Herbert V. Prochnow, Jr.) A Dictionary of Wit, Wisdom and Satire, 1962, The Public Speaker's Treasure Chest, 1976, rev. edit., 1986, The Successful Toastmaster, 1966, A Treasury of Humorous Quotations, 1969, The Changing World of Banking, 1973, The Toastmaster's Treasure Chest, 1979, rev. edit., 1988, A Treasure Chest of Quotations for All Occasions, 1983, (with Everett M. Dirksen) Quotation Finder, 1971; author: Great Stories from Great Lives (an anthology), 1944, Meditations on the Ten Commandments, 1946, The Toastmaster's Handbook, 1949, Term Loans and Theories of Bank Liquidity, 1949, Successful Speakers Handbook, 1951, 1001 Ways to Improve Your Conversations and Speeches, 1952, Meditations on the Beatitudes, 1952, The Speaker's Treasury of Stories for All Occasions, 1953, The Speaker's Handbook of Epigrams and Witticisms, 1955, Speakers Treasury for Sunday School Teachers, 1955, A Treasury of Stories, Illustrations, Epigrams and Quotations for Ministers and Teachers, 1956, The New Guide for Toastmasters, 1956, Meditations on The Lord's Prayer, 1957, The New Speaker's Treasury of Wit and Wisdom, 1958, A Family Treasury of Inspiration and Faith, 1958, The Complete Toastmaster, 1960, Speaker's Book of Illustrations, 1960, 1000 Tips and Quips for Speakers and Toastmasters, 1962, 1400 Ideas for Speakers and Toastmasters, 1964, Tree of Life, 1972, Speaker's Source Book, 1972, A Speaker's Treasury for Educators, Convocation Speakers, 1973, 1,000 Quips, Stories, and Illustrations for All Occasions, 1973, Toastmaster's Quips and Stories and How to Use Them, 1982; editor: American Financial Institutions, 1951, Determining the Business Outlook, 1954, The Federal Reserve System, 1960, World Economic Problems and Policies, 1965, The Five Year Outlook for Interest Rates, 1968, The One-Bank Holding Company, 1969, The Eurodollar, 1970, The Five Year Outlook for Interest Rates in the U.S. and Abroad, 1972, Dilemmas Facing the Nation, 1979, Bank Credit, 1981. Chmn. O.S.S., 1942-45, U.S. delegation GATT, Geneva, 1956; del. Colombo Conf., Singapore, 1955, OECD, Paris, 1956; Former lectr. Loyola U., Ind. U., Northwestern U.; dir. grad. sch. of banking U. of Wis., 1945-81; trustee, cons. McCormick Theol. Sem.; hon. trustee Chgo. Sunday Evening Club. Served with AEF, 1918-19. Decorated Order of Vasa (Sweden), comdr. Cross Order of Merit (Fed. Republic of Germany).; recipient Bus. Statesmanship award Harvard Bus. Sch. Assn. Chgo., 1965, Ayres Leadership award Stonier Grad. Sch. Banking, Rutgers U., 1966, Silver Plaque NCCJ, 1967. Mem. Chgo. Council on Fgn. Relations (pres. 1966-67), Am. Econ. Assn., Chgo. Assn. Commerce and Industry (pres. 1964-65), Beta Gamma Sigma (nat. honoree). Clubs: Commercial, Glen View; University, Chicago, Rotary, Union League (Chgo.); Executives, Bankers (past pres.). Home: 2950 Harrison St Evanston IL 60201 Office: 1 First National Plaza Chicago IL 60670

PROCHNOW, HERBERT VICTOR, JR., banker; b. Evanston, Ill., May 26, 1931; s. Herbert V. and Laura (Stinson) P.; m. Lucia Boyden, Aug. 6, 1966; children: Thomas Herbert, Laura. A.B., Harvard U., 1953, J.D., 1956; A.M., U. Chgo., 1958. Bar: Ill. 1957. With 1st Nat. Bank Chgo., 1958—, atty., 1961-70, sr. atty., 1971-73, counsel, 1973—, adminstrv. asst. to chmn. bd., 1978-81. Author: (with Herbert V. Prochnow) A Treasury of Humorous Quotations, 1969, The Changing World of Banking, 1974, The Public Speaker's Treasure Chest, 1985, The Toastmaster's Treasure Chest, 1979; also articles in legal publs. Mem. ABA, Ill. Bar Assn., Chgo. Bar Assn. (chmn. com. internat. law 1970-71), Am. Soc. Internat. Law, Phi Beta Kappa. Clubs: Harvard (N.Y.C.); Chicago (Chgo.), Legal (Chgo.), Law (Chgo.), Onwentsia, Economic (Chgo.), Executives (Chgo.), University (Chgo.). Home: 949 Woodbine Pl Lake Forest IL 60045 Office: 1 First Nat Plaza Chicago IL 60670

PROCK, MICHAEL JOSEPH, SR., funeral director; b. Merrill, Wis., Nov. 25, 1925; s. Martin John and Catherine Ann (Hubley) P.; m. Lorraine E. Knutson, Jan. 16, 1947; children—John M., Michael Joseph, Steven J., Patrick T., David A., James O., Jeffrey L. Student Marquette U., 1943-45. Cert. funeral dir. and embalmer, 1947. Owner, operator Prock Funeral Home, Gold Cross Ambulance Service and Gold Cross Van & Courier Service, Eau Claire, Wis., 1964—. City dir. March of Dimes, 1949-53, county treas., 1953-59; commr. Boy Scouts Am., 1956-57, Order of Arrow, 1953; pres. Elk Lake Improvement Assn., 1957-58; pub. relations dir. Eau Claire Drum and Bugle Corps, 1959-64; mem. parish council Immaculate Conception Catholic Ch., 1968-72, Eau Claire County Health Adv. Forum Bd., 1969; v.p. Chippewa-Eau Claire Deanery, 1970-76; v.p. pastoral council Diocese of La Crosse, 1976-78, pres. fin. and adminstrn. commn., 1980-86; chmn. EMS adv. bd. Dist. 1 Tech. Inst., 1979; pres. Triniteam Bd. Dirs., 1981-83; dir. Eau Claire County EMS Council, 1982—; pres. Regis Found., 1984-86; Recipient Service to Mankind award Sertoma, 1979. Mem. Nat. Funeral Dirs. Assn., Wis. Funeral Dirs. Assn. Club: Chippewa Valley Field Trial (pres. 1953-54); Lodge: Lions (1st v.p. 1982), K.C. (4 degree). Home: 906 Zephyr Hill Ave Eau Claire WI 54701 Office: 405 N Hastings Pl Eau Claire WI 54701

PROCTOR, CONRAD ARNOLD, physician; b. Ann Arbor, Mich., July 14, 1934; s. Bruce and Luena Marie (Crawford) P.; m. Phyllis Darlene Anderson, June 23, 1956; children: Sharon Darlene Proctor Heimbach, Barbara Jan Brown, David Conrad, Todd Bruce. MD, U. Mich., 1959, MS, 1964. Cert. Am. Bd. Otolaryngology. Intern St. Joseph Mercy Hosp., Ann Arbor, 1959-60; jr. clin. instr. Univ. Hosp., Ann Arbor, 1961-63, sr. clin. instr., 1963-65; chief dept. otolaryngology Munson Army Hosp., Ft. Leavenworth, Kans., 1965-67; mem. attending staff William Beaumont Hosp., Royal Oak, Mich., 1967—; instr. Am. Acad. Otolaryngology, Washington, 1968-82, guest examiner, Chgo., 1978-79. Author: Current Therapy in Otolaryngology, 1984-85; (booklet) Dietary Treatment of Meniere's Syndrome, 1983; (med. jour.) Abnormal Insulin Levels and Vertigo, 1981; (manual) Hereditary Sensorineural Hearing Loss, 1978. Dir. Christian edn. Bloomfield Hills (Mich.) Bapt. Ch., 1969-72, fin. chmn., 1975-78, Sunday sch. tchr., 1967—. Served to capt. U.S. Army, 1965-67. Recipient first place award for med. research Students Am. Med. Assn., 1959. Mem. AMA, Mich. State Med. Assn., Oakland County Med. Assn., Am. Bd. Otolaryngology, ACS, Triological Soc., Otosclerosis Study Group, Internat. Game Fish Assn., Phi Eta Sigma, Phi Kappa Phi, Phi Beta Kappa. Republican. Clubs: Panangling Ltd. (Chgo.); Victors and Presidents (Ann Arbor). Avocations: baseball, football, tennis, fishing, basketball. Home: 1645 Wabeek Way Bloomfield Hills MI 48013 Office: 3535 W 13 Mile Rd Royal Oak MI 48072

PROCTOR, EDWARD HAROLD, automotive executive; b. Detroit, Sept. 25, 1941; s. Donald Marvin and Winifred Martha (Seeley) P.; m. Donna M. Cousins, Aug. 8, 1964; children: Donald E., Steven C. BSME, Gen. Motors Inst., Flint, Mich., 1966; MSME, U. Mich., 1966, MBA, 1983. Engr. diesel div. Gen. Motors Corp., Detroit, 1966-70; engr. turbine ops. div. Ford Motor Corp., Dearborn, Mich., 1970-74, sales mgr. indsl. engines div., 1974-77, with heavy truck mktg., truck ops. div., 1977—; mgr. heavy truck fleet mktg. program Ford Motor Corp., Dearborn, 1985-86; mgr. heavy truck mktg. plans, truck ops. div. Ford Motor Corp., Dearborn, Mich., 1986—. Elder St. Paul's Luth. Ch., Farmington, Mich., 1070-76. Mem. Mich. Snowmobile Assn. Republican. Club: Cycle Conservation (Hart, Mich.). Avocations: dirt bike riding, snowmobiling, cross-country skiing. Home: 16818 Parklane Dr Livonia MI 48154 Office: Ford Motor Co 300 Renaissance Ctr Detroit MI 48243

PROCTOR, STANLEY IRVING, chemical company executive; b. Belleville, Ill., Dec. 23, 1936; s. Stanley I. and Eleanora N. (Seitz) P.; m. Carol J. Kroeger, June 18, 1960; children: Stephen P., James M. BSChemE, Washington U., St. Louis, 1957, MS, 1962, DSc, 1972. Registered profl. engr., Mo. Gen. supt. mfg. services Monsanto Chem. Intermediate Co., Alvin, Tex., 1976-78; mgr. process tech. Monsanto Chem. Intermediate Co., Texas City, Tex., 1978-79; dir. engring. tech. Monsanto Co., St. Louis, 1979-83; dir. biotechnology projects Monsanto Chem. Internat. Co., St. Louis, 1985, dir. engring. tech., 1986—; dir. applied scis. Monsanto Cen. Research Labs., St. Louis, 1983-84; bd. dirs. Heat Transfer Research, Inc., South Pasadena, Calif. Contbr. articles to profl. jours. Fellow Am. Inst. Chem. Engrs. (bd. dirs. 1982-84, v.p. 1986, pres. 1987); mem. Am. Chem. Soc., NSPE, Am. Soc. Engring. Edn. Lutheran. Avocation: U.S. Civil War. Home: 50 High Valley Dr Chesterfield MO 63017 Office: Monsanto Chem Co 800 N Lindbergh Blvd Saint Louis MO 63167

PROESEL, DEBORAH SUSAN, nurse, consultant; b. Chgo., Nov. 30, 1953; s. Gerald Reuben and Evelyn G. (Berg) Adelman; m. Russell John Proesel, Apr. 6, 1982; 1 child, Jonathan Edward. BS in Nursing, U. Ill., Chgo., 1980. Cert. occupational health nurse, Ill. Psychiatric nurse Mt. Sinai Hosp., Chgo., 1980-81; head nurse Mary Thompson Hosp., Chgo., 1981-82; nurse, cons. Russ Proesel, DDS, Mt. Zion, Ill., 1982—; clin. instr. Decatur (Ill.) Area Vocat. Sch., 1982-83; occupational health nurse A.E. Staley Comp., Decatur, 1983-85. Chmn. Community Enhancement Commn., Mt. Zion, 1983. Mem. Am. Nurses Assn., Ill. Nurses Assn. (panelist continuing edn. approval and rev. panel 1980, 83), Mt. Zion C. of C., Beta Beta Beta. Democrat. Jewish. Avocations: sewing, crafts, languages, reading. Home: 713 Antler Dr Mount Zion IL 62549 Office: Russ Proesel DDS 420 Broadway Mount Zion IL 62549

PROIETTI, FRANK ANTONY, financial executive, educator; b. Rome, Nov. 2, 1948; s. Eliodoro and Orilde (MAnenti) P. AB, U. Ill., Chgo., 1970; MA, Northeastern Ill. U., 1974; MBA, Loyola U., 1977. Cert. fin. planner, real estate broker. Staff auditor Servicemaster Industries Inc., Downers Grove, Ill., 1977-79; sr. auditor C.F. Industries Inc., Long Grove, Ill., 1979-81; sr. fin. analyst Schwinn Bicycle CO., Chgo., 1981-83, controller, 1983-85; v.p. fin. and adminstrn. Crystal Greetings, Waukegan, Ill., 1985-87; mng. ptnr. Investors Fin. Services, Des Plaines, Ill., 1987—; pres. Proietti, Karasek & Assocs., Wheeling, Ill., 1985. Contbr. articles to profl. jours. V.p. Wheeling Police Pension Bd., 1981—; patrolman U. Ill.-Chgo. Police, 1975. Reciepient fellowship Ellis Island Centennial Com., N.Y., 1984. Mem. Assn. MBA Execs., Inst. Internal Auditors, Ill. Fencing Club (bd. dirs. 1983). Roman Catholic. Club: Italia (treas. 1978-81). Avocations: photography, fencing, wargames.

PROKOP, JAMES JOSEPH, psychologist; b. St. Paul, Sept. 5, 1941; s. Charles John Sr. and Helen (Malecha) P.; m. Bernadine Rachel Cable, Sept. 25, 1981. BA, St. Paul Sem., 1959-63, MA, 1967-77; MSW, U. Minn., 1977-79. Lic. psychologist, Minn. Counselor East Communities Family Ctr., Maplewood, Minn., 1980-82; dir. social services family therapy ctr. St. John's Hosps., St. Paul, 1982-87, dir. family therapy services, Health East Treatment Programs, 1987—; cons. in field., St. Paul, 1982—. Recipient fed. grants, 1971, 80. Mem. Nat. Assn. Social Workers, Acad. Cert. Social Workers (clin. diplomate). Democrat. Home: 7631 Edinborough Way #5111 Edina MN 55435 Office: St John's Hosp 403 Maria Ave Saint Paul MN 55106

PROKOPEC, ROBERT PAUL, mechanical tooling engineer; b. Chgo., Mar. 27, 1960; s. Charles Joseph and Jean Veronica (Megla) P. Tool and die apprentice, Washburne Trade Sch., 1978-82; AAS in Mech. Design, Morton Coll., 1985. Tool and die maker Sunbeam Appliance, Chgo., 1978-82, tool designer, 1982-83; mfg. engr. Zenith Electronics, Chgo., 1984; tool engr. Elkay Mfg. Co., Broadview, Ill., 1985—; tool design cons. Pro Engring., Chgo., 1983—. Mem. Soc. Mfg. Engrs., Soc. Plastic Engrs., Elkay Keyman Soc. Republican. Roman Catholic. Avocations: nature and wildlife photography, automobile restoration. Home: 5416 S Kedvale Chicago IL 60632 Office: Elkay Mfg Co 2700 S 17th Ave Broadview IL 60153

PROOST, ROBERT LEE, lawyer; b. St. Louis, July 30, 1937; s. Virgil Raymond and Anna Marie (Gaeng) P.; m. Mary Jo McDonald, July 1, 1961; children: Timothy Robert, Mary Elizabeth, Thomas Edward, Daniel Joseph. BS magna cum laude, St. Louis U., 1959; JD, Washington U., St. Louis, 1962. Bar: Mo. 1962, Ill. 1962, Fla. 1979, D.C. 1987. Assoc. Peper, Martin, Jensen, Maichel & Hetlage (and predecessors), St. Louis, 1962-68, ptnr., 1968—; pres., bd. dirs. Silmasco Inc., St. Louis, 1971—, Executype Inc., St. Louis, 1971-78; chmn. bd. St. Louis Fixture Co., 1982-85; chmn. bd. dirs. St. Louis Fixture Co.; lectr. in field. Author: Financing the On-Going Business, 1973, 79, 83, Securities Regulation: Missouri Corporate Law and

Practice: Securities Regulation, 1985, 87; contbr. articles to profl. jours. Served to capt. JAGC, USAF, 1962-65. Mem. ABA, Mo. Bar Assn. (bd. govs. 1985—), Ill. Bar Assn., Fla. Bar Assn., Met. St. Louis Bar Assn. (pres. 1978-79), Washington U. Law Alumni Assn. (pres. 1972-73), Am. Judicature Soc., St. Louis U. Arts and Scis. Alumni Assn. (v.p. 1971, bd. of govs. 1987—), Order of Coif, Alpha Sigma Nu, Phi Delta Phi. Roman Catholic. Clubs: Media (St. Louis); Washington U. Faculty (Clayton, Mo.). Home: 319 Claymont Dr Ballwin MO 63011 Office: Peper Martin Jensen et al 720 Olive St Saint Louis MO 63101

PROSSER, DANIEL LEE, insurance company executive; b. Dallas, Dec. 28, 1951; s. Austin Peayand Francis Ruth (Richardson) P.; m. Nicolette Susan Indelicato, July 31, 1976; children—Zachary Lance, Christian Chase. B.S., U. Mo., 1974, M.Ed., 1981. C.L.U.; lic. secondary tchr., Mo. Tchr. pub. schs., Salem, Mo., 1974-76, Carl Junction, Mo., 1976-77; dist. sales mgr. J.I. Case Co., Racine, Wis., 1977-80, sales tng. supr., 1980-81; sales mgmt. trainee Prudential Ins. Co. Am., Newark, 1981-87, devel. mgr., St.Louis, 1982—. Named Outstanding Sales Mgr., J.I. Case Co., 1978; recipient Pres.'s Citation, Purdential Ins. Co. Am., Newark, 1984, V.P.'s trophy Prudential Ins. Co. Am., Houston, 1984. Mem. Nat. Assn. Life Underwriters, Gen. Agts. and Mgrs. Assn. Republican. Roman Catholic. Avocations: classic cars; golf. Home: 503 Falaise Dr Saint Louis MO 63141 Office: Prudential Ins Co of Am 9666 Olive Blvd Suite 700 Saint Louis MO 63132

PROSSER, DENISE LYNN, office designer; b. Norfolk, Va., Jan. 8, 1956; d. Gerald D. and Nancy L. (Hall) Stimart; m. Todd Richard Prosser, June 14, 1980; 1 child, Danielle Lyn. BS in Art and Design summa cum laude, U. Wis., Stout, 1978. Area mgr. H.C. Prange Co., Fond Du Lac, Wis., 1978-79; office designer Wausau (Wis.) Ins. Cos., 1979—. Mem. Designers Network Group. Roman Catholic. Avocations: swimming, home remodeling. Home: 1812 Roosevelt St Wausau WI 54401 Office: Wausau Ins Cos 2000 Westwood Dr Wausau WI 54401

PROVANZANA, JOHN HARMS, electrical engineer; b. Bklyn., Dec. 27, 1941; s. Edward Joseph and Cecilia Sophia (Harms) P.; m. Marie I. Anderson, Sept. 2, 1967; children—Kathleen Michelle, Beth Marie, Suzanne Marie. B.E.E., Manhattan Coll., 1967; M.E.E., Rensselaer Poly. Inst., 1968; postgrad. NYU, 1973-74; A.E.P., U. Mich. Sch. Bus. Adminstrn., 1980. With Am. Electric Power Service Corp., 1967—, staff engr., 1977, sect. head, 1978, mgr. maj. elec. equipment sect., Columbus, Ohio, 1981—, mgr. maj. transmission equipment sect., 1984—. Served with USCG, 1959-63. Sr. mem. IEEE (Bendix award 1967); mem. Eta Kappa Nu. Republican. Roman Catholic. Contbr. articles to profl. jours. Home: 304 Delegate Dr Worthington OH 43085 Office: 1 Riverside Plaza Columbus OH 43216

PROVIS, DOROTHY L., artist, sculptor; b. Chgo., Apr. 26, 1926; d. George Kenneth Smith and Ann Hart (Day) Smith Guest; m. William H. Provis, Sr., July 28, 1945; children: Timothy A., William H., Jr. Student Sch. Art Inst., Chgo., 1953-56, U. Wis.-Milw., 1967-68, 69-70. Sculptor Port Washington, Wis., 1963—; pres. bd. dirs. West Bend Gallery of Fine Arts, Wis., 1984-86, bd. dirs., 1987-89; speaker in field. Author, lobbyist Wis. Consignment Bill, Madison, 1979; panelist Women's Caucus for Art Conf., Phila., 1983; mem. adv. bd. Percent for Art Pro., 1985-87, Wis. Arts Bd. Wis. Arts Bd. Designer-Craftsmen grantee, NEA, 1981. Mem. Coalition of Women's Art Orgns. (del. to continuing com. Nat. Women's Conf. 1979, panelist conf. 1981, v.p. for membership/nominations, 1981-83, pres. 1983-85, nat. pres. 1985-87, v.p. communications 1987-89), Wis. Painters and Sculptors (pres. 1982-84, editor newsletter 1982-85), Wis. Women in Arts (legis. liaison 1978-80). Artists for Ednl. Action (corr. 1979—), Wis. Designer Craftsmen, Women's Caucus for Art, Chgo. Artists Coalition, Internat. Sculpture Ctr. Home and Studio: 123 E Beutel Rd Port Washington WI 53074

PROXMIRE, WILLIAM, U.S. senator; b. Lake Forest, Ill., Nov. 11, 1915; s. Theodore Stanley and Adele (Flanigan) P.; m. Ellen Hodges. Grad., Hill Sch., 1934; B.A., Yale, 1938; M.B.A., Harvard, 1940, M.P.A. in Pub. Adminstrn, 1948. Pres. Artcraft Press, Waterloo, Wis., 1953-57; U.S. senator from Wis., 1957—, Nominee gov., 1952, 54, 56; assemblyman Wis. Legislature, 1951. Author: The Fleecing of America. Democrat. Office: US Senate 530 Dirksen Senate Bldg Washington DC 20510 *

PRUDE, REGINA MAE, business development consultant; b. Mt. Vernon, Ohio, Sept. 9, 1942; d. Joseph Neve Brooks Jr. and Linnie Cordelia (Highwarden) Brooks Taylor; m. Floyd Prude Jr., July 9, 1961; children: Sherri Lynn Prude Neal, Randy Allen. Student, Vanderbilt U., 1972, U. Wis.-Stout, 1983-86. Adminstrv. asst. model cities project Cen. Midwest Regional Edn. Lab., Nashville, 1972-73; monitoring unit chief Rock County CETA, Janesville, Wis., 1978-83; cons. (on loan) U.S. Dept. Labor, Chgo., 1982; owner, chief exec. officer New Directions Mgmt. Services, Inc., Beloit, Wis., 1983—; cons., project dir. corps. and govtl. agys.; mem. tech. adv. council Rock County Opportunities Industrialization Ctr., Beloit, 1984—; mem. gov.'s minority adv. council, State of Wis., 1980-84; mem. gov.'s council on bus. and edn. partnerships, State of Wis., 1984-85. lectr. Christian Women's Orgns. Mem. devel. subcom. Am. Baptist Coll., 1982—; bd. dirs., mem. fin. com. Badger council Girl Scouts U.S., 1983—. Recipient Tribute to Women award, YWCA, 1982, Distinction award Greater Beloit Minority Coalition, 1987. Mem. Nat. Contract Mgmt. Assn., Am. Women Entrepreneurs. Baptist. Home: 1931 Afton Rd Beloit WI 53511 Office: New Directions Mgmt Services Inc 419 Pleasant St Suite 204 Beloit WI 53511

PRUDHOMME, LAWRENCE ARNOLD, publishing executive, retail executive; b. St. Clair, Mich., Sept. 26, 1953; s. Lawrence Camille and Marianne Therese (Arnold) P.; m. Patricia Marie Grafton, June 20, 1975; children: Julie Theresa, Mark Lawrence. BS in Acctg., Mich. State U., 1975. CPA, Mich. Tax mgr. Arthur Andersen & Co., Detroit, 1975-83; v.p. Avanti Press, Inc., Detroit, 1983—; mem. firm wide compensation team Arthur Andersen & Co., 1983. Mem. assembly United Community Services, Detroit, 1983—. Mem. Am. Inst. CPA's, Mich. Assn. CPA's, Mayo Smith Soc. Avocations: softball, racquetball. Home: 36950 Carla Ct Farmington Hills MI 48024 Office: Avanti Press Inc 800 Penobscot Bldg Detroit MI 48226

PRUDLOW, WILLIAM FRANK, otolaryngologist; b. Milw., June 12, 1944; s. Frank and Theresa E. (Claas) P.; m. Marcia A. Streich, June 13, 1970; children: Kevin, Todd A., Jason A., John R., Timothy J. BS, Marquette U., 1966, MD, 1970. Intern St. Mary's Hosp., Long Beach, Calif., 1970-71; resident in otolaryngology Med. Coll. Wis. Affiliate Hosps., Milw., 1973-77; practice medicine specializing in otolaryngology-head and neck surgery Milw., 1977—; asst. clin. prof. otolaryngology-head and neck surgery, Med. Coll. Wis., 1977—; bd. dirs. Chase Thermopanels of Wis., Inc., New Berlin. Served to capt. USAF, 1971-73. Fellow Am. Acad. Otolaryngology-Head and Neck Surgery; mem. AMA, Milw. County Med. Soc., Wis. State Med. Soc., Milw. Soc. Head and Neck Medicine and Surgery. Club: Grove (Elm Grove, Wis.) (sec. 1986-87). Avocation: tennis. Home: 14105 St George Ct Elm Grove WI 53122 Office: 3070 N 51st St Milwaukee WI 53210

PRUETT, TIMOTHY IRVING, textile executive; b. Appleton, Wis., Jan. 19, 1954; s. Richard Lawrence and Bernadine Eva (Brockman) P.; m. Meredith Julia Koski, Jan. 9, 1982. BA, Lawrence U., 1976. Br. mgr. Means Services, Inc., Portage, Wis., 1978; mgmt. info. system coordinator Means Services, Inc., South Bend, Ind., 1978-79; br. mgr. Means Services, Inc., Terre Haute, Ind., 1979-80; service mgr. Means Services, Inc., Indpls., 1980, ARA Services, Inc. (Aratex), Evansville, Ind., 1980-83; gen. mgr. ARA Services, Inc. (Aratex), East Moline, Ill., 1983—. Mem. Beta Theta Pi (pres. Gamma Phi chpt. 1974-75). Republican. Lutheran. Clubs: Big Ten Investors (East Moline); Sand Lake Musky Hunters (Big Sand Lake, Wis.). Avocations: freshwater fishing, reading, photography. Home: 2933 16th Ave Moline IL 61265 Office: Aratex Services Inc 390 42d Ave East Moline IL 61244

PRUITT, RUSSELL CLYDE, industrial and interment foundries executive; b. Damascus, Va., Aug. 31, 1927; s. R. Martin and Pearl K. (Osborne) P.; B.A., Fenn Coll., 1954; postgrad. Western Res. U., 1957-62; m. Clarice Furchess, Apr. 5, 1947; children—Phyllis (Mrs. Dwain Parks), Russell C., Mark, Daniel. Auditor, Standard Oil Co., Cleve., 1948-53; controller Nelson Worldwide div. TRW, Lorain, Ohio, 1953-83; pres., treas., dir. Oreg. Brass Works, Portland, 1983—; dir. Sheidow Bronze Co., Williamsburg Bronze Co. Notary pub., Lorain County, 1958—; cons. income tax and investment. Mem. Sheffield Lake (Ohio) Charter Commn., 1960-62; chmn. finance com. Sheffield Lake City Council, 1964-66; pres. bd. edn. Black River, Medina County, Ohio, 1973—. Bd. dirs., treas. Lorain YMCA. Served with USNR, 1944-46, 50-51; PTO, Korea. Mem. U.S. Judo Fedn., Smithsonian Inst., Ohio Sch. Bds. Assn., Nat. Assn. Accountants, Am. Inst. Corp. Controllers, Am. Accounting Assn., Am. Quarter Horse Assn., Appaloosa Horse Club. Eagle. Home: Route 58 Wellington OH 44090

PRUS, FRANCIS VINCENT, tire company executive; b. Sewickley, Pa., 1927; s. Mark Phillip and Mary Agnes P.; m. Catherine Frances Dumesic, Jan. 30, 1949; children: Cathy, Mark, Linda, David. B.S. in Elec. Engring., Carnegie Mellon U., 1949. Gen. mgr. Goodyear Aerospace Corp., Akron, Ohio, pres., chief exec. officer, until 1981; dir. mfg. services, then v.p. mfg. Goodyear Tire & Rubber Co., from 1981, now exec. v.p. research and devel.; formerly dir. prodn. Kelly Springfield Tire Co.; dir. mfg. services, then v.p. mfg. Goodyear Tire & Rubber Co., exec. v.p. corp. technology, bd. dirs., 1981—. Mem. Litchfield Park Sch. Bd., 1970-71; bd. dirs. Akron Jr. Achievement, 1974-80, pres., 1977-78. Served with USNR, 1945-46. Mem. Aerospace Industries Assn., Nat. Security Indsl. Assn., Am. Def. Preparedness Assn., Navy League U.S. Club: Portage Country (Akron). Address: The Goodyear Tire & Rubber Co 1144 E Market St Akron OH 44316

PRUZAN, IRA, consumer products company executive; b. Chgo., Dec. 6, 1940; s. Alfred A. and Sally (Goldman) P.; m. Ina Pass, June 27, 1965; children—Brian Mark, Michael Jay. B.S., U. Ill., 1962, M.B.A., 1964. Fin. analyst Gen. Foods Corp., White Plains, N.Y., 1964-66; br. mgr. Quaker Oats Co., Chgo., 1966-71; v.p. Needham, Harper & Steers, Chgo., 1971-77; v.p. mktg. Associated Mills Inc./Pollenex, Chgo., 1977—. Patentee in field. Mem. Assn. Home Appliance Mfrs. (portable appliance exec. bd.). Clubs: Merchandising Execs. (dir. 1974-77), Northshore Toastmasters (pres. 1974-75; Disting. Service award 1974). Home: 53 Fernwood Dr Glenview IL 60025 Office: Associated Mills Inc/Pollenex 111 N Canal St Chicago IL 60606

PRYCE, RICHARD JAMES, hospital adminstrator; b. Detroit, Nov. 28, 1936; s. Edward Arden and Gertrude Ella (Page) P.; m. Nancy Jean Keefer, Feb. 19, 1966; children: Andrew, Steven, Julie. B.S. in Engring., U. Mich., 1961, M.B.A., 1961. Cons. hosp. services Arthur Anderson & Co., Detroit, 1964-72; asst. adminstr. St. John's Hosp., Detroit, 1972-74, v.p. for adminstrn., 1974-79, trustee, 1974-79; exec. v.p. Aultman Hosp., Canton, Ohio, 1979-80, pres., 1980—, trustee, 1979—; dir. Central Trust Co. of N.E. Ohio. Trustee Health Found. Served to lt. (j.g.) USN, 1961-64. Mem. Am. Coll. Hosp. Adminstrs., Am. Hosp. Assn. Clubs: Brookside Country (Canton); Grosse Pointe (Hunt, Mich.) (dir. 1978-79); Lochmoor Country (Grosse Pointe). Home: 1397 Danbury Rd NW North Canton OH 44720 Office: Aultman Hosp 2600 Sixth St SW Canton OH 44710

PRYME, JOHN JOSEPH, JR., podiatrist; b. Oak Park, Ill., Dec. 1, 1950; s. John Joseph and Grace (Faro) Primozich. Student, Loyola U., Chgo., 1968-70, Ill. State U., 1971-72; BS in Biol. Scis., D. Podiatric Medicine, Ill. Coll. Podiatric Medicine, 1976. Diplomate Am. Bd. Podiatric Surgery. Preceptor Rocky Mountain Foot Clinic, P.C., Denver, 1976-77; assoc. prof. Dr. William Scholl Coll. Podiatric Medicine, Chgo., 1978—; pres. Neighborhood Foot Clinic, P.C., Homewood, Ill., 1980—; co-chmn. dissection seminar Scholl Coll. Podiatric Medicine, 1980—; sect. chief podiatry Cuneo Hosp., Chgo., 1984—, residency dir., Cuneo Hosp., 1986—. Fellow Am. Coll. Foot Surgeons; mem. Am. Podiatric Med. Assn., Ill. Podiatric Med. Assn., Am. Assn. Colls. of Podiatric Medicine (faculty chmn. 1979-84), Am. Coll. Podopediatrics, Am. Acad. Podiatry Adminstrn., Am. Assn. Podiatric Sports Medicine, Am. Assn. Hosp. Podiatry, Internat. Coll. Surgeons, Am. Assn. Physicians and Podiatrists, Scholl Coll. Podiatric Medicine Alumni Assn. (sec. 1982-85, 86—). Roman Catholic. Avocations: swimming, water polo, scuba diving, boating, skiing. Office: Neighborhood Foot Clinic PC 18025 Dixie Hwy Homewood IL 60430

PRYOR, BARBARA WRIGHT, educator, classical concert singer; b. Stamps, Ark.; d. Joseph Dudley and Bernyce Eleanor (Hayes) Wright; B.E., Chgo. State U., 1961; M.A., Roosevelt U., 1978; M.Ed., Chgo. Conservatory Music, 1967; m. Harry Leonard Pryor, Jr.; 1 son, Harry Leonard III. Tchr. Am. history and govt. Wendell Phillips Upper Grade Center, Chgo., 1961-63; 8th grade tchr. George T. Donoghue Sch., Chgo., 1963-78; contralto soloist, dir. music St. James United Meth. Ch., Chgo., 1966-74; chorale dir. Duke Ellington, 1968; soloist Quinn Chapel A.M.E. Ch., Chgo., 1978-81; guidance counselor George T. Donoghue Sch., Chgo. Public Sch. System, System, 1979—. Classical concert signer oratorio, sacred and secular, and recital repertoire; appearances with members of Chgo. Symphony and Lyric Opera Orchestras; mem. vocal duo. Recitalist Chgo. Pub. Sch. children, 1986—; dir. Sch. Black Cultural Arts, Inc., 1978-80, chmn. artist selection com., 1978—; active Chgo. Lyric Opera Guild. Recipient Outstanding Tchr. of Year award Chgo. Public Schs., 1977; Key to City, Little Rock, 1982. Nat. cert. counselor. Mem. Chgo. State U. Alumni Assn., Am. Sch. Counselor Assn., Am. Assn. Counseling and Devel., AAUW, Nat. Assn. Negro Musicians, Ill. Assn. Supervision and Curriculum Devel., Chgo. Music Assn. (bd. dirs.), Roosevelt U. Alumni Assn., Phi Delta Kappa. United Methodist. Author: Autism; Main-Streaming: Providing the Least Restrictive Environment for Handicapped Children, 1982. Composer: Hear Us, We Beseech Thee, 1968. Office: 707 E 37th St Chicago IL 60653

PRYOR, FRED HOWARD, small business owner; b. Excelsior Springs, Mo., Feb. 22, 1934; s. Charlie Arthur and Mary Malissa (Tinkle) P.; m. Shirley Jean Pryor, Dec. 16, 1955; children: Sherilyn Jean Pryor Coulter, Rebecca Ann Pryor Phillips. BA, William Jewell Coll.; BTh, So. Bapt. Theol. Sem.; MA, U. Mo. Pastor So. Bapt. Conv., Kansas City, Mo., 1960-69; tchr. Dale Carnegie Courses, Kansas City, Mo., 1970—; pres. Fred Pryor & Assocs., Kansas City, Mo., 1970-75, Fred Pryor Seminars, Kansas City, Mo., 1975—. Bd. dirs. Baptist Health Systems, Kansas City, 1984—. Recipient Achievement award, William Jewell Coll., 1980. Mem. Nat. Speaker Assn. Office: 2000 Johnson Dr Shawnee Mission KS 66205

PRZYBYLOWICZ, CAROLYN LYON, controller, personnel administrator; b. Clare, Mich., Jan. 18, 1947; d. Aaron Eugene and Alice Marie (Fall) Prout; m. Stanley George Lyon, July 13, 1968 (dec. May 1971); children: Lori Anne Lyon, Jamie Lynn Lyon; m. Dennis Karl Hunt, Jan. 1975 (div. Nov. 1977); 1 child, Julie Marie Hunt Przybylowicz; m. Arthur Roy Przybylowicz, Nov. 3, 1979. Cert. acctg., Lansing Bus. U., 1965. Bank teller Citizens Bank & Trust, Rosebush, Mich., 1965-68; bookkeeper, sec. Doyle & Smith P.C., Lansing, Mich., 1968-74; legal sec. Foster, Swift, Collins & Coey P.C., Lansing, 1974-79; mgr. office ARC, Lansing, 1979-81; controller, personnel adminstr. Mich. Protection & Advocacy Service, Lansing, 1981—. Vol. bookkeeper Citizens Alliance to Uphold Spl. Edn., Lansing, 1977-79; coordinator bingo IHM Sch., Lansing, 1979-80; mem. St. Casimir Christian Service, Lansing, 1981-84, chairperson, 1983-84; bd. dirs. Immaculate Heart of Mary Sch., Lansing, 1977-80. Democrat. Roman Catholic. Avocations: sewing, travel, photography. Office: Mich Protection & Advocacy Service 109 W Michigan Suite 900 Lansing MI 48933

PSZANKA, RICHARD THADDEUS, hospital administrator; b. Chgo., Apr. 5, 1940; s. Thaddeus C. and Julia A. (Gaura) P.; m. Lani M. Jamieson, Dec. 1, 1962; children: Richard, Theresa, Daniel, Timothy, James, David, Robert, Thomas, Michael, Anne. BA in Acctg., Loras Coll., 1964. CPA, Iowa. Mem. staff Fahey and Toohey, CPA's, Dubuque, 1965-78; bus. office dir. Iowa Lutheran Hosp., Des Moines, 1978-79; controller, 1979-81, asst. adminstr. fiscal services, 1981-87, chief fin. officer, 1987—. Treas. Little Cloud council Girl Scouts U.S.A., 1974-77. Mem. Am. Inst. CPA's, Iowa Soc. CPA's (bd. dirs., chmn. mem. in industry, chmn. healthcare facilities com.), Healthcare Fin. Mgmt. Assn. (sec. 1984-85, v.p. 1985-86, pres.-elect 1986-87, pres. 1987—). Roman Catholic. Home: 907 Cummins Pkwy Des Moines IA 50312 Office: University St and Penn St Des Moines IA 50316

PTACK, ALLEN JAMES, data processing company executive; b. Chgo., Sept. 6, 1956; s. Edward August Ptack; m. Colleen Marie Kavanagh, June 6, 1981; children: Jennifer Marie, Kristen Ann. BS, U. Ill., 1978, postgrad., 1982-84. Programmer/analyst City of Chgo., 1977-78; cons. Deloitte, Haskins, Sells, Chgo., 1978-79; sr. software specialist Digital Equipment Corp., Rolling Meadows, Ill., 1979-81; exec. dir. M.A.S. Assocs., Mt. Prospect, Ill., 1981—; ptnr. M.A.S. Assocs., Chgo., 1984—; pres. Virtuosity Inc., Chgo., 1986-87; chief exec. officer At The Top, Inc., Chgo., 1987—; instr. various seminars, 1980-86. Ill. State scholar, 1974-78. Mem. Inst. for Elec. Engrs., Ctr. Entrepreneurial Mgmt., Beta Gamma Sigma. Avocations: racquetball, golf, singing, gardening, woodworking. Office: MAS Assocs 2720 River Suite 27 Des Plaines IL 60018

PTASHKIN, BARRY IRWIN, management consultant; b. Chgo., May 6, 1944; s. Fred and Pearl (Geneles) P.; m. Roxanne Schwartz, Aug. 21, 1966; children: Jill Sheri, Joy Sandra. BA in History, U. Ill., Champaign, 1966; MBA, Loyola U., Chgo., 1969. Cert. mgmt. cons. Tchr. Chgo. Bd. Edn., 1967-68; staff officer labor relations Chgo. and Northwestern Transp. Co., 1968-70; dist. supr. labor relations Chgo. and Northwestern Transp. Co., Mpls., 1970-72; trainmaster Chgo. and Northwestern Transp. Co., Chgo., 1972-73, mgr. cost effectiveness, 1973-74; cons. ops. improvement Coopers & Lybrand, Chgo., 1974-76; mgr. transp. cons. group Coopers & Lybrand, Phila., 1976-77, human resources nat. dir. mgmt. cons. services, 1977-79, nat. dir. transp. cons. group, 1979-81; group dir. profit imprvement cons. services Coopers & Lybrand, Chgo., 1981-83; regional dir. mgmt. cons. services KMG, Chgo., 1983-84; ptnr.-in-charge mgmt. adv. services FER&S, Chgo., 1984—. Author numerous articles on mgmt. strategy, bus. ops., labor relations and rail industry, Focus on You and Your Business, 1985; contbg. editor to profl. jours. Mem. Inst. Mgmt. Cons., (v.p. 1980-86, bd. dirs. 1982—), Am. Inst. Indsl. Engrs., Am. Soc. Personnel Adminstrn., Council Logistics Mgmt. Avocations: sports, reading, travel. Home: 3110 Centennial Ln Highland Park IL 60035 Office: FER&S 401 N Michigan Chicago IL 60611

PUCHTA-BROWN, KRISTINE MARIE, osteopathic physician; b. Fort Belvoir, Va., Feb. 12, 1952; d. Randolph Everett and Eunice Marie (Rohlfing) Puchta; m. Floyd William Brown, July 5, 1951; children—Sarah Courtney, Aaron Jamison, Wayne Karlton. B.A. in Biology, U. Mo., 1975; D.O., Kansas City Coll. Osteo. Medicine, 1979. Gen. practice osteo. medicine, Troy, Mo., 1979—; mem. staff Lincoln County Meml. Hosp., chief-of-staff, 1983, 84. Fellow Internat. Coll. Gen. Practice; mem. Mo. Assn. Osteo. Physicians and Surgeons, Central Mo. Assn. Osteo. Physicians and Surgeons, Troy Bus. and Profl. Women's Orgn., NOW. Mem. United Ch. of Christ. Office: 170 W Cherry Box 289 Troy MO 63379

PUCKETT, C. LIN, plastic surgeon, educator; b. Burlington, N.C., Oct. 19, 1940; s. Harry W. And Lula C. Puckett; m. Florence Elizabeth Loy, June 18, 1961 (div. 1976); children: Loy C., Lisa A., Leslie A.; m. Patricia Louise Wells, June 17, 1984. MD, Bowman Gray Sch. Medicine, 1966. Assoc. in surgery Duke U. Med. Ctr., Durham, N.C., 1971-73; assoc. prof., head div. plastic surgery U. Mo. Med. Ctr., Columbia, 1976-81; prof., head attending plastic surgeon U. Mo. Med. Ctr., Truman VA Hosp., Columbia, 1982—. Contbr. numerous articles to profl. jours. Fellow ACS; mem. AMA, Am. Assn. Hand Surgery (bd. dirs. 1982-84, chmn. nominating com. 1985, v.p. 1987), Am. Assn. Plastic Surgeons, Am. Cleft Palate Assn., Am. Soc. Plastic and Reconstructive Surgeons Inc. (bd. dirs. 1985—), Am. Soc. Surgery of the Hand, Am. Trauma Soc., Internat. Microsurgical Soc., Lipolysis Soc. N.Am. Inc., Mo. chpt. ACS, Plastic Surgery Research Council, So. Med. Assn., Assn. Acad. Chmn. Plastic Surgery (bd. dirs. 1985—, pres. 1987), Sigma Xi, Alpha Omega Alpha. Republican. Avocation: breeding Quarter horses. Home: Rt 1 Box 146 Ashland MO 65010 Office: U Mo Div Plastic Surgery One Hospital Dr Columbia MO 65212

PUDERBAUGH, HOMER LEROY, architecture educator; b. Henrietta, Mo., May 14, 1929; s. Homer L. and Mary Edith (Mason) P.; m. Gwen Ann Mai, July 15, 1950 (div. Nov. 1977); children: Pamela Sue, Kevin Ira. BArch, Kans. State U., 1952, MS, 1959; cert., Ecole des Beaux Arts, Fontainbleau, 1960. Registered architect. Pvt. practice architecture Wichita, Kans. and Winnipeg,, Man., Can., 1952-60; prof. U. Nebr., Lincoln, 1960—, dir., 1969-70, chmn., 1970-81, asst. dean, 1982-83; pvt. practice cons., Lincoln, 1980—. Author: (with others) Structure and Architectural Design, 1965, 3d rev. ed. 1984, New Architecture in Nebraska, 1977 (Advt. Council award 1978); author 16 papers; contbr. articles profl. jours. Recipient Great Tchr. award, U. Nebr. Alumni Assn., 1972, 25th yr. teaching award, U. Nebr., 1985. Mem. AIA, Nebr. Soc. Architects (pres. 1985, bd. dirs. 1976-86, Outstanding Service award, 1981), Lincoln chpt. Nebr. Soc. Architects (pres. 1979), Architecture Found. Nebr. (bd. dirs. 1986—). Clubs: Univ., Nebr. (Lincoln). Lodge: Shriners. Avocations: photography, flying, travel. Office: U Nebr Dept Architecture Lincoln NE 68588-0107

PUDLAS, JALAYNE M., accountant; b. Freeport, Ill., Apr. 10, 1960; d. Gerald A. and Marian M. (Fegan) P. BS in Bus., Eastern Ill. U., 1982. CPA, Ill. Mgr. Gray Hunter Stenn, Marion, Ill., 1982—. Mem. Am. Inst. CPA's, Ill. CPA Soc. Roman Catholic. Avocations: bicycling, reading, animals, flowers, gardening. Office: Gray Hunter Stenn PO Box 1728 Marion IL 62959

PUELICHER, JOHN A., bankholding company executive; b. 1920. With Marshall & Ilsley Co., Milw., 1959—, exec. v.p., 1959-63, pres., 1963-79, chmn. bd. dirs., 1979-81, now chmn. bd. dirs., chief exec. officer. Office: Marshall & Ilsley Corp 770 N Water St Milwaukee WI 53201 *

PUESAN KHOURY, CESAR A., minister, Spanish coordinator, educator; b. Santo Domingo, Dominican Republic, June 3, 1938; s. César C. Puesán and Aurora Khoury; m. Nercy C. Frómeta, Oct. 15, 1958; children: César Jr., Nilda, Myrna A. AA in Bus., Colegio Las Antillas, Cuba, 1959; BBA, Antillian Coll., P.R., 1969; MBA, Inter-Am. U., P.R., 1975; MA in Edn., Loma Linda U., 1977, EDS, 1977, EdD, 1982. Pres. Dominican Coll., Santo Domingo, 1960-65; sec., treas. Dominican Conf., Dominican Republic, 1965-69; auditor Antillian Union, Puerto Rico, 1970-74; Spanish coordinator Wis. Conf. Seventh Day Adventist Ch., Milw., 1975—; also bd. dirs. Wis. Conf. Seventh Day Adventist Ch. Bd. dirs. Wis. Acad., Columbus, 1976—; bd. dirs. Spanish Seventh Day Adventist Ch., Milw., 1977—. Mem. Nat. Soc. Pub. Accts., Nat. Assn. Accts. Avocation: music. Home: 2301 W Vogel Ave Milwaukee WI 53221 Office: Wis Conf SDA 2324 S 24th St Milwaukee WI 53221

PUESCHEL, KATHLEEN MARGURITE, neuropsychologist; b. Quakertown, Pa., Aug. 20, 1943; s. Clement and Lillian (Robertson) P. BS, E. Wash. State U., 1972; MS, Memphis State U., 1974, PhD, 1979. Clin. psychologist Juvenile Diagnostic Unit, Orofino, Idaho, 1979-80; adj. prof. Ind. U. N.W., Gary, 1981-82, vis. prof., 1982-83; clin. neuropsychologist Southlake Ctr. for Mental Health, Merrillville, Ind., 1980-83; pvt. practice clin. neuropsychology Clin. Psychology Assocs. P.C., Merrillville, 1982—; mem. human rights com. Lake County Assn. for the Retarded, Gary, 1983—; presenter workshops State Ednl. Conf., Michigan City, 1983, Spl. Edn. Coop., Crown Point, Ind., 1984, Vis. Nurse Assn., Highland, Ind., 1984, St. Anthony Rehab Unit, Michigan City,1986; mem. allied health staff St. Anthony's Med. Ctr., St. Mary's Med. Ctr. Grantee Am. Psychol. Assn. Mem. Am. Psychol. Assn., Internat. Neuropsychology Assn., Nat. Head Injury Found. Avocations: swimming, needlework. Office: Clin Psychology Assocs PC 8315 Virginia St Suite 8 Merrillville IN 46410

PUETZ, JOHN DAVID, chemical executive; b. Milw., Aug. 17, 1951; s. John Henry and Mary Lou (David) P.; m. Carol Lynn Hermann, Feb. 28, 1976; children: David, Melissa. BS, U. Wis., Whitewater, 1973. Research microbiologist Great Lakes Biochemical, Milw., 1974-80, mgr. tech. services, 1980-81, head of research, 1981-82, dir. research and devel., 1982-84, v.p. research and devel., 1984—. Mem. Inst. Food Technologists (profl.), Nat. Feed Ingredients Assn. (div. v. chmn., com. chmn., v.p. research and devel. and div. bus. mgr. 1984—), Nat. Spa and Pool Inst. (chmn. chem. treatment and process com.), Assn. Am. Feed Control Officials (industry advisor 1983—). Roman Catholic. Avocations: photography, gardening, baseball, football. Office: Great Lakes Biochemical Co Inc 6120 W Douglas Ave Milwaukee WI 53218

PUGH, KENNETH DUANE, industrial supply executive; b. Sullivan, Ind., May 29, 1937; s. Damon Wilsey and Doris Esther (Harris) P.; m. Janice Kaye Southwood, Feb. 24, 1962; children: Glyna, Kenneth, William. Agrl. engring. degree, Purdue U.; bus. admin. degree, Ind. State U. Systems analyst CBS Records, Terre Haute, Ind., 1962-64; sales mgr. Powered Equipment Co., Terre Haute, 1964-69; v.p. Hydro Power Inc., Terre Haute, 1969—, also bd. dirs.; bd. dirs. HPMS Inc., Terre Haute. Mem. Terre Haute Area C. of C. Republican. Lodge: Elks. Home: Rt 2 Box 131 Shelburn IN 47879 Office: Hydro Power Inc 1221 Hulman St Terre Haute IN 47802

PUGH, SANDRA (SASS) KAY, construction and plastic and metal engraving company executive; b. Aberdeen, S.D., June 3, 1950; d. John D. and Ellabeth A. (DeYoung) P. Student Black Hills State Coll., 1968-72. Cert. electrician, S.D. Apprentice electrician Pugh Elec. Construction, Miller, S.D., 1974-81, mgr., journeyman electrician, 1981-86, elec. contractor 1986—, owner, 1984—. Contbr. poetry to West River Verses volume. Chmn. Hand County Teen Crippled Children, 1967-68; mem. Miller Civic and Commerce, 1983-87, Cen. Plains Arts Council, 1984-86. Recipient Gov.'s award in Photography S.D. State Fair, 1970. Club: Jobs Daughters (state officer 1965). Home: 620 1/2 W 4th St Miller SD 57362

PUHAKKA, LEENA KAISA, psychologist, educator; b. Helsinki, Finland, May 30, 1946; d. Risto Olli Peter and Tyyne Annikki (Maltamo) P. MA, U. Toledo, 1971, U. Toledo, 1974; PhD in Experimental Psychology, U. Toledo, 1976; diploma in clin. psychology, Adelphi U., 1983. Lic. clin. psychologist, Ohio. Asst. prof. psychology Mary Washington Coll., Fredericksburg, Va., 1977-80; postdoctorate trainee in psychology Med. Coll. Ohio, Toledo, 1982-83, clin. asst. prof. psychology, 1983—; clin. psychologist Ct. Diagnostic and Treatment Ctr., Toledo, 1984—, dir. consultation and education, 1985—; gen. practice Clin. Psychologists & Assocs., Toledo, 1984—. Author: Knowledge and Reality: A Comparative Study of Quine and Some Buddhist Logicians, 1975; contbr. articles to profl. jours. Mem. Am. Psychol. Assn., Northwestern Ohio Soc. Profl. Psychology. Avocations: reading, writing, skiing, swimming. Home: 2208 Stirrup Apt J-II Toledo OH 43613 Office: Ct Diagnostic and Treatment Ctr 1 Stranaham Sq Suite 353 Toledo OH 43604

PUKOSZEK, ELIZABETH, accountant; b. Gary, Ind., Feb. 27, 1951; d. Frank and Helen (Licheniak) P. BA, Indiana U., 1973. From staff acct. to sr. acct. Deutsch and Co. Accts., Inc., Schererville, Ind., 1973—. Mem. Ind. CPA Soc. Office: Deutsch and Co Accts Inc 833 W Lincoln Hwy Schererville IN 46375

PULFORD, ROBERT JESSE (BOB PULFORD), professional hockey team executive; b. Newton Robinson, Ont., Can., Mar. 31, 1936. Center Toronto Maple Leafs, NHL, 1956-70; center Los Angeles Kings, NHL, 1970-72, coach, 1972-77; gen. mgr. Chgo. Black Hawks, 1979—, coach, 1977-79, 82, 1984—. Office: Chgo Black Hawks Chicago Stadium 1800 W Madison St Chicago IL 60612 *

PULITZER, MICHAEL EDGAR, newspaper editor; b. St. Louis, Feb. 23, 1930; s. Joseph and Elizabeth (Edgar) P.; m. Cecille Stell Eisenbeis, Apr. 28, 1970; children: Michael Edgar, Elizabeth E., Robert S., Frederick D., Catherine D. Hanson, Christina H. Eisenbeis, Mark C. Eisenbeis, William H. Eisenbeis. Grad., St. Mark's Sch., Southborough, Mass., 1947; AB, Harvard U., 1951, LLB, 1954. Bar: Mass. 1954. Assoc. Warner, Stackpole, Stetson & Bradlee, Boston, 1954-56; reporter Louisville Courier Jour., 1956-60; reporter, news editor, asst. mng. editor St. Louis Post-Dispatch, 1960-71, assoc. editor, 1978-79; editor, pub. Ariz. Daily Star, Tucson, 1971—; pres. chief operating officer Pulitzer Pub. Co. (and subs.), 1979-84, vice chmn., 1984-86, pres., 1986—, also bd. dirs. Clubs: St. Louis Country; Mountain Oyster (Tucson). Office: St Louis Post-Dispatch Pulitzer Pub Co 900 N Tucker Blvd Saint Louis MO 63101

PULLIAM, EUGENE SMITH, newspaper publisher; b. Atchison, Kans., Sept. 7, 1914; s. Eugene Collins and Myrta (Smith) P.; m. Jane Bleecker, May 29, 1943; children—Myrta, Russell, Deborah. A.B., DePauw U., 1935, LL.D., 1973. Reporter, UP, Chgo., Detroit, Buffalo, 1935-36; news editor Radio Sta. WIRE, Indpls., 1936-41; city editor Indpls. Star, 1947-48; mng. editor Indpls. News, 1948-62; asst. publisher Indpls. Star and News, 1962-76; pub., pres. Phoenix Newspapers, 1979—; exec. v.p. Central Newspapers, Indpls., 1979—. Mem. Am. Soc. Newspaper Editors, Am. Newspaper Pubs. Assn. Found. (past pres.), Hoosier State Press Assn. (treas.), Soc. Profl. Journalists, Delta Kappa Epsilon. Club: Paradise Valley Country. Office: The Indpls Star Indpls Newspapers Inc 307 N Pennsylvania St Indianapolis IN 46204

PULLIAM, FREDERICK CAMERON, educational administrator; b. Mesa, Ariz., Jan. 5, 1936; s. Fredrick Posy and Nathana Laura (Cameron) P.; AA., Hannibal LaGrange Coll., 1955; A.B., Grand Canyon Coll., 1958; M.Ed., U. Mo., Columbia, 1966, Ed.S., 1976, Ed.D., 1981; m. Deborah Jean Botts, June 1, 1979; children by previous marriage—Cameron Dale, Joy Renee. Tchr., Centerview (Mo.) Public Schs., 1958-59; ordained to ministry So. Baptist Conv., 1955; minister Bethel Bapt. Ch., Kansas City, Mo., 1959-61; adminstr. Fiti'uta, Manu'a sch., Am. Samoa, 1966-69; cons. in fin. Mo. State Tchrs. Assn., Columbia, 1969-79; supt. schs. Midway Heights C-VII, Columbia, 1979-83; dir. elem. edn. Brentwood Pub. Schs. (Mo.), 1983—; founder, coordinator Mo. Computer-Using Educators Conf., 1982—; adj. asst. prof. ednl. studies U. Mo., St. Louis, 1986—; cons. sch. fin., curriculum improvement. Mem. Columbia Am. Revolution Bicentennial Commn. Inst. Devel. Ednl. Activity fellow, 1969, 78-84. Mem. Mo. Assn. Sch. Adminstrs., Mo. Assn. Supervision and Curriculum Devel., Nat. Assn. Supervision and Curriculum Devel. (bd. dirs. 1984—), Mo. Assn. Elem. Sch. Prins., Nat. Assn. Elem. Sch. Prins., Phi Delta Kappa (chpt. pres.). Republican. Clubs: Kiwanis, Masons, Shriners. Contbr. articles to profl. jours. Home: 5424 Kenrick Parke Dr Saint Louis MO 63119 Office: Mark Twain Sch 8636 Litzsinger Rd Brentwood MO 63144

PULLIAM, YVONNE ANTOINETTE, teacher; b. Chgo.; d. Virgil D. Sr. and Velma (Hunter) P. BA in Edn., Lane Coll., 1966; MA in Ednl. Adminstrn. and Supervision, Roosevelt U., 1987. Cert. intermediate tchr. Tchr. Howalton Day Sch., Chgo., 1968-69; actress N.Y.C., 1970-75; tchr. gifted Chgo. Bd. Edn., 1975-78, 81—; tutor Raisin in the Sun Broadway Play, N.Y.C., 1977-78, Annie Broadway Play, N.Y.C., 1980-85; coordinator Adopt-a-Sch. program, Chgo., 1984-85; tchr. rep. PTA O'Keefe Sch., Chgo., 1984-85. cartoonist 1st Nat. Bank Chgo. newsletter 1969; stand-in for Diana Ross In Mahogany, 1976; appeared on All My Children, The Hosp. and indsl. films and voiceovers. Recipient Cert. of Merit Glamour Mag., 1965; named Featured Designer V2 Fashions, Chgo., 1967, Essence Mag., 1971. Mem. AFTRA, Chgo. Tchrs. Union, Am. Film. Inst., Phi Delta Kappa. Democrat.

PULLMAN, NORMAN KEITH, plastic surgeon; b. Omaha, June 15, 1921; s. James Henry and Mildred M. DeFreece P.; m. Bette Elaine Morgan, Dec. 25, 1943; children: Norman K. Pullman Jr., Edward M., Terry L.. Grad., U. Iowa, 1942; MD, Creighton U., 1945. Cert. Am. Bd. Plastic Surgery. Asst. clin. prof. Kansas U. Sch. Medicine, Wichita; practice medicine specializing in plastic surgery Wichita. Served to lt. USNR, 1946-47, 52-53. Fellow ACS, Southwestern Surg. Congress; mem. Am. Assn. Hand Surgery, Midwestern Assn. Plastic Surgeons, Am. Soc. Plastic and Reconstructive Surgeons Inc., Am. Cleft Palate Assn. Republican. Methodist. Lodges: Masons, Shriners, Rotary. Avocations: reading, geography, music, racquetball. Office: 3007 E Central Wichita KS 67214

PULSIFER, EDGAR DARLING, leasing service and sales executive; b. Natick, Mass., Jan. 11, 1934; s. Howard George and Elvie Marion (Morris) P.; m. Alice Minarik, Feb. 13, 1957 (div. Oct. 1979); children: Mark Edgar, Audrey Carol, Lee Howard; m. Barbara Ann Chuhak, Apr. 19, 1980. BSEE, MIT, 1955. With sales and service dept. Beckman Instruments, Fullerton, Calif., 1956-59; regional sales mgr. Hewlett Packard, Palo Alto, Calif., 1959-72, Gen. Automation, Anaheim, Calif., 1973-74; exec. v.p. Systems Mktg., Elk Grove Vlg., Ill., 1975-79; pres. Consol. Funding, Mt. Prospect, Ill., 1979—. Served as 1st lt. U.S. Army, 1956. Republican. Episcopalian. Clubs: North Shore Country (Glenview, Ill.), Itasca (Ill.) Country. Avocations: coins, stamps, curling, scuba diving, golf. Home: 370 W Dulles Des Plaines IL 60016 Office: Consol Funding Corp 500 W Central Mount Prospect IL 60056

PULSIFER, THOMAS RICHARD, association executive; b. Winchester, Mass., Aug. 2, 1943; s. Frank and Janice (Goldsmith) P.; m. Eloise Ann Jones, Dec. 3, 1966; 1 child, Bethany Lynne. A.B., Wilmington Coll., 1965; M.S.M., Wittenberg U., 1967. Tchr., Xenia City Schs. (Ohio), 1967-80; pres. Ohio Assn. R.R. Passengers, Xenia, 1976—; exec. dir. Ziebart Dealers Assn., Dayton, 1983—; mgr. advt. and spl. projects Dave Marshall, Inc., Dayton, 1980-86; mgr. account services Advertising and Talent Assocs., Dayton, 1986—. Ofcl., del. Midwest High Speed Rail Compact, Columbus, 1980-83, vice chmn., 1982; bd. dirs. Ohio Rail Transp. Authority, 1976-83, chmn., 1980. Organist, composer choral music; editor The 6:53 Jour., 1973—. Bd. dirs. Community Concerts Assn., 1967-69; vice chmn. council Faith Lutheran Ch., 1980-81. Mem. High Speed Rail Assn., Assn. Ry. Communicators, Nat. Assn. R.R. Passengers, Press Club Ohio. Lutheran. Office: Ohio Assn RR Passengers PO Box 653 Xenia OH 45385

PUMMILL, CAROL SUE, business official, author; b. Springfield, Ohio, Feb. 25, 1950; d. Earl Virgil and Jacqueline Ann (Thurman) P. B.S. in Bus., Wright State U., 1975, M.B.A., 1978. Mgr. Kroger Co., Troy, Ohio, 1976-77; mktg. analyst NCR Corp., Dayton, Ohio, 1978-81, cons. relations specialist, 1981, product mgr., 1981-85, program mgr., 1985—; career bd. rep. Mademoiselle mag., N.Y.C., 1980—. Author essays, poems, newspaper articles. Active Young Democrats, Springfield, Ohio, 1984; canvasser Democratic Party, 1976. Recipient Grad. assistantship Wright State U., 1977. Mem. Recognition Techs. Users Assn., Am. Mktg. Assn., Nat. Assn. Female Execs. Roman Catholic. Office: NCR Corp 1700 S Patterson Blvd Dayton OH 45479

PUNDERSON, JOHN OLIVER, chemist; b. Northfield, Minn., Oct. 28, 1918; s. James M. and Gertrude I. (Pruett) P.; m. Frances M. Lee, Feb. 1, 1947; children: John O. Jr., Jeffrey L., Nancy C. Parr. BS, U. Chgo., 1940; PhD, U. Minn., 1950. Research chemist, research supr. E.I. DuPont de Nemours & Co., Wilmington, Del., 1950-72; research assoc. E.I. DuPont de Nemours & Co., Parkersburg, W.Va., 1972-82; pres. Punderson Cons. Inc., Marietta, Ohio, 1984—; U.S. tech. advisor Internat. Standards Orgn., Geneva, 1978—, Internat. Electrotechnical Commn., Geneva, 1977—. Patentee in field; mem. tech. adv. bd. Jour. Fire Scis., 1983—; contbr. articles to profl. jours. Adult leader Boy Scouts Am., Wilmington, 1962-72. Served with USN, 1944-46. Mem. IEEE, Am. Chem. Soc. (emeritus), Am. Soc. for Testing and Materials (sr.), Nat. Fire Protection Assn., Phi Beta Kappa, Phi Delta Theta. Avocations: computer electronics, photography. Home and Office: Punderson Consulting Inc 108 Alden Ave Marietta OH 45750

PUNDMANN, ED JOHN, JR., automotive company executive; b. St. Charles, Mo., Feb. 24, 1939; s. Ed J. Sr. and Ruth O. (Bremme) P.; m. Dolores Anne Lienau, June 15, 1963; children: Mary Ann, Steven A., Susan K. BA, Westminster Coll., 1961. Jr. accountant Peat, Marwick & Mitchell, St. Louis, 1961-62; salesman Pundmann Ford, St. Charles, 1962-82, gen. mgr., 1982—; bd. dirs. 1st State Bank, Mut. Fire Ins. St. Charles; 3d v.p., bd. dirs. Emmaus Homes Inc., St. Charles. Treas. St. Charles City Charter Commn., 1981; mem. St. Charles City Econ. Commn., Handicapped Facilities Bd. St. Charles; past pres. St. John United Ch. Christ, St. Charles City Park Endowment Bd.; past chmn. Daniel Boone dist. Boy Scouts Am.; bd. dirs. Boone Ctr. Workshops, St. Charles, Parkside Meadows Retirement, St. Charles, Family and Personal Support Ctrs. Greater St. Louis. Mem. Mo. Auto Dealers Assn. (bd. dirs. 1983—), Greater St. Louis Ford Dealers Assn. (vice chmn.), St. Charles C. of C. (past bd. dirs., past pres., Citizen of Yr. award 1986). Lodge: Rotary. Home: 3304 Lennox Saint Charles MO 63301 Office: Pundmann Ford 2727 W Clay Saint Charles MO 63301

PUNDSACK, VERN ALFRED, management and computer consultant; b. Albany, Minn., Nov. 18, 1941; s. Raymond William and Alma (Sand) P.; m. Donna Lillian Wiederin, June 15, 1968; children—Stephanie, Jonathan. B.A., St. John's U., Collegeville, Minn., 1964; M.Hosp. and Health Care Adminstrn., U. Minn., 1979. Staff assoc. Minn. Hosp. Assn., Mpls., 1966-67; adminstrv. resident Robert Packer Hosp., Sayre, Pa., 1967-69; asst. adminstr. St. Vincent Hosp., Worcester, Mass., 1969-71; dir. adminstrv. services and planning Iowa Hosp. Assn., Des Moines, 1971-74; dir. planning, v.p. Iowa Meth. Med. Ctr., Des Moines, 1974-77; v.p. St. Mary's Hosp., Rhinelander, Wis., 1977-78; adminstr. Northwood Med. Assocs., S.C., Rhinelander, 1978-85; pres. Pundsack and Assocs., Rhinelander, Wis., 1985—. Mem. Iowa Gov.'s Emergency Med. Services Adv. Council, 1972-73, Invitational Nat. Health Planning Forum, 1974-77; mem. task force on cert. of need Iowa Legislature, 1976-77; mem. task forces on orgn., open heart surgery, data collection Des Moines Hosp. Consortium, 1975-77; co-chmn. Northwoods Community United Way Campaign, 1979; pres. St. Mary of Nazareth Parish Men's Club, Des Moines, 1976-77; mem., chmn. fin. com. St. Joseph's Parish, Rhinelander, 1978-85; mem. adv. bd. Northwoods Health Careers Consortium, 1982-84; mem. Wis. adv. council Mgmt. Systems of Wausau, Inc., 1982-85. Served with USAR, 1958-65. Mem. Wis. Clinic Mgrs. Assn. (edn. com. 1982-85), Med. Group Mgmt. Assn., Am. Coll. Med. Group Adminstrs., Am. Coll. Hosp. Adminstrs.Roman Catholic. Club: Kiwanis.

PURCELL, DAVID ALONZO, hospital administrator; b. Wilmington, Ohio, Jan. 7, 1952; s. Chester A. and Elizabeth (Dalton) P.; m. Joyce Nettleton, Mar. 22, 1975; children: Andrew David, Lindsey Joy, Joel Michael. BSBA, Miami U., Oxford, Ohio, 1975. CPA, Ohio. Sr. acct. Ernst and Whinney, Cin., 1975-79; controller St. Luke Hosp., Ft. Thomas, Ky., 1979-82; corp. dir. fin. services Western Res. Care Systems, Youngstown, Ohio, 1982-86; adminstr. fin. services Ohio State U. Hosp., Columbus, 1986—. Treas. Glenwood Meth. Ch., Boardman, Ohio, 1985, trustee, 1984-86; evangelism team mem. College Hill Presbyn. Ch., Cin., 1977-82. Mem. Hosp. Fin. Mgmt. Assn. (advanced mem.), Am. Inst. CPA's. Republican. Avocations: family activities, golf, tennis. Office: Ohio State U Hosps 450 W 10th Ave Columbus OH 43210

PURCELL, TERRY ALLAN, retail executive; b. Paducah, Ky., Sept. 20, 1948; s. Allan Edward and Ruth Lorene P.; m. Marilyn Jean Robbearts, Dec. 1, 1973; children: Danielle, Gavin. BS, Murray State U., 1972. With CMC Corp., various locations, 1976-83, v.p., regional sales mgr., Atlanta, 1979, St. Louis, 1979-80, v.p. sales, St. Louis, 1980-83; regional v.p. Intrav, 1983-86, divisional v.p., 1986—. Served with USAR, 1968-76. Recipient Top Sales award Intrav, 1983-86; named Store Mgr. of Yr., Montgomery Ward Co., 1973. Mem. Am. Mgmt. Assn. Republican. Lutheran. Lodge: Masons. Home: 549 Timberridge St Saint Charles MO 63301 Office: 7711 Bonhomme Saint Louis MO 63105

PURDY, RICHARD LIONEL, orthodontist; b. Battle Creek, Mich., June 12, 1928; s. Liomel Roland and Olive Maxine (Schanzenbaker) P.; m. Olive Jean Huss, July 5, 1953; children: Margaret Ann Purdy Gatherer, Philip Richard. Student, Western Mich. U., 1946-49; DDS, Northwestern U., 1953; cert. orthodontics, Columbia U., N.Y.C., 1964. Gen. practice dentistry Kalamazoo, 1955-62; practice dentistry specializing in orthodontics Portage, Mich., 1964—. Served to 1st lt., U.S. Army, 1953-55. Mem. ADA, Am. Assn. Orthodontists. Lodge: Rotary. Home: 511 Landsdowne Dr Portage MI 49081 Office: 1822 W Milham Ave Portage MI 49081

PURKERSON, MABEL LOUISE, physician, physiologist, educator; b. Goldville, S.C., Apr. 3, 1931; d. James Clifton and Louise (Smith) P. A.B., Erskine Coll., 1951; M.D., U. S.C., Charleston, 1956. Diplomate Am. Bd. Pediatrics. Instr. pediatrics Washington U. Sch. Med., St. Louis, 1961-67, instr. medicine, 1966-67, asst. prof. pediatrics, 1967—, asst. prof. medicine, 1967-76, assoc. prof. medicine, 1976—, assoc. dean curriculum, 1976—; cons. in field. Editorial bd. Jour. Am. Kidney Diseases, 1981-87 ; contbr. articles to profl. jours. USPHS spl. fellow, 1971-72. Bd. counselors Erskine Coll., 1971—. Mem. Am. Heart Assn. (exec. com. 1973-81), Council on the Kidney, Am. Physiol. Soc., Am. Soc. Nephrology, Internat. Soc. Nephrology, Central Soc. Clin. Research, Am. Soc. Renal Biochemistry and Metabolism, Sigma Xi (chpt. sec. 1974-76). Avocations: traveling; gardening; photography. Home: 20 Haven View St Louis MO 63141 Office: Washington Univ Sch Medicine Renal Div Dept 660 S Euclid Ave St Box 8126 St Louis MO 63110

PURKHISER, STEPHEN DALE, engineer; b. Salem, Ind., Mar. 18, 1955; s. Charles and Mildred Marie (Balantine) P.; m. Glenda Marie Smith, Aug. 26, 1978. BS, Ind. State U., 1977, MS, 1978. Project engr. Kimball Piano Div., French Lick, Ind., 1978—. Organizer, umpire Little League, French Lick, 1978-86; adv. bd. South Cen. Area Vocat. Sch., Rego, Ind., 1985-87. Chastain Pickerill scholar, Region IV SME scholar, Ind. State U. scholar, 1973-77; Hon. State scholar. Mem. Soc. Mfg. Engrs., Epsilon Pi Tau. Republican. Lodge: Optimists. Avocations: photography, woodworking, model bldg., sports. Home: 212 Summit St French Lick IN 47432 Office: Kimball Piano Div Box 432 French Lick IN 47432

PUROL, SUZANNE RENEE, underwriter, customer group specialist; b. Ashland, Wis., July 30, 1956; d. Leslie Niel and Ethel Laura (Dominczek) Thibodeau; m. Matthew Francis Purol, Oct. 6, 1984. BS in Mgmt., Purdue U., 1978. CPCU. Personal lines underwriter Farm Bur. Ins. Co., Indpls., 1978-79; trainee comml. lines Chubb Group Ins. Cos., Indpls., 1979-80, assoc. underwriter then comml. underwriter, 1980-84, sr. comml. underwriter, 1985—. Parliamentarian Chatham Arch Neighborhood Assn., Indpls., 1986. Mem. Indpls. Assn. Ins. Women (chmn. various coms. 1979-84, bd. dirs. 1985-86, corr. sec. 1986—, Educator award 1985), CPCU Assn. (edn. com. 1984—). Republican. Roman Catholic. Avocations: restoring old houses, travel, reading, crafts. Home: 842 Broadway St Indianapolis IN 46202 Office: Chubb Group Ins Cos 251 Illinois St Indianapolis IN 46204

PURPURA, JOSEPH MATTHEW, gynecologist/obstetrician; b. Pitts., Mar. 8, 1950; s. Joseph Matteo and Nila (Vannucci) P.; m. Joanne Ida Narduzzi, June 3, 1973 (div. Mar. 1978); m. Nancy Patricia Smith, Sept. 1, 1979; children: Amy Nicole, Julie Michelle, Kathleen Mary, Margaret Rose, Anne Genevieve. BS summa cum laude, U. Pitts., 1972, MD, 1976. Diplomate Am. Bd. Ob-Gyn. Intern Northwestern U., Chgo., 1976-77, resident ob-gyn, 1977-80; practice medicine specializing in ob-gyn Lake Forest, Ill., 1980—; attending physician Northwest Community Hosp., Arlington Heights, Ill., 1980-82, active various coms.; attending physician Lake Forest (Ill.) Hosp., 1980—, active various coms.; attending staff Hawthorn Place Surgical Ctr., Libertyville, Ill., 1982—; chief resident Prentice Women's Hosp., Chgo. 1979-80; clin. instr. dept. ob-gyn Northwestern U. Med. Sch., 1980—. Contbr. numerous articles to profl. jours. Fellow Am. Coll. Ob-Gyn; mem. AMA, Am. Cancer Soc. (bd. dirs. Ill. div. Lake County chpt. 1985—), Am. Fertility Soc., Ill. State Med. Soc. (bd. dirs. 1985—), council on econs. 1981-83, polit. action com. 1982—, chmn. govtl. affairs council 1986—, alt. del. 1982, 85), Lake County Med. Soc. (exec. com. 1985—), Chgo. Gynecol. Soc., Crescent County Med. Found. (bd. dirs. 1987), Catholic Physicians Guild, Phi Beta Kappa, Alpha Epsilon Delta. Republican. Roman Catholic. Clubs: Knollwood (Lake Forest), Richmond (Ill.) Hunt. Avocations: golf, jogging, upland game hunting, gourmet cooking. Office: Ob Gyn Assocs Lake Forest Ltd 700 Westmoreland Rd Bldg C Lake Forest IL 60045

PURSCH, WILLIAM CLAUDE, education administrator, educator; b. Camden, N.J., Mar. 2, 1939; s. William Joseph and Emma Mae (Painter) P.; m. Lenore Donna Wilson, Aug. 26, 1967; children: Wendy Lenore, Heidi Amber. BA, Gettysburg Coll., 1960; MS, U. So. Calif., 1970; PhD, Ohio State U., 1982. Cert. profl. contracts mgr. Commd. 2d lt. U.S. Army, 1960, advanced through grades to lt. col., 1976, ret., 1981; dir. purchasing Gem Savings and Loan, Dayton, Ohio, 1981; specialist corp. purchasing Robbins and Meyers Inc., Dayton, 1981-82; dept. head, prof. AF Inst. Tech., Wright-Patterson AFB, Ohio, 1982—. Contbr. articles to profl. jours. Bd. advisors masters degree Northrup U., Los Angeles, 1986—; bd. advisors govt. contract studies Inst. for Paralegal Tng., Phila., 1986—; co-leader nat. contract mgmt. assn., del. to Peoples Republic of China Citizen's Ambassador Program, 1986. Decorated Legion of Merit. Mem. Nat. Contract Mgmt. Assn. (pres. elect 1987—, scholar 1987—), Soc. Logistics Engrs. (sr.), Nat. Property Mgmt. Assn., AF Assn. (life), Nat. Rifle Assn. (life), Nat. Purchasing Mgmt. Assn. Methodist. Club: Presidents. Lodges: Masons, Knights Templars. Avocations: travel, photography, stamp collecting. Home: 226 Brookway Rd Dayton OH 45459 Office: AF Inst Tech Sch Systems and Logistics Wright-Patterson AFB OH 45433

PURSE, CHARLES ROE, real estate company executive; b. Redhill, Surrey, Eng., May 19, 1960; came to U.S., 1960.; s. James Nathanial and Rolande Marie Louise (Redon) P.; m. Carole Sadler, July 5, 1986. BA, Dartmouth Coll., 1982; M in Mgmt., Northwestern U., 1985. Analyst Chem. Bank, Paris, 1982; comml. banking officer Northern Trust Bank, Chgo., 1982-85; sr. account officer Citicorp Real Estate, Inc., Chgo., 1985—. Treas. Belcam Condominium Assn., Chgo., 1986—. Republican. Episcopalian. Club: University (Chgo.). Avocations: golf, photography, skiing. Office: Citicorp Real Estate Inc 200 S Wacker Dr Chicago IL 60606

PURSELL, CARL DUANE, congressman; b. Imlay City, Mich., Dec. 19, 1932; s. Roy and Doris (Perkins) P.; m. Peggy Jean Brown, 1956; children: Philip, Mark, Kathleen. B.A., Eastern Mich. U., 1957, M.A., 1962; LL.D., Madonna Coll., 1977. Former educator, small bus. owner; mem. Wayne County Bd. Commnrs., 1969-70; mem. Mich. Senate, 1971-76, 95th-100th Congresses from 2d Mich. Dist., 1977—; Past mem. Mich. Crime Commn. Served in U.S. Army, 1957-59. Recipient award EPA, 1976. Republican. Address: US Ho of Reps 1414 Longworth House Office Bldg Washington DC 20515 *

PURSELL, ETHAN ELDON, architectural engineer; b. Paola, Kans., Nov. 27, 1928; s. John Van Patton and Hazel Mae (Foster) P.; m. Jeannette Baumeister, Sept. 11, 1964. BSME, U. Kans., 1959, postgrad. archtl. engring., 1960-61, postgrad. jewelry and silversmithing design, 1962-63. Gen. engr. U.S. Weather Bur., Kansas City, Mo., 1959-67; airport planning engr. FAA, Mpls., 1968-71; airport engr., instr. FAA, Okla. City, 1972-77; archtl. engr. FAA, Chgo., 1978—. Served with USN, 1951-56, Korea. Mem. Soc. N.Am. Goldsmiths, Am. Craft Council. Club: Toastmasters Internat. (adminstrv. v.p. 1970-71). Avocations: watchmaker, jeweler, silversmith. Home: 5455 N Sheridan Rd Unit 3505 Chicago IL 60640 Office: FAA AGL-436 2300 E Devon Ave Des Plaines IL 60018

PURUCKER, ERVIN FREDERICK, architect; b. South Bend, Ind., Feb. 12, 1925; s. Ervin Frederick and Bertha Christina (Armbruster) P.; m. Doris Jean Taylor, Sept. 22, 1962; children: Charles Robert, Faye Ann, Kim Edward, James Andrew. BArch, Notre Dame U., 1957. Registered architect, Ind., Ill., Mich. Draftsman C.W. Cole and Son, South Bend, 1947-58; architect Mathews & Assocs., South Bend, 1958-60; v.p. Mathews & Purucker, South Bend, 1960-72, Mathews-Purucker-Anella, Inc., South Bend, 1972—. Mem. Area Bd. Zoning Appeals, St. Joseph County, Ind., 1971—. Served as cpl. U.S. Army, 1950-52. Mem. AIA (pres. No. Ind. chpt. 1984), No. Ind. Hist. Soc. (trustee 1985—). Republican. Mem. United Ch. Christ. Lodges: Masons, Shriners. Avocation: antiques. Home: 2001 Portage Ave South Bend IN 46616 Office: Mathews Purucker Anella Inc 218 S Frances St South Bend IN 46617

PURZYCKI, DONALD ALEXANDER, small business owner; b. Flint, Mich., Feb. 25, 1932; s. Joseph John and Rose Ella (Borcsics) P.; m. Joan Teresa Delisle, July 15, 1961; children: Nancy Louise Purzycki-Engel, Gregory Joseph. BBA, Mich. State U., 1953. Office mgr. OK Plumbing & Heating, Flint, 1955—, sec., treas., 1969—. Mem. Nat. Assn. Plumbing-Heating-Cooling Contractors, Flint C. of C. Republican. Roman Catholic. Office: OK Plumbing & Heating 5317 N Saginaw St Flint MI 48505-2967

PUSCH, GLENN DARRELL, operations executive; b. Peoria, Ill., July 1, 1926; s. Leo Jay and Verle DaLena (Ogden) P.; m. Jeanne Marie Anderson, July 3, 1954; children: Gordon, Kathryn, Amy. BS, Bradley U., 1951; postgrad., Northwestern U., 1951-58, Ill. Inst. Tech., 1952, Sangamon State U., 1985. Registered profl. engr., Calif; cert. materials mgmt., cert. material handling. Sect. head Uniroyal Corp., Chgo., 1952-57; sr. project engr. Bell & Howell, Lincolnwood, Ill., 1957-63; sr. mgmt. cons. Kearney Mgmt. Cons., Chgo., 1963-74; v.p. ops. Sangamon Co., Taylorville, Ill., 1974—. Advisor Boy Scouts Am. Chgo., 1945-46; fund raiser Am. Cancer Soc., Chgo. and Taylorville, 1967-86; pres. St. Luke's United Ch. of Christ Council, Morton Grove, Ill., 1972; mem. dist. com. Campfire Girls, Maine and Niles Ill., 1973, 84; coordinating advisor, bd. dirs. Jr. Achievement, Taylorville, 1978-86; pres. Taylorville Pub. Library, 1978—; session elder 1st Presbyn. Ch., Taylorville, 1980-82, 85-86. Served to sgt. M.I., U.S. Army, 1946-48, PTO.

Mem. Internat. Material Mgmt. Soc. (life, pres. 1973), Christian County Computer Club, Pi Kappa Alpha (v.p. 1949-50). Lodges: Masons (32 degree), Shriners, Sertoma (centurian Taylorville 1981, tribune Taylorville 1985, mid-Ill. dist. gov. 1986—). Avocations: bowling, bridge. Home: 736 Big Bend Rd Taylorville IL 62568 Office: Sangamon Co W Rt 48 Taylorville IL 62568

PUSTOVAR, PAUL THOMAS, insurance agency owner; b. Chisholm, Minn., Dec. 17, 1951; s. John Anton and Perena Esther (Martini) P. AS, Hibbing Jr. Coll., 1971; BS, U. Minn., 1973; M in Curriculum and Instrn., Mankato (Minn.) State U., 1976; grad., Life Underwriting Tng. Council, 1984. Sci. tchr. Nicollet Jr. High Sch., Burnsville, Minn., 1973-74; sci. prof. Hibbing (Minn.) Community Coll., 1974-80; owner, agt. MSI Ins. Agy., Hibbing, 1980—; Nat. leader Am. Youth Hostels, Washington, 1979—; announcer World Curling Championships, 1983-84. Mem. Nat. Assn. Life Underwriters, U.S. Men's Curling Assn. (U.S. Curling Champion 1977, 80), Minn. State Curling Assn. (bd. dirs. 1980-82, State Champion 1980, 82, 87), Hibbing Jaycees. Democrat. Roman Catholic. Club: Hibbing Curling (sec. treas. 1980-82, bd. dirs. 1982-84). Avocations: bicycling, fishing. Home: 2809 1st Ave Hibbing MN 55746 Office: MSI Insurance 2310 1st Ave Hibbing MN 55746

PUTHENPURAKAL, JOSEPH MATHEW, software engineer; b. Changanacherry, India, Feb. 12, 1949; came to U.S., 1978; s. Mathew Joseph and Teresa Mathew P.; m. Mary Jose Aney, Aug. 21, 1977; children: Mathew Joseph, Thomas Joseph. BS, Kerala U., India, 1976; MS, Kerala U., 1978; AA, Dupage Coll., Glen Ellyn, Ill., 1982; BA, North Cen. Coll., Naperville, Ill., 1984. Software engr. AT&T Tech., Lisle, Ill., 1983-84; mem. tech. staff AT&T Bell Labs., Naperville, Ill., 1984-87; info. systems cons. Indecon, Inc., Chicago, 1987—. Trustee Rep. Presdl. Task Force, Washington, 1986. Mem. Data Processing Mgmt. Assn., Am. Entrepreneurs Assn., Internat. Traders. Avocations: reading, travel, swimming. Home: 326 Weatherford Ln Naperville IL 60565 Office: Indecon Inc 1210 Three First Nat Plaza Chicago IL 60602

PUTKA, ANDREW CHARLES, lawyer; b. Cleve., Nov. 14, 1926; s. Andrew George and Lillian M. (Koryta) P. Student, John Carroll U., 1944, U.S. Naval Acad., 1945-46; A.B., Adelbert Coll., Western Res. U., 1949; J.D., Western Res. U., 1952. Bar: Ohio 1952. Practice law Cleve.; instr. govt. Notre Dame Coll. for Women, South Euclid, Ohio; v.p. Koryta Bros. Coal Co., Cleve., 1952-56; supt. div. bldg. and loan assns. Ohio Dept. Commerce, 1959-63; pres., chmn. bd., chief exec. officer Am. Nat. Bank, Parma, Ohio, 1963-69; dir. fin. City of Cleve., 1971-74; dir. port control 1974-78; dir. Cleve. Hopkins Internat. Airport, 1974-78. Mem. Ohio Ho. of Reps., 1953-56, Ohio Senate, 1957-58; dep. auditor, acting sec. Cuyahoga County Bd. Revision, 1970-71; mem. exec. com. Cuyahoga County Democratic Com., 1973—, Assn. Ind. Colls. and Univs. Ohio, 1983—; bd. govs. Sch. Law, Western Res. U., 1953-56; mem. exec. com. World Service Student Fund, 1950-52; U.S. rep. Internat. Pax Romana Congress, Amsterdam, 1950, Toronto, 1952; mem. lay advisory bd. Notre Dame Coll., 1968—; mem. adv. bd. St. Andrew's Abbey, 1976—; trustee Case-Western Res. U., Newman Found. No. Ohio, 1980—; 1st v.p. First Cath. Slovak Union of U.S., 1977-80; pres. USO Council of Cuyahoga County, 1980-83. Voted an outstanding legislator Ohio Press Corrs., 1953; named to All-Star Legislative team Ohio Newspaper Corrs., 1955; named one of Fabulous Clevelanders. Mem. Am., Ohio, Cuyahoga County, Cleve. bar assns., Nat. Assn. State Savs. and Loan Suprs. (past nat. pres.), U.S. Savs. and Loan League (mem. legis. com. 1960-63), Am. Legion, Ohio Municipal League (bd. trustees 1973), Parma C. of C. (bd. dirs., treas. 1965-67), Newman Fedn. (past nat. pres.), NCCJ, Catholic Lawyers Guild (treas.), Am., Ohio bankers assns., Am. Inst. Banking, Adelbert Alumni Assn. (exec. com.), Cathedral Latin Alumni Assn. (trustee 1952—), Internat. Order of Alhambra (internat. parliamentarian 1971—, past grand comdr., supreme advocate 1973), Amvets, Pi Kappa Alpha, Delta Theta Phi (past pres. Cleve. alumni senate, master inspector 1975). Club: K.C. Home: 17013 Scottsdale Blvd Shaker Heights OH 44120 Office: 10301 Lake Ave Cleveland OH 44102

PUTNAM, DALE C., bakery products holding company executive. Pres., chief exec. officer, dir. Interstate Bakeries Corp, Kansas City. Office: Interstate Bakeries Corp PO Box 1627 Kansas City MO 64141 *

PUTNAM, MITCHELL DERWIN, utilites company executive; b. Altus, Okla., June 21, 1957; s. Gerald Ray and Thelma Jean (Witthar) P.; m. Monica Jean Billesbach, Apr. 24, 1982; 1 child, Nicholas. BSME, U. Mo., 1981. Div. engr. Panhandle Eastern Pipe Line Co., Kansas City, Mo., 1981—. Mem. ASME. Roman Catholic. Avocations: running, woodworking. Home: 305 N Hillcrest Belton MO 64012 Office: Panhandle Eastern Pipe Line Co PO Box 1348 Kansas City MO 64141

PUTNEY, MARK WILLIAM, lawyer, utility executive; b. Marshalltown, Iowa, Jan. 25, 1929; s. Lawrence Charles and Geneva (Eldridge) P.; m. Ray Ann Bartnek, May 25, 1962; children: Andi Bartnek, William Bradford, Blake Reinhart. B.A., U. Iowa, 1951, J.D., 1957. Bar: Iowa 1957, U.S. Supreme Ct. 1960. Ptnr. Bradshaw, Fowler, Proctor & Fairgrave, Des Moines, 1961-72; pres., dir. Bradford & Blake Ltd., Des Moines; pres., chief exec. officer Iowa Resources, Inc., 1984—; chmn., chief exec. officer Iowa Power & Light Co., 1984—, Iowa Gas Co.., 1984-85; dir. Norwest Bank Des Moines N.A., Allied Ins. Group. Civilian aide to Sec. Army for Iowa, 1975-77; bd. dirs. Greater Des Moines YMCA, 1976-86, Boys' Home Iowa, 1982-86 , Hoover Presdl. Library Assn., 1983—, Greater Des Moines Com., 1984—, Living History Farms, 1984—, U. Iowa Found., 1984—. chmn. Iowa Com. for Employer Support of Guard and Res., 1979-86. Served with USAF, 1951-53. Mem. Greater Des Moines C. of C. (exec. com. 1983), Delta Chi, Phi Delta Phi. Republican. Episcopalian. Clubs: Rotary, Masons, Shriners, Des Moines (pres. 1977), Wakonda (pres. 1982). Home: 6675 NW Beaver Dr Johnston IA 50131 Office: Iowa Resources Inc 666 Grand Ave Des Moines IA 50303

PUVOGEL, GREGG ALLYN, retail store operator; b. Oak Park, Ill., Mar. 31, 1951; s. T. Kenneth and Hope Edith (Tolar) Jones. Kichen steward Playboy Club, Chgo., 1979—; receiving clk., warehouse mgr., buyer Sound Video Unltd., Chgo., 1972-79; owner Mister Music Audio-Video Boutigue, Fennville, Mich., 1979—, Douglas, Mich., 1985—. Office: Mister Music PO Box 600 Fennville MI 49408

PYLE, ALLEN JACK, state agency administrator; b. Bernie, Mo., Sept. 16, 1939; s. Clarence A. and Eune (Thomas) P.; m. Connie Sue Kitzman, May 25, 1968; children: Allen Robert, Kendra Leigh. BA in Communication Arts, Mich. State U., 1961. With pub. relations staff Gen. Motors Corp., Detroit, 1961-66; pub. relations mgr. Dow Chem. Co., Midland, Mich., 1967-75; editor pub. community mag., Walnut Creek, Calif., 1976-77; sr. pub. affairs rep. Shell Oil Co., Houston, 1977-86; dir. communications Mich. Dept. Transp., Lansing, 1986—. Chmn. communications adv. com. Houston Police Dept., 1982-86; mem. gov.'s energy awareness Com. State of Mich., 1981-83; mem. leaders tng. staff Houston Golden Arrow dist. Boy Scouts Am., 1981-82; sec. Impression 5 Mus., Lansing, 1986, mem. exec. com., 1986—. Mem. Pub. Relations Soc. Am. (accredited mem., bd. dirs. Houston chpt. 1980-82, 85-86, bd. dirs. cen. Mich. chpt. 1987—, nat. assembly del. 1984—, exec. com. nat. technology sect. 1985-87, chmn. nat. communications technology task force 1986, steering com. nat. conf. 1986). Office: Mich Dept Transp Exec Bur Dir Communications Box 30050 Lansing MI 48909

PYLE, DONALD ALAN, music educator, tenor; b. Ridgewood, N.J., Jan. 12, 1933; s. Aime A. and Muriel Ann (Barbour) P.; m. Barbara Jean Sly, July 6, 1961 (dec.); m. 2d, Virginia R. Tinker, June 4, 1968. Student Juilliard Sch. Music, 1956-59; B.A. in Vocal Performance, U. So. Fla., 1969; Mus. M., Mus. D., Fla. State U., 1972. Mem. company South Shore Music Circus, Cohassett, Mass., 1958-59; tenor soloist John Harms Chorus, St. Michael's Episcopal Ch., Juilliard Opera Theatre, N.Y.C., Temple Bethel, Englewood, N.J., St. Leo Coll., Dade City, Fla., 1956-61; teaching asst. Fla. State U., Tallahassee, 1969-71, adj. faculty, 1971-72; instr. U. Mo.-Columbia, 1972-76, acting dean, Swinney Conservatory Music, Central Meth. Coll., Fayette, Mo., 1976-77, dean, prof. voice, 1977—; tenor soloist numerous U.S. colls. and univs.; tenor soloist world premiers Songs from the Ark, The Labyrinth, Of Mice and Men; performances include: Verdi Requiem, Rossini's Stabat Mater, Bach's St. Matthew's Passion, Mendelsohn's The Elijah and Les Troyens (under Sir Thomas Beecham). Served to sgt. USMC, 1951-54. U. So. Fla. scholar, 1966. Mem. Nat. Assn. Tchrs. Singing, Nat. Assn. Schs. Music, Blue Key, Gold Key, Phi Delta Kappa, Omicron Delta Kappa, Phi Mu Alpha, Pi Kappa Lambda. Roman Catholic.

PYLE, JOHN EDWARD, accountant; b. Kansas City, Mo., July 21, 1948; s. John A. and LaVonne (Marsh) P.; m. Marilyn J. Wilson, June 3, 1972; children: Douglas W., Moira L. BSBA, Rockhurst Coll., 1970; MBA, Washington U., St. Louis, 1972. CPA, Kans., Mo. Staff acct. Arthur Andersen & Co., Kansas City, Mo., 1972-73; sr. acct. Hollis Kuckleman & Van De Veer, Olathe, Kans., 1973-74; asst. controller Shaw Purdue Corp., N. Kansas City, Mo., 1974-79; mgr. bus. HNTB Architects and Engrs., Kansas City, Mo., 1979-82; adminstrv. mgr. Price Waterhouse, Kansas City, Mo., 1982—. Mem. Washington U. Bd. Govs., 1982—. Mem. Am. Inst. CPA's, Washington U. Alumni Council (chmn. 1982—). Roman Catholic. Club: Kansas City. Home: 11507 Hemlock Overland Park KS 66210 Office: Price Waterhouse 911 Main Suite 2900 Kansas City MO 64199

PYNCKEL, GARY LEE, osteopathic physician; b. Moline, Ill., Nov. 22, 1952; s. Gerard A. and Margaret F. (Wisely) P. B.A., Monmouth Coll., 1974; postgrad. U. Ill., 1976; D.O., Chgo. Coll. Osteo. Medicine, 1980. Environ. biologist U.S. Corps of Engrs., 1974-76; intern Davenport (Iowa) Osteo. Hosp.; pvt. practice gen. osteo. medicine, Bettendorf, Iowa, 1981—. Served with USMC, 1971-74. Vol. physician Arrowhead Ranch Boys Home, 1981—; mem. prins. com. Osteo. Hosp. Davenport, 1982—. Mem. Am. Osteo. Assn., Iowa Soc. Physicians and Surgeons, Scott County Soc. Osteo. Physicians and Surgeons, Am. Acad. Osteopathy, Am. Coll. Advancement Medicine (diplomat). Home: 1515 Fairland Dr Bettendorf IA 52722 Office: 201 W 2nd Ave Coal Valley IL 61240-9326

PYSH, JOSEPH JOHN, neurologist; b. Olyphant, Pa., Nov. 14, 1935; s. John Andrew and Anna Mary (Marusin) P.; m. Margaret Anne Van Dusen, Aug. 1, 1969. BA in Biology, Wayne State U., 1958; DO, Chgo. Coll. Osteo. Medicine, 1962; PhD in Neuroanatomy, Northwestern U., Chgo., 1967. From instr. to assoc. prof. anatomy Northwestern U., Chgo., 1966-86, acting chmn. cell biology and anatomy, 1978-81, resident physician in neurology, 1983-86; assoc. prof. neurology Coll. Osteo. Medicine, Mich. State U., East Lansing, Mich., 1986—; grant referee NSF, Washington, 1974—. Contbr. numerous articles to profl. jours; manuscript reviewer various orgns., Washington and N.Y.C. NIH grantee, 1969-82. Mem. Am. Acad. Neurology, Am. Coll. Neuropsychiatrists, Am. Soc. Cell Biology, Am. Assn. Anatomists, Soc. Neurosci., NIH, (mem. research grant neurology study sect. 1976-77), Sigma Xi. Republican. Avocations: blue water sailing, rare book collector. Home: 4835 Mohican Lane Okemos MI 48864 Office: Mich State U Coll Osteo Medicine Dept Internal Medicine B305 W Fee East Lansing MI 48824

PYTLIK, LEON ALVIN, entrepreneur; b. Valley City, N.D., Aug. 27, 1940; s. Alvin A. and Robert M. (Thone) P.; m. Marleen M. Miller, Feb. 17, 1961; children: L. Michael, Joseph A., Darin J. BS, Valley City State Coll., 1962. Tchr. Valley City Schs., 1963-64, Mandan (N.D.) Schs., 1964-67, North Central Schs., Rogers, N.D., 1967-71; owner Valley Oil Co. and Northwestern Inds., 1969—. Columnist: Dakota Country, 1984-86. Mem. Valley City Commn., 1986. Republican. Congregational. Clubs: Valley City Rifle and Pistol (past pres.), Barnes County Wildlife (past pres.). Lodge: Elks, Eagles.

QADIR, GHULAM, psychiatrist; b. Jahania, Pakistan, Aug. 18, 1947; s. Mohammad Yar and Karam Khatoon; m. Shirin Akbar, Jan. 4, 1979; children: Nida, Rehmat, Rabah. MBBS, Nishtar Med. Coll., Pakistan, 1971. Diplomate Am. Bd. Psychiatry, Am. Acad. Behavioral Medicine. Resident in psychiatry Norwich Hosp., Conn., 1975-76, Maimonides Med. Ctr., Bklyn., 1976-78; physician Health Ministry Iran, Tehran, 1974-75; staff psychiatrist VA Med. Ctr., Allen Park, Mich., 1978-81; chief psychiatry Oakwood Hosp., Dearborn, Mich., 1983—; cons. psychiatrist Seaway Hosp., Trenton, Mich., 1979—, Riverside Hosp., Trenton, 1981—; attending psychiatrist Heritage Hosp., Taylor, Mich., 1981—. Contbr. articles to profl. jours. Served to capt. Pakistan Army, 1971-74. Fellow Acad. Psychosomatic Medicine; mem. Am. Psychiat. Assn., Am. Acad. Clin. Psychiatrists, Am. Assn. Psychiat. Adminstrs., Assn. Pakistani Physicians, Nishtar Med. Coll. Alumni Assn. N.Am. (pres. 1986-87). Office: Oakwood Med Bldg 18181 Oakwood Suite 305 Dearborn MI 48124

QAZI, HAROON MOHAMMED, plastic surgeon; b. Abbottabad, Pakistan, Apr. 10, 1937; came to U.S., 1963; m. Sabina Constance Qazi (div. 1983); children: Shamin, Naseem, Sarah, Danyal; m. Najma Awan Qazi, July 1986. FSc, Govt. Coll., Abbott-Abad, 1956; grad., Khyber Med. Coll., 1961. Intern Lady Reading Hosp., Peshawar, Pakistan, 1961-62, Deaconess Hosp., Buffalo, 1963-64; surgical resident VA Hosp., Ft. Howard, Md., 1964-66; chief surgical resident Sisters of Charity, Buffalo, 1966-67; resident in plastic surgery Colo. Med. Ctr., Denver, 1972-74; practice medicine specializing in plastic surgery Indpls., 1974—. Contbr. articles to profl. jour. Served to lt. col. U.S. Army, 1970-72. Mem. AMA, Am. Soc. Plastic and Reconstructive Surgery, Am. Assn. Hand Surgery, Am. Burn Assn., Ind. State Med. Soc., Pakistani Friendship Assn. Home: 7552 Chablis Circle Indianapolis IN 46000 Office: Plastic & Hand Surgery PC 1935 Capitol Ave Indianapolis IN 46202

QUAAL, WARD LOUIS, broadcasting executive; b. Ishpeming, Mich., Apr. 7, 1919; s. Sigfred Emil and Alma Charlotte (Larson) Q.; m. Dorothy J. Graham, Mar. 9, 1944; children—Graham Ward, Jennifer Anne. A.B., U. Mich., 1941; LL.D. (hon.), Mundelein Coll., 1962, No. Mich. U., 1967; D.Pub. Service, Elmhurst Coll., 1967; D.H.L. (hon.), Lincoln Coll., 1968, DePaul U., 1974. Announcer-writer radio Sta. WBEO (now sta. WDMJ), Marquette, Mich., 1936-37; announcer, writer, producer Sta. WJR, Detroit, 1937-41; spl. events announcer-producer WGN, Chgo., 1941-42, asst. to gen. mgr., 1945-49; exec. dir. Clear Channel Broadcasting Service, Washington, 1949-52; pres., chief exec. officer, asst. gen. mgr. Crosley Broadcasting Corp., Cin., 1952, v.p., asst. gen. mgr., 1953-56; v.p., gen. mgr., mem. bd. WGN Inc., Chgo., 1956-61, exec. v.p., then pres., 1961-74; pres. WGN Continental Broadcasting Co., Chgo., 1961-74, Ward L. Quaal Co., 1974—; former dir. Tribune Co.; dir., mem. exec. com. U.S. Satellite Broadcasting Corp., 1982—; dir. Universal Resources Corp., Christine Valmy Inc.; chmn. exec. com., dir. WLW Radio Inc., Cin., 1975-81;. Co-author: Broadcast Management, 1968. Mem., Hoover Commn. Exec. Br. Task Force, 1949-59; mem. U.S.-Japan Cultural Exchange Commn., 1960-70; mem. Pres.'s Council Phys. Fitness and Sports, 1983—; bd. dirs. Farm Found., 1963-73, MacCormac Jr. Coll., Chgo., 1974-80; chmn. exec. com. Council for TV Devel., 1969-72; bd. dirs. Broadcasters Found., Internat. Radio and TV Found., Sears Roebuck Found., 1970-73; trustee Mundelein Coll., 1962-72, Hillsdale Coll., 1966-72. Served as lt. USNR, 1942-45. Recipient Disting. Bd. Gov.'s award Nat. Acad. TV Arts and Scis., 1966, 87, Alumnus award U. Mich., 1967; award Freedoms Found., Valley Forge, 1966, 68, 70; Loyola U. Key, 1970; Advt. Man of Yr., Gold medallion, Chgo. Advt. Club, 1968; Advt. Club Man of Yr., 1973; Disting. Service award Nat. Assn. Broadcasters, 1973; Communicator of Yr., Jewish United Fund, 1969; Ill. Broadcaster of Yr. award, 1973, Press Vet. of Yr. award, 1973; Communications award of distinction Brandeis U., 1973; first recipient Sterling Medal, Barren Found., 1985; 1st person named to Better Bus. Bur. Hall of Fame, Council of Better Bus. Burs. Inc., 1975; named Radio Man of Yr. Am. Coll. Radio, Arts, Crafts & Scis., 1961. Mem. Broadcast Pioneers (pres., bd. dirs. 1962-73), Broadcast Pioneers Library (pres. 1981-84), Broadcast Pioneers Ednl. Fund Inc., Am. Advt. Fedn. (ethics com.), Delta Tau Delta (Disting. Service chpt.). Clubs: Mid-America; Exmoor Country (Chgo.); Marco Polo (N.Y.C.); Kenwood Golf and Country; Internat. (Washington); Lakeside Golf (North Hollywood, Calif.); Boulders Golf (Carefree, Ariz.). Home: 711 Oak Winnetka IL 60093 Office: 401 N Michigan Ave Suite 3140 Chicago IL 60611

QUADE, DAVID JON, manufacturing executive; b. Monroe, Wis., Sept. 23, 1954; s. Edward Herman and Lois Marie (Schuerman) Q.; m. Dee Ann Olson, July 29, 1978; children: Mitchell, Michelle. BBA in Acctg., U. Wis., 1976. CPA, Wis. Auditor Alexander Grant & Co., Madison, Wis., 1977-80, supr., 1980-82; controller Monroe (Wis.) Truck Equipment, Inc., 1982-85, v.p., 1985—. Bd. dirs. United Way Dane County, Madison, 1980. Mem. Am. Inst. CPA's, Wis. Inst. CPA's, Monroe C. of C. (bd. dirs.). Mem. United Ch. Christ. Clubs: Monroe Mons (bd. dirs. 1986—), Monroe Country. Lodge: Lions (Monroe chpt.). Avocations: golf, softball, skiing. Office: Monroe Truck Equipment Inc 1020 3d Ave Monroe WI 53566

QUALLY, ROBERT LEE, communications executive, graphic designer, filmmaker; b. Denver, Aug. 24, 1947; s. Ebner Milton and Alberta (Jackson) Q.; A.A., Northeastern Jr. Coll., 1970; B.F.A., Colo. State U., 1972. Partner, Quill Images, Fort Collins, Colo., 1970-72; sr. designer Salesvertising, Inc., Denver, 1972-74; design dir. Stephens, Biondi, DeCicco, Chgo., 1974; v.p., creative dir., producer Lee King & Partners, Inc., Chgo., N.Y.C., Los Angeles, 1974-79; pres., creative dir. Qually & Co., Inc., Evanston, Ill., Chgo., 1979—. Served with USNG, 1968-74. Recipient over 350 awards in design, art direction, producing and writing, including Clio award; Gold medal Art Dirs. Club. Mem. Am. Inst. Graphic Arts (medal), Soc. Typographic Art, Indsl. Graphics Internat., Chgo. Advt. Club, Chgo. Soc. Communication Arts. Colo. State U. Alumni Assn. (life) (bd. dirs. Chgo. chpt.). Republican. Club: Chgo. Athletic Assn. Author: 8 1/2" x 11", The Story of a Graphic Designer, 1980; 4 patents in field. Office: Huron Plaza 30 E Huron St Suite 2502 Chicago IL 60611

QUAMME, JACK O., rubber manufacturing company executive; b. Colorado Springs, Colo., Oct. 31, 1927; s. Clarence N. and Nora C. Q.; m. Virginia Anne, Sept. 6, 1959; children—Steven J., Julie Anne. B.A., Colo. Coll., 1950. Sales engr. Goodyear Tire & Rubber Co., Denver, 1950-52, Boise, Idaho, 1952-54, Los Angeles, 1954-59; with Dayco Corp., 1959—; regional mgr. Dayco Corp., Dallas/Atlanta, 1960-64; distbn. sales mgr. Dayco Corp., 1964-66, v.p. mktg., 1966-70; div. group v.p. Dayco Corp., Dayton, Ohio, 1970-74; pres. Dayco Rubber Products Co. div., 1975—, corp. group v.p., 1979—. Office: 333 W First St Dayton OH 45402

QUANSAH, JULIANA ABA, dentist; b. Apam, Ghana, Aug. 11, 1955; d. Sinclair Tufuantsi and Elizabeth Esi (Attumbu) Q.; m. Joseph Ofori-Dankwa, Oct. 1986. BS in Zoology, U. Mich., 1976, DDS, 1980. Assoc. Lawrence D. Crawford, DDS, Saginaw, Mich., 1980-83; dentist Community Action Com., Saginaw, 1981-83, Riverfront Dental, Saginaw, 1982-83; gen. practice dentistry Saginaw, 1984—. Chmn. Internat. Trend and Services Links, Inc. of Bay City, Saginaw, 1984—; bd. dirs. Headstart Program, Saginaw, 1985—. Recipient Appreciation award Averill Career Opportunities Ctr., Saginaw, 1986. Mem. ADA, Mich. Dental Assn., Saginaw County Dental Assn., Saginaw Valley Dental Assn., Midstate Study Club, NAACP, Africans Greater Flint, Inc., Saginaw C. of C. Democrat. Methodist. Avocations: traveling, reading. Home: 774 Foxboro Rd Saginaw MI 48603 Office: 1443 E Genesee Saginaw MI 48606

QUARLES, DENISE MARIE, prison warden; b. Detroit, Jan. 26, 1950; d. Leon George McDonald and Dorothy Kimble Booker; m. Larry Quarles, June 20, 1970 (div. 1983); m. Alvin Leonidus Whitfield, May 11, 1985. BS in Sociology, Eastern Mich. U., 1971; MA in Sociology, U. Detroit, 1977. Probation agent Mich. Dept. Corrections, Detroit, 1971-74, parole agent, 1974-77, community services liason, 1977, corrections ctr. supr., 1977-79; asst. dep. warden Mich. Dept. Corrections, Marquette, 1979-81; adminstr. Riverside Reception Ctr., Mich. Dept. Corrections, Ionia, 1981; dep. dir. probation services Mich. Dept. Corrections, Detroit, 1981-83; prison warden Huron Valley Women's Facility, Mich. Dept. Corrections, Ypsilanti, 1983-85, Riverside Correctional Facility, Mich. Dept. Corrections, Ionia, 1985—; mem. criminal justice adv. bd. Montcalm (Mich.) Community Coll., 1986; del. People to People conf., Seattle, 1987, Internat. Criminal Justice Del. to China, Japan and Hong Kong. bd. dirs. Big Brothers/Big Sisters, Marquette, 1980. Named one of Young Career Women of 1980, Bus. and Profl. Women's Club, Marquette. Mem. Mich. Corrections Assn. (life) (sec. 1977-78, v.p. 1978-79, pres. 1979-80), Am. Corrections Assn. Avocations: sewing, reading, walking. Office: Riverside Correctional Facility Mich Dept Corrections 777 W Riverside Dr Ionia MI 48843

QUARLES, MARY VIRGINIA, teachers union consultant; b. Nashville, Nov. 12, 1940; d. Chester Lew and Virginia Estelle (Cooper) Q. BA, Miss. Coll., 1962; MA, Fla. State U., 1970. Tchr. Brevard County Schs., Titusville, Fla., 1962-76; dir. Fontana/Chaffey UniServ, Calif., 1976-78, Cen. Wis. UniServ Council-West, Wausau, Wis., 1978—. Sunday Sch. dir. Calvary Bapt. Ch., Schofield, Wis., 1985-86, 1st Bapt. Ch., Wausau, 1986—. Mem. Indsl. Relations Research Assn., Am. Assn. Univ. Women, Fla. Teaching. Profls. div. NEA (bd. dirs. 1974-76). Democrat. Avocations: reading, travel, sewing. Home: 726 N 1st Ave Wausau WI 54401 Office: Cen Wis UniServ Council-West PO Box 1606 Wausau WI 54402-1606

QUARLES, MERVYN VINCENT, accountant; b. Augusta, Ga., Oct. 8, 1921; s. Oscar M. and Isabella C. (Irving) Q.; m. Margaret M. Kennedy, Sept. 16, 1948; children: Margaret M. Swanton, Mervyn V., James M., Janet Q. Baker, John W. CPA, Ill. Fin. officer Olson & Bartholomay, Chgo., 1966-71; founding pres. Quarles & Swanton Ltd., Homewood, Ill., 1971-85, cons., 1986—; bd. dirs. Am. Perforator Co., Inc., Bridgeview, Ill., 1981—. Treas., pres. Hazel Crest (Ill.) Community Chest, 1966-70; treas. Village of Hazel Crest; pres. South Suburban Estate Planning Council, Hazel Crest, 1981-82. Served to sgt. U.S. Army, 1942-48. Mem. Am. Inst. CPA's, Ill. CPA Soc. Roman Catholic. Office: 2711 W 183d St Homewood IL 60430

QUARTON, JEAN ELSA RULF, psychologist; b. Hartford, Conn., Mar. 29, 1942; d. Walter Otto and Elsa Margareta (Blume) Rulf; m. David T. Quarton, Aug. 25, 1973 (div.); m. Conrad L. Bergendoff, Feb. 9, 1980. B.F.A., R.I. Sch. Design, 1964; M.A. in Home Econs., U. Iowa, 1968, Ph.D., 1974. Lic. psychologist, Ill. Staff psychologist Riverside Retreat, 1974-76; pvt. practice clin. psychology, Rock Island, Ill., 1976-81; clin. cons. to Quad-cities Indsl. Employee Assistance Programs, Internat. Harvester, 3M, John Deere, J.I. Case, Rock Island arsenal, Army C.E., 1977-81; pvt. practice clin. psychology, LaGrange Park, Ill., 1981-84; cons. Quad-Cities Alcoholism Info. Ctrs., 1977-80, Davenport (Iowa) Sch. System, 1977-78; staff psychologist ACP, Chgo., 1982-84; pres. Accredited Affiliated Psychologists, P.C.; clin. cons. Gen. Motors, Reuben Donnelley, Continental Bank AT&T; adj. prof. psychology Augustana Coll., Rock Island, 1977; mgr. Chgo. Psychol. Assn. Telephone Answering Service, 1987—. Mem. Quad-cities Career Women's Network, 1978-81, keynote speaker, 1978; lectr. in field. Spl. Research asst. U. Iowa, 1970-73. Mem. Rock Island Psychol. Assn. (sec. 1980-81), Chgo. Psychol. Assn. (chmn. newsletter com. 1982-83, editor newsletter 1982-83, pres. 1986-87, chmn. program com. 1985-86), NOW, Bus. Networking Soc. (bd. dirs. Chgo. 1983—). Lutheran. Club: Bus. and Profl. Women's (chmn. pub. relations 1983-84, named Woman of Achievement 1983). Contbr. articles to profl. jours. Home and Office: 537 S 10th Ave LaGrange IL 60525

QUAYLE, DAN, U.S. senator; b. Indpls., Feb. 4, 1947; s. James C. and Corinne (Pulliam) Q.; m. Marilyn Tucker, Nov. 18, 1972; children—Tucker Danforth, Benjamin Eugene, Mary Corinne. B.S. in Polit. Sci, DePauw U., Greencastle, Ind., 1969; J.D., Ind. U., 1974. Bar: Ind. bar 1974. Ct. reporter, pressman Huntington (Ind.) Herald-Press, 1965-69, asso. pub., gen. mgr., 1974-76; mem. consumer protection div. Office Atty. Gen., State of Ind., 1970-71; adminstrv. asst. to gov. Ind. 1971-73; dir. Ind. Inheritance Tax Div., 1973-74; mem. 95th-96th Congresses, 4th Dist. Ind., U.S. Senate from Ind., 1981—; tchr. bus. law Huntington Coll., 1975. Mem. Huntington Bar Assn., Hoosier State Press Assn., Huntington C. of C. Republican. Club: Rotary. Office: 524 Hart Senate Office Bldg Washington DC 20510

QUAYLE, JOHN CLARE, video production specialist; b. Wyandotte, Mich., Dec. 18, 1956; s. John Corlett and Elizabeth Winnie (Goward) Q. BA, Mich. State U., 1980; cert. elem. edn., Madonna Coll., 1982. Telemktg. rep. Dial America Mark, Southfield, Mich., 1980-81; videographer United Cable TV Corp. Mich., Woodhaven, Mich., 1981—; substitute tchr. Taylor (Mich.) Sch. Dist., 1981-83; staff editor, show dir. Cath. TV Network Detroit, 1983—; dir. nat., local teleconfs. Pastoral Telecommunications Ctr. Archdiocese Detroit, 1985—. Produced, dir. SCAMP Sights '82; produced Long Run '82, Pass it On; dir., edited God's Gifts; edited Way to Go!. Vol., co-chmn. cable task force Christian Communications Council Met. Detroit Chs.; scoutmaster troop 1766 Bot Scouts Am., Wyandotte, Mich., 1986—. Mem. Internat. Video Assn., Internat. TV Assn., Nat. Acad. TV Arts and Scis. (Detroit chpt.), Detroit Area Film Tchrs., Detroit Producers Assn.,. Avocations: guitar, athletics, fitness. Home: 1529 Davis St Wyandotte MI 48192 Office: Archdiocese Detroit 305 Michigan Ave Detroit MI 48192

QUEEN, KENNETH LEE, sales professional; b. Caledonia, Mo., Feb. 27, 1932; s. Robert Roy and Mary Pearl (Bean) Q.; m. Barbara A. Bayless, Feb. 11, 1955; children: Roy Lee, Joseph Frederick. Div. sales mgr. Sun Refining and Mktg. Co., St. Louis, 1965—. Pres. Tournament of Champions, St. Louis, 1974-77; bd. dirs. Mathews Dickey Boys Club, St. Louis, 1975—; chmn. St. Louis Amateur Baseball Hall of Fame, 1981—; activities chmn. nonprofit orgn. Athletic Boys Club, 1964-71, pres. 1972-76. Recipient Cool Pappa Bell award Mathews Dickey Boys Club, 1974; named Khoury League Man of Yr., St. Louis, 1973, to Athletic Boys Club Hall of Fame, 1975. Methodist. Home: 2373 Lamadera Ln Florissant MO 63031 Office: Sun Refining & Mktg Co 3006 N Raceway Blvd Box 34257 Indianapolis IN 46234

QUERESHI, MOHAMMED YOUNUS, psychology educator, consultant; b. Haripur Hazara, Pakistan, Dec. 12, 1929; came to U.S., 1953; s. Mohammed Noor and Meryam Khatoon Q.; m. Nora Jane Knapp, May 27, 1958 (div. Nov. 1979); children—Ahmed, Amna, Shukria, Shawn; m. Farzana Kaukab, May 17, 1980; children—Ajmel, Sabeeha, Azem. Ph.D., U. Ill., 1958. Lic. psychologist, Wis. Asst. prof. psychology U. Minn., Duluth, 1960-62, U. N.D., Grand Forks, 1962-64; assoc. prof. psychology Marquette U., Milw., 1964-70, prof., 1970—, chmn. dept. psychology, 1971-77; cons. psychologist. Pres. 81st Street Sch. PTA, 1968-70; merit badge counselor Milw. County council Boy Scouts Am., 1973—; pres. Islamic Assn. Greater Milw., 1978-83. NIH grantee, 1962-69; Office of Edn. grantee, 1970-71; TOPS Club grantee, 1969-76. Mem. Am. Psychol. Assn., Psychometric Soc., Am. Statis. Assn., AAAS, Sigma Xi. Author: Statistics and Behavior: An Introduction, 1980; contbr. articles to sci. and profl. jours. Home: 2759 N 68th St Milwaukee WI 53210 Office: Marquette U 497 Shcroeder Health Sci and Edn Milwaukee WI 53233

QUERRY, RALPH PIKE, dentist; b. Rensselaer, Ind., Oct. 15, 1926; s. Guilford and Effie Louise (Pike) Q.; m. Barbara Lee Gottschalk, June 17, 1951; children: Mark Alan, Kevin Dale, Kent Douglas, Janice Lynette. DDS, Ind. U., Bloomington and Indpls., 1952. Gen. practice dentistry Fowler, Ind., 1952—. Served with USN, 1945-46, ETO. Methodist. Lodge: Rotary (pres. 1962-63). Home: 604 Sharon Ave Fowler IN 47944-0307 Office: State Rd 55 N Fowler IN 47944

QUICK, ALAN FREDERICK, university director; b. Marshall, Mich., Oct. 3, 1936; s. Frederick John and Edythe Jane (Pratley) Q.; m. Arlene Doris Ramsey, Aug. 16, 1958; children: Geoffrey, Gregory, Elizabeth. BA, Western Mich. U., 1958; MA, U. Mich., 1961; EdD, U. Oreg., 1963. Tchr. English Warren (Mich.) High Sch., 1958-61; supr. univ. Cen. Mich. U., Saginaw, 1963-65; dir., chmn. Cen. Mich. U., Mt. Pleasant, 1965-74, dean, 1975-82, dir. continuing edn., 1982—. Co-author: A Partnership of Students, 1975, Critical Incidents, 1976. Mem. Isabella Community Credit Union, Mt. Pleasant, 1984—, Gen. Fedn. Woman's Club, Mt. Pleasant, 1985—; bd. dirs. Mt. Pleasant Area Vols. for Literacy, 1983—. Mem. Am. Assn. for Adult & Continuing Edn., Mich. Assn. for Adult & Continuing, Assn. Tchr. Educators (pres. 1976-77), Nat. Univ. Extension Assn., Ducks Unltd. Episcopalian. Lodges: Lions, Kiwanis. Home: 620 West Court Hiawatha Dr Mount Pleasant MI 48858 Office: Cen Mich U Continuing Edn Community Services Rowe Hall 125 Mount Pleasant MI 48859

QUINE, DOUGLAS BOYNTON, biologist; b. Boston, Dec. 20, 1950; s. Willard VanOrman and Marjorie (Boynton) Q.; m. Maryclaire Matthews, July 13, 1979; 1 child, Alexander Boynton. BA, Princeton (N.J.) U., 1973; PhD, Cornell U., 1979. Postdoctoral fellow Dalhousie U., Halifax, Can., 1979-80, research assoc., 1980-82; research asst. prof. Tulane U., New Orleans, 1982-84, vis. asst. prof., 1983-84; assoc. prof. sci. Ill. Natural History Survey, Champaign, 1984—; affiliate assoc. prof. ethology, evolution and ecology U. Ill., Champaign, 1987—; safety cons. Princeton U., 1972-73; sci. cons. W.W. Norton Books, N.Y.C., 1978-79; pres. Triskelion Ltd., Urbana, Ill., 1983—. Contbr. articles on hearing, acoustics, bird navigation and multiple sclerosis to profl. jours. Paramedic Princeton U. First Aid and Rescue, 1972-73. Mem. IEEE, AAAS, Assn. Research Otolaryngology, N.Y. Acad. Sci., Animal Behavior Soc., Acoustical Soc. Am., Sigma Xi, Phi Kappa Phi. Clubs: Champaign-Urbana Stamp (pres. 1986-87). Avocations: stamp collecting, travel, reading, computers. Home: 1507 Lincolnwood Dr Urbana IL 61801 Office: Ill Natural History Survey Wildlife Sect 172 NRB 607 E Peabody Dr Champaign IL 61820

QUINLAN, DENIS DONAL, public relations executive; b. Chgo., Dec. 9, 1933; s. Denis P. and Kathleen (Burrows) Q.; m. Eileen B. Ward, Aug. 24, 1957; children: Denis J., Margaret M., Mary E., Therese A., John P. BS in Humanities, Loyola U., Chgo., 1955. Reporter, then asst. editor Chgo. Tribune, 1956-63; v.p., then sr. v.p. Carl Byoir & Assocs., Chgo., 1963-85; sr. v.p., prin. Pub. Communications, Inc., Chgo., 1985—. Recipient William Finnegan award Loyola U., 1975, Founder's award Loyola U., 1982. Mem. Pub. Relations Soc. Am. (film fest. chmn. 1987), Publicity Club of Chgo., Chgo. Press Vets. Roman Catholic. Club: Chgo. Press. Office: Pub Communications Inc 35 E Wacker Dr Chicago IL 60601

QUINLAN, MICHAEL ROBERT, fast food franchise company executive; b. Chgo., Dec. 9, 1944; s. Robert Joseph and Kathryn (Koerner) Q.; m. Marilyn DeLashmutt, Apr. 23, 1966; children: Kevin, Michael. BS, Loyola U., Chgo., 1967, MBA, 1970. With McDonald's Corp., Oak Brook, Ill., 1966—, v.p., 1974-76, sr. v.p., 1976-78, exec. v.p., 1978-79, chief ops. officer, 1979-80, pres. McDonald's U.S.A., 1980-82, pres., chief operating officer, 1982—, chief exec. officer, 1987—, dir. Republican. Roman Catholic. Clubs: Butterfield Country, Oakbrook Handball-Racquetball. Home: 720 Midwest Corp Oak Brook IL 60515 Office: McDonalds Corp 1 McDonald Plaza Oak Brook IL 60521 *

QUINLAN, ROBERT VAIL, electronic engineer, electronics manufacturing company executive; b. N.Y.C., Sept. 11, 1932; s. Robert LaMott and Maryon Elizabeth (Callahan) Q.; m. Eleanor Meta Schwick, July 15, 1961; children: David, Karen, Susan. BEE, U. Va., 1957; MEE, Yale U., 1958; MBA cum laude, Fairleigh Dickenson U., 1973. Asst. prof. engring. Purdue U., West Lafayette, Ind., 1963-66; dept. mgr. Western Union Corp., Mahwah, N.J., 1966-72; gen. mgr. Sanders Assocs., Inc., Nashua, N.H., 1972-76; v.p. Gen. Instrument, Inc., Towson, Md., 1976-80, Arvin Industries, Inc., Carroll, Ohio, 1980-86; pres. Diamond Electronics, Inc., Lancaster, Ohio, 1986—. Contbr. articles to profl. jours.; patentee in field. Chmn. indsl. liaison Ball State U., Muncie, Ind., 1963-66; mem. adv. council Franklin U., Columbus, Ohio, 1981—; advisor Jr. Achievement, Lancaster, Ohio, 1981—. Served as cpl. U.S. Army, 1952-54. Schlumberger fellow, 1958. Mem. IEEE (regional chmn. 1966), Am. Electronics Assn., Am. Mgmt. Assn., Instrument Soc. Am., Trigon Soc., Tau Beta Pi. Republican. Presbyterian. Club: Towson Country. Lodge: Rotary. Home: 9219 Indian Mound Rd Pickerington OH 43147

QUINN, DARYL CLIFTON, chemical engineer; b. Kansas City, Mo., Dec. 18, 1958; s. Ervin Brown and Dorothy (Palmer) Q.; m. Barbara Annette Dowdy, Jan. 16, 1982. BChemE, U. Mo., Rolla, 1981. Process engr. Allied Chem. Corp., Detroit, 1981-83; mgr. energy and engring. Allied Signal, Detroit, 1983—; advisor Lambton Coll, Sarnia, Can., 1983-85. Mem. Am. Inst. Chem. Engrs., Assn. Energy Engrs. Republican. Baptist. Home: 19347 Salem Dr Woodhaven MI 48183 Office: Allied Signal 1200 Zug Island Rd Detroit MI 48209

QUINN, JOHN JOSEPH, financial executive; b. Indpls., Oct. 16, 1947; s. Francis Bernard and Barbara Jean (Flynn) Q.; m. Mary Helen Lyons, June 14, 1969; children: Katherine Mary, John Joseph Jr. B in Bus. Adminstrn., U. Notre Dame, 1969. CPA, Ind. Staff acct. Ernst & Whinney, Indpls., 1969-71, sr. acct., 1971-73, mgr., 1973-76, sr. mgr., 1976-81, ptnr., 1981. Mem. Ind. CPA Soc., Chartered Life Underwriters (Indpls. chpt.), Fellow of Life Mgmt. Inst. Soc. Indpls. Roman Catholic. Clubs: Indpls. Athletic, Skyline. Home: 7705 Candlewood Ln Indianapolis IN 46250 Office: Ernst & Whinney One Indiana Sq Suite 3400 Indianapolis IN 46204

QUINN, JOHN STEVEN, counseling psychologist; b. Lynn, Mass., Apr. 4, 1947; s. Neal Albert and Alice Caroline (White) Q. AA, Monterey Peninsula Coll., 1967; BA, U. Tenn., 1970; MS, U. N.D., 1975; EdS, U. Toledo, 1976; M. Rehab. Counseling, Bowling Green State U., 1977; Ph.D., Kent State U., 1981. Lic. psychologist, cert. rehab. counselor; nat. cert. chemical dependency counselor, clin. mental health counselor. Cons. Midwest Exec. Search, Toledo, 1976-77; rehab. counselor Ohio Bur. Vocat. Rehab., Oregon, Ohio, 1977; grad. research asst. Kent State U., 1978-80; predoctoral psychology trainee Massillon (Ohio) State Hosp., 1980-81; instr. Pyramid Career Services, Canton, Ohio, 1981-82; alcoholism counselor Interval Brotherhood Home, Akron, Ohio, 1982-85; grad. instr. Walsh Coll., Canton, Ohio, 1982-83; instr. Cuyahoga Community Coll., Cleve., 1984, Malone Coll., Canton, 1986; pvt. practice cons. psychology, 1983—; psychol./ cons. Massillon State Hosp., 1986—; continuing edn. faculty Palmer Coll. Chiropractic, Davenport, Iowa, 1985—. Served to capt. USAF, 1970-75, capt. Ohio Air N.G., 1976-80; major in res., 1986—. Mem. Am. Psychol. Assn., Soc. for Personality Assessment, Am. Assn. Counseling and Human Devel., Ohio Psychol. Assn., Air Force Assn. Office: 1201 30th St NW Canton OH 44709

QUINN, LLOYD, oil and mining company executive; b. Mt. Vernon, Ill., Feb. 28, 1917; s. Robert and Elizabeth (Lee) Q.; m. Reva Stewart, Dec. 24, 1939; children: Dee Ann Quinn Redman, Joan. Grad. high sch., Mt. Vernon. Cost acct. Mt. Vernon Furnace Mfg., 1934-39; v.p. Keek-Gonnerman Co., Mt. Vernon, Ind., 1939-54; owner Automotive Color & Supply Co., Evansville, Ind., 1954-60; ptnr. Angermeier & Quinn Oil Co., Mt. Vernon, Ind., 1960-67; pres. Ecus Corp., Mt. Vernon, Ind., 1967—, Minerex Corp., Victor, Colo., 1982—; cons. on formation of mining cos., Victor, 1979—; cons. on drilling and exporation for gold and silver, Colo., 1979—. Mem. Am. Petroleum Inst., Ill. Oil and Gas Assn., Ky. Oil and Gas Assn. Methodist. Clubs: Western Hills Country (Mt. Vernon, Ind.), Petroleum (Evansville). Lodges: Elks, Masons. Avocations: travel, fishing. Home: 114 N 4th Victor CO 80860 Office: Quinn Energy Corp PO Box 470 Mount Vernon IN 47620

QUINN, MICHAEL ALBERT, utility executive; b. Kansas City, Mo., Feb. 2, 1945; s. Lester John and Bertha Louise (Ladzinski) Q.; m. Sharon Lynn Clark, June 10, 1967; 1 child, Kristin. BBA, Rockhurst Coll., Kansas City, 1967, MBA, 1978. Controller J.L. Daw & Assoc. Architects, Kansas City, 1970-72, Oldham Meat Packing, Kansas City, 1972-74; dir. fin. Pritchard Eng Constrn., Kansas City, 1974-78; v.p. Wagner Hohns Inglis, Inc., Kansas City, 1978-84; dir. contract adminstrn. U.S. Sprint, Kansas City, 1984—; cons. constrn. and claims litigation Kansas City, 1984—. Mem. Am. Mgmt. Assn., Nat. Contract Mgmt. Assn., Am. Arbitration Assn. Democrat. Roman Catholic. Lodge: Lions. Avocations: tennis, racquetball, basketball. Home: 5838 N Spruce Kansas City MO 64119

QUINN, MICHAEL ALFRED, employment and training executive; b. Roosevelt, Utah, Sept. 15, 1946; s. James J. Quinn and Metta (Morrill) Barnes; m. Dawn Schow, Feb. 5, 1970; children: Adam Boyd, Kenneth Lee. BS in Psychology, U. Utah, 1969, MBA, 1970; MA in Edn., U. Mich., 1982. Dir. employment and tng. Ute Indian Tribe, Duchesne, Utah, 1970-74; exec. dir. Lansing (Mich.) Tri-County Employment and Tng. Consortium, 1974—. Mem. Nat. Assn. Counties (bd. dirs. 1983—), Nat. Assn. Counties Tng. and Employment Programs (bd. dirs. 1980—), Nat. Job Tng. Partnership Assn. (bd. dirs. 1984—), Mich. Assn. Employment Tng. Dirs. (pres. 1982—). Office: Lansing Tri-County Employment and Tng Consortium 1850 W Mount Hope Ave Lansing MI 48910

QUINN, NANCY LOU, kindergarten educator; b. Lafayette, Ind., Nov. 18, 1956; d. Wayne C. Carmichael and Mae Etta Cobbs; m. Joseph Loyd Quinn, Aug. 8, 1975; 1 child, Mindy Richelle. BS, Ind. U., Kokomo, 1981, MS, 1987. Cert. elem. tchr. Tchr. Delphi (Ind.) Community Sch., 1981—. Mem. Phi Lambda Theta. Republican. Avocations: swimming, reading, dogs. Home: Rural Rt 3 Box 85 Delphi IN 46923 Office: Delphi Community Sch Vine & Wabash Delphi IN 46923

QUINN, PATRICIA ANNE, telecommunications marketing manager; b. Wisconsin Rapids, Wis., Mar. 30, 1949; d. William Martin and Mary Jane (McDonald) Q.; m. Phillip Vincent Price, May 18, 1974; children: William, Richard. BA in Econs., U. Wis., 1971, MA in Library Sci., 1972; MBA, Ind. U., 1977. Librarian Ind. State Library, Indpls., 1972-74; market research analyst BDP Corp., Indpls., 1974; fin. adminstr. Ind. U.-Purdue U., Indpls., 1975-77; assoc. engr. Ind. Bell Telephone Co., Indpls., 1977-79, product mgr., 1979—. Bd. dirs. Julian Ctr., Indpls., 1980-84, treas., 1982-84; mem. Jr. League, Indpls., 1986—. Mem. Am. Soc. Tng. and Devel., Am. Mktg. Assn. (v.p. 1981-82), SKL Leadership Group (exec. bd. dirs. 1986—). Home: 2950 W 42d St Indianapolis IN 46204

QUINN, PHILIP LAWRENCE, philosophy educator; b. Long Branch, N.J., June 22, 1940; s. Joseph Lawrence and Gertrude (Brown) Q. AB, Georgetown U., 1962; MS, U. Del., 1967; MA, U. Pitts., 1968, PhD, 1970; MA (hon.), Brown U., 1972. Asst. prof. philosophy Brown U., Providence, R.I., 1969-72, assoc. prof. philosophy, 1972-78, prof. philosophy, 1978-85, William Herbert Perry Faunce prof. philosophy, 1982-85; John A. O'Brien prof. philosophy U. Notre Dame, South Bend, Ind., 1985—. Author: (book) Divine Commnad and Moral Requirements, 1978; contbr. articles to profl. jours. Fulbright fellow, 1962-63; Danforth fellow, 1967-69. Mem. Am. Philos. Assn. (sec., treas. ea. div. 1982-85, chmn. career opportunities com. 1985—), Philosophy of Sci. Assn. (nominating com. 1984-86), Soc. Christian Philosophers (exec. com. 1981-84), N.Y. Acad. Sci. Roman Catholic. Avocations: reading, swimming, film, theatre. Home: 1645 Turtle Creek South Bend IN 46637 Office: U Notre Dame Dept Philosophy Notre Dame IN 46556

QUIÑONES, CARLOS RAMÓN, computer company executive; b. Humacao, P.R., Oct. 9, 1951; s. Carlos Manuel and Thelma Gloria (Aponte) Q.; m. Patricia Ann Russom, June 10, 1975; 1 child, Carlos Daniel. BS, Rensselaer Poly Inst., 1975; MBA, Cornell U., 1979. Plant engr. Met. Edison Co. Three Mile Island Nuclear Sta., Middletown, Pa., 1975-76; nuclear safety engr. Westinghouse Electric Corp., Madison, Pa., 1976-77; bus. advisor Exxon Enterprises, Inc., Florham Park, N.J., 1978; corp. planning cons. Emerson Electric Co., St. Louis, 1979-80, asst. to pres., chief operating officer, 1980-81, dir. planning and bus. devel., 1981-82; mgmt. cons. Theodore Barry & Assoc., N.Y.C., 1982-84; sec./treas., chief fin. officer Mylee Digital Scis., Inc., St. Louis, 1984—; cons. in field. Alfred P. Sloan Found. fellow, 1977-78, Exxon grad. fellow, 1978-79. Roman Catholic. Club: Cornell. Office: Mylee Digital Scis 433 Sovereign Ct Saint Louis MO 63011

QUINTANILLA, ANTONIO PAULET, physician, educator; b. Peru, Feb. 8, 1927; s. Leandro Marino and Edel Paulet Q.; came to U.S., 1963, naturalized, 1974; Ph.D., San Marcos U., 1948, M.D., 1957; m. Mary Parker Rodriguez, May 2, 1958; children—Antonio Paulet, Angela, Francis, Cecilia, John. Asso. prof. physiology U. Arequipa, Peru, 1960-63; asso. in physiology Cornell U., N.Y., 1963-64; prof. physiology U. Arequipa, 1964-68; asso. prof. medicine Northwestern U., 1969-80, prof., 1980—; chief renal sect. VA Lakeside Hosp., 1976—; lectr.; mem. adv. bd. Kidney Found. Ill., Am. Fedn. Clin. Research. Fellow A.C.P.; mem. Chgo. Heart Assn. (hypertension council), Central Soc. Clin. Research, Am. Soc. Clin. Pharmacology and Therapeutics, Am., Internat. socs. nephrology, Chgo. Soc. Internal Medicine, Am. Physiol. Soc. Contbr. articles on renal disease to med. jours.; author books. Home: 500 Ridge Ave Evanston IL 60202 Office: 333 E Huron St Chicago IL 60611

QUINTON, GRANVILLE LEWIS, amusement and transportation manufacturing company official; b. Magazine, Ark., Nov. 23, 1941; s. William Lewis and Nancy Lucille (Holt) Q.; m. Rebecca Lee Griffith, Nov. 18, 1966; children—Brant Lewis, Misty Renea. B.S. in Acctg., Central State U., Edmond, Okla. Cert. auditor and info. systems auditor. Joint venture auditor Champlin Petroleum, Enid, Okla., 1970-72; corp. systems mgr. TG4Y Stores Co., Oklahoma City, 1972-77; EDP and operational audit mgr. Pizza Hut, Inc., Wichita, Kans., 1977-78; dir. audit Cessna Aircraft Co., Wichita, 1978-85; controller Chance Industries Inc., Wichita, 1986—. Author seminar in field. Served with USAF, 1960-64. Mem. Inst. Internal Auditors (pres. 1977-78, dir. Wichita 1978—, chmn. CIA exam. Wichita 1979—, CIA rev. chmn. 1979—), EDP Auditors Assn. Lodge: Masons. Home: 16110 Manor Rd Wichita KS 67230 Office: Chance Industries Inc 4219 Irving Wichita KS 67277

QUIRK, NEIL PATRICK, food service consultant; b. St. Louis, July 1, 1940; s. Harold Edward and Josephine Louise (Schwalm) Q.; m. Susan Marie Walck, Apr. 12, 1969; children: N. Patrick, Kathleen Marie. BS in Bus., St. Louis U., 1962; MS in Food Service and Lodging, U. Mo., 1977. Owner The Dunraven Inn, Estes Park, Colo., 1970-73; gen. mgr. Holiday Enterprises, Cleve., 1973-75; fin. officer U.S. Small Bus. Adminstrn., St. Louis, 1977-83; owner, cons. Quirk & Co., Frontenac, Mo., 1983—. Bd. dirs., exec. com. Crusade Against Crime, St. Louis, 1980—. Served to lt. USN, 1963-70, Vietnam. Mem. Restaurant Bus. Research Adv. Panel. Roman Catholic. Avocations: golf, gardening. Home and Office: 12 Glen Abby Dr Frontenac MO 63131

QUISENBERRY, BOBBY RAY, safety professional, retired military officer, consultant; b. Goodlett, Tex., July 22, 1941; s. Jesse Edward and Audra Marie (Castle) Q.; m. Patricia Ann Staples, Sept. 22, 1961; 1 child, Clinton E. BS in Agrl. Econs., Texas A&M U., 1963; postgrad., Cen. Mich. U., 1985—. Cert. occupational health and safety tech. Mgmt. trainee Sears Roebuck & Co., Amarillo, Tex., 1963-66; commd. 2d lt. USAF, 1966, advanced through grades to lt. col.; served as missile launch officer, missile systems instr., missile systems evaluator USAF, various locations, 1966-75; chief safety div. USAF, Little Rock (Ark.) AFB, 1975-79; ret. USAF, 1986; chief weapons safety div. SAC, Offutt AFB, Nebr., 1979-86; system safety mgr. Titan II deactivation, USAF, Washington, 1981-86. Recipient 4 Commendation medals, 1968-79, Meritorious Service medal, 1986, Spl. Achievment award USAF, 1981. Mem. System Safety Soc., Am. Soc. Safety Engrs., Ret. Officers Assn., Air Force Assn., Greater Omaha Commodore Users Group (pres. 1983-86). Avocations: computers, horticulture, breeding exotic birds. Home: 2932 Leawood Dr Omaha NE 68123 Office: HQ SAC/IGFW Offutt AFB NE 68113

QUTUB, MUSA YACUB, hydrogeologist, educator, consultant; b. Jerusalem, June 2, 1940; came to U.S., 1960; s. Yacub and Sarah Q.; married, July 21, 1971; children: Hania, Jennan. B.A. in Geology, Simpson Coll., Indianola, Iowa, 1964; M.S. in Hydrogeology, Colo. State U., 1966; Ph.D in Water Resources, Iowa State U. Sci. and Tech., 1969. Instr. Iowa State U., Ames, 1966-69; asst. prof., assoc. prof., prof. Northeastern Ill., Chgo., 1969—; cons. hydrogeology, Des Plaines, Ill., 1970—; sr. adviser Saudi Arabian Ministry Planning, Riyadh, 1977-78; leader U.S. environ. sci. del. to People's Republic of China, 1984; pres., founder Islamic Info. Ctr. Am. Contbr. numerous articles to profl. jours. NSF grantee, 1971; grantee State of Ill., 1974, Dept. Edn. Mem. Ill. Earth Sci. Edn. (pres. 1971-73), Nat. Assn. Geology Tchrs. (pres. central sect. 1974), Internat. Assn. Advancement of Earth and Environ Sci. (pres. 1975—). Muslim. Avocations: tennis, track, cross country, soccer.

RAABE, JANIS ASAD, educational writer and consultant; b. Lakewood, Ohio, Apr. 28, 1949; d. Theodore Charles and Jenifer Irene (Snitko) Asad; student St. John Coll. of Cleve., 1967-69; BS in Edn., Bowling Green (Ohio) State U., 1971, MEd in Reading, 1972; m. Richard A. Raabe, Aug. 11, 1972; children: Jason Richard, Mark Richard. Reading tchr. and cons. Mentor-Ridge Jr. High Sch., Mentor, Ohio, 1972-75; writer ednl. materials Modern Curriculum Press, Cleve., 1972—; freelance editorial cons. Ohio Dept. Edn., 1975-77; ednl. cons. Coronet Instructional Media, Chgo., 1976-79. Named one of Outstanding Young Women of Am., 1978. Mem. Internat. Reading Assn., Ohio Reading Assn., Kappa Delta Pi. Author: MCP Phonics Practice Readers, sets 1-4, 1974-86, MCP Kindergarten Reading Program, 1972-86; ednl. cons. Read-Along Beginning Phonics, sets 1 and 2, 1978. Home: 5901 Kerry Circle NW Canton OH 44718

RABB, GEORGE B., zoologist; b. Charleston, S.C., Jan. 2, 1930; s. Joseph and Teresa C. (Redmond) R.; m. Mary Sughrue, June 10, 1953. B.S., Coll. Charleston, 1951; M.A., U. Mich., 1952, Ph.D., 1957. Teaching fellow zoology U. Mich., 1954-56; curator. coordinator research Chgo. Zool. Park, Brookfield., Ill., 1956-64; asso. dir. research and edn. Chgo. Zool. Park, 1964-75, dep. dir., 1969-75, dir., 1976—; research asso. Field Mus. Natural History, 1965—; lectr. dept. biology U. Chgo., 1965—; mem. Com. on Evolution Biology, 1969—; pres. Chgo. Zool. Soc., 1976—; mem. steering com. Species Survival Commn., Internat. Union Conservation of Nature, 1983—, vice chmn. for N.Am., 1986—, bd. dirs. 1987—. Fellow AAAS; mem. Am. Soc. Ichthyologists and Herpetologists (pres. 1978), Herpetologists League, Soc. Systematic Zoology, Soc. Mammalogists, Soc. Study Evolution, Ecol. Soc. Am., Soc. Conservation Biology (council mem. 1986—), Am. Soc. Zoologists, Soc. Study Animal Behavior, Am. Assn. Museums, Am. Soc. Naturalists, Am. Assn. Zool. Parks and Aquariums (dir. 1979-80), Internat. Union Dirs. Zool. Gardens, Am. Com. Internat. Conservation, Chgo. Council Fgn. Relations (Chgo. com.), Sigma Xi. Club: Economic (Chgo.). Office: Chgo Zool Park Brookfield IL 60513

RABE, RICHARD FRANK, dentist, lawyer; b. Crystal Lake, Iowa, May 19, 1919; s. Otto Henry and Agnes Marie (Juhl) R.; m. Barbara Jean McNeal, Mar. 15, 1946; children—Richard Frank, Mary Elizabeth, Kathleen Ann, Michelle. A.A., Waldorf Coll., 1938; D.D.S., U. Iowa, 1942; J.D., Drake U., 1952. Bar: Iowa 1952. Practice dentistry, Des Moines, 1946—; sole practice law, Des Moines, 1952—; cons. M.F. Patterson Dental Supply Co., 1956-61, Nat. Bd. Dental Examiners, 1955-60; chmn. Iowa Bd. Dental Examiners, 1962-63, Iowa Bd. Nursing Home Examiners, 1980-84; lectr. dental assns. throughout U.S., Contbr. articles to profl. jours. Fellow Am. Coll. Dentists; mem. ADA (Vice chmn. council on legis. 1977-78), Am. Acad. Dental Practice Adminstrn., Iowa Dental Study Club (past pres.), Iowa Dental Assn. (pres. 1972, trustee 1960-71), ABA, Iowa Bar Assn., Des Moines Dist. Dental Soc. (past pres.), Milw. Dental Research Group, Central Regional Dental Testing Agy., Am. Inst. Parliamentarians., Psi Omega, Delta Theta Phi. Episcopalian. Clubs: Des Moines Golf and Country. Lodge: Masons, Shriners. Avocations: sailing; flying. Home: 5709 N Waterbury Rd Des Moines IA 50312 Office: 5709 N Waterbury Rd Des Moines IA 50312

RABIN, BARRY EDWARD, psychiatrist; b. Chgo., Oct. 1, 1942; s. Henry and Rebecca (Itzkowitz) R.; m. Nancy Joan McGonagill, Apr. 7, 1973; children: Jason, Jennifer, Jessica. Student, U. Ill., 1960-63, MD, 1967. Diplomate Am. Bd. Psychiatry and Neurology. Resident in psychiatry Loyola U., Maywood, Ill., 1970-73, dir. resident tng., 1973-75; dir. alcohol treatment Alexander Hosp., Elk Grove Village, Ill., 1975; dir. psychiatry St. Joseph Hosp., Elgin, Ill., 1975—; Cons. Ill. Dept. Pub. Health, Springfield, 1977-79. Served to capt. U.S. Army, 1968-70, Vietnam. Office: 860 Summit St Elgin IL 60120

RABOURN, WILLIAM BRADLEY, JR., marketing executive; b. Rolla, Mo., Mar. 17, 1958; s. William Bradley and Carol Jean (Smith) R.; m. Cynthia Lynn Helm, Sept. 27, 1986. BS in Mgmt., BS in Mktg., Southwest Mo. State U., 1980. Field rep. Marion Labs., Kansas City, Mo., 1980-81; v.p. mktg. Clean Car Products, Sedalia, Mo., 1981-82; 1st v.p., dir. mktg. Great So. S & L, Springfield, Mo., 1982—. Contbr. articles to profl. jours. and mags. Bd. dirs. Girls Club, Springfield, 1987—, Park Cen. Hosp., Springfield, 1982-86, Am. Cancer Soc., Jefferson City, 1984—, and Springfield, 1985—. Republican. Roman Catholic. Club: Hickory Hills Country. Avocations: jogging, swimming, golf, basketball, tennis. Home: 3535 S Weller Springfield MO 65804 Office: Great So Savs & Loan Assn 430 S Avenue Springfield MO 65806

RACE, JOHN STEPHEN, electronics executive; b. Evansville, Ind., Sept. 19, 1942; s. John Edward and Mary Rosetta (Doran) R.; children: Kimberly

Anne, John Kevin, Erin Nichole. BS in Physics, Ind. U., 1964. Adminstr. quality improvement RCA, Bloomington, Ind., 1964-70, mgr. quality control, 1971-72; mgr. prodn. engring. and quality assurance RCA, Juanez, Mexico, 1972-74, mgr. mfg. and prodn. engring., 1975-76; mgr. mfg. technology RCA, Indpls., 1976-80; pres. Hirata Corp. of Am., Indpls., 1980—, also bd. dirs. Contbr. articles to profl. jours. Appointed to Ind. dist. export council, Indpls., 1982—; subcom. chair Peace Games, Indpls., 1977—. Mem. Soc. Mfg. Engrs., Machine Vision Assn., Robotics Inst. Am., Midwest Bdminton Assn., U.S. Badminton Assn., Sigma Pi Sigma. Home: 5250 Hawthorne Dr Indianapolis IN 46226 Office: Hirata Corp of Am 3901 Industrial Blvd Indianapolis IN 46254

RACHELSON, HOWARD SAMUEL, marketing executive; b. Atlanta; s. Alexander and Henrietta (Berger) R.; m. Deborah Ann Manchak, Aug. 15, 1975. Student, Campbell Coll., 1968-70; BS in Psychology, Old Dominion U., 1972, MS in Edn., 1976; MBA, Lake Forest (Ill.) Sch. Mgmt., 1984. Product specialist Paslode div. Signode, Skokie, Ill., 1978-84; sales rep. to product specialist Lovejoy Electric, Downers Grove, Ill., 1984-86; product mktg. mgr. Johnson Controls, Naperville, Ill., 1986—. Mem. Am. Mktg. Assn. Avocations: snorkeling, bicycling, tennis.

RACIAK, RITA ROBERTA, communications company official; b. Chgo., Dec. 7, 1946; d. Stanley Joseph and Jeanne (Tokarz) R.; m. John Lasky, May 21, 1983. B.A. in Mktg., Mundelein Coll., 1980. With Sears, Roebuck and Co., Chgo., 1964-72; office mgr. Diaz & Co. Real Estate, 1972-73, Midwest Montessori Tchr. Tng. Ctr., 1973-74, Ben Friend Real Estate, 1974-75, By Jove Inc. Real Estate, Chgo., 1975-76; sec. to chmn. bd. Burke Communication Industries, Inc., Chgo., 1976-79, estimating service coordinator, 1979-80, dir. advt., producer audio/visual programs, meeting planner, 1980—; lectr. Oakton Community Coll., 1981. Clubs: Chgo. Advt., Women's Advt. of Chgo. Composer: Waves of the North Atlantic, 1982, Barbara's Waltz, 1982. Home: 279 Maureen Dr Wheeling IL 60090 Office: Burke Communication Industries 1165 N Clark St Chicago IL 60610

RACLIN, ERNESTINE MORRIS, banker; b. South Bend, Ind., Oct. 25, 1927; d. Ernest M. and Ella L. Morris; m. O.C. Carmichael, Jr., Sept. 28, 1946; children: Carmen Carmichael Murphy, O.C., III, Ernestine Carmichael Nickle, Stanley Clark; m. Robert L. Raclin, July 22, 1977. Student, St. Mary's Coll., South Bend, 1947; LL.D. (hon.), U. Notre Dame, 1978, Ind. State U., 1981; L.H.D. (hon.), Converse Coll., 1974. Chmn. Marshall County Bank & Trust Co., Plymouth, Ind., 1976—, Bremen State Bank, 1976—, FBT Bancorp., Inc., South Bend, 1976—, 1st Source Corp., 1st Source Bank; dir. First Chgo. Corp., No. Ind. Pub. Service Co.; chmn. bd. Marshall County Bank, Plymouth and Bremen State Bank, FBT Bancorp. Trustee U. Notre Dame, 1973—, Converse Coll., 1976—; bd. govs. United Way Am., UWA Internat., 1973-80; bd. dirs. Mich. Public Broadcasting, South Bend Jr. Achievement, 1978—, Ind. Vocat. Tech. Coll., United Way of Ind. Recipient E.M. Morris Meml. award Ind. Acad., Community Service award St. Mary's Coll., Ivy Tech's Excellence in Edn. award, Edmund F. Ball award Ind. Pub. Broadcasting Soc. Mem. South Bend/Mishawaka Area C. of C. (dir. 1977—, chmn.-elect 1986, Woman of Yr. award 1970). Republican. Presbyterian. Clubs: Summit (South Bend); Ocean (Delray Beach, Fla.); Signal Point (Niles, Mich.). Office: 4th Floor 100 N Michigan St South Bend IN 46601

RACZ, VICTORIA ELIZABETH, sculptress; b. Detroit, May 11, 1955; d. Victor Joseph and Elizabeth (Horvath) R.; divorced. BFA with distinction, Wayne State U., 1977. Cert. tchr., Mich. Artist and restorer Racz Art Services, Allen Park, Mich., 1973—; tchr. Allen Park Pub. Schs., 1978-82, Birmingham (Mich.) Pub. Schs., 1982-84; sculptress Gen. Motors Co., Warren, Mich., 1984—; art instr. adult edn. Melvindale (Mich.) and Northern Allen Park, 1978-82. Recipient Homemaker award Betty Crocker Co., 1973. Mem. Assn. Profl. Photographers (cert. airbrush artist). Republican. Clubs: 356 Porsche; Hamilton Place Athletic (Southfield); Vic Tanny Internat. Avocations: swimming, cooking, sports cars. Home: 18202 Beverly Birmingham MI 48009

RADCLIFFE, GERALD EUGENE, judge, lawyer; b. Chillicothe, Ohio, Feb. 19, 1923; s. Maurice Gerald and Mary Ellen (Wills) R.; m. Edythe Kennedy, Aug. 11, 1947; children—Jerilynn K. Radcliffe Ross, Pamela J. Radcliffe Dunn. B.A., Ohio U., 1948; J.D., U. Cin., 1950. Bar: Ohio 1950, U.S. Dist. Ct. 1951, U.S. Supreme Ct. 1957. Sole practice, Chillicothe, 1950-66; asst. pros. atty. Ross County, Ohio, 1966-70; acting mcpl. judge Chillicothe Mcpl. Ct., 1970-72; judge probate, juvenile divs. Ross County Ct., Chillicothe, 1973—; mem. rules adv. com. Ohio Supreme Ct., 1984; mem. Ohio Legis. Oversite com., 1974-81; trustee Ohio Jud. Coll., 1979. Editor Cin. Law Rev., 1949-50. Co-author: Constitutional Law, 1979. Contbr. articles to profl. jours. Project dir. South Central Ohio Regional Juvenile Detention Ctr., 1971-72; co-chmn. Chillicothe United Way Fund Campaign, 1972; mem. Youth Services Adv. Council, 1984. Recipient Outstanding Citizen of Yr. award, Jr. C. of C., 1972, Superior Jud. award Ohio Supreme Ct., 1976-82, Meritorious Service award Probate Ct. Judges Ohio, 1984, Dirs. award Ohio Dept. Youth Services, 1984. Mem. Ohio Juvenile Judges Assn., (pres. 1983-84), Nat. Council Juvenile and Family Ct. Judges (trustee 1982-84), Ohio Jud. Conf. Democrat. Lodges: Kiwanis (lt. gov. 1983-84, Ohio Statehood Achievement award 1979), Masons. Avocation: golf. Home: 5 Edgewood Ct Chillicothe OH 45601 Office: Ross County Juvenile and Probate Ct Corner Paint and Main Sts Chillicothe OH 45601

RADEMACHER, EARL ELVIN, educational administrator; b. Loup City, Nebr., July 8, 1933; s. Elvin J. and Wilma (Sickels) R.; m. JoAnn J. White, Dec. 27, 1959; children: Steve, Jane, Susan, John. BA, Kearney (Nebr.) State Coll., 1954; MA, U. No. Colo., 1958. Tchr. Douglas (Nebr.) Pub. Schs., 1956-58, York (Nebr.) Pub. Schs., 1958-60; asst. registrar, bus. mgr. Kearney State Coll., 1960-75, v.p., 1975-82, 83—, acting pres., 1982-83. Bd. dirs., treas. Kearney Community Ctr., 1985-86; bd. dirs. Kearney Red Cross, Kearney United Way, 1985-86, Kearney Hosp., 1986—. Served with U.S. Army, 1954-56. Named one of Outstanding Young Men Am., 1968. Mem. Nat. Assn. Coll. and Univ. Bus. Officers, Cen. Assn. Coll. and Univ. Bus. Officers. Democrat. Presbyterian. Lodges: Kiwanis (pres. Kearney, named Outstanding Club Sec.), Elks. Avocations: tennis, golf, gardening, photography. Home: 1107 W 35 Kearney NE 68847

RADEMACHER, GARY EDWARD, marketing consultant; b. Newkirk, Okla., July 7, 1938; s. Delmer Edward and Sara Anna (Komma) R.; m. Joyce Ann Woodard, June 7, 1962 (div. 1982); children: Thea, Phillip, Ross. BA, Wichita (Kans.) State U., 1962. TV and radio personality Stas. KAKE and KAKE-TV, Wichita, 1959-69; sales mgr. Swanco Broadcasting Co., Wichita, 1969-72; sales mgr., owner Sta. KLIN, Lincoln, Nebr., 1971-75; sales mgr. Sta. WREN, Topeka, 1975-76; pres. Midwest Mktg., Topeka, 1976, also bd. dirs.; cons. Christian Booksellers Assn., Colorado Springs, Colo., 1978-79, Menswear Retailers Am., Washington, 1983-84. Author: Manger's Marketing and Advertising Course, 1978. Served with U.S. Army, 1961-64. Republican. Mennonite. Office: Midwest Mktg 512 W 14th St Topeka KS 66612

RADEMACHER, HOLLIS WILLIAM, banker; b. Spencer, Iowa, Aug. 19, 1935; s. Bernard William and Helen Dorothy (Hollis) R.; m. Carolyn Alice Frisk, Sept. 21, 1957; children—William, Robert. B.B.A., U. Minn., 1957. With Continental Ill. Nat. Bank & Trust Co. Chgo., 1957—, successively 2d v.p., v.p., sr. v.p., now exec. v.p. and chief credit officer, 1984—; participant RMA Credit Policy Roundtable, 1983, 84. Mem. Am. Bankers Assn. (div. chmn. 1978-83), Nat. Futures Assn. (bd. dirs. Chgo. sect. 1982-84). Republican. Episcopalian. Clubs: Bankers, Executives, Economic (Chgo.). Avocations: golf; skiing; tennis; fishing.

RADEMACHER, RICHARD JOSEPH, librarian; b. Kaukauna, Wis., Aug. 20, 1937; s. Joseph Benjamin and Anna (Wyuts) R.; m. Mary Jane Liethen, Feb. 12, 1966; children: Alicia Mary, Ann Marie, Amy Rose. A.B., Ripon Coll., 1959; M.S., Library Sch. U. Wis., 1961. Dir. Kaukauna Public Library, 1964-66, Eau Claire (Wis.) Public Library, 1966-69; librarian Salt Lake City Public Library, 1969-76; dir. Wichita (Kans.) Public Library, 1976—. Bd. dirs. Salt Lake Art Center, Reading Room for the Blind.; mem. Kans. Com. for the Humanities, 1977-82; mem. exec. bd. Wichita Girl Scouts, 1977—. Served with AUS, 1962-64. Mem. ALA; Mem. Mountain Plains Library Assn. (sect. chmn.); mem. Kans. Library Assn. (pres. 1982-83); Mem. Wichita Library Assn. Office: 223 S Main St Wichita KS 67202

RADEN, LOUIS, tape and label corporation executive; b. Detroit, June 17, 1929; s. Harry M. and Joan (Morris) R.; m. Mary K. Knowlton, June 18, 1949; children: Louis III, Pamela (Mrs. T.W. Rea III), Jacqueline. BA, Trinity Coll., 1951; postgrad. NYU, 1952. With Time, Inc., 1951-52; with Quaker Chem. Corp., 1952-63, sales mgr., 1957-63; exec. v.p. Gen. Tape & Supply, Inc., Detroit, 1963-68, pres., chmn. bd., 1969—; pres. Mich. Gun Clubs, 1973-77. Fifth reunion chmn. Trinity Coll., 1956, pres. Mich. alumni, 1965-72, sec. Class of 1951, 81-86, pres. 1986—; trustee, v.p. Mich. Diocese Episcopal Ch., 1980-82, mem. urban evaluation com., 1975-78, chmn. urban evaluation com., 1978, chmn. urban affairs com., 1977-79; vice chmn. bd. dirs. Robert H. Whitaker Sch. Theology, 1983-85; founding sponsor World Golf Hall of Fame; mem. Founders Soc. Detroit Inst. Arts. Mem. Nat Rifle Assn. (life), Nat. Skeet Shooting Assn. (life, nat. dir. 1977-79), Greater Detroit Bd. Commerce, Automotive Industry Action Group, Mich. C. of C., U.S. C. of C., Greater Hartford Jaycees (exec. v.p. 1955-57, Key Man award 1957), Theta Xi (life; Disting. Service award 1957, alumni pres. 1952-57, regional dir. 1954-57). Republican. Clubs: Detroit Golf, Detroit Gun, Katke-Cousins Golf, Black Hawk Indians, Pinehurst Country; Oakland U. Pres.'s, Round Table. Home: 1133 Ivyglen Circle Bloomfield Hills MI 48013 Office: 7451 W Eight Mile Rd Detroit MI 48221

RADER, CHARLES MAYER, clinical psychologist, research consultant; b. Bklyn., Aug. 22, 1950; s. Milton Joseph and Edna (Saperstein) R.; m. Marcea Edith Kjervik, Sept. 8, 1985; 1 child, Kirk Martin. BA, Hamilton Coll., 1972; PhD, U. Minn., 1979. Lic. cons. psychologist, Minn. Psychol. assoc. Hennepin County Mental Health Ctr., Mpls., 1976-78; cons. Woodview Detention Home, St. Paul, 1976-77; cons. Youth Employment Programs, Mpls., 1978-79; clin. psychologist Vinson Mental Health Clinic, St. Paul, 1980-83; sr. clin. psychologist Ramsey County Mental Health Clinic, St. Paul, 1983—; guest lectr., cons. to treatment programs, group homes. Bd. dirs. Alpha House, Mpls., 1975—, v.p., 1979-81, pres., 1981-83; mem. adv. bd. Guild Hall, St. Paul, 1981—; precinct del. Dem. Farmer Labor Party, 1976-86, chmn., 1978-81; counselor Walk In Counseling Ctr., 1979-80, Neighborhood Involvement Program, 1979-80; mem. utilization rev. bd. Norhaven and Sur la Rue, 1983—; mem. planning com. Minn. Network for Disaster Stress Intervention, 1985-86, human rights com. Custom Contracts, St. Paul, 1986—. Mem. Am. Psychol. Assn., Minn. Psychol. Assn., Am. Soc. for Study Mental Imagery, Phi Beta Kappa, Sigma Xi. Jewish. Contbr. articles to profl. jours., chpt. to book. Home: 5817 Creek Valley Rd Edina MN 55435 Office: Ramsey County Mental Health Clinic 529 Jackson St Saint Paul MN 55101

RADER, TRACY LEANNE, service credit company executive, controller; b. Wichita, Kans., Aug. 7, 1961; d. Richard Allen and Kaye Sharon (Hoffman) R. Student, Dekalb Community Coll., Atlanta, Tarrant (Tex.) County Community Coll., 1979-80. Pharmacist asst. Skillern's Drugs, Garland, Tex., 1978-79; salesman Target, Ft. Worth, 1979-80; with credit and collections dept. Haverty's Furniture, Atlanta, 1980-81; adminstrv. asst. Borg-Warner Acceptance Corp., Atlanta, 1981-84; controller U.S. Credit Service Corp., St. Louis, 1984-87, v.p., controller, 1987—. Mem. Nat. Assn. Female Execs. Republican. Methodist. Home: 8837 Wrenwood Ln Brentwood MO 63144 Office: US Credit Service corp 1750 S Brentwood Blvd Saint Louis MO 63144

RADFORD-HILL, SHEILA AUDREY, community educator; b. Chgo., Dec. 12, 1949; s. James Henry and Ruth Audrey (Bolds) Radford; divorced; 1 child, Ericka Nayram Hill. BA, De Paul U., Chgo., 1972; MA in Am. Studies, U. Pa., 1973. Dir. program Drexel U., Phila., 1973, resident dir., 1974-75; dir. extended learning Cen. YMCA, Chgo., 1977-81; tng. assoc. Designs for Change, Chgo., 1981-84; dir. tng. Chgo. Area Project, 1984—; lectr. Chgo. State U., 1975-77, U. Ill., Chgo., 1986, Roosevelt U., Chgo., 1977—. Contbr. articles and reports on various civil and social change topics, 1977—. Trainer 29th Ward People's Assembly, Chgo., 1980; trainer, organizer Ill. Minority Women's Caucus, Chgo., 1982—; researcher, writer Citizens to Elect A. King, Chgo., 1986; organizer Chgo. Area Project Conv., 1985. Minority fellow Ford Found., 1972, Schmidt Acad. fellow De Paul U., 1972; recipient Disting. Contributions award Nat. Assn. Sch. Psychologists, Pa., 1984. Mem. Midwest Modern Lang. Assn. (chmn. women's studies 1983), North Shore Examiners Assn. (writer, columnist). Democrat. Lutheran. Club: Triangle Investment (pres. 1981—). Avocations: reading, feminist polit. theory. Office: Chgo Area Project 407 S Dearborn St Suite 1125 Chicago IL 60606

RADINSKY, STEPHEN HARRIS, radiologist; b. St. Louis, Jan. 8, 1942; s. Albert and Lee (Zemel) R.; m. Myra Warshafsky, Aug. 7, 1966; children: Marla, Gregory. AB, U. Mo., Columbia, 1964; DO, Kans. City Coll. Osteo. Medicine, 1969. Cert. Am. Bd. Radiology. Intern Normandy (Mo.) Osteo. Hosp., 1969-70, Barnes Hosp., St. Louis, 1970-71; resident in radiology U. Ky., Lexington, 1971-74; assoc. prof. clin. radiology St. Louis U. Sch. Medicine, 1974—; diagnostic radiologist Berland Radiology, Creve Coeur, Mo., 1977—. Mem. AMA (recognition award 1985), N.Am. Radiol. Soc., St. Louis Radiology Soc. Republican. Jewish. Home: 12267 Winrock Creve Coeur MO 63141 Office: Berland Radiology 456 N Balla St Creve Coeur MO 63141

RADKE, DALE LEE, religious association adminstrator; b. Sheboygan, Wis., July 9, 1933; s. Alfred and Viola (Aschenbach) R.; m. Diane Jean Simon, Aug. 16, 1958; children: Laura Lee, Jay Ryan. AA, Concordia Wis., 1954. Store mgr. Badger Paint Stores, Milw., 1958-65; with sales dept. Hilton Co., Butler, 1965-67; with sales and customer service depts. Century Hardware, Milw., 1967-72; exec. dir. Greater Milw. Fedn. Luth. Chs., Mo. Synod., Milw., 1973—, Luth. of Wis., Milw., 1982—. Editor The Milw. Luth., 1982—; contbr. articles to clown mags. Mem. Milw. Citizenship Commn., 1960-63; mem. religious leaders div. Nat. Safety Council, Chgo., 1980—, bd. dirs., 1987—; mem. Milw. Safety Commn., 1970—, chmn., 1983—. Served to sgt. U.S. Army, 1956-58. Mem. Milw. Advt. Club, Milw. Press Club, Milw. Jaycees (Outstanding Young Man of Yr. 1962), various clown orgns. Lutheran. Lodge: Kiwanis. Performing as Rollo, a professional clown. Home: 6410 W Melvina St Milwaukee WI 53216 Office: Greater Milw Fedn of Luth Chs 1415 Wauwatosa Ave Milwaukee WI 53213

RADMER, MICHAEL JOHN, lawyer, educator; b. Wisconsin Rapids, Wis., Apr. 28, 1945; s. Donald Richard and Thelma Loretta (Donahue) R.; children from previous marriage: Christina Nicole, Ryan Michael; m. Laurie J. Anshus, Dec. 22, 1983; 1 child, Michael John. B.S., Northwestern U., Evanston, Ill., 1967; J.D., Harvard U., 1970. Bar: Minn. 1970. Assoc. Dorsey & Whitney, Mpls., 1970-75, ptnr., 1976—; lectr. law Hamline U. Law Sch., St. Paul, 1981-84; gen. counsel, rep., sec. 38 federally registered investment cos., Mpls. and St. Paul, 1977—. Contbr. articles to legal jours. Active legal work Hennepin County Legal Advice Clinic, Mpls., 1971—. Mem. ABA, Minn. Bar Assn., Hennepin County Bar Assn. Club: Mpls. Athletic. Home: 4329 E Lake Harriet Pkwy Minneapolis MN 55409 Office: Dorsey & Whitney 2200 First Bank Pl E Minneapolis MN 55402

RADNOR, ALAN T., lawyer; b. Cleve., Mar. 10, 1946; s. Robert Clark and Rose (Chester) R.; m. Carol Sue Hirsch, June 22, 1969; children—Melanie, Joshua, Joanna. B.A., Kenyon Coll., 1967; M.S. in Anatomy, Ohio State U., 1969, J.D., 1972. Bar: Ohio 1972. Ptnr., Vorys, Sater, Seymour & Pease, Columbus, Ohio, 1972—; adj. prof. law Ohio State U., Columbus, 1979—. Contbr. articles to profl. jours. Bd. dirs., trustee Congregation Tifereth Israel, Columbus, 1975—, 1st v.p., 1983-85, pres., 1985-87. Named Boss of Yr., Columbus Assn. Legal Secs., 1983. Mem. ABA, Ohio State Bar Assn., Columbus Bar Assn. (chmn. dr.-lawyer com. 1979-80), Columbus Def. Assn. (pres. 1980-81), Def. Research Inst., Internat. Assn. Def. Counsel, Ohio Hosp. Assn. Democrat. Jewish. Avocations: reading; sculpture. Home: 400 S Columbia St Bexley OH 43209 Office: Vorys Sater Seymour & Pease 52 E Gay St PO Box 1008 Columbus OH 43216-1008

RADOMSKI, ROBYN L., public relations executive; b. Pitts., June 10, 1954; s. Robert George Sr. and Helen L. Moses; m. A. David Radomski, June 14, 1975. BA, Pa. State U., 1975. Editor, sr. reporter Mesabi Daily News, Virginia, Minn., 1975-77; dir. corporate communications Fred S. James & Co., Chgo., 1977-81; v.p., mgr. corp. fin. div. Daniel J. Edelman, Inc., Chgo., 1981-84; exec. dir. corporate communications Playboy Enterprises, Inc., Chgo., 1984—. Recipient Minn. Newspaper Assn. awards for feature writing and investigative reporting, Mpls., 1976-77. Mem. Pub. Relations Soc. Am., Soc. Profl. Journalists, Nat. Investor Relations Inst. Avocations: yacht sailing and racing. Office: Playboy Enterprises Inc 919 N Michigan Ave Chicago IL 60611

RADWANSKA, EWA, gynecologist educator; b. Wilno, Poland, Oct. 24, 1938; came to U.S., 1976; d. Stefan and Lidia (Los) Woloszyn; divorced; 1 child, Joanna Radwanska Williams. MD, Med. Acad., Warsaw, Poland, 1962, PhD, 1969; MPhil, U. London, 1975. Intern Med. Acad., Warsaw, 1962-63, asst., 1964-70; fellow Univ. Coll. Hosp., London, 1970-76; asst. prof. U. N.C., Chapel Hill, 1977-79, U. Ark., Little Rock, 1979-81; assoc. prof.gynecology Rush Med. Coll., Chgo., 1981-86; clin. dir. in vitro fertilization program Rush Med. Ctr., Chgo., 1983-86. Contbr. 52 articles on infertility to profl. jours.; also author med. columns, chpts. and revs. Fellow British Ministry Health, 1972-75. Fellow Am. Coll. Obstetricians and Gynecologists; mem. Royal Coll. Obstetricians and Gynecologists, Am. Fertility Soc. Office: Rush Med Coll 600 S Paulina St Chicago IL 60612

RAETHER, KAREN MARIE, registered nurse; b. Stanley, Wis., May 15, 1936; d. Scott Warren and Adeline Catherine (Gruber) Henderson; m. Alfred Howard Raether, June 11, 1960; children: Lorna Marie, Brian Keith. BSN in Pub. Health Nursing, U. Wis., 1960. RN, Mich., Wis.; cert. social worker, Mich. Charge nurse Univ. Hosp., Madison, Wis., 1959-60; head dept. County Health Dept., Marinette, Wis., 1960-62; head nurse St. Joseph Hosp., Menominee, Mich., 1969-70; psychiat. nurse Counseling Ctr., Marinette, 1970-81; dir. nursing Roubal Nursing Home, Stephenson, Mich., 1981—; program chmn. Mental Health Bd. Menominee County, Mich., 1980—, sec., 1986; mem. citizen's adv. com. Newberry (Mich.) Mental Health Ctr., 1984—. Council mem. St. Stephen's Luth. Ch., Stephenson, 1981-86, pres., 1982-86; vice-chmn. citizen's adv. com. Newberry, 1985-86, chmn., 1986—. Mem. Am. Legion Aux. Avocations: cross country skiing, boating, fishing, knitting. Home: PO Box 324 Stephenson MI 49887 Office: Roubal Nursing Home Rt 1 PO Box 32 Stephenson MI 49887

RAFALCO, ROY DOUGLAS, financial executive; b. Indpls., May 23, 1955; s. Marion Leroy and Barbara L. (Groves) R.; m. Susan Lawrence, June 17, 1978; children: Timothy, Lara. BS cum laude, Ind. U., 1977; JD, Ind. U., Indpls., 1983. Bar: Ind. 1983; CPA, Ind. Asst. acct. Peat, Marwick, Mitchell & Co., Indpls., 1977-78; asst. controller City of Indpls., 1978-79; adminstr. RCA Consumer Electronics div. RCA Corp., Indpls., 1980-85; mgr. Gen. Electric Consumer Electronics Bus. div. Gen. Electric Co., Indpls., 1985—. Bd. dirs. Neighborhood Assn., Indpls., 1987. Mem. ABA, Am. Inst. CPA's, Ind. State Bar Assn., Beta Gamma Sigma, Beta Alpha Psi, U.S. Chess Fedn. Avocations: chess, tennis, handball. Home: 8146 Menlo Ct W Dr Indianapolis IN 46240 Office: Gen Electric Consumer Electronics Bus PO Box 1976 Indianapolis IN 46206-1976

RAFFEL, JAMES NORMAN, social service executive; b. Milw., June 7, 1954; s. Norman Thomas and Betty Louise (Semrad) R.; m. Gail Ann Justin, Sept. 1, 1979. B.A., U. Wis.-Eau Claire, 1976. Guidance and edn. dir. Milw. Boys Club, 1976-78, teen ctr. dir., 1978-79, assoc. exec. dir., 1979-85, asst. exec. dir., Nov., Dec., 1985; dir. corp and found. support, Med. Coll. Wis., Milw, 1985—. Mem. Nat. Soc. Fund Raising Execs. (pres. 1987—). Presbyterian. Office: Med Coll of Wis 8701 Watertown Plank Rd Milwaukee WI 53226

RAFFERTY, CRAIG ELLIOT, architect, educator; b. St. Paul, Apr. 11, 1946; s. George Elliot and Betty Jane (Kates) R.; m. Kathleen Anne Riley, Feb. 14, 1969; children: Erin Marie, Anne Terese, Lynn Maureen. BA, BArch, U. Minn., 1970; MArch, MIT, 1972. Registered architect, Minn. Archtl. designer Ralph Rapson, Mpls., 1969-70, Freeman & Liston, Boston, 1971-72; architect Hugh Stubbins, Cambridge, Mass., 1972-73, Brown Daltas, Rome, 1974; prin. Rafferty Rafferty Mikutowski, St. Paul, 1975—; lectr. Boston Archtl Ctr., 1971-73; asst. prof. U. Minn., Mpls., 1975—. Contbg. to author: Building Tomorrow: The Mobile Manufactured Housing Industry, Ice Castles, The Form of Housing; contbr. articles to architecture Mags. First vice chmn. dist 17 Downtown Community Devel. Council, St. Paul, 1987; chmn. dist 17 Downtown Long Range Plan Com., St. Paul, 1985; exec. com. Small Bus. Council, St. Paul, 1985; mem. Downtown Framework Com., St. Paul, 1985; chmn. art and environment bd. Archdiocese of St. Paul, 1977-81; pres., bd. dirs. Park Square Community Theater, St. Paul. Rotch Archl. Found. scholar, 1974; recipient Fed. Design Achievement award NEA, 1984, Presidential Design award, 1985. Mem. AIA (v.p. St. Paul Chpt., past pres., Minn. Soc. (dir. 1987—, Honor award 1986, 2 Interior Architecture awards, 1987), Paper Architecture award 1986). Roman Catholic. Club: St. Paul Athletic. Avocations: photography, video, sketching. Home: 1884 Lincoln Saint Paul MN 55105 Office: Rafferty Rafferty Mikutowski 253 E 4th St Saint Paul MN 55101

RAGHUPATHI, P. S., manufacturing executive; b. Gopalasmudram, Tamilnadu, India, July 9, 1945; d. P.R. and Alamelu Seetaraman; m. Lalitha Narayanan Raghupathi, June 20, 1975; children: Ashwin R. Bharadwaj, Ajay R. Bharadwaj. BE with honors, U. Madras, India, 1966; ME with distinction, Indian Inst. Tech., Bangalore, India, 1968; PhD in Engring., U. Stuttgart, Fed. Republic Germany, 1974. Sr. engr. MICO, Bosch, India, 1975-78; tech. asst. to pres. Mico Bosch; research sci. Battelle Columbus (Ohio) div., 1978-80, principal research sci., 1981; mgr. R&D Sundram Fastners, India, 1981-82; sr. research sci. Battelle Columbus Div., Dublin, Ohio, 1982-84, assoc. section mgr., 1984-85, section mgr., 1985—; adj. prof. Ohio State U., Columbus, 1987—. Co-editor: Handbook of Metal Forming, 1985; contbr. numerous articles to profl. jours. Mem. Internat. Cold Forging Group, N.Am. Research Inst. of Soc. Mfg. Engrs. Avocations: sports, cycling, music, reading. Office: Battelle Columbus Div 505 King Ave Columbus OH 43201

RAGLAND, TERRY EUGENE, emergency physician; b. Greensboro, N.C., June 14, 1944; s. Terry Porter and Virginia Lucile (Stowe) R.; m. Marguerite Elizabeth Morton, May 15, 1976; children: Kenneth John McConnell, Ryan Lee Ragland. Student, Cen. Mich. U., 1962-66; MD, U. Mich., 1970. Diplomate Am. Bd. Internal Medicine, Am. Bd. Emergency Medicine. Intern St. Joseph Mercy Hosp., Ann Arbor, Mich., 1970-71, internal medicine resident, 1974-77, chief resident internal medicine, 1975-76; emergency physician Catherine McAuley Health Ctr., Ann Arbor, 1977—, med. dir. emergency ctr., 1985—; clin. instr. U. Mich., Ann Arbor, 1981—; examiner Am. Bd. Emergency Medicine, 1983—; med. dir. Life Support Services, Ann Arbor, 1983—. Contbr. chpts. to book. Med. examiner Washtenaw County Health Dept., Ann Arbor, 1976—; bd. dirs. Emergency Physicians Med. Group, Ann Arbor. Served to lt. USN, 1972-74. Fellow Am. Coll. Emergency Physicians; mem. Am. Coll. Physicians, Nat. Assn. Emergency Med. Technicians, Mich. State Med. Soc. (alt. del. 1982-84), Mich. Emergency Med. Technicians Assn. Democrat. Avocations: trout fishing, gardening, skiing.

RAGLEY, PHYLLIS, podiatrist; b. Painesville, Ohio, Nov. 28, 1950; d. Frank and Ina MArie (Moisio) R. BA in Biology, Wittenberg U., 1973; DPM, Ohio Coll. Podiatric Medicine, 1978. Resident in podiatry VA Hosp.m, Topeka, 1979-80; pvt. practice podiatry Lawrence, Kans., 1980—; cons. to residency V.A. Hosp., Topeka, 1981—, Leavenworth, Kans., 1983—; staff Lawrence Meml. Hosp. Named OUtstanding Young Woman of Am., 1974, 75. Fellow Am. Acad. Podiatric Sports Medicine; mem. Am. Podiatric Med. Assn., Kans. Podiatric Med. Assn., Am. Assn. for Women Podiatrists (sec. 1984-86), Am. Running and Fitness Assn. Avocations: tennis, woodworking, medical-legal issues. Office: 901 Kentucky Suite 104 Lawrence KS 66044

RAGO, NICHOLAS A., food products company executive. Pres. Conagra Consumer Frozen Food Co., Ballwin, Mo. Office: Conagra Consumer Frozen Food Co 13515 Barrett Pkwy Dr Ballwin MO 63011 *

RAHDERT, RICHARD FREDERICK, psychiatrist; b. Ft. Wayne, Ind., June 27, 1935; s. Wilmer Charles Rahdert and Rosalind Elizabeth (Rust) Osmun; m. Elizabeth Quawz, June 7, 1958 (div. Oct. 1982); children: David, Diana; m. Sharon Dee Henning, Nov. 19, 1982; children: John, Geoffrey. BS with honors, Purdue U., 1957; MD, Ind. U., 1961. Enlisted U.S. Army, 1962, advanced through ranks to lt. col., served as med. officer, 1962-71, resigned, 1971; pvt. practice Arnett Clinic, Lafayette, Ind., 1971-82; med. dir. Wabash Valley Hosp., West Lafayette, Ind., 1974—; adjunct prof. Purdue U., West Lafayette, 1985—; cons. child mental health Ind. Dept. Mental Health, Indpls., 1975—. Bd. dirs. Lafayette Pastoral Counseling Ctr., 1985. Fellow Am. Psychiat. Assn.; mem. Ind. Psychiat. Soc. (pres. 1980-81), Am. Acad. Child Pschiatry. Republican. Lutheran. Lodge: Rotary. Avocations: camping, hiking. Home: 5930 Lookout Dr West Lafayette IN 47906 Office: Wabash Valley Hosp 2900 N River Rd AP L West Lafayette IN 47906

RAHM, PETER GUSTAV, state police officer; b. Ishpeming, Mich., June 14, 1947; s. Seth August and Helen Marie (Johnson) R.; m. Susan Ann Cavanaugh, May 1, 1976; children: Erica Leigh, Stephanie Regen, Alisa Linné. Student, No. Mich. U., 1965-70. Officer Mich. State Police, New Buffalo, 1970—. Recipient Lifesaving award (2) Mich. State Police, 1977, 78, Profl. Excellence award (2) Mich. State Police, 1979, 80, Disting. Expert Shooting Badge, Mich. State Police, 1985. Republican. Presbyterian. Avocations: golfing, cooking. wood cutting, running.

RAHMAN, MOHAMMAD HAFEEZ, allergist, immunologist; b. Delhi, India, June 6, 1937; m. Anis Hakim, June 11, 1981; children: Sami, Saba, Zia. FSC, U. Karachi, Pakistan, 1952, MD, 1960. Diplomate Am. Bd. Pediatrics, Am. Bd. Allergy and Immunology. Allergy and immunology fellow U. Mo., Kansas City, 1978-80, Kans. U. Med. Ctr., Kansas City, 1978-80; instr. Washington U., St. Louis, 1980—. Fellow Am. Acad. Allergy and Immunology, Am. Coll. Allergists, Am. Assn. Cert. Allergists. Office: Washington U 6125 Clayton Suite 204 Saint Louis MO 63139

RAHN, DONALD L., accountant; b. Horicon, Wis., Oct. 5, 1952; s. Leonard Adolph and Mildred Erna (Pribnow) R. BBA, U. Wis., 1974, MBA, 1975. CPA, Wis. With Virchow Krause, Madison, Wis., 1975-86, ptnr., 1986—. Contbr. various tech. articles and presentations in govtl. acctg. Mem. Friends of 21, Madison, Wis., 1978. Mem. Am. Inst. CPA's, Wis. Inst. CPA's (chmn. various coms.), Govt. Fin. Officers Assn. (rev. com.). Lutheran. Lodge: Lions. Avocations: golf, tennis. Office: Virchow Krause & Co PO Box 7398 Madison WI 53707

RAHRMAN, GLENN HENRY, computer company executive; b. St. Paul, Apr. 14, 1932; s. Harold Frederick and Eunice Marie (Baker) R.; m. Delores Zona Wynne, Dec. 29, 1956; 1 child, Mary Catherine. BA in Polit. Sci., Coll. St. Thomas, 1954; postgrad., U. Minn., 1954-56. Supr., mktg. engr., mfg. Honeywell, Hopkins, Minn., 1957-61; mgr. product control Sperry Univac, St. Paul, 1961-64; mgr. material Control Data Corp., Mpls., 1964-70, EM&M Corp., Hawthorne, Calif., 1970-72; mgr. subcontracts Litton, Van Nuys, Calif., 1972-78; group mgr. subcontracts Unisys (merger Sperry and Burroughs), St. Paul, 1978—; cons. in field. Mem. CAble Adv. Bd., South St. Paul, 1982; commr. Police and Fire Commn., South St. Paul, 1984; del. DFL, Dist. Conv., South St. Paul, 1984. Served with U.S. Army, 1956-57. Mem. Nat. Assn. Purchasing Mgmt., Nat. Contract Mgmt. Assn., Armed Forces Communications and Electronics Assn. (v.p. 1968-70). Democrat. Roman Catholic. Club: S (South St. Paul) (sec., treas. 1960-70). Lodge: KC. Avocations: reading, sports, home restorations. Office: Unisys Corp Computer Systems Div PO Box 64525 Saint Paul MN 55164-0525

RAIBLEY, PARVIN RUDOLPH, dentist; b. Boonville, Ind., Nov. 19, 1926; s. Otto Sr. and Hallie Marie (Hedges) R.; m. Mary Helen Holder, Aug. 31, 1946; children: Bruce D., Brian L., Brent A. BS in Dentistry, Ind. U., 1951, DDS, 1954. Practice gen. dentistry Evansville, Ind., 1954—; pres. Parvin Raibley Profl. Dental Corp.; sec. Health Resources Inc., Evansville, 1986. Served with U.S. Army, 1944-45. Fellow Acad. Gen. Dentistry, Am. Soc. Dentistry; mem. ADA, First Dist. Dental Soc., Ind. Dental Assn., Pierre Fauchard Acad., Ind. Acad. Gen. Dentistry, Am. Soc. Dentistry Children. Republican. Methodist. Lodge: Masons. Avocations: farming, forestry, fishing, hunting, gardening. Home: 7100 E Olive St Evansville IN 47715 Office: 207 S Green River Rd Evansville IN 47715

RAIFSNIDER, LAURETTA JANE, library administrator and consultant; b. Detroit, Aug. 30, 1947; d. Jack Wilfred and Margaret Pearl (Shannon) Eakin; m. Ronald Dean Raifsnider, June 28, 1968; children—Geoffrey Alan, Kristina Michelle. B.A., Ind. U., 1976, M.S. in Library and Info. Sci., 1981. Reference librarian Area 3 Area Library Services Authority, Ft. Wayne, Ind., 1980-82, adminstr., 1982—. Author: Louis Fortriede Shoes: A Century of Shoemaking in Fort Wayne, 1980; editor Tri-ALSA Newsletter, 1982—. Mem. ALA, Assn. Specialized and Coop. Library Agys., Ind. Library Assn. (cons. intellectual freedom com. 1982—), Phi Beta Mu. Home: 801 Maxine Dr Fort Wayne IN 46807 Office: Tri-ALSA 900 Webster St PO Box 2270 Fort Wayne IN 46801

RAIMI, SAMUEL M., film director; b. Royal Oak, Mich., Oct. 23, 1959; s. Leonard Ronald and Celia Barbara (Abrams) R. Student in humanities study, Mich. State U., East Lansing, 1977-79. V.p. Renaissance Pictures, Ferndale, Mich., 1979—. Writer, dir. (film) Evil Dead, 1981, Crimewave, 1985 (Best Dir. award 1986), Evil Dead II, 1986; co-writer: (screenplay) The Hudsucker Proxy, 1985, Witches, 1986, Woman on Wheels, 1986. Recipient Best Horror Film, Knokke'heist Film Festival Belgium, 1982, Best Horror Film and Best Spl. Effects, Sitges Film Festival, Spain, 1982, 1st Prize of the Critics, 1st Prize of the Pub., Paris Festival Sci. Fiction, Fantasy and Horror, 1983, Best Horror Film of Yr., Fangoria Mag., 1983. Mem. Mich. State U. Soc. for Creative Film Making (founder, pres. 1978, 79).

RAIMONDI, MATTHEW STEPHEN, JR., mechanical engineer; b. Chgo., Oct. 5, 1961; s. Matt S. and Flemmie (Spilotro) R.; m. Adriana Masó, Sept. 7, 1980; children: Anna Cristine, Matthew S. III. BSME, U. Ill., Chgo., 1984. Test engr. Bodine Electric Co., Chgo., 1984-85; design engr. ECM Motor Co., Schaumburg, Ill., 1985-87; project engr. MPC Products Corp., Skokie, Ill., 1987—. Mem. Am. Soc. Mech. Engring., Phi Kappa Theta (sec. 1980-81), U. Ill. Alumni Assn. Avocations: fishing, golf, racquetball. Office: MPC Products Co 7426 N Linder Ave Skokie IL 60077

RAINE, JOHN, II, manufacturing company executive; b. Wheeling, W.Va., Dec. 15, 1954; s. John and Barbara (Nay) R.; m. Sharon Sue Healy, Apr. 26, 1986. BS in Indsl. Engring., W.Va. U., 1976; MBA in Corp. Fin., Columbia U., 1978. Fin. analyst FMC Corp., South Charleston, W.Va., 1979-80, Occidental Chem., Niagara Falls, N.Y., 1980-82; account exec. Occidental Chem., Indpls., 1982-86; pres. Raine, Inc., Indpls., 1986—. Treas. Sargent Hills Civic League, Indpls., 1984—. Home: 9420 Goodway Ct Indianapolis IN 46256 Office: Raine Inc 309 N Walnut St Daleville IN 47334

RAINES, LELAND BUFORD, manufacturing company manager, engineer; b. Corbin, Ky., Feb. 15, 1930; s. Thomas Eugene and Flora (Alsip) R.; m. Athena Deloris Hamlin, Nov. 26, 1959; 1 child, David Wayne. Diploma in engring., Allied Inst. Tech. Machine operator Ford Motor Co., Detroit, 1950-51, Chrysler Corp., Detroit, 1953-54; indsl. engr. Imperial Brass Co., Chgo., 1954-68; plant mgr. Ite-Imperial Corp., Rockford, Ill., 1968-72, Elkhart Products, Geneva, Ind., 1972—. Served with U.S. Army, 1951-53. Mem. Am. Legion, Nat. Rifle Assn. Republican. Baptist. Home: 1218 W Water St Berne IN 46711 Office: Elkart Products Box 38 700 Rainbow Rd Geneva IN 46740

RAINS, CHARLES RANDEL, industrial engineer; b. Fairland, Okla., Mar. 28, 1957; s. Charles Dempsey and Margie D'Ann (McVey) R.; m. Suzanne Davis, Dec. 19, 1976; children: Andrew Ryan, Samantha Leigh. AA, No. Ark. Community Coll., Harrison, 1977; BS, So. Ill. U., Carbondale, 1981. Sales and applications engr. Fram Corp., Tulsa, 1982-83; indsl. engr. J.I. Case, Pryor, Okla., 1983-84; mgr. standards and methods A B Chance Co., Centralia, Mo., 1984-87; mgr. indsl. engring. Sundstrand Tubular Products Inc., Camdenton, Mo., 1987—. Advisor Jr. Achievers, Centralia, 1985-86. Served with USAF, 1978-82. Mem. Inst. Indsl. Engrs., Am. Soc. Quality Control. Republican. Baptist. Avocations: basketball, softball, golf. Home: Rural Rt 1 Box 129N Linn Creek MO 65052 Office: Sundstrand Tubular Products Inc Box 636 Camdenton MO 65020

RAINS, DANIEL O'NEIL, violinist, music educator; b. Lexington, Ky., Aug. 15, 1952; s. Geneva B. (Jones) R. BM, U. Cin., 1975; MusM, U. Nebr., 1980. Orch. dir. Clark County Sch., Winchester, Ky., 1975-77, Tates Creek Sch., Lexington, Ky., 1977-78; violinist Lexington Philharmonic, 1975-78, Lincoln (Nebr.) Symphony, 1978-80, Cleve. Chamber Orch., 1985—; asst. prof. music U. Maine, Orono, 1980-85, Cleve. State U., 1985—; violinist Nebr. Chamber Orch., Lincoln, 1978-80, Maine Chamber Ensemble, Orono, 1981-85, Maine Arts Inst., Orono, 1984, 85. Named to Hon. Order Ky. Cols., 1980; named one of Outstanding Young Men in Am., 1985; recipient Outstanding Music Achievement award Lexington Jr. League, 1970. Mem. Music Educator's Nat. Conf., Am. String Tchr.'s Assn. (master tchr. 1983, 84), Nat. Sch. Orch. Assn., Bruckner Soc. Am., Am. Fedn. Musicians. Democrat. Mem. Unitarian Ch. Avocation: collecting oriental prints and ceramics. Office: Cleve State U Dept Music 907 Rhodes Tower Cleveland OH 44115

RAINS, JAMES IRA, photographer; b. St. Louis, July 25, 1956; s. Claude and Bonnie Sue (Turner) R. Grad., Sch. Modern Photography, Little Falls, N.J., 1979; AS in Bus. Mgmt., Jefferson Coll., Hillsboro, Mo., 1982. Photographer Am. Composite Corp., Kansas City, Mo., 1978-79, Def. Mapping Agy., St. Louis, 1981-82; owner/mgr./photographer The Photo Works, Hillsboro, 1982—. Leader Boy Scouts Am., Hillsboro, 1985—. Served with USN, 1974-77. Mem. Assn. Photographer's Internat., Models and Photographers Assn., Profl. Photographers Am., Wedding Photographers Internat., VFW, Am. Legion. Democrat. Lodge: Lions (sec., treas. Hillsboro chpt. 1983—). Home and Office: PO Box 520 DeSoto MO 63020

RAITER, WAYNE JOHN, psychotherapist, social services adminstrator; b. Mpls., Feb. 18, 1954; s. Russel David and Grace Jane (Herbert) R.; m. Teresa Jean Almsted, Oct. 14, 1978; children: Christopher, Alexander. BA, Coll. St. Thomas, St. Paul, 1977; MA, St. Mary's Coll., Mpls., 1986. Dir. Project New Bridge, Mpls., 1979-81; acting dir. clin. br. Johnson Inst., Mpls., 1981-83; dir. Judson Family Ctr., Mpls., 1985—; cons., adj. faculty Johnson Inst., 1983—, Community Intervention Ctr., Mpls., 1984—. Roman Catholic. Avocations: fishing, reading, climbing. Home: 1616 Demont Minneapolis MN 55109 Office: Judson Family Ctr 4101 Harriet Ave Minneapolis MN 55104

RAITHEL, FREDERICK J., information system specialist; b. Jefferson City, Mo., Nov. 20, 1949; s. Herbert C. and Mildred (Kemper) R. B.A. in Philosophy, Lincoln U., 1972; M.A. in Library Info. Sci., U. Mo., 1973. Asst. reference librarian Mo. State Library, Jefferson City, 1974; reference librarian Daniel Boone Regional Library, Columbia, Mo., 1974-78; network coordinator Mid-Mo. Library Network, Columbia, 1978-81; head access services U. Mo. Libraries, Columbia, 1981-84; info. system research analyst, dept. agrl. econs. U. Mo., 1984; dir. Mid-Mo. Library Network, Columbia, 1984—; chmn. Automation Tech. Com. of Mo. Libraries Network Bd., 1983-86; pres. U. Mo. Sch. Library Info Sci Alumni Assn., 1977-79; cons. Mem. ALA, Mo. Library Assn. (founder/organizer computer info. tech. com.). Contbr. articles to profl. jours. Home: 501H Columbia Dr Columbia MO 65201 Office: Mid-Mo Library Network 100 W Broadway Columbia MO 65203

RAJAGOPAL, ADIKKAN OANTHAN, anesthesiologist; b. Trichy, Madras, India, Mar. 27, 1941; came to U.S., June, 1972; s. Lakshmanan, Adikkan (Patchaiammal) O.; m. Vasantha Bai, Nov. 7, 1965; children—Ravi, Suresh. M.B.B.S., U. Madras, 1962. Diplomate Am. Bd. Anesthesiology. Practice medicine specializing in anesthesiology, Coimbatore Med. Coll Hosp., Madras, India, 1967-72; intern Altoona Hosp., Pa., 1972-73; resident in anesthesia, U. Ill., Chgo., 1973-75; attending in anesthesia Met. Gen. Hosp., Cleve., 1975-76; practice medicine specializing in anesthesia St. Lukes Hosp., Saginaw, Mich., 1976-86 , chmn. dept. anesthesia, 1983-85, med. dir. surg. ctr., 1986—. Century mem. Lake Huron Area council Boy Scouts Am., 1981. Mem. Am. Soc. Anesthesiologists, Mich. Soc. Anesthesiologists, Internat. Anesthesia Research Soc., Mich. State Med. Soc., Saginaw County Med. Soc. Hindu. Club: Germania. Avocations: gardening; swimming; fishing; tennis. Home: 5482 Overhill Dr Saginaw MI 48603

RAJAN, JAIRAM, obstetrician-gynecologist; b. Poona, India, Sept. 8, 1948; came to U.S., 1974; s. Ramiah and Padma Rajan; m. Sundari J. Rajan; children: Sunil, Sonali. MBBS, Kasturba Med. Coll., Mangalore, India, 1972. Chief ob-gyn Health Cen., Lansing, Mich., 1980—. Fellow Am. Coll. Ob-Gyn. Avocation: music. Home: 4238 Sandridge Okemos MI 48864 Office: 2316 S Cedar Lansing MI 48910

RAJDL, HOWARD DEWAYNE, plastics company executive; b. Glenwood, Minn.; s. Henry Joseph and Helen Mary (Tvrdik) R.; m. Dorothy Marie Ebensteiner, June 7, 1957; children: Diane, Donna, Mark, Laurie, Alan. Dist. storekeeper Air Red. Sales Co., Mpls., 1958-61; office and product mgr. Atlas Mfg. Co., Mpls., 1961-72; farmer, constrn. worker 1972-77; pres., chief exec. officer Shovel Lake Industry Inc., Remer, Minn., 1977—. Chmn. sch. bd. Hill City, Minn., 1984. Served as sgt. USAR, 1956-85. Mem. Am. Legion, Nat. Rifle Assn. Roman Catholic. Avocaitons: hunting, fishing, target shooting. Home: 7785 County Rd 67 Swatara MN 55785 Office: Shovel Lake Industries Inc Spruce St Box 230 Remer MN 56672

RAJU, NIRANJANA, physician; b. Davangere, Karnataka, India, Aug. 27, 1952; came to U.S., 1976; d. Malalkere and Parwathamma Ramappa; m. Rekha Raju, July 28, 1980. M.D., JJM Med. Coll., Davanegere, 1974; postgrad. internal medicine St. Vincent/Yale Affiliate, Bridgeport, Conn., 1977-80. Diplomate Am. Bd. Internal Medicine. Intern, Bowring Hosp., Bangalore, India, 1974-75, resident in medicine, 1975-76; resident in pathology St. Raphael Hosp., New Haven, Conn., 1976-77; resident in medicine St. Vincent/Yale Affiliate, Bridgeport, Conn., 1977-80; pvt. practice medicine, Ste. Genevieve, Mo., 1980—; cons. internal medicine and cardiology Ste. Genevieve County Meml. Hosp., 1980—. Mem. Ste. Genevieve-Perry County Med. Soc. (sec. 1984), AMA, Mo. State Med. Soc., Ste. Genevieve Med. Soc. Clubs: Rotary, Ste. Genevieve Golf. Avocations: Golfing, fishing. Home: Rural Route 2 Box 136 Lake Forest Estates Saint Genevieve MO 63670 Office: 990 Park Dr Saint Genevieve MO 63670

RAKER, J. RUSSELL, III, academic administrator; b. Phila., Nov. 18, 1941; s. J. Russell Jr. and M. Elmina (Dunkin) R.; m. Carol Barnes, June 14, 1964; children: Jonathan Russell, Timothy Paul. BA cum laude, Alderson-Broaddus Coll., 1963; MA, Columbia U., 1964, diploma, 1968. Cert. fund raising exec., Washington. Dir. devel. Moravian Sem. Girls, Bethlehem, Pa., 1964-66; assoc. dir. devel. Columbia U., N.Y.C., 1966-69, U. Rochester(N.Y.), 1969-71; dir. devel. Hiram (Ohio) Coll., 1971-75; v.p. Ottawa (Kans.) U., 1975-79; assoc. v.p. U. Redlands (Calif.), 1979-81; program dir. Campbell & Co., Chgo., 1981-82; pres. Nebr. Ind. Coll. Found., Omaha, 1982-87; chief exec. officer Kettering Med. Ctr. Found., Dayton, Ohio, 1987—; bd. dirs. Nat. Soc. Fund Raising Execs., Washington. Bd. dirs. Nebr. Women's Commn. Found., Lincoln, 1986—; v.p. Omaha Ballet Bd., 1987—; trustee Ind. Coll. Funds Am., mem. exec. com., 1986—, mem. cert. bd. Internat. Soc. Fund Raising Execs. Recipient Charles L. Foreman Dist. Performance award Ind. Coll. Funds Am., 1987. Mem. Am. Assn. Higher Edn. (life), Am. Assn. Univ. Adminstrs., Nat. Assn. Hosp. Devel., Nat. Soc. Fund Raising Execs. (chpt. pres. 1984-85, Outstanding Prof. 1985, mem. nat. com.), Phi Delta Kappa. Republican. Baptist. Club: Omaha. Avocations: travel, sports, photography. Home: 8030 Brainard Woods Dr Centerville OH 45459

RAKERS, HARRY B., accountant; b. Breese, Ill., July 13, 1946; s. John A. and Clara C. (Fuhler) R.; m. Cheryl K. Wade, Dec. 28, 1968; children: Brent, Chad. BS in Accountancy, U. Ill., 1969, MS in Bus. Adminstrn., 1986. Staff acct. Murphrey Jenne & Jones, Champaign, Ill., 1968-73; controller M&W Gear Co. Inc., Gibson City, Ill., 1973-78; v.p. fin. M&W Gear Co. Inc., Gibson City, 1978—; treas. Makor, inc., Gibson City, 1982-87, Grainstor Leasing Inc., Gibson City, 1980-86; v.p. fin. Fuerst Bros., Inc., Gibson City, 1987. Coach Little League, Champaign, 1979-87, pres. 1984-87; pres. PTA, Champaign, 1983-84. Served with USMC, 1970-72. Mem. Am. Inst. CPA's, Ill. Soc. CPA's, Ill. Mfrs. Assn., Ill. Jaycees (Outstand-ing Local Pres. 1979-80, Outstanding State Chmn. 1976-77, Officer Yr. 1978-79, v.p. Champaign-Urbana 1977-79, pres. Champaign-Urbana 1979-80, Champaign-Urbana Jaycee of Decade 1970s). Republican. Roman Catholic. Avocation: sports. Home: 906 Devonshire Champaign IL 61821 Office: M&W Gear Co Rt 47 S Gibson City IL 60936

RAKLOVITS, GREGORY OWENS, appliance manufacturing administrator; b. Kalamazoo, Feb. 2, 1957; s. Richard Frank and Nancy Ellen (Owens) R.; m. Denise Patricia Kalinas, Oct. 15, 1960. BBA in Logistics, Mich. State U., 1983; postgrad., Western Mich. U., 1985—. Mgr. Long John Silver's Restaurant, Kalamazoo, 1977-78; asst. mgr. MSU Golf Club, East Lansing, Mich., 1979-83; adminstr. transp. Whirlpool Corp., Benton Harbor, Mich., 1983-85, adminstr. order processing, 1985-86, adminstr. inventory control, 1986—. Mem. Nat. Assn. Physical Distbn. Mgrs. Republican. Roman Catholic. Club: Point O'Woods Country (Benton Harbor). Home: 4002 Atherton Coloma MI 49038 Office: Whirlpool Corp 2000 US 33 N Benton Harbor MI 49022

RAKOCZY, JACOB DAVID, steel machining and fabricating executive; b. East Chicago, Ind., Apr. 16, 1955; s. John Joseph and Josephine Elizabeth (Huss) R.; m. Gwynne Ruth Rakoczy, Aug, 21, 1975 (div. May 1984); children: Jacob John, Jillian Christine. Student, Calumet Coll., 1974, St. Joseph's Coll., 1975. Machinist, foreman Euclid Machine & Tool, Gary, Ind., 1976-78, supt., 1978-80; v.p. Euclid Machine & Tool, East Chicago, Ind., 1980—, gen. mgr., 1985—. Pres. St. John (Ind.) Fire Dept., 1983, treas. 1982, capt., 1982, bd. dirs., 1981-83. Roman Catholic. Avocations: hunting, fishing. Office: Euclid Machine & Tool PO Box 150 East Chicago IN 46312

RAKOLTA, JOHN, construction company executive; b. 1923. Student, U. Detroit. With Walbridge Aldinger Co., Livonia, Mich., 1945—, sec., treas., 1955-70, pres., treas., 1970-78, pres., 1978-80, now chmn. bd. dirs., 1980—. Office: Walbridge Aldinger Co 38099 Schoolcraft Livonia MI 48150 *

RAKSAKULTHAI, VINAI, obstetrician-gynecologist; b. Rayong, Thailand, Mar. 20, 1942; came to U.S., 1968; s. Choosak and Ngo (Koo) R.; m. Vullapa Raksakulthai, Sept. 20, 1968; children: Vipavull, Vivian, Vipat. MD, ChiengMai Med. Sch., Thailand, 1966. Diplomate Am. Bd. Ob-Gyn. Intern New Britain (Conn.) Gen. Hosp., 1969; resident St. Joseph Mercy Hosp., Pontiac, Mich., 1970-72; practice medicine specializing in ob-gyn. Fredericktown, Mo., 1973—; chief ob-gyn Madison Meml. Hosp., Fredericktown, Mo., 1986—. City physician, Fredericktown, 1986. Mem. Mo. Med. Assn., Mineral Area Med. Soc. Budhism. Home: 201 William Fredericktown MO 63645 Office: 703 N Main Fredericktown MO 63645

RALAPATI, SURESH, research chemist; b. Secunderabad, India, July 1, 1949; came to U.S., 1971; s. Ramchander and Leelavathy (Papaiah) R.; m. Asha Maroli, June 13, 1975; children: Shipra, Megha. BS with distinction, Andhra Pradesh Agrl. U., Hyderabad, India, 1971; MS, U. Mo., 1974, PhD, 1978. Postdoctoral fellow Ill. Inst. Tech., Chgo., 1978-81; research assoc. U. Chgo., 1981-82; sr. research assoc. U. Ill., Chgo., 1982-84; sr. research biochemist Inolex Chem. Co., Chgo., 1984-86; sci. dir. Pharma-Logic, Chgo., 1986; sr. research assoc. dept. chemistry Loyola U., Chgo., 1987—; research cons. Northwestern U., Evanston, Ill., 1986. Contbr. numerous articles to profl. jours. Biochemistry fellow U. Mo., 1973-74, Ill. Inst. Tech., 1978-81, neurosci. fellow U. Chgo., 1981-82, immunology fellow U. Ill., 1982-84. Fellow Am. Inst. Chemists; mem. AAAS, Am. Chem. Soc. (div. carbohydrate chemistry), Phi Lambda Upsilon (officer 1973-74). Avocations: Indian classical music, violin, tennis, jogging.

RALFS, DONALD CLARENCE, electric company administrator; b. Davenport, Iowa, Feb. 12, 1934; s. Clarence Rudolph and Mildred Ann (Murphy) R.; m. Mary Ellen Ringstad, Nov. 7, 1959; children: Scott, Mark, Ann. BBA, Augustana Coll., 1965. Various data processing mgmt. positions Alcoa, Davenport, Iowa, 1954-64, Pitts., 1965-68; various data processing mgmt. positions N.W. Computer Systems, Mpls., 1969-71, Wis. Electric Power Co., Milw., 1972—; mem. Inroads, Milw., 1976-78; presenter data processing mgmt. seminars to various orgns. Council mem. Fox Point (Wis.) Luth. Ch., 1979-82; active Big League baseball, Glendale, Wis., 1974—. Mem. Computer Ops. Mgmt. Assn. (v.p.). Republican. Lutheran. Lodge: Lions. Home: 6530 N Elm Tree Rd Glendale WI 53217

RALPH, JEFFREY JAY, manufacturing executive; b. Glen Cove, N.Y., Apr. 19, 1960; s. Gene and Jane (Mrha) R.; m. Valerie Sue Mullen, Aug. 22, 1987. BBA, Ashland (Ohio) Coll., 1982. Gen. mgr. HRZ Corp., Ontario, 1976-82; corp. office mgr. The Window Place, Inc., Mansfield, Ohio, 1982—; v.p. Bay World, Inc., Mansfield, Ohio, 1983—, also bd. dir .; fin. cons. The Window Place, Mansfield, 1983—, chmn. service com., 1985—. Mem. Phi Delta Theta (Brothership award 1982). Republican. Roman Catholic. Avocations: golf, basketball, softball. Home: 335 Marcus Pl Mansfield OH 44903 Office: Bay World Internat 49 S Illinois Ave Mansfield OH 44905

RALSTON, GERALD WESLEY, banker; b. Angola, Ind., Oct. 21, 1925; s. Wesley J. and Laura M. (Generke) R.; m. Margaret M. Hellinger, Aug. 14, 1946; children: Diane M., Cheryl A., Cathy L., G. Craig. A in Community Bank Mgmt., U. Wis., 1981. Bank teller Angola State Bank, 1955-60, asst. cashier, 1960-68, cashier, 1968-75, sr. v.p., cashier, 1975-82, pres., chief exec. officer, 1982—; v.p. Angola Indsl., 1980—. Treas. Heart Fund, Angola, 1962-82. Mem. Am. Bank Assn., Bank Adminstrn. Inst., Ind. Bankers Assn., Jaycees (pres. Angola 1961). Lodges: Rotary, Shriners, Elks, Moose. Avocations: golf, fishing, baseball. Office: Angola State Bank PO Box 120 Angola IN 46703

RALSTON, THOMAS MICHAEL, radiologist; b. Des Moines, Feb. 22, 1952; s. John James and Mary B. (McCarthy) R.; m. Isabel Pérez, Apr. 22, 1979; 1 child, Anthony. BS, Northwest Mo. State U., 1973; MD, Creighton U., 1978. Diplomate Am. Bd. Radiology. Commd. 2d lt. U.S. Army, 1974, advanced through grades to maj., 1984; intern Brooke Army Med. Ctr. U.S. Army, Ft. Sam Houston, Tex., 1978-79, resident in radiology Brooke Army Med. Ctr., 1979-82; chief radiology Munson Army Hosp., Ft. Leavenworth, Kans., 1982—. Mem. Am. Coll. Radiology, Radiology Soc. N.Am. Roman Catholic. Office: Munson Army Hosp USAMEDDAC Fort Leavenworth KS 66027

RAMACHANDRAN, AJIT KUMAR, engineering company executive; b. Calicut, Kerala, India, Mar. 17, 1952; Came to U.S., 1978; s. K.V. and Vasantha Ramachandran; m. Eleanor Wickramasekera, Oct. 27, 1980; 1 child, Vivek K. B in Engring., Coimbatore (India) Inst. Tech., 1975; M in Engring., So. Ill. U., 1980. Sr. inspection engr. Nat. Inst. Quality Assurance, Coimbatore, 1975-78; sr. mech. engr. Turbotec Products, Windsor, Conn., 1980-81, engring. mgr., 1981-82, ops. mgr., 1982-84; mgr. engring and tech. services Manoir Internat., South Holland, Ill., 1984—. Patentee in field. Mem. Am. Soc. Mech. Engrs., Am. Soc. Heating, Refrigeration and Air Conditioning Engrs. Avocations: model airplanes, boats, stamp collecting.

RAMASWAMI, DEVABHAKTUNI, chemical engineer; b. Pedapudi, India, Apr. 4, 1933; came to U.S., 1958; s. Veeriah and Rangamma Devabhaktuni; m. Vijayalakshmi, June 30, 1967; 1 child, Srikrishna. B.Sc., Andhra U., 1953, M.Sc., 1954, D.Sc., 1958; Ph.D., U. Wis., 1961. Research scholar Andhra U., Waltair, India, 1954-56, Indian Inst. Tech., Kharagpur, 1956-57; asst. prof. Benaras Hindu U., Varanasi, India, 1957-58; research asst. U. Wis., Madison, 1958-61; research engr. IBM Corp., San Jose, Calif., 1961-62; chem. engr. Argonne Nat. Lab., Ill., 1962—. Contbr. numerous articles to profl. jours. Patentee in field. Am. Chem. Soc. Disting. and Promising Asian in U.S. award Asia Found., 1960. Fellow Am. Inst. Chem. Engrs. Avocation: photography. Home: 826 Columbia Ln Darien IL 60559 Office: Engring Div Argonne National Lab 9700 S Cass St Argonne IL 60439

RAMBO, JANA LYNNE, social worker; b. Concordia, Kans., Feb. 22, 1951; d. Clifford and Lavera Mildred (Teske) R. MSW, U. Kans., 1983. Lic. master social worker. Social worker Kans. State Dept. Social and Rehabilitation Services, Augusta, 1973-81, ARC, Wichita, Kans., 1984—. Subcom. chair Interfaith Ministries, Wichita, 1986. Mem. Nat. Assn. Social Workers, Great Plains Dulcimer Alliance, Evang. Womens Caucus, Evangs. for Social Action, Bread for the World, Amnesty Internat. Office: ARC 707 N Main Wichita KS 67203

RAMER, DANIEL E., lawyer; b. Dayton, Ohio, Nov. 2, 1953; s. John L. and Margaret J. (Reese) R.; m. Kimberly Ann Montgomery, May 25, 1974; children: Brian Daniel, Valerie Rhys, Natalie Anne. BA magna cum laude, U. Miami, 1975; JD, Ohio State U., 1978. Bar: Mich. 1978, Ohio 1979. Assoc. James T. Ramer, Harbor Springs, Mich., 1978-79; ptnr. Turner & Ramer Co., L.P.A., Piqua, Ohio, 1979—; corp. sec. Terrys Cafeteria, Inc., Piqua, 1985—, Aerovent, Inc., Piqua, 1985—. Fundraiser United Fund, Piqua, sch. operating levy drives, Piqua, 1982, community swimming pool drive, Piqua, 1984; trustee Brukner Nature Ctr., Troy, Ohio, 1982. Mem. ABA, Ohio State Bar Assn., Miami (Ohio) County Bar Assn. (pres. 1987). Republican. Presbyterian. Lodge: Rotary (bd. dirs. 1982-83). Avocations: golf, reading. Home: 1511 Broadway Piqua OH 45356 Office: 320 W Water St Piqua OH 45356

RAMER, JAMES LEROY, civil engineer; b. Marshalltown, Iowa, Dec. 7, 1935; s. LeRoy Frederick and Irene (Wengert) R.; m. Jacqueline L. Orr, Dec. 15, 1957; children: Sarah T., Robert H., Eric A., Susan L. Student U. Iowa, 1953-57; MCE, Washington U., St. Louis, 1976, MA in Polit. Sci., 1978; postgrad. U. Mo., Columbia, 1984—. Registered profl. engr., land surveyor. Civil engr. U.S. State Dept., Del Rio, Tex., 1964; project engr. H. B. Zachry Co., San Antonio, 1965-66; civil and constrn. engr. U.S. Army C.E., St. Louis, 1967-76, tech. advisor for planning and nat. hydropower coordinator, 1976-78, project mgr. for EPA constrn. grants, Milw., 1978-80; chief architecture and engring. HUD, Indpls., 1980-81; pvt. practice civil engring., 1981—; civil design and pavements engr. Whiteman AFB, Mo., 1982-86; soil engr. Hdqtrs. Mil. Airlift Command, Scott AFB, Ill., 1986—; project analyst AF-1 maintenance hangar, tech. adv. C.E., 1982—; cattle and grain farmer, 1982—; expert witness; adj. faculty civil engring. Washington U., 1968-78, U. Wis., Milw., 1978-80. Ga. Mil. Coll., Whiteman AFB.; adj. research engr. U. Mo., Columbia, 1985—. Holder 25 U.S. patents in diverse art, 7 copyrights. Mem. ASCE, Nat. Soc. Profl. Engrs., Soc. Am. Mil. Engrs., AAUP. Lutheran. Club: Optimists Internat. Home and Office: Route 1 Box 50-AA Fortuna MO 65034

RAMER, LILLIAN WISSENBERG, family therapist; b. Detroit, Apr. 7, 1924; d. Herman Valdemir and Anna Matilda (Rassmussen) Wissenberg; m. William Charles Ramer, June 14, 1944; children: Karen Lee Ramer Burnette, William Charles III. BS in Psychology, Oakland U., 1975, MA in Guidance and Counsel, 1978. Cert. social worker, Mich. Therapist Groves Half Way House, Royal Oak, Mich., 1978-79; therapist Midwest Mental Health Clinic, Troy, Mich., 1979-83, on-site coordinator, 1982-83, mem. adv. bd., 1982-83; pvt. practice therapy Bloomfield Hills, Mich., 1983—. Mem. exec. com. Youth Protection Com., Hazel Park, Mich., 1956-66, Youth Aid Found., Hazel Park, 1966-67; probation officer Ferndale (Mich.) Ct., 1963-66; founder local group Al-Anon for Adult-Children of Alcoholics, Bloomfield Hills, 1984—, Al-Anon for Families of Alcoholics, Troy, 1969—. Mem. AAUW, Mich. Assn. Alcoholism and Drug Abuse Counselors. Republican. Lutheran. Clubs: Women of Wallstreet (Rochester, Mich.) (pres. 1985—); Profiteers (Birmingham, Mich.). Avocation: handwork. Home: 2206 Lost Tree Way Bloomfield Hills MI 48013

RAMEY, HENRY KYLE, data processing manager; b. Indpls., Oct. 6, 1941; s. Henry Kyle Sr. and Elsie J. (Means) R.; m. Mary Oberene Gorman, Feb. 19, 1966; children: Mary Thomasita, Jennifer Alexandra, Priscilla Anne. Student, Ind. Cen. U., 1959-61. Cons. data base adminstrn. CNA Ins., Chgo., 1974-76; asst v.p. Interstate Nat. Ins., Chgo., 1976-79, Fin. Tech., Inc., Chgo., 1979-82; regional data processing mgr. Safeguard Bus. Systems, Chgo., 1982-84; systems programming mgr. Assocs. Bancorp, Inc., South Bend, Ind., 1984—. Local and dist. corp. rep. Parent Communication Network, South Bend, Ind. Recipient cert. for Micrographics, Kodak, 1975; cert. for mgmt. Mgmt. Bd., 1978, AMA, 1980. Mem. Nat. Micrographic Assn., Data Processing Mgmt. Assn., Assn. for Systems Mgmt., Computer Ops. Mgmt. Assn. Republican. Baptist. Avocations: family activities, camping. Home: 52752 E Cypress Circle South Bend IN 46637 Office: Assocs Bancorp Inc 1720 Ruskin St South Bend IN 46604

RAMICK, CHARLES CONRAD, computer scientist; b. St. Louis, Nov. 5, 1946; s. Conrad Coburn and Marie Terese (Lodewyck) R.; m. Katherine Jameson, Oct. 1, 1983; children—Charles Coburn, Allison Lee, Amy Elizabeth; stepchildren—Jeffery Jameson, Nancy Jameson. A.A., Prairie State Coll., 1970, B.A., Governors State U., 1979; M.S., Nat. Coll. Edn., 1984. Mgr. mgmt. info. systems Brummer div. Borg-Warner Corp., Frankfort, Ill., 1973-77; mgr. prodn. control Folger Adam Co. Joliet, Ill., 1977-79; rep. communications systems Ill. Bell Co., Hinsdale, Ill., 1979-83; tech. cons. AT&T Info. Systems, Inc., Chgo., 1983-85, network design engr., 1986—. Pres., Dist. 161 Bd. Edn., 1977-82; mem. Ill. State Bd. Edn. evaluation team, 1982; treas. HFHS Found., 1985. Mem. Data Processing Mgmt. Assn., IEEE. Republican.

RAMON, JOSE GUILLERMO, orthopedic surgeon; b. Havana, June 25, 1942; came to U.S., 1979; s. Pio and Blanca Rosa (Arias) R.; m. Evangelina Tabares, May 13, 1967; children: Pio, Jose G. Premed., Havana U., Cuba, 1961; MD, Havana U., 1973. Diplomate Am. Bd. Neurol. and Orthopedic Surgery. Anatomy instr., phys. therapy instr. Havana U., 1973-74; mem. staff St. Mary's Hosp., East St. Louis, Ill., 1979—, Community Hosp., East St. Louis, Ill., 1980—, Centerville (Ill.) Hosp., 1979—, O. Anderson Hosp., Maryville, Ill., 1980—. Contbr. numerous articles to profl. jour. Mem. AMA, Soc. Orthopedic Surgeons Cuba, Physicians Assn. Clinics and Hosp. and Annex, Cuban Othopedic Soc., Inc., Latin Am. Orthopedic soc., St. Clair Med. Soc., Ill. Med. Soc., So. Med. Assn., Internat. Coll. Surgeons, Med. Utiliation Rev. So. Ill., Interamerican Coll. Physicians and Surgeons, Am. Fracture Assn., The Am. Acad. Neurol. and Orthopedic Surgeons, So. Orthopedic Assn., Arthoscopy Club St. Louis. Roman Catholic. Lodge: Rotary. Avocations: skin diving, boating. Office: 129 N 8th St East Saint Louis IL 62201

RAMON, SHARON JOSEPHINE, personnel management executive, real estate salesperson; b. Chgo., Nov. 8, 1947; d. Edward Albert and Helen Josephine (Tomasziewski) Mazur; m. Kevin John Ramon, Aug. 4, 1979. BA, U. Ill.-Chicago, 1969. Caseworker, ct. aide Social Service Dept. of Cir. Ct. Cook County, Chgo., 1969-71; investigator aide U.S. Civil Service Commn., Chgo., 1971-72, personnel staffing specialist, 1972-74, personnel mgmt. specialist, 1974-80; mgmt. cons. U.S. Office Personnel Mgmt., Chgo., 1980-82, personnel mgmt. specialist, 1982-83, personnel staffing specialist, 1983-86; salesperson First United Realtors, Barrington, Ill., 1987—. Recipient Certs. of Spl. Achievement, U.S. Office Personnel Mgmt., 1980, Cert. of Appreciation, 1981. Mem. Nat. Assn. Female Execs., AAUW. Roman Catholic. Office: First United Realtors 115 S Hough St Barrington IL 60010

RAMOS, PABLO, physician, diagnostic radiologist; b. Veracruz, Mex., June 26, 1928; came to U.S., 1954; s. Pablo and Magdalena (Ramirez) R.; m. Tija Andritis, July 28, 1956; children: Beatriz Magdalena, Dean Arthur. MD, Nat. U. Mex., 1953. Diplomate Am. Bd. Radiology. Intern St. James Hosp., Butte, Mont., 1955-56; resident in gen. surgery Bismarck (N.D.) Affiliated Hosps., 1956-59, resident in gen. radiology, 1960-63; staff radiologist diagnosis and therapy Q&R Clinic Bismarck Hosp., 1963-80, also bd. dirs., chmn. dept. radiology, 1981-83; clin. assoc. prof. U. N.D., Grand Forks, 1975-77, clin. prof. radiolgy, 1979—; diagnostic radiologist Q&R Clinic and Med. Ctr. One, Bismarck, 1980—. Bd. dirs. Bismarck-Mandan Orchestral Assn., 1974, 85, N.D. chpt. Am. Caner Soc., 1970-75, v.p. 1974-75. Fellow Am. Coll. Radiology (treas. N.D. chpt. 1973-84); mem. N.D. Med. Assn., N.D. Radiol. Soc. (pres. 1972), Radiol. Soc. N.Am., InterAm. Coll. Radiology. Republican. Baptist. Avocations: opera, classical music, travel, reading. Office: Q&R Clinic 222 N 7th St Bismarck ND 58502

RAMPAGE, BRUCE EDWARD, health care executive; b. Chgo., Mar. 5, 1947; s. Edward Joseph and Angela (Czachor) R.; m. Patricia Ann Rampage, Oct. 14, 1973; children: Tessa Ann, Joshua Seth. BA, St. Xavier Coll., 1973; M in Mgmt., Northwestern U., 1977. Dir. materials mgmt. U. Chgo., 1973-77; v.p. West Suburban Hosp. Med. Ctr., Oak Park, Ill., 1977-83; sr. v.p. Edward Hosp., Naperville, Ill., 1983—; cons. Chgo. Hosp. Council, 1985—. Mem. Am. Coll. Health Care Execs. (cons. 1986—), Edward Hosp. Assn. Avocations: ichthyology, writing, reading. Home: 13511 S Natchez Trail Orland Park IL 60462 Office: Edward Hosp 801 S Washington St Naperville IL 60566

RAMPELT, JEROME THOMAS, education association administrator; b. Cleve., Mar. 20, 1946; s. William Henry and Audrey Syvilla (Neidermeyer) R.; m. Cheryl Ann Levy, June 8, 1969; children: Jason, Michelle. BS, Ohio State, 1968, MA, 1970. Cons. univ. Ohio Edn. Assn., Cin. and Cleve., 1978-85; regional dir. Ohio Edn. Assn., Medina, 1985—. Mem. Pub. Sector Labor Relations Assn. (pres. 1986-87), Indsl. Relations Research Assn., Am. Mgmt. Assn. Democrat. Mem. Unitarian Ch. Avocations: running, classical music. Home: 6651 Edgemoor Ave Solon OH 44139 Office: Ohio Edn Assn 5000 Gateway Dr Rm 207 Medina OH 44256

RAMPERSAD, OLIVER RONALD, microbiologist, educator; b. Trinidad, W.I., Jan. 27, 1921; s. Soan Gocool and Roopnarinesingh; came to U.S., 1944; m. Peggy Ann Snellings, Mar. 19, 1955; 1 child, Gita. Oxford & Cambridge Higher Cert., St. Mary's Coll., Trinidad, 1936; Ph.B., U. Chgo., 1946; M.S., 1954, Ph.D., 1961. Teaching asst. in microbiology U. Chgo., 1954-61, research assoc. physiology and immunology, 1961-73, sr. technologist dept. pathology-clin. chemistry, 1973-86. Bd. dirs. Friends of Internat. House, Chgo., Youth Council, Trinidad; mem. Ind. Voters Ill. Mem. Fedn. Am. Socs. for Exptl. Biology, AAAS, Am. Soc. Microbiologists, Sigma Xi. Hindu. Contbr. articles to profl. jours. Home: 5531 S Kenwood Ave Chicago IL 60637

RAMPLEY, WAYNE ALLAN, pharmacist; b. El Paso, Tex., July 8, 1948; s. Oliver Coleman and Faye Gene (Davis) R.; m. Pamela Dean Young, June 7, 1967; children: Michael Wayne, Kimberly Rene, Mandy Dawn. BS, Southwestern Okla. State U., 1971. Pharmacist City Drug, Tulia, Tex., 1971-72; mgr. Sav-On Drug, Amarillo, Tex., 1972-79; co-owner, mgr. Kendall-Rampley Pharmacy, Muskogee, Okla., 1979-85; owner Muskogee Family Pharmacy, 1985—; pvt. practice real estate investor, developer Muskogee. Mem. Am. Pharm. Assn., Panhandle Pharm. Assn. (pres. 1977), Phi Delta Chi. Republican. Club: Muskogee Country. Lodges: Masons, Elks, Shriners. Avocations: sailing, flying, travelling.

RAMPP, DAVID GERALD, educator; b. St. Paul, Feb. 18, 1939; s. Theodore Joseph and Gwendolyne Marie (Mavor) R.; m. Nancy Louise Johnson, Dec. 20, 1969; children: Bethany, Emily. BA in English and History, Coll. St. Thomas, 1961; postgrad., Mankato State U., 1963, U. Minn., Hamline U., St. Catherine's Coll. Cert. jr. high sch. tchr., Minn. English tchr. Chokio (Minn.) High Sch., 1961-62, St. Odilia's Sch., St. Paul, 1963-66, Mpls. Pub. Schs., 1966—; chmn. dept. Jordan Jr. High Sch., Mpls., 1971-73, Franklin Jr. High Sch., Mpls., 1986—. Mem. Oakdale (Minn.) Human Rights Commn., 1975, Contact-Teleministry, 1982-84; del. DFL Dist. Convs., 1971—; deacon Presbyn. Ch. Served with USAAFR, 1963-68. Recipient Most Appreciated Tchr. award Franklin Jr. High Sch., 1985. Mem. Am. Fedn. Tchrs., Minn. Fedn. Tchrs. (union steward 1977-79), Minn. Council Tchrs. English. Democrat. Avocations: cross country skiing, horse riding, growing roses, walking, enjoying life.

RAMSAY, JOHN T., professional basketball team coach; b. Phila., Feb. 21, 1925; m. Jean Ramsay; 5 children. Student, St. Joseph's Coll., 1949. Coach St. Joseph's Coll., Phila., 1955-66, Phila. 76ers (Nat. Basketball Assn.), 1968-72, Buffalo Braves, 1972-76, Portland (Oreg.) Trail Blazers, 1976-86, Ind. Pacers, Indpls., 1986—. Coached winning team Nat. Basketball Assn. Championship, 1977. Office: Ind Pacer 2 W Washington St Suite 510 Indianapolis IN 46204 *

RAMSEY, DAN CLARENCE, author, marketing information analyst; b. San Fernando, Calif., Mar. 11, 1945; s. Clarence Allen and Florence May (Curtis) R.; m. Judith Kay Richards, Nov. 13, 1970; children: Heather Kay, Byron Hyun-Mo, Brendon Yun-Mo. BA in Gen. Studies, Eastern Oreg. State Coll., 1987. Dir. Ramsey & Assocs., Vancouver, 1980-85; project developer Dunn-Rowan Inc., Vancouver, 1983-84; mktg. info. analyst Fisher Controls, Marshalltown, Iowa, 1985—; author: Popular Mechanics Guide to Outdoor Structures, Effective Lighting for Home and Business, Build Your Own Fitness Center, How to Forecast Weather, The Complete Book of Fences, Budget Flying, Building a Log Cabin from Scratch or Kit, 18 others; contbr. articles to profl. jours. Mem. Nat. Assn. Home and Workshop Writers. Home: 208 N 8th St Marshalltown IA 50158

RAMSEY, DAVID SELMER, hospital executive; b. Mpls., Feb. 19, 1931; s. Selmer A. and Esther D. (Dahl) R.; m. Elinor Corfield, Aug. 15, 1953; children—Scott, Stewart, Thomas. B.S., U. Mich., 1953, M.S. in Microbiology, 1954, M.H.A., 1962. Research asst. Detroit Inst. Cancer Research, 1954-60; asst. adminstr. Harper Hosp., Detroit, 1962-68; assoc. adminstr. Harper Hosp., 1968-72; exec. v.p. Iowa Meth. Med. Ctr., Des Moines, 1972-83; pres. Iowa Meth. Med. Ctr., 1983—. chmn. bd. Des Moines Pastoral Counseling, 1981-84; bd. dirs. Arts and Recreation Council Greater Des Moines, 1983-86; group chmn. United Way Campaign, Des Moines, 1984. Fellow Am. Coll. Hosp. Adminstrs.; mem. Am. Hosp. Assn. (ho. of dels. 1982—), Iowa Hosp. Assn. (bd. dirs. 1974—). Republican. Presbyterian. Clubs: Des Moines, Wakonda. Lodge: Rotary. Avocations: golf; tennis; photography. Home: 2825 Caulder St Des Moines IA 50321 Office: Iowa Meth Med Ctr 1200 Pleasant St Des Moines IA 50308

RAMSEY, JESSE RAY, pediatrician; b. Ft. Worth, Dec. 27, 1946; s. Ray Franklin and Margie Maxine (Maley) R.; children from a previous marriage: Jessica Sue, Sheila Rae; m. Marilyn Kathreen Morgan, June 14, 1986. BS in Chemistry, Biology, Tex. Wesleyan Coll., 1970; DO, Tex. Coll. Osteopathic Medicine, 1974. Diplomate Am. Bd. Osteopathic Pediatricians. Intern U.S. Army Hosp. Med. Ctr., El Paso, Tex., 1975-76, resident in pediatrics, 1974-76, neonatal fellow, chief resident, 1976-77; chief pediatrics dept. U.S. Army Hosp., Augsburg, Fed. Republic Germany, 1977-79; pvt. practice specializing in pediatrics Cape Girardeau, Mo., 1979—; dir. neonatal ICU, regional neonatal transp. services SE Mo. Hosp., Cape Girardeau, 1980—, assoc. prof. pediatrics Washington Univ. Childrens Hosp., St. Louis, 1981—, nursing SE MO. State Univ., Cape Girardeau, 1983-85. Fellow Am. Acad. Osteopathic Pediatricians (bd. dirs.); mem. Am. Acad. Pediatrics, Am. Osteopathic Assn., Mo. State Med. Assn., Mo. Perinatal Assn., Greater Cape Girardeau Hist. Soc. (v.p. 1986—). Republican. Presbyterian. Lodge: Masons. Home: 313 Themis Cape Girardeau MO 63701 Office: Pediatric Assocs SE Mo 1435 Mount Auburn Rd Cape Girardeau MO 63701

RAMSEY, LELAND KEITH, petroleum engineer; b. Topeka, May 31, 1952; s. Keith G. and Darlene (Berndt) R.; m. Kimberly M. Milner, Mar. 31, 1979; children: Jessica Ray, Jeremy Lee. B.S., Kans. State U., 1974. Field engr. Dowell div. Dow Chem. Corp., Rock Springs, Wyo., 1975-78, dist. engr., Williston, N.D., 1978-80, sr. dist. engr., 1980-81; dist. sales supr. Dowell/Schlumberger Inc., Williston, 1981—, field service mgr., 1985— . Mem. Soc. Petroleum Engrs. (chpt. membership chmn. 1982-83, sec.-treas. 1983-84, vice-chmn., 1984-85, chmn. 85-86, scholarship chmn. 1986—), Sooner Oilmen's Club, Am. Assn. Petroleum Geologists, Am. Petroleum Inst. Republican. Baptist. Lodge: Elks. Avocations: golf, racquetball. Home: 618 15th Ave W Williston ND 58801 Office: PO Box 879 Williston ND 58801

RAMSEY, PETER MICHAEL, manufacturing executive; b. Norwalk, Conn., Dec. 1, 1943; s. John Preston and Joy Beach (Rinaldo) R.; m. Virginia Linnette Ziegler, June 18, 1966; children: Brian Patrick, Stephen Allen, Jill Elizabeth. BA, Colo. Coll., 1965; MBA, Northwestern U., 1967. With sales dept. Flexible Steel Lacing Co., Downers Grove, Ill., 1967-73, sales mgr., 1973, v.p. sales, 1974—; treas., chief fin. officer Flexible Steel Lacing Co., Downers Grove, 1987—; also bd. dirs. Flexible Steel Lacing Co., Downers Grove, Ill.; bd. dirs. Flexible Steel Lacing, Internat., Manchester, Eng., Tatch-A-Cleat Products, El Monte, Calif. Pres. United Way of Glen Ellyn, Ill., 1986—, Glen Ellyn Pub. Library, 1986—; mem. exec. bd. Glen Ellyn Youth Bd., 1986—, exec. council 1st Congl. Ch., Glen Ellyn, 1986—. Mem. Sigma Chi. Republican. Office: Flexible Steel Lacing Co 2525 Wisconsin Ave Downers Grove IL 60515

RAMSEY, WILLIAM CRITES, JR., lawyer; b. Omaha, July 31, 1912; s. William Crites and Mary Elizabeth (Cook) R.; m. Mary Jane Kopperud, Mar. 24, 1942; children—Mary Laura Ramsey Foster, Barbara Lee, Carol Elizabeth, Julie Andrea Ramsey Cutright. A.B., Dartmouth Coll., 1934; LL.B., Harvard U., 1938. Bar: Nebr. 1938. Assoc. Spier, Ramsey, Ellick, Omaha, 1940-48; v.p., sec. Am. Rd. Equipment Co., Omaha, 1948-55; v.p. N.P. Dodge Co., Omaha, 1955-60; pres. Am. Savings Co., Omaha, 1960-75; ptnr. Fellman, Ramsey, Epstein, Omaha, 1975-85, Mitchell and Demerath, Omaha, 1985-86 . Dep. county atty. Douglas County, 1947; pres. Family Service Omaha, 1951-53, Urban League, Omaha, 1954-55, Nebr. State Bd. Edn., Lincoln, 1978-87; dir. Nat. Assn. State Bds. Edn., Alexandria, Va., 1985. Mem. Nebr. Bar Assn., Omaha Bar Assn., Nebr. Assn. Indsl. Loan Cos. (pres. 1960), Am. Assn. Indsl. Banks (dir. 1962-64). Democrat. Congregationalist. Lodge: Masons (master 1950-51). Avocations: tennis; squash; reading. Home: 6481 Cuming St Omaha NE 68132 Office: 660 N 50th St Omaha NE 68132

RAMSTAD, JAMES M., state senator, lawyer; b. Jamestown, N.D., May 6, 1946; s. Marvin Joseph and Della Mae (Fode) R.; B.A., U. Minn., 1968; J.D. with honors, George Washington U., 1973. Adminstrv. asst. to speaker Minn. Ho. Reps., 1969; spl. asst. to Congressman Tom Kleppe, 1970; admitted to N.D. bar, D.C. bar, 1973, U.S. Supreme Ct. bar, 1976, Minn. bar, 1979; practiced in Jamestown, 1973, Washington, 1974-1978, Mpls., 1979—; mem. Minn. Senate, 1980—, asst. minority leader, 1983-87; instr. Am. govt. Montgomery (Md.) Coll., 1974; adj. prof. Am. U., Washington, 1975-78. Bd. dirs. Children's Heart Fund, Ridgedale YMCA, Big Bros. of Mpls.; mem. Wayzata Area Chem. Health Commn. Served as 1st lt. U.S. Army Res., 1968-73. Mem. ABA Fed., Minn., Hennepin County, D.C., N.D. bar assns., George Washington Law Assn., U. Minn. Alumni Assn. (nat. dir.), Am. Legion, Plymouth Civic League, Twin West C. of C. (dir.), Phi Beta Kappa, Phi Delta Theta. Republican. Clubs: Mpls. Athletic, Lafayette, U. Minn. Alumni (past pres. Washington). Lodge: Lions. Home: 2618 Crosby Rd Wayzata MN 55391 Office: 123 State Office Bldg Saint Paul MN 55155

RAMUNDO, MICHAEL CARMEN, marketing executive; b. Cin., Sept. 22, 1946; s. John Carmen and Mary Rose (Contino) R.; m. Beverly Anne Thomas; children: Tara Lynn, Jonathan Michael. BA in Indsl. Engring. cum laude, Miami U., Oxford, Ohio, 1969; MEd magna cum laude, U. Okla., 1971. Engr. Food Mgmt., Cin., 1971-72; instr., mgr. and trainer Cin. Milacron, Cin., 1972-85; chief exec. officer, founder MCR Mktg. Co. Inc., 1985—; bd. dirs. Cin. Bus. Connection. Author: Customer Service Training, 1985; contbr. articles to profl. jours. Chmn. alternative studies Cin. Pub. Schs., 1976, Levy sch. dist. coordinator Cin. Pub. Schs., 1978-79; campaign vice chmn. United Appeal, 1981, dist. coordinator, 1986; served in tchr. corps. Fed. Dept. HEW, 1969-71; bd. dirs. Ctr. Room Sch., 1973-74. Mem. Cin. Mktg. Club, Cin. Advt. Club, Hamilton County C. of C., Cin. C. of C., Nat. Machine Tool Bldrs. Assn. (chmn. tng. com. 1981), Chief Exec. Officer Roundtable. Avocations: theater, symphony, reading. Office: MCR Mktg Co Inc 351 Wood Ave Cincinnati OH 45220

RAMUNNI, JOSEPH SAVERIO, microcomputer manufacturing executive; b. Easton, Pa., Aug. 7, 1952; s. Joseph Anthony Ramunni and Sara (Domino) Hassan. AB in Engring., Lafayette Coll., 1976; M in Internat. Bus. with honors, U. Louvain, Belgium, 1982; MBA, U. Chgo., 1982. Sr. systems cons. Ingersoll Rand, Woodcliff Lake, N.J., 1973-80; mgr. internat. bus. devel. Gen. Elec. Co., Milw., 1982-84; dir. mktg. and sales Heurikon Corp., Madison, Wis., 1985—; Lectr. U. Chgo., 1985, U. Wis., Madison, 1985-86. Mentor Gov. of Wis. Mentor/Trustee Program, Milw., Madison, 1984-85. Recipient scholarship U. Louvain, Belgium, 1982. Avocations: French language, skiing, arts. Home: 344 W Dayton Madison WI 53703-2556 Office: Heurikon Corp 3201 Latham Dr Madison WI 53713

RAMUNNO, THOMAS PAUL, banker; b. Chgo., Sept. 13, 1952; s. Anthony Michael and Dolores (Siebert) R.; B.B.A., U. Ga., 1974, M.B.A., 1978; m. Deborah A. Pauline Benton, Jan. 31, 1976; 1 son, Michael Thomas. Treas., Concept, Inc., Atlanta, 1974-77; product dir. Johnson-Johnson, Inc., Atlanta, 1978-79; div. dir./gen. mgr. Rollins, Inc., Atlanta, 1979-80; cons. Chase Econometrics, Atlanta, 1980-83; v.p. comml. services, dir. corporate product mgmt./mktg. Union Trust Co. Md., 1983-84; prin., exec. v.p. Mktg. Scis. Group, Inc., Hunt Valley, Md., 1984-85; v.p., dir. Citicorp, Chgo., 1985—; disting. practitioner lectr. U. Ga., 1978-83; cons. in field. Exec. on loan Clarke County United Way, 1974-75. Mem. MBA Alumni U. Ga., U. Ga. Coll. Bus. Alumni (bd. dirs. 1978-83), Beta Gamma Sigma. Home: 242 W Ridge Trail Palatine IL 60067

RANCOUR, JOANN SUE, registered nurse; b. Elyria, Ohio, Nov. 10, 1939; d. Joseph and Ann (Donich) Sokol; diploma M.B. Johnson Sch. Nursing, 1960; B.S. in Profl. Arts, St. Josephs Coll., N. Windham, Maine, 1981; student in psychology Alfred Adler Inst., Chgo., 1976—, Lorain County Community Coll., 1973-75, Ursuline Coll., Cleve., 1976, Baldwin Wallace Coll., 1982; m. Richard Lee Rancour, July 29, 1961; children—Kathleen Ann, Donna Marie. Staff nurse Elyria Meml. Hosp., 1960-62, 72-75, head nurse psychiat. unit, 1975-79; sec.-treas. Alfred Adler Inst. Cleve., 1978-79; nurse Lorain County Juvenile Detention Home, Elyria, 1980; nurse VA Med. Center, Brecksville, Ohio, 1981—; mem. Cleve. VA nursing bioethics com. Active PTA, yearbook com., 1969-70, co-chmn. ways and means, 1971; Democratic poll worker, 1971-72; sec. St. Mary's Confrat. Christian Doctrine Program, 1970-71. Mem. Am. Nurses Assn. (cert. generalist practitioner psychiat. and mental health nursing practice), Ohio Nurses Assn., Nurses Orgn. of VA (NOVA), N.Am. Soc. Adlerian Psychology. Roman Catholic. Home: 205 Denison Ave Elyria OH 44035

RANCOURT, JOHN HERBERT, pharmaceutical company executive; b. Troy, N.Y., Aug. 10, 1946; s. Charles Dennis and Helen Mary (Keadin) R.; B.S. in Mgmt., Rensselaer Poly. Inst., 1968, M.S. in Mgmt., 1972, M.B.A., 1981; m. Susan Jane Koneski, Feb. 14, 1970; children—Karen Mary, John Herbert, Alison Jane, Elizabeth Anne, Maureen Ellen. Asst. to dir. research Rensselaer Poly. Inst., 1968-69; mgmt. trainee, buyer/purchasing agt., controller research div. Huyck Corp., Rensselaer, N.Y., 1969-74, corp. internat. project mgr., Wake Forest, N.C., 1974-76, adminstrv. service mgr. Formex div., 1976-77; sr. fin. analyst Abbott Labs., North Chicago, Ill., 1977-79, sect. mgr. sales acctg., 1979-80, mgr. fin. analysis, materials mgmt. div., 1980-82, mgr. fin. planning and analysis, pharm. products div., 1982-84; controller TAP Pharms subs. Abbott Labs., North Chicago, Ill., 1984—; instr. acctg. Coll. of Lake County, Grayslake, Ill., part-time, 1981—. Indian Guide/Princess Tribal leader YMCA, 1980—; solicitor United Way, 1981, 83, 85. C.P.A., Ill.; cert. mgmt. acct. Mem. Nat. Assn. Accts., Am. Acctg. Assn., Am. Inst. C.P.A.s, Ill. C.P.A. Soc. Roman Catholic. Club: Liberty Road and Track. Home: 826 Furlong Dr Libertyville IL 60048 Office: Abbott Labs 14th and Sheridan Rd North Chicago IL 60064

RAND, PETER ANDERS, architect, association executive; b. Hibbing, Minn., Jan. 8, 1944; s. Sidney Anders and Dorothy Alice (Holm) R.; m. Nancy Ann Straus, Oct. 21, 1967; children—Amy, Dorothy. B.A., St. Olaf Coll., 1966; cert. Oslo Internat. Summer Sch., Norway, 1964; student U. Minn. Sch. Architecture, 1969-72. Registered architect, Minn. Designer, architect, dir. pub. relations Setter, Leach & Lindstrom, Inc., Mpls., 1972-78; dir. bus. devel. and head Eden Prairie Office, Archtl. Design Group, Inc., Minn., 1979-80; dir. mktg. and publs. Mpls. Soc. AIA, 1981-82, exec. dir., 1982—; pub. Architecture Minn. mag.; cons., archtl. designer. Bd. dirs. Project for Pride in Living, 1979—, chmn. 1980-86; trustee Bethlehem Luth. Ch., 1980-86, chmn. bd. trustees, 1985; mem. Minn. Ch. Ctr. Commn., 1981—, chmn., 1985—; sec. Council of Component Execs. of AIA, 1987; bd. dirs. Minn. Council of Chs., 1985—, Greater Mpls. Council of Chs., 1985—, Arts Midwest, 1987—. Served with U.S. Army, 1966-69. Recipient honor award AIA Jour., 1981. Mem. AIA, Minn. Soc. AIA, Nat. Trust Hist. Preservation, Torske Klubben. Home: 1728 Humboldt Ave S Minneapolis MN 55403 Office: 275 Market St Suite 54 Minneapolis MN 55405

RANDALL, ARTHUR MUSIEL, data processing company executive; b. Pasadena, Calif., Nov. 28, 1932; s. Arthur Dunbar and Magdalena (Musiel) R.; Peri Eleanor Pratt, Sept. 11, 1954; children: Arthur Wayne, Scott Emerson, Diana Marie. AA, Pasadena City Coll., 1956; BS, Calif. State U., Los Angeles, 1958; MBA, UCLA, 1959. Br. mgr. IBM Corp., Phila., 1959-72; gen. div. mgr. System Devel Corp, Paramus, N.J., 1972-75; v.p. health info. systems McDonnell Douglas, St. Louis, 1975—; bd. dirs. Vis. Nurse Assn., St. Louis; trustee Normandy Osteo. Hosps., St. Louis. Contbr. articles to profl. jours. Speakers bur. United Way, San Gabriel, Calif., 1976; rep. campaign com. Calif., 1964—, rep. com. del., 1966; bd. dirs. U.S. Selective Service Com., Chesterfield, Md., 1983—. Served with USN, 1951-55.

Named Outstanding Citizen, City of San Gabriel, 1968, Outstanding Young Men of Am. Mem. Am. Med. Writers Assn., Am. Hosp. Assn. (speaker, educator 1983—), Sales Execs., Am. Legion. Club: Cushman of Am. (St. Louis)(pres.). Avocations: antique clocks, automobile and motor scooter restoration and collection. Home: 1693 Claymount Estates Ct Ballwin MO 63011 Office: 600 McDonnell Blvd Hazelwood MO 63042

RANDALL, DICK, advertising and public relations company owner; b. Port Chester, N.Y., Nov. 12, 1945; s. Gene and Frances (Grandazzo) Cicatelli; B.A., Marquette U., 1967; m. Maureen Russell, Aug. 17, 1966; children—Gregory, Katharine. Writer, news reporter Sta. WISN-TV, Milw., 1966-67; news reporter, anchorman Sta. WEMP, Milw., 1967-70; consumer reporter, anchorman Sta. WISN-TV, Milw., 1970-77; pres. Aquarius Prodns., Inc., Waukesha, Wis., 1977-86, Randall & Assocs., Inc., Waukesha, Milw. and Clearwater, Fla., 1986—; adj. instr. Marquette U., 1973-78. Pres. parish council. St. Anthony on the Lake, Pewaukee, Wis. Served with USNR, 1968—. Mem. Am. Fedn. TV and Radio Artists, Milw. Advt. Club, Better Bus. Bur. Milw., Variety Club of Wis., Met. Milw. Assn. Commerce, Sigma Delta Chi, Roman Catholic. Club: Pewaukee Yacht (bd. dirs., sec.). Home: W278 N2968 Rocky Point Rd Pewaukee WI 53072 Office: 225 Regency Ct Suite 200 Waukesha WI 53186

RANDALL, JAMES R., manufacturing company executive; b. 1924; married. B.S. in Chem. Engring, U. Wis., 1948. Tech. dir. Cargill Inc., 1948-68; v.p. prodn. and engring. Archer-Daniels-Midland Co., Decatur, Ill., 1968-69, exec. v.p., 1969-75, pres., 1975—, also dir. Served with AUS, 1943-46. Office: Archer-Daniels-Midland Co 4666 Faries Pkwy Decatur IL 62525 *

RANDALL, JOHN CARL, hospital official; b. Camden, N.J., July 12, 1949; s. Carl Eugene and Mary Elizabeth (Finck) R.; m. Barbara Jean Price, Oct. 30, 1971; children: Jonathan Edward, Shane William, Adam Gregory, Andrea Michal, Daniel Alan (dec.), Faith Ellen. Student Phila. Coll. Bible, 1968-71; cert. Nat. Exec. Housekeepers Assn., Akron U., 1982. Driver, salesman, Dy-Dee Services, Inc., Westmont, N.J., 1971-73; housekeeping-laundry mgr. Servicemaster Industries, Inc., Downers Grove, Ill., 1973-77; sta. mgr. Kirschner Bros. Oil Co., Inc., Haverford, Pa., 1977-78; unit mgr. ARA Services, Inc., Phila., 1978-80; dir. housekeeping and laundry Ashtabula (Ohio) Gen. Hosp., 1980-83; dir. housekeeping and laundry Lake Hosp. System, Inc., Painesville and Willoughby, Ohio, 1983—; cons. Wooster Community Hosp. (Ohio); began housekeeping depts. Bapt. East Hosp., Louisville, N.J. Rehab. Hosp., East Orange, Downstate Med. Ctr., Bklyn., Meml. Hosp. Roxborough, Pa., Burke Rehab. Ctr., White Plains, N.Y.; dir. housekeeping depts. Frankford Hosp., Phila., Burke Rehab. Ctr., Erie County Geriatric Ctr., Girard, Pa.; asst. dir. housekeeping Hopkins County Hosp., Madisonville, Ky., St. Christopher's Hosp. for Children, Phila. Named Resident Mgr. of Yr., Environ. Services Healthcare div. ARA Services, Inc., 1979. Mem. Nat. Exec. Housekeepers Assn. Office: Lake Hosp System Inc East Painesville OH 44077

RANDALL, PATRICIA LORENE, clinical social worker; b. Springfield, Mo., Nov. 14, 1942; d. James Joseph and Bertha (Sperandio) R.; B.A. in Sociology, Mt. St. Scholastica Coll., 1964; M.S.W., St. Louis U., 1966. Staff mem., clin. social worker Family and Personal Support Ctrs. of Greater St. Louis, 1966-80, dir. Clayton (Mo.) ctr. office, 1981—. Del. gov.'s adv. bd. Mo. White House Conf. on Families, 1979-80; chmn. St. Louis County Schs. Agys. Com. on Youth, 1969-71; mem. Block Partnership, 1971-72, mem. St. Francis Xavier Parish Council, 1982-83; bd. dirs. New Life Styles Orgn., 1981-84; mem. Children's Mental Health Services Council, 1981—. Cert. Acad. Cert. Social Workers. Mem. Nat. Assn. Social Workers (del. state bd. 1977-79), Am. Assn. Marriage and Family Therapy (approved supr.), Am. Group Psychotherapy Assn., Mo. Assn. Social Welfare. Roman Catholic. Club: Christian Life Community. Lodge: Soroptimists. Home: 11347 LeMonaco Ct 27A Saint Louis MO 63126 Office: 107 S Meramec St Clayton MO 63105

RANDALL, ROBERT JAMES, manufacturing company executive; b. Chandler, Ariz., Dec. 20, 1952; s. Robert James and Anna Frances (Cowen) R.; m. Christine Lee Everitt, Jan. 28, 1984; children: Kimberly Anne, Gregory Miles. BS, Rensselaer Poly. Inst., 1974, ME, 1975. Mgr. materials Colt Industries, Kansas City, Mo., 1976-79; MRP adminstr. Colt Industries, Burbank, Calif., 1979-80; mgr. materials Colt Industries, Bay Minette, Ala., 1980-84, mgr. mfg., 1984-85; dir. mktg. Colt Industries, Quincy, Ill., 1985—. Co-chmn. Episcopal Ecumenical Commn., Mobile, Ala., 1983-84; sr. warden Immanuel Episcopal Ch., Bay Minette, 1982-84. Mem. Am. Prodn. and Inventory Control Soc. (bd. dirs., pres. 1984-85), Quincy Sales and Mktg. Execs., Compressed Air and Gas Inst. Republican. Avocations: tennis, guitar. Home: 30 Ridgewood Hill Quincy IL 62301 Office: Colt Industries 36 & Wismann Ln Quincy IL 62301

RANDALL, RONALD FISHER, grocery store chain executive; b. Sioux City, Iowa, June 25, 1934; s. F. Dwain and J. Gale (Fisher) R.; m. Lavonne E. Woltoff, Dec. 27, 1961 (dec. May 1966); children—DaLinda, Ronald; m. Charlys Fern Stewart, Mar. 7, 1969. B.S. in Engring., U.S. Naval Acad., 1958. Dir. ops. Randall Stores, Mitchell, S.D., 1958-72, pres., 1972-81, pres., chmn. bd., 1981—; pres. Coca-Cola Bottling Co. of Central S.D. Inc., Mitchell; dir. Comml. Bank, Mitchell, Dakota Mfg. Inc., Mitchell. Clubs: Interlachen Country (Mpls.); Minnehaha Country (Sioux Falls, S.D.). Office: Randall Stores Inc 1705 N Main St Mitchell SD 57301

RANDALL, RUTH EVELYN, state official, educator; b. Underwood, Iowa, Mar. 4, 1929; d. Oluf and Lillie Martha (Bondo) Larsen; m. Robert Dale Randall (dec.); children—Robert, Mark, Diane. Teaching cert., Dana Coll., Blair, Nebr., 1949; B.S., U. Omaha, 1961; M.S., U. Nebr.-Omaha, 1968, Ed.S., 1972; Ed.D. in Ednl. Adminstrn., U. Nebr.-Lincoln, 1976. Various teaching positions Iowa and Nebr., 1949-67; elem. prin. Omaha Pub. Schs., 1967-75; asst. prin. Horace Mann Pub. Sch., Omaha, 1976-78; asst. supt. Rosemount Ind. Sch. Dist., Minn., 1978-81, dep. supt., 1981, supt., 1981-83; commr. of edn. State of Minn., St. Paul, 1983—; mem. Tandy Ednl. Grants Rev. Bd., planning group for Nat. Bd. Cert. of Profl. Tchrs., Carnegie Corp., Minn. State High Sch. League; lectr. in field. Mem. editorial adv. bd. Electronic Learning mag.; contbr. articles to profl. jours. Mem. exec. com. Minn. Acad. Excellence Found., adv. council for Mentally Retarded and Physically Handicapped, Higher Edn. Adv. Council, Horace Mann League of U.S., Minn. Women's Edn. Council, Jr. Achievement Bd., Citizens League, Sci. Mus., Blue Ribbon Adv. Council Campaign for Child Survival, Minn. Permanent Sch. Fund. Adv. com., Sta. KTCA Channel Two, Luth. Women's Caucus, Commn. on New Luth. Ch.; bd. dirs. Luth. Brotherhood Mut. Fund Bd.; mem. North Cen. Regional Edn. Lab. Bd., Nat. Adv. Panel Ctr. on Effective Secondary Schs.; trustee Tchrs. Retirement Assn.; mem. nat. adv. bd. Pub. Agenda Found.; mem. edn. adv. council Carnegie Corp., N.Y.; bd. dirs. SEARCH Inst., Agy. for Instrnl. Tech., Minn. Job Tng. Partnership; sec. Minn. Bd. Edn.; ex-officio mem. Minn. Indian Affairs Council; mem. Minn. High Tech. Council; mem. adv. bd. Bush Pub. Schs. Exec. Fellows; mem. Council Chief State Sch. Officers, mem. Edn. Commn. of States; mem. bd. advisors Close Up; mem. bd. Global Perspectives in Edn., Inc. Iowa Farm Bur. scholar Dana Coll., 1947-49; Franklin E. and Orinda M. Johnson fellow U. Nebr.-Lincoln, 1975-76; Bush Pub. Schs. Exec. fellow, 1980-81; recipient appreciation award Apple Valley C. of C., 1983, Award U. Nebr. Lincoln, 1983, Disting. Alumnus award Dana Coll., 1984. Mem. Minn. Valley Bus. and Profl. Women's Club (Woman of Yr. 1982), Minn. Assn. Supervision and Curriculum Devel., Minn. Assn. Sch. Adminstrs., Adminstrv. Women in Edn. Minn., LWV, AAUW, Upper Midwest Women in Edn. Adminstrn., Nat. PTA (life), Omaha Edn. Assn. (Human Relations award 1978), Women Execs. in State Govt. (founding), Nat. Council Adminstrv. Women in Edn., Am. Edn. Research Assn., Am. Assn. Sch. Adminstrs., Assn. Supervision and Curriculum Devel., Minn. Council for Gifted and Talented, Minn. Women's Econ. Roundtable, Minn. Soc. Fine Arts, U. Nebr.-Omaha Alumni (Achievement award 1987), U. Nebr. Alumni Assn. (life), Dana Coll. Alumni Assn., Phi Delta Kappa, Delta Kappa Gamma. Mem. Democratic Farm Labor Party. Lutheran. Home: 8738 Summer Wind Bay Woodbury MN 55125 Office: Dept of Edn 712 Capitol Sq Bldg 550 Cedar St Saint Paul MN 55101

RANDALL, WILLIAM SEYMOUR, electric service corporation; b. Champaign, Ill., July 5, 1933; s. Glenn S. and Audrey H. (Honnold) R.; m. Carol Mischler, Aug. 23, 1958; children—Steve, Cathy, Mike, Jennifer. B.S., Ind. State U., 1959. Controller Amana Refrigeration Co., Iowa, 1966-70; div. controller Trane Co., Clarksville, Tenn., 1970-74; corporate controller Trane Co., La Crosse, Wis., 1974-79; v.p., chief fin. officer Sta-Rite Industries, Milw., 1979-82; pres., owner Kurz Electric Service Co., Menasha, Wis., 1982—. Served with AUS, 1953-55. Mem. Financial Execs. Inst. Lodge: Rotary. Home: 807 Kay Kourt Neenah WI 54956 Office: 1400 S Oneida Rd Menasha WI 54952

RANDLES, BRUNO WILBER, musician, artist; b. Hutchinson, Kans., Jan. 17, 1928; s. Roy Sylvester and Helen May (Clark) R.; m. Mary Suzanne Orth, Jan. 3, 1950 (dec.); children—Racheal Hromadka, David, Vincent, Joseph, Mark, Peter, William, Paul, John, Julia. Grad. Hutchinson (Kans.) High Sch., 1945; student various pvt. insts. music and art, 1945-76. Player of trumpet, trombone, piano, organ with dance bands of all types, show bands, Dixieland bands, operating and recording as The Bruno Randles and The Jolly Brewers, 1951-58; played and recorded with 6 Fat Dutchmen, 1958-59; performer featured on Leo Greco TV show, Cedar Rapids, Iowa, 1959, 1969; painter landscapes, portraits, western paintings, 1950—; exhbns. include: Salone Contemporain, Paris, 1983; musician, painter, tchr. drawing Kirkwood Coll., Cedar Rapids, 1979—. Mem. Broadcast Music Inc. Republican. Roman Catholic. Composer various polkas and waltzes. Recs. for RCA Victor, Dot, Polkland, Columbia, Random. Home and office: 68 Devonwood Ave SW Cedar Rapids IA 52404

RANDLETT, RICHARD CARL, manufacturing executive; b. Hartland, Maine, May 24, 1931; s. Linwood Annis and Ada Louise (Cyr) R.; m. Gunvur Adeline Swanson, Mar. 24, 1954; children: Karen Elizabeth, Lisa Jane, Carla Annis, Erica Susan. BA, Colby Coll., 1954. Mgmt. trainee Am. Hardware Corp., New Britain, Conn., 1954-55; sales rep. Milw. Electric Tool Corp., Brookfield, Wis., 1955-62, dist. mgr., 1963-68, gen. sales mgr., 1969-72, nat. mktg. mgr., 1973-74, v.p. mktg., 1974—, also bd. dirs.; officer, bd. dirs. Milw. Electric Tool Can., Toronto, 1979—; bd. dirs. Marine Bank West, Brookfield. Mem. Am. Soc. Machine Mfrs. (bd. dirs. 1980-86). Avocations: reading, golf, gardening. Home: 855 Poplar Creek Dr Waukesha WI 53186 Office: Milw Electric Tool Corp 13135 W Lisbon Rd Brookfield WI 53005

RANDOLPH, BRUCE CHRISTIAN, accountant, training specialist; b. Glendale, Calif., June 24, 1939; s. Cecil Albert and Anna Lois (Christian) W.; m. Eugenia Lois Swarm, Sept. 6, 1964 (div. July 1971); children: Wayne Emerson, John David; m. Ila Louise Schneider, Nov. 24, 1971. BA, Pacific Union Coll., 1961. Employment interviewer Ill. State Job Service, Chgo., 1972-74, vocational counselor, 1974-75; dir. Outreach Ctr. McHenry County CETA, Woodstock, Ill., 1975-79; training specialist Ill. Dept. Employment Security, Chgo., 1979—, acct., 1986—. Bd. dirs. McHenry County unit Am. Cancer Soc., Woodstock, 1981-85, bd. dirs. Ill. div., Chgo., 1982-84, chmn. unit standards Ill. div. 1984. Served with U.S. Army, 1961-63. Mem. Ill. Tng. and Devel. Assn. Avocations: gourmet cooking, jazz, travel. Home: 319 Pleasant St Woodstock IL 60098 Office: Ill Dept Employment Security 401 S State St Chicago IL 60603

RANDOLPH, DONALD APPLEBY, building materials mfg. co. exec.; b. Biscoe, Ark., May 3, 1939; s. Almarine Leon and Bennie Lee (Appleby) R.; B.S. in Chemistry, Ark. A.M.&N. Coll., Pine Bluff, 1960; M.A. in Chemistry, Fisk U., 1962; postgrad. U. Chgo., 1971-73; m. Edna Ruth Watkins, Sept. 30, 1962; children—Donald Appleby, Daron Anthony. Analytical chemist Am. Can Co., Maywood, Ill., 1962-66; advanced analytical chemist U.S. Gypsum Co., Des Plaines, Ill., 1966-68, group leader, 1968-71, analytical testing mgr., 1971-74, research mgr., 1974-84, mgr. tech. transfer, 1984—; cons. in field. Coach Briarcliffe Community Youth Baseball & Basketball, Wheaton, Ill., 1977-84; treas. Pack 382, Dupage Area council Boy Scouts Am., Wheaton, 1977-82. Recipient Cert. of Appreciation, U.S. Gypsum Co., 1976. Fellow Am. Inst. Chemists; mem. AAAS, Am. Chem. Soc., Am. Mgmt. Assn., Kappa Alpha Psi (dir. Youth Guidance Found., Maywood-Wheaton chpt.). Methodist. Author chpt. Ency. of Indsl. Chem. Analysis, 1971; founder, editor U.S. Gypsum Co. Research Center news mag., 1968-70. Home: 1605 S Prospect St Wheaton IL 60187 Office: 101 S Wacker Dr Chicago IL 60606

RANFRANZ, ANN LOUISE, social worker; b. Rochester, Minn., Aug. 28, 1953; d. Richard Lewis and Eileen Patricia (Sullivan) R.; m. Jeffrey Alan Kremers, Sept. 27, 1985; children: Corey Elizabeth. BA in Psychology, Knox Coll., Galesburg, Ill., 1975, teaching certificate, 1976; MSW, U. Wis., Milw., 1981. Tchr. Galesburg High Sch., 1976-78; victim advocate Rapeline, Rochester, Minn., 1978-79; dir. sexual assault counseling unit Milw. County Dist. Attys. Office, 1982—; part-time instr. U. Wis., Milw., 1982-86. Chmn. Common Council Task Force on Sexual Assault and Domestic Violence, Milw., 1982-83. Mem. Wis. Pro Choice, Nat. Com. for Sane Nuclear Policy, Alpha Delta Mu. Democrat. Avocations: camping, cross country skiing, bicycling. Home: 4444 N Frederick Milwaukee WI 53211 Office: Milw County Dist Attys Office 821 W State St Milwaukee WI 53211

RANIERI, ADOLPH RICHARD, insurance company executive; b. Chgo., Sept. 24, 1946. BS, Ill. Inst. Tech., 1968; MBA, Northwestern U., 1971. CPA, CLU, CPCU, FLMI, Ill. Audit mgr. Ernst & Whinney, Chgo., 1971-77; mgr. acctg. Allstate Ins. Co., Northbrook, Ill., 1977-79; exec. v.p. United Equitable Ins. Group, Lincolnwood, Ill., 1979—; dir. United Equitable Corp., all subs., 1986—. Fellow Life Mgmt. Inst.; mem. Am. Inst. CPA's. Home: 444 Chicory Ln Buffalo Grove IL 60089 Office: United Equitable Ins Group 7373 N Cicero Ave Lincolnwood IL 60646

RANKIN, JOHN CARTER, consulting chemist; b. Knoxville, Tenn., Dec. 21, 1919; s. Nelson Henry and Rosine Bonna (Carter) R.; m. Ruth Elizabeth Kirk, Aug. 8, 1943; children—Christine, Mark, Ellen. B.S., Bradley U., 1942, M.S., 1955. Project leader derivatives and polymers, exploration research cereal products No. Regional Research Center, U.S. Dept. Agr., Peoria, Ill., 1946-79; cons. in starch chemistry, 1980—. Served with U.S. Army, 1944-46. Recipient Disting. Service award U.S. Dept. Agr., 1955, 64; Fed. Inventors award U.S. Dept. Commerce, 1980. Mem. Am. Chem. Soc., Am. Assn. Cereal Chemists, TAPPI, AAAS, Sigma Xi. Republican. Contbr. chpts. to sci. textbooks, numerous articles to profl. jours.; patentee. Home: 1734 E Maple Ridge Dr Peoria IL 61614

RANNABARGAR, MARVIN RAY, minister; b. Kansas City, Mo., Jan. 6, 1939; s. Arthur McDonald and Grace B. (Clements) R.; m. Lola I. Bailey, Aug. 10, 1960 (div. Oct. 1981); children: Paul, Ruth. BA, Culver-Stockton Coll., 1961; MDiv, Drake U., 1964. Ordained minister Christian Ch., 1964. Assoc. pastor 1st Christian Ch., Hannibal, Mo., 1966-68; sr. pastor 1st Christian Ch., DuQuoin, Ill., 1969-71, Brookfield, Wis., 1971-75; sr. pastor Univ. Christian Ch., Normal, Ill., 1975-80, Emerson Park Christian Ch., Kansas City, Kans., 1980-87, Ridgewiew Christian Ch., Kansas City, 1987—; chmn. bd. UMHE, U. Wis., Milw., 1974-75; chmn. Hosp. Chaplaincy, Bloomington-Normal, 1977. Contbr. articles to Disciple mag., 1970—. Chmn., mem. Human Relations Commn., Kansas City, 1984-87; mem. adv. bd. Public Utilities Bd., Kansas City, 1985-87; mem. bd. Planned Parenthood, Bloomington, 1978, Crosslines, Kansas City, 1987—. Psyche M. Gooden scholar, 1962-63. Mem. Tau Kappa Epsilon. Democrat. Home: 8643 E 50 St Kansas City MO 64129 Office: Ridgeview Christian Ch 8640 Sin-A-Bar Rd Kansas City MO 64129

RANNEY, RICHARD WILLIAM, data processing specialist; b. Davenport, Iowa, Nov. 2, 1944; s. Robert Lee and June Rose (Holzhausen) R.; m. Geraldine Faith Cotten, Jan. 28, 1967 (div. Sept. 1976); m. Milda Maria Dargis, Mar. 28, 1981; children: Brianna Dargis, Robert Liutauras. BS in Mktg., Okla. State U., 1967; MBA in Quantitative Analysis, So. Meth. U., 1968. Systems engr. Electronic Data Systems Corp., Dallas, 1971-77, account mgr., 1977-80; mktg. rep. Electronic Data Systems Corp., Chgo., 1980-82, account mgr., 1982—; instr., author course syllabus Computer Career Program De Paul U., Chgo., 1982-84. Served to 1st lt. USAR, 1968-71. Fellow Life Mgmt. Inst., Life Office Mgmt. Assn.; mem. Am. Prodn. and Inventory Control Soc. (cert.), Sierra Club (outing chmn. Chgo. group 1979-81). Club: Chgo. Mountaineering. Avocations: mountain climbing, skiing, kayaking, canoeing, backpacking. Home: 22 S Thurlow Hinsdale IL 60521 Office: Electronic Data Systems Corp PO Box 2047 LaGrange IL 60525-2047

RANSOM, WILLARD BLYSTONE, lawyer; b. Indpls., May 17, 1916; s. Freeman Briley and Nettie Lillian (Cox) R.; m. Gladys Lucille Miller, July 11, 1947; children—Philip Freeman, Judith Ellen. B.A. summa cum laude, Talladega (Ala.) Coll., 1936; LL.B., Harvard U., 1939. Bar: Ind. 1939. Dep. atty. gen. State of Ind., 1939-41; practice law, Indpls., 1939—; assoc. Bamberger & Feibleman, Indpls., 1971-83, of counsel, 1983—; gen. mgr. Madame C.J. Walker Mfg. Co., Indpls., 1954-71; dir. Mchts. Nat. Bank & Trust Co., Indpls. Bd. dirs. Legal Services Orgn.; mem. com., bd. dirs. Indpls. br. NAACP, former state pres. Served to capt. JAGC, U.S. Army, 1941-46; ETO. Recipient Disting. Alumnus award Talladega Coll., 1964; Traylor award Legal Services for the Poor, 1975. Mem. Ind. Bar Assn., Marion County Bar Assn., Indpls. Bar Assn., Omega Psi Phi. Democrat.

RAO, BALAKRISHNA, plant pathologist, mycologist, botanist; b. Yelluru, South Kanara, India, July 23, 1944; came to U.S., 1969; d. Y. Venkatramanayya and B. Padmavathiamma; m. Sudaxina B. Rao, Mar. 1, 1981; children: Anita B., Vinod B. BS, U. Mysore, India, 1964; MS, U. Bombay, 1966, U. N.C., 1971; PhD, Ohio State U., 1976. Postdoctoral fellow O.A.R.D.C., Wooster, Ohio, 1976-77; plant pathologist Davey Tree Expert Co., Kent, Ohio, 1977-84, dir. lawncare tech. resources, 1984-87, mgr. diagnostic lab., 1977-87, mgr. tech. resources, 1987—. contbg. editor: Landscape Mgmt. 1982—; contbr. papers to sci. jours. U. Bombay Merrit scholar, 1965, U. Madras Grant Commn. scholar, 1967. Mem. Am. Phytopathological soc. (exec. mem. diagostic com.), Am. Mycological Soc., Avocations: gardening, indoor plantscape, travel, photography, stamp collecting. Home: 3046 Stockbridge Dr Stow OH 44224

RAO, DABEERU C., genetic epidemiologist, bio-statistician; b. Santhabommali, India, Apr. 6, 1946; came to U.S., 1972; s. Ramarao Patnaik and Venkataratnam (Raghupatruni) R.; m. Sarada Patnaik, 1974; children: Ravi, Lakshmi. BS in Stats., Indian Statis. Inst., Calcutta, 1967, MS, 1968, PhD, 1971. Research fellow U. Sheffield, Eng., 1971-72; asst. prof., geneticist U. Hawaii, Honolulu, 1972-78, assoc. prof.-geneticist, 1978-80; assoc. prof., dir. div. biostats. Washington U. Med. Sch., St. Louis, 1980-82, prof. depts. biostats., psychiatry and genetics, 1982—, adj. prof. math., 1982—, dir. div. biostats., 1980—. Author: A Source Book for Linkage in Man, 1979, Methods in Genetic Epidemiology, 1983, Genetic Epidemiology of Coronary Heart Disease, 1984; editor-in-chief Genetic Epidemiology jour.; contbr. articles to profl. jours. NIMH research grantee, 1980—, NIGMS grantee, 1980—. Mem. Am. Statis. Assn., Am. Soc. Human Genetics, Behavior Genetics Assn., Am. Epidemiol. Soc. Office: Box 8067 Div Biostatistics Washington U Sch Medicine 660 S Euclid Ave Saint Louis MO 63110

RAO, LALITHA KOMMULA, psychiatrist; b. Masulipatnam, India, Sept. 22, 1954; came to U.S., 1978; d. Sreerambabu and Lakshmi Sakunthala (Kolipara) Velisetti; m. Kommula C. Rao, Mar. 12, 1978; children: Vidyak, Madhavik. Student, Stella Maris Coll., Madras, India, 1970-71; MBBS, Kilpauk Med. Coll., Madras, 1978. Resident in psychiatry Loyola U. Med. Ctr., Maywood, Ill., 1979-82, Med. Coll. Ohio, Toledo, 1982-83; practice medicine specializing in psychiatry Tiffin, Ohio, 1983—; cons. psychiatrist Tiffin Mercy Hosp., 1983—, Tiffin Devel. Ctr., 1985—. Mem. Am. Psychiat. Assn., Ohio State Med. Assn., Ohio State Psychiat. Assn. Hindu. Office: Betty Jane Ctr 65 St Francis Ave Suite 123 Tiffin OH 44883

RAO, MANIKYA ATCHUTUNI, computer executive; b. Swarna, Andhra Pradesh, India, Nov. 10, 1942; came to U.S., 1970; s. Nagakoteswara A. and Seetharavamma A. Rao; m. Radha Sankara, Aug. 30, 1973; children: Shobha, Sridhar, Prasanti. BSEE, Regional Engring. Coll., Warangal, India, 1965, MSEE, 1967; MSEE in Computers, Iowa State U., 1971. Systems programming Indsl. Television Services, Chgo., 1972-73; computer scientist Northwestern U., Chgo., 1973-74; sr. systems analyst Westinghouse Electric Co., Chgo., 1974-84; sr. project engr. Gen. Motors Corp., Warren, Mich., 1985—; cons. AMRAO, Westmont, Ill., 1984-85. Mem. IEEE, Soc. Mfg. Engrs. Avocations: swimming, reading tech. mags. Home: 546 Revere Ave Westmont IL 60559

RAO, PAL VENKATESWARA, data processing educator; b. Pedaravur, Andhra Pradesh, India, Nov. 10, 1941; came to U.S., 1965; s. Rangaiah and Sitaravamma (Kodali) R.; m. Laura Mae Bewie, Mar. 21, 1978. BA, Andhra U., Waltair, India, 1962; MLS, U. Ill., 1968; MEd, So. Ill. U., Carbondale, 1968, PhD, 1986. Cert. data processor. From instr. to assoc. prof. data processing Eastern Ill. U., Charleston, 1968-80, prof., 1980—, head Info. Systems and Media Services, 1981—. Contbr. articles in the fields of library, media and data processing to profl. jours.; developed numerous computer programs. Mem. ALA, Assn. for Ednl. Communications and Tech., Data Processing Mgmt. Assn. (internat. bd. dirs., chmn. membership com. 1986—, nominating com. 1986—), Phi Delta Kappa. Republican. Lutheran. Avocations: photography, gardening, numismatics. Home: 2213 Cortland Dr Charleston IL 61920 Office: Eastern Ill U 201 Library Charleston IL 61920

RAO, SHANKARARAO NARAYANA, psychiatrist; b. Nanjangud, India, Aug. 7, 1935; came to U.S., 1969; s. Shankararao and Devu Bai (Shankararao) Uttarkar; m. Renu Narayana, Nov. 7, 1973; children: Nikhil, Neil. Degree in intersci., St. Philomena's Coll., Mysore, India, 1956; BS in Medicine and Surgery, Mysore Med. Coll., 1963; diploma in psychol. medicine, India Inst. Neurosci., Bangalore, India, 1968. Diplomate Am. Psychiatry Assn., Am. Acad. Family Physicians. Lectr. in human anatomy Bellary (India) Med. Coll., 1965-66; registrar in psychiatry St. Lawrence Hosp., Caterham, England, 1969; resident in psychiatry Mo. Inst. Psychiatry, St. Louis, 1970-74; clin. dir. alcoholism services St. Louis State Hosp., 1975-85, psychiatrist in geriatry services, 1985—; pvt. practice psychiatry St. Ann, Mo., 1976—. Fellow Am. Acad. Family Physicians; mem. Am. Psychiatry Assn. Avocations: tennis, gardening. Home: 692 Sunbridge Dr Chesterfield MO 63017 Office: 10822 Saint Charles Rock Rd Saint Ann MO 63074

RAO, SURENDRA BALAKRISHNA, machine tool company executive; b. Ootacamund, India, July 2, 1949; came to U.S., 1977; s. Balakrishna Srinivasa and Leela Rao; m. Barbara Ann Pramik, Apr. 28, 1984. BS in Engring., Bangalore (India) U., 1970; MS in Engring., McMaster U., Hamilton, Ont., Can., 1977; PhD, U. Wis., 1980. Tech. officer Cen. Machine Tool Inst., Bangalore, 1970-75; research scientist Battelle Columbus (Ohio) Labs., 1980-83; v.p. engring. Nat. Broach & Machine, Mount Clemens, Mich., 1983—. Contbr. articles to profl. jours.; patentee in field. Mem. ASME, N.Am. Mfg. Research Inst. (sr.). Hindu. Avocations: woodworking, Bonsai. Office: Nat Broach & Machine 17500 23 Mile Rd Mount Clemens MI 48044

RAPAPORT, ROSS JAY, college educator, administrator; b. Lansing, Mich., Jan. 30, 1950; s. Ramond Harvey and A. Geraldine (Gauss) R.; m. Shelly Sue Becker, July 2, 1977; children: Lauren, Allison. BA, Mich. State U., 1972; MA, Ohio State U., 1975, PhD, 1979. Nat. cert. counselor. Sr. staff psychologist Univ. Counseling Service U. Iowa, Iowa City, 1979-82; assoc. prof. Counseling Ctr. Cen. Mich. U., Mt. Pleasant, Mich., 1983—. Co-author eight jour. articles, 1979—. Bd. mem. Mt. Pleasant Counseling Service, 1984—; mem. adv. council Mid-state Substance Abuse Commn., Clare, Mich., 1984—. Mem. Am. Assn. Counseling and Devel., Am. Coll. Personnel Assn., Mich. Assn. Counseling and Devel., Mich. Coll. Personnel Assn. Avocations: jogging, exercising, reading, playing with my children. Home: 403 E Grand Ave Mount Pleasant MI 48858 Office: Counseling Ctr Cen Mich U 102 Foust Hall Mount Pleasant MI 48859

RAPIN, LYNN SUZANNE, psychologist, educator; b. Sault Ste. Marie, Mich., Nov. 26, 1946; d. John Floyd and Ruth Antoinette (Martin) R.; m. Robert K. Conyne; children: Suzanne, Zachary. BA, Fla. State U., 1968; MEd, U. Ill., 1970, PhD, 1973. Lic. psychologist, Ohio, Ill. Resident dir. U. Ill., Champaign-Urbana, 1970-73, assoc. dir. unit one living ctr. coll. arts. and scis., 1971-73; asst. prof. edn. Ill. State U., Normal-Bloomington, 1973-78, assoc. prof. edn., 1978-80; pvt. practice psychology Cin., 1980—; staff psychologist Student Counseling Ctr., Ill. State U., 1973-76, coordinator ednl. programs., 1976-80; adj. assoc. prof. U. Cin., 1981—; cons. in field. Contbr. articles to profl. jours. and chpts. to books. Bd. dirs. Personal Assistance Telephone Help, 1979-81. Ill. State U. grantee 1975-79, State of Ill. grantee, 1978-79. Mem. Am. Psychol. Assn., Am. Assn. Counseling and

Devel., Am. Coll. Personnel Assn., Assn. for Specialists in Group Work, Assn. for Counselor Edn. and Supervision, Ohio Psychol. Assn. Home and Office: 1134 Cryer Ave Cincinnati OH 45208

RAPOPORT, KENNETH PHILLIP, accountant; b. Chgo., Nov. 3, 1960; s. Morris and Masha Rapoport. BBA, Loyola U., Chgo., 1982; postgrad., DePaul U., 1984. CPA, Ill. Acct. Soloway, Geib & Siegel, Skokie, Ill., 1982-83, Adler & Drobny, Ltd., Northbrook, Ill., 1983-85, Kessler, Orlean, Silver & Co., Skokie, 1985-86, Goldstein, Pierce & Co., Chgo., 1986-87; pvt. practice acctg. Skokie, Ill., 1987—. Mem. Sigma Alpha Mu. Jewish. Lodge: Masons. Avocations: coin and stamp collecting. Office: 4241 W Main St Skokie IL 60076

RAPP, GARY LEE, utility company executive; b. Columbus, Ohio, Oct. 7, 1947; s. Joseph W. and Marjorie E. (Noon) R.; m. Karen Lee Naughtrip, May 18, 1973; children: Adrienne, Scott, Katie. BS in Math., Ohio State U., 1969; MBA, Capital U., 1983. Programmer Columbia Gas System, Columbus, 1969-74, systems analyst, 1974-76, database analyst, 1977-82, mgr. data services, 1982-87, mgr. systems methodology, 1987—; pres. PC Rapport Co., Columbus, 1984—. Bd. dirs. Donegal Homeowner's Civic Assn., Columbus, 1986. Mem. Cen. Ohio Database Users Group (program dir. 1985-86, v.p. 1986—), Am. Mgmt. Assn. Republican. Avocations: skiing, golf, tennis, reading, pc computers. Home: 4643 Donegal Cliffs Dr Dublin OH 43017 Office: Columbia Gas System 1600 Dublin Rd Columbus OH 43215

RAPP, KIM LINDVAHL, accountant; b. Taylorville, Ill., Oct. 22, 1959; s. Ronald LeRoy and Ann Louise (Nelson) Lindvahl; m. Barry Matthew Rapp. BS, Western Ill. U., 1981. CPA, Ill. Staff acct. Price Waterhouse, Peoria, Ill., 1981-82; asst. controller Fed. Warehouse Co., East Peoria, Ill., 1982—. Mem. Am. Inst. CPA. Avocations: singing, dance. Home: 450 S Nebraska Morton IL 61550 Office: Fed Warehouse 200 Nat Rd East Peoria IL 61550

RAPPAPORT, CYRIL M., personnel administrator; b. N.Y.C., July 12, 1921; s. David M. and Saide (Newmark) R.; B.S., CCNY, 1942; M.A., Columbia U., 1943; postgrad. N.Y. U., 1943-44; m. Dorothy Pevsner, June 19, 1957 (dec. 1966); children—Stuart N., David M. Personnel cons., The Psychol. Corp., N.Y.C., 1943-44; indsl. relations asst. Emerson Radio Corp., N.Y.C., 1944-45; adminstrv. asst. A. Hollander & Son, Long Branch, N.J., 1946-52; prin. C.M. Rappaport, retailer, Hackensack, N.J., 1952-54; mem. exec. staff Martin E. Segal & Co., N.Y.C., 1954-56, Chgo., 1956-57; sec. Midcontinent Tube Service, Evanston, Ill., 1957-58; distbr. Investor's Diversified Services, Chgo., 1959-60; systems analyst Goldblatt Bros. Store, Chgo., 1960-64; personnel officer Ill. State Dept. Mental Health, 1964-69; dir. personnel Children's Meml. Hosp., Chgo., 1969-74, St. Joseph's Hosp., 1974-75, Edgewater Hosp., Chgo., 1975-76; dir. mgmt. and personnel services Jewish Vocat. Service, Chgo., 1976—; dir. Paket, Inc., 1960-61. Bd. dirs. Bernard Horwich Community Center, 1971-73; mem. personnel planning and cons. com. United Way, 1978-79; mem. Age Discrimination Sub. Com. Mayor's Coordinating Com. Old Age, 1979—; mem. rehab. com. Chgo. Hosp. Council, 1979—. Mem. Am. Public Health Assn., Am. Soc. Hosp. Personnel Adminstrn. (dir. 1971-72), Am. Soc. Mental Hosp. Bus. Adminstrn., Assn. of Mental Health Adminstrn., Am. Acad. Health Adminstrs., Indsl. Relations Research Assn., Chgo. Hosp. Personnel Mgmt. Assn., Chgo. Assn. Commerce and Industry (manpower devel. and tng. com.). Home: 4939 Coyle St Skokie IL 60077 Office: 1 S Franklin St Chicago IL 60606

RAPPE, KRISTINE ANN, utilities executive; b. Stevens Point, Wis., Oct. 16, 1956; d. Walter H. and LaVerne (Zdrojowy) Peterson; m. James A. Rappe, May 19, 1984; 1 child, Karlyn Kendall. BS, U. Wis., Oshkosh, 1978. Planner City of Appleton, Wis., 1978-82; mgr. econ. devel. Wis. Electric Power Co., Milw., 1982—. Mem. organizing com. Milw. Tennis Classic, 1986, Profl. Dimensions, Milw., 1985—; bd. dirs. Milw. Ballet Found., 1987—, Wis. Innovation Network Found., 1987—. Named one of Outstanding Young Women of Am., 1984; recipient Leadership award YWCA, Milw., 1985. Mem. Mid-Am. Econ. Devel. Assn. (bd. dirs. 1984—). Avocations: tennis, golf, sailing. Office: Wis Electric Power Co 231 W Michigan Milwaukee WI 53201

RAPPLEYE, RICHARD KENT, financial executive, consultant, educator; b. Oswego, N.Y., Aug. 10, 1940; s. Robert Edward and Evelyn Margaret (Hammond) R.; m. Karen Tobe Greenberg, Sept. 7, 1963; children: Matthew Walker, Elizabeth Marion. AB, Miami U., Oxford, Ohio, 1962; postgrad. in theology Boston U., 1962-63; MBA, U. Pa., 1964; postgrad. in law DePaul U., 1965-66. CPA, Ill. Auditor DeLoitte Haskins & Sells, Chgo., 1962-67, mgmt. cons., 1967-71; controller, United Dairy Industry Assn., Rosemont, Ill., 1971, dir. fin. and adminstrn., 1971-73, exec. v.p., 1973-74; asst. to exec. v.p. Florists' Transworld Delivery, Southfield, Mich., 1974-75, group dir. fin. and adminstrn., 1975-80; asst. treas. Erb Lumber Co., Birmingham, Mich., 1980, v.p. fin., chief fin. officer, 1981-83; sec.-treas. C.S. Mott Found., Flint, Mich., 1983—; cons. in field; instr. Oakland U., Rochester, Mich., 1981-83; bd. dirs. Mich. Nat. Bank. Treas. Council Mich. Founds. Mem. Fin. Execs. Inst., Am. Inst. CPA's, Mich. Assn. CPA's. Unitarian. Lodge: Rotary. Home: 503 Arlington Rd Birmingham MI 48009 Office: CS Mott Found 503 S Saginaw Flint MI 48502

RAPPORT, DORIS M., dancer, choreographer, educator. Studies with Theodore J. Smith, 1950-62, studies with Oswald Lemanis; studies with Valintina Pereyslovic, William Griffith, N.Y.C., studies with George Balanchine; student, Will O Way Sch. Drama, Julliard Sch., N.Y.C. Dancer Detroit City Ballet Co., 1956-63; instr. ballet, jazz, tap, head dance dept. Redford (Mich.) Community YWCA, 1965-72; owner Doris Rapport Sch. Ballet, Orchard Lake, Mich., 1972-81; instr. Vic Tanny, 1982-83; head instr. performing arts and dance Oakland Community Coll., Bloomfield Hills, Mich., 1983; instr. Rochester (Mich.) Exercise Ctr., 1983; owner Doris Rapport Sch. Dance and Fitness, Keego Harbor, Mich., 1984—; freelance choreographer, Mich. 1979—; founder Joi de Vie Dance Co., Keego Harbor, 1986—. Mem. Detroit Producers Assn. Home: 3307 Orchard Lake Rd Keego Harbor MI 48033

RARRICK, MICHAEL R., graphic designer, real estate management company executive; b. Colorado Springs, Colo., Aug. 18, 1953; s. Walter and Beverly JoAnn (Smith) R. BA, William Jewell Coll., Liberty, Mo., 1973; Diploma (MA level), Harlaxton Coll., Lincolnshire, Eng., 1974; Researcher diploma, Jesus and Regents Park Colls., Oxford, Eng., 1975. Nat. advt. dir. World Products Warehouse, Shawnee Mission, Kans., 1975-78; pres. Vantage Pub. Relations, Springfield, Mo., 1978-83; regional mgr. Marson Graphics, Balt., 1983-84; design mgr. Jewelers Bench, Inc., Kansas City, Mo., 1984-86; mgr. D&L Investments Corp., Overland Park, Kans., 1986—; midwest advt. dir. In Touch mag., Los Angeles, 1978-82; art dir., cons. Beverly Hills Embroidery Mfg. Co., Springfield, 1982-85; bd. dirs. Arts and Fantasy Internat., London. Chmn. Arts Internat. Philanthropic Found., Kansas City, Mo., 1983-85. Recipient Kansas City Best Art Dir. award, 1976, Miami Art Expo award, 1981, Major Contbg. Artist award Miami Art Expo., 1982, Delphi Artistic Excellence award Delphi Arts, Ltd., 1986. Republican. Baptist. Club: Masters (Kansas City) (bd. dirs. 1984-86). Avocations: property management, business administration. Home: 3630 Gillham Rd #15 Kansas City MO 64111

RASANSKY, RONALD JAY, gastroenterologist; b. Phila., Nov. 3, 1948; s. Harry N. and Sylvia Leah (Gilgore) R.; m. Cheryl Lynn Stoler, July 2, 1978; children: Michael Jordan, Lisa Jill. BS in Biology, Albright Coll., 1970; DO, Des Moines Coll. Osteo. Medicine, 1973. Intern Martin Place Hosp., Madison Heights, Mich., 1973-74, resident in internal medicine, 1974-76, fellow in gastroenterology, 1976-78; practice osteo. medicine specializing in gastroenterology Madison Heights, 1978—; mem. staff Huron Valley Hosp., Oakland Gen. Hosp., Redford Community Hosp., Saratoga Hosp.; adv. bd. dept. internal medicine Huron Valley Hosp., Milford, Mich.; sec.,treas. dept. internal medicine Pontiac (Mich.) Osteo. Hosp., 1982-84; cons. Doctor's Hosp., Pontiac Osteo. Hosp., N.W. Gen. Hosp. Guest editor Mich. Jour. Osteo. Medicine Gastroenterology, 1985. Vol. Allied Jewish Campaign (physicans div.). Mem. Am. Coll. Osteo. Internists (cert. internal medicine 1980, cert. gastroenterology 1981), Am. Osteo. Assn., Mich. Assn. Osteo. Physicians and Surgeons, Oakland County Soc. Osteo. Physicans, Am. Coll. Osteo. Internists (gastroenterology subsection), Am. Soc. Gastro. Endoscopy, Nat. Found. Ileitis and Colitis. Republican. Avocations: soccer coach, bridge, aerobics, reading. Home: 4246 Barn Meadow Ln West Bloomfield MI 48033 Office: 27301 Dequindre #314 Madison Heights MI 48071

RASH, JEAN LOUISE, marketing executive; b. West Bend, Wis., Nov. 8, 1949; d. Roman Michael and Audrey Katherine (Nehm) Wagner; m. Wayne Thomas Rash, Aug. 8, 1970; children: Jeffery A., Scott Lee. BS in Edn., U. Wis., Whitewater, 1970; MS in Mgmt., Cardinal Stritch Coll., 1984. Tchr. communications high schs. and vocat. schs. Richland Center, WI, 1970-74; tchr. English St. Clement Sch., Lancaster, Wis., 1975-77, St. Kilian Sch., Hartford, Wis., 1977-78; free-lance cons., substitute tchr. Southeast, Wis., 1977-79; promotions coordinator, mgr. advt. Weasler Engrng., West Bend, 1979-86; assoc. dir. mktg. and pub. relations Internat. Found. Employee Benefit Plans, Brookfield, Wis., 1986—; adj. faculty, thesis advisor Cardinal Stritch Coll., Milw., 1984—; cons. in field. Author, editor product catalogs for trade publs., 1978—. Pub. relations dir. Washington County Unit Am. Cancer Soc., West Bend, 1982-84; pres. West Bend Jaycettes, 1977-78. Named one of Outstanding Young Women Am., 1979; recipient Wis. State Speak-Up award, Wis. Jaycettes, Green Bay, 1977. Mem. Nat. Agrl. Mktg. Assn. (bd. dirs. Badger Chpt. 1983-84, treas. 1984—, nat. bd. dirs. 1984-85); Lancaster Jaycettes (treas. 1975-76, hon. life). Roman Catholic. Avocations: reading, writing, beledi dancing, sewing. Office: Internat Found Employee Benefit Plans PO Box 69 18700 Bluemound Rd Brookfield WI 53008

RASHAD, FOUAD ALY, radiologist; b. Cairo, Oct. 1, 1931; came to U.S., 1968; s. Aly Mohamed Rashad and Aziza Elhariry. MB, BCh, Ein-Shams, Cairo, 1955, DMRE, 1961. Diplomate Am. Bd. Radiology. Radiologist Ahmed Maher Hosp., Cairo, 1961-64; registrar Mt. Vernon Hosp., Middlesex, Eng., 1964-66; sr. registrar Kingston (Eng.) Hosp., 1966-67; radiologist Met. Gen. Hosp., Cleve., 1968—; assoc. dir. dept. radiology, Met. Gen. Hosp., 1973—. Fellow Am. Coll. Angiology; mem. Cleve. Radiology Soc., Cleve. Acad. Medicine, Am. Roentgen Ray Soc. Avocation: oil painting. Home: 7039 Gates Mills Blvd Gates Mills OH 44040 Office: Cleve Met Gen Hosp 3395 Scranton Rd Cleveland OH 44109

RASHILLA, RICHARD JAMES, JR., aerospace executive; b. Dayton, Ohio, Sept. 16, 1959; s. Richard James and Bonnie Lou (Kern) R. BS in Indsl. Mgmt., U. Cin., 1982. Engr. Hobart Corp., Troy, Ohio, 1978-80; mktg. rep. Brunswick Corp., Lincoln, Nebr., 1983-85; mktg. mgr. Brunswick Corp., San Francisco, 1985—; mgr. advanced programs Brunswick Corp., Skokie, Ill., 1987—. Campaign asst. Rep. Presdl. Com., Cin., 1980. Mem. Soc. Advancement Materials and Processes, USN League, Air Force Assn. Republican. Roman Catholic. Avocations: sailing, ice hockey.

RASIKAS, KERRY LEE, audio-visual specialist; b. Grand Rapids, Mich., Sept. 30, 1953; s. Albert and Mary Ann (Huizenga) R.; m. Janice Marie VanOtteren, June 29, 1974; children: Nicole, Mara. BS in Arts and Media, Grand Valley State U., Allendale, Mich., 1975. Photographer Fine Arts Communicators, Grand Rapids, Mich., 1975-78, Grand Rapids Prodn. Co., 1978-80; free-lance photographer Gand Rapids, 1980-81; producer Mendenhall, Jones, Leistra, Grand Rapids, 1981-82; producer, dir. Jones-Rasikas, Inc., Grand Rapids, 1982—. Producer, dir: (film) Michigan, You've Got A Powerful Future, 1984; (multi-image program) Ethospace Interiors, 1985; editor: (film) Kelloggs 75th Anniversary, 1981; cinematographer: Powering Michigan's Progress, 1986 (Cine Golden Eagle award), Never Before Sensor, 1986 (Cine Golden Eagle award). Home: 3303 Sunset Bluff NE Rockford MI 49341 Office: Jones-Rasikas Inc 800 Bond NW Grand Rapids MI 49503

RASIN, RUDOLPH STEPHEN, investment banker; b. Newark, July 5, 1930; s. Simon Walter and Anna (Sinovc) R.; m. Joy Kennedy Peterkin, Apr. 11, 1959; children—Rudolph Stephen, James Stenning, Jennifer Shaw. B.A., Rutgers Coll., 1953; postgrad., Columbia, 1958-59. Mgr. Miles Labs., Inc., 1959-61; devel. mgr. Gen. Foods Corp., White Plains, N.Y., 1961-62; asst. to pres., chmn. Morton-Norwich Products, Inc., Chgo., 1962-71; pres. Rasin Corp., Chgo., 1971—, GRG Interest, Chgo.; bd. dirs. GRG Interests, Inc. Bd. dirs. Center for Def. Info., 1972—; mem. Chgo. Crime Commn., 1974—; bd. dirs. Internat. Inst. for Rural Reconstrn.; bd. govs. Chgo. Zool. Soc. Served with USAF, 1954-56. Mem. Assn. for Corp. Growth, Bus. Execs. for Nat. Security. Republican. Mem. United Ch. of Christ. Clubs: Hinsdale Golf, Mid America, Chgo, Lake Geneva Country, Lake Geneva Yacht; Williams Coll. (N.Y.C.). Home: 328 E 8th St Hinsdale IL 60521 Office: 120 S La Salle St Chicago IL 60603

RASKE, ARTHUR, manufacturing executive; b. Chgo., July 3, 1921; s. Arthur and Arlene Rachel (Monger) R.; m. Elma Lydia Moody, Jan. 12, 1946; children: Arthur III, John Moody. BS, Case Western Res. U., 1948; BD, U. Chgo., 1967, MA, 1972. Clergyman Luth. Chs., Ill., 1967-72; pvt. practice family therapy Chgo., 1971-79; pres. Nu-Matic Grinders Inc., Euclid, Ohio, 1979—. Patentee in field. Bd. dirs., officer Golden Age Ctrs., Cleve., 1961-64. Served with USMC, 1942-45, PTO. Avocations: golf, computer programming. Home: PO Box 867 Lewiston MI 49756 Office: NuMatic Grinders Inc 19870 Saint Clair Ave Euclid OH 44117

RASMUSSEN, DAVID LEE, manufacturing company executive, hydraulic engineer, consultant; b. Two Rivers, Wis., Dec. 28, 1947; s. Harry and Ruth Margaret (Darrow) R.; m. Carol Jean Krejcarek, Nov. 11, 1966 (div. Nov. 1977); 1 son, Brian Lee. Student pub. schs., Manitowoc, Wis. Product engr. Imperial Eastman Corp., Manitowoc, 1968-76, engrng. mgr., Imperial Eastman UK-LTD., St. Neots, England, 1976-78; product devel. engr. Gates Rubber Co., Rockford, Ill., 1978-79; tech. mgr. Menominee Rubber Co., Milw., 1979-80; prin., v.p. Larkin Indsl. Products, Milw., 1980—; cons. product liability suits. Served with USNR, 1964-74. Mem. ASTM. Democrat. Roman Catholic. Author publs. in field. Office: Larkin Indsl Products 700 W Michigan St Milwaukee WI 53233

RASMUSSEN, LOWELL MERTON, technical institute director; b. Hutchinson, Minn., May 17, 1933; s. William Christian and Emma Louise (Duesterhoeft) R.; m. Mary June Torbeck, Apr. 27, 1957; children: Sonja, Mark, Barbara, Amy. BS, Gustavus Adolphus, 1961; MA in Ednl. Adminstrn., U. Minn., 1975. Salesperson J.C. Penney Co., Mankato, Minn., 1957-60; tchr. Wadena (Minn.) Area Vocat. Tech. Inst., 1961-65, coordinator, 1965-67, asst. dir., 1967-76, dir., 1976—. Bd. dirs. Penbina Trails, Wadena, 1979—, Share a Home, Wadena, 1986—. Mem. Area Vocat. Tech. Insts. Dirs. Assn. (pres. St. Paul chpt. 1985-86), Wadena C. of C. (bd. dirs. 1985—). Home: 611 SW Second St Wadena MN 56482 Office: PO Box 566 105 SW Colfax Ave Wadena MN 56482

RASMUSSEN, RICHARD JONES, manufacturing company executive; b. Brigham City, Utah, May 14, 1940; s. Parley Hans and Mary Ann (Jones) Rasmussen Scothern; m. Maraley Redd, Sept. 17, 1965; children: Holli, Regina, Erik, Aimee, Mark. BS, Utah State U., 1965; MBA, U. Utah, 1966. Jr. acct. Peat Marwick Mitchell, Salt Lake City, 1970; asst. gen. mgr. Christensen Diamond Service, Columbus, Ohio, 1970-74; v.p. and gen. mgr. Super-Cut, Inc., Chgo., 1974-84; pres. Rasmussen Diamond Products,Inc., Chgo., 1984—. Served to capt. USAF, 1966-70. Mem. Spl. Tool and Fastner Dist. Assn. (mfgs. liaison com. 1984-86), Am. Concrete Pavement Assn. (bd. dirs. 1981—), Concrete Sawing and Drilling Assn. (treas. 1985—). Mormon. Office: Rasmussen Diamond Products Inc 3414 N Knox Ave Chicago IL 60641

RASMUSSEN, ROBERT JOHN, computer center director, educator systems analysis; b. Oshkosh, Wis., Oct. 20, 1937; s. Ward Alvin and Charlotte Marie (Conlee) R.; m. Janice Marie Flett, Oct. 5, 1958; children: William, Anne-Marie, Christine, Catherine, Julie. BS, Colo. State U., 1959. Systems design group leader URS Data Sci. Corp., Killeen, Tex., 1967-71; prin. systems analyst Colo. State U., Ft. Collins, 1971-82; computer ctr. dir. S.D. Sch. Mines & Tech., Rapid City, 1982—; cons. Larimer County Vocat. Tech., Ft. Collins, 1978, U.S. Forest Service, Ft. Collins, 1976; speaker in field. Speaker in field. Advisor City Planning Commn., Ft. Collins, 1981-83. Served to capt. USMC, 1960-67. Mem. Coll. and Univ. Systems Exchange. Republican. Lodge: Lions (bd. dirs. Rapid City 1983—). Home: 121 San Marco Blvd Rapid City SD 57702 Office: S D Sch Mines & Tech 501 E St Joe Rapid City SD 57701

RASOVSKY, YURI, radio drama producer-director, writer, actor, consultant, teacher; b. Chgo., July 29, 1944; s. Samuel Nathan and Clarice Norma (Diamond) Rasof; 1 child, Yuri Piotr Riidl; m. Ginny Boyle, Nov. 5, 1981 (annulled 1982). Mail boy Sta. WBKB-TV, Chgo., 1963-64; drama instr. Chgo. Park Dist., 1968-70; freelance editor, writer, cartoonist, actor, dir., 1969—; founding producer, dir. Nat. Radio Theatre, Chgo., 1973-86; panelist Nat. Endowment Arts, Washington, 1976, Ill. Arts. Council, Chgo., 1983, Chgo. Office Fine Arts, 1984—, NEH, 1985; cons. Can. Broadcasting Corp., Toronto. Author radio prodns. including The Amorous Adventures of Don Juan, The Courier, Dracula, An Enemy of The People, Frankenstein, The Odyssey of Homer, A Tale of Two Cities, Three Tales of Edgar Allan Poe, The World of F. Scott Fitzgerald, numerous others. Author: The Publicity Survival Manual for Small Performing Arts Organizations, 1977. Producer, actor in Magic Circle prodn. Green Julia, 1976 (3 Joseph Jefferson Citations). Contbr. articles and revs. to Chicago Mag., Stagebill Mag., Chicago Sun-Times, other publs. Served with U.S. Army, 1964-67. Recipient Major Armstrong award, 1975, 76, 79, Ohio State award, 1975, 77, 80, 83, 85, George Foster Peabody Broadcasting award, 1978, 81, Nat. Fedn. Community Broadcasters Program award, 1981, San Francisco State Broadcast Media award, 1982, 85, Grabriel award, 1983, Corp. Pub. Broadcasting Program award, 1983, 85. Mem. Am. Inds. in Radio, Audio Inds. Inc. (founder, bd. dirs. 1979-81).

RASTOGI, ANIL KUMAR, paper company executive; b. India, July 13, 1942; came to U.S., 1969, naturalized, 1978; s. R.S. and K.V. Rastogi; m. Anjali Capur, Mar. 18, 1970; children: Priya, Sonya. B.S. with honors, Lucknow U., 1963, M.S., 1964; Ph.D. in Polymer Sci., McGill U., 1969. Mem. staff Ownes-Corning Tech. Ctr., Granville, Ohio, 1969-87; lab. supr. Owens-Corning Tech. Ctr., 1975-76; lab. mgr. materials tech. labs Ownes-Corning Tech. Ctr., Granville, Ohio, 1976-79; lab. mgr. product devel. labs. Owens-Corning Tech. Ctr., Granville, Ohio, 1979-80, research dir., 1980-83; dir. corp. diversification portfolio Ownes-Corning Tech. Ctr., Granville, Ohio, 1983-87; v.p. Mead Imaging, Miamisburg, Ohio, 1987—; mem. adv. bd. Central Ohio Tech. Coll.; lectr., cons. in field. Author of 11 bus. and tech. publs.; patentee in field. Bd. dirs. Licking County Family Services Assn.; bd. dirs. Tech. Alliance of Central Ohio; v.p. local United Way; bd. dirs. and treas. Columbus Bus. Tech. Ctr.; mem. Overview Adv. Com. Strategic Hwy. Research Program. Fellow NRC Can., 1966-69. Mem. Am. Mgmt. Assn., Am. Chem. Soc., AAAS, Soc. Plastics Engrs., Comml. Devel. Assn., Sigma Xi. Club: Toastmasters (past pres.). Lodge: Rotary. Home: 1949 Rustling Oak Ct Dayton OH 45459 Office: Mead Imaging 3385 Newmark Dr Miamisburg OH 45342

RATAJCZAK, HELEN VOSSKUHLER, immunologist; b. Tucson, Ariz., Apr. 9, 1938; d. Maximillian Philip and Marion Harriet (Messer) Vosskuhler; m. Edward Francis Ratajczak, June 1, 1959 (div. 1968); children—Lorraine, Eric, Peter, Eileen. B.S., U. Ariz., 1959, M.S., 1970; Ph.D., 1976. Asst. research scientist U. Iowa Coll. Medicine, Iowa City, 1976-78; instr. U. Pitts., 1978-80; research assoc., 1980-81; asst. prof. Loyola U. Coll. Medicine, Maywood, Ill., 1981-83; research immunologist Ill. Inst. Tech., Research Inst., Chgo., 1983-86, staff immunologist, 1986—. Fellow Am. Thoracic Soc., 1974-76, NIH, 1978; grantee Loyola U., 1981. Mem. Am. Thoracic Soc., Am. Assn. Immunologists, Chgo. Assn. Immunologists, N.Y. Acad. Scis., AAAS, Soc. Toxicology, Daus. Am. Colonists, Sigma Xi, Kappa Kappa Gamma. Republican. Roman Catholic. Avocations: Piano playing; sewing; baking. Office: Ill Inst Tech Research Inst 10 W 35th St Chicago IL 60616

RATCHFORD, ROBERT LEE, JR., insurance executive, lawyer; b. Columbus, Ohio, Sept. 23, 1944; s. Robert Lee and Sara Marshall (Sims) R.; m. Aileen Elizabeth Crawford, June 7, 1969; children: Christopher Robin, Devon Marshall. BA, Wittenberg U., 1966; JD, Capital U., 1975. Bar: Ohio 1975. Dep. asst. Gov. James A. Rhodes, Columbus, 1975-78; dep. supt. Ohio Dept. Ins., Columbus, 1978-80, supt., 1980-82; v.p. Assurex Internat., Columbus, 1982-84; pres. Dealers Alliance Corp., Columbus, 1984—, also bd. dirs.; adv. bd. Fed. Emergency Mgmt. Agy., Washington, 1985—; trustee Griffith Found. Ins. Edn., Ohio State U., 1980—. Served with U.S. Army, 1968-70. Named one of Outstanding Young Men Am., U.S. Jaycees, 1981. Mem. Assn. Ohio Commodores, Columbus Bar Assn. (bd. govs. 1980-82). Republican. Club: Toastmasters (sec. 1973-77, pres. 1977-79). Home: 1414 Reynoldsburg New Albany Rd Blacklick OH 43004 Office: Dealers Alliance Corp 3518 Riverside Dr PO Box 21185 Columbus OH 43221

RATEGAN, CATHERINE AGNES, writer; b. Oak Park, Ill., Dec. 16, 1932; d. Joseph L. and Helen A. (Russow) R. Student, U. Chgo., 1957-60; BA in Advt., Northwestern U., 1963, BA in Creative Writing, 1964, BBA in Acctg., 1975. Copy supr. Grey-North Advt., Chgo., 1964-68; writer Bozell & Jacobs, Chgo., 1968-70, Cunningham & Walsh, Chgo., 1970-73; sr. writer N.Y. Ayer ABH Internat., Chgo., 1973-76; co-creative dir. Gardner, Stein & Frank, Chgo., 1976-79; pres. Catherine A. Rategan, Writer, Inc., Chgo., 1979—. Co-editor: (book) World's Best Sales Promotions, 1983; co-writer (indsl. film) Good Look at Chgo., 1983 (Internat. Film Festival award, N.Y., 1984); writer radio commls. Girl Scouts of Chgo., 1975 (Helen Cody Baker award, 1976). Precinct capt. Ind. Voters Ill., Chgo., 1968. Mem. Independent Writers Chgo. (co-founding, v.p. 1983-84). Democrat. Avocations: running, exercise, writing short stories and plays. Home and Office: 1355 N Sandburg Terrace Chicago IL 60610

RATEKIN, DANIEL LEE, guidance counselor; b. Council Bluffs, Iowa, July 31, 1936; s. Harry E. and Dorothy L. (Grason) R.; m. Betty L. Freeman, July 25, 1959; children: Randall, Linda, Mark. BA, Parsons Coll., 1958; MA, U. Iowa, 1962. Tchr. Wapello (Iowa) High Sch., 1959-61; guidance couselor Valley High Sch., West Des Moines, Iowa, 1962—; owner Cheese Villa Restaurant, Des Moines, 1975—. Bd. dirs. Covenant Presbyn. Ch., West Des Moines, 1983-86. Mem. NEA, Am. Assn. Counseling and Devel. (sen. 1969), Iowa Assn. Coll. Admission Counselors (chmn. com. 1983-86, Iowa Counselor of Yr. 1984), Iowa Assn. Counseling and Devel. (chmn. com. 1968-70), Iowa State Edn. Assn. Republican. Home: 1711-19th St West Des Moines IA 50265 Office: Valley High Sch 1140-35th St West Des Moines IA 50265

RATH, RONALD E., educational administrator; b. Cedar Falls, Iowa, Apr. 11, 1937; s. H. Earl and Florence G. (Heironimus) R.; m. Kathryn E. Thompson, June 15, 1963; children: Thomas E., John S. BA, U. No. Iowa, 1961, MA, 1968. Mktg. salesman Bus. Machine Ctr., Waterloo, Iowa, 1959-61; dir. sales promotion and advt. Clay Equipment Corp., Cedar Falls, Iowa, 1961-64; dist. coordinator edn. Cedar Falls High Sch., 1964-68; coordinator food store mktg. Iowa Cen. Community Coll., Ft. Dodge, 1968-74; assoc. dean Kirkwood Community Coll., Cedar Rapids, 1974—; dir. Area X Planning Council for Vocat. Edn., 1986—; group leader Interstate Distributive Edn. Curriculum Consortium, 1976-78; cons. in field. Recipient Program Pioneer award Iowa Office Edn., 1986, Demontheses award Kirkwood Speakers Bur., 1983. Mem. Am. Soc. Tng. and Devel. (pres. leadership com. 1986—), Am. Vocational Assn.(nat. del. 1982), Iowa Vocat. Assn. (pres. 1982-83), Iowa City C. of C., Marion C. of C., Delta Pi Epsilon. Club: Toastmasters Internat. (named disting. toastmaster 1981). Lodge: Masons. Home: 3940 Falbrook Dr NE Cedar Rapids IA 52402 Office: Kirkwood Community Coll 6301 Kirkwood Blvd SW Cedar Rapids IA 52402

RATHKE, GEORGE EDWARD, manufacturing company executive; b. Rockford, Ill., June 2, 1945; s. Alfred G. and Alice D. Rathke; m. Debbie A. Rhodes, Sept. 11, 1965. BS, Rockford Coll., 1973. Mgr. strategic planning Sundstrand Corp., Rockford, 1973-74; dir. European Mktg. Sounstrand Corp., Dijon, France, 1974-75; group v.p., dir. Clausing Corp., Kalamazoo, 1975-81; v.p. sales and mktg. Ex-Cell-O Mfg. System Co., Rockford, 1981-85; v.p. contract services and advanced tech. programs Washington Sci. Ind., Inc., Long Lake, Minn., 1985—. Office: Washington Sci Ind Inc 2605 W Wayzata Blvd Long Lake MN 55356

RATHMAN, SUSAN KAY, data processing executive; b. Comfrey, Minn., Apr. 8, 1946; d. Jerome Joseph and Dora Ann (McNamara) R.; m. James Richard Rohrman, July 13, 1974 (div. Oct. 1983); 1 child, Anastacia. BS in Math., U. Minn., 1968. Cert. data processor. Programmer analyst No. States Power, Mpls., 1969-73; systems programmer First Bank, St. Paul, 1973-74, 3M, St. Paul, 1974-76; EDP instr. 916 Vocat. Inst., St. Paul, 1976-79; disaster recovery specialist Norwest Info. Services, Mpls., 1979-84; systems staff analyst N.W. Nat. Life Ins., Mpls., 1984-87; cons. Disaster Recovery, Inc., Mpls., 1987—; Conf. chmn. Minn. Joint Computer Conf., Mpls., 1981-83; lect. Am. Bank Inst. Conf., Washington, 1983, N.W. Contingency Group, Seattle, 1983, Alaska Expn., Anchorage, 1984, 1986. Fund drive chmn. Brownies, Girl Scouts U.S., 1984; team leader United Way Paint-A-Thon, 1986. Mem. Data Processing Mgmt. Assn. (local dir. 1981-86, region sec. 1985, region coordinator 1986, N.W. chpt. Mem. of Month 1980, N.W. Bd. Mem. Yr. 1982, Individual Performance award 1984, Silver Individual Performance award 1985, contbg. editor assoc. program curriculum 1984). Roman Catholic. Home: 2622 Innsbruck Trail New Brighton MN 55112 Office: Disaster Recovery Inc 1406 W Lake St Suite 204 Minneapolis MN 55408

RATHZ, DAVID VICTOR, school principal; b. Indpls., May 13, 1947; s. Edward Victor and Frances (Fowley) R.; m. Patricia Marie Ollom, Dec. 27, 1969; children: Kathleen, Deborah, Maureen. BS in Edn., U. Dayton, 1969; MEd, Cleve. State U., 1974, postgrad., 1976. Cert. secondary adminstrn., Ohio. English tchr., Valley Forge High Sch., Parma, Ohio, 1969-71; tchr., dept. head English, Greenbriar Jr. High Sch., 1971-76; sch. facilitator Schaaf Jr. High Sch., 1976-77; asst. prin. Chardon Middle Sch., Ohio, 1977-79; prin. Harmon Middle Sch., Aurora, Ohio, 1979-81, Aurora High Sch., 1981-86, Kenston High Sch., 1986—; cons. Cleve. State U. Sch. Edn. Contbr. articles to profl. jours. Friend of the Holden Arboretum, Cleve. Recipient Adminstrv. Leadership award Martha Holden Jennings Found., 1981; Jennings scholar, 1976. Mem. NEA, Nat. Assn. Secondary Sch. Principals, Ohio Assn. Secondary Sch. Adminstrs., Phi Delta Kappa. Democrat. Roman Catholic. Club: Legacy. Lodge: K.C. Avocations: racquetball, tennis, reading, gardening, spectator sports. Home: 11741 Christian Ave Concord Township OH 44077

RATI, ROBERT DEAN, data processing executive; b. Pittsburg, Kans., Jan. 8, 1939; s. Steve Julius Rati and Dorothy Bill (Rodebush) McWilliams; m. Margaret Fort Henry, June 7, 1969; children: Susan Margaret, Robert Henry. BA, U. Kans., 1961; MA, Northeastern U., Boston, 1970; MBA, Columbia U., 1973. Systems engr. IBM Corp., Boston, 1965-72; mgr. mgmt. services Arthur Young and Co., N.Y.C., 1973-75; mgr. client systems Touche Ross and Co., N.Y.C., 1975-76; mgr. systems and programs Walker Mfg. div. Tenneco, Racine, Wis., 1976-78; mgr. data processing Schwitzer div. Household Internat., Indpls., 1979—. Contbr. articles to fraternal orgs. newsletters. Mem. Rep. Com., Ramsey, N.J., 1972-74; vice chmn. Swimming Pool Commn., Ramsey, 1972-74; bd. dirs., exec. com. Near Eastside Multi-Service Ctr., Indpls., 1984—; fin. com. Carmel (Ind.) United Meth. Ch., 1984—. Served to lt. (j.g.) USN, 1961-64. Recipient Regional Mgrs. award, IBM Corp., 1967. Mem. Soc. Ind. Pioneers (bd. govs. 1985—), Huguenot Soc. Ind. (pres. 1985—), Pi Mu Epsilon. Republican. Avocations: genealogy, home computer. Home: 12923 Andover Dr Carmel IN 46032 Office: Schwitzer Household Internat 1125 Brookside Ave Indianapolis IN 46202

RATLEDGE, DEBRA JEAN SELL, nurse; b. Green Bay, Wis., May 23, 1957; s. Norbert Mathias and Betty Jane (DuFresne) S.; m. Earl T. Ratledge III. Diploma in Nursing, Milw. County Gen. Hosp., 1979; BS in Nursing, Med. Coll. Wis., 1985. Staff RN med. and surgical intensive care unit Milw. County Med. Complex, 1979-80; nurse Flight for Life Milw. Regional Med. Ctr., 1985-86; staff RN trauma cen. Milw. County Med. Complex, 1980-85, 86—, mem. mobile intensive care unit service, 1981-86. Mem. Emergency Nurses Assn. (cert.), Am. Heart Assn. (advanced cardiac life support provider). Democrat. Roman Catholic. Home: 2528 N 61st St Milwaukee WI 53213

RATLIFF, RALPH KENNETH, manufacturing executive; b. Sandpoint, Idaho, Nov. 25, 1930; s. Ferrell Miles and Virginia Katherin (North) R.; m. Joanne Marlene Rehn, Feb. 21, 1952 (div. Sept. 1983); children: Stephen, Kathlyn, Jaymie Lynn, Jon Karl, Kris Ann, Matthew Alex. Student, Coll. of Puget Sound, 1950, U. Wash., 1954-56. Dist. mgr. Johnson & Johnson, Mpls., 1956-67; pres. Market Sales, Minnetonka, Minn., 1967-78, Loring Labs, Inc., St. Bonifacius, Minn., 1974—. Precinct chmn. Minnetonka Reps., 1965-67. Served with USCG, 1950-54, Korea. Avocation: basketball. Office: Loring Labs Inc 4360 S County Rd 92 Saint Bonifacius MN 55375

RATNER, MARK ALAN, chemistry educator; b. Cleve., Dec. 8, 1942; s. Max and Betty (Wohlvert) R.; m. Nancy Ball, June 19, 1969; children—Stacy, Daniel. A.B., Harvard U., 1964; Ph.D., Northwestern U., 1969; Amanuensis (hon.), Aarhus U., Denmark, 1970; Akad Rat (hon.), Tech. U., Munich, W. Ger., 1971. Asst. prof. NYU, 1971-75; prof. chemistry Northwestern U., Evanston, 1975—; cons. U.S. Army, Huntsville, Ala., 1973-75; lectr. IBM, Yorktown Heights, N.Y., 1973; dir. Electrochem. Industries, Israel, 1980—; assoc. dean arts and scis. Northwestern U., Evanston, 1980-84. Contbr. numerous articles and manuscripts to profl. jours. Bd. dirs. Jewish United Fund, Chgo., 1984—, Hillel Found., Evanston, 1984—. Fellow A.P. Sloan Found., 1973-76, Inst. Advanced Study, Israel, 1979. Fellow Am. Phys. Soc.; mem. Am. Chem. Soc., Rumplestiltskin Soc., Ill. Sci. Lecture Assn. (bd. dirs. 1980—), Sigma Xi. Jewish. Avocations: scientific education; canoeing; conservation; Denmark. Home: 25 Locust Rd Winnetka IL 60093 Office: Northwestern U Chemistry Dept 2145 Sheridan Rd Evanston IL 60201

RATNY, RUTH LUCILLE, publishing executive, writer journal articles; b. Chgo., Dec. 8, 1932; d. Herman Joseph and Bertha (Levy) R. Student, De Paul U., 1950-54. Creative v.p. Niles Communications Ctrs., Chgo., 1954-64; prin. Ruth L. Ratny Mktg. Communications, Chgo., 1964-69; owner Screen mag., Chgo., 1979—. Bd. dirs. Chgo. Coalition, 1979-85. Named Advt. Women of Yr., 1979, Midwest Advt. Person of Yr., 1979; recipient Recognition award Chgo. Coalition, 1983, Clio awards, 1960-61. Mem. Women in Film, Chgo. Advt. Club, Women's Advt. Club, Acad. TV Arts and Scis., Pearl S. Buck Found. (bd. dirs. Perkasie, Pa. chpt. 1986—), Sigma Delta Chi. Mem. Christian Sci. Ch. Office: Screen Mag 720 N Wabash Chicago IL 60611

RATTUNDE, JAMES KEITH, insurance agent; b. Mauston, Wis., Dec. 20, 1953; s. Marland John and Bonnie Jean (Oakes) R.; m. Ramona Lee Polze, Aug. 28, 1976; children—Rebecca L. and Ryan J. (twins). Cert. ins. counselor. Asst. chief of police Necedah Police Dept., Wis., 1973-74; sgt. Juneau County Sheriff's Dept., Mauston, Wis., 1974-81, spl. deputy, 1982—; ins. agt. Rattunde Ins. Agy., Necedah, 1979—; bd. dirs. Mile Bluff Med. Ctr., treas. 1987—. Fireman, mem. ambulance/rescue squad Necedah Vol. Fire Dept., 1975—, capt., 1983—; mem. Necedah Area Sch. Bd., 1977-87; liturgical organist practitioner, 1985—; mem. CESA 12 Bd. Control, Portage, Wis. Mem. Wis. Assn. Sch. Bds. Alumni Assn. (charter mem.), Necedah C. of C., Profl. Ins. Agts., Homeco Life Leader's Forum, Ins. Econs. Soc. Am. Roman Catholic. Avocations: woodworking, gardening, building, piano, landscaping. Home: Rt 1 Box 572 Necedah WI 54646 Office: Rattunde Ins Agy 605 N Main PO Box 9 Necedah WI 54646

RATURI, AMITABH SARAN, business educator; b. Varanasi, India, Oct. 25, 1957; came to U.S., 1981; s. Anand Saran and Meera Raturi; m. Anita Singh, Oct. 8, 1981; 1 child, Ketan. B in Tech., Indian Inst. Tech., Kanpur, 1979; MBA, Indian Inst. Mgmt., Ahmedabad, 1981; PhD, U. Minn., 1985. Purchase exec. NTPC, New Delhi, 1981; teaching and research assoc. U. Minn., Mpls., 1981-85; asst. prof. U. Cin., 1985—. Contbr. articles to profl. jours. Mem. Am. Prodn. and Inventory Control Soc. (advisor U. Cin. chpt. 1986), Decision Scis. Inst., Ops. Research Soc. of Am., Inst. of Mgmt. Acis., Am. Soc. for Quality Control. Avocations: bridge, reading. Home: 3150 Bishop St Cincinnati OH 45220 Office: U Cin ML#130 Cincinnati OH 45221

RATZLAFF, NEAL STANLEY, radiologist; b. York, Nebr., May 25, 1937; s. Dietrich P. and Marie Rose (Friesen) R.; m. Izen Irene Stevenson, Aug. 11, 1961; children: Mark, Rebecca. BA, Nebr. Wesleyan U., 1959; MD, U. Nebr., 1963. Diplomate Am. Bd. Radiology. Intern Bryan Meml. Hosp., Lincoln, Nebr., 1963-64; staff physician Mennonite Cen. Com., Zaire, Africa, 1964-66; resident in radiology Menorah Med. Ctr., Kansas City, Mo., 1967-69; radiology fellow Cin. Gen. Hosp., 1970-71; staff radiologist Kansas City Gen. Hosp., 1971-72, Nebr. Meth. Hosp., Omaha, 1972—; clin. instr. U. Nebr. Coll. Med., Omaha, 1972—. Pres. Audubon Soc. Omaha, 1981-82, bd. dirs. 1978-83; bd. dirs. Fontenelle Forest Assn., Bellevue, Nebr., 1983-87; trustee Nebr. Wesleyan U., Lincoln, 1984-87, The Nature Conservatory, Desmoines, 1985-87. Recipient Service award Audubon Soc. Omaha, 1986. Mem. AMA, Nebr. Med. Assn., Am. Coll. Radiology, Am. Inst. Ultrasound in Med., Alpha Omega Alpha. Democrat. Methodist. Avocations: photography, botany, ornithology, reading, travel. Home: 536 Brentwood Rd Omaha NE 68114 Office: Radiologic Ctr Inc 8303 Dodge St Omaha NE 68114

RAUB, DANIEL JOSEPH, osteopathic physician, educator; b. Grove City, Pa., Dec. 3, 1947; s. Paul Lester and Miriam Geraldine (Smith) R.; m. Linda Rae Riley, Mar. 22, 1969; children: Brett, Corey. BS in Chemistry, Bethany Coll., 1969; DO, Phila. Coll. Osteo. Medicine, 1973; postgrad., Sch. Aerospace Medicine, 1977; MA in Ed., Mich. State U., 1980. Cert. Am. Osteo. Bd. of Gen. Practice; lic. osteopathic physician, Pa., Mich., Ohio; diplomate Nat. Bd. Osteo. Examiners. Emergency room physician Greenville (Pa.) Hosp., 1974-76; gen. and family practitioner Greenville, 1975-77; flight surgeon Langley AFB USAF, Hampton, Va., 1977-79; asst. prof. family medicine Mich. State U., East Lansing, 1979-82; practice medicine specializing in family practice and preventive medicine Greenville, 1982-83; asst. prof. family medicine Ohio U., Athens, 1983-86, assoc. prof. family medicine, 1987—; coordinator OCP II Ohio U. Coll. Osteo. Medicine, 1984—, overall coordinator history and phys. component of curriculum , 1984—; dir. Lifelong Wellness Program Osteo. Med. Ctr., Athens, 1985—; co-med. dir. Bassett House, Athens, 1985—; grant reviewer geriatric edn. ctrs. U.S. Dept. Health and Human Services, Rockville, Md., 1986. Mem. Greenville Bd. Health, 1975-77; active Richland Ave. United Meth. Ch., Athens, 1984—; com. mem. Kootaga council Boy Scouts Am., 1985—; mem. bd. dirs. City-County Health Dept., Athens, 1985—, acting commnr., 1986, 87. Served as capt. USAF, 1977-79. Fellow Mich. State U. Coll. Osteo. Medicine, 1979. Mem. Am. Osteo. Assn., Ohio Osteo. Assn., Am. Coll. Gen. Practitioners in Osteo. Medicine and Surgery, Ohio State Soc. Am. Coll. Gen. Practice, Assn. Tchrs. of Preventive Medicine, Pa. Osteo. Med. Assn., Beta Theta Pi, Iota Tau Sigma, Beta Beta Beta. Republican. Club: Railroad of Southeastern Ohio. Lodge: Kiwanis (chmn. youth com. 1975-76). Avocations: cooking, music, photography, cycling, water sports. Home: 483 Longview Heights PO Box 714 Athens OH 45701 Office: Ohio U Coll Osteo Medicine Dept Family Medicine 333 Grosvenor Hall Athens OH 45701

RAUCH, JOSEPH WALTER, dentist; b. Muscatine, Iowa, July 23, 1954; s. Joe Walter and Betty Louise Rauch. BS, U. Iowa, 1976, DDS, 1983. Staff dentist Community Health Care, Inc., Davenport, Iowa, 1984-85, dental dir., 1985—; dental advisor Headstart, Davenport, 1985—, Headstart, Rock Island, Ill., 1986—, Boy Scouts Am., Davenport, 1985—. Mem. ADA, Iowa Dental Assn. (young dentist del. 1985), Davenport Dist. Dental Soc., Acad. Gen. Dentistry, Illowa Study Club, Aircraft Owners and Pilot Assn., Willy's Overland Knight Registry. Roman Catholic. Club: The Outing (Davenport). Avocations: swimming, flying, skiing, scuba diving. Office: Community Health Care Inc 428 Western Davenport IA 52801

RAUNIO, MATTHEW ISAAC, controller; b. Detroit, Aug. 26, 1957; s. Isaac Cedric and Ethel Pearl (Bratt) R.; m. Holly Kristine Beck, June 19, 1982; 1 child, Duncan. BBA, Mich. Tech. U., 1979; MBA, U. Wis., Oshkosh, 1982. CPA, Mich., Wis. Sr. acct. Jonet & Fountain, CPA's, Green Bay, Wis., 1979-81; controller The Premonstratensian Fathers, De Pere, Wis., 1982—; instr. fin. acctg. St. Norbert Coll., De Pere, 1984; lectr. grad. program U. Notre Dame, South Bend, Ind., 1985-87. Fellow Wis. Inst. CPA's; mem. Am. Inst. CPA's, Nat. Assn. Treas. Religious Insts. (discussion leader fin. mgmt. workshop 1984-86). Lutheran. Avocations: golf, fishing, hunting. Home: 515 Karen Ln Green Bay WI 54301 Office: The Premonstratensian Fathers 1016 N Broadway De Pere WI 54115

RAUSCHENBERGER, JOHN MICHAEL, industrial psychologist; b. Jackson, Mich., Dec. 21, 1950; s. Richard Dale and Anastasia Theresa (Lapinski) R. Ph.D., Mich. State U., East Lansing, 1978. Personnel rep. Armco, Inc., Middletown, Ohio, 1978-80, sr. personnel rep., 1980-81, supr. personnel research, 1981-85; personnel research analyst Ford Motor co., Dearborn, Mich., 1985—. Mem. Acad. Mgmt., Am. Psychol. Assn. Roman Catholic. Office: Ford Motor Co The American Rd Room 307-WHQ Dearborn MI 11899

RAUWERDINK, WILLIAM JAY, accountant; b. Sheboygan, Wis., Mar. 3, 1950; s. Harvard M. and Dorothy M. (Duenk) R.; m. Ann Catherine Geske, July 14, 1979; 1 child, Margaret Allene. BBA, U. Wis., 1972; MBA, Harvard U., 1974. CPA, N.Y., Mich., Mass. Ptnr. Deloitte Haskins & Sells, Detroit, 1983—; bd. dirs. Mich. Growth Capitol Found., Detroit. Mem. Wis. Bus. Alumni Assn. (bd. dirs. 1980—, pres. 1984—). Club: Renaissance (Detroit); Harvard (Boston). Office: Deloitte Haskins & Sells 100 Renaissance Ctr Suite 3100 Detroit MI 48243

RAUWOLF, STEPHEN LEROY, accountant; b. Evergreen Park, Ill., May 7, 1957; s. Gerald Joseph and Audrey (Carlson) R.; m. Marlene Barrier, Oct. 17, 1981; children: Hannah, Jeremiah. BS in Acctg., Ill. State U., 1979. CPA, Ill. Sr. staff acct. Fox and Co., Elgin, Ill., 1979-83; controller BARR Vending Co., St. Charles, Ill., 1983-85; bus. mgr., asst. treas. Glencoe (Ill.) Park Dist., 1985—; chmn. fin. com. Wheaton (Ill.) Park Dist. Risk Mgmt. Agy., 1986—. Mem. Am. Inst. CPA's, Ill. Soc. CPA's, Govt. Fin. Officers Assn., Ill. Govt. Fin. Officers Assn. Messianic Jewish. Avocations: guitar playing, composing and ministering religious music. Office: Glencoe Park Dist 999 Green Bay Rd Glencoe IL 60022

RAVAS, PAUL GEORGE, secretary of corporation; b. Fremont, Ohio, Aug. 19, 1935; s. George and Clara Lydia (Buhrow) R.; m. Sally Ann Schlatter, June 17, 1961; children: James, Karen. BSME, U. Toledo, 1958, MS in Indsl. Engring., 1959, BSCE, 1971. Registered profl. engr., Ohio, Ind. Product engr. Gen. Motors Corp., Toledo, 1959-64; structural engr. Art Iron Inc., Toledo, 1964—, corp. sec., 1986—, also bd. dirs.; corp. sec. ABROS Inc., Toledo, 1986—, also bd. dirs. Mem. Jewish Community Ctr., Toledo. Named Eagle Scout, Boy Scouts Am., Toledo. Mem. NSPE, Am. Welding Soc. (pres. Toledo chpt. 1976-77), Toledo Soc. Profl. Engrs. (bd. dirs. 1976-78), Nat. Assn. Archtl. Metal Mfrs. (v.p. 1986—), Ohio Soc. Profl. Engrs. Club: Cath. (Toledo). Avocations: photography, swimming, water skiing. Home: 3949 Brockton Dr Toledo OH 43623 Office: Art Iron Inc 860 Curtis St Toledo OH 43609

RAVEN, JONATHAN EZRA, lawyer, optical chain executive; b. Chgo., Jan. 13, 1951; s. Seymour S. and Norma (Blackman) R.; m. Leslie Michelle Shapiro, Dec. 29, 1973; children: Jane Lara, David Louis. BA cum laude, Western Mich. U. 1972; JD, U. Mich., 1975. Bar: Mich. 1975. Assoc., then ptnr., bd. dirs. firm Foster, Swift, Collins & Coey, P.C., Lansing, Mich., 1975-81; sr. v.p., gen. counsel, sec., dir. NuVision, Inc., Flint, Mich., 1981—, also bd. dirs.; v.p., bd. dirs. Bell Optical Inc., Flint. Pres., bd. dirs. Stonelake Condominium Assn., East Lansing, Mich., 1978-81, Flint Jewish Fedn., 1986—, 3d v.p., 1987—; mem. franchise working group Gov.'s Cabinet Council on Jobs and Econ. Devel., Lansing, 1983. Mem. ABA, State Bar Mich., Ingham County Bar Assn., Internat. Franchise Assn. (legis. com.), Am. Arbitration Assn. (panel arbitrators 1980—), Omicron Delta Kappa. Jewish. Office: NuVision Inc 2284 S Ballenger Hwy Flint MI 48501

RAWLES, EDWARD HUGH, lawyer; b. Chgo., May 7, 1945; s. Fred Wilson and Nancy (Hughes) R.; m. Margaret Mary O'Donoghue, Oct. 20, 1979; children—Lee Kathryn, Jacklyn Ann. B.A., U. Ill., 1967; J.D. summa cum laude, Ill. Inst. Tech., 1970. Bar: Ill. 1970, U.S. Dist. Ct. (cen. dist.) Ill. 1970, U.S. Supreme Ct. 1973, U.S. Ct. Appeals (7th cir.) 1983, Colo. 1984. Assoc. Reno, O'Byrne & Kepley, Champaign, Ill., 1970-73, ptnr., 1973-84; v.p. Reno O'Byrne & Kepley P.C., Champaign, 1984—; mem. student legal service adv. bd. U. Ill., Urbana, 1982—; hearing officer Ill. Fair Employment Practice Commn., Springfield, 1972-74. Diplomate Nat. Bd. Trial Advocacy, 1983. Fellow Ill. State Bar Found., 1984. Mem. Assn. Trial Lawyers Am., Ill. Trial Lawyers Assn., Ill. Bar Assn., Colo. Trial Lawyers Assn., Bar Assn. 7th Fed. Cir., Kent Soc. Honor Men, Phi Delta Theta. Roman Catholic. Home: Rural Rt 1 Box 137 White Heath IL 61884 Office: Reno O'Byrne & Kepley 501 W Church PO Box 693 Champaign IL 61820

RAWLS, CATHERINE POTEMPA, commodity futures executive, financial futures analyst; b. Chgo., Mar. 19, 1953; d. Stanley Louis and Mary Ann (Kuczmarski) Potempa; m. Stephen Franklin Rawls, July 30, 1983. B.A., Marquette U., 1975. Mem. Chgo. Bd. Trade, 1977-79, 83—; fin. futures analyst Geldermann Inc., Chgo., 1979-82, dir. research, 1982-86 ; pres. Tiare Trading Co. 1987—; mem. Chgo. Merc. Exchange, 1982. Editor Fax & Figures newsletter, 1983, Geldermann-Peavey newsletter, 1983-86 . Recipient award Marquette U. chpt. Women in Communications, 1975. Mem. Futures Industry Assn. Roman Catholic. Home: 421-C Sandhurst Circle Glen Ellyn IL 60137 Office: O'Connor & Co 141 W Jackson 28th Floor Chicago IL 60604

RAWLS, LARRY, record company executive; b. Mansfield, Ohio, Nov. 7, 1954; s. Martin and Vera (Easley) R. 1984. A.A., North Central Tech. Coll., Ohio, 1976; B.S., Urbana Coll., Ohio, With Gen. Motors Corp., Mansfield, 1979-87; pres. Fun City Record Co., Mansfield, 1979—. Mem. Am. Soc. Tng. and Devel.

RAWLS, STEPHEN FRANKLIN, brokerage house executive; b. Tifton, Ga., Sept. 18, 1951; s. Jacob Franklin and Jean Harriet (Gamadanis) R.; m. Catherine Dorothy Potempa, July 30, 1983. BBA, Stetson U., 1973. Mgr. commodity futures Cen. Soya Co., Ft. Wayne, Ind., 1975-79; v.p. Drexel Burnham Lambert, Chgo., 1979-82, Geldermann, Inc., Chgo., 1982-85; regional dir. Delta Commodities Corp., Chgo., 1986—. Mem. Chgo. Bd. Trade. Episcopalian. Lodges: Masons, Shriners. Avocations: canoeing, scuba diving. Home: 421 C Sandhurst Cir Glen Ellyn IL 60137 Office: Delta Commodities Corp One Energy Ctr 300 E Shuman Blvd Naperville IL 60540

RAWOT, BILLIE KAY, controller, accountant; b. Sterling, Ill., Mar. 18, 1951; d. William Neal and Marilaine (Anning) Appenzeller; m. John Albert Rawot, Jan. 24, 1976; children: Brandon, Lindsay Ann. BS in Acctg., U. Ill., 1973. CPA, Ill., Ohio. Staff acct. Arthur Young & Co., Chgo., 1973-76; sr. acct. Touche Ross & Co., Akron, Ohio, 1976-77; adminstrv. reporting Eaton Corp., Cleve., 1977-80, mgr. acctg., 1980-82, asst. dir. acctg., 1982-83, asst. controller, 1983—. Mem. audit com. United Way, 1983—, allocations com., 1987—. Named Outstanding Young Woman Am., 1981; recipient Career Woman of Achievement award Cleve. YWCA, 1982, Tribute to Women in Internat. Industry award Nat. Bd. YWCA, Boston, 1986. Mem. Am. Women's Soc. CPA's (pres. elect ednl. found. 1987—, chmn. scholarship adv. council 1985-86), Fin. Execs. Inst. (bd. dirs. 1983-86). Republican. Roman Catholic.

RAWSON, JAMES RULON YOUNG, botanist, biochemist; b. Boston, July 28, 1943; s. Rulon Wells and Jane (Young) R.; m. Judy MacDonald, Aug. 15, 1970; children: Donald, David. BS, Cornell U., 1965; PhD, Northwestern U., 1969. Postdoc. fellow U. Chgo., 1969-72; asst. prof. U. Ga., Athens, 1972-78, assoc. prof., 1978-83, prof., 1983-84; research assoc. Standard Oil, Cleve., 1984-85, sr. scientist, 1985—. NIH fellow, 1969-71; NSF research grantee, 1973-84; U.S. Dept. Agr. research grantee, 1980-84. Mem. Am. Soc. Biol. Chemists, Plant Physiology Soc. (mem. editorial bd.). Office: Standard Oil 4440 Warrensville Ctr Rd Cleveland OH 44128

RAWSON, MERLE R., manufacturing company executive; b. Chgo., June 9, 1924; s. Richard W. and Flora Rawson; m. Jane Armstrong, July 5, 1947; children: David M., Jeffrey M., Laurel J. Student, U. Ill., 1946-48; B.S. in Acctg., Northwestern U., 1949; D.Pub. Service (hon.), Walsh Coll., Canton, Ohio. Asst. to plant controller John Wood Co., 1949-58; asst. controller Easy Laudry Appliances, 1958-61; controller O'Bryan Bros., 1961; with Hoover Co., North Canton, Ohio, 1961—; controller Hoover Co., 1962-64, v.p., treas., 1964-69, sr. v.p., treas., 1969-75, chmn. bd., chief exec. officer, 1975-82, chmn. bd., pres., chief exec. officer, 1982—, also dir.; exec. v.p. Hoover Worldwide Corp., 1971-75, chmn. bd., chief exec. officer, 1975—, pres., 1986—, also dir.; chmn., dir. Hoover plc, U.K., 1978—, vice chmn., dir. Chgo. Pacific Corp.; dir. Hoover Can. Inc., Hoover Mexicana, Hoover Holland, S.A. Hoover, France, Soc. Corp., Cleve., Hoover Industrial y Comercial S.A., Colombia, Phase IV Products, Inc., Juver Indsl. S.A. de C.V., Society Bank of Eastern Ohio. Trustee Ohio Found. Ind. Colls.; mem. adv. council Pace U.; mem. Aultman Hosp. Assn., Aultman Hosp. Devel. Found.; mem. sr. common room St. Edmund Hall, Oxford U., Served with F.A. AUS, 1943-46. Decorated chevalier Order of Leopold Belgium, chevalier Order of Legion of Honor; recipient Medal of City of Paris, 1983. Mem. Council Fgn. Relations, Greater Canton C. of C., Stark County Bluecoats. Clubs: Capitol Hill, Congress Lake Country. Lodge: Rotary. Office: 101 E Maple St North Canton OH 44720

RAY, ALICE MARIE, data processing executive; b. Gary, Ind., Sept. 10, 1947; d. Edmund Joseph Krzyzewski and Alice Winifred (Wilski) Kaye; m. Kevin L. Ray, Oct. 10, 1981. Data center supr. Ind. U., Gary, 1970-77; programmer, analyst Assocs. Fin.nce, South Bend, Ind., 1977-79; data base analyst Mayflower Moving, Indpls., 1979-80; data processing cons. Chgo., 1980-84; data base specialist Rayovac Corp., Madison, Wis., 1984—; systems cons., owner Tri-Star Computer Info. Specialists, Inc., Madison, 1980—. Mem. Data Processing Mgmt. Assn. (vice chmn. edn. com. 1985), Natural Spl. Interest Group (chmn. 1986—). Avocations: writing, showing horses, archery. Home: 6769 Schroeder Rd #7 Madison WI 53711 Office: Rayovac Corp 601 Rayovac Dr Madison WI 53719

RAY, CHARLES DEAN, neurosurgeon; b. Americus, Ga., Aug. 1, 1927; s. Oliver Tinsley and Katherine (Broadfield) R.; A.B., Emory U., 1950; M.S., U. Miami (Fla.), 1952; M.D., Med. Coll. Ga., 1956; m. Roberta L. Mann, Dec. 17, 1978; children—Bruce, Kathy, C. Marlene, Thomas, John, Blythe. Intern, Baptist Meml. Hosp., Memphis, 1956-57; resident, research assoc. neurosurgery U. Tenn. Hosp., Memphis, 1957-62; fellow, research asst. Mayo Clinic and Found., Rochester, Minn., 1962-64; asst. prof. neurosurgery, lectr. bioengring. Johns Hopkins U. Med. Sch., Balt., 1964-68; chief dept. med. engring. F. Hoffmann-LaRoche, Basel, Switzerland, also lectr. U. Basel, 1968-73; practice medicine, specializing in neurosurgery, Mpls., 1973—; staff Sister Kenney Inst., Children's, Abbott-Northwestern hosps., Mpls., clin. assoc. prof. medicine U. Minn., Mpls., 1973—; v.p. med research Medtronic Inc., Mpls., 1972-79; chmn. bd., pres. R-3 Devel. Corp., Cedar Surg. Inc., 1985—; cons. in field. Chmn. com. materials and devices World Fedn. Neurosurg. Socs., 1977—; vestry St. Martin's Episcopal Ch., Wayzata, Minn., 1976-79. Served with USN, 1945-49. Diplomate Am. Bd. Neurol. Surgery. Fellow ACS, Royal Soc. Health; mem. Pan-Am. Med. Assns., AMA, Am. Assn. Neurol. Surgeons, Congress Neurol. Surgeons, W. Ger. Armed Forces Med. Soc., IEEE, Internat. Fedn. Med. Biol. Engring., Internat. Soc. Stereotaxic and Functional Neurosurgery, ASTM, Internat. Orgn. Standardization, Sigma Xi, others. Clubs: Cosmos, Lafayette, Minneapolis. Author: Principles of Engineering Applied to Medicine, 1964; Medical Engineering, 1974; Lumbar Spine Surgery, 1987; contbr. articles to profl. pubs. Home: 19550 Cedarhurst Wayzata MN 55391 Office: Inst for Low Back Care Sister Kenny Inst 2737 Chicago Ave Minneapolis, MN 55407

RAY, CHARLES JOSEPH, dentist; b. South Sioux City, Nebr., June 4, 1911; s. Charles Joseph and Katherine Frances (Bridgeford) R.; m. Cecilia Estelle Radlinger, Nov. 22, 1933; children—Carole, Margie, Kathy, Jeane, Rita, Charles, Chrystal. E.E., S.D. Sch. of Mines, 1932; D.D.S., U. Minn., 1936; postgrad. Forsythe Dental Infirmary, Boston, 1936-37, Eastman Dental Dispensary, 1937-38. Pvt. practice dentistry, 1938—, with Ray Dental Group, Rapid City, S.D., 1953—; mem. S.D. Med. Adv. Bd., 1958-65, S.D. Dental Legis. Com., 1985—, chmn. 1985-86. Active USO, 1959, pres. Rapid City chpt. 1952-60; pres. S.D. Crippled Children's Assn. Mem. Am. Dental Assn. (life), S.D. Dental Assn. (Gold Tooth award 1980, pres. 1964), Am. Prosthodontic Soc. (pres. 1980-81, exec. council 1981-82), Fedn. Prosthodontic Orgn. (sec. 1976-80), Am. Assn. Hosp. Dentists, Am. Soc. Psychosomatic Dentistry and Medicine, Pierre-Fauchard Acad. (award 1980), Am. Acad. Periodontology, Acad. Internat. Dentistry and Medicine, Am. Acad. Practice Adminstrn., Am. Acad. Gen. Dentistry, Am. Acad. Dental Group Practice, Colo. Prosthodontic Soc., Rapid City Dental Soc., Black Hills Dist. Dental Soc., Dental Group Mgmt. Assn., Chgo. Dental Soc. (assoc.), Rapid City C. of C., Omicron Kappa Upsilon. Roman Catholic. Clubs: Internateonal Cosmopolitan (pres. 1972), Rapid City Cosmopolitan (pres. 1962; Disting. Service award 1977), Sioux Land Study. Lodges: K.C., Elks. Home: Rural Rt 1 Box 1040 Rapid City SD 57702 Office: Ray Dental Group PO Box 899 Rapid City SD 57709

RAY, DARRELL MORRIS, financial planning company executive, religious school administrator , educator; b. Findlay, Ohio, Mar. 22, 1959; s. Sherman Hodge and Delores (Lowe) R.; m. Julia Ann Corbin, Oct. 6, 1978; children: Jeremy James, Stephen Michael. BA, Bapt. Bible Coll., Springfield, Mo., 1981; student, Southwest Mo. State U., 1981, Pensacola (Fla.) Christian Coll., summer 1986, U. Mich., 1987; cert. in real estate fin., U. Toledo. Cert. Life Underwriting Tng. Council. Sales rep. Life Ins. Co. Va., Toledo, 1982-84; owner, pres. Darrell Ray and Assocs., Financial Planning Agy., Inc., Westland, Mich. and Toledo, 1982—; pres. Bus. Opportunity Search Partnership, Toledo, 1986—; bus. dir. United Bapt. Ch., Springfield, 1977; dir. bus., sr. citizens and children's ministries Trinity Bapt. Ch., 1978-80; adminstr., prin., tchr. chemistry, computers, history United Christian Schs., Garden City, Mich., 1986—. Vol. various Rep. polit. campaigns; past pres. Springfield area Coll. Reps.; past chmn. 7th Congrl. Dist. Coll. Reps.; past 2d v.p. Greene County Young Reps.; mgr., advisor campaigns Green County Reps. 1977-78, 80-81; candidate Findlay City Council 1979; dir. Ch. Polit. Awareness Program (forerunner Ohio Moral Majority) 1978-80; active Mo. Moral Majority 1980-81; mem. Lucas County Rep. Cen. Com. 1982-84. Mem. Nat. Assn. Life Underwriters, Ohio Assn. Life Underwriters, ToledoAssn. Life Underwriters, Nat. Bd. Realtors, Ohio Bd. Realtors, Toledo Bd. Realtors, Internat. Assn. Fin. Planning, Inst. Cert. Fin. Planners, Ohio Bapt. Bible Fellowship. Office: Darrell Ray & Assocs Fin Planning Agy Inc 33443 Fernwood Westland MI 48185 Office: United Christian Schs 29205 Florence Garden City MI 48135 Office: Bus Opportunity Search 5917 Rounding River Ln Toledo OH 43611

RAY, FRANK ALLEN, lawyer; b. Lafayette, Ind., Jan. 30, 1949; s. Dale Allen and Merry Ann (Fleming) R.; m. Carol Ann Olmutz, Oct. 1, 1982; children—Erica Fleming, Robert Allen. B.A., Ohio State U., 1970, J.D., 1973. Bar: Ohio 1973, U.S. Dist. Ct. (so. dist.) Ohio 1975, U.S. Supreme Ct. 1976, U.S. Tax Ct. 1977, U.S. Ct. Appeals (6th cir.) 1977, U.S. Dist Ct. (no. dist.) Ohio 1980, Pa. 1983, U.S. Dist. Ct. (ea. dist.) Mich. 1983; cert. civil trial adv. Nat. Bd. Trial Advocacy. Asst. pros. atty. Franklin County, Ohio, 1973-75, chief civil counsel, 1976-78; dir. econ. crime project Nat. Dist. Attys. Assn., Washington, 1975-76; assoc. Brownfield, Kosydar, Bowen, Bally & Sturtz, Columbus, Ohio, 1978, Michael F. Colley Co., L.P.A., Columbus, 1979-83; pres. Frank A. Ray Co., L.P.A., Columbus, 1983—; mem. seminar faculty Nat. Coll. Dist. Attys., Houston, 1975-77; mem. nat. conf. faculty Fed. Jud. Ctr., Washington, 1976-77. Editor: Economic Crime Digest, 1975-76. Mem. fin. com. Franklin County Republican Orgn., Columbus, 1979-84. Served to 1st lt. inf. U.S. Army, 1973. Named to Ten Outstanding Young Citizens of Columbus, Columbus Jaycees, 1976; recipient Nat. award of Distinctive Service, Nat. Dist. Attys. Assn., 1977. Fellow Columbus Bar Found.; mem. Columbus Bar Assn., Ohio State Bar Assn., ABA, Assn. Trial Lawyers Am., Ohio Acad. Trial Lawyers (trustee 1984-87, sec. 1987—, legis. coordinator 1986—, Pres.' award 1986), Franklin County Trial Lawyers Assn. (trustee 1982-83, treas. 1984-85, chmn. com. negligence law 1983-87, sec. 1985-86, v.p. 1986-87, pres. 1987—). Presbyterian. Home: 5800 Olentangy Blvd Worthington OH 43085 Office: 330 S High St Columbus OH 43215

RAY, FRANK DAVID, government agency official; b. Mt. Vernon, Ohio, Dec. 1, 1940; s. John Paul and Lola Mae (Miller) R.; B.S. in Edn., Ohio State U., 1964, J.D., 1967; m. Julia Anne Sachs, June 11, 1976. Bar: Ohio 1967, U.S. Dist. Ct. 1969, U.S. Cir. Ct. Appeals (6th cir.) 1970, U.S. Supreme Ct. 1971. Legal aide to atty. gen. Ohio, 1965-66; bailiff probate ct., Franklin County, Ohio, 1966-67, gen. referee, 1967-68; with firm Stouffer, Wait and Ashbrook, Columbus, Ohio, 1967-71; jour. clk. Ohio Ho. of Reps., 1969-71; dist. dir. SBA, 1971—; mem. Ohio Pub. Defender Commn., 1983—; mem. Columbus Mayor's Econ. Devel. Council, 1983-84; mem. Small Bus. and High Tech. adv. com. Ohio Div. Securities, 1983-84; mem. tech. alliance Central Ohio Adv. Bd., 1983—. Mem. Upper Arlington (Ohio) Bd. Health, 1970-75; pres. Buckeye Republican Club, 1970, Franklin County Forum, 1970; chmn. Central Ohio chpt. Nat. Found.-March of Dimes, 1974-77; trustee Columbus Acad. Contemporary Art, 1976. Recipient Service award Nat. Found.-March of Dimes, 1974, 75, 76, 77; Am. Jurisprudence award for Excellence; named Ohio Commodore, 1973. Mem. Delta Upsilon, Alpha Epsilon Delta. Clubs: Ohio Press, Ohio State U. Pres., Shrine. Home: 4200 Dublin Rd Columbus OH 43220

RAY, JAMES ALLEN, consultant; b. Lexington, Ky., Feb. 21, 1931; s. Allen Brice and Elizabeth Logan (Simpson) R.; m. Mary Ruth Johnston, June 8, 1958; children: James Edward, Allen Bruce, John David. BS in Geology, U. N.C., 1958; MS, N.C. State Coll., 1962. Chief petrographic research Master Builders div. Martin Marietta Corp., Cleve., 1959-73, asst. dir. research, 1973-77, dir. research, 1977-78, v.p. research, 1979-80, v.p. creative research, 1980-82; cons., 1982—; pres. James A. Ray Corp. 1986—. Patentee in field. Served with USAF, 1951-55. Recipient Jefferson cup Martin Marietta Corp., 1977. Fellow Am. Inst. Chemists, Inc.; mem. Mineral. Soc. Am., Mineral. Soc. Can., Am. Concrete Inst., ASTM, Res. Officers Assn. (life), Nat. Rifle Assn. (life), Washington Legal Found. (life), Am. Security Council. Republican. Address: 9891 Stamm Rd PO Box P Mantua OH 44255

RAY, JOHN WALKER, physician; b. Columbus, Ohio, Jan. 12, 1936; s. Kenneth Clark and Hope (Walker) Ray; A.B. magna cum laude, Marietta Coll., 1956; M.D. cum laude, Ohio State U., 1960; postgrad. Temple U., 1964, Mt. Sinai Hosp. and Columbia U., 1964, 66, Northwestern U., 1967, 71, U. Ill., 1968, U. Ind., 1969, Tulane U., 1969; m. Susanne Gettings, July 15, 1961; children—Nancy Ann, Susan Christy. Intern, Ohio State U. Hosps., Columbus, 1960-61, clin. research trainee NIH, 1963-65, resident dept. otolaryngology, 1963-65, 1966-67, resident dept. surgery 1965-66, instr. dept. otolaryngology, 1966-67, 70-75, clin. asst. prof., 1975-82, clin. assoc. prof., 1982—; active staff, past chief of staff Bethesda Hosp.; active staff, chief of staff Good Samaritan Hosp., Zanesville, Ohio, 1967—; courtesy staff Ohio State U. Hosps., Columbus, 1970—; radio-TV health commentator, 1982—. Past pres. Muskingum chpt. Am. Cancer Soc.; trustee Care One Health Systems, Ohio Med. Polit. Action Com. Served to capt. USAF, 1961-63. Recipient Barraquer Meml. award, 1965; named Ky. col., 1966. Diplomate Am. Bd. Otolaryngology. Fellow A.C.S., Am. Soc. Otolaryn. Allergy, Am. Acad. Otolaryngology (gov.), Am. Acad. Facial Plastic and Reconstructive Surgery; mem. Muskingum County Acad. Medicine, AMA (del. hosp. med. Staff sect.), Ohio Med. Assn. (del.), Columbus Ophthalmol. and Otolaryngol. Soc. (past pres.), Ohio Soc. Otolaryngology (past pres.), Pan-Am. Assn. Otolaryngology and Bronchoesophagology, Pan-Am. Allergy Soc., Am. Council Otolaryngology, Am. Auditory Soc., Am. Soc. Contemporary Medicine and Surgery, Phi Beta Kappa, Alpha Tau Omega, Alpha Kappa Kappa, Alpha Omega Alpha, Beta Beta Beta. Republican. Presbyterian. Contbr. articles to sci., med. jours. Collaborator, surg. motion picture Laryngectomy and Neck Dissection, 1964. Office: 2825 Maple Ave Zanesville OH 43701

RAY, THOMAS K., clergyman. Bishop No. Mich. region Episcopal Ch. Office: Episc Ch 131 E Ridge St Marquette MI 49855 *

RAYBURN, WILLIAM BUSBY, tool company executive; b. Canandaigua, N.Y., Mar. 31, 1925; s. Earl R. and Elisabeth I. (Busby) R.; children—John W., William D., Kathleen M., James F. Student schs., Candaigua. Nat. sales mgr. Snap-On Tools Corp., Kenosha, Wis., 1974-75; v.p. nat. sales Snap-On Tools Corp., 1975-76, sr. v.p. mktg., 1976-79, exec. v.p., 1979-82, pres., chief operating officer, 1982-84, chmn., pres., chief exec. officer, 1984—, also dir., 1976—; dir. Republic Savs. and Loan, Milw., 1979—. Served to comdr. USN, 1943-45; PTO. Mem. Hand Toll Assn. (dir. 1979-81), Mfrs. and Employers Assn. (dir. Kenosha 1984). Republican. Club: Kenosha Country (bd. dirs. 1979-81). Office: Snap On Tools Corp 2801 80th St Kenosha WI 53140

RAYL, GRANVILLE MONROE, religious association executive, founder; b. Sedalia, Mo., Aug. 21, 1917; s. Burley and Cordelia (Swope) R.; m. Hazel Arlene Gruver, June 8, 1952; children: Janet Arlene, Granville Alan. BTh, Faith Bible Coll. and Theol. Sem., 1964; DD, The Evang. Evangelism Crusades, 1962; ThD, Faith Bible Coll. and Theol. Sem., 1965. Ordained to ministry Internat. Gospel Assemblies, 1957. Regional dir. Fundamental Ministers & Chs., Inc., Kansas City, 1957-62; pres. Internat. Bible Coll. & Sem., DeSoto, Mo., 1962—, Assn. Internat. Gospel Assemblies, Inc., DeSoto, 1962—. Republican. Avocation: gardening. Office: Assn Internat Gospel Assemblies Inc 411 S Third St DeSoto MO 63020

RAYMER, DONALD GEORGE, utility company executive; b. Jackson, Mich., July 16, 1924; s. Donald Rector and Vivian Alverda (Wolfinger) R.; m. Joan Elizabeth Steck, Oct. 16, 1948; children: Mary Margaret Dorward, Dorothy Elizabeth, Charles George. B.S.E.E., U. Mich., 1948; M.S. (Sloan fellow), M.I.T., 1960. Relay engr. Central Ill. Public Service Co., Springfield, 1948-56; mgr. system ops. Central Ill. Public Service Co., 1956-65; div. mgr. Central Ill. Public Service Co., Mattoon, Ill., 1965-68; v.p. Central Ill. Public Service Co., Springfield, 1968-78; exec. v.p. Central Ill. Public Service Co., 1978-80, pres., 1980—, also dir.; dir. Electric Energy, Inc., Marine Bank of Springfield, Marine Bancorp., Inc.; vice chmn. Edison Electric Inst., 1984-87. Vice chmn. Springfield United Fund Campaign, 1964, asso. chmn., 1974; vice chmn. Mattoon United Welfare Fund, 1967; bd. dirs. Meml. Med. Center; chmn. Meml. Med. Ctr., 1987—. Served to lt. (j.g.) USNR, 1943-46. Mem. IEEE, Am. Mgmt. Assn., Ill. State C. of C. (dir. 1982—, vice chmn. 1985—), Greater Springfield C. of C. (dir. 1968-71, 85—, vice chmn. 1985—), Chi Phi. Republican. Episcopalian. Clubs: Illini Country, Sangamo (Springfield); Union League (Chgo.). Office: Cen Ill Pub Service Co 607 E Adams St Springfield IL 62701

RAYMOND, ARTHUR, university program director; b. Winner, S.D., Jan. 18, 1923; s. Enoch Wheeler and Mary (Frazier) R.; m. Rose Marie Schone, Apr. 28, 1950; children: Arthur Jr., Eric, Mary, Mark, Rebekah. BA, Dakota Wesleyan U., 1951; AM, U. Mich., 1980, postgrad., 1980-82. Reporter Daily Republic, Mitchell, S.D., 1953, city editor, 1953-62; mng. editor Herald, Williston, N.D., 1962-65; Sunday editor, legis. reporter Herald, Grand Forks, N.D., 1965-71; mem. N.D. Ho. of Reps., 1971-77; dir. Indian studies progrm U. N.D., Grand Forks, 1971-78, dir. Indian program devel., 1978—. Contbr. revs. and articles to profl. jours.; mem. editorial bd. Am. Indian Culture and Research Jour. Mem. nat. exec. council, affirmative action council Episcopal Ch., U.S. Commn. Civil Rights, adv. commn. Supreme Ct. N.D., nat. adv. bd. Am. Diabetes Assn., bd. dirs.; chmn. N.D. Commn. Alcoholism; bd. dirs. Area Manpower Planning Bd., Child Evaluation Ctr. Republican. Home: 2111 University Ave Grand Forks ND 58201 Office: U ND Box 62 Grand Forks ND 58202

RAYMOND, LAWRENCE BRIAN, retirement services company executive; b. Morristown, N.J., July 4, 1950; s. Richard Lawrence and Kay Louise (Johnson) R.; m. Mary Lee Specht, Apr. 9, 1976; children: Brian Wesley, Benjamin Lawrence. BA, U. Mich., 1973, MBA, 1975. Asst. to agy. mgr. Equitable Life Ins. Co., Ann Arbor, Mich., 1975-76; actuary Retirement Funding Corp. (name now Retirement Services Corp.), Birmingham, Mich., 1976-80, exec. v.p., 1980—. Author: (manual) Pension Workbook for CLU, 1981. Co-chmn. ann. giving Cranbrook Ednl. Community, Bloomfield Hills, Mich., 1984-87. English Speaking Union scholar, 1969. Mem. Am. Soc. Pension Actuaries, Am. Coll. CLU's (cert. 1978), Am. Coll. Cert. Fin. Cons. (cert. 1984), Million Dollar Round Table (top of table 1985-86, life), Lic. Ins. Counselors Mich. (lic.), Oakland Estate Planning Council, Cranbrook Alumni Assn. (pres. 1980), Assn. Advanced Life Underwriters. Republican. Episcopalian. Club: U. Mich. Victors (Ann Arbor). Lodge: Rotary. Avocations: golf, tennis, skiing, travel. Office: Retirement Services Corp 30100 Telegraph Suite 170 Birmingham MI 48010

RAYMOND, RUSSELL ERIC, cardiologist; b. Stamford, Conn., June 25, 1953; s. Frank Reginald and Ruth Bernice (Rundlett) R.; m. Karen Louise Shirey, Aug. 2, 1975; children: Chad Eric, Timothy Earl. BA, Asbury Coll., Wilmore, Ky., 1975; DO, Chgo. Coll. Osteo. Medicine, 1979. Diplomate Am. Bd. Internal Medicine, 1984. Intern Drs. Hosp., Columbus, Ohio, 1979-80; resident in internal medicine Cleve. Clinic, 1981-84, fellow in cardiology, 1984—; Emergency room cons. Richmond Heights (Ohio) Hosp., 1982-86. Mem. AMA, ACP, Am. Coll. Cardiology (assoc.), Am. Osteo. Assn., Christian Med. Soc. Republican. Avocations: golf, softball, reading, time with family. Home: 5160 Mayview Rd Lyndhurst OH 44124 Office: Cleve Clin Hosp 9500 Euclid Ave Cleveland OH 44106

RAYNOR, JOHN PATRICK, university president; b. Omaha, Oct. 1, 1923; s. Walter V. and Mary Clare (May) R. A.B., St. Louis U., 1947, M.A., 1948, Licentiate in Philosophy, 1949, Licentiate in Theology, 1956; Ph.D., U. Chgo., 1959. Joined Soc. of Jesus, 1941; ordained priest Roman Catholic Ch., 1954; instr. St. Louis U. High Sch., 1948-51, asst. prin., 1951; asst. to dean Coll. Liberal Arts, Marquette U., 1960, asst. to v.p. acad. affairs, 1961-62, v.p. acad. affairs, 1962-65, pres., 1965—; dir. Kimberly-Clark Corp. Mem. Greater Milw. Com.; mem. Citizens Govtl. Research Bur., Wis. Higher Ednl. Aids Bd.; corp. mem. United Community Services Greater Milw.; hon. bd. dirs. Goethe House; sponsor United Negro Coll. Fund; mem. Froedtert Luth. Meml. Hosp. Corp.; hon. com. mem. Endowment Fund Metro Milw. Luth. Campus Ministry; trustee Milw. Heart Research Found., Inc.; bd. govs. Wis. affiliate Am. Heart Assn. Recipient Disting. Service award Edn. Commn. of States, 1977. Mem. Nat. Cath. Edn. Assn., North Central Assn. (examiner, cons.), Am. Council Edn., Wis. Assn. Ind. Colls. and Univs. (past pres., exec. com.), Wis. Found. Ind. Colls. (past pres.), Assn. Jesuit Colls. and Univs. (past chmn., dir., mem. exec. com.), Internat. Fedn. Cath. Colls. and Univs., Met. Milw. Assn. Commerce, Phi Beta Kappa, Phi Delta Kappa, Alpha Sigma Nu. Office: Marquette Univ Office of President 615 N 11th St Milwaukee WI 53233

RAYNOR, SHERRY NEVANS, association administrator; b. Escanaba, Mich., Aug. 18, 1930; d. James Christopher and Ebba (Ebbesen) Nevans; married, 1949 (div. 1955); children: Robert Storrer, Christine Storrer, Sandra Storrer; married, 1959 (div. 1972); children: Ebba Raynor, Nels Raynor, Beatrice Raynor. BA, Mich. State U., 1965, MA, 1967. Cert. elem. tchr., in spl. edn., Mich., Mass. Pres., founder, dir. Blind Children's Fund (formerly Internat. Inst. for Visually Impaired, 0-7, Inc.), East Lansing, Mich. and Auburndale, Mass., 1978—; supr., initiator Perkins Presch., Watertown, Mass., 1979-80; coordinator, initiator Perkins Infant/Toddler Program, Watertown, 1980-83; project dir. Project Outreach USA, Newton, Mass., 1983-84; dir., founder Infant Program for Visually Impaired, IISD, Mason, Mich., 1972-79; pres. 1st Internat. Symposium on Infant and Presch. Visually Handicapped Infants and Young Children, Internat. Inst. for Visually Impaired, 0-7, Inc., Israel, 1981, 2d Internat. Symposium, Netherlands Antilles, 1983; mem. standing com. Annual Internat. Seminars on Presch. Blind. Author: (with others) (books for parents of blind children) Get a Wiggle On, 1975, Move It, 1977, (book for tchrs. of blind children) Mainstreaming Preschoolers: Children with Visual Handicaps, 1985. Mem. Assn. for Edn. and Rehab. of Blind and Visually Impaired (chairperson div. VIII Infants and Preschoolers 1984-86, Pauline M. Moor award 1986), Nat. Assn. Parents of Visually Impaired (1986 award for exemplary practice), Internat. Council for Exceptional Children, Internat. Council for Edn. of Visually Handicapped, World Blind Union, Am. Council for the Blind, Assn. Childhood Edn. Internat., Nat. Fedn. Blind. Lodge: Zonta. Avocations: photography, sewing, writing, traveling. Home: 1954 Hamilton Rd Okemos MI 48864 Office: Blind Children's Fund 1975 Rutgers Circle East Lansing MI 48823

RAZ, ROBERT EUGENE, librarian; b. Michigan City, Ind., Mar. 15, 1942; s. Eugene and Claradelle (Perham) R.; m. Susan Margaret Spiers, June 10, 1978; children: Richard, Philip, Christopher, Katherine. B.A., Andrews U., 1964; M.A., Western Mich. U., 1965. Librarian Library for the Blind, Mich. State Library, Lansing, 1965-67; library cons. Mich. State Library, 1967-71; dir. Willard Library, Battle Creek, Mich., 1971-79, Grand Rapids (Mich.) Pub. Library, 1979—; Trustee Library of Mich., 1982—. Mem. Grand Rapids Council for Humanities, 1980—, v.p., 1981, pres., 1983, 84. Mem. Mich Library Assn. (pres. 1979), ALA (council 1982-86). Home: 2750 7th St NW Grand Rapids MI 49504 Office: Grand Rapids Pub Library 60 Library Plaza NE Grand Rapids MI 49503-3093

RAZI, KATHLEEN ANN, human resources specialist; b. Schenectady, Jan. 12, 1950; d. Francis William and Mary Margaret (Strong) Schickel; m. Ahmad Razi, Aug. 26, 1972; 1 child, Marisa. B.A., Russell Sage Coll., 1972; M.S. in Social Adminstrn., Case Western Res. U., 1974. Lic. ind. social worker; Cert. clin. social worker. Social worker Cleve. VA Hosp., 1972-73, Fairhill Mental Health Ctr., Cleve., 1973-74; social worker, adminstr. Far West Ctr., North Olmsted, Ohio, 1976-79; adminstr. coop. edn. Baldwin-Wallace Coll., Berea, Ohio, 1979-80, adminstr. acad. advising, 1980-85; human resource devel. specialist Univ. Hosps. of Cleve., 1985-86. adj. faculty Baldwin-Wallace Coll., 1981—; bd. dirs. Hathaway Brown Corp. Developer Project Tng. Manual, 1979. Mem. Am. Soc. Tng. and Devel., Nat. Assn. Social Workers (cert.), Am. Assn. Counseling and Devel., Cleve. Assn. Jr. League, Chi Sigma Iota. Roman Catholic. Avocations: volunteer projects. Home: 21736 Aberdeen St Rocky River OH 44116

RAZINK, KRISTI KAY, communications executive; b. Mpls., Dec. 12, 1956; d. Duane Peter and Garnet Jean (Chase) R. Student, U. Minn., 1976-82, Metro State U., 1981—, Mpls. Community Coll., 1984. Asst. media buyer Capp Homes, Mpls., 1975-79; media planner, buyer Kamstra Communications, St. Paul, 1979-82; media dir. Clarke Livingston Assocs., Mpls., 1982-84, Jack Carmichael Advt., Mpls., 1984-85, John Miles Co., Mpls., 1985-87, Creative Communications Cons., Mpls., 1987—; media cons. in field, Mpls., 1985—. Mem. Advt. Fedn. Minn., Bus. Profl. Advt. Assn. Lutheran. Home: 4609 30th Ave S Minneapolis MN 55406 Office: Creative Communications Cons 1250 Internat Centre 920 Second Ave S Minneapolis MN 55402

READER, JAMES RALPH, dentist; b. Rantoul, Ill., Feb. 13, 1935; s. George H.D. and Gertrude M. (Sill) R.; m. Mary Lou Reader, Dec. 18, 1955; children: Mark E., Miriam L., Michelle M. BS, U. Ill., Chgo., 1958, DDS, 1960. Lic. dentist, Ill. Gen. practice dentistry Chrisman, Ill., 1960—. Active Ch. of the Nazarene, Chrisman, Ill., 1960—; bd. trustees Olivet Nazarene U., Kankakee, Ill., 1974—. Mem. ADA, Ill. Dental Soc. Home: 220 N Illinois Chrisman IL 61924 Office: 122 W Madison CHrisman IL 61924

REAGAN, ALAN LEE, data processing manager; b. Waterloo, Iowa, Jan. 8, 1952; s. Floyd William and Lena Florence (Adubato) R.; m. Gretchen Lorane Hess, Sept. 9, 1978; children: Benjamin James, Andrew John. BS in Math and Computer Sci., Iowa State U., 1974. System programmer Deere and Co., Moline, Ill., 1974-79, div. mgr., 1979—. Loaned exec. Quad Cities United Way, Rock Island, Ill., 1983; treas. St. James Luth. Ch., Bettendorf, Iowa, 1981, pres., 1983. Mem. SHARE, Inc. (div. mgr. 1985—). Republican. Avocations: reading, racquetball, tennis. Office: Deere & Co John Deere Rd Moline IL 61265

REAGAN, JAMES W., banking company executive. Chmn., chief exec. officer Am. Nat. Bank and Trust Co., St. Paul. Office: Am Nat Bank & Trust Co 5th & Minnesota St Saint Paul MN 55101 *

REAM, JOHN K., banker; b. 1934. Student, U. Mo. With Acceptance Fin. Corp., St. Louis, 1956-84; pres., chief operating officer Citicorp Savs. of Ill., Chgo., 1984—. Served with USMC, 1951-54. Office: Citicorp Savs of Ill a Fed Savs & Loan Assn 1 S Dearborn St Chicago IL 60603 *

REAMS, BERNARD DINSMORE, JR., lawyer, educator; b. Lynchburg, Va., Aug. 17, 1943; s. Bernard Dinsmore and Martha Eloise (Hickman) R.; m. Rosemarie Bridget Boyle, Oct. 26, 1968; children: Andrew Dennet, Adriane Bevin. B.A., Lynchburg Coll., 1965; M.S., Drexel U., Phila., 1966; J.D., U. Kans., 1972; Ph.D., St. Louis U., 1983. Bar: Kans. 1973, Mo. 1986. Instr., asst. librarian Rutgers U., 1966-69; asst. prof. law, librarian U. Kans., Lawrence, 1969-74; mem. faculty law sch. Washington U., St. Louis, 1974—, prof. law, 1976—, librarian, 1974-76, acting dean library services, 1987—. Author: Law For The Businessman, 1974, Reader in Law Librarianship, 1976, Federal Price and Wage Control Programs 1917-1979: Legis. Histories and Laws, 1980, Education of the Handicapped: Laws, Legislative Histories, and Administrative Documents, 1982, Housing and Transportation of the Handicapped: Laws and Legislative Histories, 1983, Internal Revenue Acts of the United States: The Revenue Act of 1954 with Legislative Histories and Congressional Documents, 1983 Congress and the Courts: A Legislative History 1978-1984, 1984, University-Industry Research Partnerships: The Major Issues in Research and Development Agreements, 1986, Deficit Control and the Gramm-Rudman-Hollings Act, 1986, The Semiconductor Chip and the Law: A Legislative History of the Semiconductor Chip Protection Act of 1984, 1986, American International Law Cases, 2d series, 1986, Technology Transfer Law: The Export Administration Acts of the U.S., 1987; co-author: Segregation and the Fourteenth Amendment in the States, 1975, Historic Preservation Law: An Annotated Bibliography, 1976, Congress and the Courts: A Legislative History 1787-1977, 1978, Federal Consumer Protection Laws, Rules and Regulations, 1979, A Guide and Analytical Index to the Internal Revenue Acts of the U.S., 1909-1950, 1979, The Numerical Lists and Schedule of Volumes of the U.S. Congressional Serial Set: 73d Congress through the 96th Congress, 1984, Human Experimentation: Federal Laws, Legislative Histories, Regulations and Related Documents, 1985, American Legal Literature: A Guide to Selected Legal Resources, 1985. Thornton award for Excellence Lynchburg Coll., 1986. Mem. ABA, Am. Assn. Higher Edn., ALA, Spl. Libraries Assn., Internat. Assn. Law Libraries, Am. Assn. Law Librarians, Southwestern Assn. Law Librarians (pres. 1977-78), ABA, Nat. Assn. of Coll. and Univ. Attys., Order of Coif, Phi Beta Kappa, Beta Phi Mu, Phi Delta Phi, Phi Delta Epsilon, Kappa Delta Pi., Pi Lambda Theta. Home: 2353 Hollyhead Dr Des Peres MO 63131 Office: Washington U Law Sch Box 1120 Saint Louis MO 63130

REARDON, JOHN B., III, marketing professional, educator; b. Youngstown, Ohio, Nov. 25, 1957; s. John B. Jr. and Carole Ann (Shutrump) R. BBA in Econs., Kent (Ohio) State U., 1979; MA in Econs., Youngstown State U., 1985. Mgr. sales adminstrn. Rep. Storage Systems Co., Canton, Ohio, 1980—; instr. econs. Youngstown State U., 1985—. Republican. Roman Catholic. Avocations: reading, music, sports, games, travel.

REARDON, MICHAEL JAMES, health care delivery administrator; b. Gary, Ind., Oct. 5, 1956; s. Edward Charles and Antoinette Yolanda (Saccucci) R.; m. Michele Therese Mirich, Nov. 26, 1983; children: Michael Edward, Nathaniel Charles. BA cum laude, Loras Coll., 1979; MS in Adminstrn., U. Notre Dame, 1986; MPA, U. Ind., 1987; cert. law (hon.), Drake Sch. Law, Des Moines, 1981. Cert. Emergency Med. Technician. Asst. mgr. Lukes Market, Inc., Crown Point, Ind., 1976-81; claims adjuster U.S. Fidelity and Guaranty Ins., Hammond, Ind., 1981-82; dist. mgr. Emergency Med. Service Commn., Indpls., 1982-87; account exec. Ind. Med. Ctrs., Highland, Ind., 1987—; mem. acad. adv. council U. Notre Dame, 1986; assoc. mktg. officer Mirich Med. Corp., Merrillville, Ind., 1984—. Roman Catholic. Lodge: KC. Avocations: golf, running, softball, basketball. Home: 229 Pettibone Ave Crown Point IN 46307 Office: Ind Med Ctrs 9105-A Indianapolis Blvd HIghland IN 46322

REARDON, STEVEN MICHAEL, architect, educator; b. Chgo., June 15, 1953; s. Charles Eugene and Marlys Elaine (Kuehn) R.; m. Patricia Lynn Nygaard, Apr. 24, 1971; children: Steven Michael Jr., Jennifer Lynn. AS, Moraine Valley Coll., 1973; BArch, U. Ill., Chgo., 1977. Draftsman Stewart C. Wolf & Assocs., Berwyn, Ill., 1977-78; job capt. Thomas E. Carpenter & Assocs., Evergreen Park, Ill., 1978-79; assoc. Interplan Practice, Ltd., Oakbrook Terr., Ill., 1979-86; prin. Archtl. Resource Corp., Oak Forest, Ill., 1986—; docent Chgo. Architecture Found., 1983-84; instr. Prairie State Coll., Chicago Heights, Ill., 1983-85; advisor Blue Island (Ill.) Library, Kennedy Ctr. Handicapped, Palos Hills, Ill., 1986. Edmund J. James scholar 1973-77. Mem. AIA (treas. Eastern Ill. chpt. 1983-85, v.p. 1985—), Phi Kappa Phi. Democrat. Lodge: Rotary. Avocation: photography. Office: Archtl Resource Corp 15020 S Cicero Ave Oak Forest IL 60452

REARICK, J. ARDEN, lawyer; b. Gary, Ind., Feb. 15, 1921; s. Charles and Helen (Parrott) R.; m. Jeanette Clara Schultz, Oct. 24, 1920; children: Charlotte Ann, Pamela Arden. A.B., Ind. U., 1942, LL.B., 1947. Bar: Ind. 1947, Ill. 1953. Asst. gen. atty. Monon R.R., Lafayette, Ind., 1947-48; gen. atty. Monon R.R., lafayette, Ind., 1948-50; gen. solicitor Monon R.R., Lafayette, Ind., 1950-51, gen. solicitor and sec., 1951-53; assoc. Winston & Strawn, Chgo., 1953-59; ptnr. Winston & Strawn, Chgo., Ill., 1959—; dir. Drake Oak Brook, Inc., Ill., Nat. Realty and Investment, Oak Brook; trustee AMFUND, Evanston, Ill., 1972—. Contbr. articles to profl. jours. Served to capt. U.S. Army, 1942-46. Decorated Purple Heart with 2 oak leaf clusters; decorated Bronze Star. Fellow Am. Coll. Real Estate Lawyers; mem. ABA, Ind. State Bar Assn., Chgo. Bar Assn. Republican. Presbyterian. Clubs: Michigan Shores (Wilmette); Law (Chgo.), Mid-Day (Chgo.),

Plaza (Chgo.). Office: Winston & Strawn 1 First Nat Plaza Chicago IL 60603

REBBECK, LESTER JAMES, JR., artist; b. Chgo., June 25, 1929; s. Lester J. and Marie L. (Runkle) R.; B.A.E., Art Inst. Chgo., 1953, M.A.E., Art Inst. Chgo. and U. Chgo., 1959; m. Paula B. Phillips, July 7, 1951; 1 son, Lester J. Asst. prof. art William Rainey Harper Coll., Pallatine, Ill., 1967-72; dir. Countryside Art Gallery (Ill.), 1967-73; gallery dir. Chgo. Soc. Artists, 1967-68; now artist, tchr.; one man exhbns. include Harper Jr. Coll.; group exhbns. include Univ. Club, Chgo., 1980, Art Inst., Chgo., 1953. Served with U.S. Army, 1951-52. Mem. NEA, Ill. Edn. Assn., Ill. Art Educators Assn., Chgo. Soc. Artists, Coll. Art Assn., Art Inst. Chgo. Alumni Assn. Republican. Presbyterian. Home: 2041 Vermont St Rolling Meadows IL 60008

REBECK, PAMELA JOAN, psychologist; b. Chgo., Sept. 24, 1949; d. Clarence and Jeanette Marion (De Grand) R.; m. James Eugene Clark, Sept. 5, 1981; children: Justin Reid, Colin Taylor. BA in Psychology and Edn., Calif. State U., Northridge, 1971; MS in Psychology, Ill. Inst. Tech., 1973, PhD in Psychology, 1977. Staff psychologist Westside Parents, Chgo., 1973-74; psychosocial team leader Area Services Project, Westchester, Ill., 1974-77; prof. psychology Govs. State U., Park Forest, Ill., 1977-80; assoc. Chgo. Stress Ctr., 1977—; pvt. practice clin. psychology Downers Grove and Naperville, Ill., 1980—; group leader Anorexia Nervosa and Assoc. Disorders, 1986—. Treas. Ill. Devel. Disabilities Advocacy Authority, Peoria, 1979-87. Mem. Am. Psychol. Assn., Ill. Psychol. Assn., Nat. Register Health Service Providers in Psychology. Avocations: sports, travel, photography. Office: 475 River Bend #600 A Naperville IL 60540

REBMAN, JAY RICHARD, accountant; b. Lorain, Ohio, Nov. 28, 1959; s. John Casper and Margaret Delores (Matyi) R.; m. Janice Marie Protenic, May 28, 1983; 1 child: Jason Alan. AA, Lorain County Coll., 1980; BS, Bowling Green State U., 1982. CPA, Ohio. Staff acct. Frank, Seringer and Chaney Inc., Amherst, Ohio, 1982-83, James Hirschauer and Co., Euclid, Ohio, 1983-85; acct. Fulton and Grieco Inc., Westlake, Ohio, 1985—. Mem. Ohio Soc. CPA's, Am. Inst. CPA's, Beta Gamma Sigma, Beta Alpha Psi. Democrat. Roman Catholic. Avocations: skiing, bowling. Office: Fulton and Grieco Inc 24500 Center Ridge Rd #395 Westlake OH 44145

RECHTIN, MICHAEL DAVID, lawyer, engineering and business consultant, expert witness; b. Fort Smith, Ark., Feb. 1, 1944; s. George Lester and Catherine (Holmes) R.; m. Elisabeth Ann Lloyd, Aug. 20, 1966; children: Michael David Jr., Thomas P., Matthew S. BS, U. Ill., 1966; PhD, MIT, 1970; JD, Ill. Inst. Tech.-Chgo. Kent, 1981. Bars: Ill. 1982, U.S. Patent Office, 1980, U.S. Dist. Ct. (no. dist.) Ill. 1982, U.S. Ct. Appeals (7th cir.) 1982, U.S. Ct. Appeals (fed. cir.) 1987. Instr. materials sci. MIT, Cambridge, 1970-73; research scientist Tex. Instruments Corp., Dallas, 1973-75; scientist, patent agt., Argonne Lab. and Dept. Energy, Ill., 1975-81; counsel, patent agt. Standard Oil Co. (Ind.), Chgo., 1981-83; assoc. Welsh and Katz, Ltd., Chgo., 1983-85; assoc. Niro, Scarone, Haller and Niro, Ltd., 1985—; legal counsel Holocaust Meml. Found., Ill., 1986—; adj. prof. Dawn Schuman Inst. Jewish Learning, 1987—; legal dir. Societ Jewry Legal Advocacy Ctr., 1987—; mem. exec. com., chmn. new bus. com. MIT Enterprise Forum, Chgo., 1983—; mem. adv. bd. dirs. AgraTech, Inc., 1986—. Contbr. articles to profl. jours. Chmn. ednl. council MIT, Chgo., 1978—; pres. Orgn. Children Holocaust Survivors, Chgo., 1987—. NSF fellow, 1968, IBM fellow, 1970-73; academic scholar, 1979. Mem. ABA, Patent Law Assn. Chgo. (com. on tax), Chgo. Bar Assn. (computer law, fin., new bus., and patent coms.), Nat. Strategy Forum (mem. research com. 1987—). Republican. Presbyterian. Club: MIT (bd. dirs. 1982—). Home: 2002 Coach Dr Naperville IL 60565 Office: care Niro Scavone Haller 200 W Madison Suite 3500 Chicago IL 60606

RECK, W(ALDO) EMERSON, retired university administrator, public relations consultant, writer; b. Gettysburg, Ohio, Dec. 28, 1903; s. Samuel Harvey and Effie D. (Arnett) R.; m. Hazel Winifred January, Sept. 7, 1926; children: Phyllis (Mrs. Louis E. Welch, Jr.), Elizabeth Ann (Mrs. Gabriel J. Lada). A.B., Wittenberg U., 1926; A.M., U. Iowa, 1946; LL.D., Midland Coll., 1949. Reporter Springfield (Ohio) News, 1922-26; publicity dir. Midland Coll., Fremont, Nebr., 1926-28; dir. pub. relations, prof. journalism Midland Coll., 1928-40; dir. pub. relations Colgate U., 1940-48; v.p. Wittenberg U., Springfield, Ohio, 1948-70; v.p. emeritus Wittenberg U., 1970—; pub. relations specialist Cumerford Corp., 1970-78; hist. columnist Springfield Sun, 1973-81; spl. corr. Asso. Press, 1928-38; mng. editor Fremont Morning Guide, 1939; vis. lectr. pub. relations State U. Iowa, summers 1941, 42, U. Wyo., summer 1948; lectr. pub. relations and hist. subjects. Co-dir. Seminar on Pub. Relations for High Edn., Syracuse U., summers 1944, 45, 46; Mem. commn. on ch. papers United Luth. Ch., 1951-62, cons. com. dept. of press, radio and TV, 1955-60; mem. commn. on ch. papers Luth Ch. in Am., 1962-64, 70-72, mem. exec. com., also chmn. com. periodicals of bd. publs., 1962-72; mem. mgmt. com. Office of Communications, 1972-76; chmn. pub. relations com. Council Protestant Colls. and Univs., 1961-65. Author: Public Relations: a Program for Colleges and Universities, 1946, The American College (with others), 1949, Public Relations Handbook (contbr.) , 1950, 62, 67, The Changing World of College Relations, 1976, Father Can't Forget, 1982, A. Lincoln: His Last 24 Hours, 1987; editor: Publicity Problems, 1939, College Publicity Manual, 1948; contbr. hist. and pub. relations articles to gen., ednl., profl. mags. Recipient award Am. Coll. Pub. Relations Assn. for distinguished service, 1942, for outstanding achievement in interpretation of higher edn., 1944, 47; award Council for Advancement and Support of Edn., 1977; medal of honor Wittenberg U., 1982. Mem. Am. Coll. Pub. Relations Assn. (v.p. in charge research 1936-38, editor assn. mag. 1938-40, pres. 1940-41, chmn. plans and policies com. 1944-50, dir. 1956, historian 1966-76), Luth. Coll. Pub. Relations Assn. (pres. 1951-53), Pub. Relations Soc. Am. (nat. jud. council 1952), Assn. Am. Colls. (mem. com. on pub. relations 1945-48), AAUP, Nat. Luth. Ednl. Conf. (chmn. com. pub. relations 1949-50), Ohio Coll. Pub. Relations Officers (pres. 1954-55), Clark County Hist. Soc. (pres. 1985-86), Nat. Trust for Hist. Preservation, Smithsonian Assos., Archives Assos., Nat. Hist. Soc. (founding asso.), Abraham Lincoln Assn., Blue Key, Sigma Delta Chi, Pi Delta Epsilon, Delta Sigma Phi, Omicron Delta Kappa. Home: 3148 Argonne Ln N Springfield OH 45503

RECKER, KENNETH EDWARD, accountant; b. Alpena, Mich., June 26, 1939; s. William Thomas and Marjorie (DeLaney) R.; m. Virginia Jo Ebling, Feb. 5, 1966; children: Kenneth II, Steven. BBA, Aquinas Coll., 1962; MA in Econs., Western Mich. U., 1965. CPA, Mich. Asst. auditor gen. Mich. Legis. Mcpl. Employees Retirement System, Lansing, 1966-72, mgr., 1972-80; fin. dir. Bur. Retirement Systems, Lansing, 1980—; cons. tchr. Lansing Community Coll., 1985-86. Fundraiser Pub. TV Sta., Lansing, 1985-86. Served as sgt. USNG, 1963-69. Fellow Assn. Profl. Adminstrs; mem. Govtl. Fin. Officers Assn. (exec. com. 1986—), State Assn. Accts., Auditors and Bus. Adminstrs. (pres. 1987). Roman Catholic. Club: Lansing Tennis. Avocations: bridge, tennis, boating. Home and Office: 6411 Pleasant River Dimondale MI 48821

RECKER, THERESA LOUISE, medical educator; b. Chgo., Sept. 11, 1951; d. Joseph Walter and Marjorie Irene (Crowder) Lenahan; m. William Joseph Lenahan Recker, Apr. 21, 1979. Student, Prairie State Coll., 1972; cert. in radiologic tech., Ravenswood Hosp. and Med. Ctr., 1974; student, Triton Coll., 1978, Coll. of DuPage, 1984. Cert. tchr., Ill.; cert. radiologic tech., Ill. Spl. procedures technologist Meml. Hosp. DuPageCounty, Elmhurst, Ill., 1974-79; radiologic technologist Sherman Hosp., Elgin, Ill., 1979-80; spl. procedures technologist Glendale Heights (Ill.) Hosp., 1980-82; instr. Nat. Edn. Corp., Chgo., 1982—. Contbr. articles to travel mags. and newspapers. Mem. Am. Society Radiologic Technologists. Republican. Roman Catholic. Avocations: downhill and cross-country skiing, cycling, golf, travel. Home: 310 B Milton Ct Bloomingdale IL 60108

RECTOR, DAVID RICHARD, academic administrator; b. Macon, Mo., Jan. 16, 1951; s. Elihu Graham and Bettye Carolyn (Cremer) R.; m. Carol Ann Deskin, Sept. 1, 1972; children: Stephen, Nicholas, Jonathan, Christina. BS, N.E. Mo. State U., 1973, MA, 1976; MBA, U. Okla., 1980. Asst. to registrar N.E. Mo. State U., Kirksville, 1973-74, asst. to dean instrn., 1974-79; dir. data processing U.E. Mo. State U., Kirksville, 1979-81, dir. computer services, 1981-85, dir. computer and telecommunications services, 1985—; cons. U. Ark., Monticello, 1985, Lincoln U., Jefferson City, Mo., 1982; chmn. Mo. Statewide Computer Planning Com., Jefferson City, 1986; lectr. mgmt. N.E. Mo. State U., 1979—. Coach Kirksville Little League Baseball Assn., 1986. Grantee Burroughs Corp., Detroit, 1986, Digital Equipment Corp., Maynard, Mass., 1986. Mem. Data Processing Mgmt. Assn., Assn. Instl. Research, Coll. and Univ. Systems Exchange, Higher Edn. Telecommunications Consortium. Republican. Methodist. Lodge: Kiwanis (bd. dirs. Kirksville club 1983—). Avocations: model railroads, bicycling, reading mystery novels. Home: 36 Kellwood Dr Kirksville MO 63501 Office: NE Mo State U Adminstrn Bldg Kirksville MO 63501

RECTOR, THOMAS CHARLES, dentist; b. Hartford City, Ind., Dec. 29, 1952; s. Charles Edward and Jacquelyn Nadine (Raines) R.; m. Becky Lynne Cook, Aug. 7, 1976; children: Thomas Bradley, Andrew Joseph, Alison Ashley Nadine. BS, Ball State U., 1975; DDS, Ind. U., 1979. Gen. practice dentistry Muncie, Ind., 1980—; mem. faculty Ind. U. Sch. Dentistry, Indpls., 1980—. Rep. Committeman, Muncie, 1983-84; chmn. campaign Reynard for Senate, Muncie, 1985-86. Mem. ADA, Ind. Dental Assn., East Cen. Dental Assn., Del. County Dental Assn. (pres. 1984-85), Acad. Gen. Dentistry. Methodist. Lodges: Elks, Moose, Optimists (oratorical chmn. Muncie club 1983-84). Home: 4800 N LaFern Way Muncie IN 47304 Office: 1003 W McGalliard Muncie IN 47303

RECUPIDO, DANIEL PHILIP, accountant; b. Chgo., Dec. 9, 1953; s. Donald Francis and Audrey Helen (Anderson) ReC.; m. Diana Lynn Scudella, Aug. 31, 1980; 1 child, Amanda Lauren. BBA, Coll. St. Thomas, 1975; MBA, Keller Grad. Sch. Mgmt., 1979. CPA, Ill. Gen. acctg. mgr. Centel Cable TV Co. Ill., DesPlaines, 1980-84; asst. controller Rolm Corp. of Ill., Schaumburg, 1984-85, cen. region mgr. bus. controls, 1986—. Recipient Centel Pres's. award, 1984, Rolm Leadership Club award, 1986. Mem. Am. Inst. CPA's, Ill. CPA Soc. Roman Catholic. Office: Rolm Corp 1100 Woodfield Rd Schaumburg IL 60195

REDDEN, MEG EWAN, sales and marketing executive; b. Lafayette, Ind., Aug. 2, 1944; d. Maurice Albertson and Audrey Fern (Dixon) Ewan; m. Jerry Bob Redden, Apr. 2, 1966 (div. Jan. 1979); children: Jennifer Rebecca, Molly Susannah. BA in Edn., Ottawa U., 1966. Kindergarten tchr. New Bedford (Mass.) Sch., 1966-67; elem. tchr. Davenport (Iowa) Schs., 1967-69; classified advt. mgr. Ill. Times, Springfield, 1976-79; acct. exec. Columbus (Ohio) Monthly, 1979-84; v.p. sales and marketing Bus. First, Columbus, 1984—. Mem. Nat. Assn. Profl. Saleswomen (founding), Advt. Fedn. Club: Sales Executives. Office: Business First 274 Marconi Columbus OH 43215

REDDER, ALFRED T., JR., construction executive; b. Cin., July 2, 1961; s. Alfred and Irmgard Marie (Loxterkamp) R. Assoc., U. Cin., 1982, BS in Constrn. Mgmt., 1983. Pres. A.T. Redder & Co., Cin., 1983—. Bd. dirs. Cath. Big Bros. Assn., Cin., 1987. Mem. Am. Inst. Constrn. (assoc.). Roman Catholic. Office: AT Redder & Co Inc 244 Pedretti Ave Cincinnati OH 45238

REDDIG, WALTER EDUARD, architect, master cabinet maker; b. Meldorf, Holstein, Fed. Republic Germany, Apr. 3, 1936; came to U.S., 1960; Student, Trade Sch., Meldorf, 1953-56; cert. design technician, Masters Sch., Flensburg, Fed. Republic Germany, 1959, cert. interior architect, 1960. Registered architect, Mich., Va., Md., Tex., Ill., Pa., N.H. Interior designer J. Holleman Assocs., Birmingham, Mich., 1963-66; project coordinator Levine-Alpern Assocs., Detroit, 1966-69; design and project dir. F. Stickel Assocs., Troy, Mich., 1969-73; project designer Greimel, Malcomson & James, Detroit, 1973; pvt. practice architecture Farmington Hills, Mich., 1973—. Contbr. articles to mags.; artist water colors. Appointed to Ad Hoc Hist. Dist. Com., Farmington Hills, 1979-81; vice chmn. Hist. Dist. Commn., Farmington Hills, 1981—; artist in residence Farmington Area Arts Commn., 1984. Mem. AIA, Mich. Soc. Architects, Nat. Council Archtl. Registration Bd. (cert.). Lutheran. Club: Farmington Artist (pres. 1983-85). Avocations: painting, photography, music. Home and Office: 24003 Inkster Rd Farmington Hills MI 48024

REDDY, NALLAPU NARAYAN, economics educator; b. Nagaram, India, June 22, 1939; came to U.S., 1958; s. Narasimha N. and Shantha N. Reddy; m. Saroja N. Malladi, June 1, 1957; children—Lata, Mala. B.S., Mich. Technol. U., 1961; M.S., U. Mo., 1963; Ph.D., Pa. State U., 1967; M.A., U. Notre Dame, 1973. Asst. prof. Clarkson U., Potsdam, N.Y., 1967-72, assoc. prof., 1972-74; assoc. prof. econs. U. Mich.-Flint, 1974-79, prof., 1979—, chmn. dept., 1981-84; vis. prof. London Sch. Econs., 1981. Editor: Empirical Studies in Microeconomics, 1985. Contbr. articles to profl. jours. Recipient Disting. Prof. for Teaching Excellence, 1979. Mem. Am. Econ. Assn., Eastern Econ. Assn., So. Econ. Assn., Western Econ. Assn., Phi Kappa Phi, Omicron Delta Epsilon. Home: 6250 Kings Shire Rd Grand Blanc MI 48439 Office: Dept Econs U Mich Flint MI 48502

REDEBAUGH-LEVI, CAROLINE LOUISE, senior action center coordinator, registered nurse; b. Dixon, Ill., May 23, 1910; d. Charles R. and May Caroline (Barnes) Kreger; m. Richard E. Belcher, Nov. 24, 1934 (dec. 1964); children—Richard Charles, Mary; m. Charles H. Redebaugh, Dec. 3, 1966 (dec. 1979); m. Paul Levi, July 20, 1985. R.N., Katherine Shaw Bethea Sch. Nursing, 1930. Nurse, various hosps., 1930-49; adminstr. Orchard Glen Nursing Home, Dixon, Ill., 1949-77; coordinator Sr. Action Ctr., Springfield, Ill., 1977—; mem. various adv. coms. advocating for srs. Contbr. articles to profl. jours. Mem. nat. adv. com., del. White House Conf. on Aging, 1981; v.p. Ill. Joint Council to Improve Health Care for Aged, 1953, pres., 1954. Mem. Capitol City Republican Women (v.p. 1983-84), State Council on Aging, Am. Coll. Nursing Home Adminstrs. (charter, edn. com., pres.), Am. Nursing Home Assn. (v.p. 1953), Ill. Nurses Assn. (bd. dirs.). Home: 1420 Eustace Dr Dixon IL 61021 Office: Sr Action Ctr 3 W Old Town Mall Springfield IL 62701

REDEKER, JERRALD H(ALE), banker; b. Waupun, Wis., Oct. 5, 1934; s. Samuel and Laura A. (Schinzel) R.; m. Elsie Delaine Vande Zande, June 22, 1957; children—Lisa, Joel, Cara, Allyson. B.A. in Bus. Adminstrn., Hope Coll., 1956; grad. cert. Am. Inst. Banking, 1964. Mgr., Old Kent Bank and Trust Co., Grand Rapids, Mich., 1962-65; v.p. Met. Nat. Bank of Farmington (Mich.), 1965-67; v.p. First State Bank of Charlevoix (Mich.), 1967-68, exec. v.p., 1968-69, pres., 1969-72; agt. Farm Bur. Mut. Ins. Co., Charlevoix, 1972-74; pres., chief exec. officer Old Kent Bank of Holland (Mich.), 1974—, chmn. bd., 1979—; vice chmn. Lakeshore Health Maintenance Orgn., Holland, 1985-86, bd. dirs. 1986—. Bd. dirs. Holland Econ. devel. Corp., 1974—; bd. dirs. Holland Community Hosp., 1974-86, chmn. bd., 1979-81; bd. dirs. bd. theol edn. Ref. Ch. in Am., 1978-84, bd. dirs. gen. synod exec. com., 1984—, chmn. bd. direction, 1985—; co-chmn. Holland/Zeeland area Campaign for Hope, 1985-87; chmn. Holland area Mich. Sesquicentennial, 1986-87. Served with U.S. Army, 1957-59. Named one of Outstanding Young Men Am., U.S. Jaycees, 1970. Mem. Mich. Bankers Assn., Robert Morris Assocs., Bank Adminstrn. Inst., Holland Area C. of C. (bd. dirs. 1975-84, chmn. bd. 1981-82). Republican. Mem. Reformed Ch. in Am. Lodge: Rotary (dir. 1980—) (pres. 1985-86) (Holland).

REDFORD, JANICE CAROL, secondary schools educator, management consultant, writer; b. Madison, Wis., Dec. 3, 1941. BA in English and Spanish, U. Wis., Whitewater, 1964; MS in Bus., Cardinal Stritch Coll., Milw., 1985; postgrad., U. Wis., 1967, 72, 82, Sacramento State U., 1965. Cert. secondary edn. tchr. in English, Spanish, Vocational-Technical Bus. Tchr. secondary schs. Stoughton and Ft. Atkinson, Wis., 1964-79; freelance writer newspapers and mags. Wis., 1973—; export officer Internat. Machinery Exchange, Deerfield, Wis., 1981-85; pres. Redford Cons. Group, Cambridge, Wis., 1986—; instr. Madison Area Tech. Coll., Madison and Ft. Atkinson, 1986—, Oaklawn Acad., Edgerton, Wis., 1987—. Contbr. articles to mags. Leader Dane County (Wis.) 4-H Club, Madison, 1971—; county supr. Dane County, Madison, 1975-80; Dem. candidate for Wis. state senate, 1978, 80. NDEA fellow, 1965; Brandenberg Found. scholar, 1960, Wis. Legis. scholar, 1960. Lodges: Sons of Norway, Sognafjord Laget. Avocations: figure skating, cross-country skiing, distance running, oil painting. Home: 2062 Hillside Rd Cambridge WI 53523 Office: Oaklawn Acad 432 Liguori Rd Edgerton WI 53534

REDMAN, PETER, finance company executive; b. Phila., Feb. 9, 1935; s. Hamilton Matthew and Martha (Lawson) R.; m. Julie Anne Burr, June 9, 1984; children: Kirsten, Heidi, Gretchen, Britt. B.A. in Econs., Middlebury Coll., 1958. Sr. group ins. rep. Conn. Gen. Life Ins. Co., Hartford, 1962-65; v.p. Conn. Bank & Trust Co., Hartford, 1965-73; v.p. Midlantic Nat. Bank, Newark, 1973-75, 4th Nat. Bank, Wichita, Kans., 1975-78; v.p., gen. mgr. Cessna Internat. Fin. Corp., Wichita, 1978-82, now dir.; pres., gen. mgr. Cessna Fin. Corp., Wichita, 1982—, also dir. Served to 1st lt. U.S. Army, 1958-62. Republican. Episcopalian. Home: 1408 Twisted Oak Circle Wichita KS 67230 Office: Cessna Finance Corp 5800 E Pawnee Wichita KS 67218 *

REDWING, DARWIN EUGENE, chemistry educator; b. Spring Grove, Minn., Nov. 11, 1937; s. Grant Leland and Evelyn Ione (Anderson) R.; m. Ruth Esther Luehring, Aug. 24, 1963; children: Kirsten Marie, Erika Jo. BA, Luther Coll., Decorah, Iowa, 1959; MS in Sci. Edn., Fisk U., Nashville, 1964. Cert. secondary tchr., Ill. Tchr. sci. Waldorf-Pemberton (Minn.) Pub. Schs., 1959-61, Nicollet (Minn.) Pub. Schs., 1961-62; tchr. chemistry Sch. Dist. 205, Rockford, Ill., 1963—; adj. prof. chemistry Rockford Coll., 1979—. Mem. Winnebago County Horticulture Com., Rockford, 1985-87. Mem. Nat. Sci. Tchrs. Assn., Ill. Sci. Tchrs. Assn. (Sci. Teaching award 1986), New Eng. Assn. Chemistry Tchrs., Ill. Assn. Chemistry Tchrs., Am. Chem. Soc. (named High Sch. Chemistry Tchr. of Yr. 1983, program chmn. Rock River sect. 1986-87). Republican. Lutheran. Clubs: Men's Garden of Am. (Des Moines) (regional pres. 1983-84); Men's Garden of Rockford (various offices 1974-86, Bronze medal 1983). Lodge: Moose, Ind. Order Vikings. Avocation: gardening. Home: 418 N Rockford Ave Rockford IL 61107

REECE, ROBERT DENTON, professor; b. Bonham, Tex., Oct. 25, 1939; s. Clovis D. and Bonnie (Hyatt) R.; m. Donna Reece, June 5, 1965; children: Gwendolyn, Gregory, David, Emily. BA, Baylor U., 1961; BD, So. Bapt. Theol. Sem., 1964; PhD, Yale U., 1969. Asst. prof. Wright State U., Dayton, Ohio, 1969-75, assoc. prof., 1975-87, prof., 1987—. Author: Studying People: A Primer in the Ethics of Social Research, 1986; contbr. articles to profl. jours. Elder Westminster Presbyn. Ch., Dayton, 1986—. Danforth found. fellow, 1964-68. Mem. Am. Acad. Religion, Med. Ethics Consultation (chmn. 1983-85), Soc. for Health and Human Values (chmn. program dirs. group 1982-84), Soc. of Christian Ethics. Avocation: tennis. Home: 333 Volusia Ave Dayton OH 45409 Office: Wright State U Dept Medicine in Soc PO Box 927 Dayton OH 45401

REECE, STEVE DUANE, retail executive; b. Dexter, Mo., May 16, 1955; s. Cleveland J. and Laura E. (Stafford) R.; m. Sheliah J. Allen, June 4, 1977; children: Tyler C., Jordan, Elizabeth. Grad. high sch., Malden, Mo. Dept. mgr. Magic Mart Discount, Malden, 1973-77; owner, mgr. Steve's Music City, Malden, 1977-83, The Movie Spot, Malden, 1983-86, Waterbeds & More, Malden, 1984-86, Records Plus (formerly Steve's Music & Video), Poplar Bluff, Mo., 1986—, Bedside Manor Waterbeds, Poplar Bluff, 1986—. Mem. Malden C. of C. (bd. dirs. 1982). Republican. Baptist. Lodges: Odd Fellows, Optimists, Eagles (trustee 1986). Avocations: golf, softball. Home: Rt 1 Lakeview Estates Campbell MO 63933 Office: Bedside Manor 1903 N Westwood Blvd Poplar Bluff MO 63901

REED, CHARLES FRANCIS, III, orthodontist; b. Indpls., Oct. 24, 1957; s. Charles F. II and Joan Lorraine (Nesius) R.; m. Traci Day Shaver, June 24, 1978; Sean, Kelly, Patrick, Erinn. BS, Loyola U., Chgo., 1978; DDS, Loyola U., Maywood, Ill., 1982; cert. in orthodontics, Loyola U., Maywood, 1984. Gen. practice dentistry Elk Grove, Ill., 1983-84; assoc. orthodontist Arlington Heights, Ill., 1984—; practice dentistry specializing in orthodontics Elk Grove, 1984—; cons. Berwyn (Ill.) Magnetic Resonance Ctr., 1986—. Mem. ADA, Am. Assn. Orthodontists (Sr. Orthodontist award 1982), Midwest Soc. Orthodontists, Ill. Soc. Orthodontists, Chgo. Dental Soc. Mormon. Home: 1118 Lathrop Ave Forest Park IL 60130 Office: 1100 Nerge Rd Suite 206 Elk Grove IL 60007

REED, CYNTHIA RAE, healthcare facility administrator; b. Des Moines, Mar. 12, 1956; d. James Charles and Donna Rae (DeBolt) R.; m. Thomas Joseph Shea, Aug. 30, 1986. BS in Nursing, U. Iowa, 1978, MA, 1981. Staff nurse U. Iowa Hosp., Iowa City, 1978-79; staff nurse St. Luke's Hosp., Cedar Rapids, Iowa, 1980-81, nurse clinician, 1981-82, clin. nurse specialist, 1982-83, dir. psychiatric services, 1983—; co-founder, dir. C.R. Eating Disorder Project, Cedar Rapids, 1982-84. Chairperson Adult mental Health Coalition, Cedar Rapids, 1984—; bd. dirs. Mental Health Advocates, 1985—, Community Friends Program, 1986—, Suicide Outreach Project, 1984-85, DAY Treatment Adv. Bd., 1983-85; Linn county mem. Citizens Task Force on Care Facility, Iowa, 1983-86; mem. adv. bd. Child Protection Ctr., 1986—. Recipient Outstanding New Program award Mental Health Advocates, 1986. Mem. Am. Nurses Assn., Iowa Nurses Assn., Iowa Orgn. Nurse Execs., Coe Coll. Nursing Honor Soc. Democrat. Roman Catholic. Club: Blvd. Social (v.p. 1985-87). Avocations: photography, travel, camping, biking, boating. Home: 600 Carlton Rd SE Cedar Rapids IA 52405 Office: St Lukes Hosp 1026 A Ave NE Cedar Rapids IA 52402

REED, DANIEL MICHAEL, bank loan administrator, lawyer; b. San Francisco, Feb. 9, 1945; s. Victor Pritchard and Nora Catherine (Obrien) R.; m. Candace Marie Galloway, June 30, 1979; children: Joshua Ben, Peter Deegan. BS, U. San Francisco, 1972; JD, U. Calif., San Francisco, 1975. Sole practice San Francisco, 1975-79; workout loan officer, equipment remarketing officer Colo. Nat. Bankshare, Denver, 1979-85; workout loan officer Citicorp, St. Louis, 1985—. Democrat. Roman Catholic. Avocations: bicycling, golf, gardening. Home: 307 Glyn Cagny Manchester MO 63021 Office: Citicorp Acceptance Co 666 Mason Ridge Ctr Dr Saint Louis MO 63141

REED, DAVID FRANK, controller; b. Battle Creek, Mich., July 4, 1944; s. Elwin Myron and Winifred C. (Dick) R.; m. M. Josefa Bartski, Aug. 21, 1971; 1 child, Erica. Assoc. in Bus. Adminstrn., Kellogg Community Coll., 1964; BBA, U. Mich., 1966; MBA, Western Mich. U., 1968; postgrad. in law, U. Detroit, 1972-73. Asst. mgr. gen. acctg. Nat. Machine Products, Utica, Mich., 1970-71; budget cost analyst LTV Aerospace, Dallas, 1971-74, contract pricer, 1974-75; shop mgr. AAMCO Transmissions, Berkley, Mich., 1975; v.p., controller Detroit Home Renaissance Inc., Mt. Clemens, Mich., 1975—; also chmn. bd. dirs. Detroit Home Renaissance Inc., Mt. Clemens. Vol. computer programmer Macomb Community Coll., Mt. Clemens, 1982; campaign worker Mich. State Rep., Clinton Twp., Mich., 1984, 86; committeeman Chipawa Valley Schs., Clinton Twp., 1986-87. Mem. Warren (Mich.) Astron. Soc. Republican. Avocations: astronomy, travel. Home: 15761 Schultz Mount Clemens MI 48044 Office: Detroit Home Renaissance 15761 Schultz Mount Clemens MI 48044

REED, ELINOR USHER, motel executive; b. St. Louis, June 8, 1908; d. Robert Thomas and Josephine L. T. (Boenecke) Usher; m. Clement A. Reed, Jr.; children—Robert T., Josephine, Edward. Student pub. schs., St. Louis. Owner, operator comml. dock., Kimberling City, Mo., to 1978; former owner Arrowhead Motel, Columbia Mo.; now owner, operator Lake Hills Motel & Restaurant, also recreational vehicle and mobile home park, Warsaw, Mo., 1978—. Mem. Hotel 7 Motel Assn. Lutheran. Office: Lakes Hills Motel Old Hwy 65 & White Branch Exit Warsaw MO 65355

REED, GERALD WILFRED, protective services official; b. Gary, Ind., Nov. 7, 1945; s. Lloyd Wilfred and Gertrude Ann (Nielsen) R. Student, N.E. Mo. State Tchrs. Coll., 1963-66; diploma, Control Data Inst., 1973. Cert. communications dispatcher Ind. State Police, 1980, cert. auto theft investigator, 1983. Incentive clk. U.S. Steel Corp., Gary, Ind., 1966; clk. dept. U.S. Steel Corp., Gary, 1967-73; telecommunicator Ind. State Police, Lowell, 1974—. Asst. scoutmaster troop 25 Boy Scouts Am., Kirksville, Mo., 1964-66, troop 620, Wichita, Kans., 1966-67, troop 91, Hobart, Ind., 1967-74, scoutmaster, 1974-75. Served with USAF, 1966-67. Recipient Scouters Training award Calumet Council Boy Scouts Am., 1970. Mem. Am. Numismatic Assn., Canadian Numismatic Assn., Radio Communications Monitoring Assn., No. Ind. Apple Users Group, Apple Tree Computer User Group, Michigan City Model Railroad Workshop, Ind. Police Radio Operators Club, Fraternal Order Police, Nat. Model Railroad Assn., Santa Fe Modelers Orgn. Republican. Presbyterian. Lodge: Order of DeMolay (dist. gov. Franklin Ind. 1970-79, Cross of Honor 1973, Legion of Honor 1978, life mem., master councilor Hobart Ind., 1962-63), Masons. Avocations: Apple computer, photography. Office: Ind State Police Lowell Post 1550 E 181st Ave Lowell IN 46356-9513 Mailing: PO Box 28 Hobart IN 46342-0028

REED, HAROLD WILLIAM, college administrator; b. Haigler, Nebr., July 14, 1909; s. Edwin Paul and Cleo Pricilla (Randall) R.; m. Maybelle Eleanore Ripper, June 19, 1933; 1 child, Haldor William. AB, Colo. Coll., 1932; MS, Colo. State U., 1934; ThD, U. So. Calif., 1943; DD (hon.), So. Nazarene U., 1951; LLD (hon.), Olivet Nazarene U., 1975. Pres. Bresee Coll., Hutchinson, Kans., 1936-40; prof. Pasadena (Calif.) Coll., 1940-42; v.p. Bethany (Okla.) Coll., 1942-44; pres. Olivet Nazarene U., Kankakee, Ill., 1949-75, Internat. Reed Inst., Kankakee, 1976—; trustee Lincoln Acad., Springfield, Ill., Riverside Med. Ctr., Kankakee, Riverside Med. Ctr. Found., 1977—. Author: You and Your Church, 1953, Committed to Christ, 1960, The Dynamics of Leadership, 1982. Republican. Mem. Ch. of Nazarene. Lodge: Rotary. Home: 1090 S Nelson Ave Kankakee IL 60901 Office: Box 1686 Kankakee IL 60901

REED, JAMES EDWARD, gynecologist, obstetrician; b. Ft. Dodge, Iowa, July 25, 1931; S. Robert Henry and Edna Elizabeth (Nordstrom) R.; m. Ruth Arlene Bowman, Apr. 5, 1958; children: James E. Jr., Sarah Elizabeth. Student, Iowa State Tchrs. Coll., 1950-51, U. Iowa, 1951-53; MD, U. Iowa, 1957. Diplomate Am. Bd. Ob-Gyn. Intern Hurley Hosp., Flint, Mich., 1957-58, residency in ob-gyn, 1958-59; residency in ob-gyn William Beaumont Hosp., Royal Oak, Mich., 1961-63; practice medicine specializing in ob-gyn Ft. Dodge, 1963—. Served to capt. U.S. Army, 1959-61. Fellow Am. Coll. Ob-Gyn; mem. Am. Fertility Soc., Am. Inst. Ultrasound in Medicine, Am. Assn. Gynecol. Laporoscopy. Republican. Congregationalist. Lodge: Elks. Office: Physicians Ofc Bldg 304 S Kenyon Rd Suite E Fort Dodge IA 50501

REED, JANE GARSON, accounting educator; b. Cleve., Jan. 11, 1948; d. Joseph John Guzowski and Irene Sophie (Dominic) Garson; m. Wayne Ellis Reed, May 17, 1969; children: Craig Michael, Kevin Matthew. BBA magna cum laude, Baldwin Wallace Coll., 1977; MBA, Case Western Res. U., 1983. CPA, Ohio. Letter carrier U.S. Postal Service, Brecksville, Ohio, 1966-76; sr. asst. acct. Deloitte, Haskins & Sells, Cleve., 1977-78; sr. corp. auditor White Motor Corp., Beachwood, Ohio, 1979-81; ind. contractor State of Wash., Olympia, 1982-84; dir. fin. The Montefiore Home, Cleveland Heights, Ohio, 1985-86; controller, bus. mgr. Western Res. Human Services, Inc., Akron, Ohio, 1986-87; lectr. mgmt. acctg. U. Akron, 1987—; instr. acctg. Cuyahoga Community Coll., Parma, Ohio, 1981, 82. Fin. sec. to bd. dirs. Prince of Peace Luth. Ch., Medina, Ohio, 1978-79; mem. budget and fin. com. Wooster (Ohio) dist. office United Meth. Ch., 1983-84; canvasser Democratic Club, Brunswick, Ohio, 1985; mem. Brunswick High Sch. Band and Choir Boosters, 1984—; leader Boy Scouts Am., Brunswick, 1978-79. Mem. Am. Inst. CPA's, Nat. Assn. Accts., Am. Women's Soc. CPA's, Ohio Soc. CPA's (mem.-in-industry com. 1980-82), Ohio Council Community Mental Health Agys., Soc. for Advancement Mgmt. (reactivated chpt. pres 1976-77). Methodist. Avocations: amateur radio, golf. Home: 1254 Hadcock Rd Brunswick OH 44212 Office: Univ Akron Akron OH 44325

REED, L. A., chemical company executive; b. 1939. BS, U. Minn., 1961; MS, Northwestern U., 1962; MBA, Cen. Mich. U., 1969. Research asst. U. Minn., 1960-61; with Dow Corning Corp., Midland, Mich., 1964—, chem. engr., 1964-66, staff specialist, 1967-68, econ. evaluation engr., 1968-78, v.p. chief fin. officer, controller, 1978-81, exec. v.p. bus., from 1981—, now pres., chief operating officer. Served with USN, 1962-64. Office: Dow Corning Corp Box 1767 Midland MI 48640 *

REED, LARRY LEE, chemist; b. Youngstown, Ohio, Feb. 19, 1942; s. Julia Ann (Bell) R.; m. Grace Louella Gloss, Dec. 27, 1966. BS, Ohio State U., 1965; PhD, U. Ariz., 1971. Computer scientist Argonne (Ill.) Nat. Lab., 1978—. Mem. Am. Chem. Soc., Sigma Xi. Office: Argonne Nat Lab 9700 S Cass Ave Argonne IL 60439

REED, LARRY S., chamber of commerce executive. Pres. Davenport C. of C., Davenport, Iowa. Officee: Davenport C of C 112 E Third St Davenport IA 52801

REED, MARC C., audio-visual specialist, writer; b. Plymouth, Wis., Mar. 29, 1957; s. Donn and Ruth H. (Barnes) R.; m. Cynthia Ann Campbell, Sept. 28, 1985. AA, U. Wis., Sheboygan, 1977; BS in Radio-TV-Film, U. Wis., Oshkosh, 1979. Film prodn. Ideas and Images, Iowa City, 1979; computer operator, programmer H.C. Prange Co., Sheboygan, 1979-82; video prodn. Video Trend Assocs., Oshkosh, 1982—; prodn. RSVP/Orange Prodns., Milw., 1982-85; freelance audio/visual prodn. Milw., 1985—. Contbr. film revs. to City Slicker mag., 1986. Home: 4345A N 72 St Milwaukee WI 53216

REED, RALPH CHARLES, land surveyor, genealogist; b. Dayton, Ohio, Aug. 3, 1930; s. Alonzo Newton and Mary Cecilia (Nameth) R.; m. Marjorie Ruth Hiller, Feb. 5, 1972. Registered land surveyor, Ohio. Rodman, City of Dayton, 1951-56; transit and level man Dayton Power & Light, 1956-62; engring. aide and surveyor, Miamisburg, Ohio, 1962-70; surveyor, owner RCR Land Surveying Co., Dayton, 1970—. Discoverer, Campobello Island, Great Miami River, Dayton, 1973. Served with USNR, 1965—. Mem. Internat. Platform Assn., Profl. Land Surveyors Ohio, Hist. Soc. Montgomery and Warren Counties, Am. Congress on Surveying and Mapping, Dayton C. of C., Naval Enlisted Res. Assn., Ohio Geneal. Soc., First Families Ohio, Am. Coll. Genealogy, Ohio Hist. Soc., Canal Soc. Ohio, SAR, Am. Legion. Republican. Roman Catholic. Lodge: K.C. Avocation: model railroading. Home and Office: Ralph C Reed Land Survey Co 127 Ventura Ave Dayton OH 45417

REED, RALPH DARWIN, insurance company executive; b. Tell City, Ind., Dec. 24, 1925; s. Hugh and Claudia (Leistner) R.; m. Rose Reed, Sept. 4, 1946; children: Candice, Sheila, Sam, Pamela, Tim. Grad. high sch., Tell City. Pres. Independent Agts. Ind., Indpls., 1971-72; pres. Zoercher Agy., Tell City, 1980—, also bd. dirs.; bd. dirs. Tell City Nat. Bank. Bd. dirs. Tell City Econs. com., So. Ind. Retardation Services, Handicapped Adults Workshop. Served as sgt. U.S. Army, 1944-46, ETO. Recipient Community Service award Independent Agts. Ind., 1980. Mem. Tell City C. of C. Democrat. Methodist. Club: Hoosier Heights Country. Lodge: Kiwanis. Avocations: golf, hunting, fishing. Home: 17 Tell Blvd Tell City IN 47586 Office: Zoercher Agy 723 Main St Tell City IN 47586

REED, ROBERT ERVIN, banker; b. Dayton, Ohio, Jan. 16, 1948; s. Harry E. and Mary (Gibson) R.; m. Linda Kay Whitley, June 20, 1970; 1 child, David Alan. B.S., Wright State U., 1970, M.B.A., 1973. Fin. analyst NCR Corp., Dayton, 1970-73; asst. v.p. 1st Nat. Bank, Dayton, 1973-79; sr. v.p./city exec. Huntington Nat. Bank, Cin., 1979-84; pres., chief exec. officer Miamibank, N.A., Fairborn, Ohio, 1984—. Contbr. articles to profl. jours. Chmn., Cin. Community Chest, 1983; chmn. edn. com. Hamilton County chpt. Am. Cancer Soc., 1982; trustee Wright State U. Found. 1987—, also treas.; gen. chmn. Greene County (Ohio) United Way. Mem. Am. Inst. Banking, Cin. C. of C., Fairborn C. of C. (bd. dirs. 1985). Republican. Clubs: Rotary (Fairborn); Kenwood Country (Cin.); Dayton Country. Office: Miamibank 1 W Main St Fairborn OH 45324

REED, RUTHANN, convention administrator; b. Sandusky, Ohio, Feb. 21, 1944; d. Robert Theodore and Goldie Marie (Kahler) Wheeler; m. Robert Ford Reed, Oct. 10, 1964; children: Sandra Lynn, Barbara Ann. Grad. high sch., Sandusky. Telephone sales rep. Sears, Roebuck and Co., Sandusky, 1974-79; sec., com. coordinator Sandusky Area C. of C., 1979-84; asst. dir. Erie County Visitors and Conv. Bur., Sandusky, 1985—. Fellow Lake Erie Firelands Tourist Council. Democrat. Lutheran. Largest service contract ever sold at Sears, Roebuck and Co. Avocations: reading, swimming, traveling. Office: Erie County Visitors and Conv Bur 231 W Washington Row Sandusky OH 44870

REED, SHELDON COOPER, gynecologist, obstetrician; b. Mpls., Aug. 6, 1926; s. Frank Elisha and Gladys Naomi (Cooper) R.; m. Vera Jean Grinde, July 20, 1957; children: Kimberly, Sheldon Jr., Lesley. BS, U. Minn., 1949, MD, 1952. Diplomate Am. Bd. Ob-Gyn. Intern Mpls. Gen. Hosp., 1952-53, resident, 1953-56; practice medicine specializing in ob-gyn Mpls., 1956—; chmn. dept. ob-gyn Northwestern Hosp., Mpls., 1964-66. Served with USNR, 1944-46, ETO. Mem. AMA, Minn. Med. Assn., Hennepin County Med. Soc., Minn. Soc. Obstetricians and Gynecologists, Soc. Mayflower Descendents (surgeon gen. 1969-72). Club: Mpls. Athletic. Avocations: gardening, tennis. Office: 6545 France Ave S Edina MN 55435

REEDER, DAVID SCOTT, electronics executive; b. Archbold, Ohio, Oct. 29, 1944; s. Max D. and Gayle W. (Williams) R.; m. Marianne Elfredo Hopfl, Sept. 14, 1968 (div. Apr., 1978); 1 child, Christopher Scott; m. Cynthia Lee Gresko, Nov. 24, 1980; children: Michael Scott, Stephen Scott. BSEE, U. Pitts., 1967. Sr. project mgr. Bailey Controls, Cleve., 1972-78, mgr. project mgmt., 1978-82, mgr. customer service, 1981-82; v.p., gen. mgr. systems div. Victoreen, Inc. subs. Sheller-Globe Corp., Cleve., 1982-85, v.p. mktg., 1985—. Mem. IEEE, Instrument Soc. Am., Am. Nuclear Soc. (local exec. com. 1985—). Republican. Roman Catholic. Avocations: reading, tennis. Home: 7199 Sowul Dr Painesville OH 44077 Office: Victoreen Inc 10101 Woodland Ave Cleveland OH 44104

REEDER, JAMES MARTIN, piano technician, restorer, pianist; b. Charlotte, Mich., Oct. 21, 1937; s. Elmer M. and Lora R.; m. Martha Silvia Covarrubias, July 18, 1965; children—Cindy, James, Christopher, Cheri. Student Andrews U., 1959-60, Columbian Union Coll., 1966. Owner, operator store and factory specializing in restoring pianos, 1968—; pianist, accompanist; condr. tech. workshops; piano cons. Mem. Piano Tech. Guild. Adventist. Office: PO Box 142 Grand Ledge MI 48837

REEDER, LEE, lawyer; b. LaPorte, Ind., Oct. 14, 1909; s. David Huse and Maude Angela (Warner) R.; m. Madaline Flo Brown, June 8, 1935; children: Douglas Lee, Jennifer Ann, Madaline Brown, Jr. Student, Kansas City Jr. Coll., 1926-28; J.D., U. Mo., Kansas City, 1932. Bar: Mo. 1932. Since practiced in Kansas City; dir. numerous firms; spl. counsel, dir. C.L.C. of Am., 1962-78; dir. W.S.C. Group, Inc.; Mem. spl. adv. com. to ICC. Chmn. Citizens Sch. Plant Com., Kansas City, 1950, Citizens Com. on Human Relations, 1950-52, Sch. Bond Com. Kansas City Sch. Dist., 1948; chmn. bd. Youth Symphony of Heart of Am., City Commn. Human Relations, 1952-60; bd. dirs., gen. counsel Heart of Am. council Boy Scouts Am., scoutmaster, troop committeeman, Eagle Scout, Silver Beaver award; trustee, chmn. Law Found. U. Mo., Kansas City, 1972-75; trustee, chmn. Leelanau Schs., 1972-75; bd. dirs., gen. counsel Am. Humanics. Recipient Silver Beaver award Boy Scouts Am. Mem. ABA, Mo. Bar Assn. (dir. dept. adminstrv. law 1960), Kansas City Bar Assn., Motor Carrier Lawyers Assn. (pres. 1952-53), Lawyers Assn. Kansas City, ICC Practitioners Assn. (chmn. nat. assn. ethics com. 1960-62), Kansas City Met. Bar Assn., Delta Theta Phi, Alpha Phi Omega (hon.), Bench and Robe Soc. Clubs: Kansas City (Kansas City), Carriage (Kansas City). Lodge: Rotary. Home: 824 W 53d Terr Kansas City MO 64112 Office: 4420 Madison Ave Kansas City MO 64111

REEDER, ROBERT HARRY, lawyer; b. Topeka, Dec. 3, 1930; s. William Harry and Florence Mae (Cochran) R. A.B. Washburn U., 1952, J.D., 1960. Bar: U.S. Dist. Ct. Kans. 1960, Kans. 1960, U.S. Supreme Ct. 1968. Research asst. Kans. Legis. Council Research Dept., Topeka, 1955-60; asst. counsel Traffic Inst., Northwestern U., Evanston, Ill., 1960-67, gen. counsel, 1967—; exec. dir. Nat. Com. on Uniform Traffic Laws and Ordinances, Evanston, 1982—. Co-author: Vehicle Traffic Law, 1974; The Evidence Handbook, 1980. Author: Interpretation of Implied Consent by the Courts, 1972. Served with U.S. Army, 1952-54. Mem. Com. Alcohol and Other Drugs (chmn. 1973-75). Republican. Methodist. Office: Nat Com on Uniform Traffic Laws PO Box 1409 405 Church St Evanston IL 60204

REEDER, ROGER KENT, real estate professional; b. Hammond, Ind., Sept. 21, 1950; s. Warren Arthur Jr. and June Maxine (Hershberger) R.; m. Melinda Kaye Jones, Nov. 4, 1978; children: Ryan Keith, Nathan Aaron, Warren Arthur III. BA in History, Ind. U., 1976. Cert. property mgr. Prin. Warren A. Reeder & Son Co., Hammond, 1977—. Pres. Hammond Bicentennial Commn., 1983—; pres. Calumet Goodwill Industries, Hammond, 1986. Mem. Ind. Assn. Realtors (state dir. 1980-85, dist. I v.p. state exec. com. 1985—), Calumet Bd. Realtors (pres. 1983-84), Hammond Hist. Soc. (pres. 1983-85). Baptist. Lodge: Kiwanis (bd. dirs. 1978-80). Avocation: history. Home: 7014 Forest Ave Hammond IN 46324 Office: Warren A Reeder & Son Co 260 165 th St Hammond IN 46324

REEG, KATHRYN LEGGETT, internal revenue agent; b. Grantsville, W.Va., Sept. 8, 1933; d. Hal Franklin and Cybal Jamima (Clevenger) Leggett; m. Paul Edward Reeg (dec. 1982). BS Acctg., Bus. Mgmt., Morris Harvey Coll., 1960; postgrad., Cen. IBM Programming Sch., 1960-62, Franklin U., 1970-72; student, Franklin U., 1970-72. Comptroller Charleston (W.Va.) Gen. Hosp., 1960-66; IRS field auditor U.S. Treasury Dept., Columbus, Ohio, 1966—. Mem. Bus. Profl. Women's Assn. (chmn. scholarship com. 1985-86), Internat. Acctg. Soc., Am. Soc. Women Accts. (past pres.). Avocations: golf, bowling, gardening. Home: 968 Marland Dr S Columbus OH 43224

REES, ANTHONY WARBURTON, financial executive; b. D.C., Aug. 2, 1946; s. Elias Davis and Mary Louise (Warburton) R.; m. Heide Annamaria (Weinmann); children—William Scott, Karly Annamaria. B.S., in Math., Carnegie Mellon U., 1968; M.B.A., U. Mich., 1973. Rep. marketing Westinghouse Electric Corp., Balt., 1968-71; mgr. fin. analysis Rockwell Internat., Alcester, Eng., Troy, Mich., 1973-77; dir. internat. planning, Medtronic Inc., Mpls., 1977-84; v.p. fin. and adminstrn., treas., chief fin. officer Angiomedics Inc., Mpls., 1984—. Mem. Nat. Assn. Accts., Inst. Mgmt. Acctg.; Beta Gamma Sigma (hon.). Club: YMCA. Avocations: philately; traveling; reading; athletics. Office: Angiomedics Inc 2905 Northwest Blvd Minneapolis MN 55441

REES, JACK MADISON, interior designer; b. Stanton, Iowa, May 30, 1921; s. Ross Basil and Georgene (Madison) R.; m. Joan Martz, June 19, 1949; children—John Martz, Michael Stroud. Student Iowa State U., 1940-42; B.A. cum laude, Pratt Inst., Bklyn., 1947. Interior designer William Pahlman, Assocs., N.Y.C., 1947-48; interior designer, store lectr. L. Bamberger, Newark, 1948-50, W. & J. Sloane, N.Y.C., 1950-51; pres. Jack Rees Interiors, Kansas City, Mo., 1952—, Designers Prototype, Kansas City, 1978—. Editor: Decorating with Color, 1975. Founding mem. Bacchus Ball Charity Benefit, Kansas City, 1957; bd. dirs. Kansas City Lyric Opera. Served to 2d lt. USAF, 1942-46, PTO. Named Designer of Yr., Enterprise-Kansas City Art Inst., 1975. Mem. Am. Inst. Interior Design (pres. 1981), Am. Soc. Interior Design (pres. 1981-83, founder Home of Yr. program 1982), SAR. Republican. Episcopalian. Club: Carriage (Kansas City). Home: 5508 Central St Kansas City MO 64113 Office: Jack Rees Interiors Inc 4501 Belleview St Kansas City MO 64111

REES, ROGER ALLEN, farmer; b. Lamar, Mo., Feb. 25, 1957; s. Allen Wayne and Una Mae (Pheiffer) R.; m. Debra Lynn Coppedge, July 21, 1979; children: Elizabeth Ann, Katherine Lynn, Victoria Rochelle. BS in Agr., U. Mo., 1978. Farmer Carthage, Mo., 1979—. Agr. crisis counselor United Council Churches, 1986; active ruling elder United Presbyn. Ch. Golden City, 1980-86. Mem. Young Farmers Assn. (pres. Jasper, Mo. chpt. 1983-85), Farm Bur. Republican. Lodge: Rotary. Home and Office: Rt 1 Box 254-A Carthage MO 64836

REESE, ELMER EDWARD, automotive components company executive; b. Wilkes-Barre, Pa., Mar. 17, 1928. BSME, LeHigh U., 1952; postgrad. exec. devel. program, Ohio State U., 1969; postgrad. mktg. for execs. program, Harvard U., 1971; postgrad. sr. exec. program, MIT, 1976. Engr. Delco appliance div. Gen. Motors Corp., Rochester, N.Y., 1952-58, sr. project engr., 1958-65, product mgr., 1965-66; staff engr. Delco products div. Gen. Motors Corp., Dayton, Ohio, 1966-68, asst. chief engr., 1968-70, chief engr., 1970-73, gen. sales mgr., 1973-76; chief engr. Delco Remy div. Gen. Motors Corp., Anderson, Ind., 1976-78, gen. mgr., 1978-82; gen. mgr. Packard electric div. Gen. Motors Corp., Warren, Ohio, 1982—. Patentee in field. Chmn. campaign Trumbull County United Way, Warren, 1983-84, campaign Jr. Achievement Fund Drive, Trumbull County, Ohio, 1985; bd. dirs. Trumbull Meml. Hosp., Warren. Served with USAF, 1946-48. Mem. Soc. Automotive Engrs., Youngstown (Ohio) C. of C., Warren C. of C. (bd. dirs.). Office: Gen Motors Corp Packard Electric Div PO Box 431 Warren OH 44486

REESE, JOHN CARLTON, architect; b. Cin., June 27, 1948; s. John James and Norma Agnes (Hessler) R.; m. Mary Alice Reindl, Sept. 11, 1971; children: Alicia Marie, John Michael. AA, U. Cin., 1968, BArch, 1976. Registered architect, Ohio. Intern Steed, Hammond, Paul, Architects, Hamilton, Ohio, 1976-78, Mitchell & Jensen, Architects & Engrs., Dayton, Ohio, 1978; project mgr. First Nat. Bank Cin., 1978—. Bd. dirs. Today Homeowners Assn., Fairfield, Ohio, 1975-80. Mem. AIA. Roman Catholic. Home: 1583 Hunter Rd Fairfield OH 45014 Office: First Nat Bank Cin 425 Walnut St Cincinnati OH 45202

REESE, KENNETH WENDELL, diversified company executive; b. Orange, Tex., Aug. 1, 1930; s. Richard W. and Florence (Mulhollan) R.; m. Mary A. Broom, Aug. 22, 1955; children: Jimmy, Michael, Gary. BBA, U. Houston, 1954. Asst. treas. Firestone Tire & Rubber Co., Akron, Ohio, 1968-70, treas., 1970—, v.p., 1973-75, exec. v.p. finance, 1975; sr. v.p. fin. Tenneco Inc., Houston, 1975-78, exec. v.p., 1978—, also bd. dirs.; bd. dirs. Tex. Commerce Bancshares, Inc., Fleming Cos., Inc. Bd. dirs. Better Bus. Bur. Met. Houston, Tex. Council on Econ. Edn.; nat. bd. dirs. Jr. Achievement Inc.; trustee U. Houston Found.; mem. adv. com. Coll. Bus. Adminstrn., U. Houston. Served to 1st lt. AUS, 1954-56. Mem. U. Houston Athletic Lettermans Assn. Baptist. Clubs: Petroleum, Heritage, Houston City (Houston).

REESE, TED MARION, dentist; b. Dayton, Ohio, Jan. 21, 1959; s. Virgil Marion and Elizabeth June (Holmes) R. Student, Anderson (Ind.) Coll., 1977-80; DDS with distinction, Ind. U., Indpls., 1984. Gen. practice dentistry Clinton, Ind., 1984—. Vol. Project Ptnr. in Christ, Middletown, Ohio, 1984, Good Shepherd Ministries, Rockledge, Fla., 1985, Orphans, Inc., 1984; profl. edn. chmn. Am. Cancer Soc., Vermillion County, Ind., 1986. Mem. ADA, Ind. Dental Assn., Acad. Gen. Dentistry, Am. Acad. Implant Dentistry (supporting), Internat. Congress of Oral Implantology. Republican. Avocations: travel, flying, hunting, photography. Office: 1035 N 9th St Clinton IN 47842

REESER, FREDERICK HAROLD, ophthamologist; b. Harrisburg, Pa., May 31, 1939. BA, Duke U., 1961; MD, U. Pa., 1965. Diplomate Am. Bd. Ophthalmology. Fellow in eye pathology Armed Forced Inst. Pathology, 1969-70; Heed fellow Mass. Eye and Ear Infirmary, 1970-71; asst. chief, ophthalmology services Nat. Naval Med. Ctr., Bethesda, Md., 1971-73; prof. ophthalmology Med. Coll. Wis., Milw., 1973-83; pvt. practice specializing in ophthalmology Retina and Vitreous Cons., Milw., 1983—; chmn. ophthalmology sect. St. Mary's Hosp., Milw., 1986—, laser com. St. Luke's Hosp., Milw., 1986—. Author: Physiology of the Human Eye and Visual System, 1979, Intraocular Evaluation by Computed Tomography, 1981; contbr. aticles to profl. jours. Grantee research NIH, 1978-83. Office: Retina and Vitreous Cons Ltd 2600 N Mayfair Rd Suite 901 Milwaukee WI 53226

REETZ, JAMES ARTHUR, insurance systems analyst; b. Iola, Wis., July 9, 1945; s. Orville H. and Evelyn (Polk) R.; m. Hope Ann Millard, May 31, 1969; children: Eric James, Gina Lynn. BS, U. Wis., Stevens Point, 1974. Console operator Sentry Ins. Co., Stevens Point, 1973-78, mgr. ops., 1978-83, sr. systems analyst, 1983—. Served as sgt. USAF, 1964-68. Home: PO Box 211 Plover WI 54467

REEVES, ANGELA MARIE, college administrator; b. Indpls., Feb. 23, 1949; d. Ervin V. and Mary M. Holland; m. Dale Edward Reeves, Sept. 3, 1977 (div.); children—Samuel E., Rachel A. Student C.S. Mott Community Coll., 1967-68; B.S., Cen. Mich. U., 1971; M.A., Mich. State U., 1975. Cert. social worker, Mich. Jr. therapist Rubicon House, Flint, Mich., 1971; alcoholism therapist Hurley Med. Ctr., Flint, 1972-78; advisor C.S. Mott Community Coll., Flint, 1978-83, dir. admissions, 1983—. Sec. program com. Internat. Inst.; mem. Consortium Ethnic Concerns, Consortium Ethic Concerns in Higher Edn., admissions com. United Way; bd. dirs. Mich. State U. Urban Affairs Alumni, sec. Recipient Cert. of Recognition, Gov. Blanchard, 1985; named one of Outstanding Young Women Am., 1983, Counselor of Yr., Mott Community Coll. Afro Am. Assn. 1980-81, Hon. Navy Recruiter, U.S. Navy, 1984. Mem. Mich. Personnel and Guidance Assn., Mich. Assn. Admissions Counselors, Genesee Area Personnel and Guidance Assn., Mich. Women's Studies Assn., Nat. Assn. Coll. Admissions, Nat. Assn. Negro Bus. and Profl. Women's Clubs Inc. (3rd v.p. 1982-83), Internat. Inst. (program com.), Assn. Non-White Concerns. Home: 5418 Marja St Flint MI 48505 Office: CS Mott Community Coll 1401 E Court St Flint MI 48502

REEVES, EARL JAMES, JR., college educator; b. Muskogee, Okla., Mar. 16, 1933; s. Earl James and Berneice Elizabeth (Jordan) R.; m. Wilma Gail Reece, Aug. 30, 1950; children—Barbara Gail, Gregory Alan, Carolyn Elaine. Student Kans. State U., 1950-51, Friends U., 1951-52; B.A., Wichita State U., 1954, M.A., 1959; Ph.D., U. Kans., 1962. Faculty U. Kan., Lawrence, 1961-62, U. Omaha, 1962-64, U. Mo., St. Louis, 1964-70, U. Tulsa, 1970-83; dir. urban studies program U. Tulsa, 1970-83, prof., 1971-83; pres. Mo. Valley Coll., Marshall, 1983—; cons. Cen. Midwestern Regional Edn. Lab., 1966-68, Tulsa C. of C., Leadership 1973-76, Tulsa Area Agy. on Aging, 1973-76. V.P. city council, Berkeley, Mo., 1966-70; mem. Tulsa Community Relations Commn., 1971-76, chmn., 1975; mem. Met. Tulsa Growth Strategy Com., 1975-76; bd. dirs. Indian Nations Council Govts., 1977-83; chmn. Sales Tax Overview Com., City of Tulsa, 1980-83; mem. mission direction and priorities com. Presbyn. Ch. U.S.A., 1977-81, candidate for moderator Gen. Assembly, 1982, mem. evangelism adv. com., 1982—; pres. bd. Eastern Okla. Housing Corp.; bd. dirs. Marshall Philharm. Orch. Author: Approaches to the Study of Urbanization, 1963, The Cross and the Flag: Evangelical Christianity and Contemporary Politics, 1972, Protest and Politics: Christianity and Contemporary Affairs, 1968, Back Talk: Press Councils in America, 1972, Urban Community, 1978; research editor, pres. editorial bd. Midwest Rev. of Pub. Adminstrn., 1974-76, mem. editorial bd. Jour. Urban Affairs, 1982—; contbr. articles to profl. jours. Served with USAF, 1954-58. Mem. Am. Soc. Pub. Adminstrn.; Marshall C. of C. (bd. dirs.). Lodge: Rotary. Home: 419 E College St Marshall MO 65340 Office: Missouri Valley Coll 500 E College St Marshall MO 65340

REEVES, J. DOUGLAS, retail pharmaceutical company executive; b. 1941. BS, Butler U., 1963. With Hook Drugs, Inc., Indpls., 1963—, pharmacist, 1963-70, asst. v.p. ops., 1970-73, v.p. ops., 1973-77, exec. v.p., 1977-78, pres., chief operating officer, 1978-81, chmn. bd. dirs., pres., chief exec. officer, 1981—. Office: Hook Drugs Inc 2800 Enterprise St Indianapolis IN 46226 *

REEVES, MICHAEL STANLEY, public utility executive; b. Memphis, Oct. 2, 1935; m. Patricia Ann Board, June 27, 1959; children—Michael, Michelle. Student Iowa State U., 1954-56; B.A., Roosevelt U., 1964; M.B.A., Northwestern U., 1972. With People Gas Co., Chgo., 1956—, supr., 1967-69, asst. supt., 1969-72, supt., 1972-75, gen. supt., 1975-77, v.p. mktg. and customer relations, 1977—. Bd. dirs. Chgo. Commons Assn., St. Bernard Hosp., Better Bus. Bur. Served with U.S. Army. Mem. Chgo. Assn. Commerce and Industry, Am. Gas Assn., Am. Assn. Blacks in Energy, Chgo. Econ. Club. Club: University (Chgo.). Office: 122 S Michigan Ave Suite 1525 Chicago IL 60603

REEVES, PATRICK ALOYSIUS, advertising agency executive; b. Cin., Apr. 21, 1939; s. Morris Leslie and Bernice Gertrude (Farfsing) R.; children: Patricia Pierson, Jennifer Elizabeth. BBA, U. Cin., 1963. Writer Cin. Gas & Electric Co., 1960-64; sr. copywriter Northlich Stolley, Inc., 1964-66; creative dir. Clinton E. Frank, Inc., Cin., 1966-68, Fahlgren & Swink (formerly Ralph Jones Co.), Cin., 1968-70; pres., creative dir. Reeves Advt., Inc., Cin., 1970—. Pres. Music for Kids, Inc., 1966-75; bd. dirs. Com. 100, U. Cin., 1964-67; mem. steering com. Young Rep. Club, 1962-66, Ohio steering com. Reagan for Pres., 1979-80; pub. relations mgr. Businessmen for Reagan, Cin., 1979-80. Served with U.S. Army, 1956-57. Mem. N.Y. Art Dirs. Club, Queen City Council Performing Arts (v.p., dir.), Sigma Chi (pres. 1962-63).

Methodist. Avocations: poetry, physics, handball. Home: 221 E Marion St South Bend IN 46601 Office: Reeves Advt Inc 411 Vine St. Cincinnati OH 45202

REEVES, ROY RUSSELL, osteopathic physician; b. Waco, Tex., Apr. 27, 1952; s. George A. and Doris (McKiddy) R.; m. Vicki Sharon Cain, Mar. 2, 1974 (div. May 1983); 1 child, David Nathan. BA, Union Coll., Barbourville, Ky., 1971; MS, Morehead (Ky.) State U., 1972; PhD, U. So. Miss., 1975; DO, Kirksville (Mo.) Coll. Osteo. Med., 1979. Emergency dept. physician Kirksville Osteo. Health Ctr., 1980-82, Cameron (Mo.) Community Hosp., 1982—. Contbr. articles to profl. jours. mem. Am. Osteo. Assn., Am. Coll. Emergency Physicians, Am. Coll. Osteo. Emergency Physicians, Am. Coll. Neuropsychiatrists, Drs. for Life. Republican. Avocation: astronomy. Home: 507 N Walnut Cameron MO 64429 Office: Cameron Community Hosp 1015 W 4th St Cameron MO 64429

REEVES, WALTER HAROLD, psychologist; b. Chgo., May 18, 1931; s. Harold Elmer and Betty (Cihla) R.; m. June Hubert, June 25, 1960; children: Pamela, Brenda. BA, Roosevelt U., 1953, MA, 1960; MEd, Loyola U., Chgo., 1968; PhD, Northwestern U., 1972. Psychologist Dept. Mental Health, Kankakee, Ill., 1957-60, Dept. Corrections, St. Charles, Ill., 1960-62, Sch. Assn. for Spl. Edn., Wheaton, Ill., 1962-63, 81—; chief psychologist Sch. Assn. Spl. Edn., Wheaton, Ill., 1963-80; instr. Elgin (Ill.) Community Coll., 1961-63, Nat. Coll. Edn., Evanston, Ill., 1967, 79-80, Ill. Benedictine Coll., Lisle, 1975; pvt. practice psychology, Lisle, 1973-78. Served to sgt. U.S. Army, 1953-55. Fellow Northwestern U., 1968. Mem. Am. Psychol. Assn., Midwestern Psychol. Assn., Ill. Psychol. Assn., Assn. Study of Perception. Avocations: swimming, skiing, boating. Home: 2812 Red Barn Rd Crystal Lake IL 60014 Office: Sch Assn Spl Edn 132 E Pine Roselle IL 60012

REEVES, WILLIAM HATTON, chemical company executive; b. Phila., Jan. 18, 1937; s. Jonathan Hatton and Eugene Sue (Headley) R.; m. Carole Lynne Cargal, Aug. 4, 1962; children: Mark Stephen, Jonathan Wyatt, Marion Alicia. Student, U. W.Va., 1955-56; BS in Chemistry and Zoology, Marshall U., 1959; postgrad., Universite Louis Pasteur, Strasbourg, France, 1976-81. Dir. product devel. Internat. Paper Co., N.Y.C., 1967-69; nat. sales mgr. Sherwood Med. Industries, St. Louis, 1969-73; v.p. mktg. Logos Internat., Plainfield, N.J., 1973-76; chmn., founder Vectra Corp., Columbia, Md., 1976-81, Magnum Electronics, Englewood, Ohio, 1981-86; pres., founder Chronodynamics, Ltd., Dayton, Ohio, 1986—; cons. Rhom Pharma NA, Durmstadt, Fed. Republic Germany, 1981—, QMax Tech., Dayton, 1981—; bd. dirs. MedTech Inc., Dayton, Thermology Labs., Centerville, Ohio. Holder 4 patents. Served with U.S. Army, 1959-62. Fellow Am. Acad. Thermology, Internat. Soc. Christian Counselors. Republican. Presbyterian. Avocations: tennis, fishing. Home: 1308 Norwich Ln Centerville OH 45459 Office: Chronodynamics Ltd 6012 N Dixie Dr Dayton OH 45404

REGAN, GERALD LAWRENCE, data communications analyst; b. Rochester, Minn., Sept. 20, 1942; s. Gerald Leroy and Jeannette Ronalda (Gilbertson) R.; m. Sureerat Udomlarp, Sept. 30, 1967; children: Khaimook, Nalumon Michelle, Malunee Elizabeth. Student, U. Minn., 1960-63; BA in Polit. Sci., Winona State Coll., 1971; postgrad., No. Ill. U., 1976-77. City planner City of Winona, Minn., 1971-75; city planner, chief code enforcement officer City of Dekalb, 1975-78; exec. dir. Home Owners Warranty Council Minn., St. Paul, 1978-79; programmer, analyst Cenex, Inc., South St. Paul, Minn., 1980-81; sr. systems analyst NCR Comten subs. NCR Corp. (formerly Nat. Cash Register), St. Paul, 1982—. Bd. dirs. Winona County Red Cross, 1974; Voluntary Action Ctr., Dekalb, Ill., 1977. Served as sgt. USAF, 1964-68. Avocation: youth basketball coach. Home: 6001 Shane Dr Edina MN 55435 Office: NCR Comten 2700 N Snelling Ave Saint Paul MN 55113

REGAN, JOHN EDWARD, dentist; b. Ripon, Wis., May 1, 1936; m. Delene Anne Smith; children: John, Mike, Sharon, Jennifer, Linda, David, Stephen, Stan. DDS, Ind. U., 1961. Practice family dentistry Huntington, Ind., 1961—; mem. staff Huntington Meml. Hosp.; faculty, mem. found. Huntington Coll.; sec., bd. dirs. Huntington Electric, Inc.; owner Bircraft, Inc.; cons. Ind. Dental Law Com. Contbr. articles to profl. jours. Active Boy Scouts Am.; mem. Ind. Mental Health Mental Retardation Planning Commn., Govs. Welfare Adv. Com.; pres. Huntington County Health Planning Council, 1975, Library Bd., 1975-76; past pres. Huntington County United Fund; v.p. Huntington County Med. Meml. Found., 1976; committeeman, commentator St. Mary's Cath. Ch. Served to capt. U.S. Army, 1962-64. Named Eagle Scout, Boy Scouts Am., Outstanding Young Man, Ind. Jaycees, 1969; recipient Disting. Service award Huntington Jaycees, 1969, Sagamore of the Wabash award, Ind. Gov. Orr, 1981. Fellow Am. Coll. Dentists; mem. ADA, Am. Analgesia Soc., Am. Soc. Preventive Dentistry, Am. Assn. Endodontics, Am. Orthodontic Straight Wire Assn., Am. Soc. Dentistry For Children, Acad. Gen. Dentistry (various offices and coms. including internat. pres. 1980-81, and publ. com.), Acad. Dentistry Internat., Midwest Soc. Periodontology, Ind. Bd. Dental Examiners, Ind. Dental Assn., Chgo. Dental Assn., Isaac Knapp Dental Soc. (bd. dirs., various coms.), Ind. Acad. Gen. Dentistry (founder, pres. 1979), Harry J. Healy Endodontic Study Club, Huntington County Assn. Retarded Citizens (founder, first pres.), Ind. Assn. Retarded Citizens (bd. dirs., sr. v.p., various coms.), Am. Cancer Soc. (first pres. Huntington), Huntington C. of C., Ind. U. Dental Alumni Assn., Alpha Chi Sigma, Alpha Phi Omega, Alpha Tau Omega. Lodges: Elks, Optimists, KC. Home: 11 Stoneridge Dr Huntington IN 46750 Office: 650 Cherry St Huntington IN 46750

REGAN, STEPHEN DANIEL, education consultant; b. Iowa City, Nov. 9, 1947; s. Daniel E. and Jacquelyn (Wheat) R.; m. Marianne Unnaslahti, June 23, 1973; children: Timothy, Jennifer. AA, Muscatine (Iowa) Community Coll., 1967; BA, Upper Iowa U., 1969; MS, Winona (Minn.) State U., 1975; EdD, U. S.D., 1979. Sch. counselor New Hartford (Iowa) Schs., 1975-77; instr. Sioux Falls (S.D.) Community Coll., 1977-78; adj. instr. U. S.D., Vermillion, 1978-79; edn. cons. Keystone Am. Edn. Assn., Elkader, Iowa, 1979—. Contbr. articles to profl. jours. Pres. St. Joseph's Bd. Edn., 1983. Served with USN, 1970-73. Mem. Am. Assn. Counseling and Devel., Iowa Assn. Humanistic Edn., Assn. Supervision and Curriculum Devel., Assn. Humanistic Edn. and Devel. (Leadership award 1983, Les Carlin award 1985), Four Oaks C. of C. (v.p. 1983-84). Avocation; writing naval history. Home: 801 N Main St Elkader IA 52043 Office: Keystone Area Edn Agy Box 19 Elkader IA 52043

REGENFUSS, JOHN MICHAEL, social services administrator; b. Sheboygan, Wis., June 2, 1946; s. Alphonse Robert and Mary Rose (Begush) R.; m. Linda Susan Jackson, May 2, 1970; children: Christina, John II. BA, St. Francis Sem., 1968, postgrad., 1968; postgrad., U. Wis., Milw., 1969-70, Marquette U., 1983-84. Juvenile probation officer Waukesha (Wis.) County Dept. Social Services, 1970-75, adolescent social worker, 1975-79, supr. social work, 1979-82, mgr. children's ctr., 1982-84; exec. dir. Portal Industries, Grafton, Wis., 1984—; mem. juvenile ct. adv. commn., Waukesha, 1982-84. Mem. Sch. Bd. Mukwonago (Wis.) Area Schs., 1978-84, Ozaukee County Transp. Commn., Port Washington, Wis., 1985—, Ozaukee County Council, Port Washington, 1985—; chmn. Big Bend (Wis.) Police Commn., 1980-84; campaign chmn. Ross for Sheriff, Big Bend, 1980; mem. steering com. Voss for Judge, Waukesha, 1984; bd. dirs., treas. Moraine Symphony Orch., 1986—. Mem. Mental Health Assn., Rehab. Facilities Wis., Am. Fedn. State, County and Mcpl. Employees. Avocations: running, fishing, camping, reading. Home: 4525 Hawthorne Dr Saukville WI 53080 Office: Portal Industries 420 10th Ave Grafton WI 53024

REGISTER, RICHARD OUTLER, computer systems executive; b. Marianna, Fla., Aug. 11, 1949; s. Harry and Mary Jo (Tompkins) R.; m. Joanne Mary Pasteris, June 12, 1971; 1 child, Melissa Anne. BS, U.S. Mil. Acad., 1971; MBA, U. Okla., 1976. Commd. 2d lt. U.S. Army, 1971, advanced through grades to capt., 1975, resigned, 1976; with paper products mfg. Procter & Gamble, Cape Girardeau, Mo., 1976-81; process engr. Procter & Gamble, Cape Girardeau, 1978-79, indsl. engr., 1979-81; sr. systems analyst Procter & Gamble, Cin., 1981-86, group mgr., 1986—. Sec., trustee Downtown Montessori, Inc., Cin., 1981-84. Decorated Army Commendation medal with two oak leaf clusters. Republican. Roman Catholic. Office: Procter & Gamble 2 Procter & Gamble Plaza Cincinnati OH 45201

REGLING, ANNE MARIE, hospital executive; b. Detroit, Apr. 6, 1955; d. Roland Adolph and Esther Stephanie (Le Plae) Brandau; m. Barry W. Regling, July 7, 1979. BA with honors, Mich. State U., 1977; postgrad., Wayne State U., 1985—. CPA, Mich. Auditor, cons. Ernst & Whinney, Detroit, 1977-85; dir. fiscal services N. Detroit Gen. Hosp., Hamtramyck, Mich., 1985; v.p. fin. Children's Hosp. Mich., Detroit, 1985—. Bd. dirs. Well Being Service for Aging, Detroit, 1983-85. Mem. Am. Mgmt. Assn., Am. Inst. CPA's, Mich. Assn. CPA's. Roman Catholic. Avocations: golf, needlework. Home: 4929 Deepwood Dr Troy MI 48098 Office: Children's Hosp Mich 21700 Greenfield Suite 112 Oak Park MI 48237

REGULA, RALPH, lawyer, congressman; b. Beach City, Ohio, Dec. 3, 1924; s. O.F. and Orpha (Walter) R.; m. Mary Rogusky, Aug. 5, 1950; children: Martha, David, Richard. B.A., Mt. Union Coll., 1948, LL.D., 1981; LL.B., William McKinley Sch. Law, 1952; LL.D., Malone Coll., 1976. Bar: Ohio 1952. Sch. adminstr. Stark County Bd. Edn., 1948-55; practiced law Navarre, from 1952; mem. Ohio Ho. of Reps., 1965-66, Ohio Senate, 1967-72, 93d-100th congresses from 16th Dist. Ohio, 1973—; ptnr. Regula Bros.; Mem. Pres.'s Commn. on Fin. Structures and Regulation, 1970-71. Mem. Ohio Bd. Edn., 1960-64; hon. mem. adv. bd. Walsh Coll., Canton, Ohio; Trustee Mt. Union Coll., Alliance, Ohio, Stark County Hist. Soc., Stark County Wilderness Soc. Served with USNR, 1944-46. Recipient Community Service award Navarre Kiwanis Club, 1963; Meritorious Service in Conservation award Canton Audubon Soc., 1965; Ohio Conservation award Gov. James Rhodes, 1969; named Outstanding Young Man of Yr. Canton Jr. C. of C., 1957, Legis. Conservationist of Yr. Ohio League Sportsmen, 1969. Republican. Episcopalian. Office: US Ho of Reps 2209 Rayburn House Office Bldg Washington DC 20515 *

REH, THOMAS EDWARD, radiologist, educator; b. St. Louis, Sept. 12, 1943; s. Edward Paul and Ceil Anne (Golden) R.; m. Benedette Texada Gieselman, June 22, 1968; children—Matthew J., Benedette T., Elizabeth W. B.A., St. Louis U., 1965, M.D., 1969. Diplomate Am. Bd. Radiology, Nat. Bd. Med. Examiners. Intern St. John's Mercy Med. Ctr., St. Louis, 1969-70; resident St. Louis VA Hosp., 1970-73; fellow in vascular radiology Beth Israel Hosp., Boston, 1973-74; radiologist St. Mary's Health Ctr., St. Louis, 1974—, chmn. dept. radiology, 1986—; clin. asst. prof. radiology St. Louis U. Sch. Medicine, 1978—. Mem. Am. Coll. Radiology, AMA, Radiol. Soc. N.Am., St. Louis Met. Med. Soc., Alpha Omega Alpha, Alpha Sigma Nu, Delta Sigma Phi. Republican. Roman Catholic. Clubs: St. Louis, Confrerie des Chevaliers du Tastevin. Home: 9850 Waterbury Dr Saint Louis MO 63124 Office: Bellevue Radiology Inc 6710 Clayton Rd Saint Louis MO 63117

REHA, ROSE KRIVISKY, retired business educator; b. N.Y.C., Dec. 17, 1920; d. Boris and Freda (Gerstein) Krivisky; m. Rudolph John Reha, Apr. 11, 1941; children: Irene Gale, Phyllis. BS, Ind. State U., 1965; MA, U. Minn., 1967, PhD, 1971. With U.S. and State Civil Service, 1941-63; tchr. pub. schs., Minn., 1965-66; teaching assoc., part-time instr. U. Minn., Mpls., 1966-68; prof. Coll. Bus., St. Cloud (Minn.) State U., 1968-85, chmn. bus. edn. and office adminstrn. dept., 1982-83; cons., lectr. in field. Camp dir. Girl Scouts U.S.A., 1960-62; active various community fund drives; sec., mem. relicensure rev. Com. Minn. Bd. Teaching Continuing Edn., 1984—. Recipient Achievement award St. Cloud State U., 1985; St. Cloud State U. Research and Faculty Improvement grantee, 1973, 78, 83. Mem. Am. Vocat. Assn., Minn. Econ. Assn., Minn. Women of Higher Edn., NEA, Minn. Edn. Assn. (pres. women's caucus 1981-83, award for outstanding contbns. 1983), Minn. Bus. Edn., Inc., St. Cloud U. Faculty Assembly (pres. 1975-76), St. Cloud State U. Grad. Council (chmn. 1983-84) Pi Omega Pi (sponsor St. Cloud State U. chpt. 1982—), Phi Chi Theta, Delta Pi Epsilon, Delta Kappa Gamma. Jewish. Contbr. articles to profl. jours. Home: 1725 13 Ave SE Saint Cloud MN 56301 Office: St Cloud State Univ Coll of Business Saint Cloud MN 56301

REHER, JOHN FRED, infosystems manager; b. Bensenville, Ill., Apr. 9, 1936; s. John Henry and Malinda (Schulze) R.; m. Barbara Joan Kollath, Sept. 3, 1960; children: Kaye Lynn, Gayle Anne. BA in Acctg., U. Ill., 1961. Adminstrv. services mgr. Arthur Andersen & Co., Chgo., 1961-71; v.p. mgmt. info. systems Wackenhut Corp., Coral Gables, Fla., 1971-76; office mgr. James V. Pfeiffer Co., Miami, Fla., 1976-77; dir. mgmt. info. systems Columbus-Cuneo-Cabrini Med. Ctr., Chgo., 1977-80; mgr. mgmt. info. systems William Wrigley Jr. Co., Chgo., 1980—. Pres. Chatelaine Homeowners Assn., Arlington Heights, Ill., 1980—; trustee, treas. 1st Presbyn. Ch., Arlington Heights, 1985—. Served with U.S. Army, 1954-57. Mem. Assn. for Systems Mgmt., Soc. for Info. Mgmt. Republican. Presbyterian. Avocations: boating, bicycling, landscaping, photography, travel. Home: 2314 N Evergreen Arlington Heights IL 60004-2580 Office: William Wrigley Jr Co 410 N Michigan Ave Chicago IL 60611

REHL, WILLIAM MICHAEL, III, accountant; b. Columbus, Ohio, Nov. 15, 1959; s. William Michael II and Barbara Lee (Harrington) R.; m. Lori Jean Murphy, Aug. 4, 1984. BSBA cum laude, Ohio State U., 1981. CPA, Ohio. Staff auditor Arthur Andersen & Co., Columbus, Ohio, 1981-85, Cin., 1985—. Mem. Am. Inst. CPA's, Ohio Soc. CPA's, Am. Prodn. and Inventory Control Soc. Democrat. Roman Catholic. Avocations: softball, basketball, racquetball, reading, home improvements. Home: 7301 Gammwell Dr Cincinnati OH 45230-2149 Office: Arthur Andersen & Co 425 Walnut St Cincinnati OH 45202

REHM, JACK DANIEL, media executive; b. Yonkers, N.Y., Oct. 10, 1932; s. Jack and Ann (McCarthy) R.; m. Cynthia Fenning, Oct. 18, 1958; children: Lisabeth R., Ann M., Cynthia A., Jack D. Jr. BS, Holy Cross Coll., 1954. Advt. sales trainee, asst. account exec. Batten, Barton, Burstine & Osborne, N.Y.C., 1954-59; with advt. sales Suburbia Today, N.Y.C., 1959-62; with advt. sales Better Homes and Gardens Meredith Corp., N.Y.C., 1962-66, Phila. sales mgr., 1966-67, N.Y. sales mgr., 1967-69, advt. sales dir., 1969-73, v.p., pub. dir., 1973-75, v.p., pub. Better Homes and Gardens, 1975-76, v.p. and gen. mgr. pub. group, 1976-80; pres. pub. group Meredith Corp., Des Moines, 1980-86, exec. v.p., 1986—; bd. dirs. 1st Interstate Bank of Iowa, Vernon Co., Newton, Iowa. Bd. dirs. Des Moines Civic Ctr., 1982—. Served with U.S. Army, 1956-57. Mem. Mag. Pubs. Assn. (bd. dirs. 1981—, chmn. 1983-85), Am. Council for Capital Formation. (bd. dirs. 1986—). Clubs: Pine Valley Golf (N.J.); Wakonda (Des Moines); Scarsdale Golf (Hartsdale, N.Y.). Home: 2913 Druid Hill Dr Des Moines IA 50315 Office: Meredith Corp 1716 Locust St Des Moines IA 50336

REHM, JOHN EDWIN, manufacturing company executive; b. Bucyrus, Ohio, Oct. 20, 1924; s. Lester Carl and Mary O'Dale (Myers) R.; student Heidelberg U., 1942; U. Ala., 1943-44; Ohio State U., 1946-49. Asst. plant engr. Shunk Mfg. Co., Inc., Bucyrus, 1949-53, prodn. mgr., 1951-61, plant mgr., 1961-65, mgr. prodn. services, 1965-68, mgr. customer service dept., 1968-69, ops. mgr., 1969-70, v.p. ops., 1970-71; materials mgr. Oury Engring. Co., Marion, Ohio, 1971-73, W.W. Sly Mfg. Co., Cleve., 1973-79, 84—; v.p., gen. mgr. Moody Mfg. Co., Inc., Maben, Miss., 1979-84. Bd. dirs. Bucyrus United Community Fund, 1969-70. Served with AUS, 1943-46, PTO. Decorated Bronze Star with oak leaf cluster. Mem. Am. Soc. Personnel Adminstrn., Bucyrus Area C. of C. (v.p. 1966, pres. 1967). Republican. Lodges: Elks, Rotary. Home: 5246 Manchester Circle North Ridgeville OH 44039

REHMAT, SALIM GULAMHUSSEIN, computer systems design analyst; b. Bukoba, Tanzania, June 27, 1950; s. Gulamhussein and Noorbanu (Sharif) R.; m. Shehnaz Bana, Mar. 20, 1981; children: Salman, Samir. BS, U. Ill., Chgo., 1971, MS, 1976. Research asst. U. Ill., Chgo., 1971-72; computer programmer Berry Bearing Co., Chgo., 1972-76; systems engr. Electronic Data Systems, Chgo., 1976-78; programmer, analyst Nalco Chem., Oak Brook, Ill., 1978-80; systems analyst Anaconda Ericson, Glen Ellyn, Ill., 1980-84; design analyst Navistar Internat., Oak Brook, Ill., 1984—. Recipient tuition scholarship U. Ill, Chgo., 1969-71. Mem. Am. Prodn. and Inventory Control Soc. Home: 2 N 280 Highland Ave Glen Ellyn IL 60137 Office: Navistar Corp 1901 S Meyers Rd Oak Brook Terrace IL 60148

REHMER, JOHN E., teacher; b. Kankakee, Ill., Sept. 28, 1952; s. John Francis and Shirley Jean (Lawrence) R.; m. Ellen Marie Milstead, July 2, 1977; 1 child, Aimee Beth. BS, Ill. State U., 1974; postgrad., Olivet Nazarene Coll., 1979-80; MA, Govs. State U., 1984. Registered social worker, Ill. Mental health specialist Manteno (Ill.) Mental Health Ctr., 1974-79; announcer, newsman Sta. WLCL, Lowell, Ind., 1978-80; 5th grade tchr. Momence (Ill.) Sch. System, 1980—. Sports reporter Momence Progress Reporter, 1985—. Religious edn. coordinator St. Patrick Ch., Momence, Ill., 1982—; parade marshall Momence Gladiolus Festival Assn., 1985—, bd. dirs., 1987—; football announcer Momence Village Jr. Football, 1983—. Mem. NEA, Ill. Edn. Assn., Momence Edn. Assn. Republican. Roman Catholic. Avocation: listening to records. Home: 218 St James Ct Momence IL 60954 Office: Momence Jr High Sch 801 W 2d St Momence IL 60954

REIBMAN, PAUL JEROME, occupational consultant, educator; b. Chgo., Nov. 23, 1937; s. Abraham A. and Frieda (Liner) R.; m. Susan Jane Jones, Aug. 4, 1962; children—Elizabeth, Allen. B.S.C. in Mktg., DePaul U., 1962; M.S. in Edn., No. Ill. U., 1972. Vocat. coordinator Chgo. Bd. Edn., 1962—; instr. in bus. edn. and adminstrv. services Grad. Sch., No. Ill. U., 1973—; sr. cons. Occupational Cons., Glenview, Ill., 1978—; bd. dirs. Ill. Found. Mktg. and Distributive Edn.; pres. Ill. Adv. Com. on Distributive Edn., 1970-72. Served with U.S. Army, 1960. Named Ky. col., 1975; Chgo. Ambassador, Richard J. Daley, 1976; Distributive Edn. Man of Yr., Distributive Edn. Clubs Ill., 1977; recipient Mktg. award Sears Roebuck & Co., 1977; Ill. Service award Ill. Secondary Mktg. and Distributive Edn. Assn., 1980. Mem. Am. Personnel and Guidance Assn., Nat. Vocat. Guidance Assn. (cert. profl.), Am. Vocat. Assn., Ill. Vocat. Assn., Ill. Bus. Edn. Assn., Nat. Bd. for Cert. Career Counselors (cert. profl.), Internat. Soc. Preretirement Planners. Lodge: Kiwanis (chmn. career guidance 1975-80, Career award 1982). Cons. numerous career guides for State Ill. Office: 1030 Indian Rd Glenview IL 60025

REICH, GREGORY MARC, periodontist; b. Denver, May 21, 1948; s. Philip and Helen Geraldine (Morris) R.; m. Lynn Kathleen Fazen, June 17, 1972; 1 child, Camille Lynn. BA, U. Colo., 1970; DDS, Northwestern U., 1974; MS, Northwestern U. Grad. Dental Sch., 1976. Diplomate Am. Bd. Periodontology. Practice dentistry specializing in periodontics Libertyville, Ill., 1976—; instr. Northwestern U. Dental Sch., 1974-76, Loyola U. Dental Sch., Maywood, Ill., 1976-77; staff mem. Lake Forest (Ill.) Hosp., 1976—, Hawthorne Pl. Surgical Ctr., Libertyville, 1982—. Mem. Am. Acad. Periodontics (lectr. 1985), Mid-West Soc. Periodontics, Ill. Soc. Periodontics, Am. Dental Assn., Lake County Dental Soc., Ill. Dental Assn., Chgo. Dental Assn. (lectr. mid-winter meeting, 1976, 77, 78, 83), Lake County Dental Study Club. Republican. Jewish. Club: Winter (Lake Forest). Avocations: skiing, sailing C&E scows, scuba diving, collecting Porsche cars. Home: 1100 Edgewood Rd Lake Forest IL 60045 Office: 1900 Hollister Dr Libertyville IL 60048

REICHARD, JON DIRK, architect; b. Urbana, Ill., Dec. 29, 1953; s. David Warren and Melba Rose (Frank) R.; m. Patricia Lynn Parmenter; children: Jonathan, Benjamin. BArch, U. Ill., 1976, MArch, 1978. Registered architect, Ill. Architect PACU Architects, Kailua-Kona, Hawaii, 1978-79; plumber, drafting head A & R Mechanical, Urbana, 1979-81; architect Abris Ltd. Architects & Planners, Urbana, 1981—. Recipient 2d Place award Ill. Com. for Energy and Architecture, 1977. Republican. Avocations: golf, softball. Home: 112 McHenry Urbana IL 61801 Office: Abris Ltd Architects & Planners 214 W Main Urbana IL 61801

REICHEL, LEE ELMER, mechanical engineer; b. Cin., Aug. 30, 1944; s. Elmer William and Catherine Ann (Heidlemann) R.; m. Cheryl Christine Feagans, May 7, 1966; 1 child, Geoffrey William. A in Mech. Engring., Ohio Coll. Applied Sci., 1965; BS in Engring., U. Dayton, 1980. Registered mech. engr., Ohio. Project engr. Koehring, Master Div., Dayton, 1968-77, mgr. engring., 1978-81; project engr. Micro Devices, Dayton, 1977-78; mgr. mech. engring. dept. Xetron Corp., Cin., 1985; mgr. product engring. Dayton-Walther, Dayton, 1981-85, mgr. new product devel., 1985—. Patentee in field. Mem. Alter High Sch. Booster Bd., Kettering, Ohio, 1984-86. Mem. NSPE, Soc. Automotive Engrs., Ohio Soc. Profl. Engrs. Republican. Roman Catholic. Avocations: guitar, racquetball, tennis. Home: 2325 Colony Way Kettering OH 45440

REICHELT, FERDINAND HERBERT, insurance and real estate corporation executive; b. Chgo., Jan. 26, 1941; s. Ferdinand W. and Justine E. (Schuetpelz) R.; m. Diane Bethel Peters, Nov. 14, 1964; children—Christine, Brian. B.S., U. Ill., 1963; postgrad. Loyola U., Chgo., 1964. C.P.A., Ill. Supr., mgr. Peat Marwick & Mitchell, Chgo., 1963-70; actuary, 1966-68, mgr., Omaha, 1970-72; chief fin. officer CMI Investment Corp. and subs., Madison, Wis., 1972-78; exec. v.p. Verex Corp. and subs., Madison, 1978-85, chief operating officer, 1983-86, pres., chief exec. officer, 1986—, also bd. dirs. Treas. Madison Civic Ctr. Found., 1981—; bd. dirs. Festival of Lakes; chmn. Friends of WHA-TV, Inc., 1983; trustee Edgewood Coll.; mem. bd. advisors Clin. Cancer Ctr., U. Wis., Elvehjem Art Ctr., Madison, 1986—. Served with USAF, 1963-69. Mem. Nat. Assn. Accts., Nat. Investor Relations Inst., Wis. Inst. C.P.A.s, Ill. Inst. C.P.A.s, Nebr. Inst. C.P.A.s, Nat. Assn. Ind. Insurers, Fin. Execs. Inst, Madison C. of C. (bd. dirs.). Lutheran. Clubs: PGA Nat. Golf (Palm Beach Gardens, Fla.); Nakoma Golf, Madison (Madison). Editor: Secondary Mortgage Market Handbook; guest columnist Barrons; contbr. to profl. publs. Office: Verex Corp PO Box 7066 Madison WI 53707

REICHERT, GERALD RUSSELL, accountant; b. Toledo, May 16, 1948; s. Donald Russell and Shirley Mae (Hoover) R.; m. Janet Mary Rimelspach, Aug. 10, 1974; 1 child, Jacqueline Christina. AA in Acctg., Davis Jr. Coll., Toledo, 1971; BS, Ft. Lauderdale (Fla.) U., 1973. CPA, Ohio. Asst. mgr. Hollywood Beach Country Club, Fla., 1972-74; auditor in charge Auditor of State of Ohio, Columbus, 1974-81; v.p. Buckingham & Assoc., Inc., Findlay, Ohio, 1981—. Served with U.S. Army. Mem. Am. Inst. CPA's (discussion leader 1977—), Ohio Soc. CPA's, Assn. Govt. Accts., Gov. Service Com. Ohio Soc. CPA's, Findlay Estate Planning Dem., C. of C. State and Local Govt. Com., Govt. Fin. Officer Assn. (reviewer CAFR 1984—). Lodge: KC (program chmn. Findlay club 1984). Avocations: gourmet cooking, White River rafting, racquetball. Office: Buckingham & Assocs Inc Diamond S & L Bldg 3d Floor Findlay OH 45840

REICHERT, JACK FRANK, business executive; b. West Allis, Wis., Sept. 27, 1930; s. Arthur Andrew and Emily Bertha (Wallinger) R.; m. Corrine Violet Helf, Apr. 5, 1952; children: Susan Marie, John Arthur. Cert. mktg., U. Wis.-Milw., 1957; M.A., Harvard U., 1970. Various mktg. positions Gen. Electric Co., 1948-57; with Brunswick Corp., Skokie, Ill., 1957—; pres. Mercury Marine div. Brunswick Corp., 1972-77, corp. v.p., 1974-77, group v.p. Marine Power Group, 1974-77, pres., chief operating officer, 1977—, chief exec. officer, 1982—, chmn. bd., 1983—, dir., 1977—; dir. Greyhound Corp., Phoenix. Trustee Carroll Coll., Waukesha, Wis., 1972; bd. dirs. INROADS/Chgo., Inc.; indsl. chmn. Fond du Lac United Fund, 1977. Served with C.E. U.S. Army, 1951-53. Mem. Am. Mgmt. Assn. (mem. adv. council). Presbyterian. Clubs: Knollwood (Lake Forest, Ill.); Harvard (Chgo.); Metropolitan, Mid-America. Home: 580 Douglas Dr Lake Forest IL 60045 Office: Brunswick Corp 1 Brunswick Plaza Skokie IL 60077

REICHERT, TIMOTHY J., pediatric otolaryngologist; b. Dickinson, N.D., Dec. 27, 1944; s. Henry Lawrence and Virgina Ann (Conover) R.; m. Mary Gassmann, June 8, 1968. BS in Nat. Sci., St. John's U., 1965; BS in Medicine, U. N.D., 1967; MD, U. Ill., 1969. Pediatric otolaryngologist St. Louis Children's Hosp., 1977-80, St. John's Mercy Med., St. Louis, 1980—, St. Luke's Hosp., St. Louis, 1980—; vis. surgeon Presbyn. Hosp. Korea, Kwanju, Rep. of Korea., 1982, Cath. Near East Welfare, Jerusalem, 1983, 86. Author: Pediatric Otolaryngology, 1984. Bd. dirs. St. Mary's Spl. Sch., St. Louis, 1986. Mem. Am. Soc. Pediatric Otolaryngology (fellow exec. com. subsection 1984-86), Am. Acad. Pediatrics (subsect.), St. Louis Found. for Ear Nose and Throat Problems in Children (bd. dirs.). Republican. Avocations: jogging, reading. Home: #15 Log Cabin Dr Ladue MO 63124 Office: St Lukes Hosp 777 S New Ballas Suite 129E Saint Louis MO 63141

REICHGOTT, EMBER DARLENE, lawyer, state senator; b. Detroit, Aug. 22, 1953; d. Norbert Arnold and Diane (Pincich) R. B.A. summa cum laude, St. Olaf Coll., Minn., 1974; J.D., Duke U., 1977. Bar: Minn. 1977, D.C. 1978. Assoc., Larkin, Hoffman, Daly & Lindgren, Bloomington, Minn., 1977-84; counsel Control Data Corp., Bloomington, Minn., 1984-86 ; legal cons. Home Free Battered Women's Shelter, Plymouth, Minn., 1978—; mem.

Minn. State Senate, 1983—. Chmn. Legis. Commn. on Econ. Status of Women, 1984—; Vice chmn. Senate Judiciary Com., 1983-86, Senate Edn. Com., 1987—; mem. exec. com. Minn. Job Skills Partnership; trustee, N.W. YMCA, New Hope, Minn., 1983—. Youngest woman ever elected to Minn. State Senate, 1983; recipient Woman of Yr. award North Hennepin Bus. and Prof. Women, 1983; Award for Contbn. to Human Services, Minn. Social Services Assn., 1983; Disting. Service award Mpls. Jaycees, 1984; named One of Ten Outstanding Young Minnesotans, Minn. Jaycees, 1984. Mem. Minn. Bar Assn., Hennepin County Bar Assn. Mem. Minn. Democratic Farmer-Labor Party (del. nat. Dem. conv. 1984, state exec. com. 1980-82). Home: 7701 48th Ave N New Hope MN 55428

REICIN, RONALD IAN, lawyer; b. Chgo., Dec. 11, 1942; s. Frank Edward and Abranita (Rome) R.; m. Alyta Friedland, May 23, 1965; children—Eric, Kael. B.B.A., U. Mich., 1964, M.B.A., 1967, J.D. cum laude, 1967. Bar: Ill. 1967, U.S. Tax Ct. 1967. Mem. staff Price Waterhouse & Co., Chgo., 1966; ptnr. Jenner & Block, Chgo., 1967—. Bd. dirs. Nat. Kidney Found. Ill., 1978—, Scoliosis Assn. Chgo., 1981—, Ruth Page Found. Mem. Chgo. Bar Assn., Internat. Conf. Shopping Ctrs., ABA, Ill. Bar Assn., Chgo. Mortgage Attys. Assn., Phi Kappa Phi, Beta Gamma Sigma, Beta Alpha Psi. Clubs: Executive, Legal (Chgo.). Home: 1916 Berkeley Rd Highland Park IL 60035 Office: Jenner & Block 1 IBM Plaza 43d Floor Chicago IL 60611

REICKERT, ERICK ARTHUR, automotive executive; b. Newport, Tenn., Aug. 30, 1935; s. Frederick Arthur and Reva M. (Irish) R.; m. Diane Lois Comens, June 10, 1961 (div. Jan. 1979); children: Craig A., Laura L.; m. Heather Kathlene Ross, Sept. 1, 1982. BSEE, Northwestern U., 1958; MBA, Harvard U., 1965. Various positions Ford Motor Co., Dearborn, Mich., 1965-74, exec. dir. small car planning, 1979-84; v.p. export ops. Ford Motor Co., Brentwood, Eng., 1974-79; v.p. advance product devel. Chrysler Motors, Detroit, 1984-86, v.p. program mgmt., 1986-87; v.p., mng. dir. Chrysler Mexico, 1987—. Mem. Soc. Automotive Engrs., Engring. Soc. Detroit, Harvard Bus. Sch. Club of Detroit. Avocations: photography, travel, sailing, skiing. Office: Chrysler Motors 12000 Chrysler Dr Highland Park MI 48288

REID, BAXTER ELLIS, JR., labor union representative; b. Peoria, Ill., Feb. 10, 1943; s. Baxter Ellis and Ardeane Mary (Braunagel) R.; m. Debra Kay Bowers, May 20, 1977 (div. Nov. 1983); children: Mary Linn, Baxter Ellis III; m. Charlene Teresa Badaukis, Oct. 20, 1984; 1 child, Charles Austin. Factory worker Caterpillar Tractor, Peoria, 1963-75; local rep. UAW, Peoria, 1963-75; internat. rep. v.p. staff UAW, Detroit, 1975-85, internat. rep. pres. staff, 1985-86, asst. dir. arbitration dept., 1986—, also mem. staff council internat. reps., 1977—. Contbr. articles to union jours. Mem.-at-large NAACP; Dem. precinct committeeman Peoria County, 1973-75, Dem. vice chmn., 1974-75; Dem. precinct del. Wayne County, Mich., 1986—, Dem. conv. del., 1986—. Served as cpl. USMC, 1962-64. Mem. Am. Arbitration Assn. (cons. 1987—), Indsl. Relations Research Assn. Avocation: collecting polit. paraphernalia. Home: 3239 Stuart Ln Dearborn MI 48120 Office: Internat Union-UAW 8000 E Jefferson Ave Detroit MI 48214

REID, BONNIE LEE, junior high school principal; b. St. Louis, Jan. 30, 1937; d. William Charles Lovrenic and Fern Lee (Swingler) Reiman; m. Thomas James Fitzsimmons, Aug. 16, 1958 (div. Aug. 1966); children: Susan Lee, Scott James; m. Donald Francis Reid, Nov. 18, 1966; stepchildren: Christopher Kearns, Donald Francis Jr., Connie Ann, Britton Anthony, Douglas Nye. BE, U. Mo., 1958; MA in Adminstrn., Washington U., St. Louis, 1977, postgrad., 1978-80. Cert. tchr., Mo.; cert. secondary adminstr., Mo. Tchr. Webster Groves (Mo.) High Sch., 1958-60; tchr., dept. chmn. Parkway Sch. Dist., Chesterfield, Mo., 1971-81, asst. prin., 1982-83, assoc. prin., 1984, interim prin., 1985; prin. Parkway E. Jr. High Sch., Chesterfield, 1986—; mem. governance com. Gov.'s Conf. Edn., 1978. Fellow Prin.'s Acad.; mem. Nat. Assn. Secondary Sch. Prins., Assn. Supervision and Curriculum Devel. (consortium sch. team leader 1986—) , Nat. Middle Sch. Assn. (conf. edn.), Mortar Bd., Mo. State Future Tchrs. Am., Parkway Ind. Community Tchrs. Assn., Greater St. Louis Tchrs. Assn., Delta Kappa Gamma, Kappa Alpha Theta, Pi Lambda Theta, Phi Sigma Iota, Kappa Epsilon Alpha, Sigma Rho Sigma. Republican. Presbyterian. Avocations: travel, needlepoint. Office: Parkway E Jr High Sch 181 Coeur De Ville Creve Coeur MO 63141

REID, GERALDINE WOLD (GERALDINE REID SKJERVOLD), artist; b. Portland, Oreg., Apr. 11, 1944; d. Alden Elroy and Verna (Kocinski) Wold; B.A. in Fine Art, Calif. State U., Sacramento, 1972, M.F.A., 1975; postgrad. Ind. U.-Purdue U. Instr. dental aux. edn. U. Minn., 1966-70; anthrop. research asst., 1975-76; asst. prof. dental aux. edn. Ind. U.-Purdue U., 1976-78; mng. editor Nat. Arts Guide, Chgo., 1978-80; freelance artist, Chgo., 1981—; pres. Chgo. Art Emerging Inc., 1983—; graphic artist Reid Communications, Chgo., 1981—; dir. show coordination Circle Fine Art, Chgo., 1981; seminar lectr., 1977, 86. One-woman shows include Artists' Coop. Gallery, Santa Fe, 1976, Artlink, Ft. Wayne, Ind., 1979, 84—, D.E.O. Fine Arts, Inc., Chgo., 1982-83; group exhbns. include Crocker Art Mus., Sacramento, 1975, Ft. Wayne Mus. Art, 1978, Artists Guild Chgo., 1981, Charles A. Wustum Mus., Racine, Wis., 1983, Limelight, Chgo., 1986, Neville-Sargent Gallery, 1986, 87. Mem. Artists Guild Chgo., Chgo. Artists' Coalition.

REID, JAMES SIMS, JR., automobile parts manufacturer; b. Cleve., Jan. 15, 1926; s. James Sims and Felice (Crowl) R.; m. Donna Smith, Sept. 2, 1950; children: Sally, Susan, Anne (dec.), Jeanne. A.B. cum laude, Harvard U., 1948, J.D., 1951. Bar: Mich., Ohio 1951. Practice law Detroit, 1951-52, Cleve., 1953-56; with Standard Products Co., Cleve., 1956—, pres., 1962—, now also chmn., dir.; dir. Soc. Corp., Cleve. Office: Standard Products Co 2130 W 110th St Cleveland OH 44102

REID, SHERRI JO, tax preparation company executive; b. Maquoketa, Iowa, June 22, 1941; d. William Earle and Luella Augusta (Teters) Wells; m. Gary Harrison Hicks, July 2, 1958 (dec. Apr. 1973); children: Bryon Keith, Scott Allen; m. Ronald Dwight Reid, July 21, 1977; stepchildren: Mark Douglas, Dwight David, Curtis Duane. Grad. pub. schs., Maquoketa. Enrolled to practice before IRS. Proof operator Jackson (Iowa) State Bank, 1958-61; co-owner, mgr. Hicks TV & Appliances, Maquoketa, 1961-72; tax practitioner Schoenthaler & Schoenthaler, Roberg, Maq Iowa, 1972-75; owner, tax cons. Sherri's Tax Service, Onslow, Iowa, 1975—; enrolled agt., owner, computer programmer Reid Enterprises, Onslow, 1975—. Mem. Nat. Assn. Tax Practitioners, Nat. Fedn. Ind. Bus., Nat. Assn. Enrolled Agts., Nat. Assn. Pub. Accts. Republican. Methodist. Clubs: Garden (Maquoketa); Claytonian (Onslow). Avocations: geology, science, fishing, crafts, flower arranging. Home and Office: Sherri's Tax Service Rural Rt 1 Box 27 Onslow IA 52321

REID, VALERIE LYNN, librarian; b. Cleve., Dec. 13, 1956; d. Robert Hershel and Marilyn Lucille (Hout) Timson; m. Douglas Holden Reid, July 27, 1985. BE, U. Mich., Dearborn, 1978; MLS, Wayne State U., 1980. Cert. med. librarian. Library clk. Dearborn Dept. Libraries, 1973-79; library tech. asst. Henry Ford Hosp., Detroit, 1979-80, asst. librarian, 1980—. Mem. Med. Library Assn. Home: 950 S Lafayette Dearborn MI 48124 Office: Henry Ford Hosp Sladen Library 2799 W Grand Blvd Detroit MI 48202

REIDELBACH, MICHAEL JOSEPH, SR., marketing executive; b. Columbus, Ohio, Feb. 24, 1946; s. William George and Mary Beatrice (Geis) R.; m. Vicki Lee Carter, Feb. 14, 1970 (div. Jan. 1987); children: Michael Joseph Jr., Jeffrey Allen. BS in Engring., Ohio State U., 1969; MBA, Syracuse U., 1974. Chief engr. Corning Glass, Danville, Ky., 1974-75; staff mgr. Corning Glass, Corning, N.Y., 1975-76, plant mgr., 1976-83, dir. mktg., 1983-85; v.p. mktg. Richardson Smith Inc, Worthington, Ohio, 1985-87; pres. Meretrends Inc, Columbus, Ohio, 1987—. Bd. dirs. Mon Valley Progress Council, Monesson, Pa., Charlbroi C. of C., 1979-83, Boy Scouts Am., Pitts., 1980-83; pres. United Way Monongahela Valley, Monesson, 1983. Mem. Keramos, Ohio State U. Alumni Assn. Republican. Roman Catholic. Clubs: Worthington Hills Country, Corning Country. Avocations: golf, tennis, skiing, basketball. Home: 1411 Briarmeadow Dr Worthington OH 43085 Office: Meretrends Inc 645 S Grant Ave Columbus OH 43206

REIDER, BRUCE, orthopedic surgeon; b. N.Y.C., Feb. 9, 1949; s. Edward and Blanche (Goodman) R.; m. Patricia Simmons, Nov. 30, 1985. AB magna cum laude, Yale U., 1971; MD, Harvard U., 1975. Cert. Am. Bd. Orthopaedic Surgery. Intern in gen. surgery Columbia-Presbyn. Hosp., N.Y.C, 1975-76; visiting clin. fellow Columbia U., N.Y.C., 1975-76; fellow in surgery Cornell U., Ithaca, N.Y., 1976-78; resident in orthopaedic surgery Hosp. for Spl. Surgery, N.Y.C., 1977-80; fellow in sports medicine U. Wis., Madison, 1980-81; assoc. prof. surgery U. Chgo., 1981—; instr. in surgery Cornell U., Ithaca, 1978-80; dir. sports medicine, head team physician U. Chgo. Contbr. articles to profl. jours. A.O. Internat. scholar, 1981; grantee Lilly Research Labs., Wm. H. Rorer Co., The Whitaker Found. Fellow Am. Acad. Orthopaedic Surgeons; mem. AMA, Am. Coll. Sports Medicine, Am. Orthopaedic Soc. for Sports Medicine, Orthopaedic Research Soc., Ill. Orthopaedic Soc., Chgo. Orthopaedic Soc., U.S. Powerlifting Soc., Yale Alumni Assn. (fundraiser 1971—), Phi Beta Kappa. Club: Quadrangle (Chgo.). Avocations: scuba diving, windsurfing. Home: 2500 Lakeview Apt 802 Chicago IL 60614 Office: U Chgo 5841 S Maryland Box 421 Chicago IL 60637

REIDER, JAMES WILLIAM, advertising and marketing consultant, health and safety professional; b. Mpls., June 25, 1952; s. William H. and Marilyn M. (Fish) R.; m. Mary K. Johnson, July 10, 1976; children: Christina Marie, Jessica Anne. Student Defiance Coll., 1970-72, U. Denver, 1972-74; BA, U. Minn., 1983. Cert. protection profl.; cert. health care safety profl. Safety and security mgr. K-Mart Corp., Mpls., 1974-76; ops. and safety mgr. Park Detective Agy., Inc., Mpls., 1976-77; ops. mgr. Twin City Security, 1977; security and safety officer Hennepin County Med. Ctr., Mpls., 1977-78, safety officer, 1978-81; corp. dir. security Abbott-Northwestern Hosp., Mpls., 1981; dir. tech. services Fred S. James & Co., 1982-84; pres. Write/ Comm Inc., 1984-86; pres., chief exec. officer Advt. for the Masses, Inc., 1986—; account exec. M.R. Bolin Advt., 1984-85; cons. tech. writing, loss control, advt., mktg. Active CAP, 1962-80, capt., 1978-80; mem. com. to draft city fire regulations ordinances for health care facilities Mpls. Fire Dept., 1980-81. Mem. Am. Soc. Safety Engrs., Nat. Safety Mgmt. Soc., Am. Soc. Indsl. Security, Sigma Phi Epsilon. Office: 13722 Nicollet Ave S Suite 217 Burnsville MN 55337

REIDY, BEN T., banking company executive; b. 1933. BA, U. Notre Dame, 1955; MBA, Harvard U., 1958. Sr. v.p. No. Trust Bank, Chgo., 1959-78; vice chmn. bd. dirs. Madden Group, Chgo., 1979-84; pres. Unibank Trust, Chgo., 1984—; also bd. dirs. Unibank Trust. Served with AUS, 1953-58. Office: Unibanctrust Sears Tower 233 S Wacker Dr Chicago IL 60606 *

REIDY, JOSEPH MICHAEL, lawyer; b. Cleve., Sept. 23, 1955; s. Thomas Charles and Elizabeth Jane (Haas) R.; m. Judith Kemmerling, Aug. 13, 1977; children: Meghan, Erin. BS, U. Cin., 1977; MA in Zoology, De Pauw U., 1979; JD, Capital U., 1985. Bar: Ohio 1985. Lab. asst. U. Cin., 1976-77; research assoc. DePauw U., Greencastle, Ind., 1977-79; aquatic biologist Ohio EPA, Columbus, 1979-84, legal liaison, 1984-85; assoc. Carlile, Patchen, Murphy & Allison, Columbus, 1985—. Research editor Capital U. law rev., 1984-85. Mem. pub. adv. group Ohio EPA, 1985—, ground water task force, 1986—; ground water task force Ohio Environ. Council, 1986, Ohio Alliance for the Environment, 1986. Mem. ABA (vice chmn. toxic torts, environ. litigation com. natural resources sect.), Ohio State Bar Assn., Columbus Bar Assn., Assn. Trial Lawyers Am., Order of the Curia, Phi Alpha Delta. Democrat. Roman Catholic. Club: Columbus Roadrunners. Avocations: competitive running, whitewater rafting, woodworking. Office: Carlile Patchen Murphy & Allison 366 E Broad St Columbus OH 43215

REIFEL, ALLAN JAMES, manufacturing company executive; b. St. Louis, Jan. 15, 1941; s. Harry Vernon and Luella Lydia (Linders) R.; m. Janet Patsy Lang, Sept. 14, 1963; children: Sherry, David, Julie, Michael, Stephen, Daniel, Matthew, Rebekah. BSME, U. Mo., Rolla, 1972, MSME, 1973. Registered profl. engr., Mo. Engring. rep. Carter Carburetor, St. Louis, 1962-68; devel. engr. The Trane Co., LaCrosse, Wis., 1973-77; group product engr. Watlow Electric Co., St. Louis, 1977-80; dir. engring. Intertherm, Inc., St. Louis, 1980—. Patentee in field. Bd. dirs. St. Louis Christian Sch. Soc. (fin. sec. 1984—). Served with U.S. Army, 1961-62. Mem. Am. Soc. Mech. Engrs., Am. Soc. Heating, Refrigerating and Air Conditioning Engrs. Baptist. Avocations: woodworking, church work. Home: 245 Wren Dr Florissant MO 63031 Office: Intertherm Inc 3345 Morganford Rd Saint Louis MO 63116

REIFENBERG, JOSEPH OLIVER, financial analyst; b. Evanston, Ill., Aug. 18, 1960; s. John James and Betty J. (Sherman) R. Student, Oakton Community Coll., 1978-80; BS in Acctg., No. Ill. U., 1983; postgrad., Loyola U., 1985—. CPA, Ill., cert. mgmt. accountant, Ill. Pvt. practice acctg. 1983—; staff acct. Cook Electric div. No. Telecom, Morton Grove, Ill., 1983-85; cost analyst Cook Electric div. No. Telecom, Morton Grove, 1985-86, sr. fin. analyst, 1986—. Mem. Am. Inst. CPA's, Inst. Cert. Mgmt. Accts., Ill. CPA Soc. Roman Catholic. Avocation: park dist. softball leagues.

REIFF, JAMES STANLEY, addictions physician, osteopathic physician, surgeon; b. Chgo., Mar. 17, 1935; s. Nathan Edgar and Freda Matilda (Imhoff) R.; m. Sharon Ann Kraybill, June 9, 1956 (div. Apr. 1970); children—Gregory James, James Stanley II, Cynthia Diane, Jeffery Cameron. B.A. in Chemistry, Goshen Coll., 1957; D.O., Chgo. Coll. Osteo. Medicine, 1961. Biochemist Miles/Ames Pharm. Co., Elkhart, Ind., 1955-57; gen. practice medicine, Michigan City, Ind., 1962-69; addictions physician Oaklawn Psychiat. Ctr., Elkhart, Ind. 1974-84; clin. team leader, addictions team Oaklawn Ctr., Elkhart, 1980-83. Alcohol Anonymous Cen. Service Area Inc., 1984—. Bd. dirs. Home for Runaway Kids - Victory House, Elkhart, Ind., 1974-76, 12 Step House Meth. Ch.-Halfway House, Elkhart, 1974-77; bd. dirs., treas. Caldwell Home Corp.-Social Rehab. Ctr. for Alcoholism, Elkhart, 1984-87. Mem. Am. Med. Soc. on Alcoholism, Ind. State Med. Assn. Avocations: organ and piano playing.

REIFKE, JOHN THOMAS, dentist; b. Cleve., Sept. 25, 1904; s. Henry Albert and Ellen (Keyes) R.; m. Mildred Ann Holland, Aug. 20, 1930; children: Nancy, Joan, Rosemary. Pre-dental student, John Carrol U., 1922-24; DDS, Case Western Reserve U., 1928. Gen. practice dentistry Cleve., 1928—; dental dept. staff St. Vincent Hosp., Cleve., 1928-40. Fellow Internat. Coll. Dentists (treas. 1969—); mem. ADA (del., council Ins. 1963-69), Cleve. Dental Soc. (past pres., citation 1971), Ohio Dental Assn. (past pres., del., Disting. Dentist award 1978), Case Western Reserve U. Dental Alumni Assn. (Disting. Dentists award 1981-82), Psi Omega,. Republican. Roman Catholic. Avocations: gardening, photography. Home: 2391 Lalemant Rd University Heights OH 44118

REIGEL, DON, former business executive; b. Deer River, Minn., Sept. 4, 1914; s. Jake and Marion (Shabel) R.; B.A., cum laude, Carleton Coll., 1936; postgrad. Minn. Sch. Bus., 1942; grad. Command and General Staff Coll., Fort Leavenworth, Kans., 1963; postgrad. in polit. sci. Mankato (Minn.) State U.; m. Mary Jane Scott, Oct. 24, 1942; children—Marc, Kent. Auditor, Stearns Lumber Co., Hutchinson, Minn., 1936-42; advt. mgr. U.S. Check Book Co., Omaha, 1946-50, Journ.-Chronicle Co., Owatonna, Minn., 1950-56; pub., owner Photo News, Owatonna, 1956-73; pres. Reigel Corp., 1973-79; info. officer vocat. rehab./econ. devel. State of Minn., 1974-84. Tchr. U. Omaha and Van Sant Sch. of Bus., Omaha, 1946-50, Mankato State Coll., 1972-73, Rasmussen Sch. Bus., 1978-79, Globe Bus. Coll., 1981-84. Pres. Owatonna Community Chest, 1954; dist. chmn. Wasioja dist. Boy Scouts of Am., 1955-56; chmn. long range planning and research com. Minn. United Meth. Conf. Mem. Minn. Ho. of Reps. from Steele County, 1968-70. Bd. dirs. Paul Watkins Home, Winona, 1966-72. Served to capt. AUS, 1942-46; to lt. col. Res. Mem. Minn. Newspaper Assn. (chmn. advt. com. 1962-63), Nat. Editorial Assn. Club: Sr. Active. Lodges: Rotary (sec. 1955-76), Masons. Home: 558 E South St Owatonna MN 55060

REILING, RICHARD BERNARD, physician; b. Dayton, Ohio, June 29, 1941; s. Walter Anthony Sr. and E. Dorothy (Unger) R.; m. Elizabeth Castellini, June 20, 1964; children: Maureen Elizabeth, Richard Bernard Jr. BS, U. Dayton, 1963; MD, Harvard U., 1967. Diplomate Nat. Bd. Med. Examiners. Intern, then residentin surgery Boston City Hosp., 1967-73; fellow in surgery Lahey Clinic Found., Boston, 1970; practice medicine specializing in surgery Kettering, Ohio, 1975—; assoc. clin. prof. surgery Wright State U., 1979—; chief of staff Kettering (Ohio) Med. Ctr., 1982-83. Contbr. articles to profl. jours. Scoutmaster Boy Scouts Am., Kettering, 1982-85. Served to maj. USAF, 1973-75. Fellow ACS (past pres. Ohio chpt. 1986-87); mem. AMA, Ohio Med. Assn., Montgomery County Med. Soc., Societe Internationale de Chirgerie. Avocations: tennis, sailing, skiing. Home: 441 Timberlea Trail Kettering OH 45429 Office: 5441 Far Hills Ave Kettering OH 45429

REILING, ROGER JOSEPH, insurance company executive; b. St. Paul, Aug. 3, 1937; s. George John and Theresa Marie (Hofbauer) R.; m. Gladys Marie Nielsen, Nov. 22, 1961; children: Margo Maria, Grant Randall, Jay Justin. BA, Hamline U., 1961. Mktg. rep. St. Paul Ins. Co., 1961-65, Safeco Ins. Co., Seattle, 1965-75; ins. agt., v.p. Keller Ins. Agy., St. Paul, 1975-84; ins. agt., pres. Red Carpet Ins. Agy., Mpls., 1984—. Chairperson bd. dirs. Roseville Arts Council, Minn., 1984—. Mem. Soc. Cert. Ins. Counselors (cert. 1979), Hamline U. Alumni Assn. (pres. 1982-83), Suburban Area C. of C. (pres., bd. dirs. 1983—). Unitarian. Avocations: fund-raising for non-profit orgns., travel, dining. Home: 1877 Gluek Ln Roseville MN 55113 Office: Red Carpet Ins Agy Ltd 3433 NE Broadway Minneapolis MN 55413

REILLY, PETER C., chemical company executive; b. Indpls., Jan. 19, 1907; s. Peter C. and Ineva (Gash) R.; A.B., U. Colo., 1929; M.B.A., Harvard U., 1931; m. Jeanette Parker, Sept. 15, 1932; children—Marie (Mrs. Jack H. Heed), Sara Jean (Mrs. Clarke Wilhelm), Patricia Ann (Mrs. Michael Davis). With accounting dept. Republic Creosoting Co., Indpls., 1931-32; sales dept. Reilly Tar & Chem. Corp., N.Y.C., 1932-36, v.p., Eastern mgr., 1936-52; v.p. sales, treas. both cos., Indpls., 1952-59, pres., 1959-73, chmn. bd., 1973-75, vice chmn., 1975-82, chmn., 1982—; dir. Environ. Quality Control Inc.; past dir. Ind. Nat. Corp., Ind. Union Ry., Ind. Nat. Bank. Dir. Goodwill Industries Found.; past bd. dirs. United Fund Greater Indpls., Indpls. Symphony Orch.; bd. govs. Jr. Achievement Indpls. Mem. adv. council U. Notre Dame Sch. Commerce, 1947—; mem. adv. council Winona Meml. Hosp. Recipient Sagamore of Wabash award. Mem. Chem. Spltys. Mfg. Assn. (life; treas. 1950-60, past dir.), Mfg. Chemists Assn. (past dir.), Am. Chem. Soc., Soc. Chem. Industry (past dir. Am. sect. 1979—). Clubs: Union League, Harvard, Chemist (N.Y.C.); Larchmont (N.Y.) Yacht; Indianapolis Athletic, Pine Valley Golf (N.J.), Meridian Hills Country, Columbia (Indpls.); Rotary, One Hundred (past dir.); Crooked Stick Golf. Home: 3777 Bay Rd North Dr Indianapolis IN 46240 Office: Market Square Center 151 N Delaware St Suite 1510 Indianapolis IN 46204

REILLY, RALPH ARTHUR, orthopedic surgeon; b. Cleve., June 13, 1921; s. Arthur John and Gladys Josephine (Pusch) R.; m. Ruth Ann Daniels. BA, Western Res. U., 1943; MD, Hahnemann U., 1947; postgrad. in orthopaedic surgery, U. Pa., 1949. Intern St. Luke's Hosp., Cleve., 1947-48; resident in gen. surgery Lakewood (Ohio) Hosp., 1958-49; resident orthopaedic surgery Akron (Ohio) City Hosp., 1949-50, Cleve. Clinic, 1953, Kernan Crippled Children's Hosp., Balt., 1953-54; chmn. dept. orthopaedic surgery Lakewood (Ohio) Hosp., 1970—. Contbr. articles to med. jours. Trustee West Shore Concerts Assn., Lakewood, 1965-70, Cleve. Chamber Music Soc., 1970-73. Served to capt. USAF, 1951-53. Fellow Am. Acad. Orthopaedic Surgery, bd. of councillors; mem. ACS, Cleve. Orthopaedic Club (pres. 1968—), MidAm. Orthopaedic Assn., Nat. Assn. of Disability Evaluating Physicians (charter mem.). Episcopalian. Clubs: Westwood Country (Rocky River, Ohio); Western Res. Kennel (Cleve.). Avocations: dog breeding, showing and judging. Home: 17428 Edgewater Dr Lakewood OH 44107 Office: 14601 Detroit Ave Lakewood OH 44107

REILLY, ROBERT FREDERICK, valuation consultant; b. N.Y.C., Oct. 3, 1952; s. James J. and Marie (Griebel) R.; m. Janet H. Steiner, May 17, 1975; children: Ashley Lauren, Brandon Christopher. BA in Econs., Columbia U., 1974, MBA in Fin., 1975. CPA. Sr. cons. Booz, Allen & Hamilton, Cin., 1975-76; dir. corp. planning Huffy Corp., Dayton, Ohio, 1976-81; v.p. Arthur D. Little Valuation, Inc., Chgo., 1981-85; nat. dir. valuation engring. and appraisal services Touche Ross & Co., Chgo., 1985—; adj. prof. accounting U. Dayton Grad. Sch. Bus., 1977-81; adj. prof. fin. econs., Elmhurst (Ill.) Coll., 1982—; adj. prof. fin. Ill. Inst. Tech. Grad. Sch. Bus., Chgo., 1985—; adj. prof. taxation U. Chgo. Grad. Sch. Bus., 1985—. Contbr. articles to profl. jours. Mem. Am. Soc. Appraisers (bd. examiners 1985—), Nat. Assn. Accts.(chpt. dir. 1976—), Inst. Property Taxation, Soc. Mfg. Engrs., Am. Inst. CPA's, Ill. Soc. CPA's, Ohio Soc. CPA (chpt. dir. 1978-81). Home: 427 W Walnut St Hinsdale IL 60521 Office: Touche Ross & Co 111 E Wacker Dr Chicago IL 60601

REINDERS, LEONARD HERMAN, university program administrator; b. Alliance, Nebr., May 4, 1937; s. Herman I. and Cathryn L. (Tichner) R.; m. Linda M. Shay, July 15, 1958 (div. July 1971); children: Laurie Vaugn, Daniel, Marcy Daza, Karen; m. Janet A. Schurr, Dec. 29, 1972; 1 child, Heath I. BA in Edn., Chadron State Coll., 1962; cert., U. Nebr., 1969, Northwestern U., 1970. Cert. rehab. counselor. Guidance counselor Valentine (Nebr.) Pub. Schs., 1962-66; psychiat. counselor Nebr. Dept. Edn., Norfolk and Omaha, 1966-71; dir. rehab. Cen. Nebr. Goodwill Industries, Grand Island, 1971-76; with Child Protective Services State of Nebr., Grand Island, 1976-81; personnel adminstr. USAR, Grand Island, 1981-85; advisor vocat. assessment Cen. Community Coll., Grand Island, 1985—. Served with USN,1954-58. Mem. Nat. Rehab. Assn., Nebr. Rehab. Assn., Nebr. State Edn. Assn., Nebr. Profl. Counselors Assn., Am. Legion. Democrat. Lutheran. Avocations: collectables, antiques. Home: Rural Rt 1 PO Box 55 Phillips NE 68865 Office: Cen Community Coll PO Box C Grand Island NE 68802

REINEMUND, STEVEN S., restaurant chain executive; b. Queens, N.Y., Apr. 6, 1948; s. Ott and Dora (Kramer) R.; m. Gail Timbers, Dec. 14, 1974; children: Steven S. Jr., Jonathan Craig. BS in Naval Sci., U.S. Naval Acad., 1970; MBA, U. Va., 1978. Commd. 2d lt. USMC, 1970, advanced through grades to capt., 1974, resigned, 1975; mktg. rep. IBM Corp., 1975-76; v.p., gen. mgr. Marriott-Roy Rogers, 1978-84; sr. v.p., field operator Pizza Hut, Inc., Wichita, Kans., 1984-86, exec. v.p., 1986, pres., chief exec. officer, 1986—. Sec., treas. bd. dirs. U. Va., Darden Sch. Alumni Assn.; bd. dirs. adv. bd. Bank IV Wichita Salvation Army. Named one of Outstanding Young Men Am. Republican. Presbyterian. Avocations: tennis, running. Home: 20 Colonial Ct Wichita KS 67207 Office: Pizza Hut Inc 9111 E Douglas Wichita KS 67207

REINER, JAMES ANTHONY, marketing executive; b. Orange, Calif., Sept. 12, 1958; s. Earl Arthur and Mary Ann (Cuff) R. BBA in Acctg., U. Mo., 1983, MBA in Mktg., 1984. Mktg. intern The Seven-UP Co., St. Louis, 1984-85; mktg. analyst Rawlings Sporting Goods, St. Louis, 1985-86; mktg. mgr. Rawlings Sporting Goods Co., St. Louis, 1986—. Mem. Am. Mktg. Assn., Alpha Mu Alpha (hon.). Republican. Avocations: drawing, painting, stainglass. Home: 41 W Old Watson Webster Groves MO 63119 Office: Rawlings Sporting Goods Co 1859 Intertech Saint Louis MO 63126

REINER, ROBERT WILLIAM, accountant; b. Cleve., May 14, 1957; s. William Howard and Frances Mae (Sabons) R.; m. Elizabeth Colleen Dailey, Oct. 17, 1981; 1 child, Christopher. B Adminstrv. Sci., Ohio State U., 1979. CPA, Ohio. Asst. acct. Peat, Marwick, Mitchell & Co., Cleve., 1979-80, staff acct., 1980-81, sr. acct., 1981-83, supervising sr., 1983-84, mgr., 1984-86; sr. mgr. Peat Marwick Main & Co., Cleve. and Canton, Ohio, 1986—. Vol. Cleve. Orch. Funds Dr., 1986, Cultural Ctr. for the Arts, Canton, 1987, State Devel. Bd. Small Bus. Assistance Vol. Program, Canton, 1987; loan executive United Way, Cen. Stark County, 1987. Mem. Am. Inst. CPA's, Ohio Soc. CPA's, Ohio Oil & Gas Assn., Ohio State Alumni Assn., Ind. Petroleum Assn. Am. Republican. Roman Catholic. Lodge: KC. Office: Peat Marwick Main & Co 220 Market Ave S Suite 740 Canton OH 44702

REINERS, ROCKFORD JONATHAN, military officer; b. San Tomé, Venezuela, Oct. 24, 1959; (parents Am. citizens); s. Stan D. and Nancy (Mitchell) R.; m. Ann Wylie Westbrook, July 28, 1984. BSCE, USAF Acad., 1982; MS in Internat. Relations, Troy State U., 1985; MS in Logistics Mgmt., Air Force Inst. Tech., 1986. Commd. 2d lt. USAF, 1982, advanced through grades to capt., 1986; reliability engr. armament div. USAF, Eglin AFB, Fla., 1982-85; staff officer Hdqrs. Air Force Logistics Command USAF, Wright-Patterson AFB, Ohio, 1986—. Recipient Eagle Scout award, Boy Scouts Am., 1977, commendation medal, USAF, 1985. Republican. Mo. State Wrestling Champion, 1978.

REINHARD, NORMAN ARTHUR, accountant; b. Dayton, Ohio, Feb. 6, 1939; s. Aloys J. and Rita B. (Eifert) R.; m. Edith A. Sarver, July 12, 1969; children: Pamela A., Brian J. BS in Acctg., U. Dayton, 1963. Acct. Timken Co., Canton, Ohio, 1963-69; data processing mgr. Nordson Corp., Amherst, Ohio, 1969-71; acct., ptnr. Main-Hurdman, Canton, 1971-85, Reinhard & Co., Canton, 1985—. Treas. Am. Heart Assn., Canton, 1981-86. Served with U.S. Army, 1957-59. Mem. Am. Inst. CPA's, Nat. Assn. Accts., Ohio Soc. CPA's (pres. Akron-Canton chpt. 1982-83), Planning Forum (v.p. communications 1986-87). Roman Catholic. Clubs: Canton; Congress Lake (Hartville, Ohio). Avocations: golf, reading. Office: 406 Bliss Tower Canton OH 44702

REINHARDT, JERALD WAYNE, obstetrician-gynecologist; b. Bismarck, N.D., Mar. 2, 1946; s. Raymond and Ozella Data (Ketterling) R.; m. JoAnn R. Jensen, June 1, 1968; children: Aaron, Alison, Joshua. BA, U. N.D., 1968, BS in Medicine, 1970; MD, U. Colo., 1972. Intern U. Colo., Denver, 1972-73, resident in ob-gyn, 1973-76; practice medicine specializing in ob-gyn Grand Forks, N.D., 1978—; chmn. dept. obstetrics United Hosp., Grand Forks, 1981-85, 86—. Served to maj. USAF, 1976-78. Fellow Am. Coll. Obstetricians and Gynecologists (vice chmn. N.D. sect. 1985—); mem. AMA, N.D. Med. Soc., N.D. Ob-Gyn Soc. (v.p. 1984-85, pres. 1985-86). Club: Grand Forks Country. Lodge: Elks. Home: 249 Circle Hills Dr Grand Forks ND 58201 Office: Grand Forks Clinic Ltd 1000 S Columbia Rd Grand Forks ND 58201

REINHERZ, RICHARD PHILLIP, podiatric surgeon, medical writer; b. Kenosha, Wis., Aug. 30, 1951; s. Howard R. and Faye L. (Deutch) R.; m. Sharon Rose Kimmel, July 16, 1978; children: Adam David, Benjamin Jeremy. BA in Biology cum laude, Washington U., St. Louis, 1973; D in Podiatric Medicine, Calif. Coll. Podiatric Medicine, San Francisco, 1976. Diplomate Am. Bd. Podiatric Surgery. Intern and resident in foot surgery Kern Hospital, Warren, Mich., 1976-77, chief resident, 1977-78; dir. residency program in foot surgery Am. Internat. Hosp., Zion, Ill., 1979-87; preceptor/lectr. Southeastern Wis. Family Practice Residency Program, Med. Coll. Wis., Kenosha, 1983—; now practice medicine specializing in podiatric surgery Kenosha, 1978—; mem. staff Kenosha Mem. Hosp, St. Catherine's Hosp., Kenosha, Hawthorne Med./Surgical Ctr., Libertyville, Ill.; textbook reviewer Scott, Foresman and Co., 1982; chmn. Kenosha Bd. Health, Wis., 1983-85; oral examiner for bd. cert. Am. Bd. Podiatric Surgery, 1985, 86; editorial bd. cons. Orthopedic Index (orthobase)-Med. Literature Rev., Inc., St. James, N.Y., 1986. Contbr. numerous articles to profl. jours. Scoutmaster Boy Scouts Am., San Francisco and Kenosha, 1974-76, 1978-80. Fellow Am. Coll. Foot Surgeons (editor-in-chief jour. 1980—); mem. Am. Med. Writers Assn., Am. Podiatric Med. Assn. (Jour. Writing award 1982, 84), Wis. Soc. Podiatric Medicine. Home: 1442 Chippewa Wheeling IL 60090 Office: 6801 Sheridan Rd Kenosha WI 53140

REINKE, DAVID ANTHONY, engineering manager, consultant; b. Jefferson City, Mo., July 6, 1950; s. Frank Fredric and Dorothy Regina (Bruning) R.; m. Alice Marie Schmidt, June 3, 1972; children: Michael, Timothy, Christopher. BSME, U. Mo., Rolla, 1972, MS in Engring., 1976. Registered profl. engr., Mo. Design engr. Westinghouse Electric Co., Jefferson City, 1972-77, sales engr., 1977-79, mktg. rep., 1979-81, engring. mgr., 1981—. Mem. U. Mo. Devel. Council, Rolla, 1983—; pres. Mary's Home (Mo.) Sch. Bd., 1983-86; judge Sci. and Engring. Fair, Jefferson City, 1984, 85. Named one of Outstanding Young Men Am., 1985. Mem. Nat. Soc. Profl. Engrs., U. Mo. Alumni Alliance. Republican. Roman Catholic. Lodge: Optimists (lt. gov. internat. br.St. Louis 1984-85), pres. Evening club Jefferson City 1981-82). Avocations: fishing, hunting, racquetball. Home: Rt7 2338 Lakewood Rd Jefferson City MO 65101 Office: Westinghouse Electric Corp. 500 Westinghouse Dr Jefferson City MO 65101

REINKE, LEONARD HERMAN, architect; b. Oshkosh, Wis., June 25, 1918; s. Leonard and Helen (Diestler) R.; m. Lucille Francis Fenn, Nov. 14, 1942; children—Ann Elizabeth, Mary Ellen, Joan Elaine. Student, U. Wis.-Oshkosh, 1936; B. in Architecture, Ill. Inst. Tech., 1941. Registered architect, Wis. Analyst Nat. Def. Research Commn., Princeton, N.J., 1943; architect designer Auler Irion Wertsch, Inc., Oshkosh, 1945-51; ptnr. T.H. Irion, AIA, L.H. Reinke, AIA, Oshkosh, 1951-69; sec., pres. Irion, Reinke & Assocs., Inc., Oshkosh, 1969-77; pres. Reinke, Hansche, Last, Inc., Oshkosh, 1978—; pres. Nicolet Anchorage, Inc., Oshkosh, 1962—. Architect: (library) Albertson Ctr., 1971 (Wis. AIA honor award), Polk Library, 1970; architectural designer Dartford Motor Inn, 1957(Wis. AIA honor award). Mem. Indsl. Devel. Com., Oshkosh, 1965-68, Riverfront Beautification Com., 1969-71, Parks Adv. Council, 1972-76; mem. bd. Paine Art Ctr. and Arboretum, Oshkosh, 1976-84. Served with USAF, 1944-45, ETO. Fellow AIA; mem. Wis. Soc. Architects (dir. 1959-63, 71-72, pres. 1964), Wis. Architects Found. (dir. 1978-84, pres. 1983-84). Republican. Presbyterian. Lodge: Rotary (dir. 1962-65). Avocations: cross county skiing, woodworking, travel, tree farming. Home: 937 Windward Ct Oshkosh WI 54901 Office: Reinke Hansche Last Inc 805 N Main St Oshkosh WI 54901

REINSDORF, JERRY MICHAEL, lawyer, professional athletic franchise executive, real estate executive; b. Bklyn., Feb. 25, 1936; s. Max and Marion (Smith) R.; m. Martyl F. Rifkin, Dec. 29, 1956; children: David Jason, Susan Janeen, Michael Andrew, Jonathon Milton. B.A., George Washington U., 1957; J.D., Northwestern U., 1960. Bar: D.C., Ill. 1960; CPA, Ill.; cert. specialist real estate securities, rev. appraiser; registered mortgage underwriter. Atty. staff regional counsel IRS, Chgo., 1960-64; assoc. law firm Chapman & Cutler, 1964-68; ptnr. Altman, Kurlander & Weiss, 1968-74; of counsel firm Katten, Muchin, Gitles, Zavis, Pearl & Galler, 1974-79; gen. ptnr. Carlyle Real Estate Ltd. Partnerships, 1971, 72; former pres. Balcor Co., Skokie, Ill.; chmn. bd. Balcor Co., 1974—; chmn. Chicago White Sox, 1981—, Chgo. Bulls Basketball Team, 1985—; mng. partner TBC Films, 1975—; lectr. John Marshall Law Sch., 1966-68; bd. dirs. Shearson Lehman Bros, Inc.; lectr. in real estate and taxation. Author: (with L. Herbert Schneider) Uses of Life Insurance in Qualified Employee Benefit Plans, 1970. Co-chmn. Ill. Profls. for Sen. Ralph Smith, 1970; bd. dirs. Gastro-Intestinal Research Found., 1981—, Chgo. Promotional Council, 1981-85, Ednl. Tape Recording for the Blind, 1979—; mem. Chgo. Region Bd. Anti-Defamation League, 1986—; adv. bd. Project Academus, 1987—. Mem. ABA, Ill. Bar Assn., Chgo. Bar Assn., Fed. Bar Assn., Nat. Assn. Rev. Appraisers and Mortgage Underwriters, Northwestern Law Sch. Alumni Assn. (bd. dirs.), Order of Coif, Omega Tau Rho. Office: Balcor Corp 4849 Golf Rd Skokie IL 60077

REINSTEIN, ALAN, accounting educator, consultant; b. Munich, Jan. 26, 1947; s. Solomon Reinstein and Dora (Dajches) Josephson; m. Nata-Lynn Sears, June 12, 1971; children: Franklyn, Mara, Rachelle. BA, SUNY, New Paltz, 1968, MS, 1971; MBA, U. Detroit, 1973; D of Bus. Adminstrn., U. Ky., 1980. CPA, Mich. Ednl. specialist Burroughs Corp., Detroit, 1969-70; sr. programmer Litton Industries, Detroit, 1971-73; sr. acct. Deloitte, Haskins & Sells CPA's, Detroit, 1973-76; asst. prof. U. Detroit, 1980-82; assoc. prof. Oakland U., Rochester, Mich., 1982-85; prof., chmn. dept. acctg. Wayne State U., Detroit, 1987—; research cons. Zalenko & Assoc. CPA's P.C., Southfield, Mich., 1979—; cons. various profl. orgns. and law firms. Mem. editorial bd. Advances in Acctg.; contbr. numerous articles to profl. jours. Treas. Cub Scout Pack 1672, 1985—, Cumberland Condominium Assn., 1974-77; mem. Mich. region presdl. steering com. Am. Jewish Congress, 1980-83, treas. 1974-77; mem. bus. and fin. com. Hillel Day Sch., 1982—. Mem. Am. Inst. CPA's, Am. Inst. Decision Scis., Nat. Assn. Accts. (greater Detroit chpt. assoc. dir. manuscripts 1980-85, v.p. edn. and profl. devel. 1985—), Am. Acctg. Assn. (dir. membership Mich. 1984-85), Mich. Assn. CPA's (chmn. pubs. com., mem. various coms.), Greater Detroit C. of C. (small bus. adv. council 1974-76), Beta Alpha Psi. Republican. Jewish. Avocation: racquetball.

REIS, THOMAS JOSEPH, architect; b. Columbus, Ohio, Feb. 17, 1948; s. Edmund John and Mary Magdalen (Theado) R.; m. Shermane Cressy, July 24, 1971; children: Andrew, Nina. BS in Architecture, Ohio State U., 1974. Draftsman Samborn, Steketee, Otis & Evans, Toledo, 1967-69; v.p. Karlsberger & Assocs., Columbus, Ohio, 1970-84; dir. ops., prin. URS Dalton, Columbus, 1984—. pres. Brookside Civic Assn., Worthington, Ohio, 1980-81; Y-Indian Princess chief YMCA, Worthington, 1982—; mem. parent com. Boy Scouts Am., Worthington, 1985—. Served with U.S. Army, 1969. Mem. AIA, Architects Soc. Ohio. Republican. Roman Catholic. Avocations: carpentry, coin collecting, landscaping.

REISCH, JOHN ALFRED, educator; b. Ponca City, Okla., Sept. 11, 1932; s. Warren A. and Hilda P. (Miller) R.; m. Donna J. Pratt, Apr. 29, 1961; children—Karla, Mark, Kristi, Troy. B.A., Wichita (Kans.) State U., 1970; M.Ed., 1974; Ph.D., 1983. Cert. tchr., Kans. Aux. operator Kans. Gas and Electric, Wichita, 1962-66; assembler Cessna Aircraft Co., Wichita, 1967-70; indsl. edn. tchr. Oxford (Kans.) High Sch., 1970-76, Goddard (Kans.) Jr. High Sch., 1976—; cons. Wichita State U., 1972, 1974, Wichita pub. schs., 1974; power and energy cons. Competency Project, Dept. Edn., 1976. Polit. action chmn. Goddard schs., 1981-82; bd. dirs. King's Kids Daycare Ctr. of Wichita, 1986—. Served with AUS, 1951-53. Recipient Outstanding Sr. award in Indsl. Edn., Wichita State U., 1970; Master Tchr. award Goddard Edn. Assn., 1980-81. Mem. NEA, Goddard Edn. Assn., Am. Vocat. Assn., Kans. Vocat. Assn., Kans. Indsl. Edn. Assn. Democrat. Baptist. Author hydraulics sect. in curriculum guide for power and energy Kans. State Dept. Edn., 1972. Home: 3929 Eisenhower Ct Wichita KS 67215 Office: 301 N Walnut Goddard KS 67052

REISS, DALE ANNE, investment company executive, accountant; b. Chgo., Sept. 3, 1947; d. Max and Nan (Hart) R.; m. Jerome L. King, Mar. 5, 1978; 1 child, Matthew Reiss. BS, Ill. Inst. Tech., 1967; MBA, U. Chgo., 1970. CPA, Ill. Cost acct. First Nat. Bank, Chgo., 1967; asst. controller City Colls. of Chgo., 1967-70; dir. fin. Chgo. Dept. Pub. Works, 1970-72; prin. Arthur Young & Co., Chgo., 1972-80; sr. v.p., controller Urban Investment & Devel. Co., Chgo., 1980-85, mng. ptnr. Kenneth Leventhal & Co., Chgo., 1985—; bd. dirs. Urban Diversified Properties, com. chmn. Assn. Real Estate Cos. Active Lincoln Park Zool. Soc.; fund raiser Grad. Sch. of U. Chgo.; bd. dirs., chmn. Info. Tech. Research Ctr., Mus. Sci. and Industry; bd. dirs. Urbanland Inst. Mem. Nat. Assn. Real Estate Cos., Fin. Execs. Inst., Am. Inst. CPA's, Chgo. Fin Exchange. Clubs: Econ., Metropolitan, Chgo. Yacht. Office: Kenneth Leventhal & Co 30 S Wacker Dr Suite 2414 Chicago IL 60606

REISSIG, ELVA HERROON, physical therapist; b. Toledo, June 29, 1943; d. Edwin Anthony and Mary Jane (Scribner) Herroon; m. Jake Boyde Reissig, Aug. 22, 1978; children: Edwin Kenneth, Amanda Jane. Student, Ohio U.; BS in Psychology, Ohio State U., 1965; cert. in phys. therapy, Children's Hosp. of Los Angeles, 1967. Lic. phys. therapist, Calif., Ohio. Staff therapist St. Vincent's Hosp., Los Angeles, 1967-69; pvt. practice phys. therapy Los Angeles, 1969; staff therapist Toledo Hosp., 1970; founder infant stimulation program, developer phy. threrapy program Lucas County (Ohio) Bd. Mental Retardation, 1970-73; head Dept. Phys. Therapy Flower Hosp., Cherry Hill Nursing Home, Lake Park Hillhaven Nursing Home, Parkview Hosp., 1973-74; developer phys. therapy program Monroe County Intermediate Sch., other Monroe pub. schs., 1974-76; phys. therapist Glendale-Feilbach Sch., 1976-77, 80—; pvt. practice phys. therapy 1977-78; phys. therapist Clermont County Sch. System, Batavia, Ohio, 1979-80. Avocations: music, swimming. Home: 132 E 6th St Perrysburg OH 43551

REISTER, RAYMOND ALEX, lawyer; b. Sioux City, Iowa, Dec. 22, 1929; s. Harold William and Anne (Eberhardt) R.; m. Ruth Elizabeth Alkema, Oct. 7, 1967. AB, Harvard U., 1952, LLB, 1955. Bar: N.Y. 1956, Minn. 1960. Assoc. Paul, Weiss, Rifkind, Wharton & Garrison, N.Y.C., 1955-56; sr. ptnr. Dorsey & Whitney, Mpls., 1959—; instr. U. Minn. Extension Div., 1964-66. Editor (with Larry W. Johnson): Minnesota Probate Administration, 1968. Trustee Mpls. Soc. Fine Arts, 1981-87; treas. Minn. State Hist. Soc., 1986—. Served as 1st lt. U.S. Army, 1956-59. Mem. Am. Coll. Probate Counsel (regent 1980-86), ABA, Minn. Bar Assn., Hennepin County Bar Assn. Clubs: Minneapolis, Harvard of Minn. (pres. 1969-70). Home: 93 Groveland Terr Minneapolis MN 55403 Office: Dorsey & Whitney 2100 First Bank Pl E Minneapolis MN 55402

REITER, ELIZABETH, marketing professional; b. Chgo., Dec. 23, 1956; d. George and Eugenia (Francuz) Mosarski; m. Hershel Reiter, May 16, 1980. AA with honors, Mayfair City Coll., 1976; BS in Commerce, DePaul U., 1983. Acct. Freeman United Coal Mining Co., Chgo., 1980-83, market analyst, 1983-87; asst. mktg. mgr. United Coal Mining Co., Chgo., 1987—; registered sales rep. First Investors Corp., Des Plaines, Ill., 1984-85; cons. Nat. Coal Assn., Washington, 1983—, Clarity Cons., Chgo., 1985—. Vol. Chgo. Bus. Youth Motivation Program, 1985—, Bus. Vols. for Arts, Chgo., 1986—. Mem. Nat. Assn. Security Dealers, Nat. Assn. Female Execs., Women in MIning (pres., chmn. bd. Chgo. chpt.), Phi Theta Kappa (pres. Chgo. chpt. 1975-76). Roman Catholic. Avocations: dance, film, writing, reading, physical fitness. Office: Freeman United Coal Mining Co 222 N LaSalle St Chicago IL 60601

REITER, STANLEY, educator, economist; b. N.Y.C., Apr. 26, 1925; s. Frank and Fanny (Rosenberg) R.; m. Nina Sarah Breger, June 13, 1944; children: Carla Frances, Frank Joseph. A.B., Queens Coll., 1947; M.A., U. Chgo., 1950, Ph.D., 1955. Research asso. Cowles Commn., U. Chgo., 1949-50; mem. faculty Stanford U., 1950-54, Purdue U., 1954-67; prof. econs. and math. Northwestern U., 1967—, now Morrison prof. econs. and math. Coll. Arts and Scis., Morrison prof. managerial econs. and decision scis. Grad. Sch. Mgmt.; cons. in field. Trustee Roycemore Sch., Evanston, Ill., 1969-71, treas., 1970-71. Served with inf. AUS, 1943-45. Decorated Purple Heart. Fellow Econometric Soc., AAAS; mem. Soc. Indsl. and Applied Math., Inst. Mgmt. Scis., Ops. Research Soc. Am., Am. Math. Soc., Math. Assn. Am. Home: 2138 Orrington Ave Evanston IL 60201 Office: Northwestern U Ctr for Math Studies 2001 Sheridan Rd Evanston IL 60201

REITH, PAUL EDWARD, physician; b. Carroll, Iowa, Aug. 12, 1943; s. Ferdinand and Elsie (Roschke) R. AB, U. Mo., 1965; MD, St. Louis U., 1969. Intern then resident in internal medicine St. Louis U., 1969-73; fellow in endocrinology U. Ill., Chgo., 1973-74, U. Iowa, Iowa City, 1974-76; staff physician student health services U. Kans. Watkins Meml. Hosp., Lawrence, 1976—; clin. asst. prof. medicine U. Kans., Kansas City, 1985—. Program chmn. Am. Diabetic Assn., Lawrence, 1982—. Fellow ACP; mem. Phi Beta Kappa. Lutheran. Avocations: photography, history of medicine, aerobics. Home: 1331 Naismith Rd Lawrence KS 66044 Office: U Kans Watkins Meml Hosp Student Health Ctr Lawrence KS 66045

REITZ, WILLIAM, construction company executive, mechanical engineer; b. Toluca, Ill., June 16, 1923; s. George William and Winifred Allison (Donnelly) R.; m. Ruth M. Maus, Oct. 9, 1951; 1 child, Mary Allison. BSME, U. Ark., 1950. Registered profl. engr., Tex. Mech. engr. Jewel Mining Co., Paris, Ark., 1950, Silas Mason Co., Amarillo, Tex., 1951, F.H. McGraw & Co., Hartford, Conn., 1951-62; sr. v.p. Edward Gray Corp., Chgo., 1962—, Inland Constrn. Co., Chgo., 1962—. Bd. dirs., treas. Morgan Park Improvement Assn., Chgo. Served with U.S. Army, 1942-46. Mem. ASME, Am. Nuclear Soc., Soc. Am. Mil. Engrs., ASTM, Am. Concrete Inst.

RELLE, FERENC MATYAS, chemist; b. Gyor, Hungary, June 13, 1922; came to U.S., 1951, naturalized, 1956; s. Ferenc and Elizabeth (Netratics) R.; B.S. in Chem. Engring., Jozsef Nador Poly. U., Budapest, 1944, M.S., 1944; m. Gertrud B. Tubach, Oct. 9, 1946; children—Ferenc, Ava, Attila. Lab. mgr. Karl Kohn Ltd. Co., Landshut, W.Ger., 1947-48; resettlement officer IRO, Munich, 1948-51; chemist Farm Bur. Coop. Assn., Columbus, Ohio, 1951-56; indsl. engr. N.Am. Aviation, Inc., Columbus, 1956-57; research chemist Keever Starch Co., Columbus, 1957-65; research chemist Ross Labs. div. Abbott Labs., Columbus, 1965-70, research scientist, 1970—; cons. in field. Chmn. Columbus and Central Ohio UN Week, 1963; pres. Berwick Manor Civic Assn., 1968; trustee Stelios Stelson Found., 1968-69. Mem. Am. Chem. Soc. (alt. councilor 1973, chmn. long range planning com. Columbus sect. 1972-76, 78-80), Am. Assn. Cereal Chemists (chmn. Cin. sect. 1974-75), Ohio Acad. Sci., Internat. Tech. Inst. (adv. dir. 1977-82), Nat. Intercollegiate Soccer Ofcls. Assn., Am. Hungarian Assn., Hungarian Cultural Assn. (pres. 1978-81), Ohio Soccer Ofcls. Assn., Ohio High Sch. Athletic Assn., Germania Singing and Sport Soc. Presbyterian. Club: Civitan (gov. Ohio dist. 1970-71, dist. treas. 1982-83, pres. Eastern Columbus 1962-64, 72-73; internat. gov. of yr. 1971, various awards). Home: 3487 Roswell Dr Columbus OH 43227 Office: 625 Cleveland Ave Columbus OH 43216

REMBUSCH, JOSEPH JOHN, psychologist, management consulting company executive; b. Joliet, Ill., June 29, 1939; s. Joseph Earl and Agnes Cecilia (Heinen) R. AA, Joliet Jr. Coll., 1959; BS in Psychology, U. Ill., 1962; MA in Teaching, Rockford (Ill.) Coll., 1970; postgrad., No. Ill. U., 1961-66, 70-73, Western Colo. U., 1973-75. Registered psychologist, Ill. Sci. tchr. Crete-Monee Sch. Dist., Crete, Ill., 1963-64; clin. caseworker Ill. State Sch. Boys, St. Charles, 1964-65; dir. guidance Hiawatha Unit Dist. #426, Kirkland, Ill., 1966-69; registrar Kishwaukee Community Coll., Malta, Ill., 1969-81; spl. rep., dist. mgr., regional mgr. George S. May Internat., Park Ridge, Ill., 1982-86, divisional sales mgr., 1986—; pvt. practice psychology DeKalb, Ill., 1971-80; cons. psychologist Ill. Div. Vocat. Rehab., DeKalb, 1971-79. Mem. Am. Psychol. Assn., Delta Upsilon, Phi Delta Kappa. Republican. Roman Catholic. Home: 3499 Regent Dr Palatine IL 60067

REMINGER, RICHARD THOMAS, lawyer; b. Cleve., Apr. 3, 1931; s. Edwin Carl and Theresa Henrietta (Bookmyer) R.; m. Billie Carmen Greer, June 26, 1954; children—Susan Greer, Patricia Allison, Richard Thomas. A.B., Case-Western Res. U., 1953; J.D., Cleve.-Marshall Law Sch., 1957. Bar: Ohio 1957, Pa. 1978, U.S. Supreme Ct. 1961. Personnel and safety dir. Motor Express, Inc., Cleve., 1954-58; mng. ptnr. Reminger & Reminger Co., L.P.A., Cleve., 1958—; dir. U.S. Truck Lines, Inc., Del. Cardinal Casualty Co.; mem. nat. claims council adv. bd. Comml. Union Assurance Co., 1980—; lectr. transp. law Fenn Coll., 1960-62, bus. law, Case Western Res. U., 1962-64. Mem. joint com. Cleve. Acad. Medicine-Greater Cleve. Bar Assn.; trustee Cleve. Zool. Soc., exec. com., 1984—, v.p., 1987—; trustee Andrew Sch., Huron Rd. Hosp., Cleve., Cleve. Soc. for Blind, 1987—. Served with AC, USNR, 1950-58. Mem. Fedn. Ins. and Corp. Counsel, Trial Attys. Am. (mem. sect. litigation, also tort and ins. practice), Fed. Bar Assn., ABA (com. on law and medicine, profl. responsibility com. 1977—), Internat. Bar Assn., Ohio Bar Assn. (council dels. 1987—), Pa. Bar Assn., Cleve. Bar Assn. (chmn. med. legal com. 1978-79, profl. liability com. 1977—), Transp. Lawyers Assn., Cleve. Assn. Civil Trial Attys., Am. Soc. Hosp. Attys., Soc. Ohio Hosp. Attys., Ohio Assn. Civil Trial Attys., Am. Judicature Soc., Def. Research Inst., Maritime Law Assn. U.S., Am. Coll. Law and Medicine, 8th Jud. Bar Assn. (life Ohio dist.). Clubs: Mayfield Country (pres. 1980-82), Union, Cleve. Playhouse, Hermit (pres. 1973-75) (Cleve.); Lost Tree (Fla.), Kirtland Country (Cleve.), Rolling Rock (Pa.). Home: 34000 Hackney Rd Hunting Valley OH 44022 Office: The 113 St Clair Bldg Cleveland OH 44114

REMLEY, AUDREY WRIGHT, educational administrator, psychologist; b. Warrenton, Mo., Dec. 26, 1931; d. Leslie Frank and Irene Lesetta (Graue) Wright; m. Alvin Remley, Mar. 25, 1951; children—Steven Leslie, David Mark. A.A., Hannibal-LaGrange Coll., 1951; B.S. in Edn. cum laude, U. Mo., 1963, M.A., 1969, Ph.D., 1974. Asst. prof. psychology Westminster Coll., Fulton, Mo., 1969-74, chmn. dept. psychology, 1975-78, dir. counseling services, 1975-79, dir. student devel., 1979-80, dir. acad. advising and counseling services, 1980—; cons. Serve, Inc., Fulton, 1980—, Family Service Div., 1983—. Recipient Outstanding Young Woman of Am. award Jaycettes, 1965; NDEA fellow, 1968. Mem. Am. Assn. Counseling and Devel., Am. Coll. Personnel Assn. (exec. council 1982-85, co-editor ACPA Developments, 1984-87, v.p. state divs., 1987—, Outstanding State Div. Leader 1982), Mo. Coll. Personnel Assn. (pres. 1981-82), Am. Psychol. Assn., Mo. Psychol. Assn. (lic.). Presbyterian. Avocations: singing; antique collecting; knitting. Office: Westminster Coll Fulton MO 65251

REMLEY, VIVIAN ELAINE, manufacturing company executive; b. Los Angeles, Jan. 29, 1943; d. George Grenade Toohill and Elaine Andrea (Lingwood) Fortney; m. Armand Joseph Duval Jr., Nov. 5, 1965 (div. Sept. 1975); 1 child, Andrea Elaine; m. Donald Wayne Remley, Aug. 22, 1979. Student, Hillsdale (Mich.) Coll., 1961-64; BA in Social Sci., Mich. State U., 1980, M of Labor and Indsl. Relations, 1984. Exec. asst. Roberts Corp., 1978-82; dir. personnel and quality control Simpson Industries, Inc., Litchfield, Mich., 1984-86, personnel adminstr., STS coordinator, 1986-87; mgr. employee relations div. NI Industries, Inc., Novi, Mich., 1987—; cons. PMA, Mason, Mich., 1985—; faculty Lansing (Mich.) Community Coll., 1984—. Editor Newsgram Newsletter, 1981-82, Robert's Round-Up Newsletter, 1981-82. Mem. Am. Soc. Personnel Adminstrs., Indstl. Relations Research Assn. (Lansing chpt.), Personnel Assn. Mid-Mich. Lutheran. Office: NI Industries Inc Automotive Trim Div 39600 Orchard Hill Pl Novi MI 48050

REMPLE, HENRY DIETRICH, psychologist; b. Svetloye, Ukraine, USSR, Nov. 25, 1908; s. Dietrich Remple and Aganetha Fast; m. Mariana Lohrenz, Aug. 1, 1936; children: Lucy Jean, Robert Keith. BA, U. Minn., 1932, MA, 1933; postgrad., Stanford U., 1946; PhD, U. Kans., 1950. Diplomate Am. Bd. Profl. Psychology. Asst. personnel officer Farm Credit Adminstrn., Wichita, 1934-1937; indsl. counselor Fed. Reformatory, El Reno, Okla., 1937-46, cons., 1947-50; chief psychologist regional office VA Mental Hygiene Clinic, Kansas City, 1950-55; chief psychology tng. unit VA Med. Ctr., Topeka, Kans., 1955-57; chief psychology services VA Med. Ctr., Leavenworth, Kans., 1958-81; pvt. practice psychology Lawrence, Kans., 1981—; chmn. bd. Bert Nash Community Mental Health Ctr., 1973—; bd. dirs. Advocacy Council of Aging, Lawrence, 1981—, Kansans for Improvement of Nursing Homes, Lawrence, 1985—. Co-author (book) Rehabilitation of the Chronically Institutionalized, 1970; editor (Book) Symposium on Aging, 1973. Mem. Douglas County Dem. Cen. Com., Lawrence, 1986. Served to capt. AUS, 1942-45, ETO. Fellow Am. Psychol. Assn. (council of reps. 1972-75), Kans. Psychol. Assn. (pres. 1977-78, sec. 1984—, bd. dirs. 1972-79, 84—); mem. Kans. Assn. Profl. Psychology. Democrat. Club: Ozark Waterways Wilderness (Kansas City). Avocation: canoeing. Home: 1922 Countryside Ln Lawrence KS 66044 Office: Psychol Services 901 Kentucky Suite 201 B Lawrence KS 66044

REMSBERG, CHARLES ANDRUSS, publisher, writer; b. Hutchinson, Kans., Mar. 7, 1936; s. Harmon Wilson and Laura (Andruss) R.; m. Bonnie Kohn, Sept. 14, 1958 (div. Aug. 1983); children: Jennifer Ruth, Richard Martin; m. Colleen Evans, Feb. 25, 1984. BS in Journalism, Northwestern U., 1958, MS in Journalism, 1959. Reporter Chgo. Sun-Times, 1959-60; freelance journalist Bylines, Inc., Evanston, Ill., 1960-80; pub., pres. Calibre Press, Inc., Northbrook, Ill., 1980—; instr. seminars on street surviaval. Author: Inside Badminton, 1975, Street Survival, 1980, The Tactical Edge, 1986; also over 800 articles for leading nat. mags. Bd. dirs. Family Counseling Service, Evanston, 1984-86, Evanston Property Owners Assn., 1986—. Recipient Sidney Hillman award, Penney-Missouri award, Am. Osteo. Assn. award for outstanding journalism. Mem. Am. Soc. Journalists and Authors, Authors Guild, Mystery Writers Am., Internat. Platform Assn., Justice Systems Tng. Assn., Internat. Assn. Law Enforcement Firearms Instrs., Am. Soc. Law Enforcement Trainers. Avocations: cross-country skiing, windsurfing. Home: 2114 Lincolnwood Dr Evanston IL 60201 Office: Calibre Press Inc 666 Dundee Rd #1607 Northbrook IL 60062

REMY, DAVID LEWIS, lawyer; b. Mansfield, Ohio, Sept. 6, 1949; s. Lewis Frank and Janice Beverly (McCollough) R. B.S. in Polit. Sci., Ohio No. U., 1972, J.D., 1975. Bar: Ohio 1975. Referee, Richland City Juvenile Ct., Mansfield, Ohio, 1975-77, Mansfield Mcpl. Ct., 1978-81; sole practice, Mansfield, 1975—; asst. law dir. City of Mansfield, 1984—, Pres., Pediatric Devel. Ctr. Inc., Mansfield, 1981—. Mem. Ohio State Bar Assn., Richland County Bar Assn. Republican. Lutheran. Club: Sertoma (Mansfield). Lodge: Kiwanis. Avocation: woodworking. Office: David L Remy Atty at Law 51 W First Mansfield OH 44902

RENAKER, JANE ANN, golf course executive; b. Dayton, Ohio, Dec. 3, 1922; d. Herbert Elmer and Luella Carolyn (Burkhardt) Quiggle; m. Allan Frazier Renaker, Jan. 24, 1942 (dec. Mar. 1984); children—Carol Anne, Joyce Lynn, Stephen Allan. Grad. high sch., Dayton, Ohio. Bookkeeper, Delco Products, Dayton, 1941-43; bookkeeper, part owner Al's Super Service & Used Cars, Dayton, 1945-56. Renaker Chevrolet & Oldsmobile, Brookville, Ind., 1956-67; operator, part owner Brook Hill Golf Course, Brookville, 1973-83, sole owner, 1983—. Republican. Methodist. Club: Delta Theta Tau. Lodge: Eastern Star (page 1957). Home and Office: 11090 Reservoir Rd Box 120 Brookville IN 47012

RENARD, DAVID ALBERT, paper distribution company executive; b. St. Louis, Aug. 19, 1949; s. Henri Eugene and Dorothea Angela (Massa) R.; m.

Mary Margaret Hicks, Feb. 9, 1974; children: David Michael, Mark Edward, Melanie Anne. Student, U. Mo., 1968-71. V.p., salesman Renard Paper Co., St. Louis, 1975-84, pres., 1984—. Bd. dirs. St. Elizabeth Athletic Assn., St. Louis, 1983-85, soccer coach, 1981—. Avocations: sailing, soccer, water sports, working with wood, power tools. Home: 111 Chatwood Terr Saint Louis MO 63126 Office: Renard Paper Co 4465 Manchester Ave Saint Louis MO 63110

RENDA, MICHAEL VINCENT, sales executive; b. Windsor, Ontario, Can., Nov. 10, 1953; s. Carl John and Mary Ann (Mitchell) R.; m. Susan C. Casebere, June 10, 1978; children: Matthew, Emily. BS, Miami (Ohio) U., 1976. Local salesman WTVG-TV, Toledo, 1977-79; nat. sales rep. Storer TV, Chgo., 1979-81, N.Y.C., 1981-82; nat. sales mgr. WJW-TV, Cleve., 1982—. Sta. coordinator United Way, Cleve., 1984-86; com. chmn. Boy Scouts Am., Hudson, Ohio, 1985-86. Mem. TV Bur. Advt. (advisor). Club: Tanglewood Country (Chagrin Falls). Avocations: civil war books and memorabilia, golf, photography. Home: 1732 Arbutus Dr Hudson OH 43623 Office: WJW-TV 5800 S Marginal Rd Cleveland OH 44103

RENDER, RICHARD CHARLES, dentist; b. Grand Forks, N.D., Jan. 22, 1942; s. Robert MacKenzie and Echzine Zelda (Peterson) R.; m. Mary Elizabeth Dixon, June 20, 1964; children: Rebecca Lynne, Melissa Lee. BS, U. Minn., 1965, DDS, 1967. Sec.-treas. Mpls. Dist. Dental Soc., 1982-83, v.p., 1983-84, pres. elect, 1984-85, pres., 1985-86; alternate del. to ADA Minn. Dental Assn., St. Paul, 1985—; cons. Mutual Omaha (Nebr.) Ins. Co., 1975—. Bd. dirs. Bloomington Heart Health Program, 1985—. Served to lt. USN, 1967-69. Fellow Internat. Coll. Dentists; mem. ADA, Minn. Dental Assn. (chmn. pvt. funded programs com. 1976-78, mem. mktg. com. 1984—), Am. Acad. Gen. Dentistry, Am. Soc. of Dentistry for Children. Republican. Presbyterian. Club: Minikahda. Avocations: golfing, running, reading. Office: 8900 Penn Ave S #211 Bloomington MN 55431

RENDLEN, ALBERT LEWIS, judge; b. Hannibal, Mo., Apr. 7, 1922; s. Charles E. and Norma Lewis R.; m. Dona M. Schwartz; children—Albert Lewis, Susan Virginia. Student, William Jewell Coll., 1939-41; B.A., U. Ill., 1943; J.D., U. Mich., 1948. Bar: Mo. 1948. Mem. firm Rendlen & Renalen, Hannibal, 1948-74; city atty. Alexandria, 1949-52; U.S. commr. Eastern Dist. Mo., 1953-55; judge Mo. Ct. Appeals (St. Louis dist.), 1974-77; chief justice Mo. Supreme Ct., 1982-85, assoc. justice, 1985—. Chmn. Republican State Com., 1973-74, U.S. Constn. Bicentennial Commn. of Mo.; bd. regents NE Mo. State Coll., 1973-75; mem. nat. and dist. adv. council for Small Bus. Adminstrn.; past mem. Marion County Welfare Commn.; past pres. dist. council Boy Scouts Am. Served with U.S. Army, 1943-46; served to comdr. USCG, 1951-70. Mem. Navy League, Res. Officer Assn. NE Mo. (past pres.), Am. Legion, VFW, Am. Judicature Soc. Office: Supreme Ct Bldg Jefferson City MO 65101 *

RENEHAN, JULIE ANN, pharmacist, administrator; b. Colorado Springs, Colo., July 30, 1959; d. Donald Walter and Laura Mae (Meyer) Mason; m. Jeffrey Neil Renehan, Aug. 7, 1982; 1 child, Megan Elizabeth Renehan. BS with honors in Pharmacy, Univ. Colo., Boulder, 1982. Pharmacist Mills Drugs, Rapid City, S.D., 1982-84, Boyds Drug Mart, Rapid City, 1984; head pharmacist, mgr. Boyds Pharmacy, Rapid City, 1984-86; cons. Black Hills Workshop, 1985-86; pharmacist, nursing home cons. Western Hills Pharmacy, 1986; pharmacist Parsons Bros. Rexall Drugs, Calif., 1987—. Recipient Profl. Achievement award Univ. Colo. Sch. Pharmacy, 1982. Mem. Am. Pharm. Assn., Rapid City Pharm. Assn. (sec. 1982-83), Kappa Epsilon (v.p. Univ. Colo. 1980-81), Kappa Epsilon Nat. Assn., Rho Chi (Alpha Theta chpt. 1981). Republican. Methodist. Avocations: sewing and crafts, skiing, bowling, cooking, candy-making.

RENKEN, DUANE ALLEN, real estate investment executive; b. LeMars, Iowa, Oct. 31, 1932; s. George Fredrick and Flora Freda (Kruse); m. Kathryn Ann Ohland, June 16, 1956; children: Julie Ann, David Allen, John Ohland. BS in Aero. Engring., Iowa State U., 1956; student, U. Mich., 1959-60. Cert. real estate broker. Mgr. Bendix Aerospace, Ann Arbor, 1958-68; pres. Dajac, Inc., Ann Arbor, 1968—; chmn. bd. Logo's, Ypsilanti, Mich., 1974-80; v.p. bd. Arizala Corp., 1983—; pres. Kenker, Inc., Ann Arbor, 1984—, Renken Fin. Corp., Ann Arbor, 1984—. Contbr. articles to profl. jour. Bd. dirs., fin. chmn. Huron Valley Girl Scouts USA, Mich., 1974—; pres. Ann Arbor Bd. Edn., 1971-74; founder Christian Coll. Scholarship Fund, Ann Arbor, 1981-86; mem. Mich. State Hosp. Facilities Commn., Mich., 1976-77; chmn. Mich. State Bldg. Authority, 1979-86. Served to capt. USAF, 1956-58. Mem. Real Estate Securities and Syndication Inst., Phi Gamma Delta, Sigma Gamma Tau. Republican. Lutheran. Club: Ann Arbor Golf and Outing. Lodge: Knights of Saint Patrick, Rotary. Avocations: model airplanes, golf, hiking, travel. Home: 2154 S Seventh St Ann Arbor MI 48103 Office: Dajac Inc 109 Miller Ave Ann Arbor MI 48104

RENNEKAMP, HERBERT ALPHONSE, information systems manager, educator; b. Cin., Dec. 11, 1946; s. William Lawrence and Velma Rose (Erhart) R.; m. Deborah Ann Rice, Jan. 31, 1970; children—Deana, Troy, Keith, Nathan. Computer programmer City of Cin., 1970-73; systems analyst Regional Computer Ctr., Cin., 1974-77, project mgr., 1977-79, mgr. info. systems, 1980—; instr. info. systems U. Cin. Evening Coll., 1980—; advisor on data processing curriculum Great Oaks Career Devel. Sch. System, Cin., 1981—. Soccer coach Monfort Heights Athletic Assn., 1980—; baseball coach St. Ignatius Athletic Assn., Cin., 1982—. Mem. Assn. Systems Mgmt., Delta Sigma Pi. Home: 4366 Runningfawn Dr Cincinnati OH 45247 Office: Regional Computer Ctr 138 E Court St Cincinnati OH 45202

RENNEKAMP, ROSEMARIE GREELEY, manufacturing company executive; b. Des Moines, Sept. 14, 1949; d. Bernard James and Dorothy Evelyn (Clark) Greeley; Steven Paul Rennekamp, Aug. 2, 1975; children: Kristina, Bryan. BS, Iowa State U., 1971, MS, 1973; MBA, U. Iowa, 1978. Mgr. product evaluation Amana (Iowa) Refrigeration, Inc., 1976-77, mgr. sales tng., 1977-78, product mgr., 1978-81, mktg. mgr. major appliances, 1981-83, mktg. mgr., 1983-85, v.p. product mktg. and planning, 1985—; vis. instr. U. Iowa, Iowa City, 1981—; mem. adv. bd. Iowa State U., 1987—. Contbr. articles to profl. jours. Recipient Women in Internat. Industry tribute Nat. YWCA, 1984. Mem. Internat. Microwave Power Inst. (bd. dirs. 1980-83, symposium dir. 1979-80), Am. Home Economists Assn., Home Economists in Bus., Assn. Home Appliance Mfrs. (chmn. microwave exec. bd. 1986—). Roman Catholic. Avocation: teaching adult religious education classes. Office: Amana Refrigeration Inc Amana IA 52204

RENNER, CLARENCE E., judge, artist; b. Wichita, Kans., Sept. 7, 1922; s. Charles M. and Helen (Hull) R.; m. Dorothy I. Huff, Jan. 24, 1942; children: Diane L. Renner Curtis, Cindy L. Renner Constantino, Charles M., John R., Keith E. AB, Washburn U., Topeka, Kans., 1949, JD, 1950. Bar: Kans. 1950. Sole practice, Pratt, Kans., 1950-75; atty. County of Pratt, Kans., 1957-69; assoc. dist. judge 19th Jud. Dist., 1977-81; adminstrv. judge 30th Jud. Dist., Pratt, 1982—, dist. judge, 1982—; spl. assigned judge Kans. Ct. Appeals, 1986; lectr. Pratt Community Coll. Served with USAF, 1942-46. Mem. Kans. Bar Assn., Pratt County Bar Assn., Kans. Dist. Judges Assn., Kans. Dist. and County Attys. Assn. (pres.), Am. Legion, VFW. Democrat. Methodist. Lodge: Elks. Numerous landscape and portrait paintings. Home: 415 N Main St Pratt KS 67124 Office: Pratt County Courthouse Pratt KS 67124

RENNER, ROBERT GEORGE, U.S. district judge; b. Nevis, Minn., Apr. 2, 1923; s. Henry J. and Beatrice M. (Fuller) R.; m. Catherine L. Clark, Nov. 12, 1949; children: Robert, Anne, Richard, David. B.A., St. John's U., Collegeville, Minn., 1947; J.D., Georgetown U., 1949. Bar: Minn. 1949. Pvt. practice Walker, 1949-69; U.S. atty. Dist. of Minn., 1969-77, U.S. magistrate, 1977-80, U.S. dist. judge, 1980—. Mem. Minn. Ho. of Reps., 1957-69. Served with AUS, 1943-46. Mem. ABA, Fed. Bar Assn., Minn. Bar Assn. Roman Catholic. Address: US District Court 738 US Courthouse 316 Robert St Saint Paul MN 55101 *

RENNO, RICHARD LEE, high school principal; b. Nelson, Mo., Dec. 3, 1935; s. Richard and Virginia Elizabeth (Mayfield) R.; m. Dorothea Annette Flucke, Aug. 28, 1955; children: Richard, Charles, Valerie. BS in Edn., Cen. Mo. State U., 1957, MS, 1961. Cert. tchr., Mo.; cert. adminstr., Mo. Math tchr., football coach Orrick (Mo.) High Sch., 1957-60; math tchr., football coach Lafayette County C-I Schs., Higginsville, Mo., 1961-76, jr. high sch. prin., 1976-80, jr. and sr. high prin., 1980-82, sr. high prin., 1982—; owner Lakeside Bar-B-Que, Lake of the Ozark, Lincoln, Mo. Mem. Nat. Assn. Secondary Sch. Prins., Mo. Assn. Secondary Sch. Prins., Mo. State Tchrs. Assn., Higginsville Jaycees (v.p. 1964). Democrat. Lodge: Optimists (charter pres. Higginsville 1974). Avocations: camping, fishing, golf, cooking. Home: 500 West 30 Higginsville MO 64037 Office: Lafayette County C-I Schs 31st and Highway 13 Higginsville MO 64037

RENO, OTTIE WAYNE, former judge; b. Pike County, Ohio, Apr. 7, 1929; s. Eli Enos and Arbannah Belle (Jones) R.; Asso. in Bus. Adminstrn., Franklin U., 1949; LL.B., Franklin Law Sch., 1953; J.D., Capital U., 1966; grad. Coll. Juvenile Justice, U. Nev., 1973; m. Janet Gay McCann, May 22, 1947; children—Ottie Wayne II, Jennifer Lynn, Lorna Victoria. Admitted to Ohio bar, 1953; practiced in Pike County; recorder Pike County, 1957-73; common pleas judge Probate and Juvenile divs. Pike County, 1973-79. Mem. adv. bd. Ohio Youth Services, 1972-74. Mem. Democratic Central Com. Camp Creek precinct, 1956-72, 83—; sec. Pike County Central Com., 1960-70; chmn. Pike County Democratic Exec. Com., 1971-72; del. Dem. Nat. Conv., 1972; mem. Ohio Dem. Central Com., 1969-70; Dem. candidate 6th Ohio dist. U.S. Ho. of Reps., 1966; pres. Scioto Valley Local Sch. Dist., 1962-66. Recipient Distinguished Service award Ohio Youth Commn., 1974; 6 Outstanding Jud. Service awards Ohio Supreme Ct.; 15 times Ala. horseshoe pitching champion; named to Nat. Horseshoe Pitchers Hall of Fame, 1978; mem. internat. sports exchange, U.S. and Republic South Africa, 1972, 80, 82. Mem. Ohio, Pike County (pres. 1964) bar assns., Nat. Council Juvenile Ct. Judges, Am. Legion. Mem. Ch. of Christ. Author: Story of Horseshoes, 1963; Pitching Championship Horseshoes, 1971, 2d rev. edit., 1975; Who's Who in Horseshoe Pitching, 1983. Home: 148 Reno Rd Lucasville OH 45648

RENO, PEGGY JEAN, bank executive; b. New Orleans, Aug. 8, 1952; d. Fraser Lee and Sadie (Gardner) Blanton; m. Marvin Gene Reno, Sept. 7, 1974 (div. Oct. 1985); children: Jennifer Lauren, Justin Matthew. BA, La. Coll., 1976. Manuals and forms asst. Farm Credit Banks, St. Louis, 1979-81, procedures coord., 1981-83, supr. adminstrv. services, 1983—. Mem. Assn. Records Mgrs. Adminstrs. (speaker nat. conf. 1985, chapter conf. 1986), Farm Credit System (editor Industry Action Com. 1985—). Republican. Baptist. Avocations: piano, tennis, skiing. Home: Rural Rt 1 Box 178C O'Fallon IL 62269

RENSHAW, DOMEENA C., psychiatrist, educator; b. July 20, 1929; m. Robert H. Renshaw. MB, BChir, U. Capetown, Republic of South Africa, 1960. Intern Grooteschuur Hosp. Univ. Cape Town, 1961; med. officer St. Mary's Mission Hosp., Republic of South Africa, 1964-65; resident psychiatrist Stritch Med. Sch. Loyola Univ., Maywood, Ill., 1965-68; dir. outpatient clinic Loyola U., Maywood, Ill., 1968—, dir. child program, 1969—, asst. chmn. dept. psychiatry, 1970—, dir. sex clinic, 1972—. Author: The Hyperactive Child, 1974, Incest: Understanding and Treatment, 1982, Sex Talk for a Safe Child, 1984. Fellow Am. Psychiat. Assn., Am. Coll. Psychiatry; mem. AMA (editorial adv. bd.). Avocations: photography, gardening, writing. Home: 85 S 3d Ave Lombard IL 60148 Office: Loyola U Med Sch 2160 S 1st Ave Maywood IL 60153

RENSHAW, JOHN GRAHAM, JR., data processing executive, musician/composer; b. Meriden, Conn., July 20, 1949; s. John Graham and Josephine Emily (DeMaria) R.; m. Judith Ann Morace, Dec. 24, 1972; children: Joel Adam, Jessamy Alane. BS in English Lit., So. Ill. U., 1970. Art/design cons. Cornell Galleries, Springfield, Mass., 1974-76; program mgr. Community Regional Opportunities Program, Chicopee, Mass., 1976-78; program mgr. Wabash Area Devel., Inc., Mill Shoals, Ill., 1978-80, data processing mgr., 1980—. Composer/performer: (single recording) Top of the Morning, 1968, (album recording Shadowfax, 1975; composer/performer/producer: (album record) Monkey's Uncle, 1986. Served to sgt. U.S. Army, 1970-72. Mem. Data Processing Mgmt. Assn., Nashville Songwriter's Assn., Internat. Avocation: live music performance. Home: Rt. 1 Box 105A Carmi IL 62821 Office: Wabash Area Devel Inc PO Box 89 Mill Shoals IL 62862

RENTER, LOIS IRENE HUTSON, librarian; b. Lowden, Iowa, Oct. 23, 1929; d. Thomas E. and Lulu Mae (Barlean) Hutson; B.A. cum laude, Cornell Coll., Iowa, 1965; M.A., U. Iowa, 1968; m. Karl A. Renter, Jan. 3, 1948; children—Susan Elizabeth, Rebecca Jean, Karl Geoffrey. Tchr. Spanish, Mt. Vernon (Iowa) High Sch., 1965-67; head librarian Am. Coll. Testing Program, Iowa City, Iowa, 1968—; vis. instr. U. Iowa Sch. Library Sci., 1972—. Mem. Am. Soc. Info. Sci., ALA, Spl. Libraries Assn., Phi Beta Kappa. Methodist. Home: 1125 29th St Marion IA 52302 Office: Box 168 Iowa City IA 52243

RENTSCHLER, ALVIN EUGENE, mechanical engineer; b. Havre, Mont., Oct. 24, 1940; s. Alvin Joseph and Pauline Elizabeth (Browning) R.; B.S., Mont. State U., 1964; m. Marilyn Joan Bostrom, Dec. 7, 1974; children—Elizabeth Louise, Richard Eugene, Alison Lynn. Sci. and math. instr. Helena Pub. Schs., Mont., 1964-66; dist. mgr. Woodmen Accident and Life Co., Helena, 1966-69; profl. med. rep. Abbott Labs., Great Falls, Mont., 1969-72; sales engr. Agribest, Inc., Great Falls, 1973; design engr. Anaconda Co., Mont., 1974-77; ops. and maintenance engr. Rochester Meth. Hosp., Minn., 1977-85; maintenance supervisor, 1985—; mem. engring. coordinating com. Franklin Heating Sta., 1977-85. Bd. dirs. Mont. affiliate Am. Diabetes Assn., 1975-78, pres. Butte-Anaconda chpt., 1974-77; mem. citizens adv. com. Rochester Area Vocat.-Tech. Inst., 1978—, sec., 1982-84. Recipient Greatest Achievement award Combined Tng., Inc., 1977, Pres.' Club award Woodmen Accident & Life Co., 1968. Mem. ASME, Am. Soc. Hosp. Engring., Internat. Congress Hosp. Engring. Mem. Covenant Ch.

RENTSCHLER, FREDERICK BRANT, consumer product company executive; b. N.Y.C., Aug. 12, 1939; s. George Adam and Rita (Mitchell) R.; m. Marguerite Elizabeth Shaughnessy, Nov. 20, 1971. B.A., Vanderbilt U., 1961; M.B.A., Harvard U., 1968. Dir. mktg. Armour Dial Inc., Phoenix, 1973; v.p. toiletries div. Armour Dial Inc., 1974, v.p. new bus. devel., 1975-76; pres. Armour Internat. Co., Phoenix, 1977, Armour-Dial Corp., Phoenix, 1978-80; pres., chief exec. officer Hunt-Wesson Foods Inc., 1980-84; pres., chief operating officer Farley/Northwest Industries, Inc., Chgo., 1984—; dir. Charleston Corp. Dep. dir. White House Fellows, 1971, 72; bd. dirs. Scottsdale Center for the Arts, 1974, 76, Heard Mens Council-Heard Mus., 1975, 76, United Way Ariz., from 1978; trustee Heard Mus., from 1978. Served to capt. USMC, 1961-65. Mem. Young Pres. Orgn. Republican. Roman Catholic. Clubs: Links (N.Y.C.); Racquet (Chgo.); Paradise Valley Country (Scottsdale); Ariz. (Phoenix). Office: Farley/NW Industries Inc 6300 Sears Tower Chicago IL 60606 *

RENTSCHLER, WILLIAM HENRY, business executive; b. Hamilton, Ohio, May 11, 1925; s. Peter Earl and Barbara (Schlosser) R.; A.B., Princeton U., 1949; m. Sylvia Gale Angevin, Dec. 20, 1948; children—Sarah Yorke, Peter Ferris, Mary Angevin, Phoebe Mason; m. Martha Guthrie Snowdon, Jan. 20, 1967; 1 dau., Hope Snowdon. Reporter, Cin. Times-Star, 1946; reporter, asst. to exec. editor Mpls. Star & Tribune, 1949-53; 2d v.p. No. Trust Co., Chgo., 1953-56; pres. Martha Washington Kitchens, Inc., 1957-68, Stevens Candy Kitchens, Inc., 1957-66; investor closely-held cos.; bus. and mktg. cons., 1970-81; chmn., chief exec. officer Medart, Inc., Greenwood, Miss., 1982, Jakes Mfg. Corp., Greenwood, 1983, Float Away Home Products, Inc., Atlanta, 1983, Roper Whitney Corp., Rockford, Ill., 1986, Berkley Small Corp, Medina, Ohio, 1986. Editor, pub. News Voice Newspapers, Inc., Highland Park, Ill., 1983, San Francisco Progress, Inc., 1986. Spl. adviser Pres.'s Nat. Program for Vol. Action, 1969; chmn. Ill. Low Tech./High Return Adv. Bd.; exec. com. Nat. Council Crime and Delinquency, also mem. Council of Judges; bd. dirs. Better Boys Found.; pres. John Howard Assn., 1985-87; Republican candidate U.S. Senate, 1960, 70; chmn. Ill. Citizens for Nixon, 1968; pres. Young Reps. Ill., 1957-59; exec. com. United Rep. Fund Ill., 1963-69; former trustee Rockford Coll., Goodwill Industries, Chgo. Council Fgn. Relations. Recipient 1st Ann. Buddy Hackett award for service to young men, 1968; Pulitzer prize nominee, 1985. Mem. Am. Newspaper Pubs. Assn. Clubs: Onwentsia (Lake Forest, Ill.); Execs., Economic, City, Chicago Presidents, Tavern (Chgo.); Princeton (N.Y.C.); Press (San Francisco). Home: 450 W Deerpath Rd Lake Forest IL 60045 Office: 950 N Western Ave Lake Forest IL 60045

RENZ, DAVID OWEN, state official; b. Fargo, N.D., Nov. 17, 1952; s. Leland Stanford and Janet Marion (Osell) R.; m. Sandra Kay Wessels, July 27, 1974; children: Sarah Ann, Christian David. BS, U. Minn., 1976, MA, 1978, PhD, 1981. V.p., cons. Future Systems, Inc., Mpls., 1980-81; postdoctoral research fellow U. Minn., Mpls., 1981; asst. to commr. Minn. Dept. Labor and Industry, St. Paul, 1982-83, asst. commr., 1983-87; exec. dir. Met. Council Twin Cities, St. Paul, 1987—; mem. Minn. Labor Relations Adv. Council, St. Paul, 1984. Editor book series: Systems Thinking, 1980-81; asst. editor Futurics Quar. Jour., 1981-83; contbr. articles to profl. jours. Mem. Minn. Info. Policy Council, St. Paul, 1983—; mem. Citizens League of Minn., Mpls., 1986—, bd. govs. Coffman Meml. Union, Mpls., 1979-81. Solar Energy Publ. grantee No. States Power Research, 1979, Energy Edn. grantee Norwest Bank Contbn. Program, 1980, Futures Edn. grantee Gen. Mills Found., 1980. Mem. Am. Mgmt. Assn., Am. Soc. Tng. and Devel., Nat. Pub. Employment Labor Relations Assn., World Future Soc., Minn. Futurists. Presbyterian. Avocations: photography, model railroading, woodworking. Home: 100 W 49th St Minneapolis MN 55409 Office: Minn Dept Labor and Industry 300 Metro Square Bldg Saint Paul MN 55101

RESCIGNO, JOSEPH THOMAS, conductor; b. N.Y.C., Oct. 8, 1945; s. Joseph and Leona (Llewellyn) R.; m. Jeanne Marie Lo Pinto, Aug. 9, 1971. B.A., Fordham U., 1967; M.Mus., Manhattan Sch. Music, 1969. Conducting staff Manhattan Sch. Music, N.Y.C., 1969-76; assoc. condr. Concert Orch., L.I., N.Y., 1972-79; staff condr. Dallas Opera, 1976-82; artistic dir. Artists Internat., Providence, 1979-81; artistic advisor Florentine Opera, Milw., 1981—; guest condr. Washington Opera, 1979, 84, 85, Pitts. Opera, 1983, 84, St. Louis Opera, 1984, 85, N.Y.C. Opera, 1985. Recipient 2d prize Mozarteum, Salsburg, Austria, 1969; day of honor declared in his name Gov. R.I., 1981. Roman Catholic. Home: 711 West End Ave New York NY 10025 Office: Florentine Opera 750 N Lincoln Meml Dr Milwaukee WI 53202

RESLOCK, MARY HALE, information scientist; b. Hancock, Mich., Mar. 6, 1914; d. William T. and Mary F. (Ryan) Hale; m. E. James Reslock, June 19, 1943 (dec. May 1964); children—Mary J., Martha Reiff, Sophia Konecny, Ellen Blauer, James M. B.S. in Chemistry, Mich. Tech. U., 1938; M.S. in L.S., U. Mich., 1968. With Dow Chem. Co., 1940-79, sr. logician computations research lab., 1964-70, mgr. tech. info. service, 1971-79; with Mich. Molecular Inst., Midland, 1979-82; cons. in field. Past mem. adv. bd. G.H. Dow Library, Midland; mem. aux. bd. Midland Hosp. Mem. Am. Chem. Soc., Spl. Library Assn., Chem. Notation Assn. (award 1983), Sigma Xi. Roman Catholic. Clubs: Zonta, Brownson. Editor: (with others) Wiswesser Line Formula Chemical Notation, 2d edit., 1968; contbr. articles to profl. jours. Home: 530 N Saginaw Rd Midland MI 48640

RESNICK, ALICE ROBIE, judge; b. Erie, Pa., Aug. 21, 1939; d. Adam Joseph and Alice Suzanne (Spizarny) Robie; m. Melvin L. Resnick, Mar. 20, 1970. Ph.B., Siena Heights Coll., 1961; J.D., U. Detroit, 1964. Bar: Ohio 1964, Mich. 1965, U.S. Supreme Ct. 1970. Asst. county prosecutor Lucas County Prosecutor's Office, Toledo, 1964-75, trial atty., 1965-75; judge Toledo Mcpl. Ct., 1976-83, 6th Dist. Ct. Appeals, State of Ohio, Toledo, 1983—; instr. U. Toledo, 1968-69. Trustee Siena Heights Coll., Adrian, Mich., 1982—; organizer Crime Stopper Inc., Toledo, 1981—; bd. dirs. Toledo-Lucas County Safety Council; bd. dirs. Guest House Inc. Mem. Toledo Bar Assn., Lucas County Bar Assn., Nat. Assn. Women Judges, Am. Judicature Soc., Toledo Women's Bar Assn. Ct. of Appeals Judges Assn., Toledo Mus. Art, Internat. Inst. Toledo. Roman Catholic. Home: 2407 Edgehill Rd Toledo OH 43615 Office: 6th Dist Ct Appeals 800 Jackson St Toledo OH 43604

RESNICK, MARK DAVID, bank executive, educator; b. Detroit, Feb. 2, 1957; s. Harry and Miriam (Perin) R. BA, Wayne State U., 1979, MBA, 1983. Fin. analyst Mich. Nat. Bank Detroit, Clawson, 1983-85; sr. asset/liability analyst, v.p. Mich. Nat. Corp., Farmington Hills, Mich., 1985—; instr. fin. Wayne State U., Detroit, 1985—. Mem. Bank Adminstrn. Inst. Home: 28493 Franklin Apt 319 Southfield MI 48034 Office: Mich Nat Corp 30665 Northwestern Hwy Farmington Hills MI 48018

RESNICK, THOMAS EDWARD, pediatric dentist; b. Chgo., June 1, 1946; s. William Richard and Toby (Blinder) R.; m. Barbara Sue Siegel, July 12, 1970; children: Jon Matthew, Scott Daniel. BS, U. Ill., Chgo., 1969, DDS, 1971, MS, 1975. Lic. specialist in pediatric dentistry, Ill. Pediatric dentist Ill. Masonic Med. Ctr., Chgo., 1973—; pvt. practice pediatric dentistry Chgo., 1975—; asst. prof. U. Ill., Chgo., 1975-77; lectr. Northwestern U., Chgo., 1983—; pedodontics section chief Ill. Masonic Hosp., Chgo., 1978—, cons., 1975—; cons. Evanston (Ill.) Hosp., 1983—, Delta Dental, Chgo., 1983—. Served to capt. USAF, 1971-73. Mem. ADA, Am. Acad. Pediatric Dentistry, Am. Soc. Dentistry for Children, Acad. Dentistry, for the Handicapped, Am. Assn. Hosp. Dentists. Office: 1500 Shermer Rd Northbrook IL 60062

RESTIVO, RAYMOND M., health association executive, public health consultant; b. Chgo., Aug. 19, 1934; s. Frank M. and Angeline (Franzone) R.; children: Laura, Maria, Mark, Susan, Steven, John, Tony, Matthew. BSA, Loyola U., Chgo., 1956; cert. pub. health adminstrn. U. Ill., 1968; CAE, 1978. Adminstrv. asst. to pres. of S.K. Culver Co., Chgo., 1954-59; projects coordinator Chgo. Heart Assn., 1959-66, exec. dir., 1973—; pub. health adminstr. Chgo. Bd. Health, 1966-73, mem. adv. com., 1967-73, mem. editorial rev. com. for newsletter, 1968-73; cons. community health to various pub., vol. and ofcl. health agys., 1962—; del. to Pub. Service Inst. of City of Chgo., 1973; notary pub., Cook County (Ill.), 1971—; mem. oral bd. examiners for cardiovascular technologist, City of Chgo. Civil Service Commn., 1971-73. Sec. Morris Fishbein, Jr. Meml. Fund, 1973—; mem. Zoning Bd. Appeals, Forest Park, Ill., 1964-68; mem. Health Services Task Force, Oak Park, Ill., 1974-75; bd. dirs. Chgo. Health Research Found., 1976—, vice chmn., 1985—; mem. Planning Com. 4th Nat. Congress Quality of Life AMA, 1977-78. Recipient Meritorious Service award Village of Oak Park, 1975, Recognition award Chgo. Pub. Schs., 1982, Founders award Nat. Am. Italian Sports Hall of Fame, 1987. Mem. Am. Pub. Health Assn., Ill. Pub. Health Assn. (mem. policy com. 1971-73, mem. health issues com. 1972-73), Am. Heart Assn. Profl. Staff Soc., Am. Soc. Assn. Execs., Chgo. Soc. Assn. Execs. (Samuel B. Shapiro award 1986), Am. Mgmt. Assn., Nat. Assn. of Emergency Care Technicians, Epidemiology Club of Chgo., City of Chgo. Exec. Devel., Loyola U. Alumni Assns. Clubs: Tower, Univ. Office: 20 N Wacker Dr Chicago IL 60606

RETACCO-CONNER, MARY ELLEN, sales executive; b. Bryn Mawr, Ill., Dec. 9, 1958; s. Daniel Anthony and Mary Lillian (Millard) Retacco; m. Michael Dale Conner, Nov. 23, 1985. BA, Loyola U., Chgo., 1981. Sales rep. Pitney Bowes, Chgo., 1981-84, copier team mgr., 1984, sales devel. mgr., 1984; area sales mgr. Pitney Bowes, Arlington Heights, Ill., 1984—. Mem. Nat. Assn. Female Execs. Avocation: travel.

RETON, ROBERT DANIEL, II, sales and marketing specialist; b. N.Y.C., Sept. 16, 1961; s. Robert Daniel and Magaly (Susanna) R. BA, U. Va., 1983. With sales devel. staff Oiles Am. Corp., Plymouth, Mich., 1983—. Republican. Episcopalian. Avocations: travel, reading, skiing, tennis, golf. Office: Oiles Am Corp 14941 Cleat St Plymouth MI 48170

RETSON, NICHOLAS CHRIS, plastic surgeon; b. Chgo., Apr. 27, 1949; s. Chris Nicholas and Evangeline P. (Karos) R.; m. Donna Marie Koenigshofer, June 18, 1978; children: Chris, Brian, Michelle, Laura. BA, Northwestern U., 1971, MD, 1975. Cert. Am. Bd. Plastic Surgery. Intern Baylor U. Med. Ctr., Dallas, 1975-76; resident in surgery Columbus Hosp., Chgo., 1976-78; resident plastic surgery U. Ill., Chgo., 1979-81; practice medicine specializing in plastic surgery Merrillville, Ind., 1981—; attending staff St. Anthony Hosp., Crown Point, Ind., 1981—, St. Mary Med. Ctr., Hobart, Ind., 1981—; cons. staff Porter Meml. Hosp., Valparaiso, Ind., 1981—. Mem. Am. Soc. Plastic and Reconstructive Surgeons, Am. Coll. Surgeons. Greek Orthodox. Office: 8053 Cleveland Pl Merrillville IN 46410

RETTENMAIER, MARVIN JOSEPH, manufacturing company official, mosaicist; b. Carroll, Iowa, Mar. 23, 1924; s. Edward E. and Bernadine (Bernholtz) R. Student Mpls. Inst. Art, 1945-46, U. Minn., 1947-48, Milw.

Sch. Engring., 1966. Aircraft mechanic Northwest Orient Airlines, St. Paul, 1942-45; master stencil artist Photoplating Co., Mpls., 1945-49; 3d officer, purser North Central Airlines, Mpls., 1953; chief insp. W.H. Brady Co., Milw., 1953—; exhbn. micro mosaics include: Putnam Mus., Davenport, Iowa, Milwaukee County Pub. Mus., Morristown (N.J.) Coll., Cath. U. Library, Washington, First Wis. Ctr., Milw. represented in permanent collections: Alcoa Co., Pitts., Oberlin Coll., Wildwood Mus., Cape May, N.J., Ripley Internat., Toronto. Served with AUS, 1949-53. Mem. Am. Soc. Quality Control, (charter mem. insp. div.). Roman Catholic. Lodge: Eagles. Office: 2221 W Camden Rd PO Box 2131 Milwaukee WI 53201

REUBEL, STEVEN JAY, oral and maxillofacial surgeon; b. N.Y.C., May 19, 1953; s. Roy and Elaine (Hirsch) R.; m. Carol Ann Priest, Nov. 25, 1983. BSEE, U. Pa., 1975, DMD, 1980. Resident L.I. Jewish Med. Ctr., New Hyde Park, N.Y., 1980-82, chief resident, 1983; practice dentistry specializing in oral and maxillofacial surgery Cin., 1983—. Fellow Am. Assn. Oral and Maxillofacial Surgeons, Am. Coll. Oral and Maxillofacial Surgeons; mem. ADA, Am. Soc. Dental Anesthesiology, British Assn. Oral and Maxillofacial Aurgeons. Avocations: auto restoration and racing, running, antique restoration and collecting. Office: 7724 Montgomery Rd Cincinnati OH 45236

REUM, W. ROBERT, financial executive; b. Oak Park, Ill., July 22, 1942; m. Sharon Milliken. B.A., Yale U., 1964; J.D., U. Mich., 1967; M.B.A., Harvard U., 1969. Dir. investment analysis City Investing Co., N.Y.C., 1969-72; v.p. corp fin. Mich. Nat. Corp., Bloomfield Hills, Mich., 1972-78; v.p., treas. White Motor Corp., Cleve., 1978-79; v.p. fin., chief fin. officer Lamson & Sessions, Cleve., 1980-82, The Interlake Corp., Oak Brook, Ill., 1982—. Contbr. articles to Harvard Bus. Rev. Club: Chicago Golf (Wheaton, Ill.). Office: The Interlake Corp 2015 Spring Rd Oak Brook IL 60521

REUSCHLEIN, EARL VINCENT, retired accountant; b. Plain, Wis., Aug. 6, 1921; s. Henry J. and Christina (Paulus) R.; children: Steven, Robert, Richard, Suzanne, John. BA, U. Wis., 1944. CPA, Wis. Acct. State of Wis., Madison, 1944, Ray-O-Vac Co., Madison, 1944-46, Sakrison, Rockey, Madison, 1946-50, Reuschlein & Stortroen, Madison, 1950-62; pres. Reuschlein, Strickland, Bischoff & Ragsdale, Madison, 1962-85; bd. dirs. Hursing Homes, Inc., Sauk City, Wis., Dorlee, Inc., Platteville, Wis. Bd. dirs. Am. Found. for Biol. Research, Bethesda, Md., 1970-84, Marine Bank of Dane County 1978—. Mem. Am. Inst. CPA's, Wis. Inst. CPA's. Republican. Club: Blackhawk Country (Madison) (bd. dirs. 1962-65). Lodges: Kiwanis, Elks. Home: 2225 Keyes Ave Madison WI 53711 Office: Reuschlein Strickland Bischoff & Ragsdale SC 6510 Schroeder Rd Madison WI 53711

REUSS, LLOYD EDWIN ARMIN, automobile manufacturing company executive; b. Belleville, Ill., Sept. 22, 1936; s. Lawrence Phillip and Dorthea B. (Juenger) R.; m. Maurcine Kaye Bilderback, Aug. 10, 1957; children: Charlene Faye, Mark Lyle. B.S. in Mech. Engring., U. Mo., Rolla, 1957; grad. sr. exec. course, M.I.T., 1971. With Gen. Motors Corp., 1959—, chief engr., Buick Motor div., 1975-78, dir. engring., Chevrolet div., 1978-80, v.p., gen. mgr., Buick Motor div., 1980-84, v.p., group exec., Chevrolet, Pontiac, GM of Can., 1984-86, exec. v.p., 1986—, group exec., truck & bus groups, 1987—; dir. Electronic Data Systems Corp., Tex. Trustee Lawrence Inst. Tech., Southfield, Mich., 1977—, Alma Coll., Mich., 1986—, Louisville Presbyn. Theol. Sem. Ky., 1985—. Served with C.E. AUS, 1957-59. Mem. Soc. Automotive Engrs., Pi Tau Sigma, Tau Beta Pi. Presbyterian (elder). Office: General Motors Corp Gen Motors Bldg 3044 W Grand Blvd Detroit MI 48202

REUSS, ROBERT MICHAEL, financial executive; b. Cin., Nov. 24, 1939; s. Robert Jacob and Elizabeth Lucille (Burk) R.; m. Vicki McFee, June 7, 1965 (div. Sept. 1984); children: Jeremiah, Nicholas; m. Judy Ann Nelson, Oct. 19, 1985. BSEE, Purdue U., 1961, MS in Indsl. Engring., 1962. Supr. mgmt. services Touche Ross and Co., Mpls., 1963-67; v.p. fin. planning Internat. Dairy Queen, Mpls., 1968-70; v.p., controller, treas. Standard Fabrics, Mpls., 1970-72; pres., chief exec. officer Reuss Thiss and Co., Mpls., 1972-78, H.A. Rogers Co., Inc., Mpls., 1978-82; pres. Lingate Fin. Group, Inc., St. Louis Park, Minn., 1982—; Bd. dirs., chief fin. officer Bethel Marine, Inc.; bd. dirs. Ionic Controls, Inc. Mem. Leadership Mpls.; bd. dirs. Project for Pride in Living. Clubs: 5:55, Calhoun Beach. Home: 219 Gramisie Shoreview MN 55126 Office: Lingate Fin Group 5100 Gamble Dr Saint Louis Park MN 55416

REUSS, ROBERT PERSHING, telecommunications executive; b. Aurora, Ill., Mar. 23, 1918; s. George John and Mary Belle (Gorrie) R.; m. Mildred Louise Daly, Dec. 22, 1940 (dec. May 1985); children: Lynn Ann (Mrs. David Bohmer), Robert Cameron; m. Grace K. Brady, Aug. 28, 1986. B.S., U. Ill., 1939; postgrad., Harvard Bus. Sch., 1943; M.B.A., U. Chgo., 1950; D.B.A., Blackburn Coll., 1976. Pres., chief exec. officer, dir. Centel Corp., 1972-76, chmn., 1977—; staff AT&T, 1955-58, asst. comptroller, 1958-59; v.p. Ill. Bell Telephone Co., 1959-72, dir., 1970-72; dir. Tellabs, Inc., Am. Nat. Bank and Trust Co., Chgo., Amsted Industries, Nat. Can Corp., Staley Continental, Inc. Bd. dirs. Jr. Achievement Chgo., 1970-77, pres., 1971-73; bd. govs. Midwest Stock Exchange; trustee Rush-Presbyn.-St. Luke's Med. Ctr., Chgo., Blackburn Coll., 1968-83, Aurora U., 1986—; bd. dirs. U. Ill. Found. Served to lt. (s.g.) USNR, 1943-46, PTO. Mem. Chgo. Assn. Commerce and Industry (bd. dirs. 1971-78), Phi Kappa Phi. Presbyterian (deacon, trustee). Clubs: Commercial, Mid-Am., Chicago, Economic (Chgo.); Chicago Golf (Wheaton, Ill.); Old Baldy (Saratoga, Wyo.); Ocean (Ocean Ridge, Fla.); Delray Beach Yacht, Country of Fla. (Delray Beach).

REUTZEL, ROBERT JEROME, pharmacist, pharmacology educator; b. Swea City, Iowa, Sept. 29, 1934; s. Henry John and Anna Veronica (Matheis) R.; m. Renee Marcella Neubert, May 11, 1963; children—Jerome, Thomas, Jane. B.S., S.D. State U., 1961. Registered pharmacist, Minn., S.D. Pharmacist, Paulson's Pharmacy, Fairmont, Minn., 1961-62, Thro Drug Stores, Mankato, Minn., 1962-71; owner, mgr. Mankato Clinic Pharmacy, 1971-76, Prescription Care Center, Mankato, 1976—; instr. pharmacology of emergency drugs Mankato State U., 1975—; cons. Mankato Robert E. Miller Home Inc., 1976—. Republican precinct and county del. Mankato, 1962—. Mem. Nat. Assn. Retail Druggists, Am. Acad. Pharmacy Practice, Am. Pharm. Assn., Minn. State Pharm. Assn. (bd. dirs. 1961—), Mankato Area Pharmacist Soc., Mankato Area C. of C., Rho Chi. Republican. Roman Catholic. Lodges: Hilltop Kiwanis (bd. dirs. 1964-76), K.C. Avocation: music. Home: 208 Capital Dr Mankato MN 56001 Office: Prescription Care Ctr 1057 Madison Ave Mankato MN 56001

REVEL, ANNA CARTER, school psychologist, deacon; b. Marion, Ky., June 26, 1924; d. Thomas Homer and Ruth Carlyle (Cook) Carter; m. John Clarence Revel Jr., Nov. 26, 1948 (div Aug. 1967); 1 child, Mary Linda Revel Shaw. BS in Home Econs., U. Ky., 1948; MEd in Sch. Psychology, U. Wis., Whitewater, 1973; postgrad., U. Wis., Madison, 1976-77, U. Minn., 1983; grad., Nashotah (Wis.) House Episc. Sem., 1980. Lic. sch. psychologist, Wis.; ordained deacon Episc. Ch. Home econs. tchr. various high schs., Ky., Ohio and Wis., 1948-72; sch. psychologist Janesville (Wis.) Sch. Dist., 1973—; pvt. practice sch. psychology, Madison, 1976—. Bd. dirs. Beginnings Home for Adolescent Boys, Janesville, 1974—, Janesville DayCare Ctrs., 1974-76; deacon Trinity Episc. Ch., Janesville, 1981—. Wis. Dept. Pub. Instrn. grantee, 1983. Mem. Internat. Council Psychologists, NEA, Assn. Sch. Psychologists, Wis. Sch. Psychologist Assn. (exec. bd. 1985—), Wis. Edn. Assn., Janesville Edn. Assn. (com. chair), Pi Lambda Theta. Democrat. Episcopalian. Avocations: genealogy, needlework, travel, reading, gardening. Home: 1501 Wolcott Janesville WI 53545 Office: Edn Services Ctr 527 S Franklin Janesville WI 53545

REVSINE, BERNARD WILLIAM, finance executive; b. Chgo., Feb. 27, 1936; s. Victor Boris and Pauline (Berger) R. BS, Roosevelt U., 1956; MBA, Northwestern U., 1965. CPA, Ill. Sr. acct. V.B. Revsine & Co., Chgo., 1956-64; tax supr. Baxter Travenol Labs., Deerfield, Ill., 1964-66; chief fin. officer Royal Continental Box Co., Cicero, Ill., 1966—; bd. dirs. Dynamic Container, Addison, Ill. Mem. Am. Inst. CPA's (editorial adv. com. to acctg. jour.), Ill. CPA Soc. (chmn. mgmt. adv. services com.). Avocations: reading, people.

REXING, LOUIS G., accountant; b. Evanston, Ill., Sept. 6, 1960; s. Joseph L. and Dorothy J. (Hilgenbrinck) R.; m. Candace M. Blair, Sept. 2, 1984. BS in Acctg., DePaul U., 1982, M in Acctg., 1983. CPA, Ill. Internal auditor Esmark, Chgo., 1982; pub. auditor Arthur Young & Co., Chgo., 1983-86; mgr. acctg. policy Citicorp Diners Club, Chgo., 1986—. Mem. Am. Inst. CPA's, Ill. CPA Soc., Am. Mgmt. Assn. Republican. Roman Catholic. Avocations: model railroading, travel, chess, golf. Office: Citicorp Diners Club 8430 W Bryn Mawr Ave Chicago IL 60631

REY, CARMEN ROSELLO, researcher, food scientist; b. Santiago, Cuba, Feb. 14, 1923; came to U.S., 1961, naturalized, 1968; m. Alfredo Rey, May 16, 1948 (div. 1969); children—Lauri, Roberto. B.A. in Agrl. Engring., Havana U., 1945, B.S. in Sugar Chemistry, 1946; M.S., Iowa State U., 1968, Ph.D., 1975. Head quality control Alto Songo Sugar Co., Cuba, 1947-60; lab technician dept. food sci. Iowa State U., Ames, 1963-65, research grad. asst., 1965-68, research assoc., 1968-70, assoc., 1970-75; chem. engr. Stokely-Van Camp, Inc., Indpls., 1975-76, sr. microbiologist, 1976-79, supr. microbiology labs., 1979-81, mgr. microbiology lab. services, 1981-83, mgr. research and devel., 1983-84; research scientist Quaker Oats Co., Inc., Chgo., 1984—. Contbr. articles to profl. jours. Past bd. v.p., mem. at large bd. dirs. Hispano Am. Multi Service Ctr.; bd. dirs., personnel com. Indpls. Settlements, Inc.; past sec. Indpls. Employment and Tng. Adv. Council. Recipient Profl. Achievement award Ctr. for Leadership and Devel., Inc., 1983. Mem. Inst. Food Technologists (mem. at large exec., com. microbiology div. 1979-81, chmn. nominating com. microbiology div. 1981), Am. Frozen Food Inst. (microbiology and food safety com.), Nat. Assn. Agronomic and Sugar Engrs. of Cuba in Exile, Inc., Cuban Assn. Ind., Sigma Xi, Phi Kappa Phi, Gamma Sigma Delta. Club: Toastmasters (chpt. pres.). Office: Quaker Oats Co Inc 617 W Main St Barrington IL 60010

REY, JOHN A., computer applications executive; b. Gary, Ind., Nov. 25, 1942; s. Joseph Garcia and Lillian Rose (Stefen) R.; m. Marjorie Louise Swinford, Aug. 22, 1964; children: Daniel, Timothy. BS, Purdue U., 1964; MBA, No. Ill. U., 1970. Systems programmer DeKalb (Ill.) Corp., 1964-68, seed cost acct., 1968-72, mgr. info. services, 1972-78, mgr. budget and cost, 1978-82, mgr. reporting systems, 1982-85, mgr. application programming, 1985—. Bd. dirs. Ben Gordon Mental Health Ctr. Found., DeKalb, 1981-86; mem. Dist. 428 Sch. Bd., DeKalb, 1985. Mem. Planning Execs. Forum, Sigma Iota Epsilon (hon.). Presbyterian. Home: 204 W Milner Ave DeKalb IL 60115 Office: DeKalb Corp 3100 Sycamore Rd DeKalb IL 60115

REYES, HERNAN MACABALLUG, pediatric surgeon; b. Isabela, Philippines, Apr. 5, 1933; came to U.S., 1958; s. Leonor Bulcan and Anacleta (Macaballug) R.; m. Dolores C. Cruz, Feb. 27, 1960; children: Cynthia, Michael, Maria, Patricia, Catherine. Student, U. Philippines, 1949-51; AA; MD, U. Santo Tomas Sch. Medicine, Manila, 1957. Diplomate Am. Bd. Surgery. Intern Cook County Hosp., Chgo., 1958-59, resident, 1959-64; clin. asst. dept. surgery Stritch Sch. Medicine, Loyola U., Maywood, Ill., 1964-65, 68, clin. assoc., 1969; acting pediatric surgeon Cook County Children's Hosp., Chgo., 1965; instr. surgery, chief sect. pediatric surgery U. Santo Tomas Faculty Medicine and Surgery, Manila, 1966-67; attending surgeon, chief pediatric surgery U. Santo Tomas Hosp., Manila, 1966-67; attending surgeon Little Co. of Mary Hosp., Evergreen Park, Ill., 1968—; asst. prof. dept. surgery Pritzker Sch. Medicine, U. Chgo., 1969-73, assoc. prof., 1973-76, acting chief sect. pediatric surgery, 1973-74; attending surgeon Wyler Children's Hosp., U. Chgo., 1969-76, dir. emergency surg. services, 1973-74; profl. dept. surgery, chief div. pediatric surgery U. Ill. Coll. Medicine, Chgo., 1976—, prof. clin. pediatrics, 1982—; chief div. pediatric surgery U. Ill. Hosp., Chgo., 1976—; surgeon-in-chief, chmn. div. pediatric surgery Cook County Children's Hosp., 1976—, chmn. dept. surgery, 1987—; cons. pediatric surgery Mercy Hosp. and Med. Ctr., Chgo., Mile Square Health Ctr., Chgo., Christ Hosp., Oak Lawn, Ill., Shriners Hosp. Crippled Children, Chgo. Contbr. articles to profl. publs., chpts. to books. Recipient Tchr. of Yr. award Little Co. Mary Hosp., 1969, Disting. Physician award Philippine Med. Assn. Chgo., 1972, Class recognition Pritzker Sch. Medicine, 1974-75, Leadership award Soc. Philippine Surgeons, 1976, cert. of Appreciation Philippine Med. Assn., 1977. Mem. ACS (Chgo. com. on trauma), Am. Acad. Pediatrics, Am. Assn. Surgery Trauma, AAUP, AMA, Am. Pediatric Surg. Assn., Assn. Acad. Surgery, Cen. Surg. Assn., Chgo. Med. Soc. (councilor 1975-76), Chgo. Soc. Gastro, Chgo. Surg. Soc., Ill. Pediatric Surg. Assn. (sec.-treas 1976-77, pres. 1978-79), Ill. State Med. Soc., Ill. Surg. Soc., Inst. Medicine Chgo., N.Y. Acad. Scis., Soc. Philippine Surgeons Am. (founding pres.), Western Surg. Assn., AAAS, Am. Trauma Soc., Sigma Xi. Avocation: tennis. Office: Cook County Children's Hosp 700 S Wood St Room B-40 Chicago IL 60612

REYES, ROSE MARY, teacher; b. Cleve., July 24, 1942; d. Michael A. and Clara (Almerico) Ricciardi; m. Orlando R. Reyes, June 24, 1972; children: Sean, Erica, Orlando. BS, Kent State U., 1970. Teaching sister Siters St. Dominic, Akron, 1964-69; social worker Portage Co. Social Services, Ravenna, Ohio, 1970-71; tchr. pvt. schs. 1971-84, tchr. pub. schs., 1984-87. Mem. Nat. Edn. Assn., Ohio Edn. Assn., Crestwood Edn. Assn. Democrat. Roman Cthlic. Avocations: reading, travel, bicycling, refinishing antiques. Office: 11741 Center Rd Mantua OH 44255

REYES, RUDY SAN PEDRO, real estate development and parking company executive; b. Manila, Nov. 27, 1941; s. Benito and Avelina (San Pedro) R.; m. Cecilia S.P. Suarez, Dec. 8, 1961; children: Ferdinand, Rudolf, Vanessa, Regina, Ronald. AB in Polit. Sci. cum laude,Far Eastern U., Manila, 1965; MBA, U. Philippines, 1965. Exec. asst. to exec. v.p. Air Manila, Inc., 1969, gen. mgr. traffic and sales dept., 1970; honesty checker parking ops., Edison Parking Corp. (EPC), Newark, 1970-71; supr. Newark ops., Manhattan, N.Y.C. ops., 1972-73, gen. mgr. div. B, 1976; asst. to v.p. Denison Parking, Inc., Indpls., 1977; pres. and gen. mgr. Pacific Industries, Inc., Indpls., 1978—; pres. Econo Car Rent-a-Car of Indpls., owner A-1 Car Care Ctrs. of Indpls. Bd. dirs. Indpls. Zool. Soc., 1982—, United Way Greater Ind.; bd. nat. govs. Philippine Heritage Endowment Found. at Ind. U.; liaison officer T. Sunggani dist. Boy Scouts Am., Indpls.; mem. Riley Area Revitalization Program, Internat. Ctr. Indpls. Mem. Parking Assn. Indpls., Nat. Parking Assn. Club: Barangay Philipino-Am. (Indpls.) (pres. 1982-83). Lodges: Kiwanis (dir. 1982-84), Optimists (dir. 1980-84; Community Leadership award 1980-81) (Indpls.). Roman Catholic. Home: 9737 Decatur Indianapolis IN 46256

REYMOND, RALPH DANIEL, radiologist; b. Geneva, Switzerland, Mar. 31, 1937; came to U.S. 1950; s. Ernest Reymond and Dolores (Francini) Zendali; m. Patricia Ann Bulger, Feb. 4, 1961; 1 child, Eric Daniel. BA in Physics and Egyptology, Johns Hopkins U., 1959, MA in Physics, 1963; MD, U. Md., Balt., 1967. Diplomate Am. Bd. Radiology. Intern Md. Gen. Hosp., Balt., 1967-68; resident in radiology Johns Hopkins Hosp., Balt., 1968-72; radiologist Radiology and Nuclear Medicine PA, Topeka, 1972—; clin. asst. prof. dept. radiation oncology Kans. U. Med. Ctr. Dept. Radiation Oncology, Kansas City, 1976—; physicist Harry Diamond Labs. Dept. Army, 1957-67; med. dir. St. Francis Capital Region Radiotherapy Ctr., Topeka, 1977—. Inventor med. equipment. Bd. dirs. Topeka Zoo, 1973-76. Physics fellow Aerojet Gen. Corp., 1959, Gilman fellow Johns Hopkins U., 1960-61. Mem. Am. Coll. Radiology, Am. Soc. Therapeutic Radiology and Oncology, AMA, Am. Radium Soc., Am. Phys. Soc., Am. Research Ctr. in Cairo, Egypt. Republican. Clubs: Rolls Royce Owner's, Saturday Night Literary. Avocations: Egyptology, photography, painting. Home: 2816 Mac Vicar Ave Topeka KS 66611 Office: Radiology & Nuclear Medicine Medical Park West 823 Mulvane St Topeka KS 66606

REYNES, WENDY WARNER, pub. co. exec.; b. Boston, Sept. 29, 1944; d. Philip Russell and Elizabeth (Patton) Warner; A.A., Conn. Coll., 1966; m. Jose (Tony) Antonio Reynes, III, Apr. 26, 1969; children—Jose (Tad) Antonio, Gabrielle Elizabeth. With Foote, Cone, Belding, N.Y.C., 1966-68; advt. sales rep. Cosmopolitan Mag., N.Y.C., 1968-69, Co-Ed Mag., N.Y.C., 1969-70; asst. product mgr. Avon Products, N.Y.C., 1970; advt. sales rep. Mag. Networks, N.Y.C. and Chgo., 1970-72; midwest mgr. advt. sales Girl Talk Mag., Chgo., 1972-75; div. mgr. advt. sales Pattis Group, Chgo., 1975-79; pres. Reynes & Assos., Inc., 1979—, Sales Unltd., Inc., 1985—. Bd. dirs. Multiple Sclerosis, 1974-79, St. Joseph's Sch. PTA, 1979-80, Marriage Encounter, 1976—; active Jr. League Greenwich, Conn., 1965-67, Jr. League N.Y.C., 1967-75. Mem. Agate Club (dir.), Advt. Assn., Women's Advt. Club Chgo. (co-chmn.). Clubs: Chgo. Advt., Wilmette Tennis, East Bank, Women's Advt. Chgo. Home: 460 Ash St Winnetka IL 60093

REYNOLDS, A. WILLIAM, manufacturing company executive; b. Columbus, Ohio, June 21, 1933; s. William Morgan and Helen Hibbard (McCray) R.; m. Joanne D. McCormick, June 12, 1953; children: Timothy M., Morgan Reynolds Brigham, Mary M. AB in Econs., Harvard U., 1955; MBA, Stanford U., 1957. Pres. Crawford Door Co., Detroit, 1959-66; staff asst. to treas TRW Inc., Cleve., 1957-59, asst. to exec. v.p. automotive group, 1966-67, v.p. automotive aftermarket group, 1967-70, exec. v.p. indsl. and replacement sector, 1971-81, exec. v.p. automotive worldwide sector, 1981-84; pres. GenCorp, Akron, Ohio, 1984-85, pres., chief exec. officer, 1985—, chmn., chief exec. officer, 1987—, also bd. dirs.; bd. dirs. Soc. Corp., Cleve., Eaton Corp., Cleve.; mem. dean's adv. council Stanford (Calif.) U. Grad. Sch. Bus., 1981—. Bd. dirs. N.E. Ohio chpt. INROADS, Cleve., 1985—, chmn. United Way-Red Cross of Summit County, Ohio, 1987; trustee Univ. Hosps. of Cleve., 1984—, chmn., 1987—. Mem. Soc. Automotive Engrs., Rubber Mfrs. Assn. (bd. dirs., exec. com. 1985—), Bus. Roundtable, Council on Fgn. Relations. Episcopalian. Clubs: Kirtland Country (Willoughby, Ohio); Union (Cleve.); Rolling Rock (Ligonier, Pa.); John's Island (Vero Beach, Fla.); Pepper Pike (Cleve.); Harvard (N.Y.). Avocations: hunting, fly fishing, skiing, golf. Office: GenCorp Inc 1 General St Akron OH 44329

REYNOLDS, ALLEN DEAN, media sales executive; b. Kansas City, Kans., June 27, 1957; s. Raymond O. and Irene D. (Crane) R.; m. Jill Ingram, Oct. 1, 1983. BS in Journalism and Advt., U. Kans., 1979. Mgr. advt. promotions Blue Springs (Mo.) Examiner, 1980-81; account exec. Kans. City Star and Times, Kansas City, Mo., 1981-85, Sta. KXTR-FM, Kansas City, 1985—. Bd. dirs. S Kansas City C. of C., 1983-84. Mem. Ad Club Kansas City (II div. bd. dirs. 1983—, v.p. 1986-87, pres. 1987-88). Club: Kansas City. Office: Sta KXTR-FM 1701 S 55th St Kansas City KS 66106

REYNOLDS, FRANK MILLER, minister; b. Trumansburg, N.Y., Sept. 11, 1921; s. George Andrew and Beth (Miller) R.; m. Gladys May Richards, June 15, 1946; children: Daniel, Stephen, Timothy, Mark, THomas. BS in Agriculture, Cornell U., 1944. Ordained to ministry, 1949. Pastor Assembly of God Ch., Canandaiga, N.Y., 1947-52, Medford, N.J., 1952-58; pastor El Bethel, Staten Island, N.Y., 1958-62; founder, dir. Teen Challenge Tng., Rehrersburg, Pa., 1962-73; nat. rep. Teen Challenge USA, Springfield, Mo., 1973—; sect. sec. Assemblies of God Cen. N.Y., 1948-52; dist. home missionary Assemblies of God N.J., 1953-59; sec. Teen Challenge, Bklyn., 1959-68. Co-author: Drug Bug, 1970, Somebody Help Me, 1970; contbr. articles to profl. jours. Republican. Avocation: gardening. Home: 1504 E Buena Vista Springfield MO 65807 Office: Teen Challenge 1525 Campbell Ave Springfield MO 65803

REYNOLDS, HORACE HERMAN, IV, lawyer; b. Oakland, Calif., Aug. 29, 1958; s. Horace Herman and Beverly Agnes (Tuoto) R.; m. Anne Theresa Goecke, Apr. 26, 1986. BA, Creighton U., 1977, JD, 1982. Bar: N.D. 1983, Nebr. 1983, U.S. Dist. Ct. N.D. 1983, U.S. Dist. Ct. Nebr. 1983, U.S. Ct. appeals (7th cir.) 1983, U.S. Dist. Ct. (we. dist.) Wis. 1984, U.S. Ct. Claims 1984, U.S. Ct. Internat. Trade 1984, U.S. Tax Ct. 1984, U.S. Ct. Appeals (3d, 5th, 7th, 8th, 9th, 10th, D.C. and fed. cirs.) 1984, U.S. Ct. Appeals (3d, 5th and 9th cirs.) 1985, U.S. Supreme Ct. 1986. Sole practice Bellevue, Nebr., 1983—; gen. counsel Nebr. Credit Union League, Omaha, 1983-86. Mem. ABA, Am. Trial Lawyers Assn., N.D. Bar Assn., Nebr. Bar Assn., Bellevue Jaycees (v.p. 1985-86), Pi Sigma Alpha. Democrat. Roman Catholic. Lodges: Elks, Eagles. Home: 4925 NW Radial Hwy Omaha NE 68104

REYNOLDS, JACK W., utility company executive; b. Magazine, Ark., Feb. 28, 1923; s. Robert H. and Effie (Files) R.; m. Alberta Barkett, Nov. 13, 1949; children: John, David, Steven, Thomas, Laurie. B.S. in Phys. Sci., Okla. State U., 1943, B.S. in Indsl. Engring., 1947. Registered profl. engr., Wis. With B.F. Goodrich Co., Akron, Ohio, 1947-75, dir. union relations, 1969-70, dir. indsl. relations, 1970-75; v.p. personnel Consumers Power Co., Jackson, Mich., 1975-78, sr. v.p. personnel and pub. affairs, 1978-81, exec. v.p. energy supply, 1981—; pres. Mich. gas Storage Co., Jackson, 1981—, Plateau Resources, Ltd., Jackson, 1983—. Mem. exec. bd. Land O'Lakes council Boy Scouts Am., 1975. Served to 1st lt. C.E. U.S. Army, 1943-46, CBI. Mem. Mich. Soc. Profl. Engrs., East Central Area Reliability Group (exec. bd.), Greater Jackson C. of C. Republican. Methodist. Clubs: Jackson Country; The Town (Jackson). Office: Consumers Power Co 1945 W Parnell Rd Jackson MI 49201 also: Consumers Power Co 212 W Michigan Ave Jackson MI 49201

REYNOLDS, JOHN W., federal judge; b. Green Bay, Wis., Apr. 4, 1921; s. John W. and Madge (Flatley) R.; m. Patricia Ann Brody, May 26, 1947 (dec. Dec. 1967); children: Kate M. Reynolds Lindquist, Molly A. Reynolds Jassoy, James B.; m. Jane Conway, July 31, 1971; children: Jacob F., Thomas J., Frances P., John W. III. Ph.B., U. Wis., 1946, LL.B., 1949. Bar: Wis. 1949. Since practiced in Green Ba, dist. dir. price stblzn., 1951-53, U.S. commr., 1953-58, atty. gen. of Wis., 1958-62; gov. State of Wis., 1963-65; U.S. dist. judge Eastern Dist. Wis., 1965-71, chief judge, 1971-86, sr. judge, 1986—. Served with U.S. Army, 1942-46. Mem. Am. Bar Assn., State Bar Wis., Am. Law Inst. Office: US Dist Ct Room 471 Fed Bldg 517 E Wisconsin Ave Milwaukee WI 53202

REYNOLDS, LEO THOMAS, electronics company executive; b. Mpls., May 24, 1945; s. Donald Charles and Elizabeth (Graham) R.; m. Betty Gail Herrington, Aug. 8, 1966 (div. Apr. 1978); children: William, Nathan; m. Diana Frances Boyd, Feb. 26, 1982; children: Jeffrey, Daniel. BSEE, U. Iowa, 1972; postgrad. in bus., Mankato State U., 1972-74. Mech. draftsman John Deere Co., Dubuque, Iowa, 1970-71; engring. supr. 3M Co., New Ulm, Minn., 1972-76; supt. Litton Microwave, Sioux Falls, S.D., 1976-80; founder, pres., chief exec. officer Electronic Systems, Inc., Sioux Falls, 1980—. Editor Transit mag., 1972. Served with USAF, 1963-67. Mem. Nat. Soc. Profl. Engrs., Surface Mount Tech. Assn., Sioux Falls C. of C. (leadership trainer). Republican. Avocations: reading, sailing, motorcycling, performing arts. Office: Electronic Systems Inc 600 E 50th St Box 5013 Sioux Falls SD 57117

REYNOLDS, NEAL SCOTT, data processing executive; b. Evanston, Ill., Sept. 7, 1960; s. Neal Arthur and Mary Lou (Kendrick) R. Grad. high sch., Crete, Ill. Tech. specialist R.R. Donnelley & Sons, Chicago, 1981-83; software engring. Zenith Corp., Glenview, Ill., 1984; v.p. software devel. Synth Corp., Richton Park, Ill., 1983—, co-founder, v.p. software devel., 1983—; software engr. Sun Electric, Crystal Lake, Ill., 1985—. Mem. AAAS. Clubs: L-5 Soc., Planetary Soc. Home: 1725 Birch #108 Schaumburg IL 60173

REYNOLDS, PAMELA KAY, pharmacist, pharmacy executive; b. St. Louis, Jan. 1, 1948; d. Audrey and Dorothy Katherine (Durner) Freeze; m. Gary Keith Reynolds, May 13, 1972; children: Garth Kyle, Glenna Katrina. BS in Pharmacy, St. Louis Coll. Pharmacy, 1972. Registered pharmacist Ill., Mo. Mgr., pharmacist Ross Drug, Mt. Vernon, Ill., 1972-74; staff pharmacist Pine Street Pharmacy, Eldorado, Ill., 1974-75; relief pharmacist So. Ill. area, 1975-79; co-owner, operator, Reynolds Value-Rite Pharmacy, McLeansboro, Ill., 1973—; cons. Oak View Nursing Home, McLeansboro, 1975—, Life Care Ctr. of McLeansboro, 1984—. Com. mem. Cub Scout Pack 30, Boy Scouts Am., McLeansboro, 1984-87, den leader, 1985-87, chmn. com., 1986-87, asst. cubmaster, 1986-87; chmn. troop leaders, organizer, troop leader Girl Scouts U.S., McLeansboro, 1986. Mem. Am. Pharm. Assn., SE Pharmacist Assn. Ill, Ill. Pharmacist Assn., So. Ill. Pharmacist Assn. (Ho. of Dels. 1978-83, 86-87), Hamilton County Pharmacist Assn. (treas. 1984—), Beta Sigma Phi (v.p. McLeansboro chpt. 1976-78, chmn. ways and means com. St. Louis chpt. 1971-72). Baptist. Avocations: Swimming; rose garden research; reading; sewing; working with children. Home: Route 3 McLeansboro IL 62859 Office: Reynolds Valu-Rite Pharmacy 107 North Jackson McLeansboro IL 62859

REYNOLDS, PAUL EDWARD, general engineer, real estate developer; b. Toledo, Aug. 19, 1949; s. Don Ray and Audrey Mae (Nelms) R.; m. Helen Frances Hayes, Dec. 18, 1971; 1 child, Michael Paul. BS in Gen. Engring., U.S. Mil. Acad., 1971. Commd. 2d lt. U.S. Army, 1971, advanced through grades to capt., resigned, 1977; project engr. U.S. Gypsum (Ohio) Co., 1978-

82, computer applications engr., 1982-84, plant engr., 1984—; gen. ptnr. JP Investments, Ltd., Port Clinton, Ohio, 1985—. Mem. Am. Legion. Republican. Club: Bay View Stock. Lodges: Elks, Moose. Avocation: coin collecting. Home: 2935 Cleveland Rd Port Clinton OH 43452 Office: US Gypsum Co 101 Lake St Gypsum OH 43433

REYNOLDS, ROBERT BELKNAP, psychiatrist; b. Fenchow, People's Republic of China, Nov. 8, 1922; s. Paul Russell and Charlotte Louise (Belknap) R.; m. M. Jo Hart, Feb. 10, 1951; children: Patricia, Robert Jr., Katheryn. AB, Carleton Coll., 1944; MD, Harvard U., 1947. Intern U. Chgo., 1947-48; resident in psychiatry Malcolm Bliss Hosp., St. Louis, 1948-49, VA Hosp., Jefferson Barracks, Mo., 1949-51; staff psychiatrist, chief intensive treatment service VA Hosp., Jefferson Barracks, 1954-56; staff psychiatrist VA Mental Hygiene Clinic, St. Louis, 1951-52; practice medicine specializing in psychiatry St. Louis, 1956—; clin. instr. to clin. asst. prof. psychiatry, St. Louis U. Med. Sch., 1956—; dir. Child Guidance Clinic City of St. Louis, 1956-58; attending psychiatrist, cons. Cochran VA Hosp., 1956-66; cons. Acid Rescue, Youth Emergency Service, United Meth. Children's Home. Served to capt. U.S. Army Med. Corps, 1952-54. Fellow Am. Psychiat. Assn. (life), Eastern Mo. Psychiat. Soc. (life); founding mem. Greater St. Louis Council for Child Psychiatry (sec. 1971-73, treas. 1975-77). Avocations: gardening, stamp collecting. Home: 1677 Carman Rd Manchester MO 63021 Office: 14377 Woodlake Dr Chesterfield MO 63017

REYNOLDS, SUSAN KATHLEEN, management information professional, dog breeder; b. Evergreen Park, Ill., July 11, 1950; d. George Bernard and Betty Jayne (Caughey) Reynolds; m. Richard Carl Swanson, Aug. 26, 1978 (div. June 1986). B.B.A., Loyola U., Chgo., 1972. Statis. analyst Blue Cross Assn., Chgo., 1972-75; mgr. sales adminstrn. Omron Corp. Am., Chgo., 1975-76, mgr. external accts., Schaumburg, Ill., 1976-77, mgr. systems and programming, 1977-86, sr. mgr. automated services, 1986—; speaker IBM Seminars, Rolling Meadows, Ill., 1982—. Mem. Illini Search and Rescue, 1984. Mem. Data Processing Mgmt. Assn. Republican. Roman Catholic. Club: American Chesapeake. Avocations: hunting, fishing, collecting rare books, showing dogs, bicycling. Office: Omron Business Systems 1300 N Basswood St Schaumburg IL 60195

REYNOLDS, THOMAS ELLIOTT, public relations executive; b. New Orleans, Jan. 11, 1953; s. Jack Maurice and Mary Jean (Keith) R.; m. Deborah Kay Hart, May 1, 1976; children—Heather Elizabeth, Elisabeth Anne. Student Mich. State U., 1971-72; A.B. cum laude, U. Detroit, 1975. Staff writer, feature writer New Orleans Daily Record, 1974-75; freelance writer, public relations cons., Detroit and New Orleans, 1975-76; assoc. dir. instl. advancement Detroit Coll. Law, 1977-86; account suprt. P.R. Assocs., Inc., Detroit, 1986—. Mem. Internat. Assn. Bus. Communicators, Pub. Relations Soc. Am., Detroit Sports Broadcasters Assn., Sigma Delta Chi. Author: Renaissance Center-The Symbol of a Great City's Rebirth, 1980; The Detroit College of Law Student Guide, 1980. Clubs: Adcraft, Economic of Detroit.

REYNOLDSON, WALTER WARD, state supreme court chief justice; b. St. Edward, Nebr., May 17, 1920; s. Walter Scorer and Mabel Matilda (Sallach) R.; m. Janet Aline Mills, Dec. 24, 1942; children: Vicki (Mrs. Gary Kimes), Robert. BA, State Tchrs. Coll., 1942; JD, U. Iowa, 1948; LLD (hon.), Simpson Coll., 1983. Bar: Iowa 1948. Practice in Osceola, 1948-71; justice Iowa Supreme Ct., 1971-78, chief justice, 1978—; lectr. seminar Sch. Law, Drake U., 1968; county atty., Clarke County, Iowa, 1953-57. Contbg.author: Trial Handbook, 1969. Pres. Nat. Ctr. for State Ct.s, 1984-85. Served with USNR, 1942-46. Recipient Osceola Community Service award, 1968. Mem. Iowa Bar Assn. (chmn. com. on legal edn. and admission to bar 1964-71), ABA, Am. Judicature Soc. (dir. 1983—), Iowa Acad. Trial Lawyers, Conf. Chief Justices (pres. 1984-85), Am. Coll. Trial Lawyers. Office: State Capitol Bldg Des Moines IA 50319

REZNICEK, BERNARD WILLIAM, power company executive; b. Dodge, Nebr., Dec. 7, 1936; s. William Bernard and Elizabeth (Svoboda) R.; m. Mary Leona Gallagher; children—Stephen B., Michael J., Charles W., Mary E., Bernard J., James G. BSBA, Creighton U., 1958; MBA, U. Nebr., 1979. With Omaha Public Power Dist., pres., chief exec. officer, 1981—; exec. Sierra Pacific Power, Reno, 1979-80; dir. Inst. Nuclear Power Ops., Atlanta, Atomic Indsl. Forum, Guarantee Mutual Life Ins. Co. Trustee Father Flanagans Boys' Home, 1984. Mem. C. of C. (bd. dirs. 1981, treas. 1986-87), Beta Gamma Sigma. Republican. Roman Catholic. Club: Oak Hills Country (sec. 1985, v.p. 1986). Lodge: Rotary (bd. dirs. 1984-86), Ak-Sar-Ben. Office: Omaha Pub Power Dist 1623 Harney St Omaha NE 68102-2247

REZNICK, MORRIS MARTIN, lawyer; b. Cleve., Apr. 11, 1923; s. Joseph and Miriam (Baum) R.; children: Martha, Brad. Student, Ill. Inst. Tech., 1944; BS, Ohio U., 1947; JD, Cleve.-Marshal Law Sch., 1951. Bar: Ohio, 1951, U.S. Dist. Ct. (no. dist.) Ohio, 1954, U.S. Ct. Appeals (6th cir.), 1981, U.S. Supreme Ct., 1986. Ptnr. Bernard S. Goldfarb, Cleve., 1952-58, 60-66; house counsel Midwest Builders Co., University Heights, Ohio, 1958-60; ptnr. Goldfarb and Reznick, Cleve., 1966. Served with U.S. Army, 1943-46. Decorated Bronze Star, Purple Heart with silver oak leaf cluster. Mem. ABA, Ohio Bar Assn., Bar Assn. Greater Cleve. Office: 55 Public Square #1800 Cleveland OH 44113

RHEE, YANG HO, radiologist; b. Kunsan, Republic of Korea, Mar. 22, 1943; came to U.S., 1973; s. Young Whan and Ae Wol (Rah) R.; m. Shin Ae Kang; children: Hoyeon, Thomas, Karen. MD, Chonnam Med. Sch., Kwangj, Republic of Korea, 1968. Diplomate Am. Bd. Radiology. Intern Seoul Adventist Hosp., Republic of Korea, 1972-73, Cook County Hosp., Chgo., 1973-74; resident Hines (Ill.) VA Hosp., 1974-77; staff physician Illini Hosp., Silvis, Ill., 1977—. Chmn. bd. trustees Quad City Korean Assn., Ill. and Iowa, 1986—, v.p., 1980-81; mem. adv. council on peaceful unification policy Republic of Korea, 1984—. Serve to capt. Korean Army, 1968-72, Korea and Vietnam. Mem. AMA, Am. Coll. Radiology, Radiol. Soc. N.Am., Soc. Nuclear Medicine, Am. Inst. Ultrasound in Medicine. Office: 801 Hospital Rd Silvis IL 61282

RHEIN, ELIZABETH SARAH, editor, marketing communication executive; b. Detorit, Mar. 7, 1946; d. Harold Albert and Rachel (Goldon) R. AB in English, U. Mich. Mng. editor Gallery Mag., Chgo., 1973, Sphere Mag., Chgo., 1974; editor Detroit Free Press Mag., 1978-79; chief editor Going Places Mag., Evanston, Ill., 1980-81; spl. projects editor Restaurants and Insts. Mag., Des Plaines, Ill., 1984-85; owner Sherwin Assocs., Chgo., 1974—. Edited over 50 books for various pubs., 1968—; mng. editor numerous regional and nat. mags., 1974—. Mem. Ind. Writers Chgo. (various com. and spl. projects 1981—, bd. dirs. 1982), Chgo. Women in Pub. Avocation: food, tennis, travel. Office: Sherwin Assocs 2617 N Mildred Chicago IL 60614

RHEINTGEN, FRANCES STELLA, lighting company executive; b. Chgo., Feb. 27, 1938; d. Joseph Michael and Josephine Frances (Dudziak) Bronski; m. John Joseph Rheintgen, Sept. 20, 1958; children: Steven, Michael, Robert. Secretarial cert., DePaul U., 1957. Exec., owner Oakwood Lighting, Inc., Westmont, Ill., 1971—. Mem. Ill. Electric Assn., Westmont C. of C. Office: Oakwood Lighting Inc 407 W Ogden Ave Westmont IL 60559

RHOADES, CLARA BEATRICE, teacher; b. Independance, Kans., Apr. 22, 1926; s. Daniel Ernest and Mable Alice (Livingston) R. BEd, Kans. State U., 1957; MEd, Washburn U., 1965. Cert. tchr., Kans. Grade sch. tchr. Zeandale, Kans., 1949-56, prin., 1954-56; tchr. Mckinely Grade Sch., Clay Ctr., Kans., 1956-58, Cen. Park Sch., Topeka, 1958-80, State St. Sch., Topeka, 1980—. Mem. NEA, Delta Cappa Gamma. Republican. Methodist. Club: Jeanette MacDonald Internat. Fan (pres. 1960—) (Topeka). Avocations: reading, travel, running fan club. Home and Office: 1185 Woodward Ave Topeka KS 66604

RHOADES, SHARON GRACE, business educator; b. St. Joseph, Mo., Mar. 14, 1951; d. Russell Theodore and Elizabeth Sarah (Garder) Didlo; m. Rex Bryan Rhoades, Aug. 25, 1978 (div. Jan. 1980); children: Stephanie Selecman, Sarah Grace. BS in Vocat. Bus. Edn., Mo. Western State Coll., 1977; MEd in Vocat. Bus. Edn., N.W. Mo. State U., 1983. Bookkeeper, sec. Myers Watson Florist, St. Joseph, 1963-75; bookkeeper, sec., floral designer House of Brides, St. Joseph, 1975-83; mgr. J.C. Penney, St. Joseph, 1977; instr. bus. Lafayette High Sch., St. Joseph, 1977-78, N.S. Hillyard Area Vocat. Tech. Sch., St. Joseph, 1981—; dir. Profl. Bus. Women's Seminar, St. Joseph, 1985. Author: Word Processing Applications for the IBM Displaywriter: Textpack 2 and 6, 1983. Profl. advisor Vocat. Indsl. Clubs of Am., St. Joseph, 1982—; organizer food kitchen Salvation Army, St. Joseph, 1985—; participant Crop Walk for Food, St. Joseph, 1986; ruling elder Westminster Presbyn. Ch., St. Joseph, 1983-85. Mem. Am. Vocat. Edn., Nat. Bus. Edn. Assn. (Mo. state Future Bus. Tchr., 1973), Internat. Soc. Bus. Edn. Assn., Mo. Bus. Edn. Assn., Vocat. Indsl. Clubs Am. (Outstanding Advisor, 1983, 86), North Cen. Bus. Edn. Assn., Mo. State Tchr.'s Assn., Assn. Info. Systems Profls., St. Joseph Hist. Soc., Assn. Records Mgrs. and Administrs, Inc., N.W. Mo. Bus. Edn. Assn. (pres.). Republican. Avocations: travelling, computer software applications. Home: 706 County Line Rd Saint Joseph MO 64505 Office: NS Hillyard Area Vocat Tech Sch 36th and Faraon Saint Joseph MO 64506

RHODA, ROBERT BENJAMIN, accountant; b. Valparaiso, Ind., Sept. 8, 1955; s. Roy Elmer and Lenora Katherine (Lantz) R.; m. Vicki Lynn Gutt, June 3, 1978; children: Michael, Sarah. BS, Purdue U., 1977. CPA, Ind. Mgr. Geo. S. Olive & Co., Valparaiso, 1977—. Bd. dirs. Duneland YMCA, Inc., Chesterton, Ind., 1986—. Mem. Am. Inst. CPA's, Ind. CPA Soc. (bd. dirs. Calumet chpt., pres. 1986—), Nat. Assn. Accts., Westchester C. of C. (bd. dirs. 1985—). Lutheran. Lodge: Rotary (sec. Chesterton-Porter club 1983—). Avocations: gardening, farming, golf, softball. Home: 842 N St Rd 49 Chesterton IN 46304 Office: Geo S Olive & Co PO Box 31 Valparaiso IN 46383

RHODES, CARL ANTHONY, accountant; b. Pitts., Aug. 20, 1948; s. Carl S. and Jane A. (Bodecker) R.; m. Phyllis Ann Matekuuas, Aug. 23, 1968; children: Carl A. Jr., Christopher E. BA in Liberal Arts, Wittenberg U.; MBA, Ind. U. CPA, Ind. With Ernst & Whinney, Indpls., 1972-82, ptnr., 1982—. Mem. Stanley K. Lacy Exec. Leadership, Indpls., 1983; bd. dirs., v.p. Indpls. Boys Clubs Assn., 1983—, Indpls. Zool. Soc., 1986—. Mem. Am. Inst. CPA's, Ind. CPA Soc. (chmn. fed. taxation com. 1982), Fgn. Internat. Profl. Soc., Blue Key Soc., Beta Gamma Sigma. Roman Catholic. Clubs: Indpls. Athletic, Indpls. Sailing, Indpls. Exchange (pres. 1985). Avocations: sailing, music. Home: 11940 Somerset Way E Carmel IN 46032 Office: Ernst & Whinney One Indiana Sq Indianapolis IN 46204

RHODES, FORREST TERENCE, utilities company executive; b. Mattoon, Ill., Sept. 28, 1938; s. Walter Russell and Olive (Greathouse) R.; m. Julia Waldo, Feb. 6, 1965; children: Forrest Jr., Christopher Loren. BS in Engring., U.S. Naval Acad., 1960. Commd. ensign USN, 1960, advanced through grades to lt., 1964, resigned, 1967; asst. to supt. ops. Point Beach Nuclear Plant, Two Rivers, Wis., 1967-72, supt. ops., 1972-80; plant mgr. Wolf Creek Nuclear Plant, Burlington, Kans., 1980-86; v.p. nuclear ops. Wolf Creek Nuclear Operating Corp., Burlington, Kans., 1986—. Mem. Am. Soc. Mech. Engrs. (subcom. performance testing 1974-80). Republican. Office: Wolf Creek Nuclear Operating Corp PO Box 411 Burlington KS 66839

RHODES, GEORGE HARRY, forensic aviation consultant and broadcaster; b. East Cleveland, Ohio, Jan. 4, 1925; s. Henry George and Agnes Marie (Lancefield) R.; m. Leora Ann Agnew, May 16, 1964; children: Matthew George, Jennifer Grace. Student Hope Coll., 1943-44, San Francisco State Coll., 1949-50, U. Calif.-Berkeley, 1953-54. Cert. airline transport pilot, flight instr. Commd. 2d lt. U.S. Army, 1945, advanced through grades to capt., 1953; served Japan, Pacific, Okinawa, Korea, ret. 1953; sales rep. IBM, Pitts., 1954-58; prin. Dictation Assocs., Pitts., 1959-61; dist. mgr. MacMillan Ring-Free Oil Co., N.Y.C., 1962-65; bus. planning staffer Booz-Allen & Hamilton, Cleve., 1966-67; founder, owner, pres. Aviation Tng. Seminars, Cleve., 1967—; vol. accident prevention counselor U.S. Dept. Transp., FAA, Cleve., 1969—. Author, host: (NBC 10-part TV series) Discover Flying: Just Like a Bird, 1969-81 (Earl D. Osborn Writing award 1970); producer, author, host: (weekly radio show Sta. WKYC) Discover Flight with George Rhodes, 1972-74 (Midwestern Conf. News Media award 1972); author, lectr.: (color slide presentation) A Private Pilot Ground School, 1967-69 (AFA Aerospace Award 1969). Recipient 8 Campaign Battle stars; named FAA Gold Seal Instr. Mem. Aviation and Space Writers Assn. (v.p. 1974-78), Aircraft Owners and Pilots Assn. (hon.), Internat. Soc. Air Safety Investigators. Republican. Presbyterian. Club: Willoughby Flying (pres. 1966-67). Lodges: Masons, Shriners. Avocations: military history, racquetball, old cars. Home and Office: Aviation Training Seminars 6596 Maplewood Dr Cleveland OH 44124

RHODES, JACQUELINE YVONNE, marketing executive; b. Fairfield, Ala., Mar. 3, 1949; d. Lee Oliver and Jimmye Lucille (Warren) Rhodes. Student pub. schs., Cleve. Bus. services rep. Ohio Bell Telephone Co., Cleve., 1969-73, bus. officer instr., 1973-74, spl. communications cons., 1974-76, account exec. II, 1976-80, personnel mgr., 1980-82; account exec. American Bell, Cleve., 1983; dir. sales and mktg. Psychassess, Inc., Cleve., 1983-84 ; telecommunications analyst Clev. Clinic Found., 1985—; sec. Turner & Knight, Inc., Cleve., 1981-83. Vice pres. Harambee: Services to Black Families, Cleve., 1983. Mem. Nat. Assn. Female Execs., Citizens' League, Women's City Club. Baptist. Home: 17722 Tarkington Ave Cleveland OH 44128

RHODES, RICHARD DAVID, osteopathic physician, emergency care center executive; b. East Liverpool, Ohio, Nov. 2, 1935; s. Earl E. and Gladys (Robinson) R.; m. Mary Jo Marquette, Aug. 6, 1960; children—Mary Lorraine, Wendy Lynn, Kristen Leigh. Student Kent State U., 1954-57; D.O., Iowa Coll. of Osteo. Medicine and Surgery, 1961. Intern, Warren (Ohio) Gen. Hosp., 1961-62; pres. Emergency Physicians, Inc., Orwell, Ohio, 1972—; staff mem. Warren Gen. Hosp., chmn. dept. family practice, 1965; chief of staff, 1972; chmn. dept. emergency medicine Joint Twp. Hosp., St. Mary's, Ohio, 1972—; staff mem. St. Mary's (Ohio) Hosp., 1977—; pres. Rinn Lease Inc., 1976—, Medi Kwik. Mem. Am. Coll. Osteo. Emergency Medicine, Am. Coll. Emergency Medicine, Ohio Osteo. Assn., Am. Osteo. Assn., Sigma Sigma Phi.

RHODUS, NELSON LEO, dentist, educator; b. Lancaster, Ky., Jan. 25, 1953; s. Leo Kenneth and Hallie (Green) R.; m. Patricia Ann Frederick, June 4, 1977; children: Nelson Leo II, Brianne Mary, Evan Frederick. BS, Centre Coll., 1975; DMD, U. Ky., 1979; MS, Oral Roberts U., 1984; MPH, U. Minn., 1986. Intern St. Claire Hosp., Morehead, Ky., 1978-79; gen. practice dentistry Lancaster, 1979-82; chief dental services Garrard County Meml. Hosp., Lancaster, 1980-82; asst. prof. oral medicine Oral Roberts U., Tulsa, 1982-85, U. Minn., Mpls., 1985—; dir. oral diagnosis, dir. preventive dentistry Oral Roberts U., Tulsa, 1982-85, dir. patient mgmt. U. Minn., 1985-86. Editor dental student jour., 1985-86; patentee mercury detecting device, 1984. Asst. scoutmaster St. Paul Boy Scouts Am, 1985-86; vol. Union Gospel Med. Mission, St. Paul, 1985-86; eucharistic minister St. Marks Ch., St. Paul, 1985-86; bd. dirs. Sjúgrens Synrome Found. of Minn., 1985-86. Mem. ADA, Internat. Assn. Dental Research, Am. Dental Soc. Anesthesiology (Nat. Merit award 1979), Am. Acad. Oral Medicine, Ogrn. Tchrs. Oral Diagnosis, Lancaster Jaycees. Republican. Roman Catholic. Lodges: Kiwanis (pres. 1981), Masons (sec. 1980-82). Avocations: triathlons, running, photography, golf, tennis. Home: 1887 Portland Ave Saint Paul MN 55104 Office: Oral Diagnosis U Minn 515 Delaware Minneapolis MN 55455

RHOTEN, JULIANA THERESA, school principal; b. N.Y.C., June 28; d. Julius Joseph and Gladys Maude (Grant) Bastian; B.A., Hunter Coll., 1954; M.S., 1956; Ed.S., U. Wis., Milw., 1977; m. Marion Rhoten, Aug. 7, 1956; 1 son, Don Carlos. Tchr. elem. schs., Milw., 1957-65, reading specialist, 1965-71, adminstr., 1971-80; prin. Ninth St. Sch., Milw., 1980-83, Parkview Sch., Milw., 1983—. Mem. Assn. Supervision and Curriculum Devel., Internat. Reading Assn., Nat. Assn. Elem. Sch. Principals, Nat. Council Tchrs. English, Adminstrs. and Suprs. Council, Phi Delta Kappa, Alpha Kappa Alpha. Home: 7222 N 99th St Milwaukee WI 53224 Office: 10825 W Villard Ave Milwaukee WI 53225

RIBORDY, SHEILA CATHERINE, psychologist, educator; b. Quinter, Kans., Aug. 1, 1949; d. Lenard Frances and Pauline Irene (Heinrich) R. BS, Marymount Coll., 1971; MA, U. Kans., 1974, PhD, 1975. Lic. psychologist, Ill. Staff psychologist community mental health ctr. DePaul U., Chgo., 1975—, asst. prof. psychology, 1975-82, assoc. prof. psychology, 1982—, dir. clin. training, 1987—; cons. child abuse program St. Vincent's Day Care Ctr., Chgo., 1975—, rape project Met. YMCA, Chgo., 1976-77, Pflash Tyre Residential Drug Ctr., Chgo., 1976. Contbg. author profl. books; contbr. articles to profl. jours. Recipient Disting. Service to Profession award Marymount Coll., 1981; named one of Outstanding Young Women of Am., 1972, 81. Mem. Am. Psychol. Assn. (clin. psychology, psychology of women, community and family psychology divs.), Midwestern Psychol. Assn., Assn. Advancement Behavior Therapy. Avocations: tennis, writing children's stories. Office: DePaul U Dept Psychology 2323 N Seminary Chicago IL 60614

RICCO, PHILIP A., marketing professional; b. N.Y.C., Mar. 25, 1938; s. Angelo A. and Josephine (Vitale) R.; m. Patricia A. Gerzban, July 16, 1966; children: Paul S., Alexis A. BS in Econs. and Acctg., U. Pa., 1960. Assoc. Booz, Allen & Hamilton Inc., N.Y.C., 1962-66; v.p. Dasol Corp., N.Y.C., 1966-72, Prog. Casualty Inc. Co., Mayfield, Ohio, 1973-76; assoc. dir. The Diebold Group Inc., N.Y.C., 1976-79; dir. info. resources mgmt. S.C. Johnson & Son Inc., Racine, Wis., 1979-82, corp. productivity dir., 1982-87, mgr. corp. bus. systems, 1987—; U.S. Senate appointee Wis. State Productivity Bd., Milw., 1985. Editor: Automatic Data Procssing Hand Book, 1977. Am. Productivity Mgmt. Assn. (bd. dirs. 1984-87, v.p. 1985-86, pres. 1987-88). Home: 4 Birchwood Ct Racine WI 53402 Office: SC Johnson and Son Inc 1525 Howe St Racine WI 53403

RICE, CARL VENTON, lawyer, business; b. Lovilla, Iowa, Mar. 27, 1898; s. Walter Scott and Ida Isabelle (Chamberlain) R.; LL.B., U. Kans., 1918; m. Ruth Burton, Nov. 13, 1919 (dec. 1968); children—Ruth Isabelle Rice Mitchell, Carlene V. Rice Lind, Mary E. Rice Wells, Grace L. Rice Muder; m. 2d, Virginia Docking, 1978. Admitted to Kans. bar, 1918, U.S. Supreme Ct. bar, 1933; practiced in Kansas City, Kans., 1919-85; chmn. bd., pres. Pierce Industries, Inc., Andersen, Ind., 1954-64; now v.p. Rodar Leasing Corp., Kansas City, Kans. and Tampa, Fla., Fairfax Spltys., Kansas City, Kans., Graham Tubular Specialties, 3654 Cypress Corp., Tampa, Mission Groves, Inc., Ft. Pierce, Fla.; Hwy. commr. State of Kans., 1931-33; regional counsel RFC, 1933-38, CCC, 1934-50, Def. Plant Corp., 1941-50; counsel Kans. Banking Dept., 1937-39. Mem. exec. com. Democratic Nat. Com., 1948-52. Served with F.A., U.S. Army, World War I. Named to Kans. U. Athletic Hall of Fame. Mem. Am. Bar Assn., Kans. State Bar Assn., Delta Theta Phi. Clubs: Kansas City, Indian Hills Country (Kansas City, Kans.); Pelican Yacht (Ft. Pierce). Home: 2108 Washington Blvd Kansas City KS 66102 Office: 600 Security Nat Bank Bldg Kansas City KS 66101

RICE, CHARLES EDGAR, psychology educator, editor; b. Zanesville, Ohio, Nov. 22, 1930. BA, Denison U., 1952; PhD, Fla. State U., 1962. Research psychologist Stanford Research Inst., Menlo Park, Calif., 1963-69; prof. psychology Kenyon Coll., Gambler, Ohio, 1969—. Editor: Behavior and Physiology Pennipeds, 1968, (jour.) The Psychological Record, 1975—; contbr. articles to profl. jours. Asst. chief Coll. Twp. Fire Dept., Gambler, 1971—; bd. dirs. Knox Community Hosp., Mt. Vernon, Ohio, 1980-82. Mem. Am. Psychol. Assn., Psychonomic Soc., Acoustica Soc. Am., Animal Behavior Soc., Sigma Xi. Office: Kenyon Coll Gambier OH 43022

RICE, CHRISTOPHER DOLLAR, dental educator; b. Kansas City, Mo., Sept. 6, 1954; s. Harry Dollar and Esther Lorraine (Christianson) R.; m. Janet Marie Schranz, May 31, 1980; 1 child, Collin Christopher. BS in Biology, Creighton U., 1976, DDS, 1980. Lic. dentist, Mo. Gen. practice dentistry Wichita, Kans., 1980-81, Blue Springs, Mo., 1981-86; asst. prof. dentistry U. Mo., Kansas City, 1986—. Mem. ADA, Mo. Dental Assn., Kansas City Dental Assn. Avocations: sculpture, photography, writing. Home: 15700 E 43d Terr Independence MO 64055 Office: U Mo Dental Sch 650 E 25th St Kansas City MO 64108

RICE, DAVID LEE, university president; b. New Market, Ind., Apr. 1, 1929; s. Elmer J. and Katie (Tate) R.; m. Betty Jane Fordice, Sept. 10, 1950; children: Patricia Denise Rice Dawson, Michael Alan. B.S., Purdue U., 1951, M.S., 1956, Ph.D., 1958. Dir. prof. research Ball State U., Muncie, Ind., 1958-66; v.p. Coop. Ednl. Research Lab., Inc., Indpls., 1965-67; research coordinator, bur. research HEW, Washington; dean campus Ind. State U., Evansville, 1967-71, pres. campus, 1971-85; pres. U. So. Ind., Evansville, 1985—; adminstrv. asst. Gov.'s Com. on Post High Sch. Orgn. Contbr. articles to profl. jours. Past mem. State Citizens Adv. Bd. Title XX Social Security Act; bd. dirs., past pres. United Way; mem. Goodwill Industries; past bd. commrs. Evansville Housing Authority; pres. Leadership Evansville, 1978-79; bd. dirs., past pres. S.W. Ind. Pub. TV, 1972—; bd. dirs. Villages Inc.; chmn. subcom. Met. Evansville Progress Com.; mem. Buffalo Trace council Boy Scouts Am., 1963—. Served with inf. U.S. Army, 1951-53. Decorated Combat Infantryman's Badge; recipient Service to Others award Salvation Army, 1974, Citizen of Yr. award Westside Civitan Club, 1972, Boss of Yr. award Am. Bus. Women's Assn., 1976. Mem. Am. Assn. Higher Edn., Am. Ednl. Research Assn., Am. Assn. State Colls. and Univs., Nat. Soc. Study Edn., Met. Evansville C. of C. (dir.), Alpha Kappa Psi, Alpha Zeta, Phi Delta Kappa. Methodist. Clubs: Evansville Country, Petroleum, Columbia. Lodge: Rotary (civic award Evansville club 1985). Home: 1230 McDowell Rd Evansville IN 47712 Office: U Southern Ind Office of the Pres 8600 University Blvd Evansville IN 47712

RICE, FRED, superintendent police; b. Chgo., Dec. 24, 1926; m. Thelma Martin; children: Lyle, Judith. B.S., Roosevelt U., 1970, M.S. in Pub. Adminstrn., 1977. Mem. Chgo. Police Dept., 1955—, promoted to sgt., 1961, lt., 1968, capt., 1973, dist. comdr., 1970-78, dep. chief patrol, Area Four, 1978-79, chief patrol div., 1979-83, supt. police, 1983—. Served with U.S. Army, 1950-52; Korea. Recipient numerous awards for contbns. to community. Office: Office of the Police Chief 1121 S State St Chicago IL 60605 *

RICE, GUY GARNER, lawyer; b. Kansas City, Mo., Mar. 25, 1932; s. Guy William and Elizabeth (Smith) R.; m. Marcia Louise Clines, Dec. 15, 1978; children by previous marriage—Dierk B., Brenda L., Reid R., Sandra L. Student Beloit Coll., 1949-51; A.B., U. Mo., Columbia, 1953; J.D., U. Mo.-Kansas City, 1964. Bar: Mo. 1964, U.S. Dist. Ct. (we. dist.) Mo. 1965. Asst. pros. atty. Jackson County, Mo., 1965, asst. county counselor, Jackson County, Mo., 1970-71; ptnr. Phillips, Rice & McElligott, Independence, 1968-74; sole practice, Independence, 1978-82; ptnr. Rice & Mouse, Independence, 1983-85, sole practice, 1985—; gen. counsel Med. Info. Service, Inc., 1966-80, Sugar Creek Nat. Bank, 1971-80. Served to 1st lt. U.S. Army, 1953-56. Named Outstanding Young Man, Jaycees, 1958-59; recipient Spoke award Jaycees, 1959. Mem. Estate Planning Assn. Greater Kansas City (pres. 1966-67), Independence Bar Assn. (sec. 1965-66), Eastern Jackson County Bar Assn., Independence C. of C. Office: Suite 5 3640 S Noland Rd Independence MO 64055

RICE, JEFFREY DALE, optometrist; b. Zanesville, Ohio, Feb. 24, 1955; s. Dale Eugene and Maxine F. (LeFever) R.; m. Deborah Lynn Mell, Mar. 13, 1982; children—Shawn Lee, Jamie Marie. O.D., Ohio State U., 1980. Gen. practice optometry, Zanesville, 1980—. Vice pres. Am. Cancer Soc., Muskingam County Unit, 1983-84. Mem. Am. Optometric Assn., Ohio Optometric Assn., Mid-Eastern Ohio Optometric Assn. Republican. Lodge: Kiwanis (bd. dirs. 1984-86). Avocations: sports, jogging, physical fitness. Home: 750 Fairmont Ave Zanesville OH 43701 Office: 740 Princeton Ave Zanesville OH 43701

RICE, JOHN RAY, social worker; b. Covington, Tenn., Jan. 3, 1949; s. Luttrell and Mary Alma (Walker) R. ABS, George Williams Coll., 1971, MSW, 1977. Lic. therapist, Ill. Psychiat. social worker Kane/Kendall County Mental Health Ctr., Ill., 1971-74; young adult coordinator Thresholds, Chgo., 1974-77; pvt. practice therapy, Chgo., 1977—; camp dir. Unions for Youth, Nat. Football League Players Assn., Elmhurst, Ill., 1979, Winchendon, Mass.; social worker, instr. Behavior Sci.-Family Practice Residency Tng. Program, Ill. Masonic Ctr., Chgo., 1980; child-family therapist Habilitative Systems, Inc., Chgo., 1985-86, coordinator clin. services, 1986—; field instr. George Williams Coll. Sch. Social Work Edn. Author: Thank You for Loving Me. Mem. YMCA World Service, Bogota, Columbia, 1967; mem. coms. Ill. Commn. on Children. Mem. Nat. Assn. Social Workers (cert.), Nat. Assn. Black Social Workers. Baptist. Home: 1129 W Oakdale Chicago IL 60657 Office: PO Box 14556 Chicago IL 60614

RICE, KENNETH LLOYD, financial company executive; b. St. Paul, June 17, 1937; s. Irving James and Anne Louise (Rogers) R.; m. Elizabeth Lyman Vankat, May 11, 1963 (div. June 1980); children: Anne Louise, Kenneth L. Jr., Elizabeth Ellen, Stephen James. BBA, U. Wis., 1959; postgrad., N.Y. Inst. Finance, 1960-64; completed Advanced Mgmt. Program, Harvard U., 1975. Trainee corp. finance Irving J. Rice & Co., St. Paul, 1959-64; asst. branch mgr. DB Marron & Co. Inc., St. Paul, 1964-65; mgr. corp. finance JW Sparks & Co. Inc., St. Paul, 1965-69, The Milw. Co., St. Paul, 1969-70; dir. finance Cedar Riverside Assocs. Inc., Mpls., 1970-71; prin. Kenneth L. Rice & Assocs., St. Paul, 1971—; bd. dirs. Image Premastering Corp., Falcon Heights, Minn. Founder Chimera Theatre, St. Paul, 1969; vice moderator Presbytery of the Twin Cities, Mpls., 1976; pres. Liberty Plaza Non-Profit Housing Project, St. Paul, 1975-77; judge Leadership Fellows Bush Found., St. Paul, 1985—; co-chmn. Parents Fund, Macalester Coll., St. Paul, 1985-87. Mem. Real Estate Securities Syndication Inst. (chpt. pres. 1977, disting. service award 1978). Presbyterian. Club: Harvard Bus. (local bd. dirs. 1978-83). Lodges: Optimists (local v.p. 1986-88), Masons, KT, Shriners. Avocations: aerobics, history. Office: 220 S Robert St Suite 208 Saint Paul MN 55107

RICE, MARVIN ELWOOD, dentist; b. Mexico, Mo., Nov. 18, 1951; s. Marvin Everett and Una Belle (Hogan) R.; m. Elizabeth Kay Pearl, Mar. 3, 1977; children: Nicole Josephine, Megan Elizabeth, Laura Ellen. BS in Biology, Cen. Mo. State U., 1975; med. asst., Coll. Med. and Dental Assts., 1976; MBA, Cen. Mo. State U., 1978; DDS, U. Mo., 1982. Gen. practice dentistry Mexico, Mo., 1982—. Active Community Betterment Com., Mexico, 1984-86, PTA, Mexico, 1986; bd. dirs. Mex. Sch. Bd., 1987—; deacon First Presbyn. Ch., Mexico, 1984—. Mem. ADA, Mo. Dental Assn. (communications com. 1983-86, peer rev. com. 1987—), Columbia Dental Soc., Cen. Dental Soc. (v.p.), Mexico C. of C., Sigma Tau Gamma (Outstanding Alumni 1977). Republican. Lodge: Kiwanis (treas. Mexico 1983, v.p. 1984, pres. elect 1985-86, pres. 1986—). Avocations: gardening, art, canoeing, fishing, golf. Home: 821 Woodlawn Mexico MO 65265 Office: 1000 W Old Farm Rd Mexico MO 65265

RICE, MURRY, optometrist; b. W. New York, N.J., June 27, 1922; s. Harry and Pearl (Koladner) R.; m. Sylvia Einhorn, Dec. 26, 1948; children: Robert Evan, Hollie Beth, Michelle Amy. Cert. in electronics, Rutgers U., 1943; student, Union Jr. Coll., 1946-47; OD, No. Ill. Coll. Optometry, 1949; cert. in child devel., So. Coll. Optometry, 1967. Intern Mandel Clinic Michael Reese Hosp., Chgo., 1950-51; instr. No. Ill. Coll. Optometry, Chgo., 1951-52; pvt. practice specializing in optometry Naperville and South Holland, Ill., 1952—; supr., cons. Twin Springs Camp, Berien Springs, Mich., 1969-70; lectr. Ill. Optometric Assn., 1971. Author: (procedure manual) A Simplified Approach for a Child Developmental Examination, 1971. Surgeon VFW, Naperville, 1953. Served as cpl. U.S. Army, 1942-46, PTO. Decorated Bronze Star. Fellow Coll. Optometric Vision Devel.; mem. U.S. Power Squadrons, Naperville C. of C. Jewish. Lodges: B'nai Brith, Lions. Avocations: fishing, traveling, boating. Home and Office: 15562 Woodlawn E South Holland IL 60473

RICE, NORMAN JACK, trade association executive; b. Canton, Ohio, July 18, 1936; s. Paul Emmett and Mary (Lesner) R.; m. Janet Marie Reed, June 9, 1959; children: James Arthur, John Andrew, Joseph Allen. BA, Oberlin Coll., 1958; postgrad., U. Pitts., 1959. Owner Rice Appliances, Canton, 1959-74; dir. edn. Nat. Assn. Retail Dealers Am., Chgo., 1974-75; prof. mgmt. Ottawa (Kans.) U., 1975-78; dir. edn. Nat. Retail Hardware Assn., Indpls., 1978-84, dir. mem. services, 1984—; cons. SBA Ace Program, 1975—; cons., speaker, trainer Percon, Excelsior Springs, Mo., 1981—. Co-author: Who's Next Please, 1983; contbr. articles to profl. jours. Mem. Nat. Soc. Sales Tng. Execs. Baptist. Avocations: travel, reading, classical and jazz music. Home: 3741 Shelbourne Ct Carmel IN 46032 Office: Nat Retail Hardware Assn 770 N High School Rd Indianapolis IN 46214

RICE, OTIS LAVERNE, nursing home builder and developer; b. Emerson, Iowa, June 24, 1922; s. William Reuben and Bonnie Elizabeth (Edie) R.; m. Ferill Jeane Dalton, Mar. 7, 1946; children: LeVeria June McMichael, Larry Lee. Student Fox Valley Tech. Sch., 1971-72. Lic. electrician and contractor. With Tumpane Electric, Omaha, 1949-53; ptnr., pres. Rice & Rice, Inc., Kaukauna, Wis., 1953—. Ptnr. Rice Enterprises. Served with U.S. Army, 1942-46. Decorated Bronze Stars. Mem. Associated Builders and Contractors, Fenton Art Glass Collectors of Am. Inc. (founder), Internat. Carnival Glass Collectors, Am. Carnival Glass Collectors, Heisey Collectors of Am. Republican. Clubs: Masons, Shriners, Eastern Star.

RICE, PAUL FREDERICK, structural engr.; b. Mandan, N.D., Dec. 8, 1921; s. Paul Frederick and Claire Olive (Des Jardins) R.; B.S., N.D. State Coll., 1941; postgrad. Ill. Inst. Tech., 1942; M.S., MIT, 1947; postgrad. U. Mich., 1953-57; m. Joan Carol Cannon, June 22, 1946; children—Paul Frederick, Clair Patrick, John Cassius, Richard Clay. Structural design engr. Cunningham-Limp Co., Detroit, 1947-49; structural field engr. Mich., Portland Cement Assn., Chgo., 1949-54; tech. dir. Am. Concrete Inst., Detroit, 1954-58; v.p. engring. Concrete Reinforcing Steel Inst., Chgo., 1958-86, cons. 1987—; chmn. Concrete Improvement Bd. Detroit, 1955-56; vice chmn. Reinforced Concrete Research Council, ASCE, 1974-76. Served with C.E., AUS, 1942-46; ETO. Registered profl. engr., Mich.; registered structural engr., Ill. Fellow ASCE, Am. Concrete Inst. (Lindau award 1981); mem. Am. Welding Soc., ASTM, Structural Engs. Assn. Ill., Reinforced Concrete Research Council (Arthur J. Boase award 1985). Editor, author: Concrete Reinforcing Steel Institute (CRSI) Handbook, 1968, 71, 75, 78, 80, 82, 85; co-author: Structural Design Guide to ACI Building Code, Structural Design Guide to AISI Specifications. Home: 2033 Sherman Ave Evanston IL 60201 Office: 933 N Plum Grove Rd Schaumburg IL 60173-4578

RICE, RAMONA GAIL, aquatic physiologist, ecological phycologist, educator, consultant; b. Texarkana, Tex., Feb. 15, 1950; d. Raymond Lester and Jessie Gail (Hubbard) R. B.S., Ouachita U., 1972; M.S., U. Ark., 1975, Ph.D., 1978; postgrad. Utah State U., 1978-80. Undergrad. asst. Ouachita U., Arkadelphia, Ark., 1970-72; grad. teaching asst. U. Ark., Fayetteville, 1972, 77-78, grad. research asst., 1973-77; asst. research scholar, scientist Fla. Internat. U., Miami, 1980-85; research coordinator, faculty Pratt Community Coll., Kans., 1985—; adj. instr. Miami Dade Community Coll., 1984-85, Wichita (Kans.) State U., 1986—. Contbr. articles to profl. jours. Judge Pratt County Sci. Fairs, Dade County Sci. Fair, Fla., 1981-85; tchr. Sunday Sch. First Baptist Ch., South Miami, Fla., 1982-85, leader girls in action, 1982-83, youth chaperone, 1982-85. Grantee NSF, 1981-83, Fla. Dept. Environ., 1981-83, EPA, 1983-85, So. Fla. Research Ctr., Everglades Nat. Park, 1983-86. Mem. Fla. Acad. Scis., AAAS, Phycological Soc. Am., Soc. Limnology and Oceanography, Sigma Xi. Democrat. Avocations: pianist; crochet; needlework; photography; reading. Office: Dept Biol Scis Pratt Community Coll Pratt KS 67124

RICE, RICHARD CAMPBELL, state official, retired army officer; b. Atchison, Kans., Dec. 11, 1933; s. Olive Campbell and Ruby Thelma (Rose) R.; m. Donna Marie Lincoln, Aug. 4, 1956; children—Robert Alden, Holly Elizabeth. B.A. in History, Kans. State U., 1955; M.A. in Social Studies, Eastern Mich. U., 1965; grad. U.S. Army Command and Gen. Staff Coll., 1968, U.S. Army War Coll., 1977, grad. program for sr. execs. in state and local govt., Harvard U., 1985. Commd. 2d lt. U.S. Army, 1955; advanced through grades to col., 1976; with Joint Chiefs of Staff, Washington, 1975-76; faculty U.S. Army War Coll., Carlisle Barracks, Pa., 1977-79; chief staff Hdqrs. 3d ROTC Region, Ft. Riley, Kans., 1982-83; ret. 1983; dir. Mo. State Emergency Mgmt. Agy., Jefferson City, 1983-85, dir. Mo. Dept. Pub. Safety, Jefferson City, 1985—. Mem. Gov's Commn. on Crime, Gov's Adm. Council on Driving While Intoxicated, Mo. Children's Services Commn., Blue Ribbon Commn. on Services to Youth, Campaign to Protect Our Children; chmn. adv. bd. Mo. Criminal Hist. Records; bd. dirs. Mo. Law Enforcement Meml. Found. Decorated Legion of Merit, Bronze Star (3), Meritorious Service medal (4), Air medal (2), Joint Service Commendation medal, Army Commendation medal (2); Republic of Vietnam Cross of Gallantry with Silver Star. Mem. Nat. Eagle Scout Assn., Assn. U.S. Army, Soc. First Div., Am. Legion, VFW, Internat. Assn. Chiefs of Police, Mo. Police Chiefs Assn., Mo. Peace Officers Assn., The Retired Officers Assn., Nat. Fedn. of Grand Order Of Pachyderms, Nat. Criminal Justice Assn. (bd. dirs. 1987—), Am. Soc. Pub. Administrn., Mo. Inst. Pub. Administrn. Theta Xi. Republican. Lodges: Rotary. Avocation: sailing. Office: Public Safety Dept 301 W High St Jefferson City MO 65102

RICE, RONALD JAMES, health service professional; b. Corvallis, Oreg., June 15, 1955; s. James Elliot Jr. and Catherine Ann (Raade) R.; m. Sandra Lea Richard, Aug. 14, 1976; children: Michael David, Jason Lee. AS, Kettering (Ohio) Coll. Med. Arts, 1983. Cert. physician asst. Physician asst. Dermatology and Allergy Physicians Ohio, Inc., Dayton, 1983—. Fellow Am. Acad. Physician Assts., Ohio Acad. Physician Assts. Lutheran. Club: Ohio Wander Freunde. Avocations: sports, hunting, fishing, golf. Home: 4850 Delba Dr Dayton OH 45439 Office: Dermatology and Allergy Physicians Ohio Inc 5150 Brandt Pk Huber Heights OH 45424

RICE, RONNIE JAMES, sales executive; b. Piqua, Ohio, Apr. 5, 1945; s. James Rufus and Dorothy (Dee) R.; m. Anita Marie Gentile, Sept. 6, 1969; children: Chad, Ronna, Anthony, Ann Marie. Student, Bowling Green U., Ohio U., U. Dayton, Eastern Ky. U., 1964-72. V.p. N&G Constrn. Inc., Bloomingdale, Ohio, 1969-73; v.p., sec. Ohio River Collieries Co., Bannock, Ohio, 1973-79, also bd. dirs.; pres. Lafferty Trucking Co., Bannock, 1978-80, also bd. dirs.; pres., owner A&R Devel. Corp., St. Clairsville, Ohio, 1979-83; sales rep. Reco Equipment Co., Morristown, Ohio, 1983—; bd. dirs. Bannock Coal Co. Author, narrator film documentary Energy for a Living Environment, 1977. Dir. Nat. Trail Council, Boy Scouts Am., Wheeling, W.Va., 1977-79; committeeman St. Clairsville (Ohio) Classic Run, 1983—. Served to sgt. Ohio Army N.G., 1963-72. Mem. Nat. Accts. Assn. Republican. Roman Catholic. Club: Belmont Hill Country (St. Clairsville) (committeeman). Lodge: KC. Home and Office: 47630 Morningside Dr Saint Clairsville OH 43950

RICE, VICTOR ALBERT, agricultural and industrial equipment manufacturing company executive; b. Hitchin, Hertfordshire, Eng., Mar. 7, 1941; s. Albert Edward and Rosina Emmeline (Pallant) R.; m. Sharla C. Rice, June 25, 1970; children: Gregg, Kristin, Jonathan. With Ford Motor Co., U.K., 1957-64, Cummins Engines, U.K., 1964-67, Chrysler Corp., U.K., 1968-70; comptroller N. European ops. Perkins Engines Group Ltd., Peterborough, U.K., 1970, dep. mng. dir. ops., 1974-75; comptroller world-wide Varity Corp. (formerly Massey-Ferguson Ltd.), Toronto, Ont., Can., 1975-77, v.p. staff ops., 1977-78, pres., 1978-82, chmn., chief exec. officer, 1980—, also dir. Mem. Bd. of Trade Met. Toronto, Fin. Execs. Inst., Am. Mgmt. Assn. (mem. Pres.' Assn.), Brit. Inst. Mktg., Inst. Dirs. (U.K.). Anglican. Clubs: Royal Canadian Yacht, Toronto Golf; Carlton (London). Office: Varity Corp, 595 Bay St, Toronto, ON Canada M5G 2C3 *

RICE, WALTER HERBERT, federal judge; b. Pitts., May 27, 1937; s. Harry D. and Elizabeth L. (Braemer) R.; m. Bonnie Rice; children: Michael, Hilary, Harry. B.A., Northwestern U., 1958; J.D., M.B.A., Columbia U., 1962. Bar: Ohio 1963. Asst. county prosecutor Montgomery County, Ohio, 1964-66; asso. firm Gallon & Miller, Dayton, Ohio, 1966-69; 1st asst. Montgomery County Prosecutor's Office, 1969; judge Dayton Mcpl. Ct., 1970-71, Montgomery County Ct. Common Pleas, 1971-80, U.S. Dist. Ct. So. Dist., Ohio, 1980—; adj. prof. U. Dayton Law Sch., 1976—, bd. visitors, 1976—; chmn. Montgomery County Supervisory Council on Crime and Deliquency, 1972-74; vice chmn. bd. dirs. Pretrial Release, Inc., 1975-79. Author papers in field. Pres. Dayton Area Council Alcoholism on and Drug Abuse, 1971-73; chmn. bd. trustees Stillwater Health Center, Dayton, 1976-79, Family Service Assn. of Dayton, 1978-80. Recipient Excellent Jud. Service award Ohio Supreme Ct., 1976, 77, Outstanding Jud. Service award, 1973, 74, 76; Man of Yr. award Disting. Service Awards Council, Dayton, 1977; Outstanding Jurist in Ohio award Ohio Acad. Trial Lawyers, 1986. Mem. Am. Jud. Soc., Ohio Bar Assn., Dayton Bar Assn.

RICH, JEFFREY EDWARD, manufacturing executive, consultant; b. Chgo., Sept. 14, 1943; s. Allen and Mayme (Levine) R.; m. Maureen Beth Goldstein, July 9, 1967; children: Michael, Matthew. BFA, U. Ill., 1966. Designer Montgomery Wards, Chgo., 1966-69; dir. communication services Am. Hosp. Supply Corp., Evanston, Ill., 1969-83; dir. corp. identity Beatrice Inc., Chgo., 1983-86; v.p. Lipson Alport Glass and Assocs., Northbrook, Ill., 1986—; instr. Columbia Coll., Chgo., 1981-83. Co-author, art dir.: (manual) Beatrice Graphics Standards, 1985 (Am. Corp. Identity award 1985, Art Dirs. Club of N.Y. award 1985); bd. dirs. Arts & Events Mag., 1982-83. Recipient 80 award Indsl. Design Soc. Am., N.Y., 1980, Designers Choice award Indsl. Design Mag., N.Y., 1982, Desi 9 award USA Mag., N.Y., 1986, Corp. Identity award Am. Corp. Identity, Ohio, 1986. Mem. Am. Inst. Graphic Artists (design awards 1981), Soc. Typographic Artists (1st v.p. 1978, STA100 award 1978-80, 85), Design Mgmt. Inst. Avocations: photography, music, wood sculpture. Home: 1530 Cavell Highland Park IL 60035 Office: Lipson Alport Glass and Assocs 666 Dundee Rd Suite 103 Northbrook IL 60062

RICH, JOSEPH ANTHONY, teacher, business owner; b. Ashtabula, Ohio, July 17, 1950; s. Tony D. and Celia M. (Licata) R.; m. Valerie M. Smock, July 13, 1974; children: Natalie Ann, Carrie Lee. BS in Edn., Kent State U., 1972, MEd, 1972, MA in Sports Adminstrn., 1986. Cert. tchr., Ohio. Dept. mgr. Stambaugh's, Youngstown, Ohio, 1968-76; mgr. Selected Theatre Corp., Lyndhurst, Ohio, 1973-75; tchr. Ash Area City Schs., Ashtabula, 1972—; owner The Locker Room, Inc., Ashtabula, 1980—; coach football, basketball, baseball, track Ashtabula Area City Schs., 1972-83. campaign mgr. Sheldon for State Rep. Com., Ashtabula, 1984. Named one of Outstanding Young Men in Am., Outstanding Young Ams., Inc., 1985. Mem. NEA, Ohio Edn. Assn., Ashtabula Area Tchrs. Assn., Nat. Official Assn. Democrat. Roman Catholic. Club: East Ashtabula. Lodge: Elks, KC. Avocations: golf, softball, flying, racquetball, squash. Home: 1351 Lyndon Ave Ashtabula OH 44004 Office: The Locker Room 3703 West Ave Ashtabula OH 44004

RICH, KENNETH LOUIS, management science educator, consultant; b. N.Y.C., Mar. 6, 1937; s. Leo Herbert and Margaret (Rice) R.; m. Deborah Jean Palmer, Mar. 29, 1980; children—Andrew P., Stephanie P. B.S., Purdue U., 1959; M.B.A., Harvard U., 1961; Ph.D., U. Pa., 1969. Cert. mgmt. acctg. Mgmt. cons. Rich & Assocs., Mpls., 1972-78; asst. prof. George Mason U., Fairfax, Va., 1977-78; market research mgr. Cardiac Pacemakers, Inc., St. Paul, 1978-79; pres. Rich & Assocs., Inc., Mpls., 1979—; 3M prof. mgmt. Coll. St. Catherine, St. Paul, 1981—; tech. cons. Consumer Research Corp., Mpls., 1975—. Author computer programs; also articles in mgmt. sci. Officer, del. Republican Party, Mpls., 1973-84; bd. dirs. Lowry Hills Residents Inc., Mpls., 1984—, pres., 1987—. Mem. Inst. Mgmt. Sci., Am. Inst. Decision Scis., Inst. Mgmt. Acctg., Tau Beta Pi, Eta Kappa Nu, Tau Kappa Epsilon. Universalist. Club: Purdue of Minn. (pres. 1979—). Avocations: bridge; micro-computers. Home: 1787 Colfax Ave S Minneapolis MN 55403 Office: College of Saint Catherine Dept Mgmt 2004 Randolph Ave Saint Paul MN 55105

RICH, MARY BETH, social services administrator; b. Detroit, Dec. 18, 1946; d. LeRoy and Helen Mary (Morison) Quinn; m. Robert A. Rich, June 25, 1966 (div. Oct. 1977); children: Robert A. II, Jonathan M., Scott A. BSW with highest honors, Madonna Coll., 1981; MSW, U. Mich., 1982. Therapist S.A.C. Community Mental Health, Lincoln Park, Mich., 1981-82; family therapist Boysville of Mich., Clinton, Mich., 1982-84, treatment dir., 1984—. Mem. Mich. Citizens Lobby, Southfield, 1979-84, Hope Park Assn. Block Club City of Detroit, 1966—, women's club Redford (Mich.) Presbyn. Ch., 1964—. Recipient Citizen Citation Detroit Police Dept., 1981, Vol. Mother award 1976-82. Mem. Nat. Assn. Social Workers, Acad. Cert. Social Workers. Avocations: camping with family, jogging, sports. Home: 24020 Chipmunk Trail Novi MI 48050 Office: Boysville of Mich 8744 Clinton-Macon Rd Clinton MI 49236

RICH, ROBERT JOHN, JR., computer company executive; b. Sacramento, June 4, 1943; s. Robert John and Elizabeth Jane (McDonald) R.; m. Kristine L. Hanson; children—Robert John, III, Christopher Wetherby. B.A., U. Minn.-Duluth, 1965. Mgr. comml. loan dept. Northwestern Bank, Hopkins, Minn., 1973-78; pres. Computer Maintenance and Leasing Corp., Mpls., 1978-83; pres. Use 'R Computers, Inc., Mpls., 1983—. Served to capt. USAF, 1966-72. Mem. Am. Soc. Field Service Mgmt., Am. Soc. Sales and Mktg. Execs., Greater Mpls. C. of C., Twin West C. of C. Republican. Club: Calhoun Beach. Home: 14060 Stonegate Ln Minnetonka MN 55345 Office: Use 'R Computers Inc 5929 Baker Rd Suite 490 Minnetonka MN 55345

RICHARD, EDWARD H., municipal government official, former magnetic equipment company executive; b. N.Y.C., Mar. 15, 1937; s. Henry and Ida Richard; B.A., Antioch Coll., 1959. Pres., chmn. bd. dirs. Magnetics Internat. Inc., Maple Heights, Ohio, 1967-86, exec. v.p. Stearns Magnetics S.A., Brussels, Belgium, 1974-77; prin. Edward H. Richard & Assocs., Cleve., 1967-82; pres., treas. David Round & Son, Inc., Cleve; exec. adminstrv. asst. to mayor City of Cleve., 1979—, dir. dept. pub. utilities, 1981—, dep. to mayor, chief adminstrv. officer, 1986—; chmn. Cleve. dist. adv. council Small Bus. Adminstrn., 1975-79; mem. nat. adv. council Dept. Treasury; cons. and advisor in field; del. world trade fairs. Former trustee Regional Econ. Devel. Council, Met. Cleve. Jobs Council, Cleve. Devel. Found., Cleve. Better Bus. Bur.; trustee Hiram House, Antioch U., N.E. Ohio Regional Sewer Dist., Greater Cleve. Domed Stadium Corp., Greater Cleve. Conv. and Vis. Bur.; trustee, vice-chmn. Cleve. Center Econ. Edn.; pres. Bratenahl Condominium Assn.; mem. Bratenahl Bd. Edn., 1974-80, chmn. fin. com. 1971-75. Home: 2 Bratenahl Pl Bratenahl OH 44108

RICHARD, JOHN ROBERT, geologist; b. Blackwell, Okla., Apr. 12, 1931; s. John B. and Arlene (Carter) R.; m. Nancy Joan Rush, Dec. 26, 1953; children: Mark R., Lisa K., Matthew D., Curtis J. BS, U. Kans., 1957. Cert. profl. geologist, petroleum geologist. Geologist Standard Oil Co. Calif., Houston, 1957-60, v.p., staff geologist, 1961-64; sr. geologist Sunray D-X div. Sun Oil Co., Lafayette, La., 1964-66; oil producer, cons. Richard Engring., Chanute, Kans., 1966—; owner The Richard Cos. Served with USN, 1949-53, Korea. Mem. Am. Assn. Petroleum Geologists, Am. Inst. Profl. Geologists (pres. 1983-85), Kans. Geol. Soc., Eastern Kans. Oil and Gas Assn. Avocation: vintage car restoration. Office: Richard Cos 1228 S Steuben Chanute KS 66720

RICHARD, WILLIAM RALPH, research chemist; b. Bklyn., Oct. 13, 1922; s. William Ralph and Helen (Brodie) R.; m. Joan Coombs, Aug. 23, 1947; children—Carol Lucile, Suzanne Louise, Janet Elizabeth. A.B. in Chemistry, Amherst Coll., 1943; M.S. in Chemistry, U. Mich., 1947, Ph.D. in Chemistry, 1950. Research chemist Monsanto Chem. Co., Springfield, Mass., 1943-46; DuPont fellow U. Mich., Ann Arbor, 1948-50; group leader research engring. div. Monsanto, Dayton, Ohio, 1950-63, mgr. research and devel. organic div., St. Louis, 1963-74; dir. research and devel. Monsanto Indsl. Co., St. Louis, 1974—, dir. research and devel. splty. chems., 1985—; pres. Delos Inc., Kirkwood, Mo., 1985—; mem. environ. risk com. Chem. Mfgrs. Assn., Washington, 1980-83. Contbr. articles to profl. jours. Patentee in field. Bd. dirs. Dayton Civic Ballet, 1959-61. Mem. Am. Chem. Soc., AAAS, Soc. Risk Analysis, Nat. Conf. Advancement of Research (bd. dirs. 1982—), Soc. Research Adminstrs. (indsl. div. pres. 1982, Hartford-Nicholson award 1981). Presbyterian. Avocations: tennis; sailing. Home: 729 Delchester Ln Kirkwood MO 63122 Office: Delos Inc 729 Delchester Ln Kirkwood MO 63122

RICHARDS, JACK EDWARD, medical services company executive, consultant; b. Nashville, May 29, 1945; s. E.A. and Elizabeth (Baab) R.; m. Carol Ann Missig, Sept. 30, 1967; children: Douglas Randolph, Scott Andrew. BSEE, U. Cin., 1974. V.p. Cen. Ohio Imaging, Inc., Cin., 1984—; pres. Assistance in Med. Edn., Inc., Cin., 1986—. Served with USN, 1963-66. Mem. Cin. C. of C. Businessmen's Circle. Republican. Methodist. Avocations: tennis, swimming, cycling. Office: Assistance in Med Edn Inc. 1095 Nimitzview Dr #103 Cincinnati OH 45230

RICHARDS, JOHN FLEMING, investment firm executive; b. Washington, Sept. 28, 1947; s. George and Ann Marie (Fleming) R.; B.A., U. Va., 1969; postgrad. Wesleyan U., 1969-70; M.B.A., U. Chgo., 1972; MA, U. Ill., Chgo., 1985; m. Marilyn Murray, July 22, 1972; children—Matthew J., Andrew J., Scott M. Investment analyst William Blair & Co., Chgo., 1972-81, partner investment research, 1981—. C.P.A., Ill.; chartered fin. analyst. Mem. Investment Analysts Soc. Chgo. (pres. 1983-84, dir. 1984—), Am. Inst. C.P.A.s, Ill. C.P.A. Soc., Inst. Chartered Fin. Analysts (candidate curriculum com., council examiners 1984-86), Am. Math. Soc. Club: Execs. of Chgo.; Westmoreland Country, Lasalle. Office: 135 S LaSalle St Chicago IL 60603

RICHARDS, JOHN RANDALL, pharmacist; b. Lafayette, Ind., May 21, 1958; s. Jewell Ray and Georgia Arlene (Benge) R. AS, Ferris State Coll., 1978, B Pharmacy, 1981. Registered pharmacist, Mich. Staff pharmacist Sparrow Hosp., Lansing, Mich., 1981-83; sales rep. Eli Lilly & Co., Lansing, 1983-85, hosp. sales rep., 1985—. Recipient UpJohn Achievement for Community Service award, 1981. Mem. Mich. Pharmacy Assn., Am. Soc. Hosp. Pharmacy, Capital Area Pharmacist Assn. (pres. elect. 1984-85), Phi Delta Chi (v.p. 1983-85), Omicron Delta Kappa, Rho Chi. Republican. Avocations: sports, reading, music, travel. Home and Office: 3237 Arrowhead Arms Ct Sw Grandville MI 49418

RICHARDS, LACLAIRE LISSETTA JONES (MRS. GEORGE A. RICHARDS), social worker; b. Pine Bluff, Ark.; d. Artie William and Geraldine (Adams) Jones; B.A., Nat. Coll. Christian Workers, 1953; M.S.W., U. Kans., 1956; postgrad. Columbia U., 1960; m. George Alvarez Richards, July 26, 1958; children—Leslie Rosario, Lia Mercedes, Jorge Ferguson. Psychiat. supervisory, teaching, community orgn., adminstrv. and consultative duties Hastings Regional Center, Ingleside, Nebr., 1956-60; supervisory, consultative and adminstrv. responsibilities for psychiat. and geriatric patients VA Hosp., Knoxville, Iowa, 1960-74, field instr. for grad. students from U. Mo., EEO counselor, 1969-74, 78—, com. chmn., 1969-70, Fed. women's program coordinator, 1972-74; sr. social worker Mental Health Inst., Cherokee, Iowa, 1974-77; adj. asst. prof. dept. social behavior U. S.D.; instr. Augustana Coll.; outpatient social worker VA Med. and Regional Office Center, Sioux Falls, S.D., 1978—; EEO counselor. Mem. Knoxville Juvenile Adv. Com., 1963-65, 68-70, sec., 1965-66, chmn., 1966-68; sec. Urban Renewal Citizens' Adv. Com., Knoxville, 1966-68; mem. United Methodist Ch. Task Force Exptl. Styles Ministry and Leadership, 1973-74, mem. adult choir, mem. ch. and society com.; counselor Knoxville Youth Line program; sec. exec. com. Vis. Nurse Assn., 1979-80; canvasser community fund drs., Knoxville; mem. Cherokee Civil Rights Comm.; bd. dirs., pub. relations, membership devel. and program devel. cons. YWCA, 1984-85. Named S.D. Social Worker of Yr., 1983. Mem. Nat. Assn. Social Workers (co-chmn. Nebr. chpt. profl. standards com. 1958-59), Acad. Cert. Social Workers, S.D. Assn. Social Workers (chmn. minority affairs com., v.p. S.E. region 1980, pres. 1980-82 exec. com. 1982-84, mem. social policy and action com.), Nebr. Assn. Social Workers (chmn. 1958-59), AAUW (sec. Hastings chpt. 1958-60), AMA Aux., Seventh Dist. S.D. Med. Soc. Aux., Coalition on Aging, NAACP (chmn. edn. com. 1983—). Methodist (Sunday sch. tchr. adult div.; mem. commn. on edn.; mem. Core com. for adult edn.; mem. Adult Choir; mem. Social Concerns Work Area). Home: 1701 Ponderosa Dr Sioux Falls SD 57103

RICHARDS, NOEL J., university administrator. Chancellor U. Wis.-LaCrosse. Office: U Wis Office of Chancellor LaCrosse WI 54601 *

RICHARDS, THOMAS JEFFREY, physician; b. Berwyn, Ill., Feb. 28, 1944; s. James Henry and Caroline Emily (Patha) R. B.A., Lake Forest Coll., 1966; M.A., Wake Forest U., 1968; Ph.D., St. Louis U., 1972. Sr. research engr. Caterpillar, Inc., Peoria, Ill., 1973-76, project engr., 1976-81, staff engr., 1981—. Patentee in field. Mem. Am. Phys. Soc., AAAS. Office: Research Dept TC-A Caterpillar Inc Peoria IL 61629

RICHARDS, TIMOTHY JAY, psychologist; b. Belleville, Ill., Sept. 2, 1945; s. Russell George and Helen Margaret (Thien) R.; m. Mary Ann Clyne,Aug. 14, 1971; children: Kristin Ann, Kara Marie. BA, St. Mary's U., San Antonio, 1968; MEd, U. Ill., 1975; MS, So. Ill. U., Edwardsville, 1978; PhD, So. Ill. U., Carbondale, 1982. Instr. Belleville Area Coll., 1983-86; psychologist Southwest Family Clinic, O'Fallon, Ill., 1984—; adj. asst. prof. Webster U., Webster Groves, Mo., 1987—; adj. asst. prof. grad. sch. Webster U., St. louis, 1987—. Named one of Outstanding Young Men Of Am., Jaycees, 1982. Mem. Am. Psychol. Assn., St. Mary's U. Alumni Assn. (pres. East St. Louis chpt. 1978-81), So. Ill. U. Alumni Assn., U. Ill. Alumni Assn., Phi Delta Kappa. Roman Catholic. Club: Oak Hill Racquet (Bellville). Lodge: Elks. Avocations: tennis, golf, automobile restoration. Home: 304 E 8th St O'Fallon IL 62269

RICHARDS, WARREN LEWIS, psychiatrist, consultant; b. Cin., Oct. 8, 1922; s. Daniel Smith and Alta Mathilda (Hawk) R.; m. Nancy McFarland, Feb. 4, 1941 (div. 1965); m. Wanda Lee Aikins, Apr. 27, 1966 (dec. Feb. 1979); children: Daniel, Chris, Casey, Caryn, Cathy, Kim; m. Karen DeLuca Braden, Aug. 8, 1987. BS, U. Cin., 1941, MD, 1948. Intern, then resident U. Cin. Hosp., 1948-51; practice medicine specializing in psychiatry Cin., 1954—; cons. Gen. Elec. Co., Cin., 1959—, Cin. Bar Assn., 1970—, Comprehend Inc., Maysville, Ky., 1978—; sr. staff mem. The Christ Hosp., Cin., 1969—; assoc. clin. prof. U. Cin. Hosp., 1976—. Contbr. articles to profl. jours. Mem. Cin. Civic Club, 1970—; cons. Kids Helping Kids, Cin., 1985—; lectr. Divorced and Singles Group, Hyde Park Meth. Ch., Cin., 1980—. Served to lt. col. USAFR, 1953-78. Mem. Am. Psychiat. Assn., Cin. Psychiat. Assn., Assn. Disability Examiners, Anderson Hills Swim and Tennis Club (co-founder). Avocations: choral music, amateur theater, physical fitness, athletics. Office: 250 William H Taft Rd #107 Cincinnati OH 45219

RICHARDS, WILLIAM EARL, retired state social services official; b. N.Y.C., Oct. 19, 1921; s. John Earl and Camily Pauline (Deravaine) R.; m. Ollum Elizabeth Sadler, Sept. 16, 1949; 1 son, William Earl. B.A. in Econ., Washburn U., 1972. Enlisted in U.S. Army, commd. and advanced through grades to lt. col., 1970; served in Asiatic-Pacific Theatre, World War II, 1943-46; supervised Am. engrs. and technicians in Philippine Islands, and Saipan, the Marianas Islands, 1946-49; test and evaluation officer, 1951; asst. maintenance officer and ammunition insp., Korea, 1951-52; ammunition storage officer, Nara, Japan, 1952-54; chief inspection div., Phila., 1954-58; ops. and storage officer, Pirmasens, W.Ger., 1958-61; tng. officer, Ft. Hamilton, Bklyn., 1961-62; contracting officer, Saigon, South Vietnam, 1962-63; asst. commr. and contracting officer's rep., Joliet, Ill., 1963-67; deputy dir. procurement, Worms, W.Ger., 1967-70; ret., 1970; staff dir. and legis. agt. NAACP, Topeka Kans., 1972; asst. dir. Kans. Commn. Alcoholism, Topeka, 1972-73, dir. Div. Social Services, Dept. Social and Rehab. Services, 1973-80, commr. income maintenance and med. services, 1980-83; sr. cons. Myers and Stauffer, CPA's. Adv. com. Kans. div. Services to Children and Youth, Dept. Agr. Com. on Equal Opportunity; bd. dirs. United Way of Greater Topeka, Topeka Vol. Ctr., Community resources Council. Decorated Legion of Merit. Mem. NAACP (life), Am. Pub. Welfare Assn., Nat. Council Pub. Welfare Adminstrs. (exec. com. 1982), Kans. Conf. Social Welfare, Ret. Officers Assn., Am. Def. Preparedness Assn., Assn. U.S. Army, Washburn Alumni Assn., Alpha Phi Alpha. Club: Topeka Knife and Fork. Lodges: Shriners, KT.

RICHARDSON, AVIS JUNE, minister; b. Burlington, Colo., June 20, 1931; d. Elvis Guy Foley and Sarah Margaret (Yale) Smith; m. David W. Richardson, May 19, 1949; children: Angelia J. Richardson Pfeifer, John W., Alisa J. Richardson Hoffman. AA, McKendree Coll. Ordained deacon United Meth. Ch., 1971. Minister United Meth. Ch., Beckemeyer, Ill., 1968-71, Hamburg, Ill., 1971-73, Saint Jacob, Ill., 1973-77, Waltonville, Ill., 1977-78, Patoka, Ill., 1978-85, 1985-86, Staunton, 1985-87. Home: 513 W Main Staunton IL 62088

RICHARDSON, BARBARA CONNELL, transportation research scientist; b. N.Y.C., Dec. 29, 1947; d. John Joseph and Joan Marie (Tobin) Connell; m. Rudy James Richardson, Aug. 23, 1970 (div. Dec. 1984); 1 child, Anne Elizabeth. BA, SUNY, 1969; SM, MIT, 1973; PhD, U. Mich., Ann Arbor, 1982. Programmer/analyst The Phys. Review, Upton, N.Y., 1969-70; transp. planner Mass. Exec. Office of Transp. and Constrn., Boston, 1973-74; transp. research officer Greater London Council, 1974-75; assoc. research scientist and dir. transp. planning and policy Univ. Mich., Ann Arbor, 1975-86; pres. Richardson Assocs., Inc., Ann Arbor, 1983—. Contbr. numerous articles on transp. to profl. jours. Mem. Transp. Research Bd., Nat. Assn. Bus. Economists, Am. Assn. for Automotive Medicine, Soc. for Risk Analysis, Am. Enterprise Inst. for Pub. Policy, Kappa Mu Epsilon, Signum Laudis, Sigma Xi. Roman Catholic. Office: 325 E Eisenhower Pkwy Suite 301 Ann Arbor MI 48108

RICHARDSON, CHARLES EDWARD, electronics executive; b. Columbus, Ohio, Aug. 30, 1943; s. Carl Edward and Bertha Lila (Gilkerson) R.; m. Shirley Ann Ventola, Oct. 21, 1966; 1 child, Keri Ann. BSEE, Ohio State U., 1972. V.p. mfg. Scientific Columbus (Ohio) Co., 1966-79; ops. mgr. Entronic Controls div. Cooper Energy Services, Mt. Vernon, Ohio, 1979-82; v.p. mfg. Transdata, Inc., Dublin, Ohio, 1982-83; v.p. mfg., bus. devel. Micro Industries Inc., Westerville, Ohio, 1983—. Served with USAF, 1962-66. Mem. IEEE, Surface Mount Tech. Assn. (bd. dirs. 1984—). Republican. Methodist. Avocations: reading, golf. Home: 644 Colony Dr Westerville OH 43081

RICHARDSON, DEAN EUGENE, banker; b. West Branch, Mich., Dec. 27, 1927; s. Robert F. and Helen (Husted) R.; m. Barbara Trytten, June 14, 1952; children: Ann Elizabeth, John Matthew. A.B., Mich. State U., 1950; LL.B., U. Mich., 1953; postgrad., Stonier Grad. Sch. Banking, 1965. With Indsl. Nat. Bank, Detroit, 1953-55; with Mfrs. Nat. Bank, Detroit, 1955—; v.p. adminstrn. Mfrs. Nat. Bank, 1964-66, sr. v.p., 1966-67, exec. v.p., 1967-69, pres., 1969-73; chmn., chief exec. officer Mfrs.-Detroit Internat. Corp., 1973—, also chmn. bd. dirs.; dir. Atlantic Internat. Bank, Detroit Edison Co., R.P. Scherer Corp., Fruehauf Corp., Tecumseh Products Co. Served with USNR, 1945-46. Mem. Mich., Detroit bar assns., Assn. Res. City Bankers, Am. Inst. Banking, Mens Forum, Robert Morris Assocs., Econ. Club Detroit (dir.), Newcomen Soc. N.Am. Episcopalian. Clubs: Masons, KT, Detroit Athletic, Detroit, Country of Detroit. Office: Mfrs Nat Bank of Detroit 100 Renaissance Center Detroit MI 48243

RICHARDSON, DONALD LEE, environmental engineer; b. Mt. Vernon, Ill., Aug. 26, 1954; s. Owen Lee and Shirley Jean (King) R.; m. Susan Joan Bryden, May 16, 1980; children—Lori A., Richard D., Jill R. B.S., So. Ill. U., 1977, M.S., 1981. Registered prof. engr., Ill. Engr. Ill. EPA, Springfield, 1977-81; engr. water quality Central Ill. Pub. Service, Springfield, 1981—. Adv. Jr. Achievement, 1984. Ill. State Commn. scholar, 1972. Mem. Water Polution Control Fedn., Ill. Groundwater Assn. Avocations: stereo, home remodeling. Home: 1728 S Park Springfield IL 62704 Office: Central Ill Pub Service Co 607 E Adams Springfield IL 62701

RICHARDSON, FRANK JAMES, architect; b. Toledo, Apr. 12, 1951; s. Cecil LeRoy and Virginia Mae (Stotz) R.; m. Christine Ann Barbasiewicz, Sept. 9, 1978; children: Matthew Charles, Andrew John, Victoria Rose. BArch cum laude, Kent (Ohio) State U., 1974. Registered architect, Wis. Draftsman Island Steel Bldg. Systems, Milw., 1974-77; project architect Slater Architects, Waukesha, Wis., 1977-79; architect Peter Schwabe, Inc., Milw., 1979-81; v.p., architect PSI Design, Big Bend, Wis., 1981-84; architect Inryco Constrn., Milw., 1984—; cons. downtown redevel. commn. City of Waukesha, Wis., 1983-84. Mem. AIA, Wis. Soc. Architects. Episcopalian. Lodge: Rotary. Avocations: camping, hiking, bicycling, photography, home improvements. Home: 2645 N 46th St Milwaukee WI 53210 Office: Inryco Constrn Co 2075 W Mill Rd Milwaukee WI 53209

RICHARDSON, HOWARD DEE, health and physical education and recreation educator, educational administrator; b. Salt Lake City, June 21, 1926; s. William Wilshire and Mary Emaline (Dobson) R.; m. Lorna Ann Gleave, Nov. 28, 1951; children—Wendy, Ron Howard, Mark Reed, Shelly. B.A., Westminster Coll., 1950; M.S., U. Utah, 1962, D.Ed., 1967. Life teaching cert., Utah. Instr. Salt Lake City Sch. Corp., 1951-53; assoc. prof. Westminster Coll., Salt Lake City, 1953-66; dir. athletics, phys. edn. instr. U. Utah, Salt Lake City, 1966-67; prof., dir. athletics and phys. edn. Eastern Oreg. State Coll., LaGrand, 1967-71; dean Sch. Health, Phys. Edn. and Recreation, prof., Ind. State U., Terre Haute, 1971—; editorial cons. William C. Brown Inc., Prentice Hall Inc. Author articles in field. Chmn. Ind. Gov.'s Council for Phys. Fitness, Sports Medicine, 1980—; chmn. YMCA Bldg. Fund, Salt Lake City, 1963. Served with U.S. Army, 1943-46; PTO. Honored Coll. and Univ. Adminstrs. Council, 1980; named Basketball Coach of Yr., NAIA Dist. 7, 1961, 63, 65. Mem. AAHPERD, Assn. Adminstrn. Research Profl. Council and Socs. (pres. 1981, past pres. award 1982), Nat. Assn. for Phys. Edn. in Higher Edn. (western exec. com. 1959), Phi Delta Kappa. Republican. Avocations: Writing; golf; tennis. Home: Rural Route 21 Box 422 Terre Haute IN 47802 Office: Sch Health Phys Edn and Recreation Ind State Univ Terre Haute IN 47809

RICHARDSON, JOHN AIDAN, state board administrator; b. Fargo, N.D., July 2, 1939; s. John and Norah (Jordan) R.; m. Kristin Carol Earhart, Jan. 25, 1964; children—Mark Aidan, John Joseph. B.S., U. Oreg., 1961, M.S., 1965; Ph.D., Stanford U., 1975. Counseling asst., Wash. State U., 1965-66; research asst. Stanford U. Ctr. for Research and Devel. in Teaching, 1968-69; adminstrv. intern Oreg. State System of Higher Edn., 1970-71, asst. to chancellor, 1971-75, asst. chancellor, 1975-79; commr. higher edn. Mont. U. System, Helena, 1979-81; commr. State Bd. Higher Edn. State of N.D., Bismarck, 1981—; adj. asst. prof. edn. U. Oreg., 1975-78; vis. scholar Nat. Ctr. Higher Edn. Mgmt. Systems, Boulder, Colo., 1978-79; pres. Mont. Higher Edn. Student Assistance Corp., 1980-81. Trustee, Oreg. Episcopal Sch., Portland, 1975-78; bd. dirs. Greater Mont. Found., 1979-81; commr. Western Interstate Commn. for Higher Edn., 1979-81. Served with USNR, 1961-64. Kellogg fellow, 1967-68. Mem. Am. Assn. Higher Edn., Phi Delta Theta. Office: North Dakota State Bd of Higher Edn System Office State Capitol 10th Floor Bismarck ND 58505-0154

RICHARDSON, JOHN THOMAS, clergyman, university president; b. Dallas, Dec. 20, 1923; s. Patrick and Mary (Walsh) R. B.A., St. Mary's Sem., Perryville, Mo., 1946; S.T.D., Angelicum U., Rome, Italy, 1951; M.A., St. Louis U., 1954. Prof. theology, dean studies Kenrick Sem., St. Louis, 1951-54; lectr. Webster Coll., 1954; dean Grad. Sch. DePaul U., Chgo., 1954-60, exec. v.p., dean faculties, 1960-81, pres., 1981—; also lectr. Grad. Sch. DePaul U. (Coll. Law and trustee), 1955—. Home: 2233 N Kenmore Ave Chicago IL 60614 Office: De Paul Univ Office of the President Chicago IL 60604

RICHARDSON, JOSEPH ELMER, III, dentist; b. Rolla, Mo., Sept. 4, 1951; s. Joseph Elmer II and Mary Katheryn (Ross) R.; m. Kathy Lee Kelly, Aug. 3, 1975; children: Kelly Lee, Katy Lou. AB, U. Mo., 1973, postgrad., 1974-76; DDS, U. Mo., Kansas City, 1981. Microbiology aide Fish Pesticide Research Lab. Mo. Dept. Interior, Columbia, 1974-77; pvt. practice dentistry Houston, Mo., 1981—; pres. Hospice of Care Adv. Bd., Texas County Hosp., Houston, Mo., 1984-86. Pres. Houston R-1 Sch. Bd., 1984—; active United Meth. Ch. Bd., Houston, 1984—, Houston High Alumni Assn. Bd., 1984—; chmn. Tex. County Chpt. Ducks Unlimited, Houston, 1985-86. Mem. ADA, Mo. Dental Assn., Springfield (Mo.) Dental Soc. Republican. Methodist. Lodges: Lions, Optimists. Home: HCR 4 Box 190 Houston MO 65483 Office: 321 S Second Houston MO 65483

RICHARDSON, KENNETH R., aircraft logistics executive, retired air force officer; b. Belle Rive, Ill., Nov. 28, 1943; s. James Howard and Eva Marie (Wyrick) R.; m. Priscilla Elaine Philbrick, Jan. 31, 1981; stepchildren: George B. Callow III, Adam J. Callow, Matthew M. Callow. BS, So. Ill. U., 1966; MS, U. So. Calif., 1979. Commd. 2d lt. USAF, 1965, advanced through grades to maj., 1980; propulsion project officer SAC Hdqrs., Offutt AFB, Nebr., 1971-74; maintenance supr. 9 Field Maintenance Squadron, Beale AFB, Calif., 1974-1979; chief Reconnaissance Systems Div., 15th Air Force, March AFB, Calif., 1979-81; maintenance control officer 32 Tactical Fighter Squadron, Camp New Amsterdam, Netherlands, 1981-84; maintenance supr. 410 Organizational Maintenance Squadron, K.I. Sawyer AFB, Mich., 1984-86; B-1B mgr. Rockwell Internat., Grand Forks AFB, N.D., 1986—. Decorated Bronze Star. Mem. Am. Mgmt. Assn., Retired Officers Assn., Soc. Agrl. Engrs. (assoc.), Grand Forks C. of C. (mil. affairs com.). Democrat. Baptist. Home: 2611 Olson Dr Grand Forks ND 58201

RICHARDSON, MICHAEL EDWARD, city official; b. Mpls., July 21, 1942; s. Vincent Frederick and Libby M. (Key) R.; m. Mary Ann DeMark, Aug. 29, 1964; children—Sarah, David. B.S., U. Wis.-Whitewater, 1964; M.A. (grad. asst.), Eastern Mich. U., 1967; M.P.A., No. Ill. U., 1980. Sr. planner Bi-State Plan Commn., Rock Island, Ill., 1965-67; chief planner N.E. Wis. Plan Commn., Appleton, 1971-72; dir. dept. planning City of Des Plaines (Ill.), 1972-82, dir. dept. mcpl. devel., 1982-85; dir. Dept. Community Devel., Hanover Park, Ill., 1985—. Pres., bd. dirs. N.W. Mcpl. Fed. Credit Union; lectr. Eastern Mich. U., U. Alaska. Mem. N.E. Ill. Plan Commn. Task Force; team mgr. Hoffman Estates (Ill.) Baseball Assn.; mem. planning/bldg. edn. com. Harper Coll., 1983—. Served with Intelligence, USAF, 1967-71. Decorated Bronze Star, USAF commendation medal; recipient Outstanding Grad. award USAF Officer Tng. Sch., 1967, recognition award Nat. Assn. Women in Constrn., 1985. Mem. Internat. City Mgmt. Assn., Am. Inst. Cert. Planners (charter), Am. Planning Assn., N.W. Bldg. Ofcls. and Code Adminstrs. Roman Catholic. Author: Flood Information Handbook, 1973; contbr. articles to profl. jours. Office: Dept Community Devel 2121 W Lake St Hanover Park IL 60103

RICHARDSON, MILDRED LOVINA TOURTILLOTT, psychologist; b. North Hampton, N.H., May 8, 1907; d. Herbert Shaw and Sarach Louise (Fife) Tourtillott; m. Harold Wellington Richardson, June 25, 1932; children: Elizabeth Fern Ruben, Constance Joy Van Valer, Carol Louise Dennis. AB, Bates Coll., 1930; MA, U. Mich., 1948; EdS, Butler U., 1961; PhD, Ind. U., 1965. Diplomate Am. Bd. Profl. Psychology, Nat. Register Health Service Providers in Psychology; cert. clin. and sch. psychology, Pa., Ind. Tchr. math. and sci. Norwich (Conn.) Free Acad., 1930-32, Port Huron (Mich.) High Sch., 1943-45; dir. intermediate girls Interlochen Nat. Music Camp, Mich., 1953, asst. dean univ. women, 1954; tchr., guidance counselor Community Sch. Corp., Franklin, Ind., 1956-64; supr. tng. Devereux Found., Devon, Pa., 1965-78, cons. clin. tng. in sch. and clin. psychology, 1975-78; tchr. psychology of spl. edn. Pa. State U.ext., King of Prussia, 1966-68; sch. psychologist Johnson County (Ind.) Spl. Services, 1979-82; head clin. psychology Community Psychiat. Ctrs. Valle Vista Hosp., Greenwood, Ind., 1983—; pvt. practice health service provider in psychology Greenwood, 1985—; clin. assoc. prof. Hahnemann Med. Coll., Phila., 1973-78, dir. seminar on psychodiagnostics; assoc. prof. sch. psychology Ind. U., Bloomington, 1982; pvt. practice psychology, 1970—; bd. examiners Midwest Regional Bd. Am. Bd. Profl. Psychology; bd. dirs. Johnson County (Ind.) Assn. Mentally Retarded Citizens, 1982-84; participant Internat. Sch. Psychology Colloquium, 1975. Contbr. articles to profl. jours. Recipient Headliner award Theta Sigma Phi, 1964. Fellow Am. Psychol. Assn.; mem. Inst. Clin. Tng. (hon.), Internat. Council Psychologists, Internat. Sch. Psychology Com., Soc. Ret. Execs., Devereux Found. (hon.), Phi Kappa Phi. Republican. Baptist. Avocations: needlepoint, travelling, collecting. Home: 477 Oakwood Dr S Greenwood IN 46142 Office: Community Psychiat Ctrs Valle Vista Hosp 898 E Main St Greenwood IN 46142

RICHARDSON, MYRTLE, abstracter, former judge; b. Jefferson County, Ohio, July 2, 1907; d. Thomas and Blanche (Whitecotton) Heinselman; student Kans. State Tchrs. Coll., 1926; A.A., Dodge City Community Coll., 1978; m. Harold E. Richardson, Mar. 4, 1929 (div.); 1 dau., Nancy Lee Richardson Ridgway. Tchr. public schs., Edwards County, Kans., 1924-28; reporter, advertiser Kinsley (Kans.) Graphic, 1928-35, mgr., 1937-41; editor, advt. mgr. So. Standard, McMinnville, Tenn., 1935-36; abstracter H. F. Thompson, Kinsley, 1943-54; editor Kinsley Mercury, 1954-57; abstracter, Kinsley, 1957-84; probate judge, Kinsley, 1958-69; judge Mcpl. Ct. Kinsley, 1958-69. Bd. dirs. United Drive, 1947-57, Edwards County chpt. ARC, 1940-50; community and project leader 4-H Club, 1943-52; community and project leader Edwards County 4-H Who's Who Club, 1943-52; pres. PTA, 1940-44. Vice chmn. Edwards County Democratic Com. 1956-84; pres. Edwards County Fedn. Dem. Women's Club, 1970-74, 76—; chmn. Dem. Central Com., Edwards County, 1981; dist. dir. South 1st Dist. Fedn. Dem. Women's Clubs, 1981. Mem. C. of C. (sec.-mgr. 1947-54), Edwards County Hist. Soc. (historian), S. Central Kans. Probate Judges Assn. (pres. 1966). Author: Oft Told Tales-A History of Edwards County, Kansas from 1873 to 1900, 1976; The Great Next Year Country, 1983, Changes Rode the Winds, 1986. Home: 120 N 2d St Kinsley KS 67547

RICHARDSON, PHILIP EDWIN, real estate development and construction company executive; b. Logansport, Ind., July 1, 1953; s. Omer E. and Arlette G. Richardson; m. Katherine Reishus, June 29, 1974; children: Jennifer, Kristin. Student U. Wis.-Superior, 1971-72; BS in Bus. and Econ., Gustavus Adolphus Coll., 1975. Exec. v.p. Richardson Assocs., Inc., Naperville, Ill., 1975—. Small bus. adv. bd. U.S. Rep. Thomas Corcoran, Aurora, Ill., 1983-84; pres. ch. council Geneva Lutheran Ch., 1984—. Nominated for First Decade award Gustavus Adolphus Coll., 1985. Mem. Nat. Assn. Home Builders (bd. dirs. 1984—), Home Builders Assn. Ill., (area v.p. 1985, bd. dirs. 1983-84), No. Ill. Home Builders Assn. (pres. 1984). Home: 734 Nordic Ct Batavia IL 60510 Office: Richardson Assocs Inc 1979 N Mill St Suite 201 Naperville IL 60540

RICHARDSON, REGINALD CHARLES, social services administrator; b. Chgo., May 6, 1960; s. David Milton and Bernice (Stowell) R.; 1 child, Anri J. BA in Psychology and Social Work, Coll. St. Francis, Joliet, Ill., 1982; MSW, U. Ill., Chgo., 1985. Cert. social worker, substitute tchr. Social worker youth services Guardian Angel Home, Joliet, 1980-83; adminstr. youth services Ill. Dept. Children and Family Services, Peoria, 1983-85; pvt. practice clin. social worker Chgo., 1984—; regional coordinator Gov.'s Youth Service Initiative, Chgo., 1985-86; exec. dir. The Farm Sch. Ltd., Durand, Ill., 1986—; chmn. recruitment and pub. relation com. Coll. St. Francis, 1984—, guest lectr. 1983—; assoc. faculty Residential Child Care Inst., 1986—. Mem. adv. bd. Regional Truancy Network, Parents Too Soon , 1984-85. Mem. Nat. Assn. Soc. Workers, Regional Truancy Network Council. Avocation: sports. Home: 1324 West Barry Ave First Floor Rear Chicago IL 60657 Office: The Farm Sch Ltd 10102 Farm School Rd Durand IL 61024

RICHARDSON, ROBERT EDWARD, data processing analyst; b. Ann Arbor, Mich., Dec. 13, 1955; s. Stanley G. and Frances A. (Raes) R. BBA, U. Iowa, 1978. Res. group mgr. Sears, Roebuck & Co., Des Moines, 1978-79; data processing mgmt. trainee Armstrong Dept. Store, Cedar Rapids, Iowa, 1979-81; level II programmer analyst City of Cedar Rapids, 1981-84; sr. programmer analyst Life Investors, Cedar Rapids, 1984—. Mem. Hawkeye PC Users Group, Alpha Kappa Psi (pres. Hawkeye State Alumni chpt. 1987-88, editor, pub. 1987 directory, Alumni Disting. Service Award 1981). Avocation: IBM-XT personal computer. Home: 3960 Sherman St NE Apt 24 Cedar Rapids IA 52402 Office: Life Investors 4333 Edgewood Rd NE Cedar Rapids IA 52499

RICHARDSON, ROBERT OWEN, lawyer; b. Gallatin, Mo., Sept. 7, 1922; s. Denver Oscar and Opal (Wellman) R.; m. Carroll Sparks, July 7, 1951 (div.); children—Robert Steven, Linda Colleen; m. 2d, Viola Kapantais Wempe, Dec. 22, 1977. B.S. in Physics, Drury Coll., 1946; LL.B., George Washington U., 1954, J.D., 1968; M.S., Fla. Inst. Tech., 1977. Bar: U.S. Dist. Ct. (D.C.) 1954, U.S. Patent Office 1954, U.S. Ct. Customs and Patent Appeals 1958, Calif. 1958, N.H. 1961, Iowa 1976, U.S. Supreme Ct. 1961, Can. Patent Office, 1962, U.S. Ct. Appeals (fed. cir.) 1982. Patent examiner U.S. Patent Office, Washington, 1949-54; patent atty. Navy Electronics Lab., San Diego, 1954-56, Gen. Dynamics, San Diego, 1956-60; chief patent counsel Sanders Assoc., Nashua, N.H., 1960-62; patent atty. TRW, Canoga Park, Calif., 1963-64, McDonnell Douglas, Santa Monica, Calif., 1964-75; patent counsel U.S. Army Armament Munitions Chem. Command, Rock Island, Ill., 1975-85; patent arbitrator Am. Arbitration Assn., 1984—; judge pro tem Los Angeles Mcpl. Ct., 1967-68. Author: How To Get Your Own Patent, 1981. Democratic nominee for Congress from Mo. 6th Dist., 1951. Served to lt. comdr. USNR, 1942-73. Mem. Govt. Patent Lawyer's Assn., Am. Patent Law Assn., Patent Law Assn. San Diego, Patent Law Assn. Los Angeles, Patent Law Assn. Boston, Patent Law Assn. Iowa. Lodges: Masons, Shriners.

RICHARDSON, ROBERT RONALD, neurosurgeon; b. Oak Park, Ill., Sept. 9, 1942; s. Wibert E. and Louise Mary (Macku) R.; m. Linda Marie Johnson, Mar. 3, 1984; 1 child, Robert Ray. BS in Biology, Loyola U., Chgo., 1964, MD, 1968; PhD, Nat. U., 1986. Intern U. Minn., Mpls., 1968-69, resident in gen. surgery, 1969-70; instr. neuroanatomy Northwestern U., Chgo., 1970-78, resident in neurosurgery, 1970-78; asst. prof. N.Y. Med. Sch., Valhalla, 1978-80; attending neurosurgeon Mt. Sinai Hosp. Med. Ctr., Chgo., 1980—, assoc. chief div. neurosurgery, 1980—, chief sect. physiologic neurosurgery, 1984—; asst. chief Ctr. Physiologic Neurosurgery, Valhalla, 1978-80; pres. Neurostimulation Found. Inc., Chgo., 1984-86. Contbr. numerous articles to profl. jours.; chpts. to books. Grantee Children's Meml. Hosp., Chgo., 1970-71, Precision Devices Corp., Naperville, Ill., 1976; spl. fellow NIH, 1971-73. Fellow ACS, Am. Coll. Cryosurgery, Am. Acad. Neurol. and Orthopaedic Surgery, Internat. Coll. Surgeons, Inst. Medicine; mem. Am. Acad. Neuro-muscular Thermography (charter), Am. Back Soc. (bd. dirs. 1985). Avocations: fishing, old toys, numismatics. Home: 136 Carriage Way Dr Apt C-111 Burr Ridge IL 60521 Office: Mt Sinai Hosp Med Ctr 2720 W 15th St Chicago IL 60608

RICHARDSON, ROY JOHN, health care administrator, therapist; b. St. Paul, Sept. 14, 1938; s. Charles J. and Grace E. (Sandbrink) R.; m. Bonnie Merida Sigstad, Oct. 15, 1960 (div. Feb. 1972); children—Glen, Joanne, Elizabeth, Mark, Tracy, Jon. B.A., Met. State U., St. Paul, 1981; MBA, Calif. Coast U., Santa Ana, 1986—, grad. studies, 1986—. Cert. chem. dependency practitioner. Acct., 1960-75; addictions therapist, St. Paul, 1976-81; dir. Dakota County Mental Health, South St. Paul, Minn., 1980-81, Parkview Chem. Dependency Program, Pueblo, Colo., 1981-83; exec. dir. Fountain Ctrs., Minn., Iowa, Ind., Sweden, Norway, 1983—; presenter World-Med Internat. Congress, St. Paul, 1986, Deutscher Wohlfahrtsverband, Frankfurt, Germany, 1986. Author/researcher: Adult Chemical Dependency Diagnosis, 1980; Adolescent Chemical Dependency Diagnosis, 1981. State of Minn. grantee, 1984-85. Mem. Minn. Assn. Treatment Programs (bd. dirs. 1983—, mem. exec. com. 1985—), Minn. Chem. Dependency Assn. (bd. dirs. 1984-85), Am. Coll. Addiction Treatment Adminstrs., Nat. Assn. Alcoholism Treatment Programs, Mensa. Avocations: travel, languages, weaving. Home: 799 4th Ave S Albert Lea MN 56007 Office: Fountain Lakes Ctrs 408 Fountain St Albert Lea MN 56007

RICHARDSON, RUDY JAMES, toxicology and neurosciences educator; b. Winfield, Kans., May 13, 1945; s. Irving Lavelle and Marjorie M. (Frans) R.; m. Barbara Connell, 1970 (div. Dec. 1984); 1 child, Anne Elizabeth; m. Kathleen M. Gavin, 1985. B.S. magna cum laude, Wichita State U., 1967; Sc.M., Harvard U., 1973, Sc.D., 1974. Diplomate Am. Bd. Toxicology. Research geochemist Columbia U., N.Y.C., summer 1966; NASA trainee SUNY, Stony Brook, 1967-70; research biochemist Med. Research Council, Carshalton, Eng., 1974-75; asst. prof. U. Mich., Ann Arbor, 1975-79, assoc. prof., 1979-84, prof. toxicology, 1984—; vis. scientist Warner-Lambert Co., Ann Arbor, 1982-83; cons. Nat. Acad. Scis., Washington, 1978-79, 84. Contbr. articles to profl. jours., chpts. to books; mem. editorial bd. Neurotoxicology, 1980—. Mem. Mich. Lupus Found., Ann Arbor, 1979—. Grantee NIH, 1977—, EPA, 1977—; invited speaker Gordon Conf., Meriden, N.H., 1984, Cholinesterase Congress, Bled, Yugoslavia, 1983. Mem. Soc. Toxicology (pres. neurotoxicology sect. 1987—), Soc. for Neurosci., Am. Chem. Soc., AAAS, Internat. Soc. Neurochemistry. Avocations: creative writing; classical guitar. Office: U Mich Toxicology Program M-7525/SPH-2 Ann Arbor MI 48109

RICHARDSON, SHARON LOUISE, nurse; b. Poplar Bluff, Mo., July 31, 1956; d. Alfred James and Della Pearl (Rievley) Baker; m. Gary Raymond Richardson, May 31, 1986; 1 stepson, Bron M. BS in Nursing, St. Louis U., 1980, MS in Nursing Research, 1987. Registered nurse. Staff nurse psychiatry dept. Jefferson Barracks div. VA Med. Ctr., St. Louis, 1980-85, staff nurse drug and alcohol unit, 1985—, relief supr., 1985—. Mem. Am. Nurses Assn. (cert. psychiat. mental health), Mo. Nurses Assn. (sec./treas. psychiat. spl. interest group 1986—), Sigma Theta Tau. Baptist. Avocations: piano, sewing, cooking, reading. Home: 9252 Harold Dr Saint Louis MO 63134-3567 Office: VA Med Ctr JB 118A Koch Rd Saint Louis MO 63125

RICHARDSON, THOMAS BOLLING, controller, treasurer; b. Lexington, Ky., July 23, 1951; s. William Waddle Richardson and Lois (Turner) Swartz; m. Susan Kay Sims, Apr. 25, 1981; children: Jessica Lynn, Daniel Bolling. BS in Acctg., U. Kans., 1974; MBA, Drake U., 1983. Mgr. gen. acctg. Koch Industries, Wichita, 1975-80; mgr. crude oil acctg. Pester Corp., Des Moines, 1980-85; controller Aladdin Petroleum, Wichita, 1985—, also bd. dirs.; bd. dirs. LaRobb Oil Royalties, Aladdin Middle East, Petroleum Bldg. Inc. Mem. YMCA. Fellow Kans. Ind. Oil and Gas Assn., Petroleum Accts. Soc. Kans. Presbyterian. Club: Petroleum (Wichita). Avocations: all sports, jogging, weight training, reading. Home: Rt 1 Box 192R Augusta KS 67010 Office: Aladdin Petroleum Corp 809 Petroleum Bldg Wichita KS 67202

RICHARDSON, WILLIAM HENRY, consultant civil engineer; b. Oak Park, Ill., June 10, 1929; s. Andrew William and Jean (Robinson) R.; m. Marie Therese Pembroke, July 11, 1953; children—Kevin William, Andrew William, Timothy John. Student, Wright Jr. Coll., 1947-48; B.S.C.E., U. Ill.,

1952; postgrad. student U. Louisville, 1954-57. Registered profl. engr., Ill., Ind., Ky., Mich., Wis., Ariz., Ohio, N.J. Civil engr. Alvord, Burdick & Howson, Chgo., 1952-65, ptnr., 1965—; preparer valuation studies; testified before state comms. for United Utilities Co., Ariz., Gary-Hobart Water Corp., Ind., Kokomo, Ind., Louisville Water Co., Farmers Br., Grand Prairie, Tex., Chgo., Peoria, Ill., Alton, Ill., Marion, Ohio; engr. water supply, Monrovia, Liberia, various locations through U.S.; engr. water pollution control facilities, Monrovia, various locations throughout U.S.; preparer water supply reports La Paz, Bolivia, Lagos, Nigeria, Istanbul, Turkey; preparer water rate studies Chgo. Water Dept., Gary-Hobart Water Corp., Louisville Water Co., Tarrant County Improvement Dist. No. 1, Tex., Monrovia, various towns in Ill., Flint, Mich., Virgina Beach, Va. Contbr. articles to profl. jours. Recipient Disting. Alumni award U. Ill. Civil Engring. Alumni Assn., 1984. Fellow ASCE (bd. dirs. Ill. sect. 1977); mem. Am. Water Works Assn. (pres. 1984-85, Fuller award 1984), Western Soc. Engrs. (pres. 1982-83, Octave Chanute medal 1981), Am. Acad. Environ. Engrs. (diplomate), Water Pollution Control Fedn., Nat. Soc. Profl. Engrs., Internat. Water Supply Assn. (v.p. 1986—). Clubs: Union League (Chgo.); Elgin (Ill.) Country. Lodge: Elks. Avocations: golf, sports, travel, reading. Home: 965 Webster Ln Des Plaines IL 60016 Office: Alvord Burdick & Howson 20 N Wacker Dr Chicago IL 60606

RICHEL, ALAN LEWIS, government official; b. N.Y.C., Apr. 24, 1950; s. Stanley and Rita (Englander) R. AA, Am. Coll. in Paris, 1970; BA in Internat. Affairs, George Washington U., 1972, MA in Internat. Affairs, 1974; MBA, Loyola U., Chgo., 1982. Internat. trade specialist U.S. Dept. Commerce, Washington, 1972-73; claims examiner GSA, Washington, 1973-74, property utilization specialist, 1974-75; transp. rep. Urban Mass Transp. Adminstrn., U.S. Dept. Transp., Washington, 1975-78; sr. transp. rep. Urban Mass Transp. Adminstrn., U.S. Dept. Transp., Chgo., 1978-84; dir. Office Transit Assistance Urban Mass Transp. Adminstrn., U.S. Dept. Transp., Kansas City, Mo., 1984—. Mem. Mensa. Jewish. Avocations: photography, computers, jogging.

RICHELS, JAMES KENNETH, accounting company executive; b. Breckenridge, Minn., Sept. 10, 1944; s. Kenneth Anthony and Lerna Drucilla (Snyder) R.; m. Marlene Ann Lingen, Oct. 18, 1969; children: Wade, Cody, Veeda, Rena. Assoc., N.D. State Sch. Sci., 1964; BBA, U. N.D., 1966. CPA, N.D., Minn. Auditor U.S. Gen. Acctg. Office, Denver, 1966-67, Eide, Helmeke, Boelz & Pasch, Fargo and Bismarck, N.D., 1967-71; ptnr. Richels & Easley, Wahpeton, N.D., 1971—. Treas. Red Youth Activities Assn., Wahpeton, 1981. Mem. Am. Inst. CPA's, N.D. Soc. CPA's. Home: Rt 1 PO Box 150 Wahpeton ND 58075 Office: Richels & Easley PO Box 2104 Wahpeton ND 58075

RICHERSON, HAL BATES, physician, internist, educator; b. Phoenix, Feb. 16, 1929; s. George Edward and Eva Louise (Steere) R.; m. Julia Suzanne Bradley, Sept. 5, 1953; children: Anne, George, Miriam, Julia, Susan. BS with distinction, U. Ariz., 1950; MD, Northwestern U., 1954. Diplomate Am. Bd. Internal Medicine, Am. Bd. Allergy and Immunology, Bd. Diagnostic Lab. Immunology; lic. physician, Ariz., Iowa. Intern Kansas City (Mo.) Gen. Hosp., 1954-55; resident in pathology St. Luke's Hosp., Kansas City, 1955-56; trainee in neuropsychiatry Brooke Army Hosp., San Antonio, 1956; resident in medicine U. Iowa Hosps., Iowa City, 1961-64, fellow in allergy and immunology, 1964-66; fellow in immunology Mass. Gen. Hosp., Boston, 1968-69, instr. internal medicine, 1964-66, asst. prof., 1966-70, assoc. prof., 1970-74, prof., 1974—, acting dir. Div. Allergy and Applied Immunology, dept. Internal Medicine, 1970-72, dir. Allergy and Clin. Immunology sect., 1972-78, dir. Allergy and Immunology div., 1978—; gen. practice, asst. to Gen. Surgeon Ukiah, Calif., 1958; gen. practice medicine Holbrook, Ariz., 1958-61; vis. lectr. medicine Harvard U. Sch. Medicine, boston, 1968-69; vis. research scientist Brompton Hosp., London, 1984; prin. investigator Nat. Heart, Lung and Blood Inst., 1978—; presenter lectures, seminars, continuing edn. courses; numerous univ., coll. and hosp. com. memberships, 1970—. Contbr. numerous articles and revs. to profl. jours., chpts. to books; reviewer Sci., Jour. Immunology, Jour. Allergy and Clin. Immunology, Am. Rev. Research and Disease. Served to capt. U.S. Army, 1956-58. NIH fellow 1968-69. Fellow ACP, Am. Acad. Allergy; mem. AMA, AAAS, Iowa Med. Soc., Iowa Thoracic Soc. (chmn. program com. 1964-65, 69-71, pres. 1972-73, exec. com. 1972-74), Am. Thoracic Soc. (bd. dirs. 1981-82, councillor assembly on allergy and immunology 1980-81), Iowa Clin. Med. Soc., Am. Fedn. Clin. Research, Am. Assn. Immunologists, Cen. Soc. Clin. Research (chmn. sect. on allergy-immunology 1980-81, council mem. 1981-84), Alpha Omega Alpha. Avocations: reading, swimming, handball, scuba diving. Home: 331 Lucon Dr Iowa City IA 52240 Office: U Iowa Hosps and Clinics Dept Internal Medicine Iowa City IA 52242

RICHERSON, MICHAEL E., electrical engineer; b. Wichita, Oct. 15, 1950; s. Hubert and Beverly R.; m. Roberta L. Yoho, June 30, 1972. BSEE, Wichita State U., 1972, MS, 1976. Lic. profl. engr., Kans. Engr. Boeing, Wichita, 1972-74; mgr. Boeing Computer Services, Wichita, 1977—; engr. NCR Corp., Wichita, 1974-77. Contbr. articles to profl. jours. Mem. Inst. Indsl Engrs. (sr.), IEEE. Home: 1937 N Edgemoor Wichita KS 67208 Office: Boeing Computer Services PO Box 7730 MS K79-31 Wichita KS 67277

RICHEY, THOMAS ALLEN, military officer; b. Seguin, Tex., July 18, 1949; s. Charles Wesley and Thelma Lorraine (sanders) R.; m. Theresa Marie Magliolo, May 24, 1975; children: Margaret Ann, Thomas Allen Jr. BA, U. Tex., 1971; student, Squadron Officer Sch. Air Univ., 1980, Air Command & Staff Coll. Air U., 1983; M of Aviation Mgmt., Embry-Riddle U., 1985. Commd. 2d lt. USAF, 1975, advanced through grades to maj., 1986; flight evaluator, instr. USAF, Carswell AFB, Tex., 1976-80; flight evaluator, comdr. USAF, Offutt AFB, Nebr., 1980-84, chief ops. Signal Intelligence, 1984-85, inspector reconnaissance ops. and tng., 1985—. Mem. AK-SARBEN, Omaha, 1980-86; vol. Christian Rural Overseas Program, Seguin, Tex., 1963-70, Tarrant County Leukemia Soc., Ft. Worth, 1979, Am. Cancer Soc., Papillion, Nebr., 1985-86. Decorated Air medal. Mem. Air Force Assn., Assn. Old Crows. Republican. Roman Catholic. Avocations: camping, kite flying. Office: USAF Hdqrs. SAC/IGSO Offutt AFB NE 68113

RICHMAN, DAVID WILLIAM, engineer; b. LaPorte, Ind., Aug. 3, 1940; s. Milfred William and Ethelyn Belle (Morton) R.; divorced; children: Keith, Michael, John. BSME, Purdue U., 1962; MSME, U. Mo., Rolla, 1968, MS in Engring. Mgmt., 1974. Assoc. engr. thermodynamics Aircraft div. McDonnell Douglas Astronautics Co., St. Louis, 1962-69; sr. engr. design McDonnell Douglas Astronautics Co., St. Louis, 1969-75, sr. lead engr. aerodynamics, 1975-79, unit sect. chief tech., 1979-84, br. chief tech., 1984—; cons. U. Space Research Assocs., Washington, 1984-86. Contbr. articles to profl. jours.; inventor electrophoresis chamber, hydrodynamic compensation, apparatus with flow control, electrophoresis apparatus. Mem. AIAA (nat. space processing com. 1982-84, Tech. Contbn. award 1982), Am. Assn. Engring. Mgmt., Electrophoresis Soc. Republican. Episcopalian. Club: Castle Oak (Chesterfield, Mo.). Avocations: sailing, windsurfing, skiing, running. Office: McDonnell Douglas Astronautics PO Box 516 Saint Louis MO 63166

RICHMAN, JOHN EMMETT, architect; b. East Liverpool, Ohio, June 8, 1951; s. Ethel M. (Thompson) R.; m. Susan E. Nusser, May 29, 1971; children: Stephen T., Sarah J. BArch, BS, Kent State U., 1982. Registered architect Ohio, W.Va., Pa.; ordained elder Evang. Presbyn. Ch., 1978. Draftsman Fairfield Machine Co., Columbiana, Ohio; archtl. draftsman Robert F. Beatty, Architect, East Liverpool, 1973-80; archtl. draftsman Smiths & and Assocs., Architects, Columbiana, 1981-84, architect, 1984-85, architect, v.p., 1985—. Mem. First Evang. Presbyn. Ch., chmn. Youth Camp com., 1983—, asst. dir. Youth Camp, 1982—, chmn. worship com., 1985-86, supt. Sunday sch., 1986—, mem. ch. choir; co-founder Tri-State Teen World, East Liverpool, 1978, chmn. bd. dirs. 1981—; Bible quiz dir., 1982—, coach all-star quiz team, 1985. Served with U.S. Army, 1971-73. Mem. AIA (bd. dirs. Eastern Ohio chpt. 1985—, sec. 1986—), Architect Soc. Ohio (alt. dir. 1986—), Ohio Consultive Council Nat. Inst., Youth Evangelism Assn. (Bible quiz com. 1985—). Presbyterian. Avocations: sports, music, traveling, reading. Home: 47995 Calcutta Smithferry Rd East Liverpool OH 43920 Office: Smith and Associated Architects 330 N Main St Columbiana OH 44408

RICHMAN, JOHN MARSHALL, business executive, lawyer; b. N.Y.C., Nov. 9, 1927; s. Arthur and Madeleine (Marshall) R.; m. Priscilla Frary, Sept. 3, 1951; children: Catherine, Diana H. B.A., Yale U., 1949; LL.B., Harvard U., 1952. Bar: N.Y. 1953, Ill. 1973. Assoc. Leve, Hecht, Hadfield & McAlpin, N.Y.C., 1952-54; mem. law dept. Kraft, Inc., Glenview, Ill., 1954-63, gen. counsel Sealtest Foods div., 1963-67, asst. gen. counsel, 1967-70, v.p., gen. counsel, 1970-73, sr. v.p., gen. counsel, 1973-75, sr. v.p. adminstrn., gen. counsel, 1975-79, chmn. bd., chief exec. officer, 1979—; chmn. bd., chief exec. officer Dart & Kraft, Inc (became Kraft, Inc. 1986), Northbrook, Ill., 1980—. Congregationalist. Clubs: Commercial (Chgo.), Economic (Chgo.), Mid-Am. (Chgo.); Union League (N.Y.C.); Westmoreland Country (Wilmette, Ill.). Office: Kraft Inc Kraft Ct Glenview IL 60025

RICHMAN, WILLIAM SHELDON, furniture company executive; b. Far Rockaway, N.Y., Aug. 5, 1921; s. Joseph and Mollye (Josephson) R.; m. Marilyn Melvoin, Dec. 27, 1951; children: Daniel, Elizabeth, Ruth. B.S., CCNY, 1941; M.B.A., Harvard U., 1943. Asst. buyer Kresge-Newark, 1946-49; buyer, mdse. mgr. Mandel Bros., Chgo., 1949-56; sales mgr. Futorian Corp., Chgo., 1957-64, exec. v.p., 1965-70, pres., dir., 1971-86; pres., chief exec. officer Mohasco Upholstered Furniture Corp., 1986—. Bd. dirs. NCCJ, Chgo., 1979—, nat. bd. dirs., 1982—. Recipient Champion of Youth award B'nai B'rith, 1975; recipient Brotherhood award NCCJ, 1979. Mem. Nat. Assn. Furniture Mfrs. (dir. 1975—), Upholstered Furniture Action Council. Jewish. Home: 525 Sheridan Rd Glencoe IL 60022 Office: Mohasco Upholstered Furniture Corp 666 N Lake Shore Dr Chicago IL 60611

RICHMOND, BRIAN FREDERICK, theatre director; b. Vancouver, B.C., Can., Jan. 22, 1947; s. Harry Herbert and Edith Evelyn (Smith) R.; m. Janet Fay Wright, June 6, 1970 (div. May 1979); children: Celine, Jacob. Student, Simon Fraser U., Vancouver, 1970-74. Artistic dir. Persephone Theatre, Saskatoon, Can., 1974-76; dramaturge Playwright's Workshop, Montreal, Ont., Can., 1980-82; artistic dir. Magnus Theatre, Thunder Bay, Ont., Can., 1983—; cons. Simon Fraser U., 1976-77, Concordia U., Montreal, 1980-82, McGill U., Montreal, 1981-82; freelance dir. throughout Can., 1975-86. Office: Magnus Theatre NW, 137 N May St, Thunder Bay, ON Canada P7C 3N8

RICHMOND, JAMES ELLIS, food company executive; b. Chgo., Feb. 16, 1938; s. Kenneth E. and Irene M. (Anderson) R.; m. Karen Ann Ryder, Oct. 6, 1956; children: Scott, Brian, Ann, Susan. B.B.A., Case Western Reserve U., 1960. C.P.A., Ohio. Sr. auditor Ernst & Ernst, Cleve., 1960-64; treas. Cook United, Inc., Cleve., 1964-75; treas. Fairmont Foods Co., Houston, 1975-80, v.p. ops., 1980-82; v.p., treas. U-tote-M, Inc., 1982-84; mktg. exec. Circle K Convenience Stores, 1984-86; v.p. Consolidated Products, Inc., Indpls., 1986—. Mem. Am. Inst. C.P.A.s, Ohio Soc. C.P.A.s. Lutheran. Home: 13088 Tarkington Commons Carmel IN 46032 Office: Consolidated Products Inc 36 S Pennsylvania St Indianapolis IN 46204

RICHMOND-HAWKINS, VICTORIA KATHRYN, youth association administrator; b. Rhinelander, Wis., May 24, 1949; d. Walter Harry and Marguerite Dorothy (O'Malley) Richmond; m. James M.D.R. Hawkins, July 27, 1974; children: Joseph Walter, Richard James. BS, U. Wis., 1971, MBA, 1979. Field advisor/dir. Black Hawk Council Girl Scouts, Inc., Madison, Wis., 1971-74; coordinator student recruitment Tex. State Tech. Inst., Waco, 1974-75, dir. student activities, 1975-77; adminstrv. asst. United Way Marathon County, Wausau, Wis., 1980-81; tng. dir. Birch Trails Counsel Girl Scouts Council, Inc., Wausau, 1981—. Mem. Mayor's Tax Study Commn., Wausau, 1986; intern Gov.'s Advisor on Women's Issues, Madison, 1979, Gov.'s Communication Office, Madison, 1979; chmn. 7th and 8th Ann. Antique Doll and Toy Show, Wausau, 1986-87; bd. dirs. Women of St. John's Ch., Wausau, 1985-87). Mem. Am. Soc. Tng. and Devel. (editor newsletter Cen. Wis. chpt. 1983-84). Episcopalian. Club: Altrusa (pres. 1983-85, bd. dirs. 1985—) (Wausau). Avocations: singing, sailing. Home: 640 S Fifth Ave Wausau WI 54401 Office: Birch Trails Girl Scout Council Inc 1431 Merrill Ave Wausau WI 54402-1518

RICHTER, DONALD A., transportation company executive; b. 1932. BS, St. Louis U. CPA Arthur Young and Co., St. Louis, 1952-61; with Brunswick Corp., St. Louis, 1961-68, Am. Transit Corp., St. Louis, 1968—; asst. sec. Am. Transit Corp., 1971-72, asst. treas., 1972-76, pres., chief exec. officer, also bd. dirs., 1976—. Office: Am Transit Corp 120 S Central Ave Saint Louis MO 63105 *

RICHTER, EARL EDWARD, manufacuturing company executive; b. Twin Lakes, Wis., Oct. 16, 1923; s. John Benjamin and Emma Augusta (Kautz) R.; m. Carlista Mae Dean, Sept. 12, 1943; children: Susan Dianne, Robert Dean. B.B.A., U. Wis.-Madison, 1948. C.P.A., Wis. With Modine Mfg. Co., Racine, Wis., 1948—, v.p., gen. mgr., 1963-74, pres., 1974—, chief operating officer, 1974, chief exec. officer, 1974—; dir. M&I Bank of Racine, Portec Inc. Served with USAAF, 1943-45. Mem. Racine Mfrs. Assn. (dir.), Conf. Bd., Am. Mgmt. Assn. Lutheran. Clubs: Racine Country, Milw. Athletic. Office: Modine Mfg Co 1500 DeKoven Ave Racine WI 53401

RICHTER, JOHN WILLIAM, assistant controller; b. Chgo., Feb. 3, 1946; s. William Alfred and Mary Elizabeth (Kelsey) R.; m. Patricia Renee McCann, Jan. 27, 1973; children: Tammy Renee, Kathleen Marie. BBA, Loyola U., 1969. Asst. sr. auditor Deloitte Haskins, Chgo., 1969-70; mgr. internat. acctg. Morton-Thiokol, Chgo., 1970-79; co-owner The Bump Shop Ltd., Orland Park, Ill., 1979-81; asst. controller Emro Mktg., Hazel Crest, Ill., 1981—. Trea. Catalina Homeowners Assn., Orland Park, 1980-84. Mem. Am. Inst. CPA's, Ill. CPA Soc. Roman Catholic. Avocations: hunting, coin collecting. Home: 7561 W Ponderosa Ct Orland Park IL 60462 Office: Emro Mktg Co 174th & Dixie Hwy Hazelcrest IL 60429

RICHTER, MERCER JOSEPH, manufacturing company executive; b. Ft. Dodge, Iowa, Sept. 25, 1936; s. Mercer B. and Florence A. (Walsh) R.; m. Nancy Ruth Pletcher, Sept. 7, 1963; children: Michele, Susan, Kari. BA, U. Iowa, 1959. Mktg. supr. Visual Products div. 3M, St. Paul, 1966-68; mgr. internat. mktg. Internat. div. 3M, St. Paul, 1968-73; product mgr. Bus. Products Sales Inc. div. 3M, St. Paul, 1973-78; regional mgr. Bus. Communications Products div. 3M, St. Paul, 1978-80, mktg. mgr., 1980-84; project mgr. Tartan Tooling Project div. 3M, St. Paul, 1984—. Mem. Soc. Plastic Engrs., U. Iowa Alumni Assn. Republican. Clubs: I (Iowa City). Avocations: running, biking, reading. Home: 2592 Southshore Blvd White Bear Lake MN 55110 Office: Tartan Tooling Project 3M Ctr Bldg 53-03 Saint Paul MN 55144

RICHTER, NEAL BURTON, dentist; b. Chgo., Jan. 6, 1955; s. Harold and Renee (Katz) R. AB, Ind. U., 1977, DDS, 1981. Gen. practice dentistry Merrillville, Ind., 1981—. Mem. ADA, Ind. Dental Assn., Northwest Ind. Dental Assn. (bd. dirs.), Acad. Gen. Dentistry, Merrillville C. of C., Highland C. of C., Ind. U. Alumni Assn., Ind. U. Alumni Club. (pres., v.p., bd. dirs.). Avocations: golf, running, travel, water-skiing, snow-skiing. Home and Office: 8585 Broadway Suite 851 Merrillville IN 46410

RICHTER, ROBERT LAWRENCE, minister; b. Memphis, Oct. 20, 1934; s. Edwin Michael and Hettie Elizabeth (Meek) R.; m. Suzanne Doretha Landry, Aug. 14, 1960; children: Rachael, Christian, Ingrid. BA, Concordia Seminary, 1957; MDiv, Concordia Sem., 1972; D of Ministry, Wartburg Sem., 1981. Ordained to ministry Luth. Ch., 1960. Asst. pastor Gethsemane Luth. Ch., St. Paul, 1960-62; pastor Holy Cross Luth. Ch., Tuscaloosa, Ala., 1962-64, Grace Luth. Ch., Pensacola, Fla., 1967-75; chief, chaplain service VA Hosp., Madison, Wis., 1975—. Author: Attaining Ego Integrity, 1986. Served with USN, 1964-67, to lt. comdr. Res. Recipient St. Martin of Tours Medal Mo. Synod Luth. Ch. Am., 1983. Republican. Lutheran. Avocations: skiing, biking. Home: 5866 Roanoke Dr Madison WI 53719 Office: VA Hosp 2500 Overlook Terr Madison WI 53705

RICK, DOUGLAS LEO, civil engineer; b. Peoria, Ill., Oct. 19, 1955; s. Joseph E. Kiesewetter and Carol J. Schmidt; stepfather: James T. Rick; m. Kyle René Jansen, May 13, 1978. BSCE, U. Wis., Platteville, 1978. Registered profl. engr., Iowa, Wis., Ill. Engr.-in-tng. Iowa Dept. Transp., Ames, 1978-79; sr. engr.-in-tng. Iowa Dept. Transp., Davenport, 1979-83, asst. resident constrn. engr., 1983-85; project mgr. The Schemmer Assocs., Inc., Davenport, 1985-87; transp. engr. Iowa Dept. Transp., 1987—. Mem. ASCE (sec./treas. Tri-City sect. 1984-85, v.p. 1985-86, pres. quad cities sect. 1986-87), NSPE. Home: 2623 Pershing Ave Davenport IA 52803 Office: PO Box 2646 Davenport IA 52809

RICK, JERRY RAYMOND, hydrogeologist; b. Litchfield, Minn., July 18, 1953; s. Raymond R. and Marie E. (Christenson) R.; m. Jan G. Grussendorf, June 29, 1974 (div. Jan. 1979); 1 child, Tifani. BA, St. Thomas Coll., 1975. Hydrogeologist Brevard County, Merrit Island, Fla., 1977-79, Johnson Bros. Corp., Litchfield, Minn., 1979-81; div. mgr. Twin City Testing Corp., St. Paul, 1981-86; pres. Delta Environ. Cons., Inc., New Brighton, Minn., 1986—. Tchr. St. John's Religious Edn., New Brighton, 1982-86. Mem. Assn. Groundwater Scientists and Engrs., Am. Inst. Profl. Geologists, Minn. Groundwater Assn. (pres. 1986). Republican. Roman Catholic. Avocations: triathlons, skiing, scuba diving. Office: Delta Environ Cons Inc 1801 Hwy 8 Suite 123 New Brighton MN 55112

RICKARD, CYNTHIA LEE, reporter; b. Youngstown, Ohio, Feb. 7, 1953; d. William Merrill and Muriel Jean (Ritenour) R.; m. Bertram H. de Souza, Sept. 11, 1983. BFA, Kent State U., 1978. Soc. reporter The Vindicator, Youngstown, 1978-84, Trumball news reporter, 1984-87, Warren news chief, 1987—. Baha'i. Club: Youngstown Press. Avocations: travel, bicycling, reading, exercise. Office: Vindicator Warren Bur PO Box 1127 Warren OH 44482

RICKARD, DAVID WAYNE, information systems manager; b. McKeesport, Pa., Sept. 24, 1953; s. E. Wayne and Edith Virginia (Holmbeck) R.; m. Grace Ann Squirlock, Aug. 31, 1974 (div. Nov. 1984); m. Jan Aileen Dunham, Mar. 15, 1986. BA in Math Edn., Asbury Coll., 1975; MEd., Xavier U., 1981. Computer sci. tutor Asbury Coll., Wilmore, Ky., 1971-73, math tutor, 1973-75; math tchr., coach Dayton (Ky.) High Sch., 1975-78; math tchr. Bellevue (Ky.) High Sch., 1978; infosystems mgr. Cin. Bell Infosystems, 1979—. Youth counselor Groesbeck United Meth. Ch., Cin., 1985—, coordinator computer systems installation, 1986—. Mem. Student Nat. Edn. Assn. (pres. Ky. 1974-75). Republican. Avocations: skiing, tennis, golf, sailing, classical music. Home: 9983 Pebbleknoll Dr Cincinnati OH 45247 Office: Cin Bell Info Systems 600 Vine St Cincinnati OH 45202

RICKBEIL, CLARA EVELYN SHELLMAN (MRS. RAYMOND E. RICKBEIL), club woman; b. Gibson City, Ill.; d. Kilian and Anna Marie (Johnson) Shellman; grad. Brown's Bus. Coll., Champaign, Ill., 1922; student U. Ill., 1927-28; m. Raymond Earl Rickbeil, May 8, 1930. Office sec. Ford County Farm Bur., Gibson City, 1922-26; secretarial position Raymond E. Rickbeil, C.P.A., Springfield, Ill., 1928-61, Ernst & Ernst, Springfield, 1961-65. Mem. bd. King's Daus.; adv. bd. Am. Security Council; mem. Community Concert Assn., Nat. Fedn. Republican Women, Rep. Women's Club Sangamon County, Sangamon County Farm Bur. Recipient award for work pub. acctg. legis. Ill. Soc. C.P.A.s, 1956. Mem. U. Ill. Alumni Assn., U. Ill. Pres.'s Club, Am. Legion Aux., Meml. Hosp. Aux., Sangamon County Hist. Soc. Republican. Presbyterian. Clubs: Woman's (reception com. 1962-63, social com. 1963-64, corr. sec. 1972-75, dist. program chmn. dist. 21 1968-69, dist. corr. sec. 1969-72), Mariama (vice chmn. chpt. 5 1966-67, chmn. 1967-72), Amateur Musical, Order Eastern Star, Zonta (treas. 1954-57, fin. com. 1965—, fin. chmn. 1957-63, 64, service chmn., mem. service com. 1953-62), Sangamo (assoc.); Three Hills Extension Homemakers (reporter) (Kerrville, Tex.). Home: 937 Feldkamp Ave Springfield IL 62704

RICKE, DENNIS FRANK, media educator, consultant; b. Elmhurst, Ill., July 12, 1948; s. Cyril Timothy and Helen Jane (Glancey) R.; m. Linda Ellen Schultz, Mar. 20, 1971; children—Kimberly Ann, Matthew Steven. B.A., So. Ill. U., 1970, M.A., 1972; postgrad. No. Ill. U., U. Ill. Mem. media staff Sch. Dist. 108, Roselle, Ill., 1972-73, history instr. 1973-74; media specialist Sch. Dist. 303, St. Charles, Ill., 1974—; media cons. Singer Vocat. Edn., Chgo., 1982—; curriculum developer St. Charles Sch. Dist., 1983—. Author: Struggle for Equality: Illinois Blacks through the Civil War, 1974 (Leah M. Reef award 1974). Dep. registrar Kane County Clks., Geneva, Ill., 1976—. Reef scholar So. Ill. U., 1972; Title IV Fed. grantee; mem. Gifted Council State Ill., 1975-78. Mem. Ill. State Hist. Soc. (life), NEA, Ill. Edn. Assn., St. Charles Edn. Assn. (v.p., negotiator, rep. assembly 1978). Avocations: computer science; photography. Home: 1810 Walden Circle Aurora IL 60506 Office: Dist 303 9th and Oak St Saint Charles IL 60174

RICKERT, SHIRLEY ROSE, educator; b. Huntington County, Ind., Apr. 19, 1936; d. Paul H. and Marguerite P. (Brown) Gressley; m. Garl E. Miles, Jan. 21, 1956 (div. 1969); m. Roger Mark Rickert, June 24, 1976; children by previous marriage—Terrance Wayne, Timothy Garl, Tamarah Lynne. A.A.S., Purdue U., 1969, B.S., 1973; M.A., Western Mich. U., 1974; Ed.D., Ball State U., 1977. Cert. tchr., Ind. Mobility specialist, dir. edn. blind Anthony Wayne Rehab. Ctr., Ft. Wayne, Ind., 1969-77; itinerant tchr. visually handicapped Ft. Wayne Community Schs., 1977-79; prof. dept. supervision Purdue U., Ft. Wayne, 1979—; condr. workshops in field. Mem. Mayor's Commn. on Archtl. Barriers, Ft. Wayne, 1972-78, Ft. Wayne Women's Bur., 1980—. Mem. Am. Soc. Tng. and Devel. (chpt. sec.), AAUW, Am. Assn. Workers for Blind. Lodge: Order Eastern Star. Office: Purdue U at Fort Wayne N288 2101 Coliseum Blvd E Fort Wayne IN 46805

RICKEY, LARRY FLOYD, continuing education administrator; b. Kansas City, Kans., Mar. 13, 1939; s. Glenn Maurice and Freda (Monville) R.; m. Carol Ann Ronemous, June 27, 1964. BS, U. Kans., 1961; BD, Cen. Seminary, 1964; PhD, U. Iowa, 1972. Adminstrv. asst. U. Iowa Sch. Religion, Iowa City, Iowa, 1967-69; instr., chaplain Coe Coll., Cedar Rapids, Iowa, 1969-72; career opportunities program coordinator Joint County Sch. System, Cedar Rapids, 1972-73, staff devel. coordinator, 1973-75; staff devel. coordinator Grant Wood Area Edn. Agy., Cedar Rapids, 1975-83, profl. growth mgr., 1983—; adv. com. mem. Kirkwood Community Coll., Cedar Rapids, 1975—; mem. com. on Adminstr. cert. Iowa Dept. Edn., Des Moines, 1986; assoc. dean extension program Marycrest Coll., Davenport, Iowa, 1985—. mng. editor The Linker, 1979—. Bd. dirs. Linn County Hist. Soc., Cedar Rapids, 1978-80, Seminole Valley Hist. Village, Cedar Rapids, 1980-81, Planned Parenthood Linn County, Cedar Rapids, 1984-86; precinct chair Iowa County Dem. Party, Amana, 1972-74. Mem. Am. Assn. Adult and Continuing Edn., Iowa Assn. Supervision and Curriculum Devel., Iowa Staff Devel. Coordinators (pres. 1983-86). Democrat. Baptist. Lodge: Kiwanis (pres. Cedar Rapids club 1972-73). Avocation: antique collecting and restoration, fishing, print making. Home: 202 24th St Dr SE Cedar Rapids IA 52403 Office: Grant Wood Area Edn Agy 4401 Sixth St SW Cedar Rapids IA 52404

RICKS, DREW STEPHEN, retail executive; b. Elwood, Ind., Apr. 11, 1948; s. John Andrew and Bonnie Naomi (Bouchard) R.; m. Linda Mae Sebo, July 19, 1969;children: Thomas, Keri, Timothy, Matthew, Emily. BA in Acctg. and Econs., Winona (Minn.) State U., 1970, MBA Bus. Mgmt., 1976. Store mgr. Gamble Skogma, Inc., Mpls., 1966-73; mktg. mgr. Lake Ctr. Industries, Winona, 1973-77; v.p. adminstrn. Tom Thumb Food Mkts., Hastings, Minn., 1977-81; pres. Stop-N-Go, Madison, Wis., 1981-84; v.p. retail ops. U.S. Oil Co., Combined Locks, Wis., 1984-87; founder, pres. Convenience Store Cons., Appleton, Wis., 1987—. Pres. Appleton Elem. Sch. PTA, 1986. Served to capt. U.S. Army, 1970-72, to maj. USAR. Mem. Nat. Assn. Convenience Stores, Wis. Oil Jobbers Assn. Republican. Lutheran. Avocations: sports, old house and car restoration. Home: 721 W Front St Appleton WI 54914 Office: Convenience Store Cons 721 W Front St Appleton WI 54914

RIDDLE, MAXWELL, newspaper columnist; b. Ravenna, Ohio, July 29, 1907; s. Henry Warner and Mary E. (Fitz-Gerald) R.; B.A., U. Ariz., 1929; m. Martha A. Hurd, Mar. 31, 1933 (dec. 1982); children—Betsy Riddle Whitmore, Henry W. III.; m. Lenora Romaine, 1985. Turf editor, columnist NEA Service, 1930, 39; kennel editor, columnist, pets columnist Cleve. Press, 1938-69; columnist Columbia Features, Inc., 1959-66; columnist Ledger Syndicate, 1966-73, Scott Editor Service, 1973—, Allied Feature Syndicate, 1975—; all breed dog judge, fgn. countries, 1955. U.S., 1960—. Recipient Cruikshank medal, 1941; Dog Writer of Year, 1949, 61, 83; Dogdom's Man of the Year, 1968, Dog. Journalist of Year, 1970, 72. Mem. Ohio Dog Owners Assn., Dog Writers Assn. (past pres.), Sigma Delta Chi, Delta Upsilon. Clubs: Western Reserve Kennel, Ravenna Kennel. Author: The Springer Spaniel, 1939; The Lovable Mongrel, 1954; This Is the Chihuahua, 1959; The Complete Book of Puppy Training and Care, 1962; Dog People are Crazy, 1966; Your Show Dog, 1968; A Quick Guide to the Standards of Show Dogs, 1972; (with Mrs. M.B. Seeley) The Complete Alaskan Malamute, 1976. The Complete Brittany Spaniel, 1974, The New Complete Brittany, 1987; The New Shetland Sheepdog, 1974; The Wild Dogs in Life and Legend, 1979; Your Family Dog, 1981, The Dog Through History, 1987; also articles; contbr. Hunters Ency., 1948, New Dog Ency., 1967, Internat. Dog Ency., 1972, World Book Ency.; assoc. editor Dog World Mag., 1961—. Home: PO Box 286 Ravenna OH 44266

RIDDLE, MICHAEL HOWE, military officer; b. Tulsa, Apr. 28, 1946; s. Jack Hall and Marjorie Faye (Moore) R.; m. Linda Ann Bates, Oct. 5, 1968; children: Jack Hall II, Steven Michael, Mark Scott. BA in History cum laude, U. Colo., Denver, 1976; Assoc. Applied Sci., Community Coll. of Air Force, Maxwell AFB, Ala., 1977; MA Social Sci./Pub. Administrn., U. No. Colo., 1979. Commd. 2d lt. USAF, 1977, advanced through grades to capt., 1981; telecommunications maintenance technician USAF, various locations, 1966-77; with profl. edn. USAF, Keesler AFB, Miss., 1977-78; chief maintenance USAF, Pease AFB, N.H., 1978-81; chief logistics USAF, Eielson AFB, Alaska, 1981-84; communication controller and dep. missile combat crew comdr.SAC USAF, Offutt AFB, Nebr., 1984-86, very low frequency/low frequency systems integration mgr. SAC Hdqrs., 1986—. Decorated Air medal. Mem. Armed Forces Communications Electronics Assn., Air Force Assn. Methodist. Avocations: hiking, camping, personal computers, water sports. Office: Hdqrs SAC/SCQ Offutt AFB NE 68113-6343

RIDDLE, RAYMOND ERWIN, library administrator; b. Orlando, Fla., Nov. 9, 1947; s. Theadore Leslie and Margie (Jordan) R.; m. Cecelia Yvonne Reeder, Aug. 31, 1974. BA, St. Andrews Coll., 1969; MLS, U. Miss., 1975. Dir. Humphreys County Library, Belzoni, Miss., 1975-78, Cass County Pub. Library, Harrisonville, Mo., 1978-85, Kansas City (Kans.) Pub. Library, 1985—; mem. Mo. Library Network Bd., 1981-85, pres. 1983-85; mem. Kansas City Met. Library Network Council, Independence, Mo., 1979—, pres., 1981-83, treas., 1986; bd. dirs. Blue River-Kansas City Bapt. Assn., Lee's Summit, Mo., 1980-84; bd. govs. Mo. Eye Research Found., Columbia, 1980-85; mem. SSS appellate bd. Western Mo., 1981-85, Wyandotte County Bd. #1, 1985—; mem. Kansas City Conv. and Visitor's Bur., 1985—, treas., 1986—; mem. exec. bd. Kaw Valley Arts Council, 1985—. Author: From Greasy Row to Catfish Capital, 1978, also numerous short stories for children, 1974-78; contbr. numerous articles to profl. jours. Mem. ALA (vice chmn. ALA/Pub. Library Assn. Affiliates Council 1986, chmn. 1987), Kans. Library Assn., Mo. Library Assn. (v.p. 1984-85), Kansas City Area Wide Orgn. Librarians, Phi Delta Kappa. Republican. Baptist. Lodge: Lions (dist. gov. 1982-83). Home: 7708 New Jersey Kansas City KS 66112 Office: Kans City Pub Library 625 Minnesota Ave Kansas City KS 66101-2872

RIDDLE, WILLIAM EDWARD, agricultural company executive; b. Harrisburg, Pa., June 16, 1940; s. William A. and Alice M. (Irwin) R.; m. Katherine Jackson, Sept. 10, 1960 (div. Aug. 1976); children: Eric G., Andrew D. BS in Agrl. and Biol. Sci., Pa. State U., 1963, PhD in Agrl. Econs., 1969; MS in Dairy and Food Industry, U. Wis., 1965. Economist Borden, Inc., Columbus, Ohio, 1969-70; research leader Battelle Meml. Inst., Columbus, Ohio, 1970-85; pres. AgriTech, Inc., Columbus, Ohio, 1985—; cons. U.S. Price Commn., Washington, 1972-73, Cost of Living Council, Washington, 1973-74, Consumer Product Safety Commn., Washington, 1975-77, Bur. Foods FDA, Washington, 1976; author govtl. reports, White Papers for Office Tech. Assessment., 1985. Author: (with others) Agriculture 2000: A Look at the Future, 1983. Chmn. Teen Drug Counseling Ctr., Upper Arlington, Ohio, 1972-75, Boy Scouts Am., Upper Arlington, 1975-79; founding mem. NW Mental Health Bd., Upper Arlington, 1974. Mem. Am. Soc. Agrl. Cons. (cert.), Am. Dairy Sci. Assn., Am. Agrl. Econs. Assn., Inst. Food Technologists, Columbus Jaycees (named one of Outstanding Young Men 1974), Cen. Ohio Rose Soc. (pres. 1977), Columbus Rose Club. Avocations: exhibiting roses, scuba diving. Home: 2775 Oakridge Ct Columbus OH 43221 Office: AgriTech Inc 1989 W 5th Ave Suite 6 Columbus OH 43212

RIDEN, MICHAEL DAVID, nuclear engineer; b. Maryville, Tenn., July 2, 1947; s. William Walter and Grace Ella (Elrod) R.; m. Perry Dene Thyberg, Mar. 28, 1970; children: Chad Michael, Kirk David, Eric Wesley. Cert. nuclear weapons specialist, Lowry Tng. Ctr., Denver, 1968; cert. nuclear weapons technician, Gen. Electric Co. Tng. Program, King of Prussia, Pa., 1969; BS, U. Tenn., Knoxville, 1974. Asst. engr. Duke Power Co. Oconee Nuclear Sta., Seneca, S.C., 1974-78; insp. Nuclear Regulatory Commn., Glen Ellyn, Ill., 1978-79; gen. mgr. Chgo. Barra Corp. Am., Inc., Wheaton, Ill., 1979-82; reg. mgr. Watpro, Inc., Orland Park, Ill., 1982-83; pres. ETs, Glen Ellyn, 1983—; re-entry system evaluation team mem. minuteman III missile USAF, Minot, N.D., 1969-71. Deacon Presbyn. Ch. U.S., Seneca, 1976-77. Served to sgt. USAF, 1967-71. Mem. Am. Nuclear Soc. Republican. Home and Office: 22 W 302 Hackberry Dr Glen Ellyn IL 60137

RIDENOUR, JAMES AMBURS, political party executive; b. Indpls., July 18, 1939; s. Harry and Esther Mary (Smith) R.; m. Nancy Rose Velie, June 2, 1960 (div. 1974); children: Mary, Kathy, James, Donna, Jerrold; m. Billie Jane Boswell, Oct. 1, 1977; children: Stacy Diana, Jason Alexandros. DTh, Abilene Christian Coll., 1962; ASEE Tech., Ind. Vocat. Tech. Coll., 1969. Minister Pentecostal Ministries, Indpls., 1960-67; engr. Ind. Bell Telephone Co., Indpls., 1969-84; dir. pub. relations Libertarian Party, Indpls., 1984—. Author: Prostitution and the Bible, 1960; editor: The Quill, 1986—. Candidate Gov. of Ind., 1984. Lodge: Rosicrucian (high priest 1981-82). Avocations: antique gun restoration, camping. Office: Libertarian Party Ind Box 44322 Indianapolis IN 46204

RIDEOUT, DOUGLAS WARREN, film producer, director; b. Melrose, Mass., Nov. 9, 1939; s. Warren Frederick and Marjorie Elise (Black) Rideout Mode; m. Elisabeth Antonia Brackett, Aug. 16, 1958; children: Elaine Clarice Rideout Fisher, Douglas W. Jr., Bonnie Elisabeth Rideout Shaughnessy. AA, Boston U., 1959, BS, 1961. Producer, acct. exec. D/4 Film Studios, Inc., Boston and Newton, Mass., 1961-62; film prodn. assoc. U. Mich. Audio Visual Edn. Ctr., Ann Arbor, 1962-68; film dir. and cinematographer Sight and Sound, Inc., Ann Arbor, 1967-72; media cons. and prodn. supr. Statewide Dissemination Service, Wayne, Mich., 1968-69; film prodn. supr. U. Mich. Film Unit and Mich. Media, Ann Arbor, 1969-81; pres. Liberty Films, Ann Arbor, 1981—; lectr. U. Mich., Ann Arbor, 1981, 85-87; juror Am. Film Festival, N.Y., 1970-82, 85-86, Ann Arbor Film Festival, 1965, Ann Arbor 8 millimeter Film Festival, 1983. Editor, cinematographer: The Die is Cast, 1973 (Gold Camera award 1973); writer, cinematographer, editor: The Band Director, 1975 (Golden Eagle); dir., cinematographer, editor: What We Have, 1979; writer, dir.: Continuous Performance, 1985 (Silver medal Internat. Film and TV Festival N.Y.). Mem. Assn. Visual Communicators, Detroit Producers Assn., Soc. Motion Picture TV Engrs. (active 1960—). Avocations: reading, deltiology, philately, boating, hiking, travel, antiques. Office: Liberty Films PO Box 7201 Ann Arbor MI 48107

RIDGE, STEPHEN THOMPSON, insurance company executive; b. Indpls., Oct. 7, 1942; s. Clayton Abbott and Maxine (Thompson) R.; m. Carole Sue Carter, Mar. 26, 1946; children: David T., Susan M., Philip S. Student, Miami Bible Coll., Fla., 1961-63. Founder, owner Personalized Advt. Medium, Danville, Ill., 1966-80; sales agt. Nat. Life and Accident Ins. Co., Danville, 1973-75; agy. owner Ridge Ins. Services, Danville, 1975—; mng. gen. agent Bankers United Ins., Danville, 1985—. Alderman candidate City of Danville, 1987. Mem. Nat. Ry. Hist. Soc. (local sec. 1969-72). Republican. Baptist. Avocations: photography, railroading. Home: 117 Delaware Danville IL 61832

RIDGEWAY, HOWARD GAYLE, chemical engineer; b. Mexico, Mo., Nov. 6, 1943; s. Marcus Gayle and Vivian Eggleston (Dowell) R.; m. Brooksye Sue Robinson, Nov. 1, 1966; 1 child, Stephanie. BS, NE Mo. State U., 1965. Chemist Sinclair Paint & Coatings Co., Los Angeles, 1968-69; chem. engr. Kimberly-Clark Corp., Neenah, Wis., 1969—. Served to 1st lt. U.S. Army, 1966-68, Vietnam. Mem. Am. Legion. Republican. Methodist. Avocations: reading, bicycling, cross-country skiing. Home: 1236 E Hanson Dr Appleton WI 54915

RIDGWAY, JOHN EDWARD, pharmacist, consultant; b. Aberdeen, S.D., Oct. 1, 1948; s. Edward Willard and Shirley Jane (Smith) R.; m. Linda Lee Stansbury, May 2, 1970; children—Melissa, Allison. B.S. in Pharmacy, U. Nebr., 1971. Registered pharmacist, Ind., Nebr. Head pharmacist Osco Drugs, Terre Haute, Ind., 1971-73, Turn Style, Omaha, 1973-77; pharmacist Apothecary Assocs., Omaha, 1977-83, owner, head pharmacist, 1984—; pharmacy cons. Skyline Nursing Home, Omaha, 1977—; vol. faculty instr. Coll. Pharmacy, U. Nebr. Med. Ctr., Omaha, 1978—; cons. Bristol Myers, N.Y.C., Nebr. Dept. Social Services, Lincoln. Mem. steering com. Chem. People, Omaha, 1983-84; advisor Pride, Inc.-Omaha, 1983-85; advisor to Senator Jerry Chizek, Lincoln, Nebr., 1984—; chmn. Poison Prevention Week, Omaha, 1983-84. Named Preceptor of Yr., Nebr. Med. Ctr. Coll. Pharmacy, 1981. Mem. Nat. Assn. Retail Druggists (Pharmacy Leadership award 1981), Greater Omaha Pharmacists Assn. (pres. 1983), Nebr. Pharmacists Assn. (bd. dirs. 1982-85, Pub. Relations award 1984), Coll. Pharmacy Alumni Assn. (exec. com. 1984—). Republican. Methodist. Club: Cosmopolitan. Avocations: gardening; fishing; reading. Home: 14918 Jefferson Circle Omaha NE 68137 Office: Apothecary Assocs 8300 Dodge St Omaha NE 68114

RIDGWAY, RICHARD B., public relations company executive; b. Hays, Kans., Dec. 2, 1944; s. Roy LuVerne and Margaret Elizabeth (Wollner) R.; m. Krispen Moore, June 9, 1967; children: Erin Catherine, Benjamin Barclay. BA, Kans. State U., 1966; AM, U. Mo., 1972. Account supr. W.R. Hahn Advt., Springfield, Ill., 1968-70; dir. pub. info. Ill. Dept. Pub. Health, Springfield, 1970-76; dir. pub. relations Albany (N.Y.) Med. Ctr., 1976-85, Grinnell (Iowa) Coll., 1985—; adj. prof. communications Sangamon State U., Springfield, 1972-76; lectr. Grinnell Coll., 1985—. Recipient Gold medal Atlanta Internat. Film Inst., 1972, Andy award of Excellence Advt. Club N.Y., 1973, Gold Touchstone Am. Soc. Hosp. Pub. Relations, 1984, Excellence award, Internat. Assn. Bus. Communicators, 1985. Mem. Pub. Relations Soc. Am., Council for the Advancement and Support of Edn. (Bronze medal Imagination in News and Info. 1987), Alpha Epsilon Rho, Grinnell 2000, Grinnell C. of C. Avocations: swimming, squash, cross-country skiing, gardening. Home: 1422 Broad St Grinnell IA 50112 Office: Grinnell Coll PO Box 805 Grinnell IA 50112-0810

RIDLEN, JULIAN LEON, lawyer, investment banker; b. Macon County, Ill., Feb. 4, 1940; s. Charles F. and Doris O. (Franklin) R.; m. Susanne Lee Smith, June 1, 1963. B.A., Anderson Coll., 1963; J.D., George Washington U., 1967. Bar: Ind. 1967, U.S. Dist. Ct. 1967. Tchr. Emerson Inst., Washington Hall Jr. Coll., Washington, 1966-68; legal researcher NEA, Washington, 1967-68; judge Logansport City Ct., Logansport, Ind., 1969-78; partner firm Smith & Ridlen, Logansport, 1968—; state treas. State of Ind., Indpls., 1979-87; chmn. Ind. Housing Fin. Authority, 1983-87; 1st v.p., mgr. Ind. Fin. Office of McDonald & Co. Securities, Inc., 1987—. Chmn. Cass County Bicentennial Com., 1974-76, Ind. Bond Bank, 1984-87; pres. Cass County Youth Services Bur., 1971; v.p. bd. dirs. United Fund, 1972; pres. Cass County chpt. ARC, 1971-73; v.p. Mental Health Assn., 1971-73; mem. Cass County Bd. Election Commrs., 1970; mem. staff Republican Nat. Com., 1963-64. Mem. Nat. Assn. State Treas. (pres. 1983-84, state and fed. cash mgmt. reform task force 1983-87), Nat. Assn. State Auditors, Comptrollers and Treasurers (bd. dirs. 1983-84), ABA, Ind. Bar Assn., Cass County Bar Assn., Cass County Hist. Soc. (pres. 1974-78), Phi Alpha Delta. Presbyterian. Lodges: Kiwanis, Elks, Eagles. Home: 613 Wheatland Ave Logansport IN 46947 Office: One American Sq Suite 2615 Indianapolis IN 46282

RIECKER, JOHN E(RNEST), lawyer, banker; b. Ann Arbor, Mich., Nov. 25, 1930; s. Herman H. and Elizabeth (Wertz) R.; m. Margaret Ann Towsley, July 30, 1955; children: John Towsley, Margaret Elizabeth. AB with distinction, U. Mich., 1952, JD with distinction, 1954. Bar: Mich. 1954, Calif. 1955, U.S. Tax Ct., U.S. Supreme Ct., U.S. Treasury. Assoc. Bonisteel & Bonisteel, Ann Arbor, 1954-55; ptnr. Francis, Wetmore & Riecker, Midland, Mich., 1958-65; ptnr. Gillespie Riecker & George, Midland, 1966-85; sr. ptnr. Riecker, George, Hartley & Van Dam and Camp, P.C., 1985—; chmn. bd. First Midland Bank & Trust Co., 1970-78; bd. dirs. Comerica Bank-Midland; sec., bd. dirs. numerous Mich. corps.; mem. NAM trade mission to EEC, 1964. Mem. bd. editors Mich. Law Rev., 1953-54; contbr. articles to profl. jours. Trustee, treas. Delta Coll., 1965-68; mem. bd. mgrs. United Fund Midland 1960-64, chmn., 1980—; sec. Midland City Charter Rev. Com., 1964, mem. Spl. Charter Commn., 1972; bd. dirs. Midland Found., 1974; mem. bd. Ethics State of Mich., 1976—; sec. Dow Found., Towsley Found. Ann Arbor; mem. exec. com. Mich. United Fund, 1970-72; bd. govs. Northwood Inst., 1969-71; benefactor U. Mich.; vice chmn. bd. dirs. U. Mich. Devel. Council, 1982—; chmn. bd. dirs. Cen. Mich. U. Devel. Council, 1983-86; bd. govs. Cranbrook Acad. Art, 1980-84; chmn. Matrix, Midland, 1981-83; bd. dirs. steering com. U. Mich. Grad. Sch. Bus., 1982—; mem. com. visitors U. Mich. Law Sch., 1981—; vice chmn. Campaign for Mich., 1984; bd. dirs., chmn. fin. com. Hillsdale Coll., 1985—; exec. com., trustee Mich. Hist. Soc., 1985—. Served as 1st lt., Judge Adv. Gens. Corps, AUS, 1955-58, now capt. Res. Recipient U. Mich. Outstanding Alumni award, 1984. Mem. Midland County (pres. 1962-63), ABA, Calif. Bar Assn., Mich. Bar Assn. (mem. tax council), Midland C. of C. (pres. 1971), Phi Beta Kappa, Phi Kappa Phi, Phi Eta Sigma, Sigma Iota Epsilon, Alpha Delta Phi, Phi Delta Phi. Republican. Episcopalian. Clubs: Benmark, Midland Country, Saginaw, Saginaw Valley Torch; Detroit Athletic, Renaissance; Pres.'s, Benefactors (Ann Arbor). Home: 3211 Valley Dr Midland MI 48640 Office: 414 Townsend St Midland MI 48640

RIEDEL, JOYCE LUCKE, data processing executive; b. Clinton, Iowa, May 1, 1953; s. Fred and LaVera (Reimer) Lucke; m. Thomas E. Riedel, June 25, 1977; 1 child, Brian E. BS, Iowa State U., 1975; MBA, Ill. Benedictine Coll., 1980. Programmer Montgomery Wards, Chgo., 1975-77; sr. programmer McDonald's, Oak Brook, Ill., 1977-78, programmer analyst, 1978, systems analyst, 1979-80, mgr., 1980-83, programming staff dir., 1983—. Leader Girl Scouts, Naperville, Ill., 1975-77, council del. 1978-80, fin. com. 1982-83, bd. dirs. 1980-83, Wider Opportunites com. 1980-85; fin. com. Christ Luth. Ch., Clarendon Hills, Ill., 1986—. Mem. Nat. Computer Graphics Assn. Avocations: travel, reading, stamp collecting.

RIEDEL, STEVEN DARRELL, energy management company executive; b. Eau Claire, Wis., June 2, 1943; s. Harold W. and Lucy C. (Reiter) R.; m. Fern Margaret Borum, Dec. 19, 1964; children: Phillip B., Mark S. BS in bus. admin., economics, U. Wis., Eau Claire, 1965. Project mgr. Burroughs Corp., Detroit, 1973-75, regional sales mgr., 1975-79; v.p. product mktg. No. Telecom, Mpls., 1979-82, v.p. mgr., 1982-83; pres. Betacom Corp., St. Paul, 1983-85; pres., chief exec. officer Enercon Data Corp., Mpls., 1985—, also bd. dirs.; cons. in field, 1984-85; bd. dirs. Betacom, 1983-84. Pres. St. Clares Parish Council, Detroit, 1979, sec., 1978. Mem. Nat. Tax Limitation Com., Pax Christi, Alpha Kappa Lambda. Republican. Roman Catholic. Club: Flagship Athletic (softball mgr., league champions 1986). Avocations: golf, skiing, investments. Office: Enercon Data Corp 7464 W 78th St Minneapolis MN 55435

RIEDMANN, MICHAEL LOUIS, real estate executive; b. Omaha, Feb. 17, 1953; s. Alfred Adam and Shirley Marie (Simpson) R.; m. Coleen Anne Paulison, July 15, 1977; children: Nicole, Lucas, Natalie, Jacqueline. BBA, Wayne (Nebr.) State U., 1976. Cert. residential broker. Salesman Allen Young, Omaha, 1976-83; v.p. Real Estate Profl. Group, Omaha, 1983—. Named one of Outstanding Young Men Am., 1985, Athlete of Yr., 1976. Mem. Nat. Assn. Realtors (mem. com. 1986); Soc. Ind. Developers (bd. dirs. 1983), Greater Omaha C. of C., Omaha Bd. Realtors, Met. Omaha Home Builders Assn., Nebr. Realtors Assn. Lodges: Toastmasters, River City Regents. Avocations: reading, woodworking, golf, basketball. Home: 2905 S 165th Ave Omaha NE 68130 Office: Real Estate Profl Group 4735 S 132nd St Omaha NE 68137

RIEGER, MICHAEL BERNARD, accountant, financial executive; b. Cin., Oct. 13, 1949; s. Walter Bernard and Esther M. (Fischer) R.; m. Rebecca L. Poff, May 15, 1976; children: Sarah E., David M., Thomas W. BBA, Xavier U., 1971, postgrad., 1971. CPA, Ohio. Acct., auditor Coopers & Lybrand, Cin., 1971-77; controller C.M.S.I., Cin., 1977-79; v.p. fin., chief fin. officer Hamilton Allied Corp., Harrison, Ohio, 1979—; dbd. dirs. Micro Filming of Cin., Inc. Mem. Am. Inst. CPA's, Mgmt. Info. Systems Soc. (com. iron casting). Office: Hamilton Allied Corp 200 Industrial Ln Harrison OH 45030

RIEGER, MITCHELL SHERIDAN, lawyer; b. Chgo., Sept. 5, 1922; s. Louis and Evelyn (Sampson) R.; m. Rena White Abelmann, May 17, 1949 (div. 1957); 1 child, Karen Gross Cooper; m. Nancy Horner, May 30, 1961 (div. 1972); step-children—Jill Levi, Linda Hanan, Susan Felsenthal, James Geoffrey Felsenthal; m. Pearl Handelsman, June 10, 1973; step-children—Steven Newman, Mary Ann Malarkey, Nancy Newman. A.B., Northwestern U., 1944; J.D., Harvard U., 1949. Bar: Ill. 1950, U.S. Dist. Ct. (no. dist.) Ill. 1950, U.S. Supreme Ct. 1953, U.S. Ct. Mil. Appeals 1953, U.S. Ct. Appeals (7th cir.) 1954. Legal asst. Rieger & Rieger, Chgo., 1949-50, assoc., 1950-54; asst. U.S. atty. No. Dist Ill., Chgo., 1954-60; 1st asst. No. Dist Ill., 1958-60; assoc. gen. counsel SEC, Washington, 1960-61; ptnr. Schiff Hardin and Waite, Chgo., 1961—; instr. John Marshall Law Sch. Chgo., 1952-54. Contbr. articles to profl. jours. Mem. Chgo. Crime Commn., 1965—; pres. Park View Home for Aged, 1969-71; Rep. precinct committeeman, Highland Park, Ill., 1964-68; bd. dirs. Spertus Mus. Judaica. Served to lt. (j.g.) USNR, 1943-46, PTO. Fellow Am. Coll. Trial Lawyers; ABA, Chgo. Bar Assn., Ill. State Bar Assn., Am. Judicature Soc., 7th Circuit Bar Assn., Fed. Bar Assn. (pres. Chgo. chpt. 1959-60, nat. v.p. 1960-61), Phi Beta Kappa. Jewish. Clubs: Standard, Metropolitan, Lake Shore Country, Law of Chgo., Cliff Dwellers. Avocations: photography; skiing; sailing. Home: 4950 Chicago Beach Dr Chicago IL 60615 Office: Schiff Hardin & Waite 7200 Sears Tower 233 S Wacker Dr Chicago IL 60606

RIEGER, ROB G., marketing executive; b. Toledo, Oct. 25, 1948; s. Walter E. Rieger and Joan E. (Huff) Barry; m. Sandra M. Lemerand, Nov. 10, 1967; children: Todd A., Amy L. BBA, U. Toledo, 1975; MBA, Eastern Mich. U., 1978. Dir. mktg., sales engr. AP Parts Co. div. Questor Corp., Toledo, 1968-80; dir. mktg. Atwood, Rockford, Ill., 1980-84, GC Electronics div. Household Internat., Rockford, 1984—. Sec., bd. dirs. Janet Wattles Mental Health Ctr., Rockford, 1986. Mem. Electronic Industries Assn. (chmn. distributor relations com. 1985—). Roman Catholic. Avocations: golf, running, reading. Office: GC Electronics 1801 Morgan St Rockford IL 61102

RIEGLE, DONALD WAYNE, JR., U.S. senator; b. Flint, Mich., Feb. 4, 1938; s. Donald Wayne and Dorothy (Fitchett) R.; m. Lori L. Hansen, May 20, 1978; 4 children. Student, Flint Jr. Coll., 1956-57, Western Mich. U., 1957-58; B.A., U. Mich., 1960; M.B.A., Mich. State U., 1961; postgrad., Harvard U., 1964-66; LL.D., St. Benedict's Coll., 1970, Defiance Coll. Sr. pricing analyst with IBM Corp., 1961-64; faculty Mich. State U., 1962, Boston U., 1965, Harvard U., 1965-66; cons. Harvard U. MIT Joint Center Urban Studies, 1965-66; mem. 90th-94th congresses from 7th Dist. Mich.; mem. U.S. Senate from Mich. 1977—. Author: O Congress, 1972. Named one of America's 10 Outstanding Young Men U.S. Jr. C. of C., 1967, one of Two Best Congressmen of Yr., The Nation mag., 1967. Democrat. Office: 105 Dirksen Senate Office Bldg Washington DC 20515

RIEGSECKER, MARVIN DEAN, pharmacist; b. Goshen, Ind., July 5, 1937; s. Levi and Mayme (Kauffman) R.; m. Norma Jane Shrock, Aug. 3, 1958; children: Steven Scott, Michael Dean. BA in Pharmacy, U. Colo., 1967. Pharmacist Parkside Pharmacy, Goshen, Ind., 1967-73; pharmacist, mgr. Hooks Drugs, Inc., Goshen, 1973—; coroner Elkhart County, Goshen, 1977-84; bd. dirs. Goshen Gen. Hosp., 1985—. Rep. commr. Elkhart County, 1985—; bd. commrs. pres., 1987. Mem. Elkhart County Pharm. Assn., Ind. Pharm. Assn., Ducks Unltd. Republican. Mennonite. Avocation: jogging. Home: 801 S 6th St Goshen IN 46526 Office: Adminstrv Office Bldg 117 N 2d St Goshen IN 46526

RIEMAN, ALOYSIUS PHILIP, dentist; b. Jersey City, N.J., Feb. 29, 1928; s. Aloysius Philip and Anna Marie (Davis) R.; m. Janece Marie Mollers, July 5, 1952; children: Aloysius Philip, Mark Walter. Pre-dental degree, Fordham U., 1946; DDS, Georgetown U., 1949. Dentist N.Y. State Dental Assn., Jersey City, 1949-51; pvt. practice dentistry Jersey City, 1953-61, S.D. Dental Assn., Rapid City, 1961—; assoc. prof. Seton Hall Coll. of Dentistry, Jersey City, 1958-61. Mem. S.D. Com. of Human Health Resources, 1985-86. Served to capt. USAF, 1951-53. Mem. ADA, N.J. Dental Assn., S.D. Dental Assn. (trustee 1976-85), Hudson County Dental Soc. (1959-61), Rapid City Dental Soc. Roman Catholic. Clubs: Arrowhead Country, Rapid City Yacht. Lodge: Elks. Avocations: boating, fishing, water activities, hunting. Home: 3311 Flint Dr Rapid City SD 57702 Office: 731 Meade St Rapid City SD 57701

RIEMAN, STEPHEN RALPH, manufacturing company executive; b. Lima, Ohio, Sept. 13, 1946; s. Leo John and Kathryn (Schroeder) R.; m. Carol Marie Ellerbrock, June 10, 1967; children: Michelle Rene, Stephen Ralph Jr., Scott Michael. BSBA, Bowling Green (Ohio) U., 1968. CPA, Ohio. Jr. acct. Ernst & Ernst, Toledo, 1968-69, in charge acct., 1969-70; asst. treas. Northwest Materials, Inc., Bryan, Ohio, 1970-74; acct., office mgr. Koeneman, Krouse et al, Bryan, 1974-76; asst. sec.-treas. Bard Mfg. Co., Bryan, 1977-81, sec.-treas., 1981—, also bd. dirs., 1981—. Advisor Jr. Achievement, Bryan, 1981, 85; bd. dirs., treas. Bryan Athletic Boosters, 1985—, Nat. Reyes Syndrome Found, Bryan, 1975-80; mem. parish council and fin. com. St. Patrick's Ch., 1973—. Mem. Am. Inst. CPA's, Ohio Soc. CPA's, Nat. Assn. Accts., Bryan C. of C. (fin. com. 1975-86). Republican. Roman Catholic. Club: Orchard Hills Country (Bryan). Lodges: Rotary, KC, Moose. Home: 609 Wesley Ave Bryan OH 43506

RIEMEN, DAVID CLARENCE, chief of police; b. Ft. Wayne, Ind., Mar. 8, 1944; s. Albert Joseph and Beulah Mary (Patterson) R.; m. Diane Mae Gebhard, July 11, 1964; children—David, Michael, Jennifer, Sara. A.S., Ind. U., 1981. With Ft. Wayne (Ind.) Police Dept., 1967—, chief of police, 1981—; tng. instr. Police Sch. Liaison Officers Clinic, Flint, Mich., Internat. Assn. Chiefs of Police Developing Computer Capabilities, Nashville. Mem. adv. bd. Ft. Wayne Women's Shelter. Mem. Internat. Assn. Chiefs of Police. Roman Catholic. Club: Toastmasters. Office: Office of the Police Chief 1 Main St Room 280 Fort Wayne IN 46802

RIES, JOHN GEORGE, information technology administrator; b. Sheboygan, Wis., Oct. 22, 1945; s. Leo Joseph and Anne (Gilipskey) R.; m. Paula Louise Lautz, Aug. 1, 1970; children: Krista, Gretchen, Jason, Holly. BS in Engring., U. Wis., 1969, BBA, 1971, MBA, 1972. Metall. engr. Internat. Harvester, Moline, Ill., 1969-70; systems analyst Burroughs Corp., Detroit, 1973-74; mgr. systems Badger Northland, Kaukauna, Wis., 1974-81; dir mgmt. info. systems Paragon Electric Co., Two Rivers, Wis., 1981—; instr. Silver Lake Coll., Manitowoc, 1985. Mem. Am. Prodn. Inventory Control Soc. (bd. dirs. 1969-86), Kaukauna C. of C. (bd. dirs. 1980). Roman Catholic. Avocation: outdoor activities. Home: 2623 Washington Two Rivers WI 54241 Office: Paragon Electric Co Inc 606 Parkway Blvd Two Rivers WI 54241

RIES, STUART W., product engineer; b. Wauseon, Ohio, July 12, 1959; s. William H. and Nancy E. (Ruffer) R. BSME, Tri-State U., 1982; MBA, St. Francis Coll., 1985. Product engr. King-Seeley Div., Kendallville, Ind., 1982-86, Whirlpool Corp., Benton Harbor, Mich., 1986—. Exec. advisor Jr. Achievement, Ft. Wayne, 1982-86, St. Joseph, Mich., 1986-87; vol. Blossom Land United Way. Named Outstanding Young Am., 1982. Mem. Soc. Mfg. Engrs., ASME (assocs.). Republican. Home: 2545 Dover Ln Saint Joseph MI 49085 Office: Whirlpool Corp Corporate Upon Dr Saint Joseph MI 49085

RIESS, FRANK GERALD, advertising executive; b. Detroit, Apr. 2, 1953; s. Frank Edwin and Geraldine Marie (Weber) R.; 1 son, Robert Frank; m. Sharon Patricia Nowicki, Feb. 18, 1984. A.A. cum laude, Oakland Coll., 1973; B.S. cum laude in Mktg., Central Mich. U., 1975. Field dir. Hi-Scope Research Co., Southfield, Mich., 1975-76; analyst Market Opinion Research Co., Detroit, 1976-78, Can. Opinion Research Co., Toronto, Ont., 1976-78; advt. dir. Ziebart Corp., Troy, Mich., 1978—. Contbr. articles on mktg. to profl. jours. Named Eagle Scout Boy Scouts Am., 1968; Recipient Gold medal Internat. TV & Film Festival N.Y., 1985, Clio award 1985 . Mem.

Am. Mktg. Assn., Mktg. Research Assn., Am. Assn. Pub. Opinion Research, Adcraft Club of Detroit, Founders' Soc. of Detroit Inst. Arts. Home: 2795 Bolingbroke Troy MI 48084

RIEVES, LAMAR, information systems specialist; b. Memphis, June 15, 1944; s. Selwyn Beeks and Quida May (Ross) R.; m. Johanna Golver, June 11, 1986. B in Math., Miss. State U., 1966. Mgr. mfg. systems electronics and space div. Emerson Electric Co., St. Louis, 1966-71, dir. data processing ops., 1971-76; v.p. info. services Ridge Tool Co., Elyria, Ohio, 1976—. Home: 134 California Elyria OH 44035 Office: Ridge Tool Co 400 Clark St Elyria OH 44035

RIFFE, VERNAL G., JR., state representative. m. Thelma Cooper; children—Cathy, Verna Kay, Mary Beth, Vernal III. LL.D. (hon.), Ohio State U., 1981; D. Pub. Service (hon.), Rio Grande Coll., 1983; LL.D. (hon.), Ohio U., 1977, U. Akron, 1986. State rep. Ohio House Reps., 1958—, speaker, 1975—; pres. Riffe and Bennett Ins. Agy., Inc. New Boston, Ohio; presiding officer Ohio Ho. of Reps., also leader majority party, chmn. rules com., ex officio mem. all standing coms.; chmn. Legis. Service Commn. Named Legislator of Yr. Ohio Sportsmen, 1973, Legislator of Yr. Disabled Am. Vets., 1973, Outstanding Legislator in Ohio State House Press Corps, 1974, Man of Yr. Ohio Vocat. Assn., 1979, Ohio Assn. Local Supts. Outstanding Legislator, 1984; recipient Ohio Assn. of Ins. Agents Independence award, Cert. Merit Ohio U. Alumni Assn., 1974, Meritorious Service award VFW, 1975, Achievement award Ohio Chpt. Internat. Personnel Mgmt. Assn., 1976, Phillips medal of Pub. Service Coll. Osteopathic Medicine Ohio U., 1976, Man of Yr. award Ohio Pub. Transit Assn., 1977, Legislator's award Community Mental Health and Retardation Assn., 1978, Conservation Legislator of Yr. award Ohio Sportsmen Nat. Wildlife Fedn., 1979, Gov's award, 1980, Resolution of Honor Prosecuting Attys. Assn., 1980, Commodore Elite award, 1983, Pres.'s award Ohio Youth Services Network, 1984, Disting. Service award Sec. State, 1985; inducted into State Fair Hall of Fame, 1980; named Ohioan of Yr., Ohio Civil Service Employees Assn., 1986; Disting. Service to Agriculture citation Ohio Farm Bur. Fedn., 1986. Mem. Portsmouth Area C. of C., Bus. and Profl. Men's Assn., Am. Legion, Ohio Assn. Independent Insurance Agents, Dem. Nat. Com. Lodges: Kiwanis, Shriners, Masons. Office: Ohio House of Reps State House Columbus OH 43215 *

RIFKIN, LEONARD, metals company executive; b. N.Y.C., Apr. 10, 1931; s. Irving W. and May (Goldin) R.; m. Norma Jean Smith, Aug. 22, 1954 (dec. Jan. 1983); children: Daniel Mark, Richard Sheldon, Martin Stuart; m. Ariel Kalisky, Jan. 14, 1984. B.S., Ind. U., Bloomington, 1952. Pres. Global Resources Corp., Fort Wayne, Ind., 1960—, Superior Cos. Inc., Fort Wayne, 1960—. Served with U.S. Army, 1956-58. Office: Superior Cos Inc 1610 N Calhoun St Fort Wayne IN 46808 *

RIGDON, RONALD MILTON, mgmt. cons.; b. Balt., Jan. 15, 1937; s. Leland Sanford and Betty Berniece (Roe) R.; student Kansas City (Mo.) Art Inst., 1958-60, William Jewell Coll., Liberty, Mo., 1955-58, 62-63; m. Arlene June Eddington, May 26, 1962; children—Ryan Todd, Rebecca Erin. Field adjuster CNA Ins. Corp., Kansas City, Mo., 1962-63; asst. mgr. Anchor Fin. Corp. Ins. Agy., Overland Park, Kans., 1963-64; mgr. First Mortgage Investment Co. Ins. Agy., Kansas City, Mo., 1964-67; pres. Programming Inst., Mission, Kans., 1967-70, RMR & Assos., Inc., Overland Park, 1970—; dir. Assn. Cons., Inc., Scheduling Systems, Inc. First v.p. Johnson County Mental Health Assn., 1968-70, Kans. Mental Health Assn., 1969-70. Mem. Mgmt. Cons. Inst., Profl. Ins. Mass-Mktg. Assn., Am. Mgmt. Assn., Assn. Chief Exec. Officers, Am. Profl. Assn. Group Ins. Adminstrs., U.S. Dressage Fedn., Kansas City Dressage Soc. Republican. Baptist. Author: Work Flow-Cost Reduction a Management Control System, 1978. Home: 12200 Big Bone Trail Olathe KS 66061 Office: 10875 Benson Dr Suite 103 Overland Park KS 66210

RIGGERT, ROBERT HENRY, optometrist; b. Seward, Nebr., Oct. 18, 1948; s. Harold Christopher and Emilie Elizebeth (Gieselman) R.; m. Jana Ruth Lester, Sept. 6, 1969; children: Jeffrey, Jonathan. BS in Chem. Engring. with distinction, U. Nebr., 1971; OD, U. Calif., Berkeley, 1978. Design engr. Chevron Research, Richmond, Calif., 1971-74; optometrist Seward Vision Clinic, 1978—; bd. dirs. OmniEye Services, Omaha Ctr. Elder St. John Ch., Seward, 1982-84. Served with USNG, 1971-77. Fellow Am. Acad. Optometry; mem. Nebr. Optometric Assn. (dist. pres. 1983-84). Lutheran. Lodge: Rotary. Avocations: golf, cooking, jogging. Office: Seward Vision Clinic 246 S Columbia Ave Seward NE 68434

RIGGIO, WANDA JOYCE, small business owner; b. Eastland, Tex., July 5, 1941; d. Travis Homer Sr. and Tura May (McClain) Arnold; m. Dennis Edward Buck, Dec. 12, 1959 (div. Feb. 1970); children: Michael Alan, Jacqueline Marie, David Christian, Patricia Anne; m. Lawrence Craig Riggio, July 22, 1972 (div. Feb. 1980); children: Daniel Christopher, James Patrick. Student, Nat. Sch. Dress Design, N.Y.C., 1958-59; student in computer ops., Coll. DuPage, 1971, 73. Various positions Stretch & Sew, Addison, Ill., 1978-83; owner A Stitch for All Seasons, Villa Park, IL, 1983—. Active petition com. against the demolition of schs., Elmhurst, Ill., 1979; mem. Council of Cath. Women, Mary Queen of Heaven Ch., Unity Folk Singers. Democrat. Lodge: Moose. Avocations: bird watching, painting, camping, singing, gardening. Office: A Stitch for All Seasons 201 W St Charles Villa Park IL 60181

RIGGS, JACK ALAN, lawyer; b. Brazil, Ind., Nov. 3, 1954; s. Jack Charles and Carolyn Jane (Rosser) R.; m. Katherine Ann Sandberg, Aug. 9, 1986. BS, Ind. State U., 1977; JD, Ind. U., 1985. Bar: Ind. 1985, U.S. Dist. Ct. (no. and so. dists.) Ind. 1985. Contract specialist Vigo County, Terre Haute, Ind., 1979-80; research specialist State of Ind., Inpls., 1980-85, equal employment opportunity coordinator, employment security div., 1985—; counsel/adminstrv. law. judge Ind. Dept. Hwys., 1986—; contract officer USN, Inpls., 1985. Precinct committeeman Dems., Brazil, 1972-78. Nat. Merit scholar, 1973. Mem. ABA, Ind. Bar Assn., Am. Arbitration Assn., Ind. Civil Liberties Union (mem. steering com.), Assn. Trial Lawyer of Am. Methodist. Home: 26 N Holmes Ave Indianapolis IN 46222 Office: Ind Employment Security Div 100 N Senate Ave Indianapolis IN 46204

RIGGS, JEANETTE TEMPLETON, civic worker; b. Little Rock, Mar. 13, 1933; d. Donald M. and Fay (Templeton) Brewer; student Little Rock U., 1950-51, Tex. Coll. for Women, 1951-52; B.S., U. Ark., 1955; m. Byron Lawrence Riggs, June 1955; children—Byron Kent, Ann Templeton. Founder, Rochester (Minn.) Ballet Guild, 1970, pres., 1974; mem. establishing bd., exec. bd. Rochester Arts Council, 1972, producer, dir. T.S. Elliot's The Rock, 1970; founder, performer So. Minn. Ballet Co., 1974; sponsor Nat. Ballet Cos., Rochester, 1970-75; exec. bd. for restoration 1875 Pattern Book House, Rochester Heritage Assn., 1975-77; exec. bd. Savino Ballet Nat., 1975-78; founder, exec. bd. Citizens Action Com., 1977-79; asso., commentator Women, Cable TV Program for Women, Rochester, 1979; mem. Mayor's Com. on Drug Abuse, 1979-80; mem. Olmsted County Steering Com. for George Bush, 1979-80, a founder, mem. exec. bd. Olmsted County Republican Women's Orgn., 1979—, mem. Olmsted County Rep. Central Com., 1979—, exec. bd. issues com., 1979-80. Home: 432 SW 10th Ave Rochester MN 55901

RIGHTER, WALTER CAMERON, bishop; b. Phila., Oct. 23, 1923; s. Richard and Dorothy Mae (Bottomley) R.; m. Marguerite Jeanne Burroughs, Jan. 26, 1946; children—Richard, Rebecca. B.A., U. Pitts., 1948; M.Div., Berkeley Div. Sch., New Haven, 1951, D.D., 1972. Ordained priest Episcopal Ch., 1951, consecrated bishop, 1972; lay missioner St. Michael's Ch., Rector, Pa., 1947-48; priest-in-charge All Saints Ch., Aliquippa, Pa., 1951-54; rector Ch. of Good Shepherd, Nashua, N.H., 1954-71; bishop Diocese of Iowa, Des Moines, 1972—; N.H. del. Nat. Council Chs., 1963; exec. council Protestant Episcopal Ch. U.S.A., 1979—. Mem. N.H. com. White House Conf. on Youth, 1962, Regional Crime Commn., Hillsboro County, N.H., 1969-71; trustee Nashua Library, 1968-71. Fellow Coll. Preachers, Washington Cathedral. Office: 225 37th St Des Moines IA 50312

RIGSBEE, WILLIAM ALTON, insurance company executive; b. Durham, N.C., July 10, 1926; s. Coley Leonard and Julia Hill (Hackney) R.; m. Shirley Reese Morgan, July 12, 1952. BA, Duke U., 1950. With Home Security Life, Durham, 1950-56, Franklin Life Ins., Springfield, Ill., 1956-61; pres., chmn. Midland Nat. Life Ins. Co., Sioux Falls, S.D., 1961—; pres. and chmn. Investors Life Ins. Co. of Nebr., Sioux Falls, 1968—, N.Am. Mgmt., Inc., Sioux Falls, 1968—; bd. dirs. Sammons Enterprises, Inc., Northwestern Bell Telephone Co, Norwest Bank S.D.. Bd. dirs. Downtown Devel. Corp., Sioux Falls, 1979—. Served with U.S. Army, 1944-46, ETO. Mem. Am. Council Life Ins. Home: 1200 Tomar Rd Sioux Falls SD 57105 Office: Midland Nat Life Ins Co One Midland Plaza Sioux Falls SD 57193

RIHM, PAUL CHARLES, controller; b. Cin., Dec. 23, 1953; s. Manfred John and Jean Ann (Naber) R. m. Sarah Jane Kolodziej, Sept. 10, 1977. BSBA in Acctg., Xavier U., 1976. CPA, Ohio. Audit mgr. Deloitte Haskins & Sells, Cin., 1977-86; controller Opelika Industries, Inc. (subs. Leshner Corp.), Hamilton, Ohio, 1986—. Mem. Butler County Assn. for Retarded Citizens, Hamilton, Ohio, 1978—. Recipient Four Yr. Participant award Project Bus. (div. of Jr. Achievement) 1985, Letter of Commendation Deloitte Haskins & Sells Working Paper Rev. Project, 1984. Mem. Ohio Soc. CPA's (local v.p. 1985-86), The Planning Forum (local chmn audit com. 1985-87), Assn. Mgmt. Soc. (1st v.p., local treas. 1984-88), Am. Inst. CPA's, Queen City Assn. Roman Catholic. Avocations: traveling, gardening, dogs. Home: 5450 Joey Terr Cincinnati OH 45248 Office: Opelika Industries Inc 1010 Eaton Ave Hamilton OH 45013

RIKER, DOUGLAS GEORGE, personnel director; b. Boone, Iowa, Sept. 1, 1948; s. George D. and Lois Riker; m. Marlene R. Newlin, Aug. 10, 1974; 1 child, Ture. BS, Iowa State U., 1978. Supr. coll. relations Trane, LaCrosse, Wis., 1978-82; mgr. employment CR Industries, Elgin, Ill., 1982—. Founder Concerned Citizens, Hampshire, Ill., 1985-86. Served with USN, 1969-76, Vietnam. Mem. Elgin Personnel Assn. (mem. steering com. 1982—), Am. Soc. Personnel Adminstrs., Ill. Mfrs. Assn., Midwest Coll. Placement Assn., Chgo. Rubber Group, Elgin C. of C. (ambassador 1983—), VFW. Evangelical. Lodge: Kiwanis (past v.p.). Avocations: golf, reading, working with young people, coaching. Office: CR Industries 900 N State St Elgin IL 60120

RIKIMARU, YUKI, archtl. designer, planner; b. Sacramento, Oct. 7, 1927; s. Joseph Iwasuke and Kiyono (Aramaki) R.; A.B. in Architecture, San Mateo City Coll., 1949; B.A. in Architecture Washington U., St. Louis, 1953; m. Kaoru Goto, Nov. 8, 1958; children—Raymond Kenji, Loryn Tamiko. Archtl. draftsman William B. Ittner, St. Louis, 1953-55; archtl. designer Russell, Mulgardt Schwarz, Van Hoeflin, St. Louis, 1956—; archtl. partner W.B. Kromm Asso., St. Louis, 1957—; prin. Kromm Rikimaru & Johansen Inc., architects, St. Louis, 1960—; v.p. Kromm, Rikimaru & Johansen Inc., architects, engrs. and planners, St. Louis, 1972—, Archtl. Mgmt. Group Inc. Served with AUS, 1946-47. Mem. AIA, Nat. Council Archtl. Registration Bds., Mo. Council Architects. Prin. archtl. works include: Maplewood Municipal Bldg., St. Louis, 1961; Mineral Area Coll.. Flat River, Mo., 1966; Fulton (Mo.) Juvenile Center, 1967; Delmar Gardens Nursing Home, St. Louis, 1968; Columbia (Mo.) Regional Hosp., 1972. Office: 112 S Hanley Rd St Louis MO 63105

RILEY, DAVID EVERETT, JR., insurance executive, financial counselor; b. Kansas City, Mo., Nov. 15, 1959; s. David Everett Riley Sr. and Marilyn Ann (McDonald) Peterson. B in Econs. and Speech Communications, U. Kans., 1982; cert. in Fin. Planning, Am. Coll., 1986. Ptnr. A.E. Riley & Assocs., Kansas City, 1984—, chief exec. officer, 1986; v.p. Exec. Benefits Planning Inc., Kansas City, 1984—. Hon. bd. dirs. Rockhurst Coll., Kansas City, 1984—. Mem. Nat. Assn. Life Underwriters, Mo. Assn. Life Underwriters, Million Dollar Round Table, Gamma Omicron Beta, Phi Kappa Psi Alumni Assn. (bd. dirs., v.p. 1986). Republican. Roman Catholic. Clubs: Kansas City (bd. dirs. 1984—), O.E. Ellis Soc. (founder., bd. dirs., 1984—.). Avocations: golf, tennis, skiing, gardening. Home: 2804 W 73d St Prairie Village KS 66208 Office: AE Riley Assocs 1102 Grand Ave Suite 602 Kansas City MO 64106

RILEY, DOROTHY COMSTOCK, state justice; b. Detroit, Dec. 6, 1924; d. Charles Austin and Josephine (Grima) Comstock; m. Wallace Don Riley, Sept. 13, 1963; 1 child, Peter Comstock. B.A. in Polit. Sci., Wayne State U., 1946, LL.B., 1949. Bar: Mich. 1950, U.S. Dist. Court (ea. dist.) Mich. 1950, U.S. Supreme Court 1957. Atty. Wayne County Friend of Court, Detroit, 1956-68; ptnr. Riley & Roumell, Detroit, 1968-72; judge Wayne County Circuit, Detroit, 1972, Mich. Ct. Appeals, Detroit, 1976-82; chief justice Mich. Supreme Court, Detroit, 1982-83, 85—; mem. U.S. Jud. Conf. Commn. on State-Fed. Court Relations. Co-author manuals, articles in field. Mem. adv. com. Citizenship Edn. Study, 1946-50. Recipient Disting. Alumni award Wayne U. Law Sch., 1977; Headliner award Women of Wayne, 1977; Donnelly award, 1946. Mem. ABA (family law sect. 1965—; vice chmn. gen. practice sect. com. on juvenile justice 1975-80; mem. jud. adminstrn. sect. 1973—, standing com. on fed. ct. improvements), Am. Judicature Soc., Fellows Am. Bar Found., Mich. State Bar Found., State Bar Mich. (civil liberties com. 1954-58, young lawyers sect. 1956-60, family law sect. 1966—), Detroit Bar Assn. (pub. relations com. 1955-56, author Com. in Action column, Detroit Lawyers 1955, chmn. friend of ct. and family law com. 1974-75), Nat. Women Judges Assn., Nat. Women Lawyers Assn., Women Lawyers Assn. Mich. (pres. 1957-58), Karyatides, Pi Sigma Alpha. Republican. Roman Catholic. Club: Women's Econ. Avocations: reading; gardening. Office: Michigan Supreme Court 1425 Lafayette Bldg Detroit MI 48226 *

RILEY, DOUGLAS ANTHONY, controller; b. Washington, Mo., Apr. 15, 1960; s. Julius A. Riley and Ruth (Trentmann) Lottmann; m. Donna Marie Garbs, Mar. 12, 1983; 1 child, Sarah Marie. AAS, East Cen. Coll., Union, Mo., 1980; BS, S.W. Mo. State U., 1982. CPA, Mo. Staff acct. Hochschild, Bloom & Co., CPA's, Washington, Mo., 1983-84, sr. acct., 1985-86; corp. controller The Meramec Group, Inc., Sullivan, Mo., 1986—. Mem. Am. Inst. CPA's, Mo. Soc. CPA's, Washington Jaycees (treas. 1984, v.p. 1985, bd. dir. 1986. Republican. Roman Catholic. Lodge: KC, Elks. Avocation: golf. Home: 1510 First Pkwy Washington MO 63090 Office: The Meramec Group Inc 338 Ramsey Sullivan MO 63080

RILEY, KATHLEEN ANN, consultant; b. Evanston, Ill., May 13, 1961; s. R. Donavan and Agatha Ann (Hannon) R. BA in Mktg. Mgmt., St. Thomas Coll., 1986. Cons. Small Bus. Devel. Ctr., St. Paul, 1984-87, R-W and Assocs., Minnetonka, Minn., 1980—. Mem. Gianes Profl. Feeder Plan, Pi Sigma Epsilon (top nat. salesperson), A Sigma Epsilon. Republican. Roman Catholic. Club: Kimberwick Equestrian (treas. 1980-81). Avocations: training Doberman Pinschers, horse jumping and dressage, sailing, tennis. Home: 4615 Ellerdale Rd Minnetonka MN 55345

RILEY, RICHARD, retired utility company executive; b. Des Moines, Jan. 30, 1920; s. William Francis and Catherine Mary (Green) R.; m. Betty Callan, May 23, 1942 (dec. Jan. 1983); children: Kathleen, Richard II, Mary Elizabeth, Margaret, Mark, Meaghan; m. Betty Myrl Berry, Aug. 12, 1983. BSEE, U.S. Naval Acad., 1941; MS, MIT, 1946. Registered profl. engr. Commd. ensign USN, 1941, advanced through grades to capt., 1962, retired, 1964; various positions Iowa Light & Power Co., Des Moines, 1964-85, sr. v.p., 1985. Mem. NCCJ (co-chmn. 1979-82), U.S. Naval Inst. (life), USN League (life, various offices), Western Coal Transp. Assn., Western Coal Traffic League, Iowa Engring. Soc. (bd. dirs. 1982-83), U.S. Rowing Assn. (life). Democrat. Roman Catholic. Club: Des Moines (bd. trustees 1971-73), Des Moines Rowing (v.p. 1983-84). Avocations: golf, swimming, bridge. Home: 730 51st St Des Moines IA 50312

RIMMER, KENNETH GEORGE, finance company executive; b. Detroit, Apr. 23, 1947; s. George and Eunice Mary (LeDuc) R.; m. Gretchen, Nov. 4, 1984; 1 child, Laura; 1 child from previous marriage, Kelly Joy. BBA in Mktg., Eastern Mich. U., 1969. Personnel asst. U. Mich., Ann Arbor, 1969-70; mktg. rep. IBM, Southfield, Mich., 1970-75; treas. Harlan Electric Co., Southfield, 1975-77; v.p., gen. mgr. Enterprise Oil & Gas, Detroit, 1977-83; asst. to chmn. Erb Lumber Co., Birmingham, Mich., 1983-84; v.p., chief operating officer Erb Bldg. Systems subs. Erb Lumber Co., Port Charlotte, Fla., 1984-85; mgr., cons. Peat, Marwick & Mitchell & Co., Detroit, 1985; exec. dir., chief exec. officer Total Health Care, Inc., Detroit, 1985—. Mem. YMCA, Phi Sigma Epsilon (treas. 1967-68). Republican. Roman Catholic. Clubs: Plum Hollow (Southfield). Office: 3455 Woodward Detroit MI 48201

RIMPILA, JULIAN JOHN, gastroenterologist; b. Chgo., Apr. 19, 1940; s. Charles Einar and Verna Catherine (Swanson) R.; B.A., Knox Coll., 1962; M.S., U. Chgo., 1966, M.D., 1966; m. Beverly Rose Dahlen, Apr. 30, 1966; children—John-Eric, Carl, Kari, Siiri, Heidi. Intern in medicine Northwestern U.-Evanston Hosp., 1966-67, resident in internal medicine, 1967-70; fellow in gastroenterology U. Chgo., 1973-76; practice medicine specializing in gastroenterology, Chgo., 1976—; chmn. dept. med. Henrotin Hosp., Chgo., 1984—; mem. med. staff Grant Hosp., Henrotin Hosp., Gottlieb Hosp.; mem. cons. staff Christ Hosp. Asst. scoutmaster Boy Scouts Am., Westchester, Ill., 1980—; councillor U. Chgo. Alumni Council, 1976-80. Served with M.C., U.S. Army, 1970-73. Recipient Leadership and Service award Boy Scouts Am., 1978, 79, 80. Mem. ACP, AMA, Am. Soc. Gastrointestinal Endoscopy, Chgo. Med. Soc., Assn. U.S. Army, Res. Officers Assn. U.S., Am. Scandinavian Found., Phi Beta Kappa, Tau Kappa Epsilon (Delta award Delta chpt. 1985). Sigma Xi. Republican. Lutheran. Mem. editorial bd. Medicine on the Midway, 1980—. Home: 11049 Windsor Dr Westchester IL 60153 Office: 505 N Lake Shore Dr Suite 406 Chicago IL 60611

RIMSTIDT, JAMES PAUL, manufacturing engineer; b. Owensboro, Ky., Dec. 20, 1943; s. Paul Tailor and Pauline V. (Kincade) R.; m. Sherry Jo Patridge, Dec. 20, 1962; children: James Paul, David Joseph, Stephanie Ann. BS in Mechanical Engring., U. Evansville, 1976. Tool and die maker Faultless Castor, Evansville, Ind., 1963-73, production foreman, 1973-75, tool designer, 1975-76; maintenance foreman USX, Lorain, OH, 1976-78; process engr. Ford Motor Co., Sandusky, Ohio, 1978-82; adv. mfg. engr. Ford Motor Co., Wixom, Mich., 1982—. adv. order of the arrow Boy Scouts Am., Vermillion, Ohio, 1977-85, scoutmaster Evansville and Elyria, Ohio, 1973—; marriage encounter team and flame leader, Ohio state family weekend experience team coordinator. Mem. ASME, Robotics Internat. (cert. 1983), Soc. Mfg. Engrs. (cert. 1983), Soc. Automotive Engrs. Republican. Methodist. Avocations: fishing, antique automobiles. Home: 1040 Yarmouth Rd Grafton OH 44044 Office: Ford Motor Co 3020 Tiffin Sandusky OH 44870

RINCK, JAMES RICHARD, lawyer; b. Grand Rapids, Mich., Mar. 6, 1958; s. Richard John and Ann Louise (Weening) R. BA, Calvin Coll., 1975-79; JD, U. Ill., 1979-82. Bar: Mich. 1982, U.S. Dist. Ct. (we. dist.) Mich. 1982. Asst. prosecutor Muskegon County, Muskegon, Mich., 1983-84; sole practice Grand Rapids, 1984—. Deacon Westminster Presbyn. Ch., 1985—; mem. exec. bd. Kent County Dems., 1984—; mem. exec. bd. Mich. Young Dems., 1986—. Mem. ABA, Mich. Bar Assn. (workers' compensation and negligence sects. 1987—, crminal law sect. 1983—), Grand Rapids Bar Assn. Avocations: reading, sports, photography, music. Home: 1236 Blanchard SW Wyoming MI 49509 Office: 72 Ransom NE Grand Rapids MI 49503

RINDOKS, ROLAND RAYNARD, steel company executive; b. East Chicago, Ind., June 16. 1925; s. Peter Stanley and Anna (Simon) R.; student Fenn Coll., 1944, Purdue U. Extension, 1946-47; m. Lillian Stone, Aug. 19, 1950; children—Roland Raynard, Bruce, Kurt, Brian. With M.W. Kellogg Constrn. Co., East Chicago, 1947-48; mech. designer Design Service, Inc., Chgo., 1948-49, Sumner S. Sollitt Constrn. Co., 1949-50; co-owner, mgr. Boulevard Pharmacy, East Chicago, 1950-53; mech. designer Petroleum Piping Contractors, Hammond, Ind., 1953-54; asst. plant engr. Gen. Am. Transp. Corp., East Chicago, 1954-62; project engr. Jones & Laughlin Steel Co. and precessor co., East Chicago, 1962—. Served with USAAC, 1943-46. Roman Catholic. Home: 7013 Ridgeland Ave Hammond IN 46324 Office: 3001 Dickey Rd East Chicago IN 46312

RINEHART, DANA GILLMAN, mayor of Columbus, Ohio; b. Parkersburg, W.Va., Feb. 24, 1946; s. Paul George and Kathleen (Gillman) R.; m. Nancy Carol Grant, Nov. 28, 1968; children—Dana Gillman, Jenna Michelle, Jonathan Grant. B.A., J.D., Ohio State U. Bar: Ohio. Campaign aide Roger Cloud for Gov. Ohio, Columbus, 1970; assoc. Tyack Scott & Colley, Columbus, 1970-72; ptnr. Matan Rinehart Smith, Columbus, 1972-84; treas. Franklin County, Ohio, 1977-84; mayor City of Columbus, 1984—. Co-author: Ohio in the 21st Century, 1981. Mem. Como Ave. Residents Assn., Columbus; ex-officio mem. Franklin County Republican Orgn., 1969—. Served with USN, 1984—. Recipient County Achievement award Nat. Assn. County Ofcls., 1979; award for fin. reporting achievement Nat. Mcpl. Fin. Assn., 1983. Mem. U.S. Marine League, AMVETS, Fraternal Order of Police and Assocs., Navy League (bd. dirs. 1982—). Methodist. Avocations: camping; fishing; boating; reading. Office: Office of Mayor City Hall 90 W Broad St Columbus OH 43215 *

RINEHART, JANE SOLBERG, psychologist; b. Minot, N.D., Sept. 25, 1947; d. Jerrald Vincent and Sylvia C. (Klemenhagen) Solberg; m. Dennis Jackson Rinehart, Aug. 16, 1980; 1 child, Daniel. BA, St. Olaf Coll., 1970; PhD, U. Minn., 1974. Lic. cons. psychologist, Minn. Asst. prof. U. W.Va. Med. Sch., Morgantown, 1974-75; sch. psychologist Austin (Minn.) Pub. Schs., 1975-77; staff psychologist VA Med. Ctr., Mpls., 1977—; clin. asst. prof. U. Minn., Mpls., 1977—. Cons. Stephen ministers Cen. Luth. Ch., Mpls., 1984-86. Mem. Am. Psychol. Assn. Democrat. Avocation: playing the cello. Home: 5625 Standish Ave Minneapolis MN 55417 Office: VA Med Ctr 54th St and 48th Ave S Minneapolis MN 55417

RINER, JAMES WILLIAM, lawyer; b. Jefferson City, Mo., Dec. 25, 1936; s. John Woodrow and Virginia Loraine (Jackson) R.; m. Carolyn Ruth Hicke, May 14, 1976; children—Alicia Gayle, Angela Gayle, Amity Gayle. B.A., U. Mo., 1957, LL.B., 1960. Bar: Mo. 1960, U.S. Dist. Ct. (we. dist.) Mo. 1982. Asst. atty. gen. Atty. Gen.'s Office Mo., Jefferson City, 1960; commd. 1st lt. U.S. Air Force, 1960, advanced through grades to lt. col., 1974; ret., 1981; ptnr. Inglish, Monaco, Riner & Lockenvitz, P.C., 1985-87, Jefferson City; city pros. Jefferson City, 1983—; city atty. California, Mo., 1985-87. Contbg. author: Mo. Ins. Practice Manual, 1986. Decorated Bronze Star, Meritorious service medal. Mem. ABA, Mo. Bar Assn. Democrat. Lodge: Masons. Home: 1106 Cimmaron Jefferson City MO 65101 Office: Inglish Monaco Riner & Lockenvitz 237 E High St Jefferson City MO 65101

RINER, RONALD NATHAN, cardiologist, consultant; b. Hot Springs, S.D., Mar. 7, 1949. A.B., Princeton, 1970; M.D., Cornell U., N.Y.C., 1974. Diplomate Am. Bd. Internal Medicine, Am. Bd. Cardiovascular Disease. Resident in internal medicine N.Y. Hosp., Meml. Sloan-Kettering, Hosp. for Spl. Surgery, 1974-79; resident in cardiology Mayo Grad. Sch. Medicine, Rochester, Minn., 1976-79; chmn. dept. internal medicine, St. Mary's Health Ctr., St. Louis, 1980-83, program dir. internal medicine, 1980-83; pvt. practice cardiology, St. Louis, 1983—; med. dir. BioMed. Systems, St. Louis, 1984—; asst. prof. medicine, Washington U. Med. Ctr., 1985—; pres. Ronald N. Riner and Assocs., Ltd., 1986—. Fellow N.Am. Coll. Cardiology, Am. Acad. Med. Dirs.; mem. N.Y. Acad. Scis., Mo. Soc. Internal Medicine (council), Mayo Alumni Assns., Cornell U. Alumni Assn., Princeton Alumni Assn. Club: Princeton U. Office: Univ Club Tower 1034 S Brentwood Blvd Suite 854 Saint Louis MO 63117

RING, ALVIN MANUEL, pathologist; b. Detroit, Mar. 17, 1933; s. Julius and Helen (Krolik) R.; m. Cynthia Joan Jacobson, Sept. 29, 1963; children—Jeffrey, Melinda, Heather. B.S., Wayne State U., 1954; M.D., U. Mich., 1958. Intern Mt. Carmel Hosp., Detroit, 1958-59; resident in pathology Michael Reese Hosp., Chgo., 1960-62; asst. pathologist Kings County Hosp., Bklyn., 1962-63; assoc. pathologist El Camino Hosp., Mountain View, Calif., 1963-65; chief pathologist, dir. labs. St. Elizabeth's Hosp., Chgo., 1965-72, Holy Cross Hosp., Chgo., 1972—; instr. SUNY, 1962-63, Stanford U., 1963-65; asst. prof. pathology U. Ill., Chgo., 1966-69, assoc. prof., 1969-78, prof., 1978—; adj. clin. prof. So. Ill. U., 1981—; chmn. histotech. Nat. Accrediting Agy. for Clin. Lab. Scis., 1977-81; mem. spl. adv. com. Health Manpower, 1966-71; pres. Spear Computer Users Group, 1981-82; mem. adv. com. Mid-Am. chpt. ARC, 1979-85; pres. Pathology and Lab. Cons., Inc., 1985—; originator, coordinator pathology courses Cook County Grad. Sch. Medicine, 1981—; bd. trustees Analytical Lab. for Environ. Excellence, 1987—. Author: Laboratory Correlation Manual, 1968, 82, 86, Laboratory Assistant Examination Review Book, 1971, Review Book in Pathology, Anatomic, 1986, Review Book in Pathology, Clinical, 1986; mem. editorial bd. Laboratory Medicine, 1975—; contbr. articles to med. jours. Fellow Coll. Am. Pathology (insp. 1973—),

Am. Soc. Clin. Pathology; mem. AMA, Ill. Med. Soc., Chgo. Med. Soc. (alt. councilor 1980-85, mem. adv. com. on health care delivery), Ill. Pathol. Soc., Chgo. Pathol. Soc. (censor 1980-83, exec. com. 1985—), Am. Assn. Blood Banks, Phi Lambda Kappa. Home: 6843 N Lamon St Lincolnwood IL 60646 Office: 2701 W 68th St Chicago IL 60629

RING, GARY NORMAN, market research executive; b. Chgo., June 21, 1949; s. Norman Oscar and Mildred I. (Olund) R.; m. Patricia L. Jacobs, Mar. 3, 1973; children: Brian, Kristen, John. BS cum laude, No. Ill. U., 1971, MBA, 1973. Asst. research mgr. Helene Curtis, Chgo., 1973-75, product mgr., 1975-77; client service rep. SAMI div. Time, Inc., Chgo., 1977-81, sales exec., 1981-85, v.p. sales, 1985—; cons. Trends in Food mag., 1983, Consumption Patterns in Chgo. mag, 1985. Mem. Am. Mktg. Assn. Office: Time Inc Sami Div 541 N Fairbanks Chicago IL 60611

RING, LEONARD M., lawyer; b. Taurage, Lithuania, May 11, 1923; came to U.S., 1930, naturalized, 1930; s. Abe and Rose (Kahn) R.; m. Donna R. Cecrle, June 29, 1959; children—Robert Steven, Susan Ruth. Student, N.Mex. Sch. Mines, 1943-44; LL.D., DePaul U., 1949, J.D., 1971. Bar Ill. 1949. Spl. asst. atty. gen. State Ill., Chgo., 1967-72; spl. atty. Ill. Dept. Ins., Chgo., 1967-73; spl. trial atty. Met. San. Dist. Greater Chgo., Chgo., 1967-77; lectr. civil trial, appellate practice, tort law Nat. Coll. Advocacy, San Francisco, 1971, 72; mem. com. jury instrns. Ill. Supreme Ct., 1967-71, 73—; nat. chmn. Attys. Congl. Campaign Trust, Washington, 1975-79. Author: (with Harold A. Baker) July Instructions and Forms of Verdict, 1972. Editorial bd. Belli Law Jour., 1983—; adv. bd. So. Ill. U. Law Jour., 1983—. Contbr. chpts. to books, numerous articles to profl. jours. Trustee, Roscoe Pound-Am. Trial Lawyers Found., Washington, 1978-80; chmn. bd. trustees Avery Coonley Sch., Downers Grove, Ill., 1974-75. Served with U.S. Army, 1943-46. Decorated Purple Heart. Fellow Am. Coll. Trial Lawyers, Internat. Acad. Trial Lawyers, Internat. Soc. Barristers; mem. Soc. Trial Lawyers, Am. Judicature Soc., Appellate Lawyers Assn. (pres. 1974-75), Assn. Trial Lawyers Am. (nat. pres. 1973-74), Ill. Trial Lawyers Assn. (pres. 1966-68), Trial Lawyers for Pub. Justice (founder), Chgo. Bar Assn. (bd. mgrs. 1971-73), ABA (sect. council 1983—), Ill. Bar Assn., Kans. Bar Assn. (hon. life), Lex Legio Bar Assn. (pres. 1976-78), Inner Circle Advs. Clubs: Metropolitan, Plaza, Meadow, River; Monroe (Chgo.). Home: 6 Royal Vale Dr Ginger Creek Oak Brook IL 60521 Office: 111 W Washington St Chicago IL 60602

RING, LESLIE KATHERINE, accountant; b. Dodge City, Kans., Jan. 16, 1960; d. Arthur James and Virgie Ione (Bolton) Konda; m. David Martin Ring, June 14, 1986. AA, Dodge City Community Coll., 1980; BS, Emporia (Kans.) State U., 1982. CPA, Kans. Staff acct. Oak Simon & Ott, Wichita, Kans., 1982-84; in-charge acct. Regier Carr & Monroe, Wichita, 1984—. Mem. Am. Inst. CPA's, Kans. Soc. CPA's, Nat. Assn. Accts. (bd. dirs. 1986). Republican. Roman Catholic. Avocations: needlework, camping. Home: 2150 N Meridian Wichita KS 67203 Office: Regier Carr & Monroe 200 W Douglas Suite 1000 Wichita KS 67202

RING, ROBERT A., real estate executive; b. Louisville, Jan. 10, 1950; children: Robert, David, Tracy. BS, St. Louis U., 1971; MBA, U. Mo., St. Louis, 1974. V.p. design and constrn. May Dept. Stores, St. Louis, 1976-80; v.p. Paragon Group, St. Louis, 1980—. Bd. dirs. Justice Under State Taxes, St. Louis, 1985—. Mem. Real Estate Sales and Securities Inst., Inst. Real Estate Mgmt., Nat. Apt. Assn., Nat. Assn. Accts. Republican. Roman Catholic. Avocations: running, tennis, softball, pub. speaking, skiing. Office: Paragon Group 12400 Olive Saint Louis MO 63141

RINGE, MARION KAY, non-profit organization development executive; b. Detroit, Apr. 23, 1946; d. Norman Fred and Gladys Leona (Gohlke) R. B.A., Wayne State U., 1970, M.A., 1977. Asst. to v.p. advancement Merrill-Palmer Inst., Detroit, 1971-78; asst. dir. devel. Detroit Inst. Arts, 1978-80; asst. dir. devel. Harper-Grace Hosps., Detroit, 1980-85, dir. ann. support, 1985—. Mem. Nat. Assn. Hosp. Devel., Mich. Assn. Hosp. Devel., Nat. Soc. Fund Raising Execs (cert.). Republican. Lutheran. Home: 23416 Wilmarth Farmington MI 48024 Office: Harper-Grace Hosps 3990 John R St Detroit MI 48201

RINGEL, HARVEY NORMAN, music educator; b. Peoria, Ill., Mar. 25, 1903; s. William Frederick and Mathilda Catherine (Wiesehan) R.; m. Marian E. Edwards, Aug. 30, 1931 (dec.); 1 child, Marilyn; m. Lucile H. Hertel, Sept. 1, 1945. MusB, U. Ill., 1927; MA, Columbia U., 1934; DFA, Chgo. Musical Coll., 1954; MusD (hon.), U. Mo.-Kansas City, 1949. Tchr. singing Mercersburg Acad. (Pa.), 1927-29; instr. singing Wesley Coll., U. N.D., Grand Forks, 1929-31, dir. conservatory, assoc. prof. voice, 1931-35; pvt. voice instr., Chgo., 1935-46; adminstr., instr. Chgo. Mus. Coll., 1946-54; assoc. prof. voice Chgo. Music Coll., Roosevelt U., 1954-68, prof. voice, 1968-77, prof. emeritus, 1977—, dir. summer session, 1968; tchr. singing Am. Conservatory, Chgo., 1977—; cons. and lectr. in field. Author: The History of the National Association of Teachers of Singing, 1944-84, 1984; condr. Midwest premiere The Redeemer (Martin Shaw), 1946. Fellow Nat. Assn. Tchrs. Singing (charter; mem. editor NATS bull. 1955-80, historian 1983—, v.p. NATS Found. 1976—); mem. Soc. Am. Musicians (pres. 1976-78), Chgo. Singing Tchrs. Guild (pres. 1976-78), Am. Acad. Tchrs. Singing, Phi Mu Alpha, Sigma Phi Epsilon. Club: Cliff Dwellers. Home: 1139 Leavitt Ave Apt 203 Flossmoor IL 60422 Office: Am Conservatory of Music 116 S Michigan Ave Chicago IL 60603

RINGER, JOHN WILLIAM, lawyer; b. Dexter, Mo., July 18, 1936; s. John Lee and Helen (Boyd) R.; m. Carolyn Irvin, July 18, 1954 (div. 1967); 1 child, Lisa Denise; m. Debra Lou Calhoun, Dec. 4, 1976; 1 child, James Michael; 1 stepchild, Lora Brooke Bailey. AB, William Jewell Coll., 1958; JD, U. Mo., 1960. Bar: Mo. 1960, U.S. Dist. Ct. (ea. dist.) Mo. 1964, U.S. Tax Ct. 1974. Assoc. Powell, Ringer & Bischof (and predecessor firms), Dexter, 1960-63, ptnr., 1963-79, sr. ptnr., 1979-86; assoc. judge juvenile and criminal div, Mo. 35th Jud. Cir., 1986-87; ptnr. Powell, Ringer & Bischof, Dexter, 1987—. Contbr. to Mo. Law Rev. Pres. Dexter Meml. Hosp., 1964—; campaign dir. Stoddard County March of Dimes, 1960-64, campaign treas. 1964-67; co-chmn. Community Betterment Com., 1971-73; pres., bd. dirs. Bapt. Ch., 1968-77, music dir. 1960-80; chmn. John Wesley White Areawide Evang. Crusade. Mem. Am. Trial Lawyers Assn., Mo. Assn. Trial Attys., ABA, Mo. Bar Assn., Am. Judicature Soc., Stoddard County Bar Assn., Mo. Soc. Hosp. Attys., Am. Acad. Hosp. Attys., Dexter C. of C. (past bd. dirs., Community Leadership award 1964). Democrat. Club: Kiwanis (past pres.). Avocations: yard work, model airplanes. Home: 405 N Walnut PO Box 337 Dexter MO 63841 Office: 21 Vine St PO Box 337 Dexter MO 63841

RINGNESS, RONALD CHRISTIAN, marketing executive; b. Tampa, Fla., Oct. 17, 1949; s. Curtis Woodrow and Ruth Ann (Hargis) R.; m. Margaret Ann Trebilcock, Aug. 12, 1972; children—Julie, Jeffrey, Caitlin. B.S. in Bus. Adminstrn., Oral Roberts U., 1971; postgrad. S.W. Mo. State U., 1971-72. Exec. mgmt. trainee Ednl. Devel. Corp., Tulsa, 1972; mktg. mgr. Liberty Industries, Girard, Ohio, 1972-77, v.p. mktg., 1977-81, exec. v.p., 1981—, exec. v.p., ptnr., 1983—; ptnr. Charles Christian & Assocs., Advt., Girard, 1980—, Liberty/Nutro Packaging Systems, Cleve., 1984—; dir. Liberty Industries, Girard, Kassko Enterprises, Youngstown, Ohio and Boca Raton, Fla. Republican. Club: Youngstown Country. Avocations: jogging; golfing; tennis; skiing; reading. Home: 3735 Sampson Rd Youngstown OH 44505 Office: Liberty Industries Inc 555 Tibbetts Wick Rd Girard OH 44420

RINGOEN, RICHARD MILLER, manufacturing company executive; b. Ridgeway, Iowa, May 15, 1926; s. Elmer and Evelyn Louise (Miller) R.; m. Joan Marie Brandt, June 7, 1953; children: David, John, Daniel. Student, U. Dubuque, Iowa, 1944-45, Marquette U., Milw., 1945-46; B.S. in Elec. Engring, U. Iowa, 1947, M.S., 1948. Research engr. Collins Radio, Cedar Rapids, Iowa, 1948-55; v.p. engring. Alpha Corp. subs. Collins Radio, Cedar Rapids, Iowa, 1955-59; dir. spl. projects Martin-Marietta Co., Denver, 1959-70; v.p., gen. mgr. Ball Brothers Research Corp., Boulder, Colo., 1970-74; corp. v.p. ops. Ball Corp., Muncie, Ind., 1974-78; pres., chief operating officer Ball Corp., 1978-80, pres., chief exec. officer, 1981-86; chmn., pres, chief exec. officer Arvin Industries, Inc., 1986—; dir. Am. Nat. Bank & Trust Co., CTS Corp., Arvin Industries, Inc., Am. Electric Power Co., Inc.; chief exec. officer, dir. Tally Corp., 1973-78. Patentee in communications, navigation and electronics circuitry. Pres. Arapahoe County Sch. Bd., Colo. 1963-70, dir. Arapahoe Jr. Coll. Steering Com., 1969-70; trustee Hudson Inst., Purdue U.; bd. dirs. Muncie Symphony Orch.; campaign chmn. United Way; pres., bd. dirs. United Way Delaware County; bd. dirs. Ball State Univ. Found., Meth. Hosp., Indpls., Muncie Symphony Assn., Inc. Served with USN, 1944-46. Recipient Top CEO in Container Industry award Financial World, 1982, 84. Mem. Glass Packaging Inst., Can Mfrs. Inst. (chmn. 1985-86), Ind. C. of C. (bd. dirs.). Methodist. Lodge: Rotary (bd. dirs. Muncie club). Office: Ball Corp 345 S High St Muncie IN 47302

RINGSTAD, DAVID ARTHUR, accountant, administrator; b. Chgo., Apr. 3, 1938; s. Edward Arthur and Victoria Marie (Gorek) R.; m. Joyce Lentz, Aug. 21, 1965; children: Erik Christopher, Dawn Marie. BSBA, Roosevelt U., 1962. CPA, Ill. Acct. Deloitte Haskins & Sells, Chgo., 1962-63, sr. acct., 1963-67, asst. mgr. report dept., 1967-70, adminstrv. mgr. report dept., 1970—. Bd. govs. Pepper Valley Home Assn., Geneva, Ill., 1974-79, treas., 1976-79; treas. Pepper Valley Bowling League, 1982—. Served to sgt. Ill. N.G., 1962-68. Mem. Am. Inst. CPA's, Ill. Soc. CPA's. Avocations: model railroading, swimming, bowling, water skiing. Home: 406 Essex Ct Geneva IL 60134 Office: Deloitte Haskins & Sells 200 E Randolph Dr Chicago IL 60601

RINKE, DWIGHT CLARENCE, educator; b. Mt. Clemens, Mich., Aug. 28, 1945; s. Clarence Henry William and Elsie Jane (Eddinger) R. BA, Wayne State U., 1968, MEd, 1985, postgrad., 1986—. Cert. secondary tchr., Mich. Tchr., Eng. dept. chmn. Madison High Sch., Madison Heights, Mich., 1967—; instr., dir. Cranbrook Theatre Sch., Bloomfield Hills, Mich., 1970-83; instr. Wayne State U., Detroit, 1986—. Benefits chmn. Harbinger Dance Co., Detroit, 1975; arts commr. Oakland County (Mich.) Cultural Council, 1977—; pres. Arts Council Triangle, Bloomfield Hills, 1977-79; v.p. St. Dunstan's Theatre Guild Cranbrook, Bloomfield Hills, 1986—. NEH fellow, 1985. Mem. Philosophy Edn. Soc., Midwest Philosphy Edn. Soc., John Dewey Soc., Am. Soc. Aesthetics, David MacKenzie Honors Soc. (v.p. 1986—, pres. 1987—), Phi Delta Kappa, Omicron Delta Kappa. Unitarian. Home: 555 S Woodward Ave Apt 1209 Birmingham MI 48011 Office: Madison High Sch 915 E 11 Mile Rd Madison Heights MI 48071

RINKEL, GENE KEITH, librarian, clergyman; b. Fayette County, Ill., Feb. 27, 1929; s. Walter M. and Jane E. (Dixon) R.; m. Margaret E. Causey, Aug. 4, 1950; children—Stephen D., Karen Rinkel Smith. A.B. in Philosophy and Religion, Greenville Coll., 1950; B.D., Asbury Theol. Sem., 1958; M.S. in L.S., U. Ill., 1967. Ordained to ministry Methodist Ch., 1950; minister, Free Meth. Ch., Athens, Ga., 1950-52, Davenport, Iowa, 1956-58, Aurora, Ill., 1958-63; librarian U. Ill., Urbana-Champaign, 1967—; curator spl. collections, 1985—. Author, editor bibliographies, 1973; contbr. articles to profl. publs. Pres. and dir. Mahomet (Ill.) Pub. Library Bd., 1975—; dir. Lincoln Trails Library Systems, 1986—. Mem. ALA (coms. 1975—), Assn. Coll. and Research Libraries, Library Adminstrn. and Mgmt. Assn. Lutheran. Home: 404 N Weathering Dr Mahomet IL 61853 Office: Univ Ill 346-F Rare BooK Room 1408 W Gregory Dr Urbana IL 61801

RINKEL, VERNON JOHN, electronics educator, consultant; b. Morrison County, Minn., Dec. 26, 1940; s. George and Mercedes (Beumer) R.; m. Mary Scully, July 13, 1963; children—Jeffry, Michaela, John, Andrea. BS, Bemidji State U. Installer, Western Union Co., Omaha, 1960-63, ops. tech., 1965-70, city ops. mgr., 1965-70, city mgr., 1970-72; supr. engring. services Western Union Hawaii, Honolulu, 1972-74; instr. electronics tech. Wadena (Minn.) Area Vocat. Tech. Inst., 1974—, dept. head, 1980—; cons. electronics and mgmt.; lectr. in field. Mem. Am. Vocat. Assn., Minn. Vocat. Assn., Wadena Vocat. Assn., Am. Fedn. Tchrs., Minn. Fedn. Tchrs., Wadena Fedn. Tchrs., Nat. Inst. Cert. Engring. Technologies, Minn. Trade and Industry Assn. Mem. Democratic Farm Labor Party. Roman Catholic. Office: Wadena Area Vocat Tech Inst 405 SW Colfax St Wadena MN 56482

RINKER, LARRY EUGENE, computer training coordinator; b. Wichita, Apr. 14, 1942; s. Berl Leroy and Maxene Bessie (Abshier) R.; m. LaJean Ann Stuthman, June 27, 1965; children: Barbara Lynn, Jeffrey Scott. BS in Edn., Concordia Tchrs. Coll., 1965; MBA, U. Nebr., 1972; AA, BBA, Washburn U., 1981. Cert. data processor; cert. info. systems auditor; cert. systems profl. Traffic analyst, cryptanalyst Army Security Agy., United States and Fed. Republic Germany, 1967-71; EDP auditor First Nat. Bank, Lincoln, Nebr., 1973-76; auditor First Nat. Bank, Topeka, Kans., 1976-79; programmer Santa Fe Railway, Topeka, 1979-80, instr., 1980-84, tng. coordinator, 1984—; guest lectr. Washburn U., Topeka, 1978-80. Mem. Beta Gamma Sigma. Republican. Lutheran. Home: 2215 SE 35th Topeka KS 66605 Office: Santa Fe Railway 920 Quincy Topeka KS 66612

RIOPELLE, JACK LEONARD, farmer; b. Warren, Minn., Nov. 5, 1949; s. Leonard Joseph and Madonna Jane (McGlynn) R.; m. Pam Rosalie Peterson, JUne 26, 1971; children: Tony, Tina. Grad. high sch., Argyle, Minn., 1967. Farmer Argyle, 1967—. Supr. Bloomer Twp. Bd., 1984. Served with U.S. Army, 1969-71. Mem. Minn. Wheat Growers Assn., Minn. Crop Improvement Assn. (master crop grower 1985), Minn. Seed Producers and Promotion Assn. (v.p. 1983—), Marshall County Crop Improvement Assn., Red River Valley Beet Growers (top producer 1981), Argyle Co-op Warehouse Assn., Argyle Redevel. Assn., Am. Legion (local comdr. 1985—), VFW. Roman Catholic. Lodge: Lions. Avocations: coin collecting, fishing. Home and Office: Rural Rt 1 Box 157 Argyle MN 56713

RIORDAN, RAY JOSEPH, telephone company exec.; b. Green Bay, Wis., Jan. 27, 1916; s. Daniel E. and Florence E. (Brooks) R.; student St. Norbert Coll., 1933-35; B.S., Marquette U., 1937; m. Eileen Kelly, June 25, 1941; children—Mary Eileen (Mrs. Richard Harper), Ray Joseph, Patrick D., Robert H. Editor, pub. Tri County News, Pulaski, Wis., 1938-41; salesman Yellow Pages, Mich., Wis. and Ind., 1941-42; telephone engr. Hercules Powder Co., Wilmington, Del., 1942-43; comml. mgr. Gen. Telephone Co., Wausau and Madison, Wis., 1943-46; comml. mgr. 6 state area Central Telephone Co., LaCrosse, Wis., 1946-52; exec. v.p. Wis. State Telephone Assn., Madison, 1952-81; pres. Shamrock Affiliates, Madison, 1959—; sec.-treas. Wis. State Telephone Found., Madison, 1965-81, trustee, 1981—; sec.-treas. N.E. Telephone Co., Pulaski, 1950—; mem. Wis. Emergency Number Systems Bd., 1981-82. Named to State Telephone Industry Hall of Fame. Mem. Council Telephone Execs. (pres. 1962, 70), Ind. Telephone Pioneers (pres. Badger chpt. 1954-55), Telephone Pioneers Am. (life). Clubs: Elks, Madison, Black Hawk Country. Home: 6711 N Dunlap Hollow Rd Mazomanie WI 53560 Office: 617 N Segoe Rd Suite 202 Madison WI 53705

RIORDAN, ROBERT VINCENT, archaeologist, anthropology educator; b. Newark, Sept. 19, 1946; s. Vincent John and Alice Elizabeth (Kindmark) R.; m. Sandra Elaine Neifert, Aug. 26, 1973; 1 son, Corey James. B.A., Colgate U., 1968; Ph.D., So. Ill. U., 1975. Archaeologist Md. Hist. Trust, Annapolis, 1975-76; asst. prof. anthropology Wright State U., Dayton, Ohio, 1976-82, assoc. prof. anthropology, chmn. dept. sociology and anthropology, 1982—; cons. archaeologist, Xenia, Ohio, 1976—. Author jour. articles and contracted reports. Recipient Liberal Arts Merit Teaching award Wright State U., 1981. Mem. Soc. Am. Archaeology, Soc. for Hist. Archaeology, Ohio Archeol. Council (trustee 1984—), Central States Anthrop. Soc., Sigma Xi. Avocations: collector of juvenile series books; tennis; swimming. Home: 1354 Old Springfield Pike Xenia OH 45385 Office: Dept Sociology and Anthropology Wright State U Dayton OH 45435

RIPLEY, RALPH, chemical company executive. Pres. Thompson Hayward Chem. Co., Kansas City, Mo. Office: Thompson Hayward Chem Co 5200 Speaker Rd Kansas City KS 66106 *

RIPPBERGER, GARY LEE, podiatrist, educator; b. Waukegan, Ill., Nov. 22, 1950; s. Howard Edward and Jeane Dorothea (Stroker) R.; m. Judith Lynn Veldman, Sept. 11, 1976; children: Candice, Douglas, Cassie. Sutdent, U. Wis., 1968-69, Wright Coll., 1969-71; D in Podiatry, Ill. Coll. Podiatric Medicine, 1975; grad., William M. Scholl Coll. Podiatric Medicine, 1975. Instr. William M. Scholl Coll. Podiatric Medicine, Chgo., 1976-78, asst. prof. lower extremity diseases, 1978-83, assoc. prof., 1983—, head basketball coach, 1976-85; pvt. practice podiatry Grayslake, Ill., 1975-87, Vernon Hills, Ill., 1980-85, Libertyville, Ill., 1987—; mem. staff Am. internat. Hosp., Zion, Ill., chmn. podiatric dept., 1980-83; mem. staff Hawthorn Surg. Ctr., Libertyville, Ill., 1980—; sr. surg. staff mem. McHenry (Ill.) Hosp.; guest lectr. Ind. Podiatric Med. Assn., 1986; speaker in field. Fellow Am. Acad. Podiatric Sports Medicine (bd. dirs. 1986, sci. chmn. 1983, 87); mem. Ill. Podiatric Med. Soc. (sports medicine com. 198—, speaker). Office: Gary Rippberger & Assocs Ltd 273 Peterson Rd Libertyville IL 60048

RIPPLE, KENNETH FRANCES, appellate judge; b. Pitts., May 19, 1943; s. Raymond John and Rita (Holden) R.; m. Mary Andrea DeWeese, July 27, 1968; children: Gregory, Raymond, Christopher. AB, Fordham U., 1965; JD, U. Va., 1968; LLM, George Washington U., 1972. Bar: Va. 1968, N.Y. 1969, U.S. Supreme Ct. 1972, D.C. 1976, Ind. 1984. Atty. IBM Corp., Armonk, N.Y., 1958-68; legal officer U.S. Supreme Ct., Washington, 1972-73, spl. asst. to chief justice Warren E. Burger, 1973-77; prof. law Notre Dame U., South Bend, Ind., 1977-85; judge U.S. Ct. Appeals (7th cir.), South Bend, 1985—; reporter Appellate Rules Com., Washington, 1978-85; mem. commn. on mil. justice U.S. Dept. Def., Washington, 1984-85. Author: Constitutional Litigation, 1984. Served with JAGC, USN, 1968-72. Mem. ABA, Am. Law Inst. Office: U S Ct of Appeals 208 Fed Bldg 204 S Main St South Bend IN 46601

RIPPY, FRANCES MARGUERITE MAYHEW, educator; b. Ft. Worth, Sept. 16, 1929; d. Henry Grady and Marguerite Christine (O'Neill) Mayhew; m. Noble Merrill Rippy, Aug. 29, 1955 (dec. Sept. 1980); children: Felix O'Neill, Conrad Mayhew, Marguerite Hailey. BA, Tex. Christian U., 1949; MA, Vanderbilt U., 1951, PhD, 1957; postgrad., U. London, 1952-53. Instr. Tex. Christian U., 1953-55; instr. to asst. prof. Lamar State U., 1955-59; asst. prof. English, Ball State U., Muncie, Ind., 1959-64; assoc. prof. English, Ball State U., 1964-68, prof., 1968—, dir. grad. studies in English, 1966—; editor Ball State U. Forum, 1960—; vis. asst. prof. Sam Houston State U., 1957; vis. lectr., prof. U. P.R., summers 1959, 60, 61; cons.-evaluator North Central Assn. Colls. and Schs., 1973—, commn.-at-large, 1987—; cons.-evaluator New Eng. Assn. Schs. and Colls., 1983—. Author: Matthew Prior, 1986. Contbr. articles to profl. jours., chpt. to anthology. Recipient McClintock award, 1966; Danforth grantee, summer 1964, Ball State U. Research grantee, 1960, 62, 70, 73, 76, 87, Lilly Library Research grantee, 1978; Fulbright scholar, U. London. Mem. MLA, Coll. English Assn., Ind. Coll. English Assn. (pres. 1984-85), Johnson Soc. Midwest (sec. 1961-62), AAUP, Nat. Council Tchrs. English, Am. Soc. 18th Century Studies. Home: 4709 W Jackson St Muncie IN 47304

RISCH, RICHARD WILLIAM, horticultural manager; b. Milw., Jan. 8, 1941; s. Frederick William and Sophia (Banker) R. BS, U. Wis., Milw., 1965. Asst. floriculturist Mitchell Park Conservatory, Milw., 1968-72, asst. hort. dir., 1972-81, hort. mgr., 1981—. Editor, photographer: Mitchell Park Conservatory Souvenir Booklet, 1975, 81. Mem. Am. Assn. Bot. Gardens and Arborea (chmn. conservatory com. 1984-86), Milw. Bonsai Soc. (June Kelley award 1982). Office: Mitchell Park Conservatory 524 S Layton Blvd Milwaukee WI 53220

RISER, RANDALL ERMAN, social worker; b. Marshall, Mich., Nov. 29, 1948; s. Erman William and Betty Jane (Amsler) R.; m. Cherie Elise Connelly, Sept. 30, 1978; children: Sara, Sean, Joshua, Brett. AA in Psychology, Kellogg Community Coll., 1969; BA in Psychology, Albion Coll., 1972; postgrad., Western Mich. U., 1985—. Cert. social worker, Mich. Sr. citizens counselor City of Marshall, 1975-77; social worker Coldwater (Mich.) Regional Mental Health Ctr., 1977—; cons. Codde Mgmt. Group, Marshall, 1982-84. Instr. Prepared Childbirth of Marshall, Inc., 1980-83; co-chmn. Mich. Week-Family Unity Day, Marshall, 1983; dir. acolyte program Episcopal Ch., Marshall, 1984—; v.p. bd. dirs. Help Outreach For Me, Marshall, 1986—. Club: Trinity Men's (sec. 1986—). Avocations: wildlife sports, tennis, scuba diving. Home: 221 N Gordon Marshall MI 49068 Office: Coldwater Regional Mental Health Ctr 620 Marshall Rd Coldwater MI 49036

RISK, J. FRED, banker, investment banker; b. Ft. Wayne, Ind., Dec. 1, 1928; s. Clifford and Estella (Kline) R.; m. Viola Jean Tompt, July 12, 1953; children: Nancy Jean, John Thomas. B.S. cum laude, Ind. U., 1949, LL.B., J.D., 1951; postgrad., Nortwestern U.; LL.D., Ind. State U. With Harris Trust & Savs. Bank, Chgo., 1951-54, W.T. Grimm & Co., 1954-56; with Ind. Nat. Bank of Indpls., 1956-76, exec. v.p. dir., 1965-68, pres., 1968-76, chmn., 1971-76; chmn. Forum Group, Inc., 1976—, Sargent & Greenleaf Inc., 1980—; dir. Steak n Shake, Inc., Standard Locknut, Inc., Somerset Corp., Nat. Homes Corp., Amli Realty Co., Security Group, Inc., Keystone Distbn., Inc. Lacy Diversified Industries, Inc., Excepticon, Inc., L.R. Nelson Corp., Forum Industries, Breckenridge Corp., Canterbury Corp., Cygnet Enterprises, Inc., Franklin Corp., Forum Fin., Inc.; Dir. Haag Drug Co., Inland Container Corp., Ind. Bell Telephone Co., Ransburg Corp., Hook Drug Co., Northwestern Mut. Life Ins. Co. Bd. dirs. Hanover Coll., 1966-72, Ind. U. Found., 1968—; chmn. Indpls. Center for Advanced Research; bd. dirs. United Student Aid Fund; chmn. Ind. State Scholarship Com., 1968-72. Served as capt. inf. AUS, 1950-51. Mem. Am., Ind., Res. City bankers assns., Ind., Indpls. bar assns. Methodist. Clubs: Indpls. Athletic, Meridian Hills Country (Indpls.); Royal Poinciana Golf (Naples, Fla.). Office: Forum Group Inc 8900 Keystone Crossing Indianapolis IN 46240

RISK, JAMES EDWARD, animal scientist; b. Crawfordsville, Ind., Oct. 17, 1947; s. James Allen and Delores Geraldine (Caldwell) R.; m. Carol Ann Hallock, Dec. 30, 1972; children: Jeffrey, Douglas. BS, Purdue U., 1971, MS, 1981. Vocat.-agrl. tchr. N. Montgomery Sch. Corp., Linden, Ind., 1971; farm mgr. McFadden Charolais Farm, Lafayette, Ind., 1971-79; asst. scientist Pfizer Animal Health Research, Terre Haute, Ind., 1981-85, assoc. scientist, 1985—. Author research papers. Mem. Terre Haute Concert Band, 1985—. Mem. Am. Soc. Animal Sci., Am. Registry Profl. Animal Scientists, Sigma Xi. Avocations: reading, playing musical instruments, outdoor activities. Office: Pfizer Animal Health Research PO Box 88 Terre Haute IN 47808

RISKY, FRANK ANTHONY, electrical engineer; b. Chgo., Jan. 17, 1933; s. Charles and Johanna (Svoboda) R.; m. Margaret P. Risky, Apr. 16, 1955; children: Anthony J., Gary T., Robert A., Maryann P. BEE, Ill. Inst. Tech., 1958. Registered profl. engr., Ill. Engr., supr. Stewart Warner, Chgo., 1958-61; engr. Admiral Corp., Chgo., 1961-64, GTE Communication Systems, Northlake, Ill., 1964—. Inventor telephone line cir. scanner, monitor of currents, control unit for telephone, various others. Served with U.S. Army, 1953-55, Korea. Mem. IEEE, Am. Legion, Eta Kappa Nu, Tau Beta Pi. Republican. Roman Catholic. Avocations: photography, fishing. Home: 3418 S 58th Ave Cicero IL 60650 Office: GTE Communication Systems 400 N Wolf Rd Northlake IL 60164

RISMAN, ERIK R., retail executive; b. Boston, Oct. 22, 1944; s. Edward R. and Sonja (Arven) R.; m. Susannah Baker; 1 child, Caroline; m. Cynthia Benike. B.A., U. N.C., 1966. Asst. to sr. v.p. R. H. Macy & Co., Inc., N.Y.C., 1970-72, mgr. ops. services, 1972-77; exec. v.p. Famous Footwear, Madison, Wis., 1977-84; sr. v.p. splty. retailing Brown Group, Inc., St. Louis, 1984—. Served to capt. U.S. Army, 1966-70. Office: Brown Group Inc 8400 Maryland Ave Saint Louis MO 63105

RISMILLER, DAVID A., banking company executive; b. 1936. BSBA, Ohio State U., 1958; postgrad., Rutgers U., 1973. V.p. Huntington Nat. Bank, Columbus, Ohio, 1961-74; with Commerce Bank, Kansas City, Mo., 1974—, now chmn. bd. dirs. Served to capt. USNG, 1958-67. Office: Commerce Bank of Kansas City 10th & Walnut Sts Kansas City MO 64106 *

RISSE, GAIL LEE, neuropsychologist; b. Sacramento, Aug. 17, 1948; d. Edward Lee Bristo and Carol Jean (Devine) Kennedy; m. James Patrick Risse, Jan. 27, 1968 (div. 1974); m. John D. Tobin Jr., Oct. 25, 1980; children: Emily Carol, Anna Michele. BA, U. Calif., Davis, 1971; MS, U. Mass., 1974; PhD in Psychology, SUNY, Stony Brook, 1976. Lic. cons. psychologist, Minn. Staff neuropsychologist Hennepin County Med. Ctr., Mpls., 1976—; asst. prof. neurology U. Minn. Sch. Medicine, Mpls., 1976—; cons. dept. psychology Mpls. VA Hosp., 1981—. Contbr. articles to profl. jours. Grantee Nat. Inst. Neurologic and Communicative Disorders and Stroke, 1978-91. Mem. Acad. Aphasia, Internat. Neuropsychol. Soc., Am. Psychol. Assn. Democrat. Avocations: backpacking, wilderness camping.

Home: 2733 Upton Ave S Minneapolis MN 55416 Office: Hennepin County Med Ctr Dept Neurology AB 823 701 Park Ave S Minneapolis MN 55415

RIST, PHILIP RANDALL, management consultant; b. Cleve., Sept. 15, 1956; s. Edward Louis and Josephine Elizabeth (Indriolo) R.; m. Michele Ann Mercurio Rist, Sept. 13, 1980; 1 child, Melanie Marie. BS in Econs., John Carroll U., 1974-78. Bus. mgr. Sta. WKSW-FM, Cleve., 1978-82; corp. fin. mgr. Nationwide Communications, Columbus, 1982-85; v.p., chief exec. officer Impact Resources, Columbus, 1985—. Contbr. articles to prof. jours. Mem. Broadcast Fin. Mgmt. Assn. (mgmt. info. systyem). Republican. Roman Catholic. Home: 3723 Pendlestone Columbus OH 43230 Office: Impact Resources 779 Brooksedge Blvd Columbus OH 43081

RISTUBEN, STEVEN JOHN, municipal government official; b. Winona, Minn., Jan. 7, 1944; s. Francis Vernon and Luella Isabel (Schildknecht) R.; m. JoAlice Boatright, Jan. 7, 1978; children: John, David. BA, U. Minn., 1966, MA, 1972; postgrad., U. Munich, 1971. Adminstrv. asst. Office of Mayor City of Mpls., 1974-75, admintrv. asst. budget and evaluation, 1978-79, adminstrv. asst., analyst, 1980-85, administrv. analyst, 1985-87; asst. city clk. City of Mpls., 1987—; adminstrv. asst. Dept. Human Resources City of Mpls., 1976-77. Author (book): May We Help You, 1977; co-author (books) The Historical Significance of the City Hall Courthouse, 1978, Motor Vehicle Towing, Impounding and Auctioning, 1981, Management and Operations of the Minneapolis Auditorium and Convention Center, 1985. Chmn., mem. com. Dem. Farm Labor Party, Mpls. and St. Paul, 1965—; mem. staff Mpls. City Hall Courthouse Com., 1980—; coach Youth Sports, Park and Recreation Bd., Mpls., 1986; chmn. Long Range Planning Commn., Mt. Carmel, 1983-85; mem. Northeast Planning Dist. Citizen Adv. Com., Mpls., 1978. Avocations: family activities, fishing, camping, travel, photography. Home: 3221 Garfield St NE Minneapolis MN 55418 Office: Mpls City Hall Room 304 350 S 5th St Minneapolis MN 55415

RITCHEY, DENNIS MICHAEL, financial executive; b. Columbus, Ohio, Aug. 4, 1954; s. Marianne (Holzapfel) Ritchey; m. Pamela Jo Hurley, Jan. 22, 1977; children: Brittney, Adam, Kristen. BS in Acctg., St. Joseph's Coll., Ind., 1976. CPA, Ohio. Staff acct. Arthur C. Jahn, Columbus, 1977-80; controller Scotten Dillon Tobacco Co., Gallipolis, Ohio, 1980-82; treas. Lancaster (Pa.) Leaf Tobacco Co., 1982-85; audit mgr. Hausser & Taylor, CPA, Columbus, 1985-86; chief fin. officer Hammond Electronics, Columbus, 1987—; bd. dirs. treas. O'Neil Awning Tent, Inc.; ptnr., mgr. Equity Investments. Contbr. articles to profl. jours. Baseball coach Christ the King Sch., 1987—. Mem. Am. Inst. CPA's, Ohio Soc. CPA's, Nat. Assn. CPA's. Republican. Roman Catholic. Avocations: golf, sports. Home: 870 Old Farm Rd Columbus OH 43213

RITCHEY, KENNETH WILLIAM, special education administrator; b. Washington, June 7, 1947; s. Conrad Monroe and Katherine Costance (Sheris) R.; m. Nancy Jayne Kirk, Aug. 22, 1970; children: Kirk Damon, Erin Kathryn. BS in Edn., Shippensburg U., 1969; MEd, in Spl. Edn., U. Va., 1972; MS in Ednl. Adminstrn., U. Dayton, 1980. Spl. edn. tchr. Shippensburg (Pa.) Area Sch. Dist., 1969-71; head cross country coach Shippensburg U., 1970-74; master tchr., coordinator work experience program Lincoln Intermediate Unit, New Oxford, Pa., 1971-76; adult edn. tchr. Franklin County Prison, Chambersburg, Pa., 1972-76; asst. supt. mgmt. services Montgomery County Bd. Mental Retardation and Devel. Disabilities, Dayton, Ohio, 1977-83, supt. bd., 1983—; mem. part-time faculty edn. dept. U. Dayton, 1983—; mem. community and mil. adv. com. ARC, 1986—, needs and priorities com. Human Services Levy Council, 1982-84, 87—. Former editor statewide newsletter for tchrs. and profls. in Work Experience. Vol. United Way; bd. dirs. Ohio Pub. Images, Inc. Mem. Am. Assn. Mental Deficiency, Assn. Supervision and Curriculum Devel., Am. Assn. Sch. Adminstrs., Profl. Assn. Retardation, Ohio Assn. Supts. County Bds. Mental Retardation, Supts. Assn. (exec. com.), Phi Delta Kappa. Democrat. Methodist. Home: 454 W Hudson Ave Dayton OH 45406 Office: 8114 N Main St Dayton OH 45415

RITCHIE, BONNIE LOU, psychologist; b. Pitts., Oct. 28, 1952; d. John Louis and Norma Anna (Moedinger) Schaffer; m. Sherwin Dean Ritchie, Apr. 27, 1974; children: Bethany Noël, Dirk Emerson. BA in Psychology, Wittenberg U., 1974, MA in Psychology, 1976; PhD in Psychology, Ohio State U., 1981. Lic. psychologist, Ohio. Psychologist Columbus (Ohio) Devel. Ctr., 1981-83; asst. prof. Ohio State U., Columbus, 1982-84; pvt. practice psychology Dublin, Ohio, 1984—. Mem. Am. Assn. Mental Deficiency. Home: 339 Pebble Creek Dr Dublin OH 43017 Office: 5190 Blazer Pkwy Dublin OH 43017

RITCHIE, ERIC ROBERT DAVID, materials engineering executive; b. Belfast, No. Ireland, Jan. 11, 1942; came to U.S., 1968; BME, Gen. Motors Inst., 1967; MSME, Union Coll., 1972. Registered profl. engr. Iowa, N.Y. Process engr. Gen. Motors of Can. Ltd., 1964-68; mgr. plant engring. Gen. Electric Co., Schenectady, N.Y., 1968-73, mgr. internat. facilities, 1973-78; mgr. plant engring. services John Deere Component Works, Waterloo, Iowa, 1978-85; mgr. materials engring. John Deere Component Works, Waterloo, 1985—. Active allocation panel Cedar Valley United Way, Waterloo, 1986; elder, session leader State St. Presby. Ch., Schenectady, 1972-78, Immanuel Presby. Ch., 1979-82. Mem. ASHRAE, Soc. Automotive Engrs., Am. Soc. Metals. Republican. Avocations: flying, study modern history, languages. Office: John Deere Component Works PO Box 270 Waterloo IA 50701

RITCHIE, KAREN SUE, psychiatrist; b. Louisville, Sept. 12, 1949; d. Malcolm Luther and Roberta Ann (Gossadge) R.; children: Matthew William Murphy, Megan Elizabeth Murphy. BA, Graceland Coll., 1970; MD, Ohio State U., 1973; MA, Georgetown U., 1986. Intern Mt. Carmel Hosp., Columbus, Ohio, 1973-74; resident in family practice U. Kans. Med. Ctr., Kansas City, 1974-75; resident in psychiatry U. Kans. Med. Ctr., 1977-81; emergency room physician Kansas City area hosps., 1975-77; practice medicine specializing in psychiatry Shawnee Mission, Kans., 1981-85; pres. Midwest Bioethics Ctr., Kansas City, Mo., 1985—. Mem. Am. Psychiat. Assn. Mem. Reorganized Ch. of Jesus Christ of Latter-day Saints. Office: Midwest Bioethics Ctr 1200 E 104th St #248 Kansas City MO 64131

RITCHIE, MALCOLM LUTHER, engineering psychologist; b. Desdemona, Tex., May 3, 1920; s. George Briton and Georgia March (Hinkle) R.; m. Roberta Ann Gossadge, May 30, 1947; children: Karen Sue, Jennifer Kay, William George. AA, Graceland Coll., 1947; AB, U. Calif., Berkeley, 1948, MA, 1951; PhD, U. Ill., 1953. Lic. psychologist, Ohio. Dean students Graceland Coll., Lamoni, Iowa, 1949-51; research assoc. U. Ill., Urbana, 1951-57; prof. engring. Wright State U., Dayton, Ohio, 1969-82, prof. emeritus, 1982—; pres. Ritchie Inc., Dayton, 1957—; v.p., treas. Midwest System Research Inc., Dayton, 1985—; spl. advisor FAA, 1980-82; cons. USAF, Dayton, 1974—. Contbr. nearly 100 articles to profl. jours. Served to maj. USAF, 1941-46, PTO. Fellow Human Factors Soc., Am. Psychol. Assn., AIAA (assoc.); mem. IEEE (sr.). Mem. Reorganized Ch. of Jesus Christ of Latter-day Saints. Home: 630 Brubaker Dr Dayton OH 45429 Office: Midwest Systems Research Inc 1521 Edna St Dayton OH 45431

RITCHIE, SCOTT ANDERSON, clinical psychologist; b. Cleve., Jan. 7, 1956; s. Sidney John and Lois Kathryn (Anderson) R.; m. Rhonda Lynn DeForge, Nov. 16, 1985. BA, DePauw U., 1978; MS, U. Wis., Milw., 1981, PhD, 1983. Staff psychologist Ctr. for Eating Disorders, Meth. Hosp., Madison, 1983-86; pvt. practice clin. psychology Madison, 1986—. Mem. Am. Psychol. Assn. (clin. psychology div.), Wis. Psychol. Assn., Soc. Clin. and Cons. Psychologists, Psi Chi, Sigma Xi, Lambda Chi Alpha (pres. 1973-74). Presbyterian. Avocations: swimming, travel. Office: 6425 Odana Rd Madison WI 53719

RITCHIE, WILLIAM GEORGE, manufacturing executive; b. Urbana, Ill., Aug. 18, 1954; s. Malcolm Luther and Roberta Ann (Gossadge) R.; m. Ronda Elaine Burns, Aug. 28, 1976; children: Andrea Kristine, Jessica Nicole. BA, Graceland Coll., 1975; MBA, MS, Wright State U., 1978. Planning analyst Dayton (Ohio) Power and Light Co., 1978; gen. supr. Gen. Motors Corp., Dayton, 1979—; lectr. SUNY, Brockport, 1983-84. Vice-chmn. YMCA Camp Kern, Dayton, 1986.

RITSEMA, DOUGLAS JAMES, computer programmer; b. Holland, Mich., Dec. 28, 1952; s. Herbert and Jeanne Elaine (VerBeek) R. B.A. in Math., Northwestern Coll., Orange City, Iowa, 1975; J.D., U. Iowa-Iowa City, 1978. Bar: Iowa 1979. Mem. Iowa Ho. of Reps., 1979-82; mem. Iowa Senate, 1983-86. Mem. Iowa State Bar Assn. Republican. Mem. Reformed Ch.

RITSON, SCOTT CAMPBELL, construction management consultant, real estate management and development consultant; b. New London, Conn., July 20, 1945; s. Ian Douglas and Ann Breyer (Maxwell) R.; m. Diane Kischitz, May 16, 1966 (div. Oct. 1977); children—Mark Douglas (dec.), Carrie Stewart; m. 2d, Donna Diane Nietschmann, Feb. 25, 1978. Student U. Vt., 1963-65. Field engrs. asst. Gilbane Bldg. Co., Providence, 1966-67; project control engr. Olin Corp., Stamford, Conn., 1967-73; v.p. Reed Corp., Roxbury, Conn., 1973-76; pres. Ritson & Assocs., Lake Forest, Ill., 1976—; pres. Axeman Island, Ltd., Gananoque, Ont., Can., 1978-79, v.p., 1979—, dir., 1981—; pres. Ritson, Ryan Inc., Gurnee, Ill., 1983-86. Charter mem. Congl. Adv. Com., Washington, 1982. Can. nat. sailfish champion, 1961. Mem. Internat. Assn. Profl. Planners and Schedulers (charter mem.). Clubs: Chgo. Yacht; Clayton (N.Y.) Yacht; Trident Yacht (Gananoque, Ont., Can.). Home and Office: 1084 Old Colony Rd Lake Forest IL 60045

RITTER, ARTHUR RICHARD, electrical engineer; b. Seneca Falls, N.Y., Jan. 1, 1944; s. Richard Joel and Mary Ethel (Benjamin) R.; m. Veronica Jane Buckland, Mar. 19, 1966; children: Eric, Bret, Hollie. AA, Rochester (N.Y.) Inst. Tech., 1964, BEE, 1974; MBA, Ohio U., 1982. Registered prof. engr., Ohio. Engr. Sylvania Electric, Seneca Falls, 1967-71; sr. engr. Fasco Industries Inc., Rochester, 1971-75; supr. project engring. Fasco Industries Inc., Eldon, Mo., 1975-79; supr. engring. Robbins & Myers, Gallipolis, Ohio, 1975-79; project engr. A. O. Smith, Tipp City, Ohio, 1983—; instr. Edison State Community Coll., Piqua, Ohio, 1984. Mem. IEEE (sect. chmn. 1979-83, Centennial medal 1984), Soc. Mfg. Engrs. (newsletter editor 1984-85), Accreditation Bd. Engring. and Tech. Republican. Club: Gallia Twirlers (pres. 1980-82) (Gallipolis). Avocation: square dancing. Home: 6230 Petzoldt Dr Tipp City OH 45371 Office: A O Smith 531 N Fourth St Tipp City OH 45371

RITTER, CLIFFORD LYLE, personnel manager; b. Detroit, May 7, 1947; s. Clifford Edward and Shirley Elaine (Whitsell) R.; m. Susan Tenney, Sept. 7, 1968 (div. Feb. 1979); m. Adrianne Irby, Aug. 29, 1981; 1 child, Jessica Elaine. BBA, So. Ill. U., Edwardsville, 1975. Computer operator Monsanto Co., St. Louis, 1969-75, systems analyst, 1975-79; employee relations supr. Monsanto Co., Decatur, Ala., 1979-81, tng. and communication supr., 1981-82; personnel mgr. Fisher Controls Internat., Marshalltown, Iowa, 1982-86, mgr. manpower planning, compensation, 1986—. Bd. dirs. Morgan County Mental Health Assn., Decatur, 1980-82. Served to staff sgt. USAF, 1966-69. Mem. Am. Compensation Assn., Am. Soc. Personnel Adminstrs., Marshalltown C. of C. (bd. dirs. 1986—, Pres. award 1986, pres.-elect 1987—). Republican. Lutheran. Lodges: Optimists, Rotary. Avocations: golf, reading, travel. Home: 408 Springfield Dr Marshalltown IA 50158 Office: Fisher Controls Internat Inc 205 S Center St Marshalltown IA 50158

RITTER, DAVID ALLEN, airline data processing executive; b. West Reading, Pa., Oct. 14, 1954; s. David Franklin and Marjorie A. (Long) R. BS, No. Ill. U., 1976. Programmer, analyst Continental Ill. Nat. Bank, Chgo., 1976-79; sr. cons. SRZ Services, Chgo., 1979; sr. systems analyst United Airlines, Elk Grove Village, Ill., 1979-81; pres. Progressive Mgmt. Info. Systems, Schaumburg, Ill., 1981-82; sr. planner United Airlines, Elk Grove Village, 1982—. Mem. Chgo. Area Devel. Ctr. Round Table (founder, coordinator 1984—), Pi Mu Epsilon (fellow). Methodist. Avocations: tennis, gymnastics, skiing. Office: United Airlines PO Box 66100 Chicago IL 60666

RITTER, GEORGE, cardiologist, internist; b. Detroit, Nov. 22, 1921; s. Frank Alexander and Gisela (Gottlieb) R.; m. Mary J. Coracy, Dec. 23, 1944; children—James, John, William, George Thomas, Robert. B.S., Wayne State U., 1942, M.D., 1945. Diplomate Am. Bd. Internal Medicine. Intern Detroit Gen. Hosp., 1945-46, resident Fitzsimons Gen. Hosp., Denver, 1947-48, VA Hosp., Allen Park, Mich., 1948-51; practice medicine specializing in cardiology, 1951—; mem. staff Mt. Carmel Hosp., Detroit, 1951—; mem. staff Providence Hosp., Southfield, Mich., chief, div. medicine, 1966-69, assoc. chief, div. medicine, 1969-71, chief, sect. cardiology, 1972-84, mem. exec. com., 1978-83; clin. instr. Wayne State U. Sch. Medicine, Detroit, 1956-76, clin. asst. prof., 1977—. Contbr. articles on cardiology to med. jours. Adv. mem. Oakland County Emergency Med. System, Mich., 1975-80. Served to capt. AUS, 1941-48. Fellow ACP (councilor 1984—), Am. Coll. Cardiology, Am. Heart Assn. Mich. (pres. 1981); mem. Detroit Heart Club (pres. 1967), Detroit Med. Club. Roman Catholic. Avocations; photography; travel. Home: 28420 Sunset Blvd W Lathrup Village MI 48076 Office: 28245 Southfield Rd Lathrup Village MI 48076

RITTER, LARRY RAYMOND, restaurant chain executive; b. Columbus, Ohio, Oct. 2, 1943; s. Raymond J. and Betty J. (Neutzling) R.; m. Mary Deborah DeMuth, July 1, 1972; children: Kathryn, Mary Daven. B.A., Ohio State U., 1965; M.B.A., U. Cin., 1967. Mktg. mgr. IBM, Columbus, 1967-78; exec. v.p. Rax Restaurants, Columbus, 1978-86, pres., chief operating officer, 1986—. Clubs: Scioto, Columbus Athletic (Columbus). Lodge: Rotary. Home: 4415 Langport Rd Columbus OH 43220 Office: Rax Restaurants Inc 1266 Dublin Rd Columbus OH 43220 *

RITTGARN, KENNETH LEE, construction project coordinator; b. Lexington, Nebr., May 15, 1952; s. Bob L. and Kathern H. (Arbuckel) R.; m. Gwen Jo Michel, June 10, 1972; 1 child, Nathan Lee. AA, Southeast Community Coll., 1971; student legal aspects constrn. contract, U. Wis., 1980, student constrn. and specifications, 1981. Archtl. draftsman Wilscam & Mullins, Inc., Omaha, 1972; elec. draftsman Lincoln (Nebr.) Electric System, 1972-74, constrn. project coordinator, 1975—; archtl. draftsman Thomas E. Bachtold & Assn., Lincoln, 1974-75. Instr. multimedia standard first aid ARC, Lincoln Electric System, 1979-81; instr. basic life support Am. Heart Assn., 1981-83, Instr. defensive driving program Nat. Safety Council., 1984-86. Mem. Am. Soc. Training (membership chairperson 1981-82). Presbyterian. Club: Cosmopolitan. Avocations: snow skiing, boating. Office: Lincoln Electric System PO Box 80869 Lincoln NE 68501

RIVA S., LUIS OCTAVIO, marketing company executive; b. Santiago, Dominican Republic, Mar. 9, 1949; came to U.S., 1964; s. Luis Octavio Riva Velez and Ines del Carmen (Saleta) de Riva; m. Charlene Marie, June 30, 1979; children: Teresa Marie, Johnathan Luis. BS in Psychology, U. Cin., 1971. Sales mgr. Stock Mfg., Cin., 1976-79, Ceemco, Inc., Cin., 1979-81, Internat. Micromolder, Inc., Cin., 1981-82; pres., founder Rivasal Internat., Cin., 1982—. Ordained deacon Archdiocese of Cin., 1986—; consulate Dominican Republic, Cin., 1985—; bd. dirs. Working in Neighborhoods, Cin., 1987—. Named Outstanding Ohio Naturalized Citizen, 1986. Mem. Consular Corps of Cin., Cin. C. of C. (bd. dirs. 1987—, Supplier Yr. 1985-86). Roman Catholic. Lodge: Rotary (bd. dirs. Cin. 1986—). Avocations: music, fine arts.

RIVENBARK, JAN MEREDITH, corporate executive; b. Spartanburg, S.C., Feb. 22, 1950; s. George Meredith and Audrey Isabel (Frady) R.; m. Barbara N. Newton, Sept. 25, 1976; children—Abigail, Justin, Patrick. B.S. in Math., Duke U., 1972; postgrad., Ga. State U., 1980. Mgmt. trainee Citizens & So. Nat. Bank, Atlanta, 1972, br. mgr., 1974, employee relations mgr., 1975-77, v.p. compensation, benefits, payroll and data mgmt., 1977-80; mgr. personnel First Tenn. Bank, Memphis, 1980-81; dir. compensation and benefits Hanes Group, Consol. Foods Corp. (now Sara Lee Corp.), Winston-Salem, N.C., 1981-83, exec. dir. compensation and benefits, Chgo., 1983-85—; exec. dir. corp. planning Sara Lee Corp., 1985—; dir. Health Point Preferred, Inc. Fund raiser United Way, Atlanta, 1973, Winston-Salem, 1983; active polit. campaigns 1978, 80; bd. deacons Winnetka (Ill.) Congl. Ch., 1986—. Mem. Am. Compensation Assn., (cert. compensation profl.), Am. Mgmt. Assn., Scholarship and Guidance Assn. (bd. dirs. 1986—), Alpha Tau Omega (chpt. pres. 1971-72). Republican. Home: 834 Lincoln Ave Winnetka IL 60093 Office: Sara Lee Corp Three First Nat Plaza Chicago IL 60602

RIVERA, RHONDA RAE, lawyer, educator; b. Phila., Mar. 9, 1938; d. Preston Robert and Katherine Lowe (MacSorley) Rieley; 1 child, Robert Preston. B.A. cum laude, Douglass Coll., 1959; M.Pub. Adminstrn., Syracuse U., 1960; J.D. magna cum laude, Wayne State U., 1967; cert. in urban econs. MIT, 1972. Bar: Mich. 1968, Ohio 1976, U.S. Dist. Ct. (so. dist.) Ohio 1977. Asst. prof. law Ohio State U. Law Sch., Columbus, 1976-78, assoc. prof., 1978-81, prof., 1982—, assoc. dean, 1982-86; bd. dirs. 2d Yr. Legal Writing Program, 1983—. Author: (with D.J. Whaley) Problems and Materials on Sales, 1983; also articles and revs. in legal and bus. jours. Mem. fin. com. LWV, 1971-74; lay reader St. Stephen's Episcopal Ch., Columbus, 1976—, mem. Central Ohio diocesan council, 1980-81, chancery judge So. diocese Ohio, 1982—; active Boy Scouts Am., 1976-80, Columbus Com. for Battered Women, 1979-80; pres. Stonewall Union, Columbus, 1983-84, bd. dirs. and clk., 1981—; founder Integrity Central Ohio, 1983; bd. dirs. Ohio Women Ind., 1980-82, treas., 1981-82; bd. dirs. Franklin County Legal Aid Soc., Columbus, 1983-85. Recipient Uppity Woman of Yr. award Ann Arbor chpt. NOW, 1975, Susan B. Anthony award Woman Law Students Assn. U. Mich., 1976, Evelyn Hooker Research award Gay Acad. Union, 1984, Legal Achievement award NOW Legal Def. and Edn. Fund, 1986. Mem. Am. Assn. Law Schs. (chmn. women in legal edn. sect. 1979-80, mem. sect. exec. com. 1980—, chmn. gay and lesbian legal issues sect. 1982—), Soc. Am. Law Tchrs. (mem. exec. com. of bd. govs. 1979-81, mem. bd. govs. 1978—, pres. 1984-86), ABA (mem. adv. bd. sect. individual rights and responsibilities 1979-80), Mich. Bar Assn., Ohio Bar Assn., Columbus Bar Assn., Franklin County Women Lawyers Assn., ACLU, NOW, AAUP, Nat. Lawyers Guild, Nat. Gay Task Force. Democrat. Home: 131 Price Ave Columbus OH 43201 Office: Ohio State U Law School 1659 High St Columbus OH 43210

RIVERS, DONALD LEE, marketing professional; b. Sioux City, Iowa, Feb. 10, 1943; s. Thomas Harvey and Helen Catherine (Brenner) R.; m. Robin Dee Magee, Jan. 7, 1968 (div.); m. Beverly Doss, Oct. 13, 1979; 1 child, Tiffany Rivers; 1 stepchild, Robert Brower. BS, Drake U., 1966; MA, U. Iowa, 1968. Sales rep. Holt, Rineholdt & Winston, Mpls., 1969-72; editor Holt, Rinehart & Winston, Inc., N.Y.C., 1973-76; sales rep. Rand McNally & Co., Tampa, Fla., 1972-73; editor William C. Brown Co., Dubuque, Iowa, 1976-78; sales mgr. nat. accounts Better Homes & Gardens Books, Meredith Corp., Des Moines, 1978-85, dir. nat. accounts, 1985—. Mem. Kappa Delta Pi. Republican. Avocation: jogging. Home: 4125 73d Place Urbandale IA 50322 Office: Meredith Corp 1716 Locust St Des Moines IA 50336

RIVES, STANLEY GENE, university president; b. Decatur, Ill., Sept. 27, 1930; s. James A. and Frances (Bunker) R.; m. Sandra Lou Belt, Dec. 28, 1957; children: Jacqueline Ann, Joseph Alan. B.S., Ill. State U., 1952, M.S., 1955; Ph.D., Northwestern U., 1963. Instr. W. Va. U., 1955-56, Northwestern U., 1956-58; asst. prof. Ill. State U., Normal, 1958-63; assoc. prof. Ill. State U., 1963-67; prof. Ill. State U., Normal, 1967-80, asst. dean Coll. Arts and Scis., 1968-69, Am. Council on Edn. Fellows Program, 1969-70, assoc. dean faculties, 1970-72, dean undergrad. instrn., 1972-80, dir. W.K. Kellogg Faculty and Instructional Devel. Program, 1977-80, assoc. provost, 1976-80, acting provost, 1979-80; provost, v.p. acad. affairs, prof. Eastern Ill. U., Charleston, 1981-83, pres., 1983—; vis. prof. U. Hawaii, 1963-64. Author: (with Donald Klopf) Individual Speaking Contests: Preparation for Participation, 1967, (with Gene Budig) Academic Quicksand. Trends and Issues in Higher Education, 1973, (with others) Academic Innovation: Faculty and Instructional Development at Illinois State University, 1979, The Fundamentals of Oral Interpretation, 1981; contbr. articles to profl. jours. Bd. dirs. East Cen. Ill. Devel. Corp., 1983—, Charleston Area Econ. Devel. Found., 1986—, Charleston C. of C., 1985—, Nat. Collegiate Athletic Assn. Pres.'s Commn., 1986—; trustee Nat. Debate Tournament, 1967-75. Served with U.S. Army, 1952-54. Mem. Am. Assn. State Colls. and Univs., Am. Assn. Higher Edn., Theta Alpha Phi, Pi Kappa Delta, Pi Gamma Mu. Lodge: Rotary. Home: 112 Williamsburg Charleston IL 61920 Office: Office of President Eastern Ill Univ Charleston IL 61920

RIVKIN, RICHARD ALAN, safety products company executive; b. Chgo., Oct. 13, 1947; s. Norman and Corinne (Zagorsky) R.; m. Helen Louise Low, June 26, 1971; children: Loren, Jason, Michelle. BS in Econs., U. Pa., 1969; MBA, Northwestern U., 1970. Exec. v.p. Latex Glove Co., Inc., Northbrook, Ill., 1971—; pres. Voltgard Corp., Northbrook, 1985—; mem. importers' and retailers' textile adv. com. U.S. Dept. Commerce, 1977—. Mem. various citizen adv. coms. Sch. Dists. 109, 110, Deerfield, Ill. Mem. Am. Soc. for Testing and Materials. Republican. Jewish. Avocations: photography, computers. Office: Latex Glove Co Inc 205 Huehl Rd Northbrook IL 60062

RIZOWY, CARLOS GUILLERMO, lawyer, educator, political analyst; b. Sarandi Grande, Uruguay, Mar. 5, 1949; came to U.S., 1973, naturalized, 1981; s. Gerszon and Eva (Visnia) R.; m. Charlotte Gordon, Mar. 14, 1976; 1 son, Brian Isaac. B.A., Hebrew U., Jerusalem, 1971; M.A., U. Chgo., 1975, Ph.D., 1981, J.D., Chgo. Kent Coll. Law, Ill. Inst. Tech., 1983. Bar: Ill. 1983, U.S. Dist. Ct. (no. dist.) Ill. 1983, U.S. Ct. Appeals (7th cir.) 1983. Asst. prof. polit. sci. Roosevelt U., Chgo., 1982—, chmn. dept. polit. sci., 1983-86, dir. internat. studies program, 1986—; mng. ptnr. Ray, Rizowy, Ross & Feuer, Chgo., 1983—; adj. assoc. prof. Spertus Coll. Judaica, Chgo., 1984—; weekly polit. analyst on Middle East and polit. violence issues WBEZ nat. pub. radio . Vice pres. Orgn. Children of Holocaust Survivors, Chgo., 1982; mem. community relations com. Jewish Fedn. Met. Chgo., 1983-84; mem. adv. bd., chmn. internat. affairs commn. Am. Jewish Congress, Chgo., 1983-85, chmn. subcom. for Israel, 1986—; mem. adv. bd. Chgo. Action for Soviety Jewry, 1983-85; bd. dirs. Am. Friends of Hebrew U., Chgo., 1984—, Florence Heller Jewish Community Ctr., 1986—; mem. human rights com. Anti-Defamation League, 1986. Scholar Hebrew U., 1967-72, U. Chgo., 1972-78, Hillman Found., 1978, Peter Volid Found., 1980. Mem. ABA, Ill. State Bar Assn., Chgo. Bar Assn., Assn. Trial Lawyers Am., Am. Immigration Lawyers Assn., Am. Polit. Sci. Assn., Am. Judicature Soc. Lodge: Masons. Home: 561 W Cornelia Ave Chicago IL 60657 Office: Ray Rizowy Ross & Feuer 100 N LaSalle St Chicago IL 60602

RIZZI, JOSEPH VITO, banker; b. Berwyn, Ill., Dec. 5, 1949; s. Joseph and Mary Catherine (Mancini) R.; B.S. in Commerce summa cum laude, DePaul U., 1971; M.B.A., U. Chgo., 1973; J.D. magna cum laude, U. Notre Dame, 1976; m. Candace Kunz, June 24, 1972; children—Jennifer, Joseph. Admitted to Ill. bar, 1976; law clk. to judge U.S. Dist. Ct. No. Dist. Ill., 1976-77; exec. v.p. T.B.R. Enterprises, Inc., Downers Grove, Ill., 1977-83; v.p. ABN/LaSalle Nat. Bank, Chgo., 1983—. Mem. Nat. Retail Merchants Assn., ABA, Ill. Bar Assn., Delta Epsilon Sigma. Roman Catholic. Club: Union League of Chgo. Assoc. editor Notre Dame Lawyer, 1975-76; contbr. articles to profl. publs. Home: 287 Bartram Rd Riverside IL 60546 Office: 135 S LaSalle St Room 260 Chicago IL 60690

RIZZO, ADOLFO ENRIQUE, psychiatrist; b. Buenos Aires, Mar. 2, 1930; came to U.S., 1957; married, Dec. 30, 1954. MD, Universidad de Buenos Aires, 1948-55, MD in Psychiatry, 1955-56. Diplomate Am. Bd. Psychiatry and Neurology. Intern Hosp. Penitenciario Cen., Buenos Aires, 1954-55; resident Hosp. Nat. Neuropsiquiatrico, Buenos Aires, 1955-57; resident St. Louis State Hosp., 1957-60, staff psychiatrist, 1960-62; fellow in child psychiatry St. Louis State Hosp. and Washington U., 1962-64; staff child psychiatrist St. Louis State Hosp., 1964, clin. dir. youth ctr., 1965-71, acting asst. supt., 1969; practice medicine specializing in child psychiatry St. Louis, 1971—; clin. instr. child psychiatry, Washington U., 1965-71, asst. clin. prof. 1971—; cons. child psychiatry Our Lady of Grace Clinic, St. Louis, 1965-66, child guidance clinic St. Louis County Health Dept., Clayton, Mo., 1966-74, asst. dep. dir. psychiat. services, 1975-83; cons. Spl. Sch. Dist., St. Clair County, Ill., 1971-82; clin. dir. pre-adolescent unit Weldon Spring Hosp., St. Charles, Mo., 1983-87, adolescent psychiat. unit Care Unit Hosp., St. Louis, 1987—. Author: (with E. Anthony) Adolescent Girls Who Kill or Try to Kill Their Fathers, 1973; contbr. articles to profl. jours. Fellow Am. Psychiat. Assn.; mem. Am. Acad. Child Psychiatrists, Eastern Mo. Psychiat. Assn. Office: 555 N New Ballas Creve Coeur MO 63141

RIZZO, RICHARD, psychologist; b. Detroit, Mar. 21, 1951; s. Joseph and Emma R.; m. Margaret S. Chmielewski, Sept. 8, 1973 (div. Mar. 1977); m. Judith G. Hardy, Nov. 30, 1979; children: Amanda, Elizabeth, Joseph. B, Wayne State U., 1973, postgrad.; M, Eastern Mich. U., 1977. Psychologist Wayne Ctr., Detroit, 1977-80, Mich. Human Services, Livonia, 1980-85, Bazini Psychiat. Services, Dearborn, Mich., 1980—; cons. Mich. Human Services, Livonia, 1985—, Wayne County Assn. for Retarded Citizens, Livonia, 1985—, Cruz Clinic, 1985—, Luth. Social Services, Detroit, 1986—;

instr. Henry Ford Community Coll., Dearborn, 1979—. Mem. Am. Psychol. Assn., Mich. Assn. of Profl. Psychologists. Democrat. Roman Catholic. Home: 32860 Barkley Livonia MI 48154 Office: Bazini Psychiat Services 1414 E Parklane Tower Dearborn MI 48126

ROACH, DEBRA CHARLOTTE-FEIRING, special education teacher; b. Duluth, Minn., Feb. 12, 1957; d. Robert Ernest and Mary Jane (Person) F.; m. William John Roach, July 14, 1979. B in Applied Sci., U. Minn., 1982. Nursery sch. tchr. U. Minn. Child Care, Duluth, 1983-84; spl. edn. tchr. Wash. Elemtary Sch. Ctr., Cloquet, Minn., 1984—; spl. olympics coach Cloquet Spl. Edn. Coop., 1984—; sales promotions person Camp Confidence, Brainerd, Minn., 1985—. Mem. Nat. Edn. Assn., Minn. Edn. Assn., Cloquet Edn. Assn. (exec. bd. 1986-87). Democrat. Lutheran. Home: 306 W Faribault St Duluth MN 55803 Home: Washington Elementary Sch 12th St and Doddridge Ave Cloquet MN 55720

ROACH, DENNIS LEE, elementary school teacher; b. Greensburg, Pa., Dec. 14, 1942; s. Albert Charles and Sarah (Morris) R.; m. Linda Katherine Waggoner, Mar. 21, 1975; children: Michael, Andrew. BE, California (Pa.) State Coll., 1972; MA in Ednl. Adminstrn., Ohio State U., 1975. Store mgr. G.C. Murphy & Co., Greensburg, 1958-61; enlisted USAF, 1961, advanced through grades to staff sgt., meteorologist, 1961-69, resigned, 1969; tchr. Columbus (Ohio) City Schs., 1972—; also cons. in human relations Columbus Schs., 1973—. Decorated Vietnam Air Force Honor Medal; recipient Presdl. Citation, Washington, 1967. Mem. Nat. Edn. Assn., Ohio Edn. Assn., Columbus Edn. Assn. Republican. Methodist. Avocations: building miniatures, writing prose, landscaping, flying. Home: 2479 Cranford Rd Columbus OH 43221 Office: Columbus Pub Schs 419 E 19th St Columbus OH 43201

ROACH, EUGENE GAYLE, psychiatrist, author, educator; b. Louisville, Jan. 12, 1932; s. Charles Herndon Roach and Mary (Conn) Gaines; m. Mildred Moorhouse, 1951; children—Charles, Glenna. B.S., U. Louisville, 1955, M.A., 1957; Ph.D., Purdue U., 1962; M.D., Ind. U., 1972. Diplomate Am. Bd. Psychiatry and Neurology. Resident in psychiatry Jackson Meml. Hosp., Miami, Fla., Ind. U. Med. Ctr., Indpls.; assoc. prof. Ind. U., Indpls., 1962-68, 76-80; dir. clin. psychiatry St. Francis Hosp. Ctr., Beech Grove, Ind., 1980-87; med. dir. The Anderson Ctr. of St. John's, 1987—; cons. to minister of Social Affairs Cairo, Egypt, 1966-67. Author: Purdue Perceptual Motor Survey, 1967. Bd. dirs. Am. Cancer Soc., 1980—; vice chmn. adv. bd. Salvation Army; v.p. fin. Crossroads of Am. council Boy Scouts Am. Fulbright scholar, 1966-67. Mem. AMA, Ind. State Med. Assn. (legis. commr. 1983—), Marion County Med. Soc., Am. Psychiat. Assn. Republican. Presbyterian. Clubs: Columbia Skyline (Indpls.). Avocations: photography, art collecting. Office: Anderson Ctr of St John's 2210 Jackson St Anderson IN 46014

ROACH, JOHN ROBERT, archbishop; b. Prior Lake, Minn., July 31, 1921; s. Simon J. and Mary (Regan) R. B.A., St. Paul Sem., 1946; M.A., U. Minn., 1957; L.H.D. (hon.), Gustavus Adolphus Coll., St. Mary's Coll., St. Xavier U., Villanova U. Ordained priest Roman Catholic Ch., 1946; instr. St. Thomas Acad., 1946-50, headmaster, 1951-68; named domestic prelate 1966; rector St. John Vianney Sem., 1968-71; aux. bishop St. Paul and Mpls., 1971; consecrated bishop 1971; pastor St. Charles Borromeo Ch., Mpls., 1971-73, St. Cecilia Ch., St. Paul, 1973-75; archbishop of St. Paul, 1975—; appointed vicar for parishes, 1971, vicar for clergy, 1972—; Episc. moderator Nat. Apostolate for Mentally Retarded, 1974; Mem. Priests Senate, 1968-72; pres. Priests Senate and Presbytery, 1970; chmn. Com. on Accreditation Pvt. Schs. in Minn., 1952-57; mem. adv. com. Coll. Entrance Exam. Bd., 1964; Episc. mem. Bishops and Pres.'s Com.; chmn. Bishops Com. to Oversee Implementation of the Call to Action Program, 1979-80; chmn. priestly formation com.; mem. Cath. Charity Bd. Trustee St. Paul Sem., 1971—; now chmn.; trustee Cath. U. Am., 1978-81, Coll. St. Catherine; chmn. bd. trustees St. Thomas Acad., Coll. St. Thomas, St. John Vianney Sem.; v.p. Nat. Conf. Cath. Bishops, 1977-80, pres., 1980-83, chmn. ad hoc com. on call to action, 1977. Mem. Minn. Cath. Edn. Assn. (past pres.), Assn. Mil. Colls. and Schs. U.S. (past pres.), North Central Assn. Colls. and Secondary Schs. (past mem. advisory com.), Am. Council Edn. (del. 1963-65), Nat. Conf. Cath. Bishops (adminstrv. com., priestly formation com., chmn. vocations com.), U.S. Cath. Conf., Nat. Cath. Edn. Assn. (chmn. bd. dirs.), Nat. Cath. Rural Life Conf. (chmn. rask force on food and agr., pres.). Office: Chancery Office 226 Summit Ave Saint Paul MN 55102

ROAT, GARY WAYNE, neurologist; b. Flint, Mich., Jan. 1, 1937; s. Doyle Wayne and Margaret Rose (Deitering) R.; m. Dolores Mary Wascha, Dec. 26, 1959; children—Randy J., Susan T., Dennis W., Lauree L. A.Bus., Mott Community Coll., 1956; B.A., U. Mich., 1958; D.O., Kirksville Coll. Osteo. Medicine, 1963. Diplomate Am. Osteo. Bd. Neurology and Psychiatry; cert. Am. Soc. Neuroimaging and Computerized Tomography; lic. osteo. physician, Mich., Fla., Mo. Rotating intern Flint Oste. Hosp., Mich., 1963-64; gen. practice osteo. medicine, Flint, 1964-69; resident in internal medicine Flint Osteo. Hosp., 1969-71; resident in neurology St. Louis U. Med. Sch., 1971-74; practice osteo. medicine specializing in neurology, Flint, 1974—; mem. staff Flint Osteo. Hosp., lab. dir. Scanner Diagnostic Assocs., 1983-85; mem. staff Genesee Meml. Hosp., Hurley Med. Ctr.; asst. clin. prof. Mich. State U. Med. Sch., East Lansing, 1975—; chmn. bd. Smoke Rise Vacation Resort, Davison, Mich., 1982-84; owner Flint Neurosci. Ctr., 1983—; reviewer Health Care Analysis, Inc., Med. Quality Found.; dir. Health Plus of Mich., 1981—, mem. fin. com., 1984—; mem. care/quality/cost com. Genesee Health Care, 1984—, treas., 1984—. Contbr. articles to profl. jours. Bd. dirs. Genesee Health Found.; donor St. Francis Prayer Ctr., Flint, 1980-84. Recipient award Optimist Club, 1954. Mem. Am. Neurol. Assn., Am. Acad. Neurology, Am. Osteo. Assn., Am. Coll. Osteo. Neuropsychiatry, Mich. Osteo. Soc. Physicians and Surgeons, Genesee County Osteo. Assn., Flint Neurosci. Assn., Mich. Neurol. Assn., Am. Soc. Neuropsychiatrists, Am. Soc. Neuroimaging. Roman Catholic. Avocations: flying; photography; computers; karate. Office: G3239 Beecher Rd Flint MI 48504

ROBASKA, P(HILIP) GORDON, telephone enclosures company executive; b. Hammond, Ind., Mar. 1, 1936; s. P.F. and Florence Robaska; m. June Leddy, Dec. 20, 1958; children: P. Gordon Jr., Scott L., David A. AB, Northwestern U., 1957, MA, 1960; MBA, U. Chgo., 1967. Pres. Zenith Taiwan Corp., Taipei, 1970-74; resident officer, v.p. Zenith Radio Corp. of Mo., Springfield, 1974-75; pres. Geeco, Inc., St. Joseph, Mo., 1976-81; v.p. ops. Acoustics Devel. Corp., ADCO, Northbrook, Ill., 1981-84; pres. Acoustics Devel. Corp., St. Joseph, 1984—. Republican. Episcopalian. Lodge: Rotary. Home: 5025 Briarwood Ln Saint Joseph MO 64506 Office: Acoustics Devel Corp 3800 S 48th Terr Saint Joseph MO 64503

ROBBE, GARY LEE, elementary school educator; b. Cin., Jan. 1, 1953; s. Richard Joseph and Ona Frances (Sloan) R.; m. Marcy Faye Silver, July 6, 1985; 1 child, Zachary Lee. BA, U. Cin., 1975, MEd, 1977. Instr. edn. Sinte Gleska Coll., Rosebud, S.D., 1977-78; spl. educator Green Bay (Wis.) Pub. Schs., 1978-80, Covington (Ky.) Pub. Schs., 1980-81, Cin. Pub. Schs., 1981—; pvt. tutor/edn. cons., Cin., 1980—. BEH fellow, 1976. Mem. Cin. Fedn. Tchrs. Avocations: creative writing, short fiction. Home: 3145 Ferguson Rd Cincinnati OH 45211 Office: The Childrens Home Sch 5051 Duck Creek Rd Cincinnati OH 45227

ROBBINS, ANDREW FERDINAND, JR., ophthalmologist; b. Bklyn., Dec. 28, 1947; s. Andrew F. and Fortune S. (Savarese) R.; m. Lauren Lahmann, May 22, 1976. B.S. in Natural Scis., Xavier U., Cin., 1969; M.D., U. Cin., 1973. Diplomate Am. Bd. Ophthalmology. Intern, Good Samaritan Hosp., Cin., 1973-74; resident U. Cin. Hosp., 1974-77; ptnr. Hyde Park Eye Physicians and Surgeons, Cin., 1977—; chmn. dept. ophthalmology Good Samaritan Hosp., Cin., 1983—, exec. com., 1987—; instr. dept. family practice U. Cin., 1983—; dir. internat. and regional seminars in field. Contbr. articles to profl. pubs. Fellow Am. Acad. Ophthalmology, Internat. Coll. Surgeons, ACS; mem. Am. Intraocular Implant Soc., Ohio State Med. Soc., Cin. Acad. Medicine (jud. com. 1984—, vice chmn. jud. com. 1986—), Alpha Sigma Nu. Republican. Roman Catholic. Club: Hon. Order Ky. Cols. Avocation: Dale Carnegie Motivation Course. Office: Hyde Park Eye Physicians and Surgeons Inc 3710 Paxton Ave Cincinnati OH 45209

ROBBINS, DARRYL ANDREW, pediatrician; b. Modesto, Calif., Sept. 16, 1945; s. Jerome and Grace (Bass) R.; m. Harriette Lee Eisenberg, June 12, 1971; children: Jennifer Lynn, Julie Ellen, Allison Beth. BS, Dickinson Coll., 1967; DO, Phila. Coll. Osteo. Medicine, 1971. Diplomate Am. Bd. Pediatrics. Intern Doctor's Hosp., Columbus, Ohio, 1971-72; resident in pediatrics Children's Hosp. Med. Ctr., Cin., 1972-75; practice medicine specializing in pediatrics Columbus, 1975—; vice chairperson Diocesan Child Guidance Ctr., Columbus, 1986, bd. dirs., 1983—; mem. genetics services adv. com. Ohio Dept. Health, 1978—. Recipient Samuel Dalinsky Meml. award for Outstanding Graduating Resident Cin. Children's Hosp., 1975; named Pediatrician of Yr., Columbus Children's Hosp., 1982. Fellow Am. Acad. Pediatrics (mem. fetus and newborn com. Ohio chpt.); mem. Am. Osteo. Assn. Jewish. Home: 953 Old Farm Rd Columbus OH 43213 Office: 3341 E Livingston Ave Columbus OH 43227

ROBBINS, FREDERICK CHAPMAN, physician, emeritus medical school dean; b. Auburn, Ala., Aug. 25, 1916; s. William J. and Christine (Chapman) R.; m. Alice Havemeyer Northrop, June 19, 1948; children: Alice, Louise. A.B., U. Mo., 1936, B.S., 1938; M.D., Harvard U., 1940; D.Sc. (hon.), John Carroll U., 1955, U. Mo., 1958; D.Sci. (hon.), U. N.C., 1979, Tufts U., 1983, Med. Coll. Ohio, 1983; LL.D., U. N.Mex., 1968. Diplomate Am. Bd. Pediatrics. Sr. fellow virus disease NRC, 1948-50; staff research div. infectious diseases Children's Hosp., Boston, 1948-50, assoc. physician, assoc. dir. isolation service, asso. research div. infectious diseases, 1950-52; instr., assoc. in pediatrics Harvard Med. Sch., 1950-52; dir. dept. pediatrics and contagious diseases Cleve. Met. Gen. Hosp., 1952-66; prof. pediatrics Case-Western Res. U., 1952-80, dean Sch. Medicine, 1966-80, Univ prof., dean emeritus, 1980—, Univ. prof. emeritus, 1987—; pres. Inst. Medicine, Nat. Acad. Scis., 1980-85; vis. scientist Donner Lab., U. Calif., 1963-64. Served as maj. AUS, 1942-46; chief virus and rickettsial disease sect. 15th Med. Gen. Lab. investigations infectious hepatitis, typhus fever and Q fever. Decorated Bronze Star, 1945; recipient 1st Mead Johnson prize application tissue culture methods to study of viral infections, 1953; co-recipient Nobel prize in physiology and medicine, 1954; Med. Mut. Honor Award for, 1969; Ohio Gov.'s award, 1971. Mem. Nat. Acad. Scis., Am. Acad. Arts and Scis., Am. Soc. Clin. Investigation (emeritus mem.), Am. Acad. Pediatrics, Soc. Pediatric Research (pres. 1961-62, emeritus mem.), Am. Pediatric Soc., Am. Philos. Soc., Phi Beta Kappa, Sigma Xi, Phi Gamma Delta. Office: Case Western Res U Sch Medicine 2119 Abington Rd Cleveland OH 44106 also: Case Western Reserve Univ 2119 Abirgdon Rd Cleveland OH 44106

ROBBINS, GERALD HENRY, radio broadcast executive, consultant; b. Mpls., Feb. 24, 1931; s. Arthur E. and Anna M. (Noden) R.; m. Jane Eileen Carlson, Nov. 3, 1956. Student Brown Inst. Broadcasting and Electronics, 1952-53. Radio announcer Sta. KRBA, Lufkin, Tex., sales rep./announcer Sta. KTRF, Thief River Falls, Minns., 1954-56; sales rep. Sta. KTOE, Mankato, Minn., 1956-59; sales mgr. Sta. KAGE, Winona, Minn., 1959-60; gen. mgr. Sta. KXGN TV/Radio, Glendive, Mont., 1960-67; pres., gen. mgr. WCMP Broadcasting Co., Pine City, Minn., 1967—; owner Profit Builder, pub. speaking/seminar co.; broadcasting cons. Served with U.S. Army, 1951-53; Korea. Decorated Purple Heart; recipient Ambassador of Good Will award Lions Internat., 1977; Internat. Pres. awards, 1974-81; named Citizen of Yr., Pine City C. of C., 1977; Melvin Jones fellow. Mem. Nat. Speakers Assn., Internat. Platform Assn., Nat. Radio Broadcasters Assn., Minn. Broadcasters Assn. (v.p.). Republican. Lutheran. Club: Lions (internat. dir. 1975-77). Office: Rural Rt 2 Pine City MN 55063

ROBBINS, HARRY CHRISTIAN, plant superintendent; b. Le Mars, Iowa, Feb. 27, 1941; s. Chester Ralph and Mildred Myrtle (Schultz) R.; m. Madeline Rose Mochel, May 15, 1965; children: Alyse Elizabeth, Mary Lynn, Christian Paul. BS, U. Wis., Whitewater, 1974. Plant operator Varney Chem. Co., Janesville, Wis., 1963-65; foreman No. Petrochemical Co., Janesville, 1965-69; asst. plant supt. Ashland Oil Corp., Janesville, 1969-75; plant supt. Sherex Chem. Co., Janesville, 1975—; cons. Singer Labs., Houston, 1980—. Council pres. Good Shepherd Luth. Ch., Janesville, 1980-85. Served to sgt. Army N.G., 1963-69. Recipient Sharp Shooter award U.S. Army, Fort Knox, Ky., 1963, Gov.'s Spl. Award, Madison, Wis., 1966; named Outstanding Wis. Nat. Guardsman Milw. Journal, 1966. Lutheran. Lodge: Optimist ("Just Say No" com. 1987). Avocations: rose gardening, golf, reading. Office: Sherex Chem Co 2001 Afton Rd Janesville WI 53545

ROBBINS, KENNETH CHARLES, health care executive, lawyer; b. Boston, Oct. 26, 1942; s. Charles F. and Dorothy Rae (Gillis) R.; m. Marjorie Helen Dumas, June 25, 1965; children—Kimberly, Kerri, Susan. A.B., U. Mass., 1965; J.D., Suffolk U., 1973. Bar: Mass. 1973, Ill. 1976. Research dir. Com. Govt. Regulations Mass. Legislature, 1972-73, legal counsel, staff dir., 1973-76; ptnr. Pearlman & Robbins, 1974-76; dir. med.-legal affairs Ill. Hosp. Assn., Naperville, 1976-79, v.p., asst. gen. counsel, 1979-82, pres., 1983—; exec. dir. Ill. State Cost Containment Com., 1978, lectr. health care law Northwestern U. Served to capt. USAF, 1965-70; lt. col. Ill. Air N.G., 1976—. Mem. ABA, Ill. State Bar Assn., Am. Acad. Hosp. Attys., Ill. Assn. Hosp. Attys. (state hosp. assn. execs. forum), N.G. Assn. U.S., N.G. Assn. Ill. Roman Catholic. Clubs: University, Econ. (Chgo.). Office: Ill Hosp Assn 1151 E Warrenville Rd Naperville IL 60566

ROBBINS, ROBERT JOHN, biologist, educator; b. Niles, Mich., May 10, 1944; s. Robert Addison and Aura M. (McKinney) R.; m. Coreen Amelia Kelly, July 1, 1984. AB, Stanford U., 1966; BS, Mich. State U., 1973, MS, 1974, PhD, 1977. Asst. prof. Mich. State U., East Lansing, 1979-82, assoc. prof., 1982—; postdoctoral researcher U. Calif., Davis, 1978-79. Author: Genetics: A Brief Introduction, 1981, The Sweep of Life, 1983, Chordate Development, 1985. Fellow NSF, U. Calif., Davis, 1978. Mem. Genetics Soc. Am., Am. Soc. Microbiology. Home: 1015 Morgan St Lansing MI 48912 Office: Mich State U Biol Sci Program East Lansing MI 48824

ROBE, MATTHEW WILLIAM, accountant; b. Rapids City, S.D., Apr. 22, 1961; s. John Leo and Joanne Patricia (Brennan) R. BS in Acctg., N.E. Mo. State U., 1984. CPA, Mo. Semi-sr. auditor Mo. State Auditor's Office, Jefferson City, 1984-87; internal auditor Black & Veatch, Kansas City, Mo., 1987—. Mem. Am. Inst. CPA's, Mo. Soc. CPA's, Phi Mu Alpha, Phi Lambda Chi (sec. Kirksville, Mo. 1981-83), Lambda Alumni Assn. (treas. Kirksville 1984—). Roman Catholic. Avocations: swimming, running, classical flute playing.

ROBERSON, CAROLYN A., educator; b. McComb, Miss., Jan. 12, 1950; d. Vernon and Christine (Alexander) Williams; m. Sylvester Roberson, June 17, 1975; 1 child, Carol Syleste. BS, Abilene Christian U., 1972; MS with honors, Chgo. State U., 1978, MS in Guidance and Counseling, 1987; postgrad. in policy studies, Loyola U., Chgo., 1985—. Cert. spl. educator, bus. educator, phys. edn. instr. Tchr. phys. edn. and health Waukegan (Ill.) Sch. Dist., 1972-75; phys. edn. coordinator, asst. activities dir. Hamlin House, Chgo., 1975-76; mental health therapist Ridgeway Hosp., Chgo., 1976-77; adaptive phys. tchr. phys. therapy dept. Spalding High Sch., Chgo., 1977-78; tchr. emotionally and mentally handicapped Blue Island (Ill.) Sch. Dist., 1978-79; tchr. emotionally disturbed Ray Graham Assn., Des Plaines, Ill., 1980; tchr. EMH, TMH, phys. edn., health Spalding High Sch., Chgo., 1980—, acting asst. prin. in charge of discipline, 1983-84, discipline counselor, 1984-85, sch. disciplinarian PE Dept. Spalding High Sch., 1985-86. Grantee for teaching sci. to handicapped U. Chgo., 1984-85; recipient Inst. Psychoanalysis Scholarship award, 1982-83, 83-84, Grad. Scholarship award Chgo. State U., 1986-87. Mem. Assn. Supervision and Curriculum Devel., Council of Basic Edn., Council of Exceptional Children, Ill. Assn. Health, Phys. Edn. and Recreation, NAACP, Phi Delta Kappa. Mem. Ch. of Christ. Home: 10216 S LaFayette St Chicago IL 60628 Office: 1628 W Washington St Chicago IL 60612

ROBERTS, ARTHUR STANLEY, JR., systems company executive, dentist; b. Indpls., Jan. 21, 1946; s. Arthur Stanley and Rosemary Jane (Morris) R.; m. Karen Sue Strawn, Aug. 17, 1968; children—Meredith Holly, Arthur Stanley. Student Earlham Coll., 1964-65, Ind. U., 1965-67, postgrad., 1978-80; D.D.S., Ind. U.-Indpls., 1971. Intern William Beaumont Gen. Hosp., Ft. Bliss, Tex., 1971-72; staff dental officer USARSUPTHAI, Bangkok, Thailand, 1972-73; gen. practice dentistry, Rushville, Ind., 1973-81; pres. Geneva Cons., Shelbyville, Ind., 1981-83; chmn., founder, chief exec. officer Alpha Systems Resource Co., Shelbyville, 1983-86; pres. Mgmt. Research Corp., 1986—; research assoc. oral facial genetics Ind. U. Med. Ctr., Indpls., 1981-83; faculty extramural Ind. U. Med. Ctr., Indpls., 1979-85. Co-inventor pill mill. Acad. Gen. Dentistry fellow, 1980. Fellow Royal Soc. Health, Info. Industry Assn., Acad. Gen. Dentistry Clubs: Ind. Rugby, Columbia (Indpls.) Avocations: skiing; anthropology; sailing. Home: 203 W Washington St Shelbyville IN 46176

ROBERTS, BARBARA ANN, telephone company official; b. Milw., Feb. 21, 1929; d. Andrew Max and Ersilia (Celia) Gertrude (Comparoni) Maglio; student Milw. public schs.; m. Albert Lloyd Roberts, Sept. 3, 1949; children—Marybeth, Bradley J., David L. With Wis. Telephone Co., Milw., 1961—, now group mgr. operator services; v.p., sec. Sports Dome, Inc. Mem. Bus. and Profl. Women Milw. (pres. 1979-81), Wis. Bus. and Profl. Women (dist. dir. Eastern Dist. 8 1981-82). Home: 8411 W Cheyenne St Milwaukee WI 53224 Office: 2140 Davidson Rd Waukesha WI 53186

ROBERTS, BEVERLY RANDOLPH, accounting executive; b. Alexandria, La., Jan. 28, 1948; d. William Cullen and Elizabeth Rose (Madden) R.; 1 child, Gavin. BA, Lawrence U., 1969; postgrad., Drake U., 1975. CPA, Iowa. Staff acct. McGladrey & Hendrickson, Des Moines, 1975-77; sr. auditor Deloitte, Haskins & Sells, Des Moines, 1977-79; audit mgr. Coopers & Lybrand, Denver, 1979-84; dir. corp. acctg. Tennant Co., Mpls., 1985—. Fin. advisor Faith Presbyn. Ch. Minnetonka, Minn. Mem. Am. Inst. CPA's. Avocations: stained glass windows, running, downhill skiing. Home: 3365 Shavers Lake Rd Deephaven MN 55391 Office: Tennant Co PO Box 1452 Minneapolis MN 55440

ROBERTS, BURNELL RICHARD, paper company executive; b. Wis., May 6, 1927; s. Roy C. and Ann (Jones) R.; m. Karen H. Ragatz, Aug. 8, 1953; children: Evan, Kari, Paul, Nancy. B.B.A., U. Wis., 1950; M.B.A., Harvard U., 1957. With Bendix Aviation Corp., 1953-58; with Gen. Tire & Rubber Co., 1957-62; treas., controller subsidiary A.M. Byers Co., Pitts., 1962-66; asst. to exec. v.p. Mead Corp., Dayton, Ohio, 1966-68, controller, v.p. finance, 1968-71; group v.p., pres. Mchts. group div. Mead Corp., Dayton, Ohio, 1971-74, Mead Paper div. Mead Corp., Dayton, Ohio, from 1974; sr. v.p. Mead Corp., 1979-81, pres., from 1981, chmn., chief exec. officer, 1982—, also dir.; dir. Nat. City Bank, Cleve., The Ayco Fund, Albany, N.Y., Ga. Kraft Co., Northwood Pulp & Paper, Prince George, B.C., Brunswick Pulp & Paper, Ga., Armco Corp., Perkins-Elmer, Philips Industries, DPL, Inc. Trustee Kenyon Coll., Sinclair Community Coll., Bus. Roundtable, Aspen Inst. Served with USNR, 1944-46. Mem. Fin. Execs. Inst., Am. Paper Inst. (chmn.). Office: Mead Corp Courthouse Plaza NE Dayton OH 45463

ROBERTS, CHARLES PATRICK, congressman; b. Topeka, Kans., Apr. 20, 1936; m. Franki Fann, 1970; children: David, Ashleigh, Anne-Wesley. B.A., Kans. State U., 1958. Pub. Litchfield Park, Ariz., 1962-67; adminstrv. asst. U.S. Senator Frank Carlson, 1967-68, U.S. Congressman Keith Sebelius, 1968-80; mem. 97th-98th Congresses, 1980—. Served with USMC, 1958-62. Office: Room 1314 Longworth House Office Bldg Washington DC 20515 *

ROBERTS, CRAIG MICHAEL, physician assistant; b. Madison, Wis., July 9, 1958; s. Warren Wallace and Olive Margaret (Faber) R. BS, U. Wis., 1981. Physician asst. La Clinica de los Campesinos, Wild Rose, Wis., 1981, Univ. Health Service, Madison, Wis., 1983—. Named one of Outstanding Young Men of Am., 1985. Fellow Wis. Acad. Physician Assts., Am. Venereal Disease Assn.; mem. Wis. Coll. Health Assn. Home: 2202 Kendall Ave Madison WI 53705 Office: Univ Health Service 1552 University Ave Madison WI 53706

ROBERTS, DONALD EUGENE, sports enterprise director; b. Pike County, Ohio, July 8, 1943; s. Howard Bruce and Marjorie Ann (Reno) R.; children: Sheila, Susan, Donnie. BS, Ohio U., 1968; MS, Ind. State U., 1970. Cert. elem. tchr., Ohio; cert. guidance counselor. Guidance counselor Scioto Valley Schs., Pike County, Ohio, 1970-75; supt. Pike County Schs., 1975-79; sec., treas. Nat. Horseshoe Pitching Assn., 1976—; nat. dir. ops. Sports Enterprises Inc., Munroe Falls, Ohio, 1986—. Mem. Ohio Horseshoe Assn. (Ohio of Hall Fame 1986), Nat. Horseshoe Pitchers Am. (Stokes award 1978, Hall of Fame 1986), Pike County Horseshoe Club (pres., Hall of Fame 1979). Home: PO Box 278 Munroe Falls OH 44262 Office: Sports Enterprises Inc 34 Munroe Falls Ave Munroe Falls OH 44262

ROBERTS, FLOYD K., publishing executive; b. Danville, Ill., Mar. 4, 1939; s. Ralph Charles and Sarah Irene (Brennen) R.; m. Karen Lee Bossert, Sept. 1, 1962; children: S. Keith and Brennen K. BS, U. Ill., 1964. Mktg. services mgr. Farm Jour., Phila., 1967-74; area sales mgr. A.V. Smith Harestore, Arlington Heights, Ill., 1974-78; v.p., ptnr. Freeport (Ill.) Builders, 1979-80; dir. communications Argiking, Fulton, Ill., 1981-82; pub. Johnson Hill Press, Ft. Atkinson, Wis., 1982-85; pres., founder Corp. Communications Corp., Rockford, Ill., 1985—; founder Corp. Health mag., 1985. Pres., founder Hinswood Homeowners Assn., Darrien, Ill., 1968; pres. St. John's United Ch. Christ Council, Freeport, 1983-84, chmn. long range planning com., 1986. Served with U.S. Army, 1960-62. Mem. Hinsdale (Ill.) Jaycees (bd. dirs. 1973, Outstanding First Yr. Mem. award 1965). Lodge: Masons. Avocations: reading, consulting. Home: 1439 S Deming Ave Freeport IL 61032 Office: Corp Communications Corp 333 E State Rockford IL 61104

ROBERTS, HELEN WYVONE, city official; b. Kirksville, Mo., Jan. 9, 1934; d. William Lawrence and Lectie Beryl (Boley) Chitwood; m. Philip C. Roberts, Jan. 9, 1952 (div. 1976); children—Christy, Cheryl, Gayla. Secretarial degree Chillicothe Bus. Sch., 1951; B.S., Lindenwood Coll., 1983. Exec. sec. McDonnel-Douglas Aircraft, St. Louis, 1962-65, Transit Homes, Inc., Greenville, S.C., 1970-76; exec. sec. City of St. Peters, Mo., 1976-79, asst. planning and devel. coordinator, 1979-81, adminstrv. asst. to city adminstr., 1981-84, purchasing agt., 1984, asst. to city adminstr., 85—. Mem. Nat. Assn. Female Execs., Internat. Cities Mgmt. Assn., Am. Pub. Works Assn., Am. Mgmt. Assn., Am. Bus. Women's Assn., Mo. Indsl. Devel. Council, Alpha Sigma Tau. Baptist. Avocations: horseback riding; sports; reading. Home: 329 Keran St Saint Charles MO 63301 Office: City of St Peters PO Box 9 Saint Peters MO 63376

ROBERTS, JAMES ALFRED, dentist; b. New Rochelle, N.Y., June 29, 1941; s. Lawrence David and Margaret (Vernier) R.; m. Rachel Sherwood, Apr. 1, 1966; children: Anne Margaret, Edward Hammond, Emily Allen. BS, Furman U., 1960; D of Med. Dentistry, U. Pa., 1967. Gen. practice dentistry Auburn, Ind., 1968—; mem. staff Ft. Wayne (Ind.) Hosp. and Tng. Ctr., 1968. Mem. ADA, Isaac Knapp Dist. Soc., Quarter Century Wireless Assn., Auburn C. of C., Delta Sigma Delta, Pi Kappa Phi. Republican. Presbyterian. Club: Greenhurst (Auburn) County. Lodge: Rotary (pres. 1986). Avocations: flying, amateur radio. Home: 410 Hawthorne Place Auburn IN 46706 Office: 102 N Clark St Auburn IN 46706

ROBERTS, JAMES ALLEN, obstetrician-gynecologist; b. Milw., May 6, 1947; s. John A. and Florence E. (Heil) R.; m. Rosemary Frankow. BA, UCLA, 1969; MD, Med. Coll. Wis., 1973. Cert. div. Gynecol. Oncology Am. Bd. Ob-Gyn. Acting asst. prof. ob-gyn UCLA, 1977-79; asst. prof. U. Iowa, Iowa City, 1979-80; asst. prof. U. Mich., Ann Arbor, 1980-86, assoc. prof., 1986—, dir. gynecol. oncology, 1986—; cons. Ann Arbor VA Hosp., 1981—, Oakwood Hosp., Dearborn, Mich., 1982—. Contbr. articles to profl. jours.; chpts. to books. Asst. med. advisor Boy Scouts Am., Ann Arbor, 1986. Fellow Am. Cancer Soc., 1977-79, 82-84. Fellow ACS, Am. Coll. Ob-Gyn; mem. Soc. Gynecol. Oncologists, Western Assn. Gynecologic Oncologists (sec.-treas. 1986—). Club: Travis Pointe County (Ann Arbor). Office: U Mich Dept Ob-Gyn 1500 E Medical Center Dr Ann Arbor MI 48109

ROBERTS, JAMES OWEN, financial planning executive, consultant; b. Madison, Wis., Aug. 19, 1930; s. John William and Sada (Buckmaster) R.; m. Georgianna Timmons, Jan. 30, 1954; children—Stephen, Susan, Ellen, Timmons. B.S., Ohio State U., 1952; M.B.A., Case Western Res. U., 1970. Sales trainee Owens-Ill., Inc., Toledo, 1952, 54-55, salesman, Atlanta, 1955-58, N.Y.C., 1958-62, food div. mgr., N.Y.C. and Cleve., 1963-71, br. mgr., 1966-71; mgr. corp. fin. Stone & Webster Securities Corp., Cleve., 1971-74; regional dir. Mgmt. Planning, Inc., Cleve., 1976-80, v.p., 1980-86, sr. v.p., 1986, pres., 1986—; lectr. in field. Contbr. articles to profl. jours. Chmn. bd. trustees Fairmount Presbyn. Ch., Cleve., 1984; trustee Soc. for the Blind, Cleve., 1983-86, Ohio Motorists Assn., 1985—; pres. Children's Services,

1986—; trustee Great Lakes Theater . Named Gem of a Clevelander, Cleve. Press, 1981. Mem. Fin. Analysts Fedn., Cleve. Soc. Security Analysts. Republican. Club: Cleve. Skating, Nassau (Princeton, N.J.). Avocations: sailing; skiing; hiking; photography. Home: 2323 Stillman Rd Cleveland Heights OH 44118 Office: Mgmt Planning Inc 545 Hanna Bldg Cleveland OH 44115 also: 101 Poor Farm Rd Princeton NJ 03125

ROBERTS, KAREN LOUISE, educator; b. Minco, Okla., Nov. 28, 1948; d. Hugh Jenkins and Alene Berniece (Anthony) McDaniel; m. Thomas Carrol Roberts, Dec. 21, 1968; children: Gregory Charles, Chad Daniel. BS, Kans. State U., Manhattan, 1970, MS, 1977, postgrad., 1981-83; postgrad. Emporia State U., 1980-86. Home economist Harper's Fabrics, Prairie Village, Kans., 1975-78; home economist, microwave tchr. Zenith Distbg. Corp., Lenexa, Kans., 1975-77; tchr. home econs. Paola High sch. (Kans.), 1979-82; instr. home econs. Mid-America Nazarene Coll., Olathe, Kans., 1982—. Den mother, Cub Scouts, 1982; chmn. Spl. Edn. Parent Adv. Council, 1981-84; coordinator com. First United Meth. Concerns, 1981-86. Mem. NEA, Am. Assn. Gifted Children, Kans. Assn. for Gifted Children, Council for Exceptional Children, Phi Upsilon Omicron. Republican. Home: 311 N Mesquite Olathe KS 66061 Office: USD 230 Spring Hill KS 66083

ROBERTS, KEITH EDWARD, SR., lawyer; b. White Hall, Ill., Apr. 27, 1928; s. Victor Harold and Ruby Harriet (Kelsey) R.; m. Marthan Dusch, Sept. 4, 1954; 1 son, Keith Edward. Student, Western Ill. U., 1946-47, George Washington U., 1947-48; B.S., U. Ill., 1951, J.D., 1953. Bar: Ill. 1953, U.S. Dist. Ct. (no. dist.) Ill. 1957, U.S. Dist. Ct. (so. dist.) Ill. 1961, U.S. Dist. Ct. (no. dist.) Ohio 1960, U.S. Ct. Mil. Appeals 1954, U.S. Ct. Appeals (7th cir.) 1968. Assoc. J.D. Quarant, Elizabethtown, Ill., 1953-56; staff atty. Pa. R.R. Co., Chgo., 1957-60; assoc. Henslee, Monek & Henslee, Chgo., 1960-67; sole practice, Naperville, Ill., 1967-68; ptnr. Donovan, Atten, Mountcastle, Roberts & DaRosa, Wheaton, Ill., 1968-77; pres. Donovan & Roberts, P.C., Wheaton, 1977—. Served to capt. U.S. Army, 1954-57. Mem. ABA, Assn. Trial Lawyers Am., Ill. Bar Assn., DuPage County Bar Assn. (gen. counsel 1976-86). Democrat. Presbyterian. Office: PO Box 417 Wheaton IL 60187

ROBERTS, LEO JAMES, ophthalmologist; b. Chgo., Sept. 1, 1933; s. Leo Joseph and Marjorie Elizabeth (Palmer) R.; m. Joyce Ann Woods, May 24, 1969; children—Mary, Elizabeth, Jennifer, Catherine, Leo, Jessica. B.S., Loyola U., Chgo., 1956, M.D. cum laude, 1958. Diplomate Am. Bd. Ophthalmology. Intern Cook County Hosp., Chgo., 1958-59; resident in medicine VA Hosp., Westside, Chgo., 1959-60; resident in ophthalmology U. Ill. Hosp., Chgo., 1962-65; fellow UCLA Med. Ctr., Los Angeles, 1965; practice medicine specializing in ophthalmology, Hinsdale, Ill., 1966—; instr. ophthalmology U. Ill. Med. Sch., Chgo., 1966-70; clin. assoc. prof. ophthalmology Loyola Med. Sch., Maywood, Ill., 1970—. Served to capt. USAF, 1960-62. Fellow Am. Acad. Ophthalmology, ACS, Am. Intraocular Implant Soc.; mem. AMA, DuPage County Med. Soc. (bd. dirs. 1979). Republican. Roman Catholic. Club: Hinsdale Golf. Avocations: golf, tennis. Office: Leo J Roberts MD SC 40 S Clay St Hinsdale IL 60521

ROBERTS, LUCY THEILER, family counselor; b. Indianapolis, Oct. 29, 1945; d. John Paul and Jane (Fry) Baker; m. Allen John Theiler, Oct. 20, 1967 (div. Feb. 1977); 1 child, Nicholas Andrew; m. James Edward Roberts, Nov. 4, 1977. BA in Psychology, Lindenwood Coll., St. Charles, Mo., 1967, MA in Child Psychology, 1977; postgrad., Washington U., St. Louis, Mo., 1979. Tchr. St. Ferdinand Elem. Sch., Florissant, Mo., 1967-68, Our Lady of Loretto Sch., Spanish Lake, Mo., 1968-70; pt. time St. Martin de Porres Sch., Hazelwood, Mo., 1971; tchr. St. Peters Sch., St. Charles, Mo., 1971-72, Duchesne High Sch., St. Charles, Mo., 1976; intern psychology Malcolm Bliss Mental Health Ctr., St. Louis, Mo., 1976-77, Child Ctr. of Our Lady of Grace, Normandy, Mo., 1976-77; cons. counselor Christian Psychol. and Family Services, Bridgeton, Mo., 1977-79; instr. psychology Lindenwood Coll., St. Charles, 1980-81; therapeutical counselor O'Fallon Med. Ctr., 1980-85; grief counselor Baue Funeral Home, St. Charles, 1984—; cons. Wentzville Sch. Dist., 1984—; founder Coping and Living Life widow/widower's orgn. Baue Funeral Homes, 1985—. Speaker numerous symposiums and workshops in field; developer newsletter for widow/widowers group, 1986. Chmn. publicity "Chemin de Fer" Acad. Sacred Heart, St. Charles, 1985; bd. dirs. St. Charles div. Am. Heart Assn. 1986—. Grantee "Thinkers Edge" Program Monsanto Corp., 1983. Mem. Am. Assn. Marriage and Family Therapists (clinical). Democrat. Roman Catholic. Avocations: golf, oil painting, gardening. Home: 2210 S Goebbert Rd #129 Arlington Heights IL 60005-4230 Office: Baue Funeral Home 620 Jefferson Saint Charles MO 63366

ROBERTS, MARK ANTHONY, accountant, financial consultant; b. Indpls., Mar. 4, 1959; s. William Harlan and Lois Laverne (Cunningham) R.; m. Beverly Kay Dreyer, Oct. 2, 1982; 1 child, Caitlin Brooke. BS in Bus., Ind. U., 1981. CPA, Ind. Staff acct. Finn and Co., Indpls., 1981-82; sr. acct. KMG Main Hurdman, Indpls., 1982-83; acctg. mgr. Stoops Express, Anderson, Ind., 1984—; bd. dirs. Fountain Sq.-Fletcher Pl. Investment Corp., Indpls., 1987—. Mem. community adv. bd. Sta. WIAN FM 90 Nat. Pub. Radio, Indpls., 1983-84. Mem. Am. Inst. CPA's, Nat. Assn. Accts., Inst. Cert. Mgmt. Accts., Ind. CPA Soc. (pub. relations com. 1986—). Avocations: fishing, hiking, golf, travel, reading. Office: Stoops Express Inc PO Box 287 Anderson IN 46015

ROBERTS, MERLE E., business executive; b. New Kensington, Pa., June 8, 1928; s. Merle B. and Marie E. Roberts; B.S., U. Pitts., 1949; M.B.A., Case-Western Res. U., 1952; m. Dorothy Bougher, July 1, 1950; children—Cynthia Grace, Lisa Bogumill, Keith, Courtney. Pres., owner Roberts Assocs., Inc., Columbus, Ohio, 1964—; pres. Food Group, Inc., Columbus, 1975-81; pres., dir. Luna Caster & Truck Corp., Phoenix dir. Nat. Packaging, Colamco Inc.; pres. Chrysalis Corp., Family Security Agy., Roberts Group Inc. and subs. F.O. Schoedinger Co., Columbus, L.H. Marshall Co., Columbus, Pleko Southeast Corp., Lakeland, Fla., Fosco Bldg. Products, Lakeland, Pleko Products, Inc., Tacoma, Wash.; mem. faculty Case-Western Res. U., 1953-55, Cleveland State Coll., 1954-56, Capital U., 1962-64, Ohio State U., 1964-68. Mem. U.S. Senatorial Adv. Bd., 1980-81. Republican. Presbyn. (elder, dir.). Address: 2646 Alliston Ct Columbus OH 43220

ROBERTS, RONALD CLAIR, research biochemist; b. Meadville, Pa., Jan. 28, 1936; s. Clair Roberts and Jessie Marie (Ray) R.; m. Joan Marie Gilbertson, Sept. 5, 1960 (div. June 1985); children: Steven Todd, Rhonda Jo; m. Carol Lamascus, June 19, 1985. BS, Pa. State U., 1957; PhD, U. Minn., 1964. Postdoctoral fellow Mpls. VA Hosp., 1964-66; adj. assoc. prof. dept. chemistry U. Wis., Stevens Point, 1979-83; adj. prof. dept. biology U. Wis., Oshkosh, 1979-80; vis. scientist E.I. Dupont de Nemours Co., Wilmington, Del., 1983-84; sr. research biochemist Marshfield (Wis.) Med. Found., 1966—, also bd. dirs.; mem. research com. Am. Heart Assn. of Wis., Milw. Contbr. articles to profl. jours. Sec., div. bd. dirs. Wis. div. Am. Cancer Soc.; bd. dirs. Wildwood Park Zoolog. Soc., Marshfield. Grantee Am. Cancer Soc., Am. Heart Assn., 1972-75, Cystic Fibrosis Found., 1980-81, NIH, 1972-82. Mem. AAAS, Am. Chem. Soc. (chmn. Cen. Wis. sect.), Am. Acad. Allergy, Am. Soc. Biol. Chemists. Lodges: Rotary, Elks. Home: 9457 Eagle Rd Marshfield WI 54449 Office: Marshfield Med Research Found 510 N St Joseph Ave Marshfield WI 54449

ROBERTS, RONALD WILLIAM, cattle rancher; b. Maxwell, Nebr., June 27, 1944; s. George William Jr. and Ruth Phyllis (Osborn) R.; children from previous marriage: Shane, Noelle; m. Judith Virginia Nycum, May 12, 1978; children: Kathryn, Charles, Ken. BS in Agr., U. Nebr., 1966; MS, Kearney State Coll., 1978. Sci. tchr. Maxwell Pub. Schs., 1967-70; owner, operator Roberts Ranch Co., Maxwell, 1966—; agrl. mgmt. specialist Farmers Home Adminstrn., USDA, Washington, 1978-86; assoc. Jim Harris Appraisal Service, North Platte, Nebr., 1986—; agrl. rep. Bank of Brady (Nebr.), 1984; instr. agr. pt. time Mid Plains Community Coll., North Platte, 1976-82. Pres. Sandhills Symphony Assn., North Platte, Nebr., 1981. Mem. Soc. for Range Mgmt., Nebr. Stock Growers Assn. (area pres. 1984-86). Republican. Home: HCOI Box 17 Maxwell NE 69151 Office: Jim Harris Appraisal Service 120 S Dewey PO Box 1422 North Platte NE 69103

ROBERTS, ROSS T., federal judge; b. 1938. B.A., DePauw U., 1960; J.D., U. Mo., 1963. Ptnr. Roberts & Fleischaker, Joplin, Mo., 1963; ptnr. Shook, Hardy, Ottman, Mitchell & Bacon, Kansas City, Mo., 1968-70, Roberts & Fleischaker, Joplin, 1970-82; pros. atty. Jasper County, Joplin, 1971-77; judge U.S. Dist. Ct. (we. dist.) Mo., Kansas City, 1982—. Office: U S Dist Ct US Courthouse 811 Grand Ave Room 716 Kansas City MO 64106 *

ROBERTS, STEPHEN CRAWFORD, systems consultant; b. Nashville, July 25, 1955; s. Clarence Zebedee and Carolyn (Crawford) R. BS, Vanderbilt U., 1977; MBA, U. Ala.-Tuscaloosa, 1980. Systems analyst McDonnell Douglas, St. Louis, 1980-81, sr. systems analyst, 1982; client cons. Maritz Motivation Co., Inc., St. Louis, 1982-84, sr. client cons., 1984—. Mem. Assn. for Systems Mgmt. Avocations: personal computers, raquetball, golf. Office: Maritz Motivation Co Inc 1355 N Highway Dr Fenton MO 63026

ROBERTS, TED, manufacturing executive; b. Mpls., Mar. 28, 1958; s. Walter Glen and Mary Jo (Cronin) R.; m. Lee Ann Gustafson, Nov. 9, 1985. BS in Bus., U. Minn., 1980, MBA in Mktg., 1984. Assoc. pub. Comml. West Mag., Mpls., 1980-82; v.p. mktg. Roberts Automatic Products, Mpls., 1982—. Mem. Nat. Screw Machine Products Assn., N.W. Chi Psi Ednl. Found. (v.p.). Home: 4400 Garfield Ave S Minneapolis MN 55409 Office: Roberts Automatic Products Inc 4451 W 76th St Minneapolis MN 55435

ROBERTS, THOMAS C., computer company executive. Former pres., chief exec. officer Fairchild Camera & Instrument Corp., Mountain View, Calif.; pres. internat. ops. Control Data Corp., Mpls., 1985—. Office: Control Data Corp 8100 34th Ave S Minneapolis MN 55440 *

ROBERTS, THOMAS CHARLES, food association executive, agronomist; b. Burrton, Kans., Sept. 22, 1926; s. Ernest Eugene and Mildred Lorraine (Miller) Abston R.; m. Dixie Darlene Werner, Jan. 1, 1947; children—Thomas Carroll, Bradford Charles. B.S. in Agrl. Edn., Kans. State U., 1950. Vo-ag tchr. Lebanon High Sch., Kans., 1950-53, Lyndon High Sch., Kans., 1953-56; asst. sec. Kans. Crop Improvement, Manhattan, 1956-61; gen. mgr. Frontier Hybrids, Inc., Scott City, Kans., 1961-66; exec. v.p. Wheat Quality Council, Manhattan, Kans., 1966—. Mem., chmn. Park Bd. City of Manhattan, 1969-80; pres. Friends of Sunset Zoo, Manhattan, 1979-84. Served with USAF, 1945-46. Named Friend of County Agts., Kans. County Agt. Assn., 1974. Mem. Am. Assn. Cereal Chemists, Am. Soc. Agronomy. Republican. Methodist. Lodges: Lions (pres. 1978-79, dist. gov. 1981-82), Masons. Avocation: dancing instructor. Home: 2041 Arthur Dr Manhattan KS 66502 Office: Wheat Quality Council 404 Humboldt St Suite G Manhattan KS 66502

ROBERTS, THOMAS HUMPHREY, JR., agricultural research company executive; b. DeKalb, Ill., May 23, 1924; s. Thomas Humphrey and Eleanor (Townsend) R.; m. Nancy Jean Barker, Mar. 12, 1974; children by previous marriage: Thomas Humphrey III, Catherine Roberts Tosh, Susan Shawn, Michael Joseph. B.S., Iowa State U., 1949; M.B.A., Harvard U., 1955. With DeKalb AgResearch, Inc. (name changed to DeKalb Corp.), exec. v.p., 1961-62, pres., 1961-85, chmn. bd., 1967—, also dir., former chief exec. officer; dir. Internat. Minerals & Chem. Corp., Continental Ill. Nat. Bank & Trust Co. Bd. visitors Harvard U. Bus. Sch.; trustee Rush-Presbyn.-St. Luke's Med. Ctr., other agys. Served with USAAF. Office: DeKalb Corp 3100 Sycamore Rd DeKalb IL 60115 *

ROBERTS, TIMOTHY WEAVER, retail administrator; b. St. Paul, July 23, 1942; s. Howard Weaver and Maude Eunice (Cowles) R.; m. Lynne Marie Holewa, Dec. 3, 1974. BS in Acctg., U. Minn., 1980. CPA, Minn. Controller S. Z. Wert Enterprises, Mpls., 1971-75; acct. Rochlin, Lurie, Cook & Co., CPA's, Mpls., 1976, M. J. Long Co., CPA's, Mpls., 1976-78; sr. v.p. Gene Smiley Inc., Mpls., 1978-85; gen. mgr. S & M Co., Mpls., 1985—; cons. Boras Internat. U.S., Ltd., Mpls., 1981—, Kinnasand Internat. U.S., Ltd., Mpls., 1983—. coordinator fund raising United Way, Mpls., 1987—; sgt. Bloomington (Minn.) Police Res., 1987—. Mem. Am. Soc. CPA's, Minn. Soc. CPA's. Republican. Lutheran. Club: Kanshin Ryu Karate (Mpls.). Lodge: Masons. Avocations: phys. fitness, hunting, fishing. Home: 5208 W 106th St Bloomington MN 55437 Office: S & M Co 2101 Kennedy St NE Minneapolis MN 55413

ROBERTS-MILLER, RICHARD ALEXANDER, travel industry executive; b. Manchester, Eng., Aug. 31, 1942; came to U.S., 1978; s. Alex and Doreen Garnet (Perton) R.-M.; m. Fiona Mary Deacon, June 24, 1972; children: Alexander, Joanna, Elizabeth. BS in Econs., U. Southampton, Eng., 1965. Research exec. Brit. Market Research Bur. Ltd., London, 1965-69, Times Newspapers Ltd., London, 1969-74; mktg. exec. Thomson Holidays, London, 1974-78; pres., chief exec. officer Thomson Vacations, Chgo., 1978—. Bd. dirs. Ill. Better Bus. Bur., 1980-87. Mem. Market Research Soc. United Kingdom, European Soc. for Mktg. Research.

ROBERTSON, BRIAN JAMES, architect; b. Oak Park, Ill., Apr. 10, 1951; s. Robert John and Frances LaVerne (Fleck) R.; m. Elaine Florine Bosco, May 24, 1980; 1 child, Gina. Student, Wabash Coll., Crawfordsville, Ind., 1969-71; BA in History of Architecture, U. Ill., Chgo., 1976, BArch, 1977. Registered architect, Ill. Intern Hawkweed Group, Chgo., 1977-80; job capt. Nagle, Hartray and Assoc., Chgo., 1980-85, Lohan Assocs., Chgo., 1985-86; project capt. Weton Becket Assocs., Chgo., 1987—; bd. dirs. AMC Corp., Downers Grove, Ill.; mem. Newhouse Architecture Copetition Com., Chgo., 1984—. Bd. dirs., treas. Gaslight Village Condominium Assn., Chgo., 1980-84. Mem. AIA (bd. dirs. Ill. council 1984—, bd. dirs. Chgo. 1980, state coordinator for intern devel. 1986—). Home: 4425 N Sacramento Ave Chicago IL 60625 Office: Weton Becket Assocs 200 W Adams Chicago IL 60605

ROBERTSON, BROWNING AULCEY, JR., communications executive; b. Malden, Mo., Feb. 18, 1935; s. Browning Aulcey Sr. and Georgia Ethyl (Ayres) R.; m. Tsumako Matsunaga, Sept. 27, 1957 (dec. Oct. 1980); children: Linda Matsumi, Dina Maria; m. Janet Loann Savage, Sept. 17, 1981. BFA, U. Nebr., 1976. Enlisted USAF, 1953, advanced through ranks to tech. sgt., 1967, retired, 1973; sr. tech. writer Hy-Gain Electronics, Lincoln, Nebr., 1976-77; telecommunications analyst Centel Corp., Lincoln, 1977—. Mem. Internat. Soc. Artists (regional corr. 1978-83). Democrat. Roman Catholic. Avocations: painting, drawing, classical music, ballet, photography. Home: 1645 Otoe St Lincoln NE 68502 Office: Centel Corp 1201 N St Lincoln NE 68502

ROBERTSON, DAVID LEONARD, infosystems specialist; b. Port Huron, Mich., Dec. 31, 1953; s. Robert Charles Ashpole Sr. and Brona Lee (Arnold) Watkins; m. Lynn Ann Harrison, May 15, 1982; children: Jason, David, Paul. BS in Psychology, Cen. Mich. U., 1977; cert. in computer programming, Control Data Inst., 1982. Tennis profl. Joseph Felice Enterprises, West Bloomfield, Mich., 1972-78; tech. adminstr. Soc. Mfg. Engrs., Dearborn, Mich., 1978—; computer analyst Rouge Steel div. Ford Motor Co., Dearborn, 1983—; mem. steering com. initial graphics exchange system U.S. Nat. Bur. Standards, Washington, 1981. Served with USAF, 1979. Kiwanis Internat. scholar, 1973, Mich. Competitive scholar State Mich. Dept. Edn., 1977.

ROBERTSON, DAVID PETER, management consulting company executive; b. Schnectady, N.Y., June 19, 1935; s. Peter and Frances (Cromie) R.; m. Marian Margaret Rood, Aug. 15, 1959; children: Daniel David, James Brian. BA, Coll. of Wooster, Ohio, 1957; MS, Yale U., 1961. Pastor United Ch. of Christ, Cleve. and Warren, Ohio, 1960-66; human resources exec. Sherwin-Williams Co., Cleve., 1966-83; pres. Intervention Assocs., Chgo., 1982—; sr. v.p. Patrick-Douglas, Chgo., 1983-87; pres. Robertson-Lowstuter Inc., Deerfield, Ill., 1987—. Home: 2234 Barger Ct Wheaton IL 60187 Office: Robertson-Lowstuter 104 Wilmot Deerfield IL 60015

ROBERTSON, DONELSON ANTHONY, oil company executive; b. Salina, Kans., Sept. 26, 1924; s. Donelson Caffrey Jenkins Robertson and Maudie Etholwyn (Bates) Fuhrman; m. Joan Dolores Lingo, Aug. 2, 1947; children—Bruce F. (dec.), Brian B., Bonnie A. B.S., Centenary Coll., 1949; M.S., U. Ill., 1951. Registered profl. engr., Pa. Dist. geologist Shell Oil Co., Denver, Billings, Mont., Baton Rouge and Pitts., 1951-66; v.p. ops. N.E. div. Martin Marietta Corp., N.Y.C., 1966-76; exec. v.p. P.R. Berger & Assocs., Pitts., 1976-80; div. mgr. Patrick Petroleum Co., Pitts., 1980-82, v.p., Jackson, Mich., 1982-84; v.p., regional mgr. Ladd Petroleum Corp., Jackson, 1984—. Patentee external friction coupling, 1975. Served with U.S. Army, 1943-45, ETO. Recipient Silver Cup Honors Night award Martin Marietta Corp., 1974. Mem. Am. Assn. Petroleum Geologists, Am. Inst. Profl. Geologists (cert., charter), Petroleum Engrs. Soc. AIME, Assn. Engring. Geologists. Home: 2640 Walden Woods Blvd Jackson MI 49201 Office: Ladd Petroleum Corp 744 W Michigan Ave Jackson MI 49204

ROBERTSON, EDWARD D., JR., state judge. Judge Mo. Supreme Ct., Jefferson City. Office: Missouri Supreme Ct Box 150 Jefferson City MO 65102 *

ROBERTSON, ELAINE BOSCO, nursing administrator; b. Lowell, Mass., May 4, 1945; d. Joseph and Emma (Pacillo) Bosco; m. Brian James Robertson, May 24, 1980; 1 child, Gina Elaina. B.S. in Nursing, Boston U., 1967, M.S. in Nursing, 1977. R.N., Ill., Mass., Colo. Staff nurse ICU, Univ. Hosp., Boston, 1967-68; staff and asst. head nurse nursery Malden (Mass.) Hosp., 1968-70; clinic nurse neurology/neurosurgery clinics Children's Hosp., Boston, 1971-76; pediatric practitioner-tchr. Rush U., Chgo., 1976-77; neurosurgery clin. specialist Children's Meml. Hosp., Chgo., 1978-80, clin. nurse educator, 1980-81, evening nursing adminstrv. coordinator, 1983—, cons., instr. pediatric intravenous insertion; mem. clin. faculty maternal-child dept. Northwestern U., 1986—. Served to capt., Nurse Corps, U.S. Army Res., 1978-79. Nursing fellow, 1976-78. Mem. Neurosurg. Nurses Assn., Assn. Care of Children in Health Care Settings (dir. 1979-81), Sigma Theta Tau. Democrat. Roman Catholic. Home: 4425 N Sacramento St Chicago IL 60625 Office: 2300 Children's Plaza Chicago IL 60614

ROBERTSON, FLORENCE WINKLER, public relations and advertising specialist; b. Hampton, Va., Sept. 11, 1945; s. Fred and Florence Bernice (Shamo) Felty; m. John Park Winkler, June 24, 1967 (div. 1977); m. James Milton Robertson, Oct. 21, 1982. A.A., Palm Beach Jr. Coll., 1965; B.A., U. South Fla., 1967. Reporter, Lexington (Ky.) Leader, 1967-70; freelance writer, 1971-76; TV and radio news reporter Sta. KCRG, Cedar Rapids, Iowa, 1972-73; asst. dir. pub. relations Coe Coll., Cedar Rapids, 1973-78; info. specialist Cedar Rapids (Iowa) Pub. Schs., 1979-83; adv. mgr. Smulekoff's Fine Home Furnishings, 1984—. Pres. Home Fire Safety Task Force of Ea. Iowa, 1983-86; chmn. Cedar Rapids Promotion Com., 1986—; bd. dirs. Grat Wood Area chpt. ARC. Recipient Regional award Council Advancement and Support Edn., 1975, 77, 78, nat. award CASE, 1977; Pub. Service awards Nat. Police Officers Assn., City of Shively (Ky.) and Am. Legion, 1970; Nat. award Nat. Sch. Pub. Relations Assn., 1981, 83, Gov.'s Award for Volunteerism, 1987. Home: 901 Staub Ct Ne Cedar Rapids IA 52402

ROBERTSON, JOHN ALBERT, insurance agent; b. Southampton, Eng., June 2, 1925; came to U.S., 1975; s. Harold and Allice E. (Richards) R.; m. Anne Elizabeth Andrew (div. 1967); children: Malcolm, Andrew, Tina, Sarah, Adam, Paul, Jared, David, Seth, Hannah, Mike; m. Susan M. Horlock. With Burtons Grocers, Clare, Suffolk, Eng., 1939-43; police officer Gloucesteshire (Eng.) Constabulary, 1948-59; mgr. Wessox Bus. Broker, Bristol, Eng., 1959-72; owner Robertson Ins. Agy., Oconto, Wis., 1976—. Served with RAF, 1943-47. Mem. Profl. Ins. Agys. Mormon. Lodge: Kinwanis (local chpt. pres. 1983, bd. dirs., bull. editor). Home: 1144 City M E Lena WI 54139 Office: 1028 Main St Oconto WI 54153

ROBERTSON, JOSEPH EDMOND, industrial grain processing company executive; b. Brownstown, Ind., Feb. 16, 1918; s. Roscoe Melvin and Edith Penina (Shields) R.; m. Virginia Faye Baxter, Nov. 23, 1941; 1 son, Joseph Edmond. BS, Kans. State U., 1940, postgrad., 1940. Cereal chemist Ewing Mill Co., 1940-43, flour milling engr., 1946-50, feed nutritionist, 1951-59; v.p., sec. Robertson Corp., Brownstown, Ind., 1960-80, pres., 1980—. Pres. Jackson County (Ind.) Welfare Bd., 1948-52. mem. Ind. Port Commn., 1986. Served with USAAF, 1943-45. Mem. Hardwood Plywood Mfrs. Assn. (v.p. affiliate div. 1971-73), Am. Assn. Cereal Chemists, Assn. Operative Millers, Am. Legion, Brownstown C. of C. (dir. All Am. city program 1955), Kans. State U. Alumni Assn. (life), Blue Key, Phi Delta Theta, Phi Kappa Phi, Alpha Mu. Presbyterian. Clubs: Country (Seymour, Ind.); Hickory Hills Country (Brownstown, Ind.). Lodge: Elks. Home: Route 1 Lake and Forest Club Box A Brownstown IN 47220 Office: 200 Front St Brownstown IN 47220

ROBERTSON, LEON H., transportation company executive; b. Atlanta, Jan. 25, 1934; s. Grady Joseph and Pearline (Chandler) R.; m. S. Ann Parker, Aug. 27, 1971; children: Sharon, Michael. B.S. in Indsl. Mgmt., Ga. Inst. Tech., 1957, M.S., 1959; postgrad., U. Okla.-Norman, 1958, U. Mich., 1961; Ph.D. in Bus. Adminstrn., Ga. State U., 1968. Mgr. mgmt. info. div. Arthur Anderson & Co., Atlanta, 1960-65; prof. bus. adminstrn. Ga. State U., 1965-75; corp. v.p. Tex. Gas Corp., Owensboro, Ky., 1975-78, sr. v.p., 1982-83; chmn., chief exec. officer Am. Carriers, Inc., Overland Park, Kans., 1978—. Office: American Carriers Inc 9393 W 110th St Overland Park KS 66210

ROBERTSON, LYNNE NANNEN, dietitian; b. Pierson, Iowa, Sept. 10, 1936; m. Theodore A. Robertson; children: Joyce, Brenda. BS, Iowa State U., 1958, MS, 1966, PhD, 1978; postgrad., U. Mo., 1970, Drake U., 1973. Dietitian Stouffer Corp., Cleve. and Pitts., 1958-60; chief dietitian Meth. Hosp., Sioux City, Iowa, 1960-64; therapeutic dietitian Iowa Meth. Hosp., Ankeny, 1965-66; dietary cons. Iowa Dept. Health, Ankeny, 1966-70; coordinator instrn. dept. nutrition and dietetics U. Mo. Med. Ctr., Ankeny, 1970-71; instr. food service program Des Moines Area Community Coll., Ankeny, 1971-72, dir. food services and food service programs, 1972-76; supr. bus. enterprises Iowa Commn. for Blind, Ankeny, 1976-78; asst. dir. dept. dietetics Iowa Meth. Med. Ctr., Ankeny, 1978-79; pres. Creative Concepts, Ankeny, 1979—; dietitian Friley Hall, Iowa State U., Ames, 1965-66; adv. com. Des Moines Tech. High Sch., chmn. adv. com. vocat. food service. Author: Food Service Equipment: Selection and Layout, 1973, Metric Measurement in Food Preparation and Service, 1978, Food Service Equipment, 2d edit., 1981, Purchasing for Food Service: Self-instruction, 1984, various home study courses, 1967-71; contbr. articles to profl. jours. Mem. Adminstrv. Mgmt. Soc., Am. Home Econs. Assn., Am. Hotel-Motel Assn., Am. Sch. Food Service Assn., Am. Vocat. Assn., Des Moines Assn. Dietitians and Food Mgrs., Des Moines Sch. Food Service Adv. Com., Dietetic Educators Assn., Dietitians in Bus. and Industry (treas.), Greater Des Moines Hotel-Motel Assn. (sec. 1974-76), Iowa Chefs and Culinarians Club, Iowa Dietetic Assn. (pres. elect), Iowa Health Care Assn., Iowa Home Econs. Assn., Iowa Hotel-Motel-Motor Inn Assn., Iowa Restaurant Assn., Iowa Sch. Food Service Assn., Iowa Vocat. Assn., Nat. Assn. Coll. and Univ. Food Services, Nat. Restaurant Assn., Nat. Assn. Postsecondary and Adult Vocat. Home Econs. Educators (treas.), River Valley Culinary Assn., Sioux City Dietetic Assn. (pres.), Sioux City Home Econs. Assn. (sec.), Am. Dietetic Assn., Omicron Nu. Home and Office: 814 SE Sherman Dr Ankeny IA 50021

ROBERTSON, RODNEY CHARLES, accountant; b. Eaton Rapids, Mich., July 31, 1949; s. Charles Marion and Thena Maxine (Jeffery) R.; m. Doris Ann Gillett, Dec. 19, 1970; children: Sara Marie, Brian Michael. BA, Mich. State U., 1971; MBA, Eastern Mich. U., 1977. CPA, Mich. Jr. acct. Young, Skutt & Breitenwischer, CPA, Jackson, Mich., 1971, sr. acct., 1972-73; ptnr. Robertson & Zick, CPA, Rose City, Mich., 1974-80, Robertson & Carpenter, CPA, Rose City, 1980—. Fin. chmn. and adminstrv. council Trinity United Meth. Ch., Rose City, 1983—. Mem. Am. Inst. CPA's, Mich. Assn. CPA's, Rose City-Lupton Area C. of C. (bd. dirs. 1978—), Ogemaw Valley Jaycees (bd. dirs. 1975-80). Republican. Avocations: golf, bowling, tennis.

ROBEY, LARRY WAYNE, information processing executive; b. Clayton, Wis., Sept. 23, 1939; s. Ferris M. and Josephine (Heider) R.; m. Alice J. Boomsma, June 9, 1962; children—Camille Ann, Thomas Charles. B.B.A., Northwestern U., 1971. Cert. data processing. Acct., J. I. Case Co., Racine, Wis., 1963-65; systems analyst Gen. Binding Corp., Northbrook, Ill., 1965-70; project mgr. Amoco Inc., Chgo., 1970-81; dir. mgmt. info. systems U.S. Shoe Corp., Beloit, Wis., 1981—; part-time instr. Blackhawk Tech. Inst. Mem. Data Processing Mgmt. Assn., Soc. Info. Mgmt. Republican. Mem. Evangelical Free Ch. Home: 4043 Wilshire Ln Janesville WI 53545 Office: One Freeman Ln Beloit WI 53511

ROBEY, SUSANNA HORTON, mental health counselor, educator; b. Springfield, Mo., Oct. 2, 1937; d. George Vaughan and Dorothy Dickerson (Durst) H.; m. George Earl Robey, June 18, 1960; children—Susan Marie, Margaret Eve, Cynthia Dorita. B.A., Drury Coll., 1959; M.S. in Edn., U. Wis.-Platteville, 1982. Cert. tchr., Iowa. Tchr. jr. high sch. Kansas City Community Sch. Dist., Kans., 1959-60; tchr. Dubuque Community Schs., Iowa, 1967-76; supervising counselor Substance Abuse Services, Dubuque, 1982-83; career counselor Northeast Iowa Tech. Inst., Peosta, 1983-84; family therapist Mercy Hosp., Dubuque, 1984-85; mental health counselor Jane Addams Family Counseling and Mental Health Ctr., Galena, Ill., 1985-87; promotion dir. Sibbing's Jewelry Store, Dubuque, 1987—; founding sec., Montessori Adv. Group, Dubuque, 1969-70. Founding pres. Suzuki Sch. Music, Dubuque, 1978-80; bd. dirs. Dubuque Community Schs., 1977—, Symphony Orchestra Aux., 1976-80; troop leader Little Cloud council Girl Scouts U.S.A., 1968-78; pres. council Dubuque PTA, 1974-76. Mem. Am. Assn. Counseling Devel., Am. Mental Health Counselors Assn., DAR (regent 1980-81), Kappa Delta Pi. Presbyterian. Clubs: Debonaires Dance (founding pres. 1964-66), PEO (v.p. 1980-81). Avocations: reading; golfing; singing; dancing. Home: 1130 S Grandview St Dubuque IA 52001 Office: Sibbing's Jewelry 890 Town Clock Plaza Dubuque IA 52001

ROBINS, GARY BRUCE, beverage company executive; b. Columbus, Ohio, June 6, 1946; s. Louis and Sara (Kahn) R.; student Ohio State U., 1964-66; m. Constance Kiefer, Aug. 11, 1967; children—Dean, Chad, Bret, Zach. Salesman, Excello Wine Co., Columbus, 1967-70, v.p., 1971—; pres. Hi-State Beverage Co., Columbus, 1977—, also dir.; v.p. The Robins Beverage Group, 1986—; sec.-treas. ACA JOE of Columbus, Inc., 1984—. Active United Jewish Fund, 1970—; ptnr. Cypress Beverage Co., Columbus, 1986—; bd. dirs. Jewish Family Service, 1975; mem. Columbus Conv. and Visitors Bur.; mem. Columbus Quincentennial Exposition 1992; nat. bd. dirs. Am. ORT Fedn., 1981—; bd. dirs. Columbus Jewish Fedn., 1981—, sec., 1985—, chmn. United Jewish Fund Campaign, 1985; nat. bd. dirs. Hebrew Immigrant Aid Soc., 1985—; chmn. campaign United Jewish Appeal of Columbus, 1985; co-chmn. 1987 campaign for the Bexley Edn. Fund; active Columbus Urban League. Mem. Wholesale Beer and Wine Assn. Ohio, Wholesale Beer Assn. Ohio, Nat., Beer Wholesalers Assn., Wine and Spirits Wholesalers Am., Ohio Wholesale Wine Dealers Assn., Columbus Mfrs. Reps. Assn., Columbus C. of C., Ohio C. of C. Clubs: B'nai B'rith, Winding Hollow Country (bd. dirs. 1983—), Columbus Men's ORT (vice chmn. 1983—), Capital, The Pres. Club Ohio State U. Home: 435 S Columbia Ave Columbus OH 43209 Office: 871 Michigan Ave Columbus OH 43215

ROBINS, MARJORIE MCCARTHY (MRS. GEORGE KENNETH ROBINS), civic worker; b. St. Louis, Oct. 4, 1914; d. Eugene Ross and Louise (Roblee) McCarthy; A.B., Vassar Coll., 1936; diploma St. Louis Sch. Occupational Therapy, 1940; m. George Kenneth Robins, Nov. 9, 1940; children—Carol Robins Von Arx, G. Stephen, Barbara A. Robins Foorman. Mem. Mo. Library Commn., 1937-38; mem. bd. St. Louis Jr. League, 1945, 46; mem. bd. Occupational Therapy Workshop of St. Louis, 1941-46, pres., 1945, 46; mem. bd. Ladue Chapel Nursery Sch., 1957-60, 61-64, pres. bd., 1963, 64; past regional chmn. United Fund; past mem. St. Louis Met. Youth Commn., St. Louis Health and Welfare Council; bd. dirs. Internat. Inst. of St. Louis, 1966-72, 76—82, 83—, sec., 1968, v.p., 1981; bd. dirs. Mental Health Assn. St. Louis, 1963-70, Washington U. Child Guidance and Evaluation Clinic, 1968-78; bd. dirs. Central Inst. for Deaf, 1970—, v.p., 1975-76, pres., 1976-78; bd. dirs. Met. St. Louis YWCA, 1954-63, 64-74, pres. bd., 1960-63, trustee, 1977—; mem. nat. bd. YWCA, 1967-79, nat. v.p., 1973-76; vol. tchr. remedial reading clinic St. Louis City Schs., 1968-71; trustee John Burroughs Sch., 1960-63, John Burroughs Found., 1965-80, Roblee Found., 1972—, Nat. YWCA Retirement Fund, 1979—; bd. dirs. Gambrill Gardens United Meth. Retirement Home, 1979-85, Thompson Retreat and Conf. Center, 1981—; bd. dirs. Springboard to Learning Inc., 1980—, v.p., 1980—. Mem. Archeol. Inst. Am. (bd. dirs., treas. St. Louis chpt. 1985-87). Clubs: Vassar (sec. and pres. 1939-40), Wednesday (dir. 1968-70, 77-79, 80-81) (St. Louis). Home: 45 Loren Woods Saint Louis MO 63124

ROBINS, MITCHELL JAMES, accountant; b. Detroit, May 23, 1956; s. Melvin M. Robins and Judith (Bell) Martin; m. Amy Elizabeth Green, July 2, 1978; children: Alexander Philip, Sean Lewis. BBA, U. Mich., 1977; postgrad., U. Detroit, 1979. CPA, Mich., Fla. Exec. mgr. Gen. Motors, Detroit, 1977-78; auditor nat. CPA firm, Detroit, 1979-80; founder, mng. ptnr. Robins-Assocs., P.C., Farmington Hills, Mich., 1981—; bd. dirs. Cadillac Creative Advt., Southfield, Mich., Alfonsi R.R. Constrn., Trenton, Mich., Campus Distbn., Inc., Ann Arbor, Mich., Internat. Med.-Dental Hypnotherapy Assn., Royal Oak, Mich.; mem. Restaurant Bus. Research Adv. Panel, N.Y.C., 1986-87. Mem. steering com. Rep. 300 Com. of Mich., Oakland County, 1986-87; mem. zoning bd. appeals City of Farmington Hills, 1987—. Mem. Am. Inst. CPA's Small Bus. Div. (com. mem.), Mich. Assn. CPA's (com. mem. 1986-87), Fla. Inst. CPA's (com. mem. 1987), Ind. Assn. CPA's (com. mem.), Assn. MBA Execs., U. Mich. Alumni Assn. Republican. Jewish. Club: Economic (Detroit). Lodge: B'nai B'rith (Meritorious Service award 1986). Avocations: golf, contact sports, travel. Home: 30954 Hunters Whip Farmington Hills MI 48018

ROBINSON, ALEXANDER JACOB, clinical psychologist; b. St. John, Kans., Nov. 7, 1920; s. Oscar Frank and Lydia May (Beitler) R.; m. Elsie Louise Riggs, July 29, 1942; children: Madelyn K., Alicia A., David J., Charles A., Paul S., Marietta J., Stephen N. BA in Psychology, Ft. Hays (Kans.) State U., 1942, MS in Clin. Psychology, 1942; postgrad., U. Ill., 1942-44. Cert. psychologist, sch. psychologist. Chief psychologist Larned (Kans.) State Hosp., 1948-53; sch. psychologist County Schs., Modesto, Calif., 1955-61, Pratt (Kans.) Jr. Coll., 1961-66; fed. program developer Better Edn. Services Today, Pratt., 1966-70; dir. spl. edn., researcher Stafford County Schs., St. John, 1970-81, ret., 1981; writer, asst. dir. Best Exemplary Federally Funded Program on Spl. Edn., Pratt, 1966-70; researcher, writer, study dir. Edn. for the High-Performance Child, St. John, 1970—. Minister, Ch. of Jesus Christ. Served to 2d lt. U.S. Army, 1944-46, PTO. Lodge: Lions (program chmn. St. John 1974-76). Avocations: ethnology, cultural anthropology, history, psychogenesis of the sociopathic personality. Home: Rt 1 Box 121A Saint John KS 67576

ROBINSON, BEATRICE (BEAN) ELLEN, psychologist, research scientist; b. Far Rockaway, N.Y., Sept. 29, 1950; d. Eugene and Doris (Austin) R. BA magna cum laude, SUNY, Binghampton, 1972; MA, U. Minn., 1979, PhD, 1983. Marriage and family therapist Family Consultation Ctr., Burnsville, Minn., 1976-80; research asst. U. Minn., St. Paul, 1978-83; research scientist A.H. Wilder Found., St. Paul, 1983—; instr. U. Minn., Mpls., 1979-80, 84; cons. psychologist Community Counseling Ctr., White Bear Lake, Minn., 1980—, Melpomone Inst., Mpls., 1984—. Mem. Am. Psychol. Assn., Nat. Council of Family, Am. Evaluation Assn., Am. Assn. Marriage and Family Therapists (cert.), Upper Midwest Assn. Assn. Marriage and Family Therapists, Minn. Women Psychologists (vice. chmn. steering com. 1985-87), Omicron Nu, U.S. Tennis Assn. Democrat. Avocations: tennis, racquetball, biking, jogging, movies. Home: 597 Sterling St Maplewood MN 55119 Office: Wilder Resarch Ctr 1295 Bandana Blvd Suite 210 Saint Paul MN 55108 Office: Community Counseling Ctr 4739 Division St White Bear Lake MN 55110

ROBINSON, CHERYL FRENCH, nurse; b. Louisville, Ky., Aug. 4, 1958; d. Joseph William and Dolores Marie (Graves) French; m. H. Steven Robinson, May 14, 1983; children: Jessica Lauren, Matthew Steven. BS in Nursing, Eastern Ky. U., 1981. Med. transcriptionist Am. Med. Services, Louisville, 1977-80; RN in pediatrics Kosair Children's Hosp., Louisville, 1981-85; RN in newborn nursery Clark County Meml. Hosp., Jeffersonville, Ind., 1985—. Mem. Ind. Nurses Assn. Republican. Baptist. Avocations: needlework, painting, reading, swimming, tennis. Home: 2236 Buckeye Dr Jeffersonville IN 47130 Office: Clark County Meml Hosp 1220 Missouri Ave Jeffersonville IN 47130

ROBINSON, CLAUDE DELOS, manufacturing executive; b. Hartford, Mich., Aug. 22, 1936; s. Percy E. and Marian (Schieber) R.; m. Charie C. Hunt, Sept. 7, 1957; children: Lori C., James D., Robert H. BS in Metall. Engring., U. Mich., 1959, BSChemE, 1959; MS in Metall. Engring., Ohio State U., 1965; MBA, U. Chgo., 1975. Metall. engr. Bonney Floyd Co., Columbus, Ohio, 1956-63; tech. dir. Westran Corp., Muskegon, Mich., 1963-68; v.p. mfg. Kast Metals, Shreveport, La., 1968-69; gen. mgr. Howmet Turbine Components Corp., Milw., 1969-83; pres. Robinson & Assocs., Brookfield, Wis., 1983—; pres., chief exec. officer Sivyer Steel Corp., Bettendorf, Iowa, 1985—. Contbr. articles to profl. jours. Mem. Steel Founders Soc. Am. (chmn. nat. tech. and operating com. 1978-81, Briggs award 1981), PRISEC (chmn. 1981-84), Foundry Cast (pres. 1978-81), Sigma Nu. Republican. Club: Blue Mound Country (Milw). Avocations: travel, reading, skiing, golf. Office: Sivyer Steel Corp 225 S 33d St Bettendorf IA 52722

ROBINSON, CLIFF EDMUND, real estate broker, pilot; b. Madison, Ind., Mar. 7, 1949; s. Frank Edmund and Ina Mae (Wicker) R.; m. AnnaBelle Leisure, July 14, 1972; children: Kristen Leigh, Carrie Elizabeth. BS in Bus. and Econs., Georgetown Coll., Ky., 1971. Cert. real estate broker, appraiser, comml. pilot, flight instr., aircraft mechanic. Comml. pilot Heitz Flying Service, Madison, 1972-74; real estate broker Hoosier Hills Realty, Madison and Vevay, Ind., 1974—; mgmt. broker VA, Madison, 1981—. Mem. Jefferson County Bd. Aviation Commrs., Madison, 1985—; trustee Madison Independent Bapt. Ch., 1984—. Mem. Nat. Assn. Real Estate Sales Execs. (Nat. Million Dollar Round Table), Am. Bd. Realtors, Am. Assn. Cert. Appraisers, Experimental Aircraft Assn. (trustee 1980—), Aircraft Owners and Pilots Assn., Internat. Aerobatics Club, Alpha Beta Phi. Republican. Home: 307 Golf Ridge Ln Madison IN 47250 Office: Hoosier Hills Realty 220 Clifty Dr Madison IN 47250

ROBINSON, GERALD D., food products company executive. With Kellogg Co. of Can., Ltd., 1949—, asst. mgr. sales, 1954-57, v.p., 1958-59, asst. gen. mgr., 1959-60, pres., 1960-64, chmn. bd. dirs., 1964-69; chmn. bd. dirs., chief exec. officer Kellogg Salada of Can., Ltd., 1969-76; with Kellogg Co. of G.B., Ltd., 1976—; with Kellogg Co., 1949—, vice chairman, 1982—. Office: Kellog Co 235 Porter St Box 3423 Battle Creek MI 49016 *

ROBINSON, GERALDINE MARLENE HELWIG, psychologist, psychoanalyst, computer software business executive; b. Milw., Apr. 5, 1947; d. William Frederick and Olga Wilhelmina (Syring) Helwig; m. Ian Robinson, June 21, 1969; children: Chelsea, Siobhàn, Antoinette, Krystal Georgiana Victoria, Lisa Ralet. BS in Psychology, U. Wis.-Stout, 1970, MS in Sch. Psychology, 1975. Lic. psychologist. Research assoc., psychotherapist Northwest Psychiatric Clinic, Eau Claire, Wis., 1974-77; pvt. practice psychology and psychotherapy Eau Claire, 1977-79; ptnr. Inst. Psychol. Therapies, Mpls., 1980-84; owner psychol. practice Robinson and Assoc., Mpls., 1984—; adj. asst. prof. counseling and psychol. services St. Mary's Coll. Grad. Ctr., Mpls., 1987—; psychoanaltyic preceptorship Interpersonal/Sullivanian Analysis with J.M. Tobin, M.D., Eau Claire, 1970-77; cons.; expert witness; pub. speaker, guest on TV and radio shows; allied profl. staff mem. St. Joseph's Hosp., Chippewa Falls, Wis., 1978-80; mem. med. research staff Sacred Heart Hosp., Eau Claire, 1974-77; co-owner, v.p. computer software mfg. co. Interactive Analytic Node. Contbr. articles to profl. jours.; author research papers presented to various profl. orgns. Organizer, official spokesperson, chmn. tng. com., vol. Disaster Stress Team, Twin Cities ARC and Minn. Network for Disaster Stress Intervention, 1985—; organizer Minn. Assn. Mental Health Infants; organizer vol. mental health profls. and media campaign to help serve family survivors Galaxy 204 air crash; bd. dirs. Geriatric Day Care Ctr., Luther Hosp., Eau Claire, 1975-77; v.p. pregnancy and drug prevention, intervention and edn. Concerned, Inc., Menomonie, Wis., 1971-73. Mem. Group-Without-A-Name (GWAN) Internat. Psychiat. Research Soc., Internat. Soc. Human Ethology, Internat. Assn. Infant Mental Health, Minn. Psychol. Assn. (social action com. 1984-85, author official policy statement on sexual exploitation children and teenagers, cochair entertainment com. 50th anniversary 1986), Minn. Women Psychologists, Minn. Assn. Mental Health of Infants, Midwest Assn. Comatose Care (v.p. 1984-85, pres. 1985—), Minn. Genealogical Soc., Clan Gunn Soc. N.Am. Lodge: Zonta (corp., gallery fund-raising coms. 1983-84; chair service com. 1984-85, co-chair 1985-86; co-chair corp. collection com. 1985-86, status of women com. 1987—). Avocations: Tae Kwondo Karate (Red Belt), painting, music, geneaology, writing. Home: 2345 W Medicine Lake Dr Minneapolis MN 55441 Office: 2620 Park Ave S Minneapolis MN 55404

ROBINSON, GLEN MOORE, III, optical research scientist; b. El Dorado, Ark., July 23, 1943; s. Glen Moore and Inez (Meek) R.; m. Oree Maude Hoefeld, Aug. 19, 1967; children: Mark Oscar, Luke Ian. BS, La. Tech. U., 1965; PhD, Tulane U., 1970. Sr. scientist 3M, St. Paul, 1969-76, research specialist, 1976-85, sr. research specialist, 1985—; assoc. prof. math. and chemistry Bethel Coll., St. Paul, 1973—; mem. bd. visitors U. Ariz., Tucson, 1982—. Author: Statistics for Non-Statisticians, 1974; contbr. articles to profl. and scholarly jours. Scoutmaster St. Paul council Boy Scouts of Am., 1970-77; mem. planning commn. Grant Twp., Minn., 1979—; chmn. environment com., roads com. Grant Twp., 1982—. Recipient Heinrich Hertz award Royal Soc., 1986. Mem. Am. Optical Soc., Am. Phys. Soc., Am. Chem. Soc. Presbyterian. Avocations: photography, canoeing, camping. Home: 9320 84th St N Stillwater MN 55082 Office: 3M 3M Ctr 236-3C-89 Saint Paul MN 55144

ROBINSON, HELENE SUSAN, pharmacist, manager; b. Cleve., July 10, 1956; d. Martin Stanley and Elaine (Steinhardt) Grumbach; m. Leroy Robinson, Nov. 12, 1983. BS in Pharm. Scis., U. Cin., 1979; cert. Women in Mgmt., Ursuline Coll., Pepper Pike, Ohio, 1983. Cert. pharmacy, bus. Asst. mgr. Cunningham Drugs, Cleve., 1979-80; staff pharmacist St. Luke's Hosp., Cleve., 1980-84, oncology pharmacist, 1984-85; dir. of pharmacy Care Plus-Cleve., Beachwood, Ohio, 1985—. Mem. Cleve. Soc. Hosp. Pharmacists (chmn. oncology 1984-85), Ohio Soc. Hosp. Pharmacists, Am. Soc. Hosp. Pharmacists, Kappa Epsilon. Baptist. Avocations: needlepoint, reading, sewing. Office: Care Plus-Cleve Inc 3355 Richmond Rd Suite 240 Beachwood OH 44122

ROBINSON, JACK ALBERT, retail drug stores executive; b. Detroit, Feb. 26, 1930; s. Julius and Fannie (Aizkowitz) R.; m. Aviva Freedman, Dec. 21, 1952; children: Shelby, Beth, Abigail. B in Pharmacy, Wayne State U., 1952. Founder, chief exec. officer, chmn. bd. Perry Drug Stores, Inc., Pontiac, Mich., 1957—; bd. dirs. Highland Superstores, Taylor, Mich., Entertainment Pubs. Birmingham, Mich.; v.p., bd. dirs. Mich. Merchants Council, Lansing, Harper Grace Hosps. Chmn. Wayne State Univ. Fund, Detroit, 1986; chmn. ann. fund Detroit Symphony Orch., 1986; v.p. Jewish Welfare Fedn. Detroit, 1986; bd. dirs. United Way of Pontiac, Mich., 1986, United Found. of Detroit, 1986, Pontiac Area Urban League, Community Found. SE Mich., Detroit Service Group, Save Orch. Hall, Inc., Cranbrook Inst. Sci., Jewish Fedn. Apts., Weizman Inst. Sci., Holocaust Meml. Ctr., Harper-Grace Hosp., Detroit; past dir. Pontiac Symphony, Boys Club of Pontiac, Detroit Osteo. Hosp. Recipient Disting. Alumni award Wayne State U. Coll. Pharmacy, 1975, Eleanor Roosevelt Humanities award from State of Israel, 1978, B'nai B'rith Youth Services Am. Tradition award, 1982, Wayne State U. Disting. Alumni award, 1985, Tree of Life award Jewish Nat. Fund, 1985, Disting. Citizen award Pontiac Boy Scouts Am., 1985, Corp. Leadership award Wayne State U., 1985, Booker T. Washinton Bus. Assn. Brotherhood award, 1986; named Entrepreneur of Yr. Harvard U. Bus. Sch., Detroit, 1982. Mem. Am. Pharm. Assn., Am. Found. for Pharm. Edn. (bd. dirs.), Nat. Assn. Chain Drug Stores (chmn. 1987). Club: Economic (bd. dirs. Detroit chpt.). Avocations: skiing, jogging, photography, classical music, glass collecting. Office: Perry Drug Stores Inc 5400 Perry Dr PO Box 1957 Pontiac MI 48056

ROBINSON, JACK F(AY), clergyman; b. Wilmington, Mass., Mar. 7, 1914; s. Thomas P. and Ethel Lincoln (Fay) R.; A.B., Mont. State U., 1936; D.B., Crozer Theol. Sem., 1939; A.M., U. Chgo., 1949, postgrad., 1950-52; m. Eleanor Jean Smith, Sept. 1, 1937 (dec. 1966); 1 dau., Alice Virginia Dungey; m. Lois Henze, July 16, 1968. Ordained to ministry Baptist Church, 1939; minister Bethany Ch., American Falls, Idaho, 1939-41, 1st Ch., Council Grove, Kans., 1944-49; ordained (transfer) to ministry Congregational Ch., 1945; minister United Ch., Chebanse, Ill., 1949-52, 1st Ch., Argo, Ill., 1954-58, Congl. Ch., St. Charles, Ill., 1958-64; assoc. minister Plymouth Congregational Ch., Lansing, Mich., 1964-66; tchr. Chgo. Pub. Schs., 1966-68; minister Waveland Ave. Congl. Ch., Chgo., 1967-79, interim pastor Chgo. Met. Assn., 1979—, First Congl. Ch., Des Plaines, Ill., 1979, Bethany Congl. Ch., Chgo., 1980, Eden United Ch. of Christ, Chgo., 1983-84, St. Nicolai Ch., Chgo., 1984, Grace United Ch. of Christ, Chgo., 1985-86; Christ Ch. of Chgo., 1987—; hist. cons. Bell & Howell Co., Chgo., 1981-82. Assoc. Hyde Park dept. Chgo. YMCA, 1942-44. U. Chgo. Library 1952-54; chmn. com. evangelism Kans. Congl. Christian Conf., 1947-48; city chmn. Layman's Missionary Movement, 1946-51; trustee Congl. and Christian Conf. Ill., v.p., 1963-64; mem. exec. council Chgo. Met. Assn. United Ch. of Christ, 1968-70, sec. ch. and ministry com., 1982—; mem. gen. bd. Ch. Fedn. Greater Chgo., 1969-71; mem. Library Bd. Council Grove, 1945-49; city chmn. NCCJ, 1945-49; dean Northside Mission Council United Ch. of Christ, 1975-77, sec. personnel com. Ill. Conf. United Ch. of Christ, 1986—. Mem. Am. Soc. Ch. History, Am. Acad. Polit. Sci., Am. Hist. Assn., C. of C. (past dir.), Internat. Platform Assn. Author: The Growth of the Bible, 1969; From A Mission to a Church, 1976; Bell & Howell Company: A 75 Year History, 1982, (co-author) Harza: 65 Years, 1986. Home: 2614 Lincolnwood Dr Evanston IL 60201 Office: PO Box 4578 Chicago IL 60680

ROBINSON, JERRY LEE, banker; b. Macomb, Ill., Oct. 24, 1957; s. Richard Lee Robinson and Alice Joleyn (Hightower) Arvin; m. Cythia Elaine Balch, June 28, 1987. BS in Accountancy, U. Ill., 1983. CPA, Ill.; cert. internal auditor, Ill.; cert. mgmt. auditor, Ill. Sr. auditor Dart & Kraft, Inc., Northbrook, Ill. and Atlanta, 1983-85; bus. analyst Kraft, Inc., Glenview, Ill., 1985-86; credit analyst 1st Nat. Bank Chgo., 1986-87, staff officer, mgr. credit services, 1987—. Mem. Am. Inst. CPA's, Inst. Cert. Mgmt. Accts. Republican. Jewish. Avocations: golf, tennis. Office: 1st Nat Bank Chgo 1 First Nat Plaza Chicago IL 60670-0051

ROBINSON, JOHN HAMILTON, civil engineer; b. Kansas City, Mo., Feb. 14, 1927; s. David Beach and Aileen March (Weaver) R.; m. Patricia Ann Odell, June 17, 1949; children: John Hamilton, Patricia Ann, Donna Marie, Clinton Odell. B.S., U. Kans., 1949. Registered profl. engr., Kans., Mo., Minn., Colo., N.Y., N.J., Ohio, La., Ind., Mass., Mich., N.H., Ariz., Tenn., Iowa, Va. With Black & Veatch (cons. engrs.), Kansas City, Mo., 1949—; ptnr. Black & Veatch (cons. engrs.), 1956—, exec. ptnr., 1971—, mng. ptnr., 1983—. Trustee Johnson County Community Coll.; deacon, elder 2d Presbyterian Ch., Kansas City, Mo. Served with USNR, 1945-46. Fellow ASCE; mem. Am. Cons. Engrs. Council (chmn. com. of fellows), Cons. Engrs. Council Mo. (dir. 1972—, pres. 1976-77), Mo. Soc. Profl. Engrs., Kans. Engring. Soc., Am. Water Works Assn. (dir., exec. com., chmn. standards council, v.p. 1985, pres. 1987, Fuller award 1983), Water Pollution Control Fedn., Tau Beta Pi, Sigma Tau, Omicron Delta Kappa, Beta Theta Pi. Clubs: Mission Hills Country, Vanguard, Mercury. Lodge: Rotary. Home: 3223 W 67th St Mission Hills KS 66208 Office: 1500 Meadow Lake Pkwy Kansas City MO 64114

ROBINSON, JOHN WILLIAM, electrical engineer; b. Culver, Ind., Oct. 6, 1937; s. Harold Hollis and Martha (Werner) R.; m. Barbara Ellen Williams, June 16, 1961 (div. May 1981); children: Constance, Robert, David. ASEE, Valparaiso Tech. U., 1957; BSEE, Purdue U., 1964. Technician Delco Electric, Kokomo, Ind., 1957-61; project engr. Jemco, Jasper, Ind., 1964-66; engring. mgr. Kimball Internat. Research and Devel., Jasper, 1966-73; engring. mgr. Kimball Electronics, Inc., Jasper, 1973-82, technical mgr., 1982—. Patentee in field. Mem. IEEE, Audio Engring. Soc., Acoustic Soc. Am., Computer Law Assn. (assoc.). Republican. Methodist. Club: Toastmasters (sec. 1970-72), Jasper Rifle and Gun (sec. 1980-82). Avocations: home computing, travel, reading, fine art, walking. Home: 202 Schnell Ln Jasper IN 47546 Office: Kimball Electronics Inc 1038 E 15th St Jasper IN 47546

ROBINSON, JOSIE MARA, accountant; b. Columbus, Ohio, Feb. 28, 1958; d. Donald Richard and Josephine Mary (Volpi) Britt; m. Steven Walter Robinson, Apr. 8, 1983. AS, Columbus Tech. Inst., 1978; BSBA, Franklin U., 1982. Acct., bus. U.S. Cargo & Courier Service, Columbus, 1982-86; acct. Larrimer & Warner, Columbus, 1986—. Mem. Endometriosis Assn. Roman Catholic. Avocations: gardening, home decorating, sewing, reading. Home: 428 Timber Creek Rd Reynoldsburg OH 43068

ROBINSON, LOIS HART, public relations executive; b. Freeport, Ill., Aug. 9, 1927; d. Seril N. and Cora (Stabenow) Hart; m. Noel M. Henze, Nov. 15, 1947 (div. 1964); m. Jack Fay Robinson, July 16, 1968; children—Susan Henze Bentley, Cynthia Henze Berkeley, Charles Henze. Student Oakton Community Coll., 1976-77, Northwestern U., 1977-81. Med. sec. Freeport Meml. Hosp., 1945-47; sec. No. Ill. Corp., 1947-49; adminstrv. asst. to supt. schs. Community Sch. Dist. 303, St. Charles, Ill., 1962-68; exec. sec. Bell & Howell Co., Chgo., 1969-73, supr. corp. relations, 1973-79, mgr. corp. communications, 1979-85, mgr. corp. communication services, 1985—; pres., dir. Bell & Howell Found., 1983—. Recipient Effie award Am. Mktg. Assn., 1983. Mem. Chgo. Women in Philanthropy, Corp. Volunteerism Council. Mem. Internat. Assn. Bus. Communications. Congregationalist. Home: 2614 Lincolnwood Dr Evanston IL 60201

ROBINSON, MARK E., systems auditor; b. Woodriver, Ill., Dec. 20, 1955; s. Gary E. and Mary Ann (Meyers) R. BA in Bus., U. Chgo., 1978, MBA in Fin., 1979. Cert. Data Processor. Market analyst Corning (N.Y.) Glass Works, 1979-80, account rep., 1980-81; cons. Arthur Andersen & Co., Chgo., 1982-84; systems auditor Am. Hosp. Supply, Evanston, Ill., 1984-85, Baxter Travenol Labs., Inc., Deerfield, Ill., 1985—; Presenter in field. Mem. Am. Mktg. Assn. (cert. selling skills course 1980), Inst. Internal Auditors, Psi Upsilon (trustee). Republican. Avocations: tennis, golf. Home: 1309 Elliott Ave Park Ridge IL 60068 Office: Baxter Travenol Labs Inc One Baxter Pkwy Deerfield IL 60015

ROBINSON, MEL GENE, training and development specialist; b. Stambaugh, Mich., May 15, 1948; s. Raymond Harry and Doris Marie (Borgstrom) R.; m. Patricia Marie Stafford, Dec. 7, 1968; children: Melissa Rae, Christopher Bradley. BA in Human Resource Mgmt., Met. State U., Mpls., 1981. Mgr. data services Dicomed Corp., Bloomington, Minn., 1975-76, tng. mgr., 1976-79; tng. mgr. Astrocom Corp., St. Paul, 1979-80, mgr. human resources, 1980-81; sr. instr. Comml. div. Honeywell, Mpls., 1981-86, DataServ Inc., Eden Prairie, Minn., 1986—; pres. Custom Tng., Columbia Heights, Minn., 1985—. Served with U.S. Army, 1969-71. Mem. Am. Soc. for Tng. and Devel., Internat. Assn. Quality Circles, U.S. Jaycees (ambassador 1980), Jaycees Internat. (senator 1983), Minn. Jaycees. Lutheran. Home: 1331 42 1/2 Ave NE Columbia Heights MN 55421 Office: DataServ Inc 12125 Technology Dr Eden Prairie MN 55344

ROBINSON, MELZIE LEE, chemical engineer; b. Columbia, S.C., Dec. 24, 1959; s. Roosevelt and Viola R.; m. Dianne Wilma Robinson, Apr. 6, 1985; 1 child, Nechelle. B Chem. Engring., Vanderbilt U., 1982. Chem. engr. Procter & Gamble, Cin., 1982—. Assoc. minister First Bapt. Ch.-College Hill in Cin., 1982—; mem. exec. bd. dirs. Christian Coll., Cin., 1986—. Mem. Alpha Phi Alpha. Avocations: creative writing, athletics, studying Scripture.

ROBINSON, NICHOLAS FRANK, physician; b. Kennett, Mo., Oct. 27, 1958; s. Brady Eugene and Marjorie Louise (Winters) R.; m. Deborah Kaye Pelts, Mar. 10, 1984; children: Ericca Dawn Rebstock, Amy Nicole. BA, U. Mo., Kansas City, 1978, MD, 1982. Resident in internal medicine Mayo Found., Rochester, Minn., 1982-83; staff physician Twin Rivers Regional Med. Ctr., Kennett, 1983—; med. cons. Kennett Health Care Ctr., 1984—; bd. dirs. Family Counseling Ctr., Kennett, 1984—, Tri-County Home Health, Kennett, 1984—. Mem. AMA, Am. Geriatric Soc., Mo. Med. Assn., Dunklin County Med. Soc., Airplane Owners and Pilots Assn., Mayo Alumni Assn. Democrat. Methodist. Clubs: Kennett Country, Farmers and Merchants (Holcomb). Avocations: computers, reading. Home: 204 E Lincoln Circle Kennett MO 63857 Office: Redi-Care Family Clinic 906 Saint Francis St Kennett MO 63857

ROBINSON, RICHARD EARL, federal judge; b. Omaha, Feb. 3, 1903; s. Richard and Jane (Hanna) R.; m. Florence Rich, May 22, 1929; children: Thomas E., John L. LL.B., Creighton U., 1927. Bar: Nebr. 1927. Practiced in Omaha, until 1956; U.S. dist. judge for Dist. Nebr., 1956—; chief judge 1957-72, now sr. judge. Mem. Omaha Airport Commn., 1950-51, finance commr., Omaha, 1951. Recipient Brandeis award Brandeis U. Club of Omaha, 1957; Alumni Merit award Creighton U., 1967; Man of Yr. award Omaha Club, 1986. Home: 10334 Fieldcrest Ct Apt 610 Omaha NE 68114 Office: U S Dist Ct PO Box 1457DTS Omaha NE 68101

ROBINSON, RONALD GUILFRED, minister; b. St. Louis, Nov. 9, 1955; s. Jack G. and Leoma Jean (Nelson) R.; m. Terri Jean O'Bryan, July 22, 1978; children: Joshua G., Tabitha Jean. BA, Ouachita Bapt. U., 1978; student, Midwestern Bapt. Sem., 1982-86. Ordained to ministery Bapt. Ch., 1976. Pastor Walnut St. Bapt. Ch., Arkadelphia, Ark., 1976-78; assoc. pastor Rock Hill Bapt. Ch., St. Louis, 1978-80; pastor 1st Bapt. Ch. of Cobden, Ill., 1980-82; assoc. pastor Tower Grove Bapt. Ch., St. Louis, 1982-86; pastor Bayless Bapt. Ch., St. Louis, 1986—; pastor, leader Continuous Witness Tng., St. Louis, 1982—; trainer Prayer for Spiritual Awakening, 1983—. Author: T.N.T., 1984, Show Me I'll Believe, 1984. 2d in state in baptisms Ill. Bapt. Conv., Cobden, 1981; recipient Sunday sch. growth awards Ill. State Bapt. Conv., 1981; led state in baptisms, Mo. Bapt. Conv., 1983, 84. Mem. Clear Creek Bapt. Assn. (Sunday sch. growth award, 1981), Fellowship Christian Magicians. Avocations: fishing, hunting, basketball, golf, writing. Office: Bayless Bapt Ch 8512 Morganford Saint Louis MO 63123

ROBINSON, SHELLEY ANNETTE, health service facility administrator, consultant; b. Missoula, Mont., June 4, 1960; d. William Joseph and Bertha Olive (Moen) Morton; m. Josh Leon Robinson, Nov. 2, 1985; 1 child, Panika Dawn. BA, U. Mont., 1982. Coordinator spl. service Kake (Ark.) City Schs., 1982-83; tchr. Big Sky High Sch., Missoula, 1983-84, Northland Cooperative, Virginia, Minn., 1984; behavioral cons. Mid-Range Cooperative, Chisholm, Minn., 1984-86; parent trainer/cons. State of Minn., Virginia, 1986—; dir. devel. achievement ctr. Range Ctr., Inc., Chisholm, 1987—; parent trainer/cons. Comprehensive System of Personnel Devel. Com. of Minn., Virginia, 1986—; researcher social sci., U. Mont., 1978-81. Adv. Range Women's Advs., Chisholm, 1985. North Cen. Women's Scholar Athlete scholar, 1981. Fellow Minn. Educators Assn., Psi Chi (life mem.). Congregationalist. Home: Rt 1 Box 1205 Britt MN 55710 Office: Range Ctr Inc 1001 SW 8th Ave Chisholm MN 55719

ROBINSON, STEPHEN MICHAEL, applied mathematician, educator; b. Columbus, Ohio, Apr. 12, 1942; s. Arthur Howard and Mary Elizabeth (Coffin) R.; m. Chong-Suk Han, May 10, 1968; children: Diana Marie, James Andrew. B.A., U. Wis., 1962, Ph.D., 1971; M.S., NYU, 1963. Adminstr. U. Wis.-Madison, 1969-72, asst. prof., 1972-75, assoc. prof., 1975-79, prof. indsl. engring. and computer scis., 1979—, chmn. dept. indsl. engring., 1981-84; cons. various agys. Dept. Def., 1971-86; cons. Battelle Meml. Labs., Columbus, 1980-81. Editor: Math. of Ops. Research, 1981-86; assoc. editor: Jour. Ops. Research, 1974-86, Mathematical Programming, 1986—; bd. editors Annals of Ops. Research, 1984—; contbr. numerous articles to profl. jours. Trustee Village of Shorewood Hills, Wis., 1974-76, mem. fin. com., 1973-87. Served to capt. U.S. Army, 1963-69, Korea, Vietnam. Decorated Legion of Merit; decorated Bronze Star, Air Medal, Army Commendation medal with 2 oak leaf clusters. Mem. Ops. Research Soc. Am., Inst. Mgmt. Scis., Inst. Indsl. Engrs., Soc. for Indsl. and Applied Math. Clubs: Madison. Home: 1014 University Bay Dr Madison WI 53705-2251 Office: Dept Indsl Engring U Wis 1513 University Ave Madison WI 53706

ROBINSON, THOMAS CARL, logistician; b. Cin., Jan. 17, 1954; s. Richard Paul and Wilma (Timm) R. BA in Math., Oberlin (Ohio) Coll., 1975. Systems analyst USAF, Wright-Patterson AFB, Ohio, 1976-81, logistics mgmt. specialist, 1981-86, supervisory systems analyst, 1986—. Mem. Am. Assn. Computer Machinery, Logistics Career Enhansement Program Cadre, Am. Fed. Govt. Employees Local 1138 (steward 1978-86, recording sec. 1980-81). Democrat. Avocations: hacking, rock guitar. Home: 734 Carlisle Ave Dayton OH 45410 Office: USAF Logistics Command Wright-Patterson AFB OH 45433

ROBINSON, WAYNE ANTHONY, utility company executive; b. Gallipolis, Ohio, Feb. 21, 1957; s. James William and Lydia Elizabeth (Borden) R. BA, Morehouse Coll., Atlanta, 1980. Mgmt. trainee Gallipolis Elec. Service, Ohio, 1980-82, pres., 1982—; bd. dirs. Gallco Workshops, Gallipolis, 1986—. Co-founder, bd. dirs., treas. Ohio Valley Minority Bus. Assocs., Inc.; minority rep. Ohio Valley Regional Devel. Commn., 1981; mem. Gallipolis City Planning Commn., 1983-86; mem. bd. zoning appeals, 1986—; bd. dirs. Gallco Sheltered Workshops, 1986; treas. Paint Creek Bapt. Ch., 1986—. Mem. Elec. Apparatus Service Assn., Am. Mgmt. Assn. Democrat. Baptist. Lodge: Rotary. Avocation: reading. Office: Gallipolis Elec Service 57 Pine St Gallipolis OH 45631

ROBISON, BARBARA JANE, tax accountant; b. Bkln., Oct. 17, 1924; s. Matthews and Sara (Birnbaum) Brilliant; m. Morris Moses Robison, Aug. 30, 1945; 1 child, Susan Kay. BS, Ohio State U., 1945; MBA, Xavier U., 1976. CPA. Acct. Antenna Research Lab. Inc., Columbus, Ohio, 1948-51; office mgr. Master Distributors, Inc., Columbus, 1951-57; treas. Antlab Inc., Worthington, Ohio, 1957-69; tax acct. AccuRay Corp., Worthington, 1969-76, tax mgr., 1976—. Mem. Am. Inst. CPA's, Ohio Soc. CPA's, Am. Soc. Women Accts. (pres. 1978-79), Columbus chpt. Am. Payroll Assn. Home: 1888 Jewett Rd Powell OH 43065 Office: Accuray Corp 650 Ackerman Rd Columbus OH 43202

ROBISON, HOWARD F., protective services official; b. Akron, Ohio, Mar. 4, 1935; s. Howard F. Sr. and Erna J. (Jueluison) R.; m. Maria J. Valdiviez, Mar. 10, 1956 (div. Dec. 1974); children: Donna, Cynthia, Kelly, Howard III; m. Dorothy Lee Wilkins, Mar. 4, 1975; children: Cindy, Deborah, Harry, Michelle, Melissa. Grad. high sch., London, Ohio; grad., Peace Officers Sch., London, Ohio, 1981. With juvenile missing persons unit Akron Police Dept., 1963—. Served as sgt. U.S. Army, 1953-56, Korea. Republican. Lutheran. Lodges: Moose, Masons, Faternal Order Police. Avocations: gardening, bowling, walking. Home: 2280 Eastwood Ave Akron OH 44305 Office: Akron Police Dept Missing Persons Unit 217 S High St Akron OH 44308

ROBNETT, CHRISTIE JOY, microbiologist; b. Peoria, Ill., Dec. 21, 1951; d. Paul Merlin and Virginia May (Crump) R. BA, U. Ill., 1973; MS, Ill. Inst. Tech., 1981. Microbiologist Good Humor Corp., Chgo., 1974-75; sec. Cen. Regional Lab. div. U.S. EPA, Chgo., 1975-79, aquatic biologist, 1979-81; lab. technician, microbiologist Nat. Animal Disease Ctr. USDA, Ames, Iowa, 1981-82, No. Regional Research Ctr. USDA, Peoria, Ill., 1982—. Mem. AAUW. Democrat. Methodist. Avocations: N.Am. Indian history, photography, phys. fitness, tennis, camping. Home: 110 Circle Dr East Peoria IL 61611 Office: NRRC USDA 1815 N University St Peoria IL 61614

ROBSON, JOHN EDWIN, pharmaceutical company executive, government official, lawyer; b. N.Y.C., June 21, 1930; s. Edwin O. and Elizabeth (Stone) R.; m. Margaret Elizabeth Zuehlke, Dec. 3, 1960; children: Matthew Stone, Douglas O'Neil. B.A., Yale U., 1952; J.D. with honors, Harvard U., 1955. Bar: Ill. 1955, D.C. 1955. Mem. firm Leibman, Williams, Bennett, Baird & Minow, Chgo., 1958-65; (merged with Sidley & Austin), 1969-75; staff mem. The White House, Washington, 1966-67; gen. counsel Dept. Transp., Washington, 1967-68; under sec. Dept. Transp., 1968-69; chmn. Civil Aeronautics Bd., Washington, 1975-77; exec. v.p., chief operating officer, pres., chief exec. officer G.D. Searle & Co., Skokie, Ill., 1977-85; dean, prof. mgmt. sch. bus. adminstrn. Emory U., Atlanta, 1986—; bd. dirs. AOA Corp., Chiron Corp., Continental Airlines Inc., Rand McNally Co.. Trustee St. John's Coll., Santa Fe, New Mex.; dir. Inst. Contemporary Studies, San Francisco. Served with AUS, 1955-57. Mem. Ill. State, Chgo., D.C., Fed. bar assns., Harvard Legal Aid Soc., Delta Kappa Epsilon. Clubs: Elihu, Chancery.

ROBSON, MARTIN CECIL, surgery educator, plastic surgeon; b. Lancaster, Ohio, Mar. 8, 1939; children: Karen Iredell, Douglas Spears, Martin Cecil III. Student, Northwestern U., 1957-59; B.A., Johns Hopkins U., 1961, M.D., 1964. Diplomate Am. Bd. Surgery, Am. Bd. Plastic Surgery. Intern U. Chgo. Hosps. and Clinics, 1964-65; resident in surgery Balt. City Hosps., 1965-67, Brooke Gen. Hosp., Ft. Sam Houston, Tex., 1967-69; resident in plastic surgery Yale-New Haven Hosp., 1971-73; instr. dept. surgery Yale U. Sch. Medicine, New Haven, 1973-74, asst. prof. plastic surgery, 1973-74, assoc. prof., 1974; assoc. prof. plastic surgery U. Chgo., 1974-77, prof. and chief plastic and reconstructive surgery, 1977-83, dir. Burn Center, 1976-83; prof., chmn. div. plastic and reconstructive surgery Wayne State U. Med. Center, 1983—; dir. Detroit Med. Center Burn Center, 1983—; cons. plastic and reconstructive surgery West Haven VA Hosp., Conn., 1973-74. Assoc. editor: Jour. Plastic and Reconstructive Surg.; mem. editorial bd.: Jour. Burn Care and Rehab.; editorial cons. bd.: Jour. Trauma. Served to maj. M.C. U.S. Army, 1967-71. Recipient Writing award Am. Med. Technologists, 1979, 80, 81, 82; recipient Lancer Authors' award, 1981, 82, Fisher award, 1982. Fellow ACS; mem. Soc. Univ. Surgeons (exec. council 1980-83), Plastic Surgery Research Council (chmn. 1983-84), Am. Burn. Assn. (pres. 1985-86), Am. Surg. Assn., Am. Assn. Plastic Surgery (nominating com. 1982—), Am. Soc. Plastic and Reconstructive Surgeons, Nu Sigma Nu, Phi Delta Theta, Alpha Omega Alpha. Office: 6D University Health Center 4201 St Antoine Detroit MI 48201

ROBY, DAVID JOHN, office products and gifts executive; b. Watertown, S.D., Feb. 23, 1955; s. Thomas Edmund and Ernestine (Evans) R.; m. Carla Rae Jeitz, July 23, 1977; 1 child, Christopher David. Grad., N.D. State U., 1977. Gen. salesman Cook's, Inc., Aberdeen, S.D., 1978-79; with Cook's, Inc., Watertown, S.D., 1977-78, 79—, gen. mgr., 1984-85, pres., 1985—; bd. dirs. Nutting Co., Watertown, 1985-86. Tng. dir. United Way, Watertown, 1986. Mem. Nat. Office Products Assn. (speaker 1986, retail br. stores forum 1986), Nat. Office Machine Dealers Assn., Protype Dealer Counsel, Watertown C. of C. (chmn. 1986). Republican. Roman Catholic. Club: Watertown Country (pres. 1982-83). Avocations: hunting, golf, studying business. Home: 1145 3d St NE Watertown SD 57201 Office: Cook's Inc 807 S Broadway Watertown SD 57201

ROCCHI, JEANINE LEONE, educator; b. Chgo., June 25, 1952; d. Carl William and Leona Martha (Macey) Carlson; m. Michael Bernard Rocchi, Aug. 4, 1973; children—Stephen, Melissa. B.S., DePaul U., 1974, M.S., 1976. Research asst. DePaul U., Chgo., 1971-75, teaching asst., 1973-75; research asst. Rush Presbyterian Med. Ctr., Chgo., 1975-77; chemistry tchr. Notre Dame Middle Sch., Chgo., 1977-78; chemistry instr. Triton Coll., River Grove, Ill., 1980-84; tchr. sci. St. Celestine Jr. High Sch., Elmwood Park, Ill., 1983—. State of Ill. Edn. Improvement grantee, 1984-85. Mem. Am. Chem. Soc., Nat. Sci. Tchrs. Assn. Roman Catholic. Club: Micropartners (Elmwood Park). Home: 3044 N Octavia St Chicago IL 60635 Office: St Celestine Sch Elmwood Park IL 60635

ROCCO, JAMES ROBERT, civil engineer; b. Orange, N.J., Jan. 18, 1953; s. Jerry Arnold and Anna Rocco; m. Lori Ellen Jacops, Jan. 29, 1977; children: Jerrold Edward, Jennifer Lynn. BS in Civil Engring., N.J. Inst. Tech., 1974. Jr. engr. mktg. div. Standard Oil Co., Columbus, Ohio, 1974-75, constrn. and maintenance engr., mktg. div., 1975-76, regional engr. mktg. div., 1976-77, constrn. and maintenance supr. mktg. div., 1977-79, constrn. and maintenance mgr. mktg. div., 1979-82, mgr. maintenance, retail mktg., 1983-85; mgr. constrn. and maintenance-South Standard Oil Co., Atlanta, 1985-86, mgr. maintenance and environ. services, 1986—. Councilman, Village of Reminderville, Ohio, 1982-85. Mem. ASCE (assoc.), Am. Mgmt. Assn.; Am. Petroleum Inst. (mktg. water subcom.), Nat. Water Well Assn. Roman Catholic. Home: 360 Heritage Rd Aurora OH 44202 Office: 200 Pub Sq Rm 18J 5606 Cleveland OH 44114

ROCH, RICHARD ROBERT, mining and manufacturing executive; b. Chgo., Feb. 21, 1938; s. B. John and Wanda M. (Zadlo) R.; m. Barbara Ellen Weber, Apr. 28, 1962; children: John David, Elizabeth Ann, Douglas James, Ann Kathryn. BS, Loyola U., Chgo., 1961. V.p. distbn. Internat. Minerals and Chem. Corp., Northbrook, Ill., 1978-83, v.p. transp. and distbn., 1983—; bd. dirs. Neptune Terminals, Vancouver, Can., Canpotex, Toronto, Can., Overseas Marine Services, N.Y.C. Mem. task force Park Ridge (Ill.) Sch. Bd., 1980. Served to sgt, U.S. Army, 1961-67. Mem. Nat. Freight Transp. Assn., Nat. Indsl. Transp. League, Nat. Waterways Assn., Marine Transp. Council, Fertilizer Inst. (transp. steering com. 1986—). Avocations: sailing, golf, reading, music. Office: Internat Minerals and Chem Corp 2315 Sanders Rd Northbrook IL 60062

ROCHE, JAMES RICHARD, university dean, pediatric dentist; b. Fortville, Ind., July 17, 1924; s. George Joseph and Nelle (Kinnaman) R.; m. Viola Marie Morris, May 15, 1949; 1 child, Ann Marie Roche Potter. DDS, Ind. U., 1947, MS in Dentistry, 1983. Diplomate Am. Bd. Pediatric Dentistry (exec. sec. 1982—). Prof. pediatric dentistry Ind. U. Sch. Dentistry, Indpls., 1968—, chmn. div. grad. pediatric dentistry, 1969-76, asst. dean faculty devel., 1976-80, assoc. dean faculty devel., 1980-87, assoc. dean for acad. affairs, 1987—; cons. Council Dental Edn., Hosp. Dental Service and Commn. Accreditation, Chgo., 1977-83. Served to capt. U.S. Army, 1952-54. Fellow Internat. Coll. Dentists, Am. Coll. Dentists, Am. Acad. Pediatric Dentistry (bd. dirs. 1967-70); mem. ADA (cons. Bur. Dental Health Edn. 1977—), Ind. Dental Assn. (v.p. 1973-74, chmn. legis. com. 1968-77, lobbyist 1970-77), Indpls. Dist. Dental Assn. (pres. 1967-68). Lodges: Rotary, Masons. Home: 1510 Persimmon Pl Noblesville IN 46060 Office: Ind U Sch Dentistry 1121 W Michigan St Indianapolis IN 46202

ROCHEN, DONALD MICHAEL, physician; b. Buffalo, Apr. 15, 1943; s. Leo Kent and Phoebe (Elkan) R.; m. Phyllis Helene Been, Aug. 15, 1971; children—Steven, Douglas, Deborah, Andrew. B.A., Northwestern U., 1964; D.O., Coll. Osteo. Medicine and Surgery, Des Moines, 1968. Intern, Detroit Osteo./Bi County Community Hosps., 1968-69, resident in otorhinolaryngology, 1969-73; practice otorhinolaryngology and oro-facial plastic surgery, Detroit, Warren and Mt. Clemens, Mich., 1973—; chmn. dept. otolaryngology and orofacial plastic surgery Detroit Osteo. Hosp., Highland Park and Bi County Community Hosp., Warren, Mich.; mem. staff Mt. Clemens Gen. Hosp. (Mich.); assoc. prof. Mich. State U. Coll. Osteo. Medicine and Surgery, 1975—; program dir. residency otorhinolaryngology Detroit Osteo. Hosp. and Bi-County Community Hosp.; adj. prof. Coll. Osteo. Medicine and Surgery, Des Moines, 1981—. Fellow Osteo. Coll. Ophthalmology and Otorhinolaryngology (diplomate), Am. Acad. Otolaryngology, Head and Neck Surgery; mem. Am. Osteo. Assn., Mich. Assn. Osteo. Physicians and Surgeons, N.Y. Acad. Scis., Wayne County Osteo. Assn., Macomb County Osteo. Assn. Jewish. Home: 4808 Tyndale Ct West Bloomfield MI 48033 Office: 30521 Schoenherr Warren MI 48033

ROCK, STANLEY ARTHUR, pastoral counseling educator; b. Pontiac, Mich., Apr. 22, 1937; s. Stanley Arthur Rock and Helen Cecelia (Slaybaugh) DeLongchamp; m. Nancy Beverly Rupp, Sept. 8, 1962; children: Lisa Joanne, Amy Lynne, Julie Rebecca. BA, U. Mich., 1959, MA, 1960; BD, Western Theol. Sem., 1966; EdD, Drake U., 1975. Ordained to ministry Reformed Ch. Am., 1966. Dir. Inter-Varsity, various locations in New England, 1960-63; asst. sec. translations Am. Bible Soc., N.Y.C., 1967-68; minister Blawenberg (N.J.) Reformed Ch., 1968-70; campus minister Drake U., Des Moines, 1970-76; pastoral care and counseling educator Western Theol. Sem., Holland, Mich., 1976—; chaplain USNR, Battle Creek, Mich., 1966—; cons. Reformed Ch. in Am., N.Y.C., 1976—; marriage enrich specialist, 1974—; cons. VA Hosp., Battle Creek, 1986. Author (marriage preparation): This Time Together, 1980; contbr. articles to profl. jours. Del. Govs. Conf. on the Family, Lansing, Mich., 1980; trustee Cen. Coll., Pella, Iowa, 1985—; pres. Consortium for Pastoral Counseling Tng., Western Mich., 1983-86; mem. Sr. Services Advocacy Council, Holland, 1984. Recipient Hillel Inter-Faith award, 1960; U. Mich. scholar, Ann Arbor, 1980; Danforth fellow, 1964-65. Fellow Am. Assn. Pastoral Counselors; mem. Christian Assn. Psychol. Studies, Naval Res. Assn., Am. Assn. Counseling and Devel. Home: 309 Foxcroft Circle Holland MI 49423 Office: Western Theol Sem 86 E 12th St Holland MI 49423

ROCK, THEODORE FREDRICK, banker; b. Alton, Ill., Sept. 21, 1940; s. Theodore Adolph and Jewell (Cheatham) R.; m. Carolyn J. Klasing, Feb. 21, 1963 (div. June 1984); children—Vincent James, Theodore Michael, Kevin Walter; m. Valerie M. Allen, Sept. 7, 1985. B.S., U. Wyo., 1970; M.B.A., Loyola U.-Chgo., 1976. Programmer, analyst Western Electric, Warrenville, Ill., 1970-73; systems mgr. Ofcl. Airline Guide, Oakbrook, Ill., 1973-80; sr. cons. Am. Mgmt. Systems, Chgo., 1980-81; software mgr. and v.p. Harris Bank, Chgo., 1981—; dir. Midwest Data Base/Data Communications User Group, Chgo., 1981—. Stewardship chmn. Chgo. Met. Assn., United Church of Christ, Chgo., 1984—; lay moderator First Congregational Ch., Downers Grove, Ill., 1983-84. Served with USN, 1959-68, with Res., 1969—. Mem. Phi Kappa Phi. Club: Toastmasters Internat. (pres. 1985-87). Avocations: playing English handbells; racquetball; jogging. Home: 4016 Belle Aire Ln Downers Grove IL 60515 Office: Harris Bank PO Box 755 Chicago IL 60690

ROCKE, RANDALL RICHARD, television producer, director; b. Bloomington, Ill., May 16, 1949; s. Norman Joseph and Audrey Mae (Hodel) R.; m. Betty Lou Troyer, Aug. 13, 1977. Student music edn. Ill. Wesleyan U., 1967-71; student music performance Ill. State U., 1976. Music dir. Euriskon, Inc., West Chicago, Ill., 1973-75; asst. mgr. Lowell's Distbr., Bloomington, Ill., 1976-78; photographer, salesman Salem & Click Camera, Dayton, Ohio, 1978-80; TV dir. Shiloh Ch., Dayton, 1980-84; media dir. First Community Ch., Columbus, Ohio, 1984—; mem. field faculty Capital U., Dayton, 1983-84; adviser bd. homeland ministries United Ch. of Christ, N.Y.C., 1984—. Recipient Cert. of Appreciation, Building Bridges, Inc., 1983, Wilbur award nomination Religious Pub. Relations Council, 1983. Mem. Nat. Acad. TV Arts and Scis. Avocations: photography; flying; singing; instrumental performance. Office: First Community Ch 1320 Cambridge Blvd Columbus OH 43212

ROCKEMANN, DAVID DOUGLAS, social service agency administrator; b. Jefferson City, Mo., Mar. 9, 1954; s. Raymond William and Irene Pauline (Strobel) R.; m. Margaret Ann Perkinson, June 20, 1986. BA in Sociology, U. Mo., 1976, MS in Community Devel., 1978. State health planner State Health Planning Devel. Agy., Jefferson City, 1978; health cons., research assoc. Syncaredian Health Assn., Walnut Creek, Calif., 1978-79; asst. dir. day care Jewish Home for the Aged, San Francisco, 1979; adminstr. St. Regis Retirement Ctr., Hayward, Calif., 1979-82; dir. aging services Community and Econ. Devel. Assn., Chgo., 1982-86; exec. dir. Community Nutrition Network, Chgo., 1986—; cons. Wade West Inc., San Francisco, 1979; researcher Calif. Dept. Health Services, San Francisco, 1978-79; research asst. Ctr. for Research in Social Behavior, Columbia, Mo., 1977-79. Author: Outreach to the Elderly, 1983; (with others) Health Care Trends, 1978, Consumer's Guide to Nursing Homes, 1978. Mem. adv. council Suburban Cook County Area Agy. on Aging, Chgo., 1983-84; legis. adv. State of Ill. Spl. Com. on Aging, Chgo., 1985; coordinator, moderator Mid-Am. Congress on Aging, Kansas City, Mo., 1985; mem. planning com. Mid-Am. Congress on Aging, Chgo., 1986. Adminstrn. on Aging scholar U. Mo., 1977-78; Older Americans Act grantee, 1982-87. Mem. Gerontol. Soc. Am., Am. Soc. on Aging, Nat. Council on Aging, Community Devel. Soc. Am., Nat. Assn. of Nutrition and Aging Services Programs. Lutheran. Office: Community Nutrition Network 624 S Michigan Ave Chicago IL 60605

ROCKHILL, MARVIN LYNN, infosystems specialist; b. Reedsburg, Wis., June 8, 1946; s. Everell J. and Marcella L. (Grover) R.; m. C. Ann Govan, Nov. 19, 1966; children: Edmund J., Melisa L. A in Applied Sci., Coll. Dupage, 1971; postgrad., Ind. U., 1986—. Programmer Fiat/Allis, Carol Stream, Ill., 1969-74; analyst Hook Drugs, Indpls., 1974-76; tech. support mgr. I.T.T. Pub., Indpls., 1976-85; with research and support staff Community Hosps., Indpls., 1982-85, system support analyst, 1985—; cons. I.I.T. Ednl. Services, 1982, Indpls., Indecon, Chgo., 1982, Charles Hill & Assocs., Indpls., 1984. Mem. Ways and Means com. Hamilton Southeastern Royal Guardians, Noblesville, Ind., 1986. Mem. Cen. Ind. Educators of Data Processing, Info. Ctrs. Users Group. Republican. Avocations: woodworking, soccer. Mem. gold medalist soccer team, White River State Games, 1985. Home: 11022 E 116th St Noblesville IN 46060 Office: Community Hosps Indpls 1500 N Ritter Ave Indianapolis IN 46219

RODBY, MICHAEL KEVIN, electrical engineer; b. Waterloo, Iowa, Feb. 8, 1955; s. Roy F. and Miriam A. (Steinbron) R.; m. Mischel E. Berg, May 18, 1985. BSEE, Iowa State U., 1978. Programmer NASA, Cape Canaveral, Fla., 1976-77; cons. DCO Computer Co., Waterloo, 1978-79; pres. Advanced Bus. Computers, Waterloo, 1979-84; dir. microcomputer systems Oster Communications, Cedar Falls, Iowa, 1985-86; tech. devel. mgr. Commodity Communications Corp., Lombard, Ill., 1986—. Author: (computer program) Future Source, 1986-87. Mem. IEEE, Assn. Computing Machinery. Republican. Unitarian. Home: 16W626 Honeysuckle Rose 16-24 Hinsdale IL 60521 Office: Commodity Communications Corp 420 Eisenhower Ln N Lombard IL 60148

RODDA, RICHARD EARL, writer, musician, educator; b. Bloomingdale, N.J., June 26, 1945; s. Richard and Mabel (Marion) R.; m. Donna Lee Slater, Sept. 7, 1968. B. Music Edn., Baldwin-Wallace Coll., 1967; postgrad. Yale U., 1967-68; M.A., Case Western Res. U., 1970, Ph.D., 1978. Tchr. Cleve. pub. schs., 1968-73; instr. U. Akron, 1976-77, Cuyahoga (Ohio) Community Coll., 1979, Case Western Res. U., 1975-87, Cleve. Inst. Music, 1987, Borromeo Coll. of Ohio, Blossom Music Ctr.; program annotator Dallas Symphony Orch., also orchs. of Richmond, Oklahoma City, Akron, Cedar Rapids, Austin, Springfield (Mass.), Tampa, Ottawa, Am. Symphony Orch., Orpheus Orch., N.Mex, Penunsula Music Festival; asst. program editor Cleve. Orch.; Akron Symphony Orch.; trombonist; mem. Cleve. Fedn. Musicians. Yale U. grantee, 1967-68; Case Western Res. U. grantee, 1973-78; Omicron Delta Kappa scholar, 1966-67. Mem. Am. Musicol. Assn., Internat. Trombone Soc. Contbr. Telarc, Angel Records, Stagebill mag. Address: 3330 Warrensville Rd #406 Shaker Heights OH 44122

RODDY, JOHN THOMAS, fitting manufacturing company executive; b. Cleve., Dec. 31, 1941; s. John James and Ann (Gallagher) R.; m. Andrea Paulette Scerba, Dec. 12, 1964; children—John J., William P., Julie A., Bradley J. B.B.A. in Mktg., Cleve. State U., 1973; M.B.A. in Systems Mgmt., Baldwin Wallace Coll., Berea, Ohio, 1984. Sales service coordinator Acme Cleve. Corp., Cleve., 1976-80, mgr. sales service, 1980-81, mgr. customer services, 1981-82, mktg. ops. analyst, 1982-83; mgmt. cons., Cleve., 1983-84; mgr. sales systems Crawford Fitting Co., Solon, Ohio, 1984—. Served with U.S. Army, 1964-66. Mem. Am. Mktg. Assn., Assn. Systems Mgmt., Data Processing Mgmt. Assn., Alpha Chi, Delta Mu Delta. Roman Catholic. Avocations: jogging, golf, bowling. Office: Crawford Fitting Co PO Box 39007 29500 Solon Rd Solon OH 44139

RODE, JAMES DEAN, banker; b. Cleve., Feb. 4, 1948; s. Andrew Joseph and Eileen M. (Costello) R.; m. Leslie Ann Biles, June 27, 1970. B.A. in Econs, Ohio U., Athens, 1969; M.B.A. in Fin, Case Western Res. U., 1974. With AmeriTrust Co., Cleve., 1969—; sr. v.p. consumer fin. AmeriTrust Co., 1979-80, exec. v.p. retail banking, 1980-83, sr. exec. v.p. banking services group, 1983, pres., 1984—; dir. AmeriTrust Corp. & Co., Bearings, Inc. Trustee Univ. Hosps. of Cleve., Case Western Res. U. Served with USAFR, 1969. Mem. Consumers Bankers Assn. (trustee, chmn.). Roman Catholic. Clubs: Skytop (Pa.); Union (Cleve.); Westwood Country. Office: Ameritrust Corp 900 Euclid Ave PO Box 5937 Cleveland OH 44101 Also: First Nat Supermarkets Inc 17000 Rockside Rd Cleveland OH 44137 also: Forest City EnterprisesInc 10800 Brookpark Rd Cleveland OH 44130

RODEMAN, FREDERICK ERNEST, accountant; b. Chgo., Jan. 29, 1938; s. Ernest August and Elizabeth Mae (Penrod) R.; m. Marilyn Kay Paul, June 17, 1967. BBA, Ind. U., 1959; cert. bank controllership, U. Wis., 1975; MBA, De Paul U., 1976. CPA, Ind., Wis. Auditor Arthur Andersen & Co., Chgo., 1959-67; acct. mgr. A.B. Dick & Co., Chgo., 1967-72; controller Beloit (Wis.) State Bank, 1972-77; pvt. practice acctg. Beloit, 1977—. Mem. Am. Inst. CPA's. Republican. Baptist. Home and Office: 2372 Tara Ct Beloit WI 53511

RODERICK, BARBARA HOLROYD, social worker; b. Kirin, Manchuria, China, Dec. 2, 1924 (parents Am. citizens); d. A. Waldie and Rose (Garrett) Holroyd; m. Glenn Edward Roderick, June 10, 1948; children—Carolyn, Lois. A.B., Hiram Coll., 1947; M.S.S.A., Western Res. U., 1950. Caseworker, Family Service Assn., Miami, Fla., 1950-53, Cleve., 1953-57; interim dir. Interfaith Housing Corp., Cleve., 1967-68; workshop dir. Heights Citizens for Human Rights, Cleve., 1969; housing coordinator, assoc. city planner, commr. real estate programs City of Cleveland Heights, Ohio, 1970-79; assoc. dir. Human Affairs, Inc., 1979—. Mem. bd. operation equality Urban League, 1967-74; chmn. Heights Christian Ch., 1981-83; bd. dirs. Heights Community Congress, 1972-73, Greater Cleve. Interch. Council, 1982—. Mem. Acad. Cert. Social Workers, Nat. Assn. Social Workers. Democrat. Mem. Christian Ch. (Disciples of Christ). Home: 3610 Cummings Rd Cleveland Heights OH 44118 Office: 5 Severance Circle Room 509 Cleveland Heights OH 44118

RODERICK, DOUGLAS KEITH, controller; b. St. Paul, Oct. 24, 1957; s. Richard K. and Alice M. (Johanson) R. BS in Acctg., U. Minn., 1980, MBA, 1985. CPA, Minn. Internal auditor Bemis Co., Mpls., 1980-81, asst. acct., 1981-82; acctg. mgr. MGM Liquor Warehouse Internat., Inc., St. Paul,

1982-83, controller, 1984; fin. analyst IDS Fin. Services, Mpls., 1984-85, product controller, 1985—. Bd. dirs. Northwestern Chi Psi Ednl. Found., Inc., Mpls., 1984, pres., 1987. Mem. Nat. Assn. Securities Dealers. Republican. Lutheran. Avocations: woodcraft, raquet sports. Home: 858-94th Ave NE Blaine MN 55434

RODEWALD, JAMES MICHAEL, real estate company executive, real estate syndicator; b. Waco, Tex., Apr. 20, 1942; s. Howard Fred and Dorothy Mae (Faust) R.; m. Evelynn Brown, Dec. 19, 1965; children—Kara Lynn, Kevin James. B.A., William Jewell Coll., 1964; M.A., U. Wis., 1967; postgrad. Central Mo. U., 1970. Lic. real estate broker, Mo., Kans. Vol., Peace Corps, Malawi, Central Africa, 1967-68; property mgr. William C. Haas Co., Kansas City, Mo., 1970-72; exec. v.p., co-owner Roger L. Cohen Co., Kansas, City, 1972-81; pres. James M. Rodewald Co., Kansas City, 1981-86; pres. Investment Realty Advisors, Inc.; cons. to regional stock house for real estate acquisitions. Mem. Nat. Republican Com.; mem. pres.'s adv. council William Jewell Coll.; bd. dirs. Downtown Inc., Kansas City. Served with U.S. Army, 1968-70; Vietnam. Gen. Motors scholar, 1960-64; Phi Gamma Delta scholar, 1965. Mem. Kansas City Real Estate Bd. (Comml. Realtor Assoc. of Yr.), Urban Land Inst., Nat. Assn. Office and Indsl. Parks, Real Estate Syndication Inst., Nat. Assn. Realtors, Mo. Assn. Realtors. Republican. Presbyterian. Club: Carriage. Home: 651 W 57th St Kansas City MO 64113 Office: 800 Mercantile Bank Tower 1101 Walnut Kansas City MO 64106

RODGERS, DENNIS BRUCE, lawyer; b. Decatur, Ill., Oct. 16, 1940; s. Richard Wilbur and Eleanor Frances (Cobb) R.; B.S., Trinity Coll., Hartford, Conn., 1962; J.D., Georgetown U., 1966; m. Marilynne Linda Wilson, Nov. 30, 1974; children—John, Andrew, Alainna, Aaron. Tchr., Bloomfield (Conn.) pub. schs., 1962-63; admitted to Ill. bar, 1966, since practiced in Decatur; mem. firm Denz, Lowe, Moore, Rodgers & See, 1966-77; legal planner Macon County Regional Plan Commn., 1970-76; part time prof. Richland Community Coll., 1976-79. Crusade chmn. Macon County unit Am. Cancer Soc., 1971-72, bd. dirs., 1972-77, chmn. bd., 1974-75; mem. Now and Tomorrow Council of Decatur Meml. Hosp., 1971-77; bd. dirs. Council Community Services, 1970-77, pres., 1975-77; pres. Sangamon Valley Assn., 1972-76; mem. Macon County Health Bd., 1981—; mem. Scholarships for Ill. Residents, 1970—; adminstrv. v.p. Decatur Jaycees, 1969-70; pres. Young Republican Orgn. Macon County, 1967-68; chmn. Lake Decatur Sedimentation Control Com., 1984-85. Recipient Disting. Service award Decatur Jaycees, 1971; named to Outstanding Young Men of Am., 1969-72. Mem. Ill., Decatur bar assns., Metro-Decatur C. of C. (chmn. transp. com. 1977—, dir. 1980-83, 84—; Disting. Vol. award 1983), Alpha Chi Rho, Phi Alpha Delta (cert. disting. service 1966). Co-author: Oakley Reservoir and Water Development for Central Illinois, 1968. Home: 90 John Dr Mount Zion IL 62549 Office: Suite 604 Millikin Ct 132 S Water St Decatur IL 62523

RODGERS, LOUIS DEAN, surgeon; b. Centerville, Iowa, Nov. 24, 1930; s. John James and Anna Alice (Spraguer) R.; m. Gretchen Lynn Hendershot, Feb. 19, 1954; children—Cynthia Ann, Elizabeth Dee. M.D., U. Iowa, 1960. Diplomate Am. Bd. Surgery. Intern, Broadlawns Hosp., Iowa, 1960-61; resident Meth-Hosp., Des Moines, 1961-65; practice medicine specializing in gen. surgery, Des Moines, 1965—; chmn. dept. surgery Iowa Methodist Ctr., Des Moines, 1980-84, chief gen surgery, 1982—; clin. assoc. prof. surgery U. Iowa, Iowa City, 1983—. Mem. steering com. Gov.'s Campaign, Republican Party, Iowa, 1982; bd. dirs. Iowa Meth. Med. Found., Des Moines, 1983, Des Moines Symphony, 1984—, Des Moines Children's Home, 1987. Served to staff sgt. U.S. Army, 1951-54. Named Surg. Tchr. of Yr., Iowa Meth. Med. Ctr. Dept. Surgery, 1978, 84. Fellow ACS (liaison to cancer com. 1973); mem. Western Surg. Assn. (mem. Iowa trauma com. 1983), Iowa Acad. Surgery (pres. 1982-83), Throckmorton Surg. Soc. (pres. 1986). Republican. Club: Des Moines Golf and Country. Home: 715 53d St Des Moines IA 50312 Office: Surgery PC 1212 Pleasant St #211 Des Moines IA 50309

RODGERS, RANDALL R., health services administrator; b. Monmouth, Ill., May 19, 1947; s. Lee A. and Dorothy (Baltz) R.; m. Susan Elaine Wagner; children: Jay, Jeff, Jon. BS, U. Ill., 1969, MS, 1971. Tchr., coach Champaign (Ill.) Schs., 1969-75; head football coach, athletic dir. Inver Hills Community Coll., Inver Grove Heights, Minn., 1975-79; head football coach U. Evansville, Ind., 1979-85; v.p. sales Champion Art, Indiatlantic, Fla., 1985; coordinator health promotion programs Bristol Myers, Evansville, 1985—; regional dir. White River Games, Ind., 1986—. Bd. dirs. Evansville Parks Found., 1986—. Named Outstanding Young Man of Am., 1973. Mem. Am. Assn. Health, Physical Edn. and Recreation, Am. Football Coaches Assn., Minn. Jr. Coll. Athletic Assn. (pres. 1978-79), Assn. Fitness Bus. Lodge: Optimist. Avocations: radio broadcasting, running, youth sports. Home: 1458 Bonnie View Ct Evansville IN 47715 Office: Bristol-Myers 2404 W Pennsylvania Evansville IN 47721

RODGERS, SALLY ANN, accountant; b. Alliance, Ohio, Sept. 27, 1940; d. Forrest LeRoy and Elizabeth Ann (Meinzen) Albright; m. John Dixon Tuttle, July 6, 1968 (div. June 1970); 1 child, Melanie; m. John Albert Rodgers, Nov. 16, 1974; adopted Melanie. Student, Akron U., 1966-72. Bookmobile librarian Rodman Pub. Library, Alliance, 1960-62; acctg. clk. E.W. Bliss Co., Canton, Ohio, 1962-67; bookkeeper Met. Contract, North Canton, Ohio, 1967-74; staff acct. Bruner, Cox et al, Canton, 1974-84; owner Record Mgmt. Services, Canton, 1984—. Mem. Am. Inst. CPA's, Ohio Soc. CPA's (chairperson accts. com. 1984-87), Am. Soc. Women Accts. (com. chairperson 1985—, v.p. 1985-87, pres. 1987), Network, Inc. Democrat. Presbyterian. Lodge: Eastern Star. Avocations: reading, sewing, bowling, aerobics. Office: Record Management Services 1908 Woodlawn Ave NW Canton OH 44708

RODGERS, WILLIAM CAMERON, III, marketing consulting company executive; b. East Orange, N.J., Apr. 25, 1938; s. William Cooper and Margaret (Lewis) R.; m. Judith Nancy Abbott, Aug. 19, 1966; children: Lori Cameron, William Frederick. BBA, U. Denver, 1962. Cert. mgmt. cons. Dir. mktg. Nathan's Famous, N.Y.C., 1968-71; v.p., gen. mgr. Merchant's Mktg., State College, Pa., 1971-72; pres. Wilrod Advt., State College, 1972-77; sr. v.p. trade div. Healy-Schuttle Advt., Buffalo, 1977-82; sr. v.p. Noble Mktg. Group, Springfield, Mo., 1982—. Contbr. articles to profl. jours. Recipient Effie award, 1982, Bronze Echo award, 1982; named Ky. Col. Mem. Internat. Foodservice Mfrs. Assn. (data and research com., planning com. 1981-83), Nat. Restaurant Assn., Cert. Mgmt. Cons. Republican. Club: Amiga Computer. Lodge: Masons. Avocations: food preparation, computers, carpentry. Home: 1916 E Nottingham Springfield MO 65807 Office: Noble Communications 3 Corp Ctr Springfield MO 65804

RODGERS, WILLIAM MIKLE, construction products company executive; b. Altoona, Pa., Nov. 15, 1944; s. Will and Sue (Hoffman) R.; m. Patricia R. Rodgers (div. Nov. 1985); children: Michael W. Rodgers, Liberty K. BBA in Mktg., Fla. Atlantic U., 1971. Sales rep. Master Builders, Cleve., 1973-78; br. mgr. Master Builders, Washington, 1978-81; product mktg. mgr. Master Builders, Cleve., 1981-86, gen. mgr. set products div., 1986—. Served with U.S. Army, 1965-67. Mem. Sales and Mktg. Execs. Assn. Republican. Roman Catholic. Avocations: racquetball, golf. Home: 440 Richmond Park E #003C Richmond Heights OH 44143 Office: Master Builders Set Consumer Products Div 23700 Chagrin Blvd Beachwood OH 44122

RODKEY, FREDERICK STANLEY, JR., lawyer; b. Urbana, Ill., Oct. 25, 1930; s. Frederick Stanley and Temple (Ryan) R.; m. Suzanne Ooms, June 15, 1963; children—Gretchen, Geoffrey. B.A., Stanford U., 1953; postgrad. Boalt Hall Sch. Law, U. Calif., 1954; J.D., Chgo.-Kent Coll. Law, 1956. Bar: Ill. 1957. Atty., Chgo. Title & Trust, 1956-57; assoc. Newton, Wilhelm & Kennedy, Chgo., 1957-59; atty. Household Fin. Corp., Chgo., 1959-64; counsel Res. Ins. Co., Chgo., 1964-66; ptnr. Crandall & Rodkey, Evanston, Ill., 1966-67; sole practice, Freeport and Lena, Ill., 1967—; atty. Village of German Valley, Ill., 1973—, Village of Ridott, Ill., 1974—, Village of Lena, 1977—, Village of Cedarville, Ill., 1979—; spl. asst. atty. gen. State of Ill., 1973-76; asst. pub. defender Stephenson County, Ill., 1971—; atty. Lena Park Dist., 1977—. Chmn. Central com. Stephenson County Republican Party, 1972-74. Mem. Ill. Bar Assn., Chgo. Bar Assn., Stephenson County Bar Assn., Chgo.-Kent Alumni Assn., (past treas.), Stephenson County Hist. Soc., Stanford Alumni Assn., Alpha Sigma Phi, Pi Sigma Alpha, Nu Beta Epsilon. Mem. United Ch. of Christ. Clubs: Lions (past pres.), Men's Garden Club of Freeport (past pres.), Elks. Home: 1126 S Benson Blvd Freeport IL 61043 Office: 200 Post Office Bldg Freeport IL 61032

RODKIN, DONALD T., computer consultant; b. Chgo., Apr. 15, 1939; s. Sidney and LaVerne (Hollison) R.; m. Dean S. Yellen, Aug. 6, 1961; children—Susan J., Gary A. B.S., Northwestern U., 1960; M.P.A., Ind. U., 1962. Programmer, No. Ind. Pub. Service Co., Hammond, Ind., 1961-66; ops. supr. Commonwealth Edison, Chgo., 1966-69; cons. Leasco Systems, Oak Brook, Ill., 1970-73; project dir. Tres Systems, Dallas, 1973-76; pres., cons. Mgmt. Systems Assocs., Oak Brook, Ill., 1976—. Republican. Home: 10 S 236 Birnam Trail Hinsdale IL 60521 Office: Mgmt Systems Assocs PO Box 911 Oak Brook IL 60522

RODNE, KJELL JOHN, city official; b. Haugesund, Norway, July 6, 1948; came to U.S., 1959; s. Johannes and Margit (Gautun) R.; m. Kathleen Anne Gordon, Sept. 21, 1966; children—Jay Robert, Lee Eric. B.S., U. Minn.-Duluth, 1971, M.S.W., 1985. Asst. youth dir. YMCA, Duluth, 1967-68; counselor Northwood, Duluth, 1968-71, team leader, 1971-76, social worker, 1976-77, program dir., 1977-85; personnel dir. City of Duluth, 1985-86, adminstrv. asst. City of Duluth, 1986—; bd. dirs. Minn. Council Residential Treatment Ctrs., St. Paul, 1977-85 . Mem. Duluth City Council, 1978-85, pres., 1981; bd. dirs. United Devel. Achievement Ctr., Duluth, 1978-85, Arrowhead Regional Devel. Commn., Duluth, 1981-85, United Way of Duluth, 1981—. Mem. Grandma's Marathon, Internat. City Mgrs. Assn. Democrat. Lutheran. Home: 129 N 28th Ave W Duluth MN 55806 Office: City of Duluth 406 City Hall Duluth MN 55802

RODNEY, JOEL M., provost; b. Bklyn., Nov. 9, 1937; s. Samuel Seymour and Jane (Loorya) R.; m. Madalyn Marie Okolowski; children: Jonathan, Adam, Ben. BA cum laude, Brandeis U., 1959; PhD, Cornell U., 1965. From instr. to assoc. prof. Wash. State U., Pullman, 1963-70; chmn. div. social scis., assoc. prof. history Elmira (N.Y.) Coll., 1970-72, coordinator flood relief and community planning, 1973; dean arts and sci., prof. history Widener Coll., Chester, Pa., 1973-76, acting chief acad. officer, dean, 1976-77, chief acad. officer, dean, 1977-81, dir. univ. grad. programs, 1979-81; v.p. acad. affairs Salisbury (Md.) State Coll., 1981-86; provost Rockford (Ill.) Coll., 1986—. Editor Albion, 1967-78; contbr. articles to profl. jours. Vice chmn. Md. Gov.'s Com. on Employment of Handicapped, 1985-86, chmn. and mem. Lower Shore div., 1983-86; chmn. adv. bd., mem. Crozer-Chester Med. Health Ctr., Chester, 1974-77; project evaluator NEH, 1986; mem., sec. Delaware County Mental Health/Mental Retardation Bd., 1975-81. Recipient Disting. Service award Widener Meml. Sch., 1978, Award of merit Md. Gov.'s Com. on Employment of Handicapped, 1984; named to Legion of Honor, Chapel of Four Chaplains, 1978; honoree West Phila. Vets. and Handicapped Employment Com., 1977. Mem. Am. Assn. Acad. Deans, Conf. on Brit. Studies, Am. Assn. Univ. Adminstrs., Phi Alpha Theta. Republican. Clubs: U.S. Power Squadron (Salisbury); City (Rockford). Home: 5854 Allerton Dr Rockford IL 61111 Office: Rockford Coll 5050 E State Rockford IL 61108

RODOS, JOSEPH JERRY, osteopathic physician, educator; b. Phila., July 7, 1933; s. Harry and Lisa (Perlman) R.; m. Bobbi Golden, Apr. 6, 1957; (div. 1974); m. Joyce I. Pennington, Sept. 26, 1981; children: Adam Justin, Nicole Ann. B.S., Franklin & Marshall Coll., 1955; D.O., Kirksville Coll. Medicine, Mo., 1959. Diplomate Am. Bd. Family Medicine, Am. Osteo. Bd. Pub. Health and Preventive Medicine. Intern; Grandview Hosp., Dayton, Ohio, 1959-60; gen. practice medicine, Cranston, R.I., 1960-78; exec. sec. R.I. Soc. Osteo. P/S, Cranston, 1978-79; dean New Eng. Coll. Osteo. Medicine, Biddeford, Maine, 1979-82; acting dean Chgo. Coll. Osteo. Medicine, 1982—; clin. dir. Dept. Mental Health, Providence, R.I., 1973-78; med. dir. Dept. Corrections, Providence, 1976-78; sr. cons. medicine Pub. Sector Cons., Lansing, Mich., 1980—; lectr. in field. Editor, Jour. Osteo. Annals, 1982. Bd. dirs. Cranston Red Cross, R.I. Camps, Inc., Dial Dictation, Inc., Cranston Mental Health Clinic; mem. Internat. Platform Assn., ACLU; lectr. Premarital Confs., Catholic Diocese Providence. Fellow Am. Coll. Gen. Practice, Acad. Psychosomatic Medicine; mem. Am. Coll. Osteo. and Obstetrics and Gynecology, Acad. Clin. and Exptl. Hypnosis. Avocations: breeding, showing Saint Bernards and Scottish Terriers. Licenced Am. Kennel Club judge. Home: 5204 S Lawn Ave Western Springs IL 60558 Office: Chgo Coll Osteopathic Medicine 5200 S Ellis St Chicago IL 60615

RODRIGUEZ, MOSES, neurologist; b. Havana, Cuba, Dec. 29, 1952; came to U.S., 1961; s. Chalon and Sofia (Mitrani) R.; m. Margritt Naegeli, Apr. 9, 1977; children: Esther, Adam. BS, Northwestern U., 1975, MD, 1977. Fellow in neurology Mayo Clinic, Rochester, Minn., 1977-81; fellow in exptl. neuropathology U. Calif., San Diego, 1981-83; cons. in neurology Mayo Clinic, Rochester, Minn., 1983—, asst. prof. neurology, 1983-87; assoc. prof. neurology Mayo Clinic, Rochester, 1987—; dir. exptl. neuropathology lab. Mayo Clinic, Rochester, Minn., 1983—, cons. in immunology, 1985—. Contbr. articles to profl. jours. Recipient Benard Baruch award 1979, Weil award 1983, Rappaport award Mayo Clinic, 1983, Searle award, Chgo., 1986. Mem. AAAS, Am. Soc. Neurologic Investigation, Am. Soc. Virology, Am. Assn. Neuropathology (assoc.), Am. Acad. Neurology (assoc.), Sigma Xi, Alpha Omega alpha. Avocations: tennis, music. Office: Mayo Clinic 200 First St SW Rochester MN 55905

ROE, C(LARENCE) DENNIS, retired engineer; b. Granville, Ohio, Jan. 13, 1927; s. Clarence O. and Estelle L. (Adams) R.; m. Sally A. Hunt, Mar. 19, 1948; children—Linda, Denise, David. Student Ohio State U. Sch. Engring., 1947-52. With Sta. WBNS radio and TV, Columbus, Ohio, 1953-55; with CRISE controls ACRO Div. Robertshaw Fulton, 1955-60; with AT&T Bell Labs., Columbus, 1960-87, mem. connector tech. group, 1973-87; instr. basic electronics night sch. Franklin U., 1965-69. Pres. John D. Burlie Chpt. Telephone Pioneers; co-founder electronics curriculum Fairfield Sch. for Boys, Ohio Youth Commn., 1971. Served with Signal Corps U.S. Army, 1945-47. Fellow Coll. of Relay Engrs. Nat. Assn. Relay Mfrs. Methodist. Lodge: Masons. Co-author article to mag. in field; contbr. papers to profl. confs.; patentee. Home: 2936 Johnstown Rd Columbus OH 43219 Office: 6200 E Broad St Columbus OH 43213

ROE, HAROLD RICHARD, architect, illustrator; b. Toledo, Sept. 22, 1930; s. Harvey Edward and Letha Leona (Bash) R.; m. Ramona Lee Anderson, June 7, 1952; 1 child, Rebecca Lee. BArch cum laude, Ohio State U., 1953. Registered architect, Ohio. Designer Richards Bauer & Mooreheld, Toledo, 1957-64; pvt. practice architecture Toledo, 1964-66; ptnr. Angel Roe & Mull Architects, Toledo, 1966-68; art dir. Howard Assocs., Sylvania, Ohio, 1968—; Mem. archtl. review com. Arrowhead Park, Maumee, Ohio, 1978—; archtl. adv. com. Ohio State U., 1979-84. Exhibited in group show at Leigh Yawkey Woodson Mus., Wausau, Wis., 1978, 80, 81. Served to lt. USN, 1953-57. Recipient Ohio Duck Stamp award, 1984, 87. Mem. AIA (pres. Toledo chpt. 1968), Architect Soc. Ohio (bd. dirs. 1969), Ducks Unlimited (life sponsor, Nat. Supplemental Art award 1984, Ohio Art award 1984, Nat. Artist of Yr. 1985-86, Golden Pallette and Chisel award), N.W. Ohio Water Color Soc. Republican. Mem. Ch. of Christ. Club: Torch Internat. Avocations: hunting, fishing. Home: 4439 Candlewood Ln Sylvania OH 43560 Office: Howard Assoc 5800 Monroe St Sylvania OH 43560

ROE, JAMES WILLARD, infosystems executive; b. Sacramento, Calif., June 3, 1949; s. Paul E. and Helen L. (Lockwood) R.; m. Shirley Marie Ball, June 14, 1968; children: Amy, Nathan. Computer mgr. San Jose (Calif.) Mercury-News, 1977-82; infosystems dir. Ft. Wayne (Ind.) Newspapers, 1982—. Sec. Cinema Ctr., Ft. Wayne, 1984-86. Served to sgt. USAF, 1967-71. Mem. Data Processing Mgmt. Assn., No. Ind. Telecommunications Assn. (v.p. membership, 1985-86, programs, 1986—). Avocations: boating, skiing, gardening. Home: 11415 Welsford Ct Fort Wayne IN 46804 Office: Ft Wayne Newspapers 600 W Main St Fort Wayne IN 46802

ROEBUCK, JOSEPH CHESTER, leasing company executive; b. Detroit, Feb. 6, 1946; s. Joseph Leonard and Stella (Grochocki) R.; m. Susan A. Hatala, Mar. 26, 1977; children—Christopher, Jennifer. A.A., Northwood Inst., 1966; B.S. in Bus., Central Mich. U., 1968. Sales IBM Corp., Southfield, Mich., 1968-70; prin. Roebuck, Schaden & Assoc., Detroit, 1970-73; Salesman U.S. Leasing, Birmingham, Mich., 1973-76; sales mgr. Federated Fin., Southfield, Mich., 1976-77; v.p. Corp. Funding, Inc., Birmingham, 1977-84; pres. Corp. Resources, Inc., Birmingham, 1984—; lease cons., 1984—. Mem. Am. Assn. Individual Investors. Republican. Roman Catholic. Club: Detroit Golf. Avocations: Golf, flying, travel, racquetball.

ROEHL, JANET, university official; b. Albuquerque, Mar. 25, 1953; d. A.F. and Frances H. (Mahan) Roehl. B.S. in Journalism, No. Ariz. U., 1975; M.A. in Journalism, Ariz. State U., 1976, Ph.D., 1981. Publs. coordinator Ariz. State U., Tempe, 1980-81; program specialist U. Wis.-Stout, 1981-82, assoc. dir. Office Continuing Edn., 1982—; presenter at confs. and symposia. Author: Computers for the Disabled, 1984; Teaching and Learning Basic Skills, 1984; contbr. articles to profl. jours. Bd. dirs. Menomonie Theater Guild; mem. Dunn County Sexual Assault Task Force; bd. dirs. Wis. Adult Edn. Lyceum Bd. Mem. Wis. Assn. Adult and Continuing Edn., Am. Assn. Adult and Continuing Edn., Am. Ednl. Research Assn. Home: 1002 Ingalls Menomonie WI 54751 Office: Administration Bldg U Wis-Stout Menomonie WI 54751

ROEHRICK, CHARLES T., food company executive, accountant; b. Chippewa Falls, Wis., Sept. 14, 1954; s. Robert Charles and Barbara Ann (Dreher) R.; m. Terri Ann Griese, June 2, 1979; children: Karen Elizabeth, Lisa Ann. BA in Econs., Carleton Coll., 1977; MS in Acctg., U. Wis., 1979. CPA, Minn. Mgr. Coopers & Lybrand, Mpls., 1979-86; dir. fin. reporting The Pillsbury Co., Mpls., 1986—. Treas. Greater Mpls. Day Care Assn., 1984-87; chairperson allocations panel United Way, Mpls., 1984-87. Mem. Am. Inst. CPA's (Sells award), Minn. Soc. CPA's. Avocations: golf, camping. Home: 4161 Toledo Ave S Saint Louis Park MN 55416 Office: The Pillsbury Co Pillsbury Ctr Minneapolis MN 55402

ROELOFS, ROBERT I., neurologist, educator; b. Rock Valley, Iowa, Mar. 31, 1939; s. Harold George and Cornelia (Vander Sanden) R.; m. Patricia Ann Thiel, June 24, 1962; children: Gregory Robert, Stacey Evelyn, Sarah Elizabeth. BA with honors, U. Iowa, 1961, MS, 1965, MD, 1965. Diplomate Am. Bd. Psychiatry and Neurology, Nat. Bd. Med. Examiners. Intern, med. resident Boston City Hosp., 1965-67; resident in neurology U. Minn., Mpls., 1967-69, assoc. prof. neurology, 1978—; from asst. to assoc. prof. neurology Vanderbilt U., Nashville, 1972-78. Med. advisor Muscular Dystrophy Assn. Greater Twin Cities Chpt., Mpls., 1979—. Served to sr. surgeon USPHS, 1969-72. Research Career Devel. award NIH, 1973. Mem. AAAS, Am. Acad. Neurology, N.Y. Acad. Sci., Minn. State Med. Soc., Hennepin County Med. Soc., Phi Beta Sigma, Alpha Omega Alpha. Avocations: fishing, scuba diving. Home: 1910 Toledo Ave N Golden Valley MN 55422 Office: U Minn Dept Neurology Box 269 Mayo Minneapolis MN 55455

ROEMBACH-CLARK, JEANINE LOUISE, child psychiatrist; b. Wichita, June 24, 1952; d. Theodore Leon Jr. and Donna Esther (Whitwam) R.; Gregory Darwin Roembach-Clark, Dec. 4, 1976; children: Haley Rebecca, Emily Katherine, Benjamin Michael. MD, U. Kans., 1975. Diplomate Am. Bd. Psychiatry; cert. Bd. Child Psychiatry. Staff psychiatrist The Menninger Found., Topeka, 1982—; supr. Karl Menninger Sch. Psychiatry, Topeka, 1983—. Office: The Menninger Found Box 829 Topeka KS 66601

ROEMER, JEFFREY ROY, protective services officer; b. Milw., Feb. 16, 1956; s. John Edward and Jeannette Luellen (Fleischmann) R.; m. Cindy Ann Nettesheim, Apr. 6, 1974; children: Jeremy J., Jennifer L., Jodie L. Student, Morane Park Tech. Sch., Fond du Lac, Wis., 1977-78, U. Wis., Fond du Lac, 1979-81, U. Wis., Oshkosh, 1984-85; AS in Police Sci., Northeast Wis. Tech. Coll., Green Bay, 1985. Emergency med. tech. Paratech Ambulance, Milw., 1978-80; police officer Mayville (Wis.) Police Dept., 1980-81; pub. safety sgt. Ashwaubenon Pub. Safety Dept., Green Bay, 1981—; instr. Justice System Tng. Assn., Appelton, Wis., 1986—. Mem. Wis. Firefighters Assn., Wis. Assn. Spl. Weapons and Tactics Personnel. Lodge: Optomists (bd. dirs. Ashwaubenon chpt. 1986—). Avocation: coaching high sch. football. Home: 1482 Carole Ln Green Bay WI 54303 Office: Ashwaubenon Pub Safety Dept 1310 Ponderosa Green Bay WI 54303

ROERTY, GERARD JOSEPH, financial analyst; b. Jersey City, June 2, 1943; s. Joseph Gerard and Cecelia Jeanette (Wisniewski) R.; m. Mary Tecla, Sept. 4, 1965; children—Gerard J., Michelle Anne. B.S., St. Peter's Coll., Jersey City, 1965; M.B.A., Xavier U., Cin., 1973; Cert. Inst. Exec. Leadership, Southwestern U., Memphis, 1979. Staff auditor Arthur Andersen & Co., Newark, 1965-66; with Procter & Gamble, Cin., 1968—, mgr. fin. analysis dept. cellulose and specialties div., Memphis, 1976-78, mgr. plant acctg. dept., 1978-80, mgr. fin. analysis dept. packaged soap and detergent div., Cin., 1980-83, mgr. internat. paper fin. analysis div., 1983-85, spl. assignment Comptroller's Div., 1985—; pres. RoeGer Ops. Inc., tax and investments cons.; cons. in field. Author of numerous tax advice papers. Instr. Project Bus. Program, Jr. Achievement, Memphis, 1977-78, Cin., 1984; mem. Future Forest Hills Com., Forest Hills Sch. Bd., Cin., 1983. Served to capt. U.S. Army, 1966-68. Mem. Assn. M.B.A. Execs., Property Owners Assn. Republican. Roman Catholic Clubs: Beechmont Racquet (Cin.); Turpin Swim & Racquet. Home: 7114 Royalgreen Dr Cincinnati OH 45244 Office: Comptrollers Div Procter & Gamble Co 2 Procter & Gamble Plaza Cincinnati OH 45202

ROESCH, ROBERT EUGENE, dentist; b. Falls City, Nebr., July 10, 1951; s. Wilber H. and Vivian (Reese) R.; m. Susan M. Tuttle, Aug. 25, 1973. BA, Midland Lutheran Coll., 1973; DDS, U. Nebr., 1976. Practice dentistry, Fremont, Nebr., 1979—; pub. info. officer Nebr. Acad. Gen. Dentistry, 1983—, sec., treas., 1986—. Mem. exec. bd. Dodge County Reps., Fremont, 1982—; bd. dirs., past pres. Midland Luth. Coll. Alumni Bd., Fremont, 1981—; mem. council, past pres. Sinai Luth. Ch., Fremont, 1981-83; bd. dirs. Dodge County Am. Cancer Soc., Fremont, 1984—; bd. dirs., campaign dir. United Way, 1987. Served to capt. USAF, 1976-79. Mem. ADA, Nebr. Dental Assn. (Dodge County dental health cons. 1981—), Am. Orthodontic Soc., Am. Assn. Functional Orthodontists, Acad. Gen. Dentistry, Nebr. Acad. Gen. Dentistry (sec.-treas. 1985—, pub. info. officer 1983-85), Am. Assn. Functional Orthodontics, Tri-Valley Dental Soc. (v.p. 1984-85, pres. 1985-86), Omaha Dist. Dental Soc., Fremont C. of C. (diplomat). Republican. Lodge: Optimists (Fremont) (bd. dirs. 1981-83, 84-86, pres.-elect 1986). Avocations: tennis, racquetball. Home: 750 N Clarkson St Fremont NE 68025 Office: 553 N Broad Fremont NE 68025

ROESLER, KEN EDWIN, insurance company executive; b. Merrill, Wis., Jan. 23, 1938; s. Edwin Gust and Clara Ruth (Plautz) R.; m. Lois Ann Minsart, Feb. 20, 1960; children: Robin, Lance, Holly. BS, Carroll Coll., 1959. Played with Milw. Braves, 1957-63; Cartographer Becher-Hoppe Engring., Wausau, Wis., 1963; programmer, mgr. Wausau Ins. Co., Wausau, 1964-82; v.p. Employers Health Ins., Green Bay, 1982—; dir. treas. Guide Internat., Chgo., 1975-80. Pres. Wausau PTA, 1969-70; pres., founder High Sch. Alumni Assn., Athens, Wis., 1980—, Long and Bass Lake Assn., Lincoln County, Wis., 1986—; bd. dirs. Wausau Softball Assn., 1971-73; vice chmn. Wesley Meth. Ch., Wausau, 1981. Mem. Data Processing Mgmt. Assn. (speaker award 1984), Ins. Systems Am. Usrs Group (pres. 1972-73), U.S./Can. Amdahl Users Group. Republican. Methodist. Lodge: Elks. Avocations: fishing, athletic activities, hunting. Office: Employers Health ins Box 1100 Green Bay WI 54344

ROESNER, KENDRA DOROTHY, rehabilitation consultant; b. Chgo., Aug. 6, 1949; d. George F. and Mary T. (Cavalenes) Hummel; m. William K. Roesner, June 2, 1978(div. July 1986). BA, So. Ill. U., 1972. Registered social worker, Ill.; cert. rehab. counselor, Ill., ins. rehab. specialist. Mgr. rehab. services Countryside Assn. for Handicapped, Barrington, Ill., 1973-81; rehab. cons. Internat. Rehab. Assn., Glen Ellyn, Ill., 1981-83, Midwest Rehab. Group, La Grange, Ill., 1983-84; rehab. coordinator Shore Tng. Ctr., Skokie, Ill., 1984-85; sr. rehab. cons. Conservco, Naperville, Ill., 1985—. Office: Conservco 100 Park Plaza 100 Park St Naperville IL 60540

ROESS, THOMAS JAMES, cardiologist; b. Lima, Ohio, Oct. 7, 1927; s. Otto Theodore and Martha Luella (Short) R.; m. Louise Ruth Dunn, June 25, 1976; children—Steven T., William J., Jane Roess Isley. B.A., Ohio State U., 1949; M.D., Western Res. U., 1953. Diplomate Am. Bd. Internal Medicine, Cardiovascular Disease. Intern Univ. Hosps. of Cleve., 1953-54, resident, 1954-56, teaching fellow in cardiology, 1976-77; practice medicine specializing in cardiology, Lima, Ohio, 1958—; mem. staff Lima Meml.

Hosp.; asst. prof. medicine Med. Coll. Ohio, Toledo, 1983—; dir. cardiac rehab. services Lima Meml. Hosp., 1985. Served to capt. USAF, 1956-58. Fellow ACP, Am. Coll. Chest Physicians, Am. Coll. Cardiology; mem. Am. Soc. Echocardiology, Central Ohio Heart Assn. (trustee 1981-85). Home: 2210 Oakland Pkwy Lima OH 45805 Office: Lima Meml Hosp 1001 Belle Fontaine Ave Lima OH 45804

ROGAN, JOHN FRANCIS, financial consultant; b. N.Y.C., July 10, 1926; s. John Joseph and Susan (O'Doherty) R.; m. Anna Mae Cogan, July 16, 1950; children: Suzanne, John Jr., Kathleen, Patricia, Colleen, Michael, Kevin, David, Maureen. BS with distinction, Ind. U., 1959, MBA with distinction, 1960. Enlisted U.S. Army, 1945, advanced through grades to col.; mem. faculty U.S. Army Fin. Sch., St. Louis, 1946-48; fin. disbursing officer U.S. Army, Japan, 1948; mem. faculty U.S. Army Fin. Sch., Ft. Benjamin, Harrison, Ind., 1955-58; dep. dir. fin. dept. U.S. Civil Adminstrn., Okinawa, Japan, 1960-62; fin. and acctg. officer U.S. Mil. Acad., West Point, N.Y., 1963-67; fin. and acctg. officer U.S. 8th Army, Korea, 1967, chief fin. and acctg. policy div. Office of the Comptroller, 1967-68; chief claims div. U.S. Army Fin. Ctr., Ind., 1968-70; ret. U.S. Army, 1970; state fin. dir. Wis. Dept. Adminstrn., Madison, 1970-83; pvt. practice cons. Middleton, Wis., 1983—; fin. advisor Diocese of Madison, 1971—; mem. Nat. Govt. Acctg. Research Project, Lexington, Ky., 1977-82, Nat. Council on Govtl. Acctg., Chgo., 1980-83; co-chmn. State/Fed. Cash Mgmt. Task Force, Washington, 1982-83. Chairperson adv. bd. Holy Name Seminary, Madison, 1973—; mem. Diocesan Appeals Com., Madison, 1973—; chairperson State and Univ. Employees Charity Campaign, Madison, 1975-76, bd. dirs., advisor, 1977-83; bd. dirs. St. Raphael Soc., Madison, 1975—. Featured in Know Your Madisonian, Wis. State Jour., 1983; recipient Outstanding Leadership and Service award, Wis. Gov. and State Legislature, 1983. Mem. Nat. Assn. State Auditors, Comptrlollers and Treasurers (exec. com. 1979-83, pres. 1982-83), Assn. Govt. Accts., Retired Officers' Assn., Assn. of U.S. Army, Beta Gamma Sigma, Beta Alpha Psi. Roman Catholic. Avocations: biking, walking, bowling, softball, movies. Home and Office: 6640 Boulder Ln Middleton WI 53562

ROGAN, MICHAEL PATRICK, environmental service company executive; b. Toledo, Feb. 23, 1947; s. Martin Phelan and Mary Elizabeth (Hirzel) R.; m. Linda Diane Sales, Aug. 31, 1968; children: William Daniel, Bryan Fitzpatrick. BS, Ind. U., 1969. CPA, Ill. Sr. auditor Main Hurdman, Chgo., 1969-72; controller spl. projects Waste Mgmt., Inc., Oak Brook, Ill., 1972-73; div. controller Waste Mgmt., Inc., Los Angeles, 1973-77; sr. dir. fin. and adminstrn. Waste Mgmt. Saudi Pritchard Joint Venture, Riyadh, Saudi Arabia, 1977-80; v.p. fin. Waste Mgmt. Internat., Inc., London, 1980-83; v.p. fin., treas. Waste Mgmt. Internat., Inc., Oak Brook, 1983—; bd. dirs. Gt. Lakes Coffee Inc., Chgo. Mem. Art Inst. Chgo., 1983—; sponsor Hubbard St. Dance Co., Chgo., 1986—. Mem. Am. Inst. CPA's, Ill. Soc. CPA's, Fin. Exec. Inst., Chgo. Council Foreign Relations, Ind. U. Alumni Assn. Republican. Roman Catholic. Club: Ruth Lake Country (Hinsdale), DuPage (OakBrook). Avocations: golf, tennis, gardening, reading. Office: Waste Mgmt Inc 3003 Butterfield Rd Oak Brook IL 60521

ROGERS, BRYAN ALLEN, hospital administrator; b. Akron, Ohio, Aug. 2, 1925; s. Jesse L. and Helen O. (Baker) R.; m. Jean E. Hoffman, Dec. 29, 1950; children—Mark, Amy. B.A., U. Akron, 1949; M.H.A., Washington U., St. Louis, 1954. Mem. adminstrv. staff Methodist Hosp., Indpls., 1954-72; exec. v.p., adminstr. Methodist Hosp., 1971-72; adminstr. Toledo Hosp., 1972-77, pres., 1977—; adj. instr. health care adminstrn. U. Toledo, Washington U.; charter mem. bus. adv. council Coll. Bus. Adminstrn., U. Toledo; mem. public health council Ohio Dept. Health, 1978-85; chmn. task force on cost-effectiveness Blue Cross, 1978-79; dir. Toledo Trust Co. Chmn. Pub. Health Council, 1984, Hosp. Council of Northwest Ohio, 1984. Served with AUS, 1943-46. Fellow Am. Coll. Hosp. Adminstrs.; mem. Am. Hosp. Assn. (ho. of dels. 1985-87), Ohio Hosp. Assn. (pres. 1984-85, chmn. 1984), Toledo Area C. of C. (trustee 1979-82). Presbyterian. Club: Toledo Rotary. Home: 4626 Corey Rd Toledo OH 43623 Office: 2142 N Cove Blvd Toledo OH 43606

ROGERS, CAROL JEAN, computer systems consultant; b. St. Paul, Oct. 3, 1940; d. John Edward and Luella Grace (Holland) Christensen; grad. Estelle Compton Inst., Mpls., 1964, also specialized courses; m. Donald Dee Rogers, Jan. 23, 1971; children—Sue Ann Okun, Roxanne Leigh Okun, Wade William. Data entry specialist Hennepin County Dept. Ct. Services, Mpls., 1959-63; scheduling coordinator Sta. WTCN-TV, Mpls., 1963-65; coordinator for Minn., Miss Am. Teenager, St. Paul, 1967-69; upper Midwest coordinator Miss Universe, St. Paul, 1967-69; dir., instr. Mary Lowe Modeling Sch., Mpls., 1969-70; mktg. services coordinator Naidas Girl's Modeling Agy., Mpls., 1970-72; system flow tech. analyst Super Valu Stores, Inc., Hopkins, Minn., 1974-78, systems cons., 1980—; ind. systems cons., Wayzata, Minn., 1979—; adv. council Sawyer Sch. Bus., Mpls.; inst. Minn. public schs. Sunday sch. tchr. Grace Lutheran Ch., Deephaven, 1980-84. Mem. Nat. Assn. Female Execs., Am. Bus. Women's Assn. (past pres. chpt., Woman of Yr. 1985), Internat. Platform Assn. (treas.). Office: 18326 Minnetonka Blvd Wayzata MN 55391

ROGERS, CHARLES CLAYTON, news anchor and reporter; b. Shreveport, La., Dec. 4, 1957; s. John Irwin and Ila (Milton) R.; m. Jane Elizabeth Safly, May 12, 1984. BA, U. Ark., 1979; M in Pub. Adminstrn., So. Meth. U., 1981; postgrad. in Journalism, Iowa State U. Pub. affairs rep. Exxon Co., USA, Houston, 1981-82; news anchor, reporter Sta. WOI-TV, Ames, Iowa, 1983-84, Sta. WMBD-TV, Peoria, Ill., 1984—; vol. TV cons. Ill. Dept. Children, Family Services, Peoria, 1984—. Co-producer, host TV spl., Somebody's Child, 1984— (named Best Feature AP 1986), Drunk Driving, 1986. Telethon host Muscular Dystrophy Assn., Peoria, 1986; adminstrv. bd. mem. 1st United Meth. Ch., Peoria, 1985—; adminstrv. asst. WIlliamson for Mayor Campaign, Shreveport, 1982; state campaign coordinator Williamson for Ins. Commr. Campaign, Baton Rouge, 1979. Recipient Humanitarian Service award Ill. Dept. Children Family Services, 1986, Humanitarian Service award Luth. Social Services, 1986, Humanitarian Service award Counseling and Family Services, 1986, Humanitarian Service award One Ch. One Child of Ill., 1986; Best Pub. Affairs Program Ill. Broadcasters Assn. for spl. report on drunk driving, 1986; named one of Outstanding Young Men of Am. U.S. Jaycees, 1981, 83. Mem. Ill. News Broadcasters Assn., Investigative Reporters and Editors, Delta Upsilon (bd. dirs. 1978-79). Office: WMBD-TV 3131 N University Peoria IL 61614

ROGERS, DANIEL CHRISTOPHER, psychologist; b. Lexington, Tenn., Sept. 30, 1951; s. Thomas Hal and Bonnie Faye Rogers; m. Mary Jane Zimmerman. BA, Winona (Minn.) State U., 1974; MA, Mankato (Minn.) State U., 1977. Lic. psychologist, Minn. Staff psychologist Mental Health Ctr. Mid-Iowa, Marshalltown, 1977-86, C.B. Wilson Ctr., Faribault, Minn., 1986-87, Hutchinson (Minn.) Community Hosp., 1987—. Mem. Am. Assn. Marriage and Family Therapy (clin.), Am. Psychol. Assn. (assoc.), Midwestern Psychol. Assn., Minn. Lic. Psychologists. Home: 221 Freemont Ave Apt 10 Hutchinson MN 55350

ROGERS, DARRYL D., professional football coach; b. Los Angeles, May 28, 1935. Student, Long Beach City Coll.; B.A., Fresno State U., 1957, M.S., 1964. Asst. football coach Fresno City Coll., Calif., 1961-64; football coach Hayward State U., Calif., 1965, Fresno State U., 1966-72, San Jose State U., Calif., 1973-75, Mich. State U., East Lansing, 1976-79, Ariz. State U., 1980-84, Detroit Lions, NFL, 1985—. Served with USMC, 1958-59. Office: Detroit Lions 1200 Featherstone Rd Box 4200 Pontiac MI 48057 *

ROGERS, DAVID ANTHONY, electrical engineer, educator, researcher; b. San Francisco, Dec. 21, 1939; s. Justin Anthony and Alice Jane (Vessey) R.; m. Darlene Olive Hicks, Feb. 20, 1965; 1 son, Stephen Arthur. B.S.E.E. cum laude, U. Wash., 1961, Ph.D. in Elec. Engring., 1971; M.S.E.E., Ill. Inst. Tech., 1964; M.Div. cum laude, Trinity Evangelical Div. Sch., Deerfield, Ill., 1966. Registered profl. engr., Wash., Sao Paulo, Brazil. Assoc. engr. Ford Aero., Newport Beach, Calif., 1961; tech. asst. IIT Research Inst., Chgo., 1963; predoctoral lectr. U. Wash., Seattle, 1964-71, acting asst. prof., 1971-72; asst. prof. State U. of Campinas, Brazil, 1972-77, assoc. prof., 1977-80; assoc. prof. elec. engring. N.D. State U., Fargo, 1980-86 ; prof. 1986—; researcher microwaves, fiber optics, telecommunications. Served as 2d lt. Signal Corps, U.S. Army, 1961-62. Ill. Inst. Tech. research fellow, 1963-64; NSF Summer fellow, 1965; grantee Ford Found., 1969-70, TELEBRAS (Brazil), 1973-80, N.D. State U.-Bush Found., 1981—. Mem. IEEE, Am. Soc. Engring. Edn. (grantee summer 1984), Nat. Soc. Profl. Engrs., N.D. Acad. Sci., Am. Geophysical Union, Am. Sci. Affiliation, Am. Radio Relay League (life), Order of Engr., Sigma Xi, Tau Beta Pi, Eta Kappa Nu. Evangelical. Co-author: Fiber Optics, 1984. Contbr. articles to profl. publs. Office: North Dakota State Univ Elec Engring Dept Fargo ND 58105

ROGERS, DEBORAH LOUISE, health care center administrator; b. South Bend, Ind., July 6, 1955; d. Harry T. and Lucille M. (Waumans) R. Student, U. Notre Dame, 1973; BS, Ind. U., South Bend, 1977, MS in Guidance and Counseling, 1981. Asst. house parent Sycamore Homes, Inc., South Bend, 1977-78; child care worker Family and Children's Ctr., Mishawaka, Ind., 1983-84; exec. dir. Women's Care Ctr., South Bend, 1984—; psychology tutor minority students Ind. U., South Bend, 1977-80; co-facilitator grad. sch. Ind. U., 1977-80; vol. probation planner; speaker Nat. Alternatives to Abortion Conv., Columbus, 1986. Vol. probation officer St. Joseph County Probation Dept., 1977-80; bd. dirs. Pathways to Independence, South Bend, 1980-84; mem. Community Leaders Teenage Sexuality Task Force, South Bend, 1985-86. Roman Catholic. Office: Women's Care Ctr 417 N Saint Louis St South Bend IN 46617

ROGERS, FELIX JOHN, osteopath; b. Washington, Feb. 4, 1947; s. Joseph T. and Sheila Mabel (McGown) R.; m. Caroline Bell, June 23, 1973; children: Elizabeth Quinn Rogers, Alison McGown Rogers. BA, Swarthmore (Pa.) Coll., 1969; DO, Kirksville (Mo.) Coll. Osteo. Medicine, 1973. Cert. Osteo Coll. Cardiology, Am. Coll. Osteo Internal Medicine. Staff cardiologist Riverside Osteo., Trenton, Mich., 1978—, Detroit Osteo. Hosp., Highland Park, Mich., 1978—, Seaway Hosp., Trenton. Mem. nat. exec. council Episcopal Peace Fellowship, Washington, 1985—, Cranbrook Peace Found., exec. dir., 1987—. Mem. Am. Heart Assn. (trustee 1987—), Internat. Physicians for the Prevention of Nuclear War, Physicians for Social Responsibility (exec. com. 1983—), Mich. Soc. for Echocardiography (pres. 1985—), Detroit Heart Club. Home: 15 Cambridge Blvd Pleasant Ridge MI 48069 Office: 2205 Riverside Dr Trenton MI 48183

ROGERS, FRANK HUGH, business owner; b. Steubenville, Ohio, Mar. 13, 1960; s. Frank Gordon and Elaine Ann (Furby) R. Grad., High Sch., Wintersville, Ohio, 1978. Owner, operator Frank's Body Shop, Wintersville, 1974-82; prin. Hugh's Enterprises, Wintersville, 1982—; salesman Am. Heritage Life Ins. Co., Steubenville, 1984—. Served with USNR, 1983—. Republican. Mem. Ch. of Christ. Home and Office: RD 1 Box 416 Rainbow Dr Bloomingdale OH 43910

ROGERS, GLEN DARRELL, government executive; b. Springfield, Ill., Mar. 22, 1931; s. Glen Deming and Mabel Lorraine (Farrell) R.; m. Betty Lou Pontzious, Sept. 16, 1950; children: Richard A., Robert A., Betty S. Student, Sangamon State U., 1980-82. Cert. pub. purchasing official. Purchasing agt. COE Bros. Inc., Springfield, 1953-67, pres., gen. mgr., 1967-74; sr. buyer Dept Adminstrv. Services, Springfield, 1974-81; dep. dir. Ill. Sec. State, Springfield, 1981-85, dir. purchasing, 1985—. Contbr. articles to trade pubs. Com. mem. Sangamon County Rep. Found., Springfield, 1985. Mem. Nat. Inst. Govtl. Purchasing, Ill. Assn. Pub. Purchasing Officials, Am. Soc. Pub. Adminstrn., Nat. Contract Mgmt. Assn., Jacyees, Greater Springfield C. of C. Roman Catholic. Club: Navy. Lodge: Rotary. Avocations: woodworking, carpentry. Home: 4112 Pickfair Rd Springfield IL 62703 Office: Ill Sec State 148 Centennial Bldg Springfield IL 62756

ROGERS, GREGORY HARPER, hospital administrator; b. Saginaw, Mich., Nov. 14, 1955; s. Frank F. and Elaine D. (Harper) R.; m. Candace B. Hapinstall, Aug. 14, 1976; children: Justin, Michael, Adam. BA, Albion Coll., 1978. Sr. acct. Deloitte, Haskins & Sells, Saginaw, 1979-82; acctg. mgr. Midland (Mich.) Hosp. Ctr., 1982-83, controller, 1983-86, chief fin. officer, 1986—. Bd. dirs. Midland Community Cancer Services, 1981—. Fellow Healthcare Fin. Mgmt. Assn.; mem. Am. Inst. CPA's, Mich. Assn. CPA's (healthcare com.). Lutheran. Lodge: Elks (trustee). Home: 3206 Garland Midland MI 48640

ROGERS, JANET L., nutrition project executive; b. Morris, Ill., Sept. 27, 1950; d. Edward John and Alice Carolyn (Lyon) Kulig; m. Jesse Carl Rogers, Mar. 9, 1974 (div. May 1981); 1 child, Carolyn. BEd in Econs., Ea. Ill. U., 1973. Registered social worker, Ill. Asst. dir. County of Grundy Sr. Citizens Council, Inc., Coal City, Ill., 1980-87, adminstr., 1987—. Mem. Nat. Assn. Nutrition and Aging Services Programs, Welfare Services, Inter Agy. Council, Ill. Assn. Nutrition Project Dirs. Republican. Club: Morris Jr. Women's (sr. v.p. 1986-87, pres. 1987—). Avocations: crocheting, knitting, walking. Home: 2427 Parklake Dr Morris IL 60450-1035 Office: Grundy County Sr Services 580 S Broadway Morris IL 60416-1504

ROGERS, JUDY ANN, accountant; b. Pontiac, Mich., May 25, 1948; d. Charles Michael and Virginia (Perna) Crickon; drug sci. scholar, U. Mich., 1965; B.A. summa cum laude, Oakland U., Rochester, Mich., 1978; postgrad. Wayne State U. Law Sch., 1978-79; m. Ronald Richard Rogers, Aug. 30, 1967; 1 dau., Anne Michelle. Office mgr. Holforty Assos. Inc., Rochester, 1970-76; adminstr. asst. to controller Perry Drug Stores, Inc., Pontiac, 1976-78; office mgr. Artcraft Blueprint Co., Pontiac, 1978-81; plant acct. Gates Rubber Co., Pontiac, 1981-83; mgr. VR Bus. Brokers, Troy, 1983-85; owner, operator Fantastic Sam's (3 locations); instr. Oxford Sch. of Bus.; mem. exec. adv. council Mich. region Fantastic Sams. Mem. Orion Twp. Environ. Task Force; treas. Friends of the Library; active local Republican Party. Walter Reuther Meml. Fund scholar, 1978. Recipient Silver Poet award, 1986. Mem. Nat. Assn. Exec. Females, Women's Comml. Real Estate Assn., Am. Bus. Women, Mich. Profl. Women's Network. Club: Deer Lake Racquet. Contbr. to The Poet, Our Twentieth Century's Greatest Poems, Today's Greatest Poems. Home: 4383 Morgan Rd Pontiac MI 48055 Office: 5034 Dixie Hwy Drayton Plains MI 48020

ROGERS, JUSTIN TOWNER, JR., utility executive; b. Sandusky, Ohio, Aug. 4, 1929; s. Justin Towner and Barbara Eloise (Larkin) R.; m. Virginia Logan Luscombe, May 6, 1955; children: Sarah Luscombe, Anne Larkin, Justin Towner, III. A.B. cum laude, Princeton U., 1951; J.D., U. Mich., 1954. Bar: Ohio 1954. Asso. firm Wright, Harlor, Purpus, Morris & Arnold, Columbus, 1956-58; with Ohio Edison Co., 1958—; v.p., then exec. v.p. Ohio Edison Co., Akron, 1970-79; pres. Ohio Edison Co., 1980—, dir., 1970—; chmn. bd., dir. Pa. Power Co., New Castle; dir. First Nat. Bank Ohio, First Bancorp. of Ohio. Past pres., trustee Akron Community Trusts, Akron Child Guidance Center; past chmn. Akron Associated Health Agencies, U. Akron Assocs.; bd. dirs., chmn. Gen. Med. Center; bd. dirs. Akron Devel. Corp., Assn. Edison Illuminating Cos., Ohio Electric Utility Inst., chmn. Electric Power Research Inst.; adv. com. Coll. Arts and Scis., U. Akron. Served with U.S. Army, 1954-56. Mem. Phi Delta Phi, Beta Gamma Sigma (hon.). Clubs: Akron City, Portage Country, Mayflower (Akron); Rockwell Springs Trout (Castalia, Ohio); Princeton (N.Y.C.); Capitol Hill (Washington); Union (Cleve.). Office: Ohio Edison Co 76 S Main St Akron OH 44308

ROGERS, KENNETH ALDRED, university adminstrator, consultant; b. Elizabeth, N.J., Apr. 15, 1937; s. Aldred Wilmore and Dorothy (Hickman) R.; m. Eleanor Roberta Hutchinson, May 24, 1966; children: Philip Andrew, Kevin Douglas. AB, Dartmouth Coll., 1959; M in Pub. Adminstrn., Princeton (N.J.) U., 1961. Mgmt. analyst Agy. for Internat. Devel., Washington, 1961; vol. services asst. Peace Corps, Washington, 1961-62; fgn. service officer U.S. Info. Agy., Washington, and Burma, 1962-67; asst. to dir. admissions Dartmouth Coll., Hanover, N.H., 1967-69; dir. internat. office Washington U., St. Louis, 1969-77; assoc. dean for internat. programs and dir. internat. services Ind. U., Bloomington, 1977—; cons. to bd. visitors DePauw U., Greencastle, Ind., 1982; chmn. council on internat. edn. Higher Edn. Coordinating Council Met. St. Louis, 1975-76. Contbr. chpts. to books, articles to profl. jours. Mem. St. Louis Com. on Fgn. Relations, 1974-77; mem. steering com. Nat. Project for Vietnamese and Cambodian Documents Evaluation, Washington, 1975-78; mem. internat. affairs com. Ind. Council Chs., Indpls., 1980-82; mem. governing council Ind. Office for Campus Ministries, Indpls., 1984—; pres. Ind. chpt. Soc. for Internat. Devel., Bloomington, 1981-82; trustee St. Louis Council on World Affairs, Inc., 1969-76, Latin Am. scholarship program on Am. Univs., Cambridge, Mass., 1971-73, Exptl. Campus Ministry, St. Louis, 1973-75; bd. dirs. Internat. Inst. Met. St. Louis, 1976-77. Mem. Nat. Assn. for Fgn. Student Affairs (various offices, various coms., cons. 1971—). Democrat. Episcopalian. Lodge: Rotary (v.p. Moulmein, Burma 1963-64). Office: Office Internat Services Ind Univ Bloomington IN 47405

ROGERS, KEVIN JAMES, banking executive; b. Hume, Ill., July 20, 1956; s. Dick and Effie Colleen (Kelly) R.; m. Janet Kay Hettinger, Oct. 18, 1980. BS in Secondary Edn., U. Ill., 1979; diploma in gen. banking, Parkland/Am. Banking Inst., Champaign, 1984-86; diploma in consumer lending, Bradley U., 1984; diploma in agrl. lending, Ill. State U., 1986; diploma with honors bank mgmt., So. Ill. U., 1987. Tchr., coach Shiloh High Sch., Hume, Ill., 1979-83; fin. planner IDS Am. Experess, Champaign, 1983-84; v.p. 1st Nat. Bank Villa Grove, Ill., 1984—, also bd. dirs. Mem. Villa Grove C. of C. (pres. 1985-86, bd. dirs. 1984—). Republican. Roman Catholic. Lodge: Rotary. Avocations: golf, racquetball, volleyball. Home: RR 1, Box 111-B Camargo IL 61919 Office: 1st Nat Bank Villa Grove 2 N Main Box 45 Villa Grove IL 61956

ROGERS, MICHAEL K., state senator, public relations executive; b. Winchester, Ind., June 14, 1941; s. Robert E. and Margaret Pauline M. (Kennedy) R.; m. Nancy Ellen Harter. B.S. in Radio and TV, Ind. U., 1964; M.A. in Journalism, Ball State U., 1970. News dir. Sta. WCTW, New Castle, Ind., 1964-67; asst. dir. radio and TV Ball State U., Muncie, Ind., 1967-71; v.p. Howard S. Wilcox, Inc., Indpls., 1971-75; dir. communications AMAX Coal Co., Indpls., 1975-84; pres. Rogers Communications, Inc., 1982—, Proserv., 1987—; rep. Ind. Legislature, 1966-72; mem. Ind. State Senate, 1981—. Sec. New Castle Mayor's Human Rights Commn., 1964-66; chmn. Wilbur Wright State Birthplace Commn., 1970-73; bd. dirs. Winona Meml. Found., Indpls., 1983—. Recipient Journalism award Ball State U., 1971; named Sagamore of the Wabash, 1974, 84, Ky. col., 1977. Mem. Sigma Delta Chi. Republican. Mem. Soc. of Friends. Clubs: Elks (New Castle); Skyline (Indpls.). Author: Indiana Legislative Process, 1985. Contbr. articles on legis. secrecy to periodicals. Office: PO Box 2720 Indianapolis IN 46206-2720

ROGERS, R. W., manufacturing company executive; b. Middletown, Ohio, May 9, 1943; s. Wayne Richard and Lela M. (Gillespie) R. BA, Miami U., Oxford, Ohio, 1965. Various positions Armco Inc., Middletown, 1965-78; pres. Armco Risk Mgmt., Dayton, Ohio, 1978-80; v.p. Armco Ins. Mgmt., Cin., 1980-81; various positions Crown Controls Corp., Dayton, 1982—, dir. risk mgmt. and employee benefits; pres., sec., bd. dirs. Legion Ins. Group, Dallas; bd. dirs. Empire Rattan Co., Miami; bd. dirs., cons. Dayton Chem. Corp.; bd. dirs., sec. Nat. Bloodstock and Livestock Assn. Republican. Home: 6021 Buggywhip Ln Dayton OH 45459 Office: 3201 Encrete Ln Dayton OH 45449

ROGERS, RICHARD DEAN, judge; b. Oberlin, Kans., Dec. 29, 1921; s. William Clark and Evelyn May (Christian) R.; m. Helen Elizabeth Stewart, June 6, 1947; children—Letitia Ann, Cappi Christian, Richard Kurt. B.S., Kans. State U., 1943; J.D., Kans. U., 1947. Bar: Kans. bar 1947. Partner firm Springer and Rogers (Attys.), Manhattan, Kans., 1947-58; instr. bus. law Kans. State U., 1948-52; partner firm Rogers, Stites & Hill, Manhattan, 1959-75; gen. counsel Kans. Farm Bur. & Service Cos., Manhattan, 1960-75; judge U.S. Dist. Ct., Topeka, Kans., 1975—. City commnr., Manhattan, 1950-52, 60-64, mayor, 1952, 64, county atty., Riley County, Kans., 1954-58, state rep., 1964-68, state senator, 1968-75; pres. Kans. Senate, 1975. Served with USAAF, 1943-45. Decorated Air medal, Dfc. Mem. Kans., Am. bar assns., Beta Theta Pi. Republican. Presbyterian. Club: Masons. Office: 410 Federal Bldg 444 S E Quincy St Topeka KS 66683

ROGERS, RICHARD F., construction company executive, architect, engineer; b. Chgo., July 25, 1942; s. Frank S. and Emily H. (Novak) R.; m. Christina L. Rogers, June 30, 1963; children: Mitchell, Cynthia. B in Architectural Engineering, U. Ill., Chgo., 1964. Registered architect, Ill., Wis., Mich., profl. engr., Ill. Architect Einstein Assocs. Inc., Skokie, Ill., 1963-69; v.p. Land Am. Corp., Chgo., 1969-70; project architect M.A. Lombard Constrn. Co., Alsip, Ill., 1970-73; sr. project mgr. W.E. O'Neil Constrn. Co., Chgo., 1973-78; pres. A.C.M. Assocs. Inc., Mt. Prospect, Ill., 1978—. Treas. Grace Luth. Ch., Mt. Prospect, 1985, chmn. council, 1986—. Mem. AIA, Soc. Am. Registered Architects, Am. Arbitration Assn., Builders Assn. Chgo. Lodge: Masons. Office: ACM Assocs Inc 322 N Wolf Rd Mount Prospect IL 60056

ROGERS, RICHARD JAMES, architect; b. Sharon, Conn., May 25, 1953; s. James Louis and Charlotte Ann (Hopcke) R.; m. Julie Ann McCahey, Sept. 24, 1983. BArch, Cornell U., 1976, MS, 1978; MBA, U. Chgo., 1984. Systems designer Herman Miller, Inc., Zeeland, Mich., 1978-79; assoc. ptnr. Skidmore, Owings & Merrill, Chgo., 1979—; speaker Archtl.Engring. and Constrn. Systems '86 meeting, Chgo., 1986. Contbr. articles to profl. jours. Grantee FEA at Cornell U., 1976. Mem. AIA (assoc.), Assn. Computing Machinery, Nat. Computer Graphics Assn. Avocations: computers, woodworking, sailing. Home: 1015 Whitehall Dr Northbrook IL 60062 Office: Skidmore Owings & Merrill 33 W Monroe St Chicago IL 60603

ROGERS, ROBERT ERNEST, medical educator; b. West Palm Beach, Fla., Nov. 16, 1928; s. Jessie H. and Willie L. (Bahr) R.; m. Barbara Ann Hill, May 16, 1950; children: Robert E. Jr., Stephanie Ann Thompson, Cheri Lee Heck. BS, John B. Stetson U., 1949; MD, U. Miami, 1957. Diplomate Am. Bd. Ob-Gyn. Commd. 1st lt. M.C., U.S. Army, 1952, advanced through grades to col., 1957; intern Brooke Gen. Hosp., San Antonio, 1957-58, chief resident ob-gyn, 1960-61; resident in ob-gyn Jackson Meml. Hosp., Miami, Fla., 1958-60; fellow gynocology M.D. Anderson Hosp., Houston, 1965-66; asst. chief ob-gyn Tripler Army Med. Ctr., Honolulu, 1966-69; chmn. ob-gyn Walter Reed Med. Ctr., Washington, 1969-70, Madigan Army Med. Ctr., Tacoma, Wash., 1970-74; ret. U.S. Army, 1974; prof. Ind. U. Sch. Medicine, Indpls., 1974—, also chief gynecol. div., 1974—; chief ob-gyn service Wishard Meml. Hosp., Indpls., 1983—. Contbr. articles on ob-gyn to profl. jours. Mem. AMA, Am. Coll. Ob-Gyn (chmn. gynecol. practice com., commr. practice), Soc. Gynecol. Surgeons (pres. 1983-84), Soc. Gynecol. Oncologists. Office: Wishard Hosp Dept Ob-Gyn Indianapolis IN 46202

ROGERS, ROBERT LEE, novelist, educator; b. Chgo., July 26, 1933; s. Charles and Lydia Anna (Zimmerman) R.; m. Laura Lee Scrimpsher, July 25, 1965. B.S. in History, No. Ill. U., 1955, M.Ed., 1974. Elem. tchr. pub. schs., 1955—. Author: All These Splendid Sins, 1979; Fire Bird, 1985. Home: 389 Spruce Ln Crystal Lake IL 60014

ROGERS, VAN RENSSELAER, adminstrative and sales consultant; b. nr. Lexington, Ky., Jan. 9, 1914; s. Edgar Alfred and Nellie Estella (Burton) R.; grad. Cleve. Inst. Art, 1937; m. Ruth Charlotte Reichelt, Aug. 3, 1941; 1 son, Peter Van. Commd. sculptor Walt Disney Enterprises, Hollywood, Calif., 1937-38; co-founder Rogers Bennett Studios, Cleve., 1938; pres., owner Rogers Display Studios div. NESCO, Inc. (now Rogers Displays Inc.), Cleve., 1959—; founder Van R. Rogers Prodns., Inc., 1983—; profl. sculptor, artist, designer, painter. Asst. registrar John Huntington Poly. Inst., Cleve., 1938-41, producer sculptural artwork and household decorative artifacts, 1986. Chmn. Zoning Commn., Russell Twp., Geauga County, Ohio, 1974. Served to lt. comdr. USNR, 1942-46. Mem. Exhibit Designers and Producers Assn. (pres. Ohio chpt. 1964-65), Nat. Trade Show Exhibitor Assn. (founder, citation as Godfather of orgn. 1977), Archaeol. Soc. Ohio, Dunham Tavern Soc. Collectors, Ohio Hist. Soc., Geauga County Hist. Soc., Russell Twp. Hist. Soc., Nat. Trust Hist. Preservation, Found. Ill. Archeology, North and South Skirmish Assn., Nat. Muzzle Loading Rifle Assn., Greater Cleve. Growth Assn., Nat. Hist. Soc., Western Reserve Hist. Soc., Northwestern Archaeol. Soc., Genuine Indian Relic Soc., Nat. Hist. Soc., Ohio Acad. History, Archaeology Inst. Am., Imperial German Mil. Collectors Assn., Great Lakes Hist. Soc., Exhibit Designers and Producers Assn. (pres. Ohio Chpt. 1964-65), Am. Heritage Soc., Early Am. Soc., Nat. Hist. Soc. Clubs: Hon. Order Ky. Cols.; Masons (32 deg.), K.T.; Advt. (Cleve.). Office: Rogers Displays Inc 26470 Lakeland Blvd Clevelnd OH 44132

ROGERS, WILLIAM ARTHUR, journalist, photojournalist; b. Chgo., Apr. 12, 1920; s. Edwin Arthur and Astrid (Swensen) R.; m. Pauline Elizabeth King, Apr. 6, 1945; 1 dau., Pamela Kay Rogers Jannece. Student U. Dubuque, 1937-38, also various univ. and coll. seminars, 1966-76. Reporter, newscaster, news dir. Stas.-WSAI/WCKY, Cin., 1947-48; sales promotion mgr. Frederic W. Ziv Co., Cin., 1949-52; prin. Bill Rogers, Profitable Publicity, Chgo., 1953-58; reporter, photographer Southtown Economist, Chgo., 1959-60; prin. Bill Arthur Rogers & Intermedia Picture Service, Oak Park, Ill., 1960—; instr. Triton Coll., River Grove, Ill., 1971-75, U. Ill.-Chgo. Med. Ctr., 1972-73, Coll. DuPage, Glen Ellyn, Ill., 1980-81; chmn., coordinator Chgo. 74, 1974. Exhibited in one-man shows: Chgo. Pub. Library, 1970; travelling show Am. Soc. Mag. Photographers 25th Anniversary Show, 1969-70; photog. contbns. to (books) Hemingway, 1966; Rights in Conflict, 1968; Black Americans, 1969; Sweet Medicine, 1969; Dynamics of Health Care, 1974; also miscellaneous textbooks. Vestryman, editor and bishop's penceman St. Christopher's Ch., Oak Park, 1966—, mem. Diocesan Stewardship Commn., 1969-70; mem. Oak Park Cable TV Commn., 1982—; bd. dirs., chmn. income devel. Oak Park-River Forest chpt. Am. Cancer Soc., 1983—. Served with USMCR, 1941-45; Solomons, Bismarck Archipelago. Mem. Am. Soc. Mag. Photographers (pres. chpt. 1970-77, service award 1983), Artists Guild Chgo. (council 1973-78, Service award 1978), Indsl. Editors Chgo. (treas. 67), Village Mgrs. Assn., Nat. Writers Club, DAV. Episcopalian.

ROGINSKI, JOHN LEO, marketing professional; b. Kewanee, Ill., May 9, 1945; s. Joseph George and Helen Maxine (Anderson) R.; m. Donna Jeanne Baker, June 11, 1966; children: Mary Elizabeth, Paula Lynn. B Chemistry, U. Tulsa, 1966. Research chemist Diamond Shamrock, Painesville, Ohio, 1969-74; tech. sales rep. Diamond Shamrock, Longwood, Fla., 1974-76; product mgr. Diamond Shamrock, Painesville, 1976-78; asst. sales mgr. Diamond Shamrock, Marietta, Ga., 1978-80; sales mgr. Diamond Shamrock, Naperville, Ill., 1980-82, A.E. Staley, Naperville, 1982-84; dir. mktg. A.E. Staley, Decatur, Ill., 1984—. Republican. Roman Catholic. Avocations: skiing, running, reading. Home: 2945 Lewallan Pl Decatur IL 62521 Office: A E Staley 2200 E El Dorado Decatur IL 62521

ROGNAN, LLOYD NORMAN, artist, illustrator; b. Chgo., June 14, 1923; s. John and Gertrude Sophia (Hagen) R.; student Am. Acad. Art, 1941, 50, 51; diploma Acad. de la grande Chamiere, 1949; m. Sylvia Marcella Erickson, July 18, 1953; children—Bruce Byron, Cindy Lou. Cover artist French edit. Ellery Queen, Paris, 1947-49; religious film strip artist Concordia Pubs., St. Louis, 1950-53; art dir. Jahn & Ollier Engraving Co., 1954—; sci. fiction cover artist Greenleaf Publs., Evanston, Ill., 1956-58; with Meyer and Booth Studio, Chgo., 1958-61; biol. artist Golden Books Press, N.Y.C., 1961-63; cartoonist United Card Co., Rolling Meadows, Ill., 1966-71; art dir. Gallant Greetings, Chgo., 1972; artist, advt. posters (silk screen), Chgo., 1973-75; calendar artist Brown & Bigelow, St. Paul, 1976-79, Baumgarth, Brown & Bigelow, 1976-84, with Saga, Inc., ltd. edits. Western prints Albuquerque, 1977—; ltd. edit. plates Picard, Inc., Antioch, Ill., 1983-84; art dir., creative editor United Card Co., Arlington Hts., Ill., 1978—; represented in permanent collection Vesterheim Mus., Decorah, Iowa. Art counsellor Boy Scouts Am. Served with U.S. Army, 1943-46; ETO. Decorated Purple Heart. Home and Studio: 3620 Linneman St Glenview IL 60025

ROGUSKI, RICKARD EMIL, aerospace manufacturing company executive; b. Rockford, Ill., Jan. 7, 1934; s. Emil J. and Catherine M. (Riggs) R.; m. Gail L. Arfstrom, Nov. 30, 1957 (dec. Jan. 1971); children: Randy, Jill; m. Eleanor B. Juengling, July 4, 1974 (div. 1984). Student, U. Ill., 1951-53, Rockford Coll., 1954, 57, Tex. Western Coll., 1955, Rock Valley Coll., 1981-82, U. Mich., 1983, LDD, 1985, U. Iowa, 1987. Route salesman Bluestar Foods, 1953; collector Electrolux Corp., 1953; salesman Cutco-Wearever, 1953; with Sundstrand Corp., Rockford, 1954—, group supr. graphics arts, 1960-65, group leader mktg. services, 1965-69, mgr. mktg. services, 1969-74, mgr. communication design, 1974-81, mgr. spl. events dept., 1981—; judge tech. art and tech. writing. Vol. worker United Way; bd. dirs. Rockvale Children's Home, Edn. and Research Inst.; fund raiser Rockford Hosp. Served with U.S. Army, 1955-57. Named Vol. of Yr. Montague Library; recipient appreciation award Rockford Jaycees. Mem. Soc. Tech. Communication (sr., Robert Frank award Chgo. chpt., accredited), Pub. Relations Soc. Am., Profl. Artists/Designers Guild, Rockford Advt. Club. Republican. Home: 713 Ashland Ave Rockford IL 61103 Office: Sundstrand Corp 2430 S Alpine Rd Rockford IL 61108

ROHE, DANIEL EDWARD, psychologist, educator, consultant; b. Cin., May 28, 1951; s. George Lee and Mercedes (Byrne) R.; m. Jackie Jen Silver, June 21, 1975. BA, Ohio State U., 1973; MA, PhD, U. Minn., 1980. Lic. cons. psychologist, Minn. Cons. Mayo Clinic, Rochester, Minn., 1980—; asst. prof. psychology Mayo Med. Sch., 1981—. Recipient Outstanding Research in Service to Handicapped award Mil. Order Purple Heart, Washington, 1981. Mem. Am. Psychol. Assn., Minn. Psychol. Assn., Am. Congress Rehab. Medicine. Home: 711 18th Ave SW Rochester MN 55902 Office: Mayo Clinic Sect Psychology Rochester MN 55901

ROHLFING, KENNETH EDWARD, architect; b. Paxton, Ill., May 28, 1946; s. Robert Lester and Mary Eunice (Allen) R.; m. Mary Kathleen Dunnan, June 10, 1967. Project designer Orput Assocs. Inc., Rockford, Ill., 1971-73; project dir., designer Gunnar Birkerts & Assocs., Birmingham, Mich., 1973-78; sr. designer Smith, Hinchman & Grylls, Detroit, 1978-81; prin. Gunnar Birkerts & Assocs., Inc., Birmingham, 1981—; also bd. dirs. Gunnar Birkerts & Assocs., Birmingham. Contbg. researcher archtl. monographs. Mem. AIA, Mich. Soc. Architects.

ROHRBOUGH, JOHN DAVIS, military science educator; b. Toledo, Dec. 8, 1935; s. Alvon Fortunatus and Phyllis (Davis) R.; m. Sylvia Satterthwaite, Aug. 6, 1960; children: Laurence Jackson, Gregory David. BS, U.S. Naval Acad., 1958; MS, U.S. Naval Postgrad. Sch., Monterey, Calif., 1964; MS in Adminstrn., U. Notre Dame, 1985. Commd. ensign USN, 1958, advanced through grades to capt., 1979; prof. naval sci. U. Notre Dame, South Bend, Ind., 1982—. Co-author: Sea & Air, The Marine Environment 2d edit., 1972. Mem. U.S. Naval Inst. (life). Democrat. Presbyterian. Office: U Notre Dame Naval ROTC Notre Dame IN 46556

ROHRER, DAVID J., lawyer; b. Massillon, Ohio, July 8, 1948; s. Frank J. and Frances M. (Heimann) R.; m. Noreen F. Smith, Apr. 11, 1975; children: Audrey, Daniel, Lesley, Paul. BA magna cum laude, U. Akron, 1970, JD, 1973. Bar: Ohio, U.S. Dist. Ct. (no. dist.) Ohio, U.S. Ct. Appeals (6th cir.). Staff atty. Tuscarawas Valley Legal Services, New Philadelphia, Ohio, 1973-75; asst. prosecuter Tuscarawas County, New Philadelphia, 1975-77, asst. pros., 1981-86; gen. counsel Olde Worlde Products, Inc., Canton, Ohio, 1977-79; mng. atty. Hyatt Legal Services, Canton, 1979-81; ptnr. Russell, Rohrer & Rockenfelder, North Canton, Ohio, 1981-86, Ritchie & Rohrer, Canton, 1986—; instr. real estate law Stark Tech. Coll., Canton, 1983-84. Named one of Outstanding Young Men of Am., 1985. Mem. Tuscarawas County Bar Assn., North Canton Jaycees (pres. 1984-85). Lodge: Rotary. Avocations: woodworking, gardening, computers. Home: 552 Royer Ave NW North Canton OH 44720 Office: Ritchtie & Rohrer 614 N Main St North Canton OH 44720-2007

ROHRER, JAMES WILLIAM, psychologist; b. North Manchester, Ind., Jan. 28, 1925; s. Perry L. and Ruth (Alspaugh) R.; m. Nancy Acheson, June 11, 1949; children: Richard J., Stuart A., Leslie J. BA, U. Wis., 1947; MA, Ohio State U., 1949, PhD, 1952. Staff psychologist Rohrer Hibler and Replogle, N.Y.C., 1952-53, Milw., 1959-64; mng. ptnr. Rohrer Hibler and Replogle, Cin., 1964-74; gen. practice psychology Milw., 1953-59; pres. J.W. Rohrer, Inc., Cin., 1973—. Served with U.S. Army, 1942-45. Fellow Pa. Psychol. Assn.; mem. Am. Psychol. Assn., Ohio Psychol. Assn., Phi Delta Kappa. Avocations: golf, scuba diving, photography. Office: 82 Twin Lakes Dr Fairfield OH 45014

ROHRMAN, DOUGLASS FREDERICK, lawyer; b. Chgo., Aug. 10, 1941; s. Frederick Alvin and Velma Elizabeth (Birdwell) R.; m. Susan Vitullo; children—Kathryn Anne, Elizabeth Clelia. A.B., Duke U., 1963; J.D., Northwestern U., 1966. Bar: Ill. 1966. Legal coordinator Nat. Communicable Disease Center, Altanta, 1966-68; assoc. Keck, Mahin & Cate, Chgo., 1968-73, ptnr., 1973—; exec. v.p., dir. Kerogen Oil Co., 1967—. Vice chmn., commr. Ill. Food and Drug Commn., 1970-72. Served as lt. USPHS, 1966-68. Mem. Am., Chgo. (chmn. com. on food and drug law 1972-73), 7th Circuit bar assns., Am. Soc. Law and Medicine, Selden Soc. Democrat. Episcopalian. Clubs: Legal, Metropolitan; River; Wigmore; Washington Duke. Co-author: Commercial Liability Risk Management and Insurance, 2 vols., 1978, 1986. Contbr. articles on law to profl. jours. Home: 520 Brier St Kenilworth IL 60043 Office: 8300 Sears Tower Chicago IL 60606

ROHRMAN, JOSEPH ANTHONY, art teacher; b. Indpls., Jan. 17, 1950; s. Lewis Edward and Rosenell Rita (Delatore) R.; m. Judy Lynn Wasson, July 31, 1970 (div. Dec. 1972); 1 child, Clayton Caldwell; m. Sarah Jane Quirk, July 6, 1975. BS, Ind U., 1975, M in Art Edn., 1980. Art tchr. Lebanon (Ind.) Sch. System, 1975-77, Acton Elementary Sch., Indpls., 1977—. Contg. artist (sculpture) Am. Art Clay Co. Catalog, 1984, 86, 87, Arts and Activities Mag., 1985. Faculty rep. Parent Faculty Orgn., Indpls., 1983-84; mem. Lawrence Township Citizen's Com., Lawrence, 1985—; bd. dirs. Indian Lake Improvement Assn., Indpls., 1979—. Recipient Purchase award Hoosier Salon, Indpls., 1979, Merit Cash award 1981, Award of Excellance Sheldon Swope Art Gallery, 1983. Mem. Am. Craft Council, Ind. Artist Club, Herron/Ind. U. Alumni Assn., Indpls. Mus. Art. Roman Catholic. Avocations: travel. Home: 7023 Indian Lake Blvd N Dr Indianapolis IN 46236 Office: Acton Elementary Sch 8010 Acton Rd Indianapolis IN 46259

ROHS, LARRY BERYLE, manufacturing company financial executive; b. Milw., May 15, 1950; s. Beryle Arden Rohs and Erna Clara (Hoeppner) Edwards; m. Catherine Lee Arnstein, May 30, 1968; children: Robert John, Brian Joseph. BBA in Acct. and Mgmt. Info. Systems, U. Wis., Milw., 1974. CPA, Wis. V.p. Barrel Plating Service, Inc., Milw., 1966-75; audit staff supr. Alexander Grant & Co., Milw., 1975-80; v.p. Diamond Data, Inc., Mequon, Wis., 1981-82; mgr. internal audit Kohler (Wis.) Co., 1980-86, mgr. acctg. systems, 1986—; bd. dirs. Barrel Plating Service, Inc.; instr. Lakeland Coll., Elkhart Lake, Wis., 1985. Cub scout leader Boy Scouts Am., Kohler, 1984, leader, Milw. 1978. Served to sgt. USNG, 1970-76. Mem. Inst. Internal Auditors (bd. govs. 1985—), Am. Inst. CPA's, Wis. Inst. CPA's. Republican. Lutheran. Lodge: Kiwanis (officer Kohler chpt. 1985). Avocations: camping, traveling, racquetball, outdoor sports. Home: 656 School St Kohler WI 53044 Office: Kohler Co High St Kohler WI 53044

ROIKO, RANDY LEE, controller; b. Mpls., July 19, 1954; s. Henry Richard and Donna Jean (Hempfield) R.; m. Connie Marie Larson, Jan. 3, 1976; children: Jennifer, Patti. BBA in Acctg., U. Minn., 1976. CPA, Minn. Staff auditor Touche Ross & Co., Mpls., 1976-80, audit supr., 1980-82; dir. internal audit Super Valu Stores Inc., Mpls., 1982-85; controller Shopko Stores Inc., Green Bay, Wis., 1985—. Mem. allocation panel United Way, Mpls., 1983-84; v.p. Prince of Peace Luth. Ch., Mpls., 1982-83. Mem. Am. Inst. CPA's, Minn. Soc. CPA's (mems. in industry com. 1984, outstanding com. award). Avocations: woodworking, canoeing.

ROKACH, ABRAHAM JACOB, structural engineering consultant; b. N.Y.C., Nov. 14, 1948; s. David and Sara (Biro) R.; m. Pninah Abigail Kacev, June 19, 1977; children: David, Aaron Zvi, Moshe Mordecai, Aryeh Raphael Pesach, Chaya Esther. B of Engring., CCNY, 1969; MSCE, MIT, 1970. Registered structural engr., Ill., profl. engr., N.Y. Pres. Rokach Engring. P.C., Chgo., 1984—; adj. asst. prof. U. Ill., Chgo., 1984—. Author: Guide to Load and Resistance Factor Design of Structural Steel Buildings, 1986. Fellow, grantee NSF. Mem. ASCE, AIA (Forum for Architecture), Am. Inst. Steel Construction. Jewish. Office: 6754 N Whipple St Chicago IL 60645-4123

ROLA, ANLEE MARIE, dentist; b. Sioux Falls, Sept. 4, 1952; s.James William and Rosemary Darlene (Wolterman) Kappenman; m. David Curits Rola, May 24, 1975; children: Jaclyn Marie, Angela Michelle. BA in Psychology, Mo. U., 1973; DDs, Creighton U., 1977. Gen. practice dentistry Sioux Falls, 1977—; dental cons. Good Samaritan Ctr. Nursing Home, Sioux Falls, 1978—. Advisor Creighton U. Alumni Assn., 1986-91; S.D. Dental Health Soc., 1985-86. Mem. ADA, S.D. Dental Assn., Pierre Fauchard Acad., Alpha Sigma Nu. Republican. Roman Catholic. Avocations: reading, dancing, all water sports, golf. Office: 605 S Dakota Ave Sioux Falls SD 57104

ROLAND, JIMMY DALE, civil engineer; b. Dover, Del., Apr. 19, 1959; s. Benjamin Ralph and Mary Elizabeth (Bush) R. BCE, U. Del., 1983. Designer, engr. Gerald A. Donovon & Assocs., Dover, 1983-84; project engr. D.H. Steffens Co., La Plata, Md., 1984; civil engr. Avila & Assoc., Chgo., 1985, PRC Consoer Townsend, Chgo., 1985—. Mem. NSPE (assoc.), ASCE (assoc.), Nat. Inst. for Cert. in Engring. Tech., Ill. Assn. for Floodplain and Stormwater Mgmt. Republican. Methodist. Avocations: biking, racquetball. Office: Consoer Townsend & Assocs Inc 303 E Wacker Dr Suite 600 Chicago IL 60601

ROLEWICZ, ROBERT JOHN, cost estimator; b. Chgo., Sept. 16, 1954; s. Frank Joseph and Margaret Mary (Ahlbach) R.; m. Vicki Lynn Heggeland. Sept. 1, 1985. Diploma, Washburne Trade Sch., 1977. Level II inspector Kropp Forge Co., Chgo., 1974-77, chief cost estimator, 1978—. Committeeman Citizens to Reelect Jack Kubik, Cicero, Ill., 1984—, Citizens to Reelect Judy Baar Topinka, Cicero, 1984—. Recipient Hold My Hand award Children's Ctr. of Cicero, 1982. Mem. Czechoslovak Soc. Am., Vietnow. Republican. Roman Catholic. Club: Kropp Key Club (Chgo.) (pres. 1984—). Lodges: Elks (P.E.R Plaque 1982, Exalted Ruler 1981-82), Moose. Avocations: jogging, swimming, camping, canoeing, hiking.

ROLFE, EUGENE JAMES, electrical engineer, consultant; b. St. Louis, Dec. 30, 1953; s. Eugene William and Margaret Madeline (Cooper) R.; m. Katherine Marie Hicken, Dec. 19, 1975; 1 child, Eric. BSEE, U. Mo., 1976, MSEE, 1978. Registered profl. engr., Mo. Engr. Allied Corp. div. Bendix Corp., Kansas City, Mo., 1976-80, sr. engr., 1980-84, staff engr., 1984-86, sr. project engr., 1986—; part-time instr. Longview Community Coll., Lee's Summit, Mo., 1978-85; pvt. practice cons., Kansas City, 1981—. Guitarist St. Regis Choir, Kansas City, 1982—. Recipient Allied Spl. Recognition award Allied Corp., Kansas City, 1985. Mem. Eta Kappa Nu. Roman Catholic. Club: Young Marrieds (Kansas City). Avocations: astronomy, photography, music, camping, boating. Home: 9009 Evanston Ct Kansas City MO 64138 Office: Allied Corp div Bendix Corp 2000 E 95th Kansas City MO 64141-6159

ROLFE, MICHAEL N., accounting firm executive; b. Chgo., Sept. 9, 1937; s. Mark Alexander and Antoinette (Wittgenstein) R.; m. Judith Mary Lewis, June 16, 1959; children—Andrew, Lisa, James. A.B. in Econs., U. Mich., 1959; postgrad., Grad. Sch. Bus., U. Chgo., 1963-65. Sales staff Lewis Co., Northbrook, Ill., 1961-62; systems mgmt. staff Brunswick Corp., Chgo., 1962-68; v.p. Kearney Mgmt. Cons., Chgo., 1968-81; ptnr. Peat, Marwick, Mitchell & Co., Chgo., 1981—. Author: AMA Management Handbook, 1969. Bd. dirs. Common, Chgo., 1972-75, U. Chgo. Cancer Research, 1985—, Am. Cancer Soc., Chgo., 1985—; trustee Michael Reese Med. Ctr., 1986—; pres. Sch. Bd. Dist. 113, Highland Park, Ill., 1977-83. Served to lt. (j.g.) USNR, 1959-61. Clubs: Northmoor Country (Highland Park); Standard (Chgo.), Mid Am. Home: 1730 Overland Trail Deerfield IL 60015 Office: Peat Marwick Mitchell & Co 303 E Wacker Dr Chicago IL 60601

ROLFES, JAMES WALTER, SR., lawyer; b. Providence, May 21, 1942; s. George Henry and Mary Helen (Clark) R.; m. Dorothy Patricia Robison, Sept. 10, 1966; children—John George, James Walter, Jr. B.S., U. Cin., 1971; J.D., No. Ky. State Coll. (Salmon P. Chase Coll. Law), 1975. Bar: Ohio 1975, U.S. Dist. Ct. (so. dist.) Ohio 1975, U.S. Supreme Ct. 1985. Asst. sec. Eagle Savings and Loan, Cin., 1967-70; acct. Kings Island, Kings Mill, Ohio, 1970-73, Bode-Finn, Cin., 1973-76; asst. prosecutor Madison County, London, Ohio, 1976-79, mcpl. ct. judge, 1982—; sole practice, London, 1975—; tchr. Madison County Alcohol Diversion Program, London, 1982—, Ohio Peace Officers Tng. Acad., London, 1976-79. Chmn. Madison County Heart Assn., London, 1977, Madison County Mental Health Adv. Bd., London, 1980-84; pres. Fairfield Youth Assn. Recipient Millard W. Mack Scholarship U. Cin., 1970. Mem. Ohio Bar Assn., Madison County Bar Assn. (pres. 1986), Cin. Bar Assn., ABA, London Merchants Assn., Inc. (chmn. 1983-86), Republican. Roman Catholic. Lodge: K.C. (grand Knight 1985-87). Office: 17 S Main St London OH 43140

ROLFS, BEMISS A., vehicle leasing company executive; b. New Orleans, 1935; married. Student, Tulane U., U. Minn. City mgr. Hertz Corp., 1955-56; with Nat. Car Rental System, Inc., Mpls., 1966—; city mgr. Chgo. div. Nat. Car Rental System, Inc., 1966-68, zone mgr., 1968-69, regional mgr., 1969-71, asst. v.p. car rental div., 1971-72, v.p., 1972-74, corp. v.p. car rental ops. East, 1974, corp. v.p. total car rental div., 1974-78, corp. exec. v.p. ops., 1978-81, chief exec. officer, 1981-86; pres. Nat. Car Rental System, Inc., Mpls., 1981—, also dir. Office: Nat Car Rental System Inc 7700 France Ave S Minneapolis MN 55435 *

ROLL, DELIGHT ADREAN, nurse; b. Kalamazoo, Oct. 8, 1939; d. Harold George and Bessie Pearl (Flegal) Derksen; m. Harold Wilmont Frye, Nov. 16, 1968 (div. 1971); m. Mathew B. Roll, Oct. 6, 1972. Grad., Kalamazoo Practical Nursing Sch., 1960; AS in Nursing, Southwestern Mich. Coll., 1979; BS in Nursing, U. Mich., 1982; postgrad. Western Mich. U. Indsl. nurse Electronic Supply Corp., Kalamazoo, 1964-68; staff nurse Pipp Community Hosp., Plainwell, Mich., 1967-73; charge nurse Cunningham Nursing Home, Plainwell, 1974-78; agy. nurse Quality Care, Kalamazoo, 1978-81; charge nurse Provincial House Inc., Kalamazoo, 1981-83, Ridgeview Manor, Kalamazoo, 1983-87; asst. dir. nursing Verdries Nursing Ctr., Kalamazoo, 1987—. Contbr. article to profl. jour. Mem. Kalamazoo Practical Nurses Assn. (pres. 1967-69). Baptist. Home: 10811 Boniface Point Dr Plainwell MI 49080

ROLLAND, IAN MCKENZIE, insurance executive; b. Fort Wayne, Ind., June 3, 1933; s. David and Florence (Hunte) R.; m. Miriam V. Flickinger, July 3, 1955; children: Cheri L., Lawrence D., Robert A., Carol Ann, Sara K. B.A., DePauw U., 1955; M.A. in Actuarial Sci., U. Mich., 1956. With Lincoln Nat. Life Ins. Co., Ft. Wayne, 1956—, sr. v.p., 1973-75, pres., 1977-81, chief exec. officer, 1977—, chmn., pres., 1981—; pres. Lincoln Nat. Corp., 1975—, chief exec. officer, 1977—; bd. dirs. No. Ind. Public Service, Lincoln Nat. Bank and Trust Co., Gen. Telephone Co. Ind., Inc., Tokheim Corp., Lincoln Nat. Sales Corp., Am. States Ins. Cos., Security-Conn. Life Ins. Co., Am. States Ins. Cos., Cannon Assurance Ltd., First Penn-Pacific Ins. Co., The Richard Leahy Corp., Modern Portfolio Theory Assocs., Inc.; past chmn. Am. Council of Life Ins. Agts.; exec. com. Associated Ind. Life Ins. Cos. Chmn. citizens bd. St. Francis Coll., 1978—; bd. dirs. United Way of Allen County, 1975—, S. S. Huebner Found.; exec. com. The American Coll.; mem. adv. bd. Ind. U.-Purdue U., 1977; chmn. Ind. Fiscal Policy Com.; trustee Hudson Inst.; mem. Indiana Acad. Mem. Soc. Actuaries, Acad. Actuaries, Health Ins. Assn. Am., Am. Council Life Ins. (past chmn. bd. dirs.), Assoc. Ind. Life Ins. Cos. (exec. com.), Ind. Ins. SOc. (bd. dirs.), Internat. Ins. Soc. (bd. dirs.), Ind. C. of C. (mem. exec. com.). Office: Lincoln Nat Corp 1300 S Clinton St Fort Wayne IN 46801

ROLLER, MARK CAMERON, insurance company executive; b. Springfield, Ohio, May 22, 1950; s. Cletus J. and Betty Jane (Caylor) R.; m. Karen Durica, Jan. 9, 1976; children: Peter Elliott, Lauren Kristine. B.A., Anderson Coll., 1972; M.B.A., Ball State U., 1980. Coll. rep. Anderson Coll., Ind., 1972-74, dir. admissions, 1974-79, prof. mgmt. mktg., 1980-84; mktg. mgr. Blue/Cross/Blue Shield, Indpls., 1984-86, sr. corp. planner, 1986—; cons. Mgmt. Cons. and Research Services, Anderson, 1982—; seminar speaker, 1984—. Mem. personnel com. Park Place Ch. of God, Anderson, 1980-82, Sunday sch. tchr., 1982-83; bd. dirs. Youth for Christ, Anderson, 1981-82. Mem. Am. Mktg. Assn., Midwest Bus. Adminstrn. Assn., Planning Forum, Delta Mu Delta, Beta Gamma Sigma. Republican. Avocations: golf, computers, reading. Home: 5043 Stonespring Anderson IN 46011 Office: Blue Cross/Blue Shield Inc 120 W Market St Indianapolis IN 46204

ROLLINGER, KENNETH JOHN, machinist, manufacturing company executive; b. Chgo., May 20, 1947; s. Florian Frank and Dorothy (Zdrojewski) R.; m. Myong Cha, Sept. 16, 1969; children—Kimberly, Glen. Student Triton Coll., 1973-77. Repair machinist Stanadyne Co., Bellwood, Ill., 1973—; automotive machinist Triangle Engine Rebuilders, Chgo., 1969-73; cons. V & F Engring., Itasca, Ill., 1981—; owner Impossible Engring. and Mfg. Co., 1983—. Served with U.S. Army, 1966-69; Korea. Mem. ASME, Armed Forces Communicaiton and Electronics Assn. Roman Catholic. Club: Salmon Unltd. (Chgo.). Mfr. high tech microwave antennas. Home: 635 Gladys St Elmhurst IL 60126

ROLLINS, ARLEN JEFFERY, osteopathic physician; b. Cleve., June 30, 1946; s. Lee Roy and Celia (Madorsky) R.; m. Deborah Joyce Gross, Dec. 18, 1971; children: Aaron Jason, Howard Philip, Lee Craig. AB, Miami U., Oxford, Ohio, 1968; DO, Chgo. Coll. Osteo. Medicine, 1973; MS in Occupational Medicine, Environ. Health, U. Cin., 1984. Diplomate Am. Bd. Preventive Medicine. Intern, Phoenix Gen. Hosp., 1973-74; resident in environ. health/occupational medicine Cin. Gen. Hosp.-U. Cin., 1974-77; plant physician Ford Motor Co., Cin., 1974-77, Walton Hills stamping plant div., Cleve., 1987—; assoc. med. dir. East Side Occupational Health Ctr., Cleve., 1977-79; med. dir. Ferro Corp., Cleve., 1979—, S.K. Wellman Corp., Cleve., 1979—, Piezoelectric div. Vernitron, Cleve., 1979— ;pres. Occupational Health Mgmt. Cons.; cons. occupational health Ohio Bell Telephone Co., Cleve., 1981-87; cons. Occupational Health Ctr., Univ. Hosps. of Cleve.; bd. dirs. occupational health program Bedford Hosp. Fellow Am. Acad. Occupational Medicine, Am. Occupational Med. Assn., Am. Coll. Preventive Medicine; mem. Ohio State Med. Assn., Cleve. Acad. Medicine (pub. health and immunization com., med.-legal com.), Western Res. Med. Dirs. Assn., Am. Osteo. Assn., Am. Osteo. Acad. Pub. Health and Preventive Medicine (past bd. dirs.).

ROLLYSON, CARL EDMUND, JR., academic administrator; b. Miami, Fla., Mar. 2, 1948; s. Carl Emerson and Emily (Sokolik) R.; m. Charlotte Hollander, May 17, 1969 (div. Oct. 1981); m. Lisa Olson Paddock, Nov. 4, 1981; 1 child, Amelia. BA, Mich. State U., 1969; MA, U. Toronto, Can., 1970, PhD, 1975. Instr. Agnes Irwin Sch., Rosemont, Pa., 1973-76; asst. prof. Wayne State U., Detroit, 1976-81, assoc. prof., 1981-87, prof., 1987—, asst. dean grad. sch., 1985—; cons. N. Cen. Assocs., Chgo., 1985—. Author: (literary criticism) Uses of the Past in the Novels of William Faulkner, 1984, (biography) Marilyn Monroe: A Life of the Actress, 1986. Death penalty coordinator Amnestry Internat., Detroit, 1986. Woodrow Wilson fellow, 1972, Fulbright fellow, 1979-80. Mem. Modern Lang. Assn., Popular Culture Assn., Am. Film Inst., Assn. Integrated Studies, Fulbright Alumni Assn., Phi Beta Kappa. Avocations: swimming, tennis. Home: 8100 E Jefferson 811A Detroit MI 48214 Office: Wayne State U Grad Sch Detroit MI 48202

ROLNICK, DAVID JAY, surgeon; b. N.Y.C., Oct. 7, 1943; m. Lee Kubert; children: Katie, Courtney, Brian, Kyle. BS, U. Wis., 1964; MD, SUNY, Syracuse, 1968. Cert. Am. Bd. Orthopaedic Surgery. Intern Upstate Med. Ctr., Syracuse, 1971-72; resident in orthopedics U. Wis. Med. Sch., Madison, Wis., 1973-77; surgeon Jackson Clinic, Madison, 1977—; asst. clin. prof. dept. surgery U. Wis. Med. Sch. Fellow Am. Acad. Orthopedic Surgeons; mem. Med. Soc. Wis., Wis. State Orthopedic Soc., Dane County Med. Soc., Madison Orthopedic Soc. Office: Jackson Clinic Ch 345 W Washington Ave Madison WI 53703

ROLOFF, JEFFREY JAMES, data processing executive; b. Reedsburg, Wis., Oct. 28, 1957; s. James Clarence and Jeanette Elizabeth (Schluter) R.; m. Susan Elaine Keasling, July 24, 1982; 1 child, Carolyn Elyssa. AAS, Parkland Coll., 1977. Technician Hal Communications, Urbana, Ill., 1974-76, Edn./Info. Systems, Urbana, 1976-77; pres. Cen. Data Corp., Champaign, Ill., 1977-87, chmn., 1987—. Contbr. articles to profl. jours. Mem. council Good Shepherd Luth. Ch., Champaign, 1984-85. Recipient High Tech Entrepeneur award Peat Marwick/Crains Ill. Bus., 1984, Young Entrepreneur award Ill. SBA, 1985, Nat. Top 100 Young Entrpreneur award Assn. Collegiate Entrpreneurs, 1987. Mem. IEEE, Young Pres. Orgn., Assn. Computing Machinery. Republican. Lutheran. Home: 2605 S Nottingham Ct Champaign IL 61821-7014 Office: Cen Data Corp 1602 Newton Dr Champaign IL 61821-1098

ROM, M. MARTIN, financial and real estate company executive; b. Detroit, Mar. 2, 1946; s. Jack and Thelma (Meyer) R.; m. Barbara Miller, July 12, 1970. B.A. magna cum laude, U. Mich., 1967. Founder MultiVest, Inc., Southfield, Mich., 1969; pres. MultiVest, Inc., 1969-73, chmn. bd., chief exec. officer, 1973-75; Pres. Real Estate Securities and Syndication Inst., Nat. Assn. Realtors, Washington, 1975—; dir., bd. govs. Real Estate Securities and Syndication Inst., Nat. Assn. Realtors, 1972—; pres. Martin Rom Co., Inc., 1976—, Rom Energy Corp., 1980—; vice chmn. Sports Illustrated Ct.

Clubs, Inc., 1977-79; dir. The Mocatta Corp., 1979-80, Central Savings Bank Holding Co., 1985—; mem. joint com. Nat. Assn. Securities Dealers-Nat. Assn. Realtors, 1975-76; mem. adv. com. on market instruments Commodity Futures Trading Commn.; cons. bd. dirs. Guaranty Fed. Savings Bank, 1984-87. Author: Nothing Can Replace the U.S. Dollar . . . and It Almost Has, 1975; Adv. bd.: Housing and Devel. Reporter, Washington. Mem. Nat. Assn. Securities Dealers, Com. on Gold Regulations, Phi Beta Kappa. Home: 60 Quarton Ln Bloomfield Hills MI 48013

ROMANO, JOHN LEONARD, psychology educator, consultant, counselor; b. Amsterdam, N.Y., Aug. 11, 1942; s. Daniel and Lena (Cerullo) R.; m. Dagmar Maria Langer, June 27, 1970; children: Michelle, Christopher, Jacqueline. BS, LeMoyne Coll., 1964; MEd, Pa. State U., 1968; PhD, Ariz. State U., 1976. Lic. cons. psychologist. Counselor St. Francis Coll., Loretto, Pa., 1968-69; asst. prof. Montgomery County Community Coll., Blue Bell, Pa., 1969-73; psychology intern Camelback Mental Health Ctr., Scottsdale, Ariz., 1973-74; grad. assoc. Ariz. State U., Tempe, 1974-76; assoc. prof. U. Minn., Mpls., 1976—; cons. psychologist, Janice Weiner & Assocs., St. Louis Park, Minn., 1980-82, Univ. Day Community Program, Mpls., 1981-87; evaluator and cons., Connection Program, Mpls., 1982-83; visiting assoc. prof., Ind. U., Malaysia, 1985-86. Contbr. articles to profl. jours. Vol. secondary tchr. Peace Corps, Nigeria, 1964-67; mem. St. Paul Schs. Personnel com., 1977-81, Desegregation Council, 1983-84; mem. Ramsey Ctr. Human Services Adv. Council, 1982-84. Recipient Am. Personnel & Guidance Assn. research award, 1979, Faculty Mentor award, U. Minn. Gen. Coll., 1980; U. Minn. grantee, 1979-84. Mem. Am. Psychol. Assn., Am. Assn. Counseling & Devel., Am. Coll. Personnel Assn. (mem. editorial bd. Jour. Coll. Student Personnel 1984—), Minn. Psychol. Assn., Minn. Assn. Counseling & Devel. Roman Catholic. Avocations: hiking, polit. memorabilia. Office: U Minn 216 Pillsbury Dr SE Minneapolis MN 55455

ROMANO, PASCAL MICHAEL, investment manager; b. Detroit, Dec. 13, 1955; s. Pascal Michael and Helen (Zuk) R.; m. Maureen Ann Hill, July 14, 1984. BSA, U. Mich., 1978; MBA, Wayne State U., 1982. Investment analyst City Nat. Bank, Detroit, 1979-80, Maccabees Life Ins., Detroit, 1980-82; portfolio mgr. Lincoln Nat. Investment Mgmt., Chgo., 1983-85; portfolio mgr. Alexander Hamilton Life Ins. Co., Detroit, 1985-86, chief investment officer, 1987—. Club: Dearborn Italian Am. Club. Mem. Fin. Analysts Fedn., Inst. Chartered Fin. Analysts, Dearborn Jaycees. Avocations: basketball, skydiving, bowling, home restoration. Home: 7619 Calhoun Dearborn MI 48126

ROMANOFF, MARJORIE REINWALD, educator; b. Chgo., Sept. 29, 1923; d. David Edward and Gertrude (Rosenfield) Reinwald; student Northwestern U., 1941-42, 43-45; B.Ed., U. Toledo, 1947, M.Ed., 1968, Ed.D., 1976; m. Milford M. Romanoff, Nov. 6, 1945; children—Bennett Sanford, Lawrence Michael, Janet Beth (dec.). Tchr., Old Orchard Elem. Sch., Toledo, 1946-47, McKinley Sch., Toledo, 1964-65; substitute tchr., Toledo, 1964-68; instr. Mary Manse Coll., Toledo, 1974; instr. children's lit. Sylvania (Ohio) Bd. Edn., 1977; supr. student tchrs. U. Toledo, 1968-73, 85-86, instr. advanced communications, 1977, researcher, 1973-74, instr. Am. Lang. Inst., 1978—; adj. asst. prof. elem. edn. Bowling Green (Ohio) State U., 1978—. Presenter numerous workshops and demonstrations in children lit., 1976-87; mem. research com. Am. Language Inst. U. Toledo, 1985-87. Trustee Children's Services Bd., 1974-76; pres. bd. Cummings Treatment Center for Adolescents, 1978-80; mem. Crosby Gardens Adv. Bd., 1976-82, Community Planning Council, 1980-84 , Citizens Rev. Bd. of Juvenile Ct., 1979—; mem. allocations com. Mental Health and Retardation Bd., 1980-81; mem. Bd. Jewish Edn., 1976—, pres., 1982-84; mem. Jewish Family Service, 1978-85, v.p., 1980-85; bd. dirs. Family Life Edn. Council, 1984—. Named One of Ten Women of Yr. St. Vincent's Hosp. Guild, 1985. Mem. Tchrs. English to Speakers Other Langs., Am. Assn. Supervision and Curriculum Devel., Am. Edn. Research Assn., Nat. Soc. for Study Edn., Am. Assn. Colls. Tchr. Edn., Toledo Assn. Children's Lit., Nat. Council Jewish Women, Orgn. Rehab. and Tng., Hadassah (chpt. pres. regional bd. 1961-64), Northwestern U. Alumni Assn., Phi Kappa Phi, Phi Delta Kappa, Kappa Delta Pi (pres./faculty adv. 1971-75), Pi Lambda Theta (chpt. pres. 1978-80, nat. com. 1979-84). Democrat. Home: 2514 Bexford Pl Toledo OH 43606 Office: U Toledo CEC 1006 Toledo OH 43606 Office: Bowling Green State U Coll. Education Bowling Green OH 43402

ROMANOFF, MAYA, artist, textile company executive; b. Chgo., June 30, 1941; s. William and Mildred (Danzig) R.; m. Rebecca George, Dec. 1964 (div. June 1979); m. Haruko Miyoshi, Oct. 6, 1980. BA, U. Calif., Berkeley, 1964. Freelance artist, designer 1966-78; pres. Maya Romanoff Corp., Chgo., 1978—. Exhibited in one-man shows at The Kyoto Convention Ctr., Japan, The Galleries of F.I.T., N.Y.C., The Arsenal, Chgo. Cultural Ctr., Pacific Design Ctr., Oak Lawn (Ill.) Design Ctr., Lawrence Art Ctr., Belvedere Castle; represented in numerous pvt. and corp. collections; also group shows; designer, artist wallcovering collections and drapings. Recipient 7 Best Design awards (Roscoe), 1976-82, Am. Soc. of Interior Designers award, 1982. Mem. Am. Assn. Textile Chemists and Colorists (sr.), Surface Design Assn. (Ill. rep.). Home: 1655 W Olive St Chicago IL 60660 Office: 1780 W Greenleaf Ave Chicago IL 60626

ROMANOFF, MILFORD MARTIN, building contractor, architectural designer; b. Cleve., Aug. 21, 1921; s. Barney Sanford and Edythe Stolpher (Bort) R.; student Coll. Arch., U. Mich., 1939-42; B.B.A., U. Toledo, 1943; m. Marjorie Reinwald, Nov. 6, 1945; children—Bennett S., Lawrence M., Janet Beth (dec.). Pres., Glass City Constrn. Co., Toledo, 1951-55, Milford Romanoff Inc., Toledo, 1956—. Co-founder, Neighborhood Improvement Found. Toledo, 1960; mem. Lucas County Econ. Devel. Com., 1979—; mem. citizens adv. bd. Recreation Commn. Toledo, 1973-86; mem. campus adv. com. Med. Coll. Ohio, 1980—; trustee Cummings Treatment Center for Adolescents, 1981—; mem. Children's Services Bd. Lucas County, 1981—; pres. Ohio B'nai B'rith, 1959-60; bd. dirs. Anti-Defamtion League, 1955-60, Ohio Hillel Orgns.; chmn. Toledo Amateur Baseball and Softball Com., 1979-81; mem. Democratic Precinct Com., 1975-78; trustee Temple Brotherhood, 1956-58, bd. dirs., 1981—; pres. Cherry Hill Nursing Home, 1964-85; cons. U.S. Care Corp., 1985—; mem. Crosby Gardens Bd. Adv., 1983—; bd. govs. Toledo Housing for Elderly, 1982—; bd. advisors Ret. Sr. Vol. Program, 1987—; mem. adv. bd. Salvation Army, 1984—, chmn. Mental Health Adv. Bd., 1983—; bd. dirs. Kidney Found. Northwestern Ohio, 1986—. Mem. U. Toledo Alumni Assn., Toledo Mus. Art (assoc.), U. Mich. Alumni Assn., Toledo Zool. Soc., Zeta Beta Tau. Clubs: Masons; B'nai B'rith (pres. Toledo lodge 1958-59), Hadassah (assoc. Toledo chpt.). Address: 2514 Bexford Pl Toledo OH 43606

ROMANOFF-NEWMAN, TERRI CHERYL, psychologist; b. Syracuse, N.Y., July 24, 1947; d. Saul Herbert and Irene Betty (Berlin) Bauman; divorced; 1 child, Michael. BS in Edn., Toledo U., 1971; MEd, Syracuse (N.Y.) U., 1974, PhD in Psychology, 1981. Lic. psychologist, N.Y., Minn.; cert. spl. edn. tchr., N.Y. Spl. edn. tchr. Syracuse Schs., 1971-74; spl. edn. learning disability tchr. Liverpool (N.Y.) Schs., 1974-80; psychologist Hopkins (Minn.) Schs., 1980—; pvt. practice psychology Mpls., 1982—. Contbr. articles to profl. jours., popular mags. and newspapers. Mem. Psychologist in Pvt. Practice Assn., Minn. Women's Psychologists Assn., Entrepreneur's Network. Avocations: children, reading, walking. Home: 3520 Xylon Ave S Minneapolis MN 55426 Office: 1st Western Bank Bldg 8800 Highway 7 Saint Louis Park MN 55426

ROMANOW, MARINA, contract service company executive; b. Ionia, Mich., Mar. 13, 1955; s. Harry and Jessie (Whyte) R.; m. Peter Bloom Veerhusen, Sept. 18, 1982; children: Jessica Rose, Hendrik Bloom. V.p. Romanow Bldg., Saginaw, Mich., 1979-82, pres., 1982—. Mem. Bldg. Service Contractors Assn. Internat. (bd. dirs.), C. of C. Avocations: computer programming, reading, swimming, travel. Home: 2130 Center Ave Bay City MI 48708 Office: Romanow Bldg Services 3093 Enterprise Dr Saginaw MI 48603

ROMANOWSKI, THOMAS ANDREW, educator; b. Warsaw, Poland, Apr. 17, 1925; came to U.S., 1946, naturalized, 1949; s. Bohdan and Alina (Sumowski) R.; m. Carmen des Rochers, Nov. 15, 1952; children—Alina, Dominique. B.S., Mass. Inst. Tech., 1952; M.S., Case Inst. Tech., 1956, Ph.D., 1957. Research asso. physics Carnegie Inst. Tech., 1956-60; asst. physicist high energy physics Argonne Nat. Lab., Ill., 1960-63; asso. physicist Argonne Nat. Lab., 1963-72, physicist, 1972-78; prof. physics Ohio State U., Columbus, 1964—. Contbr. articles to profl. jours. and, papers to sci. meetings, seminars and workshops. Served with C.E. AUS, 1946-47. Fellow Am. Phys. Soc., AAAS; mem. Lambda Chi Alpha. Research in nuclear and high energy physics. Home: 80 W Cooke Rd Columbus OH 43214 Office: Ohio State U Dept Physics 174 W 18th St Columbus OH 43210

ROMANS, KENNETH JOHN, nurse; b. Wayne, Mich., Mar. 13, 1954; s. Benjamin and Ruth Ellen (Lansing) R.; m. Lois Eileen Nastwold, June 3, 1984; 1 child, Ashleigh Caitlin. AA in Nursing, Wayne Community Coll., 1981. Staff emergency room specialist Heritage Hosp., Taylor, Mich., 1981-84; occupational health nurse Ford Motor Co., Dearborn, Mich., 1984—. Pres. UAW Bldg. local 600, Dearborn, 1987. Mem. Am. Heart Assn. (advanced cardiac life support provider 1986), Am. Occupational Health Assn. (treas. 1985), Am. Audiologists Assn. Republican. Presbyterian. Avocations: sky diving, photography, running, sailing. Home: 32503 Allen Ct Livonia MI 48154 Office: Ford Motor Co PO Box 1600 Miller Rd Dearborn MI 48180

ROMBS, VINCENT JOSEPH, accountant, lawyer; b. Newport, Ky., Mar. 8, 1918; s. John Thomas and Mathilda (Fromhold) R.; m. Ruth Burns, Aug. 15, 1942; 1 child, Ellen (Mrs. James P. Herman). Student Xavier U., 1936-37; BS with honors, Southeastern U., 1941; JD, Loyola U., Chgo., 1952. Bar: Ill. 1952; CPA, Ill. Tax ptnr. with local and nat. pub. acctg. firms, Chgo., 1952—; assoc. Laventhol & Horwath, Chgo., 1970-75; of counsel Edelman Chartered, 1975—; Ostrow Reisin Berk & Abrams, Ltd., 1977—; pres. Vincent J. Rombs, Ltd., 1982—. Bd. dirs. Miller Found. Served to lt. comdr., USNR, 1941-46. Recipient Scholarship Key award Delta Theta Phi, 1953. Mem. Am. Inst. CPA's, Ill. Soc. CPA's, Ill. Bar Assn. Home: 915 E Golf Rd Apt 3 Arlington Heights IL 60005 Office: 1 N LaSalle St Suite 1714 Chicago IL 60602 also: 676 Saint Clair St Suite 2100 Chicago IL 60611

ROMEO, ZACHARY JOSEPH, obstetrician-gynecologist; b. New Orleans, Apr. 26, 1912; s. Dominic A. and Laura M. (Davenport) R.; m. Mary Louise Quinn, Nov. 11, 1940; children: Judith Ann, Susan Lee, Stephen Grant, Jeffery Liam. BS, Tulane U., 1931, MD, 1935. Diplomate Am. Bd. Ob-Gyn. Intern. Touro Infirmary, New Orleans, 1936; asst. in ob-gyn Tulane Med. Sch., New Orleans, 1937; from jr. resident to sr. resident L.I. Coll. Hosp., Bklyn., 1938-39; sr. resident in ob-gyn Greenpoint Hosp., Bklyn.; practice medicine specializing in ob-gyn Rock Island, Ill., 1945—. Served to lt. col. U.S. Army, 1939-44. Office: 1705 2d Ave Rock Island IL 61201

ROMER, ANN ELIZABETH, school psychologist; b. Jamestown, N.Y., June 21, 1940; d. Andrew Martin and Ellen Jean (Chiverton) Gunnarson; m. Paul A. Romer, July 14, 1962; children: Kirsten, Daniel, Erika. BA, Alfred U., 1962; MEd, Kent State U., 1979, Ednl. Specialist, 1980. Lic. sch. psychologist. Sch. psychologist Astabual County Bd. Edn., Jefferson, Ohio, 1980-85, Trumbull County Bd. Edn., Warren, Ohio, 1985—; cons. sch. psychologist. Listener Trumbull Contact, Warren, 1972-74; co-leader Girl Scouts U.S., 1971-74. Mem. Nat. Assn. Sch. Psychologists. Mem. Christian Ch. Avocations: reading, gardening, bowling, needlework, stamp collecting. Office: Trumbull County Bd Edn 2577 Schenley NE Warren OH 44483

ROMICK, JEROME MICHAEL, health care company executive; b. Houston, May 7, 1943; s. Arthur and Lillian Y. (Smolensky) R.; B.B.A., U. Tex., 1967; m. Ina Sue Hirsch, Aug. 8, 1971; children: Stephanie Alisha, Kate Hillary. With Procter & Gamble, Corpus Christi, 1967-68; self-employed, Victoria, Tex., 1968-69; with Drustar, Inc., Grove City, Ohio, 1969-72; pres. Artromick Internat., Inc., Columbus, Ohio, 1972—. Trustee, Citizens Research, Inc., Columbus, 1978-79. Served with U.S. Army, 1964-69. Recipient Small Bus. Person of Yr. award SBA, 1977. Mem. Am. Soc. Cons. Pharmacists (asso.), Am. Soc. Hosp. Pharmacists. Jewish. Holder 4 patents in field. Home: 170 N Drexel St Bexley OH 43209 Office: 2008 Zettler Rd Columbus OH 43227

ROMP, WALTER GARY, osteopath; b. Urbana, Ill., Oct. 12, 1944; s. Arthur J. and Florence Mary (Massey) R.; m. Carole Knutson, June 10, 1967; children—Chip, Cindy, Curt. B.A. in Chemistry, Duke U., 1966; D.O., Des Moines Coll. Osteo. Medicine and Surgery, 1971. Intern, Cleve. Clinic Found., 1971-72; gen. practice osteo. medicine, Sandusky, Ohio, 1972—; team physician Sandusky High Sch. varsity football team. Pres., Sandusky Bd. Edn. Recipient Golden Medalion award Squibb Co., 1977; named Outstanding Young Man of Yr., Sandusky Jaycees, 1977. Mem. Am. Osteo. Assn., Ohio Osteo. Assn. Republican. Episcopalian. Clubs: Rotary (dist. gov. 1982-83), Masons. Office: 1313 W Bogart Rd Sandusky OH 44870

RONASZEGI, ARPAD, architect, educator; b. Budapest, Hungary, May 4, 1959; m. Ida Teuschl, July 31, 1983;. MArch, Budapest Tech. U., 1983. Designer Middough Assocs. Inc., Cleve., 1984-85; project architect Allegretti Architects, St. Joseph, Mich., 1985-86; asst. prof. Andrews U., Berrien Springs, Mich., 1986—; vis. asst. prof. Andrews U., Berrien Springs, 1985-86. Mem. AIA (assoc). Office: Andrews U Dept Architecture Berrien Springs MI 49104

RONEY, DARYL DOUGLAS, banker; b. Ottawa, Kans., June 5, 1952; s. Carl Lee and Joan Lee (Casten) R.; m. Kristine Ann Miller, July 6, 1974; children: Scott Michael, Lane Douglas. BS in Agrl. Econs., Kans. State U., 1974; grad. sch. banking, U. Colo., 1982. Sales rep. Sommer Seed Co., Topeka, Kans., 1974-75; banker Farmers Nat. Bank, Abilene, Kans., 1975—, v.p., 1982—, also bd. dirs. Chmn. exec. bd. Dickinson County Extension Council, Abilene, 1985-87. Mem. Farm Mgmt. Assn. (treas. Abilene 1983—), Dickinson County Bakers Assn. (pres. Abilene 1986—), Abilene C. of C. (bd. dirs. 1985—), Alpha Gamma Rho (sec. 1973-74), Gamma Sigma Delta. Republican. United Methodist. Lodge: Rotary (bd. dirs. 1987). Avocations: running, spectator sports, wood working. Office: Farmers Nat Bank 400 N Broadway Abilene KS 67410

RONK, RICHARD GENE, manufacturing company executive, real estate broker; b. Fredericktown, Ohio, Jan. 20, 1927; s. Alwyn Baird and Blanche Margret (Carlisle) R.; m. Bonita L. Bowman, May 27, 1950; 1 child, Richard David. BS, Ashland Coll., 1950. Lic. real estate broker, Ohio. Indsl. engr. Westinghouse Electric Corp., Mansfield, Ohio, 1951-59, staff value analyst, 1967-75, supervisory buyer, 1975-83; chief indsl. engr. Ohio Gear, Cleve., 1959-65; mgr. mfg. engring. Standard Sci. Co., Elyria, Ohio, 1965-67; dir. purchasing WCI Corp., Mansfield, 1983-85, mgr. materials, 1985—; pres. cons. firm Ronk, Warner, Patterson & Cole, Mansfield, 1960-64, Malabar Realty Co., Mansfield, 1972—. Patentee in field. Served to staff sgt. U.S. Army, 1944-49, ETO. Mem. Nat. State and Local Bd. Realtors, VFW. Republican. Jewish. Club: University. Lodges: Masons, Kiwanis. Avocation: golf. Home: 635 Ashwood Dr Mansfield OH 44906 Office: WCI Laundry Div 246 E 4th St Mansfield OH 44902

ROONEY, EDMUND JOSEPH, journalism educator; b. Chgo., June 21, 1924; s. Edmund J. and Elizabeth (MAgner) R.; m. Mary F. Flynn, Apr. 14, 1956; children: Edmund J. III, John F., Mary E., Ellen J., Peter E., Timothy. BA, Loyola U., Chgo., 1977, MA, 1981, postgrad., 1984—. Reporter Southtown Econ., Chgo., 1947-49, City News Bur., Chgo., 1951-52, Chgo. Daily News, 1952-78; asst. prof. Loyola U., 1978—; dir. Nat. Ctr. Info. for Studies Loyola U.; part-time faculty Loyola U., 1963-78; coordinator journalism program Loyola U., Chgo., 1982—. Served to corp. U.S. Army, 1943-45. Nieman fellow; recipient Pulitzer Prize, 1957. Mem. Soc. Profl. Journalists (cons.), Assn. for Edn. Journalism and Mass Communication, Ill. Freedom Info. Council. Roman Catholic. Avocations: swimming, reading. Office: Loyola U Dept Communications 820 N Michigan Chicago IL 60611

ROONEY, PHILLIP BERNARD, waste management company executive; b. Chgo., July 8, 1944; s. Christopher Thomas and Rita Ann (Mitchell) R.; m. Suzanne Victoria Perillo, Jan. 29, 1966; children: Philip B., Trisha A., Michael P., Sean B. B.A., St. Bernard Coll., 1966. Asst. to pres. Waste Mgmt., Inc., Oak Brook, Ill., 1969-71, v.p., 1971-74, sr. v.p., 1981-84, pres., 1984—, also chief operating officer, dir.; dir. First Nat. Bank LaGrange, Ill. Mem. adv. bd. Hinsdale Community House, Ill., 1984—; trustee Nazareth Acad., LaGrange, Ill., 1981—. Served to capt. USMCR, 1966-69. Decorated Bronze Star, Navy Commendation medal. Mem. Am. Pub. Works Assn., Nat. Solid Wastes Mgmt. Assn. Roman Catholic. Clubs: Butler Nat., Butterfield Country (Oak Brook, Ill.). Office: Waste Mgmt Inc 3003 Butterfield Rd Oak Brook IL 60521

ROOSA, JAN BERTOROTTA, clinical psychologist; b. Champaign, Ill., Apr. 19, 1927; s. Walter Laidlaw and Giannina (Bertorotta) R.; m. Joan Herr, Apr. 14, 1982. B.S., U. Ill., 1950; M.A., U. Denver, 1951, Ph.D., 1957. Coordinator, clin. psychologist Child Research Council, Kansas City, Mo., 1954-57; supr., psychologist State Hosp., Fulton, Mo., 1957-59; chief of psychotherapy VA Hosp., Kansas City, 1959-63; clinical psychologist in pvt. practice, Kansas City area, 1963—; dir., co-founder Learning Resource Ctr., Kansas City, 1969-79; dir. Gestalt, Social Competence Inst., Kansas City, 1969—. Active Conflict Resolution of Met. Kansas City. Served with USNR, 1945-47, 1951-52. Mem. Greater Kansas City Psychol. Assn., Mo. Psychol. Assn., Kansas Assn. Profl. Psychologists, Am. Psychol. Assn. Author: Situation-Options-Consequences-Simulation: A Technique for Teaching Social Skills, 1973; Psychological and Social Competence Model and Skills, 1975. Office: 400 E Red Bridge Rd 337 Kansas City MO 64131

ROOSE, PAUL EUGENE, osteopathic physician, orthopedic surgeon; b. Hart, Mich., Aug. 22, 1947; s. Walter Leon and Genevieve Avon (Watters) R. B.S., Wayne State U., 1969; D.O., Kirksville Coll. Osteo. Medicine, 1973. Cert. orthopedic surgery Am. Osteo. Acad. Orthopedic Surgery. Intern, Mt. Clemens (Mich.) Hosp., 1973-74; resident in orthopedic surgery Doctor's Hosp., Massillon, Ohio, 1974-78, orthopedic surgeon, 1978-79; orthopedic surgeon Mercy Hosp., Cadillac, Mich., 1979—; cons. orthopedic surgeon Reed City Hosp., Mercy Hosp. Grayling, Clare Osteo. Hosp. Recipient Geigy award, 1978. Mem. Am. Osteo. Assn., Am. Coll. Osteo. Surgeons, Am. Osteo. Acad. Orthopedic Surgeons, Wexford County Med. Soc. Contbr. articles to profl. jours.

ROOT, DONALD JUNIOR, electrical engineer; b. Coshocton, Ohio, June 14, 1955; s. Marion Donald and Anna June (Croskey) R.; m. Kathy Jo Bucklew, June 8, 1974; children: David Laurel, Michael Willis. BS in Agriculture Econs., Ohio State U., 1977; BEE, Syracuse U., 1983. Prodn. supr. Continental Grain Co., Alexander, N.Y., 1978-79; plant supt. Continental Grain Co., Sangerfield, N.Y., 1979-81, quality assurance mgr., 1981-83; project engr. Continental Grain Co., Chgo., 1983-85, sr. elec. engr., 1985—. Treas. Oneida County Right to Life Party, Utica, N.Y., 1980. Mem. IEEE (subcom. power systems design 1983—), Nat. Fire Protection Assn. Republican. Mormon. Avocations: electronics, woodworking. Office: Continental Grain Co 10 S Riverside Plaza Chicago IL 60606

ROOTES, CHARLES WESLEY, manufacturing company executive; b. Tebbetts, Mo., June 14, 1927; s. David J. and Iva R. (Adkinson) R.; m. Joanne Thesen, Feb. 1, 1951; children: David, Sue Ellen, Timothy. Student, Westminster Coll., 1947-48, Mo. U., 1949-50. CPA, Mo. Supervising acct. Ernst & Ernst, St. Louis, 1951-56; controller A.B. Chance Co., Centralia, Mo., 1956-62; asst. controller Spencer Chem. Co., Kansas City, Mo., 1962-63; v.p., treas. Rival Mfg. Co., Kansas City, 1963-77, exec. v.p., dir., 1977-85, pres., chief exec. officer, chmn. bd. dirs., 1986—; dir. Rival, Lobconco, Titan Sales Corp. Trustee, treas. Presbyn. Ch., 1967-70. Served with USAAF, 1945-47. Mem. Mo. Soc. CPA's, Fin. Execs. Inst. Clubs: Centralia Country (pres. 1960-61), Leawood (Kans.) Country. Lodge: Rotary (bd. dirs., treas. 1960-61). Home: 3509 W 92d St Leawood KS 66206 Office: 36th and Bennington Sts Kansas City MO 64129

ROOTES, PHILIP WALLACE, controller; b. Anoka, Minn., July 15, 1949; s. Earl E. and Florence M. (Beckman) R.; m. Becky Jo Stoner. BS in Bus., U. Minn., 1972. Staff auditor Arthur Young & Co., Mpls., 1972-78; treas. Info. Dialogues, Inc., Mpls., 1978-79; controller Data Card Corp., Minnetonka, Minn., 1980—. Fin. advisor Coon Rapids (Minn.) Devel. Co., 1978; chmn. fin. com. Coon Rapids Devel. Commn., 1978-81; coach Coon Rapids Youth Hockey, 1978-87, pres. 1981-82; mem. Coon Rapids Ice Arena Commn., 1981—. Served with USNG, 1969-75. Mem. Am. Inst. CPA's, Minn. State Soc. CPA's. Office: Data Card Corp 11111 Bren Rd W Minnetonka MN 55343

ROOTS, JOHN MCCOOK, author, lecturer, foreign correspondent; b. Hankow, China (parents Am. citizens) Oct. 27, 1903; s. Logan Herbert and Eliza Lydia (McCook) R. B.A. cum laude, Harvard Coll., 1925. Contbr. New York Times, Herald Tribune, Atlantic Monthly, Asia, Pace, Look, Reader's Digest, Time, Saturday Rev., others, 1927—; traveling rep., dir. Moral Re-Armament teams, S. Africa, 1929-31, U.S., 1932, Great Britain, France, Switzerland, The Netherlands, Germany, Italy, Can. Belgium, East Africa, Greece, Middle East 1932-68; lectr. U.S. and Can., 1964-81; fgn. corr. various publs., numerous countries including China, Egypt, Israel, Jordan, Lebanon, Syria, Saudi Arabia, Indonesia, Iran, 1927-80; assoc. Up With People orgn., 1968—; author: Chou: a Biography of China's Legendary Chou En-lai, 1978. Recipient Washburn Prize for History, Harvard Coll., 1925. Clubs: Harvard (N.Y.C.), Army and Navy (Washington) Home and Office: 158 Graham Ave Saint Ignace MI 49781

ROOY, JAMES ALLEN, accountant, controller; b. Hammond, Ind., Apr. 16, 1956; s. Henry Martin Rooy and Anjean Shirley (Decker) Roberts; m. Cynthia Lynn Vree, June 4, 1977; children: David, Julie, Daniel. BA, Calvin Coll., 1978; MBA, Keller Grad. Sch. Mgmt., Chgo., 1984. CPA, Ill. Staff acct. Foster & Kleiser, Chgo., 1978-79; staff acct. South Suburban Hosp., Hazel Crest, Ill., 1979-82, controller, 1985—; dir. acctg. St. Joseph Hosp., Chgo., 1982-85; dir. fin. Elim Christian Sch., Palos Heights, Ill., 1985; pvt. practice acctg., tax preparation, Lansing, Ill., 1978—. Mem. Healthcare Fin. mgmt. Assn., Ill.CPA Soc., Am. Inst. CPA's. Mem. Christian Reformed Ch. Avocations: bowling, golf. Home: 18425 Clyde Ave Lansing IL 60438

ROOZEN, MARY LOUISE, bank holding company executive; b. Milw., Mar. 31, 1921; d. Edward E. and Margaret (May) Silverman; m. Edwin Cramer Roozen, Sept. 18, 1943; children—Mary Katrina Roozen Hass, Joanna Roozen Satorius, Margaret Anne. B.A. in Speech, U. Wis., 1942. With Met. Milw. Assn. Commerce, 1942-43; adminstrv. asst. Curative Workshop of Milw., 1966-69; adminstrv. asst. mktg. Marine Corp., Milw., 1969-70, mktg. officer, 1970-73, asst. v.p., 1973-76, v.p. pub. relations, 1976-84, v.p. pvt. banking, 1984-87 ; v.p. Marine Bank, N.A., Milw., 1977-87, corp. pub. relations cons., 1987—; dir. Germantown Marine Bank, 1976-83; v.p. Marine Found., Plaza Bldg. Mgmt. Bd. dirs. Neighborhood House, Milw., 1963-78, Curative Workshop, Milw., 1970-78, Wis. Humane Soc., 1976-85, Friends of Art, Milw., 1980-84, Ozaukee Humane Soc., 1983—; bd. dirs. Vol. Ctr. Greater Milw., Met. Milw. Assn. Commerce, chmn. promotions com. 1979-80; co-chmn. capital fund drive Neighborhood House, Milw., 1984; vice chmn. 440th Tactical Air Wing Community Council, USAFR. Recipient Recognition award Nat. Ctr. for Voluntary Action, 1977. Mem. Pub. Relations Soc. Am. (chmn. fin. insts. sect. 1983-85, exec. com. 1980—), Wis. Sr. Pub. Relations Forum, Nat. Assn. Bank Women (chmn. Milw. group 1976-77), Women's Club of Wis. (mem. fin. com. 1983-85). Episcopalian. Club: River Tennis (Milw.). Home and Office: 9111 W Hawthorne Rd Mequon WI 53092

ROPA-GAIZUTIS, WANDA, personnel director; b. London, Oct. 19, 1955; came to U.S., 1964; d. Ted and Cecylia (Jajko) Ropa; m. Vytas Gaizutis, Jan. 22, 1977; 1 child, Michael David. BS in Nursing, Loyola U., Chgo., 1977; MS, U. Ill., Chgo., 1984. RN, Ill. Clin. nurse U. Ill. Med. Ctr., Chgo., 1980-82; nursing supr. Chgo. Lakeshore Hosp., 1982; asst. head nurse, float pool nurse Barclay Hosp., Chgo., 1982-83; instr. Ill. Masonic Med. Ctr. Sch. Nursing, Chgo., 1983-85; tech. recruiter Search Enterprises, Oakbrook, Ill., 1985-86; personnnel dir. Imperial Edn. Corp., Oaklawn, Ill., 1986—, tng. cons., 1986—. Avocations: writing, racquetball, tennis, art, movies, dancing. Office: 10341 S Lawler Oak Lawn IL 60453

RORER, LEONARD GEORGE, psychology educator; b. Dixon, Ill., Dec. 24, 1932; s. Leonard Gleason and Marion Emma (Geyer) R.; B.A., Swarthmore (Pa.) Coll., 1954; Ph.D., U. Minn., 1963; m. Gail Evans, Apr. 30, 1958; children—Liat, Eric Evans; m. 2d, Nancy McKimens, Jan. 9, 1969; 1 dau., Mya Noelani. Research asso., then asso. dir. Oreg. Research Inst., Eugene, 1963-75; prof. psychology Miami U., Oxford, Ohio, 1975—, dir.

clin. psychology tng. program, 1976-86; pres. Oreg. Psychol. Assn., 1973-75. NIMH spl. research fellow, 1967-68; fellow Netherlands Inst. Advanced Study, 1971-72; postdoctoral fellow Inst. for Rational-Emotive Therapy, 1982-83. Mem. Am. Psychol. Assn. (council reps. 1968-72), Ohio Psychol. Assn., Midwestern Psychol. Assn., Assn. Advancement Behavior Therapy, Soc. Multivariate Exptl. Psychology. Author articles in field, mem. editorial bds. profl. jours. Home: 327 W Sycamore St Oxford OH 45056 Office: Psychology Dept Miami U Oxford OH 45056

RORIE, CHARLES DAVID, SR., academic administrator; b. Dallas, Jan. 10, 1936; s. Oscar Lee and Sibyl Matilda (Carver) R.; m. Julia Hanora Davenport, Aug. 5, 1961; children: Julie Anne, Peter Patrick, Charles David Jr. AA, Tyler Jr. Coll., 1955; BA, Sam Houston State U., 1961; MS, East Tex. State U., 1964; PhD, U. Tex., 1973; grad. in Ednl. Mgmt., Harvard U., 1985. Counselor, instr. Southwest Tex. Jr. Coll., 1968-71; dean instruction W.Va. Northern Community Coll., 1973-75; asst. dean Cuyahoga (Ohio) Community Coll., 1975-82; dean of coll. Dyersburg State Community Coll., 1982-86; v.p. Elgin (Ill.) Community Coll., 1986—. Designing and implementing video/computer programs in the classroom. Dyersburg (Tenn.) Spl. Olympics, 1983-86. Served with U.S. Army, 1961-62, with Royal Can. Navy, 1965-68. Mem. Am. Assn. Community and Jr. Colls. (assoc.), Am. Assn. Higher Edn. (mem. Ill. council 1986—), Am. Vocat. Assn., Suburban-Chgo. Council Chief Academic Officers, Ill. Council Community Coll. Adminstrs., Council Occupational Edn., Greater Dyer C. of C. Democrat. Episcopalian. Clubs: Rolls-Royce Owner's, Dyersburg Country, Bentley Driver's. Lodge: Moose. Home: 1422 Royal Ct Elgin IL 60123 Office: Elgin Community Coll 1700 Spartan Dr Elgin IL 60123

ROSBOROUGH, JOSEPH ROBERT, lawyer; b. Moline, Ill., Jan. 13, 1911; s. Caldwell Robert and Nellie (Ball) R.; m. Jean Bowman, Oct. 7, 1939; children: Nancy, Barbara Jo, Margaret Ann. BS, U. Ill., 1933, LLB, 1935; postgrad., Harvard U., 1942. Bar: Ill. 1936, U.S. Supreme Ct. 1939. Sole practice Moline, 1936—; asst. atty. gen. State of Ill., Moline, 1968-82. Served to lt. comdr. USN, 1942-45. Mem. ABA, Ill. Bar Assn. Republican. Clubs: Rock Island (Ill.) Arsenal Golf; Davenport (Iowa) Outing; Union League (Chgo.), South Park Tennis. Lodges: Rotary, Elks. Home: 1825 29th St Moline IL 61265 Office: 1528 6th Ave Moline IL 61265

ROSE, CLAYTON W., III, accountant; b. Columbus, Ohio, Apr. 2, 1952; s. Clayton Jr. and Betty Lou (Osborn) R.; m. Lynn Ellen Jackson, June 14, 1980; children: Abigail Erin, Alex Mitchell. BS, Ohio State U., 1974. CPA, Ohio. Staff acct. Coopers & Lybrand, Columbus, 1975-81, Lee R. Headlee, P.A., Dublin, Ohio, 1981-82; pres., prin. Beall, Rose and Assocs., CPA's, Dublin, 1982—. Mem. Am. Inst. CPA's, Ohio Soc. CPA's, Ohio State Farm Sci. Rev./Farm Ops. Student Employees Mostly Peasants Alumni Assn. (bd. govs.). Lodge: Kiwanis (pres. Dublin club 1983-84, treas. 1985-87; com chmn. Div. 10-W Franklin County, Ohio 1984-87). Office: Beall Rose & Assocs CPA's Inc 5151 Post Rd Dublin OH 43017

ROSE, CLIFFORD CHAUNCEY, electronics company executive; b. Huntington, W.Va., Feb. 16, 1930; s. Clifford and Vivian (Williams) R.; m. Helen Pace, Feb. 13, 1955; children—Vivian, Karen. Student Ohio State U., 1953-58. Instrumentation specialist Westinghouse Electric, Columbus, Ohio, 1954-69, facilities engr., 1953-76; founder, chief exec. officer, pres. Contronics, Columbus, 1965—; cons. in field. Asst. gen. exec. YMCA, Columbus, 1975-78. Served as electronics specialist USAF, 1950-53. Named Outstanding Black Entrepreneur, Ohio State U., 1978. Mem. Instrument Soc. Am., Aircraft Owners and Pilots Assn., Ohio State U. Alumni Assn. Clubs: Ohio State U. Pres., Ohio State U. Buckeye. Avocations: boating; fishing; model railroad building. Home: 183 Melyers Ct Worthington OH 43085 Office: Contronics 2999 E Dublin Granville Rd Columbus OH 43229

ROSE, DANIEL HIRAM, accountant; b. Detroit, Mar. 5, 1958; s. Leonard Carrol and Elfreida (Schlese) R.; m. Karen Ann Schmidt, June 26, 1982; 1 child, Matthew Hiram. BBA, U. Mich., 1980. CPA, Mich. Sr. mgr. Peat Marwick Main & Co., Detroit, 1980-87; v.p. fin. Amsteel Internat., Inc., Farmington HIlls, Mich., 1987—. Pres. Farmington Green Homeowners Assn., Farmington Hills, Mich., 1987; com. chmn. Council Homeowners Assn. Farmington Hills, 1987; bd. dirs. Antioch Luth. Ch., Farmington Hills, 1987. Mem. Am. Inst. CPA's, Mich. Assn. CPA's, Farmington Area Jaycees (v.p. 1985), U. Mich. Alumni Assn. Republican. Avocations: tennis, softball. Home: 27821 White Plains Farmington Hills MI 48018 Office: Amsteel Internat Inc 35055 W Twelve Mile Rd Farmington Hills MI 48018

ROSE, DAVID E., lawyer; b. Columbus, Ohio, Feb. 21, 1944; s. Harvey S. and Florence (McCoy) R.; m. Virginia Lorenzen, June 3, 1967; 1 child, Suzanne. BS, Ohio State U., 1966; JD Capital U., 1977. Bar: Ohio 1978, U.S. Dist. Ct. (no. dist.) Ohio 1982, U.S. Dist. Ct. (no. dist.) Tex. 1983, U.S. Supreme Ct. 1984, U.S. Ct. Appeals (5th, 6th, 7th, 8th cirs.) 1984, U.S. Dist. Ct. Nebr. 1984, U.S. Dist. Ct. (ea. and we. dists.) Wis. 1984. Mgr. prospecting O.M. Scott & Sons, Marysville, Ohio, 1967, regional sales mgr., 1969-71, mgr. retailer services, 1971-79; corp. atty. Na-Churs Plant Food Co., Marion, Ohio, 1979—, also dir. mktg., 1986—. Served to 1st lt. U.S. Army, 1967-69. Mem. ABA, Ohio State Bar Assn., Marion County Bar Assn., Assn. Trial Lawyers Am., Comml. Law League Am., Phi Alpha Delta. Home: 2125 Olde Sawmill Blvd Dublin OH 43017 Office: Na-Churs Plant Food Co 421 Leader St Marion OH 43302

ROSE, ERNST, dentist; b. Oldenburg, Germany, July 22, 1932; s. William and Elsie (Lowenbach) R.; came to U.S., 1940, naturalized, 1946; m. Shirley Mae Galssman, Dec. 24, 1960; children: Ruth Ellen, Michele Ann, Daniel Scot, Seth Joseph. BS, Georgetown U., 1955; DDS, Western Res. U., 1963. Intern, Waterbury (Conn.) Hosp., 1964; pvt. practice dentistry, Hubbard, Ohio, 1964—; pres., treas. Dr. Ernst Rose, Inc. Lab. instr. Ohio State U., Columbus, 1956-57; dental adviser Assoc. Neighborhood Ctr. Mem. Liberty Twp. Zoning Commn., 1967-74; chmn., 1970-74; chmn. Hubbard (Ohio) Urban Renewal Com., 1968-74. Mem. brotherhood bd., 1967—, treas. 1971-73, pres. 1975-77, temple bd. dirs. 1975-84 JewishServed with AUS, 1957-59. Fellow Royal Soc. Health; mem. Chgo. Dental Soc., ADA, Ohio Dental Assn., Corydon Palmer Dental Soc. (mem. council 1983-87), Warren Dental Soc., Hubbard C. of C. (bd. dirs. 1973—), Jewish Chatauqua Soc. (life), Alpha Omega (council mem. 1968—, sec. 1970-71, v.p. 1971-72, pres. 1972-73). Lodges: B'nai B'rith (pres. 1970-71, trustee 1971—), Rotary (vice chmn. Kashrut com. 1983-85, chmn. Kashrut com. 1985—, vice chmn. Mikvah com. 1983—). Home: 418 Arbor Circle Youngstown OH 44505 Office: 30 N Main St Hubbard OH 44425

ROSE, GLADYS DORTCH, cytotechnologist; b. Memphis, Sept. 6, 1939; d. William Tell and Lillie (Thompson) Dortch; B.S., LeMoyne Coll., 1959; cert. in cytotech. U. Tenn., 1961; M.S. in Organizational Psychology, So. Ill. U., Edwardsville, 1978; m. Lucius Victor Rose, June 17, 1967; 1 dau., Gladys Ann. Substitute tchr. Memphis Public Schs., 1959, 61; supr. cytology Western Bapt. Hosp., Paducah, Ky., 1961-67; part-time cytotechnologist Cardinal Glennon Hosp., St. Louis, 1979-82; ednl. coordinator profl. edn. in cytology St. Louis U. Sch. Medicine, 1980-81; supr. cytology lab. St. Luke's Hosp., St. Louis, 1967—; assoc. dir. labs. St. Louis Regional Health Ctr., 1984—; cons. in field. Recipient various service awards. Mem. Am. Soc. Clin. Pathology, Am. Cytology Soc., St. Louis Cytology Soc., St. Louis Med. Tech. Soc., Am. Public Health Assn., LWV, Nat. Assn. Univ. Women, Sigma Gamma Rho. Mem. A.M.E. Ch. Club: Order Calanthe. Author articles in field. Home: 7006 Stanford St St Louis MO 63130 Office: 5535 Delmar St St Louis MO 63112

ROSE, JAMES RUSSELL, manufacturing company executive; b. Milw., Sept. 14, 1941; s. Russell Joseph and Elanor (Zick) R.; m. Linda Kay Quisel, July 2, 1966; children: Kevin, Derek. AAS, Milwaukee Sch. Engring., 1968, BSME, 1970. Engring. supr. 3-M Co., Bedford Park, Ill., 1981-82, coating supr., 1982-84, maintanance supr., 1984—. Mem. Soccer Adv. Bd., Naperville, Ill., 1985—; cubmaster Boy Scouts Am., Naperville, 1985-86; supt. Knox Presbyn. Sunday Sch., Naperville, 1984—. Served with U.S. Army, 1964-66. Named to Order Ky. Cols., 1975. Lodge: Lions, Masons. Home: 1755 Winola Ct Naperville IL 60565 Office: 6850 S Harlem Argo IL 60501

ROSE, JENNIFER J., lawyer; b. Dayton, Ohio, Oct. 25, 1951; d. Virginia Rose Kelly Apaydin. B.A., Tarkio Coll., 1972; J.D., Drake U., 1976. Bar: Iowa 1977, U.S. Dist. Ct. (so. and no. dists.) Iowa 1977, U.S. Ct. Appeals (8th cir.) 1978, U.S. Supreme Ct. 1980, Nebr. 1984. Adminstrv. asst. State Ombudsman, Des Moines, 1975; spl. asst. county atty. Page and Taylor Counties, Iowa, 1977-80; city atty. Imogene, Iowa, 1977-78; city atty. Essex, Iowa, 1981—; sole practice, Shenandoah, Iowa, 1977—; dir. Southwest Iowa Family Systems Project, 1978-80; adv. council southwest region Legal Services Corp. Iowa, 1983—. Contbr. articles to profl. jours. V.P. vol. council Planned Parenthood Mid Iowa, 1980-83. Fellow Am. Acad. Matrimonial Lawyers; mem. Page County Bar Assn. (pres. 1978-80), Southwest Iowa Bar Assn. (bd. govs.), Iowa State Bar Assn. (spl. com. family law, young lawyers com. law and mental health), ABA (Criminal Justice sect., Gen. Practice sect., Family Law sect., Litigation sect.), Am. Orthopsychiatric Assn., Nat. Council Juvenile and Family Ct. Judges, Nat. Assn. Counsel for Children, Nat. Assn. Vol. in Criminal Justice (bd. dirs.), Internat. Soc. Family Law, Delta Theta Phi. Jewish. Home: Rural Rt 1 Shenandoah IA 51601 Office: Rose Law Offices PO Box 616 Shenandoah IA 51601

ROSE, JERRY RICHARD, accountant; b. Yale, Mich., Sept. 10, 1956; s. Gerald Richard and Dorothy Jean (Patillo) R.; m. Patricia Jean Cleland; children: David, Laura. BS in Acctg., Cen. Mich. U., 1981. CPA, Mich. Sr. asst. Deloitte Haskins & Sells, Saginaw, Mich., 1980-83; acctg. analyst, internal auditor Comml. and Savs. Bank, St. Clair, Mich., 1983-85; cost acctg. supr. Dunn Paper, Port Huron, Mich., 1985-87, James River Corp. Dunn Paper div., Port Huron, 1987—. Mem. Am Inst. CPA's, Mich. Assn. CPA's, Nat. Assn. Accts. (v.p. communications and pub. relations Blue Water chpt. 1986-87). Home: 1211 Palmer Ct Port Huron MI 48060 Office: James River Corp Dunn Paper Div 218 Riverview Port Huron MI 48060

ROSE, JOHN MAREK, banker; b. Green Bay, Wis., May 9, 1916; s. John and Anne (Mraz) R.; m. Meredith Burke, Mar. 1, 1941; children—Polly, Alexandra, John P., Ann M., Victoria. M.B.A., Northwestern U., 1938; postgrad., Harvard Bus. Sch.; LL.D. (hon.), St. Norberts Coll., 1984. Pres. Kellogg-Citizen Nat. Bank, 1951-81, chmn. bd., 1981—; chmn. bd. Associated Bancorp., Green Bay, Wis., 1976—; dir. Wis. Pub. Service, Green Bay, Wis., Larsen Co., Green Bay. Chmn. Green Bay Redevel. Bd.; former pres. Green Bay Sch. Bd.; former mem. Green Bay Water Commn., Green Bay Met. Sewer Commn. Served to lt. comdr. USNR, 1941-46. Lodge: Masons.

ROSE, KENNETH DWIGHT, physician; b. Hastings, Nebr., Sept. 8, 1912; s. Ralph A. and Iva (Snyder) R.; B.A., U. Nebr., 1941, M.A., 1943, M.D., 1947; m. Margaret Ellen McMaster, June 13, 1943; children—Beth Marie (Mrs. Robert Dwyer), Susan Kay (Mrs. Victor Kuklin), Douglas Kenneth, Priscilla Margaret (Mrs. Barry Cross), James Allen, John Steven, Mary Elizabeth (Mrs. Douglas Unger). Instr. bacteriology U. Nebr., Lincoln, 1943, research asst. Coll. Medicine, 1943-47, clinician, dir. div. med. research Health Service, 1959-73, dir. Phys. Fitness Research Lab., 1970-73, cons. physician, 1973-86; intern Cin. Gen. Hosp., 1947-48; gen. practice medicine, Lincoln, 1948-59; mem. attending staff Bryan Meml. Hosp., staff physician emergency medicine, from 1973, now emeritus; emeritus staff Lincoln Gen. Hosp.; cons. physician to athletic dept. U. Nebr., Harris Labs., Eastmont Retirement Ctr. Served with M.C., AUS, 1943-46; to capt., M.C., AUS, 1954-56. Recipient Service citation USMC, Quantico, Va., 1969, Phys. Fitness Leadership award Nat. Jr. C. of C., 1971, Ruth Boynton award, 1974. Fellow Am. Coll. Sports Medicine (recipient Distinguished Service citation 1967, trustee 1969-73); mem. AMA (com. on med. aspects of sports 1965-73, com. exercise and phys. fitness 1965-72), Am. Acad. Family Practice, Nebr. Med. Soc., Nebr. Heart Assn., Nat. Athletic Trainers Assn. (hon.), Am. Orthopedic Soc. for Sports Medicine (hon.), Phi Beta Kappa, Sigma Xi, Phi Lambda Upsilon, Alpha Omega Alpha. Author: (with Jack Dies Martin) The Lazy Man's Guide to Physical Fitness, 1974; The Pioneer Rose Family of Adams County, Nebraska, 1983; Thoughts to Ponder While Waiting for the Doctor, 1983; A Search for Understanding—Memoirs of a Common Man, 1985. Emeritus mem. editorial bd. The Physician and Sports Medicine. Contbr. articles to med. jours. Home and Office: 10500 Yankee Hill Rd Lincoln NE 68526-9332

ROSE, LOUIS J., personnel administrator; b. Chgo., Apr. 1, 1942; s. Herbert S. Rose and Susan (Lurie) Kraus; m. Marilyn Rose, Dec. 22, 1968; children: Jeremy, Jonathan. BS in Group Work Adminstrn., George Williams Coll., 1966; degree in social work, U. Ill., Chgo., 1967; cert. in advanced mgmt., U. Chgo., 1976. Probation officer Cook County Juvenile Ct., Ill., 1966; dir. employment U. Chgo., 1966—. Mem. Dist. 161 Sch. Bd., Flossmoor, Ill., 1977—. Recipient Meritorious Service award SSS, 1972. Mem. Coll. and Univ. Personnel Assn., Chgo. Health Care Human Resource Assn. Clubs: Ravisloe Country (Homewood, Ill.), Quadrangle (Chgo.). Office: U Chgo 956 E 58th St Chicago IL 60637

ROSE, PATRICIA ANN SHULTZ, pharmacist; b. St. Louis, July 4, 1958; d. Charles E. and Clotilda A. (Beffa) Shultz; m. Douglas Scott Rose, June 8, 1979; 1 child, Paul Scott. BS in Pharmacy, St. Louis Coll., 1982. Registered pharmacist, Mo., Ill. Hosp. student pharmacist Barnes Hosp., St. Louis, 1977-79; retail student pharmacist Walgreen's Drug Stores, St. Louis, 1979-80; hosp. student pharmacist St. Mary's Health Ctr., St. Louis, 1980-82; research grad. pharmacist Norcliff-Thayer Inc., St. Louis, 1982; IV additive/staff pharmacist Barnes Hosp., 1982-84; retail pharmacist Kare Drug Store, St. Louis, 1984-86; staff pharmacist Neels Pharmacy, 1986—; IV additive pharmacist Mo. Bapt. Hosp., 1987—. Mem. St. Louis Soc. Hosp. Pharmacists, Rho Chi (mem. parish choir). Roman Catholic. Avocations: needlecrafts, volleyball, wood finishing, baking, travel. Office: Neels Pharmacy 10822 Sunset Plaza Saint Louis MO 63127

ROSE, PETER EDWARD, baseball player, manager; b. Cin., Apr. 14, 1941; s. Harry Rose; m. Karolyn Ann Englehardt (div.); children: Fawn, Peter.; m. Carol Woliung, Apr. 1984. Player Cin. Reds, 1963-78, player mgr., 1984—; player Phila. Phillies, 1979-83, Montreal Expos, 1984; mem. Nat. League All-Star Team, 1965, 67-71, 73-79, 80-81. Author: (with Bob Hertzel) Charlie Hustle, 1975, Winning Baseball, 1976, (with Peter Golenback) Pete Rose on Hitting, 1985. Named Nat. League Rookie of Year, 1963, Most Valuable Player, 1973, Most Valuable Player World Series, 1975, Nat. League Player of Year The Sporting News, 1968, Ball Player of Decade, 1979. Second player in baseball history to exceed 4,000 hits, all-time leader in hits. Office: care Cin Reds 100 Riverfront Stadium Cincinnati OH 45202 *

ROSE, RICHARD GEORGE, sales executive; b. Mpls., Sept. 26, 1946; s. George and Ellen Louise Rose; m. Annette Merritt, Dec. 16, 1967; children: Shannon Lynn, Brandi Elise. BBA, North Tex. State U., 1968. With Anderson Clayton Foods Co., Dallas, 1972-76, product mgr. cheese and dairy analogs, 1976-78; asst. gen. mgr. Automatic Buffet div. Coca Cola Bottling Co., Dallas, 1981-82; sales and mktg. mgr. chem. div. Southland Corp., Dallas, 1982-86; dir. sales Grindsted Products, Inc., Industrial Airport, Kans., 1986-87; pres. Sales Specialist Inc., Kansas City, Mo., 1987—. Mem. Inst. Food Technologists, Nat. Frozen Pizza Inst., Nat. Council Phys. Distbn. Mgmt., Am. soc. Bakery Engrs., Am. Bakers Assn. (gov.), So. Bakers Assn., Baking Assn. Carolinas, Am. Mensa Soc., North Tex. Mdse. Vendors Assn. (treas.), Phi Beta Lambda. Presbyterian. Office: Sales Specialist Inc 1156 W 103d St Suite 119 Kansas City MO 64114

ROSE, ROBERT JOHN, bishop; b. Grand Rapids, Mich., Feb. 28, 1930; s. Urban H. and Maida A. (Glerum) R. Student, St. Joseph Sem., 1944-50; B.A., Seminaire de Philosophie, Montreal, Que., Can., 1952; S.T.L., Pontifical Urban U., Rome, 1956; M.A., U. Mich., 1962. Ordained priest Roman Catholic Ch., 1955; dean St. Joseph Sem., Grand Rapids, 1966-69; dir. Christopher House, Grand Rapids, 1969-71; rector St. John's Sem., Plymouth, Mich., 1971-77; pastor Sacred Heart Parish, Muskegon Heights, Mich., 1977-81; bishop Diocese of Gaylord, Gaylord, Mich., 1981—; sec. treas. Mich. Cath. Conf., Lansing, 1983. Mem. Nat. Conf. Cath. Bishops. *

ROSE, RONALD EUGENE, electronics executive; b. Rosiclare, Ill., Mar. 19, 1929; s. Edwin Eugene and Gladys May (Joiner) R.; m. Barbara Ann Sebastian, Nov. 26, 1966; children: David, Katherine. BSEE, U. Ill., 1958. With Arvin Industries, Inc., Columbus, Ind., 1958—, tech. specialist, 1980-84, mgr. tech. support, 1985—. Served with USN, 1952-56. Avocation: electronics. Home: 4545 River Rd Columbus IN 47203 Office: Arvin Industries Inc 1531 13th St Columbus IN 47201

ROSE, ROSEMARY (S.) CATHERINE, business executive, financial consultant; b. Antigo, Wis., Jan. 2, 1931; d. Ernest J. and Rose F. Slizewski; 1 child, Ted R. Secretarial cert. Bryant-Stratton Sch., Milw., 1953; real estate course Spencerian Sch., Milw., 1964-65; Am. Inst. Paralegal Studies, 1985-86. Lic. real estate broker, Wis. Adminstrv. asst. H. R. Salen, Waukesha, Wis., 1951-55; owner, operator motel, Brookfield, Wis., 1955-65, restaurant and dry cleaning plant, Lannon, Wis., 1960-65; exec. sec. E.P. Hoyer, New Berlin, Wis., 1967-70; owner, operator Sanitation Service Inc., Menomonee Falls, Wis., 1970-75, North Twin Supper Club, Phelps, Wis., 1975-79; v.p. systems O.L. Schilffarth Co. div. Crown Industries, Milw., 1979-82; adminstr. food service Meurer Bakeries of Milw., 1984; prin., cons. R-Service Co., Germantown, Wis.; with Park East Hotel, Milw., 1984-85; office mgr. R. Service Co., 1980—, Cedar Disposal, Inc., Menomonee Falls, 1985—; gen. mgr. Hotel Rogers, Beaver Dam, Wis., 1982-83; broker, prin Alrose Realty Co.; mem. Research Bd. of Advisors Nat. Div. Am. Biographical Inst., Inc. Active Nat. Mus. Women in the Arts. Mem. Internat. Platform Assn., Nat. Assn. Female Execs., Nat. Rifle Assn. Home: N105 W15750 Hamilton Ct Germantown WI 53022 Office: N60 W16280 Kohler Ln Menomonee Falls WI 53051

ROSE, STANLEY JAY, newspaper executive; b. Kansas City, Mo., June 3, 1918; s. Joseph and Mae (Lund) R.; m. Shirley Mallin, Oct. 7, 1942; children: Roberta Susan Rose Small, Stephen F. AA, Los Angeles City Coll., 1939; BJ, U. Mo., 1941. Chmn. bd., pub. Sun Publs., Inc., Overland Park, Kans., 1950—; pub. Kansas City (Mo.) Jewish Chronicle, Inc., 1964—, College Blvd. News, 1984—, Atlanta Jewish Times, 1986—. Author: Memo from Russia, 1986. Bd. dirs. Kaw Valley Heart Assn., Heart of Am. council Boy Scouts Am.; past chmn. bd. trustees Suburban Med Ctr.; trustee William Allen White Found.; mem. adv. council U. Kans. Med. Center, K.U. Chancellor's Cabinet, 1986—. Served to lt. (j.g.) USNR, World War II; PTO. Recipient Sweepstakes, 1st place awards Kans. Better Newspaper Contest, 1968-70, 72, 73, William Allen White News Enterprise award, 1975, Bea Johnson award Am. Cancer Soc., 1st place winner for gen. excellence Suburban Newspapers Am., 1983-84; honoree Matrix Table, 1980; hon. col. Kans. Cav. Mem. Overland Park C. of C. (dir.), Kans. Assn. Commerce and Industry (dir.), Sigma Delta Chi. Club: Kansas City (Mo.) Press. Lodges: Masons, Shriners, Rotary (Paul Harris fellow 1985). Home: 8600 Mission Rd Prairie Village KS 66207 Office: Sun Publs Bldg Overland Park KS 66212

ROSE, WILLIAM, retired business executive; b. Waukegan, Ill., Nov. 7, 1919; s. Louis and Bertha Rose; m. Vivian May Gulledge, July 15, 1951; children: Whyland, Calvin, Marcia. LittD (hon.), Shimer Coll. Pres. Jobs Temporaries, Waukegan, 1951-86; ret. Jobs Temporaries, 1986. Fin. chmn. Boy Scouts Am., 1959-60, bd. dirs., 1966-71; mem. Lake County (Ill.) Mental Healt Adv. Com., 1971-80, bd. auditors Shields Twp., Ill., 1957-61; justice of peace Lake County, 1956-61, police magistrate, 1959-61; bd. dirs. Shimer Coll., Lake County Mental Health Clinic, 1957-68, United Community Services, 1964-71, Lake County Crime Commn., 1969-75; treas. Lake County Econ. Devel. Corp., 1982-83; bd. dirs., v.p. Lake County Welfare Council, 1963; bd. dirs. Pvt. Industry Council, 1977-83. Served with Signal Corps, AUS, 1944-46. Mem. Ind. Office Services Inst. (pres. 1971-73), Nat. Assn. Temporary Services (dir. 1975-78), Lake County Mental Health Soc. (pres. 1951), Waukegan-North Chgo. C. of C. (bd. dirs. 1968-74, pres. 1976), Am. Legion (comdr. 1951). Jewish (treas. congregation 1968-74, pres. 1976). Lodge: B'nai B'rith. Clubs: Waukegan Exchange (pres. 1963-64), North Shore Craftsman (pres. 1965). Home: 2439 Dunlay Ct Waukegan IL 60085 Office: 438 N Sheridan Rd Waukegan IL 60079

ROSEBERRY, DONALD MICHAEL, health care executive; b. Saginaw, Mich., Aug. 19, 1943; s. Donald Edwin and Evelyn Cecelia (Gelski) R.; m. Carolyn Jean Wilson, Dec. 18, 1971; 1 child, Gregory Neill. BS, Ferris State Coll., 1966. Advt. coordinator Baker Perkins Inc., Saginaw, 1969-72, mgr. mktg. services, 1972-74; mktg. dir. Group Health Services Mich., Inc., Saginaw, 1974-86; exec. dir. Greater Flint HMO, Mich., 1986—; mktg. cons. Blu Cross-Blue Shield Assn., Chgo., 1985; mktg. dir. Blue Care, Detroit, 1985-86. Mgmt. advisor Jr. Achievement, Saginaw, 1970-73; campaign coordinator United Way, Saginaw, 1971-72; vol. Easter Seal Soc., Saginaw, 1979. Served to U.S. Army, 1966-69. Mem. Indsl. Relations Research Assn. (sec. 1984-86), Group Health Assn. Am. Lodge: Rotary. Avocations: golf, camping, oil painting. Home: 12645 E Rathbun Rd Birch Run MI 48415 Office: Greater Flint HMO G-3245 Beecher Rd Flint MI 48504

ROSELLE, WILLIAM CHARLES, librarian; b. Vandergrift, Pa., June 30, 1936; s. William John and Suzanne Esther (Clever) R.; m. Marsha Louise Lucas, Aug. 2, 1959; 1 child, Paul Lucas. BA, Thiel Coll., 1958; MLS, U. Pitts., 1963. Lic. profl. guide State of Mont., 1978. Mem. faculty Milton Hershey (Pa.) Sch., 1960-62; trainee Pa. State Library, 1962-63; asst. catalog librarian Pa. State U., 1963-65; engring., math. librarian U. Iowa, 1965-66, library adminstrv. asst., 1966-69, asst. dir. libraries, 1969-71; prof., dir. library U. Wis.-Milw., 1971—; chmn. Morris Fromkin Meml. Lectr. Com., 1972—; chmn. planning task force on computing U. Wis. System, 1973-74, mem. library planning study com., 1978-79, co-chmn. library automation task force, 1983-85; chmn. computing mgmt. rev. team U. Wis.-Stout, 1976; chmn. Council for U. Wis. Libraries, 1981-82; library cons. Grambling (La.) State U., Viterbo Coll., LaCrosse, Wis., N.C. A&T U., Greensboro, Mt. Mary Coll., Milw., U. Ill. at Chgo., Milw. Sch. Engring., Bklyn. Coll., U. South Ala., Concordia Coll., Milw., Metrics Research Corp., Cardinal Stritch Coll., Milw., N.Y. Inst. Tech., Indiana U. of Pa., Med. Coll. Wis., Wis. Luth. Coll., Milw.; participant Library Adminstrs. Devel. Program, U. Md., 1973, micrographics seminar Nat. Microfilm Assn., 1973, Mgmt. Skills Inst., Assn. Research Libraries, Kansas City, Mo., 1977, Meadowbrook Symposium Midwest Library Network, 1976; mem. sect. geography and map libraries Internat. Fedn. Library Assns. and Instns., 1978-83; mem. bldg. com. Ctr. for Research Libraries, 1980-82. Editorial cons. The Quest for Social Justice, 1983, current geog. publs., 1978—; contbr. articles to profl. jours. Bd. dirs. Charles Allis Art Mus., 1979-84. Served with AUS, 1958-60. Named Disting. Alumnus, Thiel Coll., 1985. Hon. fellow Am. Geog. Soc.; mem. Spl. Libraries Assn. (spl. citation 1979), ALA (life), Iowa Library Assn. (chmn. audit com. 1968-70, chmn. intellectual freedom com. 1969-70), Wis. Library Assn., Midwest Acad. Librarians Conf. (chmn. 1969-71), AAUP (treas. U. Iowa chpt. 1969-70), Council Wis. Libraries (chmn. 1973-74), Soc. Tympanuchus Cupido Pinnatus, Milw. Civil War Round Table, Beta Beta Beta, Beta Phi Mu, Phi Alpha Theta, Phi Kappa Phi, Phi Delta Kappa. Lutheran. Home: 324 Sunny Ln Thiensville WI 53092 Office: U Wis Milw Golda Meir Library PO Box 604 Milwaukee WI 53201

ROSEMEYER, KENNETH ALLEN, university administrator; b. Cin., Sept. 28, 1949; s. Arnold Joseph and Mary Grace (Tenbrunsel) R.; m. Beverle Elizabeth Buttelwerth, May 14, 1975; children: Tara Ellen, Megan Elizabeth, Brynne Elyse. BBA, Thomas More Coll., Lakeside Park, 1972; postgrad, Xavier U., 1972-75. Accting supr. Northlich, Stolley, Inc., Cin., 1973-80; assoc. dir. U. Cin., 1980-83, coordinator, fin. supr. systems, 1983—. Home: 3267 Midden Cir Cincinnati OH 45238

ROSEMOND, PHILIP SALTONSTALL, dancer, choreographer; b. Miami, Fla., Feb. 2, 1955; d. St. Julien Palmer Rosemond and Patricia Saltonstall. Grad., Acad. of Washington Ballet, 1974. Apprentice Nat. Ballet of Washington, 1974; soloist Washington Ballet, 1975-76, 77-79; in corps Cleve. Ballet, 1977; soloist N.Y.C. Opera Ballet, 1979-80; in corps Milw. Ballet, 1980-82; soloist Ballet of Met. Columbus, 1982-83, Cin. Ballet, 1983—; co. rep. Ballet of Met. Columbus, 1982-83; cons. E.G.G. Studio, 1977—; cons. to dancers beginning careers, 1979—; tchr. Washington Ballet, Milw. Ballet, U. Cin. Conservatory Music, Milw. Ballet Sch. Choreographer "Dancers Tenor" U. Cin. Ensemble, 1986, Seven Deadly Sins, Augua et Vinho. Founder Evolving Art Coalition, Washington. Recipient scholarship Washington Acad. Ballet, Joffrey, Maggie Block and other Dance Schs., Washington and N.Y.C., 1976-80, conservatory scholarship U. Cin., 1985—. Mem. Dance Action Cin. (founder), Am. Guild Musical Artists (dancer 1980-86). Libertarian. Agnostic. Avocations: cooking, flute (jazz), collecting books on dance. Home: 4409 Verne Ave Cincinnati OH 45209 Office: 1216 Central Parkway Cincinnati OH 45210

ROSEN, JEFFREY K., data processing executive; b. Middletown, N.Y., Dec. 27, 1941; s. Solomon and Rose (Polk) R.; m. Huda Karaman, Mar. 21, 1970; children: Sulaima, Salwa. BS, Dartmouth Coll., Hanover, N.H., 1963; MA, Brown U., Providence, 1970, PhD, 1972. Ptnr. L.M. Kraft Assocs., Goshen, N.Y., 1968-69; asst. prof. U. Dar-es-Salaam, Tanzania, 1972-74; asst. to dir. amphibian facility Dept. Zoology U. Mich., Ann Arbor, 1974-78; procedures analyst Med. Service Plan Office U. Mich., 1978-80; programmer analyst to sr. systems analyst Hosp. Info. Services U. Mich. Hosps., 1980—. Designer, coder Med. Record Locator System U. Mich. Hosps., 1984—. Office: U Mich Hosp Info Services Taubman Ctr Ann Arbor MI 48109

ROSEN, JOHN KING, dentist; b. Columbus, Ohio, Oct. 30, 1939; s. Edwin R. and Betty (Rothman) R.; m. Rebecca Lee Rosenthal, Oct. 27, 1963; children: Bradley Dean, Christopher Jay. BS, Ohio State U., 1960, DDS, 1964. Gen. practice dentistry Reynoldsburg, Ohio, 1966—. Served to lt. USNR, 1964-66. Mem. ADA, Ohio Dental Assn., Columbus Dental Soc., Alpha Omega Alumni Assn. Republican. Jewish. Lodges: Rotary, Sertoma. Home: 1035 Barberry Ln Columbus OH 43213 Office: 7453 E Main St Reynoldsburg OH 43068

ROSEN, MATTHEW STEPHEN, botanist, consultant; b. N.Y.C., Oct. 7, 1943; s. Norman and Lucille (Cass) R.; m. Deborah Louise Mackay, June 16, 1974 (div. Feb. 1983); children—Gabriel Mackay, Rebecca Mackay. M.F.Sc., Yale U., 1972; B.S., Cornell U., 1967. Instr. ornamental horticulture SUNY-Farmingdale, 1968-69; landscape designer Manhattan Gardener, N.Y.C., 1969-70; instr. ornamental horticulture McHenry County Coll., Crystal Lake, Ill., 1972-74; coordinator agrl. studies, asst. prof. biology, chemistry Mercer County Community Coll., West Windsor, N.J., 1974-79; adminstr. Des Moines Botanical Ctr., 1979—; cons. in field. Contbr. articles to profl. jours. Com. chmn. United Way Cen. Iowa, 1982, div. chmn. 1983-86, group chmn. 1987, chmn. arts adv. com. 1985-86, pres. 1986, bd. dirs. Arts and Recreation Council, 1985-86; mem. career vocat. com. Des Moines Indsl. Sch. Dist., 1986, co-chmn., 1987. Mem. Am. Assn. Botanical Gardens and Arboreta (edn. com.), Greater Des Moines C. of C. (team leader), Phi Kappa Phi, Pi Alpha Xi. Democrat. Jewish. Avocations: photography; reading; model trains; collecting old books; writing. Home: 1042 22d St W Des Moines IA 50265 Office: Des Moines Botanical Ctr 909 E River Dr Des Moines IA 50316

ROSENBAUM, HERBERT EDWIN, neurology educator; b. Los Angeles, Dec. 11, 1924; s. Samuel P. and Rebecca (Goldberg) R.; m. Dorothy Goldner, Nov. 2, 1944 (div. Aug. 1972); children: Robert, Barbara, Nancy. BS, U. Oreg., 1947, MD, 1949. Prof. clin. neurology Washington U. Sch. Medicine, St. Louis, 1978—. Served to 1st lt. USAF, 1952-53. Fellow Am. Acad. Neurology (counselor 1970-74); mem. Am. Psychiat. Assn. (pres. Mo. chpt. 1964-65), Soc. Clin. Neurologists (pres. 1974-75). Avocation: golf. Home: 590 Sarah Lane #307 Creve Coeur MO 63141 Office: Neurological Services Inc 456 N New Ballas Rd Creve Coeur MO 63141

ROSENBAUM, JAMES MICHAEL, judge; b. Fort Snelling, Minn., Oct. 12, 1944; s. Sam. H. and Ilene D. (Bernstein) R.; m. Marilyn Brown, July 30, 1972; children: Alexandra, Victoria and Catherine (twins). BA, U. Minn., 1966, JD, 1969. Bar: Minn. 1969, Ill. 1970, U.S. Supreme Ct. 1979. VISTA staff atty. Leadership Council for Met. Open Communities, Chgo., 1969-72; assoc. Katz, Taube, Lange & Frommelt, Mpls., 1972-77; ptnr. Rosenbaum & Rosenbaum, Mpls., 1977-79, Gainsley, Squier & Korsh, Mpls., 1979-81; U.S. dist. atty. U.S. Dept. Justice, Mpls., 1981-85; judge U.S. Dist. Ct., 1985—. Author booklet: Guide to Practice Civil Rights Housing, 1972. Campaign chmn. People for Boschwitz, Minn., 1978. Mem. Hennepin County Bar Assn. (ethics com. 1980—), Minn. State Bar Assn., ABA, Fed. Bar Assn. (bd. dirs., v.p. 1981—). Republican. Jewish. Office: U S Dist Ct 669 U S Courthouse 110 S 4th St Minneapolis MN 55401 *

ROSENBAUM, KENNETH E., journalist, editor; b. N.Y.C., Aug. 30, 1942; s. Abraham Rosenbaum and Lena (Sentner) Schroeder; m. Mary Hercelia Zeller, Aug. 30, 1964 (div. 1972); children: Sandra, Steven; m. Karen Marie Tiefenbach, June 14, 1980; stepchildren: Stephanie Kay Burket and Stacey Jo Burket. BA, Ohio State U., 1965. Editor Ohio Jewish Chronicle, Columbus, 1963-64; mng. editor Medina (Ohio) County Gazette, 1965-68; copy editor, reporter Akron (Ohio) Beacon Jour., 1968; news editor Cleve. Press, 1968-82; slotman, asst. news editor St. Louis Globe-Dem., 1982-84; systems editor Toledo Blade, 1984—; photography judge Medina Country Fair, 1977-82; instr. journalism Cuyahoga Community Coll., Cleve., 1982. Democrat. Jewish. Lodges: Lions (bd. dirs. Medina chpt. 1970-71), Masons (steward 1986—). Avocations: photography, golf, motorcycling. Home: 7045 Leicester Rd Toledo OH 43617

ROSENBAUM, RICHARD C., accountant; b. Chgo., Nov. 9, 1951; s. Kurt and Jean C. (Cooper) R.; m. Ann Pharmakis, June 2, 1978. BA, Rutgers U., 1972; MBA, U. Chgo., 1974. CPA, Ill., cert. realtor. Ptnr. Coopers & Lybrand, Chgo., 1975—. Mem. adv. bd. Chgo. Civic Fedn.; bd. trustees Ill. Conservation, Parks and Recreation Found., Springfield, Ill. Mem. Chgo. Bd. Realtors (chmn. finance com.), Chgo. Soc. Assn. Execs. (mem. ann. conv. com.), Nat. Assn. Corp. Real Estate Execs., Ill. Mortgage Bankers Assn. (mem. ann. conv. com.). Club: Monroe (Chgo.) (membership com.). Office: Coopers & Lybrand 203 N LaSalle St Chicago IL 60601

ROSENBERG, DALE HENRY, plastic surgeon; b. Belleville, Ill., Sept. 13, 1927; m. Carol Rosenberg; children: Dirk, Jenny, Candra, Charles. Grad., Springfield (Ill.) Jr. Coll., 1946-48; student, U. So. Calif., 1949; BS, U. Ill., 1949; MD, U. Ill., Chgo., 1953. Cert. Am. Soc. Plastic Surgeons. Intern Sacramento County Hosp., 1953-54; resident Yuba County Hosp., Maryville, Calif., 1954-55; resident in gen. surgery Queen's Hosp., Honolulu, 1960-63; resident plastic surgery Orange Meml. Hosp., Orlando, Fla., 1963-65; fellow in hand surgery U. Louisville, 1965; practice medicine specializing in plastic surgery Plastic Surgery Cons. Ltd., Belleville, 1986—. Mem. AMA, ACS, Am. Soc. Plastic and Reconstructive Surgeons Inc., Ill. State Med. Soc., St. Clair County Med. Soc. (pres. 1976-77), So. Ill Med. Assn. (exec. sec.-treas. 1975—). Office: Plastic Surgery Cons Ltd 6401 W Main St Belleville IL 62223

ROSENBERG, DALE NORMAN, educator; b. St. Ansgar, Iowa, Dec. 12, 1928; s. Eddie Herman and Ella (Kirchgatter) R.; B.S., Mankato State Coll., 1956; M.Ed., U. S.D., 1959; postgrad. Ball State Tchrs. Coll., 1962, U. Nebr., 1961, Colo. State Coll., 1963-67; D.Arts, U. Central Ariz., 1978; m. Delrose Ann Hermanson, Sept. 10, 1950; children—Jean Marie, James Norman, Julie Ann, Lisa Jo. Tchr. public schs., Holstein, Iowa, 1956-60; prin., guidance dir., Crystal Lake, Iowa, 1960-62; prin. Grafton (Iowa) Jr. High Sch., 1962-66; psychol. tester Dept. Rehab., State of Iowa, 1960-66; prof. psychology North Iowa Area Community Coll., Mason City, 1966—; vis. lectr. Buena Vista Coll., Storm Lake, Iowa, 1984; invited speaker Inst. Advanced Philosophic Research, 1984-85. Served with USAF, 1949-53. Mem. NEA, Iowa Edn. Assn., Kappa Delta Pi, Phi Delta Kappa. Lutheran. Author multi-media curriculum for teaching disadvantaged introductory welding; author textbook-workbook, 1985. Home: Rural Route 3 Mason City IA 50401 Office: North Iowa Area Community Coll Mason City IA 50401

ROSENBERG, HAROLD, psychologist, educator; b. San Antonio, June 9, 1953; s. Seymour and Charlotte (Sackstein) R.; m. Lonnie Sampson, Oct. 3, 1981. AB, Conn. Coll., 1975; PhD, Ind. U., 1979. Lic. psychologist, Tenn., Ill. Intern in psychology VA Med. Ctr., Brockton, Mass., 1979-80; staff psychologist Dede Wallace Mental Health Ctr., Nashville, 1980-82; from asst. to assoc. prof. Bradley U., Peoria, Ill., 1982—; cons. psychologist Human Service Ctr, Peoria; clin. asst. prof. U. Ill. Med. Sch., Peoria, 1984—. Contbr. articles to profl. jours. and book revs. Bd. dirs. Neighborhood Housing Services, Peoria, 1984, 86. Distilled Spirits Council U.S. Research grantee, Washington, 1984, Bradley U. Research grantee, 1983, 85. Mem. ACLU, Assn. Advancement Behavior Therapy, Am. Psychol. Assn., Midwestern Psychol. Assn., Soc. Psychologists in Addictive Behaviors. Office: Bradley U Psychology Dept Peoria IL 61625

ROSENBERG, HOWARD LEE, marketing executive; b. Passaic, N.J., Oct. 14, 1946; s. Louis and Helen (Lavenda) R.; m. Helen Gertz, June 6, 1971; children: Lauren, Darren. Service rep. Ct. Corp. System, Chgo., 1970-79, asst. sec., 1980; br. mgr. U.S. Corp. Co., Chgo., 1980-85; dir. mktg. Prentice Hall Corp. Service, Chgo., 1986-87; dir. market devel. Prentice Hall Legal and Fin. Services, Chgo., 1987—. Edn. chmn. Northbrook Congregation Ezra Habonim, 1984-86. Mem. Am. Mktg. Assn. (profl.). Democrat. Jewish. Avocation: philately, sports. Home: 934 Leamington Glenview IL 60025 Office: Prentice Hall Legal and Fin Services 33 N LaSalle St Chicago IL 60602

ROSENBERG, MICHAEL EMANUEL, allergist, immunologist, educator; b. N.Y.C., Feb. 20, 1946; s. David and Eva (Madresh) R.; m. Janice Kaye Liebling, June 23, 1968; children: Daniel, Gabriel. BA, NYU, 1966; MD, Northwestern U., 1970. Resident in internal medicine Northwestern U., Chgo., 1970-73, fellow in allergy-immunology, 1975-77, instr. in medicine, 1976-83; practice medicine specializing in allergy and immunology Chgo., 1977—; asst. prof. medicine U. Ill., Chgo., 1984—. Contbr. articles to profl. jours. Served to maj. U.S. Army, 1973-75. Mem. AMA, Am. Acad. Allergy, Am. Coll. Allergy. Democrat. Jewish. Avocations: music, skiing, flying. Home: 540-A W Aldine Ave Chicago IL 60657

ROSENBERG, MICHAEL RAPHAEL, advertising executive; b. Honolulu, June 21, 1949; s. Joseph Moses Rosenberg and Suzanne Esther (Solomon) McCracken; m. Gayle Sosin, Feb. 24, 1974; 1 child, Joseph Benjamin. BA, San Diego State U., 1971; MA, UCLA, 1975, U. Mich., 1977. Account exec. Campbell-Ewald, Detroit, 1976-82, Ogilvy & Mather, Chgo., 1982-85; account supr. BBDO, Chgo., 1985-86; v.p., account supr. HBM/Creamer, Chgo., 1986—. Served to lt. USN, 1971-77. Mem. Am. Mktg. Assn., Detroit Adcraft Club, Mensa. Democrat. Jewish. Avocations: photography, skiing. Home: 706 Ouilmette Ln Wilmette IL 60091 Office: HBM/Creamer Chgo 400 N Michigan Ave Chicago IL 60611

ROSENBERG, NORMAN JACK, agricultural meteorologist, educator; b. Bklyn., Feb. 22, 1930; s. Jacob and Rae (Dombrowitz) R.; m. Sarah Zacher, Dec. 30, 1950; children: Daniel Jonathon, Alyssa Yael. BS, Mich. State U., 1951; MS, Okla. State U., 1958; PhD, Rutgers U., 1961. Soil scientist Israel Soil Conservation Service, Haifa, 1953-55, Israel Water Authority, Haifa, 1955-57; asst. prof. agrl. meteorology U. Nebr., Lincoln, 1961-64, assoc. prof., 1964-67, prof. agrl. meteorology, 1967—, prof. agrl. engring., 1975—, prof. agronomy, 1976—, George Holmes prof. agrl. meteorology, 1981-87; prof. emeritus U. Nebr., 1987—; leader sect. agrl. meteorology U. Nebr., Lincoln, 1975-79, acting asst. vice chancellor for research, 1983-85; sr. fellow, dir. climate resources program Resources for the Future, Washington, 1987—; bd. dirs. Center for Agrl. Meteorology and Climatology, 1979; cons. Dept. State AID, NOAA, Am. Public Health Assn.; mem. numerous ad hoc coms., and mem. standing com. on atmospheric sci. Nat. Acad. Scis./NRC, 1975-78, mem. bd. on atmospheric sci. and climate, 1982-85, mem. U.S. com. Internat. Geosphere-Biosphere Program, 1984-86; vis. prof. agrl. meteorology Israel Inst. Tech., Haifa, 1968. Author: Microclimate: The Biological Environment, 1974, 2d edit., 1983, Chinese transl., 1983; also numerous articles in profl. jours.; editor: North American Droughts, 1978, Drought in the Great Plains: Research on Impacts and Strategies, 1980; tech. editor: Agronomy Jour, 1974-79; cons. editor: Irrigation Sci., Agrl. Meteorology, Climatic Change, Jour. Climate and Applied Meteorology. Recipient Centennial medal Nat. Weather Service, 1970; NATO sr. fellow in sci., 1968, U. Nebr. research fellow, 1968, Lady Davis fellow Hebrew U., Jerusalem, 1977, Nat. Resources fellow Resources for the Future, 1986; grantee State of Nebr., 1970-73, NSF, 1971—, U.S. Dept. Commerce, 1972-74, 80-82, 83-85, NASA, 1972-73, 85-86, U.S. Dept. Interior, 1974-75, 77-79, U.S. Dept. Agr., 1979-82, U. Nebr. Found., 1982, Nat. Ctr. Atmospheric Research, 1984-85. Fellow AAAS (com. climate 1984—), Am. Soc. Agronomy, Am. Meteorol. Soc. (Outstanding Achievement in Bioclimatology award 1978, councillor 1981-84); mem. Am. Assn. State Climatologists (Nebr. rep. 1979-81), Arid Zone Soc. India, Sigma Xi, Alpha Zeta, Gamma Sigma Rho. Jewish. Club: Cosmos (Washington). Office: U Nebr 243 LWC Lincoln NE 68583

ROSENBERG, WILLIAM GERBER, real estate investment company executive; b. N.Y.C., Dec. 25, 1940; s. Leo and Lucy (Gerber) R.; m. Harriet Kuschner (div. Dec. 1973); children: Seth, Lawrence, Gabrielle; m. Mary Beth Koeze, July 26, 1975. BA cum laude, Syracuse U., 1961; MBA, JD, Columbia U., 1965. Bar: Mich. 1965. Assoc. Honigman, Miller, Schwartz & Cohn, Detroit, 1965-69; dep. dir. Dept. Commerce State of Mich., Lansing, 1969; exec. dir. Mich. State Housing Devel. Authority, Lansing, 1969-73; chmn. Mich. Pub. Service Commn., Lansing, 1973-75; asst. adminstr. energy resource devel. Fed. Energy Adminstrn., Washington, 1975-77; ptnr. Rosenberg, Freeman & Assocs., Washington, 1977-82; vice chmn. The Investment Group Capital Corp., Washington, D.C., Ann Arbor, Mich., 1982—; bd. dirs. Mich. Strategic Fund, Lansing. Mem. Mich. Bar Assn. Republican. Jewish. Avocations: tennis, horseback riding. Home: 14215 Riker Rd Chelsea MI 48118 Office: The Investment Group 150 S Fifth Ave Suite A Ann Arbor MI 48104

ROSENBLOOM, JUDY REITER, public relations/marketing consulting executive; b. Chgo., Jan. 18, 1944; d. Delbert J. and Harriet (Green) Reiter; m. Jack Alan Rosenbloom, Apr. 25, 1965; children: Douglas, Gregory, Mary. BA, Roosevelt U., Chgo., 1974, MS in Market Communications, 1978. Publicity asst. Braniff Internat., Chgo., 1962-69; asst. account exec. Janet Diederichs & Assocs., Inc., Chgo., 1971-75, account exec., 1975-79, account supr., 1979-81, v.p., 1981-84, sr. v.p., 1984-86, exec. v.p., 1987—; cons. to White House (press advance for Rosalyn Carter), 1979-80; lectr. in field. Bd. dirs. Connection Telephone Crisis Intervention and Referral Service, Libertyville, Ill., 1983. Mem. Pub. Relations Soc. Am. (counselors' sect.), Publicity Club Chgo. Democrat. Jewish. Club: Sky-Line. Office: 333 N Michigan Ave Suite 1205 Chicago IL 60601

ROSENBLUM, ARTHUR HAROLD, pediatric allergist and immunologist; b. Chgo., Feb. 11, 1909; s. Samuel and Mary (Stein) R.; m. Ruth Levine, July 12, 1938; children: Susan, Mary, Laura. SB, U. Chgo., 1930, MS in Physiology, 1932, MD in Physiology with hons., 1933. Diplomate Nat. Bd. Med. Examiners (highest score in nat. 1935), Am. Bd. Pediatrics, Am. Bd. Pediatric Allergy, Am. Bd. Allergy and Immunology. Intern then resident Michael Reese Hosp., Chgo., 1933-35, attending physician pediatric allergy clinic, 1937-66, sr. attending physician pediatric dept., 1966—, dir. allergy sect., 1971-74, co-dir. allergy and immunology div., 1974—; resident Children's Meml. Hosp., Chgo., 1935-36, Mcpl. Contagious Disease Hosp., Chgo., 1936-37; practice medicine specializing in pediatrics and allergy Chgo. area, 1937—; attending physician Infant Welfare dept. City of Chgo., 1937-42; prof. pediatrics Cook County Grad. Sch. Med., Chgo., 1946-58; attending physician pediatric dept., chief nephrology service Cook County Hosp., Chgo., 1946-58; assoc. prof. pediatrics Northwestern U., Chgo., 1950-65; prof. Chgo. Med. Sch., 1965-71; clin. prof. Pritzker Sch. Med., U. Chgo., 1974—; mem. cons. staff St. James Hosp., Chicago Heights, U. Chgo. Hosps. and Clinics, Weiss Meml. Hosp., Chgo. Served to lt. col. M.C., U.S. Army, 1942-43, PTO. Recipient Long and Devoted Service award Michael Reese Hosp., 1978. Fellow AAAS, Am. Acad. Pediatrics, Am. Acad. Allergy (chmn. penicillin study group 1965-70), Inst. Medicine, Chgo. Med. Soc. of AMA, Am. Assn. Cert. Allergists, Toyal Soc. Health (Great Britain), Internat. Congress Allergology, European Congress Allergology; mem. Chgo. Pediatric Soc. (Disting. Service award 1978, Archibald Hoyne award 1981), Chgo. Allergy Soc. (sec. 1966-67, pres. 1968-69), Internat. Coorespondence Club of Allergy, Ill. Med. Soc. (chmn. allergy sect. 1964-65, 69-70), Am. Heart Assn., Asthma and Allergy Found. Am. (Chgo. Allergist of Yr. award 1981), U. Chgo. Alumni Assn. (life), Michael Reese Hosp. Alumni Assn. (pres. 1966-67), Phi Beta Kappa, Alpha Omega Alpha. Democrat. Jewish. Avocations: piano music, photography. Home: 2231 E 67th St Chicago IL 60649 Office: 19815 Governors Hwy Flossmoor IL 60422

ROSENDAHL, JOHN MARTIN, automotive company executive; b. Lansing, Mich., Mar. 11, 1946; s. Elmer George and Alma Hermine (Schmidt) R.; m. Bonne Sue Hale, Oct. 5, 1967 (div. 1978); 1 child, John Martin; m. Brenda Sue Bishop, Aug. 2, 1980 (div. 1985). Bus. Mgmt. cum laude, Lansing Community Coll., 1975, Labor Relations, 1976. Inspector quality control Gen. Motors Corp., Lansing, Mich., 1965-73, supr. mfg., 1973-81, labor relations analyst, 1981-82, quality of work life coordinator, 1982-83, organizational devel. cons., 1983—. Bd. dirs. joint labor mgmt. com. Lansing Area Joint Labor Mgmt. Com., Inc., 1982—, Lansing br. Cystic Fibrosis Found., mem. state exec. bd. Mich. chpt. Republican. Lutheran. Avocations: golf; racquetball; bicycling. Home: 15089 Chetwyn Dr Lansing MI 48906 Office: BOC Lansing Car Assembly Body Plant 401 Verlinden St Lansing MI 48901

ROSENDALE, GEORGE WILLIAM, aircraft company executive; b. Keenan, Okla., Nov. 4, 1933; s. John Webster and Laura Lee (Schawo) R.; m. Penney Sue Tillotson, Dec. 27, 1964; children: James Christopher, Kathleen Marie, John Charles. Student Okla. Baptist U., 1957-58, U. Wichita, 1959-63; BA in English, Wichita State U., 1969, MS in Adminstrn., 1971. Diplomate Personnel Accreditation Inst., 1977-83. Engring. draftsman Skyline Corp., Wichita, Kans., 1952, Boeing Aircraft Co., Wichita, Kans., 1953, O.A. Sutton Corp., Wichita, 1956, engring. checker, 1956-57; various positions Cessna Aircraft Co., Wichita, 1958—, personnel rep., 1967-69, tng. supr., 1969-73, mgr. employee tng. and devel., 1973-84, mgr. personnel projects, 1984-85, mgr. mgmt. resource devel., 1985—; vocat. instr. Wichita Pub. Schs., 1963; personnel adviser Wichita Police Res., 1969-73; treas. Haysville Police Res., 1975—; chmn. bd. dirs. Corp. Employment Resources, Inc. Area comdr. United Fund, Wichita, 1971; sec. Haysville Jr. Football League, Haysville, Kans., 1973-75; study com. chmn. Wichita Community Planning Council, 1972-73; mem. Haysville Planning Commn., 1976-86, chmn., 1977-79, 80-84; exec. com. Kans. State Employment and Tng. Council, 1979-82, chmn. employment and tng. services com., 1981-82; mem. Kans. 107 Planning Com. for Vocat. Edn., 1981-84, chmn., 1983-84; mem. Kans. High Tech. Task Force for Vocat. Edn., 1983-84; mem. tng. adv. com. div. vocat. and continuing edn. Wichita Pub. Schs., 1974; active various Bapt. Chs., Wichita, Hominy, Okla., Mulvane, Kans., 1951—; bd. dirs. Christian Braille Found., 1971-74; bd. dirs. Amigos de SER, Wichita, 1975-77. 81—, vice chmn., 1983, chmn., 1984; bd. dirs. Kans. SER, Inc., 1981—, treas., 1983-84, vice chmn., 1985-87, chmn., 1987—; bd. dirs. Am. Cancer Soc., Sedgwick County (Kans.) unit, 1977—, Ark-Valley Jr. Football League, 1974-75. Served with U.S. Army, 1953-56. Recipient Campaign award United Fund of Wichita, 1969-71, Outstanding Service plaque award Am. Cancer Soc., 1978-79, 81-82; SER Individual Support award, 1979, others. Mem. Am. Mgmt. Assn., Am. Soc. Personnel Adminstrn. (pres. Wichita chpt. 1973-74, past pres.' plaque award 1975, chmn. nat. tng. and devel. com. 1979), Psi Chi. Republican. Lodge: Optimist (chmn. community service 1985-86, v.p. Haysville club 1986—). Home: 424 Hollywood Dr Wichita KS 67217 Office: Cessna Aircraft Div PO Box 7704 Wichita KS 67277

ROSENE, HAROLD ALFRED, JR., orthopaedic surgeon; b. Cleve., Apr. 22, 1931; s. Harold Alfred and Eleanor Maude (Myers) R.; m. Arlene Williams Wagner, Apr. 15, 1955 (div. Dec. 1967); children: Debra, Richard, William, Robert; m. Mary Elizabeth Robinson Allen, Sept. 5, 1968; 1 stepchild, Vanessa Allen. BS, Denison U., 1953; MD, Case Western Res. U., 1959. Diplomate Am. Bd. Orthopaedic Surgery. Intern. Mary Hitchcock, Hanover, N.H., 1959-60, resident gen. surgery, 1960-61; gen. practice medicine Southwest Harbor, Maine, 1961-63; resident in orthopaedic surgery U. Mich., Ann Arbor, 1963-66; assoc. E. Widener Dixon Clinic, Ellsworth, Maine, 1966-68, AP & S Clinic, Terre Haute, Ind., 1968-72; ptnr. Drs. Topping, Kabel & Rosene, Terre Haute, 1972-76; Mem. staff, past chief of staff, clin. instr. family practice Union Hosp., Terre Haute; assoc. faculty Ind. U. Sch. Medicine, Indpls.; chmn. bd. Orthopaedic Surgery of Terre Haute, Inc., 1976—. Fellow Am. Acad. Orthopaedic Surgeons; mem. Ind. Orthopedic Assn., Ind. Bone and Joint Club, Am. Fracture Soc. Clubs: Terre Haute Country; Skytop (Pa.). Avocation: tennis. Home: 93 Forest Glen Ct Terre Haute IN 47802 Office: Orthopaedic Sugery of Terre Haute 634 Beech St Terre Haute IN 47804

ROSENFELD, JOEL CHARLES, librarian; b. Bklyn., June 16, 1939. B.A., U. Mich., 1961, A.M. in L.S., 1964. Br. librarian Flint Pub. (Mich.) Library, 1962-66; adult services cons. Lincoln Trail Libraries, Champaign, Ill., 1967-68; dir. Urbana (Ill.) Free Library, 1968-74; exec. dir. Met. Library Service Agy., St. Paul, 1974-79; exec. dir. Rockford (Ill.) Pub. Library 1980—; pres. Rockford Area Literary Council, 1986—. Mem. ALA, Ill. Library Assn., Pub. Library Assn. (dir.-at-large 1980-81, pres. met. library sect. 1979-80). Office: Rockford Pub Library 215 N Wyman St Rockford IL 61101-1061

ROSENFELD, MARTIN JEROME, legal executive; b. Flint, Mich., Oct. 3, 1944; s. Israel Edward and Lillian Edith (Natchez) R.; 1 child, Joshua. BA Mich. State U., 1968; MHA, 1978, MBA with honors, Ind. No. U., 1979. Adminstr., Care Corp., Grand Rapids, Mich., 1969-70, Chandler Convalescent Ctr., Detroit, 1970-71, Grand Community Hosp., Detroit, 1971-73; exec. v.p., chief exec. officer Msgr. Clement Kern Hosp. Spl. Surgery, Warren, Mich., 1973-84; pres. M.J. Rosenfeld Assocs., 1984-85; chief operating officer Dickinson, Wright, Moon, Van Dusen & Freeman, 1985—; instr. Marygrove Coll., 1975—; assoc. prof. Mercy Coll., Detroit, 1978—; mem. faculty Inst. on Continuing Legal Edn., Ann Arbor, Mich. Vice pres. Detroit chpt. Jewish Nat. Fund, 1978—; pres. Cranbrook Village Homeowners Assn., 1977; chmn. Community Hosps. of Southeastern Mich., 1981-84; mem. tech. work group Comprehensive Health Planning Council of Southeastern Mich., 1981-84; mem. fin. mgmt. com., mem. hosp. affairs bd. Greater Detroit Area Hosp. Council, 1981-84; bd. dirs., com. chmn. Detroit Symphony Orch., 1984—; bd. dirs., mem. fund raising com. Detroit Met. Orch., 1984—. Mem. ABA, Assn. Legal Adminstrs., Am. Assn. Health Care Cons., Royal Soc. Health, Am. Podiatry Assn. (com. hosps. 1981-84). Warren C. of C. (com. chmn. 1975). Author papers in field. Mem. editorial bd. The Human-Size Hosp.; mem. panel of experts The Health Care News. Office: Dickinson Wright Moon et al 800 First Nat Bldg Detroit MI 48226

ROSENGARD, JEFFREY SCOTT, management consultant; b. Canton, Ohio, June 3, 1957; s. Herbert Hillel and Vivian Zelda (Brown) R.; m. Barbara Jean Maschke, June 15, 1980; 1 child, Amy Jill. BS, Miami U., Oxford, Ohio, 1979; MBA, U. Dayton, 1982. Fin. analyst NCR Corp., Dayton, Ohio, 1979-82, Am. Consumer Products, Cleve., 1982-83; cons. mgr. Coopers & Lybrand, Cleve., 1983—. Trustee, asst. treas. Epilepsy Found. N.E. Ohio, Cleve., 1986—. Mem. Am. Inst. CPA's, Ohio Soc. CPA's. Club: Cleve. Athletic. Home: 4500 Whitehall Dr South Euclid OH 44121 Office: Coopers & Lybrand 2800 Nat City Ctr Cleveland OH 44114

ROSENHEIM, HOWARD HARRIS, business executive; b. Williamson, W.Va., Oct. 1, 1915; s. William Spiller and Frances Minerva (Harris) R.; m. Marjorie Jane Griffin, June 30, 1945; children: Cathy (Mrs. Mark Bustamante), William Spiller. B.S., Northwestern U., 1936, M.B.A., 1954; grad., Advanced Mgmt. Program, Harvard U. Grad. Sch. Bus., 1956. Civilian dir. indsl. planning div. USAF, Dayton, Ohio, 1947; pres. Internat. Register Co., elec. mfg. co., Chgo., 1948-70; pres. home study sch. Internat. Accts. Soc., Chgo., 1971; pres. Denoyer-Geppert Co. ednl. pub. subs. Times Mirror Co., Chgo., 1972-79, Internat. Assocs., Ltd., cons., 1980—; chmn. Camelot Controls, Ltd. (Eng.), 1966-70; dir. Extel Corp., Chgo., Tele-Communication Radio Inc., Chgo., Data One, Inc., Chgo.; Vis. prof. bus. Northwestern U., Evanston, Ill., 1956-71, trustee, 1968-70; cons. Presdl. Commn. Nat. Air Policy, 1947; adv. to ministry of edn. Kingdom of Saudi Arabia, 1976-79. Pub. over 800 titles of ednl. materials in arabic for schs. in Saudi Arabia; author articles to profl. jours. Served to maj. USAF, 1942-46. Decorated Award of Merit; recipient Disting. Educator award Northwestern U., 1972. Mem. Am. Mktg. Assn., Northwestern U. Alumni Assn. (pres. 1966-67). Methodist (mem. ofcl. bd. 1965-70). Clubs: Union League (Chgo.); Park Ridge (Ill.) Country. Inventor various time switches. Home: 2411 Farrell Ave Park Ridge IL 60068

ROSENOW, JOHN EDWARD, nonprofit corporation executive; b. Lincoln, Nebr., Sept. 15, 1949; s. Lester R. and Lucille Louise (Koehler) R. BS in Agrl. Engring., U. Nebr., 1971. Dir. of tourism Nebr. Dept. Econ. Devel., Lincoln, 1971-79, interim dir., 1985; exec. dir. Nat. Arbor Day Found., Lincoln and Nebraska City, 1979—. Coauthor: (book) Tourism: the good, the bad, the ugly, 1979. Democrat. Mem. Ch. of Christ. Home: 1809 G St Lincoln NE 68508 Office: Nat Arbor Day Found 211 N 12th St Lincoln NE 68508

ROSENSTEIN, RICHARD KENNETH, physician; b. Louisville, July 31, 1951; s. Abraham Sydney and Ruth Florence (Tanenhaus) R.; m. Lynn Marla Cook, May 9, 1977; children: Yitzhok, Yehoshua, Tova, Golda. BA, Washington U., St. Louis, 1973; MD, U. Louisville, 1977. Resident ob-gyn SUNY, Buffalo, 1977-81; ob-gyn house physician Marymount Hosp., Garfield Heights, Ohio, 1981—; cons. obstetrician Womankind, Inc., Cleve.,

1985—. V.p. Congregation Zemach Zedek, Cleveland Heights, 1984—, Russian Immigrant Aid Soc., Cleveland Heights, 1982—; coordinator Israeli Widows and Orphans Fund, Cleve., 1985—. Assoc. fellow Am. Coll. Ob-Gyn; mem. Cleve. Acad. Medicine, Cleve. Soc. Ob-Gyn. Jewish. Home: 14443 Summerfield Rd University Heights OH 44118 Office: Marymount Hosp 12300 McCracken Rd Garfield Heights OH 44125

ROSENTHAL, DAVID L., account engineer; b. Stevens Point, Wis., June 30, 1961; s. Lawrence Louis and Donna Marie (Golke) R. BS in Paper Sci. and Engring., U. Wis., Stevens Point, 1984. Systems engr. AccuRay Corp., Columbus, Ohio, 1984-87; account engr. Combustion Engring. Corp., Appleton, Wis., 1987—. Mem. Stevens Point City Band, 1979-86. Mem. Tech. Assn. Pulp and Paper Industry, Paper Industry Mgmt. Assn. Clubs: Lac Du Bay Sailors (Cen. Wis.) (commodore 1986); Oshkosh Yacht. Avocations: sailing, water skiing, snow skiing, golf, bicycling. Home: 830 N Florida Ave Appleton WI 54911 Office: Combustion Engring Corp 711 N Lynndale Dr Appleton WI 54914

ROSENTHAL, EDWARD LEONARD, teacher; b. Chgo., June 15, 1948; s. Irving H. and Nina (Kritchevsky) R.; m. Hilary Rosenberg, June 29, 1969; children: Rachel, Rebecca. BS in Sci. and Letters, U. Ill., 1969; MEd in Earth Sci., Northern Ill. U., 1972. Tchr. St. Joseph Sch., Dyer, Ind., 1969-70; tchr., golf coach Joliet (Ill.) Cath. High Sch., 1970-77; tchr., girls golf coach Naperville (Ill.) N. High Sch., 1977—. Chmn. Untied Multi Family Homeowners, Bolingbrook, Ill., 1974-75; v.p. Ill. Jr. Miss Program, Bolingbrook, 1985-87; trustee Village of Bolingbrook, 1975-81; mayor , 1981-85. Named one of Outstanding Young Men Am., 1975, 82; recipient Disting. Service award, 1974. Mem. Ill. Edn. Assn.-NEA (legis. com), Ill. Earth Sci. Assn., Nat. Sci. Tchrs. Assn., Ill. Coaches Assn. for Girls and Women's (pres. sport assn.), Ill. Girls Golf Coaches Assn. (pres. 1985—), Naperville Unit Edn. Assn. (2d v.p. 1986—), Community Assn. Inst. Ill. (bd. dirs. 1980-83). Jewish. Avocation: golf. Home: 508 Clover Ln Bolingbrook IL 60439 Office: Naperville N High Sch 899 N Mill St Naperville IL 60566

ROSENTHAL, IRA MAURICE, pediatrician, educator; b. N.Y.C., June 11, 1920; s. Abraham Leon and Jean (Kalotkin) R.; m. Ethel Ginsburg, Oct. 17, 1943; children: Anne, Judith. Student, CCNY, 1936-38; A.B., Ind. U., 1940, M.D., 1943. Intern Lincoln Hosp., N.Y.C., 1943-44; resident in pathology Albert Einstein Hosp., Phila., 1947-48; resident in pediatrics Fordham Hosp., N.Y.C., 1948-49; practice medicine specializing in pediatrics Bklyn., 1950-52; instr. U. Ill. Coll. Medicine, Chgo., 1953; asst. prof. U. Ill. Coll. Medicine, 1953-55, assoc. prof., 1955-63, prof. pediatrics, 1963—, head dept., 1973-82; mem. med. service adv. com. Nat. Found. March of Dimes, 1975-80. Served to capt. U.S. Army, 1944-46. Mem. Am. Pediatric Soc., Soc. Pediatric Research, Acad. Pediatrics, Lawson Wilkins Pediatric Endocrine Soc., Endocrine Soc. Home: 5490 S Shore Dr Chicago IL 60615 Office: 840 S Wood St Chicago IL 60612

ROSENTHAL, JUDITH ELLEN LINDNER, health care facility administrator; b. N.Y.C., Oct. 16, 1954; d. Isaac Newton and Rheba (Ginsberg) Lindner; m. Ken Steven Rosenthal; 1 child, Joshua. BA with honors, U. Del., 1975; MEd, U. Ill., 1976, postgrad., 1976-77; PhD, Kent State U., 1982. Lic. psychologist, Ohio. Assoc., curriculum developer, sr. assoc. McBer & Co., Boston, 1977-79; internal cons. Fed. Res. Bank, Cleve., 1981-82; counselor, psychol. asst. U. Akron, Ohio, 1981-83; from asst. dir. to dir. ednl. services Timken Mercy Med. Ctr., Canton, Ohio, 1983-87; pvt. practice psychology 1987—; ind. cons. in field, 1981—; bd. dirs. Work/Family Life Program, Alliance, Ohio, 1986. Mem. Am. Soc. Tng. Devel., Am. Psychology Assn., Phi Beta Kappa, Phi Kappa Phi. Office: Timken Mercy Med Ctr 1320 Timken Mercy Dr NW Canton OH 44708

ROSENTHAL, LEIGHTON A., industrial laundry and apparel company executive; b. Buffalo, Jan. 27, 1915; s. Samuel and Sadie (Dosberg) R.; m. Honey Rousuck, June 30, 1940; children: Cynthia, Jane. Student, Phila. Textile Sch.; grad., U. Pa.; hon. doctorate, Cleve. Coll. Jewish Studies, 1973. Pres. Cleve. Overall Co., 1956-61, Work Wear Corp., 1961-86; pres. The Purity Uniform Service Inc., 1986—, Lars Mgmt. Corp., 1986—. Trustee Jewish Community Fedn. Cleve., Mt. Sinai Hosp. of Cleve., Samuel Rosenthal Found., Preservation Found. Palm Beach; bd. dirs. Greater Cleve. Growth Assn., Ohio Motorists Assn. Fellow Am. Assn. Jewish Edn. Clubs: Clevelander, Commerce, Oakwood, Union (Cleve.); Poinciana (Palm Beach, Fla.); Marks, Annabels, Burkes (London). Office: The Halle Bldg 1228 Euclid Ave Suite 810 Cleveland OH 44115

ROSENTHAL, MAURICE J., psychiatrist, consultant; b. Chgo., Mar. 14, 1919; s. Harry and Jennie (Cohan) R.; m. Lorraine Mellicent Groupe, May 20, 1951; children: Beth B., Monica A. Student, Wright Jr. Coll., 1936-37, U. Chgo., 1937-39; MD, U. Ill., Chgo., 1939-43. Diplomate in gen. psychiatry Am. Bd. Psychiatry and Neurology. Resident in psychiatry Bellevue Hosp., N.Y.C., 1946-47; staff psychiatrist Inst. for Juvenile Research, Chgo., 1949-52; practice medicine specializing in psychiatry Chgo., 1950—; research cons. Ill. Dept. Pub. Welfare, Springfield, 1954-57; instr. Child Therapy Program, Inst. for Psychoanalysis, Chgo., 1960-62; lectr. U. Ill., Chgo., 1964-73; faculty Rush Med. Sch., 1972-84, Chgo. Med. Sch., 1986—; cons. Inst. for Juvenile Research, Chgo., 1952—. Co-author: Psychiatric Consultation, 1959; contbr. articles to profl. jours. Fellow Am. Acad. Child Psychiatry, Am. Psychiatric Assn., Am. Orthopsychiatric Assn.; mem. Am. Soc. for Adolescent Psychiatry, Council for Child Psychiatry (pres. 1969-70). Jewish. Home: 3150 N Lakeshore Dr Chicago IL 60657 Office: 310 S Michigan Chicago IL 60604

ROSENTHAL-KRAUS, SUSAN JEAN, management consultant; b. Malden, Mass., Nov. 14, 1947; d. Morris Hirsh and Doris (Reiser) Rosenthal; m. Leslie Jay Kraus, Dec. 21, 1968; 1 child, Erica Michelle Rosenthal Kraus. BA, Simmons Coll., 1969; MA in Community Edn. Adminstrn., Coll. St. Thomas, 1974. Dir. student activities U. Bridgeport (Conn.) Hosp. Sch. Nursing, 1970-71; coordinator continuing edn. Miller Hosp., St. Paul, 1971-72; dir. South High Community Sch., Mpls., 1972-77; pres. Productive Design, Inc., Mpls., 1976—; bd. dirs. Common Space, Mpls., 1982-84, Women's Econ. Devel. Corp., St. Paul, 1983—. Bd. dirs. Regina High Sch., Mpls., 1986—. Recipient Disting. Service award Southside Sr. Citizen Council, Mpls., 1977, Orgnl. Devel. Achievement award Assn. Minn. Counties, 1979, Lake Fellowship, Excelsior, Minn., 1986. Mem. Soc. for Advancement of Mgmt., Minn. Women's Network (exec. forum), Internat. Soc. Quality Circles, Am. Soc. Performance Improvement, Minn. Community Edn. Assn. (Dir. of Yr. 1977). Jewish. Avocations: hiking, swimming, gourmet cooking, sewing, dancing. Home: 4375 Thielen Ave Edina MN 55436 Office: Productive Design Inc 4316 Upton Ave S Minneapolis MN 55410

ROSENZWEIG, LEONARD, psychiatrist; b. Manchester, England, Nov. 2, 1903; came to U.S., 1905; s. Joseph Isaac and Rose (Marks) R.; m. Dora Coopersmith, May 25, 1934; children: Monica Audrey Rosenzweig Armour, Herschel David, Harry Hillel, Susan Ruth Rosenzweig Fenster, Joseph Isaac. Student, Detroit Jr. Coll., 1922-25; AB, U. Mich, 1926, MD, 1929; postgrad. in neuropsychiatry, U. Pa., 1932. Diplomate Am. Bd. Psychiatry and Neurology, Nat. Bd. Med. Examiners. Intern Detroit Gen. Hosp., 1929-30; resident in psychiatry Warren (Pa.) State Hosp., 1930-33, jr. physician, 1933-34, sr. physician, 1935, clin. dir., 1935-40, asst. supt., 1940-45; supt. Dixmont (Pa.) State Hosp., 1945-46; dir. psychiatry Grand Valley Child Guidance Clinic, Grand Rapids, Mich., 1946-48; practice medicine specializing in psychiatry Grand Rapids, Mich., 1948—; mem. adv. bd., chief staff Forest View Hosp., Grand Rapids, 1983-84. Fellow AMA (life), Am. Psychiat. Assn.; mem. Mich. State Med. Soc., Kent County Med. Soc. (life), Mich. Psychiat. Soc. (pres. 1972-73), Western Mich. Psychiat. Soc. (pres. 1956, 75-77), Pitts. Psychiat. Soc. (founder, charter 1936), Am. Acad. Psychiatry and Law, Am. Soc. Clin. Hypnosis-Ednl. Found. (charter). Jewish. Avocations: music, ballet, lit., drama. Home: 2628 Reeds Lake Blvd SE East Grand Rapids MI 49506 Office: 205 Ramona Med Ctr 515 Lakeside Dr SE Grand Rapids MI 49506

ROSENZWEIG, NORMAN, psychiatry educator; b. N.Y.C., Feb. 28, 1924; s. Jacob Arthur and Edna (Braman) R.; m. Carol Treleaven, Sept. 20, 1945; 1 child, Elizabeth Ann. MB, Chgo. Med. Sch., 1947, MD, 1948; MS, U. Mich., 1954. Diplomate Am. Bd. Psychiatry and Neurology. Asst. prof. psychiatry U. Mich., Ann Arbor, 1957-61; from asst. prof. to prof. psychiatry Wayne State U., Detroit, 1973—; spl. cons., profl. advisor Oakland County Community Mental Health Services Bd., 1964-65; mem. protem med. adv. panel Herman Kiefer Hosp., Detroit, 1970, psychiat. task force N.W. Quadrangle Hosps., Detroit, 1971-78, planning com. mental health adv. council Dept. Mental Health State of Mich., Lansing, 1978-81, tech. adv. research com., 1978-82; psychiat. bed need task force Office Health and Med. Affairs State of Mich., 1980-84, facility bed needs task force, 1984—; bd. dirs. Alliance for Mental Health, Farmington Hills, Mich.; speaker in field. Author: Community Mental Health Programs in England: An American View, 1975; co-editor: Psychopharmacology and Psychotherapy-Synthesis of Antithesis?, 1978, Sex Education for the Health Professional: A Curriculum Guide, 1978; contbr. articles to profl. jours. and chpts. to books. Mem. profl. adv. bd. The Orchards, Livonia, Mich., 1963. Served as capt. USAF, 1955-57. Recipient Appreciation and Merit cert. Mich. Soc. Psychiatry and Neurology, 1970-71. Fellow Am. Coll. Mental Health Adminstrn., Am. Coll. Psychiatrists (hon. membership com., com. on regional ednl. programs, liaison officer to The Royal Australian and New Zealand Coll. Psychiatrists 1984-88), Am. Psychiat. Assn. (council on internat. affairs 1970-79, chmn. 1973-76, assembly liaison to council on internat. affairs 1979-80, 82-84, reference com. 1973-76, nominating com. 1978-79, internat. affairs survey team 1973-74, assoc. representing Am. Psychiat. Assn. to Inter-Am. Council Psychiat. Assns. 1973-75, others, Rush Gold Medal award 1974, cert. Commendation, 1973-76, 78-80, Warren Williams award 1986); mem. AAAS, AAUP, AMA (Physician's Recognition award 1971, 74, 77, 80-81, 84), Am. Assn. Dirs. Psychiat. Residency Tng. (nominating com. 1972-74, task force on core curriculum 1972-74), Am. Assn. Gen. Hosp. Psychiatry, Puerto Rico Med. Assn. (hon. sect. psychiatry, neurology and neurosurgery, Presdl. award 1981), Am. Hosp. Assn. (governing council psychiat. services sect. 1977-79, ad hoc com. on uniform mental health definitions, chmn. task force on psychiat. coverage under Nat. Health Ins. 1977-79, others), Brit. Soc. Clin. Psychiatrists (task force on gen. hosp. psychiatry 1969-74), Can. Psychiat. Assn., Mich. Assn. Professions, Mich. Hosp. Assn. (psychiat. and mental health services com. 1979-81), Mich. Psychiat. Soc. (com. on ins. 1965-69, chmn. com. on community mental health services 1967-68, chmn. com. on nominations of fellows 1972-73, mem. com. on budget 1973-74, task force on pornography 1973-74, chmn. commn. on health professions and groups 1978-81, chmn. com. on liaision with hosp. assns. 1979-81, chmn. subcom. on liaison with Am. Hosp. Assn. 1979-81, numerous others, Past Pres. plaque, 1978, cert. Recognition, 1980, Disting. Service award 1986), Mich. State Med. Soc. (vice chmn. sect. psychiatry 1972-73, chmn. sect. psychiatry 1974-75, mem. com. to improve membership 1977-78, alt. del for Mich. Psychiat. Soc. to House of Dels. 1978-79, del. from Wayne County Med. Soc. to Mich. Med. Soc. House of Dels. 1982-88), N.Y. Acad. Scis., Pan Am. Med. Assn., Wayne County Med. Soc. (com. on hosp. and prof. relations 1983-84, com. on child health advocacy 1983-87, med. edn. com. 1983-87, mental health com. 1983-87), Royal Australian and New Zealand Coll. Psychiatrists (hon.), Indian Psychiat. Soc. (hon. corr.). Avocations: music, films, reading. Home: 1234 Cedarholm Ln Bloomfield Hills MI 48013 Office: Sinai Hosp Detroit 6767 W Outer Dr Detroit MI 48235

ROSENZWEIG, OSCAR JOHN, obstetrician/gynecologist; b. Novisad, Yugoslavia, July 9, 1922; came to U.S., 1949; s. John A. Rosenzweig and Natalia D. Gillich. MD, U. Vienna, Austria, 1947. Diplomate Am. Bd. Ob-Gyn. Resident ob-gyn Landeskrankenhaus, Salzburg, Austria, 1947-49; intern Luth. Deaconess Hosp., Chgo., 1949-50, resident ob-gyn, 1950-52; resident ob-gyn Chgo. Maternity Ctr., 1952-53, U. Ill., Alton, 1953-54; practice medicine specializing in ob-gyn Chgo., 1957—; clin. assoc. prof. ob/gyn U. Ill.; bd. dirs. Ravenswood Hosp. Med. Ctr., Bank Ravenswood; chmn. bd. dirs. Ravenswood Pvt. Paid Med. Group. Served to maj. USAF, 1955-57. Decorated Cross of Merit (Federal Rep. Germany). Mem. ACS, Ama, Am. Coll. Ob-Gyn, Am. Coll. Abdominal Surgeons, Internat. Coll. Surgeons. Lodge: Order of St. John Jerusalem (knight). Office: 4600 N Ravenswood Ave Chicago IL 60640

ROSEVEAR, JOHN, orthodontist; b. Hammond, Ind., July 26, 1948; s. Henry J. and Helen Rae (Elledge) R.; m. Cheryl L. Swanson, Apr. 28, 1984; children—Joseph Ray, William Matthew. Student Hanover Coll., 1966-69; D.D.S., Ind. U., 1973; M.S., Northwestern U., 1976. Practice dentistry specializing in orthodontics, Lansing, Ill., 1976—; guest lectr. Northwestern U., Chgo., 1984; world lectr. on lingual orthodontic technique, 1981—. Mem. Am. Dental Assn., Am. Assn. Orthodontists (membership com. 1982—), Ill. Soc. Orthodontists (v.p. 1984—), Ill. Soc. Orthodontics (v.p.). Lodge: Rotary. Office: 18333 Burnham Ave Lansing IL 60438

ROSEVEAR, ROBERT ALLEN, orthodontist; b. Aberdeen, Wash., Mar. 11, 1943; s. Richard Clarence and Elizabeth Julia (Northgren) R.; m. Rebecca Lynn Julian, May 24, 1986; 1 child, Scott Matthew. BS, U. Puget Sound, 1965; DDS, U. Mo., Kansas City, 1968; MS, W.Va. U., Morgantown, 1971. Diplomate Am. Bd. Orthodontists. Pvt. practice Portland, Oreg., 1968-69; assoc. prof., chmn. dept. occlusion U. Mo. Sch. Dentistry, Kansas City, 1972-74; pvt. practice Overland Park, Kans., 1974—; wheat commodity trader Bd. of Trade, Kansas City, 1982—; staff cons. Wash. County Ind. Children's Clinic, Portland, 1969; cons. Jackson county Hosp., Kansas City, 1972-74, Truman Med. Ctr., Kansas City, 1980—; v.p., dir. Rosevears Music Ctr., Aberdeen, Wis., 1974—. Mem. Eagle Review com. Boy Scouts Am., Overland Park, 1981-83. Mem. Greater Kansas City Dental Soc., Am. Assn. Orthodontists, Mo. Dental Assn., Midwestern Soc. Orthodontists, Kansas City Bd. Trade, Phi Delta Theta. Episcopalian. Avocations: hunting, canoeing, backpacking. Home: 12705 Eaton Circle Leawood KS 66209 Office: 11055 Cedar Suite 112 Overland Park KS 66211

ROSHEL, JOHN ALBERT, JR., orthodontist; b. Terre Haute, Ind., Apr. 7, 1941; s. John Albert and Mary M. (Griglione) R.; B.S., Ind. State U., 1963; D.D.S., Ind. U., 1966; M.S., U. Mich., 1968; m. Kathy Roshel; children—John Albert III, James Livingston, Angela Kay. Individual practice dentistry, specializing in orthodontics Terre Haute, 1968—. Mem. ADA, Am. Assn. Orthodontists, Terre Haute C. of C., Lambda Chi Alpha, Delta Sigma Delta, Omicron Kappa Upsilon. Clubs: Terre Haute Country, Lions, Elks, K.C. Roman Catholic. Home: 1305 Royce Ave Terre Haute IN 47802 Office: 4241 S 7th St Terre Haute IN 47802

ROSKENS, RONALD WILLIAM, university system president; b. Spencer, Iowa, Dec. 11, 1932; s. William E. and Delores A.L. (Beving) R.; m. Lois Grace Lister, Aug. 22, 1954; children: Elizabeth, Barbara, Brenda, William. B.A., U. No. Iowa, 1953, M.A., 1955, L.H.D., 1985; Ph.D., State U. Iowa, 1958; LL.D., Creighton U., 1978, Huston-Tillotson Coll., 1981, Midland Luth. Coll., 1984; Litt.D., Nebr. Wesleyan U., 1981; L.H.D., Hastings Coll., 1981. Tchr. Minburn (Iowa) High Sch., 1954, Woodward (Iowa) State Hosp., summer 1954; asst. counselor to men State U. Iowa, 1956-59; dean of men, asst. prof. spl. edn. Kent (Ohio) State U., 1959-63, assoc. prof., then prof., 1963-72, asst. to pres., 1963-66, dean for adminstrn., 1968-71, exec. v.p., prof. ednl. adminstrn., 1971-72; chancellor, prof. ednl. adminstrn. U. Nebr., Omaha, 1972-77; pres. U. Nebr. System, 1977—; hon. prof. East China Normal U., Shanghai, 1985; dir. Enron Corp., Art's Way Mfg. Co., Guarantee Mut. Life Ins. Co., Am. Charter Fed. Savs. and Loan Assn.; mem. Bus.-Higher Edn. Forum, 1979—, exec. com., 1984—; mem. govtl. relations com. Am. Council Edn., 1979-83, bd. dirs., 1981-86, vice chair, 1983-84, chair, 1984-85; chmn. com. on financing higher edn. Nat. Assn. State Univs. and Land Grant Colls., 1978-83, vice chmn. com. on financing higher edn., 1983-84, chmn. com. on fed. student fin. assistance, 1981—; mem. nat. adv. com. on accreditation and instl. eligibility U.S. Dept. Edn., 1983-86, chmn., 1986; bd. dirs. Council for Fin. Aid to Edn., 1985—; exec. bd. North Central Assn., 1979-84, chmn. exec. bd., 1982-84. Co-editor: Paradox, Process and Progress, 1968; contbr. articles profl. jours. Mem. Kent City Planning Commn., 1962-66; bd. dirs. Met. YMCA, Omaha, 1973-77, Mid-Am. council Boy Scouts Am., 1973-77, Midlands United Community Services, 1972-77, NCCJ, 1974-77, Found. Study Presdl. and Congl. Terms, 1977—; trustee Huston Tillotson Coll., Austin, Tex., 1968-81, chmn., 1976-78; trustee Joslyn Art Mus., 1973-77, Nebr. Meth. Hosp., 1974-77, Brownell-Talbott Sch., 1974-77, Harry S. Truman Inst., 1977—, Willa Cather Pioneer Meml. and Ednl. Found., 1979—; pres. Kent Area C. of C., 1966. Decorated comdrs. cross Order of Merit (W. Ger.); recipient Brotherhood award NCCJ, 1977, Americanism citation B'nai B'rith, 1978; numerous others; named Nat. 4-H Alumnus, 1968, Outstanding Alumnus U. No. Iowa, 1974, King AK-Sar-Ben LXXXVI, 1980. Mem. AAAS, Am. Personnel and Guidance Assn., Am. Coll. Personnel Assn., Assn. Urban Univs. (pres. 1976-77), AAUP, Am. Ednl. Research Assn., Am. Psychol. Assn., Chief Execs. Orgn., Young Pres. Orgn., Com. Fgn. Relations, Phi Delta Kappa, Phi Eta Sigma, Sigma Tau Gamma (pres. grand council 1968-70, Disting. Achievement award 1980, Disting. Scholar award 1981), Omicron Delta Kappa (nat. pres. 1986—). Lodge: Masons (32 deg.). Home: 5930 Norman Rd Lincoln NE 68512 Office: 3835 Holdrege St Lincoln NE 68583

ROSNER, STEVEN ARNOLD, dermatologist; b. Phila., Feb. 7, 1953; s. I. Kenneth and Sally (Seidman) R.; m. Lisa Adele Miner, Oct. 13, 1985. BS, Am. U., 1974; MD, Hahnemann Med. Coll., 1978. Diplomate Am. Bd. Dermatology, Nat. Bd. Med. Examiners. Intern in internal medicine Monmouth Med. Ctr., Long Branch, N.J., 1978-79; resident in dermatology The N.Y. Hosp., N.Y.C., 1979-80, Univ. Hosp. of Cleve., 1980-82; fellow in dermatology The Royal Melbourne (Australia) Hosp., 1982-83; pvt. practice specializing in dermatology Cin., 1984—; cons. dermatology Fairfield (Ohio) Home for Mentally Retarded, 1984—; Mother Margaret Hall, Cin., 1984—; asst. clin. prof. dermatology Univ. Hosp., Cin., 1984—. Fellow Am. Acad. Dermatology, Ohio State Med. Assn., Ohio Dermatol. Soc., Cin. Dermatol., Acad. Medicine Cin. Jewish. Office: 2450 Kipling Ave Suite 107 Cincinnati OH 45237

ROSS, BARBARA HUSER, real estate company executive; b. Lamar, Colo., Nov. 13, 1943; d. Archie and Mona Belle (Robinson) Huser; m. John T. Ross, Nov. 29, 1971. Student, Drury Coll., Mo., 1982-83. Lic. real estate broker Mo., Ark. Personnel sec. Ford Aeroneutronics, Newport Beach, Calif., 1963-64; mgr. gen. Family Farm, Mt. Vernon, Mo., 1964-65; field sec. Strout Realty Inc., Springfield, Mo., 1965-67, exec. sec., 1967-79, adminstrv. asst., 1979-82, asst. v.p., 1982-85, v.p., 1985—; seminar speaker/lectr., 1982—. Author-developer: Nat. Listing System, 1983; (manual) Branch Office Computer System Manual, 1984; pub. sales and mktg. newsletters; contbr. articles to profl. jours.; pub. sales and mktg. newsletters. Mem. Nat. Assn. Realtors, Nat. Assn. Female Execs., Mo. Assn. Realtors (bd. dirs. 1986), Springfield Bd. Realtors (chair com. 1985-87), C. of C. (bd. dirs. Springfield, Mo. 1970-74). Lodge: DAR. Avocations: reading; travel; antique collector. Home: 4151 Tanglewood Rd Rogersville MO 65742 Office: Strout Realty Inc PO Box 4528 Springfield MO 65808

ROSS, CHESTER WHEELER, clergyman; b. Evansville, Ind., Nov. 3, 1922; s. Mylo Wheeler and Irma (Berning) R.; A.B. cum laude, Kans. Wesleyan U., 1952; M.Div., Garrett Theol. Sem., 1954; D. Ministry, St. Paul Sch. Theology, 1979; m. Ruth Eulaine Briney, Aug. 30, 1949; children—James W., Deborah R., Judith K., Martha S., John W. Ordained to ministry United Meth. Ch., 1953; enlisted pvt. USAAF, 1942, advanced through grades to lt. col., 1968; chaplain, Africa, Europe, Alaska, Greenland, Taiwan; installation chaplain, Columbus AFB, Miss., 1972-75; ret., 1975; pastor Unity Parish, Iuka, Kans., 1975-80, Ness City (Kans.) United Meth. Ch., 1980. Instr. Parent Effectiveness Tng., 1st aid ARC; cubmaster, scoutmaster, dist. chmn. Boy Scouts Am., recipient Silver Beaver award, 1975; vol. parolee counselor; mem. USD 303 Sch. Bd. Paul Harris fellow Rotary Internat.; Decorated Air medal (2), Meritorious Service medal (2). Mem. Ness City Ministers Assn., Conf. Council on Fin. and Adminstrn., Mil. Chaplains Assn., Acad. Parish Clergy, Ret. Officers Assn., Res. Officers Assn., Air Force Aid, Air Force Assn., Nat. Hist. Soc., Appalachian Trail Conf., Menninger Found., Kans. Sheriffs Assn. Assn. Ret. Persons, Order Ky. Col., Am. Legion, VFW. Lodge: Rotary. Address: 417 N School Ness City KS 67560

ROSS, DALE GARAND, therapist, programming consultant, speaker, writer; b. Detroit, May 31, 1948; s. Stanley Anthony and Kathleen Mary (Moore) Jamros. B.S. in Psychology, Mich. State U., 1970; M.S.W., Wayne State U., 1980. Cert. Nat. Acad. Cert. Social Workers. Ptnr. Unicorns, Detroit, 1970-76; pres. Realities, Ltd., Birmingham, Mich., 1976-78; counselor I univ. counseling Wayne State U., Detroit, 1980-82, counselor II ednl. resources/disabilities, 1982-84, counselor II, univ. counseling, 1984-85; therapist Substance Abuse Ctr., Warren, Mich., 1985 ; pvt. practice, Southfield, Mich., 1985—; founding mem. Wellness Networks, Inc., Detroit, 1983-84; cons. in field; presenter programs. Contbr. articles to profl. jours. Pres., founding mem. Wellness House Mich., 1986—; mem. steering com. Venereal Disease Action Coalition, 1986—, steering com. Macomb County AIDS Community Council, Hospice AIDS Task Force, 1986—, AIDS Related Communication Coalition, 1986—. Program chmn. Motor City Bus. Forum, 1983-84, chmn. community ctr. com., 1982-83. Recipient Am. Legion award, 1966, Library Key award Hazel Park Pub. Schs., 1966; Mich. Bd. Govs. grantee, 1978-79, 79-80. Mem. Nat. Assn. Social Workers, Am Coll. Personnel Assn., (men's task force), Nat. Orgn. for Changing Men (mental health task group, co-chmn. job-work satisfaction task group), Internat. Platform Assn., Mich. Orgn. for Human Rights, World Future Soc., Mich. Alcohol and Addiction Assn., Am. Assn. Counseling Devel. Avocations: antiques; ceramics. Home: 24818 Rensselaer Oak Park MI 48237

ROSS, DONALD, JR., English language educator, university administrator; b. N.Y.C., Oct. 18, 1941; s. Donald and Lea (Meyer) R.; m. Sylvia Berger (div.); 1 child, Jessica; m. 2d, Diane Redfern, Aug. 27, 1971; children—Owen, Gillian. B.A., Lehigh U., 1963, M.A., 1964; Ph.D., U. Mich., 1967. Asst. prof. English U. Pa., Phila., 1967-70; prof. English U. Minn.-Mpls., 1970—, dir. composition program, 1982-86, dir. Univ. Coll., 1984—. Co-author: Word Processor and Writing Process, 1984, Revising Mythologies: The Composition of Thoreau's Major Works; contbr. articles to profl. jours. Grantee Am. Council Learned Socs., 1976, NSF, 1974, Fund for Improvement of Postsecondary Edn., 1982-85. Mem. Assn. for Computers and Humanities (exec. sec. 1978), MLA, Assn. for Literary and Linguistic Computing. Office: Univ Minn Composition Program 209 Church St SE Minneapolis MN 55455

ROSS, DONALD EDWARD, film maker; b. Guymon, Okla., June 25, 1937; s. Royse Sanders and Alta Carthella (Taylor) R.; m. Betty Ruth Swieringa, Aug. 26, 1961; children: Rebecca, Stephen, Deborah, Timothy, Michael. Student, Ariz. State U., 1955-57; BS, Bob Jones U., 1961, MA, 1966; postgrad., Famous Photographers Sch., 1967-68. Editor, dir., producer Ken Anderson Films, Winona Lake, Ind., 1967-72; instr. Grace Coll., Winona Lake, 1969-72; prodn. supr. Internat. Films, Winona Lake, 1972-75; exec. dir. Harvest Prodns. (Evang. Bapt. Missions), Kokomo, Ind., 1975—; speaker Evang. Bapt. Missions, 1975—. Producer, dir. numerous evangelical films (Best Film Yr. awards Christian Film Distbrs. Assn., 1969, 78-79, 81, 86). Served to capt. USAF, 1961-67, Vietnam. Mem. Christian Film Producers Fellowship. Republican. Avocations: chess, travel. Home: Box 35 Atlanta IN 46031 Office: Harvest Prodns (EBM) Box 2225 Kokomo IN 46904

ROSS, DONALD HUGH, fraternal executive; b. Delta, Ohio, Aug. 19, 1949; s. Hugh Archbald and Margaret Baker (Harlton) R.; m. Mary Lynn Feuerborn, Dec. 21, 1974; children: Jon, Michael. BS, Miami U., Oxford, Ohio, 1971. Auditor Supreme Lodge of the World Loyal Order of Moose, Mooseheart, Ill., 1971-76, dep. supreme sec., 1976-78, asst. comptroller, 1978-83, supreme sec., 1983—; sec. Mooseheart Bd. Govs., Moosehaven Bd. Govs., 1983—. Mem. editorial bd. Moose Docket publ.; contbr. articles to newspapers and profl. jours. Republican. Club: Interact (Delta) (pres. 1966-67). Lodge: Moose (past gov. 1976, Pilgrim Degree of Merit 1983). Avocations: golf, bowling. Home: 1119 Woodland Ave Batavia IL 60510 Office: Supreme Lodge of the World Mooseheart IL 60539

ROSS, DONALD ROE, U.S. judge; b. Orleans, Nebr., June 8, 1922; s. Roe M. and Leila H. (Reed) R.; m. Janice S. Cook, Aug. 29, 1943; children—Susan Jane, Sharon Kay, Rebecca Lynn, Joan Christine, Donald Dean. LL.B., U. Nebr., 1948. Bar: Nebr. bar 1948. Practice law Lexington, Nebr., 1948-53; mem. firm Swarr, May, Royce, Smith, Andersen & Ross, 1956-70; U.S. atty. Dist. Nebr., 1953-56; gen. counsel Republican party, Nebr., 1956-58; mem. Rep. Exec. Com. for Nebr., 1952-53; nat. com. mem. Rep. Exec. Com. for Nebr., 1958-70; vice chmn. Republican Nat. Com., 1965-70; U.S. circuit judge 8th Circuit, U.S. Ct. Appeals, 1971—; Mayor City of Lexington, 1953. Home: 9936 Essex Dr Omaha NE 68114 Office: Federal Bldg Omaha NE 68101

ROSS, E. EARL, small business worker; b. St. Louis, July 3, 1942; s. Edward Earl and Ruth Randles (Loewen) R.; B.A. in Psychology, Central Mo. State U., 1965; M.A. in Corrections, Webster Coll., Webster Groves,

Mo., 1976; m. Mary Donna Moore, May 31, 1964; 1 son, Damon Moore. Reporter, Warrensburg (Mo.) Daily Star-Jour., 1965; social worker St. Louis County Welfare Div., Maplewood, Mo., 1966-68; asso. dist. scout exec. Boy Scouts Am., St. Louis, 1968; dep. juvenile officer St. Louis County Juvenile Ct., Clayton, Mo., 1969-72; program dir. St. Louis County Detention Center, Clayton, 1972—; asst. supt. St. Louis County Detention Center, Clayton, 1978—; trainer statewide detention staffs; pres. Historygram, Inc. Recipient Outstanding Detention Program award Nat. Council Juvenile and Family Ct. Judges, 1982. Mem. St. Louis County Juvenile Justice Assn., Am. Corrections Assn., Mo. Juvenile Justice Assn., Am. Mgmt. Assn. Home: 15333 Appalachian Trail Chesterfield MO 63017 Office: 501 S Brentwood Blvd Clayton MO 63105

ROSS, EDWARD, physician; b. Fairfield, Ala., Oct. 10, 1937; s. Horace and Carrie Lee (Griggs) R.; B.S., Clark Coll., 1959; M.D., Ind. U., 1963; m. Catherine I. Webster, Jan. 19, 1974; children—Edward, Ronald, Cheryl, Anthony. Intern, Marion County Gen. Hosp., Indpls., 1963; resident in internal medicine Ind. U., 1964-66, 68, cardiology research fellowship, 1968-70, clin. asst. prof. medicine, 1970; cardiologist Capitol Med. Assn., Indpls., 1970-74; pvt. practice medicine, specializing in cardiology, Indpls., 1974—; staff cardiologist Winona Meml. Hosp., Indpls.; Methodist Hosp., Indpls. Mem. Central Ind. Health Planning Council, 1972-73; dir. Ind. chpt. Am. Heart Assn., 1973-74; dir. multiphasic screening East Side Clinic, Flanner Ho. of Indpls., 1968-71; med. dir. Nat. Center for Health Service Research and Devel., HEW, 1970; dir. hyptertensive screening State of Ind., 1974. Served to capt., MC, USAF, 1966-68. Woodrow Wilson fellow, 1959; Nat. Found. Health scholar, 1955; Gorgas Found. scholar, 1955. Diplomate Am. Bd. Internal Medicine. Fellow Royal Soc. Promotion of Health (Eng.), Am. Coll. Angiology (v.p. fgn. affairs), Am. Coll. Cardiology; mem. AMA, Am. Soc. Contemporary Medicine and Surgery, Nat. Med. Assn. (council sci. assembly 1985-89), Ind. Med. Soc., Marion County Med. Soc., Am. Soc. Internal Medicine, Am. Heart Assn., Ind. Soc. Internal Medicine (pres. 1987-89), Ind. State Med. Assn. (chmn. internat. medicine sect. 1987-89), Aesculapean Med. Soc., Hoosier State Med. Assn. (pres. 1980-85), NAACP, Urban League, Alpha Omega Alpha, Alpha Kappa Mu, Beta Kappa Chi, Omega Psi Phi. Baptist. Sr. editor Jour. Vascular Medicine, 1983—. Office: 3171 N Meridian St Suite 201 Indianapolis IN 46208

ROSS, EDWIN FRANCIS, health care consultant, former hospital executive; b. Struthers, Ohio, June 19, 1917; s. Edwin Francis and Ethel Marie (Wymer) R.; m. Virginia Kerr, Apr. 26, 1941; children: Richard, David. BS, Mt. Union Coll., 1939; MHA, Washington U., St. Louis, 1949. With Republic Steel Co., Youngstown, Ohio, 1939-40; tchr. public schs. Struthers, Ohio, 1940-42; adminstrv. resident Huron Rd. Hosp., East Cleveland, 1948-49; adminstr. Doctor's Hosp., Cleveland Heights, 1949-53; asst. dir. Univ. Hosp., Cleve., 1953-62; adminstr. U. Nebr. Hosp., Omaha, 1962-66; pres., chief exec. officer Fairview Gen. Hosp., Cleve., 1966-82; health care cons. Cleve., 1983—; asst. prof. U. Nebr. Coll. Medicine, 1962-66; exec. producer TV series on hosps. and health edn. 1972-81. Pres. Cleve. Area League Nursing. Served with U.S. Army, 1942-47. Mem. Am. Hosp. Assn., Ohio Hosp. Assn., Greater Cleve. Hosp. Assn. (pres. 1972-74, chmn. exec. council 1974-75), Am. Coll. Hosp. Adminstrs. Republican. Presbyterian. Clubs: Masons, Kiwanis. Office: 14218 Lakewood Heights Blvd Lakewood OH 44107

ROSS, ESTHER, nurse, educator; b. East Chicago, Ind., Feb. 10, 1935; d. Solomon anbd Mattie Louise (Harris) R.; children—Michael and Michele Evans (twins). Diploma, St. Margaret Hosp. Sch. Nursing, 1959; B.S., Coll. St. Francis, 1979. Surgery nurse aide St. Margaret Hosp., Hammond, Ind., 1952-53, operating room technician, 1953-56, operating room staff nurse, clin. instr., 1960-65; staff nurse operating room Meth. Hosp., Gary, Ind., 1966-67; operating room head nurse, operating room supr., asst. dir. nursing services St. Catherine Hosp., East Chicago, Ind., 1968-71; dir. nursing services Gary Family Health Ctr., 1971; health occupations instr. Gary Area Career Center, 1971—. Bd. dirs. Gary Hist. and Cultural Soc.; del. Ind. State Dem. Conv., 1976, 78, 82, 86; mem. Gary Civic Chorale. Recipient Humanitarian award Women's Community Federated Club. Mem. AAHPER, Am. Vocat. Assn., Ind. Vocational Assn., NAACP, Ind. Health Occupations Assn., Gary Bus. and Profl. Women, St. Margaret Hosp. Alumnae. Democrat. Methodist.

ROSS, EUGENE I., real estate developer; b. Chgo., Dec. 30, 1934; s. Lewis and Dorothy (Levy) R.; m. Patti Ann Packman, Dec. 18, 1955; children: Kenneth, Douglas, Terri. BS in Fin. Mgmt., U. Colo., 1956. Salesman Arthur Rubloff and Co., Chgo., 1960-71; pres. Seay and Thomas, Inc., Chgo., 1972-75, Ross, Kotin and Co., Chgo., 1976-80, Ross Group, Inc., Chgo., 1981—; bd. dirs. George Evans Co., St. Louis, Treasure Lakes Co., Coral Springs, Fla., Urban Systems Co., Washington. Bd. dirs. Greater Michigan Ave. Assn., Chgo. Served to maj. USAF, 1956-59. Mem. Soc. Indsl. Realtors, Am. Soc. Real Estate Counselors, Inst. Real Estate Mgmt., Urban Land Inst., Nat. Assn. Real Estate Brokers, Chgo. Pres. Orgn., World Bus. Council, Lambda Alpha. Clubs: Arts, Tavern, Standard, Internat.; Briarwood Country (Highland Park, Ill.) (v.p. 1984—). Avocations: flying, skiing.

ROSS, FAGEY (FAYE) FRANCES, gerontologist; b. Detroit, Aug. 10, 1927; d. Morris and Margaret Marion (McDermott) Solnick; m. Elmer Ellsworth Ross, Aug. 31, 1946 (dec. Oct. 1966); children: Jeffrey Scott, Lori Paige. Student, Wayne State U., 1945-46, Oakland U., 1972; BA in Gerontology, Madonna Coll., 1978. Cert. social worker. Personal growth group leader Continuum Ctr. Oakland U., Rochester, Mich., 1971-79; dir. sr. citizens dept. Redford Twp., Mich., 1975—; instr. living creatively Wayne Community Coll., Detroit, 1976—; state del. White House Conf. Aging, Detroit, 1979; commr. Wayne County Commn. Aging, Mich., 1979-80; nat. del. White House Conf. Aging, Washington, 1980; mem. Madonna Coll. Gerontology Adv. Bd., Livonia, Mich., 1980-81. Named Most Disting. Woman of Yr., Bus. and Profl. Women's Clubs, 1980. Mem. Nat. Council Aging, Council Action Aging (chmn. 1976-79), Area Agy. Aging (bd. del. Mich. 1C, 1980—, sr. ctr. dirs. div. 1984—), Service Providers Associated Network. Recipient Madonna Coll. Lumen award, 1978. Avocations: reading, swimming, classes, travel, writing poetry. Office: Redford Twp Community Ctr 12121 Hemingway Redford Township MI 48239

ROSS, FRANK HOWARD, III, management consultant; b. Charlotte, N.C., Aug. 28, 1946; s. Frank Howard Jr. and Alma (Richardson) R.; B.S. in Engring., N.C. State U., 1968; m. Beverly Hazel Ross, June 30, 1973; children—Martha McCausland, Frank Howard IV. Cons., Fails & Assocs., Inc., Raleigh, N.C., 1968-73; ptnr. Ross-Payne & Assocs., Inc., Arlington Heights, Ill., 1973—; dir. Gilldorn Savs. Assn., Brickman Cos.; Presbyn. Ch. of Barrington. Mem. Sherman Group, Inst. Mgmt. Cons., Sigma Alpha Epsilon. Club: Barrington Hills Country. Author: More $ Through $ Management, 1975; MIS and You, 1978; Planning and Budgeting, 1979; Profit by Design, 1981; Pricing for Profit, 1983; Wealthbuilding, 1984. Home and Office: 536 Eton Dr Barrington IL 60010

ROSS, HAROLD ANTHONY, lawyer; b. Kent, Ohio, June 2, 1931; s. Jules and Helen Assumpta (Ferrara) R.; m. Elaine Louise Hunt, July 1, 1961; children—Leslie Ann, Gregory Edward, Jonathan Harold. B.A. magna cum laude, Case Western Res. U., 1953; J.D., Harvard U., 1956. Bar: Ohio 1956. Assoc. Marshman, Hornbeck, Hollington, Steadman & McLaughlin, Cleve., 1961-64; pres. Ross & Kraushaar Co., Cleve., 1964—; gen. counsel Brotherhood of Locomotive Engrs., Cleve., 1966—. Trustee Citizens League Greater Cleve., 1969-75, 76-82, pres., 1981-82; active Charter Rev. Com. North Olmsted, 1970, 75. Served with AUS, 1956-58. Mem. ABA (co-chair rwy. and airline labor law sect. 1976-78), Ohio State Bar Assn., Cleve. Bar Assn., Phi Beta Kappa, Delta Sigma Rho, Omicron Delta Kappa. Roman Catholic. Office: 1548 Standard Bldg 1370 Ontario St Cleveland OH 44113

ROSS, J. PAT, restaurant chain company executive; b. 1930. BA, Rock Island (Ill.) Coll., 1955. With Burger Chef, Indpls., 1955-72, Foodplex, Inc., 1972-78; with Rax Restaurants, Inc., 1978—, now chmn. bd. dirs., chief exec. officer. Served with AUS, 1951-53. Office: Rax Restaurants Inc 1266 Dublin Rd Columbus OH 43215 *

ROSS, JACK LEWIS, psychiatrist; b. Levelland, Tex., Sept. 3, 1932; s. Raymond T. and Mary Ann (Lewis) R.; m. Glenna M. Quillin, July 16, 1960; children: Sarah, Jennifer, Susan, Rebecca. BS, Texas Tech. Coll., 1952; MD, U. Tex., Dallas, 1956. Diplomate Am. Bd. Psychiatry and Neurology; cert. adult and child psychoanalyst. Staff psychiatrist Menninger Found., Topeka, 1962—, dir., 1984—; Tng. and supervising analyst Topeka Inst. Psychoanalysis, 1979—. Contbr. articles to profl. jours. Served to capt. U.S. Army, 1960-62. Fellow Am. Psychiat. Assn., ACP; mem. Am Psychoanalytic Assn., Alpha Omega Alpha (life). Republican. Methodist. Home: 4841 Indian Hills Rd Topeka KS 66610 Office: The Menninger Found Box 829 Topeka KS 66601

ROSS, JAMES CARL, dentist; b. Cleve., Dec. 30, 1955; s. Claiborne Carl and Grace (Willson) R.; m. Jane Carol Peterson, July 25, 1986. BS, Alma (Mich.) Coll., 1978; postgrad. in biochemistry, Oakland U., 1978-79; DDS, Case Western Res. U., 1983. Pvt. practice dentistry Southfield and Redford, Mich., 1983—. Recipient Eagle Scout award Boy Scouts Am., 1970. Mem. ADA, Mich. Dental Assn., Oakland County Dental Soc., Mich. Acad. Dentistry for the Handicapped, Detroit Dental Clinic Club (restoration sect.), Psi Omega. Republican. Presbyterian. Home: 28366 Franklin River Dr #102 Southfield MI 48034 Office: 17610 W Twelve Mile Rd Southfield MI 48076

ROSS, JANET SUE, teacher; b. Celina, Ohio, Dec. 12, 1944; d. Barnett R. and Belva Lucille (McGough) Grimm; m. Edward James Ross, June 8, 1963; 1 child, Mark Edward. BS in Edn. cum laude, Ohio State U., 1982; MS in Edn., U. Dayton, 1986. Cert. elementary edn. Tchr. Sidney (Ohio) City Schs., 1982—. Recipient Doer's award Sidney Ednl. Assn., 1986. Mem. Nat. Edn. Assn., Ohio Edn. Assn., Sidney Edn. Assn., Humane Soc., Nat. Audobon Soc., Ohio State U. Alumni Assn., U. Dayton Alumni Assn. Democrat. Lodges: Elks, Moose. Home: 411 Sunshine Dr Sidney OH 45365 Office: Sidney City Schs 232 N Miami Ave Sidney OH 45365

ROSS, JON WALLACE, health science facility administration; b. Fairmont, Minn., May 7, 1943; s. Frank Wallace Miranda Carol (Schroeder) R.; m. Patricia Ann Klein, May 4, 1968; children: Timothy Jon, Kristin Anne. BA, St. Olaf Coll., 1965; MS, Mankato State U., 1969; doctoral studies, Columbia Pacific U., 1982—. Lic. psychologist. Tchr., counselor Ind. Sch. Dist. #459, Truman, Minn., 1967-68; guidance counselor Hawaii Dept. Edn., Honolulu, 1968-70; rehab. counselor State of Minn., Marshall, 1970-74; spl. needs coord. Ind. Sch. Dist. #891, Canby, Minn., 1974-77; program dir. REM-Redwood Falls, Minn., 1977—; mem. human services tech. adv. bd. Willmar (Minn.) Area Vocat. Tech. Inst., 1978—; mem. nominating com. Health Systems Agy., Redwood Falls, 1984. Mem. spl. needs adv. bd., Canby AVTI, 1983, pres. gen. adv. bd., 1985; pres. Redwood Falls area C. of C., 1982; chmn. bd. Service Industries Rehab. Workshop, Redwood Falls, 1984-85; mem. adv. bd. Project Turnabout Outpatient Clinic, Redwood Falls, 1987. Undergrad. research grantee NIMH, 1965. Mem. Am. Assn. Mental Deficiency, Minn. assn. for Behavior Analysis, Minn. Soc. Clinical Hypnosis. Lutheran. Lodge: Rotary (bd. dirs. Redwood Falls club 1983-84, v.p. 1984-86, pres. 1987). Avocations: music (listening and performing), distance running, photography, reading, cross country skiing. Home: 109 Beachwood Ln Redwood Falls MN 56283 Office: REM-Redwood Falls Inc 1011 E Elm St PO Box 506 Redwood Falls MN 56283

ROSS, JONATHAN STEVEN, real estate developing company executive; b. Oak Park, Ill., Feb. 4, 1955; s. Robert Carl and Lillian (Haeger) R. BBA in Real Estate, BS in Constrn. Adminstrn., U. Wis., 1978. Asst. v.p., mortgage banker Richter-Schroeder Co., Milw., 1978-80; v.p., mgr., mortgage banker Norwest Mortgage, Milw., 1980-84; ptnr., exec. v.p. Divall Real Estate Devel. Co., Madison, Wis., 1985—. Mem. capital revolving fund com. Mayor's Task Force, Madison, 1986-87. Named Eagle Scout, Boy Scouts Am., 1968; Evans scholar Western Golf Assn., 1974. Mem. Nat. Assn. Realtors, Soc. Real Estate Appraisers. Republican. Lutheran. Club: Milw. Athletic. Avocations: aviation, sailing, water and snow skiing, golfing. Home: 311 N Hancock #135 Madison WI 53703 Office: Divall Real Estate Devel Co 100 N Hamilton Suite 4000 Madison WI 53703

ROSS, KAREN YVONNE, restaurant owner; b. Mankato, Kans., Jan. 4, 1940; d. E. Jack and M. Marie (Thronson) Morris; m. John R. Ross, Jan. 30, 1960; children: Leah M., Karla M., Alan J. Student, Kans. State Tchrs. Coll., 1958-60, Kans. State U., 1960. Sec. Am. Machine and Foundry, Beale AFB, Calif., 1960-62, USAF, Anchorage, Alaska, 1962-64; purchasing agt. Hallmark Cards, Kansas City, Mo., 1965; co-owner Buffalo Roam Steakhouse, Mankato, 1966—. Councilwoman City of Mankato, 1979—. Mem. Nat. Restaurant Assn., Kans. Restaurant Assn. (pres. ladies orgn. 1983), Gen. Fedn. Women's Clubs (pres. Mankato chpt. 1974-76). Republican. Lutheran. Club: PEO Sisterhood (pres. Mankato chpt. 1978-79). Home and Office: 103 N West Mankato KS 66956

ROSS, LAURA ALLISON, fraternal organization executive; b. Kansas City, Mo., June 8, 1954; d. John Joseph and Jean Marie Ross. BFA, William Woods Coll., 1972-76. Div. chmn. Beta Sigma Phi Sorority div. Walter W. Ross and Co., Inc., Kansas City, 1979-80, dir. rushing, v.p. and asst. dir. service, 1986—. Publicity chmn. Kansas City Am. Diabetes Assn. 1985-87, pres. 1986-87, bd. dirs., mem. exec. com. Heart of Am. affiliate, 1986-87, sec. state bd., chmn. pub. relations com. Mo. state affiliate, 1987—; reading tutor Project Literacy, 1986, Penn Valley Community Coll. Mem. Kansas City Internat. Assn. Bus. Communicators, Advt. Club. Republican. Avocations: house renovations, art. Office: 1800 W 91st Pl Kansas city MO 64114

ROSS, LOUIS ROBERT, automotive company executive; b. Detroit, Mar. 23, 1932; s. Louis Robert and Sadie Madge (Stobbe) R.; m. Carolyn Ann Lory, June 20, 1953; children: Stephen Charles, Philip Elliott. B.M.E., Wayne State U., Detroit, 1954; M.B.A., Mich. State U., East Lansing, 1972. With Ford Motor Co., 1955—; v.p. (Ford Brazil), Sao Paulo, 1973-75; v.p., gen. mgr. tractor div. Troy, Mich., 1975-77; exec. v.p. diversified products ops. 1977-79, exec. v.p. car product devel. N.Am. automotive ops., 1979-83, exec. v.p. tech. staffs, from 1983-85, exec. v.p. ops., 1985-86, exec. v.p. N.A. automotive ops., 1986—; dir. Ford Brazil, 1973-75, Ford Aerospace & Communications Corp., 1977—; Escorts Tractors Ltd., India, 1975-77, Hokkai Ford Tractor, Japan, 1975-77. Mem. Soc. Automotive Engrs., Phi Kappa Phi, Beta Gamma Sigma. Club: Bloomfield Hills Country. Home: Bloomfield Hills MI 48013 Office: Ford Motor Co Box 1722A Dearborn MI 48121

ROSS, MELVIN, physician; b. Mt. Vernon, Ohio, Dec. 1, 1927; s. Herman and Sadie Ross; m. Hélène Langlois, Apr. 30, 1965; children: Robert, Mike. BS, Ohio State U., 1948; MD, Case Western Res. U., 1953. Pvt. practice psychiatrist and psychoanalyst Cleve., 1953—; assoc. clin. prof. Case Western Res. U., Cleve., 1985—; cons. Dept. Labor, Hearing and Appeals div. Social Security Adminstrn. Served to capt. U.S. Army, 1955-57. Fellow Am. Psychiat. Assn., Cleve. Psychiat. Soc. (pres. 1985—), Cleve. Psychoanalytic Soc. (pres. 1984-86). Home: 3373 Kersdale Rd Pepper Pike OH 44124 Office: 28001 Chagrin Blvd Cleveland OH 44122

ROSS, MICHAEL CLAYTON, dental surgeon; b. Springfield, Ohio, Mar. 23, 1951; s. Edward and Thelma B. (Burkepile) R.; m. Julia Gill, Sept. 9, 1972; 1 child, Adam Michael. BS cum laude, Ohio U., 1973, DDS cum laude, 1976. Resident in dental surgery Miami Valley Hosp., Dayton, 1977; aviation flight instr. Ohio U., Athens, 1971-73; gen. practice dentistry Dayton, 1977—. Mem. ADA, Ohio Dental Assn., Dayton Dental Soc., Am. Acad. Implant Denstry, Dayton Implant Study Group, Omicron Kappa Upsilon. Club: Miami Valley Hsop. Staff. Office: 4049 Dayton Xenia Rd Dayton OH 45432

ROSS, NEIL L., eye surgeon; b. Chgo., Dec. 5, 1948; s. John Gunther and Doris (Serrins) R.; B.S.E.E., B.S., MIT, 1971; M.D., Northwestern U., 1975; m. Lynn Elizabeth Hauser, June 20, 1975. Resident in ophthalmology Northwestern U. Med. Sch., 1975-79, fellow in retina, 1979-80; practice medicine specializing in cataract surgery, Sycamore, Ill., 1980—; mem. staff Kishwaukee Community Hosp., DeKalb, Sycamore Mcpl. Hosp.; instr. dept. ophthalmology Northwestern U. Med. Sch., 1980—; clin. asst. prof. Ophthalmology U. Ill., 1982—; lectr. Northwestern U., 1982—; project ophthalmologist early treatment diabetic retinopathy study Nat. Eye Inst. Diplomate Am. Bd. Ophthalmology. Fellow ACS; mem. DeKalb County Med. Soc., Ill. State Med. Soc., AMA, Am. Acad. Ophthalmology, Chgo. Ophthal. Soc., Sigma Xi. Office: Gateway Dr Sycamore IL 60178

ROSS, NORMAN ALEXANDER, retired banker; b. Miami, Fla., Jan. 30, 1922; s. Norman DeMille and Beatrice (Dowsett) R.; children—Isabel, Susan Diana. A.B., Stanford U., 1946; postgrad., Trinity Coll., Oxford U., Eng., 1953; D.H.L., Lincoln Coll., Ill., 1959, Fisk U., 1978, Roosevelt U., 1979; Litt.D., Lake Forest Coll., 1967. Airport mgr. Pan Am. Airways, 1943; asst. to producer Metro-Goldwyn-Mayer, 1943-44; ptnr. Norman Ross & Co., 1947-50; owner Norman Ross Record Club, 1951-52; v.p. pub. affairs First Nat. Bank Chgo., 1968-79, sr. v.p. communications dept., 1979-81, sr. v.p. community affairs, 1981-86; pres. Ross-McElroy Prodns., Inc., 1962-68. Radio-TV commentator, NBC, ABC, Chgo., 1953-64, ABC, WGN and WBKB, Chgo., 1964-68, former columnist, Chgo. Daily News. Served with inf. AUS, World War II. Decorated cavaliere Dell Ordine Repubblica Italiana; U.S. Army Outstanding Civilian Service medal; officier and cross of chevalier Legion of Honor France; recipient Peabody award for TV program Off the Cuff 1964. Mem. Phi Gamma Delta. Clubs: Chgo., Racquet, Oxford, Econ. (Chgo.), Wayfarers.

ROSS, PATRICK CONROY, rubber company executive; b. Iron River, Mich., Aug. 27, 1929; s. William D. and Elsie A. (Thompson) R.; m. Ann M. Groves, Feb. 2, 1956; children—Stewart C., Charles E., Nancy J. A.B., U. Mich., 1951, M.A., 1976; grad., advanced mgmt. program Harvard U., 1969. Merchandising mgr. WWJ-Detroit News, 1956-57; sales mgr. Argus Cameras Co., Ann Arbor, Mich., 1957-62; area dir. Europe B.F. Goodrich Co., 1962-68; pres. internat. div. B.F. Goodrich Co., Akron, Ohio, 1969-70; pres. B. F. Goodrich Tire Group, Akron, Ohio, 1972-84; corp. exec. v.p. B.F. Goodrich Co., 1979-84, pres., 1984-86; chmn., chief exec. officer The Uniroyal Goodrich Tire Co., Akron, 1986—. Mem. Ohio Council Econ. Edn.; bd. dirs. Akron Internat. Inst.; trustee Akron Children's Hosp., Center for Econ. Edn., U. Akron.; chmn. Hwy. Users Fedn. Served with USAF, 1951-55. Mem. Rubber Mfr.'s Assn. (bd. dirs.). Club: Portage Country (Akron). Office: Uniroyal Goodrich Tire Co 600 S Main St Akron OH 44397-0001

ROSS, PETER WILLIAM, farm association executive; b. Jamestown, N.D., Jan. 7, 1946; s. William Peter and Mathilda Theresa (Kappel) L.; m. Nancy Lee Schoeder, Dec. 30, 1969; children: William, Karen. Student, N.D. State U., 1964-67. Asst. mgr. Sheels Hardware, Moorhead, Minn., 1968-71; agent Western Life, Fargo, N.D., 1971-72; salesman N.D. AAA, Fargo, 1972-74; area dir. Nat. Farmers Orgn., Jamestown, N.D., 1974-77, Beloit, Kans., 1977-83; regional mgr. Nat. Farmers Orgn., Salina, Kans., 1983—. Editor Nat. Farmers Orgn. Newsletter, 1985-86. Mem. Beloit City Council, 1982—, pres. 1985—. Served to master sgt. Army NG, 1965—. Democrat. Roman Catholic. Club: NCO (Valley City, N.D.) (pres. 1971-73) Lodge: KC (grand knight Beloit 1981-83), Eagles. Avocations: reading, hunting, public speaking. Home: 616 East Ct Beloit KS 67420 Office: Nat Farmers Orgn 1606 E Iron Ave Salina KS 67401

ROSS, REGINALD RANDOLPH, dentist; b. Dodge City, Kans., Jan. 19, 1953; s. Robert David and Velma Rose (Mackey) R.; m. Mary Ann Rackauskas, Oct. 12, 1979; children: Lindsay Ann, Amanda Jo. Student, Springfield Jr. Coll., 1971-73, U. Ill., 1973, St. Louis Coll. Pharmacy, 1974; DDS, U. Ill., 1978. Dentist Dr. L. Richards Office, Springfield, Ill., 1979-80; gen practice dentistry Springfield, 1980—. Mem. ADA, Ill. State Dental Soc., G.V. Black Dental Soc., Chgo. Dental Soc., U. Ill. Alumni Assn. Republican. Roman Catholic. Avocations: water skiing, snow mobiling, running, western united states history. Home: #5 East Lake Shore Ln Springfield IL 62707 Office: 1100 S Second Springfield IL 62704

ROSS, ROBERT E., optometrist; b. Tiffin, Ohio, Dec. 3, 1931; s. George Eldrige and Evelyn D. (Roper) R.; m. Shirley Ann Cole, Dec. 18, 1955; children—Diana Lynn, Janet Kay, Jane Ellen, Judy Ann, Dean Edward. B.S. in Optometry, Ohio State U., 1957. Diplomate State Bd. Optometry, Ohio. Gen. practice optometry, Tiffin, Ohio, 1957—. Served with USAF, 1949-53. Mem. Ohio Optometric Assn. (zone gov. 1959), Am. Optometric Assn. (25 year award). Republican. Mem. United Ch. Christ. Lodges: Rotary (bd. dirs.), Elks, Moose, VFW. Avocations: golfing, swimming, skiing. Home: 345 Coe St Tiffin OH 44883 Office: 34 W Market St Box 430 Tiffin OH 44883

ROSS, STEVEN CHARLES, business administration educator, consultant; b. Salem, Oreg., Jan. 14, 1947; s. Charles Reed and Edythe Marie (Calvin) R.; m. Meredith Lynn Buholts, June 15, 1969; children: Kelly Lynn, Shannon Marie. BS, Oreg. State U., 1969; MS, U. Utah, 1976, PhD, 1980. Cons., IRS Tng. Staff, Ogden, Utah, 1977-80; asst. prof. Marquette U., Milw., 1980—; govt. and industry cons. Author seven books and several articles in computer systems field. Mem. adv. com. Milwaukee County Mgmt., 1981-85. Served to capt. U.S. Army, 1969-75. Recipient research fellowship, U. Utah, 1977-79, Marquette U., 1981-84. Mem. Acad. Mgmt., Am. Psychol. Assn., Am. Inst. Decision Scis., Inst. Mgmt. Scis., Assn. for Computing Machinery, Mensa. Home: 1019 E Lexington Blvd Whitefish Bay WI 53217 Office: Marquette U Coll Bus Adminstrn Milwaukee WI 53233

ROSS, SUZANNE IRIS, fund raising executive; b. Chgo., Feb. 2, 1948; d. Irving and Rose (Stein) R. BA in Secondary Edn., Western Mich. U., 1971. Dir. youth employment Ill. Youth Services Bur., Maywood, Ill., 1978-79; exec. dir. Edn. Resource Ctr., Chgo., 1979-82; asst. dir. devel. Art Inst. Chgo., 1982-83, mgr. govt. affairs, 1983-84, dir. govt. affairs, 1984-85; v.p. devel. Spertus Coll. Judaica, Chgo., 1985—; lectr. Sch. Art Inst., Chgo., 1982-85, Ill. Fire Inspectors Assn., Mt. Prospect, Ill., 1982-84, Episcopalian Archdiocese, Chgo., 1984, DePaul U. Sch. for New Learning, 1987; instr. Columbia Coll., Chgo., 1980—. Mem. adv. council Citizens Com. on Media, Chgo., 1978-80; adv. panelist Chgo. Office Fine Arts, 1981-82; mem. adv. council Greater Chgo. Food Depository, 1984-85; exec. com. Chgo. Coalition Arts in Edn., 1981-82; mem. info. services com. Donors' Forum Chgo., 1986—, mem. adv. bd. Chgo. Moving Co., 1987—. Mem. Nat. Soc. Fund Raising Execs., Am. Assn. Mus., Am. Council Arts, Ill. Arts Alliance. Democrat. Jewish. Avocation: attending cultural events. Home: 3709 N Janssen #2RB Chicago IL 60613 Office: Spertus Coll Judaica 618 S Michigan Ave Chicago IL 60605

ROSS, TERRY LEE, architect; b. Sandusky, Ohio, Sept. 28, 1951; s. Ernest Wilson and Jean Margaret (Vollmer) R.; m. Phyllis Gail Molnar, Jan. 22, 1972; children: Jennifer Jae, Elizabeth Marie. AS, U. Cin., 1976. Archtl. draftsman Gartner Burdick & Bauer Nilson, Cin., 1976-77; archtl. design Baybutt Constrn., Keene, N.H., 1977-79, Feick Contractors, Sandusky, Ohio, 1979-82; engr. tech. City of Sandusky, 1982-84; mgr. arch. services Cedar Point, Sandusky, 1984—. Scoutmaster Boy Souts Am., Marlborough, N.H., 1977-79. Lodge: Masons. Home: 5709 Cambridge Circle Sandusky OH 44870 Office: Cedar Point C N 5006 Sandusky OH 44870

ROSS, WILLIAM BROOKS, insurance executive; b. Lawrenceburg, Ind., Aug. 22, 1927; s. Harvey Sherman and Rosa Lee (Mattox) R.; m. Lois Marie Kirkpatrick, June 15, 1956; children: Victoria, William Brooks, III. AB with highest honors in Econs., Ind. U., 1950; AM in Econs., Princeton U., 1952. Budget examiner U.S. Bur. Budget, Washington, 1954-64, chief fiscal economist, 1964-66; dep. under sec. U.S. Dept. HUD, Washington, 1966-70; exec. v.p. Fed. Nat. Mortgage Assn., Washington, 1970-72; pres. MGIC Mortgage Corp., Milw., 1972-76; sr. v.p. MGIC Investment Corp., Milw., 1976-85; sr. v.p. Mortgage Guaranty Ins. Corp., Milw., 1985—; dir. WPG Fund, Inc., N.Y.C., 1972—, WPG Growth Fund, N.Y.C., 1986—, trustee WPG Funds Trust, N.Y.C., 1986—; dir. Pearce, Urstadt, Mayer & Greer, N.Y.C., 1972-87, Tudor Fund Inc., N.Y.C., 1972—. Mem. Village of Shorewood (Wis.) Planning Com., 1974-83, 85—; v.p., treas. Wis. Council, Am. Youth Hostels, Inc., Wauwatosa, Wis., 1974—; treas. Wis. Phi Beta Kappa Found., Milw., 1979—. Recipient Career Service award Nat. Civil Service League, 1970; Meritorious Service award William A. Jump Found., 1963. Mem. Phi Beta Kappa. Presbyterian. Clubs: Milw. Athletic; Princeton of N.Y. Home: 2733 E Newton Ave Shorewood WI 53211 Office: MGIC Investment Corp 250 E Kilbourn Ave Milwaukee WI 53202

ROSS, WILLIAM DONALD, psychiatrist; b. Hamilton, Ont., Can., Sept. 13, 1913; came to U.S., 1948; s. Frederic William and Eleanor Margaret (McDonald) R.; m. Emily Sally Chipman (dec. Nov. 1978); 1 child, George F. Ross; m. C. Janet Gerig Newman, Dec. 27, 1979. BS in Medicine, MD, U. Manitoba, Winnipeg, Can., 1938; diploma in psychiatry, McGill U., Montreal, 1948. Diplomate Am. Bd. Psychiatry and Neurology. From instr.

to prof. various schs., Winnipeg, Vancouver, Montreal and Cin., 1939-79; prof. emeritus U. Cin., 1979—; attending physician various univ. hosp., 1939-79; cons. med. dept. Procter and Gamble, 1964—; U.S. Postal Service, 1986. Author: Understanding Ourselves, 1942, Practical Psychiatry for Industrial Physicians, 1956; contbr. articles to profl. jour. Bd. dirs. Cin. Family Services, 1955-65. Served to maj. Can. Army, 1943-46. Mem. Cin. Psychiat. Soc. (pres. 1956-57), Ohio Psychiat. Assn. (pres. 1965-66), Zeta Psi. Presbyterian. Avocations: swimming, walking, theater, personal computer. Home: 854 Rue de la Paix B 1 Cincinnati OH 45220 Office: U Cin Dept Psychiatry 7209 Coll Medicine 231 Bethesda Ave Cincinnati OH 45267-0559

ROSSI, DAVID THOMAS, chemist; b. Trenton, N.J., May 21, 1957; s. Thomas David and Lydia (Mancia) R.; m. Danell Dawn Jenkinson, June 24, 1984; 1 child, D. Aaron. BS, Lebanon Valley Coll., 1979; PhD, Purdue U., 1984. Sr. chemist Monsanto Co., St. Louis, 1984-86, Adria Labs., Columbus, Ohio, 1986—. Contbr. articles to profl. jours. Mem. Am. Chem. Soc. (Undergrad. Analytical Chemistry award 1978), Am. Fedn. of Musicians. Roman Catholic. Avocations: music, carpentry, electronics, athletics.

ROSSI, DONALD, psychoanalyst; b. Chgo., Nov. 3, 1940; s. Raymond R. and Dora R. (Rante) R.; m. J. Antoinette Chapados, Aug. 27, 1966; 1 chil, Tamara Dawn. BS, No. Ariz. U., 1964; MS, N.M. Highlands U., 1966; PhD, U. Sheffield, Eng., 1969. Licensed psychologist, Mich. Intern N. Mex. State Hosp., Las Vegas, 1965, Springfield Hosp. Ctr., Sykesville, Mo., 1968-69, dept. psychiatry Siani Hosp., Balt., 1968-69; pvt. practice psychoanalysis 1971—; dir. behavioral sci. sect. Mich. Dept. State Police, Lansing, 1978—; vis. lectr. U.S. Dept. Army, Ft. Bliss, Tex., 1979-85; vis. instr. Northwestern U. Traffic Inst., Evanston, Ill., 1978-79; adj. prof. police psychology dept. criminal justice programs Lansing Community Coll., 1983—; cons. in field. Mem. Am. Psychol. Assn. (psychology and law div.), Internat. Soc. Hypnosis, Am. Soc. Clin. Hypnosis, Greater Detroit Soc. Clin. Hypnosis, Mich. Soc. Clin. Hypnosis, Nat. Assn. for Advancement of Psychoanalysis, Internat. Assn. of Chiefs of Police, Nat. Tactical Officers Assn. Office: 600 W St Joseph St Lansing MI 48933

ROSSI, EUGENE ENRICO, insurance agent; b. Warren, Ohio, May 12, 1926; s. Anthony G. and Lena Marie (Guarnieri) R.; m. Virginia L. Porter, Sept. 18, 1948; children—Michael D., E. Jeffrey, Dennis A., Gregory L. Degree in Bus. Adminstrn., Youngstown Coll., 1953. Ins. agt. Rossi Ins. Agy., Warren, Ohio, 1951—. Treas., St. Joseph Hosp. Found., Warren, 1970—, Youngstown State Alumni Assn., 1981—; trustee YMCA of Trumbull County, 1978—. Served with U.S. Army, 1944-45. Recipient Disting. Citizen award Warren Area Jaycees, 1987. Mem. Nat. Assn. Profl. Ins. Agts., Trumbull County Assn. Life Underwriters (pres. 1956), Ind. Ins. Agts. Trumbull County (pres. 1959), Ind. Ins. Agts. Ohio (trustee 1974-77), Warren Area C. of C. (pres.), Am. Legion, V.F.W. Democrat. Roman Catholic. Clubs: Trumbull Country (trustee), Oblate Sister (trustee). Lodges: K.C. (Grand Knight 1955), Elks. Avocations: travel; golf. Home: 621 Country Club Dr Warren OH 44484 Office: Rossi Ins Agy 420 High St PO Box 630 Warren OH 44482

ROSSI, RAYMOND ERNEST, lawyer; b. Chicago Heights, Ill., Aug. 1, 1953; s. Arnold P. and Elsie S. (Nardoni) R.; m. Terri L. Wilson, June 25, 1972; children: Amanda M., Brandon M., Carmen A., Drake A. BA, N. Cen. Coll., Naperville, Ill., 1975; MBA, DePaul U., 1977; JD, John Marshall Law Sch., 1980. Bar: Ill. 1980, U.S. Dist. Ct. (no. dist.) Ill. 1980, U.S. Ct. Appeals (7th cir.) 1984. Atty. S. Suburban Law Clinic, Richton Park, Ill., 1980, Scarborough & Co., Chgo., 1980-82, Bishop & Crawford, Ltd., Oak Brook, Ill., 1982—; instr. Joliet (Ill.) Jr. Coll., 1981-82. Assoc. editor Young Lawyer's Jour., 1982. Mem. Frankfort Twp. Planning Commn., Frankfort, Ill., 1987—; area chmn. Rich Twp. Reps., Inc., Park Forest, Ill., 1982-86; v.p., treas. Prestwick Home Owner's Assn., Frankfort, 1985-86, pres., 1987—. Named one of Outstanding Young Men Am., Jaycees, 1982; recipient award Frankfort Mokena Star Pubs., 1987. Mem. ABA (gen. practice sect. 1980—, comml. law sect. 1980—), Ill. Bar Assn. (ins. sect. 1980—, civil practice sect. 1980—), Chgo. Bar Assn. (comml. law sect. 1980—, trial techniques sect. 1980—), Will County Bar Assn., Cath. Lawyers Guild, Oak Brook Execs. Roman Catholic. Club: Prestwick Country (Frankfort). Lodges: KC, Lions. Avocation: tennis. Home: 938 Shetland Dr Frankfort IL 60423 Office: Bishop & Crawford Ltd 1315 W 22d St Suite 300 Oak Brook IL 60521

ROSSKAMM, ALAN, fabric manufacturing company executive; b. 1950. With Fabri-Ctrs. of Am., Inc., 1978—, v.p., from 1980, now pres., chief exec. officer. Office: Fabri-Centers of Am., Inc 23550 Commerce Park rd Beachwood OH 44122 *

ROSSKAMM, MARTIN, fabric manufacturing company executive; b. 1915. With Fabri-Ctrs. of Am., Inc., Cleve., 1953—, first pres., chief exec. officer, now chmn. bd. dirs. Served with AUS, 1941-45. Office: Fabri-Ctrs of Am Inc 23550 Commerce Park Rd Beachwood OH 44122 *

ROSSMILLER, RICHARD ALLEN, educational administration educator, consultant; b. Burlington, Wis., May 25, 1928; s. Harold Curtis and Lydia Sophia (Keller) R.; m. Lois Catherine Koch, July 5, 1952; children—Daniel, Stuart, David. B.S., U. Wis.-Madison, 1950, M.S., 1958, Ph.D., 1960. Supt. Racine County Agrl. Sch., Rochester, Wis., 1954-57; prin. Evanston Twp. High Sch., Ill., 1960-61; supt. Muskego-Norway Schs., Wis., 1961-62; prof. ednl. adminstrn. U. Wis.-Madison, 1962—; vis. prof. U. Fla., Gainesville, 1967-68, Pontificial Cath. U., Rio de Janeiro, Brazil, 1977; cons. RAND Corp., Santa Monica, Calif., 1977-81, CAPES Ministry of Edn. and Culture, Brasilia, Brazil, 1975, OECD. Author: Opportunities Unlimited, 1959, 1983. Co-author: The Law and Public School Operation, 1969, 1978; Individual Guided Education, 1977; Dimensions of Educational Need, 1969. Dir. State Supts. Task Force on Teaching, Madison, 1983; pub. mem. Wis. Legis. Council, Madison, 1975, 1978. Recipient Benjamin Constant medal Inst. of Edn. of Rio de Janeiro, 1980. Mem. Am. Edn. and Fin. Assn. (pres. 1981), Univ. Council Ednl. Adminstrn. (pres. 1984—), Am. Ednl. Research Assn., Council for Ednl. Devel. and Research (pres. 1975-76), Nat. Orgn. Legal Problems of Edn. Democrat. Lodge: Rotary (dir. 1982-83). Avocation: photography. Home: 5806 Cable Ave Madison WI 53705 Office: Dept Ednl Adminstrn 1025 W Johnson St Madison WI 53706

ROSS-RHOADES, VICKI ANN, accountant; b. St. Ansgar, Iowa, Apr. 27, 1957; d. Darwin Ross and Alice Josephine (Wirth) Rhoades; m. Steven James Ross, Sept. 15, 1982; 1 child, Forrest Lee Ross. BS, Mankato State U., 1979. CPA, Minn. Staff acct. Clapper, Kitchenmaster & Co., CPA's, Waseca, Minn., 1980, Goldfein, Silverman & Olson, CPA's, Mpls., 1980-81; prin. Henry S. Krigbaum, Ltd., CPA's, Bemidji, Minn., 1982—. Treas. Paul Bunyan Playhouse, Bemidji, 1982—. Mem. Am. Inst. CPA's, Minn. Soc. CPA's, Jaycee Women (bd. dirs. Bemidji 1982), N.W. Minn. Woodland Owner's Assn. (treas. 1983-85). Lutheran. Avocations: theater, tree farming, cross-country skiing, hiking, canoeing. Home: Box 368 Pennington MN 56663 Office: Henry S Krigbaum Ltd 315 5th St Bemidji MN 56601

ROSSTEDT, LOIS K., computer executive; b. Paterson, N.J., July 29, 1956; s. William Frank and Patricia Marie (Doyle) Kubarewicz; m. Mark Ogden Rosstedt, Oct. 20, 1984. Radio copywriter Sta. WJRZ-FM, Manahawkin, N.J., 1978; editorial asst. Butler Service Group, Whippany, N.J., 1978-79; tech. writer Bell Labs div. AT&T, Naperville, Ill., 1979-85; product planner AT&T Data Systems, Lisle, Ill., 1985—; also chmn. subcom. affirmative action AT&T, Lisle, Ill.; chmn. subcom. affirmative action AT&T, 1986. Advance person Bill Bradley's Campaign for Senator, Toms River and Union, N.J., 1978. Mem. IEEE (computer soc. 1984, CS software engring. standards subcom. 1984—), UNIX User Group. Club: Naperville Tennis Club. Avocations: tennis, volleyball. Office: AT&T Data Systems Div 4513 Western Ave Lisle IL 60532

ROSSWAY, MELVIN WEAVER, retired railroad executive; b. Belle Plaine, Iowa, Sept. 7, 1918; s. Samuel W. and Edna (Weaver) R.; m. Marian Ruth Morehead, Oct. 31, 1946; children: Ronald Alan, Rhonda Kay, Rita Jean. Diploma in acctg., Internat. Corr. Schs., 1953. Agt. helper Chgo. and Northwestern R.R., 1937-38, telegraph sta. agt., 1938-53; traveling acct. Chgo., 1953-56; asst. controller, auditor Lake Superior & Ishpeming R.R. Co., Marquette, Mich., 1956-58, treas., controller, 1958-61, v.p., treas., controller, 1961-73, sr. v.p., 1973-79, exec. v.p., sec., treas., 1979-82; pres. Lasco Devel. Corp., 1975-86; fin. cons., 1985—. Chmn. Marquette Hosp. Bond Authority. Served with AUS, 1944-46; staff officer USCG Aux., 1969—. Mem. Tax Execs. (Wis. chpt.), Marquette Range Engrs., Am. Legion, Marquette C. of C. Republican. Lutheran. Club: Marquette (treas. 1986—). Lodges: Masons, Lions, Elks. Home: 800 W Magnetic St Marquette MI 49855

ROSTENBACH, KEVIN VICTOR, infosystems specialist, consultant; b. Davenport, Iowa, Sept. 23, 1959; s. Marvin Henry and Loisfaye (Bahr) R.; m. Jean Lee Sasser, Aug. 16, 1978 (div. June, 1980); m. Karla Lynn Bowden, Nov. 22, 1986. Postgrad., Am. Inst. Commerce, 1982. Data processing coordinator Am. Inst. Commerce, Bettendorf, Iowa, 1982—; cons. WSF, Rock Island, Ill., Weiner Realty (Caldwell Banker), Rock Island, Vera French Mental Health Ctr., Davenport. Mem. Soc. Data Educators, Data Processing Mgmt. Assn. (exec. v.p. Ill. chpt., 1985, local pres. 1986). Avocations: racing, motorcycling, billiards. Home: 1346 W 47th St Ct Davenport IA 52809 Office: Am Inst Commerce Bus Sch Duck Creek Plaza Bettendorf IA 52722

ROSTENKOWSKI, DAN, congressman; b. Chgo., Jan. 2, 1928; s. Joseph P. and Priscilla (Dombrowski) R.; m. LaVerne Pirkins, May 12, 1951; children: Dawn, Kristie, Gayle, Stacy. Student, St. John's Mil. Acad., 1942-46, Loyola U., 1948- 51. Mem. Ho. of Reps., Ill. Gen. Assembly, 1952; mem. Ill. senate, 1954, 56, 86th-100th congresses from 8th Dist. Ill.; chmn. Democratic caucus 90th-91st Congresses; chief dep. majority whip 95th-96th Congresses; chmn. com. on ways and means, joint com. on taxation. Del. Democratic Nat. Conv., 1960, 64, 68, 72, 76, 80, 84. Served with 7th Inf. Div. AUS, 1946-48. Mem. YMCA, VFW. Democrat. Clubs: K.C, Ill. Athletic. Office: 2111 Rayburn House Office Bldg Washington DC 20515

ROSWICK, ELMER J., transportation company executive. Chmn. Midwest Motor Express, Inc., Bismarck, N.D. Office: Midwest Motor Express Inc PO Box 1058 Bismarck ND 58502 *

ROSWICK, JOHN T., transportation company executive. Pres. Midwest Motor Express, Inc., Bismarck, N.D. Office: Midwest Motor Express Inc PO Box 1058 Bismarck ND 58502 *

ROSZKOWSKI, STANLEY JULIAN, judge; b. Booneville, N.Y., Jan. 27, 1923; s. Joseph and Anna (Christkowski) R.; m. Catherine Mary Claeys, June 19, 1948; children: Mark, Gregory, Dan, John. B.S., U. Ill., 1949, LL.D., 1954. Bar: Ill. 1954. Sales mgr. Warren Petroleum Co., Rockford, Ill., 1954; mem. Roszkowski, Paddock, McGreevy & Johnson, Rockford, 1955-77; judge U.S. Dist. Ct. (we. dist.), Rockford, Ill., 1977—; pres. First State Bank, Rockford, 1963-75; chmn. bd. First State Bank, 1977—. Chmn. Fire and Police Commn., Rockford, 1967-74, commr., 1974—; chmn. Paul Simon Com., 1972; active Adlai Stevenson III campaign, 1968-71, Winnebago County Citizens for John F. Kennedy, 1962, Winnebago County Democratic Central Com., 1962-64; bd. dirs. Sch. of Hope, 1960—; mem. Ill. Capital Devel. Bd., 1974—. Served with USAAF, 1943-45. Decorated Air medal with 2 oak leaf clusters.; recipient Pulaski Nat. Heritage award Polish Am. Congress, Chgo., 1982. Mem. Am., Ill., Fla., Winnebago County bar assns., Am. Coll. Trial Lawyers, Am. Judicature Soc., Am., Ill. trial lawyers assns., Am. Arbitration Assn. (arbitrator). Club: Forest Hills Country (Rockford). Office: US Dist Ct 211 S Court St Rockford IL 61101 *

ROTCHADL, DOUGLAS MARK, food company executive, accountant; b. Marshall, Minn., Mar. 25, 1955; s. Anton Joseph and Alice barbara (Carda) R.; m. Kathryn Kay Schweim, July 1, 1978; children: Lisa Marie, Lynn Nicole, Leah Kristine, Lora Kay. BS, Mankato State U., 1978. CPA, Minn. Sr. auditor Deloitte, Haskins & Sells, Mpls., 1978-81; controller Best Brands, Inc., St. Paul, 1981-87; dir. fin. Gourmet Foods, Inc., St. Paul, 1987—. Mem. Am. Inst. CPA's, Minn. Soc. CPA's. Roman Catholic. Avocations: bicycling, gardening. Office: Gourmet Foods Inc 860 Vandalia St Saint Paul MN 55114

ROTENBERG, MARK BENJAMIN, lawyer; b. Mpls., Sept. 6, 1954; s. Max and Naomi (Packer) R.; m. Beth Pearlman, Aug. 26, 1979. BA, Brandeis U., 1976; JD, Columbia U., 1979, MA, 1980, M in Philosophy, 1981. Bar: Minn. 1981, U.S. Ct. Appeals (D.C. cir.) 1981, U.S. Ct. Appeals (6th cir.) 1982, D.C. 1984, U.S. Dist. Ct. Minn. 1984. Law clk. to presiding justic U.S. Ct. Appeals (D.C. cir.), 1980-81; atty. advisor Office Legal Counsel, U.S. Dept. Justice, Washington, 1981-84; assoc. Dorsey & Whitney, Mpls., 1984—; bd. dirs. PPL Inc.; mem. commn. Mpls. Capital Improvements. Editor Columbia Law Rev., 1978-79. Press coordinator Mayor Donald Fraser's Re-election Campaign, Mpls., 1985; v.p. Adath Jeshurun Congregation. Harlan Fiske Stone scholar Columbia U., 1976-78, President's fellow, 1978-79. Mem. ABA, Minn. Bar Assn., Hennepin County Bar Assn., Am. Soc. Legal History, Orgn. Am. Historians, Columbia Law Alumni Assn., Phi Beta Kappa. Democrat. Office: Dorsey & Whitney 2200 First Bank Pl E Minneapolis MN 55402

ROTH, DIANE LOIS, accountant; b. Indpls., Jan. 9, 1961; d. Samuel Michael and Caresse Enette (Thompson) Vojnovich; m. Randall Eugene Roth, Sept. 22, 1984. BS magna cum laude, Ball State U., 1983. CPA, Ind. Acct. Ernst & Whinney, Indpls., 1983-85, Reed & Co., W. Lafayette, Ind., 1985—. Ball State scholar, 1980-83. Mem. Am. Inst. CPA's, Ind. Soc. CPA's, Am. Women's Soc. CPA's, Alpha Lambda Delta (hon.), Beta Gamma Sigma (hon.). Avocations: sewing, cooking, gardening. Home: 3250 Halfway Rd Crawfordsville IN 47433

ROTH, EDWIN MORTON, service company executive; b. Cleve., Oct. 15, 1927; s. Bernath and Lottie (Klafter) R.; m. Sarah Kennedy; children: Lacey Jan Roth Cohen, Alden Hope Guren, Corey Bruce, Cullen Andrew. Student, Ohio State U., 1946-47; B.B.A., Case Western Res. U., 1949. With Weather-Proof Co., Cleve., 1949-50; pres. E.M. Roth & Assocs., Cleve., 1950-52; sales mgr. Garland Co., Cleve., 1952-54, PlastiKote, Inc., Cleve., 1954-56; v.p. ITT Consumer Services, Cleve., 1967-75; pres., dir. ITT Service Industries, Cleve., 1970-75, Yellow Cab Co., Kansas City, Mo., 1968-75; v.p., dir. Abbey Casualty Ins. Co., Washington, 1968-75; chmn., chief exec. officer APCOA, Inc., 1975—; pres. APCOA, B.V. Amsterdam, Momentum Inc.; bd. dirs. Aerosol Systems Inc., Equity Resources, Inc. Mem. governing council Am. Jewish Congress; mem. nat. council Joint Distbn. Com.; trustee Cleve. Am. Jewish Com.; chmn. bd. dirs. Mt. Sinai Hosp., Cleve., 1979-82; bd. dirs. Menorah Park Home for Aged, Cleve. Hebrew Schs., Inst. Jewish Policy Planning and Research, No. Ohio council Camp Fire Girls; bd. overseers Case Western Res. U.; trustee No. Ohio Respiratory Disease Assn., Cleve. Ballet, United Way of Cleve.; trustee, exec. com. Jewish Community Fedn., Playhouse Sq. Found.; bd. dirs. Bellefaire Children's Home, pres., 1975-78. Served with USNR, 1945-46. Mem. Nat. Parking Assn. (pres. 1976-78, chmn. 1978-80), Musical Arts Assn. Cleve., No. Ohio Tennis Assn. Jewish (trustee, v.p. synagogue). Clubs: Commerce, Clevelander, Union, Oakwood Country, Palm Beach Country. Home: 1050 N Lake Way Palm Beach FL 33480 Office: Apcoa Inc 25550 Chagrin Blvd #300 Cleveland OH 44122 *

ROTH, LARRY GLEN, insurance company executive; b. Freeport, Ill., Dec. 1, 1944; s. Glen Clarence and Eloise Ethel (Ferguson) R.; m. LuAnn Wunsch, June 15, 1973. AA, Freeport Community Coll., 1965; BS, No. Ill. U., 1967. CPA, Wis. Sr. acct. Peat, Marwick, Mitchell & Co., Milw., 1970-73; treas. All-Star Ins. Co., Milw., 1973-75; asst. sec. Northwestern Nat. Ins., Milw., 1975-78; sec.-treas. West Bend (Wis.) Mut. Ins., 1978—. Bd. dirs. West Bend United Way, 1983—. Served to lt. USNR, 1967-69. Mem. Am. Inst. CPA's, Wis. Inst. CPA's. Avocations: golf, skiing. Office: West Bend Mut Ins Co 1115 S Main St West Bend WI 53095

ROTH, MARY JANE, marketing executive; b. Detroit, Oct. 30, 1951; d. Edward Leon and Dorothy Jane (McKay) Bagger; m. William James Roth, Apr. 16, 1971 (div. Oct. 1986); m. Richard L. Town Jr., Sept. 5, 1987. Student, Wayne State U., 1970-72; BA, U. Mich., Dearborn, 1974. Cert. secondary sch. tchr., Mich. Tchr., chmn. theater dept. Cabrini High SCh., Allen Park, Mich., 1975-80; producer DeGroot & Co., Troy, Mich., 1980; asst. program dir. Maclean Hunter Cable TV Inc., Taylor, Mich., 1981; community relations dir. Maclean Hunter Cable TV Inc., Taylor, 1981-82; regional mktg. mgr. Maclean-Hunter Cable TV Inc., Taylor, 1982—; speech cons. Detroit area, 1975—; theater programs dir. Huron Twp. (Mich.) Sch. System, 1984—; lobbyist Nat. Cable TV Assn., Washington, 1983-84. Dir. play, The Diary of Anne Frank, Allen Park, 1980 (Best Prodn. and Best Dir. awards Furay Festival 1980). Bd. dirs. Southern Wayne County C. of C., 1982-85. Mem. Adcrafters, Women In Cable Inc. (treas. Mich. chpt. 1982-83), Mich. Cable TV Assn. (lobbyist Lansing, 1983—), Southeast Mich. Cable Assn. (v.p. 1984-85, sec. 1985—). Democrat. Avocations: reading, producing community theatrical productions, photography. Office: Maclean Hunter Cable TV Inc 24744 Eureka Rd Taylor MI 48180

ROTH, MICHAEL JOHN, marketing professional; b. Chgo., Oct. 10, 1955; s. Joseph Charles and Ora Lee (Ledger) R.; m. Mary Ellen Myers, Sept. 30, 1980; children: Adrienne, Anthony. AA in Mktg., Normandale Community Coll., 1976; BS in Advt., Mankato (Minn.) State U., 1978. Production asst. Twin Communications, Mpls., 1978079; asst. advt. mgr. Crown/Auto, Inc., Mpls., 1979-83; advt. mgr. Employers Overload, Mpls., 1983-87, Quality Temp, Mpls., 1987—. Mem. Advt. Fedn. Republican. Avocations: skiing, photography, hunting, bicycling, home improvement. Home: 10500 Beard Ave Bloomington MN 55431 Office: Quality Temp 9801 Dupont Ave S Minneapolis MN 55420

ROTH, PAUL WILLIAM, nuclear services engineer; b. Park Ridge, Ill., June 29, 1960; s. Frank James and Elaine Dorothy (Wilcek) R.; m. Joan Marie Gleason, Feb, 25, 1984. BS in Nuclear Engring., U. Ill., 1982. Unit nuclear engr. Commonwealth Edison Co., Morris, Ill., 1982-84, project nuclear engr., 1984-86; radwaste systems engr. Commonwealth Edison Co., Maywood, Ill., 1986—. Gestetner scholar, 1978. Mem. Am. Soc. Mech. Engrs. (assoc.), Am. Nuclear Soc. (assoc.). Avocations: sports, music, automobiles, cooking. Office: Commonwealth Edison Co 1319 S 1st Ave Room 306 Maywood IL 60153

ROTH, ROGER ZANG, manufacturing executive; b. Johnstown, Pa., Jan. 14, 1938; s. Carl George Roth and Lorretta (Williams) Linden; m. Janet Marie Gerhardt, Feb. 14, 1959; children: Stephen F., Stuart A. BSME, Toledo U., 1969; MBA, Bowling Green State U., 1979. Project engr. Dana Corp., Toledo, 1970-73; mgr. sales accts. Dana Corp., Southfield, Mich., 1973-76; mgr. engring. Dana Corp., Edgerton, Wis., 1976-78; chief engr. Dana Corp., Auburn, Ind., 1978-81; plant mgr. Dana Corp., Detroit, 1981-86; chmn., chief exec. officer RWI, Inc., Fraser, Mich., 1986—, also chmn. bd. dirs. Patentee in field. Mem. Soc. Automotive Engrs., Engring. Soc. Detroit, Nat. Tooling Assn., Mich. C. of C. Office: Lunar Industries 34335 Groesbeck Hwy Fraser MI 48026

ROTH, TOBY, congressman; b. Strasburg, N.D., Oct. 10, 1938; s. Kasper and Julia (Roehrich) R.; m. Barbara Fischer, Nov. 28, 1964; children: Toby, Vicky, Barbie. B.A., Marquette U., 1961. Owner Toby Roth Realty, Appleton, from 1969; mem. Wis. Ho. of Reps. from 42d Dist., 1972-78, 96th-100th Congresses from 8th Wis. Dist., Fgn. Affairs Com., Banking, Fin. and Urban Affairs Com., Congl. Rural Caucus, Tourism Caucus; vice chmn. Environ. Study Conf. Served to 1st lt. USAR, 1962-69. Named Wis. Legislator of Yr. Wis. Towns Assn., 1978; Outstanding Rep. Freshman Congressman, 1979. Mem. Wis. Northside Businessmen's Assn. (pres. 1970), Am. Legion. Republican. Clubs: Optimists (hon.), Kiwanis (hon.).

ROTHENBERG, ELLIOT CALVIN, lawyer, writer; b. Mpls., Nov. 12, 1939; s. Sam S. and Claire Sylvia (Feller) R.; m. Sally Smayling; 1 child, Margaret. B.A. summa cum laude, U. Minn., 1961; J.D., Harvard U. (Fulbright fellow), 1964. Assoc. project dir. Brookings Inst., Washington, 1966-67; fgn. service officer, legal advisor U.S. Dept. State, Washington, 1968-73; nat. law dir. Anti-Defamation League, N.Y.C., 1973-74; legal dir. Minn. Public Interest Research Group, Mpls., 1974-77; admitted to Minn. bar, 1966, D.C. 1968, N.Y., 1974; pvt. practice law, Mpls., 1977—; adj. prof. William Mitchell Coll. Law, St. Paul, 1983—. State bd. dirs. YMCA Youth in Govt. Program, 1981-84 ; v.p. Twin Cities chpt. Am. Jewish Com., 1980-84 ; mem. Minn. House of Reps., 1978-82, asst. floor leader (whip), 1981-82; pres., dir. North Star Legal Found., 1983—; mem. citizens adv. com. Voyageurs Nat. Park, 1979-81. Recipient Legis. Evaluation Assembly Legis. Excellence award, 1980; North Star award, U. Minn., 1961. Mem. Am. Bar Assn., Harvard Law Sch. Assn., Minn. Bar Assn., Am. Legion, Mensa, Phi Beta Kappa. Republican. Jewish. Contbr. articles to profl. and scholarly jours., newspapers, popular magazines; author: (with Zelman Cowen) Sir John Latham and Other Papers, 1965. Home: 3901 W 25th St Saint Louis Park MN 55416 Office: 500 Plymouth Bldg Minneapolis MN 55402

ROTHENBERG, JUDY LOU, psychologist; b. Pitts., Dec. 8, 1951; s. Henry Edwin and Ruth (Anderson) R. BA, U. Rochester, 1973; MEd, Harvard U., 1974; postgrad. PhD, U. Minn. Lic. psychologist, Minn. Grant coordinator U. Minn. Ctr. for Early Edn. and Devel., Mpls., 1978-79; staff psychologist Wilder Child Guidance Clinic, St. Paul, 1979-80, Wilder Clinic, Burnsville, Minn., 1980-84; br. dir. Wilder Clinic, Mounds View, Minn., 1984—; cons. St. John's Project Pathfinder, St. Paul, 1986-87; community faculty mem. Metro State U., St. Paul, 1986-87; co-chmn. Ramsey County Am. Pub. Welfare Assn. Task Force on Family and Home Based Services, St. Paul, 1986-87; vice-chmn. ann. meeting Psychol. Assn., 1988. Mem. Am. Psychol. Assn., Minn. Psychol. Assn. (comms. coordinator 1983-86), Minn. Women's Psychologists, Nat. Assn. for Edn. of Young Children, Minn. Assn. for Edn. of Young Children (bd. dirs. 1983-85), Nat. Council Jewish Women. Democrat. Avocations: plants, cross-country skiing, dancing, music. Office: Wilder Clinic Northwest Branch 5100 NE Edgewood Dr Moundsview MN 55112

ROTHENBERG, MARC, real estate attorney; b. Cleve., Jan. 25, 1956; s. Robert and Florence (Lukin) R.; m. Cheryl E. Wolkoff, Nov. 25, 1958; children: Jessica Ann, Matthew Phillip. AB, Miami U., Oxford, Ohio, 1978; JD, Case Western Res. U., 1981. Bar: Ohio, 1983. Real estate atty. Fabri-Ctrs. of Am. Inc., Cleve., 1983—. Trustee Beachwood (Ohio) Civic League, 1985—. Mem. ABA, Cleve. Bar Assn., Cuyahoga County Bar Assn., Internat. Council Shopping Ctrs., Ohio State Bar Assn. Avocations: golf, basketball, reading, family. Office: Fabri-Ctrs of Am Inc 23550 Commerce Park Rd Cleveland OH 44122

ROTHMAN, MICHAEL DAVID, communications executive, public official; b. Chgo., Feb. 26, 1942; s. Lewis and Ann Doris (Glotzer) R.; m. Jacqueline Alice Harlow, July 16, 1967. Student U. Tulsa, Roosevelt U. Founder, pres. L&M Sales Co., Chgo., 1965—; asst. to pres., purchasing agt. Shear-Prinz Assocs. Inc., Chgo., 1967-68; asst. to pres. Weil Service Products Corp., Chgo., 1968-70; exec. v.p. PriTec; Chgo. v.p. Pvt. Telecommunications, Inc., Chgo. Rep. nominee Ill. Senate, 1976; trustee Regional Bd. Sch. Trustees, Cook County, Ill., 1974—, pres., 1976, 84, 86; Rep. committeeman 50th ward City of Chgo., 1984—. Lodges: Rotary, Masons, B'nai B'rith (pres. 1975-76). Home: 1402 W Busse Ave Mount Prospect IL 60056 Office: Pritec 5800 Lincoln Ave Chicago IL 60659 also: 2701 W Howard Chicago IL 60645

ROTHMEIER, STEVEN GEORGE, airline executive; b. Mankato, Minn., Oct. 4, 1946; s. Edwin George and Alice Joan (Johnson) R. BBA, U. Notre Dame, 1968; MBA, U. Chgo., 1972. Corp. fin. analyst Northwest Airlines, Inc., St. Paul, 1973; mgr. econ. analysis Northwest Airlines, Inc., 1973-78, dir. econ. planning, 1978, v.p. fin., treas., 1978-82, exec. v.p., treas., dir., 1982-83, exec. v.p. fin. and adminstrn., treas., dir., 1983, pres., chief operating officer, 1983; pres., chief exec. officer 1985-86, chmn., chief exec. officer, 1986—; bd. dirs. First Bank System, Honeywell, Inc.; trustee Minn. Mut. Life Ins., U. Chgo. Served to 1st lt. U.S. Army, 1969-71. Decorated Bronze Star. Mem. Air Transport Assn. Am. (chmn. econs. and fin. council 1981). Republican. Roman Catholic. Clubs: Mpls.; Minn. Office: Northwest Airlines Inc Minneapolis-Saint Paul Internat Airport Saint Paul MN 55111

ROTHROCK, JOHN STEVEN, advertising executive; b. Rahway, N.J., Sept. 14, 1954; s. John Albert and Phyllis Evelyn (Andrick) R.; m. Dru Ann Christein. AA in Visual Communications, Art Inst. Pitts., 1974. Draftsman, artist Allegheny County Dept. Planning, Pitts., 1974-76; graphic designer B.A. Graphics, Columbus, 1976-77; asst. art dir. Angeletti/Heller Advt., Columbus, Ohio, 1977-83; art dir., advt. mgr. Goal Systems Internat.,

Columbus, 1983—. Recipient Brochure Design award Scheufelen Paper Co., 1985. Columbus Soc. Communicating Arts. Avocations: World War history, mil. miniatures. Office: Goal Systems Internat 5455 N High St Columbus OH 43214-1193

ROTHSCHILD, JEFFREY L., meat packing company executive. Pres. M. Rothschild and Sons, Inc., Chgo. Office: M Rothschild & Sons Inc 311 N Aberdeen Chicago IL 60607 *

ROTHSTEIN, JAMES ANDREW, computer consultant; b. N.Y.C., Dec. 23, 1955; s. Albert Rothstein and Louise (Lehrer) Behrens. BS, MIT, 1977; MBA, U. Chgo., 1984. Ptnr. Dolce, Rothstein & Assocs., Chgo., 1984—. Mem. Chgo. Computer Soc. (bd. dirs. 1986, coordinator 1985-86), Sigma Xi. Office: Dolce Rothstein & Assocs 53 W Jackson #1636 Chicago IL 60604

ROTHWELL, RUSSELL GEORGE, controller; b. Rockville Centre, N.Y., Apr. 15, 1949; s. Robert George and Sylvia Anita (Pihlgren) R.; m. Linda Jean Tengblad, May 20, 1972 (div. June 1975); m. Susan Ruth Bloedel, July 5, 1975; children: Angela, Nicole, Stephen. BSBA, Valparaiso U., 1972. CPA, Md., W.Va. Acct. supr. Corning Glass Works, Martinsburg, W.Va., 1976-78; plant controller Paden City, W.Va., 1978-80; sr. internal auditor ITT Power Systems, Galion, Ohio, 1980-82; comptroller fluid handling div. ITT Domestic Pump, Shippensburg, Pa., 1982-84; div. controller The Vollrath Co., Sheboygan, Wis., 1984-85; corp. controller Hayssen Mfg. Co., Sheboygan, Wis., 1986—. Mem. Am. Inst. CPA's. Republican. Lutheran. Club: Sheboygan Yacht. Lodge: Masons. Avocations: sailing, reading, computers, camping, home mechanics and improvement. Home: 634 Mayflower Ave Sheboygan WI 53083 Office: Hayssen Mfg Co Hwy 42 N Sheboygan WI 53082-0571

ROTO, ROBERT RUSSELL, sales manager; b. Elgin, Ill., Aug. 1, 1958; s. Richard A. and Barbara Hellen (Angus) R.; m. Amy Lee Lechelt, Mar. 29, 1983; children: Leigh Taylor, Alexander Zachary. BS, No. Ill. U., 1980. Pres. Investrex Corp., Glenview, Ill., 1982-83; gen. sales mgr. Roto Lincoln-Mercury, Arlington Heights, Ill., 1980—. Republican. Episcopalian. Avocations: marathon running, martial arts, golf, scuba diving. Office: Roto Lincoln-Mercury 1555 E Rand Rd Arlington Heights IL 60004

ROTOLO, GWEN ELIZABETH PARDUN, interior designer; b. Oak Park, Ill., Sept. 27, 1940; d. Eugene Stewart Pardun and Elizabeth Ruth (Hafner) Pardun/Quitsch; divorced; children: Donna Marie, Michael Eugene, Elise Suzanne. AS in Interior Design, Harper Coll., 1974; student, Art Inst. of Chgo., 1958-60. Interior designer Color Councellors, Evanston, Ill., 1971-72, J.C. Penney, Schaumburg, Ill., 1972-73, Hillside Design, Saugus, Mass., 1974-77, Drexel/Heritage Showcase, Burlington, Mass., 1978-80, Homer's Furniture, Skokie and Palatine, Ill., 1980-85; prin. interior design Interiors by Gwen, Schaumburg, 1985—. Mem. Internat. Soc. Interior Designers, Am. Soc. Interior Designers, Ill. Design Soc., Harper Interior Design Assn. Home and Office: 130 Century Ct Schaumburg IL 60193

ROTTMAN, KENNETH PAUL, dentist, research technician; b. Chgo., Mar. 22, 1936; s. Morris Maxwell and Marion Esther (Marcus) R.; m. Patricia Blossom Gordon, Mar. 21, 1961 (div. 1977); children—Alan Gordon, Matthew Eric, Laura Francine. B.S., Tulane U., 1958; B.S., U. Ill.-Chgo., 1962, D.D.S., 1964. Pvt. practice dentistry, Chgo., 1964—; designer Gordon San. Systems, Chgo., 1964-65; technician Blood Bank, U. Ill. Hosp., Chgo., 1962-64, med. research technician, 1958-62; dir. dentistry Union Health Service Dental Ctr., Chgo., 1970-76. Contbr. to Quintessence Internat. Jour. Served with USAR, 1959-61. Fellow Acad. Dentistry Internat.; mem. Acad. Gen. Dentistry (master), Soc. Baromedicine and Dentistry (founder, pres. 1980—), Chgo. Acad. Gen. Dentistry (pres. 1984), Chgo. Dental Soc. (chmn. spl. patient needs com. 1985, sec. limited attendance clinic program com. 1987, pres. elect North Side br. 1987), Ill. Acad. Gen. Dentistry (pub. info. officer 1984), Am. Equilibration Soc., Internat. Congress Oral Implantologists, Am. Acad. Functional Orthodontists, U. Ill. Coll. Dentistry Alumni Assn. (bd. dirs., newsletter editor 1985). Jewish. Clubs: Sea Lancers, League Underwater Photographers. Avocations: photography, underwater photography, scuba diving, woodworking. Office: Grand Mich Dental Assoc 535 N Michigan Ave Chicago IL 60611

ROTUNDA, MARCIA ANN, lawyer; b. LaPorte, Ind., Mar. 3, 1946; d. Charles M. and Loretta M. (Luther) Mainland; m. Ronald D. Rotunda, 1969; children: Nora, Mark. BA, Valparaiso U., 1968; JD, Harvard U., 1971. Bar: Ill. 1977, D.C. 1971. Atty. congl. research service Library of Congress, Washington, 1971-74; law clk. to presiding justice U.S. Ct. Appeals (4th dist.)Ill., Urbana, 1974-77; sole practice Champaign, Ill., 1977-86; atty. office univ. counsel U. Ill., Urbana, 1986—. Mem. Nat. Assn. Coll. and Univ. Attys., LWV (bd. dirs. 1983-86), Valparaiso U. Guild (pres. 1987—). Office: U Ill Office Univ Counsel 258 Adminstrn Bldg Urbana IL 61801

ROUPP, ALBERT ALLEN, architect; b. Wichita, Kans., Sept. 12, 1930; s. Walter Roy and Bertha Pearl (Schantz) R.; m. Susan Carol Nagy, Sept. 3, 1966; children: Aimee, Christopher. Student, Staatliche Hochschule für Bildende Kunste, Hamburg, Germany; AA, Hesston Coll., 1950; BS in Architecture, Ill. Inst. Tech., 1964. Registered architect, Ill. Project architect C. F. Murphy, Chgo., 1964-74; prof. Ill. Inst. Tech., Chgo., 1966-74; tech. procedures administr. Capital Devel. Corp., Chgo., 1974-78; sr. v.p. Coder Taylor Assn., Kenilworth, Ill., 1978-82, prin., pres., 1982-85; owner, pres. Albert A. Roupp Assn., Evanston, Ill., 1985—. Plan commr. Evanston Plan Commn., 1970-74. AIA. Democrat. Office: 2530 Crawford Ave Evanston IL 60201

ROURK, JAMES ROBERT, information systems executive; b. Gary, S.D., Sept. 7, 1948; s. Robert N. and Dorothy Marie (Dinger) R.; m. Darcy Lyn Wilbur, Aug. 17, 1972; children—Winona Kathleen, Kelsey Rebecca, Claire Colleen. B.S. in Music Edn., Dakota State Coll., 1970; M.B.A., Kans. State U., 1982. Condr., dir. North Queensland Youth Orch., Innisfail, Australia, 1974-76; mgr. bus. Susan Warden Dancers, Manhattan, Kans., 1979; researcher, instr. Kans. State U., Manhattan, 1980-82; pres. Rourk Entertainment Corp., Manhattan, 1980—; programmer, analyst Kans. Farm Bur., Manhattan, 1982—. Bd. dirs. McCain Auditorium, Kans. State U. Author: Computing for Elementary School Students, 1982. Composer: Wider Horizons, 1978; columnist, crutic Manhattan Mercury. Contbr. artilces to profl. jours. Deacon, First Christian Ch., Manhattan, 1982—, dir. brass choir, 1982—; vol. United Way, 1984—; chmn. voter registration Dem. Party, 1982. Served to sgt. U.S. Army, 1970-73. Yamaha Internat. scholar, 1972. Mem. Winjammers Internat., Nat. Assn. Jazz Educators, Performing Arts Council, C. of C., Phi Mu Alpha. Club: Music Fedn. (pres. 1984) (Manhattan). Avocations: gardening, carpentry, composing. Home: 2100 Goodnow Circle Manhattan KS 66502 Office: Kansas Farm Bur Services 2321 Anderson Manhattan KS 66502

ROUSE, JOHN RATCLIFFE, fine art consultant, former art museum dir., curator; b. Cunningham, Kans., Aug. 27, 1917; s. John R. and Edith Belle (Cole) R. B.A., Bethel Coll., Newton, Kans., 1939. With Fourth Nat. Bank & Trust Co., Wichita, Kans., 1940-46; asst. and mgr. Commodore Hotel, Wichita, 1946-56; art and antique cons., 1955—; dir., curator Wichita Art Assn. Galleries and Sch. Art 1972-83; ret. 1983. Mem. Wichita Hist. Mus. Assn. (trustee 1972-78), Wichita Art Assn. (pres. bd. 1973-75), Wichita Art Mus. Mems. Found., Fine Arts Council, Am. Assn. Mus., Mountain Plains Mus. Conf., Kans. Mus. Assn., Am. Crafts Council, Midwest Enamelist Guild, Newton Art Assn., Nat. Assn. Cert. Antique and Art Appraisers, Appraisers Assn. Am. Republican. Christian Scientist. Home: 115 S Rutan St Wichita KS 67218

ROUSH-ANTES, MARY JENNIFER, ballet instructor; b. Parkersburg, W.Va., Sept. 23, 1959; d. Paul Leighton and Alice Margaret (Sheridan) Roush; m. James Steven Antes, Oct. 17, 1981; 1 child, Emily Marie. BA in Ballet, U. Akron, 1977. Teaching asst. Schrader Sch. Ballet, Belpre, Ohio, 1976-77, guest artist, 1979, guest choreographer, 1985—; spl. lectr. U. Akron, Ohio, 1979-80, instr. ballet, 1981—. Vol. United Cerebral Palsy, Akron, 1984, Sandwich Program St. Bernards, Akron, 1986. Democrat. Roman Catholic. Avocations: needlework, sewing, reading. Office: U Akron Ballet Ctr 354 E Market St Akron OH 44312

ROUSSEAU, MARK OWEN, sociologist; b. Ft. Wayne, Ind., Apr. 5, 1940; s. Richard Jackson and Wilma (Combs) R.; B.A., Ind. U., 1962, M.A., 1966; Ph.D., U. N.C., Chapel Hill, 1971; cert. III Dégré, Alliance Francaise, Paris, 1972; m. Marion Frances Pruss, Aug. 18, 1973; 1 son, Mark Owen. Asst. instr. U. N.C., 1966-68; mem. faculty U. Nebr., Omaha, 1968—, asst. prof. sociology, 1971-82, assoc. prof., 1982—, sabbatical research leave, 1985; Nat. Endowment Humanities fellow, summer 1979; funded research, Paris, 1982. Mem. Am. Sociol. Assn., AAUP, Inst. Icarian Investigations (pres. 1976-83), Midwest Sociol. Soc., Am. Assn. Tchrs. French, Conf. Group on French Politics and Soc., La Société Tocqueville, Ind. U. Alumni Assn., Alpha Kappa Delta. Contbr. articles to profl. jours. Home: 5001 Izard St Omaha NE 68132 Office: Dept Sociology Univ Nebr Omaha NE 68182

ROVAK, ABE SAMUEL, store planner; b. St. Louis, Aug. 8, 1912; s. Harry and Goldie (Rawak) R.; m. Marie Reinfeld, Nov. 24, 1938; children: Gloria (dec.), Richard. Student, Washington U., St. Louis, 1930-31. Cert. tchr., Mo. V.p. St. Louis Fixture Mfg. Co., 1931-44, 45-63; product control supr. McDonnell Aircraft, St. Louis and Memphis, 1942-45; pres. A.S.R. Designs, Ltd., St. Louis, 1963—. Mem. Inst. Store Planners (internat. sec. 1983—). Republican. Jewish. Avocations: teaching, volunteering. Home: 12338 Crystal View Ln Saint Louis MO 63131 Office: ASR Designs Ltd PO Box 31704 Saint Louis MO 63131

ROVIARO, SUSAN ELIZABETH, clinical psychologist; b. Pittsfield, Mass., Sept. 10, 1949; d. Louis Peter and Elizabeth (Angelini) R.; m. Robert Paul Wisdom, June 18, 1983. B.A., U. Mass., 1971; M.A., U. Kans., 1977, Ph.D., 1981. Lic. psychologist. Grad. research and teaching asst. dept. psychology U. Kans., Lawrence, 1974-77; psychologist in tng. VA Med. Center, Topeka, 1975-77, research asst. depts. neuropsychology and medicine, 1977-79; predoctoral fellow dept. psychiatry Mount Zion Hosp. and Med. Center, San Francisco, 1979-80; clin. dir. Pawnee Mental Health Services, Manhattan, Kans., 1980—; health profl. affiliate Meml. and St. Mary's hosps., Manhattan. Mem. Am. Psychol. Assn., Kans. Psychol. Assn. (bd. govs. 1984-86), Phi Beta Kappa. Home: 812 Colorado St Manhattan KS 66502 Office: 2001 Claflin Rd Manhattan KS 66502

ROVNER, ILANA DIAMOND, federal judge. b. 1938; m. Richard N. Rovner. AB, Bryn Mawr Coll., 1960; postgrad., U. London King's Coll., 1961, Georgetown U., 1961-63; JD, Ill. Inst. Tech., 1966. Judicial clk., Chgo., 1972-73; chief pub. protection U.S. Atty.'s Office, Chgo., 1973-77; dep. gov., legal counsel Gov. James R. Thompson, Chgo., 1977-84; dist. judge, U.S. Dist. Ct. (no. dist.) Ill., Chgo., 1984—. Recipient Spl. Commendation award U.S. Dept. Justice, 1975, 76, Ann. Nat. Law and Social Justice Leadership award The League to Improve the Community, 1975, Ann. Guardian Police award, 1977, Profl. Achievement award Ill. Inst. Tech. Chgo. Kent Coll. Law, 1986; named Today's Chgo. Woman of Yr., 1985, Woman of Yr., The Chgo. Woman's Club, 1986; honored by Midwest Women's Ctr., 1986. Mem. ABA, Ill. State Bar Assn., Chgo. Bar Assn., Women's Bar Assn. Ill., Fed. Bar Assn. (following offices with Chgo. chpt. judicial selection com. 1977-80, treas. 1978-79, sec. 1979-80, 2d v.p. 1980-81, 1st v.p. 1981-82, pres. 1982-83, nat. 2d v.p. 7th cir. 1984, v.p. 7th cir. 1986), Chgo. Council Lawyers, The Decalogue Soc., Kappa Beta Pi. Office: US Dist Ct US Courthouse 219 S Dearborn St Chambers 1988 Chicago IL 60604 *

ROVNER, RALPH ALAN, psychologist; b. Mpls., Oct. 22, 1953; s. Louis and Anne (Katzman) R. BS, U. Minn., 1976, MA, 1978, PhD, 1983. Lic. cons. psychologist, Minn. Pvt. practice psychology Mpls. and St. Paul, 1983—. Contbr. articles to profl. jours. I.S. Joseph scholar, Mpls., 1978-79. Mem. Am. Assn. Marriage and Family Therapists (cert.), Minn. Psychol. Assn., Soc. Personality Assessment, Phi Kappa Phi, Phi Beta Kappa. Avocation: travel, fishing. Office: Ramsey Profl Bldg 311 Ramsey St Saint Paul MN 55102

ROWAN, ROBERT DALE, transportation executive; b. Holland, Mich., Mar. 27, 1922; s. Joseph Henry and Mabel Barbara (Streur) R.; m. Ruth Ann Lyons, June 17, 1983; children: Richard Paul, Kristine Louise, Ruthanne Marie. BS, Mich. State U., 1947. CPA, Mich. Audit supr. Touche, Ross and Co., CPA's, Detroit, 1947-55; controller Fruehauf Corp., Detroit, 1955-63, v.p., controller, 1963-65, v.p. fin., 1965-69, exec. v.p. fin., 1969-72, also bd. dirs., pres., chief operating officer, 1972-74, pres., chief exec. officer, 1974-80, chmn., pres., chief exec. officer, 1980-81, chmn. bd., chief exec. officer, 1981—; bd. dirs. Fruehauf Internat. Ltd., Fruehauf de Mex., Fruehauf France S.A., Decatur Aluminum Co., Jacksonville Shipyards, Inc., also others. Served to capt. U.S. Army, 1942-46, 50-52. Mem. Mich. Assn. CPA's, Detroit C. of C., Nat. Def.-Transp. Assn. Republican. Presbyterian. Clubs: Oakland Hills Country, Detroit, Detroit Athletic, Econ., Renaissance (Detroit); Sky (N.Y.C.); Firestone Country (Akron, Ohio), Hundred. Lodge: Masons. Office: Fruehauf Corp 10900 Harper Ave Detroit MI 48213

ROWDEN, JOEL WAYNE, marketing analyst; b. Cedar Rapids, Iowa, June 9, 1953; s. Irvin W. and Merri F. (Bucknell) R. BA, Columbia U., 1975, MBA, 1979. Pvt. practice. mgmt. cons. N.Y.C., 1979-81; product analyst Health Care Systems, Eden Prairie, Minn., 1982-83; mktg. analyst Filmtec Corp., Mpls., 1983-85, sr. mktg. analyst, 1985—. Republican. Episcopalian. Office: Filmtec Corp 7200 Ohms Ln Minneapolis MN 55435

ROWE, HARVEY JOHN, building materials company executive; b. Oshkosh, Wis., Jan. 29, 1936; s. Harvey Jackson and Grace Linnea (Anderson) R.; B.A., U. Mo., 1959; m. Marjorie Susan Beckman, Feb. 28, 1959; children—Richard Edward, Renee Suzanne, Risa Lee. Mgmt. trainee, advt. merchandiser Walgreen Co., Chgo., 1954-63; buyer, asst. purchasing mgr. USG Industries, Chgo., 1963-72, mktg. mgr. chems. div., 1972-79, group dir. mktg. services, 1982-84, gen. mgr. metals div. USG Industries Inc., 1984-87, wall div. USG Interiors, 1987—; gen. mgr. Arrowhead Drywall Supplies, Olathe, Kans., 1979-82. Trustee Village of Deer Park, Ill., 1975-79; pres., cofounder Barrington (Ill.) Area Hockey League, 1973-74; pres. Kansas City Amateur Hockey League, 1981-82. Served with USN, 1958. Mem. Steel Service Center Inst., Sigma Phi Epsilon. Republican. Christian Scientist. Home: 25876 Tara Dr Barrington IL 60010 Office: USG Interiors 101 S Wacker Dr Chicago IL 60606

ROWE, JACK FIELD, electric utility executive; b. Minn., May 10, 1927; s. William F. and Anna (Stenborg) R.; m. Mary E. Moen, Mar. 26, 1955; 1 dau., Lizette Ann. B.E.E., U. Minn., 1950. Registered profl. engr., Minn., Wis. With Minn. Power and Light Co., Duluth, 1950—; asst. to pres. Minn. Power and Light Co., 1966-67, v.p., 1967-68, exec. v.p., 1969-74, pres., 1974-84, chief exec. officer, 1978—, chmn., 1979—, also mem. exec. com., dir.; chmn. bd., chief exec. officer FiberCore, Inc., Minn. Paper, Inc., So. States Utilities, Universal Telephone, Inc., Topeka Group, Inc., NorLight, Inc.; mem. exec. bd. Nat. Electric Reliability Council, 1970-73; vice chmn. Mid Continent Area Reliability Council, 1970-71, chmn., 1972-73; mem. bus. and econs. adv. bd. U. Minn., Duluth, 1980; bd. dirs. Waldorf Corp., St. Paul, First Bank-Duluth, Edison Electric Inst., Pub. Utilities Reports. Past bd. dirs., v.p. Duluth Jr. C. of C.; mem. exec. bd. Lake Superior council Boy Scouts Am., 1967-75, chmn., Explorers, 1968-72; comml. chmn. Duluth United Fund, 1960-61; vice chmn. Duluth United Way, 1975, chmn., 1976, pres. elect, 1981, U.S. Savs. Bond chmn., St. Louis County, Minn., 1974-77; chmn. St. Louis County Heritage and Arts Center, 1979-81; pres. NE Minn. Devel./Assn., 1981-83; mem. Minn. Bus. Partnership, 1979—; bd. dirs. Minn. Safety Council, 1979-85, Duluth Downtown Devel. Corp., 1979-81, Duluth Growth Co., 1984-85, Greysolon Mall Corp., 1980-86, Duluth Superior Area Community Found., 1984-86, Duluth Clin. Edn. and Research Found., 1985-86, Benedictine Health System, 1985—; mem. adv. bd. exec. program U. Minn., 1979; adv. council Inst. Tech., 1979; mem. Minn. High Tech. Council, 1982-87. Served with USNR, 1945-46. Recipient Distinguished Service award Duluth Jr. C. of C., 1960; Outstanding Leadership award in energy conversion scis. N.Y.C. sect. ASME, 1980, Outstanding Achievement award U. Minn. Alumni Assn., 1986; named Chief Exec. Officer of Yr., Fin. World mag., 1986; Jack F. Rowe Chair of Engring. named in his honor U. Minn., Duluth, 1986. Mem. NAM (dir. 1975-78), IEEE, Electric Info. Council (pres. 1978-82), North Cen. Electric Assn., Duluth C. of C. (pres. 1972-73, exec. com., bd. dirs.), Kappa Eta Kappa. Lutheran. Clubs: Minneapolis; Engineers (Duluth), Rotary (Duluth) (pres. 1974-75), Kitchi Gammi (Duluth) (dir. 1979—, pres. 1985—), Masons, Shriners. Home: 630 Valley Dr Duluth MN 55804 Office: Minn Power & Light Co 30 W Superior St Duluth MN 55802

ROWE, JAMES MARTIN, pottery manufacturing company executive; b. Ashland, Wis., Oct. 13, 1947; s. Oscar John and and Dorothy (Ruth) R.; m. Kristine C. Clarenbach, Sept. 28, 1974; children: Kily, Erik, Tyler. BS, U. Wis., Whitewater, 1971. Pres., founder Rowe Pottery Works, Cambridge, Wis., 1975—; bd. dirs. M&I Bank of Cambridge, Wis. Mem. Cambridge C. of C. (v.p. 1986-87). Office: Rowe Pottery Works Inc 404 England St Cambridge WI 53523

ROWE, KAREN SUE HOBBS, chemist; b. Topeka, Dec. 21, 1957; d. David Thomas and Fern (Brown) Hobbs; m. Bruce Foster Rowe, May 19, 1979. BS in Biology, Southwestern Coll., Winfield, Kans., 1979. Mgmt. info. systems specialist SER Jobs for Progress, Wichita, Kans., 1979-80, mgmt. info. officer, 1980-81; quality control chemist Cargill, Inc., Wichita, 1981-86, sr. quality control chemist, 1986—. Booth chmn. Diez y Seis Fiesta, Wichita, 1980-81. Republican. Methodist. Avocations: working with youth, gardening, reading, music, sailing.

ROWE, MAE IRENE, investment company executive; b. Gardner, Mass., Dec. 6, 1927; d. Clifford Wesley and Mertie (Moore) Mann; m. Willard Chase Rowe, June 18, 1951 (div. 1979); children—Gail B. Rowe Simons, Bruce C. B.A. with high honor, Am. Internat. Coll., 1949. Cert. real property adminstr. Social worker City of Montague, Turners Falls, Mass., 1949-51; mgr. Park Investment Co., Cleve., 1979—. Pres., v.p., bd. dirs. Park Ridge Counseling Service, Ill., 1972-76; clerk Village of Kildeer, Ill., 1977; bd. dirs. Maine Township Mental Health Service, Park Ridge, 1975-76; trustee Heathermore Condominium Assn., 1987. Mem. Cleve. Bldg. Owners Mgrs. Assn. (mem. edn. com. 1983—), Bldg. Owners Mgrs. Assn. Internat., Soc. Real Property Adminstrs. (cert.), LWV (v.p., mem. city adv. com. 1973-76), Republican. Unitarian. Club: Cleve. Racquet. Avocations: tennis; computer study and operation. Home: 34108 Chagrin Blvd Apt 5103 Moreland Hills OH 44022 Office: Park Investment Co 907 Park Bldg Cleveland OH 44114

ROWE, NATHANIEL HAWTHORNE, dentist, educator; b. Hibbing, Minn., May 26, 1931; s. Nathaniel Hawthorne and Edna (Bockler) R.; m. Norma Estelle Quinlan, June 24, 1954 (div. July 1978); children: Bradford Scott, Nathaniel Edwin, Lorna Michelle, Jonathan Alan. D.D.S., B.S., U. Minn., 1955, M.S.D., 1958. Diplomate: Am. Bd. Oral Pathology. Teaching asst. dept. oral pathology Sch. Dentistry U. Minn., 1955-56, research fellow, 1956-58, clin. instr., 1958-59; asst. prof. pathology Washington U. Sch. Dentistry, St. Louis, 1959-65; asso. prof. Washington U. Sch. Dentistry, 1965-69, prof. Grad. Sch. Arts and Scis., 1966-69, vis. prof. pathology, 1969-71, chmn. dept. gen. and oral pathology, 1959-68, coordinator oral cancer teaching, 1959-68; assoc. research scientist Cancer Research Center, Columbia, Mo., 1967-71; assoc. prof. pathology Sch. Medicine U. Mich., Ann Arbor, 1969-76; prof. pathology Sch. Medicine U. Mich., 1976—, prof. dentistry Sch Dentistry, 1968—, asso. dir. Dental Research Inst., 1970—, sr. research scientist Virus Research Group, 1977—; cons. staff Jewish Hosp., St. Louis, 1960-68; cons. Ellis Fischel State Cancer Hosp., Columbia, 1967—; sci. adv. bd. Cancer Research Center, 1975-78; cons. oral pathology U.S. VA Hosps., St. Louis, 1965-68, Ann Arbor, 1973—; cons. oral pathology Mo. Dental Assn., St. Louis, 1967-69; civilian profl. cons. Office of Surgeon 5th U.S. Army, 1967-83; cons. Bur. Medicine Adv. Panel System, HEW (dental agts. adv. com. FDA), 1968-70; mem. profl. adv. council on cancer Mich. Assn. Regional Med. Programs, 1969-73; mem. policy council Met. Detroit Cancer Control Program, 1976-82. Editor: Procs. of Symposium: Salivary Glands and Their Secretion, 1972, Procs. of Symposium: Dental Plaque: Interfaces, 1973, Procs. of Symposium: Oral and Perioral Ulcerations: Cause and Control, Emphasis on Herpes Simples Virus, 1974, Procs. of Symposium: Occlusion: Research in Form and Function, 1975, Procs. of Symposium: The Scientific Basis for Evaluation of Periodontal Therapy, 1976, Procs. of Symposium: Incipient Caries of Enamel, 1977, Procs. of Symposium: Diet, Nutrition, and Dental Caries, 1978, Procs. of Symposium: Trends in the Prevention and Treatment of Periodontal Disease, 1981, Procs. of Symposium: Dental Pulp: Reactions to Restorative Material in the Presence or Absence of Infection, 1982, Procs. of Symposium: Herpes, Hepatitis and AIDS: Current Concerns of the Health Practitioner, 1983, Procs. of Symposium: Hypersensitive Dentin: Orgin and Management, 1985, Proc. of Symposium: Insights into Dentofacial Pain: Overview, Diagnosis and Treatment, 1987; mem. editorial bd.: Journ. Mo. Dental Soc, 1963-69, Bull. Greater St. Louis Dental Soc, 1964-68, Cancer, 1967—, Oral Research Abstracts, 1967-68, Jour. Dental Research, 1971-73; contbr. articles to profl. jours., also chpts. to books. Recipient D.E. Listiac award faculty U. Minn. Sch. Dentistry, 1955, Army Outstanding Civilian Service award, 1979, Tiffany Nat. award Am. Cancer Soc., 1979, Recognition award for outstanding contbns. Mich. div., 1979; named Hon. Alumnus Washington U. Sch. Dentistry, 1966. Fellow Am. Acad. Oral Pathology (councillor 1971-74, v.p. 1976-77, pres. 1977-78), Am. Coll. Dentists, Internat. Coll. Dentists; mem. AAAS, N.Y. Acad. Scis., Am. Assn. Cancer Research, ADA (cons. Council on Dental Edn. 1971-72, 75-83, mem. commn. on accreditation 1976-80, cons. Council Hosp. Dental Service 1977-81, cons. council dental therapeutics 1984—, mem. bd. appeals commn. on dental accreditation 1982—), Mich. Dental Assn. (cons. com. on cancer control 1971-77, chmn. 1978-86), Dist. Dental Assn., Mich. Soc. Pathologists, Internat. Assn. Dental Research, Royal Soc. Health (Eng.), Fedn. Dentaire Internationale, Internat. Acad. Pathology, Internat. Acad. Oral Pathology, Am. Cancer Soc. (dir. St. Louis City and County unit 1964-68, chmn. profl. edn. com. 1967-68, v.p. 1967-68, dir. Mo. div. 1965-68, bd. dirs., mem. exec. com. Mich. div. 1970—, chmn. profl. edn. com. 1973-76, v.p. Mich. div. 1977-78, pres. 1978-79, v.p. unit 1975-76, pres. 1976-77, nat. med. del. 1987—), Sigma Xi, Xi Psi Phi, Omicron Kappa Upsilon. Home: 1042 Greenhills Dr Ann Arbor MI 48105

ROWE, RICHARD LEWIS, engineering manager; b. Freeport, Ill., July 20, 1949; s. Gregory Lloyd and Darlene (Pierce) R.; m. Reba Ridge, May 10, 1975; children: Tabatha, Jay. BS in Engring., U.S. Mil. Acad., 1971; M in Engring. Adminstrn., George Washington U., 1977. Commd. 2d lt. U.S. Army, 1971, advanced through grades to capt., 1975, resigned, 1977; sr. engr. Honeywell, Freeport, 1977-78; program mgr. Honeywell, Tampa, Fla., 1978-80; mgr. design engring. Honeywell, Freeport, 1980—. Sec. Dist. 205 Sch. Bd., Warren, Ill., 1983—; pres. Warren Youth Sports, 1980-86. Decorated Army Commendation medal with oak leaf cluster, Vietnam Cross of Gallantry. Mem. Soc. Mfg. Engrs., View-Now (bd. dirs. 1985—). Methodist. Avocation: sports.

ROWE, STANFORD HUNTINGTON, II, data processing executive; b. Boston, Nov. 13, 1942; s. Stanford Huntington Sr. and Katherine Louise (Hampe) R.; children from previous marriage: David, Jeannine, Steven; m. Pamela Jeanne Hendricks, May 26, 1984. AB, U. of Redlands, Calif., 1964; MS, U. So. Calif., Los Angeles, 1966. Software specialist Dow Corning Corp., Midland, Mich., 1966-69, mgr. computer ops., 1972-76, mgr. technical support, 1976-85, mgr. telecommunications, 1985—; supr. European EDP Dow Corning Corp., Brussels, 1969-72; instr. Delta Coll., Univ. Ctr., Mich., 1973-85. Author: Business Telecommunications, 1987. Mem. Data Processing Mgmt. Assn. (past bd. dirs., Saginaw Valley chpt., chmn. 1980, 81-83, Outstanding Performance award 1984), Assn. Computing Machinery. Republican. Lutheran. Avocation: music. Home: 306 Leonard Ln Midland MI 48640 Office: Dow Corning Corp 2200 Salzburg Rd Midland MI 48686

ROWE, STEPHEN CHRISTIAN, minister, educator. BA in Philosophy with honors, Colgate U., 1967; ThM, U. Chgo., 1969, MA, 1970, PhD, 1974. Asst. prof. William James Coll. and Grand Valley State Coll., Allendale, Mich., 1972-73, coordinator, 1973-74, faculty, 1974-83; minister Fountain St. Ch., Grand Rapids, Mich., 1976-77; prof. philosophy Grand Valley State Coll., Allendale, 1983—, also chmn. dept. liberal studies; lectr. Urban Tng. Ctr., Chgo.; cons. Chgo. Theol. Inst.; part-time faculty YMCA Community Coll., Chgo. Editor: Living Beyond Crisis, 1980. Contbr. articles to profl. jours. U. Chgo. fellow, 1971-72; Danforth Found. grantee, 1977-84. Mem. Am. Acad. Religion, Am. Philos. Assn., Am. Soc. Christian Ethics, Assn. Integrative Studies, Assn. Gen. and Liberal Studies, Ctr. Process Studies, Chgo. Social Ethics, Soc. for Values in Higher Edn., U. Chgo. Com. Religion and Am. Pub. Life, Mich. Assn. Governing Bds., Phi Kappa Phi. Home:

1625 Seminole SE Grand Rapids MI 49506 Office: Grand Valley State Coll Allendale MI 49401

ROWE, SUELLEN, auditor; b. Bremen, Ind., Sept. 9, 1956; d. Paul Otho and Patricia Ruth (Minnick) R. BBA cum laude, Hanover (Ind.) Coll., 1978. CPA. Staff auditor Ernst & Whinney, South Bend, Ind., 1979-1980, advanced staff auditor, 1980-81, sr. auditor, 1981-82; sr. internal auditor Wickes Cos., Wheeling, Ill., 1982-83, supervising sr. internal auditor, 1983-85, mgr. controls evaluation and audit, 1985—. Mem. Mus. of Sci. & Industry, 1984-87, choir St. Paul United Ch. Christ, 1982—; treas. United Religious Community, 1982, Discovery Hall Assocs., 1982; bd. fin. Zion United Ch. of Christ, 1982, tchr., mem. choir 1980-82. Mem. Am. Inst. CPA's. Republican. Avocations: sewing, biking, swimming, reading. Home: 293 N Ashland Ave Palatine IL 60067 Office: Wickes Cos Inc 1400 S Wolf Rd Bldg 200 Wheeling IL 60090

ROWE, TIMOTHY ARTHUR, lawyer; b. Mansfield, Ohio, Aug. 22, 1957; s. Donald Arthur Rowe and Phyllis Elaine (Winemiller) Rusk; m. Kathleen Ann Volk, Aug. 26, 1979. BA with distinction, Ind. U., 1981, JD cum laude, 1984; BS in Biblical Studies summa cum laude, Way Coll. of Emporia, 1981. Ptnr. Austin, Rowe & Hamilton, Indpls., 1984—; restaurant owner Sigreto's Restaurant, Carmel, Ind., 1985—. Chmn. Young Americans for Freedom, Bloomington, Ind., 1979-81, Ind. U. campaigns Reagan and Quayle, Bloomington, 1980; mem. Domestic Violence Counsel, Indpls., 1986. Mem. ABA, Ind. Bar Assn., Assn. Trial Lawyers Am., 7th Circuit Bar Assn., Ind. Restaurant Assn. Avocations: golf, racquetball, Biblical research. Home: 1016 Kessler Blvd E Indianapolis IN 46204 Office: Austin Rowe & Hamilton 22 E Washington Suite 312 Indianapolis IN 46204

ROWEKAMP, JOHN DAVID, surgeon; b. Mpls., Aug. 14, 1944; s. John Francis and Esther Helen (Yeske) R.; m. Betsy Ann Lascola, June 8, 1968; children: Todd, Eric, Scott, Adam. BS in Natural Sci. summa cum laude, St. John's U., Collegeville, Minn., 1966; MD magna cum laude, Loyola U., Maywood, Ill., 1969. Diplomate Am. Bd. gen. surgery. Commd. ensign USNR, 1966, advanced through ranks to comdr., 1976; intern USN Hosp., Portsmouth, Va., 1969-70; resident in gen. surgery USN Hosp., Portsmouth, 1970-74; staff surgeon USN, Great Lakes, Ill., 1974-77, Winona (Minn.) Clinic Ltd., 1977—; med. advisor Altura (Minn.) Ambulance Service, 1978—; chief of surgery Community Meml. Hosp., Winona, 1985—. Bd. dirs. Winona Area Hosp. Coalition, 1985; mem. Cathedral Adult Choir, Winona, 1987. Recipient Roche award Roche Co., 1969. Mem. ACS, Minn. Med. Assn., Minn. Surgical Soc., Winona County Med. Soc. (v.p. 1986-87). Republican. Roman Catholic. Avocations: hunting, tennis, camping, trap and skeet shooting. Home: 1553 Clubview Rd Winona MN 55987 Office: Winona Clinic Ltd 420 E Sarnia Winona MN 55987

ROWELL, WILLIAM FRANCIS, air force officer; b. Salem, Mass., Dec. 20, 1948; s. John Arthur and Alice Rita (Harrison) R.; m. Kathleen Ann Brody, Dec. 14, 1974; children: Bryan, Jennifer. BS in Math., U.S. Air Force Acad., 1970; MS in Ops. Research, Stanford U., 1971; PhD in Ops. Research, U. Tex., 1979. Commd. 2d lt. USAF, 1970, advanced through grades to lt. col., 1986; test analyst 3246th Test Wing, Eglin AFB, Fla., 1971-72; systems analyst Dept. Armament Systems, Eglin AFB, Fla., 1972-74; project mgr. Program Offices, Wright-Patterson AFB, Ohio, 1974-77; strategic forces analyst Pentagon, Washington, 1980-83; asst. prof. of ops. research Air Force Inst. Tech., Wright-Patterson AFB, 1984—; research assoc. Harvard U., Cambridge, Mass., 1983-84. Author Arms Control Verification: A Guide to Policy Issues for the 1980's, 1986. Mem. Inst. Mgmt. Sci., Ops. Research Soc. Am., Omega Rho, Phi Kappa Phi. Democrat. Methodist. Avocations: golf, bowling, chess, marathon running. Home: 1610 Diplomat Dr Beavercreek OH 45432 Office: Air Force Inst Tech/ENS Wright Patterson AFB OH 45433

ROWLAND, JAMES RICHARD, electrical engineering educator; b. Muldrow, Okla., Jan. 24, 1940; s. Richard Cleveland and Imogene Beatrice (Angel) R.; m. Jonell Condren, Aug. 24, 1963; children: Jennifer Lynn, Angela Janel. BSEE, Okla. State U., 1962; MSEE, Purdue U., 1964, PhD in Elec. Engring., 1966. Registered profl. engr., Okla. Instr. Purdue U., West Lafayette, Ind., 1964-65; from asst. to assoc. prof. Ga. Inst. Tech., Atlanta, 1966-71; from assoc. to full prof. Okla. State U., Stillwater, 1971-85; prof., chmn. dept. elec. and computer engring. U. Kans., Lawrence, 1985—; cons. Lockheed-Ga. Co., Marietta, 1966-71, U.S. Army Missile Command, Huntsville, Ala., 1969-79, Sandia Nat. Labs., Albuquerque, 1979. Author: Linear Control Systems, 1986; co-contbr. numerous articles to profl. jours. Mem. IEEE (edn. soc. pres. 1982-83, Centennial medal 1984, edn. soc. Achievement award 1986), Am. Assn. Engring. Edn. Republican. Methodist. Lodge: Kiwanis. Avocations: golf, gardening. Home: 2424 Free State Ct Lawrence KS 66046 Office: U Kans Dept Elec Computer Engring 1013 Learned Hall Lawrence KS 66045

ROWLAND, KENT, psychologist; b. Kittanning, Pa., Dec. 23, 1940; s. Woodrow Sanford and Jeanne Alberta (Claypool) R.; m. Constance Hope Emerson, Sept. 10, 1983; children: Holly, Jodi, Dee. BA, Mooehead State U., 1962; MEd, Wright State U., 1971; PhD, Ball State U., 1980. Lic. psychologist, Ohio. Tchr. Springfield (Ohio) Bd. Edn., 1963-69; asst. dir. Upward Bound Wittenberg U., Springfield, 1969-73; dir. ops. Springfield Opportunities Industrialization Ctr., Springfield, 1973-77; psychologist Northwest Ctr. Human Services, Lima, Ohio, 1980-83; psychologist, dir. Horizons: The Counseling Ctr Inc., Marietta, Ohio, 1983—; cons. psychologist Paulding (Ohio) Mental Health, 1982-83. Am. Psychol. Assn., Ohio Psychol. Assn., Nat. Register Health Service Providers in Psychology. Home: Rt 1 Box 56E Marietta OH 45750 Office: Horizons The Counseling Ctr Inc 822 Front St Marietta OH 45750

ROWLAND, LANDON HILL, diversified holding company executive; b. Fuquay Springs, N.C., May 20, 1937; s. Walter Elton and Elizabeth Carr (Williams) R.; m. Sarah Fidler, Dec. 29, 1959; children: Sarah Elizabeth, Matthew Hill, Joshua Carr. B.A., Dartmouth Coll., 1959; LL.B., Harvard U., 1962. Bar: Mo. Assoc. Watson, Ess, Marshall & Enggas, Kansas City, Mo., 1962-70; ptnr. Watson, Ess, Marshall & Enggas, 1970-80; v.p. Kansas City So. Industries, Inc., 1980-83, pres., chief operating officer, 1983-86, pres. chief exec. officer, 1987—, also dir.; profl. lectr. antitrust law U. Mo.-Kansas City, 1977-79; chmn. bd., dir. DST Systems, Inc., Kansas City, 1983—LDX Group, Inc., Chesterfield, Mo., 1983—, Martec Pharms., Inc., Kansas City, Mo., 1985—; dir. Boatmen's Bank & Trust Co., Kansas City, Kansas City So. Ry. Co., Am. Royal, Kansas City, Mo. Co-author: West's Mo. Practice Series. Trustee Midwest Research Inst., Kansas City, Mo.; bd. dirs. Swope Ridge Health Care Ctr., Kansas City, Lyric Opera of Kansas City; chmn. com. adv. bd. Sta. KCUR-FM, Kansas City; chmn. Met. Performing Arts Fund; bd. govs. Kansas City Art Inst., Mo., 1985—. Mem. ABA, Mo. Bar Assn., Kansas City Bar Assn., Phi Beta Kappa. Clubs: Kansas City Country, Kansas City, River. Home: Ever Glades Farm Rt 29 Kansas City MO 64166 Office: Kansas City So Industries Inc 114 W 11th St Kansas City MO 64105

ROWLISON, TERRY JAY, engineer; b. Kendallville, Ind., Aug. 9, 1958; s. Paul James and Donnabelle (Refner) R.; m. Catherine Joanne Shaner, Nov. 21, 1982; 1 child, Staci Jo. BS, Ball State U., 1982. Supr. Square D. Co., Huntington, Ind., 1982-84; quality assurance engr. Square D. Co., Huntington, 1984—. Active Big Bros. Del. County, Munice, Ind., 1981-82. Mem. Am. Soc. Quality Control, Jaycees of Huntington County, Sons of Am. Legion, Sigma Nu. Avocations: fishing, golf, boating, hiking. Home: 7117 Basel Dr Fort Wayne IN 46835 Office: Square D Co 6 Commercial Rd Huntington IN 46750

ROWND, ROBERT HARVEY, biochemistry and molecular biology educator; b. Chgo., July 4, 1937; s. Walter Lemuel and Marie Francis (Joyce) R.; m. Rosalie Anne Lowery, June 13, 1959; children: Jennifer Rose, Robert Harvey, David Matthew. B.S. in Chemistry, St. Louis U., 1959; M.A. in Med. Scis, Harvard U., 1961, Ph.D. in Biophysics, 1963. Postdoctoral fellow Med. Research Council, NIH, Cambridge, Eng., 1963-65; postdoctoral fellow Nat. Acad. Scis.-NRC, Institut Pasteur, Paris, 1965-66; prof., chmn. molecular biology and biochemistry U. Wis., Madison, 1966-81; John G. Searle prof., chmn. molecular biology and biochemistry Med. and Dental Schs., Northwestern U., Chgo., 1981—; vice chmn. Gordon Research Conf. Extra Chromosomal Elements, 1984, chmn., 1986. Contbr. numerous articles to sci. jours., books.; mem. editorial bd. Jour. of Bacteriology, 1975-81; editor, 1981—, assoc. editor plasmid, 1977—; sr. editor Advances in Plasmid Molecular Biology, 1984—; assoc. editor Jour. of Biotechnology and Med. Engring., 1986—. Mem. troop com., treas. Four Lakes council Boy Scouts Am., Madison, 1973-77, mem. People to People Program del. of microbiologists to China, 1983. Fellow NSF; Fellow NIH, 1959-66; research grantee, 1966—; tng. grantee, 1970-79; USPHS Research Career Devel. awardee, 1968-73; recipient Alumni Merit award, vis. prof. St.Louis U., 1984; hon. research prof. Biotechnology Research Ctr., Chinese Acad. Agrl. Scis., Beijing, 1987—. Mem. NIH (microbial genetics study sect. 1978-82, dir. med. scientist tng. program 1987—), Am. Soc. Microbiology, Assn. Harvard Chemists, Am. Soc. Biol. Chemists, Am. Acad. Microbiology, N.Y. Acad. Scis. Office: Northwestern University Med & Dental Schs 303 E Chicago Ave Chicago IL 60611

ROY, DENNIS ALAN, career planning administrator, social services administrator; b. Flint, Mich., Oct. 11, 1952; s. Jack B. and Phyllis J. (Hill) R.; m. Edna G. Whitter, June 1, 1973 (div. Oct. 1979); m. Nancy L. Brockway, June 19, 1982; children: Evan A., MacGregor A. BS, Cen. Mich. U., 1973, MA, 1982; MA, Ctr. Mich. U., 1984. Cert. social worker, Mich. Parole, probation officer Mich. Dept. Corrections, Flint, 1975-87; probation officer U.S. Dist. Ct., Bay City, Mich., 1987; instr. Detroit Coll. Bus., 1984—; cons. H.R.H. Assocs., Flint, 1978-80. Chairperson zoning bd. City Burton, Mich., 1985-86; council mem. UAW, Lansing, Mich., 1985-87. Mem. Am. Assn. Counseling Devel., Mich. Correctonal Assn. (trustee 1980-82), Mich. Sheriff's Assn., Fed. Probation Officers Assn. Lodge: Kiwanis (bd. dirs. Burton-Bentley chpt. 1983-87, Bay City 1987—). Home: 2254 Blackthorn Burton MI 48509

ROY, PATRICIA JANE, osteopathic physician; b. Muskegon, Mich., Feb. 27, 1956; d. Frank J. and Mary Jo (Gores) Stariha; m. Paul E. Roy, Jr., July 2, 1977; 1 dau., Jennifer Jo. Student U. Mich., 1974-75; B.S. magna cum laude, Aquinas Coll., 1978; D.O., Mich. State U., 1981. Intern, Muskegon (Mich.) Gen. Hosp., 1981-82, chief-of-staff elect, 1987, chmn. exec. staff com., 1987; practice family medicine and obstetrics, Muskegon, 1982—; mem. staff Muskegon Gen. Hosp., Muskegon Hackley Hosp. Mem. med. adv. panel Hospice, Inc.; mem. profl. edn. com. Muskegon County unit Am. Cancer Soc.; del. City of Muskegon precinct, 1979-81; chmn. citizens adv. com. reproductive health Muskegon Pub. Schs., 1985—. Named One of 5 Outstanding Young Women, Mich. Jaycees, 1984; named Bus. Woman of Yr., Quadrangle Bus. and Profl. Women, 1986. Mem. Am. Osteo. Assn., Osteo. Gen. Practitioners Mich., West Mich. Osteopathic Assn. (bd. dirs. 1984-86), Am. Med. Women's Assn., West Mich. Osteo. Assn. (dir. 1984-86), Muskegon Area Women's Med. Assn. (founder, pres.), Fedn. Bus. and Profl. Women, Muskegon Area C. of C. (bd. dirs. 1985—), Muskegon Quadrangle Club, Mich. Fedn. Bus. and Profl. Women (Young Career Woman Yr. 1983-84). Club: Century of Mich. (bd. govs.). Office: 1864 Lakeshore Dr Muskegon MI 49441

ROY, S. K., international sales executive; b. Tezpur, Assam, India; came to U.S., 1973; s. G.C. and Maya (Joarden) R.; m. Mary A. Krebs, Aug. 6, 1977. B in Math. with honors, India, 1970; M in Applied Math., Jadavpur U., Calcutta, India, 1971; MBA, Mankato State U., 1977. Dir. mktg. Katolight Corp., Mankato, Minn., 1977-80; mgr. mgmt. devel., dir. internat. sales Kato Engring. Co. div. Reliance Electric Co., Mankato, 1980—. Mem. Am. Mktg. Assn., Mankato Area C. of C. (chmn. conventions and visitors com.). Lodge: Rotary (bd. dirs.). Avocations: photography, reading, community service. Home: 142 River Hills Park Mankato MN 56001

ROY, WILFRED ELMER (WILL), educator; b. Van Buren, Maine, Aug. 7, 1935; s. Leo and Isabel (Boudreau) R.; A.B. in English, Boston U., 1961; Ed.M., Salem State Coll., 1966; Ph.D. in Urban Edn., U. Wis., Milw., 1974; m. Michaeleen Kowalkowski; children—Denise, Patrice, Michael Will. Tchr., Amesbury (Mass.) High Sch., 1962-64, North Reading (Mass.) High Sch., 1964-67; asst. supt. schs., Windsor, Vt., 1967-69; Edn. Profl. Devel. Act fellow So. Ill. U., Edwardsville, 1969-70; assoc. prof. curriculum and instrn. dept. U. Wis., Milw., 1972—; cons. Nat. Center for Gifted, 1978-81, Am. Inst. for Human Interaction, 1978-81, Good Apple Inc., 1979—, Teaching Ctrs.; speaker at convs. and confs. Served with USAF, 1953-57. NDEA fellow, 1967; fellow Robert A. Taft Inst. Practical Politics, 1967. Mem. Am. Humanist Assn., Assn. for Tchrs. Edn., N.Am. Soc. Adlerian Psychologists, World Congress of Logotherapy, Nat. Staff Devel. Council, Assn. Sch. Curriculum Devel., ACLU, Wis. Council for Gifted and Talented. Democrat. Roman Catholic. Author: Creative Coping: Ending the War with Yourself and Kids, 1980, 81; Using Language Arts to Motivate and Teach Communication Skills, 1982; Motivation and Communication, 1983, Teaching Communication and Motivating, 1985; Management Essentials: Motivation and Discipline, 1987; numerous others; editor: Using Media in the Classroom;contbr. articles to profl. publs. Home: 7772 N River Edge Dr Milwaukee WI 53209-1840 Office: University of Wisconsin Dept of Curriculum & Instrn Sch of Edn PO Box 413 Milwaukee WI 53201

ROYCE, ROBERT FARNHAM, manufacturing company executive; b. Jersey City, Dec. 9, 1931; s. Farnham Thomas and Virginia Martin (Beattie) R.; m. Dorothy Bailey Dean, Oct. 22, 1960; children: Robert Dean, Susan Virginia, Jennifer Anne. BS in Indsl. Engring., Fairleigh Dickinson U., 1957; MS in Indsl. Engring., Stevens Inst. Tech., 1961. Asst. reg. sales mgr. Union Carbide Corp., Chgo., 1967-68, mgr. mktg. services, 1968-70; asst. to gen. mgr. Union Carbide Corp., Tarrytown, N.Y., 1970-72, mgr. fin. planning, 1972-74; materials mgr. Union Carbide Corp., Florence, S.C., 1974-84, internal cons. mfg. resource planning, just-in-time, 1978-84; mgr. corp. industrial engring. and ops. systems Viskase Corp., Chgo., 1984-87; dir. materials Application Engring. Corp., Wood Dale, Ill., 1987—. Served as staff sgt. USAF, 1951-55, Korea. Mem. Am. Prodn. and Inventory Control Soc. (pres. chpt. 1984, v.p. edn. chpt. 1983, v.p. programs chpt. 1978, cert. fellow, educator MRP 1982-84). Republican. Episcopalian. Lodge: Masons (master 1963). Avocations: barbershop quartet, community theatre. Home: 22W361 Glen Valley Dr Glen Ellyn IL 60137 Office: Application Engring Corp 801 AEC Dr Wood Dale IL 60191

ROYER, MARK ALLAN, small business owner, landscaper; b. Cin., May 5, 1958; s. Donald Edward and Lois Jean (Combs) R. Student, U. Cin., 1983. Ptnr. Royer-Peloe Landscaping, Cin., 1979-85; v.p. ops. Garden Nursery, Inc., Cin., 1984-85, pres., 1985-86; ptnr. Eden Environments, Cin., 1986—; cons. Joe Faller Landscaping, Cin., 1984—, Lanco, Cin., 1985—, Landesigns, Cin., 1986—, Garden Nursery, Inc., 1986—; founding ptnr. Community Services Network, Inc. Recipient 1st place Landscape Design award City of Hamilton, Ohio, 1980. Avocations: collecting western art, farming, property renovation. Home: 6751 Sheed Rd Cincinnati OH 45247

ROYKO, MIKE, newspaper columnist; b. Chgo., Sept. 19, 1932; s. Michael and Helen (Zak) R.; m. Carol Joyce Duckman, Nov. 7, 1954 (dec. Sept. 1979); children: M. David, Robert F.; m. Judith Arndt, May 21, 1985. Student, Wright Jr. Coll., 1951-52. Reporter Chgo. North Side Newspapers, 1956; reporter, asst. city editor Chgo. City News Bur., 1956-59; reporter, columnist Chgo. Daily News, 1959-78, assoc. editor, 1977-78; reporter, columnist Chgo. Sun-Times, 1978-84; columnist Chgo. Tribune, 1984—. Author: Up Against It, 1967, I May Be Wrong But I Doubt It, 1968, Boss—Richard J. Daley of Chicago, 1971, Slats Grobnik and Some Other Friends, 1973, Sez Who? Sez Me, 1982, Like I Was Sayin', 1984. Served with USAF, 1952-56. Recipient Heywood Brown award, 1968, Pulitzer prize for commentary, 1972, Man of Yr. award City of Hope Med. Center, 1979, medal for service to journalism U. Mo. Sch. Journalism, 1979; named to Chgo. Press Club Journalism Hall of Fame, 1980. Mem. Chgo. Newspaper Reporters Assn. Club: LaSalle St. Rod and Gun. Office: Chgo Tribune 435 N Michigan Ave Chicago IL 60611

ROYSTER, DARRYL, programmer/analyst; b. Chgo., July 22, 1954; s. David and Doris (McGee) R.; m. Toni Diane Wilson, Aug. 19, 1978; 1 child, Danté Marques. BS in Psychology, MacMurray Coll., Jacksonville, Ill., 1976. Counselor River Edge Hosp., Forrest Park, Ill., 1975-76; adolescent counselor Northwestern Meml. Hosp., Chgo., 1976-78; social worker Cath. Charities, Chgo., 1978-79; counselor Ray Graham Assn., Addison, Ill., 1978-80; input/output clk. Automatic Data Processing, Oak Brook, Ill., 1980-83; computer programmer/analyst IRS, Lombard, Ill., 1983—. Basketball official Ill. High Sch. Assn., Bloomington, Ill., 1972—. Served to sgt. USAR. Mem. Ill. Notary Public Assn., Western Basketball Officials Assn., Psi Chi. Home: 105 Burlington Western Springs IL 60558 Office: IRS 350 E 22d St Lombard IL 60148

ROZANSKI, EDWARD C(ASIMIR), retired editor, manager newspapers, deacon; b. Chgo., Mar. 7, 1915; s. Casimir Joseph and Bess (Kilinski) R.; m. Leocadia Procanin, Aug. 24, 1940. O.D., Ill. Coll. Optometry, 1948; Ordained deacon Roman Cath. Ch. Photographer, Washington Photo Studio, Chgo., 1931-39; photographer-reporter Zgoda, Polish daily, Chgo., 1939-42, 45-50, gen. mgr., editor, 1975-85; deacon St. Hyacinth Ch., Chgo., 1979—; field advocate, notary Met. Tribunal, Archdiocese Chgo., 1985—; shift supr. wet plate process chart and map reprodn. for U.S. Navy, U.S. Army, and U.S. Army Air Force with U.S. Coast and Geodetic Survey, USN, Washington, 1942-45; color specialist, gravure Cuneo Press, Chgo., 1950-75; gen. mgr. Dziennik Zwiazkowy, Polish daily, Chgo., 1975-85; mem. adv. bd. Chgo. Cath., 1983. Bd. dirs. Chgo. Access Corp.; mem. sch. bd. St. Hyacinth Ch., Chgo.; mem. Ill. Hist. Records Adv. Bd.; active Polish Nat. Alliance, 1932—; v.p. PNA Youth Home Corp., 1975-86; sec. Dist. XIII Polish Nat. Alliance, 1979—. Decorated chevalier Ordre Souverain Et Militaire du Temple de Jerusalem (France); Order Polonia Restituta, Gold Cross Legion of Honor, Gold Cross of Merit, Gen. Haller's Swords, Krzyz Zaslugi Cross of Merit (Poland); comdr. Order St. Lazarus of Jerusalem (Malta); Order Lafayette (U.S.); recipient citation Polish Legion Am. Vets, 1962, 63; citation Polish Combatans World War II, (4), Silver Emblem, 1968, Gold emblem, 1983; citation Polish Welfare Council Schenectady, 1964, Polonus Philatelic Soc., 1964; Lincoln plaquette Sta. WGN-Radio-TV, 1965, Silver medal Nat. Library Poland, 1980, Bronze medal Gen. Pulaski Museum, Warka, Poland, 1981, Legion of Honor medal Polish Falcons Am., 1982. Mem. Profl. Photographers Am., Photog. Soc. Am. (cornerstone mem.), Winona Sch. Profl. Photography (cornerstone mem.), Orchard Lake Schs. Alumni Assn. (hon.), Ill. Hist. Soc. (life), Societe Historique et Litteraire Polonaise (Paris life), Polish Mus. Am. (life), Polish Am. Congress (pres. Ill. div. 1966-70, 78-79, Heritage award 1983). Democrat. Lodges: KC, Giller Zann Soc., Polish Roman Cath. Union, others. Publisher: 100 Years of Polish Press in America, 1963; The Battle That Changed The Destiny of Europe, 1982; King John Sobieski, 1983; Life of Teofila Samolinska, 1980; Memoirs of General Kriz—Krzyzanowski Civil War General, 1963; editor PNA Almanac, 1977-84, Zgoda, 1982-86. Home: 5319 N Delphia Unit 219 Chicago IL 60656 Office: St Hyacinth Ch 3636 W Wolfram Chicago IL 60618

ROZELL, JOSEPH GERARD, accountant; b. Kansas City, Kans., Mar. 20, 1959; s. Joseph Frank and Frances Elizabeth (Gojmeric) R. BSBA, Rockhurst Coll., 1981. Staff acct. Donnelly, Meiners & Jordan, Kansas City, Mo., 1981-82, Francis A. Wright & Co., Kansas City, Mo., 1982—. Mem. Am. Inst. CPA's, Mo. Soc. CPA's (legis. com., liaison com.). Republican. Roman Catholic. Avocations: basketball, soccer, volleyball. Home: 8741 Chestnut Cir #306 Kansas City MO 64131-2850

ROZELLE, LEE THEODORE, physical chemist; b. Rhinelander, Wis., Mar. 9, 1933; s. Theodore and Alice (Omholt) R.; m. Barbara J. Ingli, June 21, 1955; children—David, Steven, Carolyn, Ann, Kenneth. B.S., U. Wis., 1955, Ph.D., 1960. Research chemist DuPont Corp., Circleville, Ohio, 1960-63; prin. scientist-tech. coordinator Honeywell Corp., Mpls., 1963-67; dir. chemistry div. North Star Research Inst., Mpls., 1967-74; v.p. research and devel. USCI div. C.R. Bard, Billerica, Mass., 1974-77; dir. engring. tech. div. Mellon Inst., Pitts., 1977-78; dir. research and devel. Permutit Co., Monmouth Junction, N.J., 1978-80; v.p. research and devel. Gelman Scis., Inc., Ann Arbor, Mich., 1980-82; v.p. sci. and tech. Culligan Internat. Co., Northbrook, Ill., 1982—; cons. in field; mem. Nat. Drinking Water Adv. Council EPA, 1987—. Contbr. chpts. to books, numerous articles to profl. jours. Bd. dirs. Unitarian Ch., Andover, Mass., 1974-77. NIH fellow, 1958-60. Fellow Am. Inst. Chemists; mem. AAAS, Am. Chem. Soc., Am. Soc. Artificial Internal Organs, Health Industry Mfrs. Assn. (chmn. spl. activities com.), Water Pollution Control Fedn., Water Quality Assn. (chmn. sci. adv. com.), Am. Water Works Assn., Filtration Soc., Am. Soc. Agrl. Engring., Internat. Water Supply Assn., European Membrane Soc., N.Am. Membrane Soc., Sigma Xi, Eta Phi Alpha, Phi Lambda Upsilon. Home: 853 Sanborn Dr Palatine IL 60067 Office: 1 Culligan Pkwy Northbrook IL 60062

ROZOS, JOHN ALEXANDER, business owner, exporter; b. Havana, Cuba, May 3, 1910; s. Juan and Ramona Rozos; m. Marie G. Graff, Feb. 24, 1944. BS, LaSalle U., LLD. Owner John A. Rozos Industries, Chgo., 1950—. Served to 1st lt. U.S. Army, 1942-46. Roman Catholic. Avocations: commerce, finance, investing, horticulture. Home: 2741 W 99th St Chicago IL 60642-3696

ROZRAN, JACK LOUIS, courier service executive; b. Chgo., Mar. 4, 1939; s. Philip Reuben and Rose (Rosenberg) R.; m. Dawn Faulkner, May 25, 1986; 1 child, Claire Ashley. B.A., Northwestern U., 1960; J.D., Harvard U., 1963. Bar: Ill. 1963. Law clk. to judge U.S. Dist. Ct. Ill., 1963-64; v.p. Cannonball, Inc., Chgo., 1964-66, pres., 1966—. Trustee Hull House Assn., 1972—, v.p. 1986; sec. Erikson Inst., 1982, trustee, 1971—. Mem. Messenger Service Assn. Ill. (pres. 1987—), Air Courier Conf. Am. (treas. 1980-82, pres. 1982-84), ABA, Chgo. Bar Assn., Beta Alpha Psi. Club: Economic (Chgo.). Home: 2650 N Lakeview Ave Chicago IL 60614 Office: Cannonball Inc 875 W Huron St Chicago IL 60622

RUAN, JOHN, transportation executive; b. Beacon, Iowa, Feb. 11, 1914; s. John Arthur and Rachel Anthony (Llewellyn) R.; m. Rose Duffy, July 10, 1941 (dec. May 1943); 1 child, John III; m. Elizabeth J. Adams, Sept. 6, 1946; children: Elizabeth Jayne Ruan Fletcher, Thomas Heyliger. Student, Iowa State U., 1931-32. Pres. The Ruan Cos, Des Moines, 1932-86, chmn., 1986—; chmn. Ruan Transp. Corp., Ruan Leasing Co., Ruan Aviation Corp., Ruan Fin. Corp., Ruan Ctr. Corp.; pres. and treas. City Ctr. Corp.; chmn. bd. dirs. and chmn. exec. com. Bankers Trust Co.; bd. dirs. Heritage Communications, Inc., Northwestern States Portland Cement Co. Mem. Des Moines Devel. Corp.; past pres. Greater Des Moines Com., Iowa State Engring. Coll. Adv. Council; fin. chmn., exec. com. Northwestern U. Transp. Ctr.; bd. govs. Iowa State U. Found.; bd. dirs. Des Moines Area Council on Alcoholism, Living History Farms; trustee Hoover Presidential Library Assns., Inc. Named Des Moines Citizen Yr., Des Moines City Council, 1981; elected to Iowa Bus. Hall of Fame, 1982; recipient Disting. Iowa Citizen award Mid-Iowa Council Boy Scouts Am., 1985, Humanitarian award Variety Club of Iowa, 1986, People With Vision award Iowa Soc. Prevent Blindness, 1986. Mem. Am. Trucking Assns., Inc. (treas., exec. com., chmn. fin. com.), Am. Trucking Assns. Found. (trustee), Iowa Assn. Bus. and Industry (bd. dirs.), Des Moines C. of C. (bd. dirs.). Republican. Methodist. Clubs: Wakonda, Des Moines; Lost Tree, Old Port Yacht (North Palm Beach, Fla.); Rancho LaCosta (Carlsbad, Calif.). Avocations: golf, mushroom hunting. Home: 23 34th St Des Moines IA 52806 Office: Bankers Trust Co 7th & Locust St Des Moines IA 50309 Office: Ruan Cos 3200 Ruan Ctr Des Moines IA 50309

RUBENKING, GLEN BROEHL, architect; b. Elkhart, Ill., Nov. 15, 1916; s. John Henry and Anna Lillian (Broehl) R.; m. Barbara Jean Kindred, June 17, 1945; children: Marla, Mark, Marisa, Marcia. BArch, U. Ill., 1949. Registered architect, Ill. Pvt. practice architecture Arlington Heights, Ill., 1954-59; supt. constrn. Universal Constrn., Chgo., 1959-64; assoc. univ. architect U. Ill., Champaign, 1964-71; assoc. state architect State of Ill., 1971-73; state architect Ill. State Bd. Edn., Springfield, 1973—. Trustee 1st Presbyn. Ch., Arlington Heights; leader 4-H Club, Dewey, Ill. Served as cpl. Ordinance Corps., U.S. Army, 1946-47. Mem. Ill. State Office Educator Fedn., Council Edn. Facilities Planners Internat. Republican. Methodist. Avocations: golf, flying. Home: Greenwood Acres Box 243 Dewey IL 61840 Office: Ill State Bd Edn 100 N First St Springfield IL 62704

RUBENS, LAURENCE BROCK, controller; b. Chgo., June 9, 1939; s. Robert Leon Rubens and Esther Janet (Brock) Fell; m. Patricia Mary Fullone, Apr. 11, 1964; 1 child, Carol. BS in Econs., U. Ill., 1961; postgrad., Northeastern Ill. U., 1981-82, Oakton Community Coll., 1982-83. CPA, Ill. With Fed. Life Ins. Co. (Mut.), Chgo., Glenview and Riverwoods, Ill., 1962-73; asst. v.p. actuarial sci. Fed. Life Ins. Co. (Mut.), Riverwoods, 1973-80, asst. v.p., mgr. gen. accts., 1980-82; controller, asst. treas. The Standard of Am. Life, Park Ridge, Ill., 1982-86; controller Fort Dearborn Life Ins., Park Ridge, 1986-87, Am. Mid States Life Ins. Co., Oakbrook Terr., Ill., 1987—.

Served as pfc. N.G., 1962. Mem. Am. Inst. CPA's, Ill. CPA Soc. Avocations: bowling, golf. Home: 1249 Highland Ln Glenview IL 60025 Office: Am Mid States Life Ins Co 17 W240 22d St Oakbrook Terrace IL 60181

RUBENS, SIDNEY MICHEL, technical advisor; b. Spokane, Wash., Mar. 21, 1910; s. Max Zvoln and Jennie Golda (Rubinovich) R.; B.S., U. Wash., 1934, Ph.D., 1939; m. Julienne Rose Fridner, May 11, 1944; 1 dau., Deborah Janet. Instr. U. So. Calif., 1939-40; research asso. U. Calif. at Los Angeles, 1940-41; physicist Naval Ordnance Lab., Washington, 1941-46; physicist Engrng. Research Assos., St. Paul, 1946-52; mgr. physics Univac div. Sperry Rand, St. Paul, 1958-61, dir. research, 1961-66, staff scientist, 1969-71, dir. spl. projects, 1971-75; cons., 1975-81; technical adv. Vertimag Systems Corp., 1981—, Advanced Research Corp., 1986—; lectr. U. Pa., 1960-61; mem. adv. subcom. on instrumentation and data processing NASA, 1967-69, panel on computer tech. Nat. Acad. Sci., 1969. Hon. fellow U. Minn., 1977—. Fellow IEEE (magnetic soc. info. storage award); mem. Am. Phys. Soc., Am. Geophys. Union, AAAS, Acad. Applied Sci., Minn. Acad. Sci., Am. Optical Soc., Phi Beta Kappa, Sigma Xi, Pi Mu Epsilon. Patentee in magnetic material and devices. Author: Amplifier and Memory Devices, 1965. Contbr. articles to profl. jours. Home: 1077 Sibley Hwy Apt 506 St Paul MN 55118 Office: Vertimag Systems Corp 814 14th Ave SE Minneapolis MN 55414

RUBENSTEIN, ALBERT IRWIN, real estate developer, lawyer; b. Chgo., Mar. 28, 1927; s. William D. and Regina (Ribaysen) R.; student Herzl City Coll., 1944-46, Roosevelt Coll., 1946-48; LL.B., J.D., John Marshall Law Sch., 1951; m. Joyce Shirley Leeman, June 12, 1954; children—Jeffrey, Lauren, Jan. Bar: Ill. 1951. Sole practice law, Chgo., 1951-64; pres., chief exec. officer Fleetwood Realty Corp., Chgo., 1969—, also dir.; sr. partner Fleetwood Realty Co., Chgo., 1969-83; pres. Fleetwood Devel. Corp., 1983—; dir. Exec. Bus. Center, Inc., Fleetwood Industries; lectr. corp. real estate fin. and devel. Bd. dirs. Feinberg Charitable Found., 1969—, Hebrew Theol. Coll., 1975—; mem. Highland Park (Ill.) Planning Commn., 1980—, Highland Park Econ. Devel. Com., 1984; spl. real estate negotiator by mayoral appointment, Highland Park, 1980. Recipient Outstanding Alumnus award John Marshall Law Sch., 1982; named 1 of top 10 real estate developers Chicago mag., 1981. Mem. ABA, Ill. Bar Assn., Chgo. Bar Assn., Am. Trial Lawyers Assn., Chgo. Assn. Commerce and Industry, Nat. Real Estate Bd., Chgo. Real Estate Bd. (dir. 1980-82), Decalogue Soc. Lawyers, Nat. Realty Com., Inc., Am. Arbitration Soc. Clubs: Covenant, Execs. (Chgo.). Lodge: B'nai B'rith. Contbr. articles in field to profl. jours. Office: 200 W Jackson Blvd Chicago IL 60606

RUBENSTEIN, JEFFREY CARL, lawyer, educator; b. Chgo., Jan. 27, 1942; s. Joseph Allen Rubenstein and Mildred Florence Rothbaum; m. Susan Glazer, Sept. 23, 1967; children: Andrew H., Gordon S., Emily S. AB, U. Mich., 1963, JD, 1966; LLM, John Marshall Law Sch., 1983. Bar: Ill. 1966. Assoc. Sidley & Austin, Chgo., 1966; prin. Sachnoff, Weaver & Rubenstein Ltd., Chgo., 1966—; adj. prof. law Ill. Inst. Tech., Chgo., 1977—; bd. dirs. Selfix, Inc., Chgo., Modular Tech., Inc., Chgo., Vita Food Products, Inc., Chgo.; lectr. various profl. orgns. Author: Financial Real Estate Transactions, 1984; columnist Multi-Housing News, 1983—; chmn. editorial bd. Jour. Real Estate Securities, 1982—; contbr. articles on taxation, real estate and securities law to profl. jours. V.p., bd. dirs. Bur. Jewish Employment Problems, Chgo., 1972—; treas., bd. dirs. Jewish Family and Community Services Chgo., 1979—; mem. law sch. devel. com. U. Mich., 1968-74; del. liaison Dem. Nat. Conv., 1968. Named one of Outstanding Young Men Am., 1978. Mem. ABA (various coms.), Chgo. Bar Assn., Chgo. Council Lawyers (chmn. ethics com. 1972-74), Nat. Assn. Realtors, Jewish United Fund (bd. dirs. 1982—); HIAS Internat. (bd. dirs. 1986—). Clubs: Standard (Chgo.), Briarwood Country (Deerfield, Ill.). Avocations: running, skiing, gardening. Home: 1014 Elmwood Ave Wilmette IL 60091 Office: Sachnoff Weaver & Rubenstein Ltd 30 S Wacker Dr Suite 2901 Chicago IL 60606

RUBENSTEIN, SIDNEY JACK, dentist; b. Detroit, Dec. 10, 1931; s. Maurice Aaron and Miriam Ilene (Gutkovsky) R.; m. Miriam Deborah Levin, Nov. 24, 1954 (div. 1962); children: Judith Michelle, Suzanne Joy, Deanna Beth; m. RoseAnn Kroker, Nov. 21, 1967; 1 child, Heidi Marya. BS in Psychology, Wayne State U., 1952; DDS, U. Detroit, 1956. Gen. practice dentistry Detroit and Dearborn Heights,, Mich., 1958—; mem. operative dentistry sect. Sinai Hosp., 1960-64, mem. prosthetic sect., 1964-80, chmn. prosthetic sect., 1968-74, assoc. chmn. Dept. Dental and Oral Surgery, 1974—, prosthodontist to cleft palate team, 1966—; cons. Delta Dental Plans Mich., 1974—. Served to capt. USAR, 1956-58. Mem. Am. Dental Assn., Am. Prosthodontic Assn., Am. Assn. Hosp. Dentists, Mich. Dental Assn., Detroit Dist. Dental Assn. (ethics com. 1978—, peer rev. com. 1982—), Oakland County Dental Soc. (peer rev. com. 1978-82), B'nai B'rith, JWV, Alpha Omega (pres. Detroit chpt.). Jewish. Avocations: golf, bowling, reading, woodworking. Home: 5685 Stratford Dr West Bloomfield MI 48033 Office: Rubenstein & Eilender PC 8623 Telegraph Dearborn Heights MI 48127

RUBERG, ROBERT LIONEL, surgery educator; b. Phila., July 22, 1941; s. Norman and Yetta (Wolfman) R.; m. Cynthia Lief, June 26, 1966; children: Frederick, Mark, Joshua. BA, Haverford (Pa.) Coll., 1963; MD, Harvard U., 1967. Diplomate Am. Bd. Surgery, Am. Bd. Plastic Surgery. Instr. surgery U. Pa., Phila., 1972-75; asst. prof. Ohio State U., Columbus, 1975-81, assoc. prof., 1981—; chmn. curriculum com. Coll. Medicine, Ohio State U., 1984—; chief plastic surgery Ohio State U. Hosps., 1985—. Plastic Surgery Ednl. Found. research grantee, 1976, 78. Fellow ACS; mem. Am. Assn. PLastic Surgeons, Am. Soc. for Parenteral and Enteral Nutrition, Coordinating Council for Acad. Policies in Plastic Surgery (sec., treas. 1982—). Avocations: basketball, bicycling. Home: 6243 PeachTree Rd Columbus OH 43213 Office: Ohio State U Hosps 410 W 10th Ave #809 Columbus OH 43210

RUBIN, ABE, former college president, podiatrist; b. Winnipeg, Man., Can., Aug. 14, 1911; s. Burrows and Lily R. (Adilman) R.; m. Doris Silvia Miller, July 8, 1949; children: Mark B., Hollis Beth. Student, U. Man., 1928-32; D.P.M., Ill. Coll. Podiatric Medicine, 1937, Ed.D., 1967; postgrad., U. Chgo., 1952-55; Litt.D., Ohio Coll. Podiatry, 1968. Assoc. prof. anatomy Ill. Coll. Podiatric Medicine, 1937-42, dir. clinics, head orthopedic dept., 1947-55; sec. Am. Podiatry Assn., Washington, 1955-62; editor Am. Podiatry Assn. (Jour.), 1955-70; exec. dir. Council Podiatric Edn., 1962-70; pvt. practice 1938-42; v.p., dean Ohio Coll. Podiatric Medicine, Cleve., 1970-71; pres. Ohio Coll. Podiatric Medicine, 1971-85, pres. emeritus, 1985—; cons. N1H, Nat. Acad. Scis., Inst. of Medicine, others. Contbr. articles med. journ. encys.; co-editor: The Podiatry Curriculum; mem. editorial adv. bd.: Jour. Am. Podiatry Assn. Served to capt. USAAF, 1942-46. Recipient Gold award Wm. J. Stickel Ann. awards research podiatry, 1954. Fellow Am. Coll. Foot Orthopedists (past pres.), Am. Med. Writers Assn. (chpt. pres.), AAAS; mem. Am. Podiatry Assn., Am. Assn. Colls. Podiatric Medicine (pres. 1970), Am. Pub. Health Assn., Gerontol. Soc., Am. Inst. Parliamentarians. Home: 1511 S Interlachen Dr #126 Silver Spring MD 20900 Office: 10515 Carnegie Ave Cleveland OH 44106

RUBIN, BRENT LANE, podiatrist; b. Toledo, Feb. 26, 1954; s. Sheldon J. and JoAnne S. (Gutowitz) R.; m. Rickie Lee Solomon, Aug. 10, 1975; children: Micah, Carli, Chad. BA, Ohio State U., 1975; D of Podiatric Medicine, Ohio Coll. Podiatric Medicine, 1980. Diplomate Am. Bd. Podiatric Surgerye. Resident Detroit Cen. Hosp., 1980-81; gen. practice podiatric medicine Toledo, 1981—. Pub. edn. dir. Am. Cancer Soc., Toledo, 1983—, pub. issues dir. 1986—; sec. Etz Chayim Synagogue, Toledo, 1984—; bd. dirs. Jewish Community Ctr., Toledo, 1984—, membership chmn. 1985; bd. dirs. Jewish Welfare Fedn., Toledo, 1985—; v.p. Etz Chayim Synagogue, 1986—; active B'nai Brith. Fellow Am. Coll. Foot Surgeons, Am. Podiatric Med. Assn. Lodge: Old News Boys. Avocations: jogging, reading. Home: 4819 Princess Ct Sylvania OH 43560 Office: 3055 Sylvania Toledo OH 43613

RUBIN, CARL BERNARD, U.S. district judge; b. Cin., Mar. 27, 1920; s. John I. and Ethel (Friedman) R.; m. Gloria Weiland, Sept. 23, 1945; children: Marc W., C. Barry, Pam G., Robert S. B.A., U. Cin., 1942, J.D., 1944. Bar: Ohio 1944. Practiced in Cin., 1944-71; asst. pros. atty. Hamilton County (Ohio), Cin., 1950-60; judge U.S. Dist. Ct. So. Dist. Ohio, 1971—, chief judge, 1979—; Instr. criminal law Chase Coll. Law, Cin., 1965-67; mem. com. on ct. adminstrn. fed. cts. U.S. Jud. Conf., 1975-83; mem. Jud. Council 6th Circuit, 1985—; adj. prof. law U. Dayton Coll. Law, 1976. Mem. Cin. Civil Service Commn., 1960-66, chmn., 1965-66; pres. S.W. Ohio Regional Transit Authority, 1971. Mem. Am. Contract Bridge League (dir. 1966-73, pres. 1970-71), 6th Circuit Dist. Judges Assn. (pres. 1977-78). Office: US Courthouse 5th and Walnut Sts Cincinnati OH 45202 *

RUBIN, JOEL HARVEY, surgeon; b. Phila., June 26, 1945; s. Samuel E. and Cecelia (Breitman) R.; m. Susan L. Silverglate, Aug. 11, 1968. AB, Lafayette Coll., 1967; DO, Coll. Osteo. Medicine and Surgery, Des Moines, 1971. Diplomate Nat. Bd. Med. Examiners, Ab. Bd. Osteopathic Surgeons. Resident in gen. surgery Doctors Hosp., Columbus, Ohio, 1972-76; attending staff surgeon Muskegon (Mich.) Gen. Hosp., 1976—, chief of staff, 1982—; chmn. Burn Program, Muskegon, 1980—; owner, operator 2 self-service car wash facilities. Bd. dirs. Muskegon Exchange Club, 1980, Muskegon chpt. Am. Cancer Soc., 1980—, Mich. div. Am. Cancer Soc., 1984—, Community Alternatives Program, 1985—; pres. Temple B'nai Israel, Muskegon, 1982-86. Mem. Am. Coll. Osteo. Surgeons, Am. Osteo. Assn., West Mich. Assn. Osteo. Physicians and Surgeons, Grand Rapids Acad. Surgery, Am. Soc. Parenteral and Enteral Nutrition. Jewish. Lodge: B'nai Brith (pres. Muskegon chpt. 1980-82, sec. 1986—). Avocations: fishing, swimming, white water rafting, hot air ballooning. Office: 1790 Oak Ave Muskegon MI 49442

RUBINO, FRANK AUGUST, neurologist; b. Chgo., Feb. 19, 1933; s. Frank and Lena Lorraine (Casello) R.; m. Nancy A. Mulcahey, June, 1962 (div. 1973); children: Dorothy Ann, Patricia Louise. BA in Chemistry, Bradley U., 1955; MD, U. Ill., Chgo., 1962. Cert. Am. Bd. Psychiatry and Neurology (examiner 1972—). Resident in psychiatry Ill. State Psychiat. Inst., Chgo., 1967; resident in neurology Northwestern U., Chgo., 1969; acting chief neurology Hines (Ill.) VA Hosp., 1969-70, chief of neurology, 1970—; asst. prof. Loyola U., Maywood, Ill., 1970-74; assoc. prof. Loyola U., Maywood, 1974-79, prof., assoc. chmn. dept., 1979—. Contbr. numerous articles to profl. jours. Served with U.S. Army, 1956-58, lt. col. Res., 1985—. Named Tchr. of Yr., Loyola U., 1978. Fellow Am. Acad. Neurology; mem. AMA, Am. Epilepsy Soc., Chgo. Neurol. Soc. (sec.-treas. 1976-77, v.p./pres. 1977-79), Alpha Omega Alpha. Clubs: East Bank (Chgo.); Meadow (Rolling Meadows, Ill.). Avocations: skiing, music, art, tennis. Home: 10 S Regency Dr E Arlington Heights IL 60004 Office: Hines VA Hosp 5th and Roosevelt Hines IL 60141

RUBINYI, ROBERT MICHAEL, communications specialist, researcher; b. Los Angeles, Sept. 25, 1957; s. Benno and Jeannette (Edlen) R. BA in communications, U. Calif., San Diego, 1979; MA in Communications, U. Wis., 1981, PhD in Communications, 1985. Teaching asst. U. Wis., Madison, 1979-83; new tech. researcher Sta. WHA-TV, Madison, 1983-84; mem. staff task force U. Wis. Extension, Madison, 1984-85, research speciaist, 1985—; mem. news staff Sta. WORT-FM, Madison, 1982—. Mem. Internat. Communications Assn., Speech Communication Assn. Home: 716 Clark Ct Madison WI 53715 Office: U Wis Extension 231 Lowell Hall 610 Langdon St Madison WI 53703

RUBLE, BERNARD ROY, consultant, educator; b. Greensburg, Ind., Apr. 4, 1923; s. Jesse Emery and Marietta (Ward) R.; B.S., Ind. U., Bloomington, 1949; postgrad. transactional analysis Midwest Inst. Human Understanding, 1972-75; m. Mary Helen Rullman, Dec. 22, 1946; children—Barry Reece, Blane Rodney. Asst. mgr. Morris 5 and 10 Stores, Greensburg, 1941; store keeper Public Service Co. Ind., Greensburg, 1941-43; asst. mgr. personnel Kroger Co., Cin., 1949-51, mgr., personnel, Madison, Wis., 1951-56, Ft. Wayne, Ind., 1956-58, Cleve., 1958-73, mgr. labor relations Erie Mktg. Area, Solon, Ohio, 1973-84; faculty Kroger Edn. Center, Cin., 1978—; trustee Meat Cutters Health and Welfare Fund, 1971-79, Retail Clks. Union Health and Welfare Fund, Akron, 1970—, No. Ohio Hospice Council, 1981-84. Active United Appeal Greater Cleve., Community Chest Greater Cleve., Met. Health Planning Corp.; v.p. trustee Urban League Greater Cleve., 1968-75; adv. com. Family Health Care, Washington, 1977-78; trustee Community Health Found.; team rep. B.R. Ruble Racing, Burton, Ohio. Served with USAAF, 1943-45. Mem. Internat. Transactional Analysis Assn. (cert. clin), Photog. Soc. Am., Soc. for Advancement Mgmt. (trustee Madison chpt. 1952-55), Am. Soc. Personnel Adminstrn., Cleve. Personnel Assn., Indsl. Relations Research Assn. (pres.). Lodges: Masons, Sertoma (trustee Madison 1952-58) (charter). Lic. minister Disciples Christ, 1975. Home and Office: 8644 Ranch Dr Chesterland OH 44026

RUBLOFF, BURTON, real estate broker, appraiser; b. Chisholm, Minn., June 1, 1912; s. Solomon W. and Mary R.; m. Patricia F. Williams, July 17, 1943; 1 dau., Jenifer. Grad, Northwestern U., 1940. With Arthur Rubloff & Co. (now Rubloff Inc.), Chgo., 1930—; v.p. Arthur Rubloff & Co. (now Rubloff Inc.), 1947-76, sr. v.p., 1976—. Bd. dirs. Mcpl. Art League Chgo.; mem. Urbanland Inst. Served with U.S. Army, 1943-46, ETO. Mem. Am. Inst. Real Estate Appraisers (life mem. chpt. 6), Nat. Ill., Chgo. (hon. life mem.) assns. real estate bds., Chgo. Real Estate Bd. (ethics com.), Bldg. Mgrs. Assn. Chgo., Greater State St. Council (real estate com.), Lambda Alpha Internat. (Ely chpt.). Clubs: John Evans (Northwestern U.); City (Chgo.). Office: Rubloff Inc 111 W Washington St Chicago IL 60602

RUCKER, RICHARD S., information systems executive; b. Dayton, Ohio, Sept. 4, 1947; s. Wilbert Hunter and Estelle Janet Rucker. BBA, Wright State U., Dayton, 1976; MBA, Cen. Mich. U., Mount Pleasant, 1987. Asst. program mgr. Synergy, Inc., Dayton, 1968-78; mgr. data processing Ledex, Inc., Vandalia, Ohio, 1978-83; cons. analyst NCR Corp., Dayton, 1983-85; mgr. info. systems SelectTech Corp., Dayton, 1985; dir. info. systems services Dayton Bd. Edn., 1985—; pres. Richard S. Rucker & Assoc., Dayton, 1982—. Bd. dirs. Dakota Youth Ctr., Dayton, 1983, Dayton Urban League, 1986—; mem. exec. council Congl. Adv. Council to U.S. Congressman Tony Hall, 1986. Named one of Outstanding Young Men Am., 1984. Democrat. Avocations: painting, reading, swimming, astro-physics, basketball. Home: 2914 Forest Grove Ave Dayton OH 45406

RUCKER, RONN DEAN, clinical sociologist, AIDS consultant; b. Portsmith, Ohio, Dec. 12, 1948; s. Raleigh Kenneth and Bettie (Brigher) R.; m. Ruth Miller, Oct. 26, 1969; children: Benjamin, Andrew. BA in Sociology, Otterbein Coll., 1970; MA in Sociology, Ball State U., 1971; EdD, U. Cin., 1980. Instr. psychology and sociology U. Cin., 1972-78; pub. health educator, clin. sociologist Cin. Health Dept., 1982—; trustee Cen. Community Health Bd., Cin., mem. fin. com., 1985; trustee Citizen's Com. on Youth; mem. AIDS Task Force, U. Cin. Coll. Medicine; cons. AIDS U. Cin. Coll. Medicine, 1984, numerous hosps., 1984, Hamilton County (Ohio) Corrections Supervisory Staff, 1985, Cin. Bd. Edn., 1985, Sally Jesse Raphael Show, St. Louis, 1986, Cin. Red Cross, 1986, Our Lady of Mercy Hosp., Cin., 1987, Children's Home of Cin., 1987; lectr. AIDS numerous colls., schs., civic groups, hosps., confs., chs., 1983—. Contbr. numerous articles, papers and presentations on AIDS to profl. jours, pop. mags. and pub. health confs., 1983—. Co-founder Greater Cin. AIDS Task Force, 1983, AIDS Vols. of Cin., 1983, Ohio AIDS Coalition, 1985; mem. nat. steering com. March on Washington for Gay Rights, 1987. Mem. Am. Sociol. Assn. (named one of Outstanding Am. Sociologists 1985), Clin. Sociology Assn., Gay Mental Health Profls. (founder 1983). Democrat. Mem. Soc. of Friends. Avocations: raising borzois, sighthound coursing. Home: 2616 River Rd Cincinnati OH 45204 Office: Cin Health Dept 3101 Burnet Ave Cincinnati OH 45229

RUCKER, WILLIAM MICHAEL, psychotherapist, educator; b. Columbus, Nebr., Sept. 18, 1939; s. William Anthony and Margaret Elizabeth (Higgens) R.; m. Yvonne E. Dascher, Sept. 8, 1978; 1 child, Michael C. Reynolds. BA, Conception (Mo.) Seminary, 1961; MA in Edn., Cath. U., 1964; MSW, U. Nebr., 1979. Priest Archdiocese of Omaha, 1965-77; psychotherapist Ea. Nebr. Office Mental Health, 1977-79; clin. social worker R.D. Jones, MD, Psychiat. Practice, 1979-86; therapist The Hudson Ctr., Omaha, 1986—. Mem. Nat. Assn. Social Workers, Acad. Cert. Social Workers; clin. mem. Am. Assn. Marriage and Family Therapists. Democrat. Roman Catholic. Home: 1637 Country Club Ave Omaha NE 68104 Office: The Hudson Ctr 12111 Pacific St Omaha NE 68154

RUDD, DAVID OWEN, lawyer, lobbyist; b. Elmhurst, Ill., Mar. 4, 1955; . John Owen and Pauline (Pellitier) R.; m. Gayla Sue Smith, June 17, 1985. BA, So. Ill. U., 1977, JD, 1980. Bar: N.Mex., Ill. Research analyst Select Joint Com., Springfield, Ill., 1981-83; dep. dir. Ill. Commerce Commn., Springfield, 1983—. Contbr. articles to profl. jours. Named one of Outstanding Young Men Am., 1987. Mem. ROPB (exec. counsel 1982-87). Club: Prop (Springfield). Avocation: sailing. Office: Ill Commerce Commn 527 E Capital 7th fl Springfield IL 62708

RUDD, MARK SANTFORD, real estate executive, nuclear engineer; b. LaPorte, Ind., Nov. 14, 1950; s. Santford and Patricia (Fort) R.; m. Connie Sue Rans; children: Bethany, Brandon, Brianne, Blaine. BSE in Nuclear Engrng., Purdue U., 1972. Lic. sr. reactor operator. Reactor engr. I&M Power Co., Bridgman, Mich., 1972-75; engr. Transnucleaire SA, Paris, 1975-78; engr. ops. No. Ind. Pub. Service, Chesterton, 1978—; realtor Realty World #1, Valparaiso, Ind., 1985—; pres. Liberty Investors, Inc., Valparaiso, Ind. Investors Network, Valparaiso, 1985—; registered rep. Morris Group, Indpls., 1986—; v.p., treas. Plaza Properties, Inc. Council chmn. Valparaiso Mennonite Ch., 1985; mem. Northwest Ind. Personnel Computer Users Group, 1987; chmn. bd. dirs. Northwest Ind. Youth for Christ, 1986—. Mem. Am. Soc. Mech. Engrs. (pres. 1982-85, Officer Recognition 1985), Nat. Assn. Realtors, Nat. Assn. Security Dealers, Securities Exchange Commn. Repilican. Avocations: guitar, reading, sports, computers. Home: 2205 Penwick Dr Valparaiso IN 46383

RUDDLE, RONALD WAVERLEY, metallurgy consultant; b. London, Aug. 25, 1919; came to U.S., 1957; s. Simeon Skeate and Minnie Louisa (Stowell) R.; m. Maureen Agnes Sheen, Mar. 31, 1951; children: Susan Amanda, Simon Geoffrey, Adrian John. BA, Cambridge U., Eng., 1941, MA, 1945. Asst. metallurgist No. Aluminium Co., Birmingham, Eng., 1941-42; chief metallurgist De Havilland Forge, Ltd., South Wales, Eng., 1942-45; head melting and casting sect. British Non-Ferrous Metals Research Assn., London, 1946-56; v.p. tech., dir. spl. projects Foseco Inc., Cleve., 1957-84; cons. Cleve., 1984—. Author: Solidification of Castings, 1957, Running and Gating of Sand Castings, 1956, others; contbr. articles to profl. jours.; patentee in field. Fellow Inst. Metallurgists; mem. AIME, NSF (com.), Am. Foundrymen's Soc. (Simpson Gold medal 1967, Hoyt ann. lectr 1971), Am. Inst. Mining and Metallurgical Engrs., Am. Soc. Metals, Metals Soc., Inst. Brit. Foundrymen. Republican. Clubs: Westpark Radiops (pres. 1985), LEARA (Cleve.). Avocations: amateur radio, computer programming. Home and Office: 21660 Hilliard Blvd Rocky River OH 44116

RUDEN, VIOLET HOWARD (MRS. CHARLES VAN KIRK RUDEN), Christian Sci. tchr., practitioner; b. Dallas; d. Millard Fillmore and Henrietta Frederika (Kurth) Howard; B.J., U. Tex., 1931; C.S.B., Mass. Metaphys. Coll., 1946; m. Charles Van Kirk Ruden, Nov. 24, 1932. Radio continuity writer Home Mgmt. Club broadcast Sta. WHO, Des Moines, 1934; joined First Ch. of Christ Scientist, Boston, 1929; C.S. practitioner, Des Moines, 1934—; C.S. minister WAC, Ft. Des Moines, 1942-45; 1st reader 2d Ch. of Christ Scientist, Des Moines, 1952, Sunday sch. tchr., 1934—; instr. primary class in Christian Sci., 1947—. Trustee Asher Student Found. Drake U., Des Moines, 1973. Mem. Women in Communications, Mortar Bd., Orchesis, Cap and Gown, Theta Sigma Phi (pres. 1931). Republican. Club: Des Moines Women's. Home: 5808 Walnut Hill Dr Des Moines IA 50312

RUDES, GEORGE HARLOW, realtor, insurance agent; b. Genoa, Ohio, Dec. 16, 1923; s. Merrill Basil and Della Matilda (Meyer) R.; m. Marion Helen Bringe, Nov. 12, 1944; children: Randolph Harlow, Connie Joy Moore, Amy Margaret. Army specialized tng. program, Washington-Jefferson Coll., 1943-44. Ins. agt. Rudes & Reeder Agy., Curtice, Ohio, 1947—; mgr. Nick Stevens Motor Sales, Genoa, 1951-55; prin. George H. Rudes Realtor, Curtice, 1963—; bd. dirs. Nat. Bank of Oak Harbor (Ohio). Served to staff sgt. C.E., U.S. Army, 1943-46, PTO, ETO. Mem. Nat. Assn. Realtors, Ohio Assn. Realtors, Ottawa (Ohio) Assn. Realtors, Nat. Assn. Real Estate Appraisers, Nat. Assn. of Rev. Appraisers, Am. Legion, VFW. Republican. Methodist. Lodge: Maccabees. Avocations: fishing, golf. Office: 7165 N Lucas St Curtice OH 43412

RUDISILL, JOHN RICHARD, clinical psychologist, educator; b. Tulia, Tex., Jan. 2, 1947; s. Ray Burnley and Ruth Arlene (Blackburn) R.; m. Marla Elifritz, Aug. 30, 1969; children—John Stephen, Matthew James, Alisha Dawn. B.A. in Psychology, Denison U., 1969; Ph.D., Ind. U., 1974. Lic. psychologist, Ohio. Chief psychologist, program dir. Dayton (Ohio) Mental Health Ctr., 1977-79; dir. med. student edn. dept. psychiatry Wright State U. Sch. Medicine, Dayton, 1979—, coordinator behavioral sci. of family practice, 1979—; pvt. psychology, Dayton, 1977—; cons. Dayton VA Ctr., 1983—; cons. Wright AFB Med. Ctr., Dayton, 1982—, IAMS Co., Ohio; mem. Montgomery County Mental Health Bd., vice-chair, 1984. Served to capt. USAF, 1973-77. Denison U. Founders' scholar, 1965-69; NIMH fellow, 1971, grantee, 1972-73; named Tchr. of Yr., Wright State U. Sch. Medicine, 1981-82; recipient Wright State's Chmn. award psychiatry, 1982. Mem. Am. Psychol. Assn., Ohio Psychol. Assn., Miami Valley Psychol. Assn. (past pres.), Mental Health Assn., Am. Orthopsychiat. Assn., Assn. Behavioral Scis. in Med. Edn., Assn. Advancement Psychology, Acad. of Marital and Family Sex Therapy. Methodist. Clubs: Ind. Alumni, Denison Alumni, D-Man. Contbr. articles in field to profl. jours. Home: 5201 Pebblebrook Englewood OH 45322

RUDMAN, DANIEL S., accounting executive; b. Galesburg, Ill., Nov. 15, 1945; s. Mitchell and Rose (Levy) R.; m. Susan B. Meyer, June 22, 1964; children: Deborah, Julie. B in Acctg., U. Ill., 1969. CPA, Ill. Controller Brown Splty. Co., Galesburg, Ill., 1969-75; v.p. Doyle Gordon, Inc., Galesburg, 1975—; pres. Rudman & Assocs., Galesburg, 1975—, D & S Enterprises, Galesburg, 1975—. Author: (cassette tapes) Tax Planning, Motivation. V.p. Temple Sholem, 1984—; chmn. Mayor's com. recreation, Galesburg, 1976-79, Computers in Schs., Galesburg 1984—. Recipient Ill. Ten Outstanding Young Person's award, Jaycees, 1979, Outstanding Community award Galesburg Jaycees, 1978. Mem. Ill. CPA Soc., Am. Inst. CPA's, Galesburg Jaycees (pres. 1975). Republican. Jewish. Lodge: B'nai Brith (pres. Galesburg chpt. 1975-86, pres. Hart chpt. 1975—). Avocations: golf, bowling, reading, computers. Home: 1033 Wood Bine Circle W Galesburg IL 61401

RUDNICK, ELLEN AVA, healthcare company executive; b. New Haven; s. Harold and C. Vivian (Soybel) R.; m. Timothy J. Pettit; children: Sarah, Noah. BA, Vassar Coll., 1972; MBA, U. Chgo., 1973. Sr. fin. analyst Quaker Oats, Chgo., 1973-75; various positions Baxter Internat., Deerfield, Ill., 1975-80, dir. planning, 1980-83, corp. v.p., 1985—; pres. Travenol Mgmt. Services, Deerfield, 1983—. chief crusader Met. Chgo. United Way, 1982-85; pres. council Nat. Coll. Edn., Evanston, Ill., 1983—; circle of friends Chgo. YWCA, 1985—. Mem. Am. Coll. Healthcare Execs., Econ. Club Chgo., Chgo. Network. Office: Baxter Travenol 1 Baxter Pkwy Deerfield IL 60015

RUDNIK, SISTER MARY CHRYSANTHA, college administrator; b. Winona, Minn., Dec. 2, 1929; d. Basil John and Sarah (Knopick) Rudnik; student Loyola U., 1951-52, Felician Coll., 1952-54, Cardinal Stritch Coll., 1954-57, Coll. St. Francis, 1957; Ph.B., DePaul U., 1958; postgrad. Mundelein Coll., 1959-60, Northeastern Ill. State U., 1964; M.A., Rosary Coll., 1962. Joined Congregation of Sisters of St. Felix of Cantalice, Roman Cath. Ch., 1948; cert. fund raising exec. Nat. Soc. Fund Raising Execs. Page, clk. Hill Reference Library, St. Paul, 1946-48; tchr. Holy Innocents Sch., Chgo., 1948-49, 50-54, St. Bruno Sch., Chgo., 1954-55, Holy Family Sch., Cudahy, Wis., 1955-57, Good Counsel High Sch., Chgo., 1958-67; instr. Felician Coll., Chgo., 1963-86, head librarian, 1957-82, dir. devel. and public relations, 1975-86. Organizer, coordinator Felician Library Service, 1966-74, Arts and Crafts Festival, 1972-86; coordinator instl. self-study for accreditation North Central Assn.; mem. task force for study of instl. research for Ill. Assn. Community and Jr. Colls., 1968; library cons. St. Clement Sch., 1969. Rev. Andrew Bowhuis meml. scholar Cath. Library Assn., 1960. Cert. fund raising exec. Nat. Soc. Fund Raising Execs. Mem. Nat. Soc. Fund Raising Execs., Council for Advancement and Support of Edn., Cath. Library Assn. (life, chmn. No. Ill. unit 1968-69, exec. bd. 1981-87), Council Support and Advancement Edn., Art Inst. Chgo. (life), Council on Library Tech. (v.p. 1970, pres. 1971). Address: 3800 Peterson Ave Chicago IL 60659

RUDY, DAVID ROBERT, physician; b. Columbus, Ohio, Oct. 19, 1934; s. Robert Sale and Lois May (Arthur) R.; B.Sc., Ohio State U.,1956, M.D., 1960; m. Rose Mary Sims; children by previous marriage—Douglas D., Steven W., Katharine L. Intern, Northwestern Meml. Hosp., Chgo., 1960-61;

resident in internal medicine Ohio State U. Hosp., 1963-64; resident in pediatrics Children's Hosp., Columbus, Ohio, 1964; practice medicine specializing in family practice, Columbus, 1964-75; dir. Family Practice Center and residency program Riverside Meth. Hosp., Columbus, 1975-85; dir. Family Practice Ctr. and residency Monsour Med. Ctr., Jeannette, Pa., 1985—; clin. assoc. prof. Ohio State U., Penn. State U. Dept. Family Medicine. Served as capt., Flight surgeon, M.C., USAF, 1961-63. Diplomate Am. Bd. Family Practice (charter). Fellow Am. Acad. Family Physicians; mem. AMA, Ohio State Med. Assn., Central Ohio Acad. Family Practice (pres. 1979), Pa. Acad. Family Physicians (bd. dirs. 1985—), Columbus Maennerchor, Columbus Med. Symposium (pres. 1981), Mensa, SAR. Republican. Contbr. articles to profl. jours. Home: 1633 Timberlake Dr Delaware OH 43015

RUDZEWICZ, JOHN J., accountant; b. Detroit, Apr. 13, 1945; s. Al J. and Irene Rudzewicz; m. Victoria Rudzewicz; children: Michelle, John. Student, Walsh Coll., Detroit, 1970. CPA, Mich. Mng. ptnr. Follmer Rudzewicz & Co., P.C., Southfield, Mich., 1968—. Served with U.S. Army, 1966-68. Republican. Roman Catholic. Office: Follmer Rudzewicz & Co PC 30215 Southfield Rd Southfield MI 48076

RUEBECK, ANN ELIZABETH BOWMAN, church school executive, small business owner; b. Cleve., Apr. 25, 1939; d. Donald Edwin and Martha Jane (Reichenbach) Bowman; children: Christopher, David. Student, Cornell U., 1957-59; AB, BS, Ind. U., 1961. Pres. AB Ruebeck & Assocs., Inc., Indpls., 1980—, Tour du Jour, Indpls., 1984—; dir. sch. St. Paul's Episcopal Ch., Indpls., 1985—. Mem. Children's Mus. Guild, Indpls.; guild Indpls. Mus. Art., Jr. Aux. Indpls. Day Nursery Assn.; pres. vol. action ctr. bd. United Way, Indpls., ; bd. dirs. Jr. League of Indpls., Ind. State Symphony Soc., Inc., bd. dirs. Am. Symphony Orchestra League, Washington; trustee Indpls. Opera Co. Recipient Those Spl. People award Women in Communications, Inc., 1978. Mem. Assn. Major Symphony Orchestra (vols., pres. 1981-83). Avocations: sailing, lap swimming, skiing. Office: St Pauls Episcopal Ch 10 W 61st St Indianapolis IN 46208

RUEDEN, HENRY ANTHONY, accountant; b. Green Bay, Wis., Dec. 25, 1949; s. Bernard M. and Audrey Rueden. BS, U. Wis., Green Bay, 1971; MBA, U. Wis., Oshkosh, 1973; postgrad., Internat. Grad. Sch., St. Louis, 1984—. CPA, Ill., Wis.; cert. mgmt. acct.; cert. internal auditor; cert. info. systems auditor; cert. cost analyst. Auditor U.S. Customs Service, Chgo., 1974-86; systems acct. U.S. R.R. Retirement Bd., Chgo., 1986—. Mem. Am. Inst. CPA's, Wis. Inst. CPA's, Nat. Assn. Accts., Assn. Govt. Accts. Roman Catholic. Home: 2661 S Pine Tree Rd DePere WI 54115

RUEGEMER, DEL BERNARD, computer systems analyst; b. Richmond, Minn., Feb. 4, 1949; s. Andrew Henry and Hildegard Adelheid (Braegelmann) R. BA, St. John's U., Collegeville, Minn., 1971; cert. in mgmt. info. systems, U. Minn., 1980. System application engr. Warner & Swasey, Cleve., 1973-75; programmer City of Mpls., 1975-77; systems analyst TPF & C, Bloomington, Minn., 1977-79; programmer/analyst Gelco Corp., Eden Prairie, Minn., 1979-81; systems analyst Compucare, Mpls., 1981—. Pres. Assn. Medicine Lake Area Citizens, Plymouth, Minn., 1981. Mem. Data Processing Mgrs. Assn. Home: 2476 Hemlock Ln N Plymouth MN 55441 Office: Health Cen Corp 2810 57th Ave N Suite 520 Minneapolis MN 55430

RUEGSEGGER, DONALD RAY, JR., radiol. physicist, educator; b. Detroit, May 29, 1942; s. Donald Ray and Margaret Arlene (Elliot) R.; B.S., Wheaton Coll., 1964; M.S., Ariz. State U., 1966, Ph.D. (NDEA fellow), 1969. Diplomate Am. Bd. Radiology; m. Judith Ann Merrill, Aug. 20, 1965; children—Steven, Susan, Mark, Ann. Radiol. physicist Miami Valley Hosp., Dayton, Ohio, 1969—, chief med. physics sect., 1983—; physics cons. X-ray dept. VA Hosp., Dayton, 1970—; adj. asst. prof. physics Wright State U., Fairborn, Ohio, 1973—, clin. asst. prof. radiology, 1976-81, clin. assoc. prof. radiology, 1981—, group leader in med. physics, dept. radiol. scis. Med. Sch., 1978—. Mem. Am. Assn. Physicists in Medicine (pres. Ohio River Valley chpt. 1982-83, co-chmn. local summer sch. arrangements com. 1986), Am. Coll. Radiology, Am. Coll. Med. Physics (founding chancellor), Am. Phys. Soc., AAAS, Ohio Radiol. Soc., Health Physics Soc. Baptist. Home: 2018 Washington Creek Ln Centerville OH 45459 Office: Radiation Therapy Miami Valley Hosp 1 Wyoming St Dayton OH 45409

RUESCH, DAVID GEORGE, engineering manager; b. Berwyn, Ill., Dec. 13, 1943; s. Clarence Herman Karl and Victoria (Krystoff) R.; m. Leanne Donnis Peters, Feb. 1, 1964; children: Paul David, Mark Donald, John Carl, David Peter. BSME, Valparaiso (Ind.) U., 1966; MBA, Cen. Mich. U., 1975. Gage engr. Saginaw (Mich.) div. Gen. Motors Corp., 1966-70, tool engr., 1970-72, sr. mfg. engr., 1972-78, engring. supr., 1978-83; mgr. mfg. engring. Simpson Industries, Litchfield, Mich., 1983-85, mgr. engring. services, 1985—; mem. indsl. adv. com. Tri-State U., Angola, Ind., 1986—. Pres. Parent-Tchrs. Council, Marshall, Mich., 1985—, Saginaw Area Joint Bd. Elders, 1982. Mem. Soc. Mfg. Engrs., Sigma Iota Epsilon. Republican. Lutheran. Avocations: fishing, camping, boating, old cars. Home: 208 W Prospect St Marshall MI 49068 Office: Simpson Industries Inc 917 Anderson Rd Box 177 Litchfield MI 49252

RUFF, JESLEY CURTIS, dentist, educator; b. Des Moines, Aug. 26, 1954; s. Louis L. and Mildred Ruff; m. Sonya Jo Ruff, May 28, 1978; children: Ilana Marie, Aaron Maxwell. Student, U. Ariz., 1972-76, U. Wis., Milw., 1972-76; DDS, Marquette U., 1980; postgrad., U. Rochester, 1981-82. Fellow Eastman Dental Ctr., Rochester, N.Y., 1980-81; resident gen. practice The Genessee Hosp., Rochester, 1981-82; dir. spl. patients clinic Marquette U., Milw., 1983—; dir. Faye McBeath Sr. Citizens Oral Health Project, Milw., 1983—; asst. prof. community health Marquette U., 1983—; cons. Geriatric Dental Fellowship Programs VA, Milw., 1983-84; dir. dental sect. Good Samaritan Hosp., Milw., 1984—. Recipient ADA Geriatric Health Care award, 1984, Access award Sacred Heart Rehab. Hosp., Milw., 1985; named Outstanding Young Educator and Individual Milw. Jaycees, 1985. Mem. Nat. Found. Dentistry for the Handicapped, Am. Assn. Dental Schs. Home: 902 E Meadow Pl Milwaukee WI 53217 Office: Marquette U Sch Dentistry 604 N 16th St Milwaukee WI 53233

RUFF, RANDALL NORMAN, dentist; b. Bay, Mich., July 9, 1954; s. Clarence Leonard and Irene Marie (Gerhauser) R.; m. Judy Anne Laderach, June 10, 1978; children: Benjamin, Bradley, Daniel. Journeyman in tool and die, Bay City (Mich.) Trade Sch., 1975; student, Delta Coll., Saginaw Valley State Coll.; DDS, U. Mich., 1984. Gen. practice dentistry Nashville, Flint, Mich., 1984—. Mem. ADA, Mich. Dental Assn., Am. Acad. Implant Dentistry. Avocations: classical guitar, flying. Home: 234 W Hotchkiss Rd Freeland MI 48623 Office: Nashville Dental Clinic 604 Reed Rd Nashville MI 49073

RUFF, ROBERT LOUIS, neurologist, physiology researcher; b. Bklyn., Dec. 16, 1950; s. John Joseph and Rhoda (Alpert) R.; m. Louise Seymour Acheson, Apr. 26, 1980. BS with highest honors, Cooper Union, 1971; MD with highest honors in Medicine, U. Wash., 1976. Diplomate Am. Bd. Neurology and Psychiatry. Asst. neurologist N.Y. Hosp., Cornell Med. Sch., N.Y.C., 1977-80; asst. prof. physiology and medicine U. Wash., Seattle, 1980-84; assoc. prof. neurology Case Western Res. Med. Sch., Cleve., 1984; chief dept. neurology Cleve. VA Med. Ctr., 1984—; adv. Child Devel. and Mental Retardation Ctr., Seattle, 1980-84, Burien Devel. Disability Ctr., Wash., 1982-84; mem. med. adv. bd. Muscular Dystrophy Assn., Seattle, 1984, NE Ohio chpt. Multiple Sclerosis Soc., 1986—; chmn. med. adv. bd. NE Ohio chpt. Myasthemia Gravis Found., 1987—. Contbr. articles to profl. jours. and chpts. to books. Recipient Tchr. Investigator award NIH; NSF fellow, 1971; NIH grantee, Muscular Dystrophy Assn. grantee; N.Y. State Regents med. scholar, 1971. Fellow Am. Heart Assn. (stroke council); mem. Am. Physics Soc., Am. Acad. Neurology, AMA, Neurosci. Soc., Biophys. Soc., Am. Neurol. Assn., N.Y. Acad. Sci., Am. Geriatrics Soc., Sigma Pi Sigma (v.p. 1970-71), Alpha Omega Alpha (v.p. 1975-76). Democrat. Home: 2572 Stratford Rd Cleveland Heights OH 44110 Office: VA Med Ctr 10701 East Blvd127-W Cleveland OH 44106

RUFF, SPENCER RAYMOND, architect; b. Morris, Minn., June 13, 1944; s. Raymond and Beatrice (Zahl) R.; m. Sharon Emily Calverley, Aug. 26, 1967; children: Heather, Travis. BArch, U. Minn., 1969. Architect Cerny, Mpls., 1969-71, Haarstick and Lundgren, St. Paul, 1971-72, Weichsel Baum, Rochester, Minn., 1972-75, TSP, Sioux Falls, S.D., 1975-83; pres. Design Devel., Sioux Falls, 1983—. Pres. Aid Assn. for Luths., Sioux Falls, 1982-86; mem Hist. Preservation Commn., Sioux Falls, 1986—; bd. dirs. Historic S.D. Found, Rapid City, 1985—. Mem. AIA, S.D. Inst. Architecture, S. D. Architecture Soc. (archtl. Design award 1984,86), C. of C. (Archtl. Design award 1985). Republican. Avocations: hunting, fishing, wilderness travel. Home: 207 E 23d St Sioux Falls SD 57105 Office: Design Devel Inc 1917 S Minnesota Sioux Falls SD 57105

RUFFIN, RICHARD D(AVID), urologist; b. Cairo, Ill., July 7, 1924; s. Edward David and Alpha Mae (Curtis) R.; m. Yvonne White, May 14, 1953; children—Richard David, Patti Yvonne, Kenneth George. Student NO. Ill. U., 1940-41; student Ill. State U., 1941-43, U. Ill., 1946-47; M.D., Meharry Med. Coll., 1953. Intern Homer G. Phillips Hosp., St. Louis, 1953-54, resident in surgery, 1954-55, resident in urology, 1955-58; practice medicine specializing in urology, Columbus, Ohio, 1958—; mem. staff St. Anthony Hosp., Grant Hosp., Children's Hosp., St. Ann's Hosp.; cons. urology Ohio Dept. Rehab. and Correction, 1975-78. Served to cpl. U.S. Army, 1943-45; ETO. Recipient citation of citizenship Columbus Div. Police, 1971; Pres.'s award for 25 yrs. service Meharry Med. Coll., 1978; award for 25 yrs. Service Children's Hosp., 1984, Grant Hosp., 1984. Mem. Columbus Acad. Medicine, Ohio State Med. Assn., AMA, Central Ohio Urol. Soc. (sec.-treas. 1964-65, pres. 1967-68), Am. Urol. Assn., Columbus Assn. Physicians and Dentists. Home: 3236 E Livingston Ave Columbus OH 43227 Office: Franklin Park Med Ctr 1829 E Long St Columbus OH 43203

RUFFNER, KAREN ROSE BLAKE, English and reading educator; b. Woodstock, Ill., Jan. 21, 1952; d. Edward William and Ethel Katherine (Freund) Blake; m. Gregory Neil Ruffner, July 13, 1974; children: Blake Christopher, Amy Katherine. BA, U. Ill., 1975; MEd, No. Ill. U., 1978. Cert. secondary edn. tchr., language arts tchr., curriculum and supervision tchr. Tchr. English Harlem Sch. Dist., Loves Park, Ill., 1975-76; tchr. reading South Beloit (Ill.) Sch. Dist., 1976-78, Rockford (Ill.) Pub. Schs., 1978-84; instr. English, reading and study skills Rockford Coll., 1986—; tutor Rockford Coll., 1986; pvt. practice tutor, Rockford, 1978—. Vol. Winnebago County Ctr. for Blind, Rockford, 1982, art P.A. Peterson Nursing Home, Rockford, 1985-86. Mem. Sierra Club (exec. com. 1980-82). Roman Catholic. Avocations: bicycling, golfing, reading, playing volleyball and softball. Home: 2525 Guilford Rd Rockford IL 61107 Office: Rockford Coll 5050 E State St Rockford IL 61107

RUGG, JAMES MICHAEL, diesel engine company executive; b. Jamestown, N.Y., Nov. 27, 1952; s. Clayton Anthony Jr. and Jeanne (Pihlblad) R.; m. Jayne Greco, July 8, 1972. BA in Philosophy, SUNY, Oswego, 1974; MBA in Fin., Lehigh U., 1976. Registered securities dealer. Acct. exec. Bodell, Overcash & Anderson, Jamestown, 1977-78; fin. analyst Cummins Engine Co., Inc., Lakewood, N.Y., 1977-79, purchasing agt., 1979-82, mgr. inventory control, 1982-85; mgr. corp. strategy Cummins Engine Co., Inc., Columbus, Ind., 1985-86, mgr. internat. pricing, 1986—. Mem. team walk com. Columbus March of Dimes, 1987. Mem. U.S. Power Squadron (safety officer 1983, treas. 1984-85, 3 merit marks 1983-85). Republican. Club: Grandview Sailing Assn. (Columbus). Avocations: sailing, hunting, nordic skiing, beer brewing. Home: 10931 W Grandview Dr Columbus IN 47201 Office: Cummins Engine Co Inc Box 3005 Mail Code 60122 Columbus IN 47202-3005

RUGGIERO, JOHN ANTHONY, finance company executive; b. Jersey City, Aug. 31, 1959; s. John James and Cecilia (Paolino) R.; m. Lynn Bernadette D'Orio, Sept. 19, 1982. BA, Rutgers U., 1981. Registered investment advisor. Mgr. sales Home Life of N.Y., N.Y.C., 1981-85, Monarch Resources, Detroit, 1985-87; gen. mgr. Monarch Resources, Independence, Ohio, 1987—. Mem. Internat. Assn. Fin. Planners, Nat. Assn. Life Underwriters (cons. 1981—, polit. action com. 1981—). Republican. Roman Catholic. Avocations: photography, skiing. Home: 6272 Morning Glory Circle Solon OH 44139 Office: Monarch Resources 4500 Riverside Rd 360 Independence OH 44131

RUGGLES, MICHAEL LEE, insurance company executive; b. Danville, Ill., Dec. 30, 1938; s. Fred William and Mary Kathryn (Waltzer) R.; m. Adrienne May Spencer, Jan. 8, 1965; children—James, Gregory, David, Adrienne Michele. B.S. in Indsl. Tech., Ill. State U., 1963; postgrad. Internat. Safety Acad., 1972; cert. safety profl., 1976. Engr., Am. Mutual Liability Ins. Co., Louisville, 1964, sr. engr., 1966; safety rep. Ins. Co. of N. Am., Louisville, 1967, supr., 1972, mgr., 1974-76; malpractice loss control specialist, 1976, regional dir. loss control, Omaha, 1978, dir. home office, Phila., 1980; dir. safety mgmt. services AID Ins. Services, Des Moines, 1981—, asst. v.p. safety mgmt. service, 1982—; hosp. malpractice loss control cons. Ill. State scholar; recipient Good Samaritan award, 1972. Mem. Nat. Safety Mgmt. Soc., Am. Soc. Safety Engrs., Nat. Fire Protection Assn., Am. Contract Bridge League. Author: Principle of Half Tone Photography, 1963; Loss Control Techniques-A Success Story, 1973. Office: 701 5th Ave Des Moines IA 50304

RUGGLESS, CONNIE B., data processing executive; b. Des Moines, May 30, 1949; d. Forest Kenneth and Mildred Louise (Grubb) Borts; m. Ross Lynn Ruggless, Aug. 7, 1971; children: Claudia Marie, Stacy Lynn. BA, U. No. Iowa, Cedar Falls, 1971; MS, Iowa State U., Ames, 1980. Tchr. Bayard (Iowa) High Sch., 1972-74; coll. instr. Am. Inst. Bus., Des Moines, 1974-81; computer-based instrn. designer Allied Group, Des Moines, 1981-83, mgr. tech. edn., 1983-86, mgr. procedures and tng., 1986—. Trustee Altoona (Iowa) United Meth. Ch., 1986—, nominations com., 1985-87. Named one of Outstanding Young Women Am., 1983. Mem. Am. Soc. for Tng. and Devel. (fin. 1984-86, pres. 1986-87), Iowa Data Processing Educators Assn. (v.p. 1985, pres. 1986). Democrat. Avocations: golf, bowling, gardening. Home: 400 6th St NW Altoona IA 50009 Office: Allied Group 701 5th Ave Des Moines IA 50304

RUGO, STEVEN ALFRED, architect; b. Washington, June 1, 1953; s. Alfred Joseph and Lena (Aubrey) R.; m. Mary Lourie Blackett, Nov. 11, 1979, (div. Jan. 1984). Student, Ripon Coll., 1971-73, Harvard U., 1973; BArch, Syracuse U., 1976. Assoc. firms Booth/Hansen, Booth Nagle & Hartray, Booth & Nagle, Chgo., 1976-81; pvt. practice architecture Chgo., 1980—. Assoc. Rush Presbyn., St. Lukes Med. Ctr., Chgo. Mem. AIA. Episcopalian. Club: Racquet (Chgo.). Avocations: sailing, tennis. Office: 345 N Canal St Chicago IL 60606

RUHL, JAMES FRANCIS, printing company executive; b. Sterling, Ill., Apr. 5, 1943; s. Francis Anthony and Gladys Mary (Hamblock) R.; m. Linda Ann Schlupp, Sept. 26, 1970; children: Catherine, Kenneth, Brian, Michael. BS in Engring., U.S. Mil. Acad., 1967. Commd. 2d. lt. U.S. Army, 1967; advanced through grades to capt. U.S. Army, Fed. Republic Germany, Vietnam, 1967-74; resigned U.S. Army, 1974; indsl. engr. Personal Products, Wilmington, Ill., 1974-77, R.R. Donnelley, Dwight, Ill., 1977-85; mgr. plant engring. W.F. Hall Printing, Chgo., 1985-87; v.p. mfg. Hart Press Inc., Long Prairie, Minn., 1985—; also bd. dirs. Hart Press Inc., Long Prairie. Mem. Long Prairie C. of C. (bd. dirs. 1986—). Episcopalian. Avocations: bowling, golf, handball. Home: PO Box 162 Long Prairie MN 56347 Office: The Hart Press Inc 333 Central Ave Long Prairie MN 56347

RULAU, RUSSELL, numismatic consultant; b. Chgo., Sept. 21, 1926; s. Alphonse and Ruth (Thorsen) R.; student U. Wis., 1946-48; m. Hazel Darlene Grizzell, Feb. 1, 1968; children by previous marriage—Lance Eric, Russell A.W., Marcia June, Scott Quentin, Roberta Ann, Kyle Christopher; 1 step-dau., Sharon Maria Kenowski. Entered U.S. Army, 1944-1950, served to master sgt. USAF, 1950-62; resigned active duty, 1962; asst. editor Coin World newspaper, Sidney, Ohio, 1962-74, editor World Coins mag., 1964-74, Numis. Scrapbook mag., 1968-74; editorial coordinator How to Order Fgn. Coins guidebook, 1966-74; editor in chief World Coin News newspaper, 1974-84, Bank Note Reporter, 1983-84; fgn. editor Numis. News newspaper, 1974-77; cons. editor Standard Catalog of World Paper Money, 1975-83; contbg. editor Standard Catalog of World Coins, 1974-81; pres. House of Rulau, 1984—; v.p. Keogh-Rulau Galleries, Dallas, 1984-85, Pobjoy Mint Ltd., Iola, Wis., 1985—. Mem. U.S. Assay Commn., 1973. Sec., Numismatic Terms Standardization Com., 1966-74; vice-chmn. Waupaca County Republican party, 1977-79, chmn., 1979-82; chmn. county chairmen, 3d vice chmn. Wis. Rep. Party, 1981-83; del. Rep. Nat. Conv., 1980; exec. com. 6th Wis. Dist. Rep. Com., 1984—. Fellow Royal Numis. Soc., Am. Numis. Soc. (asso.); mem. Token and Medal Soc. (editor 1962-63), Am. Numis. Assn., Canadian, S. African numis. assns., Mont. Hist. Soc., Am. Vecturist Assn., Numis. Lit. Guild (dir. 1974-78, editor 1984—), VFW (post commdr. 1985—). Lutheran. Author: (with George Fuld) Spiel Marken, 1962-65, American Game Counters, 1972: World Mint Marks, 1966; Modern World Mint Marks, 1970; (with J. U. Rixen and Frovin Sieg) Seddelkatalog Slesvig Plebiscit Zone I og II, 1970; Numismatics of Old Alabama, 1971-73; Hard Times Tokens, 1980; Early American Tokens, 1981; U.S. Merchant Tokens 1845-1860, 1982; U.S. Trade Tokens 1866-1889, 1983, Tokens of the Gay Nineties, 1987; (with George Fuld) Medallic Portraits of Washington, 1985. Contbr. numis. articles to profl. jours. Home: Route 2 Box 11 Iola WI 54945 Office: Pobjoy Mint USA Ltd PO Box 153 Iola WI 54945

RULE-HOFFMAN, RICHARD CARL, art therapist, educator; b. Youngstown, Ohio, June 19, 1947; s. Carl Frank and Bernice Rita (Kubala) Hoffman; m. Gail Lillian Rule, Aug. 9, 1980. BA, Cleve. State U., 1973; MA, Goddard Coll., 1978. Registered Art Therapist. Art therapist Beech Brook, Pepper Pike, Ohio, 1970—; instr. art therapy Art Psychotherapy Inst. of Cleve., Cleveland Heights, Ohio, 1974-77; adj. prof. art therapy Ursuline Coll., Pepper Pike, 1978—, asst. dir. MA program in art therapy, 1986—; art therapy field faculty supr. Goddard Coll. and Norwich U., Plainfield and Montpelier, Vt., 1978—; cons. Fedn. Community Planning, Cleve., 1976-77, Case Western Reserve U., Cleve., 1976-77. Editor, creator (newsletter) The Palette, 1975-79. Mem. Am. Art Therapy Assn. (profl. credential), Buckeye Art Therapy Assn. of Ohio (publications chmn., 1975-80). Democrat. Roman Catholic. Avocations: artist, canoer, naturalist. Home: 3700 Walnut Hills Rd Orange OH 44122 Office: Beech Brook 3737 Lander Rd Pepper Pike OH 44124 also: Ursuline Coll 2550 Lander Rd Pepper Pike OH 44124

RUMELY, EMMET SCOTT, ret. automobile co. exec., banker; b. N.Y.C., Feb. 15, 1918; s. Edward A. and Fanny (Scott) R.; grad. Phillips Exeter Acad., 1935; B.S., Yale, 1939; postgrad. U. Mich., 1940-41; m. Elizabeth Hodges, July 5, 1947; children—Virginia H., Elizabeth Scott Visser, Scott Hodges. Mgr., Marenisco Farms, La Porte County, Ind., 1939-73; dir. La Porte Hotel Co., Inc., 1938-70, pres., 1965-70; pres., dir. Rumely Corp., 1970—; product planning mgr. tractor ops. Ford Motor Co., Birmingham, Mich., 1961-70, asst. to v.p., gen. mgr., 1970-75; dir., mem. exec. com. 1st Nat. Bank & Trust Co., La Porte. Mem. Detroit Inst. Arts Founders Soc., Am. Soc. Agrl. Engrs., Soc. Automotive Engrs., Am. Mktg. Assn. Clubs: Orchard Lake (Mich.) Country; Huron Mountain (Big Bay, Mich.); Yale (Detroit). Home: 207 Abbey Rd Birmingham MI 48008 Office: 800 Jefferson Ave La Porte IN 46350

RUMLEY, JAMES MICHAEL, lawyer; b. Kansas City, Kans., Apr. 30, 1953; s. James L. and Lena K. (Stoner) R.; m. Joan L. Garrison, Mar. 7, 1981 (div. Oct. 1985). BA in Adminstrn. Justice, Pub. Adminstrn., Park Coll., 1980; JD, U. Mo., 1984. Bar: Mo. 1984. Police officer North Kansas City (Mo.) Police Dept., 1975-78; spl. agt. Chgo. & Northwestern R.R., Kansas City, Mo., 1978-82; ptnr. Meise, Coen, Hutchison & Rumley, Kansas City, Mo., 1984—; adj. prof. law U. Mo., Kansas City, 1985—. Exec. editor: Urban Lawyer, 1983-84. Served to sgt. U.S. Army, 1972-75. Mem. ABA, Mo. Bar Assn., Kansas City Bar Assn., Am. Trial Lawyers Assn., Order of Barristers, Phi Delta Phi. Republican. Methodist. Office: Meise Coen Hutchison & Rumley 1125 Grand Suite 900 Kansas City MO 64106

RUNCIE, JOHN FRYER, manufacturing company executive; b. East Orange, N.J., Jan. 2, 1942; s. W. Erskine and Carol Glover (Stone) R.; m. Gail Hensley, Nov. 12, 1983; children:Pamela, Devonne, Brenda, Craig. BA, Lehigh U., 1964; MA, U. Conn., 1966; PhD, Rutgers U., 1971. Assoc. prof. U. Mich., Flint, 1969-78; dir. social research Devel. Analysis Assocs., Cambridge, Mass., 1978-80; sr. researcher Pub. Systems Evaluation, Cambridge, 1980-82; sr. orgn. devel. cons. Anheuser-Busch, St. Louis, 1982-85; v.p. human resources Doehler-Jarvis, Toledo, 1985-87; mgr. orgn. devel. and tng. Batesville (N.J) Casket Co., 1987—. Author: Experiencing Social Research, 1980. Mem. Am. Sociol. Assn., Indsl. Relations Assn., Am. Soc. Personnel Adminstrn., Alpha Kappa Delta. Home: 1511 W Stadium Blvd Ann Arbor MI 48103 Office: Batesville Casket Co Hwy 46 Batesville IN 47006

RUND, DOUGLAS ANDREW, physician; b. Columbus, Ohio, July 20, 1945; s. Carl Andrew and Caroline Amelia (Row) R.; B.A., Yale U., 1967; M.D., Stanford U., 1971. Intern in medicine U. Calif., San Francisco-Moffett Hosp., 1971-72; resident in gen. surgery Stanford U., 1972-74; Robert Wood Johnson Found. clin. scholar in medicine Stanford U., 1974-76; med. dir. Mid-Peninsula Health Service, Palo Alto, Calif., 1975-76; clin. instr. dept. medicine and preventive medicine Stanford U. Med. Sch., 1975-76, asst. dir. early clin. experience in family medicine program, 1975-76; assoc. prof., dir. div. emergency medicine Ohio State Coll. Medicine, 1982-87; dir. emergency med. services Ohio State U. Hosps., 1977—, dir. emergency medicine residency program, assoc. prof. dept. family medicine, 1976-87, assoc. prof. dept. preventive medicine; attending staff Ohio State U. Hosps., 1976-87; med. dir. CTI, Emergency Med. Services Dept.; med. dir. Columbus Emergency Med. Services System; pres. Internat. Research Inst. Emergency Medicine; examiner Am. Bd. Emergency Medicine; sr. research fellow NATO: Health and Med. Aspects of Disaster Preparedness, 1985-87; on profl. leave epidemiology and injury control, U. Edinburgh, Scotland, 1987. Lic. physician, Ohio, Calif.; diplomate Nat. Bd. Med. Examiners, Am. Bd. Family Practice, Am. Bd. Emergency Medicine. Fellow Am. Coll. Emergency Physicians; mem. Soc. Tchrs. Emergency Medicine. Soc. for Health and Human Values, Univ. Assn. for Emergency Medicine, Nat. Inst. on Alcohol Abuse and Alcoholism, IAAA, Am. Coll. Emergency Physicians (task force on substance abuse and injury control), Alpha Omega Alpha. Author: Triage, 1981; Essentials of Emergency Medicine, 1982, 2nd edit., 1986; Emergency Radiology, 1982; Emergency Psychiatry, 1983; Environmental Emergencies, 1985; editor: Emergency Medicine Ann., 1983, 84; Emergency Medicine Survey, Annals of Emergency Medicine; editor-in-chief Ohio State Series on Emergency Medicine, Emergency Medicine Observer, 1986-87; guest editor Annals of Emergency Medicine Symposium, 1986, contbr. chpt. to Family Medicine Principles and Practice, 1978, 2d edit., 1983; contbr. articles to profl. jours. Office: 450 W 10th Ave Columbus OH 43210

RUNGE, DONALD EDWARD, food wholesale company executive; b. Milw., Mar. 20, 1938; s. Adam and Helen Teresa (Voss) R.; divorced; children: Roland, Richard, Lori. Grad., Spencerian Coll., Milw., 1960. Fin. v.p. Milw. Cheese Co., Waukesha, Wis., 1962-69; dir. Farm House Foods Corp., Milw., 1966—, pres., 1966-84, chief exec. officer, 1984—, treas., 1984-85, chmn., pres., 1985—; sec. The Diana Corp., Milw., 1985-86, treas., 1986—; pres. Drug Systems Inc., Milw., 1982-84, chief exec. officer, 1984-85, treas., 1984—, chmn., 1985—; bd. dirs. Convenient Food Mart, CasaBlanca Industries, Inc., City of Industry, Calif. Adventist. Home: 2204 W Kenboern Dr Glendale WI 53209 Office: Farm House Foods Corp 111 E Wisconsin Ave Suite 1900 Milwaukee WI 53202

RUNGE, KAY KRETSCHMAR, library director; b. Davenport, Iowa, Dec. 9, 1946; d. Alfred Edwin and Ina (Paul) Kretschmar; m. Peter S. Runge Sr., Aug. 17, 1968; children: Peter Jr., Katherine. BS in History Edn., Iowa State U., 1969; MLS, U. Iowa, 1970. Pub. service librarian Anoka County Library, Blaine, Minn., 1971-72; cataloger Augustana Coll., Rock Island, Ill., 1972-74; dir. Scott County Library System, Eldridge, Iowa, 1974-85, Davenport (Iowa) Pub. Library, 1985—. Bd. dirs. River Ctr. for Performing Arts, Davenport, 1983—; mem. steering com. Quad-Cities Media for Strategic Action, 1987. Recipient Service Key award Iowa State U. Alumni Assn., 1979. Mem. ALA (vice chmn., chmn. elect library adminstrs. and mgrs. div., fundraising section 1986), Iowa Library Assn. (pres. 1983), Iowa Edn. Media Assn. (Intellectual Freedom award 1984), Alpha Delta Pi (alumni state pres. 1978). Lutheran. Office: Davenport Pub Library 321 Main St Davenport IA 52801

RUNGE, RICK DALE, sales executive; b. DuQuoin, Ill., Oct. 12, 1956; s. Richard Lee and Louise Bertha (Witbart) R.; m. Durice Dawn Hopkins, May 2, 1981. AA, John A. Logan Coll., 1976; BS, So. Ill. U., 1979. Service technician Sears Roebuck Co., Carbondale, Ill., 1976-82; contract sales div. Sears Roebuck Co., St. Louis, 1982—. Mem. Nat. Assn. Home Builders, Ill.

Home Builders Assn., Nat. Fedn. Interscholastic Officials Assn., Nat. Assn. Sports Officicals, Egyptian Officials Assn. (v.p. 1986-87), So. Ill. U. Alumni Assn. Methodist. Home: 1515 Gartside Murphysboro IL 62966 Office: Sears Contract Sales 3708 S Grand Saint Louis MO 63118

RUNKLE, MARTIN DAVEY, university library director; b. Cin., Oct. 18, 1937; s. Newton and Ilo (Neal) R.; m. Nancy Force, Aug. 7, 1965; children: Seth, Elizabeth. BA, Muskingum Coll., 1959; MA, U. Pitts., 1964, U. Chgo., 1973. Library systems analyst U. Chgo., 1970-75, head cataloging librarian, 1975-79, asst. dir. tech. services, librarian, 1979-80, dir. library, 1980—; sr. lectr. grad. library sch. U. Chgo., 1977—. Fulbright grantee, 1965. Mem. ALA. Club: Arts (Chgo.). Office: U Chgo Library 1100 E 57th St Chicago IL 60637

RUNQUIST, ALFONSE WILLIAM, chemist; b. Hibbing, Minn., Apr. 4, 1945; s. Henrik Alfonse and Eleanor Irene (Anderson) R.; m. Jennifer Agnes Jackson, July 13, 1974. BS, Hamline U., 1967; PhD, Northwestern U., 1974. Instr. Northwestern U., Evanston, Ill., 1973-74; postdoctoral researcher Johns Hopkins U., Balt., 1974-76; chemist-devel. dept. Aldrich Chem. Co., Milw., 1976-79, mgr. tech. services, 1979—. Contbr. articles to profl. jours. Served with U.S. Army, 1969-71. Recipient Scholastic award Am. Inst. Chemists, 1967; NIH fellow, Northwestern U., 1969, 71-73. Mem. Am. Chem. Soc. Office: Aldrich Chem Co 940 W St Paul Ave Milwaukee WI 53233

RUNYAN, KAREN GAIL, nurse, military officer; b. San Diego, Jan. 17, 1961; s. Bruce Alan and Novadine Eleanor (Dudley) Posey; m. James Douglas Runyan, June 1, 1985; 1 child, Ashley Nicole. A in Nursing, Ind. State U., 1981, BSN, 1986. RN Union Hosp., Terre Haute, Ind., 1982—. Served with USAFR, 1983—. Mem. Am. Mil. Surgeon, Critical Care Nurses Assn., Ind. State Nurses Assn. Democrat. Methodist. Avocations: photography, golf. Home: Rural Rt 53 N 430 Terre Haute IN 47805

RUNYON, DANIEL VIRGIL, writer; b. Zeeland, Mich., Nov. 4, 1954; s. Lawrence Virgil and Leilah (Hartgerink) R.; m. M. Renee Munn, Sept. 10, 1983; children: David, Kirby. BA, Spring Arbor Coll., 1976; MA, Wheaton Coll., 1978. Instr. journalism Spring Arbor (Mich.) Coll., 1978-81, staff writer devel., 1978-80; sr. editor Fitness Finders Inc., Spring Arbor, 1980-82, dir. mktg., 1982-84; freelance writer Spring Arbor, 1982—. Co-author: No-Diet Fitness Book, 1985, The Divided Flame, 1986, Foresight, 1986; contbr. articles to profl. jours. Methodist. Avocations: investing, financial mgmt.

RUONA, ARTHUR ERNEST, marine engineer, astronomer; b. Fairfax, Minn., Oct. 4, 1920; s. Ernest and Emma Elma (Pudas) R.; m. Darlene Debbie Nelson, Sept. 21, 1967; 1 child, Laura Tola. Student, U. Minn., 1946-47; B Laws, LaSalle U., 1963. Marine engr. MEBA, San Francisco, 1957-84; instr. engring. Lake Carriers, Cleve., 1953-56. Patentee in field. Served to sgt. U.S. Army, 1942-46, ETO. Mem. Marine Engrs., Naval Inst., Air Force Assn., Am. Legion (life). Republican. Lutheran. Avocation: tree farming. Home and Office: RFD #1 Box 62 Fairfax MN 55332

RUPEL, JAMES B., development company executive; b. Piqua, Ohio, June 17, 1954; s. James Jacob and Janet Louise (Schaffer) R.; m. Marcia Lynn Jackson, Sept. 15, 1984. BA, Wittenberg U., Springfield, Ohio, 1976; MBA, Ind. U., Bloomington, 1979. CPA, Ohio. Staff acct. Touche Ross & Co., Dayton, Ohio, 1976-77; assoc. instr. Ind. U., Bloomington, 1977-79; treas. Val Decker Packing Co., Piqua, 1979-80; exec. v.p. Lloyds Acceptance Corp. and subs., Lawrenceburg, Ind., 1980—. Mem. Am. Inst. CPA's, Ohio soc. CPA's. Club: Hidden Valley Golf (Lawrenceburg). Home: 18626 Whispering Woods Dr Lawrenceburg IN 47025 Office: Hidden Valley Lake Inc 108 Fairway Dr Lawrenceburg IN 47025

RUPERT, JOHN EDWARD, retired savings and loan executive, business and civic affairs consultant; b. Cleve., Oct. 19, 1927; s. Edward J. and Emma (Levegood) R.; m. Virginia Carlson, Oct. 27, 1951; children: Kristen, Karen, David. B.A., Cornell U., 1949, LL.B., 1951; certificate, Grad. Sch. Savs. & Loan, Ind. U., 1958. With Broadview Savs. & Loan Co., Cleve., 1953-86; v.p. Broadview Savs. & Loan Co., 1964-74, mng. officer, 1965-86, pres., chief exec. officer, 1974-86, chmn., 1979-86. Mem. Cleve. Real Estate Bd., 1955-86; Mem. Lakewood (Ohio) Bd. Edn., 1971-77, pres., 1975-78; Vice pres., trustee Lakewood Hosp., 1966-71; trustee exec. com. of Cleve. Zool. Soc., pres. 1987; trustee Cleve. Orch., WVIZ Ednl. TV; bd. dirs. West Side YMCA; mem. Lakewood Hosp. Found.; mem. Cornell U. Council, 1971—, pres., 1977. Served with USAF, 1951-53. Mem. Cleve. Interfaith Housing Corp. (pres. 1971—), Inst. Fin. Edn. (pres. 1970), Cleve. Real Property Inventory (pres. 1976—), Am., Ohio, Cleve. bar assns., Ohio Motorists Assn., Delta Kappa Epsilon, Phi Delta Phi, Sphinx Head Soc. Clubs: Westwood Country, Union; Cleve. Yachting, Cornell (Cleve.) (trustee). Home and Office: 18129 W Clifton Rd Lakewood OH 44107

RUPLEY, JEFFREY P(IDGE), electronic engineer; b. Goose Creek, Tex., May 31, 1941; s. Robert Leon and Nelle Elizabeth (Milholland) R.; m. Dianne Elizabeth Walton, Aug. 29, 1964; children: Jeffrey P. II, Gregory W. BSEE, Purdue U., 1970. Engr. integrated cir. design RCA, Somerville, N.J., 1970-74; engr. integrated cir. design Delco Electronics, Kokomo, Ind., 1974-76, engr. integrated cir. design automation, 1976-81, sr. engr., 1981—. Co-inventor glass to metal seal, 1969. Mem. Howard County (Ind.) Sci. Fair, 1975-77, chmn., 1978; chmn. Regional Sci. Fair, Ind., 1978; asst. scoutmaster Boy Scouts Am., Flemington, N.J., 1970-74, Kokomo, 1983-86, scoutmaster, 1986—. Served to petty officer 2d cl. USN, 1961-65. Mem. Kokomo Engring. Soc. Republican. Lutheran. Avocations: golf, camping. Home: 5812 Dartmouth Ct Kokomo IN 46902 Office: Delco Electronics 1600 E Lincoln Rd Kokomo IN 46902

RUPORT, SCOTT HENDRICKS, lawyer; b. Paterson, N.J., Nov. 22, 1949; s. Fred Hendricks and Juyne (Kennedy) R.; m. Linda Darlene Smith, Sept. 12, 1970; children—Brittany Lyle, Courtney Kennedy. B.S. in Bus. Adminstrn., Bowling Green State U., 1971; J.D., U. Akron, 1974. Bar: Ohio 1974, Pa. 1984, U.S. Dist. Ct. for no. dist. Ohio 1974, U.S. Ct. Appeals for 6th circuit, 1975, U.S. Supreme Ct. 1978. Assoc. firm Schwab, Sager, Grosenbaugh, Rothal, Fort, Skidmore & Nukes Co., L.P.A., Akron, Ohio, 1974-76, Skidmore & George Co., L.P.A., Akron, 1976-79, Skidmore, Ruport & Haskings, Akron, 1979-83; ptnr. Roderick, Myers & Linton, Akron, 1983-85; Ruport Co. L.P.A.,Akron, 1985—; instr. real estate law U. Akron, 1976-77, adj. asst. prof. constrn. tech. Coll. Engring., 1983—. Served as capt., Fin. Corps, USAR, 1971-79. Mem. ABA, Akron Bar Assn., Ohio Bar Assn., Ohio Acad. Trial Lawyers, Assn. Trial Lawyers Am., Beta Gamma Sigma, Sigma Chi. Republican. Presbyterian. Office: CitiCenter Bldg 6th Floor 146 S High St Akron OH 44308-1344

RUPPE, RICHARD JAMES, computer supply company executive; b. Cleve., July 18, 1938; s. Rudolf and Antonia (Petsche) R.; m. Joanne Marie Marinko, Sept. 7, 1968; children: Mark James, Christine Marie, Michael David. Student, Cleve. State U., 1958-61, 68-69, Case-Western Res. U., 1964-68. Account rep. A.B. Dick Co., Cleve., 1961-69; account mgr. Graphic Sci., Cleve., 1969-74; owner Imaging Products, Chesterland, Ohio, 1974—. Vol. project drive United Way Services, Chardon, Ohio, 1984. Mem. Nat. Assn. for Self-Employed, Nat. Office Machine Dealers Assn., U.S. Table Tennis Assn., Am. Mutual LIfe Assn. Republican. Roman Catholic. Clubs: Orchard Hills, Country, Berkshire Hills Country (Chesterland, Ohio). Avocations: table tennis, swimming, cycling, golf.

RUPPEL, PHILLIP ALLEN, restaurant executive; b. Fairbury, Ill., Nov. 7, 1942; s. Clarence E. and M. Edith (Rasmussen) R.; m. Judy A. Shirley, Sept. 12, 1964; children: Tamara Lynn, Jeffrey Phillip. BS, So. Ill. U., Carbondale, 1965. Treas., sec. Gen. Scale Corp., Morton, Ill., 1966-67; mgr. accting. A O Smith Corp., Arlington, Ill., 1967-77; v.p. Wendy's of N.C., Hickory, 1977-80; pres. Parco, Ltd., Dubuque, Iowa, 1980—; mem. Franchise Adv. Council Wendy's Internat., Inc., Dublin, Ohio, 1983—. Republican. Mem. United Ch. of Christ. Club: Dubuque Golf and Country. Lodge: Rotary. Avocations: travel, golf, business investments. Office: Parco Ltd 2625 John F Kennedy Rd Dubuque IA 52001

RUPPERT, JAYNE ANN, comptroller; b. Madison, Wis., Mar. 9, 1956; d. Wayne Henry and Annette (Garvoille) R.; m. Ian Guy Perrin, Aug. 1, 1986. BBA, U. Wis., 1978. CPA, Wis. Staff acct. Williams, Young & Assocs., Madison, 1978-79; acct. Aim, Inc., Madison, 1979-83; comptroller Lindsay & Stone Advt., Inc., Madison, 1983—. Mem. Am. Inst. CPA's, Wis. Inst. CPA's. Roman Catholic. Avocations: outdoor activities, music. Home: 160 Proudfit Madison WI 53715 Office: Lindsay & Stone Advt Inc 100 State St Madison WI 53703

RUPPERT, RUPERT EARL, lawyer; b. Middletown, Ohio, Nov. 22, 1943; s. Paul Edward and Sarah Elizabeth (Morgan) R.; B.A., Ohio State U., 1968; J.D., Capital U., 1976; children—Jason, Ryan, Bradley, Matthew. Admitted to Ohio bar, 1976; asst. to gov. state of Ohio, Columbus, 1971-74, to atty. gen., 1974-77, spl. counsel to atty. gen. and to asst. atty. gen., 1977—; partner firm Ruppert, Bronson & Chicarelli, Franklin, Ohio, 1977—, also firm Riley & Ruppert, Franklin; dir., atty. Miami Valley Bank of S.W. Ohio, Franklin, 1979—, also dir. Mem. Warren County Democratic Central Com., 1977-82 ; chmn. Warren County Dem. Com., 1978-80; chmn. Warren County Brown for Atty. Gen., 1978; dep. campaign mgr. William J. Brown for Gov. Ohio, 1982; State campaign mgr. U.S. Sen. John Glenn. mem. Franklin City Charter Commn., 1978, Franklin CSC, 1978-79; v.p. Franklin City Schs. Bd. Edn., 1978-79, pres., 1979—. Served with AUS, 1968-70; Vietnam. Decorated Bronze Star, Combat Infantryman Badge; recipient Presdl. award for outstanding civic achievement among Viet Nam vets, 1979. Mem. Ohio Bar Assn., Warren County Bar Assn., Ohio Trial Lawyers Assn., Nat. Rifle Assn., Am. Legion. Home: PO Box 70 Franklin OH 45005 Office: 313 S Main St Franklin OH 45005

RUSCH, THEODORE FREDRICK, JR., management information systems specialist; b. Black River Falls, Wis., Apr. 2, 1940; s. Theodore Fredrick Sr. and Werra Louise (Winkert) R.; m. Leanna Lorraine Helmke, Sept. 29, 1965; children: Mark, John, Krista. BS, U. Wis., Stevens Point, 1970. System programmer Sentry Ins., Stevens Point, 1970-74, system specialist, 1974-76, data communications and data base mgr., 1976-80, sr. data communications and data base mgr., 1980-84, data communications and data systems mgr., 1984-86, mgr. voice and data communications, 1986—; group mgr. GUIDE Internat., Chgo., 1980-84, dir. requirements, 1984-86, dir. divs., 1986—. Ch. sch. supt. Trinity Luth. Ch., Stevens Point, 1978-80, mem. council, 1981-83, pres., 1985—; vice chmn. Trinity Luth. Found., 1984-86. Served with U.S. Army, 1958-61. Mem. Wis. Telecommunications Assn. Avocations: fishing, hunting, bee keeping. Home: 2826 Maple Ridge Rd Stevens Point WI 54481 Office: Sentry Ins 1800 N Point Dr Stevens Point WI 54481

RUSH, DAVID RAY, pharmacy and medicine educator, consultant; b. Celina, Ohio, Dec. 14, 1946; s. Raymond Harry and Helen Catherine (Burmeister) R. B.S. in Pharmacy, Ohio No. U., 1969; Pharm.D., U. Ky., 1975. Pharmacist Davis Pharmacy, Lima, Ohio, 1969-72; resident in pharmacy U. Ky., Lexington, 1972-75; prof. medicine and clin. pharmacy U. Mo., Kansas City, 1975—; chmn. bd. Dr. of Pharmacy Cons., Inc., Kansas City, 1983—. Author: Endocrine and Metabolic Emergencies, 1984. Contbr. articles to profl. jours. Recipient numerous clin. pharmacology research grants, Achievement in Profl. Practice and Hosp. Pharmacy award, 1976, Tchr. of Yr. award Goppert Family Care Ctr., Bapt. Med. Ctr., 1985, T.J. Garrison Achievement award Mo. Soc. Hosp. Pharmacists, 1986. Mem. Am. Coll. Clin. Pharmacy, Am. Soc. Hosp. Pharmacy, Am. Assn. Colls. Pharmacy, Am. Pharm. Assn., Am. Inst. History Pharmacy. Avocations: backpacking; fishing; wilderness conservation. Office: Truman Med Ctr E U Mo Dept Family Medicine 7900 Lee's Summit Rd Kansas City MO 64139

RUSH, GERALD ELMER, food service company executive; b. New Orleans, Aug. 5, 1930; s. Elmer H. and Alta (Billig) R.; children: Diane E., Gerald E., Heidi E., David E.; m. Beverly Ann Hoffman, Apr. 20, 1985. BS, Western Mich. U., 1953; MS, U. Calif., San Fernando Valley, 1965. Designer, prodn. and executor nat. network TV shows for ABC, NBC, CBS, and ind. studios, including Dean Martin Show, Jack Benny Spl., Bob Hope Spls., Danny Thomas Spl., Laugh In, Bill Cosby Spl., Jonathon Winters Show, Let's Make a Deal, Hollywood, Calif., 1963-67; tchr. TV prodn. and stagecraft Pasadena Playhouse, Hollywood, Los Angeles, 1963-67; dir. tng. and personnel McDonald Corp., Los Angeles, 1967-73, Ky. Fried Chicken, Louisville and San Diego, 1973-77; dir. tng. Jonoth's, San Antonio, 1977-78, Interstate United Corp., Chgo., 1978-82, Hickory Farms of Ohio, Maumee, 1982-84; pres. GR Prodns., Toledo, Ohio, 1984—. Served with U.S. Army, 1953-63. Mem. Am. Soc. Tng. Dirs., Conf. Hotel and Restaurant Trainers, Nat. Restaurant Assn., Employment Mgmt. Assn., Nat. Audio-Visual Assn., Vietnam Vets. Assn., U.S. Parachute Assn. Office: 1251 S Reynolds Rd Suite 189 Toledo OH 43615

RUSH, JAMES RAYMOND, state executive; b. Chgo., Sept. 18, 1944; s. Clyde G. and Winifred M. (Campbell) R.; student So. Ill. U., Carbondale, 1965-68; m. Linda Boeser, Dec. 30, 1973; 1 dau., Amanda. With Greater Egypt Regional planning and Devel. Commn., Carbondale, Ill., 1967-84, dir. spl. programs, 1978-84; exec. Ill. Dept. Law Enforcement, 1984— (name changed to Ill. Dept. State Police). writer, lectr. in field. Mem. Nat. Council Crime and Delinquency, Ill. Assn. Chiefs of Police, Internat. Assn. Chiefs of Police, Internat. Police Assn. Presbyterian.

RUSH, RICHARD ERNEST, engineering executive; b. Phillipsburg, N.J., June 19, 1933; s. Elmer Palmer and Sadie Milcah (Morris) R.; m. Audrey Armitage Winne, Mar. 26, 1955; children: Richard Jr., Gary W., Alison A. BSME, MIT, 1955. With Bethlehem Steel Corp., 1955—; master mechanic Bethlehem Steel Corp., Chesterton, Ind., 1967-80, gen. foreman, 1980—; v.p., sec., treas. Scottees, Inc. Mich. City, 1980-85; cert. flight and ground instr. FAA, Valparaiso, Ind., 1973—. Contbr. articles to profl. jours. Bd. dirs., v.p. South Bend council Boy Scouts Am., 1964-87; pilot CAP, Valparaiso, 1978—; mem. high council Mormon Ch., Chicago Heights, Ill., 1984—. Served to capt. USAF, 1955-58. Recipient Silver Beaver award Boy Scouts Am., 1969. Mem. Assn. Iron and Steel Engrs., Aircraft Owners and Pilots Assn., Pilots Internat. Assn., Exptl. Aircraft Assn. Republican. Clubs: Valparaiso Country, Sand Creek Country. Lodge: Masons. Avocations: golf, flying, travel, stamp collecting, coin collecting. Home: 404 Powderhorn Dr Valparaiso IN 46383 Office: Bethlehem Steel Corp PO Box 248 Chesterton IN 46304

RUSHKA, ROY JOHN, Canadian diplomat, engineer; b. Esterhazy, Sask., Can., Aug. 1, 1924; came to U.S., 1969; s. Jake Edward and Mary (Hruska) R.; m. Marjorie Estelle Trainor, Aug. 5, 1950; children—Brian, Diana, Brenda, Robert. B.Sc. in Engring., U. Sask., Saskatoon, 1949. Registered profl. engr. Ont. Engring. supr. Comstock, Toronto, Windsor, Ont., Can., 1949-56; project engr. Westinghouse, Hamilton, Ont. and Toronto, 1956-62; mgr. engring. Electronic Materials, Ottawa, Can., 1966—; fgn. service officer Can. Govt., Phila., Dallas, Brussels and Dayton, Ohio, 1966—. Author, producer family history books and presentation. Mem. Profl. Engrs. Ont., Profl. Assn. Fgn. Service. Avocation: geneology research. Home and Office: 6057 Charlesgate Rd Dayton OH 45424

RUSHTON, WILLIAM EDWIN, chemical engineer; b. Blue Island, Ill., Dec. 11, 1926; s. William E. and Eva Marie (Hawkins) R.; m. Suzanne Scoville, May 19, 1951; children: Cynthia Anne, Robert William. BSChemE, U. Mo., Rolla, 1951. Pilot plant operator Armour, Chgo., 1951-53; plant engr. Tee-Pak, Chgo., 1953-56; applications engr. Swenson Process Equipment, Harvey, Ill., 1956-62, dept. mgr., 1962-80; asst. div. mgr. Swenson Process Equipment, Harvey, Ill., 1980-86, v.p., 1986—. Contbr. articles to profl. jours.; patentee in field. Served as sgt. U.S. Army, 1944-45. Mem. Am. Inst. Chem. Engrs., Alpha Chi Sigma. Republican. Presbyterian. Home: 16539 Claire Ln South Holland IL 60473 Office: Swenson Process Equipment Inc 15700 S Lathrop Ave Harvey IL 60426

RUSS, EDMOND VINCENT, JR., marketing professional; b. Washington, Feb. 14, 1944; s. Edmond V. and Thayer Kennedy (Thompson) R.; divorced; children: Jamie L., Edmond V. III; m. Tena Marie Loveland, Dec. 26, 1982; children: Christina T. Russ, Cory S. BA, Kent (Ohio) State U., 1966; MBA, U. Pitts., 1967. Dir. mktg. Borg-Warner Ednl. Systems, Niles, Ill., 1969-74; v.p. mktg. Rusty Jones Inc., Chgo., 1974-83; gen. mgr. Signed, Sealed and Delivered, Melrose Park, Ill., 1983-86; v.p. mktg. Merchant Network Inc., Chgo., 1986-87, pres., 1987—. Pres. Children's Theatre of Winnetka, Ill., 1980-81. Club: Porsche of Am. (treas. Chgo. region 1979-80). Avocations: community theater, children's theater, sports car racing. Home: 916 Ash Winnetka IL 60093 Office: Merchant Network Inc 3800 N Wilke Rd Arlington Heights IL 60004-1229

RUSSELL, BRADFORD WAYNE, dentist; b. Hannibal, Mo., Apr. 10, 1954; s. Wesley Allan and Mary Lea (Taylor) R.; m. Ann Louise Lawler, June 15, 1985; 1 child, Susanna Joy. BA, U. Mo., 1976; DMD, Washignton U., St. Louis, 1981. Gen. practice dentistry Shelbina, Mo., 1981—; dental provider Head Start, Shelbina, 1981—. Tchr. high sch. dept. Shelbina First Bapt. Ch., 1981—, dir. high sch. dept., 1982-85, bd. dirs. nominating com., 1984; participant So. Bapt. Conv., Republic of China, 1983; elected bd. dirs. Carnegie Pub. Library, Shelbina, Mo., 1987; deacon Shelbina First Baptist Ch., 1987. Mem. ADA, N.E. Mo. Dental Soc. (pres.-elect 1986-88), Mo. Dental Assn. (pres.-elect, program chmn. 1986-87). Republican. Home: 103 E Mill Shelbina MO 63468 Office: Shelbina Dental Clinic 403 S Center Shelbina MO 63468

RUSSELL, DAVID WILLIAMS, lawyer; b. Lockport, N.Y., Apr. 5, 1945; s. David Lawson and Jean Graves (Williams) R.; A.B. (Army ROTC scholar, Daniel Webster scholar), Dartmouth Coll., 1967, M.B.A., 1969; J.D. cum laude, Northwestern U., 1976; m. Frances Yung Chung Chen, May 23, 1970; children—Bayard Chen, Ming Rennick. English tchr. Talledega (Ala.) Coll., summer 1967; math. tchr. Lyndon Inst., Lyndonville, Vt., 1967-68; instr. econs. Royalton Coll., South Royalton, Vt., part-time 1968-69; asst. to pres. for planning Tougaloo (Miss.) Coll., 1969-71, bus. mgr., 1971-73; mgr. will and trust rev. project Continental Ill. Nat. Bank & Trust Co. Chgo., summer 1974; law clk. Montgomery, McCracken, Walker & Rhoads, Phila., summer 1975; admitted to Ill. bar, 1976, Ind. bar, 1983; Winston & Strawn, Chgo., 1976-83; ptnr. Klineman, Rose, Wolf & Wallack, Indpls., 1983-87, Johnson, Smith, Densborn, Wright & Heath, 1987—; cons. Alfred P. Sloan Found., 1972-73; dir., sec. Forum for Internat. Profl. Services, 1985—; lectr. Ind. Law, Gov's Ind. Trade Mission to Japan, 1986, internat. law Ind. Continuing Legal Edn. Forum, 1986. Mem. nat. selection com. Woodrow Wilson Found. Adminstrv. Fellowship Program, 1973-76; vol. Lawyers for Creative Arts, Chgo., 1977-83. Woodrow Wilson Found. Adminstrv. fellow, 1969-72. Mem. Am., Ill., Ind., Indpls., bar assns., Dartmouth Lawyers Assn., Indpls. Assn. Chinese Ams., ACLU, Chinese Music Soc., Zeta Psi. Presbyterian. Home: 10926 Lakeview Dr Carmel IN 46032 Office: 1000 Market Sq Center 151 N Delaware Indianapolis IN 46204

RUSSELL, DOUGLAS M., state agency administrator; b. Middletown, Ohio, Sept. 2, 1937; s. Riley R. and Ethel Mae (Jones) R.; m. Hope M. Kyles, Oct. 23, 1965; children: Roderique D., Jacquelyn F. AB in History and Polit. Sci., Ky. State U., 1961; postgrad., Salmon P. Chase Coll. Law, Cin., 1966-67, Xavier U., 1967-68; cert., Ohio State U., 1971. Pvt. practice legis. research, speechwriter Columbus, 1970—; dep. dir. Ohio Dept. Commerce, Columbus, 1971-75; exec. sec. Nat. Afro-Am. Mus., Columbus, 1975-80; exec. dir. Ohio Compensation Bd., Columbus, 1983-85; dep. dir. labor relations Ohio Dept. Aging, Columbus, 1985—; assoc. Joint Ctr. Polit. Studies, Washington, 1977-82; cons. Civic Action Inst., Washington, 1980. Mem. exec. com. Butler County Dems., Hamilton, Ohio, 1966, Black Elected Dems. of Ohio, 1971, Nat. Afro-Am. History and Culture Commn., Columbus, 1981. Served with U.S. Army, 1961-64. Mem. Nat. Pub. Employer Relations Assn., Ohio Pub. Employer Relations Assn., Ky. State U. Alumni Assn. (pres. Dayton, Ohio chpt. 1972-74), Ohio Valley Tennis Assn. (trustee 1979-82), NAACP. Lodges: Masons (32 degree), Shriners. Avocations: contract bridge, tennis, football, basketball, reading. Home: 612 14th Ave Middletown OH 45044 Office: Ohio Dept Aging 50 W Broad St 9th Floor LeVeque Tower Columbus OH 43215

RUSSELL, ERIC JAY, neuroradiologist; b. Bklyn., Apr. 8, 1950; s. Eugene Howard and Lillian (Rosen) R.; m. Sandra K. Fernbach, Feb. 28, 1982; 1 child, Gabrielle Robin. BS, Bklyn. Coll., 1970; MD, SUNY, Buffalo, 1974. Intern Montefiore Med. Ctr., Bronx, N.Y., 1974-75, resident in radiology, 1975-78; fellow in neuroradiology NYU Med. Ctr., N.Y.C., 1978-80; neuroradiologist Rush-Presbyn. St. Luke's Med. Ctr., Chgo., 1980-86; dir. neuroradiology Northwestern Meml. Med. Ctr., Chgo., 1986—; dir. Affiliated Radiologists, P.C., Chgo., 1984-86; cons. staff Grant Hosp., Chgo., 1980—. Contbr. articles to profl. jours. Berlex Labs grantee, 1985-86. Mem. AMA, Am. Soc. Neuroradiology (sr.), Radiol. Soc. N.Am., Am. Coll. Radiology, Am. Soc. Head and Neck Radiology. Avocations: skiing, golf, tennis, squash. Office: Northwestern U Meml Med Ctr Dept Radiology Superior and Fairbanks Sts Chicago IL 60611

RUSSELL, ERWIN DEE, management consultant; b. Salt Lake City, May 26, 1924; s. Harry James and Agnes Nancy (Gardner) R.; m. Flo Ann McMullen, Jan. 20, 1952 (div. Nov. 1970); children: Scott D., Michael E., Kent W.; m. Joan Patricia Ramsay, Sept. 29, 1973. AB, Miami U., Oxford, Ohio, 1946; MS, Purdue U., 1949, PhD, 1952. Lic. psychologist, Wis.; cert. mgmt. cons. Psychologist Butler County Juvenile Ct., Hamilton, Ohio, 1946-47; instr. Purdue U., West Lafayette, Ind., 1950-51; asst. prof. Wabash Coll., Crawfordsville, Ind., 1951-52; cons., mgr. Rohrer, Hibler & Replogle, Milw., 1952-82; sole practice E.D. Russell Co., Milw., 1982—; v.p. Wis. chpt. Inst. Mgmt. Cons., 1985—. Mem. Am. Psychol. Assn., Wis. Psychol. Assn. (treas. 1980-82), Midwest Psychol. Assn., Sigma Xi. Republican. Clubs: Milw. Athletic, North Shore Racquet (Milw.). Avocations: tennis, racquetball, jewelry, sports, remodeling. Home: 4869 N Idlewild Ave Whitefish Bay WI 53217 Office: 111 E Wisconsin Ave Milwaukee WI 53202

RUSSELL, FRANK ELI, newspaper executive; b. Kokomo, Ind., Dec. 6, 1920; s. Frank E. and Maude (Wiggins) R.; m. Dorothy M. Armstrong, Apr. 30, 1942; children—Linda Carole Russell Atkins, Richard Lee, Frank E. III, Rita Jane Russell Eagle, Julie Beth Russell Smith. A.B., Evansville Coll., 1942; cert., Internat. Accts. Soc., 1946; J.D., Ind. U., 1951; Doctor of Laws (hon.), U. Evansville, 1985. Bar: Ind. 1951; CPA, Ind. Ptnr. George S. Olive & Co., Indpls., 1947-53; exec. v.p. Spickelmier Industries, Inc., Indpls., 1953-59; bus. mgr. Indpls. Star & News, Indpls., 1959-77; v.p., gen. mgr. Central Newspapers, Inc., 1977-79, pres., 1979—; sec.-treas., dir. Phoenix Newspapers Inc., Indpls. Newspapers, Inc., Muncie Newspapers, Inc., Cen. Newspapers Found., Indpls.; chmn. adv. bd. Met. Indpls. TV Assos., Inc. Mem. task force on materiality Fin. Accounting Standards Bd.; Bd. dirs., treas., v.p., pres., chmn. bd. YMCA, Indpls., 1960-81, trustee, found. chmn., 1986—; pres. 500 Festival Assos., Inc.; treas., bd. dirs. Indpls. Bar Found.; bd. dirs. Winona Meml. Hosp., United Way, Historic Landmarks Fedn. Indpls., Meth. Hosp., Meth. Hosp.; vice chmn., mem. adv. bd., vice chmn., sec. Salvation Army; trustee Arthur Jordan Found., Marian Coll., U. Evansville; trustee, pres. Benjamin Harrison Found.; treas. Meridian St. United Meth. Ch., 1955—. Served with USMCR, 1942-45. Elected to Ind. Acad. Ind. Assn. Colls., 1984. Mem. ABA, Ind. Bar. Assn., Indpls. Bar Assn., Am. Inst. C.P.A.'s, Ind. Assn. C.P.A.'s (past dir.), Tax Execs. Inst. (past pres.), Ind. Assn. Credit Mgmt. (dir., v.p.), Inst. Newspaper Controllers and Fin. Officers (dir., past pres.), Order of Coif, Phi Delta Phi, Sigma Alpha Epsilon. Methodist. Clubs: Indpls. Athletic, Columbia, Meridian Hills Country, Skyline. Lodges: Masons, Shriners. Office: 307 N Pennsylvania St Indianapolis IN 46204

RUSSELL, GEORGE ALBERT, university chancellor; b. Bertrand, Mo., July 12, 1921; s. George Albert and Martha (Cramer) R.; m. Ruth Ann Ashby, Nov. 11, 1944; children: George Albert, Frank Ashby, Ruth Ann, Cramer Anderson. B.S. in Elec. Engring, Mass. Inst. Tech., 1947; M.S., U. Ill., 1952, Ph.D. in Physics, 1955. Assoc. prof. So. Ill. U., 1960-62; faculty U. Ill., Urbana, 1962-72; prof. physics U. Ill., 1963-72, assoc. dir. Materials Research Lab., 1963-68, assoc. head physics dept., 1968-70, assoc. dean Grad. Coll., 1970-72, vice chancellor research, dean Grad. Coll., 1972-77; chancellor U. Mo.-Kansas City, 1977—; cons. Office Naval Research, 1961-76; dir. Microthermal Applications Inc.; dir. Kansas City Power and Light Co.; mem. adv. bd. dirs. Boatman's First Nat. Bank Kansas City; mem. acad. adv. panel Com. on Exchanges. Vice chmn. Illini Union Bd., 1970; pres. Levis Faculty Center, 1972; chmn. bd. trustees AUA, 1977; mem. Mo. Sci. and Tech. Corp.; trustee Midwest Research Inst.; bd. dirs. Edgar Snow Meml. Fund. Inc. Served with USN, World War II. Mem. Am. Assn. Physics Tchrs., Am. Phys. Soc. Clubs: Champaign Country (pres. 1972), Mission Hills Country, Rockhill Tennis. Home: 5106 Cherry St Kansas City MO 64110 Office: 5100 Rockhill Rd Kansas City MO 64110

RUSSELL, GRETA JANE, comptroller; b. Columbus, Ohio, Apr. 4, 1945; d. Thomas Murrel and Angie Roberta (Wills) Hartgrove; m. Albert Russell,

June 20, 1964 (div. June 1976); children: Shelton, Marquis. BA magna cum laude, Ohio Dominican Coll., 1976. CPA, Ohio. Br. acct. Capital Fin., Columbus, 1967-70; adminstrv. specialist Ohio State U., Columbus, 1970-73; systems control analyst Anchor Hocking, Lancaster, Ohio, 1973-74; asst. v.p. Buckeye Fed. Savs. & Loan, Columbus, 1974-83; comptroller Office of Treas., State of Ohio, Columbus, 1983—; acct. KBLE, Ohio Inc., Columbus, 1978-81. Trustee S.E. Mental Health Ctr., Columbus, 1983—, Union Grove Bapt. Ch., Columbus, 1980—; treas. RAAH Women's Ministries, Columbus, 1985—; cons. Project Bus. of Jr. Achievement, Columbus, 1982—. Named an Honored Mem., Union Grove Bapt. Ch., Columbus, 1984; recipient Black History Outstanding Citizen award D.C.S.C., Columbus, 1985. Mem. Nat. Assn. Black Accts. (chpt. leadership award 1985, pres. elect 1987), Am. Inst. CPA's, Inst. Internal Auditors, Nat. Assn. Colored Women. Avocations: reading, walking. Home: 2786 Kingsrowe Ct Columbus OH 43209

RUSSELL, HARRIET SHAW, social worker; b. Detroit, Apr. 12, 1952; d. Louis Thomas and Lureleen (Hughes) Shaw; m. Donald Edward Russell, June 25, 1980; children: Lachante Tyree, Krystal Lanae. AB, Detroit Bus. Inst., 1976; BS, Mich. State U., 1974; postgrad. in pub. adminstrn., Mercy Coll. Detroit, 1986—. Cert. notary pub. Factory employee Gen. Motors Corp., Lansing, Mich., 1973; student supr. tour guides State of Mich., Lansing, 1974; mgr. Ky. Fried Chicken, Detroit, 1974-75; unemployment claims examiner State of Mich. Dept. Labor, Detroit, 1975-77, asst. payment worker, 1977-84, social services specialist, 1984—; moderator Michigan Opportunity Skills and Tng. Program, 1985-86. Vol. Mich. Cancer Soc., East Lansing, 1970-72, Big Sisters/Big Bros., Lansing, 1972-73; speaker Triumphant Bapt. Ch., Detroit, 1976-80; chief union steward Mich. Employees Assn., Lincoln Park, 1982-83. Recipient Outstanding Work Performance Merit award Mich. Dept. Social Services, 1979. Mem. Nat. Assn. for Female Execs., Am. Soc. Profl. and Exec. Women, Delta Sigma Theta. Democrat. Baptist. Office: State of Mich Dept Social Services 999 Fort St Lincoln Park MI 48146

RUSSELL, JAMES, construction engineering executive; b. Davenport, Iowa, Feb. 17, 1961; s. John vernon and Marjorie Adel (McGarvey) R.; m. Terri Ann DeBlauw, Oct. 11, 1983. BS in Constrn. Engring., Iowa State U., 1983. Project mgr. Teco Constructors, Bettendrof, Iowa, 1981-83; teaching asst. Iowa State U., Ames, 1982-83; pres. Russell Constrn. Co., Bettendrof, 1983—. Mem. Constrn. Specifications Inst. (pres. 1986), Associated Builders and Contractors Iowa (bd. dirs. 1985-86), Nat. Soc. Profl. Engrs., Iowa Engring. Soc. Republican. Methodist. Lodge: Kiwanis. Office: Russell Cos 1423 Brown St Bettendorf IA 52722

RUSSELL, JOHN THOMAS, sales executive; b. Brainard, Minn., Dec. 5, 1933; s. Francis Newell and Ruth (Gleason) R.; m. Jana Marie Slunecko, Aug. 21, 1970; children—Kevin, Christopher. Owner, pres. Wig Warehouse, Chgo., 1961-71; mil. sales mgr. Ency. Britannica, Chgo., 1971-73, sales mgr., Milw., 1973-77, eastern exhibit dir., 1977-80, nat. dir. exhibits, 1980-82, Chgo. div. sales mgr., 1982—. Mem. Joint Council Med. Confs., Eastern Fair Assn., Internat. Assn. Fairs. Republican. Roman Catholic. Home: 9 Timberline Riverwoods IL 60015 Office: Ency Britannica 5080 N Elston Ave Chicago IL 60630

RUSSELL, JUDY ANN, nurse, community health specialist; b. Chgo., Dec. 9, 1942; d. George H. and Marie B. (McCabe) Goessele; m. Theodore J. Russell, Feb. 6, 1965; children: T. Joseph, Ann-Marie. BS in Nursing, Marquette U., 1964; MS, U. Rochester, 1982. RN, Ill., Wis., N.Y. Hosp. staff nurse Ill., Wis., N.Y., 1964-68; labor and delivery specialist Northwest Community Hosp., Arlington Heights, Ill., 1971-73; labor and delivery instr. Loyola U., Chgo., 1973-74; village nurse Village of Arlington Heights, 1978; dir. edn. Custom Health Services, Buffalo Grove, Ill., 1981-83; corp. hdqrs. nurse C.F. Industries, Long Grove, Ill., 1982—; mem. Bd. Health, City of Rolling Meadows, Ill., 1981—; CPR instr. Am. Heart Assn., Chgo., 1981—; multi-M 1st aid instr. ARC, Chgo., 1983—. Mem. Am. Nurses Assn., Am. Assn. Occupational Nurses, Nat. Wellness Assn., Marquette U. Alumni Assn. (bd. dirs. 1983-86). Roman Catholic. Club: Arlington Heights RN's (bd. dirs. 1969-86). Avocations: skiing, diving, bicycling, antiques, real estate investment. Home: 6 Rosewood Rd Rolling Meadows IL 60008 Office: CF Industries Salem Lake Dr Long Grove IL 60047

RUSSELL, KEITH CUSHMAN, investment banker, conservationist; b. Andover, Ohio, Apr. 30, 1920; s. Ford Bliss and Ruth Evelyn (Satterlee) R.; m. Marjorie Miriam Wilkins, Nov. 28, 1941; 1 child, Jacqueline Sue. B.A., Ohio Wesleyan U., 1941. Exec. v.p. Hayden, Miller & Co., Cleve., 1946-69; ptnr. McDonald & Co., Cleve., 1969-81; v.p. McDonald & Co., Securities, Cleve., 1981—; gov. Midwest Stock Exchange, Chgo., 1968-71; chmn. bd. dirs. Boise Basin Gold, Inc., Cin. Author, editor: The Duck-Huntingest Gentlemen, 1979, For Whom the Ducks Toll, 1984, The Fly-Fishingest Gentlemen, 1986. Served to lt. (j.g.) USNR, 1942-46, PTO. Named Man of Yr., Woods and Waters Club, Cleve., 1983. Mem. Ohio C. of C. (bd. dirs. 1980—), African Wildlife Found. (trustee 1979—), Am. Mus. Fly Fishing (bd. dirs. 1984—), Ducks Unltd. (sr. v.p. 1978-80, trustee emeritus 1981—), Trout Unltd. (nat. dir. 1981—), Canvasback Soc. (nat. pres. 1978-85, chmn. bd. dirs. 1985—). Republican. Presbyterian. Clubs: Union (Cleve.), The Country; Rolling Rock (Ligonier, Pa.). Avocations: fly fishing, waterfowl and upland bird hunting, conservation. Office: McDonald & Co Securities 2100 Soc Bldg Cleveland OH 44114

RUSSELL, LEONARD ALONZO, dentist; b. Paris, Ky., Dec. 27, 1949; s. Joseph Bailey and Celia Russell. BS in Indsl. Edn., Eastern Ky. U., 1971; BS in Biology, Cen. State U., Wilberforce, Ohio, 1978; DDS, Case Western Res. U., 1982. Indsl. arts tchr. Dayton (Ohio) Bd. Edn., 1972-76; assoc. Hawes Realty, Dayton, 1974-83; resident in dentistry Med. Coll. of Ohio, Toledo, 1982-83; gen. practice dentistry Shaker Heights, Ohio, 1983-84, Cleveland Heights, Ohio, 1984—. Recipient Kenneth W. Clement award Cleve. City COuncil, 1981; named one of Outstanding Young Men of Am., U.S. Jaycees, 1984. Mem. Acad. Gen. Dentistry, Ohio Dental Assn., Forest City Dental Assn. (program dir. 1984, pres. 1986—), Nat. Assn. Career Women (bd. dirs. civic club 1982), Kappa Alpha Psi (founder, pres. Ea. Ky. U. chpt. 1969, Leonard A. Russell award 1971). Office: 2204 S Taylor Rd Cleveland Heights OH 44118

RUSSELL, MARY HELEN, publishing company executive, youth counselor; b. St. Louis, Aug. 9, 1939; d. George Kelly and Sarah Mae (Belion) Fugh; m. Charles David Russell, June 6, 1968; children—Sararetha, Anthony, Cedric. Student Thornton Community Coll., Harvey, Ill., 1958-59; Southwestern Coll., Dowagiac, Mich., 1981. Technician, Consol. Lab., Chicago Heights, Ill., 1960-64, Sue Ann Food Labs., Chgo., 1964-65; med. sec. Huntington Meml. Hosp., Pasadena, Calif., 1965-68; pub. Society mag., Harvey, Ill., 1968-70; youth dir., counselor Cass Youth Service Bur., Cass County, Mich., 1970-81; pres. C & M Pub., Kalamazoo, 1983—. Author: Black Achievers Vol. I. 1983, Vol. II, 1985; (plays) Old Time Religion, 1967, Our People, 1968. Treas. Cass Mental Health Bd., Cassopolis, Mich., 1970-81; dir. efectiveness tng. Youth Service Bur., Cassopolis, 1970-81; mem. Cass Zoning Bd., Cassopolis, 1974-81; mem. Kalamazoo Human Relations Bd., 1981-82; chmn. action audit com., bd. dirs. YWCA, Kalamazoo, 1984—; sec., program and music dir. 2d Baptist Ch., Harvey, Ill., 1959-73; campaign dir. Harvey Democratic Com., 1975. Recipient plaque YMCA, Harvey, 1975; cert. YWCA, Kalamazoo, 1985, Human Relations Commn., Kalamazoo, 1981. Mem. Kalamazoo Women's Network. Presbyterian. Avocations: singing; fashion coordinator; tennis; sewing; ceramics. Office: C & M Publishing Inc 270 N O'Keefe St Cassopolis MI 49031

RUSSELL, MAURICE ROBERT, farm credit association executive; b. Cedar Rapids, Iowa, Dec. 19, 1948; s. Richard C. and Mary A (Pospisil) R.; m. Mardene R. Kramer, Oct. 5, 1974; children—Jared Russell, Tana Russell. B.S., Iowa State U., 1971. Area credit supr. FICB of Omaha, Ames, Iowa, 1974-78, v.p., Mitchell, S.D., 1978-84; pres. Central Iowa Prodn. Credit Assn., Newton, Iowa, 1984-85; pres. Farm Credit Region, Newton, 1985—. Pres. YMCA, Mitchell, 1982-84; bd. dirs. St. Joseph's Hosp., Mitchell, 1983-84. Served to sgt. Army N.G., 1969-75. Republican. Roman Catholic. Club: Mitchell Exchange (pres. 1983-84). Avocations: running; reading; management studies; gardening; wine making. Home: 120 Pioneer Lambs Grove Newton IA 50208 Office: Farm Credit Region Box 887 Newton IA 50208

RUSSELL, RICHARD L., van line executive; b. Evansville, Ind., Mar. 10, 1946; s. Frank E. and Dorothy (Armstrong) R.; m. Jan C. Russell, Sept. 1, 1963; children—Roderick, Mark, Brian, Amanda. B.S. in Transp., Ind. U., 1968. Comml. account salesman Mayflower Agy., Chgo., 1968-69; comml. account salesman Mayflower Agy., Indpls., 1969-70, office mgr., 1970-71, v.p., gen. mgr., 1971-72; v.p., gen. mgr. Mayflower Agy., Detroit, 1972-73; v.p. wholesale div. Aero Mayflower Transit Co., Indpls., 1973-74, v.p., 1977-78, exec. v.p., chief operating officer, 1978-79, pres., chief operating officer, 1980-82, pres., chief exec. officer, 1982—, also dir.; exec. v.p. Mayflower Group, Indpls., 1979—; chmn. bd. Household Goods Carriers Bur. Officer Indpls. 500 Festival; bd. dirs. Indpls Conv. and Visitors Bur. Mem. Am. Movers Conf. (bd. dirs. 1982-86), Am. Trucking Assn. (conf. v.p.), Young Pres.' Orgn., Am. Bus. Club. Republican. Presbyterian. Clubs: Crooked Stick Golf (Carmel, Ind.); Meridian Hills Country (Indpls.). Office: Mayflower Transit Inc PO Box 107 Indianapolis IN 46206-0107 also: Mayflower Group Inc 9998 N Michigan Rd Carmel IN 46032

RUSSELL, ROBERT EMERSON, JR., marketing and fund raising services executive, consultant; b. Indpls., Aug. 1, 1937; s. Robert E. and Nancy Schwenk (Kalleen) R.; B.A., Wabash Coll., 1959; postgrad. Nat. Indsl. Conf. Bd., 1965; m. Ruth Ellen Drake, May 26, 1967; children—Kristen Kalleen, Robert Emerson III. Advt. and pub. relations Armstrong Cork Co., Lancaster, Pa., 1963-67; devel. officer Wabash Coll., Crawfordsville, Ind., 1967-68, dir. devel. and alumni affairs, 1968-71; div. devel. Rosary Coll., River Forest, Ill., 1971-72; dir. devel. and pub. affairs Rehab. Inst. of Chgo., 1972-76, assoc., 1976—; pres. Robert Russell & Assocs., Inc., Chgo. and Hillsdale, Mich., 1976—; v.p. mktg. Hillsdale Coll., 1983-86; devel. counsel The Heritage Found., 1987—; mem. adv. bd. Inst. Ednl. Affairs, 1987—; John T. McCarty Meml. Found., 1986—. Mem. task force Chgo. Community Trust Edn. Network, 1977; chmn. conf. Nat. Assn. Hosp. Devel., 1975; pres., bd. dirs. operation ABLE Chgo., 1977-80;pres. Wabash Club of Chgo., 1974-78. Served with U.S. Army, 1960-63. Recipient Capital Funds award Nat. Assn. Hosp. Devel., 1975; Golden Trumpet award Chgo. Pub. Assn., 1974. named Outstanding Young Man of Mem. Nat. Soc. Fund Raising Execs., Nat. Assn. Hosp. Devel., Council Advancement and Support of Edn., Am. Mktg. Assn., SAR, Nat. Assn. Wabash Men (dir.), Blue Key, Sigma Chi, Alpha Psi Omega. Republican. Episcopalian. Club: University (Chgo). Office: PO Box 206 Naperville IL 60540 Office: Hillsdale Coll Hillsdale MI 49242

RUSSELL, ROBERT JAY, accountant, infosystems specialist; b. Hudson, Mich., Aug. 2, 1961; s. Robert Nathan and Sharon Shirley (Laubaugh) R. BA in Acctg., Hillsdale Coll., 1983. CPA, Mich. Computer programmer Hillsdale (Mich.) Computer Services, 1979-83; acct. Howell Osbourne & Co., Hillsdale, 1983—; prof. acctg. Jackson (Mich.) Community Coll., 1986—. Mem. Am. Inst. CPA's, Mich. Assn. CPA's. Mem. Assembly of God Ch. Avocations: reading, golf. Home: 49 S Howell Hillsdale MI 49242 Office: Howell Osbourne & Co 184 W Carleton Rd Hillsdale MI 49242

RUSSELL, TERENCE RAYMOND, architect; b. Chgo., Jan. 29, 1959; s. Irene Lottie (Paske) R. BArch, U. Ill., 1981, MArch, 1983. Registered architect, Ill. Grad. tchg. asst. U. Ill., 1982-83; architect Opus Corp., Mt. Prospect, Ill., 1983-86, Hansen, Lind, Meyer, Chgo., 1986—. Mem. AIA. Roman Catholic. AvocationsL gardening, cooking. Office: Hansen Lind Meyer 350 N Clark Chicago IL 60610

RUSSELL, THOMAS FRANK, manufacturing company executive; b. Detroit, Apr. 7, 1924; s. Frank W. and Agnes V. (Kuhn) R.; m. Ruth Helen Costello, June 25, 1949; children: R. Brandon, Scott K. B.S. in Acctg., U. Detroit, 1948. Cost acct. Fed.-Mogul Corp., Southfield, Mich., 1946-47, internal auditor, 1948-49, asst. controller, 1950-58, controller, 1959-64, v.p. fin., 1964-68, group mgr. adminstrn., 1968, v.p., group mgr. service group, 1968-69, exec. v.p., 1969-72, pres., 1972-76, chief exec. officer, 1975—, chmn. bd., 1976—; dir. Comerica Inc., Detroit, Comerica Bank-Detroit, Consumers Power Co., Cross & Trecker Corp., Bloomfield Hills, Mich., A.O. Smith Corp., Milw. Mem. exec. bd. Detroit Area council Boy Scouts Am., 1972—, treas., 1976-77, 1st v.p., 1978-79, pres., 1979-80; bd. dirs. United Found., 1975—, exec. com., 1977—, v.p., 1978—; trustee Detroit Symphony Orch., Bus./Edn. Alliance, Com. for Econ. Devel., St. John Hosp. Served to sgt. U.S. Army, 1943-45. Mem. Machinery and Allied Products Inst. (fin. council 1967-71, exec. com. 1973—, v.p., treas. 1978—, treas. Council for Technol. Advancement 1976—), Greater Detroit C. of C. (bd. dirs. 1978-80, asst. treas. 1978-79), Automotive Info. Council (bd. dirs. 1973—, 1st vice chmn. 1976-77, vice chmn. 1977-78), Citizens Research Council (trustee), Hwy. Users Fedn. (bd. dirs. 1975—), Assn. Ind. Colls. and Univs. (trustee 1976-81). Republican. Roman Catholic. Clubs: Bloomfield Hills Country; Country of Detroit (Grosse Pointe Farms, Mich.); Detroit Athletic, Renaissance (chmn. bd. govs.); Country of Fla. (Golf). Avocation: golf. Office: Fed-Mogul Corp 26555 Northwestern Hwy Southfield MI 48034

RUSSELL, TWILA JANE, lawyer; b. Vandalia, Ill., Sept. 4, 1960; d. Glenn S. and Jessie C. (Wright) R.; m. David L. Orr, Apr. 10, 1986. BS, Western Ill. U., 1981; JD, St. Louis U., 1984. Bar: Ill. 1984, U.S. Dist. Ct. (so. dist.) Ill. 1986. Asst. state's atty. Effingham (Ill.) County, 1984-85; assoc. Schniederjon, Weber, Harvey & Stephens, Effingham, 1985—; tchr. Lakeland Coll., Mattoon, Ill., 1985. Spl. prosecutor Effingham County, 1985; bd. dirs. United Way Effingham County, 1986—, pres., 1987. Mem. ABA, Assn. Trial Lawyers Am., Ill. Bar Assn., Effingham County Bar Assn., Nat. Dist. Attys. Assn., Am. Judicature Soc., Beta Sigma Phi. Home: PO Box 73 Effingham IL 62401 Office: Schniederjon Weber Harvey et al 304 E Jefferson Effingham IL 62401

RUSSELL, WILLIAM STEVEN, finance executive; b. Evanston, Ill., Aug. 5, 1948; s. John W. and Lillian H. Russell; m. Susan M. Hanson, Aug. 20, 1972. BS, So. Ill. U., 1970. CPA, Ill. Sr. staff auditor Arthur Andersen & Co., Chgo., 1972-76; acctg. mgr., controller, asst. sec. and treas. Lawter Internat., Inc., Northbrook, Ill., 1976-86, sec., 1986-87, v.p. fin., treas. and sec., 1987—. Served with U.S. Army, 1970-72. Mem. Am. Inst. CPA's, Beta Alpha Psi, Beta Gamma Sigma. Roman Catholic. Home: 1225 S Grove Ave Park Ridge IL 60068 Office: Lawter Internat Inc 990 Skokie Blvd Northbrook IL 60062

RUSSICK, BERTRAM WARREN, marketing research comapany executive; b. Des Moines, Oct. 29, 1921; s. David Frank and Blanche (Weiser) R.; m. Harriet Helen Halperin, Oct. 5, 1950; children: Betsy Louise, Constance Eve, Bertram W. Jr. BS, U. So. Calif., Los Angeles, 1946; MA, U. Minn., 1960. Lic. cons. psychologist, Minn. Market analyst Gen. Mills, Inc., Mpls., 1946, M&O Paper, Mpls., 1947-84; pres. Mid-Continent Surveys, Inc., Mpls., 1985-86; chmn. Mid-Continent Research, Mpls., 1987—; cons. Russick Research, Inc. Chmn. Better Bus. Bur. Minn., St. Paul, 1979-80. Served to lt. USAF, 1943-45, PTO. Mem. Am. Psychol. Assn., Am. Mktg. Assn., Minn. Mktg. Assn. (pres. 1956-57), Advt. Fedn. Minn. (bd. dirs. 1971-72). Jewish. Club: Mpls. Home: 6566 France Ave S #405 Edina MN 55435 Office: Russick Research 1001 Foshay Tower Minneapolis MN 55402

RUSSO, HELEN, psychologist; b. Cin., July 30, 1939; d. Frank and Lucy (Pellegrino) R. BA magna cum laude, Xavier U., 1963, MEd, 1965; postgrad., Xavier U., U. Cin., Miami U. Lic. psychologist, Ohio. Tchr. St. Francis Seraph Sch., Cin., 1959-65; tchr., counselor Reading (Ohio) Mid. Sch., 1965-69; psychologist Hamilton Office of Edn., Cin., 1969—; instr. Spl. Edn. Regional Resource Ctr., Cin., 1972—, U. Cin., 1976—, Coll. Mt. St. Joseph, Cin., 1981—; originator Operation Reachout Workshop; contbr. numerous parent study groups and PTA programs. Author, editor (tabloid) Early Entrance Eval. Program, 1977, (booklet) The ABC's of Workshop Planning; columnist Northside News. Recipient Vol. award Mental Health Assn. Cin., 1986, Amaranth award Roger Bacon Alumni Bd., 1986. Mem. Nat. Assn. Sch. Psychologists, Ohio Sch. Psychologists Assn., Southwestern Ohio Sch. Psychol. Assn. Roman Catholic. Club: Northside Round the Clock Block (initiator, pres. 1982—). Avocations: hiking, singing, dancing, writing, travel. Home: 4129 Kirby Ave Cincinnati OH 45223 Office: Hamilton County Office Edn 11083 Hamilton Ave Cincinnati OH 45231

RUSSO, JOHN FRANCIS, small business executive; b. Grand Rapids, Mich., Jan. 22, 1949; s. Frank David and Mary Carmela (Amante) R.; m. Loreen Anne Hencir, Aug. 8, 1970; children: Gina, Michael, Gregory. Announcer WERX and WLAV Radio, Grand Rapids and Wyoming, Mich., 1965; announcer, program dir. WJPW, Rockford, Mich., 1966-68; with mktg. and sales Viviano Wine Importers, Detroit, 1972-74; pres. G.B. Russo & Son Ltd., Grand Rapids, 1974—; cons. wine mktg. to various vinters, wholesalers and restaurants. Author: Wine Memories Album, 1982. Active in fundraising for various civic and polit. orgns., Grand Rapids. Mem. West Mich. Lodge Order Sons of Italy in Am. (v.p. 1983-84). Republican. Roman Catholic. Office: G B Russo & Son 2770 29th SE Grand Rapids MI 49508-1719

RUSSO, JOSE, pathologist; b. Mendoza, Argentina, Mar. 24, 1942; came to U.S., 1971; s. Felipe and Teresa (Pagano) R.; m. Irma Haydee, Feb. 8, 1969; 1 child, Patricia Alexandra. B.S., Agustin Alvarez Nat. Coll., 1959; M.D., U. Nat. Cuyo, 1967. Instr. Inst. Gen. and Exptl. Pathology Med. Sch., Mendoza, 1961-66; asst. prof. Inst. Histology and Embryology, 1967-71; Rockefeller Found. postdoctoral fellow Inst. Molecular and Cellular Evolution U. Miami, 1971-73; chief exptl. pathology lab. Mich. Cancer Found., Detroit, 1973-81; assoc. clin. prof. pathology Wayne State U., Detroit, 1979—, chmn. dept. pathology, 1981—; mem Mich. Cancer Found., 1982. Author: Tumor Diagnosis by Electron Microscopy, 1986, Immunocytochemistry in Tumor Diagnosis, 1985; contbr. over 150 articles to profl. jours. USPHS grantee, 1978, 80, 84; grantee Am. Cancer Soc., 1982; NRC Argentina fellow, 1967-71. Mem. Am. Assn. Cancer Research, Am. Soc. Cell Biology, Soc. Exptl. Biology and Medicine, Tissue Culture Assn., Am. Soc. Clin. Pathology, Internat. Acad. Pathology, Am. Coll. Pathology, Sigma Xi. Roman Catholic. Office: 110 E Warren Ave Detroit MI 48201

RUSSO, MARTIN A., congressman; b. Chgo., Jan. 23, 1944; s. Anthony and Lucille R.; m. Karen Jorgensen; children: Tony, Dan. BA, DePaul U., 1965, JD, 1967. Bar: Ill. 1967, U.S. Supreme Ct. 1974, D.C. 1977. Law clk. to presiding justice Ill. Appellate Ct., 1967-68; asst. state's atty. Cook County, Ill., 1971-73; sole practice law Chgo., 1973—; mem. 94th-100th congresses from 3d dist., Ill.; mem. ways and means com., com. on budget, dep. whip; mem. Dem. Steering and Policy Com. Mem. Joint Civic Com. of Italian-Ams., citizens bd. Ill. Masonic Med. Center. Recipient Disting. Service award Pinta Neri KC, Appreciation award Vietnam Era Vets. in Congress, 1986, Michelangelo award Italo-Am. Nat. Union, 1986, Congl. Humanitarian award Coalition Suburban Bar Assn., 1985, Leadership award Greater Southwest Revitalization Program, 1982, Law Enforcement award Fraternal Order Police, 1982,; named Outstanding Legis. Leader, Soc. Little Flower, 1975, Man of Yr., Chgo. Chpt. Magen David Adom, 1977, One of Ten Outstanding Young People, Harvey (Ill.) Jaycees, 1977, Legislator of Yr., United Hellenic Voters of Am., 1981, Century Mem. of Boy Scouts Am., 1982-85, Legislator of Yr., United Irish-Am. soc. Ill., 1985-86, Man of Yr., New Hope Ctr., 1986. Mem. ABA, Fed. Bar Assn., Ill. Bar Assn., D.C. Bar Assn., S. Suburban Bar Assn., Justinian Soc. Lawyers (Man of Year 1976), Alpha Phi Delta Alumni Assn. Roman Catholic. Lodges: KC, Elks, Order Sons of Italy. Office: 2233 Rayburn House Office Bldg Washington DC 20515

RUSSO, MICHAEL JOHN, manufacturing engineer, manufacturing company executive; b. Cin., Apr. 3, 1960; s. George Edward and Ann Marie (Cianciolo) R. BS in Indsl. and Systems Engring., Ohio State U., 1983. Indsl. engr. Liebert Corp., Columbus, Ohio, 1983-84, Fremont, Calif., 1984-85, Cork, Ireland, 1985; sr. mfg. engr. Tracewell Enclosures, Inc., Columbus, 1985-86, mgr. mfg. engring., 1986—. Avocations: golf, boating, model building, nautilus, basketball. Home: 2932 Wildflower Trail Dublin OH 43017 Office: Tracewell Enclosures Inc 567 Enterprise Dr Columbus OH 43083

RUSSO, ROBERT RITTER, electronics company executive; b. N.Y.C., Aug. 19, 1926; s. Anthony and Dorothy (Ritter) R.; m. Dorothy Foster; children—Thomas, Steven, Judith. B.N.S., Tufts U., 1946, B.S. in Mech. Engring., 1948. Mgr. devel. engring. RCA Corp., Indpls., 1950-61, mgr. process devel., 1964—. Patentee in field. Served with USN, 1944-47. Methodist. Avocations: old and rare book collecting. Home: 3820 E 61 St Indianapolis IN 46220 Office: RCA Corp 600 N Sherman Dr Indianapolis IN 46201

RUST, EDWARD BARRY, JR., insurance company executive, lawyer; b. Chgo., Aug. 3, 1950; s. Edward Barry Sr. and Harriett B. (Fuller) R.; m. Sally Buckler, Feb. 28, 1976; 1 child, Edward Barry III. Student, Lawrence U., Appleton, Wis., 1968-69; BS, Ill. Wesleyan U., Bloomington, 1972; JD and MBA, So. Meth. U., Dallas, 1975. Mgmt. trainee State Farm Ins. Cos., Dallas, 1975-76; atty. State Farm Ins. Cos., Bloomington, 1976, sr. atty., 1976-78, asst. v.p., 1978-81, v.p., 1981-83, exec. v.p., 1983-85, pres. and chief exec. officer, 1985—; pres. and bd. dirs. State Farm Investment Mgmt. Corp., State Farm Internat. Services, Inc., State Farm Cos. Found.; bd. dirs., exec. and investment coms. State Farm Annuity and Life Ins. Co., State Farm Mut. Automobile Ins. Co., State Farm Life Ins. Co., State Farm Fire and Casualty, State Farm Gen. Trustee Ill. Wesleyan U., 1985—. Mem. ABA, Tex. State Bar Assn., Ill. Bar Assn., Am. Inst. Property and Liability Underwriters (trustee 1986—), Ins. Inst. Am. (trustee 1986—), Assn. Commerce and Industry (bd. dirs. 1981—). Office: State Farm Ins Cos 1 State Farm Plaza Bloomington IL 61710

RUSTEN, ELMER MATHEW, dermatologist; b. Pigeon Falls, Wis., Oct. 5, 1902; s. Ener E. and Clara L. (Benrud) R.; B.A., St. Olaf Coll., 1925; B.S., U. Minn., 1928, B.M., 1928, M.D., 1929, postgrad., 1929-31, U. Vienna, 1932; m. Helen Marthine Steidl, July 19, 1930; 1 son, Elmer Michael. Intern, Mpls. Gen. Hosp., 1929, resident, 1929-31; practice medicine specializing in dermatology, Mpls., 1933-82; instr. dermatology U. Minn., Mpls., 1934-38, clin. instr., 1938-42, clin. asst. prof., 1942-71; mem. cons. staff Mpls. Gen. Hosp., 1933-40, 51-60, Glen Lake Sanatorium, Oak Terrace, Minn., 1936-60; mem. attending staff Methodist Hosp., St. Louis Park, Minn., 1959-77, Abbott Hosp., Mpls., Minn., 1935—, Asbury Hosp., Mpls., 1934-50. Del. to 14th Internat. Tb Conf., New Delhi, India, 1957. Mem. Minn. Citizens Council, 1963-66; bd. dirs. Correctional Service of Minn., pres., 1963-67; bd. dirs. Minn. Dermatol. Found., 1950-54, Central Luth. Found., 1952-84. Diplomate Am. Bd. Dermatology. Mem. Am., Minn. med. assns., Mpls. Acad. Medicine (past pres.), Am. Acad. Dermatology, Soc. for Investigative Dermatology, Minn. (past pres.), Chgo. Dermatol. Socs., Internat. Soc. Tropical Dermatology, Am. Acad. Allergy, Internat. Corrs. Soc. of Allergists, Hennepin County Med. Soc., Alaska Territorial Assn. (hon.), Phi Beta Kappa, Phi Beta Pi (past pres. North Central chpt.). Republican. Lutheran. Clubs: Rotary (pres. 1961, Paul Harris fellow 1983), Boone and Crockett (hon. life mem., chmn. Big Game Competition 1961, 64, v.p. 1965-74), Big Game (pres. 1940, dir. Spl. Projects Found. 1970—). Author: Wheat, Egg and Milk-Free Diets, 1932; contbr. to Ofcl. Scoring System for N. Am. Big Game, 1971. Home: 18420 D 8th Ave N Plymouth MN 55447

RUSYNYK, DENNIS JOHN, former industrial executive; b. Cleve., May 6, 1948; s. Sam and Victoria (Gluszik) R.; B.B.A., Ohio U., 1970. Laborer, Union Carbide Corp., Cleve., summers 1966-70; press operator Airco Welding Products, Cleve., 1971-73; indsl. engr. Lamson & Sessions Co., Cleve., 1973-75; supr. Gen. Industries, Elyria, Ohio, 1975-81, plant mgr., 1981-84; supr. Premier Mfr., Cleve., 1985-86. Treas. Little League North, Elyria, 1977-78; advisor Jr. Achievement Assn., Cleve., 1974-75. Greek Catholic. Developer one resin formulations in bulk molding compounds. Home: 327 Canterbury Ct Elyria OH 44035

RUTENBERG-ROSENBERG, SHARON LESLIE, journalist; b. Chgo., May 23, 1951; d. Arthur and Bernice (Berman) R.; m. Michael J. Rosenberg, Feb. 3, 1980; children—David Kaifel and Jonathan Reuben (twins). Student, Harvard U., 1972; B.A., Northwestern U., 1973, M.S.J., 1975; cert. student pilot. Reporter-photographer Lerner Home Newspapers, Chgo., 1973-74; corr. Medill News Service, Washington, 1975; reporter-newsperson, sci. writer UPI, Chgo., 1975—. Interviewer: exclusives White House chief of staff, nation's only mother and son on death row; others. Vol. Chgo.-Read Mental Health Ctr. Recipient Peter Lisagor award for exemplary journalism in features category, 1980, 81; Golden Key Nat. Adv. Bd. of Children's Oncology Service Inc., 1981; Media awards for wire service feature stories, 1983, 84, wire service news stories, 1983, 84, all from Chgo. Hosp. Pub. Relations Soc. Mem. Profl. Assn. Diving Instrs., Nat. Assn. Underwater Instrs., Hon. Order Ky. Cols., Hadassah, Sigma Delta Chi, Sigma Delta Tau. Home: 745 Marion Ave Highland Park IL 60035

RUTH, GLORIA ANN, management consultant; b. Cleve., Apr. 17, 1950; d. Lucio Augustino and Catherine (Schepis) Regalbuto; m. Michael Angelo DiLauro, June 1973 (div. June 1974); m. Douglas Peter Ruth, Aug. 21, 1976; children: Eoin Richard, Erin Joyce. BA in English, Ohio U., 1974, MA in English, 1975; PhD, Ohio State U., 1980. Instr. Cen. Ohio Tech., Newark, 1979-80; employee communications officer United McGill Corp., Columbus, Ohio, 1980-82; instr. Hocking Tech. Coll., Nelsonville, Ohio, 1982-83; corp. tng. mgr. Anchor Hocking, Lancaster, Ohio, 1983-85; sr. mgmt. advisor Battelle Meml. Inst., Columbus, 1985-86; pres. Strategic Performance Systems, Inc., Amanda, Ohio, 1986—. Mem. Am. Soc. for Tng. and Devel. (nat. bd. dirs. 1987—, v.p. external affairs 1985-86), Nat. Soc. for Performance and Instrn. (founding pres. Heartland chpt. 1986—), Sports Car Club Am. (licensee 1976-87, publicity chairperson Ohio Valley region 1980-81). Avocations: poetry, sports car racing. Home and Office: Strategic Performance Systems Inc 9015 Westfall Rd Amanda OH 43102

RUTHEMEYER, THOMAS JAMES, hospital administrator; b. Cin., May 10, 1947; s. Charles Joseph and Barbara Marie (Stoffel) R.; m. Patricia Jean Muszynski, Sept. 6, 1975; children: Todd Andrew, Kristen Marie. BBA in Acctg. and Fin., U. Cin., 1971; MBA in Mgmt., Xavier U., 1984. CPA, Ohio. Acct. William H. Mers & Co., Cin., 1970-73; sr. v.p., treas. Clermont Mercy Hosp., Batavia, Ohio, 1973—; cons. in field. Bd. dirs. Cin. Chpt. ARC, 1977-84, Community Chest Cin., 1977-86; active Greater Cin. Hosp. Council. Fellow Ohio Soc. CPA's (lectr.); mem. Am. Inst. CPA's, Fin. Execs. Inst., Nat. Assn. Accts., Health Care Fin. Mgmt. Assn., Am. Hosp. Assn., Delta Sigma Pi, Beta Alpha Psi. Roman Catholic. Lodge: Rotary. Home: 2130 Hunterspoint Ln Cincinnati OH 45244 Office: Clermont Mercy Hosp 3000 Hospital Dr Batavia OH 45103

RUTHER, MARK STEPHEN, systems design engineer; b. Rockford, Ill., Oct. 19, 1951; s. Edward E. and Virginia (Gray) R.; m. Barbara J. Ruther, Oct. 18, 1986. BA, Cornell Coll., 1973; MBA, No. Ill. U., 1980. Lab technician Woods div. Hesston Corp., Oregon, Ill., 1973-75, engrng. test supr., 1975-79, indsl. engr., 1979-83, paint finishing engr., 1983-85; systems design engr. The Sherwin-Williams Co., Chgo., 1985—. Mem. Soc. Mfg. Engrs. (Assn. Finishing Processes), Chemical Coating Assn., Am. Auto Racing Writers Broadcasters Assn. Methodist. Club: Tebala Honda Patrol (Rockford, Ill.); Lodge: Shriners, Masons. Avocations: golf, photography. Home: 2121 Anson Way West Covina CA 91792 Office: The Sherwin-Williams Co 11541 S Champlain Ave Chicago IL 60628

RUTHERFORD, L. A., coal company executive. Pres., chief exec. officer Baukol-Noonan, Inc., Minot, N.D. Address: 1117 7th St NW Minot ND 58702 Office: Baukol-Noonan Inc Box 879 Minot ND 58702 *

RUTHMAN, THOMAS R., manufacturing company executive; b. Cin., May 24, 1933; s. Alois H. and Catherine (Gies) R.; grad. LaSalle U., 1970; m. Audrey J. Schumaker, Mar. 17, 1979; children—Thomas G., Julia C., Theresa K. With Ruthman Pump and Engring. Inc. (formerly Ruthman Machinery Co.), Cin., 1953—, gen. mgr., 1964-70, v.p., 1970-74, pres., 1974—, pres., owner, 1981—; pres. Gusher Pumps Inc., Fulflo Spltys. Co., Gusher Pumps of New Castle, Cin., Grant County, Dry Ridge, Calif. Served with U.S. Army, 1953-55. Mem. Cin. Council World Affairs, Navy League U.S. Club: Rotary. Home: 6858 Dimmick Rd West Chester OH 45069 Office: 1212 Streng St Cincinnati OH 45223

RUTSTEIN, ALEXANDER, engineering consultant; b. Kharkov, USSR, Oct. 18, 1929; Came to U.S., 1974; s. Lev Rutstein and Tatiana Shechter; m. Sedmara Zakarian, Aug. 28, 1958; 1 child, Alla. MSME, Kharkov Poly. Inst., 1952. Chief turbine dept. Energochermet, Leningrad, USSR, 1965-73; pres. Compressor Controls Corp., Des Moines, 1974-77; staff cons. Energy Mgmt. Engring., Lorain, Ohio, 1977-81; pres. Energy Mgmt. Controls, Elyria, Ohio, 1981-83; owner Alex Rutstein & Assocs., Oberlin, Ohio, 1983—. Patentee in field; contbr. articles to profl. jours. Mem. ASME, Instrument Soc. Am., Am. Soc. Heating Refrigeration and Air Conditioning Engrs., Nat. Soc. Profl. Engrs. Avocations: records, tapes, books, swimming.

RUTTENBERG, HARVEY NOLAN, marketing executive; b. Chgo., May 8, 1942; s. Simon and Tillie (Trembot) R.; m. Phyllis Rubin, Jan. 5, 1964 (div. July 1981); children: Melissa Dawn, Gina Nicole; m. Leah Joanne Adelman, Apr. 25, 1982. BA, U. Ill., 1964. Sales mgr. Mfr. Rep. Agy., Chgo., 1964-71; nat. acctg. mgr. Dow Chem. Co., Midland, Mich., 1971-74; v.p. mktg. Style Wood Co., Arlington Heights, Ill., 1974-79; mktg. mgr. Ekco Houseware Co., Franklin Park, Ill., 1979-82; mktg. mgr. Safety Kleen Co., Elgin, Ill., 1982-87, gen. mgr, 1987—; design cons. in field. Mem. Automotive Service Ind. (officer 1980-84), Automotive Chem. Mfrs. Council (steering com. 1985, chmn. environ. interest com. 1985, exec. com. 1987, council chmn. 1987, chmn. industry affairs com. 1987). Design Cons. (officer 1976-82), Nat. Retailer Assn. (officer 1980-82). Jewish. Avocations: design, lecturing, writing. Home: 47 Longridge Ct Buffalo Grove IL 60089 Office: Safety Kleen Co Big Timber Rd Elgin IL 60120

RUYLE, ELIZABETH SMITH (BETH), association executive; b. Atlanta, Oct. 26, 1946; d. Daniel Lester and Mae (Coley) Smith; B.A., U. Fla., 1968; M.P.A., U. Ga., 1975; m. Craig Harlan Hullinger, Oct. 24, 1985; children: Clint, Brett, Leigh Ann. Health planner Met. Council for Health, Atlanta, 1970-72; govtl. relations coordinator Atlanta Regional Commn., 1972-76, govtl. affairs coordinator, 1976-78; exec. dir. South Suburban Mayors' and Mgrs. Assn., Homewood, Ill., 1978—; exec. dir. South Towns Agy. Risk Mgmt., 1980—, South Towns Area Benefits Coop., 1983—, South Towns Bus. Growth Corp., 1983—; cons. Planning Devel. Service, University Park, Ill., 1986—. Sec., bd. dirs. FOCUS Council on South Suburbs, Homewood, 1981-87; mem. World's Fair Adv. Com., Chgo., 1986, Met. Planning Council, Cook County Housing Adv. Com., Cook County Tax Reform Adv. council, Fiscal Adv. Council, Austerity and Urban Innovation Project, S. Suburban Arts Council, Ill. Airport Adv. Council, Council Urban Econ. Devel., Chgo. Council Fgn. Relations, 1986, tax study com. Cook County, Chgo., 1987, adv. council Urban Innovations, Chgo., 1987; bd. dirs. S. Suburban Hosp. Mem. Internat. City Mgmt. Assn., Ill. City Mgmt. Assn., Met. City Mgrs. Assn. (bd. dirs.), Ill. Pub. Employer Labor Relations Assn., Pub. Risk Ins. Mgmt. Assn., S. Suburban Chiefs of Police Assn., S. Suburban C. of C., Chgo. C. of C., Chgo. Assn. Commerce and Industry, Plank Rd. Trail Assn. Methodist. Contbr. articles to profl. and devel. mags. Home: 1415 Pinewoods Ct University Park IL 60466 Office: South Suburban Mayors/Mgrs Assn 1154 Ridge Rd Homewood IL 60430

RUYLE, ROBERT LLOYD, engineer, fire and security consultant; b. Liberty, Nebr., Mar. 26, 1934; s. Oliver William and Dorothy Margaret (Graham) R.; m. Bernice Fay Vitosh, Aug. 17, 1957; children: Sherri, Nanci, Patricia, Joan, Robert II, Steven. AS in Elec. Engring., Cen. Tech. Inst., 1959. Teaching engr. RCA Field Service, various locations, 1959-63; sales engr. Hy-Gain Electronics, Lincoln, 1963-66; teaching engr. Nebr. ETV and Notifier Co., Lincoln, 1966-82; pvt. practice computer applications Boca Raton, Fla., 1983-85; cons. engr. Ruyle & Assocs., Lincoln, 1985—; cons. CASI, Boca Raton, 1983—. Contbr. articles on electronics security to various tech. publs. Mem. com. Nebr. Fire Marshal, Lincoln, 1985—. Served with USN, 1953-57, Korea. Mem. Fire Protection Assn. (mem. coms. 1982—), Nat. Assn. Atomic Vets., Am. Legions. Republican. Roman Catholic. Avocations: speaking, writing, computer software, flying. Home and Office: 420 Steinway Rd Lincoln NE 68505

RUZEK, ROBIN REEDY, plastics molding engineer; b. San Francisco, Mar. 2, 1941; s. Charles V. Jr. and Maurine (Reedy) R.; m. Joanne Luenberger, July 18, 1964; children: Melanie C., Bryan C. BS in Civil Engring., Stanford U., 1963, MS in Civil Engring., 1964. Maintenance engr. Crown Zellerbach, Portland, Oreg., 1969-74; plant engr. Crown Zellerbach, Newcastle, Del., 1974-76, Kansas City, Mo., 1976-79; plastic molding engr. AT&T Tech., Lees Summit, Mo., 1979—. Pres. Blue Springs (Mo.) Powderpuff Softball, 1978-80. Served to lt. USN, 1964-69,. Mem. Soc. Plastic Engrs. (bd. dirs. 1984—, v.p. 1986-87, pres. 1987—), Am. Inst. Plant Engrs., Instrument Soc. Am. Avocation: tuba playing. Home: 1313 S 21st St Blue Springs MO 64015 Office: AT&T Tech 2220 777 N Blue Pkwy Lees Summit MO 64063

RUZIC, DAVID NEIL, nuclear engineering educator; b. Michigan City, Ind., Feb. 10, 1958; s. Neil Pierce and Carol Wilhelmina (Kalsbeek) R.; m. LeAnn Michelle Ormsby, Dec. 30, 1979; 1 child, Ryan David. BS in Physics and Applied Math. with honors, Purdue U., 1979; MS in Physics, Princeton U., 1981, PhD in Physics, 1984. Mem. research staff Princeton U. Plasma Physics Lab., 1984; asst. prof. nuclear engring. U. Ill., 1984—. Contbr. articles to profl. jours. Mem. Am. Vacuum Soc. (chmn. edn. com., plasma sci. and tech. div. 1986—), Am. Phys. Soc., Am. Nuclear Soc. Home: Rural Rt 1 Box 128 Sadorus IL 61872-9735 Office: U Ill 103 S Goodwin Ave Urbana IL 61801

RUZICK, SAM, JR., finance executive; b. Deadwood, S.D., Sept. 22, 1945; s. Sam Sr. and Frances (Hargraves) R.; m. Delores M. Jones, June 20, 1972; children: Lily A., Ben. BS, Black Hills State Coll., 1969. Driver Coca Cola, Pierre, S.D., 1960-69; auditor Amsted Industries, Chgo., 1969-71; staff acct. Am. Steel Foundry, Chgo., 1971-75; plant controller Am. Steel Foundry, Alliance, Ohio, 1975-80; sec./treas. Litho-Strip Co., Chgo., 1980—. Auditor Free Meth. Ch., Aurora, 1980-86. Republican. Methodist. Avocations: bowling, basketball, hunting, fishing.

RUZICKA, VICKI PATRICIA, marketing executive; b. Chgo., Apr. 30, 1945; d. Victor Hugo and Ellyn Marie (Doyle) Reid. B.S., Northeastern Ill. U., Chgo., 1976. Prodn. mgr. Signature Direct Response Mktg., Evanston, Ill., 1981-82, purchasing mgr., 1983-84; credit promotions media mgr. Montgomery Ward, Chgo., 1982-83; fulfillment purchasing mgr. The Signature Group, Schaumburg, Ill., 1984-87; sr. credit analyst CitiCorp DinersClub, Chgo., 1987—. Author: Trips: Head, Bod and Side, 1968, Poetry Magazine, 1970. Served with USAF, 1979-83. Mem. Nat. Assn. Purchasing Mgrs., Direct Mail Mktg. Assn., Printing Inst. Ill., Women's Direct Response Group, Chgo. Assn. Direct Mktg. Roman Catholic. Avocations: sailing; golf; classical piano; baseball. Office: CitiCorp Diners Club 8430 W Bryn Mawr Chicago IL 60631

RYALL, JO-ELLYN M., psychiatrist; b. Newark, May 25, 1949; d. Joseph P. and Tekla (Paraszczuk) R.; B.A. in Chemistry with gen. honors, Douglass Coll., Rutgers U., 1971; M.D., Washington U., St. Louis, 1975. Resident in psychiatry Washington U., 1975-78, psychiatrist Student Health, 1980-84, clin. instr. psychiatry, 1978-83, clin. asst. prof. psychiatry, 1983—; inpatient supr. Malcolm Bliss Mental Health Center, St. Louis, 1978-80, psychiatrist outpatient clinic, 1980-82; pvt. practice medicine specializing in psychiatry, St. Louis, 1980—. Bd. dirs. Women's Self Help Center, St. Louis, 1980-83. Diplomate Am. Bd. Psychiatry and Neurology. Mem. Am. Psychiat. Assn. Soc. (pres. Eastern Mo. Dist. Br. 1983-85, sect. council Am. MED Assn. 1986—), Am. Med. Women's Assn. (pres. St. Louis Dist. br. 1981-82, regional gov. VIII 1986—), AMA, St. Louis Met. Med. Soc. (del. to state conv. 1981—councilor 1985—), Mo. State Med. Assn. (vice speaker ho. of dels. 1986—), Manic Depressive Assn. St. Louis (chmn. bd. dirs. 1985—). Club: Washington U. Faculty. Office: 9216 Clayton Rd Saint Louis MO 63124

RYAN, ALLAN JAMES, publishing executive, editor; b. Bklyn., Dec. 9, 1915; s. Lorne McDonnell and Valerie (Britton) R.; m. Agnes Louise Nelson, July 4, 1942; children: Brendan Michael, James Allan, Robert Edward. BA, Yale U., 1936; MD, Columbia U., 1940; D in Sports Sci., U.S. Sports Acad., 1983. Diplomate Am. Bd. Gen. Surgery. Intern in gen. surgery Kings County Hosp., Bklyn., 1940-42, research fellow surgery, 1942-43; asst. resident surgery Grace New Haven (Conn.) Hosp., 1943-45; chief resident surgery Long Island (N.Y.) Coll. Hosp., Bklyn., 1945-46; attending surgeon Meriden (Conn.) Hosp., 1947-1965; assoc. prof. U. Wis., Madison, 1965-70; prof. U. Wis., 1970-76; editor-in-chief Postgrad. Medecine, Mpls., 1976-79, The Physician & Sports Medicine, Mpls., 1973=85; dir. Sports Medicine Enterprise, Edina, Minn., 1985—; athletic teams physician U. Wis., Madison, 1965-76. Author: Medical Care of Athlete, 1962, Guide to Running, 1980; editor: Sports Medicine, 1974, Dance Medicine, 1986. Mem. Commn. Mil. Accidents, Washington, 1964-69; med. examiner City of Meriden, 1947-65; trustee U.S. Sports Academy, Mobile, 1985—. Recipient Silver Medal award City of Paris, 1983, Nat. Phys. Fitness Leadership award Jr. C. of C., 1971. Fellow Am. Coll. Sports Medicine (pres. 1963—), Am. Orthopaedic Soc. Sports Medicine (assoc.); mem. Am. Alliance Health, Phys. Edn., and Recreation Devel., Council Phys. Fitness and Sports (cons., pres. 1960—), AMA (commn. on med. aspects of athletics), Internat. Fedn. Sports Medicine (sec. gen. 1980-86), Phi Beta Kappa, Sigma Xi. Republican. Roman Catholic. Avocations: racing bicycles, attending veterans class. Office: Sports Medicine Enterprise 4510 W 77 St Edina MN 55435

RYAN, DANIEL LEO, Roman Catholic bishop; b. Mankato, Minn., Sept. 28, 1930; s. Leonard Bennett and Irene Ruth (Larson) R. B.A., Ill. Benedictine Coll., 1952; J.C.L., Pontificia Università Lateranense, Rome, 1960. Ordained priest Roman Cath. Ch., 1956, consecrated bishop, 1981. Parish priest Roman Catholic Diocese Joliet, Ill, 1956-82, chancellor, 1965-78, vicar gen., 1977-79, aux. bishop, 1981-84; bishop Roman Catholic Diocese Springfield, Ill., 1984—. Trustee Pope John XXIII Sem., Weston, Mass., 1984—, N. Am. Coll., Louvain, Belgium, 1984—. Office: Diocese of Springfield PO Box 1667 Springfield IL 62705

RYAN, DONALD PATRICK, contractor; b. Janesville, Wis., July 13, 1930; s. William H. and Myrtle (Westrick) R.; B.S. in Civil Engring., U. Wis., 1953, B.S. in Naval Sci., 1953; m. Diana Houser, July 17, 1954; children—Patrick, Susannah, Nancy, David, Josephine, Rebecca, Polly, Adam. Partner, Ryan Bros. Co., Janesville, Wis., 1949—; pres. Ryan, Inc. Cen., Janesville; dir. Valley Bank, Janesville, Valley Bncorp, Appleton U. Wis. Cancer Ctr. Adv. Bd., Elvehjem Mus. Art Council, U. Wis. Found. Served with USNR, 1953-55. Registered profl. engr., Wis., Ill. Mem. Nat. Soc. Profl. Engrs., Wis. Meml. Union Bldg. Assn. (trustee), U. Wis. Alumni Assn., Chi Epsilon, Phi Delta Theta. Home: 703 St Lawrence Ave Janesville WI 53545 Office: PO Box 1079 Janesville WI 53545

RYAN, GEORGE, state lieutenant governor, pharmacist; b. Maquoketa, Iowa, Feb. 24, 1934; s. Thomas J. and Jeanette (Bowman) R.; m. Lura Lynn Lowe, June 10, 1956; children: Nancy, Lynda, Julie, JoAnne, Jeanette, George. B.S. in Pharmacy, Ferris State Coll., Big Rapids, Mich. Vice-pres. Ryan Pharmacies, Kankakee, Ill.; mem. Ill. Ho. of Reps., 1972-83, minority leader, 1977-81, speaker, 1981-83; lt. gov. State of Ill., 1983—. Mem. Kankakee County Bd., 1966-72, chmn., 1971-72; hon. chmn. Ill. Easter Seal Kickoff, UN Internat. Year of Disabled Persons, 1981. Served with U.S. Army. Recipient Humphrey award Am. Pharm. Assn., 1980. Mem. Am. Pharm. Assn., Ill. Pharm. Assn., One Hundred Club. Republican. Methodist. Lodges: Elks, Moose, Shriners. *

RYAN, HOWARD CHRIS, state chief justice; b. Tonica, Ill., June 17, 1916; s. John F. and Sarah (Egger) R.; m. Helen Cizek, Oct. 16, 1943; children: John F., Elizabeth Ellen, Howard Chris. B.A., U. Ill., 1940, LL.B., J.D., 1942; LL.D. (hon.), John Marshall Law Sch., 1978. Bar: Ill. 1942. Practice in Decatur, 1946-47, Peru, 1947-57; asst. state's atty. LaSalle County, 1952-54, county judge, 1954-57, circuit judge, 1957-68; chief judge 1964-68; judge appellate ct. 3d Jud. Dist. Ill., 1968-70; justice Ill. Supreme Ct., 1970—, chief justice, 1981-84. Served with USAAF, 1942-45. Mem. Am., Ill., LaSalle County bar assns., Am. Judicature Soc., Am. Legion, Phi Alpha Delta. Republican. Methodist. Lodges: Masons; Elks; Odd Fellows. Home: Box 397 Tonica IL 61370 Office: 111 E Jefferson St Ottawa IL 61350

RYAN, JACK, physician, hospital corporation executive; b. Benton Harbor, Mich., Aug. 26, 1925; s. Leonard Joseph and Beulah (Southworth) R.; m. Lois Patricia Patterson; children: Michele, Kevin, Timothy, Sarah, Daniel. AB, Western Mich. U., 1948; postgrad., U. Mich. Law Sch., 1949-50, Emory U., 1950-51; MD, Wayne State U., 1955. Pres. Meml. Med. Ctr., Warren, Mich., 1956-77; v.p. med. affairs Detroit-Macomb Hosp. Corp., 1976-77, pres. and chief exec. officer, 1977—; assoc. prof. medicine Wayne State U., Detroit, 1974—. Recipient Disting. Alumnus award Wayne State U. Med. Sch., 1974, Wayne State U., 1979, Disting. Key award Mich. Hosp. Assn., 1986. Fellow Am. Coll. Family Physicians, Am. Coll. Physician Execs., Detroit Acad. Medicine; mem. Internat. Health Econs. and Mgmt. Inst. (charter), Econ. Club Detroit. Clubs: Detroit Athletic, Renaissance. Avocations: Civil War, history, golf, tennis. Home: 175 Hendrie Blvd Royal Oak MI 48067 Office: Detroit-Macomb Hosp Corp 7815 E Jefferson Ave Detroit MI 48214

RYAN, JAMES EDWIN, plastics company executive, real estate company executive; b. San Antonio, June 23, 1943; s. Edwin F. and Margaret L (Hale) R.; m. Connie S. Roseberry, Nov. 30, 1966; children—Rebecca Morrow, Rachel Morgan. B.A. in Psychology, Ohio State U., 1965. Registered profl. engr., Ohio. Br. mgr. Dayton Plastics, Ohio, 1965-71, sec.-treas., 1971-85, pres., 1985—; pres. Metro Group, Dayton, 1977—; dir. Ohio Products, Inc., Dayton. Editor: Handbook of Plastics, 1973, Plastics Engineering Guide, 1986. Bd. dirs. Soccer Internat., Dayton, 1979—. Mem. Soc. Plastics Engrs., Soc. Plastics Industry, Nat. Assn. Plastics, Nat. Assn. Land Developers, Young Pres. Am. Avocations: tournament tennis playing. Office: Metro Group 860 W Centerville Rd Dayton OH 45459

RYAN, JAMES JOSEPH, lawyer; b. Cin., June 17, 1929; s. Robert J. and Marian (Hoffman) R.; m. Mary A. Noonan, Nov. 25, 1954; children: Kevin, Timothy, Nora, Daniel. AB, Xavier U., 1951, JD, U. Cin., 1954. Bar: Ohio 1954. Teaching assoc. Northwestern U., Chgo., 1954-55; ptnr. Dolle, O'Donnell & Cash, Cin., 1958-71, Taft, Stettinius & Hollister, Cin., 1971—; lectr. U. Cin. Coll. Law, 1960-65. Chmn. Health Planning Assn. Ohio River Valley, Cin., 1978-85; bd. dirs. Hamilton County Bd. of Mentally Retarded, 1968-80; trustee Resident Home for Mentally Retarded, 1980—. Mem. ABA, Ohio Bar Assn., Cin. Bar Assn. Republican. Roman Catholic. Clubs: Queen City, Western Hill. Avocations: reading, sports. Home: 1386 Wynnburne Dr Cincinnati OH 45238 Office: Taft Stettinius & Hollister 1800 1st Nat Bank Ctr Cincinnati OH 45202

RYAN, JAMES LEO, federal judge; b. Detroit, Nov. 19, 1932; s. Leo Francis and Irene Agnes Ryan; m. Mary Elizabeth Rogers, Oct. 12, 1957; children: Daniel P., James R., Colleen M., Kathleen A. LL.B., U. Detroit, 1956; LL.D. (hon.), Madonna Coll., 1976, Detroit Coll. Law, 1978, Thomas M. Cooley Law Sch., Lansing, Mich., 1986, U. Detroit Sch. Law, 1986. Justice of peace Redford Twp., Mich., 1963-66; cir. judge 3d Jud. Circuit Mich., 1966-75; justice Mich. Supreme Ct., 1975-86; judge U.S. Ct. Appeals (6th cir.), 1986—; faculty U. Detroit Sch. Law, Nat. Jud. Coll., Reno, Am. Acad. Jud. Edn., Washington. Contbr. article to legal jour. Served with JAGC, USNR, 1957-60; to capt. JAGC, Res. 1960—. Mem. Am. Judicature Soc., ABA, Detroit Bar Assn., Naval Res. Lawyers Assn., Nat. Conf. Appellate Ct. Judges, Fed. Judges Assn., State Bar Mich. Roman Catholic. Club: KC. Office: U S Ct of Appeals 20793 Farmington Rd Suite 24 Farmington Hills MI 48024

RYAN, JAMES RAYMOND, orthopaedic surgeon, educator; b. Benton Harbor, Mich., Apr. 25, 1936; s. Leonard J. and Beulah M. (Southworth) R. Student, Western Mich. U., 1957; MD, Wayne State U., 1961. Diplomate Am. Bd. Orthopaedic Surgery. Resident in orthopaedics U. Ark., Little Rock, 1967, asst. prof. orthopaedics, 1968; instr. Wayne State U., Detroit, 1970-75, asst. prof., 1976-77, assoc. prof., 1977—; vice chmn. S.W. Oncology Group Nat. Cancer Inst., 1985—. Author: Orthopedic Surgery, 1977, rev. edit., 1980; author, coordinator: (sound slide series) Fractures Parts I and II, 1979; reviewer: Annals of Emergency Medicine, 1983—; contbr. articles to profl. jours. Served to comdr. USPHS, 1967-69. Mem. Am. Bd. Orthopaedic Surgeons (bd. examiner), Orthopaedic Research and Edn. Found. (state chmn. fund raising), Detroit Orthopaedic Soc. (pres. 1982). Avocation: tennis. Office: Wayne State U Sch Medicine Dept Orthopaedic Surgery 4201 Saint Antoine 7C Detroit MI 48201

RYAN, JOHN WILLIAM, university president; b. Chgo., Aug. 12, 1929; s. Leonard John and Maxine (Mitchell) R.; m. D. Patricia Goodday, Mar. 20, 1949; children: Kathleen Elynne Ryan Acker, Kevin Dennis Mitchell, Kerrick Charles Casey. B.A., U. Utah, 1951; M.A., Ind. U., 1958, Ph.D., 1959; LL.D. (hon.), U. Notre Dame, 1978, Oakland City Coll., 1981, St. Joseph Coll., 1981, Hanover Coll., 1982, DePauw U., 1983, Manchester Coll., 1983, U. Evansville, 1985, Wabash Coll., 1986; D.Litt., Coll. St. Thomas, 1977. Research analyst Ky. Dept. Revenue, Frankfort, 1954-55; vis. research prof. Ind. U. project at U. Thammasat, Bangkok, Thailand, 1955-57; asst. dir. Inst. Tng. for Public Service, Ind. U., 1957-58; successively asst. prof., asso. prof. polit. sci., asso. dir. Bur. Govt., U. Wis., 1958-62; exec. asst. to pres., sec. of univ. U. Mass., Amherst, 1962-63; chancellor U. Mass., Boston, 1965-68; v.p. acad. affairs Ariz. State U., 1963-65; v.p., chancellor regional campuses Ind. U., Bloomington, 1968-71, pres., 1971—; also now prof. polit. sci. Ind. U.; dir. Ind. Bell Telephone Co.; chmn. Nat. Adv. Bd. on Internat. Edn. Programs, 1985—. Author papers and reports in field. Pres. Newman Found. Ind., 1969-71, bd. dirs., from 1969; pres. Ind. Conf. Higher Edn., 1977-78; bd. govs. Riley Meml. Assn., from 1971, Public Broadcasting Service, from 1973; bd. dirs. Ind. Center Advanced Research, 1977-80; bd. govs. Univ. Field Staff Internat., from 1971; chmn. bd. Am. U. field staff, 1972-77; chmn. bd. dirs. Ind. U. Found., from 1972; bd. dirs., mem. exec. com. Ind. Corp. for Sci. and Tech., from 1984; trustee Coll. St. Thomas, from 1975; bd. visitors Air U., 1974-81; chmn. Air Force Inst. Tech Subcom., 1976-81; mem. univ. adv. com. Am. Council Life Ins.; mem. White River Park Devel. Commn., from 1979; mem. council pres's Midwest Univs. Consortium for Internat. Activities, from 1971, chmn., 1976-78; bd. dirs. Nat. Inst. Campus Ministries, 1975-78, Corp. Community Council, 1976, Council Fin. Aid to Edn., 1981; Council of Ten, Common Instl. Coop. rep. to NCAA, from 1980, pres. President's Commn., 1984; mem. nat. adv. council Pan Am. Games, 1985; mem. adv. bd. Assocs. for Religious and Intellectual Life, from 1984; mem. United Way of Ind. Centennial Commn. Mem. Am. Soc. Public Adminstrn. (pres. Ind. chpt. 1969-70, nat. chpt. 1972-73, nat. council from 1970, Ind. Soc. Chgo. (non-resident v.p. from 1976, Am. Polit. Sci. Assn., Assn. Asian Studies, Am. Council Edn., Am. Judicature Soc., Assn. Am. Univs. (exec. com. from 1978, chmn. com. on coms. 1984, health edn. com. from 1978, chmn. 1981-82), Ind. Soc. N.Y.C., Ind. Soc. Washington, Nat. Acad. Public Adminstrn., Ind. Acad., Explorers Club, Adelphia (hon.), Phi Kappa Phi, Phi Alpha Theta, Pi Sigma Alpha, Beta Gamma Sigma, Kappa Sigma (worthy grand master 1985-87). Club: Circumnavigators, N.Y. Lodges: K.C., Rotary, Elks. Office: Central Adminstrn Ind U Bryan Hall Bloomington IN 47405

RYAN, JOYCE NICHTERN, animator, art director; b. New Rochelle, N.Y., July 29, 1951; d. Leo and Violet (Luckacs) Nichtern; m. John Robert Ryan, Aug. 21, 1971; 1 child, Lucas Craig. BFA, Rhode Island Sch. Design, 1973; MFA, Washington U., St. Louis, 1979. Exhibits artist Mus. Sci., St. Louis, 1974-78; artist, animator Ryan 2 Studio, St. Louis, 1979-83; creative dir. Design Network, St. Louis, 1983-84; v.p. Ryan and Friends, Inc., St. Louis, 1984—; sculpture instr. Jewish Community Ctr., St. Louis, 1986—; art lectr. Washington U., 1987—. Art dir. for TV spots include Miss Egg Am., Schnucks Pumpkin Patch; creative dir. TV spot Steakhouse Charcoal, 1985 (Flair award 1985). Mem. Advt. Fedn. St. Louis. Avocations: sculpture, singing, reading, racquetball. Office: Ryan & Friends Inc 4740 A McPherson Saint Louis MO 63108

RYAN, LEO VINCENT, university dean; b. Waukon, Iowa, Apr. 6, 1927; s. John Joseph and Mary Irene (O'Brien) R. B.S., Marquette U., 1949; M.B.A., DePaul U., 1954; Ph.D., St. Louis U., 1958; postgrad., Catholic U. Am., 1951-52, Bradley U., 1952-54, Northwestern U., 1950. Joined Order Clerics of St. Viator, 1950; mem. faculty Marquette U., Milw., 1957-65; dir. continuing edn. summer sessions, coordinator evening divs. Marquette U., 1959-65, prof. indsl. mgmt., 1964; prof. and chmn. dept. mgmt. Loyola U., Chgo., 1965-66; adj. prof. mgmt. Loyola U., 1967-69; dep. dir. Peace Corps, Lagos, Nigeria, 1966-67; dir. Western Nigeria Peace Corps, Ibadan, 1967-68; asst. superior gen. and treas. gen. Clerics of St. Viator, Rome, 1968-69; dir. edn. Am. province Clerics of St. Viator, Arlington Heights, Ill., 1969-74; pres. St. Viator High Sch., 1972-74; dean Coll. Bus. Adminstrn. U. Notre Dame, Ind., 1975-80, Coll. Commerce, DePaul U., 1980—; dir. Peace Corps. tng. programs Marquette U., 1962-65; adj. prof. human devel. St. Mary's Coll., Winona, Minn., 1972-74; mem. sch. bd. Archdiocese Chgo., 1972-75, vice chmn., 1973-75; mem. nat. edn. com. U.S. Cath. Conf., 1971-75, mem. exec. com., 1973-75; mem. nat. adv. bd. Benedictine Sisters of Nauvoo, 1973— ; mem. nat. adv. council SBA, 1982-85, vice chmn. minority bus., 1982-85, exec. com. Chgo. chpt., 1982-84; vis. prof. U. Ife, Ibadan, 1967-68; bd. dirs. 1st Bank-Milw., chmn. trust audit com., 1980-85, chmn. audit and trust com., 1985—; bd. dirs. 1st Bank-LaCrosse, Vilter Mfg. Co., McHugh-Freeman Assos., Filbert Corp., Vilter Sales & Service, Vilter Internat., Henricksen & Co., Inc., Gebhardt Refrigeration Co.; mem. fin. commn. Clerics of St. Viator, 1978—, mem. provincial chpt., 1985—; cons. Pontifical Commn. on Justice and Peace, 1968-70. Mem. Pres.'s Com. on Employment Handicapped, 1959-65, Wis. Gov.'s Com. on Employment Handicapped,

1959-65, Wis. Gov.'s Com. on UN, 1961-64, Burnham Park Planning Commn., 1982—; bd. dirs. Ctr. Pastoral Liturgy U. Notre Dame, 1976-79; trustee St. Mary of Woods Coll., 1978-81; regent Seton Hall U., 1981-87, mem. acad. affairs com., 1981-87, chmn., 1983-87. Recipient Freedom award Berlin Commn., 1961; chieftaincy title Asoju Atoaja of Oshogbo Oba Adenle I, Yorubaland, Nigeria, 1967; Brother Leo V. Ryan award created in his honor Cath. Bus. Edn. Assn., 1962; named Man of Year Jr. C. of C. Milw., 1959, Marquette U. Bus. Adminstrn. Alumni Man of Year, 1974, Tchr. of Yr. U. Notre Dame, 1980; recipient B'nai B'rith Interfaith award Milw., 1963; Distinguished Alumnus award DePaul U., 1976; Tchr. of Yr. award Beta Alpha Psi, Notre Dame U., 1980; Centennial Alumni Achievement award Marquette U., 1981; Milw. Bd. Realtors travelling fellow, 1964; Nat. Assn. Purchasing Agts. faculty fellow, 1958; German Am. Acad. Exchange Council fellow, summer 1983. Mem. Cath. Bus. Edn. Assn. (nat. pres. 1960-62, nat. exec. bd. 1960-64), Assn. Sch. Bus. Ofcls. (nat. com. chmn. 1965-67), Am. Assembly Collegiate Schs. Bus. (com. internat. affairs 1977-84, chmn. 1981-84, bd. dirs. 1981-87, program chmn. 1979-80, exec. com., chmn. projects/service mgmt. com. 1984-86), Am. Fgn. Service Assn., Acad. Internat. Bus., Acad. Mgmt., August Derleth Soc., Econ. Club Chgo., Chgo. Counvil Fgn. Relations, Council Fgn. Relations (Chgo. com.), Nigerian Inst. Mgmt., Alpha Sigma Nu, Alpha Kappa Psi (Bronze Disting. Service award 1949, silver Disting. Service award 1958), Beta Alpha Psi, Beta Gamma Sigma (co-chair 75th Anniversary committee), Delta Mu Delta, Pi Gamma Mu, Tau Kappa Epsilon. Club: Milw. Press (hon.). Office: DePaul U Dean's Office Coll Commerce 25 E Jackson Blvd Chicago IL 60604

RYAN, MARY ELLEN, advertising materials distributing business official; b. Chgo., Oct. 24, 1951; d. Albert John and Helen Mary (Heinlein) Gubricky; m. Patrick M. Ryan. Cert. Arts, Richard J. Daley Jr. Coll., Chgo., 1972; B.S.Ed., No. Ill. U., 1974; M.A. in Curriculum Devel., U. Conn., 1977, postgrad., 1980-84. With Ill. Bell Telephone Co., Chgo., 1969-71; internat. acct. Mex. br. Ency. Brit. Ednl. Corp., Chgo., 1974-76; advt. cons. Buzz Barton & Assos., Inc., Chgo., 1977-78; varied advt. positions Dimensional Mktg. Inc., Chgo., 1978; tchr. Nativity of Our Lord Sch., Chgo., 1979; tchr. Mother McAuley High Sch., Chgo., 1979-82; substitute tchr. Oak Lawn and Evergreen Park, Ill., 1983-84; tchr. Montessori Elem. Sch., Blue Island, Ill., 1984; customer service rep. Martin Brower (M-B Sales), Chgo., 1985—.

RYAN, MICHAEL JOSEPH, veterinary pathologist; b. Santa Ana, Calif., Apr. 11, 1945; s. Daniel Stephen and Rosemary (Schuster) R.; m. Mara Susan Gales, Nov. 26, 1971; 1 child, Pamela Claire. BA, U. Minn., 1967, DVM, 1977; PhD, U. Conn., 1982. Diplomate Am. Bd. Vet. Pathologists. Pathologist Sterling-Winthrop Research Inst., Rensselaer, N.Y., 1982-84; vet. pathologist Battelle, Columbus, Ohio, 1984—. Contbr. articles to profl. jours. Mem. Am. Soc. Toxicolic Pathologists, Phi Zeta. Home: 6832 Hill Rd NW Canal Winchester OH 43110 Office: Battelle 505 King Ave Columbus OH 43110

RYAN, PATRICK G., insurance company executive; b. Milw., May 15, 1937; m. Shirley Welsh, Apr. 16, 1966; children—Patrick III, Robert J., Corbett M. B.S., Northwestern U., 1959. Sales agt. Penn Mut., 1959-64; founder Pat Ryan & Assocs., Chgo., 1964-71; chmn., pres. Ryan Ins. Group Inc., Chgo., 1971-82; pres., chief exec. officer Combined Internat. Corp., Northbrook, Ill., 1982—, dir., 1982—; dir. Commonwealth Edison, Chgo., First Chgo. Corp., First Nat. Bank, Chgo., Gould Inc., Rolling Meadows, Ill. Past pres. Chgo. Boys Clubs; trustee Rush-Presbyterian-St. Luke's Med. Ctr., Chgo., Northwestern U., Field Mus. Natural History, Chgo. Recipient Disting. Mgr. award, Lake Forest Coll., Ill., 1983. Roman Catholic. Office: Combined Internat Corp 123 N Wacker Dr Chicago IL 60606 also: Combined Ins Co of America 222 N Dearborn Chicago IL 60601 *

RYAN, RAYMOND RICHARD, JR., optometrist; b. Anchorage, Alaska, July 13, 1954; s. Raymond Richard and Carol Rose (Cummings) R.; m. Marcia Leslie Pogue, June 30, 1979; children—Erin Kathleen, Kelly Rae, Brianna Jean. B.S. in Psychology, Pacific U., Forest Grove, Oreg., 1976. O.D., 1979; M.S.Ed., U. Wis.-Oshkosh, 1985. Staff optometrist Shopko Stores, Inc., Kimberly, Wis., 1979-85; pvt. practice, 1985—; guest lectr. U. Wis-Oshkosh, 1980—; presenter in field. Vice pres. bd. dirs. Kinderhaus Day Care Ctr., Kaukauna, 1980-84; bd. dirs. Kaukauna Assembly of God, 1980-83, Kaukauna Bowling Assn., 1984-85; fund raiser Cerebral Palsy, Kimberly, 1983-85. Recipient appreciation award Amigos de las Americas, 1978; named Outstanding Jaycee of Quarter, 1980. Mem. Kaukauna Jaycees (v.p., pres. 1979-81), Antigo Optimists. Lodge: Elks. Avocations: fishing, bowling, reading. Home: W8964 Hwy 64 Antigo WI 54409 Office: The Vision Ctr 810 5th Ave Antigo WI 54409

RYAN, RICHARD MICHAEL, data processing executive; b. Aurora, Ill., Apr. 30, 1952; s. Richard John and Mildred Janet (Dieke) R.; m. Sharon Ann Daniels, Aug. 25, 1973; children: Jennifer Lynn, Steven Michael. B Bus., Western Ill. U., 1974. Computer facilities analyst Amoco Corp., Chgo., 1974—; cons. Deltak Corp., Naperville, Ill., 1979-80. Communications specialist Naperville Emergency Services, 1986. Ill. State Scholar, 1970. Mem. Amoco Microcomputer User's Group (pres. 1984-86). Avocation: amateur radio. Office: Amoco Corp MC 0401 200 E Randolph Dr Chicago IL 60601

RYAN, ROBERT COLLINS, lawyer; b. Evanston, Ill., Sept. 15, 1953; s. Donald Thomas and Patricia J. (Collins) R.; m. Joanne Kay Holata, Nov. 5, 1983. B.A. in Econs., B.S.I.E. with high honors, U. Ill., 1976; J.D., Northwestern U., 1979. Bar: Ill. 1979, U.S. Dist. Ct. (no. dist.) Ill. 1980, U.S. Ct. Appeals (Fed. cir.) 1982, U.S. Supreme Ct. 1984. Assoc., Allegretti, Newitt, Witcoff & McAndrews, Ltd., Chgo., 1979-83, ptnr. 1983—; lectr. engring. law Northwestern U. Tech. Inst., Evanston, Ill., 1981-85, adj. prof. engring. law, 1985—. Exec. editor Northwestern Jour. Internat. Law & Bus., 1978-79. Contbr. articles to profl. jours. James scholar U. Ill., 1976. Mem. ABA, Fed. Cir. Bar Assn., Intellectual Property Law Assn. Chgo., Tau Beta Pi, Alpha Pi Mu, Phi Kappa Phi. Home: 2650 N Lakeview #3501 Chicago IL 60614 Office: Allegretti Newitt Witcoff & McAndrews Ltd 125 S Wacker Dr Chicago IL 60606

RYAN, ROBERT GILBERT, dentist; b. Duluth, Minn., Dec. 22, 1945; s. Gilbert C. and Genevieve (Edholm) R.; m. Maureen Kay Stapleton, Aug. 10, 1968; children: Colleen K., Patrick G., Bridgit K. Student, St. John's U., 1963-65; BS, DDS, U. Minn., 1969. Gen. practice dentistry Duluth, 1970-80, Lake Superior Dental Assocs., Duluth, 1980—. Served to lt. (J.G.) USPHS, 1969-70. Fellow Am. Acad. Gen. Dentistry (bd. dirs. 1978-84, v.p. 1984-85, pres-elect 1985-86, pres. 1986—), Am. Coll. Dentists; mem. Am. Dental Assn., Omricon Kappa Upsilon. Roman Catholic. Avocations: golf, skiing. Office: Lake Superior Dental Assocs 1225 E 1st St Duluth MN 55805

RYAN, ROBERT L., manufacturing executive; b. Cleve., Nov. 8, 1942; s. Eugene F. and Phyllis E. (Kriner) R.; m. Mary Beth Heidenreich, July 3, 1965; children: Mark, Tim, Greg, Bob, Matt. Student, Fenn Coll., 1960-63, John Carroll U., 1963-68. Asst. engr. Gould Inc., Bedford, Ohio, 1967-70; product supr. Austin Powder Co., McArthur, Ohio, 1970-73; foreman Am. Safety, Medina, Ohio, 1973-74; engr. Channel Products, Chesterland, Ohio, 1974-78; chief product engr. Speed Selector, Chagrin Falls, Ohio, 1978-85; gen. mgr. Torque Transmission, Fairport Harbor, Ohio, 1985—. Avocations: canoeing, camping. Office: Torque Transmission 1246 High St Fairport Harbor OH 44077

RYAN, THOMAS EDWARD, school system administrator; b. Chgo., Sept. 29, 1951; s. Thomas Bernard and Connie Lavergne (Kreher) R.; m. Eloise Marie Gaetner, June 29, 1974; children: Rosemary, Jane, Anne. BS, St. Ambrose Coll., 1973; MEd in Adminstrn., Loyola U., Chgo., 1977, cert. in advanced study, 1979. Asst. supt. Edn. Service Region of Cook County, 1977-82; asst. adminstr. Cook County Hosp., Chgo., 1982-84; dep. appraiser Cook County Appraiser's Office, 1984-85; prin. Patton Sch. Dist. 133, Riverdale, Ill., 1985-86; comptroller, fin. adminstr. Posen (Ill.)-Robbins Sch. Dist. 143 1/2, 1986—; instr. Moraine Valley Community Coll., Palos Hills, Ill., 1982—. Mem. Ill. Assn. Sch. Adminstrs., South Cook County Sch. Adminstrs., Bremen Assn. Sch. Adminstrs., Ill. Assn. Sch. Bus. Ofcls., Ill. Prins.' Assn., Phi Delta Kappa. Avocations: travel, athletics, performing arts. Home: 15558 S Narcissus Ln Orland Park IL 60462 Office: Posen-Robbins Sch Dist 143 1/2 14025 Harrison Ave Posen IL 60469

RYAN, WILLIAM FRANK, management consultant, insurance and risk consultant; b. Inkster, Mich., May 6, 1924; s. William Henry and Gertrude Mary (Kling) R.; m. Loke Waiau Akoni, Oct. 5, 1963; children—Ilima, Lokelani, Eugene. Student Georgetown U., 1948-49, Columbia U., 1951-52, U. Padua (Italy), 1950-51; B.A., U. Mich., 1948. Diplomatic assignments in Russia, Italy and Japan, 1949-53; investment broker N.Y.C., Detroit and Honolulu, 1953-63; mgmt. cons. Bus. Mgmt. Internat., Honolulu, 1963-68; officer, dir. numerous corps.; ins. and risk mgr. U. Mich., Ann Arbor, 1969—; mem. Nat. Univ. Property Pool Ins. Study Group, 1969-70; chmn. ins. com. Mich. Council State Coll. Pres., 1971-73; mem. Nat. Task Force on Instl. Liability, 1974-76; exec. cons. William Ryan Risk Mgmt. Assocs., 1984—; chmn. adv. com. Assoc. Degree program in health care risk mgmt. Oakland Community Coll., 1984—; pres. Veritas Ins. Corp, 1986—; pres. Risk Mgmt. Internat. Ltd., 1986—. Trustee Assn. Ind. Colls. and Univs. Mich. Workers Compensation Self-Ins. Fund. Served to lt. (j.g.) USN, 1943-46. Recipient Instl. Risk Mgr. of Yr. award Bus. Ins. mag., 1981, Disting. Service award Assn. Ind. Colls. and Univs. of Mich., 1986. Mem. Am. Soc. Hosp. Risk Mgmt. (bd. dirs. 1981-84, pres. 1983), Univ. Risk Mgmt. and Ins. Assn. (dir.), Mich. Coll. and Univ. Risk Mgmt. Officers Assn. (chmn. 1973-75), Midwest Univ. Risk and Ins. Mgmt. Assn. (chmn. 1977-78), Hist. Soc. Mich., Nat. Trust for Hist. Preservation, Irish Georgian Soc., Am. Com. for Irish Studies. Democrat. Roman Catholic. Home: 801 Center Dr Ann Arbor MI 48103 Office: 326 E Hoover St Ann Arbor MI 48109

RYBARCZYK, HEIDI MARY, accountant; b. Chgo., May 17, 1957; d. Iwan and Katharina (Frahammer) Paszko; m. Richard J. Rybarczyk, Aug. 29, 1981. AA in Fgn. Langs., Wright Jr. Coll., 1978; BS in Acctg., U. Ill., Chgo., 1981. CPA, Ill. Sr. staff acct. Arthur Andersen & Co., Chgo., 1981-85, Morrison & Morrison, Ltd., Chgo., 1985—. Mem. Am. Inst. CPA's, Ill. CPA Soc. Avocations: snow and water skiing, travel, aquatic gymnastics. Home: 1731 Monmouth Pl Downers Grove IL 60516 Office: Morrison & Morrison Ltd 105 W Adams St Chicago IL 60603

RYDSON, MARLYN DEAN, real estate executive; b. Britt, Iowa, Oct. 30, 1930; s. Milburn L. and Esther T. (Tweeten) R.; m. Laura C. Turner, July 21, 1962; children: Matthew T., Michael L. AA, Britt (Iowa) Jr. Coll., 1950; BA, U. Iowa, 1955, postgrad., 1956. Mgmt. trainee Sears, Chgo. and Elkhart, Ind., 1956-59; sales mgr. Monteith Bros., Inc., Elkhart, 1959-63; pres. Northern Ind. Mortgage Co., Elkhart, 1963-81; owner The Chamberlain. Agy., Elkhart, 1963-86. Mem. adv. bd. Salvation Army; mem. Elkhart Redevel. Com., Elkhart, 1976-82, Elkhart City Planning Com., 1986—. Served to sgt. USAF, 1951-53. Mem. Elkhart Bd. Realtors (Realtor of Yr. 1985), Profl. Ins. Agents Assn., Elkhart C. of C. (streets and highways com., 1959-86, legisl. affairs com., 1963-86). Lutheran. Lodges: Rotary (bd. dirs. Elkhart), Masons, Shriners. Avocations: golf, travel. Home: 1824 Brookwood Dr Elkhart IN 46514 Office: The Chamberlain Agy 314 S 4th St Elkhart IN 46516

RYERSON, PETER JAMES, health care consultant; b. Bryn Mawr, Pa., Dec. 3, 1939; s. Philip Nelson and Octivia (Hamilton) R.; m. Nanette Glidden, Mar. 30, 1963; children: Steve, David. BSBA, LaSalle U., 1974, MBA, 1980. Indsl. engr. Standard Press Steel, Jenkintown, Pa., 1966-72; mgmt. engr. Pa. Hosp., Phila., 1972-78; sr. mgmt. engr. Albert Einsteins Med. Ctr., Phila., 1978-80; dir. AGMC, Akron, Ohio, 1980-86; mgr. Peat Marwick Main Co., Cleve., 1986—. Contbr. articles to profl. jours. Chmn. energy com. United Way, Akron, 1980-83. Served with U.S. Army, 1959-63. Recipient Richard Allen Lit. award Respiratory Therapy Assn., 1986. Mem. Health Care Info Mgmt. and Systems Soc. (sr., bd. dirs. 1979, 83-85, nat. pres. 1985), Health Care Fin. Mgmt. Assn., Am. Coll. Health Care Execs. (affilliated), Inst. Indsl. Engrs. (sr., pres. 1981). Office: Peat Marwick Main and Co 1600 National City Ctr Cleveland OH 44114

RYHERD, LARRY EARL, insurance executive; b. Garnett, Kans., Sept. 16, 1940; s. Earl Enos Ryherd and Halcie Belle (Johnson) Brown; m. Dorothy LouVae Harr, May 5, 1962; children: Shari Lynnette, Derek Scott, Jarad John. Grad. high sch., Iola, Kans. Agt., mgr. The Grolier Soc., Kansas City, Mo., 1959-65; agt., state mgr. Farm & Ranch Life Ins., Wichita, Kans., 1965-73; state mgr., asst. to pres. Investors Trust Assurance Cos., Indpls., 1973-84; agy. dir. sales Liberty Am. Assurnace Co., Lincoln, Nebr., 1981-84; founder, pres., chmn. United Trust, Inc., Springfield, Ill., 1984—; pres., chief exec. officer Trust Assurance Co., Springfield, 1986—. Charter mem. Rep. Task Force, Washington, 1983. Served with Kans. Nat. Guard, 1962-68. Mem. Nat. Assn. Life Cos. (Gold Plaque Award 1968, 69, 71, 72, 74, 79, 80, 81). Republican. Lutheran. Lodge: Elks. Avocations: football, golf, tennis, fishing, hunting. Home: Rt 1 Box 1 Rochester IL 62563 Office: Trust Assurance Co 725 S Second St Suite 236 Springfield IL 62718

RYMAN, TERRI L., trucking company financial executive; b. Newton, Kans., Feb. 25, 1954; d. Merle Duane and Elda May (Witt) Pulaski; m. Jerry Jay Ryman, Mar. 21, 1975; 1 child, Jeremy Daniel. B.A. in Bus. Adminstrn. cum laude, Southwestern Coll., Winfield, Kans., 1976; M.B.A. in Mgmt., Rockhurst Coll., 1983. Clk., No. Natural Gas, Holcomb, Kans., 1976-78; with Butler Mfg. Co., 1978-80, budget analyst, Kansas City, Mo., 1980-81, div. acctg. supr., 1981-82, controller, Garden City, Kans., 1982-87; fin. exec. Nat. Cariers, Liberal, Kans., 1987—. Mem. Nat. Accts. Assn. Republican. Methodist. Home: 804 N Sherman Ave Liberal KS 67901 Office: Nat Carriers 1501 E 8th St Liberal KS 67901

RYMAR, JULIAN W., manufacturing company executive; b. Grand Rapids, Mich., June 29, 1919; student Grand Rapids Jr. Coll., 1937-39, U. Mich., 1939-41, Am. Sch. Dramatic Arts, 1946-47, Wayne U., 1948-52, Rockhurst Coll., 1952-53; Naval War Coll., 1954-58; m. Margaret Macon Van Brunt, Dec. 11, 1954; children—Margaret Gibson, Gracen Macon, Ann Mackall. Entered USN as aviation cadet, 1942, advanced through grades to capt., 1964; chmn. bd., chief exec. officer, dir. Grace Co., Belton, Mo., 1955—; chmn. bd. dirs. Shock & Vibration Research, Inc., 1956-66; chmn. bd., chief exec. officer Bedtime Story Fashions; dir. Am. Bank & Trust; comdg. officer Naval Air Res. Squadron, 1957-60, staff air bn. comdr., 1960-64. Mem. Kans. Hist. Soc., Kans. Art Inst.; bd. dirs. Bros. of Mercy, St. Lukes Hosp.; adv. bd. dirs. St. Joseph Hosp.; trustee Missouri Valley Coll., 1969-74; pres. Rymar Found. Mem. Mil. Order World Wars, Navy League U.S. (pres. 1959-60, dir. 1960-70), Rockhill Homes Assn. (v.p.) Friends of Art (pres., chmn. bd. govs. 1969-70, exec. bd. 1971-74), Soc. of Fellows of Nelson Gallery Found. (exec. bd. 1972-77), Soc. Profl. Journalists, Sigma Delta Chi. Episcopalian (dir., lay reader, lay chalice, vestryman, sr. warden, diocesan fin. bd., parish investment bd.). Clubs: Press, University of Mich. (Kansas City); Arts (Washington); Quiet Birdman. Home: 1228 W 56th St Kansas City MO 64113 Office: 614 W Mill St Belton MO 64012

RYMER, TERRIE ADRIENNE, lawyer; b. Chgo., May 23, 1946; d. David Maurice and Myrna (Zaremsky) Rymer; m. Frank R. Vozak. B.A. with distinction, U. Mich., 1968; J.D., Northwestern U., 1981. Bar: Ill. 1981, U.S. Dist. Ct. (no. dist.) Ill. 1981. Social services worker various locations, Chgo. and N.Y.C., 1968-78; tutor Stanley Kaplan Ednl. Ctr., Chgo., 1978-79; assoc. Fischel & Kahn, Chgo., 1981-83; staff atty. AMA, Chgo., 1983—. Author: Physician-Hospital Contracts, 1983, Physician-Hospital Joint Ventures, 1987; also articles. Bd. dirs. Protection & Advocacy, Inc., Chgo., 1985—. Mem. ABA (mem. sect. individual rights and responsibilities 1981—, health law forum 1983—), Ill. Bar Assn., Chgo. Bar Assn. (hosp. and health law com. 1983—). Jewish Office: Office of Gen Counsel AMA 535 N Dearborn Chicago IL 60610

RYNDERS, PERRY MICHAEL, financial officer; b. Rapid City, S.D., Apr. 21, 1958; s. Robert John and Charlotte Matilda (Marto) R.; m. Carolyn Marie Geneva, Feb. 25, 1978; children: David Ryan, Michael William, John Fredrick. BS in Acctg., St. John's U., Collegeville, Minn., 1980. CPA, Minn. Supr. sr. Peat, Marwick, Mitchell, St. Paul, 1980-83; v.p. fin. and adminstrn. Best, Inc., St. Paul, 1983—. Mem. Am. Inst. CPA's, Minn. Soc. CPA's. Republican. Roman Catholic. Lodge: KC (fin. sec. White Bear Lake, Minn. 1984—). Avocations: golf, tennis. Home: 1145 Augusta Ln Eagan MN 55123 Office: Best Inc 563 Payne Ave Saint Paul MN 55101

RYNE, JOSEPH EDWARD, dentist; b. Kettering, Ohio, Nov. 30, 1951; s. William Russell and Victoria Caroline Ryne; m. Julie Ann Miller, june 25, 1977; 1 child, Aaron Michael. BA, Ohio State U., 1973, DDS, 1976. Gen. practice dentistry Hinsdale, Ill., 1978—; dental staff LaGrange (Ill.) Hosp., 1978—, Hinsdale (Ill.) Hosp., 1982—; cons. Americana Nursing Home, Westmont, Ill., 1978—. Homebound Dental Care, Hinsdale, 1978—. Served to capt. USAF, 1976-78. Recipient Cert. Commendation, Suburban Health Systems Agy., 1983. Mem. ADA, Chgo. Dental Soc. (chmn. access to care nursing home, homebound com. 1984-85), West Suburban Dental Soc., acad. Gen. Dentistry. Republican. Roman Catholic. Avocations: skiing, water skiing, landscape architecture, gardening. Home: 35 Orchard Pl Hinsdale IL 60521 Office: 522 Chestnut St Hinsdale IL 60521

RYSER, CAROL ANN, physician, director mental health organization; b. Kansas City, Mo., Apr. 24, 1937; d. Leland Farley and Mary Francis (Roberts) Carter; m. A. Thomen Reece, June 17, 1963; Stephanie, Andrea; m. 2d, Michael E. Ryser, Apr. 25, 1980. A.B. in Chemistry, William Jewell Coll., Liberty, Mo., 1959; M.D., U. Kans., 1963. Intern, U. Kans., Kansas City, 1963-64, resident in pediatrics, 1964-65, 67-68; asst. prof. Children's Rehab. Unit, U. Kans., 1967-76; pediatric cons. USAF, 1965-67; mem. staff Research Hosp., Gardner Med. Ctr.; pres., exec. dir. Matrix, Kansas City, Mo., 1977—. Named Outstanding Alumnus, William Jewell Coll. Fellow Am. Acad. Pediatrics; mem. AMA, Johnson County Med. Soc., Metro. Med. Soc. Greater Kansas City, Internat. Transactional Analysis Assn. Republican. Baptist. Office: Matrix 7447 Holmes Suite 1 Kansas City MO 64131

SA, CHUNG-YEH, automotive executive; b. Kaoshiung, Taiwan, Republic of China, Oct. 1, 1955; came to U.S., 1980; s. Shih-Hong and Roeing (Teng) S.; m. Rey Fu, Aug. 11, 1980; 1 child, Daniel. BS, Nat. Taiwan U., Taipei, 1977; MS, Northwestern U., 1981, PhD, 1985. Teaching asst. Nat. Taiwan U., 1979-80; sr. project engr. Gen. Motors Tech. Ctr., Warren, Mich., 1985—. Mem. ASME, Am. Soc. Metals, Soc. Automotive Engrs. Home: 2551 Dorchester Rd N Apt #204 Troy MI 48084-3726 Office: Gen Motors Tech Ctr Mfg A/MD-29 30300 Mound Warren MI 48090-9040

SAALE, DANIEL ALLEN, dentist; b. Alton, Ill., July 14, 1958; s. Carl Felix and Patricia Ann (Astroth) S. BS, Millikin U., 1980; DDS, Northwestern U., 1984. Practice gen. dentistry Chen & Assocs., Granite City, Ill., 1985, St. Charles, Mo., 1986—. Participant Leadership St. Charles '86. Mem. ADA, Mo. Dental Assn., Greater St. Louis Dental Soc., Acad. Gen. Dentistry, St. Charles C. of C. Roman Catholic. Club: Alton Road Runners, St. Louis Bicycle Touring Soc. Lodge: KC. Avocations: running, bicycling, swimming, golf, waterskiing, camping. Office: 2408 Hwy 94 S Saint Charles MO 63303

SABAU, CARMEN SYBILE, chemist; b. Cluj, Romania, Apr. 24, 1933; naturalized U.S. citizen; d. George and Antoinette Marie (Chiriac) Grigorescu; m. Mircea Nicolae Sabau, July 11, 1956; 1 dau., Isabelle Carmen. M.S. in Inorganic and Analytical Chemistry, U. C.I. Parhon, Bucharest, Romania, 1955; Ph.D. in Radiochemistry, U. Fridericiana, Karlsruhe, W.Ger., 1972. Chemist, Argonne (Ill.) Nat. Lab., 1976—. Internat. Atomic Energy Agy. fellow, 1967-68; Humboldt fellow, 1970-72. Mem. Am. Chem. Soc., Am. Nuclear Soc., Am. Romanian Acad. Arts and Sci., Assn. for Women in Sci., N.Y. Acad. Sci., Sigma Xi. Author: Ion-exchange Theory and Applications in Analytical Chemistry, 1967; contbr. articles to profl. jours. Home: 6902 Martin Dr Woodridge IL 60517 Office: Argonne Nat Lab 9700 S Cass Ave Bldg 205 Argonne IL 60439

SABBANN, ROBERT BRUCE, podiatrist; b. Monona, Iowa, Aug. 12, 1925; s. Ewald and Hilma M. (Klinge) S.; m. Jean Pederson, Oct. 28, 1960; children: Mark, Kimberly, Michael, Heidi. Student, Wartburg Coll., 1946-47; D in Podiat. Medicine cum laude, Ill. Coll. Podiat. Medicine, 1951. Diplomate Am. Bd. Podiat. Surgery. Pvt. practice podiatry Red Wing, Minn., 1951-53, Rochester, Minn., 1953—; mem. staff Olmsted Community Hosp., Rochester, 1962—; lectr. in field. Contbr. articles to profl. jours. Served with USN, 1942-46. Fellow Am. Coll. Foot Surgeons; mem. Minn. Hosp. Podiatrists (pres. 1971-81), Minn. Podiatry Assn. (pres. 1966-67). Republican. Lutheran. Clubs: Ducks, Unltd. (nat. trustee 1981), Am. Kennel (lic. judge), Kiwanis (pres. 1966, dist. lt. gov. 1967). Home: 182318 1/2 NW Rochester MN 55901 Office: 915 3d Ave SE Rochester MN 55901

SABERS, RICHARD WAYNE, justice; b. Salem, S.D., Feb. 12, 1938; s. Emil William and Elrena Veronica (Godfrey) S.; m. Colleen D. Kelley, Aug. 28, 1965; children: Steven Richard, Susan Michelle, Michael Kelley. BA in English, St. John's U., Collegeville, Minn., 1960; JD, U. S.D., 1966. Bar: S.D. 1966, U.S. Dist. Ct. S.D. 1966, U.S. Ct. Appeals (8th cir.) 1983. From assoc. to ptnr. Moore, Rasmussen, Sabers & Kading, Sioux Falls, S.D., 1966-86; justice Supreme Ct. S.D., Pierre and Sioux Falls, 1986—. Mem. editorial bd. U. S.D. Law Rev., 1965-66. State rep. March of Dimes, Bismarck, N.D., 1963; bd. dirs. St. Joseph Cathedral, Sioux Falls, 1971-86; trustee, bd. dirs. O'Gorman Found., Sioux Falls, 1978-86; mem. sch. bd. O'Gorman High Sch., Sioux Falls, 1985-86. Served as 1st lt. U.S. Army, 1960-63. Named Outstanding Young Religious Leader, Jaycees, Sioux Falls, 1971. Mem. ABA, S.D. Bar Assn., Inst. Jud. Adminstrn., St. John's Alumni Assn. (pres. Sioux Falls chpt. 1975-86). Republican. Roman Catholic. Lodge: Elks. Avocations: tennis, skiing, sailing, sports. Home: 401 N DuLuth Ave Sioux Falls SD 57104 Office: SD Supreme Ct 415 N Dakota PO Box 84726 Sioux Falls SD 57118

SABERS, TERRY JOSEPH, accountant, controller; b. Mitchell, S.D., Mar. 20, 1955; s. Edgar A. and Tillie A. (Bartscher) S.; m. Debra Kay Giesler, Sept. 6, 1975; children: Eric, Blake. Student, Mitchell Area Voact.-Tech. Inst., 1973-75. Acct. Muth Electric, Inc., Mitchell, 1874-83, controller, 1983—; bd. dirs. Mitchell Area Fed. Credit Union. Bd. dirs. Holy Family Sch. Bd., Mitchell, 1986—. Named one of Outstanding Young Men of Am., 1985. Mem. Mitchell Jaycees (pres. 1980-81, S.D. pres. 1985-86). Republican. Roman Catholic. Home: 1321 Firesteel Dr Mitchell SD 57301 Office: Muth Electric Inc 730 N Kimball Mitchell SD 57301

SABESAN, SHARDHA KUPPUSWAMY, psychiatrist, educator; b. Madras, India, Apr. 22, 1948; came to U.S., 1974; d. Tirumangalam Krishnaswamy and Janakiammal (Narayanan) Kuppuswamy; m. Mandakolathur N. Sabesan, Jan. 25, 1974; 1 child, Vani. MB, BS, Madras (India) U., 1972. Cert. Am. Bd. Neurology and Psychiatry. Staff psychiatrist Community Hosp. Inc., Indpls., 1979-81; faculty psychiatrist Ind. U. Sch. Medicine, Indpls., 1981—; med. dir. Midtown Meridian Adult Mental Health Clinic, Indpls., 1981—, Midtown Child and Adolescent Mental Health Sources, Indpls., 1982—. Mem. Am. Psychiat. Assn., Am. Acad. Child and Adult Psychiatry (sec. 1985—, v.p. 1986—, del. for Ind. 1986—), Am. Assn. Physicians from India (life), Am. Assn. Psychiatrist from India, Orthopsychiatric Assn., Ind. Psychiatric Assn., India Assn. Indpls. Avocations: gourmet cooking, music, reading, gardening, knitting. Office: U Ill Sch Medicine Wishard Hosp 1001 West 10th St Indianapolis IN 46202

SABINE, JOHN JAMES, JR., leasing representative; b. Bklyn., Aug. 18, 1954; s. John James Sr. and Mary Elizabeth (Smyth) S.; m. Mary Therese Bush; 1 child, John Michael. BA, St. Anselm Coll., Manchester, N.H., 1976; MA, St. Louis U., 1978; MBA, So. Meth. U., Dallas, 1987. Dean students Woodside Priory Sch., Portola Valley, Calif., 1978-81; account exec. Levi Strauss & Co., Atlanta, 1981-83, LeClair Sutton Assoc., Dallas, 1983-84; leasing rep. Med. City Dallas-Crow/Wright, 1984—. Mem. St. Vincent dePaul Soc. (bd. dirs. 1985-87). Democrat. Roman Catholic.

SABLACK, GILBERT GEORGE, social worker; b. Manistique, Mich., Aug. 30, 1940; s. Sylvester and Esther (Hacquist) S.; m. Rosemary Ann Leach, Aug. 8, 1964; children: Sherry Lynn, Wendy Lou. BS, No. Mich. U., 1963, MA, 1966. Tchr. Engadine (Mich.) Consol. Schs., 1963-69; social worker State of Mich., Manistique, 1969-74, supr. social work, 1974—; instr. adult edn. Manistique Area Schs., 1972-75. Mem. Mich. Assn. Govt. Employees (pres. 1985—), Mich. County Social Service Workers (del. 1984-86). Roman Catholic. Lodge: KC (various offices), Elks. Avocation: studying to be a lay minister. Home: Box 83 Gulliver Lake Gulliver MI 49840 Office: State of Mich PO Box 339 Manistique MI 49854

SABLE, JOHN E., bank executive; b. Wamego, Kans., Sept. 15, 1939. BA in Accounting, Kans. State U., 1967. CPA. Exec. v.p. First Commerce Bancshares, Inc., Lincoln, Nebr.; bd. dirs. Commerce Savs. Lincoln, Inc., NBC Computer Services Corp., Lincoln. Office: Box 82408 Lincoln NE 68501

SABO, JOHN BENJAMIN, pharmacist; b. Herminie, Pa., Nov. 11, 1927; s. Julius Louis and Lottie Belle (Eckenrod) S.; B.S. in Pharmacy, Purdue U., 1950; m. Helen Marie Calhoun, June 30, 1951; children—Cynthia Jean, Michael John. Mgr., Hook's Drugs, Gary, Ind., 1950-53; pharmacist Black Oak Pharmacy, Gary, 1953-58; owner Park Plaza Pharmacy, Merrillville, Ind., 1958-62; mem. staff Methodist Hosp., Gary, 1962-81, chief pharmacist, 1968-69, dir. pharmacy, 1969-75, dir. pharmacy services, 1975-81; dir. pharmacy services Broadway Meth. Hosp., Merrillville, 1975-81; pharmacy staff Our Lady of Mercy Hosp., Dyer, Ind., 1981—; cons. Norwich Lab., Eaton Lab.; clin. instr. Purdue U. Sch. Pharmacy. Served with USNR, 1945-46. Recipient service and recognition awards. Mem. Am. Soc. Hosp. Pharmacists, Ind. Soc. Hosp. Pharmacists (pres. 1968-69). Methodist. Home: 1830 Dale Dr Merrillville IN 46410

SABO, MARTIN OLAV, congressman; b. Crosby, N.D., Feb. 28, 1938; s. Bjorn O. and Klara (Haga) S.; m. Sylvia Ann Lee, June 30, 1963; children: Karin, Julie. B.A. cum laude, Augsburg Coll., Mpls., 1959; postgrad., U. Minn., 1961-62. Mem. Minn. Ho. of Reps. from 57B Dist., 1960-78, democratic-farmer-labor party minority leader, 1969-72, speaker, 1973-78, chmn. joint legis. coordinating com., 1973, 75, 77; mem. 96th to 100th congresses from 5th Minn. Dist.; mem. Nat. Adv. Commn. on Intergovtl. Relations; past pres. Nat. Legis. Conf.; bd. regents Augsburg Coll. Named One of 200 Rising Young Leaders in Am. Time mag., 1974; recipient Disting. Alumni citation Augsburg Coll.; named Man of Yr. Mpls. Jr. C. of C., 1973-74, One of Ten Outstanding Young Men of Yr. Minn. Jr. C. of C., 1974. Mem. Nat. Conf. State Legis. Leaders (past pres.). Office: 2201 Rayburn House Office Bldg Washington DC 20515

SABOL, MARY PUNGERCAR, education association administrator; b. Milw., Aug. 8, 1959; s. Roger Joseph and Maria Katherine (Armbruster) Pungercar; m. Thomas Bernard Sabol, Aug. 9, 1986. BJ, Marquette U., 1981. Asst. dir. alumni relations Marquette U., Milw., 1981-83, assoc. dir. alumni relations, 1983-84, coordinator nat. clubs, 1984-85, dir. alumni programs, exec. dir. assn. univ. women, 1986—; mem. adminstrv. search coms. Marquette U., 1985—, com. on adminstrs.; bd. dirs. Marquette Admissions Nat. Adv. Bd., Milw., 1987—. Vol. ARTREACH Milw., 1981—; founder Milw. Barre Assn., 1984; mem. Intergroup Council Milw. Mem. AAUW, Dominican High Sch. Alumni Assn., Council for Advancement and Support of Edn., Wis. Independent Coll. Alumni Assns., Alpha Sigma Nu, Kappa Tau Alpha, Sigma Tau Delta, Sigma Delta Chi. Roman Catholic. Avocations: golf, swimming, vol. activities, sewing, profl. baseball. Home: 11524 Watertown Plank Rd #3 Wauwatosa WI 53226 Office: Marquette U Alumni Relations 1212 W Wisconsin Ave Milwaukee WI 53233

SABOUPIN, RODNEY WOOD, hotel management company executive; b. Bay City, Mich., Apr. 1, 1949; s. Roger James and Helen E. (Wood) S.; m. Lane S. Lesnick, Aug. 19, 1973; 1 child, Evan F. BA, Mich. State U., 1971; JD, Wayne State U., 1973. Assoc. Lawson and Anderson P.C., Farmington, Mich., 1973-75; sole practice Farmington, 1975-79; pres. Valley Properties, Farmington, 1979—. Chmn. Mich. lodging fundraiser for Gov., Lansing, 1986. Mem. Mich. Bar Assn., Am. Lodging Assn., Mich. Lodging Assn., Southwest Oakland County Bar Assn. (pres. 1982-84). Democrat. Club: Macatowa Yacht (Holland, Mich.). Avocations: skiing, travel. Office: 22500 Orchard Lake Rd Farmington MI 48170

SABSAY, BORIS IOSEPH, physician, medical researcher; b. Moscow, Nov. 9, 1932; came to U.S., 1979; s. Ioseph Israel and Gitel (Israelson) S.; m. Julia M. Mirkin, Mar. 24, 1962; 1 son, Vitaly. M.D., 1st Moscow Med. Sch., 1957; Ph.D., Inst. Normal and Path. Physiology, Acad. Med. Scis., 1963. Intern, Clinics and Hosps. 1st Moscow Med. Sch., 1956-57; resident Central City Hosp., Moscow, 1957-57; fellow in gastroenterology Clinic for Med. Nutrition, Inst. Nutrition, Acad. Med. Scis., Moscow, 1961-64; practice medicine specializing in surgery/oncology, Moscow, 1957-59; research assoc. Inst. Physiology, Acad. Med. Scis., Moscow, 1959-66; sr. cons. gastroenterology, City Hosp., 1966-78; sr. research assoc. Northwestern U. Dental Sch., Chgo., 1979—. Mem. Sigma Xi. Contbr. numerous articles to sci. publs. Office: Northwestern U Dental Sch 303 E Chicago St Ward 13-049 Chicago IL 60611

SACCO, GEORGE JOSEPH, JR., rubber company executive; b. Pitts., July 20, 1942; s. George Joseph and Thelma Virginia (Cannistra) S.; m. Madeleine Gail Curry, June 5, 1965; children—Kimberly Ann, Anthony Brennan. B.S. in Personnel Mgmt., U. Dayton, 1964. With Goodyear Tire & Rubber Co., 1967—, employment mgr., North Chicago, Ill., 1969-73, mgr. personnel and purchasing, San Angelo, Tex., 1973-76, personnel mgr., Sun Prairie, Wis., 1976-77, mgr. research and devel. for personnel devel., Akron, Ohio, 1978-80, research adminstr., Akron, 1980-85, mgr. research adminstrn. and services, 1985—; guest lectr. colls. and univs. Jr. Achievement coordinator, Rotary Club, North Chicago, 1969-73; corp. solicitor United Way, 1970-73; pres. PTA Holy Angels Sch., San Angelo, 1974-75; trustee Towpath Homeowners' Assn., Akron, 1982-86. Served to capt. U.S. Army, 1965-67. Named Bus. Assoc. of Yr., Beacon chpt. Am. Bus. Women's Assn., 1983. Mem. Am. Soc. Personnel Adminstrn., Personnel Mgrs. Assn., Goodyear Mgmt. Club (sec.-treas. 1980-81, pres. 1981-82), Soc. for Research Adminstrs. Clubs: Goodyear Racquet (pres. 1981). Contbr. articles to profl. jours. Home: 2426 Laurel Valley Dr Akron OH 44313 Office: 142 Goodyear Blvd Akron OH 44305

SACHA, ROBERT FRANK, osteopathic physician, allergist; b. East Chicago, Ind., Dec. 29, 1946; s. Frank John and Ann Theresa Sacha; m. Carolyn Sue Levon, June 21, 1969; children—Joshua Jude, Josiah Gerard, Anastasia Levon, Jonah Bradley. B.S., Purdue U., 1969; D.O., Chgo. Coll. Osteo. Medicine, 1975. Diplomate Am. Bd. Pediatrics, Am. Bd. Allergy and Immunology. Pharmacist, asst. mgr. Walgreens Drug Store East Chicago, Ind., 1969-75; intern David Grant Med. Ctr., San Francisco, 1975-76, resident in pediatrics, 1976-78; fellow in allergy and immunology Wilford Hall Med. Ctr., 1978-80; staff pediatrician, allergist Scott AFB (Ill.), 1980-83; practice medicine specializing in allergy and immunology Cape Girardau, Mo., 1983—; assoc. clin. instr. St. Louis U., 1980—; clin. instr. Purdue U., 1971-72, Pepperdine U., 1975-76, U. Tex.-San Antonio, 1978-80. Pres., Parent Tchrs. League. Served to maj. M.C., USAF, 1975-83. Fellow Am. Coll. Allergy, Am. Coll. Chest Physicians, Am. Acad. Pediatrics, Am. Acad. Allergy-Immunology, Am. Assn. Cert. Allergists; mem. AMA, Am. Acad. Allergy, Assn. Mil. Allergists, ACP, Am. Coll. Emergency Physicians, Mil. Surgeons and Physicians. Republican. Roman Catholic.

SACHS, HOWARD F(REDERIC), U.S. judge; b. Kansas City, Mo., Sept. 13, 1925; s. Alex F. and Rose (Lyon) S.; m. Susanne Wilson, 1960; children: Alex Wilson, Adam Phinney. B.A. summa cum laude, Williams Coll., 1947; J.D., Harvard U., 1950. Bar: Mo. bar 1950. Law clk. U.S. Dist. Ct., Kansas City, Mo., 1950-51; pvt. practice Kansas City, 1951-79; U.S. dist. judge Western Dist. Mo., Kansas City, 1979—. Contbr. articles to various publs. Mem. Kansas City Commn. Human Relations, 1967-73; chmn. Jewish Community Relations Bur., 1968-71, Kansas City chpt. Am. Jewish Com., 1963-65; mem. exec. com. Nat. Jewish Community Relations Adv. Council, 1968-71; pres. Urban League Kansas City, 1957-58, Kansas City chpt. Am. Jewish Congress, 1974-77; co-chmn. Kansas City chpt. NCCJ, 1958-60; mem. Kansas City Sch. Dist. Desegregation Task Force, 1976-77; pres. Jackson County Young Democrats, 1959-60; treas. Kennedy-Johnson Club, Jackson County, 1960. Served with USNR, 1944-46. Mem. Am. Bar Assn., Am. Judicature Soc., Mo. Bar, Kansas City Bar Assn., Lawyers Assn. Kansas City, Phi Beta Kappa. Home: 816 W 68th Terr Kansas City MO 64113 Office: US Dist Ct US Courthouse 811 Grand Ave Room 443 Kansas City MO 64106

SACK, JAMES MCDONALD, JR., radio and television producer; b. London, Ky., Oct. 11, 1948; s. James McDonald and Ruth Elmore (Bryant) S.; m. Cheryl S. Gremaux, July 13, 1969 (div. June 1974); 1 child, Graehm McDonald. BA in History, Ind. U., 1974, MS in Telecommunications, 1975. Coordinator Latin Am. Ednl. Ctr., Ft. Wayne, Ind., 1979-81, Mayor's Office, Ft. Wayne, 1981-83; producer WMEE-WQHK Radio, Ft. Wayne, 1983-85; owner, operator Festival Mgmt. and Devel., Ft. Wayne, 1984—. Producer radio documentary, 1985 (First Place award Ind. Broadcasters Assn., 1985). Founder, pres. Germanfest of Ft. Wayne; pres. cable TV program adv. council City of Ft. Wayne. Served with U.S. Army, 1970-73. Mem. Ind. Festival Assn., Ind. German Heritage Soc. (bd. dirs. 1983-84, Gov.'s Commendation award 1983), N. Am. Sängerbund (sec. 1985-87). Republican. Lutheran. Clubs: Männerchor (Ft. Wayne), Ft. Wayne Sport (sec. 1985-86). Avocations: fencing, canoeing, soccer, politics, linguistics. Home and Office: 720 Union St Fort Wayne IN 46802

SACKS, RONALD L., restaurant chain executive. Pres. Baker's Square Restaurants, Inc., Mpls. Office: Bakers Square Restaurants Inc 300 S Country Rd 18 Minneapolis MN 55426 *

SADD, JOHN ROSWELL, plastic surgeon; b. Chgo., Apr. 18, 1933; s. Sumner Harry and Louise Elizabeth (Beardsley) S.; m. Valrie Crim Lavery; children: Elizabeth, Katherine, Virginia, Dorothy. BS, Purdue U., 1955; MD, U. Rochester, 1959. Diplomate Am. Bd. Plastic Surgery. Resident in plastic surgery U. Wis., 1959-67; attending suregon Toledo Hosp., 1967—, chmn. surgery, 1972-86; asst. clin. prof. Med. Coll. Ohio, Toledo, 1972—; bd. dirs. P.I.E. Mut. Ins. Co., Cleve. Contbr. articles to med. jours. Served to lt. USN, 1961-63. Fellow Am. Coll. Surgeons; mem. Am. Soc. Plastic and Reconstructive Surgeons, Ohio Valley Plastic Surgery Soc. Republican. Episcopalian. Lodge: Rotary. Avocations: trout fishing, golf. Home: 4612 Farmington Rd Toledo OH 43623 Office: 2121 Hughes Dr Toledo OH 43606

SADEK, SALAH ELDINE, consulting pathologist; b. Cairo, Egypt, June 9, 1920; s. Ahmad A. and Zienab (Zahran) S.; D.V.M., U. Cairo, 1945; M.R.C.V.S., U. Edinburgh, 1948; M.S., Mich. State U., 1950; Ph.D., U. Ill., 1956; m. Helen Ann Phoenix, Apr. 12, 1952; children—Craig, Ramsay, Mark. Asst. prof. U. Cairo, 1945-48; asst. U. Ill., Urbana, 1953-55; pathologist Dow Chem. Co., Midland, Mich., 1956-67; head of pathology Hoffmann La Roche, Nutley, N.J., 1967-85, also asst. dir.; clin. prof. pathology N.J. Coll. Medicine and Dentistry, Newark; cons. in exptl. pathology and toxicology. Pres., Midland County Humane Soc., 1965-67. Diplomate Am. Bd. Indsl. Hygiene. Mem. Am. Vet. Med. Assn., N.Y. Acad. Sci., British Vet. Assn., Royal Coll. Veterinary Surgeons, Mich. Soc. Pathologists, N.Y. Pathol. Soc., Soc. Toxicology, Soc. Toxicologic Pathologists, Internat. Acad. Pathology, AAAS, Am. Acad. Indsl. Hygiene. Club: Midland Country. Home and Office: 3910 Valley Dr Midland MI 48640

SADER, NEIL STEVEN, attorney; b. Torrington, Conn., Oct. 10, 1958; s. Harold M. and Carol Hope (Shimkin) S. AB, Columbia U., 1980; JD, U. Kans., 1984. Bar: Mo. 1984. Asst. White House Domestic Policy Staff, Washington, 1980-81; assoc. Brown & Thiessen, P.C., Kansas City, Mo., 1986—. Planning commr. Johnson County, Olathe, Kans., 1983-87, City of Overland Park, Kans., 1986—; precinct committeeman Johnson County Dem., Overland Park, 1983—, exec. com. 1984—. Mem. ABA, Mo. Bar Assn., Lawyer's Assn. Kansas City. Jewish. Avocations: travel, sports. Home: 10210 W 86th Terr Overland Park KS 66212 Office: Brown & Thiessen PC 2405 Grand #300 Kansas City MO 64108-2510

SADJADI, FIROOZ AHMADI, electrical engineer, consultant, researcher; b. Tehran, Iran, Mar. 18, 1949; came to U.S., 1968; s. Akbar Ahmadi and Fakhri (Mohsen) S.; m. Carolyn JoAnne Elkins; 1 child, Farzad. B.S.E.E., Purdue U., 1972, M.S.E.E., 1974; E.E.E., U. So. Calif., 1976; postgrad. U. Tenn., Knoxville, 1983. Research asst. Image Processing Inst., U. So. Calif., Los Angeles, 1974-76; cons. Oak Ridge Lab., Knoxville, 1980; researcher dept. elec. engring. U. Tenn., 1977-83; research scientist Honeywell Systems and Research Ctr., 1983—. Mem. IEEE (sr.), Soc. Photo-Optical Instrumentation Engrs., Am. Assn. for Artificial Intelligence, Sigma Xi. Contbg. author numerous profl. publs. Office: Honeywell Systems and Research 3660 Technology Dr MN65-2300 Minneapolis MN 55418

SADJADPOUR, KAMAL, neurologist; b. Tehran, Iran, Mar. 19, 1932; came to U.S., 1957; s. Jafar Sadjadpour and Ehsan Resai-Rafii; m. Shahnaz Azari, Mar. 27, 1949; children: Nina, Reza, Karim, Leila. MD, Tehran U., 1957. Cert. Am. Bd. Psychiatry and Neurology. Rotating intern Binghamton (N.Y.) City Hosp., 1958-59; resident in neurology Buffalo Gen. Hosp. U. Buffalo, 1959-60, Presbyn. St. Luke's Hosp. U. Chgo., 1960-61; fellow in neurology U. Mich. Med. Ctr., Ann Arbor, 1961-63; instr. neurology Harper Hosp. Wayne State U. Med. Ctr., Detroit, 1963-64; asst. prof. U. Teheran Med. Sch. Pahlavi Hosp., 1964-67, SUNY Upstate Med. Ctr., Syracuse, 1967-70; chief neurology VA Hosp., Syracuse, 1968-70; assoc. prof. U. Nebr., Omaha, 1970-73; practice medicine specializing in neurology Midland (Mich.) Hosp. Assn., 1973—; research fellow Anatomical Inst. U. Oslo, 1966-67; dir. Muscular Dystrophy Assn. Clinic at Midland Hosp. Ctr., Multiple Sclerosis Clinic. Contbr. numerous articles and abstracts to profl. jours. Fellow ACP, Am. Acad. Neurology; mem. AMA, Can. Neurol. Soc., Am. Assn. Study of Headache, Am. Epilepsy Soc., Mich. State Med. Soc., Midland County Med. Soc., Am. Acad. Clin. Neurophysiology, Am. Electroencephalographic Soc., N.Y. Acad. Scis., Nat. Migraine Found., Nat. Ataxia Found., Nat. Amyotrophic Lateral Sclerosis Found., Tourette Syndrome Assn., Mich. STate Multiple Sclerosis Soc. (med. adv. bd.), Com. to Combat Huntington's Disease. Home: 4601 James Dr Midland MI 48640 Office: 4005 Orchard Dr Midland MI 48640

SADLER, JAMES BERTRAM, psychologist, clergyman; b. Albuquerque, Mar. 29, 1911; s. James Monroe and Mary Agnes (English) S.; m. Vera Ellen Ahrendt, Apr. 10, 1938. A.B., U. N.Mex., 1938; B.D., Crozer Theol. Sem., 1941, Th.M., 1948; M.A., U. Pa., 1941, Ed.D., 1959. Lic. psychologist, S.D. Ordained to ministry Baptist Ch., 1941; pastor First Bapt. Ch., Mt. Union, Pa., 1941-42; chaplain USAF, 1943-48; pastor Hatboro (Pa.) Bapt. Ch., 1948-61; chmn. dept. psychology Sioux Falls (S.D.) Coll., 1961-75; pvt. practice psychology, Sioux Falls, 1975—; cons. in psychology and religion. Mem. ministers council Am. Bapt. Conv. Mem. Am. Psychol. Assn., Am. Assn. Counseling and Devel., Soc. for Sci. Study Religion. Clubs: Mason, Rotary (pres. 1960). Contbr. articles to profl. jours. Home: 4312 Glenview Rd Sioux Falls SD 57103

SADLER, JON J, bank executive; b. Dayton, Ohio, Nov. 2, 1958; s. James Lloyd and May (Pierson) S. BA, Miami U., Oxford, Ohio, 1981. Br. mgr., asst. treas. State Savs. Bank, Columbus, Ohio, 1981—. Bd. dirs. Operation Feed, Columbus United Way, 1984-87; mem. Columbus Symphony Chorus, 1981—. Republican. Office: State Savs Bank 7520 E Main St Reynoldsburg OH 43068

SADOVE, ALAN MICHAEL, physician; b. Chgo., Oct. 8, 1948; s. Max Samuel and Ethel (Segall) S.; m. Armin Altshuler, June 1, 1974; 1 son, Scott Lawrence. A.B., Washington U., 1970; M.D., Loyola U., Maywood, Ill., 1974; M.S., U. Ill.-Chgo., 1977. Intern, Presbyn.-St. Luke's Hosp., Chgo., 1974-75, resident in gen. surgery, 1975-79; resident in plastic surgery U. Va., Charlottesville, 1979-81; fellow in plastic surgery NYU-Inst. Reconstructive Plastic Surgery, N.Y.C., 1981-82; assoc. prof. surgery Ind. U. Sch. Medicine, 1982—; chief plastic surgery service James Whitcomb Riley Hosp. for Children, Ind. U. Med. Ctr., 1982—, med. dir. Burn Ctr., 1982—, dir. Oral-Facial Clinic, 1983—, med. dir. Craniofacial Anomalies team, 1982—; cons. VA Med. Ctr., Indpls.; mem. attending staff Wishard Meml. Hosp., Indpls. Mem. Chgo. Med. Soc., Ill. Med. Soc., AMA, ACS, Am. Soc. Plastic and Reconstructive Surgeons, Am. Cleft Palate Assn., Am. Burn Assn., Assn. Acad. Surgery, Am. Soc. Maxillofacial Surgeons, Marion County Med. Soc., Ind. State Med. Soc., Ohio Valley Soc. Plastic and Reconstructive Surgery, Sigma Xi. Office: Ind U Med Ctr Dept Plastic Surgery 702 Barnhill Dr Riley Hosp Room 1172 Indianapolis IN 46223

SADUR, PAUL RICHARD, translator, interpreter; b. Miami, Jan. 28, 1947; s. Saul and Tekla (Bernat) S.; m. Maria Mercedes Torres, May 1, 1971; 1 child, Justino Alejandro. BA, U. Cen. Fla., 1980; postgrad., U. Fla., 1980-84. Cert. ct. interpreter in Spanish. Translator Astilleros Españoles, Cádiz, Spain, 1974-77; copy editor Daytona Beach (Fla.) News-Journal, 1977-80; translator, interpreter World Council of Credit Unions, Madison, Wis., 1984—; freelance translator Southeastern Translating Services, 1981-83. U. Fla. fellow, 1980-81. Mem. Am. Translators Assn. (accreditation com. 1985—). Jehovah's Witness. Avocations: cross country skiing. Home: 4337 Somerset Ln Madison WI 53711 Office: World Council of Credit Unions 5810 Mineral Point Rd Madison WI 53701

SAFFELS, DALE EMERSON, federal judge; b. Moline, Kans., Aug. 13, 1921; s. Edwin Clayton and Lillian May (Cook) S.; m. Margaret Elaine Nieman, Apr. 2, 1976; children by previous marriage: Suzanne Saffels Gravitt, Deborah Saffels Knorr, James B.; stepchildren: Lynda Cowger Harris, Christopher Cowger. A.B., Emporia State U., 1947; LL.B., J.D. cum laude, Washburn U., 1949. Bar: Kans. 1949. Individual practice law Garden City, Kans., 1949-71, Topeka, 1971-75, Wichita, Kans., 1975-79; U.S. dist. judge Dist. of Kans., Kansas City, 1979—; chmn. bd. Fed. Home Loan Bank of Topeka, 1978-79. Bd. govs. Sch. Law Washburn U.; pres. Kans. Dem. Club, 1957; Dem. nominee Gov. of Kans., 1962; county atty., Finney County, Kans., 1951-55; mem. Kans. Ho. of Reps., 1955-63, minority leader, 1961-63; mem. Kans. Corp. Commn., 1967-75, chmn., 1968-75; mem. Kans. Legis. Council, 1957-63; Kans. rep. Interstate Oil Compact Commn., 1967-75, 1st vice chmn., 1971-72; pres. Midwest Assn. Regulatory Commn., 1972-73, Midwest Assn. R.R. and Utilities Commrs., 1972-73; trustee Emporia State Univ. Endowment Assn.; bd. dirs. Nat. Assn. Regulatory Utility Commrs., 1972-75. Served to maj. Signal Corps U.S. Army, 1942-46. Recipient Disting. Alumnus award Emporia State U., 1974, Disting. Alumnus award Washburn U., 1983. Fellow Am. Bar Found.; mem. ABA, Kans. Bar Assn., Sedgwick County Bar Assn., Am. Judicature Soc. Lutheran. Home: 8901 Maple Dr Overland Park KS 66207 Office: US Dist Ct 118 US Courthouse PO Box 1278 Kansas City KS 66117

SAFFIOTI, CAROL LEE ANN, humanities educator; b. Paterson, N.J., Nov. 24, 1949; d. Joseph Francis and Dorothy Grace (Porter) Saffioti. B.A. in English magna cum laude, U. N.C., 1971; M.A., Princeton U., 1973, Ph.D., 1975. Instr. communication skills, Princeton U., 1974-75; vis. asst. prof. U. Victoria, B.C., Can., 1976; asst. prof. humanities div., U. Wis.-Parkside, Kenosha, 1976-82, assoc. prof., 1983—. Author: (with Patricia Berge) Basic College Research, 1986; author poetry; contbr. articles, revs., abstracts to profl. jours. Grantee Danforth Found., 1975, NEH, 1978; Danforth Found. fellow, 1971-75. Mem. Nat. Council Tchrs. English, Wis. Council Tchrs. English, Assn. Tchrs. Tech. Writing (bibliog. com.), Assn. Profl. Writing Cons., Root River Voices Poets Coop., U. N.C. Golden Chain Honor Soc., Phi Beta Kappa. Mem. Unity Ch.

SAGADIN, MERIDEE J., accountant, financial planner; b. Milw., Aug. 19, 1955; d. Edward James and Beverly Doris (Cherney) S. BBA in Acctg., U. Wis., Milw., 1977. Sr. mgr. Seidman & Seidman, Milw., 1977—, dir. fin. planning services, 1986—. Contbr. articles to profl. jours. Asst. treas. Jim Moody for Congress, 1982. Mem. Am. Inst. CPA's, Wis. Inst. CPA's, Ill. Assn. Fin. Planners, Wis. Women Entrepreneurs, Meta House (bd. dirs.). Republican. Lutheran. Club: Tempo (treas.). Avocations: snow skiing, aerobics, jogging. Home: 4235 N 84th St Milwaukee WI 53222 Office: Seidman & Seidman 330 E Kilbourn Ave Suite 950 Milwaukee WI 53202

SAGADY, DANIEL VICTOR, automotive engineer, engineering consultant; b. Saginaw, Mich., May 16, 1949; s. Fred and Lydia (Leichner) S.; m. Donna Lorraine Budzinski, May 18, 1973; children—Jessica Lorraine, Erika Jane. B.S. in Mech. Engring., Gen. Motors Inst., Flint, Mich., 1972; M.B.A., Oakland U., Rochester, Mich., 1980; M.S. in Indsl. Engring., Wayne State U. Registered profl. engr., Mich. Gen. Motors Inst. coop. student Saginaw Steering Gear div. Gen. Motors, Saginaw, 1967-71, engr., 1971-75, devel. engr., 1975-78; project engr. Ford Motor Co., Dearborn, Mich., 1978-85; staff project engr. Saginaw div. Gen. Motors, Saginaw, Mich., 1985—; engring. cons. Recipient Product Engring. award Saginaw Steering Gear div. Gen. Motors, 1978. Mem. Soc. Automotive Engrs. Republican. Lutheran. Patentee in automotive engring. field. Home: 3858 Marilyn Lane Midland MI 48640-8816 Office: Saginaw Div Gen Motors 3900 Holland Saginaw MI 48602

SAGAN, JOHN, former automobile company executive; b. Youngstown, Ohio, Mar. 9, 1921; s. John and Mary (Jubinsky) S.; m. Margaret Pickett, July 24, 1948; children: John, Linda, Scott. B.A. in Econs, Ohio Wesleyan U., 1948; M.A., U. Ill., 1949, Ph.D., 1951; Fellow, Ohio Wesleyan U., 1946-48; scholar, fellow research, U. Ill., 1948-51. With Ford Motor Co., 1951-86, v.p., treas., 1969-86; pres. John Sagan Assocs., 1986—; bd. dirs. Comerica Bank of Detroit, Discount Corp., N.Y., T. Rowe Price Mut. Funds, Kahler Corp. Trustee Ohio Wesleyan U., 1964—, Com. Econ. Devel. U.S.A., Oakwood Hosp., Dearborn, Mich., YMCA Found., Detroit Fund for Henry Ford Hosp. Served with USNR, 1943-46. Mem. Am. Econ. Assn., Phi Beta Kappa, Phi Kappa Phi, Delta Sigma Rho. Home and Office: 22149 Long Blvd Dearborn MI 48124

SAGARIN, JAMES LEON, rabbi; b. Oceanside, N.Y., Dec. 31, 1951; s. Lawrence and Ethel (Wallace) S.; m. Lori Beth Baumblatt, Aug. 31, 1986. BA, SUNY, Albany, 1974; MA in Hebrew Letters, Hebrew U. Coll. Jewish Inst. Religion, 1978. Ordained rabbi, 1979. Hillel dir., congl. rabbi So. Ill. U., Carbondale, 1979-80; dir. Young Judaea Jewish Community Ctrs. Assn., St. Louis, 1980-82; dir., sr. adult coordinator adult edn., chaplain Cen. Agy. for Jewish Edn., St. Louis, 1982—; prof. Hebrew langs. and lit. Washington U., St. Louis, 1985—. Author: Hebrew Noun Patterns, 1987. Mem. Cen. Conf. of Am. Rabbis, Nat. Assn. Professors of Hebrew. Lodge: B'nai Brith. Avocations: running, weight-lifting, writing. Home: 6300 Southwood I-E Saint Louis MO 63105 Office: Cen Agy Jewish Edn 12 Millstone Campus Dr Saint Louis MO 63146

SAGE, LEE ALFRED, accounting firm executive; b. Fremont, Ohio, Aug. 9, 1949; s. Hugh Edward Janette Gertrude (Krotzer) S.; m. Carol Jo Dewey, June 14, 1975; children: Justin Hill, Jonah Drew. BS in Fin., Bowling Green State U., 1973. Mgr. prodn. planning White Consol., Mansfields, Ohio, 1974-79; mgr. mfg. Ex-Cell-O, Cocoa, Fla., 1979-85; ptnr. Arthur Young & Co., Detroit, 1985—. Served with USNG, 1971-77. Mem. Am. Prodn. Cinventory Control Soc. (cert.), Assn. Mfg. Excellence, Automotive Industry Action Group. Republican. Methodist. Clubs: Athletic (Detroit); Forest Lake Country (Bloomfield Hills). Avocations: golfing, swimming, reading. Office: Arthur Young & Co 100 Renaissance Ctr Detroit MI 48243

SAGE, MYRON ALVIN, construction company executive; b. Cardington, Ohio, July 8, 1920; s. Walter J. and Inez S. (Caris) S.; m. Vivian Gaynell Conley, May 30, 1970; children: Judith Sage Laughbaum, Michael Allen, Cynthia Sage Engler, James T., Pamela Sage Dougherty. Student, Marion Bus. Coll., 1937-38, Ohio State U. Purchasing agt. Gledhill Road Machinery Co., Galion, Ohio, 1939-42, v.p., 1945-49; bd. chmn. Iberia (Ohio) Earthmoving Service, 1949—; co-owner Sagier Realty Co., Iberia, Iberia Mining Co., Cliffshire Estates, Galion; bd. dirs. Wire Assemblies, Inc., Bucyrus, Ohio; chmn. bd. dirs. Saber Equipment Corp., Iberia, Earthworm Constrn., Iberia. Bd. dirs. Harding Area Council Boy Scouts Am., Marion, Ohio, Hope Line, Mt. Gilead, Ohio, Galion Community Hosp. Served as sgt. U.S. Army, 1942-45, ETO. Decorated Bronze Star. Mem. Ohio Contractors Assn. Republican. Baptist. Lodge: Mason (32 degree). Avocations: fishing, exploring. Home: 8662 State Rt 61 Galion OH 44803

SAGER, ALLEN RANDOLPH, business educator; b. Rogers City, Mich., Apr. 6, 1945; s. Frank E. and Mildred (Larner) S.; m. Jeanne M. Darling, July 31, 1966; children: Sarah, Jonathan. BS in Edn., Cen. Mich. U., Mt. Pleasant, 1967; M in Divinity, Princeton Theol. Sem., 1970. Ordained to ministry Presbyn. Ch., 1970. Pastor Kinde (Mich.) and Chandler Presbyn. Ch., 1970-74, Flora (Ind.) Presbyn. Ch., 1974-79; inst., project supr. Ind. Vocat. Tech. Coll., Lafayette, 1980-85, chmn. bud. div., 1985—, acting dir. instrn., 1986—. Mem. Ind. Soc. CPA's, Tippecanoe Chpt. Nat. Assn. Accts. (sec. 1986). Lodge: Lions. Avocations: reading, bicycling. Home: 204 W Columbia Flora IN 46929 Office: Ind Vocat Tech Coll 3208 Ross Rd PO Box 6299 Lafayette IN 47903

SAGER, DONALD JACK, librarian; b. Milw., Mar. 3, 1938; s. Alfred Herman and Sophia (Sagan) S. B.S., U. Wis., Milw., 1963; M.S. in L.S, U. Wis., Madison, 1964. Sr. documentalist AC Electronics div. Gen. Motors Corp., Milw., 1958-63; teaching asst. U. Wis., Madison, 1963-64; dir. Kingston (N.Y.) Pub. Library, 1964-66, Elyria (Ohio) Pub. Library, 1966-71, Mobile Pub. Library, 1971-75, Pub. Library Columbus and Franklin County, Ohio, 1975-78; commr. Chgo. Pub. Library, 1978-81; dir. Elmhurst Pub. Library, Ill., 1982-83, Milw. Pub. Library, 1983—; sec. Online Computer Library Center, 1977-78; disting. vis. scholar, 1982; chmn. ALTA/PLA investment com., 1985-87, PLA nat. conf. com., 1986—; bd. dirs. Council Wis. Libraries, 1982—; adj. faculty U. Wis.-Milw., 1984—; cons. in field. Author: Reference: A Programmed Instruction, 1970, Binders, Books and Budgets, 1971, Participatory Management, 1981, The American Public Library, 1982,

Public Library Administrators Planning Guide to Automation, 1983, Managing the Public Library, 1984; also articles. Bd. dirs. Goethe House, 1985—, v.p. Milw. Civic Alliance, 1986—; chmn. Milw. United Way Campaign, 1984; pres. Milw. Westown Assn., 1987—. Served with inf. AUS, 1956-58. Mem. ALA, Pub. Library Assn. (dir., v.p., pres.-elect, pres. 1982-83), Chgo. Library Club, Library Info. and Tech. Assn., Library Adminstrn. and Mgmt. Assn., Wis. Library Assn., Wis. Library Assn. Found. (chmn. 1986—), Library Adminstrn. Assn. of Wis. (chmn. 1987—), Early Music Soc. (treas. 1987—). Unitarian. Club: Exchange of Milw. (v.p. 1987—, pres.-elect). Home: 2943 N Cramer Milwaukee WI 53211 Office: Milwaukee Pub Library 814 W Wisconsin Ave Milwaukee WI 53233

SAGER, ROBERT DAVID, dentist, lectr., cons.; b. Manhattan, Kans., May 17, 1950; s. Robert Frank and Betsy Jane (Otey) S.; B.S. cum laude in Biology, Kans. State U., 1972; D.M.D. with honors, Washington U., St. Louis, 1975. Mem. faculty Dental Sch., Washington U., St. Louis, 1975-76; gen. practice dentistry, St. Louis, 1975-76; resident gen. dentistry Ill. Masonic Med. Ctr., Chgo., 1976-77; outpatient clinic mgr., dept. dentistry Ill. Masonic Med. Center, Chgo., 1977-78, mem. staff, 1977—; hosp. gen. dentistry practice, Chgo., 1977-80; clinician, lectr. hosp. dentistry, 1978—; pres. Dentcare Ltd., hosp. dentistry cons., Chgo., 1978—, Dentsystems, Inc., 1979—; pres. Sager Dental Assocs., P.A., 1984—; pres., originator Dr. Toothbrush and Friends Products Co.; mem. staff Swedish Am. Hosp., Rockford, Ill., 1979—, St. Mary's Hosp., Manhattan, 1980—, chmn. dept. of dentistry, 1986—, Meml. Hosp., Manhattan, 1980—; cons. Cook County Hosp., 1979—; guest instr. hosp. gen. practice residency U. Colo. Sch. Dentistry, 1980—; consulting dentist hosp. gen. practice dental residency St. Joseph Hosp., Denver, 1985—; attending dentist Sunset Zoo. Bd. dirs. Riley County Heart Assn. br. Am. Heart Assn., 1980—, v.p., 1984—; pres.-elect, 1986—; chmn. Manhattan Arts Council; mem. curriculum com. Kans. State Univ. Sch. of Interior Design, 1983—. Lic. comml. pilot. Recipient Dentsply Internat. Prosthetic award Dentsply Internat., 1975; Edward R. Hart clin. dentistry award Washington U., 1975. Fellow Am. Assn. Hosp. Dentists; mem. ADA, Am. Acad. Dental Radiology (award 1975), Flying Dentists Assn., Acad. Gen. Dentistry, Acad. Sports Dentistry (founding mem.), Am. Soc. Dentistry for Children, Pierre Fauchard Acad., Acad. Dentistry for Handicapped (dir. 1980—, treas. 1982—, membership chmn., rep. to ADA Council on hosps. and instl. care 1980—, v.p. 1984, pres. 1986—), Kans. Ind. Profl. Assn. (pres. 1983—). Lodges: Masons, Shriners, Odd Fellows. Author: Hospital Dentistry, 1979, Dr. Tooth Brush and Friends Childrens' Books, 1981, Preventive Dentistry Shopper (TV). Home: 1919 Poyntz Manhattan KS 66502 Office: 514 Humboldt Plaza Manhattan KS 66502

SAGER, STEPHEN CHARLES, accountant; b. Detroit, Oct. 2, 1949; s. Charles Jackson and June Eileen (Davidson) S.; m. Mary Joan Leahy, Apr. 28, 1974; children: Randall Charles, Beth Marie, Megan Joan. B Bus. Adminstrn., Western Mich. U., 1971; postgrad., Northwestern U., 1974-76; MBA, De Paul U., 1980. CPA, Ill. Acct. Checkers, Simon & Rosner, Chgo., 1971-73; controller Williams-Bowman, Cicero, Ill., 1973-76, Beckman Instruments, Schiller Park, Ill., 1976-80; ptnr. Sager, Maly & Co., St. Charles, Ill., 1980—; instr. Waubonese (Ill.) Community Coll., 1981-83; speaker to various profl. groups. Bd. dirs. St. Charles Community Chest, 1982-86; pres. Fox Valley Concerned Citizens Orgn., St. Charles, 1983—. Recipient St. Charles Community Chest award, 1983-86. Mem. Am. Inst. CPA's, Ill. Soc. CPA's. Avocations: photography, sports. Office: Sager Maly & Co 102 W Illinois St Saint Charles IL 60174

SAGO, LANCE WILLIAM, horticulturist, small business owner; b. Festus, Mo., Nov. 9, 1958; s. Darrell Gene and Lela Joe (Shy) S. AS in Mech. Drafting, Jefferson Coll., 1978; BS in Horticulture, U. Mo., 1982. Draftsman McDonnell Douglas Aircraft Co., St. Louis, 1978-79; plant propagator Edden Island Nursery, Naples, Fla., 1982-83; owner AAA Nursery, Festus, 1983—; tchr. Jefferson Coll., Hillsboro, Mo., 1985. Office: AAA Nursery 1240 American Legion Dr Festus MO 63028

SAHARA, STEVEN CHARLES, accountant; b. Chgo., Nov. 10, 1962; s. Charles Thomas and Diane Patricia (Moraske) Czochara. BS in Commerce, DePaul U., 1984, M Acctg., 1985. CPA, Ill. With computer system documentation Equity Group, Chgo., 1984; software analyst, instr. Computech Systems Inc., Chgo., 1984-85; staff acct. Price Waterhouse, Chgo., 1985—. Advisor Boy Scouts Am. Explorers, Chgo., 1986. Mem. Am. Inst. CPA's, Ill. CPA Soc. Avocations: tennis, bicycling, reading. Home: 6034 W Byron Chicago IL 60634 Office: Price Waterhouse 200 E Randolph Chicago IL 60601

SAHLBERG, CHARLES VICTOR, manufacturing company executive; b. Oak Park, Ill., July 2, 1935; s. Carl Victor and Lucile Lynette (Dunn) S.; m. Ruth Erma Stenger, June 22, 1957; children: Jeffrey Lee, Cynthia Lynn, Jennifer Ruth. BS, Miami U., Oxford, Ohio, 1957, MBA, 1963. Indsl. engr. Champion Paper Co., Hamilton, Ohio, 1957-61; supr. cen. services Miami U., 1961-64; office supr. Moderncote Co., New Castle, Ind., 1964-69; purchasing mgr. New Castle Products, 1969-79; material mgr. Modernfold, New Castle, 1979-83, v.p. material mgmt. Modernfold, 1983-85; v.p. MATL'S/Services, 1985—. Contbr. articles to bus. jours. Pres. First Nighters, New Castle, 1978, YMCA, New Castle, 1980; elder Presbyn. Ch., New Castle, 1984—. Recipient Best Article award Am. Purchasing Soc., 1973, Good Citizenship award Mut. Trust Ins. Co., 1969; Nat. Assn. of Purchasing Mgmt. Presdl. scholar Indpls., 1979. Mem. Indpls. Purchasing Mgmt. Assn. (sec. 1983-84, treas. 1984, 2d v.p. 1985, 1st v.p. 1986, pres. 1987-88), New Castle C. of C. (v.p. 1985—, pres. 1986-87), Jaycees (v.p. 1960-61). Republican. Lodge: Rotary (pres. 1980-81). Avocations: racquetball, photography, water skiing, softball, reading. Office: Modernfold Inc 1711 I Ave New Castle IN 47362

SAHS, ADOLPH LOUIS, neurologist; b. Charles City, Iowa, 1906; s. Herman John and Bertha Emma (Dahse) S.; m. Margaret Alice Sahs, Feb. 8, 1936; children: Margaret, Carolyn, Mary. Student, U. Iowa, 1925-27, MD, 1931. Prof. neurology, head dept. U. Iowa Coll. Medicine, Iowa City, 1948-74, prof. emeritus, 1974—. Co-author: Textbook of Neurology, 6 ed., 1966. Mem. AMA, Am. Acad. Neurology (pres. 1961-63), Am. Neurol. Assn. (1967-68). Republican. Avocation: amateur radio. Home: 300 N Lee St Iowa City IA 52240 Office: Univ Hosps Newton Rd Iowa City IA 52242

SAIA, ALBERT STEVE, advertising executive; b. Chicago Heights, Ill., Nov. 19, 1933; s. Anthony and Rose (Lobue) S.; m. Joan Primavera, Sept. 3, 1955; children: Mark, Daniel, Andrea, Matthew. BFA, U. Ill., 1956. Designer Thomas A. Schutz Co., Morton Grove, Ill., 1959-66, estimator, 1966-68, v.p., 1968-73, pres., chief exec. officer, 1973—; bd. dirs. Point-of-Purchasing Advt. Inst., vice chmn., 1984-86. Coordinator Arts & Riverwoods (Ill.), 1980. Served to 1st lt. U.S. Army, 1956-58. Republican. Roman Catholic. Club: Thorngate Country (dir., v.p. 1980-82). Avocations: painting, photography, golf, fishing. Home: 410 Thornmeadow Riverwoods IL 60015 Office: Thomas A Schutz Co 8710 N Ferris Morton Grove IL 60053

SAID, MOHSIN M., insurance company executive, consultant; b. Cairo, Egypt, Nov. 7, 1954; came to U.S., 1978, naturalized 1981; s. M. Said and Hanem (Hagag) Mohamoud; m. Therese Hanson, Nov. 7, 1977; children: Sharif Mohsin, Summer. BA in Phys. Edn., Cairo U., 1976. Fin. planner Aetna Ins., Milw., 1978-79; ins. exec. Lincoln Fin. Resources, Milw., 1979—; dir. Lincoln Fin. Resources Fin. & Investment Corp., Milw., 1979—. Active Republican Party, Washington, 1983—. Mem. Internt. Assn. Fin. Planners (accredited), Nat. Assn. Life Underwriters (life, Nat. Sales Achievement award, 1981-85), Nat. Assn. Health Underwriters (life, leading producer roundtable, Nat. Quality award 1981-85). Club: Athletic. Avocations: soccer, bicycling, traveling, tennis, stamp collecting. Home: 14505 Watertown Plank Rd Elm Grove WI 53122 Office: Lincoln Fin Resources Bishops Woods W 150 S Sunnyslope Rd Suite 101 Brookfield WI 53005

SAILER, ALLEN JOHN, military officer, engineer; b. Beulah, N.D., Nov. 26, 1939; s. Herbert Emil and Louise Ernestena (Merkle) S.; m. Patricia Kathryn Retterath, Nov. 28, 1963; children: David, Amy, Daniel. BSME, N.D. State U., 1961; MS in Indsl. Engring., U. Pitts., 1966. Registered profl. engr., Ohio. Commd. 2d lt. USAF, 1962, advanced through grades to col., 1981; engr. USAF, Offutt AFB, Nebr., 1962—. Contbr. articles to profl. jours. Pres. Homeowners Assn., Quail Creek, Omaha, 1986-87. Decorated Bronze Star. Mem. Soc. Am. Milit. Engrs. (bd. dirs. 1984-85, v.p. 1980-81, 86—, pres. elect 1987-88), Nat. Soc. Profl. Engrs. Roman Catholic. Club: Rod and Gun (Hawaii) (pres. 1967-68). Avocations: golf, home improvement, stained glass, hunting, fishing. Home: 4412 Anderson Grove Omaha NE 68123 Office: USAF Hdqrs Strategic Air Command/DE Offutt AFB NE 68113

ST. AMAND, GERALD EDWARD, real estate development company executive; b. Detroit, June 5, 1944; s. Edward Gerald and Mary (Kreskosky) St. A. B.S. in Fin., U. Detroit, 1966, M.A. in Econs., 1968. Coordinator computer activities Mich. State U. Grad. Sch. Bus. Adminstrn., 1968-82; asst. mgmt. info. systems dir. Melvin Simon and Assocs., Inc., Indpls., 1982—; cons. in field. Recipient Fitzgerald award U. Detroit, 1966. Office: PO Box 7033 Indianapolis IN 46207

ST. CLAIR, JOHN CHARLES, SR., construction executive; b. Indpls., Aug. 26, 1940; s. Jesse H. and Margaret (Wismeier) St. C.; m. Karen Marie Jensen, Oct. 3, 1962; children: John Charles, Michelle Marie. Student Purdue U., 1959-60, Ind. U.-Purdue U., Indpls., 1960-62. Pres. Classic Pool & Patio, Indpls., 1965—. Served with USAF, 1962-67. Mem. Nat. Spa and Pool Inst. (bd. dirs. 1983—, chpt. v.p. and treas. 1976-80, regional v.p. 1985—, judge internat. design awards 1984, Gold Medal Design award 1984-85, Silver medal 1985, Bronze medal 1984-85, 87, award of Merit 1979, 84, 87), Cen. Ind. Pool Service Assn. (charter; v.p. 1970-71, pres. 1971-72, treas., bd. dirs. 1983-85), Nat. Retail Mchts. Assn., Nat. Sporting Goods Assn., Nat. Assn. Home Builders, Ind. Home Builders Assn., Indpls. Landscape Assn., Indpls. C. of C., Better Bus. Bur. Republican. Methodist. Club: Columbia, Hillcrest Country (Indpls.). Avocations: golf, boating, skiing. Home: 6306 Hillcrest Ln Indianapolis IN 46220 Office: 5294 E 65th St Indianapolis IN 46220

ST. JOHN, CHARLES VIRGIL, pharmaceutical company executive; b. Bryan, Ohio, Dec. 18, 1922; s. Clyde W. and Elsie (Kintner) St. J.; m. Ruth Ilene Wilson, Oct. 27, 1946; children: Janet Sue St. John Amy, Debra Ann St. John Mishler. AB, Manchester Coll., 1943; MS, Purdue U., 1946. Asst. gen. mgr., dir. ops. Eli Lilly and Co., Clinton, Ind., 1971-75; gen. mgr. Eli Lilly and Co., Lafayette, Ind., 1975-77, v.p. prodn. ops. div., 1977—; bd. dirs. Bank One of Lafayette, Lafayette Life Ins. Co. Bd. trustees Lafayette Symphony Found.; past chmn. lay adv. council St. Elizabeth Hosp.; mem. Purdue U. Pres. Council; trustee Manchester Coll., North Manchester, Ind. Recipient Elizabethan award, St. Elizabeth Hosp., Lafayette, 1985. Mem. Am. Chem. Soc., Purdue Research Found., Greater Lafayette C. of C. (past bd. dirs.). Republican. Methodist. Club: Lafayette Country (Ind.). Home: 320 Overlook Dr West Lafayette IN 47906

ST. JOHN, DOUGLAS ALLEN, advertisig executive; b. Detroit, June 20, 1939; s. Donald Ross and Ruth Evangeline (Allen) S.; m. Sandra Jean Lamphear, July 6, 1963 (div. Mar. 1971); m. Lynn Margaret Erickson, July 24, 1971; children: Kristin Lynn, Dana Lauren. BA in Advt., Mich. State U., East Lansing, 1982. Cert. bus. communicator. Advt. mgr. Redwood & Ross, Inc., Kalamazoo, Mich., 1965-67; v.p. Russell T. Gray, Inc., Chgo., 1967-75, Indsl. Mktg. Service ,Inc., Chgo., 1975-80, M.G. Walther Advt., Inc., Oak Brook, Ill., 1980-84; exec. v.p. E.R. Hollingsworth & Assocs., Rockford, Ill., 1984—. Contbr. numerous articles to profl. jours. Mem. Community Caucus, Clarendon Hills, Ill., 1982-83, Rockford C. of C., 1985-87. Served as 1st lt. U.S. Army, 1963-65. Mem. Bus./Profl. Advt. Assn., No. Ill. Advt. Council (v.p., 1985-87), Phi Kappa Psi. Republican. Clubs: Newcomers (Rockford); The Anvil (East Dundee, Ill.). Lodge: Rotary. Avocations: bridge, skiing, golf. Home: 4587 Olde Lyme Dr Rockford IL 61111 Office: E R Hollingsworth & Assocs 6067 Strathmoor Dr Rockford IL 61107

ST. JOHN, JUDY KAY, food company executive; b. Carthage, Mo., Jan. 29, 1949; d. George Samuel and Jewell Marjorie (Simmons) Byers; m. Henry David St. John, Aug. 9, 1969; children: Amber Kiki, Samuel David. BS in Edn., Mo. So. State Coll., Joplin, 1970. Cert. elem. tchr., Mo. Tchr. Jasper (Mo.) Pub. Schs., 1970-72, Carthage (Mo.) Pub. Schs., 1972-73, Adult Basic Edn., Carthage, 1982; pres. Water Wheel Foods Ltd., Carthage, 1981—. Contbr. articles to profl. jours. Mem. Nite Writers (pres. 1984-86). Mem. Ch. of Christ. Avocations: arts and crafts. Home: 1009 S Maple Carthage MO 64836 Office: Water Wheel Foods Ltd Route 6 Box 344A Carthage MO 64836

ST. JOHN, MICHAEL HAROLD, health services administrator, consultant; b. Erie, Pa., June 1, 1944; s. Harold S. and E. Ruth (Smith) St. J.; m. Jane Ann Russell, Sept. 1, 1967; children—Sharon, Elizabeth, Steven. B.A. in Applied Sociology, Ohio Wesleyan U., 1965; M.S.W. in Social Welfare, U. Wis.-Milw., 1969, postgrad., 1976-79. Correctional counselor Lebanon (Ohio) Correctional Inst., 1966-67; social worker div. corrections State of Wis., 1967-70; liaison tchr. Wis. Sch. for Boys, Wales, 1970-72; community services coordinator Bur. Probation and Parole, Milw., 1972-73; program dir. Jewish Vocat. Services, Milw., 1973-80; dir. dept. social services Sacred Heart Rehab. Hosp., Milw., 1980-81, dir. rehab. services, 1981-85; dir. research and devel. Sacred Heart Services Network, 1986; dir. rehab. services Community Meml. Hosp., Menomonee Falls, Wis., 1987—; treas. Rehab. Facilities Wis.; lectr., cons. in field. Pres. bd. dirs. Youth Policy and Law Ctr., Milw.; mem. Exceptional Edn. Task Force, Milw.; bd. treas. Council for the Spanish-Speaking. Mem. Soc. Hosp. Social Work Dirs., Wis. Assn. Rehab. Social Workers (past pres.), Soc. Hosp. Risk Mgmt., Sherman Park Community Assn. (bd. pres.), Wis. Adult Daycare Assn. (pres.). Home: 2662 N Grant Blvd Milwaukee WI 53210 Office: Community Meml Hosp W 180 N 8085 Town Hall Rd Menomonee Falls WI 53051

ST. JULIAN, GRANT, JR., microbiologist; b. Beaumont, Tex., Feb. 13, 1931; s. Grant and Leah (Hebert) St. J.; m. Cora Jeanne Wood, Dec. 26, 1955; children: Grant, Andrea Renee, Tanya Suzanne. BS, Samuel Huston Coll., 1951; BA, Huston-Tillotson Coll., 1954; MS, U. Tex., 1957; postgrad. Bradley U., 1964-65, MIT, 1967. Research microbiologist agrl. microbiology unit, fermentation lab. No. Regional Research Ctr., U.S. Dept. Agr., Peoria, Ill., 1961—. Cons. dept. biochemistry U. Oxford (Eng.), Internat. Ctr. Insect Physiology and Ecology, Nairobi, Kenya, 1982. Chmn. Human Relations Commn. Peoria, 1960-64, mem. Fire and Police Commn., 1964-70; chmn. bd. dirs. Peoria Tri-County Urban League, 1969-71; mem. Mayor's Drug Abuse Task Force, 1970-71; bd. dirs. Ill. Arthritis Found, 1970-71, Tri-County Comprehensive Health Planning Commn., 1977; mem. priorities com. Heart of Ill. United Way, 1972-73, adv. bd. Salvation Army. Served with U.S. Army, 1952-54. Recipient Cert. of Merit, Human Relations Commn. Peoria, 1963; Humanitarian award State of Ill., 1965; Ralph Bunche Humanitarian award Peoria Bus. Assn., 1966; Paul Schlink Good Govt. award Peoria C. of C., 1968; Disting. Citizen award Urban League, 1976; Cert. of Merit, No. Regional Research Ctr., Peoria, 1979; Disting. Speaker award Am. Chem. Soc., 1980. Mem. N.Y. Acad. Scis., Ill. Acad. Sci., Internat. Invertebrate Pathology, Am. Soc. Microbiology, Ill. Soc. Microbiology, Entomol. Soc. Am., Sigma Xi. Democrat. Roman Catholic. Contbr. 60 articles to profl. jours. Home: 5609 Stephen Dr Peoria IL 61615 Office: 1815 University Peoria IL 61604

ST. OURS, SANDRA LOU, banker; b. Escanaba, Mich., Nov. 30, 1957; d. Wayne Anthony and Roberta Lou (Hardy) Jacques; m. Thomas J. St. Ours, Apr. 30, 1977. Student No. Mich. U. Sch. Banking, 1981-82, Am. Inst. Banking, 1982. Bookkeeper, First Nat. Bank, Escanaba, 1975, teller, 1975-76, head teller, 1977-79, br. mgr., 1980-82, asst. cashier, 1983-85, asst. v.p., 1985-86, asst. v.p., br. adminstr., 1987—. Mem. Mich. Bank Pac, Bus. and Profl. Women's Orgn. (bd. dirs. 1984-85, found. chmn., 1985-86, sec. 1986-87), Nat. Assn. Female Execs., Am. Inst. Banking (sec. Bay de Noc chpt. 1979-82), Altrusa (publicity chmn. 1986-87), U.S. tae Kwon-Do Assn., Cho's Black Belt Acad. Democrat. Roman Catholic. Avocations: cake decorating, cross country skiing. Office: First Nat Bank and Trust Co 1205 Ludington St Escanaba MI 49829

SAINT-PIERRE, MICHAEL ROBERT, funeral director, consultant; b. Indpls., July 12, 1947; s. Robert Ross and Gaile Russell (Cousins) S.; m. Betty Carolyn Wilhoit, Jan. 14, 1967; children: Michelle René, Paul Christopher. Student Milligan Coll., 1965-67, Butler U., 1966; B.S., East Tenn. State U., 1969; diploma Ind. Coll. Mortuary Sci., 1970; postgrad. Nat. Found. Funeral Service, 1970, 71, 73, 74, 76, Ind. U., Indpls., 1977. Intern, Hamlett-Dobson, Kingsport, Tenn., 1967-69; pres. J.C. Wilson & Co., Inc., Indpls., 1969—, St. Pierre Funeral Mgmt. Corp., 1984—; evaluator/practitioner rep. Am. Bd. Funeral Service Edn., 1980—; prof., trustee Ind. Coll. Mortuary Sci., 1971-76; prof. Nat. Found. Funeral Service, 1987—; bd. advisors Nat. Bank Greenwood (Ind.), 1978-80. Contbr. articles to profl. jours. Bd. dirs. Central Ind. Better Bus. Bur., Indpls., 1982-86, Adult/Child Mental Health Ctr., Indpls., 1982-85, Allied Meml. Council, Indpls., 1979—; elder Greenwood (Ind.) United Presbyn. Ch., 1976; past mem., treas. bd. dirs. Consumer Info. Bur., Inc.; past mem. bd. dirs. Center for Life/Death Edn., Indpls. Recipient Nat. Bd. Cert., Conf. Funeral Service Exam. Bd., 1970; Disting. Service awards Ind. Coll. Mortuary Sci., Indpls., 1978, Mid Am. Coll. Funeral Service, Jeffersonville, Ind., 1982. Fellow Nat. Found. Funeral Service (pres. alumni assn. 1978); mem. Associated Funeral Dirs. Service Internat. (pres. 1981), Nat. Selected Morticians, Nat. Funeral Dirs. Assn. (practitioner, resource and outreach, edn., supplementary speakers bur. and arbitration coms., chmn. employee/employer task force, chmn. mgmt. practice com.), Acad. Profl. Funeral Service Practice, Ind. Funeral Dirs. Assn. (bd. dirs., pres. 1982-83), Funeral Dirs. Forum, Prearrangement Assn. Am., Marion County Funeral Dirs. Assn. (pres. 1974), Nat. Eagle Scout Assn. Republican. Presbyterian. Clubs: Valle Vista Country, Skyline. Lodges: Rotary (past pres.; Paul Harris fellow); Masons; Shriners; Order Eastern Star. Office: Wilson St Pierre Funeral Service PO 147 481 W Main St Greenwood IN 46142

SAKAGUCHI, RONALD LOUIS, dental educator and researcher; b. Los Angeles, Aug. 3, 1955; s. Louis and Hatsy (Kosha) S.; m. Nancy Pilgrim, Sept. 13, 1986. BS, UCLA, 1976; DDS, Northwestern U., 1980; MS, U. Minn., 1984. Optical service technician McBain Inst., Chatsworth, Calif., 1972-74; research asst. UCLA, Los Angeles, 1974-76, ADA, Chgo., 1976-80; dentist Chgo. Osteopathic Hosp., 1980-82; research assoc. U. Minn., Mpls., 1984-86, asst. prof. dentistry, 1986—; cons. Research Triangle Inst., N.C., 1981, 3M Co., St. Paul, 1987—. Grantee Nat. Inst. Dental Research, 1986. Mem. Am. Coll. Prosthodontists, Minn. Assn. Prosthodontists, Internat. Assn. for Dental Research, Am. Assn. for Dental Research, Acad. Dental Medicine. Avocations: photography, computer graphics, tennis. Office: U Minn 16-212 Moos Tower Minneapolis MN 55455

SAKEY, ROBERT WILLIAM, personnel director; b. Sharon, Pa., June 29, 1930; s. Alex Zahariah and Martha (Popp) S.; m. Myrna Mae Livingston, June 29, 1968; 1 child, Robert A. BS in Bus. Edn., Youngstoen (Ohio) U., 1956; MS in Edn., Westminster Coll., New Wilmington, Pa., 1957. Indsl. engr. Westinghouse, Sharon, Pa., 1951-57; tchr., coach Vernon (Ohio) Sch., 1957-59; instr. Gen. Motors Inst., Flint, Mich., 1959-60; supr. training and safety Sawhill Cyclops, Sharon, 1960-66; dir. personnel Comml. Shearing, Youngstown, 1966—; instr. Pa. State U., Sharon, 1963—. Mem. adv. com. Choffin Vocat. Sch., 1981-84, Youngstown State U. Bus. and Tech., 1982—; mem. labor mgmt. com. Woodside Receiving Hosp., Youngstown, 1980—. Mem. Am. Soc. Personnel Adminstrn., Youngstown Area C. of C. Episcopalian. Avocations: jogging, handball, reading, gardening. Office: Comml Shearing Inc 1771 Logan Ave Youngstown OH 44501

SAKRY, CLIFF R., writer, publicist, film writer, speaker, trainer, consultant; b. St. Cloud, Minn., Aug. 27, 1914; s. Paul Edward and Monica Sophy (Thomalla) S.; m. Donna Cecilia Barthelemy, Oct. 11, 1946; children—Michelle Marie, Donna Lynnelle, Clifford Mark, Brian John. Student, St. Cloud State U., 1932-38, U. Minn., 1942-43, Harvard U., 1944, St. John's U., 1947, Stanford U., 1951. Reporter, proof reader St. Cloud Daily Times, Minn., 1935-37, columnist, spl. features writer, regional and farm editor, pub. relations dir., 1946-51; spl. features writer/editor AP, 1937-38, regional news corr., 1938-41; news writer, editor, announcer Sta. KFAM (now KNSI), 1938-41, sta. mgr., pub. relations dir., commentator, 1946-51; co-founder, exec. sec. Midwest Conservation Alliance, 1933-34; co-founder, organizer, exec. dir. Minn. Conservation Fedn., 1952-55; radio-TV dir. Olmstead and Foley Advt., Mpls., 1954; founder Minn. Youth Firearms Safety Tng. Program, 1954-55, creative dir., sales, script writer, film dir., musical coordinator Promotional Films, Inc., 1955-66; pub. relations dir. Coll. St. Benedict, dir. Benedicta Arts Ctr., 1966-71; programming mktg. research sales, program coordinator Personal Dynamics, Inc., Mpls., 1971-76; bd. dirs. Cen. Minn. Group Health Plan, 1986—; cons. in incentive tng., mktg., 1975—; free-lance writer, 1975—. Author, editor: Boondocks Baseball, 1980; founder, editor: Minn. Out-of-Doors, 1953-55; author, composer, producer stage musical: Minnesota!, 1949-51, 58, 76, 83 (state award 1949); author, dir. over 80 documentary films; author poem, The Titan Lake Encounter, 1986; lyricist/composer songs tributing cen. Minn.; contbr. numerous articles to newspapers and magazines, 1934—. TV panelist Sportsmen's Round Table and Minn. Outdoors, 1958-63; co-founder, organizer St. Cloud Blood Donors Guild, 1939-41; vol. Retired Srs. Vol. Program, 1984—; mem. adv. bd., sr. advocate Whitney Sr. Ctr., St. Cloud, 1981—; mem. St. Cloud's Human Rights Commn., 1983—, St. Cloud Library Bd., 1984—, congressman A. Stangeland Legis. Adv. Com., St. Cloud, 1984—; co-founder, 1st pres. St. Cloud Community Arts Council, 1970-71; mem. Stearns County Hist. Soc.; active Nat. Wildlife Fedn., del. convs., 1954, 55, 58; founder 2 scholarships St. Cloud State U. Served to lt. (j.g.) USNR, 1941-46; ETO. Recipient Alumni Service award St. Cloud State U., 1983; Robert G. Green Disting. Service award Mpls. Jaycees, 1953; Disting. Service award St. Cloud Jaycees, 1950; Hon. Life Mem. Minn Conservation Fedn., 1955; Governor's Citation Senior of the Yr. award Stearns County, 1986; 50th Anniversary Minn. Conservation Fedn. Founders award, 1986; World of Poetry Golden Poet award, 1987; named Congl. intern, 1983. Roman Catholic. Mem. Minn. Film Producers Assn. (co-founder, pres. 1966). Avocations: music; literature; poetry; golf; politics. Lodge: Kiwanis (Golden K pres. 1983-84, Senior of Yr. Citation 1986). Home and Office: 663 Roosevelt Rd St Cloud MN 56301

SALABOUNIS, MANUEL, computer information scientist; b. Salonica, Greece, Apr. 15, 1935; came to U.S., 1954; s. Anastasios and Marietta (Mytonidis) Tsalabounis; m. Mary Louise Turk, Apr. 26, 1966 (div. Sept. 1978); children: Stacy, Mary E., John. Cert., Anatolia Coll., Salonica, Greece, 1954; student, Morris Harvey Coll., 1954-56; BS in Engring. Sci., Cleve. State U., 1960; MS in Math., Akron U., 1964. Master Univ. Sch., Shaker Heights, Ohio, 1960-62; mathematician Babcock and Wilcox, Alliance, Ohio, 1962-66; dir. computer ctr. John Carroll U., University Heights, Ohio, 1966-68; pres. Electronic Service Assocs. Corp., Euclid, Ohio, 1968-73; v.p. North Am. Co., Chgo., 1974-79; sr. project leader Hibernia Bank, New Orleans, 1979-83; project mgr. Compuware Corp., Birmingham, Mich., 1984—. Vol. Saint Constantine Ch., Saint Helen Ch., Cleve., 1956-58, Saint Nicholas, Detroit, 1986. Avocations: classical music, opera, golf, fishing, cooking. Home: 28238 Westerleigh Farmington Hills MI 48018 Office: Compuware Corp 32100 Telegraph Rd Birmingham MI 48010

SALAS, ALAN ROBERT, auditor; b. Chgo., Aug. 22, 1956; m. Joann LaBuda, May 9, 1981; 1 child, Jennifer. BS in Commerce, DePaul U., 1978, M in Fin., 1984. CPA, Ill. Staff acct. Coopers & Lybrand, Chgo., 1978-80; acctg. mgr. Quaker Oats, Chgo., 1980-83; budget analyst Montgomery Ward, Chgo., 1983-85; sr. internal auditor Marshall Field's, Chgo., 1986—. Served to capt., USAR, 1977—. Mem. Am. Inst. CPA's, Ill. Soc. CPA's, Delta Sigma Pi. Roman Catholic.

SALAZAR, NINFA ALICIA REYES, janitorial services company executive; b. Dexter, Mo., May 27, 1959; d. Juan Q. and Eloisa (Rodriguez) Reyes; m. Julian Salazar Sr., Sept. 10, 1979; 1 child, Julian Jr. Ed. Prarie State Coll., Sawyer Coll. Bus., Med. Career Inst. With Davis Temporaries, Chicago Heights, Ill., 1980-82; office mgr. E&B Painting, Harvey, Ill., 1981-82; owner, pres. J&N's Janitorial Services, Chicago Heights, 1982—. Court watcher Cook County Ct. Watcher's Project, Chicago Heights, 1985. Mem. Women in Mgmt., Women's Referral Services, Entrepreneur Assn. Am., Notaries Assn. Am., Am. Cardiology Tech. Assn., Chicago Heights C. of C. Avocations: bicycle riding; skating; dancing. Home: 175 Thelma Ln Chicago Heights IL 60411 Office: J&N's Janitorial Service PO Box 353 Park Forest IL 60466

SALDAN, NICHOLAS, lawyer; b. N.Y.C., Apr. 6, 1955; s. Hnat and Mary (Wihak) S.; m. Alice Ann Adams, Oct. 8, 1982. BA, Fairleigh Dickinson U., 1977, M of Pub. Adminstrn., 1979; JD, Washburn U., 1982. Bar: Kans. 1983, Nebr. 1983, U.S. Dist. Ct. Kans. 1983, U.S. Ct. Appeals (10th cir.) 1985. Atty. League of Kans. Municipalities, Topeka, 1983-85; asst. county counselor Johnson County (Kans.) Legal Dept., Olathe, 1985—. Contbr.

articles to profl. jours. Scholar Fairleigh Dickinson U., 1973. Mem. ABA, Kans. Bar Assn., Nebr. Bar Assn., Johnson County Bar Assn., Am. Trial Lawyers Assn., Washburn Law Sch. Assn., Phi Omega Epsilon, Phi Zeta Kappa. Republican. Home: 2111 Kasold Dr Apt #G-102 Lawrence KS 66046 Office: Johnson County Legal Dept 110 S Cherry Suite 8 Olathe KS 66061

SALESKE, ALLEN EDWARD, trust tax officer; b. Milw., May 30, 1957; s. Theodore Edward and Beverly Jane (Bailey) S.; m. Joy Darlene Krueger, Apr. 30, 1983; 1 child, Matthew Allen Saleske. BBA, U. Wis., 1975-79. CPA, Wis. Tax analyst Marshall & Ilsley Trust Co., Milw., 1980-84, trust tax officer, 1984—. Fellow Am. Inst. CPA's, Wis. Inst. CPA's. Mem. Assembly of God. Avocations: baseball, volleyball, skiing. Home: 5239 N 108 Ct Milwaukee WI 53225

SALIGMAN, HARVEY, consumer products and services company executive; b. Phila., July 18, 1938; s. Martin and Lillian (Zitin) S.; m. Linda Powell, Nov. 25, 1979; children: Martin, Lilli Ann, Todd Michael, Adam Andrew, Brian Matthew. B.S., Phila. Coll. Textiles and Sci., 1960. With Queen Casuals, Inc., Phila., 1960—; v.p. Queen Casuals, Inc., 1966-68, pres., chief exec. officer, 1968-81, chmn., 1981—; pres., chief operating officer Interco Inc., St. Louis, 1981—, chief exec. officer, 1983—; chmn. Interco Inc., 1985—, also dir.; dir. Merc. Bank. Trustee St. Louis Children's Hosp., Jewish Hosp. St. Louis, Washington U., St. Louis; bd. dirs. St. Louis Symphony Soc.; commr. St. Louis Art Mus. Mem. Young Pres. Orgn. Club: St. Louis. Lodges: Locust, Masons. Office: Interco Inc 101 S Hanley Rd Saint Louis MO 63105

SALISBURY, ALICIA LAING, state senator; b. N.Y.C., Sept. 20, 1939; d. Herbert Farnsworth and Augusta Belle (Marshall) Laing; m. John Eagan Salisbury, June 23, 1962; children—John Eagan Jr., Margaret Laing. Student Sweet Briar Coll., 1957-60; B.A., Kans. U., 1961. Mem. Kans. Senate, 1985—, chmn. adminstrv. rules and regulations com., vice chmn. edn. com., mem. assessment and taxation com., legis. and congl. apportionment com., legis. econ. devel. commn. local govt. com., pub. health and welfare com. Elected mem. State Bd. Edn., Topeka, 1981-85; mem. edn. task force Midwestern Conf. of Council State Govts.; pres. Jr. League of Topeka, 1961—; trustee Leadership Kans., 1982—; bd. dirs. Topeka Community Found., 1983—, Kans. Council on Employment and Tng., 1985—; mem. adv. commn. Juvenile Offenders Program, Kans., 1985—; mem. adv. bd. Kans. Action for Children, 1982—, Kans. Ins. Edn. Found., 1984—; former bd. dirs. Topeka C. of C., United Way Greater Topeka, ARC, Family Service and Guidance, Topeka, Shawnee County Mental Health Assn., Florence Crittenton Services, Topeka, Kans. Action for Children, Topeka City Commn. Govtl. Adv. Com. Mem. Nat. Conf. State Legislators, Nat. Republican Legislators' Assn., Shawnee County Rep. Women, Kappa Kappa Gamma. Episcopalian. Avocations: tennis; downhill skiing; water sports; horseback riding; spectator sports. Office: Kans State Senate State Capital Bldg Topeka KS 66612

SALITERMAN, LAURA SHRAGER, pediatrician; b. N.Y.C., June 26, 1946; d. Arthur M. and Ida (Wildman) Shrager; A.B. magna cum laude (Greenberg Sci. award 1967), Brandeis U., 1967; M.D. (med. scholarship for merit 1967), N.Y. U., 1971; m. Richard Arlen Saliterman, June 15, 1975; 1 son, Robert Warren. Intern, Montefiore Hosp. and Med. Center, Bronx, N.Y., 1971-72, resident in pediatrics, 1972-74; pediatrician Morrisania Family Care Center, N.Y.C., 1974-75; pediatrician Share Health Plan, St. Paul, 1975-85 , dir. pediatrics, 1976-82; pediatrician Aspen Med. Group, St. Paul, 1985; —clin. asst. prof. U. Minn. Med. Sch. Mem. Am. Acad. Pediatrics, Phi Beta Kappa. Club: Oak Ridge. Home: 11911 Live Oak Dr Minnetonka MN 55343 Office: 1020 Bandana Blvd W Saint Paul MN 55108

SALITERMAN, RICHARD ARLEN, lawyer, educator; b. Mpls., Aug. 3, 1946; s. Leonard Slitz and Dorothy (Sloan) S.; m. Laura Shrager, June 15, 1975; 1 son, Robert Warren. B.A. summa cum laude, U. Minn., 1968; J.D., Columbia U., 1971; LL.M., N.Y.U., 1974. Bar: Minn. 1972, D.C. 1974. Mem. legal staff U.S. Senate Subcom. on Antitrust and Monopoly, 1971-72; acting dir., dep. dir. Compliance and Enforcement div. Fed. Energy Office, N.Y.C., 1974; mil. atty. Presdl. Clemency Bd., White House, Washington, 1975; sr. ptnr. Saliterman & Alden Law Firm, Mpls., 1975—; adj. prof. law Hamline U., 1976-81. Chmn. Hennepin County Bar Jour., 1985—. Bd. dirs. Mpls. Urban League, 1987—. Served with USN, 1972-75. Mem. ABA, Minn. State Bar Assn., Hennepin County Bar Assn. (governing council 1985-87). Clubs: Oakridge Country (Hopkins, Minn.); Mpls.

SALLEN, MARVIN SEYMOUR, banking and mortgage company executive; b. Detroit, Oct. 15, 1931; s. Jack Samuel and Sara Sallen; m. Nancy Susan Berke; 1 child, Jack Samuel II. AB in Econs., U. Mich., 1952. V.p. Sonnenblick-Goldman Corp., Detroit, 1967-83; sr. v.p. Comerica Bank, Detroit, 1983—; pres. Comerica Mortgage Corp., Detroit, 1983—. Office: Comerica Mortgage Corp 280 W Maple Rd Birmingham MI 48010

SALM, EDWARD RAYMOND, bank executive; b. Chgo., Feb. 1, 1948; s. Edward Peter and Mary Lois (Waters) S.; m. Bobby L. Sykes, Aug. 31, 1969; children: Russel E., Andrew R. BS in Engring., U. Ill., 1969; MBA in Fin., Ind. U., 1974. With Ind. Nat. Bank, Indpls., 1975—, successively mgr. proof & transit, mgr. deposit ops., programming mgr., mgr. tech. strategic planning, now mgr. info. planning and affiliate support; chmn. computer scis. adv. com. Franklin (Ind.), 1983-85. Treas. Ind. Nat. Officers Polit. Action Com., Indpls., 1986. Served to lt. USN, 1971-74. Home: Rt 1 PO Box SW240 New Palestine IN 46163 Office: Ind Nat Bank 1 Indiana Sq M460 Indianapolis IN 46266

SALM, RENEE JOY, electrologist; b. Engelwood, N.J., Apr. 9, 1958; d. Curt and Nellie (Lieberman) S. Student, U. Hartford, 1976-78; BS, Purdue U., 1980; postgrad., Roosevelt U., 1983—. Front desk mgr. Marriott Corp., Chgo., 1979-83; systems analyst Carson Pirie Scott, Chgo., 1983-85; pvt. practice electrolysis Skokie, Ill., 1985—; cons. Alert Mktg., Skokie, 1985—. Mem. Soc. Clin. and Med. Electrologists, Internat. Guild Profl. Electrologists, Assn. Children of Holocaust Survivors. Avocations: sailing, nautilus, aerobics, horseback riding. Home and Office: 516 Madison St Glencoe IL 60022

SALMI, DARLENE MARIE, teacher; b. L'Anse, Mich.; d. Urho Theodore and Esther Susan (Johnson) Wuori; m. Allen Frederick Salmi, Aug. 27, 1966; children: Allen, Michael, Sarah, Bradley. BS, No. Mich. U., 1968. Tchr. 3d grade North Sashabaw Sch., Clarkston, Mich., 1967-68; tchr. 2d grade Soo Hill Sch., Escanaba, Mich., 1968-69; tchr. 1st grade Mid-Peninsula Sch., Rock, Mich., 1978—. Delta Kappa Gamma. Republican. Lutheran. Avocations: reading, knitting. Home: 10637 Q 5 Ln Rapid River MI 49878

SALMON, ROBERT NEAL, college fund president; b. Springfield, Mo., Dec. 25, 1944; s. Arthur Donald and Cleta Glee (Way) S.; m. Judith Lynn Williams, Sept. 2, 1967; children: Christopher Neal, Patrick Allen. BA, Washburn U., 1969. Prodn. mgr. Sta. WIBW-TV, Topeka, 1966-70; mgr. dist. sales Investors Diversified Services, Inc., Mpls., 1070-73, Mantek, Dallas, 1973-74; gen. mgr. Topeka Met. Transit Authority, 1974-84; v.p. mktg. Mchts. Nat. Bank, Topeka, 1984-85; exec. dir. univ. relations Washburn U., Topeka, 1985-86; pres. Kans. Ind. Coll. Fund, Topeka, 1986—. Contbr. numerous articles to jours. Chmn. state awards Kans. Com. for Employer Support of Guard and Res., Topeka, 1986—; vice-chmn. Future Heritage of Topeka, 1986—; mem. Downtown Improvement Dist., Topeka, 1987—. Recipient Adminstrs. award Urban Mass Transp. Adminstrn., Washington, 1983; named Officer of Yr., Topeka Police Dept., 1984; numerous other awards. Mem. Kans. Soc. Assn. Execs., Sales and Mktg. Execs. Assn., Greater Topeka C. of C., Downtown Topeka, Inc. (chmn. 1987—). Republican. Episcopalian. Lodge: Rotary. Avocations: reading, golf, writing, family activities, church activities. Home: 3919 SE 31st Topeka KS 66603 Office: Kans Ind Coll Fund 700 Kansas Ave Suite 511 Topeka KS 66603

SALMON, STUART CLIVE, manufacturing engineer; b. London, 1952. B in Prodn. Engring. Tech. and Mgmt. with honors, Loughborough U., 1975; PhD, Bristol U., 1979. Apprentice Rolls-Royce Ltd., Derby, Eng., 1969-79; with Gen. Electric Aircraft Engine Group, Cin., 1979-80; engr. Gen. Electric Aircraft Engine Group, Evendale, Ohio, 1980-83; prin. Advanced Mfg. Sci. and Tech., 1983—. Author: Abrasive Machining Handbook; contbr. articles to profl. jours., McGraw-Hill Encyclopoedia, 1982-83; also numerous seminars; patenee in field. Research grantee Rolls-Royce and British Sci. Research Council; recipient Sir Walter Puckey Prize. Office: Advanced Mfg. Sci. and Tech. PO Box 40469 Cincinnati OH 45240

SALOMON, DONNA JEAN, optometric assistant, artist; b. Chgo., Jan. 9, 1940; d. Eugene Vernon and Virginia E. (Roe) Rogers; m. Robert Lee Snavely, June 3, 1961 (div. Feb. 1965); m. John Fredrick Salomon, Aug. 28, 1965; children: Pamela Christine, Kathryn Nannette. Student, Trinity Coll., Clearwater, Fla., 1957-60; cert. in emergency med. tech., Ivy Tech. Coll., 1975; student, Ind. Paraoptometric Assn., 1980-86. Cert. optometric asst. Emergency med. technician, vol. firefighter Monticello (Ind.) Fire Dept., 1974-87; optometric asst. Dr. John C. Corbin, Monticello, 1979-86; owner, operator Salomon Industries, Monticello, 1986; substitute tchr. Twin Lakes Sch. Corp. Artist numerous pastel-oil paintings, designer mayoral stationary, 1980 (Commendaton), exhibited in state-wide Art-in-History contest, 1985 (Purchase award); inventor ruler concept; patentee in field. Campaign coordinator Blair for Mayor, Monticello, 1978-80; White county coordinator Dan Quayle for Senate, 1978-80; mem. White County Hosp. Aux., White County Rep. Women; sec.-treas. paramedic equipment fund Monticello Fire Dept.; past supt. Sunday sch. Methodist Ch., former Sunday sch. tchr., youth "life" coordinator. Mem. Monticello Artist Assn. (sec. 1985-86). Club: Monticello Booster. Avocations: sports, horseback riding, cake decorating, traveling. Office: John C Corbin OD 115 W Marion Monticello IN 47960

SALSITZ, MALLORY GWYNNE, police officer; b. Bethesda, Md., Apr. 9, 1960; s. Richard Burton and Tanya (Ruskin) S. BA, Duke U., 1982; M in Pub. Policy Adminstrn., U. Wis., Madison, 1983—. Mktg. research coordinator, asst. product mgr., sales rep. Ohmeda Med. Products, Madison, 1982-85; police officer Madison Police Dept., 1986—. Mem. Wis. Profl. Police Assn., Madison Profl. Police Officers Assn. Democrat. Avocations: photography, athletics, horseback riding. Home: 2123 Rosenberry Rd #7 Madison WI 53711

SALTER, EDWIN CARROLL, physician; b. Oklahoma City, Jan. 19, 1927; s. Leslie Ernest and Maud (Carroll) S.; m. Ellen Gertrude Malone, June 30, 1962; children—Mary Susanna, David Patrick. B.A., DePauw U., 1947; M.D., Northwestern U., 1951. Intern Cook County Hosp., Chgo., 1951-53; resident in pediatrics Children's Meml. Hosp., Chgo., 1956-58, Cook County Hosp., Chgo., 1956-58; practice medicine specializing in pediatrics Lake Forest, Ill., 1958—; attending physician Lake Forest Hosp., 1958—, pres. med. staff, 1981-82; attending physician Children's Meml. Hosp., Chgo.; clin. faculty mem. dept. pediatrics Northwestern U. Med. Sch. Served to capt. M.C., U.S. Army, 1954-56. Mem. AMA, Ill. State Med. Soc., Lake County Med. Soc. (pres. 1984), Phi Beta Kappa. Republican. Methodist. Home: 19 N Maywood Rd Lake Forest IL 60045 Office: 800 Westmoreland Rd Lake Forest IL 60045

SALTER, RICHARD JAY, accountant, lawyer; b. Chgo., June 26, 1955; s. Marvin Jerome and Grace (Overall) S.; m. Anne Elizabeth Schutz, Oct. 16, 1982; 1 child, Matthew. BS, DePaul U., 1977; JD, Ill. Inst. Technology, 1981. CPA, Ill. Mem. tax staff Lester Witte, Chgo., 1976-83; tax supr. Oppenheimer, Appel, Dixon, Chgo., 1983-84; tax mgr. Friedman, Eisenstein, Raemer & Schwartz, Rolling Meadows, Ill., 1984—. Mem. ABA, Ill. Bar Assn., Am. Inst. CPA's, Ill. CPA Soc. Avocations: road rallies, tennis, bowling. Office: Friedman Eisenstein et al 1701 Golf Rd Rolling Meadows IL 60008

SALZMAN, ARTHUR GEORGE, architect; b. Chgo., June 20, 1929; s. Russell Harvey Salzman and Mildred Olive (Olsen) Erickson; m. Joan Marie Larson, Aug. 16, 1952; children: Lisa Jo Salzman Braucher, David Ralph. BS in Archtl. Engring., U. Ill., 1952; MArch, Ill. Inst. Tech., 1960. Registered architect, Ill. Architect Skidmore, Owings & Merrill, Chgo., 1960, Mies van der Rohe, Arch., Chgo., 1960-69; assoc. The Office of Mies Van Der Rohe, Chgo., 1969-81; v.p. FCL Assocs., Chgo., 1981-86; ex. v.p. Lohan Assocs., Chgo., 1986—. Mem. Chgo. Com. on High Rise Bldgs.; bd. dirs. Savoy Aires, Evanston, 1985—; v.p. Chgo. area Unitarian-Universalist Council, Chgo., 1974-76. Served to corp. U.S. Army, 1952-54. Mem. AIA, Constrn. Specifications Inst., Bldg. Ofcls. and Code Adminstrs. Internat., Inc. (profl.). Club: Cliff Dwellers. Avocations: community theater, choral singing, sailing. Home: 1018 Greenwood St Evanston IL 60201 Office: Lohan Assocs 225 N Mich Ave Chicago IL 60601

SALZMAN, STANLEY E., health science facility administrator; b. Shawano, Wis., Mar. 23, 1941; s. Elmer R. Salzman; m. Diane C. Schroeder, June 9, 1962; children: Michael, Wade. BS, Wis. State U., 1964; MBA, U. Tulsa, 1970. Ins. claim rep. Mutual of Wausau (Wis.), Inc., 1964-66; adminstr. Orthopedic Clinic, Tulsa, 1966-70; asst. adminstr. Duluth (Minn.) Clinic, Ltd., 1971-75, adminstr., 1976-81, exec. dir., 1982—; bd. dirs., mem. exec. com. Duluth Growth Corp. Fellow Am. Coll. Med. Group Adminstrs.; mem. Accreditation Assn. for Ambulatory Health Care (bd. dirs. 1985—), Med. Group Mgmt. Assn. (pres. midwest section 1986-87). Lutheran. Clubs: Kitchi Gammi (Duluth), Northland Country. Avocation: golf. Home: 2704 E 5th St Duluth MN 55812 Office: The Duluth Clinic Ltd 400 E 3d St Duluth MN 55805

SALZMAN, STEVEN SAMUEL, architect, health consultant; b. Chgo., Jan. 20, 1957; s. Wallace and Geraldine (Dintzis) S.; m. Lisa Ruttenberg, Aug. 24, 1985. BAS, U. Ill., 1979. Owner, mgr. Salzman Constrn., Chgo., 1979-83; sr. ptnr. Archetype, Chgo., 1981-83; pres. S.S. Syntec, Ltd., Chgo., 1983—; pres., health cons. L.I.F.E. Group, Inc., Chgo., 1986—; cons. real estate Salzman Assocs., Chgo., 1982—. Mem. Ravenswood Community Coalition, Chgo., 1987. Jewish. Avocations: skiing, reading, woodworking, music, writing. Office: S S Syntec Ltd 114 S Racine Ave Chicago IL 60607

SALZMANN, DONALD FREDERICK, manufacturing executive; b. St. Louis, Aug. 7, 1930; s. Frederick H. and Norma J. (Schmidt) S.; m. Lois Ann Blatt; children: Cynthia, Christian, John, Anne. BS in Indsl. Engring., Washington U., St. Louis, 1952. Registered profl. engr., Mo. Salesman Wagner Electric, Chgo., 1954-59; original equipment sales mgr. Wagner Electric, St. Louis, 1959-67, mktg. dir., 1967-77; dir. sales and mktg. Brake Parts Co. subs. Echlin Inc., McHenry, Ill., 1977-80; pres. Blackstone Mfg. Co. Inc. subs. Echlin Inc., Chgo., 1980—; chmn. Brake Systems Parts Mfrs. Council, Washington, 1975-77. Served to sgt. U.S. Army, 1952-54. Mem. Soc. Automotive Engrs., Mo. Soc. Profl. Engrs. Republican. Lutheran. Avocations: boating, hunting, fishing. Home: 815 Woodbine Ln Northbrook IL 60062 Office: Blackstone Mfg Co Inc 4630 W Harrison Chicago IL 60644

SALZMANN, ROBERT DONALD, dentist; b. Fond du Lac, Wis., Jan. 5, 1948; s. Peter Walter and Beatrice Elizabeth (Dellger) S.; m. Johanna Marie Kaiser, Aug. 8, 1970; children: Tracy Debra, Jill Elizabeth. Student, U. Wis., Oshkosh, 1966-68; DDS, Marquette U., 1972. Practice dentistry Madison, Wis., 1972—; treas. Profl. Dental Plan, Inc., 1985—; program chmn. Greater Madison Dental Study Group, 1979-80; cons. Group Health Coop., Madison, 1985. Mem. PTO bd. Orchard Ridge Middle Sch., Madison, 1982-85; speaker Jefferson Middle Sch., Madison, 1985, 86, Huegle Elem. Sch., Madison, 1976-86. Mem. ADA, Wis. Dental Assn. (alt. del. to state conv. 1985, Continuing Edn. award 1982-84), Dane County Dental Soc. (chmn. program adminstrn. 1985-86, chmn. mktg. program 1986, new dentists com. 1978, trustee 1982), Sigma Tau Gamma, Delta Sigma Delta. Clubs: Madison Curling, Cen. Wis. Porsche of Am. (Madison). Avocations: scuba diving, curling, running, tennis, softball. Home: 2314 Prairie Rd Madison WI 53711 Office: 5520 Medical Circle Madison WI 53719

SAMBORN, J. WARREN, corporate executive; b. Hollywood, Calif., Dec. 12, 1931; s. Jack A. and Margaret (Langdon) S.; m. Patricia Sperry, Aug. 21, 1955; children—Anne Melinda, Amy Elizabeth. B.S., U. Calif.-Berkeley, 1953; M.B.A., Golden Gate U., 1960. Pres. GATX Leasing Corp., San Francisco, 1969-85; pres., chief operating officer GATX Corp., Chgo., 1985—. Office: GATX Corp 120 S Riverside Plaza Chicago IL 60606

SAMDAHL, DAVID ANTHONY, micro-electronic manufacturing executive; b. Eau Claire, Wis., Oct. 10, 1958; s. Carl David and Eda Karen (Stokke) S.; m. Allison Gail Swanson, June 1, 1985. BS, U. Wis.-Stout, Menomonie, 1981. Dist. sales engr. Eaton Corp., Edina, Minn., 1981-84; with investment sales Metropolitan, St. Paul, 1984-85; product mgr. Wilbrecht Electronics, St. Paul, 1985-87; nat. sales mgr. H.E.I. Opto-Electronics Inc., Victoria, Minn., 1987—. Author: songs. Recipient 1st Place Photo Posing award Model Assn. Am. Internat., 1984, 1st Place Regional Image award Model Assn. Am. Internat., 1984. Mem. Minn. Music Acad., Nashville Songwriters Assn., Basement Investors Club of Am. Republican. Lutheran. Avocations: singing, talent competitions, songwriting, physical fitness. Home: 3625 Gettysburg Ave S #42 White Oak Saint Louis Park MN 55426 Office: HEI Opto-Electronics Inc 1495 Steiger Lake Ln Victoria MN 55386

SAMELSON, CHARLES FREDERICK, psychiatrist; b. Milw., Nov. 10, 1917; s. William and Sarah Samelson; m. Natalie Rudeis, May 1, 1949; children: Lawrence E., Daniel. MD, U. Ill., Chgo., 1943. Diplomate Am. Bd. Neurology and Psychiatry. Intern U.S. Naval Hosp., San Diego, 1944; resident in psychiatry Michael Reese Hosp., Chgo., 1946-49, sr. attending psychiatrist, 1949—; resident in psychiatry Inst. for Psychoanalysis, 1955-60; practice medicine specializing in psychiatry Chgo., 1962—; cons. psychiatrist Schwab Rehab. Ctr. Mt. Sinai, Chgo., 1962—, pres. med. staff, 1982-86; asst. prof. psychiatry Rush-Presbyn. St. Luke's Med. Ctr., Chgo., 1975—, sleep research service, 1979—; cons. local nursing homes, Chgo., 1985—. Inventor oral appliance for sleep apnea. Bd. dirs. Save the Dunes Council, Ind., 1962-85, Open Lands Projects, Chgo., 1962-86. Served to lt. USNR, 1944-46, PTO. Mem. AMA, Ill. Psychiat. Soc., Ill. Med. Assn., Chgo. Med. Assn. Avocations: concerts, plays, hiking, reading, cycling. Home: 5712 S Kenwood Ave Chicago IL 60637 Office: 30 N Michigan Ave Chicago IL 60602

SAMPLES, IRIS LYNETTE, teacher; b. Ravenna, Ohio, July 28, 1948; d. Enzo Joseph and Iris Lynette (Wiley) Lanari; m. Charles Victor Samples, Aug. 24, 1968. BS in Edn., Kent State U., 1973; postgrad. in Reading Instruction, U. Akron, 1977-79. Cert. tchr., Ohio. Tchr. first grade Highland Local Schs., Medina County, Ohio, 1968-72; tchr. first grade Barberton (Ohio) City Schs., 1973-77, reading tchr., 1977—; mem. faculty adv. com. Woodford Sch., 1982—, sch. levy com. Barberton City Schs., 1982. tchr. Bible sch., Sunday Sch. First Lutheran Ch., 1978-82, coordinator Christmas program, 1979-80; vol. various health founds., 1975—. Jennings Scholar 1984—. Mem. NEA, Ohio Edn. Assn., NE Ohio Tchrs. Assn., Barbeton Tchrs. Assn. (past bldg. rep.), Woodford PTA (past program chmn.), Internat. Reading Assn. (Akron area council), Kappa Delta Pi, Delta Kappa Gamma. Lutheran. Avocations: seminars, gardening, fitness. Home: 670 E Paige Ave Barberton OH 44203 Office: Woodford Elementary Sch 315 E State St Barberton OH 44203

SAMPSON, GEORGE H., flower delivery company executive. Pres. Florists' Transworld Delivery Assn., Southfield, Mich. Office: Florists' Transworld Delivery Assn 29200 Northwestern Hwy Southfield MI 48037 *

SAMPSON, JEFFERY DILLARD, information systems engineer; b. Dayton, Ohio, May 17, 1959; s. Robert Eugene and Zoie Louise (Grayer) S.; m. Charlene Marie Butler, June 14, 1986. B Indsl. Adminstrn., Gen. Motors Inst., 1982. Assoc. programmer Delco Moraine div. Gen. Motors Corp., Dayton, Ohio, 1982-83, programmer, analyst, 1983-85, systems engr. Electronic Data Systems, 1985—. Democrat. Baptist. Avocations: basketball, model cars, reading, photography, music. Office: Delco Moraine div Gen Motors 1420 Wisconsin Blvd Dayton OH 45401

SAMPSON, ROGER M., manufacturing company executive; b. 1933. BS, U. Minn., 1956, MBA, 1958. With Mpls. Honeywell, 1953-59, Kirst & Sampson, 1959-68; with Barber-Colman Co., 1968—, group v.p., 1973-75, pres., chief exec. officer, 1975—, also chmn. bd. dirs., 1984—. Office: Barber-Colman Co 555 Colman Center Dr Rockford IL 61125 *

SAMPSON, ROGER WAYNE, transportation company executive; b. Long Prairie, Minn., Mar. 23, 1947; s. Millard and Ardelle (Anderson) S.; m. Susan Elizabeth Orton, Sept. 12, 1970; 1 child, Aaron. BA in Acctg., St. Cloud State U., 1972. CPA, Wis. Staff acct. Main Hurdman Co., Mpls., 1973-74, sr. auditor, 1975-77; auditor CW Transport, Inc., Wisconsin Rapids, 1977-79, comptroller, 1979-85, v.p., sec., treas., 1985—. Served to sgt. U.S. Army, 1965-68, Vietnam. Mem. Am. Inst. CPA's, Vietnam Vets. Am. (treas. Wis. Rapids chpt. 1984-86). Home: 2511 Country Ln Wisconsin Rapids WI 54494 Office: CW Transport Inc 610 High St Box 200 Wisconsin Rapids WI 54494

SAMPSON, WILLIAM ROBERT, JR., communication and theater arts educator, administrator; b. Detroit, Apr. 23, 1942; s. William Robert and Alice Juanita (Jones) S.; m. Sharon Kay Miner, Feb. 27, 1970 (div. Jan. 1982); children: William Robert, Michael Stanton; m. Karin Lee Menzel, Jan. 31, 1983; 1 child, Andrew Peter. BA, Western Mich. U., 1964; MA, Wayne State U., 1967, PhD, 1973. Tchr. Utica (Mich.) Community Schs., 1964-66; instr. Macomb County Community Coll., Mich., 1966-68; asst. prof. Ferris State Coll., Big Rapids, Mich., 1968-72, assoc. prof., 1972-76; assoc. prof. Ea. Mich. U., Ypsilanti, 1976-80; dir. grad. bus. programs, 1978-80, assoc. dean Coll. Bus., 1979-80; chmn., prof. dept. communication and theater arts U. Wis., Eau Claire, 1980—; organizational communication tng. and devel. cons. Editor Wis. Communication Assn. Jour. Bd. dirs. Chippewa Valley Theatre Guild. Recipient Ferris State Coll. Bd. Control, 1972. Mem. Acad. Mgmt., Am. Soc. Tng. and Devel., Internat. Communication Assn., Speech Communication Assn. Congregationalist. Home: 6650 South Shore Dr Altoona WI 54720 Office: U Wis Dept Communication and Theatre Arts Eau Claire WI 54701

SAMTER, MAX, physician, educator; b. Berlin, Germany, Mar. 3, 1908; came to U.S., 1937; s. Paul and Claire (Rawicz) S.; m. Virginia Svarz Ackerman, Oct. 17, 1947; 1 dau., Virginia Claire. Student, U. Freiburg, Germany, 1926, U. Innsbruck, Austria, 1928; M.D., U. Berlin, 1933. Diplomate: Am. Bd. Internal Medicine (past chmn. bd. allergy), Am. Bd. Allergy and Immunology. Intern, resident Medizinische Universitätsklinik der Charité, Berlin, 1931-33; practice medicine Berlin-Karow, Germany, 1933-37; asst. dispensary physician hematology Johns Hopkins Hosp., 1937-38; guest fellow anatomy U. Pa. Sch. Medicine, 1938-43; research asso. dept. biochemistry U. Ill., Chgo., 1946-47; instr. asst. prof., asso. prof., prof. dept. medicine, 1948-69; prof. medicine Abraham Lincoln Sch. Medicine, 1969—, asso. dean for clin. affairs, 1974-75; chief staff U. Ill. Hosp., 1974-75; sr. cons. allery and clin. immunology Max Samter Inst., Chgo., 1975—; cons. in allergy U.S. VA, 1962—. Editor: American Lectures in Allergy, 1950, (with Oren C. Durham) Regional Allergy, 1954, (with Harry L. Alexander) Immunological Diseases, 1965, 71, 78, Excerpts from Classics in Allergy, 1969, (with Charles W. Parker) Hypersensitivity to Drugs, 1972; also articles in field. Served to capt. M.C. AUS, 1943-46, ETO. Recipient Disting. Faculty award U. Ill. Coll. Med. 1987. Fellow ACP; mem. AMA, Am. Acad. Allergy (past pres.), Internat. Assn. Allergology (past pres.), Phila. Coll. Physicians (hon.), Interasma (hon.), Sigma Xi, Alpha Omega Alpha. Home: 645 Sheridan Rd Evanston IL 60202 Office: 550 W Webster Ave Chicago IL 60614

SAMUEL, ROBERT THOMPSON, optometrist; b. Kansas City, Mo., June 27, 1944; s. Manlius Thompson and Helen Evelyn (Syverson) S. B.A., William Jewell Coll., 1966; postgrad. U. Mo.-Kansas City, 1967, M.S. U. Mo., 1968; D. Optometry, U. Tenn.-Memphis, 1971. Cert. optometrist, Mo. Buyer Recco, Inc., Kansas City, Mo., 1963-67; histology lab. instr. William Jewell Coll., Liberty, Mo., 1965-66; pvt. practice optometry Gladstone, Mo., 1972—; panel doctor Ford Motor Co., Claycomo, Mo., 1985—, Union Pacific R.R., Kansas City, 1985—. Publicity coordinator Republican Party, Kansas City, Mo., 1975-76; chmn. Save Your Vision Week, Kansas City, 1977; mem. Theatre League of Kansas City, 1976—, Friends of Art, 1985. Recipient Outstanding Young Men of Am. award Jaycees, 1978. Mem. Am. Optometric Assn., Mo. Optometric Assn., Heart of Am. Contact Lens Congress, Am. Acad. Sports Vision, Smithsonian Assocs. Republican. Lutheran. Lodge: Lions (exec. bd. dirs. Lions Eye Clinic 1974-84, bd. dirs. Lions Eye Clinic 1982—, Outstanding Service award 1973, 74, editor Lions Optometric Ctr. Quar., 1974-84). Avocations: photography, music, piano, swimming.

Home: 6325 N Monroe St Gladstone MO 64119 Office: 2700 Kendallwood Pkwy Suite 109 Gladstone MO 64119

SAMUELS, GARY ALAN, financial consultant; b. Detroit, Nov. 1, 1958; s. Aubrey Theodore and Dorian (Hirsch) S. BEE summa cum laude, U. Mich., 1979, MS in Indsl. Engring., 1980. Salesman Olson Electronics, Detroit, 1978-79; resident advisor U. Mich., Ann Arbor, 1978-79; systems engr. IBM Corp., Dearborn, Mich., 1980-83; mktg. rep. IBM Corp., Detroit, 1984-87; fin. cons. Merrill Lynch, Bloomfield Hills, Mich., 1987—. Regents Alumni scholar U. Mich., 1976; Rackham Grad. Sch. scholar U. Mich., 1980. Mem. Tau Beta Pi (treas. 1979-80), Eta Kappa Nu (v.p. 1979-80). Avocations: tennis, squash, swimming, skiing. Office: Merrill Lynch 2100 N Woodward Suite 265 Bloomfield Hills MI 48013

SAMUELS, JANET IRENE, nurse; b. Mexico, Mo., Apr. 14, 1957; d. Marion Edmund and Ella Elizabeth (Knecht) Schoning; m. Grover Thomas Samuels, Jan. 14, 1983; stepchildren: Jeff, Amy, Jason, Kristen. Diploma in nursing, St. Luke's Sch. Nursing, Kansas City, 1978; BS in Nursing, Webster U., 1986. RN; cert. neurosci. RN. Staff nurse Boone Hosp., Columbia, Mo., 1978-79, asst. head nurse, 1979-80, head nurse neurology, 1980-86, med. surg. float nurse, 1986, coordinator dementia screening, 1986—. Co-author (video) Alzheimer's Disease: Tips for Caregivers, 1987; author brochures. Mem. Citizens for Adult Day Care, Columbia, 1984—, Mid-Mo. chpt. Alzheimer's Disease and Related Disorders, 1987. Mem. Am. Assn. Neurosci. Nurses (sec.-treas. Cen. Midwest chpt. 1983-85), Am. Nurses Assn., Mo. Nurses Assn., Assn. Rehab. Nurses, Mo. League Nursing. Avocations: softball, bowling, sewing, cooking, canoeing. Home: 301 Broadview Ct Columbia MO 65201 Office: Boone Hosp Ctr 1600 E Broadway Columbia MO 65201

SAMUELS, MARSHALL WILLIAM, manufacturing company executive, accountant; b. Cleve., Jan. 22, 1941; s. John Arnold and Miriam Lee (Wolf) S.; m. Rochelle Joyce Gerritt, July 22, 1962; children: David, Caroline. BS, Northwestern U., 1962; MBA, U. Chgo., 1967. CPA, Ill., N.Y. Acct. Coopers & Lybrand, Chgo. and N.Y.C., 1962-75; treas. Cerro Corp., Chgo., 1975-76; pvt. practice cons. Chgo., 1977-78, pvt. practice acctg., 1979-86; v.p. fin. and adminstrn. Riverside Mfg. Co., Chgo., 1979—; bd. dirs. Westbank, Inc., Westchester, Ill. Author: (several chapters in) Montgomery's Auditing, 1973. Mem. Am. Inst. CPA's, Ill. CPA Soc., N.Y. State Soc. CPA's, Am. Acctg. Assn. Jewish. Avocation: piano. Home: 550 Sheridan Rd Highland Park IL 60035 Office: Riverside Mfg Co 2846 W North Ave Chicago IL 60647

SAMUELS, ROBERT T., supermarket chain executive; b. 1934. Student, Case Western Res. U. Pres. M.H. Hausman Co., 1978; sr. v.p. corp. mgmt. First Nat. Supermarkets Inc., Cleve., 1978-79, sr. v.p. adminstrn., 1979-81; sr. v.p., pres. Eastern div. First Nat. Supermarkets Inc., 1981; then exec. v.p., pres. Eastern div. First Nat. Supermarkets Inc., Cleve.; now corp. pres., chief operating officer Maple Heights, Ohio; also dir. Office: 1st Nat Supermarkets Inc 17000 Rockside Rd Maple Heights OH 44137 *

SAN, NGUYEN DUY, psychiatrist; b. Langson, Vietnam, Sept. 25, 1932; s. Nguyen Duy and Tran Tuyet (Trang) Quyen; came to Can., 1971, naturalized, 1977; M.D., U. Saigon, 1960; postgrad. U. Mich., 1970; m. Eddie Jean Ciesielski, Aug. 24, 1971; children—Megan Thuloan, Muriel Mylinh, Claire Kimlan, Robin Xuanlan, Baodan Edward. Intern, Cho Ray Hosp., Saigon, 1957-58; resident Univ. Hosp., Ann Arbor, Mich., 1968-70, Lafayette Clinic, Detroit, 1970-71, Clarke Inst. Psychiatry, Toronto, Ont., Can., 1971-72; chief of psychiatry South Vietnamese Army, 1964-68; staff psychiatrist Queen St. Mental Health Center, Toronto, 1972-74; unit dir. Homewood San., Guelph, Ont., 1974-80; cons. psychiatrist Guelph Gen. Hosp., St. Joseph's Hosp., Guelph; practice medicine specializing in psychiatry, Guelph, 1974-80; unit dir. inpatient service Royal Ottawa (Ont., Can.) Hosp., 1980-84, dir. psychiat. rehab. program, 1985-87; asst. prof. psychiatry U. Ottawa Med. Sch., 1980-85, assoc. prof. psychiatry, 1985-87; bd. dirs. East-West Mental Health Ctr., Toronto; cons. UN High Commr. for Refugees, 1987—. Served with Army Republic of Vietnam, 1953-68. Mem. Can. Med. Assn., Can., Am. psychiat. assns., Am. Soc. Clin. Hypnosis, Internat. Soc. Hypnosis, N.Y. Acad. Scis. Buddhist. Author: Etude du Tetanos au Vietnam, 1960; (with others) The Psychology and Physiology of Stress, 1969, Psychosomatic Medicine, theoretical, clinical, and transcultural aspects, 1983, Uprooting, Loss and Adaptation, 1984, Southeast Asian Mental Health, 1985.

SANCHEZ, ROSIE LEE, business educator; b. St. Joseph, La., Apr. 7, 1944; d. Ike Bellows, Jr. and Ophelia (Hartley) Bellows McDonald; div., 1 child, Darryl. B.S. in Bus. Edn., Langston U., 1967; M.A. in Bus. Edn., Govs. State U., University Park, Ill., 1981. Cert. bus. edn. instr., Ill. Tchr. 4th and 5th grades McClellan Sch., Chgo., 1967-68; tchr. coordinator Headstart Sch., Hominy, Okla., 1972-74, PREP Progam, Joliet, Ill., 1978-79; instr. STAT-TAB Tng. Ctr., Chgo., 1982-83, curriculum specialist, 1983-86; employment assessor Govs. State U., 1985-86; dir. placement Ill. Med. Tng. Ctr., Chgo., 1986—; instr. summer youth program in career edn. Govs. State U., 1979. Recipient Coop. Vocat. Edn. commendation Chgo. Bd. Edn., 1983. Baptist. Avocations: reading, sports, horticulture. Home: 709 Burnham Dr Apt 4B University Park IL 60466 Office: Ill Med Tng Ctr 162 N State St Chicago IL 60601

SAND, RICHARD EUGENE, allergy and immunology physician; b. Cin., Feb. 2, 1931; s. Harry Joseph and Lulu Louise (Schray) S.; m. Margaret Catanzaro, Feb. 21, 1975 (div. Sept. 1984); children: Barbara Melissa, Jonathon Parker; m. Cynthia Ratté, Oct. 19, 1985. BS, U. Cin., 1953, MD, 1957. Diplomate Am. Bd. Allergy and Immunology, Am. Bd. Pediatrics. Intern, then resident U.S. Naval Hosps., Portsmouth, Va. and Phila., 1957-61; chief dept. pediatrics U.S. Naval Hosps., Key West, Fla., 1961-63; staff physician St. Paul Allergy Clinic, 1963—, Children's Hosp., St. Paul, 1963—, United Hosps., St. Paul, 1964—; co-chmn. pediatric allergy clinic Children's Hosp., 1974—; chief of staff Children's Hosp., 1974; clin. asst. prof. U. Minn. Med. Sch., Mpls., 1977—; pres., chief exec. officer St. Paul Allergy Clinic, Mpls., 1985—. Bd. dirs. People, Inc., St. Paul, 1978-81, Am. Lung Assn. Asthma Camp Hennepin County, 1970-80. Served to lt. commdr. USN, 1957-63. Mem. AMA, Am. Coll. Allergists, Am. Acad. Allergy and Immunology, N.Cen. Allergy Soc., Am. Acad. Pediatrics, Am. Acad. Family Physicians (Teaching award 1975-83). Avocations: tennis, camping, sailing, travel. Office: St Paul Allergy Clinic 565 Snelling Ave S Saint Paul MN 55116

SANDAGE, ELIZABETH ANTHEA, advertising educator; b. Larned, Kans., Oct. 13, 1930; d. Curtis Carl and Beulah Pauline (Knupp) Smith; student Okla. State U., 1963-65; B.S., U. Colo., 1967; M.A., 1970; Ph.D. in Communications U. Ill., 1983; m. Charles Harold Sandage, July 18, 1971; children by previous marriage—Diana Louise Danner White, David Alan Danner. Pub. relations rep., editor Martin News, Martin Marietta Corp., Denver, 1960-63, 65-67; retail advt. salesperson Denver Post, 1967-70; instr. advt. U. Ill., 1970-71, vis. lectr. advt., 1977-84; v.p., corp. sec., dir. Farm Research Inst., Urbana, 1984—. Exec. dir. Sandage Charitable Trust, 1986—. Mem. Am. Acad. Advt., Am. Assn. Edn. in Journalism and Mass Communications, Sigma Delta Chi, Kappa Tau Alpha. Republican. Presbyterian. Editor: Occasional Papers in Advertising, 1971; The Sandage Family Cookbook, 1976; The Inkling, Carle Hosp. Aux. Newsletter, 1975-76. Home: 106 The Meadows Urbana IL 61801

SANDBERG, RYNE, professional baseball player; b. Spokane, Wash., Sept. 19, 1959; s. Derwent and Elizabeth S.; m. Cindy White; children—Lindsey, Justin. Profl. baseball player Phila. Phillies, 1981; profl. baseball player Chgo. Cubs, 1982—. Recipient Gold Glove, 2d base, Nat. League, 1983, 84; named Nat. League Most Valuable Player, 1984; Sporting News Players of Yr., 1984. Participant Nat. League All-Star Team, 1984, 85. Office: care Chgo Cubs Wrigley Field 1060 W Addison St Chicago IL 60613 *

SANDBULTE, AREND JOHN, utility executive; b. Sioux Center, Iowa, Dec. 9, 1933; s. Ben and Rena (Rensink) S.; m. Verna VanDeBerg, June 30, 1953; children: Ruth Marie, Gregory Bern, Kristin Ann, Rachel Lynn. B.S. in Elec. Engring., Iowa State U., 1959; M.B.A., U. Minn., 1966. Registered profl. engr., Minn., N.D., Wis. Rate engr. No. State Power Co., Mpls., 1959-64; with Minn. Power & Light Co., Duluth, 1964—; asst. v.p. budgets and corp. planning Minn. Power & Light Co., 1972-74, v.p. corp. planning, 1974-76, v.p. fin., chief fin. officer, 1976-78, sr. v.p. fin. and adminstrn., chief fin. officer, 1978-80, exec. v.p., chief fin. officer, 1980-83, exec. v.p., chief operating officer, chief fin. officer, dir., 1983-84, pres., chief operating officer, 1984—; bd. dirs. Norwest Bank, Duluth. Bd. dirs. Iowa State Regulatory Conf., 1986—, Northeastern Minn. Devel. Assn., 1987—, Minn. C. of C. and Industry, 1984—, St. Luke's Found., 1985—; mem. econ. devel. steering com. City of Duluth, 1984—; chmn. bd. trustees Coll. St. Scholastica, Duluth, 1984—, vice chmn. bd., 1983, trustee, 1979—; trustee St. Luke's Hosp., Duluth, 1977—, 1st v.p., 1980-82, chmn. bd., 1982-84; trustee Duluth YMCA, 1977—; bd. dirs. Ordean Found., 1983—, Duluth 1200 Fund, Inc., 1985—, Duluth Growth Co., 1983—, Minn. Safety Council, 1986—, bd. dirs. United Way, 1984—, campaign chmn., 1986; chmn. Duluth Indsl. Devel. Task Force, 1984—. Served with AUS, 1954-55. Recipient Nikola Tesla award Midwest Area Power Utilities, 1975; named Boss of Year, Duluth Jaycees, 1974. Mem. Edison Electric Inst., IEEE, Duluth Area C. of C. (pres. 1982). Republican. Presbyterian. Clubs: Mpls. Athletic (Mpls.); Kitchi Gammi (Duluth); Northland Country. Lodge: Kiwanis. Home: 2930 London Rd Duluth MN 55804 Office: Minn Power & Light Co 30 W Superior St Duluth MN 55802 *

SANDER, IVAN LEE, forester; b. Cape Girardeau, Mo., Mar. 13, 1928; s. Henry Frank and Marie (Kiehne) S.; m. Betty Ann Wendel Sander, June 12, 1949; children: Saundra, Deborah, Michael. BS in Forestry, U. Mo., 1952, MS in Forestry, 1953. Research forester USDA Forest Service, Berea, Ky., 1955-61, Athens, Ohio, 1961-66, Columbia, Mo., 1967—. Contbr. articles to profl. jours. Scoutmaster Boy Scouts Am., Columbia, 1957-77. Mem. Soc. Am. Foresters, Xi Sigma Pi. Lodge: Lions. Office: USDA Forest Service 1-26 Agrl Bldg U Mo Columbia MO 65211

SANDERFOOT, THOMAS ALOYSIUS, flexible packaging manufacturing executive; b. Appleton, Wis., July 17, 1954; s. Aloysius Jacob and Alice Jean (Meloen) S.; m. Eugenia Patricia Mueller, June 1, 1974; children: Natalie, Erica, Matthew. Student, USAF Acad., 1972-73; AAS, De Vry Inst. Tech., Chgo., 1975; student, Maricopa Community Coll., 1976-78, U. Wis., Green Bay, 1982-86. Quality control technician Sperry Flight Systems, Phoenix, 1975-78, electronics specialist, 1978-79; electrician Curwood, Inc., New London, Wis., 1979-80, elec. draftsman, 1980, elec. designer, 1980-84, supr. elec. maintenance, 1984—. Mem. Nat. Arbor Day Found., Nat. Audubon Soc., Electorial Bd. City of New London. Avocations: gardening, reading, camping, golf. Home: Rt 3 PO Box 396 New London WI 54961 Office: Curwood Inc 718 High St New London WI 54961

SANDERS, BARBARA ANN, materials engineer, scientist; b. New Orleans, Oct. 20, 1947; d. Otis and Arma (Atkins) Miles; m. Joe Sanders Jr., June 10, 1972. BS, So. U., Batan Rouge, 1969; MS, Rutgers U., 1972. Exptl. physicist materials engring. Gen. Motors, Warren, Mich., 1972, sr. project engr. materials engring., 1974, supr. materials engring., 1976-78, mgr. composites, 1978-83, dir. CAD/CAM, 1983-85, dir. artificial intelligence, 1985—. Contbr. articles to profl. jours. Mem. adv. bd. U. Delaware, Newark, 1982—; bd. dirs. Minority Tech. Council of Mich., Detroit, 1985—. Mem. Soc. Mfg. Engrs., Engring. Soc. Detroit, Am. Assn. Artificial Intelligence, So. U. Alumni Assn. (Outstanding Alumni 1982, 86), Women's Econ. Club of Detroit. Avocations: tennis, photography, reading. Office: Gen Motors Corp 30300 Mound Rd Warren MI 48090-9040

SANDERS, C. JANE, psychologist; b. San Marcos, Tex., Apr. 3, 1941; d. E. J. Hendon and Catherine Jane (Herndon) Wiegand; m. J. C. Sanders, Apr. 4, 1960 (div. Sept. 1962); 1 child, Mary Catherine Sanders Stoll. BS in Psychology, U. Iowa, 1970, MA in Rehab. Counseling, 1973, PhD in Counseling Psychology, 1980. Instr. Coll. Dentistry U. Iowa, Iowa City, 1973-75, intern Counseling Service, 1975-77; counselor VA Upward Bound program Kirkwood Community Coll., Cedar Rapids, Iowa, 1977-79, dir., 1979-80; owner, exec. officer Herndon Assocs., Cedar Rapids, 1980—; pvt. practice psychology Cedar Rapids, 1982—; cons. Iowa Merit Employment Mgmt. Tng. system, Cedar Rapids, 1980—. Contbr. articles to profl. jours. Bd. dirs. Linn County Human Resources Mgmt., Cedar Rapids, 1986—, Mental Health Advs., Cedar Rapids, 1986. Mem. AAUW, Am. Psychol. Assn., Iowa Psychol. Assn. (chair women in psychology 1986), Profl. Women's Network, Phi Delta Kappa, Pi Lambda Theta. Club: Quota. Avocations: gardening, reading, traveling, woodworking, community services. Office: 150 1st Ave NE Suite 350 Cedar Rapids IA 52401

SANDERS, DAVID JAMES, marketing professional; b. Norfolk, Nebr., Nov. 10, 1952; s. Leo Andrew and Frances Nina (Williss) S. BS, U. Nebr., 1975. Copywriter Swanson Sinkey Agy., Lincoln, 1974-75; mng. editor Behavioral Engring. Mag., Grand Island, Nebr., 1976-79; media buyer Gloria Aleff Agy., Waverly, Iowa, 1979-80; mgr. advt. Independence (Iowa) Newspaper, 1980-82; coordinator sales promotions Omaha World-Herald, 1982-86; dir. mktg. Papillion (Nebr.) Times, 1986—. Creator ads (1st Pl. award 1976, 82). State singles dir. Ch. of Nazarene, Nebr., 1985—; grad. Omaha C. of C. Leadership Omaha Program. Mem. Am. Mktg. Assn., Omaha Fed. Advt., Iowa Jaycees (state editor 1982-83), Nebr. Jaycees (state editor 1977-79). Democrat. Avocations: writing poetry, tennis, reading. Home: 2207 S 32d Ave Omaha NE 68105 Office: Papillion Times Printing Co 138 N Washington Papillion NE 68046

SANDERS, DIANE KATHLEEN, dietician; b. Kansas City, Mo., Oct. 26, 1950; d. C.R. and E.E. (Ernst) Sanders. BS, Kans. State U., 1973, MS, 1974. Registered dietician; cert. culinary educator. Clin. dietician St. Mary Hosp., Manhattan, Kans., 1973-75; instr. U.S.D. #383, Manhattan, 1975—; cons. Manhattan area nursing homes, 1974—; vol. nutritionist Head Start, Manhattan, 1973-74; coordinator Food Service Supr. Program, Manhattan, 1977—, continuong edn. course food service workers, Manhattan, 1982—. Bd. dirs. Wharton Manor Nursing Home, 1973-81, chmn., 1979. Avocations: water skiing, sailing. Home: 5012 Vista Acres Dr Manhattan KS 66502 Office: Manhattan Vocat Sch 3136 Dickens Ave Manhattan KS 66502

SANDERS, DONALD ROBERT, ophthalmologist; b. Chgo., Dec. 29, 1948; s. Herman and Barbara (Pinz) S.; m. Wanda Sanders; 1 child, Monica. BS in Biology, U. Ill., Chgo., 1971, MD, 1973, PhD in Pharmacology, 1984. Deiplomate Am. Bd. Ophthalmology. Intern and resident Eye and Ear Infirmary, Chgo., 1975-77; asst. prof. ophthalmology U. Ill., Chgo., 1977-81, assoc. prof., 1981—; chief VA Westside Hosp., Chgo., 1977—. Chief med. editor Ocular Surgery News, 1982—; editor: Principles and Practice of Ophthalmology, 1980, Refractive Corneal Surgery, 1986; author: Manual of Implant Power Calculation, 1982. Mem. Am. Acad. Ophthalmology, Am. Intraocular Implant Soc., Chgo. Ophthal. Soc., Am. Med. Writers Assn. Office: Univ Illinois 1855 W Taylor St Chicago IL 60612

SANDERS, GERALD HOLLIE, communications educator; b. Mt. Vernon, Tex., Dec. 10, 1924; s. Elmer Hugh and Velma Mae (Hollowell) S.; m. Mary Dean Crew, July 18, 1947; children: Michael Dwaine, Rose Ann, Susan Kathleen, Randall Wayne. BA, Southeastern Okla. U., 1947; MA, Tex. Tech U., 1969; PhD, U. Minn., 1974. Program dir. WEWO, Laurenburg, N.C., 1947-49; sports dir. KFYO, Lubbock, Tex., 1949-50; gen. mgr. KLVT, Levelland, Tex., 1950-51, 53-54; sports dir. KCUL, Ft. Worth, 1954-55; asst. mgr. KDAV, Lubbock, 1955-57; mgr. KCBD, Lubbock, 1957-58; with numerous broadcasting stas. Tex. and Okla., 1958-67; lectr. communications The Coll. of Wooster, Ohio, 1967-68; asst. prof. The Coll. of Wooster, 1968-75, assoc. prof., 1975-81; chmn. dept. communication The Coll. of Wooster, Ohio, 1974-81, Miami U., Oxford, Ohio, 1981—; cons. in field., Oxford, 1982—. Author: Introduction to Comtemporary Academic Debate, 1983; also articles. Active Dem. Political Campaigns. Served to col. USMC, 1943-46, PTO, 1951-53, Korea. Mem. Am. Forensic Assn. (pres. 1978-82), Speech Communication Assn., Speech Communication Assn. of Ohio (pres. 1976-77, Disting. Service award 1978), Cen. States Speech Assn. Presbyterian. Avocations: sports, political campaigns. Home: 200 Country Club Ln Oxford OH 45056 Office: Miami U Dept Communication Oxford OH 45056

SANDERS, JAMES RUSSELL, anesthesiologist; b. Vandalia, Ill., Nov. 9, 1952; s. Lawrence Kendall and Mildred Pearl (Hunter) S.; m. Brenda Susan Behnke, Sept. 14, 1973. BA cum laude, Greenville (Ill.) Coll., 1975; MD, U. Ill., Rockford, 1980. Diplomate Am. Bd. Anesthesiology, Nat. Bd. Med. Examiners. Intern Barnes Hosp., St. Louis, 1980-81, resident in anesthesiology, 1981-83; chief resident anesthesiology Barnes Hosp., 1982-83; fellow Children'S Hosp., Phila., 1983-84; anesthesiologist Rockford Anesthesiologists Assoc., 1984—. Mem. AMA, Am. Soc. Anesthesiologists, Ill. State Med. Soc., Internat. Anesthesia Research Soc. Avocations: camping, scuba diving, snorkeling, photography. Home: 5297 McFarland Rd Rockford IL 61111 Office: Rockford Anesthesiologists Associated 2929 N Main Rockford IL 61125

SANDERS, JUDITH CHAPLINE, psychotherapist; b. Chgo., Mar. 2, 1941; d. John Robert and Elsie Alice (Downing) Chapline; m. Philip Richard Terrill, Aug. 17, 1963 (div. Sept. 1983); children: John, Jeffrey; m. Bill L. sanders, Apr. 21, 1984. BA, Ind. U., 1963, MS, 1964. Cert. sex therapist and counselor, Ind. Psychotherapist Child Guidance Ctr., Ft. Wayne, Ind., 1965-68, Park Ctr., Ft. Wayne, 1975—. Bd. dirs. Jr. League Ft. Wayne, 1975-78, McMillen Ctr. Health Edn., Ft. wayne, 1977—. Mem. Internat. Transactional Analysis Assn., Am. Group Psychotherapy Assn., Am. Assn. Sex Educators, Counselors and Therapists, Phobia Soc. Am., Phi Beta Kappa. Office: Park Ctr 909 E State Blvd Fort Wayne IN 46805

SANDERSON, KEITH WAYNE, advertising executive; b. Albany, N.Y., Apr. 23, 1945; s. Lester Stanley and Elizabeth Amy (Paine) S.; m. Helen Marie Pedersen, Sept. 12, 1970; children: Christine Marie, Keith Michael. BA, Monmouth (Ill.) Coll., 1969. Advt. mgr. Bucyrus-Erie Co., South Milwaukee, Wis., 1971-79; advt. and sales promotion mgr. Koehring Co., Milw., 1979-82; acct. supr. Grant/Jacoby, Inc., Chgo., 1982-84; gen. mgr. Andrews/Mautner, Inc., Northbrook, Ill., 1984-87; v.p. Andrews/Mautner, Inc., Northbrook, 1987—; also bd. dirs. Andrews/Mautner, Inc. Mem. Bus. Profl. Advt. Assn. (bd. dirs. 1977-79), Constrn. Equipment Advertisers Assn. Avocations: sailing, reading, writing fiction. Home: 211 Willow Ave Deerfield IL 60015 Office: Andrews/Mautner Inc 5 Revere Dr Suite 200 Northbrook IL 60062

SANDERSON, ROBERT LESTER, printing executive; b. Dixon, Ill., Dec. 7, 1952; s. Lester Eber and Rogene Eleanor (Ulferts) S. BA, Rockford Coll., 1974. Adminstrv. mgr. Combined Communication Services, Inc., Oreg., Ill., 1974-77; exec. v.p. Combined Communication Services, Inc., Mendota, Ill., 1977-80, pres., 1980—. Mem. Phi Beta Kappa. Office: Combined Communication Services Inc 901 Warrenville Rd Suite 206 Lisle IL 60532

SANDLER, ALBERT N. (ALBERT NATHAN SANDLER), radiologist; b. St. Louis, Dec. 1, 1930; s. Lewis N. and Dorothy (Zimmerman) S.; m. Lillian Jean Muchnick, Aug. 1965; children: Scott Louis, Bradley Jay. BS, MA in Edn., Northeast Mo. State U., 1962; DO, Kirksville Coll. Osteopathic Medicine, 1970. Diplomate Am. Bd. Radiology. Tchr., coach Webster Groves Sch., Mo., 1961-62, Parkway Sch. Dist., Chesterfield, Mo., 1962-66; emergency physician Normandy (Mo.) Osteopathic Hosp., 1970-73, resident in radiology, 1973-76; radiologist Radiol. Cons., Des Peres, Mo., 1977—; head resident program Radiol. Cons., 1982-83, 85—, chief radiology dept. Active Am. Cancer Soc., St. Louis; mem. Friends of St. Louis Art Mus., 1984, Mo. Hist. Soc., 1984, Wildlife Soc, St. Louise, 1984. Served to cpl. U.S. Army, 1952-54. Mem. Am. Coll. Osteopathic Radiology (cert.), Am. Coll. Radiology, Mo. Osteopathic Assn., St. Louis Osteopathic Assn., Mo Osteopathic Radiologists. Republican. Home: #7 Clayton Hills Ln Town and Country MO 63131 Office: Normandy Osteopathic Hosp S 530 Des Peres Rd Des Peres MO 63131

SANDLIAN, LANCE BRADFORD, real estate developer; b. Wichita, Kans., Apr. 13, 1956; s. Colby B. and Jane Sandlian; children: Darah, Colby. Grad., High Sch., Wichita, 1975. Asst. Mico Investment Co., Kansas City, Mo., 1977-78; site supr. Sandlian Realty Co., Clearwater, Fla., 1978-83; comml. developer Sandlian Investment Co., Indpls., 1983—; cons. self storage industry, 1983—, comml. market analyst, 1983—. Mem. Builder's Assn. Indpls., Ind. Forum Civil Justice, Indpls. C. of C., Nat. Rifle Assn. Republican. Club: Columbia (Indpls.). Lodge: Masons. Avocations: skeet, tennis, hunting, fishing, backpacking. Office: Sandlian Investment Co 5637 Georgetown Rd Indianapolis IN 46254

SANDLIN, BARBARA JEAN, accountant; b. Richmond, Ind., Apr. 17, 1958; d. Robert Leon and Jean Anne (Hartman) Gard; m. George Sandlin, Nov. 19, 1983. BS, Ball State U., 1980. CPA, Ind. Staff acct. George S. Olive & Co., Richmond, 1980-82, sr. acct., 1982—. Mem. Nat. Assn. Accts., Am. Inst. CPA'S, Ind. CPA Soc. Home: 7903 US 127 N Lewisburg OH 45338 Office: George S Olive & Co 808 South A St Richmond IN 47374

SANDMIRE, HERBERT, physician; b. Richland Ctr., Wis., Apr. 9, 1929; m. Crystal Jane Ainsworth, Sept. 15, 1951; children: Cheryl, Yvonne, Kevin, Michael, David. BS, U. Wis., 1950, MD, 1953. Intern William Beaumont Army Hosp., El Paso, Tex., 1953-54; practice medicine specializing in ob-gyn Green Bay, Wis., 1959—; staff, lectr. Bellin Meml. Hosp., Green Bay, 1959—; staff St. Vincent Hosp., Green Bay, 1959—; clin assoc. prof. dept. family medicine and practice U. Wis. Med. Sch., Madison, 1984, preceptor, 1966-85, assoc. preceptor, 1985—; lectr. Coll. Human Biology U. Wis. Med. Sch., Green Bay, 1967—, dir. family practice obstet. rotation, 1980—; dir. Continuing Med. Edn. Ctr. Health Scis., Madison, 1985—; lectr. ob-gyn Bellin Sch. Nursing, 1959-80, various colls. and profl. socs.; chmn. physicians operating com. U. Wis. Green Bay Health Protection Plan, 1980-82; cons. Northeast Wis. Perinatal Ctr., Green Bay. Contbr. numerous ob-gyn articles to profl. jours. Bd. dirs. Lakeland chpt. ARC, 1975-81; mem. human growth and devel. ad hoc adv. com. Wis. Dept. Pub. Instrn., 1982—, mem. urology, ob-gyn panel peer review com. Blue Cross-Blue Shield United Wis., 1980-82. Recipient Zero Population Growth of Wis. Humanitarian award, 1974, Green Bay Area Free Cilnic award, 1978, Erwin R. Schmidt Interstate Teaching award Interstate Postgrad. Med. Assn., 1985, Max Fox Preceptorship award, 1985, Clin. Teaching award U. Wis. Med. Sch., 1986. Mem. Am. Pub. Health Assn., AMA, Am. Coll. Surgeons (Wis. chpt.), Am. Coll. Obstetricians and Gynecologists, Cen. Assn. Obstetricians and Gynecologists (trustee 1983-86, nominating com. 1982, Community Hosp. award 1984), Wis. Pub. Health Assn., Wis. State Med. Soc. (chmn. pub. info. 1972-82, maternal mortality com. 1966—, presdl. citation 1979), Wis. Soc. Ob-Gyn, Iowa Soc. Ob-Gyn (hon.), Wis. Assn. Perinatal Care, Nat. Perinatal Assn., Great Plains Perinatal Assn., Physicians for Social Responsibility, U. Iowa Ob-Gyn Alumni Assn., Med. Alumni Assn. Home: 201 St Marys Blvd Green Bay WI 54301 Office: 704 S Webster Ave Green Bay WI 54301

SANDONATO, CLAUDIA ELLEN, professional develoment specialist, social worker; b. Chgo., May 31, 1947; d. Frank Paul and Dorothy (Crost) Bourgin; divorced; children: Steven, Aaron. BA, U. Mich., 1968; MSW, Washington U., St. Louis, 1970. Psychiat. social worker, clin. supr. Hamot Community Mental Health, Erie, Pa., 1970-77; clin. social worker Detroit Edison, 1981-86, profl. devel. specialist, 1986—; dist. mgr. A. L.Williams, Detroit, 1985-87; Bd. dirs. ALMACA, Detroit. Contbr. articles to profl. jours. Group facilitator Space-Room to Grow, Southfield, Mich., 1983-86. Mem. Am. Soc. Tng. and Devel., Assn. Cert. Social Wokers, Women's Econ. Club, Phi Beta Kappa. Democrat. Club: Jewish Parents Inst. Home: 28156 Berkshire Southfield MI 48076 Office: Detroit Edison Co 2000 Second Ave #210 GO Detroit MI 48226

SANDS, HERBERT TERRANCE, fence supply company executive; b. Indpls., June 20, 1945; s. Herbert and Rose Margaret (Wilson) S.; B.A. in Acctg., Marian Coll., Indpls., 1967; m. Francie J. Brockslager, Aug. 26, 1967; children—Stacie Marie, Michael Terrance. Audit sr. George S. Olive & Co., C.P.A., Indpls., 1967-71; controller Cloverleaf Devel. Co., Indpls., 1971-73; partner Henry A. Woods & Co., C.P.A., Indpls., 1973-77; treas. J & W Fence Co., Inc., Indpls., 1977—. Mem. Am. Inst. C.P.A.s, Ind. Assn. C.P.A.s. Roman Catholic. Home: 1660 Royalton Dr Carmel IN 46032 Office: 1740 W Epler Ave Indianapolis IN 46217

SANDS, ROBERT A., military officer; b. Jacksonville, Fla., Jan. 27, 1937; s. Allen and Gertrude (Johnson) S.; m. Shirley Jean Moore, Oct. 10, 1956; children: Allen, Lisa, April. Student, U. Ga., 1958; AS in Bus. Adminstrn., Macon Jr. Coll., 1974; BA in Mgmt., Park Coll., 1977. Commd. USAF, 1974; br. chief procurement policy HQ AFLC, Wright Patterson AFB, Ohio, 1974-76, chief procurement policy, 1976, chief pricing and fin., 1977-81, dep. asst. to comdr. for competition, 1984—; chief pricing and fin. USAF, Washington, 1981-84. Mem. Youth Bd. City, Centerville, Ga., 1971-73,

Centerville, Ohio. Recipient Meritorious Citation, Joint Logistic Comdrs., 1976. Mem. Nat. Contract Mgmt. Assn. (bd. dirs. 1986—), Inst. Cost Analysis (v.p. 1982-84), Air Force Mgmt. Assn. (chief pricing team 1983), Am. Def. Preparedness Assn. Avocations: restoring cars, collecting coins, gardening. Home: 1016 Fleming Ct Spring Valley OH 45370 Office: Air Force Logistic Command HQ/CR Wright Patterson AFB OH 45433

SANDSNES, ARDEN T., engineering company executive, land surveyor; b. Westby, Wis., May 21, 1934; s. Alf. G. and Beverly B. (Hoff) S.; m. Reeta F. Smith, Aug. 9, 1952; children—Carl M., Terri E. Sandsnes Zimmerman, Eric W. Student Hutchinson Jr. Coll., 1956-57, U. Wis.-Madison, 1957-61. Party chief U.S. C.E., Kansasville, Wis., 1958; land surveyor Alex W. Ely Co., Madison, 1960-64; v.p. Royal Oak Engring. Inc., Madison, 1964—; dep. surveyor, Dane County, 1957-82. Charter mem. Wis. Land Records Com., 1985—. Recipient appreciation award U. Wis.-Stout, 1976, appreciation award Madison Bd. Realtors, 1979, appreciation award U. Wis.-Stevens Point, 1980, 81. Mem. Wis. Soc. Profl. Engrs., Am. Congress on Surveying and Mapping, Madison Area Surveyors Council (sec.-treas. 1968-69, pres. 1970), Wis. Soc. Land Surveyors (legis. chmn. 1975-84, pres. 1984, appreciation award 1978), Madison Sports Car Club (chief steward), Midwestern Council Sports Car Clubs (pres.). Lutheran. Avocation: home built aircraft. Home: 4705 Shore Acres Rd Monona WI 53716 Office: Royal Oak Engring Inc 5610 Medical Circle Suite 6 Madison WI 53719

SANDWICK, DAVID DEAN, dentist; b. Canon City, Minn., Aug. 3, 1937; s. Willie and Thelma Carol (Durfey) S.; m. Janice Lee Vincent, June 27, 1959 (div. 1985); children: Michael, Michelle, Maija, MyLynn, Robyn, Sherry, Todd, Jill; m. Valada Marie Driver, June 20, 1986. AA, Bemidji State U., 1958; BS, U. Minn., 1960, DDS, 1962. Gen. practice dentistry Bagley, Minn., 1964—. Mem., chmn. Bagley (Minn.) Sch. No. 162, 1972-83; chmn. Bagley Indsl. Devel. Corp., Bagley, 1965—; chmn. Bemidji Alumni Assn., 1976. Served to lt. USN, 1962-64. Mem. ADA, Minn. Dental Assn. (pres. N.W. dist. 1965-71). Republican. Home: PO Box 299 Bagley MN 56621

SANDY, WILLIAM HASKELL, training and communications systems company executive; b. N.Y.C., Apr. 28, 1929; s. Fred and Rose S.; A.B., U. Md., 1950, J.D., 1953; postgrad. Advanced Mgmt. Program, Harvard Bus. Sch., 1970-71; m. Marjorie Mazor, June 15, 1952; children—Alan, Lewis, Barbara. Admitted to Md. bar, 1953; planner-writer, account exec., account supr. Jam Handy Orgn., Detroit, 1953-64, v.p., 1964-69, sr. v.p., 1969-71; pres. Sandy Corp., Troy, Mich., 1971—. Bd. govs. Northwood Inst., 1976-80; bd. dirs. Cranbrook Sci. Inst.; mem. nat. exec. council Harvard Bus. Sch., 1985—. Mem. Am. Mktg. Assn. (pres. Detroit chpt. 1975), Am. Soc. Tng. and Devel., Southeastern Mich. Better Bus. Bur. (bd. dirs.), Adcraft Club, Nat. Assn. Ednl. Broadcasters. Clubs: Harvard Bus. Sch. (pres. Detroit club 1983-85), The Hundred. Home: 596 Rudgate Bloomfield Hills MI 48013 Office: Sandy Corp 1500 W Big Beaver Rd Troy MI 48084

SANEHOLTZ, ROGER LEE, optometrist; b. Napoleon, Ohio, Nov. 6, 1950; s. Wilber J. and Grace E. (Carter) S.; m. Melinda Jane Denney, July 5, 1975; children: Brent, Austin. OD, Ohio State U., 1974. Pvt. practice optometry Montpelier, Ohio, 1977—. pres. Montpelier United Fund, 1979—; mem. bd. dirs. Montpelier Pub. Library, 1980-85, Montpelier Schs., 1986. Served to capt. USAF, 1974-77. Mem. Am. Optometric Assn., Nat. Fedn. Ind. Businessmen, Ohio Optometric Assn., Toledo Area Optometric Assn., Ohio Sch. Bd. Assn., Montpelier C. of C. (pres. 1978-79). Methodist. Lodge: Rotary. Avocations: skiing, camping, golf, fishing, racquetball. Home: 419 N Pleasant Montpelier OH 43543 Office: 306 W Main Montpelier OH 43543

SANFORD, RUTH EILEEN, data processing company administrator; b. Two Harbors, Minn., Mar. 15, 1925; d. John Arvid and Helene (Lind) Bostrom; m. Keith N. Sanford, Sept. 21 1950 (div. Sept. 1960); m. Michael R. Notaro, Mar. 10, 1984. Degree in bus., Cable's Secretarial Coll., 1944; student, Northwestern U., 1966. Exec. sec. 1st Am. Nat. Bank, Duluth, Minn., 1944-48; pvt. sec. Adam Thomson, Duluth, Minn., 1948-52; exec. sec. and administrv. asst. Res. Mining Co., Silver Bay, Minn., 1952-62, United Calif. Bank, San Francisco, 1963-64; office mgr. Poly-Tech, Mpls., 1964-66; corp. sec. and administrv. asst. to pres. Statis. Tabulating Corp., Chgo., 1966—. Mem. Chgo. Council Fgn. Relations. Mem. Nat. Assn. Exec. Secs. Roman Catholic. Club: Butterfield Country (Hinsdale, Ill.). Lodge: Women of Moose. Avocations: golf, fishing, gardening, cooking, embroidery. Home: 500 Linden Ave Oak Park IL 60302 Office: Statis Tabulating Corp 2 N Riverside Plaza Chicago IL 60606

SANGHVI, MANOJ KUMAR DALICHAND, oil company executive; b. Morvi, India, Sept. 13, 1928; s. Dalichand Hakubhai and Navalben Jagannath (Sanghani) S.; B.S. with honors, U. Bombay, 1949, B.S. in Tech., 1951; M.S. (Fulbright fellow, Ford Found. scholar), Ohio State U., 1953, Ph.D., 1956; m. Shobha Hiralal Shah, Apr. 1, 1958; children: Sunil, Parag, Pulin. Came to U.S., 1952. Research fellow Govt. India Council Sci. and Indsl. Research, Bombay, 1951-52; research fellow Ohio State U., Columbus, 1953-55, research asso., 1955-56; project chem. engr. Standard Oil Co. (Ind.), Whiting, Ind., 1956-60; economiste conseil Société Civile Amoco, Paris, 1960-62; chief economist Amoco (U.K.) Ltd., London, 1962-63; econ. adviser-Far East, Amoco Internat. Oil Co., N.Y.C., 1963-65; sr. tech. coordinator Amoco India, Inc., New Delhi, 1965-68; coordinator corporate planning Standard Oil Co. (Ind.), Chgo., 1968-74, sr. coordinator planning and econs., 1974-83, now dir.; dir. Industry Analysis (Internat.), 1983—. Vis. fellow Ohio State U., 1956-57; trustee ILA Found., 1981—, pres., 1984—. Mem. Am. Inst. Chem. Engrs. (chmn. nat. program com., mgmt. sci. 1972-78, chmn. mgmt. group 1980-82), India League Am. (v.p., dir. 1974-81; pres. 1978), Ill. Asian Am. Adv. Council to Gov., Sigma Xi, Phi Lambda Upsilon. Club: Rotary (Chgo.). Contbr. articles to profl. jours. Home: 1024 Heatherfield Lane Glenview IL 60025 Office: 200 E Randolph Dr Chicago IL 60601

SANGMEISTER, GEORGE EDWARD, lawyer, state senator; b. Joliet, Ill., Feb. 16, 1931; s. George Conrad and Rose Engaborg (Johnson) S.; B.A., Elmhurst Coll., 1951; LL.B., John Marshall Law Sch., 1960, J.D., 1970; m. Doris Marie Hinspeter, Dec. 1, 1951; children—George Kurt, Kimberly Ann. Admitted to Ill. bar, 1960, since practiced in Joliet; partner firm McKeown, Fitzgerald, Zollner, Buck, Sangmeister & Hutchison, 1969—; justice of peace, 1961-63; states atty. Will County, 1964-68; mem. Ill. Ho. of Reps., 1972-76, Ill. Senate, 1977-87 . Chmn. Will County chpt. Salvation Army; chmn. Frankfort Twp. unit Am. Cancer Soc.; former trustee Will County Family Service Agy.; bd. dirs. Joliet Jr. Coll. Found. Served with inf. AUS, 1951-53. Mem. ABA, Ill., Will County bar assns., Am. Trial Lawyers Assn., Am. Legion, Frankfort (past pres.), Mokena chambers commerce, Old Timers Baseball Assn. Lion. Home: S Wolf Rd Mokena IL 60448 Office: 2455 Glenwood Ave Joliet IL 60435

SANISLO, PAUL STEVE, lawyer; b. Cleve., Feb. 8, 1927; s. Paul and Bertha (Kasa) S.; m. Mary Ellen P. Conroy, May 7, 1949; 1 child, Susan J. B.A., Baldwin-Wallace Coll., 1948; J.D., Cleve. State U., 1961. Bar: Ohio 1961, U.S. Dist. Ct. (no. dist.) Ohio 1964. Order clk. Am. Agrl. Chem. Co., Cleve., 1948-52; safety engr. Park Drop Forge Co., Cleve., 1952-62, personnel mgr., 1954-62; assoc. then ptnr. Spohn & Sanislo, L.P.A., Cleve., 1962-81, pres., 1981-86; ptnr. Sanislo & Assocs. LPA, Cleve., 1987—; spl. counsel Atty. Gen. Ohio, 1971; arbitrator Am. Arbitration Assn., 1972-78. Mem. Cleve. City Council, 1964-67; trustee Cleve.-Marshall Law Sch., 1962-63; trustee Cleve.-Marshall Ednl. Found., 1963—, pres., 1980-83; mem. Solon City Bd. Edn., Ohio, 1972-83, pres., 1974-83; chmn. Solon Charter Rev. Commn., 1971; past mem., organizer, legal adv. Solon Drug Abuse Ctr.; mem. Cuyahoga County Democratic Exec. Com.; ward leader 29th Ward Dem. Club, 1965-71, also past pres.; trustee Solon Dem. Ward Club, 1972-75. Recipient Disting. Service award City of Solon, 1984, Solon Bd. Edn., 1984, Solon Edn. Assn., 1984. Mem. Bar Assn. Greater Cleve. (Merit Service award 1978-79; chmn. workers compensation sect. 1975—), Ohio Bar Assn., Cuyahoga County Bar Assn., Assn. Trial Lawyers Am., Cleve.-Marshall Law Sch. Alumni Assn. (pres. 1968-69), Hungarian Bus. and Trademen's Club (pres. 1967-68), Cleve. Assn. Compensation Attys. (pres. 1973-76). Democrat. Roman Catholic. Club: Aurora Country (v.p. 1983—) (Ohio). Lodge: KC. Avocations: golf; travel. Office: 710 Standard Bldg Cleveland OH 44113

SANKEY, CLAYTON DAVID, clinical social worker, psychologist; b. Mpls., Oct. 18, 1947; s. Jack Carson and Alta Helena (Thompson) S.; m. Dorothy Jeanne Nollet, Mar. 27, 1976; children: Carrie Lynn, Aaron Thomas, Jack Clayton. Student, Macalester Coll., St. Paul, 1965-67; BA, U. Minn., 1969; MSW, Western Mich. U., 1975. Cert. clin. social worker, Minn.; lic. psychologist, Minn. Sr. corrections agt. Minn. Dept. Corrections, Mpls., 1969-72; social worker Ct. Diagnostic and Treatment Ctr., Toledo, 1972-76; social services supr. Minn. State Prison, Bayport, 1976-77; clin. social worker Arlington House, St. Paul, 1977-82, Kiel Clinics, Inc., St. Paul, 1982-85; clin. social worker, dir., owner River City Mental Health Clinic, St. Paul, 1985—; clin. social worker Luth. Social Services, St. Paul, 1979-82, N. Suburban Family Services, Coon Rapids, Minn., 1982-83; rep. Coalition Legal Regulation Social Workers in Minn., 1984-87. Mem. Nat. Assn. Social Workers (diplomate 1986), Acad. Cert. Social Workers, Minn. Soc. Clin. Social Workers (sec. 1980-82, v.p. 1984-86, pres. 1986—). Presbyterian. Avocations: softball, physical fitness, running, biking, hunting. Office: River City Mental Health Clinic 2265 Como Ave Suite #201 Saint Paul MN 55108

SANKPILL, LESTER ALAN, manufacturing company executive; b. Mexico, Mo., Jan. 6, 1942; s. James Harold and Clarice Marie (Caldwell) S.; m. Susan Parmelee, Nov. 2, 1963; children: Dorothy, Kimberly, Cynthia, J.P. BSME, U. Kans., 1968; student, U. Mo., 1963-65, 69-72. Various mgmt. positions Parmelee Industries, Inc., Kansas City, Mo., 1963-77, v.p., 1977-85, pres., 1985—, also bd. dirs. Mem. Indsl. Safety Equipment Assn. (chmn. future standards com. 1983), Greater Kansas City Arabian Horse Assn. (bd. dirs.), Internat. Arabian Horse Assn. (nat. del. 1985—), Am. Royal Assn. (gov. 1979—). Clubs: Kansas City, Carriage. Office: Parmelee Industries Inc 1535 Walnut PO Box 417237 Kansas City MO 64141-7237

SANNELLA, JOSEPH LEE, industrial science company executive; b. Boston, July 27, 1933; s. Theodore and Anna (Barone) S.; m. Nancy Marshall, June 6, 1959; children—Joseph, SueAnne, Stephen. A.B., Harvard U., 1955; M.S., U. Mass., 1958; Ph.D., Purdue U., 1963; M.B.A., U. Del., 1969. Research chemist FMC, Am. Viscose Div., Marcus Hook, Pa., 1962-67; supr. organic research Ball Corp., Muncie, Ind., 1967-69, mgr. graphic arts, 1969-71, supr. chem. research, 1971-74, dir. research, 1974-85, dir. corp. lab. services, 1985—. Contbr. articles to profl. jours. Patentee in field. Bd. dirs. Big Bros./Big Sisters E. Cen. Ind., 1969-78, Easter Seal Soc., 1977-85, 86—, Ball Employees Credit Union, 1981—, Ball Polit. Action Com., 1976—. Recipient Community Service award Ball Corp., 1984. Mem. Am. Chem. Soc., Soc. Plastic Engrs., Nat. Metal Decorators Soc. Republican. Roman Catholic. Clubs: Del. Country, Muncie (Muncie). Lodge: Kiwanis. Home: 2803 W Woodbridge Muncie IN 47304 Office: Ball Corp 1509 S Macedonia Muncie IN 47302

SANSCRAINTE, WILLARD ALLEN, JR., computer systems executive; b. Kenmore, N.Y., Jan. 19, 1960; s. Willard Allen and Mary Anne (Dietrich) S.; m. Michelle Kay Mehne, Feb. 21, 1986. BS in Biomed. Engring., Rensselaer Poly. Inst., 1981, MS in Indsl. Engring., 1982; MBA, Xavier U., 1985. Project leader Procter & Gamble, Cin., 1982-86; sr. mgr. Kraft Inc., Glenview, Ill., 1986—. Committeeman Conservative Party, Tonawanda, N.Y., 1979-81; mem. P&G Ptnrs. in Edn., Cin., 1982-85. Mem. AAAS, Assn. Systems Mgmt. (profl.), Rensselaer Poly. Inst. Alumni. Republican. Roman Catholic. Home: 1291 Longacre Ln Wheeling IL 60090 Office: Kraft Inc One Kraft Ct Glenview IL 60025

SANSOUCIE, LARRY ALLEN, pastor, theology educator; b. DeSoto, Mo., Dec. 23, 1951; s. John Joseph and Eileen Mae (Smith) S.; m. Cheryl Annette Burton, July 21, 1979. BS in Physics, U. Mo., Rolla, 1973; MDiv, Chgo. Theol. Sem., 1978; DMin, Christian Theol. Sem., 1983. Ordained minister United Ch. of Christ, 1979. Asst. pastor Living Peace Bapt. Ch., Chgo., 1974-77; supply preacher United Ch. Christ churches, Ill. and Mich., 1977-78; pastor Waterford United Ch. Christ, Goshen, 1978-79, Plymouth United Ch. Christ, Dunkirk, Ind., 1979-83, Pleasant Valley United Ch. Christ, Osceola, Ind., 1983-87, Nashville United Ch. of Christ, West Milton, Ohio, 1987—; bd. dirs. Ind.-Ken. Conf. United Ch. of Christ, 1978-79. Author: The Ecumenical Lectionary: Theological Foundations, Liturgical Use, Congregational Usefulness, 1985; contbr. articles to profl. jours. Vol. various hosps., Chgo., Ind., nursing homes, Ind. 1979—; coordinator Plymouth Community Concerns Fund, Dunkirk, Ind., 1980-83; mem. religious arts steering com. United Religious Community St. Joseph County, Ind., 1983-86. Mem. Ind.-Ken. Conf. of the United Ch. of Christ (Ch. in Soc. commn. 1979-83, peace and justice task force 1981-83, exec. com. Eastern Assn. 1982-83), Jay County Chaplains, Dunkirk Ministerial Assn. (pres. 1979-83), Osceola Ministerial Assn., Phi Theta Kappa, Kappa Mu Epsilon, Sigma Pi Sigma. Avocations: geneology, aerobics, travel, writing, walking. Home and Office: 4665 West State Rd 571 West Milton OH 45383

SANTANGELO, MARIO VINCENT, dentist, association executive, educator; b. Youngstown, Ohio, Oct. 5, 1931; s. Anthony and Maria (Zarlenga) S.; student U. Pitts., 1949-51; D.D.S., Loyola U. (Chgo.), 1955, M.S., 1960. Instr. Loyola U., Chgo., 1957-60, asst. prof., 1960-66, chmn. dpt. radiology, 1962-70, dir. dental aux. utilization program, 1963-70, assoc. prof., 1966-70, chmn. dept. oral diagnosis, 1967-70, asst. dean, 1969-70; practice dentistry, Chgo., 1960-70; cons. Cert. Bd. Am. Dental Assts. Assn., 1967-76, VA Research Hosp., 1969-75, Chgo. Civil Service Commn., 1967-75; counselor Chgo. Dental Assts. Assn., 1966-69; mem. dental student tng. adv. com. Div. Dental Health USPHS, Dept. Health, Edn. and Welfare, 1969-71; cons. dental edn. rev. com. NIH, 1971-72; cons. USPHS, HEW, Region IV, Atlanta, 1973-76, Region V, Chgo., 1973-77; mem. Commn. on Dental Edn. and Practice, Fedn. Dentaire Internationale, 1984—. Bd. visitors Sch. Dental Medicine, Washington U., St. Louis, 1974-76. Served to capt. USAF, 1955-57. Recipient Dr. Harry Strusser Meml. award NYU Coll. Dentistry, 1985. Fellow Am. Coll. Dentists; mem. AMA (mem. edn. work group 1982-86), Assembly Specialized Accrediting Bodies (council on postsecondary accreditation 1981—), Am. Assn. Dental Schs., Odontographic Soc. Chgo., Am. (asst. sec. council dental edn. 1971-81, acting sec. 1981-82, sec. 1982—, asst. sec. commn. on dental accreditation 1975-81, acting sec. 1981-82, sec. 1982—, acting sec. commn. on continuing dental edn. 1981-82, sec. 1982-85), Ill., Chgo. dental assns., Am. Acad. Oral Pathology, Am. Acad. Dental Radiology, Am. Acad. Oral Medicine, Omicron Kappa Upsilon (pres. 1967-68), Blue Key, Xi Psi Phi. Contbr. articles to profl. jours. Home: 1440 N Lake Shore Dr Chicago IL 60610 Office: 211 E Chicago Ave Chicago IL 60611

SANTI, EUGENE ARNOLD, furniture company executive; b. Chgo., Nov. 15, 1938; s. V.R. and D.H. Santi; m. Mary Guilbeault, Oct. 3, 1964; children: Andrew, Steven, John, E. Michael. BS in Statistical Econs., U. Ill., 1960; grad. exec. devel. program, Ohio State U., 1979. Mgr. internat. adminstrn. U.S. Gypsum Co., Chgo., 1963-69; dist. mgr. Keene Corp., Northville, Mich., 1969-70; product mgr. Keene Corp., Princeton, N.J., 1970-72; sales mgr., div. mgr. Conwed Corp., St. Paul, 1972-84, v.p. to pres., 1984—. Mgr. Little League Baseball, White Bear Lake, Minn., 1974—; mem. Long Range Planning Com. St. Mary's Ch., White Bear Lake, 1978—. Served to capt. U.S. Army, 1961-63. Roman Catholic. Home: 5935 Otter Lake Rd White Bear Lake MN 55110

SANTUCCI, MICHAEL LOUIS, dentist; b. Oak Park, Ill., Sept. 16, 1949; s. Mario Ansalmo and Antoinette Marie (Coppola) S.; m. Barbara Gene Souyoul, Apr. 11, 1948; children: Beth, Laura. DDS, Northwestern U., 1974. Resident gen. practice VA Research Ctr., Chgo., 1975; staff dentist Va. Hosp., Iron Mountain, Mich., 1975-77; gen. practice dentistry Belvidere, Ill., 1977—; staff dentist Swedish Am. Hosp., Rockford, Ill., 1979—, St. Joseph Hosp., Belvidere, Ill., 1979—, Highland Hosp., Belvidere, Ill., 1979—. Bd. dirs. Boone County Bd. Health. Mem. ADA, Ill. Dental Assn., Winnebago Dental Assn. (bd. dirs. 1985), Boone County C. of C. Republican. Roman Catholic. Lodge: Rotary (bd. dirs. 1986). Avocation: amateur radio. Office: 121 S State Belvidere IL 61008

SANTULIS, KEVIN CHARLES, insurance company executive; b. New Eagle, Pa., Mar. 12, 1954; s. Michael and Patricia Ann (Rarick) S.; m. Carol Ann Everett, Aug. 13, 1983. BA in Polit. Sci., History, U. Pitts., 1976. Mgr. Mgmt. Systems Inc., Pitts., 1976-78; mgmt. cons., mgr. Scheduling Corp. Am., Oakbrook, Ill., 1978-83; dir. profl. claims Blue Cross/Blue Shield No. Ohio, Cleve., 1983-85; mgr. CHAMPUS ops. Wis. Physicians Service, Madison, 1985—. Scholar NSF, 1971. Republican. Home: 1343 Hobby Horse Rd Oregon WI 53575 Office: Wis Physicians Service PO Box 7927 Madison WI 53707

SAPARETO, STEPHEN ALAN, cancer research scientist, educator; b. Haverhill, Mass., Oct. 30, 1949; s. Frank Vincent and Alice Loraine (Lambert) S.; m. Sheila Kay Schmeling, June 21, 1972 (div. 1976). B.S. in Physics, U. Mass., 1971; M.S. in Health Physics, Colo. State U., 1973, Ph.D. in Radiation Biology, Cell and Molecular Biology, 1978. Postdoctoral fellow dept. radiology and radiation biology Colo. State U., Ft. Collins, 1977-78; postdoctoral fellow in cancer biology dept. radiology Stanford U., 1978-80; asst. prof. sect. cancer biology, div. radiation oncology Washington U., St. Louis, 1980-82; asst. prof. medicine div. med. oncology Wayne State U., Detroit, 1982-85, assoc. prof. medicine div. med. oncology 1985—; asst. mem. dept. exptl. therapeutics Mich. Cancer Found., Detroit, 1982—, mem. safety com., radiation safety officer, 1982-86; dir. Ben Kasle Lab. for Flow Cytometry, 1982—. Recipient Nat. Research Service award USPHS, 1978-79; NSF grantee, 1971; FDA radiation health trainee, 1972-75; mem. exec. com. N.Am. Hyperthermia Group, 1985-86. Mem. Radiation Research Soc., Am. Soc. Therapeutic Radiologists, Am. Assn. Cancer Research, Am. Soc. Analytic Cytology, Sigma Xi. Contbr. articles to profl. publs. Office: Wayne State Univ Sch Medicine Oncology/Hematology 540 E Canfield Detroit MI 48201

SAPER, CLIFFORD B., neurology and pharmacology educator; b. Chgo., Feb. 20, 1952; s. Julian and Susan Menkin S.; m. Barbara Susan Farby, Aug. 26, 1973; children: Rebecca Michelle, Leah Daniele. BS, U. Ill., 1972, MS, 1972; MD, Washington U., 1977, PhD, 1977. Diplomate Am. Bd. Psychiatry and Neurology. Intern Jewish Hosp., St. Louis, 1977-78; resident New York Hosp., N.Y.C., 1978-81; asst. prof. Washington U., St. Louis, 1981-84, assoc. prof., 1984-85; assoc. prof. U. Chgo., 1985—. contbr. articles to profl. jours. Mem. Am. Acad. Neurology, Am. Physiological Soc., Soc. for Neuroscience. Office: U Chgo 947 E 58th St Chicago IL 60637

SAPIENZA, MICHAEL SANTO, industrial microbiologist; b. Chgo., Apr. 4, 1937; s. Michael and Frances (Tomaselli) S.; m. Arlene Agnes Clemente, June 10, 1961; children: Michael A., Cynthia A., Mark C., Suzanne M., Robert S. BS, Loyola U., Chgo., 1959; postgrad., Ill. Inst. Tech., 1960-61. Group leader Nalco Chem. Co., Chgo., 1968-70, tech. mgr., 1970-76, dir. quality assurance, 1976-83, plant mgr., 1983—. Contbr. articles to profl. jours.; patentee in field. Chmn. bus. industry council Moraine Valley Community Coll., Palos Hills, Ill., 1982-83; pres. Bedford Park (Ill.) Clearing Indsl. Assn., 1981-82. Mem. Research Soc. Am. (pres. Nalco chpt.). Republican. Roman Catholic. Avocations: golf, swimming, camping, jogging. Home: 7737 Cashew Dr Orland Park IL 60462 Office: Nalco Chem Co 9165 S Harbor Ave Chicago IL 60617

SAPORTA, JACK, clinical psychologist, educator; b. N.Y.C., Oct. 27, 1927; s. David and Victoria (Fils) S.; m. Judith Hammond, May 28, 1967 (div. 1979); children: David, Victoria. AB cum laude, Adelphi U., 1951; PhD, U. Chgo., 1962. Diplomate Am. Bd. Profl. Psychology; registered psychologist. Supt. Tinley Park (Ill.) Mental Health Ctr., 1975-78; chief manpower tng. and devel. Ill. Dept. Mental Health, Chgo., 1978-82; dean, prof. Forest Inst. Profl. Psychology, Des Plaines, Ill., 1982-85; core faculty Fielding Inst., Santa Barbara, Calif., 1984—, Ill. Sch. Profl. Psychology, Chgo., 1985—; pvt. practice in psychology Bresler & Dugo. Ltd., Hoffman Estates, Ill., 1985; Mem. Ill. State Psychology Exam Com., Springfield, Ill., 1984—, profl. staff Forest Hosp., Des Plaines, 1977—, Luth. Gen. Hosp., Park Ridge, Ill., 1986—. Served with U.S. Army, 1946-47, Germany. Named Educator of Yr., Forest Inst., 1982. Mem. Am. Acad. Psychotherapists, Am. Psychol. Assn. (accreditation site vis. team), Ill. Psychol. Assn.; fellow Nat. Tng. Labs. Inst. (adj. staff). Avocations: tennis, sailing, do-it-yourself home projects. Home: 3201 California Ave Rolling Meadows IL 60008 Office: Bresler & Dugo Ltd 2500 W Higgins Rd Hoffman Estates IL 60195

SAPPENFIELD, CHARLES MADISON, architect, educator; b. Columbia, S.C., Mar. 17, 1930; s. Charles Madison and Elizabeth Olive (Moss) S.; m. Mary Frances McGowan Dec. 14, 1963; children—Charles Ross, Sarah Kathleen. B.Arch., N.C. State U., 1956; Cert., Denmark's Royal Acad., Copenhagen, 1961. Registered architect, Ind., Tenn., N.C. Asst. prof. N.C. State U., Raleigh, 1956-57, asst. prof., 1961-63; head archtl. firm C.M. Sappenfield, Asheville, N.C., 1961—; assoc. prof. Clemson U., S.C., 1963-65; prof. architecture Ball State U., Muncie, Ind., 1965—, dean, 1965-81, dir. Design Indiana, 1983—; awards juror Interfaith Forum on Religious Art and Architecture, 1981, Am. Cons. Engrs. Council, 1982; mem. accreditation team Nat. Archtl. Accrediting Bd., 1967-82. Archtl. works include: Dormitories, U. N.C., Gumpert residence, Dave residence. Pres. Asheville Art Mus., N.C., 1964-65; chmn. Ind. Commn. on Aging, Indpls., 1983-85; pres. Alpha Day Care Ctr. for Elderly, Muncie, 1985; mem. State Planning Adv. Commn., Indpls., 1974-82. Served with U.S. Army. Recipient Gold medal for service Ball State U., 1983; named Sagamore of the Wabash, Gov. of Ind., 1982. Fellow AIA; mem. Ind. Soc. Architects (pres. 1976), Ind. Archtl. Found. (chmn. 1975), Am. Soc. Landscape Architects (awards juror 1983), Fulbright Alumni Assn., Alpha Rho Chi. Republican. Episcopalian. Lodges: Rotary, Civitan. Avocations: bicycling; racquetball/ photography; classic cars. Home: 2322 W Berwyn Rd Muncie IN 47304 Office: Design Indiana Ball State U Muncie IN 47306

SAPUTO, VINCENT ANTHONY, publishing executive, consultant; b. St. Louis, Oct. 21, 1953; s. Salvator and Rose Marie (Taff) S.; m. Melody Lynn Downen, Nov. 7, 1981; 1 child, Adrienne Leigh. AA, Belleville Area Col., 1974; BS, So. Ill. U., 1975. Avdt. salesperson Press Record, Granite City, Ill., 1975-78; mgr. advt., 1978-80; mgr. advt. sales Southern Illinoisan, Carbondale, 1980-81; pub. The Register, Sandoval, Ill., 1981-82, Ledger-Star, Sandoval, 1982-83, Mineola (Tex.) Monitor, 1983-86; gen. mgr. The Chgo. Cath., 1986—crw. Author: Key Course Sales Training, 1983. Mem. Collinsville (Ill.) Planning and Zoning Commn., 1978-80; treas. Madison County Reps., Collinsville, 1978-80; candidate Collinsville Sch. Dist., 1979; chmn. Mineola Devel. Com., 1984-86. Named one of Outstanding Young Men Am. Mem. Cath. Press Assn., Delta Chi. Republican. Roman Catholic. Lodges: Elks, Lions. Avocations: guitar, poetry, softball, bicycling, aerobics. Home: 1849 N Newland Ave Chicago IL 60635

SARABIA, ANTONIO ROSAS, lawyer; b. Chihuahua, Mex., June 29, 1913; s. Rafael Rosas and Maria S.; children—Antonio Rosas II, Sean Rosas. B.S. in Chem. Engring., Ind. Tech. Coll., 1942; J.D., U. Chgo., 1949. Bar: Ill. 1950. Assoc. Baker, McKenzie & Hightower, Chgo., 1949-52, ptnr., 1952-62; sole practice, Chgo., 1962-64; sr. assoc. Lord, Bissell & Brook, Chgo., 1964-65, ptnr., 1966-83; faculty mem. Lawyers Inst. John Marshall Law Sch., Chgo., 1962-73. Mem. legis. com. Chgo. Crime Commn., 1971—; bd. dirs. Geographic Soc. of Chgo., 1970-78, 3d v.p., 1978—. Mem. ABA (internat. law sect. 1970—, council 1971-75, budget officer 1972-78), Inter-Am. (membership com.), Ill. State Bar Assn. (internat. law sect. chmn. 1965-66, council 1974-75), Chgo. Bar Assn. (charter flight com. 1961-82, internat. and fgn. law com. 1982—, internat. human rights 1978—, chmn. 1980—), Am. Fgn. Law Assn. (pres. Chgo. br. 1952-59), Am. Arbitration Assn., Mexican Am. Lawyers Assn. Clubs: Univ., Mid-Am. Contbr. articles to profl. jours. Home: 175 E Delaware Pl Apt 7805 Chicago IL 60611 Office: 79 W Monroe St Suite 1320 Chicago IL 60603

SARAMA, DAVID THEODORE, marketing professional; b. Cleve., Mar. 11, 1953; s. Max Theodore and Rita (Dlzynski) S. BS, Christopher Newport Coll., 1976. Area mgr. Busch Gardens, Williamsburg, Va., 1975-78; project supr. Anheuser-Busch, Inc., St. Louis, 1978, sales trainer, 1979-80, mgr. mobile tng., 1980-83, mgr. sales tng./devel., mktg. communications, 1983-86, mgr. sales devel., 1986—. Mem. Am. Soc. Tng. and Devel., Am. Mktg. Assn., Am. Mgmt. Assn., St. Louis Advt. Club, UN Assn. (bd. dirs. 1986-87), St. Louis Beta Theta Pi Alumni (bd. dirs. 1984). Clubs: Mo. Athletic, Variety (bd. dirs. 1984-87), Young Variety (pres. 1983-84, bd. dirs. 1983-85). Avocations: fundraising work for charity orgns., internat. travel. Office: Anheuser-Busch Inc 1 Busch Pl Saint Louis MO 63118

SARANTAKIS, ANTHONY JAMES, advertising executive, consultant; b. St. Louis, Dec. 14, 1949; s. James George and Georgia (Geroulis) S.; m. Christine Carol Dziukala, July 25, 1981. B.S., U. Wis., 1972. Salesman advt. Pubs. Devel. Corp., Skokie, Ill., 1972-75; dist. mgr. Nat. Sch. Bd. Assn.,

Washington, 1975-77; regional mgr. Cahners Pub., Boston, 1977-80; regional mgr. Irving Cloud Pub., Lincolnwood, Ill., 1980-85; regional mgr. Do-it-Yourself Retailing mag. Nat. Retail Hardware Assn., 1986—, Arlington Heights, Ill. Democrat. Greek Orthodox. Home and Office: 1404 Afton Circle Inverness IL 60010 Office: Nat Retail Hardware Assn 1424 Allison Ct Arlington Heights IL 60005

SARAPATA, SUSAN LEE, senior human resources development specialist; b. Fairborn, Ohio, Dec. 21, 1950; d. Stephen and Orma Lee (Palmer) S. BS, Ohio State U., 1973; MA, Northwestern U., 1974. Tchr. early childhood edn. Spl. Edn. Dist. Lake County, Ill., 1974-78; tchr. of hearing impaired Lincolnwood (Ill.) Dist. 75, 1979; tchr. computers Twp. High Sch. Dist. 214, Mt. Prospect, Ill., 1979-85, adminstr., 1984-85; cons. Emery Air Freight, Dayton, Ohio, 1985-87; sr. human resources development specialist Monarch Marking, Dayton, 1987—; tchr. of gifted students Friends of the Gifted, Mt. Prospect, 1983; tchr. cons. computers Brevard County (Fla.) Pub. Schs., 1982; retail mgr. Best and Co., Vernon Hills, Ill., 1978-79; intern play therapy Ohio State U., Columbus., 1976. Author: Elements of Mathematics Software, 1982; editor: The Truth About You, 1978. Avocations: bird watching, cross country skiing, art collecting, decorating, opera and film. Home: 2618 Orchard Run Rd Dayton OH 45449 Office: Emery Worldwide One Emery Plaza Vandalia OH 45377

SARBER, JOYE LYNNE, measurement company execuitve; b. Laredo, Tex., Mar. 6, 1954; d. Jesse Cosby and Louise Orloff (Pickus) Mason; m. William Robert Sarber, July 19, 1974; children: William Jacob, Justin Abram. Student, Ohio State U., 1972-74; AA, Sinclair Community Coll., 1976, student, 1979—; student, Edison State Coll., 1976. Clk. purchasing Extra Help Inc., Dayton, Ohio, 1978, Bendix/Allied/Sheffield, Dayton, 1978-84; buyer Sheffield Measurement subs. Cross and Trecker Corp., Dayton, 1984—. Asst. coach, referee Mad River Soccer Assn., Dayton, 1985. Jewish. Avocations: camping, swimming, golf, soccer, volleyball. Home: 5298 Access Rd Dayton OH 45431

SARBINOFF, JAMES ADAIR, periodontist, consultant; b. Indpls., Dec. 29, 1947; s. James Gill and Eileen Sarbinoff; m. Tamara Lynn Griffith, June 6, 1971. A.B. in Zoology, Ind. U., 1970; D.D.S., Ind. U.-Indpls., 1974, M.S. in Dentistry, 1981. Gen. practice dentistry, Indpls., 1974-79; gen. practice periodontics, Indpls., 1981—; cons. Marion County Home, Indpls., 1975-79; instr. clin. dentistry Ind. U. Sch. Dentistry, Indpls., 1974-79, assoc. prof., 1981-82. Editor: Perio Probe, 1981. Chmn. dental div. United Way, Indpls., 1983, 84. Recipient Mosby Scholarship Book award Mosby Pub. Co., 1974. Mem. ADA, Am. Acad. Periodontology, Ind. Dental Assn. (alt. del. to conv. 1986, 87), Indpls. Dist. Dental Soc. (bd. dirs. 1987—). Avocations: skiing; computers. Office: 6801 Lake Plaza Dr A-111 Indianapolis IN 46220

SARDAS, JACQUES RAPHAEL, rubber company executive; b. Alexandria, Egypt, Sept. 18, 1930; came to U.S., 1974, naturalized, 1981; s. Raphael Leon and Dora (Beja) S.; m. Esther Pesso Sardas, July 29, 1956; children: Dora, Marianne, Isabella, Claudia. Student, Egypt and France, Harvard U., 1974. With Companhia Goodyear do Brasil, Sao Paulo, 1957-67; pres., gen. mgr. Compagnie Francaise Goodyear, France, 1967-74; exec. v.p. Goodyear Internat. Corp., Akron, Ohio, 1974-81; group exec. v.p., dir. Goodyear Tire & Rubber Co., 1981-84, exec. v.p., 1984—, also bd. dirs.; pres. Goodyear Internat. Corp. Trustee Akron City Hosp., 1982—; trustee Ohio Council on Econ. Edn., Columbus, 1981—; div. chmn. United Way Summit County, Akron, 1982. Republican. Club: Portage Country (Akron, Ohio). Home: 1287 Country Club Rd Akron OH 44313

SARDONI, LAWRENCE WHITMAN, corporate communications specialist; b. Grand Junction, Colo., Dec. 15, 1936; s. Lawrence Whitman Sr. and Ilene (Oldroyd) S.; m. Myrna Deinert, Sept. 6, 1960; children: Kenneth, Thomas, David, John, Christina. BS in Math., U. Nebr., Omaha, 1969. Mgr. spl. project Mut. of Omaha, 1968-78; dir. time sharing HDR, Inc., Omaha, 1978-83; v.p. systems DRM, Inc., Omaha, 1983-85; v.p. services CMI, Inc., Omaha, 1985—; pres., chief fin. officer Midland Assistance Programs, Omaha, 1984—. Served with USAF, 1959-63. Mem. Am. Nat. Standards Inst., Internat. Standards Orgn., Assn. for Computer Machinery, Internal Fin. Planning Soc., Corp. Planning Soc. of U.S. Republican. Mormon. Avocation: concert cellist. Home: 15018 Brookside Circle Omaha NE 68144 Office: CMI 13211 F St 10701 Mockingbird Dr Omaha NE 68137

SAREINI, SUZANNE, restaurant executive; b. Detroit, May 4, 1951; d. Houssain Ali Taleb and Skiney Jaffar (Assad) Mallad; m. Toufic Ali Sareini, Aug. 11, 1968; children: Nowal, Michael, Houssain, Ali. Student, Detroit Coll. Bus., 1985. Owner, mgr. Neighborhood Store, Dearborn, Mich., 1973-75, Uncle Sam's Restaurant, Dearborn, Mich., 1977-81, Uncle Sam's Village Cafeé, Dearborn, Mich., 1979—; pres. Arabian Village Devel. Corp., Dearborn, 1979-84; dir. Gen. Devel. Council of Dearborn, 1982-85. Mem. Pvt. Industry Council, Dearborn, 1981-83; mem. adv. council Mich. Dept. Mental health, 1984—, Northville Psychiat. Hosp., 1986; bd. dirs. Pvt. Industry Council Wayne County, 1986—, YWCA, 1986—, Dearborn Arts Council, 1986—. Recipient Women in Politics award Supreme Ct. Justice Boyle, 1983, citation City of Dearborn, 1985. Mem. Dearborn C. of C. (bd. dirs.), League of Women Voters, Springwell Bus. Assn. (v.p.), Nat. Fedn. Ind. Bus., Arab Am. Inst. Republican. Moslem. Club: Civitan. Office: Uncle Sam's Village Café 3337 Greenfield Rd Dearborn MI 48121

SARGEL, SCOT D., controller; b. Galion, Ohio, June 25, 1960; s. Frederick E. and Betty J. (Craner) S.; m. Lisa A. Kestler, Sept. 25, 1982. BS in Adminstrv. Sci., Ohio State U., 1982. CPA, Ohio. Sr. acct. Kenneth LEventhal & Co., Columbus, Ohio, 1982-86. Mem. Am. Inst. CPA's, Ohio Soc. CPA's. Home: 6487 Skywae Dr Columbus OH 43229 Office: Provident United Inc 5597 Sierra Ridge Columbus OH 43229

SARGENT, THOMAS ANDREW, educator; b. Indpls., Apr. 24, 1933; s. Thomas Edward and Inez (Secrest) S.; m. Cecily Constance Fox-Williams, 1965 (dec.); children: Sarah Beatrice, Andrew Fox; m. 2d Frances Petty, 1987. BA, DePauw U., Greencastle, Ind., 1955; MA, Fletcher Sch. Law and Diplomacy, Tufts U., 1959, MA in Law and Diplomacy, 1968, PhD, 1969. With First Nat. City Bank, N.Y.C., 1959-64; asst. accountant First Nat. City Bank, 1963-64; asst. sec. Irving Trust Co., N.Y.C., 1964-66; mem. faculty Ball State U., Muncie, Ind., 1969—, dir. London Ctr., 1973-74, chmn. polit. sci. dept., 1977-80, prof. polit. sci., 1979—, acting asst. to dean Coll. Scis. and Humanities, 1981-82, assoc. dean Coll. Scis. and Humanities, 1982-85, dir. spl. programs Minnetrista Ctr., 1985-87; dir. E.B. Ball Ctr., Muncie, 1987—. Contbg. editor: Ripon Forum, 1973-78. Bd. dirs., exec. v.p. Eastern Ind. Community TV, Muncie, 1974-76, pres., 1976-77; mem. nat. bd. govs. Ripon Soc., Washington, 1976-84; mem. Indpls. Com. Fgn. Relations, 1977—; bd. dirs. Hist. Muncie, Inc., 1979-85, pres., 1980; bd. dirs. Muncie Civic Theatre Assn., 1978-81, 1st v.p., 1979-80, sec., 1980-81; exec. dir. Ind. Consortium for Internat. Programs, 1982—; mem. Ind. Real Estate Commn., 1983—; trustee DePauw U., 1983—; bd. dirs. Muncie Symphony Orch., 1985—. Served to 1st lt. USAF, 1955-58. Mem. Am. Polit. Sci. Assn., Am. Soc. Internat. Law, Am. Acad. Polit. Sci., Delaware County Hist. Soc. (bd. dirs. 1980-86), Sigma Delta Chi, Phi Delta Theta. Republican. Methodist. Clubs: Delaware Country, Muncie; Columbia (Indpls.); Maxinkuckee Yacht (Culver, Ind.). Address: 2207 W Wiltshire Rd Muncie IN 47304

SARKISIAN, EDWARD GREGORY, dentist; b. Detroit, Oct. 6, 1952; s. Albert Nicholas and Nina (Doctorian) S.; m. Anna Svirid, July 12, 1975; children: Sara, Aram. BS, cert. in med. tech., U. Mich., 1974; DDS, U. Detroit, 1978. Lic. Bd. Dentistry, Mich. Gen. practice dentistry Dearborn, Mich., 1978—; mem. staff Harper Grace Hosp., Detroit, 1978—; clin. instr. dept. otolaryngology Wayne State U. Dept. Medicine, Detroit, 1982—. Mem. ADA, Mich. Dental Assn., Detroit Dist. Dental Assn., Armenian Gen. Benevolent Union Am., Francis Vedder Soc. Crown and Bridge Prosthodontics. Armenian Orthodox. Clubs: U. Mich. Pres.'s, U. Mich. Victors. Lodge: Knights of Vartan (Nareg chpt. comdr. 1984-85, midwest rep. 1986—). Office: 22190 Garrison Suite 201 Dearborn MI 48124

SARNI, MARC ROBERT, investment banker, accountant; b. St. Louis, Sept. 16, 1958; s. William F. and Bette J. (Anderson) S.; m. Mary K. Tull, June 22, 1985. BSBA in Acctg., U. Mo., 1981; MBA in Fin., U. Chgo., 1986. CPA, Mo. Sr. acct. Price Waterhouse, St. Louis, 1981-84; assoc. investment banker A.G. Edwards, St. Louis, 1986—. Vol. Am. Heart Assn., St. Louis, 1983. Mem. Am. Inst. CPA's, Mo. Soc. CPA's, Nat. Assn. Accts. Republican. Club: Chicago (St. Louis). Avocations: sports, reading, music, travel, fin. planning. Home: 2086 Winterhaven Ct Chesterfield MO 63017

SARNO, JOSEPH ADRIAN, store proprietor; b. Chgo., Feb. 17, 1939; s. Joseph Frederick and Ann Marie (Zaconne) S.; m. June Carol Vaznonis, July 25, 1965; children—Laura Jenine, Jamieson Joseph, Adrienne Joyce. Student, DePaul U., 1965, Amundson City Coll., 1968. With Putman Pub., Chgo., 1957-60; with Sun Electric, Chgo., 1960-61; asst. credit mgr. Wallace Bus. Forms, Chgo., 1964-68; credit supr. Armor-Dial, Inc., Chgo., 1968-73; propr. The Fantasy Shop, Chgo., 1971-78, The Nostalgia Shop, Chgo., 1973-79, Original Comic Art Emporium, Chgo., 1975-78, Comic Kingdom, Chgo., 1979—; pub. The Nostalgia Shop Newsletter, 1975-79, Chgo. Collectors Chronicles, 1978-80, Collectors Bull., 1981-82, Space Acad. Newsletter, 1978—. Contbr. articles and poetry to jours. Author: Poems, 1968; Shattered Dreams, 1978. Served with U.S. Army, 1961-64. Club: Fantasy Collectors of Chgo. Office: Joe Sarno Pub 5941 W Irving Park Rd Chicago IL 60634

SARTHER, LYNETTE KAY, accountant; b. Terre Haute, Ind., Mar. 16, 1947; d. William Horace and Margaret Jane (Bennett) Alsman; m. William Patrick Sarther, June 7, 1974; children: Kristen Casey, Joseph Bennett. B.S., Ball State U., 1969. C.P.A., Ohio. Staff acct., office mgr. Arthur Young & Co., Cin., 1969-74; ptnr. Fowler, Alsman & Co., Cin., 1974-75; sr. acct. small bus. John Sullivan, C.P.A., Reston, Va., 1975-77; mgr. small bus. dept. Rippe, Strickling, Kingston & Co., Cin., 1977-79; prin. Lynette K. Sarther, C.P.A., Cin., 1979—; bus. mgr. jour. Woman C.P.A. Mem. Am. Inst. C.P.A.s, Ohio Soc. C.P.A.s, Am. Soc. Women Accts. (bd. dirs., past pres. Cin. chpt., nat. editor Coordinator), Am. Woman's Soc. C.P.A.s, Kindervelt Children's Hosp. Aux. Republican. Methodist.

SARVAY, JOHN THOMAS, sales executive; b. Weirton, W.Va., Apr. 29, 1937; s. George and Anna (Kasich) S.; m. Beth Ann Ogan, July 15, 1961; children: Margaret Louise, Anna Beth, Scott Andrew. BS in Design, U. Cin., 1961; postgrad. Case Western Res. U., 1963. Plant mgr., dir. design Altech div. Ravens Metals Products, Parkersburg, W.Va., 1960-63; mgr. applied research Ohio Rubber Co. div. Eagle-Pitcher Corp., Willoughby, Ohio, 1963-65; devel. mgr. Standard Products Co., Cleve., 1965-70; dir. tech. info. group Stirling Homex Corp., Avon, N.Y., 1970-72; dir. corp. design and mktg. services Schlegel Corp., Rochester, N.Y., 1972-77; v.p. mktg. Modernfold div. Am. Standard Co., New Castle, Ind., 1977-79; sr. sales rep. Midwest Area, Computervision Corp., Bedford, Mass., 1979-86, ADRA Systems, Lowell, Mass., 1986—; planning cons. Wirt County (W.Va.), 1962-63. Contbr. articles to profl. jours.; patentee in field. Mem. Am. Inst. Aeros. and Astronautics, ASTM, Soc. Automotive Engrs., Am. Soc. Metals, Aircraft Owners and Pilots Assn., Confederate Air Force, Nat. Muzzle Loading Rifle Assn., Indsl. Designers Soc. Am. Byzantine Catholic. Lodge: Kiwanis. Home: 1200 Ivywood Ct New Castle IN 47362

SARWAR, MOHAMMAD, neuroradiologist, educator; b. Pakistan, June 7, 1945; came to U.S., 1968; s. Mohammad and Hajiran Bibi (Bashir) S.; m. Zahida Ahmad, Apr. 14, 1974; children: Huma, Sadiya, Sina. FSc, Govt. Coll. Lahore, Pakistan, 1962; MBBS, King Edward Med. Coll., Lahore, 1967. Lic. physician. Resident in radiology St. Luke's Hosp., N.Y.C., 1969-72; fellow in neuroradiology Albert Einstein Coll. Medicine, N.Y.C., 1972-74; assoc. prof. neuroradiology U. Tex., Galveston, 1974-80, Yale U., New Haven, Conn., 1980-85; prof., chief neuroradiology dept. U. Ill., Chgo., 1985—. Author: Basic Neuroradiology, 1983, Computed Tomography of Congenital Brain Malformation, 1985; editor-in-chief Neuroradiology Clinics mag.; contbr. numerous articles to profl. jours. Mem. AAAS, Am. Soc. Neuroradiology, Radiol. Soc. N.Am., Am. Roentgen Ray Soc. Home: 120 St Francis Circle Oakbrook IL 60521

SATARIANO, HARRY JOHN, family therapist; b. Pitts, Nov. 30, 1950; s. Anthony Joseph and Grace Veronica (Bowles) S. BA, St. Thomas Coll., Sem., 1973; MSW, U. Kans., 1977. Lic. specialist clin. social worker Kans.; cert. clin. social worker Nat. Bd. Cert. Social Work; cert. family therapist; cert. mediator. Mem. staff Cath. Social Service, Kansas City, Mo., 1977-79; clin. researcher Community Outreach Program for the Deaf, Tucson, 1979; clin. instr. Children Rehab. Unit, Kans. U. Med. Ctr., Kansas City, 1979—, dir. social work, 1981—, co-founder Neonatal ICU Family Study Inst., 1985; project coordinator Handicapped Child Abuse Prevention Program, RAP Fed. Region VII, 1983-84; staff cons. Head Start Programs, Kansas City, 1980-82; pvt. practice mediator; fed. grant. reviewer HHS. Fellow Menninger Found. Mem. Am. Assn. Mental Deficiencies, Nat. Assn. Auctioneers, Kansas. Assn. Auctioneers. Club: Toastmasters. Home: 4422 W 69th Terr Prairie Village KS 66208 Office: U Kans Med Ctr Children's Rehab Unit Room 137 Olathe Blvd at Rainbow Blvd Kansas City KS 66103

SATERNOW, PAULINE VIRGINIA, college administrator; b. Johnstown, Pa., Dec. 3, 1946; d. Charles Joseph and Alice Jeanne (Hesketh) Schech; m. Robert William Noe II, June 1, 1968 (div. 1974); 1 child, Robert William Noe III; m. Paul Herbert Saternow, Oct. 3, 1981. BS in Edn., Slippery Rock Coll., 1968; MS in Edn., U. Pitts., 1975. Tchr. New Castle (Pa.) Schs., 1968-69, Allegheny Valley Schs., Cheswick, Pa., 1969-73; instr., coach Thiel Coll., Greenville, Pa., 1973-76; asst. dir. athletics Youngstown (Ohio) State U., 1976-87, assoc. dir. athletics, 1987—; coach state championship softball teams Youngstown State U., 1978-79, mem. speakers' bur., 1976—. Mem. Ohio Assn. Intercollegiate Sports for Women (sec., treas 1985—), Mahoning Valley Coaches Assn., Nat. Assn. Female Execs., Zeta Tau Alpha (advisor 1985—). Avocations: golf, reading. Home: 124 Massachusetts Ave Youngstown OH 44514 Office: Youngstown State U Stambaugh Stadium Youngstown OH 44514

SATO, SHOZO, artist, educator; b. Kobe City, Japan, May 18, 1933; came to U.S., 1964; s. Takami and Midori Sato; m. Alice Y. Ogura, June 19, 1975. Degree in Fine Arts, Bunka Gakuin Coll., 1955; diplomas in traditional arts. Dir. Kamakura Ryusei Sch. Fine Arts, Japan, 1959-64; faculty U. Ill., Urbana, 1964-66, 68—, artist-in-residence, prof. art, 1968—, dir. Japan House, 1976—; vis. lectr. colls., univs., 1964—; dir. opera, theatre prodns., 1965—; faculty U. Wis., 1966-67. Author: The Art of Arranging Flowers, 1966, The Appreciation of Oriental Art, 1967, The Art of Sumi-E, 1984. Co-recipient Prints Regional Design award for Kabuki Macbeth, Casebook 4, 1979; recipient Joseph Jefferson awards for prodn., direction and costume design for Kabuki Macbeth Chgo. Theatre Assn., 1982, award for best costuming for Kabuki Medea, 1984, Designers award for Kabuki Medea poster N.Y. Arts Dirs., 1984, Bay Area Theatre Critics award for best prodn., direction, tech. achievement for Kabuki Medea, 1985, Hollywood Drama-Logue Critics award for outstanding achievement in theatre for Kabuki Medea, 1985, 1st Burlington No. Found. Faculty Achievement award, 1985, Prints Regional Design award for Kabuki Faust poster, 1986; U. Ill. research grantee on Middle Eastern, Southeastern Asian performing arts, 1974, Hoso Bunk Found. grantee, 1983. Mem. Am. Theatre Assn., Am. Guild Mus. Artists, AAUP, Gold Key (hon.). Office: U Ill 124 Fine Arts Bldg Champaign IL 61820

SATTERWHITE, JON THOMAS, dentist; b. Danville, Ill., Apr. 4, 1953; s. George Byron and Florence Hortense (Henderson) S.; m. Carla Ann Sommerville, June 30, 1973; children: Kelly Jean, Melinda Beth. AS, Danville Jr. Coll., 1973; BS, Ea. Ill. U., 1980; DDS, So. Ill. Sch. Dental Medicine, 1984. Lab. technician Lauhoff Grain Co., Danville, 1973-78; orderly Alton (Ill.) Meml. Hosp., 1980-84; gen. practice dentistry Rossville, Ill., 1984—. Mem. ADA, Chgo. Dental Soc., Danville Dist. Dental Soc., Mensa. Lodges: Masons, Elks. Avocations: scuba diving, aquariology, hunting. Home: 124 1/2 S Chicago Rossville IL 60963 Office: 124 S Chicago Rossville IL 60963

SATTLER, JOAN LINDA, education educator, dean; b. Adrian, Mich., Oct. 21, 1947; d. Allen Henry and Ruth Alice (Beyer) M.; m. Edward Lee Sattler, June 7, 1969; children—Linda Grace, Allen Edward, Michael Edward. B.S., Western Mich. U., 1969; Ed.M., U. Ill., 1974, Ed.D., 1977. Cert. elem. and spl. edn. tchr., Nebr., Miss., Ill. Tchr. pub. schs. Springfield, Wis., 1969-70; spl. edn. tchr. Lincoln Pub. Schs., Nebr., 1970-71, Jackson Pub. Schs., Miss., 1971-72; assoc. prof., then chmn. spl. edn. Bradley U., Peoria, Ill., 1977—, assoc. dean Coll. Edn. and Health Scis., 1985—. Assoc. editor Tchr. Edn. and Spl. Edn. jour. 1983—; contbg. editor Ill. Council for Exceptional Children Quar. jour. 1981—. Mem. higher edn. adv. com. Ill. Bd. of Edn., 1979—; mem. sch. bd. Montessori Sch., Peoria, Ill., 1980-81; bd. dirs. Allied Agys., Peoria, 1981-82, Easter Seal Soc., Peoria, 1985. U.S. Office of Edn. fellow, 1972-76; U. Ill. fellow, 1974-76. Mem. Council for Exceptional Children (faculty adviser 1969—), Am. Council for Learning Disabilities, Nat. Council for Accreditation of Tchr. Edn. (team evaluator 1978—), AAUP, Am. Edn. Research Assn, Phi Delta Kappa (del. 1983—, research 1984). Unitarian Universalist. Avocations: reading, family activities, piano, organ. Home: 2302 W Bainter Ln Peoria IL 61615 Office: Bradley U Westlake Hall Peoria IL 61625

SATYAPRIYA, COMBATORE KESHAVAMURTHY, geotechnical engineer; b. Bangalore, Mysore, India, Jan. 27, 1949; came to U.S., 1972; s. C. V. and C. V. (Vedamma) Keshavamurthy; m. Indira Muthanna, Nov. 1, 1976; children: Ajay S., Anand A. BCE, Bangalore U., 1969, MCE, 1971; MS, Worcester (Mass.) Poly. Inst., 1972. Registered profl. engr., Ohio, Md., Va., W.Va., Washington, Pa., Ind., Ky., Fla. Staff engr. Mason & Ray Inc., Columbus, Ohio, 1976-77; sr. geotech. engr. Resource Internat. Inc., Columbus, 1977-78; staff engr. CTL Engring. Inc., Columbus, 1978-79, dept. head geotech. engring., 1979-80, v.p., 1981-83, exec. v.p., 1983-86; mgr. ops. Washington Testing, Inc., Fairfax, Va., 1981-82; pres. CTL Engring. Inc., Columbus, 1986—; mem. control group Placement & Improvement, Columbus, 1982—. Contbr. articles to profl. jours. Mem. ASCE (pres. cen. Ohio 1978-79, tech. com. on placement and improvement of soils 1982—), Am. Soc. Testing Materials (coms. E-06, D-18, D-20), Indian Geotechnical Soc., Chi Epsilon. Lodge: Rotary. Avocation: tennis. Home: 799 Tweed Ct Worthington OH 43085 Office: CTL Engring Inc 2860 Fisher Rd Columbus OH 43204

SAUDER, MARILYN ANNE TRELFORD, surgeon; b. Toronto, Ont., Can., Apr. 13, 1937; naturalized, 1983; d. John Edward Alexander and Anne Katherine (Von Maur) Trelford; m. Oran A.J. Sauder (div.). BSCN, U. Western Ont., 1961; BA, Wayne State U., 1965, MD, 1970. Diplomate Am. Bd. Surgery. Asst. dir. nursing services Windsor (Ont.) Met. Hosp., 1961-62; instr. med.-surg. nursing Harper Hosp. Sch. Nursing, Detroit, 1965-66; intern Oakwood Hosp., Detroit, 1970-71; resident in gen. surgery Sinai Hosp., Detroit, 1971-72; physician Gen. Med. Indsl. Clinic, East Detroit, Mich., 1972-73; asst dir. emergency room Outer Dr. Hosp., Lincoln Park, Mich., 1972-74; resident in gen. surgery Grace Hosp., Detroit, 1974-77; attending physician Harper-Grace Hosp., Detroit, 1977—; practice medicine specializing in gen. surgery South Lyon, Mich., 1977—; med. dir. N.W. Med. Arts, Livonia, Mich., 1984—, South Lyon Med. Arts, 1985—; mem. steering com. Huron Valley Hosp., Milford, Mich., 1985-87, attending physician, mem. exec. com., 1986-87; mem. cons. and courtesy staff in gen. surgery Rehab. Inst., Detroit, 1981-87; mem. affiliate staff Detroit Receiving Hosp. and Univ. Med. Ctr., 1981—. Contbr. numerous articles to med. jours., 1977-86. Mem. Mayor's Adv. Com. for Indsl. Devel., South Lyon, 1980-82. Named People to People Ambassador to Russia, 1987. Fellow ACS, Internat. Coll. Surgeons; mem. Oakland County Med. Soc. (med. examiner 1978—, mem. pub. relations com. 1986), Southeastern Mich. Surg. Soc., Profl. Standards Rev. Orgn., South Lyon C. of C. (bd. dirs. 1977-82). Home: 25500 Belladonna South Lyon MI 48178 Office: Northwest Med Arts 32410 Five Mile Rd Livonia MI 48178

SAUER, DALE JOSEPH, marriage and family therapist; b. Lorain, Ohio, July 11, 1940; s. John Frank and Evelyn Ann (Kastl) S.; divorced; children: Andrea, Jonathan, Gretchen, Sean. BA, Otterbein Coll., 1962; MDiv, United Theol. Sem., 1966; MST, Boston U., 1968; DMin., Christian Theol. Sem., 1979. Pastor Belmont (Ohio) United Meth. Ch., 1970-73; counselor, educator Buchanan Counseling Ctr. Meth. Hosp. Ind., Inc., Indpls., 1973-87, counselor, group practice, 1987—; pastor First Presbyn. Ch., Danville, Ind., 1975-80, Bethel Presbyn. Ch., Knightstown, Ind., 1980-86; supr. field edn. Christian Theol. Sem., Indpls., 1975-81. Editor: (newsletter) Bridgebuilder, 1982-85. Chmn. steering com. Bethesda (Ohio) Learning Ctr., 1971-73; elder East Ohio Conf. United Meth. Ch., 1966. Mem. Am. Assn. Pastoral Counselors (diplomate, chair profl. concerns 1975-80), Am. Assn. for Marriage and Family Therapy (clin., approved supr. 1976), Ind. Assn. for Marriage and Family Therapy (bd. dirs., treas. 1984—), Am. Group Psychotherapy Assn. Republican. Home: 6125 N Meridian St Indianapolis IN 46208 Office: Buchanan Counseling Ctr 8350 N Craig St Suite 225 Indianapolis IN 46250

SAUER, FREDERICK ALBERT, JR., lawyer; b. Pontiac, Mich., Mar. 7, 1929; s. Frederick Albert and Martha Lavina (Witters) S.; m. Frances Louise Jackson, Dec., 1953 (div. June 1960); 1 son, Stephen Dana; m. 2d, Anne Marie Kruizenga, Sept. 7, 1962; children—Stephanie Ann, Mark Frederick. B.A., Albion Coll.-Kalamazoo Coll., 1955; J.D., Detroit Coll. Law, 1958. Bar: Mich. 1958. Ptnr. Sauer & Sauer, Kalamazoo, 1958-60; sole practice, Kalamazoo, 1960-69, 74—; ptnr. Sauer & Tucker, Kalamazoo, 1969-74; lectr. Inst. Continuing Legal Edn., U. Mich. Served as lt. comdr. N.G., 1943-44, USMC, 1947-50, USAR, 1950-53. Mem. State Bar Mich. (councilman family law sect.), County Bar of Kalamazoo, U.S. Coast Guard Assn., Sigma Chi, Sigma Rho Sigma. Lutheran. Home: 2455 Kensington Dr Kalamazoo MI 49008 Office: 827 W South St Kalamazoo MI 49007

SAUER, HAROLD JOHN, physician, educator; b. Detroit, Dec. 1, 1953; s. Peter and Hildegard (Muehlmann) S.; m. Kathleen Ann Iorio, Sept. 4, 1982; children: Angela Karin Fermante, Peter Rolf Jan Muehlmann. BS, U. Mich., 1975; MD, Wayne State U., 1979. Diplomate Am. Bd. Ob-Gyn. Resident in ob-gyn William Beaumont Hosp., Royal Oak, Mich., 1979-83; fellow in reproductive endocrinology and infertility William Beaumont Hosp., Royal Oak, 1983-85; asst. prof. dept. ob-gyn and reproductive biology Mich. State U., East Lansing, 1985—; mem. staff St. Lawrence Hosp., Lansing, Mich., 1985—, E.W. Sparrow Hosp., Lansing, 1985—; cons. Mich. Dept. Social Services, Lansing, 1985—; researcher in field. Mem. AMA, Mich. State Med. Soc., Ingham County Med. Soc., Lansing Oby-Gyn Soc., Am. Fertility Soc., Wayne State U. Med. Alumni Assn. Roman Catholic. Avocations: classical piano, microcomputers, skiing. Home: 4101 Spinnaker Ln Okemos MI 48864-3477 Office: Mich State U Dept Ob-Gyn Reproductive Biology B-316 Clin Ctr East Lansing MI 48823-1315

SAUER, JANE GOTTLIEB, artist, educator; b. St. Louis, Sept. 16, 1937; d. Leo and Sally (Walpert) Gottlieb; m. Martin Rosen, June 6, 1959 (div. 1967); children: Julie, Leo, Rachel; m. Donald Carl Sauer, Oct. 31, 1972; children: Jeffrey, Diane. BFA, Washington U., St. Louis, 1960; pvt. study with Leslie Laskey, 1976-78. Artist in residence New City Sch., St. Louis, 1976-78; artist in schs. Mo. Arts Council, St. Louis, 1979; studio artist St. Louis, 1979—; tchr. Craft Alliance Art Ctr., St. Louis, 1979-82; cons. Harris Stowe Tchrs. Coll., St. Louis, 1980-84; lectr. and workshop leader various orgns. throughout country, 1979—. Represented in collections Joseph & Emily Rauh Pulitzer, St. Louis, Nordenfjeldske Kunstindustrimuseum, Trondnheim, Norway, Vera Mott U. Mo., Columbia, Prudential Ins. Co. Am., Dallas, others; one and two person exhibits Craft Alliance Gallery, St. Louis, 1981, The Hand and the Spirit Gallery, Scottsdale, Ariz., 1982, 85, Linda Einfeld Gallery, Chgo., 1987; others; numerous selected exhibitions, 1979—; contbr. articles to profl. publs. Recipient Critic's Choice award Christmas exhibit Craft Alliance Gallery, 1979-80, Vera Mott Purchase award, 1981, various others; Nat. Endowment for Visual Arts grantee, 1984, Mo. Arts Council grantee, 1986. Mem. Am. Craft Council, Area Coordinating Council (sec. 1984-86, past bd. dirs.), St. Louis Weavers Guild. Home and Office: 6332 Wydown Saint Louis MO 63105

SAUER, JEFFERY JOSEPH, accountant; b. Iowa City, Aug. 3, 1956; s. Gerald and Peggy J. S. BA in Acctg., U. No. Iowa, 1979; postgrad. in taxation, U. Minn., 1982-84. CPA, Minn. Supr. Fox and Co., Mpls., 1979-85; mgr. Larson, Allen, Weishar & Co., Mpls., 1985—; adv. council acctg. faculty U. No. Iowa, 1982—. Vol. Susan Lindgren Sch. Site Mgmt. Program, 1985; bd. dirs. New Classic Theater, 1986—. Mem. Am. Inst. CPA's, Nat. Assn. Accts., Minn. Soc. CPA's (pub. relations com., 1983-84, chmn. acctg. careers com. 1983-84, bd. dirs. 1984—), Pi Kappa Alpha Housing Assn. (treas. 1985—). Republican. Roman Catholic. Avocations: reading, writing, tennis, travel. Home: 4200 Toledo Ave S Saint Louis Park MN 55416 Office: Larson Allen Weishair & Co 1200 Interchange Tower 600 S County Rd 18 Minneapolis MN 55426

SAUER, KENNETH H., bishop. Bishop Luth. Ch. Am., Columbus, Ohio. Office: Luth Ch 1233 Dublin Rd Columbus OH 43215 *

SAUER, ROBERT WILLIAM, engineering company executive; b. Indpls., Sept. 14, 1941; s. Carl M. and Erma R. (Swaim) S. B.S., Purdue U., 1963; Ph.D., Northwestern U., 1968. With Reuas Engring. Co., Inc., Indpls., 1968—, pres., 1972—; pres. Sauer Realty Co., 1980—. Mem. Am. Soc. Metals, Sigma Xi, Phi Eta Sigma, Alpha Sigma Nu, Sigma Alpha Epsilon, Tau Kappa Beta. Clubs: Columbia; Contemporary. Office: 555 W 16th St Indianapolis IN 46208

SAUERBURGER, DAVID PAUL, lawyer, accountant, tax consultant; b. St. Louis, July 11, 1956; s. Paul E. and Mary A. (Schroeder) S.; m. Jamie Lynn Smigieski, Nov. 10, 1984. BSBA, St. Louis U., 1977, MBA, JD, 1980. Bar: Mo. 1981; CPA, Mo. Acct. Zielinski & Wolff CPA's, St. Louis, 1977-80; ptnr. Stelmacki, Cochran & Sauerburger, P.C., St. Louis, 1981—. Mem. ABA, Am. Inst. CPA's, Mo. Soc. CPA's, Mo. Bar Assn., St. Louis Met. Bar Assn. Roman Catholic. Office: Stelmacki Cochran & Suerburger One Insurance Plaza Ctr #101 Saint Louis MO 63141

SAUERS, JAMES BYRON, allergist, clinical immunologist; b. Willard, Ohio, Nov. 14, 1930; s. Charles Sylvester Sauers and Margaret Helen (Dungan) Dellinger; m. Ruth Parry Owens, June 28, 1962 (div). BA, Ohio Wesleyan U., 1952; MD, Ohio State U., 1958. Diplomate Am. Bd. Pediatrics. Intern Cleve. Met. Gen. Hosp., 1958-59, resident in pediatrics, 1959-60; resident in pediatrics Univ. Hosp. Cleve., 1961; fellow in allergies and immunology U. Colo. Med. Ctr., Denver, 1961-63; practice medicine specializing in allergy and clin. immunology Cleve., 1963—; head pediatrics and allergies St. Luke's Hosp., Cleve., 1963—; assoc. clin. prof. pediatrics U. Hosp. Cleve., 1963—, Case Western Res. U., Cleve., 1963—. Served with U.S. Army, 1952-54. Fellow Am. Acad. Pediatrics; mem. Am. Acad. Allergy and Clin. Immunology, AMA, Ohio State Med. Assn., Cleve. Acad. Medicine, Cleve. Allergy Soc. (past pres.). Avocations: antiques, agriculture. Office: 3619 Park East Cleveland OH 44122 Office: 1218 Cleveland Rd Sandusky OH 44870

SAUL, BRADLEY SCOTT, communications and entertainment executive; b. Chgo., June 29, 1960; s. Richard Cushman and Yolanda (Merdinger) S. BS, Northwestern U., 1981, MA, 1982; postgrad., Loyola U., 1983-84. With info. services dept. Sta. CBS/WBBM Radio, Chgo., 1979-80; gen. mgr. Sta. WEEF Radio, Highland Park, Ill., 1979-81, Sta. WONX, Evanston, Ill., 1981-83; faculty advisor Sta. WNUR Radio, Evanston, 1981-83; pres., ptnr., co-founder Pub. Interest Affiliates, Chgo., N.Y., 1981—; pres. Chgo. Antique Radio Corp., 1986—; prof. Columbia Coll., Chgo., 1985-87; bd. dirs. Lake View Mental Health Ctr., Chgo. Contbr. articles to prof. jours. Named Outstanding Investigative Journalist, Warner Books, 1977. Mem. Nat. Assn. Broadcasters, Nat. Radio Broadcasters Assn. Jewish. Club: East Bank (Chgo.). Avocations: reading, weight lifting, old movies, boxing, old time radio shows. Office: Pub Interest Affiliates 666 N Lake Shore Dr Suite 800 Chicago IL 60611 also: 12 W 31st St New York NY 10001

SAUNDERS, GEORGE LAWTON, JR., lawyer; b. Mulga, Ala., Nov. 8, 1931; s. George Lawton and Ethel Estell (York) S.; m. Joanne Rosa Helperin, Dec. 4, 1959 (div.); children: Kenneth, Ralph, Victoria; m. Terry M. Rose, Sept. 21, 1975. B.A., U. Ala., 1956; J.D., U. Chgo., 1959. Bar: Ill. 1960. Law clk. to chief judge U.S. Ct. Appeals (5th cir.), Montgomery, Ala., 1959-60; law clk Justice Hugo L. Black, U.S. Supreme Ct., Washington, 1960-62; assoc. Sidley & Austin, Chgo., 1962-67, ptnr., 1967—. Served with USAF, 1951-54. Mem. ABA, Ill. State Bar Assn., Chgo. Bar Assn., Chgo. Council Lawyers, Order of Coif, Phi Beta Kappa. Democrat. Baptist. Clubs: Chicago, Saddle and Cycle, Mid-Am., Quadrangle, Law, Legal (Chgo.). Home: 179 E Lake Shore Dr Chicago IL 60611 Office: Sidley & Austin 1 First National Plaza Chicago IL 60603

SAUNDERS, LESLIE MCCALL, architect; b. Lubondai, Kasai, Belgian Congo, Dec. 14, 1955; came to U.S., 1960; s. Manford Harding and Lenore (McCall) S.; m. Cynthia Ann Sams, Dec. 29, 1978; children: Elizabeth, Leslie Jr., Lenore. BArch, Clemson U., 1978, MArch, 1980. Registered architect, Ohio. Med. facility planner Bohm-NBBJ, Columbus, Ohio, 1980-82, sr. med. facility planner, 1982-84, dir. med. facility planning, 1984—, v.p., 1987—. Am. Hosp. Assn. fellow, 1979-80, Langley scholar, 1980. Mem. AIA (Silver medal 1980), Soc. for Hosp. Planning, Com. Architecture for Health (corp., subcom. chmn. 1980). Presbyterian. Home: 537 Fallis Rd Columbus OH 43214 Office: NBBJ Group 55 Nationwide Blvd Columbus OH 43215

SAUNDERS, LONNA JEANNE, lawyer, newscaster; b. Cleve., Nov. 26, 1952; d. Jack Glenn and Lillian Frances (Newman) Slaby. Student, Dartmouth Coll., 1972-73; AB, Vassar Coll., 1974; JD, Northwestern U., 1981. Bar: Ill. 1981. News dir., morning news anchor Sta. WKBK-FM, Keene, N.H., 1974-75; reporter Sta. KDKA-FM, Pitts., 1975; pub. affairs dir., news anchor Sta. WJW-FM, Cleve., 1975-77; morning news anchor Sta. WBBG-FM, Cleve., 1978; talk host, news anchor Sta. WIND-AM, Chgo., 1978-82; atty. Arvey, Hodes, Costello & Burman, Chgo., 1981-82; host, news anchor WCIU-TV, Chgo., 1982-85; staff atty. Better Govt. Assn., Chgo., 1983-84; news anchor, reporter Sta. WBMX-FM, Chgo., 1984-86; sole practice Chgo., 1985—; news anchor Sta. WKQX-FM, Chgo., 1987—; guest talk host Sta. WMCA, N.Y.C., 1983; host, producer "The Lively Arts" Cablevision Chgo., 1986; atty. Lawyers for Creative Arts, Chgo., 1985—. Contbg. editor Chgo. Life mag., 1986—; contbr. articles to profl. jours.; creator (pub. affairs program) "Ask The Schools" WBBM-AM. Recipient Akron Press Club award (best pub. affairs presentation); Scripps Howard found. grantee, 1978-79, 79-80; AFTRA George Heller Meml. scholar, 1980-81. Mem. Dartmouth Lawyers Assn., Women's Bar Assn. Ill., Investigative Reporters and Editors, Nat. Acad. TV Arts and Scis., ABA (exec. coms. Lawyers and the Arts, Law and Media), Sigma Delta Chi. Roman Catholic. Clubs: Chgo. Vassar, Vassar (N.Y.C.), Chgo. Dartmouth. Avocations: theater, piano. Home: 1212 S Michigan Ave #2206 Chicago IL 60605 Office: 134 N LaSalle St Suite 1220 Chicago IL 60602

SAUNDERS, MONTE KEITH, communications executive; b. Salina, Kans., May 3, 1955; s. Keith Donald and Patricia Lynn (Beck) S.; m. Marie Rose Mies, June 19, 1985. AA, Hutch County Jr. Coll., 1975; BS, Ft. Hays State U., 1977. Acct. Dub Johnsons & Sons Inc., Mpls., 1977-80; asst. controller Great Empire Broadcasting, Wichita, Kans., 1980-85; chief fin. officer Long-Pride Broadcasting, Wichita, 1985—. Avocations: weight lifitng, aerobics, jogging, softball, skiing. Home: 3970 N Porter Wichita KS 67204 Office: Long-Pride Broadcasting Inc 2829 Salina Wichita KS 67204

SAUNDERS, RICHARD FAYE, distribution company executive; b. Minot, N.D., Oct. 3, 1919; s. Captain Henry and Mayne Minerva (Bella) S.; married; children: Jill Susanne, Joan Denise. Student, Minot State Coll., 1938, 39; BS in Pharmacy, U. Minn., 1943. Pres., gen. mgr. Dakco Distbrs., Inc., Minot, 1946—; bd. dirs. NorWest Bank. Elder First Presbyn. Ch., Minot, 1986—. Served as cpl. U.S. Army, 1943-46. Mem. Nat. Wholesale Druggist Assn. (bd. dirs., adv. bd. 1986—), Minot Alumni Assn. (pres. 1983-84, bd. dirs. 1986—), State U. N.D. Regents Alumni Assn. (bd. dirs. 1986—). Lodges: Rotary, Elks, Inquisitors. Avocations: hunting, fishing, photography, tennis, golf. Office: Dakco Distbr Inc PO Box 5009 Minot ND 58502

SAUNDERS, THOMAS H., architect; b. Lincoln, Nebr., July 12, 1941; s. Lovell Glenn and Kathryn Margaret (Schleining) S.; m. Jill Theirl, Sept. 12, 1981; children: Jennifer, Christine, Maureen. Student, U. Nebr., 1959-61, Frank Lloyd Wright Sch. Architecture, 1967. Registered architect, Mo., Ky., Nev., Minn., Colo., Nebr. Draftsman Taliesin Assocs. Architects, Scottsdale, Ariz., 1961-67; draftsman, designer Bernoudy Assocs., St. Louis, 1967-70; architect Peckham-Guyton Architects, St. Louis, 1970-71; architect, owner Saunders-Thalden Assocs., St. Louis, 1971-85; prin. Thomas H. Saunders Assocs., St. Louis, 1985—; chmn. bd. advisors Meramec Coll., St. Louis, 1975—. Designer Nat. Bowling Hall of Fame, apartments, condominiums. Mem. Traffic Study Commn., St. Louis County, 1984, Long Range Housing Task Force, Webster Groves, Mo., 1985, Archtl. Rev. Bd., Webster Groves. Mem. AIA, Am. Soc. Landscape Architects. Republican. Mem. Unitarian Ch. Avocations: gardening, building, backpacking, skiing, cooking. Office: 7711 Bonhommie Saint Louis MO 63105

SAUNDERS, TONI LYNNE, construction company executive; b. Columbus, Ohio, Aug. 19, 1949; d. Larry Brook Wells and Mildred Carole (Talbott) Souders; m. William Kenneth Riley, May 13, 1969 (div. Apr. 1971); m. Albert Eugene Saunders, Sept. 28, 1971; 1 child, Randy Lee Saunders. Grad. high sch., Xenia, Ohio, 1967. Corp. sec. Ind. Horizontal Boring, Inc., Indpls., 1981-82; pres., chmn. bd. Ind. Horizontal Boring, Inc., New Palestine, Ind., 1982—; also bd. dirs. Ind. Horizontal Boring, Inc., Indpls.; founder Pride Cons., New Palestine, Ind., 1986—. Mem. Nat. Assn. Women in Constrn. (fund raiser 1984, 85, 86, chmn. Women's Bus. Enterprise com. 1984-86), Nat. Assn. Female Execs., Nat. Assn. Self-Employed. Avocations: reading, writing, swimming, oil painting, refinishing old furniture. Office: Ind Horizontal Boring Inc PO Box 197 New Palestine IN 46163

SAUTTER, RICHARD DANIEL, physician, administrator; b. Ord, Nebr., Dec. 30, 1926; s. Daniel August and Theresa May (Ries) S.; m. Rosemary Elizabeth Graham, Aug. 4, 1952; children—Ann Elizabeth, Daniel Richard, Michael Graham, Mark Allen. B.S., U. Nebr., Lincoln, 1948; M.D., U. Nebr., Omaha, 1953. Diplomate Am. Bd. Surgery, Am. Bd. Thoracic Surgery. Intern Highland Alameda County, Oakland, Calif., 1953-54; resident, instr. in gen. surgery State Univ. of Iowa, Iowa City, 1954-61; thoracic and cardiovascular surgeon Marshfield Clinic, Wis., 1961—, dir. med. edn., 1975—; exec. dir. Marshfield Med. Research Found., Wis., 1977—; asst. dean for clin. affairs U. Wis., Madison, 1984—; mem. alcohol and other drug abuse research adv. com. Dept. Health and Social Services, State of Wis., 1985—. Contbr. numerous articles to profl. jours., chpts. to books; patentee in field; mem. editorial bd. Wis. Med. Jour., 1977—, assoc. editor, 1986-87, med. editor, 1987—. Served with U.S. Army, 1944-45; PTO. Grantee NIH, 1968-70, 70-71, Nat. Heart-Lung Inst., 1971, 71-72, 73-83, 74-77, others. Fellow ACS (nat. and Wis. chpt.); mem. Am. Assn. Thoracic Surgery, Soc. Thoracic Surgeons, Central Surg. Assn., Wis. Surg. Soc., Wis. Heart Club, Wood County Med. Soc., Am. Heart Assn. (council on thrombosis), Wis. State Med. Soc., Western Surg. Assn., Soc. for Clin. Trials Inc. Lodge: Elks. Avocations: fishing; gardening. Home: 221 S Schmidt Ave Marshfield WI 54449 Office: Marshfield Med Found 510 N St Joseph's Ave Marshfield WI 54449

SAUTTER, ROBERT GERHARD, human resources development executive; b. Highland, Ill., Apr. 17, 1941; s. Milton Norman and Sylvia Ida (Feutz) S.; children: David Lewis, Matthew Peter. BS in Indsl. Mgmt., So. Ill. U., Carbondale, 1963; MA in Behavioral Scis., So. Ill. U., Edwardsville, 1973. Design engr. McDonnell Douglas Corp., St. Louis, 1963-71; mgmt. edn. specialist Tng. and Devel. Inst., U.S. Postal Service, Chgo., 1974-77; mgr. assessment and devel. Owens Corning Fiberglas, Toledo, Ohio, 1977—. V.p., steward Good Shepherd Luth. Ch., Toledo, 1983-85; co-founder, treas. Chgo. Orgn. Devel. Assn. Mem. Am. Soc. Tng. and Devel., Psi Chi. Home: 4525 Nantucket Dr Toledo OH 43623 Office: Owens Corning Fiberglas Toledo OH 43659

SAVAGE, BARRY EMERY, lawyer; b. Jackson, Mich., Apr. 19, 1940; s. Herbert E. and Marva V. (Schultz) S.; B.A. in Econ., U. Mich., 1962, J.D., 1965; m. Joyce A. Diaz, Oct. 6, 1977; 1 son by previous marriage, Steven Vincent. Admitted to Ohio bar, 1965, Mich. bar, 1966; practice in Toledo, 1965—; with firm Savage & Lindsley, P.A., Toledo; engaged in real estate investment, 1968—. Mem. Mich. Bar Assn., Toledo Bar Assn. (chmn. unauthorized practice com. 1970-72), ABA. Club: Toledo Yacht. Home: 1663 Wyandotte Maumee OH 43537 Office: Savage & Lindsley Co 405 Madison Suite 1850 Toledo OH 43604-1294

SAVAGE, FRED WILLIAM, sales executive; b. Cleve., May 28, 1939; s. Frank W. and Anne (Sypos) S.; children: Frank Fredric, Kirsten Erna. Student Ohio U., 1957-58, Baldwin-Wallace Coll., 1966-69. Dist. sales mgr. Hertz Truck Div., Cleve., 1970-75; lease account mgr. Ryder Truck Rental, Cleve., 1976-80; rental mgr. Lend Lease Truck Rental, Cleve., 1980-81, sta. mgr., 1981-82, regional sales mgr., Worthington, Ohio, 1982—; sales cons. Leaseway Transp., Cleve., 1975. Served with M.I., U.S. Army, 1962-66. Republican. Baptist. Avocations: history; golf; jogging. Home: 8213 Chinook Pl #2B Worthington OH 43085

SAVAGE, GUS, congressman; b. Detroit, Oct. 30, 1925; s. Thomas Frederick and Molly (Wilder) S.; m. Eunice King, Aug. 4, 1946 (dec. Feb. 1981); children: Thomas James, Emma Mae. B.A., Roosevelt U., 1951, postgrad., 1951; postgrad., Chgo.-Kent Coll. Law, 1952-53. Editor Am. Negro mag., Chgo., 1954, Woodlawn Booster newspaper, Chgo., 1961-64, The Bulletin, Chgo., 1963-64; asst. editor Ill. Beverage Jour., Chgo., 1955-57; editor, pub. Westside Booster newspaper, Chgo., 1958-60, Citizen newspapers, Chgo., 1965-79, The Chgo. Weekend newspaper, 1973-79; mem. 97th-100th Congresses from 2d Ill. Dist., 1981—. Author: Pamphlets How to Increase the Power of the Negro Vote, 1959, Political Power, 1969. Active civil rights leader; a founder, campaign mgr. Chgo. League Negro Voters, 1958-59; founder, chmn. Protest at the Polls, 1963-64; pres. Orgn. S.W. Communities, 1968-69; founder, 1st chmn. Chgo. Black Pubs. Assn., 1970. Served with USAAF, 1943-46. Named Ind. Journalist of Year Washington Park Improvement Assn., 1965; recipient medal of merit City of Chgo., 1976; award of merit Operation PUSH, 1976; Businessman of Year award Dollars and Sense mag., 1978; Freshman of Year award NAACP, Evanston, Ill., 1981; Presdl. award Cook County Bar Assn., 1981. Office: US House of Representatives 1121 Longworth House Office Bldg Washington DC 20515 *

SAVAGE, JOHN PAUL, educator; b. Detroit, July 12, 1946; s. Neil Saxton and Josephine Alice (Ettinger) S.; m. Mary Margaret Bermel, Nov. 27, 1971; 1 child, John Paul Jr. BA, U. Mich., 1968; MEd, Wayne State U., 1980, EdS, 1986. Tchr. Lincoln Park (Mich.) Pub. Schs., 1968—, Huff Jr. High, 1968-79, Carr Elem. Sch., 1979-82, Le Blanc Elem. Sch., 1982-83, Raupp Elem. Sch., 1983-87; dist. computer coordinator, tchr. computer sci. Lincoln Park High Sch., 1987—. Asst. scoutmaster Boy Scouts Am., 1964-76, commr., 1972-74, asst. dist. commr., 1974-76, dist. dir. tng., 1977-84, dist. commr., 1984—. Served with AUS, 1970-71. Recipient Order of Arrow, Boy Scouts Am., 1974, Dist. Merit award, 1976, Silver Beaver award, 1984; recipient Disting. Service award Lincoln Park PTA Council, 1977; named Outstanding Young Educator, Lincoln Park Jaycees, 1976. Mem. NEA, Mich. Edn. Assn., Lincoln Park Edn. Assn., Mich. Council Tchrs. Math., Mich. Assn. Computer Users in Learning, Assn. Supervision and Curriculum Devel., Mich. Assn. Supervision and Curriculum Devel., Mich. Jaycees (super Saturday portfolio mgr. 1982-83, leadership series portfolio mgr. 1983-84, senator 1984, Outstanding State Chmn. award 1983, chmn. senate speakers bur. 1985-87, treas. senate 1987, Doc Huldin award 1986), Dearborn (Mich.) Jaycees (v.p. individual devel. 1981-82), Phi Delta Kappa. Home: 7840 Calhoun St Dearborn MI 48126 Office: Lincoln Park High Sch 1701 Champaign Lincoln Park MI 48146

SAVAGE, ROBERT WILLIAM, marriage and family counselor; b. Detroit, Dec. 23, 1933; s. Frank Savage and Margaret Cruikshank; m. Shirley Jane Barker, Aug. 12, 1955; children: Rebecca Diane, Timothy Shaun. BA, No. Bapt. Theol. Sem., 1963; MA, Eastern Mich. U., 1970. Ordained to ministry Greendale Bapt. Ch. Social worker State of Mich., Detroit, 1959-66; rehab. counselor Vocat. Rehab. Services, Pontiac, Mich., 1966-68; blind rehab. counselor Service for Blind, Kalamazoo, Mich., 1968-73; counselor First Bapt. Ch., Elkhart, Ind., 1973-76; dir. Christian Counseling, Goshen, Ind., 1976—; conf. speaker, lectr. Christian Counseling Services, Goshen, 1976—; radio speaker, cons. Sta. WFRN, Elkhart, 1976—; cons. Crown Internat., Elkhart, 1976—. Contbr. articles to profl. jours. Served as cpl. U.S. Army, 1953-55. Recipient Cert. Appreciation Optimist Club, 1982, Kiwanis Club, 1984. Mem. Menninger Found. Republican. Club: Exchange (Goshen) (bd. dirs. 1982-84). Avocations: automobile body repairing, woodcarving, walking. Home: 66258 Hartzler Blvd Goshen IN 46526 Office: Christian Counseling Services 333 E Madison Goshen IN 46526

SAVAGEAU, ROBERT GEORGE, ink manufacturing executive; b. Oak Park, Ill., Mar. 5, 1935; s. George Joseph and Anne (Hegnar) S.; m. Sally E. Stukel, Sept. 21, 1957; children: Susan, Sondra, Robert T., Richard, Rory, Sharon, Ron, Russell. BSChemE, Ohio State U., 1958. Coating chemist inks div. Interchemical, Chgo., 1954-64; group leader research and devel. Interchemical, Elizabeth, N.J., 1964-68; lab mgr. research and devel. Inmont (formerly Interchemical), Clifton, N.J., 1968-74; mgr. research and devel. Inmont, Cin., 1974-77; dir. research and devel. Flint Ink Corp., Detroit, 1977-84, tech. dir., 1984—. Patentee inks. trustee Pompton Lakes (N.J.) Bd. Edn., 1966-75; cubmaster, asst. scoutmaster Boy Scouts Am., Northville, Mich., 1971—. Mem. Soc. Mfg. Engrs., Tech. Assn. Pulp and Paper Industry, Nat. Assn. Printing Ink Mfrs. (chmn. conf. com. 1982—, Pres. Service award 1983, Printing Ink Pioneer award 1985), Tech. Assn. Graphic Arts (bd. dirs. 1980-83). Roman Catholic. Office: Flint Ink Corp Research Ctr PO Box 8609 Ann Arbor MI 48107

SAVARD, DENIS, professional hockey player; b. Pointe Gatineau, Que., Can., Feb. 4, 1961. Profl. hockey player Chgo. Black Hawks, 1980—. Office: Chgo Blackhawks 1800 Madison Ave Chicago IL 60612 *

SAVO, DOMINICK SALVATORE, marketing executive; b. Syracuse, N.Y., Dec. 21, 1938; s. Dominick Anthony and Mary Lou (Fiato) S.; m. Roseanne Donato, Apr. 20, 1963; children: Sunday-Ann, Star-Lee. B-SChemE, Tri-State U., Angola, Ind., 1960; MS in Physics and Chemistry, Loyola U., Chgo., 1968; MBA, Northwestern U., 1982. Engring. mgr. Zenith Radio Corp., Niles, Ill., 1963-68; prodn. engring. mgr. Zenith Radio Corp., Melrose Park, Ill., 1976-78; mktg. mgr. Gen. Electric Co., Syracuse, N.Y., 1969-76; product mgr. Molex, Inc., Lisle, Ill., 1979-84; dir. mktg. Allied Amphenol, Lisle, 1984-86; dir. bus. planning Amp. Inc., 1986—. Mem. Chgo. Council Fgn. Relations, Chgo. High Tech. Soc., Chgo. Council Commerce and Industry. Home: 102 Blackstone St LaGrange IL 60525

SAVOIE, LEONARD MITCHELL, business administration educator; b. Cuyahoga Falls, Ohio, Mar. 25, 1923; s. Leonard and Anna May (Gardner) S.; m. Barbara Sites, Apr. 14, 1951; children: Leonard J., Joan, Paul, Donald, Robert, Mary, James, John, William, Carol. Student Stanford U., 1943; BS in Accountancy, U. Ill., 1946; postgrad. Inst. for Mgmt., Northwestern U., 1959. C.P.A., Ill. Dickinson fellow Harvard U., Boston, 1962-63; ptnr. Price Waterhouse, Chgo., 1960-62, N.Y.C., 1962-67; exec. v.p. Am. Inst. C.P.A.s, N.Y.C., 1967-72; v.p., controller Clark Equipment Co., Buchanan, Mich., 1972-79; prof. bus. administrn. U. Notre Dame, Ind., 1980—; dir. Hach Co., Loveland, Colo., LaSalle Fed. Savs. and Loan, Buchanan, Mich., Prudential-Bache, Moneymart Assets, N.Y.C., Prudential-Bache Research Fund, N.Y.C., Prudential-Bache Time Target Trust, N.Y.C. Contbr. articles to profl. jours. Pres. Gateway, Berrien Springs, Mich., 1979-81, Niles-Buchanan YMCA, 1975-77; govt. com. U.S. C. of C., Washington, 1973-76; bd. govs. Accts. Club of Am., 1969-72. Served with U.S. Army, 1943-46. Recipient Highest Univ. award U. Ill., 1946; Disting. Accountant award U. Hartford, 1970. Mem. Am. Inst. C.P.A.s (exec. v.p. 1967-72), Fin. Execs. Research Found. (trustee), Am. Acctg. Assn., Nat. Assn. Accts., Fin. Execs. Inst. (pres. Michiana 1980-81), Beta Alpha Psi, Beta Gamma Sigma. Republican. Roman Catholic. Clubs: Chicago, University. Home: 13721 S Indian Springs Rd Buchanan MI 49107 Office: U Notre Dame Coll Bus Adminstrn Notre Dame IN 46556

SAVOY, SUZANNE MARIE, nurse; b. N.Y.C., Oct. 18, 1946; d. William Joseph and Mary Patricia (Moclair) S. BS, Columbia U., 1970; M in Nursing, UCLA, 1978. RN. Staff nurse MICU, transplant Jackson Meml. Hosp., Miami, Fla., 1970-72; staff nurse MICU Boston U. Hosp. (Mass.), 1972-74; staff nurse MICU VA Hosp., Long Beach, Calif., 1974-75; staff nurse MIRU Cedars-Sinai M.C., Los Angeles, 1975-77; critical care clin. nursing specialist Anaheim Meml. Hosp., (Calif.), 1978-81; practitioner, instr. and assoc. neurosurgery research Rush-Presbyn.-St. Luke's Med. Ctr. Coll. Nursing, Chgo., 1982-86; research assoc. dept. neurosurgery, 1986—; edn. cons. Critical Care Services, Inc., Orange, Calif., 1979-81. Co-author articles on Alzheimers drug research and diagnosis to profl. jours. Mem. Am. Assn. Neurosci. Nurses (treas. Ill. chpt. 1983-85, pres. 1986-87), Am. Assn. Critical Care Nurses (bd. dirs. Long Beach chpt. 1981-82), No. Am. Nursing Diagnosis Assn., Sigma Theta Tau. Roman Catholic. Office: Rush-Presbyn St Luke's Med Ctr 1725 W Congress Pkwy Chicago IL 60612

SAWAYA, RAYMOND, neurosurgeon; b. Latakia, Syria, May 5, 1949; s. Emile and Josephine (Boulos) S.; m. Madeleine Boskovitz, Mar. 24, 1979; children: Marc-Emile, Corinne Marguerite. MD, St. Joseph U., Beirut, 1974. Diplomate Am. Bd. Neurol. Surgery. Intern Beeckman-Downtown Hosp., N.Y.C., 1974-75; resident in surgery SUNY, Syracuse, 1975-76; resident in neurosurgery U. Cin., 1976-80, Johns Hopkins Hosp., Balt., 1981; vis. scientist NIH, Bethesda, Md., 1981-82; assoc. prof. U. Cin., 1983—, dir. div. neuro-oncology, 1983—; neurosurgeon Mayfield Neurol. Inst., Cin., 1983—. Contbr. numerous articles on neurosurgery to profl. jours. research Adv. Group grantee VA Med. Ctr., 1984. Mem. AAAS, AMA, Am. Assn. Neurol. Surgeons, Nat. Assn. VA Physicians, Ohio State Med. Assn., Cin. Acad. Medicine, Found. for Advanced Edn. in Scis., Cin. Soc. Neurology and Neurosurgery, Congress of Neurosurgeons, Ohio State Neurol. Soc., Assn. Brain Tumor Research, McMicken Soc., Johns Hopkins Alumni Assn. Democrat. Roman Catholic. Avocations: music, bridge, swimming. Home: 5800 Donjoy St Cincinnati OH 45242 Office: Mayfield Neurol Inst 506 Oak St Cincinnati OH 45219

SAWCHUK, SANDRA ALLISON, veterinarian; b. Peterborough, Ont., Can., June 13, 1956; d. Samuel Allen Sawchuk and Marilyn Wayne (Schrader) Monette; m. Steven Robert Struss, Mar. 26, 1983. DVM, Ontario Vet. Coll., 1980; MS, U. Ill., 1983. Intern U. Ill., Urbana, 1980-81, resident, 1981-84; pvt. practice staff veterinarian Waterloo, Iowa, 1984-85, Community Animal Hosp., Fond du Lac, Wis., 1985—. Contbr. articles to profl. jours., chpts. to books. Recipient Andrew Smith award Ont. Vet. Coll., 1980, Proficiency award Ont. Vet. Coll., 1978, 80, Large Animal Medicine & Surgery award Ont. Vet. Coll., 1979, Ayerst award Ont. Vet. Coll., 1980, Frank Cote Meml. award Ont. Vet. Coll., 1980. Mem. AVMA, Am. Animal Hosp. Assn., Am. Vet. Soc. of Animal Behavior, Feline Practitioner Assn. Women Veterinarians, Vet. Neurology Assn., Audubon Soc. (treas. 1986—). Avocations: crafts, sailing, hiking, birding. Home: 3704 DeNeveu Ln Rt 3 Fond du Lac WI 54935 Office: Community Animal Hosp N6611 Rolling Meadows Dr Fond du Lac WI 54935

SAWINSKI, VINCENT JOHN, chemistry educator; b. Chgo., Mar. 28, 1925; s. Stanley and Pearl (Gapinski) S.; m. Florence Whitman, Aug. 24, 1952; children—Christine Frances, Michael Patrick. B.S., Loyola U., 1948, M.A., 1950, Ph.D., 1962. Instr., asst. prof. chemistry, physiology and pharmacology Loyola U., Chgo., 1949-67; supervisory research chemist VA, Hines, Ill., 1961-66; assoc. prof. chemistry, phys. sci. City Colls. Chgo., 1967-71, prof., 1971—, chmn. phys. sci. dept. Wright campus, 1971—. Contbr. articles to profl. jours. Served with U.S. Army, 1945-46. Fellow AAAS, Am. Inst. Chemists; mem. Am. Chem. Soc., N.Y. Acad. Sci., Nat. Sci. Tchrs. Assn., Sigma Xi. Home: 1945 N 77th Ct Elmwood Park IL 60635 Office: 3400 N Austin Ave Chicago IL 60634

SAWMILLER, TIMOTHY JOHN, data processing executive; b. Detroit, Dec. 14, 1952; s. Darrell Edward and Jean Marie (Meyer) S.; m. Donna Ruth Mays, May 6, 1978; children: Andrew George, Kathleen Ann. BS in Computer Sci., Wayne State U., 1975. Data processing supr. Good Housekeeping Shops, Detroit, 1975-77; programmer/analyst Darin & Armstrong, Southfield, Mich., 1977-81; systems coordinator Woodland Med. Group, Novi, Mich., 1981—. Mem. Nat. Assn. Honeywell Users, Honeywell Users Group of Mich. (pres. 1986-87), Mich. Chess Assn. (sec. 1985—). Presbyterian. Club: Trenton (Mich.) Chess (pres. 1985—). Avocations: chess, dining, civil war. Home: 24480 Riverview Ln Novi MI 48050 Office: Woodland Med Group Inc 41935 W 12 Mile Rd Novi MI 48050

SAWYER, JOHN, professional football team executive. s. Charles S.; m. Ruth Sawyer; children: Anne, Elizabeth, Catherine, Mary. Pres., part owner Cin. Bengals, Nat. Football League; pres. J. Sawyer Co., Ohio, Miss., Mont., Wyo. Home: Cincinnati OH Office: J Sawyer Co Provident Tower Cincinnati OH 45202 *

SAWYER, NANCY ANN HABIG, nurse, educator; b. Indpls., Aug. 29, 1946; d. Frank J. and Nancy (Trimble) Habig; m. James Woempner Sawyer, Dec. 4, 1976; children: Melissa Ann, Stephen James. BSN, Ind. U., 1969, MSN, 1975. Head nurse obstetrics Ind. U., Indpls., 1969-74; asst. dir. maternal child health St. Vincent Hosp., Indpls., 1975-81, assoc. dir. Nursing, 1981, nursing supr., 1982-86; instr. St. Vincent Wellness Ctr., Carmel, Ind., 1983—, St. Vincent Breast Diagnostic Ctr., 1985—; adv. bd. for 13-30 Corp. Bd. dirs. March of Dimes, Indpls., 1976-86; mem. adv. bd.

Neo-fight, Inc., Indpls. Mem. Ind. U. Alumni Assn., Sigma Theta Tau, Pi Beta Phi Alumni Assn. Avocations: snowskiing, gardening, boating.

SAWYER, THOMAS C., congressman; b. Akron, Ohio, Aug. 15, 1945; m. Joyce Handler, 1968; 1 child, Amanda. BA, U. Akron, 1968, MA, 1970. Pub. sch. tchr. Ohio; adminstr. state sch. for delinquent boys; legis. agt. Ohio Pub. Utilities Commn.; mem. Ohio House Reps., Columbus, 1977-83; mayor City of Akron, 1984-86; mem. 100th Congress from Ohio, Washington, 1987—. Office: US House of Representatives Office Office of House Members Washington DC 20510 *

SAWYER, THOMAS HARRISON, health, physical education and recreation educator; b. Norwich, N.Y., Apr. 5, 1946; s. Harrison Donald and M. Daughn (Geer) S.; m. Kathleen Ann Daly, July 5 1969; children: Shawn Thomas, Meghan Daly. BS, Springfield Coll., 1968, MPE, 1971; EdD, Va. PolyTech Inst., 1977. Instr. health, phys edn., recreation Va. Mil. Inst., Lexington, 1969-72, asst. prof., 1972-75, assoc. prof., 1975-79; dir. recreation ctr. U. Bridgeport, 1979-81; assoc. prof., head dept. Mont. Tech. Inst., Butte, 1981-84; prof., chmn. phys. edn. dept. Ind. State U., Terre Haute, 1984—; cons. Mont. Fitness, Butte, 1981-84, ARC, Mont., 1981-83, Wellness-Pillsbury Co. Mem. edit. bd. Jour. for Employee Health and Fitness, Mag. for Health Mgrs.; contbr. articles to profl. jours. Bd. dirs. YMCA, Butte, 1981-84; mem. Sch. Bd. Dist. 1, Butte, 1982-84; mem. bd. dirs. Vocation Edn. Council Mont., 1983-84. NDEA scholar, 1968; recipient Founder's award Alcohol Services, Buena Vista, Va., 1979, Vol. Safety award ARC, Conn., 1981, Red Triangle, YMCA, Butte, 1982. Mem. Am. Alliance for Health, Phys. Edn., Recreation and Dance, ARC (bd. dirs. Terre Haute 1985-87), Ind. Alliance for Health, Phys. Edn., Recreation and Dance (editor jour.), Nat. Assn. Sports Offcls., Assn. Fitness in Bus., Nat. Employees Recreation Service Assn., Am. Coll. Sports Medicine, Nat. Recreation and Park Assn. Office: Ind State U Sch Phys Edn Terre Haute IN 47809

SAX, MARY RANDOLPH, speech pathologist; b. Pontiac, Mich., July 13, 1925; d. Bernard Angus and Ada Lucile (Thurman) TePoorten; B.A. magna cum laude, Mich. State U., 1947; M.A., U. Mich., 1949; m. William Martin Sax, Feb. 7, 1948. Supr. speech correction dept. Waterford Twp. Schs., Pontiac, 1949-69; lectr. Marygrove Coll., Detroit, 1971-72; pvt. practice speech and lang. rehab., Wayne, Oakland Counties, Mich., 1973—; adj. speech pathologist Southfield, Mich.; mem. sci. council stroke Am. Heart Assn. Grantee Inst. Articulation and Learning, 1969, others. Mem. Am. Speech-Lang.-Hearing Assn., Mich. Speech Pathologists in Clin. Practice, Mich. Speech-Lang.-Hearing Assn. (com. community and hosp. services), Am. Heart Assn. of Mich., AAUW, Internat. Assn. Logopedics and Phoniatrics (Switzerland), Founders Soc. of Detroit Inst. Arts, Mich. Humane Soc., Theta Alpha Phi, Phi Kappa Phi, Kappa Delta Pi. Contbr. articles to profl. jours. Home and Office: 31320 Woodside Franklin MI 48025

SAXER, RICHARD KARL, metallurgical engineer, retired air force officer; b. Toledo, Aug. 31, 1928; s. Alexander Albert and Gertrude Minnie (Kuebeler) S.; m. Marilyn Doris Mersereau, July 19, 1952; children—Jane Lynette, Robert Karl, Kris Renee, Ann Luette. Student, Bowling Green State U., 1946-48; B.S., U. S. Naval Acad., 1952; M.S. in Aero. Mechanics Engring., Air Force Inst. Tech., 1957; Ph.D. in Metall. Engring., Ohio State U., 1962; grad., Armed Forces Staff Coll., 1966, Indsl. Coll. Armed Forces, 1971. Commd. 2d lt. U.S. Air Force, 1952, advanced through grades to lt. gen., 1976; electronics officer, mech. officer (4th Tactical Support Sqadron, Tactical Air Command), Sandia Base, N.Mex., 1953-54; electronics and mech. officer, spl. weapons assembly sect. supr. (SAC 6th Aviation Depot Squadron), French Morocco, 1954-55; project engr. mech. equipment br. Air Force Spl. Weapon's Center, Kirtland AFB, N.Mex., 1957-59; project officer Nuclear Safety div., 1959-60; assoc. prof. dept. engring. mechanics Air Force Inst. Tech., 1962-66; asso. prof., dep. dept. head USAF Acad., 1966-70; comdr., dir. Air Force Materials Lab., Wright-Patterson AFB, Ohio, 1971-74; dep. for Reentry System Space and Missile Systems Orgn., 1974-77; dep. for aero equipment Aero. Systems Div., 1977-80, dep. for tactical systems, 1980, vice comdr., 1981-83; aero. systems div. dir. Def. Nuclear Agy., 1983-85, ret., 1985; pres. R.K. Saxer & Assocs., Dayton, Ohio, 1985—; research and tech. com. materials and structures NASA, 1973-74; chmn. planning group aerospace materials Interagy. Council Materials, 1973-74; mem. Nat. Mil. Adv. Bd., 1971-74, NATO adv. group for research and devel., 1973-74. Contbr. articles to profl. jours. Decorated Def. Disting. Service medal, Legion of Merit, Meritorious Service medal, D.S.M., Joint Service Commendation medal, Air Force Commendation medal with 3 oak leaf clusters, Army Commendation medal U.S., Def. Superior Service medal, Cross of Gallantry with palm Vietnam, Def. Meritorious Service medal; recipient Disting. award for systems mgmt. Air Force Assn., 1979; Disting. Alumnus award Ohio State U., 1986. Mem. Air Force Assn., Am. Def. Prepare-dness Assn. (pres. Dayton 1977-78), Sigma Xi, Phi Lambda Epsilon, Alpha Sigma Mu. Mem. United Ch. of Christ. Clubs: Masons, Shriners. Home and Office: 5916 Yarmouth Dr Dayton OH 45459

SAXON, KEITH GORDON, surgeon; b. Ann Arbor, Mich., Apr. 15, 1951; s. Gordon Edward and Janet (Buckwater) S.; m. Mary Dugan, June 25, 1983; 1 child, Katherine Dugan. BA, U. Tex., 1973; MD, U. Tex., San Antonio, 1977. Diplomate Am. Bd. Otolaryngology, Am. Bd. Med. Examiners.b. Intern surgery U. Tex. Hosp., San Antonio, 1977-78; resident U. Mich., Ann Arbor, 1978-83; instr. U. Mich. Sch. Music, Ann Arbor, 1981-82, adj. prof., 1982-84; gen. practice otolaryngology Liberty, Mo., 1983—; resident laryngologist Aspen (Colo.) Music Festival, 1983—; pres. Hearing Specialists, Inc., Liberty, 1984—; chmn. patient care Liberty Hosp., 1984-86, mem. exec. com. Liberty Hosp., 1984-86. Merit scholar Tex. Legis., San Antonio, 1976. Fellow Am. Acad. otolaryngology; mem. AMA, Am. Acad. Facial Plastics and Reconstructive Surgery (assoc.), Mo. Med. Assn., Kans. City Soc. Opthamology and Otolaryngology, Alpha Omega Alpha (award). Republican. Presbyterian. Club: Clayview Country. Lodge: Rotary. Avocations: professional voice, piano. Office: Westowne IV Suite 205 Liberty MO 64068 Other: 6420 Prospect T0313 Kansas City MO 64132

SAXON, SAMUEL ALBERT, III, educator, consultant; b. Albany, Ga., Apr. 6, 1936; s. Samuel Albert and Sarah Jo (Murray) S.; m. Mary Ella Hodges, June 6, 1965; children—John Brooks, Robert Dale, Gus Murray. A.B., LaGrange Coll., 1964; postgrad. U. Nev., 1965-67; M.Ed., Brigham Young U., 1974, Ed.D., 1981. Tchr. several Nev. schs., 1964-76; prin. Petersen Sch., Sunnyside, Utah, 1976-81; ednl. adminstr. Francis Howell Sch. Dist., St. Charles, Mo., 1981-84; supt. schs. Joint Sch. Dist. 418, Murtaugh, Idaho, 1984-86; prin. Mo. Mil. Acad., Jr. Sch., Mexico, Mo., 1986—; cons. Saxon Ednl. Enterprises, 1981—, New Parents as Tchrs., St. Charles, Mo., 1981-84. Author: A Manual of School Policy and School Regulations, 1979; A Music Curriculum Guide, 1981. Co-author: Missouri Military Academy Junior School Teachers Handbook; Missouri Military academy Junior School Cadet Handbook, 1987; contbr. articles to profl. jours. Sec. Young Democrats Club, U. Fla., 1961; sec. Logandale Town Bd., Nev., 1972-76; adult leader Boy Scouts Am., Nev., Utah, Mo., Idaho, 1965—. Served with USAF, 1955-59. Recipient Woodbadge award Boulder Dam Area council Boy Scouts Am., 1973; intern doctoral program fellow Brigham Young U., 1977; research grantee Utah State Office Edn., Salt Lake City, 1980. Mem. centennial com. Mo. Mil. Acad., 1986—. Mem. Am. Assn. Sch. Adminstrs., Independent Schs. Assn. Cen. States, Idaho Sch. Supts. Assn., La Grange Coll. Alumni Assn., Mo. Mil. Acad. Faculty Club. Phi Delta Kappa, Pi Kappa Phi. Mormon. Office: Mo Mil Acad 204 Grand Ave Mexico MO 65265

SAY, MARLYS MORTENSEN (MRS. JOHN THEODORE SAY), supt. schs.; b. Yankton, S.D., Mar. 11, 1924; d. Melvin A. and Edith L. (Fargo) Mortensen; B.A., U. Colo., 1949, M.Ed., 1953; adminstrv. specialist U. Nebr., 1973; m. John Theodore Say, June 21, 1951; children—Mary Louise, James Kenneth, John Melvin, Margaret Ann. Tchr. Huron (S.D.) Jr. High Sch., 1944-48, Lamar (Colo.) Jr. High Sch., 1950-52, Norfolk Pub. Sch., 1962-63; Madison County supt., Madison, Nebr., 1963—. Mem. N.E.A. (life), Am. Assn. Sch. Adminstrs., Dept. Rural Edn., Nebr. Assn. County Supts. (pres.), Nebr. Elementary Prins. Assn., AAUW (pres. Norfolk br.), N.E. Nebr. County Supts. Assn. (pres.), Assn. Sch. Bus. Ofcls., Nat. Orgn. Legal Problems in Edn., Assn. Supervision and Curriculum Devel., Nebr. Edn. Assn., Nebr. Sch. Adminstrs. Assn. Republican. Methodist. Home: 4805 S 13th St Norfolk NE 68701 Office: Courthouse Madison NE 68748

SAYEEDI, ABDUL MULIK, infosystems specialist, civil engineer; b. Hyderabad, Deccan, India, Apr. 4, 1933; came to U.S., 1959; s. A. Munim and Azeema (Begum) S.; m. Nancy Jane Nelson, June 6, 1961 (div. Jan. 1970); m. Shahanaz Talat Qazi, June 12, 1975; children: Mani, Naeem, Bari. BS in Math., Karachi U., Pakistan, 1952; BCE, Karachi U., 1956; MCE, U. Minn., 1963. Registered profl. engr. Assoc. programmer Scientific Computers, Mpls., 1960-63; sr. programmer IBM Corp., Poughkeepsie, N.Y., 1963-65; mgr. advance planning Gen. Electric Corp., Bethesda, Md., 1966-70; dir. info. systems Fed. Govt., Washington, Chgo., 1970—. Editor: The Letter, 1985—. Trustee, v.p. Hyderabad Found., Chgo., 1984—. Mem. ASCE, Am. Pub. Works Assn., Assn. for Computing Machinery. Republican. Mem. Christian Ch. Club: Toastmasters. Avocations: bridge, writing. Home: 2859 W Touhy Chicago IL 60645

SAYLES, RONALD LYLE, computer executive; b. Waukesha, Wis., Oct. 12, 1936; s. Burton Lyall and Sophia (Lapaz) S.; m. Fumiko Soeda, Jan. 15, 1957. B.S. in Secondary Edn., U. Wis.-Milw., 1978. Computer operator Mortgage Assocs., Milw., 1966-71, Kohl's Food Stores, Wauwatosa, Wis., 1971-83; supr. computer ops. Kohl's Dept. Stores, Brookfield, Wis., 1983-86, prodn. coordinator, 1986—. Author articles on old time radio programs. Vol. Jim Moody for Congress 1984, 86, Shirley Krug for State Asembly, 1984, 86. Served with USN, 1954-57. Mem. Milw. Zool. Soc., Am. Film Inst., Smithsonian Instn., Wis. Hist. Soc., Milw. Area Radio Enthusiasts, U. Wis.-Milw. Alumni Assn. (life). Democrat. Mormon. Home: 4278 N 53d St Milwaukee WI 53216 Office: 2315 N 124th St Brookfield WI 53005

SAYLOR, JIMMY D., auditor, manufacturing and retailing company executive; b. Berea, Ky., Sept. 21, 1950; s. James W. and Corrine Joy (Cope) S.; m. Pamela Kay Morath, Aug. 21, 1971; children: Jeremy D., Jessica Kay. BS in Bus. Adminstrn., Miami U., Oxford, Ohio, 1972; MBA, Xavier U., 1976. CPA, Ohio. Asst. br. auditor Fed. Res. Bank, Cin., 1972-79; mgr. internal audit U.S. Shoe Corp., Cin., 1979—; cons. tax and acctg. West Chester, Ohio, 1972—. Mem. Inst. Internal Auditors, Am. Inst. CPAs, Ohio Soc. CPAs. Office: US Shoe Corp One Eastwood Dr Cincinnati OH 45227-1197

SAYLOR, LARRY JAMES, lawyer; b. Biloxi, Miss., Nov. 7, 1948; s. Rufus Don and Alice Julia (Kidd) S.; m. Mary L. Mullendore, Dec. 27, 1975; children: David James, Stephen Michael. AB in Political Sci., Miami U., Oxford, Ohio, 1970; M in City and Regional Planning, Ohio State U., 1976; JD, U. Mich., 1976. Bar: D.C. 1976, Mich. 1977, U.S. Ct. Appeals (D.C. cir.) 1977, U.S. Ct. Appeals (6th cir.) 1978, U.S. Supreme Ct. 1981, U.S. Ct. Appeals (10th cir.) 1982. Law clk. to presiding judge U.S. Ct. Appeals (D.C. cir.), Washington, 1976-77; ptnr. Miller, Canfield, Paddock and Stone, Detroit, 1977—. Article editor Mich. Law Rev., 1975-76; contbr. articles to profl. jours. Served to 1st lt. USAF, 1970-72. Mem. ABA (antitrust and litigation sects.), Mich. Bar Assn., D.C. Bar Assn., World Trade Club. Club: Detroit Econ. Avocations: skiing, woodworking. Home: 424 Lincoln Rd Grosse Pointe MI 48230 Office: Miller Canfield Paddock & Stone 2500 Comerica Bldg Detroit MI 48230

SCACCIA, CARL R., chemical engineering executive; b. Turin, Italy, Aug. 23, 1946; came to U.S., 1961; s. Patrick R. and Josephine (Baroero) S.; m. Ellen K. Hohlstein, Apr. 5, 1974; 1 child, Lynn. BS in Aero. Engring., SUNY, Buffalo, 1968, PhD in Chem. Engring., 1973; MS in Engring. Mechanics, U. Rochester, 1970. Registered profl. engr., N.Y., Ohio. Coop. engr. Lockheed Missiles div. Lockheed Corp., Marietta, Ga., 1968-69; supr. process product devel. Union Carbide, Tonawanda, N.Y., 1973-79; sr. mgr. engring. techs. Combustion Engring., Wellsville, N.Y., 1979-81; research mgr. research and devel. Ashland Chem. Co., Dublin, Ohio, 1981—; adj. prof. Ohio State U., Columbus, 1981—, SUNY, Buffalo; bd. dirs. Cen. Ohio Tech. Coll., Newark, 1981—. Reviewer for NSF, SUNY, Buffalo, 1970-73; contbr. chpts. to books and articles to profl. jours.; patentee in field. Bd. dirs. Wellsville Pub. Library, 1979; dir. career tng. Boys Scouts Am., Dublin, 1986; fund raiser Jr. Achievement, Columbus, 1987—. NSF fellow, 1969-70. Mem. Am. Inst. Chem. Engrs., Am. Chem. Soc., ASME, Soc. for Advancement Material and Process Engring., Nat. Soc. Profl. Engrs. Avocations: tennis, long-distance running, electronics, weightlifting. Home: 8422 Tibbermore Ct Dublin OH 43017 Office: Ashland Chem Co 5200 Blazer Pkwy Dublin OH 43017

SCALLEN, THOMAS KAINE, broadcasting executive, lawyer; b. Mpls., Aug. 14, 1925; s. Raymond A. and Lenore (Kaine) S.; children: Thomas, Sheila, Patrick, Eileen, Timothy and Maureen (twins). BA, St. Thomas Coll., 1949; JD, U. Denver, 1950. Bar: Minn. Asst. atty gen. State of Minn., Mpls., 1950-55; sole practice Mpls., 1955-57; pres. Med. Investment Corp., Mpls., 1957—, Internat. Broadcasting Corp., Mpls., 1977—; owner Harlem Globetrotters; pres., exec. producer Ice Capades; bd. dirs. Northwest Sports Enterprises, Ltd., Vancover, B.C., Can., Advance Machine Tool, Mpls.; chmn. bd. dirs. Blaine-Thompson Co., Inc., N.Y.C. Served with AUS. Mem. Young Pres. Orgn. Clubs: University (St. Paul, Mpls.), Rochester (Minn.) Golf and Country, Edina (Minn.) Country, Athletic (Mpls.). Home: 2950 Dean Pkwy Minneapolis MN 55416 Office: Internat Broadcasting Corp 5101 IDS Ctr Minneapolis MN 55402

SCANLAN, FRANK ALLEN, component engineer; b. Evanston, Ill., July 30, 1929; s. Allen Joseph and Marie Magdalen (Merk) S.; m. Marilyn Elenor Heuel, June 27, 1964; children—Kevin Francis, Brian William. Component engr. Oak Industries, Crystal Lake, Ill., 1956-83, T.R.W. Electronics Assemblies Div., Schaumburg, Ill., 1983-86, AT&T Bell Labs, Naperville, Ill., 1986-87, Rockwell Internat., Downers Grove, Ill., 1987—. Com. chmn. Blackhawk council Boy Scouts Am., 1979-84. Served to sgt. U.S. Army, 1951-53, Korea. Recipient Disting. Community Service award Crystal Lake Jaycees, 1982, Founders award Boy Scouts Am., 1982, Cert. of Achievement, Am. Heart Assn., 1981. Republican. Roman Catholic. Home: 434 Porter Ave Crystal Lake IL 60014 Office: AT&T Bell Labs Room 15228 1200 E Warrenville Rd Naperville IL 60566

SCANLAN, JOHN MICHAEL, accountant; b. Evergreen Park, Ill., Dec. 8, 1954; s. Edmund James and Margaret Mary (Dever) S.; m. Jeanne Marie Tew; children: Laura Patricia, Jenna Lee. BS, U. Santa Clara, Calif., 1977. CPA, Ill. Acct. Bansley & Kiener, Chgo., 1977-79; ptnr. Smith & Culumber, Oak Brook, 1979—. Mem. Am. Inst. CPA's. Office: Smith & Culumber 1110 Jorie Blvd Oak Brood IL 60521

SCANLAN, THOMAS MICHAEL, computer software executive; b. Rochester, Minn., Dec. 7, 1941; s. Martin Jerimiah and Marian Geneive (Walsh) S.; m. Joyce Eileen Hoffa, Sept. 14, 1974. BA in Bus., St. Thomas U., 1966. Research analyst State of Minn., St. Paul, 1966-67, computer programmer, 1967-69, system programmer, 1969-73, senior programmer, 1974-77, supr., 1977-80, software mgr., 1980—. Mem. Nat. Fedn. of the Blind (Minn. treas. 1974—). Roman Catholic. Home: 4445 Grand Ave Minneapolis MN 55409 Office: State of Minn 658 Cedar St IMB Saint Paul MN 55155

SCANLIN, PATRICIA BOARINI, registered nurse; b. Elkhorn, Wis., Aug. 8, 1958; d. James Joseph and Margaret Patricia (Idstein) Boarini; m. Kenneth John Scanlin, May 30, 1981; 1 child, Kelly Patricia. AS, Coll. of Lake County, 1982. Medical surgical nurse No. Ill. Med. Ctr., McHenry, 1982, emergency room nurse, 1982-86; flight nurse Flight for Life, Milw., 1986; trauma nurse-Life Support Ctr. U. Hosp., Madison, Wis., 1986—; trauma nurse specialist Am. Heart Assn., Rockford, Ill., 1984—, advanced cardiac life specialist, 1983—; support instr., co. dir. Emergency Nurses CARE, McHenry, 1985-86. Roman Catholic. Avocations: water skiing, hiking, canoeing, gardening, family. Home: 5139 Caton Ln Waunakee WI 53597 Office: U Hosp 600 Highland Ave Madison WI 53706

SCANLON, TERENCE J., publisher; b. St. Joseph, Mo., July 26, 1931; s. Byron Bernard and Margaret Susan (Zirkle) S.; m. Doris Jean Blasdel, Mar. 8, 1969; children: Kerry, Brooke, Erin, Thomas, Duffy, Tanner. BA, Wichita (Kans.) State U., 1956. Mem. mgmt. dept. City of Wichita, 1956-66; dir. adminstrn. State of Kans., Topeka, 1966-70, dir. econ. devel., 1972-73; pres. Cen. Devel., Inc., Topeka, 1970-71, Coors of Kans., Inc., Wichita, 1973-79, Scanlon Enterprises, Wichita, 1980-85; pres. and publisher Wichita Bus. Jour., 1986—; bd. dirs. Kans. Gas and Electric Co.; chmn. bd. trustees St. Joseph Med. Ctr. Vice chmn. bd. trustees Wichita State U., 1981—; chmn. Dem. State Com., Topeka, 1977-79. Roman Catholic. Home: 3912 E Douglas Wichita KS 67208 Office: Wichita Bus Jour 138 Ida Wichita KS 67211

SCANLON, TERRENCE WILLIAM, physician; b. Cleve., Oct. 9, 1948; s. Howard William and Elaine Scanlon; m. Patricia Ann Patterson, May 16, 1970; children: Kelly Lynn, Sheryl Lynn, Bret William. BS, U. Dayton, 1970; DO, Chgo. Coll. Osteo. Medicine. Diplomate Am. Osteo. Bd. Gen. Practioners; lic. osteopath, Ohio, Fla. Gen practice osteo. medicine Cleve., 1974—; mem. staff Brentwood Hosp., Cleve., 1974—, Parma Hosp., Cleve., 1985—, Deaconess Hosp., Cleve., 1986—; asst. clin. prof. Ohio U. Coll. Osteo. Medicine, Athens, 1981—; pres. med. staff Brentwood Hosp., Cleve., 1982, chmn. dept. gen. practice, 1983-84. Recipient Upjohn Academic Achievement award, 1974. Mem. Am. Osteo. Assn., Am. Coll. Osteo. Gen. Practitioners, Ohio Osteo. Assn., Ohio State Med. Assn., Cleve. Acad. Osteo. Medicine (pres. 1985-86), Cleve. Acad. Medicine, Alpha Epsilon Delta, Sigma Sigma Phi. Roman Catholic. Club: Tanglewood Country. Avocations: golf, swimming, basketball. Home: 10910 Sunrise Trail Brecksville OH 44141 Office: Drs Saridakis Scanlon & Saridakis Inc 7530 Carter Rd Sagamore Hills OH 44067

SCARRITT, RICHARD WINN, lawyer; b. Enid, Okla., Dec. 13, 1938; s. Nathan Spencer and Rilla Fayette (Winn) S.; m. Gloria June Gaba, Nov. 7, 1966 (div. Nov. 1971); m. Deborah Louise Guillemot, Sept. 3, 1986. BA, Okla. U., 1960; JD, Harvard U., 1963. Bar: Mo. 1963, U.S. Dist. Ct. (we. dist.) Mo. 1964, U.S. Supreme Ct. 1971. Assoc. Spencer, Fane, Britt & Browne, Kansas City, Mo., 1963-68, ptnr., 1969—; guest lectr. real estate law U. Mo. Extension Ctr., Independence, 1966-68; mem. panel of arbitrators Am. Arbitration Assn., chmn. standard forms com., mem. govtl. affairs council, zoning law com., legis. com. Real Estate Bd. Kansas City; panelist Plaza West Assn., Kansas City, 1971-78. Fellow AM. Coll. Real Estate Lawyers; mem. ABA (real property, probate and trust law sect., subcom. significant real property decisions, environ. law com. subcom. on energy law and real property, corp., banking and bus. law sect.), Mo. Bar Assn. (property law com., adv. council, energy law com.), Kansas City Bar Assn., Lawyers Assn. Kansas City, Mo. C. of C., Downtown Inc. of Kansas City, Mensa, Phi Delta Theta. Republican. Presbyterian. Avocations: photography, collecting art, pocket billiards, handball. Home: 825 W 53d Terr Kansas City MO 64112 Office: Spencer Fane Britt & Browne 1000 Commerce Bank Bldg 1000 Walnut Kansas City MO 64106-2140

SCHAAF, JAMES HOWARD, professional football club executive; b. Erie, Pa., May 22, 1938; s. Raymond and Marion Coletta S.; m. Julia Kay Brockmeier, Feb. 2, 1963; children: Jill Marie, James Michael. B.S. in Econs, U. Notre Dame, 1959. Stockbroker A.C. Allyn & Co., 1960-61; traveling sec., public relations dir. Kansas City Athletics Baseball Club, 1961-66; public relations dir. Kansas City Chiefs Football Club, 1966-68, asst. gen. mgr., public relations dir., 1969-74, v.p., asst. gen. mgr., 1974-78, v.p., gen. mgr., 1978—. Mem. Kansas City Sports Commn. Served with U.S. Army, 1959. Mem. Greater Kansas City C. of C. Club: Kansas City. Office: Kansas City Chiefs 1 Arrowhead Dr Kansas City MO 64129 *

SCHAAF, LINDA ANN, nurse, educator; b. Balt., Feb. 15, 1944; d. Wilbert Frederick and Rosina Catherine (Lutz) S. Diploma, St. Agnes Hosp. Sch. Nursing, 1967; BSN, U. Md., 1971; MSN, Cath. U. Am., 1973. RN. Staff nurse, charge nurse St. Agnes Hosp., Balt., 1967-71; staff nurse Provident Hosp., Washington, 1972-73; pvt. duty nurse Med. Personnel Pool, Washington, 1973; practitioner, tchr. Rush-Presbyn. St. Luke's Med. Ctr., Chgo., 1973-80; staff nurse Critical Care Services, Inc., Chgo., 1980-82; assoc. prof. Ill. Benedictine Coll., Lisle, 1980—; clin. educator, cons. Glendale Heights (Ill.) Community Hosp., 1983—; cons. curriculum Trinity Coll., Washington Hosp. Ctr., Washington, 1976. Bd. dirs. Woodridge (Ill.) Unit Am Cancer Soc., 1984—; mem. Chgo. Heart Assn., 1973—. Mem. Am. Nurses Assn. (cert.), Ill. Nurses Assn., Am. Assn. Critical Care Nurses (cert. critical care RN), Nat. League for Nursing, Ill. League for Nursing (program developer 1976), Am. Heart Assn. (council on cardiovascular nursing 1970—). Democrat. Roman Catholic. Avocations: handicrafts, travel, cultural events, ch. activities. Home: 6513 Puffer Rd Apt #310 Downers Grove IL 60516 Office: Ill Benedictine Coll 5700 College Rd Lisle IL 60532

SCHACHT, HENRY BREWER, diesel engine manufacturing company executive; b. Erie, Pa., Oct. 16, 1934; s. Henry Blass and Virginia (Brewer) S.; m. Nancy Godfrey, Aug. 27, 1960; children: James, Laura, Jane, Mary. B.S., Yale U., 1956; M.B.A., Harvard U., 1962. Sales trainee Am. Brake Shoe Co., N.Y.C., 1956-57; investment mgr. Irwin Mgmt. Co., Columbus, Ind., 1962-64; v.p. finance Cummins Engine Co., Inc., Columbus, 1964-66; v.p., central area mgr. internat. Cummins Engine Co., Inc., London, Eng., 1966-67; group v.p. internat. and subsidiaries Cummins Engine Co., Inc., 1967-69; pres. Cummins Engine Co., Inc., Columbus, 1969-77; chmn., chief exec. officer Cummins Engine Co., Inc., 1977—; bd. dirs. AT&T, CBS, Chase Manhattan Corp., Chase Manhattan Bank N.A. Mem. Bus. Council, Council Fgn. Relations; mem. The Assocs., Harvard Bus. Sch.; trustee Brookings Instn., Com. Econ. Devel., Conf. Bd.; trustee The Ford Found.; bd. dirs. Nat. Exec. Service Corps. Served with USNR, 1957-60. Mem. Mgmt. Execs. Soc., Assocs. Harvard Bus. Sch. (bd. dirs.), Tau Beta Pi. Republican. Office: Cummins Engine Co Inc MC-60910 Box 3005 Columbus IN 47202

SCHACHT, JAMES WILLIAM, state insurance regulation executive; b. Aurora, Ill., Nov. 24, 1941; s. Robert William and Violet Elnora (Sandholm) S.; m. Carol Mae Kleinwachter, June 25, 1966; children—Susan, Justina, Edward, Max and James. B.S. in Acctg., Walton Sch. Commerce, 1964; student Northwestern U., 1965-67, No. Ill. U., 1959-60, Elmhurst Coll., 1960-62. Adminstr., Ill. Ins. Dept., Springfield, 1964—, dep. dir., 1974-78, chief dep. dir., 1978-82, 83—, acting dir., 1982-83. Editor: Accounting Practices Manual-Fire & Casualty Cos., 1974; Accounting Practices Manual-Life and Health Cos., 1974. Contbr.: Financial Regulation in Illinois, 1977, Financial Regulation in Illinois: An Update, 1981. Contbr. articles to profl. jours. Cubmaster Boy Scouts Am., Springfield, 1981-83. Served with U.S. Army, 1966-72. Methodist. Avocations: golf; tennis; running. Home: RR 1 Box 265C Petersburg IL 62675 Office: State of Ill Dept Ins 320 W Washington Springfield IL 62767

SCHAD, JASPER G., librarian; b. Los Angeles, July 29, 1932; s. Robert Oliver and Frances (Gripper) S.; m. Alice Hsu, Nov. 7, 1969; children: Robert H., Caroline Y. BA in History, Occidental Coll., 1954; MA in History, Stanford (Calif.) U., 1957; MLS, UCLA, 1961. Social sci. librarian Calif. State U., Northridge, 1961-64, head acquisitions librarian, 1964-69, asst. prof. history, 1966-67, assoc. dir. libraries, 1970-71; dean of libraries Wichita (Kans.) State U., 1971—; del. Kans. Conf. Library and Info. Services, Topeka, 1979; chmn. Kans. Library Network Bd., Topeka, 1981-86; mem. adv. council sch. library and info. mgmt. Emporia (Kans.) State U., 1984—; cons. in field. Author: (with others) Problems in Developing Academic Library Collections, 1974; editor Collection Mgmt., 1981-83; editorial bd. Choice, 1986—; contbr. articles to profl. jours. Served with U.S. Army, 1954-56. Mem. ALA (chmn. standards com. 1979-83), Kans. Library Assn., Assn. Coll. and Research Libraries (chmn. standards and accreditation com. 1970-76). Home: 1214 N Pinecrest Wichita KS 67208 Office: Wichita State U Ablah Library Box 68 Wichita KS 67208

SCHADE, GEORGE FRANCIS, government agency administrator; b. Chgo., Oct. 4, 1936; s. George Walter Schade and Eileen Agnes (Turner) Anderson; m. Jaynee Lorene Anderson; June 20, 1959; children: Eileen, George, Frank, John, Paul, Maureen. AA, Coll. DuPage, 1972; MA magna cum laude, Ill. Benedictine Coll., 1978. CPA. Revenue agt. IRS, Chgo., 1974-82, regional analyst, 1982-83, group mgr., 1983—. Served with USAF, 1955-58. Recipient Disting. Performance award IRS, 1984, 86. Mem. Am. Inst. CPA's, Ill. Soc. CPA's., Am. Legion. Republican. Roman Catholic. Avocations: outdoors, traveling.

SCHADE, KEVIN TIMOTHY, auditor; b. St. Louis, Sept. 28, 1959; s. Clinton Harold and Carolyn Mae (Huning) S.; m. Lois Ann Eddleman, Sept. 17, 1982. BSBA, S.E. Mo. State U., 1981. CPA, Mo. Staff acct. Conner, Ash & Co., St. Louis, 1982-85; internal audit sr. Drury Industries, Inc., Cape Girardeau, Mo., 1985—. Mem. Am. Inst. CPA's, Mo. Soc. CPA's.

Lutheran. Home: 1911 Sherwood Cape Girardeau MO 63701 Office: Drury Industries Inc 200 S Farrar Cape Girardeau MO 63701

SCHADE, STANLEY GREINERT, JR., medical educator; b. Pitts., Dec. 21, 1933; s. Stanley G. and Charlotte (Marks) S.; m. Sylvia Zottu, Mar. 24, 1966; children: David Stanley, Robert Edward. BA in English, Hamilton Coll., 1955; MD, Yale U., 1961. Diplomate Am. Bd. Internal Medicine, Am. Bd. Hematology, Am. Bd. Oncology. Intern, resident, hematology fellow U. Wis., Madison, 1962-66; chief hematology Westside VA Hosp., Chgo., 1971-77; prof. medicine U. Ill., Chgo., 1978—. Contbr. articles to profl. jours. Served to maj. U.S. Army, 1967-69. Fulbright fellow Tubingen, Fed. Republic of Germany, 1956. Fellow Am. Coll. Physicians; mem. Am. Soc. Hematology. Presbyterian. Avocation: medical ethics. Home: 189 N Delaplaine Rd Riverside IL 60546 Office: Hematology Sect Dept Medicine U Ill Health Scis Ctr 840 S Wood St Chicago IL 60612

SCHAECHER, DAVID LAURENCE, architect; b. Newman Grove, Nebr., Feb. 26, 1953; s. Roland Anthony and Alice Margaret (Wilhelm) S.; married; children: Jaime, Jordan. AA, Platt Jr. Coll., 1973; BS in Archtl. Studies, U. Nebr., 1976. Detailer Thomas Buchtold & Assocs.,, Lincoln, Nebr., 1976-77; architect State of Nebr., Lincoln, 1978-85, State of Kans., Topeka, 1985—. Mem. YMCA, Topeka, 1982—, citizens adv. bd. Washburn/Auburn Sch. Dist. #437. Mem. AIA (bd. dirs. Lincoln chpt. 1985-86), Constrn. Specifications Inst. Democrat. Roman Catholic. Office: Kans Dept Corrections 700 Jackson Topeka KS 66603

SCHAEFER, DONALD JOHN, computer center executive, educator; b. Sioux Falls, S.D., Dec. 9, 1932; s. Gustav Rheinhold and Lydia (Hartig) S.; m. Alice Lutterman, Sept. 24, 1955; children: Mark A., Stuart A. BA, San Jose State Coll., 1957; MA, Ohio State U., 1958, PhD, 1963. From asst. prof. to prof. Wright State U., Dayton, Ohio, 1966—, dir. research and instruction computation ctr., 1969—. Contbr. articles to profl. jours. Served to sgt. USMC, 1951-54. Mem. Math. Assn Am. (scholarship 1966), Am. Math. Soc., Assn. for Computing Machinery. Avocations: golf.

SCHAEFER, GEORGE ANTHONY, manufacturing company executive; b. Covington, Ky., June 13, 1928; s. George Joseph and Marie Cecelia (Sandheger) S.; m. Barbara Ann Quick, Aug. 11, 1951; children: Mark Christopher, Sharon Marie. BS in Commerce, St. Louis U., 1951. With Caterpillar Inc., Peoria, Ill., 1951—, div. mgr., 1968-73; plant mgr. Caterpillar Inc., Decatur, Ill., 1973-76, v.p., 1976-81, dir., 1981-84; vice chmn., exec. v.p. Caterpillar Inc., Peoria, 1984-85, chmn., chief exec. officer, 1985—; fin. and acctg. mgr. Caterpillar France S.A., Grenoble, 1962-68; bd. dirs. Towmotor Corp., Mentor, Ohio, Solar Turbines Inc., San Diego, 1st Chgo. Corp.; mem. bus. council Emergency Com. for Am. Trade Negotiations. Mem. adv. council Coll. Commerce and Bus. Adminstrn. U. Ill, Champaign, 1979; trustee Bradley U.; econ. devel. com. Proctor Community Hosp. Served with USMC, 1946-48. Mem. Conf. Bd., Bus. Roundtable. Republican. Roman Catholic. Club: Peoria Country. Office: Caterpillar Inc 100 NE Adams St Peoria IL 61629

SCHAEFER, JON PATRICK, lawyer; b. Fremont, Ohio, Nov. 20, 1948; s. Ellsworth Joseph and Lois Ann (Fought) S.; m. Kathryn Louise Koch, Aug. 21, 1971; children—Heather Marie, Matthew Thomas. B.S., Bethel Coll., 1971; J.D., Memphis State U., 1974. Bar: Ohio 1974, U.S. Dist. Ct. 1977, U.S. Ct. Appeals 1977. V.p. McKown, Schaefer & McKown Co., Shelby, Ohio, 1974-84; sole practice, Shelby, 1984—; judge Shelby Mcpl. Ct., 1982-86, mcpl. judge, 1986—; dir. Rodon Inc., Shelby, 1982—; law dir. City of Shelby, 1976-80. Exec. com. Richland County Democratic Club, Mansfield, Ohio, 1977; mem. Shelby Dem. Club, 1974—; bd. dirs. Shelby Heart Assn., 1976-77, Shelby Red Cross, 1986—; sec. Most Pure Heart of Mary Parish, 1985—. Mem. ABA, Ohio State Bar Assn., Ohio Trial Lawyers Assn., Richland County Bar Assn., Huron County Bar Assn. Lodges: Shelby Sertoma (pres. 1981-82, dist. gov. 1985-86), K.C. (council 1968, Grand Knight 1982-84), Jr. Order Mechanics. Avocations: Fishing; boating; reading. Home: 65 Independence Dr Shelby OH 44875 Office: 68 W Main St Shelby OH 44875

SCHAEFER, JOSEPH JAY, optometrist; b. Milw., Apr. 28, 1934; s. Joseph John and Elsie (Porath) S.; m. Glenyce Ann Bathke, Nov. 18, 1961; children: Janean Ann, Karry Lynn. BS, Marquette U., 1955; OD, Ill. Coll. Optometry, 1958. Cert. Wis. Bd. Optometry. Gen. practice optometry Milw., 1958, Menomonee Falls, Wis., 1962—, Hartford, Wis., 1980—, West Bend, Wis., 1982—. Served to 1st lt. U.S. Army, 1958-62. Mem. Kettle Moraine Optometric Soc., Jaycees. Republican. Roman Catholic. Lodge: Lions. Avocations: golf, camping, antique autos. Home: N84 W31170 Kilbourn Rd Hartland WI 53064 Office: PO Box 363 N86 W 16275 Appleton Ave Menominee Falls WI 53051

SCHAEFER, MARK KENNETH, accountant; b. Madelia, Minn., Dec. 14, 1956; s. Edwin Walter and Blanche Irene (Larsen) S.; m. Dianna Lee Deppe, Mar. 18, 1978; children: Kathryn Adele, Laura Jayne. BS, Mankato (Minn.) State U., 1978; postgrad. in Taxation, U. Minn., 1981—. CPA, Minn. Acct. Vekich, Arkemm & Cp., Mpls., 1978-83; acct., tax mgr. Schweitzer, Rubin, Gottlieb & Karon, Mpls., 1983-87; tax mgr. Hansen, Jergenson & Co., Mpls., 1987—. Editor: State Tax Action Coordinator, 1981. Treas. Luth. Ch. Redemption, Bloomington, 1983-84. Mem. Minn. Soc. CPA's (sec. estate, fin. planning com. 1987—), CPA Tax Roundtable. Republican. Club: Edina Investment (Mpls.) (v.p. 1980-87), Corvettes of Minn. Home: 3308 W 102d St Bloomington MN 55431 Office: Hansen Jergenson & Co NW Financial Ctr Suite 515 7900 Xerxes Ave Minneapolis MN 55431

SCHAEFER, PATRICIA, librarian; b. Ft. Wayne, Ind., Apr. 23, 1930; d. Edward John and Hildegarde (Hormel) Schaefer; B. Music, Northwestern U., 1951; M.Music, U. Ill., 1958; A.M.L.S., U. Mich., 1963. With U.S. Rubber Co., Ft. Wayne, Ind., 1951-52; sec. to promotion mgr. Sta. WOWO, Ft. Wayne, Ind., 1952, sec. to program mgr., 1953-55; coordinator publicity and promotion Home Telephone Co., Ft. Wayne, 1955-56; sec. Fine Arts Found., Ft. Wayne, 1956-57; library asst. Columbus (Ohio) Pub. Library, 1958-59; audio-visual librarian Muncie (Ind.) Pub. Library, 1959-86, asst. library dir., 1981-86; library dir., 1986—; chmn. Ind. Library Film Circuit, 1962-63; treas. Ind. Library Film Service 1969-70, 83-85; mem. exec. com. Eastern Ind. Area Library Services Authority; now pres.; mem. trustees adv. council Milton S. Eisenhower Library, Johns Hopkins U.; cons. in field; weekly columnist Library Lines, Muncie Evening Press, 1981-83; dir. Franklin Electric Co., Inc. Bd. dirs. Muncie Symphony Assn., 1964-74, 85—; bd. trustees Masterworks Chorale, Muncie Mcpl. Band; bd. dirs. Downtown Bus. Council. Choral mem. adv. com., bookshop dir. Midwest Writers Workshop, 1976-77; sec. Del. County Council for the Arts, 1978-79, pres., 1979-81, bd. dirs., 1985—; bd. dirs. Muncie YWCA, 1977-82, 84—, treas., 1981-82; gen. chmn. Ind. Renaissance Fair, 1978-79; program annotator Muncie Symphony Orch., 1963—, East Central Ind. Community Singers, 1980—; pres. Muncie Matinee Musicale, 1965-67; past pres. Ind. Film and Video Council; mem. community adv. com. Ball Bros. Found. Mem. Ind. Library Assn. (pres.), ALA, Nat. League Am. Pen Women (pres. Muncie br. 1974-78), Am. Recorder Soc., Northeastern Ind. Recorder Soc., Delta Zeta, Mu Phi Epsilon. Republican. Roman Catholic. Clubs: Riley-Jones, Altrusa (Muncie) (pres. 1986-87). Contbr. articles to profl. jours. Home: 405 S Tara Ln Muncie IN 47304 Office: 301 E Jackson St Muncie IN 47305

SCHAEFER, ROBERT STEPHEN, engineering executive; b. Fox Lake, Ill., Mar. 21, 1934; s. Stephen Joseph and Regina Christina (May) S.; m. Barbara Jean Hogue, July 6, 1957 (div. 1979); children: Stephen, Kathleen, Jennifer, Elizabeth; m. Rena Constance Moustaris, Aug. 12, 1979; children: Philip, Anthony. BS, U. Ill., 1960. Plant engr. Owens-Corning Fiberglas Corp., Newark, Ohio, 1968-71; mgr.T&I process Owens-Corning Fiberglas Corp., Toledo, 1971-73, dir. process engring., 1973-75, dir. design engr., 1975-86, chief engr., 1986—; cons. various cos.,1985—. Author numerous articles. Patentee zinc sterate application, 1967. Served with USN, 1952-54, PTO. Mem. Am. Soc. Civil Engring., Am. Assn. Engring. Socs. (adv. bd. 1981—), Phi Kappa Phi (hon.), Phi Eta Sigma (hon.). Republican. Greek Orthodox. Avocations: golfing, flying, fishing. Home: 1718 Glendel Ln Toledo OH 43614 Office: Owens-Corning Fiberglas Corp Fiberglas Tower Toledo OH 43659

SCHAEFER, STEVEN JOHN, accountant; b. St. Louis, Feb. 2, 1957; s. John Joseph and Carole Ann (Faulkner) S.; m. Cynthia May Thoenes, Jan. 20, 1979; children: Michael, Lauren, Sarah. BBA, U. Mo., St. Louis, 1979. CPA, Mo. Staff auditor Clayton Bancshares Corp., St. Louis, 1979-80; sr. acct. Schott & Co., Inc., St. Louis, 1980-82; staff acct. Schmitt, Biermann, Spitznagel, Inc., St. Louis, 1982-83; sr. acct. Group Health Plan, Inc., St. Louis, 1983-84, controller, 1984—; pvt. practice acctg. St. Louis, 1980—. V.p. St. John's Toppers, St. John's Ch., St. Louis, 1984-85, pres. 1985-86. Mem. Am. Inst. CPAs. Avocations: softball, spectator sports, reading. Home: 3074 Woodbridge Estates Dr Saint Louis MO 63129 Office: Group Health Plan Inc 11475 Olde Cabin Rd Saint Louis MO 63141

SCHAEFER, SUSAN MARIE, psychologist; b. New Ulm, Minn., Jan. 31, 1952; d. Henry Roland and Marjorie Lillian (Gilbertson) S. BA in Psychology summa cum laude, U. Minn., 1974, MA in Psychology, 1978. Lic. psychologist, Minn.; cert. chem. dependency counselor. Counselor, program mgr. Chrysalis Ctr. Women, Mpls., 1975-80; instr. U. Minn., Mpls., 1975-78; counselor Relate Counseling Ctr., Minnetonka, Minn., 1981-83; pvt. practice psychology Mpls., 1983—; adj. prof. St. Mary's Coll., Mpls., 1984-86; co-chmn. tng. insts. com. State Task Force Sexual Exploitation by Counselors and Therapists, 1985-86; bd. dirs. Sojourner Shelter, Hokins, Minn., 1982-85; trainer, cons. Program in Human Sexuality, U. Minn. Med. Sch., 1979-85. Contbr. articles to profl. jours. and books. Mem. Minn. Women Psychologists, Minn. Chem. Dependency Assn., Minn. Psychol. Assn. Democrat. Roman Catholic. Office: 2400 Blaisdell Ave S Minneapolis MN 55404

SCHAEFFER, BRENDA MAE, psychologist; b. Duluth, Minn., Jan. 7, 1946; s. Ralph J. Bernice M. (Johnson) Furtman; m. Gordon Schaeffer, Aug. 17, 1963 (div.); children: Heidi, Gordon III. Student, Coll. St. Scholastica, 1958-59; BA in Sociology, Psychology and English cum laude, U. Minn., 1962; postgrad., U. Wis., Eau Claire, 1972; MA in Human Devel., St. Mary's Coll., Winona, Minn., 1976. Cert. psychologist, psychotherapist, Minn. Social worker St. Louis County Welfare Dept., 1962-64; adoption coordinator, marriage and family counselor Cath. Social Services, Eau Claire, 1965-73; staff trainer Bethany Children's Home, Eau Claire, 1974-76; faculty Coll. St. Scholastica, Mpls., 1976—; pvt. practice group and family therapy Mpls., 1977—; psychotherapist Inst. for Therapy and Behavior Change, Mpls., 1984—; trainer, therapist, communications cons. Transactional Analysis Inst., Mpls., 1984—; vis. prof. U. Minn., Duluth, 1976—; guest lectr. Dept. Counseling U. Wis., Superior, 1980-81; lectr. numerous presentations to various profl. and social orgns. Author (ednl. materials) Signs of Healthy Love, Signs of Addictive Love, Power Plays, Addictive Love, Help Yourself Out. Planner Lake Superior Task Force, Duluth, 1980-83. Mem. Internat. Transactional Analysis Assn. (various coms.), Transactional Anaylsis Inst. (founding) (pres. 1984-86), U.S. Assn. Transactional Analysis (founding) (chmn. social activities com.), Nat. Assn. Social Workers, Northeast Minn. Transactional Analysis Seminar (founding) (chairperson 1977-83), Minn. Lic. Psychologists. Office: 6100 Green Valley Dr Suite 150 Bloomington MN 55438

SCHAEFFER, BRUCE WAYNE, engineer; b. Sturgis, Mich., Oct. 9, 1935; s. Peter H. and Pauline B. (Van Aken) S.; m. Ruth E. Pierson, Oct. 23, 1954; children: Norman W., Peter A., Diana J. Machine designer Kirsch Co., Sturgis, 1957-63, product engr., 1963-65, research engr., 1965-74, tech. mgr., 1974-82, mgr. product devel., 1982—. Patentee in field. Lutheran. Avocations: coins, raising pigs. Home: 24465 W Fawn River Rd Sturgis MI 49091 Office: Kirsch Co 309 N Prospect St Sturgis MI 49091

SCHAEFFER, DONALD PAUL, pharmacist; b. Beardstown, Ill., Apr. 1, 1956; s. George Warren and Margaret Eunice (Knippenberg) S.; m. Catherine Aileen Conerty, Aug. 31, 1985. BS in Pharmacy, U. Colo., 1981; MBA, Western Ill. U., 1985. Registered pharmacist. Staff pharmacist Cottage Hosp., Galesburg, Ill., 1982-83, Mercy Hosp., Urbana, Ill., 1983-84; dir. pharmacy services HPI Health Care, Inc., Champaign, Ill., 1986—; pharmacy cons. Systems Pharm., Peoria, Ill., 1986—. Am. Soc. Hosp. Pharmacists, Assn. MBA Execs. Republican. Lodges: Optimists, Elks. Avocations: golf, snow skiing, basketball officiating. Home: 1110 Frank Dr Champaign IL 61821 Office: Dir Pharmacy Services 809 W Church St Champaign IL 61820

SCHAEFFER, RICHARD CHARLES, priest; b. Grayling, Mich., Feb. 20, 1952; s. Richard Cradick and Donna Marie (Scott) S. AA, Kirtland Community Coll., 1972; BA, Oakland U., 1974; MDiv, St. John's Provincial Sem., 1983. Ordained priest Roman Cath. Ch., 1983. Assoc. pastor St. Peter's Cathedral, Marquette, Mich., 1983-84, St. Mary Queen of Peace, Kingsford, Mich., 1984-85; pastor St. Stanislaus Kostka, Goetzville, Mich., 1985—; charter mem. project Rachel Diocese of Marquette, 1985—, assoc. dir. vocations, 1987—. Mem. Am. Friends of Vatican Library (charter), Oakland U. Alumni Assn. Lodge: KC. Avocations: study of patristics, foreign languages, travelling, jogging, swimming. Home and Office: PO Box 207 Goetzville MI 49736

SCHAEFFER, WANDA MARIE, nurse, nursing educator; b. Rhineland, Mo., Nov. 3, 1950; d. Victor Louis and Ida Lidwina (Struttman) Van Booven; m. Donald Steven Schaeffer, Oct. 4, 1980; children: Brandy Alicia, Jared Victor. AA, St. Mary's Coll., O'fallon, Mo., 1973, AS in Nursing, 1983; BSBA, Lindenwood Coll., 1981. Registered profl. nurse, Mo. Gen. mgr. Aloysius McGillicuddy Co., St. Charles, Mo., 1978-81; student nurse asst. St. Joseph's Hosp., St. Charles, 1981-83; dir. of nursing Wentzville (Mo.) Park Care Ctr., 1984-85; asst. adminstr. Country Manor Home, Creve Coeur, Mo., 1985-86; instr., dir. in-service Marymount Manor, Eureka, Mo., 1986—; bd. dirs. infection control Riley, Spence Inc., Ellisville, Mo. Republican. Roman Catholic. Avocation: writing. Home: 143 Lamplighter Way O'Fallon MO 63366 Office: Mary Mount Manor 313 Augustine Rd Eureka MO 63025

SCHAERER, JACQUES PAUL, neurosurgeon; b. Zurich, Switzerland, Aug. 14, 1917; came to U.S., 1948, naturalized 1951; s. Georg Paul and Anna (Hiestand) S.; m. Cheryl L. Pulis, Jan. 31, 1974; children: Anne Carole, Marguerite Janet, Elizabeth Eleanor, Maria Amy, Paul Jacques. MD, U. Zurich, 1942, PhD, 1944. Diplomate Am. Bd. Neurol. Surgery, Am. Acad. Neurol. and Orthopaedic Surgeons. Rotating intern Hosp. Waedenswil, Switzerland, 1942-43; asst. instr. Inst. Anatomy, U. Zurich, 1943-44; surg. intern. Children's Hosp., U. Zurich, 1944-45; surg. resident Kantonsspital Winterther Suval Winterthur, Switzerland, 1947-48; rotating intern Luth. Hosp., St. Louis, 1948-49; resident in psychiatry Binghamton (N.Y.) State Hosp., 1949-51; resident in neurosurgery SUNY, Syracuse, 1951-54, instr. neurosurgery, 1954-55; acting chief neurosurgery VA Hosp., Syracuse, 1954-55; practice medicine specializing in neurosurgery St. Louis, 1957—; mem. acting staff Mo. Bapt. Hosp.; mem. courtesy staff Incarnate Word Hosp., St. Joseph's Hosp., Kirkwood, Mo. Hon. consul Switzerland, 1973—; sec., treas. St. Louis Consular Corps, 1978, v.p., 1979, pres., 1980. Served to 1st. lt. M.C., Swiss Army, 1942-48; served to maj. M.C., U.S. Army, 1955-57. Fellow Internat. Coll. Surgeons, Internat. Coll. Angiology, Am. Geriatrics Soc.; mem. Congress Neurol. Surgeons, Neurosurg. Socs. Germany and Switzerland, Am. Soc. Stereotactic and Functional Neurosurgery, Assn. Research Nervous Mental Diseases, AMA, Acad. Neuromuscular Thermography, Pan Am. Med. Assn., Swiss Neurol. Soc., Swiss Med. Soc., So. Med. Assn., Mo. State Med. Assn. Office: 777 S New Ballas Rd Saint Louis MO 63141

SCHAFER, ARTHUR WALTER, JR., real estate corporation executive; b. Chgo., Mar. 3, 1937; s. Arthur W. Sr. and Margaret (Busse) S.; 1 child, Dane Andrew. BS, Ferris State Coll., 1964. Asst. group leader Champion Home Builders, Dryden, Mich., 1955-59; v.p., gen. mgr. Merc-O-Tronic Insts Corp, Almont, Mich., 1959—; ptnr. Clinton River Dist., Almont, 1975—; bd. dirs. Unisen, Inc., Almont. Clubs: Detroit Yacht (Belle Isle, Mich.); German Am. (Detroit). Lodges: Elks, Masons. Avocations: boating, skiing, hunting, flying, travel. Home: 53014 Scenic Dr Rochester MI 48064 Office: Merc-O-Tronic Insts Corp 215 Branch St Almont MI 48003

SCHAFER, GARLAND JEFFREY, small business owner; b. Ashland, Ky., Oct. 4, 1953; s. Garland Edwin and Edith (Blazer) S. Student, Ohio U., 1971-75. Publicity chmn. Sunny Brook Farms, Kitts Hill, Ohio, 1971-86; pres. Schafer & Price Ltd., Huntington, W. Va., 1984-87; pres., sec. Schafer Farms, Kitts Hill, Ohio, 1984-87; pres. Schafer Ltd., Huntington, 1985-87, Your Image Co., Ironton, Ohio, 1986-87; owner, mgr. Exec. Limo Service, Ashland, Ky., 1986-87; owner Impressions-3030 Limousine, Ashland, 1987—. Contbr. articles to local newspapers. Pres. UMYF, Kitts Hill, 1969-71; pres. Jr. Leadership Lawrence County, 1970-71, Young Rep. council, 1972-74, chmn. advisor Tri-State, 1974-87; chmn. Heart Fund, 1979-80; dist. chmn. Lawrence County Cancer Drive, 1979-81; chmn. Lawrence County Fair Queen Assn., Proctorville, 1969-81. Recipient Buckeye Leadership award. Mem. Nat. Limousine Assn., Am. Polled Hereford Assn., Buckeye Polled Hereford Assn., Lawrence County New Ctr. Show Club (pres. 1972-76). Mormon. Lodge: Kiwanis (past dir.). Avocations: antique autos, gemology, comtemporary music. Office: Schafer Ltd Mount Crest Farms of Galliopdlis Scottown OH 45678-9801

SCHAFER, MICHAEL EUGENE, surgeon; b. Beloit, Kans., Feb. 27, 1940; s. Arthur Eugene and Marceline (Gallagher) S.; m. Candace Kittle, June 17, 1967; children: Erika, Joshua, Gabrielle. BA, Kans. State U., 1962; MD, U. Kans., 1967. Diplomate Am. Bd. Plastic Surgery. Surg. intern Rush Presbyn. St. Lukes Hosp., Chgo., 1967-68, surg. resident, 1968-69, gen. surgery resident, 1972-73; resident in plastic surgery Northwestern U., Chgo., 1973-75; craniofacial surg. fellow with Dr. Paul Tessier, Paris, 1976; craniofacial surg. and pediatrics surg. fellow Hosp. for Sick Children, Toronto, Can., 1976-77; chief div. plastic surgery U. Ill., Chgo., 1985—. Editor Clinics in Plastic Surgery, 1983; contbr. articles on plastic surgery to profl. jours. Served to maj. USAF, 1969-71. Eberhard-Karls U. fellow, 1962-63. Mem. AMA, Am. Coll. Surgeons, Am. Soc. Plastic and Reconstructive Surgeons, Am. Cleft Palate Assn., Midwest Soc. Plastic Surgeons, Ill. State Med. Assn., Chgo. Soc. Plastic Surgery. Roman Catholic. Office: U Ill Div Plastic Surgery 840 S Wood St Chicago IL 60612

SCHAFF, HARTZELL VERNON, cardiac surgeon; b. Holdenville, Okla., Feb. 24, 1948; s. Hartzell Vernon and Ruth N. (Stuckey) S.; m. Voni Faith Schafer, Mar. 3, 1973; children: Brynn, Leslie, Sarah, Matthew. Student U. Okla., 1966-69, MD, 1973. Diplomate Am. Bd. Surgery, Am. Bd. Thoracic Surgery. Intern dept. surgery Johns Hopkins Hosp., Balt., 1973-74, asst. resident, 1974-75, fellow cardiovascular surg. research lab., 1975-76, sr. asst. resident, 1976-78, resident cardiac and thoracic surgery, 1978-80; cons. thoracic and cardiovascular surgery, Mayo Med. Sch., Rochester, Minn., 1980—, asst. prof. surgery, 1980-85, assoc. prof., 1985—, co-dir. cardiovascular surg. research lab., 1985—. Mem. editorial bd. Jour. Thoracic and Cardiovascular Surgery; contbr. articles to profl. jours., chpts. to books. Recipient L.G. Moorman award, 1973; George D. Zuidema Resident Research award, 1980; Fulbright Vis. Prof. Cardiac Surgery, 1986. Fellow ACS, Am. Coll. Cardiology, Assn. for Acad. Surgery, Am. Heart Assn., Soc. Univ. Surgeons, Soc. for Thoracic Surg. Edn.; mem. AMA, Am. Assn. Clin. Anatomists, Internat. Assn. Cardia Biol. Implants, Priestley Soc., Johns Hopkins Med. And Surg. Assn., Sigma Xi, Phi Eta Sigma, Alpha Omega Alpha. Republican. Episcopalian. Home: 425 SW 9th Ave Rochester MN 55902 Office: Mayo Clinic 200 1st St SW Rochester MN 55905

SCHAFFER, DONALD JOE, accountant, finance manager; b. Des Moines, May 2, 1956; s. William and Violet Julia (Sundvall) S.; m. Barbara Ann Shanker, June 21, 1980; children: Michael, Robert. BS, Ill. State U., 1978. CPA, Ill. Staff acct. Price Waterhouse, Chgo., 1978-80, sr. acct., 1980-82; mgr. external reporting GATX Corp., Chgo., 1982-84, mgr. spl. projects, 1984-86, mgr. fin., 1986—. Mem. Am. Inst. CPA's, Nat. Assn. Accts. Republican. Roman Catholic. Avocations: jogging, golf. Home: 4045 Grand Ave Western Springs IL 60558 Office: GATX Corp 120 S Riverside Plaza Chicago IL 60606

SCHAFFER, HARWOOD DAVID, clergyman; b. Dayton, Ohio, Oct. 15, 1944; s. Phillip David and H. Ruth (Scheid) S.; B.S. in Math., Ohio State U., 1965; M.Div., Hartford Sem. Found., 1969; m. Polly Anna Francis, May 6, 1983; children—Rosita, Virginia, Chandra, Karen, Amy, Laura. Ordained to ministry United Ch. of Christ, 1969; chaplain, tchr. Austin Sch., Hartford, Conn., 1967-71; asst. pastor S. Congl. Ch., Middletown, Conn., 1967-71; pastor Trinity United Ch. of Christ, Hudson, Kans., 1971-79, Emma Lowery United Ch. of Christ, Luzerne, Mich., 1979-82, First Congregational United Ch. of Christ and Scambler Union United Ch. of Christ, Pelican Rapids, Minn., 1982-86, United Ch. of Mapleton, Minn., 1986—; area counselor 17/76 Achievement Fund of United Ch. of Christ, 1974-75; mem. Western Assn. council Kans.-Okla. Conf., United Ch. of Christ, 1971-74, 76-79, sec.-treas., 1971-74, chmn. ch. and ministry com., 1976-79; mem. various bds. Mich. Conf., United Ch. of Christ, 1979-82; Am. camp mgr. Joint Archaeol. Expdn. to Tel Aphek/Antipatris, Israel, 1978, 80. Bd. govs. Austin Sch., Hartford, 1970-71; mem. Stafford County Democratic Central Com., 1976-79, Dem. Farm Labor precinct chairperson House dist. 10B, 1984-86; Oscoda County Dem. Com., 1980-82; mem. Stafford Council Overall Econ. Devel. Planning Com., 1976-79, chmn., 1977-79; mem. Oscoda County Housing Commn., 1979-82, Pelican Rapids Library Com., 1986. Home: 300 Truendle SW Mapleton MN 56065 Office: PO Box 413 Mapleton MN 56065

SCHAFFER, MARK A., excavating firm executive; b. Norwalk, Ohio, Oct. 28, 1955; s. John A. and Doris A. (White) S.; m. Diane M. Cutnaw, Nov. 27, 1976; children: Jason A., Amy M., Julie B. Pres., mgr. Mark Schaffer Excavating and Trucking Inc., Norwalk, 1983—. Home and Office: 1623 Old State Rd Norwalk OH 44857

SCHAFFER, PAMELA JANE, vocation education administrator; b. Detroit, May 14, 1949; d. George Reichland and Deleta (Pauley) S. BS, Western Mich. U., 1971; MA, Mich. State U., 1976. Cert. Mich. vocat. authorization; cert. continuing edn. Tchr. Hemlock (Mich.) Pub. Schs., 1971-74, Delta Coll., Bay City, Mich., 1974; tchr. Utica (Mich.) Community Schs., 1974-86, adminstr., 1986—; cons. Judy Schaffer Enterprises, Birmingham, Mich., 1985—. Mem. Am. Vocat. Assn. (Tchr. of Yr. Region I 1986), Mich. Home Econs. Educator (legis. chairperson 1978-79, pres. 1980-82, Outstanding Tchr. 1981-82), Mich. Occupational Edn. Assn. (bd. dirs. 1980-82, pres.'s council 1980-81, co-chairperson membership com. 1986—, Tchr. of Yr. 1983-84), Mich. Council Vocat. Adminstrs., Mich. Indsl. Edn. Soc., Macomb Vocat. Edn. Adminstr. Assn., Macomb County Assn. Sch. Adminstrs. (sub-com. vocat. edn.). Office: Utica Community Schs 51041 Shelby Rd Utica MI 48087

SCHALLIOL, THOMAS EDGAR, municipal government official; b. South Bend, Ind., Jan. 29, 1951; s. Edgar R. and Patricia J. (Crawford) S.; m. Barbara J. Black, Sept. 28, 1974; 1 child, Laura Anne. BS in Park Adminstrn., Ind. U., 1974, cert. Pub. Mgmt., 1980, M in Pub. Affairs, 1981. Asst. dir. South Bend Recreation Dept., 1979—. Contbr. articles to profl. jours. Vol. Spl. Olympics, South Bend, 1974—; adv. bd. St. Joseph County Council for Retarded, South Bend, 1980. Recipient Garrett Epply Honors award Ind. U., 1981, Founder's Day Honors award, 1981. Mem. Nat. Recreation and Park Assn. (various coms. Great Lakes Regional Council 1985), Ind. Park and Recreation Assn. (various offices, pres. 1984-85, Outstanding Service award 1983, Pres.'s award 1986). Avocations: running, swimming, biking, golfing, camping. Home: 1520 E LaSalle Ave South Bend IN 46617 Office: South Bend Recreation Dept 727 S Eddy St South Bend IN 46615

SCHAMEL, RAYMOND DEL, radiologist; b. Wheatland, Wyo., Nov. 25, 1940; s. Henry Albert and Evelyn Miriam (Anderson) S.; m. Jan C. Cummings, Aug. 13, 1966; children: Robert Donovan, Sonja Lee. AA, Eastern Wyo. State Coll., 1961; BA, U. Wyo., 1963; MD, U. Colo., 1967. Diplomate Am. Bd. Radiology. Intern St. Lukes Hosp., Denver, 1967-68, resident in radiology, 1971-74; chief radiologist Trinity Regional Hosp., Ft. Dodge, Iowa, 1974—. Commr. Prairie Gold Area council Boy Scouts Am., Sioux City, Iowa, 1985, 86. Served to lt. comdr. USN, 1968-71. Recipient Dist. Merit award Boy Scouts Am., 1982, Silver Beaver award Boy Scouts Am., 1984. Mem. AMA, Iowa Med. Soc., Webster County Med. Soc. (pres. 1980), Radiol. Soc. N.Am., Iowa Radiol. Soc. Republican. United Methodist. Home: 1423 N 14th St Fort Dodge IA 50501 Office: Trinity Regional Hosp South Kenyon Rd Fort Dodge IA 50501

SCHANCK, JORDAN THOMAS, manufacturing company executive; b. Portland, Oreg., Feb. 5, 1931; s. Francis Raber and Kathryn (Short) S.; m. Barbara Burgoyne, Apr. 27, 1957; children: Karen, William, Rebecca. BA, Dartmouth Coll., 1952. With Signode Industries, Inc., 1954—, sales engr.,

1958-60, asst. sales mgr., Paslode div., 1960-61, gen. sales mgr., 1961-65, asst. v.p., gen. sales mgr., 1965-66, gen. sales mgr., Eastern div., 1966-67, asst. to corp. pres., 1967-68, dir. corp. planning, 1968-69, asst to v.p. corp. planning, 1969-70, v.p. corp. planning, 1970-71, exec. v.p. corp. planning and phys. distribn., 1971-73, pres., from 1973, chief exec. officer, 1975—, now also chmn., dir.; former dir. Amsted Industries, Chgo., Walter Heller Internat. Corp., Chgo.; dir. Am. Nat. Bank and Trust Co., Chgo., Maytag Co., Newton, Iowa, Lindberg Corp., Chgo. Past bd. govs. United Republican Fund Ill., 1974—, Chgo. Symphony Orch.; pres. York Woods Community Assn., 1971; mem. adv. bd. YMCA of Met. Chgo., Kellogg Grad. Sch. Mgmt., Northwestern U.; past mem. bd. dirs. United Charities of Chgo.; former trustee, former chmn. George Williams Coll.; active Christ Ch. of Oak Brook, Ill. Served with AUS, 1952-54. Mem. Chgo. Assn. Commerce and Industry (past dir.), Ill. Mfrs. Assn. (past dir.), Dartmouth Alumni Assn. Chgo. (past dir.). Clubs: Hinsdale (Ill.) Golf (dir.); Economic, Chicago, Commercial (Chgo.); Macatawa Bay Yacht (Mich.); Lobloley Bay Yacht, Mariner Sands (Fla.). Home: 38 Croydon Ln Oak Brook IL 60521 Office: Signode Industries Inc 3600 W Lake Ave Glenview IL 60025 *

SCHANDER, CONNIE MARIE, educator; b. Wagner, S.D., Sept. 21, 1943; d. George Joseph and Adeline Ann (Cihak) Rokusek; m. John Frederick Schander, Oct. 23, 1965; children: Chad, Jason. BS, U. S.D., Springfield, 1968; MA in Teaching, Augustana Coll., 1979. Elem. tchr. Sioux Falls (S.D.) Pub. Schs., 1963—. Mem. PTA (life) Laura B. Anderson Sch., Sioux Falls, 1980. Mem. NEA, S.D. Edn. Assn., Sioux Falls Edn. Assn., Alpha Delta Kappa. Democrat. Roman Catholic. Home: 2312 Tamarac Dr Sioux Falls SD 57103

SCHANUEL, SCOTT MATTHEW, economic developer; b. Richmond Heights, Mo., Oct. 9, 1958; s. Lee Arthur and Marjorie Ann (Long) S. BS, U. Ill., 1980; MS, So. Ill. U., Edwardsville, 1981; grad., U. Oklahoma Econ. Devel. Inst., 1984-86. Econ. developer Office of Area Devel. So. Ill. U., Edwardsville, 1982-84; coordinator econ. devel. St. Clair County, Belleville, Ill., 1984-86; dir. econ. devel. Belleville Econ. Progress, Inc., 1986—; bd. dirs. Southwestern Ill. Devel. Corridor, Inc., Belleville, 1986—. Mem. Artrain, Belleville, 1985. Named one of Outstanding Young Men Am., 1985. Mem. Ill. Devel. Council, Leadership Council Southwestern Ill. (assoc.), Belleville Downtown Optimists, Gamma Theta Upsilon, Phi Kappa Phi. Presbyterian. Lodge: Rotary. Avocations: volleyball, softball. Office: Belleville Econ Progress Inc 334 W Main St Belleville IL 62220

SCHARF, MAX RAYMOND, corporate executive; b. St. Louis, Sept. 1, 1933; s. Fischelle Halpern and Sonia (Sunshine) S.; m. Eileen Madeline Ziglin, June 14, 1964; children: Hal Samuel, David Michael. Grad., Harvard U., 1986. Pres. Thelmax, Inc., St. Louis, 1963-66, Incentives Corp., St. Louis, 1966-72; pres., chief exec. officer, chmn. bd. Diversified Graphics, Ltd., St. Louis, 1972—. Served to cpl. U.S. Army, 1953-55. Mem. St. Louis Advt. Splty. (cert. advt. specialist, pres. 1979), Splty. Advt. Assn. Internat. (bd. dirs. 1981). Republican. Jewish. Avocations: racquetball, classical cars. Office: Diversified Graphics Ltd Internat 5433 Eagle Indsl Ct Hazelwood MO 63042

SCHARINGER, DALE HERBERT, business educator; b. Sheboygan, Wis., Nov. 20, 1934; s. Herbert Chester and Frances Eleanor S.; m. Carole Donna Porter, June 15, 1957; children: Anne Elisabeth, Steven Dale. BEd, U. Wis., Whitewater, 1957; MBA, Ind. U., 1958, D Bus. Adminstrn., 1965. Asst. prof. Coll. Bus. U. Wis., Whitewater, 1964-66, asst. dean, 1966-67, acting dean, 1967-68, assoc. dean, 1968-76, prof. mgmt., 1976—. Contbr. articles to profl. jours. Served with U.S. Army, 1958-60. Named one of Disting. Alumni, U. Wis., Whitewater, 1979. Republican. Methodist. Avocation: golf. Home: 407 Douglas Ct Whitewater WI 53190 Office: Univ Wis-Whitewater Whitewater WI 53190

SCHASER, ROBERT JOHN, medical biostatistician; b. Chgo., Mar. 7, 1956; s. Robert Frank and Anne Theresa (Milekant) S. BA in Biology, Western Mich. U., 1979, MS in Biostatistics, 1983. Clin. biostatistician The Upjohn Co., Kalamazoo, Mich., 1983—. Mem. Mich. Kidney Found., Ann Arbor, 1973—, Nat. Kidney Found., Washington, 1973—. Mem. Am. Stats. Soc., SW Statis. Soc., Biometric Soc. Roman Catholic. Avocations: soccer, softball, music. Home: 2180 Albatress Apt 2A Portage MI 49002 Office: The Upjohn Co 7000 Portage Rd Kalamazoo MI 49001

SCHATZ, MARC WILLIAM, electrical engineer; b. Chgo., Feb. 20, 1942; s. Sidney and Lois Rita (Stein) S.; m. Carol Ann Jakaitis, July 10, 1966; children: Jeffrey, David, Timm. BSEE, U. Denver, 1964, MBA, 1965. Profl. engr., Wis. Application engr. Square D Co., Milw., 1965-75, mgr. programmable controllers, 1976-79, mgr. systems products, 1980-85, mgr. product mktg. dept., 1985—. Youth soccer and hockey coach, Milw. Mem. Instrument Soc. Am. Jewish. Avocations: photography, racquetball, skiing. Home: 4123 W LeGrande Mequon WI 53092 Office: Square D Co 4041 N Richards Milwaukee WI 53212

SCHATZMAN, BARD IRWIN, psychologist; b. St. Louis, Feb. 13, 1950; s. Herman Murray and Eugenia (Bierman) S.; m. Linda Sally Brasch, Mar. 22, 1980 (div. Oct. 1980); 1 dau., Laura Ann. B.S., Westminster Coll., 1972; M.S., Central Mo. State U., 1974. Registered, lic. psychologist, Mo.; cert. tchr., Mo. Intern psychologist Farmington State Hosp. and Presbyn. Home for Children, 1974; clin. psychologist Fulton State Hosp. (Mo.), 1974-75; vol. Butterfield Youth Services, Marshall, Mo., 1976-78; clin. psychologist Marshall State Sch. and Hosp., 1976-79; clin. psychologist II, St. Louis Developmental Disabilities Treatment Ctr., 1979-80; surrogate parent Judivine Ctr. for Autistic Children, St. Louis, 1980; cons. psychologist St. John's Mercy Med. Ctr. chem. dependency dept., 1979-81; psychologist Div. Family Services, St. Louis, 1979—, Columbia, 1986—; pvt. practice psychology, St. Louis, 1978—, Columbia, 1986—; research, teaching asst. U. Mo., Columbia, 1986—; asst. prof., vocat. resource educator and counselor disabled students St. Louis Community Coll., Forest Park, 1982—. Mem. Gov.'s Com. Employment of Handicapped, 1982—. Named Counselor of Yr., St. Louis Community Coll. at Forest Park, 1983. Mem. Am. Assn. Counseling and Devel., St. Louis Assn. Counseling and Devel. (past pres.), Mo. Vocat. Spl. Needs Assn. (Outstanding Achievement award for Jr. Colls. 1984-85), Am. Psychol. Assn., Mo. Psychol. Assn., Soc. St. Louis Psychologists, Mo. Coll. Personnel Assn., Assn. Labor-Mgmt. Adminstrs. Jewish.Assn. Labor-Mgmt. Adminstrs. Jewish. Home: 64 Smith Hall Columbia MO 65201 Office: 111 Townsend Hall Columbia MO 65201

SCHAUBEL, HOWARD JAMES, orthopaedic surgeon; b. Grand Rapids, Mich., May 20, 1916; s. Charles Theodore and Jennie (Slager) S.; m. Marjorie Faye Moody, June 19, 1943; children: Candice, Janice, Wendy, Gayla. AS, Grand Rapids Jr. Coll., 1936; AB, Hope Coll., 1938; MD, U. Mich., 1942; cert. orthopaedic surgery, Duke U., 1946. Diplomate Am. Bd. Orthopaedic Surgeons. Intern Duke U. Hosp., Durham, N.C., 1942-43, chief orthopaedic resident, 1944-46; chief resident N.C. Orthopaedic Hosp., Gastonia, 1943-44; practice medicine specializing in orthopaedic surgery Grand Rapids, 1946—, Brownsville, Tex., 1982—; hosp. appointments Butterworth Hosp., Grand Rapids, 1946— (emeritus), Ferguson Hosp., Grand Rapids, 1946— (cons.); chief orthopaedic surgeon Saladin Temple Crippled Children's Clinic, 1947-73; orthopaedic cons. Shriner's Hosp., Chgo., 1950-73, U.S. Dept. Labor, Tex., 1985; dep. examiner Tex. div. Disability Determination, 1984—. Contbr. articles to profl. jours. Served to maj. M.C., U.S. Army, 1953-54. Recipient Disting. Service award Saladin Shrine Temple, Appreciation award Shriner's Hosp. of Chgo., Service award Ferguson Hosp., 1962-73, Service award Fishermen's Hosp., 1974, 75, 76, Disting. Service award Monroe County Med. Soc., 1977, Service award Key's Meml. Hosp., 1977, Disting. Alumni award Grand Rapids Jr. Coll., 1967. Fellow Am. Acad. Orthopaedic Surgeons (emeritus), Internat. Coll. Surgeons; mem. AMA (Physician's Recognition award 1973-88), Mich. Orthopaedic Soc., Piedmont Orthopaedic Soc. (chmn. 1963), Eastern Orthopaedic Assn. (emeritus), So. Med. Assn. (life), Galens Hon. Med. Soc. U. Mich., So. Orthopaedic Assn. (charter), Tex. Orthopaedic Soc., The World Med. Assn., Mich. State Med. Soc., Ottawa County Med. Soc., Tex. Med. Assn., Cameron-Willacy County Med. Soc., Am. Occupational Med. Assn., Mich. Occupational Med. Assn., Monroe County Med. Soc. (pres. 1976), Internat. Soc. Aquatic Medicine, Phi Rho Sigma (officer1941-42). Republican. Congregationalist. Avocations: golfing, scuba diving, internat. travel. Home: 10843 Lake Shore Dr West Olive MI 49460 Office: 456 Cherry St SE Grand Rapids MI 49503

SCHAUER, FREDERICK FRANKLIN, legal educator; b. Newark, Jan. 15, 1946; s. John Adolph and Clara (Balayti) S.; m. Margery Clare Stone, Aug. 25, 1968 (div. June, 1982); m. Virginia Jo Wise, May 25, 1985. AB, Dartmouth Coll., 1967, MBA, 1968; JD, Harvard U., 1972. Bar: Mass. 1972, U.S. Supreme Ct. 1976. Assoc. Fine & Ambrogne, Boston, 1972-74; asst. prof. law W.Va. U., Morgantown, 1974-76, assoc. prof. law, 1976-78; assoc. prof. law Coll. William & Mary, Williamsburg, Va., 1978-80, Cutler prof. law, 1980-83; prof. law U. Mich., Ann Arbor, 1983—; vis. scholar, mem. faculty law Wolfson Coll. Cambridge (Eng.) U., 1977-78. Author: The Law of Obscenity, 1976, Free Speech: A Philosophical Enquiry, 1982 (ABA cert. merit 1983), Supplements to Gunther, 1985-87; co-author: (with Gunther) Constitutional Law, 1983-84; contbr. articles to profl. jours. Mem. Atty. Gen.'s Commn. on Pornography, 1985-86. Served with Mass. Army N.G., 1970-71. NEH fellow, summer 1980. Mem. Am. Philos. Assn., Am. Soc. for Polit. and Legal Philosophy, Assn. Am. Law Schs. (chmn. sect. constl. law 1984-86). Home: 1208 Wells Ann Arbor MI 48104 Office: U Mich Law Sch Hutchins Hall Ann Arbor MI 48109

SCHAUER, MARK HAMILTON, urban planner; b. Howell, Mich., Oct. 2, 1961; s. Robert Charles and Myra (Trafton) S. BA in Sociology and Spanish, Albion Coll., 1984; MPA, Western Mich. U., 1986. Assoc. planner Calhoun County Planning Dept., Marshall, Mich., 1984-85; sr. planner Calhoun County Planning Dept., Marshall, 1985-86; planning dir. Community Action Agy. of Southcen. Mich., Battle Creek, 1987, exec. dir., 1987—. Active Big Brother Big Bros./Big Sisters of South Cen. Mich., 1985-86; vol. coach Marshall Recreation Dept., Marshall, 1986. Methodist. Lodge: Optimist Internat. (sgt.-of-arms 1986—). Home: 216 N Eagle #1 Marshall MI 49068

SCHAUER, THOMAS ALFRED, insurance company executive; b. Canton, Ohio, Dec. 24, 1927; s. Alfred T. and Marie A. (Luthi) S.; B.Sc., Ohio State U., 1950; m. Joanne Alice Fay, Oct. 30, 1954; children—Alan, David, Susan, William. Ins. agt., Canton, 1951—; with Schauer & Reed Agy., 1951—, Kitzmiller, Tudor & Schauer, 1957—, Webb-Broda & Co., 1971—, Foglesong Agy., 1972—; pres. Ind. Ins. Service Corp. Akron, Dover and Canton, Canton, 1964—, Laurenson Agy., 1978—, Wells-Williams, 1978—, J.D. Craig Agy., 1981—dir. Central Trust Co. NE Ohio (N.A.). Chmn., Joint Hosp. Blood Com., 1974; bd. dirs. Better Bus. Bur., Canton, 1970-81, chmn., 1979-80; bd. dirs. area YMCA, 1974, v.p., 1975-82, pres., 1982-84; bd. dirs. Hosp. Bur. Central Stark City, 1972-78; vice chmn. bd. Aultman Hosp., 1981-84, chmn., 1984-87; pres. Aultman Hosp. Found., 1987—; chmn. bd. JMS Found., 1968—; bd. dirs. United Way, 1974-84, pres., 1976-78; mem. distbn. com. Stark County Found., 1977-87, chmn. distbn. com.; 1984-87; adv. bd. Malone Coll., 1979—; trustee Kent State U., 1980—, N.E. Ohio Univs. Coll. Medicine, 1983—; past trustee Canton Urban League, Boys Village (Smithville, Ohio), Canton Art Inst., Buckeye Council Boy Scouts Am. Served with USNR, 1946-48. C.L.U., C.P.C.U. Mem. Chartered Ins. Inst. London, Nat. Assn. Mfg., Am. Soc. C.P.C.U.'s, Am. Soc. C.L.U.s, Am. Mgmt. Assn., Assn. Advanced Life Underwriters, Am. Risk and Ins. Assn., Am. Soc. Pension Actuaries, Stark County Accident and Health Underwriters (past pres.). Clubs: Canton, Brookside Country, Atwood Yacht. Home: 1756 Dunbarton Dr NW Canton OH 44708 Office: Carnegie Library Bldg 236 3d St SW Canton OH 44702

SCHAUER, WILBERT EDWARD, JR., lawyer, manufacturing company executive; b. Milw., Oct. 28, 1926; s. Wilbert Edward and Gertrude (Nickel) S.; m. Genevieve Stone, June 23, 1951; children—Jeffrey Edward, Constance Emily, Gregory Wilbert, Martha Ann, Jennifer Caroline. B.B.A., U. Wis., 1949, M.B.A., 1950, J.D., 1950. Bar: Wis. 1950. Accountant Pub. Service Commn. Wis., 1950-52; with Rexnord, Inc., Milw., 1952—; v.p. finance, treas. Rexnord, Inc., 1968-76, v.p. fin. and law, 1977-78, exec. v.p. fin. and adminstrn., 1978-86, vice chmn., 1986—. Alderman, Brookfield, Wis., 1958-68; pres. Common Council, 1966-68. Clubs: Milwaukee; Westmoor Country (Brookfield, Wis.); Bluemound Golf and Country. Home: 14865 Woodbridge Rd Brookfield WI 53005 Office: Rexnord Inc 350 N Sunny Slope Brookfield WI 53005

SCHAUM, JAMES HOWARD, hospital administrator; b. Lodi, Ohio, Apr. 4, 1946; s. Howard Leroy and Effie Irene (Jacot) S.; m. Kathryn Anderson, June 20, 1970; children—Jonathan James, Benjamin Anderson, Robert Howard. B. in Pharmacy, West Va. U., 1969; M.S. in Hosp. and Health Service Adminstrn., Ohio State U., 1979. Registered pharmacist, Ohio, Ind. Pharmacist, store mgr. Revco Discount Drug Stores, Van Wert, Ohio, 1969-71, Akron, Ohio, 1972, Massillon, Ohio, 1972-73, Wooster, Ohio, 1973-77; asst. adminstr. profl. services Med. Center Hosp., Chillicothe, Ohio, 1979-83, assoc. adminstr., 1983-84, sr. assoc. adminstr., 1985—. Pres. YMCA, 1982, 83; mem. ARC. Named Jaycee of the Yr., 1982, Outstanding Dist. Dir.; Named Citizen of Yr. Ross County, 1985. Mem. Am. Coll. Hosp. Adminstrs., Am. Hosp. Assn., Ohio Hosp. Assn., Central Ohio Health Adminstrs. Assn. Republican. Presbyterian. Clubs: Elks, Jaycees (assoc., past state dir., treas.), Rotary. Home: 377 Shannon Dr Chillicothe OH 45601 Office: Medical Center Hospital 272 Hospital Way Chillicothe OH 45601

SCHAUT, LEO LOUIS, engineering firm executive; b. LaBranch, Mich., June 6, 1931; s. Louis Joseph and Edna Margaret (Niquette) S.; m. Patricia Addison Simon, Aug. 29, 1953; children: John, James, Paul, Mary, William, Joseph, Patricia, Barbara. BS in Civil Engring., Wayne State U., 1954, MS in Civil Engring., 1955. Registered profl. engr., Mich. Sr. design engr. Giffels of Can., Windsor, Ont., 1957-60; mgr. ops. Giffels of Can., Ottawa, Ont., 1960-63; sr. project mgr. Giffels of Can., Windsor, 1963-67, Phoenix Contractors, Grand Rapids, Mich., 1967-71, Williams & Works, Grand Rapids, 1971-81; pres. Schaut Assocs. Inc., Grand Rapids, 1981—. Leader Cub Scouts Am., Grand Rapids, 1967-74; troop and dist. chmn. Boy Scouts Am., Grand Rapids, 1968-77; chmn. fin. commn. Holy Spirit Parish, Grand Rapids, 1973-77. Mem. Mich. Soc. Profl. Engrs., Water Pollution Control Fedn. Roman Catholic. Lodge: Elks. Avocation: sailing. Home and Office: Schaut Assocs Inc 2530 Leonard NW Grand Rapids MI 49504

SCHAUVLIEGE, PERRY ALLEN, architect; b. Spearville, Kans., Aug. 15, 1960; s. Clifford Roy Schauvliege and Peggy Jane (Speck) Elder; m. Leslie Ann Smith, Mar. 16, 1985. BS in Environ. Design, U. Okla., 1983. Archtl. intern Jeff Krehbiel & Assocs., Wichita, Kans., 1984-86; designer Law-Kingdon, Inc., Wichita, 1986—. Mem. AIA (active intern directorship program Kans. chpt. 1984—), Kans. AIA. Roman Catholic. Avocations: golfing, tennis, softball, fishing, hunting. Home: 2447 Wilson Dr Wichita KS 67204 Office: Law-Kingdon Inc 345 Riverview Wichita KS 67203

SCHEANWALD, MARJORIE DIANA, medical office administrator; b. Toledo, Sept. 27, 1926; d. August G. and Henrietta H. (Helbing) S.; student public schs., Saginaw, Mich. Bookkeeping machine operator Sugar Beet Products, Gen. Office, Saginaw, 1944-46; bookkeeping machiner operator Heavenrich's, Saginaw, 1946-53, sec. to pres., 1953-56; receptionist/sec. pvt. med. office, Saginaw, 1956-72; office mgr., asst. corp. sec. Valley Ob-Gyn Clinic, Saginaw, 1972—, also dir. Mem. Med. Group Mgrs. Assn., Am. Assn. Med. Assts., Mich. Med. Group Mgmt. Assn. Republican. Presbyterian. Home: 311 S Wheeler St Saginaw MI 48602 Office: 926 N Michigan St Box 3216 Saginaw MI 48605

SCHECHTER, ALLEN E(DWARD), publishing company executive; b. Chgo., Dec. 17, 1935; s. Oscar A. and Sarah (Silberman) S.; m. Esther M. Schiller, June 11, 1961; children—Deborah, Daniel. A.B., U. Chgo., 1955; J.D., Northwestern U., 1958. With Commerce Clearing House, Inc., Chgo., 1959—; now v.p., sr. mng. editor Commerce Clearing House, Inc. Mem. Am., Fed., Ill. bar assns. Home: 6747 S Constance Ave Chicago IL 60649 Office: Commerce Clearing House Inc 2700 Lake Cook Rd Riverwoods IL 60015

SCHECHTER, HERBERT SHERMAN, accountant; b. St. Paul, Nov. 11, 1937; s. Irving E. and Ceil (Rabinovitz) S.; m. Marta Jane Lazarus, Dec. 22, 1983; children: Heidi, Michael, Scott. BBA, U. Minn., 1958. CPA. Staff acct. Wolkoff, Effress and Co., St. Paul, 1958-62, ptnr., 1962-65; mgr. Lybrand, Ross Bros. and Montgomery, Mpls., 1965; ptnr. Klane Gillman and Schechter, Mpls., 1965-84, Laventhol and Horwath, Mpls., 1984—; lectr. in acctg. U. Minn., Mpls., 1962-67. Author: Audit Guide, 1971, Computer Accounting Systems, 1981; editor: Software Contract Negotiations, 1984; author, tech. editor Guide to Small Business Consulting, 1987; tech. editor various works. Chmn. planning commn. City of St. Louis Park, Minn., 1982—, fin. adv. com. Sch. Dist. #283, St. Louis Park, 1973-77; chmn. group services panel Mpls. Fedn. for Jewish Services, 1983—. Served to 1st lt. USAF, 1960-65. Mem. Am. Inst. CPA's (Mgmt. Adv. Services exec. com. 1985—), Minn. Soc. CPA's (chmn. auditing com.), Beta Gamma Sigma, Beta Alpha Psi. Republican. Jewish. Lodge: B'nai Brith (pres.). Home: 8621 W 29th St Saint Louis Park MN 55426 Office: Laventhol and Horwath 100 Washington Sq Minneapolis MN 55401

SCHEEL, RODNEY CLAIR HANS, energy company executive; b. Grand Forks, N.D., June 4, 1949; s. Clarence and Delores Irene Hazel (Pederson) S.; m. Jolene Kay Johnson, Apr. 28, 1979; children: Lindsey Joy, Courtney Jo, Jesse Hans, Abby Jaclyn. BSEE, N.D. State U., 1971; MS, S.D. State U., 1973. Registered profl. engr., Minn. Engr. Otter Tail Power Co., Fergus Falls, Minn., 1973-78; supr. system engring. Otter Tail Power Co., Fergus Falls, 1978-80, mgr. system engring., 1980-84, dir. info. services, 1984—. V.p. Fergus Falls Childrens' Services Bd., 1980; pres. bd. dirs. United Fund, 1984, patron chmn., 1986. Mem. IEEE, NSPE (pres. Height of Land br. Minn. soc. 1984). Methodist. Club: Lake Region Amateur Radio (Fergus Falls) (pres. 1984-85). Lodge: Elks. Avocations: hunting, trap shooting, classic cars, amateur radio. Home: 1215 N Concord St Fergus Falls MN 56537 Office: Otter Tail Power Co 215 S Cascade Fergus Falls MN 56537

SCHEELE, ROY MARTIN, educator; b. Houston, Jan. 10, 1942; s. Elmer Martin and Hazel Ilene (McChesney) S.; m. Frances McGill Hazen, June 26, 1965; children—Evan Mathew, Christof Andrew. B.A., U. Nebr., 1965, M.A. in English, 1971; postgrad. U. Tex.-Austin, 1965-66. Instr. English, U. Tenn., Martin, 1966-68; research librarian Weldon Kees collection Bennett Martin Pub. Library, Lincoln, Nebr., 1969-70; instr. English, Theodor Heuss Gymnasium, Waltrop, W. Ger., 1974-75; lectr. Classics, Creighton U., 1977-79; vis. instr. Classics, U. Nebr., Lincoln, 1980-81; instr. English as a second lang. Midwest Inst. for Internat. Studies, Doane Coll., Crete, Nebr., 1982—; poet-in-the-schs. program, Nebr. Arts Council, 1976—. Pres. Lincoln chpt. Save the Niobrara River Assn., 1980-81. Recipient Ione Gardner Noyes poetry awards U. Nebr., Lincoln, 1962, 64; 1st prize for poetry John G. Neihardt Found., 1983. Mem. Nebr. Tchrs. English to Speakers of Other Langs./Nebr. Assn. Bi-lingual Educators, Acad. Am. Poets, Royal Oak Found., Smithsonian Assocs., Nature Conservancy, Sierra Club. Democrat. Presbyterian. Author: (poetry) Grams and Epigrams, 1973; Accompanied, 1974; Noticing, 1979; The Sea-Ocean, 1981; Pointing Out the Sky, 1985. Home: 2020 S 25th St Lincoln NE 68502

SCHEER, GEORGE EDWARD, orthopedic surgeon; b. Wichita, Kans., Dec. 12, 1918; s. George William and Grace Ethyl (McIlvain) S.; m. Margaret Dee, Aug. 29, 1942 (div.); children: DeeAnn Ivey, George E. Jr.; m. Oleta Frances Bennett, July 28, 1978; 1 child, James Paul. BA, Wichita U., 1940; MD, Washington U., St. Louis, 1943. Diplomate Am. Bd. Orthopedic Surgeons. Intern St. Louis Hosp., 1944; resident in orthopedic surgery Jefferson Barracks VA Hosp., St. Louis, 1946-49; resident children's orthopedic surgery Shriners Hsop. Crippled Children, St. Louis, 1949-50; chief surgeon St. Louis Shrine Hosp., 1949-76; orthopedic surgeon St. Louis-Clayton Orthopedic Group, 1976—. Served to lt. USN, 1942-46, PTO. Fellow AMA, Am. Bd. Orthopedics; mem. Am. Acad. Orthopedic Surgeons. Republican. Avocations: flying, fishing. Home: 53 Berkshire Saint Louis MO 63117 Office: St Louis-Clayton Orthopedic Group 1034 S Brentwood Saint Louis MO 63117

SCHEETZ, GEORGE HENRY, library director; b. Columbus, Ohio, July 27, 1952; s. Donald Jean and Betty Jane (Killeen) S.; m. Kathy Charlotte Durley, Apr. 28, 1979; 1 child, Trevor Killeen. AB, U. Ill., 1974, MS, 1976. Reference librarian Bradley U., Peoria, Ill., 1977-78; bus. librarian Peoria Pub. Library, 1978-79, br. mgr., 1979-82; asst. dir. Ames (Iowa) Pub. Library, 1982-85; dir. Sioux City (Iowa) Pub. Library, 1985—. Author: Place Names of Story County, 1985, Trevor, 1986; editor: Riverworld War, 1980; contbr. articles to profl. jours. Rep. Jr. League Community Adv. Council, Sioux City, 1985—; bd. dirs. Ames Heritage Assn., 1985, Ames Community Arts Council, 1984-85, Open Line Inc., Ames, 1982-83. Named one of Outstanding Young Men of Am., Jaycees, 1979. Mem. ALA, Iowa Library Assn. (legis com., local history round table), Am. Name Soc., Sci. Fiction Research Assn., Am. Interprofl. Inst., Sigma Tau Delta, Omicron Delta Kappa. Roman Catholic. Lodge: Rotary. Avocations: books and bibliographies, Sherlock Holmes, onomastics, logology, philately. Home: 2814 Summit St Sioux City IA 51104-3743 Office: Sioux City Pub Library 705 Sixth St Sioux City IA 51105-1998

SCHEIBACH, MICHAEL EVAN, publishing executive; b. Orlando, Fla., June 13, 1949; s. Bernard Frederick Scheibach and Grace Pearl (Cady) Laribee; m. Tami Lane Neal, Feb. 27, 1970; 1 child, Jessica Shaan. BA in English, U. Mo., Kansas City, 1974, MA in History, 1976; postgrad., U. Kans., 1981-82. Asst. to pub. The Westport Reporter, Kansas City, 1970-75; asst. editor Am. Indian Hist. Soc., San Francisco, 1976-77; managing editor Intertec Pub., Overland Park, Kans., 1977-78; v.p. ops. Globecom Pub., Overland Park, 1978—; English tchr., Graceland Coll., Independence, Mo., 1977—. Editor Mag. Design and Prodn. Mem. Am. Mgmt. Assn., Am. Soc. Bus. Press Editors, Nat. Computer Graphics Assn., Western Publ. Assn. Avocations: jogging, softball, reading, photography. Office: Globecom Pub Unlimited 4551 W 107th St Suite 343 Overland Park KS 66207

SCHEIDT, DON RANDELL, real estate appraisal company executive; b. Columbus, Ind., Oct. 27, 1950; s. Virgil D. and Bettie L. (Todd) S.; m. Jill Louise Coleman, June 2, 1979; children: Leslie, Katie. BA, Ind. U., 1972. Designated real estate instr. Pres. Don R. Scheidt & Co. Inc., Columbus, Ind., 1977—; instr. Ctr. for Real Estate Edn. & Research, Bloomington, Ind., 1982—, GRI Program for Ind. Assn. Realtors, Indpls., 1985-86. Pres. Disting. Visitors Series, Columbus, 1982; chmn. fund drive Driftwood Valley Arts Council, Columbus, 1983; bd. pres. Retirement Found. Bartholomew County, Columbus, 1986. Mem. Am. Inst. Real Estate Appraisers (bd. dirs. 1986), Soc. Real Estate Appraisers (sec. 1986), Appraisal Inst., Sr. Real Property Appraisers, Columbus Bd. Realtors (treas. 1976, bd. dirs. 1983-84). Republican. Lutheran. Lodge: Rotary (bd. dirs. Columbus club 1985-87). Office: 434 4th St Suite 4 Columbus IN 47201

SCHELIN, PEGGY, personnel director; b. Ossining, N.Y., Feb. 4, 1956; d. E. Wayne and Jane (Wight) S. BS in Zoology, Iowa State U., 1978; MBA, U. Mich., 1980. Assoc. organizational research and devel. Gen. Motors, Detroit, 1979-80; productivity analyst Gen. Mills, Mpls., 1980-81, productivity cons., 1981-83, personnel mgr. Yoplait USA div., 1983-85, personnel dir. mktg. services, 1985—; bd. dirs. Gen. Mills Vol. Action Council, 1984—. Mem. adminstrv. council Eden Prairie Meth. Ch., chmn. outside concerns, sec. bldg. fund, asst. lay leader; del. Dem. Nat. Conv., 1984; bd. dirs. Dem. 3d. Congressional Dist., 1986—; bd. dirs. Minn. Geneal. Soc., 1986—. Mem. Am. Soc. Tng. and Devel., Am. Soc. Personnel Adminstrn., Twin Cities Personnel Assn. (profl. devel. com. 1985—), Mortor Bd., Cardinal Key. Democrat. Avocations: genealogy, travel. Home: 14371 Fairway Dr Eden Prairie MN 55344 Office: Gen Mills Mktg Services PO Box 1113 Minneapolis MN 55440

SCHELL, DAVID LAURENCE, health care administrator; b. Cleve., Dec. 16, 1954; s. Paul Lewis and Winifred Rose (Cermak) S.; m. Annette G. Lorenz, June 5, 1976; children—Joshua David, Jeremy Ryan. B.S. in Health Services Mgmt., Ferris State Coll., 1977; M.B.A., Grand Valley State Coll., 1983. Lic. nursing home adminstr., Mich. Mental health adminstr. Cambridge Devel. Ctr., Ohio, 1977-78; facilities planner Cambridge Mental Health & Devel. Ctr., 1978-81; adminstr. Meadowbrook Care Ctr., Holland, Mich., 1981-82; dir., adminstr. Resthaven Patrons, Inc., Holland, Mich., 1982—; adminstrv. intern Reed City Hosp., Mich., 1977; gerontology instr. Muskingum Tech. Coll., Zanesville, Ohio, 1980. Mem. Mich. Non-Profit Homes Assn. (com. chmn.), Am. Hosp. Assn., Mich. Gerontology Assn., Holland Area C. of C. (rep.). Republican. Club: Golconda Investment (asst. fin. advisor). Avocations: sailing; skiing. Home: 15414 141st Ave Holland MI 49423 Office: Resthaven Patrons Inc 5 E 8th St Holland MI 49423

SCHELLENBERG, JAMES ARTHUR, sociology educator, university official; b. Vinland, Kans, June 7, 1932; s. Isaac F. and Tena (Franz) S.; m. Diana B. Sadler, July 29, 1956 (div.); children: Robert L. , Franklin M.; m. Christine A. Alberti, Dec. 28, 1974; children: Amy J., Stephen A. AB, Baker U., 1954; MA, U. Kans., 1955, PhD, 1959. Asst. prof. sociology Western Mich. U., Kalamazoo, 1959-63, assoc. prof. sociology, 1963-67, prof. sociology, 1967-76; prof. sociology Ind. State U., Terre Haute, 1976—, asst. v.p. acad. affiars, 1980—. Author: An Introduction to Social Psychology, 1970, rev. edit., 1974, Masters of Social Psychology, 1978, The Science of Conflict, 1982. Mem. Am. Sociol. Assn., Am. Psychol. Assn., AAAS, Assn. Univ. Profs. Methodist. Home: 87 Heritage Dr Terre Haute IN 47803 Office: Ind State U Terre Haute IN 47809

SCHEMA, DOUGLAS, educator; b. Rapid City, S.D., Dec. 3, 1953; s. Ernest Anton and Nima (Bursik) S. B.A. in History and Art, Bellevue Coll., 1977; M.A., U. Mo., 1981; postgrad. Creighton U., 1982. Mfrs. rep. Midwest Supply Co., Des Moines, 1974-75; library staff U. Nebr., Omaha, 1977-79; staff supr. Health Scis. Library, Creighton U., 1979-81, cons. corp. communications, 1981—; teaching asst. Am. History Studies, U. Mo., Columbia, 1979-81; instr. European history Bellevue Coll., 1981-82; instr. continuing edn. div. U. Nebr., Omaha, 1983—. Producer Pub. Broadcasting System TV program When Boulder Power Came to Los Angeles, 1986; contbr. articles to profl. jours. Tech. Advisor Dakota Territorial Mus., 1981-84; mem. speakers bur. Nishnabotna Girl Scout Council. Named Toastmaster of Yr., 1976. Mem. Illuminating Engring. Soc. North Am., State Hist. Soc. Mo., Nat. Trust for Historic Preservation, Am. Council Pub. Policy, Am. Qtr. Horse Assn. Methodist. Lodge: Toastmasters (pres. 1974). Home: 711 Grace St Council Bluffs IA 51501

SCHEMMEL, RACHEL ANNE, food science and human nutrition educator, researcher; b. Farley, Iowa, Nov. 23, 1929; d. Frederic August and Emma Margaret (Melchert) Schemmel. B.A., Clarke Coll., 1951; M.S., U. Iowa, 1952; Ph.D., Mich. State U., 1967. Dietitian, Children's Hosp. Soc. Los Angeles, 1952-54; instr. Mich. State, U., East Lansing, 1955-63, from asst. prof. to prof. food sci., human nutrition, 1967—. Author: Nutrition Physiology and Obesity, 1980. Contbr. articles on obesity, clin. nutrition to profl. jours. Recipient Disting. Alumni award Mt. Mercy Coll., 1971, Borden award for research in applied nutrition, 1986. Mem. Am. Inst. Nutrition, Inst. Food Technologists, Am. Diet Assn. (pres. Mich. and Lansing 1975-76), Brit. Nutrition Soc., Soc. for Nutrition Edn., Sigma Xi (sr. research award 1986). Roman Catholic. Home: 1341 Red Leaf Ln East Lansing MI 48823 Office: MI State U Dept Pediatrics Dept Food Sci and Human Nutrition East Lansing MI 48824

SCHENK, BOYD F., holding company executive; b. Providence, Utah, 1922. Student, U. Utah, 1942, U. Idaho, 1943. With Pet, Inc., St. Louis, 1947—, now pres., chief exec. officer; with IC Industries, Inc. (parent co.), Chgo., 1978—, exec. v.p., 1984-85, pres., chief operating officer, 1985, vice-chmn., 1985—, dir.; dir. Laclede Gas Co., Ill. Power Co., Staley Continental, Inc. Office: IC Industries Inc One Illinois Ctr 111 E Wacker Dr Chicago IL 60601 *

SCHENK, JONELL ANN, social worker; b. McPherson, Kans., July 24, 1948; d. John Harrison and Cora Cynthia (Bernstorf) Farver; m. Jerald Dee Schenk, July 26, 1975; 1 child, Cameron Anthony. Adoption specialist Salina Area SRS, Beloit, Kans., 1975-79; social worker juvenile offender programs Youth Ctr. at Beloit, 1979—. Mem. Acad. Cert. Social Workers, No. Cen. Kansas Welfare Assn. (v.p., pres.), Beta Sigma Phi (sec. 1985-86). Republican. Methodist. Clubs: Andromeda (treas., sec. 1986—), Beloit Booster (treas. 1985-86).

SCHENK, QUENTIN FREDERICK, social work educator, mayor; b. Fort Madison, Iowa, Aug. 25, 1922; s. Fred Edward John and Ida (Sabrowsky) S.; m. Patricia J. Kelley, Aug. 6, 1946 (div. Apr. 1970); children: Fred W. (dec. 1972), Patricia, Karl, Martha; m. Emmy Lou Willson, May 23, 1970. B.A., Willamette U., 1948; M.S., U. Wis., 1950, M.S. in Social Work, 1953, Ph.D., 1953. Asst. prof. social work U. Wis.-Madison, 1953-55, prof., chmn. extension social work, 1961-63; prof., former dean Sch. Social Welfare, Milw., 1963—; assoc. prof. U. Mo., 1955-61; project specialist Ford Found., 1968-71; Spl. cons. on urban mission in Africa United Presbyn. Ch., 1971—, World Council Chs., 1971—; adviser to Haile Sellassie I U., Addis Ababa, Ethiopia, 1968-71; Alderman City of Cedarburg (Wis.), 1974-82, mayor, 1982-86. Author: (with Emmy Lou Schenk) Pulling Up Roots, 1978, Welfare Society and the Helping Professions, 1981; editor sect. on Ethiopa, Welfare in Africa, 1987; contbr. articles, bulls., reports to profl. lit. Mem. Wis. Historic Preservation Negotiating Bd.; chmn. bd. Guest House, Milw., 1987—. Served as pilot USNR, 1942-46. Decorated Air medal with 3 gold stars, DFC. Mem. AAUP, Nat. Trust for Historic Preservation, Am. Sociol. Assn., Council on Social Work Edn., Aircraft Owners and Pilots Assn., Cessna Pilots Assn., Am. Legion. Home: Box 31 W61 N 439 Washington Ave Cedarburg WI 53012 Office: Sch Social Welfare U Wis Milwaukee WI 53201

SCHENK, ROBERT EUGENE, civil engineer; b. Waterloo, IA, Jan. 10, 1925; s. Ernest Eugene and Edna Belle (Alton) S.; m. Sarah Emogene Bridges, Jan. 3, 1952; children: Robert E. Jr., Glee Acor, Anne. BS, U.S. Naval Acad., 1946. Registered profl. engr., Iowa, Wis. Commd. lt. (j.g.) USN, 1946, resigned, 1953; ptnr. Schenk Engring. Co., Waterloo, Iowa, 1953-66, pres., 1966—. Mem. NSPE, Iowa Engring. Soc. Lutheran. Lodge: Rotary. Avocations: hiking, canoeing. Home: 441 Kingbard Blvd Waterloo IA 50701 Office: Schenk EngringCo 216 Brookeridge Dr Waterloo IA 50702

SCHENK, RONALD, publishing executive; b. Elizabeth, N.J., Feb. 25, 1945; s. Albin F. and Mary (Nash) S.; m. Donna Napoli, Aug. 19, 1967; children: Kristen, Jennifer. BA, Rutgers Coll., 1967; MA, Columbia U., 1969, M in Philosophy, 1972. Assoc. dir. admission tchrs. coll. Columbia U., N.Y.C., 1967-73; acting dean Marymount Manhattan Coll., N.Y.C., 1973-75; v.p. Prentice Hall Devel. Learning Ctrs., West Paterson, N.J., 1976-84; gen. mgr. Reading Resources, Inc., Worthington, Ohio, 1984-87; pres. Schenk Assocs. Inc., Dublin, Ohio, 1984—; dir. mktg. Sch. Book Fairs Inc., Worthington, 1987—; mem. adj. faculty County Coll. Morris, Randolph, 1981-85. Contbr. articles to ednl. jours. Home: 182 Waterford Dr Dublin OH 43017

SCHENK, THOMAS LEE, data processing executive; b. Great Bend, Kans., July 9, 1954; s. Edwin Joseph and Norma Jean (Rose) S.; m. Julie Padilla, Apr. 15, 1978; children: Eric, Valerie, Tom Jr. Grad. high sch., Otis, Kans. Asst. mgr. data communications Norwest Fin. Info. Services Group, Des Moines, 1976—. Capt. EMT-A Granger Community Ambulance, Granger, Iowa, 1978—. Served to sgt. USAF, 1972-76. Republican. Roman Catholic. Lodge: KC. Avocations: jogging, coin and stamp collecting. Home: 2100 Court Granger IA 50109 Office: Norwest Fin Info Services Group 206 8th St Des Moines IA 50309

SCHENKEL, JAMES JOSEPH, architect; b. Ft. Wayne, Ind., Mar. 21, 1933; s. William Francis and Georgia Ruth (haaga) S.; m. Janice Mary Hillyard, June 23, 1956; children: Ellen, Scott, Linda, Rita, Stewart. BArch, U. Notre Dame, 1956. Architect, ptnr. Schenkel & Lawrence, Ft. Wayne, 1959-66; architect, pres. Schenkel & Shultz Inc., Ft. Wayne, 1966—. Served to capt. U.S. Army, 1957-60. Mem. Ind. Archtl. Found. (bd. dirs. 1981—, pres. 1970-71; Edward D. Pierre Meml. medal 1978), No. Ind. Chpt. Ind. Soc. Architects (pres. 1969-70), Ft. Wayne C. of C. Republican. Roman Catholic. Club: Ft. Wayne Country. Lodge: Rotary. Avocations: golf, fishing, trumpet. Home: 5022 Midlothian Dr Fort Wayne IN 46835 Office: Schenkel & Shultz Inc 3702 Rupp Dr Fort Wayne IN 46815

SCHENKEN, JERALD RUDOLPH, pathologist, educator; b. Detroit, Oct. 11, 1933; s. John Rudolph and Lucile (Jerald) S.; m. Charlotte Elizabeth Sutherland Parker, Aug. 8, 1959; children—John Rudolph II, Elizabeth Jerald, Thomas Parker. B.A., Tulane U., 1954, M.D., 1958. Diplomate Am. Bd. Pathology, Spl. Comp. in Clin. Chemistry. Resident in pathology Charity Hosp., New Orleans, 1959-63, assoc. pathologist, 1963-65; pathologist Methodist and Children's Hosp., Omaha, 1965-74, dir. dept., 1974—; pres. Pathology Ctr., P.C., Omaha, 1981—; instr. Tulane U. Med. Sch., 1962-65; instr. U. Nebr. Coll. Medicine, 1965-67, asst. prof., 1967-72, assoc. prof., 1972-75, mem. grad. faculty, 1975—, clin. prof. pathology, 1975—; clin. prof. pathology Creighton U. Sch. Medicine, Omaha, 1978—; pres. Am. Bd. Pathology, 1983-84. Editor (with J.B. Fuller) Instrumentation Workshop Manual, 1967; (with others) Laboratory Instrumentation, 1980; Clinical Pathology Case Studies, 3d edit., 1975. Contbr. articles to profl. jours. Mem. Nebr. State Nursing Home Adv. Council, 1982-83; bd. dirs. Nebr. Meth. Hosp. Found., 1983—; mem. pres.'s adv. council U. Nebr., 1984—; vice-chmn. com. White House Conf. on Aging, 1981; mem. adv. com. Office of Tech. Assessment, 1984—. Fellow ACP, Am. Soc. Clin. Pathologists, Coll. Am. Pathologists; mem. AMA (trustee 1985—), Coll. Am. Pathologists (Pathologist of Yr. 1983, nat. legis. com. 1971-80, chmn. 1972-80), Am. Soc. Clin. Pathologists (chmn. council clin. chemistry 1969-71, commn. edn. 1982—), Nebr. Assn. Pathologists (pres. 1971-72), Met. Omaha Med. Soc. (chmn. program com. 1971-72, 83—, exec. bd. 1982—, legis. com. 1970-72, pres. 1987), Nebr. Med. Assn., AMA (vice-chmn. council legis. 1982-84, chmn. 1984—), Am. Assn. Blood Banks, Am. Soc. Cytology, Internat. Acad. Pathology, Internat. Life Scis. Inst., Soc. Pediatric Pathology, Nebr. Assn. Commerce and Industry (bd. dirs. 1986—), Omaha C. of C. (bd. dirs. 1982-85, v.p. govt. relations 1986—), Alpha Omega Alpha. Republican. Episcopalian. Avocations: tennis; golf. Home: 115 N 54th St Omaha NE 68132 Office: PO Box 14424 Omaha NE 68114

SCHERBERG, GOLDIE RUTH, social worker, educator; b. Kovna, Lithuania, Mar. 14, 1909; came to U.S., 1914; m. Max Scherberg, Jan. 1, 1930; children: Lee Carl, Neal Hersh. BS, U. Minn., 1937, MS, 1937. Cert. social worker, Ohio. Caseworker, research dir. Children's Services, Inc., St. Paul, 1937-42; intake supr. Dayton (Ohio) Child Guidance Ctr., 1956-59; dir. social services Green County Guidance Ctr., Ohio, 1959-64, Children's Med. Ctr., Dayton, 1964-67; pvt. practice clin. social work Columbus, Ohio, 1967-75; pvt. practice Dayton, 1975—; asst. clin. prof. dept. psychiatry Wright State U., Dayton, 1975—; cons. Ohio Dept. Mental Health, Columbus, 1967-75. Mem. children's cultural programming com. Jewish Fedn., Dayton, 1986—; mem. Pub. Issues Forum, Dayton, 1985, Hadassah, 1946—; pres. LWV, Dayton, 1954-56, trustee, 1985—; trustee Sinclair Coll., Dayton, 1975—. Fellow Am. Orthopsychiat. Assn.; mem. Acad. Cert. Social Workers, Nat. Assn. Social Workers (chmn. continuing edn. program 1986, protective services for adults com. 1986—). Avocations: fiction writing, golf, theater. Home and Office: 4334 Seiber Ave Dayton OH 45405

SCHERECK, WILLIAM JOHN, retired historian, consultant; b. Chgo., Dec. 22, 1913; s. Frank and Adele (Schubert) S.; student Wofford Coll., 1950-51; B.S. in Sociology, U. Wis., 1952, postgrad., 1952-53; m. Flora Blanche George, May 19, 1943; children—Linda, William John, Ralph, George. With Crawford County (Wis.) Welfare Dept., 1938-42; with State Hist. Soc. Wis., Madison, 1953-79, research asst., 1954-55, field services supr., 1956-59, head Office Local History, 1960-79, Wis. Council Local History, from 1961, ret.; now researcher ancient histories and religions. Active Girls Scouts U.S.A., Spartanburg, S.C., 1947-48, Boy Scouts Am., Madison, 1956-58; established William J. Schereck Local History Promotional Fund, Inc., 1986. Served to 2d lt. U.S. Army, 1942-45. Decorated Bronze star medal; recipient 1st place award S.C. State Coll. Press Assn., 1951, Crusade for Freedom awards, 1951, 1st place award for Sounds of Heritage, Am. Exhbn. Ednl. Radio and Television, 1955. Mem. Am. Legion, Ret. Officers Assn., Am. Fedn. State, County and Mcpl. Employees, Wis. Alumni Assn., Smithsonian Instn., Madison Civic Opera Guild, Costeau Soc., Field Mus. Natural History, Am. Assn. Ret. Persons. Episcopalian. Author numerous publs. State Hist. Soc. Am. Contbr. articles to mags. and newspapers. Home: W 11013 Harmony Dr Lodi WI 53555

SCHERER, ANITA (STOCK), advertising agency executive; b. Cleve., Sept. 20, 1938; d. William John Stock and Gertrud Clara (Kaufmann) Bacher; m. Richard Phillip Scherer, Nov. 25, 1961; children—William Richard, Christopher Howard. Student U. Cin., 1956-57; Assoc.Bus., Jones Bus. Coll., 1958. Account sec. Northlich, Stolley, Inc., Cin., 1978-79, account asst., 1979-80, asst. account mgr., 1980-81, account mgr., 1981-84, mktg. service assoc., 1984—; lectr. local schs., univs., Cin. 1980—. Co-editor: monthly newsletter Badge, 1967-72; designer, created assorted notepads, 1986. Lector, Our Lady of Victory Roman Cath. Ch., Cin., 1972—; pres. Delhi Hills Community Council, Cin., 1974-75; adv. bd. mem. Coll. Mount St. Joseph, Ohio, 1974-80; v.p. adminstrn. Stagecrafters, Cin., 1983-85, publicity chmn., 1984—; mktg. bd. mem. Contemp. Arts Ctr., 1985—. Winner nat. competition Am. Assn. Advt. Agys., 1980; recipient Outstanding Performance award Assn. Community Theatres, Cin., 1983, Excellence in Acting award Ohio Community Theatres Assn., 1984. Mem. Nat. Assn. Female Execs., Cin. Direct Mktg. Assn., Am. Mktg. Assn., Acad. Health Services Mktg., Cin. C. of C. (lectr. 1984—). Avocations: travel, reading, medieval/rennaissance history, community theater. Office: Northlich Stolley Inc 200 W 4th St Cincinnati OH 45202

SCHERER, VICTOR RICHARD, physicist, computer specialist; b. Poland, Feb. 7, 1940; came to U.S., 1941, naturalized, 1951; s. Emanuel and Florence B. Scherer; B.S. magna cum laude, CCNY, 1960; M.A., Columbia U., 1962; Ph.D., U. Wis., Madison, 1974; m. Gail R. Dobrofsky, Aug. 11, 1963; children—Helena Cecille, Markus David. Health physics asst. Columbia U., N.Y.C., 1961-63; research asst. dept. physics U. Wis., Madison, 1967-74, project assoc., project mgr. Inst. for Environ. Studies, World Climate-Food Research Group, 1974-78, specialist computer systems Acad. Computing Center, 1978—; cons. in computer graphics and supercomputing applications. Concert pianist; tchr., promoter contemporary composers. AEC fellow, 1960-61. Mem. Am. Phys. Soc., Am. Meteorol. Soc., Am. Soc. Agronomy, Assn. Computing Machinery, Nat. Computer Graphics Assn., AAAS, Sigma Xi, Phi Beta Kappa. Researcher in particle physics, agroclimatology, soil-yield relationships and computer graphics; cons. on computer graphics and supercomputing applications. Office: U Wis Acad Computing Ctr 1210 W Dayton St Madison WI 53706

SCHERICH, ESTHER ANNE, educator, editor; b. New Haven, Dec. 15, 1943; d. Millard and Esther (Petersen) Scherich. BA, Oreg. State U., 1966; MA, U. Oreg., 1970, D in Arts, 1973, PhD, 1975. Sec. dept. English, U. Oreg., Eugene, 1966-69, research asst., 1969-70, teaching fellow in English, 1970-75; manuscript editor Moody Bible Inst., 1977-83, 84—; vis. asst. prof. English, Wheaton (Ill.) Coll., 1983-84. Assoc. editor Moody Press. Mem. Women in Communications, Am. Bus. Women's Assn., MLA, Am. Soc. Eighteenth Century Studies, Conf. on Christianity and Lit., P.E.O., Kappa Delta. Republican. Episcopalian. Home: 821 N Washington Wheaton IL 60187 Office: Moody Bible Inst 820 N LaSalle St Chicago IL 60610

SCHERNITZKI, PAUL THOMAS, hospital pharmacy administrator; b. Omaha, Sept. 22, 1951; s. Thomas G. and Edith A. S.; m. Ann Maria Chappell, Aug. 18, 1973; children—Rebecca Ann, Paul Scott. B.S. in Pharmacy, U. Mo.-Kansas City, 1974; M.S. in Pharmacy, U. Ariz., 1979. Registered pharmacist, Mo., Iowa, S.D., Ariz. Staff pharmacist Methodist Med. Ctr., St. Joseph, Mo., 1974-78; postgrad. resident Ariz. Health Scis. Ctr., Tucson, 1978-79; dir. pharmacy Des Moines Gen. Hosp., 1979-85; dir. pharmacy Rushmore Nat. Health Systems, Rapid City, S.D., 1985—; mem. pharmacy adv. bd. Iowa Healthcare Purchasing Council, Am. Healthcare Systems. Am. Assn. Poison Control Ctrs. research fellow, 1978. Mem. Am. Soc. Hosp. Pharmacists. Lutheran. Office: 353 Fairmont Blvd Rapid City SD 57701

SCHEU, JAMES RICHARD, appliance company official; b. Evansville, Ind., Mar. 3, 1944; s. Leo J. and Mary Ruth (Lannert) S.; m. Patricia Glenn Grant, Sept. 7, 1943; children: Teresa Ann, Tamara Kaye, Jeffrey Michael. BA in Chemistry, U. Evansville, 1969, MBA, 1972. Lab. technician Whirlpool Corp., Evansville, 1963-69, environ. engr., 1969-72, facilities and environ. engr., 1972-74, supr. quality lab., 1974-75, supr. final assembly quality control, quality engr., 1975-77, supr. customer assurance, 1977-80, mgr. customer assurance, 1980-82, dir. refrigeration group products, sales, 1982-84, mgr. retail mktg. Benton Harbor, Mich., 1984-86, dir. food preservation products Kitchen Aid div., 1986—. Contbr. numerous articles to profl. publs. Mem. vis. council Newburgh Medco Ctr., 1977; bd. dirs. Newburgh Youth Sports Assn.; pres. Soccer Bd., 1979-84. Mem. Am. Soc. Quality Control, Assn. Home Appliance Mfrs., Sigma Xi. Roman Catholic. Clubs: Whirlpool Mgmt.; Foremans. Office: Whirlpool Corp 701 Main St Saint Joseph MI 49085

SCHEUBLE, PHILIP ARTHUR, JR., controls and valve company executive, management consultant; b. N.Y.C., Sept. 25, 1919; s. Philip Arthur and Elsa (Kunkel) S.; m. Katharine Paul Aman, Jan. 19, 1946; children—James, Paul, Katharine, Pamela. B.Engring., CUNY, 1939; M.B.A., U. Toledo, 1950. Registered profl. engr., Ohio, Wis. Asst. group exec. A.O. Smith Corp., Milw., 1951-54, mgr. mfg. staff, 1954-57; with Vapor Corp. subs. Brunswick Co., Niles, Ill., 1957—, corp. v.p., 1959—, group exec., 1969-78; pres. GPE Controls Co., Morton Grove, Ill., 1978-84 ; chmn. P.A. Scheuble Assocs., Glenview, Ill.; dir. Nihon Regulator Co., Tokyo. Mem. naval air adv. council Office Asst. Sec. Navy, 1949-62. Served to comdr. USNR, 1941-46. Mem. ASME, Am. Mktg. Assn., Indsl. Mktg. Assn. (chmn. 1967-68, pres. 1966-67), Sci. Apparatus Makers Assn. (dir.), Fgn. Policy Assn. N.Y. (dir.). Episcopalian. Clubs: Glenview (Golf, Ill.), Union League (Chgo.); Michigan Shores (Wilmette, Ill.). Office: 1701 E Lake Ave Suite 140 Glenview IL 60025

SCHEY, RALPH EDWARD, manufacturing executive; b. Cleve., 1924; married. B.S., Ohio U., 1948; M.B.A., Harvard U., 1950. Sales trainee Leisy Brewing Co., 1950-51; indsl. engr. Gen. Motors Corp., 1951; exec. v.p. Clevite Corp., 1951-69; pres. Joseph Mellen & Miller Inc., 1959-71; venture capital activities 1971-74; with Scott & Fetzer Co., Westlake, Ohio, 1974—; pres. Scott & Fetzer Co., 1974-83, chmn. and chief exec. officer, dir., 1976—, pres., 1985-86; dir. Hauserman Co. Served with U.S. Army, 1943-45. Office: Scott & Fetzer Co 28800 Clemens Rd Westlake OH 44145 *

SCHIAPPACASSE, RICHARD HENRY, physician; b. Warren, Mich., June 9, 1948; s. Henry Louis and Eva (Kurdilla) S.; m. Dee Ann Lynn Houdek, Dec. 1, 1973; children—Michael, Angela. B.S., Wayne State U., 1969, M.D., 1973. Diplomate Am. Bd. Internal Medicine, Am. Bd. Tropical Medicine. Intern St. John's Hosp., Detroit, 1973, resident internal medicine 1973-76; fellow in infectious disease William Beaumont Hosp., Royal Oak, Mich., 1976-78; practice medicine Meml. Med. Ctr., Sterling Heights, Mich., 1978—; chief Div. Infectious Disease, Detroit Macomb Hosps., 1980—, chmn. infection control, 1979—; cons. Macomb County Health Dept., Mt. Clemens, Mich., 1978—; FAA med. examiner, 1985—. Author computer program First Aid, 1983; contbr. articles to profl. jours. Bd. dirs. Families for Children, Southfield, Mich., 1985—, Humane Soc. Southeastern Mich., 1983—. Haemophilus Grantee Eli Lily and Co., 1984. Fellow ACP; mem. AMA (Physican Recognition award 1977, 80, 83, 86), Am. Coll. Tropical Medicine, Infectious Disease Soc. Am., Am. Soc. Internal Medicine, Aircraft Owners and Pilots Assn., Phi Beta Kappa. Club: Mich. Atari Computer Enthusiasts (Southfield). Avocation: computers. Home: 12916 Easton Ct Utica MI 48087 Office: 36300 Van Dyke Sterling Heights MI 48077

SCHICK, ROBERT LEROY, fire chief; b. Davenport, Iowa, July 13, 1940; s. Lester Roy Schick and Annabel Marzee (Bonbrake) Kirkman; m. LaVern Florence Rhode, Aug. 9, 1960 (dec. June 1972); children—Sheryl Lee, Lynn Marie; m. Mary Louise Smith, Oct. 2, 1973. Student Palmer Jr. Coll., 1970, Scott Community Coll., 1976, Muscatine Community Coll., 1977. Chief Davenport Fire Dept., 1983—. Bd. dirs. Illowa chpt. ARC, Rock Island, Ill., 1983—. Mem. Internat. Assn. Fire Chiefs, Mo. Valley Fire Chiefs (state v.p. 1984—), Iowa Paid Fire Chiefs Assn., Nat. Fire Prevention Assn., Iowa Soc. Fire Service Instrs. (past bd. dirs.). Lutheran. Lodges: Rotary (com. chmn. 1985), Moose (bldg. chmn. 1965—). Home: 2230 W Columbia St Davenport IA 52804 Office: Office of the Fire Chief 331 Scott St Davenport IA 52801

SCHICKERT, JACK G., controller, accountant; b. Milw., Apr. 26, 1944; s. Edmund A. and Catherine A. Schickert; m. Patricia Ann Reshel, May 10, 1969; children: Matthew, Anne. BS, Marquette U., 1966; MBA, U. Wis., Milw., 1970. CPA, Wis. Auditor Price Waterhouse & Co., Milw., 1968-70; sr. auditor Am. City Bank, Milw., 1970-75; controller Data View Inc., Milw., 1975-77, Humphries-Hansen Inc., Milw., 1977-79, Liturgical Publs. Inc., Milw., 1979—. Served with USAR, 1967-73. Mem. Am. Inst. CPA's, Nat. Assn. Accts. Roman Catholic. Home: 14355 Beechwood New Berlin WI 53151 Office: Liturgical Publs Inc 1025 S Moorland Rd Brookfield WI 53005

SCHIELER, CALVIN LOUIS, laundry equipment manufacturing executive; b. Athens, Wis., Sept. 2, 1932; s. Egon Erasmus and Irma Anna Bertha (Laehn) S.; m. Margaret Elizabeth Jess, Aug. 27, 1955; children: Susan, Steven, Shane. BA, Ripon Coll., 1954; MBA, Ind. U., 1955. Underwriter Kemper Ins. Co., Chgo., 1955-57; agt. State Farm Ins. Co., Ripon, Wis., 1957-60; dist. salesman Speed Queen Co., Ripon, 1960-65, div. sales mgr., 1965-75, v.p. sales, 1975—. Served to 2d lt. inf. U.S. Army, 1956. Recipient Achievement award Sales and Mktg. Mgmt. mag., 1976, Gov's. Export award State of Wis., 1984. Republican. Avocations: gardening, reading, stamp collecting, small game hunting, camping. Home: 545 Fairview Ave Ripon WI 54971 Office: Speed Queen Co Shepard St PO Box 990 Ripon WI 54971

SCHIERL, PAUL JULIUS, paper company executive, lawyer; b. Neenah, Wis., Mar. 28, 1935; s. Julius Michael and Erna (Landig) S.; m. Carol Schierl; children: Michael, Kathryn, Susan, David, Daniel. B.S. in Polit. Sci, U. Notre Dame, 1957, LL.B., 1961. Mem. Wickham, Borgelt, Skogstad & Powell (attys.), Milw., 1961-64; with Fort Howard Paper Co., Green Bay, Wis., 1964—; sec., gen. counsel Fort Howard Paper Co., 1967-74, pres., chief exec. officer, 1974-84, chmn. bd., 1984—; pres., bd. dirs. Fort Howard Paper Found. Inc.; bd. dirs. Fed. Res. Bank Chgo., Green Bay Packers, Wis. Trustee St. Norbert Coll.; mem. adv. council Sch. Law U. Notre Dame; bd. regents Milw. Sch. Engring.; bd. dirs. Green Bay Area Cath. High Sch. Found., Ltd. Served with AUS. Mem. ABA, State Bar Wis, Nat. Assn. Mfrs. (bd. dirs.). Clubs: Union League, University (Chgo.). Office: Ft Howard Paper Co 1919 S Broadway PO Box 19130 Green Bay WI 54307

SCHIERLINGER, KEVIN NICKOLAS, dentist; b. Detroit, Mar. 6, 1955; s. Nickolas and Dolores A. (Zabinski) S.; m. Teresa Miskiewicz, Sept. 7, 1985. BS, U. Detroit, 1977, DDS, 1981. Resident gen. dentistry St. Joseph Mercy Hosp., Pontiac, Mich., 1981-82; gen. practice dentistry Troy, Mich., 1982—; clin. prof. U. Detroit Sch. Dentistry, 1984-85; mem. med. staff St. Joseph Hosp., 1985—. Mem. Oakland County Young Reps., Mich., 1979-82. Mem. ADA, Am. Student Dental Assn., Mich. Dental Assn., Tricounty Dental Health Council (treas. 1984-85), Mich. Assn. Profls., Jaycees, Delta Sigma Delta, Alpha Epsilon Delta. Republican. Roman Catholic. Lodge: Lions. Avocations: snow skiing, volleyball, outdoor sports, travel. Home: 3751 Bristol Troy MI 48083 Office: 5895 John R Troy MI 48098

SCHIFF, DANIEL, psychiatrist; b. Chgo., June 6, 1929; s. Emil Joseph and Rebecca (Block) S.; m. Gloria Copeland, June 17, 1956 (dec. Aug. 1985); children: Melissa Ann, Elliot Joseph, Stuart Copeland; m. Valerie Schwartz, June 15, 1985. BS, U. Ill., Chgo., 1952, MD, 1954. Diplomate Am. Bd. Psychiatry and Neurology. Intern Cook County Hosp., Chgo., 1954-55; resident in psychiatry Michael Reese Hosp., Chgo., 1955-58; chief adolescent service Forest Hosp., Des Plaines, Ill., 1965-67; practice medicine specializing in psychiatry Chgo., 1960—, Evanston, Ill., 1970—; attending physician Michael Reese Hosp., 1960—; cons. Juvenile Temp. Detention Ctr., Cook County, 1961—, Libra Spl. Sch., Riverdale, Ill., 1982—, Ill. State Psychiat. Inst., Chgo., 1985—. Served to capt. USAF, 1958-60. Fellow Psychiat. Assn.; mem. Am. Soc. for Adolescent Psychiatry, Am. Ortho Psychiat. Assn., Chgo. Adolescent Soc. (founding, clin. discussion group). also: 636 Church Evanston IL 60201

SCHIFF, HERBERT HAROLD, consulting and personal investment company executive; b. Columbus, Ohio, Oct. 6, 1916; s. Robert W. and Rebecca (Lurie) S.; m. Betty Topkis, June 19, 1938; children: Suzanne (Mrs. Murray Gallant), Patricia (Mrs. Richard Hershorin), Jane Ann Schiff. Grad., Peddie Sch., 1934; BBS, U. Pa., 1938; LHD, Ohio Dominican Coll., 1984, Yeshiva U., 1985. With SCOA Industries Inc. (formerly Shoe Corp. Am.), Columbus, 1938-85; salesman SCOA Industries Inc. (formerly Shoe Corp. Am.), 1938, asst. mgr., 1939-41, mgr., 1941-45, asst. merchandise mgr., 1945-46, v.p.-merchandise mgr., 1946-60, v.p. charge coordination, 1960-62, exec. v.p., 1962-65, pres., 1965-68, chmn. bd., chief exec. officer, 1968-85; chmn., pres. Schiff Co., Columbus, 1986—. Past mem. adv. council Grad. Sch. Adminstrn., Capital U.; bd. dirs. Am. ORT Fedn.; past trustee, past pres. United Jewish Fund and Council; trustee United Jewish Appeal, Peddie Sch.; past trustee Children's Hosp., Temple Israel Found.; fellow, mem. exec. com. Brandeis U.; exec. com., budget and fin. com., chmn. audit com., bd.

dirs. Am. Jewish Joint Distbn. Com.; nat. exec. bd. Am. Jewish Com.; pres. Columbus Jewish Found.; chmn., bd. govs. Wurzweiler Sch. Social Work, Yeshiva U.; trustee, dir. Am. Friends of Hebrew U.; nat. campaign cabinet State of Israel Bonds; mem. legacy endowment fund com. Council of Jewish Fedns. Recipient 28th ann. award T. Kenyon Holly/Two-Ten Assn., 1976, Spirit of Life award City of Hope, 1977, Milton Weill Human Relations award Am. Jewish Com., 1979, Patriots award U.S. Savs. Bonds Campaign, 1979, Israel Prime Minister's medal, 1979, Community Achievement award Am. ORT Fedn., 1984, Founders award Am. Jewish Com., 1985, Kesser Shem Tov award, 1986. Mem. Nat. Retail Mchts. Assn. (past dir.), Nat. Council Fgn. Policy Assn., Newcomen Soc. N.Am. Jewish. Clubs: B'nai B'rith, Pres.'s of U. Miami; Winding Hollow Country, Pres.'s of Ohio State U., Athletic, Capital (Columbus); Long Boat Key Golf, Univ. (Sarasota, Fla.). Office: Schiff Co 41 S High St Suite 3310 Columbus OH 43215 *

SCHIFF, JOHN JEFFERSON, financial corporation executive; b. Cin., Apr. 19, 1916; s. John Jefferson and Marguerite (Cleveland) S.; B.Sc. in Commerce, Ohio State U., 1938; m. Mary Reid, July 26, 1941; children: John Jefferson, Suzanne, Thomas R. Vice chmn. Cin. Ins. Co., 1979—; pres. Cin. Fin. Corp., 1979-86, chief exec. officer, 1986—; chmn. bd. Inter-Ocean Ins. co., Cin., 1979. Vice pres. Deaconess Hosp. of Cin., Griffith Found. for Ins. pres. Cin. Art Mus.; trustee Am. Inst. for Property and Liability Underwriters. Served to lt. comdr. Supply Corps, USNR, 1942-46. Named Ins. Man of Year in Cin., Cin. Ins. Bd., 1977. Mem. Cin. C. of C. (v.p. 1972). Republican. Methodist. Clubs: Queen City, Western Hills Country, Cin. Country, Royal Poinciana Golf. Home: 1926 Beech Grove Dr Cincinnati OH 45238 Office: Cincinnati Financial Corp 6200 S Gilmore Rd Cincinnati OH 45014

SCHIFF, SHELDON KIRSNER, psychiatrist; b. Bklyn., Sept. 29, 1931; s. Albert and Judith (Kirsner) S.; m. Louise Antoinette Latsis, June 29, 1957; 1child, Nicholas. BA, NYU, 1952; MD, U. Chgo., 1956. Diplomate Am. Bd. Neurology and Psychiatry (examiner 1969), Nat. Bd. Med. Examiners, Pan Am. Med. Assn. Intern Kings County Hosp., Bklyn., 1956-57; psychiat. resident Yale U. Sch. Medicine, New Haven, 1957-60, instr. psychiatry, 1962-63; chief psychiat. resident Grace-New Haven Hosp., 1959-60; asst. prof. psychiatry U. Ill. Sch. Medicine, Chgo., 1963-66; assoc. prof. psychiatry U. Chgo., 1967-71; practice medicine specializing in psychiatry Chgo., 1971—; mental health instr. City New Haven Police Dept., 1959; co-founder and co-founder Woodlawn Metal Health Ctr., Chgo, 1963-70; examiner N.Y. State Dept. Mental Hygiene, 1970; pres. Children's Ctr. Learning Capacities, Chgo., 1970—; dir. sch. intervention and tng. program dept. psychiatry Chgo. Med. Sch., 1970-71, clin. prof. psychiatry, 1974-76; chief of psychiatry Downey (Ill.) VA Hosp., 1973—; cons. in field. Contbr. articles to profl. jours. Mem. Woodlawn Urban Progress Ctr. Adv. Bd., City of Chgo. Com. Urban Opportunity, 1964, Greater Chgo. Com. Rehab. Welfare Council Met. Chgo., 1964-66; mem. systems analysis com. Ill. Mental Health Planning Bd., Ill. State Dept. Mental Health, 1966-67; adv. health com. City of Chgo. Commn. Human Relations, 1966-70; chmn. Service Agys. Council on Woodlawn, 1967-69. Served to capt. USMC, 1960-62. Grantee Ill. State Dept. Mental Health, 1964-65, Research Authority, 1965-68, NIMH, 1966-70, van Amerigen Found., 1968-69, Wieboldt Found., 1968-69, Field Found., 1968-69, Maurice Falk Med. Fund, 1968-69, 70, Iowa State Mental Health Authority, 1971. Fellow Am. Psychiat. Assn. (sec. task force on poverty 1968-70), Am. Orthopsychiat. Assn. (mem. com. community mental health ctrs. 1967-71, children's mental health services com. 1968-70), Am. Pub. Health Assn.; mem. AAUP (pres. U. Chgo. chpt. 1967-70, com. accrediting colls. and univs. 1969-71, ad hoc investigating com. U. Fla. 1969), Am. Acad. Polit. and Social Sci., Am. Ednl. Research Assn., Am. Sch. Health Assn., NY. Acad. Sci., Organisation Mondiale pour l'Education Prescholaire, U.S. Nat. Com. Early Childhood Edn., World Fedn. Mental Health, Phi Chi. Home: 6901 S Bennett Ave Chicago IL 60649 Office: 111 N Wabash Chicago IL 60602

SCHIFMAN, EDWARD JOSEPH, marketing executive; b. Kansas City, Mo., Mar. 10, 1949; s. Herman H. and Dorothy (Price) S.; m. Vicki F. Wellner, Aug. 8, 1971; children—Michael Aaron, Lori Ann. B.F.A., U. Kans., 1972; M.B.A., Internat. U., 1978. Product coordinator Aladdin Industries, Nashville, 1972-76; mgr. devel. Kenner Products, Cin., 1976-78; product mgr. Clopay Corp., Cin., 1978-80; v.p. mktg. I.D.I., Kansas City, Kans., 1981-84, pres., 1984—. Patentee mailbox, game board apparatus (2), cart, mounted planter box. Recipient awards Samsonite Corp., Indsl. Design Soc. Am. Mem. Sales and Mktg. Execs. Republican. Jewish. Club: Kansas City (Mo.). Lodge: B'nai B'rith. Avocations: photography, weightlifting, woodworking. Home: 9017 W 113th St Overland Park KS 66210 Office: 5101 Richland Ave Kansas City KS 66106

SCHILD, JOYCE ANNA, otolaryngologist, surgeon; b. Chgo., May 26, 1931; d. William Paul and Helen (Kammer) S.; m. John A. Hegber, Dec. 15, 1973. BS, U. Ill., Chgo., 1954, MD, 1956. Diplomate Am. Bd. Otolaryngology. Intern St Francis Hosp, Peoria, Ill., 1956-57; residency in otolaryngology U. Ill., 1958-61, fellow in bronchoesophagology, 1961-62, clin. instr. to assoc. prof. otolaryngology, 1958-82, interim acting head dept. otolarygology, 1978-79; prof. otolaryngology head and neck surgery Coll. Medicine U. Ill., 1982—; mem. staff U. Ill. Hosp.; otolaryngologist, surgeon Ill. Eye and Ear Infirmary, Chgo.; from adj. to assoc. attending otolaryngologist Presby. St. Luke's Hosp., Chgo., 1964-76; acting head bronchoesophagology dept. Children's Meml. Hosp., Chgo., 1972-76, cons. staff, 1976—; courtesy staff dept. surgery sect. otolaryngology St. Joseph's Hosp., Chgo., 1961-74; numerous presentations and lectrs. in field. Mem. AMA, Ill State Med. Soc., Ill Med. Soc., Am. Laryngol., Rhinol. and Otol. Soc., Am. Soc. Pediatric Otolaryngolgy, Chgo. Laryngological and Otological Soc. (pres. elect 1983-84, pres. 1984-85, council mem. 1985-86), Am. Broncho-Esophagological Assn. (v.p. 1976-77, pres. elect 1978-79, pres. 1979-80, thesis com. 1981-82), Am. Council Otolaryngology, Soc. Ear, Nose and Throat Advances in Children, Am. Acad. Pediatrics (com. on accident and poison prevention 1982-85), Pan-Am. Assn. Oto-Rhino-Laryngology, Head and Neck Surgery, Am. Laryngol. Assn. Office: Ill Eye and Ear Infirmary 1355 W Taylor St Chicago IL 60612

SCHILKE, JOAN MOSSONG, financial planner; b. Fond Du Lac, Wis., Mar. 16, 1943; d. Arthur G. and Mildred (Krautsch) Mossong; m. Michael D. Schilke, Dec. 29, 1973; children: Sarah, Erica. BA, Marian Coll., 1965; MBA, Marquette U., 1982. Cert. fin. planner. Tchr. various cities, 1965-70; budget dir. Marquette U., Milw., 1976; fin. planner Investment Strategies, Ltd., Waukesha, Wis., 1982—, also bd. dirs.; bd. dirs. Automated Systems Inc., Brookfield, Wis., Investment Strategies, Ltd., Waukesna, Wis. contributing editor CPA Digest, 1986. Chmn. Christian edn. commn. St. Pius Ch., 1982-83, stewardship commn., 1985-86. Mem. Internat. Assn. for Fin. Planning, Marian Alumnae Assn. (pres., v.p., treas. 1976-86). Roman Catholic. Home and Office: Investment Strategies Ltd 1846 N 81st St Wauwatosa WI 53213

SCHILLER, LES J., psychologist, mental health administrator; b. N.Y.C., Sept. 5, 1946; s. Harry and Florence (Joslin) S. BBA, CCNY, 1967; MS, Ind. U., 1969; PhD, U. Md., 1974. Tchr. N.Y.C. Pub. Schs., 1969-72; exec. dir. Greenbelt (Md.) Youth Services Bur., 1974-76; psychologist Psychol. Services Ctr., Clinton, Md., 1975-77; v.p. Southlake Ctr. Mental Health, Merrillville, Ind., 1977—; Mem. Child Abuse Protection Team Lake County, 1979—; bd. dirs. Lake County Mental Health Assn. Office: Southlake Ctr Mental Health 8555 Taft St Merrillville IN 46410

SCHILLHORN-VAN-VEEN, TJAART WILLEM, veterinary parasitology educator, college dean; b. Uithuizen, Netherlands, Dec. 6, 1940; came to U.S., 1979; m. Karla Suzanna, 1971. Student Agrl. U., Wageningen, Netherlands, 1958-61; D.V.Sci., State U. Utrecht, Netherlands, 1968, D.V.M., 1970, D.V. Sci., 1981. Postdoctoral fellow State U. Utrecht, 1970; vet. expert Fgn. Aid Dept., Netherlands, assigned to Zaria, Nigeria, 1970-78; vis. asst. prof. Mich State U., East Lansing, 1979-81, assoc. prof., 1981-85 , prof. 1985—, asst. dean Coll. Vet. Med., 1983-85; co-founding dir. Probe-tek Inc., Lansing, Mich., 1982—; cons. USAID, World Bank, Internat. Atomic Energy Agy.; cons. in field. Contbr. articles to profl. jours. Pres. Dutch Vet. Student Orgn., Utrecht, Netherlands, 1966-67; founding sec. Nigerian Assn. Parasitology, 1977. Recipient agrl. and indsl. grants, 1975—. Mem. World Assn. Advancement of Vet. Parasitology, Am. Assn. Vet. Parasitology, AAAS, Overseas Devel. Inst. Club: Samaru Sports and Social (Zaria, Nigeria) (sec. 1974-76). Office: Mich State U A-12 Vet Clinic East Lansing MI 48824

SCHILLING, CATHERINE ANN, accountant; b. Red Bud, Ill., Sept. 3, 1958; d. Leo Ignatius and Rose Marie (Schaefer) S. AS, Belleville (Ill.) Area Coll., 1977; BBA with honors, McKendree Coll., 1979. CPA, Ill, Mo. Staff auditor 1st Nat. Bank, Belleville, 1979-80; acct. R. C. Fietsam & Co., CPA's, Belleville, 1980-85; sr. acct. Rubin, Brown, & Gornstein, CPA's, St. Louis, 1985—. Mem. Ill. Soc. CPA's, Mo. Soc. CPA's, St. Louis Soc. Women CPA's. Republican. Roman Catholic. Avocations: guitar, volleyball, reading. Office: Rubin Brown & Gornstein CPA's 230 S Bemiston Saint Louis MO 63105

SCHILLING, JANET NAOMI, dietitian; b. North Platte, Neb., Mar. 1, 1939; d. Jens Harold and Naomi Frances (Meyer) Hansen; m. Allan Edward Schilling Jr., June 1, 1969; children: Allan Edward III, Karl Jens. BS, U. Neb., 1961; MS, Ohio State U., 1965. Registered dietitian. Tchr. home econs. Peace Corps., Dimbokro, Ivory Coast, 1962-64; cons. nutrition Wis. Div. Health, LaCrosse, 1966-67, 69; dietary cons. Cozad (Neb.) Community Hosp., 1968; instr. Viterbo Coll., LaCrosse, 1974-81; lectr. U. Wis., LaCrosse, 1982-84; teaching asst. English as second language Sch. Dist. LaCrosse, 1984-87; nutrition cons. LaCrosse, 1987—. Author: Life in the Nutrition Community, 1980, Life on the Nutrition Cycle II, 1980; co-author: Nutrition Activities, 1984, Recipe Book of Nutritious Snacks, 1985. Mem. LaCrosse Sch. Dist. Nutrition Task Force, 1976—; sunday sch. tchr., supr. Our Saviors Luth. Ch., 1976-86, chmn., Mobile Meals, 1982-86; v.p. membership booster club Cen. High Sch., LaCrosse, 1985-87, pres. 1987-88; bd. dirs. YMCA, LaCrosse, 1982—. Mem. AAUW (pres. 1978-80, Name Grant scolar 1981), LaCrosse Area Dietetic Assn. (1st pres. 1968-69, Outstanding Dietitian Yr. 1985), Wis. Dietetic Assn. (chmn. educators 1983-85), No. Wis. Dietetic Assn. (pres. 1982), Am. Dietetic Assn. (educators practice group 1978—), LaCrosse Jaycees (Carol award 1973), French Discussion Group. Democrat. Avocations: running, swimming, biking. Home: 2120 Orchard Valley Dr LaCrosse WI 54601

SCHILLING, JOHN MICHAEL, golf course association executive; b. Hiawatha, Kans., Nov. 23, 1951; s. George H. and Darlene J. (Wachter) S.; m. Pamela S. Hischke, Sept. 5, 1969; children—John II, James. Student Highland Coll., 1971-72; B.S. in Journalism, U. Kans., 1974. Assoc. editor Kans. Electric Coops., Topeka, 1975-76, editor, 1976-79; editor Golf Course Supts. Assn. Am., Lawrence, Kans., 1978-79, mktg. dir., 1979-83, exec. dir., 1983—. Contbr. articles to profl. jours. Mem. Am. Soc. Assn. Execs., Nat. Assn. Expn. Mgrs., Am. Advt. Fedn., Topeka Advt. Club, U.S. Golf Assn., Nat. Golf Found. (bd. dirs.), Internat. Assn. Golf Adminstrs. Republican. Lutheran. Club: Alvamar Country (Lawrence). Avocations: golf, boating, coaching, breeding dogs, reading, computers. Home: 3934 NW Morley S Topeka KS 66618 Office: Golf Course Supts Assn Am 1617 St Andrews Dr Lawrence KS 66044

SCHILLING, KAREN MAITLAND, psychology educator; b. Webster, Mass., June 21, 1949; d. James Edward and Ann Magdelan (Szumal) Maitland; m. Karl Lewis Schilling, Aug. 25, 1973; 1 child, Erin Maitland. BS, Tufts U., 1971; MA, U. Fla., 1972, PhD, 1975. Clin. intern U. Fla., 1974-75; asst. prof. Miami U., Oxford, Ohio, 1975-79, assoc. prof. psychology, 1980—, asst. chair, 1979-82, coordinator women's studies, 1985—; cons. Oxford Crisis and Referral, 1977-79, Cin. VA Hosp., 1982-86. Contbr. articles to profl. jours. Bd. dirs. Camilla B. Dunn Mental Health Ctr., Richmond, Ind., 1976-78; trustee Planned Parenthood Butler County, Hamilton, Ohio, 1979-85. Mem. Am. Psychol. Assn., Midwestern Psychol. Assn., Ohio Psychol. Assn., Nat. Women's Studies Assn., Assn. For Women in Psychology. Home: 613 White Oak Dr Oxford OH 45056 Office: Miami U Dept Psychology Oxford OH 45056

SCHILLING, KATHERINE LEE TRACY, educator; b. Mitchell, S.D., May 31, 1925; d. Ernest Benjamin and Mary Alice (Courier) Tracy; B.A., Dakota Wesleyan U., 1947; M.A., U. S.D., 1957; postgrad. U. Wyo., U. Nebr., Kearney State Coll.; m. Clarence R. Schilling, Oct. 14, 1951; 1 dau., Keigh Leigh. Tchr. elem. and secondary schs., also colls., S.D. and Nebr.; with specially funded project for disadvantaged children Winnebago Indian reservation, Nebr. Mem. staff S.D. Girls' State, 1950-51; mem. S.D. Gov.'s Com. on Library, Nebr. Gov.'s Com. on Right to Read. Recipient Outstanding Tchr. award S.D. High Sch. Speech Tchrs., 1966. Mem. NEA, Nebr., Thurston County (pres.) edn. assns., Winnebago Tchrs. Assn., Delta Kappa Gamma. Clubs: Internat. Toastmistress (internat. dir. 1963-65, Mitchell Toastmistress of Year 1959), Order Eastern Star. Contbr. articles to profl. jours., also poetry. Home: 39 S Harmon Dr Box 578 Mitchell SD 57301

SCHILSON, ELIZABETH ALLAN, counseling psychology educator; b. Washington, Mo., Aug. 1, 1930; s. Harry John and Gladys Amanda (Maher) Warnebold; m. Donald Lee Schilson, July 20, 1968; children: Elizabeth Allan, Kathryn Allan, Donald Lee Jr. AB, Drury Coll., 1952; MEd, U. Mo., 1965; PhD, Ohio U., 1968. Lic. psychologist, Ind.; diplomate Am. Bd. Med. Psychotherapists; cert. health service provider. Tchr. Springfield (Mo.) Elementary Schs., 1961-64; counselor Parkway Sch. Dist, Chesterfield, Mo., 1964-65; instr. Ohio U., Athens, 1965-68; prof. counseling, clin. prof. sch. medicine U. N.D., Grand Forks, 1969-81; prof. counseling psychology Ind. State U., Terre Haute, 1981—; behavior sci. coordinator Family Practice Ctr. Union Hosp., Terre Haute, 1985—; cons. Assoc. Psychologists and Counselors Clinic, Inc., Terre Haute, 1986—. Author: Educating Young Child: Early Childhood Education in North Dakota, 1971, Guidance in North Dakota Schs., 1974; editor Issues in Human Development and Behavior, 1970; contbr. articles to profl. jours. Bush Found. fellow, 1981-83. Mem. Am. Psychol. Assn., Am. Assn. for Marriage and Family Therapists (supr.), Am. Mental Health Counselors Assn. (cert.), Assn for Counseling and Devel. (cert.), Delta Kappa Gamma. Lodge: Elks. Home: 4620 Summerset Dr Terre Haute IN 47803 Office: Ind State U Terre Haute IN 47809

SCHILZ, YVONNE ELIZABETH, military officer; b. Waco, Tex., Nov. 23, 1958; d. John David and Charleen Kay (Leaverton) Wilhelm; m. Michael Thomas Schilz, May 29, 1981. BS, USAF Acad., 1981; MEd, S.D. State U., 1985. Commd. 2d lt. USAF, 1981, advanced through grades to capt., 1985; chief air traffic control tng. 2148 Communications Squadron, Ellsworth AFB, S.D., 1982-84; chief air traffic control ops. 2148 Info. Systems Squadron, Ellsworth AFB, S.D., 1984, dep. chief air traffic control ops., 1984-85; chief air traffic control ops. officer 390 Info. Systems Ops., Offutt AFB, Nebr., 1985—. Tchr. catechism Cath. Ch., Offutt AFB, 1985-86. Named one of Outstanding Young Women of Am., 1983, 84, 86. Mem. USAF Assn. (life), USAF Acad. Assn., Profl. Women Controllers, Armed Forces Communications Electronics Assn., Air Traffic Control Assn. Republican. Roman Catholic.

SCHIMMOLLER, RICHARD EDMUND, osteopathic physician; b. Dayton, Ohio, Apr. 4, 1929; s. Raymond Louis and Anna Mae (Hartley) S.; m. Gay Lee Mahan, Dec. 29, 1956; children—Terry, Cristy, Becky. Student U. Dayton, 1946-47, Kent State U., 1953-55; D.O., Chgo. Coll. Osteopathy (now Chgo. Coll. Osteo. Medicine), 1960. Diplomate Am. Coll. Gen. Practitioners in Osteo. Medicine and Surgery. Intern, Still Meml. Hosp., Jefferson City, Mo., 1960-61; gen. practice osteo. medicine, Camdenton, Mo., 1961-63, Columbus, Ohio, 1963—; mem. staff Doctors Hosp., Columbus; mem. health adv. bd. Blue Cross, Blue Shield, Ohio. Served to sgt. USAF, 1948-52. Mem. Am. Osteo. Assn., Ohio Osteo. Assn., Chgo. Coll. Osteo. Medicine and Surgery Alumni Assn. Am. Coll. Osteo. Gen. Practitioners, Columbus Acad. Osteo. Medicine, Iota Tau Sigma. Club: Brookside Country (Worthington, Ohio). Home: 6694 Merwin Rd Worthington OH 43085 Office: 5109 W Broad St Columbus OH 43228

SCHINAGLE, ALLAN CHARLES, consulting firm executive; b. Cleve., June 7, 1930; s. Elmer William and Mildred (Handlir) S.; B.S. in Bus. Adminstrn., Miami U., Oxford, Ohio, 1953; m. Cynthia Volz Robinson, Apr. 21, 1956; children—Cheryl Lynn, Allan Charles, Holly Anne, Penny Sue. Home office rep. group div. Aetna Life Ins. Co., Cleve. and Louisville, 1953-65, mgr. group div., Cleve., 1965-70; sr. account exec. Aetna Life & Casualty Co., Cleve., 1970-76; v.p. Rollins Burdick Hunter of Ohio, Inc., Cleve., 1976-82; pres. Consulting Services, Inc., 1982—; chmn. pres.'s adv. council Central Res. Life Ins. Co. N.Am. Mem. Republican state candidate screening com., 1974; chmn. Rep. exec. and central coms., Geauga County, Ohio, 1970-76; del. to Rep. Nat. Conv., 1976; mem. Geauga County Bd. Elections, 1974-78. Served with USN, 1948-49. Named Ky. col. Mem. Am. Mgmt. Assn., Internat. Platform Assn., Nat. Life Underwriters Assn., Ohio Life Underwriters Assn. Presbyterian. Clubs: Rotary (dir.), Hunting Creek Country (Louisville), Hillbrook, Chagrin Valley Athletic, Cotillion Soc., Cleve. BlueBook, Fork and Fiddle. Home: Hillbrook Estate Lane E Hunting Valley OH 44072 Office: 45 Bell St Chagrin Falls OH 44022

SCHINDLER, JOEL MARVIN, scientist, medical educator; b. N.Y.C., Oct. 27, 1950; s. Herbert and Margot (Rosenberg) S.; m. Myra Ellen Krupkin, Aug. 9, 1974; 1 child, Abbe Meryl. BS, Hebrew U., 1973, MS, 1975; PhD, U. Pitts., 1978; student U. Rochester, 1969-71. Postdoctoral fellow Roche Inst. Molecular Biology, Nutley, N.J., 1978-81; mem. grad. program in devel. biology Children's Hosp. Research Found., Cin., 1981—; asst. prof. dept. anatomy and cell biology U. Cin. Coll. Medicine, 1981-85, assoc. prof., 1985—. Contbr. articles to profl. jours. Mem. exec. bd. dirs. Leadership Council, Jewish Fedn. Cin., 1982—, pres. 1985—; pres. Israel Programs Cabinet, 1985—; bd. dirs. Israel Programs Cabinet, Jewish Community Relations Council, 1986—, Jewish FAmily Service, 1984—. Recipient Acad. awards Faculty Sci., Hebrew U., 1973-75, Allen Cowett Leadership award, 1984—, Kate S. Mack Leadership award, 1986; Irwin Cohen scholar, 1974-75; Mellon fellow, 1977-78; Roche postdoctoral fellow, 1978-81; Am. Cancer Soc. grantee, 1986—, 84-85; Elsa U. Pardee Found. grantee, 1983-84; NSF grantee, 1983—. Mem. Soc. for Devel. Biology, Am. Assn. Anatomists, Am. Soc. Cell Biology, AAAS, Am. Israel Pub. Affairs Com. Office: Univ Cin Coll Medicine ML 521 231 Bethesda Ave Cincinnati OH 45267

SCHINDLER, RICHARD JOSEPH, engineering executive; b. Cleve., Mar. 4, 1940; s. Robert William and Josephine Florence (Janko) S.; m. Anita Maria Arenas, Feb. 19, 1966; children: Meredith Lee, Richard Michael. BEE, Cleve. State U., 1963; grad. exec. program, Ind. U., 1980, 81. Registered profl. engr., Ohio. Dist. mgr. tech. planning Ohio Bell Corp., Cleve., 1970-73, dist. mgr. outside plant engineering, 1973-76, dist. mgr. circuit provision bur., 1976-77, dist. mgr. network staff, 1977-84, dist. mgr. rates and costs, 1984—. Group chmn. Cleve. United Way, 1976; judge Internat. Sci. and Engring. Fair, Cleve., 1977; div. chmn. Jr. Achievement Fund Drive, Cleve., 1982-83. Mem. IEEE (sr., sect. chmn. 1975-76, Centennial medal 1984), Cleve. Engring. Soc. (chmn. pub. utilities div. 1972-73, Outstanding Service award 1986, bd. dirs. 1987—), Cleve. State U. Engring. Alumni Assn. (pres. 1980-81). Republican. Roman Catholic. Club: Broadview Heights Soccer (treas. 1985-86). Avocations: tennis, softball, touch football. Home: 8753 Falls Ln Broadview Heights OH 44147 Office: Ohio Bell Rates and Costs 45 Erieview Plaza Rm 1523 Cleveland OH 44114

SCHINDLER, STEVEN J., television producer; b. Bronx, July 26, 1954; s. John and Ruth (Paoilecelli) S. BS magna cum laude, CUNY, 1978. Freelance TV writer, producer Washington, 1980-82; tv writer, producer WUSA-TV, Washington, 1982-83, WLS-TV, Chgo., 1983-85, WFLD-TV, Chgo., 1985-86; freelance writer, producer Chgo., 1986—; instr. Columbia Coll., Chgo., 1984-86. Producer Bears '86, 1986; co-writer, producer Chgo. Stuff, 1985, Rock'n'Roll Legacy, 1986. Named Newscaster of Yr. Chgo. chp. Critical Care Nurses, 1984; recipient Emmy award Chgo. TV Arts and Scis., 1986. Democrat. Roman Catholic. Avocations: jogging, playing rock and roll music, crooning. Home: 2102 W Giddings St Chicago IL 60625

SCHINNER, JOHN LAWSON, savings and loan executive; b. Cin., Jan. 1, 1942; s. John A. and Jane M. (Lawson) S.; m. Linda K. Tiley, May 4, 1966 (div.); children: John L. Jr., Paul E.; m. Carolyn A. Schmit, Sept. 17, 1977. BBA, U. Cin., 1966. Asst. sec. Cottage Savs. Assn., Cin., 1966-74, v.p., treas., chief fin. officer, 1974—. Republican. Office: Cottage Savs Assn 9635 Montgomery Rd Cincinnati OH 45242

SCHIRMER, HENRY WILLIAM, architect; b. St. Joseph, Mo., Dec. 8, 1922; s. Henry William and Asta (Hansen) S.; m. Jane Irene Krueger; children: Andrew Lewis, Monica Sue, Daniel F. Carr. AS, St. Joseph Jr. Coll., 1942; BArch Design, U. Mich., 1949. Staff architect Eugene Meier, Architect, St. Joseph, 1939, Neville, Sharp & Simon, Kansas City, Mo., 1946, 49, Ramey & Himes, Wichita, Kans., 1950-57; ptnr. Schaefer & Schirmer, Wichita, 1957-60, Schaefer, Schirmer & Eflin, Wichita, 1960-72, Schaefer, Schirmer & Assocs. P.A., Wichita, 1972-76; prin. Henry W. Schirmer, Wichita, 1976—. Editor: Profile Ofcl. Directory of AIA, 1978, 80, 83, 85, 87; contbr. AIA Handbook; works include Burn Ctr. U. Kans. Med. Ctr., Allen County Community Jr. Coll., Iola, Kans., Rainbow Mental Health Ctr., Kansas City, Kans., Capitol area Plaza Project, Topeka. Pres. East Br. YMCA, 1954—; bd. dirs. Wichita YMCA, 1956-73. Served with C.E. U.S. Army, ETO. Decorated Purple Heart. Fellow AIA (past pres. Kans. chpt., seminar leader, chmn. nat. com. office mgmt.1976, nat. bd. dirs. 1979-81, treas. 1982-86, nat. documents com. 1978, chmn. nat. com. on project mgmt. 1977); mem. Kans. Bd. Tech. Professions (chmn. bd. 1986—), Tau Sigma Delta. Lutheran. Home: 20 Pepper Tree Ln Topeka KS 66611 Office: Henry W Schirmer FAIA Architect PO Box 4403 Topeka KS 66611

SCHIRO-GEIST, CHRISANN, rehabilitation counselor; b. Chgo., Dec. 31, 1946; d. Joseph Frank and Ethel (Fortunato) Schiro; m. John J. Conway Sr., Aug. 26, 1985; children: Jennifer, Daniel; stepchildren: Patricia, Nicole, John Jr., Denice, Christine. BS, Loyola U., Chgo., 1967, MEd, 1970; PhD, Northwestern U., 1974. Registered psychologist, Ill.; cert. sex edn. cons. Tchr. sci. Northbrook (Ill.) Jr. High Sch., 1967-70; dir. career counseling and placement Mundelein Coll., Chgo., 1972-74; counselor human devel. Regional Service Agy., Skokie, Ill., 1974-75; assoc. prof. psychology, rehab. counselor Ill. Inst. Tech., Chgo., 1975—. Co-author: Placement Handbook for Counseling Disabled Persons, 1982. Research grantee Northwestern U., 1974; Region V Short-Term Tng. grantee Rehab. Services Adminstrn., 1978-79, Long-Term Tng. grantee, 1986-89. Mem. Am. Psychol. Assn., Am. Personnel and Guidance Assn., Nat. Rehab. Assn., Nat. Council Rehab. Edn., Ill. Rehab. Counseling Assn. (pres. 1979-80), Council on Rehab. Edn., (pres. 1982-84), Kappa Beta Gamma Alumni Assn. (nat. officer). Office: Psychology Dept Ill Inst Tech 3101 S State St Chicago IL 60616

SCHLADER, DAVID ANTHONY, accountant; b. Dubuque, Iowa, Oct. 1, 1958; s. Donald Richard and Mary Olive (Derkert) S.; m. Susan Kay Stuedeman, May 31, 1986. BA in Acctg., Loras Coll., 1981. CPA, Iowa. From staff acct. to audit mgr. Schnurr & Co., P.C., Ft. Dodge, Iowa, 1981—. Mem. Am. Inst. CPA's, Iowa Soc. CPA's, Nat. Assn. Accts., Ducks Unlimited (asst. treas. Ft. Dodge 1985—), Sigma Phi Epsilon. Roman Catholic. Clubs: Ft. Dodge Country, EFP Investment (treas. 1987). Lodge: Elks. Avocations: golf, fishing, hunting, camping, sports. Home: 2626 4th Ave N Fort Dodge IA 50501 Office: Schnurr & Co PC 822 Central Ave Suite 400 Fort Dodge IA 50501

SCHLAEBITZ, WILLIAM DONALD, architect, artist; b. Lincoln, Nebr., Apr. 9, 1924; s. William Alfred and Ruth Lucille (Halley) S.; m. Shirley Maxine Brigham, Aug. 8, 1945; children: William Bruce, Terri Lynn, Jodi Beth, Carol Joyce. BArch, BA, U. Nebr., 1949. Registered architect Nebr., S.D., Colo., Wyo., Kans. Project architect Clark & Enersen, Lincoln, 1949-56; prin. Wight & Co., Downers Grove, Ill., 1956-58; assoc. architect Clark, Enersen, olsson, Burroughs & Thomsen, Lincoln, Nebr., 1958-63, prin., 1963-72; prin. v.p. The Clark Enersen Ptrns., Lincoln, 1972—; sec. treas. Council Ednl. Planners, Midwest Region, 1981-84, pres., 1985-86. Artist Nebraska Land Mag., 1980. Pres. Community Arts Council, Lincoln, 1977; mem. City Hall Renovation com., Lincoln, 1977-86, Mayors Task Force for Codes, Lincoln, 1984-86; v.p. Wesleyan Art Council, Lincoln, 1986; chmn. bd. Salvation Army, Lincoln, 1985—, adv. com., 1984—. Served as navigator USAF, 1943-45. Mem. AIA (pres. Lincoln chpt. 1960), Nebr. Art Assn., Lincoln Artist Guild (pres. 1985), Am. Legion. Republican. Methodist. Club: Univ. (Lincoln). Lodge: Elks. Avocations: water color painting, car restoration, skiing. Home: 2947 Park Place Dr Lincoln NE 68506 Office: The Clark Enersen Ptnrs 600 NBC Ctr Lincoln NE 68508

SCHLAEPFER, CYNTHIA JANE, computer operations administrator; b. Ithaca, N.Y., Aug. 12, 1956; d. Walter Woodley and Esther Susan (Youker) S. Student, Principia Coll., 1974-75; BS, Cornell U., 1978. Co-mgr. The Kroger Co., Columbus, Ohio, 1978-81; asst. mgr. Wendy's Internat., Columbus, 1981; computer operator Warner-Amex, Columbus, 1981-84;

supr. computer ops. Online Computer Library Ctr., Dublin, Ohio, 1984—. Umpire Ohio High Sch. Athletics, Columbus, 1986—. Inducted into Athletic Hall of Fame, Cornell U., Ithaca, 1985. Mem. Sierra Club. Democrat. Mem. Christian Sci. Ch. Club: Toastmasters (sgt. at arms). Home: 129 E Beaumont Rd Columbus OH 43214 Office: OCLC Ind 6565 Frantz Rd Dublin OH 43017

SCHLAFLY, PHYLLIS STEWART, author, lawyer; b. St. Louis, Aug. 15, 1924; d. John Bruce and Odile (Dodge) Stewart; m. Fred Schlafly, Oct. 20, 1949; children: John F., Bruce S., Roger S., Phyllis Liza Forshaw, Andrew L., Anne V. B.A., Washington U., St. Louis, 1944, J.D., 1978; M.A., Harvard U., 1945; LL.D., Niagara U., 1976. Bar: Ill. 1979, D.C. 1984, Mo. 1985. Syndicated columnist Copley News Service, 1976—; pres. Eagle Forum, 1975—. Author, pub.: Phyllis Schlafly Report, 1967—; broadcaster, Spectrum, CBS Radio Network, 1973-78, commentator, Cable TV News Network, 1980-83, Matters of Opinion, radio sta. WBBM, Chgo., 1973-75; author: A Choice Not an Echo, 1964, The Gravediggers, 1964, Strike From Space, 1965, Safe Not Sorry, 1967, The Betrayers, 1968, Mindszenty The Man, 1972, Kissinger on the Couch, 1975, Ambush at Vladivostok, 1976, The Power of the Positive Woman, 1977, Child Abuse in the Classroom, 1984, Pornography's Victims, 1987; editor: Equal Pay for UNequal Work. Del. Republican Nat. Conv., 1956, 64, 68, 84, alt., 1960, 80; pres. Ill. Fedn. Rep. Women, 1960-64; 1st v.p. Nat. Fedn. Rep. Women, 1964-67; mem. Ill. Commn. on Status of Women, 1975-85; nat. chmn. Stop ERA, 1972—; mem. Ronald Reagan's Def. Policy Adv. Group, 1980; mem. Commn. on Bicentennial of U.S. Constn., 1985—; mem. Adminstrv. Conf. U.S., 1983-86. Recipient 10 Honor awards Freedoms Found.; Brotherhood award NCCJ, 1975; named Woman of Achievement in Pub. Affairs St. Louis Globe-Democrat, 1963, one of ten most admired woman in world Good Housekeeping poll, 1977—. Mem. DAR (nat. chmn. Am. history 1965-68, nat. chmn. bicentennial com. 1967-70, nat. chmn. nat. def. 1977-80, 83—), Am., Ill. bar assns., Phi Beta Kappa, Pi Sigma Alpha. Address: 68 Fairmount Alton IL 62002

SCHLAKE, DENISE LYNETTE, educational administrator; b. Beatrice, Nebr., July 30, 1957; d. Wilmer Harlan and Eleanor Tina (Folkerts) S. B.S. in Home Econs., U. Nebr., 1979, M.S. in Ednl. Psychology, 1981. Activities advisor Tex. Tech U., Lubbock, Tex., 1981-84, activities advisor student orgn., 1984-85; coordinator orientation and orgns. U. Mo.-Columbia, 1986—; asst. ednl. services coordinator Nat. Assn. Campus Activities, South Central Regional Conf., 1984. Contbr. articles to profl. jours. Mem. leadership devel. com. Nat. Assn. Campus Activities, 1981, evaluation coordinator, 1982, mem. host com., Lincoln, Nebr., 1980; mem. health of life com., Tex. Tech. U., 1983—, mem. student affairs staff devel. com., 1981-82. Mem. Am. Coll. Personnel Assn. (conf. coordinator 1981), Am. Assn. Counseling and Devel. Lutheran. Avocation: creative activities. Office: U Mo-Columbia A022 Brady Commons Columbia MO 65211

SCHLAKE, JAMES JOSEPH, electronics company executive; b. East St. Louis, Ill., Aug. 11, 1954; s. Richard John and Marian (Graham) S.;m. Valerie Jean Hitsman. BS, So. Ill. U., 1976. Mgr. lab. Meml. Hosp., Belleville, Ill., 1976-81; mgr. territory Am. Hosp. Supply Co., Chgo., 1981-84; product mgr. Watlow Elec., St. Louis, 1984—; clin. instr. St. Louis U., 1979-80. Chmn. East St. Louis March of Dimes, 1970; edn. coordinator Belleville Area Coll., 1979-81; dist. comdr. Belleville council Boy Scouts Am., 1985. Named Eagle Scout Boy Scouts Am., 1970; Henry L. Ettman fellow Jewish Hosp. So. Ill. U., 1977. Mem. Am. Soc. Clin. Pathologists (cert.). Roman Catholic. Club: President's. Avocations: golf, skiing. Office: Watlow Elec Mfg Co 12001 Lackland Rd Saint Louis MO 63146

SCHLAMERSDORF, JOHN MICHAEL, mechanical engineer; b. Indpls., June 12, 1943; s. Norman Frederick and Helen Virginia (Murphy) S.; m. Dawn LaRae, July 18, 1964; children: David, Richard, Susan. BSME, Purdue U., 1965. Assoc. project engr. Miles Labs. Inc., Elkhart, Ind., 1965-72, project engr., 1972-77, supr. plant engring., 1977—. Mem. Ind. Soc. Profl. Engrs., Nat. Soc. Profl. Engrs., Am. Soc. Heating Refrigeration and Air Conditioning Engrs. Republican. Roman Catholic. Club: 4 Flags (Niles, Mich.) (pres. 1981-83). Avocations: amateur radio, antique cars. Home and Office: 66788 Conrad Rd Edwardsburg MI 49112-9630

SCHLARMAN, STANLEY GERARD, bishop; b. Belleville, Ill., July 27, 1933. Student, St. Henry Prep. Sem., Belleville, Gregorian U., Rome, St. Louis U. Ordained priest Roman Catholic Ch., 1958, consecrated bishop, 1979. Titular bishop of Capri and aux. bishop of Belleville 1979-83; bishop of Dodge City Kans., 1983—. Office: The Roman Cath Ch 1608 Ave C Dodge City KS 67801 *

SCHLATTER, DONALD ALLAN, metal company executive, lawyer; b. Toledo, Ohio, Aug. 25, 1929; s. Ezra Andrew and Alpha Ida (Bornhoft) S.; m. Barbara Louise Reichert, June 18, 1955; children: Louise, Edward, Richard, Ann, Robert, Thomas. SB, MIT, 1951; LLB, M in Indsl. Engring., U. Toledo, 1956. Bar: Ohio, 1956. Priorities dir. Art Iron, Inc., Toledo, 1951-52, asst. prodn. mgr., 1952-54, mgr. sales distbn., 1954-64, mgr. metal services ctr. div., 1964-73, pres., 1973—; treas., mem. exec. com. Steel Service Ctr. Inst., Cleve., 1981-87. V.p., exec. com. YMCA, Toledo, 1979—; chmn. employee div. United Way, Toledo, 1984; exec. com. St. Luke's Hosp., Toledo, 1981—. Mem. ABA, Ohio Bar Assn., Toledo Bar Assn., Am. Soc. Metals, Am. Soc. Testing Materials, Soc. Automotive Engrs., Am. Welding Soc. Lutheran. Club: Toledo. Office: Art Iron Inc 860 Curtis St Toledo OH 43609

SCHLATZER, ROBERT KARL, chemical company research executive; b. Roanoke, Va., Apr. 18, 1935; s. Robert Karl and Ann (Holtzman) S.; m. Christine Elmes, Oct. 13, 1956; children: R. Karl III, T. Kurt, E. Brant. Student, Coll. of William and Mary, 1953-55, Shepherd Coll., Shepherdstown, W.Va., 1955; BS, U. Va., Charlottesville, 1960, PhD, 1966. Research chemist B.F. Goodrich Corp. Research, Brecksville, Ohio, 1964-67, sr. research chemist, 1967-74; research assoc. B.F. Goodrich Chem. Co., Brecksville, Ohio, 1974-75, group leader research and devel., 1975-76, research and devel. mgr., 1976-81; dir. research and devel. speciality products B.F. Goodrich Chem. Group, Cleve., 1981-85; dir. research and devel. Specialty Polymers and Chems. div. BFGoodrich Co., Cleve., 1985-87, dir. comml. devel., 1987—. Holder (separately and with others) seven patents. Trustee Bainbridge Twp., Ohio, 1974-77, 80—; pres. Health Dist. Adv. Council, Geauga County, Ohio, 1985—; mem. Geauga County Bd. of Health, 1978-80. Served as sgt. USMC, 1955-58. Shell Found. fellow in chemistry, 1963. Mem. Am. Chem. Soc., Sigma Xi, Pi Kappa Alpha. Home: 8501 Pilgrim Ave Chagrin Falls OH 44022 Office: B F Goodrich SP & C Div 6100 Oak Tree Blvd Cleveland OH 44131

SCHLAUTMANN, JOHN ALVIN, accountant; b. Germantown, Ill., July 8, 1946; s. Frank J. and Clementine (Jansen) S.; m. Patricia Ann Kuhl, Sept 9, 1972; children: Scott, Stacey, Jason, John R. BS in Acctg. magna cum laude, Rockhurst Coll., 1968; MBA in Fin., So. Ill. U., Edwardsville, 1976. Cert. mgmt. acct. 1978. Cost acctg. mgr. Monsanto Co., Sauget, Ill., 1968-71; sr. internal auditor Monsanto Co., St. Louis, 1971-74; plant controller Monsanto Co., Yardville, N.J., 1974--76; fin. systems specialist Monsanto Co., St. Louis, 1976-77, mgr. internat. acctg., 1977-79; corp. controller Raskas Inc., St. Louis, 1979-80, v.p. fin., 1982—; Tchr. acctg. Parkway Community, St. Louis, 1986—. Mem. com. United Way, St. Louis, 1977; mgr. Ascension Athletic Assn. Served with U.S Army, 1969-70, Vietnam. Mem. Inst. Cert. Mgmt. Accts., Nat. Assn. Accts. (assoc. dir. 1984-86), Assn. for Systems Mgmt., Am. Soc. for Personnel Adminstrn., Am. Inst. CPA's. Roman Catholic. Avocations: flying, photography, sports, gardening. Home: 17917 Wild Horse Creek Rd Chesterfield MO 63017 Office: Raskas Inc 25 N Brentwood Saint Louis MO 63105

SCHLECHTE, DAVID WILLIAM, sales executive, consultant; b. St. Louis, Sept. 4, 1949; s. Wilfred Theodore and Violet Marie (Morgan) S.; m. Linda Rae Middendorf, Aug. 29, 1970; children: Jacob Christopher, Jamie Elizabeth. Student, Augustana Coll., Rock Island, Ill., 1967-69; BA magna cum laude, St. Louis U., 1980. Salesman Southwestern Bell Telephone Co., St. Louis, 1969-76, sales mgmt., 1976-81; pres. Personal Skills Devel., St. Louis, 1981—, also bd. dirs.; cons. Dick Miller & Assocs., Grand Island, Nebr. Recipient Blue Blazer Club, Wilson Learning Corp., Mpls., 1984, Gray Blazer Club, 1986. Lutheran. Avocations: athletics, reading, boating.

SCHLEGEL, DICK REEVES, lawyer, judge; b. Bloomfield, Iowa, Mar. 4, 1922; s. Verne John and Helen Elizabeth (Reeves) S.; m. Maxine Glenn, Apr. 4, 1943; children—Richard R., Mary Patricia Wilson, Robert Glenn. B.A., U. Iowa, 1948, J.D., 1950. Bar: Iowa 1950. Ptnr. Barnes & Schlegel, Ottuma, Iowa, 1950-78; judge 8th Jud. Dist. Iowa, 1978-82, Iowa Ct. Appeals, 1982—. Served with USAF, 1942-50. Decorated Air medal. Mem. ABA, Iowa Bar Assn., Ottumwa Bar Assn., Iowa Acad. Trial Lawyers, Iowa Def. Counsel, Assn. Trial Lawyers Iowa, Iowa Judges Assn. Presbyterian. Club: Ottumwa Country. Lodge: Masons. Office: State Capitol Court of Appeals Des Moines IA 50319

SCHLEGEL, EDWARD JOHN, heavy machinery manufacturing company executive; b. Peoria, Ill., Apr. 7, 1922; s. Edward John and Anna (Endres) S.; m. Teresa Ann Radosevich, Apr. 17, 1948; children—Christine, Susan. B.S.B.A., Bradley U., 1947. Mng. dir. Caterpillar of Australia Ltd., Melbourne, 1966-70, chmn. Caterpillar Mitsubishi Ltd., Sagamihara-shi, Japan, 1970-73, v.p. Caterpillar Inc., Peoria, Ill., 1973-75, exec. v.p., 1975—, dir., 1978—; dir. NCR Corp., Dayton, Ohio, Comml. Nat. Bank, Peoria. Trustee, Bradley U., Meth. Med. Ctr. Ill., Peoria. Office: Caterpillar Inc 100 NE Adams St Peoria IL 61629

SCHLEGEL, WESLEY PETE, farmer; b. Ness City, Kans., July 26, 1928; s. Henry Conrad and Scharlotta (Kerbs) S.; m. Grace Nadine Tuttle, Feb. 12, 1956; children: Stephanie Jan, Patricia Kim, Betty Jo. Grad. high sch., Ness City, Kans., 1945. Farmer Ness City, 1945—. Twp. treas. Twp. Governing Body, Ness County, Kans., 1972—; mem. sch. bd. Served as cpl. U.S. Army, 1951-53, Korea. Mem. Kans. Livestock Assn., Kans. Assn. Wheat Growers, Am. Legion, VFW. Methodist. Avocations: watching football, car races. Home and Office: HC 61 Box 16 Ness City KS 67560

SCHLEITWILER, DAVID MARTIN, bank executive; b. Chgo., June 19, 1951; s. Harold Joseph and Rose Barbara (Porod) S.; m. Margaret Ann Voight, Nov. 21, 1981; children: Nikolaus Axel, Karl Manfred, Gretchen Elizabeth, Benjamin Martin. BBA, Loyola U., Chgo., 1974. Asst. cashier Cicero (Ill.) State Bank, 1973-82; audit and compliance officer ops. 1st Nat. Bank, Cicero, 1982-86; comml. loan rep. Drexel Nat. Bank, Chgo., 1986—. Mem. Morton Coll. Alumni Assn. (bd. dirs. 1985—). Home: 1826 S 60 Ct Cicero IL 60650-1636 Office: Drexel Nat Bank 3401 S King Dr Chicago IL 60616

SCHLENDER, WILLIAM ELMER, management sciences educator; b. Sawyer, Mich., Oct. 28, 1920; s. Gustav A. and Marie (Zindler) S.; m. Lela R. Pullen, June 9, 1956 (dec. June 1983); m. Margaret C. Krahn, Mar. 3, 1987. A.B., Valparaiso U., 1941; M.B.A., U. Denver, 1947; Ph.D., Ohio State U., 1955. With U.S. Rubber Co., 1941-43, 46; asst. prof., assoc. prof. bus. adminstrn. Bowling Green State U., 1947-53; asst. prof. bus. orgn., prof. Ohio State U., 1954-65, asst. dean, 1959-62; assoc. dean Ohio State U. (Coll. Commerce and Adminstrn.), 1962-63; prof. mgmt. U. Tex., 1965-68, chmn. dept., 1966-68; dean Cleve. State U. Coll. Bus. Adminstrn., 1968-75, prof. mgmt., 1975-76; Internat. Luth. Laymen's League prof. bus. ethics Valparaiso (Ind.) U., 1976-79, Richard E. Meier prof. mgmt., 1983-86, Richard E. Meier prof. emeritus, 1986—; vis. asso. prof. mgmt. Columbia, 1957-58; vis. prof. mgmt. U. Tex., Arlington, 1981-82; cons. in field; Bd. govs. Internat. Ins. Seminars. Author: (with M.J. Jucius) Elements of Managerial Action, 3d edit, 1973, (with others) Management in Perspective: Selected Readings, 1965; Editor: (with others) Management in a Dynamic Society, 1965; Contbr. (with others) articles to profl. jours. Served with AUS, 1943-45. Decorated Bronze Star. Fellow Acad. Mgmt.; mem. Indsl. Relations Research Assn., Am. Mgmt. Assn., Internat. Council Small Bus., Assn. Ohio Commodores, Tau Kappa Epsilon, Beta Gamma Sigma, Sigma Iota Epsilon, Pi Sigma Epsilon, Alpha Kappa Psi, Phi Kappa Phi. Club: Rotarian. Home: PO Box 96 Sawyer MI 49125 Office: Coll Bus Adminstrn Valparaiso U Valparaiso IN 46383

SCHLENKER, ALBIN ELDO, farm owner; b. Jud, N.D., Sept. 7, 1936; s. Theodore and Anna (Elhard) S.; m. Clara Miller, July 21, 1955; children: Pamela Kay, Cheryl Marie, Lori Ann, Mark Albin, Lisa Kristine, Sonja Rae. Ed. pub. sch., Jud, N.D. Farmer Alfred, N.D., 1955—. Mem. Glenn Twp. Bd., 1965; bd. dirs. Farmers-Home Adminstrn., Lamoure County, 1986. Avocation: snowmobiling. Address: PO Box 91 Alfred ND 58411

SCHLENKER, EMILY CATHERINE, nurse; b. Moline, Ill., Feb. 18, 1939; d. Charles O. and Cora B. Diehl; m. George John Schlenker, Apr. 28, 1962; children: Charles Eric, Lisa Anne. BA in Psychology, Augustana Coll., Rock Island, Ill., 1962; RN, Luth. Hosp. Sch. Nurses, 1974; BSN, Marycrest Coll., 1977; MS, No. Ill. U., 1979. Lic. nurse, Iowa, Ill. Instr. nursing Luth. Hosp. Sch. Nurses, Moline, 1975-76, Marycrest Coll., Davenport, Iowa, 1977-78; coordinator family planning Rock Island County Health Dept., 1978-79; asst. prof. nursing Marycrest Coll., Davenport, 1979-84; quality assurance mgr. Davenport Med. Ctr., 1984-85; prin. cons. Health Mgmt. Assocs., Rock Island, 1985—; lectr. USAMETA, Rock Island Arsenal, 1981—, Midwest Regional Tng. Ctr., Ft. Benjamin, Harrison, Ind., 1986; cons. Resource Applications, Balt., 1984—; pvt. couselor, Rock Island, 1982—. USPHS grantee. Mem. AAAS, Am. Mgmt. Assn., Nat. Assn. Female Execs., Ill. Nurses Assn. (5th dist. pres. 1979, commn. edn. 1979-81), Career Womens Network, Sigma Theta Tau. Home and Office: 3611 33d Ave Rock Island IL 61201

SCHLENSKER, GARY CHRIS, landscaping company executive; b. Indpls., Nov. 12, 1950; s. Christian Frederick and Doris Jean (Shannon) S.; m. Ann Marie Tobin, Oct. 27, 1979; children: Laura Patricia, Christian Frederick II. Student, Purdue U., 1969-71, 73; A Bus. Adminstrn., Clark Coll., 1979; cert. emergency med. technician, Ind. Vocat. Tech. Inst., Lafayette, 1974. Salesman Modern Reference, Indpls., 1971; orthopaedic technician St. Elizabeth Hosp., Lafayette, 1973-75, asst. mgr. ambulance service, 1975; sales asst. Merck, Sharpe & Dohme, Oakbrook, Ill., 1975-77; v.p. Turfco, Inc., Zionsville, Ind., 1977-84; pres. Turfscape, Inc., Zionsville, 1984—. Served with U.S. Army, 1971-73. Mem. Nat. Fedn. Ind. Bus., Midwest Turf Found., Better Bus. Bur., Indpls. C. of C., Zionsville Jaycees (Jaycee of Yr. 1986). Avocations: woodworking, golf, bowling.

SCHLEPPENBACH, RAYMOND JOHN, dentist; b. Cold Spring, Minn., May 12, 1919; s. Anton and Gertrude (Baltes) S.; m. Agnes Louise Hoffmann, Aug. 12, 1949; children: Robert, Joan, Tim, Tom, Ann, Gene, Mary, Mike, Gary, Julie, Greg. Student, St. John's U., 1937-40; DDS, Creighton U., 1943. Gen. practice dentistry Schuyler, Nebr., 1974-85, Pierce, Nebr., 1947—. Pres. Pierce Sch. Bd., 1965-68, pres. 1966-68. Served to capt. U.S. Army, 1942-46. Mem. ADA (life), Nebr. Dental Soc. (del. to state dental soc. 1965-71), North Dist. Dental Soc. (pres. 1970-71, cons.), Pierce C. of C. (past. pres.), Am. Legion (comdr. and adj.). Roman Catholic. Avocations: golfing, bowling, Boy Scouts, church activities.

SCHLEPPI, ANN ELIZABETH, child welfare training consultant; b. Queens, N.Y., Mar. 11, 1953; d. Albert August and Marie Louise (Hall) Welge; m. Craig Alan Schleppi, Jan. 5, 1980. BSW, Cornell U., 1975; MSW, Va. Commonwealth U., 1976. Lic. ind. social worker. Drug program coordinator Crawford County Council on Alcohol and Drugs, Bucyrus, Ohio, 1976; alcoholism counselor, cons. Columbus (Ohio) Health Dept., 1976-78; custody mediator Franklin County Ct. Domestic Relations, Columbus, 1978-83; tng. coordinator Ohio Mediation Seminars Inc., Columbus, 1983-84; coordinator children's resource program Franklin County Children Services, Columbus, 1984-87; tng. cons. Ohio welfare tng. program Inst. for Human Services, Columbus, 1987—; cons. to mental health agys., clergy, attys. Ohio Mediation Seminars Inc., Columbus, 1983-84; child welfare trainer Inst. Human Services, Columbus, 1986-87. Mem. Nat. Assn. Social Workers. Episcopalian. Avocations: home renovation, needlework, crafts, cross-country skiing, jogging. Home: 880 S Champion Ave Columbus OH 43206 Office: Inst for Human Services 1247 S High St Columbus OH 43206

SCHLETTY, STEVEN BRIAN, dentist; b. Red Wing, Minn., June 7, 1951; s. Fred John and Maxine Claire (Van Guilder) S.; m. Donna Rae Brust, Dec. 27, 1975; children: John Brian, Michael Ray, Daniel Fred. BA, BS, U. Minn., 1974, DDS, 1976. Practice gen. dentistry, mem. staff Osceola (Wis.) Hosp., 1978—, St. Croix Hosp., St. Croix Falls, Wis., 1979—; cons. dentist Osceola Extended Care Facility, 1985—. Mem. Five County Dist. Dental Soc., Osceola Jaycees (pres. 1979), Osceola Civic and Commerce Assn. (pres. 1980). Republican. Lutheran. Lions (v.p. Osceola club). Home: PO Box 366 Osceola WI 54020 Office: 215 Cascade St Osceola WI 54020

SCHLEY, AMY MARGARET (GLOE), child psychologist; b. Manitowoc, Wis., Feb. 19, 1947; d. Robert August and Edith Mae (Queram) Gloe. BS, Carroll Coll., 1969; MS, U. Wis., Whitewater, 1970; PhD, Marquette U., 1985. Lic. psychologist, Wis. Counselor Waukesha County Assn. for Retarded Citizens, Wis., 1979-80; teaching asst. Marquette U., Milw., 1979-80; pvt. practice child psychology Waukesha, 1980—; provider contract Waukesha County Dept. of Human Services, 1982—; lectr. various colls. and univs. Vol. Assn. for Retarded Citizens, 1980—; mem. adv. com. Adult Activity Ctr., 1982; bd. dirs. Kern Found., 1987. Named Profl. Person of Yr., Waukesha County Assn. for Retarded Citizens, 1984. Mem. Am. Psychol. Assn., Phi Delta Kappa. Club: Sports Car of Am. Avocation: sports car racing. Home and Office: 204 Wisconsin Ave Waukesha WI 53186

SCHLICHTER, JEROME JOSEPH, attorney; b. Belleville, Ill., Aug. 13, 1948; s. Olyn Rodolph and Margaret (Bechtoldt) S. BS, U. Ill., 1969; JD, UCLA, 1972. Bar: Calif. 1972, Ill. 1973, Mo. 1973. Assoc. Cohn, Carr, Korein, Kunin & Brennan, East St. Louis, Ill., 1973-78; ptnr. Carr, Korein, Schlichter, Kunin & Montroy, East St. Louis, 1978—. Mem. ABA, Ill. State Bar Assn., St. Clair County Bar Assn., Bar Assn. Met. St. Louis, Calif. Trial Lawyers Assn., Ill. Trial Lawyers Assn., Assn. Trial Lawyers Am., Mo. Assn. Trial Attys. Office: 701 Market Suite 300 Saint Louis MO 63101

SCHLICK, THOMAS LEROY, marketing executive; b. Red Wing, Minn., Mar. 18, 1950. BS in Engring. and Mktg., U. Minn., 1972, MBA, 1977. Design engr. Gen. Electric Co., Erie, Pa., 1972; product service specialist Gen. Electric Co., Bridgeport, Conn., 1973; industry mktg. specialist Gen. Electric Co., Fort Wayne, Ind., 1974; mktg. engr. Rosemount, Inc., Mpls., 1974-77, mgr. bus. planning, 1977-81, dir. planning and new bus. devel., 1981—; bd. dirs. Azonix Corp., Burlington, Mass. Author: Product Development Guidelines, 1980. Recipient Outstanding Tech. Mktg. award Gen. Electric Co., 1973, 74. Mem. Instrument Soc. of Am. (sr.), Am. Mgmt. Assn., Planning Forum. Lutheran. Avocations: reading, nautilus exercise, jogging, racquetball. Home: 15213 Edgewater Circle Prior Lake MN 55372 Office: Rosemount Inc 12001 W 78th St Eden Prairie MN 55344

SCHLIMM, FREDERICK BERNARD, academic administrator; b. Cin., Aug. 8, 1935; s. Joseph Richard and Nellie Katherine (Prentice) S.; m. Patricia Martha Simon, May 30, 1958; children: Frederick Jr., Maryann, Margaret, Joseph, Christopher, Steven. BS in History, Xavier U., 1957, MEd, 1959. Tchr. Taylor High Sch., Cin., 1957-60; counselor Western Hills High Sch., Cin., 1960-68; admissions counselor Cin. Tech. Coll., 1968-69, v.p., 1969-76, pres., 1976—. Chmn. St. Alaysius Gonzara Bd. Edn., Cin., 1972-75, Cin. Minority Bus. Assistance Corp., 1980-86; mem. City of Hope, Cin., 1981—; vice chmn. LaSalle High Sch. Bd. Trustees, Cin., 1978-81. Mem. Am. Assn. Community and Jr. Colls. (pres.'s acad. 1983, 86), Am. Council on Edn., Nat. Council Resource Devel., Ohio Tech. and Community Coll. Assn. (chmn. 1986—), Greater Cin. Consortium Colls. and Univs. (chmn. 1976—). Avocations: golf, lit., writing, civic activities. Home: 3971 Race Rd Cincinnati OH 45211 Office: Cin Tech Coll 3520 Central Pkwy Cincinnati OH 45223

SCHLOBOHM, KENNETH OTTO, infosystems specialist; b. Macomb, Ill., Sept. 23, 1961; s. William George and Mary Wieland (Taylor) S.; m. Irene Ann DeMarlie, Aug. 1, 1981; children: Kenneth Otto Jr., Kristin Rae. BA in Physics, Statistical Math, Computer Sci., Monmouth Coll., 1983. Programmer analyst A.C. Nielson Co., Clinton, Iowa, 1983—. Republican. Presbyterian. Avocations: electronics, motorcycle and automobile racing. Office: AC Nielson Co 1900 N 3d St Clinton IA 52732

SCHLOEMER, PAUL GEORGE, diversified manufacturing company executive; b. Cin., July 29, 1928; s. Leo Bernard and Mary Loretta (Butler) S.; m. Virginia Katherine Grona, Aug. 28, 1954; children—Michael, Elizabeth, Stephen, Jane, Daniel, Thomas. B.S. in Mech. Engring., U. Cin., 1951; M.B.A., Ohio State U., 1955. Research and devel. engr. Wright Patterson AFB, Dayton, Ohio, 1951-52, R&D officer, 1952-57; resident engr. Parker Hannifin Corp., Dayton, also Eastern area mgr., Huntsville, Ala., 1957-65, v.p. aerospace group, Irvine, Calif., 1965-77, pres. aerospace group, 1977, corp. v.p., 1978-81, exec. v.p., 1981, pres., Cleve., 1982-84, chief exec. officer, 1984—, also bd. dirs.; bd. dirs. Leaseway Transp. Corp., Cleve., Ameritrust Corp. and Ameritrust Nat. Co., Cleve. Chmn. St. Vincent Charity Hosp. and Health Ctr.; vice chmn. Cleve. Tomorrow, Inc.; bd. dirs. United Way Services, Cleve.; active Friends of Scouting campaign, Cleve. council; trustee John Carroll U., University Heights, Ohio, 1982—. Served to capt. USAF, 1952-53. Recipient Silver Beaver award Boy Scouts Am., 1976. Mem. Aerospace Industries Assn. (bd. govs.), Machinery and Allied Products Inst. (exec. com.). Republican. Roman Catholic. Club: The Country, Big Canyon Country, The Pepper Pike. Office: Parker Hannifin Corp 17325 Euclid Ave Cleveland OH 44112

SCHLOSS, NATHAN, real estate research corporation executive; b. Balt., Jan. 14, 1927; s. Howard L. and Louise (Levi) S.; B.S. in Bus., Johns Hopkins U., 1950; m. Rosa Montalvo, Mar. 1, 1958; children—Nina L., Carolyn D. Buyer, Pacific Coast merchandise office Sears Roebuck & Co., Los Angeles, 1955-60, staff asst. econ. research dept., Chgo., 1960-63; sr. market analyst corp. research dept. Montgomery Ward & Co., Chgo., 1963-65; research mgr. real estate dept. Walgreen Co., Chgo., 1970-72; v.p. research and planning Maron Properties Ltd., Montreal, Que., Can., 1972-74; corp. economist, fin. analyst Real Estate Research Corp., Chgo., 1974—, sr. v.p., 1986—, treas., chief fin. analyst, 1982—; cons. economist, since 1965—; mem. com. on price indexes and productivity Bus. Research Adv. Council of Bur. Labor Stats., Dept. Labor, 1979—, also chairperson (1985-86), com. on employment and unemployment. Mem. Plan Commn., Village of Wilmette, Ill., 1975-77, tech. adv. com. on employment and tng. data Ill. Employment and Tng. Council, 1979-82; mem. tech. adv. com. Ill. Job Tng. Coordinating Council, 1983-87. Mem. Am. Mktg. Assn., Nat. Assn. Bus. Economists, Lambda Alpha. Contbr. articles on fin. and market analysis of real estate to profl. jours. Home: 115 Hollywood Ct Wilmette IL 60091 Office: 72 W Adams St Chicago IL 60603

SCHLOSSER, SISTER BLANCHE MARIE, religious educator; b. Arkansaw, Wis., Feb. 13, 1919; d. William George Schlosser and Ella Catherine Denning. Grad., Viterbo Coll., 1950, BS, 1955; MEd, De Paul U., 1964. Cert. tchr., Wis.; joined Franciscan Sisters of Perpetual Adoration, Roman Cath. Ch., 1937. Tchr., cathechist elem. schs. Wis., Iowa, 1939-52, adminstr. elem. schs., 1953-70; music tchr., religious coordinator St. Mary's Assumption Parish and Sch., Durand, Wis., 1978-87, coordinator Confraternity Christian Doctrine programs, 1978-85. Parish del. Deanery Pastoral Council, Durand, 1973-82; deanery del. Diocesan Pastoral Council, La Crosse, Wis., 1976-82; active Parish Council, Durand, 1973-85. Recipient Martha Peck award Music Assn., Durand, 1984. Mem. Music Tchrs. Nat. Assn., Inc., Wis. Music Tchrs. Assn., Nat. Cath. Edn. Assn. (tchr. assoc.). Avocations: fishing, art, music, travel. Home and Office: St Marys Assumption Parish and Sch 901 W Prospect St Durand WI 54736

SCHLOSSMAN, GEORGE BRADLEY, controller; b. Fargo, N.D., July 6, 1954; s. William Alexis and Anna Jane (Black) S.; m. Jene Elaine Nartnik, Jan. 3, 1981; children—B. Elliott, Jennifer Jane. B.B.A., So. Meth. U., 1976. C.P.A., Tex. Audit staff Arthur Andersen & Co., Dallas, 1976-78; treas. George M. Black Co., Fargo, 1978-86; controller West Acres Devel. Co., Fargo, 1978—. bd. dirs. First Bank of N.D. (N.A.), Fargo. Bd. dirs., officer at large Fargo-Moorhead YMCA, 1985—; bd. dirs., treas. Am. Gold Gymnastics, Fargo, 1986—; campaign cabinet United Way of Cass Clay, Fargo, 1980; mem. Fargo, Cass County Econ. Devel. Corp. Membership Com; C-400 bus. div. com. Concordia Coll., Moorhead, Minn., 1982-84; others. Mem. Nat. Assn. Accts. (bd. dirs. 1980-82), Am. Inst. C.P.A.s, N.D. Soc. C.P.A.s (Fargo Moorhead chpt.). Internat. Council Shopping Ctrs. (chmn. N.D. state govt. affairs com.) Republican. Presbyterian. Clubs: Kiwanis, Pelican Lake Yacht. Home: PO Box 701 Fargo ND 58107 Office: West Acres Devel Co 305 Black Bldg Fargo ND 58102

SCHLOSSMAN, JOHN ISAAC, architect; b. Chgo., Aug. 21, 1931; s. Norman Joseph and Carol (Rosenfeld) S.; m. Shirley Goulding Rhodes, Feb. 8, 1959; children—Marc N., Gail M., Peter C. Student, Grinnell Coll., 1949-50; B.A., U. Minn., 1953, B.Arch., 1955; M.Arch., MIT, 1956. Registered architect, Ill., Fla. Archtl. designer The Architects Collaborative, Cambridge, Mass., 1956-57; architect Loebl Schlossman & Hackl and predecessors, Chgo., 1959-65, assoc., 1965-70, prin., 1970—; founding bd. dirs. Chgo. Archtl. Assistance Ctr., 1974-79. Chmn. Glencoe Plan Commn., Ill., 1977-82; trustee Com. for Green Bay Trail, Glencoe, 1970-77, Chgo. Architecture Found., 1971-75; bd. dirs. Merit Program, Chgo., 1983—. Named dir. for life Young Men's Jewish Council, Chgo., 1971; Rotch traveling scholar, 1957. Fellow AIA (trustee ins. trust 1971-76, chmn. ins. com. 1974-75, v.p. Chgo. chpt. 1975, chmn. architects liability com. 1976, 80-82); mem. Alpha Rho Chi (life). Clubs: Tavern, The Arts (Chgo.). Office: Loebl Schlossman and Hackl Inc 845 N Michigan Ave Chicago IL 60611

SCHLOTTERER, WILLIAM LEE, osteopathic physician; b. Shelby, Ohio, Mar. 6, 1955; s. Karl Leo and Phyllis Ray (Stewart) S.; m. Debra Kay Hohman, Aug. 23, 1986. B.S. in Zoology with honors, Kent State U., 1976; D.O., Ohio U. Coll. Osteo. Medicine, 1980; postgrad. U. Toledo, 1983—. Intern, Parkview Hosp., Toledo, 1980-81; dir. Rainbow Clinic, Woodville, Ohio, 1981-83; emergency dept. physician Central Ohio Emergency Services, 1983-84; med. dir. After Hours Health Care, Sundusky, Ohio, 1984-86, Huron (Ohio) Healing Arts, 1986-87; gen. practice osteomed., Sandusky, Ohio, 1987—; clin. instr. Ohio U. Coll. Osteo Med. Civilian draft and mil. counselor, 1973-74; water safety instr., Akron, Ohio, 1973-75; dir. Radix Christian Workshop Relief Program for Skeels-McElrath, 1975-76. Summer fellow in disaster contingency planning in Appalachian Ohio, 1977; mem. exec. bd. Muskingum Valley Boy Scout Council, 1983-86. Recipient Sandoz award for scholarship and community service, 1978. Mem. Am. Osteo. Assn., Ohio Osteo. Assn. Am. Coll. Emergency Physicians, Toledo Acad. Osteo. Medicine (sec.), Sandusky Acad. Osteo Med. Jewish. Club: Mensa. Home: 3019 Truman Rd Perrysburg OH 43551

SCHLUTTER, LOIS COCHRANE, psychologist; b. Indpls., Oct. 18, 1953; d. Roy and Mavis (Wolfe) Cochrane; m. Dennis James Schlutter, Oct. 30, 1976; 1 child, Nathan Paul. BS, U. S.D., 1974, MA, 1975, PhD, 1978. Licensed cons. psychologist, Minn. Psychologist, asst. Neurol. Inst. and Pain Ctr., Sioux City, Iowa, 1975-77; staff Mpls. Psychotherapy Inst., St. Louis Park, Minn., 1978-80; pvt. practice psychology St. Louis Park, 1980-81; bd. dirs. Vail Pl.; allied health staff, cons. Meth. Hosp., St. Louis Park., 1978—, mem. hospice adv. com., 1984—, child abuse consortium, 1985—; staff psychologist, Sister Kenny Inst., Mpls., 1980-81; cons. Dept. Vocat. Rehab., St. Paul. 1984—; supr. Pastoral Care/AAPC, St. Louis Park, 1984—; lectr. St. Mary's Hosp. and Coll., Mpls., 1984—; psychologist, dir. Family Dynamics, St. Louis Park., 1980—. Co-author: (play) The Extrapolator, 1968; contbr. articles to profl. jours. Recipient research grant Lederle Pharms., 1979. Mem. Minn. Psychol. Assn., Am. Assn. Pastoral Counselors (profl. affiliate), Brookside Condominium Assn., The Blvd. Condominium Assn., Phi Beta Kappa, Kappa Alpha Theta, Alpha Lambda Delta, Psi Chi. Avocations: family, friends, reading, circuit weight tng., cooking. Office: Family Dynamics 4039 Brookside Ave S Saint Louis Park MN 55416

SCHMEDA, JOHN ANTHONY, dentist; b. Chgo., Mar. 1, 1941; s. John Peter and Constance (Palmeri) S.; m. Sue Anne Stuckey, Aug. 8, 1964; children—Jill, Peter, Kelly Anne. D.D.S., Loyola U., Chgo., 1965. Gen. practice dentistry, Des Plaines, Ill., 1967—; cons. Mazarethville Nursing Home, Des Plaines, 1978—, Holy Family Health Ctr., Des Plaines, 1982—; staff Holy Family Hosp., Des Plaines, 1980—; dir. Legis. Interest Com. Ill. Dentists, Springfield, 1982—. Served to capt. USAF, 1965-67. Fellow Acad. Gen. Dentistry, Odontographi Soc. Chgo.; mem. Am. Dental Assn. (alt. del. to ho. of dels. 1986, del., 1987), Ill. State Dental Soc. (exec. council 1985-88), Chgo. Dental Soc. (pres. Northwest suburban br. 1984-85). Roman Catholic. Avocations: golf; skiing. Home: 1027 W Mallard Dr Palatine IL 60067 Office: 1400 Golf Rd #125 Des Plaines IL 60016

SCHMETZER, ALAN DAVID, psychiatrist; b. Louisville, Sept. 3, 1946; s. Clarence Fredrick and Catherine Louise (Wootan) S.; m. Janet Lynn Royce, Aug. 25, 1968; children—Angela Beth, Jennifer Lorraine. B.A., Ind. U., 1968, M.D., 1972. Diplomate Am. Bd. Psychiatry and Neurology. Intern, Ind. U. Hosps., Indpls., 1972-73, resident, 1972-75; dir. clinics PCI, Inc., Anderson, Beech Grove and Kokomo, Ind., 1975-79; psychiat. cons. Community Addiction Services Agy., Indpls., 1975-80; instr. psychiatry in primary care Family Practice Residency Programs, St. Francis Hosp., St. Vincent's Hosp. and Ind. U. Hosps., Indpls., 1975—; med. dir. Child Guidance Clinic of Marion County, Indpls., 1980-81; chmn. psychiatry dept. St. Francis Hosp., Beech Grove, 1980-82; med. dir. Crisis Intervention Unit, Midtown Mental Health Center and coordinator emergency psychiat. services Ind. U. Med. Ctr., Indpls., 1980—, also asst. prof. psychiatry. Served to maj. Ind. N.G., 1972-79. Decorated Army Commendation medal; recipient Physicians Recognition award AMA, 1978; Residents award for outstanding teaching 1985. Fellow Am. Psychiat. Assn.; mem. AMA, Ind. Med. Assn., Marion County Med. Soc., Am. Psychiat. Assn., Ind. Psychiat. Soc., Am. Orthopsychiat. Assn., Am. Acad. Clin. Psychiatry, Alpha Phi Omega, Phi Beta Pi, Psi Chi, Alpha Epsilon Delta. Presbyterian. Club: Athenaeum Turnverein. Author: Crisis Intervention: The Psychotic Assaultive Patient, a videotape and workbook, 1981; Crisis Intervention: The Suicidal Patient, 1981. Office: 1001 W 10th St Indianapolis IN 46202

SCHMID, CRAIG NICHOLAS, lawyer; b. St. Louis, July 14, 1959; s. Bill Bernard and Adele Louise (Daniels) S. BA magna cum laude with honors, St. Louis U., 1981, JD cum laude, 1984. Bar: Mo. 1984, U.S. Dist. Ct. (ea. dist.) Mo. 1985, Ill. 1985, U.S. Ct. Appeals (8th cir.) 1985. Assoc. Schlafly, Griesedieck et al, St. Louis, 1984-86, Armstrong, Teasdale et al, St. Louis, 1986—. Active Vol. Lawyer Program, 1985—, grievance com. 22d Jud. Cir., 1985—; mem. Cupples Ho. Aux., St. Louis, 1982—; bd. mem. Carondelet Community Sch., 1986—,Aid for Victims Crime, 1985—, Grand Marquette Arts Council, 1986—; mem. Dutchtown South Community Corp., 1980—, pres. 1985-86. Coro Found. Leadership fellow, 1987. Home: 4917 S Compton Saint Louis MO 63111 Office: Armstrong Teasdale et al 611 Olive Suite 1900 Saint Louis MO 63102

SCHMIDL, MARY KATHERINE, nutrition company executive; b. Marysville, Calif., Aug. 11, 1951; d. Joseph and Katherine Charolette (Schnell) S.; m. Theodore Peter Labuza, Nov. 30, 1985. BS, U. Calif., Davis, 1973; MS, Cornell U., 1976, PhD, 1978. Dept. head Cutter Labs., Berkeley, Calif., 1978-82; group leader Sandoz Nutrition Corp., Mpls., 1982—; chmn. Midwest Food Processors Conf., La Crosse, Wis., 1985. Patentee in field. Mem. Inst. Food Technologists (exec. com. 1984-86, sci. lectureship com. 1984-87, nat. sec., treas. nutrition div. 1986-87, chmn.-elect Minn. chpt. 1986-87), Am. Dietetic Assn., Am. Assn. Cereal Chemists, Am. Soc. Parenteral and Enteral Nutrition. Home: 1870 Stowe Ave Saint Paul MN 55112 Office: Sandoz Nutrition Corp 5320 W 23d St Minneapolis MN 55440

SCHMIDLIN, PAUL ROBERT, insurance agent; b. Toledo, Dec. 30, 1948; s. Oscar Fredrick and Mary Lucille (Byers) S.; m. Gaylynn Mc Curdy, Oct. 18, 1970 (div. Aug. 1978); children: Amber Dawn, Eric Paul, Arron Michael, Hans Fredrick. BA, Ohio State U., 1970; M Div., Trinity Sem. Counseling, 1976. Mem. Ti-Cats Profl. Football Team, Hamilton, Ont., Can., 1970-72; pastor Bethel Luth. Ch., Toledo, 1976-78; mgr. Bob Evans Farm Foods, Cleve., 1978-79; agt. State Farm Ins., Perrysburg, Ohio, 1979—. Coach Perryburg Youth Soccer, 1985—; trustee Abundant Life Ret. Ctr., Perrysburg, 1986—. Mem. Ohio State U. Alumni (pres. 1986). Lodge: Rotary (chmn. fin. Perrysburg). Home: 27772 Oregon Rd Toledo OH 43551 Office: State Farm Ins 27457 Holiday Ln Perrysburg OH 43551

SCHMIDT, ALBERT DANIEL, utility executive; b. Alpena, S.D., Nov. 16, 1925; s. Ernest Otto and Dorothea Marie Augusta (Hansohm) S.; m. Joyce Bernice Anderson, Nov. 24, 1946; children—Roxanne Rae Schmidt Eisen, Janet Jaye Schmidt Foss. Student, Miami U., Oxford, Ohio, 1943-45; B.S.E.E. with honors, S.D. Sch. Mines and Tech., 1949. With Northwestern Public Service Co., 1949—; v.p. opns. Northwestern Public Service Co., Huron, S.D., 1958-65; pres. Northwestern Public Service Co., 1965-80, chief exec. officer, 1965—, chmn., 1980—, also dir.; mem. adv. bd. No. dist. Norwest Bank of S.D.; mem. exec. com., past chmn. Mid-Continent Area Power Pool. Trustee Huron Coll., 1970-73. Served with USNR, 1943-46. Named Man of Yr. S.D. Electric Council, 1979; Boss of Yr. Huron Jaycees, 1979. Mem. North Central Electric Assn. (exec. com., past chmn.), N.Am. Elec. Reliability Council (past trustee), Food and Energy Council (past chmn.), Nat. Assn. Over-the-Counter Cos., U.S. Indsl. Council (dir.), S.D. C. of C. (past dir.), S.D. Council Econ. Edn. (dir.), Nat. Assn. Electric Cos. (past dir.), Am. Gas Assn. (past dir.), Midwest Gas Assn. (past pres.), S.D. Electric Council, S.D. Engring. Soc., Huron C. of C. Republican. Lutheran. Clubs: Elks, Masons, Huron Country. Office: Northwestern Pub Service Co 3d St and Dakota Ave S Huron SD 57350

SCHMIDT, ARTHUR IRWIN, steel fabricating company executive; b. Chgo., Sept. 9, 1927; s. Louis and Mary (Fliegel) S.; m. Mae Rosman, July 25, 1950; children: Jerrold, Cynthia, Elizabeth, Richard. Student, Colo. A. and M. Coll., 1946-47; BS in Aero. Engring., U. Ill., 1950. Sec. Rosman Iron Works, Inc., Franklin Park, Ill., 1950-86; pres. Rosman-Schmidt Steel Corp., 1986—. Served with USNR, 1944-46, 51-52. Mem. U. Ill. Alumni Assn. Lodge: B'nai B'rith (trustee, past pres. Lincolnwood chpt.). Home and Office: 3601 Golf Rd Evanston IL 60203

SCHMIDT, BENEDICT JOSEPH, nurse; b. Battle Creek, Mich., Nov. 12, 1956; s. Arthur Joseph and Irene Elizabeth (Rosenberry) S.; m. Sharon Joy Teske, Aug. 4, 1984. BS in Nursing cum laude, Nazareth Coll., Kalamazoo, 1986. RN, Mich. Nurse Borgess Med. Ctr., Kalamazoo, 1984—. Served with USN, 1975-80. Mem. Mich. Nurses Assn. Avocations: playing guitar, running, cross-country skiing, camping.

SCHMIDT, C. OSCAR, JR., manufacturing company executive; b. Cin.; s. C. Oscar Sr. and Charlotte A. (Fritz) S.; m. Eugenia Hill Williams, June 29, 1944 (dec.); children: Carl O., Christoph R., Milton W., Eugene H., Juliann R.; m. Georgia Lee, Aug. 1977. BSME, U. Cin.; MBA, Harvard U.; student in animal husbandry Rutgers U.; LHD, Sterling Coll. Registered profl. engr., Ohio. Apprentice Am. Can Co.; engr. Cin. Shaper; held several exec. positions with Cin. Butchers' Supply Co., asst. to pres., v.p. prodn., v.p., gen. mgr., exec. v.p., pres., treas., chmn. bd. dirs.; pres. BEC, Inc., Cin. Renderers Assn., Winger Boss Co.; bd. dirs. Cin. Refrigerator and Fixture Works, Dixie Rendering Co., Ky. Chem. Industries, Inc., Mille Lacs Products Co., Queen City Scale, Boss Pack Co., many others. Contbr. articles to profl. jours; patentee in field. Trustee Deaconess Hosp.; ruling elder Wyo. Presbyn. Ch.; ruling elder, commr. Cin. Presbytery, Ecclesiastical Order Com.; mem. Cin. Art Mus., Friends Pub. Library, Hamilton County Soc. Crippled Children, Hamilton County Soc. Prevention Cruelty to Animals, Ohio Aubudon Soc.; mem. fin. com. Nat. United Cerebral Palsy Assn.; mem. rev. com. United Funds, Cin., many others. Served to capt. U.S. Army, 1940-45. Recipient Silver Beaver award Boy Scouts Am., 1969, Herman award, Disting. Engring. Alumnus award U. Cin., 1969, others. Mem. Process Equipment Mfg. Assn., Ga. Ind. Meat Packers Assn. (bd. dirs.), Meat Machinery Mfgrs. Inst. (bd. dirs., past pres.), Meat Industry Supply and Equipment Assn. (bd. dirs., past chmn.), Nat. Assn. Mfgrs. (indsl. problems com.), Miami Purchase Assn., Am. Oil Chemist Soc. (life); Nat. Parks Assn. (life), Ohio Hist. Soc.(life), Aircrafts Owners and Pilots Assn., Am. Ordnance Assn., Engr. Soc. Cin., Am. Assn. Indsl. Mgmt., Air Pollution Soc., Cin. Indsl. Inst., Nat. Metal Trades Assn., Harvard U. Alumni Assn., U. Cin. Alumni Assn. (life), Cin. C. of C., Zool. Soc. Cin., Kappa Sigma Pi (bd. dirs., nat. sec.), many others. Club: Wyoming Golf. Lodges: Masons, Rotary (various offices), Shriners. Home: 405 Meadow Ln Cincinnati OH 45215 Office: Cin Butchers Supply Co Box 16098 5601 Helen St Elmwood Place Cincinnati OH 45216

SCHMIDT, CHARLES LARRY, utility executive; b. Cin., Jan. 6, 1930; s. Charles Henry and Erna Selma (Scholz) S.; m. Mary Jane Heher, Nov. 28, 1953 (div. Oct. 1973); children: Gregory, Robert, Laura, Lisa, David; m. Linda Mae Ferguson, Oct. 15, 1976. BS, U. Cin., 1960, MBA, 1962. V.p. Cin. Gas and Electric Co., 1949—; Trustee Ind. Gas Assn., Ohio Gas Assn., Ky. Gas Assn. Contbr. articles to profl. jours. Mem. Am. Gas Assn. (chmn. operating sect. 1973-75, Disting. Service award 1975), Delta Mu Delta, Alpha Sigma Lambda, Delta Sigma Pi. Republican. Roman Catholic. Clubs: Kenwood Country (Cin.), Cin. Avocations: golf, numismatics. Home: 8100 S Clippinger Dr Indian Hill OH 45243 Office: Cin Gas and Electric 4th and Main Sts Cincinnati OH 45202

SCHMIDT, DANIEL JOSEPH, radio broadcasting executive; b. Madison, Wis., July 6, 1954; s. Karl Frances and Vera Joan (Dougan) S.; m. Julia Brewster, Aug. 30, 1975; children: Karl Andrew, Sarah Joan. Student, Boston U. Tanglewood Inst., 1971, 72; MusB, U. Wis., 1976, MBA, 1978. Pvt. practice music tchr. Madison, 1971-76; broadcast engr. Sta. WHA, Madison, 1973-77; asst. dir., spl. projects & devel. Sta. WHA-Radio and TV, Madison, 1977-79; devel. assoc. Minn. Pub. Radio, Inc., St. Paul, 1979-81, dir., grants adminstrn., 1981-83, dir. adminstrv. services, 1983-87; gen. mgr. WSCO/WIRR/WGGL, Duluth, Minn., 1987—; presenter, lectr. Chamber Music Am., N.Y.C., 1981. Co-Author: Administration in the Arts: Annotated Bibliography of Selected References. Bd. dirs. Dane County Arts Council, Madison, 1978-79; council mem. St. Michael's Luth. Ch., Roseville, Minn., 1985—. U. Wis. Grad. Sch. Bus. fellow, 1976-77, 77-78. Mem. Beta Gamma Sigma. Home: 3009 E 1st St Duluth MN 55812 Office: WSCD-FM 1200 Kenwood Ave Duluth MN 55811

SCHMIDT, DUANE ARTHUR, dentist; b. Brookings, S.D., Aug. 30, 1929; s. Arthur and Eunice Lucina (Clifford) S.; m. Shirley Fontelle Finefield, Aug. 6, 1950 (div. May 1977); children: Cyndee Schmidt Ferris, Catherine Ann. Student in pre-dentistry, Coe Coll., 1947-49; DDS, U. Iowa, 1954; cert. in pedodontics, Iowa State U., 1956. Gen. practice pedodontics Ft. Dodge, Iowa, 1957-70; gen. practice dentistry Self-Dental East P.C., Cedar Rapids, Iowa, 1970—; mem. faculty Iowa State U. Coll. Dentistry, 1956-57; mem. med.-dental staff Mercy Hosp., St. Luke's Hosp.; chief dental services, sec. med.-dental staff Luth. Hosp., Ft. Dodge; founder, chmn. Drs. With A Heart, Inc. Author: Tu-Tu and the Joy Bell, 1963, The Late J.C., 1973, Sneaky Snake Goes Dancin', 1975, 3 Steps to a Million Dollar Practice, 1984, Earn More-Work Less, 1985; author: (tapes) The Challenger File, 1985; mem. various editorial bds. profl. jours.; contbr. articles to profl. jours. Past bd. dirs. Ft. Dodge Bd. Edn. Served to lt. USN, 1954-56. Named Eagle Scout Boy Scouts Am.; recipient Disting. Service award Jaycees, 1965, Golden Rule award Kiwanis, Ft. Dodge, 1963, Home Town Builder award Eagles Lodge, 1983; disting. fellow Iowa State U. Coll. Dentistry. Fellow Am. Acad. Pedodontics; mem. ADA, Iowa Dental Soc., Linn County Dental Assn., Webster County Dental Soc. (past pres.), Ft. Dodge Dist. Dental Soc. (past pres.), Iowa Soc. Dentistry for Children (past pres.), Mensa. Republican. Methodist. Club: President's (So. Ill. U.); Cedar Rapids Country. Lodges: Masons, Shriners. Avocations: bridge, travel, gourmet dining, golf, writing. Office: Dental East PC 3700 1st Ave NE Cedar Rapids IA 52402

SCHMIDT, FRANKLIN T., design engineer; b. N.Y.C., Nov. 3, 1936; s. Julius and Anne (Macher) S.; m. Glenda Jane Nelson, July 21, 1964; children: Julie, Chris, Brian, Heather. AA, Westchester Coll., 1956; BS, N.Y.U., 1959. Tech. engr. Sperry-Rand, Wichita, Kans., 1962-64; systems engr. Boeing, Wichita, 1964; design engr. Lear-Jet, Detroit, 1964-67; project engr. Edo-Air, Inc., Wichita, 1967-69, Coleman Co., Wichita, 1969—. Patentee in field. Chmn. Boy Scouts Am., Mulvane, Kans., 1978-82. Served with USAF, 1958-62. Mem. Am. Soc. Plastic Engrs. (sr.), Am. Gas Assn., Am. Soc. Testing and Materials, Am. Mgmt. Assn. Republican. Methodist. Lodge: Optimists. Avocations: boating, camping, photography. Home: 1203 Sunset Mulvane KS 67110 Office: The Coleman Co 250 N Saint Francis Wichita KS 67201

SCHMIDT, GRANT, reproductive endocrinology and obstetrics/gynecology educator; b. Kansas City, Mo., Nov. 23, 1949; s. Paul and Cathryn Louise (Erffmeyer) S.; m. Debra Colleen Covington, Mar. 18, 1978; children: Joshua Morgan, Ashley Blair. BS, Bethel Coll., 1971; MD and PhD in Biochemistry, U. Mo., 1976. Diplomate Am. Bd. Ob-Gyn, Am. Bd. Reproductive Endocrinology and Infertility. Resident in pathology U. Mo., Columbia, 1976-77; resident in Ob-Gyn U. N.C., Chapel Hill, 1977-81, visiting asst. prof. Ob-Gyn, 1981; fellow in reproductive endocrinology Ohio State U., Columbus, Ohio, 1981-82; asst. prof. Ob-Gyn Ohio State U., Columbus, 1982—, dir. Human Embryo Labs, 1983—. Contbr. various and articles to scientific jours. Fellow Am. Coll. Ob-Gyn; mem. Am. Fertility soc., Columbus Ob-Gyn Soc., Robert Ross Ob-Gyn Soc., Sigma Xi. Methodist. Avocations: softball, volleyball, woodworking. Office: Ohio State U Dept Ob-Gyn Room 525 Means Hall Columbus OH 43210

SCHMIDT, GUNTER, dentist; b. Nuremberg, Germany, Aug. 22, 1913; s. Willy and Irma (Treumann) S.; m. Corinne Mitchell, May 26, 1944; children: Carol, Linda. Student, U. Munich, 1932-33, U. Wurzburg, 1933; DDS, Washington U., St. Louis, 1937. Gen. practice dentistry, St. Louis, 1937-59, Clayton, Mo., 1959—; dentist Shriner's Hosp. for Crippled Children, 1938-43; staff dentist Jewish Hosp., 1938-78, sr. dentist, 1978—. Past editor Newsletter of Am. Acad. of Oral Medicine, Greater St. Louis Dental Soc. Bull.; contbr. articles to profl. jours. Past chmn. United Fund Dental Div., Arts and Edn. Fund Dental Div.; mem. adv. com. on dental technologies St. Louis Community Coll. Served to maj. AUS, 1943-46. Recipient Diamond Pin award Am. Acad. Oral Medicine, 1976, Gold medal Greater St. Louis Dental Soc., 1985, Herschtus Meml. award Am. Acad. Oral Medicine, 1986; Am. Acad. Oral Medicine fellow, 1964, Am. Coll. Dentists fellow, 1980. Mem. ADA, Am. Acad. Oral Medicine (past pres., sec., trustee), Am. Soc. Geriatric Dentistry (past pres.), Pierre Fauchard Acad., Acad. Gen. Dentistry, Fedn. Dentaire Internat., St. Louis Soc. Dental Sci., Mo. Dental Assn. (chmn. council on legislation, Disting. Service award 1985). Clubs: Temple Emanuel Men's (founder), Temple Israel Men's (past pres.). Home: 15 Princeton Pl University City MO 63130 Office: 222 S Bemiston Clayton MO 63105

SCHMIDT, HARRY JUSTUS, surgeon; b. Humberstone, Ont., Can., Sept. 17, 1924; came to U.S., 1929; s. Wilfried A. Schmidt and Luella Schaus; m. Rhoda Skindlov, Apr. 5, 1953; children: Maren, Andrew, Reed, Robert. BS, Mich. State U., 1945; MD, U. Mich., 1948. Diplomate Am. Bd. Surgery. Intern Rochester (N.Y.) Gen. Hosp., 1948-53; resident in gen. surgery U. Mich. Hosps., 1953-57; staff Sperrow Hosp., Lansing, Mich., 1957—; exec. bd. Sparrow Hosp., Lansing, 1958-70. Esec. bd. Univ. Luth. Ch., Mich., 1970-74. Served to capt. U.S. Army, 1951-53. Fellow Am. Coll. Surgeon; mem. AMA, Pan Pacific Surg. Soc., Coll. Surgery Soc. Republican. Club: Walnut Hill Golf. (Mich.). Avocations: golf, travel, gardening. Home: 625 Belmonte Circle East Lansing MI 48823 Office: 2909 E Grand River Lansing MI 48823

SCHMIDT, JAKOB EDWARD, medical and medicolegal lexicographer, physician, author, inventor; b. Riga, Livonia, Latvia, June 16, 1906; came to U.S., 1924, naturalized, 1929; s. Michael E. and Rachel I. (Goldman) S. Grad., Balt. City Coll., 1929; Ph.G., U. Md., 1932, BS in Pharmacy, 1935, MD, 1937, postgrad., 1939. Intern Sinai Hosp., Balt.; gen. practice medicine Balt., 1940-53; resident Charlestown, Ind., 1953—; indsl. physician Ind. Ordnance Works, 1953-54; med. and medicolegal lexicographer 1950—; pres. Sculptural Med. Jewelers, 1973-76; mem. revision com. U.S. Pharmacopeia XI. Columnist What's the Good Word, Balt. Sun; Sharpen Your Tongue, Am. Mercury; The Medical Lexicographer, Modern Medicine; Medical Semantics, Medical Science; Underworld English, Police; Medical Vocabulary Builder, Trauma; English Word Power and Culture, Charlestown Courier, Understanding Med. Talk; assoc. med. editor, Trauma, 1959—; editor: Medical Dictionary, 1959—; compiler: 50,000-word vocabulary test, 1956; contbr. numerous articles to med. jours., lay press, including Esquire, Playboy, also to press services, including UPI, NANA, others; cons. JAMA on med. terminology, also cons. med. terminology to legal profession and cts., to mfrs. on med. tradenames and trademarks; Author: Terminology of Sensual Emotions, 1954, Medical Terms Defined for the Layman, 1957, REVERSICON, A Physician's Medical Word Finder, 1958, Medical Discoveries, Who and When, 1959, Dictionary of Medical Slang and Related Expressions, 1959, Narcotics, Lingo and Lore, 1959, The Libido, Its Scientific, Lay, and Slang Terminology, 1960, Baby Name Finder—The Source and Romance of Names, 1961, Schmidt's Illustrated Attorneys' Dictionary of Medicine and Word Finder, 1962, One Thousand Elegant Phrases, 1965, Medical Lexicographer A Study of Medical Terminology, 1966, The Cyclopedic Lexicon of Sex Terminology, 1967, Police Medical Dictionary, 1968, Practical Nurses' Medical Dictionary, 1968, A Paramedical Dictionary, 1969, 2d edit., 1973, Structural Units of Medical and Biological Terms, 1969, English Word Power for Physicians and other Professionals, 1971, English Idioms and Americanisms, 1972, English Speech for Foreign Students, 1973, Textbook of Medical Terminology, 1973, Visual Aids for Paramedical Vocabulary, 1973, Analyzer of Medical-Paramedical Vocabulary, 1973, Index of Medical-Paramedical Vocabulary, 1974, Schmidt Diccionario para Auxiliares de la Medicina, 1976, Literary Foreplay, 1983, Schmidt's Illustrated Attorneys' Dictionary of Medicine and Word Finder, 18th edit., 4 vols., 1981, 19th edit., 1985, 21th edit., 1987. Recipient Owl gold medal Balt. City Coll., 1929; Rho Chi gold medal U. Md. Sch. Pharmacy, 1932; gold medal for excellence in all subjects, 1932; cert. of honor U. Md. Sch. Medicine, 1937; award and citation N.Y. met. chpt. Am. Med. Writers' Assn., 1959. Mem. Am. Dialect Soc., Natural History Soc., Am. Name Soc., Am. Med. Writers' Assn., Internat. Soc. Gen. Semantics, AMA, Med. and Chirurgical Faculty of Md., Balt. City Med. Soc., Nat. Assn. Standard Med. Vocabulary, Nat. Soc. Lit. and Arts, Authors' Guild, Authors' League Am., Mus. Natural History, Cousteau Soc., Smithsonian Instn., Planetary Soc., Nat. Writers' Club, Rho Chi, others. Inventor iodine-pentoxide-shunt method and apparatus for detection of carbon monoxide in oxygen, atmosphere, and medicinal gases; shock-proof electric fuse; magnetic needle finger ring; prosthetic mammary papilla; discovered effect of cesium and related metals on oxidation of organic matter in lakes, ponds and drinking water; the TV eye phenomenon; others. Home: Monroe St nr Park Charlestown IN 47111 Office: 934 Monroe St Charlestown IN 47111

SCHMIDT, JAMES DALE, mechanical engineer; b. Alton, Ill., Dec. 8, 1956; s. Earl Dale and Shirley Ann (Chappell) S.; m. Dana Carol Saueresen, May 30, 1981; children: Mark, Edward. BS, Northwestern U., 1980. Registered profl. engr., Ill. Project engr. Shell Oil Co., Wood River, Ill., 1977-79; design engr. W.F. Hall Printing Co., Chgo., 1980; process engr. Koppers Co., Cicero, Ill., 1980-82; mech. engr. CPC Internat., Summit, Ill., 1983-87; project supr. Quaker Oats Co., Chgo., 1987—. Mem. ASME (assoc.), NSPE. Avocations: golf, racquetball, numismatics, hunting. Office: Quaker Oats Co PO Box 9001 Suite 23-11 Chicago IL 60604-9001

SCHMIDT, JAMES GARDINER, manufacturing company executive; b. Berwyn, Ill., Feb. 19, 1947; s. Raymond John and Margaret (Gardiner) S.; m. Martha Evelyn Crews, June 19, 1971; children—Steven, Sarah. B.S.M.E., Purdue U., 1969; M.B.A., U. Chgo., 1980. Mgr. contracts Rockwell Internat., Chgo., 1974-76, dir. customer credit, 1976-77, controller newspaper, 1977-79, dir. fin. ops., 1979-81, controller, dir. Ikegai-Goss Corp., Tokyo, 1981-83; v.p. corp. devel. Fed. Signal Corp., Oak Brook, Ill., 1983-84, v.p. fin. and adminstrn., Burr Ridge, Ill., 1984-86; v.p. fin. Interlake Material HAndling div., BurrRidge, Ill., 1986—. Office: 100 E Tower Dr Burr Ridge IL 60521

SCHMIDT, JOHN JOSEPH, consultant; b. Chgo., Jan. 13, 1928; s. William Fred and Mildred C. (Petrone) S.; m. Gail Bormann, Oct. 8, 1955; children: Cathleen M., Karen B., Linda G. B.S., DePaul U., 1951; J.D., Loyola U., Chgo., 1955. Bar: Ill. 1955. Trial atty. The Atchison, Topeka and Santa Fe Ry., Chgo., 1955-69; asst. v.p. exec. dept. The Atchison, Topeka and Santa Fe Ry., 1969-73; v.p. Santa Fe Industries, Inc., Chgo., 1969-73; exec. v.p. Santa Fe Industries, Inc., 1973-78, pres., 1978-83; chmn. bd., chief exec. officer Santa Fe So. Pacific Corp. (formerly Santa Fe Industries, Inc.), 1983-87; pvt. practice cons. Chgo., 1987—; bd. dirs. Harris Trust & Savs. Bank, Harris Bankcorp Inc. Mem. Zoning Bd. Appeals, Planning Commn. Village of Burr Ridge, Ill., 1973-84. Served with U.S. Army, 1945-47. Mem. Am., Ill., Chgo. bar assns., Soc. Trial Lawyers (past dir.), Ill. Def. Council (past pres.), Nat. Assn. R.R. Trial Counsel (past pres.). Clubs: Chgo. Athletic, Chgo. Economic. Home: 6401 County Line Burr Ridge IL 60521 Office: 135 S LaSalle St Chicago IL 60603

SCHMIDT, JOHN LOUIS, architect, trade association executive; b. Kansas City, Mo., Oct. 31, 1931; s. John Louis and Helen Edna (Stuntz) S.; m. Sally Louise Schmidt, Aug. 15, 1953; children: John Eric, Peggy Lynn, Kathy Louise, Jo Ann. BArch, U. Ill., 1955. Registered profl. architect, Ill. Sr. architect Clark, Dailey & Dietz, Urbana, Ill., 1959-61; dir. archtl. research U.S. League Savs. Instns., Chgo., 1961-72; v.p. Environ. Systems Internat., Los Angeles, 1972-74; pres. Berkus Group, Los Angeles, 1974-76; v.p. Inst. Fin. Edn., Chgo., 1976—; lectr. various indsl. and ednl. orgns., 1970—. Co-author: Construction Principles Materials and Methods, 1966, Construction Lending Guide, 1964; author (monthly column) Housing Report, 1964-72. Mem. Riverwoods (Ill.) Planning Commn., 1967; pres. Riverwoods Residents Assn., 1968; mem., vice chmn. Lake County (Ill.)

Regional Planning Commn., 1977-86). Served to 1st lt. USAF, 1956-59. Named Top Performer House and Home mag., N.Y.C., 1964. Mem. AIA, Urban Land Inst., Sigma Pi (bd. dirs. 1977-81). Republican. Club: Tennaqua (Deerfield, Ill.) (bd. dirs. 1984-86). Avocations: tennis, photography. Home: 2627 Gemini Ln Riverwoods IL 60015 Office: Inst Fin Edn 111 E Wacker Dr Chicago IL 60601

SCHMIDT, JOSEPH MICHAEL, veterinarian; b. Youngstown, Ohio, July 24, 1954; s. Richard Neil and Marilyn Louise (McCallen) S.;. BS in Agr., Ohio State U., 1976, DVM, 1980. Veterinarian Springmeadow Vet. Clinic, Ashland, Ohio, 1980-81, Ft. Recovery (Ohio) Vet. Clinic, 1981-82, Dresden (Ohio) Vet. Clinic, 1982-83, Belmont Vet. Clinic, Youngstown, 1983—. Mem. AVMA, Am. Animal Hosp. Assn., Ohio Vet. Med. Assn., Ea. Ohio Vet. Med. Assn. Republican. Roman Catholic. Avocations: bicycling, backpacking, skiing, photography. Office: Niles Vet Clinic 134 Vienna Ave Niles OH 44446

SCHMIDT, JOY INEZ, business educator; b. Spencer, Iowa, Jan. 2, 1928; d. John Arends and Fay Inez (Guy) Heikens; m. Henry Fred Schmidt, Jan. 8, 1949; 1 child, Robyn Fay Linn. BS, Mankato State U., 1949; MA, U. No. Iowa, 1973. Sec. Hamline U., St. Paul, 1944-45; instr. bus. edn. Waterville (Iowa) Pub. Schs., 1946-47; with Mankato (Minn.) State U., 1948-49; instr. Ridgeway (Iowa) Pub. Schs., 1949-52; with Eastern Allamakee Community Sch., Lansing, Iowa, 1956-67; dept. chmn. NE Iowa Tech. Inst., Calmar, 1967—. Chmn. Zalmona Presbyn. Ch. Christian Edn., Waukon, Iowa, 1980—; elder Zalmona Presbyn. Ch., Waukon, 1985—; mem. Rep. com., Iowa. Mem. Am. Vocat. Assn. (life), Iowa Vocat. Assn. (dist. rep.), Iowa Bus. Edn. Assn. (dist. rep.), Office Edn. Coordinators of Iowa (sec.), Searchlight Lit. Club, TOPS, Delta Phi Epsilon (sec. 1973-75), Phi Delta Kappa (v.p., sec., treas., newsletter editor 1975-80). Lodge: Order Eastern Star (assoc. conductress, assoc. matron 1973-83). Avocations: bridge, playing the organ, raising African Violets. Home: Rt 3 Box 311 Waukon IA 52172 Office: NE Iowa Tech Inst Hwy 150 S Max Clark Hall Calmar IA 52132

SCHMIDT, KENNETH PAUL, financial planner; b. Highriver, Alta., Can., June 24, 1954; s. Harold J. and June M. (Louden) S.; m. Robin J. Merrick, Aug. 18, 1978; 1 child, Emily. BA in Math and Social Scis., N.W. Nazarene Coll., 1976; JD, U. Oreg., 1979; MS in Fin. Services, Am. Coll., 1983. Bar: Ind. 1980. Atty. Mut. Security Life, Ft. Wayne, Ind., 1979-83; owner Fin. Planning Services, Ft. Wayne, 1983—. Mem. Ft. Wayne Estate Planning Council. Mem. ABA, Ind. Bar Assn., Am. Soc. CLU's and Chartered Fin. Cons.'s (v.p. Ft. Wayne chpt. 1985-86, pre. 1987—). Republican. Nazarene. Lodge: Rotary. Home: 8925 Village Grove Dr Fort Wayne IN 46804 Office: Financial Planning Services One Summit Sq Suite 726 Fort Wayne IN 46804

SCHMIDT, NEIL JOSEPH, pharmacist, educator; b. St. Louis, Dec. 16, 1949; s. Waring Edward and Angalina Mary (Colton) S.; m. Margaret Susan Nack, July 31, 1971; children—Christopher, Tracy, Stephen. B.S. in Pharmacy, St. Louis Coll. Pharmacy, 1973; M.A., Webster U., 1986. Registered pharmacist, Mo., Ill. Staff pharmacist Venture Pharmacy, Kirkwood, Mo., part-time 1975-81, St. John's Mercy Med. Ctr., Creve Coeur, Mo., 1973-85; dir. pharmacy and ancillary services St. Mary's Hosp., East St. Louis, Ill., 1985—, hosp. adminstr., 1986; instr. hosp. pharmacy St. Louis Coll. Pharmacy, 1983—; guest speaker radio and TV. Mgr. Ballwin Athletic Assn., Mo., 1980-84, div. coordinator, 1981-84; chmn. com. Cub Scout Pack 627, Boy Scouts Am., Ballwin, 1981-83, cubmaster, 1985; soccer coach Holy Infant Parish, 1978-80. Mem. St. Louis Soc. Hosp. Pharmacists (Hosp. Pharmacist of Yr. 1979, pres. 1977-78), Mo. Soc. Hosp. Pharmacists (pres. 1983-84, pres. research and edn. found. 1984-85), Am. Soc. Hosp. Pharmacists (student adv. panel 1984), Mo. Pharm. Assn., Metro East Soc. Hosp. Pharmacists, Kappa Psi. Democrat. Roman Catholic. Club: Holy Infant Men's. Avocations: Sherlock Holmes, Civil War novels, baseball, soccer, scouting. Home: 532 Golfwood Dr Ballwin MO 63021 Office: St Mary's Hosp 129 N 8th St East Saint Louis IL 62201

SCHMIDT, RETA MAE, educator; b. Sturgeon Bay, Wis., Oct. 15, 1933; d. Vernon Edward Olson and Gertrude Jennie Johnson; m. Frederick James Schmidt, June 28, 1968 (div. 1975); 1 dau., Mary Ann. Student U. Wis., 1952-53, Prospect Hall Secretarial Sch., Milw., 1953-54; B.S. in Elem. Edn., U. Wis.-Oshkosh, 1958. Tchr., Racine (Wis.) Pub. Schs., 1958-59, Neenah (Wis.) Pub. Schs., 1959-68, Broward Pub. Schs., Ft. Lauderdale, Fla., 1968-69; tchr. Sturgeon Bay (Wis.) Pub. Schs., 1978—, 1st grade tchr. Sunrise Elem. Sch., 1978—. Mem. Wis. Edn. Assn., NEA, Internat. Platform Assn. Republican. Mem. Moravian Ch. Club: Order Eastern Star. Home: 845 S 16th Ct Sturgeon Bay WI 54235 Office: Sunrise Sch Sturgeon Bay WI 54235

SCHMIDT, ROBERT, mechanicist, civil engineer; b. Ukraine, May 18, 1927; came to U.S., 1949, naturalized, 1956; s. Alfred and Aquilina (Konotop) S.; m. Irene Hubertine Bongartz, June 10, 1978; 1 child, Ingbert Robert. B.S., U. Colo., 1951, M.S., 1953; Ph.D., U. Ill., 1956. Engr., C.E.; Engr. U.S. Army, Omaha, 1951-52; asst. prof. mechanics U. Ill., 1956-59; assoc. prof. U. Ariz., Tucson, 1959-63; prof. mechanics and civil engring. U. Detroit, 1963—, chmn. dept., 1978-80. Editor: Indsl. Math., 1969—; contbr. 110 articles to profl. jours. NSF grantee, 1960-78. Mem. ASCE, ASME (cert. recognition 1977), Am. Acad. Mechanics (a founder), Indsl. Math Soc. (pres. 1966-67, 81-84, 1st Gold award 1986), AAUP, Sigma Xi. Research on linear and nonlinear theory of elasticity. Address: Coll Engring Univ Detroit Detroit MI 48221-9987

SCHMIDT, ROBERT EDWARD, optometrist; b. Melrose Pk., Ill., Mar. 2, 1936; s. Gustav Schmidt and Amelia (Steigerwald) Zeier; m. Janeece E. Slover, June 8, 1963 (div. Oct. 1985); children: Marcia, Jennifer, Laura; m. Patricia Ann Hoffman, May 16, 1987. Student, U. Ill., 1959-62; BS, Ill. Coll. Optometry, Chgo., 1963; OD, Ill. Coll. Optometry, 1964. Pvt. practice optometry Nokomis, Ill., 1965-68; practice optometry Granite City, Ill., 1968-69; pvt. practice optometry Pekin, Ill., 1969—; cons. Holiday Sch., Pekin, 1969-75. Pres. Ambucs, Pekin, 1972-73. Served with USN, 1954-59. Fellow Am. Acad. Optometry, Coll. Optometrists in Vision Devel. (treas. 1981-83, Midwest Region dir. 1987—); mem. Am. Optometric Assn., Ill. Optometric Assn. (v.p. 1978-79), Tazewell-Mason County Spl. Edn. Assn. (Disting. Service award 1971), Nokomis Jaycees (pres. 1966-67). Lutheran. Lodge: Rotary (pres. Pekin 1979-80). Avocations: gardening, swimming, golf, reading. Home: 75 Northern Oaks Estates Pekin IL 61554 Office: 1491 Valle Vista Pekin IL 61554

SCHMIDT, RONALD JOSEPH, dentist; b. Milw., July 28, 1959; s. Josef and Cecilia (Strigens) S.; m. Laurie Mae Liegel, Oct. 27, 1984. DDS, Marquette U., 1984. Gen. practice dentistry Menomonee Falls, Wis., 1984—; assoc. clin. prof. Marquette U. Sch. Dentistry, Milw., 1986—. Mem. ADA, Acad. Gen. Dentistry, Am. Soc. Dentistry for Children (sec., treas.), Wis. Dental Assn., Chgo. Dental Soc. Roman Catholic. Avocations: hunting, fishing, skiing, golfing. Home and Office: N89 W15680 Main St Menomonee Falls WI 53051

SCHMIDT, RONALD T., organizational development director; b. Chgo., Feb. 2, 1936; s. John G. and Margaret K. (Weber) S.; m. Theresa C. Rago, July 1, 1977. BA, St. Mary's Coll., Mundelein, Ill., 1959, MA, 1962; MA, Lateran U., Rome, Italy, 1968. Tng. coordinator, cons. Michael Reese Hosp. and Med. Ctr., Chgo., 1978-81; asst prof. Rush U., Chgo., 1981—; dir. tng., organizational devel. Rush Presbyn St. Luke's Med. Ctr., Chgo., 1981-86, Bethany Meth. Hosp., Chgo., 1986—; cons. Martha Washington Hosp., Chgo., 1984, Shriner's Children's Hosp., Chgo., 1985. Mem. Am. Soc. Tng. and Devel., Human Resources Mgmt. Assn. Chgo. Office: Bethany Meth Hosp 5015 N Paulina Chicago IL 60612

SCHMIDT, ROSEMARIE FRANCES, chemical company executive; b. Chgo., Nov. 18, 1936; s. Max Robert and Harriet (Grejczyk) Baum; m. William Arlen Schmidt, Feb. 20, 1960; children: Laura, Daniel. Student, U. Wis., Kenosha, 1953-56. V.p. 7 Oaks Motel, Kenosha, 1967—, Easterday Paint Co., Milw., 1982—. Roman Catholic. Clubs: Bristol Oaks Wednesday Golf League (Kenosha) (pres. 1986—). Avocations: reading, golf, bowling, needlework. Office: Easterday Paint Co 1306 E Bolivar Milwaukee WI 53207

SCHMIDT, THOMAS LEE, pediatric orthopedic surgeon; b. Pratt, Kans., July 9, 1948. BA, Elmhurst Coll., 1970; MD, U. Ill., Chgo., 1974. Diplomate Nat. Bd. Med. Examiners, Am. Bd. Orthopaedic Surgery. Gen. surgery intern Akron (Ohio) City Hosp., 1974-75, resident in orthopaedic surgery, 1975-79; fellow pediatric orthopaedic surgery Alfred I. DuPont Inst. of Nemours Found., Wilmington, Del., 1979-80; dir. orthopaedic surgery Children's Mercy Hosp., Kansas City, Mo., 1980—; assoc. prof. U. Mo., Kansas City, 1984—. Contbr. articles to profl. and scholarly jours. Bd. dirs. Mo. Easter Seal Soc., 1982—, Heartland's Sch. Riding for Handicapped, Shawnee Mission, Mo., 1982—. Fellow Am. Acad. Orthopaedic Surgeons; mem. AMA, Pediatric Orthopaedic Soc. of N.Am., Am. Acad. Cerebral Palsy and Devel. Medicine, Mid-Am. Orthopaedic Assn. Office: Children's Mercy Hosp 24th at Gillham Rd Kansas City MO 64108

SCHMIDT-JANOSIK, WENDY TERESA, therapist; b. Green Bay, Wis., Apr. 13, 1951; d. Arthur William and Armella Elizabeth (Rieneger) Schmidt; m. Richard Barry Janosik, May 28, 1982. BS, U. Wis., Green Bay, 1978; MA, Northeastern Ill. U., 1985. Dir. restitution project of Green Bay 1978-80; family therapist Bellin Meml. Hosp., Green Bay, 1980-82, Martha Washington Hosp., Chgo., 1982-83; health educator North Care Med. Group, Des Plaines, Ill., 1983-85; therapist Parkside Lodge of Mundelein, Ill., 1985—. Author: Stress Management, Weight, 1983, Management, Lifestyle, 1983; coauthor: Jenny Takes Charge Coloring Book, 1983. Vol. Ill. Masonic Hospice, Chgo., 1985.

SCHMIDTKE, STEVEN R., sales executive; b. Wausau, Wis.; s. Robert William and Blanche Louise (Swan) S.; m. Jean Louise Sylvester, Aug. 25, 1973; children: Heidiann, Heather. BA in Psychology, Valparaiso U., 1972. Sales rep. Graham Paper Co., Maywood, Ill., 1972-74, Breon Labs,, N.Y.C., 1974-75; sales rep. Jobst Inst., Inc., Toledo, Ohio, 1975-80, regional sales mgr., 1980—. Republican. Avocations: computer science, golf. Office: Jobst Inst Inc 653 Miami St Toledo OH 43694

SCHMIG, DARWIN DUANE, auditor, accountant; b. Aberdeen, S.D., July 1, 1957; s. Harold Robert and Alta Lorraine (Misslitz) S.; m. Dianna Jean Underberg, June 3, 1978; children: Raychall, Keith, Nicole. BS in Bus. Adminstrn., U. S.D., 1979. CPA. Auditor Dept. Legis. Auditing, State of S.D., Pierre, 1979-82; acct. Commerce Commn., Des Moines, 1982-85; internal auditor Des Moines Area Community Coll., 1985—; bd. dirs. State Employees Credit Union, Des Moines, 1983—, chmn. auditing com., 1985—. Mem. Am. Inst. CPAs, S.D. Soc. CPAs, S.D. Bd. Accts., Iowa Bd. Accountancy. Pentecostal. Avocations: fishing, boating, coin collecting, flying. Home: 3015 Cambridge Des Moines IA 50313 Office: Des Moines Area Community Coll 2006 S Ankeny Blvd Ankeny IA 50021

SCHMISEK, JOHN MICHAEL, JR., deputy city auditor; b. Grand Forks, N.D., Aug. 5, 1946; s. John Michael Sr. and Loretta Margaret (Lacey) S.; m. Wanda Rae Littlejohn, Nov. 4, 1972; children: Ryan Michael, Tara Lyn. BBA in Acctg., U. N.D., 1969. CPA, N.D. Acct. City of Grand Forks, 1971-76, dep. city auditor, 1976—. Served with U.S. Army, 1969-71. Mem. Am. Inst. CPA's, N.D. Soc. CPA's, Govt. Fin. Officers Assn. Avocations: model railroading, fishing, golfing, hunting. Office: City of Grand Forks PO Box 1518 Grand Forks ND 58206

SCHMIT, DAVID HERMAN, priest, religious organization administrator; b. Fairmount, N.D., May 3, 1925; s. Mathias and Matilda Elizabeth (Smith) S. BA in Philosophy and Classical Languages, St. John's U., Collegeville, Minn., 1950; postgrad., St. John's Sem., Collegeville, 1951-54. Ordained priest Roman Cath. Ch., 1951. Asst. pastor St. Mary Parish, Grand Forks, N.D., 1954-61, co-pastor, 1970-75; pastor St. Bernard Parish, Oriska, N.D., 1961-62; staff Cardinal Muench Sem., Fargo, N.D., 1962-64; pastor St. Vincent DePaul Parish, Leeds, N.D., 1962-70, St. Margaret Mary Parish, Drake, N.D., 1975—; with N.D. Conf. Chs., Bismarck, 1981-86, pres., 1985-86; pres. Diocesan Ecumenical Commn., Fargo, 1981-84. Served with U.S. Army, 1943-45, ETO. Mem. Nat. Assn. Diocesan Ecumenical Officers (bd. dirs. 1982-84). Avocations: jogging, golf. Home: PO Box 197 Drake ND 58736 Office: ND Conf of Chs 218 N Fourth St Bismarck ND 58501

SCHMIT, KENNETH WILLIAM, manufacturing executive; b. Sheboygan, Wis., Mar. 16, 1935; s. William Michael and Catherin Mary (Weber) S.; m. Geraldine Louise Parker, Oct. 5, 1957; Children: Andrew, Marten, William, Tina Marie, Barbara. Machinist Rice Pump & Machine Co., Belgium, Wis., 1954-55, purchasing agt., 1955-58, sales mgr., 1959-63, 1959-63; sales mgr. Medalist State Foundry, Cedar Grove, Wis., 1963-70; pres. Medalist Rein Leitzke, Hustisford, Wis., 1970—. Trustee Belgium Village Bd., 1962-63. Lodge: Lions (pres. 1967). Avocations: hunting, fishing. Home: 532 Main St Belgium WI 53004

SCHMITT, DENNIS LEE, veterinarian; b. Springfield, Mo., Nov. 25, 1947; s. Ivan Lee and Helen Elizabeth (Dickens) S.; m. Phyllis June Sell, July 14, 1967; children: Brian Lee, Brock Alan. BS in Agrl. Edn., U. Mo., 1969, MS in Dairy Husbandry, 1974, DVM, 1978, PhD in Reproductive Physiology, 1986. Diplomate Am. Coll. Theriogenology. Instr. vocat. agriculture, Forsyth, Mo., 1969-71, Willard, Mo., 1972-73; pvt. practice vet. medicine ltd. to bovine reprodn., Republic, Mo., 1978—; staff veterinarian Dickerson Park Zoo, Springfield, Mo.; ptnr. S&S Transplants, 1982-85; owner Reproductive Resources, 1985—; adj. faculty S.W. Mo. State U. Mem. AVMA, Am. Assn. Zoo Veterinarians, Am. Fertility Soc., Mo. Vet. Med. Assn., Theriogenology Soc., Internat. Embryo Transplant Soc. Mem. Ch. of Christ. Home and office: Route 2 Box 188 Republic MO 65738

SCHMITT, MARK F., bishop; b. Algoma, Wis., Feb. 14, 1923. Ed., Salvatorian Sem., St. Nazianz, Wis., St. John's Sem., Collegeville, Minn. Ordained priest Roman Cath. Ch., 1948; titular bishop of Ceanannus Mor and aux. bishop of Green Bay 1970-78, bishop of Marquette (Mich.), 1978—. Office: Chancery Office 444 S 4th St PO Box 550 Marquette MI 49855 *

SCHMITT, MARK JAMES, social worker; b. Algoma, Wis., Feb. 4, 1950; s. John J. and Marjorie (Koss) S.; m. Nola Ann Satrom, June. 2, 1973; children: Julie Ann, Sara Marie. BA, Saint John's U., Collegeville, Minn., 1972; M in Social Work, Western Mich. U., Kalamazoo, 1976. Registered social worker, Wis. Forensic social worker Mendota Mental Health Inst., Madison, Wis., 1976-78; social worker VA Med. Ctr., Eau Claire, Wis., 1978—. Pres. St. Olaf's Parish Council, Eau Claire, 1982-85; sec. bd. dirs. Cath. Charities Inc. Diocese La. Crosse, Wis., 1986-89. Mem. Nat. Assn. Social Worker (assembly del. 1981, 84, 87, sec. Wis. chpt. 1984-85, pres. elect 1985-86, pres. 1986-88), Eau Claire Jaycees (Outstanding Young Pub. Servant award 1984). Club: Saint Olaf's Mens (treas. 1980-82, bd. dirs. 1980-86, v.p. 1983-86, pres. 1987-88). Avocations: racquetball, photography, fishing, traveling. Home: 2831 Wellington Dr E Eau Claire WI 54703 Office: VA Med Ctr Fed Bldg 500 S Barstow B-1 Eau Claire WI 54701

SCHMITT, THOMAS ALLEN, psychologist; b. Joplin, Mo., Oct. 16, 1945; s. Clarence Fredrick and Marian Helen (Fier) S. BS in Biology, Mt. Union Coll., 1967; MS in Psychology, U. Akron, Ohio, 1976; EdS in Guidance and Counseling, U. Toledo, 1978. Cert. sch. psychologist, Ohio; lic. psychologist, Ohio. Psychologist Christian Psychol. Assn., Toledo, 1977—; practice psychology in assn. with psychiatrist C. Bhat Sylvania, Ohio, 1986—; cons. psychologist severe behavioral handicapped psychiat. unit St. Vincent's Hosp., Toledo, 1984-85; tchr. bus. communications U. Toledo, 1987—. Vol. Toledo Mus. Art, Toledo Symphony. Republican. Unitarian. Avocations: piano, organ, harpsichord, oil painting, collecting classic cars. Home: 2138 Dana Toledo OH 43609-1850

SCHMITZ, ANN MAUREEN, academic administrator; b. Milw., Jan. 27, 1959; d. Donald Michael and Jean Ellen (Dooley) S. Mgr. ops. Carroll Coll., Waukesha, Wis., 1980-85, purchasing agt., 1985—. Mem. Nat. Assn. Ednl. Buyers, Nat. Assn. Purchasing Mgrs., Milw. Assn. Purchasing Mgrs. Roman Catholic. Avocations: gourmet cooking, golf, travel. Home: 1218 The Strand Waukesha WI 53186 Office: Carroll Coll 100 N East Ave Waukesha WI 53186

SCHMITZ, JAMES D., osteopath; b. Bellville, Ind., Aug. 28, 1957; s. James Gerhard and Ruth Jeanine (Davis) S.; m. Lisa Marie Schmitz, May 26. 1979; 1 child, David. BS summa cum laude, Northeast Mo. State U., 1979; DO, Kirksville (mo.) Coll. Osteo. Medicine, 1983. Co-owner Big Jim's Trash Hauling and Landfill, Chgo. and East St. Louis, Ill., 1976—; dir. Steelville (Mo.) Family Practice Clinic, Inc., 1984—. Mem. Am. Osteo. Assn., Am. Acad. Osteo. Gen. Practitioners, Mo. Assn. Osteo. Physicians. Democrat. Methodist. Club: Kirksville Coll. Osteo. Medicine Rams (Right Wing 1979-83). Avocations: fishing, hunting, hockey. Home: Rt 2 573 Steelville MO 65565 Office: Steelville Family Practice PO Box 189 Steelville MO 65565

SCHMITZ, KEITH ROBERT, advertising executive; b. Port Washington, Wis., July 13, 1950; s. Wallace George and Beverly Jean (Loukes) S.; m. Judith L. SanFelippo, May 19, 1974. BA, U. Wis., Milw., 1972, MA, 1979; MS, U. Wis., 1979—. Tech. editor Johnson COntrols, Milw., 1974-77; advt. asst. Enerpac, Butler, Wis., 1977-81, advt. supr., 1981-86, mgr. mktg. communications, 1986—. Author The Milwaukee Black Community 1930-41, 1979. Dir. Black Heritage Program., Milw., 1981; cons. Black Arts Summer Experience, Milw., 1981-82; com. mem. Planned Parenthood, Milw., 1980-82. Mem. Bus. and Profl. Advt. Assn. (bd. dirs. 1986), Am. Demographic Assn., YWCA. Democrat. Roman Catholic. Avocations: reading, swimming, corss country skiing, clarinet.

SCHMITZ, MARY ELLEN, executive housekeeper; b. Centerville, Iowa, Dec. 11, 1938; d. Leonard J. and Thelma LaVelle (Thompson) Clarke; m. Lawrence H. Schmitz, Feb. 17, 1962. Student, Drake U., 1957-58, Okla. Ctr. for Continuing Edn., Okla. U., 1976. Registered exec. housekeeper. Sec., McHale, Cook & Welch, law offices, Indpls., 1964-66, U.S. Steel, Bettendorf, Iowa, 1966-67; sec. to personnel dir. Ottumwa Hosp. (Iowa), 1968-72, dir. housekeeping, 1972—; part time instr. community coll. Named Laundry Mgr. of Yr., Iowa chpt. Nat. Assn. Instl. Laundry Mgrs., 1977. Mem. Nat. Exec. Housekeepers Assn. (registered). Roman Catholic. Office: Ottumwa Regional Health Ctr 1001 E Pennsylvania Ave Ottumwa IA 52501

SCHMITZ, RICHARD FRANK, oral and maxillofacial radiologist; b. Chgo., Nov. 30, 1934; s. John Earl and Leota S. (Alstad) S. BS in Zoology, U. Ill., 1955, BS in Dentistry, 1961, DDS, 1963, MS in Radiology, 1966. Diplomate Am. Bd. Oral and Maxillofacial Radiology. Instr. U. Ill., Chgo., 1963-65, asst. prof. radiology and oral diagnosis, 1966; pvt. practice radiology La Grange, Ill., 1971—; adj. asst. prof. U. Ill., Chgo., 1975—; research assoc. ADA, Chgo., 1966-67, asst. sec., 1967-68; asst. prof. Loyola U., Chgo., 1968-69; examiner Ill. Dental Examining Com., 1971-72. Editor: Guide to Dental Materials and Devices, 1969. Served with U.S. Army, 1957-59. Fellow Am. Acad. Dental Radiology, Sigma Xi. Roman Catholic. Home and Office: 1035 S Waiola Ave La Grange IL 60525

SCHMITZ, ROGER ANTHONY, chemical engineering educator, academic administratitor; b. Carlyle, Ill., Oct. 22, 1934; s. Alfred Bernard and Wilma Afra (Aarns) S.; m. Ruth Mary Kuhl, Aug. 31, 1957; children—Jan, Joy, Joni. B.S. in Chem. Engring., U. Ill., 1959; Ph.D. in Chem. Engring., U. Minn., 1962. Prof. chem. engring. U. Ill., Urbana, 1962-79; Keating-Crawford prof. chem. engring. U. Notre Dame, Ind., 1979—, chmn. dept. chem. engring., 1979-81, dean engring., 1981-87; v.p., assoc. provost U. Notre Dame, 1987—; cons. Amoco Chems., Naperville, Ill., 1966-77; vis. prof. Calif. Inst. Tech., Los Angeles, 1968-69, U. So. Calif., Los Angeles, 1968-69. Contbr. articles to profl. jours. Served with U.S. Army, 1953-55. Guggenheim Found. fellow, 1968. Mem. Nat. Acad. Engring., Am. Inst. Chem. Engrs. (A.P. Colburn award 1970, R.H. Wilhelm award 1981), Am. Chem. Soc., Am. Soc. for Engring. Edn. (George Westinghouse award 1977). Roman Catholic. Home: 16865 Londonberry Ln South Bend IN 46635 Office: U Notre Dame 202 Adminstrn Bldg Notre Dame IN 46556

SCHMITZ, STEPHEN LOUIS, accounting executive; b. Kansas City, Kans., July 19, 1953; s. Albert Joseph and Helen Adelaide (Dulle) S.; m. Mary Ann Simpson, Aug. 12, 1972; children: Christine Marie, Sara Elizabeth. AA, Kans. City (Kans.) Community Coll., 1973; BA, Pittsburg (Kans.) State U., 1975. CPA, Kans., Mo. Sr. acct. Peat Marwick& Mitchell, Kansas City, Mo., 1975-78; controller Harmon Industries, Inc., Blue Springs, Mo., 1978—, v.p., 1983—; Bd. dirs. Modern Industries, Inc., Louisville, Electro Pneumatic, Riverside, Calif., Harmon Electronics, Grain Valley, Mo. Recipient Outstanding Young Bus. Alumnus Pittsburg State U., 1986. Mem. Am. Inst. CPA's, Nat. Assn. Accts., Mo. Soc. CPA's. Lodge: KC (treas. Blue Springs chpt. 1983-85). Avocation: racquetball. Office: Harmon Industries Inc 1900 Corp Ctr Blue Springs MO 64015

SCHMITZ, THOMAS MATHIAS, lawyer; b. Cleve., June 1, 1938; s. Augustine A. and Lenora C. (Gerhart) S.; m. Gloria E. Sabo, June 6, 1964; children: Christopher T., Susan T. BS in Chem. Engring., Case Inst. Tech., 1961; JD, Cleve.-Marshall Law Sch., 1967; MBA in Internat. Mgmt., Baldwin-Wallace Coll., 1985. Bar: Ohio 1967, U.S. Patent Office 1968; registered profl. engr., Ohio. Sr. engr. E.F. Hauserman Co., Cleve., 1964-67; patent atty. B.F. Goodrich Co., Akron, Ohio, 1967-69; assoc. Slough & Slough, Cleve., 1969-72; sr. patent atty. SCM Corp., Cleve., 1972-84, gen. patent counsel, 1984-86; gen. patent counsel, asst. gen. counsel The Glidden Co. (formerly SCM Corp.), Cleveland, 1986—. Contbr. articles to profl. jours. Bd. dirs. Fontbonne Home, Lakewood, Ohio, 1981—. Mem. ABA, Cleve. Patent Law Assn. (bd. dirs. 1975-83, 85—, pres. 1985-86), Am. Patent Law Assn. Avocation: golf. Home: 17228 Ernadale Ave Cleveland OH 44111 Office: The Glidden Co 900 Huntington Bldg 925 Euclid Ave Cleveland OH 44111

SCHMOHE, DIANNE LEE, travel agency owner; b. East St. Louis, Ill., Nov. 30, 1946; d. Arthur Auvenshine and Catherine Marcella (Sodders) Conner; m. Leo Edward Schmohe June 17, 1967 (dec. May 1979); children: Todd Edward, Debi Lynn. Student, St. Ambrose Coll., Davenport, Iowa, 1985. Lic. real estate broker, Iowa. Owner S&S Supply Co., Inc., Clinton, Iowa, 1972-85, DLS, Ltd., Davenport, 1986—. Bd. dirs. YWCA, Clinton, 1986. Republican. Lutheran. Avocations: traveling, real estate. Home: 1724 Westminster Circle Davenport IA 52807 Office: Travel Agents Internat 2136 E Kimberly Davenport IA 52807

SCHMUCKER, RUBY ELVY LADRACH, nurse, educator; b. Sugarcreek, Ohio, Nov. 17, 1923; d. Walter F. and Carrie M. (Mizer) Ladrach; R.N., Aultman Hosp., Canton, Ohio, 1945; B.S. in Nursing, U. Akron, 1970, M.S. in Edn., 1973; children—Gary, David, Barbara, Steven. Gen. duty nurse, head nurse Aultman Hosp., 1945-47, part-time, 1950-62, instr. nursing, 1962-64, 69-74; instr. nursing Coll. Nursing, U. Akron (Ohio), 1974-76; instr. div. nursing edn. Children's Hosp., Akron, 1976-78; psychiat. nurse and supr. Massillon (Ohio) State Hosp., 1978-80, cons. to nursing dept., 1980—, dir. nursing edn., 1981-84; supr. Molly Stark Hosp. and charge nurse Cuyahoga Falls Gen. Hosp., 1984—; cons. Stark-Tuscarawas Counties Student Nurses Assn., 1973-74. Health chmn. Avondale Sch. PTA, Canton, 1956, mem. coms., 1954-70; vol. instr. home nursing courses ARC, 1959-62, instr. CPR, 1979—. Cert. psychiat. nurse. Mem. Aultman Hosp. Sch. Nursing Alumni Assn., Am. Nurses' Assn., Nat. League Nursing, Am. Personnel and Guidance Assn., Am. Coll. Personnel Assn., U. Akron Alumni Assn., Alpha Sigma Lambda. Mem. Ch. of Christ. Home: 12501 Whitewater Canton OH 44708 Office: 1900 23d St Cuyahoga Falls OH 44221

SCHNACK, LARRY GENE, university chancellor; b. Harlan, Iowa, Mar. 19, 1937; s. Alvin and Twyla (Kulbom) S.; m. Carol Jean Hansen, Sept. 1, 1955; children—Lorrie, Kevin, Mark, Rachelle. B.S. in Gen. Sci., Iowa State U., 1958, Ph.D. in Organic Chemistry, 1965. Tchr. Emmons High Sch., Minn., 1958-61; mem. faculty, adminstr. U. Wis.-Eau Claire, 1965—, prof. chemistry, 1981—, chancellor, 1985—. Recipient DuPont Teaching award Iowa State U., 1965, Disting. Service award Nat. Residence Hall Hon., Eau Claire, Wis., 1984. Club: Hillcrest Country (past v.p., bd. dirs.) (Eau Claire, Wis.). Lodge: Rotary (past pres. local club).

SCHNECK, DALE ARTHUR, accountant; b. Seymour, Ind., Aug. 1, 1947; s. Maurice Arthur and Margaret Louise (Haines) S. BA, Ind. U., 1969; MBA, U. Houston, 1986. CPA, Tex., Ill. Asst. controller Nat. Ben Franklin Life, Chgo., 1978-81; acctg. mgr. Am. Gen. Corp., Houston, 1981-85; controller Nat. Fidelity Life, Overland Park, Kans., 1986—. Mem. Am. Inst. CPA's, Tex. Soc. CPA's. Home: 701 E 77th St Kansas City MO 64131 Office: National Fidelity Life 7171 W 95th PO Box 2986 Overland Park KS 66201

SCHNECKLOTH, EDWIN DONALD, photographer; b. Davenport, Iowa, June 26, 1949; s. Donald Herbert and Elaine Ann (Meewes) S.; m. Teresa Lynn Dolan, June 25, 1981; children: Joseph, Megan. BS in Indsl. Edn., Iowa State U., 1971. Self-employed farmer Davenport, 1971-73; owner, mgr. Big Ed's Photos, Davenport, 1973—; mem. adv. bd. McKenna Color Lab, Waterloo, Iowa, 1985—; supt. Miss. Valley Fair Photos, Davenport, 1985—. Mem. Profl. Photographers Am. Republican. Lutheran. Avocations: woodworking, skiing, golf, metalworking, travel. Home and Office: Rural Rt 1 Box 109 Davenport IA 52804

SCHNEE, WILLIAM JOSEPH, computer systems analyst; b. Akron, Ohio, Feb. 13, 1943; s. William Joseph and Betty Avis (Jerrow) S.; m. Patricia Lynn Rennie, July 31, 1965; children: Michael, Susan, Deborah, Christopher. AAS in Computer Sci., U. Akron, 1974, BS in Tech. Edn., 1979. Computer programmer Am. Greetings, Cleve., 1966-68; computer programmer Firestone Tire and Rubber Co., Akron, 1962-66, computer programmer, analyst, 1968-84, bus. systems analyst, 1984—. Dir. Snowfall Ministries; active Boy Scouts Am., Akron, 1964—. Democrat. Roman Catholic. Avocations: reading, classical music, hiking, gardening. Home: 987 Stadelman Ave Akron OH 44320 Office: Firestone Tire and Rubber Co 1200 Firestone Parkway Akron OH 44317

SCHNEIDER, C. REX, illustrator; b. Butler, Pa., Feb. 22, 1937; s. Cyril Leo and Alice Elizabeth (Jewell) S. BS in Edn., Ball State U., 1959. Art tchr. North Branch (Mich.) High Sch., 1959-60, Sparrows Point High Sch., Balt., 1960-61; caseworker Dept. Social Services, Balt., 1961-62; program dir. Logan Sch. for the Retarded, South Bend, Ind., 1962-64; employment counselor Balt. Assn. for the Retarded, 1964-72; graphic arts editor Performance, Balt., 1972-73; freelance illustrator Balt., 1972-79; illustrator Blue Mouse Studio, Union, Mich., 1979—; producer, set designer WNIT-TV, Elkhart, Ind., 1980-83. Co-author, graphic designer (film) Peace Talks, 1969 (Silver Medal award 1969); illustrator (books) Tom Sawyer, 1976, Call of the Wild, 1976, I'm Nobody, Who Are You?, 1978, Baltimore Nc, 1978, Big Fire in Baltimore, 1979, Movie Posters of the Silent Era, 1981, Water, 1982, Caves, 1984, Transportation, 1984, Jog, Frog, Jog, 1984, I Want A Pet, 1984; (film strip) Mexican Christmas, 1984, Halloween, 1986 (Silver Screen award), Magnets, 1986, Balance, 1986, Heat, 1986; illustrator, author (books) The Wide-Mouthed Frog, 1980, Ain't We Got Fun, 1982, That's Not All, 1984. Mem. Bonsai Soc. Kalamazoo (Mich.). Avocation: bonsai. Home: 70038 Treasure Island Union MI 49130 Office: Blue Mouse Studio Box 312 Union MI 49130

SCHNEIDER, DONALD FREDERIC, banker; b. N.Y.C., Nov. 12, 1939; s. Charles and Lillian (Anton) S.; m. Mary Patricia McCafferty, Sept. 7, 1963; children—Laurie, John. B.S., Lehigh U., 1961; M.B.A., N.Y. U., 1968. Mgmt. trainee Marine Midland Bank, N.Y.C., 1961-65; asst. sec. Marine Midland Bank, 1965-68, asst. v.p., 1968-69, v.p., 1969; v.p. 1st Nat. Bank Chgo., 1979-87; fin. cons. Cigna Individual Fin. Services Co., Chgo., 1987—; mem. corp. trust activities com. Am. Bankers Assn., fiduciary and securities ops. exec. com. Mem. Am. Soc. Corporate Secs. (pres. Chgo. region 1987), Stock Transfer Assn. Home: 399 N Valley Rd Barrington IL 60010 Office: Cigna Individual Fin Services 8700 W Bryn Mawr Suite 800 Chicago IL 60631

SCHNEIDER, DONALD NORMAN, pharmacist, educator; b. Point Clinton, Ohio, Jan. 7, 1945; s. Norman Edward and Leilia Luela (Lamalie) S.; m. Sharon Kay Asbury, Dec. 23, 1972; children—Kristen Renee, Erinn Dawn. B.S., U. Toledo, 1969; M.S., Ohio State U., 1971. Registered pharmacist, Ohio. Asst. dir. pharmacy Riverside Hosp., Columbus, Ohio, 1971-77, assoc. dir. pharmacy, 1977—; adj. asst. prof. U. Toledo, Ohio, 1979—; asst. clin. prof. Ohio State U., Columbus, 1981—. Contbr. articles to profl. jours. Co-chmn. Ohio Pharmacy's Centennial Celebration, Columbus, 1984. Recipient Merck award Merck & Co., 1969. Mem. Am. Soc. Hosp. Pharmacists, Ohio Soc. Hosp. Pharmacists (pres. 1984-85), Ohio State Pharm. Assn., Central Ohio Soc. Hosp. Pharmacists (pres. 1975-76), Rho Chi. Republican. Roman Catholic. Avocations: woodworking; gardening; cross country skiing; guitar playing. Home: 7254 Davis Rd Hilliard OH 43026 Office: Riverside Meth Hosp 3535 Olentangy River Rd Columbus OH 43214

SCHNEIDER, FERD RICHARD, accountant; b. Cin., Apr. 10, 1938; s. Ferd George and Mildred Frances (Phillips) S.; m. Barbara Ann Wenz, May 28, 1966; children: Ferd M., Matthew E., Martin A. BBA, U. Cin., 1962. Internal auditor Procter & Gamble Corp., Cin., 1962-65, cost acct., 1965-69, fin. analyst, 1969-72, mgr. gen acctg., 1972—. Roman Catholic. Home: 3373 Treasure Ct Cincinnati OH 45211 Office: Procter & Gamble 2 Procter & Gamble Plaza Cincinnati OH 45202

SCHNEIDER, FREDERICK P., food products company executive. Chmn., chief exec. officer Schneider Corp., Waterloo, Ont., Can. Office: Schneider Corp, 175 Columbia St W, Waterloo, ON Canada N2J 4M3 *

SCHNEIDER, GARY PAUL, accountant educator; b. Cin., July 16, 1952; s. Anthony J. and Elaine M. (Silbernagel) S.; m. M. Linda Tracy, June 1972 (div. June 1977); m. Donna Behler, Nov. 14, 1978 (div. Nov. 1986). BA, U. Cin., 1973; postgrad., U. Cin, 1980—; MBA, Xavier U., Cin., 1975. CPA, Ohio. Trust officer Provident Bank, Cin., 1975-76; pvt. practice acctg. Cin., 1976-80; instr. acctg. U. Cin., 1980-82; asst. prof. acctg. No. Ky. U., Highland Heights, 1982-85; asst. prof. Xavier U., 1985—; bd. dirs. Morrison Greenhouses, Inc., Loveland, Ohio. Author: Fundamentals of Estate Planning, 1980; contbg. editor: (book series) Solutions to the Uniform CPA Examination, 1979, 80, 81, 82. Mem. Am. Acctg. Assn. (doctoral consortium fellow), Am. Inst. CPA's, Mensa, Beta Gamma Sigma. Home: 1149 Devils Backbone Rd Cincinnati OH 45238 Office: Xavier U Hinkle Hall Cincinnati OH 45207

SCHNEIDER, GEORGE HENRY, chemical engineer, electronics executive; b. Anchorage, Dec. 30, 1952; s. Lloyd William and Mary Ellen (Lewellen) S.; m. Cynthia Lynn Bartlett, Aug. 14, 1973; children: Erin Joy, Kathryn Ann, Patrick Reed, Susan Nicole. BSChemE, U. Nebr., 1975; MSChemE, W.Va. Coll. Grad. Studies, 1977; MBA, Rider Coll., 1980. Prodn. supr. Mallinckrodt, Inc., St. Louis, 1980-83; prodn., engr. mgr. Mallinckrodt, Inc., Paris, Ky., 1983-84; mgr. prodn. engring. Dale Electronics, Inc., Norfolk, Nebr., 1984—. Pres. Dist. 3 Sch. Bd., Norfolk, 1985-88; area coordinator Operation Brightside, St. Louis mayor's office, 1981, 82. Mem. Am. Inst. Chem. Engrs. Republican. Baptist. Avocations: auto mechanics, home repair. Home: 4301 W Benjamin Ave Norfolk NE 68701 Office: Dale Electronics Inc PO Box 74 Norfolk NE 68701

SCHNEIDER, HAROLD JOEL, radiologist; b. Cin., Aug. 9, 1923; s. Henry W. and Sarah Miriam (Hauser) S.; m. Mary Zipperstein, Dec. 23, 1945; children—Jill, Elizabeth, Ann, Jane. M.D., U. Cin., 1947. Diplomate: Am. Bd. Radiology. Intern Cin. Gen. Hosp., 1947-48, resident in radiology, 1953-56; resident in surgery Holzer Hosp. and Clinic, Gallipolis, Ohio, 1948-49; gen. practice medicine Dayton, Ohio, 1949-50; asst. prof. radiology U. Ala. Med. Sch., Birmingham, 1956-59; assoc. prof. radiology U. Cin. Med. Center, 1959-69, prof. radiology, 1969—; dir. diagnostic radiology Christian R. Holmes Hosp., 1959—; cons. Cin. VA Hosp. Contbr. articles to profl. jours. Served to lt. USNR, 1950-52. Fellow Am. Coll. Radiology; mem. Radiol. Soc. N. Am., Am. Roentgen Ray Soc., Assn. Am. Med. Coll., AAUP, Am. Geriatrics Soc., Ohio Radiol. Soc., Ohio Med. Soc., Greater Cin. Radiol. Soc., Cin. Acad. Medicine, Brit. Inst. Radiology. Home: 7290 Elbrook Ave Cincinnati OH 45237 Office: Holmes Hosp Eden and Bethesda Ave Cincinnati OH 45219

SCHNEIDER, HENRY WOLFGANG, real estate developer; b. Stutgart, Republic of Germany, July 17, 1946; s. Joseph and Ellen (Seider) S.; m. Barbara Lee Zuber, June 9, 1967; children: Benjamin, Stephen. BBA, U. Cin., 1969. V.p. Housing Mgmt. Corp., Cin., 1968-75; pres. E. Galbraith Health Care Ctr., Cin., 1976—, R.H. Investments, Cin., 1977—. Mem. Am. Health Care Assn., Acad. Nursing Homes (exec. com. 1979—). Home: 6980 Given Rd Cincinnati OH 45243 Office: RH Investments 3801 E Galbraith Rd Cincinnati OH 45236

SCHNEIDER, JAMES FREDERICK, lawyer; b. St. Paul, Oct. 10, 1953; s. Frank Jr. and June Margaret (Hensel) S.; m. Sandra Thompson, Sept. 16, 1983; 1 child, Leigh Katherine. BA, Coll. St. Thomas, 1975; JD, Hamline U., 1978. Bar: Minn. 1978. Ptnr. St. Paul, 1978—. Served to 2d lt. USAFR, 1976-77. Mem. Minn. Trial Lawyers Assn., Minn. Bar Assn., Ramsey County Bar Assn. Democrat. Roman Catholic. Club: Forest Hills Golf (pres.), Arden Hills Tennis. Avocations: golf, tennis, bridge, hunting, fishing. Home: 1136 Summer St Saint Paul MN 55113 Office: Butts Sandberg & Schneider 155 S Lake St Forest Lake MN 55025

SCHNEIDER, MARVIN WALTER, engineer; b. Appleton, Wis., Apr. 21, 1936; s. Joseph Peter and Christina (Vander Zanden) S.; m. Ramona Julia Schneider, Aug. 16, 1972; children: Timothy, Katherine, Terrence. BSEE, U. Wis., 1970. Project engr. Unico Inc., Racine, Wis., 1970-73; sales engr. Struthers Dunn Inc., Bettendorf, Iowa, 1973-75; chief elec. engr. Ametek Inc., East Moline, Ill., 1975-77; project engr. Essex Corp., Ft. Wayne, Ind., 1977-78; prodn. engr. Honeywell, Mpls., 1978—. Served with U.S. Army, 1959-62. Mem. IEEE. Avocations: tennis, investments, card games. Home: 5208 Birchcrest Dr Edina MN 55436 Office: Honeywell Twin Cities Arsenal New Brighton MN 55112

SCHNEIDER, PHILIP JAMES, pharmacist, educator, editor; b. Toledo, Aug. 29, 1947; s. Stanley Dale and Marcella (Degan) S.; m. Candace Gentile, May 27, 1972; children Gretchen, Karl. B.S., U. Wis., 1970; M.S., Ohio State U., 1975. Assoc. dir. pharmacy Ohio State U. Hosp., Columbus, 1975-78, assoc. dir., 1978—; pres. Clin. Pharm. Cons., 1982—; Assoc. clin. prof. pharmacy and surgery Ohio State U. Editor-in-chief Nutrition in Clin. Practice. Mem. Am. Soc. Hosp. Pharmacists, Am. Soc. Parenteral and Enteral Nutrition (bd. dirs. 1982-86), Central Ohio Soc. Hosp. Pharmacists (pres. 1983-84), Ohio Soc. Hosp. Pharmacists, Am. Pharm. Assn. Avocations: sailing, golf. Home: 835 Chelsea Ave Columbus OH 43209 Office: Ohio State U Hosp 410 W 10th Ave Columbus OH 43210

SCHNEIDER, SALLY LORRAINE, obstetrician-gynecologist, anesthesiologist; b. Friend, Nebr., Sept. 22, 1943; s. Lloyd William and Mary Ellen (Lewellen) Schneider; m. Roger William Smith, Aug. 16, 1979; 1 child, John Roger. BS, U. Nebr., Lincoln, 1965; MD, U. Nebr., Omaha, 1968. Cert. Am. Bd. Ob-Gyn., Am. Bd. Anesthesia. Resident in ob-gyn. U. Nebr., Omaha, 1969-72; practice medicine specializing in ob-gyn. Olmstead Med. Group, Rochester, Minn., 1972-76; resident in anesthesia U. Iowa, Iowa City, 1976-78; practice medicine specializing in obstetrical anesthesia St. John's Mercy Hosp., St. Louis, 1978—. Fellow Am. Coll. Ob-Gyn.; mem. Am. Soc. Anesthesiologists, St. Louis Met. Med. Soc. Office: St Johns Mercy Med Ctr 621 S New Ballas Rd Saint Louis MO 63141

SCHNEIDER, STEVEN EUGENE, training counselor, educator; b. Swansea, Ill., Nov. 9, 1952; s. Alvin Peter and Marie M. (Wimmer) S.; m. Sheryl Marie Deitz, May 8, 1976; children—Sarah Abigail, Benjamin Issac. A.A. in English, Belleville Area Coll., 1972; B.A. in Teaching of English, U. Ill., 1974. Cert. secondary tchr., Ill. Tchr. St. Dominic Sch., Breese, Ill., 1975-79, St. Albert Sch., Fairview Heights, Ill., 1979-81; chief deputy county clk. St. Clair County, Belleville, Ill., 1981-82, dir. property mgmt. Housing Authority, 1982-83, tng. counselor, Intergovernmental Grants Dept., 1983-85, recruitment specialist, 1985-87, supr. client relations, 1987—; instr. Belleville Area Coll., 1987—; mem. steering com. Belleville Diocesan Speech League, 1979-80, chmn., 1980-81; sgt. at arms, St. Clair County Young Dems., 1986—; mem. Belleville News-Dem. Citizen Adv. Bd., 1986—, Kaskaskia Reading Council, Centralia, Ill., 1975-79. writer, dir. (play) A Christmas Play, 1977, The Christmas Caper, 1978. Pres. Belleville Community Theatre, 1974; bd. dirs. Comet Productions Inc.-Community Entertainment Services, 1983, pres., 1984-86; dir. community theatre prodns., 1983, 86, 87. Mem. U. Ill. Alumni Assn., Ill. Employment and Tng. Assn., St. Clair County League of Women Voters, So. Ill. Arts Assn. (resource devel. com. 1985, bd. dirs. 1986—). Roman Catholic. Club: St. Peter Cathedral Men's Choir (Belleville) (sec. 1984). Avocations: camping; reading; amateur/community theater. Home: 301 Anna St Swansea IL 62221 Office: Saint Clair County Intergovtl Grants Dept 512 E Main St Belleville IL 62221

SCHNELL, THEODORE ALLEN, insurance company officer, architect; b. Evanston, Ill., Feb. 16, 1948; s. Theodore Alphonse and Francis Elizabeth (Danley) S.; m. Barbara Elizabeth Shivvers, Sept. 29, 1973. Student, No. Mich. U., Marquette, 1966-68; BArch, U. Ill., 1973. Registered architect, Ill. Architect Consoer/Townsend, Chgo., 1974-78; project mgr. Allstate Ins. Co., Northbrook, Ill., 1978-82, investment mgr., 1983-85, dir. real estate investments, 1985-86, asst. treas. investments, 1986—. Mem. AIA, Red Ribbon Soc., Sigma Alpha Epsilon. Avocations: photography, racquetball, basketball. Home: 345 Park Ave Glencoe IL 60022 Office: Allstate Ins Co Allstate Plaza E-4 Northbrook IL 60062

SCHNELLER, GEORGE CHARLES, chiropractor; b. St. Louis, Feb. 22, 1921; s. Michael Alois and Eleanora Christine (Weber) S.; m. Dorothy Virginia Doran, Mar. 6, 1943; children—George Charles, Judith Ann. D. Chiropractic, Mo. Chiropractic Coll., 1946, Ph.Chiropractic, 1946. Ordained priest Anglican Orthodox Ch., 1973. Gen. practice chiropractic, St. Louis, 1946—; chiropractic staff Lindell Hosp., St. Louis; faculty Mo. Chiropractic Coll., 1947-51, dean, 1957-61. Fellow Internat. Chiropractors Assn.; mem. Mo. Acad. Chiropractors (pres. 1970-75), Dist. One Mo. State Chiropractic Assn. (pres. 1952). Clubs: Kiwanis (past pres. Maplewood, Mo.), Moose. Office: 3538 Jamieson Ave Saint Louis MO 63139

SCHNOBRICH, FORREST PAUL, insurance agent, realtor; b. Avery, Iowa, Nov. 22, 1942; s. Everal Arther and Winona Kathleen (Gailey) S.; m. Carolyn Gwen Smith, Aug. 6, 1966; children: Amy, Tracy. BS in Secondary Edn., N.W. Mo. State U., 1965; MA in Secondary Edn., N.E. Mo. State U., 1972. Tchr., coach Atlantic (Iowa) Community Schs., 1965-67, English Valleys Schs., North English, Iowa, 1967-68, 70-71, North Fayette Community Schs., West Union, Iowa, 1971-73; ins. agt., agy. owner Ins. Store Ltd., Adair, Iowa, 1973—. Pres. Casey (Iowa) Service Club, 1985-86, Adair C. of C., 1975, Good Shepherd Luth. Ch., Adair, 1984. Served with U.S. Army, 1968-70, Vietnam. Mem. Ins. Agts. Am., Ins. Agts. Iowa (bd. dirs., instr. 1981-83), Farmers Mut. Fire Ins. Assn. Guthrie County (bd. dirs. 1982-86). Republican. Lodges: Masons, Order Eastern Star. Avocations: hunting, fishing, camping. Home: 708 4th St Adair IA 50002 Office: Ins Store Ltd 318 Audubon Adair IA 50002

SCHNOERING, JAMES ALLEN, professional society administrator; b. Lakewood, Ohio, Feb. 26, 1948; s. William E. and Shirley G. (Bowman) S.; m. Fernabelle K. Schnoering, Sept. 3, 1966; children: Melissa Ann, Michelle Jennet. Student, Miami-Dade Community Coll., 1965-66. Asst. exec. v.p. Nat. Exchange Club, Toledo, 1970-83, exec. v.p., 1983—, also bd. dirs.; sec., treas. Nat. Exchange Club Found. Prevention Child Abuse, 1982—. Editor-in-chief The Exchangite mag. Active Northwest Ohio Jr. Achievement, Young Life; bd. dirs. Nat. Crime Prevention Coordinating Com.; mem. Toledo Mayor's com. Neighborhood Block Watch, Community Relations Com. Boy Scouts Am., Toledo Mus. Art. Mem. Am. Soc. Assn. Execs., Am. Mgmt. Assn., Toledo Area C. of C. Republican. Roman Catholic. Avocations: gardening, antique autos. Home: 1828 Parkside Blvd Toledo OH 43607 Office: Nat Exchange Club 3050 Central Ave Toledo OH 43606

SCHNUCK, CRAIG, grocery stores company executive; b. 1948. MBA, Cornell U., 1971. With Schnuck Markets, Inc., Hazelwood, Mo., 1971—, v.p., 1975-76, exec. v.p., sec., 1976-83, pres., 1983—, also bd. dirs. Office: Schnuck Markets Inc 12921 Enterprise Way Bridgeton MO 63044 *

SCHNUCK, DONALD O., retail grocery store company executive; b. 1922. V.p. Schnuck Markets, Inc., Hazelwood, Mo., 1957-70, pres., chief exec. officer, 1970-83, chmn. bd. dirs., 1983—. Office: Schnuck Markets Inc 12921 Enterprise Way Bridgeton MO 63044 *

SCHODOWSKI, JOHN JOSEPH, sales executive, mathematician; b. Detroit, Sept. 10, 1928; s. Frank A. and Julia Veronica (Marjezon) S.; m. Helen Elizabeth Frank, May 5, 1956; children: Anne, John, Robert, Michael, Frank, Joseph, Joan. BS, St. Mary's Coll., Winona, Minn., 1951. Pres. Shelving Inc., Auburn Hills, Mich., 1961—. Served to lt. (j.g.) USCG, 1951-53. Mem. Detroit Engring. Soc. Republican. Roman Catholic. Home and Office: 175 Grosse Pines Ct Rochester MI 48063

SCHOELD, CONSTANCE JERRINE, financial planner, investment broker; b. Wichita, Kans., July 20, 1935; d. Joe Delos and Volna May (Liston) Lumbert; m. Edmund Allan Schoeld, Oct. 4, 1953 (div. Dec. 1974); children: Nancy Ann., Elsa Charlene, Jennie Marie, Brian Shelton, Richard Zweibruck. Student, St. Olaf Coll., 1953-54, Lindenwood Coll., 1960-62, U. Mich., 1967-68, Harper Jr. Coll., 1970. Cert. fin. planner. Mgr. Walden Books, Schaumburg, Ill., 1972-74; owner Books, Etc., Mt. Prospect, Ill., 1974-77; sales rep. Fawcett Books/CBS, N.Y.C., 1977-78, Lawyers Cooperative Pub., Rochester, N.Y., 1978-83; owner Associated Lawyers Service, Palatine, Ill., 1982-86; broker investments A.G. Edwards & Sons, Aurora and Roselle, Ill., 1983—. Sec. Rep. Orgn. Schaumburg Twp., 1970, Northwest Mental Health/Retardation Ctr., Arlington Hts., Ill., 1971, Mental Health Ctr. Elk Grove/Schaumburg Twp., Ill., 1970-72, vice chmn., bd. dirs.; v.p. PTA, St. Charles, Mo., 1964; pres. St. Charles Girl Scouts Am., 1965-66; mem. com. Dist. 54 Bd. Edn., Schaumburg, 1969-72; bd. dirs. Mental Health Ctr. St. Charles, 1963-66, Mental Health Ctr. Schaumburg Twp., chmn. 1969-72. Named one of Outstanding Young Women Am., 1964. Mem. Internat. Bd. Cert. Fin. Planners, League Women Voters (bd. dirs. St. Charles 1964-66, Hoffman Estates/Schaumburg 1969-71), DAR (outstanding mem. award 1964), Greater O'Hare Assn., Nat. Assn. Women in Careers, Nat. Assn. Female Execs., Epsilon Sigma Alpha (outstanding mem. award 1970). Republican. Episcopalian. Avocations: bridge, travel, sewing, art. Office: 1350 W Lake St Roselle IL 60172

SCHOELLHORN, ROBERT A., pharmaceutical company executive; b. Phila., 1928. Grad., Phila. Coll. Textiles and Sci., 1957. With Am. Cyanamid Co., 1947-73; pres. Lederle Labs., 1971-73; with Abbott Labs., North Chicago, Ill., 1973—; exec. v.p. hosp. group Abbott Labs., 1973-76, pres., 1976-81, chief operating officer, 1976-79, 85—, chief exec. officer, 1979—, chmn. bd., 1981—, also dir. Office: Abbott Labs Abbott Park 22d and Waukegan Rd North Chicago IL 60064 *

SCHOEMEHL, VINCENT CHARLES, JR., mayor; b. St. Louis, Oct. 30, 1946; s. Vincent Charles and Lucille (Miller) S.; m. Lois Brockmeier, Sept. 18, 1971; children—Timothy Martin, Joseph Vincent. B.A. in History, U. Mo., 1972. Alderman 28th Ward, St. Louis, 1975-81; mayor City of St. Louis, 1981—. Democrat. Roman Catholic. Office: Mayor's Office Room 200 Tucker and Market St St Louis MO 63103

SCHOEN, CARL EDGAR, inventor, model builder, baseball researcher; b. St. Louis, Sept. 11, 1936; s. Carl Bernard and Mary Mildred (Heath) S. Inventor baseball related games, designer and builder baseball stadium models Sulphur Springs, Mo., 1963—. Designer Fenway Park model for baseball historian Paul MacFarlane, St. Louis, 1985-86; builder several baseball stadium models for St. Louis area writer, 1980-86; designer stadium model displays in Belleville, Ill., 1985 and Webster Groves, Mo., 1986; patentee mech. baseball game, 1968; inventor baseball card games, 1982-84; designer, builder (with Tim Heitman) model of N.Y. Polo Grounds, 1981. Home and Office: PO Box 52 Sulphur Springs MO 63083

SCHOEN, JANICE LU, business educator; b. Herrin, Ill., July 31, 1946; d. Wayne Pulley and Helen Ivy (Rendleman) Sirles; m. Paul Gerald Schoen, June 11, 1967 (div. Jan. 1985); 1 child, Suzanne Kay. BS, So. Ill. U., 1968; MEd, U. Ill., 1970; PhD, So. Ill. U., 1987. Cert. bus. tchr., Ill. Tchr. Cen. High Sch., Champaign, Ill., 1968-70; instr. John A. Logan Coll., Carterville, Ill., 1970-75; instr. So. Ill. U., Carbondale, 1974-79, asst. prof. bus., 1979—; teletypist, sec. Lamson Brother and Co., Carbondale, 1968; coordinator shorthand So. Ill. U., Carbondale, 1981—. Author: Business Education World, 1985; co-author: Index to Doctoral Dissertations in Business Education, 1980-85. Pres., sec., bd. dirs. pta Winkler Elem. Sch., Carbondale, 1976-79; sec. area Girl Scout Council, Carbondale, 1981-83; sec. pta Lincoln Jr. High Sch., Carbondale, 1984-85. William E. Nagel award Voc. Edn. Studies, 1985. Mem. Am. Vocat. Assn., Ill. Vocat. Assn., So. Ill. Bus. Edn. Assn., Ill. Bus. Edn. Assn., Beta Gamma Phi, Delta Pi Epsilon. Democrat. Congregationalist. Club: Women's Aux. (Carbondale), So. Ill. U. Women's (Carbondale). Avocations: waterskiing, cooking. Home: 615 Terrace Dr Carbondale IL 62901

SCHOEN, WILLIAM PHILIP, retired dentist; b. Chgo., Aug. 18, 1906; s. William P. and Eugenie (Steckel) S.; m. Isabel R. Summers, Apr. 9, 1932; children: Ellen Schoen Schneider, Jerome, John. DDS, Loyola U., Chgo., 1929, BS, 1938, DMS, 1943, ScD (hon.), 1983. Prof., chmn. dept. dentistry Loyola U., Chgo., 1929-73, dean Sch. Dentistry, 1956-73, dean emeritus, 1973—; gen. practice dentistry Evanston, Ill., 1973-86. Editor Ill. Dental Jour., 1942, 77; author dental materials, lab manual, 1930, 73. Mem. ADA, Ill. State Dental Soc., Wis. State Dental Soc., Chgo. Dental Soc., Odontographic Soc. (pres. 1930), Am. Assn. Dental Editors (pres. 1951), Omicron Kappa Upsilon. Avocations: boat bldg., art. Home: 9540 Hamlin Evanston IL 60623

SCHOENBECK, PAUL JOHN, transportation executive; b. Hinsdale, Ill., June 3, 1959; s. Delbert Louis and Joyce Marie (Kolzow) S. Pres., owner Uni-Carrier Inc., Willowbrook, Ill., 1977—. Asst. fin. sect. Good Shepherd Ch., Downers Grove, Ill., 1984—. Mem. Am. Mktg. Assn. (cons.1985—), Fleet Owners (Community Service award 1985), Willowbrook C. of C., Ill. C. of C. Lutheran. Home: 218 Brookside Ln C Willowbrook IL 60514 Office: Uni Carrier Inc 7886 S Quincy St Willowbrook IL 60521

SCHOENEBECK, KAREN PEARL, accountant, educator; b. Ripon, Wis., Aug. 17, 1954; d. Robert Elroy and Carol Mae (Flugum) Meyer; m. Dennis Mark Schoenebeck, July 19, 1975; children: Casey, Grant. MBA, U. Minn., 1982. Acct. Shinners, Hucouski, & Co., S.C., Green Bay, Wis., 1981-86; asst. prof. acctg. St. Norbert Coll., DePere, Wis., 1986—. Gen. Mills. Corp. fellow, 1979. Mem. Wis. Inst. CPA's., Am. Assn. Univ. Women (activity group chairperson 1982-83). Republican. Presbyterian. Avocations: travel, arts and crafts, singing. Home: 725 Eau Claire Place DePere WI 54115 Office: St Norbert Coll DePere WI 54115

SCHOENEBERG, DEBRA SUE, graphic designer; b. Amory, Miss., Nov. 30, 1953; d. Kenneth Walter and Margaret Christina (Linville) S. Assoc. of tech., Am. Acad. Art, 1974. Artist J & J Publs., Evanston, Ill., 1974-75; dir. art Ken Roush & Assocs., Lincolnwood, Ill., 1975-76, Hahn, Crane Advt., Chgo., 1976-82; owner Schöeneberg Design, Evanston, 1982—. Recipient Chgo. Addy award Am. Advt. Fedn. 6th Dist., 1980, Cert. of Excellence Direct Mktg. Echo, 1980, Cert. of Achievement Chgo. Assn. Direct Mktg., 1984, Desi award Graphic Design USA, 1987; named Ad Woman of Yr. nominee, 1982. Mem. Women in Design/Chgo. (designer/coordinator newsletter 1986—, bd. dirs. 1986—, Cert. Excellence, 1985), Women's Advt. Club Chgo. Presbyterian. Avocations: knitting, travel, antiques, art galleries, cooking. Home and Office: 337 Sherman Ave Evanston IL 60202

SCHOENENBERGER, TOM ALAN, publisher; b. Canton, Ill., Dec. 19, 1940; s. John Harold and Mary Grace (Morgan) S.; m. Virginia Caroline Potratz, Sept. 29, 1962; children: Scott, Heidi, Denise, Paula. Grad. high sch., Maynard, Iowa, 1958. Operator Westgate (Iowa) DX, 1959-61; dist. mgr. Rockford (Ill.) Life Ins., 1961-63; area mgr. Old Northwest Co., Mpls., 1963-76; state mgr. Rockford Map Publ., 1976-78; chief exec. officer M.A.P.S. Midwestern, Oelwein, Iowa, 1978—; co-founder Re-Unite Inc., 1987; owner, chief exec. officer Upper Midwest Pubs., 1987. Precinct chmn. Fayette County Dem. Party, Oelwein, 1980; officer Oelwein Jaycees, 1970-76; sect. chmn., edn. chmn. Peace Luth. Ch., Oelwein, 1964-72; mktg. chmn. Fayette County Tourism Assn., 1987. Named one of Outstanding Young Men of Am., 1976; recipient various awards Oelwein Jaycees, 1972-76. Democrat. Lutheran. Avocations: reading, travel. Home: 203 5 Ave SW Oelwein IA 50662 Office: M A P S Midwestern City Park Rd Oelwein IA 50662

SCHOENMAN, KIRK LEE, chiropractor; b. Mansfield, Ohio, Apr. 29, 1957; s. Kenneth J. and Joan A. (Snyder) S.; m. Nancy E. Fasz, June 20, 1980; children: Ryan, Christopher. BS, Ohio State U., 1979; postgrad., U. Miami, Coral Gables, Fla., 1975-77; D Chiropractic magna cum laude, Life Chiropractic Coll., 1983. Diplomate Am. Bd. Chiropractic Examiners. Gen.

practice chiropractic medicine Columbus, Ohio, 1983—. Mem. Am. Chiropractic Assn., Fla. Chiropractic Assn., Ohio Chiropractic Assn. Lodge: Optimists. Avocations: hunting, outdoor activities. Home: 6250 Emberwood Rd Dublin OH 43017 Office: 2965 Donnylane Blvd Columbus OH 43220

SCHOENNAUER, ALFRED W.W., business professor, management consultant; b. Seattle, Sept. 3, 1923; s. Arthur C.J. and Ida A. (Welk) S.; m. Nelda A. Meyer, Feb. 15, 1958; children: Mark W., Cheryl, Sandra, Debra. BA, U. Wash., 1950, MBA, 1959; PhD, UCLA, 1962. Asst. prof. bus. Ariz. State U., Tempe, 1961-63; prof. Portland (Oreg.) State U., 1963-75, Mankato (Minn.) State U., 1975—; mgr. traffic Superior Portland Cement Corp., Seattle, 1955-58; div. traffic mgr. Lone Star Cement Corp., Seattle, 1955-58; lectr. U. Adelaide, South Australia, 1972-74. Author: Problem Finding and Problem Solving, 1981, (booklet) The Formulation and Implementation of Corporate Objectives and Strategies, 1972; contbr. articles to profl. jours. Rep. precinct chmn., Mankato, Minn., 1986. Served with U.S. Army, 1943-46. Mem. Phi Beta Kappa, Beta Alpha Psi. Republican. Lutheran. Home: 105 Thro Ave Mankato MN 56001 Office: Mankato State U Coll Bus Mankato MN 56001

SCHOENOFF, ARTHUR WILLIAM, music educator, consultant; b. Waverly, Iowa, Apr. 24, 1930; s. Arthur Frederick and Evaline Maragetha (Stahl) S.; m. Ann Louise Lane, Feb. 24, 1952; children: Jon Frederic, Joanna Louise, Ellen Elisabeth. Tchr. vocal, instrumental, gen. music. Pub. Schs., Kans., Iowa, Wis., Ga., Minn., 1952—; asst. prof. music Carthage Coll., Kenosha, Wis., 1967-73; assoc. prof. music Mercer U., Macon, Ga., 1973-77; adj. asst. prof. Ga. Coll., Milledgeville, 1974-77 part-time instr. Bethel Coll., St. Paul and Anoka, Minn., Anoka-Ramsey Community Coll., Coon Rapids, Minn., 1983—; adminstr. music edn. Anoka-Hennepin Sch. dist., Coon Rapids, 1977—; pvt. instr. music., 1950—; adjudicator, clinician instrumental and vocal music., 1958. Composer, arranger instrumental music, 1953—; instrumental/vocal soloist. Bd. dirs. Racine (Wis.) Symphony Orch., 1965-72, personnel mgr., 1965-69, pres. , 1970-71; dir. Anoka-Ramsey Community Chorus, 1978-79; bd. dirs. Blaine (Minn.) Community Theater, 1987—; minister of music, chmn.Luth. Ch., Iowa, Wis., Ga., Minn., 1953—. Served with USAF, 1953-57. Doctoral fellow Luth. Ch. Am., 1969; Iowa Research grantee, 1972; recipient Cert. Recognition, Alpha Psi Omega, 1971, Mercer Spirit award, 1975. Mem. Minn. State High Sch. League (regional com., state fine arts com. 1978—), Music Educators Nat. Conf., Minn. Music Educators Assn., Minn. Music Coordinators Orgn. (pres. 1984), Soc. Research in Music Edn., Nat. String Orch. Assn., Am. Choral Dirs. Assn., Internat. Horn Soc., Nat. Assn. Coll. Wind and Percussion Instrs., Coll. Music Soc., Assn. Supervision and Curriculum Devel., Nat. Fedn. Music, Adjudicators Assn., Am. Topical Assn., Nat. Ret. Tchrs. Assn., Found for Christian Living. Republican. Club: Kogudus. Lodge: Kiwanis (bd. dirs., sec., editor bull, v.p.). Home: 1203 Norwood Ln Anoka MN 55303 Office: 11299 Hanson Blvd NW Coon Rapids MN 55433

SCHOENROCK, TRACY ALLEN, airline pilot, stock broker; b. Oshkosh, Wis., Jan. 11, 1960; s. Elder Roy and Shirley Mae (Rutz) S.; m. Kathleen Mary Neumann, Oct. 8, 1983. BS in Geography summa cum laude, U. Wis., Oshkosh, 1982. Charter pilot Basler Airlines, Oshkosh, 1977-82; pilot Simmons Airlines, Marquette, Mich., 1982-84, Northwest Airlines, St. Paul, 1984—; stockbroker Howe, Barnes & Johnson, Oshkosh, 1986—. Republican. Lutheran. Avocations: golf, travel, flying, electronics. Home: 111 Westbrook Dr Oshkosh WI 54904 Office: Howe Barnes & Johnson 21 Washington Ave Oshkosh WI 54904

SCHOENWETTER, WILLIAM FREDERICK, allergist, clinical immunologist; b. Milw., Mar. 10, 1935; s. William Martin and Ann L. Schoenwetter; m. Barbara Lee Barney; children: Jeffrey Martin, Laura Lee, Charles Joseph. BS, U. Wis., 1956, MD, 1959. Diplomate Am. Bd. Internal Medicine, Am. Bd. Allergy and Immunology. Intern Hennepin County Med. Ctr., Mpls., 1959-60; resident in internal medicine U. Minn. Hosps., Mpls., 1960-63; fellow in allergy and clin. immunology Hosp. of U. Pa., Phila., 1963-64; allergist Park Nicollet Med. Ctr., Mpls., 1964—, also bd. dirs., 1972—; clin. prof. medicine U. Minn., Mpls., 1975—; pres., bd. dirs. Medctr. Health Plan, Mpls., 1983—; pres. med. staff Meth. Hosp., Mpls., 1977. Contbr. articles to profl. jours.; mem. bd. editors Minn. Medicine. Bd. dirs. Am. Lung Assn. Hennepin County, Mpls., 1969-74. Served to capt. U.S. Army, 1966-68. Fellow Am. Coll. Physicians, Am. Acad. Allergy and Clin. Immunology; mem. Asthma and Allergy Found. Am. (v.p. Minn. chpt. 1983), Minn. Allergy Soc. Republican. Roman Catholic. Clubs: Daybreaker Breakfast (Mpls. pres. 1971-72), Decathlon (Mpls.). Avocations: fishing, waterfowl hunting. Home: 4502 Edina Blvd Edina MN 55424 Office: Park Nicollet Med Ctr 5000 W 39th St Minneapolis MN 55416

SCHOEPHOERSTE, GEORGE ELDON, physician; b. Sumner, Iowa, July 22, 1952; s. Eldon William and Marjorie (Clark) S.; m. Kathy Lynn Gorman, May, 1973 (div. Sept. 1975); m. Jeanie Cunningham, Jan. 2, 1982; 1 child, Anthony Michael. BA, U. Iowa, 1975, MD, 1979. Resident Akron (Ohio) Gen. Med. Ctr., 1979-82; general physician St. Cloud Assoc. Med. Practice, St. Joseph, Minn., 1982-83, St. Cloud Med. Group, Cold Spring, Minn., 1983—. Mem. Minn. Med. Assn., Minn. Acad. Family Physicians (pres. cen. chpt. 1983-86, bd. dirs. 1986-87), Stearns-Benton County Med. Soc. Democrat. Unitarian. Avocations: bicycling, skiing, reading, chess, raquetball. Home: 29281 Kraemer Lake Rd Saint Joseph MN 56374

SCHOEPHOERSTER, LORIN KEITH, insurance company executive; b. Prairie du Sac, Wis., Jan. 10, 1923; s. Edwin Carl and Ruth (Preuss) S.; m. Lillian McGilvra, June 3, 1944; children: Douglas E., Linda J., Christine A. BS, Marquette U., 1945; MBA, U. Wis., 1951. CPCU, CLU; cert. assoc. research and planning, cert. assoc. risk mgmt.; registered health underwriter. Underwriter Farmers Mut., Madison, Wis., 1948-52, dir. edn. and research, 1952-56; supr. sales and tng. Nationwide Ins. Co., Columbus, Ohio, 1956-59; asst. sec. research State Auto Cos., Columbus, 1959-65, v.p. devel., 1966—; pres. Columbus Security Life, 1983—; v.p. Southern Home Ins. Co., Greer, S.C., 1986—; pres. Assoc. Services Agy., Columbus, 1983—. Editor: Guide to Leadership, 1975, Insurance Training and Education a Digest, 1976, vol. II 1982, Research Review 1st Decade, 1981; exec. editor (bi-monthly periodical) Edn. Exchange, 1969-85. Treas. Bd. Edn., Prairie du Sac, Wis., 1952-55; trustee Overbrook Presbyn. Ch., Columbus, 1966-68; advisor Boy Scouts Am., Columbus, 1962-65; pres. PTA, Prairie du Sac, 1952-53. Served as lt (j.g.) USNR, 1943-46. Recipient Merit award Nat. Assn. Mut. Ins. Cos., 1979; named Nat. Man of Yr., Internat. Assn. Health Underwriters, 1975, Commr. Gen. Internat. Ins. Seminars, 1976. Mem. Ohio Ins. Guarantee Assn. (chmn. bd. dirs. 1986—), Ohio Ins. Inst. (v.p. 1967-69, treas. 1976-78, bd. dirs.), Soc. Ins. Research (founder, exec. editor 1970—, Founders award 1972, bd. dirs.), Ins. Co. Edn. Dir. Soc. (life, pres. 1967-68, bd. dirs.), Gamma Iota Sigma (bd. dirs. Grand chpt. 1966—). Republican. Avocations: woodworking, editing, writing. Office: State Auto Cos 518 E Broad St Columbus OH 43216

SCHOFIELD, WILLIAM, educator, psychologist; b. Springfield, Mass., Apr. 19, 1921; s. William and Angie Mae (St. John) S.; m. Geraldine Bryan, Jan. 11, 1946; children: Bryan St. John, Gwen Star. B.S., Springfield Coll., 1942; M.A., U. Minn., 1946, Ph.D., 1948. Diplomate: Am. Bd. Profl. Psychology. Instr. U. Minn., Mpls., 1947-48; asst. prof. U. Minn., 1948-51, asso. prof., 1951-59, prof. psychology, 1959—; vis. prof. U. Wash., 1960, U. Colo., 1965; Cons. VA Hosp., Mpls., child study dept.; Mpls. Pub. Schs.; examiner, instr. USCG Aux., 1968—; mem. adv. council VA, 1970-75; Mem. med. policy adv. com. Dept. Pub. Welfare Minn., 1960-68; mem. mental health services research rev. com. NIMH, 1969-73; bd. dirs. Profl. Exam. Service, 1976-81; mem. editorial bd. Roche Psychiat. Service Inst.; mem. Minn. State Bd. Psychology, 1983-86. Author: Psychotherapy: The Purchase of Friendship, 1964, 2d edit., 1986, Pragmatics of Psychotherapy, 1987; contbr. articles to profl. jours. Served with USAAF, 1943-46. Fellow Am. Psychol. Assn. (com. on health ins. 1968-71, membership com. 1968-71, sec.-treas. clin. div. 1969-72, chmn. task force on health research 1973-75, chmn. sect. health research div. psychologists in pub. service 1977, mem. com. profl. standards 1982-85, chair com. 1984-85); mem. Midwestern Psychol. Assn., Minn. Psychol. Assn. (exec. sec. 1954-59), AAAS, AAUP, Assn. Am. Med. Colls. (chmn. com. on measurement of personality 1970-74), Sigma Xi, Pi Gamma Mu. Club: St. Croix Yacht. Home: 1441 E River Pkwy Minneapolis MN 55414 Office: U Minn Hosp 420 Delaware SE Minneapolis MN 55455

SCHOLFIELD, KEITH WALTER, real estate broker, insurance agent; b. Eldorado, Kans., Sept. 29, 1936; s. Gene L. and D. Earlyne (Shaw) S.; m. Rochelle Lane English, June 9, 1957; children—Mark K., Julie Lee. B.S. in Bus., U. Kans., 1959. Owner, pres. Keith Scholfield Agy., Inc., Augusta, Kans., 1960—. Pres. Augusta Unified Sch. Dist. 402, 1983-85; Augusta Md. Complex, 1980-82; chmn. Butler County Planning Bd., Kans., 1974. Mem. Nat. Assn. Realtors, Butler County Bd. Realtors, Augusta C. of C. (pres. 1969). Republican. Lodge: Optimist. Avocation: tennis. Home: 1922 Moyle Ave Augusta KS 67010 Office: 606 Walnut St Augusta KS 67010

SCHOLFIELD, MAX WENDELL, electronics executive, engineer; b. Elkhart, Ind., Feb. 22, 1930; s. Charles Sylvester and Minnie Leona (Keith) S.; m. Doris Ann Hartzler, May 17, 1952; children: Steve, Lynn, Ann, Brent. BEE, Purdue U., 1952; MS, Mich. State U., 1956; postgrad., Ind. U., 1965. Engr. Bendix Corp., Ann Arbor, Mich., 1956-57; engr. Crown Internat., Inc., Elkhart, Ind., 1957-59, chief engr., 1959-61, v.p. engring., 1961-71, sr. v.p., 1971-79, pres., 1979—, also bd. dirs. Bd. dirs. Youth for Christ, Elkhart, 1973-83, Hubbard Hills Estates, Elkhart, 1986—. Served to 1st lt. USAF, 1952-56. Mem. IEEE, Audio Engring. Soc., Elkhart C. of C. (bd. dirs. 1985—). Avocations: photography, fishing, flying, computers. Home: 24596 County Rd 126 Goshen IN 46526 Office: Crown Internat Inc 1718 W Mishawaka Rd Elkhart IN 46517

SCHOLL, BARBARA SUE, academic psychologist; b. Columbus, Ohio, Jan. 2, 1952; d. William Spitler Poff and Ramona Mae (Welch) DeBoor; m. Timothy P. Scholl; 1 child, Moriah. AB, Ohio U., 1974, MS, 1976. Sch. psychology intern Lancaster (Ohio) City Sch., 1975-76; sch. psychologist Perry County Bd. Edn., New Lexington, Ohio, 1976—; pvt. practice sch. psychology and counseling Lancaster, Ohio, 1979—. Mem. Ohio Sch. Psychologists, Southeastern Sch. Psycholgists (legis. rep. 1980-84, sec. treas. 1986—, lic.). Democrat. Avocations: baking, cooking, sewing. Home: 727 E 5th Lancaster OH 43130 Office: 114 N High Box 307 New Lexington OH 43764

SCHOLL, IDAMAE, bank administration executive; b. St. Paul; d. Louis Gotlieb and Isabelle Mae (Campbell) Reeck; m. Lloyd Leonard Scholl; children: Thomas, Steven, Jerome. BA, U. Mo., Carthage, 1954; postgrad. bus. mgmt., Mgmt. Ctr., 1970; postgrad. mgmt. sci., Mpls. Tech. Inst., 1971; postgrad. telecommunications, Drake U., 1984. Savs. supr. First Nat. Bank, St. Paul, 1963-69; with Norwest Bank, St. Paul, 1969—, adminstrv. services mgr., 1982—. Pres., bd. dirs. Capitol Community Services, St. Paul, 1983—; bd. dirs. Nat. Coll. Bd., St. Paul, 1982—; vol. Battered Women's Shelter, St. Paul, 1983-86; float chmn. St. Paul Winter Carnival Assn., 1983, 85; solicitor St. Paul United Way,1985-86, ARC, 1983-86, Am. Cancer Soc., 1985-86. Recipient Theme awards, St. Paul Winter Carnival Assn., 1983, 86, 87, YWCA Leadership award, Norwest Corp., 1984, 86. Mem. Internat. Women in Telecommunications (charter), Nat. Fedn. Bus. and Profl. Women (nat. task force, 1985-86, Minn. 2d v.p. 1986-87, Minn. 1st v.p. 1987—, named Bus. Woman of Yr., 1983, Minn. Woman of Achievement award 1987), Nat. Assn. Bank Women, Am. Inst. Banking, Minn. Women's Consortium, Minn. Econ. Devel. Assn., Female Execs. Minn., Minn. Minority Purchasing Council. Avocation: breeding and raising registered horses. Home: 6301 Oak Knoll Plaza Woodbury MN 55125

SCHOLTEN, HENRIETTA BLEEKER, physical therapist; b. Sioux Center, Iowa, Jan. 8, 1943; d. Cornelius and Jennie (Herweyer) Bleeker, m. Herman David Scholten, June 19, 1965; children: Samuel Jonathan, Susanne Janene. Student, Northwestern Coll., Orange City, Iowa, 1961-62; BS, U. Minn., Mpls., 1965. Physical therapist Easter Seals, Sioux City, 1965-79, St. Lukes Regional Med. Ctr., Sioux City, 1979—; cons. Sioux City area Nursing Homes, 1965-79; cons., speaker Am. Lung Assn., Sioux City, 1980-84; speaker, educator Burn Edn., Sioux City, 1979—; utilization review Beverly Nursing Homes, Sioux City, 1986—. Pres. Women for Christian Service, Sioux City, 1986. Mem. Am. Physical Therapy Assn., Am. Burn Assn. Continuing Edn. award 1986), Iowa Physical Therapy Assn., Am. Univ. Women. Lodge: Soroptimist. Avocations: reading, spectator sports, bike riding. Home: Rural Route 337 Sioux City IA 51108 Office: St Lukes Regional Med Ctr 2720 Stone Park Blvd Sioux City IA 51104

SCHOLTEN, JEFFREY JOHN, industrial engineer; b. Port Washington, Wis., Oct. 15, 1959; s. Jerome Clarence and Tamako (Noda) S.; m. Patricia Ann Heiser, Apr. 11, 1980; children: Maria Lynn, Angela Mary Sue. AAS in indsl. engring., Milw. Sch. Engring., 1981, BS in indsl. mgmt., 1984, postgrad., 1986—. Indsl. engr. Allen-Bradley Co. div. Rockwell Internat., Milw., 1981-85, prodn. engr., 1985—; career counselor Southeastern Wis. middle and high schs., 1984—. Port Washington Kiwanis scholar, 1978, Sprague Electric Acad. scholar, 1978, Milw. Sch. Engring. scholar, 1978. Mem. Inst. Indsl. Engrs. Republican. Roman Catholic. Clubs: Toastmaster's, Windjammer Drum and Bugle Corp. Avocations: history, reading of tech. advances, model building, nature.

SCHOLZ, JANE, publisher; b. St. Louis, July 31, 1948; d. Robert Louis and Mildred Virginia (Hudgins) S.; m. Jay W. Johnson, June 1979 (div. Dec. 1981); m. Douglas C. Balz, Jan. 1, 1983. B.A., Mich. State U., 1970; M.B.A., U. Miami, 1981. Reporter Jour.-Gazette, Fort Wayne, Ind., 1970-73; reporter The Miami Herald, Fla., 1973-77, asst. city editor, 1977-80; advanced mgmt. devel. participant Knight-Ridder Inc., Miami, Fla., 1980-85; pres., pub. Post-Tribune, Gary, Ind., 1985—. Bd. dirs. United Way of Lake county, Ind., Gary chpt. Urban League, Ind., NW Ind. Forum, Tradewinds Rehab. Ctr. Mem. Am. Newspaper Pubs. Assn., Ind. C. of C. (bd. dirs.), Sigma Delta Chi. Home: 7118 Forest Ave Hammond IN 46324 Office: Post-Tribune Post-Tribune Pub Inc 1065 Broadway Gary IN 46402

SCHOMAKER, JOHN BERNARD, accountant; b. Breese, Ill., Sept. 5, 1958; s. Herman Clemens and Sophie Veronica (Frerker) S.; m. Nancy Jean Schmidt, June 15, 1985. BBA in Acctg. and Bus. Administrn., McKendree Coll., 1980. CPA, Ill. Staff acct. Rice, Sullivan & Co., Ltd., Belleville, Ill., 1980-83, supr., 1984—. Sec. New Baden (Ill.) Vol. Fire Dept., 1985—. Mem. Am. Inst. CPA's, Ill. CPA Soc. (so. chpt.), St. George Holy Name Soc. (pres. 1984-85). Roman Catholic. Lodge: KC (treas. Trenton, Ill. chpt. 1987—). Avocations: photography, walking. Home: 9 Tanbark Dr New Baden IL 62265 Office: Rice Sullivan & Co Ltd 202 S High St Belleville IL 62220

SCHOMAKER, SHERRY LEE, accountant; b. Spicer, Minn., June 30, 1940; d. Arthur Elroy and Hazel Eldora (Olson) Johnson; m. Larry Dailey, Oct. 25, 1957(div. 1971); children: Jeff, Vicky Tuel, Terry, Kevin. Student, Spencer (Iowa) Bus. Sch., 1972, student in acctg. mgmt., 1982. Pvt. practice acctg. Royal, Iowa, 1982—. Foster parent Clay County Social Services, Spencer, 1969-71; councilperson City of Royal, 1986. Mem. Nat. Fedn. Bus., Nat. Assn. Female Execs. Democrat. Lutheran. Avocations: reading, painting.

SCHOMER, FRED K., manufacturing executive; b. Chgo., June 21, 1939; s. Harold M. and Jeanette (Gerchikov) S.; m. Sharon Ann Schear, Feb. 8, 1964; children: Marcy, Amy. BA, U. Chgo., 1960, JD, 1962, MBA, 1982. With Beatrice Cos., Chgo., 1963-83; v.p. fin. and adminstrn. Acco World Corp., Northbrook, Ill., 1984—; bd. dirs. Exec. Program Club. Mem. adv. council U. Chgo. Grad. Sch. Bus.; v.p. Mens' Club, Congregation Beth Shalom, Northbrook, 1985—. Served with U.S. Army, 1962, 63. Mem. Fin. Mgrs. Assn. (vice chmn.), Fin. Execs. Inst. Avocations: music, theater, golf.

SCHON, NANCY CATHERINE, manufacturing engineer; b. Cleve., Nov. 17, 1961; d. Willis Logan and Catherine Ann (Stearns) Ballew; m. Timothy Gerard Schon, June 22, 1985. BS in Engring., Ohio State U., 1985. Engr. Delco Products div. Gen. Motors, Dayton, 1985—. Chmn. Miami Valley Freedom of Choice, Dayton, 1986. Owens-Corning scholar, 1982-84. Mem. Miami Valley Mgmt. Assn. Home: 412 Harman Blvd Dayton OH 45419 Office: Delco Products Gen Motors PO Box 1042 Dayton OH 45401

SCHONFELD, PETER JEFFREY, hospital executive, consultant; b. Detroit, Mar. 6, 1953; s. Jack Harold and Miriam Luella (Hougom) S.; m. Luanne Smith, Oct. 24, 1975; children: Matthew Jeffrey, Kathleen Elizabeth. BA, Kalamazoo Coll., 1975; M in Mgmt., Northwestern U., 1977. Cons. Med. Computer Scis. Assn., Seattle, 1975; asst. to pres. Henrotin Hosp., Chgo., 1975-77, exec. v.p., 1982-84; adminstr. asst. then asst. adminstr. Skokie (Ill.) Valley Hosp., 1977-82; pres., chief exec. officer McPherson Community Health Ctr., Howell, Mich., 1984—; treas. Health Ventures Corp., Howell, 1985—; vice chmn. bd. dirs. Vol. Hosps. Am.-Mich., Grand Rapids, sec., treas. Vol. Hosps. Am. Mich. Preferred Providers. Contbr. articles to profl. jours. Chmn. Citizens Adv. Council Pub. Schs., Howell, 1986; co-chmn. Howell United Way, 1986. Mem. Am. Coll. Health Execs., Mich. Hosp. Assn. (vice chmn. fin. com. 1986—), Northwestern U. Hosp. Mgmt. Lodge: Rotary (sgt. of arms Howell club, 1986—). Avocations: cross country skiing, canoeing, hunting, hiking, sports. Office: McPherson Community Health Ctr 620 Byron Rd Howell MI 48843

SCHOOFS, GERALD JOSEPH, pilot; b. Kewaskum, Wis., May 11, 1954; s. Francis Christ and Bernice Mary (Kowanda) S.; m. Nancy Lynn Thompson, June 7, 1975; children: Matthew, Katherine. AS in Aeronautics, Gateway Tech. Inst., 1974. Lic. airline transport pilot., ground instr. Asst. chief flight instr. West Bend flying Service, 1974-78; dir. ops. Brennan Air Flight, Clintonville, Wis., 1978-80; capt. pilot Mss. Valley Airlines, Moline, Ill., 1980-85, Air Wis., Appleton, Wis., 1985—; chief pilot Advanced Tech. Aircraft Design, Hartford, Wis., 1984—. Mem. Airline Pilot Assn., Experimental Aircraft Assn. Roman Catholic. Avocations: cabinet making, hiking, scuba diving. Home: 11 Park Ave Eldridge IA 52748

SCHOOLMAN, ARNOLD, neurological surgeon; b. Worcester, Mass., Oct. 31, 1927; s. Samuel and Sarah (Koffman) S.; m. Gloria June Feder, Nov. 10, 1964; children: Hugh Sinclair, Jill. Student, U. Mass., 1945-46; BA, Emory U., 1950; PhD, Yale U., 1954, MD, 1957. Diplomate Am. Bd Neurol. Surgery, Nat. Bd. Med. Examiners. Intern U. Calif. Hosp., San Francisco, 1957-58; resident in neurol. surgery Columbia-Presbyn. Med. Ctr., Neurol. Inst. N.Y., N.Y.C., 1958-62; instr. neurol. surgery U. Kans. Sch. Medicine, Kansas City, 1962, asst. prof. surgery, 1964; assoc. prof. U. Mo. Sch. Medicine, Kansas City, 1976; chief sect. neurosurgery Research Med. Ctr., Kansas City, 1982; dir. Midwest Neurol. Inst., 1982-83. Patentee in field. Served with USN, 1946-48. Fellow ACS (mem. Mo. chpt.); mem. AMA, Mo. State Med. Assn., Kansas City Med. Soc., Kansas City Neurosurg. Soc. (pres. 1984-85), Kansas City Neuro-radiol. Soc., Rocky Mountain Neurosurg. Soc., Am. Assn. Neurol. Surgeons, AAAS, Mo. Neurol. Soc., Internat. Coll. Surgeons, Congress Neurol. Surgeons, Brit. Royal Soc. Medicine, Phi Beta Kappa, Sigma Xi. Jewish. Avocation: pilot. Home: 8705 Catalina Prairie Village KS 66207 Office: 6420 Prospect Suite T411 Kansas City MO 64132

SCHOONBECK, LINDA HARMON JOHNSON, mathematics educator; b. Hammond, Ind., Jan. 19, 1945; d. Claude Harmon and Evelyn Agnes (Haupt) Johnson; m. Robert Richard Schoonbeck, Feb. 14, 1967; children: Evelin Kay, Alana Joi, Dayhe Alan. BA with honors, Mich. State U., 1964; MS, U. Mich., 1967. Tchr. Okemos (Mich.) Pub. Schs., 1964, Willow Run Pub. Schs., Ypsilanti, Mich., 1964-67, Grosse Pointe (Mich.) Pub. Schs., 1967—; instr. methods U. Detroit, 1973; instr. math. Wayne State U., Detroit, 1974. Sec.-treas. Educators Parents Open Classroom, Ann Arbor, Mich., 1971-74; corp. vol. Jr. League, Detroit, 1984, active Sibley house restoration, 1987. Republican. Presbyterian. Clubs: Silver Lake Sail (commodore 1982-83), Pentwater (Mich.) Yacht. Avocations: sailing, computers. Home: 8131 Thorntree Ct Grosse Ile MI 48138-1517

SCHORGL, THOMAS BARRY, art commission administrator; b. St. Louis, Mar. 1, 1950. BFA, U. Iowa, 1973, MA in Drawing, 1974; MFA in Printmaking, Miami U., Oxford, Ohio, 1976; apprenticeship, Atelier, Garrigue, France, 1976; postgrad., U. Notre Dame, 1979. Comml. artist R.H. Donnelly, Chgo., 1977; curator Art Ctr. Inc., South Bend, Ind., 1977-78, dir. acting, 1978, exec. dir., 1978-81; account exec. James Carroll Assocs., South Bend, 1981-83; exec. dir/ Ind. Arts. Commn., Indpls., 1983—; cons. in field. Author: Twentieth Century American Masters, 1978, European Paintings from the Collection of Richard Zeisler, 1978, Michiana Collects, 1979, Works on Paper, 1980; contr. articles to profl. jours. Active Hudson-Dayton Found., South Bend, 1981, Ednl. Services Project, 1981, Inst. Mus. Services, 1980-81. Mem. Great Lakes Arts Alliance (sec., treas. 1983-85, merger com.), Affiliated State Arts Agys. Upper Midwest (chmn. program com. 1985—). Office: Ind Arts Commn 32 E Washington Indianapolis IN 46204

SCHOTT, MARGE, professional sports team owner; b. 1928; d. Edward and Charlotte Unnewehr; m. Charles J. Schott, 1952 (dec. 1968). Owner Schottco, Cin.; ltd. ptnr. Cin. Reds, 1981-84, gen. ptnr., 1984-85, owner, pres., 1985—, chief exec. officer. Office: Cin Reds 100 Riverfront Stadium Cincinnati OH 45201 *

SCHOTTELKOTTE, ALBERT JOSEPH, broadcasting executive; b. Cheviot, Ohio, Mar. 19, 1927; s. Albert William and Venetta (Mentrup) S.; student pub. and parochial schs.; m. Virginia Louise Gleason, July 2, 1951; children—Paul J., Carol Ann, Linda Louise, Joseph G., Matthew, Louis A., Martha Jane, Amy Marie, Mary Jo, Ellen Elizabeth, William H., Michael E. Wtih Cin. Enquirer, 1943-61, successively copy boy, city-wide reporter, columnist, 1953-61; news broadcaster Sta. WSAI, Cin., 1953-59; news broadcaster Sta. WCPO-TV, 1959—, dir. news-spl. events, 1961-83, sta. dir., 1983—; gen. mgr. news div. Scripps-Howard Broadcasting Co., 1969-81, v.p. for news, 1971-81, sr. v.p., 1981—; pres., chief exec. officer, trustee Scripps Howard Found., 1986—. Served with AUS, 1950-52. Recipient Nat. CD award for reporting on subject, 1958. Mem. Radio-TV News Dirs. Assn. Roman Catholic. Clubs: Bankers, Maketewah Country, Cin. Home: 7647 Pineglen Dr Cincinnati OH 45224 Office: 500 Central Ave Cincinnati OH 45202

SCHOTTENHEIMER, MARTIN EDWARD, professional football coach; b. Canonsburg, Pa., Sept. 23, 1943; m. Patricia; children—Kristen, Brian. B.A., U. Pitts., 1964. Football player Buffalo Bills, NFL, 1965-68; football player Boston Patriots, 1969-70; real estate developer Miami and Denver, 1971-74; asst. coach World Football League, Portland, 1974, N.Y. Giants, 1975-77, Detroit Lions, 1978-79; asst. coach Cleve. Browns, 1980-84, head coach, 1985—. Office: Cleve Browns Cleve Stadium Cleveland OH 44114

SCHRADER, ALFRED EUGENE, lawyer; b. Akron, Ohio, Nov. 1, 1953; s. Louis Clement and Helen Maye (Eberz) S.; m. Cathy Diane Fincher, Apr. 17, 1982; children—Eric Brian, Angela Diane. B.A. in Polit. Sci. magna cum laude, Kent State U., 1975; J.D., Ohio State U., 1978. Bar: Ohio 1978, U.S. Dist. Ct. (no. dist.) Ohio 1978, U.S. Ct. Appeals (6th cir.) 1985, U.S. Supreme Ct. 1985. Dep. clk. Summit County Clk. of Cts., Akron, 1972-74; sole practice, Akron, 1978—; spl. counsel Bath Twp., Ohio, 1980—; law dir. Northampton Twp., Ohio, 1983-86, Franklin Twp., Ohio, 1984—, Twinsburg Twp., Ohio, 1981—; spl. counsel Richfield Twp., Ohio, 1983-85; consulting counsel law dept. City of Cuyanoga Falls, 1986; spl. annexation counsel Bath, Perry and Shawnee Twps., Allen County, Ohio, 1986—; spl. counsel Carlisle Twp., Lorain County, 1986-87; spl. annexation counsel Brimfield Twp., Portage County, 1986—. Trustee Springfield Twp., Ohio, 1973—, pres., 1975, 79, 82; mem. adv. com. Community Devel. Block, Summit County, 1985—, Summit County Annexation Com., Ohio, 1981-85; mem. Summit County Jail Study Commn., 1983, 84; mem. adv. bd. Springfield Schs., 1975. Mem. Akron Bar Assn. (v.p. legis. com. 1981-82), Ohio Acad. Trial Lawyers, Assn. Trial Lawyers Am., Ohio Bar Assn., Summit County Twp. assn. (exec. com. 1983—), Ohio Twp. Assn. (exec. com. 1983—). Democrat. Roman Catholic. Home: 3344 Brunk Rd Akron OH 44312 Office: Dalessio Shapiro Manes et al 441 Wolf Ledges Pkwy Suite 400 Akron OH 44311-1054

SCHRADER, DAVID ALAN, minister; b. South Bend, Ind., Dec. 14, 1954; s. Raymond Harvey and Arlene Elizabeth (Griminus) S.; m. Pamela Kay Knox, July 23, 1977; 1 child, John David. AB, Ind. U., South Bend, 1976; M in Div., Garrett-Evang. Theol. Sem. at Northwestern U., 1982. Ordained to ministry United Meth. Ch. as deacon, 1980, as minister, 1984. Assoc. pastor Norwood Park United Meth. Ch., Chgo., 1980-82; pastor Door Village United Meth. Ch., LaPorte, Ind., 1982-86; assoc. pastor, Coll. Ave. United Meth. Ch. at Ball State U., Muncie, Ind., 1986—; rep. to No. Ind. Conf. of Bd. Global Ministries United Meth. Ch., Marion, Ind., 1983-86;

cons. pastoral care program LaPorte Hosp., 1984-86, Muncie Substance Abuse Task Force, 1987—. Mem. Ministerial Assn. Delaware County, Conf. Council Camps and Confs. (dean 1986). Club: Exchange (Muncie). Avocations: angler, naturalist, classical music, history, literature. Office: Coll Ave United Meth Ch 1968 W Main Muncie IN 47303

SCHRAGE, JOHN FREDERICK, information systems educator; b. Granite City, Ill., Mar. 5, 1947; s. Raymond Joe and Rose Marie (Luksan) S.; m. Diane Louise Dressel, Sept. 8, 1973; children—Jason Christopher, Mariam Elizabeth. B.S., So. Ill. U., 1969, M.S., 1973; Ph.D., Mich. State U., 1978. Programmer, analyst So. Ill. U., Edwardsville, 1972-73, assoc. prof. mgmt. info. systems 1978—, scis. coordinator MIS faculty, 1978-84, chmn. dept. mgmt. info. systems, 1984—; asst. mgr., operator Mobile CAI Lab. Penn State U., University Park, 1973; data processing instr. Muskegon (Mich.) Community Coll., 1973-76; asst. prof. computer tech. Purdue U., Ft. Wayne, Ind., 1976-78; word processor Computer Systems, Resource Mgmt. U.S. Army. Sec., treas. Aid Assn. for Lutherans, Troy, Ill., 1979-81; elder St. Paul Lutheran Ch., Troy, 1982-85 . Served with U.S. Army, 1969-71; USAR, 1971-86 . Recipient Cert. Merit Am. Legion, 1968; cert. systems profl. Mem. Am. Inst. Decision Scis., Assn. for Computing Machinery, Assn. Ednl. Data Systems, Assn. Systems Mgmt., Am. Mgmt. Assn., Data Processing Mgmt. Assn., EDP Auditors Assn., Pi Omega Pi, Sigma Pi, Alpha Phi Omega (advisor 1979—). Lutheran. Contbr. articles to profl. jours. Home: 617 Brentmoor Dr Troy IL 62294 Office: Campus Box 1106 Bldg II Edwardsville IL 62026

SCHRAGE, PAUL DANIEL, fast food executive; b. Chgo., Feb. 25, 1935; s. William and Rose Marie (Bruell) S.; m. Janet Carolyn Sievers, June 15, 1957; children: Paul Daniel, Gordon Clark. B.A., Valparaiso U., 1957; M.S. in Advt., U. Ill., 1959. Media buyer Young & Rubicam Advt., Chgo., 1959-61; brand mgr. Quaker Oats Co., Chgo., 1961-65; salesman This Week mag., Chgo., 1965-66; asso. media dir. D'Arcy Advt., Chgo., 1966-67; sr. exec. v.p., chief mktg. officer McDonald's Corp., Oak Brook, Ill., 1967—; dir. Century Co. Am., Safety-Kleen Corp. Mem. president's council Valparaiso (Ind.) U. Lutheran. Club: Butterfield Country. Office: McDonald's Corp 1 McDonald Plaza Oak Brook IL 60521

SCHRAMM, DAVID NORMAN, astrophysicist, educator; b. St. Louis, Oct. 25, 1945; s. Marvin and Betty (Math) S.; m. Melinda Holzhauer, 1963 (div. 1979); children: Cary, Brett.; m. Colleen Rae, 1980 (div. 1981); m. Judith J. Zielinski, 1986. S.B. in Physics, MIT, 1967; Ph.D. in Physics, Calif. Inst. Tech., 1971. Research fellow in physics Calif. Inst. Tech., Pasadena, 1971-72; asst. prof. astronomy and physics U. Tex., Austin, 1972-74; assoc. prof. astronomy, astrophysics and physics Enrico Fermi Inst. and the Coll., U. Chgo., 1974-77, prof., 1977—, Louis Block prof. phys. scis., 1982—, prof. conceptual founds. of sci., 1983—, acting chmn. dept. astronomy and astrophysics, 1977, chmn., 1978-84; resident cosmologist Fermilab, 1982-84; cons., lectr. Adler Planetarium; organizer numerous sci. confs.; frequent lectr. in field; bd. dirs. Aspen Ctr. for Physics; pres. Big Bang Aviation, Inc. Contbr. over 200 articles to profl. jours.; co-editor: Explosive Nucleosynthesis, 1973; editor: Supernovae, 1977; assoc. editor: Am. Jour. Physics, 1978-81; co-editor: Phys. Cosmology, 1980, Fundamental Problems in Stellar Evolution, 1980, Essays in Nucleosynthesis, 1981; editor: U. Chgo. series Theoretical Astrophysics; Physics Reports, 1981—; editorial bd.: Ann. Revs. Nuclear and Particle Sci., 1976-80; columnist: Outside mag.; co-author: Advanced States of Stellar Evolution, 1977. Nat. Graeco-Roman wrestling champion, 1971; recipient Robert J. Trumpler award Astron. Soc. Pacific, 1974, Gravity Research Found. awards, 1974, 75, 76, 80. Fellow Am. Phys. Soc., Meteoritical Soc.; mem. Nat. Acad. Sci. (elected), Am. Astron. Soc. (Helen B. Warner prize 1978, exec. com. planetary sci. div. 1977-79, sec.-treas. high energy astrophysics div. 1979-81), Am. Assn. Physics Tchrs. (Richtmeyer prize 1984), Astron. Soc. Pacific, Internat. Astron. Union (commns. on cosmology, stellar evolution, high energy astrophysics), Aircraft Owners and Pilots Assn., Am. Alpine Club, Austrian Alpine Club, , Sigma Xi. Club: Quadrangle. also: 1163 Cemetery Ln Aspen CO 81611 Office: 5640 S Ellis Ave AAC-140 Chicago IL 60637

SCHRAMM, FREDERIC BERNARD, lawyer; b. Cleve., June 3, 1903; s. A. Bernard and Flora Frederica (Leutz) S. B.S., Case Inst. Tech., 1925; J.D., George Washington U., 1931; LL.M., Western Res. U., 1955. Bar: U.S. Patent Office 1930, D.C. 1931, Ohio 1944, N.Y. 1933, Calif. 1957. Patent atty. Gen. Electric Co., Schenectady, 1925-42; ptnr. Richey & Watts, Cleve., 1942-54, Kendrick, Schramm & Stolzy, Los Angeles, 1954-60, Schramm, Kramer & Sturges, Cleve., 1960-72, Schramm & Knowles, Cleve., 1972-80; instr. Fenn Coll., 1973-74, Cleve. Marshal Law Sch., Cleve. State U., 1974-75. Mem. ABA, Cleve. Bar Assn., Am. Patent Law Assn., Cleve. Patent Law Assn., IEEE, Sigma Xi, Eta Kappa Nu, Tau Beta Pi. Clubs: Kiwanis (Shaker Heights, Ohio); Univ., Torch (Cleve.). Author: Handbook on Patent Disputes, 1974; contbr. articles to law jours. Office: 3570 Warrensville Center Rd Suite 201 Cleveland OH 44122

SCHRAMM, RICHARD MARTIN, sales and marketing executive; executive; b. Bklyn., Apr. 15, 1940; s. Harold Matthew and Elizabeth Ann (Hitt) S.; m. Camille K. Khoury, Apr. 24, 1964; children—Christine, Carolyn, Catherine. Student U. San Francisco, 1957-59; B.A., Columbia U., 1961. Nat. sales mgr. 3M Co., 1970-75; dir. mktg. Hollingsworth Co., 1975-79; coach N.Y. Nets profl. basketball, 1967-69; pres. Sol. Term. Mfrs. Assn., N.Y.C., 1972-75; dir. sales and mktg. Mega diamond Industries Inc., 1979-83; v.p. Baumgold Diamond Co. Inc., 1983—; pres. Indsl. Diamond Assn., Columbia, S.C., 1987—. Mem. Am. Mgmt. Assn., Chgo. Execs. Club. Author: Marketing - Keys to Successful Selling, 1983.

SCHREIBER, EDWARD JOSEPH, business tax executive; b. Dayton, Ky., Dec. 5, 1946; s. Edward Joseph and Dorothy Mae (Saner) S.; m. Mary Jo Roedersheimer, July 15, 1967; children: Kimberly, Karen, Renee. BS, U. Ky., 1968. CPA, Ky. Auditor Ernst & Whinney, Cin., 1969, tax supr., 1973-81; linguist USN, Washington, 1969-73; tax mgr. Winegardner & Hammons, Cin., 1981—. Panelist TV program, Talking Taxes, 1985. Treas., auditor Health, Sci. and Industry Mus., Cin., 1980. Mem. Am. Inst. CPA's, Ohio Soc. CPA's (chpt. dir. 1986-87, sec. 1987-88), Inst. Property Taxation (com.), Internat. Assn. Assessing Officers. Republican. Roman Catholic. Avocation: fishing. Home: 859 Suncreek Ct Cincinnati OH 45238 Office: Winegardner & Hammons 4243 Hunt Rd Cincinnati OH 45242

SCHREIBER, JAMES RALPH, obstetrics-gynecology researcher; b. Rosebud, Tex., May 29, 1946; s. Lester B. and Jane Elinore (Hodges) S.; m. Mary Celia Schmit, Aug. 19, 1968; children: Lisa, Joseph, Laura, Cynthia. BA, Rice U., 1968; MD, Johns Hopkins U., 1972. Cert. Am. Coll. Ob-Gyn, Am. Bd. Reproductive Endocrinology. Asst. prof. ob-gyn U. Calif., San Diego, 1978-82; assoc. prof. U. Chgo., 1982—. Contbr. articles to profl. jours. Grantee NIH, 1978—. Mem. Endocrine Soc., Soc. Gynecologic Investigation. Home: 715 N Linden Oak Park IL 60302 Office: U Chgo Dept Ob-Gyn Box 446 5841 S Maryland Ave Chicago IL 60637

SCHREIER, LEONARD, allergist, immunologist; b. Detroit, June 3, 1934; s. Alexander and Fanny (Wayne) S.; M.D., U. Mich., 1959, M.S. in Internal Medicine, 1965; m. Barbara Gay Hirsch, Aug. 11, 1956 (div. June 1980); children—Eric Marvin, Jordan Scott, Barry Andrew; m. Raquel Lucia Cruz, July 11, 1981. Intern, Sinai Hosp., Detroit, 1959-60, resident in internal medicine, 1960-63; fellow in allergy and immunology U. Mich., 1963-65; practice medicine specializing in allergy and immunology, Detroit, 1965-66, Pontiac, Mich., 1968—; staff St. Joseph Mercy Hosp., Pontiac, acting chmn. dept. medicine, 1980-81; asst. clin. prof. medicine Wayne State Coll. Medicine, 1976—. Served with M.C., U.S. Army, 1966-68. Diplomate Am. Bd. Internal Medicine, Am. Bd. Allergy and Immunology. Fellow Am. Acad. Allergy. Jewish. Contbr. articles to med. jours. Office: 1555 Woodward Ave Suite 101 Bloomfield Hills MI 48013

SCHRENK, W(ILLI) JUERGEN, chemical executive; b. Dachau, Fed. Republic of Germany, June 19, 1945; came to U.S., 1972; s. Willi Schrenk and Irmgard (Urbanek) Meinhardt; m. Ruth Halfenberg, Nov. 10, 1971; 1 child, Ralph Michael. PhD, Cologne U., Fed. Republic of Germany, 1972. Research fellow Harvard Med. Sch., Boston, 1972-73; guest scientist Nat. Cancer Inst., Bethesda, Md., 1972-73; asst. research prof. U. Calif., Santa Barbara, 1974-77; sr. scientist Abbott Labs., North Chicago, Ill., 1977-79; sci. dir. Boehringer Mannheim, Tutzing, Fed. Republic of Germany, 1979-85; dir. research and devel. Boehringer Mannheim Corp., Indpls., 1986—. Contbr. articles to profl. jours; patentee in field. Established 5 nature preserves in U.S. and Fed. Republic of Germany, 1975-85. Fellow Fed. Republic of Germany, 1964-70, Deutsche Forschungs-Gemeinschaft, 1972-74. Mem. Audubon Soc., The Nature Conservancy, World Wildlife Fund, Bund f. Naturschutz i. Deutschland. Avocations: nature photography, skiing, hiking. Home: 1424 Douglas Dr Carmel IN 46032 Office: Boehringer Mannheim Corp 9115 Hague Rd PO Box 50100 Indianapolis IN 46250-0100

SCHRINER, JON LESLIE, sports medicine physician; b. Flint, Mich., Mar. 9, 1937; s. Alva Niel and Helena Ione (McLean) S.; m. Mary Patricia O'Keefe, May 25, 1963 (div. Oct. 1980); children: Jon, Lindsay, Laura, Joan; m. Delores Korb, Mar. 2, 1985. AS, Flint Community Coll., 1957; BA, Eastern Mich. U., 1959; DO, Kirksville Coll., 1963. Intern Flint Osteo. Hosp., 1963-64, staff; physician Flushing (Mich.) Med. Ctr., 1963-81; physician, pres. Sports Medicine Rehab. Ctr., Flushing, 1981—; assoc. prof. clin. medicine Mich. State U., East Lansing; staff St. Joseph's Hosp., Genesee Meml. Hosp.; team physician Flushing Community Schs., 1963—, Flint Gens. Hockey Club, 1980-84, Flint Spirits Hockey Club, 1986—. Contbr. articles to profl. jours. Pres. Bd. Edn. Flushing schs., 1968-76; dir. med. services Bobby Crim Road Race Spl. Olympics, Flint, 1978-86, Buick City Road Race, Flint, 1984-86; bd. dirs. United Way Genesee County, Mich., 1979. Recipient 23 Yr. Service award Flushing Community Schs., 1986, numerous community awards. Fellow Am. Coll. Sports Medicine; mem. Am. Osteo. Assn., Canadian Am. Med. Dental Assn. (bd. trustees 1986—), Profl. Ski Instrs. Assn. Roman Catholic. Club: Bruin of Genesee County (Sports Med. award 1987). Avocations: skiing, tennis, running, sailing. Home: 8022 Fawn Valley Dr Clarkston MI 48106 Office: Sports Medicine Rehab Ctr 6045 Pierson Rd Flushing MI 48433

SCHROCK, RICHARD DAVID, health care executive; b. Columbus, Ohio, Jan. 1, 1939; s. Robert Thomas and Isabel (Wightman) S.; m. Sharon L. Thompson, Aug. 13, 1966; children: Melissa Alane, Richelle Dawn. BS in Acctg., Ohio State U., 1964, MBA, 1978. CPA, Ohio. Staff acct. Coopers & Lybrand, N.Y.C. and Columbus, 1964-69; asst. adminstr. Mt. St. Mary Hosp., Nelsonville, Ohio, 1969-71, St. Anthony Hosp., Columbus, 1971-79; dir. fin. Med. Coll. of VA Hosp., Richmond, Va., 1979-85; sr. v.p. fin. Luth. Hosps. and Homes, Fargo, N.D., 1985—; bd. dirs. Interhealth, Mpls., 1985—; adj. faculty mem. Ohio State U., Columbus, 1978-79; faculty Va. Commonwealth U., Richmond, 1980-85. Served with U.S. Army, 1958-61. Fellow Healthcare Fin. Mgmt. Assn. (pres. cen. Ohio chpt. 1975, Buckeye Achievment award 1975, pres. Va. chpt. 1984-85); mem. Am. Inst. CPA's, Am. Coll. Healthcare Execs. Club: Kiwanis (bd. dirs. Berwick, Ohio chpt. 1978-79). Avocations: travel, sports. Home: 3127 Peterson Pkwy Fargo ND 58102 Office: Luth Health Systems 1202 Westrac Dr PO Box 2087 Fargo ND 58107

SCHRODER, BARRY CHARLES, lawyer; b. New Buffalo, Mich., Apr. 26, 1955; s. Charles William and Veronica Helen (Bigda) S.; m. Nancy Lee Vincent, Sept. 6, 1980. B.A. with high honors, Mich. State U., 1977; J.D., Wayne State U., 1980. Bar: Mich. 1980, U.S. Dist. Ct. (we. dist.) Mich. 1980, U.S. Ct. Appeals (6th cir.) 1983. Assoc., Rhoades, McKee & Boer, Grand Rapids, Mich., 1980-86; mem. Mich. Worker's Compensation Appeal Bd., Grand Rapids, 1986-87; magistrate, Mich. Worker's Compensation Bd. Magistrates, Grand Rapids, 1987—. Democrat. Roman Catholic. Office: Workers Compensation Bd Magistrates Office 350 Ottawa NW 3d Floor Grand Rapids MI 49503

SCHROECK, MICHAEL JOSEPH, management consultant; b. Cin., Jan. 20, 1956; s. Herbert George and Betty J. Elizabeth (Federle) S.; m. Susan Marie Schlanser, July 3, 1982; 1 child, Lisa Marie. BBA, U. Cin., 1979; MBA, Xavier U., 1982. CPA, Ohio, cert. in prodn. and inventory mgmt., Ohio. Supr. cost acctg. U.S. Shoe Corp., Cin., 1979-81; cons. Price Waterhouse, Cin., 1981-82, sr. cons., 1982-84, mgr., 1984-86, sr. mgr., 1986—. Contbr. articles to trade mags. Chmn. bd. dirs. Cin. Restoration, Inc., 1985—; bd. dirs. The Charter Com., Cin., 1985—. Mem. Nat. Assn. Accts. (v.p. 1984—, pres. 1987-88), Am. Inst. CPA's, Inst. Cert. Mgmt. Accts. (cert.), Cincinnatus Assn., Young Friends of the Arts, U. Cin. Alumni Assn. Roman Catholic. Home: 3671 Moonridge Dr Cincinnati OH 45248 Office: Price Waterhouse 1900 Central Trust Ctr Cincinnati OH 45202

SCHROEDER, CHARLES EDGAR, bank executive, investment management executive; b. Chgo., Nov. 17, 1935; s. William Edward and Lelia Lorraine (Anderson) S.; m. Martha Elizabeth Runnette, Dec. 30, 1958; children: Charles Edgar, Timothy Creighton, Elizabeth Linton. B.A. in Econs., Dartmouth Coll., 1957; M.B.A., Amos Tuck Sch., 1958. Security analyst Miami Corp., Chgo., 1960-69, treas., 1969-78, pres., 1978—, dir., 1969—; security analyst Cutler Oil & Gas Corp., Chgo., 1960-69; treas. Cutler Oil & Gas Corp., Chgo., 1969-78, pres., 1978—, dir., 1969—; chmn. bd., dir. Blvd. Bank of Chgo., 1981-86; dir. Nat. Blvd. Bank of Chgo., 1969—; dir. Nat.-Standard Co., Niles, Mich., 1973—. Assoc. Northwestern U., 1975—; trustee First Presbyterian Ch. of Evanston, Ill., 1968—; bd. dirs. Presbyn. Home, Evanston, 1979—; trustee Wayland Acad., Beaver Dam, Wis., 1982—, Northwestern Meml. Hosp., 1985—. Served to lt. (j.g.) USN, 1958-60. Mem. Fin. Analysts Soc. of Chgo., Beta Theta Pi. Clubs: Chicago, Glen View, Mid-America, Michigan Shores, Casque and Gauntlet, Comml. Office: Nat Blvd Bank of Chgo 410 N Micigan Ave Chicago IL 60611

SCHROEDER, DOUGLAS FREDRICK, architect; b. Omaha, June 12, 1935; s. Walter Elmer and Ellen Ruth (Niles) S.; m. Joanne Vlecides, July 5, 1980. B.Arch., U. Mich., 1959. Registered Architect, Ill., N.C., Mich. Designer, draftsman C.F. Murphy Assocs., Chgo., 1959-63; architect, sr. architect Skidmore, Owings & Merrill, Chgo., 1964-67; architect, ptnr. Schroeder, Yamamoto & Schreiber, Chgo., 1968-69; ptnr. Hinds & Schroeder, Ltd., Chgo., 1972-74; propr. Douglas Schroeder Assocs., Chgo., 1974-83; ptnr. Siegel & Schroeder, P.C., Chgo., 1983—; v.p. Yacht Harbor Mgmt. Co., South Haven, Mich., 1983—; dir. Inland Architect Mag. Contbr. articles to profl. jours. Bd. dirs. Chgo. Archtl. Assistance Ctr., 1982-84; chmn. Mass. Transp. Crisis Com., Chgo., 1973, Ill. Futures Forum, 1976-77; pres. Ill. Planning and Conservation League, Chgo., 1971-74. Named Outstanding Alumnus Lake Superior State Coll., 1971. Fellow AIA; mem. Am. Arbitration Assn. (arbitrator). Unitarian. Club: Cliff Dwellers (dir. 1971-74). Home: 700 W Irving Park Rd Apt A4 Chicago IL 60613 Office: Siegel & Schroeder PC 230 N Mich Ave Chicago IL 60601

SCHROEDER, FRED ERICH HARALD, humanities educator; b. Manitowoc, Wis., June 3, 1932; s. Alfred William and Sissel Marie (Lovell) S.; m. Janet June Knope, Aug. 21, 1954; 1 child, Erich Karl. BS, U. Wis., 1960; MA, U. Minn., 1963, PhD, 1968. Elementary sch. tchr. various locations, Wis., 1952-60; asst. prof. English U. Minn., Duluth, 1968-71, assoc. prof. English, 1971-74, prof. behavioral sci., 1977-82, prof. humanities, 1974—, dir. Ctr. for Am. Studies, 1986-87, dir. Inst. Interdisciplinary Studies, 1987—. Lectr., writer Nat. Humanities Series, 1969-71; author Joining the Human Race: How to Teach Humanities, 1972, Outlaw Aesthetics: Arts and the Public Mind, 1977; editor Humanities Edn. jour., 1983—, (book) 5000 Yrs. of Popular Culture, 1980, 20th Century Popular Culture in Mus. and Libraries, 1981. Mem. Minn. Humanities Commn., 1985—. Woodrow Wilson Nat. Found. fellow, 1960-61, dissertation fellow 1963; NEH scholar, 1969-70; Inst. for Human Values in Medicine fellow, 1976. Mem. Am. Culture Assn (pres. 1984-87), Popular Culture Assn., Am. Studies Assn., Nat. Assn. for Humanities Edn. (pres. 1987—, exec. com. 1982—), Am. Assn. for State and Local History (seminar instr. 1978-82). Avocations: collecting art, woodworking. Home: 10700 North Shore Dr Duluth MN 55804 Office: U Minn Duluth Humanities Program 10 University Dr Duluth MN 55812

SCHROEDER, MARK A., assistant dean; b. Clinton, Iowa, Jan. 24, 1950; s. Wesley L. and Harriet K. (Mess) S. AA, Mt. St. Clare Coll., 1970; BA, U. No. Iowa, 1972; MS, Western Ill. U., 1984, postgrad., 1986—. Mgr. inventory control Chgo. NorthWestern R.R., Green Bay, Wis., 1973-74; tchr., coach Clinton Schs., 1975-79; asst. dean Clinton Community Coll., 1980—. Loaned exec. Gateway United Way, Clinton, 1983; trustee Found. Ednl. Excellence, Clinton Schs., 1984—; bd. dirs. Am. Cancer Soc., Clinton, 1985—. Mem. Am. Assn. Sch. Bus. Officials (research com. 1985—), Jaycees (Presdl. award Honor 1984, bd. dirs. 1981-84), Clinton C. of C. (chmn. community activities com. 1985—). Republican. Lutheran. Clubs: Westwood Sports Ctr. (Sterling, Ill.). Office: Clinton Community Coll 1000 Lincoln Blvd Clinton IA 52732

SCHROEDER, MARK JAMES, agricultural educator; b. West Point, Nebr., Aug. 17, 1953; s. James F. and Marlys (Bettenhausen) S.; m. Debra E. Lee, Aug. 18, 1979; 1 child, David. B in Agrl. Econs., U. Nebr., 1976, M in Agrl. Edn., 1982. Agrl. tchr. Blair (Nebr.) Community Schs., 1977-79, Wisner (Nebr). Pilger Schs., 1979—; coach meats team Cuming County 4-H Clubs, West Point, 1984—; advisor Future Farmers of Am., Wisner, 1977—. Sunday sch. tchr. Grace Luth. Ch., West Point, 1984. Mem. Nat. Vocat. Agr. Assn., Wisner Pilger Edn. Assn. (v.p.), Nat. Vocat. Assn., Cuming County Pork Producers, Cuming County Feeders. Democrat. Home: 230 S Farragut West Point NE 68788 Office: Wisner Pilger Schs Box 580 Wisner NE 68791

SCHROEDER, MARK LOUIS, retail company executive; b. Cleve., Apr. 24, 1951; s. Robert Louis and Elaine Lois (Thunhorst) S.; m. Roberta Jo Brandt, July 2, 1977; children: Michael, Jacqueline. BA in Econs. and Bus., Muskingum Coll., 1973. Market analyst Sherwin Williams, Cleve., 1973-76, dir. real estate, 1976-79; real estate rep. Revco Drug Stores Inc., Twinsburg, Ohio, 1979-81, dir. real estate, 1981-83, asst. v.p. real estate, 1983—. Mem. Internat. Council Shopping Ctrs. Lutheran. Avocations: reading, boating.

SCHROEDER, MICHAEL LAWRENCE, chemistry, physics educator; b. Bridgewater, S.D., May 29, 1943; s. Lawrence Michael and Marie Eliabeth (Schroeder) S.; m. Pamela Ann Hill, July 26, 1985; children: Thomas, Mark. BS in Edn., Black Hills State U., 1965; postgrad., U. S.D., 1968, 69, U. Tex., 1972. Sci. instr., coach Jasper (Minn.) Pub. Schs., 1967-74; sales mgr. Internat. Multifoods, Mpls., 1975-84; sci. prof. Estelline (S.D.) Pub. Schs., 1985—; cooperating tchr., trainee instr. Dakota State Coll., Madison, S.D., 1986-87; co-owner Schroeder Elevator Inc., Bridgewater, S.Dak. Mem. long term planning com. Brooking Sch. Bd., Brookings, S.D., 1986—. Named State Conservation Tchr. of Yr., 1987. Mem. Nat. Sci. Tchrs. Assn., Estelline Edn. Assn., S.D. Friends of Pub. TV, S.D. Coaches Assn. Republican. Roman Catholic. Lodge: Elks. Avocations: gardening, fishing, golfing. Home: 918 6th Ave Brookings SD 57006 Office: Estelline Pub Schs Box F Estelline SD 57234

SCHROEDER, NICHOLAS VICTOR, accountant; b. Lima, Ohio, Oct. 1, 1953; s. Robert August and Alice Theresa (Verhoff) S. BS, St. Joseph's Coll., Rensselaer, Ind., 1975. CPA, Ohio. Staff acct. Buckingham, Donaldson and Knueven, Inc., Findlay, Ohio, 1975-77; data processing mgr. Data Processing Services of Findlay, 1977-78; ptnr. Schroeder and Co., CPA's, Ottawa, Ohio, 1978—. Recipient Ernst & Ernst Acctg. Achievement award, St. Joseph's Coll., 1974. Mem. Ohio Soc. CPA's (Lima chpt. treas. 1979-80, sec. 1980-81, bd. dirs. 1984-87, v.p. 1987—), Ottawa Area C. of C. Republican. Roman Catholic. Lodge: KC. Avocations: basketball, swimming, reading. Office: Schroeder and Co 315 E Main St PO Box 307 Ottawa OH 45875

SCHROEDER, PAUL HILLER, JR., shoe company executive; b. Melrose, Mass., Sept. 3, 1942; s. Paul H. and Elizabeth (Soule) S.; m. Judith Lea Ide, June 13, 1964; 1 child, Susan. B.A., Beloit Coll., 1964. Cert. data processor. Programmer, Northwestern Mutual Life Ins., Milw., 1964-66; instr. Inst. Computer Programming, Milw., 1966-67; dir. data processing, real estate, ops. Weyenberg Shoe Co., Milw., 1967—; cons. Mfrs. Box Co., Milw., Mfrs. Chem. Co., Milw. Unit chmn. United Fund, Milw., 1976; bus. advisor Milw. Art Mus., 1982-83. Mem. Am. Contract Bridge League (life master), Mensa. Avocations: bridge; gravity theory; sailing. Home: 16820 Sundown Ct New Berlin WI 53151 Office: Weyenberg Shoe Co 234 E Reservoir Ave Milwaukee WI 53201

SCHROEDER, PHILIP, campus pastor; b. Lansing, Mich., Jan. 24, 1937; s. Philip and Esther Anna (Ude) S.; m. Sharon Ruth Scherer, June 11, 1960; children: Sarah J., Rachel E., Maria J. BD, MDiv, Concordia Sem., 1960; STM, Union Theol. Sem., 1965. Ordained to ministry Luth. Ch., 1961. Campus pastor Ohio State U., Columbus, 1965-74; asst. to exec. dir. Luth. Council in USA, Chgo., 1978-83; dir. Ctr. for Study of Campus Ministry, Valparaiso, Ind., 1974-83; campus pastor Augustana Coll., Rock Island, Ill., 1983—; pres. Columbus Luth. Pastors Conf., 1972-73. Author: Ministry With The Community College: A Lutheran Perspective, 1982; editor CSCM Yearbooks, 1975-80. Mem. Luth. Campus Ministry Assn., Luth. Acad. Scholarship (v.p. 1977-83). Avocation: tennis. Home: 2705 34th St Rock Island IL 61201-5622 Office: Augustana Campus Ministry Augustana Coll Rock Island IL 61201

SCHROEDER, REINHOLD, accountant, consultant; b. Chgo., Nov. 16, 1956; s. Albert and Lena Schroeder; m. Lisa Schmaltz, Aug. 12, 1978; children: Jennifer Lynn, Kristen Karrin. BS in Acctg., Valparaiso U., 1977; MS in Taxation, DePaul U., 1985. CPA, Ind., Mich. Staff acct. Crowe, Chizek, South Bend, Ind., 1978-80; tax specialist Holdeman, Chiddister, Elkhart, Ind., 1980-83; pres., owner Rein Schroeder CPA, South Bend, 1984—; pvt. practice tax cons., bus. valuation, South Bend, 1984—. Bd. dirs. Christian Businessman's Com., South Bend and Elkhart, 1981—. Mem. Internat. Assn. Fin. Planners (bd. dirs. South Bend chpt. 1983, 86), Am. Inst. CPA's, Ind. CPA Soc., Mich. CPA Soc., Bus. Valuation Assn. Republican. Mem. Evang. Free Ch. Lodge: Rotary. Avocation: golf. Office: 501 E Monroe Suite 350 South Bend IN 46601

SCHROEDER, TERRI LEA, city manager, educator; b. Elgin, Ill. Mar. 11, 1955; d. Earl and Caroline Louise Christensen. Student William Rainey Harper Coll., summers, 1973-77; BSEd, No. Ill. U., 1977, MA in Pub. Adminstrn., 1979. Lic. pub. water supply operator Ill. EPA Class C; cert. water treatment plant operator Iowa Dept. Environ. Quality Grade I. Tchr., English, Sch. Dist. 202, Plainfield, Ill., 1977-78; adminstrv. asst. to village mgr. Village of Deerfield (Ill.), 1978-79; asst. village mgr. Village of Lincolnshire (Ill.), 1979-81, village mgr., 1981-82; city mgr. City of Iowa Falls (Iowa), 1982—; cons. exec. dir. Lake County Youth Service Bur., Lake Villa, Ill., 1979-80; communications and pub. relations coordinator Univ. Health Ctr., DeKalb, Ill., 1977-78; legal asst. Winnebago County Legal Aid, Rockford, Ill., spring 1979; feature speaker KIFG Radio Sta., fall 1982. Trustee, mem. budget com., bd. dirs. Iowa conf. 1st Congl. Ch., Iowa Falls, 1982—; bd. dirs., mem. leadership com. Com. of 80's Iowa Falls, 1982—; mem. DeKalb Human Relations Commn., 1977-79; lobbyist for Student Assn. on Higher Edn. Appropriations, 79th Gen. Assembly, Washington; chairperson for polit. awareness week, DeKalb, 1977; mem. Gov.'s Com. on Future of Econ. Growth of Iowa, 1984; mem. Gov.'s Ptnrship Econ. Progress, 1985—; mem. Iowa Electric's Indsl. Adv. Panel, 1986; mem. direct dialonge Northwestern Bell Telephone, 1984-86; founder Iowa Falls 2000, 1985, Iowa Falls Area Arts Council, 1985. Named Iowa's Young Career Woman of 1982-83, Iowa Fedn. Bus. Profl. Women, 1983; named Outstanding Young Working Woman, Glamour Mag., 1984; Esper A. Peterson Found. scholar, 1976-79; Gen. Assembly scholar. Mem. Bus. Profl. Women (Young Career Woman, chmn. dist. IV northwest Iowa 1983-84), Internat. City Mgmt. Assn. (assoc.), Iowa City Mgmt. Assn. (newsletter editor 1983-84), North Cen. Iowa City Mgmt. Assn. (founder, exec. bd. dirs.), Mcpl. Fin. Officers Assn., Am. Pub. Works Assn., Am. Econ. Devel. Council. Home: 315 Estes St Iowa Falls IA 50126 Office: City of Iowa Falls IA 315 Stevens St PO Box 698 Iowa Falls IA 50126

SCHROEDER, WAYNE HAROLD, engineer; b. Milw., Feb. 23, 1944; s. Harold and Carice (Duval) S.; m. Mary Lynn Comerford, June 16, 1971; stepchildren: Kelly, Steven; children: Phillip, Amy. AA, U. Wis., Oshkosh, 1984, BA cum laude, 1987. Draftsman Rasche Schroeder Spransy Architects, Milw., 1963-65, Shattuck Siewert Architects, Neenah, Wis., 1965-66; draftsman, engring. technician, project engr. Appleton (Wis.) Papers Inc., 1966-82, sr. project engr., 1982-84, engring. support services supr., 1984-87, adminstrv. services mgr. Research and Devel. Engring. Dept., 1987—. Pres. Park Commn., Menasha, 1976; v.p. Tri County Ice Arena, Menasha, 1979; adv. bd. mem. Appleton Area Sch. Dist. Drafting Com., 1984-85. Mem. Internat. Facility Mgmt. Assn., Am. Mgmt. Assn. Home: 1268 Mayer St Menasha WI 54952 Office: Appleton Papers Inc 825 E Wisconsin Ave Appleton WI 54911

SCHROEDER, WILLIAM LOUIS, architect; b. Oconto, Wis., Jan. 20, 1935; s. Edmund Roy Schroeder and Roemilda Mercedes (Martens) Hickman; m. Barbara Jean Reed, July 16, 1981; children by previous marriage: Catherine Susanne, Linda Diane. Student, U. Kans., 1958-65, BArch, 1965. Registered architect, Wis., Minn. Inspector ultra precision mech. div. Bendix Corp., Kansas City, Mo., 1959-62; architect in training Dana Dowd Architect, Lawrence, Kans., 1962-65, Hackner, Schroeder, Architects and Engrs., La Crosse, Wis., 1965-68; architect, design dir. Schubert, Schroeder Architects and Engrs., La Crosse, 1968-72; staff architect Hennepin County Dept. Property Mgmt., Minn., 1972-79, mgr. archtl. and engring. services, 1979—. Designer Stout Home Econs. Bldg., U. Wis., 1972. Designer judge La Crosse Pub. Sch. Design Competition, 1968, La Crosse Beautification Com., 1969-70. Served with USN, 1953-57. Mem. AIA (north central regional rep. architects in govt. com. 1977-78), Minn. Soc. Architects (Spl. Merit award 1982). Home: 6400 Barrie Rd Apt 1602 Edina MN 55435 Office: Hennepin County Dept Property Mgmt A2208 Govt Ctr 300 S 6th St Minneapolis MN 55487

SCHROER, EDMUND ARMIN, utility company executive; b. Hammond, Ind., Feb. 14, 1928; s. Edmund Henry and Florence Evelyn (Schmidt) S.; children: James, Fredrik, Amy, Lisa, Timothy, Suzanne. BA, Valparaiso U., 1949; JD, Northwestern U., 1952. Bar: Ind. 1952. Sole practice Hammond, 1952—; assoc. Crumpacker & Friedrich, 1952; ptnr. Crumpacker & Schroer, 1954-56; assoc., then ptnr. Lawyer, Friedrich, Petrie & Tweedle, 1957-62; ptnr. Lawyer, Schroer & Eichhorn, 1963-66; sr. ptnr. Schroer, Eichhorn & Morrow, Hammond, 1967-77; pres., chief exec. officer No. Ind. Pub. Service Co., Hammond, 1977—, chmn., 1978—, also bd. dirs.; asst. dist. atty., No. Ind., 1954-56; bd. dirs., mem. exec. com. Ind. Electric Assn.; bd. dirs. Harris Bank Corp., Assoc. Electric and Gas Ins. Services, Ltd, Bankmont Fin. Corp. Trustee Sch. Bd., Munster, Ind., 1969-71, pres., 1971; fin. chmn. Rep. Party, Hammond, 1958-62; del. Ind. Rep. Conv., 1958, 60, 64, 66, 68. Mem. ABA, Fed. Bar Assn., Ind. Bar Assn. (bd. mgrs. 1969-71), Hammond Bar Assn. (pres. 1966-67), Am. Gas Assn. (various coms., bd. dirs.), Edison Electric Inst. (bd. dirs.). Lutheran. Lodge: Rotary (pres. Hammond club 1968). Office: No Ind Pub Service Co 5265 Hohman Ave Hammond IN 46320

SCHROER, WILLIAM LOUIS, engineering manager; b. Cin., Dec. 9, 1927; s. William Louis and Henrietta Louise (Strothman) S.; m. Ethel Louis Breithold, Sept. 3, 1949; children: William, Dale, Joel. BSME, Purdue U., 1952. Profl. engr., Ont., Can. Engring. mgr. Tecumseh (Mich.) Product Co., 1952-61; mgr. of engring. Westinghouse Electric Co., Columbus, Ohio, 1961-66; v.p. sales Shelmark Industry Inc., Columbus, 1966-69; mgr. corp. devel. Reading (Pa.) Industries, 1969-71; dir. engring. Keeprite Products Ltd., Brantford, Ont., Can., 1971-78; mgr. engring. Elkay Mfg. Co., Lanark, Ill., 1978—. Served as cpl. USMC, 1946-48. Mem. ASHRAE. Avocations: photography, woodcrafting. Home: 2494 Shepard Dr Freeport IL 61032 Address: Elkay Mfg Co 105 N Rochester Lanark IL 61046

SCHROETER, DONALD GARRISON, oil company executive; b. Cin., Nov. 16, 1921; s. Garrison B. and Dorothy Carter (Kendal) S.; m. Phyllis Jean Hannah, July 7, 1945; 1 child, Paul Allen. BS in Chemistry, U. Cin., 1943; MS ChemE, Ohio State U., 1947. Asst. dean of men Ohio State U., Columbus, 1946-48; chem. engr., other positions Amoco Corp., Tex., Ind. and Ill., 1949-69; mgr. employee and pub. relations Amoco Research Ctr., Naperville, Ill., 1970-79; exec. dir., sec. Amoco Found. and Amoco Corp., Chgo., 1980-86; retired 1986; bd. dirs. JETS, N.Y.C. Dir. Donors Forum Chgo., 1983-86, Naperville Community Fund, 1987—; pres. Naperville YMCA, 1973, former bd. dirs.; bd. dirs. Naperville United Way, 1987—. Served to lt. USN, 1943-46. Mem. AAAS, Am. Chem. Soc., Am. Inst. Chem. Engrs. (chmn. fuels & petrochems. div. 1968), Am. Assn. Engring. Socs. (chmn. engring. manpower commn. 1985-86). Republican. Presbyterian. Club: Cress Creek (Naperville). Avocation: golf. Home: 1013 Heatherton Naperville IL 60540

SCHROETTER, PAUL DAVID, insurance agent; b. St. Paul, Minn., Mar. 10, 1947; s. Paul Schroetter and Delores Eileen (Murray) Miller; m. Ann Marie Aultfather, Mar. 22, 1975; 1 child, Paul David Jr. Student, U.S. Naval Acad., 1966-68; cert. bus. adminstrn., U. Minn., 1980. Devel. mgr. Prudential Ins. Co., St. Paul, 1981-84; gen. agt. Crown Life Brokerage Inc., Fargo, N.D., 1984—. Bd. dirs., chmn. fundraising com. N.D. Make-a-Wish Found., Fargo, 1986-87. Mem. Nat. Assn. Life Underwriters, N.D. Life Underwriters Assn. (bd. dirs. polit. action com. 1986—), Fargo/Moorhead Assn. Life Underwriters (bd. dirs. 1986—), Estate Planning Council, Fargo C. of C. (ambassador). Republican. Roman Catholic. Club: Fargo Country. Lodge: Kiwanis. Avocations: racquetball, golf, swimming. Home: Rural Rt 1 Heritage Hills Estates Fargo ND 58103 Office: Crown Life Brokerage Inc 811 Black Bldg Fargo ND 58102

SCHROPP, MARY ANN, medical association executive; b. Fremont, Mich., June 24, 1957; d. Robert Jacob and Dorothy (Ekkel) S.; m. Frank H. Samples, May 5, 1984. Student, U. Mich., 1975-76, Lansing Community Coll., 1979-82. Mem. staff Am. Coll. Emergency Physicians, Lansing, Mich., 1976-80; exec. dir. Univ. Assn. for Emergency Medicine, Lansing, 1980—. Mem. Am. Soc. Assn. Execs., Women in Assn. Mgmt. Office: Univ Assn Emergency Medicine 900 W Ottawa Lansing MI 48915

SCHROTENBOER, DIRK, optometrist; b. Holland, Mich., Jan. 30, 1951; s. Jason John and Olga Jean (Baar) S.; m. Marla Andra Coggins, Aug. 10, 1974; children: Jason Sean, Ryan Lee. Student, Mich. State U., 1969-71, Grand Valley State Coll., 1971-72; OD, Ill. Coll. Optometry, 1976. Pvt. practice optometry Holland, Mich., 1976—. Mem. Am. Optometric Assn. (Optometric Recognition award, 1986), Mich. Optometric Assn., West. Mich. Optometric Ann. (sec. 1981-82), Better Vision Inst., Holland C. of C. Republican. Lodge: Optimists. Avocations: golf, nature, family. Home: 30 S Lee St Zeeland MI 49464 Office: 285 James St Holland MI 49424

SCHROTT, JANET ANN, social work administrator, consultant; b. Cleve., Dec. 11, 1941; d. Louis Vincent and Amelia Jane (Lauko) Cupolo; BA, Flora Stone Mather Coll. of Case Western Res. U., 1963, MS in Social Adminstrn., 1974; MBA, Baldwin-Wallace Coll., Berea, Ohio, 1986; m. Norman Schrott, July 25, 1964. Research asst. Aging Baseline Study, HEW Grant, Miami, Fla., 1964-65; caseworker Div. Social Services, Cuyahoga County Welfare Dept., Cleve., 1965-72, protective services supr., 1974-78; dir. social services Luth. Housing Corp., Cleve., 1973-74; dir. travelers aid services and quality assurance Ctr. for Human Services, Cleve., 1978-86; tng. analyst Cleve. Electric Illuminating Co., Perry, Ohio, 1985-86, supr. support services, 1986—. Bd. dirs. adv. council Adult Rehab. Services, Salvation Army, 1978-85. Cuyahoga County Welfare Dept. grantee, 1972-74. Mem. Assn. MBA Execs., Acad. Cert. Social Workers, Nat. Assn. Social Workers, Am. Evaluation Assn., Nat. Geographic Soc., Travelers Aid Assn. Am. (bd. dirs., Steering com. 1982-85), Theta Phi Omega. Club: Zonta. Home: 25925 Lake Rd Bay Village OH 44146 Office: Perry Tng Ctr PO Box 97 Mail Zone TEC Perry OH 44081

SCHROTT, NORMAN, clinical social worker; b. N.Y.C., Jan. 26, 1938; s. Walter Quido Otto and Anna (Klein) S.; B.A. in Sociology, Cleve. State U., 1972; M.S. in Social Planning and Adminstrn. (grantee State of Ohio 1974-76), Case Western Res. U., 1976; m. Janet Ann Cupolo, July 25, 1964. Lic. Ind. Social Worker, Ohio. Adminstrv. specialist div. social services Cuyahoga County Welfare Dept., Cleve., 1972-74, foster care specialist, 1976-79, child abuse supr., 1979-80, protective services supr., 1980—. Served with U.S. Army, 1962-65. Mem. Acad. Cert. Social Workers, Nat. Assn. Social Workers, Nat. Conf. Social Welfare, Am. Public Welfare Assn., Am. Acad. Polit. and Social Scis., Nat. Audubon Soc., Am. Orchid Soc. Club: Kiwanis. Home: 25925 Lake Rd Bay Village OH 44140 Office: 3955 Euclid Ave Cleveland OH 44115

SCHROUD, DONALD FRANK, real estate development executive; b. Madison, Wis., Aug. 20, 1943; s. Roger Frank and Domenica (Gianunzio) S.; m. Saundra Lee Minnick, June 6, 1968 (div. Jan. 1977); m. Robin Lee Buttala, Dec. 26, 1981; 1 child, Sarah Ann. BS, U. Wis., 1965; postgrad., John Marshall Law Sch., 1977-80. Exec. v.p. Maple Manor, Inc., Fond du Lac, Wis., 1965-68; pres. Pine Manor, Inc., Iron Mountain, Mich., 1968-71; v.p. Van C. Argiris, Chgo., 1971-79; v.p., ptnr. Harrington, Tideman & O'Leary, 1977-84; exec. v.p., ptnr. Hiffman, Shaffer, Anderson, Oakbrook Terrace, Ill., 1984—. Rep. candidate for senator 13th Legis. Dist., 1972. Served with USNG, 1966-72. Mem. Soc. Office and Indsl. Realtors, Indsl. Devel. Research Council, Chgo. Real Estate Bd., Alpha Chi Rho. Avocations: flying, golf, skiing, fishing, hunting. Home: 1030 N State St 47 E Chicago IL 60610 Office: Hiffman Shaffer Anderson One Oakbrook Terr Oakbrook Terrace IL 60181

SCHROYER, WILLIAM KEITH, teacher; b. Vincennes, Ind., July 12, 1955; s. Donovan Wright and Mary Charlene (Mominee) S. AS, Vincennes U., 1977; BS, Ind. State U., 1979. Tchr., coach Flat Rock (Ill.) Grade Sch., 1979-86; tchr. Lincoln Grade Sch., Robinson, Ill., 1986—. Author: For Beginning Autograph Collectors, 1986. Mem. Old Cathedral Basilica Ch., Vincennes. Mem. NEA, Ill. Edn. Assn., Travelers Protective Assn., Universal Autograph Collectors Club. Avocations: autographs, traveling, writing, collecting sports memorabilia. Home: 1505 Broadway St Vincennes IN 47591

SCHRUM, JOHN MARTIN, investment company executive, educator; b. Woodward, Iowa, Dec. 6, 1932; s. Peter Friedrich and Anita (Warner) S.; m. Marilyn Jean Lister, Aug. 9, 1975; children—Rachel Ann, Heidi Marie, Joshua Martin. B.S. in Agrl. Edn., Iowa State U., 1959; M.S. in Agrl. Econs., Purdue U., 1961. Cert. sch. adminstr., Iowa, 1966. Tchr. jr. high and high sch., Coggon, Iowa, 1962-63, Parkersburg, Iowa, 1963-68; broker R.G. Dickinson Co., Cedar Falls, Iowa, 1968-71, Packers Trading Co., Waterloo, Iowa, 1971-72, A.G. Edwards, Waterloo, 1972—. Rep. precinct chmn., Cedar Falls, 1976—. Served with U.S. Army, 1954-56. Lutheran. Avocations: travel, politics, reading. Home: 3703 McClain Dr Cedar Falls IA 50613

SCHUBERT, ELIZABETH M(AY), paralegal adminstrv. asst.; b. Hamilton, Ohio, Sept. 10, 1913; d. A(ndreas) Gordon and Grace Symmes (Laxford) S.; B.S. in Edn. cum laude, Miami U., 1933. Sec., Beta Kappa Nat. Frat., Oxford, Ohio, 1931-38; adminstrv. asst. to dir. Ohio State Employment Service, Columbus, 1938-45, supr. procedures, 1945-47; adminstrv. asst. to pres. Schaible Co., Cin., 1948-50; paralegal adminstrv. asst. to Gordon H. Scherer, Atty.-at-Law, mem. U.S. Congress, U.S. del. to UN, U.S. rep. to exec. bd. UNESCO, Paris, 1950—. Mem. Phi Beta Kappa. Republican. Presbyn. Home: 1071 Celestial St Apt 1701 Cincinnati OH 45202 Office: 1071 Celestial St Suite 2103 Cincinnati OH 45202

SCHUBERT, GREGORY PAUL, dentist; b. St. Louis; s. Raymond William and Mildred Eleanor (Albers). BS in Biology, Med. Sci., So. Ill. U., Edwardsville, 1980; DDS, U. Ill., Chgo., 1984. Gen. practice dentistry Justice, Ill., 1984—. Health service emergency med. technician Miss. River Festival, Edwardsville, Ill., 1977-80. Mem. ADA, Ill. Dental Assn., Chgo. Dental Assn. Lutheran. Avocations: music playing and listening, jogging, biking. Home: 1001 W Belmont #611 Chicago IL 60657 Office: 8008 W 84th St Justice IL 60458

SCHUBERT, JOHN O., pollution control equipmentexecutive; b. Denver, Mar. 29, 1950; s. John Schubert II and Victoria Marosan Tilton; m. Rhonda L. Schulze, Sept. 9, 1978. BSCE, U. Cin., 1973. With sales dept., then engring. mgr. United Air Specialists, Cin., 1974-79; owner, operator Schubert Environ. Equipment, Inc., Glendale Heights, Ill., 1979—. Author: Celestial Navigation with Publication #229, 1979; contbr. articles on air pollution control equipment systems to profl. jours. Office: Schubert Environ Equipment Inc 714 E Fullerton Ave Glendale Heights IL 60108

SCHUBERT, NANCY ELLEN, beauty industry executive, management consultant, franchise director; b. Chgo., June 25, 1945; d. Raymond James and Kathleen Mary (Gibbons) Nugent; m. Emil Joseph Schubert, Jan. 14, 1967; children—James Bryant, Erin Heather, Shannon Kathleen. B.F.A., Mundelein Coll., 1968. Freelance artist, Chgo., 1968; tchr. St. Pius X Sch., Lombard, Ill., 1975-76; pres., treas., dir. Super Style, Inc., Hoffman Estates, Ill., 1981—, Super Six, Inc., Glendale Heights, Ill., 1983—, N.E.S. Mgmt. Inc., Schaumburg, Ill., 1985—, Super Style III, Inc., Berwyn, Ill., 1985—; created and developed Super Style concept and system of operation; created SuperStyle logo and design trademarked in 1983. Mem. Cermak Plaza Mcht. Assn. (bd. dirs.). Republican. Roman Catholic. Avocations: painting, sculpting, downhill skiing, horseback riding, flying. Office: Super Style Inc 707 W Golf Rd Hoffman Estates IL 60194

SCHUBERT, PAUL WM., consulting psychologist; b. Chgo., Jan. 19, 1930; s. Fred Max and Helen Martha (Klank) S.; m. Constance G. Noecker, May 11, 1957; children: Julia, Kristin, Kurt. BA, Wartburg Coll., Waverly, Iowa, 1952; M of Div., Luth. Sch. Theology, Chgo., 1956, MA, 1967; PhD, Purdue U., 1971. Lic. psychologist, Mich.; ordained to ministry Luth. Ch., 1986. Admissions counselor Wartburg Coll., 1951-54; chaplain Luth. Social Missions Soc., Chgo., 1956-57; pastor Luth. Ch. Am., Wis., Ill., Ind., U.S. Virgin Islands, 1957-71; staff psychologist Met. Guidance Ctr., Southfield, Mich., 1971-72; clin. dir. Psychol. Insts. Mich., Franklin, 1972—; exec. dir. Psychol. Studies and Consultation Program, Inc., Franklin, 1976—; psychol. cons. Cranbrook/Kingswood Sch., Bloomfield Hills, Mich., 1974—; pres. Psychol. Health Mgmt., Inc., Farmington Hills, Mich., 1983—. Pres., trustee Plymouth (Mich.) Fife and Drum Corps, 1976—; pres. Wartburg Coll. Alumni Bd., 1977-80. Fellow Am. Assn. Marriage and Family Therapy; mem. Am. Psychol. Assn., Mich. Psychol. Assn., Am. Assn. Counseling and Devel., Psychol. Insts. Mich. (pres. 1976-85). Home: PO Box 206 Franklin MI 48025 Office: Psychol Studies and Consultations Program 26111 W 14 Mile Rd #104 Franklin MI 48025

SCHUBERT, WILLIAM HENRY, educator; b. Garrett, Ind., July 6, 1944; s. Walter William and Mary Madeline (Grube) S.; B.S., Manchester Coll., 1966; M.S., Ind. U., 1967; Ph.D., U. Ill., 1975; m. Ann Lynn Lopez, Dec. 3, 1977; children: Heidi Ann, Henry William; children by previous marriage—Ellen Elaine, Karen Margaret. Tchr., Fairmount, El Sierra and Herrick Schs., Downers Grove, Ill., 1967-75; clin. instr. U. Wis., Madison, 1969-73; teaching asst., univ. fellow U. Ill., Urbana, 1973-75; asst. prof. U. Ill., Chgo., 1975-80, assoc. prof., 1981-85, prof., 1985—, coordinator secondary edn., 1979-82; coordinator instructional leadership, 1979-85, dir. grad. studies Coll. Edn., 1983-85, coordinator grad. curriculum studies, 1985—; vis. assoc. prof. U. Victoria (B.C., Can.), 1981; disting. vis. prof. U. S.C., 1986. Mem. Profs. of Curriculum (factotum 1984-85), Soc. for Study of Curriculum History (founding mem., sec.-treas. 1981-82, pres. 1982-83), Am. Ednl. Research Assn. (chmn. creation and utilization of curriculum knowledge 1980-82, program chmn. curriculum studies div. 1982-83), John Dewey Soc. (bd. dirs. 1986—), Assn. for Supervision and Curriculum Devel. (steering com. of curriculum com. 1980-83, pubs. com. 1987), Am. Ednl. Studies Assn., World Council for Curriculum and Instrn., Soc. for Profs. of Edn., Nat. Soc. for Study of Edn., Inst. Dem. Edn., Phi Delta Kappa, Phi Kappa Phi (pres. U. Ill.-Chgo. chpt. 1981-82). Clubs: Masons, Scottish Rite. Author: Curriculum Books: The First Eighty Years, 1980; editor: (with Ann Schubert) Conceptions of Curriculum Knowledge: Focus on Students and Teachers, 1982; (with Short and Willis) Toward Excellence in Curriculum Inquiry, 1985; Curriculum: Perspective, Paradigm, and Possibility, 1986; mem. editorial bd. Ednl. Studies, Ednl. Theory, Phenomenology Pedagogy, Teaching Edn.; cons. editor Jour. Curriculum and Supervision; contbr. articles to profl. publs. Home: 1642 E 56th St Chicago IL 60637 Office: U Ill at Chgo Coll Edn Box 4348 Chicago IL 60680

SCHUCHART, JOHN ALBERT, JR., utility executive; b. Omaha, Nov. 13, 1929; s. John A. and Mildred Vera (Kessler) S.; m. Ruth Joyce Schock, Dec. 2, 1950; children: Deborah J. Kelley, Susan K. Felton. B.S. in Bus, U. Nebr., 1950; grad., Stanford U. Exec. Program, 1968. With No. Natural Gas Co., Omaha, 1950-71, asst. sec., 1958-60, mgr. acctg., 1960-66, adminstrv. mgr., 1966-71; v.p., treas. Intermountain Gas Co., Boise, Idaho, 1972-75, chief fin. officer, 1973-75; fin. v.p. and treas., chief fin. officer Mont.-Dakota Utilities Co. (now MDU Resources Group, Inc.), Bismarck, N.D., 1976-77, pres., chief operating officer, 1978—, pres., chief exec. officer, 1980—, chmn. bd., 1983—, also dir.; dir. First Bank Bismarck, Knife River Coal Mining Co., Bismarck, Williston Basin Interstate Pipeline Co., Bismarck; mem. adv. bd. Arkwright-Boston Ins. Co., Waltham, Mass.; mem. adv. com. Mountain States Legal Found., Denver. Contbr. articles to profl. jours. Mem. budget com. United Way, Omaha, 1969-70; mem. Council U.S. Savs. Bonds Vols.; bd. dirs. Girl Scouts U.S.A., Boise, 1975; trustee Bismarck YMCA, 1980—, N.D. chpt. Nature Conservancy; mem. lay adv. bd. St. Alexius Med. Ctr., Bismarck; bd. regents U. Mary, Bismarck. Served with AUS, 1951-53. Recipient Scroll and Merit award Adminstrv. Mgmt. Soc., 1972, U. Nebr. at Omaha citation for Alumnus Achievement, 1987. Mem. Am. Gas Assn. (past bd. dirs., Merit award 1968), Midwest Gas Assn., Edison Electric Inst., North Central Elec. Assn., Fin. Execs. Inst., Delta Sigma Pi. Republican. Methodist. Clubs: Elks, Apple Creek Country. Home: 1014 Cottage Dr Bismarck ND 58501 Office: MDU Resouces Group Inc 400 N 4th St Bismarck ND 58501

SCHUCHTER, SIDNEY LAZARUS, physician; b. N.Y.C., June 9, 1925; s. Philip and Beatrice (Teplitz) S.; m. Doris Brown, Mar. 24, 1954 (div. 1978); children—Lynn, Janet, Philip. A.B., Syracuse U., 1948; M.D., Chgo. Med. Sch., 1952. Diplomate Am. Bd. Internal. Medicine, Nat. Bd. Med. Examiners. Intern, Phila. Gen. Hosp., 1952-53; resident physician Cleve. Clinic, 1953-56, asst. staff physician, 1956-57; staff internist VA Hosp., Nashville, 1957-58; staff internist Met. Hosp., Detroit, 1958-63, chief dept. medicine, 1963-69; internist Detroit Indsl. Clinic, Southfield, Mich., 1969—; clin. instr. Frank E. Bunts Ednl. Inst., Cleve., 1956-57; adj. clin. instr. Dept. Medicine, Wayne State U., 1960—. Contbr. articles to med. jours. Served to 1st lt. U.S. Army, 1943-46. Fellow Am. Coll. Physicians; mem. Am. Heart Assn., AMA, Am. Rheumatism Assn., Wayne County Med. Soc. Home: 2370 Somerset Blvd Troy MI 48084 Office: 20755 Greenfield Southfield MI 48075

SCHUCK, STEVEN PHILLIP, podiatrist; b. Bethesda, Md., Feb. 10, 1954; s. Roland Peter and Elizabeth Anne (Robinson) S.; m. Petra Lange, Nov. 20, 1982. BS, Loyola U., Chgo., 1976; D in Podiatric Medicine, Ill. Coll. Podiatric Medicine, 1981. Practice medicine specializing in podiatry Cuba City, Wis., 1981—. Fellow Acad Ambulatory Foot Surgeons; mem. Am. Podiatric Med. Assn., Wis. Podiatric Med. Assn. Republican. Roman Catholic. Avocation: music.

SCHUELLER, DAVID NORBERT, accountant; b. Dubuque, Iowa, Mar. 24, 1950; s. Norbert Frank and Marcella Philomena (Cummer) S.; m. Madonna Jane Phillips, Aug. 6, 1972; children: Scott, Jason. BA, Loras Coll., 1972. CPA, Iowa. Acct. Fahey and Toohey CPA's, Dubuque, 1972-82, ptnr., 1983—. Mem. Am. Inst. CPA's, Iowa Soc. CPA's, Serra Club. Avocation: golf. Home: Box 35F Peosta IA 52068 Office: Fahey & Toohey CPAs Box 815 Dubuque IA 52001

SCHUENEMAN, ARTHUR LATTZ, neuropsychologist; b. Tullahoma, Tenn., Apr. 5, 1943; s. Arthur Henry and Verna Olive (Lattz) S.; divorced; children: Derek Herman, Alec Douglas. BA, Calif. State U., Long Beach, 1965; MA, La. State U., 1971, PhD, 1973. Registered psychologist, Ill. Asst. prof. psychology Loyola U., Chgo., 1973-78; chief psychol. alcohol program Inst. of Psychiatry, Chgo., 1978-79; assoc. prof. psychology Northwestern U., Chgo., 1978-84, assoc. prof. phys. medicine and rehab., 1982-84; sr. clin. psychologist Rehab. Inst. Chgo., 1979-83; asst. prof. surgery Loyola U., Maywood, Ill., 1984—; supervising psychologist Loyola Child Guidance Ctr., Chgo., 1973-77; med. staff Northwestern Meml. Hosp., Chgo., 1982-84, Loyola U. Med. Ctr., 1985—; cons. Rehab. Services of Chgo., Downers Grove, Ill., 1985—. Contbr. articles to profl. jours. Bd. dirs. Pilsen-Little Village Community Mental Health Ctr., Chgo., 1975-77. Mem. Am. Psychol. Assn., Internal Neuropsychol. Soc., Assn. Med. Sch. Psychology Profs., Soc. Psychophysiol. Research, Nat. Rehab. Caucas (mem. steering com., chmn. edn. subcom., 1984—). Avocations: skeet shooting, sports cars, camping, piano. Home: PO Box 1177 Saint Charles IL 60174 Office: Loyola U Med Ctr Neuropsychology Lab Dept Surgery 2160 S 1st Ave Maywood IL 60153

SCHUENKE, DONALD JOHN, insurance company executive; b. Milw., Jan. 12, 1929; s. Ray H. and Josephine P. (Maciolek) S.; m. Joyce A. Wetzel, July 19, 1952; children: Ann, Mary. Ph.B., Marquette U., 1950, LL.B., 1958. Bar: Wis. 1958. Spl. agt. Nat. Life of Vt., 1958-59; real estate rep. Standard Oil Co. of Ind., Milw., 1959-63; atty. Northwestern Mut. Life Ins. Co., Milw., 1963-65; asst. counsel Northwestern Mut. Life Ins. Co., 1965-67, asst. gen. counsel, 1967-74, v.p., gen. counsel, sec., 1974-76, sr. v.p. investments, 1976-80, pres., 1980—, chief operating officer, 1981-83, pres., chief exec. officer, 1983—; bd. dirs. Mortgage Guaranty Ins. Corp., No. Telecom Ltd., Regis Group. Bd. dirs. Milw. Symphony Orch., Com. Econ. Devel., Marquette U., United Way of Greater Milw., Med. Research Fund, Milw. Redevel. Fund, Badger Meter, Milw. Regional Med. Ctr., Milw. Art Mus., Milw. Boys and Girls Club, Grand Ave Corp., Greater Milw. Com., Wis. Taxpayers Alliance, Med. Coll. Wis.; mem. adv. council Am. Heart Assn.; mem. Competitive Wis. Milw. Redevel. Corp. Mem. Wis. Bar Assn., Am. Council Life Ins. (bd. dirs.), Met. Milw. Assn. Commerce (bd. dirs.). Club: University (local bd. dirs.). Home: 3704 N Lake Shore Dr Shorewood WI 53211 Office: Northwestern Mut Life Ins Co 720 E Wisconsin Ave Milwaukee WI 53202

SCHUERHOLZ, JOHN BOLAND, JR., professional baseball executive; b. Balt., Oct. 1, 1940; s. John Boland and Maryne (Wyatt) S.; m. Ellen Louise Lawson, June 21, 1963; 1 dau., Regina Marie Reagan; m. Karen Louise Wiltse, Sept. 18, 1978; 1 son, Jonathan Lawrence. B.E., Towson State U., 1962; student Loyola Coll. (Md.), 1964-66. Tchr., 1962-66; adminstrv. asst. Balt. Orioles, 1966-68; adminstrv. asst. Kansas City Royals, 1968-70, asst. farm dir., 1970-75, farm dir., 1975, dir. scouting and player devel., 1976-79, v.p. player personnel, 1979-81, exec. v.p., gen. mgr., 1981—. Served with AUS, 1966-72. Lutheran. Office: Kansas City Royals PO Box 1969 Kansas City MO 64141 *

SCHUERMAN, NORBERT JOEL, superintendent of schools; b. DeWitt, Nebr., Dec. 26, 1934; s. Edwin J. and Martha (Finkbeiner) S.; m. Charlette Ann Detling, Aug. 6, 1960; children: Robert, Brenda, Todd. B of Music Edn., U. Nebr., 1957, MEd, 1961, EdS in Ednl. Mgmt. and Supervision, 1964, EdD, 1967. Cert. profl. tchr. (life), Nebr. Tchr. Clatonia-Bennett (Nebr.) Pub. Sch., 1955-58; tchr., prin. Mullen (Nebr.) Pub. Sch., 1958-61; prin. Ainsworth (Nebr.) Pub. Sch., 1961-63; sr. high sch. vice prin. Lincoln (Nebr.) Pub. Sch., 1963-66, 67-69; sr. high sch. prin. Arapahoe County Sch. Dist. 6, Littleton, Colo., 1969-74; from asst. supt. to assoc. supt. to supt. Omaha Pub. Schs., 1974—; trustee exec. com. Nebr. Council Econ. Edn., 1985—; bd. dirs. Nat. Study Sch. Evaluation, 1986—, Charles Drew Health Ctr., Fontenelle Forest Assn. Adv. com. Mid-Am. Council Boy Scouts Am., Omaha, 1984—; council regents Big Bros./Big Sisters of Midlands, Omaha, 1986—; bd. dirs. United Way of Midlands, 1985—, chmn. edn. div. campaign, 1985. Mem. Am. Assn. Sch. Adminstrs., Nebr. Council Sch. Adminstrs., Omaha Sch. Adminstrs. Assn., N. Cen. Assn. (bd. dirs. 1983—, chmn. 1987-88, vice chmn. 1986-87), Large City Schs. Supts., Nebr. Schoolmasters Club, Phi Delta Kappa. Home: 4007 N 94th St Omaha NE 68134 Office: Omaha Pub Sch Dist 3902 Davenport St Omaha NE 68131

SCHUERMEYER, FRITZ LUDWIG, physicist, engineer; b. Munich, Mar. 1, 1935; came to U.S., 1963; s. Heinz Ludwig and Lucia (Rastetfer) S.; m. Maria D. Garcia Estrada, Aug. 30, 1969; children: Isabel, Michael, Joseph. Diploma in Engring., Tech. U., Munich, 1959, PhD, 1961. Resident physicist Tech. U., Munich, 1961-62, Lindes Eismashineu, Hollriegels, Kreuth, Fed. Republic of Germany, 1962-63, Wright Aero. Labs., Wright-Patterson AFB, Ohio, 1963—. Soccer referee Yellow Springs (Ohio) Schs., 1983—, judge sci. project, 1985—. Mem. IEEE (Harold V. Noble award 1979, numerous coms.). Avocations: skiing, tennis. Home: 1759 Southview Dr Yellow Springs OH 45387 Office: Aeronautical Labs Wright Patterson AFB OH 45387

SCHUETTE, BILL, congressman; b. Sanford, Mich., Oct. 13, 1953. Student, U. Aberdeen, 1974-75; B.S.F.S., Georgetown U., 1976; J.D., U. San Francisco, 1979. Bar: U.S. Supreme Ct. 1985. Atty. Midland, Mich., 1981—; Mich. field coordinator George Bush for Pres., 1979; Mich. polit. dir. Reagan/Bush for Pres., 1980; mem. 99th Congress from 10th Mich. dist., Washington, 1985—, sophomore Rep. whip; rep. from Region 5 to Rep. Policy Com. Named Outstanding Legislator of Yr., Mich. Assn. of Professions; recipient Leadership award Peace Through Strength Caucus, 1986, Golden Eagle award Am. Fedn. Police, Golden Bulldog award Watchdogs of Treasury. Mem. Midland Hosp. Assn., Midland C. of C., Nat. Rifle Assn. Office: US House of Reps 415 Cannon House Office Bldg Washington DC 20515

SCHUETTPELZ, ALVIN HARLAN, insurance company executive; b. Suring, Wis., Dec. 7, 1944; s. Harold Ervin and Gertrude Margaret (Schuettpelz) S.; m. Ellen Ann Cavil, May 5, 1973; 1 child, Chadwick Jeremy. BS, U. Wis., Green Bay, 1973. Gen. mgr. Maple Valley Mut. Ins. Co., Lena, Wis., 1975—; pres. Town Mut. Services, Sun Prairie, Wis., 1986—; bd. dirs. Guilderland Mut. Reinsurance Co., Delmar, N.Y., 1982—. Pres. Lena Civic Devel. Corp., 1985-86. Served with U.S. Army, 1965-67, Vietnam. Lutheran. Lodge: Lions (pres. Lena 1980-81). Office: Maple Valley Mut Ins Co 304 N Rosera Hwy 141 Lena WI 54139

SCHUH, JAMES PAUL, broadcast executive; b. Milw., May 26, 1938; s. George Joseph and Leona Marie (Lauer) S.; m. Martha Elizabeth Hampton, June 29, 1968. BA, Marquette U., 1962. Announcer, newsman Sta. WFOX, Milw., 1962, Sta. WRIT, Milw., 1963; announcer, news dir. Sta. WSPT, Stevens Point, Wis., 1963-64, program and news dir., 1965-72; gen. mgr. Stas. WSPT and WXYQ-FM, Stevens Point, 1973—; chmn. Stevens Point Telecommunications Commn., 1979-85. Sec. Newman Parish Fin. Council, Stevens Point, 1976-87; mem. Stevens Point Fire and Police Commn., 1986-87. Recipient Disting. Alumni award Marquette U., 1969, Friend of Communication award U. Wis. at Stevens Point, 1986. Mem. Nat. Assn. Farm Broadcasters, Wis. Broadcast Assn. (v.p. radio sect. 1986), Broadcast Pioneers. Roman Catholic. Lodge: Lions (pres. Stevens Point chpt. 1985-86). Avocations: computers, art, collecting recors and stamps. Office: Stas WSPT-AM and WXYQ-FM 500 Division St PO Box 247 Stevens Point WI 54481

SCHUL, BILL DEAN, psychological administrator, author; b. Winfield, Kans., Mar. 16, 1928; s. Fred M. and Martha Mildred (Miles) S.; B.A., Southwestern Coll., 1952; M.A., U. Denver, 1954; Ph.D., Am. Internat. U., 1977; m. Virginia Louise Duboise, Aug. 3, 1952; children—Robert Dean, Deva Elizabeth. Reporter and columnist Augusta (Kans.) Daily Gazette, 1954-58, Wichita (Kans.) Eagle-Beacon, 1958-61; Kans. youth dir. under auspices of Kans. Atty. Gen., 1961-65; Kans. state dir. Seventh Step Found., Topeka, 1965-66; mem. staff Dept. Preventive Psychiatry, Menninger Found., Topeka, Kans., 1966-71; dir. cons. Center Improvement Human Functioning, Wichita, 1975—; author: (with Edward Greenwood) Mental Health in Kansas Schools, 1965; Let Me Do This Thing, 1969; (with Bill Larson) Hear Me, Barabbas, 1969; How to Be An Effective Group Leader, 1975; The Secret Power of Pyramids, 1975; (with Ed Pettit) The Psychic Power of Pyramids, 1976, Pyramids: The Second Reality, 1979; The Psychic Power of Animals, 1977; Psychic Frontiers of Medicine, 1977. Bd. dirs. Recreation Commn., Topeka, United Funds, Topeka, Adamic Inst., Trees for Life; v.p. Pegasus Way; mem. adv. bd. Clayton U. Served with USN, 1945-46. Recipient John H. McGinnis Meml. award for Nonfiction, 1972, Am. Freedom Found. award, 1966, Spl. Appreciation award Kans. State Penitentiary, 1967. Mem. Acad. of Parapsychology and Medicine, Kans. Council for Children and Youth (pres. 1965-66), Assn. for Strenghtening the Higher Realities and Aspirations of Man (pres. 1970-71), Smithsonian Inst. Club: Lions (pres. 1957). Address: Rural Route 3 Winfield KS 67156

SCHULCZ, JOHN HENRY, human resources executive; b. Phila., Jan. 16, 1943; s. Joseph Andrew and Patricia Henry (Griffin) S.; m. Charleen Ann McCann, Feb. 17, 1973; children: John Henry Jr., Timothy Patrick, Matthew McCann, Benjamin Joseph. BA, Villanova U., 1967; MA in Bus., Webster U., St. Louis, 1979. Cert. sr. profl. human resources, Personnel Accreditation Inst., 1983, 1986. Tchr. Hartford County Bd. Edn., Bel Air, Md., 1969-70; office mgr. Phoenix Mut. Life, Hartford, Conn., 1970-74; personnel mgr., corp. indsl. relations mgr. S-R Inc., St. Louis, 1974-79; personnel div mgr. Nashua (N.H.) Photo Products, 1979-80; dir. human resources Southwest Ohio Regional Transit Authority, Cin., 1980—. Mem. Am. Soc. Personnel Adminstrn., Greater Cin. Human Resources Assn. (sec. bd. dirs. 1985-86). Roman Catholic. Avocations: tennis, gardening, reading. Home: 2095 Endovalley Dr Cincinnati OH 45244 Office: Southwest Ohio Regional Transit Authority 6 E 4th St Cincinnati OH 45202

SCHULD, DONALD JOHN, psychologist; b. Dickinson, N.D., May 27, 1953; s. John Francis and Alvera Margaret (Brilz) S.; m. Charlotte Ann Marquart, Aug. 14, 1973; children: Eric, Sarah. BS cum laude, St. John's U., 1974; MS, Eastern Mich. U., 1977. Lic. psychologist, Minn. Psychologist F-M-W Human Services, Blue Earth, Minn., 1977-79; sch. psychologist Martin County Spl. Edn. Coop., Fairmont, Minn., 1979—; pvt. practice Blue Earth, 1980-85; cons. Assissi Residence, Blue Earth, 1980—; interim dir. Friendship Haven, Sherburn, Minn., 1981. St. John's U. grantee, 1972-74. Mem. Am. Psychol. Assn. (assoc.), Minn. Sch. Psychologists, S. Cen. Minn. Psychol. Assn. (sec., treas. 1978-80), Martin County Spl. Edn. Assn. (pres. 1984-85), Minn. Edn. Assn. (mem. task force 1985-86), Psi Chi. Roman Catholic. Avocations: singing, gardening, fishing. Office: Martin County Spl Edn Coop 115 S Park St Fairmont MN 56031

SCHULDENREIN, JOSEPH, archeologist; b. Bad Nauheim, Germany, Nov. 12, 1949; came to U.S., 1952; s. Salomon and Nina (Schiffer) S. BA in Anthropology, SUNY, Stony Brook, 1971; MA in Anthropology, U. Chgo., 1976, PhD in Anthropology, 1983. Sr. cultural resource mgr. Gilbert/Commonwealth, Jackson, Mich., 1980—; archeol. cons. Oriental Inst., Chgo., 1980-86; paleo-ecology cons. Ariz. State U., 1984—; cons. prehistoric environl. All-Am. Pipeline Co., Las Cruces, N.M., 1985—; adv. hist. preservation office tech. assessment U.S. Dept. Interior, Washington, 1985—. Contbr. articles to profl. jours. Israel Govt. grantee, 1977-79; Field Mus. fellow, 1976-77, Fulbright-Hays fellow, 1977-79. Mem. Am. Anthrop. Assn., Soc. Am. Archaeology, Internat. Soc. Sedimentologists, Am. Quaternary Assn., Mich. Acad. Sci. Democrat. Jewish. Club: Jackson (Mich.) Ski. Avocations: photography, skiing, running, softball, backpacking. Office: Gilbert/Commonwealth 209 E Washington Jackson MI 49201

SCHULDT, JOHN CHARLES, SR., safety director, consultant; b. Blue Island, Ill., Apr. 16, 1937; s. Elmer A. and Marion G. (Meier) S.; m. Alice Marie Biedronski, Sept. 13, 1958; children—John, Joe, Christine. B.B.A., U. Toledo, 1966. Cert. safety profl. Supr. Malanco Inc., Blue Island, 1958-61; gen. supr. Alton Boxboard, Chgo., 1961-64; safety supr. Gen. Motors Co., Defiance, Ohio, 1964—; cons.; tchr. four county vocat. sch. Mem. Northwestern Ohio Safety Council. Mem. Nat. Safety Council, Am. Foundrymen Soc., Am. Soc. Safety Engrs., Defiance C. of C. Republican. Roman Catholic. Club: Kettenring Country. Lodges: Rotary, Elks. Office: Central Foundry Defiance OH 43512

SCHULDT, LAURA DUBAICH, corporate manager, human resources consultant; b. Duquesne, Pa., Oct. 12, 1929; d. Nicholas Sava and Deanna (Petrovich) Dubaich; m. Robert R. Schuldt, June 24, 1952; children: Karen, Robert R. III. BA, U. Dayton, 1976. Placement dir. U. Dayton Sch. Law, Ohio, 1977-79; personnel recruiter The White House, Washington, 1980; adminstr., dir. personnel U.S. Dept. Labor, Washington, 1981-82; cons. Robert R. Schuldt & Assocs., Ltd., Fairfax, Va., 1982-85, also bd. dirs.; mgr. human resources Household Internat., Prospect Heights, Ill., 1985—; adv. bd. Northeastern Ill. U. Coll. Bus. and Mgmt., Chgo., 1986-87. Exhbn. chmn. Westchester Art Soc., White Plains, N.Y., 1971-72; founder The Collectors, Dayton Art Inst., 1976. Recipient Disting. Service award Student Bar Assn., U. Dayton Sch. Law, 1978. Mem. Am. Soc. for Tng. and Devel., Exec. Council on Fgn. Diplomats, Human Resources Mgmt. Assn. Chgo. Republican. Avocations: art, golf, tennis. Home: 1932 Mission Hills Ln Northbrook IL 60062 Office: Household Internat 2700 Sanders Rd Prospect Heights IL 60070

SCHULER, CAROL SUE, candy store owner; b. Flint, Mich., Jan. 17, 1953; d. Vernon William And Dorothy Jean (Stacey) S. Restaurant mgr. W.T. Grant, Fenton, Mich., 1972-75; mgr. young men's dept. Hughes & Hatcher, Flint, Mich., 1975-78; asst. mgr. Vitality Foods, Flint, 1978-79; asst. mgr. Long John Silver's, Sylvan Lake, Mich., 1979-81, Troy, Mich., 1981-82; owner Sweet Variations, Fenton, 1982—. Mem. Retail Confectioners Internat., Am. Fedn. Ind. Bus., Dibbleville Merchants Assn. Roman Catholic. Avocations: travel, concerts, gardening, philately. Office: Sweet Variations 101 W Shiawassee Ave Fenton MI 48430

SCHULER, JACK WILLIAM, healthcare company executive; b. N.Y.C., Sept. 17, 1940; m. Renate Rosita Schuler; children—Tino, Tanya, Tessi. B.S. in Mech. Engring., Tufts U., 1962; M.B.A., Stanford U., 1964. Various positions Tex. Instruments, France, W.Ger. and Japan,, 1964-72; dir. sales and market diagnostics Abbott Labs., North Chicago, Ill., 1972-74, div. v.p. sales and mktg., 1974-76, v.p. diagnostic ops., 1976-83, group v.p., 1983-85, exec. v.p., 1985-86; pres. Abbott Labs., North Chicago, 1987—, also bd. dirs. Bd. dirs. Lake Forest Hosp., Ill., 1983—. Office: Abbott Labs Abbott Park IL 60064

SCHULERT, SANFORD CHARLES, chemical company executive; b. Camden, N.J., Aug. 21, 1943; s. Sanford Oscar and Patricia Adams (Flack) S.; m. Gretchen Louise Schneider, May 10, 1968; children: Grant Sanford, Suzanna Banks. Research chemist Liquid Carbonic, Chgo., 1965-66, The Richardson Co., Melrose Park, Ill., 1966-67; advt. writer Amoco Chems., Chgo., 1967-83, mgr. advt., 1983-84, dir. mktg. communications, 1984—; chmn. pub. relations SPI Composites Inst., N.Y.C., 1985-87. Mem. Bus. Profl. Advt. Assn. (cert.). Club: Tibetan Terrier of Greater Chgo. (pres., founder 1978-79). Avocations: photography, dog obedience tng. Office: Amoco Chems Co 200 E Randolph Chicago IL 60601

SCHULKE, C. PATRICK, chain food and drug store company executive. Pres., chief exec. officer Red Owl Stores, Inc., Hopkins, Minn. Office: Red Owl Stores Inc 215 E Excelsior Ave Hopkins MN 55343 *

SCHULLER, CAROLE ADELE, nurse; b. Youngstown, Ohio, Dec. 15, 1941; d. Raymond Thomas and Isabelle Mae (Woods) Logan; m. Donald Edward Schuller, June 22, 1963; children—D. Geoffrey, T. Douglas, J. Eric. Diploma St. Luke's Hosp., Cleve., 1962, cert. cen. service tech., Purdue U., 1984, cen. service mgr., 1987. Night charge nurse psychiatry St. Luke's Hosp., Cleve., 1962; head nurse psychiatry, 1963; charge nurse med.-surgery Timken Mercy Med. Ctr., Canton, Ohio, 1964, charge nurse orthopedics, 1970, nurse, 1973-76, charge nurse gynecology, 1976-81, asst. dir. materials mgmt. cen. sterile supply, 1981, staff nurse Upjohn Health Care Services, 1986, pvt. duty nurse, 1968—; ARC nurse, Canton, 1970—; indsl. nurse Hoover Co., North Canton, 1971-74. Mem. Assn. Advancement Med. Instrumentation, Am. Hosp. Assn., Internat. Assn. Hosp. Cen. Service Mgrs., St. Luke's Alumna Assn. Republican. Lutheran. Clubs: Branhaven Tennis, Lake Cable Recreation Assn. Office: Timken Mercy Med Ctr 1320 Timken Mercy Dr Canton OH 44708

SCHULMAN, ALAN MICHAEL, business owner; b. Chgo., Feb. 5, 1946; s. Aaron and Anne (Bendersky) S.; m. Barbara Picard, May 27, 1984. BBA, Roosevelt U., 1968. Salesman Dictaphone Corp., Chgo., 1968-69; sales engr. Boston Gear, Chgo., 1969-70; mgr. Imperial Packaging, Chgo., 1970-71; owner A.M.S. Distbg., Skokie, Ill., 1971-77; owner, pres. Greater Distbn. Services, Glenview, Ill., 1977—, The Battery Bank (formerly Jalco Inc.), Glenview, 1982—. Author newspaper column Gardening Information, 1980. Mem. Entrepreneurs Network. Club: Men's Garden of North Shore (Highland Park) (pres. 1984-85). Avocations: gardening, fishing, photography. Office: Jalco Inc 2011 John's Dr Glenview IL 60025

SCHULMAN, FREDERICK ROBERT, data processing executive; b. Chgo., Apr. 16, 1939; s. Sidney Nathan and Rose (Cohen) S.; m. Sheila Barbara Kominsky; children: Brian, Laura. BS in Indsl. Mgmt., Purdue U., 1961. Sr. programmer Kitchens of Sara Lee, Deerfield, Ill., 1963-69; mgr. systems tng. Travenol Labs., Deerfield, 1969—; instr. Oakton Community Coll., Des Plaines, 1978—, advisor, 1982—. Served with USAR. Mem. Am. Soc. Tng. and Devel. Home: 3434 W Meadow St Northbrook IL 60062 Office: Travenol Labs 1 Baxter Pkwy Deerfield IL 60015

SCHULMAN, SIDNEY, neurologist, educator; b. Chgo., Mar. 1, 1923; s. Samuel E. and Ethel (Miller) S.; m. Mary Jean Diamond, June 17, 1945; children—Samuel E., Patricia, Daniel. B.S., U. Chgo., 1944, M.D., 1946. Asst. prof. neurology U. Chgo., 1952-57, asso. prof., 1957-65, prof., 1965-75, Ellen C. Manning prof., div. biol. scis., 1975—. Served with M.C. AUS, 1947-49. Mem. Am. Neurol. Assn., U. Chgo. Med. Alumni Assn. (pres. 1968-69), Chgo. Neurol. Soc. (pres. 1964-65). Home: 5000 East End Ave Chicago IL 60615 Office: U Chgo Culver Hall 1025 E 57th St Chicago IL 60637

SCHULTE, C., mineral company executive; b. 1927. Student, U. S.D., 1951. With L.G. Everist, Inc., Sioux Falls, S.D., 1951—, v.p., 1973—, sr. v.p., 1978-81, pres., 1981—, also bd. dirs. Office: L G Everist Inc 313 S Phillips Ave Sioux Falls SD 57102 *

SCHULTE, CRAIG ANDREW, insurance executive; b. Cedar Rapids, Iowa, Dec. 8, 1952; s. Melvin Andrew and Marjorie Fay (Tecklenburg) S. BA, Loras Coll., 1975; MA, Marquette U., 1977. Coordinator Rockford (Ill.) Bd. Edn., 1977-78; underwriter Life Investors, Inc., Cedar Rapids, 1978-83, employment specialist, 1983—; Bd. dirs. Light Co. Credit Union, Cedar Rapids; mem. adv. council Goodwill industries, Cedar Rapids, 1986—. Recipient Cert. Appreciation U.S. Small Bus. Assn., 1986. Mem. Am. Soc. Personnel Adminstrn., Midwest Coll. Placement Assn. Roman Catholic. Avocations: sports, photography, reading, travel. Office: Life Investors Inc 4333 Edgewood Rd NE Cedar Rapids IA 52499

SCHULTHEIS, WILLIAM JOSEPH, manufacturing executive; b. Rochester, N.Y., Jan. 24, 1930; s. Joseph J. and Mary M. (Laux) S.; m. Jo Ann Wilkinson, Sept. 19, 1970; children: William J. Jr., Andrew. BSME, Notre Dame U., 1952. Mech. engr. Sandia Corp., Albuquerque, 1952-54; mgr. Missile div. Chrysler Corp., Detroit, 1958-62, 3-M Co., Rochester, N.Y., 1962-73; gen. mgr. Colorcraft Corp., Rockford, Ill., 1973—. Chmn. Am. Cancer Soc., Rockford, 1986-87, Parochial Sch. Bd., Rockford, 1982-85. Served to lt. USNR, 1955-58. Mem. Soc. Photography Scientists and Engrs., Photo Mktg. Assn., Am. Bus. Clubs (pres. 1983). Home: 2874 Woodhill Dr Rockford IL 61111 Office: Colorcraft Corp 214 N Church St Rockford IL 61105

SCHULTZ, ALAN HERBERT, civil engineer, water resources consultant; b. Long Beach, N.Y., May 25, 1936; s. Irving Jack and and Esther Vivian (Nager) S.; m. Harriet Carol Spar, Aug. 24, 1958; children: Dana L., Reid B. BCE, Cornell U., 1958; MS, U. Iowa, 1959. Registered profl. engr., Ill., N.Y., N.J. Civil engr. Harza Engring. Co., Chgo., 1959-62, sect. head, 1965-69, dept. head, 1970-72, assoc., 1975—; field engr. Harza Engring. Co., Lahore, Pakistan, 1962-65; plan engr. Harza Engring. Co., Accra, Ghana, 1969-70; resident engr. Harza Engring. Co., Medellin, Colombia, 1972-75. Contbr. articles to profl. jours. Chmn. Flood Adv. Com., Deerfield, Ill., 1983. Mem. Internat. Water Resources Assn. (v.p. 1980-83, pres. 1983-86, treas. 1986—), Am. Water Resources Assn., Chgo. Assn. Commerce and Industry (Mex. com. 1983), U.S. Hispanic C. of C. Home: 241 Forestway Dr Deerfield IL 60015 Office: Harza Engring Co 150 S Wacker Dr Chicago IL 60606

SCHULTZ, BETTY LITTLEJOHN, banker, accountant; b. Starkville, Miss., June 5, 1945; d. William Wylie and Mary Ruth (Laney) Littlejohn; m. Joseph John Schultz, Jr., Oct. 24, 1965 (div. Apr. 1974); 1 child, Theresa Lynn. BS in Acctg., Miss. State U., 1966; postgrad. in commerce, U. Ill., 1978-82. CPA, Ill. Chief fin. officer Prairie Opportunity, Starkville, 1967-69; staff acct. Peat, Marwick & Mitchell Co., Austin, Tex., 1969-72; tax mgr. Clifton Gunderson & Co., Champaign, Ill., 1972-87; v.p. 1st Nat. Bank, Champaign, 1987—. Contbr. articles to profl. jours. Treas. Planned Parenthood, Champaign County, Ill., 1981-87; v.p. Estate Planning Council, 1986-87. Mem. Am. Inst. CPA's, Ill. Soc. CPA's (pres. fin. planning com. 1986—), Internat. Assn. Fin. Planners, Am. Women CPA's, Phi Mu. Avocations: photography, music, snorkeling, reading. Home: 707 S McCullough Urbana IL 61801 Office: 1st Nat Bank 30 E Main St Champaign IL 61820

SCHULTZ, BRYAN CHRISTOPHER, dermatologist, educator; b. Evergreen Park, Ill., June 29, 1949; s. Warren H. and Norinne A. (McNamara) S.; m. Cathleen T. Fitzgerald, May 14, 1977; children—Carrie T., Megan C., Erin L. B.S., Loyola U., Chgo., 1971; M.D., Loyola Stritch Sch. Medicine, 1974. Diplomate Am. Bd. Dermatology. Intern St. Joseph's Hosp., Chgo., 1975; resident Northwestern U., Chgo., 1976-79; asst. clin. prof. Loyola U., Maywood, Ill., 1979—; practice medicine specializing in dermatology, Oak Park, Ill., 1979—; cons. dermatologist West Suburban Hosp., Oak Park Hosp., Gottlieb Hosp., Westlake Hosp., 1979—. Author: Office Practice of Skin Surgery, 1985. Patentee surgical instrument. Contbr. articles to sci. publs. Supr., founder pub. awareness program for skin cancer Loyola U. Stritch Sch. Medicine, 1983—. Mem. Am. Acad. Dermatology, Am. Soc. Dermatologic Surgery, Internat. Soc. Dermatologic Surgery, Soc. Investigative Dermatology, Chgo. Dermatologic Soc., AMA (del. intern and resident sect. 1975), Ill Dermatologic Soc. (exec. com. 1981, chmn. membership com. 1983-84), N.Y. Acad. Scis., Soc. Cosmetic Chemists, Royal Soc. Medicine, Alpha Sigma Nu. Office: Affiliates in Diseases and Surgery of Skin S C 1159 Westgate Oak Park IL 60301

SCHULTZ, CARL HERBERT, retail chain executive; b. Chgo., Jan. 9, 1925; s. Herbert V. and Olga (Swanson) S.; m. Helen Ann Stevesson, June 6, 1948; children: Mark Carl, Julia Ann. B.S. in Gen. Engring., Iowa State U., 1948. With Schultz Bros. Co., 1948—; mdse. mgr. and store planner Schultz Bros. Co., Chgo., 1962-70; v.p. Schultz Bros. Co., Lake Zurich, Ill., 1968-72; pres. Schultz Bros. Co., 1972—, Ill. Schultz Bros. Co., Ind. Schultz Bros. Co., Iowa Schultz Bros. Co., Wis. Schultz Bros. Co. Mem. Lake Bluff (Ill.) Zoning Bd. Appeals, 1976-85, chmn., 1978-85. Served with U.S. Army, 1944-46. Mem. Lake Zurich Indsl. Council (sec. 1976), Assn. Gen. Mdse. Chains (dir. 1975-86, exec. com. 1983-86, chmn. nat. conv. 1982), Ill. Retail Mchts. Assn. (dir. 1984—), Wis. Retail Fedn. (dir. 1981—). Presbyterian. Club: Bath and Tennis (Lake Bluff). Home: 701 Center St Lake Bluff IL 60044 Office: 800 N Church St Lake Zurich IL 60047

SCHULTZ, CHARLES ALBERT, theatre educator, historian, director; b. Seattle, Mar. 4, 1941; s. Edmund Anton and Helen D. (Beall) S.; m. Patricia Bowers, June 1, 1963; children—Todd Matthew, Vaughn Andrew, Cynthia Kristine. B.S., Bowling Green U., 1963, Ph.D. (teaching fellow), 1970; M.A., U. Ill., 1964. Profl. actor Wagon Wheel Playhouse, Ind., 1963; tchr., speech dir. Northmont High Sch. (Ohio), 1964-66; dir. theatre, assoc. prof. speech Dickinson (N.D.) State Coll., 1970-74; head theatre div. U. Dayton (Ohio), 1974-76; chmn. dept. theatre N.W. Mo. State U., Maryville, 1976—, chmn. grad. council for programs, policies, and degrees, 1986-88; mng. dir. Sosondowah-Gov.'s Players of N.D., 1972-74; founder, mng. dir. Popcorn Playhouse, Dayton, 1974-76; artistic and coordinating dir. Creative Arts Prodns., St. Joseph, Mo., 1983, 84; dir. children's theatre; cons. Mem. State bd. Area Commn. on Higher Edn., 1985; chmn. bd. Wesley Found., 1985-88. Lay leader Methodist chs., Mo., N.D.; chmn. Univ. Div. United Way of Nodaway County, 1986-88. Recipient Disting. Achievement in Theatre award Bowling Green U., 1963, Outstanding Achievement in TV Directing, 1962, Outstanding Educator award Fireland campus, 1970; Disting. Faculty Service award Dickinson State Coll., 1974; Outstanding Contbr. to Drama award, Dayton, 1976; Mo. Com. for Humanities grantee, 1977, 82; Ohio Arts Council grantee, 1975. Mem. Am. Theatre Assn., Speech Communications Assn., Speech and Theatre Assn. Mo., Mid-Am. Theatre Alliance, Omicron Delta Kappa, Alpha Psi Omega, Theta Alpha Phi, Rho Sigma Mu. Lodge: Rotary (dir. club service) (Maryville). Scholarly writer Am. Theatre Cos. Publ., 1986; contbr. articles to profl. jours. Home: 1004 W Cooper Maryville MO 64468 Office: NW Mo State U Maryville MO 64468

SCHULTZ, DON EDWARD, academic administrator; b. Wewoka, Okla., Jan. 20, 1934; s. Carl Edward and Donna Loretta (Welch) S.; m. Margaret Ann Putman, Aug. 28, 1956 (div. Mar. 1978); children: Steven D., Bradley E., Jeffrey P. BBA, U. Okla., 1957; MA, Mich. State U., 1975, PhD, 1977. Sales mgr. Associated Pubs., Dallas, 1957-59; advt. dir. Tyler (Tex.) Courier-Times, 1959-64; sr. v.p. Tracy-Locke Advt., Dallas, 1965-74; asst. prof. Mich. State U., 1975-77; assoc. dean, dir. grad. advt. programs Northwestern U., 1978—; pres. Agora, Inc., Evanston, 1982—. Author: Essentials of Creative Strategy, 1982; co-author: Strategic Advertising. Campaigns, 1985, Essentials of Sales Promotion, 1984, Sales Promotion Management, 1984; editor: Journal of Direct Marketing, 1986—. Mem. Promotion Mktg. Assn. Am. (bd. dirs. 1986), Internat. Advt. Assn. (edn. chmn. 1984), Am. Mktg. Assn., Assn. Edn. in Journalism, Dir. Mktg. Assn. Episcopalian. Home: 412 Lee St Apt 1 Evanston IL 60202 Office: Northwestern U 1813 Hinman Ave Evanston IL 60201

SCHULTZ, FREDERICK CARL, die casting company executive; b. Toledo, Sept. 23, 1929; s. Oswald Charles and Margarete Joanne (Schoeneberg) S.; m. Anita Margarete Lueller, Sept. 10, 1955; children: David, Elisabeth, Mary, Martha. BSChemE, U. Mich., 1951, MS in Indsl. Engring., 1952. Research engr. LECO Corp., St. Joseph, Mich., 1956-61, dir. research, 1961-67, market research mgr., 1967-71; exec. v.p. Benton Harbor (Mich.) Malleable, 1971-75; pres. Cast-Matic Corp., Stevensville, Mich., 1975—. Patentee in field. Bd. dirs. Community Concerts Assn., St. Joseph, 1960-69, S.W. Mich. Symphony, St. Joseph, 1965—, Blossomland Area Safety Council, St. Joseph, 1972-79, Krasl Art Ctr., St. Joseph, 1985—. Served to cpl., U.S. Army, 1951-54. Republican. Lutheran. Avocations: photography, travel. Home: 2816 Evergreen Dr Saint Joseph MI 49085 Office: Cast-Matic Corp 2800 Yasdick Dr Stevensville MI 49127

SCHULTZ, JEFFREY ERIC, optometrist; b. Cleve., Jan. 28, 1948; s. Albert I. and Lenore (Aster) S.; m. Nancy Lynne Wachs, July 5, 1970; children—Brian David, Amy Robin. B.S. in Zoology, Ohio State U., 1970, O.D., 1974, M.S. in Physiol. Optics, 1974. Lic. optometrist, Ohio, Fla. Research asst. Ohio State U. Coll. Optometry, Columbus, 1970-74, clin. instr., 1974-75; gen. practice optometry, Cleve., 1975—. Contbr. articles to profl. jours. Nikon scholar. Mem. Ohio Optometric Assn. (continuing edn. com. 1976—, chmn. sports vision com. 1977-79, Optometric Recognition award 1978), Fla. Optometric Assn., Am. Optometric Assn. (Optometric Recognition award 1980, 82—, charter mem. contact lens sect. 1982—, mem. sports vision sect. 1983—), Am. Acad. Optometry, Nat. Eye Research Found., Council Sports Vision, Vision Conservation Inst., Better Vision Inst., Ohio Contact Lens Soc., Cleve. Optometric Assn. (trustee 1985—), Beta Sigma Kappa, Phi Eta Sigma. Lodge: Masons. Avocations: philately, fine art collecting. Office: 5706 Turney Rd Garfield Heights OH 44125 also: 5395 Mayfield Rd Lyndhurst OH 44124

SCHULTZ, JOHN ARTHUR, accountant; b. Jackson, Mich., Jan. 8, 1954; s. Arthur L. and Margaret M. (Anderson) S. BA, Mich. State U., 1976. CPA, Mich. Tax and audit mgr. Bond & Co., P.C., Jackson, 1977—. Mem. Am. Inst. CPA's, Nat. Assn. Accts., Mich. Assn. CPA's. Roman Catholic. Lodge: Civitan (treas. Jackson chpt. 1986-87, Civitan of Yr. award 1986). Avocations: golf, skiing. Home: 1005 W Morrell Jackson MI 49203 Office: Bond & Co PC 706 W Michigan Jackson MI 49201

SCHULTZ, JOHN LEO, univ. adminstr.; b. Cape Girardeau, Mo., Feb. 1, 1931; s. Louis J. and Norma E. (Shivelbine) S.; B.S. magna cum laude, Southeast Mo. State Coll., 1954, B.S. in Edn. magna cum laude, 1957; M.S. in Edn., So. Ill. U., 1959, Ed.S., 1965; Ph.D. Open U., 1977; postgrad. U. Chgo., 1960-63, U. Tenn., 1954, Louisville Sem., 1953, U. Mo., 1977; m. Carole Nelle Sparks, Aug. 19, 1959; children—Elizabeth Ann (dec.), Deborah Lorraine. Asst. in guidance and counseling Community High Sch., Downers Grove, Ill., 1959-60; dir. curriculum research Sch. Dists. 58 and 59, Downers Grove, 1960-64; adminstrv. supr. student employment program So. Ill. U., Carbondale, 1964-65; adminstrv. asst. and prof. psychology Jefferson Coll., Hillsboro, Mo., 1965-66; registrar Cornell Coll., Mt. Vernon, Iowa, 1966-67, asst. prof. edn., 1966-67; registrar, sec. to exec. faculty Sch. Medicine, Washington U., St. Louis, 1967—, asst. prof., 1967—, asst. dean acad. adminstrn., 1976—, registrar Barnes Hosp. Med. Staff, 1967—, lectr. resident program in orthodontics Sch. Dental Medicine, 1970—; cons. Fed. Aid Coordinating Services, Inc., Chgo., 1965-67, Washington, 1966-67; dist. rep. to sch. improvement program U. Chgo., 1960-63; evaluative cons. Health Care Specialists, Inc., St. Louis. Pres. Internat. Forum, Open U., 1977-79; bd. dirs. St. Louis Neighborhood Health Ctr., Inc. Served with U.S. Army, 1954-56. Mem. Am. Ednl. Research Assn., Am. Assn. Coll. Registrars and Admissions Officers (nat. chmn. profl. schs. group 1975-76), Midwestern Psychol. Assn., Mo. State Tchrs. Assn., NEA, Nat. Soc. for Study Edn., Am. Assn. U. Adminstrs., Am. Assn. Higher Edn., Am. Assn. Med. Colls. (group on student affairs), Phi Kappa Phi, Kappa Delta Pi, Phi Delta Kappa. Lutheran. Author: (with George J. Fuka) New Education Interaction Curriculum Model, 1966; author curriculum studies; contbr. articles to profl. publs. Office: Washington Univ School Medicine 660 S Euclid Ave Saint Louis MO 63110

SCHULTZ, LEE E., manufacturing company executive; b. 1941. With Yardman Inc., Jackson, Mich., 1969-76, Allsons Corp., Hillsdale, Mich., 1976-78; with Lozier Corp., Omaha, 1978—, v.p. ops., 1978-82, pres., bd. dirs., 1982—. Office: Lozier Corp 4401 N 21st St Omaha NE 68110 *

SCHULTZ, LOUIS WILLIAM, justice Supreme Ct.; b. Deep River, Iowa, Mar. 24, 1927; s. M. Louis and Esther Louise (Behrens) S.; m. D. Jean Stephen, Nov. 6, 1949; children: Marcia, Mark, Paul. Student, Central Coll., Pella, Iowa, 1944-45, 46-47; LL.B., Drake U., Des Moines, 1949. Bar: Iowa. Claims supr. Iowa Farm Mut. Ins. Co., Des Moines, 1949-55; partner firm Harned, Schultz & McMeen, Marengo, Iowa, 1955-71; judge Iowa Dist. Ct. (6th dist.), 1971-80; justice Iowa Supreme Ct., 1980—; county atty. Iowa Couty, 1960-68. Served with USNR, 1945-46. Mem. Am. Bar Assn., Iowa Bar Assn. (bd. govs.), Iowa Judges Assn. (pres.). Republican. Lutheran. Office: Univ Iowa Coll of Law Iowa City IA 52242 *

SCHULTZ, MARTIN C., hearing and speech pathologist, educator; b. Phila., Aug. 29, 1926; s. George D. and Belle (Seidman) S.; m. Beatrice Golder, June 17, 1951; children: Claudia, Richard, Jeffrey, Amy. BA, Temple U., 1950; MA, U. Mich., 1952; PhD, U. Iowa, 1955. Instr. speech and hearing Northwestern U., Evanston, Ill., 1954-55; dir. speech and hearing Hosp. of U. Pa., Phila., 1955-58; supr. research lab. Cleve. Hearing and Speech Ctr., 1958-60; prof. speech and hearing U. Mich., Ann Arbor, 1960-66, Ind. U., Bloomington, 1965-72; dir. hearing and speech Children's Hosp., Boston, 1972-85; prof. communication disorders and scis. So. Ill. U., Carbondale, 1985—; dir. Audiological Engring. Corp., Somerville, Mass., 1982—; cons. MIT, 1973-85, Wrentham State Home and Tng. Sch., Mass., 1975-85. Author: Analysis of Clinical Behavior in Speech and Hearing, 1972, Laboratory Instrumentation for Speech and Hearing, 1986, Maps and Territories, 1986. Served with U.S. Army, 1944-46, ETO. Grantee NIH, 1959, 62, U.S. Dept. Edn., 1979, E.S. and J.M. Shapiro Found., 1979, 86. Mem. Am. Speech-Lang. Hearing Assn. (Editor's award 1974), Acoustical Soc. Am., AAUP, AAAS, Sigma Xi. Home: Rural Rt 1 Spring Arbor Box 389A Carbondale IL 62901 Office: So Ill U Carbondale IL 62901

SCHULTZ, NANCY LYNN, data processing manager; b. Minot, N.D., Feb. 12, 1957; d. Alfred Carl and Evangeline (Benson) S.; foster children: Cora McCarter, Julie Davidson. AA, N.D. State U., 1978, BBA, 1980; postgrad., Tenn. State U., 1984-85. Systems engr. devel. CNA Life Ins. Co., Chgo., 1980; project leader, systems engr. Excalibur Ins. Co., Dallas, 1981-83; account mgr. Parthenon Ins. Co., Nashville, 1983-85; adminstr. Gen. Motors Truck and Bus., Detroit, 1985—. Bd. dirs. Meadowbrook Racquet and Fitness Ctr., Rochester, Mich., 1986-87; v.p. Bloomfield Orchards Civic Assn., Auburn Hills, Mich., 1986-87. Fellow Life Mgmt. Inst.; mem. Jaycees. Republican. Baptist. Avocations: sailing, photography, skiing. Home: 616 Sheffield Rd Auburn Hills MI 48057 Office: Electronic Data Systems 5555 New King St PO Box 7019 Troy MI 48007

SCHULTZ, RICHARD CARLTON, plastic surgeon; b. Grosse Pointe, Mich., Nov. 19, 1927; s. Herbert H. and Carmen (Huebner) S.; m. Pauline Zimmermann, Oct. 8, 1955; children: Richard, Lisa, Alexandra, Jennifer. McGregor scholar, U. Mich., 1946-49; M.D., Wayne State U., 1953. Diplomate Am. Bd. Plastic Surgery. Intern Harper Hosp., Detroit, 1953-54; resident in gen. surgery Harper Hosp., 1954-55, U.S. Army Hosp., Fort Carson, Colo., 1955-57; resident in plastic surgery St. Luke's Hosp., Chgo., 1957-58, U. Ill. Hosp., Chgo., 1958-59, VA Hosp., Hines, Ill., 1959-60; practice medicine specializing in plastic surgery Park Ridge, Ill., 1961—; clin. asst. prof. surgery U. Ill. Coll. Medicine, 1966-70, assoc. prof. surgery, 1970-76, prof., 1976—, head div. plastic surgery, 1970-87; pres. med. staff Lutheran Gen. Hosp., Park Ridge, 1977-79; vis. prof. Jikei U. Coll. Medicine, Tokyo, 1976. Author: Facial Injuries, 1970, 2d edit., 1977, Maxillo-Facial Injuries from Vehicle Accidents, 1975, Outpatient Surgery, 1979. Mem. sch. bd., Lake Zurich, Ill., 1966-72, pres., 1968-72; pres. Chgo. Found. for Plastic Surgery, 1966—. Served to capt. M.C., AUS, 1955-57. Recipient research award Found. Am. Soc. Plastic and Reconstructive Surgery, 1964-65, Med. Tribune Auto Safety award, 1967, Robert H. Ivy award, 1969, Disting. Sci. Achievement award Wayne U. Coll. Medicine Alumni, 1975; Sanvenero-Rosselli award, 1981; Fulbright scholar U. Uppsala, Sweden, 1960-61. Fellow ACS (pres. local commn. on trauma 1985—); mem. Am. Assn. Plastic Surgeons, Am. Soc. Plastic and Reconstructive Surgeons, Midwestern Assn. Plastic Surgeons (pres. 1978-79), Chgo. Soc. Plastic Surgeons (pres. 1970-72), Midwestern Assn. Plastice Surgeons (pres. 1978-79), Am. Soc. Maxillo-Facial Surgeons (award of hon. 1986), Am. Assn. Automotive Medicine (pres. 1970-71, A. Merkin award 1982), Am. Cleft Palate Assn., Tord Skoog Soc. Plastic Surgeons (pres. 1971-75). Home: 21150 N Middleton Dr Kildeer IL 60047 Office: 1875 Dempster St Park Ridge IL 60068

SCHULTZ, ROBERT KENNETH, minister; b. Mpls., July 29, 1947; s. Kenneth Theodore and Lillian G. (Wohlfeil) S.; m. Pamela Jean Schmiesing, Nov. 11, 1966; children: Cindi Lee, Abi Elisabeth, Caleb Robert. Student, U. Minn., 1965-67; BA with honors, Bear Valley Sch. Biblical Studies, 1976; student, Clemson U., 1976-77, U. Alaska, Soldotna, 1979-80. Minister Ch. of Christ, Clemson, S.C., 1976-77, Soldotna, 1977-80; minister and elder Ch. of Christ, Bismarck, N.D., 1982—; dir. Dakota Christian Camp, Bismarck, 1984—; lectr. in field. Active Y's Men Internat., Bismarck, 1984—. Recipient Vol. Leader award YMCA, 1984. Mem. Western Christian Found., Bismarck/Mandan symphony Orch. Assn. (bd. dirs. 1986—), Bismarck Chem. Health Found. (bd. dirs. 1986—), Sons of Norway, 3 Crowns. Republican. Lodge: Kiwanis (com. chmn. Bismarck chpt. 1985, bd. dirs. 1987—). Avocations: golf, walking, cycling, volleyball. Office: Ch of Christ 1914 Assumption Dr Bismarck ND 58501

SCHULTZ, TERRY ALLEN, architectural consultant; b. Elmhurst, Ill., May 18, 1946; s. Clarence Frederick Theodore and Elvera Stella (Landmeier) S. BArch, U. Ill., 1970, MS, 1971; MBA, Keller Grad. Sch. Mgmt., 1980. Registered architect, Wis. Sr. project structural engr. Skidmore Owings & Merrill, Chgo., 1971-75; gen. mgr. Archtl. Engring. Cons., Arlington Heights, Ill., 1975-77; project engr. Gillum-Colaco, Chgo., 1977-79; prin. A/E Consulting, Arlington Heights, 1979—; Bd. dirs. Evang. Health Systems Corp., Oak Brook, Ill., 1978—; chmn. bd. dirs. Evang. Care Corp., Oak Brook, 1985—. Mem. bd. govs. Good Sheperd Hosp., Barrington, Ill., 1978-83; trustee Bethany Hosp., Chgo., 1980—; v.p. Good Sheperd Manor, Barrington, 1985—; pres., treas. St. John United Ch. of Christ, Arlington Heights, 1976-80. Mem. AIA, Nat. Assn. Corp. Dirs. Republican. Club: American (Hong Kong). Lodge: Lions. Home and Office: 316 E Euclid St Arlington Heights IL 60004

SCHULTZ, THEODORE WILLIAM, retired educator, economist; b. Arlington, S.D., Apr. 30, 1902; s. Henry Edward and Anna Elizabeth (Weiss) S.; m. Esther Florence Werth; children: Elaine, Margaret, T. Paul. Grad., Sch. Agr., Brookings, S.D., 1924; B.S., S.D. State Coll., 1927, D.Sc. (hon.), 1959; M.S., U. Wis., 1928, Ph.D., 1930; LL.D. (hon.), Grinnell Coll., 1949, Mich. State U., in 1962, U. Ill., 1968, U. Wis., 1968, Cath. U. Chile, 1979, U. Dijon, France, 1981; LL.D., N.C. State U., 1984. Mem. faculty Iowa State Coll., Ames, 1930-43; prof., head dept. econs. and sociology Iowa State Coll., 1934-43; prof. econs. U. Chgo., 1943-72, chmn. dept. econs., 1946-61, Charles L. Hutchinson Disting. Service prof., 1952-72, now emeritus; econ. adviser, occasional cons. Com. Econ. Devel., U.S. Dept. Agr., Dept. State, Fed. Res. Bd., various congl. coms., U.S. Dept. Commerce, FAO, U.S. Dept. Def., Germany, 1948, Fgn. Econ. Adminstrn., U.K. and Germany, 1945, IBRD, Resources for the Future, Twentieth Century Fund, Nat. Farm Inst., others.; dir. Nat. Bur. Econ. Research, 1949-67; research dir. Studies of Tech. Assistance in Latin Am.; bd. mem. Nat. Planning Assn.; chmn. Am. Famine Mission to India, 1946; studies of agrl. developments, central Europe and Russia, 1929, Scandinavian countries and Scotland, 1936, Brazil, Uruguay and Argentina, 1941, Western Europe, 1955. Author: Redirecting Farm Policy, 1943, Food for the World, 1945, Agriculture in an Unstable Economy, 1945, Production and Welfare in Agriculture, 1950, The Economic Organization of Agriculture, 1953, Economic Test in Latin America, 1956, Transforming Traditional Agriculture, 1964, The Economic Value of Education, 1963, Economic Crises in World Agriculture, 1965, Economic Growth and Agriculture, 1968, Investment in Human Capital: The Role of Education And of Research, 1971, Human Resources, 1972, Economics of the Family: Marriage, Children, and Human Capital, 1974, Distortions of Agricultural Incentives, 1978, Investing in People: The Economics of Population Quality, 1981; co-author: Measures for Economic Development of Under-Developed Countries, 1951; editor: Jour. Farm Econs., 1939-42; contbr. articles to profl. jours. research fellow Center Advanced Study in Behavioral Sci., 1956-57; recipient Nobel prize in Econs., 1979. Fellow Am. Acad. Arts and Scis., Am. Farm Econs. Assn., Nat. Acad. Scis.; mem. Am. Farm Assn., Am. Econ. Assn. (pres. 1960, Walker medal 1972), Royal Econ. Soc., Am. Philos. Soc., others. Home: 5620 Kimbark Ave Chicago IL 60637 Office: Unov of Chgo Dept of Economics 5801 Ellis Ave Chicago IL 60637 *

SCHULTZ, WARREN ROBERT, aerospace engineer; b. Chgo., June 29, 1949; s. Warren Gimbel and Helen Catherine (Mattes) S.; m. Mary Elise Nunnally, Mar. 31, 1973; children: Warren Thomas, Gregory James. BS in Aerospace Engring., U.S. Naval Acad., 1971. Commd. ensign USN, 1971, advanced through grades to lt., 1975, resigned, 1976; process engr. Corning Glass Works, Harrodsburg, Ky., 1976-78, quality control supr., 1978; project engr., elec. supr. Manville Corp., Etowah, Tenn., 1978-82; plant engr. Manville Corp., Waterville, Ohio, 1982-86, prodn. supt., 1986—. Religious tng. instr. St. Joseph's Ch., Maumee, Ohio, 1984-85; little league coach Anthony Wayne Area Baseball Assn., Waterville, 1983-86. Republican. Roman Catholic. Avocations: raquetball, golf. Home: 39 Mattatuck Way Waterville OH 43566 Office: Manville Corp PO Box 517 Toledo OH 43693

SCHULTZ, WILLIAM ARNOLD, marine surveyor, consultant; b. Racine, Wis., Apr. 3, 1942; s. Arnold H. and Grace Ann (Olson) S.; m. Ann Louise Petersen, Oct. 24, 1970; children: Kurt, Karin. BS in Marine Transp., U.S. Mcht. Marine Acad., 1964. Marine surveyor Midwest Adjustment Co., Milw., 1970-81; pres. Marine Service Bur., Franklin, Wis., 1981—. Served with U.S. Mcht. Marine, 1964-69; served to lt. USNR, 1964-72, Vietnam. Mem. Internat. Oceanagraphic Found., Wis. Marine Hist. Soc., Boat Owners Assn. U.S., Am. Boat and Yacht Council, Maritime Seaway Users Council. Baptist. Avocations: hunting, fishing, travel. Home and Office: Marine Service Bur 7131 S 68th St Franklin WI 53132

SCHULZ, DALE METHERD, retired pathologist; b. Fairfield, Ohio, Oct. 20, 1918; s. Jerome Charles and Minnie Irene (Metherd) S.; m. Dorothy Ann Hartman, June 14, 1947; children—Ann Huston, Stephen Metherd. B.A., Miami U., Oxford, Ohio, 1940; M.S., Washington U., St. Louis, 1942, M.D., 1949. Diplomate Am. Bd. Pathology, 1954. Research chemist Tretolite Co., St. Louis, 1942-45; intern, then resident in pathology Barnes Hosp., St. Louis, 1949-51; fellow in pathology Ind. U., Indpls., 1951-53, asst. prof. pathology Sch. Medicine, 1953-58, assoc. prof., 1958-62, prof., 1962-66, clin. prof., 1966-85; pathologist Meth. Hosp., Indpls., 1966-85. Bd. dirs. Allisonville Civic Assn.; past pres. Cedar Knolls Assn. Served as capt. U.S. Army, 1955-57. Grantee Riley Meml. Assn., 1954-64, USPHS, 1964-71. Mem. Am. Assn. Pathologists, Internat. Acad. Pathology. Republican. Presbyterian. Author: (with others) Principles of Human Pathology, 1959; patentee. Home: 9540 Copley Dr Indianapolis IN 46260

SCHULZ, JEROME ALLEN, information systems director; b. Milw., Sept. 2, 1950; s. Robert Louis and Mary Margaret (Watry) S.; m. Dianne Elizabeth Olson, July 29, 1978; children: David, Mary Beth, Amy. BA, Cornell U., 1972; MA in Teaching, Northwestern U., 1974; M of Pub. Adminstrn., Roosevelt U., 1977. Tchr. Chgo. Bd. Edn., 1972-78; computer programmer U. Wis., Milw., 1978-81; staff analyst Northwestern Nat. Ins., Milw., 1981-85; info. systems dir. Milw. county Dept. Social Services, Milw., 1985—. Contbr. articles to profl. jours. Mem. Assn. Systems Mgmt. (bd. dirs.). Roman Catholic. Avocation: family activities. Home: 506 E Day Ave Whitefish Bay WI 53217 Office: Milw County Dept Social Services 1220 W Vliet St Milwaukee WI 53205

SCHULZE, ARTHUR ROBERT, JR., food company executive; b. LaCrosse, Wis., Jan. 31, 1931; s. Arthur Robert and Elizabeth Margaret (Showers) S.; m. Joan M. Hanifan, June 25, 1955; children: Brett, Mark, David, Anne. BA, Carleton Coll., Northfield, Minn., 1952; MBA with distinction, Harvard U., 1958. With IBM Corp., until 1959; from sales trainee to product mgr. Procter & Gamble Co., Cin., 1959-62, product mgr., 1961-62; product mgr. angel cake mixes Gen. Mills, Inc., Mpls., 1962-63, product mgr. cake mixes, 1963-65, mktg. mgr. baking mixes, 1965-66, mktg. mgr. cereals, 1966-69, asst. gen. mgr. Big G div., 1969-70, v.p., gen. mgr. Golden Valley div., 1970-73, group v.p. consumer foods, 1973-80, exec. v.p., 1981-85, also pres. grocery products food group; exec. v.p., pres. Grocery Products Food Group, 1985—; bd. dirs. Tennant Co., Inc., Gen. Mills, Inter-regional Fin. Corp. Trustee Carleton Coll., Northfield, Minn., 1977—; bd. govs. Meth. Hosp., St. Louis Park, Minn., 1980—. Served with AUS, 1953-56. Recipient Merit award Mpls. United Way. Mem. Cereal Inst. (mem. exec. com., bd. dirs.), Civic League Mpls. Republican. Clubs: Mpls.; Harvard Bus. Sch.; Interlachen Country (Edina, Minn.). Avocation: tennis. Office: General Mills Inc 9200 Wayzata Blvd Minneapolis MN 55440

SCHULZE, ERWIN EMIL, manufacturing company executive, lawyer; b. Davenport, Iowa, May 4, 1925; s. Erwin F. and Hazel (Sorensen) S.; m. Jean E. Steele, June 21, 1952; children: Suzanne Schulze Walker, William Steele, Donna Schulze Ballard, Stephen Johnson. B.A., De Pauw U., 1947; LL.B., Yale, 1950. Bar: Ill. 1950. Practiced in Chgo.; partner firm Rooks, Pitts, Fullagar & Poust (and predecessor firms), 1950-67, counsel, 1967-80; pres., dir. Standard Alliance Industries, Inc., 1967-79; pres., chief operating officer, dir. Ceco Industries, 1985—; chmn. The Ceco Corp., 1984—, Ceco Industries, Inc., 1986—; chief counsel Standard Forgings Corp., Chgo., 1963-65; exec. v.p. Standard Forgings Corp., 1965-67; treas., dir. Transue & Williams Steel Forging Corp., Alliance, Ohio, 1965-66; dir. AAR Corp., Interlake, Inc.; mem. com. on specialist assignment and evaluation and space planning com. Midwest Stock Exchange, bd. govs., 1979—; Mem. Adv. Council Zoning, Chgo., 1955-57. Bd. visitors De Pauw U., 1979-81, trustee, 1981—; co-chmn. Joint Com. Codify Ill. Family Law, 1958-61; mem. Mayor Chgo. Adv. Council Juvenile Delinquency, 1958-62; v.p., dir. Midwestern Air Pollution Prevention Assn., 1958-72, chmn. legal com., 1960-63; Vice pres., dir. Chgo. Tennis Assn., 1964-71; sec., dir. Chgo. Tennis Patrons, 1960-74; chmn. men's ranking com. U.S. Lawn and Tennis Assn., 1961-71. Served as lt. (j.g.) USNR, 1943-46, PTO. Mem. ABA, Ill. Mfrs. Assn. (bd. dirs. 1983—, vice chmn. 1986—), Phi Beta Kappa. Presbyterian (deacon, elder trustee). Clubs: Chicago, Economics, Chicago Golf, Legal; Shoreacres. Office: Ceco Industries Inc 1400 Kensington Rd Oak Brook IL 60521 *

SCHULZE, ERWIN FRED C., engring executive; b. Chgo., Nov. 14, 1921; s. Fred C. and Marie (Sedlmeier) S.; m. Joyce Ione Bergee, June 20, 1948; children: Kurt, Christine, Karen, Barbara, Eric. BSME, Ill. Inst. Tech., 1943. Project engr. Engring. Research Assocs., St. Paul, 1946-49, Sperry-Rand, South Norwalk, Conn., 1949-57, Underwood Corp., Hartford, Conn., 1957-60, Addressgraph-Multigraph Co., Cleve., 1960-70; product mgr. Waynco, Winona, Minn., 1970-71; v.p. purchasing N.Am. Systems, Inc., Bedford Heights, Ohio, 1971—. Patentee in field. Served to Lt. (j.g.) USN, 1947-52. Avocations: golf, woodworking. Home: 14027 E Willard Dr Novelty OH 44072 Office: N Am Systems Inc 24700 Miles Rd Bedford Heights OH 44146

SCHULZE, JOHN HENRY, photographer, educator; b. Scottsbluff, Nebr., June 7, 1915; s. Henry and Josephine (Westerholdt) S.; m. M. Lavonne Foster, Oct. 5, 1940; 1 child, Tascha J. BE, Emporia (Kans.) State U., 1940; MFA, U. Iowa, 1948. From instr. to prof. U. Iowa, Iowa City, 1948-85, prof. emeritus, 1985—; Artist in residence Western Ill. U., 1967, U. Ala., Tuscalooosa, 1969, Washburn U., Topeka, 1972, Western Ky. U., 1973, SUNY Geneseo, 1973, Cleve. Inst, Arts, 1974, U. Mo., Kansas City, 1982, Gallery Talk Art Mus. 1985, Tisch Ctr. for the Arts NYU, 1985, Northeast La. U., 1986. One man shows include Davenport Mcpl. Art Gallery, 1965, 82, The U. of Iowa Cedar Rapids Art Ctr., 1967, U. Ala. Fine Arts Festival, 1969, Exposure Gallery N.Y.C., Sun Valley (Idaho) Ctr. for the Arts, Springfield (Ill.) Art Mus., 1983, Kathryn Nash Gallery U. Minn., 1985, The Mus. Contemporary Photography Columbia Coll., Chgo., 1985; group shows include Cornell Coll. Fine Arts Festival, 1964, U. Sask., Can., 1965, Nihon U. Tokyo, 1964, Met. Mus. Art, 1967, 68, 69, Hayden Gallery MIT, 1968, Ohio State U., 1973, Chgo. Peace Mus., 1981, Sioux City (Iowa) Art Ctr. 1983, Harman Fine Arts Ctr Drake U., 1983, Mich. State U., East Lansing, 1984, Centre Internat. D'Art Contemporain, Paris, 1985; permanent collections include Oakland Mus., U. Calif.-Davis, Western Ill. U., La. State Coll., Hatden Gallery MIT, Coll. St. Benedict, St. Joseph, Minn., Ednl. Facilities Lab N.Y.C., Crocker Art Gallery, Sacramento, Calif., Smithsonian Inst., Library of Congress. Mem. Nat. Soc. for Photographic Edn. (founding, Honored Educator award 1985). Home: 5 Forset Glen Iowa City IA 52240 Office: U Iowa Art Bldg Iowa City IA 52242

SCHUMACK, JOAN MARIA, magazine publisher, journalist; b. Methoni, Greece, Nov. 4, 1953; came to U.S., 1958; d. Eugene John and Lydia Mary (Stellpflug) S. BA, Marquette U., 1976. Editor Post Newspapers, West Allis, Wis., 1975-79; freelance writer Wauwatosa, Wis., 1979-81; info. officer Common Council, Milw., 1981-84; founder, editor, publisher ETHNOS mag., Wauwatosa, 1985—; community programmer Viacom Cablevision, Glendale, Wis., 1983—. Assoc. editor Am. Cyclist sect. Bicycling mag., 1980. Active Adoption Info. and Direction, Milw., 1982—; Friend of Milw. Symphony, 1985—, Milw. Art Museum, 1984—; sponsor Cyprus Childrens' Fund, N.Y.C., 1985—; established (with Mrs. Lydia M. Schumack) Eugene J. Schumack Meml. Journalism Fund in the Coll. of Journalism at Marquette U. for grad. study, 1986. Recipient Spl. Award Nat. Council Tchrs. of English, 1972. Mem. Soc. Profl. Jours. (Mark of Excellence award 1975), Milw. Press Club, Women in Communication, Inc., Nat. Assn. Female Execs., Marquette Journalism Alumni Assn. (bd. dirs. 1976-78, 1980-82), Nat. Fedn. Local Cable Programmers, Phil-Hellenic Greek Profl. Soc., Alpha Sigma Nu, Kappa Tau Alpha. Democrat. Eastern Orthodox. Club: Florentine Opera (Milw.). Avocations: foreign language, art, world travel, soap carving, kite flying. Office: ETHNOS Mag PO Box 25805 Milwaukee WI 53225-0805

SCHUMANN, HAROLD ELMER, telephone service analyst; b. Pinconning, Mich., Nov. 19, 1939; s. Elmer William and Regina (Rezler) S.; m. Patricia Hycki, Feb. 8, 1958; children—Rick, Randy, Rodney, Roger, Ronald. Graduate Pinconning High Sch. Line man Contel Telephone Co., Pinconning, 1958-60, repairman, 1960-69, plant supr., 1969-75, service ctr. supr., 1975-81, telephone service anaylst, 1985—. Emergency med. technician No. Bay Ambulance Service, 1969; chief fire dept., Pinconning, 1971, pres. Booster Club, 1965. Roman Catholic. Lodge: Lions (pres. 1969). Home: 3805 Fraser Rd Pinconning MI 48650

SCHUNA, ARTHUR ALLEN, pharmacist; b. Clear Lake, Wis., June 11, 1950; s. Arthur W. and Ruby I. (Riley) S.; m. Cher Steiner, July 30, 1983. BS, U. Wis., Madison, 1973, MS, 1975. Registered pharmacist. Resident in pharmacy Univ. Hosp., Madison, 1973-75; clin. coordinator William S. Middleton VA Hosp., Madison, 1975—; assoc. prof. U. Wis. Sch. Pharmacy, Madison, 1975—. Contbr. articles to profl. jours. Bd. dirs. so. dist. Wis. Arthritis Found., Madison, 1983—. Mem. Am. Soc. Hosp. Pharmacists, Wis. Soc. Hosp. Pharmacists, Ambulatory Care Sig Group (chmn.). Avocations: music, reading, horticulture, bicycling, cross country skiing. Office: William S Middleton VA Hosp 2500 Overlook Terr Madison WI 53705

SCHUNK, WILLIAM ALLEN, military officer; b. Omaha, Sept. 27, 1942; s. Orville Edwin and Beulah Fern (Andersen) S.; m. Diane Adele Brodbeck, July 25, 1964; children: Eric, Kelly, Karen. BA in English, U. Nebr., Omaha, 1964; MA in Police Adminstrn., Troy State U., 1981. Commd. 2d lt. USAF, 1964; dep. dir. tng. disciplinary barracks USAF, Ft. Leavenworth, Kans., 1969-72; instr. security police acad. USAF, Lackland AFB, Tex., 1972-76; chief security police USAF, Yokota AFB, Japan, 1976-79; mgmt. cons. USAF, Montgomery, Ala., 1979-82; advanced through grades to lt. col. USAF, 1981; chief security police USAF, Offutt AFB, Nebr., 1982—. Mem. Internat. Assn. Chiefs of Police, Air Force Soc. Mgmt. Cons., Air Force Assn., Bellevue, Nebr. C.of C. (mil. affairs com. 1982-86, Pres.' special service award 1984, Vol. of Yr. award 1985). Republican. Lutheran. Avocations: golf, bridge, reading. Home: 12509 S 30th St Omaha NE 68111 Office: USAF 55 Security Police Squadron Offutt AFB NE 68113-5000

SCHURING, J(AMES) KIRK, insurance company executive; b. Canton, Ohio, Sept. 17, 1952; s. James A. and D. Margaret (Felton) S.; m. Darlene K. Newkirk, Mar. 2, 1976; children: J. Derrick, Kristin. Student, Kent State U., 1970-74. Sec., treas. The Schuring Agy., Inc., Canton, 1978-80, pres., 1980—; ins. cons. Stark Devel. Bd., Canton, 1985—. Bd. dirs. Canton Urban League, 1983—, Stark/Wayne Am. Lung Assn., 1984—, Canton Players Guild, 1986; mem. exec. bd. Stark County Rep. Orgn., Canton, 1981—; chmn. Stark County Reagan-Bush Com., Canton, 1984. Mem. Ind. Ins. Agents Canton (bd. dirs. 1982-85), Jaycees Internat. (Sen. 1984), U.S. Jaycees (Charles Kulp, Jr. award 1983, Gordon B. Thomas award 1983), Ohio Jaycees (James Lammermier award 1982), Canton Jaycees (pres. 1982-83). Republican. Mem. Ch. Christ. Clubs: Canton (bd. dirs. 1986—), Brookside Country. Avocations: golf, swimming, tennis. Home: 1817 Devonshire Dr NW Canton OH 44708 Office: The Schuring Agy Inc 401 W Tuscarawas Canton OH 44702

SCHURMEIER, L. JON, health systems executive; b. Elgin, Ill., Feb. 17, 1937; s. LeRoy H. and June (Zorn) S.; B.A., DePauw U., Greencastle, Ind., 1959; M.B.A., U. Pitts., 1960, M.H.A., 1970; m. Donna Kay Cunningham, Apr. 1, 1961; children—Kristin, Darla, Steffany. From merchandiser to mgr. Carson, Pirie, Scott & Co., Chgo., 1963-67; adminstrv. extern Presbyn.-St. Luke's Hosp., Chgo., 1967-68; adminstrv. resident, then asst. adminstr. Cin. Gen. Hosp., 1969-72; asso. adminstr. S.W. Gen. Hosp., Middleburg Heights, Ohio, 1972-81, adminstr., 1981-85, system pres., 1985—; asst. clin. prof. U. Pitts.; regent OSDVS; dir., officer Hudson Younglife, 1981-85; dir., officer Emerald Health Network, Westside Imaging Ctr.; bd. dirs. Hospac, Dual Diagnostic Ctr.; mem. Hudson (Ohio) Com. Emergency Health Care. Pres. Olde Towne Colony Homeowners Assn., 1979; ch. lay leader, Hudson, 1973-76, trustee, 1981-84, adminstrv. bd.; bd. dirs. Hudson Girls-Womens Softball League, 1980—, treas.; officer Hudson Girls Softball; chmn. Shared Services Council; village councilman, 1984; trustee Greater Cleve. Hosp. Assn., Greater Cleve. Hosp. Assn. Served with U.S. Army, 1961-63. Recipient recognition award Seven Hills Neighborhood Houses, Cin., 1972. Fellow Am. Coll. Hosp. Adminstrs.; mem. Hosp. Fin. Mgmt. Assn., Am. Public Health Assn., Health Care Adminstrs. N.E. Ohio, DePauw U. Alumni Assn., U. Pitts. Alumni Assn. Health Adminstrn. (pres. 1976), Middleburg C. of C. Clubs: Hudson, Western Res. Tennis. Author articles in field. Home: 49 Keswick Dr Hudson OH 44236 Office: SW Gen Hosp 18697 E Bagley Rd Middleburg Heights OH 44130

SCHUSSELE, MICHAEL JON, accountant; b. Canton, Ill., Feb. 25, 1947; s. Robert Petrini and Rosemary (Sutton) Schussele; adopted s. Halbert A. Schussele; m. Ingeborg Marie Thompson, Jan. 19, 1979 (div. May 1981). BA in Philosophy and Math., Shimer Coll., 1968; MA in Social Change, Sangamon State U., 1972. CPA, Ill. Social econ. program specialist Gov.'s Office State of Ill., Springfield, 1968-70; pvt. practice cons. Springfield, 1970-78; asst. dir. legislation Ill. Sec. State, Springfield, 1977-83; dir. fin. adminstrn. Ill. State Library, Springfield, 1983-84; pres., owner Byte ComputerPower, Inc., Springfield, 1984—, also bd. dirs.; pvt. practice acctg. Springfield, 1980—; cons. curriculum planning So. Ill. U. Sch. Medicine, Springfield, 1971-72; microcomputer instr. Lincoln Land Community Coll., Springfield, 1986-87. Precinct committeeman Sangamon County Dem. Orgn., Springfield, 1972-80, vice chmn., 1974-80; pres. Woodside Twp. Dem. Orgn., 1974-80; founding mem. governing bd. Common Cause-Ill., Chgo., 1974-81; dist. coordinator Common Cause-20th Congl. Dist., Springfield, 1976-79. Mem. Am. Inst. CPA's (mgmt. adv. services div., personal fin. planning div.), Ill. CPA Soc. (com. mem. 1982-85), Assn. Govt. Accts. Presbyterian. Avocations: writing, tennis. Home: 207 Commerce Box 239 Rural Rt #1 Curran IL 62670 Office: 3695 S 6th St Springfield IL 62703

SCHUSTER, EUGENE IVAN, venture capital executive; b. St. Louis, Dec. 8, 1936; s. David Theodore and Anne (Kalisher) S.; B.A., Wayne State U., 1959, M.A., 1962; postgrad. U. Mich., 1959-62, (Fulbright scholar) Warburg Inst., U. London, 1962-65, Courtauld Inst., U. London and London Sch. Econs., 1962-65; m. Barbara Zelmon, June 22, 1958 (div.); children—Joseph, Sarah, Adam. Lectr. art history Wayne State U., Detroit, 1959-62, Eastern Mich. U., Ypsilanti, 1960, Rackham extension U. Mich., 1961, Nat. Gallery, London, 1962-65; owner London Art Gallery, Detroit, 1965—; chmn. bd. Venture Funding Ltd.; chmn. bd. dirs., pres., founder Quest Biotechnology Inc., The Claridge Art Gallery, Inc.; founder, bd. dirs. Univ. Sci. Ptnrs., Inc. Recipient Distinguished Alumni award Wayne State U., 1968. Mem. Founders Soc., Detroit Inst. Arts, Detroit Art Dealers Assn., Art Appraisers Assn. Am. Home: 25425 Dennison Franklin MI 48025 Office: Venture Funding Ltd 321 Fisher Bldg Detroit MI 48202

SCHUSTER-EAKIN, CYNTHIA ANNE, editor, freelance writer; b. Sharon, Pa., Sept. 15, 1952; d. John Richard and Marianne (Holodnak)

Schuster; m. Eric Judson Eakin, May 26, 1979; children: Marah Anne, Judson Pierce. BJ, Kent (Ohio) State U., 1975. Assoc. editor Modern Tire Dealer mag., Akron, Ohio, 1977-80; editor Where mag., Cleve., 1980-82; contbg. editor Ohio Restaurant News, Columbus, 1982—; assoc. pub. Athletic Adminstrn. mag., Cleve., 1982—; editor This Week In Cleve., 1982—. Mem. Cleve. Press Club. Democrat. Roman Catholic. Avocations: reading, gourmet cooking. Home: 440 Bradley Rd Bay Village OH 44140 Office: 1501 Euclid Ave #736 Cleveland OH 44115

SCHUTT, GORDON JOHN, accountant; b. Toledo, Nov. 13, 1933; s. Harold John and Virginia Ellen (Gordon) S.; m. Janet K. Zimmerman, Feb. 3, 1956; 1 child, Jana. BBA, U. Toledo, 1956; postgrad., Bowling Green State U., 1965-66. CPA, Ohio. Jr. acct. C. Richard Fruth, Fostoria, Ohio, 1955-56; mgr. C. Richard Fruth and Assocs., Fostoria, 1958-70; ptnr. Fruth & Co., Fostoria, 1970-77, mng. ptnr., 1977—. Pres. Riley Sch. PTA, Fostoria, 1968; v.p. Findlay Sch. Official Assn., 1972; bd. dirs. Fostoria Athletic Boosters, 1975-82, St. Wendelin Sch. Endowment Fund, Fostoria, 1986—. Served with U.S. Army, 1956-58. Mem. Am. Inst. CPA's, Ohio Soc. CPA's, Ohio High Sch. Athletic Assn. (football official 1965-86), Findlay Ohio Football Official Assn. (v.p. 1972), Ohio Athletic Conf. (officiating staff). Republican. Methodist. Clubs: Fostoria Country (bd. dirs. 1972), Valley Creek. Lodge: Rotary, Elks (exalted ruler 1965). Home: 407 West Ridge Dr Fostoria OH 44830 Office: Fruth & Co PO Drawer CR Fostoria OH 44830

SCHUTTE, PAUL CLARK, healthcare finance executive; b. Cin., Dec. 3, 1950; s. Walter Ford and Winnie Lou (Clark) S.; m. Karen Suzanne Koenig, Sept. 6, 1975; children: Emily Suzanne, Erin Marie. BBA, U. Cin., 1973, MBA, 1986. CPA, Ohio. Gen. mgr. Lebanon (Ohio) Concrete, 1973-75; staff acct. Coopers & Lybrand, Cin., 1975-77; asst. controller Children's Hosp., Cin., 1977-79, controller, 1979-83, v.p. fin., 1984-86; v.p. fin. Huron Rd. Hosp., East Cleveland, Ohio, 1983-84; sr. mgr. Deloitte, Haskins & Sells, Cin., 1986—; mem. fin. com. Greater Cin. Hosp. Council, 1985—. Mem. Ohio Hosp. Assn. (fin. com. 1984—), Am. Inst. CPA's, Ohio Soc. CPA's, Healthcare Fin. Mgmt. Assn. Avocations: golfing, woodworking, photography. Home: 1005 Willow Ln Mason OH 45040 Office: Children's Hosp Med Ctr Elland & Bethesda Ave Cincinnati OH 45229

SCHUTZ, JOHN THOMAS, real estate developer; b. Jasper, Ind., Jan. 3, 1932; s. William Ludwig and Marcella Elizabeth (Schneider) S.; m. Mary Alice Gramelspacher, Sept. 5, 1953; children: Sandra, Stephen, Scott, Stanley, Stuart, Sarah. BSEE, Purdue U., 1955. Engr. H.D. Tousley, Indpls., 1955; purchsing agt. DeCamp Reality, Indpls., 1959-60; gen. mgr. R.V. Welch, Indpls., 1960-64; construction supr. Brendon Park, Indpls., 1964-68; pres., owner Quadrant Devel. Co., Carmel, Ind., 1968—; part owner Chandelle Enterprises, Carmel, 1983—, Eden Devel., Carmel, 1985—, Peak Group, Carmel, 1986—. Mem. pres. council, Purdue U., West Lafayette, Ind., 1980. Served to capt. USAF, 1956-59. Republican. Roman Catholic. Clubs: Gold Coats, John Purdue (West Lafayette). Lodge: KC. Avocations: fishing, sports, traveling. Home: 3234 McLaughlin St Indianapolis IN 46227 Office: PO Box 864 445 Gradle Dr Carmel IN 46032

SCHUTZ, RONALD JAMES, lawyer; b. Adrian, Minn., Nov. 15, 1955; s. Harold Henry and Joanne Dorothy (Peters) S.; m. Janet Jayne Jensen, June 4, 1977; children—Matthew, Erik. B.S. in Mech. Engring., Marquette U., 1978; J.D., U. Minn., 1981. Bar: Minn. 1981, U.S. Dist. Ct. Minn. 1981, U.S. Ct. Mil. Appeals 1984, U.S. Supreme Ct. 1986. Commd. capt. U.S. Army, 1981; atty. JAGC, Ft. Ord, Calif., 1981-85; atty. Merchant & Gould, Mpls., 1985-87, Robins, Zelle, Larson & Kaplan, Mpls., 1987—; lectr. U. Minn. Law Sch., 1986-87. Contbr. articles to profl. jours. Mem. N.W. Suburbs Cable Commn. Recipient Army Achievement medal, 1983, 84. Mem. ABA, Minn. Bar Assn., Judge Advocates Assn., Assn. Trial Lawyers Am. Republican. Home: 6532 Meadowlark Ln Maple Grove MN 55369 Office: Robins Zelle Larson & Kaplan 1800 International Centre Minneapolis MN 55402

SCHUYLER, DANIEL MERRICK, lawyer, educator; b. Oconomowoc, Wis., July 26, 1912; s. Daniel J. and Fannie Sybil (Moorhouse) S.; m. Claribel Seaman, June 15, 1935; children: Daniel M., Sheila Gordon. A.B. summa cum laude, Dartmouth Coll., 1934; J.D., Northwestern U., 1937. Bar: Ill. 1937, U.S. Supreme Ct. 1942, Wis. 1943. Tchr. constl. history Chgo. Latin Sch., 1935-37; assoc. Schuyler & Hennessy (attys.), 1937-42, ptnr., 1946-48; partner Schuyler, Richert & Stough, 1948-58, Schuyler, Stough & Morris, Chgo., 1958-76, Schuyler, Ballard & Cowen, 1976-83, Schuyler, Roche & Zwirner, P.C., 1983—; treas., sec. and controller B-W Superchargers, Inc. div. Borg-Warner Corp., Milw., 1942-46; lectr. trusts, real property, future interests Northwestern U. Sch. Law, 1946-50, asso. prof. law, 1950-52, prof., 1952-80, prof. emeritus, 1980—. Author: (with Homer F. Carey) Illinois Law of Future Interests, 1941; supplement, 1954; (with William M. McGovern, Jr.) Illinois Trust and Will Manual, 1970; supplements, 1972, 74, 76, 77, 79, 80, 81, 82, 83, 84; contbr. to profl. jours. Republican nominee for judge Cook County Circuit Ct., 1958; bd. dirs. United Cerebral Palsy Greater Chgo.; bd. mgrs. Bartelme Homes and Services. Fellow Am. Bar Found.; mem. Chgo. Estate Planning Council (past pres., Disting. Service award 1977), Am. Coll. Probate Counsel (past pres.), Internat. Acad. Estate and Trust Law, ABA (past mem. ho. dels., past chmn. sect. real property, probate trust law), Chgo. Bar Assn. (past chmn. coms. on trust law and post-admission edn., past bd. mgrs.), Ill. Bar Assn. (past chmn. real estate and legal edn. sects., past bd. govs.), Wis. Bar Assn., Phi Beta Kappa, Order of Coif, Phi Kappa Psi. Clubs: Legal (Chgo.), Law (Chgo.), Chicago (Chgo.), University (Chgo.). Home: 324 Cumnor Rd Kenilworth IL 60043 Office: 3100 Prudential Plaza Chicago IL 60601

SCHWAB, MARK FRANCIS, advertising executive, film and video producer; b. Buffalo, Aug. 11, 1953; s. Joseph Francis Schwab Sr. and Alice Margaret (McCord) Boles. BA in English cum laude, SUNY, Buffalo, 1975. Cert. tchr., N.Y. Journalist Oakland (Calif.) Tribune, 1976-77; dir. pub. affairs Zool. Soc. Buffalo, 1979-80; exec. dir. Schwab Internat., Buffalo, N.Y., 1979—; dir. pub. relations and acctg. services Finley H. Greene Advt., Buffalo, 1980-82; acct. supr. Hallmark Advt., Pitts., 1984-85; v.p. creative services Mktg. Advt. and Promotion, Inc., Dublin, Ohio, 1986-87; pres. Schwab & Assocs., Dublin, Ohio, 1987—; mktg. cons. Seaway Trail Mag., Buffalo, 1985-86. Author: (poetry) The Woman Not Known, 1973. Sec. press Rep. campaign Mayoral election, Buffalo, 1978; mem. Buffalo Zoo Publ. com., 1979-82, Niagara Frontier Tourist adv. task force, Buffalo, Niagara Falls, N.Y., 1981-83; chmn. I Love N.Y. Summer Festival, N.Y. State Dept. Commerce, 1981. Mem. Advt. Fedn. Columbus, Pub. Relations Soc. Am. Republican. Club: Blue Blazer (Buffalo) (social chmn. 1981-82). Avocations: tennis, skiing, golf. Home and Office: Schwab & Assocs 2845 Ravine Way Dublin OH 43017

SCHWAB, STEPHEN MICHAEL, steel company executive; b. Denver, Mar. 12, 1960; s. John and Marilyn (Hanna) S.; m. Melissa Stephens Foster, May 24, 1980; children: Rachel, Jessicah, Charlotte. BSc MetallE, Colo. Sch. Mines, 1982; MBA, U. Chgo., 1986. Pvt. practice cons. Golden, Colo., 1981-82; project engr. Inland Steel Co., East Chicago, Ind., 1982—; gen. ptnr. B.I. Services, Crown Point, Ind., 1986—. Advisor Jr. Achievement, Ind., 1986; teen leader Bethel Bapt. Ch., Ind., 1986. Avocations: sports, piano. Home: 4238 Westover Dr Crown Point IN 46307

SCHWANHAUSSER, ROBERT ROWLAND, aerospace industry executive, engineer; b. Buffalo, Sept. 15, 1930; s. Edwin Julius and Helen (Putnam) S.; m. Mary Lea Hunter, Oct. 17, 1953 (div. 1978); children—Robert Hunter, Mark Putnam; m. Beverly Bohn Allemann, Dec. 31, 1979. S.B. in Aero. Engring., MIT, 1952. V.p. aerospace systems, then v.p. programs Teledyne Ryan Aero., San Diego, 1954-74, v.p. internat. requirements, 1977-79, v.p. Remotely Piloted Vehicles programs, 1979-81; pres. Condur, La Mesa, Calif., 1973-74; v.p. bus. devel. All Am. Engring., 1976-77; v.p. advanced programs Teledyne Brown Engring., Huntsville, Ala., 1981-83; pres. Teledyne CAE, Toledo, Ohio, 1983—; bd. dirs. Ohio Citizen's Bank, Toledo, 1987. Bd. dirs. Riverside Hosp., Toledo, 1985. Served to lt. USAF, 1952-54. Fellow AIAA (assoc., Outstanding Contbn. to Aerospace award 1971); mem. Assn. Unmanned Vehicle Systems (Pioneer award 1984), Nat. Mgmt. Assn. (Silver Knight of Mgmt. award 1972, Gold Knight of Mgmt. award 1987), Air Force Assn., Am. Def. Preparedness Assn., Nat. Rifle Assn., Navy League, Theta Delta Chi. Republican. Presbyterian. Clubs: Greenhead Hunting (Pine Valley, Calif.), Inverness (Toledo), Maumee River Yacht (Ohio), Gulf Shores Country (Ala.), The Crew's Nest (Ohio). Avocations: boating; hunting, skiing, golf. Home: 28765 East River Rd Perrysburg OH 43551 Office: Teledyne CAE 1330 Laskey Rd Toledo OH 43612

SCHWANZ, H(ERMAN) LEE, publishing company executive; b. Lorimor, Iowa, Apr. 29, 1923; s. Arthur I. and Elva Rae (Caffery) S.; m. Kathleen J. Belland, Sept. 1, 1947; children: Michael L., Leslie Anne Schwanz Satran, Stephen E., Susan E. Schwanz Pigorsch. B.S. in Agrl. Journalism, Iowa State U., 1947. Farm editor Cedar Rapids (Iowa) Gazette, 1947-50; asso. editor Country Gentleman mag. Curtis Pub. Co., Phila., 1950-55; editor, pub. Agrl. Pubs., Milw., 1955-70; pres., pub. Market Communications, Milw., 1970-81, Elmbrook Publishing Co., Brookfield, Wis., 1981—. Editor: Farmer's Digest, 1970—, Buying for the Farm. Served with 90th inf. div. AUS, 1943-46. Decorated Silver Star. Mem. Sigma Delta Chi. Republican. Methodist. Clubs: Milw. Press, Westmoor Country. Home: 2645 Maple Hill Ln Brookfield WI 53005 Office: 21100 Capital Dr Pewaukee WI 53072

SCHWARK, AUGUST CARL, banker; b. Cape Girardeau, Mo., Jan. 10, 1948; s. August C. and Mabel A. (Roth) S.; m. Mary Ruth Brauer, July 5, 1975 (div. Jan. 1983); m. Janette Wiley Field, Sept. 21, 1985; 1 child, Ashley Catherine. BA, Valparaiso (Ind.) U., 1970; MBA, Washington U., 1972; diploma, Stonier Grad. Sch. Banking. Comml. banking officer Continental Ill. Nat. Bank, Chgo., 1972-76; asst. v.p. Bank One, Milford, Ohio, 1976-79, v.p., 1979-84, sr. v.p., 1984—, sec. bd. dirs.; instr. Am. Inst. Banking, Cin., 1986—. Mem. adv. com. Cancer Family Care, 1980-83; treas. Clermont County YMCA, Batavia, Ohio, 1983-85; chmn. Clermont Mercy Hosp. Devel. Council, 1984-85; asst. chmn. United Way Campaign, Clermont and Brown Counties, 1982, asst. v.p. 1987. Recipient Community Service award Greater Cin. Community Chest, 1982. Mem. Clermont County C. of C. (chmn. 1986—). Club: Terrace Park Country. Avocation: aerobics. Home: 2902 Saddleback Dr Cincinnati OH 45244 Office: Bank One I-275 and State Rt 28 Milford OH 45150

SCHWARK, HOWARD EDWARD, civil engineer; b. Bonfield, Ill., Aug. 31, 1917; s. Edward F. and Florence M. (Schultz) S.; student St. Viators Coll., Bourbonnias, Ill., 1935-37; B.S., U. Ill., 1942; m. Arlene M. Highbarger, Sept. 28, 1940. Asst. to county supt. hwys. Ford County (Ill.), 1941-43; engr. E. I. DuPont de Nemours Co., 1942; asst. county supt. hwys. Kankakee County (Ill.), 1946-52, county supt. hwys., 1952-82; dir. 1st Bank of Meadowview, Kankakee Devel. Corp.; adviser county rds. FHWA, 1973-82; spl. cons. ESCA Consultants, Urbana, Ill., 1982—. Co-chmn., Republican Finance Com., 1962-66; pres. Kankakee Park Dist., 1959-70; mem. tech. adv. com. to Ill. Transp. Study Commn., 1975-82; trustee, pres. Azariah Buck Old People's Home; mem. exec. bd. Rainbow council Boy Scouts Am.; bd. dirs. Soil and Water Conservation Service, 1967-74. Served with AUS, 1943-46. Recipient Disting. Alumnus award Civil Engring. Alumni Assn. U. Ill., 1975; Disting. Service award U.S. Dept. Transp., 1982; Spl. Achievement award as road adv. for Region 5, FHWA, 1982 Mem. Nat. Assn. County Engrs. (life mem., v.p. North Central region 1979-81, Urban County Engr. of Yr. award 1982), Ill. Soc. Profl. Engrs., Ill. Assn. County Supts. Hwys. (life mem., pres. 1970), Ill. Engring. Council (pres. 1971-72), Am. Road and Transp. Builders Assn. (life mem., dir. county div. 1969-75, dir. 1975-81, pres. county div. 1975; Outstanding Service award transp. ofcls. div. 1981, Ralph R. Bartelsmeyer award 1983), Kankakee Area C. of C. (dir. 1960-74), Am. Soc. Profl. Engrs., Western Soc. Engrs., Twp. Ofcls. Ill., Freelance Photographers Assn., Ill. Wildlife Fedn. Lutheran. Clubs: Rotary, South Wilmington Sportsman. Home: 1051 W Vanmeter Kankakee IL 60901

SCHWARTZ, BRUCE ROBERT, infosystems specialist; b. Greenfield, Mass., Mar. 7, 1944; s. Ralph Syvester and Doris (Sidman) S.; m. Diane Corday Koerner, Mar 23, 1968; children: Christine Corday, Brie Anne. AA, Norwalk U., 1968; BA, U. Md., 1971; grad., N.Y. Inst. Photography, 1975; postgrad., Washington U., St. Louis, 1982-85. Dean of boys The Principia, St. Louis, 1972-81, asst. purchasing agt., 1981-82, mgr. ops., 1982-84, adminstrv. mgr., 1984-85, personal computer mgr., 1985—; tchr. Forest Park Coll., St. Louis, 1984-85; cons. disaster recovery, halon fire systems, uninterrupted power, 1984—. Supt. Sunday sch., St. Louis, 1986—. Served to sgt. U.S. Army, 1967-71. Decorated Vietnamese Cross of Gallantry. Mem. Adminstrv. Mgmt. Soc. (speaker 1984-86). Republican. Christian Scientist. Club: Principia Dad's (Liaison officer)(St. Louis). Avocations: photogrpahy, coaching. Home: 821 Country Meadow Ln Saint Louis MO 63141 Office: The Principia 13201 Clayton Rd Saint Louis MO 63131

SCHWARTZ, GERHART ROBERT, university dean and vice president; b. Berne, Ind., Apr. 11, 1917; s. Peter D. and Elizabeth (Nussbaum) S.; m. Josephine Ruth Zehr, Aug. 15, 1944; children—Robert Arthur, Susan Jo Schwartz Lavin. B.S., Ball State U., 1942; M.S., Ind. U., 1948, Ed.D., 1952. Asst. to registrar Ball State U., Muncie, Ind., 1939-42; staff counselor Ind. U., Bloomington, 1946-48, dean of students office, 1946-51, asst. dir. student activities, 1949-50, acting dir. student activities, 1950-51; dean students Mankato State U., Minn., 1951-62; dean of students Western Ill. U., Macomb, 1963-68, v.p. student affairs, 1969-76, prof. grad. faculty, 1977—; participant profl. confs. Author: The Effect of a Reading Deficiency on a Student's Scholastic, Social and Emotional Adjustment in College, 1952; The Prospective Teacher Looks at Guidance, 1961. Mem. exec. bd. Mankato Adult-Youth Council, 1955-60; bd. dirs. Mankato YMCA, 1956-62, United Fund, Mankato, 1960-63, Macomb, 1965-67; mem. adv. com. on guidance, counseling and testing State Dept. Edn., Minn., 1959-62. Recipient Outstanding Service award Mankato State YMCA, 1956-63, Outstanding Contbn. award Mankato State U., 1962-63; honored as founder Ind. Coll. Personnel Assn., 1973. Served to lt. comdr. USNR, 1943-46. Mem. Am. Assn. Counseling and Devel. (life mem.), Ill. Assn. Counseling and Devel. (parliamentarian 1981-83), Nat. Assn. Student Personnel Adminstrs. (Commn. III; editor newsletter), Am. Coll. Personnel Assn. Nat. Vocat. Guidance Assn., Ill. Coll. Personnel Assn. (founding mem., treas. 1966-67, pres. 1967-68), NEA, Assn. Higher Edn., Blue Key, Phi Delta Kappa, Pi Gamma Mu, Pi Omega Pi, Sigma Tau Delta, Alpha Phi Gamma, Theta Chi. Presbyterian. Lodges: Elks, Rotary, Masons. Avocations: photography; sailing; horseback riding. Home: West Adams Rd Rural Rt 1 Macomb IL 61455

SCHWARTZ, HAROLD ALBERT, retired newpaper company executive; b. Troy Center, Wis., July 7, 1913; s. Albert Andrew and Mae (Flanagan) S.; m. Anne Lynch Powers, Aug. 22, 1938; children: Weldon Harold, Lynn Siobhan Schwartz Donoghue. Ph.B., Marquette U., 1935. Reporter Associated Press, Milw., 1935; clk. circulation dept. Milw. Jour., 1935-40; asst. traffic mgr., ast. state circulation mgr., asst. circulation mgr. Jour. Co. Milw., 1940-70, v.p. and circulation dir. Milw. Jour., 1970-85; v.p., dir. Newspapers Inc., Milw., 1970-85, Jour. Co., 1970-87. Mem. Wis. Equal Rights Council, Madison, 1968—, chmn., 1984-87; vice chmn., bd. mgrs. Central YMCA, Milw., 1979-84, chmn., 1984-86; gen. chmn. youth participation program Metro. YMCA, 1986; bd. dirs. Commando Project I, 1968—, Sunrise Nursing Home for Blind, 1978—, Marquette U. Alumni Assn.; pres., bd. dirs. Bokkfellows of Milw., 1970—; trustee Wis. Marine Hist. Soc., 1985—. Decorated Order of North Star Sweden; recipient Editor and Pub. Disting. Service award Internat. Circulation Mgrs. Assn., 1970, By Line award Marquette U. Col. Journalism, 1974, award Wis. region NCCJ, 1986; named Alumnus of Yr. Marquette U., 1981. Mem. Internat. Circulation Mgrs. (bd. dirs., pres. 1979-80); mem Am. Newspapers Pubs. Assn. (edn. com. 1969-78); mem. Central State Circulation Mgrs. Assn. (bd. dirs. exemplary service award). Roman Catholic. Clubs: Wis. Milw. Press; South Shore Yacht (Milw.). Lodge: Lions (pres. 1986). Home: 3800 N Newhall St Shorewood WI 53211

SCHWARTZ, HOWARD JULIUS, allergy educator; b. N.Y.C., Nov. 24, 1936; s. Henry and Edna Betty (Herman) S.; m. Gertrude H. Blody, July 1, 1962; children: Adam David, Kaila Jessica, Michael Jonathan. BA, Bklyn. Coll., 1956; MD, Albert Einstein Coll. Medicine, 1960. Diplomate Am. Bd. Allergy and Immunology, Am. Bd. Internal Medicine; lic. allergist Mass., N.Y., Ohio, Nat. Bd. Med. Examiners. Intern, then asst. resident NYU Med. Services, Bellevue Hosp., N.Y.C., 1960-63, chief resident medicine, psycho-med. div., 1963-64; teaching asst. dept. medicine NYU, N.Y.C., 1961-66; clin. and research fellow in allergy and immunology Mass. Gen. Hosp., Boston, 1966-68; USPHS trainee in medicine Case Western Res. U., Cleve., 1967-71, asst. prof. medicine, 1971-74, mem. Phase II respiratory com., 1971—, mem. hosp. utilization and rev. com., 1975-77, assoc. clin. prof. medicine, 1977-87, clin. prof. medicine, 1987—; asst. physician Univ. Hosps. Cleve., 1968-71, assoc. physician, 1971—, chief allergy clinic, 1972—; staff physician pulmonary sect. Cleve. VA Med. Ctr., 1974-80, cons. in allergy, 1980—; attending physician and cons. in allergy Hillcrest Hosp., Cleve.; cons. staff medicine Mt. Sinai Hosp., Cleve. Author: Hospital Management of the Adult with Status Asthmaticus in Current Therapy of Allergy, 1974, Acute Asthma, Hospital Management-Adult in Current Therapy of Allergy, 1978, Allergic Reactions to Insect Stings in Current Therapy, 1983, also book chpts. and abstracts; contbr. several articles to profl. jours. Served to capt. U.S. M.C., 1964-69. Fellow Am. Acad. Allergy (cutaneous allergy com. 1972-73, penicillin allergy study group 1972—, insect allergy com. 1974—, com. on alternate forms of therapy 1977—, audio-visual com. 1979-81, edn. council 1979-81, chmn. sci. and workshop com. 1982-83, chmn. com. on Am. insects 1980—), Am. Coll. Chest Physicians (com. on allergy 1976—), Am. Coll. Allergy; mem. AMA, Am. Assn. Immunology, Am. Thoracic Soc. (ad hoc com. on definition asthma, allergy, clin. immunology assembly 1979—, program com. 1979-80), Am. Acad. Allergy and Immunology (research council 1980—, sci. and workshop com. 1982—, com. on allergen standardization 1983—, com. on awards, meml. and commemorative lectureships 1984), Am. Coll. Allergists (com. on insect reactions 1984), Am. Soc. Internal Medicine (com. on internal medicine subspltys. socs. 1984), Asthma and Allergy Found. Am. (med. sci. council 1985), Cen. Soc. Clin. Research, Cleve. Acad. Medicine (health ins. rev. com. splty. panel 1979—), Cleve. Allergy Soc. (sec. treas. 1971, v.p. 1971-72, pres. 1972-74), Cleve. Chest Soc., Cleve. Course in Pulmonary Disease (planning com. 1971-77), Med. Advances Inst. Ohio (allergy com. 1972-73), Midwest Allergy Forum (chmn. 1974, exec. com. 1973-77), Ohio Soc. Allergy and Immunology (program com. 1973-75). Office: Univ Suburban Health Ctr 1611 S Green Rd Cleveland OH 44121

SCHWARTZ, IRVING LLOYD, history educator. m. Rosanne S. Schwartz; children: Barth D., Regina Mara. BA, U. Dayton, 1942; Diplomate, U. Florence, Italy, 1946, Coll. Armed Forces; MA in History, Miami U., 1948. Instr. U.S. Office Edn., Wright-Patterson AFB, Ohio, 1940-43; historian USAF, 1946-47; edn. and tng. specialist, chief spl. rehab. unit VA, Ohio, 1947-50; chief of protocol aeronautical systems USAF, Wright Patterson AFB, 1950-78; prof. history Sinclair Community Coll., Dayton, Ohio, 1978—; faculty Patterson High Sch., Dayton, 1949-53, history dept. U. Dayton 1953-56. Contbr. articles to profl. jours. Chmn. Gov.'s Help a Disabled Vet. Com., 1945; mem. Mayor's Sister City Com., 1969—; sec. City Plan Bd., Dayton, 1970—; chmn. bd. trustee Dayton and Montgomery County Public Library System, 1971—; prin. Temple Israel Religious Sch., 1956-68; bd. dirs. Temple Israel, 1972—, Dayton Council on World Affairs, 1982—. Mem. Am. Hist. Assn. Home: 2033 Burroughs Dr Dayton OH 45406 Office: Sinclair Community Coll Dept History 444 W 3d St Dayton OH 45402

SCHWARTZ, LAWRENCE ELLIOT, consulting financial economist; b. Chgo., Feb. 16, 1935; s. Louis and Eleanor (Mazor) S. BA, Northwestern U., 1956; MA, Harvard U., 1960, PhD, 1963. Assoc. prof. U. Utah, Salt Lake City, 1970-74, Northwestern U., Evanston, Ill., 1974-75; dir. econ. dept. AMA, Chgo., 1974-76; pres. Econ. Cons., Chgo., 1976—; cons. Rand Corp., Santa Monica, Calif., 1961-62, Triton Corp., Springfield, Va., 1969-70. Contbr. articles to profl. jours. Recipient Woodrow Wilson Fellowship Harvard U., 1958-59. Mem. Am. Econ. Assn., Am. Statis. Assn. Avocation: computers. Home and Office: 6292 N Leona Ave Chicago IL 60646

SCHWARTZ, LEO G., JR., architect; b. St. Louis, July 26, 1957; s. Leo G. Sr. and Mathilda L. (Heimos) S.; m. Kathleen L. Hahn, Aug. 19, 1983; 1 child, Sarah L. AArch, Meremac Community Coll., 1977; student, U. Kans., 1978-79; BArch, Kans. State U., 1982. Registered architect, Mo. Intern Wahlberg Morales & Wright Assoc., Houston, 1981; project mgr. Carl E. Day, Architect, Houston, 1982-84; architect Mackey & Assocs., ST. Louis, 1984—. Counselor Ephiphaney Sr. Youth Group, St. Louis, 1984-86. Mem. AIA (assoc.). Lutheran. Club: Executive. Avocations: model trains, antique refinishing, historic preservation, athletics. Office: Mackey & Assocs 5585 Pershing Saint Louis MO 63112

SCHWARTZ, LEONARD PAUL, management consultant; b. N.Y.C., Feb. 16, 1934; s. Theodore M. and Rose (Diamond) S.; m. Harriet Gale Meltz, Sept. 7, 1958 (div. Feb. 1966); children—Andrea Pearl, Gary Martin; m. 2d, Carolyn Rand, May 1, 1970; children—Sarah Roselyn, Daniel Lee. A.B., U. Miami, 1956, student law, 1958-59; student Inst. Fin., N.Y.C., 1959-60. Cert. Inst. Cert. Profl. Bus. Cons. Registered rep., Walston & Co., Miami, Fla., 1959-62; owner, operator shoe store, Margate, N.J., 1962-65; regional mgr. Gulf Am. Land Corp., Miami, 1965-70; pres. Adminstrv. Health Mgmt., Inc., Cin., 1970—; condr. seminars; tchr. residency programs. Pres. North Miami Beach Jaycees, 1961. Served to 2d lt. USAF, 1956-58. Recipient 2d place Spoke award Fla. Jaycees, 1961, Achievement in Editorial Excellence award Physician's Mgmt. Mag., 1978, Mem. Nat. Assn. Bus. Economist, Soc. Med.-Dental Mgmt. Cons. (dir. 1976-78, pres. 1980-81, Pres.' award 1983 Outstanding Mgmt. Cons of Yr. 1983), Inst. Cert. Profl. Bus. Cons. (trustee 1983-84, v.p. 1985). Democrat. Jewish. Clubs: Mercedes Benz (Cin.); K.P. (Atlantic City). Contbg. editor Physician's Mgmt. and Dental Mgmt. mags.; monthly byline question and answer comumn; contbr. articles to profl. jours. Office: Adminstrv Health Mgmt Inc 10361 Spartan Dr Cincinnati OH 45215

SCHWARTZ, MICHAEL, university president, sociology educator; b. Chgo., July 29, 1937; s. Norman and Lillian (Ruthenberg) S.; m. Ettabelle Slutsky, Aug. 23, 1959; children: Monica, Kenneth, Rachel. BS in Psychology, U. Ill., 1958, MA in Indsl. Relations, 1959, PhD in Sociology, 1962. Asst. prof. sociology and psychology Wayne State U., Detroit, 1962-64; asst. prof. sociology Ind. U., Bloomington, 1964-66, assoc. prof. sociology, 1966-70; chmn. dept. sociology Fla. Atlantic U., Boca Raton, 1970-72, dean Coll. Social Sci., 1972-76; v.p. grad. studies and research Kent (Ohio) State U., 1976-78, interim pres., 1977, acting v.p. acad. affairs, 1977-78, v.p. acad. and student affairs, 1978-80, provost, v.p. acad. and student affairs, 1980-82, pres., 1982—; acting dir. Inst. for Social Research, Ind. U., 1966-67; tng. cons. Operation Head Start in Ind., 1964-70; cons. Office of Manpower, Automation and Tng., U.S. Dept. Labor, 1964—. Cons. editor: Sociometry, 1966— , assoc. editor, 1970; reader: Am. Sociol. Rev. papers; author: (with Elton F. Jackson) Study Guide to the Study of Sociology, 1968; contbr. articles to profl. jours., chpts. to books. Chmn. Mid-Am. Conf. Council Pres.; rep. Nat. Coll. Athletic Assn. Pres.'s Commn.; bd. dirs. Akron (Ohio) Regional Devel. Bd., N.E. Ednl. TV of Ohio, Inc., N.E. Ohio Univs. Coll. Medicine; trustee Akron Symphony Orch. Assn. Recipient Disting. Tchr. award Fla. Atlantic U., 1970-71. Mem. Ohio Tchr. Edn. and Cert. Adv. Commn., Akron Press Club, Cleve. Press Club. Club: Twin Lakes Country. Office: Kent State U Adminstrv Offices Office of Pres Kent OH 44242

SCHWARTZ, MICHAEL, personal computer analyst; b. Park Falls, Wis., Aug. 8, 1950; s. Louis Peter and Kathrine Ann (Kundinger) S. BS in Communications, Grand Valley State U., Allendale, Mich., 1975. Personal computer analyst Am. Can, Neenah, Wis., 1975—; lectr. computer clubs, bus. computer groups. Mem. Midwest Interactive Computer Groups, Valley Bus. Computer Users (v.p. 1986-87). Roman Catholic. Home: 34 Pleasantview Ct Appleton WI 54914 Office: Am Can 155 Western Ave Neenah WI 54956

SCHWARTZ, MICHAEL B., psychotherapist; b. N.Y.C., Jan. 3, 1938; s. Julius and Rose Marie (Rubinstein) S.; m. Gloria Pudick, Aug. 11, 1968; 1 child, Jean-Paul. AB, Goddard Coll., 1962; MSW, Adelphi U., 1964; DSW, Tulane U., 1971. Diplomate Am. Bd. Psychotherapy. Clin. social worker U.S. VA, N.Y.C., 1964-66; pvt. practice psychotherapy N.Y., Fla., Ill., 1964—; coordinator Suicide Prevention Ctr. Bellevue Hosp., N.Y.C., 1966-68; asst. dir. Suicide Prevention Ctr., New Orleans, 1969-70; asst. prof. Fla. State U. Sch. Social Work, Tallahassee, 1971-75; assoc. prof. psychotherapy So. Ill. U. Sch. Medicine, Springfield, 1975—. Talk show host Sta. WSSR-FM, 1981; contbr. articles to profl. publs. Vol. Springfield Jewish Fedn., 1975. Vis. scholar U. Hawaii, 1977. Fellow Am. Orthopsychiat. Assn.; mem. Am. Assn. Marriage and Family Therapists, Am. Acad. Psychotherapists, Am. Group Psychotherapy Assn., Assn. Applied Psychoanalysis. Office: So Ill U Sch Medicine PO Box 3926 Springfield IL 62708

SCHWARTZ, RICHARD CARL, biochemistry researcher; b. N.Y.C., Nov. 25, 1952; s. Jacob Anton and Sydelle Francis (Stelzer) S. BS, U. Calif., Irvine, 1974; PhD, MIT, 1980. Post-doctorate fellow U. Calif., San Diego, 1980-83; research fellow Calif. Inst. Tech., Pasadena, 1983; post-doctorate fellow UCLA, 1983-86; asst. prof. Mich. State U., 1986—. Contbr. articles to profl. jours. NIH fellow, 1974-80,80-83; Calif. Inst. Cancer Research fellow, UCLA, 1983-84; Cancer Research Coordinating Com. fellow, UCLA, 1985-86. Mem. AAAS, Phi Beta Kappa. Democrat. Avocations: hiking, mountaineering. Office: Mich State U Dept Microbiology and Pub Health East Lansing MI 48824-1101

SCHWARTZ, ROBERT HERMAN, gynecologist/obstetrician; b. Cleve., Nov. 28, 1934; s. Leo and Sadie (Danziger) S.; m. Sandra Diane Rogovin, June 14, 1959; children: Steven M., Karen L., Lora B., Lisa J. BS, Ohio State U., 1957, MD, 1961. Diplomate Am. Bd. Ob-Gyn. Intern Mt. Sinai Hosp., Cleve., 1961-62, resident in ob-gyn, 1962-65; practice medicine specialing in ob-gyn Cleve., 1965—. Fellow Am. Coll. Ob-Gyn. Jewish.

SCHWARTZ, S. E., provincial judge. Judge Ct. of Queen's Bench, Winnipeg, Man., Can. Office: Court of Queen's Bench, Law Courts Bldg, Winnepeg, MB Canada R3C 0V8 *

SCHWARTZ, SELWYN BERNARD, commercial finance company executive; b. Chgo., July 3, 1939; s. Theodore and Pearl (Gelfand) S.; m. Sheila Kaye Miller, May 25, 1967; children: Steven, Jeffrey. BA, U. Ill., 1961. Area mgr. Gen. Electric CreditCorp., Des Plaines, Ill., 1971-78; regional mgr. A.J. Armstrong, Chgo., 1978-79; v.p., regional credit mgr. CIT/Bus. Credit, Chgo., 1979—. Pres. Beth Tikvah Congregation, Hoffman Estates, Ill., 1985-87. Served with USAR, 1962-68. Named Citizen of Yr. Lerner Newspaper Co., 1984. Avocations: coaching basketball, serving as community vol. Home: 1500 Cnartwell Rd Schaumburg IL 60195

SCHWARTZ, STANLEY ALLEN, pediatrician; b. Newark, N.J., July 20, 1941; s. Jack D. and Betty (Katz) S.; m. Diane I. Gottlieb, June 20, 1965. AB, Rutgers U., 1963, MS, 1965; PhD, U. Calif., San Diego, 1968; MD, Albert Einstein Coll., 1972. Diplomate Am. Bd. Med. Examiners, Am. Bd. Pediatrics, Am. Bd. Allergy and Immunology. Intern, then resident Bronx (N.Y.) Mcpl. Hosp. Ctr., 1972-74; asst. attending pediatrician Meml. Hosp. Cancer and Allied Diseases, N.Y.C., 1977-78, N.Y. Hosp., 1977-78; assoc. Sloan-Kettering Inst. Cancer Research, N.Y.C., 1977-78; asst. prof. pediatrics, biology Cornell U. Med. Coll., N.Y.C., 1977-78; prof. pediatrics, epidemiology, microbiology U. Mich., Ann Arbor, 1978—; mem. sci. adv. bd. Proteins Internat., Rochester, Mich. Contbr. articles to profl. jours.; mem. editorial bd. Jour. Allergy and Clin. Immunology, 1986—; editor immunology sect. Birth Defects Ency. Recipient Meller award Meml. Sloan-Kettering Cancer Ctr., 1977, Research Career Devel. award NIH, 1983, grantee 1978—; Henry Rutgers scholar Rutgers U., 1963, Am. Cancer Soc. scholar Albert Einstein Coll. Med., 1969-72; research grantee Am. Cancer Soc. 1977-79. Fellow Am. Acad. Allergy Immunology; mem. Am. Soc. Clin. Investigation, Am. Assn. Immunologists, Am. Pediatric Assn., Am. Fedn. Clin. Research. Office: U Mich 109 Observatory St Ann Arbor MI 48109

SCHWARTZ, SUSAN HIRSCH, book publisher; b. N.Y.C., Mar. 30, 1946; d. Edwin Waixel and Patricia (Lamm) Hirsch; m. Charles P. Schwartz, Jr., Dec. 18, 1976; stepchildren—Alex, Ned, Debra, Emily. B.A., Skidmore Coll., 1968. Sr. publicist ABC-TV, Chgo., 1968-72; advt. and promotion dir. Follett Pub. Co., Chgo., 1972-75; pres. Susan Hirsch Pub. Relations, Chgo., 1975-81, Surrey Books, Inc., Chgo., 1981—. Author: How To Get a Job in Chicago, 1983. Bd. dirs. Michael Reese Hosp. Med. Research Inst., 1975—. Mem. Chgo. Advt. Club, Publicity Club Chgo., Publicity Club N.Y., Pub. Relations Soc. Am., Women's Bd. Univ. Chgo., Midwest Writers, Women in Communications, Pubs. Publicity Assn. Jewish. Clubs: Chgo. Press, Arts, Quadrangle (Chgo.). Home: 5546 S Dorchester Ave Chicago IL 60637 Office: Surrey Books 500 N Michigan Ave Chicago IL 60611

SCHWARTZEL, FRANK ANTHONY, accountant; b. Tell City, Ind., Sept. 18, 1959; s. Frank Bertram and Sarah Ann (Quinn) S. BS in Acctg., Ball State U., 1981. CPA, Ind., Ohio. Acct. Brady, Ware & Co., Inc., Richmond, Ind., 1981—. Bd. dirs. and v.p. fin. Richmond Area Rose Festival, inc., 1985—; bd. dirs. Scott Boy's Club, Richmond, 1985—. Mem. Nat. Assn. Acct's (pres. Ind. E. chpt. 1986—), Am. Inst. CPA's, Ind. CPA Soc. (Muncie chpt. adv. forum rep. 1985—). Roman Catholic. Lodge: Kiwanis. Avocations: golf, racquetball, backpacking, motorcycles.

SCHWARTZHOFF, JAMES PAUL, finance company executive; b. Waukon, Iowa, June 24, 1937; s. Harold J. and Mary (Regan) Schwartzhoff; m. Mary Lou Hess, Apr. 23, 1964; children: Tammara, Eric, Stephanie, Mark, Laurie, Michelle, Steven. B, U. Iowa, 1962. Asst. cheif auditor Wis. Dept. Tax, Madison, 1962-67; mgr. treas. dept. Mead Johnson and Co., Evansville, Ind., 1967-69; v.p., treas. Kettering Found., Dayton, Ohio, 1969—; chmn., treas. bd. Pastoral Counceling Ctr., Dayton, 1975-81; treas. Ohio River Rd. Runners, Dayton, 1986—. Served as cpl. U.S. Army, 1957-59. Mem. Am. Inst. CPA's, Found. Fin. Officers Group, Southwestern Ohio Pension Fund Group. Avocations: bicycling, backpacking, photography, woodworking. Office: Kettering Found 200 Commons Rd Dayton OH 45459

SCHWARZ, EITAN DANIEL, physician, psychiatrist. AB, Cornell U., 1965; MD, Johns Hopkins U., 1969. Intern Boston City Hosp., 1969-70; resident in psychiatry U. Chgo., 1970-73, chief resident, 1972-73, fellow in child psychiatry, 1972-73; chief fellow in child psychiatry Michael Reese Hosp., Chgo., 1973-75; clin. asst. prof. U. Chgo., 1976—; attending physician Michael Reese, Highland Park (Ill.), Evanston (Ill.) Hosps.; cons. Evanston Twp. High Sch. Contbr. sci. papers; developer computer programs. Mem. Am. Psychiat. Assn. Avocations: cello, computer. Office: 735 St Johns Ave Highland Park IL 60035

SCHWARZ, ROBERT LESSING, advertising agency executive; b. Chgo., Feb. 23, 1918; s. Sol Robert and Marie (Goldstein) S.; m. Eleanor R. Lowenson, Oct. 5, 1941; children: David S., Steven D. Student, Northwestern U., 1937-41, Ray Sch. Art, 1943, Ill. Inst Tech., 1943-44, Ill. Inst. Tech. Sch. Design, 1955-56. Mgr. Greggory, Inc., Chgo., 1937-43; asst. engr. Motorola, Inc., Chgo., 1943-49; copywriter Montgomery Wards, Chgo., 1944, supr. display publs., 1945-51; procedure editor Spiegel's, Inc., Chgo., 1944; advt. mgr. Match Corp. Am., Chgo., 1951-58; owner Bertram, Blake & Russell Advt., Chgo., 1958—. Treas. Chgo. Fedn. of the Union Am. Hebrew Congregations, 1974-75, mem. nat. membership com. 1974-75, nat. bd. 1976-78; trustee Michael Reese Hosp. Health Plan, 1977-82; life trustee Temple Beth Israel of Chgo., pres., 1970-72, 83-85. Mem. Audit Bur. Circulation, Bus. and Profl. Advt. Assn. (editor Copy/ Chgo. 1976-77, treas. 1977-78), Men's Garden Clubs Am. (regional dir. New Trier Township, chmn. nat. pub. relations com., flower show judge, 3d v.p. 1987—). Jewish. Home: 4953 N Tripp Ave Chicago IL 60630 Office: 4001 W Devon Ave Chicago IL 60646

SCHWARZE, MARTIN WILLIAM, cardiologist; b. St. Louis, Nov. 14, 1946; s. William C. and Mary Constance (Glaser) S.; m. Janet Louise Musial, June 9, 1973; children: Julie, Brian. BS, St. Louis U., 1968; DO, Kirksville Coll. Osteopathic Medicine, 1973. Instr. medicine St. Louis U., 1978-81, asst. clin. prof., 1981—; dir. cardiac rehab. Normandy Osteopathic Hosp., St. Louis, 1978—, chmn. dept. internal medicine, 1984-85. Mem. Am. Osteopathic Assn., Am. Coll. Osteopathic Internists, Am. Heart Assn. (bd. dirs. St. Louis chpt.), St. Louis Met. Med. Soc., St. Louis Cardiac Club. Roman Catholic. Avocations: antique convertible automobiles, model trains, horticulture. Office: 2200 W Port Plaza Dr Suite 212 Saint Louis MO 63146

SCHWEIKERT, DEBRA LYNN, counseling administrator and evaluator; b. New Castle, Pa., July 30, 1955; d. George Joseph and Joyce Aileen (McGaffic) S. BA, Ohio Wesleyan U., 1977; MA, Ohio State U., 1979. Recruiter Coll. Pharmacy Ohio State U., Columbus, 1980-83, asst. fin. aid. dir., 1983-85; program consultation and assessment specialist USA Funds, Indpls., 1985—. Mem. Alpha Chi Omega (alumni chpt. pres. 1983-85). Democrat. Methodist. Clubs: Twig 84 (pres. 1983-85). Avocations: reading, crafts, photography, traveling. Home: 10262 Thames Ct W Indianapolis IN 46229 Office: USA Funds PO Box 50827 Indianapolis IN 46250-0827

SCHWEIZER, PAUL ALLEN, agricultural products executive; b. Sterling, Kans., Feb. 23, 1937; s. Albert D. and Pearl B. (Zimmerman) S.; m. Barbara D. Jones, Aug. 17, 1961; children: Dan, Shirley, Ruth, Diane. Farmer Sterling, 1961—; bd. dirs. Nickerson (Kans.) Co-Op. Bd. dirs. Reno County, Kans., 1977-80. Served to sgt. U.S. Army, 1959-60. Home and Office: Rt #1 Box 79 Sterling KS 67579

SCHWELLER, DONALD GEORGE, lawyer; b. Dayton, Ohio, Oct. 13, 1930; s. Edmund Francis and R. Helen (Trace) S.; m. Mary Elizabeth Jauch, Sept. 1, 1956; children—Susan S., Stephen G., Ellen M., Peter C. B.A., U. Dayton, 1952; J.D., U. Cin., 1957; LL.M. in Taxation, NYU, 1958. Bar: Ohio 1957. Officer, ptnr. Pickrel, Schaeffer & Ebeling, Dayton, 1958—. Contbr. articles to profl. jours. First pres. Dayton Opera Assn., 1961-62. Served to 1st lt. U.S. Army, 1953-55, Korea. Fellow Am. Coll. Probate Counsel; mem. Ohio State Bar Assn. (bd govs. probate and trust law sect.). Republican. Roman Catholic. Club: Dayton Bicycle. Avocations: tennis; antique collecting. Home: 1819 Southwood Ln Dayton OH 45419 Office: Pickrel Schaeffer & Ebeling 2700 Kettering Tower Dayton OH 45423

SCHWEMM, JOHN BUTLER, printing company executive, lawyer; b. Barrington, Ill., May 18, 1934; s. Earl M. and Eunice (Butler) S.; m. Nancy Lea Prickett, Sept. 7, 1956; children: Catherine Ann, Karen Elizabeth. A.B., Amherst Coll., 1956; J.D., U. Mich., 1959. Bar: Ill. 1959. With Sidley & Austin, Chgo., 1959-65; with legal dept. R.R. Donnelley & Sons Co., Chgo., 1965-69; gen. counsel R.R. Donnelley & Sons Co., 1969-75, v.p., 1971-75, dir. Mattoon Mfg. div., 1975-76, group v.p., 1976-79, sr. group v.p., 1980-81, pres., 1981-87, chmn., 1983—, dir., 1980—; dir. Growth Industry Shares, Inc., Square D Co., Walgreen Co. Adv. bd. O.I.C. Am., Inc.; bd. dirs. Newberry Library, The Conf. Bd., United Fund/Crusade of Mercy, Chgo., Evangel. Health Systems, Northwestern U. Mem. Law Club Chgo., Ill. C. of C. (dir. 1981—), Order of Coif, Phi Beta Kappa. Clubs: Chicago, University, Mid-Am., Commercial, Commonwealth (Chgo.); Hinsdale (Ill.) Golf, Old Elm, Blind Brook. Home: 2 Turvey Ln Downers Grove IL 60515 Office: R R Donnelley & Sons Co 2223 Martin Luther King Dr Chicago IL 60616

SCHWENDEMANN, DONALD EUGENE, manufacturing executive; b. Otho, Iowa, May 21, 1919; s. Francis and Mildred (Lundgren) S.; m. Barbara M. Brueck, Nov. 13, 1948; children: Sandra Kay, Sheryl Lee. BS, Iowa State U., 1941; postgrad., Pa. State Coll., 1942. With Detroit Diesel Engine div. Gen. Motors Corp., 1946-68, successively sales engr., zone sales rep., zone sales mgr., sales promotion mgr., 1946-56; regional mgr. Detroit Diesel Engine div. Gen. Motors Corp., Chgo., 1956-57; mgr. market research Detroit Diesel Engine div. Gen. Motors Corp., Detroit, 1958-59; mgr. orgn. and bus. devel. Detroit Diesel Engine div. Gen. Motors Corp., 1957-68; v.p., gen. mgr. Baker div. Reef-Baker Corp., Mt. Clemons, Mich., 1968—, also corp. dir., successively v.p., mgr., 1968-80, corp. exec. v.p., 1980-81, pres., 1981—; pres., chief exec. officer Reef Baker Corp., Mt. Clemens, Baker Mfg. Inc., Marine City, Mich., Reef Gear Inc., Mt. Clemens; bd. dirs. Arrow Mfg. Inc., Richmond, Mich., Stark Mfg. Inc., Farmington Hills., Mich. Trustee Downriver Community Services, Inc., Alganac, Mich. Served to lt. USNR, 1941-46. Mem. Alpha Gamma Rho. Republican. Presbyterian. Clubs: Roundtable Internat., Univ., Recess, Economy (Detroit). Lodge: Masons. Home: 2444 St Clair River Dr Algonac MI 48001 Office: 27322 23 Mile Rd Mount Clemens MI 48045

SCHWERIN, JUDITH ILLENE, nurse; b. Tacoma, Mar. 16, 1954; d. Gerald August and Bonnie Jean (Schull) Groskreutz; m. James Stephen Schwerin, Aug. 28, 1976; children: Terra Trichelle, Liesl Marie. BA in Nursing and Psychology magna cum laude, Augustana Coll., Sioux Falls, S.D., 1976; MS in Nursing summa cum laude, S.D. State U., 1984. Staff nurse McKennan Hosp., Sioux Falls, 1976-78, 1982-85; diabetes edn. coordinator McKennan Hosp., Sioux Falls., 1986—; clin. instr. Augustana Coll., Sioux Falls, 1978-81, substitute instr., 1981—; cons. United Cerebral Palsy, Sioux Falls, 1978-79; diabetes edn. cons. McKennan Hosp., 1986. Active with Peace Luth. Ch., Sioux Falls, 1978—. Mem. S.D. Nurse's Assn. (numerous dist. coms. 1976—, state sec. 1984-86), Phi Kappa Phi, Sigma Theta Tau, Zeta Zeta (chpt. sec. 1982—). Republican. Club: Christian Women's (progress sec. 1985-86). Home: 4401 Hypointe Circle Sioux Falls SD 57105 Office: McKennan Hosp 800 E 21st St Sioux Falls SD 57105

SCHWILCK, GENE LEROY, foundation administrator; b. Corydon, Iowa, Dec. 2, 1925; s. Gerald Alfred and Hazel (Woods) S.; m. Sara Celeste Anderson, June 11, 1950; children: Carol, Cathy. AB, Knox Coll., 1948; MS, U. Wis., 1949; EdD, Ind. U., 1956, hon. doctorate; hon. doctorate, Hanover Coll., Coll. Idaho, Rocky Mountain Coll., Lincoln U. Dir. guidance Park Prep. Sch., Indpls., 1949-55; prin., asst. supt. North Cen. High Sch., Indpls., 1959-62; supt. Oak Park (Ill.) and River Forest High Sch., 1963-67; v.p. Danforth Found., St. Louis, 1967-73, pres., 1973—; speaker in field, 1957—; mem. Council on Edn., Commn. on Equal Edn., Mo. Arts and Edn. Bd., Mo. Gov.'s Commn. on Edn.; mem. testing com. Coll. Entrance Exam Bd., 1965—, adv. bd. Mo. Commn. on Higher Edn.; chmn. vis. com. Ednl. Testing Service; mem. bd. Mark Twain Sch. and Lakeside Sch. Contbr. articles ednl. publs. Mem. Nat. Com. on U.S.-China Relations; vice chmn. bd. dirs. Mo. Div. Youth Services; trustee Nat. Merit Scholarship Corp., Ednl. Records Bur., Nat. Council on Philanthropy, YMCA Bd., Meth. Ch., Harris-Stowe State Coll.; bd. dirs. Mark Twain Inst., Conf. on Edn., Arts and Edn. Council, Little Symphony, Fair Housing, Boy Scouts Am.; bd. dirs., chmn. nat. program com. Council on Founds.; trustee, sec. to bd. Found. Ctr.; mem. Mayor's Council on Youth, Mo. Conf. on Youth; campaign div. chmn. United Way; chmn. bd. visitors Ind. U. Served with USAAF, World War II. Recipient Alumni Achievement award Knox Coll., 1965. Mem. Am. Psychol. Assn., Nat. Assn. Secondary Sch. Prins., Nat. Vocat. Guidance Assn., Assn. Supervision and Curriculum Devel., Am. Assn. Sch. Adminstrs., C. of C., Headmasters Assn., Met. Assn. Philanthropy (pres.), St. Louis Met. Assn. Philanthropy (pres.), Assn. Community Coll. Trustees (bd. dirs. Resource Ctr.), Phi Beta Kappa, Delta Sigma Rho, Phi Delta Kappa. Methodist. Lodge: Rotary Internat. (bd. dirs.). Home: 77 Webster Woods Webster Groves MO 63119 Office: 231 S Bemiston Ave Saint Louis MO 63105

SCHWORM, CURTIS PAUL, radiologist; b. Omaha, Feb. 2, 1947; s. Richard Paul and Vida Marie (Hipple) S.; m. Connie Jeanne Bruce, Jan. 31, 1970; children: R. Marcus, Kimberly Jeanne. BS, U. Nebr., Lincoln, 1973; MD, U. Nebr., Omaha, 1973. Diplomate Am. Bd. Radiology. Intern Scott and White Clinic, Temple, Tex., 1973-74; resident Mayo Clinic, Rochester, Minn., 1974-77; radiologist Providence St. Margaret Health Ctr., Kansas City, Kans., 1977—. Office: 155 S 18th St Kansas City KS 66102

SCIARRA, JOHN J., physician, educator; b. West Haven, Conn., Mar. 4, 1932; s. John and Mary Grace (Sanzone) S.; m. Barbara Crafts Patton, Jan. 9, 1960; children: Vanessa Patton, John Crafts, Leonard Chapman. BS, Yale U., 1953; MD, Columbia U., N.Y.C., 1957, PhD, 1963. Asst. prof. Columbia U., N.Y.C., 1964-68; prof., dept. head U. Minn. Med. Sch., Mpls., 1968-74; prof. Northwestern U. Med. Sch., Chgo., 1974—; chmn. ob-gyn Northwestern Meml. Hosp., Chgo., 1974—. Editor Gyn-Ob Journ., 1973—, Internat. Jour. Gyn-Ob, 1985—. V.p. med. affairs Chgo. Maternity Ctr., Chgo., 1974—. Fellow Internat. Fedn. Gyn-Ob, Assn. Profs. Gyn-Ob (sec. 1976-79, pres. 1980), Am. Assn. Maternal and Neonatal Health (pres. 1980—), Am. Fertility Soc. (Hartman award 1965), Cen. Assn. Ob-Gyn. (bd. trustees 1986—). Club: Yale (N.Y.C.); Carleton (Chgo.). Avocation: photography, food, wine. Office: Northwestern U Med Sch 333 E Superior Chicago IL 60611

SCIPIONE, JOSEPH JOHN, financial analyst; b. Altoona, Pa., Aug. 9, 1959; s. Frank John and Carol Ann (Ajemian) S.; m. Sue Ann McCutcheon, May 3, 1985. AB in History, Harvard U., 1981; postgrad. in acctg., Ohio State U., 1986. Corp. tax auditor State of Ohio, Columbus, 1981-86; corp. fin. planner The Kissell Co., Springfield, Ohio, 1986—; prin. Scipione Investments, Dublin, Ohio, 1985—. Mem. St. Peters Folk Choir, Worthington, Ohio, 1982-86. Republican. Roman Catholic. Club: St. Peter's Italian (Worthington). Lodge: Moose. Home: 6268 Bannister Dr Dublin OH 43017 Office: The Kissell Co 30 E Warner St Springfield OH 45501

SCLOVE, STANLEY LOUIS, statistics educator; b. Charleston, W.Va., Nov. 25, 1940; s. Abraham Bernard Sclove and Dorothy Ruth (Gold) Broh; m. Suzan Tash, June 14, 1962 (div. Mar. 1983); children: Sarabeth, Benjamin. AB, Dartmouth Coll., 1962; PhD, Columbia U., 1967. Math. statistician USPHS, Cin., Summers 1962-64; research assoc. Stanford U., Palo Alto, Calif., 1966-68, vis. asst. prof., 1971-72; asst. prof. stats. Carnegie-Mellon U., Pitts., 1968-72; assoc. prof. U. Ill., Chgo., 1972-81, prof., 1981—; vis. assoc. prof. Northwestern U., Evanston, Ill., 1980-81; statis. cons. for various firms; expert witness in fed. ct.; contracted prin. investigator USAF Office Scientific Research, 1976, Office of Naval Research, 1980-82, Army Research Office, 1982-85. Co-author 2 textbooks on statis. data analysis; contbr. 28 articles to statis. publs. Mem. exec. bd. Friends of Library, Highland Park, Ill., 1976-77; saxophone player, historian Highland Park Jazz/Dance Band, 1976—. Mem. Am. Statis. Assn., Classification Soc., Computer Soc. of IEEE, Inst. Math. Stats., Ops. Research Soc. (elected). Democrat. Reform Jewish. Avocations: play clarinet, saxophone and flute. Office: Univ Ill Info and Decision Scis Dept PO Box 4348 Chicago IL 60680-4348

SCOFIELD, SANDRA KAY, state legislator; b. Chadron, Nebr., June 16, 1947; d. Maurice William and Mildred Elizabeth (Connell) S. BS, U. Nebr., 1969, MA, 1974. Tchr. Westside High Sch., Omaha, 1969-71; tech. writer, coordinator Kentron Hawaii, Honolulu, 1971-73; script writer Nebr. Dept. Edn., Lincoln, 1974-75, U. Mid-Am., Lincoln, 1975, Nebr. Ednl. TV Consortium for Higher Edn., Lincoln, 1975-79, Nebr. Ednl. TV, Lincoln, 1975-79; dir. planning Chadron State Coll., 1979-81, career counselor, 1979, 82-83, dir. career devel. ctr., 1983; mem. Nebr. Legislature, Lincoln, 1983—; vice chair com. on agriculture, food policy and rural devel. Nat. Conf. State Legislators. Bd. dirs. Nebr. Preservation Council, Nebr. Groundwater Found., Nebr. Tourism Council, Nebr. 4-H Devel. Found.; mem. Environmental Control Council, Lincoln, 1983; pres. Dawes County Hist. Soc., Chadron, 1981-83. Mem. Nat. Order Women Legislators, Bus. and Profl. Women, AAUW, Delta Kappa Gamma. Democrat. Lodge: Eagles. Office: Nebr State Legislature State Capitol Bldg Lincoln NE 68509

SCOGGINS, SHIRLEY LOIS, typographical engineer; b. Dearborn, Mich., Mar. 27, 1929; d. Frederick August Andrew and Anna Marie Elizabeth (Pletz) Morris; student Slippery Rock Tchrs. Coll., 1948, Ind. State Tchrs. Coll., 1949-50; children—Bruce Edward, Michael Albert. Detailer, atomic power div. Westinghouse, Pitts., 1956-64, detailer, research, 1961-64; designer Computer Peripherals, Inc., Rochester, Mich., 1964-78, mgr. documentation control, 1978-82; engr. Centronics Data Computer Corp., Rochester, 1982-86; owner, cons. engr. Assign It, Inc., Farmington Hills, Mich., 1986—. Mem. Am. Soc. Profl. and Exec. Women, Am. Bus. Womens Assn. Republican. Lutheran. Home: Assign It Inc 30134 Fink St Farmington Hills MI 48024

SCOLES, CLYDE S., library director; b. Columbus, Ohio, Apr. 14, 1949; s. Edward L. and Edna M. (Ruddock) S.; m. Diane Francis, July 14, 1976; children: David, Kevin, Karen, Stephen. BS, Ohio State U., 1971; MLS, U. Mich., 1972. Librarian Columbus Pub. Library, 1972-74; library dir. Zanesville (Ohio) Pub. Library, 1974-78; asst. dir. Toledo-Lucas County Pub. Library, 1978-85, dir., 1985—. Mem. ALA, Ohio Library Assn., Jaycees. Club: Torch (Toledo). Lodge: Rotary.

SCOLLIN, JOHN AMBROSE, provincial judge; b. Edinburgh, Scotland, Oct. 6, 1927; s. John Benedict and Mary Veronica (McGhee) S.; m. Rita McGregor, Oct. 21, 1950; children: John Charles, Lorraine Maria. MA, U. Edinburgh, 1948, LLB, 1950. Magistrate British Colonial Service, East Africa, 1954-57; ct. atty. Man., Can., 1957-60; ptnr. Pitblado and Hoskin, Winnipeg, Man., 1960-66; dir. criminal law sect., asst. dep. atty. gen., then chief gen. counsel Ontario Dept. Justice, Ottawa, 1966-81; judge Ct. of Queen's Bench, Man., 1981—. Office: Court of Queen's Bench, Law Courts Bldg, Winnipeg, MB Canada R3C 0V8 *

SCOTT, ALICE H., librarian; b. Jefferson, Ga.; d. Frank D. and Annie D. (Colbert) Holly; m. Alphonso Scott, Mar. 1, 1959; children—Christopher, Alison. A.B., Spelman Coll., Atlanta, 1957; M.L.S., Atlanta U., 1958; Ph.D., U. Chgo., 1983. Librarian Bklyn. Pub. Library, 1958-59; br. librarian Chgo. Pub. Library, 1959-72, dir. Woodson Regional Library, 1974-77, dir. community relations, 1977-82, dep. commr., 1982—. Doctoral fellow, 1973. Mem. ALA (councilor 1982-85), Ill. Library Assn., Chgo. Library Club, Chgo. Spelman Club, Chgo. Art Inst., DuSable Mus., Chgo. Urban League. Democrat. Baptist. Office: Chgo Pub Library 425 N Michigan Ave Chicago IL 60611

SCOTT, BETTY ANN, advertising agency executive; b. Canton, Ohio, May 23, 1949; d. Charles M. and Betty M. (Barthel) S. Student Kent State U., 1967-75. Asst. art dir. Goodway Pub., Ft. Lauderdale, Fla., 1968-69; layout and design artist Creative Universal, Detroit, 1969—; owner, pres., account exec. Scott & Assocs., Canton, 1971—; owner, pub. Focus mag., 1978—; owner Beauty Master, Inc., 1984—; owner Nail Place, 1982-87; pres., stockholder Profl. Bingo Players Assn. Co., Inc. Chmn. enshrinee com. Pro Football Hall of Fame, 1979-82, active display com., 1971-82; bd. dirs. Canton Ballet. Recipient Pub. Service award Mayor Stanley Cmich, Canton, 1980. Mem. Indsl. Marketers of Cleve., Network of Akron/Canton, Canton C. of C., Internat. Advt. Assn., Am. Mktg. Assn., Internat. Platform Assn., Akron/Canton Advt. Club. Republican. Home: 5601 Liberty Rd Bentleyville OH 44022

SCOTT, BRUCE LEWIS, chemical company executive; b. San Diego, June 4, 1949; s. Reid Montague and Billie Jean (Lewis) S.; m. Mary Bennett Botkin, Nov. 20, 1974; 1 child, Bennett Lewis. BBS, Gonzaga U., 1972; MBA, Purdue U., 1977. Mgr. fin. analysis B.F. Goodrich Co., Akron, Ohio, 1979-81, product mgr., 1981-83, dir. mktg., 1983-85, dir. bus. devel., 1986—; chmn. CAPI, 1984-85. Served with U.S. Army, 1972-76. Republican. Avocations: triathlons, golf, travel. Home: 1987 Wiltshire Rd Akron OH 44313 Office: BF Goodrich Co 6100 Oak Tree Blvd Cleveland OH 44115

SCOTT, CARL JAMES, architect; b. Oconomowoc, Wis., Apr. 7, 1944; s. Evertt and Laura (Nelson) S.; m. Fredericka Carol Wisneski, Sept. 12, 1964; children: Kimberly, Matthew, Samantha. Cert. in archtl. tech., ICS Schs., 1966; cert. in structural tech., Internat. Correspondence Schs., 1969; cert. in masonry design considerations, Milw. Sch. Engring., 1979; cert. solar design, Waukesha County Tech. Inst., 1981; cert. renovation and rehab. of bldgs., U. Wis., 1984, cert. facility planning, 1985; cert. small office building devel., NW Ctr. Profl. Edn., 1986. Registered architect, Wis. Architect Wenzel-Zoller-Gunn, Elm Grove, Wis., 1973-76, Howard & Assoc., Lake Geneva, Wis., 1976-77, M.H.J.S & Assoc., Milw., 1977-79, Slater & Assoc., Waukesha, Wis., 1979-82, Scott & Assoc., Oconomowoc, 1982-84, Mid-State Assoc., Inc., Baraboo, Wis., 1984—. Leader Boy Scouts Am., Oconomowoc, 1977-85, Baraboo, 1985-86. Recipient Wood Badge, Boy Scouts Am., 1979, Scouters Tng. award, 1980. Mem. AIA, Wis. Soc. Architects, Wis. Assn. Nursing Homes, Wis. Innkeepers Assn. Republican. Lutheran. Lodge: Kiwanis. Avocations: cross-country skiing, scouting, speed skating, model airplanes. Home: 1525 Amundson Dr Baraboo WI 53913 Office: Mid-States Assocs Inc 1230 South Blvd Baraboo WI 53913

SCOTT, CHERYL L., retail executive; b. Portland, Ind., Sept. 4, 1946; d. Don G. and Marjorie L. (Hutchens) S.; children: Chris, Teresa. AA, Stephens Coll., 1966. V.p. Scott's Food Stores, Inc., Ft. Wayne, Ind., 1962—. Bd. dirs. Allen County Crippled Children and Adult Soc., Ft. Wayne, 1986—. Mem. Am. Soc. for Personnel Adminstrn. Democrat. Lutheran. Lodges: Civitan (charter mem.). Avocations: sports, music, travel. Office: Scott's Food Stores Inc 4118 N Clinton St Fort Wayne IN 46805

SCOTT, DARREL JOSEPH, hospital executive; b. Indpls., Sept. 12, 1947; s. Hubert Norris and Beverly June (Hiatt) S.; m. Janice L. Meredith, June 21, 1969; children: Andrew, Brennan. BA, Ind. U., 1969, MHA with high honors, 1971. Planning assoc. Ind. Hosp. Assn., Indpls., 1970-72; asst. dir. Welborn Bapt. Hosp., Evansville, Ind., 1972-77, AMA, Chgo., 1977-78; pres., chief exec. officer King's Daus. Hosp., Madison, Ind., 1978—; mem. Ind. Emergency Med. Services Commn., 1974-75. Bd. dirs. Jefferson County United Way, 1979-85; chair coms. Trinity United Methodist Ch., Madison, 1982—. Fellow Am. Coll. Healthcare Execs. Republican. Home: Rt 5 Madison IN 47250 Office: King's Daughters' Hosp 112 Presbyterian Ave Madison IN 47250

SCOTT, DAVID KNIGHT, physicist, university administrator; b. North Ronaldsay, Scotland, Mar. 2, 1940; married, 1966; 3 children. B.Sc., Edinburgh U., 1962; D.Phil. in Nuclear Physics, Oxford U., 1967. Research officer Nuclear Physics Lab. Oxford U., 1970-73; research fellow nuclear physics Balliol Coll., 1967-70, sr. research fellow, 1970-73; physicist Lawrence Berkeley Lab. U. Calif., 1973-75, sr. scientist nuclear sci., 1975-80; prof. physics, astronomy and chemistry Nat. Superconducting Cyclotron Lab. Mich. State U., East Lansing, 1979—, disting. Hannah prof. physics Nat. Superconducting Cyclotron Lab., 1979-86, assoc. provost, 1983-86, provost, v.p. acad. affairs, 1986—. Fellow Am. Phys. Soc.; mem. AAAS, European Phys. Soc. Office: Office of the Provost Mich State U East Lansing MI 48824

SCOTT, GEORGE MATTHEW, state supreme court judge; b. Clark, N.J., Sept. 14, 1922; s. Francis Patrick and Harriet Ann (O'Donnell) S.; m. Joyce E. Hughes, July 26, 1947; children: Dan, Neil, Brian, George Matthew, Sheila. B.S., U. Minn.; J.D., William Mitchell Coll. Law. Bar: Minn. Practice law 1951-55; dep. atty. gen. State of Minn., 1955; atty. Hennepin County, Mpls., 1955-73; justice Minn. Supreme Ct., St. Paul, 1973—. Contbr. articles to profl. jours. Trustee William Mitchell Coll., 1960; del. Democratic Nat. Conv.; campaign chmn. Hubert H. Humphrey for Senator, 1960. Served with AUS, 1942-45. Mem. ABA, Minn. Bar Assn., Nat. Dist. Atty's. Assn. (pres. 1964-65), Am. Legion. Roman Catholic. Club: Optimists. Office: Minn Supreme Ct 228 Minnesota State Capitol Saint Paul MN 55155 *

SCOTT, GERTRUDE ROSE, metals co. exec.; b. Pitts., Oct. 12, 1932; d. Leroy Lewis and Dorothea Margaret King; m. William B. Ward, 1984. B.A. magna cum laude, U. Pitts., 1969, M.A., 1971. Public relations supr. Allegheny Gen. Hosp., Pitts., 1971-73; mgr. communications Jones & Laughlin Steel Corp., Pitts., 1973-76; v.p. corp. communication Meldrum & Fewsmith, Cleve., 1976-81; v.p. Steel Service Center Inst., Cleve., 1981—. Mem. Public Relations Soc. Am. (chpt. pres. 1982-83). Office: Steel Service Center Inst 1600 Terminal Tower Cleveland OH 44113

SCOTT, IRENA MCCAMMON, neurophysiologist, writer; b. Delaware, Ohio, July 31, 1942; d. James Robert and Gay (Nuzum) McCammon; m. John Watson Scott, Dec. 6, 1969; 1 child, Rosa. B.Sc., Ohio State U., Columbus, 1965; M.S., U. Nev., Las Vegas, 1972; Ph.D., U. Mo., Columbia, 1976. Teaching and research asst. U. Nev., 1970-72; research asst. U. Mo., 1972-76; researcher Cornell U., 1977-78; asst. prof. biology St. Bonaventure (N.Y.) U., 1978-79; researcher Ohio State U., 1979—, Batelle Meml. Inst., 1980-86; correspondent Popular Mechanis mag., 1985—; contbr. articles to profl. jours., mags., newspapers. Vol. Ohio State U. Radio Telescope, 1981—, Lewis Ctr. Meth. Ch., Ohio State U. Hosp. Grantee St. Bonaventure U. Mem. AAAS, Am. Physiol. Soc., Am. Dairy Sci. Assn., Mo. Acad. Sci., Ohio State U. Astronomy Club, Verse Writers Guild Ohio, Olentangy Poets, Mensa (newsletter editor), Sigma Xi, Gamma Sigma Delta. Contbr. articles to profl. jours. Home: 6520 Bale Kenyon St Galena OH 43021 Office: Ohio State U 310 Hamilton Hall Columbus OH 43210

SCOTT, JAMES EDWARD, sales and marketing professional; b. Oak Park, Ill., Oct. 15, 1937; s. Charles Edwin and Muriel (Battey) S.; m. Anna-Lena Sundberg, 1960; children: Katherine Ann, Pamela Lynn, Kimberly Ann. BA, Denison U., 1959. Sales rep. Diamond Nat., Chgo., 1962-70; dist. mgr. Rockwell Internat., Cin., 1970-77; mktg. mgr. Rockwell Internat., Chgo., 1977-81; gen. sales mgr. Independent Machinery, Addison, Ill., 1981-83; mktg. mgr. Komori Am., Rolling Meadows, Ill., 1983—. Served to 1st lt. USAF, 1959-62. Mem. Graphic Arts Tech. Found., Nat. Printing Equipment and Supply Assn. (rep.). Republican. Lutheran. Club: Meadow. Avocations: reading, music, camping. Office: Komori Am Corp 5520 Meadowbrook Ct Rolling Meadows IL 60008

SCOTT, JOE LEE, health organization administrator; b. Milburn, W.Va., Dec. 26, 1934; s. Earl Walter Scott and Dorothy Blanche (Cameron) Burke; m. Virginia Crookshanks, June 29, 1957 (div. Nov. 1969); m. Sandra Kay Earl, July 2, 1970; children: Jeffrey Brent, Jennifer Sue Scott Seidner. BS, Marshall U., Huntington, W.Va., 1957; MS, Butler U., 1967; MHA, Ind. U., Indpls., 1971; cert. physical therapy, Mayo Clinic Sch. of Phys. Therapy, Rochester, Minn., 1959. Phys. therapist Beckley (W.Va.) Meml. Hosp., 1959-61, St. Francis Hosp., Beech Grove, Ind., 1961-69; pres. Restorative Services of Ind., Indpls., 1969-81; sr. v.p. Basic Am. Med., Inc., Indpls., 1981—; chmn. P.T. adv. com. Med. Licensing Bd. Ind.; cons. Blue Cross/Blue Shield, Indpls., 1980-86. Named to Order Ky. Cols., Gov. of Ky., 1986. Mem. Am. Assn. Healthcare Execs. Republican. Lodge: Masons, Shriners (officer Indpls. club 1986), Murat Temple. Office: Basic Am Med Inc 4000 E Southport Rd Indianapolis IN 46237

SCOTT, JULES FRANKLIN, advertising executive; b. Chgo., May 22, 1920; s. Jules Franklin and Helen Veronica (Kasmer) S.; 1 child, Mark S. BS, Northwestern U., 1942; postgrad. U.S. Naval Acad., 1941. Copywriter Montgomery Ward & Co., 1946-47, catalog advt. mgr., 1947-56; creative dir. Carter & Galantin Advt. Agy., 1956-59; creative dir., account supr. Hammett & Gillespie Advt. Agy., 1964-68; corp. dir. advt., sales promotion, and pub. relations Vaughan-Jacklin Corp., Downers Grove, Ill., 1968-84; pres. Advantage Promotions, Chgo., 1984—; mktg. cons., Naperville, Ill., 1985—. Writer short stories; contbr. articles to hort. trade publs. Former scoutmaster Boy Scouts Am.; former treas. PTA; pres. Homeowner Assn. Served to lt. comdr., USNR, 1941-45, ETO, PTO. Home: 1428 Queensgreen Circle Naperville IL 60540

SCOTT, LORRAINE ANN, association executive; b. Cleve., Dec. 14, 1947; d. Harry F. and Ann Mae (Dolecek) Dufek; m. John William Scott, Jan. 4, 1969; 1 son, Bruce. B.B.A., Dyke Coll., Cleve., 1967. Acct., Fulton, Reid & Staples, Cleve., 1967-69; acct., data control Nat. City Bank, Cleve., 1969-70; asst. treas. Independence (Ohio) Bd. of Edn. 1978-80; exec. dir. Nat. Frat. of Phi Gamma Nu, Cleve., 1980—. Mem. Am. Soc. Assn. Execs. Republican. Lutheran. Editor Phi Gamma Nu mag., 1980—.

SCOTT, MARIANNE ELIZABETH, lawyer; b. Cin., Mar. 24, 1959; d. Ralph C. and Rosemary Ann (Schultz) S. BA, U. Cin., 1981, JD summa cum laude, 1984. Bar: Ohio 1984, U.S. Dist. Ct. Ohio 1985. Assoc. Santen, Shaffer & Hughes, Cin., 1984—. Contbr. articles to profl. jours. Recipient Outstanding Female award U. Cin., 1981. Mem. Cin. Bar Assn., Ohio Bar Assn., ABA, Phi Beta Kappa, Omicron Delta Kappa, Alpha Lambda Delta, Kappa Alpha Theta (chmn. scholarship com., Sr. Activity award 1981). Republican. Roman Catholic. Home: 2955 Alpine Terr Cincinnati OH 45208 Office: Santen Shaffer & Hughes 105 E 4th St Suite 1800 Cincinnati OH 45202

SCOTT, MARK E., food products executive; b. San Diego, May 15, 1953; s. Gerald R. and Eileen C. (Nelson) S.; m. Susan Lynn Burns, May 24, 1975; children: William, Melanie. BA, U. Wash., 1976. CPA, Wash. Sr. auditor Arthur Andersen & Co., Seattle, 1976-80; v.p. planning and adminstrn. Brittania Sportswear, Seattle, 1980-83; v.p. Merlino's Macaroni, Kent, Wash., 1983-86; pres. New Tech Snacks, Inc., Joliet, Ill., 1986—. Mem. Am. Inst. CPA's, Wash. Soc. CPA's., Ill. Soc. CPA's. Republican. Home: 2909 Autumn Dr Woodridge IL 60517 Office: New Tech Snacks PO Box 2668 Joliet IL 60434

SCOTT, MILDRED HOPE, nurse; b. Miami, Fla., July 5, 1926; d. Enos R. and Ruth (Sommers) Eby; m. Thomas Wayne Scott, Dec. 19, 1958; children: Linda Joy Scott Day, Daniel Dean. B in Bible Theology, Internat. Bible Inst. and Sem., Plymouth, Fla., 1982. Lic. practical nurse, Fla. Lic. practical nurse various hosps., Fla. and Mo., 1969-86; sch. nurse Orange County Sch. Bd., Orlando, Fla., 1974-78; pvt. duty nurse Upjohn Healthcare Services, Kansas City, Mo., 1985—. Served as cpl. USMC, 1957-59. Mem. Assn. Internat. Gospel Assemblies, Inc. (ordained minister), Tyler Crusades, Inc. (ordained minister). Democrat. Mem. Nazarene Ch. Avocation: poet. Home: 105-C Hargis St Belton MO 64012

SCOTT, PATRICIA LOUISE, sign manufacturing executive; b. Chgo., Feb. 13, 1946; d. Gerald E. and Grace B. (Hauser) Doyle; m. Gregory L. Marshall (dec. 1967); 1 child, Gregory L. II; m. Don Scott, May 13, 1978. Student Harper Jr. Coll., 1978-82. Adminstrv. asst. Sweda Internat., Chgo. and Des Plaines, Ill., 1969-73; asst. credit mgr. Oce Industries, Chgo., 1974-77; gen. office clk. Nutheme Co., 1977-78, gen. mgr. 1978-83, pres., 1983—. Office: Nutheme Co 1461-D Lunt Ave Elk Grove Village IL 60007

SCOTT, R. J., provincial judge. Judge Ct. of Queen's Bench, Winnipeg, Man., Can. Office: Court of Queen's Bench, Law Court Bldg, Winnipeg, MB Canada R3C 0V8 *

SCOTT, RALPH C., physician, educator; b. Bethel, Ohio, June 7, 1921; s. John Carey and Leona (Laycock) S.; m. Rosemary Ann Schultz, June 26, 1945; children: Susan Ann, Barbara Lynne, Marianne. B.S., U. Cin., 1943, M.D., 1945. Diplomate: Am. Bd. Internal Medicine (subspecialty cardiovascular disease). Intern Univ. Hosps., U. Iowa, 1945-46; resident, asst. dept. pathology U. Cin. Coll. Medicine, 1948-49, fellow internal medicine, 1949-53, fellow cardiology, 1953-57, mem. faculty, 1950—, prof. medicine, 1968—; staff clinics Cin. Gen. Hosp., 1950-75, clinician in internal medicine, 1952-75, dir. cardiac clinics, 1965-75, attending physician med. service, 1958—; staff VA Hosp., Cin., 1954-86, cons., 1961-86; attending physician Med. Service, Christian R. Holmes Hosp., Cin., 1957—; attending staff USAF Hosp., Wright Patterson AFB, 1960—; staff Good Samaritan Hosp., Cin., 1961—, cons., 1967—; staff Jewish Hosp., Cin., 1957—, cons., 1968—; cons. Children's Hosp., Cin., 1968—; attending physician Providence Hosp., Cin., 1971—. Contbr. articles to med. jours.; Editorial bd.: Am. Heart Jour, 1967-79, Jour. Electrocardiology, 1967—; editor: Electro-Cardiographic-Pathologic Conf., Jour. Electrocardiology, 1967—, Clin. Cardiology and Diabetes, 5 vols, 1981. Served to capt. AUS, 1946-48. Nat. Heart Inst. grantee, 1964-68, 67-74, 76-82, 1985—. Fellow A.C.P. Am. Coll. Cardiology, Am. Coll. Chest Physicians; mem. AMA, Ohio State Med. Assn., Cin. Acad. Medicine, Cen. Soc. Clin. Research, Am. Heart Assn. (Fellow Council Clin. Cardiology), Cin. Soc. Internal Medicine, Heart Assn. Southwestern Ohio, Am. Fedn. for Clin. Research, Internat. Cardiovascular Soc., Sigma Xi, Alpha Omega Alpha, Phi Eta Sigma, Phi Chi. Home: 2955 Alpine Terr Cincinnati OH 45208 Office: U Cin Med Ctr Med Scis Bldg Rm 7157 231 Bethesda Ave Cincinnati OH 45267

SCOTT, RALPH SAMUEL, psychologist; b. Portage, Wis., July 31, 1927; s. Ralph Martin and Mabel Doris (Quamme) S.; m. Liesel Luise Sattel, Oct. 21, 1961; children: Kristina, Ingrid, Heidi. BS, Luther Coll., 1950; MSW, U. Wis., 1953; PhD, U. Chgo., 1964; hon. degree, Chinatown Freedom Schs., San Francisco, Calif., 1977. Diplomate Am. Bd. Profl. Psychologists. Social worker Joliet (Ill.) Pub. Schs., 1953-55, West Aurora (Ill.) Schs., 1955-58; guidance counselor Frankfurt (Fed. Rep. of Germany) Am. Schs., 1958-59; social worker West Chicago (Ill.) Pub. Schs., 1959-61; clin. psychologist Med. Sch. Northwestern U., Chgo., 1963-65; prof. ednl. psychology, dir. edn. clinic U. No. Iowa, Cedar Falls, 1965—; vis. scholar Nat. Acad. Scis., Poland, 1980, 83, 84, Internat. Research Inst. Yugoslavia and Poland, 1982; cons. Home Start, Waterloo, Iowa, 1966-77; chairperson Iowa adv. com. U.S. Commn. Civil Rights, Washington, 1984—. Author: Learning Readiness System, 1967, Fun at the Pond, 1968, The Busing COverup, 1976, Rebuilding American Education, 1978. Served to sgt. U.S. Army, 1945-47. Recipient Key to City, Corpus Christi, Tex., 1977, commendation Mass. State Senate, 1977, spl. recognition City of Warren, Mich., 1976. Fellow Soc. Personality Assessment; mem. Univ. Profs. for Acad. Order (v.p. 1983—). Home: 1515 Columbia Dr Cedar Falls IA 50613 Office: U No Iowa Ednl Ctr Cedar Falls IA 50614

SCOTT, REBECCA ANDREWS, biology educator; b. Sunny Hill, La., June 4, 1939; d. Hayward and Dorothy (Nicholson) Andrews; m. Earl P. Scott, June 8, 1957; children—Stephanie Scott Dilworth, Cheryl L. B.S., So. U., 1962; M.S., Eastern Mich. U., 1969. Biology tchr., Detroit, 1966-68; sci. tchr. Ann Arbor (Mich.) Pub. Schs., 1968-69; biology tchr. North High Sch., Mpls., 1972—, advisor Jets Sci. Club. Pres. LWV of St. Anthony County, 1981-83, treas., 1984-86. Mem. Nat. Sci. Tchrs. Assn., Minn. Sci. Tchrs. Assn., LWV St. Anthony (treas. 1984—), Nat. Assn. Biology Tchrs., Iota Phi Lambda. Democrat. Presbyterian. Home: 3112 Wendhurst Ave Minneapolis MN 55418 Office: 1500 James Ave N Minneapolis MN 55411

SCOTT, RICHARD LYNN, data processing executive; b. Ora, Ind., Mar. 1, 1941; s. Harold Hophius and Maxine Louise (Strevey) S.; m. Karen Louise Kamp, Aug. 9, 1963; 1 child, Jonathon William. Student, Purdue U., 1959-61. Design engr. Kaydon, Muskegon, Mich., 1961-63; mgr. data processing Bastian Blessing, Grand Haven, Mich., 1963-79; dir. data programming Oliver Machine Co., Grand Rapids, Mich., 1979-82; mgr. CAD/CAM-CIM Steelcase, Inc., Grand Rapids, 1983—. Cons. United Way Kent County, Grand Rapids, 1986. Mem. Data Processing Mgmt. (pres. 1984-85), Am. Prodn. and Inventory Control Soc. (regional dir. 1984-85). Avocations: hiking, reading. Home: 18063 Lake Hills Dr Spring Lake MI 49456 Office: Steelcase Inc 901 44th St Grand Rapids MI 49508

SCOTT, ROBERT GENE, lawyer; b. Montague, Mass., Aug. 29, 1951; s. Edwin Ray and Barbara Agnes (Painchaud) S.; m. Laura Beth Williams, May 27, 1978; children: Jason Robert, Amanda Marie, Leah Beth. BS, U. Notre Dame, 1973, MS, 1975; postgrad. U. Tex. Med. Br., 1975-76; JD, U. Notre Dame, 1980. Bar: Ind. 1980, Mo. 1981, U.S. Dist. Ct. (no. dist.) Ind. 1980, U.S. Dist. Ct. (we. dist.) Mo. 1981, U.S. Patent Office 1980, U.S. Ct. Appeals (11th cir.) 1986, U.S. Ct. Appeals (8th cir.) 1987. Asst. women's basketball coach U. Notre Dame, Ind., 1977-80; assoc. atty. Oltsch, Knoblock & Hall, South Bend, Ind., 1980-81; atty. Swanson, Midgley, et al, Kansas City, Mo., 1981-82; exec. adminstr. Council of Fleet Specialists, Shawnee Mission, Kans., 1982-83; atty. Levy and Craig, Kansas City, Mo., 1983—. Precinct Committeeman Johnson County Rep. Party, Kans., 1983-84. Mem. ABA, Ind. Bar Assn., Mo. Bar Assn., Kansas City Bar Assn., Kansas City Lawyers Assn. Republican. Roman Catholic. Club: Notre Dame of Kansas City (pres. 1985-86). Home: 9405 Dice Ln Lenexa KS 66215 Office: Levy and Craig 916 Walnut St Suite 400 Kansas City MO 64106

SCOTT, ROBERT JAMES, accountant; b. Detroit, Apr. 9, 1949; s. Robert Nelson and Virginia Margaret (Love) S.; m. Karen Lee Wood, Feb. 20, 1971; children: Christopher, Jennifer, Daniel, Lindsey. BSBA, Mich. Tech. U., 1971. Staff acct. Shuttie & Floersch, Southfield, Mich., 1971-73; sr. acct. Seidman & Seidman, Traverse City, Mich., 1973-76; controller, v.p. Sheffer Collet Co., Traverse City, Mich., 1976-83; proprieter Robert J. Scott, CPA, Traverse City, Mich., 1983—. Mem. Am. Assn. CPA's, Mich. Assn. CPA's, Interlochen C. of C. (treas. 1974-75). Avocations: softball, bowling, golf. Home: 1804 Outer Dr Interlochen MI 49643

SCOTT, ROGER DAN, insurance company executive; b. Ottawa, Kans., Feb. 25, 1951; s. True Roger and Helen Louise (Mages) S.; m. Sally Jo Cox, Apr. 8, 1972; children—Christopher, Marcy, Amy. Student Clark's Bus. Coll., Topeka, 1969-70. Asst. underwriter Taylor & Co. Gen. Agy., Topeka, 1970-73; personal lines mgr. Northwestern Nat. Ins. Co., Topeka, 1973-76; underwriting mgr. Kans. Mut. Ins. Co., Topeka, 1976-80, exec. mgr., 1980-86, pres., exec. mgr., 1986—; sec.-treas. Midwest Rating and Service Bur., Inc., McPhearson, Kans., 1984-86, v.p., treas., 1986—. Fund raising com. Kans. Ins. Edn. Found., Topeka, 1983-84; chmn. Kans. Com. on Arson Prevention, Topeka, 1983-87 ; co. fund raising chmn. United Way of Topeka, 1980—. Mem. Kans. 1752 Club, Profl. Ins. Agts., Ind. Ins. Agts. Kans., Kans. Assn. Property and Casualty Ins. Cos. (pres. 1982-83), Topeka Underwriters Assn. Republican. Roman Catholic. Home: 6335 W 11th Topeka KS 666615 Office: Kans Mut Ins Co PO Box 1247 Topeka KS 66601

SCOTT, RONALD HUBERT, physician, surgeon; b. Rocky Ford, Colo., Jan. 3, 1912; s. Robert Hetherington and Bessie Estelle (Searls) S.; m. Hazel Louise Wiler, Aug. 15, 1937; 1 child Ronalyn Louise Scott Yeary. A.B., Western State Coll., 1935; D.O., Kirksville Coll. Osteo. Medicine, 1945; postgrad. Kans. U-Med. Ctr., 1970-82. Practice osteo. medicine specializing in geriatrics, Sullivan, Mo., 1947—; Sullivan Community Hosp. Dir. Presbyn. Chancel Choir, Sullivan Community Chorus, 1956-85; bd. dirs. Dist. CII Sch., Sullivan, Mo., 1957-72, pres. bd., 1960-70. Fellow Internat. Coll. Gen. Practitioners; mem. Am. Acad. Osteopathy, Nat. Assn. Watch and Clock Colletors Assn., Am. Osteo. Assn., (life), Mo. Osteo. Assn. (life; trustee 1957-72), Am. Coll. Gen. Practitioners, Psi Sigma Alpha. Republican. Presbyterian. Lodges: Rotary (pres. 1959-60, dist. gov. 1965-66), Odd Fellows. Home: 131 Meredith Lane Sullivan MO 63080

SCOTT, RONALD HUGH, chemical company executive; b. Jefferson City, Mo., Nov. 22, 1936; s. Ray B. and Carleen Ialeen (Fisher) S.; m. Jennie L. Sinnett, Dec. 24, 1959; children: Martin, Susan, Brian, Sarah. AA, Jefferson City Jr. Coll., 1956; BCE, U. Mo., 1960; MBA, U. Akron, 1966. Engr. chem. div. Pitts. Plate & Glass, Barberton, Ohio, 1960-64; supr. prodn. Amoco Chem., Joliet, Ill., 1964-66; area supt. Cen. Soya, Chgo., 1966-68; gen. mgr. Midwest Carbide, Keokuk, Iowa, 1968—. Moderator 1st Bapt. Ch., Keokuk, 1976-81; bd. dirs. Keokuk Community Schs., 1970-76, Area Edn. Agy., Burlington, Iowa, 1979-85. Mem. Am. Inst. Mech. Engrs. Republican. Lodges: Lions, Elks. Avocations: running, racquetball, fishing, golf, softball. Home: 1767 Fairlane Keokuk IA 52632 Office: Midwest Carbide Corp Box 607 Keokuk IA 52632

SCOTT, THEODORE R., lawyer; b. Mount Vernon, Ill., Dec. 7, 1924; s. Theodore R. and Beulah (Flannigan) S.; m. Virginia Scott, June 1, 1947; children: Anne Sheyka, Sarah Buckland, Daniel, Barbara Gomon. AB, U. Ill., 1947, JD, 1949. Bar: Ill. 1950. Law clk. to judge U.S. Ct. Appeals, 1949-51; sole practice Chgo., 1950—; assoc. Spaulding Glass, 1951-53, Loftus, Lucas & Hammand, 1953-58, Ooms, McDougall, Williams & Hersh, 1958-60; ptnr. McDougall, Hersh & Scott, Chgo., 1960-87; of counsel Jones, Day, Reavis & Pogue, 1987—. Served to 2d lt. USAAF, 1943-45. Decorated Air medal. Fellow Am. Coll. Trial Lawyers.; mem. ABA, Ill. Bar Assn., Chgo. Bar Assn., 7th Circuit Bar Assn. (past pres.), Legal Club Chgo., Law Club Chgo., Patent Law Assn. Chgo. (past pres.), Phi Beta Kappa. Clubs: Union League (Chgo.); Exmoor Country (Highland Park, Ill.). Home: 1569 Woodvale Ave Deerfield IL 60015 Office: 225 W washington St Chicago IL 60606

SCOTT, WALTER, JR., construction company executive; b. 1931. BS, Colo. State U., 1953. With Peter KiewitSons, Inc., Omaha, 1953—, mgr. Cleve. dist., 1962-64, v.p., 1964, exec. v.p., 1965-79, chmn. bd. dirs., pres., 1979—. Served with USAF, 1954-56. Office: Peter Kiewit Sons Inc 1000 Kiewit Plaza Omaha NE 68131 *

SCOTT, WILLIAM PAUL, lawyer; b. Staples, Minn., Nov. 8, 1928; A.L.A., U. Minn., 1949; B.S.L., St. Paul Coll. Law, 1952, J.D., 1954; m. Elsie Elaine Anderson, Feb. 7, 1968; 1 son, Jason Lee; children by previous marriage—William P., Mark D., Bryan D., Scott; stepchildren—Thomas J. (dec.), Terri L. Berg. Bar: Minn. 1954. Atty. right of way div. Minn. Hwy. Dept., 1945-52, civil engr. traffic and safety div., 1953-55; practice law Arlington, Minn., 1955-61, Gaylord, Minn., 1963-67; sr. partner firm Scott Law Offices and predecessors, Pipestone, Minn., 1967—; probate, juvenile judge Sibley County, Minn., 1956-61; Minn. pub. examiner, 1961-63; county atty. Sibley County, 1963-68, city atty., Pipestone, 1978—. Formerly nat. committeeman Young Rep. League; Sibley County Rep. chmn., 1961. Served with USMCR, 1946-50; from 2d lt. to lt. col. USAF Res., 1950-77; ret. Recipient George Washington Honor medal Freedoms Found., 1970, 72. Mem. Am., Minn. bar assns., Mensa, V.F.W., DAV, Am. Legion, Air Force Assn., Res. Officers Assn., U.S. Supreme Ct. Bar Assn. Mason (32 deg., Shriner). Home: Box 704 Pipestone MN 56164 Office: Park Plaza Offices Pipestone MN 56164

SCOTT, WINFIELD JAMES, marketing executive; b. Worcester, Mass., Jan. 4, 1933; s. Gherald Dean and Helen L. S.; B.A., Norwich U., 1955; postgrad. Marquette U., 1961-62; m. Betty Joan Price, June 29, 1957; children—Mary Jo, Susan Elizabeth. With sales dept. Norton Co., Worcester, 1956, sales rep. Chgo. dist., 1957, sales supr. Wis. dist., 1960-71; founder, pres. The Abrasive Group, Wauwatosa, Wis., 1971—; ad hoc prof. mktg. U. Wis. Extension. Mem. Abrasive Engring. Soc. (co-gen. chmn. internat. conf.), Nat. Small Bus. Assn., Wis. Mfrs. and Commerce, Ind. Bus. Assn. Wis., Met. Milw. Assn. Commerce, Nat. Fedn. Ind. Bus. Republican. Episcopalian. Author: Modern Machine Shop, 1967. Home: 11037 W Derby Ave Wauwatosa WI 53225 Office: PO Box 13244 Wauwatosa WI 53213

SCOVEL, ROGER LARRY, investment analyst; b. Oelwein, Iowa, July 30, 1940; s. Leon E. and Nettie B. (Mitchell) S.; m. Susan V. Peters, Oct. 17, 1970; children: Lori S., Amy L. BA, Cornell Coll., Mt. Vernon, Iowa, 1962; MBA, U. Ill., 1978. Supt. data processing State Farm Ins. Co., Bloomington, Ill., 1967-80, investment analyst, 1980—. Served with U.S. Army, 1962-65. Methodist. Office: State Farm Ins Co One State Farm Plaza Bloomington IL 61701

SCOVIL, SAMUEL KINGSTON, mining company executive; b. Cleve., June 15, 1923; s. R. Malcolm and Dorothy Lee (Brown) S.; m. Barbara C. Baker, May 22, 1944; children—Emily, Malcolm (dec.), Samuel, Alexander. B.S., Yale U., 1945; grad., Advanced Mgmt. Program, Harvard, 1962. With Republic Steel Corp., 1947-50; with Cleveland Cliffs Inc., 1950—, mgr. sales, 1960-63, v.p. sales, 1963-69, sr. v.p. sales, 1970-72, sr. v.p., 1972-74, pres., 1974-83, chief exec. officer, 1976—, chmn. bd., 1983—, also dir.; dir. Eaton Corp., Nat. City Bank Cleve., Dundee Cement Co. Trustee Univ. Sch., Cleve., Cleve. Clinic Found. Office: Cleveland-Cliffs Inc Huntington Bldg Cleveland OH 44115

SCREETON, GARY LEONARD, accountant; b. Ft. Wayne, Ind., Nov. 23, 1956; s. Marvin Leonard Screeton and Jeneth Carol (Waltz) Dubé; m. Linda Lucille Myers, Aug. 9, 1975; children: Amanda, Matthew, Heather. BS, Ind. U., 1982. CPA, Ind. Dep. treas. Allen County, Ft. Wayne, 1979-83; field examiner State of Ind., Indpls., 1983-86; sr. auditor Lincoln Fin. Corp., Ft. Wayne, 1986—. Served as sgt. USAF, 1975-79. Mem. Am. Inst. CPA's, Ind. CPA Soc., Inst. Internal Auditors. Republican. Mem Ch. Christ. Avocations: racquetball, basketball. Home: 6124 Millhollow Ln Fort Wayne IN 46815-6234 Office: Lincoln Financial Corp 2123 Lincolnway Ct Fort Wayne IN 46816

SCRIBNER, MARGARET ELLEN, school evaluator and administrator, consultant; b. Pana, Ill., Oct. 20, 1948; d. William M. and Bertrice Faye (Springman) S.; m. John E. McNeal, Aug. 15, 1977 (div. Oct. 1981); m. Leonard P. Basak Jr., Mar. 13, 1986. B.S. in Social Work, Spaulding U., 1970. Coordinator Gov.'s Inaugural Com., Springfield, Ill., 1972; sch. evaluation specialist Ill. State Bd. of Edn., Chgo., 1970—; dir. on bd. and corp. sec. Ventura 21, Inc., Roselle, Ill., 1984—. Mem. Uptown Community Orgn., Chgo., 1978-80; charter mem. and organizer Margate-Ainslie Block Club, Chgo., 1979-80. Recipient cert. of Recognition, Ill. State Bd. of Edn., Springfield, 1975, 77, 78. Mem. Bus. and Profl. Women of Chgo., (historian 1978-79), Internat. Leadership Training Inst. (cert. 1974). Republican. Roman Catholic. Clubs: Ill. Athletic (Chgo. 1983—), Brookwood Country (Wood Dale, Ill. 1977-81, 83—). Avocations: golf, clarinet, water colors, racquetball. Office: Ill State Bd of Edn 100 W Randolph Suite 14-300 Chicago IL 60601

SCRIVNER, JOYCE KAY, design engineer; b. Denver, June 12, 1950; d. Mansil Wayne and Harriet Lorraine (Webster) S. SSTP, Colo. Sch. Mines, 1967; student U. Colo., 1968-72, Mich. State U., 1974, Clarion (Pa.) State Coll., 1974; BSCS, Purdue U., 1976. Clk. U.S. Book Exchange, Washington, 1972-73, Govt. Printing Office, Washington, 1973-74; programmer SCADA group Leeds & Northrup Corp., North Wales, Pa., 1976-78; programmer/analyst Energy Mgmt. Systems div. Control Data Corp., Mpls., 1979-84; sr. design automation engr. Mercury div. Unisys Corp. (formerly Sperry Corp.), Mpls., 1984—; adminstr. Down Under Fan Fund, 1981-83; chmn. Plergbcon, Mpls., 1982, Notanokon, 1986; mem. staff SIGGRAPH, 1985, SIGPLAN, 1987. Editor: (mags.) Gypsy, 1979—, Of Such are Legends Made, 1978—. Mem. World Sci. Fiction Conv. Staff, 1977-78, 80-81, 85-85; chairperson art show Minicon, Mpls., 1980-81, 83, 86. Down Under Fan Fund grantee, 1981. Mem. Assn. Women in Computing (program v.p. 1982-83), Assn. for Computing Machinery, Minn. Sci. Fiction Assn., IEEE Computer Assn.

SCRIVO, JERRY VANCE, marketing executive; b. Highland Park, Mich., Aug. 18, 1941; s. John R. and Martha A. (Woodcox) S.; m. Carole Ann Lillstrang, June 20, 1964; children: Michelle Marie, Robert John. BSME, Mich. Tech. U., 1963; MBA, Wayne State U., 1966. Devel. engr. Gen. Motors Truck and Bus Co., Pontiac, Mich., 1963-67; exptl. supr. Teledyne Continental Motors, Muskegon, Mich., 1967-72; mgr. application engr. Excello Corp., Dover, N.H., 1972-80; reaction injection molding Fireston Tire & Rubber, Romeo, Mich., 1980-82; v.p. planning Romeo-Reaction Injection

Molding, 1982-83; mgr. plastic machinery Excello Corp., Holland, Mich., 1983—. Contbr. articles to profl. jours.; patentee reaction injection molding mix head, vehicle bumper assembly. Mem. Soc. Automotive Engrs. (readers com. 1982—), Soc. Plastic Engrs. (standards com. 1985—), Soc. Plastics Industry, Soc. for Advancement Material and Process Engring., Sigma Iota Epsilon, Beta Sigma Psi (past pres.). Republican. Lutheran. Avocations: bowling, skiing, swimming. Home: 1374 Heather Dr Holland MI 49423 Office: Excello Corp 345 E 48th St Holland MI 49423

SCRUGGS, SHARON ANITTA, counselor; b. Chgo., Aug. 3, 1958; m. Frank T. Scruggs, Apr. 23, 1983; 1 child, Danielle Alexandria. BS in Sociology, Ill. State U., 1980; cert. in law, John Marshall Law Sch., 1983. Counselor, adv. Orchard Village, Skokie, Ill., 1981-83; job devel., youth coordinator Alternatives, Inc., Chgo., 1983-84; freelance writer Chgo., 1981—; child care worker, counselor Habilitative Systems, Chgo., 1986—; adv. Brother Tech. Writer Co., Chgo., 1983—; treas. Systems & Elites, Inc., Chgo., 1976-80. Author: Job Talk Newsletter, 1984. Bldg. code vol. Rogers Park Tenant Com., Chgo., 1985. Recipient Tenant Hotline Appreciation award Rogers Park Tenant Com., Chgo., 1985; named one of Outstanding Young Women Am., 1985. Avocations: painting, sketching, photography, symphony concerts.

SCUDAMORE, HAROLD HUNTER, internist; b. Wayne City, Ill., Dec. 8, 1915; s. Fay Walter and Edith Alice (Hunter) S.; m. Virginia Gordon Haskins, Dec. 26, 1942; children: James Allen, Gordon Hunter, Susan Edith, Walter Edwin. AS, Rocky Mountain Coll., 1935; BS, Mont. State Coll., 1937; MS in Zoology, Northwestern U., 1940, PhD, 1942, MB, 1945, MD, 1946. Practice medicine specializing in internal medicine and gastroenterology Mayo Clinic, Rochester, Minn., 1951-71; practice medicine specializing in internal medicine and gastroenterology The Monroe (Wis.) Clinic, 1971—, med. dir., 1986—; assoc. prof. medicine, Mayo Grad. Sch., 1965-71; clin. assoc. prof. med., U. Wis. Med. Sch., 1972—. Contbr. numerous articles to profl. jours. Cubmaster, scoutmaster, chmn. Zumbro Valley Dist., pres. Gamehaven Council, Boy Scouts Am., Rochester, 1956-71, recipient Eagle Scout award. Served to capt. M. C., U.S. Army, 1946-48. Fellow Am. Coll. Physicians, Am. Coll. Gastroent.; mem. AMA, Internat. Soc. Internal Medicine, Am. Soc. Internal Medicine, Am. Gastroent. Assn., Wis. Soc. Internal Medicine, Wis. Soc. Gastrointestinal Endoscopy, Wis. State Medical Soc., Green County Med. Soc. Republican. Mem. United Ch. of Christ. Lodge: Kiwanis. Office: The Monroe Clinic 1515 10th St Monroe WI 53566

SCUDAMORE, SHULAR RAYMOND, marketing executive; b. Evansville, Ind., Nov. 8, 1948; s. Raymond Luther and Joyce (Whetstone) S.; m. Theresa Joy Schaleger, June 14, 1970; children: Amalia, Katherine. BS in Gen. Engring., U. Ill., 1972; MBA with distinction, Ill. Benedictine Coll., 1980. Application engr. Henry Pratt Co., Aurora, Ill., 1972-74; sales engr. Reinken Engring./Calcorp., North Aurora, Ill., 1974-77; mgr. engineered products and others Stephens-Adamson subs. Allis-Chalmers Co, Aurora, 1977—. Contbr. articles to profl. jours. Chmn. Fox Valley Leadership Prayer Breakfast, Aurora, 1986—. Named Eagle Scout Boy Scouts Am., Des Moines, 1964. Office: Stephens-Adamson/Allis-Chalmers Co PO Box 1367 Aurora IL 60507

SCUDDER, THEODORE TOWNSEND, III, lawyer; b. Oak Park, Ill., June 26, 1939; s. Theodore Townsend Jr. and Joan (Kerr) S.; m. Eileen Hesmondhalgh, May 31, 1974; children—Caroline Sarah, Robert Cameron. A.B., Harvard U., 1961; J.D., U. Mich., 1964; postgrad. John Marshall Law Sch., 1965-67, Northwestern Law Sch., 1971. Bar: Ill. 1964, U.S. Dist. Ct. (no. dist.) Ill. 1965. Ct. reporter Ill. Army N.G., Chgo., 1964-70; assoc. willian, Brinks, Olds, Hofer, Chgo., 1963-67, Wilson & McIlvaine, Chgo., 1967-68, Jacobs, Williams & Montgomery, Chgo., 1968-70, asst. U.S. atty. U.S. Dept. Justice, Chgo., 1970-79; ptnr. Ruff Weidenaar & Reidy, Chgo., 1979-87; sole practice, Hoffman Estates, Ill. 1987—; trustee, counsel Pacific Garden Mission, Chgo., 1967—; advisor Ill. Selective Service, Springfield, 1973-79. Editor: Pike-Schaefer Dialog, 1969. Canvasser, Republican Party, Chgo., 1964-67. NEH scholar U. Wis., 1974. Mem. ABA, Christian Legal Soc. (bd. dirs. 1965-67), Am. Judicature Soc., Ill. Bar Assn., Chgo. Bar Assn. Episcopalian. Clubs: Harvard (Chgo.) (asst. treas. 1968-72); Philadelphia Soc. (North Adams, Mich.). Home: 362 Marion St Glen Ellyn IL 60137 Office: 2300 N Barrington Rd Hoffman Estates IL 60195

SCULLY, JOHN EDWARD, JR., banker; b. Chgo., Jan. 18, 1943; s. John Edward and Ann Berenice (Allenbrand) S.; m. Mary Julia Purvin, June 11, 1966; children—Melissa, Julie, John Edward III. B.A., U. Notre Dame, 1964; M.A., DePaul U., 1966. Supr., No. Trust Co., Chgo., 1968-69, with personnel dept., 1969-74, personnel officer, 1974-77, bond investment officer, 1977-80; asst. v.p. First Nat. Bank of Chgo., 1980-82, v.p., 1982—; instr. Am. Inst. Banking, 1972—. Served with USAR, 1964—, col. Res. Mem. Am. Soc. Personnel Adminstrs., Employment Mgrs. Assn., Res. Officers Assn., Mil. Order World Wars, Assn. U.S. Army. Republican. Roman Catholic. Club: Riverside Swim. Avocations: running, stamp collecting. Home: 258 Lawton Rd Riverside IL 60546 Office: First Nat Bank of Chicago Chicago IL 60670

SCULLY, MICHAEL, educator, consultant; b. Detroit, Sept. 12, 1942; s. Robert Edward and Jean Lenore (Carmichael) S. BA in Bus., Parsons Coll., 1967; MS, Ind. U., 1970; PhD in Higher Ed., So. Ill. U., 1981. Head resident U. Wis., Oshkosh, 1970-73, Western Ill. U., Macomb, 1973-76; asst. dir. housing So. Ill. U., Carbondale, 1976-80; tchr. Kenosha (Wis.) Unified Sch. Dist., 1981-82; instr. Catherine Coll., Chgo., 1982—. Dir. AIDS Hotline Ill. Dept. Health, 1982-86; cons. AIDS lectr., Chgo., 1982—. Mem. Great Lakes Assn. Coll. and Univ. Housing Officers (editor 1976-80, Achievement award 1979), Nat. Assn. Student Personnel Adminstrs. Methodist. Home: 2620 N Halsted Chicago IL 60614 Office: Catherine Coll 2 N LaSalle Chicago IL 60602

SEABURY, STEPHEN L., control system engineer; b. Portland, Maine, Sept. 6, 1944; s. Joseph W. and Barbara (Winslow) S.; m. Leslie Jean Sanborn, July 27, 1968; children: Derek, Dana. BS in Chem. Engring., U. Maine, 1967, MS in Chem. Engring., 1967; JD, New England Sch. Law, 1979. Bar: Mass. Mgr. application engring. Beloit (Wis.) Corp., 1967-70; cons. in field Beloit, 1970-71; design sect. mgr. Weyerhauser, Tacoma, Wash., 1971-73; mgr. fin. ops. Foxboro, Mass., 1973-83; dir. process mgmt. systems Bailey Controls Co., Wickliffe, Ohio, 1983-85, v.p. engring., 1985-87; v.p., gen. mgr. electronic info. systems div. McDermott, Inc., Chagrin Falls, Ohio, 1987—. Mem. Beloit City Council, mem. research com. U. Maine Pulp and Paper Found. Mem. Tech. Assn. of the Pulp and Paper Industry (past chmn. nat. process control com.), Instrument Soc. Am., Soc. Mfg. Engrs., Armed Forces Communications and Electronics Assn., Am. Assn. Artificial Intelligence. Office: Bailey Controls Co 29801 Euclid Ave Wickliffe OH 44092

SEACHRIST, WILLIAM EARL, holding company executive; b. Columbia, Pa., Jan. 31, 1931; s. Simon Earl and Madelyn Grace (Stiger) S.; m. Marjorie Leone Raab, June 20, 1953; children: Frederick, Sibyl, David, Eric, Marjorie. AB in Polit. Sci., Franklin and Marshall Coll., 1952; M of Govt. Adminstrn., U. Pa., 1958. City mgr. City of Ridgway, Pa., 1958-62; pres. Kent (Ohio) Industries, Inc., 1966-82; pres., prin. W.E. Seachrist Assocs., Hudson, Ohio, 1967—; pres. Seachrist Real Estate, Kent, 1968-83; pres., chief exec. officer Tekcore, Inc., Hudson, 1982—, also bd. dirs.; pres., chief exec. officer Adventek Corp., Hudson, 1982—, also bd. dirs.; chmn., chief exec. officer Prodex, Inc., Hudson, 1987—, also bd. dirs.; cons. Heritage Fin. Corp., Hudson, 1986—, Physicians Diagnostics of Am., 1986—; adj. instr. Franklin & Marshall Coll., Kent State U. Author: The Role of the State Planning Agency, 1953; contbr. articles to profl. jours. Cons. State of Pa., Harrisburg, 1959-61; bd. dirs. United Fund, Kent, 1963; sr. warden Episcopal Ch., Kent, 1972; trustee, overseer Franklin and Marshall Coll., Lancaster, Pa., 1972—. Served to lt. USN, 1953-57. Recipient Alumni Disting. Service Medal award Franklin and Marshall Coll., 1984; Fels fellow U. Pa., 1953. Mem. Am. Acad. Polit and Social Sci., Acad. Polit. Sci., Soc. Plastic Engrs., N.Y. Acad. Scis., Internat. City Mgrs. Assn., Beta Alpha Psi. Republican. Club: Cascade (Akron, Ohio). Lodge: Masons. Avocations: reading, music. Home: 1655 Woodway Kent OH 44240 Office: Park Pl 10 W Streetsboro Rd Hudson OH 44236

SEAGER, GLENN MARVIN, otolaryngologist; b. Rutland, Vt., Jan. 31, 1934; m. Lila Ann Hart, Aug. 24, 1957; children: Glenn Mark, Scott Arthur, Brent Craig. BS, U. Vt., 1956, MD, 1959. Diplomate Am. Bd. Med. Examiners, Am. Bd. Otolaryngology; lic. physcian Ohio, Vt., N.Y., Wis. Intern Guthrie Clinic, Sayre, Pa., 1959-60; fellow otolaryngology Cleve. Clinic, 1960-61, U. Vt., Burlington, 1962-64; fellow otolaryngology and thoracic surgery U. Pa., 1963-64; instr. otolaryngology NYU, N.Y.C., 1964-67; asst. chief otolaryngology Madigan Gen. Hosp., Tacoma, Wash., 1968-69; otorhinolaryngologist Gundersen Clinic Ltd., Lacrosse, Wis., 1969—; asst. otorhinolaryngology Univ. Hosp., N.Y., 1964-65; clin. asst., vis. surgeon Bellevue Hosp., New York, 1964-65, asst. vis. surgeon, 1965-67; otologist in charge Hearing and Speech Ctr. Univ. Hosp., 1966-6; cons. pediatric dept. Bellevue Hosp., 1966-68; asst. clin. prof. otorhinolarnygology NYU Sch. Medicine, 1967, U. Wash. Sch. Medicine, 1968, U. Wis. Sch. Med., 1986; dir. edn. and tng., asst. chief otolaryngology Madigan Gen. Hosp., 1968-69; chmn dept. otolaryngology Gundersen Clinic Ltd., 1984-86. Contbr. articles to profl. jours. Bd. outreach 1st Congregational Ch., LaCrosse, 1970-76, pres. bd. dirs. 1971-75; mem. youth and camping com. YMCA of LaCrosse, 1971-75; bd. dirs. Chgo. Theol. Sem., 1976-80, bd. assocs., 1980—. Fellow ACS; mem. AMA, AAAS, Am. Acad. Otolaryngology, Nat. Assn. Hearing and Speech Agencies, Wis. Soc. Otolaryngology, (sec., treas. 1981-85, pres. elect 1985—0), N.Y. Acad. Scis., Med. Soc. N.Y., Med. Soc. Wis., Med. Soc. County of N.Y., Med. Soc. County of LaCrosse, Wis. Soc. of Otolaryngology-Head and Neck Surgery (pres. 1986-87), Wis. Physicians Polit. Action Com. (bd. dirs. 1981), Sierra Club (pres. Coulee Region Group John Muir chpt. 1975-77). Avocations: boating, waterskiing, hiking, indoor plant gardening, photography. Office: Gundersen Clinic 1836 South Ave LaCrosse WI 54601

SEAL, DARRELL GREG, prosthodontist; b. Artesia, N.Mex., Nov. 26, 1951; s. Darrell Grey and Shirley Irene (Hanthorne) S. BS summa cum laude, Graceland Coll., 1973; DDS magna cum laude, U. Mo., Kansas City, 1975, cert. fixed prosthodontics, 1977. Asst. prof. dept. fixed prosthodontics U. Mo., 1977-80; practice dentistry specializing in prosthodontics Kansas City, 1977—; dir. grad. fixed prosthodontics tng. program U. Mo. Kansas City, 1978-80; active staff, mem. head and neck pain team Truman Med. Ctr., Kansas City, 1978—; cons. prosthodontics Calcitek, Inc., San Diego, Calif., 1985—. Pastor Ridgewood Reformed Ch. Jesus Christ of the Latter Day Saints, Kansas City, 1979-82. Mem. ADA, Am. Coll. Prosthodontics, Prosthodontics Soc., Internat. Coll. Prosthodontics. Home: 6170 Sni-A-Bar Rd Kansas City MO 64129 Office: 2440 Pershing Rd Kansas City MO 64108

SEAL, GREGORY MORRIS, management consultant; b. Buffalo, Feb. 23, 1948; s. Maynard A. and Sally (Latak) S.; m. Victoria Ghearing, Mar. 30, 1974; children—Allyson Marie, Alexander Michael. B.A. in Econs., Colgate U., 1970. Cert. mgmt. cons., systems profl. Systems analyst Procter & Gamble, Cin., 1970-73, group mgr., 1973-76; ptnr. Touche Ross & Co., Cleve., 1976—. Contbr. articles retail and mfg. systems Regional pres. Big Bros./Big Sisters Am., Cin., 1976, bd. dirs., Phila., 1975-76, v.p., Cin., 1973-76. Mem. Inst. Mgmt. Cons., Soc. Info. Mgmt. Home: 3175 Montgomery Rd Shaker Heights OH 44122 Office: Touche Ross 1801 E 9th St Cleveland OH 44114

SEAL, JACK RAMON, construction executive; b. Ottumwa, Iowa, Nov. 9, 1927; s. Jacques and Charlotte Marie (Cline) S.; m. Phyllis Ilene Pitts, May 16, 1948; children: Richard, Barry, Janice. BCE, Findley Engring. Sch., 1952. Chief estimator Sharp Bros. Contractors, Kansas City, Mo., 1952-57; pres. Seal-Wells Constrn., Kansas City, 1957-70, Pugh & Assoc., Pensacola, Fla., 1970-79, Apt. Contracting Corp., Miami, Fla. and East Lansing, Mich., 1982—; dir. constrn. Deltona Corp., Miami, 1979-82. Served with USN, 1945-46, PTO. Mem. Assn. Builders and Contractors (bd. dirs. cen. Mich. chpt., state, nat. 1984—, pres.-elect cen. Mich. chpt., chief exec. officer com., cost effective ops. com.). Republican. Methodist. Club: Walnut Hills Country (East Lansing). Lodges: Masons, Shriners. Avocations: boating, golf. Home: 260 Wind N Wood Okemos MI 48864 Office: Apt Contracting Corp 4970 Northwind Dr Suite 120 East Lansing MI 48823

SEALSCOTT, J. RICHARD, accountant, educator; b. Van Wert, Ohio, Apr. 19, 1954; s. Doyle Morris and Virginia (Martin) S.; m. Deborah J. Adam, Nov. 26, 1977; 1 child, Emily Anne. BS, Bowling Green (Ohio) State U., 1976; MBA, U. Dayton, 1981. CPA, Ohio. Pvt. practice acctg. Van Wert, 1981—; acctg. instr. Northwest Tech. Coll., Archbold, Ohio, 1981—. Mem. Ohio Soc. CPA's, Ohio Edn. Assn., Office Edn. Assn. Methodist. Avocations: jogging, racquetball, tennis, cycling. Home: 764 Williams St Van Wert OH 45891 Office: Northwest Tech Coll Box 246A Archbold OH 43502

SEALY, ZOE WEST, artistic director, dance instructor, choreographer; b. Mobile, Ala., Dec. 19, 1939; d. Henry Carver and Margaret (Griffith) West; m. William Francis Sealy, Dec. 12, 1968; children—Charles Lee, Michael Henry. Student U. Ala., 1958-59. Dancer, Mobile Civic Ballet, 1963-65, Crescent City Ballet, New Orleans, 1957-59; tchr./dancer Arthur Murray Studios, Mobile, Pensacola, Fla., 1966-68; co-dir. Studio Dance Arts, Mpls., 1970-72, founder, artistic dir. Zoe Sealy Dance Ctr., Mpls., 1972—, Minn. Jazz Dance Co., Mpls., 1976—; dance tchr. U. Minn. Mpls., 1984—; choreographer Morris Park Players, Mpls., 1970-75; dance instr. Gulf Coast Dance Seminar, Mobile, Ala., 1980-84; panel mem. Minn. Ind. Choreographers Alliance/McKnight Fellowship, Mpls., 1984-85. Choreographer: Rhapsody in Blue, 1977; Classique Moderne, 1978; Tribute, 1979; XI Commandment: Dance, 1982; Under the Influence, 1985; bd. dirs. Minn. Dance Alliance, 1986—. Pres., PTA, Mpls., 1971-72. Recipient 1st Place Tchrs. trophy (regional competition) Arthur Murray Studios, 1968, 2d Place Tchrs. trophy (world competition), 1968. Mem. Profl. Dance Tchrs. Assn., Minn. Ind. Choreographers Alliance. Republican. United Methodist. Avocations: tennis, swimming. Office: Zoe Sealy Dance Ctr 1815 E 38th St Minneapolis MN 55407

SEAMAN, LINDA K., restaurant owner; b. Wichita, Kans., May 22, 1958; d. Floyd Freeman and Harriet Lorea (Holden) Blakely; m. Thomas Joseph Jones, Jan. 28, 1978 (div. Nov. 1980); m. Terry Lynn Seaman, May 22, 1981; children: Heather Rae, Danielle Marie. Student, Cowley County (Kans.) Community Coll., 1976—. Owner Kountry Kitchen Restaurant, Winfield, Kans., 1983—. Mem. Ind. Bus. Persons. Home: Rural Rt 4 Box 202 Winfield KS 67156 Office: Kounty Kitchen 1414 Main Winfield KS 67156

SEAMAN, WILLIAM RICE, lawyer; b. Newton, Mass., Sept. 3, 1909; s. William Grant and Laura Owen (Rice) S.; m. Martha Elizabeth Steed, May 14, 1949; children—Diana Whitten, John Terrell. A.B., DePauw U., 1930; LL.B., Harvard U., 1933. Bar: Ohio 1933, U.S. Dist. Ct. (so. dist.) Ohio 1935, U.S. Ct. Appeals (6th cir.) 1935. Assoc., Frost & Jacobs, Cin., 1933-42, 46-49, ptnr., 1950-79, of counsel, 1980—. Councilman Indian Hill Village, Cin., 1943-54, vice mayor, 1955; trustee Citizens Devel. Com., 1952-53. Served to lt. Comdr. USN, 1942-46, ETO. Decorated Bronze Star. Mem. Cin. Bar Assn., Ohio Bar Assn., ABA, Cincinnatus Assn. (pres. 1951). Republican. Methodist. Club: University. Lodge: Rotary. Home: 8875 Fawn Meadow Ln Cincinnati OH 45242 Office: Frost & Jacobs 2500 Central Trust Ctr Cincinnati OH 45202

SEARLE, DANIEL CROW, financial corporation executive, former pharmaceuticals executive; b. Evanston, Ill., May 6, 1926; s. John Gideon and Frances Louise (Crow) S.; m. Dain Depew Fuller, Sept. 2, 1950; children: Anne Searle Meers, Daniel Gideon, Michael Dain. B.S., Yale U., 1950; M.B.A., Harvard, 1952. With G.D. Searle & Co., Chgo., 1938-85, successively staff asst. to v.p. charge fin. and mfg., asst. sec., sec., 1952-63, v.p., 1961-63, exec. v.p., 1963-66, pres., chief ops. officer, 1966-70, pres., chief exec. officer, 1970-77, chmn. bd., 1977-85, dir., 1964-85; dir. Earl Kinship Capital Corp., 1982—; bd. dirs. Ethics & Pub. Policy Ctr., Chgo., Utilities Inc., Maynard Oil Co., Jim Walter Corp., Multimix Systems, Inc. Bd. dirs. Evanston Hosp.; trustee Northwestern U., Art Inst. Chgo., WTTW, Hudson Inst., 1980—; assocs. bd. dirs. Harvard U. Bus. Sch. Served with USNR, World War II. Republican. Episcopalian (vestry). Clubs: Glen View (Golf, Ill.); Indian Hill (Winnetka, Ill.); Shoreacres (Lake Bluff, Ill.); Chicago (Chgo.); Seminole Golf, Augusta Nat. Golf; Old Elm (Highland Park, Ill.); Jupiter Island (Fla.). Office: 400 Skokie Blvd Suite 675 Northbrook IL 60062

SEARLE, DANIEL GIDEON, venture capital executive; b. Evanston, Ill., Jan. 23, 1953; s. Daniel Crow and Dain Depew (Fuller) S.; m. Nancy Roberta Schneider, Aug. 15, 1976; children—Kristin Anne, Gideon Paul, Frederick Todd. B.S. in Sociology, Vanderbilt U., 1975; M.M. in Fin., Northwestern U., 1983. Mgmt. trainee G.D. Searle & Co., Skokie, Ill., 1975-77; asst. product mgr. Searle Pharms., Chgo., 1977-78, pharm. sales rep., 1978-79; mem. mktg. research staff Searle Pharms., Chgo., 1979; mgr. internal control Searle Pharm. Group, Skokie, 1979-83, mgr. records mgmt., 1983-84; assoc. Earl Kinship Capital Corp., Skokie, 1984-86; pres. The Serafin Group, 1986—. Trustee Allendale Sch., Lake Villa, Ill., 1977—, Shedd Aquarium, Chgo., 1982—. Mem. Chgo. Venture Capital Club, Ducks Unlimited (chmn. North Shore sponsor chpt. 1983—). Republican. Episcopalian. Clubs: Glen View (Golf, Ill.); Indian Hill (Winnetka, Ill.). Avocations: wine collecting; duck hunting; golf; reading in management.

SEARLE, STEWART A., transportation equipment holding company executive; b. Winnipeg, Man., Can., 1923; s. Stewart Augustus and Sally Elizabeth (Appleyard) S.; m. Maudie Jessiman, Nov. 9, 1949; children: Stewart A., David J. Student, Trinity Coll., Port Hope, Ont., Queen's U., Kingston, Ont. Chmn. bd. dirs. Fed. Industries, Ltd., Winnipeg. Served to lt. RCAF. Office: Fed Industries LTD, 1 Lombard Pl, Winnipeg, MB Canada R3B 0X3 *

SEARLES, ROBERT MONROE, accountant; b. Berkshire, Ohio, Sept. 22, 1934; s. Arlo Monroe and Alice May (Augestine) S.; m. Deana May Ball, Nov. 18, 1955 (div. Feb. 1970); children: Terresa, Tamara, Robert Craig; m. Linda Joyce Neal, June 27, 1981. BS in Bus. Adminstrn., Ohio State U., 1974. Pvt. practice hair styling Sunbury, Ohio, 1959-74; acctg. mgr. and controller Ohio Agrl. Services, Inc., Powell, Ohio, 1974-83; pvt. practice acctg. Sunbury, 1983—. Mem. Nat. Soc. Pub. Accts., Pub. Accts. Soc. Ohio. Republican. Methodist. Lodges: Lions (pres. 1977), Masons (worship master Sunbury 1984, pres. Delaware County 1985, exec. com. Columbus). Avocations: golf, fishing, sports car rallying. Home: 197 N Columbus St Sunbury OH 43074 Office: 25 S Columbus St Sunbury OH 43074

SEARLES, STEVEN DOUGLAS, industrial engineer; b. Mpls., Nov. 14, 1955; s. Clayton Roger and Phyllis Ann (Kistler) S.; m. Kathryn Jean Balcer, June 18, 1977; children: Douglas Steven, Kari Frances. AA in Tech. Illustration, Ferris State Coll., Big Rapids, Mich., 1975, AA in Tech. Drafting, BS in Edn. with distinction., 1977; postgrad., Western Mich. U. Tchr., coach Bellevue (Mich.) Schs., 1977-79; draftsman Eaton Corp., Marshall, Mich., 1979-82, indsl. engr., 1983—; Woodworking tchr. Marshall Pub. Schs., 1980—. Mem. Marshall Jaycees, Inst. Indsl. Engring. Roman Catholic. Avocations: restoring classic cars, woodworking, motorcycling, basketball, sports. Home: 14932 W Michigan Ave Marshall MI 49068 Office: Eaton Corp 1101 W Hanover Marshall MI 49068

SEARSON, THOMAS EARL, psychologist; b. Deming, N.Mex., Oct. 4, 1943; s. Earl T. and Wilma C. (Lykke) S.; m. Jeanette M. Stulken, Aug. 7, 1964; children: Thomas L., Michael T., Stephanie M. BA, Hastings Coll., 1965; MEd, U. Ill., 1966, EdD, 1970. Cert. dlin. psychologist. Counseling psychologist Creighton U., Omaha, 1971-75; dir. Mid Nebr. Community Mental Health Ctr., Grand Island, 1975-79; psychologist Nebr. Div. Rehab., Omaha, 1979—; psychologist St. Joseph Hosp., Omaha, 1982—. Presl. scholar Hastings Coll., 1961-65; U. Ill. fellow, Urbana, 1965-67. Mem. Am. Psychol. Assn., Nebr. Psychol. Assn. (bd. dirs. 1985-86, Epilepsy Assn. Nebr. (adv. bd. 1985—), Douglas County Hist. Soc. Lutheran. Club: Fairs and Squares (Omaha). Avocations: history, square dancing. Home: 6111 S 92d Ave Omaha NE 68127 Office: Nebr Div Rehab 1313 Farnam Omaha NE 68103

SEASE, GENE ELWOOD, university president; b. Portage, Pa., June 28, 1931; s. Grover Chauncey and Clara Mae (Over) S.; m. Joanne D. Cherry, July 20, 1952; children: David Gene, Daniel Elwood, Cheryl Joanne. A.B., Juniata Coll., 1952; B.D., Pitts. Theol. Sem., 1956, Th.M., 1959; Ph.D., U. Pitts., 1965, M.Ed., 1958; LL.D., U. Evansville, 1972, Butler U., 1972; Litt.D., Ind. State U., 1974. Ordained to ministry United Methodist Ch., 1956; pastor Grace United Meth. Ch., Wilkinsburg, Pitts., 1952-63; conf. dir., supt. Western Pa. Conf. United Meth. Ch., Pitts., 1963-68; lectr. grad. faculty U. Pitts., 1965-68; mem. staff U. Indpls., 1968—, asst. to pres., 1968-69, pres., 1970—; dir. Indpls. Life Ins. Co., Mchts. Nat. Bank and Trust Co., WYFI Channel 20, Overland Express; bd. dirs., chmn. Howard S. Wilcox. Author: Christian Word Book, 1968; also numerous articles. Pres. Greater Indpls. Progress Com., 1972-75; pres. Marion County Sheriff's Merit Bd.; mem. Ind. Scholarship Commn., 1970—; Chmn. Am. Cablevision of Indpls.; bd. dirs. Indpls. Conv. Bur., Ind. Law Enforcement Tng. Acad., 500 Festival, Crossroads council Boy Scouts Am., Community Hosp. Indpls., St. Francis Hosp. Mem. Internat. Platform Assn., Indpls. C. of C. (bd. dirs.), English Speaking Union, Ind. Schoolmen's Club, Phi Delta Kappa, Alpha Phi Omega, Alpha Psi Omega. Clubs: Mason (Indpls.) (33 deg., Shriner), Kiwanian. (Indpls.), Columbia (Indpls.). Home: 4001 Otterbein Ave Indianapolis IN 46227

SEATON, GEORGE LELAND, former utility co. exec., civic worker; b. Sunny South, Calif., Feb. 9, 1901; s. Frank H. and Charity Jane (Lee) S.; B.S.E.E., Iowa State U., 1923; A.A. (hon.), Coll. DuPage; m. Mildred Irene Sandall, Aug. 14, 1926 (dec. Nov. 1984); children—Robert Lee, James Mann, Mary Seaton Martin. Engr., Gen. Electric Co., Ft. Wayne, Ind., 1923; with Ill. Bell Telephone Co., Chgo., 1923-66, asst. v.p., 1952-64, v.p., 1964-66, ret., 1966. Mem. Hinsdale (Ill.) Bd. Edn., 1941-47; chmn. Chgo. council Boy Scouts Am., 1958-63; chmn. exec. com. Gt. Books Found., Chgo., 1965—; treas. Disciples Div. House, U. Chgo., 1945—, mem. vis. com. U. Chgo. Div. Sch., 1977—; mem. Ill. Fair Employment Com., 1961-69; chmn. Coll. DuPage, 1966-72. Served to 2d lt. C.E., USAR, 1923-28. Recipient Silver Beaver award Boy Scouts Am., Silver Antelope award. Mem. Western Soc. Engrs., Am. Statis. Assn. Republican. Mem. Christian Ch. (Disciples of Christ). Clubs: Union League (Chgo.); Hinsdale Golf, Econ. Home: 6110 S County Line Burr Ridge IL 60521

SEATON, JOHN RICHARD, distribution company executive; b. Boone, Iowa, Nov. 30, 1934; s. Donald F. and Florence (Park) S.; m. Elizabeth Kirch, Sept. 20, 1961; children: Catherine, Elizabeth, Anne. BS in Indsl. Adminstrn., Gen. Sci., Iowa State U., 1958; MBA, U. Pa., 1961. CPA, N.Y., Mo. Group ins. salesman Conn. Gen., Des Moines, 1958-60; with Arthur Young, N.Y.C., 1961-82, gen. ptnr., 1970-82; v.p. Graybar Electric Co., St. Louis, 1982—, also bd. dirs. trustee, v.p. Lawrence Hosp. Bronxville, N.Y., 1977-82. Served to 2nd lt. U.S. Army, 1958-59. Mem. Am. Inst. CPA's, N.Y. Soc. CPA's, Mo. Soc. CPA's. Clubs: Siwanoy Country (Bronxville), (treas. 1975-82); Old Warson Country, St. Louis. Avocations: platform tennis, golf. Office: Graybar Electric Co Inc 34 N Meramec Saint Louis MO 63105

SEATON, SCOTT LEE, SR., architect; b. Chgo., Apr. 1, 1935; s. Charles Theo and Flora M. (Coplin) S.; m. Beverly A. Lambert, Nov. 24, 1956 (div. Sept. 1980); children: Scott L. Jr., Susan M., Kathryn A., Sandra J., Michael J., Patrick M., Mark W., Christopher M; m. Jeanette L. Hill, Oct. 1981. Diploma engring., Thornton Jr. Coll., 1954; BArch, U. Ill., 1959; C.E.U.'s, U. Wis., Madison, 1970-80. Registered profl. architect., Ill. Draftsman Holabird, Root, Burgee, Chgo., 1956-57; designer Glen G. Frazier AIA, Urbana, Ill., 1957-59; sr. architect Clark Daily Smith, Urbana, Ill., 1959-63; ptnr. Smith, Seaton, Olach, Urbana, Ill., 1963-70, Moline & Seaton AIA, Kankakee, Ill., 1970-84; project architect, mgr. Balsamo/Olson, Oak Brook Terrace, Ill., 1984—; ptnr. MSP Developers, Crawfordsville, Inc., 1970-74, ECV Ptnrs., Kankakee, 1970-78; asst. prof. U. Ill., Urbana, 1966-67. Graphic artist: Construction Lending Guide, U.S. Savs. and Loan League, 1968—. Mem. AIA (Outstanding Bldg. award 1969-70, 81, design/planning award 1973-80). Roman Catholic. Club: Gargoyle (Urbana). Avocations: canoeing, cooking, travel. Office: Balsano/Olson Group 1 S 376 Summit Oak Brook Terrace IL 60181

SEAWORTH, MARY ELLEN, lawyer; b. Bismarck, N.D., Oct. 28, 1947; d. George H. and Margaret M. (Fortune) S.; m. Henry H. Howe, Dec. 4, 1976; children: Oren, Deborah, Tavia, Christopher. Student, Coll. St. Teresa, 1965-68; BA in Speech and Theatre, U. N.D., 1971, BS in Edn., 1973, JD, 1983. Bar: Minn. 1983, N.D. 1984, U.S. Dist. Ct. N.D. 1984. Ptnr. Howe and Seaworth, Grand Forks, N.D., 1983—. Editorial staff N.D. Law

Review, 1982-83. Trustee Grand Forks Symphony, 1984—; bd. dirs. Greater Grand Forks Community Theatre, 1983—, LWV, 1985—; mem. com. Gov's Commn. Children Adolescents at Risk, 1985-86; commr. for Commn. Uniform State Laws, 1985-89. Recipient Women Who Care award U. N.D. Women's Ctr., 1986. Mem. N.D. Bar Assn., Minn. Bar Assn., Trial Lawyers Nat. & State, ABA (family law sect.), ACLU. Office: Howe and Seaworth Law Offices PO Box 34 Grand Forks ND 58201

SEBASTIAN, ALEC ALDRICH, political organization administrator; b. Flint, Mich., Nov. 2, 1948; s. Patrick Clinton and Kay (Bajo) S.; m. Linda J. Bronowski, Oct. 15, 1977. BA, U. Notre Dame, 1970; MA, U. Mich., 1972. Exec. dir. Nat. Hamiltonian Study Group, Flint, 1964-66; nat. chmn. Nat. Hamiltonian Party, Flint, 1966—; bd. dirs. Nat. Hamiltonian Library, Flint, 1970—, New Progressive Coalition, Flint, 1972—. Office: Nat Hamiltonian Party 3314 Dillon Rd Flushing MI 48433

SEBASTIAN, JOHN FRANCIS, chemistry educator; b. San Diego; s. John Francis and Martha Klazina (Van der Linde) S.; children: Byron David, Colin Alan. BS, San Diego State U., 1961; PhD, U. Calif.-Riverside, 1965. NIH postdoctoral fellow Northwestern U., Evanston, Ill., 1965-67; asst. prof. chemistry Miami U., Oxford, Ohio, 1967-72, assoc. prof. chemistry, 1972-80, prof. chemistry, 1980—. Research Corp. grantee, 1968; NSF grantee, 1972. Mem. Am. Chem. Soc., Royal Chem. Soc., AAAS, Sigma Xi. Contbr. articles to sci. jours. Office: Dept Chemistry Miami U Oxford OH 45056

SEBASTIAN, MICHAEL JAMES, diversified manufacturing company executive; b. Chgo., July 8, 1930; s. Michael and Larraine (DeAmicis) S.; m. Sally Ervin, Nov. 29, 1953; children: Michael, Mark, Lisa. B.S. in M.E., Santa Clara U., 1952; A.M.P., Harvard U., 1972. Div. mgr. FMC Corp, Indpls., 1953-77; pres. Rotek, Aurora, Ohio, 1977-78; v.p. Gardner-Denver, Dallas, 1978-79; group pres. Cooper Industries, Dallas, 1979-81; exec. v.p. ops. Cooper Industries, Houston, 1981—; dir. Weatherford, Houston, 1984—. Republican. Roman Catholic. Clubs: Petroleum, Lakeside Country (Houston). Avocations: golf; gardening; tennis. Home: 8973 Briar Forest Dr Houston TX 77024 Office: Cooper Industries PO Box 4446 1001 Fannin 40th Floor Houston TX 77210

SEBEK, JOSEPH JOHN, accountant; b. Evergreen Park, Ill., Mar. 11, 1950; s. Joseph B. and Anna T. (Pavlinec) S.; m. Susan M. Hansen, Oct. 23, 1971; children: Joseph J. Jr., Dawn M., Jennifer A., Nicholas E. BS in Acctg., DePaul U., Chgo., 1975, MS, 1982. CPA, Ill. Programmer, analyst Chgo. Title and Trust, Chgo., 1968-75; acct. Village of Oak Park, Ill., 1975-77; asst. fin. dir. Village Oak Lawn, Ill., 1977-79; dir. fin. mgmt. Mcpl. Fin. Officers Assn., Chgo., 1979-81; dir. fin. Transit Mgmt., Oak Park, 1981-84; dir. bus. affairs Ill. Cancer Council, Chgo., 1984—; pvt. practice acctg. and income tax services, Oak Lawn, Ill., 1975—. Mem. St. Gerald Sch. Bd., Oak Lawn, 1986—, athletic dir., 1983—; treas. S.W. Cath. Conf., Oak Lawn, 1987. Mem. Am. Inst. CPA's, Ill. CPA Soc. Republican. Roman Catholic. Avocations: coaching youth sports, playing golf, reading. Home: 9319 S Tulley Oak Lawn IL 60453 Office: Ill Cancer Council 36 S Wabash Suite 700 Chicago IL 60453

SEBERG, JOHN RAYMOND, dentist; b. Upland, Nebr., Feb. 18, 1921; s. Louis Alfred and Annie (Schaaf) S.; m. Marion Hazel Johnson, Sept. 6, 1949; children: Eric, Leslie Seberg Neuhaus, Lance. BS, DDS, U. Nebr., 1944. Gen. practice dentistry Hastings, Nebr., 1947-48; resident in dentistry Fla. State Hosp., Chattahooche, 1948-49; gen. practice dentistry Seberg, Seberg & Holm, Hasting, 1949—; cons., mem. adv. bd. Good Samaritan Village, Hastings, Nebr., 1979—. Served to capt. U.S. Army, 1942-47. Mem. ADA, Nebr. Dental Assn. (Hall of Fame, bd. trustees), Adams County Dental Assn. (pres.), Southwest Dental Assn. (past. pres.), Am. Acad. Dental Practice Adminstrn. (pres. 1976), Am. Equilibration Soc., Pierre Fauchard Acad., U. Nebr. Alumni Assn. (Merit award 1980, Disting. Service award 1982), Am. Legion. Republican. Methodist. Lodges: Lions, Masons. Avocations: golf, jogging, reading, travel. Home: 150 Forest Blvd Hastings NE 68901 Office: Central Dental Group PC 515 W 9th St Hastings NE 68901

SECOR, GARY LEE, utility company executive; b. Decatur, Ill., Oct. 30, 1947; s. George Alexander and Elizabeth P. (Frantz) S.; m. Susan Jo Reich, July 19, 1969; 1 child, Sara Lyn. BS in Communications, U. Ill., 1969. Asst. supr. customer service Ill. Power Co., Champaign, 1969-73; supr. customer service Ill. Power Co., Ottawa, 1973-75; supr. customer service Ill. Power Co., Belleville, 1975-76, asst. to mgr., 1976-78; dir. customer relations Ill. Power Co., Decatur, 1978-83, asst. treas., dir. risk mgmt., 1983—. Bd. dirs. Cen. Ill. Easter Seal Soc., Decatur, 1983—, treas., 1984-86, state bd. mem., 1985—, pres., 1986—. Served with NG, 1970-76. Mem. Am. Mgmt. Assn., Jaycees (v.p. Decatur chpt. 1980-81, named Jaycees Internat. Senator, 1983, recipient Keyman award Ottawa chpt., 1975, named Officer of Yr., Ottawa chpt., 1974, Officer of Yr., Champaign-Urbana chpt., 1973), IBM Compatible Club (sec. 1983-85), Cen. Ill. Lotus Software Group (pres. 1985—). Home: 1145 Veech Ln Decatur IL 62521 Office: Ill Power Co 500 S 27th St Decatur IL 62525

SECOR, RICHARD EUGENE, manufacturing company executive; b. Ottumwa, Iowa, Sept. 12, 1930; s. Raymond Eugene and Lola Mae (Clements) S.; m. Jean Putney, Nov. 28, 1951 (div. Apr. 1973); children: Mark, Darcy, Richard Jr., Thomas; m. Heidi Marie Fritz, Mar. 28, 1984; 1 child, Christopher Fritz McGinness. Student, Iowa State U., 1948-50; BA in Journalism, U. Iowa, 1953; LHD (hon.), Tarkio Coll., 1986. Acct. exec. Sperry-Boom, Inc., Davenport, Iowa, 1953-54; with Northwestern Bell, Omaha, 1954-60, employee info. mgr., 1960-64, pub. relations prodn. mgr., 1964-71, advt. mgr., 1972-80; exec. v.p. Rainmatic Corp., Omaha, 1983—; pres. Secor & Assocs., Omaha, 1980—. Author (weekly newspaper column) Traveling Correspondent, 1975-79. Founder, dir. Omaha Civic Opera, 1959; communications chmn. United Community Services, Omaha, 1966, 68; com. chmn. Omaha Symphony, 1968; bd. dirs. Tarkio (Mo.) Coll., 1980—; elder Wheeler Presbyn. Ch., Omaha, 1986. Republican. Club: Quad. Home: 10423 Hansen Ave Omaha NE 68124

SEDER, STEVE DENNIS, food distribution executive; b. Flint, Mich., Apr. 14, 1955; s. J.B. and Wilima L. (Eaker) S. BA, Mich. State U., 1977; MBA, U. Mich., 1979. CPA, Mich. Acct. Deloitte Haskins & Sells, Detroit, 1979-82; controller, asst. treas. Cert. Grocers Midwest Inc., Chgo., 1982—. Mem. Jaycees (treas. Detroit chpt. 1981). Republican. Methodist. Office: Cert Grocers Midwest Inc 4800 S Central Ave Chicago IL 60638

SEDGWICK, RAE, psychologist, lawyer; b. Kansas City, Kans., Apr. 7, 1944; d. Charles and Helen (Timmons) Sedgwick. R.N., Bethany Sch. Nursing, 1965; B.S., U. Iowa, 1967; M.A., U. Kans., 1970, Ph.D., 1972, JD, 1986. Cert. psychologist, Kans.; bar: Kans. 1986. Med./surg., orthopedic and obstet. nurse, Iowa City, Iowa, 1965-67; with Community Mental Health Nursing, Kansas City, Kans., 1967-68; specialist Lab. Edn., Washington, 1971-72; adj. clin. staff community psychiatry, 1975-76; coordinator Health C.A.R.E. Clinic, Pa. State U., 1974-76; head grad. program in community mental health nursing and family therapy, Pa. State U., 1974-76, asst. prof., 1972-76; pvt. practice psychology, Bonner Springs, Kans., 1976—; cons. in field.; staff Bethany Med. Ctr., Kansas City, Kans., Cushing's Meml. Hosp., Leavenworth, Kans., St. John's Hosp., Leavenworth; del. Internat. Council Nurses, Frankfurt, Germany, People for People, People's Republic of China, 1982. Active Am. Heart Assn.; city councilwoman Bonner Springs, 1981—, pres. pro tem, 1983-87; mem. Kans. Internat. Women's Yr. Commn. Recipient Outstanding Young Woman award, U. Kans., Bus. and Profl. Women's Club scholar; elected to Kans. U. Women's Hall of Fame, 1987. Fellow Am. Orthopsychiat. Assn.; mem. AAAS, ABA, Kansas Bar Assn., Am. Assn. Psychiatric Services for Children, Am. Group Psychotherapy Assn. (dir.), Am. Nurses Assn., Am. Psychol. Assn., Anthrop. Assn. for Study of Play, Council of Advanced Practitioners in Psychiat. Mental Health Nursing, Kans. Psychol. Assn., Council Nurse Researchers, Sigma Theta Tau. Republican. Methodist. Club: Pilot. Author: Family Mental Health, 1980; The White Frame House, 1980; contbr. articles to profl. jours.

SEDLAK, RICHARD, naprapath; b. Berwyn, Ill., July 7, 1944; s. Richard and Alice H. (Tejcek) S. D in Naprapathy, Nat. Coll. Naprapathy, Chgo., 1966; D in Phys. Therapy, Am. Inst. of Sci., 1967; D in Chiropractic Medicine, Palmer Coll. Chiropractic Medicine, 1970; PhD (hon.), Community Ch. Coll., Wheatfield, Ind., 1979. Diplomate Nat. Bd. Chiropractic and Phys. Therapy, Diplomate Am. Bd. Phys. Therapy Examiners; bd. cert. naprapath. Phys. therapist West Suburban Hosp., Oak Park, Ill., 1964-66; pvt. practice naprapath, phys. therapist Cicero, Ill., 1970—; cons. phys. therapist Pershing Convalescent Home, Stickney, Ill., 1985—; assoc. dean Nat. Coll. Naprapathy, 1966-69. Spl. police officer City of Cicero, 1968—. Recipient Cert. of Merit, Am. Massage Therapy Assn., 1969, Cert. of Achievement Palmer Coll. of Chiropractic Medicine, 1970, Cert. Achievement AMA, 1980. Fellow Soc. for Nutrition and Preventive Medicine; mem. Am. Naprapathic Assn., United Naprapathic Assn. (sec. 1972-73). Democrat. Roman Catholic. Avocations: fishing, hunting. Home: 5537 W 24th Pl Cicero IL 60650 Office: Cicero Naprapathic Ctr 6003 W Cermak Rd Cicero IL 60650

SEDON, LEONARD CHARLES, dentist; b. Canton, Ohio, Aug. 23, 1951; s. George and Julia (Cherepko) S.; m. Kathy Brisley, June 25, 1977; children: L. Charles, Justin O'Neill, Brenton Michael, Katherine B. BS, Kent (Ohio) State U., 1974; DDS, Ohio State U., 1976. Resident in dentistry Med. Coll. Ohio, 1976-77; resident in oral surgery UCLA, San Francisco, 1977-78; gen. practice dentistry Canton, Ohio, 1978—. Mem. ADA, Am. Assn. Functional Orthodontics, Acad. Gen. Dentistry, Stark County Dental Soc. Lodge: Rotary. Avocations: wood working, plumbing, hunting, fishing. Office: 4141 Martindale Rd Canton OH 44705

SEEBERT, KATHLEEN ANNE, international trade consultant; b. Chgo.; d. Harold Earl and Marie Anne (Lowery) S.; BS U. Dayton, 1971, M.A., U. Notre Dame, 1976; M.M., Northwestern U., 1983. Publs. editor ContiCommodity Services, Inc., Chgo., 1977-79, supr. mktg., 1979-82; dir. mktg. MidAm. Commodity Exchange, 1982-85; internat. trade cons. to Govt. of Ont., Can., 1985—; guest lectr. U. Notre Dame. Registered commodity rep. Mem. Futures Industry Assn. Am. (treas.). Republican. Roman Catholic. Clubs: Young Executives, Notre Dame of Chgo., Northwestern Mgmt. of Chgo. Office: 208 S LaSalle St Suite 1806 Chicago IL 60604

SEEBOHM, JEFFREY CURTIS, optometrist; b. Cin., July 1, 1954; s. Walter Douglas and Beatrice Maxine (Harvey) S.; m. Roberta Kay Johnson, June 18, 1977; children: Joshua Jeffrey, Jeremiah Robert, Nathaniel Walter. BS, Defiance Coll., 1976; OD, Ohio State U., 1981. Pvt. practice optometry Reading, Ohio, 1981-86. Commr. Boy Scouts Am., Cin., 1981-86; counselor Cin. Crisis Pregnancy Ctr., 1985-86; trustee Grace Brethren Ch., Cin., 1983-86. Mem. Am. Optometric Assn. (Recognition award 1986), Ohio Optometric Assn. Avocations: geneaology, fishing, backpacking. Home: 3550 Verbena Dr Cincinnati OH 45241 Office: 9016 Reading Rd Cincinnati OH 45215

SEED, ANIESE EDWARD, engineer, electronics company executive; b. Toledo, June 21, 1924; s. Edward George and Marie (Shewary) S.; m. Neysa Ellen Imhof, June 21, 1952; children: Kathryn, Susan, Edward. BEE, U. Toledo, 1949; MS, U. Mich., 1951. Registered profl. engr., Ohio. Tchr. Detroit Inst. Tech., 1949-50; engr. Owens-Ill., Toledo, 1951-54, Auto Lite, Toledo, 1954-57, Toledo Scale, 1957-73; mgr. Helm Instruments, Toledo, 1973-76; pres. and chmn. bd. dirs. Toledo Transducers, Inc., 1976—. Patentee in field. V.P. St. Paul's Luth. Ch., Toledo, 1978. Served to staff sgt. U.S. Army, 1943-46, ETO and PTO. Recipient Disting. Alumnus award U. Toledo, 1983. Mem. Soc. Mfg. Engrs., Soc. Experimental Mechanics. Republican. Lodge: Rotary. Avocations: woodworking, reading, golf. Home: 4155 Berwick Ave Toledo OH 43612 Office: Toledo Transducers 3525 Monroe Toledo OH 43612

SEEDER, RICHARD OWEN, infosystems specialist; b. Chgo., May 4, 1947; s. Edward Otto and Betty Jane (Reamer) S.; m. Deborah Jo Michaelsen, Mar. 15, 1983. BA, Trinity U., 1969; M in Mgmt., Northwestern U., 1979; postgrad., DePaul U., 1985—. Programmer, analyst R.R. Donnelley & Sons Co., Chgo., 1972-76, project mgr., 1977-80; mgr. systems devel. Joint Commn. Accreditation of Hosps., Chgo., 1980-84, dir. mgmt. info. systems, 1985—; cons. Internat. Printworks, Newton, Mass., 1981-82. Served to 1st lt. U.S. Army, 1969-71, Korea. Mem. Assn. MBA Execs., Data Processing Mgmt. Assn., Am. Mgmt. Assn., Mensa. Club: Northwestern U. Mgmt. Avocations: sports, gardening. Home: 2208 Wesley Evanston IL 60201 Office: Joint Commn Accreditation Hosps 875 N Michigan Ave Chicago IL 60611

SEEFLUTH, AUGUST RAYMOND, business consultant; b. Geridge, Ark., Aug. 7, 1922; s. August Theodore and Clara Eunice (Dunham) S.; m. Nan L. Morgan, Oct. 3, 1942; children: Nancy, Ted, Karen, Scott. Student, Air Force tech. and flying schs., 1943, 48, 52, Wright State U., 1961-65. Commd. 2d lt. USAF, 1942, advanced through grades to maj., 1965, electronic warfare instr., Keesler AFB, Miss., 1952-57, served in Federal Republic of Germany and Eng., 1958-61, group leader aero. system div., Wright-Patterson AFB, Ohio, 1961-65, ret., 1965; mgr. new bus. devel. TRACOR, Inc., Austin, Tex., 1965-70; regional mktg. mgr. Lundy Electronics & Systems, Pompano Beach, Fla., 1970-73; prin. Seefluth & Assocs., Dayton, Ohio, 1973—, Raymond Tech., Inc., Dayton, 1983—. Author various tech. studies and reports on USAF electronic ops. Tchr. adult classes 1st United Meth. Ch., Troy, Ohio. Decorated Air medal; recipient Commendation award RAF, 1960, Luftwaffe, 1959, NATO, 1960. Mem. Air Force Assn., Am. Def. Preparedness Assn., Assn. Old Crows. Home and Office: 1080 Dorchester Rd Troy OH 45373

SEEHAUSEN, RICHARD FERDINAND, architect; b. Indpls., Mar. 17, 1925; s. Paul Ferdinand and Melusina Dorothea (Nordmeyer) S.; student DePauw U., 1943-44, Wabash Coll., 1944, State U. Iowa, 1944; B.Arch., U. Ill., 1949; m. Phyllis Jean Gates, Dec. 22, 1948; children—Lyn, Dirk. Ptnr., Johnson, Kile, Seehausen & Assocs., Inc., architects, engrs., Rockford, Ill., 1949-82, pres., 1974-82; pres. Richard F. Seehausen-Architect, Inc., 1983—. Mem. com. jail planning and constrn. standards Bur. Detention Facilities, Ill. Dept. Corrections, 1970-73; analyst Fed. Fall-Out Shelter, 1962—. Bd. dirs. Rockford Boys Club. Served with USNR, 1943-45, USAF, 1949. Mem. AIA (dir. No. Ill. chpt. 1966-68, 75—, pres. chpt. 1978—), Lambda Chi Alpha. Lutheran. Mason (Shriner), Kiwanian. Club: Forest Hills Country (gov. 1970-72), Prin. works include No. Ill. U. Center, also Health Service Bldg., DeKalb, Winnebago County Courthouse, Rockford, St. Mark Luth. Ch., Rockford, Christ Meth. Ch., Rockford, 1st Presbyn. Ch., Rochelle, Ill., McHenry County Ct. House, Woodstock, Ill., Stephenson County Courthouse, Freeport, Ill., Ogle County Pub. Safety Bldg., Rochelle, DeKalb High Sch., Page Park Spl. Edn. Sch., Rockford, Social Security bldgs. in Racine, Sheboygan, Oshkosh and Janesville, Wis., Freeport YWCA Bldgs., renovation of Carroll County Ct. House, DeKalb Area Retirement Center; renovation Old Winnebago County Courthouse. Rockford, Rockford Mut. Ins. Home Office Bldg., Willows Personal Care Ctr., Rockford, others. Home: 36 Briar Ln Rockford IL 61103 Office: Am Nat Bank Bldg Rockford IL 61104

SEEKELY, MARTIN SCOTT, accountant; b. Cleve., Dec. 7, 1956; s. Martin William and Marilyn Bernice (Keller) S.; m. Patricia Ann Simon, Jan. 7, 1978; children: Michael, Lauren. BSBA, John Carroll U., 1979. CPA, Ohio. Staff acct. Fisher Foods Inc., Bedford Heights, Ohio, 1979-81; acctg. supr. Fisher Foods Inc., Bedford Heights, 1981-84, acctg. mgr., 1984-86, asst. controller, 1986—; dir., pres. Fisher Foods Employees Credit Union, Bedford Heights, 1983 . Mem. Am. Inst. CPA's, Ohio Soc. CPA's. Republican. Home: 1783 Westwood Dr Twinsburg OH 44087 Office: Fisher Foods Inc 5300 Richmond Rd Bedford Heights OH 44146

SEELANDER, JOHN MARSHALL, engineering executive; b. Chgo., Feb. 20, 1940; s. John Marshall and Edith Johanna (Madison) S.; m. Marilyn Jean Erickson, Sept. 10, 1960; 1 child, John Marshall. Student, Chgo. Tech. Coll., 1961-66, Bradley U., 1958-59. Mech. design engr. Harza Engrng. Co., Chgo., 1960-64; project engr. Maccabee & Assocs., Chgo., 1964-67; mgr. engrng. Copeland Systems, Oak Brook, Ill., 1967-70; pres. The SEC Cos., Oak Brook, 1970—; bd. dirs. The SEC Co., Oak Brook, Intracon Services, Oak Brook, Salem Tech. Services, Oak Brook, Salem Services, Oak Brook, The Oak Brook Design Group. Ch. council Gloria Dei Luth. Ch., Downers Grove, Ill., 1965-72. Served with USNR, 1962-70. Mem. Nat. Tech. Services Assn. (pres. 1985-86). Republican. Avocations: flying, snow skiing, water skiing, golf. Office: The SEC Cos 1000 Jorie Blvd Oak Brook IL 60521

SEELEY, KIMBERLEY ANN, police officer; b. Urbana, Ill., Oct. 21, 1960; d. William Edward and Patricia Ann (Philbeck) Tarte; m. Ronald Eugene Seeley, Jan. 21, 1985. Assoc. Sci., Parkland Coll., 1981; B.S., U. Ill., 1982. Sec., bookkeeper Tarte's TV and Marine, Rantoul, Ill., 1972-78; police dispatcher City of Champaign, Ill., 1978-82, police officer, 1982—, mem. tactical unit, 1985-86. Recipient Merit award Champaign Police Dept., 1984, 86. Mem. Police Protective and Benevolent Assn., Nat. Assn. Female Execs., Ill. Police Assn. Republican. Lutheran. Avocations: downhill snow skiing; target shooting. Office: Champaign Police Dept 82 E University Champaign IL 61820

SEELEY, MARY FRANCES, social services adminstrator; b. Joliet, Ill., Oct. 4, 1931; d. Mary (Rittof) Derlinga. BA, Coll. St. Francis, Joliet, Ill., 1965; MEd, De Paul U., 1971; PhD (hon.), Lewis U., 1980. Prin. St. Michael Sch., Siegel, Ill., 1962-67, Corpus Christi Elem. Sch., Columbus, Ohio, 1967-71; guidance counselor Cardinal Gibbons High Sch., Ft. Lauderdale, Fla., 1971-73; asst. dir. Crisis Line Palm Beach, West Palm Beach, Fla., 1973-75; exec. dir. Crisis Line of Will County, Joliet, 1975—; exec. dir. Crisis Line Internat., Joliet, 1985—, cons., 1985—. Co-author (manual) Procedural Manual for Volunteers, 1975. Pres. Community Services Council, Will County, Ill., 1978-80. Recipient Profl. Achievement award Alumni Assn. Coll. St. Francis, 1985. Mem. Am. Assn. Suicidology, Am. Assn. I&R System (v.p. 1984—), Ill. Assn. I&R System (v.p. 1984-87, pres. 1987—), Ill. Assn. Suicidology (pres. 1984-87), Sisters of St. Francis of Mary Immaculate. Lodge: Zonta. Avocations: classical music, sewing, reading. Home: 120 Woodlawn Ave Joliet IL 60435 Office: Crisis Line of Will County PO Box 2354 Joliet IL 60434

SEELOFF, GREGORY SCOTT, mechanical engineer; b. Detroit, Feb. 7, 1954; s. Donald William and Marcella Ann (Fresard) S.; m. Marcella Kaye Modin, Apr. 2, 1977; children: Megan, Erin, Scott. BSME, Gen. Motors Inst., Flint, Mich., 1977. Lic. residential builder, 1980—. Assoc. system analyst Fisher Body, Warren, Mich., 1977-78, systems analyst, 1978-82, sr. systems analyst, 1982-83; sr. systems analyst Gen. Motors Advanced Engrs. Staff, Warren, 1983-84; sr. systems engr. Electronic Data Systems, Southfield, Mich., 1984—; owner Home and Energy Enterprises. Trustee chmn. macomb Baptist Ch., Mt. Clemens, Mich., 1983-85. Mem. Nat. Rifle Assn. (life), Sigma Nu (house mgr. 1973-75). Home: 6810 Rattle Run Rd Saint Clair MI 48079 Office: Electronic Data Systems 28333 Telegraph Southfield MI 48086

SEEWALD, ELSBETH M., law firm executive, fraternal organization administrator; b. Hamburg, Fed. Republic of Germany, Aug. 24, 1927; came to U.S., 1953; d. Heinrich and Klara (Wohltorf) Bierkarre; m. Bosko Vasich, July 3, 1954 (dec. Dec. 1974); m. George Seewald, Feb. 4, 1978; 1 stepchild, Gerbert. Student, Comml. Coll., Fed. Republic of Germany. With Modine Mfg. Co., Racine, Wis., 1957-60, Brach & Wheeler, Attys., Racine, 1960-63; mgr. real estate div. Heide, Hartley, Thom, Wilk & Guttormsen, Attys., Kenosha, Wis., 1963—; nat. pres. German Am. Nat. Congress, Chgo., 1981—. Editor Der Deutschamerikaner, 1981—. Named Honored Am., Ams. By Choice, 1986; recipient Ellis Island Medal of Honor, U.S. Congress, 1986. Home: 9804 8th Ave Kenosha WI 53140 Office: German Am Nat Congress 4740 N Western Ave 2d Floor Chicago IL 60625 Office: Heide Hartley Thom Wilk & Guttormsen 611 56th St PO Box 635 Kenosha WI 53140

SEFCIK, DAVID NICHOLAS, packaging consultant; b. Bridgeport, Conn., May 12, 1956; s. John and Alicia Ann (Robergé) S.; m. Debra Loraine Parker, Dec. 4, 1981; children: Christopher, Rachel. Student, Sacred Heart U., Bridgeport, 1976-80. Extruder operator Mobil Chem. Co., Stratford, Conn., 1974-78, maintenance scheduler, 1978-82; tech. cons. Mobil Chem. Co., Pittsford and N.Y., 1982; now with Borden Chem. Co., North Andover, Mass. Inventor hot hole punch, 1984 (tech. achievement award 1984), deionized air assist manifold, 1985. Republican. Avocations: horticulture, wood working.

SEFTON, CYNTHIA DOREEN, business education educator, financial broker, consultant; b. Cin., Oct. 21, 1947; d. Archie and Ruth (Jollie) Bolton; m. James Richard Sefton, Mar. 15, 1969 (div.). BEd, U. Cin., 1969, MEd in Bus. Edn., 1975. Tchr. high sch. vocat. bus., Cin., 1969-75; asst. prof. bus. edn. U. Cin., 1975-83; bus. and office tchr. educator Ohio Dept. Edn., 1975-83; owner CDS Enterprises, human resources devel. cons., 1980—; ptnr. Transcendence, 1981-84; broker, bus. edn. instr., Al Williams First Am. Nat. Securities, 1985—; corp. trainer, fin. cons., Gen. Electric Co., 1986—; adv. Office Edn. Assn., Cin. Inst. Career Alternatives; ctr. mgr. Loving Relationships Tng., 1981-84; seminar leader; awareness cons. Mem. Am. Vocat. Assn., Ohio Vocat. Assn., Am. Soc. Tng. and Devel., Ohio Bus. Tchrs. Assn., S.W. Ohio Word Processing Adminstrv. Support Group (hon.), Women's Network, Delta Pi Epsilon (pres. Delta chpt.), Zeta Tau Alpha. Home: 3438 Ferncroft Dr Cincinnati OH 45211

SEGAL, ARLENE ESTA, radiologist; b. N.Y.C., Nov. 12, 1937; s. Moe and Fanny (Schlussel) S.; m. Richard Thomas Logan, Aug. 14, 1969. BA, Duke U., 1958; MD, Albert Einstein Coll. Medicine, 1962. Diplomate Am. Bd. Radiology, Am. Bd. Nuclear Medicine. Intern Bronx Mcpl. Hosp. Ctr., N.Y.C., 1962-63, resident in radiology, 1963-66; instr. radiology Albert Einstein Coll. Medicine, N.Y.C., 1966-68, asst. prof., 1968-71; practice medicine specializing in gen. diagnostic radiology Rye, Naneret and Hornell, N.Y., 1971-82; assoc. prof. U. Mo. Sch. Medicine, Kansas City, Mo., 1982—; staff radiologist Children's Mercy Hosp., Kansas City, 1982-83, radiologist-in-chief, 1983—. Mem. Soc. for Pediatric Radiology, Radiol. Soc. N.Am., AM. Coll. Radiology. Office: Children's Mercy Hosp 24th & Gillham Kansas City MO 64108

SEGAL, MALLORY P., sales executive; b. Chgo., July 28, 1950; s. Dave A. and Beatrice B. (Barnett) S.; m. Joy C. Peters, June 21, 1972; children: Danielle, Bryan. BS, So. Ill. U., 1972. Sales rep. A-M Corp., Chgo., 1972; dist. mgr. Burroughs Corp., Chgo., 1974-82; regional mgr. Pitney Bowes, Arlington Heights, Ill., 1982-85; v.p. sales Telesphere Internat., Oak Brook, Ill., 1985-86; sales dir. Interand Corp., Chgo., 1986—; cons. in field, Glenview, Ill., 1985—. Author (manual) Creative Training, 1984. Mem. Am. Mgmt. Assn. Avocations: plant care, boating, golf, baseball, art. Office: Interand Corp 3200 W Peterson Ave Chicago IL 60659

SEGGEBRUCH, DANIEL FREDERICH, architect; b. Chicago Heights, Ill., June 14, 1958; s. Frederich John Paul and Shirley Ann (Chester) S.; m. Rhonda Jean Glasenapp, Oct. 10, 1981. BArch, U. Ill., 1980; MArch, U. Fla., 1985. Draftsman Philip Braden AIA, Stuart, Fla., 1981, Fenton, Hoon & White Architects, Stuart, 1981-82, Interactive Resources, Point Richmond, Calif., 1982-83, Dompe, Paluzzi, Vyverberg & Taylor AIA, Gainesville, Fla., 1983-84, Al Dompe AIA, Gainesville, 1984-85; assoc. Dixon Assocs. AIA, St. Charles, Ill., 1985—. Mem. AIA (assoc., hist. resources com. Northeast Ill. chpt.), Nat. Trust Hist. Preservation, Phi Eta Sigma. Methodist. Lodge: Moose. Avocations: reading, photography, sports. Home: 143 Spuhler Dr Batavia IL 60510 Office: Dixon Assocs 636 Seneca Dr Aurora IL 60506

SEGHI, PETER RICHARD, health adminstrator; b. Chgo., Oct. 17, 1946; m. Carolyn, Aug. 31, 1968; children: Christine, Jeffrey. BBA, Gov.'s State U., 1982; MBA, Columbia-Pacific U., 1987. X-ray technician Mercy Hosp., Chgo., 1967-68; asst. dept. mgr. St. Francis Hosp., Blue Island, Ill., 1968-73; dept. mgr. Chgo. Osteo. Hosp., 1973-76; v.p. St. Anthony Med. Ctr., Crown Point, Ind., 1976—; bd. dirs. Tech. Fed. Credit Union, Crown Point, 1984—. Mgr. Crown Point Little League, Crown Point Girls Softball. Mem. Am. Coll. Healthcare Execs., Am. Coll. Healthcare Mktg. Lodge: Rotary. Avocations: boating, golf, tennis. Office: St Anthony Med Ctr Inc 201 Main St Crown Point IN 46307

SEGRAVES, DONALD WARREN, research organization executive; b. Madison County, Ga., June 11, 1932; s. Bennie Harber and Lera (Swindle) S.; m. Janet Brill, Feb. 28, 1959; children: Dixie Jean, Carol Diane, Katherine Ann. AB, U. Ga., 1953; postgrad., Columbia U., 1955-57. News corr. UPI, Raleigh, N.C., 1953-54; TV-radio editor UPI, N.Y.C. and Chgo.,

1956-59; mag. editor Alliance of Am. Insurers, Chgo., 1959-65, dir. pub. affairs, 1966-68, v.p. research, 1969-82; exec. dir. All-Industry Research Adv. Council, Oakbrook, Ill., 1982—. Author: Automobile Injuries and Their Compensation in the United States, 1979; contbr. to profl. research publs. Served with U.S. Army, 1953-55. Mem. Am. Risk and Ins. Soc., Ins. Inst. Highway Safety (bd. dirs. 1973-79). Club: Lombard Camera (v.p. 1985—). Avocations: photography, travel. Home: 245 N Craig Lombard IL 60148

SEHN, MARVIN DANIEL, accountant; b. Bismarch, N.D., Jan. 23, 1951; s. Leo and Valeria (Wagner) S.; m. Nancy Warren, June 25, 1977; children: Nicholas, Amy Caroline. BA in Computer Sci., North Dakota State U., 1973; MBA in Mgmt. Control, Lynchburg Coll., 1980. CPA, Ohio. Programmer, analyst Babcock & Wilcox, Lynchburg, Va., 1973-77; sr. buyer Babcock & Wilcox, Lynchburg, 1977-80, mgr. fin. forecasting, 1980-84; mgr. group acctg. service Babcock & Wilcox, Barberton, Ohio, 1984-86; mgr. power system acctg. Babcock & Wilcox, Barberton, 1987—. Treas. Cub Scouts, Canton, Ohio, 1986-87. Mem. Am. Inst. CPA's, Ohio Soc. CPA's, Nat. Assn. Accts. (fin. community relations program 1986-87). Mem. Disciples of Christ. Avocations: computers, gardening. Home: 6789 Ponteberry St NW Canton OH 44718 Office: The Babcock & Wilcox Co 20 S Van Buren Barberton OH 44203

SEHNERT, WALTER E., small businessman; b. Huron, S.D., Mar. 13, 1928; s. Walter M. and Lenita B. (Ackerman) S.; m. Jean K. Leisy, June 10, 1951; children: Susan, Marie, Matthew. BS, U. Nebr., 1949; grad., Am. Inst. Baking, 1953. Baker Sehnert Bakery, Plainview, Nebr., 1953-57; owner, operator Sehnert Bakery, McCook, Nebr., 1957—. Chmn. Red Willow County Reps., McCook, 1962-64. Served as sgt. U.S. Army, 1951-52; bd. dirs. McCook Coll., 1970-72, Pres.'s Adv. Council U. Nebr., Lincoln, 1984—; pres. bd. dirs. McCook Pub. Library, 1980—. Mem. Retail Bakers Am. (chmn. membership com. Nebr. chpt. 1975), Nebr. Bakers Assn. (pres. 1962, bd. dirs. 1960-70). Lutheran. Lodges: Rotary, Elks, Kiwanis (pres. 1962-63). Avocations: civil war enthusiast, anthropology, football, antique cars, travel. Home: 401 E 1st St McCook NE 69001 Office: Sehnert Bakery 312 Norris Ave McCook NE 69001

SEHNKE, ERROL DOUGLAS, geologist; b. Superior, Wis., Mar. 14, 1943; s. Henry Herman and Athlyn Marion (Westlund) S. B.S., U. Wis., 1965; M.S., U. Mich., 1969. Jr. geologist Aluminum Co. of Am., Phoenix, 1971-72, exploration mgr. Alcoa-Fairview Mining, Derbyshire, Eng., 1972-74, project geologist Alcoa-Cimca, San Jose, Costa Rica, 1974-77, sr. geologist Alcoa-Chelsea Properties, Phoenix, 1977-80, staff geologist Alcoa-Suralco, Moengo, Suriname, 1980-83, projects mgr. Alcoa-Western Mining Ltd., Rio de Janiero, Brazil, 1983-86; cons. Superior, Wis., 1986—. Mem. Soc. Mining Engrs. of AIME, Geol. Soc. Am., Am. Soc. Photogrammetry. Home: 6122 John Superior WI 54880 Office: PO Box 3007 Superior WI 54880

SEIBERLING, JOHN F., former congressman, law educator; b. Akron, Ohio, Sept. 8, 1918; s. J. Frederick and Henrietta (Buckler) S.; m. Elizabeth Pope Behr, June 4, 1949; children—John B., David P., Stephen M. AB, Harvard U., 1941; LLB, Columbia U., 1949. Bar: N.Y. bar 1950, Ohio bar 1955. Assoc. mem. firm Donovan, Leisure, Newton, Lumbard & Irvine, N.Y.C., 1949-53; atty. Goodyear Tire & Rubber Co., Akron, 1954-71; mem. 92d-99th Congresses from 14th Ohio Dist.; mem. com. on judiciary, com. on interior and insular affairs, chmn. subcom. on public land; vis. prof. law U. Akron. Served to maj. AUS, 1942-46. Mem. Akron Bar Assn. Mem. United Ch. of Christ. Office: 2 S Main St Akron OH 44308 Office: U Akron Sch Law Akron OH 44325

SEIBERT, MARK ERIC, accountant; b. Cleve., Apr. 29, 1957; s. Michael Charles and Martha Joan (Youschak) S.; m. Gloria Jean Kissel, Sept. 17, 1983; 1 child, Lauren. BS, U. Dayton, Ohio, 1979. Staff acct. Arthur Andersen & Co., Cleve., 1979-81; sr. acct. Kopperman & Wolf Co., Cleve., 1981-83; acct. Ohio Bell Telephone Co., Cleve., 1983—. Named one of Outstanding Young Men of Am., 1982. Mem. Am. Inst. CPA's, Ohio Soc. CPA's, Cleve. Jaycees (pres. 1984-85, senatorship 1986). Roman Catholic. Avocations: handball, bicycling, investments. Home: 23961 Devoe Ave Euclid OH 44123-2221 Office: Ohio Bell Telephone Co 45 Erieview Plaza Room 1052 Cleveland OH 44114

SEIBERT, STEVEN WAYNE, periodontist; b. Belleville, Ill., Jan. 2, 1955; s. Cletus Francis and Elizabeth Jean (Meyers) S.; m. Cheryl Ellen Mellinger, Aug. 18, 1979; children: Matthew Aaron, Christina Renee. BS in Biomed. Sci. and Biology, So. Ill. U., Edwardsville, 1977, MS in Biology, 1982; D of Dental Medicine, So. Ill. U., Alton, 1982; Cert. in Periodontics, U. Nebr., 1984. Practice dentistry specializing in periodontics Champaign, Ill., 1984; instr. dentistry Parkland Jr. Coll., Champaign, 1984—. Contbr. articles to profl. jours. Mem. ADA, Am. Acad. Periodontology, Sigma Xi (assoc.). Republican. Roman Catholic. Avocations: golf, basketball, racquetball, camping, skiing. Home: 2305 Aspen Dr Champaign IL 61821 Office: 303 W Springfield Champaign IL 61820

SEIBERT, VERN FREDERICK, JR., electronics executive; b. Kansas City, Mo., June 30, 1938; s. Vern Frederick Sr. and Mary Elizabeth (Overstreet) S.; m. Gaina LaJean Clark, Aug. 14, 1960; children: Tammy L., Teresa L., Tanya L. BSME, Gen. Motors Inst., 1960. Jr. engr. Gen. Motors Corp., Kansas City, 1956-60, foreman, 1960-62; engr. Gen. Motors Corp., Detroit, 1962-64, sr. engr., 1964-71; staff supr. Gen. Motors Corp., Warren, Mich., 1971-84, mgr., 1984—. Exec. producer multi-media Expanding Tech. Excellence, 1984 (Silver medal N.Y. Film and TV Festival 1985). Recipient Eagle Scouts award Boy Scouts Am., 1951. Mem. Internat. TV Assn., U.S. Amateur Confederation of Roller Skating (judge Lincoln chpt. 1979—). Republican. Presbyterian. Avocations: roller skating, golf, music. Office: GM Product Service Tng 30501 Van Dyke Warren MI 48090

SEIBOLD, RONALD LEE, sociologist, writer; b. Kansas City, Mo., May 8, 1945; s. Dean Phillip and Helen H. (Haney) S.; m. Christine Herbst, June 23, 1971 (div. July 1975). BS, Emporia State U., 1967; MA, Colo. State U., 1969. Dir. cbpt. services Alpha Kappa Lambda, Ft. Collins, Colo., 1969-71; v.p. Siever & Assocs., Ft. Collins, 1971-72; pvt. practice sociology research Colo., 1972-75; coodinator Pines Internat., Lawrence, Kans., 1975—, sec., treas., 1976—; pres. Live Foods Co., Lawrence, 1978—. Author: AKL Manual, 1969, Pines...The Wheat Grass People, 1982, Condominium Farming, 1986; contbr. articles to profl. mags. Founder, pres. Midwestern Interfraternity Council, Emporia, Kans., 1966; pres. Interfraternity Council, Emporia, 1965; v.p. Collegiate Young Reps., Emporia, 1965; mem. Kans. Organic Producers, 1978—. George Meredith scholar Emporia State U., 1963. Mem. Nat. Nutritional Foods Assn., Lawrence C. of C., U.S. C. of C., Kappa Mu Epsilon, Xi Phi. Presbyterian. Home and Office: Pines Internat Inc PO Box 1107 2120 Tennessee Lawrence KS 66044

SEIDEL, RICHARD JAMES, chemical company executive; b. Olean, N.Y., May 28, 1941; s. Roderick F. and Muriel (Stapley) S.; m. Susan Arthur, Aug. 15, 1964; children: Gary, Kevin, Brian, Julie. BS in Chem. Engring., Lehigh U., Bethlehem, Pa., 1963. V.p. petrochems. Korea Oil Corp., 1974-76; plant mgr. Gulf Jayhawk Plant, 1977-78; explosives ops. mgr. 1979-80; gen. mgr. performance chems. Gulf Chems., Kansas City, Kans., 1981-1983; mgr. fin., ops. Gulf Chems., Houston, 1983; mgr. profit forecasting Gulf Oil Products Co., Houston, 1983-85; v.p. mfg. Petrolite Corp., St. Louis, 1985-86, v.p. materials mgmt., 1986—. Com. chmn. Boy Scouts Am., Leawood, Kans., 1980-82, camping chmn., Houston, 1983-84; pres. Jr. Achievement, Joplin, Mo., 1979; v.p. Joplin C. of C., 1979. Republican. Roman Catholic. Club: Greenbriar Country (Kirkwood, Mo.). Lodge: Rotary. Office: Petrolite Corp 369 Marshall Saint Louis MO 63119

SEIDEN, ALLEN MARK, otolaryngologist; b. N.Y.C., Dec. 18, 1953; s. George and Pearl (Koltun) S.; m. Peachy Diaz, June 28, 1986. BA in Psychology, U. Pa., 1976; MD, N.J. Coll. Medicine, 1980. Diplomate Am. Bd. Otolaryngology, Nat. Bd. Med. Examiners. Resident, instr. U. Ill. Med. Ctr., Chgo., 1980-81, U. Ill. Med. Ctr. Eye and Ear Infirmary, Chgo., 1981-84; asst. prof. U. Cin., 1984—; dir. div. otolaryngology VA Hosp., Cin., 1986—; dir. swallowing ctr. dept. otolaryngology U. Cin. Med. Ctr., 1986—. Contbr. articles to profl. jours. Fellow Am. Acad. Otolaryngology, Cin. Otolaryngology Soc. Avocations: cooking, jogging. Office: U Cin Coll Med 231 Bethesda Ave ML528 Cincinnati OH 45229

SEIDL, MICHAEL JAMES, sales executive; b. Huntingburg, Ind., Sept. 29, 1950; s. Jerome Edward and Ardella Kahern (Deindorfer) S.; m. Lavonne Ann Schuetter, Nove. 3, 1973; 1 child, Brandon Michael. AAS, Vincennes U., 1972. Draftsman Kimball Internat. Research and Devel., Jasper, Ind., 1972-73; foreman mill Ind. Hardwoods div. Kimball Internat., Chandler, Ind., 1973-76; with sales Ind. Hardwoods div. Kimball Internat., Chandler, 1976-78, asst. gen. mgr., 1978—; Sec., v.p. Newburgh Youth Sports Assn., v.p. Newburgh Park and Recreation, 1985-87. Mem. Ind. Hardwood Lumber Assn. (bd. dirs. 1976-83, chmn. ednl. com. 1978-86, hon. dir. 1985—), Newburg Jaycees (pres., v.p. bd. dirs. 1982—). Roman Catholic. Lodges: Lions (2d v.p. 1984-85), KC. Avocations: travel, fin. mgmt. Home: 7533 Marywood Dr Newburgh IN 47630 Office: Ind Hardwoods PO Box 309 Chandler IN 47610

SEIGER, DANIEL ALTER, pharmaceutical research and development company executive, real estate company executive; b. Cleve., Aug. 9, 1932; s. Isidore and Lillian (Kritzer) S.; m. Marcia Suzanne Levine, Aug. 21, 1955; children—Sherri Beth Seiger Davis, Sanford Bernard. B.Sc., Toledo U., 1954; B.B.A., Fenn Coll., 1957; M.Sc., Northwestern Coll., Tulsa, 1976, Pharm. D., 1979. Registered pharmacist, Ohio. Mgr., Miller's Inc., Cleve., 1955-63; pres. Seiger Realty, Cleveland Heights, Ohio, 1963—; pres. Southside Drugs, Inc., Cleve., 1972-80, Andanco Labs., Inc., Cleveland Heights, 1980—; v.p. The Am. Dietics Co., Cleve., 1984—cons. pharms.; dir. EJBL Pharm., Cleve., 1972-80, Evans Devel., Aurora, Colo., 1976—, Natanya Properties, Cleve., 1977-79. Patentee cough and cold medication for cardiac and diabetic patients, preventative for herpes; author: Preventing S.T.D.'s., 1982; author abstracts, clin. papers, 1960—. Vice pres. Am. Red. Magen David, Ohio, 1976-78; chmn. Ohio Council Gov.'s Phys. Fitness, 1978; pres. Village Residents, Inc. Ohio, 1979; vice chmn. Ohio Ednl. Drug Council, 1981. Recipient Presdl. citation HEW, 1977, commendation Cleve. City Council, 1979, Breath of Life award Am. Red Magen David, 1980. Fellow AAPP; mem. Am. Pharm. Assn. (pres. Toledo chpt. 1953-54, Gavel award 1954), Alpha Zeta Omega (pres. Toledo chpt. 1954-55), Ohio State Pharm. Assn., Greater Cleve. Growth Assn. Lodge: B'nai B'rith. Home: 3830 Severn Rd Cleveland Heights OH 44118

SEIKEL, GEORGE R., engineer; b. Akron, Ohio, Nov. 30, 1933; s. George R. and Lucile (Riley) S.; m. Alice Hudak, Mar. 2, 1957 (div. 1982); children—Linda Ann Seikel Slife, Mary Elizabeth, George R. B.S. magna cum laude, U. Notre Dame, 1955, M.S. in Engring. Mechanics, 1957. With NASA, 1956-81, mgr. MHD Systems and MHD Project office, 1978-81; founder, pres. SeiTec, Inc., Cleve., 1982—; organizer, chmn. sessions for various nat., internat. meetings; lectr. in field; faculty U. Notre Dame, 1955-57. Active Boy Scouts Am., Rocky River, Ohio, 1975-79; pres. St. Christophers PTA, Rocky River, 1973-74; prin., tchr. religion program St. Christopher High Sch., 1965-70. Recipient NASA Outstanding Achievement and Group Achievement awards; U. Notre Dame teaching fellow, 1955-57; ASME Grad. Study award, 1955; U. Notre Dame scholar, K.C. Ednl. Trust Fund, 1950-55. Mem. AIAA (chmn. plasmadynamics and lasers tech. com. 1980-83), Sigma Xi. Democrat. Roman Catholic. Club: Notre Dame Alumni. Contbr. articles to profl. jours. Office: PO Box 81264 Cleveland OH 44181

SEILER, CHARLOTTE WOODY, ret. educator; b. Thorntown, Ind., Jan. 20, 1915; d. Clark and Lois Merle (Long) Woody; A.A., Ind. State U., 1933; A.B., U. Mich., 1941; M.A., Central Mich. U., 1968; m. Wallace Urban Seiler, Oct. 10, 1942; children—Patricia Anne Bootzin, Janet Alice Seiler Sawyer. Tchr. elem. schs., Whitestown, Ind., 1933-34, Thorntown, Ind., 1934-37, Kokomo, Ind., 1937-40, Ann Arbor, Mich., 1941-44, Willow Run, Mich., 1944-46; instr. English div. Delta Coll., University Center, Mich., 1964-69, asst. prof., 1969-77, ret., 1977; organizer, dir. Delta Coll. Puppeteers, 1972-77. Treas., Friends of Grace A. Dow Meml. Library, 1974-75, 77-79, corr. sec., 1975-77; mem. Midland Art Assn.; adv. bd. Salvation Army, 1980-87, sec., 1984-87; leader Sr. Ctr. Humanities program Midland Sr. Ctr., 1978—. Mem. Am., Mich. Library Assn., AAUW (fellowship honoree 1979), Midland Symphony League, Pi Lambda Theta, Chi Omega. Presbyterian. Clubs: Tuesday Review (pres. 1979-80), Seed and Sod Garden (pres. 1986-87). Home: 5002 Sturgeon Creek Pkwy Midland MI 48640

SEILER, WALLACE URBAN, chem. engr.; b. Evansville, Ind., Aug. 31, 1914; s. Samuel Alfred and Anna Beatrice (Grossman) S.; student U. Evansville, 1932-34; B.S., Purdue U., 1937; postgrad. U. Mich., 1945-46; m. Charlotte Woody, Oct. 10, 1942; children—Patricia Anne, Janet Alice. With Dow Chem. Co., 1937-80, engr., Midland, Mich., 1937-39, cons. research engr., Ann Arbor, Mich., 1939-49, tech. service engr., Midland, 1950-55, mgr. solvents field service, 1955-64, contract research and devel. specialist, 1964-80. Mem. Am. Chem. Soc., AAAS, Am. Inst. Chemists, Sigma Xi, Tau Beta Pi, Phi Lambda Upsilon. Home: 5002 Sturgeon Creek Pkwy Midland MI 48640

SEILER, WALTER ADOLPH, banker; b. Grand Island, Nebr., Dec. 2, 1941; s. Walter Armin and Mary Anne (Fritz) S. B.A., U. Nebr., 1963. Asst. trust officer Guardian State Bank and Trust Co., Alliance, Nebr., 1967-80, trust officer, 1980—, dir. Guardian Banshares, Inc., 1980—; v.p. Slagle Fund, 1986—. Mem. Alliance Pub. Library Bd., 1982—; treas. Alliance Pub. Library Found., 1983—; mem. Am. Field Service Com., Alliance, 1980—; chmn. Box Butte County chpt. ARC, Alliance, 1970-73; chpt. advisor Order of DeMolay, 1971—; chmn. program adv. com. Nebr. Ednl. TV, Alliance, 1981—; co-chmn. fund dr. Box Butte Gen. Hosp., Alliance, 1974. Decorated Legion of Honor, Internat. Supreme Council, Order of DeMolay, 1973. Mem. Kappa Sigma (Grand Master, No. Platte Valley Alumni chpt. 1975—). Republican. Presbyterian Ch. (treas. Alliance 1969—). Lodges: Kiwanis (pres. Alliance 1973), Masons, Eastern Star, Scottish Rite (Alliance-Consistory 1973—, rank of insp. gen. 33 deg. Supreme Council) Nebr. Scottish Rite Found. (bd. dirs. 1983—). Office: Guardian State Bank Trust Co 224 Box Butte St Alliance NE 69301

SEILOFF, MICHAEL ROBERT, systems analyst; b. Battle Creek, Mich., Sept. 20, 1951; s. Robert Francis and Lucille Hope (Shively) S.; m. Lizbeth Ann Adams, Sept. 2, 1978; 1 child, Shawna. BS in Engring., Western Mich. U., 1974; MBA, Grand Valley State U., 1987. Work standards analyst Amway Corp., Ada, Mich., 1974-78, forecast analyst, 1978-80, strategic forecast analyst, 1980-84; sr. bus. analyst Foremost Ins., Grand Rapids, Mich., 1984-86, ops. planning, research analyst, 1986—; cons. Alto, Mich., 1984—. Mem. Inst. Indsl. Engrs. (chpt. pres. 1978-79, treas. 1977-78, bd. dirs. 1979-81, Nat. Award of Excellence 1979), Inst. Mgmt. Sci., Mensa. Avocations: chess, golf, personal computers, trout fishing. Office: Foremost Ins PO Box 2450 Grand Rapids MI 49501

SEIPEL, RICHARD ALAN, insurance agent; b. Columbus, Ohio, Mar. 11, 1953; s. William J. and Mary J. (Tompkins) S.; B.S. in Agr., Ohio State U., 1975, M.S. in Agr., 1980; m. Debra Sue Hand, June 9, 1973; 1 son, Joseph. Designated fraternal ins. counselor. Vocat. agr. tchr., Future Farmers Am. advisor Greenville (Ohio) High Sch., 1976-81; 4-H agt. Darke County, Ohio Coop. Extension Service, 1981-83; field agt. K.C. Ins., Greenville, 1983-86, Prudential Fin. Services, Greenville, 1987—; tchr. adult hort. classes, Youth Employment Tng. Program. Parliamentarian Village of Wayne Lakes, Ohio, also mem. rules com., 1981-83; bd. dirs., sec. Darke Econ. Found.; initiated neighborhood watch program, Wayne Lakes; dist. advancement chmn. Boy Scouts Am. Named one of 5 Outstanding Young Agr. Tchrs., State of Ohio, 1980; recipient awards for publs. Ohio Vocat. Agr. Tchrs. 30 Minute Club, 1978-80. Mem. Ohio State U. Alumni Assn. (life), Nat. Assn. Security Dealers (registered rep.), Life Underwriter Tng. Council (grad.). Roman Catholic. Home: 3612 Scenic Dr Greenville OH 45331 Office: 1315 Chippewa Greenville OH 45331

SEITANAKIS, GEORGE PETER, chemical company executive; b. Latrobe, Pa., Apr. 12, 1932; s. Nicholas Aristides and Mary (Kariosifides) S.; m. Christine Patrinos, May 8, 1960; children—Anne Maria, Nicholas John. B.S. in Metall. Engring., Carnegie-Mellon U., 1954. Sr. devel. engr. Allegheny Ludlum Steel, Pitts., 1954-70; sales mgr. Arnold Engring. Co., Marengo, Ill., 1970-73; mgr. product devel. Airco Temescal, Berkeley, Calif., 1973-77; v.p. sales Park Chem. Co., Detroit, 1977—; dir. Du Tone, Waukegan, Ill., 1978—. Patentee alloy application. Mem. Am. Soc. for Metals. Office: Park Chem Co 8074 Military Ave Detroit MI 48204

SEITNER, RITA A., researcher, consultant; b. Milw., July 11, 1940; d. Robert and Esther (Steren) Seitner; m. Alfred F. Huete, Nov. 3, 1973 (div.). B.A., Beaver Coll., 1962; M.S., U. Wis.-Milw., 1977. Mktg. asst. Advanced Learning, Milw., 1972-75; adminstv. asst. J. Walter Thompson, N.Y.C., 1962-67; assoc. planner David M. Walker, Phila., 1967-68; urban analyst HUD, Phila., 1968-70; market analyst Gen. Electric, Milw., 1977-82; mgr. research Hoffman, York & Compton, Milw., 1982-84, pres. RS Research Cons., Inc., Milw., 1984—. Fellow Am. Mktg. Assn., Am. Mgmt. Assn., Direct Mktg. Club. Jewish. Office: 1219 N Jackson St Milwaukee WI 53202

SEITZ, MELVIN CHRISTIAN, JR., distributing company executive; b. Indpls., Aug. 9, 1939; s. Melvin Christian and Francis Sue (Lee) S.; m. Bette Louise Pierson, May 5, 1941; children—David, Mark, Keith, Cindy. Student Butler U., 1957-60. Salesman, Service Supply Co., Inc., Indpls., 1963-71, sec.-treas., 1971-74, v.p., 1974-81, exec. vp., 1981-83, pres., 1983—. Treas., Franklin Twp. High Sch. Bldg. Corp., Franklin Central High Sch. Booster Club. Served with U.S. Army, 1960-63. Mem. Nat. Fastener Distributor Assn., Sigma Nu. Republican. Mem. Disciples of Christ. Lodges: Masons, Shriners. Home: 4716 Northeastern Ave Wanamaker IN 46239 Office: 603 E Washington St Indianapolis IN 46202

SEKOWSKI, ROBERT STEVEN, architect; b. Chgo., June 10, 1960; s. Norbert John and Theresa M. (Kholen) S.; m. Jean Mary Jasionka, Aug. 9, 1986. BArch, Ill. Inst. Tech., 1983. Registered architect, Ill. Draftsman Errol J. Kirsch Architects, Chgo., 1980-82; draftsman Continental Bank, Chgo., 1982-84, project mgr., 1984-85; architect The Austin Co., Chgo., 1985—. Prin. works include three pvt. residences, Ill. Mem. AIA. Republican. Roman Catholic. Club: Irish Clowns. Avocation: team sports. Home: 3954 W Dakin Apt 1A Chicago IL 60618 Office: The Austin Co 401 S LaSalle St Chicago IL 60005

SELBE, JANE WILLIAMS, dentist. Student, U. Colo., 1947; student coll. dentistry, U. Nebr., 1948; DDS, Northwestern U., 1951. Gen. practice dentistry Glenview, Ill., 1951—; lectr. various profl. and civic groups. Contbr. articles to profl. jours. Elder Winnetka (Ill.) Presby. Ch.; chmn. dental exhibit Glenview Days Health Fair, 1978; co-leader People-To-People Dental Del. to China, 1982. Fellow Am. Coll. Dentists; mem. ADA (chmn. pedodontic sec. Scientific Session 1976, alt. del. 1982, 84, cons. video continuing edn. com. 1980-85), Am. Assn. Women Dentists (trustee, pres. 1975-76, treas. 1979-80, various com. chairs, Lucy Hobbs Taylor award 1983), Am. Soc. Dentistry for Children, Ill. Soc. Dentistry for Children (pres. 1960-61, sec. 1981-83, various coms., Disting. Service award 1981), Ill. State Dental Soc. (com. dental health and continuing edn. 1975-78, chmn. Nat. Children's Dental Health Week 1976-78, exec. council mem. 1982-85, witness for Ill. Council on Nutrition, Junk Foods 1980), Chgo. Dental Soc. (chmn. dental health edn. 1977-78, 80-81, chmn. pub. relations com. 1983-84, chmn. course div., program com. Midwinter Meeting, 1986-87, chmn. North Suburban Br. Dinner Programs 1960-61, editor 1977-78, chmn. speakers bur. 1985—, others), Odontographic Soc. Chgo. (program chmn. 1976-77, chmn. credentials com. 1979-80), Am. Assn. Functional Orthodontics (founder, del. 1987), Northwestern U. Dental Alumni Assn. (bd. dirs. 1970-77, pres. 1972-73), Northwestern U. Alumni Assn. (dir.-at-large 1972-74), Iota Sigma Pi, Alpha Chi Omega. Home: 938 Kenilworth St Glenview IL 60025

SELBO, RAY GORDON, training director; b. Jamestown, N.D., Mar. 23, 1940; s. Arthur Gordon Selbo and Helen Evelyn (Peterson) Johnson; m. Joy Marget Bostrom, May 29, 1964; children: Jon Gordon, James Everett. Student, U. Minn., 1958-59. Various positions Am. Hardware Mut. Ins. Co., Mpls., 1959-70, dir. tng., 1970-77; dir. tng., regional v.p. Collateral Control Corp., St. Paul, Chgo., 1977-79; sales cons. Universal Tng. Systems, Wilmette, Ill., 1980-81; dir. training Schwan's Sales Enterprises Inc., Marshall, Minn., 1981—; cons. in field, 1973—. Rep. precinct chmn., Bloomington, Minn., 1974-77; pres. Marshall United Fund, 1985—. Served with U.S. Army, 1963-65, Vietnam. Mem. Am. Soc. for Tng. and Devel. (local pres. 1974-75, Torch award 1974). Republican. Lutheran. Avocations: reading, crossword puzzles, golf. Home: RR 1 Box 3F Lynd MN 56157 Office: Schwan's Sales Enterprises Inc 115 W College Dr Marshall MN 56258

SELBY, ROBERT IRWIN, architect, educator; b. Evanston, Ill., Jan. 26, 1943; s. William Martin and Alice (Irwin) S.; m. Barbara Jean Kenaga, June 19, 1965; 1 child, Michael Scott. BArch, U. Ill., 1967, MArch, 1985. Registered architect, Ill., Wis., Ind., Colo., Fla., Pa., Idaho, N.C., Mich., Mo., Ohio. V.p. The Hawkweed Group, Ltd., Chgo., Soldiers Grove and Ossed, Wis., 1971-84; prin. Robert I. Selby, Architect, Champaign, Ill., 1984—; asst. prof. architecture U. Ill., Champaign, 1984—; cons. housing research and devel. program U. Ill., Urbana, 1985—; bd. editors U. Ill. Sch. Architecture jour., 1986—. Author: (with others) The Hawkweed Passive Solar House Book, 1980; contbr. articles to profl. jours. Served with USAFR, 1966-72. Mem. AIA (corp., sec. Champaign sect. 1985, pres. Champaign sect. 1987), Environ. Design Research Assn. Avocations: music, photography, jogging. Home: 909 W Union Champaign IL 61821-3323 Office: U Ill Sch Architecture 608 E Lorado Taft Dr Champaign IL 61820-6969

SELFRIDGE, CALVIN, lawyer; b. Evanston, Ill., Dec. 20, 1933; s. Calvin Frederick and Violet Luella (Bradley) S. BA, Northwestern U., 1956; JD, U. Chgo., 1960. Admitted to Ill. bar, 1961; trust officer Continental Ill. Nat. Bank & Trust Co. Chgo., 1961-71; individual practice law, Chgo., 1972-76; mem. firm Howington, Elworth, Osswald & Hough, Chgo., 1976-79; individual practice law, 1979—; pres., dir. Des Plaines Pub. Co., Northwest Newspapers Corp. Pres., bd. dirs. Scholarship Fund Found., 1965—; trustee Lawrence Hall Sch. for Boys, 1982—. Served with AUS, 1959. Mem. Chgo., Am., Ill. bar assns., Law Club Chgo., Legal Club Chgo., Chi Psi, Phi Delta Phi. Republican. Congregationalist. Clubs: Attic (gov., sec.), Univ. Racquet (Chgo.); Balboa (Mazatlan, Mexico); Indian Hill Country (Winnetka, Ill.). Home: 1320 N State Pkwy Chicago IL 60610 Office: 135 S LaSalle St Suite 2120 Chicago IL 60603

SELGREN, PHILIP MORTON, dentist; b. Janesville, Wis., July 22, 1930; s. Clarence Henry and Myrtle Fayetta (Morton) S.; m. Faith Valorice Olsen, June 26, 1954; children: Stacey, Susan, Sandra, Sara. Undergrad., St. Olaf Coll., 1950; DDS, Marquette U., 1954. Pvt. practice Janesville, Wis., 1954—. Scout master Boys Scouts Am., 1967—, pres. Sinnissippi Council; pres. First Luth. Ch., Janesville, 1982-83. Served to lt. USN, 1954-56. Recipient Silver Beaver award Boy Scouts Am., 1968; Lamb award Luth. Ch., 1973, 84. Mem. Wis. Dental Assn. (bd. dirs. 1971-80), Rock County Dental Soc. (pres. 1965). Club: Y's Men (pres. 1963). Lodge: Kiwanis (v.p. Janesville 1985-86, pres. elect 1986-87, pres. 1987—). Home: 430 Mohawk Rd Janesville WI 53545 Office: 101 S Main St Janesville WI 53545

SELIG, ALLAN H. (BUD), professional baseball team executive; b. Milw., July 30, 1934; s. Ben and Marie S. Grad., U. Wis.-Madison, 1956. With Selig Ford (became Selig Chevrolet 1982), West Allis, Wis., 1959—; pres. Selig Ford, 1966—; part owner Mlw. Braves (became Atlanta Braves 1965), 1963-65; co-founder Teams, Inc., 1964; co-founder Milw. Brewers Am. League (baseball team), 1965, owner, pres., 1970—. Served with U.S. Army, 1956-58. Address: Milwaukee Brewers Milwaukee County Stadium Milwaukee WI 53214

SELIGMAN, ROSLYN, psychiatrist; b. Augusta, Ga.. BS, U. Ga., 1957; MD, Med. Coll. Ga, 1961. Diplomate Am. Bd. Psychiatry and Neurology. Intern Michael Reese Hosp., Chgo., 1961-62; resident in gen. psychiatry U. Cin., 1962-64, fellow in child psychiatry, 1964-66, fellow community child psychiatry, 1966-67, instr., 1966-69, asst. prof. psychiatry, 1969-74, assoc. prof. psychiatry, 1974—; cons. div. adolescent medicine Children's Hosp. Med. Ctr., 1966—; psychotherapist children, adolescents and adults, U. Cin., 1966—, psychiatrist dept. pediatrics U. Cin., 1967—; witness Ct. Domestic Relations, Cin., 1982 ; mem. Friends of Womens Studies, U. Cin., 1986—. Mem. com. for responsible devel. Mt. Adams Civic Assn., 1986—. Fellow Am. Psychiatric Assn., Am. Acad. Child Psychiatry; mem. Ohio State Med. Assn., Ohio Psychiatric Assn. (legis. com., pres. 1981-82, legis. com. 1986), Cin. Psychiat. Soc. (legis. com., pres. 1975, legis. com. chairmn. 1986). Home: 2401 Ingleside Cincinnati OH 45206 Office: U Cin Coll Med Dept Psychiatry 231 Bethesda Ave Cincinnati OH 45267-0559

SELIGSON, THEODORE H., architect, urban designer, art consultant; b. Kansas City, Mo., Nov. 10, 1930; s. Harry and Rose (Haith) S.; m. Jacqueline Rose, Dec. 27, 1964 (div. 1976). B.Arch., Washington U., St. Louis, 1953. Registered architect, Mo., Kans. Intern Marshall & Brown, Kansas City, Mo., 1949-54; designer, head design Kivett & Myers, Kansas City, Mo., 1954-62; prin. Atelier Seligson, Kansas City, Mo., 1962-64; pres. Seligson, Eggen, Inc., Kansas City, 1964-73, Seligson Assocs., Inc., Architects Planners, Kansas City, 1973—; tchr. adult edn. U. Mo.-Kansas City, 1958-61; tchr., critic Kansas City Art Inst., Mo., 1961-64, 71-72; vis. prof. Washington U., 1975, 77, 78, 81, 86, U. Kans., Lawrence, 1978, 79, 80; art cons. Design Assocs., Kansas City, Mo., 1955—. Vice pres. Friends of Art Nelson-Atkins Mus. Art, Kansas City, 1965-67, chmn. selections com., 1981, vis. curator, 1987; chmn. Capitol Fine Arts Commn. Mo., 1983—; bd. dirs. Westport Tomorrow, Kansas City, 1973—, Hist. Kansas City Found., 1984—. Recipient Urban Design award Kansas City Mcpl. Art Commn., 1968, 74, 78; Nat. Archtl. award Am. Inst. Steel Constrn., 1970. Fellow AIA, Kansas City chpt. AIA (pres. 1983, bd. dirs. 1959—, Design Excellence award 1966, 68, 70, 74, Cen. States Regional award 1974, 78, Honor award for outstanding service to chpt. and profession 1982-83); mem. Mo. Council Architects, Am. Soc. Interior Designers, Soc. Archtl. Historians (pres. 1973-75), Native Sons (bd. dirs. 1978—). Republican. Jewish. Clubs: Rockhill Tennis, Kansas City (Kansas City). Office: Seligson Assocs Inc 106 W 14th St Kansas City MO 64105

SELIM, JENNIE MAE, social worker, guidance couselor; b. Caruthers, Mo., Aug. 9, 1944; d. Manuel and Jennie Estella (Graham) Higgins; m. Jahangir Selim, June 22, 1982 . AS in law enforcement cum laude, Washtenaw Community Coll., 1972; BSW, Eastern Mich. U., 1974, M in Counseling magna cum laude, 1981. Cert. social worker. Grad. asst. Ea. Mich. U. Guidance and Counseling Dept., Ypsilanti, 1980-81; child care worker Child and Parent Ctr., Jackson, Mich., 1984; law clk. to presiding justice U.S. Ct. Appeals (3d cir.), Detroit, 1986; law clk. Gregory Reed & Assoc., Detroit, 1986—; social worker Ingham County Med. Care Facility, Okemos, Mich. 1981-82; corrections supr. State Prison of S. Mich., Ypsilanti, 1972-80; housemother and counselor Browndale Group Homes, Ann Arbor, 1972; dietetic clerk VA Med. Ctr., Allen Park, Mich. Vol. Dept. Social Services, 1973-75, 84-85, Aware Shelter and Emergency Counseling Ctr. Recipient Cert. Appreciation, Dept. Social Services, 1973-75, 84-85. Mem. ABA, Mich. Bar Assn., Nat. Notary Assn., Am. Personnel and Guidance Assn., Black WOmen in Corrections (pres. 1977-79). Democrat. Baptist. Avocations: avid reading, creative cooking, letter writing, music, sewing. Home: 11806 Corbett Detroit MI 48213

SELINGER, DAVID, architect; b. Petach-Tikva, Israel, Aug. 26, 1945; came to U.S., 1967; s. Naftali and Hanna (Kaliski) S.; m. Ilana Fishler, Jan. 21, 1968; children: Tal P., Ronit R., Hanna O. BS in Environ. Design, Syracuse U., 1971, B in Land Architecture, 1972; MArch, Washington U., St. Louis, 1977. Registered architect, Fla., Israel. Landscape architect Harland Bortholomew Assocs., St. Louis, 1972-75; architect, designer and planner Bank Bldg. Corp. Health Care, St. Louis, 1977-80; architect, med. planner, assoc. Hellmuth, Obata & Kassabaum, St. Louis, 1980-86; project mgr. Pearce Corp., St. Louis, 1987—. Mem. AIA. Avocations: travel, photography, art, sports. Home: 9752 Lindley Dr Saint Louis MO 63132

SELLECK, ROBERT WILCOX, soft drink bottling company executive; b. 1921; married. Student, Flint Jr. Coll. Salesman Coca-Cola Co., Inc., 1941-45, sales mgr., 1945-52; propr. R.W. Selleck Distbg. Co., 1953-56; mktg. dir. Pepsi-Cola Gen. Bottlers, Inc., Chgo., 1956, v.p. sales, 1956-59, sr. v.p. mktg., 1959-68, exec. v.p. mktg., 1968-70, sr. exec. v.p., chief operating officer, 1970-72, pres., chief operating officer, 1972-75, pres., chief exec. officer, 1975-86, chmn. bd. dirs., chief exec. officer, 1986—; bd. dirs. IC Products Co. div IC Industries., Dad's Root Beer Co., Bubble Up Co., Midas Internat. Corp., Mt. Prospect State Bank, United Nat. Bank. Served with AUS, 1942-45. Mem. Nat. Soft Drink Assn. (bd. dirs.), Ill. Soft Drink Assn. (past bd. dirs.). Office: 1745 N Kolmar Ave Chicago IL 60639

SELLERS, MARGARET REGULAR, personnel administrator; b. Pendleton, S.C., Sept. 28, 1935; d. Daniel and Annie Mae (Morris) Regular; m. Thomas James Sellers, Jan. 22, 1955; children: Loren Sellers Jackson, Sharon Elizabeth. BA, Wayne State U., 1979; MPA, Western Mich. U., 1983. Various positions Detroit Pub. Library, 1951-72, asst. dir. personnel, 1972-74, assoc. dir. personnel, 1974-77; dir. personnel Wayne County Community Coll., Detroit, 1977-80, Mich. Dept. Natural Resources, 1980-86; chief examiner, dir. human resources City of Grand Rapids, Mich., 1986—; asst. mgr. adminstrv services City of Grand Rapids, 1987—; chmn. Mich. Personnel Dirs. Council, 1981-82; mem. adv. com. Classified Exec. Service, State of Mich.; lectr. in field. Trustee, Rehab. Inst., 1980-81; bd. dirs. minority apprentice program Mich. State U., Dwelling Place of Grand Rapids, Inc., 1986—, United Way Boardwalk, 1986—. U. Md. fellow, 1973. Mem. ALA (adv. office library personnel resources), Internat. Personnel Mgmt. Assn. U.S. (exec. bd. Mich. chpt. 1977—, pres. Mich. chpt. 1978, v.p. central region 1980-81, pres. region 1981, exec. council, central region rep. 1983-85), Mich. Pub. Employer Labor Relations Assn. (exec. bd. 1977, program com. 1980). Baptist. Office: City of Grand Rapids 300 Monroe NW Grand Rapids MI 49503

SELLS, BOAKE ANTHONY, retail company executive; b. Ft. Dodge, Iowa, June 24, 1937; s. Lyle M. and Louise (Gadd) S.; m. Marian S. Stephenson, June 20, 1959; children: Damian, Brian, Jean Ann. B.S.C., U. Iowa, 1959; M.B.A., Harvard U., 1969. Bus. office mgr. Northwestern Bell Telephone, Des Moines, 1959-63; salesman Hydraulic Cos., Ft. Dodge, Iowa, 1964-67; pres. Cole Nat. Corp., Cleve., 1969-83; vice chmn. Dayton Hudson Corp., Mpls., 1983-84; pres. Dayton Hudson Corp., 1984—; dir. Holiday Corp., 1985—; treas. Retail Industry Trade Action Coalition. Trustee Mpls. Soc. Fine Arts, 1983—; regional chmn. Midwest U.S. Olympic Com., 1983—; bd. dirs. Guthrie Theater, 1984, Dale Warland Singers, 1984, Macalester Coll., 1985. Office: Dayton Hudson Corp 777 Nicollet Mall Minneapolis MN 55402 Home: 2670 Woolsey Ln Wayzata MN 55391 *

SELM, ROBERT PRICKETT, architectural engineering executive; b. Cin., Aug. 9, 1923; s. Frederick Oscar and Margery Marie (Prickett) S.; m. Rowena Imogene Brown, Nov. 25, 1945 (div. Jan. 1975); children: Rosalie C. Selm Pace, Linda R. Selm Partridge, Robert F., Michael E.; m. Janis Claire Broman, June 24, 1977. BS in Chem. Engring., U. Cin., 1949. Enlisted U.S. Army, 1943; advanced through grades to sgt. U.S. Army, CBI, 1943-46; commd. capt. U.S. Army, 1949, resigned, 1954; design engr. Wilson & Co., Salina, Kans., 1954-67, gen. ptnr., 1967-81, sr. ptnr., 1981—; ptnr. in charge Wilson Labs., Salina, Kans., 1956—. Contbr. articles to profl. jours.; patentee in field. Named Engr. of Yr. Kans. Engring. Soc., Topeka, 1986. Mem. Am. Chem. Soc., NSPE (state chmn. environ. resource com.), Am. Inst. Chem. Engrs., Am. Water Works Assn., Water Pollution Control Fedn. Republican. Episcopalian. Clubs: Petroleum (Wichita, Kans.); Salina Country (pres. 1986). Lodges: Elks, Shriners. Avocations: golf, lapidary arts. Home: 135 Mt Barbara Rd Salina KS 67401 Office: Wilson & Co 631 E Crawford Salina KS 67402-1640

SELMEIER, LEWIS WILLIAM, advertising agency executive; b. Covington, Ky., June 21, 1912; s. Harry Herman and Carrie Leona (Brossenne) S.; m. Marjory Moore, July 20, 1946; children: Jane, Joel, Ross. BA, Principia Coll., 1934; postgrad., U. Cin., 1937. Dir. advt. and promotion RCA Estate Appliance Corp., Hamilton, Ohio, 1947-55; account supr. Farson, Huff & Northlich Advt., Cin., 1955-56; pres. Lewis W. Selmeier Co., Advt., Cin., 1956-68; v.p. Early/Selmeier Advt., Cin., 1969-71, Stockton-West-Burkhart, Inc., Advt., Cin., 1972-83; pres. Selmeier & Assocs. Advt., Cin., 1984—. Editor and monthly contbr. articles to Home Appliance Builder, 1957-68; contbr. 20 articles to various mags. chmn. bd. trustees First Ch. of Christian Scientist, Wyoming, 1951-56, first reader, 1952-55. Served with AUS, 1942-46. Recipient Nat. Idea Man award Indsl. Mktg. mag., 1960, also 37 awards for top-scoring ads in readership studies. Mem. Cin. Execs. Assn. (past pres.), Cin. Advertisers Club (past mem. bd. dirs.). Republican. Club: Queen City Racquet (Cin.). Avocations: writing, tennis, condo in Fla. Home: 3 Woodcreek Cincinnati OH 45242 Office: Selmeier and Assocs 10999 Reed Hartman Hwy Suite #238 Cincinnati OH 45242

SELTMAN, GARY MYRON, psychiatrist; b. Pitts., Mar. 13, 1951; s. Seymour Nathan and Miriam (Fagen) S.; m. Constance Lenis, Dec. 27, 1977; children: Sara, Andrea, Ted. BS, U. Mich., 1973; MD, U. Pitts., 1977. Diplomate Am. Bd. Psychiatry and Neurology. Resident in psychiatry Letterman Hosp., San Francisco, 1978-81; chief psychiatry Munson Army Hosp., Ft. Leavenworth, Kans., 1981-83; psychiatrist Hertzler Clinic, Halstead, Kans., 1983—; chief cons. Alcohol Drug Abuse Program, Ft. Leavenworth, Kans., 1981-83, U.S. Disciplinary Barracks, Ft. Leavenworth, 1981-83; clin. cons. Kans. Hemophilia Treatment Ctr., Halstead, 1984—; advisor Harvey County Spl. Edn. Coop., Newton, Kans., 1985—. Contbr. articles to profl. jours. Served to maj. U.S. Army, 1977-83. Mem. Am. Psychiat. Assn., Kans. Psychiat. Soc., Assn. Mil. Surgeons of U.S. Avocations: jogging, hunting, arts. Home: 916 Ridge Dr Halstead KS 67056 Office: Hertzler Clinic PA Fourth and Chesnut Halstead KS 67056

SELTZ, PAUL HERMAN, insurance executive; b. McInstosh, Minn., Oct. 28, 1921; s. Paul Julius and Regina Margaret (Nibbe) S.; m. Mildred Dehaan, Aug. 16, 1947; children—Paul, Kathryn, Karen, Sandra. A.A., U. Minn., 1942; student, St. Paul Coll. Law, 1946-48. Asst. sec. St. Paul Hosp. and Casualty Co., 1946-48; sec. Des Moines Casualty Co., 1948-56; pres. Nat. Travelers Life Co., Des Moines, 1979—, Am. Travelers Assurance Co., Des Moines, 1985—. Bd. control Concordia Coll., St. Paul, 1958-72; trustee Luth. Ch. Found., St. Louis, 1983. Served with U.S. Army, 1943-46. Mem. Des Moines C. of C., Am. Council Life Ins. Republican. Lutheran. Clubs: Des Moines, Des Moines Golf and Country. Home: 1909 74th St Des Moines IA 50322 Office: 820 Keosauqua Way Des Moines IA 50309

SELVAKUMAR, VEDHAGIRI, gastroenterologist; b. Kurinjipadi, India, Jan. 20, 1945; came to U.S., 1975; s. Vaiyapuri Kolandivel Vedhagiri Chettiar and Vedhagiri Chakkarai Dhanabakiyam; m. Jane Elizabeth Costello, Sept. 17, 1977; children: Sumantha Rani, Pamela Priya, Raj Vel. Student, A.V.C. Coll., Mayuram, India, 1962-63; BS and MB, Madras (India) Med. Coll., 1972. Diplomate Am. Bd. Internal Medicine, Am. Bd. Gastroenterology. Rotating intern G.G. Hosp., Madras, 1971-72; resident in internal medicine Madurai (India) Med. Coll., 1972-75; resident in internal medicine Bronx-Lebanon Hosp. Ctr., N.Y., 1975-78, fellow in gastroenterology, 1978-80, chief resident in internal medicine, 1979; practice medicine specializing in gastroenterology Council Bluffs, Iowa, 1980—; clin. instr. sch. medicine Creighton U., Omaha, 1981-83, asst. clin. prof., 1983—. Fellow Am. Coll. Gastroenterology, Am. Coll. Internat. Physicians; mem. AMA (state and county socs.), ACP, Am. Soc. for Gastrointestinal Endoscopy, Am. Gastroent. Assn., U.S. Chess Fedn. Club: Iowa State Chess. Avocations: chess, backgammon. Home: 9 Horizon Dr Council Bluffs IA 51501 Office: 801 Harmony Suite 301 Council Bluffs IA 51501

SELZER, CHARLES LOUIS, retired educational administrator; b. Homestead, Iowa, Dec. 21, 1914; s. Louis Carl and Caroline (Shoup) S.; m. Louise Kippenhan, Mar. 9, 1935; 1 dau., Patricia Madelyn Selzer Carstensen. BA cum laude, Coe Coll., 1935; MA, State U. Iowa, 1950, postgrad., 1951—. Notary public. Tchr., prin., coach Amana (Iowa) High Sch., 1935-50; supt. Amana Community Schs., 1950-83; guest lectr. U. Iowa, summers 1977-79; bd. dirs. Amana Telephone Co., Amana Woolens, Inc. Contbr. to Amana News Bull.; translator Amana documents and testimonies; author: Amana Coop. Edn. Plan; TV appearance: (Amana segment) 60 Minutes. Former justice of peace, Iowa County; mem. Iowa County Crime Commn.; pres. Amana Community Chest, 1951-53; mem. adv. bd. Kirkwood Coll., Amana Service Co.; mem. Iowa County Soc. Aging, Area X Grant Wood Spl. Edn. Bd., Amana Travel Council, Amana Hist. Landmark Charter and Constn. Commn., 1977—; pres. Amana Bicentennial; mem. bicentennial com. Coe Coll. Mem. Am. Assn. Sch. Adminstrs., Iowa Assn. Sch. Adminstrs., NEA, Iowa Edn. Assn., Amana Young Men's Bur. (hon. past pres.), Iowa Poweshiek County Supts. Assn., Sr. Supts. Iowa, Joint County Area X Supts. Assn. (legis. com.), Iowa Benton Supts. Assn. (legis. com.), Amana Soc. (bd. dirs.), Iowa Peace Officers Assn., Amana Hist. Soc., Nat. Notary Assn., Amana Men's Chorus, Iowa County Hist. Soc. (pres. 1965-67), Iowa County Schoolmasters Assn. (past pres.), Amana Landmark Soc. (mem. constn. com.), Coe Coll. Alumni Assn., U. Iowa Alumni Assn., Phi Beta Kappa. Mem. Amana Ch. Soc. (trustee, elder, pres. 1971—). Clubs: Elks, Masons (32 deg.), Shriners, El Kahir, Homestead Welfare (past pres., sec.), Cedar Rapids Toastmasters (hon.). Home: Homestead IA 52236

SEMELSBERGER, KENNETH J., household products company executive; b. 1936. BBA, Ohio State U., 1970; MBA, Cleve. State U., 1972. Product mgr. Holan Corp., 1954-66; mgr. sales and contracts Barts Corp., 1966-73; with Scott Fetzer Corp., Cleve., 1973—, v.p. mfg., 1974-75, div. pres., 1975-78, group v.p., 1978-83, sr. v.p. fin. adminstrn., 1983-86, pres., chief operating officer, 1986—. Served with AUS, 1959-62. Office: Scott & Fetzer Co 28800 Clemens Rd Westlake OH 44145 *

SEMERENA, PIERRE, automobile corporation executive; b. June 20, 1927; married; 3 children. D.Bus., Hautes Etudes Commmerciales, Paris, 1949. Various positions Renault, 1950-78; mgr. Renault Brazil, until 1978, dir. mktg. Latin Am., until 1978; mng. dir. Renault Spain, until 1978; v.p. Renault Internat. Automobile Div., 1978-80; v.p. planning and control Renault Automobile Ops., 1982; pres., chief exec. officer Renault Vehicules Industriels, 1982-84; chief exec. officer Renault Automobile Div., 1984-85; exec. v.p. Renault, 1985; dir. Am. Motors Corp., Southfield, Mich., 1980-82, chmn. bd., 1985—. Office: Am Motors Corp 27777 Franklin Rd Southfield MI 48034

SEMKE, CHARLES WESLEY, psychology educator, dean; b. Oklahoma City, Iowa, Dec. 11, 1924; s. John August and Tillie C. (Schroeder) S.; m. Harriet Dorothea Mugler, June 6, 1946; children: Mark Wesley, Kathleen Renee. BA, Western Union Coll., Le Mars, Iowa, 1945; BD, Evang. Theol. Sem., Naperville, Ill., 1948; postgrad., Philips U., 1954-55; MA, Boston U., 1959; PhD, U. Colo., 1967. Ordained to ministry Meth. Ch., 1948; lic. psychologist, Iowa. Minister Highland Ch., Tieton, Washington, 1949-54, German Congl. Ch., Clinton, Mass., 1955-59; research psychologist Mass. Gen. Hosp., Boston, 1956-59; psychologist Mental Health Inst., Cherokee, Iowa, 1960, 62; prof. psychology, assoc. dean Westmar Coll., Le Mars, 1959—. Vice chmn. Iowa Mental Hygiene Com., Iowa City, 1977-81, Mental Health/Mental Retardation Com., Des Moines, 1981-85; chmn. bd.dirs. Plains Area Mental Health, Le Mars, 1971-81; bd. dirs. Iowa Health System Agy., Des Moines, 1976-82, Hospice of Plymouth County, Le Mars, 1984—. Recipient Merit award Assn. Coll. and Univs. for Internat.-Intercultural Studies, 1975, Appreciation award Community Mental Health Ctrs., 1976, Community Service award Iowa Health Systems Agy., 1982; Fulbright scholar, 1954-55. Mem. Am. Psychol. Assn., Midwest Psychol. Assn., Iowa Psychol. Assn., Am. Assn. Counselling and Devel., Am. Assn. Univ. Profs. (local pres. 1978-81), Nat. Assn. Fgn. Student Affairs (regional chmn. 1965-66), Psi Chi. Democrat. Lodge: Lions. Avocations: traveling, photography, skiing, reading. Home: 221 2d Ave SE Le Mars IA 51031 Office: Westmar Coll 1002 3d Ave SE Le Mars IA 51031

SEMM, HOWARD RUSSELL, otolaryngologist; b. Mitchell, S.D., Aug. 17, 1950; s. Charles Ronald and Ruth Elizabeth (Naser) S.; m. Sally Irene LeBaron, May 19, 1973; children: Nathan Russell, Jacob Alexander. BS, U. Nebr., Lincoln, 1972, MA, 1974; MD, U. Nebr., Omaha, 1974. Cert. Am. Bd. Otolaryngology. Surg. intern U. Oreg., Portland, 1978-79; resident in otolaryngology Ohio State U., Columbus, 1979-82; practice medicine specializing in otolaryngology Lincoln, 1982—. Asst. editor Textbook of Otolaryngology, 1982. Fellow ACS, Am. Acad. Otolaryngology; mem. Am. Acad. Facial Plastic and Reconstructive Surgery. Democrat. Avocations: skiing, travel. Home: 2845 Woodsdale Lincoln NE 68502 Office: 630 N Cotner Lincoln NE 68505

SEN, ASHISH KUMAR, urban scientist, educator; b. Delhi, India, June 8, 1942; came to U.S., 1967, naturalized, 1985; s. Ashoka Kumar and Arati Sen; m. Colleen Taylor. B.S. with honors, Calcutta U., 1962; M.A., U. Toronto, Ont., Can., 1964, Ph.D., 1971. Research assoc., lectr. dept. geography Transp. Center, Northwestern U., 1967-69; mem. faculty Center Urban Studies, U. Ill., Chgo., 1969—; prof. Center Urban Studies, U. Ill., 1978—; dean Center Urban Studies, U. Ill. (Sch. Urban Scis.), 1977-78; mem. Transp. Research Forum, Transp. Research Bd.; pres. Ashish Sen, and Assocs., Chgo., 1977—. Contbr. articles to profl. jours. Mem. Am. Statis. Assn., Inst. Math. Stats., Am. Soc. Planning Ofcls., Regional Sci. Assn. Hindu. Home: 2557 W Farwell Ave Chicago IL 60645

SENDRY, DOUGLAS JOHN, lawyer; b. N.Y.C., Feb. 6, 1946; s. William Alphonse and Dorothy (Renna) S.; m. Sara Lee Brobst, Aug. 17, 1968 (div. Nov. 1983); children: Stacey Lee, Lindsay Anne; m. Carolynne Krebs, Jan. 21, 1984. BA in History, Kent State U., 1969; JD, U. Akron, 1974; cert., Nat. Judicial Coll., 1977, Ohio Judicial Coll., 1979. Bar: Ohio 1974, U.S. Dist. Ct. (no. dist.) Ohio 1975, U.S. Supreme Ct. 1980, U.S. Tax Ct. 1982. Ptnr. Ulrich & Sendry, Ravenna, Ohio, 1973-77; municipal referee Portage Municipal Ct., Ravenna, 1976-81; acting judge Kent, Ravenna Mcpl. Cts., Ohio, 1976; domestic relations referee Portage County Common Pleas Ct., Ravenna, 1982—; lectr. Kent State U., 1973-75. Mem. exec. com. Mental Health Retardation Bd., Portage County, 1974-76; trustee Western Res. Legal Services, Akron, 1981-83. Mem. Ohio State Bar Assn., Akron Bar Assn., Portage County Bar Assn. (lectr. 1973—), Jaycees (bd. dirs. 1974-76), Delta Theta Phi. Lodge: Optimists, Elks. Avocations: sailing, golf, building model ships and aircraft. Home: 308 Bryn Mawr Ravenna OH 44266 Office: Portage County Common Pleas Ct 201 W Main St Ravenna OH 44266

SENEKER, STANLEY A., automobile manufacturing company executive; BS Santa Clara U., 1953, MBA U. Pa., 1957. With Ford Motor Co., 1957—, mgr. investment & system analysis, 1963-65, regional fin. mgr. fin. staff, 1965-66, mgr. facilities & property dept., fin. staff, 1966-69, exec. v.p. Ford real estate ops. fin. staff, 1969-71, exec. v.p. Ford land devel., 1971-77, dir. pension & ins. analysis fin. staff, 1977-84, pres. fin. & ins. subs. (Ford Motor Credit Co.) 1984-86, corp. v.p. & treas., 1986—. Served to 1st lt. U.S. Army, 1953-55. Office: Ford Motor Co American Rd Dearborn MI 48121 *

SENEKJIAN, ELIZABETH KITTY, obstetrician, gynecologist; b. Feb. 11, 1950; d. Oshin and Jamie (Shukry) S. BA, CUNY, 1970; MD, Med. Coll. Pa., 1974. Diplomate Am. Bd. Ob-Gyn, Am. Bd. Oncology. Resident in surgery Baylor Coll. Medicine, Houston, 1974-76, 77-78, fellow in pediatric surgery, 1976-77; resident in ob-gyn U. Tex., San Antonio, 1978-81; fellow in gynecologic oncology, instr. U. S.C., 1981-83; asst. prof. U. Chgo., 1983—. Contbr. articles to profl. jours. Recipient Career Development award Am. Cancer Soc., 1985. Fellow Am. Coll Obstetricians and Gynecologists; mem. M.E. DeBakey Internat. Surg. Soc., Am. Soc. Colscopy and Cervical Pathology, Gynecol. Laser Soc., Soc. Gynecol. Oncologists, Am. Soc. Clin. Oncologists. Office: U Chgo/Chgo Lying-In Hosp 5841 S Maryland Ave Box 446 Chicago IL 60637

SENER, JOSEPH PAUL, mechanical engineering executive; b. Chgo., May 20, 1953; s. Charles J. and Helen Jane (Whitehead) S.; m. Linda Marie Walters, June 11, 1977; 1 child, Christina. Registered profl. engr., Ill. Nuclear design engr. GPE Controls, Morton Grove, Ill., 1978-79; project engr. W.J. Woolley Co., Oak Brook, Ill., 1979-84; sr. project engr. Miller Fluid Power, Bensenville, Ill., 1984-85, mgr. engineered products, 1985-86, dir. engring. and quality assurance, 1986—; pres. SDA Tech. Services, Naperville, Ill., 1983—. Served to sgt. U.S. Army, 1973-76, Korea. Mem. ASME, Am. Nuclear Soc., Owasippe Staff Assn. (pres. 1986). Roman Catholic. Avocation: karate. Home: 1399 River Oak Dr Naperville IL 60565 Office: Miller Fluid Power 800 N York Rd Bensenville IL 60106

SENGPIEHL, PAUL MARVIN, former state official, lawyer; b. Stuart, Nebr., Oct. 10, 1937; s. Arthur Paul and Anne Marie (Andersen) S.; B.A., Wheaton (Ill.) Coll., 1959; M.A. in Pub. Adminstrn., Mich. State U., 1961; J.D., Ill. Inst. Tech.-Chgo. Kent Coll. Law, 1970; m. June S. Cline, June 29, 1963; children—Jeffrey D., Chrystal M. Bar: Ill. 1971, U.S. Supreme Ct. 1982. Adminstrv. asst. Chgo. Dept. Urban Renewal, 1962-65; supr. Ill. Municipal Retirement Fund, Chgo., 1966-71; mgmt. officer Ill. Dept. Local Govt. Affairs, Springfield, 1971-72, legal counsel, Chgo., 1972-73; spl. asst. atty. gen. Ill. Dept. Labor, Chgo., 1973-76; asst. atty. gen. Ct. of Claims div. Atty. Gen. of Ill., 1976-83; hearing referee Bd. Rev., Ill. Dept. Labor, 1983-84; local govt. law columnist Chgo. Daily Law Bull., 1975-84; instr. polit. sci. Judson Coll., Elgin, Ill., 1963. Republican candidate for Cook County Recorder of Deeds, 1984. Mem. Ill. Bar Assn. (local govt. law sect. council 1973-79, vice chmn. 1976-77, co-editor local govt. newsletter 1976-77, chmn. 1977-78, editor newsletter 1977-78, state tax sect. council 1979-82, 84-85), Chgo. Bar Assn. (local govt. com., chmn. legis. subcom. 1978-79, sec. 1979-80, vice chmn. 1980-81, chmn. 1981-82, state and mcpl. tax com.),Internat. Platform Assn., John Ericsson Republican League Ill. (state sec. 1983-85), sec. Cook County 1982—). Republican. Baptist (vice chmn. deacons 1973-76, 79-80, moderator 1983-86, supt. sunday sch. 1986—). Home: 727 N Ridgeland Ave Oak Park IL 60302

SENGSTACKE, JOHN HERMAN HENRY, publishing company executive; b. Savannah, Ga., Nov. 25, 1912; s. Herman Alexander and Rosa Mae (Davis) S.; 1 son, Robert Abbott. B.S., Hampton (Va.) Inst., 1933; postgrad., Ohio State U., 1933. With Robert S. Abbott Pub. Co. (publishers Chgo. Defender), 1934—, v.p., gen. mgr., 1934-40, pres., gen. mgr., 1940—; chmn. bd. Mich. Chronicle, Detroit; pres. Tri-State Defender, Defender Publs., Amalgamated Pubs., Inc.; pub. Daily Defender; pres. Sengstacke Enterprises, Inc., Sengstacke Publs., Pitts. Courier Newspaper Chain; dir. Ill. Fed. Savs. & Loan Assn., Golden State Mut. Life Ins. Co. Mem. exec. bd. Nat. Alliance Businessmen; bd. govs. USO; mem. Ill. Sesquicentennial Commn., Pres.'s Com. on Equal Opportunity in Armed Services; mem. pub. affairs adv. com. Air Force Acad.; trustee Bethune-Cookman Coll., Daytona Beach, Fla., Hampton Inst.; bd. dirs. Washington Park YMCA, Joint Negro Appeal; chmn. bd. Provident Hosp. Recipient Two Friends award Nat. Urban League, 1950; Hampton Alumni award, 1954; 1st Mass. Media award Am. Jewish Com. Mem. Negro Newspaper Pubs. Assn. (founder), Nat. Newspaper Pubs. Assn. (founder, pres.), Am. Newspaper Pubs. Assn., Am. Soc. Newspaper Editors (dir.). Congregationalist. Clubs: Royal Order of Snakes, Masons, Elks, Econs, Chgo. Press. Office: Chgo Defender Robert S Abbott Pub Co 2400 S Michigan Chicago IL 60616

SENGSTOCK, CHARLES AUGUST, JR., public relations executive; b. Chgo., Aug. 21, 1932; s. Charles August and Vivian Louise (Comstock) S.; m. Norma Joann Halseth, Oct. 24, 1959. B.S. in Journalism, U. Ill., 1954; postgrad. U. Chgo., 1959-61. Radio announcer, news reporter Sta. WSOY, Decatur, Ill., 1954, 1956-57; news writer, editor Sta. WGN, Chgo., 1957-59; pub. relations assoc. Ill. Inst. Tech. Research Inst., Chgo., 1959-61; dir. pub. relations, dir. mktg. Cenco Instruments Corp. subs. Soiltest, Inc., Chgo., 1961-68; dir. corp. pub. relations Motorola, Inc., Western Region, 1968-73, dir. corp. pub. relations Motorola, Inc., 1973—. Served to lt. U.S. Army, 1954-56. Mem. Pub. Relations Soc. Am. Presbyterian. Office: 1303 E Algonquin Rd Schaumburg IL 60196

SENICA, JAMES PETER, accountant; b. LaSalle, Ill., May 4, 1951; s. Adolph Joseph and Mary Rose (Parola) S. AA, Ill. Valley Community Coll., Oglesby, 1971; BS, U. Ill., 1973; MBA, No. Ill. U., 1978. CPA, Ill. Internal auditor Marshall Field & Co., Chgo., 1973-76; lead fin. analyst Union Oil Calif., Schaumburg, Ill., 1976-77; sr. acct. Hofmann, Imig & Gemberling, LaSalle, 1979-84; mgr. retail acctg. Chris Hoerr & Son Co., East Peoria, Ill., 1984-85; sr. internal auditor Kitchens of Sara Lee, Deerfield, Ill., 1985—; pvt. practice acctg., cons. Oglesby, 1984—; auditor Ill. Valley chpt. ARC, Peru, 1984—. Mem. Am. Inst. CPA's, Ill. Soc. CPA's, Phi Theta Kappa. Democrat. Roman Catholic. Lodge: Elks. Home: 233 E 1st St Oglesby IL 61348

SENN, KATHLEEN ANN, marketing professional; b. La Crosse, Wis., Dec. 7, 1943; d. Hugo George and Sherley Anna (Kroll) S. BS in Sociology and Psychology, U. Wis., La Crosse, 1975; cert. in civil lit., Inst. Paralegal Tng., Phila., 1976. Field rep. Mkt. Research, La Crosse, 1976-81; cons. New Ventures Cons. and Assocs., La Crosse, 1981-86; dir. mktg. Colors for Success, La Crosse, 1986—. Charter mem. Statue of Liberty-Ellis Island Found., N.Y.C., 1984-86; precinct committeewoman La Crosse Dem. Party, 1984; chairperson La Crosse Community Action Program, 1986—; bd. dirs. Wis. Coulee Region Community Action Program, Westby, 1986. Named one of Outstanding Young Women Am., 1979. Mem. La Crosse C. of C. (com. mem. 1984—). Democrat. Adventist. Home: 1817 Kane St La Crosse WI 54603 Office: Colors for Success Rural Rt 3 Viroqua WI 54665

SENNOTT, JOHN STEPHEN, marital and family therapist; b. Richmond Heights, Mo., Jan. 31, 1946; s. John Stephen and Martha Mae (Kern) S.; m. Marcia Joan Lawrence, Aug. 4, 1973; children: John Stephen, Christie Amber, Shane Lawrence, Mark Eric, Kellie Renee. BA, U. Notre Dame, 1969; MSW, St. Louis U., 1975; PhD, Purdue U., 1981. Licensed profl.

counselor, Clin. Mem. Am. Assn. Marriage and Family Therapy, diplomate Am. Acad. Behavioral Medicine; cert. social worker. With Mo. Div. Family Services, Hillsboro, 1969-71; supervisor Mo. Div. Family Services, Union, 1971-73; dist. supr. Mo. Div. Family Services, Boonville, 1975-78; sole practice Jefferson City, 1981—; dir. Profl. Therapy Ctr., Jefferson City, 1986—; Mem. adv. bd. Compassionate Friends, Jefferson City, 1982-86, Chronic Pain Outreach, 1986—; bd. dirs. Council for Drug Free Youth, Jefferson City, 1982—; cons. Cath. Diocese, Jefferson City, 1985-87; mem. staff St. Mary's Health Ctr., Meml. Community Hosp., Charles Still Hosp. YMCA Soccer and basketball coach, 1986—; Little League coach, Jefferson City, 1985. Mem. Am. Assn. for Marriage and Family Therapy, Nat. Assn. Social Workers, Acad. Cert. Social Workers, Mo. Assn. for Marriage and Family Therapy, Mo. Assn. of Social Workers, Gamma Sigma Delta, Omicron Nu. Roman Catholic. Avocoations: travel, racquetball, waterskiing, swimming. Home: 957 Westwood Dr Jefferson City MO 65101 Office: Profl Therapy Ctr 1303 Edgewood Dr Jefferson City MO 65101

SENO, GARY F., accountant; b. Evanston, Ill., Oct. 5, 1956; s. Sebastian B. and Ruth M. (DeJeski) S. BBA, Marquette U., 1978, M in Acctg. Sci., 1986. CPA, Ill. Internal auditor Sunbeam Corp., Oak Brook, Ill., 1978-80; plant acct. Oak Industries, Elkhorn, Wis., 1980-81, acctg. mgr., 1981-82; acct. various orgns., Milw., 1983-86, Bulk Petroleum Corp., Milw., 1986—. Mem. Am. Inst. CPA's, Wis. Inst. CPA's (com. mem. 1981-85, 87—). Roman Catholic. Club: Milw. Fagowee Ski (v.p. 1984-86, pres. 1986-87). Avocations: skiing, Alpine racing, softball, volleyball, reading, bowling. Home: 4141 S 60th St #25 Greenfield WI 53220 Office: Bulk Petroleum Corp PO Box 23427 Milwaukee WI 53224

SENSENBRENNER, FRANK JAMES, JR., congressman; b. Chgo., June 14, 1943; s. Frank James and Margaret Anita (Luedke) S.; m. Cheryl Lynn Warren, Mar. 26, 1977; children: Frank James III, Robert Alan. A.B. in Polit. Sci, Stanford U., 1965; J.D., U. Wis., 1968. Bar: Wis. 1968, U.S. Supreme Ct. 1972. Mem. Wis. Assembly, 1969-75; mem. firm McKay and Martin, Cedarburg., Wis., 1970-75; mem. Wis. State Senate, 1975-79, asst. minority leader, 1977-79; mem. 96th-100th Congresses from 9th Wis. Dist.; mem. House Jud. Com., Select Com. on Narcotics, Sci., Space and Tech. Com. Mem. Am. Philatelic Soc. Republican. Episcopalian. Club: Capitol Hill. Office: 2444 Rayburn House Office Bldg Washington DC 20515

SENSENBRENNER, KENNETH CLARK, dentist; b. Spokane, Wash., Dec. 8, 1948; s. Ralph Debold and Georgia Fern (Clark) S.; m. Joan Elizabeth Froom, June 17, 1972; children: William Kenneth, Kenneth Clark Jr. BS in Aero. and Astronautical Engring., U. Ill., 1972; D of Dental Medicine, So. Ill. U., Edwardsville, 1978. Aero. engr. Rockwell Internat., Los Angeles, 1972-73; engr. Clifford-Jacobs, Champaign, Ill., 1974-75; gen. practice dentistry Champaign, 1978—. Deacon 1st. Presby. Ch., Champaign, 1983-86; bd. dirs. Gamma Zeta chpt. Alpha Tau Omega House Corp., Urbana, Ill., 1983—. Mem. ADA, Ill. state Dental Soc., Illini Dist. Dental Soc. (treas. 1985-86, sec. 1986—). Republican. Lodge: Rotary. Avocations: tennis, physical fitness, travel. Home: 1002 Page Dr Champaign IL 61821 Office: 919 W Kirby Ave Champaign IL 61821

SENSER, SANDRA GERSON, accountant; b. Ashland, Ohio, June 14, 1954; d. Fred M. and Thelma Doris (Kohnop) Gerson; m. Bernard L. Senser, May 29, 1977; children: Aaron Jacob, David Matthew. BS, Miami U., Ohio, 1976. CPA, Ohio. Auditor Ernst & Whinney, Columbus, Ohio, 1976-79; fin. asst. Galion (Ohio) Community Hosp., 1978-80; asst. controller Crestline (Ohio) Hosp., 1981-84, Richland Hosp., Mansfield, Ohio, 1982-84; v.p. CycleMET, inc., Columbus, 1984—; controller MMS, internat., Columbus, 1986—. Early childhood mem. Leo Yassenoff Jewish Ctr., Columbus, 1985-87. Mem. Am. Inst. CPA's, Ohio Soc. CPA's. Jewish. Home: 415 Seranade St Reynoldsburg OH 43068 Office: CycleMET Inc 1061 McKinley Ave Columbus OH 43222

SENTANY, MARKI SUWITA, plastic surgeon; b. Bandung, Indonesia, May 28, 1939. MD, Pajajaran U., Bandung, 1965. Diplomate Am. Bd. Plastic Surgery. Intern Marion County Gen. Hosp., Indpls., 1969-70, resident in gen. surgery, 1970-74; resident in plastic surgery Ind. U. Med. Ctr., Indpls., 1974-76; practice medicine specializing in plastic surgery Indpls., 1976—. Fellow ACS; mem. AMA, Am. Soc. Plastic and Reconstructive Surgeons. Office: 3530 S Keystone Indianapolis IN 46227 Office: 1550 E County Line Rd Indianapolis IN 46227

SENTURIA, RICHARD HARRY, financial planning company executive; b. West Frankfort, Ill., Aug. 14, 1938; s. Irwin J. and Frances (Persow) S.; student So. Ill. U., 1956-57; student Bus. Sch., Washington U., St. Louis, 1957-59, 60-61, Law Sch., 1959-60; m. Ilene M. Bluestein, Dec. 24, 1961; children—Beth, Philip, Laura. From registered rep. to asst. mgr. Dempsey-Tegeler & Co., Inc., St. Louis, 1961-70; asst. mgr. E.F. Hutton & Co., Inc., St. Louis, 1970; sales promotion, research analyst Stix & Co., St. Louis, 1970-74; v.p. in charge sales promotion, tng., seminars, product acquisition, br. mktg. for tax shelter dept. R. Rowland & Co., St. Louis, 1976-79; pres., chief exec. officer Investment Capital Assocs., Creve Coeur, Mo., 1979—; mem. faculty continuing edn. seminar U. Kansas City Dental Sch., 1978; gen. partner Downtown Devel. Assocs., Ltd., 1980—, Riverside Hotel Investments, Ltd., 1981—; v.p. Wharfside Devel. Co., Riverside Landing Parking Systems, Inc.; v.p. mktg. The REal Estate Channel; tchr. numerous adult evening schs., St. Louis area, 1961—. Founding mem., dir. Traditional Congregation of Creve Coeur, 1964-72; bd. dirs. St. Louis chpt. Am. Jewish Congress, 1981—. Served with U.S. Army, 1961-62. Home: 425 Shadybrook Dr Creve Coeur MO 63141 Office: 707 N 2d St Saint Louis MO 63102

SENZAI, MOHAMMAD DAUD, agronomist, educator, researcher; b. Kabul, Afghanistan, Oct. 14, 1941; s. Mir Ahmad and Bibi (Hanifa) S.; m. Hamida Gulpana Kaboojan, June 19, 1969; children—Farid, Fahim, Farhad. B.S., Kabul U., 1965; M.S., Am. U., Beirut, Lebanon, 1968; Ph.D., U. Wis., 1978; postgrad. Internat. Tng. Ctr., Delft, Netherlands, 1970. Teaching and research asst. Kabul U., 1965, instr., 1968-69, asst. prof., 1970-73; agrl. stats. cons., interpreter USAID, Kabul, 1973-74; assoc. prof. agronomy Kabul U., 1978-80; assoc. prof. Wilmington (Ohio) Coll., 1981-83; crop and soil cons., 1984—; cons. IDEA Ctr., Jeddah, Saudi Arabia, 1980. Afghan Govt. scholar, 1961-65; U.S. Govt. scholar, 1965-68, 75-78; Dutch Govt. fellow, 1969-70; FAO fellow, 1973. Mem. Am. Soc. Agronomy, Soil Sci. Soc. Am., Weed Sci. Soc. Am., Afghan Natural Sci., Delta Tau Alpha (advisor). Moslem. Contbr. articles to profl. jours.

SEPPALA, KATHERINE SEAMAN (MRS. LESLIE W. SEPPALA), business executive, clubwoman, b. Detroit, Aug. 22, 1919; d. Willard D. and Elizabeth (Miller) Seaman; B.A., Wayne State U., 1941; m. Leslie W. Seppala, Aug. 15, 1941; children—Sandra Kay, William Leslie. Mgr. women's bldg. and student activities adviser Wayne State U., 1941-43; pres. Harper Sports Shops, Inc., 1947-85, chmn. bd., treas., sec., v.p. 1985—; ptnr. Seppala Bldg. Co., 1971—. Mich. service chmn. women grads. Wayne State U., 1962—, 1st v.p., fund bd., active Mich. Assn. Community Health Services, Inc., Girl and Cub Scouts; mem. Citizen's adv. com. on sch. needs Detroit Bd. Edn., 1957—, mem. high sch. study com., 1966—; chmn., mem. loan fund bd. Denby High Sch. Parents Scholarship; bd. dirs., v.p. Wayne State U. Fund; precinct del. Rep. Party, 14th dist., 1956—, del. convs.; mem. com. Myasthenia Gravis Support Assn. Recipient Am. Women's Service award Wayne State U., 1963. Recipient Alumni award Wayne State U., 1971. Mem. Intercollegiate Assn. Women Students (regional rep. 1941-45), Women Wayne State U. Alumni (past pres.), Wayne State U. Alumni Assn. (dir., past v.p.), AAUW (dir. past officer), Council Women as Public Policy Makers (editor High lights) Denby Community Ednl. Orgn. (sec.), Met. Detroit Program Planning Inst. (pres.), Internat. Platform Assn., Detroit Met. Book and Author Soc. (treas.), Mortar Bd. (past pres.), Karyatides (past pres.), Anthony Wayne Soc., Alpha Chi Alpha, Alpha Kappa Delta, Delta Gamma Chi, Kappa Delta (chmn. chpt. alumnae adv. bd.). Baptist. Clubs: Zonta (v.p., dir.); Detroit Boat; Les Cheneaux. Home: 22771 Worthington Saint Clair Shores MI 48081 Office: 17157 Harper Detroit MI 48224

SEQUEIRA, LUIS, plant pathology educator; b. San Jose, Costa Rica, Sept. 1, 1927; s. Raul and Dora (Jenkins) S.; m. Elizabeth Steinvorth, May 27, 1954; children: Anabel, Marta, Robert, Patricia. AB, Harvard U., 1949, AM, 1950, PhD, 1952. Plant pathologist United Fruit Co., Coto, Costa Rica, 1953-60; research assoc. N.C. State U., Raleigh, 1960-61; prof. plant pathology U. Wis., Madison, 1961-82, J.C. Walker prof., 1982—; cons. Agracetus, Madison, 1982—; mgr. competitive grants program USDA, Washington, 1984-85. Contbr. over 200 articles to profl. jours. Fellow Am. Phytopathological Soc. (editor-in-chief jour. 1979-81, St. Paul sect. v.p. 1984, pres. elect 1985, pres. 1986); mem. Nat. Acad. Scis. Democrat. Roman Catholic. Home: 10 Appomattox Ct Madison WI 53705 Office: U Wis Dept Botany 1630 Linden Dr Madison WI 53706

SEREDA, JOHN WALTER, JR., lawyer, adult education educator; b. Chgo., Dec. 27, 1952; s. John W. and Theresa M. (Karlowicz) S.; m. Sharon Anne Bonior; 1 child, Melissa Ann Therese. BA, DePaul U., 1975, JD, 1978. Bar: Ill. 1978, U.S. Dist. Ct. (no. dist.) Ill. 1978, U.S. Dist. Ct. (no. dist.) Ind. 1978. Assoc. S. David Friedlander, Calumet City, Ill., 1978-81; sole practice, Chgo., 1981— ; instr. adult edn. Prairie State Coll., 1983-85 . Mem. ABA, Ill. State Bar Assn., Chgo. Bar Assn., South Suburban Bar Assn., South West Bar Assn., Trial Bar of U.S. Dist. Ct. Roman Catholic. Office: 11732 S Western Ave Chicago IL 60643

SERGER, GERRY RICHARD, infosystems specialist; b. Cin., May 19, 1959; s. Paul David and Patricia Clair (Adams) S. BS in Psychology, Xavier U., 1981; BS in Computer Sci., 1986. Specialties mgr. Kenna Metal, Cin., 1981-84; systems mgr. Moore, Owen, Thomas & Co., Cin., 1984-87, First Ind. Holding Corp., Cin., 1987—. Club: Parachute (Waynevile, Ohio). Home: 6303 Lisbon Ave Cincinnati OH 45213

SERNETT, RICHARD PATRICK, publishing company executive, lawyer; b. Mason City, Iowa, Sept. 8, 1938; s. Edward Frank and Loretta M. (Cavanaugh) S.; m. Janet Ellen Ward, Apr. 20, 1963; children: Susan Ellen, Thomas Ward, Stephen Edward, Katherine Anne. BBA, U. Iowa, 1960, JD, 1963. Bar: Ill. 1965. With Scott, Foresman & Co., Glenview, Ill., 1963-80, house counsel, asst. sec., 1967-70, sec., legal officer, 1970-80; with SFN Cos. Inc., Glenview, Ill., 1980—, v.p. law, sec., 1980-83, sr. v.p., sec., gen. counsel, 1983-86, exec. v.p. and gen. counsel, 1986—; mem. adv. panel on internat. copyright U.S. Dept. State, 1972-75; bd. dirs. Iowa State U. Broadcasting Corp. Mem. ABA (chmn. copyright div. sect. patent, trademark and copyright law 1972-73), Ill. Bar Assn. (chmn. copyright law com. 1978-79), Chgo. Bar Assn., Am. Patent Law Assn. (chmn. copyright matters com. 1972-73, bd. mgrs. 1981-84), Patent Law Assn. Chgo. (chmn. copyright com. 1972-73, 77-78, bd. mgrs. 1979-81), Copyright Soc. U.S.A. (trustee 1972-75, 77-80), Am. Judicature Soc., Am. Soc. Corporate Secs., Assn. Am. Pubs. (chmn. copyright com. 1972-73, vice chmn. 1973-75), Phi Delta Phi, Phi Kappa Theta. Clubs: Met. (Chgo.); North Shore Country (Glenview, Ill.). Home: 2071 Glendale Ave Northbrook IL 60062 Office: 1900 E Lake Ave Glenview IL 60025

SERPICO, JOSEPH JAMES, distribution company financial officer, accountant; b. Chgo., June 15, 1951; s. Frank and Irene (Sacco) S.; m. Theresa Serpico, Oct. 6, 1979 (div. Feb. 1987); 1 child, Tiffany Lauren; m. Linda Serpico, July 1987. CPA, Ill. Mem. staff, sr. audit acct. Peat, Marwick, Mitchell, Chgo., 1973-77; corp. acctg. mgr. Beeline Fashions, Bensenville, Ill., 1977-81; controller Beeline Fashions, Bensenville, 1981-83, v.p. fin., treas., 1983-85; controller P.C. Network, Inc., Chgo., 1985-86; treas., v.p. ops. Atlas Distbg., Inc., Chgo., 1986—; exec. v.p., bd. dirs. Artistic Impressions, Inc., Lombard, Ill., 1986—; fin. advisor Holy Cross High Sch., River Grove, Ill., 1978—. Treas. St. Williams Parish, Chgo., 1987; advisor Jr. Achievement, Chgo., 1973-78, Coll. Commerce DePaul U., Chgo., 1978-85; pres. St. Williams Sch. Bd., Chgo., 1977-83. Mem. Am. Inst. CPA's, Ill. CPA Soc., Notary Pub. Assn., Lic. Ill. CPA's. Roman Catholic. Club: Chgo. Blackhawks Standby (treas. 1971-75, pres. 1975-78). Avocations: hockey, sports. Office: Atlas Distbg Inc 2122 N Western Chicago IL 60647

SERRA, ANTHONY MICHAEL, nursing home administrator; b. Willoughby, Ohio, June 22, 1940; s. Enrico and Paulina (Schiaffino) S.; m. Carol Frances Heintz, July 22, 1962; children: Lisa Marie, Steven Anthony. BBA, Fenn Coll., 1965. CPA, Ohio. Staff acct. Walthall and Drake CPA's, Cleve., 1962-67; adminstr., exec. dir. Health Hill Hosp., Cleve., 1967-80; adminstr. Madison (Ohio) Village Manor, 1978—; gen. practice acctg., Madison, 1980—. Adminstr. Child Abuse and Neglect Project, Cleve., 1972-74. Mem. Am. Inst. CPA's, Ohio Soc. CPA's, Ohio Health Care Assn., Cleve. Area League for Nursing (bd. dirs. 1976-79). Republican. Roman Catholic. Home: 1845 Ridgewick Dr Wickliffe OH 44092 Office: PO Box 17080 Euclid OH 44117

SERSTOCK, DORIS SHAY, microbiologist, educator; civic worker; b. Mitchell, S.D., June 13, 1926; d. Elmer Howard and Hattie (Christopher) Shay; B.A., Augustana Coll., 1947; postgrad. U. Minn., 1966-67, Duke U., summer 1969, Communicable Disease Center, Atlanta, 1972; m. Ellsworth I. Serstock, Aug. 30, 1952; children—Barbara Anne, Robert Ellsworth, Mark Douglas. Bacteriologist, Civil Service, S.D., Colo., Mo., 1947-52; research bacteriologist U. Minn., 1952-53; clin. bacteriologist Dr. Lufkin's Lab., 1954-55; chief technologist St. Paul Blood Bank of ARC, 1959-65; microbiologist in charge mycology lab. VA Hosp., Mpls., 1968—; instr. Coll. Med. Scis., U. Minn., 1970-79, asst. prof. Coll. Lab. Medicine and Pathology, 1979—. Mem. Richfield Planning Commn., 1965-71, sec., 1968-71. Fellow Augusta Coll.; named to Exec. and Profl. Hall of Fame; recipient Alumni Achievement award Augustana Coll., 1977; Superior Performance award VA Hosp., 1978, 82; Golden Spore award Mycology Observer, 1985. Mem. Am. Soc. Microbiology, N.Y. Acad. Scis., Minn. Planning Assn. Republican. Lutheran. Clubs: Richfield Women's Garden (pres. 1959), Wild Flower Garden (chmn. 1961). Author articles in field. Home: 7201 Portland Ave Richfield MN 55423 Office: VA Hosp Minneapolis MN 55417

SERVER, GREGORY DALE, state legislator, guidance counselor; b. Mpls., Jan. 27, 1939; m. Sandra Witherspoon; 3 children. BA, U. Evansville, Ind., 1962; MS, Ind. State U., 1968, Ind. State U., 1970; EdS, Ind. State U., 1981. Guidance counselor Cen. High Sch., Evansville, 1976; mem. Ind. State Senate, 1973—; bd. dirs. Sta. WNIN-TV. Mem. New Harmony (Ind.) Commn. Served with USN. Mem. Edn. Commn. of States, Evansville Tchrs. Assn., VFW, Phi Delta Kappa. Republican. Methodist. Home: 640 Dexter Ave Evansville IN 47714

SERVOSE, DOUGLAS MICHAEL, oil company executive; b. Detroit, Sept. 10, 1953; s. Albert George and Pauline (Menoian) S.; m. Irene Elizabeth Daszkiewycz, Aug. 25, 1984. Student, Northwestern U., 1971-74; BS ChemE, U. Mich., 1975; MBA, Baldwin-Wallace Coll., 1984. Engr. Standard Oil Co., Cleveland, 1975-77; sr. engr. Standard Oil Co., Cleve., 1977-79, sr. supply planning analyst, 1979-81, tech. project leader, 1981-83, mgr. linear programming applications, 1983—. Advisor Jr. Achievement, 1982, 83; active local pub. television, Cystic Fibrosis Found. mem. Westwood Acres Homeowners Assn., Westlake, Ohio. Roman Catholic. Home: 24627 Wildwood Dr Westlake OH 44145 Office: The Standard Oil Co 200 Public Sq Cleveland OH 44114

SERWY, ROBERT ANTHONY, accountant; b. Chgo., Mar. 26, 1950; s. Anthony J. and bernice (Zubek) S.; m. Margaret A. Smejkal, Aug. 12, 1972; children: Karen, Steven. BS in Engring., U. Ill., 1972; M Mgmt., Northwestern U., 1974. Mgr. cons. Arthur Andersen & Co., Chgo., 1974-83; dir. fin. planning Teepak, Inc., Oak Brook, Ill., 1983-85; sr. mgr. cons. Peat Marwick & Mitchell, Chgo., 1985-86; dir. cons. Warady & Davis, Lincolnwood, Ill., 1986—. F.C. Austin scholar, 1972. Mem. Am. Inst. CPA's, Ill. CPA Soc. Roman Catholic. Avocations: amateur radio, microcomputers, football. Home: 721 Valley Rd Lake Forest IL 60045 Office: Warady & Davis 7383 N Lincoln Ave Lincolnwood IL 60646

SESTINA, JOHN E., fin. planner; b. Cleve., Mar. 17, 1942; s. John J. and Regina Sestina; B.S., U. Dayton, 1965; M.S. in Fin. Service, Am. Coll, 1982; m. Mary Barbara Jezek, Dec. 20, 1970; 1 dau., Alison. Cert. fin. planner, chartered fin. cons. With Sestina and Assocs., Inc., Columbus, Ohio, 1967—. Mem. Soc. Ind. Fin. Advisers (past pres., Fin. Planner of Yr. award 1982), Internat. Assn. Fin. Planners, Nat. Assn. Personal Fin. Advisors (pres.), Inst. Cert. Fin. Planners. Author: Complete Guide to Professional Incorporation, 1970; contbr. articles to profl. jours.; contbr. weekly fin. planning segment AM Columbus, WOSU-AM, 1979—. Office: 3726 Olentangy River Rd Columbus OH 43214

SESTRIC, ANTHONY JAMES, lawyer; b. St. Louis, June 27, 1940; s. Anton and Marie (Gasparovic) S.; student, Georgetown U., 1958-62; JD, Mo. U., 1965; m. Carol F. Bowman, Nov. 24, 1966; children: Laura Antonette, Holly Nicole, Michael Anthony. Bar: Mo. 1965, U.S. Ct. Appeals (8th cir.) 1965, U.S. Dist. Ct. Mo., 1966, U.S. Tax Ct. 1969, U.S. Supreme Ct. 1970, U.S. Ct. Appeals (7th cir.) 1984, U.S. Dist. Ct. (no. dist.) Tex. 1985, U.S. Claims Ct. 1986. Law clk. U.S. Dist. Ct., St. Louis, 1965-66; ptnr. firm Sestric, McGhee & Miller, St. Louis, 1966-77, Fordyce & Mayne, 1977-78; spl. asst. to Mo. atty. gen., St. Louis, 1968; hearing officer St. Louis Met. Police Dept. Contbr. articles to profl. jours. Mem. St. Louis Air Pollution Bd. Appeals and Varience Rev., 1966-73, chmn., 1968-73; mem. St. Louis Airport Commn., 1975-76; dist. vice chmn. Boy Scouts Am., 1970-76; bd. dirs. Full Achievement, Inc., 1970-77, pres., 1972-77; bd. dirs. Legal Aid Soc. of St. Louis, 1976-77, Law Library Assn. St. Louis, 1976-78; v.p. bd. St. Elizabeth Acad., 1985-86. Mem. ABA (state chmn. judiciary com. 1973-75, circuit chmn. com. condemnation, zoning and property use 1975-77, standing com. bar activities 1982—), Mound City Bar Assn., Chgo. Bar Assn., Fed. Bar Assn., Lawyers Assn., Mo. Assn. Trial Attys., Am. Judicature Soc., Mo. Bar (vice chmn. young lawyers sect. 1973-76, bd. govs. 1974-77), Bar Assn. Met. St. Louis (chmn. young lawyers sect. 1974-75, exec. com. 1974-83, pres. 1981-82). Club: Mo. Athletic. Home: 3967 Holly Hills Blvd Saint Louis MO 63116 Office: 1015 Locust St Saint Louis MO 63101

SETHNESS, CRAIG ALLAN, software engineer; b. Evanston, Ill., Feb. 22, 1952; s. William Henry and Margaret (Jeffery) S.; m. Donna Christine Sansone, July 5, 1975; children: Lauren, Jennifer, Christopher, Daniel. Student, Tex. Christian U., 1970-73. Asst. to v.p. ops. Great Lakes Corp., Chgo., 1973-74; systems analyst NCR Corp., Niles, Ill., 1974-78; pres., chief exec. officer CAS Enterprises, Inc., Northbrook, Ill., 1978—; bd. dirs. Data Services-The Bureans. Explorer advisor Boy Scouts Am., Wilmette, Ill., 1974-82, mem. dist. com., 1982—. Republican. Avocations: camping, computers, photography, scouting. Office: CAS Enterprises Inc 1717 Central Evanston IL 60201

SETTLES, JERI LYNN (ENGLE), food services executive; b. Oklahoma City, Dec. 23, 1955; d. Jerry and Darlene (Woodside) E. BS in Community Heath, Pub. Safety and Sch. Health and Safety, U. Ill., 1979. Prevention/edn. specialist Aurora (Ill.) Drug Program, 1979-80; case worker family intervention program Grundy/Kendall Ednl. Service Region, Morris, Ill., 1980-84; asst. mgr. Wendy's Internat., Morris, 1984-85; account exec. Federated Foods Inc., Arlington Heights, Ill., 1985—. Chmn. youth com. ARC, Morris, 1984-85; bd. dirs. Joliet (Ill.) Area Operation Snowball, 1980—, Morris, Joliet, Yorkville, Ill.; chairperson personnel policy revision comn. Guardian Angel Home, Joliet, 1983—. Named one of Outstanding Young Women of Am., 1982-84; Pub. Affairs scholar Ill. Gen. Assembly, 1974-77. Mem. Nat. Assn. Female Execs. Avocations: sailing, clothing, design, cross-country skiing, backpacking. Office: Federated Foods Inc 3025 W Salt Creek Ln Arlington Heights IL 60005-1096

SETTLES, JOSEPH HAYS, chemical engineer; b. Clarksville, Ind., May 14, 1954; s. Paul Wathen and Betsy Ann (Hays) S. BA in Chemistry, Vanderbilt U., 1976; MS in Chem. Engring., U. Ky., 1981. Research assoc. CPC Internat., Argo, Ill., 1981-83, chem. engring. team leader, 1983-84, instrumentation engr., 1985, team leader, 1986. Vol. League of Women Voters, 1979. Mem. Am. Inst. Chem. Engrs., Nat. Honor Soc., Nat. Beta Club. Republican. Avocations: student piloting, stamp collecting, classic car collecting, electronics, tennis. Home: 1539 S 61st Ave Cicero IL 60650 Office: CPC Internat 6500 Archer Ave Summit-Argo IL 60501

SEWALL, EDWARD REEVES, manufacturing company executive; b. Mpls., Dec. 20, 1927; s. Edward Bradstreet and Lorena (Reeves) S.; m. Barbara Overton, Apr. 21, 1951; children—Stephen, Katherine, David. B.S., Yale U., 1950. With Sewall Gear Mfg. Co., St. Paul, 1951—, v.p., 1965-80, exec. v.p., 1980—; dir. GMI, Ltd., Bermuda. Bd. dirs. YMCA. Mem. Am. Gear Mfrs. Assn. (pres. 1983-84). Republican. Presbyterian. Clubs: North Oaks Golf (St. Paul). Home: 148 W Pleasant Lake Rd North Oaks MN 55110 Office: 705 Raymond Ave Saint Paul MN 55114

SEWARD, JEFFREY JAMES, lawyer, protective services official; b. Rochester, Pa., Aug. 21, 1953; s. Kelson Charles and Virginia Emma (McConnell) S. BA, Ohio No. U., 1975, JD, 1986; MS, U. Nebr., 1979. Bar: Nebr. 1987. Security cons. North Hills Passavant Hosp., Pitts., 1975-77; state trooper Nebr. State Patrol, Omaha, 1977-84; sole practice Omaha, 1986—; cons. Fire Photo Corp., Omaha, 1980—; instr. law enforcement State Nebr., 1979—; technician hazardous material Nebr. State Patrol, 1979—; investigator accidents Nebr. State Patrol, 1978—; adj. faculty U. Nebr., Omaha. Law Enforcement Assistance Adminstrn. scholar, 1978; recipient Life Saving award Am. Heart Assn., 1982, Am. Jurisprudence award Bancroft-Whitney Co., 1986, 87. Mem Nat. Assn. Chiefs of Police, State Troopers Assn. Nebr., Peace Officers Assn. Nebr., Am. Trial Lawyers Assn., ABA, Delta Theta Phi. Republican. Methodist. Lodge: Masons. Avocation: car collecting. Home and Office: 9921 Broadmoor Rd Omaha NE 68114

SEWARD, JOHN EDWARD, JR., insurance company executive; b. Kirksville, Mo., June 12, 1943; s. John Edward and Ruth Carol (Connell) S.; B.S. in Fin., St. Joseph's Coll., 1968; children—Mitch, Justina. Mgr. acctg. services Guarantee Res. Life Ins. Co., Hammond, Ind., 1964-69; asst. controller Gambles Ins. Group, Mpls., 1969-71, N.Am. Cos., Chgo., 1971-73; pres., dir. mem. exec. com. Home & Auto. Ins. Co., Chgo., 1975-83; pres. and chief exec. officer, dir., mem. exec. com. Universal Fire & Casualty Ins. Co., 1983—; Park Lane Ins. Agy., Bd. dirs. Calumet Council Boy Scouts Am., 1979-85, Teddy Bear Club for Shriners Hosp., 1979-81, Chgo. Baseball Cancer Charities, 1981—. F.L.M.I., C.L.U., C.P.C.U. Home: 9549 Prairie Ave Highland IN 46322 Office: 730 W 45th St Munster IN 46321

SEWARD, STEVEN LEMAR, optometrist; b. Ft. Wayne, Ind., Oct. 26, 1946; s. George Winn and Eva (Olive) S.; m. Dorothy Lamar, Mar. 17, 1968 (div. 1977); children: Heidi Elaine, James Lemar; m. Debra Stickles, Nov. 11, 1978; 1 child, Robert Nathaniel. AB in Math., Knox Coll., 1968; OD, Ohio State U., 1972, MS in Physiol. Optics, 1972. Cert. Ocular Disease and Treatment. Pvt. practice optometry North Manchester, Ind., 1972—. Bd. dirs. Wabash County United Fund, pres., 1978; sec. North Manchester Community Found., 1982-84, pres., 1985—; mgr. Kiwanis Little League baseball team, 1981-83; active Zion Luth. Ch. Council, 1974-80, sec., 1977. Fellow Am. Coll. Optometric Physicians, Am. Acad. Optometry; mem. Am. Optometric Assn. (adv. com. 1979-83, recognition award), Gesell Inst. Child Devel., Ind. C. of C., Ind. Pub. Health Assn., Am. Pub. Health Assn., Better Vision Inst., Vol. Optometric Services for Humanity, Wabash Valley Optometric Soc. (pres. 1977-78), Nat. Acad. Sports Vision, Ind. Optometry Assn. (v.p. 1981-82, pres. 1983-84, chmn. and del. various coms., citation 1978), Coll. Optometrists Vision Devel. (assoc.), Beta Sigma Kappa. Republican. Lodges: Masons, Shriners, Optimists (chmn. 1985). Avocation: golf. Home: 1604 Hillcrest Dr North Manchester IN 46962 Office: Optometric Assocs Inc State Rd 114E RR3 North Manchester IN 46962

SEWELL, JAMES THOMAS, minister, educator; b. Lubbock, Tex., Jan. 8, 1942; s. O.D. and Mary Jane (McMahon) S.; m. Linda Kay Morgan, June 8, 1963; children: Kathryn, Mark, Sharon. Grad. theology, Bapt. Bible Coll., Springfield, Mo., 1963; BA, Garland (Tex.) Bible Coll., 1965; MRE, MDiv, Temple Bapt. Theol. Sem., Chattanooga, 1968; PhD, Bob Jones U., Greenville, S.C., 1972. Prof. Bapt. Bible Coll., 1972—, chmn. edn. dept., 1975-79, dir. div. bibl. studies, 1979—; minister edn. Park Crest Bapt. Ch., Springfield, 1973—. Author: The Lesser Lights, 1977, Degrees For The Christian Ministry, 1980. Mem. Bapt. Bible Coll. Alumni Assn. (favorite faculty 1975, 79). Avocations: computers, fishing, camping. Home: 3033 S Ferguson Springfield MO 65807 Office: Bapt Bible Coll 628 E Kearney Springfield MO 65807

SEXAUER, ROBERT S., agricultural products company executive. Pres., treas. Sexauer Co., Brookings, S.D. Office: Sexauer Co 100 Main Ave Box 58 Brookings SD 57006 *

SEXSON, RICHARD WAYNE, accountant; b. Indpls., Apr. 26, 1949; s. Richard Wayne Sr. and Norma Jean (Lloyd) S.; m. Peggy Lee Brown, June

21, 1979. BS, Purdue U., 1971. CPA, cert. fin. planner. Revenue agt. IRS, Indpls., 1975-79; acct. various acctg. firms, Indpls., 1979-82, R.W. Sexson, CPA, Indpls., 1982—. Mem. Am. Inst. CPAs, Ind. CPA Soc. (chmn. tax com. 1987—), Internat. Assn. Fin. Planners, Mensa. Avocations: karate, tennis. Home: 3729 Barrington Dr Carmel IN 46032 Office: 10333 N Meridian St #120A Indianapolis IN 46290

SEXTON, DAVID LLOYD, family therapist; b. Toronto, Ont., Can., Mar. 20, 1937; came to U.S., 1958; s. Walter D. and Dorothy (Bennet) S.; m. Brenda C. Lawlor, Jan. 17, 1961; children: Heather, Cynthia, Mary Elizabeth. BS, George Williams Coll., 1962; MSW, U. Ill., Chgo., 1964. Chief social work dept. Our Lady of Mercy Hosp., Dyer, Ind., 1964-68; clinical social worker Valparaiso (Ind.) U., 1967-71; pvt. practice psychology Cen. for Psychol. Services, Chicago Heights, Ill., 1964-71, Valparaiso Neuropsychiat. Inst., 1967-75; owner, psychotherapist family counseling clinic Valparaiso, 1975—. Fellow Am. Orthopsychiat. Assn., Am. Assn. Marital and Family Therapy; mem. Nat. Assn. Social Workers, Acad. Cert. Social Workers. Office: 1507 Roosevelt Rd Valparaiso IN 46383

SEYMOUR, CHARLES WILLIAM, computer systems analyst; b. Greensboro, N.C., June 27, 1928; s. William Baulch and Pearle J. (Desper) S.; m. Anne Piskla, Dec. 15, 1951 (div. July 1980); children: Charles William, Paul Randolph; m. Sharon Lynn Gruenberg, July 14, 1980; children; Brian Daniel, Travis Aaron. Student, Coll. Hampton Rds., 1965-69, Coll. William and Mary, 1969-70, Keys Bus. Coll., 1979-83. Computer specialist U.S. Army Civil Service, Ft. Monroe, Va., 1952-83; systems analyst Dept. Mental Health, Lansing, Mich., 1984—; instr. Davenport Coll., Lansing, 1983-84, Lansing Community Coll., 1984-85. Served as cpl. USAF, 1947-50. Avocations: spectator sports, video taping, music. Home: 3406 Danbury Crossroad Lansing MI 48910 Office: Dept Mental Health Lewis Cass Bldg Lansing MI 48926

SEYMOUR, ROBERT KENNETH, architect; b. Detroit, Nov. 27, 1948; s. Kenneth John and Ann Margaret (Nikolits) S. BArch magna cum laude, U. Detroit, 1973, MArch, 1974. Draftsman W.P. Lindhout, Livonia, Mich., 1965-66; draftsman, designer Architects Assoc., Southfield, Mich., 1970-71, 73; designer Hubble, Roth & Clark, Bloomfield Hills, Mich., 1971-72; designer, job capt. Clark W. Corey, Westland, Mich., 1973; cons. designer Cement Enamel Devel., Redford, Mich., 1973-74; prin. Robert K. Seymour, Architect, Livonia, 1975—. Author: Hill House Documentation, 1978. Archtl. advisor Hist. Commn., Livonia, 1976-81; chmn. Detroit United Railway Sta. Restoration Com., Livonia, 1977-79; chmn. Hist. Preservation Commn., Livonia, 1978-80; adv. Bldg. Trades Adv. Com., Livonia, 1980—. Recipient Mayor's proclamation City of Livonia, 1982, cert. of honor Am. Soc. Body Engrs., Detroit, 1966, Design award City of Southfield (Mich.), 1987. Mem. AIA, Mich. Soc. Architects, Assn. for Preservation Tech., Nat. Council Archtl. Registration Bds. (cert.), Livonia Hist. Soc. (Heritage award 1984), Blue Key (life). Club: 1st Pa. Regiment (Livonia) (founder, pres. 1974-83). Avocations: hunting, fishing, wood carving, photography.

SHABAZ, JOHN C., federal judge; b. West Allis, Wis., June 25, 1931; s. Cyrus D. and Harriet T.; children: Scott J., Jeffrey J. Student, U. Wis., 1949-53, Marquette U., 1953-54; LL.B., Marquette U., 1957. Sole practice West Allis, Wis., 1957-81; mem. Wis. Ho. of Reps., 1967-81; judge U.S. Dist. Ct. (we. dist.) Wis., 1981—. Office: US District Court PO Box 2687 Madison WI 53701 *

SHACKEL, NEAL FREDERICK, program director; b. Chgo., Nov. 17, 1951; s. Lester Clifford and Dorothy Alice (Morlock) S., m. Nancy Jo Stanton, Dec. 16, 1977; children: Jaime Elizabeth, Erin Lynne. BS in Math, Western Ill. U., 1973, MS in Student Personnel Services, 1975; MBA, Rosary Coll., 1984. Mgr. fin., ins. Joe Jacob Chevrolet, Wilmette, Ill., 1975-76; dir. student residential program Concordia Coll., River Forest, Ill., 1977-79, ops. mgr., 1979—. Chmn. bd. stewardship St. John Luth. Ch. Mo. Synod, Forest Pk., Ill., 1985-86. Named one of Outstanding Young Men of Am., 1985. Mem. Assn. Physical Plant Adminstrs., Nat. Assn. Coll. & U. Bus. Officers. Avocations: residential remodeling, softball, bowling, golf.

SHACKELFORD, DOUGLAS ANDREW, industrial contracting and distributing company executive; b. Columbus, Ohio, Jan. 13, 1948; s. Joseph Andrew and Juanita Belle (Welling) S.; B.A. in Biology and Chemistry, Ohio Dominican Coll., 1973; m. Mary Jo Hatem, Dec. 14, 1968; children—Joseph Jonathan, Andrew. Maintainance mgr. Allen Refractories Co., Columbus, 1970-74, job foreman, 1974-76; tech. adv. refractories CE Cast Indsl. Products, Inc., Oak Park, Ill., 1976-78, sales rep., Wis., 1978-80; br. mgr. Jay L. Angel, Inc., Lima, Ohio, 1980—, corp. sales mgr., 1981—; now dist. rep. indsl. water treatment div. Nalco Chem. Co., Naperville, Ill. Bd. dirs. St. Vincent's Children's Center, Columbus, 1976-78, St. Francis Children's Activity and Achievement Center, Milw., 1978-80; mem. endowment com. St. Coletta Sch., Jefferson, Wis. Mem. Am. Foundrymen's Soc. (chmn. apprenticeship com. Southeastern Wis. chpt. 1979-80).

SHACKELFORD, JAMES HUBERT, counseling center administrator; b. Durham, N.C., Feb. 18, 1945; s. Emmett William and Mary (Herring) S.; m. Mary Jane Bolton, Sept. 6, 1966 (div. Dec. 1975); m. Darlene Mae Mackeben, Dec. 17, 1983; children: Julie Christine, Elizabeth Ann. BA, Davidson Coll., 1967; M in Theology, U. Chgo., 1969, MA, 1970, PhD, 1975. Diplomate Am. Assn. Pastoral Counselors; lic. psychologist, Ill. Asst. prof. religion and psychology McMurray Coll., Abilene, Tex., 1972-75; resident Inst. Religion and Human Devel., Houston, 1975-76; sr. staff counselor Pastoral Psychotherapy Inst., Park Ridge, Ill., 1976-79, coordinator Perissos Inst., 1978-81, dir. edn. tng., 1981-84, dir., 1984-86; dir. Parkside Counseling and Psychotherapy Ctr., Park Ridge, 1986—. Contbr. articles to profl. jours. Mem. Am. Assn. Marriage and Family Therapy (supr.). Democrat. Presbyterian. Home: 215 Elm Ct Livertyville IL 60048 Office: Pastoral Psychotherapy Inst 1875 Dempster Suite 360 Park Ridge IL 60068

SHADDID, W(OODROW) WILLIAM, manager; b. Bloomington, Ill., June 10, 1945; s. Woodrow George and Gertrude Ellen (Whitenack) S.; m. Jean Carol Ward, June 25, 1966; 1 child, Bonnil Jill. Student, Ill. State U., 1963-85. Draftsman Eureka Co., Bloomington, 1966-68; designer Harris Corp., Quincy, Ill., 1968-73; mech. engr. Sono-Mag Corp., Bloomington, 1973-76; purchasing mgr. DMI, Inc., Goodfield, Ill., 1976-84, Internat. Tapetronics Corp. div 3M Co., Bloomington, 1984—. Served with U.S. Army, 1967. Mem. Nat. Assn. Purchasing Mgrs. (bd. dirs. Cen. Ill. chpt. 1984-87), Am. Radio Relay League. Republican. Episcopalian. Lodge: Masons. Avocations: amateur radio, astronomy, music. Office: Internat Tapetronics Corp 3 M 2425 S Main St Bloomington IL 61761

SHADIS, VINCENT FRANCIS, advertising executive; b. Chgo., June 9, 1962; s. Frank Stanley and Dolores Elizabeth (Rusin) S. BA, No. Ill. U., 1984. Sr. copywriter Standard Rate & Data Service, Wilmette, Ill., 1984—; cons. Agent Prodns., Chgo., 1982—. Democrat. Roman Catholic. Avocations: bicycling, golfing, writing. Office: Standard Rate & Data Service Inc 3004 Glenview Rd Wilmette IL 60091

SHADUR, MILTON I., judge; b. St. Paul, June 25, 1924; s. Harris and Mary (Kaplan) S.; m. Eleanor Pilka, Mar. 30, 1946; children: Robert, Karen, Beth. B.S., U. Chgo., 1943, J.D. cum laude, 1949. Bar: Ill. 1949, U.S. Supreme Ct. 1957. Sole practice Chgo., 1949-80; assoc. Goldberg, Devoe & Brussel, 1949-51; ptnr. Shadur, Drupp & Miller and predecessor firms, 1951-80; judge U.S. Dist. Ct. (no. dist.) Ill., Chgo., 1980—; commr. Ill. Supreme Ct. Character and Fitness, 1961-72, chmn., 1971; gen. counsel Ill. Jud. Inquiry Bd., 1975-80. Editor-in-chief: U. Chgo. Law Rev., 1948-49. Chmn. visiting com. U. Chgo. Law Sch., 1971-76, bd. dirs. Legal Assistance Found. Chgo., 1972-78; trustee Village of Glencoe, 1969-74, Ravinia Festival Assn., 1976—, mem. exec. com. Served to lt. (j.g.) USNR, 1943-46. Fellow Am. Bar Found.; mem. ABA (spl. com. on youth edn. for citizenship 1975-79), Ill. State Bar Assn. (joint com. on rules of jud. conduct 1974), Chgo. Bar Assn. (chmn. legis. com. 1963-65, jud. com. 1970-71, profl. ethics com. 1975-76, sec. 1967-69), Chgo. Council Lawyers, Order of Coif. Office: US Dist Ct 219 Dearborn St Chicago IL 60604 *

SHADWICK, STEVEN ALEXANDER, optometrist; b. Newark, Ohio, Feb. 20, 1958; s. Jan and Emily (Smajkiewicz) S.; m. Beth Belinda Brooks, June 25, 1983. BA in Zoology, Miami U., Oxford, Ohio, 1980; BS in Physiological Optics, Ohio State U., 1982, OD, 1984. Assoc. Dr. Frank Bickle & Assoc., Mansfield, Ohio, 1984-85; pvt. practice optometry Middletown, Ohio, 1985—. Mem. Am. Optometric Assn., Ohio Optometric Assn. Avocations: racquetball, tennis, swimming, camping. Home: 337 Wexford Way Monroe OH 45050 Office: 701 N University Blvd Middletown OH 45042

SHAFER, DENNIS W., management consultant, small business owner; b. Des Moines, Oct. 10, 1945; s. Floyd H. and Mildred (Sydness) S.; m. Patricia Jo Patrice, Sept. 9, 1967; children: Michael, Steven, David. BSEE, Iowa State U., 1967; MBA, U.S. Internat. U., 1969. Territory mgr. Memorex, Mpls., 1969-70; dir. mktg. Sci. Computers, Mpls., 1971-73, Van Dale Inc., Mpls., 1974-77, Toro Inc., Mpls., 1977-80; group v.p. Wagner Inc., Mpls., 1980-85; gen. ptnr. Venture Resource Group, Mpls., 1986-87; pres. Ameripro, Inc., Mpls., 1987—. Author: Pioneering New Products, 1986-87; also articles. Served to lt. (j.g.) USN, 1967-69. Mem. Am. Mktg. Assn. Avocations: sailing, skiing, jogging. Office: Ameripro Inc 684 Excelsior Blvd Excelsior MN 55331

SHAFER, JON MERVIN, writer, farm manager; b. Lima, Ohio, Nov. 15, 1944; s. Howard Lewis and Emma Lois (Day) S.; m. Linda Jo Smith, July 3, 1968 (div. 1972); m. Rebecca Ellen McDowell, Jan. 1, 1983. Student, Regional Council for Internat. Edn., Basel, Switzerland, 1965-66; B.A., Ohio No. U., 1967; M.A., U. Minn., 1977. Mem. community faculty Metro State U., St. Paul, 1972-77; dir. cable project Am. Friends Service Com., Mpls., 1973; dir. communications program Metro Council, St. Paul, 1974-77; farmer Shafer Family Farm, Cloverdale, Ohio, 1979-86 ; instr. Defiance Coll., Ohio, 1980; dir. Putnam County Council on Aging, Ottawa, Ohio, 1983-85; fundraiser Neighbors East and West, Richmond, Ind., 1987—; cons. in field. Author: Annotated Bibliography on Cable Television, 1972, 6 edits.; (booklet) Education and Cable TV: A Guide, 1973; Toward A Sustainable Ohio, 1982; co-editor The Continental Centennial Book, 1986. Contbr. chpts. to books, articles to profl. jours. Trustee, Community Action Commn., Findlay, Ohio, 1983-85. Ohio No. U. Acad. scholar, 1963-67; named Hon. Ohio Green Thumber, Ohio Green Thumb, 1984. Mem. Ohio Farmers Union (state del. 1984-85), Ohio Ecol. Food and Farm Assn. (v.p. 1980, 85). Democrat. Quaker. Address: 207 Lincoln St Richmond IN 47374

SHAFF, MARLYS ANNA, librarian, media coordinator; b. Alvord, Iowa, June 14; d. Louis Matthew and Anna Hilda Margaret (Mundt) Kroger; m. Harold A. Shaff, June 18, 1947; children: William Louis, Robert Harold, Lynda LuAnne Shaff Lee. BA, Sioux Falls (S.D.) Coll., 1972; MA, U. S.D., 1979. Tchr. Lyon County Sch., Inwood, Iowa, 1944-48; librarian Winner Pub. (S.D.) Sch., 1972—. Cub Scout Leader Boy Scouts Am., Sioux Falls, 1959-62, Girl Scouts Am., Sioux Falls, 1960-69; Sunday Sch. tchr. St. John's Luth. Ch., Sioux Falls, 1962-76; vol. Meals on Wheels, Sioux Falls, 1984; v.p. S.D. State Reading Council, 1983-86, pres. 1986—. Recipient Literacy award Mo. Valley Reading Council, Winner, 1982, S.D. State Reading Council, 1982. Mem. NEA, S.D. Edn. Assn., Winner Edn. Assn. (sec. 1978-79), Bus. and Profl. Women Assn. (scholarship com. 1986), Alpha Delta Kappa. Lodge: Lioness.

SHAFFER, ALFRED GARFIELD, service organization executive; b. Sunbury, Pa., Jan. 5, 1939; d. Alfred G. and Betty Marjorie (Vogel) S.; m. Nancy Jane Dawson, Aug. 29, 1976. B.S., Susquehanna U., 1961. Cert. tchr., Pa. Tchr., Danville Sch. Dist. (Pa.), 1962-69; mgr. club service Kiwanis Internat., Chgo., 1969-74, dir. program devel., 1974-81, dir. program services, Indpls., 1982-85, dir. spl. services, 1985—; corp. affairs cons. Nat. Easter Seal Soc., Chgo., 1981-82; adminstr. Circle K Internat., Chgo., 1982; mem. Pres.'s Com. on Employment of Handicapped, 1983-86; sec. Kiwanis Club of Northwest Indpls., 1983-86. Chmn. adv. council 70001 Ltd., Indpls., 1984—. Named Kiwanian of Yr., 1966, 85; recipient Gold Key of Service, Pa. Dist. Key Clubs, 1964; Outstanding Service Kiwanis Club, Chgo., 1981. Lutheran. Lodges: Kiwanis (Selinsgrove, Pa.; pres. 1964; lt. gov. Pa. 1966-67; pres. Chgo. 1970-72). Home: 5688 N Broadway Indianapolis IN 46220 Office: Kiwanis Internat 3636 Woodview Trace Indianapolis IN 46268

SHAFFER, CLIFTON EUGENE, JR., bank executive; b. Akron, Aug. 10, 1931; s. Clifton Eugene Sr. and Flossie Ruth (Whippo) S.; m. Karole Lee Shank, Feb. 22, 1985; children: Lisa Marie, Jennifer K., C. Andrew. BA in Music, U. Akron, 1954. Asst. v.p. Evans Savs. Assn., Akron, 1957-69; v.p. Centran Bank, Akron, 1969-86, Society Bank, Akron, 1986—. Student adv., U. Akron, 1980—. Mem. Bldg. Owners and Mgrs. Assn. (bd. dirs. 1980—). Republican. Avocation: amateur radio. Home: 1837 Guss Ave Akron OH 44312 Office: Society Bank 157 S Main St Akron OH 44308

SHAFFER, HARRY GARD, JR., advertising executive; b. Clearfield, Pa., Apr. 6, 1932; s. Harry Gard and Harriet (McCloskey) S.; m. Janet Evelyn Bayliss, Nov. 10, 1961 (div. Apr. 1972); children—Lynne, Harry Gard III, Karen; m. Geraldine Louise Adams, Dec. 12, 1976. B.S., U. Hawaii, 1957. Account exec. K.M. & G., Inc., Pitts., 1959-61; account supr. Sykes Advt., Inc., Pitts., 1961-64; v.p., media dir. Carlton Advt. Co., Pitts., 1964-70; account supr. M & F Advt., Inc., Cleve., 1970-72; exec. v.p. Palm & Patterson, Cleve., 1972-78; pres. Shaffer Shaffer Shaffer, Cleve., 1979—; exec. sec. Florists Assn. of Greater Cleve., 1976—. Creative dir. TV program Singing Angels Sing America, 1975 (Best TV Entertainment Spl. award). Recipient 6 Nat. Telly awards, 7 Silver dNat. Microphone awards, various others in field. Capt. Hawaii Olympic Ocean Swimming and Surfing Team, Melbourne, Australia, 1956; pub. relations dir. Swimming Hall of Fame, Fort Lauderdale, Fla., 1967-71. Served with USMC, 1951-54. Recipient Bronze medal Australian Surf Life Sav. Assn. Mem. Mensa. Republican. Presbyterian. Clubs: Singing Angels, Cleve. Ad; Pitts. Ad, Pitts. Athletic. Lodge: Masons, Shriners. Home: 10301 Lake Ave Apt 222 Cleveland OH 44102 Office: Shaffer Shaffer Shaffer Inc 226 Hanna Bldg Cleveland OH 44115

SHAFFER, JANE REGINA, association executive; b. Peoria, Ill., June 4, 1933; d. Archie Henry and Ethel Ruth (Pedreyra) Hall; student Bradley U., Peoria, 1951-53; m. Roy Alvin Shaffer, Jan. 31, 1955; children—Jamie, Roy, Shawn. Sec.-treas., Diverco Corp., Winter Haven, Fla., 1957-70, Mansysco Corp., Peoria, 1970-72; dir. adminstrn. and mktg. Winona Sch. Profl. Photography, Mt. Prospect, Ill., 1972—. Chmn., Beautification Com. Winter Haven, 1968-69. Mem. Am. Photog. Artistans Guild, Nat. Assn. Female Execs., Nat. Soc. Assn. Execs., Nat. Mgmt. Assn. Democrat. Roman Catholic. Club: St. Mary's Women's. Home: 7500 Elmhurst Rd #30 Des Plaines IL 60018 Office: 350 N Wolf Rd Mount Prospect IL 60056

SHAFFER, JERRY LEE, data processing executive; b. Rochester, Ind., Mar. 2, 1958; s. Dee Ward and Aletha Marcielle (Sanders) S.; m. Sharon Elaine Wallace, Aug. 13, 1977; children: Amanda Sue, Christopher Michael. AAS in Computer Tech., Purdue U., 1981, AAS in Supr., 1982. Data control clk. Parkview Hosp., Ft. Wayne, Ind., 1979-81, data control specialist, 1981-82, info. ctr. cons., 1982-86, info. ctr. mgr., 1986-87; microcomputer cons. Software Shoppe (Shaffer Industries), Ft. Wayne, 1984-87; specialist micro-computers Trans World Airlines, Kansas City, Mo., 1987—. Mem. No. Ind. Info. Ctr. Users Group (pres. 1985-87). Home: 4901 NW 67th St Kansas City MO 64151

SHAFFER, KAREN KNICK, information management educator; b. Piqua, Ohio, July 12, 1942; s. Donald Delos and Eunice Vernaine (Jenkins) Knick; m. David Allen Shaffer, Feb. 1, 1964; children: Kelly Renae, David Bradley, Kristin Marie. BS, Miami U., Oxford, Ohio, 1964; MS, Miami U., 1978; MBA, U. Dayton, 1983. Exec. sec. Armco Steel Corp., Middletown, Ohio, 1964-66; fin. dir. Carousel Nursery Sch., Middletown, 1970-72; ins. specialist Maupin Ins. Agy., Middletown, 1972-74; instr. Miami U., Oxford, 1974-84, asst. prof., 1984—; cons. NCR World Hdqrs., Dayton, 1984-85, Bank One, Middletown, 1984, Cert. Parts, Germantown, Ohio, 1978—. co-chmn. cancer crusade Am. Cancer Soc., Middletown, 1983, chmn. 1984, bd. dirs. 1982—; cons. Assn. for Retarded Citizens, Cin., 1985; pres. Pastoral Counseling, Middletown, 1978-79. Named one of Outstanding Young Women of Am., 1976. Mem. Assn. of Records Mgrs. and Adminstrs. (v.p. 1983-84, pres. 1984-85, bd. dirs. 1985—, chmn. 1985-86), Assn. for Info. and Image Mgmt., Assn. Info. System Profls. Avocations: raising and showing registered quarter horses. Home: 7000 Hamilton-Middletown Rd Middletown OH 45044 Office: Miami U 1601 Peck Blvd Hamilton OH 45011

SHAFFER, ROBERT OTTO, psychologist, company executive; b. Phila., Jan. 1, 1921; s. Robert Sydney and Marie Agnus (Woerner) S.; m. Marilyn Benfer Eppley, Dec. 8, 1945 (dec. 1984). AB, Bucknell U., 1942; MS, Cornell U., 1948, PhD, 1951. Lic. psychologist, Ill., Ind., N.Y., Okla., Colo., Kans., Mo. Asst. dean of men Cornell U., Ithaca, N.Y., 1948-50, asst. pres., 1950-52; dean students SUNY, Oswego, 1952-54; staff psychologist Rohrer, Hibler & Replogle, Chgo., 1954-63, office mgr., 1963-84, region mgr., 1984—; also bd. dirs. Pres. Wholistic Health Ctrs., Inc., Hinsdale, Ill., 1975-83; treas. Aspen-in-Chgo., 1982—; bd. dirs. Plymouth Pl. Retirement Ctr., 1981—, Urban Gateways, 1981—, Sch. Bd. Matthew, Ill., 1960-63. Served to lt. USN, 1942-46. Mem. Am. Psychol. Assn. Republican. Mem. United Ch. Christ. Avocations: tennis, biking, skiing, music, art. Home: 158 Briarwood N Oak Brook IL 60521 Office: Rohrer Hibler & Replogle 2021 Spring Rd Oak Brook IL 60521

SHAFFER, ROGER LEE, educator; b. Norfolk, Nebr., Mar. 1, 1947; s. La Verne Wishert and Darlene J. (Milligan) S.; m. Sherry Kaye Schweishow Kramer; children: Jenny, Heidi. BA, U. Nebr., 1969, MA, 1972. Estimator Simpsons Structures, Norfolk, Nebr., 1973-74; instr. NE Community Coll., Norfolk, 1974—. Mem. Norfolk Community Theatre, 1976-77, Norfolk Planning Commn., 1981-84, Nebr. Dem. Cen. Com., Lincoln, 1986; chmn. Madison County Dem. Cen. Com. 1981-85. Methodist. Lodge: Elks.

SHAFFER, RONALD LEE, architect; b. Kansas City, Kans., June 1, 1947; s. Charles Edward and Ruth Marie (Mitchell) S.; m. B. Jeannine Hensley, May 1, 1971; children: Whitney Leigh, Drew Mitchell. BArch, Kans. State U., 1970. Registered architect Kans., Mo., Tex., Okla., Colo., La., Miss., Ariz., N.Y. Architect, Duncan Architects, Kansas City, Mo., 1970-77; assoc. James E. Taylor & Assocs., Kansas City, 1977-79; owner, pres. RLS Architects, P.A., Shawnee Mission, Kans., 1979—. Mem. adv. bd. Johnson County (Kans.) Econ. Research Inst.; bd. dirs. Mid-Continent Small Bus. United, Kansas City, 1984. Mem. AIA, Kans. Soc. Architects, Mo. Council Architects, Mat. Council Archtl. Registration Bds., Internat. Council Bldg. Ofcls., Internat. Relations Council, Kans. State U. Alumni Assn., Merriam C. of C. (bd. dirs., pres. elect),, Kansas City C. of C., Pi Kappa Alpha Alumni Assn. Club: Pika Investment (pres.). Lodge: Kiwanis (chpt. pres. 1982-83, dist. lt. gov.-elect 1985-86, chmn. 1986-87, past pres. student assistance program). Home: 4113 W 67th Terr Prairie Village KS 66208 Office: RLS Architects PA 6750 Antioch Rd Suite 110 Shawnee Mission KS 66204

SHAFFER, RONALD LOWREY, broadcasting executive; b. Hutchinson, kans., Feb. 13, 1951; s. Frederick I. Jr. and June Louise (Lowrey) S.; m. Brenda Gay Miller, July 7, 1973; children: Stephanie Anne, Christopher Toban. BS, U. Kans., 1973. V.p. Shaffer Oil & Gas Co., Hutchinson, 1973-76; exec. v.p. Kans. Crude Inc., Hutchinson, 1976-78, pres., 1978-85; chmn. bd. Consolidated Communications Network, Inc., Hutchinson, 1986—; bd. dirs. Mar-wa-ka Broadcasting Co., Lawrence, Dimension Fin. Corp., New Caanan, Conn., Traditional Bldgs., Inc., Hutchinson, Kan-Cal Spyglass Hills, Inc., San Francisco and Hutchinson. Fund raiser YMCA, Boy Scouts Am., Am. Cancer Soc., 1973—. Named one of Outstanding Young Men Am., 1984. Mem. Nat. Assn. Broadcasters, Kans. Ind. Oil and Gas Assn. Democrat. Presbyterian. Clubs: Prairie Dunes Country (Hutchinson), Biltmore Country (Phoenix). Avocations: tennis, skiing, bicycling. Office: Consolidated Communications Network Inc 200 Wolcott Bldg Hutchinson KS 67501

SHAFFER, SUSAN ELIZABETH, real estate executive, retailer; b. Detroit, Oct. 30, 1949; d. Robert William and Eleanor (Schwartz) Shaffer; m. Peter Nogueras, June 26, 1982. B.A., U. Mich., 1971; M.B.A. in Fin., Wayne State U., 1979. Asst. sec. Citizens Mortgage Corp., Southfield, Mich., 1972-75; mortgage officer Lambrecht Realty Co., Detroit, 1975-79; dir. fin. Maisel and Assocs., Southfield, 1979-81; ptnr. Nogueras and Assocs., Madison, Wis., 1981—; pres., dir. Shopping Ctr. Mgmt., Madison, 1984—; pres. Flair, Wisconsin Rapids, 1985—; ptnr. WR Joint Venture, Madison, 1984—. Mem. Internat. Council Shopping Ctrs., Mortgage Bankers Assn. (mem. young mortgage bankers com. 1978). Republican. Methodist. Home: 835 Richmond Way Nekoosa WI 54457 Office: Nogueras and Assocs 100 E Riverview Expressway Wisconsin Rapids WI 54494

SHAFRON, MELVIN, neurological surgeon; b. Cleve., Mar. 9, 1931; s. Harry and Lillian (Friedman) S.; m. Maude Suzanne Nichthauser, June 26, 1960; children: Steven D., David H., Karen E. BS, Case Western Res. U., 1952; MD, Harvard U., 1956. Intern U. Mich. Hosps., 1956-57; resident in gen. surgery Cleve. VA Hosp., 1959-60; resident in neurosurgery U. Hosp. of Cleve., 1960-64; assoc. clin. prof. neurosurgery Case Western Res. U., Cleve.; dir. neurosurgery Mt. Sinai Med. Ctr., Cleve.; practice medicine specializing in neurological surgery Beachwood, Ohio. Trustee Jewish Family Service Assn. of Cleve.; v.p., mem. exec. com., bd. dirs. Acad. Medicine of Cleve. Served to lt. USN, 1957-59. Fellow ACS; mem. AMA, Am. Assn. Neurol. Surgeons, Neurosurg. Soc. Am., Ohio State Med. Assn., Acad. Medicine Cleve. (bd. dirs. 1983—, exec. com. 1985—, v.p. 1986-87), Jewish Family Service Assn., Phi Beta Kappa, Delta Sigma Rho, Omicron Delta Kappa. Jewish. Home: 5538 Harleston Dr Lyndhurst OH 44124 Office: 26900 Cedar #324 Beachwood OH 44122

SHAH, ANIL RAMANLAL, foreign currency and precious metals dealer, accountant; b. Sojitra, Gujarat, India, Sept. 1, 1950; came to U.S., 1976; s. Ramanlal and Vinod (Shah) S.; m. Ranjan Shah, June 6, 1974; 1 child, Rupesh. BS in Acctg., Sarder Patel U., V.V. Nagar, India, 1971; postgrad., DePaul U., 1977. Cert. acct. Inst. Chartered Accts. of India. Staff acct. A.B. Modi & Co.-C.A., Bombay, 1971-75, C.B. Shah & Co.-C.A., Ahmedabad, India, 1975-76; gen. acct. A&P Tea Co., Des Plaines, Ill., 1976-78; sr. staff acct. Allen & Assocs. CPA's, Chgo., 1978-81; v.p., regional controller Deak Internat., Chgo., 1981-87; cons. Deak Internat., N.Y.C., 1987; pres. Shah & Assocs., Norridge, Ill., 1984—, World's Money Exchange, Inc., Chgo., 1987—. Editor Monthly Mag. for Univ., 1966; author: How the Hindu Religion Was Developed, 1970. Social worker Indians in U.S., Chgo., 1976—. Served with Indian Army, 1967-69. Mem. Nat. Assn. Acctg., Chgo. C. of C. (world trade com. 1982-87). Avocations: reading, sports. Home: 7912B W Lawrence Ave Norridge IL 60656 Office: World's Money Exchange Inc 6 E Randolph St Chicago IL 60601

SHAH, KUSH KRISHNALAL, mechanical engineer; b. Bombay, Mar. 8, 1960; came to U.S., 1982; s. Krishnalal Mansukhlal and Madhuben Krishnalal (Madhuben) S.; m. Sunita Shah, Jan. 18, 1985; 1 child, Nirav Shah. B in Engring., Maharaja Sayajirao U., 1982; MS in Mech. Engring., U. Mich., 1984. Advanced mfg. engr. Gen. Motors Corp., Saginaw, Mich., 1984—. Recipient Nat. Scholarship Govt. of India. Assoc. mem. Soc. Mfg. Engrs., ASME. Hindu. Avocations: music, tennis, short wave listening, badmitton. Home: 6201 Fox Glen Dr #278 Saginaw MI 48603 Office: Gen Motors Corp 1629 N Washington Ave Saginaw MI 48601

SHAH, LALIT JAYANTILAL, pediatrician; b. India, Feb. 4, 1938; came to U.S., 1965; s. Jayantilal and Kusum J. (Shah) S.; m. Shobha Shah, Oct. 14, 1969; 1 child, Nikhil. Grad., Wilson Coll., Bombay, 1957; MBBS, Topiwala Nat. Med. Coll., Bombay, 1962. Resident L.T.M. Gen. Hosp., Bombay, 1962-65; intern Highland Park (Mich.) Gen. Hosp., 1966; resident Pontiac (Mich.) Gen. Hosp., 1966-68; fellow hematology William Beaumont Hosp., Royal Oaks, Mich., 1968-71; pvt. practice Benton Harbor, Mich., 1971-72, Royal Oak (Mich.) Pediatrics, 1972—. Mem. Mich. State Med. Soc., Am. Med. Assn., Am. Acad. Pediatrics, Oakland County Med. Soc. Home: 5151 Hollow Ct Bloomfield Hills MI 48013 Office: Royal Oaks Pediatrics 1307 S Washington Royal Oak MI 48067

SHAH, MAHENDRA (MIKE) CHHOTUBHAI, manfacturing engineer; b. Amalasad, Gujarat, India, May 20, 1941; came to U.S., 1964; s. Chhotubhai S. and Shantaben L. S.; m. Kusum Mapilal, Sept. 30, 1967; children: Amit, Monica, Ketan. BEE, Baroda (India) U., 1963; MS in Indsl. Engring., Okla. State U., 1965. Registered profl. engr. in quality. Mgr. mfg. engring. Litton Microwave, Mpls., 1982-85, Barry Blower div, Snyder Gen., Mpls., 1985—. Mem. Inst. Indsl. Engrs. (sr.), Am. Soc. Quality Control (membership chmn. 1985—), Soc. Mfg. Engrs. (sr.). Home: 10525 Lancaster Maple Grove MN 55369 Office: Barry Blower 99 NE 77th way Minneapolis MN 55432

SHAH, RAJANIKANT PRANLAL, civil engineer, motel executive; b. Lunawada, India, Mar. 16, 1941; Came to U.S., 1973; s. Pranlal C. and Nirmala P. Shah; m. Kalpana Ratilal, Mar. 3, 1968; 1 child, Nisha. Diploma in civil engring., Maharaja Sayajirao U. of Baroda, India, 1961; BSCE, Chgo. Tech. Coll., Chgo., 1974. Registered profl. engr., Wis. Supr. Ahmedabad (India) Mcpl. Corp., 1961-62; civil engr. Oil & Natural Gas Commn., Ahmedabad, 1962-74; balancer direct deposit accounts Cen. Nat. Bank, Chgo., 1976-80; engr., mgr. Down Town Motel, Cape Girardeau, Mo., 1982—. Mem. Assn. Structural Engrs. Ill. (assoc.).

SHAH, RAMESH PREMCHAND, entrepreneur; b. Bardoli, Gujarat, India, Feb. 24, 1937; came to U.S., 1959; s. Premchand L. and Mangiben P. S.; m. Jaya B. Patel, Aug. 21, 1966; children: Baiju, Bella. BE, U. Bombay, 1959; MSEE, U. Ill., 1960; MBA, Marquette U., 1965. Pres. Alpha Devel. Corp., Mentor, Ohio, 1976—; chief exec. officer, v.p. Computer Resources, Cleve., 1986—, also bd. dirs.; chmn. New Ventures Mgmt. Lake Erie Coll., Painesville, Ohio, 1976-82. Mgr. Greater Cleve. Growth Assn., 1973-76. Mem. Cleve. Engring. Soc. (chmn. tech. edn. sect. 1974-76). Hindu. Avocations: volleyball, boating, tennis, reading. Office: Alpha Profl Bldg 8925 Mentor Ave Mentor OH 44060

SHAH, SATISH C., aerosol manufacturing executive; b. Bombay, India, Sept. 5, 1941; came to U.S., 1962.; s. Chanduled S. Shah; 1 child, Amish. BS, 1964. Former chemist Faberge, Inc.; pres., chief exec. officer Accra Pac Group, Inc. Office: Accra Pac Inc 2730 Middlebury St Elkhart IN 46516

SHAH, SURESH MANEKLAL, merchandising executive; b. Baroda, India; came to U.S., 1969; s. Maneklal and Manorama Shah; m. Vanlila S. Shah, Feb. 10, 1965; children: Sagar, Manish. BS in Engring., Maharaja Sayajirao U. Baroda, 1960; MBA, Northwestern U., 1974. Project engr. Cimmco, Gwalior, India, 1960-63, Indequip Engring., Ahmedabad, India, 1963-68, Continental Can Co., Toronto, Ont., Can., 1968-69; research supr. Continental Can Co., Chgo., 1969-76; mgr. merchandise McMaster-Carr Supply, Elmhurst, Ill., 1976—. Mem. Am. Soc. Non-Destructive Testing, Am. Quality Control Instn., Laser Inst. Am. Avocation: reading. Home: 9947 S Leavitt Chicago IL 60643 Office: McMaster-Carr Supply 600 Countyline Rd Elmhurst IL 60126

SHAH, UPENDRA CHHITUBHAI, endocrinologist. married; 1 child, Rishi. MD, Baroda Med. Coll., India, 1975. Diplomate Am. Bd. Internal Medicine, Am. Bd. Endocrinology and Metabolism. Intern Weiss Meml. Hosp., Chgo., 1978-81; resident in endocrinology U. Ill. Hosp., Chgo., 1981-83; practice medicine specializing in endocrinology Chgo., 1983—. Mem. AMA, Am. Diabetes Assn. Office: 7447 W Talcott Ave Suite 403 Chicago IL 60631

SHAH, VIBHAKAR SHANTILAL, physician; b. Petlad, India, Oct. 7, 1944; came to U.S., 1968; s. Shantilal Manilal and Chandrika A. (Parikh) S.; m. Sheela Mukundlal Patwa, Dec. 13, 1969; children: Meetul, Siddhartha. MD, Baroda (India) Med. Coll., 1968. Diplomate Am. Bd. Otolaryngology. Intern Beth Israel Med. Ctr., Newark, 1968-69, residency gen. surgery, 1969-70; residency otolaryngology United Hosps., Newark, 1970-73; practice medicine specializing in otolaryngology Waukegan, Ill., 1978—; asst. prof. U. Ill. Sch. Med., Chgo., 1976-81. Otolaryngology fellow Lenox Hill Hosp., N.Y.C., 1973-74, Mt. Edgecumbe Hosp., Alaska, 1974-75. Fellow Am. Coll. Surgeons, Am. Acad. Otolaryngology Head and Neck Surgery; mem. AMA. Hindu. Home: 723 Kendler Ct Lake Forest IL 60045 Office: 2645 Washington St Suite 305 Waukegan IL 60085

SHAH, VIJAY PRAVINCHANDRA, mechanical engineer; b. Ahmedabad, Gujarat, India, Apr. 23, 1957; Came to U.S., 1981; s. Pravinchandra D. and Chandravati P. S. BS in Mech. Engring., L.D. Coll. Engring., Ahmedabad, 1978; MS in Mech. Engr., Ill. Inst. Tech., 1983. Mech. engr. SLM-Maneklal, Ahmedabad, 1978-81; design engr. Dayton Industries, Northbrook, Ill., 1984—. Home: 661 Piper Ln 1A Prospect Heights IL 60070 Office: Dayton Industries 1657 Shermer Rd Northbrook IL 60062

SHAHAN, NORMAN DEAN, machinery company executive; b. San Angelo, Tex., Nov. 29, 1934; s. Roy Bynum and Gertrude (Hagelstein) S.; divorced; children: Scott, Robin. BSChemE, U. Tex., 1958. Process engr. Mobil Oil Co., Beaumont, Tex., 1958-60, Tex. Eastman Co., Longview, 1960-63; sr. propellant engr. Rocketdyne div. N.Am. Aviation, McGregor, Tex., 1963-66; mgr. European div. Howe-Baker Engrs., Inc., London and Tyler, Tex., 1966-70; v.p. devel. Intech div. LTV, Tyler, 1970-71; planning analyst Cooper Industries, Houston, 1971-73, v.p. mktg. and engring. Ajax div. Cooper Industries, Corry, Pa., 1973-77; v.p., gen. mgr. Superior div. Cooper Industries, Springfield, Ohio, 1977-79; v.p. mktg. Energy Services Group Cooper Industries, Mount Vernon, Ohio, 1979-84, pres., 1984—; pres., bd. dirs. Cooper-Bessemer S.A., Zug, Switzerland, 1979—; chmn., bd. dirs. Cooper-Vulkan GmbH, Dusseldorf, Fed. Republic Germany, 1979—; bd. dirs. Cooper Energy Services U.K., Ltd., Liverpool., Eng., Gascomij, Hengelo, The Netherlands, Servicios Energeticos Cooper SA de CV, Mexico City, Cooper Energy Services Nigeria Ltd., Lagos. Bd. dirs. United Way Knox County, Mount Vernon, Jr. Achievement, Mount Vernon. Republican. Methodist. Office: Cooper Industries Inc Energy Services Group N Sandusky St Mount Vernon OH 43050

SHAKE, JOHN GILBERT, restaurateur; b. Vincennes, Ind., Sept. 23, 1951; s. Gilbert S. and Mary Alice (Klemeyer) S.; m. Kaethe A. Pohle, Apr. 2, 1977; 1 child, Ryan. BA, Hanover Coll., 1973. Intern U.S. Ho. Reps., Washington, 1973-75; assoc. fundraiser Republican Nat. Com., Washington, 1975; dir. sales and mktg. Galt House Hotel, Louisville, 1975-80; v.p. Sparmal Enterprises, Muncie, Ind., 1980-85; pres. Ind. Food Ventures, Muncie, 1986—. Named Salesman of Yr. Sales and Mktg. Execs., 1978. Methodist. Lodge: Elks. Avocations: golf, tennis, camping, reading. Home: 2803 Burnell Dr Muncie IN 47304 Office: Ind Food Ventures 4709 N Wheeling Muncie IN 47304

SHALLCROSS, ELIN J., infosystems specialist; b. Ridley Park, Pa., Feb. 4, 1944; d. Thomas Paul and Ramona Fredricka (Higgins) S. BS in Biology, Antioch Coll., 1967; MS, U. Tenn., 1975. Lit. scientist Am. Cyanamid Co., Princeton, N.J., 1970-74, bibliographer, 1975-77; information scientist The Upjohn Co., Kalamazoo, 1977-81, mgr. tech. documents, 1981—. Mem. Assn. Records Mgrs. and Adminstrs. (sec. 1983-85, pres. 1985-86, bd. dirs. 1986—, Chpt. Mem. of Yr. 1985), Pharm. Mfrs. Assn. (proprietary info. mgmt. com., 1985—), NOW (Woman of Yr. Kalamazoo chpt. 1986). Home: 1019 Sheridan Dr Kalamazoo MI 49001 Office: The UpJohn Co 7222-126-8 Kalamazoo MI 49001

SHAMBAUGH, GEORGE ELMER, III, internist; b. Boston, Dec. 21, 1931; s. George Elmer and Marietta Susan (Moss) S.; m. Katherine Margaret Matthews, Dec. 29, 1956 (dec.); children—George, Benjamin, Daniel, James, Elizabeth; m. Martha Repp Davis, Jan. 3, 1987. B.A., Oberlin Coll., 1954; M.D., Cornell U., 1958. Diplomate Am. Bd. Internal Medicine. Gen. med. intern Denver Gen. Hosp., 1958-59; research fellow physiologic chemistry U. Wis.-Madison, 1968-69; asst. prof. medicine Northwestern U. Med. Sch., Chgo., 1969-74, assoc. prof., 1974-81, prof., 1981—; mem. Ctr. for Endocrinology, Metabolism and Nutrition, 1969—; chief endocrinology and metabolism VA Lakeside Med. Ctr., Chgo., 1974—; attending physician Northwestern Meml. Hosp., Chgo., 1969—. Contbr. articles to text books and profl. jours. Served with M.C., U.S. Army, 1959-67. NIH spl. postdoctoral fellow, 1967-69; Schweppe Found. fellow, 1972-75. Fellow ACP; mem. Am. Fedn. Clin. Research, Sci. Research Soc. Am., Endocrine Soc., Am. Thyroid Assn., Am. Inst. Nutrition, Am. Soc. Clin. Nutrition, Am. Physiol. Soc., Central Soc. Clin. Research, Inst. Medicine Chgo., Taipei Internat. Med. Soc. (pres. 1960), Sigma Xi, Nu Sigma Nu. Home: 530 S Stone Ave LaGrange IL 60525 Office: Northwestern Med Faculty Found Inc 222 E Superior St Chicago IL 60611 also: VA Lakeside Med Ctr 333 E Huron Chicago IL 60611

SHAMES, MICHAEL CHARLES, stock options trading company executive; b. Omaha, Sept. 15, 1938; s. Frank Aaron and Anne (Smolowitz) S.; m. Abby Louise Graff, May 21, 1967; 1 dau., Amanda Anne. Student Pace U., 1957-60, N.Y. Inst. Fin., 1960-61. Registered rep. N.Y. Stock Exchange. Page, reporter N.Y. Stock Exchange, N.Y.C., 1955-61; account exec. Newburger Loeb & Co., N.Y.C., 1966-70; stock trader Godnick, Inc., 1970-73; pres., chief exec. officer M.C.S. Options, Inc., Chgo., 1973—; mem. N.Y. Futures Exchange, N.Y.C., 1980—, Chgo. Bd. Options Exchange, 1973—. Served with USAF, 1961-65. Mem. Fretted Instrument Guild Am. (bd. dirs. 1973—), Train Collectors Assn. Am., Am. Numismatic Assn., Planetary Soc. Am. Republican. Methodist. Home: 3240 Lake Shore Dr Chicago IL 60657 Office: MCS Options Inc 327 S La Salle St Chicago IL 60604

SHAMP, JOHN CASHON, dentist; b. Zanesville, Ohio, Nov. 5, 1951; s. John Howard and Mildred Louise (Cashon) S.; m. Nancy Lee Kreager, June 14, 1975; children: Jennifer Lee, John Christopher, Elizabeth Anne. BS, Ohio State U., 1973, DDS, 1976. Pvt. practice dentistry Zanesville, Ohio, 1978—; dental staff Bethesda Hosp., Good Samaritan Med. Ctr. Bd. dirs. YMCA, Zanesville, Grace Methodist Ch., Zanesville. Served to lt. USN, 1976-78. Mem. ADA, Ohio Dental Assn., Muskingum Valley Dental Soc., Acad. Gen. Dentistry. Lodge: Kiwanis. Office: 145 Sunrise Ctr Zanesville OH 43701

SHANAHAN, THOMAS M., state supreme court justice; b. Omaha, May 5, 1934; m. Jane Estelle Lodge, Aug. 5, 1956; children: Catherine Anne Shanahan Trofholz, Thomas M. Jr., Mary Elizabeth, Timothy F. A.B. magna cum laude, U. Notre Dame, 1956; J.D., Georgetown U., 1959. Bar: Nebr. Mem. McGinley, Lane, Mueller, Shanahan, O'Donnell & Merritt, Ogallala, Nebr.; assoc. justice Nebr. Supreme Ct., Lincoln, 1983—. Mem. Nebr. State Bar Assn. (Legal Services Lawyers Referral Service, ho. of dels. 13th jud. dist. 1983, rep. exec. council 1979-83), ABA, Western Nebr. Bar Assn. (pres. 1975-76, sec.-treas. 1969-70), Nebr. Assn. Trial Attys., Assn. Trial Lawyers Am. Office: Nebr Supreme Ct State Capitol Bldg 1445 K St Lincoln NE 68509 *

SHANDS, COURTNEY, JR., lawyer; b. St. Louis, Mar. 17, 1929; s. Courtney and Elizabeth W. (Jones) S.; m. Frances Jean Schellfeffer, Aug. 9, 1952; children—Courtney, E.F. Berkley, Elizabeth; m. Nancy Bliss Lewis, Oct. 25, 1980. A.B., Washington U., St. Louis, 1951; LL.B., Harvard U., 1954. Bar: Mo. 1954, U.S. Supreme Ct. 1962. Assoc. Thompson and Mitchell, St. Louis, 1954-62, ptnr., 1962-63; ptnr. Thompson, Walther and Shewmaker, St. Louis, 1963-69, Kohn, Shands, Elbert, Gianoulakis and Giljum, St. Louis, 1970—; dir. Daniel and Henry Co., Tripos Assocs., Inc. Trustee Frank G. and Florence V. Bohle Scholarship Found., Edward Chase Garvey Meml. Found.; bd. dirs. Mark Twain Summer Inst., St. Louis Fund. Mem. ABA, Mo. Bar Assn., Bar Assn. of St. Louis, Selden Soc. Republican. Episcopalian. Clubs: Noonday, Racquet, St. Louis. Home: 507 Taylor Ave Kirkwood MO 63122 Office: Kohn Shands Elbert Gianoulakis & Giljum 411 N 7th St Saint Louis MO 63101

SHANE, JEWELL LEWIS, accountant; b. Park City, Ky., Jan. 26, 1940; d. Wilson Bryant and Louise (Jewell) Lewis; children: William Michael Cissell, Mark Aubrey Cissell, Jonathan Robert Shane. BS in Acctg., U. Ky., 1976; MBA, U. Cin., 1984. CPA, Ohio. Acct. Deloitte Haskins and Sells, Cin., 1976-82, Price Waterhouse, Cin., 1980-82; owner Lewis-Shane CPA's, Cin., 1982—. Del., state chairperson procurement com. White House Conf. Small Bus., 1986; acct. exec. United Appeal Campaign, 1984, 86; family allocations com. Community Chest, 1985; mem. Hyde Park Community long-range planning task force, 1978-83, bd. dirs. Hyde Park Neighborhood Council, 1980-84; bd. dirs., fin. com. Comprehensive Community Child Care, 1984-87; bd. dirs., bldg. and grounds com. Cin. Art Mus., 1986—; bd. dirs., treas., exec. com. CIn. Bicentennial Commn., 1986—. Recipient Advocate award Women in Communications, 1986. Mem. Nat. Assn. Women Bus. Owners (steering com., treas. 1986—), Am. Soc. Women Accts. (various coms.), Am. Inst. CPA's, Am. Women's Soc. CPA's (rev. editor jour. 1978—), Cin. C. of C. (govt. com. Inst. Small Bus. 1983—), Leadership Cin. Alumni, U. Ky. Alumni Assn. (bd. dirs., various coms. 1980—). Club: Bankers. Avocations: jogging, swimming, collecting art and antique furniture, gardening, civic and volunteer activities. Office: Lewis Shane CPAs Suite 1200 36 E 4th St Cincinnati OH 45202

SHANK, DAVID L., public relations executive; b. Muncie, Ind., Mar. 22, 1949; s. George Myers and Sidney Augusta (Shroyer) S.; m. Marilyn Louise Chance, June 6, 1971; children—Brendon, Andrew. B.S. in Edn., Ind. U., 1972. Acct. exec. Sta. KSSS, Colorado Springs, Colo., 1972-75, Henry & Henry Advertising, 1975-76; dir. pub. relations Garrison, Jasper, Rose, Indpls., 1976-79, BDP Co., 1979—; freelance writer, photographer. Bd. dirs. Central Ind. Better Bus. Bur., 1979—, Indpls. Symphony Orch.; mem. Wayne Twp. Schs. Human Rights Com. Recipient Community Relations award E. Central Pub. Relations Soc., 1978. Mem. Public Relations Soc. Am. (past pres. Hoosier chpt.). Mem. Christian Ch. (Disciples of Christ).

SHANK, STEPHEN GEORGE, lawyer, toy manufacturing executive; b. Tulsa, Dec. 6, 1943; s. Louis Warren and Lillian Margaret Shank; m. Judith Frances Thompson, July 17, 1966; children: Susan, Mary. BA, U. Iowa, 1965; MA (Woodrow Wilson fellow), Fletchers Sch., Tufts U., 1966; JD, Harvard U., 1972. Bar: Minn. 1972. Ptnr. Dorsey, Marquart, Windhorst, West & Halladay, Mpls., 1972-74, 78-79, Dorsey, Windhorst, Hannaford, Whitney & Halladay, Mpls., 1978-79; gen. counsel Tonka Corp., Hopkins, Minn., 1974-78, sec., 1974-79; pres., chief exec. officer Tonka Corp., 1979—, also bd. dirs.; asst. prof. law William Mitchell Coll. Law, 1974-77; bd. dirs. Nat Computer Systems, Inc., Eden Prairie, Minn. Assoc. editor: Harvard Law Rev., 1971-72. Bd. dirs. Loring-Nicollet-Bethlehem Center, Mpls., 1977; bd. govs. Meth. Hosp., 1982-85; trustee Mpls. Soc. Fine Arts, 1986—, Minn. Med. Found., 1986—; chmn. Vanguard A div., Mpls. United Way Campaign, 1986. Served with U.S. Army, 1966-69. Decorated D.S.M. Mem. ABA, Minn. State Bar Assn., Nat. Assn. Mfrs. (bd. dirs. 1985, 87—), Toy Mfrs. Am. (vice-chmn. 1983, adv. com. 1983—, chmn. 1984), Young Pres.'s Orgn. Home: 330 Peavey Ln Wayzata MN 55391 Office: 6000 Clearwater Dr Minnetonka MN 55343

SHANK, WESLEY IVAN, architect, educator; b. San Francisco, Mar. 1, 1927; s. Ivan Wesley and Lenore (Futernick) S.; m. Georgene Morrison, Aug. 13, 1949; children: Jennifer Jean Casstevens, Matthew Wyatt, Edmund George. BA, U. Calif., Berkeley, 1951; MArch, McGill U., Montreal, Que., Can., 1965. Registered architect, Calif., Iowa. Draftsman, architect various archtl. and engring. firms, San Francisco Bay area, 1951-63; prof. architecture Iowa State U., Ames, 1964—; architect, archtl. historian Hist. Am. Bldg. Survey, Nat. Park Service, various locations, 1967-84; mem. nominations rev. com. Iowa Nat. Register Hist. Places, 1973-86. Author, compiler: The Iowa Catalog: Historic American Buildings Survey, 1979. Mem. AIA, Soc. Archtl. Historians. Democrat. Episcopalian. Office: Iowa State U Dept Architecture Ames IA 50011

SHANKEL, CAROL JO, publishing executive, photographer; b. Chehalis, Wash., Jan. 30, 1935; d. Basil Ellsworth Mulford and Elaine (Warner) Dorrah; m. Delbert Merrill Shankel, Sept. 10, 1962; children: Merrill, Jill, Kelley. BA, BE, Western Wash. U., Bellingham, 1956; postgrad., U. Kans., 1959—. Tchr. Eugene (Oreg.) Sch. Dist., 1956-58, Elmira (Oreg.) Sch. Dist., 1958-59, Lawrence (Kans.) Sch. Dist., 1960-62; with pub. relations Spencer Mus. of Art, Lawrence, 1977-84, mng. editor, 1984—. Author: (biography) Sallie Casey Thayer, 1976. Co-founder, bd. dirs. Kans. Women's Sports, Lawrence, 1978—, Historic Mt. Oread Fund, U. Kans., Lawrence, 1981—, co-chmn. Lawrence Sister City Steering Commn., 1986—. Honorable mentioned for photography contbn. Kans. City Star Mag., 1980. Home: 1618 Cypress Point Lawrence KS 66046 Office: Spencer Mus Art U Kans Lawrence KS 66045

SHANKS, THOMAS MICHAEL, structural engineer; b. Cin., Apr. 2, 1954; s. Daniel James and Josephine (Castelluccio) S.; m. Mary Josephine Ell, Oct. 2, 1982; children: Michael Thomas, Joseph Thomas. BCE, Purdue U., 1976. Registered profl. engr., Ohio. Structural engr. Graham-Obermeyer, Cin., 1977-81; project structural engr. THP, Ltd., Cin., 1981-85, Pedco E&A Services, Cin., 1985—. Mem. ASCE, Am. Inst. Steel Constrn., Am. Concrete Inst., Chi Epsilon. Avocation: sports. Home: 33 Sugarmaple Ct Cincinnati OH 45236 Office: Pedco E&A Services 11499 Chester Rd Cincinnati OH 45246

SHANLEY, MICHAEL FRANCIS, accountant; b. Chgo., Dec. 13, 1942; s. Frank and Anne Marie (Barlow) S.; m. Dianne Evelyn Stack, Aug. 30, 1969. BSC, De Paul U., 1964. CPA, Ill. Auditor, mgr. Arthur Young & Co., Chgo., 1965-78, ptnr., 1978-81, 1986—; ptnr. Groupe HSD, Paris, France, 1981-86. Trustee Prairie State Coll., 1980-81. Mem. Am. Inst. CPA's (Elijah Watt Sells award 1965), Ill. CPA Soc. Roman Catholic. Clubs: Am. (Paris); Plaza. Avocations: sailing, whitewater canoeing. Office: Arthur Young & Co One IBM Plaza Chicago IL 60611

SHANLINE, RIX DONALD, clinical social worker; b. Turon, Kans., Apr. 29, 1926; s. Clarence John and Tillie Anice (Nelson) S.; m. Phyllis Nadine Semisch, June 5, 1949; children: Teresa, Ellen, Susan, Lynne, Amy. BS, Kans U., 1951, MSW, 1953. Lic. clin. social worker. Staff social worker VA, Kansas City, Mo., 1953-56; exec. dir. N. Cen. Kans. Guidance Ctr., Manhattan, Kans., 1956-67; pvt. practice counseling Manhattan, 1967—; clin. cons. Kans. Girls Indsl. Sch., Beloit, 1975-78; asst. prof. Kans. State. U., Manhattan, 1971-80. Author: (play) A.E., 1985, Spirit of The Trail, 1986. Pres. Manhattan Civic Theatre, 1975-77. Mem. Nat. Assn. Social Workers, Acad. Cert. Social Workers. Methodist. Club: Toastmasters (area gov. 1984). Home: 2406 Rebecca Rd Manhattan KS 66502 Office: 121 A S 4th Suite 213 Manhattan KS 66502

SHANNON, DONALD SUTHERLIN, accounting educator; b. Tacoma Park, Md., Dec. 28, 1935; s. Raymond Corbett and Elnora Pettit (Sutherlin) S.; B.A., Duke, 1957; M.B.A., U. Chgo., 1964; Ph.D., U. N.C., 1972; m. Virginia Ann Lloyd, June 24, 1961 (div.); children—Stacey Eileen, Gail Allison, Michael Corbett; m. 2d, Kay Powe, Dec. 30, 1977; stepchildren—Christopher, Bonnie Bertelson. Mem. auditing staff Price Waterhouse & Co., N.Y.C., 1957-61; sr. accountant Price Waterhouse, Chgo., 1964-65; instr. Duke U., Durham, N.C., 1964-69; asst. prof. bus. adminstrn. U. Ky., Lexington, 1969-76, assoc. prof., 1976-81; assoc. prof. acct. Depaul U., Chgo., Ill., 1981-87; 1958-59, 61-62; prof. acctg., 1987—. Mem. Ky. Soc. C.P.A.s, Am. Inst. C.P.A.s, Western Finance Assn., Bus. Valuation Assn. (pres. 1986—), Am. Finance Assn., Beta Gamma Sigma. Office: DePaul U Acct Dept 25 E Jackson Blvd Chicago IL 60604

SHANNON, KENNETH FRANCIS, manufacturing plant executive; b. Wichita, Kans., May 17, 1955; s. Dwayne H. and Dorothy E. (Smith) S.; m. Janet A. Swails, Jan. 3, 1976; children: David J., Julie E. Student, Graceland Coll., 1973-75; BBA, Wichita State U., 1979. Salesperson Beecham Lab., Wichita, 1980-81; sales mgr. Newark Electronics, Wichita, 1981-82; purchasing mgr. Metal-Fab Inc., Wichita, 1982-84, plant mgr., 1984-86, v.p., 1986—; bd. dirs. Employee Assistance Cons., Wichita. Elder Reorganized Ch. of Jesus Christ of Latter Day Saints, Wichita. Mem. Wichita Mfrs. Assn., Purchasing Mgmt. Assn. Republican. Avocations: woodworking, fishing, boating. Home: 9000 Suncrest Wichita KS 67212 Office: Metal-Fab Inc PO Box 1138 Wichita KS 67201

SHANNON, WENDY S., teacher, consultant; b. Grand Rapids, Minn., Feb. 3, 1954; d. Bernadine K. Simons; m. Larry J. Shannon, Dec. 26, 1976. BS in Social Studies and Econs., U. Minn., 1976, MA, 1981, postgrad., 1981—. Social studies tchr. Stewartville (Minn.) High Sch., 1976-84; facilitator ctr. for instnl. excellance SE Minn. Ednl. Coop. Service Unit, Rochester, 1984—; cons. sch. improvement programs, effective schs. Performax Instruments, Minn. Dept. Edn., St. Paul, 1984—. Chmn. deacons First Presbyn. Ch., Rochester, 1986. Recipient Econ. awards Minn. Council for Econ. Edn., 1980, 81. Mem. Alliance for Invitational Edn., Am. Assn. for Supervision and Curriculum Devel., AAUW (program v.p. Rochester 1983-85, pres. 1986—), NOW, Phi Delta Kappa. Dem. Farm Labor Party. Avocations: golf, reading, skiing. Home: 2187 Silver Creek Ct NE Rochester MN 55904 Office: Southeast Minn Ednl Coop Service Unit 5930 Bandel Rd NW Rochester MN 55901

SHANNON, WILLIAM NORMAN, III, food service executive, marketing educator; b. Chgo., Nov. 20, 1937; s. William Norman Jr. and Lee (Lewis) S.; m. Bernice Urbanowicz, July 14, 1962; children: Kathleen Kelly, Colleen Patricia, Kerrie Ann. BS in Indsl. Mgmt., Carnegie Inst. Tech., 1959; MBA in Mktg. Mgmt., U. Toledo, 1963. Sales engr. Westinghouse Electric Co., Detroit, 1959-64; regional mgr. Toledo Scale, Chgo., 1964-70; v.p. J. Lloyd Johnson Assoc., Northbrook, Ill., 1970-72; mgr. spl. projects Hobart Mfg., Troy, Ohio, 1972-74; corp. v.p. mktg. Berkel, Inc., La Porte, Ind., 1974-79; gen. mgr. Berkel Products, Ltd., Toronto, Can., 1975-78; chmn. Avant Industries, Inc., Wheeling, Ill., 1979-81; pres. Hacienda Mexican Restaurants, Mishawaka, Ind., 1978—, Hacienda Franchising Group, Inc., South Bend, Ind., 1987—; chmn. Ziker Shannon Corp., South Bend, Ind., 1982—; assoc. prof. mktg. Saint. Mary's Coll., Notre Dame, Ind., 1982—. Co-author: Laboratory Computers, 1971; contbr. articles to profl. jours. V.p. mktg. Jr. Achievement, South Bend, Ind., 1987—; pres. Small Bus. Devel. Council, South Bend., 1987—; bd. dirs. Ind. Small Bus. Council, Indpls., Mental Health Assn., South Bend, 1987—; chmn. bd. trustees, Holy Cross Jr. Coll., Notre Dame, Ind., 1987—. Named Small Bus. Person of Yr., City of South Bend, 1987, Small Bus. Advocate of Yr., State of Ind., 1987. Mem. Am. Mktg. Assn. (chmn. Mich./Ind. chpt., pres. 1985-86), South Bend C. of C. (bd. dirs. 1987—), Assn. for Bus. Communication (nat.conf. program chmn. 198—). Roman Catholic. Club: University of Notre Dame (vice chmn.). Lodge: Rotary. Home: 2920 S Twyckenham South Bend IN 46614 Office: Saint Mary's Coll Notre Dame IN 46556

SHANSKY, CAROLBETH R., psychologist; b. Chgo., May 22, 1944; d. Lawrence and Harriet (Lewis) Rosner; m. Robert M. Pope, Sept. 20, 1986; 1 child, Ava Louise. MS, Ill. Inst. Tech., Chgo., 1970, PhD, 1976. Lic. psychologist, Ill. Pvt. practice psychology Chgo., 1976—; cons. psychologist Lakeview Mental Health, Chgo., 1980—; chief psychologist TASC Inc., Chgo., 1981—. Mem. Internat. Psychol. Assn., Am. Psychol. Assn., Nat. Register. Office: 230 N Michigan Ave Chicago IL 60601

SHAPIRO, DANIEL, psychiatrist; b. Chgo., July 6, 1926; s. Isadore H. and Goldie (Rosenthal) S.; m. LaVerne Ann Bicek, May 9, 1930; 1 child, Joan Nancy. BS, U. Ill, 1949, MD, 1953. Diplomate Am. Bd. Psychiatry and Neurology, Am. Bd. Psychiatry. Resident in psychiatry Michael Reese Hosp., Chgo., 1955-58; practice medicine specializing in psychiatry Chgo., 1958—; sr. attending physician Michael Reese Hosp., 1958—. Active troop 94 Girl Scouts Am., Evanston, Ill., 1972-79. Served with USAF, 1945. Fellow Am. Psychiatry Assn.; mem. AMA, Ill. Psychiatry Soc., Chgo. Med. Soc. Democrat. Jewish. Avocation: skiing. Office: 111 N Wabash Ave Chicago IL 60602

SHAPIRO, HAROLD DAVID, lawyer, educator; b. Chgo., Apr. 15, 1927; s. Charles Bernard and Celia Deborah (Nierenberg) S.; m. Beatrice Cahn, June 6, 1950; children—Matthew D., Michal Ann, Nicholas J. BS, Northwestern U., 1949; JD, Northwestern U., Chgo., 1952. Adminstrv. asst. State of Ill. Dept. Fin., Springfield, 1952; assoc. Sonnenschein Carlin Nath & Rosenthal, Chgo., 1953-59; ptnr. Sonnenschein Carlin Nath & Rosenthal, 1959—; Edward A. Harriman adj. prof. law Northwestern U., Chgo., 1970—. Trustee, mem. exec. com., sec. Jr. Achievement of Chgo.; bd. dirs. Schwab Rehab. Ctr., Chgo.; pres. Northwestern U. Law Alumni Assn., Chgo., 1984-85. Served with Seabees, USN, 1945-46, PTO. Mem. Ill. Bar Assn., ABA, Chgo. Bar Assn., Chgo. Council Lawyers, Legal Club of Chgo. (pres.), Law Club of Chgo., Order of Coif, Wigmore Key. Democrat. Jewish. Clubs: Standard, Metropolitan, Cliff Dwellers, Lake Shore Country. Home: 34 Linden Ave Wilmette IL 60091 Office: Sonnenschein Carlin Nath and Rosenthal 8000 Sears Tower Chicago IL 60606

SHAPIRO, HOWARD S., accountant; b. Chgo., Sept. 14, 1938; s. Ben and Ida (Kriloff) S.; m. Lorie M. Blum, Oct. 26, 1960; children: Russel, MItchell, Suzanne. BSBA, Roosevelt U., 1964. Ptnr. Oppenheim Appel Dixon & Co., Chgo., 1973—. Mem. Am. Inst. CPA's, Ill. CPA Soc. (bd. dirs. 1986—), Am. Israel C. of C. (bd. dirs. 1985—), Am. Ort Fedn. (bd. dris. Chgo. chpt. 1985—). Home: 2139 Woodview Ln Park Ridge IL 60068

SHAPIRO, JOAN ISABELLE, laboratory administrator, nurse; b. Fulton, Ill., Aug. 26, 1943; d. Macy James and Frieda Lockhart; m. Ivan Lee Shapiro, Dec. 28, 1968; children—Audrey, Michael. R.N., Peoria Methodist Sch. Nursing, Ill., 1964. Nurse, Grant Hosp., Columbus, Ohio, 1975-76; nurse Cardiac Thoracic and Vascular Surgeons Ltd., Geneva, Ill., 1977—, mgr. non-invasive lab., 1979—; owner, operator Shapiro's Mastiff's 1976-82; sec.-treas. Sounds Services, 1976—, Mainstream Sounds Inc., 1980-84; co-founder, sec.-treas. Cardio-Phone Inc., 1982—; v.p., dir. Computer Specialists Inc., 1986—. Mem. Soc. Non-invasive Technologists, Soc. Peripheral Vascular Nursing (community awareness com. 1984—), Kane County Med. Soc. Aux. (pres. 1983-84, adviser, 1984-85). Lutheran. Office: Suite 100 Cardiac Thoracic and Vascular Surgeons Ltd 123 South St PO Box 564 Geneva IL 60134

SHAPIRO, MARSHALL ALLEN, plastic and reconstructive surgeon; b. Toledo, June 9, 1940, s. William and Jeanette (Golob) S.; m. Deann L. Waldman, Dec. 22, 1963; children: Mark Louis, Stacie Lynne. BS, Ohio State U., 1963; DO, Kansas City Coll. Osteo. Medicine, 1968. Diplomate Nat. Bd. Plastic and Reconstructive Surgery. Intern Botsford Gen. and Providenc Hosp, Farmington Hills, Mich., 1968-69, gen. surgery resident, 1969-72; practice osteo. medicine specializing in plastic and reconstructive surgery West Bloomfield, Mich., 1975—; cons. plastic surgery sect. Am. Osteo. Bd. Surgery. Patentee in field; contbr. articles to profl. jours. Past team physician little league football teams, Farmington, W. Bloomfield, Southfield, Mich.; bd. dirs. Harrison High Sch. Football Boosters. Fellow Am. Coll. Osteo. Surgeons (founding mem. plastic surgery sect., bd. cert. examiner, insp. residency program in plastic and reconstructive surgery, past chmn., past vice chmn.), Am. Osteo. Assn., Mich. Assn. Osteo. Physicians and Surgeons, Oakland County Osteo. Soc., Am. Arbitration Assn. Jewish. Avocations: classical music, travel, gardening. Office: 7001 Orchard Lake Rd Suite 120 B West Bloomfield MI 48322

SHAPIRO, MAYNARD IRWIN, physician, educator; b. Chgo., Dec. 18, 1914; 1 child, Juli Ann. B.S., U. Ill., 1937, C.M., 1939, M.D., 1940. Intern Mt. Sinai Hosp., Chgo., 1939-40; resident Mt. Sinai Hosp., 1940-41; practice medicine specializing in family practice Chgo., 1946—; active staff dept. family practice Jackson Park Hosp., dir. dept. phys. medicine and rehab., pres. med. staff, 1975-77, also v.p. acad. affairs; past clin. asst. surgery Mt. Sinai Hosp.; prof. family medicine Chgo. Med. Sch.; past. bd. dirs. Family Health Found. Am.; past pres., past bd. dirs. Inst. Sex Edn.; past mem. regional adv. group Ill. Regional Med. Program; past chmn. profl. adv. council Nat. Easter Seal Soc.; bd. dirs. Citizens Alliance for VD Awareness, Jackson Park Hosp. Found. Fellow Am. Occupational Med. Assn., Acad. Psychosomatic Medicine, Am. Geriatrics Soc., Central States Soc. Indsl. Medicine and Surgery, Inst. Medicine Chgo.; mem. AMA (ho. of dels.), Ill. Med. Soc. (ho. of dels.), Chgo. Med. Soc. (council), Chgo. Found. Med. Care (pres.), Am. Acad. Family Physicians (pres. 1968-69), Ill. Acad. Family Physicians (past pres.), Am. Acad. Med. Adminstrs., Pan Am. Med. Assn., Am. Congress Rehab. Medicine, Assn. Hosp. Med. Edn., Assn. Am. Med. Colls., Soc. Tchrs. Family Medicine, Ill. Soc. Phys. Medicine and Rehab., Chgo. Soc. Phys. Medicine and Rehab., Chgo. Soc. Indsl. Medicine and Surgery (past pres.), Nat. Med. Vets. Soc. Home: Apt 3609 1700 E 56th St Chicago IL 60637 Office: 7531 Stony Island Ave Chicago IL 60649

SHAPIRO, NEAL MARK, art gallery executive, appraiser; b. St. Louis, June 8, 1946. BS in Econs., U. Ariz., 1968. Stock broker A.G. Edwards & Sons, St. Louis, 1968-70; leasing mgr. Neal Chevrolet, Inc., Crystal City, Mo., 1970-73; pres., art appraiser Art Directions, Inc., St. Louis, 1973—. Served with U.S. Army, 1968-74. Mem. Delta Sigma Pi. Avocations: snow skiing, racquetball. Office: Art Directions Inc 6120 Delmar Blvd Saint Louis MO 63112

SHAPIRO, ROBERT D., soap company executive; b. St. Louis, Dec. 10, 1928; s. Harry Gregory and Rosalind Esther (Dick) S.; m. Aileen B. Behrendt, Mar. 22, 1953; children: Rand Allen, Lynn Ellen. BS, U. Ill., 1951. Pres., chief exec. officer Indsl. Soap Co., St. Louis; pres. Barry Atlas Investment Co.; bd. dirs. Tregaron Galleries, St. Louis. Served as sgt. USAF, 1951-53. Mem. Internat. Sanitary Supply Assn. Republican. Jewish. Avocations: collector of fine art and antiques, tennis. Home: 436 Tregaron Pl Saint Louis MO 63131 Office: Indsl Soap Co 2930 Market St Saint Louis MO 63103

SHAPIRO, ROBERT DONALD, management consultant; b. Milw., Sept. 11, 1942; s. Leonard Samuel and Adeline Ruth (Arnovitz) S.; m. Karen Jean Hubert, Apr. 14, 1979; children: Lee Evan, Stacy Ellen, Jenifer Erin, Tracy Elizabeth, Jeffrey Eric. BS with honors, U. Wis., 1964. CLU. Cons. actuary Milliman & Robertson, Inc., Milw., 1965-80; dir. Life Ins. Cons., TPF&C, Milw., 1980-85; mng. dir. Merrill Lynch Capital Markets, Milw., 1986-87; pres. The Shapiro Network, Inc., 1987—. Contbr. articles to profl. lit. Fellow Soc. Actuaries, Conf. Actuaries in Pub. Practice; mem. Am. Acad. Actuaries. Home: 4923 N Oakland Ave Milwaukee WI 53217 Office: 312 E Wisconsin Ave Suite 700 Milwaukee WI 53202

SHAPIRO, ROBYN SUE, lawyer, educator; b. Mpls., July 19, 1952; d. Walter David and Judith Rae (Sweet) S.; m. Charles Howard Barr, June 27, 1976; children: Tania Shapiro-Barr, Jeremy Shapiro-Barr, Michael Shapiro-Barr. BA summa cum laude, U. Mich., 1974; JD, Harvard U., 1977. Bar: D.C. 1977, Wis. 1979. Assoc. Foley, Lardner, Hollabaugh & Jacobs, Washington, 1977-79; ptnr. Barr & Shapiro, Menomonee Falls, Wis., 1980—; adj. asst. prof. law Marquette U., Milw., 1979-83; assoc. dir. bioethics ctr. Med. Coll. Wis., Milw., 1982-85, dir., 1985—; asst. clin. prof. health law Med. Coll. Wis., 1984—. Contbr. articles to profl. jours. Mem. ethics com. St. Luke's Hosp., Milw., 1983—, Elmbrook Meml. Hosp., Milw., 1983-86, Community Meml. Hosp., Menomonee Falls, 1984—, Good Samaritan Hosp., Milw., 1986—, Milw. County Med. Complex, 1985—; mem. subcom. organ transplantation Wis. Health Policy Council, Madison, Wis., 1984, bioethics com., 1986—; mem. com. study of bioethics Wis. Legis. Council, Madison, 1984-85. James B. Angell scholar, 1971-72. Mem. ABA (forum com. health law), Am. Soc. Law and Medicine, Wis. Bar Assn. (mem. council health law sect.), Assn. Women Lawyers, Phi Beta Kappa. Home: 7360 N Seneca Rd Milwaukee WI 53217 Office: Barr & Shapiro N88 W17015 Main St Menomonee Falls WI 53051 also: Med Coll Wis Bioethics Ctr 8701 Watertown Plank Rd Milwaukee WI 53226

SHAPIRO, STANLEY, research executive; b. Bklyn., Jan. 3, 1937; s. George Israel and Dora (Richman) S.; m. Janet Skolnick, Aug. 24, 1958; children: Shari Lynne, David Elliot, Jill Diane. B.Chem. Engring., CCNY, 1960; M.S., Rensselaer Poly. Inst., Troy, N.Y., 1964; Ph.D. in Metallurgy and Materials Sci, Lehigh U., Bethlehem, Pa., 1966. Research engr. Pratt & Whitney Aircraft Co., 1960-61, United Aircraft Corp., 1961-64; instr., research asst. Lehigh U., 1964-66; research scientist, supr. metals research lab. Olin Corp., New Haven, 1966-79; dir. research, pres., dir. Revere Research Inc. subs. Revere Copper & Brass, Inc., Edison, N.J., 1979-84; v.p. research and devel. Nat. Can Corp. Research Ctr., Des Plaines, Ill., 1984-87; v.p. research and devel. ops. Am. Nat. Can Co., Barrington, Ill., 1987—. Mem. Metall. Soc., Am. Soc. Metals, AAAS, ASTM, Am. Mgmt. Assn., Electron Microscopy Soc., Inst. Metals, Sci. Research Soc., N.Y. Acad. Scis., Packaging Inst., PI/USA, Inst. Food Technologists, Research Dirs. Chgo., Indsl. Research Inst. Patentee in field. Office: Am Nat Can Co 433 N Northwest Hwy Barrington IL 60010

SHAPIRO, STEVEN ROBERT, osteopathic physician, hospital executive; b. N.Y.C., Oct. 6, 1942; s. Mack and Sylvia (Warshaw) S.; m. Dawn Michelle Vermette, Oct. 19, 1980; children—Jacqueline, Robyn, Marnie, David. B.S., U. Mich.-Ann Arbor, 1965; D.O., Coll. Osteo. Medicine and Surgery, Des Moines, 1969. Intern, Flint (Mich.) Osteo. Hosp., 1969-70; practice osteo. medicine, Flint, 1970—; mem. Flint Osteo. Hosp., 1970—, chmn. dept. gen. practice, 1976-78, vice chief of staff, 1978-82, chief, 1982-84, v.p. for med. affairs, 1984—; assoc. prof. family medicine Mich. State U. Mem. Am. Osteo. Assn., Mich. Assn. Osteo. Physicians and Surgeons, Am. Coll. Gen. Practitioners, Osteo. Gen. Practitioners Mich. Jewish. Office: G-3422 Flushing Rd Flint MI 48504

SHAREEF, AMEER ABDUL-KHABEER, entrepreneur; b. Flint, Mich., Oct. 30, 1950; s. John A. and Annie (Strozier) Marks; m. Teresa Ann McClendon, May 24, 1974 (div. 1976); 1 child, Nekida Markel Burns; child from 2d marriage, Zikea Naeema Marks. Student, Mott Community Coll., Flint, Mich., 1969-70, 75-76, Baker Coll. of Bus., Flint, 1978-79. Owner, mgr. Al-Aswad, Flint, 1972-75; dir. community service Beecher Community, Flint, 1979-80; mgr. Genesee Co. Wendy's, Flint, 1980-82; market researcher Marvel Enterprises, Flint, 1980-85, dir., 1985—; pvt. practice cons. human devel., Flint, 1970—, success motivation, 1975—, dietary consultation, Flint, 1970—; mktg. cons. Marvel Enterprises, Flint, 1980—. Organizer Community and Econ. Bazaar, Flint, 1986. Fellow Life Dynamics Fellowship; mem. Astara, Met. C. of C. Islam. Lodge: Mayan. Avocations: roller-skating, swimming, chess, reading. Home: 1092 W Princeton Ave Flint MI 48505 Office: Marvel Enterprises 2712 N Saginaw Suite 212 Flint MI 48505

SHARMA, PIYARE LAL, electrical engineering educator, researcher; b. Srinagar, Kashmir, India, Apr. 17, 1945; s. Nand Lal and Yachawati S.; m. Sarojini Handoo, Aug. 9, 1969; children—Rajesh, Reetu. B.E.E., J and K U., India, 1967; M.Tech. in Elec. Engring., Indian Inst. Tech., New Delhi, 1973; Ph.D.E.E., U. Akron, 1982. Assoc. lectr. elec. engring. Regional Engring. Coll., India, 1967-71, lectr., 1973-78; asst. prof. elec. engring. U. Detroit, 1982-86; assoc. prof., researcher U. Wis., Platteville, 1986—. Mem. IEEE, Sigma Xi. Hindu. Home: 30 Maple Dr Platteville WI 53818 Office: Univ Wis Dept Elect Engring Platteville WI 53818

SHARMA, RAM RATAN, physics educator, researcher; b. Jaipur, Rajasthan, India, Oct. 6, 1936; came to U.S., 1962; s. Kalyan Mal and Ramanandi Devi Sharama; m. Shakuntala Sharma, July 16, 1967; 1 child, Raja. BS, U. Rajasthan, Jaipur, India, 1958; MS, U. Bombay, India, 1962; MA, U. Calif., Riverside, 1964, PhD, 1965. Sci. officer atomic energy establishments, Trombay, India, 1958-62; assoc. prof. U. Ill., Chgo., 1968-72, prof. physics, 1972—; vis. prof. U. Liverpool, Eng., 1975, Atomatic Energy Res. Est., Harwell, Eng., 1974-75; equal oppertunity officer U. Ill. Chgo., 1980—. Contbr. sci. articles to profl. jour. Fellow Am. Phys. Soc. (mem. biophysics div.). Avocations: writing poems, fine arts, gardening, electronics. Home: 6809 S Bentley Darien IL 60559 Office: U Ill Chgo Dept Physics Box 4348 Chicago IL 60680

SHARMA, SATISH CHANDER, chemist; b. Bhatinda, Punjab, India, Sept. 1, 1944; came to U.S., 1968; s. Shiv Parkash and Dayawanti (Sharma) S.; m. Veena Sharma, Jan. 1, 1976; children: Sabina Bharati, Shalu Bharati, Samir Dev. BSChemE, Indian Inst. Tech., Kanpur, India, 1966; MSChemE, U. Waterloo, Ont., Can., 1968; PhD in Polymer Sci., Case Western Res. U., 1973. Sr. research chemist Gencorp Inc., Akron, Ohio, 1973-79, group leader, 1979-85, head sect., 1985—. Patentee in field. Mem. Am. Chem. Soc., The Adhesion Soc., Tire Soc. Home: 4441 Leewood Rd Stow OH 44224 Office: Gencorp Inc Research Div 2990 Gilchrist Rd Akron OH 44305

SHARP, ALLEN, judge; b. Washington, Feb. 11, 1932; s. Robert Lee and Frances Louise (Williams) S.; m. Sara J. Roberts, Dec. 7, 1982; children: Crystal Catholyn, Scarlet Frances. Student, Ind. State U., 1950-53; A.B., George Washington U., 1954; J.D., Ind. U., 1957; postgrad., Butler U., 1970-73. Bar: Ind. 1957. Practiced in Williamsport, 1957-68; judge Ct. of Appeals Ind., 1969-73; U.S. dist. judge No. Dist. Ind., Hammond, 1973—. Bd. advisers Milligan (Tenn.) Coll. Served to JAG USAFR. Mem. Ind. Judges Assn., Blue Key, Phi Delta Kappa, Pi Gamma Mu, Tau Kappa Alpha. Republican. Mem. Christian Ch. Club: Mason. Office: U S Dist Ct 325 Fed Bldg 204 S Main St South Bend IN 46601 *

SHARP, CARL EDWIN, podiatrist; b. Findlay, Ohio, Aug. 15, 1942; s. Roscoe William and Donna Delores (Schade) S.; student Bowling Green State U., 1960-62; B.S. in Anatomy, Ohio State U., 1965, B.S. in Pharmacy, 1970; D.P.M., Ohio Coll. Podiatric Medicine, 1975; m. Kathleen Blanche O'Connell, Dec. 28, 1968; children—Geoffrey Alan, Ryan Devon, Cameron Grannon. Med. and surg. resident Foot Clinic, Youngstown, Ohio, 1975-76; pvt. practice podiatric medicine, Worthington, Ohio, 1976—; mem. surg. staff Doctors Hosp., Columbus, Ohio, 1980-85; assoc. staff Riverside Meth. Hosp.; cons. Friendship Village Dublin/Columbus, Mayfair, Columbus Colony, Wesley Glen. Trustee Central Ohio Diabetes Assn., chmn. constitution com. Mem. Am. Podiatry Assn., Am. Acad. Podiatric Sports Medicine, Am. Pharm. Assn., Ohio Podiatry Assn. (chmn. public edn. and info. com. 1979-81, pres. central acad. 1980-81), Alpha Epsilon Delta. Republican. Clubs: Sawmill Athletic, Arlington Court, Breakfast Sertoma. Home: 2392 Sovron Ct Dublin OH 43017 Office: 37 E Wilson Bridge Rd Worthington OH 43085

SHARP, HOMER GLEN, dept. store exec.; b. Cleve., July 3, 1927; s. Homer David and Kathleen (Hawkins) S.; diploma Parsons Sch. Design, 1945; student Am. Acad. Art, 1947; m. JoAnn Harbour, Aug. 29, 1947; children—David Lee, Terry Glen. Trimmer window display Marshall Field & Co., Chgo., 1946-55, mgr. interior display, 1955-68, display dir., 1968-70, store design and display dir., 1970—, v.p. design and display div., 1971—. Served with USMCR, 1945-46. Recipient Nat. Assn. Display Industries award outstanding achievements, 1973; named to Hall of Fame Nat. Assn. Display Industries, 1986. Mem. Chgo. Assn. Commerce and Industry, Chgo. Council Fgn. Relations, Chgo. Athletic Assn., Nat. Retail Mchts. Assn. (visual merchandising com.), Western Assn. Visual Merchandising (retail adv. com.). Methodist (chmn. pastor parish relations com.). Office: Marshall Field & Co 111 N State St Chicago IL 60690

SHARP, MARY LUCILLE PEDEN, educational administrator; b. Kansas City, Mo., May 29, 1929; d. Clarence Allen and Laura Winifred (Henley) Peden; m. Richard Calvin Sharp, June 23, 1951; children—Richard Calvin, Robert Parker, Allen Russell Howland. B.S., Missouri Valley Coll., 1950; M.Ed., Central Mo. State U., 1970. Classroom tchr., Kans., Mo., Wash., 1950-69; reading specialist Kansas City (Mo.) Pub. Schs., 1969-74, adminstr. remedial reading program, 1974-76, cons. K-6 grades, 1976-77, instr. facilitator, 1977-80; prin. elem. schs., Kansas City, 1980—. Active local Boy Scouts Am., 1960-68, PTA, 1950—; sec. Elem. Schs. Meml. Fund Com., 1985—. Mem. Internat. Reading Assn. (treas. Kansas City chpt. 1975), Nat. Assn. Elem. Sch. Prins., Mo. Assn. Elem. Sch. Prins., Kansas City Assn. Elem. Sch. Prins. (pres. 1984-85), Assn. Supervision and Curriculum Devel., Kansas City Sch. Adminstrs. Assn., Delta Kappa Gamma (editor 1978-80, chmn. chpt. profl. affairs com. 1980-82, chmn. selective recruitment com. 1982-84, program com. 1984—). Episcopalian. Office: 11424 Gill St Sugar Creek MO 64054

SHARP, PHILIP R., congressman; b. Balt., July 15, 1942; s. Riley and Florence S.; m. Marilyn Kay Augburn, 1972; children: Jeremy Beck, Justin Riley. B.S. cum laude, Sch. Fgn. Service, Georgetown U., 1964; Ph.D. in Govt, 1974; postgrad., Exeter Coll., Oxford (Eng.) U., summer 1966. Legis. aide to Senator Vance Hartke of Ind., 1964-69; from asst. to assoc. prof. polit. sci. Ball State U., Muncie, Ind., 1969-74; mem. 94th-97th Congresses from 10th Ind. Dist., 1975-83, 98th-99th Congresses from 2d Ind. Dist., 1983—, Com. Energy and Commerce, Com. Interior and Insular Affairs. Democrat. Methodist. Office: US House of Reps 2452 Rayburn House Office Bldg Washington DC 20515 *

SHARPE, GARY LEWIS, medical equipment company executive; b. Circleville, Ohio, Feb. 19, 1947; s. Harold Eugene and Erma Marie (Lathouse) S.; m. Connie Mae Hahn, Nov. 27, 1971; children—Bethany Lynn, Kyle Lewis. B.A., Ohio State U., 1970; M.B.A., Xavier U., Cin., 1978. With Philips Roxane Labs., Inc. subs. N.Am. Philips, Columbus, Ohio, 1970-78, dir. govt. and contract sales, 1971-78; v.p., treas. Health Care Logistics, Inc., Circleville, Ohio, 1978-82 pres., treas. 1983—; hosp. cons.; sec. Nat. VA Pharm. Adv. Council, 1979-81. Chmn., pres., bd. dirs. Brown Meml. Nursing Home, Circleville; pres. Bethel Lutheran Ch., Grove City, Ohio, 1978-79. Served to 1st lt. Med. Service Corps, U.S. Army, 1967-68. Mem. Am. Hosp. Assn., Am. Soc. Hosp. Pharmacists. Republican. Compiler, editor: Pharmacy Management Systems, 1977; inventer, designer new lines of hosp. carts, cabinets, and spl. packaging. Office: PO Box 25 Circleville OH 43113

SHARPE, LESLIE ALLEN, obstetrician-gynecologist; b. Springfield, Ohio, Aug. 24, 1947; s. Elmer Robert and Lucille Rose (Moorman) S.; m. Marilyn Jane Hagstrum, June 13, 1970; children: Alison Elizabeth, Kathryn Nicole, Jonathan Adam. AB, Harvard U., 1969; MD, Johns Hopkins U., 1973. Diplomate Am. Bd. Ob-Gyn. Resident in ob-gyn. U. Minn., Mpls., 1973-77, asst. prof. ob-gyn., 1977-78; practice medicine specializing in ob-gyn. Group Health Inc., Mpls., 1978—; chmn. ob-gyn. dept. Fairview Hosp., Mpls., 1980-85; bd. dirs. Shelter Tech., Inc., Mpls., 1983—. Asst. cubmaster Cub Scouts, Edina, Minn., 1986. Mem. Minn. Med. Assn., Hennepin County Med. Assn., Minn. Ob-Gyn. Soc., Mpls. Council Ob-Gyn. Republican. Lutheran. Avocations: hunting, fishing, skiing, ballet, theater. Home: 6501 Cherokee Trail Edina MN 55435 Office: Group Health Bloomington 8600 Nicollet Ave Bloomington MN 55420

SHARPE, MELVIN LEE, JR., public relations educator, consultant; b. Oklahoma City, Apr. 9, 1936; s. Melvin L. and Dorothy Jean (Shipman) S. B.S., Okla. State U., 1958, M.S., 1962; Ed.D., U. Fla., 1973. Info. specialist U.S. Dept. Agr. Mktg. Info. Service, Dallas, 1953; reporter Guthrie (Okla.) Daily Leader, 1960; publs. editor Okla. State U. Info. Services, Stillwater, 1961-62; news editor Inst. Food and Agrl. Scis., U. Fla., Gainesville, 1962-64, asst. to pres., 1964-69, asst. to dir. Inst. Higher Edn., 1970-73, instr. journalism, 1973; asst. to chancellor, assoc. dir. personnel and faculty relations State Univ. System of Fla., Tallahassee, 1974-76; asst. prof. journalism, coordinator pub. relations sequence U. Tex., Austin, 1976-81; assoc. prof. journalism, coordinator pub. relations sequence Ball State U., Muncie, Ind., 1981-85, prof. 1986—; named judge J. Carroll Bateman Nat. Pub. Relations Student Soc. Am. Case Study Competition, 1987, Ameritech Mid-Am. Awards Program, Chgo., 1986; invited lectr. 2d World Congress for Pub. Relations Educators, 1985, Canadian Pub. Relations Assn., 1987. Bd. dirs. Muncie Area ARC, 1982—; mem. Muncie Clean City Adv. Com., 1981. Served with U.S. Army, 1958-60. Kellogg fellow, 1973; Alcoa Faculty fellow, 1980; recipient spl. recognition for contbns. to Dept of Journalism, U. Tex., 1981; award for contbn. to student govt. U. Fla. Faculty and Adminstrn., 1967. Mem. Pub. Relations Soc. Am. (accredited, Hoosier, Indpls. and NE Ind. chpts., nat. task force 1980, Outstanding Achievement in Teaching Pub. Relations award Austin chpt. 1981, pres.'s citation 1985, chmn. continuing edn. bd. 1985, sr. cons. continuing edn. bd. 1986, newsletter editor educators' sect. 1984-86, bd. dirs. educators sect. 1985—, chmn. profl. devel. com., mem. planning group, task force Hoosier chpt. 1987—), Tex. Pub. Relations Assn., Assn. Educators in Journalism and Mass Communications, Internat. Pub. Relations Assn., Edward L. Bernays Com. of Ninety-Five, Muncie-Delaware County C. of C. (pub. relations and research com. 1981—), Delta Upsilon. Democrat. Methodist. Author: (with Sam Black) Practical Public Relations, 1983; edn. editor IPRA Rev., 1983—; mem. editorial rev. com. Pub. Relations Rev., 1983—; mem. edit. bd. Cen. States Speech Jour., 1987; contbr. over 20 articles to nat. and internat. profl. jours. Home: 1806 N Alden Rd Muncie IN 47304 Office: Dept of Journalism Ball State U Muncie IN 47306

SHARPE, VERLOS G., engineering company executive; b. Keystone, Ind., May 5, 1924; s. Homer and Treva Laverne (Fisher) S.; m. Rosemary Ann Lee, June 6, 1943 (div. June 1960); children: Rita Kay Turnbach, David Alan, Pamela Lee; m. Patricia Jean Crews, May 13, 1961. Student in engring., Purdue U., 1946, U. Pa., 1946, Cornell U., 1946; student in bus., Harvard U., 1973. Asst. chief engr. Frigidaire div. Gen. Motors Corp., Dayton, Ohio, 1948-70; corp. dir. engring. Addressograph/Multigraph, Cleve., 1970-71; v.p. ops. Addressograph/Multigraph, Chgo., 1971-77; v.p. group engring. Admiral/Norge, Galesburg, Ill., 1977-87, v.p. bus. devel., 1987—; bd. dirs. Bus. Tech. Ctr., Galesburg, 1986—. Inventor, patentee in field. V.p. adv. bd. St. Marys Hosp., Galesburg, 1986—; dir. industry adv. bd. So. Ill. U., Carbondale, 1984—; bd. dirs. Monmouth (Ill.) Coll., 1987. Served with USN, 1943-46, ETO. Republican. Presbyterian. Club: Knox Study (Galesburg) (v.p. 1987—). Avocations: golf, travel. Home: 19 Park Lane Dr Galesburg IL 61401 Office: Admiral div Maytag Corp Galesburg IL 61401

SHARPSTEIN, SIDNEY J., shoe co. exec.; b. Boston, Mar. 26, 1926; s. Joel A. and Ethel S.; student U. Mass., 1946-48; m. Marilyn Weitzman, Oct. 31, 1948; children—Richard A., Robert A. Prodn. mgr. Lucky Shoe Co., Trieste, Italy, 1950-52; field supr. H. Scheft Co., Boston, 1952-57; sales mgr. Stride Rite Shoe Co., Boston, 1961-62; pres. Weber Shoe, Tipton, Mo., 1963-65; pres., chief exec. officer men's div. U.S. Shoe Corp., Beloit, Wis., 1979—, corp. v.p. U.S. Shoe Corp., 1980—. Served with U.S. Army, World War II. Decorated Purple Heart. Office: Freeman Shoe Co Mill St Beloit WI 53511 *

SHARTLE, STANLEY MUSGRAVE, civil engineering executive, land surveyor; b. Brazil, Ind., Sept. 27, 1922; s. Arthur Tinder and Mildred C. (Musgrave) S.; m. Anna Lee Mantle, Apr. 7, 1948 (div. 1980); 1 child, Randy. Student Purdue U., 1947-50. Registered profl. engr., land surveyor, Ind. Chief dep. surveyor Hendricks County, Ind., 1941-42; asst. to hydrographer Fourteenth Naval Dist., Pearl Harbor, Hawaii, 1942-44; dep. county surveyor Hendricks County (Ind.), Danville, 1944-50, county engr., surveyor, 1950-54, county hwy. engr., 1975-77; staff engr. Ind. Toll Rd. Commn., Indpls., 1954-61; chief right of way engring. Ind. State Hwy. Commn., Indpls., 1961-75; owner, civil engr. Shartle Engring., Stilesville, Ind., 1977—; right of way engring. cons. Gannett Fleming Transp. Engrs., Inc., Indpls., 1983—; part-time lectr. Purdue U. for Ind. State Hwy. Commn., 1965-67. Author: Right of Way Engineering Manual, 1975, Musgrave Family History, 1961, Shartle Genealogy, 1955; contbr. tech. articles in sci. jours. Ex-officio mem., charter mem. exec. sec. Hendricks County (Ind.) Plan Commn., 1951-54. Recipient Outstanding Contbn. award Hendricks County Soil and Water Conservation Dist., 1976. Mem. Am. Congress Surveying and Mapping (life), Nat. Soc. Profl. Surveyors, Ind. Soc. Profl. Land Surveyors (charter, bd. dirs. 1979), Nat. Geneal. Soc. (Quarter Century club), Ind. Toll Road Employees Assn. (pres. 1959-60), The Pa. German Soc. Republican. Avocations: astronomy, genealogy, geodesy. Home and Office: Shartle Engring Rural Route 1 Box 33 Stilesville IN 46180

SHAUM, LOREN EUGENE, engineering executive; b. Elkhart, Ind., Jan. 16, 1942; s. Ernest Bemiller and Agnes Myrtle (Housour) S.; m. Gayle Louise Overholser, Nov. 23, 1961; children: Scott, Steven. BSEE, Purdue U., 1964; MSEE, U. Wis., 1967. Registered profl. engr. Wis., Ind. Devel. engr. Allen-Bradley Co., Milw., 1964-67, sr. devel. engr., 1967-69; chief engr. Tenor Co., New Berlin, Wis., 1969-72; mktg. mgr. Control System Research, Pitts., 1972-76; prin. Ind. Control Systems, Elkhart, 1976-80; pres. Shaum Mfg. Inc., Elkhart, 1980—; instr. Milw. Sch. Engr., 1967-69; cons. Compumotor Corp., Petaluma, Calif., United Tech., Gerber Scientific, Hartford, Conn.; del. to Small Bus. Conf., Indpls., 1986. Patentee in field; contbr. articles to profl. jours. Purdue U. Merit scholar, 1963-64. Mem. Robotics Industry Assn., Machine Vision Assn. Republican. Club: Elcona Country (Elkhart). Avocations: golf, sports, electronics. Office: Shaum Mfg Inc 1127 N Nappanee Elkhart IN 46514

SHAW, BARTON ROBERT, manufacturing executive; b. Kalamazoo, Apr. 15, 1933; s. Robert Nichols and Louise Merideth (Newton) S.; m. Eloise Frances Matthews, Oct. 5, 1952 (div. Sept. 1969); m. Sheila Ann Louden, Sept. 27, 1969; children: Kenneth, Peter, Brian, Aimee. Grad. high sch., Kalamazoo, 1951. Operator hydro electric power plant City of Allegan, Mich., 1957-59; fabricator machinery Hammond Machinery Builders, Kalamazoo, 1959-61; mgr. prodn. Tru Heat Corp., Allegan, 1961-63, v.p. mfg., 1965—; sales rep. Davenport Coll., Grand Rapids, Mich., 1963-65. Chmn. bd. vintage program Substance Abuse Services, Allegan, 1978—. Served with USAF, 1953-57. Mem. Allegan C. of C. (bd. dirs. 1983). Republican. Avocations: running, photography, biking, traveling. Home: 602 Beechwood Dr Allegan MI 49010

SHAW, DANNY WAYNE, educator; b. Detroit, Jan. 18, 1947; s. George L. and Nina Margarete (Smith) S.; m. 2d Nancy Rivard Shaw, Feb. 29, 1980; 1 dau., Christina Marie. B.S., Wayne State U., 1973, M.Mus., 1975, Ed.S., 1979, Ph.D., 1982. Tchr. Dearborn Pub. Schs. (Mich.), 1973-74, Lincoln Park (Mich.), Schs. 1974—; pres. System Support Services, Lincoln Park, 1982—; research asst. Wayne State U., 1980-81, now adj. faculty; adj. faculty Marygrove Coll., Detroit, 1984. Mem. music adv. panel Mich. Council Arts, 1976-84. Served with USMC, 1965-68; Vietnam. Decorated Vietnam Service medal, Nat. Def. Service medal Presdl. Unit citation, Campaign medal Republic of Vietnam; recipient cert. for outstanding acad. achievement Mich. Ho. Reps., 1975. Mem. NEA, Am. Mgmt. Assn., Wayne State U. Alumni Assn., Phi Delta Kappa. Lodge: Masons. Home: 1999 Church Pl Trenton MI 48183

SHAW, EDWARD JAMES, physician; b. N.Y.C., Oct. 22, 1914; s. Samuel Johnson and Adele (Herndon) S.; B.A., Columbia U., 1934; M.D., Yale U., 1937; m. Huguette Adele Herman, Apr. 19, 1965; children—Edward James, Emily K., Barbara A. Intern Bellevue Hosp., N.Y.C., 1937-38, resident surgery, 1938-39; resident surgery N.Y. Post Grad. Sch. and Hosp., N.Y.C., 1939-41; chief surg. services U.S. Army Sta. Hosp., Plattsburg Barracks, N.Y., 1941-42, chief gen. surg. sect. 69th Sta. Hosp., North Africa, 1942-44, comdg. officer and chief surgeon 16th Sta. Hosp., Wiesbaden, Ger., 1945-46; chief resident surgery New Rochelle (N.Y.) Hosp., 1946-47; practice medicine specializing in gen. surgery, New Rochelle, 1947-52; chief resident surgery Lawrence and Meml. Hosp., New London, Conn., 1952-53; chief resident and surgery resident Doctors Hosp., N.Y.C., 1953-54, attending surgeon, 1954-65; practice medicine specializing in gen. surgery, N.Y.C., 1954-65, St. Louis, 1965-67; chief surgeon Sutter Clinic, St. Louis, 1967-71; practice medicine specializing in surgery and occupational medicine, St. Louis, 1971—; mem. surg. staffs Luth. Hosp., St. Louis, Incarnate Word Hosp., St. Louis, St. Elizabeth Hosp., Granite City; asst. clin. prof. N.Y. Med. Coll., N.Y.C., 1954-65; asst. attending surgeon Flower Fifth Ave. Hosp., N.Y.C., 1954-65; assoc. attending surgeon Met. and Bird S. Coler hosps., N.Y.C., 1954-65; pres. Shaw Surg. Clinic, St. Louis and Granite City, 1975-85. Served with AUS, 1941-44, U.S. Army, 1944-46. Diplomate Am. Bd. Surgery, Am. Bd. Abdominal Surgery. Fellow ACS, Southwestern Surg. Congress, Internat. Coll. Surgeons, St. Louis Soc. Colon and Rectal Surgeons, N.Y. Acad. Medicine; mem. Am. Soc. Colon and Rectal Surgeons, Am. Occupational Med. Assn., Am. Geriatrics Soc., Central States Soc. Occupational Medicine, Aerospace Med. Assn., Pan Am. Med. Assn., St. Louis Met. Med. Assn. (del. to Mo. Med. Assn. 1978-83), Mo. Med. Assn., AMA, Mo. Surg. Soc., Assn. Mil. Surgeons U.S., N.Y. Acad. Gastroenterology, Club: Yale of St. Louis. Home: 3105 Longfellow Blvd Saint Louis MO 63104 Office: Barnes Sutter Healthcare Inc 819 Locust St Saint Louis MO 63101

SHAW, HARRY ALEXANDER, III, manufacturing company executive; b. Tacoma, Sept. 27, 1937; s. Harry Alexander and Gladys (Reynolds) S.; m. Phoebe Jo Crouch, Nov. 27, 1966; children: Harry Alexander IV, Austin R., Christine N. A.B., Dartmouth Coll., 1959; grad., Advanced Mgmt. Program, Harvard Bus. Sch., 1978. Various sales positions U.S. Steel Corp., 1962-69; div. mktg. v.p. Huffy Corp., 1969-73, corp. mktg. v.p., 1973-75, Calif. div. pres., 1975-77; group v.p. Huffy Corp., Dayton, Ohio, 1977-78; pres., chief operating officer Huffy Corp., 1979-82, chief exec. officer, 1982-85, chmn. bd., chief exec. officer, 1986—; dir. Citizens Fed. Savs. & Loan Assn., Dayton. Trustee, pres. bd. Dayton Art Inst., 1986—; sr. warden St. Paul's Ch.; past Dayton area chmn. U.S Olympic Com., United Negro Coll. Fund; chmn. Dayton area Boy Scouts Am.; trustee Wilberforce U. Served with USN, 1959-62. Mem. Bicycle Mfrs. Assn. (chmn.), Young Presidents Orgn.(chmn.), Dayton C. of C.(bd. dirs.). Club: Rotary. Home: 1135 Ridgeway Rd Dayton OH 45419 Office: Huffy Corp PO Box 1204 Dayton OH 45401

SHAW, JACK PARKS, computer software company executive, consultant; b. Lockhart, Tex., Mar. 8, 1941; s. Millard and Janie (Parks) S.; m. Merrillyn Griffith, Aug. 24, 1963; children—Myra, Mark. Cons. System Devel. Corp., Milw., 1978-80; pres. Diamond Software, Inc., Cedarburg, Wis., 1980—. Mem. Assn. Computing Machinery, Am. Mensa. Office: Diamond Software Inc W73 N726 Locust Ave Cedarburg WI 53012

SHAW, JOHN ROBERT, project engineer; b. Fondulac, Wis., Sept. 23, 1956; s. Henry Robert and Lorraine Hellen (Hagedorn) S. BSME, U. Wis., 1981; MBA, Coll. St. Thomas, St. Paul, 1986. Registered mech. engr., Minn., Mich., Iowa, Wis. Project engr. Ellerbe Inc., Mpls., 1981-83; facilities engr. Sperry, St. Paul, 1983-85; project engr. Planmark, Eden Prairie, Minn., 1985—. Avocations: sailing, biking, fitness, travel, reading. Home: 8797 Jasmine Ln Eden Prairie MN 55344 Office: Planmark 11840 Valley View Rd Eden Prairie MN 55344

SHAW, JUDITH MARILYN, hospital association executive; b. Newark, Aug. 19, 1944; d. Louis H. and Sara C. (Wilson) Kaye; m. John M. Shaw, Sept. 5, 1965; children—Michael, Steven. B.A., Smith Coll., 1966. Pub. relations dir. ARC Blood Program, Phila., 1974-76; mgr. pub. relations services Am. Hosp. Assn., Chgo., 1978-80, pub. relations dir., 1980—. Named Communicator of Yr., Internat. Assn. Bus. Communicators, Chgo., 1982. Mem. Pub. Relations Soc. Am., Publicity Club of Chgo. Office: Am Hosp Assn 840 N Lake Shore Dr Chicago IL 60611

SHAW, MARY CATHERINE, home economics educator; b. Austin, Minn., Nov. 24, 1949; d. Nicholas Bernard and Katherine Anne (Kasel) Dinneen; m. Robert John Shaw, Dec. 18, 1971; children: Nicole, Jessica, R. John. BS in Vocat. Home Econs. Edn., U. Wis.-Stout, 1971. Cert. tchr., Minn. Tchr. home econs. Hill City (Minn.) Pub. Schs., 1971-72; tchr. home econs. Austin (Minn.) Pub. Schs., 1975-85, summer sch. coordinator, 1985, dir. early childhood family edn., 1985—; Editor (newsletter) Early Childhood Family Edn. News, 1986-87. coordinator teen parent programs Austin High Sch. State of Minn. grantee, 1986, Mower County (Minn.) grantee, 1986, First Bank of Minn. grantee, 1987. Mem. Home Econs. Assn., Minn. Assn. for Edn. Young Children, Betas, 4-H. Roman Catholic. Avocations: reading, camping, outdoors, tennis. Home: Rural Rt 2 Box 271 Austin MN 55912 Office: Early Childhood Family Edn 1601 19th Ave SW Austin MN 55912

SHAW, MARY KAY, bank executive; b. East Liverpool, Ohio, June 21, 1958; d. William John and Margaret Ann (McDonald) Milby; m. Timothy James Shaw, July 4, 1980. BBA, Marshall U., 1980. CPA, Ohio. Staff acct. to supr. Coopers & Lybrand, Columbus, Ohio, 1980-85; mgr. corp. acctg. Huntington Bancshares, Columbus, 1985—. Sec. exec. com., bd. dirs. Camp Fire Boys and Girls, Inc., Columbus, 1984—. Mem. Am. Inst. CPA's, Nat. Assn. Accts., Ohio Soc. CPA's. Avocations: travel, photography, reading. Office: Huntington Bancshares Inc 41 S High St Columbus OH 43287

SHAW, MAYNARD DEVOTIE, engineer; b. Oxford, Miss., Apr. 18, 1930; s. Oliver Abbott and Alma Clyde (Billingsley) S.; m. Marybec Miller, June 8, 1951; children: Maynard DeVotie Jr., Charlotte Page, Wynne Aylette. BA in Geology, U. Miss., 1953, BS in Mech. Engring., 1958. Registered profl. engr., Mich., Ind. Surveyor Nat. Geophysical, Dallas, 1951-52; computer Gen. Geophysical, Houston, 1953-55; draftsman Allis Chalmers Corp., Springfield, Ill., 1958-60; mech. engr. TVA, Knoxville, Tenn., 1960-64; project engr. Formex Co., Greeneville, Tenn., 1964-65, Bowser Co., Greeneville, Tenn., 1966-67; lab. mgr. Brunswick Corp., Kalamzoo, Mich., 1967-71; plant engr. Ozite Corp., Libertyville, Ill., 1971-72; research and devel. mgr. Inter-Royal Inc., Michigan City, Ind., 1972-73; product engr. Sears Roebuck and Co., Chgo., 1973—; E.T.I.P. Program, Gen. Service Adminstrn. Served with USAF, 1950-51. Mem. Bus. and Inst. Furniture Makers Assn. (cons.), CONFER, GSA. Avocations: canoeing, hiking, camping, fishing. Home: 5272 Robbins Ave Portage IN 46368 Office: Sears Roebuck and Co D817 BSC2331 Sears Tower Chicago IL 60684

SHAW, MELVIN ROBERT, lawyer, public affairs consultant, educator; b. Bklyn., Nov. 23, 1948; s. Arthur and Pearl (Gutterman) S. B.A. in Polit. Sci., L.I. U., 1970; M.P.A., U. Ill., 1972; B.S. in Law, Western State U., 1984, J.D., 1984; M.A. in Human Behavior, Nat. U., 1985; LL.D. (hon.), Roman Coll., Rome, 1974; Let.D., London Inst. Applied Research, 1973. Bar: Ind. 1985, U.S. Dist. Ct. (no. and so. dist.) Ind. 1985, U.S. Dist. (no. dist.) Calif. 1985, U.S. Dist. Ct. (ea. dist.) Wis. 1985, U.S. Dist. Ct. Hawaii 1985, U.S. Ct. Appeals (3d, 5th, 7th, 9th, D.C., fed. cirs.) 1985, U.S. Ct. Internat. Trade 1985, U.S. Ct. Mil. Appeals 1985, U.S. Ct. Claims 1985, U.S. Tax Ct. 1985. Exec. asst. N.Y. State Senate, Albany, 1969-71; polit. cons. Kirson & Shaw, Ltd., N.Y.C., 1972-76; pres. Master Pubs., Inc., Chgo., 1976-80; lectr. Inst. for Internat. Affairs, Washington, 1978—; sr. ptnr. Littlejohn & Shaw Assocs., N.Y.C., Chgo., San Diego, 1980-85; gen. ptnr. Shaw, Smith and Schimek, Indpls., South Bend, Ind., San Diego, N.Y.C., Phila., 1985—; instr. law Calif. Community Colls., 1985—; dir. Hudson Industries, San Diego, Master Communications, N.Y.C., Inst. for Internat. Affairs, 1979—. Contbr. articles to profl. jours. Editor Internat. Relations Jour., 1982. Active Am. Jewish Com., Jewish Nat. Fund, Dem. Nat. Com. Mem. ABA, Fed. Bar Assn., Ind. State Bar Assn., N.Y. State Bar Assn., San Diego County Bar Assn., Am. Soc. Internat. Law, (chpt. pres. 1983—), Assn. Trial Lawyers of Am., Am. Judicature Soc., Am. Arbitration Assn., Am. Soc. Communications and Media Execs., Nat. Mgmt. Execs., Am. Polit. Sci. Assn., ACLU, Delta Theta Phi. Clubs: N.Y. Pub. Relations, N.Y. Publicity, Chgo. Pub. Relations. Democrat. Jewish. Lodges: Odd Fellows, B'nai B'rith. Office: Shaw Smith and Schimek 3925 N College Ave Indianapolis IN 46205

SHAW, PAUL CHARLES, III, psychotherapist, educator; b. Charleston, W.Va., Mar. 16, 1938; s. Paul Charles and Mildred Gail (Ray) S.; m. Nancy Mathias, June 3, 1981; 1 son, Patrick. B.A., Morris Harvey Coll., 1962; M.A., Mich. State U., 1964; Ph.D., Pa. State U., 1973. Research dir. U. Pitts., 1970-73; assoc. prof., dir. Wright State U., Dayton, Ohio, 1973-83; psychotherapist Good Samaritan Hosp. and Health Ctr., Dayton, 1982—. Bd. dirs. Daymont West Community Mental Health Ctr., 1978; mem. City of Trotwood Action Commn., 1975-79. Trainee NIH, 1966. Mem. Am. Psychol. Assn., Am. Soc. Clin. Hypnosis, Am. Assn. Sex Educators, Counselors and Therapists. Contbr. articles to profl. jours. Home: 305 W Sherry Dr Trotwood OH 45426 Office: Good Samaritan Hospital Dayton OH 45406

SHAW, RANDY LEE, social services adminstrator; b. Revenna, Ohio, Oct. 18, 1945; s. Robert and Dorothy Mae (Turner) S.; m. Karen Jean Murar Mar. 4, 1967 (div. June 1978). BTh, Ridgedale Sem., 1975, ThM, 1977. Cert. social worker. Exec. dir. Boy's Recovery Home, Detroit, 1979; clin. dir. Boniface, Detroit, 1979-83; unit dir. Problem Daily Living, Detroit, 1983-84; clin. dir. Calvin Woll, Detroit, 1984-86; exec. dir. Children Youth Equal Rights Adv. House, Pontiac, Mich., 1986—; exec. dir. Nat. Inst. Hypertension Studies, Detroit, 1979—. Mem. Soc. Am. Magicians. Lodge: Jaycees (Mich. portfolio mgr., Outstanding Pres. award 1973, Named one of ten most outstanding men, 1969).

SHAW, RICHARD COWEN, plastic surgeon; b. Wichita, Kans., Mar. 21, 1935; s. James W. and Amelia (Cowen) S.; m. Ruth J. Shaw, Aug. 24, 1957; children: Robert K., James M., John W. BA, U. Kans., 1957, MD, 1961. Diplomate Am. Bd. Surgery, Am. Bd. Plastic Surgery. Commd. 2d lt. U.S. Army, 1961, advanced through grades to col., resigned, 1975; practice medicine specializing in plastic surgery Wichita, Kans., 1975—; asst. clin. prof. surgery George Washington U., 1959-61, U. Kans. Sch. Medicine, Wichita, 1975—; med. dir. surg. intensive care unit Wesley Med. Ctr., Wichita, 1980—. Contbr. articles to profl. jours. Fellow ACS. Lodges: Masons, Shriners. Office: Plastic and Reconstructive Surgery PA 825 N Hillside Wichita KS 67214

SHAW, ROBERT EUGENE, minister, administrator; b. Havre, Mt., Apr. 8, 1933; s. Harold Alvin and Lillian Martha (Kruse) S.; m. Marilyn Grace Smit, June 14, 1957; children—Rebecca Jean, Ann Elizabeth, Mark David, Peter Robert. B.A., Sioux Falls Coll., 1955; M.Div., Am. Baptist. Sem. of West, 1958; D.D. (hon.), Ottawa U., 1976, Judson Coll., 1984. Ordained to ministry Am. Bapt. Chs. U.S.A., 1958; pastor First Bapt. Ch., Webster City, Ia., 1958-63, Community Bapt. Ch., Topeka, Kans., 1963-68; sr. pastor Prairie Bapt. Ch., Prairie Village, Kans., 1968-78; pres. Ottawa U, Kans., 1978-83; exec. minister Am. Bapt. Chs. Mich., East Lansing, 1983—; mem. gen. bd. Am. Bapt. Chs. U.S.A., Valley Forge, Pa., 1972-80, nat. v.p., 1978-80; nat. v.p. Am. Bapt. Minister Council, Valley Forge, 1969-72, nat. pres., 1972-75; trustee Northern Bapt. Theol. Sem., Lombard, Ill., 1983—; mem. nat. exec. com. Am. Bapt. Adminstrs. Colls. and Univs., 1980-82; bd. dirs. Kans. Ind. Colls. Assn., 1980-82. Trustee Kalamazoo Coll., Mich., 1983—, Judson Coll, Elgin, Ill., 1983—; dir. Webster City C. of C., 1961-62, Ottawa C. of C., 1980-82. Office: Am Baptist Chs of Mich 4610 S Hagadorn Rd East Lansing MI 48823

SHAW, ROBERT T., banking company executive. Chmn., chief exec. officer Bankers Life and Casualty Co., Chgo. Office: Bankers Life & Casualty Co 4444 W Lawrence Ave Chicago IL 60630 *

SHAW, RUSSELL CLYDE, lawyer; b. Cleve., Mar. 19, 1940; s. Clyde Leland and Ruth Arminta (Williams) S.; B.S., Ohio State U., 1962; J.D., Ohio State U., 1965; m. Jane Ann Mohler, Feb. 15, 1969; children—Christopher Scott, Robin Nicole, Curtis Russell. Bar: Ohio 1965, U.S. Supreme Ct. 1968. assoc. mem. firm Thompson, Hine & Flory, Cleve., 1965, 69-74, ptnr., 1974—. Mem. Geauga United Way Services Council, 1980-87, officer, 1982-87, chmn. (chief vol. officer), 1984-87; trustee United Way Services of Cleve., 1983—, assoc. v.p., 1986—. Trustee Cleve. Community Fund, 1986—, Ohio Citizen's Council, Ohio United Way, 1986—, v.p., 1987—. Served to capt. AUS, 1965-69. Mem. ABA (employee benefits com. taxation sect.), Fed. Bar Assn., Ohio Bar Assn., Nat. Lawyers Club, Internat. Found. Employee Benefit Plans, Employee Benefits Attys. Forum Cleve., Old English Sheepdog Club Am. (nat. officer 1972-74), Fedn. Ohio Dog Clubs (pres. 1978-82), Sugarbush Kennel Club (pres. 1975-78, 81—), Midwest Pension Conf., Delta Sigma Phi (nat. officer 1975—, nat. officer Found. 1978—, trustee Found. 1983—). Club: President's (Ohio State U.). Office: 1100 National City Bank Bldg Cleveland OH 44114

SHAW, THOMAS DOUGLAS, newspaper executive; b. Dixon, Ill., Jan. 2, 1948; s. Benjamin Douglas and Lucy Bates (Denny) S.; m. Tamsin Johanna Davis, May 9, 1971; children: Jesse Thomas, Benjamin Davis, John Peter Morgan, Katerine Johanna, Mary Alice Powell. BBA, Colo. Coll., 1970. Owner Dixon Cable TV, 1970-81; asst. gen. mgr. Dixon Telegraph, 1974-75, gen. mgr., 1975-86; chief ops. officer Shaw Newspaper, Dixon, 1986—; owner Durango (Colo.) Stockman, 1976—; bd. dirs. Dixon Nat. Bank. Bd. dirs., pres. Dixon Family YMCA, 1972-78; pres. Dixon Rural Fire Dist., 1972-76; pres. Katherine Shaw Bethea Hosp. Found., Dixon, 1985—; bd. dirs. KSB Hosp., Dixon, 1979-85; Alternate del. Rep. Nat. Conv., Detroit, 1980, 84. Mem. Inland Daily Press Assn., Ill. Press Assn., Suburban Newspapers Am., Am. Newspaper Pub. Assn. Avocations: skiing, swimming, jogging. Home: 8399 S Green St Dixon IL 61021 Office: Shaw Newspaper 113 Peoria Ave Dixon IL 61021

SHEA, DONNA MIKELS, public relations company executive; b. Marion, Ind., Sept. 27, 1924; d. Ora Elmer and Susan (Dinius) Mikels; m. Cortland William Shea, Apr. 27, 1951; children—Kevin, Kelly. Student Ind. U.-Butler. Reporter Leader-Tribune, Marion, 1941-45; stringer UPI, Ind. and Midwest, 1941-45; asst. city editor, reporter Indpls. Times, 1945-54; writer various syndicated publs., 1945-54; pub. relations dir. Community Service Council, Indpls., 1956—; pres. D.M. Shea, Inc., pub. relations firm, Indpls., 1979—; cons. Indpls. Marriott; cons. communications/pub. relations field to various agys., seminars and courses; charter com. mem., adminstr. ann. CASPER awards to central Ind. news media, community service agys., 1953—; creator, charter com. mem. ABACUS awards, Indpls., 1983—; dir. spl. projects United Way of Cen. Ind. Civic worker, 1956—; former mem. bd. Family Service Assn., Brebeuf Prep. Sch.; mem. Vis. Nurse/Home Health Alliance; mem. Subcom. Nat. Sports Festival Opening Ceremony, 1981, Pan Am Games, 1987; com. mem. Internat. Conf. on Cities, 1973. Recipient numerous state, regional, nat. journalism awards, 1940's, 50's; Big Story award, 1956; hon. CASPER award, Indpls. Mayor's proclamation Donna Mikels Shea Day, 1979; Nat. Pub. Relations award Marriott Hotels, 1977. Mem. Pub. Relations Soc. Am., People of Vision (mutual service life mem.), Alliance to Vis. Nurse Home Health Care Assn. (charter). Episcopalian. Clubs: Indpls. Press (dir., hon. life 1986), Skyline, Players, Lambs Contemporary (Indpls.) Editor, pub. News Media Handbook, 12th edit., 1985. Home: 245 E Westfield Blvd Indianapolis IN 46220 Office: 1828 N Meridian St Indianapolis IN 46202

SHEA, ELAINE EVANS, civic association executive; b. Ithaca, N.Y., Aug. 1, 1935; d. William Arthur and Genevieve (Covert) Evans; m. Michael Henry Shea, June 28, 1956; children: Elizabeth Ann, Linda Evans, William Michael. AA, Stephens Coll., 1955. Writer, film previewer Sta. KWTV, Oklahoma City, 1955-56; exec. dir. Save the Tallgrass Prairie, Inc., Shawnee Mission, Kans., 1974-84. Bd. dirs. Kans. Natural Resource Council, 1982-83; registered lobbyist, 1980-82; pres. Porter Sch. PTA, 1969; leader Girl Scouts; tchr. Sunday Sch., Shepherd deacon Village United Presbyn. Ch.; tract chmn. Am. Cancer Soc., 1982; exec. dir. Grassland Heritage Found., 1982-85, bd. dirs., 1985—; mem. Kans. Gov.'s Adv. Commn. on Environ., 1983-86 . Recipient Environ. Quality award EPA, 1978. Clubs: Stephens Coll. Dinner (pres. 1966), Prairie Planters Garden (pres. 1972), Kansas City Country. Editor: Tallgrass Prairie News, 1974-84. Home: 6025 Cherokee Dr Shawnee Mission KS 66205 Office: 5450 Buena Vista Shawnee Mission KS 66205

SHEA, FRANCIS RAYMOND, clergyman; b. Knoxville, Tenn., Dec. 4, 1913; s. John Fenton and Harriet (Holford) S. A.B., St. Mary's Sem., Balt., 1935; B.S.T., N.Am. Coll.- Gregorian U., Rome, 1939; M.A., Peabody Coll., Nashville, 1942; D.D., 1969. Ordained priest Roman Catholic Ch., 1939; tchr. Christian Bros. Coll. and Siena Coll., Memphis, 1940-45; prin. Father Ryan High Sch., Nashville, 1945-46; pastor Immaculate Conception Ch., Knoxville, 1956-69; named bishop Evansville, Ind., 1969; consecrated 1970. Mem. planning bd. United Fund Agys., Knoxville, 1968-69; bd. dirs. Buffalo Trace council Boy Scouts Am., Evansville, Child and Family Services, Knoxville. Office: The Roman Cath Ch 4200 N Kentucky Ave Evansville IN 47711 *

SHEA, JOHN J., catalogue and retail company executive; b. 1938. BS, La Salle Coll.; MBA, U. Pitts. With John Wanamaker, Phila., 1953-80; pres., chief exec. officer Spiegel, Inc., Hinsdale, Ill., 1981—. Office: Spiegel Inc 1515 W 22nd St Oak Brook IL 60522 *

SHEA, KATHLEEN VIRGINIA, psychologist; b. Waukegan, Ill., Mar. 18, 1944; d. George Shea and Eleanor Meyer. BA, Southern Ill. U., 1966, MA, 1972; PhD, Northwestern U., 1979. Lic. psychologist, Ill. Pvt. practice psychology Libertyville, Ill., 1979—. Author: Psychological Health of High-Achieving Executives. vol. to pres. ARC, Washington. Mem. Am. Psychol. Assn. (media rep. exec. mental health 1986), Ill. Psychol. Assn., Am. Soc. Clin. Hypnosis. Republican. Avocations: sailing, golf, tennis. Home: 42275 N Crawford Rd Antioch IL 60002 Office: Forum Square Suite 10 1117 S Milwaukee Ave Libertyville IL 60048

SHEA, MICHAEL EDWARD, geochemist; b. Bangor, Maine, Dec. 15, 1953; s. Edward John and Evelyn (McCollum) S. AA, Riverside (Calif.) City Coll., 1974; BS, N.Mex. Inst. Tech., 1976; MS, U. Calif., Riverside, 1982. Jr. geologist Rocky Mountain Geochem. Corp., Salt Lake City, 1976-79; project mgr. office of nuclear waste isolation Battelle Meml. Inst., Columbus, Ohio, 1982-84; lead project mgr. Battelle Meml. Inst., Columbus, 1984-86; project mgr. office of waste tech. devel. Battelle Meml. Inst., Willowbrook, Ill., 1986—. Contbr. articles to profl. jours. Club: Hewitt (pres. Riverside 1981-82). Office: Battelle/OCRD 7000 S Adams St Willowbrook IL 60521

SHEAR, TIMOTHY ALLEN, computer programmer; b. Grand Rapids, Mich., May 15, 1950; s. Thomas Arthur and Lois (Clark) S. BS in Indsl. Design, U. Mich., 1972. Pres. Telesource Corp., Ann Arbor, Mich., 1975-80; programmer Willmark Enterprises, Birmingham, Mich., 1983-84; mgr. advanced products Parameter Driven Software, Inc., Birmingham, 1984—. Mem. Assn. Computing Machinery. Home: 35927 Woodridge Circle Apt 34209 Farmington Hills MI 48018 Office: Parameter Driven Software Inc 30800 Telegraph Rd Suite 3820 Birmingham MI 48010

SHEARER, MARSHALL L., psychiatrist; b. Athens, W.Va., Mar. 1, 1933; s. Marshall L. Sr. and Jane Mildred (Carpenter) S.; m. Marguerite Raft, June 24, 1961; children: Mildred, Christine, Thomas. BS in Medicine, Coll. of Charleston, S.C., 1956; MD, Med. U. S.C., 1958. Diplomate Am. Bd. Psychiatry and Neurology, Am. Bd. Psychiatry and Neurology in Child Psychiatry. Intern St. Louis City Hosp., 1958-59; resident in psychiatry U. Mich., Ann Arbor, 1959-62, fellow in child psychiatry, 1963-64, faculty dept. psychiatry, 1964-70; clin. and research assoc. Masters and Johnson Inst., St. Louis, 1970-72; practice medicine specializing in psychaitry Ann Arbor, 1972—; lectr. sch. social work U. Mich., 1972-78; clin. assoc. prof. dept. psychiatry U, Mich., 1972—; cons. State Prison So. Mich., Jackson, 1962-63, Ann Arbor Pub. Schs., 1965-70, Washtenaw County Detention Home, Ann Arbor, 1966-68, Wayne-Westland (Mich.) Community Schs., 1972-74. Author: (with M.R. Shearer) Rapping About Sex, 1972; syndicated columnist, Knight/Ridder Wire Service, 1973—; contbr. articles to profl. jours. Mem. AMA, Mich. State Med. Soc., Washtenaw County Med. Soc., Am. Psychait. Assn., Mich. Soc. Neurology and Psychiatry. Home: 8044 Dexter-Pinckney Rd Dexter MI 48130 Office: 400 Maynard St Ann Arbor MI 48104

SHEARIN, JOHN WILLIS, JR., librarian, educator; b. Norfolk, Va., Apr. 19, 1950; s. John Willis Sr. Shearin; 1 child, Evan Russell. BS, U. So. Miss., 1974; MLS, Ind. U., 1980. Substitute librarian Meridian (Miss.) Pub. Schs., 1974, media specialist, 1976-78; English tchr. and librarian Wayne County Schs., Waynesboro, Miss., 1974-76; audiovisual dir. Carmel-Clay)Ind.) Schs., 1978-81; cons. Ind. Dept. Edn., Indpls., 1981—; cons. media workshops U. So. Miss., Hattiesburg, 1979-80; substitute instr. Ind. U., Ft. Wayne and Indpls., 1982-85; bd. dirs. Aime Media Fair, Ind., 1979-85. Editorial staff Ind. Media Jour., 1982-84; contbr. articles to profl. jours. Named one of Outstanding Young Men of Am., 1984, 85. Mem. ALA, Am. Assn. Sch. Librarians, Nat. Assn. State Ednl. Media Profls. (bd. dirs. 1986—), Assn. Ind. Media Educators (exec. bd. dirs. 1982-83), Ind. Film and Video Council. Club: Mecca (Indpls.). Avocations: music, photography, scuba diving. Home: 5134 N College Ave Indianapolis IN 46205 Office: Ind Dept Edn State House Room 229 Indianapolis IN 46204

SHEARS, RENEÉ MARIE, systems analyst; b. Cleve., May 6, 1960; d. Peter Jr. and Eleanor (Hedesh) S. BS in Mgmt. Info Systems, BS in Prodn. and Ops. Mgmt., Bowling Green State U., 1982. Programmer/ analyst I Monsanto Research Corp., Miamisburg, Ohio, 1982-84, programmer/analyst II, 1984—. Small bus. coordinator, United Way, Miamisburg, 1985. Mem. Am. Production and Inventory Control Soc. Office: Monsanto Research Corp PO Box 32 Miamisburg OH 45342

SHEASBY, KEVIN LEE, financial planner; b. Mt. Vernon, Ohio, Aug. 30, 1953; s. Daniel Irving and Vonetta Lee (Landis) S.; m. Brenda Sue Sharp, Jan. 8, 1978; children: Nathan Daniel, Nikolas David. Student, Bowling Green State U., 1976-78. Life ins. agt. Harvest Life Ins. Co., Cleve., 1981-82; regional mgr. Bestline Agy. Inc., Columbus, Ohio, 1982-84; fin. planner Marshall Smith Agy., Ashland, Ohio, 1984—; ins. cons. Samaritan Hosp., Ashland, 1986—. Mem. Ashland City County Council, 1986, Ashland Ins. Bd., 1984-86. Republican. Avocations: reading, model airplanes, tennis, water skiing, basketball. Home: 226 Highland Ave Ashland OH 44805 Office: Marshall Smith Agy 310 College Ave Ashland OH 44805

SHEBILSKY, PAUL MARTIN WALTER, optometrist; b. Argentine, Kans., Sept. 30, 1895; s. John and Pauline Wihelmina (Moltz) Przybylski; grad. Needles Inst. Optometry, 1923; D. Optometry, No. Ill. Coll. Ophthalmology and Otolaryngology, 1926; m. Esther Margaret Wortman, Dec. 27, 1931. Practice optometry, Fairbury, Nebr., 1923-26, Strong City, and Burlington, Kans., 1926-29, Emporia, 1929-77. Served with USNR, 1917-19. Mem. Am., Kans. optometric assns., Am. Legion, Vets. World War I, Kans. Hist. Soc. (life), Beta Sigma Kappa. Congregationalist. Mason, Kiwanian (pres. 1937). Club: Outlook. Editor: Kans. Optometric Journal, 1944-52. Home: 1502 Sherwood Way Emporia KS 66801

SHEBSES, LEONARD WILLIAM, real estate developer; b. Detroit, Sept. 17, 1939; s. Ben and Bella (Grosz) S.; m. Sharon Berkowitz, Dec. 11, 1977; 1 child, Amy. Grad., High Sch., Detroit, 1957; student, Eastern Mich. U., 1957-58, Wayne State U., 1958-71. Lic. real estate broker, Mich. Surveyor City of Detroit, 1960-62; civil engr. Neree D. Alix, Southfield, Mich., 1963-64; estimator Barton-Malow Co., Oak Park, Mich., 1965-67; mgr. constrn. project Cronk & Tocco, Oak Park, 1967-69; dir. devel., property mgr. Maisel & Assocs., Southfield, 1969-82; prin. L.W. Shebses & Assocs., West Bloomfield, Mich., 1982—; cons. Borman's Inc., Detroit, 1983—. Mem. Internat. Council Shopping Ctrs. (cert. mgr.), Urban Land Inst., Am. Concret Inst., Mich. Soc. Registered Land Surveyors. Club: Economic (Detroit). Home: 5657 W Maple Rd West Bloomfield MI 48033 Office: LW Shebses & Assocs PO Box 8068 West Bloomfield MI 48304

SHEDD, JOHN CHARLES, pharmacist; b. Coldwater, Mich., June 1, 1947; s. John Goff and Marjorie Dawn (Sizeland) S.; m. Janice Kay Gertz, Sept. 13, 1969; children: John Bradley, Michael Ryan, Trevor James. BS in Pharmacy, Ferris State Coll., 1970. Registered pharmacist. Pharmacist Parks Drug Store Inc, Albion, Mich., 1970-74; mgr. Parks Drug Store Inc, Albion, 1974-86, ptnr., 1986—; bd. dirs. Homestead Savings and Loan Assn., Albion. Chmn. Downtown Devel. Assn., Albion, 1982; co-chmn. Community Hosp. Charity Ball, Albion, 1981; trustee Albion Civic Found.,

1983—, St. Johns Sch., Albion, 1980—. Mem. Am. Pharm. Assn., Mich. State Pharm. Assn., Nat. Assn. Retail Druggists. Lutheran. Avocations: physical training. Home: 10708 29 Mile Rd Albion MI 49224 Office: Parks Drug Store Inc 318 S Superior St Albion MI 49224

SHEEHAN, DANIEL EUGENE, bishop; b. Emerson, Nebr., May 14, 1917; s. Daniel F. and Mary Helen (Crahan) S. Student, Creighton U., 1934-36, LL.D. (hon.), 1964; student, Kenrick Sem., St. Louis, 1936-42; J.C.D., Cath. U. Am., 1949. Ordained priest Roman Cath. Ch., 1942; asst. pastor Omaha, 1942-46; chancellor Archdiocese Omaha, 1949—; aux. bishop Archdiocese Omaha, Omaha, 1964-69; archbishop of Omaha 1969—; Pres. Canon Law Soc. Am., 1953; chaplain Omaha club Serra Internat., 1950—. Office: Chancery Office 100 N 62d St Omaha NE 68132 *

SHEEHAN, DENNIS WILLIAM, lawyer, business executive; b. Springfield, Mass., Jan. 2, 1934; s. Timothy A. and H. Marjorie (Kelsey) S.; m. Elizabeth M. Hellyer, July 27, 1957; children: Dennis William, Catherine Elizabeth, John Edward. BS, U. Md., 1957; JD, Georgetown U., 1960, LLM, 1962. Bar: D.C., Md. 1960, Mo. 1976, Ohio 1977. Legal asst. to chmn. NLRB, Washington, 1960-61; trial atty. U.S. SEC, Washington, 1962-63; corp. atty. Martin Marietta, Balt., N.Y.C., 1963-64; v.p., gen. counsel, sec. Bunker Ramo Corp., Oak Brook, Ill., 1964-73; exec. v.p., gen. counsel, dir. Diversified Industries, Inc., St. Louis, 1973-75; v.p., gen. counsel, dir. N-ReN Corp., Cin., 1975-77; v.p., gen. counsel, sec., dir. AXIA Inc., Oak Brook, Ill., 1977-84, chmn., pres., chief exec. officer, 1984—; bd. dirs. Ames Taping Tools of Can. Ltd., Ont., Andamios Atlas, Mexico City, Jensen Tools & Alloys Inc., Phoenix, Compagnie Fischbein (S.A.), Brussels, Tex Tenn Corp., Johnson City, Tenn., B&L Steel Co., Chgo., Ednl. Mgmt. Corp., Pitts. Bd. dirs. Associated Employers Ill., Evang. Hosp. Found., Mid-Am. Inst., Nat. Council on Crime and Delinquency. Served with AUS, 1954-56. Mem. ABA, Fed. Bar Assn., Phi Delta Phi, Pi Sigma Alpha, Delta Sigma Phi. Republican. Clubs: St. Louis; Econ., Met., Carlton (Chgo.); Bankers (Cin.); Met., Nat. Lawyers (Washington); Downtown (Richmond, Va.). Home: 450 Lexington Dr Lake Forest IL 60045 Office: Axia Corp 122 W 22d St Oak Brook IL 60521

SHEEHAN, JOHN PATRICK, automotive company executive; b. N.Y.C., Feb. 25, 1933; s. Patrick Joseph and Briget Veronica (Downing) S.; m. Helen Patricia McCarthy, May 25, 1957; children: John P. Jr., Dennis M., Joseph B. BS, Fordham U., 1955; student exec. program, Stanford U., 1980. Sales rep. AC spark plug div. Gen. Motors Corp., N.Y.C., 1960-66; product mgr. Carter Automotive div. ACF, St. Louis, 1966-68, sales planning mgr., 1968-72, dir. mktg., 1972-81, sr. dir. aftermarket ops., 1981-83; exec. v.p., gen. mgr. Everco Industries, Inc., Skokie, Ill., 1983—. Served with U.S. Army, 1955-57. Mem. Automotive Sales Council, Automotive Service Industry Assn., Nat. Inst. Automotive Service Excellence, Automotive Elect. Assn. Republican. Roman Catholic. Home: 1160 Old Mill Rd Lake Forest IL 60045 Office: Everco Industries Inc 8324 N Skokie Blvd Skokie IL 60077

SHEEHAN, MARK CHARLES, computer service executive; b. Hamilton, Ohio, Sept. 10, 1948; s. John Paul and Elinor Adel (Popkins) S.; m. Kathy Ann Barnes, 1976; children: David, Michael. AB, Ind. U., 1970, MA, 1972, PhD, 1979. Assoc. instr. Ind. U., Bloomington, 1970-76, paleoecol. cons., 1976-82, computer programmer, 1982-83, mgr. microcomputer support, 1983—; organizer Midwest Regional Acad. Microcomputer Conf., Indpls., 1985-87. Contbr. articles on paleoecology to profl. jours. Trustee The Nature Conservancy, Indpls., 1985—. Research grantee Nat. Geographic Soc., 1972. Mem. Assn. Computing Machinery. Avocations: homesteading, children. Office: Ind U Acad Computing Service 750 N State Rd 46 Bypass Bloomington IN 47405

SHEEHAN, MICHAEL FRANCIS, marketing agency executive; b. Beaufort, S.C., July 19, 1951; s. Vincent M. and Catherine A. (O'Donnell) S.; m. Patricia A. Hochwarth, Oct. 1, 1983; 1 child, Patrick M. BS in Indsl. Mgmt., U. Akron, 1979, MBA, 1985. Product mgr. Contours Inc., Orrville, Ohio, 1976-81; editor Penton Pub., Cleve., 1982-84; mktg. mgr. Nestaway div. Axia Inc., Cleve., 1984-87; pres. Tyfiant Mktg Communications, Cleve., 1987—. Assoc. editor Precision Metal, 1982-84; also papers in field. Mem. Inst. Indsl. Engrs., Soc. Mfg. Engrs. Roman Catholic. Club: Toastmasters Inernat. (sgt. of arms local club 1984, ednl. v.p. 1985). Avocations: running, racquetball. Home: 3461 Doris Rd Cleveland OH 44111 Office: Tyfiant Mktg Communications 3461 Doris Rd Cleveland OH 44111

SHEEHAN, MICHAEL GILBERT, utilities executive; b. Peoria, Ill., Oct. 26, 1952; s. Jerry James and Mary Ellen (Murrin) S.; m. Debra Lynn England, Apr. 12, 1975; children: Mark Michael, Lisa Michele. AS, Ill. Cen. Coll., 1972; BS, Bradley U., 1974. Cert. purchasing mgr., Nat. Assn. Purchasing Mgmt. Sta. clk. Cen. Ill. Light Co., Canton, 1975, office and stores supr., 1975-79; purchasing agt. Cen. Ill. Light Co., Peoria, 1979-81, bldg. mgr., 1981-85, investment mgr., 1985-87, sr. investment recovery adminstr., 1987—. Advisor Jr. Achievement, Peoria, 1980; mem YWCA, Pekin, Ill., 1983—. Mem. Bldg. Owners and Mgrs. Assn., Invesment Recovery Assn. Republican. Roman Catholic. Avocations: swimming, reading, fishing. Office: Cen Ill Light Co 300 Liberty St Peoria IL 61602

SHEEHAN, WILLIAM RICHARD, banker; b. Columbus, Ohio, Sept. 2, 1946; s. William Richard and Mary June (Strickfaden) S.; m. Linda Frances Case, Jan. 16, 1969; children: Christopher, Suzanne. BA, Ohio State U., 1968; MA, Ball State U., 1972. Employment mgr. Bancohio Nat. Bank, Columbus, 1976-79, lending officer, 1979-81, team mgr., 1981-85, v.p., sect. mgr., 1985—; prof. bus. and mgmt. sch. Columbus Tech. Inst., 1981—. V.p. bd. dirs. Choices for Victims Domestic Violence, Columbus, 1987. Served to capt. USAF, 1969-73. Roman Catholic. Avocations: reading, walking, traveling. Office: Bancohio Nat Bank 155 E Broad St Columbus OH 43229

SHEETS, DAVID LLOYD, fundraising executive; b. Olney, Ill., Dec. 19, 1945; s. Franklin Lloyd and Edna Mary (Hyndman) S.; m. Barbara Browning Allen, May 19, 1968; children: Catherine Browning, Nathan Allen. BS, Miami U., 1967; MS in Pub. Relations, Am. Univ., 1972. Dir., pub. relations and advt. Aerojet Chem. Corp., Sacramento, 1972-75; dir. devel. WFYI Ch. 20 Pub. TV, Indpls., 1975-81, WOSU-TV AM-FM Ohio State U., Columbus, 1981-84; pres. David L. Sheets & Assocs., Columbus, 1984-87. Served to capt. USAF, 1967-72. Recipient Devel. awards (3) Corp. for Pub. Broadcasting, 1976, 77, 78; named Pub. Affairs Officer of Yr. 10th USAF Reserve, 1981. Mem. Nat. Soc. Fund Raising Execs. (pres. cen. Ohio ch., 1985, dir. 1985), Indpls. Speech & Hearing Ctr. (bd. dirs., 1980-81), Reserve Officers Assn., Pub. Relations Soc. Am., Columbus Ohio Area C. of C. Republican. Episcopalian. Lodges: Indpls. Downtown Kiwanis (Indpls.); Downtown Kiwanis (Columbus). Avocations: sailing, backgammon, youth activities coach. Home: 4151 Gavin Ln Columbus OH 43220 Office: 4900 Reed Rd PO Box 20532 Columbus OH 43220

SHEETS, JOSEPH L., obstetrician-gynecologist; b. Marietta, Ohio; s. Joseph Donald and Agness (Holst) S.; m. Janice B. Sheets, Nov. 6, 1959; children: J. Donald II, David Scott, Timothy John. BS with honors, Denison U., 1954; MD, Temple U., 1958; MS in Ob-Gyn, U. Minn., 1962. Diplomate Am. Bd. Ob-Gyn. Practice medicine specializing in ob-gyn Lansing, Mich., 1964—; asst. prof. Mich. State U., East Lansing, Mich., 1964, assoc. prof., 1968, clin. prof. ob-gyn, 1972—. Fellow Am. Coll. Ob-Gyn, Am. Coll. Surgeons; mem. Cen. Assn. Ob-Gyn. Office: Lansing Ob Gyn Assn 2509 E Grand Dr Lansing MI 48912

SHEETZ, ERNEST AUSTIN, college administrator, educator; b. McKeesport, Pa., June 23, 1929; s. Ernest Austin and Grace Manley S.; m. Betty Ann Hixenbaugh, Nov. 24, 1956; children: Craig Thomas, Kenneth Lee, Brian Douglas. BS, Mt. Union Coll., 1951. Alumni sec. Mt. Union Coll., Alliance, Ohio, 1955-62, asst. to pres., 1962-68, dir. devel., 1968-82, v.p. devel., 1982—. Campaign coordinator Ohio Found. Ind. Coll., Columbus, 1979; bd. dirs. Alliance City Hosp., 1982—, ARC, Alliance, 1975-80; chmn. bd. Alliance Area United Way, 1981; mem. exec. com. Buckeye council Boy Scouts Am., 1984—. Named Citizen of Yr. Alliance Area United Way, 1981. Mem. Nat. Soc. Fund Raiser Execs., Council for Advancement and Support Edn. (cons. 1977-79, dist. bd. dirs. 1983-84, fund raising com., summer faculty). Republican. Methodist. Club: Alliance Country (bd. dirs. 1982). Lodges: Filibusters (pres. 1979-80), Alliance Ruritans (Service to Youth award 1983). Avocations: reading, camping. Home: 2500 Crestview Alliance OH 44601 Office: Mt Union Coll 1972 S Clark Alliance OH 44601

SHEFFER, BRENT ALAN, accountant; b. Canton, Ohio, Nov. 7, 1957; s. Dwight W. and JoAnne Sheffer. BS, Ohio State U., 1979; postgrad., Capital U. Law Sch., 1986—. CPA, Ohio. Contract specialist Ohio State U., Columbus, 1978-79; supr. auditing Coopers & Lybrand, Columbus, 1979-85; internal auditor Cen. Ohio Transit Authority, Columbus, 1985-86, mgr. fin. planning, 1986—. Advisor Jr. Achievement, 1980-85. Named one of Outstanding Young Men of Am., 1986. Mem. Am. Inst. CPA's, Nat. Assn. Accts. (asst. treas. 1985-86, dir. spl. activities 1986-87, dir. orientation 1987—), Ohio Soc. CPA's, Columbus Jaycees (dir. pub. relations 1985-86, dir. membership 1986-87, dir. community events 1987—, Presdl. Achievement award 1986, Membership award 1987), Sports Car Club Am. (chmn. membership 1982-83, regional exec. 1984-85, dir. Columbus 500 Rd. Race ops. 1987—, Regional Exec. Worker award 1983, Regional Exec. award 1984), Ohio State U. Sports Car Club (pres. 1978-80). Avocations: sports car racing, rallying, bicycling, reading. Home: 2229-H Hedgerow Rd Columbus OH 43220-2358 Office: Cen Ohio Transit Authority 1600 McKinley Ave Columbus OH 43222

SHEFFIECK, MICHAEL CHARLES, auditing manager; b. Mt. Clemens, Mich., Dec. 27, 1958; s. Charles Favriaux and Marjorie Ann (Tallieu) S.; m. Julie Christina Rusanoff, Nov. 27, 1980; children: David Michael, Gregory Charles. BS in Acctg. Adminstrn., U. Mich., Dearborn, 1980. CPA, Mich. Audit staff acct. Coopers & Lybrand, Detroit, 1980-82, audit sr. acct., 1982-84, audit supr., 1984-85, audit mgr., 1985—. Chmn. adminstrn. commn. St. Edith Ch., Livonia, Mich., 1984—. Recipient Branstrom award U. Mich., Ann Arbor, 1978. Mem. Am. Inst. CPA's, Mich. Assn. CPA's, U. Mich. Dearborn Mgmt. Alumni Assn. (bd. govs.). Roman Catholic. Avocations: golf, basketball, reading. Home: 31714 Penn Livonia MI 48150 Office: Coopers & Lybrand 400 Renaissance Ctr Detroit MI 48243

SHEFFIELD, LESLIE FLOYD, agricultural educator; b. Orafino, Nebr., Apr. 13, 1925; s. Floyd L. and Edith A. (Presler) S.; B.S. with high distinction in Agronomy, U. Nebr., 1950, M.S., 1964; postgrad. U. Minn., summer 1965; Ph.D., U. Nebr., 1971; m. Doris Fay Fenimore, Aug. 20, 1947; children—Larry Wayne, Linda Faye (Mrs. Bernard Eric Hempelman), Susan Elaine (Mrs. Randy Thorman). County extension agt. Lexington and Schuyler, Nebr., 1951-52; exec. sec. Nebr. Grain Improvement Assn., 1952-56; chief Nebr. Wheat Commn., Lincoln, 1956-59; exec. sec. Great Plains Wheat, Inc., market devel., Garden City, Kans., 1959-61; asst. to dean Coll. Agr., U. Nebr. at Lincoln, 1961-66, supt. North Platte Expt. Sta., 1966-71, asst. dir. Nebr. Coop. Extension Service, Nebr. Agrl. Expt. Sta., Lincoln, 1971-75, asst. to vice chancellor Inst. Agr. and Natural Resources, 1975-84, also extension farm mgmt. specialist and assoc. prof. agrl. econs., 1975—; v.p. U. Nebr. Found., 1982—; sec.-treas. Circle 4S-L Acres, Wallace, Nebr., 1973—. Cons. econs. of irrigation in N.D., Minn., S.D. and Brazil, 1975, Sudan, Kuwait and Iran, 1976, People's Republic of China, 1977, 81, Can., 1977, 78, 79, 80, Mex., 1978, 79, Argentina, 1978, Hong Kong, 1981, Japan, 1981, Republic of South Africa, 1985. Served with U.S. Army, 1944-46; ETO. Recipient Hon. State Farmer award Future Farmers Am., 1955, Hon. Chpt. Farmer award, North Platte chpt., 1973; fellowship grad. award Chgo. Bd. Trade, 1964; Agrl. Achievement award Ak-Sar-Ben, 1969; NASA research grantee, 1972-77; Citizen award U.S. Dept. Interior Bur. Reclamation, 1984; Pub. Service award for contbns. to Nebr. agr. Nebr. Agribus. Club, 1984. Mem. Am. Agrl. Econs. Assn., Am., Nat., Nebr. (Pres.'s award 1979) water resources assns., Nebr. Irrigation Assn., Nebr. Assn. Resource Dists., Am. Soc. Farm Mgrs. Rural Appraisers, Orgn. Profl. Employees of U.S. Dept. Agr., Lincoln C. of C. (chmn. agrl. com. 1974-77), Gamma Sigma Delta, Alpha Zeta. Club: Rotary (dir. 1965-66). Editor: Procs. of Nebr. Water Resources and Irrigation Devel. for 1970's, 1972; contbg. editor Irrigation Age Mag., St. Paul, 1974—. Contbr. articles to various publs. Home: 3800 Loveland Dr Lincoln NE 68506 Office: U Nebr-Lincoln 223 Filley Hall Lincoln NE 68583

SHEFFIELD, SUZANNE JOAN, corporate trainer; b. Dearborn, Mich., Aug. 6, 1944; d. David Lees and Joan Lois (Caswell) Jackson; m. Elbert Lowell Sheffield, May 7, 1966; children: Scott Edward, Jason Derek. BA in English Lang. and Lit., Eastern Mich. U., 1966. Tchr. Allen Park (Mich.) Schs., 1966-67, Romulus (Mich.) Schs., 1967-70; engring. tng. coordinator Bechtel Power, Ann Arbor, Mich., 1980-84; corp. trainer Bookcrafters, Inc., Chelsea, Mich., 1984—. Mem. Am. Soc. Tng. Devel. Avocations: skiing, boating, reading. Office: Bookcrafters Inc 140 Buchanan Chelsea MI 48118

SHEFT, MARK DAVID, market analyst; b. Racine, Wis., Dec. 10, 1953; s. Max Morris and Ruth (Milman) S.; m. Susan Barbara Fisher, Sept. 16, 1984. BSEE, Purdue U., 1976; MBA in Mktg., Loyola U., Chgo., 1982. Proposal engr. ITT Telecommunications, Des Plaines, Ill., 1977-78, software engr., 1978-80; software engr. Motorola, Inc., Schaumburg, Ill., 1980-83; product planner AT&T Teletype, Skokie, Ill., 1983-86; bus. analyst Ill. Inst. Tech. Research Inst., Chgo., 1986—. Mem. Am. Mktg. Assn., U.S. Chess Fedn., Am. Radio Relay League. Avocations: chess, amateur radio. Office: IIT Research Inst 10 W 35th St Chicago IL 60616

SHEHADI, SAMEER IBRAHIM, plastic surgeon; b. Zahle, Lebanon, Mar. 3, 1931; came to U.S., 1984; s. Ibrahim A. and Mounira D. (Dumit) S.; m. Leila A. Nassif, June 18, 1960; children: Ramzi Richard, Kamal Sameer, Imad Edward. BA, Am. U. Beirut, 1952, MD, 1956. Diplomate Am. Bd. Surgery, Am. Bd. Plastic Surgery. Intern. Am. U. Hosp., Beirut, resident gen. surgery, 1956-59, chief resident gen. surgery, 1959-60; resident plastic surgery St. Louis U. Hosps., 1960-62; fellow hand surgery Pitts. U. Hosps., 1962; resident head and neck surgery Roswell Park Meml. Inst., Buffalo, N.Y., 1963; clin. asst. prof. Am. U. Beirut, 1963-79, clin. prof. surgery, 1979-84, chmn. dept. surgery, 1976-79, 81-84; prof., dir. div. plastic surgery St. Louis U., 1984—. Contbr. articles to profl. jours. Recipient Chevaliers award Order of the Cedars, Govt. Lebanon, 1968. Fellow ACS (gov. at large Lebanon chpt. 1981-84); mem. AMA, St. Louis Met. Med. Soc., St. Louis Surg. Soc., Mo. Med. Assn., Lebanese Order of Physicians, Am. U. Beirut Med. Alumni Assn., Am. Soc. Plastic and Reconstructive Surgeons, Am. Soc. Maxillofacial Surgeons, Am. Assn. Chmn. Plastic Surgery, Lebanese Soc. Plastic and Reconstructive Surgeons (pres. 1974-84), Internat. Soc. Burn Injuries (Lebanon rep. 1968-84). Home: 205 S McKnight Rd Saint Louis MO 63124 Office: St Louis U Med Ctr 1325 S Grand Blvd Saint Louis MO 63104

SHEHAN, PATRICK VINCENT, broadcast executive; b. Kansas City, Mo., Oct. 28, 1942; s. Allen McMellan and Lorraine Laverne (Doudna) S.; m. Sharon L. Wilson, July 21, 1963; children: Patrick V. Jr., Kelly, Kimberly. Student, Columbia Sch. Broadcasting, 1970, Neosho County Community Coll., Chanute, Kans., 1979. Staff announcer Sta. KDMO, Carthage, Mo., 1971-74; staff announcer Stas. KKOY and KQSM-FM, Chanute, 1974-82, program dir., 1982—; with pub. relations George Churchill Co., Chanute, 1976-82. Bd. dirs. Neosho County Community Coll. Endowment Found., 1985—, Neosho County Chpt. ARC, 1985—, Drug and Alcohol Abuse Council, Chanute, 1985—. Recipient Outstanding Service award Chanute Area C. of C., 1984, Pub. Awareness award Kans. Assn. Broadcasters, 1984. Democrat. Mem. Assembly of God Ch. Avocations: golf, fishing, bowling. Home: RR 3 Box 293C Liberty MO 64806-9451 Office: Stas KKOY and KQSM-FM PO Box 788 Chanute KS 66720

SHELDON, NANCY WAY, management consultant; b. Bryn Mawr, Pa., Nov. 10, 1944; d. John Harold and Elizabeth Semple (Hoff) W.; m. Robert Charles Sheldon, June 15, 1968. B.A., Wellesley Coll., 1966; M.A., Columbia U., 1968, M.Philosophy, 1972. Registered pvt. investigator, Calif. Mgmt. cons. ABT Assocs., Cambridge, Mass., 1969-70; mgmt. cons. Harbridge House, Inc., 1970-79, Los Angeles, 1977-79, v.p., 1977-79; mgmt. cons., pres. Resource Assessment, Inc., 1979—; ptnr., real estate developer Resource Devel. Assocs., 1980—; ptnr. Anubis Group, Ltd., 1980—. Author: Social and Economic Benefits of Public Transit, 1973. Contbr. articles to profl. jours. Columbia U. fellow, 1966-68; recipient Nat. Achievement award Nat. Assn. Women Geographers, 1966. Mem. Am. Mining Congress, Am. Inst. Mining, Metall. and Petroleum Engrs., Nat. Wildlife Fedn., Nat. Audubon Soc., Nature Conservancy, World Wildlife Fund (charter mem.), Nat. Assn. of Chiefs of Police, Grad. Faculties Alumni Assn. Columbia U., DAR, Am. Wildlife Soc. Club: Wellesley (Los Angeles). Office: Resource Assessment Inc 1431 Washington Blvd Suite 2108 Detroit MI 48226

SHELDON, STEPHEN, osteopathic pediatrics educator, researcher; b. Miami Beach, Fla., Nov. 4, 1947; s. Murray M. and Sally (Lee) S.; m. Eugenia Edwina Korona, Dec. 5, 1976; children: David Patrick, Susan Victoria. BS, U. Fla., 1969; DO, Chgo. Coll. Osteo. Medicine, 1975. Diplomate Am. Bd. Physicians and Surgeons, Am. Bd. Pediatrics. Resident in pediatrics Rush-Presbyn.-St. Luke's Med. Ctr., Chgo., 1975-78, chief pediatric resident, 1977-78, coordinator pediatric residency, 1978-80, dir. pediatric residency, 1980-83; dir. pediatric research Mt. Sinai Hosp. Med. Ctr., Chgo., 1983-85; chmn. dept. pediatrics Chgo. Coll. Osteo. Medicine, 1985—; cons. pediatrician Rush-Presby.-St. Lukes Med. Ctr., 1983—, Mt. Sinai Hosp. Med. Ctr., 1980—, Christ Hosp., Oak Lawn, Ill., 1980—; vis. faculty U. Ill. Coll. Dentistry, Chgo., 1982—. Author: Pediatric Differential Diagnosis, 1979, 2d edit. 1986, Manual of Practical Pediatrics, 1981, Diagnosis and Management of the Hospitalized Child, 1984. Fellow Am. Acad. Pediatrics (cert. merit 1985); mem. AMA, Am. Osteo. Assn. (research grantee 1986), Ambulatory Pediatric Assn. Avocations: painting, ship building, cabinetry, writing. Office: Chgo Coll Osteo Medicine 5200 S Ellis Ave Chicago IL 60615

SHELDON, TED PRESTON, library director; b. Oak Park, Ill., July 5, 1942; s. Preston and Marjorie Sheldon; m. Beverly Stebel; children: Kathy, Mark. BA, Elmhurst (Ill.) Coll., 1964; MA, Ind. U., 1965, PhD, 1976; MLS, U. Ill., 1977. Asst. archivist U. Ill., Urbana, 1976-77; reference librarian U. Kans., Lawrence, 1977-79, head collection devel., 1979-81; assoc. dir. libraries SUNY, Binghamton, 1981-83; assoc. dir. libraries U. Mo., Kansas City, 1983-85, dir. libraries, 1985—. Author: Population Trends, 1976, Kans. Coll. Devel. Policy, 1978, SUNY Coll. Devel. Policy, 1983, History, Sources Social Science, 1985. Mem. ALA, Mo. Library Assn., Assn. Recorded Sound Collection. Office: U Mo Libraries 5100 Rockhill Rd Kansas City MO 64110-2499

SHELL, GARY STEPHEN, systems analyst; b. Cin., Nov. 27, 1951; s. James Howard and Anna Jean (Phillips) S.; m. Diane Pritchard, May 12, 1972 (div. Apr. 1979). AS, Cin. Tech. Coll., 1971. Programmer City of Cin., 1969-72; systems analyst Cin. Bd. Edn., 1972-76; tchr. Great Oaks Vocat. Sch., Cin., 1976; pres. Microworks, Cin., 1976-79; systems integrater MB Computing, Cin., 1979-86, Tominy Inc., Cin., 1986—. Bd. dirs. Stepchild Radio Cin, 1975-83, chmn. bd., 1982. Club: Applesiders (Cin.) (system operator 1985—). Avocations: music, auto racing. Home: 3414 Whitfield Suite 1 Cincinnati OH 45220 Office: Tominy Inc 4221 Malsbary Rd Cincinnati OH 45242

SHELLEY, V(IRGIL) DALE, oil equipment company financial executive; b. Goddard, Kans., Oct. 17, 1926; s. Thomas E. and Irene E. (Jones) S.; m. Irma Lee Ready; children: Nancy, Amy. BSBA in Acctg., U. Wichita, 1950. CPA, Kans. From jr. to sr. acct. Moberly, West & Calvin, Wichita, 1950-55; internat auditor Mountain Iron & Supply Co., Wichita, 1955-56; v.p., treas. MISCO Industries, Inc., Wichita, 1956—. Mem. Am. Inst. CPA's, Nat. Assn. Accts., Kans. Soc. CPA's. Republican. Baptist. Home: 5480 Sullivan Ct Wichita KS 67204 Office: MISCO Industries Inc 257 N Broadway Wichita KS 67202

SHELLHAAS, TAMARA KLOCKNER, art director, artist; b. Cin., July 8, 1957; d. Richard Wilbur and Ruby Ellen (Yount) Klockner; m. John Roger Shellhaas, May 14, 1983; 1 child, Benjamin Elliot. Student, U. Cin., 1975-76, Wright (Ohio) State U., 1977-78, Columbus Coll. Art and Design, 1978-80. Prod. mgr. Lancelot Advertising, Piqua, Ohio, 1981-84; art dir. Star Labels, Inc., Troy, Ohio, 1984—; free-lance artist Robert Keppel, Piqua, 1985-86, Characters, Inc., Troy, 1987—. Painter oil and acrylic paintings, 1975—; exhibited in group shows at Hayner Cultural Ctr., Troy, 1981. Republican. Mem. United Ch. of Christ. Avocation: collector of Impressionist art. Home: 101 Littlejohn Rd Troy OH 45373 Office: Star Labels Inc 1390 Lytle Rd Troy OH 45373

SHELLY, ROBERT KEITH, sociology educator; b. Jackson, Mich., Jan. 5, 1943; s. Keith Herbert and Doris Marian (Wardwell) S.; m. Ann Crowell Converse, Sept. 12, 1964; children: Marshall Keith, Elizabeth Louise. BA, Mich. State U., 1965, MA, 1968, PhD, 1972. Asst. prof. sociology Ohio U., Athens, 1971-77, assoc. prof., 1977—, chmn. dept., 1981-86; cons. Vinton County Schs., McArthur, Ohio, 1986, Community Bank, Lancaster, Ohio, 1984, Area Agy. on Aging, Marietta, Ohio, 1976. Contbr. articles to profl. jours. Adult leader Boy Scouts Am., Athens, 1983-85; vestry mem. Good Shepherd Episcopal Ch., Athens, 1980-83. Grantee Agy. on Aging, 1979. Mem. Am. Sociol. Assn., North Cen. Sociol. Assn. Home: 468 Nu Rad Rd Athens OH 45701 Office: Ohio U Dept Sociology & Anthropology Lindley Hall Athens OH 45701

SHELTON, CHARLES EDWIN, military educator and officer; b. Greeneville, Tenn., Feb. 16, 1955; s. Dove Walter and Mildred Mercitious (Shelton) S.; m. Beverly Jo Williams, Sept. 10, 1977; children: Jennifer, Jason. BS, East Tenn. State U., 1977; MA, Webster U., 1982. Platoon leader CBtry 2 Battalion 57 Air Def. Artillery, Hohenfels, Fed. Republic of Germany, 1977-81; weapons systems officer Air Def. Artillery Combat Devels., El Paso, Tex., 1981-83; tactical ops. officer 1st Battalion, 65th Air Def. Artillery, El Paso, Tex., 1983, system comdr. improved Hawk missile, 1983-85; asst. prof. mil. sci. Kans. State U., Manhattan, 1985, Lawrence, 1985; asst. prof. mil. sci. U. Kans., Lawrence, 1985—; vol. income tax asst. IRS, El Paso, 1985. Served to capt. U.S. Army, 1977—. Mem. Assn. U.S. Army. Avocations: karate, weightlifting, sports. Home: 213 YY Dover Sq Lawrence KS 66044-2083 Office: U Kans Mil Sci Dept Lawrence KS 66045

SHELTON, GEORGE HALLETT, investment banking executive; b. Paducah, Ky., Oct. 18, 1933; s. George Hallett and Mary Ellen (Rogers) S.; m. Carol Marie Hurley, Dec. 28, 1957; children—George Hallett III, John Rogers II, Michael Joseph, Margaret Ellen, Susan Anne. B.S. cum laude in Commerce, U. Notre Dame, 1955. Sr. staff Ernst & Ernst, New Orleans, 1958-61; controller R.P. Farnsworth & Co., Inc., New Orleans, 1962-63; treas., dir. A.L. Jackson Co., Chgo., 1963-68; pres., chief operating officer, dir. Howe, Barnes & Johnson, Inc., Chgo., 1968—; bd. dirs. Midwest Securities Trust Co. Active numerous polit. campaigns; mem. New Trier Republican Orgn.; chmn. Wilmette Sch. Bd. Caucus, Wilmette Forum Adv. Com.; mem. Wilmette Recreation Adv. Com., St. Francis Sch. Bd., St. Francis Parish Council, New Trier Sch. Bd. Caucus; bd. dirs. Wilmette Baseball Assn. Served with USN, 1955-58. Mem. Am. Inst. C.P.A.s, Ill. Soc. C.P.A.s, Securities Industry Assn., N.Y. Stock Exchange. Roman Catholic. Clubs: Union League, Econ., Bond. Office: Howe Barnes & Johnson Inc 135 S LaSalle St Suite 2040 Chicago IL 60603-4477

SHELTON, JEFFERY RANDOLPH, logistics management specialist; b. Chester, S.C., Aug. 29, 1957; s. Claudie Mack and Carrie Mae (Feaster) S. BA, S.C. State Coll., 1979; M of Pub. Adminstrn., Atlanta U., 1981. Program analyst Dept. of Air Force, Robins AFB, Ga., 1981-84, Dept. of Army, Gentile AFS, Ohio, 1984-87; logistics mgmt. specialist Dept. Air Force, Gentile AFS, Ohio, 1987—. Named one of Outstanding Young Men of Am., Jaycees, 1981, 84, 85. Mem. Better Mgmt. Assn. (2d v.p. 1983, 1st v.p. 1984), Omega Psi Phi. Baptist. Home: 5061 Laguna Rd Trotwood OH 45426 Office: Joint Depot Maintenance Analysis Group 1507 Wilmington Pike Gentile Air Force Station Dayton OH 45444-5370

SHELTON, L(OUIS) AUSTIN, clergyman, psychologist; b. Shreveport, La., July 28, 1927; s. Benjamin Lee and Hazel Mae (Russell) S.; m. Bonnie May Curry, July 25, 1952; children: Janice Lynn, Kristel Joy, Marc Austin Lee, Camille Caye. BS in Edn., U. S.D., 1962, MA, 1963, EdD, 1968. Pastor Assembly of God Ch., Vernonia, Oreg., 1954-58, Vermillion, S.D., 1959—; psychologist Area Edn. Agy., Sioux City, Iowa, 1965—. Author: An Analysis of C.H. Spurgeon's Lectures on the Art of Preaching, 1962, A Comparative Study of Educational Achievement in One-Parent and Two-Parent Families, 1968. Bd. dirs. Vermillion Ind. Sch. Dist., 1971-76; pres. PTA, 1971. Served with USNR. Mem. Am. Psychol. Assn., Iowa Psychol. Assn., Phi Delta Kappa. Republican. Avocations: hunting, tennis, racquetball. Home: 1218 Valley View Dr Vermillion SD 57069

SHELTON, SANDRA MARY, medical supplies company official; b. Knoxville, Tenn.; d. Claude Earl and Mary Jane (Eblen) Hudson; m. John E. Shelton, Feb. 17, 1973; children—Ingrid, Eric, David. Community health rep. health and welfare div. Met. Life Ins. Co., N.Y.C., 1968; dist. mgr. statis. research div. Research Triangle Inst., Research Triangle Park, N.C., 1968-73; sales rep. Lederle Pharms. div. Am. Cyanamid Co., Pearl River, N.Y., 1973-76; with Mallinckrodt Inc., St. Louis, 1976-86, S.E. regional mgr. diagnostic div., 1979, assoc. product mgr., 1981-82, product mgr., 1982-84, sr. product mgr., 1984-85, bus. dir., 1985-86; zone mgr. cen. U.S. & Canada Advanced Med. Systems subs. Fidelity Med., 1987—. Home: PO Box 12596 Creve Coeur MO 63141

SHELTON, STEPHEN EDWARD, auditor; b. Columbus, Ohio, Jan. 18, 1955; s. Robert Francis and Jean Cecile (Belt) S.; m. Joy Ann Armbruster, July 8, 1978. BBA, U. Toledo, 1978, MBA, 1983. Internal auditor Sheller-Globe Corp., Toledo, Ohio, 1978-79, auditor data systems, 1979-82; sr. EDP auditor Owens-Ill., Toledo, 1982-83; EDP audit specialist Republic Airlines, Mpls., 1983-86; mgr. EDP auditing Northwest Airlines, St. Paul, 1986—. Mem. EDP Auditors Assn. (membership dir. 1984-85), Inst. Internal Auditors. Republican. Roman Catholic. Avocations: travel, gourmet cooking, skiing. Home: PO Box 11752 Saint Paul MN 55111

SHEMA, WILLIAM C., corporate executive; b. Pitts., Mar. 18, 1944; s. William C. and Catherine M. (Bentz) S.; m. Sheila Ann Shema. BA, U. Wis., Parkside; MBA, U. Wis., Milw. Pres. Midwest Control Systems Inc., Kenosha, Wis.

SHENEFELT, PHILIP DAVID, dermatologist; b. Colfax, Washington, July 31, 1943; s. Roy David and Florence Vanita (Cagle) S.; m. Debrah Ann Levenson; children—Elizabeth, Sara. B.S. with honors, U. Wis.-Madison, 1966, M.D., 1970, M.S. in Adminstrv. Medicine, 1984. Intern U.S. Naval Hosp., Bethesda, Md., 1970-71; general practice Oregon (Wis.) Clinic, 1975; resident in dermatology U. Wis. Hosp., Madison, 1975-78, staff, 1985—; dermatologist Univ. Health Service, U. Wis.-Madison, 1978—, VA Hosp., Madison, 1982-85. Mem. vestry St. Andrews Ch., Madison, 1980-83. Served to lt. comdr. USN, 1969-74. Kellogg fellow, 1980-82. Mem. AMA, State Med. Soc. Wis., Am. Acad. Dermatology, Chgo. Dermatol. Soc., Wis. Dermatol. Soc. Episcopalian. Home: 2759 Florann Dr Madison WI 53711 Office: Univ Health Service 1552 University Ave Madison WI 53705

SHENKAROW, BARRY, professional hockey team executive. Pres., gov. Winnipeg (Man.) Jets (NHL), Can., 1983—. Office: care Winnipeg Jets, 15-1430 Maroons Rd, Winnipeg, MB Canada R3G 0L5 *

SHENKER, DAVID M., physician, neurologist; b. Middletown, Conn., Oct. 14, 1942; s. Benjamin M. and Edna Rose (Newberg) S.; m. Judith E. Polish, Aug. 7, 1966; children: Amy, Abby, Noah. AB, Bowdoin Coll., Brunswick, Maine, 1964; MD, Tufts U., 1968. Diplomate Am. Bd. Neurology. Intern Presbyn.-St. Luke's Hosp., Chgo., 1968-69, resident neurology, 1969-72; lt. commdr. U.S. Pub. Health Service, Washington, 1972-74; asst. prof. neurology Rush Med. Coll., Chgo., 1974—; attending neurologist Presbyn.-St. Luke's Med. Ctr., 1974—, Grant Hosp., Chgo., 1974—. Contbr. articles to profl. jours. Mem. Am. Acad. Neurology, Phi Beta Kappa. Jewish. Avocation: tennis. Office: 845 N Michigan Chicago IL 60611

SHEON, ROBERT PHILIP, rheumatologist; b. Canton, Ohio, Nov. 7, 1934; s. Benjamin William and Kate (Rappoport) S.; m. Irma Jean Shainberg, July 14, 1957; children: Sarah, Amy, David. BS, U. Toledo, 1955; MD, St. Louis U., 1958. Diplomate Am. Bd. internal medicine. Intern St. Louis City Hosp., 1958-59; resident in rheumatology Cleve. Clinic, 1959-62; rheumatologist Toledo Clinic Inc, 1964—; cons., rheumatologist Toledo Hosp., 1964—; mem. staff Flower Hosp., Sylvania, Ohio, 1964—; clin. prof. medicine Med. Coll. Ohio, Toledo, 1987. Author: Soft Tissue Rheum Pain, 1982, Coping with Arthritis, 1987; also articles; mem. edit. bd. Postgrad. Medicine, 1984—. Mem. adv. bd. Vis. Nurse Assoc., 1983—; trustee Arthritis Found., Atlanta, 1986—, founder Northwestern Ohio chpt., 1967. Recipient Lion of Judah, State of Israel, 1981; named Gold T Outstanding Alumnus U. Toledo, 1983. Fellow ACP; mem. Am. Rheumatism Assn. (founding), N.Y. Acad. Scis. Jewish. Avocations: fishing, tennis. Office: Toledo Clinic Inc Toledo OH 43623

SHEPARD, CHARLES ALFRED III, equity guild administrator; b. Bath, Maine, July 5, 1952; s. Charles Alfred Jr. and Barbara (Legard) S.; m. Susan K. Beedle, Apr. 15, 1972. BA, U. Maine, Orono, 1982; MA in Art History, Williams Coll., Williamstown, Mass., 1984. Dir. Workspace Gallery, Orono, 1981-82; research asst. Clark Art Inst., Williamstown, Mass., 1982-83; adminstrv. asst. to dir. Williams Coll. Mus., Williamstown, 1983-84, exec. dir. Mich. Guild Artists and Artisans, Ann Arbor, Mich., 1984—. Contbr. art revs. and essays to profl. publs. Mem. Am. Assn. Mus., Phi Beta Kappa, Phi Kappa Phi. Home: 1678 Murfin Ave Ann Arbor MI 48105

SHEPARD, D. C., wood products manufacturing company executive; b. 1924. BA, Yale U., 1950. With Menasha (Wis.) Corp., Neenah, Wis., 1945—, v.p., 1953-80, pres., chief exec. officer, 1980—, also bd. dirs. Served with USMC, 1943-46. Office: Menasha Corp PO Box 367 Neenah WI 54956 *

SHEPARD, EARL EMANUEL, orthodontist; b. Marine, Ill., Sept. 3, 1908; s. Earl W. and Elma (Sutter) S.; m. Wilma Schwartz, Dec. 26, 1931. D.D.S. cum laude, Washington U., St. Louis, 1931. Diplomate: Am. Bd. Orthodontics (dir. 1970-77, sec.-treas. 1971-77, exec. dir. 1977—; Albert H. Ketcham Meml. award 1979). Gen. practice dentistry Edwardsville, Ill., 1931-38; orthodontic practice St. Louis, 1938—; mem. staff Barnes Hosp., 1954—; mem. staff, mem. cleft palate team St. Luke's Hosp., 1979—; mem. faculty Sch. Dentistry, Washington U., 1931—, prof. orthodontics, chmn. dept., 1953-75, prof. emeritus, lectr., 1975—; pres. Denver Summer Meeting for Advancement Orthodontic Practice and Research, 1970, President's award, 1976. Author: Technique and Treatment with Twin Wire Appliance, 1961, History of Marine, Illinois, 1975; also articles; asst. editor: Am. Jour. Orthodontics, 1953—; editor: Pictures That Hang on Memories Wall, 1965. Alumni rep. bd. dirs. Washington U., 1956-59; bd. dirs. Boys Town Mo., 1961—, Playgoers, St. Louis, 1966-72. Served to lt. col., Dental Corps AUS, World War II, ETO. Decorated Bronze Star, Army Commendation medal; recipient Alumni Faculty award Washington U., 1964; Distinguished Alumnus award Washington U. Sch. Dentistry, 1968; Albert H. Ketcham award, 1979; Disting. Alumni award Washington U., 1984. Fellow Am. Coll. Dentists, Internat. Coll. Dentists; mem. Am. Assn. Orthodontists (sec. treas. 1957-62, pres. 1964, Disting. Service scroll 1983), Midwestern Soc. Orthodontists (sec-treas. 1947-51, pres. 1953), ADA (life), Mo. Dental Assn. (council 1958-61, 1st v.p. 1965), St. Louis Dental Soc. (council 1950-54), Pierre Fauchard Acad., Omicron Kappa Upsilon, Delta Sigma Delta (grand master Upsilon chpt. 1931, Grad. chpt. 1952). Club: University (life). Home: 900 S Hanley Rd Saint Louis MO 63105 Office: 225 S Meramec Ave Saint Louis MO 63105

SHEPARD, LAWRENCE ELWOOD, osteopath; b. Attleboro, Mass., Apr. 11, 1954; s. Elwood Bert and Priscilla Louise (Mott) S.; m. Deborah Ann Sullivan, Aug. 1, 1981; children: Lauren, Kyle, Kaitlan. BS magna cum laude, Fla. So. Coll., 1976; DO, Kirksville (Mo.) Coll. Osteo. Medicine, 1984. Gen. practice osteo. medicine Normandy (Mo.) Osteo. Hosp., 1984-85, Doctor's Clin. Group, Normandy, 1985—. Mem. Am. Osteo. Assn., Mo. Osteo. Assn., St. Louis Med. Assn., Am. Coll. Gen. Practitioners. Episcopalian. Office: Doctors Clin Group Med N 8225 Florissant Rd Normandy MO 63121

SHEPARD, RANDALL TERRY, state supreme court justice; b. Lafayette, Ind., Dec. 24, 1946; s. Richard S. and Dorothy I. (Donlen) S.; B.A. cum laude, Princeton U., 1969; J.D., Yale U., 1972. Admitted to Ind. bar, 1972, U.S. Dist. Ct. for So. Dist. Ind., 1972; spl. asst. to under sec. U.S. Dept. Transp., Washington, 1972-74; exec. asst. to mayor City of Evansville (Ind.), 1974-79; judge Vanderburgh Superior Ct., Evansville, 1980-85; justice Ind. Supreme Ct., 1985—; instr. U. Evansville, 1975-78; chmn. bd. advisors Nat. Trust for Historic Preservation, 1980-85, now chmn. bd. advisors, trustee; chmn. State Student Assistance Commn. of Ind., 1980-85; vice chmn. Vanderburgh County Republican Central Com., 1977-80; mem. state adv. com. Vincennes U., 1983—, Acad. Arts and Scis., U. Evansville, 1983—. Recipient Friend of Media award Cardinal States chpt. Sigma Delta Chi, 1979; Disting. Service award Evansville Jaycees, 1982. Mem. Fed. Bar Assn., Ind. Bar Assn., Ind. Judges Assn. Republican. Methodist. Clubs: Princeton (N.Y.); Capitol Hill (Washington); Columbia(Indpls.). Author: Preservation Rules and Regulations, 1980; contbr. articles to profl. publs. Home: 4057 N Meridian St Indianapolis IN 46208 Office: 304 State House Indianapolis IN 46204

SHEPARD, ROBERT CARL, association executive; b. Durand, Mich., Mar. 22, 1945; s. Donald A. and Florance Marie (Tillstrom) S.; m. Ruth Ellen Woodman, Sept. 10, 1966; children: John Carl, Mary Suzanne. BS, Mich. State U., 1967. Mgr. mem. service Mich. Farm Bur., Lansing, 1971-76; exec. v.p. N.D. Farm Bur., Fargo, 1976-84; asst. dir. tng. Am. Farm Bur., Park Ridge, Ill., 1984—; sec. Nodak Mut. Ins., Fargo, 1976-84. Elder Presbyterian Ch., Fargo, 1982. Mem. Am. Soc. Assn. Execs. (com. mem.), Chgo. Soc. Assn. Exec. (com. mem.), Mem. Am. Soc. Tng. and Devel., Future Farmers Am. (Hon. State Farmer award 1983). Club: Toastmasters (ednl. v.p. 1987). Lodge: Free And Accepted Masons. Home: 56 Fairfield Ave Cary IL 60013 Office: Am Farm Bur 225 Touhy Ave Park Ridge IL 60068

SHEPHERD, DAVID H., management consultant; b. Indpls., June 13, 1943; s. Mary C. Shepherd; BBA, U. Cin., 1966; MBA, Butler U., 1969; m. Jonnie L. Sandlin, Aug. 31, 1974; children: Kellie, Mary Martha. Systems analyst Link Belt div. FMC, Indpls., 1966-68, supr. standard cost acctg., 1968-69; with Touche Ross Co., Detroit, 1970-79, Cleve., 1979-83, ptnr., 1979-83; v.p. Milton Allen & Assocs., 1983-86; v.p. Cleve. Cons. Assocs., 1986—; Trustee, Bus. Edn. Alliance, Detroit. Bd. dirs. Town of Westchester (Mich.), 1977-78. Cert. mgmt. cons. Mem. Inst. Mgmt. Cons., Am. Prodn. and Inventory Control Soc., Am. Mgmt. Assn., Fin. Execs. Inst., Assn. Accts. Clubs: Detroit Athletic (fin. com.), Oakland Hills Country, Shaker Heights Country. Office: 23925 Commerce Park Rd Cleveland OH 44122

SHEPHERD, ELSBETH WEICHSEL, operations engineer; b. Youngstown, Ohio, Dec. 5, 1952; d. Richard Henry and Lesley Frances (Lynn) Weichsel; BS in Math., Carnegie-Mellon U., 1974; MBA, U. Cin., 1978; m. Gordon Ray Shepherd, Aug. 28, 1976. Asst. indsl. engr. Armco, Inc., Middletown, Ohio, 1974-76, asso. indsl. engr., 1976-78, indsl. engr., 1978-82, sr. ops. engr., 1982-86, supr. process planning, 1986—. Mem. news mag. staff Jr. League Cin., 1980-81; vol. Miami Purchase Assn. Am. Iron and Steel Inst. fellow, 1978-81. Mem. Soc. Women Engrs. (pres. sect. 1981-82, provisional regional dir. 1983-84), Assn. Computing Machinery, Am. Inst. Indsl. Engrs. (v.p. services, pres. 1985-86), Tech. Socs. Council of Cin. (pres. 1986-87, 1st v.p. 1985-86, 2d v.p. 1984-85, treas. 1983-84), Engrs. and Scientists of Cin. (sec. 1986—). Home: 6255 Howe Rd Middletown OH 45042 Office: 1801 Crawford St Middletown OH 45043

SHEPHERD, JOHN DAVID, communications executive, counselor; b. Salt Lake City, July 10, 1943; s. John Morgan and Genevieve (Mitchell) S.; m. Bonnie Jean Allen, Mar. 16, 1968; children: Todd, Tyler, Amy, John Adam, JayDee. BS, Brigham Young U., 1967; postgrad., Redlands (Calif.) U., 1969; MA, Ariz. State U., 1970; postgrad., Pepperdine Coll., 1972, U. So. Calif., 1974. Lic. profl. counselor, Calif., Va. Tchr., debate coach Fontana (Calif.) High Sch., 1968-70; prin., tchr. Kino Jr. High Sch. Seminary, Westwood High Sch., Mesa, Ariz., 1970-72; inst. dir. L.D.S. Insts., Los Angeles, 1972-75; area dir. Ch. Edn. System, No. Va., 1976-79; counselor, cons. Ch. Edn. System, No. Va., Washington, 1979-84; chief exec. officer Target Directories Inc., Manitou Beach, Mich., 1984—; lectr. civic, marketing and youth groups. Talk show host radio Sta. WGTS., College Park, Md., 1983-84. Named Outstanding Young Men Am., Jaycees, 1978. Mem. Am. Assn. Marriage Family Therapists (screening com. 1975—), Counseling Devel. Assn., Midwestern Ind. Pubs. Assn. (v.p. 1985). Republican. Mormon. Avocations: racquetball, tennis, drafting, woodwork. Home: 2873 Amsler Dr Adrian MI 49221 Office: Target Directories Inc 6155 US 223 Manitou Beach MI 49253

SHEPHERD, PAUL DOUGLAS, data processing executive; b. Paintsville, Ky., Mar. 12, 1956; s. Tony and Beatrice (Bailey) S. AAS in Computer Tech., Purdue U., 1976; AAS in Supervision, Ind. U.-Purdue U., Ft. Wayne, 1979; BS in Computer Tech., Ind. U., Ft. Wayne, 1979; postgrad., St. Francis Coll., 1985—. Mgr. computer ops. Dilgard Frozen Foods, Ft. Wayne, 1979-81; programmer, analyst Magnavox Electronic Systems, Ft. Wayne, 1981-84, sr. programmer, analyst, 1984—. Named one of Outstanding Young Men Am., 1986. Mem. Avilla (Ind.) Jaycees (charter) (v.p. 1985, treas. 1984-85). Club: Magnavox Mgmt. Ind. Home: 311 Ley St Avilla IN 46710 Office: Magnavox Electronic Systems Co 1415 Profit Dr Fort Wayne IN 46808

SHEPHERD, ROY JAMES, III, campaign director; b. Jacksonville, Fla., Dec. 27, 1942; s. Roy James, II and Willie Martha Marion (Griffith) S.; student Ohio State U., 1960, Rio Grande (Ohio) Coll., 1962-63; m. Patricia Ann Taggart, Nov. 1, 1980. Area mgr. Massey Ferguson, Ltd., Lansing, Mich., 1970-72; ordinary agt. Prudential Ins. Co., Columbus, Ohio, 1972-76, brokerage mgr., 1976-77; ptnr. Davis Agy., Pomeroy, Ohio, 1977-78; owner, operator Arlington Ins. Service, Columbus, 1978-84; owner, prin. Canterbury Fin. Strategies, 1985-86; assoc. dir. Ward, Dreshman & Reinhardt, Inc., 1987—; cons. Minority Devel. Corp., Inc.; composer gospel music. Served with Army N.G., 1964-85. Decorated Army Commendation Medal; recipient DeMolay Cross of Honor; named Outstanding Sales Underwriter, also recipient Nat. Quality award Nat. Assn. Life Underwriters; named hon. Ky. Col. Mem. Profl. Ins. Agts. Assn. Am., Nat. Assn. Life Underwriters, Ins. Econs. Soc. Am., Enlisted Assn. Army N.G., Amvets. Episcopalian. Clubs: Masons, Odd Fellows. Playwright: (with others) Life of Christ, 1982. Home: 5687 Brinkley Ct Columbus OH 43220 Office: Ward Dreshman & Reinhardt PO Box 448 Worthington OH 43085

SHEPHERD, WAYNE LEIGH, industrial engineering executive; b. Barnesville, Ohio, Sept. 22, 1941; s. Donald Wayne and Geneva Mary (Coleman) S.; m. Jane Louise Davidson, Dec. 28, 1962; children: Lesley, Andrew, Mathew. BSME, Ohio U., 1963; MBA, Ohio State U., Columbus, 1971. Registered profl. engr., Ohio. Staff engr. Caterpillar Tractor Co., Peoria, Ill., 1963-66; mgr. prodn. Webster Mfg. Co., Tiffin, Ohio, 1971-73; plan mgr. Webster Mfg. Co., Tiffin, 1976-82, mktg. mgr., 1982-84, v.p. mktg. and sales, 1984-86; mgr. mfg. NRM Corp., Talmadge, Ohio, 1973-76. Pres. United Way Seneca County, Tiffin, 1982, Tiffin Jr. Achievement, 1983. Served to lt. U.S. Army, 1966-69. Mem. Tiffin Indsl. Mgmt. Council (pres. 1981-82), Am. Chain Assn. (bd. dirs. 1983-86). Republican. Methodist. Lodge: Elks. Avocations: fishing, hunting, mechanics, construction. Home and Office: 349 Sycamore St Tiffin OH 44883

SHEPLER, JOHN EDWARD, engineering manager; b. Freeport, Ill., June 23, 1950; s. Edward Charles and Joyce Margaret (Wagner) S.; m. Barbara Jeanne Heinrich, Sept. 11, 1976. BSEE, Milw. Sch. Engring., 1972. Broadcaster Sta. WACI, Freeport, 1972-75; chief engr. Sta. WROK, Rockford, Ill., 1975-79; project engr. Martin Automatic, Rockford, 1979-80; sr. design engr. Sundstrand Corp., Rockford, 1980-84, mgr., 1986—; engring. mgr. Pacific Scientific, Rockford, 1984-86; tech. instr. Rock Valley Coll., Rockford, 1981-84; tech. cons. various broadcasters, 1979—. Author: Sensational Sound Handbook, 1981; columnist Radio World mag., 1982—; also articles; patentee in field. Roman Catholic. Avocation: nature photography. Home: 5653 Weymouth Dr Rockford IL 61111

SHEPPS, R(EGINALD) RONALD, management consultant; b. N.Y.C., Jan. 11, 1939; s. I. Robert and Lillian (Halprin) S.; m. Florence Pearl Zahn, June 4, 1966; children: David, Sari. BA, Queens Coll., 1960; MS, Yale U., 1962; PhD, Case Western Res. U., 1967. Lic. psychologist, N.J., N.Y. USPHS fellow Yale U., New Haven, 1960-62; dir. personnel research and planning Metro. Ins. Cos., N.Y.C., 1967-82; dir. edn. design and evaluation Coopers & Lybrand, Newark, 1983-84; pres. Productivity Strategies, Jamaica Estates, N.Y., 1984-85; dir. mgmt. devel. Sandy Corp, Troy, Mich., 1985-86; v.p. Drake Beam Morin, Birmingham, Mich., 1986—. Contbr. articles to profl. jours. Founding sec. Holliswood (N.Y.) Civic Assn., 1972-74; bd. dirs. Temple Israel, Holliswood, 1980-84. Mem. Am. Psychol. Assn., Met. N.Y. Assn. Applied Psychology (pres. 1982-83), Soc. Indsl./Organizational Psychology, Life Ins. Mgmt. and Research Assn. (chmn. bd. 1979, ins. ind. research planning com.). Democrat. Avocations: tennis, bridge. Home: 4390 Ramsgate Ln Bloomfield Hills MI 48013 Office: Drake Beam Morin 5505 Corporate Dr Troy MI 48098

SHERBIN, MICHAEL, osteopath; b. Mich., Dec. 2, 1937; 1 child, Julie Nicole. BS, Detroit Inst. Tech., 1962; DO, Kansas City (Kans.) Coll. Osteo. Medicine, 1967. Diplomate Am. Bd. Osteo. Medicine. Intern Detroit Osteo. Hosp. and B.C.C.H., Detroit and Warren, Mich., 1968, resident in ear, nose and throat, 1968-71; practice osteo. medicine specializing in facial plastic surgery Warren, 1976—; physician Amateur and Profl. Boxing Assn., Detroit, 1975—; dept. chmn. and trainer Detroit Osteo. hosp. and B.C.C.H., 1976-82; dept. chmn. Mt. Clemens (Mich.) Gen. Hosp., 1981—, trainer 1982—. Served with U.S. Army, 1957. Home: 309 N Gratiot Mount Clemens MI 48043 Office: 13355 10 Mile Rd Room 210 Warren MI 48089

SHERBURNE, PAUL VERNON, educational organization executive; b. Menomonie, Wis., Jan. 2, 1948; s. Marvin Dale and Irene Ann (Steinbring) S.; m. Patricia Jo Armstrong, Sept. 23, 1977; 1 son, Andrew Armstrong. B.A., Macalester Coll., 1974; cert. of completion, Humphrey Inst., U. Minn., 1982. Photographer St. Paul, 1972-76; program dir. World Press Inst., St. Paul, 1976-80, exec. dir., 1980—; founder, pub., Topic mag., 1982—. Home: 1283 Dayton Ave Saint Paul MN 55104 Office: World Press Institute Macalester Coll 1600 Grand Ave Saint Paul MN 55105

SHERE, DENNIS, publisher; b. Cleve., Nov. 29, 1940; s. William and Susan (Luskay) S.; m. Maureen Jones, Sept. 4, 1965; children: Rebecca Lynn, David Matthew, Stephen Andrew. B.S. in Journalism, Ohio U., 1963, M.S. in Journalism, 1964. Staff writer Dayton (Ohio) Daily News, 1966-69; asst. prof. Sch. Journalism Bowling Green (Ohio) State U., 1969-70; fin. editor Detroit News, 1970-72, city editor, 1973-75; editor Dayton Jour. Herald, 1975-80; pub. Springfield (Ohio) Newspapers Inc., 1980-83, Dayton Newspapers, Inc., 1983—. Served with AUS, 1964-66. Mem. Sigma Alpha Epsilon, Omicron Delta Kappa. Office: The Journal Herald Dayton Newspaper Inc 4th & Ludlow Sts Dayton OH 45401

SHERFEY, GERALDINE RICHARDS, educational administrator; b. Pontiac, Mich., Dec. 11, 1929; d. William and Ethel (Spurr) Richards; m. William E. Sherfey, Aug. 4, 1950 (div.); children—Emily J., Laura A., Susan E., William E. B.S., Ind. State U., 1963, M.S., 1965; Ed.S., U. Ga., 1973, Ed.D., 1978. Biology and gen. sci. instr. Hammond (Ind.) Tech.-Vocat. High Sch., 1963-65; advanced biology instr. Griffith (Ind.) Sr. High Sch., 1965-70, dept. chmn. grades K-12, acting sci. cons., 1968-70; mgr. sch. programs (asst. supt. for curriculum and instrn.) Greenville (S.C.) Pub. Schs., 1972-73; instr. edn. Purdue U., Calumet Campus, Hammond, Ind., 1973-75; guest lectr. Purdue U. Calumet Campus and Ind. U. N.W., Gary, 1975-78; sci. instr. grades 7 and 8, Spohn Middle Sch., Hammond, 1975-78, prin. A.L. Spohn Elem./Middle Sch., 1978-80, adminstrv. asst. for curriculum and instruction Hammond Schs., 1980-82, coordinator vocat. program devel. and extended programs 1982-85, dir. curriculum/operation, area career ctr., 1985—; dir. Curriculum and Plant Mgmt., 1985—. Ind. State U. teaching fellow, 1964-65; U. Ga. grad. asst., 1970-72. Co-editor, Ind. State newsletter for adult and continuing edn., 1985. Recipient IAACE State award for Outstanding Contbn., 1986. Mem. World Council for Curriculum and Instruction, Assn. for Supervision and Curriculum Devel., Nat. Sci. Tchrs. Assn., Nat. Middle Schs. Assn., Ind. Middle Schs. Assn. Democrat. Roman Catholic. Contbr. articles to profl. jours. Home: 540 W 56th Ave Merrillville IN 46410 Office: 5727 Sohl Ave Hammond IN 46320

SHERIDAN, MICHAEL BERNARD, publishing company executive; b. Washington, Sept. 13, 1945; s. Brian I. and Mary A. (Watson) S.; m. Linda Susan Jurek, Sept. 27, 1980. Student, Silver Springs Community Coll., 1966. Race car driver U.S. Auto Circuit, Nat. Hot Rod Assn., Nat. Assn. Stock Car Auto Racing, various locations in N.Am., 1968-76; show mgr. Group Promotions, Detroit, 1976-83; pres. GP Pub., Detroit, 1983—. Author: Showtime, 1980; editor (ann. pub.) Hot Rod Show World, 1978—; pub.. Harrahs Auto Collection, 1984; producer: Meadowbrook His. Races, Waterford, Mich., 1985, 86. Mem. com. Meadow Brook Hall Concours, Rochester, Mich., 1985—; producer Automotive Fine Arts Soc. Art Exhibit Benefits United Way, Pebble Beach, Calif., 1986. Served with USCG, 1967. Named Producer of Yr., Internat. Auto Show Producers Assn., Altantic City, 1982. Republican. Roman Catholic. Avocation: racing and restoring vintage autos. Home: 39 Maryknoll Rochester MI 48063 Office: GP Pub 4140 S Lapeer Rd Pontiac MI 48057

SHERIDAN, TIMOTHY PHILIP, college administrator; b. Monmouth, Ill., Jan. 18, 1954; s. Robert Eugene and Pauline (Leafgreen) S.; m. Gina Marie Burgan, Aug. 9, 1980; children: Corey Robert, Kelly Marie. BA, DePauw U., 1976; MS in Edn., Ind. U., 1979. Dir. residence hall, asst. coach basketball Elmhurst (Ill.) Coll., 1979-81; asst. dean students MacMurray Coll., Jacksonville, Ill., 1981-82; asst. dean student affairs Davis and Elkins (W.Va.) Coll., 1982-85; asst. dir. residential life, coordinator jud. affairs Western Ill. U., Macomb, 1985-87, adj. asst. prof., 1986—, asst. to v.p. student affairs, 1987—. Mem. steering com. Bicentennial Pool, Monmouth, 1976-77; mem. mcpl. band, 1973-75; coach Little League Baseball, 1973-75; mem. task force C. of C. Bus. Service, 1981-82; bd. dirs. Randolph County Blood Bank, 1983-85; counselor Meth. Youth Fellowship, 1987—. Mem. Nat. Assn. Student Personnel Adminstrs., W.Va. Assn. Student Personnel Adminstrs. (exec. com. 1983—, task force prevention sexual assault, 1986). Republican. Methodist. Avocations: tennis. golf, woodworking, bridge. Address: Western Ill U 315 Sherman Hall Macomb IL 61455

SHERIDAN, WILLIAM COCKBURN RUSSELL, bishop; b. N.Y.C., Mar. 25, 1917; s. John Russell Fortesque and Gertrude (Magdalene) Hurley) S.; m. Rudith Treder, Nov. 13, 1943; children—Elizabeth Sheridan Noak, Margaret Sheridan Wilson, Mary Sheridan Janda, Peter, Stephen. Student, U. Va.; B.A., Carroll Coll., 1939; S.T.M., Nashotah House Sem., 1968, D.D., 1966, D.C.L., 1984. Ordained priest Episcopal Ch., 1943, consecrated bishop, 1972; asst. priest St. Pauls Ch., Chgo., 1943-44; rector Gethsemane Ch., Marion, Ind., 1944-47, St. Thomas Ch., Plymouth, Ind., 1947-72; Anglican chaplain Culver Mil. Acad., Ind., 1953-58, 70-72; bishop Diocese of No. Ind., South Bend, 1972-87, ret., 1987; clerical dep. to Gen. Conv., Nat. Synod, 1952-70. Author: Journey to Priesthood, 1950, For High School Boys Only, 1955, Between Catholics, 1968. Pres. bd. trustees Howe Mil. Sch., Ind., 1972-86, Nashotah House Sem., 1972-87. Mem. Alumni Assn. Nashotah House Sem. (pres. 1953-55, pres. bd. trustees 1985-87).

SHERIFF, KENNETH WAYNE, social services administrator; b. Carthage, Mo., Dec. 27, 1942; s. Albert Edward and Veda Marie (Holcomb) S.; m. Shirley Ann Wingler, Oct. 3, 1964; children: Wendy Ann, Bradley Wayne. BA, Greenville Coll., 1965; MSW, U. Mo., 1970; M in Pub. Adminstrn., Sangamon State U., 1983. Cert. social worker. Social worker Ill. Dept. Pub. Aid, Centralia, 1965-70, social services cons., 1970-71; asst. regional dir. Ill. Dept. Pub. Aid, Springfield, 1971-72, sect. supr., 1972-79, program mgr., 1979-82, asst. bur. chief, 1982 ; bd. dirs. Woodstock (Ill.) Christian Care Inc., 1981—; exec. dir. Christian Counseling and Ednl. Ministries, Springfield, 1985—; pvt. practice counseling and cons., Tallula, Ill., 1983—. Bd. edn. Community Unit Dist. 8, Pleasant Plains, Ill., 1981—; com. chmn. Citizens Com. for Better Schs., Pleasant Plains, 1979-80; bd. dirs. ministerial edn. and guidance Free Meth. Cen. Ill. Conf., Greenville, 1980—; alumni bd. mem. Greenville Coll., 1975-78. Mem. Nat. Assn. Social

Workers, Am. Soc. for Pub. Adminstrn. Free Methodist. Avocations: canoeing, camping. Home: RR 1 PO Box 8 Tallula IL 62688

SHERMAN, BROCK VAN EVERY, allergist, immunologist; b. Buffalo, Mar. 9, 1944; s. William Blunt and Frances (Van Every) S.; m. Judith Ann Davidson, May 23, 1970; children: Kathryn, Caroline, Andrew. BA, Yale U., 1966; MD, Tufts U., 1970. Diplomate Am. Bd. Allergy and Immunology, Am. Bd. Pediatrics. Chief pediatrics Columbia Point Health Ctr., Boston, 1974-76; physician dept. allergy Milw. Med. Cen. S.C., 1978—; sec., treas. Milw. Med. Clinic S.C., 1982—. Mem. Am. Acad. Allergy and Immunology. Episcopalian. Avocations: running, sailing, bridge. Office: Milw Med Clinic SC 3003 W Good Hope Milwaukee WI 53217

SHERMAN, FRANK WILLIAM, engineer; b. Ft. Dodge, Iowa, Nov. 15, 1946; s. Frank LaSalle and True Rosemary (Miller) S.; m. Joan Francis Van Bruaene, Aug. 21, 1971; children: Emma Daun, Joshua Frank. BS, Iowa State U., 1970. Registered profl. engr., Ill. Air pollution engr. Ill. Environ. Protection Agy., Springfield, 1970-84; mgr. Ill. Vehicle Emission Test Program, Springfield, 1984—; chmn. Air Quality Adv. Com. Chgo. Area Transp. Study, 1976-84. Contbr. articles to profl. jours. Pres. Pasfield Neighborhood Assn., Springfield, 1979; active with First Congl. Ch., Springfield, 1985-86. Avocations: bicycling, bridge. Office: Ill Environ Protection Agy 2200 Churchill Rd Springfield IL 62706

SHERMAN, GEORGE M., executive manufacturing company; b. N.Y.C., Aug. 6, 1941; s. Joseph B. and Fredericka (Hand) S.; m. Betsy Rae Bicknell, Nov. 26, 1966; children: Jonathan, David, Michael, Matthew. B.S., L.I. U., 1963; M.B.A., U. Louisville, 1970. Product gen. mgr. Gen. Electric Co., Bridgeport, Conn., 1966-79; pres. Weed Eater Inc., Emersen Electric Co., Houston, 1979-80; pres. Skil Corp. Emersen Electric Co., Chgo., 1980—. Office: Skil Corp 4801 W Peterson Ave Chicago IL 60646 *

SHERMAN, HUNTER B., clergyman, educator; b. Long Beach, Calif., Aug. 30, 1943; s. Hunter B. and Mary Rawls (French) S.; B.A., Calif. State U., Long Beach, 1965; postgrad. Bapt. Bible Coll., 1965-66; M.Div., Talbot Theol. Sem., 1970; Ph.D., Calif. Grad. Sch. Theology, 1976; m. Louisa Ann Stahl, June 27, 1964; children—Whitnae Nicolle, Garrett Hunter. Prof., Bapt. Bible Coll., Springfield, Mo., 1970—, chmn. Bible dept., 1975-78, acad. dean, 1979-83; pastor Bellview Bapt. Ch., Springfield, 1983—. Mem. Soc. Bibl. Lit., Am. Assn. Collegiate Registrars, Am. Schs. Oriental Research, Israel Exploration Soc., Oriental Inst. U. Chgo. Author: Must Babylon Be Rebuilt, 1970; The Biblical Concept of Babylon, 1976. Recipient Audrey Talbot Meml. award Talbot Theol. Sem., 1970. Office: 628 E Kearney St Springfield MO 65802

SHERMAN, JAMES RICHARD, publisher; b. Luverne, Minn., Aug. 20, 1935; s. Russell Alfred and Blanche Leona (Peterson) S.; m. Merlene Gail Thorson, June 6, 1957; children: Christopher James, Eric Emerson, Lincoln Everett. BA, U. Colo., 1963, MPS, 1964; PhD, U. No. Colo., 1967. Dir. student housing U. Minn., Mpls., 1967-68; asst. chancellor Mnn. Community Coll. System, St. Paul, 1968-73; sr. cons. Ednl. Mgmt. Services, Edina, Minn., 1973-79; owner, pub. Pathway Books, Golden Valley, Minn., 1979—. Author, pub.: (book) Stop Procrastinating-Do It, 1981, How to Overcome a Bad Back, Rejection, Get Set.. Go, Escape to the Gunflint, Middle Age is Not a Disease. Mem. Pubs. Mktg. Assn., Minn. Ind. Pubs. Assn. (sec. 1983-86, treas. 1986—). Republican. Episcopalian. Avocations: cross country skiing, canoeing, hiking, fishing, gardening. Home and Office: 700 Parkview Terr Golden Valley MN 55416

SHERMAN, JULI ANN, psychologist; b. Akron, Mar. 25, 1934; d. Roy V. and Edna Helen (Schultz) S.; m. Stanley George Payne, June 16, 1961; 1 child, Michael George Sherman. BA, Case Western Res. U., 1954; PhD, U. Iowa, 1957. Diplomate Am. Bd. Psychology. Dir. Women Research Inst. Wis., Madison, 1974-79; preceptor psychology dept. U. Wis., 1979-87; practice psychology Madison Psychiatric Assn., 1980-87; psychologist Mental Health Assn., Madison, 1987—. Author: Psychology of Women, 1971, Sex Related Cognitive Differences, 1978; editor: Prism of Sex, 1979, Psychology of Women, 1978; also articles. Rockefeller grantee NSF, 1972-79. Fellow Am. Psychol. Assn. (chmn. fellowship commn. 1979-81, pres.-elect clin. div. 1986); mem. Wis. Psychol. Assn., Wis. Women in Psychology (pres. 1984). Lutheran. Avocation: nature study. Home: 3917 Plymouth Circle Madison WI 53705 Office: Mental Health Assn 20 S Park Madison WI 53715

SHERMAN, KERMIT GLEN, automotive company executive; b. Rolla, Mo., May 12, 1927; s. Shelby and May (Satterfield) S.; m. Violet Fern Roberts, Aug. 9, 1947; children: Gary, Robert, Chris. Mgr. Hausam Co., Sedalia, Mo., 1957-59, Hermann-Brownlow Co., Rolla, 1959-68; v.p., treas. Hermann-Brownlow Co., Springfield, Mo., 1968-70, pres., 1970-72; pres., gen. mgr. Empire Automotive Distbrs., Inc., Springfield, 1972—. Served with USN, 1945-46, PTO. Named to Automotive Hall of Fame, 1986-87. Mem. Mo./Kans. Automotive Wholesalers, Automotive Service Industry, Springfield C. of C. Democrat. Baptist. Lodge: Masons. Avocations: fishing, hunting, boats, travel. Home: 224 E Crestview Springfield MO 65807 Office: Empire Automotive Distributors Inc 1477 E Trafficway St Springfield MO 65802

SHERMAN, KEVIN CARL, juvenile Court administrator; b. Mt. Clemens, Mich., Nov. 9, 1954; s. Harold Kenneth and Marion Ann (Gerds) S.; m. Cheryl Ann Galavage, Nov. 3, 1979. AS, Macomb Community Coll., 1977; BS, Lake Superior State Coll., 1979; MA, Cen. Mich. U., 1983. Registered social worker, Mich. Probation officer Antrim Probate Ct., Bellaire, Mich., 1979-85, adminstr., 1985—. Bd. dirs. Big Bros. and Sisters of Antrim and Kalkaska Counties, Inc., 1980-84, A-Cry, Bellaire, 1983; chmn. Antrim County Dept. Vet. Affairs, Bellaire, 1986. Served With U.S. Army, 1973-75. Mem. Juvenile Officers Assn. Mich. and Ontario, Juvenile Justice Assn. Mich. (bd. dirs. 1981-86, v.p. 1985-86, pres. 1986—), Top Mich. Children's Assn., Am. Legion. Republican. Lutheran. Avocations: sports, reading, music. Home: 11839 Ridgeview Dr Rapid City MI 49676 Office: Antrim County Probate Ct Courthouse PO Box 276 Bellaire MI 49615

SHERMAN, MARILYN C., financial analyst; b. Chgo., Mar. 3, 1961; d. Irvin Sheldon and Marlene Pearl (Altman) S. BS in Acctg., U. Ill., 1983; postgrad., Northwestern U., 1986—. CPA, Ill. Auditor, sr. tax analyst Peat, Marwick, Mitchell and Co., Chgo., 1983-85; fin. analyst Harris Trust and Savs. Bank, Chgo., 1985—. Mem. Am. Inst. CPA's, Ill. Soc. CPA's, Chgo. Soc. Women CPA's, Phi Kappa Phi. Avocations: designing jewelry, tennis, jogging, biking. Office: Harris Trust & Savs Bank 111 W Monroe 200/19 Chicago IL 60606

SHERMAN, MARK, horticulturist; b. New London, Conn., July 21, 1949; s. Byron Stanley and Lillian Mary (Brennan) S.; m. Patricia Ruth Vollrath, Oct. 18, 1969; children: Zachary Elden, Emily Rose. Student, Elgin Community Coll., 1971-72; BS in Plant and Soil Sci., Southern Ill. U., 1975, MS in Plant and Soil Sci., 1976; PhD in Vegetable Crops, Cornell U., 1980. Research asst. So. Ill. U., Carbondale, 1975-76, Cornell U., 1976-80; asst. prof. U. Fla., Gainesville, 1980-85, assoc. prof., 1985-86; research scientist Pillsbury Co., Mpls., 1986—; cons. Nature Fresh Inc., Dominican Republic, 1985-86. Author (with others) (chpt.) Preripening and Ripening, 1987; also articles. Mem. council United Ch. Gainesville, Fla., 1985, Christian enlistment, 1985. Served with U.S. Army, 1967-71. Fla. Tomato Exchange grantee, 1983, 85, Fla. Lettuce Found. grantee, 1985. Mem. AAAS, Am. Soc. for Hort. Sci., Am. Soc. for Plant Physiology, Fla. State Hort. Soc. (v.p. 1984-85). Avocations: running, music, volleyball. Office: The Pillsbury Co 311 Second St SE Minneapolis MN 55414

SHERMAN, MARK A., insurance company executive; b. Buffalo, Nov. 16, 1924; m. Kathleen Ann Laughlin, Feb. 17, 1951; children: Ann, John. AB, Oberlin Coll., 1948; MBA, U. Mich., 1949. CPCU, CLU. Office mgr., dir. tng. and personnel Citizens Ins. Co. Am., Howell, Mich., 1949-59; program developer Allstate Ins. Group, Skokie, Ill., 1959-60; sec./treas. Farmland Ins. Group, Des Moines, Iowa, 1960-67; dir. orgn. planning, regional dir. mktg. Country Cos., Bloomington, Ill., 1967-80; v.p. mktg. Union Ins. Group, Bloomington, 1980—, bd. dirs. Editor quar. in-house publ.; contbr. articles to profl. jours. V.p. planning United Way of McLean County, Bloomington, 1973, bd. dirs., 1972-81; v.p. Bloomington-Norman Symphony Soc., 1985-86, pres., 1986—; elder Presbyn. Ch. Served as sgt. U.S. Army, 1943-46, ETO. Mem. Soc. Ins. Trainers and Educators (life, pres. 1975-76), Soc. CPCU's, Nat. Assn. Ind. Insurers,. Club: Coll. Alumni (Bloomington) (pres. 1972). Lodge: Rotary (v.p. Howell, Mich. chpt. 1959) (bd. dirs. 1984—). Home: 1013 Barton Dr Normal IL 61761 Office: Union Ins Group 303 E Washington Bloomington IL 61701

SHERMAN, MARY ANN CIMRMANCIC, dentist; b. Milw., July 14, 1956; d. Joseph and Antonia (Kraljic) Cimrmancic; m. Michael James Sherman, Oct. 27, 1984. BS, Marquette U., 1978, DDS, 1984. Resident Zablocki VA Med. Ctr., Milw., 1984-85; gen. practitioner Office of Dr. Michael Vitense, Hartland, Wis., 1985-86, Office of Dr. JoAnna Geldner, Delavan, Wis., 1986-87; pvt. practice dentistry Wauwatosa, Wis., 1985—; pvt. practice with husband Dr. Michael J. Sherman Delavan, 1987—; adj. clinical instr. Marquette U., Milw., 1985—. Active Bach Chamber Choir and Orch., Milw. Mem. ADA, Wis. Dental Assn., Greater Milw. Dental Assn., Acad. Gen. Dentistry, Slovenian Cultural Soc. Triglav, Delta Sigma Delta. Roman Catholic. Avocations: folk dancing, cross-country skiing. Home: 526 Sugar Creek Rd Delavan WI 53115 Office: 10425 W North Ave Suite 116 Wauwatosa WI 53226 also: 1221 E Phoenix St Delavan WI 53115

SHERMAN, MITCHELL BRIAN, psychologist; b. Bklyn., Mar. 11, 1947; s. Harry Jacob and Ida (Brenner) S.; m. Colette Monica Klasic, July 27, 1970; 1 child, Lara Jo. BS, Bklyn. Coll., 1968; MA, U. Ill., 1970; PhD, U. Minn., 1983. Lic. cons. psychologist. Psychologist State of Minn., St. Paul, 1976-80, Hennepin County, Mpls., 1980-81; mgmt. cons. Fairview Hosp., Mpls., 1981-82; pres. Rater, Inc., Mpls., 1982—; clin. instr. U. Minn. Med. Sch., Mpls., 1984—; asst. prof. U. Wis. Stout, Menomonie, 1986—; psychology licensure course instr. St. Mary's Coll., Mpls., 1986—; staff psychologist Prodn. Improvement, Hopkins, Minn., 1986. Author: Self Evaluation Handbook, 1976, Employment Catalogue, 1984. Vol. coordinator YMCA, Edina, Minn., 1986; bd. dirs. Youth Emergency Service, Mpls., 1976, Nexus, Inc., Hopkins, 1984. Recipient Suggestion award Dept. of Commerce, 1970; grantee, U. Minn., 1980, Dept. Health and Human Services, 1986; Nat. Computer Systems fellow, 1978. Mem. Am. Psychol. Assn. Office: U Wis Stout Dept Psychology Menomonie WI 54751

SHERMAN, SAUL S., manufacturing company executive; b. 1917. BA, U. Chgo., 1939. Profl. football player Chgo. Bears, 1939-40; pres., treas. Emerson Machinery Corp., 1937-66; with Davis & Thompson Corp., 1948—; pres. Am. Eagle Corp. merged Allied Products Corp., 1962-65; with Allied Products Corp., 1963—, chmn. bd. dirs., 1973—. Office: Allied Products Corp 10 S Riverside Plaza Chicago IL 60606 *

SHERREN, ANNE TERRY, chemistry educator; b. Atlanta, July 1, 1936; d. Edward Allison and Annie Ayres (Lewis) Terry; m. William Samuel Sherren, Aug. 13, 1966. B.A., Agnes Scott Coll., 1957; Ph.D., U. Fla.-Gainesville, 1961. Grad. teaching asst. U. Fla., Gainesville, 1957-61; instr. Tex. Woman's U., Denton, 1961-63, asst. prof., 1963-66; research participant Argonne Nat. Lab., 1973-80; assoc. prof. chemistry N. Central Coll., Naperville, Ill., 1966-76, prof., 1976—. Clk. of session Knox Presbyn. Ch., 1976—, ruling elder, 1971—. Mem. Am. Chem. Soc., Am. Inst. Chemists, AAAS, AAUP, Ill. Acad. Sci., Sigma Xi, Delta Kappa Gamma, Iota Sigma Pi (nat. pres. 1978-81, nat. dir. 1972-78). Presbyterian. Contbr. articles to field to profl. jours. Office: N Central Coll Naperville IL 60566

SHERRILL, THOMAS BOYKIN, III, newspaper executive; b. Tampa, Fla., Nov. 19, 1930; s. Thomas Boykin Jr. and Mary Emma (Addison) S.; m. Sandra Louise Evans, Dec. 27, 1969; children—Thomas Glenn, Stephen Addison. Circulation dir. Tampa Tribune, Fla., 1962-67; circulation dir. Sarasota Herald-Tribune, Fla., 1967-75; v.p. circulation Dispatch Printing Co., Columbus, Ohio, 1975-78, v.p. mktg., 1978—, also dir.; v.p. dir. Ohio Mag., Inc. Bd. dirs. Salvation Army, 1975—, Central Ohio Ctr. for Econ. Edn., 1978—, Ohio Council on Econ. Edn., 1981—, Better Bus. Bur., 1983—; v.p., trustee Columbus Dispatch Charities; pres. Wesley Glen United Meth. Retirement Home, 1986—; mem. pres.'s adv. bd. The Meth. Theol. Sch. Served with USN, 1951-56, Far East, Europe. Recipient Disting. Service award Editor and Pub. Mag., 1978; named hon. pres. Troy State U., 1979, hon. Ky. col., 1980, hon. lt. col. aide-de-camp to gov. Ala., 1984. Mem. Internat. Circulation Mgrs. Assn. (pres. 1975), Internat. Newspaper Mktg. and Advt. Execs., Ohio Newspaper Assn. (pres. 1986—), So. Circulation Mgrs. Assn. (pres. 1967-68, C.W. Bevinger Meml. award 1972), Audit Bur. Circulation (bd. dirs. 1980—), Am. Advt. Fedn., Ohio Newspapers Found., Columbus Area C. of C., SAR. Republican. Methodist. Clubs: Execs. of Columbus, Athletic of Columbus, Muirfield Village Country. Lodge: Kiwanis (pres. 1982). Home: 1569 Langston Dr Upper Arlington OH 43220 Office: Dispatch Printing Co 34 S 3d St Columbus OH 43216

SHERWIN, JOHN, JR., venture capitalist; b. Cleve., Aug. 19, 1938; s. John and Frances (Wick) S.; m. Clara DeMallie, June 30, 1962; children: Heather, John III, Laura, Tyler. BSBA, John Carroll U., 1967. Dir. corp. auditing Diamond Shamrock Corp., Cleve., 1972-76, mgr. internat. planning, 1980-82, v.p. planning, 1982-83; dir. fin. adminstr. Diamond Shamrock Europe, Manchester, Eng., 1976-80; cons. in field Cleve., 1983-84; pres. Heartland Group Inc, Cleve., 1985—; bd. dirs. Brush Wellman Inc., Cleve., 1981—. Trustee Hawken Sch., Cleve., 1973—, Westminster Sch., Simsbury, Conn., 1980—, Cleve. Clinic Found., 1982—, John Carroll U., Cleve., 1985—. Served with U.S. Coast Guard, 1958-60. Republican. Episcopalian. Clubs: Kirtland Country (bd. dirs. 1973-76), Tavern (pres. 1985-87), Union (Cleve.). Avocations: fishing, hunting, reading. Office: Heartland Group Inc 545 Hanna Bldg Cleveland OH 44115

SHERWOOD, DIANE ELIZABETH, personnel director; b. Wichita, Kans., Nov. 26, 1960; d. Howard Kenneth and Joan Karolyn (Sargent) S. BA in Psychology, Colo. Coll., 1983. Group life counselor Nat. Children's Rehab. Ctr., Leesburg, Va., 1983-84; dir. personnel, safety Sherwood Constrn., Wichita, 1984—. Mem. Wichita Updowntowner, 1987. Mem. Kans. Contractors' Assn. (edn. and tng. com. 1985—, convention entertainment com. 1986—). Avocations: athletics, knitting, photography. Home: 3023 W Maple Wichita KS 67213 Office: Sherwood Constrn PO Box 9163 Wichita KS 67277

SHERWOOD, NORMAN PAUL, army education administrator; b. Spokane, Wash., Feb. 10, 1943; s. Lynn Marvin and Ethel Belle (Miller) S.; children—Suni, Jody. B.A. in Polit. Sci., U. Wash., 1966; D.Edn., U. So. Calif., 1982. Pub. relations officer Korea Regional Exchange, Seoul, 1969-71; editor, writer Dept. Navy, Honolulu, 1972-73; edn. services officer Dept. Army, Korea., 1973-79; edn. coordinator Army Recruiting Command, Portland, Oreg., 1979-81, dir. edn., Honolulu, 1981-83; mgr. testing program Hdqrs. U.S. Army Recruiting Command, Fort Sheridan, Ill., 1983—; tchr. ESL, adviser Asia-Pacific Social Cultural Found., Seoul, 1969. Served to sgt. U.S. Army, 1966-69. Recipient Journalism award Dept. Navy, 1971; commendation Dept. Army, 1980, 81, 82, 83; nominated Fed. Employee of Yr., 1982. Mem. Am. Personnel and Guidance Assn., Oriental Inst. Union of Chgo., Mil. Edn. Counselors Assn., Phi Delta Kappa. Methodist. Editor, writer The Pointer, Barbers Point, Hawaii, 1971-73; newspaper columnist Korea Herald, Seoul, 1970; contbr. Korea Times, Seoul, 1969-71. Office: PO Box 203 Education Programs Br Hdqrs US Army Recruiting Command Fort Sheridan IL 60037

SHESGREEN, MARY, psychotherapist; b. Chgo., May 27, 1941; d. James Edward and Rosalind (LaBreche) O'Gallagher; m. Sean Shesgreen, Aug. 8, 1964 (div. 1974); 1 child: Deirdre Roisin; m. Tom Powers, May 2, 1981; stepchildren: Bert, Jack. BS in English, Loyola U., 1963; MS in Linguistics, Northeastern U., 1970; MS in Family Therapy, No. Ill. U., 1979. English tchr. various high schs., Chgo., 1963-68; English instr. Waubonsee Coll., Sugar Grove, Ill., 1970-77; psychotherapist Ctr. for Psychotherapy, Geneva, Ill., 1977-80; pvt. practice psychotherapy St. Charles, Ill., 1981—. Chairperson Kane County (Ill.) ACLU, 1983. Mem. Am. Assn. Marriage and Family Therapists (clin.). Avocation: reading. Office: Assocs in Psychotherapy 12 S 1st Ave Saint Charles IL 60174

SHESTOKAS, JILL BARBARA, beverage distributing company executive; b. Chgo., Oct. 21, 1955; d. John Thomas and Charlotte Christine (Boguch) S. BS in Human Ecology, U. Md., 1979. Program dir. Future Homemakers Am., Washington, 1975-77; editor Intersection Assocs., Cambridge, Mass., 1977-79; gen. mgr. Shestokas Distbg., Inc., Chgo., 1979—; cons. March of Dimes, White Plains, N.Y., 1975-78, Performance Achievement, Chgo., 1983-84. Editor: Wanted: Healthy Babies, 1977, Healthy Babies: Chance or Choice, 1978. Mem. Pres.' Com. Employment of Handicapped, Washington, 1975-76; vol. Infant Welfare Soc., Chgo., 1980—; bd. dirs. Wellness Found., Lemont, Ill., 1985—. Mem. Nat. Beer Wholesalers Assn., Cath. Youth Orgn., Kappa Kappa Gamma.

SHETH, RAMESH D., electrical engineer, high-tech research company executive; b. Bombay, Oct. 31, 1942; came to U.S., 1963; s. Devchand R. and Mandakini D. Sheth; m. Neela P. Mehta, Apr. 5, 1967; children: Sandeep, Sameeta, Sonal. BSEE, Victoria Jubilee Tech. Inst., Bombay, 1963; postgrad., U. Cin., 1965; MBA with honors, Miami U., Oxford, Ohio, 1969. Cons. engr. Marbon Chem., Parkersburg, W.Va., 1965-66, Union Carbide, Charleston, W.Va., 1965; product devel. engr. Belden Corp., Richmond, Ind., 1966-74, product devel. mgr., 1974-78; product and material devel. mgr. Belden Corp., Geneva, Ill., 1978-83; pres. S.I. Tech., Geneva, 1983—; Chmn. Electronic Industry Assn., Washington, 1978-84; tech. advisor Internat. Electrotech. Commn., 1982-85. Patentee in field. Mem. IEEE, Am. Mgmt. Assn. Hindu. Avocations: photography, tennis. Home: 224 Cambridge Dr Geneva IL 60134 Office: SI Tech PO Box 609 Geneva IL 60134

SHETTY, SHANKARA, senior project planning engineer; b. Mangalore, India, Apr. 1, 1945; s. M. Kochappa and Sanjeevi K. (Mally) S.; m. Poornima S. Bhandary, June 25, 1976; children: Nima S., Chethan G. BSEE, K.R.E.C., Surathkal, India, 1968; MS in Indsl. Engring., Ill. Inst. Tech., 1977; MBA, DePaul U., 1982. Registered profl. engr., Wis. Elec. engr. NGEF ltd., Bangalore, India, 1970-74; design engr. Sargent & Lundy, Chgo., 1974-77, project planning engr., 1978-81, sr. project planning engr., 1981—; with station nuclear engring. dept. La Salle (Ill.) Nuclear Project Commonwealth Edison Co., 1986—. Recipient grad. tng. grant Govt. India, 1968-69. Mem. Alpha Phi Mu. Hindu. Avocations: reading, photography. Home: 850 Case Dr Roselle IL 60172 Office: Sargent & Lundy Engrs 55 E Monroe St Chicago IL 60603

SHIBLEY, FREDERIC JAMILE, glass company executive; b. Copperhill, Tenn., May 7, 1946; s. George Toufic and Adele (George) S.; B.S. cum laude in Mktg., U. Tenn., 1968; m. Andrea Mannal Haug, Sept. 27, 1969; children—Robert Liggett, Andrew Williamson. Sales trainee Owens Corning Fiberglas, Raleigh, N.C., Miami, Fla., 1968-69, salesman, Cleve., 1969-72, salesman, Chgo., 1973-74, nat. mktg. mgr., Toledo, 1974-77, mgr. shingle mktg. sect., 1977-78, product line mgr. residential roofing, 1978-79, product and facilities devel. mgr. residential roofing, 1979-80, product and market mgr., residential roofing, 1980-84, venture specialist new bus. ops., 1984-85, venture mgr., 1985—; asst. mgr. Shibley's Fabric Center, Dayton, Tenn., 1972-73. Scoutmaster, Boy Scouts Am., Dayton Tenn., 1973; advisor Jr. Achievement, Toledo, 1978-80; deacon Christ Presbyterian Ch., Toledo, 1987—. Mem. Asphalt Roofing Mfrs. Assn. (residential roofing com. 1980-84), Phi Sigma Kappa, Phi Kappa Phi, Delta Sigma Pi, Beta Gamma Sigma. Club: Masons. Home: 3738 Edgevale Rd Toledo OH 43606 Office: Owens Corning Fiberglas Corp 1 Levis Sq Toledo OH 43659

SHIEH, CHING LONG, structural engineer, researcher; b. Tainan, Taiwan, Jan. 24, 1948; came to U.S., 1973, naturalized, 1983; s. Yen-Chy and Jean (Tsai) S.; m. Shu-Hui Chuang, June 24, 1978; 1 dau., Lisa. B.S. in Civil Engring., Cheng Kung U.-Taiwan, 1970; M.S. in Civil Engring., Nat. Taiwan U., 1973; Ph.D. in Structural Engring., U. Fla., 1975. Registered profl. civil engr., Republic of China; registered profl. structural engr., Ill. Fla. Research asst. U. Fla., Gainesville, 1973-75; vis. scholar Northwestern U., Evanston, Ill., 1976-77; structural engring. specialist Sargent & Lundy Engrs., Chgo., 1978-80, sr. structural engring. specialist, 1980—, assigned trainer for engrs. analysis and design nuclear power plants People's Republic of China, 1983. Mem. ASCE, Mid.-Am. Chinese Sci. and Tech. Assn. (bd. dirs.). Contbr. tech. papers and reports to internat. jours. Home: 1316 Nichols Rd Arlington Heights IL 60004 Office: 55 E Monroe St 21T57 Chicago IL 60603

SHIELDS, GORDON ADAMS, manufacturing company executive; b. Pitts., Apr. 12, 1957; s. Bruce Maclean and Nancy (Adams) S.; m. Karen Ann Doyle, June 9, 1984. BS in Mktg. and Mgmt., Miami U., Oxford, Ohio, 1979. Nat. sales rep. Ferno Washington, Inc., Wilmington, Ohio, 1980-84, product mgr., 1984-86, mktg. mgr., 1986—. Republican. Presbyterian. Home: 1155 Peggy Ln Wilmington OH 45177 Office: Ferno Washington Inc 70 Weil Way Wilmington OH 45177

SHIELDS, PATRICK THOMAS, JR., property tax manager; b. San Antonio, Sept. 5, 1935; s. Patrick Thomas and Mary Belle (Carson) S.; m. Mary Lou Sechrist, Mar. 28, 1964; children: Llewellyn Sechrist, Patrick Terrence. BBA in Real Estate, U. Tex., 1959. Loan officer Oak Cliff Savs., Dallas, 1962-65; appraiser assessor's office City of Richmond, Va., 1965-68; tax mgr. Sears Roebuck and Co., Chgo., 1968—. Plan commr. Village of Buffalo Grove, Ill., 1973-85, chmn., 1978-85, trustee, 1985—; bd. dirs. Wheeling Twp. Rep. Orgn., Arlington Heights, Ill., 1984—. Mem. Inst. Property Taxation (cert., membership com. 1985, CMI com. 1986), Soc. Real Estate Appraisers (cert.), Am. Inst. Real Estate Appraisers (cert.), Internat. Assn. Assessors Officers (chmn. subscribing mem. com. 1985-87, membership service com. 1984, Harry Galkin award 1984, Presdl. Citation 1985). Republican. Presbyterian. Avocation: reading. Home: 1016 Whitehall Dr Buffalo Grove IL 60089 Office: Sears Roebuck & Co Sears Tower D/970 Chicago IL 60084

SHIER, JOHN DAVID, charitable organization executive; b. Madison, Wis., Jan. 23, 1935; s. Harold Bernard and Rachel Marie (Reitan) S.; m. Rosalie Ann Holden, Aug. 19, 1961; 1 child, Elizabeth Anne. BA, St. Olaf Coll., 1956; MA in Philosophy, U. Wis., 1968, PhD, 1972. Asst. prof. U. Wis., Green Bay, 1965-74; exec. dir. Area Agy. on Aging, Green Bay, 1974-78, United Way of Brown County, Green Bay, 1978—; mem. adv. bds. social work and nursing U. Wis., Green Bay, 1984—; pres. Wis. Assn. Agys. on Aging, 1974-78, nat. bd. dirs. 1976-78. Vice-chairperson, then chairperson planning adv. com. Wis. State Dept. Transp., 1976-80; community lectr. U. Wis., Green Bay, 1975; pres. Voluntary Action Ctr., 1976-78; bd. chairperson Juvenile Ct., 1979-80; mem. De Pere and Allouez Planning Commns., 1974—; pres. Scholarships, Inc., 1985—; bd. dirs. Green Bay Symphony 1980—; v.p. Friends of Green Bay Wildlife Sanctuary, 1982-84; vol. Bellin Hosp. Hospice, 1982—;blacksmith and weaver Heritage Hill State Pk., 1978—, bd. dirs. 1985—; actor Theater of Concern, 1970-82, Evergreen Prodns., 1985—; curriculum com. Leadership Green Bay program Greater Green Bay C. of C. Recipient Outstanding Tchr. award Standard Oil Co., U. Wis., 1968, Brotherhood award B'naiB'rith Green Bay, 1974, Liberty Bell award Brown County Bar Assn., 1980. Lodge: Optimists (sec. Green Bay 1981-82). Avocations: blacksmithing, weaving, bicycle touring. Home: 309 Arrowhead Dr Green Bay WI 54301 Office: United Way Brown County 123 S Webster Ave Green Bay WI 54301

SHIERHOLZ, JOHN DEE, radiologist; b. Ft. Dodge, Iowa, Dec. 29, 1943. BA, Grinnell (Iowa) Coll., 1966; MD, U. Iowa, 1970. Diplomate Am. Bd. Radiology. Intern Highland Gen. Hosp., Oakland, Calif., 1970-71; resident in radiology U. Iowa, 1973-76; radiologist McFarland Clinic, Ames, Iowa, 1976—, also bd. dirs. Served to lt. comdr. USPHS, 1971-73. Mem. AMA, Iowa Med. Soc., Story County Med. Soc. (pres. 1986-87), Am. Coll. Radiology, Radiology Soc. of N.Am., Izaak Walton League. Episcopalian. Avocations: tennis, water sports. Home: 1926 George Allen Ave Ames IA 50010 Office: McFarland Clinic 1215 Duff Ave Ames IA 50010

SHIH, CHIA HSIN, electrical power engineer; plasma physicist; b. Peking, China, Mar. 8, 1941; s. Shao and Hen Feng (Wen) S.; came to U.S., 1966, naturalized, 1977; B.S., Nat. Taiwan U., 1963; M.S., U. Toronto, 1966; Ph.D., Poly Inst. Bklyn., 1971; m. Grendy P. Wang, Oct. 10, 1970; children—Willard C., Loren C. Registered profl. engr., Ohio. Asst. engr. Stanford Linear Accelerator Center, summer 1967; engr., sr. engr. Am. Electric Power Service Corp., 1970, 76-77; mgr. elec. research, N.Y.C., now Columbus, Ohio, 1978—; lectr. math. dept. Chinese Naval Acad.; adj. lectr. elec. engring. dept. CCNY; NRC Can. research asst. Mem. IEEE (sr.), Bioelectromagnetics Soc., Chinese Am. Assn. Cen. Ohio (exec. sec. 1985-86, pres. 1986-87), Sigma Xi. Contbr. chpts. to Handbook of Electrical and

Computer Engineering, articles to engring. jours. Office: AEP 1 Riverside Plaza Columbus OH 43216

SHIMALA, JOSEPH MICHAEL, industrial engineer; b. Hammond, Ind., Aug. 15, 1954; s. Anthony Thomas and Helen Dolores (Solamon) S.; m. Annette Marie Girman, June 24, 1978; 1 child, Kurt Joseph. BS, Purdue U., Hammond, 1977; MBA, Ind. U., Gary, 1985. Asst. mgr. Kitchens of Sara Lee, Whiting, Ind., 1974-77; supr. Am. Maize Prodn. Co., Whiting, 1977-79; indsl. engr. Oscar Mayer & Co., Chgo., 1979-81, Vulcan Mold & Iron Co., Lansing, Ill., 1981-85; sr. indsl. engr. Allied Tube & Conduit Co., Harvey, Ill., 1985—; bd. dirs. FGS Enterprises, Inc. Mem. Inst. Indsl. Engring., Beta Gamma Sigma. Roman Catholic. Lodge: KC. Avocation:golf. Home: 822 Appletree Dr Schererville IN 46375 Office: Allied Tube & Conduit Co 16100 S Lathrop Ave Harvey IL 60426-6021

SHIMANDLE, FRANCIS EDWARD, advertising agency executive, writer, illustrator; b. Chgo., Nov. 20, 1942; s. Leonard Thomas and Margaret Frances (Voda) S.; m. Sally Ann Callanan, Sept. 5, 1963 (dec. July 1975); children—Shannon Mary, Del Francis, Tara Janine; m. Constance D. Baker, June 26, 1976 (div. Feb. 1984); 1 child, Christopher Jaime. Student Chgo. Acad. Fine Arts, 1960-61. Prin. v.p., The Art Guys, Inc., Evansville, Ind., 1967-69; art dir. Albert Jay Rosenthal & Co., Chgo., 1969-70; exec. art dir. Rothenberg, Feldman & Moore, Chgo., 1970-73; creative dir. Scussell/Miller, Chgo., 1973-76, PGM, Inc., Chgo., 1976-83; prin. Our Co., Inc., Chgo., 1983—. Co-author, illustrator: Chocolate Mooselaneous, 1984. Songwriter popular songs. Recipient awards in field. Roman Catholic. Club: Naturals Social and Athletic (sec. 1981-83) (Chgo.). Home and Office: 411 S Sangamon St Apt 6-D Chicago IL 60607

SHIMMEL, ROBERT GILHAM, dermatologist; b. Jackson, Mich., Feb. 23, 1930; s. Earl Clinton and Alta Stewart (Reid) S.; m. Janice Marie Evely, Oct. 12, 1957; children—Anne E., Thomas R., Amie S., Elizabeth A. B.A., Albion Coll., 1951; D.O., Chgo. Coll. Osteopathic Medicine, 1955. Diplomate Am. Osteo. Bd. Dermatology. Intern Chgo. Osteo. Hosp., 1955-56; dermatology preceptor Chgo. Osteo. Hosp., 1956-59; pvt. practice dermatology, Riverview, Mich., 1959—; cons. Riverside Osteo. Hosp., Trenton, Mich., 1959—; clin. prof. Mich. State U. Coll. Osteo. Medicine, Lansing, 1972—. Diplomate Nat. Bd. Examiners for Osteo. Physicians and Surgeons. Fellow Am. Osteo. Coll. Dermatology (pres. 1963-64, sec. 1969-74); mem. Am. Osteo. Assn., Mich. Osteo. Soc. Dermatologists (pres. 1969-70), Mich. Assn. Osteo. Physicians and Surgeons, Inc., Acad. Dermatology, Wayne County Osteo. Assn. Republican. Presbyterian. Avocation: running. Home: 19891 Parke Ln Grosse Ile MI 48138 Office: 17171 Fort Box 2070 Riverview MI 48192

SHIMURA, FUMIO, materials scientist; b. Tokyo, July 19, 1948; s. Hidetaro and Hiroko (Ueda) S.; m. Mutsuko Ishimori, July 19, 1978. BS, Nagoya Inst. Tech., Japan, 1972, MS, 1974; PhD, Nagoya U., Japan, 1982. Research scientist NEC Corp., Kawasaki, Japan, 1974-80; sr. research scientist NEC Corp., Kawasaki, 1980-83; mgr. research applications Monsanto, St. Louis, 1983-87, sci. cons., 1987—; adj. prof. N.C. State U., 1986-87, vis. prof., 1987—. Author: Sand to Electronics, 1986, (chpt.) VLSI handbook, 1985. Mem. Electrochem. Soc., Japan Applied Physics Soc., Japan Crystallography Soc., Japan Crystal Growth Assn. Avocations: golfing, travelling, tennis, skiing, movies. Home (temporary): 7220 Bluffside Ct Raleigh NC 27615 Office: Monsanto Electronic Materials Co 800 N Lindbergh Saint Louis MO 63167

SHINDLER, SCOTT L., podiatrist; b. Yankton, S.D., May 5, 1956; s. Edward Isadore and Sue (Daskovsky) S.; m. Karen Davidson, June 6, 1982. BS, U. Iowa, 1978; D of Podiatric Medicine, Ill. Coll. Podiatric Medicine, 1982. Gen. practice podiatric medicine Yankton, 1982—; team podiatrist Mt. Marty Coll., Yankton, 1982—, U. S.D., 1983—. Contbr. articles to profl. jours. V.p. Community Concert Bd., Yankton, 1986. Mem. Am. Podiatric Med. Assn., S.D. Podiatric Med. Assn. (v.p. 1985—). Democrat. Club: Quarterback (treas. 1986). Avocations: golf, basketball, tennis, running. Home: 508 James Pl Yankton SD 57078 Office: Shindler Foot Clinic 220 W 3d St Yankton SD 57078

SHINDLER, STEVEN HUNT, lawyer, political consultant; b. Yankton, S.D., Nov. 26, 1954; s. Edward Isadore and Suzanne (Daskovsky) S.; m. Roxanne Louise Foresman, May 25, 1986. BS, Drake U., 1977; JD, Calif. Western Sch. Law, 1982. Bar: Mo. 1983, Iowa 1984, Nebr. 1984. Atty. Jackson County, Kansas City, Mo., 1982-83; exec. asst. Iowa Supreme Ct., Des Moines, 1983-84; assoc. Wimer, Hudson, Flynn & Neugent, Des Moines, 1984—. Democrat. Jewish. Avocations: athletics, golf, softball. Office: Wimer Hudson Flynn & Neugent 222 Equitable Bldg Des Moines IA 50309

SHINE, BARBARA, advertising executive; b. Mpls., July 22, 1938; d. Monroe J. and Charlotte K. Shine. Ph.B. in Communications, Northwestern U., 1982; A.A., U. Minn., 1960. With Dow Jones & Co., Inc., Wall St. Jour., Denver, Los Angeles, Silver Spring, Md. and Chgo., 1962—. Midwest advt. coordinator Travel for Bus. and Pleasure, office mgr. classified advt. sales, 1980—. Com. mem. Mental Health Assn. Montgomery County, Kensington, Md., 1973-77; mem. mental health edn. adv. com. State of Md., Balt., 1975-77; com. mem. Mental Health Assn. Greater Chgo., 1977-78; mem. leadership com. U. Minn. Alumni Assn., Chgo., 1980-86. Recipient Crystal Prism award Advt. Club, 1974. Mem. Am. Advt. Fedn. (recipient Citations for Meritorious Service 1972, 74, dir. 2d dist. 1971-76), Midwest Bus. Travel Assn. (bd. dirs. 1984—), Advt. Club Met. Washington (com. mem., dir. 1974-77, pres. 1973-74). Office: 1 S Wacker Chicago IL 60606

SHINKLE, NORMAN DOUGLAS, state senator, lawyer; b. Toledo, Oct. 4, 1950; s. Ted V. and Marge Shinkle; m. Linda K. Pompi, Oct. 1976; 1child, Theodore Michael. BS, Mich. State U., 1972; JD, U. Toledo, 1979. Commr. Monroe County, Mich., 1972-76; supr. Bedford Twp., Temperance, Mich., 1976-78; ptnr. Shinkle & Shinkle, Temperance, 1980-85; mem. Mich. State Senate, Lansing, 1985—. Mem. Toledo Area Council Govts., 1973-78, Mich. Adv. Commn. Juvenile Justice, Lansing, 1976-78; chmn. Bedford Twp. Civil Preparedness Bd., Temperance, 1976-78, Monroe County Reps., 1978-82. Episcopalian. Avocations: tennis, basketball, bicycling. Home: 7499 Canterbury Dr Lambertville MI 48144

SHINN, ARTHUR FREDERICK, pharmaceutical company medical director, business executive, educator; b. N.Y.C., May 23, 1945; s. A. Frederick and Eleanor (McDonald) S.; m. Margaret See, Aug. 12, 1978; children: Jeffrey, Kara Nicole, Caitlin Jennifer. BS, L.I. U. Bklyn. Coll. Pharmacy, 1968; PharmD, U. Mich., 1972. Lic. pharmacist, Tenn., Mo., Mich. Supr., dir. drug info. ctr. William Beaumont Hosp., Royal Oak, Mich., 1972-76; asst. prof. clin. pharmacy Wayne State U., Detroit, 1972-76; asst. prof., dir. drug info. ctr. St. Louis Coll. Pharmacy, 1976-78; mgr. profl. relations med. dept. Beecham Labs., Bristol, Tenn., 1978-82; med. dir., exec. v.p. Profl. Drug Systems, St. Louis, 1982—, also bd. dirs.; adj. assoc. prof. family practice Quillen Dishner Sch. Med., Johnson City, Tenn., 1979-82; staff cons. clin. pharmacology Faith Hosp., Creve Coeur, Mo., 1983—; bd. dirs. Trimel Corp., Toronto, Ont., Can. Editor: Evaluations of Drug Interactions, 1985; cons. clin. editor: Mosby's Pharmacology in Nursing, 1986; contbr. numerous articles to profl. jours. Fellow NIH, 1968. Mem. Am. Coll. Clin. Pharmacy, Am. Pharm. Assn., Am. Soc. Hosp. Pharmacists, Drug Info. Assn., Rho Chi, Iota Mu Pi. Avocations: fishing, gardening. Home: 630 Clover Trail Dr Chesterfield MO 63017 Office: Profl Drug Systems Inc 2388 Schuetz Rd Suite A56 Saint Louis MO 63146

SHIPKA, RONALD BRUCE, business executive; b. Chgo., Dec. 1, 1938; s. John and Mildred (Kubala) S.; m. LaVerne Young, May 6, 1961; children: Ronald Bruce Jr., John Young. BS, U. Ill., 1959. Lic. real estate broker, Ill.; lic. gen. contractor, Chgo. Pres. Enterprise Devel. Co., Chgo., 1961—; bd. dirs. Home Improvement Council, Chgo., 1977-80. Vestryman St. Paul's Ch., Delray Beach, Fla., St. Richards, Chgo., Holy Comforter, Kenilworth, Ill. Recipient Northside Real Estate Bd. award, Chgo., 1985, 87; Sun Times Apt. Tribute award, Chgo., 1985, Commendation for Pioneering Devel. Work, Ill. Ho. Rep., 1984. Mem. Lakeview Businessmens Assn. (bd. dirs. 1985—). Clubs: Skokie Country (Glencoe, Ill.); Quail Ridge Country (Boynton Beach, Fla.); I Men's Assn. (Champaign, Ill.). Avocations: tennis, fishing.

SHIPLEY, EDWARD GENE, vocational assessment specialist; b. Hamersville, Ohio, Apr. 24, 1930; s. Edmond F. and Enid M. (Steele) S.; m. Bobbie J. Edwards, June 30, 1951; children: Randall G., Brenda K. Whitman. BS in Edn., Wilmington Coll., 1953; MEd, Miami U., Oxford, Ohio, 1957; postgrad., Ohio State U., 1971; EdD, U. Sarasota, Fla., 1978. Lic. psychologist, Ohio; cert. counselor and sch. psychologist, Ohio. Sch. psychologist Adams County Schs., West Union, Ohio, 1971-80; ednl. cons. Ohio Dept. Edn., Columbus, 1980; counselor, psychologist Clinton County Mental Health Ctr., Wilmington, Ohio, 1980-83; sch. psychologist Circleville (Ohio) City Schs., 1983-84; vocat. assessment specialist Pickaway Ross Vocat. Ctr., Chillicothe, Ohio, 1984—. Served with USAF, 1951-55. Mem. Am. Psychol. Assn., Am. Vocat. Assn. Republican. Methodist. Home: 7 Zander Dr Chillicothe OH 45601 Office: Pickaway Ross Vocat Ctr 895 Crouse Chapel Rd Chillicothe OH 45601

SHIPLEY, TONY LEE, software company executive; b. Elizabethton, Tenn., July 19, 1946; s. James A. and Edith J. (Crowder) S.; m. Lynda Anne Jenkins, Nov. 19, 1971; children: Blake Alan, Sarah Robyn. BS in Indsl. Engring., U. Tenn., 1969; MBA, U. Cin., 1975. Indsl. engr. Monsanto Co., Pensacola, Fla., 1969-72; mktg. mgr. SDRC, Cin., 1972-76; v.p. sales and mktg. Anatrol Corp., Cin., 1977-81; pres. Entek Sci. Corp., Cin., 1981—. Mem. ASME, Soc. Automotive Engrs., Vibration Inst. Republican. Club: Terrace Park (Ohio) Country. Avocations: golf, family activities. Home: 7 Laurelwood Dr Milford OH 45150 Office: Entek Sci Corp 4480 Lake Forest Dr Suite 316 Cincinnati OH 45242

SHIPMAN, CHARLES DARREL, university dean; b. Kilgore, Nebr., Apr. 19, 1924; s. Marion Samuel and Margaret Louise (Hill) S.; m. Eva June Holm, Aug. 24, 1952; children—Gregory Kent, Brian Dean; m. 2d, Dorothy Ann Pringle, Aug. 27, 1978; 1 stepson, Dana Drew. B.S., U. Nebr.-Lincoln, 1950, M.E., 1951, Ed.D., 1957. Supt., Thomas County High Sch., Thedford, Nebr., 1951-56; asst. prof. tchr. edn. Dana Coll., Blair, Nebr., 1957-58; asst. prof. ednl. adminstrn. Ball State U., 1958-61, adminstrv. asst. to chmn. div. edn., 1961-65, asst. dean Tchrs. Coll., 1965-74, 76—; dep. dir. Nat. Right to Read Program, Office of Edn., Washington, 1974-75, acting dir., 1975-76; cons. Dept. of Def. Schs., W.Ger., 1967, Am. Schs., Bolivia, 1969-70; dir. 12 state tech. asst. team Office of Edn., 1972-74; mem. nat. adv. bd. Fund for Improvement of Postsecondary Edn., U.S. Dept. Edn., 1983-86. Served with USNR, 1943-46. Recipient Outstanding Service award Phi Delta Kappa, 1973; Outstanding Service award Right to Read Program, P.R., 1976; named Hon. Sec. of State, State of Ind., 1983, Sagamore of the Wabash, Gov. Ind., 1986. Mem. Assn. Supervision and Curriculum Devel., Nat. Assn. Tchr. Educators, Phi Delta Kappa. Methodist. Lodges: Elks, Kiwanis. Author: (with others) American Cooperative Schools in Bolivia, The Ball State Report, 1970; Kindergarten Overseas, a Study of the Requirements for Establishing Kindergarten as Part of the Department of Defense Overseas Dependent Schools, 1967; A Look at the Administrative Structure of Education in England, An Onsite Report, 1980. Office: Ball State University 1008 Teachers College Muncie IN 47306

SHIPP, JEFFREY CRAIG, lawyer; b. Louisville, Jan. 20, 1959; s. Darl B. and Linda (Blackburn) S.; m. Marjorie Elizabeth Sweet, Aug. 14, 1982; 1 child, Matthew Alexander. BA, No. Ky. U., 1981, JD, 1984. Bar: Ky. 1985, U.S. Dist. Ct. (ea. dist.) Ky. 1985, Ohio 1986, U.S. Dist. Ct. (so. dist.) Ohio 1987, U.S. Ct. Appeals (6th cir.) 1987. Assoc. Meredith L. Lawrence & Assocs., Covington, Ky., 1984-85, Lindhorst & Dreidame, Cin., 1985—. Mem. ABA, Ky. Bar Assn., Ohio State Bar Assn., Cin. Bar Assn., Assn. Trial Lawyers Am., No. Ky. U. Alumni Assn., Salmon P. Chase Law Alumni Assn. Democrat. Mem. Christian Ch. Avocations: golf, hunting, fishing, softball, reading.

SHIPP, TRAVIS, education educator, author; b. Waycross, Ga., Jan. 10, 1940; s. Travis and Pernia (Ellis) S.; m. Barbara Diane Blake, Oct. 9, 1964 (div. Mar 1980). BS in Engring., Auburn U., Auburn, Ala., 1962, MBA, 1971; EdD, U. Ga., 1974. Registered profl. engr. Dean Auburn U., Montgomery, Ala., 1971-72; prof. Marshall U., Huntington, Ind., 1974-77, Ind. U., Bloomington, 1977—; pres. Waycross Corp., Ga., 1973—; v.p. EAP, Inc., Ind., 1981-84. Author 3 non-fiction books, 9 novels, 12 short stories and over 40 articles. Served to maj. U.S. Army, 1962-70, Vietnam. Decorated DSC, Silver Star with 1 bronze oak leaf cluster, Bronze Star with V Device with 2 bronze oak leaves, Purple Heart with silver oak leaf cluster, DFC with 2 bronze oak leaves. Mem. Am. Assn. Adult and Continuing Edn. (controller 1979-81), Am. Soc. Tng. and Devel. CLub: Columbia. Avocation: sailing.

SHIPPERT, STAN HARRY (TONY), retired telephone company executive, real estate broker; b. Dixon, Mo., July 11, 1930; s. Harry Winfield and Livonia (Humphrey) S.; m. Betty Louise Good, Dec. 30, 1950; children—Garry, Terry, Shari, Cary. B.A., Rockhurst Coll., 1970. Installation foreman Southwest Bell Telephone Co., Kansas City, Mo., 1963-65, wire chief, Liberty, Mo., 1965-70, outside plant foreman, Liberty, 1970-77, installation force mgr., Independence, Mo., 1977-81, plant foreman, Parkville, Mo., 1981-84, plant foreman, community relations mgr., Liberty, 1984-86; real estate broker Loren Chasteen E.R.A., Liberty, 1986—. Trustee Liberty Hosp. Dist.; bd. dirs. New Liberty Hosp. and Med. Corp. Served with U.S. Army, 1951-53, Far East. Recipient State Farmer Degree, Future Farmers Am., 1947. Mem. Telephone Pioneers (bd. dirs. 1978-79). Democrat. Baptist. Lodge: Kiwanis (v.p. 1970-77, mem. bd. dirs., 1970—, pres. 1977, 84—). Avocations: fishing, hunting, beekeeping, farming, gardening. Home: 812 Park Ln Liberty MO 64068 Office: Southwest Bell Telephone Co Liberty MO 64068

SHIRER, MARTHA QUISENBERRY, feed grains company executive; b. Louisville, Mar. 3, 1915; d. Thomas Edwin and Quinlan (Hanna) Quisenberry; m. Richard V. Pelton, 1935 (div. 1955)); m. William L. Shirer, 1972 (div. 1977); children—Martha Pelton Lanier, E. Williams Pelton, Catherine E. Pelton, Suzanne Walker Pelton. B.A., Mt. Holyoke Coll., 1936. Dir., officer Neveridle Corp., Wilmette, Ill., 1963—, pres., treas., 1980—, mgr., 1983—. Mem. NOW. Office: 816 4th St Wilmette IL 60091

SHIRK, CYNTHIA MARIE (MAZURKIEWICZ), voice instructor; b. St. Paul, Sept. 16, 1954; d. Donald Peter and Doris Margaret (Thurmes) Mazurkiewicz; m. Craig Roger Shirk, Oct. 25, 1975; children: Ryan Craig, Laurie Marie. BS, St. Cloud State U., 1977; MusM, Mankato State U., 1984. Lic. tchr., Minn. Music instr. Sts. Peter and Paul Sch., Mankato, Minn., 1977-86; voice instr. Mankato State U., 1983-84, Bethany Coll., Mankato, 1986—; high potential music instr. Mankato Pub. Schs., 1985—; mem. Minn. Valley Chorale, Mankato, 1978—, treas. 1984—. Concert Choir scholar St. Cloud State U., 1974, 75. Mem. Music Educators Nat. Conf. Democrat. Roman Catholic. Avocations: composing, writing, singing. Home: 150 Stoney Creek Rd Mankato MN 56001 Office: Bethany Luth Coll 734 Marsh St Mankato MN 56001

SHIVELY, DANIEL JEROME, transportation executive; b. Akron, Ohio, Sept. 2, 1924; s. Richard Miles and Josephine (Pellicer) S.; m. Pamela Marion Kurfess, July 31, 1954; children: Jennifer, Laurie, Thomas. Grad., U.S. Mcht. Marine Acad., King's Point, N.Y., 1945. Chief officer (tanker) Trinidad Corp., N.Y.C., 1946-51; co-owner, mgr. Shively Bros. Jersey Farm, Quaker City, Ohio, 1952-54; staff asst. Gulf Oil Corp., Phila., 1955-57; mgr. mktg. budget and planning Standard Oil Co., Cleve., 1957-85; owner, mgr. Shively & Assocs., Cleve., 1985—. Served to lt. (j.g.) USNR, 1945-61. Mem. Transp. Practitioners Assn. (exec. com. 1984—, pres. local chpt. 1984-85);. Republican. Roman Catholic. Club: King's Point. Lodge: KC (chancellor 1986). Avocations: farming, sailing. Home: 21347 Erie Rd Rocky River OH 44116

SHIVES, THOMAS CLYDE, orthopedic surgeon; b. Newton, Iowa, Dec. 28, 1947; s. Everett Ross and Helen Louise (Jacobs) S. BA, Cornell Coll., 1970; MD, U. Iowa, 1974. Resident Mayo Grad. Sch. Med., Rochester, Minn., 1975-79; orthopedic surgeon Mayo Clinic, Rochester, 1979—; instr. orthopedic surgery Mayo Grad. Sch. Med., Rochester, 1979-83, asst. prof. orthopedic surgery, 1983—. Contbr. articles to profl. jours. Fellow Am. Acad. Orthopedic Surgeons; mem. Musculoskeletal Tumor Soc. (sec.). Republican. Presbyterian. Avocations: golf, tennis, woodworking. Home: Rural Rt 8 Box 38 Rochester MN 55904 Office: Mayo Clinic 200 First St SW Rochester MN 55905

SHLAES, JARED, real estate consultant; b. Chgo., July 7, 1930; s. Harry Lurie and Ruth Brill Shlaes; divorced; children: Amity, Noah, Jane. BA in Liberal Arts, U. Chgo., 1948, MBA in Fin., 1950. Sr. v.p. Arthur Rubloff & Co., Chgo., 1971-74; pres. Shlaes & Co., Chgo., 1975—. Co-author Rehab for Profit, 1984; editor-in-chief Real Estate Issues, 1976—. V.p. The Bright New City, Chgo., 1983-85; civic activist, Chgo., 1966—. Served to cpl. U.S. Army, 1952-54. Mem. Am. Soc. Real Estate Counselors (v.p. 1978), Am. Soc. Real Estate Appraisers (Louise and Y.T. Lum award, 1974, Robert H. Armstrong award, 1984), Urban Land Inst., Am. Planning Assn., Chgo. Bd. Realtors, Lambda Alpha. Avocation: reading. Office: Shlaes & Co 20 N Michigan Ave Chicago IL 60602

SHLENSKY, LOUIS RICHARD, accountant; b. Milwaukee, Wis., Jan. 5, 1954; s. Herschel Jerome and Selma Joy (Berman) S.; m. Karen Lori Miller, Nov. 12, 1983; 1 child, Heidi Jo. BBA, U. Wis., 1976; JD, Marquette U., 1979. CPA. Tax mgr. Arthur Andersen, Milw., 1979-85, Detroit, 1985—. Loaned exec. United Way, Milw., 1982; chmn. budget com. Congregation Shalom, Milw., 1983-85. Mem. Wis. Bar Assn., Jewish Community Ctr. Avocations: golf, parenting. Home: 37850 Greenwood Dr Northville MI 48167 Office: Arthur Andersen & Co 400 Renaissance Ctr. Detroit MI 48243

SHNURMAN, BENJAMIN Z., physician; b. Hamburg, Fed. Republic of Germany, June 21, 1946; came to U.S., 1949; s. Meyer and Frances (Choka) S.; m. Sandra Lee Phillips, Oct. 21, 1968; children: Robbin, Scott. BA, Drake U., 1975; DO, U. Osteopathic Medicine and Surgery, 1984. Intern Des Moines Gen. Hosp., 1984-85, resident, then chief resident in family practice, 1985-87; practice medicine specializing in family practice Des Moines, 1984—; med. dir. Iowa Vocat. Rehab., Des Moines, 1984—. Contbr. articles to profl. jours. Bd. dirs. Iowa Found. Handicapped, Des Moines, 1984—. Mem. Am. Osteopathic Assn., Iowa Osteopathic Med. Assn., Psi Chi. Jewish. Home: 3009 E Tiffin Ave Des Moines IA 50317 Office: 603 E 12th St Des Moines IA 50309

SHOAFSTALL, EARL FRED, entrepreneur, consultant; b. Des Moines, Jan. 26, 1936; s. Ralph Paul and Josephine E. (Carnes) S.; m. Sharon I. Vannoy, Mar. 21, 1962 (div. 1980); children: Michael E., Angela R.; m. Carlene Christenson, Dec. 11, 1980. BA, MBA, Drake U., 1962. Enlisted USAF, Des Moines, 1954; advanced through grades to sgt. USAF, 1961, resigned, 1962; underwriter Hawkeye Security Ins., Des Moines, 1962-65; mgr., owner B & B Transfer and Storage Inc., West Des Moines, Iowa, 1965—; cons., owner B & B Mini Storage Inc., West Des Moines, 1975—, Iowa Truck Driving Sch., West Des Moines, 1976—, Great Expectations Salon, West Des Moines, 1978—. Inventor pressure gage, control valve for air and liquid. Republican. Club: Des Moines Golf and Country. Lodges: Masons (32 degree), Shriners. Avocations: flying, golf, hunting, fishing. Home: 103 W Ridge Dr West Des Moines IA 50265 Office: B & B Transfer and Storage Inc 536 S 19th West Des Moines IA 50265

SHOEMAKER, DUANE CHARLES, office equipment company executive; b. Bloomington, Ill., Mar. 16, 1928; s. Lyle Adam and Besie May (Van Scyoc) S.; m. Grace Marie Sidwell, Nov. 12, 1949; children: Denis, Diana, Darrell, Dean. Grad. high sch., Peoria, Ill., 1947. Salesman, serviceman Comptometer Corp., Chgo., 1948-61; owner, operator Mid-West Office Equipment Co., Peoria, 1961—. Served with USN, 1946-48, PTO. Decorated Victory medal. Mem. Nat. Offices Services Assn. (pres. 1978-82), Nat. Office Products Assn., Nat. Office Machine Dealers Assn.

SHOEMAKER, HELEN E. MARTIN ACHOR, civic worker; b. Houston, Mar. 24, 1915; d. Earl L. and Blanche L. (Williams) Martin; A.B., Anderson (Ind.) Coll., 1960, LL.D., 1978; m. Harold E. Achor, Oct. 11, 1935; children—Dianne Achor Johnston, Lana Achor Dean; m. Robert N. Shoemaker, May 19, 1972. Resident dir. Anderson Coll., 1967-69, dir. alumni services, 1969-72; legis. counsel Ind. Colls. and Univ. Ind., 1970-72; spl. asst. Center Public Service, Anderson, 1973-77, spl. asst. to dean for acad. devel., 1977-78. Sec.-treas. Ind. State Library and Hist. Bldg. Expansion Commn., 1973-78; mem. com. region VII, Girl Scouts U.S.A., 1958-66; adv. council fin. aid to students Office Edn. HEW, 1976-78. Mem. Ind. Ho. of Reps. from Madison County, 1968-70; v.p. Ind. Fedn. Women's Republican Clubs, 1945-46; treas. Nat. Fedn. Women's Rep. Clubs, 1947-51; Rep. precinct vice chmn. Madison County, 1946-68, vice chmn., Anderson, 1967-68; bd. dirs. Urban League Madison County, 1969-76; adv. com. Georgetown U. Grad. Sch. Acad. in Public Service, 1976-83; mem. adv. com. on sex discrimination Ind. Civil Rights Commn., 1978-83; bd. dirs. Anderson Symphony Orch., 1987 trustee Anderson Coll., 1978-85; bd. dirs. Opportunities Industrialization Center, Inc., Madison County, 1980-84, Ind. Acad. Public Service, 1981-83, Women's Alternatives Inc., Anderson, 1982—(Elizabeth Howard McMahan award, 1987); mem. exec. com. devel. bd. St. John's Med. Center, Anderson, 1981—. Recipient William B. Harper award Urban League Madison County, 1975,

SHOEMAKER, JOHN CALVIN, aeronautical engineer, engineering company executive; b. Portland, Ind., Dec. 21, 1937; s. Homer Vaughn and Thelora Maxine (Avey) S.; m. Ruby Nell Johnson, Aug. 3, 1957; children: Gena Rebecca, Lora Rachele, John Calvin II; foster child, Jeanine Louise Patterson. BS in Aero. Engring., Ind. Inst. Tech., Ft. Wayne, 1960. Project engr. Wayne Pump Co., Ft. Wayne, 1960-63, Daybrook Ottawa Co., Bowling Green, Ohio, 1963-65; engring. mgr. Globe Wayne div. Dresser Industries, Ft. Wayne, 1965-67; sales engr. Taylor-Newcomb Engring., Ft. Wayne, 1967-74; prin. Shoemaker, Inc., Ft. Wayne, 1974—. Patentee in field. Served with USAR, 1960-67. Mem. Am. Inst. Plant Engrs. Republican. Lodge: Lions (pres. local chpt. 1972). Avocations: gospel music, ch. choristering, directing choir. Home and Office: 12120 Yellow River Rd Fort Wayne IN 46818

SHOEMAKER, PAUL SATTERFIELD, engineer; b. Detroit, Feb. 26, 1937; s. Paul S. Sr. and Mary A. (Bendure) S.; m. Patricia E. Olds, Sept. 29, 1966 (div. Aug. 1983); children: Michelle, Anne; m. Peggy J. Bickett, Nov. 1, 1985; 1 stepchild, Heather Boltz. BS in Mech. Engring, Mich. State U., 1960, MS in Mech. Engring., 1961. Structure engr. Gen. Dynamics, San Diego, 1961-62; research engr. Chemstrand, Durham, N.C., 1962-65; mgr. OTR engring. Uniroyal Tire Inc., Detroit, 1965-80; mgr. advanced engring. Gen. Tire Inc., Akron, Ohio, 1980—. Mem. Tire Soc. (program chmn. 1986-87), Soc. Automotive Engring., Akron Rubber Group. Avocation: tennis. Home: 3630 Darrow Rd Stow OH 44224 Office: Gen Tire Inc 1 General St Akron OH 44329

SHOEMAKER, ROBERT LAWRENCE, mechanical engineer, researcher; b. Wauseon, Ohio, Nov. 3, 1949; s. Delbert Arthur and Darlene Mae (Young) S.; m. Karen Ann Juillard, June 6, 1970; children: Benjamin David, Rachel Renee. BS, Taylor U., 1971; MS, Purdue U., 1973, PhD, 1978. Postdoctoral researcher Purdue U., West Lafayette, Ind., 1978-80, asst. sr. researcher, 1980-82, assoc. sr. researcher, 1982—; cons. Theta Industries, Port Washington, N.Y., 1979—; cons. in field, Lafayette, Ind., 1985—; pres. CARS, West Lafayette, Ind., 1981—. Elder Upper Christian Fellowship, West Lafayette, 1983—. Mem. Sigma Pi Sigma, Sigma Xi, Eta Sigma Gamma. Avocations: hunting, fishing, tennis, golf. Office: TPRL 2595 Yeager Rd West Lafayette IN 47906

SHOEMAKER, ROBERT LEWIS, optometrist; b. Elkhart, Ind., Dec. 22, 1928; s. W. Albert and Annetta (Wilson) S.; m. Alice Marie Amick, Aug. 7, 1954; children—Mark Amick, Scott Robert. Student DePauw U., 1946-48, Ind. U., 1948-49; O.D., Pa. Coll. Optometry, 1953. Diplomate Nat. Bd. Optometry. Cons. Wayne Twp. Sch. System, Indpls., 1970-73, Warren Twp. Sch. System, 1972-73, Ind. Dept. Pub. Instrn., 1974-84, Ind. Boy's Sch., Ind. Dept. Correction, Indpls., 1972-86; guest lectr. Butler U., Ind. U., Ind. Central Coll., 1972-80, U. Ill., Bradley U., Congress European Optometric Socs., Paris, 1975. Mem. editorial council Jour. Optometric Vision Therapy, 1970-72. Contbr. articles to profl. jours. Bd. dirs. Prisoners Aid By Citizens' Effort, Indpls., 1968-72, Meridian St. Methodist Ch., 1982—. Served as cpl. U.S. Army, 1953-55. Named Optometrist of Yr., 1970—. Fellow Am. Acad.

Optometry (pres. Ind. chpt. 1979-81); mem. Coll. Optometrists in Vision Devel. (bd. dirs. 1971-73). Republican. Avocation: photography. Home: 7204 Harbour Isle Indianapolis IN 46240 Office: 6214 N Broadway Indianapolis IN 46220

SHOEMAKER, ROBERT SHERN, architect, real estate investment consultant; b. Omaha, Sept. 9, 1953; s. Donald Shern and Peggy (Farnam) S. Student, Bethany Coll., 1971-72; pvt. pilot cert., Penn Valley Coll., 1975; BArch, Kans State U., 1977. Cert. architect Nat. Cert. Archtl. Registration Bd. Assoc. planner W.G. Roeseler, Kansas City, Mo., 1973-76; asst. project mgr. McCloskey Devel., Phila., 1976-77; project architect Fullerton Carey & Oman Architects, Kansas City, 1977-79; project mgr. HNTB Architect/Engineer/Planner, Kansas City, 1979-86; prin. Robert S. Shoemaker & Assocs., Kansas City, 1986—. Mem. council City of Fairway, Kans., 1979-80. Mem. AIA (pres. Kans. State U. 1975-76, jurer Homes for Better Living 1976), Mo. Council Architects, Constrn. Specifications Inst., Kans. Soc. Architects (assoc.), Phi Kappa Tau. Avocations: real estate, golf. Home: 450 W 68th St Kansas City MO 64113 Office: PO Box 22477 Kansas City MO 64113

SHOGREN, DANIEL CHARLES, accountant, human resource director; b. Oak Park, Ill., Nov. 1, 1952; s. Edward William and Beatrice Elaine (Breen) S.; m. Karen Elizabeth Lindstrom, Sept. 25, 1983; children: Jonathan Edward, Jennifer Elaine. BA in Polit. Sci., Western Ill. U., 1973. CPA, Ill. Supr. audits Touche Ross & Co., Chgo., 1973-79; sr. v.p. ASC, Inc., Chgo., 1979-81; cons. Ernst & Whinney, Chgo., 1981-83; human resources dir. Altschuler, Melvoin and Glasser, Chgo., 1983—. Sr. warden Christ Episcopal Ch., River Forest, Ill., 1987, asst. treas. The Church Home, 1987—. Fellow Wacker Inst. (audit com. 1982—); mem. Ill. CPA Soc. (various coms. 1974—), Am. Inst. CPA's. Avocations: building wooden boats, sailing. Office: Altschuler Melvoin and Glasser 30 S Wacker Dr Chicago IL 60606

SHOLL, WILLIAM BRYAN, advertising agency executive; b. Defiance, Ohio, Apr. 16, 1958; s. Gerald M. and Leta Rosalie (Bryan) S.; m. Jill Darlene Carr, June 25, 1983. BS, Bowling Green State U., 1981. Owner, pres. Sholl Advt. Pub. Relations Services, Toledo, Ohio, 1981—. Author monthly advt. column Toledo Bus. Jour., 1985—. Adv. council mem. Salvation Army Adult Rehab. Ctr., Toledo, 1980-85. Roman Catholic. Club: Toledo Advt.

SHONS, ALAN RANCE, plastic surgeon, educator; b. Freeport, Ill., Jan. 10, 1938; s. Ferral Caldwell and Margaret (Zimmerman) S.; A.B., Dartmouth Coll., 1960; M.D., Case Western Res. U., 1965; Ph.D. in Surgery, U. Minn., 1976; m. Mary Ella Misamore, Aug. 5, 1961; children—Lesley, Susan. Intern, U. Hosp., Cleve., 1965-66, resident in surgery, 1966-67; research fellow transplantation immunology U. Minn., 1969-72; resident in surgery U. Minn. Hosp., 1972-74; resident in plastic surgery NYU, 1974-76; asst. prof. plastic surgery U. Minn., Mpls., 1976-79, assoc. prof., 1979-84, prof., 1984; dir. div. plastic and reconstructive surgery U. Minn. Hosp., St. Paul Ramsey Hosp., Mpls. VA Hosp., 1976-84; cons. plastic surgery St. Louis Park Med. Center, 1980-84; prof. surgery Case Western Res. U., Cleve., 1984—; dir. div. plastic and reconstructive surgery Univ. Hosps. Cleve., 1984—. Served to capt. USAF, 1967-69. Diplomate Am. Bd. Surgery, Am. Bd. Plastic Surgery. Fellow ACS (chmn. Minn. com. on trauma); mem. Am. Soc. Plastic and Reconstructive Surgeons, Am. Assn. Plastic Surgeons, Minn. Acad. Plastic Surgeons (pres. 1981-82), AMA, Soc. Head and Neck Surgeons, Am. Assn. Surgery Trauma, Transplantation Soc., Plastic Surgery Research Council, Am. Soc. Aesthetic Plastic Surgery, Am. Soc. Maxillofacial Surgeons, Am. Assn. Immunologists, Soc. Exptl. Pathology, Am. Burn Assn., Am. Cleft Palate Assn., Am. Soc. Nephrology, Assn. Acad. Surgery, Pan Am. Med. Assn., Central Surg. Assn., Minn. Med. Assn., Mpls. Surg. Soc., Ramsey County Med. Soc., Sigma Xi. Office: 2074 Abington Rd Cleveland OH 44106

SHOOK, DALE RAY, radiologist; b. Bismarck, N.D., Jan. 18, 1946; s. Lester D. and Ann Evelyn (Bergeson) S.; m. Mona G. Quale, Aug. 10, 1968; children: Kirsten, Dale, Cassandra. BS in Physics cum laude, Jamestown Coll., 1968; BS in Medicine, U. N.D., 1970; MD, Tufts U., 1972. Diplomate Am. Bd. Radiology, Nat. Bd. Med. Examiners. Intern Hennepin County Gen. Hosp., Mpls., 1973; chief resident U. Minn. VA Hosps., Mpls., 1976; mem. staff Neuropsychiat. Inst. Hosp., Fargo, N.D., 1976—, exec. com., 1982—, vice-chief of staff, 1982-84, chief of staff, 1984-86, chmn. edn. com., 1981-83, active various coms.; neuroradiologist Radiologists Ltd., Fargo, 1976—, also bd. dirs.; cons. staff St. John's Hosp., St. Angsar Hosp., 1978—, VA Hosp., St. Luke's Hosp., Fargo, 1976—; planning com. St. Luke's Hosp. Patient Care Task Force, 1982; lectr. various academic and profl. groups; asst. clin. prof. to assoc. clin. prof. dept. radiology U. N.D. Sch. Medicine, Grand Forks, 1976—, southeast area health edn. ctr. coordinator, 1979-80, asst. clin. prof. to assoc. clin. prof. dept. neurosci., 1982—. Elder Presbyn. Ch., 1980—, active various coms.; advisor Statewide Health Coordinating Council, 1980; program chmn. 25th Anniversary Neurosci. Conf., 1980, 3d Annual Neurosci. Conf., 1981; CT scanning task force Health Dept., N.D., 1980. Psychiatry fellow U. N.D. Sch. Medicine, 1969, neuropsychiatric fellow, Fargo, 1970. Mem. AMA, Am. Soc. Neuroradiology, Am. Coll. Radiology (sec. N.D.chpt. 1982-86), Radiologic Soc. N.Am., Jamestown Coll. Alumni Assn. (bd. dirs. 1978-80, chmn. 1979-80, Gold Medal Scholarship fund), Alpha Chi. Republican. Club: Fargo Country. Office: Radiologists Ltd 606 Professional Bldg 100 S 4th St Fargo ND 58103

SHORES, DAVID LLOYD, clearinghouse executive; b. Newton, Iowa, Aug. 23, 1952; s. Denver Lloyd and Dora Elizabeth (Rash) S.; m. Sharon Lynn Croissant, Aug. 1974 (div. Dec. 1979); m. Nicki Lu Davidson, Nov. 20, 1984; 1 child, Colin David. BS, Iowa State U., 1974, PhD, 1984; MEd, Miami U., Oxford, Ohio, 1976. Mgr. Manpower, Inc., Ames, Iowa, 1979-81; asst. to pres. Seminar Clearinghouse Internat., Inc., St. Paul, 1982-83, pres., 1983—. Contbg. author: Facilitator's Manual: Quality Cirlces, 1982, Driving Forces of Creativity Leadership, 1983; editor: Selected Readings in Quality Circles, 1986. Mem. Soc. Advancement Mgmt. (v.p. 1984-86, pres. 1986-87), Am. Soc. Tng. and Devel., Am. Soc. Personnel Adminstrn., Programmers, Analysts, Computer Trainers. Avocations: camping, hiking, music, gardening, cooking. Office: Seminar Clearinghouse Internat Inc 630 Bremer Tower Saint Paul MN 55101

SHORLEY, STEVEN CHARLES, accountant; b. Kansas City, Kans., Jan. 8, 1954; s. Marlin D. and Beatrice M. (Brinton) S.; m. Christine G. Collins, June 30, 1973 (div. Mar. 1980); 1 child, Andy. BBA, Cen. Mo. State U., 1978. CPA, Mo. V.p. St. John & Mersmann, Inc., Chesterfield, Mo., 1979—. Mem. Mo. Soc. CPA's, Am. Inst. CPA's (mem. tax div.). Office: St John and Mersmann Inc 640 Cepi Dr Suite A Chesterfield MO 63017

SHORT, BRIAN PATRICK, real estate executive; b. Mpls., Feb. 17, 1950; s. Robert Earl and Marion Dolores (McCann) S.; m. Kathleen Mary Desmond, Apr. 24, 1982; children—Kathryn Mary, Robert Desmond, Michael Edward. B.A., U. Notre Dame, 1972, J.D., 1975. Bar: Minn. 1975, Fla. 1976, U.S. Dist Ct. Minn., 1975, U.S. Ct. Appeals (8th cir.) 1976. Law clk. to chief judge U.S. Dist. Ct. Minn., 1975-77; ptnr. Foster, Jensen & Short, Mpls., 1977-80; magistrate U.S. Dist. Minn. St. Paul, 1980-85; exec. v.p. 1014 Property Co., Mpls., 1985—. Adv. bd. Notre Dame Law Sch., 1984—; bd. dirs. Robert E. Short Found., St. Paul, Cath. Charities of Archdiocese of St. Paul and Mpls, St. Joseph's Home for Children. Mem. ABA, Minn. Bar Assn., Fla. Bar, Fed. Bar Assn., Hennepin County Bar Assn., Am. Judicature Soc. (bd. dirs.), St. Thomas Acad. (alumni bd. 1986—). Democrat. Roman Catholic. Home: 1165 Summit Ave Saint Paul MN 55105 Office: 1014 Property Co 215 S 11th St Minneapolis MN 55403-2520

SHORT, HOWARD NEWTON, surgeon, ophthalmologist; b. St. Louis, Dec. 27, 1951; s. Newton Hickman and Ann Marie (Bassett) S.; m. Kathleen Ann Capps, Aug. 9, 1978; children: John, Elizabeth, Thomas. AB, Wash. U., St. Louis, 1974; MD, St. Louis U., 1978; cert. opathalmology, Duke U., Durham, N.C., 1983. Diplomate Nat. Bd. Med. Examiners, Am. Bd. Ophthalmology. Pres., med. dir. Tri County Eye Ctr., Inc., Wash., Mo., 1983—; asst. clin. prof. Dept. Ophthalmology, U. Mo., Columbia, 1985—. Fellow ACS, Am. Acad. Ophthalmology, Am. Soc. Catract and Refractive Surgery; mem. Franklin-Warren-Gasconade Counties Med. Assn. (pres. 1985—), Omicron Delta Kappa. Republican. Roman Catholic. Lodge: Lions. Avocations: tennis, golf, skiing. Office: Tri County Eye Ctr Inc 800 E Fifth Washington MO 63090

SHORT, JAMES DAVID, electronics executive; b. Abington, Pa., Mar. 1, 1942; s. William Howard Jr. and Rita Mary (kaufman) S.; m. Suzanne Poter, Nov. 23, 1963; children: Krisana Kay, Suzanne Pauline, Joanna Nicol. BEE, So. Meth. U., 1964, MS in Engring. Adminstrn., 1967. Engr. Collins Radio Co., Dallas, 1967-70; pres. Electric Data Corp., Garland, Tex., 1970-77; v.p. E-Systems Inc, Dallas, 1977-83; group mgr. strategic planning Eaton Corp., Cleve., 1983—; bd. dirs. Short Investment Co., Sarasota, Fla. Active Greater Clev. Growth Assn. Mem. Inst. Elec. Engrs., Ass. Old Crows, Air Force Assn., Phi Gamma Delta. Republican. Club: Lakeside Yatch (Cleve.). Avocations: sail racing, tennis. Home: 6620 Antree Park Dr Mayfield Village OH 44143 Office: Eaton Corp Eaton Ctr Cleveland OH 44114

SHORT, JEFFREY ROBSON, III, grain milling company executive; b. Chgo., Nov. 21, 1940; s. Jeffrey R. Jr. and Barbara (Allen) S.; m. Françoise Tabary, June 21, 1963; children: Tricia, David, Andrew, Graham. Grad., Phillips Exeter Acad., 1958; AB in French and Lit., Harvard U., 1962. Asst. to dir. statistical sampling A.C. Nielson Co., Paris, 1963-64; v.p. J.R. Short Can. Mills Ltd., Toronto, Ont., 1964-72; sr. v.p. J.R. Short Milling Co., Chgo., 1972—, also bd. dirs. Co-inventor foundry molding machinery, 3 patents. Mem. Master Brewers Assn. of the Ams., Am. Foundrymen's Soc., Am. Soc. Bakery Engrs. Clubs: Univ. (Chgo.); Badminton & Raquet (Toronto). Avocation: clock making. Home: 6 Whitby Ct Lincolnshire IL 60015 Office: JR Short Milling Co 233 S Wacker Dr Chicago IL 60606

SHORT, KENNETH LOWELL, JR., controller; b. Kankakee, Ill., Nov. 11, 1956; s. Kenneth Lowell and Gladys Sharon (Spence) S.; m. Diane Lynette Poland, May 14, 1983; 1 child, Brian Lowell. BS in Acctg., Olivet Nazarene U., 1979. CPA, Ind. Supr. auditing Coopers & Lybrand, Indpls., 1979-84; v.p., controller Investors Trust Assurance Co., Indpls., 1984-86, Bankers Nat. Life subs. Conseco, Inc., Carmel, Ind., 1986—. Trustee Westside Nazarene Ch., Indpls., 1986-87. Mem. Am. Inst. CPA's, Ind. CPA Soc., Ins. Acctg. and Systems Assn. Republican. Avocations: tennis, golf, baseball, basketball. Home: 728 Kokomo Ln Indianapolis IN 46241 Office: Bankers Nat Life/Conseco Inc 11815 N Pennsylvania Carmel IN 46032

SHORT, KEVIN MICHAEL, financial consulting company executive; b. Louisville, Sept. 5, 1956; s. Michael Smith and Carolyn (Lockard) S.; m. Patti Anne Cannon, May 31, 1980; children: Brittney Lauren, Jennifer Anne. V.p. Security Research Assocs., St. Louis, 1978-80; pres. Clayton Fin. Group, St. Louis, 1980—. Bd. dirs. Bd. Edn. St. Louis Archdiocese, 1985—, found. bd., 1985—; treas. bd. edn. St. Louis Archdiocese, 1986—. Mem. Nat. Soc. Pub. Accts., Ind. Accts. Soc. Mo. Roman Catholic. Club: Clayton (St. Louis). Office: Clayton Fin Group Inc 230 S Bemiston Saint Louis MO 63105

SHORT, PAULA MYRICK, educational administration educator; b. Pinehurst, N.C., Feb. 25, 1945; d. John Howard and Ruby Pauline (Fields) Myrick; m. Rick Jay Short, Feb. 2, 1980; children—Jeffrey Brent, John Ryan, Rick Jay Jr. B.A., U. N.C.-Greensboro, 1967, M.Ed., 1970; Ph.D., U. N.C., Chapel Hill, 1983. Tchr., Greensboro City Schs., N.C., 1967-68, Orange County Schs., Hillsborough, N.C., 1968-69; media coordinator Alamance County Schs., Mebane, N.C., 1970-71; tchr. Neal Jr. High Sch., Durham, N.C., 1971-74, Chewing Jr. High Sch., Durham, 1977-79; system level media supr. Chapel Hill-Carboro City Schs., 1979-80; ednl. cons. div. ednl. N.C. Dept. Pub. Instrn., Raleigh, 1980-82; asst. prof. ednl. adminstrn. Coll.Edn., Tex. Woman's U., Denton, 1984-85, Centenary Coll., Shreveport, La., 1985-86, U. Nebr. at Omaha, 1986—. Chmn. day care com. Chapel Hill Service League, 1977-78. Delta Kappa Gamma state scholar 1982. Mem. SW Ednl. Research Assn., La. Assn. Sch. Execs., Tex. Assn. Supervision and Curriculum Devel., Nebr. Assn. Sch. Adminstrs., Nebr. Assn. for Supervision and Curriculum Devel., Nebr. Assn. Student Councils (asst. exec. dir.), Soc. Sch. Librarians Internat. (bd. dirs. 1985-86), Assn. Supervision and Curriculum Devel., N.C. Media Council (pres. 1982), Delta Kappa Gamma, Phi Delta Kappa, Pi Lambda Theta. Methodist. Home: 11677 Capitol Ave Omaha NE 68154 Office: U Nebr Dept Ednl Adminstrn 314 Kayser Hall Omaha NE 68182

SHOTWELL, VIRGINIA LAMBETH, career education administrator; b. N.Y.C., Dec. 2, 1924; d. Edgar Leigh and Marion Arleen (Maddrea) Lambeth; m. John Ralph Shotwell, June 22, 1947; children—Donna Lynn, JoAnn. B.A., U. Richmond (Va.), 1946; M.A., Trinity Coll., 1972; postgrad. U. Hartford, Governors State U. Asst. buyer Thalhimers Dept. Store, Richmond, 1946-47; adminstrv. asst. Kodak Park, Rochester, N.Y., 1947-49; tchr., Rocky Hill and Hartford (Conn.), 1967-75; prof. Prairie State Coll., Chicago Heights, Ill., 1975-77, Ind. U. Northwest, Gary, 1975—; career edn. dir. Rich Career Ctr., Matteson, Ill., 1979—; career cons. Region 9 Career Guidance Ctr., Thornton Coll., Ill. Author: Passage: An Individual Career Planning Program, 1986. Bd. dirs. Family Service and Mental Health; coordinator Network Clergy Spouses Internat. Mem. Am. Assn. Counseling and Devel., Am. Vocat. Assn., Ill. Assn. Local Adminstrs., NEA, Vocat. Edn. Assn. (bd. dirs. work-edn. council), Nat. Council Tchrs. English, AAUW, LWV, Mortar Bd., Phi Delta Epsilon. Office: 242 S Orchard Dr Park Forest IL 60466

SHOULDERS, PATRICK ALAN, lawyer; b. Evansville, Ind., Mar. 26, 1953; s. Harold Ray and Jeanne Marie (Nicholson) S.; m. Lisa Lou Iaccarino, July 12, 1975; children—Samantha Alain, Andrew Patrick. B.A., Ind. U., 1975, J.D. magna cum laude, 1978. Bar: Ind. 1978, U.S. Dist. Ct. (so. dist.) Ind. 1978, U.S. Ct. Appeals (7th cir.) 1979, U.S. Supreme Ct. 1985, Ky. 1986, U.S. Dist. Ct. (we. dist.) Ky. 1987. Assoc. Kahn, Dees, Donovan & Kahn, Evansville, Ind., 1978-81, ptnr., 1981-87; ptnr. Early, Arnold & Ziemer, Evansville, 1987—; adj. prof. law of evidence U. Evansville, 1980-82; mem. instl. rev. bd. St. Mary's Med. Ctr., Evansville, 1980—. Pres. Evansville Parks Found., 1982-83, Vanderburgh Law Library Found., Evansville, 1983-84; bd. dirs. Evansville Mus. Arts and Sci., 1982—; mem. Bd. Park Commrs., Evansville, 1984—; bd. dirs. Democrats for Better Govt., 1981-83. Recipient Cert. of Achievement, City of Evansville, 1982, Civic Service award Ind. Assn. Cities and Towns, 1983. Mem. ABA (litigation sect.), Ind. Bar Assn., Ind. Trial Lawyers Assn., Seventh Cir. Bar Assn., Evansville Bar Assn. (pres. 1984-85). Methodist. Home: 417 S Alvord Blvd Evansville IN 47714 Office: Early Arnold & Ziemer 1507 Old National Bank Bldg PO Box 916 Evansville IN 47706

SHOVAN, W(ILLIAM) RICHARD, accounting executive; b. St. Clair, Mich., Aug. 26, 1948; s. Verne and Alice Irene (Mackley) S.; m. Barbara Jean Mowery, Mar. 4, 1972; children: Kathleen Irene, Kristopher Allan. BS in Acctg., Ferris State Coll., 1969; MS in Taxation, Walsh Coll., 1981. CPA, Mich. Revenue auditor Mich. Dept. Treas., Port Huron, 1970-76; sr. revenue auditor Bloomfield Hills, 1977-81; mgr. James Ross, CPA, Mt. Clemens, Mich., 1976-77; tax supr. Fox & Co., Southfield, Mich., 1981-82; tax mgr. J. B. Webb Co., Farmington Hills, Mich., 1982—. Fellow Am. Inst. CPA's, Tax Execs. Inst., Inc. (chmn. state and local taxation 1986-87, asst. sec. 1987), Mich. Assn. CPA's (asst. chmn. memberships 1985-87, chmn. 1987—), Inst. Property Taxation. Republican. Baptist. Avocations: camping, computers.

SHOWALTER, HOWARD DANIEL HOLLIS, medicinal chemist; b. Broadway, Va., Feb. 22, 1948; s. Owen Franklin and Edith (Rhodes) S.; m. Martha Jane Augsburger, Aug. 18, 1973; children: Howard Daniel Hollins, Daron Christopher. BA, U. Va., 1970; PhD, Ohio State U., 1974. NIH postdoctoral fellow Rice U., Houston, 1974-76; research scientist Pharm. Research div. Warner-Lambert Parke-Davis, Ann Arbor, Mich., 1976-80, sr. research scientist, 1980-83, research assoc., 1983-86, sr. research assoc., 1986—. Patentee in field. S.B. Penick Meml. fellow Am. Found. Pharm. Edn., 1971-74. Mem. Am. Chem. Soc. (Excellence in Indsl. Chem. Research award 1983), Internat. Soc. Heterocyclic Chemistry, Am. Assn. Cancer Research. Mennonite. Home: 3578 Lamplighter Dr Ann Arbor MI 48103-1702 Office: Warner Lambert Parke Davis 2800 Plymouth Rd Ann Arbor MI 48106

SHREVE, GREGORY MONROE, university administrator; b. Munich, West Germany, Aug. 3, 1950; came to U.S., 1951; s. Joyce L. and Rosa (Zerweiss) S.; m. Joan Marie Nelson, Dec. 29, 1971; 1 child, Jessica Corrine. BA, Ohio State U., 1971, MA, 1974, PhD, 1975; cert. advanced study info. sci., U. Pitts., 1980. Asst. prof. anthropology Kent State U., East Liverpool, Ohio, 1975-80, assoc. prof., East Liverpool, Burton and Ashlabula, 1980—, asst. dean, 1978-80, dean, 1981-85; pres. Structured Software Systems, Burton, 1982—, coordinator cooperative program in applied linguistics, 1987—; vis. prof. Karl Marx U., Leipzig; pres. Logitech, Inc., Chesterland, 1985—. Author: Genesis of Structures, vols. I and II, 1975, 83; contbr. articles to profl. jours. Fellow Am. Anthrop. Assn., Am. Folklore Soc., Assn. for Computing Machinery, Soc. Hist. Archaeology. Lodge: Rotary. Advocation: collector 19th century Am. ceramics. Home: 14649 Evergreen Dr Burton OH 44021 Office: Kent State U Ashtabula Campus 3325 W 13th St Ashtabula OH 44004

SHREWSBURY, CAROLYN ANN, political science educator; b. Wichita, Kans., Mar. 28, 1943; d. Richard Charles and Virginia Lee (Martin) Mundell; m. Walton Scott Shrewsbury, July 18, 1969. BA, U. Chgo., 1965; MA, U. Okla., 1968, PhD, 1974. Asst. prof. polit. sci. Mankato (Minn.) State U., 1968, assoc. prof., 1975-79, prof., 1979—, chmn. women's studies, 1978-83. Mem. Region Nine Subcom. on Human Resources, 1981—; mem., vice chmn. North Mankato Cable Adv. Com., 1986-87, Mankato Cable Communications Commn., pres. LWV, 1987. Recipient Outstanding Faculty award Mankato State Student Ambassadors, 1982, Faculty Salute award Am. Assn. Higher Edn. and Carnegie Found. Advancement Teaching, 1986; grantee Bush Found., 1983-84. Mem. Am. Polit. Sci. Assn., Nat. Women's Studies Assn. (nat. task force on service-learning), Midwest Polit. Sci. Assn., Minn. Polit. Sci. Assn. (pres. 1986'3), Minn. Women in Higher Edn. (dir. 1980-82), NOW, Delta Kappa Gamma. Contbr. articles to profl. jours. Home: 135 Hawaiian Dr Mankato MN 56001 Office: Mankato State U PO Box 7 Mankato MN 56001

SHRIMPTON, JAMES ROBERT, controller; b. St. Louis, Dec. 13, 1956; s. Robert Franklin and Mildred Lucille (Baxter) S.; m. Rhonda Jo Crabtree, July 23, 1983; children: Phillip Sean, Bradley James. BS, S.W. Bapt. Coll., 1978; MBA, So. Ill. U., 1983. CPA, Mo. Inventory supr. Edison Bros. Stores, St. Louis, 1978-79, asst. internal auditor, 1982-83, sr. acct., 1984; acctg. supr. Hill-Brehan Lumber Co., St. Louis, 1979-81; sr. regional auditor TG&Y Stores, Oklahoma City, 1984-85; asst. controller J&J Holding Co., Paola, Kans., 1985—. Mem. Am. Inst. CPA's, Mo. Soc. CPA's, Inst. Mgmt. Acctg. Home: Rural Rt 3 Box 275 Paola KS 66071

SHRINER, WILLIAM CUPPY, psychiatrist, educator; b. Terre Haute, Ind., Sept. 11, 1937; s. Walter Owen and Virginia (Cuppy) S.; m. Nancy Lou McKee, Dec. 30, 1959; children: Virginia Ann, Walter McKee, Eric William. BA, Ind. State U., 1958; MD, Ind. U., 1962. Cert. Am. Bd. Neurology and Psychiatry. Resident in psychiatry Ind U., 1966-69; chief exec. officer, sr. psychiatrist Hamilton Ctr., Inc., Terre Haute, 1969-83; practice medicine specializing in psychiatry Terre Haute, 1983—; clin. assoc. prof. psychiatry Ind. U. Sch. Medicine, Terre Haute, 1973—; adj. assoc. prof. psychology Ind. State U., Terre Haute, 1971—, mem. instl. rev. bd., 1980-86; med. dir. chem. dependency unit Union Hosp., Terre Haute, 1986—. Mem. community adv. bd. Ind. U. Sch. Medicine, 1982—; mem. devel. council Rose Hulman Inst., Terre Haute, 1971-86; bd. dirs. Goodwill Industries, Terre Haute, 1984—. Recipient Labor Day award Wabash Valley Labor Council, 1977, Mental Health award Community Mental Health Services, 1977. Fellow Am. Psychiat. Assn; mem. AMA, Ind. Psychiat. Soc., Vigo County Med. Soc. Lodge: Rotary. Avocations: music, travel, gardening, reading. Home: 123 Woodbine Dr Terre Haute IN 47803 Office: 501 Hospital Ln Terre Haute IN 47802

SHROUT, DEBRA JO, journalism educator; b. Ypsilanti, Mich., Nov. 11, 1953; d. William Howard and Beverly Joice (Baer) Kitts; m. Thomas R. Shrout, Dec. 21, 1974; children: Thomas Reuben III, Rachael Elizabeth. BS in Edn., N.E. Mo. State U., 1974, MA, 1978, edn. specialist, 1986. Cert. tchr., Mo. Tchr. Kirksville (Mo.) High Sch., 1975-77; instr. communications N.E Mo. State U., Kirksville, 1977-86; tchr. journalism Kirkwood (Mo.) High Sch., 1986—; dir. summer journalism program N.E. Mo. State U., 1982-86; judge Coll. Media Advisors, 1984-86, Columbia Scholastic Press, 1985-86. Committeewoman Dem. Twp. Walnut, Kirksville, 1980—; sec. Adair County Den. Com., Kirksville, 1982—; mem. YMCA. Named one of Outstanding Young Women of Am., 1981. Mem. NEA, Delta Kappa Gamma, Phi Delta Kappa (past pres.); Univ. Dames (pres. 1980-81). Methodist. Avocations: reading, jogging. Home: 815 Hawbrook Glendale MO 63122 Office: Kirkwood High Sch Essex Ave Kirkwood MO 63122

SHUCK, D(EE) R(OSS), industrial exhibit designer, illustrator; b. Logansport, Ind., Oct. 19, 1941; s. Donald Ray and Dorothy (Ross) S.; m. Martha Scott, Feb. 14, 1975. Diploma, Ind. U., 1963; postgrad., Art Ctr. Coll. Design, 1967-68. Pres. Dimensional Designs, Inc., Indpls., 1971-75; designer/model builder Giltspur Exhibits, Chgo., 1979-81; designer, model builder Exhibitgroup Chgo., 1981-86; pres. D.R. Shuck and Assocs., Elburn, Ill., 1986—; cons. Exhibitgroup, Chgo., 1986—. Advisor J. Everett Light Career Ctr., Indpls., 1974-79, Ind. Evaluation Team on Higher Edn., 1979, Ind. Vocat. Tech. Coll., South Bend, 1979-81; bd. dirs. Elburn/Countryside (Ill.) Community Ctr., 1985—. Served with U.S. Army, 1963-66. Mem. Soc. Illustrators (Nat. Exhibition Cert. of Merit 1972, 75), Art Dirs. Club Ind. (pres. 1976), Oak Park/Forest River Art League (bd. dirs. 1981-82), Herron Sch. Art Alumni Assn. (pres. 1975). Republican. Methodist. Avocation: auto racing, photography. Home and Office: PO Box 1202 Elburn IL 60119

SHUEY, HERBERT ERSLA, protective services official; b. Peola, Kans., Feb. 15, 1942; s. Herbert Henry and Elizabeth Louise (Craig) S.; m. Julianne Charno, Aug. 22, 1975 (div. Dec. 1, 1980); m. Gene Marie Patterson, Oct. 3, 1981. B.A., U. Mo.; M.A., U. Mo.-Kansas City, postgrad.; postgrad. U. Kans. Work evaluator Johnson County Mental Retardation Dept., Lenexa, Kans., 1970-71, houseparent, Olathe, Kans., 1971-72, dir. recreation, Lenexa, 1971-74; tchr. Kansas State Sch. Deaf, Olathe, 1973-76; adv. bd. 1981—; policeman, detective Johnson County Sheriff's Dept., Olathe, 1976—; chmn. adv. bd. Johnson County Mental Health, Olathe, 1980—; cons. Child Protection, Johnson County, 1982—; part-time faculty Johnson County Community Coll., 1984—. Contbr. articles to profl. jours. Mem. Friends of Zoo, Kansas City, 1976, Friends of Art, Kansas City, 1977; bd. dirs. Olathe Library, 1984—. Served with U.S. Army, 1963-67. Recipient Cert. of Appreciation, Child Protection, Johnson County, 1984, Service award Lion's Club, 1977, Service award Optimist Club, 1979, Law Enforcement award, 1987. Mem. Nat. Sheriff's Assn. Republican. Club: Viet Nam Vets. (Kansas City). Avocations: history, bridge. Office: Johnson County Courthouse Sheriff's Dept Olathe KS 66061

SHUFELT, JOHN MARSHALL, psychologist; b. Campbell, N.Y., Nov. 13, 1913; s. Jesse Fremont and Nettie Louise (Reed) S.; m. Aug. 11, 1943; children—John Marshall, Lynne Shufelt Cook. B.A., Colgate U., 1936; Ed.D., Wayne State U., 1963; grad. Episc. Theol. Sem., 1946. Cert. psychologist, Mich. Tchr. sci., high sch., Caguas, P.R., 1936-37; tchr. sci. Grace High Sch., N.Y.C., 1938-40; tchr. sci., asst. prin. Lago High Sch., Aruba, N.W.I., 1941-43; assoc. St. Andrew's Episcopal Ch., Ann Arbor, Mich., 1946-48; canon Cathedral Ch. of St. Paul, Detroit, 1948-60; rector St. John's Epis. Ch., Royal Oak, Mich., 1960-69; cons. psychologist in pvt. practice, 1969-77; dir. research PMH, Inc., Bloomfield Hills, Mich., 1977—. Served to ensign USNR, 1943-45. Mem. Phi Beta Kappa. Clubs: Econ. (Detroit); Rotary (Bloomfield Hills). Home: 3120 Coolidge Hwy Royal Oak MI 48072 Office: PMH Inc 2550 Telegraph Rd Suite 200 Bloomfield Hills MI 48013

SHUGAN, STEVEN MARK, marketing educator; b. Chgo., Apr. 21, 1952; s. David Lester and Charlotte Rose Shugan; B.S. in Chemistry, So. Ill. U., 1973, M.B.A., 1974; Ph.D. in Managerial Econs. and Decision Scis. (fellow), Northwestern U., 1978; m. Irene H. Ginter, Dec. 16, 1973; 1 son, Adam Joshua. Lectr. Grad. Sch. Mgmt., Northwestern U., Evanston, Ill., 1976-77; asst. prof. bus. adminstrn. Grad. Sch. Mgmt., U. Rochester (N.Y.), 1977-79; asst. prof. mktg. Grad. Sch. Bus., U. Chgo., 1979-82, assoc. prof., 1982-87, prof., 1987—; chmn., organizer sessions numerous nat. confs., 1979—; cons. various cos., 1976—; chmn. Mktg. Sci. Conf., 1983; pres. Coll. Mktg., The Inst. of Mgmt. Scis.. Mem. Am. Mktg. Assn., Ops. Research Soc. Am.,

Assn. for Consumer Research, Inst. Mgmt. Scis., Am. Statis. Assn. Contbr. articles and revs. to profl. jours., chpts. to books; assoc. editor Mgmt. Sci.; mem. editorial bd. Mktg. Sci. Jour. Office: 1101 E 58th St Chicago IL 60637

SHULA, ROBERT JOSEPH, lawyer, medical clinic executive; b. South Bend, Ind., Dec. 10, 1936; s. Joseph Edward and Bertha Mona (Buckner) S.; m. Gaye Ann Martin, Oct. 8, 1978; children: Deirdre Regina, Robert Joseph II, Elizabeth Martin. BS in Mktg., Ind. U., 1958, JD, 1961. Bar: Ind. 1961; Diplomate Ind. Def. Trial Counsel. Ptnr. Bingham Summers Welsh & Spilman, Indpls., 1965-82, sr. ptnr., 1982—; mem. faculty Nat. Inst. Trial Advocacy; guest lectr. Brit. Medicine and Law Soc., 1979, Ind. U. Sch. Law; medico-legal lectr. Ind. U. Schs. Medicine, Dentistry, and Nursing. Bd. dirs. Arts Insight, Indpls.; pres. Oriental Arts Soc., Indpls., 1975-79, Meridian Women's Clinic, Inc., Indpls.; trustee Indpls. Mus. Art, 1975-78, life trustee, 1984—; bd. dirs Ind. Repertory Theatre, Indpls., 1982—, chmn. bd., 1985—; v.p., bd. dirs. Flanner House of Indpls., Inc., 1977—. Served to maj. JAGC, USAFR, 1961-65. Mem. ABA, Fed. Bar Assn., Ind. State Bar Assn., Indpls. Bar Assn., Bar Assn. 7th Fed. Circuit, Assn. Trial Lawyers Am., Am. Law Inst. Democrat. Episcopalian. Clubs: Indpls. Athletic, Woodstock Country. Home: 4137 N Meridian St Indianapolis IN 46208 Office: Bingham Summers Welsh & Spilman One Indiana Sq 2700 Ind Tower Indianapolis IN 46204

SHULKIN, MICHAEL HOWARD, accountant; b. Sioux City, Iowa, Mar. 7, 1948; s. Joe and Harriet (Wolsky) S.; m. Louise Kiefer, June 20, 1970; children: Jonathan, Jeffrey. BBA, U. Iowa, 1970; MS in Taxation, DePaul U., 1974. CPA, Ill. Staff acct. Price Waterhouse, Chgo., 1970-72; staff acct. Altschuler Melvoin & Glasser, Chgo., 1972—, tax mgr., tax ptnr., 1980; dir. tax services Altschuler Mehoin & Glasser, Chgo., 1983. Bd. dirs. Am. Jewish Com., Chgo., 1986—; regional bd. dirs. Anti-Defamation League, Chgo., 1985—; bd. dirs., treas. Young Men's Jewish Council, Chgo., 1978-83. Mem. Am. Inst. CPA's, Ill. Soc. CPA's. Club: Standard (Chgo.). Office: Altschuler Melvoin & Glasser 30 S Wacker Chicago IL 60606

SHULL, ROGER LOWELL, association administrator; b. Girard, Ill., June 9, 1934; s. Ralph Lowell and Bertha Elizabeth (Miller) S.; m. Suzanne Blessing, Aug. 13, 1955 (div. 1971); 1 child, Thomas Allen. BS, Manchester Coll., 1956; MBA, Ind. U., 1961. Tchr. Marion (Ohio) Harding High Sch., 1957-62, Dyke Coll., Cleve., 1962-63; pub. acct. Walthall & Drake, Cleve., 1963-69; office mgr. The Cleve. Fedn. Musicians, 1969—; bd. dirs. Local 4 Musicians Fed. Credit Union, Cleve. Mem. Data Processing Mgmt. Assn. (bd. dirs. 1986—), Adminstrv. Mgmt. Soc., Delta Pi Epsilon. Methodist. Home: 3328 Euclid Ave Cleveland OH 44115-2576 Office: The Cleve Fedn Musicians 2200 Carnegie Ave Cleveland OH 44115-2675

SHULMAN, CAROLE KAREN, professional society administrator; b. Mpls., Nov. 25, 1940; d. Allen Eldon and Beulah Ovidia (Blomsness) Banbury; m. David Arthur Shulman, Mar. 26, 1962; children: Michael, Krista, Tracy, Robbyn. Student, Colo. Coll., 1958-61. Profl. instr. Rochester (Minn.) Figure Skating Club, 1962-84, dir. skating, 1964-79, cons., 1979—; exec. dir. Profl. Skaters Guild, Rochester, 1984—, master rating examiner, 1971—, world profl. judge, 1976, 79. Editor Professional Skater mag., 1984—. Pres. Rochester Arts Council, 1983. Named triple gold medalist, U.S. Figure Skating Assn., Colorado Springs, Colo, 1959, 63, Master Rated Coach Profl. Skaters Guild, 1970, Sr. Rated Coach in Dance Profl. Skaters Guild, 1970. Mem. Am. Harp Soc. Mem. Covenant ch. Avocations: harp, skiing. Office: Profl Skaters Guild Am PO Box 5904 Rochester MN 55903

SHULSTAD, (RONALD) CRAIG, food company executive; b. Fargo, N.D., Sept. 28, 1942; s. Arvid Roland and Delia Iola (Stensrud) S.; m. Mariana Margaret Roca, June 28, 1968; children: Sara, Matthew. BA, U. Minn., 1964; MBA, Harvard U., 1968, M in Pub. Adminstrn., 1977. Asst. dir. adminstrn. U.S. Peace Corps, Washington, 1968-70; with mktg. dept. Gen. Mills, Inc., Mpls., 1970-78, dir. pub. issues, 1978-82, dir. consumer and pub. affairs, 1982-86, dir. media and fin. relations, 1986—. Councilman Chanhassen (Minn.) City Council, 1967; bd. dirs. Better Bus. Bur. Minn., Mpls., 1982—. Fellow Ford Found., 1967, Bush Found., 1976-77. Mem. Bach Soc. Minn. (pres. 1985—). Club: Apollo (Mpls.) (bd. dirs. 1979-82). Avocations: music, singing. Home: 19026 Carsonwood Ave Deephaven MN 55391 Office: Gen Mills Inc B 1113 Minneapolis MN 55440

SHUMAKER, STEVEN DONALD, college administrator; b. Auburn, Ind., Dec. 5, 1948; s. Donald E. and Helen Jeanette (Gary) S.; m. Delores Jean Weik, Oct. 7, 1972; children: Kimberly, Todd. BS in Acctg., Manchester Coll., 1971. Cert. internal auditor, Ind., N.Y., Wis. Acct. Graber Homes, Auburn, 1971-73, acctg. supr. Gen. Telephone Co., Ft. Wayne, Ind., 1973-74, internal auditor, 1974-77; internal audit mgr. Gen. Telephone Co., Johnstown, N.Y., 1977-78; customer acctg. mgr. Gen. Telephone Co., Sun Prairie, Wis., 1978-80, gen. acctg. mgr., 1980; property acctg. mgr. Gen. Telephone Co., Bloomington, Ill., 1980-83; treas. and bus. mgr. Manchester Coll., N. Manchester, Ind., 1983—. Gen. chmn. Wabash County United Fund, 1985; bd. dirs. Jr. Achievement Project Bus., 1985—. Mem. Nat. Assn. Accts., Inst. Internal Auditors, Manchester Coll. Acctg. Alumni Assn. (Alumni Service award 1979), North Manchester C. of C. (bd. dirs.). Republican. Lodges: Optimists (internat. sec. 1984-86), Shriners (local pres. 1985), Masons. Avocations: golf, bicycling, racquetball, reading. Home: 503 College Ave North Manchester IN 46962 Office: Manchester Coll 604 College Ave North Manchester IN 46962

SHUMSKI, HARRIET KRISTINE, insurance company executive; b. Chgo., May 27, 1952; d. Michael Joseph and Josephine Marie (Piela) Kowalski; m. Robert A. Shumski, Mar. 26, 1977. AA, Western Wis. Tech. Inst., 1972; paralegal cert., Roosevelt U., 1984. Lic. property/casualty broker, Ill. Legal sec. Steele, Klos & Flynn, La Crosse, Wis., 1972-77; sec. Complete Equity Markets, Inc., Wheeling, Ill., 1977-78, program adminstr., 1978-81, sr. account exec., 1981-82, dir. lawyers profl. liability ins. dept., 1982—. Co-author: textbook for legal secretarial sci. course, 1977. Mem. Nat. Legal Aid and Defender Assn., Nat. Assn. Female Execs. Roman Catholic. Avocations: traveling, reading, dancing. Office: Complete Equity Markets Inc 1098 S Milwaukee Ave Wheeling IL 60090

SHUMWAY, SPENCER THOMAS (TOM), usiness and acquisition broker; b. Bronxville, N.Y., May 31, 1943; s. Floyd Mallory Shumway and Margaret (Rabling) Shumway McAvoy; m. Alicia Fain, Apr. 10, 1965 (div. Dec. 1970); 1 dau., Erin Linn; m. 2d Bonnie Lee Shuppert, Dec. 20, 1975; children—Kristen Marie, Megan Nichole. Student pub. and pvt. schs., Lake Forest, Ill., Culver, Ind., Morristown, N.J. Adminstrv. asst. City of Lake Forest, 1960-64; corp. buyer Rogers Park Auto Parts (Ill.), 1964-66; br. mgr. Bearing Hdqrs. Co., Broadview, Ill., 1966-71; dist. mgr. Berry Bearing Co., Chgo., 1971-86; bus. broker Corp. Investment Internat., Mishawaka, Ind. Mem. South Bend Purchasing Mgmt. Assn. (sec. 1980-82), Nat. Assn. Purchasing Mgrs. Republican. Presbyterian. Lodge: Soc. Cin. (successor mem.). Home: 11002 Maumee Dr Granger IN 46530 Office: Corp Investment Internat 3702 N Main St Suite 101 Mishawaka IN 46544

SHUR, MICHAEL, electrical engineer, educator, consultant; b. Kamensk-Vralski, Sverdlovsk, USSR, Nov. 13, 1942; came to U.S., 1976.; s. Saul and Anna (Katz) S.; m. Paulina Gimmelfarb, Sept. 25, 1966; children: Luba, Natasha. MS, Leningrad Electrical Tech. Inst., 1965; PhD, Ioffe Inst., Leningrad, 1967. Scientist Ioffe Inst., 1965-75; asst. prof. Wayne State U., Detroit, 1976-77, Oakland U., Rochester, Mich., 1978; prof. U. Minn., Mpls., 1979—; cons. Honeywell Corp., 1978—, Xerox, 1986—. Author four books; also articles. Mem. IEEE (sr.), Am. Physics Soc. Office: U Minn Minneapolis MN 55455

SHUSTERICH, FREDERICK LAWRENCE, energy company executive; b. Virginia, Minn., Oct. 7, 1954; s. Frederick Lawrence and Patricia Marian (Barta) S.; m. Sheila Ann Kilbride, Aug. 6, 1983. BS, U. Minn., Duluth, 1977, MBA, 1985. Lab. supr. Inland Steel Mining Co., Virginia, Minn., 1977-79, ops. engr., 1979-81, sr. ops. engr., 1981-84, gen. maintenance engr., 1984-86; asst. gen. mgr. Midwest Energy Resources, Superior, Wis., 1986—. Author: Design and Implementation of a Maintenance Management System for A Taconite Mine, 1985; contbr. articles to profl. jours. Mem. Am. Inst. Mining Engrs., Soc. Naval Architects and Marine Engrs. (affiliate), Am. Soc. Quality Control,Am. Soc. Tng. Devel., Instrument Soc. Am. Roman Catholic. Avocations: running, golf, fishing, reading, scale boat and plane building. Home: 314 W Lewis St Duluth MN 55803 Office: Superior Midwest Energy Terminal PO Box 787 Superior WI 54880

SHUTER, MARC ANDREW, building products executive; b. Milw., Dec. 30, 1950; s. Irwin James and Ruth (Langley) S.; m. Mary Ellen Gressman, Oct. 27, 1973; children: Steven Andrew, Brian James. BS, U.S. Naval Acad., 1973; MBA, U. Wis., Whitewater, 1977. Commd. ensign USN, 1973, advanced through grades to lt. (j.g.), 1975, resigned, 1976; sales mgr. Builders World, Inc., Waukesha, Wis., 1977-82; gen. mgr. Builders World, Inc., Waukesha, 1982-87, exec. v.p., 1987—; lectr. fin. U. Wis., Whitewater. Mem. Lumberman's Frat. (bd. dirs. 1981—). Republican. Club: Skyway Flying (Waukesha) (sec.-treas. 1983-86). Lodge: Rotary (bd. dirs. Hartland, Wis. chpt. 1983-86). Avocations: flying, golf. Home: W297 N6227 Creekside Ct Hartland WI 53029 Office: Builders World Inc PO Box 881 Waukesha WI 53029

SHUTER, MARY ELLEN GRESSMAN, educator, writer, editor; b. Milw., Sept. 10, 1951; d. Walter F. and Marilyn (Daley) Gressman; m. Marc A. Shuter, Oct. 27, 1973; 1 child, Steven Andrew. BA, Hamline U., 1973; MEd, U. Wis., Whitewater, 1976. Reading specialist North Lake (Wis.) Pub. Schs., 1976-83; freelance writer, editor Scott Foresman Pub. Co., Glenview, Ill., 1982—; lectr. U. Wis., Whitewater, 1984-86; cons. various Wis. sch. dists., 1984—; aerobic instr., 1983—. Author children's stories. Mem. Women for Midwest Athletes Against Childhood Cancer, Milw., 1986—. Mem. Internat. Reading Assn., Wis. Edn. Assn. Republican. Roman Catholic. Club: Lake County Women's. Avocations: racquetball, aerobics. Home: W297 N6227 Creekside Ct Hartland WI 53029

SHUTZ, BYRON CHRISTOPHER, realtor; b. Kansas City, Mo., Feb. 16, 1928; s. Byron Theodore and Maxine (Christopher) S.; m. Marilyn Ann Tweedie, Mar. 30, 1957; children: Eleanor S. Gaines, Byron Christopher, Collin Reid, Allison Reid, Lindley Anne Baile. A.B. in Econs, U. Kans., 1949. Partner Herbert V. Jones & Co., Kansas City, Mo., 1953-72; pres. Herbert V. Jones Mortgage Corp., Kansas City, 1967-72, The Byron Shutz Co., Kansas City, 1973—; dir. Bus. Men's Assurance Co. Am., 1st Am. Financial Corp., Rothschild's, Inc. Chmn. bd. trustees U. Kansas City, 1979-81; trustee Pembroke-Country Day Sch., 1974-77, Midwest Research Inst., 1980—; bd. dirs. Kansas City Crime Commn. Served to 1st lt. USAF, 1951-53. Mem. Mortgage Bankers Assn. Am. (bd. govs. 1966-74), Am. Inst. Real Estate Appraisers. Clubs: Kansas City Country, Kansas City, University, Mercury (pres. 1978-79); Fla. Yacht (Jacksonville). Home: 1001 W 58th Terr Kansas City MO 64113 Office: 800 W 47th St Kansas City MO 64112

SHY, JIH-SHEN, architect; b. Taipei, Taiwan, Rep. of China, Jan. 17, 1954; came to U.S., 1978; s. Wei-Hsing and Shuh-Nein (Sheen) S.; m. I-Hsien Teng, July 31, 1979; children: Eddie, P.J. BArch, Chung-Yuan Christian Sci. and Engring. Coll., Chung-Li, Taiwan, 1977; MArch, Ill. Inst. Tech., 1980. Registered architect, Mo. Designer C.K. Chen & Assocs., Taipei, 1977-78, Skidmore, Owings & Merrill, Chgo., 1980-81; architect Kromm, Rikimaru & Johansen, St. Louis, 1982-84; project architect Smith & Entzeroth, St. Louis, 1984-85, Jones-Mayer, St. Louis, 1985, Hellmuth, Obata & Kassaabaum, Inc., St. Louis, 1985-86, Booker Assocs., Inc., St. Louis, 1986—. Bd. dirs. Free Chinese Assembly Greater St. Louis, 1984—. Mem. AIA, Nat. Council Archtl. Registration (bd. dirs. 1986—), Mo. Council Architects, Internat. Chinese Architect Soc. Roman Catholic. Home: 78 Manson Dr Chesterfield MO 63017 Office: Booker Assocs Inc 1193 Olive St Saint Louis MO 63101

SIBLEY, RUSSELL MARTIN, management information systems specialist; b. Gouverneur, N.Y., Dec. 7, 1944; s. Russell Martin and Rose (Refici) S.; m. Rosemary McBroom, Aug. 3, 1963 (div. July 1983); children: Robin, Scott. BBA, SUNY, Canton, 1966. Cert. systems profl. Mgr. systems and programming Cyro Industries, Sanford, Maine, 1980-84; dir. mgmt. info. systems Schlumberger, Ann Arbor, Mich., 1984—; exec. com. Software Internat. Users Group, Boston, 1984—. Recipient Outstanding Citizen award Rotary Club, Gouverneur, N.Y., 1977. Mem. Assn. for Systems Mgmt., COMMON. Roman Catholic. Avocations: reading, bicycling, travel. Office: 3330 Surrey Dr Saline MI 48176

SIBLEY, WILLIAM FRANCIS, accountant; b. Sioux City, Iowa, Sept. 5, 1947; s. Edward Heathcote and Clara Marie (Munger) S.; m. Cora Francine Howard, July 11, 1970. BBA, U. Iowa, 1969. CPA, Iowa. Staff acct. Nichols, Rise and Co., Sioux City, 1969-74, pvt. practice acctg., 1974—. Past officer Sioux Land Chpt. ARC, Sioux City, 1980—; sec., treas. Sioux City Concert Course, 1986. Mem. Am. Inst. CPA's, Iowa Soc. CPA's (pres. N.W. Chpt. 1980-81). Presbyterian. Lodges: Rotary, Masons (fin. com. 1986—). Avocations: model railroading, astronomy, bird watching. Home: 3615 Cheyenne Sioux City IA 51104 Office: Nichols Rise & Co PO Box 3529 Sioux City IA 51102

SICHERMAN, MARVIN ALLEN, lawyer; b. Cleve., Dec. 27, 1934; s. Harry and Malvina (Friedman) S.; m. Sue Kovacs, Aug. 18, 1957; children: Heidi Joyce, Steven Eric. B.A., Case Western Res. U., 1957, LL.B., 1960, J.D., 1968. Bar: Ohio 1960. Since practiced in Cleve.; mng. prin. Dettelbach & Sicherman Co., L.P.A., 1971—. Editorial bd.: Case-Western Res. Law Rev, 1958-60; Contbr. articles to legal jours. Mem. Beachwood (Ohio) Civic League, 1972—; mem. Beachwood Bd. Edn., 1978-86, pres., 1981, 85, v.p., 1984; trustee Beachwood Arts Council, 1977-84. Mem. ABA, Ohio Bar Assn. (lectr. truth in lending 1969, lectr. bankruptcy 1972, 81, 84; Meritorious Service awards 1971, 77, 78, 79, 83, 84, 85, 86, 87), Cleve. Bar Assn. (lectr. practice and procedure clinic 1960-80, 82-87, chmn. bankruptcy ct. com. 1971-73), Jewish Chautauqua Soc., Tau Epsilon Rho, Zeta Beta Tau. Jewish (trustee Temple brotherhood 1968-76, sec. 1971-73). Home: 24500 Albert Ln Beachwood OH 44122 Office: Ohio Savs Plaza Cleveland OH 44114

SICZEK, ROMAN WOJCIECH, mechanical engineer; b. Warsaw, Poland, July 14, 1951; s. Bernard Witold and Jadwiga Danuta (Myszkowska) S.; m. Joanna Turska, June 28, 1986. MS MechE, Poly. U., Warsaw, Poland, 1976; postgrad., Keller Grad. Sch. Mgmt., 1985—. Engr. OBRTT (Research and Devel. Ctr.), Warsaw, 1976-80; owner, mgr. Lab. Equipment Mfg. Co., Warsaw, 1979-81; equipment designer Wilson Sporting Goods Co., River Grove, Ill., 1981-83; design engr. Gaertner Sci. Corp., Chgo., 1983-85; project engr. Stoelting Co., Chgo., 1986—; project mgmt. and design cons., various cos. in Chgo. area, 1982—. Patentee lab. rotator. Avocations: skiing, windsurfing, tennis, travel. Home: 1426 Portsmouth Westchester IL 60153 Office: Stoelting Co 1350 S Kostner Ave Chicago IL 60623

SIDDIQI, TARIQ AHMED, physician, educator; b. Rawalpindi, Pakistan, Feb. 21, 1952; came to U.S., 1976; s. Zahur Ahmed and Zohra (Mufti) S. MB, BS, King Edward Med. Coll., Lahore, Pakistan, 1975; FSc, Govt. Coll., Lahore, 1969. Diplomate Am. Bd. Ob-Gyn. Instr. dept. ob-gyn U. Cin., 1981-83, asst. prof., 1983—, asst. prof. dept. pediatrics, 1984—. Contbr. articles to sci. jours. NIH grantee, 1986. Fellow Am. Coll. Ob-Gyn; mem. Am. Inst. Ultrasound in Medicine (sr.), Soc. Perinatal Obstetricians, Ohio State Med. Assn., Assn. Pakistani Physicians N.Am. Moslem. Office: U Cin Dept Ob-Gyn 231 Bethesda Ave Cincinnati OH 45267-0526

SIDDONS, JAMES KENNETH, fuel company executive, mechanical engineer; b. Milw., June 15, 1928; s. James Kenneth and Loretta (Bush) S.; m. Dolores Gardner, Sept. 9, 1950; children: Jeffrey, Sarah Siddons Bowers, Paul David. BSME, Marquette U., 1951. Project engr. Am. Airlines, Tulsa, 1966-80; exec. v.p. Nat. Chassis, Kansas City, Mo., 1981; pres. Tri-State Refueler Co., Kansas City, Kans., 1981—. Mem. Soc. Automotive Engrs. Democrat. Avocations: sculpture, gourmet cooking. Home: 4905 Mercier Kansas City MO 64112 Office: Tri State Refueler Co 539 S 10th St Kansas City KS 66105

SIDERS, WILLIAM DALE, academic program director; b. Hillsboro, Ohio, Dec. 3, 1941; s. Charles A. and Esther Long (Fels) S.; m. Nancy C. Cluff, June 16, 1961; children: Melissa, Colleen, Craig. BS, Ohio State U., 1963, MA, 1965, postgrad., 1971-74. Tchr. math. Worthington (Ohio) High Sch., 1968-71; asst. prof. math. Findlay (Ohio) Coll., 1975-81, dir. computer ctr., 1980-81; dir. Wing Computer Ctr. Kenyon Coll., Gambier, Ohio, 1981—. Mem. Assn. Computing Machines, Data Processing Mgmt. Assn., Poise User Group (chmn. VAX com. 1986). Avocation: camping. Home: 1111 E Chestnut Mount Vernon OH 43050 Office: Kenyon Coll Wing Computer Ctr Gambier OH 43022

SIDWELL, ELI ROSCOE, JR., real estate broker; b. Casey, Ill., Nov. 22, 1932; s. Eli Roscoe Sr. and Opal (Howe) S.; m. Laura Ann Gray, June 29, 1958; children: Melanie Ann, Eli R. III, Jamie Leann. BS in Edn., Eastern Ill. U., 1958. Cashier Coles County Nat. Bank, Charleston, Ill., 1961-66; from asst. dir. to dir. Embarra River Basin Agy., Greenup, Ill., 1966-67; salesman Leland Hall real Estate, Charleston, 1967-77; broker, prin. Eli Sidwell & Assoc., Charleston, 1977—; pres. Coles County Bd. Realtors, Charleston, 1975. Chmn. Citizens for Jim Edgar for State Rep., 1974, 76, 78; pres. Jefferson Sch. PTA, 1978; mem. steering com. to Re-elect Rep. Harry "Babe" Woodyard, 1980, chmn. 1982; mem. State of Ill. Balance of State Planning Council, Coles County Bd. Dist. 10, 1982, chmn. pro tem, 1984, chmn. 1986—; bd. dirs. Charleston Community Theatre, 1963-64, v.p., 1965; bd. dirs. Charleston Area Econ. Devel. Found., 1986—; bd. dirs. Eastern Ill. Found., 1965-75, mem. dean's adv. bd. Eastern Ill. U.sch. bus., 1987; adminstrv. bd. dirs. Charleston Wesley United Meth. Ch., meml. chmn., 1981—, stewardship and fin. chmn., 1985. Named one of Outstanding Young Men Am., Charleston Jaycees, 1967. Mem. Nat. Assn. Realtors, Ill. Assn. Realtors, Charleston C. of C. (bd. dirs., treas. 1964, Small Bus. of Yr. 1987), Sigma Pi (internat. pres. 1984—). Republican. Club: Eastern Ill. U. Panther (pres. 1982). Home: Rural Rt 4 Box 29 Charleston IL 61920 Office: Eli Sidwell & Assoc 409 Buchanan St Charleston IL 61920

SIEBENMANN, NANCYLEE ARBUTUS, hospital administrator, nurse; b. Ladysmith, Wis., Oct. 12, 1933; d. Herbert O. and Arbutus H. (Ruckdashel) Hartig; m. John F. Siebenmann, Apr. 13, 1957; children—John Hart, Lori Jean. Diploma St. Luke's Sch. Nursing, Duluth, Minn., 1954; B.S. in Nursing Adminstrn., U. Minn., 1957; M.A. in Nursing Adminstrn., U. Iowa, 1971. R.N., Iowa. Staff nurse St. Luke's Hosp., 1954, U. Minn., Mpls., 1955-57, Iowa Meth. Hosp., Des Moines, 1957; head nurse pre/post surg. unit St. Luke's Hosp., Cedar Rapids, Iowa, 1957-59, instr., asst. dir. St. Luke's Sch. Nursing, 1960-71, assoc. adminstr. St. Luke's Hosp., 1974-80, v.p. corp. devel. adminstrn., 1980-82, staff asst. to pres.; v.p. St. Luke's Health Resources; founding chmn. and dir. B.S. in Nursing Program, Coe Coll., Cedar Rapids, 1972-74; lectr. in field. Mem. Small Bus. Adv. Council; commr. Iowa Environ. Protection Commn., 1986—; bd. dirs. ARC (local chpt.). USPHS grantee, 1956, 57, 71. Mem. Am. Coll. Hosp. Adminstrs., Am. Hosp. Assn. (del.-at-large 1979-82, mem. council on nursing 1980-83), Sigma Theta Tau. Republican. Lutheran. Contbr. articles to profl. publs. Office: St Lukes Methodist Hosp 1026 A Ave NE Cedar Rapids IA 52402

SIEBERT, KARL JOSEPH, research biochemist; b. Harrisburg, Pa., Oct. 29, 1945; s. Christian Ludwig and Katharine (Springer) S.; m. Sui Ti Atienza, Mar. 14, 1970; children: Trina, Sabrina. BS in Biochemistry, Pa. State U., 1967, MS in Biochemistry, 1968, PhD in Biochemistry, 1970. Chemist Applied Sci. Labs., State College, Pa., 1968-70; research assoc. Stroh Brewery Co., Detroit, 1971, head research and devel. sect., 1971-73, mgr. research and devel. lab., 1973-82, dir. research, 1982—. Contbr. articles to profl. jours. Bd. visitors Oakland U. Biology Dept., Rochester, Mich., 1985—. Served to capt. USAR, 1967-75. Fellow NSF, 1967. Mem. Am. Chem. Soc., Master Brewer Assn. Ams., Am. Soc. Brewing Chemists (chmn. tech. com. 1986—, mem. editorial bd. 1983—). Avocations: computers, electronics. Home: 3661 Root Troy MI 48083 Office: Stroh Brewery Co 100 River Pl Detroit MI 48207

SIEBERT, WILLIAM ALAN, lawyer; b. Royal Oak, Mich., Jan. 25, 1955; s. William Edward and Mary Elizabeth (Northrup) S. BA, Albion Coll., 1977; JD, U. Detroit, 1980. Bar: Mich. 1980, U.S. Dist. Ct. (ea. dist.) Mich. 1981. Gen. counsel RARE Realty, Beaverton, Mich., 1983-85; sole practice Gladwin, Mich., 1985—. Exec. com. Gladwin County Reps., 1983—; candidate for Gladwin County Prosecuting Atty., 1984. Mem. ABA, Mich. Bar Assn. (real property sec. title ins. com. 1984—), Clare-Gladwin Trial Lawyers, Albion Coll. Alumni Bd., Phi Alpha Delta (chpt. clk. 1980). Methodist. Lodge: Masons. Office: 1105 1/2 W Cedar Ave Gladwin MI 48624

SIEBRASSE, JONATHAN DAVID, dentist; b. Hamilton, Ohio, Dec. 20, 1957; s. Edwin Andrew and Joan (Miller) S.; m. Vicki Kathleen Marsh, Dec. 27, 1981; 1 child, Erica Anne. BS, U. Mo., 1980, DDS, 1984. Gen. practice dentistry Parsons, Kans., 1984—. V.p. Trinity Luth. Ch., Parsons, 1986. Mem. ADA, Kans. Dental Assn., Southeast Kans. Dental Assn. Lodge: Rotary. Avocations: golf, water skiing, bicycling. Office: 109 s 27th St Parsons KS 67357

SIEDBAND, GERALD N., physician, radiologist; b. Chgo., Sept. 21, 1933; s. Michael William and Roslyn (Carman) S.; m. Sandra Jule Kowalski, Nov. 27, 1965; children: Michael, Stephanie, Julie, Mark. BS, Roosevelt U., 1959; MD, U. Basel, Switzerland, 1965. Diplomate Am. Coll. Radiology. Intern then resident St. Luke's Hosp., Milw., 1965-69; radiologist Bryan Meml. Hosp., 1969-73; radiologist Lincoln (Nebr.) Radiology Group, 1973—, treas., 1973-84, pres., 1984—. Served as staff sgt. U.S. Army, 1953-56. Fellow Am. Coll. Radiology; mem. Am. Coll. Nuclear Physicians (pres. Nebr. chpt. 1984-85). Office: Lincoln Radiology Group PC 1600 S 48th St Lincoln NE 68506

SIEFERT, ROBERT GEORGE, vehicle components manufacturing executive; b. Elizabeth, N.J., 1931; s. George Christian and Gertrude Marian (Duff) S.; m. Betty Lee Ritter, July 11, 1959; children: Cynthia, Margaret, Judith, Barbara, Sarah. BSME, Purdue U., 1955; MBA, Harvard U., 1957. Project mgr. Standard Oil N.J., 1957-58; gen. mgr. Wanson de Mexico, 1958-63; with Kelsey-Hayes Co., Inc., 1963—, engr., 1963-65, asst. chief engr., 1965-67, chief research engr., 1967-68, mgr. Jackson Mich. plant, 1968-69, v.p. ops., 1969-71, 78-81, dir. material mgmt., 1971-72, v.p. diversified products, 1972-78, pres. automotive, 1981-84, pres., chief exec. officer, 1984—; trustee Auotmobile Hall Fame; chmn. bd. dirs. Kelsey-Hayes Can., Windsor; bd. dirs. Fruehauf Corp., Detroit, Kelsey-Hayes Espana, S.A., Barcelona, Spain, Brembo, Bergamo, Italy, Cen. Mfg. Co., Paris, Ky., Kelsey-Hayes de Mexico, , FPS Italy, Sarezzo. Served as corp. U.S. army, 1950-52. Mem. Soc. Automotive Engrs., Automotive Pres. Council, Am. Supplier Inst. (bd. dirs. 1986), Econ. Club. Republican. Presbyterian. Clubs: Bloomfield Hills (Mich.) Country; Barton Hills Country, Exchange (Ann Arbor, Mich.). Avocations: hunting, golf. Office: Kelsey-Hayes Co 38481 Huron River Dr Romulus MI 48174 Other Office Address: Kelsey-Hayes Canada Ltd, 309 Ellis Ave E, Windsor, ON Canada

SIEGAL, BURTON LEE, product designer, consultant; b. Chgo., Sept. 27, 1931; s. Norman A. and Sylvia (Vitz) S.; m. Rita Goran, Apr. 11, 1954; children—Norman, Laurence Scott. B.S. in Mech. Engring., U. Ill., 1953. Torpedo designer U.S. Naval Ordnance, Forest Park, Ill., 1953-54; chief engr. Gen. Aluminum Corp., Chgo., 1954-55; product designer Chgo. Aerial Industries, Melrose Park, Ill., 1955-58; chief designer Emil J. Paidar Co., Chgo., 1958-59; founder, pres. Budd Engring. Corp., Chgo., 1959—; dir. Dur-A-Case Corp., Chgo.; design cons. to numerous corps. Contbr. articles to tech. publs.; patentee in field. Mem. math., sci. and English adv. bds. Niles Twp. High Schs., Skokie, Ill., 1975-79; electronic cons. Chgo. Police Dept., 1964. Winner, Internat. Extrusion Design Competition, 1975; nominated Presdl. Medal Technology Sen. Paul Simon and Rep. Dan Rostenkowski, 1986; named Inventor of Yr. Patent Law Assn. Chgo., 1986. Mem. No. Ill. Indsl. Assn., Inventor's Council, Soc. Automotive Engrs, Ill. Mfg. Assn. Office: 8707 Skokie Blvd Skokie IL 60077

SIEGAL, RITA GORAN, engineering company executive; b. Chgo., July 16, 1934; d. Leonard and Anabelle (Soloway) Goran; student U. Ill., 1951-53, B.A., DePaul U., 1956; m. Burton L. Siegal, Apr. 11, 1954; children—Norman, Laurence Scott. Tchr. elem. schs. Chgo. Public Schs., 1956-58; v.p. Easy Living Products Co., Chgo., 1960-62, pres. and founder, 1980—; freelance interior designer, Chgo., 1968-73; dist. sales mgr. Super Girls, Chgo., 1976; v.p and founder Budd Engring., Skokie, Ill., 1974—; lectr. Mem. adv. council Skokie High Schs., 1975-79; advisor Cub Scouts Skokie Council Boy Scouts Am.; bus. mgr. Nutrition for Optimal Health

Assn., 1980-82, pres., 1982-84, v.p., med./profl. liaison, 1985—. Recipient Cub Scout awards Boy Scouts Am., 1971-72; Sales award Super Girls, 1976. Mem. Women in Mgmt. (bd. dirs. 1986-87, pres. 1987—), Nat. Assn. Female Execs., No. Ill. Indsl. Assn., Ill. Mfrs. Assn., Inventors Council, North Shore Art League. Club: Profit Plus Investment (founder 1970). Contbr. articles to profl. jours. Office: 8707 Skokie Blvd Skokie IL 60077

SIEGEL, CALVIN, clothing company executive; b. 1924. Student, Yale U., 1948. With Calvin Clothing Co., 1948-68, Calvin Clothing Corp., 1968-82; with Palm Beach Co., Cin., 1982—, now pres., chief exec. officer, also bd. dirs. Served with AUS, 1942-45. Office: Palm Beach Inc 400 Pike St Cincinnati OH 45202 *

SIEGEL, GARY HOWARD, accountant, sociologist, educator; b. Chgo., Jan. 30, 1944; s. Sam Bernard and Miriam Arlene (Poster) S.; m. Beverly Kolodny, Sept. 14, 1968; children: Adam, Joshua, Sunny, Gabriel, Johanna, Samantha. BA in Acctg. with honors, U. Ill., 1966, PhD in Sociology, 1977; MBA in Acctg., DePaul U., 1967; postgrad., U. Chgo., 1967-68. CPA, Ill. Lectr. U. Ill., Chgo., 1967-70, asst. prof., 1977-80; research asst. U. Ill., Urbana, 1971-73; asst. prof. Ill. Inst. Tech., Chgo., 1974-77; assoc. prof. DePaul U., Chgo., 1980—; staff cons. 1st Nat. Bank Chgo., 1968-70; cons. pvt. practice, Chgo., 1975-85; pres. Gary Siegel Orgn., Chgo., 1985—. Assoc. editor Advances in Acctg., 1982-83; referee Decision Scis., 1984—; contbr. articles to profl. jours. Bd. dirs. Yeshiva Migdal Torah, Chgo.; pres. Jewish Burial Soc. Mem. Am. Inst. CPA's, Am. Acctg. Assn. (acctg., behavior and orgns. sect. 1982—), Ill. CPA Soc. (pub. relations council 1973-80, chmn. internal communications subcom. of pub. service and info. com. 1975-77, study team profl. specialization 1976-78), Am. Assn. Pub. Opinion Research, Decision Scis. Inst., Beta Alpha Psi, Delta Mu Delta. Office: DePaul U 25 E Jackson Chicago IL 60659

SIEGEL, JACK MORTON, biotechnology company executive; b. Sioux City, Iowa, June 11, 1922; s. Harry and Rose (Perlman) S.; m. Betty Virginia Collins, Feb. 22, 1946 (dec. Feb. 1986); children: Jennifer L. Mastricola, Marjorie G., Thomas A. BS in Chemistry, UCLA, 1944; PhD in Chemistry, Washington U., St. Louis, 1950. Chemist The Clinton Labs., Oak Ridge, Tenn., 1944-46; asst. prof. chemistry U. Ark. Sch. Medicine, Little Rock, 1950-55; chemist, v.p. P-L Biochems. Inc., Milw., 1955-82; v.p., gen. mgr. Pharmacia P-L Biochems. Inc., Milw., 1982-87, pres., 1987—. Contbr. articles to profl. jours. Mem. AAAS, Am. Chem. Soc. Democrat. Jewish. Avocation: watercolor painting. Office: Pharmacia P-L Biochems Inc 2202 N Bartlett Ave Milwaukee WI 53202

SIEGEL, LLOYD H., architect, real estate developer, consultant; b. N.Y.C., Nov. 27, 1928; s. Saul M. and Lillian (Bell) S. B.A. in Architecture, Princeton U., 1949; M.Arch., MIT, 1953. Registered architect, N.Y., N.J., Conn., Ohio, Ill., Mich. Designer Skidmore, Owings & Merrill, then I. M. Pei & Assocs., then Antonin Raymond, N.Y.C., 1955-60; assoc. Kelly & Gruzen, N.Y.C., 1960-66; dep. health services adminstr. City of N.Y., 1966-70; dep. exec. dir. health and hosps. governing com. Cook County, Chgo., 1970-76; prin. L.H.S. Cons. in Health Planning, Facility Design & Mgmt., Chgo., 1976—, Siegel & Schroeder, P.C., Chgo., 1983—; prin. Yacht Harbor Devel. Co., South Haven, Mich., 1983—, Siegel & Schroeder Developers Inc., Chgo., 1984—; mem. adv. coms. HEW; mem. pub. adv. panels GSA; mem. adv. com. Legislature State of Ill.; mem. fellowship evaluation com. AIA-Am. Hosp. Assn.; mem. tech. adv. com. to Northeastern Ill. Planning Commn.; chmn. Com. on Architecture for Health, 1984. Author: Hidden Asset? Interstitial Space, A Critical Evaluation, 1986; photography in permanent collections Met. Mus. Art, N.Y.C., Mus. Modern Art, N.Y.C., others; prin. works include N.Y. World's Fair Spanish Pavillion, N.Y.C. (N.Y. chpt. AIA award 1964), Williams Meml. Residence, Flushing, N.Y. (Queens C. of C. award 1964), Hebrew Home for Aged, Riverdale, N.Y. (Bronx C. of C. award 1966). Fulbright fellow Università di Roma, 1954, Politecnico di Milano, 1955. Fellow AIA (v.p. Chgo. chpt. 1972-74); mem. Urban Land Inst. Clubs: The Arts, University (Chgo.). Avocations: micology; microphagy; oenology. Home: 431 S Dearborn St Chicago IL 60605 Office: Siegel & Schroeder PC 230 N Michigan Ave Chicago IL 60601

SIEGEL, MARVIN, accountant; b. Bklyn., May 8, 1940; s. Harry and Freda (Schaffel) S.; m. Sara Pearl Widelitz, July 4, 1965; children: Marla, Marc. BBA, U. Miami, Fla., 1961. Mem. staff Murray J. Cohen, Miami, Fla., 1957-58; sr. acct. Mermell, Cherkas & Co., Miami, 1958-62, Mallah, Furman & Co., Miami, 1962-66, Miller Beer & Co., Miami, 1966-69; ptnr. Alexander Grant & Co., Chgo., 1969-79, Laventhol & Horwath, Chgo., 1979—. Editor: (tech. manual) Accounting & Auditing Manual. Treas. Bus. Vols. for the Arts, Chgo.; bd. dirs. Chgo Theatre Group. Served with U.S. Army, 1963-69. Mem. Am. Inst. CPA's, Fla. Inst. CPA's, Dade County Chpt. CPA's, Ill. CPA Soc., French-Am. C. of C. (bd. dirs.). Clubs: Metropolitan, River (Chgo.). Office: Laventhol & Horwath 300 S Riverside Plaza Chicago IL 60606

SIEGEL, SAUL MARSHALL, psychoanalyst, psychiatrist; b. Chgo., July 16, 1923; s. Morris and Lena (Adler) S.; m. Ann Solon, July 9, 1951 (div. Mar. 1969); children: Cara Beth Siegel Levinson, Stephen J.; m. Janis Fey, Dec. 25, 1969; children: Matthew, Amie. BA, U. Chgo., 1942, PhD, 1951, MD, 1955. Diplomate Am. Bd. Psychiatry and Neurology.; cert. psychoanalyst, Chgo. Practice medicine specializing in psychiatry Chgo., 1959—; dir. psychiatry clinic Michael Reese Hosp., Chgo., 1959-74, sr. cons., 1974—; supervising. analyst, mem. faculty Inst. Psychoanalysis, Chgo., 1980—, also chmn. Psychotherapy Conf., Chgo., 1985—. Contbr. articles to profl. jours. Am. Psychoanalytic Assn. Research grantee, 1981. Fellow Am. Psychiat. Assn.; mem. Am. Psychoanalytic Assn., Am. Psychol. Assn., Soc. for Psychotherapy Research. Office: 151 N Michigan Ave 1002 Chicago IL 60601

SIEGEL, W. WILLIAM, restaurateur; b. Chgo., Nov. 3, 1947; s. Arthur Brown and Rochelle (Wolfson) S.; m. Kathleen Carol Williams, Apr. 3, 1978 (div. Mar. 1987); 1 child, Jaclyn Morgan. Student, U. Chgo., 1965-67, Ill. Inst. Tech., 1966-67. Gen. mgr. 1137 Meat Co., Chgo., 1965-67; exec. Gold Seal Liquor Co., Chgo., 1967-75; owner That Steak Joynt, Chgo., 1975—. Chmn., trustee Sky Ranch fo Boys, N.D., 1979; chmn. Com. for Hunger, Chgo., 1986. Recipient Cert. Appreciation Lincoln Park C. of C., Chgo., 1976, hon. diploma Italian Wine Ctr., 1976, Honor award St. Jude's Research Hosp., Chgo., 1984. Mem. Ill. Restaurant Assn. Jewish. Avocations: antiques, wine collecting, sports. Office: That Steak Joynt 1610 N Wells Chicago IL 60614

SIEGLE, MICHAEL DUANE, marketing profl.; b. Springdale, Ohio, July 3, 1947; s. Joseph D. and Nina Jane (Carmichael) S. Student, Miami U., Oxford, Ohio, 1965-67; BA, Century U., 1983. Cert. med. technologist. Med. technician St. Jude's Children Res. Hosp., Memphis, 1975-76; adminstrv. supr. St. Louis Children's Hosp., 1976-79; product mgr. ICL Scientific, Fountain Valley, Calif., 1980-83; mktg. mgr. St. Louis U. Hosp., 1984; mktg. div. mgr. Rupp and Bowman, Schaumburg, Ill., 1985-86; pres. Creative Services, St. Louis, 1987—; clin. instr., faculty advisor Forest Park Community Coll., St. Louis, 1977-79. Contbr. articles to profl. jours. Served with USN, 1966-75. Mem. Nature Conservancy, Nat. Audubon Soc. Republican. Avocations: baseball, bicycling, art, wildlife, nature. Office: Creative Services 7536 Forsyth Suite 125 Clayton MO 63105

SIEHL, DONALD, osteopathic surgeon; b. Cin., Mar. 30, 1917; s. Walter H. and Flora L. (Sontag) S.; m. Ruth Gardiner, Aug. 22, 1944 (dec. May 1946); m. Susan A. Kultenbach, Sept. 13, 1947; children: Charles, Joh, Joseph, Patrick, Michael, Timothy, Susanne Amy. AB, Miami U., Oxford, Ohio, 1939; DO, Kirksville Coll. Osteopathic Medicine, 1943. Intern Doctors Hosp., Columbus, Ohio, 1943-44, resident osteopathic medicine, 1946-49; mem. staff Kirksville Coll. Osteopathic Medicine, 1949-51; practice osteopathic medicine Dayton, Ohio, 1951—. Served to 2d lt. USPHS, 1945-46. Fellow Am. Coll. Osteopathic Surgeon (pres. 1977-78, Disting. Service award 1984), Am. Osteopathic Acad. Orthopedics (pres. 1958-59, Appreciation medal 1970); mem. Am. Osteopathic Assn. Office: 1217 Salem Dayton OH 45406

SIEKERT, ROBERT GEORGE, neurologist; b. Milw., July 23, 1924; s. Hugo Paul and Elisa (Kraus) S.; m. Mary Jane Evans, Feb. 17, 1951; children: Robert G. Jr., John E., Friedrich A.P. BS, Northwestern U., 1945, MS, 1947, MD, 1948. Cert. Am. Bd. Psychiatry and Neurology. Instr. anatomy U. Pa., Phila., 1948-49; fellow neurology Mayo Found., Rochester, Minn., 1950-54; cons. Mayo Clinic, Rochester, 1954—, head neurology sect., 1966-76, bd. govs., 1973-80, prof. neurology med. sch., 1969—. Contbr. articles to profl. jours. Trustee Mayo Found., Rochester, 1973-81; editor Mayo Clinic Proceedings, 1982-86. Served to lt. j.g. M.C., USNR, 1950-52. Fellow Am. Coll. Physicians; mem. Am. Neurol. Assn., Northwestern U. Med. Sch. Alumni Assn. (Service award 1983), Alpha Omega Alpha. Avocation: philately. Office: Mayo Clinic 200 1st St SW Rochester MN 55905

SIEKMAN, ELIZABETH NANCY ANN, corporate executive; b. Cin., Aug. 19, 1942; s. Lawrence G. and Mabel R. (Staudt) Kampe; m. James W. Siekman, Oct. 7, 1961; children: Anthony J., Daniel P., Jeffrey A., Matthew L. A in Bus., Xavier U., 1963. Sec., Mac Piping & Constrn., Cin., 1975-79, Adath Israel Synagogue, Cin., 1979-80; book keeper Normandy Swim CLub, Loveland, Ohio, 1977-79; pres., owner Artic Heating and Air Conditioning, Inc., Loveland, 1980—. Den leader Boy Scouts Am., Loveland, 1970-75; bd. dirs. Loveland Youth Orgn., 1975-80, Empires and Educators, 1976-80. Mem. Allied Constrn. Industries, Loveland PTA (officer 1965-68). Democrat. Roman Catholic. Lubs: Normandy Swim (Loveland) (judge 1977-86); YMCA (Blue Ash, Ohio) (judge 1977-82).

SIEKMANN, DONALD CHARLES, accountant; b. St. Louis, July 2, 1938; s. Elmer Charles and Mabel Louise (Blue) S.; m. Linda Lee Knowles, Sept. 10, 1966; 1 child, Brian Charles. BS, Washington U., St. Louis, 1960. CPA, Ohio. Ptnr., practice dir. Arthur Andersen & Co., Cin., 1960—. Columnist Cin. Enquirer, 1983-86, Gannett News Services, 1983-86; editor "Tax Clinic" column Tax Advisor mag., 1974-75. Mem. bd. Cin. Zool. Soc., 1985—; officer, bd. dirs. Cin. Found. for Pub. TV, 1984—, Cin. Symphony Orch., 1973-85, Cin. Ballet Co., 1973—. Served with U.S. Army, 1961. Mem. Am. Inst. CPA's, Ohio Soc. CPA's, Cin. Estate Planning Council. Lutheran. Club: Cin. Country (trustee 1983—). Lodge: Optimists (pres. Queen City chpt. 1986). Home: 8160 N Clippinger Dr Cincinnati OH 45243 Office: Arthur Andersen & Co 425 Walnut St Cincinnati OH 45202

SIEKMANN, REM OWEN, business developer; b. Grosse Pointe Farms, Mich., Dec. 15, 1954; s. Harold John and Joan Hoffman (Henritzy) S.; m. Kathleen Eleanor Lake, Jan. 20, 1979; 1 child, Sarah Lake. B.S.E. cum laude, Duke U., 1976; M.B.A., U. Chgo., 1983. Registered profl. engr. Mfg. devel. engr. Baxter Travenol Labs., Deerfield, Ill., 1976-78, sr. devel. engr., 1978-79, prin. engr., 1979-80, dir. spl. projects, 1987—; project engr. Am. Covertors div. Am. Hosp. Supply Corp., Evanston, Ill., 1980-83; new product planning mgr. Am. Hosp. Supply Corp., 1983-84, sr. bus. analyst, 1984-85, mgr. bus. devel., 1985-86; sr. bus. assoc. Baxter Travenol Labs., 1986; spl. project dir. Busken Bakery, 1987—. Patentee in field. Patroller Nat. Ski Patrol System, 1969—. Mem. Inst. Environ. Sci., Nat. Soc. Profl. Engrs., ASTM (contbr. F01.10 subcom. 1981-84). Presbyterian. Home: 7060 Mt Vernon Ave Cincinnati OH 45227 Office: Busken Bakery 2675 Madison Rd Cincinnati OH 45208

SIEMASKA, SAULIUS JONAS, electronics company sales professional; b. Bklyn., Jan. 5, 1954; s. Liutaveras Antanas and Danute Janina (Daniunas) S.; m. Sophie VanWinkle, Feb. 5, 1977; children: Kristin Alexandra, Nicholas Paul. BS, U.S. Mil. Acad., 1976; MBA, Rockhurst Coll., 1985. Commd. 2d lt. U.S. Army, 1976, advanced through grades to capt., 1980, resigned, 1981; design engr. Butler Mfg. Co., Kansas City, Mo., 1981-83; sales rep. Digital Equiptment Corp., Kansas City, 1983—. Republican. Roman Catholic. Avocations: racquetball, skiing. Home: 9721 W 121st Terr Overland Park KS 66213 Office: Digital Equipment Corp 1300 E 104th St Kansas City MO 64131

SIERAKOWSKI, ROBERT LEON, engineering educator; b. Vernon, Conn., Apr. 11, 1937; s. Stanley F. and Amelia C. (Misiaszek) S.; m. Nina A. Shopa, May 2, 1975; children—Steven R., Sandra M. B.S. in Engring, Brown U., 1958; M.S., Yale U., 1960, Ph.D., 1964. Engr. Sikorsky Aircraft, Stratford, Conn., 1958-60; research engr. United Techs Corp., 1963-67; research asst. Yale U., New Haven, 1960-63; adj. asst. prof. engring. mechanics Rensselaer Poly. Inst. Hartford Grad. Center, 1965-67; vis. asst. prof. engring. mechanics U. Fla., 1967-68, assoc. prof., 1968-72, prof., 1972-83; chmn. dept. civil engring. Ohio State U., 1983—. Contbr. numerous articles and revs. to profl. publs. Mem. Vernon Bd. Edn., 1965-67; mem. Vernon City Commn., 1967, Gainesville (Fla.) Citizens Adv. Council for Elementary Schs., 1973-75, St. Andrews Sch. Bd., Columbus, Ohio, 1985—; vis. prof. AFOSR, 1982. NRC sr. research fellow, 1972-73. Fellow AIAA (asso.), ASME; mem. Soc. Exptl. Stress Analysis, Soc. Engring. Sci. (editor procs. 1978), Soc. Materials Process Engrs., Yale Engring. Assn., Sigma Xi, Sigma Tau, Tau Beta Pi, Phi Kappa Phi. Roman Catholic. Club: K.C. Home: 2725 Lymington Rd Columbus OH 43220 Office: Dept Civil Engring Ohio State U Columbus OH 43220

SIERLES, FREDERICK STEPHEN, psychiatrist, educator; b. Bklyn., Nov. 9, 1942; s. Samuel and Elizabeth (Meiselman) S.; m. Laurene Harriet Cohn, Oct. 25, 1970; children: Hannah Beth, Joshua Caleb. AB, Columbia U., 1963; MD, Chgo. Med. Sch., 1967. Diplomate Am. Bd. Psychiatry and Neurology. Intern Cook County Hosp., Chgo., 1967-68; resident in psychiatry Mt. Sinai Hosp., N.Y.C., 1968-69, 1969-71, chief resident, 1970-71; staff psychiatrist U.S. Reynolds Army Hosp., Ft. Sill, Okla., 1971-73; assoc. attending psychiatrist Mt. Sinai Hosp., Chgo., 1973-74; instr. psychiatry Chgo. Med. Sch., North Chicago, 1973-74, dir. undergrad. edn. in psychiatry, 1974—, asst. prof., 1974-78, assoc. prof., 1978—; chmn. ednl. affairs com., 1983-85, 86—; cons. psychiatry Cook County Hosp., 1974-79, St. Mary of Nazareth Hosp., 1979-84; chief Mental Health Clinic, North Chicago VA Hosp., 1982-85, chief psychiatry service, 1983-85. Author: (with others) General Hospital Psychiatry, 1985, Behavioral Science for the Boreds, 1987; editor: Clinical Behavioral Science, 1982; contbr. articles to profl. jours. Served to maj., M.C., U.S. Army, 1971-73. Recipient Ganser Meml. award Mt. Sinai Hosp., 1970; named Prof. of Yr., Chgo. Med. Sch., 1977, 80, 83; N.Y. State Regents scholar, 1959-63; NIMH grantee, 1974-83, Chgo. Med. Sch. grantee, 1974-83. Fellow Am. Psychiat. Assn.; mem. Ill. Psychiat. Soc. (fellowship com. 1985—), Assn. Interns and Residents Cook County Hosp., Assn. Dirs. Med. Student Edn. in Psychiatry (exec. council 1985—, chmn. ins. program com. 1987—), Nat. Assn. VA Physicians (sec.-treas. North Chgo. chpt. 1984-85), Alpha Omega Alpha, Phi Epsilon Pi. Office: Chgo Med Sch 3333 Green Bay Rd North Chicago IL 60064

SIERMINSKI, GREGORY V., dentist; b. Chgo., Aug. 25, 1951; s. Walter Anthony and Sophie (Magnowski) S.; m. Kathy L. (Thorne), Mar. 28, 1981; 1 child, Rachel. BA, St. Joseph's Coll., Renssel, Ind., 1973; BS, U. Ill., Chgo., 1975, DDS, 1977. Gen. practice dentistry Wonder Lake, Ill., 1977—, Chgo., 1984-86. Mem. ADA, Ill. State Dental Soc., McHenry (Ill.) County Dental Soc. (sec., treas. 1985-86, v.p. 1986—); Chgo. Dental Soc. (assoc.), Wonder Lake Jaycees. Roman Catholic. Avocations: jogging, golf, collector of golf related antiques. Office: 7432 Hancock Dr Wonder Lake IL 60097

SIEVERS, HARRY JOHN (JACK), marketing executive; b. Waterloo, Iowa, Sept. 11, 1930; s. Harry L. and Grace L. (Butcher) S.; m. Patricia H. Hewins, Dec. 27, 1953; children: Rodney L., Holly A., Rebecca L. BS, U. Iowa, 1953, MA, 1956. Personnel adminstr. Oscar Mayer & Co., Madison, Wis., 1956-58; employment mgr. Oscar Mayer & Co., Davenport, Iowa, 1958-62; sales engr. The Kartridg Pak Co., Atlanta, 1962-69, Chgo., 1969-81; internat. mgr. The Kartridg Pak Co., Davenport, 1981—. Mem. dist. export council State of Iowa, 1986. Served to 1st. lt. USMC, 1953-56. Avocation: amateur radio.

SIEVERT, ROBERT ALBERT, clergyman, development manager; b. Watertown, Wis., May 20, 1935; s. Hubert A. and Ada L. (Frey) S.; BA, Northwestern Coll., 1958; MDiv, Wis. Lutheran Sem., 1963; MA, Coll. of St. Thomas, 1980; m. Jean Ann Ihde, Oct. 11, 1964; children: Julie Ann, Sharyn Jean, Scott Robert, Deanne Lyn. Instr., Northwestern Luth. Acad., Mobridge, S.D., 1960-61; ordained to ministry Wis. Evang. Luth. Synod, 1964; pastor Luth. chs. Montrose, Minn., 1964-68, Onalaska, Wis., 1968-71; prin. Saint Croix Luth. High Sch., West St. Paul, Minn., 1971-84, supt., 1984-86; mgr. devel. Wis. Luth. Child and Family Services, Milw., 1986—; mem. Minn. Dept. Edn. Nonpublic Sch. Study Com., 1972-82, 85-86; dir. pub. relations Western Wis. Dist., Wis. Evang. Luth. Synod, 1969-71. Mem. bd. control Luther High, Onalaska, Wis., 1969-71, chmn., 1970-71; mem. Minn. Dist. Bd. for Info. and Stewardship, Wis. Evang. Luth. Synod, 1965-68; bd. dirs. Minn. Ind. Sch. Fund, 1976-79, 84-86, treas., 1985-86. Mem. Nat. Assn. Secondary Sch. Prins., Minn. Assn. Pvt. Sch. Adminstrs., Assn. Luth. High Schs. (pres. 1976-78), Assn. for Supervision and Curriculum Devel., Assn. Luth. Devel. Execs.

SIEVERTSEN, RHONDA LYNN, elementary and remedial reading educator; b. Denison, Iowa, Dec. 17, 1959; d. Leslie Harry and Marguerite Jane (Dunlap) Rath; m. Jeffrey Alan Sievertsen, July 27, 1985. BS with high honors, U. S.D., 1982, MA with highest honors, 1987. Cert. tchr. Iowa, Nebr. Tutor English for bilingual, remedial reading Denison (Iowa) Community Schs., 1982-83; tchr. elem. and summer sch. Maple Valley Community Sch., Mapleton, Iowa, 1983-87; tchr. elem. remedial reading Irwin (Iowa) -Kirkman Community Sch., 1987—; asst. dir. fund-raising campaign Am. Heart Assn., Maple Valley Schs., Castana, Iowa, 1986; monitor gifted students program Maple Valley Schs., 1986-87; sponsor cheerleading Irwin-Kirkman Community Schs., 1987—. Mem. AAUW, Internat. Reading Assn., Iowa and W. Cen. Iowa Reading Assn. Republican. Lutheran. Clubs: Women's City Bowling League (Denison), Women's City Slowpitch Softball Team (Denison). Avocations: sewing, aerobics, softball, bowling, tennis. Home: 113 Ave B Denison IA 51442 Office: Irwin-Kirkman Community Schs Irwin IA 51446

SIGAL, KASS F., psychiatric social worker; b. Ft. Lewis, Wash., Feb. 7, 1943; d. Edward Michael and Gertrude Lavinia (McNeill) Flaherty; m. Michael S. Sigal, May 16, 1971; 1 child, Sarah Caroline. BA, U. Colo., 1965; post grad., Roosevelt U., 1966-68; MSW, U. Ill., 1970. Cert. social worker, Ill; diplomate Am. Bd. Social Work. Research asst. dept. genetics Fels Research Inst., Antioch Coll., Yellow Springs, Ohio, 1965-66; social worker Cook County Dept. Pub. Aid, Chgo., 1966-68; psychiat. social worker Northwestern Meml. Hosp., Chgo., 1970-74; pvt. practice family therapy Chgo., 1974-85; teaching cons. Inst. Family Studies, Chgo., 1985—; instr. Northwestern U. Med. Sch., Chgo., 1971-87; cons. Northwestern Meml. Hosp., Chgo., 1974-87. bd. dirs. Friends Handicapped Riders, Chgo., 1986; active Friends of Second City Ballet. Mem. Nat. Assn. Social Workers, Acad. Cert. Social Workers, Lincoln Park Zool. Soc., Hooved Animal Humane Soc. (aux.), U. Ill. Alumni Assn., U. Colo. Alumni Assn., Alpha Chi Omega. Club: Mill Creek Hunt (hon. sec. 1986—). Home: 2821 N Pine Grove Ave Chicago IL 60657

SIGAL, MICHAEL STEPHEN, lawyer; b. Chgo., July 9, 1942; s. Carl I. and Evelyn (Wallack) S.; m. Kass M. Flaherty, May 16, 1971; 1 child, Sarah Caroline. B.S., U. Wis.-Madison, 1964; J.D., U. Chgo., 1967. Bar: Ill. 1967, U.S. Dist. Ct. (no. dist.) Ill. 1967. Assoc. firm Sidley & Austin and predecessor firm, Chgo., 1967-73, ptnr., 1973—. Mem. U. Chgo. Law Rev., 1965. Bd. dirs. EMRE Diagnostic Services, Inc., affiliate Michael Reese Hosp., Chgo., 1982—, The Mary Meyer Sch., Chgo., 1986—. Mem. Chgo. Bar Assn., Ill. State Bar Assn., ABA, Phi Beta Kappa, Phi Kappa Phi, Phi Eta Sigma. Jewish. Clubs: Law, Monroe (Chgo.); Mill Creek Hunt (Wadsworth, Ill.). Home: 2821 N Pine Grove Ave Chicago IL 60657 Office: Sidley & Austin 1 First National Plaza Chicago IL 60603

SIGLAR, HAROLD L., hospital administrator; b. Kansas City, Mo., Mar. 18, 1950; s. Harold L. and Gertrude Marie (Schinze) S.; m. Pamela Jo Norman, Apr. 13, 1985. BS, St. Mary's of the Plains, Dodge City, Kans., 1972; M Pub. Adminstrn. in Health Adminstrn., U. Mo., Kansas City, 1983; MA in Mktg., Webster U., 1985. Nat. rep. ARC, Peoria, Ill., 1972-78; assoc. exec. dir. Crittenton Ctr., Kansas City, Mo., 1978-81; adminstrv. asst. St. Mary's Hosp., Kansas City, 1981-84; asst. exec. dir. St. Mary's Hosp., Blue Springs, Mo., 1985—. Treas. The Learning Ctr., Kansas City, 1981-84; mem. Centerions, Kansas City, 1984-86; bd. dirs. Mid-Am. chpt. Nat. Multiple Sclerosis Soc., Kansas City, 1984-86, Westport Ballet Theatre, Kansas City, 1984-86. Named one of Outstanding Youn Men Am., 1986; named Outstanding Coll. Athlete of Am., 1971-72. Mem. Am. Coll. Healthcare Execs., Greater Kansas City Council of Health Care Execs., Greater Kansas City Soc. of Health Planners and Marketers (v.p. 1986), Raytown (Mo.) Jr. C. of C. (bd. dirs. 1978-83). Roman Catholic. Avocations: travel, basketball, cycling. Home: 516 SE Adobe Lee's Summit MO 64063 Office: St Mary's Hosp 201 R D Mize Rd Blue Spring MO 64015

SIGLER, CAROL JEAN, educator; b. New Castle, Ind., July 29, 1949; d. Robert Sheldon and Ruth (Brooks) S. B.S., Ball State U., 1971, M.A., 1974. Elem. sci. tchr. Greenfield-Central Community Schs., Greenfield, Ind., 1971—. Chancel choir dir. Wilkinson United Methodist Ch., Ind., 1972-80; dir. music Trinity Park United Meth. Ch., Greenfield, 1981-86, Amity United Meth. Ch., Greenfield, 1986—. Students recipient 50 awards including 6 overall championships Central Ind. Regional Sci. Fair, 1974-84; recipient Tchr. of Yr. award Ind. Computer Educators' Assn., 1987. Mem. Alph Delta Kappa (pres. Ind. Alpha Delta chpt. 1984-86). Avocation: computer programming. Home: 3904 N State Rd 9 Greenfield IN 46140 Office: Lincoln Park Sch North and School Sts Greenfield IN 46140

SIGOLOFF, SANFORD CHARLES, retail executive; b. St. Louis, Sept. 8, 1930; s. Emmanuel and Gertrude (Breliant) S.; m. Betty Ellen Greene, Sept. 14, 1952; children: Stephen, John David, Laurie. B.A., UCLA, 1950. Cons. AEC, 1950-54, 57-58; gen. mgr. Edgerton, Germeshausen & Grier, Santa Barbara, Calif., 1958-63; v.p. Xerox Corp., 1963-69; pres. CSI Corp., Los Angeles, 1969-70; sr. v.p. Republic Corp., Los Angeles, 1970-71; chief exec. officer Kaufman & Broad, Inc., Los Angeles, 1979-82; chmn., pres., chief exec. officer Wickes Cos. Inc., Santa Monica, 1982—. Contbr. articles on radiation dosimetry to profl. jours. Bd. govs. Cedars-Sinai Hosp. Served in USAF, 1954-57. Recipient Tom May award Nat. Jewish Hosp. and Research Ctr., 1972. Mem. AAAS, Am. Chem. Soc., AIAA, Am. Nuclear Soc., IEEE, Radiation Research Soc.

SIKMA, JACK, professional basketball player; b. Kankakee, Ill., Nov. 14, 1955; m. Shawn Strickland, 1984; 1 child, Jacob. Student, Ill. Wesleyan U. Player Seattle Supersonics, 1977-86, Milwaukee Bucks, 1986—; mem. NBA championship team, 1979; player NBA All-Star, Game, 1979, 80, 81, 82, 83, 84, 85, 86. Office: care Milwaukee Bucks 901 N Fourth St Milwaukee WI 53203 *

SIKORA, SUZANNE MARIE, dentist; b. Kenosha, Wis., Dec. 4, 1952; d. Leo F. and Ida A. (Dupuis) S. BS, U. Wis., Parkside, 1975; DDS, Marquette U., 1981. Assoc. Paul G. Hagemann, DDS, Racine, Wis., 1981-84; pvt. practice dentistry Racine, 1984—; cons. Westview Nursing Home, Racine, 1981—, Lincoln Luth. Home, Racine, 1981—, Becker-Shoop Ctr., Racine, 1981—, Lincoln Village Convalescent Ctr., Racine, 1986—. Mem. ad hoc study com. County Health Dept., Racine, 1982-83. Mem. ADA, Wis. Dental Assn. (council on access prevention and wellness com. 1984-86), Racine County Dental Assn. Office: 1900 Lathrop Ave Racine WI 53405

SIKORSKI, GERRY, congressman; b. Breckenridge, Minn., Apr. 26, 1948; s. Elroy and Helen S.; m. Susan Jane Erkel, Aug. 24, 1974; 1 dau., Anne. B.A., U. Minn., 1970, J.D., 1973. Bar: Minn. 1973. Mem. Minn. Senate, 1976-82, majority whip, 1980-82; mem. 98th-100th Congresses from Minn., 1983—; freshman whip 98th-99th Congresses from Minn., mem. Energy Com., Commerce Com., Post Office and Civil Service Com., Select Com. on Children, Youth and Families. Mem. Minn. Adv. Commn. on Internat. Trade; mem. Spl. Minn. Task Force on China; past chmn. legis. com. Minn. Gov.'s Citizens Council on Aging; past treas. Legal Assistance Minn. Mem. Stillwater and Bayport Jaycees, Assn. for Retarded Citizens. Office: US House of Representatives 414 Cannon House Office Bldg Washington DC 20515 *

SILAKOSKI, ANTHONY FRANK, utility company; b. N.J., Dec. 19, 1952; s. Anthony John and Jeanette Silakoski; m. Linda G. Pinkava, Aug. 9, 1974; children: Kristin, Ryan. BSME, BS in Aerospace Engring., U.S. Naval Acad., 1974; MBA, John Carroll U., 1984. Registered profl. engr., Ohio. Commd. ensign USN, 1974, advanced through grades to lt., 1978; served on USS Andrew Jackson Groton, Conn., 1975-78; served on USS Birmingham Norfolk, Va., 1978-79; resigned now lt. commdr. Res. USN, 1979—; ops. engr. Cleve. Electric Illumination Co., 1979-81, dir. tng., 1981-86, gen.

supervising engr., 1986—. Mem. ASME, IEEE, Naval Res. Assn., Midwest Nuclear Tng. Assn. (chmn. mem. com. 1983-85). Republican. Roman Catholic. Office: Cleve Electric Illuminating Co E140 PO Box 97 Perry OH 44081

SILBERBERG, NORMAN ESAU, psychologist, consultant; b. Bklyn., Sept. 12, 1931; s. Hyman L. and Bessie M. (Lasky) S.; m. Margaret Carlson (dec. Nov. 1982); children: Amy, Sarah, Ann. BA, Syracuse U., 1953; MA, U. Minn., 1957; student, U. Paris, 1957-58; PhD, U. Iowa, 1965. Lic. cons. psychologist, Minn. Sch. psychologist North St. Paul Schs., 1963-65; dir. research Sister Kenny Inst., Mpls., 1967-73, v.p., 1973-77; psychol. cons. Mpls., 1977-85; psychologist Minn. Indian Women's Resource Ctr., Mpls., 1985—; advisor Red Sch. House, St. Paul, 1973, Nat. Urban League, 1974-75; evaluator AIM Schs., Mpls., St. Paul, 1969-76; mem. Govs. COuncil on Aging, 1973-75; cons. Mpls. Head Start, 1977—. Author: Who Speaks for the Child, 1974; editorial advisor Jour. Learning Disabilities, 1967—; contbr. articles to profl. jours. Bd. dirs. St. Paul Urban League, 1965-74; trustee Northlands Med. Program. 1974-77. Recipient Appreciation awards St. Paul Indian Clinic, 1983, Women's Advocates, 1983, Mpls. Head Start, 1984. Mem. Am. Psychol. Assn. Democrat. Home and Office: 920 Lincoln Ave Saint Paul MN 55105

SILBERMAN, CARL MORRIS, physician; b. Phila., Aug. 7, 1946; s. Emanuel Harry and Sylvia (Cohen) S.; B.A., Temple U., 1968; M.D., Jefferson Med. Coll., 1972. Resident, Cooper Med. Center, Camden, N.J., 1974-76; fellow in cardiology Northwestern U. Hosp., Chgo., 1977-79; practice medicine specializing in cardiology, Chgo., 1979—; asst. prof. medicine dept. cardiology Chgo. Med. Sch., 1979—; dir. cardiology unit Naval Regional Med. Center, North Chicago, Ill.; dir. coronary care unit Cook County Hosp., Chgo.; mem. staff Hofy Family Hosp.; cons. in internal medicine and cardiology and cardiologist for EKG interpretation and quality of care assurance, Humana Corp., 1986—; cons. in cardiology 11th Naval Dist., Cook County Hosp. Diplomate Am. Bd. Internal Medicine, Sub-bd. Cardiovasular Disease. Fellow Am. Coll. Chest Physicians, Am. Coll. Angiographers, Am. Coll. Cardiology; mem. AMA, Chgo. Med. Assn., Ill. Med. Assn., ACP. Home and Office: 2734 N Seminary Ave Chicago IL 60614

SILER, JAMES FRANCIS, vocational educator; b. Defiance, Ohio, June 23, 1942; s. Victor Francis and Margaret Louise (Holman) S.; m. Jean Ellen Kemerer, June 24, 1967; children—Heather Lynne, Kelby James, Perry Wynn. Student Bowling Green State U., 1962-64; B.S. in Edn., U. Toledo, 1982. Electric motor repairman Bryan Electric Co. (Ohio.), 1960-64; maintenance man B.F. Goodrich Co., Woodburn, Ind., 1969-77; vocat. educator in indsl. elecricity Vantage Joint Vocat. Sch., Van Wert, Ohio, 1977—; journeyman instrument maintenance United Rubber Works Union; asst. football coach Hicksville High Sch. Pres. Hicksville Little League, 1980—, Hicksville Athletic Boosters, 1982—; coach pony league baseball, 1974—; high sch. baseball and basketball ofcl., Ohio. Served with USAF, 1964-68; Vietnam. Decorated Air Force Commendation, Air medal. Recipient Am. Math. Assn. medal, 1960. Mem. Am. Vocat. Assn., Ohio Vocat. Assn., Vocat. Indsl. Clubs Am., Nat. Assn. Trade and Indsl. Educators, Kappa Delta Phi, Iota Lambda Sigma. Democrat. Roman Catholic. Clubs: KC, Kiwanis, VFW, Am. Legion, Nat. Rifle Assn.

SILK, SPENCER ANTHONY, academic administrator; b. South Bend, Ind., Oct. 7, 1943; s. Leonard P. and Dorothy M. (Roth) S.; m. Sherry L. Smith, June 22, 1980; 1 child, Stephanie A. BA, Mich. State U., 1967. Cert. data processor, Mich.; cert. mgmt. cons., Mich. With mktg. dept. IBM, Detroit, 1967-71, Singer-Friden, Columbus, Ohio, 1971-74; cons. mgr. Price Waterhouse & Co., Columbus, 1974-80; mgr. mktg. info. systems Core Industries, Bloomfield Hills, Mich., 1981-83; dir. mktg. info. systems Wayne State U., Detroit, 1983—. Mem. Data Processing Mgmt. Assn. Home: 4004 Parkwood Ct Birmingham MI 48010 Office: Wayne State U 5950 Cass Ave Detroit MI 48202

SILKA, GERARD PAUL, management consultant; b. Detroit, June 8, 1952; s. S. Michael and Genevieve (Padzieski) S. BA, U. Mich., Dearborn, 1977; M Sci. and Adminstrn. Bus., Madonna Coll., 1986. Owner, operator Made In The Shade, Canton, Mich., 1974-77; acct. Ford Motor Co., Dearborn, 1977-78; funding coordinator City of Dearborn Heights, Mich., 1978-80; sr. contract mgr. Wayne (Mich.) City Area Agy., 1980-84; cons. Allied Research, Dearborn, 1984—. Author, editor (with others): In Home Service Providers Manual, 1982. Mem. Assn. In Home Service Providers (chmn. 1980-84), Nat. Conf. on Aging (bd. dirs. 1982), Am. Soc. Pub. Adminstrn. (bd. dirs. 1983-84), Mich. Assn. Adult Day Care Providers (bd. dirs. 1983-85), Greater Detroit Health Council (bd. dirs. 1984). Home: 1813 N Gulley Dearborn Heights MI 48127

SILKAITIS, RAYMOND PAUL, medical device company executive, pharmacist; b. St. Charles, Ill., Dec. 22, 1949; s. Mitch and Irene S.; m. Rasa Maria Domarkas, June 5, 1976; children—Rimas, Danius. B.S. in Pharmacy, U. Ill.-Chgo., 1973; Ph.D. in Pharmacology, U. Health Scis./Chgo. Med. Sch., 1977. Registered pharmacist, Ill. Formulation chemist R.I.T.A. Chem. Corp., Crystal Lake, Ill., 1971-73; clin. pharmacist U. Ill. Hosp., Chgo., 1974-77; asst. dir. pharmacy MacNeal Meml. Hosp., Berwyn, Ill., 1977-78; sr. clin. research assoc. Abbott Labs., North Chicago, Ill., 1978-80; assoc. dir. clin. affairs Zimmer, Inc., Warsaw, Ind., 1980—; cons. Huron Prodns., Burbank, Calif., 1976. Editorial staff mem., photographer Ateitis Mag., 1976. Contbr. articles on cosmetics and perfumery, brain research, life scis. to profl. jours. Sprague scholar U. Health Scis./Chgo. Med. Sch., 1976. Mem. Soc. Clin. Trials, Bioelectromagnetics Soc., Am. Soc. Hosp. Pharmacists (alt. del. 1975). Roman Catholic Avocations: photography; woodworking; dancing; electronics; arts. Home: 5326 Kindig Dr South Bend IN 46614 Office: Zimmer Inc PO Box 708 Warsaw IN 46580

SILL, LARRY ROBERT, physics educator; b. Fairmont, Minn., Sept. 10, 1937; s. Robert Ellis and Marie Victoria (Keeler) S.; m. Judith Ann Larson, Aug. 29, 1959; children: Jennifer, Stephen. BA, Carleton Coll., 1959; PhD, Iowa State U., 1964. Prof. physics No. Ill. U., DeKalb, 1964—, assoc. dean Coll. Liberal Arts and Scis., 1969-80, dir. Tech. Commercialization Ctr., 1986—; scientist-in-residence Argonne (Ill.) Nat. Lab., 1983-84. Contbr. articles to profl. jours. Mem. Am. Assn. Physics Tchrs., Am. Inst. Physics, Soc. Univ. Patent Adminstrs., Licensing Execs. Soc. Presbyterian. Lodge: Lions (local pres. 1981-82). Avocations: reading, photography. Office: No Ill U Dept Physics DeKalb IL 60115

SILL, WILLIAM FRAZIER, physician; b. Grand Rapids, Mich., June 13, 1944; s. William Hervey and Emogene Margaret (Perschbacher) S.; m. Bette Louise Armentrout, Aug. 25, 1968; children: Jonathan Bagshaw, Tara Louise. Grad., Millikin U., 1966; DO, Kirksville (Mo.) Coll. Osteopathic Medicine, 1970; chief family practice, St. Peters Hosp., 1983, chief dept. medicine, 1985. Diplomate Am. Bd. Family Practice. Intern Normandy Osteopathic Hosp., St. Louis, 1970-71; resident in family practice USAF Med. Ctr., Scott AFB, Ill., 1973-75; physician St. Charles (Mo.) Clinic, 1976-81; physician family practice St. Peters, Mo., 1982—; chief family practice St. Peters Hosp., 1984, chief dept. medicine, 1985; chief family practice dept. St. Joseph Health Ctr., St. Charles, 1986; assoc. clin. instr. family practice residency program, Scott AFB, Ill., 1975-76. Served to maj. USAF, 1971-76. Fellow Am. Acad. Family Phyicians; mem. Mo. Acad. Family Physicians, St. Louis Acat. Family Physicians, Mo. State Med. Assn. Presbyterian. Avocations: downhill snow skiing, boating. Home: 12 Berkshire Saint Charles MO 63301 Office: 6 Jungerman Circle Saint Peters MO 63376

SILLING, S(TEPHEN) MARC, psychologist; b. Charleston, W.Va., Dec. 14, 1950; s. Cyrus Edgar and Margaret (Moore) S.; m. Martha Aileen Stevenson, Aug. 23, 1978. BA, Marietta (Ohio) Coll., 1974; MA, Cleve. State U., 1977; PhD, Kent State U., 1981. Lic. psychologist, Ohio. Asst. project dir. Ohio Mental Health Devel. Research Ctr., Cleve., 1974-80; intern Cleve. State U., 1980-81; coordinator testing U. Akron (Ohio), 1981—; cons. Akron Family Inst., 1983—, Edwin Shaw Hosp., Akron, 1986—. Contbr. articles to profl. jours. Mem. Am. Psychol. Assn. Home: 6532 N Pleasant Ave Kent OH 44240

SILLS, WILLIAM HENRY, III, investment banker; b. Chgo., Jan. 2, 1936; s. William Henry II and Mary Dorothy (Trude) S.; m. Ellen Henriette Gervais, Apr. 24, 1971; children: William Henry IV, David Andrew Henry. AB, Dartmouth Coll., 1958; MA, Northwestern U., 1961. Stockbroker Bache & Co., Chgo., 1961-65; investment banker Chgo. Corp., 1965-79; gen. ptnr. Algenia Ranch, Island Park, Idaho; chmn. S&S Lines, Inc., Zenda, Wis., 1986—; bd. dirs. Pacific Enteprises GSW Corp. Author papers in field. Mem. Geneva Lake (Wis.) Area Joint Transit Commn., 1974—; pres. Wis. Coalition for Balanced Transp., 1976—; chmn. exec. com. Rep. Party Wis., 1978-82. Served with USMCR, 1956-59. Mem. Am. Soc. Traffic and Transp., Am. Short Line R.R. Assn., Am. Soc. Equipment Lessors, Am. Public Transit Assn., Ill. Public Transit Assn., Nat. Rifle Assn. (benefactor mem.), Wis. Rifle and Pistol Assn., Idaho State Rifle and Pistol Assn., Ill. State Rifle Assn., Field Mus., Art Inst. Chgo., Am. Mensa Assn., Internat. Soc. Philosophic Enquiry, Kappa Beta Phi, Delta Kappa Epsilon. Episcopalian. Clubs: Lake Geneve Country, Lake Geneva Yacht (commodore), U.S. Yacht Racing Union Cert. Judge, Skeeter Ice Boat, Delavan Sportsman; Chgo. Lions Rugby Football, Chgo. Area Rugby Football Union Referees Soc. Home: Rural Rt #1 Box 150 Lake Geneva WI 53147-9503 Office: S&S Steamship Lines Inc PO Box 100 Zenda WI 53195

SILVER, GEORGE, metal trading and processing company executive; b. Warren, Ohio, Dec. 17, 1918; s. Jacob and Sophie (Bradlyn) S.; m. Irene Miller, Aug. 5, 1945. Student U. Ala., 1938; BA, Ohio U., 1940, postgrad. law sch., 1940-41; grad. Adj. Gen. Sch., 1944. Pres., Riverside Indsl. Materials, Bettendorf, Iowa, 1947-70, Metalpel subs. Continental Telephone Co., Bettendorf, 1970-71, Riverside Industries Inc., Bettendorf, 1971—; now pres. Scott Resources Inc., Davenport, Iowa; founder Iowa Steel Mills (name changed to North Star Steel), Cargill and Wilton. Contbr. articles to profl. jours. Mem. Nat. UN Day Com., 1975-83. Served to capt. AC, U.S. Army, 1941-46, 50-51; Korea. Mem. Nat. Assn. Recycling Industries (co-chmn. nat. planning com., bd. dirs.), Copper Club, Paper Stock Inst. Am. (mem. exec. com.), Bur. Internat. de la Recuperation (chmn. adv. com.), Mining Club N.Y.C., Phi Sigma Delta. Republican. Jewish. Clubs: Outing, Hatchet Men's Chowder and Protective Assn., Rock Island Arsenal Officer's, Chemist (N.Y.C.), Crow Valley Country. Lodge: Elks (Davenport).

SILVER, JAMES ALLEN, military physician; b. Tracy, Minn., Apr. 7, 1933; s. Bernard J. and Nora J. (Bustad) S.; m. Regina Alohanohea Lover, June 15, 1964; children: Maile, Moana, Gregory, Telu, James K. BA, St. John's U., 1955; BS, MD, U. Minn., 1958; MPH, U. Mich., 1873. Diplomate Am. Bd. Occupational Medicine. Asst. med. dir. Marathon Oil Co., Findlay, Ohio, 1973-74; commd. USAF, 1974, advanced through grades to col., 1976; chief preventive medicine HQPACAF, Hickam AFB, Hawaii, 1974-78; comdr. USAF Hosp., Kirtland AFB, N.Mex., 1978-83; dir. med. inspection div. HQAFISC, Norton AFB, Calif., 1983-85. Fellow Am. Coll. Preventive Medicine; mem. Am. Acad. Occupational Medicine, Aerospace Med. Assn., Soc. Air Force Flight Surgeons. Republican. Roman Catholic. Lodge: ELks. Avocations: computer, bowling, bridge, photography. Home: 651 Yount Dr Wright-Patterson AFB OH 45433 Office: HQAFLC/SGP Wright-Patterson AFB OH 45433

SILVER, RALPH DAVID, distilling company executive; b. Chgo., Apr. 19, 1924; s. Morris J. and Amelia (Abrams) S.; m. Lois Reich, Feb. 4, 1951; children: Jay, Cappy. B.S., U. Chgo., 1943; postgrad., Northwestern U., 1946-48; J.D., DePaul U., 1952. Bar: Ill. bar 1952. Staff accountant David Himmelblau & Co. (C.P.A.'s), 1946-48; internal revenue agt. U.S. Dept. Treasury, 1948-51; practice in Chgo., 1952-55; atty. Lawrence J. West, 1952-55; exec. v.p. fin., dir. Barton Brands, Ltd., Chgo., 1955—. Bd. dirs., pres. Silver Found. Served to lt. (j.g.) USNR, 1943-46. Mem. Am., Chgo. bar assns., Am. Inst. C.P.A.s. Clubs: Green Acres Country; University (Chgo.). Home: 1124 Old Elm Ln Glencoe IL 60022 Office: Barton Brands Ltd 55 E Monroe St Chicago IL 60603

SILVER, SUSAN LEE, television writer, producer and director; b. Tulsa, July 9, 1952; d. Jack C. and Sammye (Castle) S.; m. Mendes J. Napoli, Nov. 29, 1981. BS, U. Tulsa, 1974. News anchor Sta. KTUL-TV, Tulsa, 1974-76, Sta. WFRV-TV, Green Bay, Wis., 1976-79; news dir. Sta. KJRH-TV, Tulsa, 1979-81; pres. and chief creative officer Silver Projects, Inc., Cleve., 1983—. Recipient Gold Addy award San Antonio Advt. Fedn., 1985, Silver Addy award, 1985, Graphex Silver award Okla. Art Dirs.' Clubs, 1986, Graphex Bronze award, 1986, Nori award Ad Club Upstate N.Y., 1986, Telly award Telly Assn., 1986, Addy Regional Gold award Am. Advt. Fedn., 1986, Bronze award Utah Ad Club, 1986, Finalist award 28th Ann. Internat. Film and TV Festival N.Y., 1986. Mem. Broadcast Promotion and Mktg. Execs. Assn. (Gold Medallion award 1986). Avocations: painting, reading, writing, traveling. Office: Silver Projects Inc 21520 Kenwood Ave Cleveland OH 44116

SILVERI, PETER WAYNE, principal; b. Detroit, Feb. 4, 1951; s. Conrad and Clarice (Pacific) S.; m. Sharon Wagner, Feb. 23, 1985. BS, Western Mich. U., 1973; MA, U. Mich., 1980, postgrad., 1986—. Cert. tchr., Mich. Tchr. Romulus (Mich.) Community Schs., 1973-85, prin. elem. sch., 1985—. Mem. Mich. Opera Theatre Guild, Founders Soc. Detroit Inst. of Arts. Mem. Nat. Assn. Elem. Sch. Prins., Am. Edn. Research Assn., Assn. for Supervision and Curriculum Devel. Democrat.

SILVERMAN, DEBORAH ANN WAIDNER, dietitian, educator, consultant; b. Columbus, Ohio, July 8, 1950; d. Otto Charles and Eileen C. (Herderick) Waidner; m. Gary Harvey Silverman, Dec. 18, 1977. BS in Med. Dietetics, Ohio State U., 1972; MS in Health Planning/Adminstrn., U. Cin., 1979; postgrad. Eastern Mich. U., 1981-83, Ohio State U., 1987—. Registered dietitian. Chief project nutritionist Ohio Dept. Health, Columbus, 1972-78; clin. dietitian Mt. Carmel East Hosp., Columbus, 1973-77 (part-time); instr. pediatric nurse assoc. program Mt. St. Joseph Coll., Cin., 1974-78; nutritionist Drs. Hallet, Bressler and Schaeffer, Columbus, 1975-78; nutritionist maternal and child health Ind. State Bd. Health, Indpls., 1978-79; relief clin. dietitian U. Mich. Hosps., Ann Arbor, 1980—; nutrition cons. St. Joseph Mercy Hosp., Ann Arbor, 1983—; instr. coordinated undergrad. curriculum in gen. dietetics Eastern Mich. U., Ypsilanti, 1979—; cons., lectr. in field. Recipient Josephine Nevins Keal award Eastern Mich. U., 1981. Mem. Am. Dietetic Assn., Am. Pub. Health Assn., Am. Soc. Parenteral and Enteral Nutrition, Nutrition Today Soc., Soc. Nutrition Edn., Mich. Dietetic Assn. (Registered Dietitian of Yr., 1986), Ann Arbor Dist. Dietetic Assn., Dietetic Educators Practice Group of Mich. Dietetic Assn., Dietetic Educators Practice Group and Dietitians in Nutrition Support of Am. Dietetic Assn. Jewish. Author manuals for dietetic courses at univ.; contbr. articles to profl. jours. Office: Ea Mich U Dept Environ and Consumer Resources Ypsilanti MI 48197

SILVERMAN, HOWARD BURTON, banker; b. Chgo., July 20, 1938; s. Jack B. and Pearl (Solomon) S.; m. Sharon L. Shanoff, June 4, 1967; children: Julie, Jill. B.S., Northwestern U., 1959, M.B.A., 1970. C.P.A., Ill. Internal auditor Toni Co., Chgo., 1959-60; acct. Apeco Corp., Evanston, Ill., 1960-62; with Continental Bank, Chgo., 1964-70; chmn., chief exec. officer First Ill. Corp., Evanston, Ill., 1970—; also bd. dirs. First Ill. Corp. and affiliates, Evanston, Ill.; bd. dirs. Facility Systems, Inc., Schaumburg, Ill. Bd. dirs., treas. St. Francis Hosp., Evanston; bd. dirs. Nat. Lekotek Ctr. Served with U.S. Army, 1962-64. Recipient Civic Leadership award Am. Jewish Com., 1986. Mem. Ill. C.P.A. Soc., Bankers Club of Chgo., Economic Club of Chgo. Republican. Jewish. Clubs: Ravinia Green (Riverwoods, Ill.); University (Evanston). Office: First Illinois Corp 800 Davis St Evanston IL 60204

SILVERMAN, JERALD, veterinarian; b. Bklyn., Mar. 23, 1942; s. Herbert Louis and Martha (Bernstein) S.; m. Sara Kay Zwerling, Dec. 17, 1967 (div.); children: Adam, Daniel. BS, Cornell U., Ithaca, N.Y., 1964, DVM, 1966; MPS, New Sch. for Social Research, N.Y.C., 1986. Diplomate Am. Coll. Lab. Animal Medicine. Clin. veterinarian Humane Soc. N.Y., N.Y.C., 1966-67, L.I. Pet Hosp., Bklyn., 1967-69, Rockland Vet. Med. Ctr., Pearl River, N.Y., 1969-75; dir. research animal facility Am. Health Found., Valhalla, N.Y., 1975-85; dir. lab. animal ctr. Ohio State U., Columbus, 1985—; cons. Revlon Health Care Group, Tuckahoe, N.Y., 1980-85, Avon Products, Suffern, N.Y., 1982—, Eugene Tech. Internat., Allendale, N.J., 1984—, Am. Health Found., Valhalla, 1985—. Contbr. articles to profl. jours. Recipient cancer research grants. Mem. AVMA, Am. Assn. Cancer Research, Am. Assn. Lab. Animal Sci. (cen. Ohio br.), Am. Coll. Lab. Animal Medicine, Vet. Cancer Soc. Avocations: birdwatching, stamp collecting, track and field. Office: Ohio State U 6089 Godown Rd Columbus OH 43220

SILVERMAN, RAYMOND MAYER, psychiatrist, health science facility administrator; b. Detroit, Mar. 17, 1945; s. Joseph Maurice and Ruth (Oppenheim) S.; m. Alice Jane Green, Sept. 12, 1971; children, Michael, Joseph. BS, Wayne State U., 1968, MD, 1970. Asst. dir. adolescent program Northwestern U., Chgo., 1976-78; dir. psychiat. services Highland Park (Ill.) Hosp., 1978—; cons. Internat. Minerals and Chem. Corp., Mundeline, Ill., 1983-86. Served to lt. commdr. USN, 1974-76. Mem. Am. Psychiat. Assn., Assn. Adolesent Psychiatry, Phi Beta Kappa, Alpha Omega Alpha. Avocations: Am. history, steroegraphy. Home: 913 Rollingwood Highland Park IL 60035 Office: Highland Park Hosp 718 Glenview Highland Park IL 60035

SILVERMAN, RICHARD BRUCE, chemist, biochemist, educator; b. Phila., May 12, 1946; s. Philip and S. Ruth (Simon) S.; m. Barbara Jean Kesner, Jan. 9, 1983; children: Matthew, Margaret, Philip. BS, Pa. State U., 1968; MA, Harvard U., 1972, PhD, 1974. Postdoctoral fellow Brandeis U., Waltham, Mass., 1974-76; asst. prof. Northwestern U., Evanston, Ill., 1976-82, assoc. prof., 1982-86, prof., 1986—; cons. Procter and Gamble Co., Cin., 1984; mem. adv. panel NIH, Bethesda, Md., 1981, 83, 85, 87—. Contbr. articles to profl. jours.; patentee in field. Served with U.S. Army, 1969-71. Recipient Career Devel. award USPHS, 1982-87; DuPont Young Faculty fellow, 1976, Alfred P. Sloan Found. fellow, 1981-85; grantee various govt. and pvt. insts., 1976—. Mem. AAAS, Am. Chem. Soc., Am. Soc. Biol. Chemists, Am. Inst. Chemists. Avocations: tennis, family interactions. Office: Dept Chemistry Northwestern U 2145 Sheridan Rd Evanston IL 60208

SILVERMAN, SHELDON LEON, accounting company executive; b. Chgo., Apr. 29, 1937; s. Nathan and Jean (Wald) S.; m. Dale Ann Feltman, Aug. 26, 1962; 1 child, Deborah Joy. BS, U. Ill., 1958. CPA, Ill. Staff acct. Silver, Millman & Co., Chgo., 1958-63, Kaplan, Biederman & Stetter, Chgo., 1963-68; ptnr. Biederman, Stetter, Silverman & Co., Northfield, Ill., 1968—; mem. faculty New Ventures Workshop, Northfield, 1985; speaker Nat. Sch. Bd. Assn., 1985-86; bd. dirs. Pub. Petroleum Co., Chgo. Bd. mem. Northbrook (Ill.) Sch. Dist. #27, 1979—, pres. 1985—; commr. Northbrook Plan Commn., 1984—. Mem. Am. Inst. CPA's, Nat. Soc. Pub. Accts., Ill. CPA Soc. Jewish. Home: 4032 Picardy Dr Northbrook IL 60062 Office: Biederman Stetter Silverman & Co 550 Frontage Rd Northfield IL 60093

SILVERSTEIN, GERALD HENRY, social services agency administrator; b. Chgo., Sept. 20, 1934; s. Irving and Evelyn (Tatkin) S. BA, U. Minn., 1956, MA, 1958. Cert. rehab. counselor. Vocat. rehab. counselor Elizabeth Kenny Inst., Mpls., 1958-59; vocat. counselor Jewish Vocat. Service, Chgo., 1959-66, rehab. supr., 1966-69, adminstrv. supr., 1969-78, asst. exec. dir., 1978-80, assoc. exec. dir., 1980—; regional field rep. Commn. on Accreditation of Rehab. Facilities; lectr. Rehab. Mgmt. Program Roosevelt U., Chgo., 1983; mem. council Edgewater Uptown Mental Health Ctr., 1972-80. Recipient Nat. Citation award Nat. Rehab. Counseling Assn., 1978. Mem. Am. Psychol. Assn., Am. Personnel and Guidance Assn., Nat. Rehab. Assn., Assn. Jewish Vocat. Service Profls. Office: 1 S Franklin St Chicago IL 60606

SILVERSTEIN, STEPHEN HOWARD, corporate executive; b. Lowell, Mass., July 5, 1948; s. Jerry L. and Gertrude S. (Buyarsky) S.; m. Linda Gerhardt, Aug. 16, 1970; children: David, Daniel. BBA in Econs., U. Mass., 1970; MBA, U. Chgo., 1972. Assoc. J. Lloyd Johnson Assocs., Northbrook, Ill., 1972-75; v.p., treas. Playboy Enterprises, Inc., Chgo., 1977-80, sr. v.p. fin. ops., 1980-82, sr. v.p., chief fin. officer, 1982-84; pres., chief exec. officer The Balcor Co., Skokie, Ill., 1985—, also chief operating officer. Served to lt. USAF, 1970-72. Mem. Am. Mgmt. Assn., Fin. Execs. Inst., Nat. Assn. Rev. Appraisers and Mortgage Underwriters, Econ. Club Chgo., Beta Gamma Sigma. Club: Green Acres. Office: The Balcor Co 4849 Golf Rd Skokie IL 60077

SILVIA, JOHN EDWIN, financial economist; b. Providence, Sept. 22, 1948. B.A., magna cum laude, in Econs., Northeastern U., 1971, Ph.D. in Econs., 1980. M.A. in Econs., Brown U., 1973. Research asst. Boston Mcpl. Research Bur., 1969-70; cons. Mass. Pub. Finance Project, 1973; assoc. tech. staff Mitre Corp., Bedford, Mass., 1974-75; instr. econ. St. Anselm's Coll., Manchester, N.H., 1977-79; asst. prof. Ind. U., Indpls., 1979-82; econ. research officer Harris Bank, Chgo., 1982-83; v.p., fin. economist Kemper Fin. Services, Chgo., 1983—. Contbr. numerous articles to Wall Street Jour., others. Mem. Am. Econ. Assn., Am. Fin. Assn., Nat. Assn. Bus. Economists, Chgo. Assn. Bus. Economists (sec./treas.). Home: 913 Turnbridge Circle Naperville IL 60540 Office: Kemper Fin Services 120 S LaSalle St Chicago IL 60603

SILVOSO, JOSEPH ANTON, accounting educator; b. Benld, Ill., Sept. 15, 1917; s. Biagio and Camilla (Audo) S.; m. Wilda Lucille Miller, Nov. 16, 1942; children—Joseph A., Gerald R. B.Ed., Ill. State U., 1941; A.M., U. Mo., 1947, Ph.D., 1951. C.P.A., Mo., Kans. Instr. U. Mo., 1947-48, 50-51; asst. U. Ill., 1948-49; staff accountant Touche Ross & Co. (and predecessor, C.P.A.s), Kansas City, Mo., 1951-55; ednl. dir. Touche Ross & Co. (and predecessor, C.P.A.s), Detroit, 1956; mem. faculty U. Mo., 1955-56, 57—, prof. accountancy, 1958—, Peat Marwick Mitchell prof. profl. acctg., 1978—, chmn. dept. accountancy, 1964-75; dir. Sch. Accountancy, 1975-79; cons. in field, 1956—. Author: Auditing, 1965, Illustrative Auditing, 1965, Audit Case, 1966. Chmn. Joint Adv. Council Accounting, 1962-64. Served with USAAF, 1942-45. Recipient Shutz Award U. Mo., 1985. Mem. Am. Acctg. Assn. (chmn. membership com. Mo. 1956-58, nat. chmn. accounting careers com. 1961-63, sec. treas. 1971-73, pres.-elect 1979-80, pres. 1980-81), Am. Inst. C.P.A.s (contbg. editor jour. 1958-61, editorial bd. 1970-72, mem. council 1981-86, bd. dirs. 1983-86, Outstanding Acctg. Educator award 1986, Distin g. Service award 1986), Mo. Soc. C.P.A.s (chmn. acctg. careers com. 1966-67, dir., sec. ednl. found. 1968-70, bd. dirs. 1983-86, Max Myers Disting. Service Award 1984), Central States Conf. C.P.A.s (treas. 1975, sec. 1976, v.p. 1977, pres. 1978), Fedn. Schs. Accountancy (dir. 1977-78, v.p./pres.-elect 1981-82, pres. 1982-83), Nat. Assn. Accts., Inst. Internal Auditors, Fin. Exec. Inst., Midwest Econs. Assn., Delta Sigma Pi, Beta Gamma Sigma, Alpha Pi Zeta., Beta Alpha Psi (named Nat. Acad. Accountant of Yr. 1977). Methodist. Avocations: exercise, reading, gardening. Home: 818 Greenwood Ct Columbia MO 65203 Office: U Missouri 340 Sch Accountancy Columbia MO 65211

SIMACEK, MILO JAMES, woodcrafter, retired industrial technology educator; b. Montgomery, Minn., June 6, 1930; s. Matt and Emma (Koldin) S.; B.S., Mankato State U., 1952, also postgrad.; M.S., Eastern Ky. U., 1969; postgrad. St. Cloud State U., Winona State U., River Falls State U.; m. Lois Mae Davis, Dec. 26, 1955; children—Michele, Mark, David, Scott. Tchr., St. Anns Sch., Wabasso, Minn., 1955-56; tchr. indsl. tech., chmn. dept. Hastings (Minn.) High Sch., 1956-87; owner, mgr. Artistry With Wood, Hastings, 1960—; also designer, builder houses. Mem., chmn. Hastings City Planning Commn., 1979—; founding pres. Hastings United Fund. Served with M.C. AUS, 1952-54. Silver Beaver award Boy Scouts Am., 1980, Minn. Indsl. Arts Tchr. of Yr. award, 1981. Mem. Am. Legion (comdr. 1976), Jaycees (senator), Minn. Indsl. Arts Assn. (pres. 1985-86), Am. Indsl. Arts Assn., Minn. Edn. Assn., NEA, Internat. Wood Collectors Soc., DAV, VFW. Roman Catholic. Clubs: Lions, Hastings Snowmobile, Snow Patrol. Home: 1041 W 4th St Hastings MN 55033 Office: 11th and Pine Sts Hastings MN 55033

SIMCOE, BARBARA CARRIE, advertising executive; b. Mpls., Mar. 6, 1956; d. Donald Lee and Joan Helen (Wood) S. BS in Journalism and Mktg., No. Ill. U., 1978. Employee relations dir. Free Press Newspapers, Carpentersville, Ill., 1978-80; advt. mgr. Oak Switch Systems Inc., Crystal Lake, Ill., 1980—. Adviser Jr. Achievement, Crystal Lake, 1982-85; bd. dirs. Lake Region YMCA, Crystal Lake, 1983. Mem. Internat. Assn. Bus. Communicators, Electronics Industry Assn. (planning com. 1985-87). Office: Impact Communications 730 S McHenry Ave Crystal Lake IL 60014

SIMCOX, EDWIN JESSE, state official; b. LaPorte, Ind., Jan. 12, 1945; s. J. Willard and Rachel (Gibbs) S.; m. Sandra Sue Stephenson, Aug. 30, 1970; children: Edwin J., Stephen R. and Ethan J. (twins). BS, Ind. U., 1967, JD, 1971. Bar: Ind. 1971. Sec. Ind. State Hwy. Commn., 1969-71, Public

Service Commn. of Ind., 1971; chief dep. Office of Reporter of Supreme Cts. and Jud. Ct. of Appeals, State of Ind., 1973-78; sec. of state State of Ind., Indpls., 1978-86; pres. Ind. Electric Assn., Indpls., 1986—; sec. Ind. State Rep. Cen. Com., 1972-77. Chmn. adminstrv. bd. White Harvest United Meth. Ch., 1975-76; mem. adv. council Peace Corps. Mem. ABA, Ind. Bar Assn., Indpls. Bar Assn., Nat. Assn. Secs. of State (pres. 1984-85). Lodges: Masons, Shriners, Kiwanis. Office: Ind Electric Assn 1375 One American Sq Indianapolis IN 46282

SIMCOX, MARTHA ELAINE, psychologist; b. Harrisburg, Ill., Jan. 7, 1937. BA, Park Coll., 1958; MS in Edn., So. Ill. U., 1964; PhD, Ind. U., 1980. Elem. sch. tchr. U.S. Army Dependent Schs., various locations, 1964-79; psychol. services dept. chmn. RISE Spl. Services, Indpls., 1979—. Mem. Nat. Assn. Sch. Psychologists, Ind. Psychol. Assn. Republican. Baptist. Home: Rural Rt 1 Box SW166 New Palestine IN 46163 Office: Rise Special Services 5391 Shelby Indianapolis IN 46227

SIME, CLAUDE IRVIN, orthodentist; b. Beaver Dam, Wis., May 12, 1933; s. Claude Irvin Sr. and Estelle Ette (Bunders) S.; m. Geraldine Mae Smith, Sept. 20, 1956; children: Jeffrey, Lianne, Sharon, Dianne, Leslie. BS, U. Ill., 1956, DDS, 1959. Gen. practice dentistry Freeport, Ill., 1962-65; practice dentistry specializing in orthodontics Madison, Wis., 1967—. Scoutmaster Boy Scouts Am., Madison, 1973-76. Served to capt. U.S. Army, 1958-62. Fellow Am. Coll. Dentists, Pierre Fauchard Acad.; mem. ADA, Wis. Dental Assn. (pres. 1984-85), Am. Assn. Orthodontists, Omicron Kappa Upsilon. Republican. Avocations: flying, fishing, hunting, canoeing, skiing. Office: 6618 Mineral Point Rd Madison WI 53705

SIMKINS, LAWRENCE DAVID, psychology educator; b. Phila., Jan. 18, 1933; s. Samuel and Ida (Fagin) S.; m. Paula Gertrude Katz, June 17, 1959 (div. July 1975); children: Lee, Jeffery; m. Kristine Marie Eskesen Nov. 5, 1977. BA, Temple U., 1954; MA, Lehigh U., 1956; PhD, U. Houston, 1959. Lic. psychologist, Kans., Mo., Ga. Asst. prof. psychology Fla. State U., Tallahassee, 1959-64; assoc. prof. psychology U. Mo., Kansas City, 1964-69, prof., 1969—; dept. chmn. U. Mo. Kansas City, 1971-74, 85-86; research cons. Met. Orgn. to Counter Sexual Assault, Kansas City, 1985—. Author Basis of PSychology, 1969; editor Alternative Sex Lifestyles, 1986; contbr. articles to profl. jours. Sr. Fulbright lectr., 1970-71. Mem. Am. Psychol. Assn., Soc. Sci. Study of Sex, Assn. Advancement of Behavior Therapy. Home: 6142 E 127th St Grandview MO 64030 Office: U Mo 5319 Holmes St Kansas City MO 64110

SIMMA, RICHARD CHARLES, accountant; b. New Richmond, Wis., May 13, 1946; s. Everett Paul and Leota M. (Stoltz) S.; m. Judith Lorene Lewerer, Sept. 13, 1969; children: Joshua, Joseph, Jacob, Zachary. BS, U. Wis., River Falls, 1972. CPA, Wis. Tax specialist Alexander Grant & Co., Mpls., 1972-75; pres., dir. taxation Simma Flottemesch & Orenstein, Ltd., New Richmond, Wis., 1975—. Leader Boy Scouts Am., New Richmond. Served with U.S. Army, 1968-70. Mem. Am. Inst. CPA's (task force chmn. 1984-87), Wis. Soc. CPA's, Minn. Soc. CPA's. Avocations: family, reading. Office: Simma Flottemesch & Orenstein PO Box 158 111 N Knowles Ave New Richmond WI 54017-0158

SIMMONS, ALLAN KENNETH, oral surgeon; b. Winnipeg, Can., Sept. 25, 1951; came to U.S., 1971; s. John Louis and Anna (Smando) S.; m. Jeanne Marie Potter, Sept. 1, 1973 (div. Apr. 1984). BS, U. Manitoba, 1977; DDS, Ohio State U., 1980; oral surgery cert., Ind. U., 1986. Profl. hockey player Calif. Seals, Oakland, 1971-73, Boston Bruins, 1973-75, N.Y. Rangers, N.Y.C., 1975-76; gen. practice dentistry Dublin, Ohio, 1980-83; practice dentistry specializing in oral surgery Columbus, 1986—; asst. hockey coach Ohio State U., 1977-78; head hockey coach Upper Arlington High Sch., Columbus, 1978-80; instr. Paul C. Hayes Dental Asst. Sch., Columbus, 1980-81. Named to All-Star Team Am. Hockey League, Providence, 1976. Mem. ADA, Ohio Dental Assn., Columbus Dental Soc., Am. Assn. Oral and Maxillofacial Surgeons. Roman Catholic. Club: Sawmill Athletic, Ohio State Golf (Columbus). Avocations: golf, skiing, weight training, jogging, bicycling, music. Home: 2638 Cedar Lake Dr Dublin OH 43017 Office: 1707 Bethel Rd Columbus OH 43220

SIMMONS, BARBARA ANN, editorial services company executive; b. Indpls., May 8, 1941; d. Robert Donald and Mary Elizabeth (Fitzpatrick) Munro; m. Edward E. Simmons Jr., Aug. 8, 1964; 1 child, Kathryn Mary. BA, Purdue U., 1963. Editor IIT Research Inst., Chgo., 1963-67; ops. service supr. applied research div. Booz, Allen & Hamilton Inc., Chgo., 1968-69; editor Warren King & Assocs., Chgo., 1969-70; staff editor Am. Hosp. Assn., Chgo., 1970-73; tech. editor Inst. Gas Tech., Chgo., 1973-76; owner Tech. Editing Services, Skokie, Ill., 1976—; presenter 21st Internat. Tech. Communications Conf., 1974. Editor (booklet) Typing Guide for Mathematical Expressions, 1976. Pres. Dist. 72 Bd. Edn., Skokie, 1983—. Mem. AAAS, Soc. Tech. Communication (chmn. Chgo. chpt., sec. standards council, various awards), Phi Mu. Roman Catholic. Avocations: needlepoint, ice skating. Home and Office: 4943 Fairview Ln Skokie IL 60077

SIMMONS, CLINTON CRAIG, construction company executive; b. Cleve., Nov. 25, 1947; s. Benjamin F. and Catharin (Thornton) R.; m. Cheryl LeRoy, June 16, 1973; 1 child, Eric. BBA, Miami U., Oxford, Ohio, 1969; grad. quality mgmt. course Winter Park, Fla., 1986. Cert. quality edn. system instr. Specialist employee and community relations Euclid Lamp Plant, Gen. Electric Co., Cleve., 1970-75; employee and indsl. relations rep. Bailey Controls Co., Wickliffe, Ohio, 1975-78; mgr., coll. recruiting Gen. Tire and Rubber, Akron, Ohio, 1978-81, profl. staffing coordinator, 1981-82; regional human resource mgr. Gilbane Bldg. Co., Cleve. 1982-86, human resource mgr. Western regions, 1987—. Past chmn. orgn. and extension com. Newton D. Baker Dist., Greater Cleve. council Boy Scouts Am., 1970-71; Bd. Edn. commr. Villa Angela High Sch., Cleve., 1983—, pres., 1986—; founder, advisor Explorer Post, Gilbane Bldg. Co., Cleve., 1984—; mem. adv. bd. Cath. Social Services Cuyahoga County; mem. urban regional bd. Cath. Edn. Cleve., 1986; trustee Marta Montessori Sch, Harambee Services Orgn. Cleve., 1987—. Recipient commendation Nat. Alliance of Bus., Akron, 1979, Community Service award WJW-Northwest Orient Airlines, 1975. Mem. Cleve. Employee's Equal Opportunity Assn., Am. Soc. Personnel Adminstrn., Mid-West Coll. Placement Assn. (chmn. rubber industry com. 1979-81), Ctr. for Human Services (v.p., trustee), Indsl. Relations Research Assn., NAACP, Urban League of Cleve., Alpha Phi Alpha. Democrat. Roman Catholic. Home: 24400 Emery Rd Warrensville Heights OH 44128 Office: Gilbane Bldg Co Central Region 2000 E 9th St Cleveland OH 44115

SIMMONS, EDWARD CLAY, dentist; b. Ashland, Kans., July 19, 1925; s. Earl Clay and Leona Bessie (Hughes) S.; m. Joan Redding, Dec. 26 1946; children: Rick, Tanya, Randy. Student, Kans. Wesleyan U., 1947-49; DDS, U. Mo., Kansas City, 1953. Gen. practice dentistry Salina, Kans., 1953—; adj. prof. dental hygiene Wichita (Kans.) State U., 1981—; instr. Kans. Wesleyan U., Salina, 1957-59. Mem. insdl. com. Salina C. of C., 1957-65; trustee St. John's Mil. Sch., Salina, 1964-68; mem. cen. regional testing state bd. of dental examiners U. Mo., Kansas City, 1973-80. Served with U.S. Army, 1944-46, ETO. Mem. Kans. State Dental Assn. (pres. 1981-82), Kans. Soc. Dentistry for Children (pres. 1972-74), Acad. Gen. Dentistry (pres. 1975-76, Man of Yr. award 1983), Am. Assn. Endodontics, Golden Belt Dist. Soc. (pres. 1957-58). Republican. Episcopalian. Club: Salina Country (bd. dirs. 1973-76). Lodges: Rotary, Masons, Shriners. Home: 771 Victoria Heights Terr Salina KS 67401 Office: 645 S Ohio Salina KS 67401

SIMMONS, FRED HARRISON, JR., pediatric dentist; b. Portland, Ind., Feb. 27, 1944; s. Fred Harrison Sr. and Mary Jane; m. Marilyn Elaine Ross, July 31, 1971; children: Greg, Andrew, Scott. AB in Zoology, Ind. U., 1966, DDS, 1972, MS in Pedodontics, 1974. Practice dentistry specializing in pedodontics Terre Haute, Ind., 1975—. Served with USAF, 1966-68. Mem. ADA, Am. Acad. Pediatric Dentistry, Am. Soc. Dentistry for Children. Presbyterian. Avocations: camping, jogging. Home: 110 Berkeley Dr Terre Haute IN 47803 Office: 3404 S 7th St Terre Haute IN 47802

SIMMONS, JACK LELAND, corporate tax executive; b. Colorado Springs, Colo., May 18, 1947; s. Robert King and Birdie Maxine (Hughes) S.; m. Kyle Jean Smith, June 5, 1971; children: Shannon Leigh, Scott McFarland. BBA, U. Mo., 1970, JD, 1973. Bar: Mo. 1973; CPA, Mo. Tax sr. Arthur Andersen & Co., St. Louis, 1973-75; asst. tax counsel Gen. Dynamics Corp., St. Louis, 1975-82; asst. treas. Fisher Controls Internat., Inc., St. Louis, 1982-84, Monsanto Co., St. Louis, 1985-86; mgr. corp. tax R.R. Donnelley & Sons Co., Chgo., 1986—. Mem. Tax Exec. Inst. (chmn. state and local tax sect. St. Louis chpt. 1985-86, co-chmn. internat. tax sect. 1983-85), Mo. Bar Assn., Am. Inst. CPA's. Republican. Baptist. Avocation: sports. Home: 608 North 3d Ave Saint Charles IL 60174 Office: RR Donnelley & Sons Co 2223 King Dr Chicago IL 60616

SIMMONS, JAMES EDWIN, child psychiatrist, educator; b. Toledo, July 13, 1923; s. Guy B. and Ruth S. Simmons; m. Kathryn Witt, Feb. 26, 1972; children: Christina C., James M., Anne E., Katherine L., Martha E., Sarah J., John A. B.S., Toledo U., 1945; M.D., Ohio State U., 1947. Diplomate: Am. Bd. Psychiatry and Neurology, also Sub-Bd. Child Psychiatry. Intern St. Vincents Hosp., Toledo, 1947-48; resident in psychiatry Menninger Found., Topeka, 1948-51; psychiatrist, dir. Child Guidance Clinic of Marion County, Indpls., 1953-57; fellow in child psychiatry U. Louisville, 1957-58; instr. Ind. U. Sch. Medicine, Indpls., 1954-56; asst. prof. Ind. U. Sch. Medicine, 1956-58, assoc. prof., 1958-62, prof., coordinator child psychiatry services, 1962-74, prof., dir. child psychiatry services, 1975-79, Arthur B. Richter prof., dir. child psychiatry, 1979—, acting chmn. dept. psychiatry, 1972, 74-75; cons. in field. Contbr. articles to med. jours. Bd. dirs. Ind. Assn. Mental Health, 1961-71, 1st v.p., 1965-66; bd. dirs. Waycross, Inc., 1964-75, pres., 1965-67. Served with USN, 1951-53. Fellow Am. Psychiat. Assn., Am. Acad. Child Psychiatry; mem. AMA, Ind. State Med. Soc., Marion County Med. Soc., Ind. Psychiat. Soc., Soc. Profs. of Child Psychiatry (founding mem.), Am. Acad. Pediatrics (Ind. chpt.), Ind. Regional Council for Child and Adolescent Psychiatry, Nu Sigma Nu. Episcopalian. Office: Ind U Sch Medicine Dept Psychiatry 702 N Barnhill Dr Indianapolis IN 46223

SIMMONS, JOSEPH THOMAS, business educator; b. Forest Lake, Minn., Jan. 23, 1936; s. Roland Thomas and Erma (Rabe) S.; m. Winola Ann Zwald, Aug. 18, 1962; children: Thomas E, Kevin M. BS in Bus. and Econs., Morningside Coll., 1964; MBA, U. S.D., 1965; PhD in Bus., U. Nebr., 1974. CPA, S.D. Prof. acctg. and fin. U. S.D., Vermillion, 1966-69, 75—, dir. sch. bus., 1975—; prof. U. Nebr., Lincoln, 1969-71, U. Man., Winnipeg, Can., 1971-75; prin. Simmons and Assocs. Mgmt. Cons., Rapid City, S.D., 1981—; pvt. practice acctg. Rapid City, 1982—; pres. Simmons Profl. Fin. Planning, Rapid City, 1983—; bd. dirs. Mont. Dakota Utilities Resources, Inc., Bismarck, N.D., High Plains Genetics, Rapid City, Black Belt Inc., Rapid City, Remvac, Spearfish, S.D. Served with U.S. Army, 1958-60. Mem. Am. Acctg. Assn., Am. Inst. CPA's, Fin. Mgmt. Assn., Investment Co. Inst., S.D. Soc. CPA's. Republican. Methodist. Home: 3603 Scenic Dr Rapid City SD 57702 Office: PO Box 9526 Rapid City SD 57709

SIMMONS, LINDA NACHTIGALL, therapist; b. Newton, Kans., Apr. 20, 1954; d. George F. and Norma J. (Walker) N.; m. Randy L. Simmons, May 7, 1983. BA, Tabor Coll., 1976; MSW, U. Kans., 1983. Lic. specialist, clin. social worker. Social worker State of Kans., Newton, 1976-82; crisis therapist Horizons Mental Health, Hutchinson, Kans., 1984-85; therapist Family Consultation Services, Wichita, 1985-86; pvt. practice therapist Home Counseling Care, Wichita, 1986—. Mem. Nat. Assn. Social Workers. Office: 1999 N Amidon Suite 100 Wichita KS 67203

SIMMONS, REGINALD, business consultant; b. Camden, N.J., Oct. 28, 1954; s. Mamie Delores Simmons; m. Denise Aytoinette Williams, Nov. 15, 1980; 1 child, Dänielle Esprit. BBA, U. Tex., 1984; MBA, U. Chgo., 1987. Electro-mech. assembler IMCO Services-Halliburton, Houston, 1979-80; br. mgr. trainee Household Fin. Internat., Houston, 1980-81; software cons. Execucom Systems Corp., Austin, Tex., 1983-84; mgmt. cons. World Book, Inc., Chgo., 1986; mgmt. cons. Town & Country Montessori, Austin, 1983-85, Bluebonnet Montessori, Austin, 1984-85; software cons. Kallestad Labs., Austin, 1985. Author: Gentle Power, 1986. Vol. Houston Symphony Orch., 1978-82; co-founder/chmn. Town & Country Montessori Parents' Orgn., Austin, 1983-85. Martin Luther King scholar, 1974; fellow Citibank Corp., 1985-87. Mem. Assn. MBA Execs., Inc. Avocations: poetry, songwriting, chess sports, reading.

SIMOM, MICHAEL ALLAN, surgery and oncology educator; b. Detroit, Jan. 13, 1943; s. Morris and Bertha (Knee) S.; m. Barbara Leslie Simon, Dec. 19, 1965; children: Susan, Dyan, Renee. MD, U. Mich., 1967. Resident U. Mich., Ann Arbor, 1967-74; mem. faculty U. Chgo., 1975—. Contbr. articles to profl. jours. Served to capt. USAF, 1969-71, Vietnam. Fellow Am. Orthopedic Assn. (Traveling felow), Am. Acad. Orthopedic Surgery, Surg. Oncology Soc.; mem. Am. Soc. Clin. Oncology. Office: 5841 S Maryland Box 102 Chicago IL 60637

SIMON, BERNIE, municipal official. Mayor city of Omaha, 1987—. Office: Office of the Mayor Omaha-Douglas Civic Ctr Suite 300 1819 Farnam St Omaha NE 68183 *

SIMON, DANA LESLIE, anesthesiologist, pain consultant; b. Halifax, N.S., Feb., 9, 1952; came to U.S., 1962, naturalized, 1972; s. Stanley M. and Joyce (Aronoff) S.; m. Ronit Dermansky, June 19, 1977; 2 children—Ariel, Shira. B.S. with highest distinction, valedictorian, U. Ariz., 1972; M.D., Northwestern U., 1977. Diplomate Am. Bd. Anesthesiology. Anesthesia resident Northwestern U., Chgo., 1977-80; pain fellow U. Va. Pain Ctr., Charlottesville, 1980-81; dir. pain block ctr. Mercy Hosp., Des Moines, 1983—, pain cons., 1981—, med. staff, 1981—. Contbr. articles to profl. jours. NIH grantee, 1984—. Mem. Am. Soc. Anesthesiologists, Iowa Soc. Anesthesiologists (sec. 1987—), Am. Soc. Regional Anesthesia, Internat. soc. Study of Pain, AMA, Am. Israel Polit. Action Com. Lodge: B'nai B'rith Hillel. Avocations: Mid-East history; philately; reading; music; sports. Office: Med Ctr Anesthesiologists PC 421 Laurel #202 Des Moines IA 50314

SIMON, HERBERT, professional sports team owner; b. Bronx. Grad., CCNY. With Albert Frankel Co., Indpls., 1959; co-founder Melvin Simon and Assocs., Inc., Indpls., 1959—, pres., 1973—; owner Ind. Pacers (Nat. Basketball Assn.), Indpls., 1983—. Office: Ind Pacers 2 W Washington St Suite 510 Indianapolis IN 46204 *

SIMON, JOHN WILLIAM, lawyer; b. Hamburg, Iowa, July 25, 1949; s. Chris Howard and Wilma Marian (Silence) S.; m. Carole Mae Dornhoff, June 7, 1971; children: Thomas Michael, Mary Elizabeth. AB in Philosophy, Polit. Sci. summa cum laude, Boston U., 1971; AM in Polit. Sci., Harvard U., 1974, PhD in Polit. Sci., 1978; JD, Yale U., 1984. Bar: Mo. 1985, U.S. Dist. Ct. (we. dist.) Mo. 1985, U.S. Ct. Appeals (8th cir.) 1986. Adminstrv. asst. State of Nebr., Lincoln, 1970-71; teaching fellow in govt. Harvard U., Cambridge, Mass., 1973-75; instr., asst. prof. Bates Coll., Lewiston, Maine, 1975-81; lectr. polit. sci. Yale U., New Haven, Conn., 1982; assoc., clk. Spencer, Fane, Britt & Browne, Kansas City, Mo., 1984-86; asst. atty. gen. State of Mo., Jefferson City, 1986—. Alt. Maine State Dem. Conv., Augusta, 1976, del., Portland, Augusta, Bangor, Lewiston, 1978, 80, 82, 84, sec. platform com., 1980; state rep. State of Maine, 1979-80; alt., platform whip Dem. Nat. Conv., N.Y.C., 1980. Grad. fellow NSF, 1972-75. Mem. ABA, Assn. Trial Lawyers Am., Phi Beta Kappa. Episcopalian. Lodge: Rotary. Avocations: music, swimming. Office: Asst Atty Gen PO Box 899 Jefferson City MO 65102

SIMON, LEWIS BRYANT, financial executive; b. Chgo., Oct. 12, 1940; s. M. Phillip and Rosalyne L. (Ballin) S.; m. Sherrill A. Miller, Feb. 2, 1963; children: Scott Terrence, Johanne Michele. BSCE, U. Ill., 1963; MBA in Fin., Calif. State U.-Long Beach, 1967. Pres., chief exec. officer, dir. TigerAir, Chgo., 1971-76; exec. v.p., dir. AAR Corp., Elk Grove Village, Ill., 1976-78; group v.p. Avis, Inc., Garden City, N.Y., 1978-79; pres. S-J Fin. Corp., Barrington, Ill., 1978—; chmn. SR Industries Corp., Schaumburg, Ill., 1984—; v.p., ptnr. Realty Unltd., Inc., Barrington, Ill., 1980—; fin. cons. Bombardier, Inc., Que., Can., 1984; sr. v.p., cons. Winthrop Fin. Corp., Boston, 1981-84; cons. FSC Corp./FS Airlease, Inc., Pitts., 1979-84; bd. dirs. Am. Risk Transfer Ins. Co., Bermuda, Presdl. Airways, Inc., Washington, ARTEX Ins., Dallas. Bd. dirs. Chgo. Jesters Hockey Orgn. Mem. Internat. Soc. Transport Aircraft Traders (founding officer). Jewish. Clubs: Riding of Barrington Hills (Ill.); Bit and Bridle (Barrington, Ill.); Barrington Area Figure Skating (pres., bd. dirs.); Lake Barrington Shores Golf. Avocations: show horses, men's hockey, racquetball. Office: S-J Fin Corp 114 E Main St Barrington IL 60010

SIMON, MELVIN, real estate developer, professional basketball executive; b. Oct. 21, 1926; s. Max. and Mae Simon; m. Bren Simon, Sept. 14, 1972; children: Deborah, Cynthia, Tamme, David, Joshua. BS in Acctg., CCNY, M in Bus., Real Estate; PhD (hon.), Butler U., 1986. Leasing sgt. Albert Frankel Co., Indpls., 1955-60; pres. Melvin Simon & Assocs., Indpls., 1960-73, chmn. bd., 1973—; co-owner Ind. Pacers, Indpls.; mem. adv. bd. Wharton's Real Estate, Phila., 1986—. Mem. adv. bd. dean's council Ind. U., Bloomington; bd. dirs. United Cerebral Palsy, Indpls., Muscular Dystrophy Assn., Indpls., Jewish Welfare Found., Indpls.; trustee Urban Land Inst., Internat. Council Shopping Ctrs. Recipient Horatio Alger award Boy's Club Indpls., 1986; named Man of Yr., Jewish Welfare Found., 1980. Democrat. Jewish.

SIMON, PAUL, senator, educator, author; b. Eugene, Oreg., Nov. 29, 1928; s. Martin Paul and Ruth (Troemel) S.; m. Jeanne Hurley, Apr. 21, 1960; children: Sheila, Martin. Student, U. Oreg., 1945-46, Dana Coll., Blair, Nebr., 1946-48; 27 hon. degrees. Pub. Troy (Ill.) Tribune, 1948-66, and other So. Ill. weeklies; mem. Ill. Ho. of Reps., 1955-63, Ill. Senate, 1963-69; lt. gov. Ill. 1969-73; fellow John F. Kennedy Inst. Politics Harvard, 1972-73; prof. public affairs Sangamon State U., Springfield, Ill., 1973; mem. 94th-98th Congresses from 24th Dist. Ill.; U.S. Senator from Ill. 1985—. Author: Lovejoy: Martyr to Freedom, 1964, Lincoln's Preparation for Greatness, 1965, A Hungry World, 1966, You Want to Change the World, So Change It, 1971, The Tongue-Tied American, 1980, The Once and Future Democrats, 1982, The Glass House, Politics and Morality in The Nation's Capitol, 1984, Beginnings, 1986, Let's Put America Back to Work, 1986; (with Jeanne Hurley Simon) Protestant-Catholic Marriages Can Succeed, 1967; (with Arthur Simon) The Politics of World Hunger, 1973. Bd. dirs. Dana Coll. Served with CIC, AUS, 1951-53. Recipient Am. Polit. Sci. Assn. award, 1957; named Best Legislator 7 times. Mem. Luth. Human Relations Assn., Am. Legion., VFW, NAACP, Urban League. Lutheran. Office: 462 Dirksen Senate Bldg Washington DC 20510

SIMON, RAY, utilities company executive. Chmn. Met. Utilities Dist., Omaha. Office: Met Utilities Dist 1723 Harney St Omaha NE 68102 *

SIMON, ROBERT MICHAEL, manufacturing company executive; b. Chgo., Aug. 24, 1947; s. Frank Michael and Emily Eleanor (Malinauskas) S.; m. Wendelin Theresa Lang, May 17, 1969; 1 child, Heather Lee. BS in Chemistry, John Carroll U., 1969; MBA, Roosevelt U., 1972. Account exec. Richardson Corp., Madison, Conn., 1973-76; sr. mktg. specialist Mobay div. Bayer A.G., Pitts., 1976-79; v.p. Transmet div. Battelle, Columbus, Ohio, 1979-85; pres., sr. cons. Indsl. Mktg. Mgmt. Systems, Dublin, Ohio, 1985-87; pres. USTEK Inc., Dublin, 1987—. Editor, author Designing with Flake Filled Plastic, 1986. Mem. Soc. Plastic Engrs. (bd. dirs.), Soc. Plastics Industry (chmn. N.Y.C. 1974), Bus. Tech. Ctr. (bd. dirs. 1986—), Technology Alliance Cen. Ohio. Republican. Avocations: sports, flying, scuba diving, music.

SIMON, RONALD HAROLD, insurance company executive; b. Fowler, Mich., July 31, 1945; s. Oscar C. and Bernita (Sontag) S.; m. Mary E. Harr, June 11, 1966; children: Denise A., Karla J. BS in Math., Mich. State U., East Lansing, 1967. Cert. Fellow Life Mgmt. Inst. Mgr. Auto-Owners Ins. Co., Lansing, Mich., 1971-79, dir., 1979-85, asst. v.p. corp. systems, 1985, asst. v.p. applications devel., 1985—. Pres. ednl. com. St. Therese Ch., Lansing, 1983-85, also choir mem. Mem. Consol. Functions Ordinary User Group (pres.), Assn. Systems Mgrs. Roman Catholic. Avocations: traveling, hunting, gardening. Home: 1003 E Dill Dr DeWitt MI 48820 Office: Auto-Owners Ins Co 6101 Anacapri Blvd Lansing MI 48917

SIMON, SEYMOUR, Illinois supreme court justice; b. Chgo., Aug. 10, 1915; s. Ben and Gertrude (Rusky) S.; m. Roslyn Schultz Biel, May 26, 1954; children: John B., Nancy Harris, Anthony Biel. B.S., Northwestern U., 1935, J.D., 1938; LL.D. (hon.), John Marshall Law Sch., 1982, North Park Coll., 1986. Bar: Ill. 1938. Spl. atty. Dept. Justice, 1938-42; practice law Chgo., 1946-74; judge Ill. Appellate Ct., Chgo., 1974-80; presiding justice Ill. Appellate Ct. (1st Dist., 3d Div.), 1977, 79; justice Ill. Supreme Ct., 1980—; former dir. Nat. Gen. Corp., Bantam Books, Grosset & Dunlap, Inc., Gt. Am. Ins. Corp. Mem. Cook County Bd. Commrs., 1961-66, pres., 1962-66; pres. Cook County Forest Preserve Dist., 1962-66; mem. Pub. Bldg. Commn., City Chgo., 1962-67; Alderman 40th ward, Chgo., 1955-61, 67-74, Democratic ward committeeman, 1960-74; bd. dirs. Schwab Rehab. Hosp., 1961-71, Swedish Covenant Hosp., 1969-75. Served with USNR, 1942-45. Decorated Legion of Merit; recipient citation for disting. service North Park Coll., Chgo., 1967, 9th Ann. Pub. Service award Tau Epsilon Rho, 1963, alumni award of merit Northwestern U., 1982, Hubert L. Will award Am. Vets. Com., 1983, Decalogue Soc. of Lawyers award of Merit, 1986, Freedom award John Marshall Law Sch., 1987. Mem. ABA, Ill. Bar Assn., Chgo. Bar Assn., Chgo. Hist. Soc., Decalogue Soc. Lawyers (Merit award 1986), Izaak Walton League, Chgo. Hort. Soc., Phi Beta Kappa Assocs., Phi Beta Kappa, Order of Coif. Clubs: Standard, Variety (Chgo.). Home: 1555 N Astor St Chicago IL 60610 Office: Supreme Ct Bldg Springfield IL 62706 also: 3088 Richard J Daley Center Chicago IL 60602

SIMON, THOMAS ALAN, accountant; b. Wichita, Kans., Oct. 5, 1947; s. Edward M. and Rita M. (Lodes) S.; (div. June 1979); children: Jennifer, Kelly; m. Toni Macias, Sept. 6, 1980; children: Holly, Paul, Tiffany. BS, Wichita State U., 1970. Staff acct. Elmer Fox & Co., Wichita, 1969-74; ptnr. Oak Simon & Ott, Wichita, 1975-84, Regier Carr & Monroe, Wichita, 1984—. Bd. dirs. Sedgewick County Heart Assn., Wichita, 1979-83, Ctr. City Steering Com., Wichita, 1977-78. Mem. Am. Inst. CPA's, Nat. Associated CPA Firms (SW region coordinator, 1984-85), Kans. Soc. CPA's (pres. Wichita chpt. 1985). Republican. Roman Catholic. Club: Wichita Ski (bd. dirs. 1984-85), Terradyne Country. Avocations: golf, racquteball, skiing. Office: Regier Carr & Monroe 200 W Douglas Suite 1000 Wichita KS 67202

SIMONDS, JOHN ORMSBEE, landscape architect; b. Jamestown, N.D., Mar. 11, 1913; s. Guy Wallace and Marguerite Lois (Ormsbee) S.; m. Marjorie C. Todd, May 1, 1943; children: Taye Anne, John Todd, Polly Jean, Leslie Brook. B.S., Mich. State U., 1935, D.Sc. hon.; M.Landscape Architecture (Eugene Dodd medal), Harvard U., 1939. Landscape architect Mich. Dept. Parks, 1935-36; ptnr. Simonds and Simonds, Pitts., 1939-70, Collins, Simonds and Simonds, Washington, 1952-70; ptnr. The Environ. Planning and Design Partnership, Pitts., also Miami Lakes, 1970-82, emeritus, 1983—; lectr., vis. critic urban and regional planning Carnegie-Mellon U., 1955-67; vis. critic Grad. Sch. Planning, also Sch. Architecture, Yale, 1961-62; Cons. Chgo. Central Area Com., 1962, Allegheny County Dept. Regional Parks, 1961-74; U.S. cons. community planning Inter-Am. Housing and Planning Center, Bogota, Colombia, 1960-61; mem. jury Am. Acad. Rome, 1963, 65, 66, 69; mem. Nat. Adv. Com. on Hwy. Beautification; chmn. panel on parks and open space White House Conf. on Natural Beauty; mem. Interprofl. Commn. on Environ. Design, Joint Com. on Nat. Capital; mem. urban hwy. adv. bd. U.S. Bur. Pub. Rds., 1965-68; mem. landscape architecture adv. panel U.S. C.E., 1968-71, Pres.'s Task Force on Resources and Environment, 1968-70; mem. design adv. panel Operation Breakthrough, HUD, 1970-71; mem. Mid-Atlantic regional adv. bd. Nat. Park Service, 1976-78; assoc. trustee U. Pa., 1962-66, mem. bd. fine arts, 1962-66; chmn. joint com. planning Carnegie-Mellon U. and U. Pitts., 1959-60; overseer's vis. com. Harvard Grad. Sch. Design, 1962-68, exec. council alumni assn., 1960-63; adv. com. Sch. Design, N.C. State U., 1965-67; mem. Fla. Gov.'s Task Force on Natural Resources, 1979-80. Author: Landscape Architecture, the Shaping of Man's Natural Environment, 1961, rev. edit., 1983, Earthscape, a Manual of Environmental Planning, 1978, revised edit. 1986 ; editor: Virginia's Common Wealth, 1965, The Freeway in the City, 1968. Maj. works include master plans for Chgo. Bot. Garden, (with others) Mellon Sq., Pitts., (with others) Miami Lakes New Town, Va. I-66 Corridor, Fairfax and Arlington counties, Va., Pelican Bay Community, Fla., Weston New Town, Fla. Bd. dirs. Hubbard Ednl. Trust, 1974—; bd. govs. Pitts. Plan for Arts. Recipient citation Top Men of Year Engring. News-Record, 1973; Charles L. Hutchinson medal Chgo. Hort. Soc., John R. Bracken medal Dept. Landscape Architecture, Pa. State U., 1985. Fellow Am. Soc.

Landscape Architects (mem. exec. com. 1959-67, pres. 1963-65, pres. Found. 1966-68, recipient medal 1973), Royal Soc. Arts (Gt. Britain); mem. NAD (assoc.), Archtl. League N.Y., Royal Town Planning Inst. (hon. corr.); hon. assoc. Pa. chpt. AIA. Presbyn. (ruling elder). Clubs: Harvard-Yale-Princeton (Pitts.). Home: 17 Penhurst Rd Pittsburgh PA 15202 Office: The Loft 17 Penhurst Rd Pittsburgh PA 15202 also: Admiralty 9415 Gulfshore Dr Naples FL 33963

SIMONETT, JOHN E., state supreme court justice; b. Mankato, Minn., July 12, 1924; m. Doris Bogut; 6 children. B.A., St. John's U., 1948; LL.B., U. Minn., 1951. Practice law Little Falls, Minn., 1951-80; asso. justice Supreme Ct. of Minn., 1980—. Office: Supreme Ct State Capitol Saint Paul MN 55155 *

SIMON-HARRIS, TERESA VIRGINIA, market analyst; b. Hannibal, Mo., Mar. 4; d. Reginald Randal and Juanita Virginia (Houston) Simon; m. Larry Eugene Miles, Nov. 4, 1967 (div. Aug. 1972); children: Traci, Larry, Angela; m. Frederick Leon Harris, Jan. 9, 1982; children: Melissa, Frederick III, Justin. AA, Palmer Jr. Coll., Davenport, Iowa, 1978; BA, St. Ambrose Coll., 1982, MBA, 1987. Coordinator overseas div. John Deere & Co., Moline, Ill., 1971-82; price analyst John Deere & Co., Moline, 1982-86, sr. price and market analyst, 1986—. Cons. Jr. Achievement Project Bus., Davenport, 1986—; adv. Principal's Scholars Program Cen. High Sch., Davenport, 1986; mem. Polit. Action Fund, Moline, 1986—. Mem. Assn. MBA Execs., MBA Senate, Career Womens Network, Womens Adv. Council, St. Ambrose U. Grad. Sch. Alumni. Democrat. Baptist. Home: 218 E Central Park Davenport IA 52803 Office: John Deere & Co John Deere Road Moline IL 61265

SIMONS, JOANNE ALICE, marketing communications company executive; b. St. Paul, Oct. 3, 1946; d. Lawrence James and Lauretta Sophia (Hopp) S.; m. Ronald L. Christianson, Aug. 2, 1969 (div. July 1978); m. R. Bruce Allyn, Nov. 12, 1983; 1 child, Matthew. BA, Hamline U., 1968; MA, U. Minn., 1977. Instr. journalism and English Edina, Glencoe and Blaine Sr. High Schs., Minn., 1969-80; asst. pub. Hastings (Minn.) Gazette, 1980-81; mktg. mgr. Kroy, Inc., Woodbury, Minn., 1981-83; dir. mktg. planning Duncan Mktg., Mpls., 1983-84; pres. Simons Allyn Mktg. Communications, Mpls., 1984—. Mem. Hamline U. Alumni Bd. (pres. 1986). Avocations: distance running, skiing. Office: Simons Allyn Mktg Communications 708 N 1st St Suite 238 Minneapolis MN 55401

SIMONS, ROBERT WEBSTER, manufacturing company executive; b. Cleve., Mar. 3, 1962; s. John Whiton and Nancy (Pyle) S. BA in Polit. Sci., Pub. Adminstr., Econ., Miami U., Oxford, Ohio, 1984. V.p. sales Advanced Peripherals, Inc., Cleve., 1984-85, v.p., chief exec. officer, 1985—. Episcopalian. Avocations: cycling, historical reading, stamp collecting. Office: Advanced Peripherals Inc 11000 Cedar Ave 4th Floor Cleveland OH 44106

SIMONS, SUZANNE EILEEN, foundation executive; b. Garfield Heights, Ohio, Nov. 9, 1959; d. Edwin Charles and Delores Jean (Muck) S. BS, Kent (Ohio) State U., 1981. Mktg. asst. Control Data Bus. Ctrs. Inc., Cleve., 1981-83; asst. dir. alumni relations Kent State U., 1983-86; dir. adminstrn. and devel. Nat. Headache Found., Chgo., 1986—. Fundraising adv. com. Kent Environtl. Counil, 1986; vol. Animal Protective League, Kent, 1986. Mem. Nat Soc. Fundraising Execs., Kent State U. Alumni Assn., Ind. Sector. Avocations: tennis, traveling, horseback riding, cultural arts. Home: 407 Happfield #302 Arlington Heights IL 60004 Office: Nat Headache Found 5252 N Western Ave Chicago IL 60625

SIMONSEN, ROBERT ALAN, marketing executive; b. Cherokee, Iowa, Apr. 8, 1956; s. Earl Dean and Betty (Gabrielson) S.; m. Shawn Marie Beck, June 11, 1983; children: Adam David, Patrick Robert. BS in Bus. with honors, Iowa State U., 1978, BA in Econs. with honors, 1978; MBA in Mktg. with honors, U. Colo., 1982. Cost acct. Simonsen Mfg. Co., Quimby, Iowa, 1978-81, mktg. mgr., 1983—; bd. dirs. Simonsen Mill, Inc., Simonsen Propane, Inc.; v.p. Dr. Simonsen's Pet Food, Inc., Quimby, 1985—. Chmn. Quimby Centennial Com., 1983-87; precinct chmn. Cherokee County Reps., Quimby, 1980; trustee Quimby United Meth. Ch., 1983—. Mem. Iowa State U. Alumni Assn., Beta Gamma Sigma. Home: Rt 1 Box 123 Quimby IA 51049 Office: Simonsen Mfg Co Box 247 Quimby IA 51049

SIMONSEN, V., provincial judge. Judge Ct. of Queen's Bench, Winnipeg, Man., Can. Office: Court of Queen's Bench, Law Courts Bldg, Winnipeg, MB Canada R3C 0V8 *

SIMONSEN, VERNER MARVIN, osteopathic ophthalmologist and otorhinolaryngologist; b. Rome, N.Y., Nov. 3, 1931; s. Verner Marvin and Pauline Ann (Whitmeyer) S.; m. Cleona Eleanor Brooks, June 2, 1959; children—Kristine Pauline Simonsen Monas, Karin Diane. B.S., St. Lawrence U., 1953; D.O., Kirksville Coll. Osteopathy and Surgery, 1959. Intern Greencross Gen. Hosp., Cuyahoga Falls, Ohio, 1959-60; resident in ophthalmology and otorhinolaryngology Detroit Osteo. Hosp., 1962-65; practice osteo. medicine specializing in ophthalmology and otorhinolaryngology, Toledo and Perrysburg (Ohio), 1965—; mem. staff Parkview Hosp., also chmn. dept. ophthalmology and otorhinolaryngology; mem. staff Riverside Hosp., St. Luke's Hosp., Maumee, Ohio; instr. Ohio U. Coll. Osteopathy. Fellow Osteo. Coll. Ophthalmology and Otorhinolaryngology (cert.); mem. Toledo Dist. Osteopathy, Am. Osteo. Assn., Ohio Osteo. Assn., Ohio Med. Assn., Physician for Golden Gloves Boxing of Toledo. Republican. Methodist. Club: Brandywine Country. Lodges: Elks, Masons, Shriners. Home: 2865 Byrnwyck W St Maumee OH 43537 Office: 27121 Oakmead Dr Suite B Perrysburg OH 43551

SIMONSON, MARILYN DIANE, business educator; b. Buffalo County, Wis., Feb. 11, 1936; d. Walter S. and Hilda (Hilgert) Schlawin; m. Byron Dean Simonson, May 23, 1970; children—Tia, Carisa. B.E., Wis. State U.-Whitewater, 1957; postgrad. Winona State U., 1963; M.A., U. Minn., 1969. Cert. tchr., Wis., Minn. Sec., registrar Wis. State U.-Superior, 1957-58; tchr. pub. schs., Wis. and Minn., 1958-70; instr. Lakewood Community Coll., White Bear Lake, Minn., 1970—, head dept. secretarial sci., 1970—, mem. curriculum task force, 1983-84, search com. for dean of instrn., 1986-87. Publicity chair St. Anthony Middle Sch. PTA, Minn., 1984-85, pres. elect, 1985-86; pres. Wilshire Park PTA, St. Anthony, 1985-86, pres. St. Anthony Middle Sch., 1986-87; mem. St. Anthony Lang. Arts Evaluation Com., 1984-85, Dist. #282 Planning Com, 1986-87, Christian edn. com. Christ the King Luth. Ch., New Brighton, Minn. Mem. Minn. Community Coll. Faculty Assn., Delta Pi Epsilon. Democrat. Lutheran. Avocations: needlework; reading. Home: 3327 Skycroft Dr Saint Anthony MN 55418 Office: 3401 Century Ave N White Bear Lake MN 55110

SIMOWITZ, FREDRIC MALCOLM, neurologist; b. Augusta, Ga., Oct. 4, 1937; s. Joseph and Thelma (Levy) S.; m. Beverly Seigal, Jan. 29, 1966; children: Lynn Cheryl, Mark Alan. Student, Ohio State U., 1955-58; MD, Med. Coll. Ga., 1962. Cert. Am. Bd. Psychiatry and Neurology. Chief resident in neurology U. Mich., Ann Arbor, 1968-69; instr. neurology St. Louis U., 1969-72, asst. clin. prof. neurology, 1972-80, assoc. clin. prof. neurology, 1980—; cons. Sandoz Pharmacies, Hanover, N.J., 1970—. Contbr. articles to profl. jours. Served to lt., USN, 1963-65. Fellow Am. Acad. Neurology; mem. AMA, Mo. Med. Assn., Med. Amateur Radio Council (pres. 1986—). Jewish. Home: 20 Vouga Ln Saint Louis MO 63131 Office: 2850 W Clay St Saint Charles MO 63301

SIMPKINS, JOE ALBERT, oil company executive; b. St. Louis, Sept. 15, 1905; s. Leo and Ella Simpkins; m. Florence Putnam, Oct. 7, 1978; 1 child from previous marriage, Linda. Owner Joe Simpkins Oil Devels., St. Louis, 1942—, Joe Simpkins Ford Agy., St. Louis, 1946-56, Tiffany Industries, St. Louis, 1944—. Supporter Mother Dickey Boy's Club, St. Louis, 1960—, Herbert Hoover Boy's Club, St. Louis, 1980—, Multiple Sclerosis Soc., Cardinal Glenmor Children's Hosp., 1980—. Recipient Silver Torah award St. Louis Rabinnical Coll., 1975, Eleanor Roosevelt Humanities award, State of Israel, 1970, Disting. Humanitarian award Nat. Jewish Hosp. & Research Ctr., 1981, Citizen award St. Louis Police Wives Assn., 1982, Generosity award St. Mary's Spl. Sch., 1977, Helping Hands award Luth. Family & Children's Services, 1983, Nat. award Boys Club Am. Home: 2220 S Warson Rd Saint Louis MO 63124

SIMPSON, DANIEL WAYNE, engineer; b. Ewing, Va., Aug. 25, 1947; s. Curtiss and Bessie (Rowlette) S.; m. Beverly Kay Charlton, June 19, 1970; children: Matthew, Danielle. BS, Ea. Ky. U., 1971. Designer Mosler Safe Co., Hamilton, Ohio, 1970-72; project engr. Big Four Automotive, Mainville, Ohio, 1972-73; design engr. Water Refining Indsl., Middletown, Ohio, 1973-74, tech. service engr., 1974-78, custom engring. mgr., 1978-83, engring. mgr., 1983—. patentee deionizer process. Avocation: auto mechanics. Home: 1353-A Corydale Dr Fairfield OH 45014 Office: Water Refining Indsl 500 N Verity Pkwy Middletown OH 45042

SIMPSON, DAVID ALLEN, osteopath; b. Highland Park, Mich., Mar. 29, 1955; s. Fred Raymond and Mary Theresa (Rossi) S.; m. Anne M. Pawlak, Oct. 20, 1984. BS in Biology with distinction, Wayne State U., 1977, MS in Anatomy, 1979; DO, Kirksville Coll. Osteo. Medicine, 1983. Commd. to med. corps U.S. Army, 1984, advanced through grades to capt., osteopath health clinic, 1984—. Patentee in field; contbr. articles to profl. jours. Mem. Am. Osteo. Assn.; Mich. Assn. Osteo. Physicians and Surgeons, Assn. Military Osteo. Physicians and Surgeons, Psi Sigma Alpha, Sigma Sigma Alpha. Roman Catholic. Avocation: golf. Home: 19550 Laurel Livonia MI 48152 Office: US Army Health Clinic Bldg 310 Selfridge ANG Base Mount Clemens MI 48045

SIMPSON, DONALD BRUCE, library director; b. Ithaca, N.Y., Dec. 13, 1942; s. Francis Alfred and Drusilla Lucille (Dickson) S.; m. Evangeline Foster Bower, Jan. 7, 1967 (div. Feb. 1977); 1 child, Michael John; m. Lupe Mary Rodriquez, Nov. 9, 1977; 1 stepson, Matthew Glenn. AA, Corning (N.Y.) Community Coll., 1962; BA, Alfred (N.Y.) U., 1964; MS, Syracuse (N.Y.) U., 1970; PhD, Ohio State U., 1974. Asst. librarian Keuka Coll., Keuka Park, N.Y., 1970-71; head catalog ctr. State Library Ohio, Columbus, 1971-75; exec. dir. Bibliog. Ctr. for Research, Denver, 1975-80; pres. Ctr. for Research Libraries, Chgo., 1980—; mem. adv. bd. Satellite Library Network, Denver, 1976-77, Telefacsimile Library Network, Denver, 1978-80; mem. adv. com. Online Computer Library Ctr., Dublin, Ohio, 1980-86, v.p., del. to users council, 1978-80. Editor: The State Library Agencies, 1972, 4th edit., 1978; contbr. articles to profl. jours. Mem. adv. bd. Rosary Coll., River Forest, Ill., 1984—. Served to capt. USAF, 1965-69, Vietnam. Fellow Beta Phi Mu; mem. Assn. State Library Agys. (pres. 1977-78), ALA (various coms. 1972—), Internat. Fedn. Library Assocs. (various coms. 1978—), Am. Soc. for Info. Sci., Am. Mgmt. Assn. Republican. Roman Catholic. Clubs: University, Quadrangle (Chgo.). Avocation: personal computer software devel. Home: 6103 N Lenox Ave Chicago IL 60646-4819 Office: Ctr for Research Libraries 6050 S Kenwood Ave Chicago IL 60637

SIMPSON, EDWIN L., environmental chemist; b. Jackson, Ohio, Feb. 29, 1948; s. Edwin F. and Doris B. Simpson; m. Sonja L. Simpson, May 10, 1974; children: Jerimiah E., David T. BS, Ohio U., 1971. With Austin Power, 1971-77, Mead Research, 1977-82, Goodyear Automic, 1982—. Author: Home Business Guide, 1984; pub., editor: Home Bus. News. Mem. Internat. Assn. Ind. Pubs. Republican. Adventist. Avocation: micro computers. Home and Office: 12221 Beaver Pike Jackson OH 45640

SIMPSON, FLOYD DUANE, psychiatrist, health services facility administrator; b. Sac City, Iowa, Aug. 6, 1944; s. Clive Arlo and Gertrude Arleen (Mason) S.; divorced; m. Diane Lyn Fick, Feb. 14, 1986; children: Amy, Shea, Matthew, Nicole, Scott. AA, Ellsworth Jr. Coll., 1964; cert., Worsham Coll. Mortuary Sci., 1965; BS, Buena Vista Coll., 1968; DO, Coll. Osteo. Medicine Surgery, 1972. Practice medicine specializing in psychiatry Sedona, Ariz., 1973-74, Chandler, Ariz., 1974-80; physician emergency room Scottsdale (Ariz.) Community Hosp., 1982-83; resident psychiatrist Cherokee (Iowa) Mental Health Inst., 1983-86; psychiatrist, med. dir. Northwest Iowa Mental Health Ctr., Spencer, 1986—. Served to maj. USAF, 1980-82. Mem. Am. Psychiat. Assn., Iowa Psychiat. Assn. Mormon. Avocations: snow skiing, water skiing, horticulture, Am. Indian anthropology. Home: 604 4th St SW Spencer IA 51301 Office: Northwest Iowa Mental Health Ctr 201 E 11th St Spencer IA 51301

SIMPSON, HOWARD MATTHEW, textbook publisher; b. Peoria, Ill., Apr. 29, 1918; s. Laurens Luther and Pearl Claudia (Howard) S.; m. Kathryn Lucia Jacquin, Nov. 25, 1948; children—John Niehaus, James Patrick (dec.), Cory Jane, Michael Howard, David Matthew, Dana Kathleen. Student U. Ill., 1937-41. Shipping clk. Manual Arts Press, Peoria, Ill., 1933-37, advt., 1945-49, salesman, 1946-53, dir., 1949-83; advt. mgr. Chas. A. Bennett Co., Inc. (formerly Manual Arts Press), 1949-53, sales mgr., 1953-64, treas., 1962-72, v.p., 1970-75, pres., 1975-83, cons., 1983-85, dir., 1949-83, cons., 1983-85; organizer, dir., sec., pres. CABCO, Inc., Peoria, 1964-76. Mem. exec. bd. W.D. Boyce council Boy Scouts Am., Peoria, 1966—, rep. nat. council, 1985—; mem. capital projects com. United Way Peoria, 1978-80, spl. fund raising com., 1978-80; mem. YMCA Leader Luncheon Com., 1981-83; mems. chmn.'s council Crow Canyon Archeol. Ctr., Cortez, Colo., 1987—. Served to capt., cav. armor U.S. Army, 1941-46; Africa, Italy. Decorated Purple Heart, 6 battle stars; recipient Silver Beaver award Boy Scouts Am., Peoria, 1969, also Order of Arrow. Mem. Am. Legion, Pi Beta Alpha, The Ship, Sigma Alpha Epsilon. Clubs: Kiwanis (dir. 1966-68) Willow Knolls Country (Peoria).

SIMPSON, JACK BENJAMIN, medical technologist, business executive; b. Tompkinsville, Ky., Oct. 30, 1937; s. Benjamin Harrison and Verda Mae (Woods) S.; student Western Ky. U., 1954-57; grad. Norton Infirmary Sch. Med. Tech., 1958; m. Winona Clara Walden, Mar. 21, 1957; children—Janet Lazann, Richard Benjamin, Randall Walden, Angela Elizabeth. Asst. chief med. technologist Jackson County Hosp., Seymour, Ind., 1958-61; chief med. technologist, bus. mgr. Mershon Med. Labs., Indpls., 1962-66; founder, dir., officer Am. Monitor Corp., Indpls., 1966-77; mng. partner Astroland Enterprises, Indpls., 1968—, 106th St. Assocs., Indpls., 1969-72, Keystones Ltd., Indpls., 1970-82 Delray Rd. Assoc., Ltd., Indpls., 1970-71, Allisonville Assocs. Ltd., Indpls., 1970-82, Grandview Assocs. Ltd., 1977—, Rucker Asso., Ltd., Indpls., 1974—; mng. partner Raintree Assos., Ltd., Indpls., 1978—, Westgate Assos., Ltd., Indpls., 1978—; pres., dir. Topps Constrn. Co., Inc., Bradenton, Fla., 1973—, Acrouest Corp., Asheville, N.C., 1980—, Alpha Systems Resource, Inc., Shelbyville, Ind., 1985—; dir. Indpls. Broadcasting, Inc. Mem. Am. Soc. Med. Technologists (cert.), Indpls. Soc. Med. Technologists, Ind. Soc. Med. Technologists, Am. Soc. Clin. Pathologists, Royal Soc. Health (London), Internat. Platform Assn., Am. Mus. Natural History. Republican. Baptist. Clubs: Columbia of Indpls.; Harbor Beach Surf, Fishing of Am., Marina Bay (Fort Lauderdale, Fla.). Lodge: Elks.

SIMPSON, NANCY PROCTOR, retail executive; b. Stockbridge, Mich., Apr. 10, 1936; d. Stanley Edwin and Lucille (Latson) Proctor; m. Richard L. Simpson, Dec. 28, 1957; children: Reid, Cindy, Sally. BS, Mich. State U., 1958, MA, 1977. Cert. tchr., Mich. Program dir. YWCA, Rockford, Ill., 1958-64; dir. drown proofing Rockford (Mich.) Pub. Schs., 1969-73, East Grand Rapids (Mich.) Sch., 1972-77; counselor Pub. Schs., Sparta & Rockford, Mich., 1977-80; store mgr. Clothesworks, Rockford, 1980-84; regional mgr. Jack Winter, Rockford, 1984—; drownproofing program cons. Mich. Dept. Natural Resources, Lansing, Mich., 1970-77. Recipient 25 Yr. award ARC, 20 Yr. award Girl Scouts Am. Lutheran. Home and Office: 5103 Surf Dr Rockford MI 49341

SIMPSON, PAMELA JO, accountant; b. Springfield, Ill., July 19, 1954; d. Leonard Eugene and Ruby Alice (Burgin) S.; m. Gary Barton, Sept. 18, 1976 (div. Dec. 1982). BS, Eastern Ill. U., 1976, MBA, 1982. CPA, Ill. Acctg. clk. Wyman-Gordon, Danville, Ill., 1976-77; accountant Kesler & Co., Ltd., Danville, 1977-82; mgr. Graves & Graves, PC, Decatur, Ill., 1982-84; ptnr. J. Richard Howe, PC, Decatur, 1984—. Chmn. personnel policy com. Community Home Environ. Learning, Decatur, 1985, chmn. project nominating com., 1986. Named one of Outstanding Young Women Am., 1985. Mem. Ill. Soc. CPA's, Am. Inst. CPA's, Am. Women's Soc. CPA's, Cen. Ill. Women's Soc. CPA's., Am. Legion, Delta Zeta. Mem. Christian Ch. Clubs: Jr. Women's (v.p. 1981-82), St. Elizabeth Jr. Aux. (Danville). Home: 2965 Primrose Ln Decatur IL 62526 Office: J Richard Howe PC 628 Millikin Ct Decatur IL 62523

SIMPSON, PAUL FOIGHT, management consultant; b. New Kensington, Pa., Dec. 16, 1935; s. Robert Steel and Ruth Wilson (Foight) S.; m. Ann R. Goodman, June 18, 1966; children: Hope, Meredith Ann. BSBA in Mgmt., Ind. U., 1980. Co-dir. EDP Coral Gables (Fla.) Fed. Savs. & Loan, 1959-62; dir. EDP Standard Fed. Savs. & Loan, Chgo., 1962-66; systems and programming mgr. Symons Mfg. Co., Des Plaines, Ill., 1966-70; corp. project mgr. Marlennan Corp., Chgo., 1970-72; cons. mgr. Arthur Young & Co., Chgo., 1972-76; dir. data processing Wheelabrator Frye Inc., Mishawaka, Ind., 1976-79; corp. dir. mgmt. info. systems Euclid, Inc. subs. Daimler Benz Agy., Cleve., 1980-83; dir. mgmt. cons. services-info. systems for cen. and so. Ohio and W.Va. Coopers & Lybrand, Columbus, Ohio, 1984; dir. info. systems and services Bendix Aircraft Brake and Strut div. Allied-Signal Corp., South Bend, Ind., 1985—. Served with USMC, 1956-58. Mem. Data Processing Mgmt. Assn. (bd. dirs. local chpt. 1977-79, 81-83). Office: Bendix Aircraft Brake and Strut div Allied-Signal Corp 3520 W Westmoor St South Bend IN 46624

SIMPSON, ROBERT EDWARD, sales executive; b. St. Louis, Nov. 2, 1948; s. Charles Edward and Orvilla Celeste (Bernhardt) S.; m. Sharon Ann Vickers, Aug. 9, 1975; children: Thomas Robert, Kate Ann. BS in Edn., U. Mo., 1970; MA in Teaching (Social/Behavioral Scis.), Webster U., 1975. Cert. elem. and secondary edn. tchr., Mo. (life). Tchr., dept. chmn. Riverview Gardens Sch., St. Louis, 1971-78; sales rep. Laidlaw Bros. Pubs., Chgo., 1978-84; communications cons. Trans-Lux Corp., Norwalk, Conn., 1984-85; regional sales mgr. Milliken Pub. Co., St. Louis, 1985-86, nat. sales mgr. computer courseware div., 1986—. Mem. bus. mgmt./mktg. adv. council St. Charles County Community Coll. Mem. Mo. Textbook Pubs. Assn. (v.p. 1983-84), U. Mo. Alumni Assn. Roman Catholic. Avocations: Miss. River boating, profl. musician. Home: #3 Nugget Ct Saint Peters MO 63376 Office: Milliken Pub Co 1100 Research Blvd Saint Louis MO 63132

SIMPSON, VINSON RALEIGH, manufacturing company executive; b. Chgo., Aug. 9, 1928; s. Vinson Raleigh and Elsie (Passeger) S.; m. Elizabeth Caroline Matte, Sept. 9, 1950; children: Kathleen Simpson Jackson, Nancy Simpson Ignacio, James Morgan. S.B. in Chem. Engring, Mass. Inst. Tech., 1950; M.B.A., Ind. U., 1955. With Trane Co., LaCrosse, Wis., 1950-75; mgr. mktg. services Trane Co., 1957-64, mgr. dealer devel., 1964-66; mng. dir. Trane Ltd., Edinburgh, Scotland, 1966; v.p. internat. Trane Ltd., LaCrosse, 1967, exec. v.p., 1968-70; exec. v.p., gen. mgr. comml. air conditioning div. Trane Ltd., 1970-73, pres., 1973-75; pres. Simpson and Co., La Crosse, 1975-76; pres., chief operating officer Marathon Electric Mfg. Corp., Wausau, Wis., 1976-80; chmn., pres., chief exec. officer Marion Body Works, Inc., Wis., 1980—; dir. RTE Corp. Regional chmn. edn. council MIT; trustee Northland Coll.; past pres. Wausau Area Jr. Achievement, bd. dirs.; mem. Marion Minutemen, adv. team U. Wis. Served to 1st lt. USAF, 1951-53. Decorated Korean War ribbon. Mem. Fire Apparatus Mfrs., Am. Prodn. and Inventory Control Soc., Kappa Kappa Sigma, Alpha Tau Omega, Beta Gamma Sigma (dirs. table). Methodist. Clubs: Clintonville Riverside Golf, U. Chgo. Lodges: Masons, Shriners, Jesters, Rotary (pres. Marion club). Avocations: running, handball, snorkeling, water skiing, cross country skiing. Home: 419 W Ramsdell St Marion WI 54950 Office: Marion Body Works Inc 211 W Ramsdell PO Box 500 Marion WI 54950-0005

SIMPSON, WILLIAM GLEN, accountant; b. Princeton, Mo., Oct. 15, 1949; s. John Henry and Betty Lu (Stottlemyre) S.; m. Cynthia Louise Kelly, May 21, 1977; children: Rebecca Lynn, Michael Ryan, Meaghan Louise. BS in Bus. Adminstrn., U. Mo., Kansas City, 1974. CPA, Mo. Pvt. practice acctg. Overland Park, Kans., 1977-80; staff acct. Gasper & Co., St. Joseph, Mo., 1981-84; ptnr. Sumner, Carter, Hardy & Simpson, St. Joseph, Mo., 1984—. Bd. dirs. Green Acres, Inc., St. Joseph, 1983-84. Mem. Mo. Soc. CPAs (sec. NW chpt. 1986-87, trea. 1985-86, strategic planning com.), Am. Inst. CPAs (tax div., pvt. practice sect.). Clubs: Sertoma (Overland Park) (bd. dirs. 1978-80), Downtown Sertoma (St. Joseph) (bd. dirs. 1982—). Home: 3921 W Haverill Saint Joseph MO 64506 Office: Sumner Carter Hardy & Simpson 3110 Karnes Saint Joseph MO 64506

SIMPSON, WILLIAM STEWART, psychiatrist, sex therapist; b. Edmonton, Alta., Can., Apr. 11, 1924; came to U.S., 1950, naturalized, 1963; s. William Edward And Ethel Lillian (Stewart) S.; m. Eleanor Elizabeth Whitbread, June 17, 1950; children—David Kenneth, Ian Stewart, James William, Bert Edward. B.Sc., U. Alta., 1946, M.D., 1948. Diplomate Am. Bd. Psychiatry and Neurology. Rotating intern U. Alta. Hosp., 1948-49, resident in internal medicine, 1949-50; resident in psychiatry Topeka State Hosp., 1950-53, cons., 1967-68, asst. sect. chief, 1953-54; fellow Menninger Sch. Psychiatry, Topeka, 1950-53; clin. dir. Menninger Sch. Psychiatry, 1954-59, 68-72; sect. chief C.F. Menninger Meml. Hosp., 1959-66, dir. edn., 1963-66; assoc. dir. Menninger Sch. Psychiatry, 1966-68; dir. field services Menninger Found., 1972-74, sr. staff psychiatrist adult outpatient dept., 1977-84, assoc. dir. adult outpatient dept., 1984—; chief psychiatry service, residency tng. program Topeka VA Hosp., 1974-77; mem. faculty Menninger Sch. Psychiatry, 1953—, Ann. Seminar Inst. on Alcoholism, U. Wis., 1973-74; cons. Osawatomie State Hosp., 1954-68, Colmery-O'Neill VA Hosp., 1983—; mem. staff Stormont-Vail Hosp., Topeka, Meml. Hosp., Topeka, St. Francis Hosp., Topeka; cons. in sex therapy Colmery-O'Neil VA Hosp., Topeka, 1983—. Assoc. editor Bull. Menninger Clinic, 1963-70. Bd. dirs. Topeka Civic Symphony Soc., 1953-55, Topeka People to People Council, 1963-66; mem. Kans. Citizens' Adv. Com. on Alcoholism, 1973-78; founder Topeka affiliate Nat. Council on Alcoholism, 1964, pres., bd. dirs., 1964, bd. dirs. N.Y.C., 1967, v.p., 1971-73, pres., 1973-75, mem. exec. com., 1967. Recipient Bronze Key award, Topeka affiliate Nat. Council on Alcoholism; 1972, Silver Key award, 1975, Outstanding Achievement award U. Alta. Med. Alumni Assn., 1975. Fellow Am. Psychiat. Assn.; mem. Topeka Inst. Psychoanalysis (cert.), Am. Assn. Sex Educators, Counselors and Therapists (cert. sex therapist), Am. Psychoanalytic Assn. (cert.), AMA, Kans. Psychiat. Soc., Kans. Med. Soc., Shawnee Med. Soc., Topeka Psychoanalytic Soc., Menninger Sch. Psychiatry Alumni Assn. (pres. 1979-80), Soc. for Sci. Study of Sex, Soc. for Sex Therapy and Research. Democrat. Presbyterian. Club: Saturday Night Literary. Lodge: Rotary. Avocations: reading, classical music, photography, traveling. Home: 834 Buchanan Topeka KS 66606 Office: PO Box 829 Topeka KS 66601

SIMPSON, WILLIAM TILDEN, engineer, consulting company executive; b. Martinsburg, Mo., Nov. 25, 1934; s. Huron Preston and Frances Hazel (Morris) S.; m. Beverly Jane Taylor, Aug. 18, 1956; children: William, Cheryl, Catherine. AA, Hannibal-LaGrange (Mo.) Coll., 1955; BSME, U. Mo., 1958; postgrad., Ga. Inst. Tech., 1968; postgrad. Mgmt. Inst., U. Miami (Fla.), 1977. Design/reliability engr. McDonnell Aircraft, St. Louis, 1958-60; systems engr. Am. Airlines, Tulsa, 1960-67; mgr. structures engring. Eastern Airlines, Miami, Fla., 1967-77, dir. aircraft engring., 1977-81; v.p. ops. Indsl. Mgmt. Services, Inc., Hannibal, 1981-83, pres., 1983—, also bd. dirs.; pres. Bevco, Inc., Hannibal, 1981—, also bd. dirs.; cons. NASA, Miami, 1972-77, Ralls County Water Dist., Hannibal, 1983, Dee Howard Co., San Antonio, 1982; cons., mgr. Clarcom Receiver, Inc., Vandalia, Mo., 1986. Author: (with others) (govt. aviation rules) Far 121 Fatigue Rules, 1977, Far 121 Composite Structures, 1978. Mem. AIAA (Cert. for Service 1980). Republican. Baptist. Avocations: golf, painting, reading, fishing. Home: 2 Mockingbird Ln Hannibal MO 63401 Office: Indsl Mgmt Services Inc 101 A N 3d Hannibal MO 63401

SIMS, ROBERT ALAN, educator; b. Cheboygan, Mich., Aug. 2, 1949; s. Eugene R. and Betty R. (Grody) S.; m. Kaye Lorainne D'Arcy, June 12, 1971; children: Stacy, Angela, Wendi. BA, Bethel Coll., Mishawaka, Ind., 1971; postgrad., Saginaw (Mich.) Valley State U., 1977, Cen. Mich. State U., 1977. Cert. elem. tchr., Mich. Tchr. Kingston (Mich.) Schs., 1971—; co-dir. sch. plays Kingston Schs., computer specialist Kingston Schs., 1986. Youth dir. Lamotte Missionary Ch., Marlette, Mich., 1973—, bd. dirs., 1984—; zoning adminstr. Kingston Twp., 1983—; bd. dirs. Brown City Camp, 1986. Avocations: camping, spelunking, carpentry, art, poetry. Home: 7686 Rossman Rd Kingston MI 48741 Office: Kingston Community Schs Sanilac Rd Kingston MI 48741

SINCLAIR, DOUGLAS RAY, mechanical engineer; b. Detroit, Nov. 17, 1958; s. James Ray and Irene Patricia (Mager) S.; m. Kimberly Ann Young, May 12, 1984. BSME, Wayne State U., 1981. Combustion engr. Detroit Diesel Allison div. Gen. Motors Corp., 1981-83; engine design engr. Pontiac Motor div. Gen. Motors Corp., Mich., 1983-86; vision applications engr. Perceptron, Farmington Hills, Mich., 1986-87, project engring mgr., 1987—. Mem. Soc. Automotive Engrs., Soc. Mfg. Engrs. Home: 37270 Chesapeake Farmington Hills MI 48018 Office: Perceptron 23855 Research Dr Farmington Hills MI 48024

SINCLAIR, JEFFREY LYLE, actuary; b. Campbellsville, Ky., Oct. 27, 1949; s. Harold F. and Delores (Rimer) S.; m. Deborah A. Bohlinger, Aug. 21, 1971; children: Brooke E., Jennifer E. AA, Oakland Coll., 1969; BS, Walsh Coll., 1972, B in Acctg., 1974, MS, 1977. Actuary, cons. Midwest Pension Actuaries, Farmington Hills, Mich., 1976-82; chief actuary, pres. Jeffrey L. Sinclair & Co., Livonia, Mich., 1982—; cons. in field. Contbr. articles to profl. jours. Office: 27476 W Five Mile Rd Livonia MI 48154

SINCLAIR, LLOYD GIFFIN, psychotherapist, sex educator; b. Racine, Wis., Aug. 13, 1949; s. Amos Lloyd and Susan Hazel (Giffin) S.; m. Anne Davidson Keller, Sept. 26, 1981; children: Jason Lloyd, Daniel Keller. MSSW, U. Wis., 1973. Cert. sex edu. and therapist. Psychotherapist, instr. Midwest Psychotherapy Ctr., Madison, 1973—; lectr. U. Wis., Whitewater, 1976—; dir. Family Sexual Abuse Treatment, Madison, 1983—. Contbg. author numerous book chpts. Mem. Assn. Sex Therapists and Counselors (v.p. 1986—), Am. Assn. Sex Educators, Counselors and Therapists, Nat. Assn. Social Workers, Acad. Cert. Social Workers, Sex Info. and Edn. Council of U.S. Office: 9 Odana Ct Suite 202 Madison WI 53719

SINCLAIR, LONNIE RAY, architect; b. Brookings, S.D., Apr. 22, 1952; s. Gerald J. and Lorraine V. (Anderson) S.; m. Monica L. Dolezal, June 16, 1973. BArch, Iowa State U., 1974. Registered architect, Iowa; cert. Nat. Council Archtl. Registration Bds. Intern architect Tinsley, Higgins, Lighter & Lyon, Des Moines, 1974-76, James Paxton & Assoc., Des Moines, 1976-79; architect, project mgr. Kendall Griffith Russell Artiaga, Des Moines, 1979—. Editor Specifically Speaking Newsletter, 1982-85. Steering com. Leadership Iowa, 1986—; bd. dirs. Com. of 200, 1986-87. Mem. AIA, Des Moines Architects Council, Constrn. Specifications Inst. (bd. dirs. Cen. Iowa chpt. 1984-88, pres. 1987-88; publ. com. chmn. North Cen. Region chpt. 1986-87). Democrat. Roman Catholic. Clubs: Waveland Golf Assn. (bd. dirs. 1977-83, pres. 1981); Hyperion Field. Avocation: golf. Office: Kendall Griffith Russell Artiaga 3030 Ruan Ctr Des Moines IA 50309

SINCLAIR, RICHARD B., school system adminstrator; b. Chgo., Jan. 12, 1936; s. Barney Michael and Harriet (Kowalczyk) Kamowski; m. Barbara Ann Sturomski, June 30, 1958; children: René Janean, Suzanne Lea, Lisa Corryn, Samantha Beth. BS, Chgo. State U., 1966; MA, Roosevelt U., 1968; EdD, No. Ill. U., 1974. Tng. dir. North Am. Rockwell, Chgo.; asst. prin. Nathan Hale Sch., Schaumburg, Ill.; asst. prof. Voldosta (Ga.) State U.; cons. Posen (Ill.)-Robbins Sch. Dist., dir. state and fed. programs, adminstrv. asst., bus. mgr., supt. of schs.; bd. dirs. Moraine Valley Credit Union, Palos Hills, Ill. Author 42 booklets. Bd. dirs. Trans Allied Med. Edn. Service, Homewood, Ill., 1984—, Eisenhower Spl. Edn. Program, Alsip, Ill., 1984—. Mem. Nat. Assn. Sch. Adminstrs., Ill. Assn. Sch. Adminstrs., Bremen Assn. Sch. Adminstrs., Supts.' Roundtable of Ill., Internat. Show Car Assn., Phi Delta Kappa. Club: Willow Basin Yacht (Colon, Mich.) (pres. 1986—). Avocations: boating, show car design, old car restoration. Home: 6331 N Normandy Chicago IL 60631 Office: Sch Dist 143 1/2 14025 Harrison Posen IL 60469

SINCLAIR, WINFIELD JAMES, lawyer; b. Balt., Mar. 10, 1954; s. James Edward and Pauline Louise (Shoemaker) S.; m. Julianne Moores Williams, Dec. 16, 1978. BA cum laude, U. of the South, 1975; JD, Samford U., 1978. Bar: Ala. 1978, U.S. Ct. Appeals (11th cir.) 1981, U.S. Supreme Ct. 1982, Mo. 1986, U.S. Ct. Appeals (8th cir.) 1986. Asst. dist. atty. U.S. Dist. Atty.'s Office, Selma, Ala., 1978-79; asst. atty. gen. State of Ala., Montgomery, 1979-83; spl. agt. FBI, Washington, 1983-86; asst. atty. gen. State of Mo., Jefferson City, 1986-87, 1987—. Mem. Ala. Bar Assn., Mo. State Bar Assn., Ala. Peace Officers Assn., FBI Agts. Assn., Fraternal Order Police. Avocation: golf. Office: Atty Gen's Office Wainwright Office Bldg 111 7th St 9th Floor Saint Louis MO 63101

SINGER, STANLEY THOMAS, JR., engineering administrator; b. Detroit, June 29, 1933; s. Stanley Thomas and Agnes Frances (Maciejewski) S.; m. Iris Josephine Bandmann, Nov. 12, 1960; children: Stanley Thomas III, Eric Herms. BBA, U. Detroit, 1966; MA Cen. Mich. U., 1977. Tool designer Gen. Motors Corp., Detroit, 1951-55, prodn. engr., 55-62; prodn. engr. Ford Motor Co., Utica, Mich., 1962-64, research engr., 1964-67, engring. mgr., Dearborn, 1967—, mgr. quality assurance, 1986. Mem. exec. bd. Detroit Area Council Boy Scouts of Am., 1967—, mem. East Cen. region exec. bd.; trustee Greater Detroit Cath. Youth Orgn.; mem. Macomb County Community Relations Com. Recipient Silver Beaver award Boy Scouts Am., 1984, St. George Emblem, Cath. Ch., 1984, Ed Crowe award for service to youth, 1986. Mem. Soc. Automotive Engrs., Engring. Soc. of Detroit, Soc. Mfg. Engrs., Am. Soc. Quality Control, Delta Sigma Pi. Republican. Roman Catholic. Clubs: Detroit Yacht, Hillcrest Country. Lodge: K.C. Avocations: skiing, flying, boating.

SINGH, SHYAM NARAYAN, engineering company executive; b. Basantpur, India, Jan. 1, 1952; came to U.S., 1977; s. Sitaram and Dhanwantari (Devi) S.; m. Sheela Singh, June 3, 1975; children: Shantanu, Sachin, Shilpee. BS in Tech. Chem. Engring., Banares Hindu U., Varansi, India, 1975; MS in Fuel Sci., Pa. State U., 1982. Engr. research and devel. Cleaver-Brooks, Milw., 1981-84; project mgr. Energy Systems, Milw., 1984-85; dir. research and engring. WB Combustion, Inc., Milw., 1985-87; mgr. research engring. Combustion div. Eclipse, Inc., Rockford, Ill., 1987—; cons. Froedtert Malt Corp., Milw., 1986; adj. lectr. mech. engring. U. Wis., Milw., 1987—. Mem. ASME (tech. com. petroleum div. 1983), Combustion Inst. Avocations: jogging, dancing, tennis. Home: 1020 E Glendale Ave Shorewood WI 53211 Office: Eclipse Inc 1665 Elmwood Rd Rockford IL 61103

SINGH, SURENDRA NARAIN, business educator; b. Varanasi, India, July 1, 1952; s. Awadh Narain and Kamla (Rai) S.; m. Namrata Rai; 1 child, Anish. BS, Banavas Hindu U., Varanasi, India, 1972, MBA, 1975; MBA, U. Wis., 1980, PhD, 1982. Instr. mktg. U. Wis., Madison, 1982; asst. prof. bus. U. Kans., Lawrence, 1982—; coordinator vis. scholar series Sch. Bus. U. Kans., 1985—, chmn. colloquium com., 1984-85, mem. external affairs com., 1983-84; cons. U. Wis. Mus. Fine Arts, 1982. Ad hoc reviewer Jour. Mktg.; contbr. articles to profl. jours. Named one of Outstanding Young Men Am., 1985. Mem. Am. Mktg. Assn., Assn. Consumer Research. Hindu. Office: U Kans Sch Bus Summerfield Hall Lawrence KS 66045

SINGLETARY, MICHAEL, professional football player; b. Houston, Oct. 9, 1958; m. Kim Singletary. B.A., Baylor U., 1981. Middle linebacker Chgo. Bears, 1981—. Named Defensive Most Valuable Player for 1985 season; participated in Pro Bowl, 1984, 85, 86. Office: Chgo Bears 55 E Jackson Suite 1200 Chicago IL 60604 *

SINGLETON, GARY WILLIAM, hospital administrator, psychologist; b. DeKalb, Ill., Jan. 29, 1945; s. James and Lois Marie (Thompson) S.; m. Kathleen Diana Singleton, July 10, 1982; children: Kristen, Christopher, Kristi. BS in Psychology, U. Ill., 1967, MA in Labor and Indsl. Relations, 1969; MA in Clin. Psychology, Wayne State U., 1974, PhD in Clin. Psychology, 1976. Lic. psychologist, Mich.; cert. sex therapist, Mich. Staff psychologist Rehab. Inst., Detroit, 1975-76, dir. psychology, 1976-79, div. dir., 1979-82, chief operating officer, 1982-83, exec. v.p. and chief operating officer, 1983—; adj. asst. prof. psychology Wayne State U., Detroit, 1978—. Contbr. articles to profl. jours. Mem. Detroit Econ. Club. Mem. Am. Psychol. Assn., Am. Congress Rehab. Medicine, Am. Hosp. Assn., Mich. Hosp. Assn. (com. assn. governance 1983-85, southeast Mich. hosp. council com. govt. relations 1983—, com. pub. relations 1985—), Nat. Assn. Rehab. Facilities (com. med. rehab. facilities 1983—), Greater Detroit Area C. of C. (com. labor law 1985—). Mormon.

SINGLETON, JAMES ALBERT, gynecologist/obstetrician; b. Mannington, W.Va., Nov. 14, 1930; s. Albert Horace and Helen Carolyn (Phillips) S.; m. Mary Anne Evans, Aug. 8, 1953; children: James, John, Patrick. AB, W.Va. U., 1951; MD, Thomas Jefferson U., 1955. Diplomate Am. Bd. Ob-Gyn. Intern Delaware Hosp., Wilmington, 1955; resident in obgyn U. Ill. Hosp., Chgo., 1958-61; practice medicine specializing in ob-gyn Springfield, Ill., 1961—. Served to capt. USAF, 1956-58. Fellow Am. Coll. Obstetricians and Gynecologists; mem. Cen. Assn. Obstetricians and Gynecologists, Am. Fertility Soc. Republican. Presbyterian. Avocations: sailing, skiing, scuba diving. Home: 1750 Illini Rd Springfield IL 62704 Office: 701 N Walnut St Springfield IL 62702

SINGLETON, JOHN ALAN, military officer; b. Louisville, Ky., Dec. 31, 1959; s. Floyd G. Singleton and Doris Mae (Klefot) S.; m. Mary Elizabeth Fitzpatrick, Jan. 9, 1982; children: Sean Michael, Nicholas Joseph. BS in Acctg., U. Ky., 1981; postgrad., Okla. U., 1984-86. Field rep. Ky. Revenue Cabinet, Louisville, 1982-83; commd. 2d lt. USAF, Lackland, Tex., 1983; advanced through grades to capt. USAF; officer trainee, navigator tng. 1983; electronic warfare officer 343 Strategic Reconnaissance Squadron Initial Qualification Tng., Offutt AFB, Nebr., 1986; instr. electronic warfare 343 Strategic Reconnaissance Squadron Initial Qualification Tng., Offutt AFB, 1986-87, exec. officer, 1987—. Chmn. Recon Booster Club, Omaha, 1985. Decorated Air medal; named one of Outstanding Young Men Am., 1986. Mem. Air Force Assn., Assn. Old Crows, Hon. Order Ky. Cols. Republican. Roman Catholic. Club: Offutt Officers. Home: 5021 Davenport St Omaha NE 68132 Office: USAF 343 SRS DOTI Offutt AFB NE 68113-5000

SINGSIME, GRACE SMOCK, catering company executive; b. Chgo., Nov. 22, 1924; d. Albert William and Martha Krueger (Manke) Smid; m. Alvin E. Singsime, Apr. 16, 1966 (dec.); 1 dau., Stacey G. Smock, stepchildren—Delores Singsime De Lellis, Mardi Singsime Schlondrop, Deane A. Owner mgr. Smock's Yankee Doodle Restaurant-Gracious Catering, Milw., 1953-59, Grace Smock-Gracious Catering Corp., Elm Grove, Wis., 1959—. Mem. Internat. Food Service Exec. Assn. (Food Service Exec. of Yr. Milw. br. 1978), Elm Grove Bus. Assn. Lodge: Order Eastern Star. Home: S 36 W 26579 Velma Dr Waukesha WI 53186 Office: Grace Smock Gracious Catering 890 Elm Grove Rd Grove WI 53122

SINHA, DEVENDRA PRASAD, veterinarian, state laboratory administrator; b. Patna, India, Jan. 3, 1936; came to U.S., 1968, naturalized, 1971; s. Mohan Lal and Prameshwari (Devi) S.; m. Chandra Kanta, June 9, 1957; children—Renu, Ajit, Daisy; B.V.Sc. and A. H., Bihar U. (India), 1959; M.S., U. Mo., 1969; Ph.D., Ohio State U., 1973. Lic. veterinarian, Ohio. Veterinarian, State Govt. Bihar, 1959-68; research asst. U. Mo., 1968-70; research assoc. Ohio State U., 1970-73; microbiologist Ohio Dept. Agrl. Labs., Reynoldsburg, 1973-74, veterinarian, 1974—, dir. vet. microbiology lab., animal diseases diagnostic lab., 1974—. Bihar U. merit acad. scholar, 1955-59. Mem. Ohio Vet. Med. Assn., Am. Soc. Vet. Clin. Pathology, Am. Assn. Vet. Lab. Diagnosticians, Am. Soc. Microbiology, Gamma Sigma Delta. Research and publs. in field. Home: 696 Stow Pl Reynoldsburg OH 43068 Office: 8995 E Main St Reynoldsburg OH 43068

SINICROPI, STEPHEN ANTHONY, radio station executive; b. Olean, N.Y., June 9, 1957; s. Anthony Vincent and Margaret Frances (Michienzi) S.; m. Laura Marie Schwaigert, Jan. 8, 1983. BBA in Indsl. Relations, U. Iowa, 1983. Account exec. Sta. KKRQ-FM, Iowa City, Iowa, 1982-83, sales mgr. Cedar Rapids, 1983-84, gen. sales mgr., 1984-86; gen. mgr. KKRQ-FM and KXIC-AM, Iowa City, Iowa, 1987. Republican. Roman Catholic. Avocations: cooking, travel, spectator sports, reading, computers. Home: 1116 Franklin St Iowa City IA 52240 Office: Sta KKRQ-KXIC Interstate 80 and N Dubuque Iowa City IA 52240

SINK, BRUCE R., banking systems executive; b. Piqua, Ohio, Sept. 22, 1955; s. Jack R. and Pat. L. (Swartz) S.; m. Mary E. Fender, Jan. 11, 1975; children: Andrew T., Adam T., Scott E. Student, Columbus Coll. Art and Design, 1973-79, Otterbein Coll., 1986-87. Computer operator Blue Shield/Blue Cross, Worthington, Ohio, 1974-75, systems programmer, 1975-79; systems programmer Bank One, Columbus, Ohio, 1979-82, systems mgr., 1982-86; v.p. systems Chase Bank Ohio, Columbus, 1986—. v.p. Worthington Art League, 1979. Mem. Assn. Systems Mgmt. (cert.), Watercolor Soc. Columbus. Republican. Roman Catholic. Club: Art Gallery. Lodge: Lions. Avocation: painting.

SINKA, ARVI, musician; b. Tallinn, Estonia, USSR, May 6, 1938; came to U.S., 1949; s. August and Miralda (Idnurm) S.; m. Brenda Pauline Rettmer, June 26, 1965; children: Erik, Aaron. MusB, Oberlin (Ohio) Conservatory, 1960; MusM, Ind. U., 1962, MusD, 1965. Instr. music Huron (S.D.) Coll., 1963; asst. prof. U. So. Minn., Mankato, 1965-67; instr. Herderschule U., Rendsburg, Fed. Republic of Germany, 1968-69; pianist Detroit Symphony Orch., 1975—; opera coach Bremen Opera, Fed. Republic of Germany, 1969; mus. dir. The Fantasticks, Bern, Switzerland, 1968; choirmaster, organist various chs., Detroit, 1960-87. Solo recitals in Boston, N.Y., Toronto, Ont., Can. and Chgo., 1960-87; appears in recs. for Voice of Am., 1970-78, Coronet and Crystal Records, 1980-84; appears in video rec. for Sterling Heights (Mich.) Pub. Library, 1985; contbr. articles to profl. jours. Concert mgr. Cultural Arts Council, Utica, Mich., 1982-87. Served with USNG, 1952-66. Recipient Young Artist award Nat. Fedn. Music Clubs, Chgo., 1967. Mem. AAUP, Music Tchrs. Nat. Assn. (cert.). Lutheran. Home: 407 Randall Troy MI 48098

SINNER, GEORGE ALBERT, governor of North Dakota, farmer; b. Fargo, N.D., May 29, 1928; s. Albert and Katherine (Wild) S.; m. Elizabeth Jane Baute, Aug. 10, 1951; children: Robert, George, Elizabeth, Martha, Paula, Mary Jo, Jim, Jerry, Joe, Eric. BA in Philosophy, St. Johns U., St. Cloud, Minn., 1950. Farmer Sinner Bros. and Bresnahan, Casselton, N.D., 1952—; mem. N.D. Senate, 1962-66, N.D. Ho. of Reps., 1982-84; chmn. fin. and tax com., 1983; gov. State of N.D., Bismarck, 1985—; founder N.D. Crops Council, Fargo, 1978-83; U.S. del. Inter-Am. Food and Agrl. Conf., 1966; founder, chmn. N.D. Crops Council, Fargo, 1978-83; chmn. No. Crops Inst. Council, Fargo, 1980-83, Interstate Oil Compact Commn., 1986—. Candidate for U.S. Congress, 1964; chmn., co-founder bd. dirs. Southeast Region Mental Health and Retardation Clinic, Carrington, N.D., 1964-66; mem. N.D. Broadcasting Council, 1968-73, N.D. Bd. Higher Edn., Bismarck, 1966-75, chmn. 1970; del. N.D. Constl. Conv., Bismarck, 1972; mem. Casselton Planning and Zoning Commn., 1982-85; co-founder bd. dirs. Tri-Coll. Univ. Bd., Fargo/Moorhead, N.D., 1970-84; chmn. Interstate Oil Compact Commn., 1986—. Served as pvt. USNG, 1950-51. Recipient Diversified Family award Fargo Rotary, 1960, Agrl. award N.D. State U., 1974, L.B. Hartz Profl. Achievement award Moorhead (Minn.) State U., 1982. Mem. Nat. Gov.'s Assn., N.D. Cattle Feeders' Assn. (farm prodn.), Red River Valley Sugarbeet Growers Assn. (pres. bd. dirs. 1975-79), Greater N.D. Assn. (bd. dirs. 1981), N.D. Farm Bur. (farm prodn.), N.D. Wheat Producers (farm prodn.), N.D. Crop Improvement Assn. (farm prodn.), N.D. Stockmen's Assn. (farm prodn.), Am. Soybean Assn. (farm prodn.), N.D. Barley Council (farm prodn.), N.D. Farmers Union (farm prodn.), Am. Legion. Democrat. Roman Catholic. Club: Casselton Community (pres. 1969). Avocations: family, tennis, racquetball, reading, boating. Office: Governor's Office State Capitol Bismarck ND 58505

SINOR, DONNA KAY, lawyer; b. Cozad, Nebr., Sept. 5, 1952; d. Floyd Virgil and Arlene Caroline (Morris) S.; m. Steve E. Bowen, Oct. 27, 1984. B.S., U. Nebr., 1973, J.D., 1984. Bar: Nebr. 1984, U.S. Dist. Ct. Nebr. 1984. Tchr. Lincoln Pub. Schs., Nebr., 1973-81; researcher student Research Service, Lincoln, 1982-84; student coordinator Community Legal Edn., Lincoln, 1982-84; assoc. Nelson and Harding, Lincoln, 1984-85; asst. dir. advanced underwriting Bankers Life Nebr., 1985—, Gen. Securities registered rep., 1986; Recipient Outstanding Sophomore Woman award U. Nebr., 1971-72. Mem. Lincoln Bar Assn., Nebr. State Bar Assn., ABA, Nebr. Assn. Trial Attys., Assn. Trial Lawyers Am., Alpha Lambda Delta. Office: Bankers Life Neb 5900 O Street Lincoln NE 68510

SIRCY, JOHN EDWARD, banker; b. Waukegan, Ill., Aug. 5, 1956; s. Hubert Edward and Patricia Mary (Struve) S.; m. Deborah Catherine Caraway, Mar. 18, 1978; children: Jonathan Lawrence, Elisha James. BA magna cum laude, Knox Coll., 1978. CPA, Ill. Controller 1st Galesburg (Ill.) Nat. Bank, 1981-83, v.p., controller, 1983-85; chief fin. officer First Illini Bancorp, Inc., Galesburg, 1985—; bd. dirs. Madison Park Bank, Peoria, Ill. Mem. Am. Inst. CPA's, Ill. CPA Soc., Phi Beta Kappa. Apostolic Pentecostal. Avocation: participating in sports. Home: 587 E Third St Galesburg IL 61401 Office: First Illini Bancorp Inc 200 E Main St Galesburg IL 61401

SIRKIS, ROBERT LANE, foodservice company executive; b. Washington, Nov. 5, 1951; s. Joseph A. and Eleanor B. (Block) S.; m. Kendall Kay Whitham, Aug. 30, 1986. BA, Johns Hopkins U., 1973; MBA, Harvard U., 1975. Dir. mktg. Dobbs Houses Inc., Memphis, 1975-79; cons. Arthur D. Little Inc., Cambridge, Mass., 1979-81; v.p. ops. services Pizza Hut Inc., Wichita, Kans., 1981-86; v.p. east cen. region Pizza Hut Inc., Downers Grove, Ill., 1987—. Contbr. articles on foodservice industry. Home: 1133 Dartmore Ct Naperville IL 60540 Office: Pizza Hut Inc 1100 W 31st St Downers Grove IL 60512

SIROCKY, KENNETH MICHAEL, dentist, consultant; b. Cleve., Oct. 18, 1952; s. Paul John and Dolores Marie (Spisak) S.; m. Diana Marie Sirocky, Aug. 7, 1976 (div. Dec. 1986); 1 child, Allison Nicole; m. Andrea Amico, June 13, 1987. DDS, Ohio State U., 1976. Gen. practice dentistry Strongsville, Ohio, 1976—. Fellow Acad. Gen. Dentistry, Am. Edodontic Soc.; mem. Am. Dental Soc., Cleve. Dental Soc., Ohio Dental Soc., S.W. Hosp. Study Group., Bd. Govs. (bd. dirs.). Roman Catholic. Club. Medina Country. Avocations: skiing, golf, landscaping. Home: 13744 Brigadon Way Strongsville OH 44136 Office: 16360 Pearl Rd Strongsville OH 44136

SIROCKY, MICHAEL PAUL, chemical executive; b. Cleve., Feb. 19, 1948; s. Michael Edward and Dorothy Ann (Desoffy) S.; m. Pamela Jean Carr, Feb. 26, 1971. BA, Cuyahoga Community Coll., Cleve., 1968; BBA, Cleve. State U., 1977; MBA, Baldwin Wallace, Berea, Ohio, 1980. Devel. chemist Glidden, Cleve., 1972-76; plant mgr. Foseco, Inc., Cleve., 1976-82; sales rep. G. Coureaux, Inc., Indpls., 1982-84; pres., chief exec. officer B.W.T., Inc., Cleve., 1985—; cons. Insul Corp., East Palestine, Ohio, Diamonite Products, Shreve, Ohio. Counselor Jr. Achievement, Cleve., 1981-82. Served as capt. U.S. Army, 1985. Mem. BMER Foundryman's Soc. Lodges: Masons, Shriners. Avocation: boating. Home: 17729 Hampton Pl Strongsville OH 44136 Office: BWT Inc PO 36718 Cleveland OH 44136

SIRRIDGE, MARJORIE SPURRIER, physician, educator; b. Kingman, Kans., Oct. 6, 1921; d. Frank R. and Fannie (Watson) Spurrier; m. William Thomas Sirridge, Oct. 28, 1944; children: Mary Jeannette, Stephen Thomas, Patrick Michael, Christopher Frank. BS, Kans. State U., 1942; MD, U. Kans., 1944. Gen. practice medicine Kansas City, Kans., 1955-71; asst. clin. prof. sch. medicine U. Kans., Kansas City, 1958-71; docent, prof. sch. medicine U. Mo., Kansas City, 1971—, asst. dean, 1985—; mem. chancellor's adv. bd. U. Mo. Women's Ctr., Kansas City. Author: Laboratory Evaluation of Hemostasis and Thrombosis, 3d edit., 1983. Bd. dirs. Greater Kansas City (Mo.) Mental Health Found., 1982—. Named Med. Alumnus of Yr., U. Kans. Sch. Medicine, 1983; recipient Woman of Achievement award Kansas City Girl Scouts U.S., 1984, Mentor award U. Mo., Kansas City, Women's Ctr., 1984, Outstanding Kansas Citian award Kansas City mag., 1984, 85. Mem. AMA, Mo. State Med. Assn., Met. Med. Soc. Greater Kansas City, Am. Soc. Hematology, Am. Med. Women's Assn., Alpha Omega Alpha, Kappa Kappa, Gamma. Club: Cen. Exchange (Kansas City, Mo.) (v.p. bd. dirs. 1986—). Home: 2510 Grand Kansas City MO 64108 Office: U Mo Sch Medicine 2411 Holmes St Kansas City MO 64108

SISK, GREGORY BLAINE, psychologist; b. Poplar Bluff, Mo., Aug. 22, 1953; s. Herschel C. and Faye (Boyers) S.; m. Deborah Ann Drury, Jan. 2, 1983; 1 child, Rebecca Faye. BA cum laude, U. Mo., 1974; MA, La. State U., 1976, PhD, 1980. Lic. psychologist, Mo. Staff psychologist Western Mo. Mental Health Ctr., Kansas City, 1978-81; program dir. Transitional Living Consortium, Kansas City, 1981-85; psychologist Briscoe-Carr Cons., Inc., Kansas City, 1984—; instr. U. Mo., Kansas City, 1985-86. Mem. Am. Psychol. Assn., Greater Kansas City Psychol. Assn., Am. Assn. Counseling and Devel., Phi Beta Kappa, Phi Kappa Phi. Avocation: filmmaking. Office: Briscoe-Carr Cons Inc 3519 Walnut Kansas City MO 64111

SISK, LAWRENCE THEODORE, musicologist, conductor; b. Toccoa, Ga., Jan. 31, 1950; s. Theodore Roosevelt and Virginia Lee (Dalton) S.; m. Caryl Jane Worthington, Oct. 7, 1971 (div. Nov. 18, 1979); m. Jill Margaret Ballotti, Mar. 27, 1982. MusB, Roosevelt U., 1977; MusM, Northwestern U., 1983, PhD, 1986. Dir. of music Bryn Mawr Community Ch., Chgo., 1972-82, Wilmette (Ill.) Luth. Ch., 1982-84, Northbrook (Ill.) Meth. Ch., 1985-86, Good Shepherd Luth. Ch., Naperville, 1986—; choirmaster Congregation Shaare Tikvah, Chgo., 1979-84; editor The Instrumentalist, Northfield, Ill., 1986—; solo tenor Chgo. Monteverdi Singers, 1974—; asst. conductor DePaul U. Symphony, Chgo., 1979; founder, dir. The Dowland Consort, Chgo., 1980-84; lectr. Northwestern U., Evanston, Ill., 1987—. Eckstein grantee, 1981-84; Fulbright scholar, 1984-85. Mem. Am. Musicological Soc., Coll. Music Soc. Republican. Avocations: Italian cuisine, bicycling. Home: PO Box 48931 Chicago IL 60648-0931 Office: The Instrumentalist 200 Northfield Rd Northfield IL 60093

SISK, MARK SEAN, priest, seminary dean, religious educator; b. Takoma, Md., Aug. 18, 1942; s. Robert James and Alma Irene (Davis) S.; m. Karen Lynn Womack, Aug. 31, 1963; children: Michael A., Heather K., Bronwyn E. BS, U. Md., 1964; MDiv, Gen. Theolog. Sem., 1967, DD, 1985. Asst. Christ Ch., New Brunswick, N.J., 1967-70; assoc. Christ Ch., Bronxville, N.Y., 1970-73; rector St. John's Ch., Kingston, N.Y., 1973-77; archdeacon Diocese of N.Y., N.Y.C., 1977-84; dean, pres. Seabury-Western Theol. Sem., Evanston, Ill., 1984—; sec. Council Episcopal Sem. Deans, 1984-85; mem. task force for recruitemnt, tng. and deployment of black clergy. Pres. Anglican Theol. Rev. Named Hon. Canon Cathedral of St. John the Divine, N.Y.C., 1977. Mem. Soc. Biblical Lit., Conf. Diocesan Execs., Assn. Chgo. Theol. Schs., Soc. St. Francis (third order). Home: 625 Garrett Pl Evanston IL 60201 Office: Seabury-Western Theol Sem 2122 Sheridan Rd Evanston IL 60201

SISKA, RICHARD STANLY, marketing professional; b. Chgo., June 6, 1948; s. Stanly J. and Anna Marie (Czelka) S.; m. Christine Alexandria Plodzin, Sept. 7, 1969; children: Cara, Kylene. BSBA, Christian Bros. Coll., 1969. Tech. sales rep. Advance Process Supply, Chgo., 1971-73; nat. sales mgr. premium/incentives R.A. Briggs Co., Lake Zurich, Ill., 1974-77, nat. sales mgr. retail div., 1977-80, dir. sales, mktg., 1980-82, v.p., 1983—. Contbr. articles to profl. jours. Campaign dir. Rep. Com. to Elect Jim Kay for Lake Zurich Mayor, 1982. Served to sgt. U.S. Army, 1970-71. Mem. Nat. Premium Sales Execs., Chgo. Textile Assn., Bed and Bath Linen Assn., Lake Zurich Indsl. Council, Christian Bros. Coll. Alumni Assn. (sec. 1980-81), Delta Sigma Pi. Avocations: tennis, sport fishing, hunting, numismatics, bicycling. Home: 3 Hickory Ln Hawthorn Woods IL 60047 Office: RA Briggs Co Box 468 Lake Zurich IL 60047

SISKEL, GENE (EUGENE KAL SISKEL), film critic; b. Chgo., Jan. 26, 1946; s. Nathan W. and Ida (Kalis) S.; m. Marlene Iglitzen, 1980; children: Kate Adi, Callie Gray. B.A., Yale U., 1967; postgrad. Coro Found. fellow 1968, Dept. Def. Info. Sch., 1968. Film critic Chgo. Tribune, 1969—; movie critic WBBM-TV, Chgo., 1974—. Co-host: Sneak Previews, PBS Network, 1977-82, At the Movies, syndicated TV, 1982-86, Siskel & Ebert & The Movies, syndicated TV, 1986—. CORO Found. fellow, 1968. Mem. Acad. TV Arts and Scis., Sigma Delta Chi. Clubs: Yale, Culver; Arts (Chgo.). Office: care Chicago Tribune 435 N Michigan Ave Chicago IL 60611

SISSON, EVERETT ARNOLD, diversified industry executive; b. Chgo., Oct. 24, 1920; s. Emmett B. and Norma (Merbitz) S.; m. Betty L. DeGrado, Apr. 7, 1984; children: Nancy Lee Sisson Rassbach, Elizabeth Anne Sisson Levy. A.B., Valparaiso U., 1942. Sales mgr. Ferrotherm Corp., Cleve., 1946-51, Osborn Mfg. Co., Cleve., 1951-56; dir. sales Patterson Foundry & Machine Co., East Liverpool, Ohio, 1956-58; mgr. sonic energy products Bendix Corp., Davenport, Iowa, 1958-60; pres., chief exec. officer, dir. Lamb Industries, Inc., Toledo, 1960-65, Lehigh Valley Industries, Inc., N.Y.C., 1965-66, Am. Growth Industries, Inc., Chgo., 1966—, Workman Mfg. Co., Chgo., 1966-69, Am. Growth Devel. Corp., Chgo., 1968—; chmn. bd., chief exec. officer G.F.I. Inc., 1976—; pres. Peru Properties, Inc., Oak Brook, 1976—; chmn. bd., chief exec. officer Pringle & Booth, Inc., Chgo., 1986—; dir. Century Life of Am., Waverly, Iowa, Telco Capital Corp., Hickory Furniture Co., N.C., Opelika Mfg. Co., Chgo., Sunstates Corp., Jacksonville, Fla., Century Life Ins. Co., Waverly, Iowa, Indiana Fin. Investors Inc., Indpls., Acton (Mass.) Corp.; trustee Wis. Real Estate Investment Trust, 1980—. Pres. council, Mayfield Heights, Ohio, 1952-57; adviser to bd. trustees Valparaiso (Ind.) U., 1960-69; bd. regents Calif. Lutheran Coll., 1968—, fellow, 1969. Served pres. capt. USAAF, 1943-46. Mem. Am. Mgmt. Assn., Cleve. Engring. Soc., President's Assn., Tau Kappa Epsilon. Clubs: Burr Ridge, Gt. Lakes Yachting, Ocean Reef. Home: 1405 Burr

Ridge Club Burr Ridge IL 60521 Office: Am Growth Devel Co 547 S Clark St Suite 300 Chicago IL 60605

SISSON, RAYMOND ARTHUR, real estate management and mortgage company executive; b. St. Joseph, Mo., May 8, 1937; s. Howard Roosevelt and Wilma (Jones) S.; m. Louise Tomlinson, Aug. 6, 1960; children: Lynette, Sara, Rick. BS in Fin., U. Kans., 1959. Pres. The Sisson Group, St. Joseph, 1965—, Sisson Co., Realtors, St. Joseph, 1965—, Am. Properties, St. Joseph, 1971—, Heritage Mortgage Co., St. Joseph, 1981—; chmn. Mo. Real Estate Commn., Jefferson City, 1985. Mem. United Way, St. Joseph; councilman City of St. Joseph, 1986—. Mem. Nat.Assn. Realtors (bd. dirs. 1986), Mo. Assn. Realtors (bd. dirs., pres. 1984, Realtor of Yr. award 1982), Mo. Comml. Investment Assn. (pres. 1981), Kansas City Bd. Realtors, St. Joseph Bd. Realtors (Realtor of Yr. award 1972, 83, pres. 1972), St. Joseph C. of C. Republican. Presbyterian. Club: Country. Lodges: Rotary, Moila. Avocations: golf, flying, tennis. Home: 4326 Stonecrest Dr Saint Joseph MO 64506 Office: The Sission Group 3715 Beck Rd Bldg B Suite 203 Woodlawn Village Office Condo Saint Joseph MO 64506

SISSON, VERDA M., state corrections official; b. Ann Arbor, Mich., Dec. 16, 1945; d. Clyde M. and Vollie M. (Robinson) S.; divorced; children: Alan, Maria. AS, Washtenaw Community Coll., 1972, paralegal cert., 1976; BS, Eastern Mich. U., 1978. Cert. social worker. Head counselor S.T.O.P., Lansing, Mich., 1981; program coordinator Indsl. Step-Up Pre-Apprenticeship for Women Ingham Intemed. Sch., Mason, Mich., 1982; corrections officer Mich. Dept. Corrections, Ionia, Mich., 1983-84, housing officer, 1984-85, asst. housing mgr., 1985; classification dir. Mich. Dept. Corrections, Jackson, 1985—. Mem. Am. Corrections Orgn., Mich. Corrections Orgn., Nat. Assn. Negro Women. Democrat. African Methodist. Avocations: sewing, camping. Home: 36 S Hewitt Rd Apt #103 Ypsilanti MI 48197 Office: Jackson Temp Facility 3500 N Elm Rd Jackson MI 49201

SIT, EUGENE C., investment executive; b. Canton, China, Aug. 8, 1938; s. Hom Yuen and Sue (Eng) S.; B.S.C., DePaul U., 1960, postgrad. Grad. Sch. Bus., 1962-65; m. Gail V. Chin, Sept. 14, 1958; children—Ronald, Debra, Roger, Raymond, Robert, Richard. Fin. analyst Commonwealth Edison, Chgo., 1960-66, fin. asst. to chmn. finance com., 1966-68; asso. portfolio mgr. Investors Stock Fund, Investors Diversified Services, Mpls., 1968-69; portfolio mgr. IDS New Dimensions Fund, Mpls., 1969, v.p., portfolio mgr., 1970-72; v.p., sr. portfolio mgr. IDS New Dimensions, IDS Growth Fund, Mpls., 1972-76; pres. IDS Adv., 1976-77, pres., chief exec. officer, 1977-81; chief exec. officer IDS Trust Co., 1979-81; chmn., chief exec. officer IDS Adv./Gartmore Internat. Ltd., 1979-81; pres., chief exec. officer Sit Investment Assos., Inc., Mpls., 1981—; chmn., pres., dir. New Beginning Income and Growth Fund, New Beginning Growth Fund, New Beginning Investment Res. Fund, New Beginning Yield Fund. C.P.A., Ill.; chartered fin. analyst. Bd. pensions Presbyterian Ch. Mem. Am. Inst. C.P.A.s, Inst. Chartered Fin. Analysts (vice chmn., trustee), Fin. Analysts Fedn., Twin Cities Soc. Security Analysts, Investment Analysts Soc. Chgo. Clubs: University (N.Y.C.); Chicago; Minneapolis; Edina Country; World Trade (San Francisco). Home: 6216 Braeburn Circle Edina MN 55435 Office: 1714 First Bank Pl West Minneapolis MN 55402

SITA, MICHAEL JOHN, pharmacist, educator; b. St. Louis, Apr. 28, 1953; s. Julianne Gail Sita; m. Nora Ann Dillon, June 1, 1974; children: Michael John, Paul Thomas. BS, St. Louis Coll. Pharmacy, 1976; MBA, So. Ill. U., 1983. Registered pharmacist, Mo., Ill. Staff pharmacist Luth. Med. Ctr., St. Louis, 1976-78, asst. chief pharmacist, 1978-81, adminstrv. coordinator pharmacy services, 1981-85; dir. pharmacy services Jefferson Meml. Hosp., 1985—; instr. St. Louis Coll. Health Careers, 1983-86; adj. clin. instr. pharmacy St. Louis Coll. Pharmacy, 1980—; relief pharmacist Dolgins Apothecary, St. Louis, 1976-86, Best Pharmacy, 1986—. Author/editor Pharmacy Capsule quar., 1977-85. Mem. St. Louis Soc. Hosp. Pharmacists (treas. 1985-87, pres.-elect. 1987—), Mo. Soc. Hosp. Pharmacists, Am. Soc. Hosp. Pharmacists, Am. Pharm. Assn., Am. Soc. Parenteral and Enteral Nutrition, Hosp. Assn. Met. St. Louis (chmn. pharmacy tech. adv. com. 1985-86). Avocations: carpentry; rehabbing. Home: 6325 Pernod Ave Saint Louis MO 63139 Office: PO Box 350 Crystal City MO 63019

SIVE, REBECCA ANNE, public affairs company executive; b. N.Y.C., Jan. 29, 1950; d. David and Mary (Robinson) S.; m. Clark Steven Tomashefsky, June 18, 1972. B.A., Carleton Coll., 1972; M.A. in Am. History, U. Ill., Chgo., 1975. Asst. to chmn. of pres.' task force on vocations Carleton Coll., Northfield, Minn., 1972; asst. to acquisitions librarian Am. Hosp. Assn., Chgo., 1973; research asst. Jane Addams Hull House, Chgo., 1974; instr. Loop Coll., Chgo., 1975, Columbia Coll., Chgo., 1975-76; cons. Am. Jewish Com., Chgo., 1975, Ctr. for Urban Affairs, Northwestern U., Evanston, Ill., 1977, Ill. Consultation on Ethnicity in Edn., 1976, MLA, 1977; dir. Ill. Women's History Project, 1975-76; founder, exec. dir. Midwest Women's Ctr., Chgo., 1977-81; exec. dir. Playboy Found., 1981-84; v.p. pub. affairs/pub. relations Playboy Video Corp., 1985; v.p. pub. affairs Playboy Enterprises, Inc., Chgo., 1985-86; pres. The Sive Group, Inc., Chgo., 1986—; guest speaker various ednl. orgns., 1972—; instr. Roosevelt U., Chgo., 1977-78; dir. spl. projects Inst. on Pluralism and Group Identity, Am. Jewish Com., Chgo., 1975-77; cons. Nat. Women's Polit. Caucus, 1978-80; bd. dirs. NOVA Health Systems, Woodlawn Community Devel. Corp.; trainer Midwest Acad.; mem. adv. bd. urban studies program Associated Colls. Midwest; proposal reviewer NEH. Contbr. articles to profl. jours. Commr. Chgo. Park Dist., 1986—; mem. steering com. Ill. Commn. on Human Relations, 1976; mem. structure com. Nat. Women's Agenda Coalition, 1976-77; del.-at-large Nat. Women's conf., 1977; mem. Ill. Gov.'s Com. on Displaced Homemakers, 1979-81, Ill. coordinating com., Internat Womens Yr.; coordinator Ill. Internat. Women's Yr. Photog. Exhbn., 1977; mem. Ill. Employment and Tng. Council; mem. employment com. Ill. Com. on Status of Women; bd. dirs. Nat. Abortion Rights Action League and NARAL Found., Ill. div. ACLU, Midwest Women's Ctr. Recipient award for outstanding community leadership YWCA Met. Chgo., 1979. Mem. ACLU; mem Women's Inst. for Freedom of Press (assoc.). Home: 3529 N Marshfield Chicago IL 60657 Office: The Sive Group 359 W Chicago Ave Suite 300 Chicago IL 60610

SIZEMORE, DONALD DEAN, statistician; b. Detroit, Oct. 21, 1951; s. Charles Stanley and Rilda Marie (Schoneman) S.; m. Rhonda Lynn Smith, May 12, 1973; children—Rebecca Lynn, Christopher Dean. B.S., U. Mich., 1973; M.B.A., Eastern Mich. U., 1982. Geog. analyst Hwy. Safety Inst., Ann Arbor, Mich., 1970-73; staff asst. Mich. Bell Telephone Co., Southfield, 1973-76, statistician, Detroit, 1976-78, sr. statistician, 1978—; high sch. vis. lectr., Ann Arbor, 1983—. Chmn. adv. bd. Northside Community Ch., Ann Arbor, 1976-77. Mem. Am. Statis. Assn., Math. Assn. Am., Beta Gamma Sigma. Republican. Baptist. Avocations: speleology; space exploration; computing, tennis, geography. Home: 3216 Baylis Dr Ann Arbor MI 48108 Office: Mich Bell Telephone Co 444 Michigan Ave Room 1440 Detroit MI 48226

SKAALERUD, BJORN DAVID, retail furniture design executive; b. Feiring, Norway, Oct. 7, 1931; came to U.S. 1948, naturalized 1954; m. Anne Signe Solberg, Aug. 1, 1953 (div. 1975); children—Karin Signe Deger, Lisbeth, Pia Ann; m. Sunny Orlina, Sept. 13, 1975. Student Bklyn. Coll., 1952, Bklyn. Poly. U., 1953-55. Sales mgr. Royal System, Inc., N.Y.C., 1959-61, Dux, Inc., Burlingame, Calif., 1961-63; pvt. practice, N.Y.C., 1963-73; product mgr. Standard Oil Ind., Chgo., 1973-76; sales mgr. Eidsvold Mobel, Norway, 1976-79; tng. coordinator Scandinavian Design, Evanston, Ill., 1979—; bd. dirs. Norway Am. Hosp., Chgo., 1971-73. Recipient Woodbadge Tng. award Boy Scouts Am., 1964. Republican. Lutheran. Clubs: Norwegian (Bklyn.) (pres. 1969); Sons of Norway (Chgo.). Lodge: Masons. Avocations: golf, Norwegian language instruction. Home: 4720 Madison St Skokie IL 60076 Office: Scandinavian Design Inc 820 Church St Evanston IL 60201

SKALL, TERRY ROBERTSON, newspaper editor; b. Chgo., May 3, 1943; d. Robert Irving and Beatrice Hannah (Winter) Robertson; m. Richard A. Skall, May 23, 1963; children—Barbara, Jeffrey, David. Student Northwestern U., 1961-63; B.S., Western Res. U., 1966. News editor Chagrin Valley Pub. Co., Chagrin Falls, Ohio, 1974-80; editor-in-chief Chagrin Valley-Solon Times, Chagrin Falls, 1980—; freelance travel writer, 1983—. Mem. Sigma Delta Chi (award for editorial writing 1980, award for news reporting 1981). Office: Chagrin Valley/Solon Times Box 150 34 S Main St Chagrin Falls OH 44022

SKATZES, DAWERANCE HORACE, retired educator; b. Delaware, Ohio, Aug. 21, 1914; s. Carl Henry and Eulalia (Strickler) S.; B.S., Ohio U., 1951, M.Ed., 1954; postgrad. Ohio State U., 1958-59, 67-73, Muskingum Coll., 1965-66; m. Ruth Helen Jones, Apr. 1, 1941 (div. June 1949); children—Thelma Ruth Skatzes Moore, Elta Anne Skatzes George, Carl Alvin, Neatha Elaine Skatzes Marler, August Brent; m. 2d, Mildred M. Stillion, Feb. 18, 1975. Transient laborer, 1932-36; enrollee Civilian Conservation Corps, Price, Utah, 1936-37; unit clk. Soil Conservation Service, Price, 1938-41; field office mgr. Hunt & Frandsen, Gen. Contractors, Elko, Nev., 1942-44; boiler operator, supt. bldgs. and property Delaware (Ohio) City Schs., 1946-49; tchr. South Zanesville (Ohio) High Sch., 1951-54, 58-59; supt. Wills Local Sch. Dist., Old Washington, Ohio, 1954-58, Somerset (Ohio) Sch., 1959-60; prin. Adamsville (Ohio) Elem. Sch., 1960-61; supt. Quaker City (Ohio) Sch. Dist., 1961-62; prin. Valley High and Elementary Sch., Buffalo, Ohio, 1962-66; tchr. Columbus City Schs., 1967-74. Mayor, Old Washington, Ohio, 1975-79, clk.-treas., 1982—; Democratic candidate state rep., 1960-74. Served with U.S. Army, World War II. Mem. Nat. Soc. Study of Edn., Am. Assn. Sch Adminstrs., Nat. Council Tchrs. of Math., Acad. Polit. and Social Sci., Ohio Hist. Soc., Am. Legion, Am. Def. Preparedness Assn., Assn. U.S. Army, 37th Div. Vets. Assn., Kappa Delta Pi. Clubs: Eagles, Elks, Moose, Masons, Shriners. Home: Old Washington OH 43768

SKEA, NEIL EUGENE, podiatrist; b. Hot Springs, S.D., Feb. 18, 1955; s. Harry Ross and Phyllis Marie (Stearns) S.; m. Julie Kay Van Etten. BS, Evangel Coll., 1977; DPM, Ill. Coll. of Podiatric Medicine, 1981. Diplomate Nat. Bd. Podiatry Examiners. Podiatrist Rapid City, S.D., 1981—; cons. Ft. Meade V.A. Med. Ctr., 1981—, City Nursing Homes, Rapid City, 1981—. Mem. S.D. Podiatric Med. Assn. (v.p. 1981-82, sec./treas. 1982-86, nat. del. 1986—), Am. Podiatric Med. Assn. (S.D. del. 1986—, Podiatry Recognition award 1985), Am. Acad. Podiatry Administrn., Am. Acad. Podiatric Sports Medicine (assoc.), S.D. Bd. Podiatry (v.p. 1985-86, sec./treas. 1987—), Jaycees (chaplain 1983). Republican. Mem. Assembly of God Ch. Avocations: photography, skiing, hiking, bicycling, fly fishing. Home: 3602 Meadowbrook Dr Rapid City SD 57702 Office: 505 Kansas City St #301 Rapid City SD 57701

SKEANS, CAROLOU, education educator; b. Dayton, Ohio, Nov. 26, 1932; s. Ledford and Sue Ann (Brown) Smith; children: Max Howard, Mark Timothy. BA, Georgetown Coll., 1964; MEd, U. Cin., 1969, EdD, 1980. Cert. tchr. bus. and music; cert. supr. bus. office edn. Tchr. Johnsonville New Lebanon (Ohio) High Sch., 1964-65; coordinator Trotwood (Ohio)-Madison High Sch., 1965-75; assoc. prof. Miami U., Middletown, Ohio, 1975—; cons. Nat. Adv. Council, Columbus, Ohio, 1967, Armco Steel Corp., Middletown, 1977-78, Fifth Third Bank, Cin., 1979-80. Co-author: Advanced Information Processing, 1980; editor (book) Office Procedures, 1984. Choir dir. Triumphant Luth. Ch., Trotwood, 1964-66, Ft. McKinley Meth. Ch., Dayton, 1967-75. Georgetown U. scholar 1961, U. Cin. scholar 1977. Mem. Adminstrv . Mgmt. Soc. (coll. advisor), Beta Gamma Sigma, Delta Omicron (scholarship coordinator 1981-83), Delta Pi Epsilon. Republican. Baptist. Office: Miami U 4200 E University Blvd Middletown OH 45042

SKELTON, ISAAC NEWTON, IV (IKE SKELTON), congressman; b. Lexington, Mo., Dec. 20, 1931; s. Isaac Newton and Carolyn (Boone) S.; m. Susan B. Anding, July 22, 1961; children: Ike, Jim, Page. AB, U. Mo., 1953, LLB, 1956. Bar: Mo. 1956. Sole practice Lexington; pros. atty. Lafayette County, Mo., 1957-60; spl. asst. atty. gen. State of Mo., 1961-63; mem. Mo. Senate from 28th dist., 1971-77, 95th-100th Congresses from 4th Mo. Dist., 1977—. Active Cub Scouts. Mem. Phi Beta Kappa, Sigma Chi. Democrat. Mem. Christian Ch. Clubs: Masons, Shriners, Elks. Home: 2008 South St Lexington MO 64067 Office: 2453 Rayburn House Office Bldg Washington DC 20515

SKENDER, LAVERNE JANET, electric motor services co. exec.; b. Berwyn, Ill., Aug. 28, 1935; d. Edward Louis and Philamina Tillie (Baumruk) Stedron; A.A., Morton Jr. Coll., 1955; m. George Joseph Skender, June 9, 1956 (dec.); children—Jeffrey Scott, Patricia Diane, Edward George, Jacalyn Louise, Amy Lynn. Sec., Sears Roebuck, 1952-58; asst. purchasing agt. Prater Industries, 1967-69; sec. Dykema & Dykema, 1970-71; outside salesman DeBar Electric Motors, Chgo., 1971-83; pres. City Suburban Electric Motors, Inc., 1983—; dir. Stedcor Corp. Pres. U.S. Navy League, Forest Park, 1976, 77, 79, 81, 82; active NOW; bd. dirs. Fillmore Family Services. Named to scroll of honor U.S. Navy League. Mem. Elec. Apparatus Service Assn. (mem. mgmt.), Elec. Motor Distbrs., Elec. Assn., Cicero Assn. Bus. and Industry, Greater O'Hare C of C., Northwest Suburban Assn. Commerce and Industry, Women in Elec. Trades, Women in Bus., Nat. Assn. Women Bus. Owners, Am. Soc. Profl. and Exec. Women, Nat. Assn. Female Execs. Clubs: West Suburban Exec., West Suburban Breakfast (dir. 1980-82), Bus. and Profl. Women (legis. chmn. Cicero, 1976-77, 80-81, pres. 1974-75, 79-71, Nike award, dist. dir. 1976, state expansion chmn., 1980-81). First woman in outside motor sales, first woman shop foreman, first woman pres. of motor shop, first woman pres. U.S. Navy League Council. Home: 2211 W Clifton Pl Hoffman Estates IL 60195 Office: 2740 N Pulaski Rd Chicago IL 60639

SKERRY, PHILIP JOHN, English educator; b. Boston, May 6, 1944; s. Angelina (Creilson) S.; m. Amy Simon, June 15, 1968; children: Jessica Blythe, Ethan Amadeus. BA in English, U. Mass., 1966; MA in English, Case Western Res. U., 1968; PhD, Ind. U. of Pa., 1975. Instr. English Lakeland Community Coll., Mentor, Ohio, 1968-69; prof. Lakeland Community Coll., Mentor, 1973—; assoc. prof. Tarrant County Jr. Coll., Hurst, Tex., 1971-73; project dir. Early English Composition Assessment Program Ohio Bd. Regents, Columbus, 1985—. Contbr. articles to profl. jours.; host TV talk show Western Res. Connection, 1980-86. Chmn. Jump Rope for your Heart program Am. Heart Assn., Cleve., 1980-83, mem. adv. com., 1984. NEH grantee, 1983. Mem. Nat. Council Tchrs. English, Am. Film Inst., Modern Language Assn., Popular Culture Assn. Democrat. Avocations: rope jumping, collecting movies. Home: 3655 Sutherland Rd Shaker Heights OH 44122 Office: Lakeland Community College Mentor OH 44060

SKIBINSKI, ARNOLD F., industrial engineer; b. Chgo., Dec. 24, 1950; s. Arnold G. and Marie V. (Bufano) S.; m. JoAnne Politano, Nov. 8, 1975; children: Brian, Joseph. AA, Thornton Community Coll., 1970; BS, No. Ill. U., 1972, MS, 1973. Cert. mfg. engr. Process engr. automotive assembly div. Ford Motor Co., Allen Park, Mich., 1973-74; mgr. mfg. engring. Graver Energy Systems div. Aero-Jet Gen. Corp., East Chicago, Ind., 1974-82; sr. indsl. engr. Andrew Corp., Orland Park, Ill., 1982—. Mem. Soc. Mfg. Engrs. (cert.), Computer and Automated Systems Assn., Robotics Inst. Am., Am. Inst. Indsl. Eng. (sr.). Roman Catholic. Avocation: tennis. Home: 3402 191st St Lansing IL 60438 Office: Andrew Corp 10500 W 153d St Orland Park IL 60462

SKIE, CHARLES MARTIN, transportation executive; b. Chgo., July 19, 1938; s. Carl Oliver and Edith (Otten) S.; m. Diane Chiappe, Sept. 1, 1962; children: Martin, Lisa, David, Jason. BBA, Roosevelt U., 1963; MBA, Xavier U., 1983. CPA, Ill. Budget dir. Gillette Corp., Chgo., 1963-74; regional dir. SCA Services, Chgo., 1974-78; dir. corp. devel. Midland Enterprises, Cin., 1978-83, v.p. transp., 1983—. Served with USN, 1956-59. Mem. Am. Inst. CPA's, Assn. Corp. Growth. Republican. Roman Catholic. Lodge: Rotary. Office: Midland Enterprises Inc 580 Walnut Cincinnati OH 45202

SKIERKIEWICZ, ALAN JOHN, broadcast and maintenance and design engineer; b. Chgo., Apr. 15, 1951; s. Eugene James and Mary Frances (Bava) S.; m. Dorothy Mae Pelz, Oct. 20, 1973; children: Mark Alan, Karen Elaine. BS, Bradley U., 1973. Engr. Sta. WPTVúTV, Peoria, Ill., 1969-73, Sta. WTTW-TV, Chgo., 1973—. Mem. Soc. Broadcast Engrs. (cert. broadcast technologist), Audio Engring. Soc., Internat. Brotherhood Electrical Workers (bd. dirs. local 1220 1984-86, pres. local 1220 1986—). Roman Catholic. Avocations: ham radio, personal computers, studying acoustics and studio sound systems. Home: 316 Robert Wheeling IL 60090 Office: Sta WTTW-TV 5400 N Saint Louis Chicago IL 60625

SKIEST, EUGENE NORMAN, chemical company executive; b. Worcester, Mass., Feb. 2, 1935; s. Hyman Arthur and Dorothy Ida (Brickman) S.; m. Toby Ann Aisenberg, Aug. 14, 1957 (div. 1973); children—Jody, Daniel, Nancy; m. Carol Tata, Nov. 26, 1974. B.S., Mass. Coll. Pharmacy, 1956; M.S., U. Mich., 1958; Ph.D., 1961. Research chemist Foster Grant Co., Leominster, Mass., 1961-62; sr. research chemist Thompson Chem. Co., Atteboro, Mass., 1962-64; pres. C&S Polymers, Westminster, Mass., 1965-66; group leader Borden Chem. Co., Leominster, 1966-69, devel. mgr., 1969-77, dir. devel. and applications, 1976-78; assoc. dir. quality assurance and compliance Borden, Inc., Columbus, Ohio, 1978-79, dir. quality assurance and compliance, 1979-81, corp. tech. dir. chems., 1981-84, corp. tech. dir., 1984—, co. rep. to Ind. Research Inst., 1983—. Contbr. articles, papers to profl. publs. Patentee in field. Bd. dirs. Pickawillany Assn., Westerville, Ohio, 1981. Mem. Am. Chem. Soc., Soc. Plastics Engrs., Formaldehyde Inst. (chmn. tech. com. 1979-84, bd. dirs. 1981, vice chmn. exec. com. 1986—), Chem. Mfrs. Assn. (chmn. task force 1983—), Nat. Paint and Coating Assn., Synthetic Organic Chem. Mfg. Assn. (govt. affairs com. 1979-83), Soc. Plastics Industries (vinyl toxicology subcom. 1978-82, vinyl acetate task force 1980-82, chmn. ad hoc packaging risk assessment com. 1978-81). Club: Continental Tennis. Avocations: tennis, reading, sports. Home: 134 Green Springs Dr Worthington OH 43085 Office: Borden Inc 960 Kingsmill Pkwy Columbus OH 43229

SKILLING, DAVID VAN DIEST, manufacturing executive; b. St. Louis, Sept. 16, 1933; s. David Miller Jr. and Eloise Margaret (van Diest) S.; m. Barbara Jo Chaney, Aug. 4, 1956; children: Kimberly Alice, Mark Chaney. BS, Colo. Coll., 1955; MBA, Pepperdine U., 1977. With TRW, Inc., Los Angeles, 1970—, dir. mktg. energy group, 1978-83, v.p. planning and devel., 1983—, also bd. dirs. Norton-TRW Ceramics subs.; bd. dirs. Metals Exploration Corp, St. Louis. Bd. dirs. Cleve. State U. Found., 1984—. Served to lt. USN, 1955-58. Mem. IEEE, Am. Petroleum Inst., Nat. Ocean Industries Assn. (bd. dirs. 1984—), Petroleum Equipment Suppliers Assn., (bd. dirs. 1982—). Republican. Clubs: Petroleum (Los Angeles); Mayfield Country (Cleve.); Garden of Gods (Colorado Springs, Colo.). Office: TRW Inc 1900 Richmond Rd Cleveland OH 44124

SKILLMAN, RODNEY, manufacturing company executive. Pres. Am. Western Corp., Sioux Falls, S.D. Office: Am Western Corp 1208 W. Elkhorn St Sioux Falls SD 57104 *

SKINNER, DAVID BERNT, surgeon, educator; b. Joliet, Ill., Apr. 28, 1935; s. James Madden and Bertha Elinor (Tapper) S.; m. May Elinor Tischer, Aug. 25, 1956; children: Linda Elinor, Kristin Anne, Carise Berntine, Margaret Leigh. B.A. with high honors, U. Rochester, N.Y., 1958, Sc.D. (hon.), 1980; M.D. cum laude, Yale U., 1959. Diplomate: Am. Bd. Surgery (dir. 1974-80), Am. Bd. Thoracic Surgery. Intern, then resident in surgery Mass. Gen. Hosp., Boston, 1959-65; sr. registrar in thoracic surgery Frenchay Hosp., Bristol, Eng., 1963-64; teaching fellow Harvard U. Med. Sch., 1965; from asst. prof. surgery to prof. Johns Hopkins U. Med. Sch., also surgeon Johns Hopkins Hosp., 1968-72; Dallas B. Phemister prof. surgery, chmn. dept. U. Chgo. Hosps. and Clinics, 1972—; dir. Omnis Surg. Inc., 1984-85; mem. President's Biomed. Research Panel, 1975-76; past cons. USPHS, Office Surgeon Gen. U.S. Navy. Co-author: Gastroesophageal Reflux and Hiatal Hernia, 1972; editor: Current Topics in Surg. Research, 1969-71, Jour. Surg. Research, 1972—; co-editor: Surgical Treatment of Digestive Disease, 1985, Esophageal Disorders, 1985, Reconstructive Surgery of the Gastrointestinal Tract, 1985; mem. editorial bd.: Jour. Thoracic and Cardiovascular Surgery, Annals of Surgery, Surg. Gastroenterology; contbr. profl. jours., chpts. in books. Elder Fourth Presbyn. Ch., Chgo., 1976—, clk. of session, 1978-82, 84—; bd. visitors Cornell U. Med. Coll., 1980—. Served to maj. M.C. USAF, 1966-68. John and Mary Markle scholar acad. medicine, 1969-74. Fellow ACS; mem. AMA, Internat. Surg. Group, Am., Western, So. surg. assns., Soc. Univ. Surgeons (pres. 1978-79), Am. Soc. Artificial Internal Organs (pres. 1977), Soc. Surg. Chmn. (pres. 1980-82), Am. Assn. Thoracic Surgery (council 1981-86), Soc. Vascular Surgery, Soc. Thoracic Surgery, Soc. Pelvic Surgeons, Soc. Surgery Alimentary Tract, Société Internationale de Chirurgie, Collegium Internationale Chirurgiae Digestivae, Am. Coll. Chest Physicians, Central Surg. Soc., Internat. Soc. Diseases Esophogus (v.p. 1983-86, pres. 1986—), Assn. Acad. Surgery, Halsted Soc., Soc. Clin. Surgery, Phi Beta Kappa, Alpha Omega Alpha. Clubs: Quadrangle (Chgo.); Cosmos (Washington). Home: 5490 South Shore Dr Chicago IL 60615 Office: 5841 S Maryland Ave Chicago IL 60637

SKINNER, DAVID ERREST, management consultant; b. Detroit, Dec. 21, 1954; s. James H. and Ruth M. (Hart) S. BA in Econs. and Psychology with honors, U. Mich., 1978, MBA, 1980. Product mktg. mgr. Stanley Automatic Openers, Detroit, 1980-84; mktg. mgr. Tribune div. United Cable Communications, Royal Oak, Mich., 1984-86; pres. Mktg. and Planning Systems, Rochester, Mich., 1986—. Avocations: music, cycling, woodworking. Home and Office: 316 W 3d St Rochester MI 48063

SKINNER, NED LLOYD, grain merchandising executive; b. Ames, Iowa, Aug. 16, 1952; s. Robert Lee and Joy Joan (Lloyd) S.; m. Paula Sue Moll, Nov. 22, 1975; children: Sarah Elizabeth, Andrea Joy. BS in Indsl. Adminstrn., Iowa State U., 1974; MBA, Harvard U., 1981. Auditor Deere & Co., Moline, Ill., 1974; grain merchandiser Gen. Mills Inc., Mpls., 1974-79; exec. v.p. Kerr Pacific Corp., Portland, Oreg., 1981-82; mgr. Western region Pillsbury Co., Mpls., 1982—; cons. HFM Inc., Honolulu, 1980. Alt. del. Rep. Nat. Conv., Miami, Fla., 1972; del. State Rep. Conv., Des Moines, 1972, St. Paul, 1976; Rep. Precinct chmn., Ames, Iowa 1972, Crystal, Minn., 1976; bd. dirs. Stockton (Calif.) Symphony Orchestra, 1979, Harvard Coop. Soc. 1980-81; pres. New Rose Theatre, Portland, Oreg., 1981-83. Named one of Outstanding Young Men of Am., Jaycees, Cambridge, Mass., 1980; named one of Outstanding Young Alumnus, Iowa State U., 1987—. Mem. N.W. Terminal Elevator Assn. (bd. dirs. 1985—, pres. 1987—), Nat. Grain and Feed Assn. (country elevator com. 1986—), Mpls. Grain Shippers Assn. (bd. dirs. 1983—), Mpls. Grain Exchange (arbitration com. 1983—), Iowa Grain and Feed Assn. (arbitration com. 1983—), Grain Engring. and Processing Soc., Harvard Bus. Sch. Club Minn. (bd. dirs. 1987). Mem. Ch. of Christ. Clubs: Wayzata (Minn.) Country; Mpls. Athletic (squash com.), Northwest Racquet. Avocations: squash, rugby, golfing, tennis, skiing. Home: 18915 4th Ave N Plymouth MN 55447 Office: Pillsbury Co 480 Grain Exchange Minneapolis MN 55415

SKINNER, ROLLAND GENE, electric company executive; b. Ogallala, Nebr., Apr. 15, 1941; s. Neal Ray S. and Mildred Fay (Dowlar) Brill; m. Patricia Ann Worley, June 18, 1965; children: Shardel Shae, Brett Deon, Keri Lynn. Student, U. Wyoming. 1960-62. Lineman, meter reader Nebr. Pub. Power Dist., Ogallala, 1964-69, local rep., 1969-73; lineman Northwest Rural Pub. Power Dist., Hay Springs, 1973-74, ops. mgr., 1974-81, mgr., 1981—; speaker in field. Chmn. Tri-State Strategic Load Bldg. Comn., Denver, 1982—; mem. mgmt. adv. com. Basin Electric G&T., Bismark, N.D., 1984—. Mem. Hay Springs Fire Dept., 1965-83, pres., 1972. Served to sgt. USNG, 1963-69. Mem. Nebr. REA Mgrs. Assn. (past pres.), Tri-State G&T Mgrs. Assn. (pres. 1986-87), Hay Springs C. of C. (pres. 1972), Nebr. Job Tng. and Safety Com., Nebr. Inter-Industry Electric Council, Nebr. Rural Electric Assn. (legis. com.), Am. Legion. Democrat. Methodist. Lodges: Masons, Elks. Home: 224 N Post St PO Box 416 Hay Springs NE 69347 Office: Northwest Rural Pub Power Dist S Hwy 87 PO Box 249 Hay Springs NE 69347

SKIRBALL, RICHARD LEWIS, family therapist; b. Columbus, Ohio, July 2, 1951; s. Alan and Betty Jean (Greene) S.; m. Donna Sue Danco, Dec. 23, 1972; children: Alicia, Richard Jr. BS, Bradley U., 1972; MEd, So. Ill. U., 1978; PhD, St. Louis U., 1985. Cert. substance abuse counselor. Mental health specialist Madison County Mental Health Ctr., Granite City, Ill., 1978-81; alcoholism counselor Nat. Council on Alcoholism, St. Louis, 1981-85; Familycare coordinator Family and Personal Support Ctrs. Greater St. Louis, 1985—; v.p. Coalition on Alcoholism and Other Chem. Dependencies, St. Louis, 1986-87, pres., 1987—. Bd. dirs. Coordinated Youth Services, Granite City, 1980—. Assoc. mem. Am. Assn. Marriage and Family Therapists. Presbyterian. Avocations: swimming, racquetball, golf, home computers, photography. Home: 2572 Westmorland Dr Granite City IL 62040 Office: Family and Personal Support Ctrs Greater St Louis 9109 Watson Rd Saint Louis MO 63126

SKJORDAHL, EMILY SUE, nurse; b. Clinton, Ind., Mar. 20, 1944; d. Paul Kenneth and Esther Louise (Frist) Foltz; m. Jeffrey Wayne Skjordahl, Sept. 12, 1964; children: Heidi W., Martin Scott. Student, Ind. U., Terre Haute, 1962-64; A in Applied Sci. and Nursing, Coll. of Lake County, 1982; student, Barat Coll., Lake Forest, Ill., 1984. Registered nurse. Staff nurse SCCU Victory Meml. Hosp., Waukegan, Ill., 1982-84; nurse Victory Immediate Care Ctr., Gurnee, Ill., 1984-85, adminstrv. asst., 1985, nursing supr., 1985—; mem. radiology adv. com. Coll. Lake County, Grayslake, Ill., 1985-86. Mem. Women in Mgmt., Phi Theta Kappa. Republican. Methodist. Avocations: sewing, needlework. Home: 18490 W Washington St Gurnee IL 60031

SKOIEN, GARY J., state agency administrator; b. Chgo., Jan. 27, 1954; s. Willard J. and Shirley R. (Tess) S.; m. Maureen Mullady. AB cum laude, Colgate U., 1976; M of Pub. Policy, U. Mich., 1978. Budget analyst Ill. Bur. Budget, Springfield, 1978-80; asst. for human services Office of Gov. of Ill., Springfield, 1980-83; exec. dir. Ill. Capital Devel. Bd., Springfield and Chgo., 1983—. Rep. precint committeeman Palatine (Ill.) Twp., 1984—. Lutheran. Club: Colgate of Chgo. Avocations: politics, racquetball, reading. Home: 248 E Briarwood Ln Palatine IL 60067 Office: Ill Capital Devel Bd 100 W Randolph St 14th Floor Chicago IL 60601

SKOLNICK, VIVIAN BLAIR, clinical psychologist; b. Norfolk, Va., Apr. 20, 1929; d. Morris L. and Pauline (Kleinstein) Blair; m. Irving H. Skolnick, Aug. 16, 1949; children—Blair, Sarelle. B.A., Chgo. State U., 1969; M.S., Ill. Inst. Tech., 1971, Ph.D. in Psychology, 1974. Registered psychologist, Ill. Psychologist, chief withdrawal section Ill. Drug Abuse Program, Chgo., 1971-73; head psychologist drug withdrawal program, U. Chgo., 1973-74; clin. assoc. U. Ill., Chgo., 1981—; pvt. practice psychology, Chgo., 1974—; cons. in field. Mem. Chgo. Psychoanalytic Psychology Assn., Am. Personnel and Guidance Assn., Am. Psychol. Assn., Chgo. Assn. Psychoanalytic Psychology, Am. Soc. Clin. Hypnosis, Soc. Clin. and Exptl. Hypnosis, Nat. Register Health Service Providers, Am. Mental Health Aid to Israel (nat. bd. mem.). Contbr. articles to prof. jours. in field. Office: 180 N Michigan Ave Chicago IL 60601

SKOLNIK, DAVID ERWIN, financial systems analyst; b. Cleve., Oct. 31, 1949; s. Marvin and Ruth (Kovit) S.; m. Linda Susan Pollack, Mar. 31, 1973; children: Carla Denise, Robyn Laurel. BS in Acctg., Ohio State U., 1971. CPA, Ohio. Chief acct. Gray Drug Fair, Cleve., 1976-82, mgr. acctg. systems, 1982-84; fin. systems analyst Soc. Corp., Cleve., 1984, fin. systems officer, 1984-86, fin. systems research officer, 1986—. Scoutmaster Boy Scouts Am., Cleve., 1971-77. Mem. Ohio Soc. CPA's, Am. Inst. CPA's, Am. Inst. Banking. Jewish. Avocations: golf, bowling, home repairs. Home: 4130 Stonehaven Rd South Euclid OH 44121 Office: Soc Corp 2025 Ontario Cleveland OH 44115

SKONEY, SOPHIE ESSA, educational administrator; b. Detroit, Jan. 29, 1929; d. George Essa and Helena (Dihmes) Cokalay; Ph.B., U. Detroit, 1951; M.Ed., Wayne State U., 1960, Ed.D., 1975; postgrad. Harvard Grad. Sch. Edn., 1986-87; m. Daniel J. Skoney, Dec. 28, 1957; children—Joseph Anthony, James Francis, Carol Anne. Tchr. elem. sch. Detroit Bd. Edn., 1952-69, remedial reading specialist, 1969-70, curriculum coordinator, 1970-71, region 6 article 3 title I coordinator, 1971-83, area E curriculum devel. specialist, 1984—; cons. in field. Mem. Wayne State U. Edn. Alumni Assn. (pres. bd. govs. 1979-80, newsletter editor 1975-77, 80—), Macomb Dental Aux. (pres. 1969-70), Mich. Dental Aux. (pres. 1980-81), Am.-Assn. Sch. Adminstrs., Wayne State U. Alumni Assn. (dir., v.p. 1985-86), Internat. Reading Assn., Mich. Reading Assn., Mich. Assn. State and Fed. Program Specialists, Profl. Women's Network (newsletter editor 1981-83, pres. 1985-87), Assn. for Supervision and Curriculum Devel., Delta Kappa Gamma, Beta Sigma Phi, Phi Delta Kappa. Roman Catholic. Home: 20813 Lakeland St St Clair Shores MI 48081 Office: Detroit Pub Schs 1121 E McNichols Detroit MI 48203

SKORA, ALAN PATRICK, osteopath, surgeon; b. Detroit, Mar. 10, 1947; s. Charles and Ann M. (Roman) S.; m. Susan Sundman, May 1, 1977. BS, Wayne State U., 1970; DO, Chgo. Coll. Osteo. Medicine, 1975. Diplomate Am. Bd. Surgery. Intern Chgo. Osteo. Hosp., 1975-76, resident, 1976-80; practice medicine specializing in surgery Grand Rapids, Mich., 1983—; mem. staff Chgo. Osteo. Hosp., 1975-83, Met. Hosp., Grand Rapids, 1983—; resident trainer Met. Hosp. ,1983—. Mem. Am. Osteo. Assn., Mich. Assn. Osteo. Physicians and Surgeons, Kent County Assn. Osteo. Physicians and Surgeons, Am. Coll. Osteo. Surgeons, Chgo. Coll. Osteo. Medicine Alumni Assn., Polish Heritage Soc. Clubs: Sportsman's (Berrien Springs, Mich.), Steelheaders (St. Joseph, Mich.). Avocations: fishing, photography, travel, audio, video.

SKOVHOLT, THOMAS MEYER, psychology educator; b. St. Paul, Sept. 11, 1943; s. Joseph William and Elvera Helen (Meyer) S.; m. Catherine Louise Juve, June 18, 1967; children: Rachel, David. BA, St. Olaf Coll., 1966; MEd, U. Mo., 1971, PhD, 1973. Lic. cons. psychologist, Minn.; diplomate Am. Bd. Profl. Psychology. Asst. prof. U. Fla., Gainesville, 1973-77; asst. prof. U. Minn., Mpls., 1977-80, assoc. prof., 1980-85, prof., 1985—; cons. in psychology, Mpls., 1977—. Contbr. articles to profl. jours. Fulbright prof. Council for Internat. Exchange of Scholars, 1982. Mem. Am. Psychol. Assn., Am. Assn. for Counseling and Devel., Nat. Career Devel. Assn., Fulbright Alumni Assn. Mem. United Ch. of Christ. Avocations: physical fitness, photography, travel. Home: 2084 Juliet Ave Saint Paul MN 55105 Office: U Minn 106 Nicholson Hall Minneapolis MN 55455

SKOW, ROBERT JOSEPH, insurance and real estate executive; b. Des Moines, Feb. 1, 1952; s. Leonard James and Rosemary Joan (Hermsen) S.; m. Connie Jean Van Horn, Aug. 18, 1973; children: Emily, Laura. BS, Drake U., 1974. Cert. CPCU. Claims adjuster Employer Mut., Des Moines, 1974-75, IMT Ins. Co., Des Moines, 1975-78; prin., owner Skow Ins. and Real Estate, Guthrie Ctr., Iowa, 1978—; ins. cons. Iowa area colls., 1980—. Rep. State of Iowa, Des Moines, 1982—; co-chair Guthrie Dems., 1980—. Mem. Ind. Ins. Agts., Iowa Ind. Ins. Agts. (Young Agt. Yr. 1985), Realtors Assocs., CPCU Assoc., Guthrie Ctr. C. of C. (v.p. 1981, pres. 1982). Democrat. Roman Catholic. Lodges: Lions, KC. Avocations: gardening, canoeing. Home: 604 Division St Guthrie Center IA 50115 Office: Skow Ins & Real Estate PO Box 38 Guthrie Center IA 50115

SKOWRONSKI, RAYMOND, JR., dentist; b. Detroit, Oct. 23, 1956; s. Raymond Leonard and Antoinette Liberty (De Palma) S.; m. Mary Ann Brasile, Oct. 19, 1985. BS in Biology summa cum laude, U. Detroit, 1978, DDS, 1982. Assoc. dentist Dr. Patrick Angott, Waterford, Mich., 1982-83, Dr. Mullen Barrett, Grosse Pointe, Mich., 1982-83; pvt. practice dentistry St. Clair Shores, Mich., 1983—; clin. instr. dental hygiene Oakland U., Waterford, 1983; pre-clin. dental instr. U. Detroit, 1982—. Vol. musician Muscular Dystrophy Benefit, Warren, Mich., 1978-80, Retarded Children's Benefit for Christmas, Detroit and Warren, 1978-83, Leukemia Found., Macomb County, 1976—. Mem. ADA, Acad. Gen. Dentistry, U.S. Dental Inst., Assn. Functional Orthodontics, Macomb County Dental Assn., Psi Omega, Omicron Kappa Upsilon, Alpha Epsilon Delta, Alpha Sigma Nu. Roman Catholic. Avocations: saxophone, tennis, photography. Home: 36576 Melbourne Sterling Heights MI 48079 Office: 31512 Harper Saint Clair Shores MI 48082

SKOWRONSKI, VINCENT PAUL, concert violinist, classical recording company executive; b. Kenosha, Wis., Jan. 22, 1944; s. Vincent Edward and Eleonore Wanda (Solewska) S.; m. Helen-Kay Marie Eberley, July 15, 1972. MusB, Northwestern U., 1966, MusM, 1968. V.p. Eberley-Skowronski, Inc., Evanston, Ill., 1973—; broker rare instrument Strings & Things, Evanston, 1973, internat. sales coordinator, 1974; instr. violin Northwestern U., 1969-71; asst. prof. violin U. Wyo., 1971-72; dir. media communications E-S Mgmt., Evanston, 1985. Solo violinist deput Chgo. Youth Orch., 1959, Civic Orch., 1968; performing artist Am. Artist Gala, Puerto Rico, 1960, Young Am. Musicians, U. Mich. 1966, Artist Showcase, Sta. WGN-TV, 1966-71, A.M. Am., Sta. ABC-TV, 1977-79; numerous concert and recital in Europe, Cen.Am., Mex. and U.S.; artist, producer: Separate but Equal, 1976, All Brahms, 1977; artist, exec. producer Gentleman Gypsy, 1978, Strauss and Szymanowski, 1979, (sonata) Franck and Szymanowski, 1982; producer, annotator Opera Lady I, 1978, Eberley Sings Strauss, 1980, Am. Girl, 1983, Opera Lady II, 1984; guest performances numerous TV stas. Bd. dirs. Chgo. Youth Orch., 1973-77, v.p., 1974-77; adjudicator ice skating shows and competition Wilmette Park Dist., 1985-86; mem. mayor's founding com. Evanston Arts Council, 1974-75. Recipient Am. Fedn. Musicians award, 1961, McCormick Found. award Chicago Tribun1965. Mem. Am. Fedn. Musician, Sigma Nu. One of seven violinists chosen to represent U.S. in the IV Internat. TchaikovskyCompetition in Moscow. Office: EB-Sko Prodn 1726 1/2 Sherman Ave Evanston IL 60201

SKULAS, IRENE MICHELLE, science and health educator; b. Toledo, July 21, 1951; s. Michael Anthony and Christina Jean (Cherpas) S. BEd, U. Toledo, 1973, MA in Edn., 1975, PhD, 1982. Cert. tchr., Mich. Instr. Bedford Sr. High Sch., Temperance, Mich., 1973—, chmn. scis. dept., 1978—; homebound tchr. Washington Schs., Toledo, summer sch. tchr., 1978; cons. in field, 1982—. Vol. cons. Lucas County Rep. Party, Toledo, 1984; campiagn worker Bedford Pub. Schs., 1986. Grantee Argonne Nat. Lab, 1984, NSF, 1985. Mem. Am. Chemical Soc. (treas. 1984-85), Am. Pub. Health Assn., NEA, Mich. Edn. Assn., Bedford Edn. Assn., Mich. Sci. Tchrs. Assn., Kappa Delta Pi, Pi Lamda Theta, Phi Kappa Phi. Republican. Greek Orthodox. Office: Bedford Sr High Sch 8285 Jackman Temperance MI 48182

SKULINA, THOMAS RAYMOND, lawyer; b. Cleve., Sept. 14, 1933; s. John J. and Mary B. (Vesely) S. A.B., John Carroll U., 1955; J.D., Case Western Res. U., 1959, LL.M., 1962. Bar: Ohio 1959, U.S. Supreme Ct. 1964, ICC 1965. Ptnr. Skulina & Stringer, Cleve., 1967-72, Riemer Oberdank & Skulina, Cleve., 1978-81, Skulina, Fillo, Walters & Negrelli, 1981-86, Skulina & McKeon, Cleve., 1986—; atty. Penn Cen. Transp. Co., Cleve., 1960-65, asst. gen. atty., 1965-78, trial counsel, 1965-76; with Consol. Rail Corp., 1976-78; dir. High Temperature Systems, Inc., Active Chem. Systems, Inc.; tchr. comml. law Practicing Law Inst., N.Y.C., 1970. Contbr. articles to legal jours. Income tax and fed. fund coordinator Warrensville Heights, Ohio, 1970-77; spl. counsel City of N. Olmstead, Ohio, 1971-75; pres. Civil Service Commn., Cleve., 1977-86, referee, 1986—, fact-finder SERB, Ohio, 1986—; spl. counsel Ohio Atty. Gen., 1983—. Served with U.S. Army, 1959. Mem. Nat. Assn. R.R. Trial Counsel, Internat. Assn. Law and Sci., ABA, Cleve. Bar Assn., Ohio Bar Assn. (bd. govs. litigation sect. 1986—), Fed. Bar Assn., Pub. Law Practitioners Assn., Ohio Trial Lawyers Assn., Pub. Sector Labor Relations Assn. Democrat. Roman Catholic. Clubs: River Run Racquet, Lakewood Country. Home: 3162 W 165th St Cleveland OH 44111 Office: Skulina & McKeon 709 Ohio Savings Plaza 1801 E 9th St Cleveland OH 44113

SKUTT, RICHARD MICHAEL, lawyer; b. Pontiac, Mich., Sept. 25, 1947; s. Milton E. and Esther R. (Kayner) S. BS, Ea. Mich. U., 1969; JD cum laude, Wayne (Mich.) State U., 1972. Bar: Mich. 1972. Dir. Food Task Force, N.Y.C., 1974-76; atty. Food Research and Action Ctr., Washington, 1976-78; dir. Mich. Legal Services, Detroit, 1978-82; sole practice Detroit, 1982-85; ptnr. Glotta, Rawlings & Skutt, Detroit, 1985—. Author: (textbook) Materials on Legal Assistance to Migrant Farmworkers. Pres. LaSalle Townhouses Coop., Detroit, 1982-84. Mem. ABA, Nat. Lawyers Guild, Nat. Legal Aid and Defender's Assn., Mich. Bar Assn. (chmn. com. pro bono involvement, past chmn. standing com. civil liberties), Mich. Trial Lawyers Assn., Fedn. Fly Fishers, Trout Unltd. Democrat. Avocation: fly fishing. Home: 1366 Joliet Pl Detroit MI 48207 Office: Glotta Rawlings & Skutt 220 Bagley Suite 808 Detroit MI 48207

SKUTT, THOMAS JAMES, insurance company executive; b. Omaha, Nov. 1, 1930; s. Vestor Joseph and Angela (Anderson) S.; m. Jeanne Cecille Plunkett, Sept. 3, 1955; children: Mary Elizabeth Skutt Sutton, Kimberly Ann Skutt Norwood, Thomas V. J. BA, Yale U., 1952; LLB, Creighton U., 1957; postgrad., Harvard U., 1979. Ptnr. Spire, Morrow & Skutt, Omaha, 1961-69; with Mut. of Omaha, 1969—, exec. v.p., sec., 1980-81, vice chmn. bd. dirs., 1981-84, 1st vice chmn. bd. dirs., chief exec. officer, 1984-86, chmn. bd. dirs., chief exec. officer, 1986—, chmn. bd. dirs., chief exec. officer United of Omaha subs., 1986—; bd. dirs. United of Omaha, Norwest Bank Omaha. Mem. exec. bd. Mid-Am. Council Boy Scouts Am., 1980—; mem. consultation com. SAC, Omaha, 1984; bd. dirs. Boys Town, Omaha Zool. Soc., 1978—; gen. chmn. campaign United Way of Midlands, 1979-80, bd. dirs., 1981—; bd. dirs. Creighton U., Omaha, 1983—. Served to 1st lt. U.S. Army, 1952-54, Korea. Mem. Omaha C. of C. (bd. dirs. 1979—, chmn. 1983). Republican. Roman Catholic. Clubs: Mpls.; Yale of N.Y. (N.Y.C.). Lodge: Knights of Ak-Sar-Ben (bd. govs. 1985). Avocations: golf, tennis. Home: 656 N 57 St Omaha NE 68132 Office: Mut of Omaha Ins Co Mutual of Omaha Plaza Omaha NE 68175

SKUTT, VESTOR JOSEPH, insurance executive; b. Deadwood, S.D., Feb. 24, 1902; s. Roy N. and Catherine (Gorman) S.; m. Angela Anderson; children: Donald Joseph (dec.), Thomas James, Sally Jane (Mrs. John G. Desmond, Jr.). LLB, Creighton U., 1923; LLD (hon.), U. Omaha, 1958, U. Nebr. Coll. Medicine, 1964, Creighton U., 1971, Bellevue Coll., 1985, Coll. of St. Mary, 1986; LHD (hon.), U. S.D., 1977. Bar: Nebr. 1923. With Mut. of Omaha Ins. Co., 1924-86, various capacities, chmn. bd., 1953-86, chmn. emeritus, 1986; chmn. bd. United of Omaha Life Ins. Co., 1963-86, chmn. emeritus, 1986—; chmn. bd. Companion Life Ins. Co. of N.Y., 1963—, Mutual of Omaha Fund Mgmt. Co., 1968—; bd. dirs. emeritus FirsTier Bank, Omaha. Mem. pres.'s com. on Employment of the Handicapped, World Rehabilitation Fund, Inc., Nat. Council Boy Scouts Am., Am. Life Conv.; nat. co-chmn. NCCJ, 1978-87; nat. crusade chmn. Am. Cancer Soc., 1967; chmn. Nat. Alliance of Businessmen, 1976-77; Nebr. chmn. United Negro Coll. Fund, 1975, nat. distinguished service award, 1977; bd. dirs. Health Ins. Inst., 1972-75, trustee Creighton U., 1968-76, Nat. Little League Found., 1976—. Recipient Harold R. Gordon Meml. award, 1950; Air Force Exceptional Service medal, 1963; Golden Sword of Hope Am. Cancer Soc., 1966; named Scouting Man of Year, 1971, Man of Year Fedn. Ins. Counsel, 1971; recipient Disting. Nebraskalander award, 1984, Golden Plate award Am. Acad. Achievement, 1976, Disting. Service award World Rehabilitation Fund, 1983 Silver Buffalo award Boy Scouts Am., 1982, Corp. Leadership award, Nebr. chapter Arthritis Found., 1984; Citations Pres. Gerald Ford, Pres. Jimmy Carter. Mem. Nebr., Tex., Okla. bar. assns., Internat. Assn. Health Underwriters, Ins. Fedn. Nebr. (exec. council), Ins. Econs. Soc. Am., Fedn. Ins. Counsel. Clubs: Omaha Country, Omaha, Chicago, Marco Polo, Newcomen. Home: 400 N 62d St Omaha NE 68132 Office: Mut of Omaha Ins Co Mutual of Omaha Plaza Omaha NE 68175

SKYPAKEWYCH, ROMAN ADRIAN, mental health facility administrator; b. Detroit, Jan. 31, 1957; s. Stephan and Jaroslava (Andruszkiw) S.; m. Eugenia Vera Jurkiw, Oct. 5, 1979. BA in Psychology, Wayne State U., 1979, postgrad. Law Sch., 1987—; MS in Psychology, Eastern Mich. U., 1984. Lic. social worker, Mich. Psychiatric attendant Glen Eden Hosp., Warren, Mich., 1976-77, mental health worker, 1977-82, dir. quality assurance, recipient rights' advisor, 1982—; psychol. testing asst. to pvt. psychologist, Mich., 1981. Performer, arranger (record) Koliada, 1981. Active Com. for Def. of Human Rights in Ukraine, Warren, 1985—; co-chmn. dept. mental health subcom. Community Rights Adv. Council, 1986—. Mem. Southeastern Mich. Assn. Quality Assurance Profls., Nat. Assn. Quality Assurance Profls., Community Mental Health-Recipient Rights Officers Assn. Mich. Republican. Ukrainian Catholic. Avocations: music (composing, arranging), travel. Home: 28537 Cunningham Warren MI 48092 Office: Glen Eden Hosp 6902 Chicago Rd Warren MI 48092

SLABAUGH, ROBERT DEAN, radiologist; b. Topeka, Ind., Jan. 1, 1943; s. David Henry and Verna Vietta (Hooley) S.; m. Georgia Kopchinski, Aug. 7, 1965; children: Stephanie, Andrea. Cert. in radiologic tech., Elkhart (Ind.) Gen. Sch. Radiologic Tech., 1963; AB, Ind. U., South Bend, 1973; MD, Ind. U., Indpls., 1977. Intern, then resident in radiology Ind. U., Indpls., 1977-81; diagnostic radiologist Radiology Inc., South Bend, 1981—. Contbr. articles to profl. jours. Bd. dirs. St. Joseph County Cancer Soc., South Bend, 1982—; mem. radiation cert. com. Ind. State Bd. Health, 1985—. Mem. Am. Coll. Radiology, Radiologic Soc. N.Am., Soc. for Pediatric Radiology (assoc.), Ind. State Med. Assn., Ind. Roentgen Soc. (chmn. technologist adv. com. 1985—, mem. manpower com. 1985). Office: 707 N Michigan St South Bend IN 46601

SLABY, FRANK, business educator, consultant, writer; b. South Bend, Ind., Aug. 3, 1936; s. Frank A. and Alice E. (Michalec) S.; m. Carolyn Kay Carr, Jan. 20, 1960 (div. Sept. 1977); children: Cami Lynn, Keriann; m. Kristi Lynn Courtright, May 18, 1978, 1 child, Joy Marie. BS, Ind. U., 1961, MBA, 1963; postgrad., U. Cin., 1967-70. Prof. bus. adminstrn. Ill. Inst Tech., Chgo., 1970-72; from spl. asst. to pres. St. Mary's Coll., Notre Dame, Ind., 1972-74; dir. grad. program Ind. U. Northwest, Gary, 1974-78; prof. bus. adminstrn. Valparaiso (Ind.) U., 1978-81, St. Joseph's Coll., Rensselaer, Ind., 1981—; sr. assoc. Mark-Killian Assocs., Collegeville, Ind., 1978—. Author: (monograph) Safety and The Needs of Man, 1982, National Programming, 1984; also articles to profl. jours. Del. Rep. State Conv., Indpls., 1972-86; mem. Rep. Cen. Com., Jasper County, Ind., 1982—, adv. council Union Twp., Jasper County, 1982—. Served to comdr. USNR, 1963—. Named Ky. Col. by Gov. State of Ky., 1968, Ky. Admiral, 1969; Sagamore of the Wabash by Gov. State Ind., 1981. Mem. Ind. U. Alumni Assn. (life), Midwest Bus. Adminstrn. Assn., Midwest Bus. Econ. Assn. (adv. com.), Alpha Kappa Psi (life), Beta Gamma (life, chpt. pres.), Kappa Delta Rho (life, alumni pres.). Lodge: Masons. Avocations: golf, farming. Home: Stonehedge Glen Rt 6 Box 54 Rensselaer IN 47978 Office: St Joseph's Coll Collegeville IN 47978

SLADE, LLEWELLYN EUGENE, lawyer, engineer; b. Carroll, Iowa, May 1, 1911; s. Llewellyn and Mary (Veach) S.; m. Jane England Dickinson, June 8, 1945; 1 dau. by previous marriage, Yvonne Slade Tidd. B.S. in Elec. Engring., Iowa State U., 1938, M.S., 1942; J.D., Drake U., 1951. Registered profl. engr., Iowa. With Iowa Power & Light Co., Des Moines, 1940-68; exec. v.p. ops., dir. Iowa Power & Light Co., 1964-68; cons. Nebr. Public Power Dist. nuclear project; pvt. practice as exec. counsellor, atty., profl. engr.; fed. ct. bankruptcy trustee; past mgmt. adv. and dir. Wright Tree Service Cos.; mem. panel arbitrators U.S. Fed. Mediation and Conciliation Service, Iowa Pub. Employees Relations Bd., Am. Arbitration Assn. Former chmn., trustee Des Moines Metro Transit Authority; bd. dirs. Iowa Luth. Hosp., West Des Moines Devel. Corp., Iowa Arboretum, Theta Chi Corp. Mem. Fed., Am., Iowa, Polk County bar assns., IEEE, Iowa Engring. Soc. (Anson Marston award for outstanding service 1957, Outstanding Service award 1987), Nat. Soc. Profl. Engrs., Engrs. Club Des Moines, Atomic Indsl. Forum, Greater Des Moines C. of C., Iowa Hist. Soc. (bd. dirs.), Iowa Arboretum (bd. dirs.). Lutheran. Clubs: Des Moines, Embassy, Bohemian (Des Moines); Men's Garden of Am. Lodges: Masons (32 deg.), Shriners, Rotary. Home: 5833 Pleasant Dr Des Moines IA 50312-1211

SLADEN, BERNARD JACOB, psychologist; b. Chgo., Mar. 30, 1952; s. Mayer and Anne S. BA, U. Ill., 1974; PhD, Washington U., St. Louis, 1979. Intern U. Minn., Mpls., 1976-77; psychologist Mental Health Ctr., Inc., Ft. Wayne, Ind., 1978-80, Hines (Ill.) VA Hosp., 1980—; pvt. practice psychology Chgo., 1982—; asst. prof. Northwestern U. Med. Sch., Chgo., 1983—; cons. Riveredge Hosp., Forest Park, Ill., 1984—, Assocs. in Adolescent Psychiatry, Forest Park, 1984—, Assocs. in Clin. Psychology, Westchester, Ill., 1985—. VA traineeship, 1974-76; NIMH fellow, 1977-78. Mem. Am. Psychol. Assn., Am. Orthopsychiat. Assn., Ill. Psychol. Assn. (chmn. speakers bur.). Home: 201 E Chestnut 20-A Chicago IL 60611 Office: Assoc Cert Psychologists 625 N Michigan Chicago IL 60611

SLAGLE, JAMES ROBERT, computer science educator; b. Bklyn., 1934; married; 5 children. B.S. Summa Cum Laude, St. John's U., 1955; M.S. in Math., MIT, 1957, Ph.D. in Math., 1961. Staff mathematician Lincoln Lab. MIT, 1955-63; group leader Lawrence Livermore Radiation Lab. U. Calif., Livermore, 1963-67; chief heuristics lab., Div. Computer Research and Tech. NIH, Bethesda, Md., 1967-74; chief computer sci. lab., Communication Scis. div. Naval Research Lab., Washington, 1974-81, spl. asst. Navy Ctr. for Applied Research in Artificial Intelligence, 1981-84; Disting. prof. computer sci. U. Minn., Mpls., 1984—; mem. faculty dept. elec. engring. MIT, 1962-63; mem. faculty dept. computer sci. and elec. engring. U. Calif.-Berkeley, 1964-67; mem. faculty dept. computer sci. Johns Hopkins U., 1967-74; cons. in field. Author: Artificial Intelligence: The Heuristic Programming Approach, 1971. Contbr. articles to profl. jours. Named one of Ten Outstanding Young Men of Am., U.S. Jaycees, 1969; recipient Outstanding Handicapped Fed. Employee of Yr. award, 1979; Mary P. Oenslager Career Achievement award, Recording for the Blind, 1982. Mem. Assn. Computing Machinery, Am. Assn. Artificial Intelligence, IEEE (sr., former chmn. subcom. on AI of pattern analysis and machine intelligence com of Computer Soc.), Mil. Ops. Research Soc. (chmn. 51st artificial intelligence working group 1983). Office: Univ Minn Computer Sci Dept 136 Lind Hall 207 Church St SW Minneapolis MN 55455

SLAGLE, THOMAS DEEN, dentist; b. China Lake, Calif., May 12, 1956; s. Lowell Elwood Sr. and Francine (Greene) S.; m. Jacqueline Sue Humphreys, Sept. 18, 1981; children: Jennifer Marie, Joshua Thomas. BS, Case Western Res. U., 1978, DDS, 1980. Gen. practice dentistry Minot, N.D., 1983—. Bd. dirs. First Dist. Health Unit, Minot, 1985—. Served to capt. USAF, 1980-83. Mem. ADA. Lodges: Lions, Eagles. Avocations: swimming, jogging, racquetball, fishing, camping. Home: 303 25th St Minot ND 58701 Office: 309 Trinity Profl Bldg Minot ND 58701

SLANE, HENRY PINDELL, broadcasting executive; b. Peoria, Ill., Dec. 29, 1920; s. Carl P. and Frances (Pindell) S.; children by previous marriage: John, Elizabeth Jean, Henry Pindell, Barbara. A.B., Yale U., 1943. Became pub. Peoria Newspapers, Inc., Peoria Broadcasting Co.; now pres. Peoria Jour. Star, Inc.; pres. PJS Publs., Inc. (Sew News, Shooting Times and Rotor & Wing, Profitable Crafts Merchandising and Crafts mags.). Served with USNR, 1943-46. Mem. Am. Soc. Newspaper Editors, Chi Psi, Sigma Delta Chi. Clubs: Peoria Country, Creve Coeur (Ill.) Country, Sturgeon Bay (Wis.). Home: 5188 N Prospect Rd Peoria IL 61614 Office: Peoria Journal Star Inc 1 News Plaza Peoria IL 61643

SLATER, FREDERICK WILMOT, newspaper editor; b. St. Joseph, Mo., Feb. 25, 1913; s. Pembrook Ward and Mary Josephine (Wilmot) S.; m. Ann Phyllis Bundick, Nov. 6, 1943; children: Michael Ward, Stephen Russell. AA, St. Joseph Jr. Coll., 1933. Reporter Kansas City Jour. Post, Mo. and Kans., 1936-42; correspondent UP, Kans., 1941-42; govt. and polit. affairs reporter St. Joseph News-Press, 1941-42, 45-82, editorial page editor, 1982—. Contbr. articles to popular mags. Served to tech. sgt. U.S. Army, 1942-45, ETO. Mem. Am. Legion (comdr. St. Joseph chpt. Post 396 1956). Roman Catholic. Avocations: print collecting, camera collecting. Home: 2309 Mulberry St Saint Joseph MO 64501 Office: St Joseph News Press 9th and Edmond Sts Saint Joseph MO 64501

SLATER, GEORGE RICHARD, banker; b. Indpls., Feb. 13, 1924; s. George Greenleaf and Chloe (Shoemaker) S.; m. Mary Catherine Brown; children: George Greenleaf, Kathleen Slater Hamar, John Goodwill, Frederick Richard. B.S., Purdue U., 1946, M.S., 1957, Ph.D., 1963. Chief economist Allis-Chalmers Mfg. Co., Milw., 1957-60; v.p. Citizens Nat. Bank of Decatur (Ill.), 1960-64; sr. v.p., group exec. Met. Group, Harris Trust & Savs. Bank, Chgo., 1964-76; pres., chief exec. officer Marine Bank, N.A., Milw., 1976-78; chmn., chief exec. officer Marine Corp., Milw., 1978—. Bd. dirs. Greater Milw. Com., Marquette Univ., Milw. Symphony Orch. Served to 1st lt. F.A. U.S. Army, 1943-46. Mem. Assn. Res. City Bankers, Assn. Bank Holding Cos. (bd. dirs.), Internat. Fin. Conf., Met. Milw. Assn. Commerce (bd. dirs.). Episcopalian. Clubs: Milw. Country, Milwaukee, Town; Chicago (Chgo.), Economic (Chgo.). Office: Marine Corp 111 E Wisconsin Ave Milwaukee WI 53201 *

SLATER, JAMES MICHAEL, surgeon; b. Fort Wayne, Ind., Jan. 18, 1947; s. Fred Lyman and Vera (Van Houten) S.; m. Sue Ellen Anderson, Sept. 6, 1969; children—Jessica Sue, Emily Michael. B.S., Purdue U., 1969; M.S., cum laude in Inorganic Chemistry, Eastern Mich. U., 1971; D.O., Kirksville Coll. Osteo. Medicine, 1975. Diplomate Am. Bd. Surgery. Intern, Flint (Mich.) Osteo. Hosp., 1975-76, resident in gen. surgery, 1977-81; practice medicine specializing in gen. surgery; pvt. practice Whitley County Gen. Hosp., Columbia City, Ind., 1975-76; pres. Whitley Med. Assocs., Columbia City, 1975-76; attending physician Gen. Hosp., Lapeer, Mich., 1979-80; mem. staff Jackson (Mich.) Osteo. Hosp., 1982—, chief of staff, 1983-84, 85-86, chmn. dept. surgery, 1983-84. Named Outstanding Surg. Resident, Flint Osteo. Hosp., 1981; March of Dimes fellow; Stewart fellow. Mem. Am. Osteo. Assn., Genesee County Osteo. Soc., Southeastern Mich. Osteo. Assn., Sigma Sigma Phi. Contbr. articles to profl. jours.

SLATER, JOHN GREENLEAF, manufacturing company executive; b. Milw., Mar. 25, 1935; s. Thomas McIndoe and Margaret Mary (McAnarney)

S.; m. Colleen Mary Conway, July 19, 1958; children: James C., John T., Ann E. BS in Econs, Marquette U., 1958, MA, 1960. With First Wis. Nat. Bank, Milw., 1960-69; with First Wis. Nat. Bank, Madison, 1969-79, exec. v.p., dir., 1973-79; sr. v.p. Fifth Third Bank, Cin., 1979-82; pres., chief exec. officer Slater Carley Group, Inc., Cin., 1982-85; exec. v.p., bd. dirs. E. W. Buschman Co., Cin., 1985—; bd. dirs. L'Har, Inc., Cin. Mem. Madison Adv. Com. Drug Abuse, 1970-71; mem. long-range planning com. Edgewood High Sch., Madison, 1972-75; mem. long-range planning task force OKI Regional Planning Commn., 1980-81; bd. dirs. First Offenders Sch., 1975-79. Mem. Wis. Bus. Economists Assn. (pres. 1973), Nat. Assn. Bus. Economists, Cin. Inst. for Small Enterprise, Fin. Execs. Inst., Nat. Venture Capital Assn., Conveyer Equipment Mfrs. Assn., Phi Gamma Mu. Roman Catholic. Home: 10606 Orinda Dr Montgomery OH 45249 Office: EW Buschman Co 10045 International Blvd Cincinnati OH 45246

SLATER-DITTRICH, LYNN MARIE, communications executive; b. St. Paul, July 25, 1961; d. George William and Beverly Jane (Mader) Slater; m. Thoams Allen Dittrich, Sept. 26, 1986. BS in Mktg., St. Cloud State U., 1983. Media analyst Bozell & Jacobs Advt., Mnpls., 1983-84, asst. media planner, 1984-85; media dir. Creative Communications Cons., Mpls., 1985-87, William L. Baxter Advt., Mpls., 1987—. Office: William L Baxter Advertising 821 Marquette Ave Suite 100 Minneapolis MN 55402

SLATKIN, LEONARD, conductor; b. Sept. 1; s. Felix Slatkin and Eleanor Aller. Began violin study, 1947; piano study with, Victor Aller and Selma Cramer, 1955; composition study with, Castelnuovo-Tedesco, 1958; viola study with, Sol Schoenbach, 1959; conducting study with, Felix Slatkin, Amerigo Marino and Ingolf Dahl; attended, Ind. U., 1962, Los Angeles City Coll., 1963, Juilliard Sch.; attended (Irving Berlin fellow in musical direction), beginning 1964; student of, Jean Morel and Walter Susskind. founder, music dir. and condr. St. Louis Symphony Youth Orch., beginning 1969; musical adv., 1979-80; mus. dir., condr., St. Louis Symphony Orch., 1979-80, 80-81; former vis. asst. prof. music Washington U., St. Louis; initiated Friday afternoon lecture series; hosted weekly radio program. Guest condr. orchs. throughout world; Conducting debut as asst. condr., Youth Symphony of N.Y., Carnegie Hall, 1966; asst. condr., Juilliard Opera Theater and Dance Dept., 1967, St. Louis Symphony Orch., 1968-71, assoc. condr., 1971-74, assoc. prin. condr., 1979—; debut with, Chgo. Symphony Orch., 1974, N.Y. Philharmonic, 1974, Phila. Orch., 1974, European debut with, Royal Philharmonic Orch., 1974, debut with, USSR orchs., 1976-77; prin. guest condr. Minn. Orch., beginning 1974; summer artistic dir., 1979-80, music dir., New Orleans Philharmonic Symphony Orch., 1977-78. Office: St Louis Symphony Orch Powell Symphony Hall 718 N Grand Blvd Saint Louis MO 63103 *

SLATON, PAUL GEORG, optometrist; b. Vienna, Austria, Oct. 25, 1923; came to U.S., 1946; s. Emil and Wilhelmine (Schladnich) Eckstein; m. Susan Weiss, Oct. 22, 1950 (dec. 1973); children: Eric, Ellen; m. Suzanne Brandon, Aug. 26, 1983; children: Margaret, Donna, David, Daniel. Applied optics degree, U. Manchester (Eng.) Inst. Tech., 1942; OD, No. Ill. Coll. Optometry, Chgo., 1949. Practice medicine specializing in optometry Hopkins, Minn., 1953—; optometrist Group Health, Mpls., 1980—. Active planning and zoning commn., Hopkins, 1971-75; mem. CSC, Hopkins, 1984—; bd. dirs. Jewish Family and Childrens Service, Mpls., 1980-86; bd. dirs. Vail Place, 1985—; councilman City of Hopkins, 1975-81. Fellow Brit. Coll. Optometry, Am. Acad. Optometry; mem. Am. Optometric Assn., Minn. Optometric Assn. (pres. 1962-63, Optometrist of Yr. 1964, Disting. Service award 1978). Democrat. Jewish. Lodges: Rotary (pres. Hopkins club 1965-66, Rotarian of Yr. 1974, Paul Harris fellow), B'nai Brith, Masons. Home: 108 Farmdale Rd E Hopkins MN 55343 Office: 905 1st St N Hopkins MN 55343

SLATTERY, JAMES CHARLES, congressman, real estate executive; b. Atchison, Kans., Aug. 4, 1948; s. Charles and Rose S.; m. Linda Smith, May 18, 1974; children: Jason, Michael. B.S. in Polit. Sci., Washburn U., Topeka, 1970; J.D., Washburn U., 1974; student, Netherlands Sch. Internat. Bus. and Econs., 1969-70. Mem. Kans. Ho. of Reps., Topeka, 1973-79, speaker pro team, 1977-78; pres. Brosius, Slattery & Meyer, Inc., Topeka, 1979-83; mem. 98th-99th Congresses from 2d Dist. Kans., 1983—; acting sec. of revenue State of Kans., 1980. Former bd. regents Washburn U. Served to 2d lt. Army NG, 1970-75. Democrat. Roman Catholic. Home: 2220 SW Terrace #32 Topeka KS 66611 Office: 1440 Longworth House Office Bldg Washington DC 20515

SLATTERY, THOMAS CARL, real estate executive; b. LaCrosse, Wis., July 31, 1935; s. Thomas Lawrence and Esther Katherine (Spinner) S.; m. Clare Lynn Durr, Apr. 4, 1964; children: Thomas Michael, James Patrick. MusB, U. Rochester, 1958; MA, U. Iowa, 1964, PhD, 1966. Clarinetist Eastman Symphonic Wind Ensemble, Rochester, N.Y., 1954-58; prof., conductor Coe Coll., Cedar Rapids, Iowa, 1966-72, chmn. dept. music, 1972-79; exec. v.p. Heritage Assocs. Corp., Cedar Rapids, 1979-84, pres., 1984—; cons. N. Cen. Assn. Colls. Univs., 1973-79, various bus. 1985—; mgr., conductor internat. concert tours, 1966-79. Author: The Biography of Percy A. Grainger-The Inveterate Innovator, 1974; contbr. articles to profl. jours. Bd. dirs. YMCA, 1985—. Served with U.S. Army, 1959-61. Grantee Nat. Found. Arts and Humanities, 1968, Iowa Humanities Bd., 1979. Mem. Iowa Bandmaster Assn. (pres. 1971-72). Club: Elmcrest Country, Picwick (Cedar Rapids). Avocations: writing, business, golf. Home: 650 30th St Dr SE Cedar Rapids IA 52403 Office: Heritage Assocs Corp Brenton Fin Ctr Cedar Rapids IA 52401

SLAUGHTER, DIANA TERESA, educator; b. Chgo., Oct. 28, 1941; d. John Ison and Gwendolyn Malva (Armstead) S.; B.A., U. Chgo., 1962, M.A., 1964, Ph.D., 1968. Instr. dept. psychiatry Howard U., Washington, 1967-68; research asso., asst. prof. Yale U. Child Study Center, New Haven, 1968-70; asst. prof. dept. behavioral scis. and edn. U. Chgo., 1970-77; asso. prof. edn. and African Am. studies Northwestern U., Evanston, Ill., 1977—; mem. nat. adv. bd. Fed. Center for Child Abuse and Neglect, 1979-82, Ednl. Research and Devel. Center, U. Tex., Austin; chmn., dir. public policy program com. Chgo. Black Child Devel. Inst., 1982-84; dir. Ill. Infant Mental Health Com., 1982-83; mem. res. adv. bd. Chgo. Urban League, 1986—. Mem. Am. Psychol. Assn. (bd. ethnic and minority affairs), Soc. for Research in Child Devel. (governing council 1981-87), Am. Ednl. Research Assn., Assn. Black Psychologists, Groves Conf. Family, Nat. Acad. Scis. (com. on child devel. and publ. policy, 1987—), Delta Sigma Theta. Contbr. articles to profl. jours. Home: 835 Ridge Ave Evanston IL 60202 Office: 2003 Sheridan Rd Evanston IL 60201

SLAUGHTER, JAMES LUTHER, III, graphic designer; b. Jenkins, Ky., Aug. 22, 1944; s. James Luther and Loretta (Winchester) S.; m. Susan Lee Brundige, Sept. 16, 1972. BS in Graphic Design, U. Cin., 1967. Graphic designer Shaw Studio Advt., Cin., 1967-69, E.F. MasDonald, Dayton, Ohio, 1969-70; ptnr., designer Slaughter & Slaughter, Inc., Cin., 1970—; cons. NIOSH, Cin., 1979; adj. faculty mem. No. Ky. U., Highland Heights, 1978-80. Contbr. articles to profl. jours. Mem. Concours Com. Arthritis Found., Cin., 1980-86; trustee Unity Ctr. Cin., 1986; bd. dirs. Appalachian Com. Devel. Assn., Cin., 1985-86, A Day In Eden Community Festival, Cin., 1986. Recipient Silver and Bronze medals The Advt. Club, Cin., 1980, Design Excellence award Internat. Typographic Composition Assn., 1980. Mem. Bus. and Profl. Advt. Assn. (workshop chmn. 1986), The Art Dirs. Club (Merit award 1970-85), Am. Inst. Graphic Arts, Nat. Model RR Assn. Avocations: model building, photography.

SLAVEN, ROY, chemical company executive. Pres., gen. mgr. Potter & Brumfield Inc., Princeton, N.J. Office: Potter & Brumfield Inc 200 Richland Creek Dr Princeton IN 47671 *

SLAVIN, JOHN JEREMIAH, lawyer, corporation director; b. Yonkers, N.Y., Apr. 5, 1921; s. John Lawrence and Carolyn (Lyons) S.; m. Jean Celeste Murphy, Aug. 23, 1943; children: Jean, Susan, Paul, Thomas, Margaret. BA, Manhattan Coll., 1943; JD, Harvard U., 1949. Bar: Mich. 1949. Atty. Detroit Edison Co., Detroit, 1949-51; ptnr. Freud, Markus, Slavin & Galgan and predecessor firms, Troy, Mich., 1951—; bd. dirs. Fed. Screw Works, Detroit, Mac Valves, Inc., Wixom, Mich., various other corps. Served to 1st lt. USAAC, 1942-46, ETO. Mem. ABA, Mich. Bar Assn., Detroit Bar Assn., Oakland County Bar Assn., Am. Judicature Soc. Clubs: Birmingham (Mich.) Athletic (pres. 1967-68), Hillsboro (Fla.). Avocations: tennis, squash, flying. Home: 4688 Haddington Ln Bloomfield Hills MI 48013 Office: Freud Markus Slavin & Galgan PC 100 E Big Beaver Rd Suite 900 Ameritech Bldg Troy MI 48083

SLAVIN, RAYMOND GRANAM, allergist, immunologist; b. Cleve., June 29, 1930; s. Philip and Dinah (Baskind) S.; m. Alberta Cohrt, June 10, 1953; children: Philip, Stuart, David, Linda. A.B., U. Mich., 1952; M.D., St. Louis U., 1956; M.S., Northwestern U., 1963. Diplomate: Am. Bd. Internal Medicine, Am. Bd. Allergy and Immunology (treas.). Intern U. Mich. Hosp., Ann Arbor, 1956-57; resident St. Louis U. Hosp., 1959-61; fellow in allergy and immunology Northwestern U. Med. Sch., 1961-64; asst. prof. internal medicine and microbiology St. Louis U., 1965-70, assoc., 1970-73, prof., 1973—, dir. div. allergy and immunology, 1965—; mem. NIH study sect., 1985—; cons. U.S. Army M.C. Contbr. numerous articles to med. publs.; editorial bd.: Jour. Allergy and Clin. Immunology, 1975-81, Tice Practice Medicine, 1973-84, Jour. Club of Allergy, 1978-80. Chmn. bd. Asthma and Allergy Found. Am., 1985—Served with M.C. U.S. Army, 1957-59. NIH grantee, 1967-70, 84—, Nat. Inst. Occupational Safety and Health grantee, 1974-80. Fellow ACP, Am. Acad. Allergy and Immunology (exec. bd., historian, pres. 1983-84); mem. Am. Assn. Immunologists, Central Soc. Clin. Research, AAAS, Alpha Omega Alpha. Democrat. Jewish. Home: 631 E Polo Dr Clayton MO 63105 Office: 1402 S Grand Blvd Saint Louis MO 63104

SLAWIAK, SHEILA IAQUINTO, manufacturing corporation executive; b. Erie, Pa., Nov. 1, 1956; d. Salvatore and Carrie (Veneziano) Iaquinto; m. Thomas Arthur Slawiak, Oct. 23, 1976. Cert. lab. asst., Hamot Med. Ctr., 1975; B.S. in Chemistry, Gannon U., 1981, M.B.A., 1981. M.S. in Communications, Rensselaer Poly. Inst., 1983. Tech. rep. Hughson Chems. Co., Erie, 1976-81; sales assoc. J.C. Penney Co., Erie, 1981-82; tech. writer Allen-Bradley Corp., Highland Heights, Ohio, 1983-84, product engr., 1984-87; office automation cons. First Nat. Bank, Erie, 1985—; demand mgr. Digital Equipment Corp., Westfield, Mass., 1987—. Contbr. articles to tech. jours. Mem. Soc. Tech. Communications (research grant com.), Nat. Assn. Female Execs., Am. Soc. for Profl. and Exec. Women, Phi Sigma Sigma. Republican. Roman Catholic.

SLAYTON, ALICE HOGAN, educator; b. Florence, Ala., Oct. 7, 1944; d. Milton Earl and Mary Edith (Horsfield) Hogan; m. Arthur Joseph Slayton, Feb. 19, 1966; children—Arthur, Amy Catherine. B.A., Converse Coll., 1967. Tchr. AB4 Skol Bridgeport, W.Va., 1972-76; tchr., San Benito Sch., Humacao, P.R., 1976-80; tchr. Wesley Pre-Sch., Fostoria, Ohio, 1980-86; mem. Fostoria City Sch. Bd., 1982-86; Fostoria rep. to Sentinel Vocat. Sch. Bd., 1985; founder Fostoria Tchr. of Yr. award, 1983; candidate Fostoria Hosp. Bd., 1987, Fostoria City Sch. Bd., 1987; mem. Fostoria Econ. Devel. Assn. Excellence in Edn. Com., 1983—. Author (booklet) Moving to Puerto Rico, 1976. Mem. Fostoria City Sch. Bd. 1982—, v.p., 1983, pres., 1984. Recipient 1st place award W.Va. Fedn. of Women's Clubs, 1975, 76. Mem. AAUW, Ohio Sch. Bd. Assn. Republican. Episcopalian. Avocations: reading, needlework, photography. Home: 1206 Woodrow Wilson Dr Fostoria OH 44830

SLAYTON, RANSOM DUNN, consulting engineer; b. Salem, Nebr., Mar. 10, 1917; s. Laurel Wayland and Martha Ellen (Fisher) S.; B.S. with distinction, U. Nebr., 1938; postgrad. Ill. Inst. Tech., 1942, DePaul U., 1945-46; m. Margaret Marie Ang, Sept. 25, 1938; children—R. Duane, David L., Sharon J. Slayton Manz, Karla M. Slayton Fogel, Paul L. With Western Union Telegraph Co., Lincoln, Nebr., 1937-38, St. Paul, 1938-40, Omaha, 1940, Chgo., 1940-45; asst. prof. elec. engring. Chgo. Tech. Coll., 1945-46; with Teletype Corp., Chgo. and Skokie, Ill., 1946-82, lectr., China and Japan, 1978, 79, 80. Active vol. civic orgns., numerous ch. offices. Mem. IEEE (sr.; numerous coms.), IEEE Communications Soc. (parliamentarian 1972-80, 82—, vice chmn. terminals com. 1980-82, chmn. 1983-84). Patentee in field. Home: 1530 Hawthorne Ln Glenview IL 60025

SLAYTON, ROBERT ALLEN, social services researcher; b. N.Y.C., Apr. 6, 1951; s. A. David and Sylvia J. (Rogosin) S.; m. Rita LaVerde, July 25, 1982. BA magna cum laude, SUNY, Buffalo, 1973; MA, Northwestern U., 1977, PhD, 1982. Research specialist Chgo. Urban League, 1984—; cons. Ill. Humanities Council, Chgo., 1986-87; mem. adv. com. on SRO Hotels, Chgo. Dept. Housing, 1985-86. Fellow Hearst Found., 1976-77. Mem. Am. Hist. Assn., Phi Beta Kappa. Democrat. Jewish. Avocations: reading, movies, mystery novels. Home: 3632 N Janssen Chicago IL 60613 Office: Chgo Urban League 4510 S Michigan Ave Chicago IL 60613

SLEDGE, CARLA ELISSA, auditor, educator; b. Detroit, July 20, 1952; s. Thomas Biggs Sr. and Zephrie (Heard) Griffin; m. Willie Frank Sledge, July 20, 1974; children: Arian Darkell, Ryan Marcel. B in Music Edn., Eastern Mich. U., 1973, MA, 1982. Tchr. Taylor (Mich.) Bd. Edn., 1974-81, Met. Detroit Youth Found., 1981-86; auditor Touche Ross & Co., Detroit, 1986—. Coordinator Tiger Cub Boy Scouts Am., Detroit, 1985—. Mem. Nat. Assn. Black Accountants. Democrat. Avocations: reading, music, travel. Home: 18434 Curtis Detroit MI 48219 Office: Touche Ross & Co 200 Renaissance Ctr Detroit MI 49243

SLEEMAN, MARY (MRS. JOHN PAUL SLEEMAN), librarian; b. Cleve., June 28, 1928; d. John and Mary Lillian (Jakub) Gerba; B.S., Kent State U., 1965, also M.L.S.; m. John Paul Sleeman, Apr. 27, 1946; children—Sandra Sleeman Swyrydenko, Robert, Gary, Linda. Supervising librarian elementary schs. Nordonia Hills Bd. Edn., Northfield, Ohio, 1965—; children's librarian Twinsburg (Ohio) Pub. Library, 1965-66. Mem. ALA, Ohio Sch. Librarians Assn., NEA, Summit County Librarians Assn., Storytellers Assn., North Eastern Ohio Tchrs. Assn. Methodist. Home: 18171 Logan Dr Walton Hills OH 44146 Office: 115 Rushwood Ln Northfield OH 44067

SLEIGHT, STANLEY DAVID, accountant; b. Lansing, Mich., Nov. 30, 1951; s. Spencer David and Otha Donadean (Emmons) S.; m. Nancy Lyn Sterritt, July 23, 1977; children: Steven, Jonathan. BA, Mich. State U., 1974. CPA, Mich. Supr. audit staff Ernst & Whinney, Detroit, 1974-78; mgr. audit Ernst & Whinney, Grand Rapids, Mich., 1978-81; sr. mgr. cons. Ernst & Whinney, Grand Rapids, 1981-85, ptnr. West Mich. mgmt. cons., 1986—. contbr. articles to profl. jours.; developer (software) MicroMix, 1984. Treas. Community Vis. Nurses, Grand Rapids, 1979-82. Mem. Am. Assn. CPA's, Mich. Assn. CPA's, Health Care Fin. Mgrs. Assn. (advanced, v.p. 1986), Hosp. Council West Mich. (fin. com. 1985-86), Mich. State U. Pres. Club, Lambda Chi Alpha Alumni Assn. Republican. Presbyterian. Avocations: tennis, golf. Home: 7777 Timber Canyon Ada MI 49301 Office: Ernst & Whinney 171 Monroe Suite 1000 Grand Rapids MI 49503

SLEMMONS, ROBERT SHELDON, architect; b. Mitchell, Nebr., Mar. 12, 1922; s. M. Garvin and K. Fern (Borland) S.; B.A., U. Nebr., 1948; m. Dorothy Virginia Herrick, Dec. 16, 1945; children—David (dec.), Claire, Jennifer, Robert, Timothy. Draftsman, Davis & Wilson, architects, Lincoln, Nebr., 1947-48; chief designer, project architect Office of Kans. State Architect, Topeka, 1948-54; asso. John A. Brown, architect, Topeka, 1954-56; partner Brown & Slemmons, architect, Topeka, 1956-69; v.p. Brown-Slemmons-Kreuger, architects, Topeka, 1969-73; owner Robert S. Slemmons, A.I.A. & Assos., architects, Topeka, 1973—. Cons. Kans. State Office Bldg. Commn., 1956-57; lectr. in design U. Kans., 1961; bd. dirs. Kaw Valley State Bank & Trust Co., Topeka, 1978—. Bd. dirs. Topeka Civic Symphony Soc., 1950-60, Midstates Retirement Communities, Inc., 1986—; v.p. Ministries for Aging, Inc., Topeka, 1984—. Served with USNR, 1942-48. Mem. AIA (Topeka pres. 1955-56, Kans. dir. 1957-58, mem. com. on architecture for justice), Topeka Art Guild (pres. 1950), Kans. Council Chs. (dir. 1961-62), Greater Topeka C. of C., Downtown Topeka, Inc. Presbyn. (elder, chmn. trustees). Kiwanian (pres. 1966-67). Prin. archtl. works include: Kans. State Office Bldg., 1954, Topeka Presbyn. Manor, 1960-74, Meadowlark Hills Retirement Community, 1979, Shawnee County Adult Detention Facility, 1985. Office: 1515 1 Townsite Plaza Topeka KS 66603

SLICK, JEWEL CHERIE, consulting service administrator, nurse; b. Poplar, Mont., June 13, 1934; d. Ralph and Charity Ruth (Reddoor) Wing; m. Virgil Slick, May 31, 1970; 1 child, Cherie Ann. RN St. Luke's Hosp., Kansas City, Mo., 1955. Pvt. duty nurse, 1958—; advocate for Am. Indians, 1969—; owner Am. Indian Cons. Service, Des Moines, 1980—; mem. Des Moines Human Rights Commn., 1974-77, 82—, Gov. Iowa Interstate Indian Council, 1975-77, Nat. Indian Bd. Alcoholism, 1975-78; bd. dirs. Des Moines YWCA, 1981—. Recipient Iowa Gov.'s Vol. award, 1987. Mem. Iowa Nursing Assn., Nat. Assn. Female Execs. Democrat. Address: 3610 Columbia St Des Moines IA 50313

SLIVE, STEVEN HOWARD, lawyer; b. Queens, N.Y., July 1, 1950; s. Theodore Hertzel and Jean Rhoda (Blatt) S.; m. Harriet Weinmann, Sept. 3, 1982. B.G.S., Ohio U., 1972; J.D., Cleve. State U., 1976. Bar: Ohio 1976. Dir. legal clinic Free Med. Clinic of Greater Cleve., 1977-81; ptnr. Slive & Slive, Cleve., 1981—. Trustee Guardian Ad Litem Adv. Bd. Cuyahoga County, Cleve., 1982-84, mem. adv. bd. Domestic Relations Ct., mem. adv. bd. Cuyahoga County Juvenile Ct., 1984—; vol. atty. Free Med. Clinic Greater Cleve., 1981—; mem. advocacy com. Divorce Equity, Inc.; bd. dirs. ACLU, 1983-84; trustee Cleve. State U. Mem. Greater Cleve. Bar Assn. (treas. family law sect.), Ohio State Bar Assn., Cuyahoga County Bar Assn., Cleve. Marshall Coll. Law Alumni Assn. (trustee 1984—). Democrat. Avocations: basketball; jogging; photography. Home: 2648 Eaton Dr University Heights OH 44118 Office: 800 Engrs Bldg 1365 Ontario St Cleveland OH 44114

SLIWINSKI, ALFRED JOHN, savings and loan executive; b. Wyandotte, Mich., Jan. 1, 1947; s. Alfred and Mary Ruth (Thomason) S.; m. Linda Sue Rudnicki, Aug. 2, 1969; children: Marcy, Richard, Benjamin. BS, Mich. State U., 1970. Br. mgr. Down River Fed. Savs., Taylor, Mich., 1972-77; br. mgr. 1st Fed. Savs. & Loan Assn. of Livingston County, Howell, Mich., 1977-80, data ctr. coordinator, 1980-85, v.p. sales and ops., 1985—. Mem. Fin. Insts. Mktg. Assocs., Fin. Mgrs. Soc., Inst. Fin. Edn. (pres. local chpt. 1982-83), Pinckney C. of C. (pres. 1978-79). Lodges: Lions (treas. 1980-87), Elks. Avocations: jogging, coaching Little League football, baseball. Office: 1st Fed Savs & Loan Assn Livingston County 611 E Grand River PO Box 740 Howell MI 48843

SLOAN, ADAM, advertising executive; b. Chgo., July 22, 1942; s. Morton David and Leah (Robin) S.; m. Jean Lois Sloan, May 15, 1971. B in Edn., Cen. Mo. State U., 1969; MA, U. Md., 1971, postgrad., 1971-73. Media dir. HFG&M, Peoria, Ill., 1979-81, acct. exec., 1981-83, acct. supr., 1983-84, v.p., 1984-86; sr. v.p. Hult, Fritz, Matuszak & Assocs. Advt., Peoria, 1986—. mktg. cons. Peoria Symphony, 1985—, bd. dirs. Served to sgt. USAF, 1963-67. Mem. Pub. Utility Commns. Assn., Retail Advt. Council, Bank Mktg. Assn. Jewish. Avocation: painting, music history. Home: 9324 Grimm Rd Edwards IL 61528 Office: Hult Fritz Matuszak & Assocs 245 NE Perry Peoria IL 61603

SLOAN, ELIZABETH ANLOUISE, music educator; b. Indpls., Jan. 10, 1948; d. William Evart and Margaret Louise (Dickens) Beck; m. James Robert Sloan, Apr. 29, 1967; children: Amy Renée, James Abram. BME, Butler U., 1969, MME, 1975, postgrad., 1987—. Cert. elem. and secondary music edn. tchr. (life). Tchr. Indpls. Pub. Schs., 1969-71, 72-73, 74-78, 79-84, Washington Twp. Schs., Indpls., 1973-74; tchr. music early childhood Jewish Community Ctr., Indpls., 1977-79; pvt. tchr. Suzuki piano method Indpls., 1979-87; tchr. music magnet program Shortridge Jr. High Sch., Indpls. Pub. Schs., 1984—; Chmn. Jazz Tchrs. Indpls. Pub. Schs., 1980-82, dir. All-City Jazz/Vocal Combo, 1981-82; workshop clinician Indpls. Montessori Schs., 1979, Marian Coll., 1979. Contbr. to various music curriculum guide and textbooks; devel. early childhood music methods. Mem. Ind. Music Educators Assn. (planning com., 1980, 87), Suzuki Assn. Ams., Mu Phi Epsilon (v.p. 1968-69, scholarship award 1967). Office: Shortridge Jr High Sch 3401 N Meridian Indianapolis IN 46208

SLOAN, JERRY LEE, public relations executive; b. Cleve., Dec. 10, 1936; s. John Thomas and Winifred (Seale) S.; m. Jeanne Helen Chapin, Apr. 19, 1958; children: Timothy, Jeffrey, David, Betsy. BS, Ohio U., 1959. Editor Cleve. Stamping Plant Ford Motor Co., 1960-62; pub. relations rep. Ford Motor Co., Cleve., 1962-64; pub. relations rep. Ford Internat. Ford Motor Co., Wixom, Mich., 1964-65; pictoral editor news dept. Ford Motor Co., Dearborn, Mich., 1965-68, pub. relations rep.-labor news dept., 1968-70, press relations rep. news dept., 1970-72, asst. mgr. news dept., 1972-74, mgr. news dept., 1974-77, asst. dir. corp. info. office, 1977-80, dir. corp. info. office, 1980-83; v.p. pub. relations American Motors Corp., Southfield, Mich., 1983—. Mem. name/symbol task force United Found. Met. Detroit; pub. relations advisory com. Detroit Renaissance; fund raiser United Found., YMCA; soccer coach; elder, fundraiser, Sunday sch. tchr. United Presbyn. Ch. Mem. Pub. Relations Soc. Am. (past. chmn. accreditation com. Detroit chpt.), Internat. Motor Press Assn., Motor Vehicle Mfrs. Assn. (pub. info. policy com.), Sigma Delta Chi. Home: 165 Puritan Birmingham MI 48009 Office: Am Motors Corp 27777 Franklin Rd Southfield MI 48034

SLOAN, MARY LOVE STRINGFIELD, interior designer; b. Waynesville, N.C., Aug. 7, 1947; d. Thomas and Harriet (Coburn) Stringfield; m. Hugh Johnston Sloan, III, Feb. 12, 1982; 1 stepchild, Kathleen Sloan Gebhart. B.S., U. Tenn., 1973. Staff designer Omnia Design, Inc., Charlotte, 1973-79; dir. planning and design Counterpoint, Inc., Knoxville, 1979-81; coordinator interior design Ohio State U. Hosps., Columbus, 1981—; instr. Central Piedmont Community Coll., Charlotte, 1978, U. Tenn., Knoxville, 1980, trustee Coalition for Interior Design Licensing Ohio, 1987—. Bd. dirs., pres. ECO, Inc., Charlotte, 1977, 79; sec. Young Democrats Club, Charlotte, 1978; rep. to state bd. Women's Polit. Caucus, Knoxville, 1980; mem. Columbus Com. for UNICEF, 1982—; mem. centennial com. King Ave. United Meth. Ch., 1985—. Recipient Assn. of Univ. Interior Designers Interior Design Competition award. Mem. Inst. Bus. Designers (nat. trustee 1978-79, v.p. Tenn. chpt. 1980, edn. chair Ohio regional chpt. 1985-86, Cert. of Appreciation 1980), Assn. Univ. Interior Designers (sec. 1983-85, v.p. 1985—), U. Tenn. Alumni Assn. (sec. 1984-86). Republican. Methodist. Clubs: Women's Guild Opera/Columbus, World Future Soc., Sierra, Nat. Trust Hist. Preservation, Ohio Preservation Alliance. Avocations: travel; gardening; opera; theatre; philately. Home: 758 N Park St Columbus OH 43215 Office: Ohio State U Hosps 410 W 10th Ave Columbus OH 43210

SLOAN, MICHAEL LEE, computer consultant, author; b. Chgo., Jan. 24, 1944; s. Robert Earl Sloan and Cyril (Lewis) Glass; m. Claudia Ann Schultz, Sept. 27, 1969. B.S. in Physics, Roosevelt U., 1966, M.S., 1971. Tchr. physics Glenbard West High Sch., Glen Ellyn, Ill., 1966-79; computer cons. Midwest Visual, Chgo., 1979-82; sr. engr. Apple Computer, Rolling Meadows, Ill., 1982-85; asst. prof. Roosevelt U., 1971-73; instr. Harper Coll., Palatine, Ill., 1984. Author: AppleWorks: The Program For the Rest of Us, 1985, Working with Works, 1987. Bd. dirs. Youth Symphony Orch., Chgo., 1977-78; trustee Body Politic Theatre, Chgo., 1981-82. Home: 411 W Park Ave Wheaton IL 60187

SLOCUM, CHARLES MERTON, financial analyst; b. Echo, Minn., July 9, 1922; s. Charles Paul and Elsie Ruth (Johannsen) S.; m. Joan Dows, Sept. 3, 1947; children: Linda, Jeffrey, Holly, James, Marion. BA, Carleton Coll., 1948. Trainee Gen. Electric Co., Schenectady, N.Y., 1948-50; pres. Paramount Reading Club, Mpls., 1950-55; salesperson Conn.-Gen. Life Ins. Co., Mpls., 1956-66; pres. Chuck Slocum & Assocs., Inc., Mpls., 1966—; pres. Unisource Corp., Mpls., 1970-79. Trustee Carleton Coll., Northfield, Minn., 1976-80. Served to capt. USAF, 1941-45. Recipient Outstanding Achievement award Carleton Coll., 1980. Mem. Minn. Assn. Life Underwriters (pres. 1968-69), Nat. Assn. Life Underwriters (sec., treas. polit. action com. 1968-80), Minn. Life Leaders (pres. 1969-70), Million Dollar Round Table (life). Club: Great Books (Mpls.). Avocations: golf, reading, jogging. Home: 9506 Woodbridge Rd Bloomington MN 55438 Office: Chuck Slocum & Assocs Inc 10000 Hwy 55 W Suite 430 Minneapolis MN 55441

SLOCUM, DONALD WARREN, chemist. BS in Chemistry, BA in English, U. Rochester; PhD in Chemistry, NYU, 1963. Asst. prof. chemistry Carnegie Inst. Tech., 1964-65; from asst. to assoc. prof. chemistry So. Ill. U., 1965-72, prof., 1972-81, adj. prof., 1981-84; program dir. Chem. Dynamics sect. Chemistry div. NSF, Washington, 1984-85; program leader div. ednl. programs Argonne (Ill.) Nat. Lab., 1985—; sr. scientist Gulf Research and Devel. Co., Pitts., 1980-82; vis. prof. U. Ill., 1970, U. Bristol, Eng., 1973, U. Cin., 1976; vis. fellow U. Bristol, 1972; vis. lectr. Carnegie-Mellon U. and U. Pitts., 1983-84; cons. in field. Contbr. more than 50 articles to profl. jours.;

also papers, book chpts., and editorshops. Mem. AAAS, Am. Chem. Soc., Chem. Soc. Great Britain, Phi Lambda Upsilon, Sigma Xi. Avocations: music, literature, sports. Office: Argonne Nat Lab 9700 S Cass Argonne IL 60439

SLOCUM, PATRICIA JOANNE, psychology educator; b. Chgo., Sept. 19, 1946; d. Joseph John and Theresa Eve (Sanford) Matula; m. Rex Vaenar Slocum, Jan. 25, 1970; children: Jenna, Daniel. BA, No. Ill. U., 1969, MS, 1970, postgrad., 1986—. Alcoholism counselor Singer Zone, Rockford, Ill., 1970-73; pvt. practice therapy Ft. Wayne, Ind., 1974-77; instr. Concordia Coll., Ft. Wayne, 1976-77; instr. Coll. of DuPage, Glen Ellyn, Ill., 1982—, program evaluator, 1985—. Bd. dirs. Ill. Deaf Blind Sch., Glen Ellyn, 1979-81. Mem. Am. Diabetes Assn. (cons. and chair Chgo. chpt. 1979—), Am. Evaluation Assn. Republican. Avocation: tennis. Office: Coll of DuPage 22d & Lambert Rd Glen Ellyn IL 60137

SLOWINSKI, DAVID ALLEN, software engineer, financial investor; b. Willimantic, Conn., Sept. 1, 1953; s. Emil John Jr. and Emily (Dayton) S. BS, Mich. State U., 1976, MS, 1980. Systems analyst Burroughs Corp., Lansing, Mich., 1973-76, Cray Research, Inc., Livermore, Calif., 1978-79; systems programmer Mpls., 1977-78; software engr. Chippewa Falls, Wis., 1980—; ptnr. Woodwind, Chippewa Falls, 1984—; instr. mgmt. info. systems U. Wis., Eau Claire, 1984-85. Designer posters. Mission pilot Civil Air Patrol, Chippewa Falls, 1982—. Mem. IEEE, Usenix. Republican. Avocations: flying, sculling. triathlons. Home: Rt 5 Box 583 Chippewa Falls WI 54729 Office: Cray Research Inc 900 Lowater Rd Chippewa Falls WI 54729

SMALE, JOHN GRAY, diversified industry executive; b. Listowel, Ont., Can., Aug. 1, 1927; s. Peter John and Vera Gladys (Gray) S.; m. Phyllis Anne Weaver, Sept. 2, 1950; children: John Gray, Catherine Anne Smale Caldemeyer, Lisa Beth, Peter McKee. B.S., Miami U., Oxford, Ohio, 1949, LL.D. (hon.), 1979; LL.D. (hon.), Kenyon Coll., Gambier, Ohio, 1974; D.Sc. (hon.), DePauw U., 1983; D.C.L. (hon.), St. Augustine's Coll., 1985; LL.D., Xavier U., 1986. With Vick Chem. Co., 1949-50, Bio-Research, Inc., N.Y.C., 1950-52; pres. Procter & Gamble Co., 1974-86, chief exec., 1981—, chmn. bd., 1986—, dir., 1972—; dir. Eastman Kodak Co., Gen. Motors Corp.; mem. internat. council Morgan Guaranty Trust Co. Bd. dirs. United Negro Coll. Fund, United Way Am., Nat. Park Found.; mem. nat. adv. bd. Goodwill Industries Am., Inc.; trustee Kenyon Coll., Cin. Inst. Fine Arts. Served with USNR, 1945-46. Mem. Grocery Mfrs. Am. (bd. dirs.), Conf. Bd. (trustee), Bus. Council (grad.), Bus. Roundtable, Nat. Ctr. State Cts. (bus. and profl. friends com.), Internat. Life Scis. Inst. (CEO Council), Nutrition Found., Cin. Bus. Com. Clubs: Commercial, Commonwealth, Queen City, Cincinnati Country. Office: Procter & Gamble Co PO Box 599 Cincinnati OH 45201

SMALL, EDWARD WILLIAM, accountant; b. Lawrence, Kans., Sept. 13, 1946; s. Joe Richard and Virginia Alice (Shertzer) S.; m. Nancy Sue Starnes. BS, So. Ill. U., 1972, MBA, 1984. CPA, Ill. Auditor Ill. Agrl. Auditing Assn., Bloomington, 1968-72, Arthur Andersen & Co., St. Louis, 1972-76, Teel, Heller & Wentzel, Belleville, Ill., 1976-78; pvt. practice acctg. Edwardsville, Ill., 1978—; instr. So. Ill. U., Edwardsville, 1980-87; treas., bd. dirs. Edwardsville Investment Co., Automation Facilitators, Inc., Edwardsville. Scout master Boy Scouts Am., Edwardsville, 1973-76. Served with USMC, 1964-67, Vietnam. Recipient award Edwardsville Optmists, 1964. Mem. Am. Inst. CPAs, Ill. Soc. CPAs. Mem. Christian Ch. (Disciples of Christ). Avocations: golf, softball, hiking, canoeing, tennis. Home: Rural Rt #1 Box 122 Edwardsville IL 62025 Office: 142B N Main Edwardsville IL 62025

SMALL, ELIZABETH ANNE, dermatologist; b. Streator, Ill., Jan. 9, 1951; d. John Davis and Mary Elizabeth (Gleim) S.; m. Randall Blaine Huggins, Apr. 28, 1984; 1 child, Emily Rebecca. BA, Wellesley (Mass.) Coll., 1973; MD, John Hopkins U., 1977. Intern Northwestern Meml. Hosp., Chgo., 1977-78; resident John Hopkins Hosp., Balt., 1978-81; dermatologist Zachary, La., 1981-86, Springfield (Ill.) Clinic, 1986—; cons. Meml. Med. Ctr., Springfield, 1986—, St. John's Hosp., Springfield, 1986—. Durant scholar Wellesley Coll., 1973. Fellow Am. Acad. Dermatology; mem. AMA, So. Med. Assn., Ill. Dermatology Soc., St. Louis Dermatology Soc., Phi Beta Kappa, Sigma Xi. Presbyterian. Office: Springfield Clinic 1025 S Seventh Springfield IL 62703

SMALL, JEROME KUHN, JR., clinical psychologist; b. Nashville, Dec. 6, 1947; s. Jerome K. and Eleanor (Bloch) S.; m. Holly Cohen, Sept. 4, 1977. BA in Psychology, U. Va., 1969; MA, U. Ga., 1970, PhD, 1972; postgrad., Med. U. S.C., 1972-73, U. S. Fla., 1974-75. Lic. clin. psychologist, Tenn., Ohio. Clin. psychologist VA Ctr., Hampton, Va., 1973-74; pvt. practice psychology Tenn. and Ohio, 1974—; prof. psychology U. Tenn., Martin, Tenn., 1975-76, Youngstown (Ohio) State U., 1976—; lectr. numerous presentations to local civic and social orgns. Contbr. articles to profl. jours. Mem. B'nai B'rith (bd. dirs. Youngstown chpt.). Mem. Am. Psychol. Assn., NEA. Home: 6000 Greenbrier Dr Girard OH 44420 Office: Youngstown State U Youngstown OH 44555

SMALL, LARRY ALAN, medical center official; b. Springfield, Ill., Nov. 23, 1946; s. Walter Alan and Kathleen Joyce (White) S.; m. Barbara Leona Murphy, Aug. 14, 1971; children—Patrick Alan, Erin Leona. Student Springfield (Ill.) Coll., 1965-67, George Williams Coll., Downers Grove, Ill., 1968-69; B.A. in Biol. Sci., So. Ill. U., Carbondale, 1971, M.S. in Edn., 1975. Cert. tchr., Ill. Media specialist Ill. Office Edn., Springfield, 1971-73; grad. asst. So. Ill. U., 1973-75; media specialist Lake-McHenry Regional Project, Gurnee, Ill., 1975-76; dir. media resources Meml. Med. Ctr., Springfield, 1976-86, dir. ednl. resources, 1987—; free lance media producer video, slides and photography; cons. equipment. Mem. adv. bd. communications program Capital Area Vocat. Ctr., Springfield. Recipient hon. mention award Kodak Internat. Snapshot Contest, 1973, Best of Show award in employee photography Meml. Med. Ctr., 1979, 1st place award, 1980. Mem. Internat. TV Assn. (sec. local chpt.), Health Scis. Communications Assn., Am. Cancer Soc. for Healthcare Edn. and Tng., Springfield Advt. Club, Meml. Med. Ctr. Mgmt. Club (pres.). Office: 800 N Rutledge St Springfield IL 62781

SMALL, LESLIE ALAN, accountant; b. St. Louis, Oct. 17, 1945; s. Albert D. and Martha (Katz) S.; m. Leslee R. Silverman, June 8, 1969 (div. June 1980); children: Jeffrey B., Michael S.; m. Marilyn J. Berger, Nov. 3, 1984; stepchildren: Bradford P. Hohenberg, Jennifer A. Hohenberg. BS in Acctg., So. Ill. U., 1970. CPA, Mo. Staff acct. Arthur Andersen & Co., St. Louis, 1970-74, mgr., 1974-79, ptnr., 1979—; adj. prof. taxation So. Ill. U., Edwardsville. Served with U.S. Army, 1967-69. Mem. Am. Inst. CPA's, Mo. Soc. CPA's, Nat. Retail Merchant's Assn. (taxation com.). Jewish. Clubs: Media, Meadowbrook Country (St. Louis). Office: Arthur Andersen & Co 1010 Market St Saint Louis MO 63101

SMALL, RICHARD ALLAN, radiologist; b. Detroit, Jan. 31, 1941; s. Henry and Sadie (Nuchims) S.; m. Leanne Dorothy Trost, June 11, 1963; children—Brian Joel, Scott Andrew. B.A. in Psychology, U. Mich., 1963; M.D., Chgo. Med. Sch., 1968. Diplomate Am. Bd. Radiology. Intern, William Beaumont Hosp., Royal Oak, Mich., 1968-69, resident in diagnostic radiology, 1969-72; practice medicine specializing in diagnostic radiology Woodland Med. Group, Inc., Detroit, 1972—, dir. div. diagnostic ultrasound, 1982—. Served with USAR, 1960-66. Mem. AMA, Mich. State Med. Soc., Wayne County Med. Soc., Am. Coll. Radiology, Mich. Radiol. Soc., Am. Inst. Ultrasound in Medicine. Club: Wabeek Country (Bloomfield Hills, Mich.) Office: 41935 W Twelve Mile Rd Novi MI 48050 Office: 22341 W Eight Mile Rd Detroit MI 48219

SMALL, RICHARD DONALD, travel company executive; b. West Orange, N.J., May 24, 1929; s. Joseph George and Elizabeth (McGarry) S.; A.B. cum laude, U. Notre Dame, 1951; m. Arlene P. Small; children—Colleen P., Richard Donald, Joseph W., Mark G., Brian P. With Union-Camp Corp., N.Y.C., Chgo., 1952-62; pres. Alumni Holidays, Inc., 1962—, AHI Internat. Corp., Des Plaines, Ill., 1962—, All Horizons, Inc., 1982—, chmn. AHI, Inc., 1982—. Club: University (Chgo.). Home: 191 Sheridan Rd Winnetka IL 60093 also: 2202 Wailea Elua Wailea Maui HI 96753 Office: 1st Nat Bank Bldg 701 Lee St Des Plaines IL 60016

SMALLWOOD, GLENN WALTER, JR., utility company marketing representative; b. Jeffersonville, Ind., Oct. 12, 1956; s. Glenn Walter and Darlene Ruth (Zeller) S.; B.S. in Bus. Adminstrn., SE Mo. State U., 1978. Customer service advisor Union Electric Co., Mexico, Mo., 1979—; instr. Mexico Vo-Tech Sch., 1981; panelist on home design Mo. Extension Service, 1984. Coordinator local United Way, 1984. Mem. Am. Mktg. Assn., Nat. Eagle Scout Assn., Copper Dome Soc., Boy Scouts Am. Alumni Family, Mexico area C. of C. Lodges: Optimist (cert. appreciation 1982, youth appreciation award 1974), Kiwanis (cert. appreciation 1984). Avocations: music; spectator sports; baseball; basketball; tennis. Office: Union Electric Co 321 W Promenade Mexico MO 65265

SMART, DOROTHY, purchasing agent; b. Memphis, Mar. 4, 1935; d. James and Emily (Morris) Gilmore; m. Lewis Smart Jr., June 16, 1955; 4 children. Student Lincoln Corr. Sch., 1963-64 supervisory trainee Elkhart Area Career Ctr., 1980. With Clarke's Discount, Elkhart, Ind., 1963-66; billing mgr., inventory control Nat. CROP Office, Elkhart, 1966-72; asst. purchasing agt., dep. controller, mgr. Barrett Law Dept., City of Elkhart, 1972-80, dir. purchasing and materials mgmt., 1980-86. Bd. dirs. Elkhart Community Day Care, 1969-76, pres. policy and intake, 1969-75; precinct capt. Dem. Central Com., 1968-70, treas., 1970-72. Recipient Disting. Service award Elkhart Day Care Ctr., 1976; Golden Service award Ind. Black Polit. Assembly, 1975, Outstanding Contribution award City Elkhart Govt., 1983, Hon. Cert. St. James AME Ch., 1983. Mem. Elkhart Urban League Guild, NAACP, LWV. Baptist. Club: Amicus Christian Guild. Home: 54657 County Road 101 N Elkhart IN 46514 Office: City of Elkhart 229 S 2d St Elkhart IN 46514

SMART, ELNORA SUE, psychologist; b. Kansas City, Mo., Nov. 20, 1953; d. Carl J. and Bernice (Benner) Smart. BS in Edn., Cen. Mo. State U., 1974, MS in Psychology, 1976; EdS, Pittsburg (Kans.) State U., 1985. Lic. psychologist, Mo. Psychology intern Fulton (Mo.) State Hosp., 1975-76; clin. psychologist I and II Nevada (Mo.) State Hosp., 1976-81; sch. psychologist Shawnee Mission (Kans.) Sch. Dist., 1981—; family and individual psychologist Shawnee Mission Schs. Clinic, 1983—. Named Young Career Woman of Yr., Bus. and Profl. Women's Assn., Nevada, Mo., 1978. Avocations: needle craft, reading. Office: DO Cherokee 8714 Antioch Shawnee Mission KS 66212

SMART, GREG LEE, insurance executive; b. Springdale, Ark., Aug. 13, 1956; s. Danny L. Smart and Sylvia (Johnson) Carr; m. Brenda Marie Paxton, Mar. 7, 1980; children: Cole, Hunter. BS in Acctg. and Bus., U. Kans., 1979. Pres., chief exec. officer Doug Ruedlinger, Inc., Topeka, 1982—, also bd. dirs.; pres., bd. dirs. Sports Risks Purchasing Group, Topeka, Kansas City, Mo., 1982—; pres., chief exec. officer, bd. dirs. Linda Lee Design Assn., Topeka, 1984—; v.p., treas., bd. dirs. United Internat. Ins. Co., Providence, 1986—; pres., chief exec. officer, bd. dirs. Wheatland Group Holding, Inc., Providence, First Benefits, Inc., Providence, Sunflower Intermediaries, Inc., Providence; bd. dirs. Fund Ins. Co. Ltd., Hamilton, Bermuda. Mem. Fund Adminstrs. Assn. (exec. v.p., treas.). Presbyterian. Club: Topeka Active 20/30 (bd. dirs.). Home: 940 NW Menninger Rd Topeka KS 66618 Office: PO Box 2159 1420 SW Arrowhead Rd Topeka KS 66601

SMART, PAUL M., utility company executive, lawyer; b. Middleport, Ohio, Jan. 6, 1929. A.B. summa cum laude, Capital U., 1952; J.D. summa cum laude, Ohio State U., 1953. Bar: Ohio 1953. Ptnr. firm Fuller & Henry, Toledo, 1959-84; v.p. Toledo Edison Co., 1974-78, sr. v.p., gen. counsel corp. devel., 1984-85, pres., chief operating officer, 1985—, also dir. Fellow Ohio State Bar Found.; mem. Am. Bar Found., Order of Coif, Phi Delta Phi. Office: Toledo Edison Co 300 Madison Ave Toledo OH 43652 *

SMEARSOLL, ALAN PAUL, retail executive; b. Bowling Green, Ohio, Apr. 17, 1963; s. George Henry and Mary Lou (Henschen) S. A in Applied Bus., Kent State U., 1985. Asst. dept. mgr. Best Products, Inc., Niles, Ohio, 1985-86; asst. mgr. Gray Drug Fair, Inc., Warren, Ohio, 1986-87; mgr. Rite Aid Pharmacy, Ravenna, Ohio, 1987—. Sec. ch. council Prince of Peace Lutheran, Cortland, Ohio, 1985-87. Mem. Alpha Beta Gamma, Alpha Rho. Avocations: collecting old bottles, bicycling.

SMEDAL, DAVID OLAF, dentist; b. Madison, Wis., July 20, 1932; s. Agnar Tengel and Edith Marie (Oldenburg) S.; m. Janice Ruth Kirby, July 30, 1955; children—Susan, Eric, Kristi. Student U. Wis.-Madison, 1950-53; D.D.S., Northwestern U., 1957. Instr. Northwestern U. Dental Sch., Chgo., 1957-58; pvt. practice dentistry Stoughton, Wis.; chief dental staff Stoughton Community Hosp., 1970-71. Treas. Stoughton Bd. Edn., 1963-68; pres. Christ Luth. Endowment Found., 1968-75, 80-85. Mem. Dane County Dental Assn., ADA, Northwestern U. Dental Study Club Wis. (pres. 1970-71), Stoughton C. of C. Clubs: Stoughton Lions (pres. 1967-68), Stoughton Country (rep. 1983-87). Lodge: Sons of Norway. Home: 724 Pine St Stoughton WI 53589 Office: 218 S Forrest St Stoughton WI 53589

SMELSER, THOMAS ALBERT, accountant; b. Hartford City, Ind., Feb. 19, 1947; s. Albert Franklin and Martha Ellen (Hinkle) S.; m. Linda Sue Taylor, Dec. 23, 1967; children: Brandon, Michelle, Michael. BS in Acctg., Ball State U., 1970. CPA, Ill. Acct. Deloitte Haskins & Sells, CPA's, Chgo., 1969-71, Grey, Hunter, Stenn, CPA's, Chgo., 1971-72; sr. acct. Simmons & Co. CPA's, Muncie, Ind., 1972-74; gen. acctg. mgr. Borg-Warner Automotive, Muncie, 1974-78; ptnr. R.J. Whitinger & Co., Muncie, 1978—; bd. dirs. Precision Printing, Inc., Muncie. Mem. Muncie Soccer Club, 1985-86; chmn. fin. com. Gethsemane United Meth. Ch., Muncie, 1981-85, lay leader, 1985-86; treas. Muncie Area Red Cross, 1981—, chmn. bd., 1984-85. Mem. Am. Assn. CPA's, Ind. CPA Soc. Republican. Club: Muncie. Lodge: Rotary. Office: RJ Whitinger and Co 114 S Franklin St Muncie IN 47305

SMERCINA, CHARLES JOSEPH, mayor, accountant; b. Cleve., Sept. 18, 1932; s. Edward Steven and Barbara Rose (Vincik) S.; m. Dorothy Rita Pazdernik, May 9, 1953; children: Cynthia Bomeli Smercina, David. ABA in Acctg., Fenn Coll.; ABA in Mgmt., BBA in Acctg., Cleve. State U.; postgrad., Kent State U., Case Western Res. U., Youngstown (Ohio) State U. Chmn. CSC, Solon, 1956-66; councilman City of Solon, Ohio, 1966-68, vice mayor, 1966-67, income tax adminstr., 1968-73, mayor, 1974-75, 78—; cons. taxation, mcpl. fin. various Ohio communities, 1970—; lectr. polit. sci., corp. fin. Case Western Res. U. Trustee Suburban Community Hosp. Mem. Am. Soc. Pub. Adminstrs., Mayors Assn. Ohio, Cuyahoga County Mayors and City Mgrs. Assn., Mcpl. Fin. Officers Am., Nat. League of Cities, Nat. Soc. Pub. Accts., Ohio Assn. Pub. Safety Dirs., Ohio Assn. Tax Adminstrs. (past pres.), Ohio Mcpl. League, Water Pollution Control Fedn., Solon C. of C., VFW, Council on Human Relations, Ohio Nature Conservancy, Nat. Arbor Day Found. Democrat. Roman Catholic. Lodges: Rotary, KC. Home: 5075 Brainard Rd Solon OH 44139 Office: City of Solon City Hall Solon OH 44139

SMILEY, THOMAS WALTER, dentist; b. Marion, Ohio, Aug. 9, 1953; s. Walter Thomas and Jean Jenny (Benedetti) S.; m. Sara Joyce Stangel, May 15, 1982; 1 child, Jared Ahn. BS in Biology and Chemistry, St.Joseph's Coll., Rensselear, Ind., 1975; DDS, Loyola U., Maywood, Ill., 1979. Gen. practice dentistry Marshfield, Wis., 1979—. Bd. dirs. Big Bros. and Big Sisters of Marshfield, 1984-86, Visitor and Promotion Bur., Marshfield, 1986. Mem. ADA, Cen. Wis. Dental Assn., Wood County Dental Assn. (pres. 1983-84). Presbyterian. Office: 333 S Central Ave Marshfield WI 54440

SMITH, ALICE ELIZABETH SWILLEY, hospital services executive, consultant, clinical educator; b. Coral Gables, Fla., Sept. 24, 1948; d. Thomas and Alva (Zebendon) Swilley; m. Philip Edward Smith, June 26, 1971, 1 child, Eve Elizabeth. Cert. elementaire Le Cordon Bleu, Paris, 1969; B.A. in Home Econs., The Western Coll., 1970; postgrad. U. Dayton, 1972-73; dietetic intern Miami Valley Hosp., Dayton, Ohio, 1973-74; M.S. in Nutrition, No. Ill. U., 1978. Tchr. Miami Dade Jr. High, Opa Locka, Fla., 1970-71; food service coordinator Mercy Med. Ctr., Springfield, Ohio 1972-73; pub. health nutritionist Chgo. Bd. Health, 1974-78; assoc. dir. clin. dietetics Children's Meml. Hosp., Chgo., 1980-84, asst. clin. prof. U. Ill., Chgo., 1983—; dir. clin. dietetics Children's Meml. Hosp., Chgo., 1985—; liaison rep. Am. Acad. Pediatrics Com. on Nutrition, Am. Dietetic Assn., Chgo., 1981—. Contbr. articles to profl. jours. Vol. 8th Day Ctr. for Justice, Chgo., 1976-77. Grantee Mead Johnson Nutritional Co., 1983-86. Mem. Am. Dietetic Assn., AAAS, Clin. Nutrition Mgmt. Practice Group (newsletter editor, 1983-84), Chgo. Dietetic Assn., Am. Soc. Parenteral and Enteral Nutrition, Dietitians in Pediatric Practice. Avocations: Creative cookery, indoor gardening. Office: Children's Meml Hosp 2300 Children's Plaza Chicago IL 60614

SMITH, ANDREW JEPTHA KINCANNON, neurosurgeon; b. Houston, Sept. 28, 1942; s. A.J. Kincannon and Helen (Townes) S.; m. Mary Ethlyn Hill, July 10, 1965; children: Emily, Andrew, Bradley. BA, U. Tex., Austin, 1964; MA, U. Tex. Southwestern Med. Sch., Dallas, 1968, MD, 1969; PhD, U. Minn., 1977. Diplomate Am. Bd. Neurol. Surgeons. Staff assoc. NIH, Bethesda, Md., 1970-72; clin. instr. U. Minn., Mpls., 1977—; practice medicine specializing in neurosurgery Mpls. Neurol. Surgeons Ltd., 1977—; chmn. laser and critical care com. Meth. Hosp., Mpls., 1986; bd. dirs. West Metro. Ind. Physicians Assocs., Mpls.; mem. negotiations and reimbursement methodologies com. Council of State Neurosurg. Socs. Served to lt. comdr. USPHS, 1970-72. Mem. Minn. Med. Assn. (chmn. communications com. 1986-88, del. 1984-86, ad hoc com. on worker's compensation 1983, chmn. task force on risk mgmt. 1985, mem. task force on rural health 1986, Minn. rep. to Council of State Neurosurg. Socs. 1982-84, profl. liability com. 1987), Minn. Neurosurg. Soc. (pres.-elect 1987), Am. Assn. Neurol. Surgeons, Congress of Neurol. Surgeons. Republican. Episcopalian. Avocations: fishing, boating, reading, gardening, travelling. Home: 515 N Ferndale Rd Wayzata MN 55391 Office: Mpls Neurol Surgeons Ltd 911 Medical Arts Bldg Minneapolis MN 55402

SMITH, ARTHUR E., counseling educator, vocational psychologist; b. St. Louis, Feb. 28, 1926; s. Lee L. and Dorothea M. (Debrecht) S.; m. Jane C. Dooley; children—Greg, Laura, Terry, Chris. B.S., St. Louis U., 1949, M.Ed., 1951, Ph.D., 1962. Diplomate Am. Bd. Vocational Experts; lic. psycholgist. Tchr., counselor St. Louis Pub. Schs., 1949-60; Evening Coll. dir. and assoc. prof., St. Louis U., 1960-66; grad. dean St. Mary's Coll., Notre Dame, Ind., 1966-68; chmn. behavioral studies U. Mo., St. Louis, 1968—; pres. Clayton Bus. Sch., St. Louis, 1983—; dir. Affiliates in Psychology and Counseling, St. Louis, 1970-78. Contbr. articles to profl. jours. Served with USNR, 1944-46, PTO. Recipient Recognition award Am. Soc. Tng. Dirs. and Am. Personnel and Guidance Assn. Mem. Am. Assn. Counseling and Devel. (pres. St. Louis 1965), Nat. Voc. Guidance Assn., Assn. Counselor Educs. and Supvs., Am. Coll. Voc. Experts, Nat. Rehab. Assn. (pres. St. Louis 1979-80, Recognition award 1980). Office: Univ Mo-St Louis 8001 Natural Bridge St Louis MO 63121

SMITH, BETTY ANNE, rehabilitation specialist; b. Pekin, Ill., Nov. 18, 1934; d. Ernest A. and Josephine M. (Hines) Davis; m. David Philip Davis Smith, Jan. 10, 1952; children: Steven David, Jeffrey Alan, Bruce Philip, Rebecca Anne. BS, U. Wis., River Falls, 1974, MS, 1980. Cert. clin. competence in speech/lang. pathology. Sec. 3M Co., St. Paul, 1966-69; speech/lang. pathologist Hudson (Wis.) Schs., 1974-80, River Ridge Assocs., Hudson, 1980-83; pres. River Ridge Rehab., Stillwater, Minn., 1983—, Croix Home Care, Inc., Stillwater, Minn., 1984—, Minn. Acad. of Minn. Rehab. Agys., Inc., 1986—; Communication chmn. Nat. Assn. Rehab. Agys. Village Council Trustee Village Bd., Hudson, Wis., 1980-83. Mem. Am. Speech, Lang., Hearing Assn., ASHA Congl. Action Contact (mem. network com. 1984—), U. S. C. of C., Entrepreneur Network Group, Minn. League for Nursing, Minn. Alliance of Nursing Services (treas. 1985), Wis. Assn. Rehab. Agys., Wis. Assn. Speech, Lang. Pathologists, Nat. Fedn. Bus. and Profl. Women, Hudson C. of C., Stillwater C. of C. Republican. Methodist. Club: Hudson Garden (pres. 1979-80). Home: Rt 3 Box 23A River Ridge Rd Hudson WI 54016 Office: River Ridge Rehab Inc 275 S #d St PO Box 407 Stillwater MN 55082

SMITH, BRENDA JO, accountant; b. Charles City, Iowa, Mar. 9, 1955; d. Parker Allen and Mary Joan (Schmadeke) S.; m. Joel David Topp, June 2, 1974 (div. Aug. 1979); 1 child, Justin David. BA in Acctg., Wartburg Coll., 1981. CPA. Tax and subs. acct. Rolscreen Co., Pella, Iowa, 1981-83, budget analyst, 1983-85, fin. analyst, 1985-87, internal auditor, 1987—; tchr. Des Moines Area Community Coll., 1986. Com. appointee State Welfare Reform, 1987. Regents scholar Wartburg Coll., 1973. Mem. Iowa Soc. CPA's, Am. Inst. CPA's, Inst. Internal Auditors, Iowa Inst. Internal Auditors. Mem. Trinity Reformed Ch. Avocations: reading, aerobic exercise. Home: 1211 1/2 Boone St Pella IA 50219 Office: Rolscreen Co 102 N Main Pella IA 50219

SMITH, BRICE REYNOLDS, JR., engineering company executive; b. St. Louis; s. Brice Reynolds and Frances Matilda (Cook) S.; m. Jane Medart; children: Brice Reynolds III, Victoria D. Smith Trauscht, Hollis M., Karen C., Todd E. B.C.E., U. Mo., Columbia, 1951; M.C.E., MIT, 1952; Cert. advanced mgmt. program, Harvard U., Hawaii, 1961. Registered profl. engr., D.C., Fla., Kans., Md., Mass., Mich., Mo., N.D., Ohio, Oreg., Tenn., Va. Resident engr. Sverdrup & Parcel, St. Louis, 1954-59, asst. to v.p. fgn. ops., 1959-64, treas., 1964-69, v.p., treas., 1970-75; exec. v.p. Sverdrup Corp., St. Louis, 1976-81, pres., 1982-86, pres., chief exec. officer, 1986—, also dir.; dir. Centerre Trust Co., St. Louis; chmn. bd. dirs. Convention Plaza Redevel. Corp., St. Louis. Served to 1st lt., USAF, 1952-54. Recipient Mo. Honor award for Disting. Service to Engring., U. Mo., 1979; Levee Stone award, Downtown St. Louis, Inc., 1982. Fellow Am. Cons. Engrs. Council; mem. ASCE, Cons. Engrs. Council Mo. (past pres.), Mo. Soc. Profl. Engrs., Nat. Soc. Profl. Engrs. Clubs: Bellerive Country, Log Cabin, Mo. Athletic, Noonday, St. Louis (St. Louis). Home: 15 Fielding Rd St Louis MO 63124 Office: Sverdrup Corp 801 N 11th St St Louis MO 63101

SMITH, CARL EDWIN, electronics company executive; b. Eldon, Iowa, Nov. 18, 1906; s. Seldon L. and Myra (Hutton) S.; B.S. in E.E., Iowa State U., Ames, 1930; M.S. in E.E., Ohio State U., 1932, E.E., 1936; m. Hannah B. McGuire, Sept. 3, 1932; children—Larc A., Darvin W., Barbadeen Jo, Margene Sue, Ada Kay, Ramona Lee. Draftsman, Iowa Electric Co., Fairfield, summer 1929; student engr. RCA Victor Co., Camden, N.J., 1930-31; engr. Radio Air Service Corp., Cleve., 1932; radio operator WGAR, Cleve., 1933; engr. United Broadcasting Corp., Cleve., 1933-36, asst. chief engr., 1936-41, chief engr., 1941-45, v.p., 1946-53; owner, mgr. Carl E. Smith Consulting Radio Engrs., Cleve., 1953-80; pres. Smith Electronics, Cleve., 1956—; founder Cleve. Inst. Electronics Inc., 1934, chmn. ednl. com., 1970—. Recipient Dist. Achievement citation Iowa State U., 1980. Served with Office of Chief Signal Officer, U.S. Army, World War II. Recipient Dist. Alumnus award Ohio State U., 1974, Disting. Achievement award, Iowa State U., 1980, Disting. Service award Nat. Religious, 1984, Engring. Achievement award Nat. Assn. Broadcasters, 1985. Registered profl. engr., Ohio. Fellow IEEE (life), Radio Club Am.; mem. Cleve. Engring. Soc., Brecksville C. of C. Republican. Presbyterian. Ch. Am. Author 51 books including: Directional Antenna Patterns, Theory and Design of Directional Antennas, Applied Mathematics, Communications Circuit Fundamentals; Contbr. articles to tech. jours. Patentee electromech. calculators; elliptical polarization electromagnetic energy radiation systems; slotted cylindrical antenna; three-slot cylindrical antenna; spiral slot antenna; low loss antenna system. Home: 8704 Snowville Rd Cleveland OH 44141 Office: 8200 Snowville Rd Cleveland OH 44141

SMITH, CARLYLE SHREEVE, anthropologist; b. Great Neck, N.Y., Mar. 8, 1915; s. Harold William and Lulu (Allen) S.; m. Judith Eva Pogany, May 2, 1942; children: Evan Shreeve, Pamela Anne. BA, Columbia U., 1938, PhD, 1949; LittD (hon.), U. S.D., 1979. Unit supr. archaeol. survey W.P.A. of Nebr. and La., 1939, 40-41; asst. Hudson Valley Archeol. Survey, Vassar Coll., 1940; curator div. anthropology Mus. Natural History, U. Kans., Lawrence, 1947-68, prof. anthropology, 1947-80, prof. and curator emeritus, 1981—; archaeologist Norwegian Archaeol. Expdn. to Easter Island and East Pacific, 1955-56; participant internat. anthrop. congresses, 1949-64; cons. Lindblad Travel, Inc., 1967-80; mem. Kans. Hist. Sites Bd. of Rev., Topeka, 1970-83; lectr. Norwegian Am. Line, Prudential Cruises, Royal Viking Line, 1972—; mem. div. behavioral scis. NRC, 1961-64. Editor: U. Kans. Publs. in Anthropology, 1969-73; adv. editor N.Am. Archaeologist, 1979—; contbr. articles and revs. to scholarly jours.; author: Archaeology of Coastal New York. Served with USAF, 1943-46. Carlyle S. Smith Archaeol. Labs. named in his honor at Nassau County Mus. Natural History, Glen Cove, N.Y., 1967; NSF grantee, 1960-67, Nat. Park Service grantee, 1950-76, Am. Philos. Soc. grantee, 1960, 64. Fellow Am. Anthrop.

Assn., Co. Mil. Historians; mem. Soc. for Am. Archaeology (1st. v.p. 1954-55), Soc. for Hist. Archaeology, Am. Ethnol. Soc., Sigma Xi. st, 1979—; contbr. articles and revs. to scholarly jours.; author: Archaeology of Coastal New York; Carlyle S. Smith Archaeol. Labs. named in his honor at Nassau County Mus. Natural History, Glen Cove, N.Y., 1967. Home: 2719 Harvard Rd Lawrence KS 66044

SMITH, CAROLE PROCHASKA, clinical psychologist, consultant; b. Cleve., Mar. 21, 1940; d. Charles J. and Harriet (Behm) Prochaska; m. Walter E. Smith, Dec. 27, 1961; children—Gregory, Patrick, Thomas. B.A. summa cum laude, Notre Dame Coll.-Ohio, 1961; M.A. John Carroll U., Cleve., 1965; Ph.D., Kent State U., Ohio, 1980. Lic. psychologist, Ohio. Tchr. social studies South Euclid-Lyndhurst Ohio Sch. Dist., 1961-62; lectr. history Notre Dame Coll.-Ohio, South Euclid, 1965-66; registrar Old Colony Montessori Sch., Hingham, Mass., 1970-73; practice clin. psychologist, Stow, Ohio, 1980—. Mem. Hudson (Ohio) bd. edn., 1980—, v.p., 1982—. Mem. Am. Psychol. Assn., Ohio Psychol. Soc., Cleve. Psychol. Assn., Am. Soc. Clin. Hypnosis. Democrat. Roman Catholic. Office: Western Res Psychol Assn 3435 Kent Rd Stow OH 44224

SMITH, CHARLES MORGAN, nurse; b. Cedar Falls, Iowa, Oct. 12, 1951; s. Elliot Adward and Ercell Marie (Nation) S.; m. Sandra Anne Rashke, Mar. 4, 1978; children: Marcus Andrew, Elliot Edward, Kenneth James. BA, Graceland Coll., 1977; diploma nursing, Research Med. Ctr., 1980. Emergency room technician Independence (Mo.) Hosp., 1976-77, 78-80, RN intensive care unit, 1980-81; tech. Sears, Inc., Waterloo, Iowa, 1977-78; RN Armco Steel Inc., Kansas City, Mo., 1981-86; coordinator inservice edn. Armco Steel Inc., Kansas City, 1982-86, chmn. dept. quality plus, mem. labor mgmt. participation, 1985; RN Marion Labs, Kansas City, 1986-87; v.p. Supportive Staffing Agy. Inc., Kans. and Mo. Mem. PTA, Independence, 1974—. Served with USN, 1970-73. Mem. Naval Reserve Assn., Occupational Nurses Assn. Republican. Reorganized Ch. of Latter Day Saints. Lodge: Masons. Mailing Address: PO Box 7848 Sugar Creek MO 64054

SMITH, CHARLES PHILIP, state official; b. Chgo., June 18, 1926; s. William Arthur and Lillian Christine (Christensen) S.; m. Bernadette C. Carroll, Aug. 23, 1947; children: Charles Philip, II, Stephen, Megan, Haley. B.S., Milton Coll., 1950. Field rep. Guardian Life Ins. Co., Coll. Life Ins. Co., 1958-67; prodn. supr. Olin Corp., Baraboo, Wis., 1967-71; treas. State of Wis., Madison, 1971—. Pres. Madison Rivers and Lakes Commn., 1965-71; vice chmn. Dane County (Wis.) Democrats., 1969-70; McGovern del. Nat. Dem. Conv., 1972, Kennedy del., 1980; Hart del., 1984; bd. dirs. Big Bros. of Dane County, pres., 1981; bd. dirs. Madison Opportunity Center, treas., 1980-81, v.p., 1984—; bd. dirs. Wis. Spl. Olympics., sec., 1980-82. Served with USMC, 1944-45. Decorated Purple Heart. Mem. Nat. Assn. State Treasurers (regional v.p., sec.-treas.), Nat. Assn. Unclaimed Property Adminstrs. (treas.). Roman Catholic. Home: 509 S Spooner St Madison WI 53711 Office: 125 S Webster St Room 134 Madison WI 53703

SMITH, CHARLES SCOTT, commercial photographer, foundation administrator; b. Sheboygan, Wis., Nov. 21, 1960; s. Robert Fredrick and Dorothy Ann (Heller) S. Cert., New Eng. Sch. Photography, Boston, 1982. Photographic asst. Marvy Advt., Hopkins, Minn., 1982-83; photographer Malisa Martina Photography, Mpls., 1983; comml. photographer Collective Concepts, Inc., Minnetonka, Minn., 1983-85; sr. photographer Dayton-Hudson Dept. Store Co., Mpls., 1985—; pres. The World Timecapsule Fund, Mpls., 1986—. Exhibited works at Walt Disney World's Epcot Ctr., 1984, Cleve. Mus. Natural History, 1984. Founder, pres. World Timecapsule Fund. Recipient Steuben Tetrahedron award Eastman Kodak, 1984. Lutheran. Avocations: science, space tech., education, fitness, entrepeneurialship. Home and Office: 3300 Louisiana Ave So Suite 415 Saint Louis Park MN 55426

SMITH, CHRISTINE, early childhood educator, counselor; b. St. Louis, July 26, 1948; d. James Bryant and Mamie Lee (Stewart) Bryant; m. John Jefferson, Oct. 5, 1968; children—Michelle Lynn, Andrea Denise, Jevon Jefferson. B.S. in Edn., So., Ill. U., 1976, M.S., 1980. Cert. tchr., Ill. Mem. staff Southwestern Bell Telephone Co., St. Louis, 1966-68; with Union Electric, St. Louis, 1968-71; acct. Monsanto Chem. Co., Sauget, Ill., 1971-73; tchr. early childhood edn., counselor social service East St. Louis Bd. Edn., Ill., 1976—; mem. steering com. early childhood edn. So. Ill. U., 1976—. Vol. Hospice for Cancer Patients, East St. Louis, 1984—; mem. Mo. State Choir, St. Louis, 1981—, sec., 1981—. Mem. Zeta Phi Beta. Democrat. Home: 4720 S Spring Apt 6 Saint Louis MO 63116

SMITH, CHRISTOPHER JAMES, electrical engineering technology educator, consultant; b. Youngstown, Ohio, July 13, 1952; s. Bernard Francis and Mary Regina (McCambridge) S.; m. Pamela Kay Leichtman, Mar. 2, 1983; children: James Robert, Christina Marie, Mary Katherine, Jamie Marie. BA, BSEE, U. Notre Dame, 1979, MSEE, 1983. Data processing instr. Michiana Coll., South Bend, Ind., 1982-84; asst. prof. elec. engring. tech. Purdue U., Westville, Ind., 1984—; cons., Westville, 1984—; campus rep. elec. engring. tech. steering com. Purdue U., West Lafayette, Ind., 1984—; moderator Purdue Statewide Elec. Engring. Tech. Colloquium, Ft. Wayne, Ind., 1986. Author: Programming for Scientists and Engineers in Basic, 1984; also articles. Officer St. Peter's Parish Parents Club, La Porte, Ind., 1986—. Mem. IEEE, Am. Soc. Engring. Educators (campus rep. 1986), Data Processing Mgmt. Assn., Educators Spl. Interest Group of Data Processing Mgmt. Assn. (bd. dirs. 1985—), Soc. Profl. Journalists. Democrat. Roman Catholic. Home: 1540 Michigan Ave La Porte IN 46350 Office: Purdue U North Cen Campus Westville IN 46391

SMITH, CLIFFORD VAUGHN, JR., academic administrator; b. Washington, Nov. 29, 1931; s. Clifford Vaughn and Jean (Murray) S.; m. Nina Marie Smith, Aug. 22, 1953; children: Sharon, Debra, Patricia. BSCE, State U. Iowa, 1954; MS Engring., Johns Hopkins U., 1960, PhD, 1966. V.p. Oreg. State U., Corvallis, 1978-81, spl. asst. to chancellor, dir. Council Adv. Sci. and Engring. Edn., 1983-85, dir. Radiation Ctr., 1985-86; exec. engr. Bechtel Nat. Inc., Oak Ridge, Tenn., 1981-83; chancellor U. Wis., Milw., 1986—; cons. NSF, Washington, 1985—, Envirodyne Engrs., St. Louis, 1985—; mem. radiation adv. com. to sci. adv. bd. U.S. EPA, Washington, 1984—; bd. dirs. Astronautics Corp. Am., Milw. Bd. dirs. Milw. County Research Park, 1987—, Greater Milw. Com., 1987—, Columbia Hosp. Health System Inc., Milw., 1987—; at-large-gov. Am. Heart Assn., Milw., 1987—. Recipient Gold medal for exceptional service EPA, 1973; named Eminent Engr., Tau Beta Pi, 1979; hon. faculty mem. Blue Key Nat. Honor Fraternity, 1980. Mem. ASCE, NSPE, Am. Soc. Engring. Edn., Am. Assn. Higher Edn. Roman Catholic. Club: Univ. (Milw.). Avocations: reading historical novels, travel. Home: 4430 North Lake Dr Shorewood WI 53211 Office: Univ of Wisc-Milw PO Box 413 Milwaukee WI 53201

SMITH, COLLEEN SUE, bank executive; b. Mt. Pleasant, Mich., Dec. 27, 1946; d. Max Edmond and Susanna Wilhelmina (Scharf) S. A of Applied Sci. and Tech., Ferris State Coll., 1967; BS in Edn., Cen. Mich. U., 1970. Mgr. Elegante Enterprises, Okemos, Mich., 1971-76; forms analyst Mich. Nat. Bank, Lansing, 1976-78, forms mgr., 1978-81, product mgr., 1981-82, sales trainer, mgr., 1982-85, sales devel. mgr., 1985—. Chmn. Christian Women's Bus. and Profl. Council, 1976-78, hostess chmn., 1978-80; class officer Single Focus Sunday Sch. and Ch. Ministry, 1978-84. Mem. Am. Soc. Tng. and Devel., Bus. Forms Mgmt. Assn. (treas. 1978-80. Meritorious award 1980), Alpha Gamma Delta Alumni Assn. Avocations: gardening, reading, fishing, Bible studies. Home: 2815 Mersey Ln Apt A Lansing MI 48911 Office: Mich Nat Corp 30445 Northwestern Hwy Farmington Hills MI 48018

SMITH, CRAIG MALCOLM, architect, consultant; b. Bloomington, Ind., Nov. 4, 1952; s. Ned Myron and Virginia (Reuter) S.; m. Carolyn Guth, Sept. 3, 1983; 1 child, Natalie Fern. BArch, U. Ill., 1974, MArch, 1976. Registered architect, Chgo. Design instr. U. Ill., Urbana, 1974-76; intern Piano & Rogers, Paris, Ill., 1974; designer Bertrand Golberg, Chgo., 1976-77; architect Schipporeit Inc., Chgo., 1977-83; prin. Smith-Smith, Chgo., 1983; assoc. Bevins Cons., Chgo., 1983—; chmn. Mem. Friends of Downtown, Chgo. 1981—. planner City of Hammond and Ind. Arts Council, 1977. Mem. AIA (grantee 1977, chmn. office practice commn. 1985—, chmn. exhibit Chgo. chpt. housing trends, 1986), Nat. Council Archtl. Accreditation Bds (cert.). Democrat. Avocations: painting, photography, hist. restoration, skiing, tennis. Home: 3905 N Hamilton Chicago IL 60618 Office: Bevins Cons 70 W Madison Chicago IL 60602

SMITH, CRAIG WARREN, marketing executive; b. Elkhart, Ind., Jan. 21, 1947; s. Albert Lee and Phyllis (Wenger) S.; m. Madeline Ann Erdelyi, Oct. 15, 1966; children: Stephanie Ann, Jennifer Ann. BS, Ind. U., 1973. V.p. mktg. B&B Interiors Inc., Bristol, Ind., 1976—. Pres. Baugo Twp. Sch. Bd., Elkhart, 1981—. Served as staff sgt. USAF, 1966-69. Republican. Mem. Brethren Ch. Club: Four Lakes Country (Elkhart). Avocations: golfing, basketball. Home: 30948 Woods-n-Water Dr Elkhart IN 46517

SMITH, CURTIS S., corporate professional; b. Chickasha, Okla., Jan. 15, 1944; s. Ralph C. and Mary D. (Reeves) S.; m. Cheryl Wood, June 20, 1964 (div. Dec. 1973); m. Susan R. Montgomery, Dec. 20, 1976. B in Aerospace Engring., Okla. U., 1972. Mgr. Procter and Gamble, Cape Girardeau, Mo., 1972-85; pres., chief exec. officer Cusan Corp., Cape Girardeau, 1985—. Mem. city council, mayor pro tem, City of Cape Girardeau, 1982—; bd. dirs. United Way, Cape Girardeau, 1976—. Served with USN, 1963-67. Named to Hon. Order Ky. Cols. Mem. Jaycees (Ten Outstanding Missourians, Disting. Service award 1979). Republican. Lodge: Optimists (pres. 1986—). Avocation: golf. Home: 1210 Hilldale Circle Cape Girardeau MO 63701 Office: Cusan Corp 2121 William St Cape Girardeau MO 63701

SMITH, CYNTHIA ANNE, information specialist; b. Akron, Ohio, Nov. 28, 1944; d. Thomas and Lois Eileen (Lowry) Ignizio; m. Michael Wallace Smith, Aug. 26, 1967; children—Andrea Lynne, Jessica Clare. B.S., Kent State U., 1966; postgrad. Akron U., 1967-68. Asst. research librarian Goodyear Tire & Rubber Co., Akron, 1966-70, asst. to dir. research, 1971-77, staff research lit. chemist, 1978-82, staff info. specialist, 1983—. Office: Goodyear Tire & Rubber Co 1144 E Market St Dept 450D Akron OH 44316

SMITH, D. RICHARD, academic administrator; b. Lafayette, Ind., Dec. 27, 1930; s. Guy Macilvane Smith and Hilde Emily Sattler; m. Virginia Lehker, Aug. 24, 1957; children: Richard Lehker, Steven Henry. BS, Purdue U., 1953, MS, 1957, PhD, 1960; postdoctoral study, Mich. State U., 1960-62, U. Mich., 1970, Harvard U., 1971, Cambridge U., 1971, Baruch Coll., 1972, CUNY, 1972, 74, 76; grad., Cuauhnahuac Instituto Colectivo de Lengua y Cultura, Cuernavaca, Morelos, Mexico, 1977. Dean, dir. Purdue U., Ft. Wayne, 1965-70; asst. to v.p. regional campus, dean continuing edn Purdue U., West Lafayette, Ind., 1970-74, asst. to exec. v.p. and provost, prof. gen. studies, 1974-76, asst. dir. Internat. edn. and research, prof. gen. studies, 1976-79, assoc dir. internat. edn. and reaserch and internat. programs in agr., prof. gen. studies, 1979—; con. accreditation examiner N.Cen. Commn. Higher Edn., Chgo. 1970—; bd. rep. Ind Consortium for Internat. Programs., 1976-87; accreditation chairperson The Am. Bd. Edn., Fairmount, W.Va., 1980—; del. White House Conf. Libraries and Info. Services, Washington, 1979; liaison officer Midwest U. Consortium for Internat. Activities, 1976-77; dir. U.S. Presdl. Commn. World Hunger Symposium, 1981; supr. U.S. Peace Corps Counselling Office, 1986—; seminar speaker Chinese Acad. Sci, Beijing, 1981, Nanjing, People's Republic of China, 1981. Editor: An Inventory of Non-Traditional Instructional Activities, Patterns of Innovation. Bd. dirs. Ft. Wayne Fine Arts Assn., 1966-70, Ft. Wayne YMCA, 1968-70, Northeastern Ind. Mental Health Ctr., 1966-70, pres. Lafayette Symphony Found., 1985—. Served to cpl. U.S. Army, 1953-55. Purdue Research Found. fellow, 1958-60; vis. scholar Horace G. Racknam Sch. Grad. Studies, U. Mich., 1977. Mem. AAUP (assoc.), Assn. U.S. Univ. Dirs. of Internat. Agr. Programs., Patners of The Americas, Purdue Alumni Assn. (life). Lutheran. Clubs: Ft. Wayne Quest, Ft. Wayne Forthnightly. Avocation: timpanist Lafayette Symphony. Home: 2851 Ashland West Lafayette IN 47906 Office: Purdue U AGAD Room 26C West Lafayette IN 47907

SMITH, DANIEL LARSEN, financial planner; b. Richmond, Va., Mar. 14, 1929; s. Henry Benton and Vivian (Larsen) S.; m. Patricia Jean McLaughlin, May 27, 1953; children: Mark, Susan, Jan, Paul, James. Degree in Modern Langs. and Naval Sci., U. Louisville, 1951. CLU; cert. fin. planner; chartered fin. cons. Agt. Commonwealth Life, Louisville, 1953-60, N.W. Nat. Life Ins. Co., Overland Park, Kans., 1964-70; mgr. Pacific Mut. Life, Overland Park, 1960-64; pres. Daniel L. Smith Assocs., Overland Park, 1970—. Trustee Suburban Med. Ctr., Lenexa, Kans., 1979-80. Served to capt. USMC, 1951-53, Korea. Mem. Internat. Assn. Fin. Planners, Life Underwriters Assn. Republican. Roman Catholic. Lodge: Rotary (pres., v.p., sec., treas. 1977-78, Paul Harris fellow 1982). Avocation: yachting. Home: 9801 Glenwood Overland Park KS 66212

SMITH, DANIEL R., bank holding company executive; b. 1934. With First of Am. Bank of Mich., 1955-82, sr. v.p., 1971-77, pres., then pres., chief exec. officer, 1977-82; with First of Am. Bank Corp., Kalamazoo, 1982—, pres., 1982-85, chmn. bd., chief exec. officer, 1985—. Served to capt. USAR, 1955-64. Office: First of Am Bank Corp 108 E Michigan Ave Kalamazoo MI 49007 *

SMITH, DARRELL WAYNE, metallurgical engineering educator, consultant; b. Long Beach, Calif., July 31, 1937; s. Joseph Sidney and Bethel Irene (Monroe) S.; m. Marilyn Margaret Meese, Dec. 20, 1958; children: Mark Kevin, Barbara Dean, Paul Edwin. BS MetE, Mich. Technol. U., 1959; MS in Metallurgy, Case Western Res. U., 1965, PhD, 1969. Process metallurgist Babcock & Wilcox, Beaver Falls, Pa., 1959-62; project engr. Gen. Electric Co., Cleve., 1962-68, research metallurgist, 1968-70; prof. metall. engring. Mich. Technol. U., Houghton, 1970—; pres. SCS Assocs. Inc., Houghton, 1984—; bd. dirs. Peninsula Copper Industries, Hubbell, Mich., 1983—; metall. engring. cons. various corps. Contbr. 50 reports and papers in field. Mem. Am. Soc. Metals Internat., Am. Powder Metall. Inst. Republican. Avocations: flying, sport fishing, piano playing. Home: 111 W Edwards Ave Houghton MI 49931 Office: Mich Technol U Dept Metall Engring Houghton MI 49931

SMITH, DAVID ANTHONY, motor manufacturing company executive; b. Spring Grove, Ill., Nov. 4, 1941; s. Elmer P. and Isabelle M. (Meyer) S.; m. Beverly J. Hildinger, July 6, 1963; children—Sheryl, Kimberly, Michael. B.S. in Elec. Engring., Milw. Sch. Engring., 1964. Quality and inspection supr. to design engr. Heppner Mfg., Round Lake, Ill., 1959-68; design engr. Boding Electronic, Chgo., 1968-69; design engr., gen. product mgr. RAE Corp., McHenry, Ill., 1969—. Pres. bd. edn. Richmond Burton Community High Sch., 1981—. Mem. Small Motor Mfrs. Assn. (pres.), Northwest Internat. Trade Club. Roman Catholic. Lodge: Moose. Home: 3909 Overton Dr Richmond IL 60071 Office: RAE Corp 5801 W Elm St McHenry IL 60050

SMITH, DAVID ODELL, public administrator, developer; b. Lebanon, Ohio, Oct. 3, 1951; s. Walter and Mildred (Hager) S.; m. Sherry Sue Osborn, Jan. 7, 1977; children: Justin, Taylor. BA, Furman U., 1974. Personnel dir. City of Mason, Ohio, 1977-78; city mgr. City of Mason, 1978-80; exec. dir. Countryside YMCA, Lebanon, 1980-83; dir. devel. Warren County, Lebanon, 1983-86, dir. adminstrn. and devel., 1986—; exec. dir. Warren County Community Improvement Corp., Lebanon, 1983—; dir., chmn. Southwest Ohio Ohio Indsl. Training Program, Hamilton, 1983—; vice chmn. Mason Planning Commn., 1980—; bd. mem. Warren County Planning Commn., 1978-79, Clermont-Warren Pvt. Industry Council, Batavia, Ohio, 1983—; bd. dirs. Warren County Area Progress Council, 1983—, Cert. Devel. Corp. Mem. allocations com. Warren County United Way, 1985-86. Mem. World Trade Assn., Ohio Devel. Assn. Republican. Lodge: Kiwanis. Avocations: golf, woodworking. Home: 448 Cloverwood Dr Mason OH 45040 Office: Warren County Offices 320 E Silver St Lebanon OH 45036

SMITH, DAVID SHAWN, pharmacist; b. Coshocton, Ohio, Feb. 3, 1960; s. John Elmer and Donna Ethel (Plotner) S.; m. Bunni Lee George, June 4, 1983; 1 child, Larissa Marie. BS in Pharmacy, Ohio State U., 1983. Registered pharmacist, Ohio, Fla. Mgr. K-Mart Pharmacy, Cape Coral, Fla., 1983-84, Columbus, Ohio, 1984—. Preceptor extern program Ohio State U. Mem. Cen. Ohio Cactus and Succulent Soc., Phi Eta Sigma, Alpha Lambda Delta, Kappa Psi (past v.p. Xi chpt.). Republican. Methodist. Avocations: cultivation of rare and endangered plants, freshwater tropical fish. Home: 2113 Zollinger Rd Upper Arlington OH 43221-1927 Office: K-Mart Pharmacy 3800 W Broad St Columbus OH 43228

SMITH, DAVID STEWART, aquatic safety educator; b. Wilmington, Del., Apr. 5, 1938; s. Alfred Ezekiel and Grace Mildred (Stewart) S.; m. Sara Jane Thomas, Dec. 30, 1961; children: Michael Carl, Debbie Sue. BS in Naval Sci., U.S. Coast Guard Acad., 1960; MEd, Am. U., 1970; PhD in Edn., St. Louis U., 1981. Commd. ensign USCG, 1960, advanced through grades to comdr., 1981, ret., 1981; pres. Smith Aquatic Safety Services, St. Charles, Mo., 1981—; mem. nat. adv. com. sea exploring. Author: Handbook of Cold Water Survival, 1978, Smith's Teaching Tips, 1981, Waterwise, 1983. Pres. SEAL Found., Gallatin, Tenn., 1987. Recipient George Washington Honor medal Freedoms Found., 1968, Improved Pub. Relations award Washington Treasury Dept., 1970; Cokesbury scholar Washington Meth. Ch., 1969. Mem. Nat. Safety Council, Nat. Assn. State Boating Law Adminstrn. (Nat. award 1981), Nat. Transp. Safety Assn. (bd. dirs. Dania, Fla. chpt. 1983—), USCG Alumni Assn. Methodist. Lodge: Masons. Home and Office: 61 Broken Oak Ct Saint Charles MO 63303

SMITH, DAVID WESLEY, orthopedic surgeon; b. Piqua, Ohio, Sept. 21, 1937; s. Richard and Harriet Smith; student Ohio Wesleyan U., 1958; D.O., Kirksville Coll. Osteo. Medicine, 1962; m. Tanzy J. Smith, May 21, 1962 (dec. 1986); children—Douglas M., Dyanna; m. Margaret Lynn Smith, Jan. 3, 1987. Intern, Doctors Hosp., Columbus, Ohio, 1962-63, resident in orthopedic and traumatic surgery, 1963-66; practice medicine specializing in orthopedic surgery, Columbus, 1966-67, Massillon, Ohio, 1967—; pres. Tri County Orthopedic Surgeons, Inc.; mem. staff, chmn. dept. surgery Doctors Hosp.; clin. asso. prof. orthopedics Ohio U.; adj. clin. instr. orthopedic surgery Kansas City Coll. Osteo Medicine. Diplomate Am. Osteo. Bd. Surgery. Fellow Am. Coll. Osteo. Surgeons, Am. Osteo. Acad. Orthopedics (past pres.); mem. Eighth Dist. Acad. Osteo. Medicine. Office: 3244 Bailey St NW Massillon OH 44646

SMITH, DAVID WILLIAM, research engineer; b. Lebanon, Ind., Aug. 6, 1945; s. Milburn Francis and Mildred Lois (Bowman) S.; m. Sharon Ann Pritchett, Aug. 28, 1971; children—Beth Ann, Kara Lynn. B.S., Purdue U., 1967, M.S., 1969; Ph.D., U. Ill., 1974. Registered profl. engr., Ill. Research engr. Deere & Co. Tech. Ctr., Moline, Ill., 1973—. Served with U.S. Army, 1969-71. Mem. Am. Soc. Agrl. Engrs. (Young Researcher award 1982), Soc. Automotive Engrs., Sigma Xi, Tau Beta Pi. Republican. Methodist. Co-author: Tractors and Their Power Units. Home: 120 39th Ave East Moline IL 61244 Office: Deere & Co Tech Ctr 330 River Dr Moline IL 61265

SMITH, DELANEY GERARD, JR., computerized automation company professional; b. Versailles, Ky., Aug. 10, 1954; s. Delaney Gerard and Lottie America (Burns) S. B.E.E., Cleve. State U., 1977; postgrad. Case Western Res. U., 1985—. Report writer Polytech Inc., Cleve., 1972; systems engring. trainee Motorola, Inc., Parma, Ohio, 1973-76; product engr. Gould Instrument Co., Cleve., 1977-79; sr. application engr. Allen-Bradley Co., Highland Heights, Ohio, 1979-82, sr. product engr., 1982—; sr. controls engr. Controlled Power Corp. Inventor (algorithm) PLC-3 PID Controller, 1982. Guitarist (record album) Nat. Conv. Gospel Choirs and Choruses, Orlando, Fla., 1982, Chgo., 1983. Dep. registrar Cuyahoga County Bd. Elections, Ohio, 1984. Mem. Instrument Soc. Am., Nat. Tech. Assn. (chmn. 1976-77), Greater Cleve. Choral Chpt. (young adult treas. 1982-83). Baptist. Avocations: bicycling, martial arts, guitar playing, songwriting, wood working. Home: 4361 Clarkwood Pkwy Warrensville OH 44128 Office: Allen-Bradley Co 747 Alpha Dr Highland Heights OH 44143

SMITH, DENNIS DONALD, architect; b. Fairbury, Nebr., Sept. 10, 1948; s. Donald Raymond and Leona Mae (Pelesly) S.; m. Jenell Marie Matson, May 20, 1972; children: Ty Donald, Trent Ryan. BArch, Kans. State U., 1972. Reg. architect, Kans., Colo., N.Mex., Calif., Wyo., Mont., Idaho, Tex. Draftsman Calvin, Kingdon & Berger, Wichita, Kans., 1973-74; job capt. Law/Kingdon P.A., Wichita, 1974-77, project arch., 1977-83, sr. project architect, 1983—. Mem. State of Kans. AIA/AGC Liason com., Topeka, 1985—. Mem. AIA, Kans. Am. Inst. Architects (membership chmn. Wichita sect. 1978-79), Kans. State U. Alumni Assn. Presbyterian. Avocations: archtl. photography, softball, hunting, collecting antique tractors. Home: 1602 Mesa Ct Wichita KS 67212 Office: Law/Kingdon Inc 345 Riverview Wichita KS 67203

SMITH, DONALD ARCHIE, religion business executive, consultant; b. Dayton, Ohio, Feb. 23, 1934; s. Archie Ford and Catherine Rosella (Rabold) S.; m. Joan Sandra Speedie, May 18, 1955; children—Douglas Alan, Keith Cameron, Deirdre Lynn, Neal Ramsey. B.A. in Sci. and Math., Harvard U., 1956; cert. Indsl. Coll. of Armed Forces, 1971. Nuclear research and project engr. N.Am. Aviation Co., 1956-62; fin. software specialist Nat. Cash Register, 1962-63; mgr. systems engring. N.Am. Aviation, 1963-67; mgr. bus. planning, mktg. services and pub. relations N.Am. Rockwell, Columbus, Ohio, 1967-72, mgr. internat. sales and mktg., 1968-73; mgr. stratetic planning Rockwell Internat. Corp., Columbus, 1973-76, program mgr. Condor weapons system, 1976-77, dir. guided bomb programs, 1977-78, dir. bus. devel. and legis. liaison, 1978-80; v.p. fin. applied tech. group Arvin Industries, Columbus, Ind., 1980-84; v.p. fin. Calspan Corp., Columbus, 1980-82, v.p. fin. and adminstrn., 1982-84, chief fin. officer, treas., dir., 1983-84; bus. dir. Franklin United Meth. Home, 1984-86; dir. fin. and adminstrn. North Ind. Conf. of the U.S. Meth. Ch., 1986—; ops. research cons., 1962-64; instr. math. Sinclair Coll., Dayton, Ohio, 1961-63; mem. U.S.-U.K. Bipartite Com. on Nuclear Weapons, 1958-61; industry chmn. Mil. Specifications and Standards Rev. Com., 1972-79; mgmt. cons., 1984—. Pres., trustee Columbus Arts Guild, 1980-83; treas., dir. Franklin United Methodist Home, 1982-84; auditor First United Meth. Ch., 1981-84; past pres., treas., trustee Players Theatre of Columbus, 1975-80; v.p. Ohio Assn. of U.S. Army, 1979-80; dist. commr. Boy Scouts Am., 1970-73, cubmaster, 1965-70; squadron comdr. CAP, 1976; chmn. Commn. on Racism in Columbus Pub. Schs., 1972. Recipient Nat. award Jr. Achievement, Inc., 1954; Letters of Commendation govt. agys., Am. Def. Preparedness Assn., Boy Scouts Am., 1958-78; Leadership award Nat. Mgmt. Assn., 1979. Mem. AIAA (nat. chmn. soc. and aerospace tech. com. 1980-83, nat. pub. policy com.), Royal Inst. Nav., Nat. Mgmt. Assn. (v.p., trustee), Nat. Rifle Assn. (life mem.), SAR, Palatines to Am. Clubs: Harvard of Ind.; Army and Navy. Lodges: Masons, Shriners. Contbr. articles to profl. jours. Home: 3811 Penbrook Dr Marion IN 46952 Office: 1105 N Western Ave Marion IN 46952

SMITH, DONALD EUGENE, banker; b. Terre Haute, Ind., Nov. 4, 1926; s. Henry P. and Ruth I. (Bius) S.; m. Mary F. Ryan, June 25, 1947; children: Virginia Lee, Sarah Jane. Student, Ind. U., 1945-47, Ind. State U., 1947-48. With Deep Vein Coal Co., Terre Haute, Ind., 1947-60, R.J. Oil Co., Inc., 1948-69; sec. Princeton Mining Co., Terre Haute, 1947—; pres. Terre Haute Oil Corp., 1947—; pres., chief exec. officer Terre Haute First Nat. Bank, 1969—; bd. dirs. So. Ind. Gas and Electric Co., Gen. Tel. Co. of Ind.; trustee Ind. State U. Bd. mgrs. Rose-Hulman Inst. Tech., 1978—; mem. exec. com. Alliance for Growth and Progress, 1985—, pres., 1987—; treas. Terre Haute Econ. Devel. Commn., 1982—. Mem. Terre Haute C. of C. (bd. dirs. 1982—). Club: Country of Terre Haute. Lodge: Elks. Home: 52 Allendale St Terre Haute IN 47802 Office: Terre Haute First Nat Bank 643 Wabash Ave Terre Haute IN 47808

SMITH, DONALD EUGENE, financial analyst; b. Norfolk, Nebr., July 25, 1953; s. Albert Lee and Blanche Anna (Koski) S.; m. Nancy Lynn Moeller, May 26, 1979; children: Stephanie Dawn, Brittany Lea. BSBA, U. Nebr., 1980, MBA, 1981. Pvt. practice fin. analysis and planning Lincoln, Nebr., 1981—; fin. feasability analyst Nebr. Dept. Health, Lincoln, 1984—. Served with USN, 1971-75, Vietnam. Republican. Methodist. Avocation: water-skiing. Home: 6249 Briar Rosa Dr Lincoln NE 68516

SMITH, DONALD WILLIAM, accountant; b. Des Moines, Apr. 11, 1949; s. William Paul and Maxine Doris (Lust) S.; m. Diana Lynn Powell, June 27, 1969; children: Timothy, Michael, Kimberly, Mathew. BS in Acctg., Drake U., 1971. Audit ptnr. Touche Ross & Co., Milw., 1972—. Com. mem. Boy Scouts Am., Milw., 1977—; treas. Am. Cancer Soc., Milw., 1984—. Served with Iowa N.G., 1971-77. Mem. Am. Inst. CPA's, Wis. Inst. CPA's. Republican. Home: 458 W Ellsworth Ln Bayside WI 53217 Office: Touche Ross & Co 250 E Wisconsin Ave Milwaukee WI 53202

SMITH, DORIS YVONNE, physical education teacher; b. Inverness, Fla., June 11, 1943; d. Eddie and Viola (White) Green; m. Robert Lee Smith, June 26, 1965. BS, Bennett Coll., 1964; MS, Ind. U., South Bend, 1978. cert. tchr. phys. edn. K-12. Tchr. Woodrow Wilson Jr. High Sch., South Bend, Ind., 1964-67; tchr., coach THomas Jefferson Elem.-Jr. High Sch., South Bend, 1967-81, Edward Eggleston Elem. Sch., South Bend, 1981—; mem. South Bend Community Sch. Corp. Intermediate Athletic Dirs. Council, 1978-79. Judge U. Notre Dame Cheerleaders, 1981; mem., coop. dir. Young Adult Choir Pilgrim Bapt. Ch. Named Tchr. of Yr., Thomas Jefferson Elem.-Jr. High Sch., 1981, Tchr. of Yr., Edward Eggleston Elem. Sch., 1982, Tchr. of Yr., South Bend Community Sch. Corp., 1982. Mem. NEA, Ind. State Tchrs. Assn., Delta Sigma Theta (South Bend Alumnae chpt., sec. 1986—, rep. to black coll. seminar). Democrat. Avocations: reading, sports, cooking, gardening, sewing. Home: 17460 Fleetwood Ln South Bend IN 46635 Office: Eggleston Elem Sch 19010 Adams Rd South Bend IN 46637

SMITH, ELDRED REID, librarian; b. Payette, Idaho, June 30, 1931; s. Lawrence E. and Jennie (Reid) S.; m. Judith Ausubel, June 25, 1953; children: Steven, Janet. B.A., U. Calif.-Berkeley, 1956, M.A., 1962; M.L.S., U. So. Calif., 1957. Aquisition reference librarian Long Beach State Coll. Library, 1957-59; reference librarian San Francisco State Coll. Library, 1959-60; bibliographer U. Calif.-Berkeley Library, 1960-65, head search div. acquisition dept., 1966-69, head loan dept., 1969-70, asso. univ. librarian, 1970-72, acting univ. librarian, 1971-72; dir. libraries, also prof. SUNY, Buffalo, 1973-76; univ. librarian U. Minn., 1976-87, prof., 1976—; lectr. Sch. Library Sci., U. Wash., 1972; bd. dirs. Center for Research Libraries, 1975-77. Editor: Outlook on Research Libraries; contbr. articles to library jours. Council on Library Resources fellow, 1970. Mem. ALA, Assn. Research Libraries (dir. 1979-85, pres. 1983-84), Assn. Coll. and Research Libraries (pres. 1977-78, dir. 1976-79, com. on academic status 1969-74, chmn. univ. libraries sect. 1974-75). Home: 576 Montcalm Pl Saint Paul MN 55116 Office: 499 O Meredith Wilson Library 309 19 th Ave S Minneapolis MN 55455-0414

SMITH, ELLEN OLIVER, microbiology educator; b. Nashville, June 3, 1945; d. Floyd Edward and Virginia Roselyn (Dosé) Oliver; m. John Robert Smith, Jan. 23, 1971. BS, La. State U., 1967, PhD, 1972. Vis. lectr. Eastern Mich. U., Ypsilanti, 1977-82; asst. prof. microbiology Madonna Coll., Livonia, Mich., 1983-86; assoc. prof. Madonna Coll., Livonia, 1986—. Mem. AAAS, Am. Soc. Microbiology. Avocations: travel, sewing, quilting, computers. Office: Madonna College 36600 Schoolcraft Livonia MI 48150

SMITH, EMILY LOUISE, radiologist; b. Madison, Wis., Sept. 11, 1943; d. William Charles Smith and Melba Emily (Grossmann) Lidisky. BA, Washington U., 1964, MD, 1968. Diplomate Am. Bd. Diagnostic Radiology. Intern Parkland Meml. Hosp., Dallas, 1968-69; resident Mallinckrodt Inst. Radiology, St. Louis, 1969-72; instr. in radiology Washington U., St. Louis, 1972-75, asst. prof. radiology, 1975—; practice medicine specializing in radiology St. Louis, 1972—. Mem. Am. Coll. Radiology, Radiologic Soc. N.Am., Mo. State Med. Assn., St. Louis Met. Med. Soc., Am. Assn. Univ. Radiologits. Republican. Avocation: needlepoint. Office: Mallinckrodt Inst Radiology 510 S Kingshighway Saint Louis MO 63110

SMITH, EVA BLANCHE, school psychologist; b. Rosendale, Wis., Apr. 10, 1914; d. Frank and Anna Augusta (Konow) S. BS, U. Wis., Oshkosh, 1965; MS, U. Wis., Madison, 1965; postgrad., U. Wis., Milw., 1967-68, U. No. Colo., 1968, 78, 82. Tchr. various schs., Rosendale, 1933-49; prin. Alice Callen Elem. Sch., Ripon, Wis., 1949-61; tchr. Oshkosh (Wis.) Pub. Schs., 1961-67; sch. psychologist Coop. Ednl. Service Agy. #6, Oshkosh, 1967—. Mem. Nat. Assn. Sch. Psychologists, Wis. Sch. Psychologists Assn., Delta Kappa Gamma, Phi Beta Sigma. Republican. Lodge: Pilgrim Rebecca. Home: 201 LaFayette St PO Box 174 Rosendale WI 54974 Office: Coop Ednl Service Agency #6 2300 Ripon Rd Oshkosh WI 54904

SMITH, FRANCIS THOMAS, III, health center administrator; b. Detroit, June 14, 1934; s. Francis Thomas Jr. and Maxine (Greene) S.; A.B., Hope Coll., Holland, Mich., 1960; M.H.A. (Nat. Tuberculosis Assn. grad. fellow 1960), Wayne State U., Detroit, 1961; m. E. Jane Fawcett, July 30, 1983; children—Thomas John, Karen Marie. Program devel. cons., dir. patient service programs Ill. Tuberculosis Assn., Springfield, 1961-63; exec. dir. Peoria (Ill.)-Stark County Tuberculosis Assn., 1963-66; adminstr. Allied Agys. Ctr.-Peoria County Bd. Care and Treatment Mentally Deficient Persons, Peoria, 1966—; cons. exec. dir. Ill. Assn. Maternal and Child Health, 1972-84; cons. exec. sec. Downstate Ill. Pediatric Soc.; mem. tri-county project rev. com. Ill. Health Systems Agy. Mem. program and budget com. Heart of Ill. United Way, 1970-78; mem. Forest Park Found., 1971—; bd. dirs. Tower Park, Inc., 1975, Council Responsible Driving, 1976-79; lay leader First United Meth. Ch., Peoria, 1979-80, chmn. adminstrv. bd., 1981-82. Served with USNR, 1953-57. Mem. Am. Soc. Public Adminstrn. (chpt. charter mem., past chpt. pres.), Am. Assn. Mental Deficiency, Nat. Rehab. Counseling Assn., Bldg. Owners and Mgrs. Assn., Nat. Rehab. Assn., Ill. Rehab. Assn., Ill. Public Health Assn. Republican. Lutheran. Clubs: Peoria Rotary, Masons, Shriners. Contbr. articles to profl. jours. Office: 320 E Armstrong Ave Peoria IL 61603

SMITH, FRANK EARL, association executive; b. Fremont Center, N.Y., Feb. 4, 1931; s. Earl A. and Hazel (Knack) S.; m. Caroline R. Gillin, Aug. 14, 1954; children—Stephen F., David S., Daniel E. B.S., Syracuse U., 1952. With Mellor Advt. Agy., Elmira, N.Y., 1954-55; asst. mgr. Assn. of Commerce, Elmira, 1955-56, C. of C., Binghamton, N.Y.; and mgr. Better Bus. Bur., Broome County, N.Y., 1956-60; exec. v.p. C. of C., Chemung County, Elmira, 1960-65, Schenectady County (N.Y.) C. of C., 1965-69, Greater Cin. C. of C., 1969-78; pres. Greater Detroit C. of C., 1978—. Served to 1st lt. USAF, 1952-54. Named Young Man of Yr. Jr. C. of C. Elmira, 1964. Mem. C. of C. Execs. Mich., Am. C. of C. Execs. (past chmn.), N.Y. State C. of C. Execs. (past pres.), Ohio C. of C. Execs. (past pres.), C. of C. of U.S. (past bd. dirs., past chmn. nat. bd. regents Insts. for Orgn. Mgmt.), Ctr. Internat. Pvt. Enterprise (bd. dirs.). Presbyterian. Clubs: Detroit, Detroit Athletic, Renaissance, Lochmoor Golf, Hidden Valley-Otsego Ski. Home: 45 Renaud Rd Grosse Pointe Shores MI 48236 Office: 600 W Lafayette Blvd Detroit MI 40220

SMITH, GARY RICHARD, development company executive; b. Niagara Falls, N.Y., Feb. 21, 1943; s. Donald R. and Faith (May) S.; m. Jan M. Nelson, Sept. 9, 1961; children: Tim, Christine, Chad, Lane. BA, St. Cloud (Minn.) State U., 1965; exec. program, Stanford U., 1980. Various sales mgr. positions Horrner Waldorf/Champion Internat., St. Paul, 1963-76; exec. dir. sales Cummins Engine Co., Columbus, Ind., 1976-84; v.p. sales and mktg. White Engines Inc., Canton, Ohio, 1984-87; pres., chief operating officer Vancorp, Indpls., 1987—, also bd. dirs.; pres., bd. dirs. Eye Guards Inc., Canton, 1982—; bd. dirs. West Wind Packaging, Grand Rapids, Mich. Named to Hall of Fame, Nat. Assn. Intercollegiate Athletics, 1981, St. Cloud State U., 1984. Republican. Methodist. Avocations: racquetball, antiques, officiating collegiate wrestling.

SMITH, GENE GORDON, accountant; b. Alma, Mich., Dec. 29, 1957; s. George J. and Virginia I. (Akin) S.; m. Wendy Jo Clarke, Feb. 23, 1980; children: Morgan Leigh, Carlie Anne. BSBA, Cen. Mich. U., 1979. Owner Landscape & Wood Design, Mt. Pleasant, Mich., 1980-82; sr. corp. acct. Panhandle Ea. Corp., Houston, 1983-85; sr. acct. Karl J. Leppien, P.C., Alma, 1986-87; prin. Leppien & Smith, Alma, 1987—; Advisor Denver Bapt. Bible Coll., 1986. Mem. Am. Inst. CPA's, Mich. Soc. CPA's, Alma C. of C. (bd. dirs. 1987—). Republican. Baptist. Club: Exchange. Avocations: golf, woodworking. Home: 308 Orchard Alma MI 48801 Office: Leppien & Smith PC 7810 N Alger Rd Alma MI 48801

SMITH, GEORGE CURTIS, lawyer, judge; b. Columbus, Ohio, Aug. 8, 1935; s. George B. and Dorothy R. S.; m. Barbara Jean Wood, July 10, 1963; children—Curt, Geof, Beth Ann. B.A., Ohio State U., 1957, J.D., 1959. Bar: Ohio 1959. Asst. city atty. City of Columbus, 1959-62; exec. asst. to Mayor of Columbus, 1962-63; asst. atty. gen. State of Ohio, 1964; chief counsel to pros. atty. Franklin County, Ohio, 1965-70, pros. atty., 1971-80; judge Franklin County Mcpl. Ct., Columbus, 1980-85; judge Franklin County Common Pleas Ct., 1985—. faculty Ohio Jud. Coll.; Bd. elders Covenant Ch., trustee Central Ohio sect. Am. Lung Assn.; trustee Leukemia Soc. Central Ohio; men's bd. Project Hope; trustee Crime Solvers Anonymous, Teen Challenge, Inc.; pres. Young Republican Club, 1963, Buckeye Rep. Club, 1968; exec. com. Franklin County Rep. Party, 1971-80. Recipient Superior Jud. Service award Supreme Ct. Ohio, 1980, 81, 82, 83, 84; Resolution of Honor, Columbus Bldg. and Constrn. Trades Council, 1980; award Eagles, 1980; Mem. Ohio Common Pleas Judges Assn., Ohio Pros. Attys. Assn. (life, pres., Ohio Prosecutor of Yr, Award of Honor, Leadership award), Columbus Bar Assn., Ohio Bar Assn., Assn. Trial Lawyers Am., Ohio Common Pleas Judges Assn., Ohio Mcpl.-County Judges Assn. 2d v.p., trustee). Presbyterian. Clubs: Columbus Athletic (pres., dir.), Columbus Maennerchor, Germania, Lawyers Club of Columbus (pres. 1975), Shamrock. Lodges: Fraternal Order Police Assocs., Eagles, Masons, Shriners. Office: Franklin County Common Pleas Ct 369 S High St Columbus OH 43215

SMITH, GERALD ROBERT, financial executive; b. Detroit, Sept. 3, 1956; s. Harold Franklin and Jolan Helen (Hrabosky) S.; m. Deborah Jo Gunter, Sept. 8, 1979; 1 child, Brian Andrew. BBA, Eastern Mich. U., Ypsilanti, 1978; postgrad., U. Mich., 1985—. CPA, Mich. Accnt. Ernst and Whinney, Detroit, 1979-84; corp. controller Fed. Screw Works, Detroit, 1984-86, sec., treas., chief fin. officer, 1986—. Mem. bd. cons. Eastern Mich. U. Career Horizons, Ypsilanti, 1983-86. Recipient Wall Street Jour. award, 1978. Mem. Fin. Exec. Inst., Am. Inst. CPA's, Mich Assn. CPA's. Avocations: golf, hockey. Home: 9748 Normandy Dr Plymouth MI 48170

SMITH, GLENN MORGAN, dentist; b. Gary, Ind., Mar. 12, 1947; s. Morgan B. and Virginia E. (Shepherd) S.; m. Diane Ruth Bontrager, June 3, 1973; 1 child, Erick Glenn. B.S., Ind. U.-Bloomington, 1969; D.D.S., Ind. U.-Indpls., 1972. Councilman, Montpelier City Govt., Ind., 1980—, council pres., 1984—. Fellow Internat. Coll. Dentists; mem. Am. Soc. Geriatric Dentistry, Pierre Fauchard Acad., Am. Dental Assn., Am. Soc. of Dentistry for Children, Am. Soc. Dentistry for Children, Ind. Dental Assn. (trustee 1981—), Ind. U. Alumni Assn. (life), Montpelier C. of C., Ind. U. Varsity Club (loyalty), Psi Omega. Republican. Methodist. Lodge: Kiwanis (pres. 1976-77). Avocations: photography; hiking; reading. Home: 533 S Adams St Montpelier IN 47359

SMITH, GRACIE BERNON, dress designer, tailor; b. Hyden, Ky., Aug. 1, 1932; d. Joe and Eva Lee (Howard) Maggard; m. William Robert Smith, June 10, 1972; children by previous marriage—Donald Eugene Turpin, Jr., Daniel Edwin Turpin; stepchildren: Steven Carson Smith, Vicki Lynn Booth. Student Nat. Sch. Dress Design-Chgo., 1955-58; student in real estate Purdue U., 1973. Tailor Sovern Tailors, Lafayette, Ind., 1965-68; mgr. Millers Sportswear, Lafayette, 1968-70; with Benker Realty, Lafayette, 1973-75; service contract dept. head Montgomery Ward, Lafayette, 1975-77; alteration dept. head Montgomery Ward, 1977-80; owner, operator Bernon Custom Fashions, Lafayette, 1955—; cons. local 4-H Clubs, 1983—; local sales rep. Leiters Designer Fabrics, Kansas City, Mo., 1982-86; local sales mgr. House of Laird Fabrics, Lexington, Ky., 1985-86. Com. mem. Tippecanoe County Fair, Lafayette, 1983-85. Fellow The Custom Tailors and Designers Assn. Am., Nat. Assn. Female Execs. Baptist. Avocations: bowling; gardening; knitting; cooking; crocheting. Home and Office: 2350 N 23d St Lafayette IN 47904

SMITH, GREGORY JOSEPH, psychologist; b. N. Canton, Ohio, Dec. 27, 1951; s. Joseph Ernest and Dorothy (Uber) S.; m. Marcia K. Broemsen, June 9, 1973. B.A., Kent State U., 1975; M.A., SUNY-Binghamton, 1978, Ph.D., 1981. Jr. research asst. Kent (Ohio) State U., 1973-75; sr. research asst. SUNY-Binghamton, 1975-79, intern Office of Provost for Grad. Studies, 1979-80; asst. prof. Case Western Res. U., Cleve., 1980-84; managerial psychologist PRADCO, 1983—; asst. prof. Kent State U., Ohio, 1984—; cons. in field. Mem. Am. Psychol. Assn., Am. Assn. Sci., Eastern Psychol. Assn., Internat. Soc. Devel. Psychobiology, Midwestern Psychol. Assn., N.Y. Acad. Sci. Contbr. articles to profl. jours. Office: PRADCO 30195 Chagrin Blvd Pepper Pike OH 44124

SMITH, GUY W., health care executive; b. Alton, Ill., May 31, 1940; s. Guy and Claudine (Young) S.; m. Nancy Smith; children: Guy W., Lynn, Teresa, Michael. Cert. restaurant mgmt., INT Industries, Pasadena, Calif., 1964; nursing home adminstrn. tng., Milw. Area Tech. Coll.-Unicare Health Program, 1969; continuing edn., Marquette U., Milw., 1980-83. Owner, mgr. Internat. House of Pancakes Restaurant, Milw., 1964-67; nursing home adminstr. Unicare Health, Milw., 1967-69, adminstr., 1969-72, v.p., 1972-80, exec. v.p., 1980-83; pres. United Health, Milw., 1983-86; bd. dirs. Universal Savs. Bank; mem. adv. bd. IN-Speech, Phila., 1982-84. Fund Raiser Hunger Task Force, Milw., 1986; mem. boy's club Am. Boosters, Milw., 1967-86, Ranch Bd., Milw., 1982-86; bd. dirs. Art Reach, 1987. Mem. Assn. Healthcare Adminstrs. (mem. multiple facility commn. 1983-86), Am. Mgmt. Assn. Republican. Roman Catholic. Club: Milw. Athletic. Avocations: horses, sports, reading. Home: W140 N7668 Lilly Rd Menomonee Falls WI 53051 Office: United Health Inc 105 W Michigan St Milwaukee WI 53203

SMITH, H. DOUGLAS, communications company executive; b. Lansing, Mich., May 26, 1938; s. Hallie Lilburn and Ruth Amelia (McDonald) S.; m. Mary Elizabeth Bround, June 11, 1961; children: Scott M., Craig D., Daniel B. BS in Mech. Engring., Mich. State U., 1960; SM in Indsl. Mgmt., MIT, 1963. Dir. planning and materiel Whirlpool, St. Paul, 1967-73; dir. planning., material and data processing BMC Industries, St. Paul, 1973-75, gen. mgr. MICRO div., 1975-82, dir. quality, ops. supr., 1982-86; v.p., chief operating officer OmniCom Data, Mendota Heights, Minn., 1986—. Chmn. Rep. precinct, St. Paul, 1967-71, treas., North Oaks, Minn., 1981-85. Served to staff sgt. USAFR. Mem. Am. Soc. Quality Control. Avocation: tennis. Home: 1 Nord Circle Saint Paul MN 55110 Office: OmniCom Data 1408 Northland Dr #206 Mendota Heights MN 55120

SMITH, HAROLD HASKEN, university administrator; b. Cin., Mar. 16, 1942; s. Harold C. and Ruth V. (Hasken) S.; m. Karen A. Willis, Dec. 20, 1969; children—Amy Elizabeth, Andrew David, Anne Cameron. A.B., Centre Coll., 1964; M.B.A., Am. U., 1968. Admissions counselor Centre Coll., Danville, Ky., 1964-66, assoc. dir. admissions, 1968-70, dir. admissions, 1970-73, dean admissions, 1973-80, v.p., dean students, 1980-83, lectr. econs. mgmt., 1973-80; v.p. devel. Muskingum Coll., New Concord, Ohio, 1983—; cons. in edn. Dir. Boyle-Mercer County (Ky.) YMCA, 1979-83; mem. bd. trustees Guernsey Meml. Hosp., 1987—; bd. dirs. Southeast Ohio. Symphony Orch., 1983—, Renew Environment of New Concord, 1983—. Recipient Disting. Chmn. awards Rotary Found., 1981-82. Mem. Council Ind. Ky. Colls. and Univs., Nat. Assn. Student Personnel Adminstrs., Am. Coll. Personnel Assn., Cambridge C. of C. (bd. dirs. 1984—), Nat. Assn. Coll. Admissions Counselors. Presbyterian (elder). Lodge: Rotary (pres. 1979-80, dist. gov.'s rep. 1981-82). Office: Muskingum College New Concord OH 43762

SMITH, HARRY BUCHANAN, JR., graphic designer, photographer, writer; b. Springfield, Ill., Aug. 30, 1924; s. Harry Buchanan and Cordelia Warren (Birchall) S.; divorced; 1 child, Mark Savolainen. B of Design, U. Mich., 1947; MS in Design, Ill. Inst. Tech., 1948. Designer Chgo. Plan Commn., 1948-49, Warren Wetheral & Assocs., Chgo., 1949-50; dir. design Dekovic-Smith Design Orgn., Chgo., 1951-58; prin. H.B. Smith & Assocs., Chgo., 1959-87. Works include graphic design (with Mortimer Adler) Encyclopaedia Britannica, 15th edit., 1975, 176 exhibitions, 1951-87; redisigned YMCA internat. symbol, numerous corporate identity programs, pubs. Served to lt. (j.g.) USNR, 1943-47, PTO. Mem. Am. Inst. Graphic Arts, Soc. Typographic Arts (steering com.). Home and Office: 415B Grant Pl Chicago IL 60614

SMITH, ISABEL FRANCIS, financial planner; b. Detroit, May 21, 1935; d. Edward Hugh and Isabel Francis (Winegar); m. Lawrence Smith, June 7, 1958; children—Mark, Hugh, Claire. Student, Newton Coll., 1953-54; B.A., U. Mich., 1957, M.A., 1958, postgrad., 1975-76. Registered investment adviser, SEC; cert. fin. planner. Tchr., Edison Sch., Hazel Park, Mich. and Warren Valley Sch., Dearborn, Mich., 1958-61; counselor Riverside High Sch., Dearborn Hts., Mich., 1961-62; pres. Isabel Francis Smith Ltd., Birmingham, Mich., 1980—, Integrated Fin. Strategies, Ltd., Birmingham, 1980—; registered rep., dist. mgr. Investors Diversified Services, Oak Park, Mich., 1978-80; instr. Henry Ford Community Coll., Oakland County Community Coll., Schoolcraft Community Coll. (all Mich.), 1979—; cons. to women's orgns., 1977—; writer, radio and TV personality. Lectr., trustee Bloomfield Twp. Library; founder Interlochen Friends, Vol. Network for Women. Recipient Heart of Gold award United Found., 1976; Outstanding New Rep. award Investors Diversified Services, 1979. Mem. Registry Fin. Planning Practitioners, AAUW, League Women Voters, Nat. Assn. Profl. Saleswomen, Internat. Assn. Fin. Planners (past pres. S.E. Mich. chpt.), Inst. Cert. Fin. Planners (regional dir., nat. dir. 1983-87), Nat. Assn. Life Underwriters, Nat. Assn. Women Bus. Owners, Birmingham-Bloomfield C. of C., Interlochen Alumni Assn. (award, past pres.), U. Mich. Alumni Assn., Detroit Symphony League, Phi Beta Kappa (nat. chmn., past pres. Detroit assn., mem. exec. com., Pres.'s award Detroit assn.), Pi Lambda Theta. Clubs: Women's Economic, Village Women's, Birmingham Women's Ctr. Home: 7110 Paterese St Birmingham MI 48010 Office: 30200 Telegraph Rd Suite 466 Birmingham MI 48010

SMITH, J. ALBERT, JR., banking executive; b. Indpls., June 26, 1940; s. J. Albert Se. and Bernice (Brennan) S.; m. Maribeth Ann Albers, Aug. 20, 1964; children—J. Albert, III, Kathleen, Edward. B.B.A., U. Notre Dame, 1962; M.B.A., NYU, 1967. Asst. sec. Chem. Bank, N.Y.C., 1964-69; v.p. Ind. div. Am. Fletcher Nat. Bank, Indpls., 1969, sr. v.p. corp., 1969-77; exec. v.p. real estate Bank One, Indpls., 1977—; pres. Banc One Mortgage Corp., Indpls., 1977—. Bd. dirs. Brebeuf Prep. Sch., Indpls., Jr. Achievement Central Ind., Indpls., Little Sisters of Poor, Indpls., U.S. Shelter Corp., Greenville, S.C., Cath. Social Services, Indpls. Served with USN, 1962-64. Mem. Robert Morris Assocs., Mortgage Bankers Assn., Am. Bankers Assn., Ind. Bankers Assn., Indpls. Athletic Club, Am. Bus. Club. Republican. Clubs: Meridian Hills, Woodstock Country, Columbia, 702, Notre Dame, 100. Home: 7524 N Pennsylvania St Indianapolis IN 46240 Office: Banc One Mortgage Corp 333 N Pennsylvania Indianapolis IN 46277

SMITH, J. G., provincial judge. Judge Ct. of Queen's Bench, Winnipeg, Man., Can. Office: Court of Queen's Bench, Law Courts Bldg., Winnipeg, MB Canada R3C OV8 *

SMITH, J. HAROLD, II, oral and maxillofacial surgeon; b. Fort Wayne, Ind., Feb. 20, 1947; s. J. Harold Sr. and Lorraine (Miller) S.; m. Janet Grigsby, June 6, 1969; children: Jill Suzanne, Meg Elizabeth. AB, Ind. U., 1969, DDS, 1973. Pvt. practice oral and maxillofacial surgery Indpls., 1976—; bd. dirs. J. Everett Light Career Ctr., Indpls. Recipient Oral Surgery award Great Lakes Soc. Oral Surgeons, 1973. Fellow Am. Soc. Oral and Maxillofacial Surgeons (com. chmn. 1986, del. 1984-86); mem. ADA, Ind. Soc. Oral and Maxillofacial Surgeons (pres. 1984, treas. 1986—), Ind. Dist. Dental Soc. (editor newsletter 1979-82, sec. 1982-83, pres. 1984-85, Plaque of Excellence 1982). Republican. Methodist. Avocations: sports, tennis, golf, skiing, skydiving. Home: 8738 Sawleaf Rd Indianapolis IN 46260 Office: 652 N Girls School Rd Indianapolis IN 46214

SMITH, JAMES DOUGLAS, architect; b. Chgo., May 14, 1943; s. Lyman Douglas and Hallie Marie (Sanders) S.; m. Anita Louise Metzger, June 24, 1967; 1 child, Elisa Marie. BArch with honors, U. Ill., 1968; cert. with honors Ecole des Beaux Arts, Fontainbleau, France, 1967. Registered architect, Ill., Ind., Mich., Mo. Planner, Northeastern Ill. Planning Commn., Chgo., 1966, Dept. Devel. and Planning, Chgo., 1968-69; archtl. designer A. Epstein Internat., Chgo., 1969-72; architect-planner, ptnr. Smith-Kureghian & Assos., Chgo., 1972-77; architect City of Gary (Ind.), 1977-79; v.p. H. Seay Cantrell Assos., Inc., Architects, 1979—; planning dir. Indsl. Council/N.W. Community, Chgo., 1972; urban planning cons. Nathan-Barnes & Assos., Chgo., 1972—; prin. works include Sheraton Hotel, Gary, Gary Hotel Renovation, Pub. Safety Bldg., Gary, Adam Benjamin Jr. Metro Ctr., Gary; co-designer Hyatt Regency Hotel, Chgo.; other city and comml. rehab. plans; co-author bldg. code; bd. dirs. Ind. Archtl. Found., 1981—. Precinct del. 44th Ward Assembly, Chgo., 1973—, chmn. services com., 1973-74, chmn. steering com., 1974—, campaign area chmn., 1974-76; bd. dirs. Ind. Archtl. Found., Lake Ct. House Found., Crown Point, Ind., 1985—, City of Crown Point Hist. Rev. Bd., 1985—; mem. grant rev. jury Ind. Arts Commn., 1983, adv. panel design arts, 1982-83, 84-85. Named an Outstanding Young Man Am., 1974; recipient Outstanding Achievement award Ind. Soc. Profl. Engrs., 1986, Outstanding Concrete Achievement award Ind. Concrete Council, 1986. Mem. AIA (sec. planning com. 1972-75, dir. chpt., bd. dirs. 1983-84, First Honor award Ind. chpt. 1986, pres.-elect Northwest Ind. chpt.), Ind. Soc. Architects (bd. dirs. 1984—), Internat. Platform Assn., Prestressed Concrete Inst., Constrn. Specifications Inst., Nat. Council Archtl. Registration Bds., Chgo. Assn. Commerce and Industry, Gargoyle Soc. (membership chmn. 1968), Scarab, Sigma Tau. Home: 1001 Merrillville Rd Crown Point IN 46307 Office: 522 Broadway Suite 212 Gary IN 46402

SMITH, JAMES MARSHALL, biophysicist, government official; b. Charleston, W.Va., Sept. 28, 1942; s. Louis Benton and Edna Christine (Norman) S.; m. June Wright, July 26, 1965; children: James Jr., Timothy, Kym. BS, W.Va. U., 1964, MS, 1966, PhD, 1969. Cert. Am. Bd. Health Physics, 1981—. Physicist RCA, Princeton, N.J., 1969-71; sr. research fellow Inst. Molecular Biophysics, Tallahassee, 1971-74; research prof. U. Utah Sch. Medicine, Salt Lake City, 1974-83; suprvisory research physicist Nat. Inst. Occupational Safety and Health/CDC, Cin., 1983—; adj. asst. prof. math. Rider Coll., Lawrenceville, N.J., 1969-71; bd. dirs. Early Success Inst., Inc., Cin., 1986—. Editor: (assoc.) Health Physics Jour., 1986—; contbr. articles to profl. jours. Fellow NASA, 1964-67, NSF, 1967. Mem. Health Physics Soc., Radiation Research Soc., N.Y. Acad. Scis., Bioelectromagnetics Soc., Internat. Nuclear Tracks Soc. Avocations: fly fishing, alpine skiing, writing. Home: 7158 Goldengate Dr Cincinnati OH 45244 Office: Nat Inst Occupational Safety & Health 4676 Columbia Pkwy Cincinnati OH 45226

SMITH, JAMES PERRY, educator; b. Southwest City, Mo., Aug. 15, 1933; s. Eual Clay and Susan Marie (Perry) S.; m. Molly Jayne Smith, Aug. 21, 1955; children—James Duston, Rebecca Dawn. B.S., Okla. State U., 1960; M.S., Ark. U., 1963. Cert. life vocat. agr. tchr., Mo. Instr. animal sci. dept. Okla. State U., Stillwater, 1964-69; sec. Okla. Quarter Horse Assn., 1969-73, vocat. agr. instr. McDonald County High School, Anderson, Mo., 1978—; technician, Eagle-Picher Industries, 1985—; processor Teledyne, Neosho, Mo., 1974-78. Show supt. McDonald County Fair Bd.; mem. McDonald County Extension Council, Econ. Security Corp., road commr. Buffalo spl. dist.; bd. dirs., Sunday Sch. supt. Goodman United Meth. Ch. Served to sgt. U.S. Army, 1955-57. Recipient Pres.'s award for outstanding vocat. agr. tchr., 1979. Mem. Am. Vocat. Assn., Mo. Vacat. Assn., Mo. Cattleman's Assn. Contbr. articles to profl. jours. Office: Eagle Picher Industries Joplin MO 64801

SMITH, JAMES T., electronics company executive. Chmn., pres., chief exec. officer, dir. Magnavox Govt. and Indsl. Electronics Co., Ft. Wayne, Ind. Office: Magnavox Govt & Indsl Electronics Co 1313 Production Rd Fort Wayne IN 46808 *

SMITH, JANE SCHNEBERGER, city clerk; b. Chgo., Aug. 9, 1928; d. Frank R. and Marion (Durante) Schneberger; m. Z. Erol Smith, Jr., Oct. 28, 1950 (div. 1974); children—Suzan McCue Kuester, Tracy Smith Cawley, Cameron Farley, Z. Erol III, Kimberly, Scott. B.A. in Chemistry, U. Colo., 1950; M.A. in Communication, Mich. State U., 1978, PhD, 1987, in ednl. adminstrn. Mich. State U., 1987. Chemist, Kellogg Switchboard, Chgo., 1950-51; tchr. Crab Orchard Sch., Palos Heights, Ill., 1969-70; staff advisor South Cook County Girl Scouts, Harvey, Ill., 1970-72; program and tng. dir. Mich. Capitol council Girl Scouts U.S., Lansing, 1972-75; dir. service learning ctr. Mich. State U., East Lansing, 1975-81; city clk. City of Ashland, Wis., 1981—; cons. vol. adminstrn., Mich., Wis., 1975—. Co-editor Looking Backward Moving Forward; contbr. articles to profl. jours. Vice pres. South Cook County Girl Scout Council, Harvey, Ill., 1967-69 (Thanks badge 1972), Mich. Capitol Girl Scout Council, Lansing, 1976-78 (cert. appreciation 1975); bd. dirs. Lansing RSVP, 1976-81, Ashland Mus., 1985—, Ptnrs. in Recovery, 1985—, New Horizons, 1985—. Mem. Internat. Assn. Municipal Clks., Wis. Municipal Clks. Assn. (dist. dir. 1984-86). Roman Catholic. Club: Am. Bus. Women's Assn. (scholarship chmn. 1985) (Ashland). Lodge: Zonta (pres. 1979-81). Avocations: stained glass, gardening. Home: 700 MacArthur St Ashland WI 54806 Office: City Ashland 601 W 2nd St Ashland WI 54806

SMITH, JEFFREY DEAN, accountant; b. Milw., May 2, 1958; s. Robert Francis and Betty (Owen) S.; m. Victoria Jean Andreas, Apr. 25,

1986. BBA, U. Wis., Oshkosh, 1980. CPA, Wis. Staff acct. Schumaker, Romenesko & Assocs., Appleton, Wis., 1980-82; cost acctg. supr., sr. acct. Menasha Corp., Neenah, Wis., 1982-86; treas., controller Castle-Pierce Printing Co., Oshkosh, 1986—; cons. in field, Neenah, 1982—. Mem. Am. Inst. CPA's, Wis. Inst. CPA's, Oshkosh Acctg. Club (v.p. 1980). Lodge: Rotary. Avocations: martial arts, sports. Home: 1497 Windmar Dr Neenah WI 54956 Office: Castle-Pierce Printing Co Oshkosh WI 54000

SMITH, JEFFREY HOWARD, accountant; b. Des Moines, Dec. 3, 1956; s. Richard Howard and Helen Louise (Shepley) S.; m. Carol Sue Lippens, Sept. 7, 1985; 1 child, Crystal. AA in Liberal Arts, Des Moines Area Community Coll., 1977; BA in Acctg., U. No. Iowa, 1979. CPA, Iowa. Sr. staff acct. Dee, Gosling and Co., Maquoketa, Iowa, 1980-84; pvt. practice tax acctg. Jeffrey H. Smith, Tax Practice, Maquoketa, Iowa, 1984-85; acct. West Des Moines (Iowa) Water Works, 1985—. Mem. Am. Inst. CPA's, Iowa Soc. CPA's, Maquoketa Jaycees. Democrat. Avocations: jogging, coin collecting, music, landscaping. Home: 1035 22d St West Des Moines IA 50265 Office: West Des Moines Water Works PO Box 65505 West Des Moines IA 50265

SMITH, JEFFREY PETER, auditor, consultant; b. Detroit, Oct. 4, 1956; s. William H. and Patricia Marie (LePage) S.; m. Jeanne Elizabeth Rose, Aug. 17, 1974; children: Christine Marie, Jeffrey Peter Jr., Brian Patrick, Kathryn Elizabeth. Assoc. in Bus. Adminstrn., St. Clair County Community Coll., 1976; BBA, Eastern Mich. U., 1978; MBA, Wayne State U., 1986. Acct. Commn. on Profl. and Hosp. Activities, Ann Arbor, Mich., 1976-79, Ford Motor Co., Milan, Mich., 1979-82; fin. procedure analyst Ford Motor Co., Dearborn, Mich., 1982-84, corp. auditor, 1984—; cons. Henry H. Smith & Co., Algonac, Mich., 1985—. Roman Catholic. Lodge: KC. Home: 2205 Grindley Park Dearborn MI 48124 Office: Ford Motor Co- WHQ American Rd Room 162 Dearborn MI 48121

SMITH, JEREMY JON, data processing company executive; b. Chicago Heights, Ill., Nov. 25, 1951; s. Jay W. and Ruth Elizabeth (Cull) S. Student, Ind. U., 1969-70. Software specialist Howard Sams's div. ITT, Indpls., 1978-80; gen. mgr. Kaltronics Corp., Northbrook, Ill., 1980-82; pres., chief exec. officer PC Distbg., Northbrook, 1982—; bd. dirs. Nat. Micro Inc., Wheeling, Ill., PCX Corp., Northbrook. Avocation: photography. Home: 2902 N Dunton Arlington Heights IL 60004 Office: PC Distbg Inc 3520 Milwaukee Ave Northbrook IL 60062

SMITH, JERRY LUMRY, real estate developer; b. Sioux City, Iowa, July 3, 1929; s. Harold Leland and Catherine (Lumry) S.; m. Patricia Marie Orr, Dec. 22, 1955; children: Kenneth Orr, Harold Randall, Julie Anne. BS, U. Colo., 1951, LLB, 1956. Leasing rep. J.C. Penney Co., Denver, N.Y.C., Pitts., 1963-70; mgr. regional real estate J.C. Penney Co., Pitts., 1970-76; mgr. nat. real estate J.C. Penney Co., N.Y.C., 1976-78; ptnr., dir. devel. Oxford Devel. Co., Pitts., 1978-82; leasing ptnr. The Mall Co., Alliance, Ohio, 1982—; owner, cons. JLS Assocs., Pitts., 1982—. Mng. editor Rocky Mountain Law Rev., 1955-56. Rep. precinct capt., Upper St. Clair, Pa., 1980—. Served with U.S. Army, 1951-53, Korea. Mem. Internat. Council Shopping Ctrs. Presbyterian. Clubs: Rolling Hills Country (bd. dirs. 1985-86), St. Clair Country. Avocations: golf, tennis, theater. Home: 1590 Pinetree Dr Pittsburgh PA 15241 Office: Mall Co 2500 W State St Alliance OH 44601

SMITH, JOHN ALEXANDER, dentist; b. Balt., Sept. 30, 1954; s. John Walter Jr. and Joan Ann (Boswell) S.; m. Jerri Lee Muskopf, Aug. 6, 1977; children: Elizabeth Ann, Charles Alexander. BA mgna cum laude, U. Mo., St. Louis, 1976; DMD, Washington U., St. Louis, 1981. Practice dentistry St. Louis, 1984—. Served to capt. USAF, 1981-84. Mem. ADA, Mo. Dental Assn., St. Louis Dental Soc. (trial council 1985—). Lodge: Kiwanis (chmn. activities com. 1985-86). Home: 1106 Pinrun Dr Saint Louis MO 63011 Office: 610 N Geyer Rd Kirkwood MO 63122

SMITH, JOHN BURNSIDE, business executive; b. Indpls., 1931; m. Barbara J.; children: John S., Lynn B., Nancy L. Grad., U. Ind., 1957, postgrad. Sch. Bus. Adminstrn., 1958; LL.D. (hon.), Butler U., 1984. Pres., chmn., chief exec. officer, dir. Mayflower Group, Indpls.; dir. Citizens Gas & Coke Utility, Ind. Nat. Corp. Bd. govs. James Whitcomb Riley Assocs.; bd. dirs. Wholesale Club. Mem. Ind. State C. of C. (bd. dirs.). Office: Mayflower Group Inc PO Box 107 Indianapolis IN 46206-0107

SMITH, JOHN J., manufacturing company executive; b. Woodland, Mich., Dec. 9, 1911; s. Owen Benjamin and Ethyl (Katherman) S.; m. Elinor S. Lamoreaux, Dec. 10, 1938. Student, Argubright Coll., 1929-31. C.P.A., 1940. Sr. partner Smith & Skutt (C.P.A.s), 1942-50; dir. Sparton Corp., now chmn.; chmn. (Sparton Can. Ltd.), London, Ont.; dir. Lake Odessa Machine Products, Inc., Mich., Kent Products, Inc., Grand Haven, City Bank Trust Co., Jackson., DU-WEL Metal Products. Mem. Chief Execs. Forum, Mich. Assn. C.P.A.s, Am. Inst. C.P.A.s. Club: Detroit Athletic (Detroit). Home: 1839 S Walmont Jackson MI 49203 Office: Sparton Corp 2400 E Ganson St Jackson MI 49202

SMITH, JOHN T., real estate development company executive; b. Liberal, Kans., Apr. 18, 1941; s. Roy E. and Margaret E. Smith; m. Nancy J. Schmidt, Mar. 30, 1978; children: William T., James T. BA, Southwestern Coll., Kans., 1964; BS, Mich. State U., 1966, M in Urban Planning, 1966. City planner City of East Lansing, Mich., 1965-67, Wichita-Sedgwick Co., Kans., 1967-71; cons. planning and devel. J.T. Smith Assoc., Liberal, Kans., 1971-76; dir. pres. John T. Smith Assocs. Inc., Liberal, 1971—. Bd. dirs. Seward County United Way, 1974; chmn. fund-raising drive; bd. dirs. Liberal Area Crime Commn., 1981, treas., 1981; 1st pres., bd. dirs. Liberal Air Mus. Mem. Am. Inst. Cert. Planners, Internat. Council Shopping Ctrs., Am. Planning Assn., Urban Land Inst. Club: Liberal Country. Lodge: Rotary (pres. bd. dirs. 1978). Avocations: flying, snow skiing, hunting. Office: 150 Plaza Dr Liberal KS 67901

SMITH, JOHN WALLACE, surgeon, educator; b. Hutchinson, Kans., Feb. 18, 1931; s. W. Donald and Claramary (Smith) S.; m. Margaret Lee, Dec. 26, 1959; children: John Wallace Jr., Frances, George MacDonell. AB, Harvard U., 1952; MD, U. Nebr., 1956. Diplomate Am. Bd. Surgery. Intern San Francisco Hosp., 1956-57; resident Stanford U. Hosps., San Francisco, 1957-60, U. Calif. Hosps., San Francisco, 1960-62; gen. practice surgery Omaha, 1964-70; practice specializing in vascular surgery, ptnr. Vascular Services, Omaha, 1970—; clin. assoc. prof. surgery Coll. Medicine U. Nebr., Omaha, 1966—; pres. med. staff Meth. Hosp., Omaha, 1986-87. Contbr. articles to profl. jours. Bd. dirs. Omaha Symphony Assn. Served to capt. Med. Corps U.S. Army, 1962-64. Fellow ACS (gov. 1987—); mem. Midwestern Vascular Surg. Soc. (chmn. membership com. 1982), Internat. Soc. Cardiovascular Surgery, Western Surg. Assn., Alpha Omega Alpha (pres. 1982-83). Office: Vascular Services 8300 Dodge St Omaha NE 68114

SMITH, JULIAN PAYNE, gynecological oncologist, educator; b. Portsmouth, Ohio, Mar. 23, 1930; s. Emory Farl and Blanche Lola (Payne) S.; m. Eleanor G. Stankunas, June 5, 1954; children—Susan Sharon, Charles Douglas, Geraldine Gigi, David James. Student, U. Mich., 1947-48; B.A., Ohio Wesleyan U., 1951; M.D., Columbia U., 1955. Diplomate: Am. Bd. Ob-Gyn. Intern Univ. Hosps., Cleve., 1955-56; resident in Ob-Gyn, Cornell N.Y. Hosp., 1956-57, Columbia Presbyn. Med. Ctr., N.Y.C., 1957-59; fellow in gynecology-oncology U. Tex., Houston, 1963-66; private medicine specializing in (Ob-Gyn), Portsmouth, 1961-63; prof. U. Tex. System Cancer Center, M.D. Anderson Hosp. and Tumor Inst., Houston, 1973-77; prof., dir. gynecologic oncology Wayne State U. Med. Sch., Detroit, 1977-83; prof. of ob-gyn Loyola U., Chgo., 1986—; practice medicine specializing in oncology Southfield, Mich., 1983-86; prof., dir. gynecol. oncology Loyola U. Med. Ctr., Maywood, Ill., 1986—. Editor: (with Gravlee) Endometrium, 1977, A Review of the World Literature, 1977, (with Delgado) Management of Complications in Gynecologic Oncology, 1982, (with Hafez) Carcinoma of the Cervix, 1982; contbr. articles to profl. jours. Bd. dirs. Am. Cancer Soc., Wayne County, Mich., 1980-81. Served to capt. M.C., USAR, 1959-61. Mem. Am. Coll. Obstetricians and Gynecologists, Am. Radium Soc., Am. Assn. Obstetricians and Gynecologists, Felix Rutledge Soc. (pres. 1969-70), Am. Gynecol. Soc., Am. Gynecol. and Obstet. Soc., AMA, Soc. Gynecologic Oncologists (pres. 1984-85), Soc. Pelvic Surgeons, Tex. Med. Assn., Mich. State Med. Soc., Ill. State Med. Soc., Chgo. Med. Soc., Wayne County, Med. Soc., others. Republican. Methodist. Home: 1201 Burr Ridge Club Dr Burr Ridge IL 60521 Office: Loyola U Med Ctr Dept Ob-Gyn 2160 S 1st Ave Maywood IL 60153

SMITH, KAROL KLOOTS, information systems specialist; b. Cleve., Jan. 13, 1940; d. Walter Fred and Marion Florence (Linder) Kloots; m. Roy Harold Smith Jr., May 6, 1961; children: Mark, Catherine, Laura. Student, Ohio State U., 1958-60, Schoolcraft Coll., 1976-78; cert., Oakland (Mich.) Community Coll. Cert. office automation mgmt. instr., Mich. Sec. Amstar Corp., Chgo., 1976-78; office mgr. Dependable-Fordath, Portland, Oreg., 1978-89; info. ctr. specialist Flint Ink Corp., Detroit, 1980—; instr. Oakland Community Coll., Farmington Hills, Mich., 1986. Den leader Cub Scouts, Livonia, Mich., 1972-74; active Rep. Women's Club, Livonia, 1972-74; leader Camp Fire Girls, Livonia, 1979. Recipient Hon. Mention award Baycrafters Juried Art Show, Bay Village, Ohio, 1968. Mem. Assn. Info. Systems Profls. (bd. dirs. 1984-85, v.p. 1985-86). Avocations: stained glass work, reading, needlework. Home: 3398 McCluskey Pinckney MI 48169 Office: Flint Ink Corp 25111 Glendale Detroit MI 48239

SMITH, KENT ERNEST, non-profit organization executive; b. Oak Park, Ill., May 21, 1939; s. James Paul and Jane Louise (Gardner) S.; m. Pamela Ann Streich, Sept. 11, 1965; children—Julie Ellen, Stephen Paul. B.S. in Journalism, U. Ill., 1961. Producer, writer pub. service programming Sta. WLW-TV, Cin., 1965-67; radio/TV news writer producer Sta. WGN, Chgo., 1967-69; TV news producer, writer, project planner Sta. WLS-TV, Chgo., 1969-78; exec. dir. Spina Bifida Assn. Am., Chgo., 1978-86; exec. dir. Community Counseling Service Co. Inc., Chgo., 1986—. Chmn. bd. Council For Disability Rights, Chgo.; bd. mem. Chgo. Youth Symphony Orch.; treas. Elmhurst Instrumental Music Boosters. Served with U.S. Army, 1961-65. Mem. Am. Soc. Assn. Execs., Chgo. Soc. Assn. Execs., Chgo. Headline Club, Sigma Delta Chi. Mem. United Ch. of Christ (elder). Home: 472 Prairie Ave Elmhurst IL 60126 Office: 8420 Bryn Mawr #858 Chicago IL 60631

SMITH, KEVIN BENJAMIN, mechanical engineer; b. Chgo., Feb. 6, 1957; s. Robert Emmett and Edith May (Falcon) S.; m. Cheryl Lyn Bruce, Oct. 12, 1985. BSME, Purdue U., 1979; MBA, U. Chgo., 1986. Registered profl. engr., Ill., Mo. Engrng. analyst Sargent & Lundy, Chgo., 1981-82, mech. engr., 1982-85, project engr., 1985; project mgr. Midwesco, Inc., Niles, Ill., 1985-86. Mem. Chgo. Council Fgn. Relations, 1986; pres. Lakewood Commons Condominium Assn., Chgo., 1986. Mem. Am. Soc. Mech. Engrs., Western Soc. Engrs. Roman Catholic. Home: 2310 Lakewood Ave Chicago IL 60614 Office: Midwesco Energy Systems 7720 N Lehigh Ave Niles IL 60648

SMITH, KEVIN CHARLES, lawyer; b. Lima, Ohio, July 24, 1954; s. Thomas F. and Dorothy (Holtkamp) S.; m. Sharon Sousley, Aug. 8, 1981; children: Jeffrey, Joseph. BS, USCG Acad., 1976; JD, Cleve. State U., 1982. Bar: Ohio 1983, U.S. Dist. Ct. (no. dist.) Ohio 1983. Assoc. Betts, Miller & Russo, Findlay, Ohio, 1983—; instr. Paralegal Inst., Findlay, 1985—; asst. prosecutor Hancock County, Findlay, 1983—; mediator Divorce Mediation Project, Findlay, 1985—. Dist. commr. Hancock County council Boy Scouts Am., Findlay, 1986; bd. dirs., officer Safetytown Inc., Findlay, 1986, Hancock County Spl. Olympics, Findlay, 1986; v.p. Hospice of Hancock County; bd. dirs. Findlay Area Youtheatre, Crimestopper and Block Watch; trustee Glendora Mills Scholarship fund, Findlay, 1984—. Served to lt. (j.g.) USCG, 1976-81. Mem. Ohio Bar Assn., Findlay/Hancock County Bar Assn., Northwest Ohio Bar Assn., Acad. Family Mediators, Findlay Area C. of C. Lodge: Kiwanis (pres.-elect, bd. dirs., chmn. com.). Home: 131 Highland Findlay OH 45840 Office: Betts Miller & Russo 101 W Sandusky Findlay OH 45840

SMITH, KEVIN LEYON, pastor, teacher; b. Charleston, Ill., Aug. 19, 1956; s. Paul Earl and Mary Etta (Cummins) S.; m. Susan Lorraine Taylor, July 8, 1978 (div. Nov. 4, 1985). Student, Eastern Ill. U., 1974-76; BA, Bob Jones U., 1979. Ordained to ministry Bapt. Ch., 1981. Minister of music Hearon Circle Freewill Bapt. Ch., Spartanburg, S.C., 1979-80; sr. pastor Rock Prairie Bapt. Ch., Tipton, Ind., 1980-86; bd. dirs. No. Ind. Youth Activity Bd., 1982-86; substitute tchr. Tri-Cen. Schs., Sharpsville, Ind., 1981-86. Republican. Baptist. Home: Rural Rt #2 Box 123 Tipton IN 46072 Office: Rock Prairie Ch Rural Rt #2 Box 222 Sharpsville IN 46068

SMITH, KIM LEROY, lawyer; b. Boone, Iowa, June 17, 1955; s. George LeRoy Smith and Karen Jean (Price) Nystrom; m. Carol Ann Chapman, Mar. 25, 1978; children: Stephanie Nicole, Austin Jameson. BS in Acctg., Iowa State U., 1977; JD, U. Iowa, 1980. Bar: Iowa 1980; CPA, Iowa. Law clerk Stanley Lande Coulter & Pearce, Muscatine, Iowa, 1978, Claypool & Claypool, Williamsburg, Iowa, 1980; tax mgr. Peat, Marwick, Mitchell & Co., Des Moines, 1980-85; pres. K.L. Smith, P.C., West Des Moines, 1985—. Mem. Des Moines Estate Planning Council, 1984—; pres. Employee Retirement Income Security Act Forum, 1984—. Mem. ABA, Iowa Bar Assn., Internat. Assn. for Fin. Planning (mem. local program com. 1985—), Am. Soc. CPAs, Iowa Soc. CPAs. Presbyterian. Avocations: popular music, tennis, science fiction. Office: 3737 Woodland Ave Suite 130 West Des Moines IA 50265

SMITH, LARRY GORDON, educator, business consultant; b. Gary, Ind., Aug. 14, 1944; s. Gordon Henry and Loretta Elaine (Reglein) S.; m. Joyce Evelyn Lohrman, June 11, 1966; 1 son, Kenneth Gordon. B.S.Ed., N.E. Mo. State U., 1966, M.A., 1976; Ed.Sp., U. Mo., 1986. With U.S. Steel Co., Gary, Ind., 1964-66; asst. mgr. B. Dalton Booksellers, St. Louis, 1967-69; tchr. Riverview Gardens Schs., St. Louis, 1968-81; mgr. Mid-Am. Theatres, St. Louis, 1980-83, cons., 1983-86; tchr., adminstr. Ft. Zumwalt Sch. Dist., O'Fallon, Mo., 1980—. NSF grantee, 1971-72; Allen Scovell scholar, 1977; N.E. Mo. State U. Music scholar, 1962-65. Mem. Nat. Assn. Secondary Sch. Prins., Mo. Assn. Secondary Sch. Prins., Mo. Middle Sch. Assn., Phi Delta Kappa (pres. 1986), Alpha Phi Sigma, Kappa Delta Pi, Blue Key. Republican. Home: 2416 Saint Robert Ln Saint Charles MO 63301 Office: Fort Zumwalt Sch Dist 110 Virgil St O'Fallon MO 63366

SMITH, LAURENCE WAYNE, manufacturing company executive; b. Aurora, Ill., July 29, 1928; s. Laurence Thorton and Ethyl Grace (Davis) S.; m. Donna Lucille Shales, June 2, 1948 (div. 1975); children: Candice Lee, Bruce Wayne, Scott Allan; m. Sheila Ann Dorsett, Dec. 20, 1975. Student, Am. Acad. Art, 1948-49. Account exec. Connor-Sager Advt., Aurora, 1951-68; pres. L. Smith Assocs., Elgin, Ill., 1964-68; v.p. mktg. TRNK Advt., Aurora, 1968-70; dir. mktg. W.R. Meadows, Inc., Elgin, 1970—. Pres. Parkwood Village Assn., Elgin, 1980-85. Served with U.S. Army, 1946-47, 49-50. Republican. Lutheran. Avocations: boating, golf, gardening. Home: 1946 Portage Way Elgin IL 60123 Office: WR Meadows Inc PO Box 543 Elgin IL 60121

SMITH, LAWRENCE CHURCH, manufacturing company executive; b. Akron, Ohio, May 4, 1946; s. Robert Benjamin and Barbara Ann (Patry) S.; m. Carol Dee Canfield, June 20, 1982; children: Christine, Tonya Zimmer. BSEE, Case Inst. Tech., 1968; MS in ChemE, Case Western Res. U., 1976. Registered profl. engr., Ohio. Engr. Bunker-Ramo, Cleve., 1968-70; sr. engr. Allen Bradley, Cleve., 1970-76; supr. engrng. Warner & Swasey, Cleve., 1976-79; ptnr. Custom Automation, Cleve., 1979-81; chmn. North Coast Automation, Inc., Cleve., 1981—. Mem. IEEE, NSPE (pres. local chpt. 1984), Assn. Computing Machinery, Machine Vision Assn. Republican. Episcopalian. Office: North Coast Automation Inc 71 Alpha Park Highland Heights OH 44143-2202

SMITH, LINDA DRUMMOND, accountant; b. Kansas City, Mo., Apr. 12, 1954; d. William Kenneth and Shirley Jean (Stevens) Drummond; m. Craig Alan Smith, June 5, 1976; 1 child, Sean Alan. BS, U. Mo., Columbia, 1976. CPA, Mo. Data processing mgr. Williams & Keepers, CPA's, Columbia, 1977-86; mgmt. cons. Rubin, Brown, Gornstein & Co., St. Louis, 1986—. Mem. Accts. Computer Users Tech. Exchange, Am. Inst. CPA's, Mo. Soc. CPA's. Avocation: travel. Home: 7326 Goff Ave Saint Louis MO 63117 Office: Rubin Brown Gornstein & Co 230 S Bemiston Ave Saint Louis MO 63105

SMITH, LISA ELAINE, food products executive; b. Cleve., Aug. 18, 1959; s. Richard Lee and Patricia Jean (Grace) S. BS, Ohio State U., 1981; postgrad., Case Western Res. U., 1985—. Travel coordinator Ohio State U., Columbus, 1979-81; store mgr. Cole Nat. Corp., Cleve., 1981-82; adminstrv. asst. Fabri-Centers Am., Cleve., 1982-83; support staff supr. Touche Ross & Co., Cleve., 1983-84; office mgr. McDonald's Corp., Cleve., 1984-86, adminstrv. mgr., 1986—. Named Internat. Office Mgr. of Yr., McDonald's Corp., 1987. Mem. Adminstrv. Mgmt. Soc., Nat. Assn for Female Execs., Young Profls. of Cleve., Case Western Res. U. Grad. Bus. Assn., Ohio State U. Alumni Assn. Republican. Methodist. Home: 1182 Cook Lakewood OH 44107 Office: McDonalds Corp 28253 Lorain Rd North Olmsted OH 44070

SMITH, LOIS ANN, real estate executive; b. Chgo., Jan. 1, 1941; d. Alburn M. and Ruth A. (Beaver) Beaudoin; m. Dickson K. Smith, Mar. 24, 1962 (div. May 1982); children: Michelle D., Jeffrey D. BA, U. Utah, 1962; MBA, Marquette U., 1972. Asst. mgr. prodn. Northwestern Mut. Life Ins. Co., Milw., 1979-83, asst. mgr., asset mgr., 1983—. Cons. Girl Scouts Am., Milw., 1986, YWCA, Milw., 1986, bd. dirs. YWCA, 1981-87; bd. dirs. Wis. Rep. Orgn., 1985-87. Mem. Internat. Council Shopping Ctrs., Profl. Dimensions, Beta Gamma Sigma. Unitarian. Home: 2555 N Lake Dr #1 Milwaukee MI 53211 Office: Northwestern Mut Life Ins Co 720 E Wisconsin Ave Milwaukee WI 53202

SMITH, LYLE BENSON, data processing executive; b. Hartford, Conn., Dec. 1, 1934; s. Everton Benson and Elizabeth (Baker) S.; children: David Lyle, Scott William. BA, Hiram (Ohio) Coll., 1956; MS, Case Western Res. U., 1960; PhD, Stanford (Calif.) U., 1969. Vis. scientist Conseil Eurpeen pour la Recherch Nucleaire, Geneva, Switzerland, 1969-71; asst. dir. computer ctr. U. Colo., Boulder, 1971-73, Stanford U., 1973-76; assoc. prof. No. Ill. U., DeKalb, 1976-85; mem. tech. staff AT&T, Naperville, Ill., 1985—. Contbr. articles on computer graphics and man-machine interaction to profl. jours. Regional commr. Am. Youth Soccer Orgn., DeKalb, 1977-85; coordinator Annual Crop Walk to End Hunger, DeKalb, 1982-86. Mem. IEEE (computing sect.), Assn. for Computing Machinery (chmn. Swiss chpt. 1970-71, vice chmn. Boulder chpt. 1972-73), Ill. Assn. Data Processing Edn. (pres. 1981-83). Clubs: Ski of DeKalb (various offices 1980—), Running (Naperville). Avocations: travel, reading, cycling. Home: 204 W Locust DeKalb IL 60115 Office: AT&T 1100 E Warrenville Rd IW2Z356 Naperville IL 60566

SMITH, LYNN HOWARD, manufacturing company executive; b. Ft. Wayne, Ind., Mar. 9, 1936; s. Lester Earl and Catherine Lois (McCurdy) S.; student Ind.-Purdue U. Extension, Ft. Wayne, 1956-57; grad. Internat. Harvester Tech. Sch., 1961; m. Jean Marie Bauman, Sept. 2, 1955; children—Julie, Linnett, Jeffery, Lisa. Methods engr. Jervis Corp., Grandville, Mich., 1964-67; project engr. Twigg Industries, Martinsville, Ind., 1967-70; project engr. Tri Industries, Terre Haute, Ind., 1970-74; tool and mfg. engr. Berko Electric Mfg. Co., Peru, Ind., 1974-77, fabrication supt., 1977-78, mgr. mfg. engring., 1978-79, plant supr., 1979; chief project engr. Tube Processing Corp., Indpls., 1979-85, Tube Forming and Mfg. Corp., Lebanon, Ind., 1985-87; prin., pres. Lynsco Mfg. Co., Inc., Peru, 1987—; cons. Groteness Machine Works, Chgo. Pres. Harlan (Ind.) Days Assn., 1962; adv. Jr. Achievement, Terre Haute, Ind., 1972-73. Named Jr. Achievement Adv. of Yr., Terre Haute Jr. Achievement, 1973. Methodist. Clubs: Berko Mgmt., Masons (Harlan lodge master 1964), Shriners. Developed proprietary spot welding process and equipment, 1966, proprietary high temperature brazing process, 1970-74; developer, editor Berko Electric Mfg. Procedures Man., 1975-79. Home: Rural Route 1 Box 269-A Peru IN 46970 Office: Lynsco Mfg Co Inc 19 W 2d St Peru IN 46970

SMITH, MARK BURTON, electronic engineer; b. Louisville, May 1, 1960; s. Fred Lewis and Loretta (Burton) S.; m. Pamela Sue Wisner, Aug. 6, 1983; children: Stephanie Nicole. BS, U. Louisville, 1982, MSEE, 1983; postgrad., Washington U., St. Louis, 1986. Electronics engr. McDonnell-Douglas Corp, St. Louis, 1983—. Avocation: gardening, automobiles, gardening, golfing. Home: 609 Watkins Glen Saint Charles MO 63303 Office: McDonnell-Douglas Corp B105 D315 L3 POST B2 Saint Louis MO 63166

SMITH, MARTHA ANN, special education educator; b. Wallis, Tex., May 2, 1938; foster d. Bert Randolph Abendroth Sr. and Ruby Faye Ayers; m. Homer Alvin Smith Jr., Aug. 26, 1959; children: Melinda Anne, Matthew Brian. BA in Speech and Dramatics, Okla. State U., 1961; MS in Spl. Edn., Ind. U., 1978. Cert. tchr. pre-sch. handicapped, Va., learning disabilities, Va., Ill., Dramatics and costume design, Va., speech and pub. speaking, Va., Mo. Substitute tchr. Prince Edward County Pub. Schs., Farmville, Va., 1969-75; tchr. handicapped presch. Buckingham Pub. Schs., Dillwyn, Va., 1979-85; tchr. learning disabilities Decatur (Ill.) Pub. Schs., 1985-86; tchr. early childhood spl. edn. Tuscola (Ill.) Pub. Schs., 1986—; Mem. Monroe County Parent Adv. Bd. for Exceptional Children, Bloomington, Ind., 1977-78; vol. regional rep. Devel. Disabilities Protection and Advocacy Office, Va., 1978-80. Deacon, mem. numerous coms. Coll. Prebyn. Ch., Hampden-Sydney, Va. Mem. Ill. Edn. Assn., Millikin Assn. Women, Kappa Kappa Iota. Avocations: quilting, reading. Home: 346 S Wooddale Decatur IL 62522

SMITH, MARTIN BROOKS, JR., health care executive; b. Whiteville, N.C., Feb. 14, 1947; s. Martin Brooks and Pearl Louise S.; m. Regina Patricia Stopczywski, Dec. 18, 1971; m. Carolyn Marie Vogt, Apr. 14, 1981; 1 son, Martin Brooks III; 1 stepdau. Allison Rebecca Williams. Commd. U.S. Air Force, 1966, advanced through grades to capt., 1977; chief ops. 1st aeromed. squadron Pope AFB, N.C., 1975-77; resigned, 1977; v.p., gen. mgr. Indsl. Health Services, Cin., 1977-79; pres. M.B. Smith & Assocs., Cin., 1979-81; v.p. United Healthcare Systems, Inc., Kansas City, Mo., 1981-82, pres., 1983—; pres. EquiMed, Inc., Overland Park, Kans., 1985—. Mem. Am. Hosp. Assn., Am. Mktg. Assn., Emergency Medicine Mgmt. Assn. (charter). Republican. Club: Blue Hills Country.

SMITH, MARY LOUISE, real estate salesperson; b. Eldorado, Ill., May 29, 1935; d. Joseph H. and Opal M. (Shelton) S.; m. David Lee Smith, June 18, 1961; children: Ricky Eugene, Brenda Sue. Student, So. Ill. U., 1954-56, 57-58. Cert. tchr., Mo.; cert. real estate broker/salesperson, Mo. With acctg. dept. Cen. Hardware Co., St. Louis, 1958-61; mgr. income tax office Tax Teller Inc., St. Louis, 1967-69, H&R Block Co., St. Louis, 1970-76; with acctg. dept. Weis Neumann Co., St. Louis, 1976-79; sales assoc. Century 21 Neubauer Realty, Inc., St. Louis, 1981-83, John R. Green Realtor, Inc., St. Louis, 1983-85; sales assoc. Century 21 Action Properties, St. Louis, 1985-86, real estate broker/salesperson, 1986—; substitute tchr., St. Louis Bd. Edn., 1967—. Children's dir. Lafayette Park Bapt. Ch., St. Louis, 1981—. Mem. St. Louis Metro Realtors Assn., Real Estate Bd. Met. St. Louis, Nat. Assn. Realtors, Mo. Assn. Realtors. Avocation: writing children's stories. Home: 2627 Nebraska Saint Louis MO 63118

SMITH, MARYANN PATRICIA YODELIS, academic administrator, journalism educator; b. Sioux City, Iowa, Dec. 19, 1935; d. Joseph Anthony and Mary Sophie (Galas) Yodelis; m. Kim Rhodes Smith, May 14, 1977; 1 stepchild, Lisa. B.A., Briar Cliff Coll., 1963; M.A., U. Wis.-Madison, 1969, Ph.D., 1971. Tchr. St. Mary High Sch., Remsen, Iowa, 1960-62; asst. dir. admissions Briar Cliff Coll., Sioux City, 1962-64, asst. to acad. dean, 1964-65, dir. publs. and publicity, 1965-67; from teaching asst., lectr. to assoc. prof. U. Wis.-Madison, 1967-81, prof. journalism, 1981-87 , assoc. vice chancellor of academic affairs, prof., 1978-86 ; prof., dir. Sch. Journalism and Mass Communication, U. Minn., Mpls., 1986—; asst. prof. Ind. U., Bloomington, 1971-72; mem. media-law relations com. Wis. State Bar, 1976—. Contbr. articles to profl. jours. and book chpts. Recipient Chancellors award U. Wis., 1975. Mem. Journalism Council (pres. 1983-85), Assn. for Edn. in Journalism and Mass Communication (exec. com. 1977-79), Internat. Communications Assn., Orgn. Am. Historians, Soc. Profl. Journalists. Roman Catholic. Clubs: Weavers Guild, Minn. Press Club, Minn. Press Women. Office: U Minn Sch Journalism/Mass Communic 111 Murphy Hall 206 Church St SE Minneapolis MN 55403

SMITH, MERCY A(NN), insurance agent, consultant; b. Akron, Ohio, Aug. 26, 1953; d. Bryant Ralph and Mary Ann (Mettle) S.; m. Randall C. Allen, Oct. 21, 1977 (div. Dec. 1979). Student pub. schs., Salem, Ohio. Claims clk. Prudential Ins. Co., Youngstown, Ohio, 1971-73, Grange Casualty, Niles, Ohio, 1973-75; ins. agt. Moreman-Yerian Co., Youngstown, 1975-79, Met. Life Ins. Co., Warren, Ohio, 1979-81; account asst. F.B. Hall & Co., Youngstown, 1981-83; account exec. M.W. Early Ins. Assocs., Canton, Ohio, 1983—. Mem. Nat. Assn. Ins. Women (asst. regional dir. region IV 1982-83), Ins. Women Youngstown (Ins. Woman of Yr. 1982), Ohio Ins. Inst. (speakers bur.). Republican. Episcopalian. Office: Musick Ins 639 High NE Warren OH 44483

SMITH, MICHAEL DALE, insurance agency executive; b. Rensselaer, Ind., Sept. 17, 1953; s. Hamlin Henry and Phyllis Joan (Hall) S.; m. Gretchen Zuege, Sept. 1, 1973; children—Mandy, Joshua. Grad. Internat. Coll., 1973. Mem. mgmt. program Household Fin. Corp., 1973-74; owner Credit Bur. Rensselaer, 1974-79; pres. Smith Realty, Rensselaer, 1974—; v.p., owner Consol. Ins. Agy., Rensselaer, 1975—. Precinct committeeman Reps., Rensselaer, del. state conv., 1978, 82. Mem. Ind. Ins. Agts. Assn. (bd. dirs.), Soc. Cert. Ins. Counselors (cert.), Profl. Ins. Agts. Assn., Rensselaer C. of C. (past v.p.). Lodges: Rotary (dir. 1982—), Masons, Shriners (Rensselaer). Home: PO Box 1 Rensselaer IN 47978 Office: 116 W Washington St Rensselaer IN 47978

SMITH, MICHAEL GREGORY, computer software company executive; b. Mpls., July 27, 1960; s. Gregory B. and Ruth Ann (Klosterman) S. BA in Computer Sci., St. Thomas Coll., 1982, BA in Bus., 1983; MBA, U. Minn., 1986—. Programmer, analyst Sperry Corp., Eagan, Minn., 1983-84; pres. Advanced Office Systems, Mpls., 1984—; cons. Control Data Corp., Bloomington, Minn., 1984; adj. instr. St. Mary's Coll., Mpls., 1984-85. Contbr. articles to Workstation mag., 1984-85. Del. Minn. Ind. Reps., St. Paul, 1982; coach Minn. Ski Council, 1985-86. Mem. Data Processing Mgmt. Assn. Roman Catholic. Avocations: golf, sailing, skiing. Home: 11028 Territorial Dr Burnsville MN 55337 Office: Advanced Office Systems Hyatt Trade Mart suite 3093 1300 Nicollet Mall Minneapolis MN 55403

SMITH, MURRAY T., transportation company executive; b. 1939. V.p. Overland Express Inc., Indpls., 1978-82; v.p. ops. R.T.C. Transp. Inc., Forest Pk., Ga., 1982-83; with Midwest Coast Transport Co., Sioux Falls, S.D., 1983—, sr. v.p., 1983-84, pres., 1984—, also bd. dirs. Office: Midwest Coast Trasport Inc 1600 E Benson Rd Sioux Falls SD 57104 *

SMITH, NEAL EDWARD, Congressman; b. Hedrick, Iowa, Mar. 23, 1920; s. James N. and Margaret M. (Walling) S.; m. Beatrix Havens, Mar. 23, 1946; children—Douglas, Sharon. Student, U. Mo., 1945-46, Syracuse U., 1946-47; LL.B., Drake U., 1950. Bar: Iowa 1950. Farmer Iowa, 1937—; sole practice Des Moines, 1950-58; atty. 50 sch. bds. in, Iowa, 1951-58; asst. county atty. Polk County, Iowa, 1951; mem. 86th-100th Congresses from 4th Dist. Iowa., 1959—. Chmn. Polk County Bd. Social Welfare, 1954-56; pres. Young Democratic Clubs Am., 1953-55. Served with AUS, World War II. Decorated Air medal with 4 oak leaf clusters, Purple Heart. Mem. Am. Bar Assn., Farm Bur., Farmers Union, DAV. Clubs: Masons, Moose. Home: RFD 1 Altoona IA 50009 Office: 2373 Rayburn House Office Bldg Washington DC 20515

SMITH, OTHA WILLIAM, softball association administrator; b. Omaha, Aug. 31, 1925; s. Otha William and Alice Hattie (Clark) W.; m. Audra Ellen Barnes, June 27, 1943; children—Michael Eugene, Pamela Jo, Rocella Ann. Grad. high sch., Wisner, Nebr. Ptnr. Smith & Clark Trucking, Brekendrige, Colo., 1947-49; dept. mgr. Gamble Skogmo, Inc., Fremont, Nebr., 1952-67; dist. mgr. Century Mfg. Co., Mpls., 1968-80; ecex. dir. Nebr. Softball Assn., Fremont, 1980—, also pres., 1965-76; v.p. Amateur Softball Assn. Am., 1971-72, 81-82, 85-86 ; founder, pres. Nebr. Sports Council, 1984-86 . Founder, Women's Coll. World Series, 1969, Nebr. Softball Scholarship Program, 1974, Nebr. Softball Hall of Fame, 1977. Served as pvt. U.S. Army, 1941-45. Named Admiral, Great Navy of Nebr., State of Nebr., 1977; named to Nebr. Softball Hall of Fame, 1980. Mem. Nebr. Congress Parents and Tchrs. (life) Nebr. Parks and Recreation Assn. (spl. award 1983), Am. Legion (comdr. 1955-56). Republican. Lodges: Lions (pres. 1984-85). Avocations: fishing; golf. Home: 1840 N C St Fremont NE 68025

SMITH, PAUL DANIEL, dentist; b. Cin., May 6, 1947; s. Clarence Vernon and Mary Rogers (Myers) S.; m. Stephanie A. Apthorp, Dec. 20, 1969; children: Lauren Christine, Andrea Kaye, Daniel Stephen. BA, Coll. of Wooster, 1969; DDS, Ohio State U., 1974. Practice dentistry Canton, Ohio, 1977—; mng. ptnr. Belpar Profl. Bldg. Ptnrship., Canton, 1979—. Advisor Boy Scouts Am., Canton, 1979-84; pres. PTA, Plain Twp., Ohio, 1983-86; bd. dirs. Next Step Inc., Canton, 1985-87. Served to capt. U.S. Army. Mem. ADA, Ohio Dental Assn., Acad. Gen. Dentistry, Stark County Dental Soc. Presbyterian. Lodge: Rotary. Home: 256 Everhard Rd North Canton OH 44709 Office: 4565 Dressler Rd Canton OH 44718

SMITH, PAUL GREGORY, tax consultant; b. Lafayette, Ind., Dec. 6, 1959; s. Norton Eugene and Beverly Ann (Daivs) S.; m. Beth Lynn McKibben, Oct. 1, 1983. BS in Indsl. Mgmt., Purdue U., 1983. CPA, Ind. Staff auditor Touche Ross and Co., Chgo., 1982-83; comml. auditor, tax cons. Crowe Chizek and Co., Indpls., 1984—. Contbr. articles to profl. jours. Mem. pres. council Purdue U. Mem. Am. Inst. CPA's, Builders Assn. Greater Indpls., Nat. Assn. Home Builders, Ind. CPA Soc. Roman Catholic. Clubs: John Purdue. Home: 319 Scarborough Way Noblesville IN 46060 Office: Crowe Chizek & Co 1 American Square Indianapolis IN 46282

SMITH, PETER WILLIAM, financial executive; b. Portland, Maine, Feb. 23, 1936; s. Walt S. and Harriet S. (Hawkins) S.; m. Janet S. Langenfeld, Sept. 20, 1958; children: Linda M., William M., David A. MBA, Syracuse U., 1959. Congressional asst. U.S. Ho. of Reps., Washington, 1960-62; assoc. exec. dir. Assn. Am. Pubs., N.Y.C., 1963-69; sr. v.p. Field Enterprises, Inc., Chgo., 1969-80; pres. Peter W. Smith & Co., Inc., Chgo., 1980; bd. dirs. Manchester Tool Co., Akron, Ohio, Lancaster (Pa.) Press, Hunter Melnor, Memphis, Xaloy Inc., Pulaski, Va., CWT Specialty Stores, Inc., S. Attleboro, Mass., WGM Safety Corp., Framingham, Mass. Assoc. mem. bd. dirs. Rush Presbyn. St. Luke's Med. Ctr., Chgo., 1976; investment com. Met. YMCA council, Chgo., 1976; chmn. Coll. Young Reps. div. Rep. Nat. Com. Club: Mid-Day (Chgo.). Home: 596 E Cherokee Rd Lake Forest IL 60645 Office: 401 N Wabash Ave Suite 521 Chicago IL 60611

SMITH, PHILIP RONALD, commodities trader, accountant; b. Cleve., Jan. 30, 1947; s. Leo Ralph and Ida (Barnett) S.; m. Margot Ann Phillips, Oct. 4, 1975; children: Erin, Zachary. AB, MBA, Wash. U., 1970. CPA, Ill. Assoc. dir. Midwest Stock Exchange, Chgo., 1970-74; ptnr. Rosenbloom &Smith, Accts., Chgo., 1974-75; trader Ferguson Grain Co, Chgo., 1975—. Sec. North Suburban Jewish Community Ctr., Highland Park, Ill., 1984, mem. exec com., 1985, v.p., 1986; Washington U. Chgo. mem. com. for Eliot Soc.,, 1986; mem. Chgo. Bd. Trade, 1975—, Chgo. Bd. Options Exchange, 1974—. Mem. Am. Inst. CPA's, Ill. Soc. CPA's. Club: Highland Park Country. Avocations: gardening, tennis. Home: 1790 Ridge Rd Highland Park IL 60035 Office: Ferguson Grain Co 141 W Jackson Blvd Room 3250 Chicago IL 60604

SMITH, REGAN GRANVILLE, sociology educator; b. Kalamazoo, Aug. 13, 1938; s. Granville Blemyuer and Frances Marion (Little) S.; m. Lillian Sanders, July 27, 1968; children: Philip Michael, Steven Albert, Ethan Joel, Robert Jay. BA in Philosophy, Kalamazoo Coll., 1960; AM, PhD in Sociology, U. Ill., 1970. Probation officer Juvenile Ct., Pueblo, Colo., 1964-65, Calhoun County, Marshall, Mich., 1965-67; asst. prof. U. Wyoming, Laramie, 1970-72; asst. prof. sociology Sangamon State U., Springfield, Ill., 1972-76, assoc. prof., 1976—, dir. theatre, 1983-85, chmn dept. sociology, 1972-79, 86—; vis. sr. lectr. Poly. of the Southbank, London, 1981-82; mem. univ. adv. com. Ill. Bd. Regents, Springfield, 1973-77, chmn. 1974-75. Producer TV documentaries, 1984-86. Chmn. citizen's adv. com. to Sangamon County Juvenile Justice, Springfield, 1986—; exec. sec. Springfield Area AIDS Task Force, 1982—; bd. dirs Springfield Area Arts Council, 1982—, resident artists guild Springfield Theatre Ctr., 1986—. NIMH traineeship, 1967-70. Mem. Ill. Sociol. Soc. (session organizer), Midwest Sociol. Soc. (recruiting chmn. 1975-79), Soc. for Study of Symbolic Interaction (corr. sec. 1975-82, sec./treas.), ACLU (bd. dirs., exec. com. 1977-79). Democrat. Avocations: reading, weight lifting, films. Home: 140 N Douglas Springfield IL 62702-4814 Office: Sangamon State U Shepher Rd Springfield IL 62794-9243

SMITH, RICHARD CARL, manufacturing executive; b. Wilkes-Barre, Pa., June 8, 1946; s. Walter Franklin Sr. and Agnes May (Young) S.; m. Bonita Lee Motel, Aug. 17, 1968; children: Kathleen Renee, Janis Elaine, Lori Christine. BS in Aerospace Engrng., Pa. State U., 1968. Mem. tech. staff Rockwell Internat., Columbus, Ohio, 1968-70; mechanization engr. Owens-Ill., Inc., Atlanta and Fairmont, W.Va., 1970-72; asst. selecting supr. Owens-Ill., Inc., Fairmont, 1972-76; forming select and pack supr. Owens-Ill., Inc., Toledo, 1976-78, machine prodn. supt., 1978-83; v.p. mfg. Toledo Plate and Window Glass Co., 1983—. V.P. council All Saints Luth. Ch., Toledo, 1985—, chmn. social ministry, 1980-82, chmn. stewardship, 1982-84, mem. fin. and future ministry coms., 1980—. Mem. Internat. Assn. Quality Circles, Aircraft Owners and Pilot Assn., Exptl. Aircraft Assn. Republican. Club: Weekend Flyers, Inc., Toledo (pres. 1985-86). Avocations: flying, gardening, camping, skiing. Home: 2102 Sawyer Ct Holland OH 43528 Office: Toledo Plate and Window Glass Co 1042 Utica St Toledo OH 43608

SMITH, RICHARD HAMILTON, professional photographer; b. Taunton, Mass., June 15, 1950; s. Philip Frances and Antoinette (Furmanik) S.; m. Janet Ann Bliss, Oct. 16, 1975. BA, BS summa cum laude, U. N.D., 1971. Staff educator Environ. Learning Ctr., Isabella, Minn., 1972-73; staff educator Northwoods Resource Ctr., Ely, Minn., 1973-75, dir., 1975-77; adminstrv. staff YMCA Camp Widjiwagan, Ely, 1975-78; naturalist St. Croix State Parks, Hinckley, Minn., 1974; freelance photographer St. Paul, 1978—; leader photography workshops Telemark Lodge, Cable, Wis., 1978, Sci. Mus. Minn., St. Paul, 1980; cons. to arts River Falls (Wis.) High Sch., 1980; cons. to humanities Orono (Minn.) High Sch., 1984-86; treas., bd. dirs. Frozen Images, Mpls., 1983—. Photographer: Creative Edge in Photography, 1983, Minnesota II, 1984 (Communication Arts award of excellence 1985); photographer for various mags. including Nat. Geog., Time, Newsweek. Recipient Excellence award Advt. Fedn. Minn., 1980, 86. Mem. Am. Soc. Mag. Photographers, Profl. Photographers of Am., Minn. Comml. Indsl. Photographers Assn., Minn. Graphic Designers Assn. Avocations: canoeing, windsurfing, skiing, camping, running. Home and Office: 1021 W Montana Ave Saint Paul MN 55117

SMITH, RICHARD JAY, orthodontist, educator; b. Bklyn., Aug. 10, 1948; s. Benjamin and Miriam (Cohen) S.; m. Linda Sharon Harris, Aug. 22, 1970; children—Jason Andrew, Owen Harris, Hilary Rachele. B.A., Bklyn. Coll., CUNY, 1969; M.S. in Anatomy, Tufts U., 1973, D.M.D., 1973; Ph.D. in Anthropology, Yale U., 1980. Asst. clin. prof. orthodontics U. Conn., Farmington, 1976-79; asst. prof. U. Md., Balt., 1979-81, assoc. prof., 1981-84; prof. orthodontics, biomed. sci., chmn. dept. orthodontics, adj. prof. anthropology Washington U., St. Louis, 1984—, assoc. dean, 1987—, cons. orthodontics Cleft Palate and Craniofacial Anomalies Team, 1984—; vis. assoc. prof. cell biology Sch. Medicine, Johns Hopkins U., Balt., 1980-84; orthodonic cons. St. Louis VA Med. Ctr., 1986—; staff Barnes Hosp., 1986—, St. Louis Children's Hosp., 1985—. Editor-in-chief Jour. Balt. Coll. Dental surgery, 1981-84. Contbr. numerous articles in orthodontics, anthropology, comparative biology to profl. jours. Am. Fund for Dental Health dental tchr. tng. fellow, 1977-78; NIH postdoctoral fellow, 1978-79. Fellow Internat. Coll. Dentists; mem. ADA, Alumni Assn. Student Clinicians (bd. govs. 1984—, Alan J. Davis award 1983), Am. Assn. Orthodontists, Am. Assn. Phys. Anthropologists, Internat. Assn. Dental Research. (pres. St. Louis sect. 1985—), Am. Assn. Dental Schs. Home: 816 S Bemiston Ave Clayton MO 63105 Office: Washington U Sch Dental Medicine 4559 Scott Ave Saint Louis MO 63110

SMITH, RIETTE DORIS THOMAS, family and marriage therapist; b. Canton, Ohio, June 4, 1936; d. Samuel Smith and Della Gertrude (Kessler) Thomas; m. Sidney Russell Smith, Apr. 6, 1958; children: Sharon Luise, Steven Mitchell. AA, Stephens Coll., 1956; BS, Ind. U., 1958, MS, 1967. Pvt. practice marriage and family therapy Bloomington, Ind., 1974—. Mem. regional adv. bd. Anti-Defamation League, Columbus, Ohio, 1983; bd. dirs. Comunity Service Council, Bloomington, 1985. Mem. Am. Assn. for Marriage and Family Therapy (clin., supr.), Am. Assn. Sex Educators, Counselors and Family Mediators (cert. sex therapist), Acad. Family Mediators (cons.), Soc. for the Sci. Study of Sex. Jewish. Office: PO Box 1965 Bloomington IN 47402

SMITH, ROBERT CHARLES, banker; b. Waco, Tex., Sept. 4, 1953; s. David Richard and Martha Loretta (Johnson) S.; m. Cynthia Louise Morey, Dec. 20, 1975; children: Sean Morey, Trevor David. BS in Indsl. Engrng., Millikin U., 1975; MBA in Fin., Mich. State U., East Lansing, 1977; grad., Decatur (Ill.) Leadership Inst., 1987. Loan officer Nat. Bank of Detroit, 1977-81; v.p. 1st Nat. Bank Decatur, 1981—. Bd. dirs., treas. Cen. Ill. Easter Seal Soc., Decatur, 1981-83; mem. exec. com. Small Bus. Council, Decatur, 1982-84. Mem. Robert Morris Associates, Met. Decatur C. of C. (asst. treas. 1987—). Republican. Presbyterian. Clubs: Country of Decatur, Decatur. Lodge: Rotary. Avocations: golf, gardening, travel.

SMITH, ROBERT E., computer systems manager; b. Sunflower, Miss., May 12, 1946; s. Bessie Spears; m. Sheila M. Smith, Nov. 7, 1968; children: Lori, Kim. AA, Owens Tech. U., 1975; BS, Lourdes Coll., 1985. Computer coordinator Toledo Edison, 1978-82, computer supr., 1982-86, computer system mgr., 1986—. Treas. Toledo Old West End Redevel., 1980; pres. Alpha Community Devel. Corp., 1984; bd. dirs. ARC, Toledo, 1982-84, Toledo Planning Council, 1984-86; treas. Third Baptist Ch., Toledo, 1985. Democrat. Office: Toledo Edison 300 Madison Ave Toledo OH 43652

SMITH, ROBERT GEORGE, manufacturing executive; b. St. Clair, Mich., Feb. 3, 1935; s. G. Grant and Mildred L. (McConkey) S.; m. Janet McHenry, June 3, 1961; children: Jennifer L. Smith Wolfkiel, Cheryl, Gail, Amy. BS in Engrng., U. Mich., 1958; MBA, U. Chgo., 1985. Plant mgr. Conolite div. Woodall Industries, Carpentersville, Ill., 1972-76; v.p. mfg. All Am. Plastics Co., Chgo., 1976, pres., 1976-79; plant supr. Furnas Electric Co., Chgo., 1979-85; v.p. mfg. Zenith Controls Inc., Chgo., 1986—.

SMITH, ROBERT JOEL, hospital administrator; b. Chgo., Dec. 29, 1955; s. Maurice and Elaine (Roseth) S.; m. Nancy Beth Kupper, May 28, 1978; 1 child, Michelle Gail. BS, Bradley U., 1977; MSW, Washington U., St. Louis, 1979. Cert. social worker, Ill. Social worker ECHO, St. Louis, 1979-83, CompCare/Care Unit, St. Louis, 1983-84, Forest Hosp., Des Plaines, Ill., 1984-85, CompCare/Care Unit, Skokie, Ill., 1985-86; mgr. programs CompCare BMC Unit, Glenview, Ill., 1986—. Mem. Glenview Citizens Against Drug and Alcohol Abuse, Northbrook Citizens Against Drug and Alcohol Abuse, Parents Against Alcohol and Drug Abuse. Mem. Nat. Assn. Social Workers (cert.), Acad. Cert. Social Workers. Avocations: family activities, sports, reading. Home: 8905 Lyons St Des Plaines IL 60016 Office: Glenbrook Adolescent Care Unit 2100 Pfingsten Rd Glenview IL 60025

SMITH, ROBERT LEE, psychologist; b. Massillon, Ohio, Oct. 24, 1955; s. Warren Henry and Gloria Ann (Scharver) S.; m. Linda Kay Martin, June 19, 1976. BA in Psychology magna cum laude, Kent (Ohio) State U., 1978, MA in Clin. Psychology, 1980, PhD in Clin. Psychology, 1983. Lic. psychologist, Ohio. Asst. dir. Metro Chem. Dependency Treatment Service, Cleve., 1982-84, dir., 1984—; asst. prof. sch. medicine case Western Res. U., Cleve., 1984—; psychol. cons. Parmadale Family Treatment Program, Parma, Ohio, 1984—. Vol. Big Bros. Am., Kent, 1978-81; religious instr. St. Luke's Cath. Ch., Lakewood, Ohio, 1983-84. Mem. Am. Psychol. Assn., Ohio Psychol. Assn., Assn. Med. Edn. and Research in Substance Abuse. Democrat. Avocations: photography, hiking, sailing. Office: Metro Chem Dependency Treatment Services Cleve Met Gen Hosp 3395 Scranton Rd Cleveland OH 44109

SMITH, ROBERT LOUIS, property development company executive; b. Eau Claire, Wis., Dec. 15, 1947; s. Robert Francis and Betty Ellen (Owen) S.; m. Mary Elizabeth Thompson, Aug. 22, 1970; children: Tracey, Michael, Douglas. BS, U. Wis., Milw., 1971. Claims rep. State Farm Ins., Milw., 1971-72; mgr. Marshall Field & Co., Milw., 1972-74, Jacobs, Visconsi & Jacobs Co., Milw., Madison, Wis. and Merrillville, Ind., 1974-82; v.p. Park Plaza of Oshkosh, Wis., 1982—; pres., bd. dirs. Oshkosh Comml. Devel. Co. Pres. Oshkosh Symphony Orch., 1985-86; bd. dirs. Oshkosh Boy's Clubs, 1984-85; bd. dirs. Oshkosh Big Bros. and Big Sisters, 1985—; bd. dirs.Oshkosh Bus. Sch. Adv. Bd., U. Wis., 1985-86. Mem. Internat. Council Shopping Ctrs., Oshkosh C. of C. (v.p. 1984-86). Lodge: Rotary (community service officer 1985-86). Avocations: skiing, sailing, painting, golf. Office: Park Plaza 246 Park Plaza Oshkosh WI 54901

SMITH, ROBERT STEVE, refinery construction project manager; b. Springfield, Mo., June 29, 1943; s. Fred A. and Helen G. (Whitehead) S.; m. Linda Ann Payne, Jan. 8, 1966; children—Barry S., Gregory J., Sean F. B.S. in C.E., Mo. Sch. Mines and Metallurgy, 1965. Registered profl. engr., Kans. Project engr. Shell Oil Co., Deer Park, Tex., 1965-69; sales mgr. air pollution control Koch Engrng. Co., Inc., Wichita, Kans., N.Y.C., 1972-74; pres. R. S. Smith & Assoc., Wichita, 1974-77; sr. project egr. Litwin Engrs., Wichita, 1977-84, project mgr., 1984-86, Koch Refining Co., 1986—. V.p. Third Order St. Francis, Wichita, 1979-81, pres. Midwest region, 1981; v.p. St. Anthonys Parish Council, Wichita, 1983-84, pres., 1984-85. Mem. Tau Beta Pi, Phi Kappa Phi, Republican. Roman Catholic. Home: 1844 N Turquoise St Wichita KS 67212 Office: Koch Refining Co Box 2256 Wichita KS 67201

SMITH, ROGER BONHAM, automotive manufacturing executive; b. Columbus, Ohio, July 12, 1925; s. Emmet Quimby and Bess (Obetz) S.; m. Barbara Ann Rasch, June 7, 1954; children: Roger Bonham, Jennifer Anne, Victoria Belle, Drew Johnston. Student, U. Mich., 1942-44, B.B.A., 1947, M.B.A., 1949. With Gen. Motors, Detroit, 1949—; treas. Gen. Motors, 1970-71, v.p. charge fin. staff, 1971-73; v.p., group exec. in charge of non-automotive and def. group 1973-74, exec. v.p., 1974-80, vice chmn. fin. com., 1975-81, chmn., chief exec. officer, 1981—. Trustee Cranbrook Ednl. Community, Bloomfield Hills, Mich., Mich. Colls. Found., Detroit, Calif. Inst. Tech., Pasadena. Served with USNR, 1944-46. Mem. Bus. Council, Bus. Roundtable, Motor Vehicle Mfrs. Assn. (dir.). Clubs: Detroit, Detroit Athletic, Orchard Lake (Mich.) Country, Bloomfield Hills Country; Links (N.Y.C.). Home: Bloomfield Hills MI 48013 Office: Gen Motors Corp Gen Motors Bldg 3044 W Grand Blvd Detroit MI 48202

SMITH, ROLAND EMERSON, accountant; b. Kalkaska, Mich., Jan. 9, 1918; s. Ernest C. and Sybil M. (Planck) S.; m. Lois F. Frontjes, Feb. 11, 1950; 1 child, Richard. Student, Mich. State U., 1935-36; BA, Olivet Coll., 1939; cert., Walsh Coll., 1942. CPA, Mich., Ill. Acct. Coopers & Lybrand, Detroit, 1942-46, Chgo., 1946-52; ptnr. Moore, Smith & Dale, Detroit and Southfield, Mich., 1952—. Mem. Am. Inst. CPA's, Mich.Assn. CPA's. Mormom. Clubs: Franklin Racquet, Torch Lake Yacht. Home: Piety Hill Pl 600 W Brown St Apt 110 Birmingham MI 48009 Office: 24700 Northwestern Hwy 206 Southfield MI 48075

SMITH, RONALD LUVERNE, marketing manager; b. Des Moines, Oct. 16, 1933; s. Russell L. and Mary Ada (Cook) S.; m. Janice Edna Kahler, July 2, 1955; children: Suzanne, Matthew, Glenn. BSEE with high distinction, State U. Iowa, 1961. Electrical engr. Motorola, Phoenix, 1961; publs. engr. Collins Radio, Cedar Rapids, Iowa, 1961-63; electrical engr. Sperry-Univac, St. Paul, 1963-68; program mgr. Control Data, Bloomington, Minn., 1968—, Magnetic Peripherals, Inc., Minnetonka, Minn., 1986—. Served with USN, 1953-57. Methodist. Club: CDC/MPI Mgmt. Avocations: fishing, hunting, tennis, bowling, gardening. Home: 2604 River Hills Dr Burnsville MN 55337 Office: Magnetic Peripherals Inc 12701 Whitewater Dr Minnetonka MN 55343

SMITH, RONALD NOEL, facilities manager; b. Beech Grove, Ind., Oct. 10, 1946; s. Clayton Marion and Fannie Lee (Ashley) S.; m. Susan Jean Lauterborn, Dec. 15, 1972; children: Jennifer Lynn, Jessica Lee. A in Archtl. Engrng. Tech., Sams Tech. Inst., 1966; cert., Ind. U., 1978, BS, 1980. Draftsman Elliot-William Co., Indpls., 1967-68; chief designer Acme Corp., Indpls., 1973-77; supr. contract maintenance, improvements and alterations Indpls. Pub. Schs., 1977-82; dir. physical plant to dir. facilities planning and constrn. Sinclair Community Coll., Dayton, 1982—. Leader Royal Rangers, Beech Grove, 1972-74; coll. rep. Miami Valley River Corridor Com., Dayton, 1982. Served to staff sgt. USAF, 1968-72. Mem. Assn. Physical Plant Adminstrs. of Univs. and Colls. (Instl.), Am. Inst. Plant Engrs. (editorial bd. 1984—), Profl. Grounds Mgmt. Soc., Internat. Facility Mgmt. Assn. Republican. Mem. Assembly of God Ch. Club: Engrs. (Dayton). Avocations: golf, bowling, music. Office: Sinclair Community Coll 444 W Third St Dayton OH 45402

SMITH, RUTH HUNTER, lawyer; b. Columbus, Ohio, Dec. 23, 1949; d. Richard F. and Bernice E. (Strawser) Hunter; m. J. T. Smith, Jan. 23, 1970 (div. May 1972); 1 son, Jason C. B.S. in Edn., Ohio State U., 1973, J.D., 1977. Bar: Ohio 1977. Tchr. English, Columbus Pub. Schs., 1973-74; cons. Franklin County Mcpl. Ct., Columbus, 1975-76; research asst. Coll. Law, Ohio State U., Columbus, 1976; law clk. Vorys, Sater, Seymour & Pease, Columbus, 1976-77; legal counsel John W. Galbreath & Co., Columbus and Denver, 1977—; lectr. N.W. Ctr. for Profl. Edn., Portland, Oreg., 1984. Vol. Am. Cancer Soc., Columbus, 1984, March of Dimes, Columbus, 1984. Coll. Law scholar Ohio State U., 1974-76; Milton R. Bierly scholar Ohio State U., 1972. Mem. ABA, Ohio State Bar Assn., Columbus Bar Assn., Franklin County Women Lawyers Assn. Republican. Roman Catholic. Office: John W Galbreath & Co 188 E Broad St Columbus OH 43215

SMITH, SAM DEVERE, industrial engineer; b. Rolla, Mo., Oct. 24, 1936; s. Levi P. and Eula G. (Christensen) S.; m. Norma Jean Leonard, Dec. 22, 1957; 1 child, Samra Dee. M of Engrng., Mo. Sch. of Mines, 1960. Registered profl. engr., Kans. Designer Gen. Steel Ind., Granite City, Ill., 1961-68; design engr. Rockwell Mfg., Atchison, Kans., 1968-76; project engr. Rockwell Internat., Troy, Mich., 1976-79, Youngstown (Ohio) Steel Door, 1979-82; pvt. practice engr. transp. industry 1982—; pres. Smith Tranco Service Ltd., Richton Park, Ill., 1987—. Inventor intermodal transp. vehicle. Mem. ASME, Am. Soc. Quality Control (cert. reliability engr. 1981, quality engr. 1984), Assn. Am. R.Rs.(track train dynamics task force 1979-82). Home: 22418 Butterfield Dr Apt 107 Richton Park IL 60471

SMITH, SAMUEL LIONEL, data processing executive, consultant; b. Chgo., Dec. 27, 1946; s. Hiawatha Clarence Sr. and Vashtie (Jones) S.; m. Valerie Dixon, Nov. 16, 1968 (div. June 1980); children: Michael, Donna. Student, Roosevelt U., 1972-78. Cert. data processor. Project mgr. Ryan Ins., Chgo., 1979-81; sr. staff programmer Info Industries, Inc., Kansas City, Mo., 1981-83, Allstate Ins., Northbrook, Ill., 1983-86; contractor Progressive Systems, Woodridge, Ill., 1986; engr. software Cutler-Williams, Chgo., 1986—; pres. Progressive Devel. Systems, Inc., Downers Grove, Ill., 1986—. Served with USNR, 1986—. Mem. Black Data Processing Assocs., Systems Programmers Soc. (pres. 1978). Avocations: photography, books, cars. Home: 2260 Country Club Dr Woodridge IL 60517-3029 Office: Progressive Devel Systems Inc 5117 Main St Suite D Downers Grove IL 60515

SMITH, SPENCER BAILEY, business and engineering educator; b. Ottawa, Ont., Can., Jan. 31, 1927; s. Sidney B. and Etta (Bailey) S.; m. Mildred E. Spidell, Dec. 31, 1954. B.Eng., McGill U., 1949; M.S., Columbia U., 1950, Eng.Sc.D., 1958. Adminstrv. engr. Mergenthaler Linotype Co., N.Y.C., 1953-58; ops. research mgr. Raytheon Co., Newton, Mass., 1958-61; ops research mgr. Montgomery Ward & Co., Chgo., 1961-66; assoc. prof., then prof. Ill. Inst. Tech., 1966—, chmn. dept. indsl. and systems engring., 1971-77, dir. Stuart Sch. Office of Research, 1977-82. Contbr. articles to profl. jours.; patentee on order quantity calculator, 1964. Vol. cons. on sch. redistricting Elem. Sch. Dist., Evanston, Ill., 1972-74. Research grantee Harris Trust and Savs. Bank, 1968-70, Ill. Law Enforcement Commn., 1972-74, U.S. Army C.E., 1981, Am. Prodn. and Inventory Control Soc., 1980. Mem. Ops. Research Soc. Am., Inst. Mgmt. Sci., Am. Inst. Indsl. Engrs., Am. Statis. Assn., ASME, Am. Prodn. and Inventory Control Soc., Soc. Mfg. Engrs. Presbyterian. Club: University (Chgo.). Home: 2530 Lawndale Ave Evanston IL 60201 Office: Ill Inst Tech Chicago IL 60616

SMITH, STANLEY EDWARD, JR., obstetrician-gynecologist; b. Cooks Falls, N.Y., Mar. 20, 1923; s. Stanley Edward and Sarah Louise (Treyz) S.; m. Marie Perry, June 23, 1945; children: Roger Perry, Susan Laura. BS, Cornell U., 1943, MD, 1946. Diplomate Am. Bd. Ob-Gyn. Practice medicine specializing ob-gyn Norfolk, Va., 1951-55; mem. staff Carle Clinic Assn., Urbana, Ill.; asst. prof. ob-gyn U. Ill., Urbana, 1975—. Contbr. articles to profl. jour. Served to capt. M.C. U.S. Army, 1942-49. Fellow Am. Coll Ob-Gyn; mem. Am. Med. Soc., Am. Fertility Soc., Cen. Assn. Ob-

Gyn, Ill. Ob-Gyn Soc. (pres. 1965). Avocations: wood carving, stamps collecting. Home: 1001 Harrington Dr Champaign IL 61821

SMITH, STANLEY JAMES, accountant; b. Winterset, Iowa, Aug. 18, 1952; s. James Berl and Mabel Lucile (Stanley) S.; m. Linda Jean Griffith, May 28, 1977; children: Kari Lynn, Ellen Dyan. BS in Indsl. Adminstrn., Iowa State U., 1974. CPA, Iowa. Acct. Coopers & Lybrand, Des Moines, 1974-81; pvt. practice acct. Winterset, 1981—; bd. dirs. Wesley Day Advt., Des Moines. Asst. commr. Soil Conservation Service, Madison County, 1982-87. Mem. Am. Inst. CPA's, Iowa Soc. CPA's. Republican. Lodges: Lions (pres. 1987), Optimists. Home: Rural Rt 2 Box 104 Earlham IA 50072 Office: 116 W Court PO Box 326 Winterset IA 50273

SMITH, STANLEY VLADIMIR, economist, financial service company executive; b. Rhinelander, Wis., Nov. 16, 1946; s. Valy Zdenek and Sylvia (Cohen) S.; m. Diane Sue Green, Aug. 8, 1979; children: Cara, David. BS in Ops. Research, Cornell U., 1968; MBA, U. Chgo., 1972, postgrad., 1973. Lectr. U. Chgo., 1973; economist bd. govs. Fed. Res. System, Washington, 1973-74; assoc. December Group, Chgo., 1974—; founding pres. Seaquest Internat., Chgo., 1977-81; mgr., ptnr. Ibbotson Assocs., Chgo., 1981—; pres. Corp. Fin. Group, Ltd., Chgo., 1981—; bd. dirs. Seaquest, Chgo., Alternatives, Chgo.; chmn. Corp. Investment Bus. Brokers, Chgo., 1986—. Founding editor Stocks, Bonds, Bills and Inflation yearbook, 1984; also contbr. articles in field. Fellow Allied Chem., 1967, John McMullen Trust, 1969; grantee Ford Found., 1972, U.S. Fed. Res., 1973. Mem. Fin. Analyst Fedn., Ea. Fin. Assn., Am. Econ. Assn., Alpha Delta Phi. Republican. Home: 1318 N Sandburg Terr Chicago IL 60610 Office: Corp Fin Group 1165 N Clark Suite 650 Chicago IL 60610

SMITH, STELLA ELIZABETH, multi-housing company executive; b. Springfield, Mo., July 6, 1931; d. Russell Lena and Oma Oble (Stockstill) Baber; m. Arthur A. Smith, May 30, 1952 (div. 1981); children: Michael A., Barbara A., James Edward, Cynthia Sue. Student St. Louis U., 1981-83. Office mgr. Consumers Warehouse Markets, Springfield, 1948-52; acctg. clk. Mathieson Chem. Corp., Little Rock, 1952-54; group leader McDonnell Aircraft Corp., St. Louis, 1954-59; office mgr. Arthur A. Smith, M.D., O'Fallon, Ill., 1968-74; pres., chief exec. officer Mantek, Inc., Springfield, 1981—. Bd. dirs. Signal Hill United Meth. Ch., Belleville, Ill., 1973-87. Mem. Nat. Assn. Women Bus. Owners, Nat. Assn. Female Execs., P.E.O. (treas. 1983-84, v.p. 1986-87, pres. 1987-88), Springfield Apt. Assn., Mo. Apt. Assn., Nat. Apt. Assn., St. Clair County LWV (bd. dirs. 1978-84), Women's Aux. Ill. Med. Soc. (bd. dirs. 1968-72), Women's Aux. St. Clair County Med. Soc. (safety chmn. 1963-69), Greater Springfield C. of C., St. Clair County Genealogy Soc. (charter 1977). Republican. Avocations: travel, theater, reading, collecting cook books. Home and Office: 64 Oak Hill Dr Belleville IL 62223

SMITH, STEPHEN FOSTER, manufacturing company executive; b. Seward, Nebr., May 21, 1940; s. Herbert R. and Mary Elizabeth (Foster) S.; m. Susan Louise Sahn, Oct. 26, 1967; children: Mary Elizabeth, Stephen Foster II. BSME, U. Nebr., 1965. Engr. Hughes Bros., Inc., Seward, 1965-70, asst. to chief engr., 1970-76, asst. chief engr., 1976-78, v.p. engring, 1978-85, exec. v.p., 1985—, also bd. dirs. Pres. Seward Vol. fire Dept., 1978-82; v. chmn. Seward Airport Authority, 1984—; bd. dirs. Seward Community Scholarship Bd., 1966—, Seward Housing Authority, 1976—. Served to capt. Air N.G., 1965-85. Mem. ASME, IEEE, Am. Soc. Testing Materials, Am. Wood Preservers Inst. (bd. dirs. 1986). Republican. Methodist. Club: Seward Country. Lodge: Rotary. Avocations: golf, fishing, hunting, camping, home computers. Office: Hughes Bros Inc Box 159 Seward NE 68434

SMITH, STEPHEN WALTER, school system administrator; b. Callicoon, N.Y., Aug. 24, 1946; s. Robert Stephen and Hilda Katherine (Moller) S.; m. Kandace Lou Haugh, Dec. 23, 1968; children: Eric, Paul. BA, Eastern Nazarene Coll., 1968; MA, U. Akron, 1974. Tchr. math. and psychology Claymont City Schs., Uhrichsville, Ohio, 1969-73; sch. psychologist Perry Local Schs., Massillon, Ohio, 1973-82, dir. pupil services, 1982—. Mem. Ohio Assn. Pupil Personnel Administrs., Council Exceptional Children, Assn. Retarded Citizens, Stark County Guidance Assn., Phi Delta Kappa. Lodge: Rotary. Home: 3333 Crownpoint NW Massillon OH 44646 Office: Perry Local Schs 4201 Harsh Ave SW Massillon OH 44646

SMITH, STEVEN BROOKS, food products executive; b. Paris, Tenn., Apr. 11, 1949; s. Everett H. and Louane C. (Brooks) S.; m. Julie Kathryn Eng, July 20, 1979; children: Steven Brian, Bradford Michael. BS in Bakery Sci. and Mktg., Kans. State U., 1971. Tech. sales rep. Pillsbury Co., Dallas, 1972-74; nat. account exec. Pillsbury Co., N.Y.C., 1974-76, regional sales mgr., 1977; v.p., nat. sales mgr. The Ph. Orth Co., Milw., 1977-80, sr. v.p., 1980-84, exec. v.p., 1984-87, pres., 1987—. Milw. Citizens' Govtl. Research Bur., mem. steering com. Milw. Assn. Commerce/Council Small Bus. Execs. Served to capt. U.S. Army, 1971-72. Mem. Am. Bakers Assn. (co-chmn. young execs. 1982-84), Bakers Nat. Edn. Found. (bd. dirs. 1980-86), Bakers Ambassadors (sec., treas. 1980-86), Kans. State U. Bakery Sci. and Mgmt. Alumni Assn. (pres. 1977-80), Tuckaway C. of C., Milw. Assn. Commerce/Council Small Bus.Execs. (mem. steering com.). Club: University (Milw.). Avocation: golf. Home: 4415 N Lake Dr Shorewood WI 53221 Office: Ph Orth Co 7350 S 10th St Oak Creek WI 53154

SMITH, STEVEN DICKINSON, electronics co. exec.; b. Indpls., Sept. 13, 1953; s. Gerald Dickinson and Dorothy Jane S.; m. Carol G. B.S. in Bus., Ind. U., 1976. Mech. engr., ops. mgr. Mouron & Co., Indpls., 1972-74; mech. engr. Carson Mfg. Co., Indpls., 1974-75; mfg. mgr. Internat. Energy Mgmt. Corp., Indpls., 1975-78; founder, 1978, since pres. Manutek, Inc., Indpls. Mem. IEEE, Indpls. C. of C., Sports Car Club Am. Republican. Lutheran. Office: 8076 Woodland Dr Indianapolis IN 46278

SMITH, STEVEN GENE, statistician, consultant; b. Joplin, Mo., May 28, 1947; s. Charles Christopher and Virginia Lee (Copher) S.; m. Sharon Ann Smith, June 1, 1966; children: Steven Gene, Mischelle Angenette. Student, Crowder Coll. Mgr. One Hour Cleaners, Joplin, 1965-72; supr. prodn. Lozier Corp., Joplin, 1972-75; supr. prodn. Fasco Ind., Cassville, Mo., 1975-76, gen. foreman, 1976-81, staff quality control facilitator, 1981—; cons. Cassville, 1984—; instr. Crowder Coll., Neosho, Mo., 1984—. Author: Introduction to SPC, 1984; contbr. articles to profl. mags. Recipient cert. merit Bur. Nat. Affairs, 1985. Mem. Internat. Assn. of Quality Circles (facilitator, pres. Joplin chpt. 1985—), DAV (jr. commdr. Cassville chpt. 1983—). Avocations: golf, fishing. Home: HC01 Box 83 Cassville MO 65625 Office: Fasco Industries PO Box 548 Cassville MO 65625

SMITH, SYDNEY DAVID, computer information scientist; b. San Antonio, Tex., Nov. 25, 1947; s. Sydney Philip and Doris Annette (King) S.; m. Helen Louise Smith; 1 child, Anne. BBA, Baylor U., 1969; MBA, Northwestern U., 1973. CPA, Ill. Sr. adminstrv. services Arthur Andersen & Co., Chgo., 1973-76; sr. systems engr. Bd. Edn., Chgo., 1976-77; applications mgr. Estech, Inc., Chgo., 1977-84; info. ctr. mgr. GATX Corp., Chgo., 1984-85; sr. cons. Artificial Intelligence Corp., Chgo., 1986—. Served with U.S. Army, 1969-71. Mem. Am. Inst. CPA's, Ill. CPA soc., Am. Assn. Artificial Intelligence. Office: Artificial Intelligence Corp 444 N Michigan Ave Suite 3656 Chicago IL 60611

SMITH, TERRENCE RONALD, science educator, farmer; b. Cin., June 16, 1941; s. Woodrow Wilson and Viola Marie (Sellers) S.; m. Elizabeth Jane Tracy, May 23, 1964. BS in Agriculture, Ohio State U., 1969; MEd, Xavier U., 1975; postgrad., U. Cin. Cert. tchr., Ohio. Sci. tchr. Bethel (Ohio) Tate Local Schs., 1969—, sci. curriculum chmn., 1983; owner, operator Bet-Ter Farms, Mt. Orab, Ohio, 1971—. Mem. steering com. Regional Agricultural Alternatives, So. Ohio, 1985-86. Mem. NEA, Ohio Edn. Assn., Southwestern Ohio Edn. Assn., Bethel-Tate Tchrs. Assn., Ohio Sci. Edn. Assn., Ohio Fruit Growers Soc., Highland County Farm Bur., Ohio Valley Fruit and Vegetable Growers Assn. (pres. 1977-79), Ducks Unlimited, Ohio State U. Alumni Assn. Avocation: natural resource conservation. Home: 1971 Sicily Rd Mount Orab OH 45154 Office: Bethel Tate Middle School Fossyl Dr Bethel OH 45106

SMITH, TERRY LYNN, information scientist; b. La Porte, Ind., Dec. 8, 1944; s. Paul F. and Ferne R. (Eplett) S.; m. Mary Jo Hartley, Jan. 31, 1970; children: Todd Alan, Timothy Eric. BS, Butler U., 1968. Programmer LTV Steel Co., East Chicago, Ind., 1971-74; systems analyst Allis Chalmers Co., Harvey, Ill., 1974-76; mgr. finished inventory La Salle Steel Co., Hammond, Ind., 1976-80; internal cons. Wheelabrater-Frye Co., Harvey, 1980-82; dir. mgmt. info. systems Trailmobile, Inc., Chgo., 1982-83; prin., cons. Arthur Young & Co., Chgo., 1983-86; sr. mgr. Peat Marwick, Chgo., 1986—; mem. client strategy com., Arthur Young & Co., Chgo., 1986, peer rev. team, Orange County, Calif., 1986. Served as sgt. U.S. Army, 1968-71. Mem. Am. Prodn. and Inventory Control Soc. (edn. com. 1981, cert.), Data Processing Mgmt. Assn., Spl. Interest Group for Cert. Data Processors, Assn. Inst. Cert. Group Computer Profls. (cert.). Republican. Methodist. Club: East Bank (Chgo.). Avocations: tennis, basketball, softball, reading autobiographies. Home: 8752 Lantern Dr Saint John IN 46373

SMITH, THOMAS ANTHONY, architect, engineer; b. Chgo., Sept. 22, 1926; s. Thomas L. and Florence May (Hill) S.; divorced; children: Susan D., Steven T., Cindy A., Janice G., Cheri L. BS in Archtl. Engring., U. Ill., 1950. Archtl. engr. Stanley Engring. Co., Muscatine, Iowa, 1950-54, C. Edward Ware & Assocs., Rockford, Ill., 1954-55; archtl. designer Allen Patton Bates, Architects, Rockford, 1955-58; ptnr. Knowland Smith, Architects, Rockford, 1958-80; pres. Smith Tyson & Assocs., Inc., Rockford, 1980-86, cons., 1986—. Contbr. articles on antique guns research to profl. jours. Mem. Rockford zoning bd., 1979-85. Served with Air Corps USN, 1944-46, PTO. Mem. AIA (chpt. treas. 1970, pres. 1972-73, mem. Ill. state com. on legis. 1971, nat. com. on legis., 1972-73, creative detailing and contract documents award 1960, emeritus, cons.), Constrn. Specification Inst. Republican. Mem. United Ch. of Christ. Avocations: golf, writing poetry, collecting antique guns, world travel. Home: 209 Bienterra Trail Unit 2C Rockford IL 61107 Office: 400 N First St Rockford IL 61107

SMITH, THOMAS DWIGHT, telephone company executive; b. Chariton, Iowa, Nov. 30, 1938; s. Harold and Carrie Smith; m. Janet E. Hess; 1 child, Michael S. B.B.A., U. Iowa, 1962; M.B.A., Creighton U., 1968. With Northwestern Bell Telephone Co., 1962—, mgmt. trainee, Des Moines, 1962, asst. toll supr., 1963, asst. acct., Omaha, 1963, acctg. supr., 1965, 66, 67, dist. acctg. mgr. revenue, Omaha, data processing, Omaha, 1969, data systems cons., Omaha, 1971, gen. data systems supr., Omaha, 1972-75, asst. comptroller, Omaha, 197-80, treas., Omaha, 1980-83, v.p. advanced info. markets, Omaha, 1983, v.p., chief exec. officer-Iowa, Des Moines, 1983-86; exec. v.p. Bankers Trust Co., Des Moines, 1986—. dir. internal auditing AT&T, 1978, Bankers Trust, Des Moines, mem. audit com., loan com. Trustee Drake U.; bd. dirs. United Way, Des Moines Metro YMCA, Social Settlement Assn. of Omaha, Omaha Awareness and Action; mem. Greater Des Moines Com; chmn. Des Moines YWCA Strategic Adv. Com.; exec. bd. dirs. Mid Iowa Council Boy Scouts Am.; mem. Am. Heart Assn. Corp. Cabinet; mem. utilities adv. com. Iowa Coll. Found.; v.p. Omaha Symphony Council; mem. exec. com. program, planning and budget com. United Way of the Midlands. Mem. Iowa Telephone Assn. (bd. dirs.), Greater Des Moines C. of C. (bd. dirs., exec. com. of bus. and urban devel.), Am. Mgmt. Assn., Beta Gamma Sigma. Avocations: golf; hunting; physical fitness. Home: 2417 70th Pl Des Moines IA 50322 Office: Bankers Trust Co 665 Locust PO Box 897 Des Moines IA 50304

SMITH, THOMAS EDWARD, social welfare educator; b. Kamakura, Japan, Dec. 5, 1951; came to U.S., 1968; s. Robert L. and Aki (Sato) S. B.S., U. Wash., 1975, M.S.W., 1978, Ph.D., 1982. Crisis counselor Valley Gen. Hosp., Renton, Wash., 1975-76; research asst. Child Devel. and Mental Retardation Ctr., Seattle, 1977-81; instr. Sch. Social Welfare, U. Wis.-Milw., 1981-82, asst. prof., 1982-85, assoc. prof., 1985—; tng. dir. Family Therapy Inst. Milw. Seattle Drug Commn. grantee, 1981-82; bd. dirs. Family Therapy Training Inst., 1985—. Mem. Am. Assn. Behavior Therapy, Nat. Council Family Relations, Nat. Assn. Social Workers (cert.), Council on Social Work Edn., Am. Assn. Marriage and Family Therapy (clin. mem.). Contbr. numerous articles to profl. jours. Office: U Wis Milw Dept Social Welfare PO Box 786 Milwaukee WI 53201

SMITH, THOMAS EUGENE, optometrist; b. Seymour, Ind., Nov. 20, 1955; s. Ray T. and Marilyn (Cummings) S.; m. Terri Morgan, Aug. 17, 1980. BS, Purdue U., 1978, MS, 1980; OD, Ind. U., 1983. Pvt. practice optometrics Seymour, 1983—. Mem. Am. Optometric Assn. Lodge: Lions (v.p. Brownstown, Ind. 1985—). Office: Eye Clinic 319 W 3d St Seymour IN 47274 Office: Eye Clinic 405 N Main St Brownstown IN 47220

SMITH, THOMAS GORDON, architect; b. Oakland, Calif., Apr. 23, 1948; s. Sheldon Wagers and Margaret (Prendergast) S.; m. Marika Wilson, Dec. 19, 1970; children—Alan, Stuart, Demetra, Andrew, Philip. A.B., U. Calif.-Berkeley, 1970, M.Arch., 1975. Lic. architect, Calif. Prin. Thomas Gordon Smith, Architect, Chgo., 1980-86; instr. archtl. history Coll. of Marin, Kentfield, Calif., 1976-77; guest instr. archtl. design So. Calif. Inst. Architecture, Santa Monica, 1983; guest lectr., seminar leader Kunstgeschichtlieches Institut der Philipps Universitat, Marburg, W.Ger., 1983; guest tchr. U. Ill., Chgo., UCLA, 1984; assoc. prof. U. Ill., Chgo. Exhibited art in shows at Santa Barbara Mus. Art, 1977, Cooper-Hewitt Mus., Chgo. Art Inst., 1980, Louisiana Mus. Modern Art, Copenhagen, 1981, Venice Biennale, 1980, Smith Coll. Mus. Art, 1981, La Jolla Mus. Modern Art, Calif., 1982, Deutsches Architekturmuseum, Frankfurt, W.Ger., 1984; revision of Modern IBM Gallery, N.Y., 1987; author: Classical Architecture: Rule and Invention, 1987. AIA Grad. fellow, 1973, U. Calif. grad. fellow, 1974, John K. Branner fellow, 1975, Rome Prize fellow, 1979; grantee Graham Found. Advanced Study in Fine Arts, 1984, 87, Am. Philos. Soc., 1987. Mem. Soc. Archtl. Historians (bd. dirs. 1979-81), AIA, San Francisco Archtl. Club. Home and Office: 121 Park Ave River Forest IL 60305

SMITH, THOMAS GREGORY, manufacturing executive; b. Aurora, Ill., May 18, 1959; s. Dwight Emerson and Margaret Eloise (Garrett) S.; m. Lisa Jo Middleton, Jan. 27, 1979 (div. Mar. 1980); Stacey Lynn Marcum, Feb. 27, 1982; 1 child, Michelle Lynn. Grad. high sch., West Aurora, Ill. Sales engr. Dwight Smith and Assocs., Aurora, 1980-81, v.p., gen. mgr., 1981-84, pres., gen. mgr., 1984—; pres., gen. mgr. Gregory Thomas, Inc., Aurora, 1981—; static cons. RCA Video Disk, Indpls., 1981-84. Mem. Nat. Electronics Distbr. Assn., Am. Fedn. Musicians, U.S. Ind. Telephone Assn., Elect. Overstress/Electro Static Discharge Assn. Republican. Roman Catholic. Avocation: profl. musician. Office: 834 N Highland Ave Aurora IL 60506

SMITH, THOMAS HAMILTON, IV, optometrist; b. Cedar Rapids, Iowa, Dec. 20, 1943; s. Thomas Hamilton and V. Darlene (Foster) S.; m. Sheryl Ann Cochran, June 17, 1967; children—Tom, Chad, Lynn. O.D., Ill. Coll. Optometry, 1968. Pvt. practice optometry, Chgo., 1968-69, Fergus Falls, Minn., 1969-76, 81—; optometrist Profl. Corp., Fergus Falls, 1976-81. Pres. Otter chpt. Izaak Walton League, 1983. Fellow Coll. Optometrists in Vision Devel.; mem. Am. Optometric Assn., Minn. Optometric Assn., Am. Acad. Optometry. Republican. Baptist. Avocation: photography. Home: 314 N Whitford Fergus Falls MN 56537 Office: 210 N Cascade Box 96 Fergus Falls MN 56537

SMITH, VANN ARTHUR, neuropsychologist; b. San Bernardino, Calif., Feb. 18, 1949; s. William Alfred and Genevieve Margaret (White) S.; m. Bonnie Ann Hanson, Apr. 24, 1982. BS, Idaho State U., 1972, MA in Edn., 1973; PhD, U.S. Internat. U., 1975. Lic. psychologist, Ill.; cert. alcoholism counselor, Ill. Clin. neuropsychologist Libertyville, Ill., 1980—; dir. psychol. services New Beginnings Adolescent Alcohol Treatment Program, Chgo., 1984—; clin. dir. Specialty Care Devel. Corp., Chgo., 1987—; exec. dir. Nat. Acad. Specialists in Addictive Disorders, Libertyville, Ill., 1987—; cons. psychologist Parkside Lodge Adolescent Alcohol Treatment Program, Mundelein, Ill., 1980-84. Author: (ednl. audiotapes) Why Do I Keep Hurting Myself? 1985; developed psychodiagnostic test instruments; contbr. articles to profl. jours. Served to lt. comdr. USN, 1976-80. Mem. Am. Psychol. Assn., Ill. Psychol. Assn., Nat. Acad. Neuropsychologists. Democrat. Roman Catholic. Nat. bluegrass fiddling champion. Avocations: musician, martial arts, pistol shooting, racquetball. Home: 400 N Greenbay Waukegan IL 60085 Office: 1123 S Milwaukee Ave Libertyville IL 60048

SMITH, VIRGINIA DODD (MRS. HAVEN SMITH), congresswoman; b. Randolph, Iowa, June 30, 1911; d. Clifton Clark and Erville (Reeves) Dodd; m. Haven N. Smith, Aug. 27, 1931. A.B., U. Nebr., 1936. Nat. pres. Am. Country Life Assn., 1951-54; nat. chmn. Am. Farm Bur. Women, 1954-74; dir. Am. Farm Bur. Fedn., 1954-74, Country Women's Council; world dep. pres. Asso. Country Women of World, 1962-68; mem. Dept. Agr. Nat. Home Econs. Research Adv. Com., 1960-65. Mem. Crusade for Freedom European inspection tour, 1958; del. Republican Nat. Conv., 1956, 72; bd. govs. Agrl. Hall of Fame, 1959—; mem. Nat. Livestock and Meat Bd., 1955-58, Nat. Commn. Community Health Services, 1963-66; adv. mem. Nebr. Sch. Bds. Assns., 1949; mem. Nebr. Territorial Centennial Commn., 1953, Gov.'s Commn. Status of Women, 1964-66; chmn. Presdl. Task Force on Rural Devel., 1969-70; mem. 94th-98th Congresses from 3d Dist. Nebr.; mem. appropriations com., ranking minority mem. agrl. appropriations subcom., appropriations subcom. on energy and water devel. 94th-98th Congresses from 3d dist. Nebr.; v.p. Farm Film Found., 1964-74, Good Will ambassador to Switzerland, 1950. Apptd. adm. Nebr. Navy. Recipient award of Merit, DAR, 1956; Disting. Service award U. Nebr., 1956, 60; award for best pub. address on freedom Freedom Found., 1966; Eyes on Nebr. award Nebr. Optometric Assn., 1970; Internat. Service award Midwest Conf. World Affairs, 1970; Woman of Achievement award Nebr. Bus. and Profl. Women, 1971; selected as 1 of 6 U.S. women Govt. France for 3 week goodwill mission to France, 1969; Outstanding 4H Alumni award Iowa State U., 1973, 74; Watchdog of Treasury award, 1976, 78, 80, 82; Guardian of Small Bus. award, 1976, 78, 80, 82, 84,86; Nebr. Ak-Sar-Ben award, 1983. Mem. AAUW, Delta Kappa Gamma (state hon. mem.), Beta Sigma Phi (internat. hon. mem.), Chi Omega, PEO (past pres.), Eastern Star. Methodist. Club: Business and Professional Women. *

SMITH, WADE WILLIS, marketing professional; b. Madison, Wis., May 21, 1950; s. Willis William and Miriam Alice (Triggs) S.; m. Patrica Ann Grahlman, June 16, 1973. BS in Civil and Environ. Engring., U. Wis., 1972. Registered professional engr., Wis. Sales engr. Trane Co., La Crosse, Wis., 1972-75, product mgr., 1975-83, mgr. market devel., 1983-86, mktg. mgr., 1986—; adv. bd. Tex. A&M Engring. Sch., College Station, Tex., 1984-86, Bldg's mag. Expn. and Conf., Cedar Rapids, Iowa, 1986—. Contbr. articles to profl. jours. Mem. ASHRAE, Nat. Assn. Indsl. and Office Parks, Bldg. Owners and Mgrs. Assn. Republican. Lutheran. Avocations: sailing, skiing. Home: 2510 Hillcrest La Crosse WI 54601 Office: Trane Co 3600 Pammel Creek Rd La Crosse WI 54601

SMITH, WALLACE BUNNELL, physician, church official; b. Independence, Mo., July 29, 1929; s. William Wallace and Rosamond (Bunnell) S.; m. Anne M. McCullough, June 26, 1956; children—Carolyn, Julia, Laura. A.A., Graceland Coll., Lamoni, Iowa, 1948; B.A., U. Kans., 1950, M.D., 1954. Diplomate: Am. Bd. Ophthalmology. Intern Charity Hosp. of La., 1955; resident in medicine U. Kans. Med. Center, 1958, resident in ophthalmology, 1959-62; pvt. practice medicine specializing in ophthalmology 1962-76; ordained to ministry Reorganized Ch. of Jesus Christ of Latter Day Saints, 1945; asso. pastor Walnut Park Congregation, Independence, Mo., 1966-70, Pleasant Heights Congregation, Independence, 1975-76; president-designate Reorganized Ch. of Jesus Christ of Latter Day Saints, 1976-78, pres., 1978—; clin. assoc. U. Kans. Med. Center, 1962-76; dir. Pacific Land Devel. Assn. Bd. dirs. Mo. State Hist. Soc., Am. Lung Assn. W. Mo.; chmn. Independence Sanitarium and Hosp. Corp. Served to lt. M.C. USNR, 1955-58. Fellow Am. Acad. Ophthalmology, A.C.S.; mem. AMA, Jackson County Med. Soc., Independence C. of C., Phi Beta Pi. Club: Rotary. Home: 337 Partridge Independence MO 64055 Office: Auditorium Box 1059 Independence MO 64051

SMITH, WALTER DELOS, accountant; b. Rensselaer, Ind., June 7, 1936; s. Walter Myron and Evelyn Geraldine (Murphy) S.; m. Yvonne Marie Dietz, Sept. 24, 1960; children—Michele, Michael, Kevin, Bryan, Denise, Derek. B.S. in Acctg., Walton Sch. Commerce, Chgo., 1960. C.P.A., Wis., Ill. Acct. Frazer & Torbet C.P.A.s, Chgo., 1960-66; asst. controller Rath-Packing Co., Waterloo, Iowa 1966-68; controller, treas. DeLeuw, Cather & Co., Chgo., 1968-72; corp. controller Mohawk Data Scis., Utica, N.Y., 1972-75; mgmt. cons. Walter D. Smith & Assocs., New Hartford, N.Y., 1975-76; v.p., gen. mgr. Flambeau-Plastics, Baraboo, Wis., 1976-83; prin. Walter D. Smith, C.P.A., Baraboo, 1983—; owner, pres. Fine Cabinet Shop, Inc., Baraboo, 1983—; mem. adv. panel U. Wis., Madison and Whitewater, 1981—; dir. Trachte Bldg. Systems, Sun Prairie, Wis. Pres. Downers Grove Drug Abuse Council, Ill., 1972; mem. Baraboo Area Opportunity Devel. Com., 1983—; bd. dirs. New Hartford Sch. Dist., 1974-76, Baraboo Sch. Dist., 1980-83. Served with AUS, 1955-56, Korea. Mem. Nat. Assn. Accts. (bd. dirs. 1966-67), Baraboo Toastmasters. Republican. Roman Catholic. Lodge: Kiwanis. Home: 809 Iroquois Circle Baraboo WI 53913 Office: Walter D Smith CPA 222 4th Ave Baraboo WI 53913

SMITH, WALTER KENT, marketing executive; b. Shelbyville, Ill., Mar. 2, 1942; s. D. Kenneth and Helen J. (Law) S.; m. Karen S. Grossaint, Aug. 27, 1961 (div. Dec. 1979); children: Kreig S., Kelly J.; m. Sheila L. Shuett, Jan. 27, 1980; children: Maribeth L. Fry, Steven B. Fry. BSBA, Bradley U., 1964. Mktg. trainee Caterpillar Inc., Peoria, Ill., 1964-66, supr., 1978-85, Electric Power Generation Bus. Mgr. U.S. and Can., 1985—; indsl. products rep. Caterpillar Americas, Lima, Peru, 1966-70, dist. mgr., 1970-73; supr. Caterpillar Americas, Peoria, 1973-78; gen. mgr., ptnr. C&S Rentals, Peoria, 1976—; gen. mgr., owner K&S Rentals, Peoria, 1980—; v.p., chief exec. officer K&S Farming Corp., 1984—. Pres. Delta Upsilon Alumni Corp., 1965-66. Mem. Omicron Delta Kappa. Republican. Lodges: Masons, Shriners. Avocations: stamp collecting, boating.

SMITH, WARD, manufacturing company executive, lawyer; b. Buffalo, Sept. 13, 1930; s. Andrew Leslie and Georgia (Ward) S.; m. Gretchen Keller Diefendorf, Oct. 29, 1960; children: Jennifer Hood, Meredith Ward, Jonathan Andrew, Sarah Katherine. Student, Georgetown U., 1948-49; AB, Harvard, 1952; JD, U. Buffalo, 1955. Bar: N.Y. 1955, Mass. 1962, Ohio 1977. Assoc. Lawler & Rockwood, N.Y.C., 1959-62; sec., gen. counsel Whitin Machine Works, Whitinsville, Mass., 1962-66; sec. White Consol. Industries, Inc., Cleve., 1966-69, v.p., 1967-69, sr. v.p., 1969-72, exec. v.p., 1972-76, pres., chief adminstrv. officer, 1976-84, pres., chief operating officer, 1984-86, pres., chief exec. officer, 1985-86, chmn., 1986; pres., chief exec. officer NACCO Industries, Inc., Cleve., 1986—, also bd. dirs.; bd. dirs. Soc. Bank and Soc. Corp., Sundstrand Corp., Rockford, Ill. Pres., trustee The Musical Arts Assn.; op. trustee The Cleve. Orch., Case Western Res. U., Cleve., others. Served to lt. USNR, 1955-59. Mem. ABA, N.Y. State Bar Assn. Clubs: Pepper Pike (Ohio) Country; Union, Tavern (Cleve.). Home: 19701 N Park Blvd Shaker Heights OH 44122 Office: NACCO Industries Inc 12800 Shaker Blvd Cleveland OH 44120

SMITH, WILBUR COWAN, lawyer; b. Aledo, Ill., July 16, 1914; s. Fred Harold and Anna Elizabeth (Cowan) S.; m. Teressa Phyllis Stout, Sept. 10, 1938; children—Roger Allen, Judith Ellen Smith Adams; m. Florence Ann Mackie, June 21, 1964; 1 dau., Donna Lee Pinkes; step-children—Diane Marie Linhart, Wayne Douglas Griffith, Nancy Ann LaFraugh. Student Colo. U., 1932-33, N.Mex. U., 1933; B.A., U. Iowa, 1937; J.D., Creighton U., 1954. Bar: Nebr. 1954, U.S. Dist. Ct. Nebr. 1954, U.S. Ct. Appeals (8th cir.) 1974. Salesman Gen. Foods Corp., 1939; civilian chemist U.S. Naval Ordnance, 1942-45; mgr. Omar Flour Mills, 1945-47; account exec. C.A. Swanson & Sons, 1948-49; dist. mgr. Brown-Forman Distillery, 1950-51; adminstrv. asst. to judge Douglas County, 1954-55; asst. city prosecutor Omaha, 1956; sole practice, Omaha, 1956-73; ptnr. Smith & Hansen, Omaha, 1973—. Pres., North High Sch. PTA, 1959-61, Belvedere Sch., 1954-56, Oak Valley, 1965-67; mem. bldg. com. YMCA, 1954-56; membership com. Boy Scouts Am., 1956-61; county del. Republican Party, 1962-82. Mem. ABA, Nebr. Bar Assn., Omaha Bar Assn., Am. Judicature Soc., Phi Alpha Delta. Methodist. Clubs: Odd Fellows, Masons, Shriners, United Comml. Travelers Protective Assn., Order Eastern Star. Office: Smith & Hansen 1st Nat Bank Bldg 1603 Farnam St Omaha NE 68102

SMITH, WILLIAM BASIL, manufacturing executive; b. Kansas City, Mo., Mar. 9, 1936; s. Theodore Winningham and Vera Ureth (Webb) S.; m. Nancy Lee Barker, June 22, 1957; children: Mark William Lee, Theodore Robert James. BSBA, U. Mo., 1958. cert. orthotist. Purchasing agt. Knit-Rite, Inc., Kansas City, 1959-67, distbn. mgr., 1967-68, exec. v.p., 1968-70, chmn. bd. dirs., 1970—, pres., 1973—; pres. Am. Bd. for Cert. in Orthotics and Prosthetics, Alexandria, Va., 1974-75. Mem. Am. Orthotic and Prosthetic Assn. (pres. elect 1984-85, pres. 1985-86), Internat. Soc. Orthotists and Prosthetists. Home: 11000 Alhambra Leawood KS 66211 Office: Knit-Rite Inc PO Box 410208 Kansas City MO 64141

SMITH, WILLIAM C., bank holding company executive. Pres. Firstier Inc., Omaha. Office: Firstier Inc 1700 Farnam St Omaha NE 68102 *

SMITH, WILLIAM SIDNEY, lawyer; b. Clearwater, Fla., Feb. 25, 1944; s. Sidney Bankhead and Daphne (Guptile) S.; m. Caroline L. Holley, June 12, 1967 (div. Jan. 1982); children: Cynthia Ann, Charles W., Craig W.; m. Bobbi Ann Trachta, Sept. 18, 1983. BBA, U. Iowa, 1966, JD, 1968. Bar: Iowa 1968, U.S. Tax Ct. 1972, U.S. Dist. Ct. (so. dist.) Iowa 1976, U.S. Dist. Ct. (no. dist.) Iowa 1977, U.S. Ct. Claims 1978, U.S. Ct. Appeals (8th cir.) 1978, U.S. Supreme Ct. 1979, U.S. Ct. Appeals (fed. cir.) 1982; CPA, Ill., Iowa. Tax acct. Price Waterhouse & Co., Chgo., 1968-70; tax ptnr. Sidney B. Smith & Co., Des Moines, 1970-75; prin. Smith, Schneider & Stiles, P.C., Des Moines, 1975—. Mem. ABA (litigation sect.), Iowa State Bar Assn. (tax com.), Polk County Bar Assn., Am. Inst. CPA's (Elijah Watt Sell award 1969), Jaycees (pres. 1971-72), Order of Coif. Episcopalian. Home: 4301 Walnut West Des Moines IA 50265 Office: Smith Schneider & Stiles PC 4717 Grand Ave Des Moines IA 50312

SMITH, WILLIAM STANLEY, construction company executive; b. Chgo., July 7, 1933; s. Stanley William and Lillie Lou (Peck) S.; m. Susan D. Dixson, Dec. 21, 1957; children—Cynthia Elizabeth, Nancy Anne, Christine Louise. B.A., Beloit Coll., 1955. Indsl. relations mgr. Container Corp. Am., Chgo., 1955-60; v.p. Crampton, Inc., 1960-78, pres., 1978—. Mem. Archtl. Woodworkers Inst., Nat. Club Assn. Republican. Presbyterian. Clubs: Glen Oak Country, Perry Park Country. Home: 844 Woodland Dr Glen Ellyn IL 60137 Office: Crampton Inc 7437 S Vincennes Chicago IL 60621

SMITH-BLACKMER, DEBORAH, psychotherapist, social worker; b. Los Angeles; d. J. Livingston and Miriam Sarah (Osness) Smith; m. Benjamin Blackmer. BA, U. Cin., 1970; MSW, Smith Coll., 1974. Psychotherapist N. Essex Mental Health Ctr., Haverhill, Mass., 1975-78; pvt. practice psychotherapy Cin., 1978—; psychotherapist Cen. Psychiat. Clinic, U. Cin. Med. Sch., 1978—, supr. 1978—; tchr. U. Cin., 1979—; cons. PH.D Psychologists, Cin., 1979—. Mem. Nat. Assn. Social Workers, Ohio Soc. Clin. Social Workers, Smith Coll. Alumni Club (treas.). Avocations: music, dance. Office: 2607 Burnet Ave Cincinnati OH 45219

SMITHBURG, DONALD ROWAN, city administrator; b. Pomona, Calif., Oct. 18, 1960; s. Donald Winston and Mary Harper (McAnlis) S.; m. Susan Jane Swafford, July 7, 1984; 1 child, Devon Marie. BA in Anthropology, Colo. Coll., 1983; MA in Pub. Adminstrn., U. N.Mex., 1985. Asst. to chief adminstr. City of Albuquerque, 1983-85; dir. adminstrv. affairs sch. medicine U. Mo., Kansas City, 1986-87; city adminstr. City of Mission Hills, Kans., 1987—; vice chmn. adv. bd. Health Care for Homeless, Albuquerque, 1984-85. Exec. producer pub. service announcement, pub. affairs program Ditches Are Deadly, 1984. Mem. Lenexa (Kans.) Safety Council, 1986—. Newberry Library fellow Colo. Coll., 1983. Mem. Am. Soc. Pub. Adminstrn. (elected council, N.Mex. chpt.), Assn. Am. Med. Colls., Kans. Assn. City Mgrs., Phi Alpha Alpha, Phi Kappa Phi, Phi Delta Theta. Democrat. Episcopalian. Avocations: tennis, skiing, fishing, soccer, racquetball.

SMITHBURG, WILLIAM DEAN, food manufacturing company executive; b. Chgo., July 9, 1938; s. Pearl L. and Margaret L. (Savage) S.; m. Alberta Hap, May 25, 1963; children: Susan, Thomas. BS, DePaul U., 1960; MBA, Northwestern U., 1961. With Leo Burnett Co., Chgo., 1961-63, McCann-Erickson, Inc., Chgo., 1963-66; various positions Quaker Oats Co., Chgo., 1966-71, v.p., gen. mgr. cereals and mixers div., 1971-75, pres. food div., 1975-76, v.p. U.S. grocery products, 1976-79, pres., 1979-83, chief exec. officer, 1979—, chmn., 1983—, also bd. dirs. Served with USAR, 1959-60. Roman Catholic. Office: Quaker Oats Co 345 Merchandise Mart Plaza Chicago IL 60654 *

SMOLEN, JAMES EDWARD, biochemist; b. Greenfield, Mass., Apr. 8, 1949; s. Joseph and Edith May (Spaulding) S.; m. Roberta Sawyer, June 19, 1971 (div. 1982). AB, Harvard U., 1971, PhD, 1976. Assoc. research scientist NYU Sch. Medicine, N.Y.C., 1976-81, res. asst. prof., 1981-82; assoc. research scientist U. Mich. Med. Ctr., Ann Arbor, 1982-86, assoc. prof., 1986—. Arthritis Found. fellow 1981-86. Mem. AAAS, Am. Assn. of Pathologists, Am. Fedn. for Clin. Research, Am. Soc. for Cell Biology, N.Y. Acad. Scis. Avocations: flying, rock climbing, squash, swimming. Home: 679 Watersedge Dr Ann Arbor MI 48105 Office: U Mich Med Ctr Div Pediatrics-Hematology/Oncology 7510 C MSRB I Ann Arbor MI 48109

SMOLENSKI, JOHN JOSEPH, obstetrician-gynecologist; b. Detroit, Jan. 18, 1925; s. Joseph Marjan and Elsa Helen (Connolly) S.; m. Joanne Falk, Sept. 8, 1951; children: John Jr., Thomas, James, Robert, Edward, Richard. BS, Coll. of the Holy Cross, 1946; MD, Marquette U., 1950. Diplomate Am. Bd. Ob-Gyn. Practice medicine specializing in ob-gyn. Detroit, 1954-68; assoc. Med. Arts Clinic, Minot, N.D., 1968—; asst. clin. prof. U. N.D. Med. Sch., Grand Forks, 1975—. Mem. bd. Bishop Ryan High Sch., Minot, 1969-73. Served to lt. USN, 1943-46. Fellow Am. Coll. OB-Gyns. (N.D. sect. chmn. 1985—); mem. AMA, N.D. Ob-Gyn. Soc., Minn. Ob-Gyn. Soc., Nebr. Ob-Gyn. Soc. Roman Catholic. Lodge: KC (faithful navigator 1981-82), Elks. Home: 1120 Robert St Minot ND 58701 Office: Med Arts Clinic PC 600 17th Ave SE Minot ND 58701

SMOOT, DAVID PAUL, software company executive; b. Guthrie, Okla., Jan. 9, 1947; s. Jerry Edward and Katherine Ann (Doyle) S.; m. Marie Kathleen Stokes, Aug. 6, 1971; children: Aimee, Melissa. Student, Cumberland Coll., 1965-67, Glassboro State Coll., 1967, U. Cin., 1968-69. Regional mgr. Dennison Mfg., Chgo., 1969-77, Wordstream, Chgo., 1978-79; dist. mgr. AM Jacquard, San Francisco, 1979-82; co-founder, v.p. sales Phaser Systems Pub. Co., San Francisco, 1980-82; dir. cen. ops. Digital Research, Schaumburg, Ill., 1982-85; founder, chmn. bd., chief exec. officer Software Funding Internat., Deerfield, Ill., 1985—. Vol. Little City Home for Retarded, Palatine, Ill., 1986. Served with U.S. Army, 1969-75. Mem. Assn. Data Processing Services Orgns., Software Pubs. Assn., Syntopicaon XII, IBM PC User's Group. Avocations: basketball, sailing, camping, fishing, tennis. Home: 1435 Camden Ct Buffalo Grove IL 60089 Office: Software Funding Internat 2 Northfield Plaza #230 Northfield IL 60093 also: 111 Pfingsten Rd #115 Deerfield IL 60015

SMOOT, JOSEPH GRADY, academic administrator; b. Winter Haven, Fla., May 7, 1932; s. Robert Malcolm and Vera (Eaton) S.; m. Florence Rozell, May 30, 1955 (dec.); m. Irma Jean Kopitzke, June 4, 1959; 1 son, Andrew Christopher. B.A., So. Coll., 1955; M.A., U. Ky., 1958, Ph.D., 1964. Tchr., Ky. Secondary Schs., 1955-57; from instr. to asso. prof. history Columbia Union Coll., Takoma Park, Md., 1960-68, acad. dean, 1965-68; prof. history Andrews U., Berrien Springs, Mich., 1968-84, dean Sch. Grad. Studies, 1968-69, v.p. acad. adminstrn., 1969-76, pres., 1976-84; v.p. for devel. Pittsburg State U., Kans., 1984—; exec. dir. Pittsburg State Univ. Found., 1985—; commr. North Cen. Assn., 1987—, cons., evaluator; cons. internat. edn. Contbr. articles to profl. jours. Bd. dirs. Pittsburg United Way, 1987— bd. advisors Pitts. Salvation Army. Recipient Disting. Pres. award Mich. Coll. Found., 1984. Fellow Inst. Early Am. History and Culture; mem. Am., So. hist. assns., Orgn. Am. Historians, soc. for Historians of Early Am. Republic, Phi Alpha Theta. Club: Crestwood Country. Lodge: Rotary (chmn. scholarship com. 1986) Home: 1809 Heritage Rd Pittsburg KS 66762 Office: Pittsburg State U Pittsburg KS 66762

SMORAG, DOUGLAS JOHN, accountant, law firm administrator; b. Cleve., July 23, 1958; s. John Stanley and Olga Marie (Briselli) S.; m. Carol Lynn Smorag, June 4, 1982; 1 child, Marissa Lynn. BBA, Kent State U., 1979; MBA, Cleve. State U., 1987. CPA, Ohio. Jr. acct. Lewandowski & Co., Cleve., 1980-81; mgr. partnership tax Towner Petroleum Co., Lorain, Ohio, 1982-83; fin. and tax analyst McCarthy, Lebit, Crystal & Haiman, Cleve., 1984, adminstr., 1984—. Mem. candidate selection com. Citizens League Cleve., 1981, Greater Cleve. Growth Assn., Cleve. Council Smaller Enterprises. Mem. Am. Inst. CPA's, Ohio Soc. CPA's, Am. Assn. Legal Adminstrs., Beta Gamma Sigma, Beta Alpha Psi. Avocations: photography, investments, travel. Home: 28520 Stonegate Circle Westlake OH 44145 Office: McCarthy Lebit Crystal & Haiman 900 Illuminating Bldg Cleveland OH 44113

SMURFIT, MICHAEL W. J., manufacturing company executice; b. 1936. With Jefferson Smurfit Group PLC, Dublin, Ireland, 1961—, pres., 1966—; pres. Jefferson Smurfit Corp., Alton, Ill., 1979-82, now chief exec. officer, chmn. bd., 1982—. Office: Jefferson Smurfit Corp 401 Alton St Alton IL 62002 *

SMYNTEK, JOHN EUGENE, JR., newspaper editor; b. Buffalo, Aug. 24, 1950; s. John Eugene Sr. and Leona (Kluczynski) S.; m. Barbara Murphy, Oct. 23, 1972 (div. Mar. 1980); m. Rebecca Anne Van Dine, June 4, 1982. BA, U. Detroit, 1972. Features editor Detroit Free Press, 1985—; asst. instr. Mich. State U., east Lansing, 1981. Recipient Fine Arts Reporting award Detroit Press Club, 1985. Roman Catholic. Office: Detroit Free Press 321 W Lafayette Blvd Detroit MI 48231

SMYTH, SAMUEL MARLOWE, automotive executive; b. Cin., Aug. 28, 1959; s. Samuel M. and Doreen (Weir) S.; m. Sherry Lynn Schaudig, Feb. 14, 1981 (div. Sept. 1985); 1 child, Christine Amanda. Grad. high sch., Cin. Salesman Mercedes Benz, Casper, Wyo., 1977-78; pynt. Sam Smyth Imports Ltd., Cin., 1978-84; pres. Sam Smyth Imported Car Service Inc., Cin., 1984—. Republican. Presbyterian.

SMYTHE, JEFFREY HALL, real estate developer; b. Cleve., Apr. 2, 1934; s. Charles Loomis and Madeline (Nellis) S.; m. Jane Elise Raisbeck, July 27, 1957; children: Christopher E., Alison L., Dana K. BA, Williams Coll., 1956. V.p., treas. A.B. Smythe Co., Cleve., 1959-65; prin., sr. v.p. Cragin Lang Free & Smythe Inc., Cleve., 1965—; bd. dirs. Point Breezy Inc., Cleve; bd. dirs. CLFS Securites, Cleve. Mem. United Appeal Campaign, Cleve., 1970-80. Served to capt. USAF, 1956-59. Mem. Cleve. Bldg. and Mgrs. Orgn. (pres. 1974-76), Inst. Real Estate Mgmt., Cleve. Inst. Real Estate Mgmt. (v.p. 1972), Cleve. Area Bd. Realtors, Nat. Assn. Securities Dealers, Soc. Indsl. and Office Realtors (exec. com. 1980), Nat. Real Estate Bd., Willimas Coll. Alumni of Northeast Ohio (pres. 1980, adv. council 1980-86). Republican. Episcopalian. Clubs: Kirkland Country (bd. dirs. 1980-86), Union. Avocations: skiing, sailing, travel, golf, college recruiting. Office: Cragin Lang Free & Smythe Inc 1801 E 9th Cleveland OH 44114

SNAGE, ALEXANDER MICHAEL, II, chemical engineer; b. Detroit, June 18, 1948; s. Edward and Helen Louise (Ammar) S.; B.S. in Chem. Engring., Wayne State U., 1970; m. Loretta Strenk, May 2, 1970; 1 son, Bryan Alexander. Asst. chemist Nelson Chems., Detroit, 1965-69; process chem. engr. Monsanto Co., Trenton, Mich., 1970-74, mfg. chem. process supr., Augusta, Ga., 1974-78, process chem. engring. supr., Trenton, 1978-82, also chmn. supervisory com. Monsanto Fed. Employees Credit Union, 1980-82; supt. custom chem. mfg. plant Monsanto Co., Dayton, Ohio, 1982-85, product mgr. new tech. devel. dept., 1985-86, mgr. bus. devel., 1986—. Mem. Am. Inst. Chem. Engrs. (sec. Dayton chpt), Inst. Food Technologists, Inst. Environ. Scis., Tau Beta Pi. Roman Catholic. Home: 15917 Country Ridge Dr Chesterfield MO 63017 also: 281 Whistling Pine Rd Severna Park MD 21146-2173 Office: Monsanto-Permea 11444 Lackland Rd Saint Louis MO 63146

SNEED, MARIE ELEANOR WILKEY, ret. educator; b. Dahlgren, Ill., June 12, 1915; d. Charles N. and Hazel (Miller) Wilkey; student U. Ill., 1933-35; B.S., Northwestern U., 1937; postgrad. Wayne State U., 1954-60, U. Mich., 1967; m. John Sneed, Jr., Sept. 18, 1937; children—Suzanne (Mrs. Geoffrey B. Newton), John Corwin. Tchr. English, drama, creative writing Berkley (Mich.) Sch. Dist., 1952-76. Mem. Mich. Statewide Tchr. Edn. Preparation, 1968-72, regional sec. 1969-70; mem. Pleasant Ridge Arts Council, 1982—, Pleasant Ridge Parks and Recreation Commn., 1982—. Mem. NEA, Mich., Berkley (pres. 1961-62, 82-87) edn. assns., Oakland Tchr. Edn. Council (exec. bd. 1973-76), Student Tchr. Planning Com. Berkley (chmn. 1971-72), Phi Alpha Chi, Pi Lambda Theta, Alpha Delta Kappa, Alpha Omicron Pi. Club: Pleasant Ridge Woman's (pres. 1980-83). Home: 21 Norwich Rd Pleasant Ridge MI 48069

SNEED, SHERRIE LYNN, clergy, educator, psychotherapist; b. Knoxville, Tenn., Apr. 17, 1954; d. Charles Herbert and Ann Marie (Maloney) S. B.A., U. Tenn., 1975; postgrad. Hamma Sch. Theology, 1975-78; M.Div., Trinity Luth. Sem., 1979; D.Min. in Pastoral Care and Counseling, Luth. Sch. Theology, 1983. Ordained to ministry Lutheran Ch., 1979. Counselor, Clark County Mental Health Satellite, New Carlisle, Ohio, 1975-76; bookstore bibliographer Hamma Sch. Theology, Springfield, Ohio, 1976-77; asst. to pastor Wittenberg U., Springfield, Ohio, 1977-78; interim pastor Rocky Point Chapel, Springfield, 1978-79; pastor Robinson-Sulphur Luth. Parish, St. Paul Luth. Ch., North Robinson, Ohio, 1979-81, St. John Luth. Ch., Sulphur Springs, Ohio, 1979-81; vice-pastor First Luth. Ch., Galion, Ohio, 1980-81; tchr. Unity Cath. High Sch., Chgo., 1981-82; tchr., dept. head Acad. of our Lady, Chgo., 1982-84; interim pastor St. Thomas Luth. Ch., Chgo., 1983-84, pastor, 1984-86; marriage and family therapist West Suburban Counseling and Ednl. Service, Luth. Social Services Ill., Wheaton, 1984-86; mem. Ohio Synod Task Force on Women in the Ch., 1979-81, Ohio Synod Ednl. Ministry Team, 1980-81, Ill. Synod Ednl. Ministry Team, 1984—; retreat dir. various chs. in Ohio and Ill., 1981—; stewardship cons. Ohio Synod Stewardship Team, 1980-81; supply pastor Ill. Synod, Luth. Sch. Theology, 1981-83; marriage and family therapist. Cons., instr. Contact, 24-hour hotline, Bucyrus, Ohio, 1980-81; CPR instr., area coordinator Mid-Am. chpt. ARC, Chgo., 1983—; chaplain Rehab. Inst. Chgo., 1986—. Vol. dep. registrar Cook County Bd. Elections, 1984—. Mem. Am. Acad. Religion, Soc. Bibl. Lit., Bucyrus Area Ministerial Assn., South Shore Ministerial Assn., South Shore Council Chs. Democrat. Lutheran. Home: 1606 E Hyde Park Blvd Chicago IL 60615 Office: Rehabilitation Inst Chgo 345 E Superior Chicago IL 60611

SNEIDER, NORMAN HARRY, electrical engineer; b. Evanston, Ill., Oct. 5, 1951; s. Edward and Anna (Bembers) S. AA in Bus., Coll. of Du Page, 1972; BSEE, DeVry Inst. Tech., 1979. With Rockwell Internat., Downers Grove, Ill., 1972-75; engr. Associated Research, Skokie, Ill., 1978-81, Breuer Electric Mfg. Co., Chgo., 1982—. Republican. Lutheran. Avocations: target shooting, photography, video filming. Home: 602 E Lemoyne Lombard IL 60148 Office: Breuer Electric Mfg Co 7401 W Lawrence Ave Chicago IL 60656

SNELL, ALAN HAROLD, optometrist; b. Liberty, Nebr., June 22, 1940; s. J. Harold and Elizabeth (Finney) S.; m. Phyllis Lea Moses, Aug. 25, 1963; children—Lennah, Michelle, Dawn. B.A., Tarkio Coll., 1963; O.D., Pacific U., 1966. Optometrist, Dr. Watts-Snell, Leavenworth, Kans., 1966-69; practice optometry, Leavenworth, 1969-72, Lansing, Kans., 1972—. Mem. sch. bd. Lansing Sch. Dist. #469, Kans., 1981—, pres., 1985. Mem. Am. Optometric Assn. (sports sect., contact lens sect.), Kans. Optometric Assn., Heart Am. Contact Lens Assn., Leavenworth Area C. of C. (bd. dirs., 2d v.p. 1985). Republican. Home: Rural Route 3 Box 216 C Leavenworth KS 66048 Office: Holiday Plaza Box 210 Lansing KS 66043

SNELL, D. RICHARD, pharmacist; b. Denver, Dec. 15, 1934; s. William Edward and Thelma Loraine (Leeds) S.; m. Alice Jane Joachim, Sept. 5, 1954; children: Carol Marie Snell Yarnall, Susan Jane Snell Reifschneider, Thomas Edward. BS in Pharmacy, U. Colo., 1956. Pharmacist Link Drug, Ainsworth, Nebr., 1957-58, Wimberley Drug, Kearney, Nebr., 1958-60; owner, pharmacist Snell Pharmacy, Scottsbluff, Nebr., 1960-85; mgr., pharmacist Med. Ctr. Pharmacy, Scottsbluff, 1985—. Bd. dirs. West Nebr. Gen. Hosp., Scottsbluff, found. com.; adv. bd. KCMI Christian radio, Scottsbluff; mem. state bd. dirs. Fellowship Christian Athletes. Recipient Service award YMCA, 1969, Service award United Way, 1968. Fellow Nat. Assn. Retail Druggists. Republican. Lodges: Elks, Rotary (pres. Scottsbluff club 1984-85), Masons, Shrine (pres. scottsbluff club 1975-76). Avocations: golf, fishing, hunting, camping, travel. Home: 4714 Cardinal Dr Scottsbluff NE 69361 Office: Med Ctr Pharmacy 3802 Ave B Scottsbluff NE 69361

SNELL, FRANCIS JUDSON, avionics executive, educator; b. Chgo., May 11, 1920; s. Roy Judson and Lucile Grace (Ziegler) S.; m. Elizabeth Savage, Aug. 12, 1968 (dec. Oct. 1972); children: Teri, Gregory, Roy, Cindy; m. Dorothy Holmes, Mar. 31, 1973; children: Virginia, Paul. Student, Eastern Ill. U., 1937-39, Coll. St. Thomas, 1967-68. Adminstr. Honeywell, Minn., 1942-61; gen. mgr. Control Data Corp., Minn. and Mich., 1961-67, 70-75; assoc. dir. Coll. St. Thomas, Minn., 1967-70; pres. Montevideo (Minn.) Tech., Inc., 1975—. Scout master Boy Scouts Am., Minn.; planning commr. City of Bloomington, Minn., 1950; supt. Ch. Sch., Minn.; co-chmn. Minn. div. crusade Am. Cancer Soc., 1981-82; Hennipen County Justice of Peace, Minn., 1952. Lodge: Order Eastern Star. Home: 1402 N 4th St Montevideo MN 56265 Office: Montevideo Tech Inc 204 N 4th St Montevideo MN 56265

SNELL, JOSEPH FREDERICK, accountant; b. Union City, Ind., Mar. 30, 1938; s. Richard Clark and Bernice Evelyn (McEowen) S.; m. Judith Anne Randall, Aug. 9, 1958; children: Joy Louise, Jeffery Randall, James David. BSBA, Wright State U., 1976. Lic. pub. acct. Staff coordinator Frigidaire, Dayton, Ohio, 1974-79, mgr. mktg. analysis, 1979-81, mgr. customer acctg., 1981-83, mgr. gen. acctg., 1983-85; gen. ptnr. Dayton Tax and Acctg. Service, 1985—; treas.-controller Imnetec, Inc., 1984—. Mem. Pub. Accts. Soc. Ohio, TALS Businessmen's Orgn. Presbyterian. Lodge: Optimists. Avocation: antique collecting and restoration. Office: Dayton Tax & Acctg Service 1935 E 3d St Dayton OH 45403

SNELL, THADDEUS STEVENS, III, retired building materials manufacturing company executive, lawyer; b. Ida Grove, Iowa, Feb. 23, 1919; s. Thaddeus Stevens and Catharine (Noble) S.; m. Mary Ward, Nov., 1951 (div. 1965); children: William, Kathleen, Pamela, Debra, Robert; m. Gloria Cramer Brent, July, 1966 (dec. 1981); m. Eleanor Larson Hawes, Nov. 24, 1982. BS, Northwestern U., 1941, postgrad. Law Sch., 1941-42; postgrad. U.S. Naval Acad. Postgrad. Sch., 1944-45; LLB, Yale U., 1947. Bar: Ill. 1948, Iowa 1948. Assoc. Keck, Mahin & Cate and predecessors, Chgo., 1947-58, ptnr., 1959-71; v.p., corp. counsel U.S. Gypsum Co., Chgo., 1971-82, v.p., gen. counsel, 1982-84; v.p., gen. counsel USG Corp., 1984-85; sole practice, Chgo., 1986—. Deacon Glenview (Ill.) Community Ch., 1958-61; pres. Kenilworth (Ill.) Citizens Adv. Com., 1973-74; mem. Chgo. Crime Commn. Served to lt. USNR, 1942-46. Mem. ABA, Ill. Bar Assn., Iowa Bar Assn., Chgo. Bar Assn., Legal Club Chgo., Am. Judicature Soc. Clubs: University, Metropolitan (Chgo.); Sunset Ridge Country (Northbrook, Ill.); Quail Ridge (Boynton Beach, Fla.). Lodge: Masons. Home: 1901 Somerset Ln Northbrook IL 60062 Office: 101 S Wacker Dr Chicago IL 60606

SNELLER, ROBERT CALVIN, optometrist; b. Hastings, Nebr., Dec. 25, 1926; s. Floyd Calvin and Lydia Sourezny; m. Marjorie Jeann Kurfman, Feb. 17, 1951; children: Todd, Jeff, Peggy, Scott, Sally. OD, No. Ill. Coll. Optometry, 1950. Practice optometry Hastings, Nebr.; pres. bd. examiners Nebr. Dept. Health, Lincoln, 1968-77. Author: Vision and Driving, 1962. Served to lt. comdr. USNR. Fellow Am. Acad. Optometry; mem. Am. Optometric Assn. (trustee St. Louis chpt. 1962-64), Nebr. Optometric Assn. (optometrist of yr. 1978), Heart of Am. Contact Lens Soc. (pres. 1976), Royal Soc. Health. Republican. Episcopalian. Club: Lochland Country (Hastings, Nebr.). Lodge: Elks. Avocations: hunting, fishing, sailing. Home: 406 University Hastings NE 68901 Office: 605 N Denver Hastings NE 68901-5189

SNIDER, C. STEVEN, school administrator; b. Terre Haute, Ind., May 16, 1947; s. Charles L. and Barbara M. (Figg) S. B.S., Ind. State U., 1969, M.S., 1972, Ph.D., 1977. Tchr./adminstr. North Newton Sch. Corp., Morocco, Ind., 1969-73; prin. South Central Sch. Corp., Union Mills, Ind., 1973-75; asst. prin./instrn. Penn High Sch., Mishawaka, Ind., 1977-79, prin., 1979-83; supt. schs. FRHC Sch. Corp., Hope, Ind., 1983-85; supt. schs. LaPorte Community Sch. Corp., 1985—; Ind. State U. adminstrv. intern; conf. speaker; lectr., condr. workshops in field. Bd. dirs. Jr. Achievement, 1980—, Bartholomew County unit ARC, YMCA, 1985—; adv. mem. No. Ind. Sch. Band, Orch. and Vocal Assn., 1979-82, Ind. U.-South Bend Sec. Sch., 1979-82; mem. chancellor's adv. com. Purdue North Central U., 1985—. Recipient award of merit Jr. Achievement, 1982. Mem. Nat. Assn. Secondary Sch. Prins., Nat. Soc. Study Edn., Assn. for Supervision and Curriculum Devel., Am. Assn. Sch. Adminstrn., Nat. Assn. Student Activity Advisors, Ind. Assn. for Supervision and Curriculum Devel., Nat. Orgn. Legal Problems In Edn., LaPorte C. of C. (bd. dirs. 1985—), Phi Delta Kappa. Presbyterian. Lodges: Elks, Kiwanis, Lions. Contbr. articles to profl. jours.

SNIDER, DAVID LESLIE, financial analyst; b. Marceline, Mo., Feb. 10, 1957; s. Max Lee and Camilla Jane (Cameron) S. BS in Acctg. and Fin., N.W. Mo. State U., 1980, MBA in Acctg., 1983. CPA, Mo. Instr. acctg. N.W. Mo. State U., Maryville, Mo., 1980-85; fin. analyst Gilbert/Robinson, Inc., Kansas City, Mo., 1985—. Mem. Am. Soc. CPA's, Mo. Soc. CPA's (mem. program com. N.W. chpt. 1982-84, membership com. 1985). Republican. Methodist. Club: Kansas City Ski (mem. audit com. 1986-87). Lodge: Masons. Avocations: skiing, charitable work. Home: 1112 Wornall Rd Excelsior Springs MO 64024 Office: Gilbert/Robinson Inc 47th and Main PO Box 16000 Kansas City MO 64112

SNIDER, PATRICIA ANN, college counselor; b. Fremont, Ohio, Sept. 7, 1937; d. Millard Alfred and Mary (Danchisen) Snider. B.S. in Edn., Bowling Green State U., 1959; M.Ed., Ohio U., 1963. Instr. St. Joseph Coll., Emmitsburg, Md., 1959-61; grad. asst. tchr. Ohio U. Athens, 1961-63; head resident advisor Western Ill. U., Macomb, Ill., 1963-67; counselor Morton Coll., Cicero, Ill., 1967—. Author: (with others) Community College Career Alternatives Handbook, 1979; Women on their Way-A Guide for Women Returning to School, 1984. Contbr. articles to profl. jours. Bd. dirs. Cicero chpt. Am. Cancer Soc.; flotilla vice comdr. U.S. Coast Guard Aux., 1969-82. Recipient Faculty Mem. of Yr. award Morton Coll. Endowment Found., 1982. Mem. Am. Assn. for Counseling and Devel., Nat. Acad. Advisors Assn., Nat. Assn. for Women Deans, Adminstrs. and Counselors, Ill. Assn. for Counseling and Devel., Nat. Coll. Personnel Assn., Ill. Coll. Personnel Assn. Roman Catholic. Avocations: Reading; fishing. Home: 1540 S 59th Ct Cicero IL 60650 Office: Morton Coll 3801 S Central Ave Cicero IL 60650

SNODGRASS, JAMES M., holding company executive. Pres., chief exec. officer Estronics Inc., Oak Brook, Ill. Office: Estronics Inc 711 Jorie Blvd Oak Brook IL 60521 *

SNOOK, ORRIE MCVEY, dentist; b. Independence, Kans., Jan. 17, 1929; s. Orrie Vernon and Emma Lucile (McVey) S.; m. Marcia Clare Speer, June 10, 1956; children: Karen Elizabeth, David Michael, Jennifer Lynn, Amy Diane. AA, Wentworth Mil Acad., Lexington, Mo., 1951; BS, U. Kans., 1953; DDS, U. Mo., 1957. Served with U.S. Army, 1946-47. Mem. ADA, Mo. Dental Assn., Cen. Dist Dental Soc., Am. Soc. Clin. Hypnosis, Biofeedback soc. Am., Am. Soc. Profl. Hypnotherapists. Republican. Lodge: Kiwanis, Masons, Shriners. Avocations: tennis, swimming. Home: 1028 Bourn Columbia MO 65203 Office: PO Box 30139 Columbia MO 65203

SNORF, LOWELL DELFORD, JR., insurance executive, lawyer, farm operator; b. Chgo., Aug. 4, 1919; s. Lowell Delford and Marcellene Harris (Roberts) S.; m. Nancy Heath, Aug. 7, 1943; children: Paula Henderson, Margaret, Lowell Delford. Student U. Ill., 1937-39; B.S., Northwestern U., 1941, J.D., 1947. Bar: Ill. 1947, U.S. Dist. Ct. (no dist.) Ill. 1947, U.S. Ct. Appeals (7th cir.) 1947, U.S. Supreme Ct. 1960. Sole practice Chgo., 1947; asst. counsel Kemper Ins., Chgo., 1947, sr. officer, exec., 1951-58; gen. counsel Lansing B. Warner Inc. (Wausau Ins. Group), Chgo., 1958—, sr. v.p., 1966-85, dir., 1979—; pres. Lansing B. Warner Inc. (Wausau Ins. Group), 1985—. Served to maj. U.S. Army, World War II. Decorated Purple Heart, Bronze Star (2). Fellow Am. Bar Found. (life); mem. ABA (council tort ins. practice sect., chmn. traffic ct. com.), Chgo. Bar Assn., Ill. Bar Assn., Fed. Ins. Counsel, Internat. Assn. Ins. Counsel, Wigmore Found. Northwestern U., Counsel Internat. Law, Am. Reciprocal Ins. Assn. (exec. com.). Clubs: Glen View Golf, John Evans. Office: Lansing B Warner Inc 7411 Lake St River Forest IL 60305

SNOW, ARTHUR DEAN, JR., physician; b. Springfield, Mo., Feb. 20, 1945; s. Arthur D. and Louise E. (Stevens) S.; m. Sarah J. Williamson, Aug. 25, 1967; children: Christine R., Jennifer L., Brian D. BS, Wichita State U., 1967; MA in Math., U. Kans., Lawrence, 1969; MD, U. Kans., 1975. Resident in gen. medicine U. Kans. Med. Ctr., Kansas City, 1975-78; gen. practice medicine Shawnee Mission, Kans., 1974—; mem. med. staff Shawnee

Mission Med. Ctr., 1976—, chmn. dept. family practice, 1985-86, courtesy med. staff Humana Hosp. Overland Park, Kans., 1978—. Served with U.S. Army, 1969-72. Fellow Am. Acad. Family Physicians, Am. Coll. Emergency Physicians; mem. Kans. Acad. Family Physicians (pres. 1986—), Kansas City Southwest Clin. Soc. (sec./treas. 1986—). Republican. Episcopalian. Home: 3616 W 122 Terr Leawood KS 66209

SNOW, JOHN WILLIAM, railroad executive; b. Toledo, Aug. 2, 1939; s. William Dean and Catharine (Howard) S.; m. Fredrica Wheeler, June 11, 1964 (div. 1973); children: Bradley, Ian; m. Carolyn Kalk, Aug. 31, 1973; 1 child, Christopher. B.A., U. Toledo, 1962; Ph.D., U. Va., 1965; LL.B., George Washington U., 1967. Asst. prof. econs. U. Md., College Park, 1965-67; assoc. Wheeler & Wheeler, Washington, 1967-72; asst. gen. counsel Dept. Transp., Washington, 1972-73, asst. sec. for govtl. affairs, 1974-75, dep. under sec., 1975-76; dep. asst. sec. for policy U.S. Plans of Internal Affairs, Washington, 1973-74; adminstr. Nat. Hwy. Traffic Safety Adminstrn., Washington, 1976-77; v.p. govt. affairs Chessie System Inc., Washington, 1977-80; sr. v.p. corp. services CSX Corp., Richmond, Va., 1980-84, exec. v.p., 1984-85; pres., chief exec. officer Chessie System R.R.s, Balt., 1985—; adj. prof. law George Washington U., 1972-75; vis. prof. econs. U. Va., Charlottesville, spring 1977; vis. fellow Am. Enterprise Inst., Washington, spring 1977. Bd. dirs. Sch. Pub. Affairs, U. Md. Disting. fellow Yale U. Sch. Mgmt. Mem. ABA, D.C. Bar Assn., Va. Bar Assn. Episcopalian. Clubs: Chevy Chase, Metropolitan (Washington); Commonwealth, Country of Va. (Richmond). Home: 1003 Winding Way Baltimore MD 21210 Office: Chesapeake & Ohio RY PO Box 6419 Cleveland OH 44101 *

SNOW, RICHARD H., chemical engineer; b. Worcester, Mass., Apr. 26, 1928; s. Arthur F. and Elsie I. (Tunison) S.; m. Rosemary Mixon, Aug. 2, 1952; children: Anita, Luther, Sarah. AB in Chemistry, Harvard U., 1950; MS in Chem. Engring., Va. Poly. Inst., 1952; PhD in Chem. Engring., Ill. Inst. Tech., 1956. Sr. engr. IIT Research Inst., Chgo., 1956-73, engring. advisor, 1973-77, mgr. chem. engring. research, 1977-83, engring. advisor, 1985—; dir. Nat. Inst. Petroleum and Energy Research div. Ill. Inst. Tech. Research Inst., Bartlesville, Okla., 1983-85; pres. Ill. Engring. Council, 1973. Contbr. numerous articles to profl. jours. Fellow Am. Inst. Chem. Engrs.; mem. AAAS, AIME, Am. Chem. Soc., Ill. Soc. Profl. Engrs. Unitarian. Avocations: skiing, sailing. Home: 5000 S Cornell Ave Chicago IL 60615 Office: IIT Research Inst 10 W 35th St Chicago IL 60616

SNYDER, ALLEN DEAN, data processing executive; b. Wadsworth, Ohio, Sept. 3, 1946; s. Edwin D. and Faith D. (Beery) S.; m. Janet M. Hochstetler, June 14, 1970; children: Jeffrey A., Mark E., Beth Ann. BSA, Ashland Coll., 1976-79. Computer programmer Rubbermaid Inc., Wooster, Ohio, 1968-72, systems analyst, 1972-74, ops. mgr., 1974—. V.p. Smithville (Ohio) Zoning Appeals Bd., 1980-86; mem. adv. com. career ctr. date processing Wayne County Schs., 1985-86; pres. Smithville Bd. Pub. Affairs, 1985-86; treas. Grace Brethren Ch., Wooster, 1979-86. Served to sgt. U.S. Army, 1965-67. Democrat. Avocations: fishing, antiques. Home: 295 S Summit St Box 31 Smithville OH 44677

SNYDER, ANN CATHERINE, exercise physiologist, educator; b. Lansing, Mich., July 16, 1951; d. Warren G. and Ann Catherine (Dearing) S. B.S., Western Mich. U., 1973; M.Ed., Bowling Green State U., 1975; M.A., Mich. State U., 1979; Ph.D., Purdue U., 1982. Asst. prof. exercise physiology, Ball State U., Muncie, Ind., 1982-86; asst. prof., dir. exercise physiology lab. U. Wis., Milw., 1986—. Contbr. articles to tech. jours. Internat. Inst. Sports Medicine research grantee, 1984-86. Mem. Am. Coll. Sports Medicine, Am. Alliance of Health, Phys. Edn., Recreation and Dance, Muncie Jaycee Women (pres. 1984). Methodist. Avocations: Cross-country skiing; bicycling; running. Home: 2202 N 68th St Wauwatosa WI 53213 Office: U Wis-Milw Dept Human Kinetics Milwaukee WI 53201

SNYDER, BERNADETTE MCCARVER, columnist, author; b. L.I., N.Y., Dec. 6, 1930; d. William Columbus and Zella Hazel (Davids) McC.; m. John William Snyder, Sept. 28, 1963; 1 child, Matthew Joseph. Ad. copywriter, TV producer Gardner Advt., 1960-64; free-lance ad. writer, designer 1978-85; advt. copywriter Liquori Publications, 1985—. Columnist Our Sunday Visitor, 1981—; author: Hoorays & Hosannas, 1980, Graham Crackers, Galoshes and God, 1982, Dear God I Have This Terrible Problem, 1983, The Kitchen Sink Prayer Book, 1984, Everyday Prayers for Everyday People, 1984, Heavenly Hash, 1985, MORE Graham Crackers, Galoshes and God, 1985. Mem. Advt. Fedn. St. Louis, Nat. Platform Assn., United Daughters of the Confederacy. Roman Catholic.

SNYDER, CHARLES ROYCE, sociologist, emeritus educator; b. Haverford, Pa., Dec. 28, 1924; s. Edward D. and Edith (Royce) S.; m. Patricia Hanson, June 30, 1951; children—Stephen Hoyt, Christiana Marie, Constance Patricia, Daniel Edward. BA, Yale U., 1945, M.A., 1949, Ph.D., 1954. Mem. staff Ctr. Alcohol Studies Yale U., 1950-60, asst. prof. sociology, 1956-60; prof. sociology So. Ill. U., Carbondale, 1960-85; chmn. dept. So. Ill. U., 1964-75, 81-85, prof. emeritus, 1985—; vis. prof. human genetics Sackler Sch. Medicine, Tel Aviv U., 1980; cons. behavioral scis. tng. com. Nat. Inst. Gen. Med. Scis., NIH, 1962-64; mem. planning com., chmn. program 28th Internat. Congress Alcohol and Alcoholism, 1964. Author: Alcohol and the Jews, 1958; editor: (with D.J. Pittman) Society, Culture and Drinking Patterns, 1962; editorial bd. Quar. Jour. Studies on Alcohol, 1957-83; assoc. editor Sociol. Quar., 1960-63. Mem. theol. commn. United Ch. of Christ, 1964-71. Served with USNR, World War II. Fellow Am. Sociol. Assn.; mem. Soc. Study Social Problems (v.p. 1963-64, rep. to council Am. Sociol. Assn. 1964-66), Midwest Sociol. Soc. (bd. dirs. 1970-71), AAUP. Home: 705 Taylor Dr Carbondale IL 62901

SNYDER, COOPER, state senator; b. Blanchester, Ohio, July 10, 1928; s. Harry C. and Marion E. (Sprague) S.; m. Dorothy B. Blakeney, 1949; children—Marianne Snyder Macke, Phillip, Emily Snyder Steer, Harry, Elizabeth. Student Ohio U., 1947, Wilmington Coll., 1948-49. Mem. Ohio State Senate from Dist. 14. Mem. Phi Kappa Tau. Republican. Methodist. Lodges: Rotary, Masons. Home: 6508 Springhill Rd Hillsboro OH 45133

SNYDER, GARY RONALD, hospital administrator; b. Akron, Ohio, May 7, 1946; s. Harry H. and Zola S.; B.A., Calif. State Coll., Northridge, 1970; M.P.H., U. Mich., 1972; m. Francine Susan Snyder, Sept. 2, 1972; children—Mark Kenneth, Joel Martin. Dir. for health New Detroit, Inc., 1972-74; dir. planning Comprehensive Health Planning Council, 1974-76; cons. HEW, Chgo., 1976-78; mem. Chgo. Bd. Trade, 1976-78; dir. plan devel. and coordination Comprehensive Health Planning Council, Detroit, 1978-83; exec. v.p. Warren Hosp. Corp., 1983—. Chmn., Am. Cancer Soc., Detroit, 1973-76; bd. dirs. Neighborhood Service Orgn., Jewish Family Service, Warren Hosp. Ctr. Recipient Exceptional Service citation Calif. State Colls., 1970. Mem. Am. Public Health Assn., Am. Health Planning Assn., Am. Mgmt. Assn., Am. Hosp. Assn., Am. Coll. Health Care Execs., ACLU, Anti-Defamation League. Home: 6185 Worlington Rd Birmingham MI 48010 Office: 21230 Dequindre Rd Warren MI 48091

SNYDER, JAMES WILLIAM, JR., sales exec.; b. South Bend, Ind., Mar. 16, 1948; s. James William and Marjorie Jane (Blakeman) S.; B.B.A., Northwood Inst., 1970; postgrad. Oakland U., 1985; m. Sharon Ann Wallace, Aug. 22, 1970; children—Erin Elizabeth, Stephanie Wallace. Sales mktg. rep. Jim Snyder Sales Co., Grosse Pointe Woods, Mich., 1970-72, v.p., 1972-75, sr. v.p., treas., 1975—, dir., 1972—; v.p. sales and mktg., dir. Country Sales, Inc., 1983-85; v.p. Thomas S. Maentz, Inc., Troy, Mich., 1985—. Bd. dirs. Northwood Inst. Alumni; active St. John Men's Hosp. Guild, 1971—, Grosse Pointe Woods Police and Fire Aux., 1971—. Mem. Am. Mgmt. Assn., Soc. Advanced Mgmt., Soc. Plastic Engrs., Am. Soc. Body Engrs., Founders Soc. Detroit Inst. Arts, Automotive Old Timers. Clubs: Detroit Athletic, Grosse Pointe Yacht, Grosse Pointe Crisis; Oakland Hills Golf; White Hall (Chgo.). Home: 16814 St Paul Grosse Pointe MI 48230 Office: Thomas S Maentz Inc 2075 W Big Beaver Rd Suite 300 Troy MI 48084

SNYDER, JOEL JAY, architect; b. Columbus, Ohio, Feb. 21, 1949; s. Joel Rice and Gloria (Mertz) S.; m. Christine Ann Wittmann, Mar. 13, 1982; 1 child, Austin Wittmann. BS, Ohio State U., 1972; postgrad. U. Ky., 1977, Harvard U., 1982. Registered architect, U.K., Ohio, N.Y., Pa., Ky., W.Va. Intern architect Eschliman & Assocs., Columbus, 1968-70, Acock, Trees & White, 1970, County Architects Office of Northamptonshire, Northampton, Eng., 1971, Ireland & Assocs., Columbus, 1972-73, Holroyd & Myers, 1973; architect Brubaker/Brandt, Inc., 1974-75, Feinknopf, Feinknopf, Macioce & Schappa, 1976; prin. Joel J. Snyder Assocs. Architecture and Planning, 1977—; pres. JS Assocs., 1982—; assocs. Sims Cons. Group, Lancaster, Ohio, 1983—; adj. prof. Ohio State U., Columbus, 1985—, bd. govs. Sch. Architecture Ohio State U., 1986—; mem. bd. advisors Ohio Bank and Savs. Co. Mem. AIA (chpt. pres. 1987—), Architects Soc. Ohio, Urban Land Inst., Am. Planning Assn., Constrn. Specifications Inst., Royal Inst. Brit. Architects, Inst. Urban Design., Ohio State U. Alumni Assn. (bd. govs.). Republican. Clubs: Columbus, Scioto Country. Avocations: travel; tennis; history. Home: 1892 Suffolk Rd Columbus OH 43221 Office: 744 S High St Columbus OH 43206

SNYDER, JOHN TODD, restaurant owner, operator; b. Mansfield, Ohio, Aug. 18, 1962; s. Charles Frederick and Constance Jean (Derr) S.; m. Deborah K. Hatfield, July 19, 1986. AA, Johnson & Wales Coll., 1981. Counter helper, cook McDonalds, Mansfield, 1979-80, 81-81; cook, mgr. Country Corners, Lakeville, Ohio, 1982-83; cook Evergreens Restaurant, Upper Sandusky, Ohio, 1983-84; head night cook The Carriage House Restaurant, Findlay, Ohio, 1983-84; owner, operator The Cottage Inn Restaurant, Upper Sandusky, 1985—. Mem. United Ostomy Assn. (sec. 1981-82, v.p. 1982-83), Mansfield-Ashland United Ostomy Assn. (cofounder, v.p. 1979). Democrat. Roman Catholic. Lodges: St. Maximilian-Kolby, Order St. Francis, Moose. Avocations: taking care of horses, computer programming, cooking, reading. Home: Rt #1 Box 76 Wharton OH 43359 Office: The Cottage Inn Restaurant 109 N Sandusky Ave Upper Sandusky OH 43351

SNYDER, LOUIS GEORGE, non profit association administrator; b. Jersey City, N.J., May 6, 1931; s. Louis George and Josephine (Cossolini) S.; m. Phyllis Gene Vallaster, June 25, 1955; children: Louis, Susan, Kathleen, Walter, Stephen, Ida, Andrew. BS, St. Peters Coll., Jersey City, N.J., 1952; MA, Webster U., 1974. Commd. 2d lt. USMC, 1952, advanced through grades to lt. col., 1972, ret., 1979; exec. dir. ARMA Internat., 1979—; pres. MASAE, Kansas City, Mo., 1986—. Decorated Bronz Star. Mem. Assn. Records Mgrs. and Administrs., Mid Am. Soc. Assn. Execs. Roman Catholic. Office: 4200 Somerset Dr Room 215 Shawnee Mission KS 66208

SNYDER, NANCY E., rental manager; b. Dayton, Ohio, Apr. 25, 1938; d. Calvin Sylvester and Marjorie M. (Keener) Eby; m. Duane L. Snyder, June 27, 1959; children: Sheryl, Lynn. Diploma in Dental Hygiene, Ohio State U., 1960. Dental hygienist various dental offices, Dayton, 1960-72; rental mgr., investor Centerville, Ohio, 1972—. Precinct chmn. Montgomery County Rep. Party, Dayton, 1976—, mem. cen. and exec. coms., 1976—; mem. sister city com. for City of Centerville. Mem. Chi Omega Alumnae Assn. Clubs: Centerville Women's Civic, Federated Women's. Avocations: antiques, boating, travel, Amazon parrotts, bridge. Home: 31 Glencroft Pl Centerville OH 45459

SNYDER, PAUL LEON, accountant; b. Urbana, Ill., Dec. 3, 1948; s. Whalen Christian and Mary Josephine (Quinlan) S.; m. Katherine Ann Kreis, June 17, 1972; children: Elizabeth, Kimberly, David. BS in Bus., Ea. Ill. U., 1970. CPA, Minn. Ptnr. Peat, Marwick, Main & Co., Chgo., 1970-86, Mpls., 1986—; vis. instr. ins. acctg. U. Wis., Madison, 1983—. Mem. fin. com. Naperville (Ill.) Sesquicentennial Com., 1978-84; treas. Good Shepherd Luth. Ch., 1984-86, mem. council, 1985-86; bd. dirs., mem. fin., nominating coms. Edward Hosp., Naperville, 1984-86. Mem. Am. Inst. CPA's, Minn. Soc. CPA's. Republican. Home: 11532 Zion Rd Bloomington MN 55437 Office: Peat Marwick Main & Co 1600 MeritorTower Saint Paul MN 55101

SNYDER, ROBERT LEE, anesthesiologist; b. Midland, Mich., Aug. 26, 1952; s. Robert M. and Kathleen M. (Bogan) S.; m. Shelley Ann Marquiss, June 29, 1974; children: Kenneth Robert, Kacie Lee Ann. BS in Zoology, Mich. State U., 1974, D of Osteopathy, 1979. Diplomate Am. Bd. Anesthesiology. Intern Saginaw (Mich.) Osteo. Hosp., 1979-80, cons., 1982—; resident in anesthesia Flint (Mich.) Osteo. Hosp., 1980-82; staff anesthesiologist McPherson Community Health Ctr., Howell, Mich., 1982—, chief of anesthesia services, 1986—, chmn. dept. anesthesia, 1986-87; cons. Herrick Meml. Hosp., Tecumseh, Mich., 1982—; assoc. clin. prof. Mich. State U., East Lansing, 1982—; lectr. Mich. Osteo. Med. Ctr., Detroit, 1986. Legis. asst. to Thomas Holcomb State Rep., 1974-75; physician liaison United Way, Livingston County, Mich., 1986. Recipient Richard P. Alper Meml. award for Community Service, Mich. State U., 1979. Mem. Am. Osteo. Assn. (alt. del. 1986), Mich. Assn. of Osteo. Physicians and Surgeons (del. 1985—), Livingston County Osteo. Assn. (sec.-treas. 1984-86), Am. Osteo. Coll. of Anesthesiologists, Mich. Soc. of Osteo. Anesthesiologists (sec.-treas. 1985—), Mich. Soc. Anesthesiologists, Am. Soc. Anesthesiologists, Mich. State U. Alumni Assn., Jaycees (internal v.p. Holt, Mich. chpt. 1975-76), Sigma Sigma Phi (founding chpt. pres. 1977). Presbyterian. Clubs: Chemung Hills Country, Bay Valley Corvette. Avocations: golfing, snow skiing, corvette restoration, hunting, fishing. Home and Office: 103 Fordney Pl Howell MI 48843

SNYDER, THOMAS JOHN, osteopath; b. Monticello, Iowa, June 19, 1950; s. John Arvid and Laura Emma (Dirks) S.; m. LuAnne Carole Horner, June 17, 1972; children—Rachael, Mark, Andrea. B.A., Coe Coll., 1975; D.O., U. Osteo. Medicine, 1978. Cert. in internal medicine. Intern, Davenport Osteo. Hosp., Iowa, 1978-79; resident in internal medicine Normandy Hosp., St. Louis, 1979-82; asst. prof. U. Osteo. Medicine, Des Moines, 1982-83; staff physician Davenport Med. Ctr., Iowa, 1983—; staff physician Mercy Hosp., Davenport, 1984—, St. Lukes Hosp, Davenport, 1984—, Illini Hosp., Silvis, Ill., 1984—. Contbr. articles to profl. jours. Bd. dirs. Am. Cancer Soc., Scott County, 1984. Served with USMC, 1968-71. Mead Johnson fellow, 1982. Mem. Am. Heart Assn., Am. Lung Assn., Am. Diabetes Assn., Iowa Osteo. Med. Assn., Scott County Osteo. Assn. Mem. Reformed Ch. Am. Lodge: Rotary. Avocations: running, decoy collecting. Office: 3801 Marquette Suite 202 Davenport IA 52806

SNYDER, WILLARD BREIDENTHAL, lawyer; b. Kansas City, Kans., Dec. 18, 1940; s. Nona E. and Ruth (Breidenthal) S.; m. Lieselotte Dieringer, Nov. 10, 1970 (dec. Nov. 1975); m. Christa Wittman, June 1, 1978; children: Kim Green, Jackie Green, Rolf. BA, U. Kans., 1962, JD, 1965; postgrad., Hague Acad. Internat. Law, The Netherlands, 1965-66, U. Dijon, France, 1966; grad., Command and Gen. Staff Coll., Ft. Leavenworth, Kans., 1977. Sole practice Kansas City, Kans., 1970-80, 85—; trust officer, corp. trust officer Security Nat. Bank., Kansas City, 1980-83, corp. sec., 1983-85; pres. Real Estate Corp. Inc., 1984—; bd. dirs. Providence St. Margaret Health, Kansas City, Kans.; adv. bd. dirs. United Mo. Bankshares, Kansas City; West German consul for Kans., Western Mo., 1972—. Mem. Platte Woods (Mo.) City Council, 1983-84. Served with U.S. Army, 1967-70, Kans. Army N.G. Mem. Mo. Bar Assn., Kansas City Bar Assn., Kans. Attys. Assn., Kansas City Hosp. Attys. Assn., Mil. Order of World Wars (regional commdr. 1983-84). Avocations: scuba, shooting, Notgeld collections, cartridge collection. Office: care Security Bank of Kansas City PO Box 1250 Kansas City KS 66117

SOBEL, HOWARD BERNARD, osteopathic physician; b. N.Y.C., May 15, 1929; s. Martin and Ella (Sternberg) S.; m. Ann Louise Silverbush, June 16, 1957 (dec. May 1978); children—Nancy Sobel Schumer, Janet Sobel Medow, Robert; m. Irene S. Miller, June 8, 1980; stepchildren—Avner Saferstein, Daniel Saferstein, Naomi Saferstein. A.B., Syracuse U., 1951; D.O., Kansas City Coll. Osteopathy and Surgery, 1955. Intern Zieger Osteo. Hosp., Detroit, 1955-56; gen. practice osteo. medicine Redford Twp., Mich., 1956-74, Livonia, Mich., 1974—; chief of staff Botsford Gen. Hosp., Farmington, Mich., 1978; mem. faculty Mich. State U. Coll. Osteo. Medicine, 1969—, clin. assoc. prof. family practice, 1973—; mem. exec. and med. adv. coms. United Health Org. Mich.; mem. Venereal Disease Action Com., Mich.; apptd. to asst. impaired osteo. physicians Mich., 1983. Mem. Am. Osteo. Assn. (ho. of dels. 1981—), Mich. Assn. Osteo. Physicians and Surgeons (ho. of dels.), Am. Coll. Osteo. Rheumatologists, Coll. Am. Osteo. Gen. Practitioners, Osteo. Gen. Practice Mich., Wayne County Osteo. Assn. (pres.). Jewish. Home: 6222 Northfield St West Bloomfield MI 48322 Office: 28275 Five Mile Rd Livonia MI 48154

SOBOLESKI, RENEE MAXINE, educator; b. International Falls, Minn., Jan. 27, 1937; d. Max Paul and Elaine Josephine (LaValley) Goulet; m. Frank Joseph Soboleski, Jan. 12, 1973; children—Beth E. Madison, Bonnie I. LaJambe, Barbara L. Cassibo. A.S., Rainy River Community Coll., 1968; B.S., Bemidji State U., 1970, M.S. in Edn., 1975. Spl. edn. tchr. International Falls (Minn.) Sch. Dist. 361, 1970-78, elem. edn. tchr., 1978-84; now spl. edn./EMH tchr. Backus Middle Sch. Sunday Sch. tchr. Sr. high sch. students; mem. Council for Exceptional Children. Mem. Minn. Fedn. Tchrs. (bd. dirs., negotiating com. 1980-84), Cat Fanciers Assn. AAUW. Clubs: Gen. Federated Women's (v.p. 1972-74, pres., 1974-76), Ice Box Twirlers Square Dance (International Falls, Minn.). Office: Alexander Baker Backus Middle School International Falls MN 56649

SOBOTA, WALTER LOUIS, clinical psychologist, neuropsychologist; b. Detroit, Oct. 30, 1946; s. Walter Paul and Martha Dorothy (Czapski) S.; m. Dianne Mary Brent, May 9, 1969; children: Christopher, Jennifer. BA magna cum laude, U. Detroit, 1968, PhD, 1973. Diplomate in Clin. Neuropsychology Am. Bd. Profl. Psychology; lic. psychologist, Mich. Therapist Wake Psychology Clinic, Royal Oak, Mich., 1974-81; pvt. practice psychology Royal Oak, 1981—; staff psychologist Sinai Hosp., Detroit, 1973—; instr. U. Windsor, Ont., Can., 1977-78; adj. instr. Wayne State U. Med. Sch., Detroit, 1982—; cons. Providence Hosp., Southfield, Mich., 1978-82. Recipient Psi Chi award, U. Detroit, 1968. Mem. AAAS, Nat. Acad. Neuropsychologists, Am. Psychol. Assn., Mich. Psychol. Assn. (pres. 1986), Mich. Interprofl. Assn. (pres. 1981, Disting. Service award 1984). Democrat. Roman Catholic. Avocations: reading, jogging, swimming. Office: Sinai Hosp Dept Psychiatry 14800 W McNichols Rd Detroit MI 48235

SOBOTKA, MARK JOSEPH, computer infomation scientist; b. Mt. Ayr, Iowa, Aug. 4, 1954; s. Walter Joe and Lois Bernadine (Linkvis) S. BS in Computer Science, Iowa State U., 1976. Computer programmer Mo. Pacific R.R., St. Louis, 1976-78; systems analyst Centel Corp., Lincoln, Nebr., 1978-80; systems programmer Centel Corp., Lincoln, 1981-84; systems cons. AT&SF Railway, Topeka, Kans., 1980-81; project leader Citibank S.D. N.A., Sioux Falls, 1984—. Republican. Methodist. Avocation: sports official. Home: 900 E 65th St N Sioux Falls SD 57104 Office: Citibank SD NA 701 E 60th St N Sioux Falls SD 57117

SOBRALSKE, BARBARA NILA, educator; b. Wild Rose, Wis., May 10, 1949; d. Kenneth John and Beverly Janice (Rasmussen) Graydon; m. Michael John Sobralske Jr., Oct. 17, 1970; 1 child, Mark Michael. Cert. in Teaching, Waushara County Tchrs. Coll., Wautoma, Wis., 1969; BS, U. Wis., Oshkosh, 1974. Cert. elem. tchr., Wis. Tchr. elem. schs. Waupun (Wis.) Sch. Dist., 1969-72; title I aide Wild Rose Sch. Dist., 1975, tchr. elem. schs., 1975—. Mem. NEA, Wis. Edn. Assn., Wis. Assn. Environ. Edn., Internat. Reading Assn., Wis. State Reading Assn., Fox Valley Reading Council. Home: Rt 1 Box 88 Wild Rose WI 54984 Office: Wild Rose Sch Dist PO Box 276 Wild Rose WI 54984

SODAWALLA, ANITA B., nurse, training and development consultant; b. Quezon City, Philippines, Dec. 5, 1942; came to U.S., 1972; d. Jose Canete Bustamante and Esperanza Manzano Carino; m. Badruddin Hussain Sodawalla, Dec. 26, 1975; 1 child, Ibrahim Badruddin. Diploma in Nursing, U. Philippines, 1968, MS in Nursing, 1971; BS in Nursing, Philippine Women's U., 1970; postgrad. Wayne State U., 1977-80. Charge nurse neonatal and pediatric ICU, Henry Ford Hosp., Detroit, 1972-73; instr., coordinator critical care Grace Hosp., Detroit, 1973-76; sr. instr. Harper Hosp. div. Harper-Grace Hosps., 1976-79, asst. dir. nursing Grace Hosp. div., 1980; pres., exec. dir. Critical Care Unltd., Inc., Southfield, Mich., 1979-84; dir. nursing services and continuing edn. Critical Care Profl. Services, 1980-84; pres., exec. dir. Profl. Success Systems, Inc., 1982-85, dir. human resources tng. and devel., 1986—; program coordinator, cons. Critical Care Edn. Ctr., 1984—; instr. Am. Heart Assn. Mich., Detroit, 1974—, bd. dirs. Macomb County Chpt., 1981-84. Mem. Am. Assn. Critical Care Nurses, Nat. Assn. Female Execs., Nat. Assn. Nurse Cons. and Entrepreneurs. (founder, pres.), Philippine Nurses Assn. Mich. (life, pres., cons. 1975-78). Mem. Ch. of Christ. Avocations: swimming, singing, reading.

SODERQUIST, GEORGE DAVID, actuary; b. Des Moines, Sept. 29, 1937; s. George Elmer and Bertha Isis (Alvis) S.; m. Madeline Joan McKenna, Aug. 29, 1958; 1 child, Erin Ann McMullen. BSBA, Drake U., 1958. Assoc. actuary Woodmen Accident and Life Ins., Lincoln, Nebr., 1960-64; asst. actuary Columbus (Ohio) Mut. Life, 1964-67; actuary Olympic Nat. Life Ins., Seattle, 1967-72; prin. Tillinghast, Columbus, 1972-83; 2d v.p., assoc. actuary Paul Revere Co., Worcester, Mass., 1984-85; sr. v.p., chief actuary Capitol Am. Fin. Corp., Cleve., 1985—. Served to capt. USAFR. Fellow Soc. Actuaries (Edn. and Exam CMTE 1972-76), Conf. Actuaries Pub. Practice,; mem. Am. Acad. Actuaries, Actuaries Club of Ind., Ky., and Ohio (v.p. 1981-82), Columbus Actuarial Club (pres. 1977-78). Avocations: bridge, backgammon, photography. Office: Capitol Am Fin Corp 1300 E 9th Cleveland OH 44114

SOELTER, ROBERT R., retail sales company executive; b. 1926. BBA, Kans. State U., 1949. With S.S. Kresge & Co., 1949-50; with Duckwall-Alco Stores Inc., Abilene, Kans., 1950—, v.p., 1974-75, exec. v.p., 1975-77, now pres., chief exec. officer. Served with AUS, 1943-46. Office: Duckwall-Alco Stores Inc 40 Cottage Abilene KS 67410 *

SOENKE, EDWARD LEONARD, architect; b. Davenport, Iowa, July 1, 1943; s. Louis George and Ruth Frances (Carr) S.; m. Bette Jane Jensen, June 8, 1968; children: Teresa Marie, Dena Elizabeth. BArch, Iowa State U., 1966. Registered architect, Iwa. Architect in tng. Emery-Prall, Des Moines, 1967-69; architect Frevert-Ramsey, Des Moines, 1969-71, Charles Herbert, Des Moines, 1971-74; architect, owner The Design Partnership, West Des Moines, Iowa, 1974—; edn. chmn. U. Wis., Madison, 1982—. editorial staff Iowa Architect Mag., 1967—. Bd. dirs. Des Moines Art Ctr., 1986. Mem. AIA, Constrn. Specifications Inst. (region officer 1972-86, bd. dirs. 1972—, Cert. Appreciation 1985), Am. Arbitration Assn. (arbitrator 1977-86, Meritorius Service award 1984), Internat. Comanche Soc., Am. Bonanza Soc., Delta Upsilon. Republican. Methodist. Club: FMR (Boston). Avocations: hunting, tennis, golf, photography, travel with family. Home and Office: 1637 Thornwood Rd West Des Moines IA 50265

SOENS, LAWRENCE D., bishop; b. Iowa City, Aug. 26, 1926. Student, Loras Coll., Dubuque, Iowa, St. Ambrose Coll., Davenport, Iowa, Kenrick Sem., St. Louis, U. Iowa. Ordained priest Roman Catholic Ch., 1950, consecrated bishop, 1983. Bishop of Sioux City Iowa, 1983—. Office: Chancery Office PO Box 3379 1821 Jackson St Sioux City IA 51102 *

SOGG, ALAN JAY, physician, surgeon; b. Cleve., Mar. 30, 1931; s. Jack and Atha (Minsky) S.; m. Judith Marcia Kline, Dec. 22, 1957; children: Richard, Elise, Daniel. BA, Miami U., Oxford, Ohio, 1953; MD, U. Cin., 1957. Practice medicine specializing in otolaryngology Drs. Sogg & Smith, Cleve., 1967—; dir. Ear, Nose & Throat Allergy Clinic, Univ. Hosp., Cleve., 1986—, mem. com. on paranasal sinus disease, 1986—. Contbr. articles to med. jours. Mem. Am. Acad. Otolaryngology Head and Neck Surgery (Honor award 1986), Acad. Facial Plastic and Reconstructive Surgery, Triological Soc. Inc. Republican. Jewish. Club: Cleve. Civil War Roundtable. Avocations: cooking, gardening, tennis, trout fishing. Home: 2771 Chesterton Rd Shaker Heights OH 44122 Office: 21100 Southgate Park Cleveland OH 44137

SOGNEFEST, PETER WILLIAM, manufacturing company executive; b. Melrose Park, Ill., Feb. 4, 1941; s. Peter and Alvera E. Sognefest; m. Margaret Brunkow, Aug. 15, 1964; children: Scott, Brian, Jennifer. BSEE, U. Ill., 1964, MSEE, 1967. Elec. engr. Magnavox Corp., Urbana, Ill., 1964-67; sr. fellow, mgr. research, United Techs. fellow Mellon Inst., Pitts., 1967-71; gen. mgr. for semicondr. ops. United Techs., Pitts., 1971-77; v.p. indsl. electronics unit Motorola Inc., Schaumburg, Ill., 1977-84; pres., chief exec. officer Digital Appliance Controls, Inc., Hoffman Estates, Ill., 1984—, also bd. dirs.; bd. dirs. Two-Six Inc. Patentee in field. Pres. bd. deacons Presbyn. Ch., 1981-82. Mem. IEEE, U. Ill. Elec. Engring. Alumni Assn. (pres. 1986-87), Coves Property Owners Assn. (pres. 1982). Republican. Clubs: Meadow, Barrington Hills Country. Home: 4 Back Bay Rd Barrington IL 60010

SOKOL, DAVID MARTIN, educator, art historian, consultant; b. N.Y.C., Nov. 3, 1942; s. Harry and Ruth (Waldman) S.; m. Sandra H. Schorr, June 15, 1963; children: Adam Jonathan, Andrew Levi. AB, Hunter Coll., 1963; MA, NYU, 1966, PhD, 1970. Lectr. Bronx (N.Y.) Community Coll., 1965-66; instr. Kingsborough Community Coll., Bklyn., 1966-68; asst. prof. Western Ill. U., Macomb, Ill., 1968-71; from assoc. prof. to prof. U. Ill., Chgo., 1971—; curator Terra Mus., Evanston, Ill., 1981-85; interim dir. Spertus Mus., Chgo., 1985-86. Author: American Architecture of Art, 1976, Am. Decorative Arts and Old World Influences, 1979; co-author: American Art, 1979. Commr. Oak Park (Ill.) Hist. Preservation Com. 1985—; trustee Village of Oak Park, 1977-81. NEH grantee 1973, research grantee Graham Found., 1987. Mem. Assn. Historians Am. Art (ediotr newletter 1977—), Chgo. Arts Club. Lodge: Masons. Avocations: chamber music, reading, running, photography. Home: 330 S Taylor Ave Oak Park IL 60302 Office: U Ill Chgo History of Architecture Art Dept Chicago IL 60680

SOKOL, DENNIS ALLEN, hospital administrator; b. Chgo., May 3, 1945; s. Stanley John and Mildred Veronica (Krenslake) S.; m. Gwen Noble, Dec. 19, 1971 (div.); children: Anne, Ellen. BS in Bus., No. Ill. U., 1968; MBA, U. Nebr., Omaha, 1974; M of Hosp. Adminstrn., U. Minn., 1976. Radio personality various stas., Ill., Iowa and Nebr., 1968-72; pub. relations officer Children's Meml. Hosp., Omaha, 1972-73, Meth. Hosp., Omaha, 1973-74; v.p. adminstrn. Golden Valley (Minn.) Health Ctr., 1976-82; pres. Sacred Heart Hosp., Yankton, S.D., 1982—; instr. health care mgmt. Mt. Marty Coll., 1986-87, U. Minn., 1986-87. Pres. Respiratory Care Services, Inc., 1984—, Health Mgmt. Services, 1987—. Swerved with U.S. Army N.G., 1970-71, USAF N.G., 1971-77. Mem. Am. Coll. Health Care Execs., S.D. Hosp. Assn., Mo. Valley Health Network (v.p. 1986—). Republican. Roman Catholic. Lodge: Rotary. Office: Golden Valley Health Ctr 501 Summit Yankton SD 57078

SOKOL, ROBERT JAMES, obstetrician, gynecologist, educator; b. Rochester, N.Y., Nov. 18, 1941; s. Eli and Mildred (Levine) S.; m. Roberta Sue Kahn, July 26, 1964; children: Melissa Anne, Eric Russell, Andrew Ian. B.A. with highest distinction in Philosophy, U. Rochester, 1963, M.D. with honors, 1966. Diplomate Am. Bd. Ob-Gyn (assoc. examiner), Sub-Bd. Maternal-Fetal Medicine. Intern Barnes Hosp., Washington U., St. Louis, 1966-67, resident in ob-gyn, 1967-70, asst. in ob-gyn, 1966-70, research asst., 1967-68, instr. clin. ob-gyn, 1970; Buswell fellow in maternal fetal medicine Strong Meml. Hosp.-U. Rochester, 1972-73; fellow in maternal-fetal medicine Cleve. Met. Gen. Hosp.-Case Western Res. U., Cleve., 1974-75, assoc. obstetrician and gynecologist, 1973-83, asst. prof. ob-gyn, 1973-77; asst. program dir. Perinatal Clin. Research Ctr., 1973-78, co-program dir., 1978-82, program dir., 1982-83, acting dir. obstetrics, 1974-75, co-dir., 1977-83, assoc. prof., 1977-81, prof., 1981-83, assoc. dir. dept. ob-gyn., 1981-83; prof. ob-gyn Wayne State U., Detroit, 1983—, chmn. dept. ob-gyn, 1983—; mem. grad. faculty dept. physiology Wayne State U., 1984—; chief ob-gyn Hutzel Hosp. 1983—; dir. C.S. Mott Ctr. for Human Growth and Devel., 1983—; past pres. med. staff Cuyahoga County Hosps.; mem. profl. adv. bd. Educated Childbirth Inc., 1976-80; cons. Nat. Inst. Child Health and Human Devel., Nat. Inst. Alcohol Abuse and Alcoholism, Ctr. for Disease Control, NIH, Health Resources and Services Adminstrn., Nat. Clearinghouse for Alcohol Info.; mem. alcohol psychosocial research rev. com. Nat. Inst. Alcohol Abuse and Alcoholism, 1981-86; mem. ob/gyn adv. panel U.S. Pharmacopeial Conv., 1985—. Contbr. articles to med. jours., chpts. to books; reviewer med. jours.; mem. editorial bd. Jour. Perinatal Medicine; researcher computer applications in perinatal medicine, alcohol-related birth defects, perinatal risk and neurobehavioral devel. Mem. Pres.'s leadership council U. Rochester, 1976-80. Served to maj. M.C. USAF, 1970-72. Mem. AMA, Am. Coll. Obstetricians and Gynecologists (chmn. steering com. drug and alcohol abuse contract 1986-87), Soc. Gynecologic Investigation, Perinatal Research Soc., Assn. Profs. Ob-Gyn, Royal Soc. Medicine, Mich. Med. Soc., Wayne County Med. Soc., Central Assn. Obstetricians-Gynecologists, Research Soc. Alcholism, Soc. Perinatal Obstetricians (v.p., pres. elect 1987-88), Behavioral Teratology Soc., Am. Pub. Health Assn., Am. Med. Soc. on Alcoholism and Other Drug Dependencies, Internat. Platform Assn., Detroit Physiol. Soc. (hon.), Phi Beta Kappa, Sigma Xi, Alpha Omega Alpha. Republican. Jewish. Home: 5200 Rector Ct Bloomfield Hills MI 48013 Office: Dept Ob-Gyn Hutzel Hosp 4707 St Antoine Blvd Detroit MI 48201

SOKOL, SHERRY LYNN, controller, accountant; b. Chgo., Sept. 11, 1960; d. Jack and Rita Rose (Miller) Plenner; m. Steven Scott Sokol, June 6, 1982; 1 child, Elizabeth Anne. BA, Northeastern Ill. U., 1982. CPA, Ill. Staff acct. Laventhol & Horwath, Chgo., 1982-84; supply controller Cooper's Plumbing & Heating, Chgo., 1984—. Mem. Soc. Advancement Mgmt., Am. Inst. CPA's, Ill. CPA Soc. Office: Skokie Plumbing Supply Inc 3714 W Oakton Skokie IL 60076 Office: Cooper's Plumbing and Heating Supplies Inc 3401 W Madison Skokie IL 60076

SOLBERG, NELLIE FLORENCE COAD, artist; b. Sault Ste. Marie, Mich.; d. Sanford and Mary (McDonald) Coad; m. Ingvald Solberg, Aug. 24, 1930; children—Jeanne Elaine Solberg Unruh, Walter Eugene, Kay Louise Solberg Link. B.A., Minot State Tchrs. Coll., 1930; M.A., N.D. State U., 1963; postgrad. Wash. State U., 1960, U. Wyo., 1964, St. Cloud Coll., 1971. Tchr. Bismarck Elem. Schs., N.D., 1954-63, art dir. high sch., 1963-72; instr. art Bismarck Jr. Coll., 1964-67; cons. Bismarck Art Assn. Galleries, 1973-79, State Capitol Galleries, 1973-78; dir. arts festivals including Statewide Religious Arts Festival, Bismarck, 1969-85, State Treas.'s Gallery, 1977, N.D. State Capitol, Bismarck, 1973-78; co-dir. Indian Art Show, Nat. Congress Am. Indians, Bismarck, 1963. One-woman shows include Minot State Coll., 1963, Dickinson State Coll., 1964, Jamestown Coll., 1964, U. N.D., Valley City State Coll., Bismarck Jr. Coll., 1963, 65, 68, 69, N.D. State U., 1970, 74, Linha Gallery, Minot N.D., 1972, 74-77, Bank of N.D., 1972-74, 76-77, Elan Gallery, 1982; exhibited in group shows at Gov. John Davis Mansion, 1960, Concordia Coll., Moorhead, Minn., 1965, N.D. Capitol, 1968, 69, Gov. William Guy Mansion, 1971, Internat. Peace Gardens, 1969. Mem. Indian Culture Found., 1964—, Civic Music Assn., 1942—; works included in numerous pvt. collections U.S., Can., Europe; religious arts com. Conf. Chs., 1973; bd. dirs. Citizens for Arts, 1978-81. Recipient numerous awards including Gov.'s award for arts, 1977, Gov. Allen Olson award, 1982, Gov.'s award Bismarck Art Show, 1982, Dakota Northwestern Bank award, 1983, Dr. Shari Orser Purchase award Religious Arts Festival, 1984, William Murray award Religious Arts Festival, 1984, Manadan Art Assn. award, 1986, 18th ann. 3d prize weaving Festivcal of Arts, 1987, Dr. Cy Rinkel watercolor purchase award, 1987; named N.D. Woman Artist of Yr., 1974. Mem. Bismarck Arts and Galleries Assn. (membership com.), Bismarck Art Assn. (charter, Honor award 1960, pres. 1963-64, 71-72), Jamestown Art Assn., Linha Gallery (Minot), Nat. League Am. Pen Women (pres. N.D. 1964-66, pres. Medora br. 1972-74, treas. 1975-86), Mpls. Soc. Fine Arts, P.E.O. (pres. chpts. 1967-69), Bismarck Vets, Meml. Library (life), Soc. Preservation Gov.'s Mansion (charter, bd. dirs.), Sigma Sigma Sigma. Republican. Lodges: Zonta, Order of Eastern Star. Home: 925 N 6th St Bismarck ND 58501 Office: 1021 N 6th St Bismarck ND 58501

SOLBERG, NORMAN SIGURD, gynecologist/obstetrician; b. Crookston, Minn., Mar. 31, 1940; s. Ragnvald S. and Signe (Pearson) S.; m. Thais Price, Apr. 27, 1969; children: Rebecca Ann, Leah Catherine. BA, U. Minn., 1962, MD, 1966. Diplomate Am. Bd. Ob-Gyn. Intern Fresno (Calif.) Gen. Hosp., 1966-67; resident in ob-gyn Highland County Hosp., Oakland, Calif., 1970-72; resident in ob-gyn Kaiser Found. Hosp., San Francisco, mem. staff, 1972-74; gynecologist/obstetrician Park Nicollet Med. Ctr., Mpls., 1975—. Fellow Am. Coll. Ob-Gyn; mem. Minn. Ob-Gyn Soc., Mpls. Council Ob-Gyn. Avocations: running, tennis, music. Home: 5017 Chowen S Minneapolis MN 55410 Office: Park Nicollet Med Ctr 5000 W 39th St Minneapolis MN 55416

SOLBERG, RONALD DEAN, bank public relations executive; b. Tracy, Minn., Jan. 20, 1941; s. Adolph Tedeman and Helen Marie (Swanjord) S.; m. Norma Shearon Dick, Aug. 3, 1962; children—Barrett R., Jerrell C. Student, St. Olaf Coll., 1958-60; B.S., Mankato State U., 1962, B.A., 1962. Tchr. English and journalism Tech. High Sch., St. Cloud, Minn., 1962-69; dir. publs. and pub. relations Central Minn. Ednl. Research and Devel. Council, St. Cloud, 1969-70; coordinator sch. info. Downers Grove Schs., Ill., 1970-73; dir. communications Inst. Real Estate Mgmt., Chgo., 1973-75; dir. pub. relations Million Dollar Round Table, Des Plaines, Ill., 1975-77; staff media rep. Standard Oil Co. of Ind., Chgo., 1977-79; press relations adminstr. Continental Bank, Chgo., 1979-81, corp. affairs officer, mgr. retail advt., 1981-83, 2d v.p., 1983—. Chmn. fin. com., first asst. treas. Woodhaven Lakes Assn., 1982, v.p., 1984. Mem. Pub. Relations Soc. Am. (chpt. pres.-elect 1984, chpt. pres. 1985, nat. chmn. technologies task force 1985). Democrat. Unitarian. Founder sytems operator public relations and mktg. forum. Home: 1032 61st St Downers Grove IL 60516 Office: Continental Bank 231 S Lasalle St Chicago IL 60697

SOLEM, MAIZIE ROGNESS, educator; b. Hendricks, Minn., Nov. 8, 1920; d. John A. and Nora Adeline (Engelstad) Rogness; B.A., Augustana Coll., 1942; postgrad. George Washington U., 1955-57, Wright State U., 1970-71; M.Ed., Miami U., Oxford, Ohio, 1970-71; Ed.D., U. S.D., 1976; postgrad. U. Calif., 1978. Tchr., LeMars, Iowa, 1942-43, Internat. Children's Centre, Bangkok, Thailand, 1952-53, George Washington U., Washington, 1957, Fairfax (Va.) schs., 1956-58, Maxwell AFB Sch., Montgomery, Ala., 1963-66; tchr., librarian Central High Sch., Madison, S.D., 1943; dir., tchr., supr. remedial reading tchrs. City schs., Fairborn, Ohio, 1966-71; Title I resource tchr. L.B. Anderson Elem. Sch., Sioux Falls, S.D., 1971-73; primary coordinator Instructional Planning Center, Sioux Falls, 1973-77; curriculum coordinator Sioux Falls public schs., 1973—. Mem. adv. bd. Ret. Sr. Vol. Program, 1974-78, publicity chmn., 1975-78; mem. adv. bd. Vol. Action Center, 1976-78, mem. service com., 1974-78; chmn. exec. bd. Augustana Fellows, 1979-81; scholarship chmn. LaSertoma, 1979-80; active various drives including Heart Fund, Muscular Dystrophy, Cancer Fund; bd. regents Augustana Coll., 1984—. Recipient Vol. Yr. in Edn. awardGov. S.D, 1984, Leader Luncheon award YWCA, 1984, Alumni Achievement award Augustana Coll., 1986, IRA Literacy award, 1987; named S.D. Adminstr. of Yr., 1987. Mem. AAUW, DAR (bd. dirs. found. 1986-87, chmn. publicity com. 1986-87, chmn. grants com. 1986-87), Sch. Adminsrs. S.D. (v.p. 1977-78), Assn. Supervision Curriculum Devel. (pres. 1976-78, nat. exec. council 1979-82), Nat. Assn. Supervision Curriculum Devel. (bd. dirs. 1977-79; mem. nat. selection com. 1977-78), Assn. Childhood Edn. Internat., S.D. Assn. Elem. Prins., Elem., Kindergarten, Nursery Sch. Edn., Nat. Assn. Edn. Young Children, Sioux Land Assn. for Edn. Young Children, NEA, S.D. Edn. Assn., Nat. Council Social Studies, Internat. Reading Assn., S.D. Tchrs. Maths. Orgn., S.D. Assn. Supervision and Curriculum Devel., Orton Soc. Republican. Lutheran. Home: 1600 North Dr Box 911 Sioux Falls SD 57101 Office: 201 E 38th St Sioux Falls SD 57102

SOLIMAN, ANWAR S., restaurant company executive. Chmn. Gilbert/Robinson, Inc., Kansas City, Mo. Office: Gilbert/Robinson Inc Warnall Rd & Ward Pkwy Kansas City MO 64112 *

SOLIUNAS, WALTER, food products executive; b. Vilaikiai, Lithuania, Sept. 15, 1933; came to U.S., 1949; s. Florijonas and Anele (Viscinis) S.; m. Lydia Irene Reklaitis, Feb. 20, 1965; children: Thomas Anthony, Peter Paul. BS in Commerce, DePaul U., 1962; cert., A. Hamilton Bus. Sch., 1971. Chief bookkeeper N.Y. Cen. R.R., Chgo., 1954-64; paymaster Transoceanic Terminal, Chgo., 1964-65; asst. controller Am. Meat Packing Corp., Chgo., 1965-73, controller, 1973-75, v.p. controller, 1975-80, v.p. fin. and adminstrn., 1980—; chmn. unsecured creditors com. Winchester Foods, Hutchinson, Kans., 1986—. Pres. Lithuanian Christian Dem. Union Exile, Willow Springs, Ill., 1974-86, Pope Leo XIII Lit. Fund, Willow Springs, 1976—, Lithuanian Council Chgo., 1986-87. Served with U.S. Army, 1957-59. Republican. Roman Catholic. Avocation: political causes for the restoration of independence to Lithuania. Office: Am Meat Packing Corp Div Kane Miller 3946 S Normal Chicago IL 60609

SOLLARS, FRANK B., automobile insurance company executive. Chmn., dir. Nationwide Mut. Ins. Co., Columbus, Ohio. Office: Nationwide Mut Ins Co 1 Nationwide Plaza Columbus OH 43216 *

SOLOMON, GLEN DAVID, internist, researcher, medical educator; b. Jersey City, Mar. 24, 1955; s. Ernest and Shirley (Schlosky)S.; m. Barbara Ann Metzger, May 27, 1984. BA, Northwestern U., 1976; MD, Rush Med. Coll., 1980. Diplomate Am. Bd. Internal Medicine, Nat. Bd. Med. Examiners. Intern and resident in internal medicine USAF Med. Ctr., Wright-Patterson AFB, Ohio, Wright State U. Affiliated Hosps., Dayton, Ohio, 1980-83; physician Diamond Headache Clinic, Chgo., 1986—; adj. asst. prof. Chgo. Med. Sch., 1987—; attending staff Louis A. Weiss Hosp., Chgo., 1986—; lectr. sci. and lay orgns. in field of headaches, pain mgmt., internal medicine, pharmacology. Contbr. chpts. to books and articles to profl. jours. Served to maj. USAF, 1980-86. Named one of Outstanding Young Men Am., 1986; recipient teaching award Am. Acad. Family Physicians, 84, 85, 86. Fellow Am. Coll. Physicians; mem. Am. Fedn. Clin. Research, Am. Assn. for Study of Headache, Internat. Headache Soc., Am. Soc. Clin. Pharmacology and Therapeutics, Alpha Omega Alpha, Psi Upsilon. Avocations: travel, reading, films. Office: Diamond Headache Clinic 5252 N Western Ave Chicago IL 60625

SOLOMON, MARK RAYMOND, law educator, lawyer; b. Pitts., Aug. 23, 1945; s. Louis Isadore and Fern Rhea (Josselson) S. BA, Ohio State U., 1967; MEd, Cleve. State U., 1971; JD with honors, George Washington U., 1973; LLM in Taxation, Georgetown U., 1976. Bar: Ohio, Mich. Tax law specialist corp. tax br. Nat. Office of IRS, 1973-75; assoc. Butzel, Long, Gust, Klein & Van Zile, Detroit, 1976-78; dir., v.p. Shatzman & Solomon, P.C., Southfield, Mich., 1978-81; prof., chmn. tax and bus. law dept., dir. MS in Taxation Program, Walsh Coll., Troy, Mich., 1981—; of counsel in tax matters Meyer, Kirk, Snyder and Safford, Bloomfield Hills, Mich., 1981—; adj. prof. law U. Detroit, 1977-81. Editor: Cases and Materials on Consolidated Tax Returns, 1978. Mem. ABA, Mich. Bar Assn., Phi Eta Sigma. Lodge: Kiwanis (bd. dirs). Avocation: bridge (life master). Home: 2109 Golfview Dr Apt 102 Troy MI 48084 Office: Meyer Kirk Snider and Safford 100 W Long Lake Rd Suite 100 Bloomfield Hills MI 48013

SOLOMON, RICHARD JAY, architect; b. Chgo., May 20, 1943; s. Louis Richard and Jeanne (Handelman) S.; children: Aaron Louis, Jonathan Daniel. Student, Brandeis U., 1961-63; BArch, MIT, 1967; MA in Environ. Design, Yale U., 1969. Registered architect, Ill. Pvt. practice architecture Chgo., 1974—; adj. asst. prof. archtl. design U. Ill., Chgo., 1980—. Contbr. articles to profl. jours. Bd. dirs. F. Heller Jewish Community Ctr., Chgo., 1985—; bd. trustees Francis W. Parker Sch., Chgo., 1987—. Mem. AIA, Chgo. Archtl. Club, Arts Club. Avocations: writing, collecting. Home: 501 W Oakdale Chicago IL 60657

SOLTI, SIR GEORG, conductor; b. Budapest, Hungary, Oct. 21, 1912; naturalized Brit. citizen, 1972; s. Mor Stern and Theres (Rosenbaum) S.; m. Hedi Oechsli, Oct. 29, 1946; m. Anne Valerie Pitts, Nov. 11, 1967; 2 daus. Ed., Budapest Music High Sch.; Mus.D. (hon.), Leeds U., 1971, Oxford U., 1972, DePaul U., Yale U., 1974, Harvard U., 1979, Furman U., 1983, Sussex U., 1983, London U., 1986, Rochester U., 1987, London U., 1986, Rochester U., 1987. Mus. asst., Budapest Opera House, 1930-39, pianist, Switzerland, 1939-45; gen. music dir., Munich (Germany) State Opera, 1946-52, Frankfurt (Germany) City Opera, 1952-60, mus. dir. Royal Opera House Covent Garden, London, 1961-71, Chgo. Symphony Orch., 1969—, Orchestre de Paris, 1972-75; prin. condr. and artistic dir. London Philharm., 1979-83, condr. emeritus, London Philharm., 1983—; pianist Concours Internat., Geneva, 1942; guest condr. various orchs. including N.Y. Philharm., Vienna Philharm., Berlin Philharm., London Symphony, New Philharmonia, Bayerischer Rundfunk, Norddeutscher Rundfunk, Salzburg, Edinburgh, Glyndebourne, Ravinia and Bayreuth Festivals, Vienna State, Met. Opera; condr. concert tours with Chgo. Symphony to Europe, 1971, 74, 78, 81, 85, Chgo. Symphony to Japan, 1977, 86; prin. guest condr. Paris Opera Bicentennial Tour, 1976, rec. artist for London Records. Decorated Great Cross of the German Republic, knight comdr.'s cross, 1986 with Badge and Star; knight comdr. Order Brit. Empire; comdr. Legion of Honor, France; recipient grand prix du Disque Mondiale, 1959, 62, 63, 64, 66, 70, 77, 82; Grammy award (26) Silver medal of Paris, 1984. Hon. fellow Royal Coll. Music (London). Office: Chgo Symphony Orch 220 S Michigan Ave Chicago IL 60604

SOLTIS, ROBERT ALAN, lawyer; b. Gary, Ind., Jan. 30, 1955; s. George William and Frances Marie (Jakob) S. AB (scholar), Ind. U., 1977; JD, DePaul U., 1982. Bar: Ill. 1982, Ind. 1982, U.S. Dist. Ct. (no. dist.) Ill. 1982, U.S. Dist. Ct. (no. and so. dists.) Ind. 1982, U.S. Ct. Apls. (7th cir.) 1983, U.S. Dist. Ct. Trial (no. dist.) Ill. 1984, Ind. Indsl. Bd. 1982; lic. instrument-rated pilot. Photographer Herald Newspapers, Merrillville, Ind., 1971-72; dep. coroner Lake County, Ind., 1972-78, spl. dep. sheriff, 1972-78; dep. coroner, Monroe County, Ind., 1975-76; area dir. Mayors Office of Urban Conservation, Gary, 1977-80; title examiner Law Bull. Title Services, Chgo., 1980; field clm. rep. Employers Ins. of Wausau, River Forest, Ill., 1980-82; assoc. Perz & McGuire, P.C., Chgo., 1982-84, McKenna, Storer, Rowe, White & Farrug, Chgo., 1984—. Co-host twice weekly TV show: Cancer and You, Bloomington, Ind., 1975-76; contbr. articles in field of cancer. Dir. pub. info. Am. Cancer Soc., Gary, 1977-79, Monroe County unit, 1975-76; pres. Gary Young Dems., 1977-78; precinct committeeman Dem. Party, Gary, 1978-82; bd. dirs. N.W. Ind. Urban League; chmn. Com. to Retain State Rep. William Drozda, 1978-82. Recipient Outstanding Reporter award Lake County Mar. of Dimes, 1973, Disting. Service award Am. Cancer Soc. Ind. Div., 1975-76. Mem. Ill. Bar Assn., Chgo. Bar Assn., Ind. Bar Assn., Lawyer-Pilots Bar Assn., Aircraft Owners and Pilots Assn., Glen Park Jaycees (founder, charter pres. 1977), Nat. Press Photographers Assn., Am. Soc. Mag. Photographers, Ind. U. Alumni Assn. (life). Roman Catholic. Club: Slovak (Gary). Home: 1711 W 105th Pl Chicago IL 60643 Office: McKenna Storer Rowe White & Farrug 135 S LaSalle St #4200 Chicago IL 60603

SOLTYKIEWICZ, DARIUSZ JOSEPH, mechanical engineer; b. Chgo., May 10, 1961; s. Joseph and Wanda Maria (Zawlocki) S. BSME, BS in Thermo-Mech. Engring., U. Ill., Chgo., 1984, MS in Mech. Engring., 1987. Sales engr. No. Ill. Gas, Naperville, 1984-85, devel. engr., 1985-86; mem. tech. staff AT&T Info. Systems, Naperville, 1986—. Mem. ASME (vice chmn. student chpt. 1983-84). Avocations: football, softball, photography, golf. Office: AT&T Info Systems 1100 E Warrenville Naperville IL 60566

SOLTYSIAK, SANDRA KANTNER, automotive company executive; b. Dearborn, Mich., Aug. 19, 1948; d. John Henry and Ileine Lucille (Merz) Kantner; m. Gregory Peter Soltysiak, June 20, 1970; 1 son, John. B.A., Mich. State U., 1971, M.Labor and Indsl. Relations, 1978. Dissertation sec. U. Mich., Ann Arbor, 1970-72, research asst. Survey Research Ctr., 1972-73; placement rep., compensation rep. and labor relations rep. Ford Motor Co., Dearborn, Mich., 1973-76; compensation adminstr., mgr. compensation, dir. compensation, benefits and services Mich. Consol. Gas Co., Detroit, 1976-78; dir. compensation and benefits Mich. Nat. Bank, Lansing, 1979; supr. salaried personnel Oldsmobile div. Gen. Motors Corp., Lansing, 1979-80, adminstrv. coordinator, 1981-85; supt. material prodn. control Buick-Oldsmobile-Cadillac group, 1985—; supt. materials, quality, 1986-87; instr. Lansing Community Coll, 1980-81; seminar leader Mich. State U. Bus. Sch., 1980-81. Vol. Capital Area United Way, Lansing, 1981-82, team capt., 1983; chmn. personnel and adminstrv. com., 1985. Maj. irms div., bd. dirs., 1985—, Lansing Health Found., 1986—; chmn. vocations com. St. Mary's Cathedral, Lansing, 1982-87; adv. bd. Sch. Labor and Indsl. Relations Mich. State U., 1983—. Recipient Chmn.'s Excellence in Community Activities award GM, 1987. Roman Catholic. Office: Buick-Oldsmobile-Cadillac Group 920 Townsend Lansing MI 48921

SOMER, BEN MARTIN, dentist; b. Walnut, Nebr., Feb. 11, 1922; s. Joseph John and Augusta Henrietta (Block) S.; m. Phyllis Jean Bradwell, Dec. 26, 1948; children: Douglas, Cindy, Lisa, Randy. BS, U. Nebr., 1948, DDS, 1950. Pvt. practice dentistry Grand Island, Nebr., 1950—. Served to lt. (j.g.) USN, 1942-46. Mem. ADA, Nebr. Dental Assn., VFW (commdr. 1957). Republican. Lodges: Lions (pres. Grand Island club 1983), Elks (exalted ruler Grand Island club 1960). Avocations: bowling, golf, fishing, water skiing. Home: 2222 W Oklahoma Grand Island NE 68803

SOMERS, ALAN BROUNELL, neurologist; b. Indpls., July 30, 1941; s. Earl J. and Roberta D. (Dilling) S.; m. Kathryn J. Kenealy, Nov. 27, 1965; children: Lissa, Amy, Megan. AB, Ind. U., Bloomington, 1963; MD, Ind. U., Indpls., 1968. Diplomate Am. Bd. Psychiatry and Neurology. Intern Blodgett Meml. Hosp., Grand Rapids, Mich., 1968-69; resident U. Iowa, 1971-74, instr. neurology, 1974-75; practice medicine specializing in neurology Bloomington, 1975—; asst. prof. neurology Ind. U., Bloomington, 1975—; bd. dirs. Bloomington Hosp. Bd. dirs. The Am. Spectator Ednl. Found., Arlington, Va., 1972—. Fellow Am. Acad. Neurology. Republican. Methodist. Home: 1100 S High St Bloomington IN 47401 Office: 719 W 2d St Bloomington IN 47401

SOMERS, CANDY LEE, management consultant; b. Ypsilanti, Mich., Oct. 16, 1947; s. Ted and Edna Maxine (McClish) Whitt. BS, Ind. U., 1985. Organizational devel. cons. Delco Electronics Corp. div. Gen. Motors, Kokomo, Ind., 1970—. Alumni bd. dirs. Ind. U., Bloomington, 1985—. Mem. Am. Soc. Tng. and Devel., Assn. for Psychol. Type. Home: 1700 East Alto Rd Kokomo IN 46902 Office: Delco Electronics Corp div Gen Motors 700 E Firmin St Kokomo IN 46902

SOMERVILLE, PERRY WILSON, accountant, educator; b. Akron, Ohio, Dec. 8, 1940; d. Dawson Perry and Effie Pauline (Hanes) Wilson; m. David L. Somerville, Feb. 8, 1964 (div. Jan. 1973); children: David L. Jr., Thomas A. BSBA in Edn., U. Akron, 1983, MBA, 1985. CPA, Ohio. Pres. Somerville Entertprises, Inc., Akron, 1982-86; v.p., ptnr. Dietz, Somerville & Co., Medina, Ohio, 1986—; instr. Malone Coll., Canton, Ohio, 1986. Mem. Nat. Assn. Accts (newsletter editor, dir. communications, 1983-85, bd. dirs., sec. 1980-83), Am. Inst. CPA's, Ohio Soc. CPA's. Republican. Home: 2939 Smith Rd Bath OH 44210 Office: Dietz Somerville and Co 124 W Washington Medina OH 44258

SOMIT, ALBERT, political educator; b. Chgo., Oct. 25, 1919; s. Samuel and Mary (Rosenblum) S.; m. Leyla D. Shapiro, Aug. 31, 1947; children: Scott H., Jed L. A.B., U. Chgo., 1941, Ph.D., 1947. Prof. polit. philosophy N.Y. U., 1945-65; chmn. dept. polit. sci. State U. N.Y. at Buffalo, 1966-69, exec. v.p., 1970-80; acting pres. SUNY, Buffalo, 1976-77, pres. So. Ill. U., Carbondale, 1980-87, disting. service prof., 1987—; fellow Netherlands Inst. Advanced Study, 1978-79; Nimitz prof. polit. philosophy U.S. Naval War Coll., 1961-62. Author: (with Joseph Tanenhaus) The Development of American Political Science: From Burgess to Behavioralism, 1967, expanded edit., 1982, (with Tanenhaus) American Political Science: A Profile of A Discipline, 1964, Political Science and the Study of the Future, 1974, Biology and Politics: Recent Explorations, 1976, (with others) The Literature of Biopolitics 1963-1977, 1978, 1980, 1983, 1986. Served with AUS, 1950-52. Home: 1314 Meadowbrook Carbondale IL 62901

SOMMER, JOSEPH THOMAS, magnetic coil company executive; b. Chgo., Apr. 23, 1941; s. Joseph J. and Solveig E. Sommer; children: Joseph Thomas, Jeffrey Todd. BS, U. Ill., 1964. With Magnetic Coil Mfg. Co., Chgo., 1964—, exec. v.p., 1972-87, pres. 1987—; mgmt. cons. Mem. Sigma Chi (bd. dirs. chpt.).

SOMMERFELD, DAVID WILLIAM, lawyer, educator; b. Detroit, Jan. 21, 1942; s. Henry Anthony and Hilda (Diffley) S.; m. Anne Marlaine Toth, June 27, 1964; children: Catherine, David Jr., Michael, Caroline. BS, U. Detroit, 1963; JD, Detroit Coll., 1967. Trust officer Nat. Bank Detroit, 1963-68; tax supr. Ernst & Ernst, Detroit, 1968-73; ptnr. Monaghan, Campbell, LcPrete & McDonald, Detroit, 1973-77; prof. Detroit Coll., 1977—; ptnr. Butzel Long Gust Klein & Van Zile, Detroit, 1987—; lectr. Ind. Soc. CPA's, Indpls., 1980-87, Ohio Soc. CPA's, Columbus, 1987, W.Va. Soc. CPA's, Charleston, 1983-86. Editor Mich. Probate and Trust Law Jour., 1981-83. Mem. Mich. Bar Assn., Detroit Bar Assn., Am. Inst. CPA's, Mich. Assn. CPA's. Roman Catholic. Club: Detroit Athletic. Avocations: bowling, spectator sports, gardening. Home: 272 N Cranbrook Rd Birmingham MI 48009 Office: Butzel Long Gust Klein & Van Zile Prof Corp 1881 First Nat Bldg Detroit MI 48226

SOMMERS, DANA EUGENE, insurance agency executive; b. Marion, Ind., Oct. 15, 1953; s. Darlton L. and Martha F. (Bontrager) S.; m. Judy L. Grotenhuis, Aug. 21, 1976; children: Erin L., Danae N. BA in Social Work, Taylor U., 1976; MA in Student Personnel Adminstrn., Ball State U., 1977. Resident dir., coordinator Calvin Coll., Grand Rapids, Mich., 1977-79; ins. agt. F.W. Grotenhuis Underwriters, Grand Rapids, 1979-80, ops. mgr., agt., 1980-81; v.p. adminstrn., treas. F.W Grotenhuis Underwriters, Inc., Grand

Rapids, 1981-82, exec. v.p., treas., 1982-83, pres., treas., 1983—; chmn. Mich. agts. adv. com. Firemans Fund Ins. Co., Detroit, 1986—; mem. Jonathan Trumball council Hartford Ins. Co., Grand Rapids, 1986—, agts. adv. council Aetna Ins. Co., Grand Rapids, 1986—. Vice-chmn., bd. dirs. Grand Rapids Area Youth for Christ, 1986—; chmn. Grand Rapids campaign Mich. Colls. Found., Southfield, 1985-87, chmn. program com. 1987— ; bd. dirs. Maranatha Bible Conf., chmn. personnel com., Muskegon, Mich. 1986—; Mem. Devel. Council St. Mary's Hosp., Grand Rapids, 1987—. Mem. Greater Grand Rapids C. of C. (co-chmn. program com. 1986—). Republican. Club: Cascade Hills Country (Grand Rapids). Lodge: Grand Rapids Downtown Rotary. Avocations: reading, biking, golf. Office: F W Grotenhuis Underwriters Inc 660 Cascade W Pkwy SE Grand Rapids MI 49516-6407

SOMMERS, DAVID LYNN, architect; b. Salem, Ohio, June 17, 1949; s. Carl Ervin and Jean (Mohr) S.; m. Linda Loretta Eves, Aug. 28, 1982. BArch, Kent State U., 1974. Registered architect, Ohio. Designer, draftsman Rice & Stewart, Architects, Painesville, Ohio, 1974-76; assoc. architect Prentiss Brown Assoc., Kent, Ohio, 1977-81; project architect Edward W. Prusak, Assoc., Ravenna, Ohio, 1982-83; pvt. practice Kent, 1983—. Mem. archtl. adv. com. Kent Planning Commn., 1985—; bd. dirs. Townhall II Drug and Crisis Intervention Ctr., Kent, 1986. Named one of Outstanding Young Men of Am., 1979-81. Mem. AIA, Architects Soc. Ohio, Kent Jaycees (pres. 1981-82, Jaycee of Yr. 1980, Keyman of Yr., 1981). Lodge: Rotary. Home: 760 N Main St #106 Kent OH 44240 Office: 136 N Water St #208 Kent OH 44240

SOMMERS, PAUL ALLEN, health care executive; b. Marshfield, Wis., Apr. 9, 1945; s. Frank Albert and Rosalie Bertha (Steffen) S.; B.S., U. Wis., 1967; M.S., So. Ill. U., 1969, PH.D., 1971; m. Carol Ann Newsom, June 10, 1967; children—Eric Paul, Marc Allen. Instr. health/phys. edn. Wisconsin Rapids (Wis.) public schs., 1967-68; instr. dept. health/phys. edn. So. Ill. U., Carbondale, 1968-69, research asso. dept. spl. edn., 1969-70, instr., 1970-71; evaluation cons. Minn. State Dept. Edn., St. Paul, 1971-72; dir. Spl. Edn. Services-Coop. Edn. Service Agy. 4, Cumberland, Wis., 1972-73; dir. spl. edn. services Wausau (Wis.) Dist. public schs., 1973-75; dir. liaison edn. affairs Comprehensive Child Care Center, Marshfield (Wis.) Clinic and Med. Found., 1975-80; instr. exeptional children U. Wis., Stevens Point, 1973-79, Milton (Wis.) Coll., 1973-79; exec. dir. Comprehensive Child Care Center, asst. adminstr. Gundersen Clinic, LaCrosse, Wis., 1980-85; chief adminstrv. officer Ramsey Clinic, St. Paul, 1985—; field editor div. spl. edn. and rehab. U.S. Dept. Edn., 1982—. Bd. dirs. Midstate Epilepsy Ctr., 1976-78, Neurodevel. Inst. for Cerebral Palsy, Wausau Med. Center, 1973-80; bd. dirs., mem. edn. policy com. Sunburst Youth Homes for Emotionally Disturbed, 1975-80, Wis. Assn. Perinatal Centers, 1976-79. Recipient Disting. Service award Epilepsy Assn., 1980; Nat. Doctoral Honors fellow, 1970-71; State of Ill. Masters Honors fellow, 1969-70; State of Wis. scholar, 1966-67, many grants. Mem. Am. Public Health Assn., Nat. Council Adminstrs. of Spl. Edn., Wis. Council Adminstrs. of Spl. Edn. (exec. officer 1975-76), Council for Exceptional Children, Am. Assn. on Mental Deficiency, United Cerebral Palsy Assn. Am., United Cerebral Palsy Assn. Wis., Nat. Epilepsy Assn., Wis. Epilepsy Assn. (pres. Midstate Ctr. 1978-80), Easter Seal Soc. Wis. (v.p. 1978-79), Wis. Assn. Perinatal Centers, Wis. Assn. Children with Learning Disabilities (profl. adv. bd. 1983-85), Am. Med. Group Practice Assn. (mktg. com. 1983-85), Med. Group Mgmt. Assn. Lutheran. Contbr. articles to profl. jours. and books. Office: Ramsey Clinic 640 Jackson St Saint Paul MN 55101

SOMS, ANDREW PETER, mathematics educator; b. Riga, Latvia, Mar. 7, 1938; came to U.S., 1950, naturalized, 1956; s. Peter and Elsa S.; B.S. with high honors in Math. (Disting. Alumni fellow 1956-60), Mich. State U., 1960; M.S. in Math. (Woodrow Wilson fellow 1960-61), U. Wis., Madison, 1961, M.S. in Statistics (Wis. Alumni Research Found. fellow 1968-70), 1970, Ph.D. in Statistics (fellow 1970-71), 1972. Statistician, Mich. State Dept. Health, Lansing, 1961-62, Delco Electronics, Milw., 1962-68; computer scientist Burroughs, Wayne, Pa., 1973; sr. statistician G.D. Searle & Co., Skokie, Ill., 1973-75; asso. prof. dept. math., U. Wis., Milw., 1975—; vis. asst. prof. Math. Research Center, summer 1978, fall 1979; cons. pharm. firms. Research grantee U. Wis., Milw., 1976-77, 77-78; Office Naval Research co-grantee, 1979-82. Mem. Am. Statis. Assn., Biometrics Soc., Inst. Math. Stats., Statis. Soc. Can. Contbr. papers in field to sci. publs. Home: 401 N Eau Claire Madison WI 53705 Office: Dept Math U Wis-Milw PO Box 413 Milwaukee WI 53201

SONDEREGGER, THEO BROWN, psychology educator; b. Birmingham, Ala., May 31, 1925; s. Ernest T. and Vera M. (Sillox) B.; children: Richard Paul, Diane Carol, Douglas Robert. BS, Fla. State U., 1946; MA in Chemistry, U. Nebr., 1948, MA in Exptl. Psychology, 1960; PhD in Clin. Psychology, U. Nebr., 1965. Lic. psychologist, Calif; clin. lic., cert. Nebr. Asst. prof. U. Nebr. Med. Ctr., Omaha, 1965-71, Nebr. Wesleyan U., Lincoln, 1965-68; asst. prof. U. Nebr., Lincoln, 1968-71, assoc. prof., 1971-76, prof., 1976—; vol. assoc. prof. U. Nebr. Med. Ctr., 1972-77, courtesy prof. med. psychology, 1977—. Editor Nebr. Symposium on Motivation, 1984, Problems of Perinatal Drug Dependence: Research and Clinical Implications, 1986, Neurobehavioral Toxicology and Teratology Vol. 8, editor (with others) Nebr. Symposium on Motivation, 1974, Problems of Perinatal Drug Dependence, 1979, 1982, 1984, (with E. Zimmermann) Neurobehavioral Toxicology and Teratology. Tribute to Women award Lincoln YWCA, 1985. Mem. Am. Psychol. Assn., Midwestern Psychol. Assn., Internat. Soc. Devel. Psychobiology, Internat. Soc. Psychoneuroendocrinolty, Nebr. Psychol. Assn. (pres. 1972—), Soc. Neuroscis., Phi Beta Kappa (sec. Nebr. chpt. 1974), Sigma Xi (pres. 1986). Club: Altrusa YWCA. Avocations: painting, photography. Office: U Nebr 229 Burnett Hall Lincoln NE 68588

SONDHI, ANOOP, orthodontics educator; b. New Delhi, Feb. 15, 1952; came to U.S., 1975; s. Bal Raj and Kamla (Sein) S.; m. Rani Singh, Feb. 10, 1980; children: Jason Raj, Sara Renee. B of Dental Surgery, U. Lucknow, India, 1974; MS, U. Ill., Chgo., 1977; DDS, Ind. U., Indpls., 1982. Lectr. orthodontics Ind. U. Sch. Dentistry, Indpls., 1977, asst. prof., 1977-81, assoc. prof., 1981—, mem. grad. com., 1979—, chmn. 3d yr. promotions com., 1984. Contbr. articles to profl. jours. Mem. ADA, Am. Assn. Orthodontists, Am. Assn. Dental Research, Internat. Assn. Dental Research, Ind. Soc. Orthodontists (pres. 1987—), Mensa, Omicron Kappa Upsilon (chmn. membership com. 1983-84). Home: 12958 Brighton Ave Carmel IN 46032 Office: Ind Univ Sch of Dentistry Dept of Orthodontics 1121 W Michigan St Indianapolis IN 46202

SONG, AGNES YOUNG, psychologist; b. Pusan, Korea, July 28, 1937; came to U.S., 1957; d. Kee-Yon Bae and Ko-Soon Kim; m. Ralph H. Song , July 28, 1968; children: Lisa, Sandra, Thomas. Student, St. Francis Coll., 1960; PhD, The Cath. U. Am., 1965. Lic. Psychologist. Intern Md. Dept. Mental Hygiene, 1964-65; sch. psychologist Coop. Ednl. Service Agy. #18, Burlington, Wis., 1968-71; staff psychologist So. Wis. Ctr., Madison, 1971-76, chief psychologist, 1976—. Author Wis. behavior rating scale, 1967; contbr. articles to profl. jours. NIMH grantee 1967. Fellow Am Assn. Mental Deficiency (v.p. psychology sect. 1978-80); mem. Am. Psycholo. Assn., Soc. Clin. Consulting Psychology, 1982—, Wis. Psychol. Assn., Child Birth and Parent Edn. Assn. (adv. bd. 1983—). Avocations: camping, traveling. Home: 925 Burningwood Way Madison WI 53704

SONG, TAE-SUNG, real estate appraiser, consultant; b. Seoul, June 11, 1941; came to U.S., 1967; s. Won Do Song and Un Hae Lim; m. Chae-Ryong Moon, Dec. 27, 1969; children: Edward, Sumie. BBA in Acctg. and Mgmt., Yonsei U., Seoul, 1964; MBA in Real Estate and Urban Land Econs., U. Wis., 1971. Appraiser, analyst Am. Appraisal Co., Milw., 1971-74, Real Estate Research Corp., St. Louis, 1974-78; regional v.p. Marshall and Stevens, Inc., St. Louis, 1978—; cons. in field. Mem. Am. Inst. Real Estate Appraisers (nat. grader demonstration report 1983-87); Mo. and Am. Real Estate and Urban Econs. Assn.(membership chmn.). Office: Marshall and Stevens Inc 818 Olive St Saint Louis MO 63101

SONI, VARUN, health care products facility administrator; b. Amritsar, Punjab, India, Nov. 13, 1954; came to U.S., 1977; s. Ved Prakash and Kanta (Chopra) S.; m. Lisa P. Meagher, Dec. 13, 1986. BA in Tech., Indian Inst. Tech., 1975; MA in Mgmt., Northwestern U., 1979. Research assoc. Indsl. Devel. Services, New Delhi, India, 1975-77; pres. Accucare Div. Medline Industries, Inc., Mundelein, Ill., 1979—. Avocations: tabletennis, racquetball, swimming, reading, travel. Office: Medline Industries Inc 1 Medline Place Mundelein IL 60062

SONNE, THOMAS ERIC, surgeon, otolaryngologist; b. Louisville, Aug. 19, 1951; s. Irving Hamilton and Agnes Louise (Johnson) S.; m. Kim Taylor, June 7, 1986; children: Thomas, Chris, Jaclyn. AB, Ind. U., 1973; MD, U. Louisville, 1977. Diplomate Am. Bd. Otolaryngology, Am. Bd. Head and Neck Surgery. Resident in gen. surgery Mich. State U., Grand Rapids, 1977-79; resident in ear, nose, throat and neck surgery Ind. U., Indpls., 1979-82; practice medicine specializing in otolaryngological surgery New Albany, Ind., 1982—; surgeon Floyd County Hosp., New Albany, 1982—, Harrison County Hosp., Corydon, Ind., 1982—, Clark County Hosp., Jeffersonville, Ind., 1982—; bd. dirs. Otology Clinic southern Ind. Fellow: ACS, Am. Coll. Head and Neck Surgeons; mem. AMA (del. Chgo. chpt.). Republican. Roman Catholic. Office: 1919 State St New Albany IN 47150

SONNINO, CARLO BENVENUTO, elec. mfg. co. exec.; b. Torino, Italy, May 12, 1904; came to U.S., 1952, naturalized, 1959; s. Moise and Amelia S.; m. Mathilde Girodat, Jan. 21, 1949; children—Patricia, Frederic, Bruno. Ph.D., U. Milano, Italy, 1927, LL.B., 1928. Dir. research Italian Aluminum Co., Milano, 1928-34; pres. Laesa Cons. Firm, Milano, 1934-43; tech. adviser Boxal, Fribourg, Switzerland, 1944-52, Thompson Brand, Rouen, France, 1972-76; materials engring. mgr. Emerson Electric Co., St. Louis, 1956-72; staff scientist Emerson Electric Co., 1973—; prof. metall. engring. Washington U., St. Louis, 1960-68, U. Mo., Rolla, 1968—; cons. Monsanto Chem. Co., Wagner Co., other maj. firms, U.S., Europe. Decorated knight comdr. Italian Republic. Fellow Am. Soc. Metals, ASTM (hon.), Alpha Sigma Mu. Patentee process for synthetic cryolite; patentee in field of metallurgy, corrosion; mfr. 1st aluminum cans in world, 1940. Home: 7206 Kingsbury Blvd Saint Louis MO 63130 Office: Emerson E and S Div Emerson Electric Co 8100 Florissant St Saint Louis MO 63136

SONTAG, M. SUZANNE, human ecology educator; b. Erie, Pa., July 20, 1944; d. George Joseph and Myrtle Marian (Davis) S.; m. Richard Shields Hurst, Sept. 7, 1985. BA, Mercyhurst Coll., 1966; MS, Cornell U., 1969; PhD, Mich. State U., 1978. Asst. prof. home econs. Mercyhurst Coll., Erie, 1969-76; prof. clothing and textiles Mich. State U., East Lansing, 1979—. Contbr. articles to profl. jours. Grantee Mich. State U., 1987. Mem. Am. Home Econs. Assn., Nat. Council on Family Relations, Assn. Coll. Profs. of Textiles and Clothing (mem. council cen. region), Soc. for Human Ecology (2d v.p. 1987—). Club: University. Avocations: running, genealogy, needlework, reading. Home: 1238 Ivanhoe Dr East Lansing MI 48823 Office: Mich State U Coll Human Ecology Dept Human Environment Design East Lansing MI 48824-1030

SOORIYAARACHCHI, GAMINI S., oncologist, hematologist, internist. MB, BS with honors, U. Ceylon; LRCP, MRCS, Royal Coll. Physiciansof London; MRCP, Royal Coll. Physicians of U.K. Diplomate Am. Bd. Internal Medicine, Am. Bd. Med. Oncology, Am. Bd. Hematology. Research assoc., fellow U. Wis. Comprehensive Cancer Ctr., Madison, 1975-77; clin. asst. prof. U. Ill. Coll. Medicine, Rockford, 1977-83; assoc. clin. prof. Creighton U. Sch. Medicine, Omaha, 1983—; cons. hematologist-oncologist Bergan Mercy Hosp., Omaha, 1983-86, St. Joseph's Hosp., Omaha, 1983-86, Luth. Gen. Hosp., Omaha; dir. nutritional support service Bergan Mercy Hosp., Omaha. 1983—. Contbr. articles to profl. jours. Fellow ACP; mem. Am. Soc. Clin. Oncology, Am. Soc. Hematology, Royal Coll. Physicians U.K., Am. Soc. for Parenteral and Enteral Nutrition.

SOORYA, NARENDIR TOLARAM, psychiatrist; b. Karachi, Pakistan, May 10, 1939; s. Tolaram Khemchand and Savitri T. Soorya; m. Sarla Rangwani, July 16, 1967; children: Geeta Nitin, Sandeep. Intermediate sci. degree, D.J. Sci. Coll., Karachi, 1958; med. degree, Dow Med. Coll., 1964. Intern Deaconess Hosp., St. Louis, 1964-65; resident in psychiatry Cen. State Hosp., Milledgeville, Ga., 1965-68, staff psychiatrist, 1968-71; child psychiatrist Washington U./Malcolm Bliss, St. Louis, 1971-72; pvt. practice psychiatry St. Louis, 1974—. Mem. Am. Psychiat. Assn., Am. Acad. Child Psychiatry, Am. Medicine Soc. on Alcoholism and Other Drug Dependencies, Am. Coll. Internat. Physicians, Eastern Mo. Psychiat. Soc., St. Louis Med. Soc. Office: 6651 Chippewa Saint Louis MO 63109

SOPER, GEORGE EBEN, hospital administrator, physical therapist; b. Mason City, Iowa, July 3, 1938; s. George Eben and Helen Margaret (Towle) S.; m. Jannis Esther Boardman, Aug. 15, 1959; childen—Jennifer, Jonathon; m. 2d, Sandra Kapff, Apr. 18, 1970; children—Teresa, Jessica. B.A., U. No. Iowa, 1961; M.A., U. Iowa, 1967, Ph.D., 1976. Cert. phys. therapy, U. Iowa. Tchr., coll. community schs., Cedar Rapids, Iowa, 1961-64; chief, phys. therapist Myrtue Meml. Hosp., Harlan, Iowa, 1966-69; supr. phys. therapy U. Iowa Hosp. Sch., Iowa City, 1969-71; dir. phys. therapy U. Iowa Hosps. and Clinics, Iowa City, 1971-80; v.p. Meml. Hosp. of South Bend (Ind.), 1980—; clin. instr. phys. therapy Washington U., St. Louis, 1973-80, Northwestern U., 1974-80; mem. multipurpose arthritis ctr. rev. com., NIH, Dept. HEW, 1978-80; mem. Hawkeye Arena/Recreation Campaign Nat. Com., U. Iowa, 1979-80; mem. Allied Health Professions Research Com. Nat. Arthritis Found., 1981-83; lectr. in field. Bd. dirs. St. Joseph Council for Retarded, South Bend, 1982-87, United Health Services, 1986-87. Recipient Olive Farr Disting. Service award Iowa Phys. Therapy Assn., 1978. Mem. Am. Phys. Therapy Assn. (dir. 1977-80, sec. 1980-83), Am. Phys. Therapy Assn. (Ind. Chpt.), Am. Hosp. Assn. Republican. Club: Knollwood Country (Granger, Ind.). Contbr. articles to profl. jours.; cons. editor Allied Health and Behavioral Scis., 1977-81. Office: Meml Hosp 615 N Michigan St South Bend IN 46601

SOPHER, EDWARD ORRIN, accountant; b. Balt., July 28, 1954; s. Albert Jerome and Betty M. (Dubow) S.; m. Roseanne Schloss, Aug. 27, 1978; children: Jodie Beth, Michelle Arin. BChemE, Ga. Tech. U., 1976; MBA, U. Chgo., 1979. CPA, Ill., Ind. Chem. engr. E.I. DuPont, East Chicago, Ind., 1976-79; mgr. EDP audits Arthur Young, Chgo., 1979—. Treas. Northwest Ind. Jewish Welfare Fedn., Highland, 1986-87, bd. dirs. 1985-87; bd. dirs. Beth Israel Synogogue, Hammond, Ind., 1984-87. Recipient Young Leadership award Northwest Ind. Jewish Welfare Fedn., 1985. Mem. Am. Inst. CPA's, Ill. Soc. CPA's, Ind. Soc. CPA's. Democrat. Home: 9512 Primrose Ln Munster IN 46321 Office: Arthur Young 1 IBM Plaza Chicago IL 60611

SOREM, JAMES RUSSELL, SR., farmer; b. Spearville, Kans., July 7, 1932; s. Roy and Mae (Abel) S.; m. Mary Joanne Schauvliege, Nov. 25, 1954; children: James R. Jr., Richard J., William A., Jennifer J., Robert M. Sorem. BS in Aero. Engring., U. Kans., 1955. Engr. Douglas Aircraft, Tulsa, 1955-56; farmer Jetmore, Kans., 1956—; bd. dirs. Farmers State Bank, Jetmore, Lane-Scott Rural Electrification Coop., Dighton, Kans.; mem. Agrl. Stabilization & Conservations Service County Com., Hodgeman County, 1980—. Chmn. bd. trustees Hodgeman County Health Ctr., Jetmore, 1982—; mem. Area Council on Aging, Jetmore, 1982—; mem. Bd. County Commrs., Hodgeman County, Jetmore, 1964-72. Mem. U. Kans. Alumni Assn., Aircraft Owners and Pilots Assn. Democrat. Roman Catholic. Avocations: hunting, fishing, flying. Address: RR 1 Jetmore KS 67854

SORENSEN, EARL RICHARD, manufacturing company executive; b. Castana, Iowa, Nov. 9, 1919; s. Chris and Emmy (Jensen) S.; m. Phyllis Patton McMurdo, June 13, 1942; children: Lynn Ellen Sorensen Ripley, Gail Ann. BS, Iowa State U., 1941. Mgmt. tng. Internat. Harvester, Mason City, Iowa, 1941-42; mgr. exptl. farms H.D. Hudson Mfg. Co., Fennville, Mich., 1946-78; mgr. pub. affairs H.D. Hudson Mfg. Co., Chgo., 1974-78, v.p., 1978-81, exec. v.p., 1981—, also bd. dirs. Chmn. bd. dirs. Community Hosp., Douglas, Mich., 1960-74; chmn. Harbors Health Care Inc., Douglas, 1982-86; mem. Nat. Bd. Missions United Meth. Ch., N.Y.C., 1965-72; mem. Conf. Bd. Edn., Bd. Lay Activities, Area Commn. Higher Edn. United Meth. Ch., Grand Rapids, Mich., 1956-64; v.p. bd. trustees Adrian (Mich.) Coll., 1974—; bd. dirs. Ctr. for Parish Devel., Chgo., 1972—. Served to capt. USMCR, 1941-46. Decorated Bronze star. Mem. Nat. Migraine Found. (bd. dirs. 1984—), Am. Soc. Farm Mgrs. (1st v.p.), Nat. Cattlemen's Assn., Farm & Indsl. Equipment Inst. (chmn. Nat. Sprayer and Duster Assn. 1980-82, bd. dirs.), Chgo. Farmers Club, Psi Chi, Phi Kappa Tau (pres. 1937). Lodge: Rotary. Home: 2326 68th St Fennville MI 49408 Office: HD Hudson Mfg Co 500 N Michigan Ave Chicago IL 60611

SORENSEN, JIMMY LOUIS, management information services executive, consultant; b. Chgo., June 11, 1927; s. Soren Johannes and Jensine Elizabeth (Jensen) S.; m. Esther Nancy Sorensen, Nov. 27, 1954; children: Nancy, Mark, Karen, Ruth. BA cum laude, Dana Coll., 1951. CPA, Ill. Asst. dir. data processing Continental Assurance Co., Chgo., 1951-57; spl. rep. UARCO, Chgo., 1957-59; asst. treas. Signode Steel, Glenview, Ill., 1959-60; ptnr. Arthur Young & Co., Chgo., 1960-84; dir. mgmt. info. services Cotter & Co., Chgo., 1984—; chmn. Luth. Gen. Health Care System, Park Ridge, Ill., 1985—; bd. dirs. Parkside Health Mgmt. Corp., Parkside Home Health Services, Inc., Luth. Gen. Hosp., Augustana Hosp. chmn. bd. trustees Danish Old People's Home. Chgo., 1976—; chmn. bd. dirs. Pioneer Ministries, Inc.; bd. dirs. Great Lakes Dist. Evang. Free Ch. in Am. Mem. Am. Inst. CPA's, Ill. Soc. CPA's, Midwest Danish Am. C. of C. (treas.). Club: Medinah (Ill.) Country. Home: 329 W Carter Ave Wood Dale IL 60191 Office: Cotter & Co 2740 N Clybourn Chicago IL 60614

SORENSEN, JOHN BRENT, recording studio owner; b. Council Bluffs, Iowa, Sept. 14, 1961; s. Jerry P. Sorenson and Sandy J. (Collins) Brown; m. Denise M. Kopecky, Sept. 25, 1981. Student, Ozark Bible Coll., 1978-80, Creighton U., 1980—. Air personality Sta. KFSB, Joplin, Mo., 1978-80, Sta. WOW, Omaha, 1980-82; prodn. dir. Sta. WOW/KEZ0, Omaha, 1982-85; owner, mgr. Sorenson Sound Studios, Omaha, 1985—. Mem. Audio Engring. Soc. Avocations: hiking, skiing. Home: 3326 S 133rd St Omaha NE 68144 Office: 11319 P St Suite C Omaha NE 68137

SORENSON, DAVID PAUL, architect; b. Rice Lake, Wis., Sept. 2, 1955; s. Neil and Marie (Zimmerman) S,; m. Bette Jean Stodola, Feb. 20, 1982, 1 child, Andrew. Registered architect, Wis. Landscape designer Dewaynes, Cumberland, Wis., 1977-79; architect intern Northern Sun, Eau Claire, Wis., 1979-81, Rice Lakes, 1981-83, Cooper Engring., Rice Lake, 1983-85; architect Cooper Engring., Rice Lakes, 1985—. Mem. AIA. Club: Trout Unltd. (Rice Lake). Avocations: fishing, camping, softball, golf. Home: 1061 22 7/8 St Chetek WI 54728 Office: Cooper Engring 100 W Orchard Beach Rice Lake WI 54868

SORENSON, MICHAEL ROBERT, accountant; b. Sheboygan, Wis., Apr. 3, 1960; s. Herbert A. and Myrtle M. (Sauer) S.; m. Kristi K. Pietsch, July 21, 1984. AS, U. Wis., Sheboygan, 1980; BBA, U. Wis., Whitewater, 1982. CPA, Wis. Staff acct. Gerald R. Van De Kreeke, CPA, S.C., Sheboygan, 1983—; instr. Lakeshore Tech. Inst., Cleve., 1985—. Mem. Am. Inst. CPA's, Wis. Inst. Cert. CPA's. Lutheran. Avocations: camping, tennis. Office: Gerald R Van De Kreeke CPA SC 1530 S 12th St Sheboygan WI 53081

SORGEN, RICHARD JESSE, architect; b. Toledo, Ohio, Aug. 4, 1945; s. William C. and Frances Louise (Lederhaus) S.; m. Ellen Kathleen Mumma, Aug. 19, 1972; children—Brian Richard, Neal Andrew. B.S. in Arch., U. Mich., 1972, M.Arch. with high distinction, 1973, postgrad. U. Toledo, 1974, 80. Registered architect, Ohio, Pa. Designer, Schauder & Martin, Architects, Toledo, Ohio, 1972; project mgr. Sanborn, Steketee, Otis and Evans, Toledo, 1972-76; v.p. Harris Builders, Inc., Toledo, 1977; assoc. Sanzenbacher, Miller, Troy, Dansard, Ltd., Toledo, 1977; partner The Richard Troy Partnership, Toledo, 1977-83; prin. Richard Jesse Sorgen, AIA, Toledo, 1983; dir. archtl. services Donald A. Johnson Architects, Monroe, Mich., 1983—; instr. archtl. tech. Monroe County Community Coll., 1987—. Solicitor, United Way Campaign com., 1981; adminstrv. bd. Epworth United Meth. Ch., 1981-82. Served with USN, 1965-69. Recipient Scholastic award AIA and AIA Found., 1972. Mem. AIA (nat. design com.), Architects Soc. Ohio (trustee 1980), Toledo Mus. Art, Nat. Council Archtl. Registration Bds. Republican. Lodges: Rotary, Elks. Maj. works incl.: Toledo Engring. Co. Hdqrs., YMCA, Oregon, Ohio, Ohio Citizens Bank, Owens Tech. Coll., Jefferson High Sch., Monroe. Office: 25 Washington St Monroe MI 48161

SORIANO, DANILO BUENAFLOR, neurosurgeon; b. Manila, May 15, 1938; s. Restituto F. and Leonisa (Buenaflor) S.; B.S., U. Phillippines, 1957, M.D., 1962; m. Lydianila S. San Pedro, Sept. 5, 1964; children—Brian, Perry, Jennifer. Intern, St. Francis Hosp., Pitts., 1962-63; teaching fellow, resident in neurosurgery U. Pitts., 1964-66; asst. instr. neoranatomy Albert Einstein Coll. Medicine, 1966-67, neurosurgery, 1968-69, instr. neurosurgery, 1969-70; chief of neurosurgery Queens Hosp. Center, N.Y., 1970-73; asst. prof. neurosurgery SUNY-Stony Brook, 1972; chief of neurosurgery Hempstead Gen. Hosp., 1972-74; chief of surgery Palos Community Hosp., Palos Heights, Ill.; cons. neurosurgeon Christ Hosp., Oak Lawn, Ill., Central Community Hosp., Chgo. Trustee Avery Coonley Sch., Downers Grove, Ill. Recipient William C. Menninger award; NIH research fellow. Diplomate Am. Bd. Neurosurgery. Fellow ACS; mem. Am. Assn. Neurol. Surgeons, Congress Neurol. Surgeons, Internat. Coll. Surgeons, AMA, Chgo., Ill. med. socs., Central Neurosurg. Soc., Soc. Functional Neurosurgery, Mensa, U.S. Chess Fedn., Phi Kappa Phi, Phi Sigma. Republican. Roman Catholic. Contbr. articles profl. jours. Research on spinal cord physiology, spasticity, pain. Composer: I Endure (Voice and Piano), 1960; Silangan Quartet (2 Violins, Viola, Cello), 1976. 1st violinist SW Symphony Orch.; mem. Chamber Music Players, Chinquapin Hills String Quartet; concertmaster St. Xavier Chamber Orch. Office: 6600 W College Dr Palos Heights IL 60463

SORTEBERG, KENNETH WARREN, agriculture and real estate sales executive; b. Mpls., July 26, 1945; s. Kenneth L. and Ellen L. (Moynihan) S.; m. Karon L. Burmeister, Dec. 2, 1972; children: Samuel T., Garrett W. BA in Acctg., St. Cloud (Minn.) State U., 1967, MBA in Mgmt. and Fin., 1968. CPA, Minn. Sr. auditor Arthur Andersen & Co., Mpls., 1969-72; asst. v.p. Eberhardt Co., Edina, Minn., 1972-75; pvt. practice acctg. Edina, 1975-80; pres. Diamond S. Livestock Eguipment, Watertown, Minn., 1981-84; ter. mgr. Snell Systems, San Antonio, 1985—; grazing and agr. cons., Watertown, 1980—; real estate cons., Watertown, 1985—; pres. Entry One, Inc. Mem. Minn. Assn. of Realtors, Minn. Cattlemen's Assn., Twin Cities Newfoundland Club, Watertown C. of C., Ducks Unlimited (com. chmn. 1972-80). Roman Catholic. Avocations: skiing, hunting, dog training. Home and Office: 14825 County Rd 122 Watertown MN 55388

SORTO, LOUIS ANTHONY, JR., podiatrist; b. N. Tonawanda, N.Y., Feb. 2, 1946; s. Louis A. and Margaret Sorto; m. Karen B. Dell, Sept. 6, 1969; children: Alexis, Christopher. BS, Western Ill. U., 1969; D of Podiatric Medicine magna cum laude, Ill. Coll. Podiatric Medicine, 1973. Diplomate Am. Bd. Podiatric Surgery. Resident Northlake (Ill.) Community Hosp., 1973-75; practice medicine specializing in foot surgery and sports medicine Des Plaines, Ill., 1975—; mem. staff Northwest Surgicare Ctr., Arlington Heights, Ill., 1975—, Lincoln W. Med. Ctr., Chgo., 1980—, Mt. Sinai Hosp., Chgo., 1984—, Holy Family Hosp., Des Plaines, 1987—; adj. clin. prof. Scholl Coll. Podiatric Medicine, Chgo., 1975—; cons. Westside VA Hosp., Chgo., 1982—, Suburban Sports Medicine Ctr., Des Plaines, Ill., 1983—, Sue Thompson Exercize, Arlington Heights, Ill., 1983—, Chgo. Sports Medicine and Dance Injury Ctr., 1984—, Exercise RX, Arlington Heights, 1984—; team podiatrist Chgo. Sting Profl. Soccer Team, 1986—. Host radio and cable sports medicine shows; contbr. articles to profl. jours. Recipient William J. Stickel award Northlake Community Hosp., 1975. Fellow Am. Coll. Foot Surgeons; mem. Am. Coll. Sports Medicine, Am. Podiatry Assn., Am. Podiatric Med. Assn., Ill. Podiatry Soc. Home: 126 Saddlebrook Dr Oak Brook IL 60521 Office: Podiatry Assocs Ltd 420 Lee St Des Plaines IL 60016 also: 25 E Washington Chicago IL 60602

SORTOR, DONALD CHARLES, computer security executive; b. Chgo., May 21, 1956; s. Charles Joah and Nancy Jean (Weinfeld) S.; m. Donna L. Douglass, Apr. 28, 1984. Analyst Mich. Bell, Detroit, 1979-86; computer security mgr. Mich. Bell, Redford, 1986—. Del. Nat. Reps., 1984—. Served with USN, 1975-79. Mem. Am. Soc. Indsl. Security, Computer Security Inst., Digital Users Soc., Mich. Bell End Users Computing Group (founder, vice chmn. 1985-86, program dir. 1986—). Office: Mich Bell 24251 Acacia Room 201 Redford MI 48239

SOSNOWSKY, WILLIAM PAUL, education educator; b. Hamtramck, Mich., May 6, 1928; s. Michael and Kathryn (Uzych) S.; m. Frances Marie

LaPlante, Oct. 29, 1976; children: William M., Marynell K. B.S. in Edn., Wayne State U., 1955, MA, 1958, EdD, 1965. Lic. psychologist, Mich. Tchr. Detroit Pub. Schs., 1955-57, psychologist, 1957-63; chief psychologist Grosse Pointe (Mich.) Schs., 1963-69; asst. prof. Wayne State U., Detroit, 1969-74, assoc. prof., 1974-78, prof., 1978—; hearing officer State of Mich., 1978—; spl. asst. Detroit Desegregation Case Monitoring Commn., 1976-84. Author: Policy Foundations of Special Education, 1978. Served with USN, 1945-50. Named Educator of Yr., Edn. Alumni Assn., 1985. Mem. Mich. Assn. Profs. Ednl. Adminstr. (sec.-treas.). Greek Catholic. Home: 16813 Cranford Ln Grosse Pointe MI 48230 Office: Wayne State U 385 Education Detroit MI 48202

SOSTROM, SHIRLEY ANNE, organizational communications cons. co. exec., educator; b. Billings, Mont., Dec. 22, 1933; d. Jack Kenneth and Edith Ester (Bates) Thompson; student U. Wyo., 1951-59; B.Sc., No. Ill. U., 1966; M.A., Central State U., Ohio, 1970; Ph.D., Ohio State U., 1976; m. John Philip Sostrom, July 11, 1950; children—John David, Kristen Ingrid, Edith May. Tchr. various high schs., Ohio, Mont., 1966-74; with Carroll Coll., Helena, Mont., 1972-74; lectr. linguistics and writing Sinclair Coll., 1976-78; program coordinator Sch. Public Adminstrn., Ohio State U., Columbus, 1978-80; lectr. English and journalism Muskingum Coll., 1980-81; pres. Sostrom Assocs., pub. relations cons., Columbus, 1979—; prin., dir. human resource services, officer The Sims Cons. Group, Lancaster, Ohio, 1983—; prof. Grad. Sch. Adminstrn., Capital U., Columbus, 1980-86; acting exec. dir. Internat. Materials Mgmt. Soc., Schaumburg, Ill., 1986-87; exec. dir. Health Care Mgmt. Soc., Columbus, 1988—. Mem. Women's Poetry Workshop, Am. Assn. for Tng. and Devel., Internat. Assn. Bus. Communicators, Am. Soc. Public Adminstrn., Ohio State U. Alumni Assn., Phi Delta Kappa. Republican. Club: Zonta. Author chpts. and articles on pub. relations and bus.; contbr. poetry to mags. Home: 99 E Weber St Columbus OH 43202 Office: 2199 E Main St Columbus OH 43209

SOUCY, GERALD PAUL, psychologist, mental health program developer; b. Emunston, N.B., Can., July 29, 1949; came to U.S., 1949; s. Roger and Theresa (Lausier) S. BA with honors, Boston U., 1971; MA with distinction, DePaul U., 1979, PhD with distinction, 1982. Lic. psychologist, Ill. Psychologist Northwest Mental Health, Arlington Heights, Ill., 1982-85; dir. Horizons Psychotherapy, Chgo., 1982-83; support services dir. AIDS project Howard Brown Clinic, Chgo., 1983-85, cons. NIH project, 1985—; dir. Met. Psychotherapy, Chgo., 1983—; cons. Chgo. Dept. Health, 1985—; chmn. Mental Health Group, AIDS Interdisciplinary adv. council State of Ill., 1985—. Author: Psychological Aspects of Asthma, 1983; contbr. articles to profl. jours. Schmitt fellow, 1977, 81. Mem. Am. Orthopsychiat. Assn., Am. Pub. Health Assn., Ill. Pub. Health Assn. Avocations: swimming, skiing, tennis. Home: 909 W Gunnison Chicago IL 60640 Office: Met Psychotherapy 1000 W Diversey Chicago IL 60614

SOUCY, PATRICIA CALLISON, personal property appraiser, educator; b. Lafayette, Ind., Apr. 11, 1950; d. Charles F. and Eileen P. (Neville) Callison; m. John C. Soucy Jr., July 10, 1965; children: Maureen, John. BS in Nursing, Loretto Heights Coll., 1962; MA in Valuation Sci., Lindenwood Coll., 1982, MA in Art History, 1986—. Antique dealer Country Rd. Antiques, Centralia, Mo., 1975-86; antique and decorative arts appraiser Mid-Mo. Appraiser Services, Centralia, 1977—; faculty Lindenwood Coll., St. Charles, Mo., 1983—. Mem. Am. Soc. Appraisers (sr., chpt. sec. 1985, treas. 1986, chmn. valuation scis. program, 1985—, personal property com. 1985, designation in antiques, decorating arts, splty. designation furniture, Valuation Scis. medal 1982). Home and Office: Rt 1 Box 178 Centralia MO 65240

SOUDER, PAUL CLAYTON, banker; b. Greencastle, Ind., Dec. 2, 1920; s. Dewey C. and Julia (Dowell) S.; m. Doris E. Elliott, Sept. 27, 1941; children—Douglas Paul, Julie Jan. A.B., DePauw U., 1941; grad., Harvard Grad. Sch. Bus. Adminstrn., 1943, Grad. Sch. Banking, Rutgers U., 1951. Office mgr. Comml. Credit Corp., 1941; credit mgr. Mich. Nat. Bank, 1946; asst. v.p. Mich. Nat. Bank, Saginaw, 1947-52; v.p. Saginaw, 1952-62, sr. v.p., dir., 1961-71, exec. v.p., 1971-72, pres., dir., 1972-80, vice chmn., 1980-85; chmn. MNC Outstate Banks, 1980; chmn. bd. dirs. Mich. Nat. Bank; bd. dirs. MNB Valley Bank, MNB-West Bank, MNB-Michiana Bank, Mich. Bank-Huron, Mich. Bank-Mid South, Auto-Owners Ins. Co., Auto-Owners Life Ins. Co. Mich. Nat. Bank, Mich. Nat. Corp., Detroit & Mackinac R.R. Co., Jameson Corp., Lake Huron Broadcasting Corp., Homeowners Mut. Ins. Co., Mich. Nat. Bank Midland, Property Owners Ins. Co., Owners Ins. Co., W.F. McNally Co., Inc., Mich. Nat. Bank Detroit, Mich. Nat. bank-Mid Mich.; past chmn. bd. dirs. First Nat. Bank, East Lansing. Author: Financing Oil Production in Michigan, 1951. Past pres. Greater Mich. Found.; trustee Mich. Wildlife Found., Mich. State U. Devel. Fund; bd. dirs., v.p. Frank N. Andersen Found.; bd. dirs. Woldumar Nature Center. Served from ensign to lt. comdr. USNR, 1942-46. Recipient Distinguished Service awards; Saginaw's Outstanding Young Man. Mem. Robert Morris Assos., Am., Mich. bankers assn., Ind. Petroleum Assn., Am., Mich. oil and gas assns., C. of C. (dir.). Methodist. Clubs: Saginaw (Detroit), Bankers (Detroit), Econ. (Detroit); Otsego Ski. Home: 2800 Maurer Rd Charlotte MI 48813 Office: Mich Nat Bank 124 W Allegan St Lansing MI 48901

SOUDERS, WILLIAM LAWRENCE, architect; b. Clarksburg, W.Va., Feb. 23, 1955; s. William Lloyd and Sara Diane (Swisher) S.; m. Janet Lynne Riley, Aug. 14, 1976; children: Aaron Lawrence, Jennifer Ann, Stephanie Lauren. AA, Daytona Beach (Fla.) Community Coll., 1975; B of Design with high honors, U. Fla., 1978; MArch, Ohio State U., 1980. Registered architect, Ohio. Architect Coke Harpham, Inc., Columbus, Ohio, 1980-83; architect and facility mgr. Grant Med. Ctr., Columbus, 1983—; cons. in field; teaching assoc. design and graphic arts Ohio State U., 1978-80; active award-winning urban design case study, Clarksburg, W.Va., 1978-80. Designer: one of first laser ctrs. in U.S. (Presdl. recognition), 1985, obstetrics birthing suites, Ohio, 1985; designer, adminstr: largest ch. in Ohio, 1986. Vice chmn. Planning and Zoning Commn., Pickerington, Ohio, 1985—; mem. Nat. Trust for Hist. Preservation. Mem. AIA, Columbus Chpt. AIA, Architects Soc. Ohio, Tau Sigma Delta (life).

SOUTHWICK, CHRISTOPHER LYN, anesthesiologist; b. Salina, Kans., Jan. 12, 1956; s. Forrest Arthur II and Carolyn Kay (Kauth) S.; m. Laura Lee Stuck, Nov. 17, 1984; 1 child, Andrew William. BS in Chem. Sci., Kans. State U., 1979; MD, U. Kans., 1984. Diplomate Am. Bd. Anesthesiology. Intern Western Res. Care System, Youngstown, Ohio, 1984-85, resident, 1985-87; anesthesiologist Columbia (Mo.) Regional Hosp., 1987—. Mem. AMA, Am. Soc. Anesthesiologists, Ohio Med. Soc., Theta Xi, Alpha Delta Epsilon (pres. 1976-78). Republican. Avocations: racquetball, skiing, basketball. Home: 2911 Bluegrass Ct Columbia MO 65201 Office: Anesthesiologists Inc PO Box 975 Columbia MO 65205

SOVEY, WILLIAM PIERRE, manufacturing company executive; b. Helen, Ga., Aug. 26, 1933; s. Louis Terrell and Kathryn Bell (White) S.; m. Kathryne Owen Doyle, Dec. 28, 1958; children: Margaret Elizabeth, John Todd. B.S.I.E., Ga. Inst. Tech., 1955; grad., Advanced Mgmt. Program, Harvard U., 1976. Gen. mgr. automotive div. Atwood Vacuum Machine Co., Rockford, Ill., 1963-68; v.p. internat. A.G. Spalding & Bros., Inc., Chicopee, Mass., 1968-71; pres. AMF Inc., Ft. Worth, 1971-77; corp. v.p., group exec. Indpls. products group AMF Inc., Stamford, Conn., 1977-79; pres., chief operating officer, dir. AMF Inc., White Plains, N.Y., 1982-85; pres., chief operating officer Newell Co., Freeport, Ill., 1986—, also bd. dirs. Served with USN, 1955-58. Home: 5349 Winding Creek Dr Rockford IL 61111 Office: Newell Co Newell Center Freeport IL 61032

SOVINE, DAVID LOUIS, psychiatrist; b. Indpls., June 12, 1946; s. Joe W. and Lena Pearl (Moss) S.; m. Lydia Frances Hallay, Oct. 21, 1972; children: Erik, Vanessa, Cory, Monika. AB, Ind. U., Bloomington, 1968; MD, Ind. U., Indpls., 1972. Diplomate Am. Bd. Psychiatry and Neurology. Intern, then resident in psychiatry U. Cin., 1972-75; pvt. practice Milw., 1975-82; pres. Associated Mental Health Services, Inc., Milw., 1982—; dir. geriatric psychiatry program St. Anthony's Hosp., Milw., 1982—, Columbia Hosp., Milw., 1984—, St. Michael's Hosp., 1986—. Author: (with others) Textbook of Biological Feedback, 1980. Served to lt. comdr. USN, 1975-77. Fellow Am. Psychiat. Assn. (local pres. 1984); mem. AMA, Milw. Acad. Medicine, Biofeedback Soc. Am. Office: Associated Mental Health Services Inc 250 W Coventry Ct Suite 101 Milwaukee WI 53217

SOWDER, FRED ALLEN, foundation administrator, alphabet specialist; b. Cin., July 17, 1940; s. William Franklin and Lucille (Estes) S.; m. Sandra Ann Siegman, July 15, 1961 (div. Sept. 1963); 1 child, William. Founder World Union for a Universal Alphabet, Cin., 1981—. State dir. Soc. Separationists, Cin., 1967-70; bd. dirs. ACLU of Ohio, ACLU Found., 1984—. Democrat. Home: 4020 Rose Hill Ave Cincinnati OH 45229 Office: World Union Universal Alphabet PO Box 252 Cincinnati OH 45201-0252

SOWERS, RONALD LEE, lawyer; b. Dover, Mo., Apr. 20, 1938; s. John Lee and Mary Katherine (Dysart) S.; m. Launa R. Stayer, June 11, 1960 (div. 1980); children—Julie Ann Sowers de Palomares, Jennifer Lee Sowers Nichols, Jill Susan; m. Cynthia J. Delagrange, Oct. 13, 1984. B.A., U. Notre Dame, 1960, LL.B., 1965, J.D., 1969. Bar: Ind. 1965, U.S. Dist. Ct. (no. and so. dists.) Ind. 1965, U.S. Ct. Appeals (7th cir.) 1970, U.S. Supreme Ct. 1982. Assoc. Torborg, Miller & Moss, Ft. Wayne, Ind., 1965-68; ptnr. Torborg, Miller, Moss, Harris & Sowers, 1968-77; ptnr. Sowers & Benson, 1977-83; prin. Ronald L. Sowers & Assocs., 1983-85; ptnr. Sowers, Larson, Riebenack & Connolly, 1985—. Mem. rehab. com. ARCH, Inc., 1979—; bd. dirs. Downtown Fort Wayne Assn., 1979—; bd. dirs. Notre Dame Law Assn., 1965-75. Served with USMC, 1960-62, to col. USMCR, 1960—. Fellow Belli Soc.; mem. ABA, Assn. Trial Lawyers Am., Ind. Trial Lawyers Assn., Am. Arbitration Assn., Ind. Bar Assn., Allen County Bar Assn., Am. Bd. Trial Advocates (chpt. pres. 1986, bd. dirs. 1986). Republican. Roman Catholic. Office: The Landing 1 Rose Maries Alley Fort Wayne IN 46802-1710

SOWINSKI, ROBERT ALAN, real estate association executive; b. Hobart, Ind., Apr. 21, 1945; s. Frank Alan and Anastasia Rose (Mihalic) S.; m. Vicki Margo Miller, June 8, 1968; children: Gant Miller, Nathan Marcus, Dane Joseph, Jerah Ashley. BS in Psychology, Mo. State U., 1967, MA in Counseling Psychology, 1968; JD, Valparaiso U., 1972. Chmn., chief exec. officer The Combined Capital Group, South Bend, Ind.; founder Combined Capital Corp., Combined Capital Securities Corp., Combined Capital Devel. Corp., Acquisition Assocs., Inc. and Real Estate Mgmt. Corp. Mem. Ind. State Bar Assn. (real estate and taxationsect.), Nat. Assn. Securities Dealers (cert.), Real Estate Securities and Syndication Inst. Home: 10605 Nutmeg Rd Plymouth IN 46563 Office: The Combined Capital Group 211 W Washington Suite 2112 South Bend IN 46601

SPACE, CHRISTOPHER, endodontist; b. Brookville, Pa., Dec. 24, 1952; s. Boggs William and Sue (McAbier) S.; m. Lauren Ann Bollenbacher, Sept. 12, 1981; 1 child, Bryan Christopher. BS, Allegheny Coll., 1974; DDS, Case Western Reserve U., 1978; Cert. in Endodontics, Albert Einstein Med. Ctr., Phila., 1981. Practice dentistry specializing in endodontics Medina, Ohio, 1982—; clin. instr. endodontics Case Western Reserve U., Cleve., 1986—. Mem. ADA, Ohio Dental Assn., Medina County Dental Assn., Am. Assn. Endodontists, Ohio Assn. Endodontists, Case Western Reserve U. Dental Alumni Assn. (bd. dirs. 1986—). Avocations: running, skiing, water skiing. Home: 401 Hampden Ct Medina OH 44256 Office: 257 S Court St Medina OH 44256

SPACHT, JON CRAIGE, medical photography department manager, videotape producer; b. Peoria, Ill., Jan. 31, 1956; s. Ivan Ray and Ruth Leone (Flechsig) S.; m. Wanda Sue Miller, Apr. 12, 1980; children: Craig Alan, Lauren Michele. BS in Journalism, U. Ill., 1978. Cert. profl. photographer, Ill. Photographer Peoria Jour. Star, 1975-78, UPI, Champaign, Ill., 1977-78; media services coordinator Meth. Med. Ctr., Peoria, 1978-83, media services mgr., 1983—. Mem. Internat. TV Assn., Assn. for Multi-image, Profl. Photographers Am. Lutheran. Avocations: racquetball, bicycling, computer graphics.

SPADONI, ROSELLA JUDY, dentist; b. Chgo., Aug. 31, 1958; d. Dominick Reno and Rachele Zita (Lombardi) S. BS, Loyola U., Chgo., 1980, DDS, 1984. Assoc. dentist Albert Castellan DDS, Melrose Park, Ill., 1984—; gen. practice dentistry Schaumburg, Ill., 1986—; cons. Delta Dental Plan Ill., River Forest, 1985—, BMS Services, Inc., Rosemont, Ill., 1985-86. Vol. state rep. election com., Melrose Park, 1984. Mem. ADA, Ill. State Dental Soc., Ill. Assn. Women Dentists, Chgo. Dental Soc., Acad. Gen. Dentistry, Hanover Park Community C. of C. Republican. Roman Catholic. Office: 873 S Roselle Rd Schaumburg IL 60193

SPAETH, CARL F., JR., bank holding company executive. Pres. CB Fin. Corp., Jackson, Mich. Office: CB Finacial Corp One Jackson Sq Jackson MI 49201 *

SPAETH, MARY ARRAGON, information specialist; b. Portland, Oreg., Jan. 30, 1932; d. Reginald Francis and Gertrude Tower (Nichols) Arragon; m. Joe Lamont Spaeth, Aug. 28, 1954; children: Donald A., Alan T. BA, Reed Coll., 1953; MLS, Columbia U., 1954. Asst. cataloger Chgo. Hist. Soc., 1954-56; editorial dir. Nat. Opinion Research Ctr., Chgo., 1967-71; research asst. survey research lab. U. Ill., Urbana, 1971-73, publs. editor survey research lab., 1973-79, info. coordinator survey research lab., 1979—. Co-editor: The Collection and Analysis of Economic and Consumer Behavior Data, 1984; co-editor Pub. Opinion Quar. Index, 1984; editor Survey Research newsletter, 1971—; contbr. articles to profl. jours. Mem. Am. Assn. Pub. Opinion Research (chmn. publicity and info. com. 1981-83), Soc. Scholarly Pub. Avocation: reading. Home: 1708 Henry St Champaign IL 61821 Office: U Ill Survey Research Lab 1005 W Nevada St Urbana IL 61801

SPAETH, NICHOLAS JOHN, state attorney general; b. Mahnomen, Minn., Jan. 27, 1950. A.B., Stanford U., 1972, J.D., 1977; B.A., Oxford U., Eng., 1974. Bar: Minn. 1979, U.S. Dist. Ct. (Minn.) 1979, U.S. Ct. Appeals (8th cir.) 1979, N.D. 1980, U.S. Dist. Ct. (N.D.) 1980, U.S. Supreme Ct. 1984. Law clk. U.S. Ct. Appeals (8th cir.), Fargo, N.D., 1977-78; law clk. to Justice Byron White U.S. Supreme Ct., Washington, 1978-79; pvt. practice 1979-84; atty. gen. State of N.D., Bismarck, 1984—; adj. prof. law U. Minn., 1980-83. Rhodes scholar, 1972-74. Democrat. Roman Catholic. Office: Office of Atty Gen State Capitol Bismarck ND 58505 *

SPAIN, JOHN NICHOLLS, JR., television network executive; b. Memphis, July 30, 1947; s. John Nicholls and Mary Elizabeth (Wilson) S.; m. Sally Cary Clarke, Apr. 12, 1969; children: John N. III, Patrick Wilson. Student, Southwestern U., Memphis, 1966-67, Memphis State U., 1967-68, Wayne State U., 1972-75. With Sta. WWJ-TV, Detroit, 1972-79; nat. sales mgr. WDSU-TV, New Orleans, 1980-81; acct. exec. NBC, Detroit, 1981-83; v.p. Detroit sales NBC, 1983—. Trustee Found. for Exceptional Children, Grosse Pointe, Mich., 1973—; mem. exec. bd. Detroit Area council Boy Scouts Am., 1985—. Served with USAF, 1968-72, Vietnam. Mem. Detroit Advt. Assn., Adcraft Club of Detroit. Club: Detroit Econ. Office: NBC TV Network 2855 Coolidge Suite 216 Troy MI 48084

SPAINHOUR, DALLAS KYLE, financial analyst; b. Winston-Salem, N.C., Oct. 8, 1960; s. Dallas Marvin and Rachel Lee (Jones) S. BS in Acctg., U. N.C., 1982; postgrad., U. Chgo., 1987—. Auditor U.S. Dept. Defense, Washington, 1983-85; cons. Peat, Marwick, Mitchell & Co., Washington, 1985-86; fin. analyst Motorola, Inc., Schaumburg, Ill., 1986—. Author, editor: PMM & Co. Government Contracts Hotline newsletter, 1985-86. Vol. U.S. Spl. Olympics, Washington, 1986, Chgo., 1987. Mem. Am. Inst. CPA's, Nat. Assn. Accts. Democrat. Methodist. Avocations: running, swimming, horseback riding. Home: 2663 College Hill Circle Schaumburg IL 60195 Office: Motorola Inc IL01-10 1303 E Algonquin Rd Schaumburg IL 61096

SPALDING, ALBERT DOMINIC, JR., attorney, accountant; b. Grand Rapids, Mich., Dec. 11, 1951; s. Albert D. Sr. and Mary Barbara (Jastifer) S.; m. Sharon Berman, May 7, 1972 (div. May 1974); m. Nancy Winkler, June 24, 1978; 1 child, Richard Lee. Student, Grand Rapids Jr. Coll., 1970-72; BBA, U. Mich., 1974; MBA, George Washington U., 1978, JD, 1979. Bar: Mich. 1979; CPA, Mich. Tax law specialist IRS Nat. Office, Washington, 1977-79; tax cons. Arthur Young & Co., Detroit, 1979-80, Plante & Moran, CPA's, Southfield, Mich., 1980-81; sole practice Detroit, 1981—; ptnr. Flickinger, Gockerman, Wilson & Spalding, P.C., Detroit, 1983—; lectr. Wayne State U., Detroit, 1983—; gen. counsel, bd. dirs. Denver Group, Inc., 1986—; gen. counsel Ann Arbor, Mich., 1985—; author small bus. workshop materials, 1987; bd. dirs. Fringe Benefit Specialists, Inc., St. Clair Shores, Mich., Small Computer Installations, Inc., Roseville, Mich., Winkler Found., Detroit. Author: Deferred Compensation, 1985. Named Account Advocate of Yr. for Mich., U.S. Small Bus. Adminstrn., 1983. Mem. Am. Acctg. Assn., Am. Bus. Law Assn., Mich. Assn. CPA's, Inst. for Study of Christian Values (bd. dirs. 1986—). Republican. Baptist. Club: Christian Bus. Men's Com. (St. Clair Shores); Grosse Pointe Econ. (bd. dirs. 1987—). Avocations: fishing, computers. Office: Flickinger Gockerman Wilson & Spalding PC 17190 Denver Detroit MI 48224

SPALDING, FRANKLIN MATTHEW, dentist; b. Peoria, Ill., Oct. 17, 1942; s. Franklin M. and Mary Rose (Conklin) S.; m. Sandra E. Woodward, July 3, 1971. Student, Marquette U., 1960-62, U. Ill., 1963; DDS, U. Ill., 1967. Gen. practice dentistry Peoria, 1969—. Served to commdr. USN, 1967-69. Mem. ADA, Ill. State Dental Assn., Chgo. Dental Assn., Peoria Dental Soc. Avocation: astronomy. Office: 2305 S Jefferson Peoria IL 61605

SPALDING, JOHN ARTHUR, architect; b. Chgo., Sept. 29, 1948; s. Arthur Rudolph and Bernice Matilda (Bork) S.; m. Victoria Jean Dillon, June 22, 1968; 1 dau., Lisa Marie. Student Ill. Inst. Tech., 1966-70; B.S. in Archtl. Engring., Chgo. Tech. Inst., 1971. Registered architect, Wis., Minn. Apprentice architect Arnold May Builders, Inc., Richmond, Ill., 1971-75; v.p. archtl. div. Cooper Architects/Engrs., Rice Lake, Wis., 1976-82; owner Spalding Architects, Rice Lake, 1983—. Mem. Diocese of Superior Commn. on Art and Architecture. Mem. AIA, Wis. Soc. Architects, Constrn. Specifications Inst., Am. Arbitration Assn. Roman Catholic. ch. renovation project pub. in Wisconsin Architect mag. Home: Route 5 Woodland Vista Rice Lake WI 54868 Office: 431 S Main St Rice Lake WI 54868

SPALDING, THOMAS CLAYTON, JR., investment banker; b. Oakland, Calif., July 31, 1951; s. Thomas Clayton and Katharine (Van Sant) S.; m. Martha Jean Knecht, June 25, 1977; 1 child, Charles Thomas. AB, U. Mich., 1973, MBA, 1975. Chartered fin. analyst. Investment analyst Lincoln Life Ins. Co., Ft. Wayne, Ind., 1975-76; asst. portfolio mgr. John Nuveen & Co., Chgo., 1976-78; portfolio mgr. Nuveen Adv. Corp., Chgo., 1978—. Mem. Inst. Chartered Fin. Analysts, Investment Analysts Soc. Chgo., Chgo. Mcpl. Analysts Soc. Home: 142 Sterling Ln Wilmette IL 60091 Office: Nuveen Adv Corp 333 W Wacker Dr Chicago IL 60606

SPANGLER, EDWARD EUGENE, electrical company executive; b. Connersville, Ind., Feb. 15, 1949; s. Jesse Edward and Lily Margaret (Bickel) S.; m. Lynn Ellen Shoemaker, June 26, 1971; children: Kelly Lynn, Margaret Anne. BS MechE, Rose Poly. Inst., 1971. Registered profl. engr., Ind. Design engr. Avco Corp., Richmond, Ind., 1971-73; mfg. engr. Copeland Corp., Sidney, Ohio, 1973-77; mfg. engr. Reliance Electric Co., Columbus, Ind., 1977-82, supr. mfg. engring., 1982-83, mgr. mfg. services, 1983—. Student liaison coordinator Columbus chpt. AFS Internat., 1986. Mem. Ind. Soc. Profl. Engrs. Roman Catholic. Avocations: tennis, golf, basketball, softball, woodworking. Home: 1510 Locust Dr Columbus IN 47203 Office: Reliance Electric Co 3300 10th St Columbus IN 47201

SPANGLER, JIMMY LEE, city official; b. Hillsdale, Mich., Dec. 5, 1950; s. Eben L. and Jean (Rothlisberger) S.; m. Joyce E. Heller, July 22, 1972; children: Christopher E., Joshua R. BCE, Mich. State U., 1973. Registered profl. engr., Mich. Plant engr. Wash. Suburban Sanitary Commn., Hyattsville, Md., 1973-76; asst. supt. City of Pontiac, Mich., 1976-79; wastewater div. supt. City of Lansing, Mich., 1979—. Mem. Water Pollution Control Fedn. (Hatfield award 1983), NSPE, Mich. Water Pollution Control Assn. (J.R. Rumsey award 1987). Methodist. Avocations: camping, hunting, playing with children. Office: Wastewater Div 1625 Sunset Ave Lansing MI 48917

SPANIER, EDWARD JACOB, academic administrator; b. Phila., May 13, 1937; s. Jacob F. and Elizabeth M. (Bogansky) S.; m. Helene M. Moeltner, May 25, 1968; children: Christopher E., David E. BA, La Salle U., 1959; PhD, U. Pa., 1964. Chemist E.J. Du Pont, Wilmington, Del., 1964-65; asst. prof. Seton Hall U., South Orange, N.J., 1965-70, assoc. prof., 1970-72; asst. dean sci. Wright State U., Dayton, Ohio, 1972-73, assoc. dir. planning and health affairs, 1973-74, from asst. dean to assoc. dean adminstrn. Sch. Medicine, 1974-80, asst. v.p. health affairs, 1980-81, asst. dir. then asst. v.p. fin. services, 1981-85, treas., 1984—, v.p. bus. and fin., 1985—. Home: 1966 State Rt 725 Spring Valley OH 45370 Office: Wright State U Dayton OH 45435

SPANN, BETTYE JEAN PATTERSON, educational administrator; b. East St. Louis, Ill., Nov. 16, 1930; d. LeRoy H. and Minnie P. (Ford) Patterson; m. Patric N. Spann, June 25, 1952 (dec.); children: Derrick Leroy, Monique Renata. BS, U. Ark., 1952; MA, U. Mo., 1967. Tchr. grade sch. and high sch. Dist. 189, East St. Louis, 1952-65, supr. reading clinics, 1966, reading supr., 1967-69; dir. Project Conquest (reading clinics), East St. Louis, 1969-82; cons. Ill. Office Edn., East St. Louis, 1972—, RMC Research, Palo Alto, Calif., 1977-78, Learning Achievement Corp., Calif., 1975-77. Active United Fund, East St. Louis, 1968-70, March of Dimes, East St. Louis, 1979—; trustee Mt. Olive Bapt. Ch. Recipient Cert. Merit U.S. Office Edn., 1976-85, Outstanding Contribution to Edn. award U.S. Office Edn., 1976-79, Cert. Recognition (Understanding, Considerate Leadership) Sch. Dist. 189, 1974-75, Ednl. Excellence award Ill. State Bd. Edn., 1979. Mem. Ill. Edn. Assn., Ill. reading Assn., Internat. Reading Assn., Assn. for Supervision and Curriculum Devel., Ill. Women's Assn., Nat. Council Negro Women, Am. Cancer Soc., United Way, Phi Delta Kappa. Democrat. Office: Board of Education 1005 State St East Saint Louis IL 62205

SPANOGLE, ROBERT WILLIAM, foundation administrator; b. Lansing, Mich., Nov. 13, 1942; s. William Prune and Mary Ann (Lenneman) S.; m. Ruth Ann Long; Jan. 14, 1967; children: John Paul, Stephen Donald, Amy Lynn. AB, Lansing Community Coll., 1969; BA, Mich. State U., 1971. Cons. Nat. League Cities, U.S. Conf. Mayors, Washington, 1971-72; mem. cons. Am. Legion, Indpls., 1972-75, asst. dir., 1975-76, dir. mem. and post activities, 1976-78, dir. internal affairs, 1978-79; exec. dir. Am. Legion, Washington, 1979-81; nat. adjutant Am. Legion, Indpls., 1981—; also hon. life mem. and past dept. commd. Am. Legion; pres. Hale Fed. Credit Union, Indpls. Pres., chmn. United Service Orgn. Greater Indpls.; bd. dirs. 500 Festival Assocs., Queen's Selection com., 1983-84, vice chmn. Meml. Day com., 1985; bd. dirs. Crossroads of Am. Council Boy Scouts Am., Inc. Served with U.S. Army, 1962-65, Vietnam. Named Outstanding Young Man Am., U.S. Jr. C. of C., 1978, Outstanding Vietnam Vet. Ind., Gov. Otis Bowen, 1979. Mem. Am. Mgmt. Assn., Nat. Assn. Collegiate Vets. Assn. (pres. 1970-71 exec. dir. 1971-72), Profl. Secs. Internat. (exec. adv. bd. Crossroads Am. chpt., Ind. chpt.), Greater Washington Soc. Execs., Mich. State Alumni Assn. Roman Catholic. Club: Army, Navy and Air Force Vets. in Can. (ex-officio sec.). Lodge: Kiwanis. Avocations: golf, hunting, fishing, reading. Office: Am Legion Nat Hdqrs 700 N Pennsylvania St Indianapolis IN 46204

SPANSKI, GARY STEPHEN, financial consultant; b. Bad Axe, Mich., July 26, 1953; m. Eugene Vincent and Doris E. S.; B.S., Mich. State U., 1975; M.B.A., Pepperdine U., 1981. Engine research technician Gen. Motors Corp. Oldsmobile div., Lansing, Mich., 1975-78; pres. Fast Lane Swimwear, Manhattan Beach, Calif., 1978-80; account exec. Dean Witter Reynolds, Inc., Torrance, Calif., 1980-82; investment specialist Sutro & Co., Inc., Beverly Hills, Calif., 1982-83, Dean Witter Reynolds, Inc., Marina del Rey, Calif., 1983-85; mng. dir., Hamilton Rhodes Group, Inc., Hamilton Rhodes Capital Mgmt., Inc., Birmingham, Mich., 1985—. Mem. Intra-Sci Research Found.; co-founder, bd. dirs., treas. Beverly Hills Bus. Forum. Recipient Goal Buster award Torrance YMCA, 1982. Mem. Am. Mktg. Assn., Am. Mgmt. Assn., Assn. Registered Reps. Republican. Roman Catholic. Clubs: Wind 'n' Sea Sailing, Beverly Hills Mens, Beverly Hills Kiwanis (bd. dirs. 1983), Sierra. Contbr. investment column Healthcare Horizons, cable TV program How's Business?; co-host, exec. producer Westinghouse Cable Systems. Home: 743 Woodchester Dr Bloomfield Hills MI 48013 Office: 300 Park St Suite 375 Birmingham MI 48009

SPARGO, WILLIAM GILBERT, mechanical engineer; b. St. Louis, May 9, 1925; s. Roy and A. Margaret (Schneider) S.; m. Erna K. Nottmeier, June 6, 1954; children—Janice, Darryl. B.M.E., Tulane U., 1947. Registered profl.

engr., Mo. Mgr. engring. Anheuser Busch Cos., Inc., St. Louis, to 1983, mgr. packaging equipment devel., 1983—. Patentee process for filling beer containers. Served to lt. (j.g.) USNR, 1945-47, PTO. Mem. ASME (chmn. beverage subcom. of food drug and beverage equipment com. 1972—), Master Brewers Assn. Am., Soft Drink Technologists Assn. Lodges: Masons, Elks. Home: 9154 Cordoba Ln Saint Louis MO 63126

SPARKS, ALLEN KAY, electronics company executive; b. Chgo., Sept. 26, 1933; s. Allen Kay and Violet Elsie (Lindstrom) S.; m. Nina Suzanne Bade, Nov. 5, 1955; 1 child, Alison Claire. A.B. in Chemistry, Ripon Coll., 1955; Ph.D. in Chemistry, Case Inst. Tech., 1960. Dir. chem. research Signal Co., Des Plaines, Ill., 1972-75, v.p. tech. chem. div., East Rutherford, N.J., 1975-76, v.p. ops. Chem. div., 1976-78; v.p., gen. mgr., 1978-80, v.p., gen. mgr. Norplex Div., LaCrosse, Wis., 1980-85, pres., 1985-86, Eng. Materials Group Crane Co., Manhattan, Ill., 1986—; dir. Norplex Hong Kong, Ltd., Norplex France SARL, Paris, Norplex U.K. Ltd., Northampton, Eng. Contbr. articles to profl. jours. Patentee in field. Bd. advisors Viterbo Coll., LaCrosse, Wis., 1982-86; bd. dirs. Elk Grove Twp. Republicans, Ill., 1971-74; pres Dist. 59 Bd. of Edn., Elk Grove, 1968-74; area chmn. Des Plaines Community Chest, 1964. Allied Corp. fellow Case Inst. Tech., 1958-60. Mem. Sigma Xi. Avocations: travel, photography, swimming, golf. Home: Rural Rt 2 Carriage Ln Manhattan IL 60442 Office: Signal Co Norplex Div 1300 Norplex Dr PO Box 1448 La Crosse WI 54601

SPARKS, BILLY SCHLEY, lawyer; b. Marshall, Mo., Oct. 1, 1923; s. John and Clarinda (Schley) S.; A.B., Harvard, 1945, LL.B., 1949; student Mass. Inst. Tech., 1943-44; m. Dorothy O. Stone, May 14, 1946; children—Stephen Stone, Susan Lee Sparks Raben, John David. Admitted to Mo. bar, 1949; partner Langworthy, Matz & Linde, Kansas City, Mo., 1949-62, firm Linde, Thomson, Fairchild Langworthy, Kohn & Van Dyke, 1962—. Mem. Mission (Kans.) Planning Council, 1954-63; mem. Kans. Civil Service Commn., 1975—. Mem. dist. 110 Sch. Bd., 1964-69, pres., 1967-69; mem. Dist. 512 Sch. Bd., 1969-73, pres., 1971-72; del. Dem. Nat. Conv., 1964; candidate for representative 10th Dist., Kans., 1956, 3d district, 1962; treas. Johnson County (Kans.) Dem. Central com., 1958-64. Served to lt. USAAF, 1944-46. Mem. Kansas City C. of C. (legis. com. 1956-82), Am., Kansas City bar assns., Mo. Bar, Law Assn. Kansas City, Harvard Law Sch. Assn. Mo. (past dir.), Nat. Assn. Sch. Bds. (mem. legislative com. 1968-73), St. Andrews Soc. Mem. Christian Ch. (trustee). Clubs: Harvard (v.p. 1953-54), The Kansas City (Kansas City, Mo.); Milburn Golf and Country. Home: 8517 W 90th Terr Shawnee Mission KS 66212 Office: City Center Sq 12th & Baltimore Sts Kansas City MO 64105

SPARKS, DONALD EUGENE, interscholastic activities association executive; b. St. Louis, May 26, 1933; s. Lloyd Garland and Elsie Wilma (Finn) S.; m. Gloria Mae Helle, Sept. 22, 1951; children: Robert, Michael, Donna Lyn. BS in Edn., N.E. Mo. Univ., 1956, MA, 1959, postgrad., 1962-63. Cert. tchr. and principal, Mo. High sch. coach, athletic dir. The Parkway Sch. Dist., Chesterfield, Mo., 1959-77; assoc. dir. Mo. High Sch. Activity Assn., Columbia, 1977-81; asst. dir. Nat. Fedn. State High Sch. Assns., Kansas City, Mo., 1981—. Recipient spl. Nat. Athletic Dir.'s citation Nat. Fedn. State High Sch. Assns., 1972. Mem. Nat. Interscholastic Adminstrs. Assn. (Disting. Service award 1979). Home: 5204 NW 84th Terrace Kansas City MO 64154 Office: Nat Fedn State High Sch Assns 11724 Plaza Circle Kansas City MO 64195

SPARKS, EARL EDWIN, consumer products company executive; b. Topeka, May 6, 1920; s. Earl Edwin and Utah Gertrude (Rice) S.; children: Patrick M., Monty E., Dianne M., Daniel E., Jack D.; m. Marjorie Joyce Voorhees, Oct. 26, 1974. B.S., U. Nebr.-Omaha, 1952. Enlisted as pvt. USAAF, 1940; advanced through grades to col. USAF, 1963; served in North Africa-Italy 15th Air Force, World War II; as sr. navigator SAC combat crew mem.; guided missile staff officer; dep. chief staff 8th Air Force SAC, Westover AFB, Mass., 1961-63; ret. 1963; with IBM, 1963-66; mgr. market planning and adminstrn. Electronic Systems Center, Owego, N.Y.; with Chamberlain Mfg. Corp., Elmhurst, Ill., 1967-71; sr. v.p. marketing, consumer products Chamberlain Mfg. Corp., 1969-71; v.p. consumer products USG Industries, Inc. subs. USG Corp., Chgo., 1972-75; v.p. mktg. USG Industries, Inc. subs. USG Corp., 1975—. Decorated Legion of Merit, Soldiers medal with oak leaf cluster, Commendation medal with oak leaf cluster. Mem. AIAA, Air Force Assn., Ret. Officers Assn., Am. Marketing Assn., Am. Mgmt. Assn. Club: K.C. Mem. Joint Am.-Brit. Program to set up first operational Ballistics Missile System in free world, THOR, 1958-61. Home: 1323 Tall Oaks Ln Wheaton IL 60187 Office: USG Industries Inc subs US Gypsum Co 101 S Wacker Dr Chicago IL 60606

SPARKS, JACK DAVID, appliance company executive; b. Chgo., Nov. 24, 1922; m. Fredda Sullivan; children: Suzanne, Cinde Marie, Katherine S., Jack David. With Whirlpool Corp., Benton Harbor, Mich., 1940—; beginning as laborer, successively asst. dir. personnel, sales dept. staff, advt. and promotion mgr., sales mgr., gen. sales mgr., dir. mktg., 1940-59, v.p., 1959-66, group v.p., 1966-77, exec. v.p., 1977-81, vice chmn., chief mktg. officer, from 1981, chmn. bd., 1982—, chief exec. officer, 1982-87, former pres., also dir.; dir. Meredith Corp., Des Moines, Peoples State Bank, St. Joseph, Mich. Formerly chmn. bd. trustees Olivet Coll. Served frpm pvt. to capt. USAAF, 1941-46. Mem. Mich. Acad. Arts and Scis. Clubs: Racquet (Chgo.); Point O'Woods Golf and Country (Benton Harbor, Mich.). Office: Whirlpool Corp Administrative Center Benton Harbor MI 49022 *

SPARKS, (LLOYD) MELVIN, appraiser; b. Putnam County, Mo., Sept. 12, 1921; s. Whitlow Vane and Anna Jane (Hart) S.; m. Naomi Nadine Wiles, Jan. 3, 1942; children: Beverly, Richard, Jill. Grad. high sch., Unionville, Mo. Farm operator Unionville, 1942-77; pres. Northeast Mo. Telephone Co., Green City, Mo., 1961-77; asst. cashier Farmers Bank, Unionville, 1967-77; appraiser Sparks Appraisal, Inc., Unionville, 1983—. Mem. school bd. Putnam County Rt. I, Unionville, 1967-72. Membership Quincy Chpt. Nat. Assn. Ind. Fee Appraisers. Republican. Mem. Ch. of Christ. Lodge: Rotary (pres. Unionville chpt. 1982-83). Home: Rt 2 Box 38 Unionville MO 63565 Office: Sparks Appraisals Inc Route 2 Box 38 Unionville MO 63565

SPARKS, (THEO) MERRILL, entertainer, translator, poet; b. Mount Etna, Iowa, Oct. 5, 1922; s. David G. and Ollie M. (Hickman) S.; student U. Besancon (France), 1945; B.A., U. So. Calif., 1948; postgrad. U. Iowa, 1948-51, Columbia U., 1951-52. Entertainer as singer, pianist, Los Angeles, Midwest, Fla., N.Y., N.J. areas, 1953—. Served with AUS, 1942-46. Co-recipient P.E.N. transl. award, 1968, Cross of Merit with Vernon Duke for cantata Anima Eroica, Order of St. Brigida, Rome, 1966. Mem. Am. Fedn. Musicians, Authors Guild, Am. Guild Authors and Composers, Icarian Players, Modern Poetry Assn., Iowa Friends of the Library, Iowa Geneal. Soc. Composer songs including Sleepy Village, 1942, A Heart of Gold, 1956, Anima Eroica, 1971, An Italian Voyage, 1976, O Come and Join the Angels, 1982, Ballad of Ollie and Bart, 1983, Elegy, 1987. poems pub. in mags. including Western Rev., Choice, Coastlines, South & West, N.Y. Rev. Books; poems included in: Arts of Russia, Primer of Experimental Poetry; play (musical) Icaria, 1986; co-editor, co-translator (with Vladimir Markov) Modern Russian Poetry, 1967. Club: Rotary. Home: Mount Etna IA 50855 Office: 4620 SE 4th St #104 Des Moines IA 50315

SPARKS, PHILIP WAYNE, banker, construction company executive; b. Dayton, Ohio, Nov. 25, 1952; s. Travis Earl and Nannie (Martin) S.; m. Susan Eileen Lang, Aug. 18, 1973. Student, Wright State U., 1974; diploma, Grad. Sch. Banking, 1980. Sr. v.p. The Cen. Trust Co., Dayton, Ohio, 1974—; v.p. Lang and Sons Builders, Beavercreek, Ohio, 1985—; Bd. dirs., treas. Eastway Community Mental Health Ctr., 1978-80. Bd. dirs. Evangelical Retirement Villages of Dayton, 1983—; mem. econ. devel. commn. City of Beavercreek; mem., v.p. Dayton Bd. Edn., 1976-79; chmn. Serving Our Schs. Com., Dayton, 1978-80. Recipient Americanism award Am. Legion, 1969, Outstanding Citizenship award Elks, 1970, Resolution of Appreciation Dayton Bd. Edn., 1979. Mem. Miami Valley Mgmt. Assn., Beavercreek Jaycees (pres. 1982-83). Republican. Presbyterian. Lodge: Sertoma. Avocations: antique autos, collecting political memorabilia. Home: 3058 Lantz Rd Beavercreek OH 45432 Office: The Cen Trust Co 112 W 2d St Dayton OH 45432

SPARROW, ALBERT WILLIAM, physician, medical educator, researcher; b. Balt., Feb. 7, 1933; s. Albert William and Vera (Teano) S.; m. Virginia Devereux, May 10, 1958 (div. 1982); children: Christine, Theresa, Michelle, Kathleen, Suzanne. AB, Holy Cross Coll., 1955; MD, Georgetown U., 1959; MPH in Epidemiology, Harvard U., 1979. Diplomate Am. Bd. Pediatrics, Am. Bd. Pediatric Cardiology. Asst. prof. pediatrics U. Va. Med. Sch., Charlottesville, 1967-72; assoc. prof. pediatrics Mich. State U., East Lansing, 1972-76, prof. pediatrics and human devel., 1976—, dir. preventive cardiology and pediatric cardiology, 1972—; cons. Mich. Dept. Pub. Health, Lansing, 1978—, Lansing Community Coll., 1979-83. Served to capt. USAF, 1958-63. Grantee NIH, Mich. State U. Fellow Am. Coll. Cardiology, Am. Acad. Pediatrics; mem. Am. Heart Assn. (pres. Mich. chpt. 1985-86, bd. dirs. 1983—, grantee). Republican. Roman Catholic. Club: Faculty. Avocations: skiing, swimming, sailing. Home: 5391 Wild Oak Dr East Lansing MI 48823 Office: Mich State U B-401 Clin Ctr East Lansing MI 48824

SPARROW, VINCENT ROBERT, accountant; b. Hertford, Eng., June 3, 1956; came to U.S., 1957; s. Vincent P. and Joan R. (Russell) S. BA in Econs., Vanderbilt U., 1978; MBA, U. Mich., 1980. CPA, Ill. Staff acct. Arthur Andersen & Co., Chgo., 1980-82, sr. acct., 1982-85, acctg. mgr., 1985—. Bd. dirs. MetroHelp Crisis Line, Chgo., 1986—. Mem. Am. Inst. CPA's, Ill. Soc. CPA's. Roman Catholic. Avocation: racquetball. Home: 3150 N Sheridan Rd 20 D Chicago IL 60657 Office: Arthur Andersen & Co 33 W Monroe St Chicago IL 60603

SPATHELF, STEPHEN EDWARD, financial executive; b. Phila., June 12, 1947; s. Walter Edward and Margaret Ada (Shuttleworth) S.; m. Susan Kathaleen Hall, Sept. 14, 1974; children—Jennifer Susanne, Jonathan Edward. B.S. in Acctg. and Math., U. Dubuque, 1969. C.P.A., Ill. Asst. sr. acct. Deloitte, Haskins & Sells, Chgo., 1969-70; sr. acct. Friedman, Galen & Co., Chgo., 1970-72; asst. treas., sec. Nat. Student Mktg. Corp., Chgo., 1972-76; controller, treas. Arthur Frommer Enterprises, Inc., N.Y.C., 1976-78; asst. treas. Playboy Enterprises, Inc., Chgo., 1978-84, treas., 1984—. Chmn. bd. dirs. Transitional Living Programs, Inc., 1979-81. Mem. Am. Inst. C.P.A.s.

SPATZ, CHARLES ALEXANDER, gift company executive; b. Amityville, N.Y., Mar. 16, 1951; s. Albert Charles and Katherine Emma (McGough) S.; m. Diane Marie Brockmeyer, July 26, 1975; children: Paul Albert, Gwen Michelle. BFA, Lindenwood Coll., Saint Charles, 1979. Gen. mgr. Sculptor's Guild, Ltd., St. Louis, 1980-83; owner Glastonbury Studios, Ltd., 1982—. Served with USAF, 1970-74. Democrat. Roman Catholic. Lodge: KC. Home: 106 Henry St Saint Peters MO 63376 Office: PO Box 212 Saint Peters MO 63376

SPATZ, WILLIAM LEE, real estate developer and manager; b. Chgo., Sept. 11, 1948; s. David and Hazel Davis (Englander) S.; m. Wendy Becker, May 26, 1974; children: Bryan Joshua, Alexis Nicole. Student, U. Wis., 1966-69. Pres. Alpert & Spatz, Chgo., 1970-71, Spatz Internat. Trading Co., Chgo., 1971-72; sr. v.p. Enterex Commodities, N.Y.C., 1972-75; pres. Spatz & Co., Chgo., 1975—. Avocations: tennis, bowling, football, golf, baseball. Office: 500 Skokie Blvd Northbrook IL 60062

SPAUN, WILLIAM BECKER, lawyer, retired; b. Atchison, Kans., Aug. 22, 1913; s. Floyd and Bertha (Becker) S.; J.D., U. Mo., Kansas City, 1936; m. Sidney Clyde Collins, Sept. 13, 1930 (dec.); 1 dau., Theon Spaun Martin; m. 2d, Mary Louise Robinson, Aug. 5, 1948 (dec.); children—William Becker, Mary Lou Spaun Montgomery, Robert R., Sarah Jean Fletcher, Shirley Anne. Admitted to Mo. bar, 1937; U.S. Supreme Ct., 1960; practice law, Hannibal, Mo., 1937-86; charter mem. World Peace Through Law Center, participant Washington conf., 1965. Regional fund chmn. ARC, 1961, nat. staff mem., 1943-44, nat. vice chmn. fund campaigns, 1963-64, local chpt. chmn., 1977-82; govt. appeal agt. SSS, 1968-72, chmn., 1972—. Recipient award for meritorious personal service WW II from ARC. Fellow Am. Coll. Probate Counsel, Harry S. Truman Library Inst. (hon.); mem. Am., Tenth Jud. Circuit (pres. 1958-60) bar assns., Mo. Bar (chmn. Law Day 1961, asso. editor jour. 1942-43), Am. Judicature Soc., Scribes. Republican. Home: PO Box 1169 Hannibal MO 63401 Office: 617A Broadway Hannibal MO 63401

SPEAK, KARL DENNIS, marketing company executive; b. St. Paul, Feb. 1, 1951; s. Karl S. and Janis E. (Brenner) S.; 1 child, Kathryn. BS in Econs., U. Minn., 1975, MS in Applied Econs., 1976. Sr. market analyst Cargill Investor Service, Chgo., 1976-77; grain buyer Joseph Schulz Brewing Co., Milw., 1977-78; grain buyer and trader CPC Internat., Chgo., 1978-79; v.p. sales Control Data Corp., Mpls., 1979-84; pres. Bus. Mktg. Technologies, Mpls., 1985—. Mem. Sales and Mktg. Execs. Assn. Avocations: tennis, golf. Office: Bus Mktg Technologies 8000 Town Line Ave Bloomington MN 55438

SPEAKS, MARTHA BENNETT, funeral director, mental health counselor; b. Springfield, Mo., Feb. 27, 1937; d. Howard Franklin and Virginia Frances (Turner) Bennett; m. William Frederick Lawrence, Aug. 23, 1958 (div. Jan. 1973); children: Catherine Lee Lawrence Schanze, Andrew William; m. Roland Robert Speaks Jr., June 26, 1981. BA in Speech Pathology, U. Kans., 1959, MA in Speech Pathology, 1961, MA in Human Relations, 1975. Lic. funeral dir., Mo.; cert. tchr., Mo. Speech pathologist Davisson Sch., Atlanta, 1970-73; asst. dir. vols. in ct. Douglas County Ct., Lawrence, Kans., 1974-77; coordinator info. and referral ctr. United Way, Kansas City, Mo., 1977-79; exec. dir. Heart of Am. Affiliate of Am. Diabetes Assn., Kansas City, 1979-82; coordinator grief resource ctr. Speaks Meml. Chapels, Inc., Independence, Mo., 1982—; bd. dirs. Community Mental Health Ctr. S., Kansas City, Widowed Persons Service of Kansas City; mem. adv. bd. Mo. Dept. Health, 1980-82; appointee citizens avd. com. Dist. Attys. Office, Johnson County, Kans., 1977-78; mem. Govs. Com. on the Yr. the Child, Mo., 1981. Bd. dirs. Am. Cancer Soc., Independence. Mem. Am. Assn. Counseling and Devel., Am. Mental Health Counseling Assn., Assn. Death Edn. and Counseling, Nat. Funeral Dirs. Assn., Independence C. of C. Avocations: reading, hiking, music, theater. Office: Speaks Meml Chapel Inc Lexington at Walnut Independence MO 64050

SPEAR, LARRY ROSS, minister; b. Indpls., Sept. 16, 1941; s. Horace Ross and Evelyn Alice (Lynn) S.; m. Brenda Eveline Sexton, June 22, 1963; children: Lynnelle, Michele. BS in Mil. Sci., U.S. Mil. Acad., 1963; MS in Systems Mgmt., Air Force Inst. Tech., 1974; MDiv., So. Bapt. Theol. Sem., 1983. Ordained to ministry So. Bapt. Ch., 1978. Commd. 2d lt. USAF, 1963, advanced through grades to maj., 1973, resigned, 1976; assoc. pastor First Bapt. Ch., Englewood, Ohio, 1976-77; minister of youth First Bapt. Ch. of Dent, Cin., 1977-78; pastor Calvary Bapt. Ch., Lebanon, Ill., 1978—. Vol. fireman City of Lebanon, 1986—; mem. Lebanon Zoning Bd., 1986—. Recipient 1987 Community Builder's award Lebanon Masonic Lodge. Republican. Avocations: bowling, counted cross stitch, tennis. Home: 409 Summerfield Lebanon IL 62254 Office: Calvary Bapt Ch 225 N Monroe Lebanon IL 62254

SPEAR, PHILIP DUANE, controller; b. Marietta, Ohio, Nov. 4, 1957; s. Zail Everett and Shelah Cristine (Cain) S.; m. Meg Diane Evilsizer, July 24, 1982; children: Samuel Zane, Julie Anna. Student, U. Cin., 1976-77; BBA in Bus. Econs., Ohio U., 1981. Bond analyst AmeriTrust, Cleve., 1981; mgr. Able Cleaning Co., Macksburg, Ohio, 1981; sec./treas. Able, Inc., Macksburg, 1982-86, ops. mgr., 1982-83; controller Tastee Apple, Inc., Newcomerstown, Ohio, 1984—. Republican. Methodist. Lodge: Elks. Avocations: gardening, golf, softball, football, piano. Home: 203 Westview New Concord OH 43762 Office: Tastee Apple Inc 60810 CR 9 Newcomerstown OH 43832

SPEARS, JANET E., educator; b. Chambersburg, Ill., Sept. 5, 1933; d. Enoch E. and Marguerite Irene (Riley) Downey; A.A., Black Hawk Coll., 1978; B.S. (Chris Hoerr scholar), Bradley U., 1980; postgrad., St. Ambrose Coll., 1981-84; postgrad., Nova U., 1987; m. Keith A. Spears, July 6, 1952; children—Bruce, Roger, Darci, Paul. Secretarial positions Kewanee Machinery Conveyor (Ill.), 1951-52, William E. Trinke, atty., Lake Geneva, Wis., 1952-53, Walworth Co., Kewanee, 1968-72; adminstrv. asst. Kewanee Pub. Hosp., 1972-75; asst. personnel dir. Davenport (Iowa) Osteo. Hosp., 1980-81; bus. mgr. Franciscan Med. Center, Rock Island, Ill., 1981; bus. prof. Black Hawk Coll., Kewanee, 1981—, Henry County Rep. Women; liturgist, Sunday sch. tchr., mem. adminstrv. council). Mem. Am. Mgmt. Assn., AAUW, Nat. Assn. for Female Execs., Kewanee Pub. Hosp. Assn., Kewanee Art League, Phi Chi Theta. Republican. Clubs: Annawan Jr. Women's (pres. 1964-65), United Fairview Women. Home: Rural Route 1 Sheffield IL 61361 Office: Black Hawk Coll East Campus PO Box 489 Kewanee IL 61443

SPEAS, R. A., insurance company executive. Chmn. Equitable Life Ins. Co. of Iowa, Des Moines. Office: Equitable Life Ins Co of Iowa 604 Locust St Des Moines IA 50306 *

SPECK, HILDA, social worker; b. Stalybridge, Cheshire, England, Mar. 2, 1916; came to U.S., 1923; d. John Robert and Rose Ethel (Tymns) Smith; m. Willmot Hilton Speck, Sept. 4, 1937 (dec. Jan 1968); foster children: Barbara Ann Beranek Renfrow, Winifred June Aguilar. Grad. high sch., Flint, Mich. Lic. social worker, Mich. Dir. social services The Salvation Army, Flint, 1945—. Assisted in establishing Safe House for Victims of Domestic Violence, Flint, 1976-80. Recipient Hands of Mercy award The Salvation Army, 1967, Centennial Youth award The Salvation Army, 1965, 20 Year Service award Big Brothers of Genesee County. Mem. Council of Social Agys., Genesee County Commn. on Aging (v.p. 1971—), GLS Counties Health Planning Council Bd., Genesee County Emergency Task Force. Lodge: Zonta. Avocations: ch. work, vol. work, reading, sewing. Home: 2015 Stoney Brook Ct Flint MI 48507

SPECK, STEVEN LEE, engineer; b. Wichita, Kans., Oct. 19, 1956; s. James Lee and Caroleen Ann (Smith) S.; m. Nancy Louise Cole, Aug. 1, 1976; children: Michelle, Scott, Shawn, Samuel. AA, AAS, Crowder Coll., 1977. Cert. mech. engr. Draftsman Allgier & Martin, Joplin, Mo., 1975-77; draftsman, tool and die Dwyer Enterprises, Neosho, Mo., 1977-81; sr. draftsman, engr. Sunbeam Leisure, Neosho, 1981-85; design engr. Lear Siegler, Seymour, Ind., 1985—; chmn. Crowder Coll. Design/Drafting Com., Neosho, 1983-85. Mem. Am. Inst. Design and Drafting, Am. Soc. for Testing Materials, Soc. Computer-Aided Engring. Republican. Avocations: reading, tennis, jogging, softball, computers. Home: 624 N Ewing Seymour IN 47274 Office: Lear Siegler 885 N Chestnut Seymour IN 47274

SPECTER, MELVIN H., lawyer; b. East Chicago, Ind., July 12, 1903; s. Moses and Sadie (Rossuck) S.; A.B., U. Mich., 1925; J.D., U. Chgo., 1928; m. Nellie Rubenstein, Feb. 1, 1927; children—Lois, Michael Joseph. Admitted to Ind. bar, 1928; individual practice law, East Chicago, Ind. 1928—. Bd. dirs. ARC (chpt. chmn. 1940-46), Community Chest Assn., Salvation Army Adv. Bd., pres., 1930-35; bd. dirs. Vis. Nurse Assn., pres., 1943-44; bd. dirs. East Chgo. Boys Club, 1958-65; trustee East Chicago Pub. Library, 1956-80, pres., 1957-67; pres. Anselm Forum, 1957-58; chmn. Brotherhood Week NCCJ, East Chicago, 1958-61; exec. bd. Twin City council Boy Scouts Am.; city chmn. U. Chgo. Alumni Found. Fund, 1951-55. Awarded James Couzen Medal for Inter-collegiate debate, U. Mich., 1924; citation for distinguished pub. service, U. Chgo. Alumni Assn., 1958. Citizenship award Community Chest Assn., 1965. Mem. Am. Ind. (del.), East Chicago (pres. 1942-44) bar assns., Am. Judicature Soc., Comml. Law League Am., Community Concert Assn. (dir. 1950-55), Wig and Robe Frat., Phi Beta Kappa, Delta Sigma Rho. Elk (exalted ruler 1945), K.P., Kiwanian (dir. 1946, 49-51, 52-55, pres. 1961); mem. B'nai B'rith. Home: 4213 Baring Ave East Chicago IN 46312 Office: 804 W 145th St East Chicago IN 46312

SPEICHER, JACQUELYN LOU, educator; b. Holdrege, Nebr., May 18, 1946; d. Jack Louis and Norma Fern (Corder) McKenzie; m. David Ross Speicher, Oct. 7, 1972; children—Jill Marie, Tracey Ann, Stepanie Jane. B.S., U. Nebr., 1969. Tchr. pub. schs., Holdrege, 1969-70; urban services worker United Meth. Ch. Bd. Global Ministries, N.Y.C., 1970-74; tchr. John F. Kennedy Sch., Berlin, 1974-77; trainer Inst. Cultural Affairs Internat., Chgo., 1977-79; instr. Central YMCA Community Coll., Chgo., 1979-80; dir., program set-up Inst. Cultural Affairs, Indpls., 1980-81; program dir. Ind. U.-Purdue U./Tng., Inc., Indpls., 1981-83; program dir. Ind. Vocat.-Tech. Coll./Tng. Inc., Indpls., 1983—. Chmn. Women's programs com. YWCA, Indpls., 1985-86, bd. dirs., 1984-86; trustee, treas. Mobile Homes Trust, 1984-87. Mem. Am. Soc. Personnel Adminstrs., Am. Soc. Tng. and Devel., Am. Vocat. Assn., Ind. Vocat. Assn., Community Service Council, Ind. Employment and Tng. Assn. (sec. 1985-86, v.p. membership 1986—), Profl. Secs. Internat. (exec. adv. bd. 500 chpt. 1985-86), Network of Women in Bus., Ind. Women and Work Conference Com. (program chmn. 1987) Republican. Methodist. Office: Training Inc 47 S Pennsylvania St Suite 801 Indianapolis IN 46204

SPEIGEL, I. JOSHUA, neurosurgery educator; b. Ft. William, Ont., Can., Aug. 16, 1915; came to U.S., 1937; s. Jeremiah and Dora (Slobed) S.; m. Rosalynde Speigel, June 25, 1942; children: Virginia, Jonathan, Petra. MD, U. Toronto, 1937. Diplomate Am. Bd. Neurol. Surgery. Rotating intern Mt. Sinai Hosp., Cleve., 1937-38; asst. resident Neuropsychiatry State Hosp., Howard, R.I., 1938-39; asst. resident in neurol. surgery Boston City Hosp., 1939-40; sr. resident St. Luke's Hosp., Chgo., 1940-41; chief resident Cook County Hosp., Chgo., 1941-42; chief resident in neurology and neurol. surgery Neuropsychiat. Inst., Chgo., 1942; clin. prof. emeritus neurol. surgery U. Chgo., 1974-85; sr. neurological surgeon Michael Reese Hosp. and Med. Ctr., Chgo., 1985—; cons. neurol. surgeon Thorek Hosp., South Chgo. Community Hosp., South Shore Hosp., Jackson Park Hosp.; med. advisor U.S. Dept. Health and Human Services; mem. med. adv. council Assn. Brain Tumor Research. Contbr. articles to profl. jours. Served to maj. MC, AUS, 1942-46. Mem. AMA, Internat. Coll. Surgeons (chmn. U.S. div. neurosurg. sect. 1960—, vice regent U.S. div. 1983), Internat. Bd. Surgery (chmn. U.S. div. 1960—), Ill. State Med. Soc., Chgo. Neurol. Soc., Cook County Med. Soc., Chgo. Med. Soc., Assn. Mil. Surgeons of U.S., Am. Assn. Neurol. Surgeons, Am. Bd. Neurol. Surgeons, Neurosurg. Soc. Am. (treas. 1948-55, pres. 1957, Disting. Service award 1976), Congress Neurol. Surgeons, Interurban Neurosurg. Soc., Cen. Neurosurg. Soc. Royal Soc. Medicine, Ill. State Neurosurg. Soc., Soc. Neurovascular Surgery. Democrat. Jewish. Clubs: Explorer's (N.Y.C.); Standard, The Art, Adventurer's (Chgo.). Avocations: hunting, fishing, sculpture, prehistoric paintings and sculpture. Home: 1420 N Lakeshore Dr Chicago IL 60610 Office: Neurol Surgery 55 E Washington St Chicago IL 60602

SPEISER, JAMES WARREN, engineer; b. N.Y.C., Sept. 2, 1949; s. Warren Henry and Eileen Catherine (Lupo) S.; m. Phoebe Louise Winholt, Nov. 25, 1977; children: Selene Elizabeth, Samantha Emily, Jonathan David. BEE, U. Mo., Rolla, 1977, MEE, 1979. Engr. McDonnell-Douglas Astronautics Co., St. Louis, 1979-81, sr. engr., 1981-83, lead engr., 1983-86, unit chief, 1986—. Served with USCG, 1970-74. Mem. IEEE, AIAA, Eta Kappa Nu. Republican. Presbyterian. Avocations: fishing, boating, cars, personal computers. Home: 721 Stone Canyon Manchester MO 63021 Office: McDonnell Douglas Astronautics Co Po Box 516 Saint Louis MO 63166

SPELLACY, WILLIAM NELSON, physician, educator; b. St. Paul, May 10, 1934; s. Jack F. and Elmyra L. (Nelson) S. B.A., U. Minn., 1955, B.S., 1956, M.D., 1959. Diplomate: Am. Bd. Ob-Gyn, subsplty. cert. in maternal and fetal medicine. Intern Hennepin County Gen. Hosp., Mpls., 1959-60; resident U. Minn., Mpls., 1960-63; practice medicine, specializing in ob-gyn Mpls., 1963-67, Miami, Fla., 1967-73, Gainesville, Fla., 1973-79, Chgo., 1979—; prof. dept. obstetrics and gynecology U. Miami, 1967-73; prof., chmn. dept. U. Fla., 1974-79; prof., head U. Ill. Coll. Medicine, Chgo., 1979—. Contbr. articles to med. jours. Mem. Am. Gynecol. Soc., Am. Assn. Obstetricians and Gynecologists, Am. Gynecol. and Obstet. Soc., Soc. Gynecol. Investigation, Am. Coll. Obstetricians and Gynecologists, Endocrine Soc., Am. Fertility Soc., Assn. Profs. Gynecology and Obstetrics, Am. Diabetes Assn., Perinatal Research Soc., South Atlantic Soc. Obstetrics and Gynecology, Central Assn. Obstetrics and Gynecology, Soc. Perinatal Obstetricians, AMA, Ill. Med. Soc. Episcopalian. Club: Rotary. Office: 840 S Wood St Chicago IL 60612

SPELTZ, GEORGE HENRY, bishop; b. Altura, Minn., May 29, 1912; s. Henry and Josephine (Jung) S. BS, St. Mary's Coll., Winona, Minn., 1932, LLD, 1963; student theology, St. Paul Sem., 1936-40; MA, Cath. U. Am., 1942, PhD, 1944; DD, Holy See, Italy, 1963. Ordained priest Roman Cath. Ch., 1940. Vice chancellor Diocese Winona, 1944-47, supt. schs., 1946-49, aux. bishop, 1963-66; pastor St. Mary's Ch., Minneiska, Minn., 1946-47;

tchr. St. Mary's Coll., 1947-63; rector Immaculate Heart of Mary Sem., Winona, 1948-63; co-adjutor bishop St. Cloud, Minn., 1966-68; bishop 1968-87; Pres. Nat. Cath. Rural Life Conf., 1970-72; mem. bishops' com. for pastoral on Cath. social thought and U.S. economy Nat. Council Cath. Bishops, 1981-86; cons. NCCB/USCC Task Force on Food and Agriculture Chpt. Economy Pastoral, 1987—.

SPELTZ, JOHN RALPH, investment manager; b. Albert Lea, Minn., Dec. 26, 1954; s. Thomas Theodore and Mary Jean (Donovan) S.; m. Lisa Marie McDonough, July 14, 1984 (div. Mar. 1986); 1 child, Evan. BS, St. John's U., 1977; BCE, U. Minn., 1979, MBA, 1984. Design engr. Sargent & Lundy Engring., Chgo., 1979-81; fin. cons. Merrill Lynch, Mpls., 1984-85; investment mgr. Speltz Inc., Albert Lea, 1981-84, 1985—. Avocations: investments, microcomputers, sailing, swimming, biking. Home: 311 Garden Rd Albert Lea MN 56007

SPENCE, JOHN DANIEL, real estate broker; b. Lethbridge, Alberta, Can., May 18, 1915; came to U.S., 1915, naturalized, 1943; s. Benjamin Abner and Clara May (Fullerton) S.; m. Phyllis Saxton Johnson, Feb. 4, 1939; children: Susan Kathleen Spence-Glassberg, John Daniel. A.B., Grinnell (Iowa) Coll., 1938; LL.D. (hon.), Rockford Coll., 1979. With Container Corp. Am., 1938-54, v.p., 1949-54; exec. Lanzit Corrugated Box Co., Chgo., from 1954; v.p. Consol. Paper Co., 1963; dir. devel. Rockford Coll., 1964-65, v.p., 1965-77, acting pres., 1977-79, cons., 1979—; bus. and ednl. cons., 1980—. Pres. Woodcrest Assn., Rockford, 1974-78; mem. adv. com. Forest Preserve Dist., Winnebago County, 1974—; chmn. adv. council Severson Dells Forest Preserve, 1976—; bd. dirs. John Howard Assn., to 1974-76; trustee Keith Country Day Sch., 1971-81, Children's Home of Rockford, 1973-76, Lake Forest Acad., to 1975, Pecatonica Prairie Path, 1975-85, Rockford Art Assn., 1980-83, Ctr. for Sight and Hearing Impaired, 1986—; trustee Highview Retirement Home, 1983—, pres., 1986—; mem. community adv. bd. WNIV-FM, No. Ill. U., 1984—. Recipient Karl L. Williams award Rockford Coll. Alumni Assn., 1980, Service Above Self award Rockford Rotary Club, 1980. Mem. Profl. Secs. Internat. (adv. com.), Rockford C. of C. (dir. 1966-71, v.p.). Clubs: Lion. (Chgo.), University (Chgo.). Home and Office: 6710 Woodcrest Pkwy Rockford IL 61109

SPENCE, MICHELE JEANNE, editor, writer; b. Smithville, N.C., July 14, 1940; d. Grant Fletcher Mollring and Margaret Mary (Kuhl) Baker; m. Stan Stephen Spence, Apr. 14, 1960; children: Scott David, Robert Lewis. BA summa cum laude, U. Md., 1970. Editor Cliffs Notes, Inc., Lincoln, Nebr., 1979—. Author: Shadow Play, 1981, Rebekka Moon, 1983. Democrat. Club: Lincoln Camera (editor 1985—). Avocation: photography. Home: 5147 S 37th St Lincoln NE 68516 Office: Cliffs Notes Inc 4851 S 16th St Lincoln NE 68512

SPENCER, ALAN GERALD, film and audiovisual entertainment producer, genealogist; b. Youngstown, Ohio, Mar. 16, 1941; s. David and Esther (Sohmer) Shwartz; m. Marylin Joyce Camberg, June 16, 1968; children—Bennett Colin, Ronna Lynn. B.S. in Edn., Ohio U., 1963; M.A., Central Mich. U., 1966. Cert. tchr., Ill. Tchr., Paul C. Bunn Sch., Youngstown, 1963-65; radio newscaster WBBW Radio, Youngstown, 1963-65; tchr. Coleman Intermediate Sch. (Mich.), 1965-66; tchr., resource dir. Crow Island Sch., Winnetka, Ill., 1966-74; producer, dir. The Spot Shop, Chgo., 1974-81; exec. producer Williams/Gerard Prodns., Chgo., 1981—. Editor: Search, 1981—, Internat. Quar. Researchers Jewish Geneaology; producer, dir. ednl. films, documentaries; contbr. articles to mags. Recipient Best Ednl. Film award Chgo. Internat. Film Festival, 1975. Mem. Jewish. Geneal. Soc. of Ill. (bd. dirs. 1981—). Jewish. Office: Williams/Gerard Prodns 420 N Wabash 5th Floor Chicago IL 60611

SPENCER, C. STANLEY, insurance executive; b. Canton, Pa., Sept. 24, 1940; s. Clarence N. and Maude E. (Phipps) S.; m. Carol M. Vest, Aug. 23, 1962; children: Greg, Mike. BS in Agrl. Engring., Pa. State U., 1961. Regional sales mgr. W.T. Grant Co., N.Y.C., 1966-76; engr. Hoover Well Service, Zion, Ill., 1976-80, Nielson Iron Works, Racine, Wis., 1980-82; spl. agent Prudential Ins. Co., Racine, 1982-84, div. mgr., 1984—. Recipient 1st Place Barbershop Chorus award, Racine, 1984, Kenosha, 1985, Manitowoc, 1986, 1st Place Barbershop Quartet award, Kenosha, Wis., 1986. Mem. Life Underwriters Assn. (v.p. 1985-86), Soc. for the Preservation and Encouragement of Barber Shop Quartet Singing in Am. (pres. Racine 1984-85). Republican. Club: Toastmasters (1st Place 1985). Home: 6234 Larchmont Dr Racine WI 53406 Office: 4401 Taylor Ave Racine WI 53405

SPENCER, CAROLE JANE MEARDY, educational administrator; b. Chgo., Nov. 27, 1935; d. Silas and Frances (Grabiec) Meardy; m. Fred Brown Spencer, May 4, 1957; children: Karyn Spencer Regitz, Susan Spencer Schwartz, Scott Martin. BS in English, Ill. State U., 1957, MS in English, 1968, EdD in Adminstrn., 1975. Dir. gifted student program, head English dept. LeRoy (Ill.) High Sch., 1965-71; asst. prof. Ill. State U., Normal, 1971-73; edn. cons., analyst Ill. State Senate, Springfield, 1973-77; asst. to state supt. edn. Ill. Dept. Edn., Springfield, 1977-81; research liaison officer Ill. State Bd. Edn., Springfield, 1981—; assoc. coordinator ednl. policy fellowship program Inst. Ednl. Leadership, Washington, 1975-79; dir. Nat. Assembly on Juvenile Justice, St. Charles, Ill., 1978; cons. Nat. Sch. Transp. Assn., Springfield, Va., 1976-82; state dir. edn./mil. liaison com. Dept. Def., Washington, 1977-83. Co-author (booklet) Educator's Guide to Career Military Resources, 1981; editor (monograph) The Courts Seek Fiscal Neutrality, 1972; mem. editoral bd. (jour.) Planning and Changing, 1971-73. Bd. dirs. Ill. Caucus on Teenage Pregnancy, Chgo., 1982—; mem. exec. service corps Project Life, Chgo., 1984; mem. planning com. Govs. Conf. on Edn., Chgo., 1978, state adv. com. Hugh O'Brian Youth Found., Ill., 1980—. Recipient Disting. Service Alumni award Ill. State U., 1980. Mem. Am. Assn. Sch. Adminstrs. (Outstanding Service award 1984), Am. Ednl. Research Assn., Ill. Women Adminstrs., Nat. Sch. Transp. Assn., Phi Delta Kappa. Avocations: travelling, genealogy. Home: 2 Duncan Park Jacksonville IL 62650 Office: Ill State Bd Edn 100 N First Springfield IL 62777

SPENCER, EDSON WHITE, computer systems company executive; b. Chgo., June 4, 1926; s. William M. and Gertrude (White) S. Student, Princeton, 1943, Northwestern U., U. Mich., 1944; B.A., Williams Coll., 1948, Oxford (Eng.) U., 1950; M.A., Oxford (Eng.) U., 1950. With Sears, Roebuck & Co., Chgo., 1951-54, Honeywell, Inc., Mpls., 1954—; Far East regional mgr. Honeywell, Inc., Tokyo, 1959-65; corp. v.p. internal ops. Honeywell, Inc., Mpls., 1965-69, exec. v.p., 1969-74, pres., chief exec. officer, 1974-78, chmn. bd., chief exec. officer, 1978—. Mem. Phi Beta Kappa. Office: Honeywell Inc Honeywell Plaza Minneapolis MN 55408 *

SPENCER, ETTA LORRAINE, nurse; b. East St. Louis, Ill., July 3, 1928; d. Leonard and Matilda Leola (Wiggins) Richie; R.N., St. Mary's Infirmary, 1949; BS St. Joseph's Coll., North Windham, Maine; m. Thomas Lee Spencer, Aug. 20, 1960; 1 son, Kevin. Staff, operating room nurse St. Mary's Infirmary, East St. Louis, 1949-55; night charge nurse Firmin Deslage Hosp., St. Louis, 1955-59; operating room nurse John Cochran VA Hosp., St. Louis, 1957-62; operating room supr. Centreville Twp. Hosp., East St. Louis, 1962-86; nurse infant mortality reduction services East Side Health Dist., East St. Louis, Ill., 1986—. Active East St. Louis Charities Day Organ. Mem. Am. Nurses Assn., Ill. Nurses Assn., 10th Dist. Nurses Assn., Assn. Operating Room Nurses, Black Nurses Assn. Democrat. Baptist. Lodge: Lioness. Home: 519 N 22d St East Saint Louis IL 62205 Office: East Side Health Dist 638 N 20th St East Saint Louis IL 62205

SPENCER, GARY DALE, chief police; b. Monte Vista, Colo., Sept. 3, 1949; s. Bob and Helen Eloise (Martz) Simpson; m. Myrna Ellen Willmore, July 6, 1969; children: Daniel Dale, Jeffrey Paul, Sheila Diane. Student various schs., intermittently, 1968—. Shop foreman Tripple M Chinehilla Cage Co., Omaha, 1964-67; acct. Commodore Corp., Omaha, 1967-70; patrolman Fremont Police Dept., Nebr., 1970-78; dir. Southeast Nebr. Ct. Alcohol Program, Beatrice, Nebr., 1978-79; chief of police Falls City, Nebr., 1979—. Den leader Falls City Webelos, 1981-82; bd. dirs. Southeast Nebr. Alcohol Program, 1978-85, mem. adv. council, 1980-85; vice-chmn. retirement com. Falls City Police and Firefighters, 1980—, adv. com. Nebr. Bingo and Pickle Card, 1985; mem. exec. com. Mid-States Organized Crime Info. Ctr., 1986. Recipient State of Nebr. Gov.'s award, 1980, Dist. Experts award Nat. Rifle Assn., 1981, Disting. Service award, 1985; Pedestrian Safety awards AAA Motor Club, 1979-84, Outstanding Young Law Enforcement award 1981; named one of Outstanding Young Men of Am., 1982, 85. Mem. Am. Guild of Hypnotherapists, Internat. Assn. Chiefs of Police, Nat. Assn. Chiefs Police (Safety and Edn. award 1986), Police Officers Assn. Nebr., Nebr. Assn. Notary Pubs., Nebr. Assn. Alcoholism Counselors, Falls City Jaycees (pres. 1984—, Outstanding Service award 1982, 83, Keyman award 1983-84, Presdl. award 1982, Jaycee of Yr., 1986). Republican. Mem. Christian Ch. Club: Foresters. Lodges: Eagles, Lions (local v.p.), Masons, Kiwanis (bd. dirs. Beatrice Early Risers club 1978) Home: 2618 Schoenheit St Falls City NE 68355

SPENCER, KATHLEEN MARY, small business owner; b. Trenton, N.J., Feb. 19, 1944; d. Angelo and Rose Marie (Nanni) Correnti; m. Thomas James Spencer, Nov. 30, 1963; 1 child, Lenore Rebecca. Exec. sec. 1st United Life Ins. Co., Gary, Ind., 1963-65, Swartz, Retson, Lindholm & Kettas, CPA's, Gary, 1966-69; legal sec. Hoeppner, Wagner, and Evans, Lowell, Ind., 1976-79; agt. New York Life Ins. Co., Merrillville, Ind., 1982-86; owner, operator Spencer Sewing Machine Service, Lowell, 1972—. Chmn. Home Econs. Adv. Bd., Lowell, 1978; mem. Intensive Office Lab. Adv. Bd., Lowell, 1985. Mem. South Lake County Bus. and Profl. Women (charter pres. Lowell 1979—, bd. dirs. 1979—), Retail Merchants (sec. 1976-79), N.W. Ind. Coalition of C. of C.'s (sec. 1978-80), Lowell C. of C. (bd. dirs., sec. 1976-81, v.p. 1981), Blind Vets. Assn., Disbaled Am. Vets. (co-state service officer 1986). Avocations: swimming, cooking, reading. Home and Office: 1651 E Commercial Ave Lowell IN 46356

SPENCER, LARRY LEE, industrial engineer; b. Cumberland, Md., Dec. 8, 1946; s. Ervin Davin and Virginia Mae (Holloway) S.; m. Carol Ann Cecil, Sept. 16, 1972; children: MarLisa Ann, LeAnna Shay. BSME, W.Va. U., 1969; MBA, U. Cin., 1983. Plant engr. Kelly Springfield Tire Co., Cumberland, 1969-75; project engr. Swedcast Corp., Florence, Ky., 1975-77, Stearns & Foster Co., Cin., 1977-80; mgr. project engring. Batesville (Ind.) Casket Co., 1980-83; robot project mgr. indsl. robot div. Cin. Milacron, 1983—. Coach and referee Youth Soccer, Landen, Ohio, 1986. Served to 1st lt. U.S. Army, 1969-71, Vietnam. Republican. Roman Catholic. Club: Engineers (Cumberland) (v.p. 1972-73). Avocations: golf, jogging, woodworking. Home: 8724 S Cove Dr Maineville OH 45039 Office: Cin Milacron Indsl Robot div 4701 Marburg Ave Cincinnati OH 45209

SPENCER, MICHAEL SHEA, author, educator, business executive; b. Oak Park, Ill., Sept. 12, 1949; s. Frank L. and Helen T. (Zezulak) S.; m. Susan C. Switzer, Dec. 27, 1971; children: Kathleen M., Cynthia M., Kelsey S., Andrew J. BS, So. Ill. U., Carbondale, 1971; MBA, So. Ill. U., Edwardsville; MA, U. No. Iowa, 1980. Cert. tchr., Iowa. Supr. inventory planning John Deere Engine Works, Waterloo, Iowa, 1976-78, systems analyst, 1978-80, master scheduler, 1980-81, mgr. inventory control, 1982-86; supr. materials mgmt. Deere Waterloo Engine Works, 1986-87; with John Deere Engine Works, Waterloo, 1987—; ptnr. Lancer Cons. Group, Cedar Falls, Iowa, 1983—; adj. prof. econs. U. No. Iowa, 1978-83. Served to capt. USAF, 1972-76. Decorated Air Force Commendation medal; named an Outstanding Young Am., 1986; So. Ill. U., Carbondale resident fellow, 1970, 71. Mem. AAUP, Am. Prodn. and Inventory Control Soc. (bd. dirs. 1987, v.p. Region V). Home: 421 W Seerley Blvd Cedar Falls IA 50613 Office: Deere Inc Waterloo Engine Works Box 5100 Waterloo IA 50704

SPENCER, SHARON DENISE, systems analyst; b. Washington, Feb. 2, 1961; d. Willie Spencer and Hattie Mae (Washington) Cockrell. BBA in Mgmt. Info. Systems, Howard U., 1983. Assoc. systems analyst Gen. Motors, Warren, Mich., 1984—. Product advisor Jr. Achievement, 1985-86, exec. advisor 1986—; mem. Big Bros./Big Sisters, 1986; asst. troup leader Girl Scouts U.S., 1986—. Mem. Focus User Orgn., Pre-MBA Assn. (cert. 1986). Democrat. Baptist. Club: Anspené (Detroit) (coordinator 1984—). Avocations: biking, reading magazines. Home: 5800 Annapolis Rd #411 Bladensburg MD 20710 Office: Gen Motors 30001 Van Dyke Ave Warren MI 48090

SPENCER, THEODORE RAY, engineering administrator; b. Pearl City, Ill., Nov. 1, 1935; s. Meryl Eugene Spencer and Helen Marie (Katzenberger) Hammond; m. Donna Fern McDearmon, May 5, 1957; children: Michael Ray, Mitchell Jon, Matthew Thomas, Mark Evan, Molly Anna. Student, Western Ill. U., 1961. Draftsman Beloit (Wis.) Corp., 1961-65, supr. engring. services, 1965-80, mgr. engring. support divs., 1980—. Creator of 35mm micrographics systems, 1970. Master Cub Scouts of Am., Newark Twp., 1968-71; leader 4H Newark Pioneers, 1969-75; coach Orfordville Little League, 1971-80; advisor Luth. Ch. Luther League, 1975-86. Served with U.S. Army, 1959-61. Mem. Assn. Image and Info. Mgmt. (pres. Rockford, Ill. Blackhawk micrographics chpt. 1979-80). Office: Beloit Corp 1 St Lawrence Ave Beloit WI 53511

SPENCER, WILLIAM EDWIN, telephone company executive, engineer; b. Kansas City, Mo., Mar. 22, 1926; s. Erwin Blanc and Edith Marie (Peterson) S.; student U. Kansas City, 1942; A.S., Kansas City Jr. Coll., 1945; B.S. in E.E., U. Mo., 1948; postgrad. Iowa State U., 1969; m. Ferne Arlene Nieder, Nov. 14, 1952; children—Elizabeth Ann, Gary William, James Richard, Catherine Sue. With Southwestern Bell Telephone Co., Kansas City, Mo., 1948-50, Topeka, 1952-61, sr. engr., 1966-69, equipment maintenance engr., 1969-76, engring. ops. mgr., 1976-79, dist. mgr., 1979—; mem. tech. staff Bell Telephone Labs., N.Y.C., 1961-62, Holmdel, N.J., 1962-66; U.S. Senatorial Club, 1985—. Mem. Rep. Presdl. Task Force, 1984—. Served with AUS, 1950-52. Recipient best Kans. idea award Southwestern Bell Telephone Co., 1972, cert. of appreciation Kans. Miss Teen Pageant, 1984. Registered profl. engr., Kans. Mem. Kans. Engring. Soc., Nat. Soc. Profl. Engrs., IEEE, Topeka Engrs. Club (past pres.), Telephone Pioneers Assn., Nat. Geog. Soc., Kans. Hist. Soc., Am. Assn. Ret. Persons, U. Mo.-Columbia Alumni Assn., Nat. Travel Club. Republican. Patentee in field. Home: 3201 MacVicar Ct Topeka KS 66611 Office: 220 E 6th St Topeka KS 66603

SPENGLER, KAREN ANN, accountant; b. Los Angeles, June 7, 1952; d. Robert I. and Jean K. (Steinbacher) S. BSBA, Rockhurst Coll., 1974. CPA, Mo., Kans. Staff tax acct. Arthur Andersen & Co., Kansas City, Mo., 1974-78; ptnr. Schmidt, Carrico & Spengler, Overland Park, Kans., 1979-81; pres. K.A. Spengler, Chartered, Overland Park, 1981-86; v.p. Wolff, Spengler & Co., Fairway, Kans., 1985-86; prin. Karen A. Spengler, CPA, Kansas City, Mo., 1986—. Chmn. Shawnee Mission Regional Leadership Council, ARC, Prairie Village, Kans., 1984-87, bd. dirs. Kansas City chpt., 1984—. Mem. Am. Inst. CPA's, Mo. Soc. CPA's, Estate Planning Assn. Kansas City. Roman Catholic. Avocations: detective novels, fgn. langs. Office: 20 E Winthrope Kansas City MO 64113

SPERLICH, HAROLD KEITH, automobile company executive; b. Detroit, Dec. 1, 1929; s. Harold Christ and Elva Margaret (Stoker) S.; m. Polly A. Berryman, May 22, 1976; children: Sue, Scott, Terry L.; stepchildren: Laurie, Brian, Scott, Colleen. B.S. in Mech. Engring, U. Mich., 1951, M.B.A., 1961. With Aluminum Co. Am., 1951-54; v.p. car ops. Ford Motor Co., Detroit, 1957-77; v.p. product planning and design Chrysler Corp., Highland Park, Mich., 1977-78; group v.p. engring., product devel. Chrysler Corp., Highland Park, 1978-81, pres. N.Am. ops., 1981-84; pres. Chrysler Corp., 1984—, also dir. Active Detroit Community Fund. Served with USNR, 1954-57. Presbyterian. Club: Orchard Lake (Mich.) Country. Home: 3333 W Shore Dr Orchard Lake MI 48033 Office: Chrysler Corp 12000 Chrysler Dr Highland Park MI 48288 *

SPERLING, MARC LEWIS, accountant; b. Chgo., Feb. 28, 1951; s. Aaron Arky and Helen (Zolotar) S.; m. Judith Louise Zibell, July 9, 1977; children: John Benjamin, Allison Leah. BA, U. Ill., 1973, MAS, 1976. CPA, Ill. Staff acct. Katch Tyson & Co., Chgo., 1976-77; staff auditor Bell Fed. Savs. and Loan, Chgo., 1977-78; internat. acct. Borg Warner Acceptance, Chgo., 1978-80; advanced staff acct. Ernst & Whinney, Chgo., 1980-83; sr. acct. Laventhol & Horwath, Chgo., 1983-86; acct. Inland Steel Co., Chgo., 1986—. Mem. Am. Inst. CPA's, Ill. CPA Soc. Democrat. Jewish. Avocations: TV, movies, sports, music. Home: 122 S Washington Westmont IL 60559

SPERLING, RICHARD LYLE, plastic surgeon; b. Chgo., Jan. 15, 1939; s. Nathan Stanley and Ethel (Tuller) S.; m. Harlene Joy Fagot, Dec. 17, 1961; children: Marci Sue, Beth Ann, Michael Scott. Student, U. Ill., Chgo., 1956-59, MD, 1963. Intern Cook County Hosp., Chgo., 1963-64; resident in gen. surgery West Side VA Hosp., Chgo., 1964-68; resident in plastic surgery Presbyn.-St. Luke's Hosp., Chgo., 1968-69, U. Ill., Chgo., 1969-70; practice medicine specializing in plastic surgery Skokie, Ill., 1970—. Contbr. articles to profl. and scholarly jours. Served to maj. Ill. NG, 1964-70. Fellow ACS; mem. Am. Soc. Plastic and Reconstructive Surgeons, Am .Soc. Trauma, Am. Burn Assn., Chgo. Soc. Plastic Surgery (pres. 1981-82), Am. Cleft Palate Assn., Am. Soc. Aesthetic Plastic Surgery, Am. Soc. Maxilofacial Surgery, Am. Assn. Hand Surgery, Midwest Surgical Assn., Midwest Assn. Plastic Surgery, Am. Assn. for Hand Surgery. Office: 64 Old Orchard Suite 210 Skokie IL 60077

SPERO, KEITH ERWIN, lawyer; b. Cleve., Aug. 21, 1933; s. Milton D. and Yetta (Silverstein) S.; m. Carol Kohn, July 4, 1957 (div. 1974); children—Alana, Scott, Susan; m. 2d, Karen Weaver, Dec. 28, 1975. B.A., Western Res. U. 1954, LL.B., 1956. Bar: Ohio 1956. Assoc. Sindell, Sindell & Bourne, Cleve., 1956-57, Sindell, Sindell, Bourne, Markus, Cleve., 1960-64; ptnr. Sindell, Sindell, Bourne, Markus, Stern & Spero, Cleve., 1964-74, Spero & Rosenfield, Cleve., 1974-76, Spero, Rosenfield & Bourne, L.P.A., Cleve., 1977-79, Spero & Rosenfield Co. L.P.A., 1979—; tchr. bus. law U. Md. overseas div., Eng., 1958-59; lectr. Case-Western Res. U., 1965-69; instr. Cleve. Marshall Law Sch. of Cleve. State U., 1968—; nat. panel arbitrators Am. Arbitration Assn. Trustee Western Res. Hist. Soc., 1984—. Served as 1st lt. JAGC, USAF, 1957-60; capt. Res., 1960-70. Mem. ABA, Ohio Bar Assn., Cleve. Bar Assn., Cuyahoga County Bar Assn., Ohio Acad. Trial Lawyers (pres. 1970-71), Assn. Trial Lawyers Am. (state committeeman 1971-75, bd. govs. 1975-79, sec. family law litigation sect. 1975-76, vice-chmn. 1976-77, chmn. 1977-79), Order of Coif, Phi Beta Kappa, Zeta Beta Tau, Tau Epsilon Rho. Jewish (trustee, v.p. congregation 1972-78). Clubs: Cleve. Racquet, Dugway Creek Yacht (commodore 1984—). Lodge: Masons. Author: The Spero Divorce Folio, 1966; Hospital Liability for Acts of Professional Negligence, 1979. Home: 2 Bratenahl Pl Bratenahl OH 44108 Office: Suite 500 113 St Clair Cleveland OH 44114

SPERRY, JAMES ALLEN, farmer; b. Aberdeen, S.D., Sept. 24, 1930; s. Allen R. and Marjorie (Jones) S.; m. Jo Ann Burnham, Sept. 20, 1953; children: Kathy, Scott, John. BS, S.D. State U., 1952. Ptnr. Sperry Farms Inc., Bath, S.D., 1960-70; gen. mgr. Sperry Farms Inc., Bath, 1970-84; pres. Sperry Farms Inc., 1984—. Bd. dirs. Aberdeen Pub. Sch. System, 1974-83, Hub Area Vocat. Sch., 1980-83; adv. bd. St. Lukes Hosp. Aberdeen, 1977-83; chmn. bd. First United Meth. Ch., 1982-85. Named Outstanding Young Farmer, Aberdeen Jaycees, 1957. Mem. S.D. Crop Import Assn., Brown County Livestock Import Assn. (pres. 1961-62), S.D. Livestock Assn., N. Cen. Livestock Feeders, Profl. Famrers Am, Aberdeen C. of C. Democrat. Lodge: Elks. Avocation: home computer. Home and Office: Rt 1 Box 99 Bath SD 57427

SPERRY, JAMES EDWARD, anthropologist; b. Weeping Water, Nebr., May 17, 1936; s. John Edward and Augusta Anea (Frandsen) S.; m. Gail Louise Killen, Sept. 26, 1964; 1 child, Patrick Reuben. Student, Bethany Coll., Lindsborg, Kans., 1953-55; A.B. in Art and Anthropology, U. Nebr., Lincoln, 1962, M.A. in Anthropology, 1965. Teaching asst. U. Neb., 1961-63, instr. anthropology, 1964-65; research archeologist State Hist. Soc. N.D., Bismarck, 1965-69; supt. State Hist. Soc. N.D., 1969—; sec. N.D. Heritage Found., 1973-76; sec. N.D. Lewis and Clark Trail Council, 1970, chmn., 1971; N.D. hist. preservation officer 1969—, N.D. State records coordinator, 1975—; mem. Theodore Roosevelt Rough Rider award com., 1969—, N.D. Natural Resources Council, 1969—. Editor: North Dakota History: Journal of the Northern Plains, 1969-1973; contbr. numerous articles profl. jours. Served with USAF, 1956-59. Am. Assn. State and Local History fellow, 1967; Bush summer fellow, 1984. Mem. Sigma Xi, Delta Phi Delta, Sigma Gamma Epsilon. Home: Rt 2 Bismarck ND 58501 Office: North Dakota Heritage Center Bismarck ND 58505

SPERRY, LEN T., psychiatry and preventive medicine educator; b. Milw., Dec. 1, 1943; s. Leonard V. and Wanda R. (Sadowski) S.; m. Patricia L. Garcia, June 11, 1977; children: Tracy, Christen, L. Timothy, Steven, Jonathon. BA, St. Mary's Coll., Winona, Minn., 1966; PhD, Northwestern U., 1970; MD, Centro Estudios Tecnologicos Universidad, Dominican Republic, 1981. Diplomate Am. Bd. Profl. Psychology. Asst. prof. Marquette U., Milw., 1971-74; assoc. prof. U. Wis., Milw., 1974-75, U.S. Internat. U., San Diego, 1976-78; resident in psychiatry and preventive medicine Med. Coll. Wis., Milw., 1982-85, clin. prof. psychiatry, preventive medicine, 1986—; cons. Northeastern Ill. U., Chgo., 1970-71, Am. Appraisal Assn., Milw., 1972-76, Calif. Sch. Profl. Psychology, San Diego, 1977-79. Author: Learning Performance and Individual Differences, 1972, Together Experience, 1978; (with others) Contact Counseling, 1974, You Can Make It Happen: Self-Actualization and Organization, 1977, Adlerian Counseling and Psychotherapy, 19876. Cons. mayoral campaign, South Bend, Ind., 1971. Northwestern U. fellow, 1969, Med. Coll. Wis. grantee, 1980. Mem. Am. Psychol. Assn. (sci. affair com. 1975-76), N. Am. Soc. Adlerian Psychology, Am. Psychiat. Assn., Assn. Christian Therapists, Wis. Psychiat. Assn. for Counselor Edn. and Supervision (chmn. publs. com., 1974-77), Assn. Counseling and Supervision. Avocations: reading, racquet sports, music.

SPEZIA, MICHAEL JOSEPH, osteopathic physician and surgeon, educator; b. St. Louis, Sept. 8, 1950; s. Anthony Louis and Annabelle (Schauer) S.; m. Joyce Louvre Henson, Oct. 28, 1978; 1 child, Michelle. BA, U. Mo., 1972; DO, Kansas City Coll. Osteo. Medicine, 1977. Intern Normandy Osteo. Hosp., St. Louis, 1977-78, clin. teaching faculty, 1978—; practice medicine specializing in family practice and osteo. medicine, St. Louis, 1977—; adj. clin. faculty Kirksville Coll. Osteo. Medicine, 1978—, Tulsa Coll. Osteo. Medicine, 1978—, Kansas City Coll. Osteo. Medicine, 1978—. Adv. bd. Forest Park Community Coll., St. Louis, 1984—; patron St. Louis Zool. Assn., 1984—. Mem. Am. Osteo. Assn., St. Louis Assn. Osteo. Physicians and Surgeons, Mo. Assn. Osteo. Physicians, Am. Coll. Osteo. Gen Practioners, Am. Osteo. Assn. of Scleprotherapy, Fraternal Order Police (assoc.). Roman Catholic. Lodge: K.C. (4th degree). Avocations: classic auto restoration, road rallys. Home: 46 Bellerive Acres Saint Louis MO 63121 Office: 23 N Oaks Plaza Saint Louis MO 63121

SPHIRE, RAYMOND DANIEL, anesthesiologist; b. Detroit, Feb. 12, 1927; s. Samuel Raymond and Nora Mae (Allen) S.; m. Joan Lois Baker, Sept. 5, 1953; children—Suzanne M., Raymond Daniel, Catherine J. B.S., U. Detroit, 1948; M.D., Loyola U., Chgo., 1952. Diplomate Am. Bd. Anesthesiology. Intern Grace Hosp., Detroit, 1952-53, attending anesthesiologist, 1955-72, dir. dept. inhalation therapy, 1968-70; dir. dept. inhalation therapy Harvard Anesthesia Lab.-Mass. Gen. Hosp., 1953-55; sr. attending anesthesiologist, dir. dept., dir. dept. respiratory therapy Detroit-Macomb Hosps. Assn., 1970—, trustee, 1978—, chief of staff, 1980—; clin. asst. prof. Wayne State U. Sch. Medicine, 1967—; clin. prof. respiratory therapy Macomb County Community Coll., Mount Clemens, Mich., 1971—; examiner Am. Registry Respiratory Therapists, 1972—; insp. Joint Rev. Com. Respiratory Therapy Edn., 1972—. Co-author: Operative Neurosurgery, 1970, First Aid Guide for the Small Business or Industry, 1978. Served with AUS, 1944-45; as 1st lt. M.C., USAF, 1952. Fellow Am. Coll. Anesthesiologists, Am. Coll. Chest Physicians; mem. AMA, Am. Soc. Anesthesiologists, Wayne County Soc. Anesthesiologists (pres. 1967-69), Am. Assn. Respiratory Therapists, Soc. Critical Care Medicine. Clubs: Detroit Athletic, Country of Detroit, Otsego Ski. Lodge: Severance. Home: 281 Lake Shore Rd Grosse Pointe Farms MI 48236 Office: 119 Kercheval St Grosse Pointe Farms MI 48236

SPICE, DENNIS DEAN, state university official, financial consultant; b. Rochester, Ind., Feb. 7, 1950; s. Donnelly Dean and Lorene (Rhodes) S.; m. Linda Kay Buehler, Oct. 1, 1971; children: Kristie Lorene, Danielle Deanne. A.A., SUNY, Albany, 1974, B.A., Eastern Ill. Univ., 1978; M.B.A., Univ. Ill., Urbana, 1985. Cert. systems profl., 1984. Employee benefits mgr. Eastern Ill. Univ., Charleston, 1977-80; disbursements officer State Univs. Retirement System, Champaign, Ill., 1980-81, assoc. exec. dir. adminstrn., 1981—; pres., cons. Spice and Assocs., Champaign, 1984—. Served to staff sgt. USMC, 1968-77; Vietnam. Mem. Data Processing Mgmt. Assn. (v.p. 1982-83), Nat. Assn. Accts. Assn. Systems Mgmt., Govt. Fin. Offices Assn., Internat. Found. Employee Benefits Plans, Nat. Conf. Pub. Employee Retirement Systems, Am. Cons. League. Republican. Home: Rural Route 3 Box

39 Champaign IL 61821 Office: State Univs Retirement System 50 Gerty Dr Champaign IL 61820

SPICER, JAMES WARREN, pharmaceuticals company executive; b. Massillon, Ohio, July 22, 1953; s. Warren Harding and Eileen Mary (McLaughlin) S.; m. Antonia Marie Andriotto, Dec. 4, 1976; children: James Warren, Andrew Barclay. BA cum laude, W.Va. U., Morgantown, 1975. Instr. lab. human physiology, cellular molecular biology W.Va. U., Morgantown, 1974-75, surg. technician (Am. Heart Assn. Dept. Pharmacology grantee), 1975-76; trainee med. sales Bowman Drug Co., Canton, Ohio, 1976-77; rep. med. sales Pennwalt Corp., Rochester, N.Y., 1977-80, hosp. sales rep., sales trainer, various locations, 1980-82, dist. sales mgr., Pitts., Canton, W.Va., Columbus, Youngstown, 1982—. Pres., Massillon (Ohio) Young Reps. Club, 1971-72; mem. Canton Council for Exceptional Children, 1976—. Mem. Pres.'s Club, Beta Beta Beta, Alpha Epsilon Delta. Republican.

SPIEGEL, MICHAEL GILBERT, optometrist; b. Chgo., Feb. 2, 1948; s. Oscar and Marlene (Warsaski) S.; m. Elaine Biblin, Aug. 18, 1974; 1 child, Marisa. BA, Bradley U., 1970, OD, Pacific U., 1974. Pvt. practice optometry Evanston, Ill., 1981—. Mem. Am. Optometric Assn. Contact Lens Div., Chgo. Northside Optometric Soc. (v.p. info. 1984—). Jewish. Lodge: Lions (pres. local chpt. 1986-87). Avocations: triathlons, marathons, tennis, golf. Home: 5005 N Lawndale Chicago IL 60625 Office: 1008 W Church St Evanston IL 60201

SPIEGEL, S. ARTHUR, judge; b. Cin., Oct. 24, 1920; s. Arthur Major and Hazel (Wise) S.; m. Louise Wachman, Oct. 31, 1945; children—Thomas, Arthur Major, Andrew, Roger Daniel. B.A., U. Cin., 1942, postgrad., 1949; LL.B., Harvard U., 1948. Assoc. Kasfir & Chalfie, Cin., 1948-52; assoc. Benedict, Bartlett & Shepard, Cin., 1952-53, Gould & Gould, Cin., 1953-54; ptnr. Gould & Spiegel, Cin., 1954-59; assoc. Cohen, Baron, Druffel & Hogan, Cin., 1960; ptnr. Cohen, Todd, Kite & Spiegel, Cin., 1961-80; judge U.S. Dist Ct. Ohio, Cin., 1980—. Served to capt. USMC, 1942-46. Mem. ABA, Ohio Bar Assn., Cin. Bar Assn., Fed. Bar Assn. Democrat. Jewish. Club: Cin. Lawyers. Home: 4031 Egbert Ave Cincinnati OH 45220 Office: US Dist Ct 838 US Courthouse Cincinnati OH 45202 *

SPIGLANIN, ROBERT JAY, chemist; b. Racine, Wis., Apr. 13, 1959; s. John Vitold and Olga Alexis (Luka) S. BS, U. Wis., 1981. Chemist Abbott Labs., Abbott Park, Ill., 1982—. Recipient Chemistry Achievement award Chem Rubber Co., 1978. Mem. Am. Chem. Soc., Chgo. Chromatography Discussion Group. Avocations: golf, racquetball, skiing, softball. Home: 518 Lakehurst Rd #2R Waukegan IL 60085 Office: Abbott Labs Routes 137 and 43 Abbott Park IL 60064

SPILBELER, LARRY NEIL, automotive executive, mechanical engineer; b. Indpls., July 23, 1954; s. Donald George Spilbeler and Carol Elaine (Miller) Locke; m. Pamela Sue Dover, Aug. 23, 1975; children: Brian Neal, Kyle Allen, Jason Aaron. BSME, Rose Hulman Inst. Tech., 1976. Process engr. Packard Electronics div. Gen. Motors Corp., Warren, Ohio, 1976-80; mfg. foreman Packard Electronics div. Gen. Motors Corp., Warren, 1980-81, process engr., 1981-84; sr. mfg. engr., mfg. engr. supr. Ford Electronics and Refrigeration Corp., Bedford, Ind., 1985—. Active YMCA, Bloomington, Ind., U.S. Jaycees, Warren. Mem. Soc. Mfg. Engrs. Avocations: softball, golf, skiing, automobile rebuilding. Office: Ford Electronics 3120 W 16th St Bedford IN 47421

SPILSETH, PAUL, physician; b. Kensington, Minn., June 25, 1943; s. Palmet Anthony and Esther Pauline (Gunderson) S.; m. Claire Morgan, Feb. 17, 1973; children: Emily, Ted, Sarah. BA, Concordia Coll., 1965; MD, U. Minn., 1969. Intern St. Mary's Hosp., Duluth, Minn., 1969-70; resident in family practice U. Okla. Hosps., 1970-71; practice medicine specializing in family practice Stillwater, Minn., 1971—. Recipient Mead Johnson award, 1970; Smith Kline Fgn. fellow, 1968, Bush Found. fellow, 1986. Mem. Minn. Med. Assn., Wakota County Med. Assn. (pres. 1978-79), Minn. Assn. Nursing Home Med. Dirs. (pres. 1984-85), Am. Acad. Family Physicians, Am. Med. Dirs. Assn., Am. Coll. Allergy, Acad. Allergists and Immunologists. Lutheran. Lodge: Lions. Office: St Croix Valley Clinic 921 S Greeley Stillwater MN 55082

SPINAZZE, DENNIS JOSEPH, oral and maxillofacial surgeon; b. Detroit, Oct. 22, 1950; s. Angelo and Ernestine (Manzon) S.; m. Nancy Mallow, Dec. 18, 1976; children: Mark, Jaime, Anne. BS, U. Mich., 1972; postgrad., Western Mich. U., 1972-74; DDS, U. Detroit, 1978. Diplomate Am. Bd. Oral and Maxillofacial Surgery. Resident in gen. dentistry Hines (Ill.) VA Hosp., 1978-79; resident oral and maxillofacial surgery Detroit Macomb Hosps., 1979-82; practice dentistry specializing in oral and maxillofacial surgery Assocs. for Oral Surgery Ltd., Mt. Prospect, Chgo. and Bartlett, Ill., 1982—; instr. Am. Heart Assn., Chgo., 1983—; clin. instr. Northwestern U., Chgo., 1984—. Fellow Am. Assn. Oral and Maxillofacial Surgeons; mem. ADA, Ill. Soc. Oral and Maxillofacial Surgeons, Great Lakes Soc. Oral and Maxillofacial Surgeons, Chgo. Dental Soc. (Northwest Surburban Br.), Chgo. Soc. Oral and Maxillofacial Surgeons. Roman Catholic. Office: Assocs for Oral Surgery Ltd 110 S Oak Bartlett IL 60103 Office: 10 N Ridge Mount Prospect IL 60056 Office: 4935 W Irving Park Rd Chicago IL 60641

SPINDEL, ROBERT J., financial consultant, investment advisor; b. St. Louis, June 19, 1946; m. Joyce Ann Sharp. A.A., St. Louis Community Coll., 1970; C.L.U., Am. Coll. 1978, Chartered Fin. Cons., 1980. Acctg. and fin. specialist U.S. Air Force, 1960-64; acct. Siegel, Robert, Plating and Co., St. Louis, 1965-70; life underwriter New England Life, St. Louis; 1970-75; pres., owner Spindel, Van Ittersum & Co., St. Louis, 1976—; mem. Estate Planning Council of St. Louis, 1975—. Contbr. articles on fin. and tax planning to profl. jours. Served to sgt. USAF, 1964-70. Life and quality mem. Million Dollar Round Table; charter mem. Registry Fin. Planning Practioners; mem. Internat. Assn. for Fin. Planning, Fin. Profls. Adv. Panel. Republican. Mem. United Ch. of Christ. Club: Mo. Athletic. Avocation: fishing

SPINK, GORDON CLAYTON, osteopathic physician; b. Lansing, Mich., Jan. 6, 1935; s. John Clayton and Marian (Taylor) S.; m. Jane Miller Frisbee, Nov. 26, 1960; children—John, Anne. B.S., Mich. State U., 1957, Ph.D., 1966, D.O., 1975. Instr. Research Electron Microscope Lab., Mich. State U., 1962-66, dir., 1966-72, asst. prof. Pesticide Research Ctr., 1966-71, dir., Electron Microscope Lab. Osteo Medicine 1972-74, clin. asst. prof. dept. family medicine, 1975-76, assoc. prof., 1976—, unit III coordinator osteo. medicine, 1977-80, co-dir. preceptor program, 1978-80; acting asst. dean grad. and continuing med. edn. in osteo. medicine, 1980; research collaborator Brookhaven Nat. Lab., Upton, N.Y., 1969; intern Osteo. Hosp., Flint, Mich., 1976, dir. med. edn., 80-82; dir. med. edn. Lansing Gen. Hosp., Mich., 1982-84. Bd. dirs. devel. fund Mich. State U., 1981-85; mem. Okemos Sch. Bd., Mich., 1983. Served with USAF, 1958-60. NIH fellow 1972-73. Mem. Am. Osteo. Assn., Mich. Osteo. Physicians and Surgeons Assn., Maine Osteo Assn., Assn. Osteo. Dirs. Med. Edn., Am. Heart Assn. (Mich. affiliate), Mich. Sch. Health Assn., Am. Med. Soccer Assn. (sec., treas.), Am. Soc. Cell Biology, AAAS, Electron Microscope Soc., Mich. Assn. Osteo. Dirs. Med. Edn., Mich. Council Grad. Med. Edn., Mich. State U. Coll. Osteo. Med. Alumni Assn. (past chmn.), Sigma Xi. Home: 3910 Sandlewood Dr Okemos MI 48864 Office: Mich State U Fee Hall East Lansing MI 48824

SPINNER, LEE LOUIS, accountant; b. Hillsboro, Ill., Nov. 9, 1948; s. John Louis and Clara Mae (Brown) S. B.S. in Acctg., U. Ill., 1971, M.A.S. in Acctg., 1972; M.S. in Taxation, DePaul U., 1983. C.P.A., Ill. Sr. tax acct. Ernst & Whinney, Chgo., 1972-78; dir. tax returns and audits Sunbeam Corp., Chgo., 1978-82; dir. tax compliance Sara Lee Corp., Chgo., 1982-83; mgr. tax compliance AM Internat., Inc., Chgo., 1983-85; mgr. taxes Household Mfg., Inc., Prospect Heights, Ill., 1985—; instr. tax tng. program Ernst & Whinney, 1975-78. Tax advisor Sta. WIND, Call Your Act., Chgo., 1977-78; sec. Grant Park Accts. Softball League, Chgo., 1976-77. Mem. Ill. C.P.A. Soc., Am. Inst. C.P.A.s. Democrat. Roman Catholic. Club: Top Social Athletic (Chgo.). Lodges: Moose, K.C. Home: 9332 Landings Ln Des Plaines IL 60016 Office: Household Mfg 2700 Sanders Rd Prospect Heights IL 60070

SPIRE, ROBERT M., attorney general of Nebraska; b. Omaha, Sept. 20, 1925. B.S., Harvard U., 1949, J.D., 1952; student, Juilliard Sch. Music, 1952; D.H.L. (hon.), U. Nebr.-Omaha, 1971. C.P.A., Nebr. Ptnr. Ellick, Spire & Jones, Omaha; atty. gen. State of Nebr., Lincoln, 1985—; adj. assoc. prof. med. jurisprudence U. Nebr. Coll. Medicine, 1968-84; mem. Nebr. Fourth Jud. Dist. Com. on Inquiry, 1959-81, vice chmn., 1974-81. Contbr. articles to profl. jours. Mem. Gov.'s Citizens Comm. for Study Higher Edn. in Nebr., 1984. Served with U.S. Army, 1943-46. Recipient numerous awards for profl. and civic contbns., including Spl. Contbn. to Black Heritage award Omaha Black Heritage Series, 1983, Whitney M. Young Meml. award Urban League Nebr., 1983. Fellow Am. Bar Found.; mem. Am. Judicature Soc. (bd. dirs. 1983-84), ABA (spl. com. on lawyers' pub. service responsibility 1983-84), Am. Guild Organists, Nebr. State Bar Assn. (pres. 1981-82), Nebr. Continuing Legal Edn. (pres. 1978-80), Urban League Nebr. (bd. dirs. 1977-80), Omaha Bar Assn. (pres. 1978-79), Legal Aid Soc. Omaha (bd. dirs. 1971-79, pres. 1972-75). Office: Nebr Dept Justice Office Atty Gen Lincoln NE 68509 *

SPITZ, RANDY JOSEPH, comptroller; b. Urbana, Ill., Aug. 26, 1958; s. Charles Samuel and Colleta Mary (Zwilling) S. BS in Acctg., U. Ill., 1981. CPA, Ill. Audit supr. Kesler & Co., Ltd., Urbana, 1981-86; comptroller Hicks Oils and Hicksgas Inc., Roberts, Ill., 1986—. Parade chmn. Champaign County Freedom Celebration com., Ill., 1986. Mem. Am. Inst. CPA's, Ill. CPA Soc., St. Joseph Jaycees (pres. 1982-83). Roman Catholic. Lodge: KC. Avocation: pvt. pilot. Office: Hicks Oil and Hicksgas Inc PO Box 98 Roberts IL 60962

SPLINTER, WILLIAM ELDON, agricultural engineering educator; b. North Platte, Nebr., Nov. 24, 1925; s. William John and Minnie (Calhoun) S.; m. Eleanor Love Peterson, Jan. 10, 1953; children: Kathryn Love, William John, Karen Ann, Robert Marvin. BS in Agrl. Engring., U. Nebr., 1950; MS in Agrl. Engring., Mich. State U., 1951, PhD in Agrl. Engring., 1955. Instr. agrl. engring. Mich. State U., East Lansing, 1953-54; assoc. prof. agrl. engring. N.C. State U., Raleigh, 1954-60, prof. biology and agrl. engring., 1960-68; prof., chmn. dept. agrl. engring. U. Nebr., Lincoln, 1968-84, George Holmes Disting. prof., head dept. agrl. engring., 1984—; cons. engr. Mem. exec. bd. Am. Assn. Engring. Socs.; hon. prof. Shengyang (People's Republic of China) Angrl. U. Contbr. articles to tech. jours. Served with USNR, 1946-51. Recipient Massey Ferguson Ednl. award; named to Nebr. Hall of Agrl. Achievement. Fellow AAAS, Am. Soc. Agrl. Engrs. (pres., adminstrv. council, found. pres.); mem. Nat. Acad. Engring., Soc. Automotive Engrs., Am. Soc. Engring. Edn., Nat. Soc. Profl. Engrs., Sigma Xi, Sigma Tau, Sigma Pi Sigma, Pi Mu Epsilon, Gamma Sigma Delta, Phi Kappa Phi, Beta Sigma Psi. Patentee in field. Home: 7105 N Hampton St Lincoln NE 68506 Office: U Nebr Dept Agrl Engring 223 LWC Lincoln NE 68583-0726

SPODEN, JAMES EDWARD, otolaryngologist; b. Guttenburg, Iowa, Jan. 16, 1949; s. John M. and Elinor E. (Adams) S.; m. Janet Lynn Thompson, Apr. 22, 1978; children: Elizabeth Christine, Erika Berniece. BA, U. Iowa, 1971, MD, 1974. Diplomate Am. Bd. Otolaryngology. Intern Butterworth Hosp., Grand Rapids, Mich., 1954-75; mem. staff emergency room Cottage Hosp., Galesburg, Ill., 1975-76; resident in otolaryngology Maxillo Facial Surgery, U. Iowa, 1976-79; assoc. fellow dept. otolaryngology U. Iowa, 1979-80; mem. staff head and neck surgery Dubuque (Iowa) Otolaryngology P.C., 1980-84; Otolaryngologist Eastern Iowa Head and Neck Surgery, P.C., Cedar Rapids, Iowa, 1984—; mem. staff St. Luke's Hosp., Cedar Rapids, 1984-86, Mercy Hosp., 1984-86; cons. Del. Co. Hosp., Manchester, Iowa, 1981-86, Anamosa Community Hosp., 1984-86. Mem. Cedar Rapids YMCA, 1985—, Greater Downtown Assn, Cedar Rapids, 1985—; bd. dirs. Dubuque Symphony Orch., 1980-84. Fellow ACS; mem. AMA, Am. Acad. Otolaryngology Head and Neck Surgery, Iowa Med. Soc., LinnCounty Med. Soc., Dubuque County Med. Soc., Knox County Med. Soc., Am. Coll. E.R. Physicians, Cedar Rapids C. of C., Phi Betta Kappa, Phi Eta Sigma. Republican. Roman Catholic. Clubs: U. Iowa Pres., Elcrest Country, Dubuque Golf and Country. Avocations: literature, theatre, art, dancing, spectator sports.

SPOLUM, ROBERT NIC, equipment company executive; b. Aberdeen, S.D., Jan. 8, 1931; s. Arthur and Marvelyn S.; m. Diane Spolum; children: Victoria Ann, Lynne Elizabeth. Student, Grinnell Coll., 1950-51; C.P.A., Acad. Accountancy, Mpls., 1952-53; A.M.P., Harvard U., 1983. Pub. acct. Broeker & Hendrickson, Mpls., 1953-63; comptroller, v.p. Melroe Co., Gwinner, N.D., 1963-69; v.p. Clark Equipment Co.; pres., gen. mgr. Melroe div. Clark Equipment Co., Fargo, N.D., 1969—. Recipient Greater N.D. Sci. and Industryaward N.D. C. of C., 1976. Mem. N.D. Soc. C.P.A.s, Minn. Soc. C.P.A.s, Farm and Indsl. Equipment Inst. (dir.), NAM (dir.), Greater N.D. Assn. (dir.), Am. Legion. Republican. Episcopalian. Club: Fargo Country (dir. 1979-82). Lodge: Elks. Home: 818 Southwood Dr Fargo ND 58103 Office: Melroe Div Clark Equipment Co 112 N University Dr Fargo ND 58102 *

SPONSELLER, MARY ANN, manufacturing company executive; b. Canton, Ohio, Aug. 9, 1955; d. J. Dennis and Caroline (Conrad) Spragg; m. John W. Sponseller, July 15, 1978. BS, Bowling Green State U., 1977; MBA, U. Akron, 1985. CPA, Ohio; cert. mgmt. acct. Adv. staff acct. Ernst & Whinney, Canton, 1978-80; sr. tax analyst Diebold Inc., Canton, 1980-81, mgr. tax research, 1981-82, tax mgr., 1982-86, mgr. tax and risk financing, 1986—; instr. Stark Tech. Col., Canton, 1986. Publicity mgr., judge Hugh Obrien Youth Found., Alliance, Ohio, 1984-86. Mem. Nat. Assn. Accts. (v.p. 1986, pres. 1987, mem. of yr. 1986), Ohio Soc. CPA's (pub. relations com. mem. 1984-86), Beta Alpha Psi, Beta Gamma Sigma. Republican. Roman Catholic. Clubs: Quota, College (Canton). Avocation: travel. Home: 6463 Blossomwood North Canton OH 44721 Office: Diebold Inc PO Box 8230 Blossomwood Canton OH 44711

SPOOR, WILLIAM HOWARD, retired food company executive; b. Pueblo, Colo., Jan. 16, 1923; s. Charles Hinchman and Doris Field (Slaughter) S.; m. Janet Spain, Sept. 23, 1950; children—Melanie G., Cynthia F., William Lincoln. A.B., Dartmouth Coll., 1949; postgrad., Denver U., 1949, Stanford U., 1965. Asst. sales mgr. N.Y. Export div. Pillsbury Co., 1949-53, mgr. N.Y. Office, 1953-62; v.p. export div. Pillsbury Co., Mpls., 1962-68; v.p., gen. mgr. internat. ops. Pillsbury Co., 1968-73, chmn bd., chief exec. officer, 1973-85, also bd. dirs., 1973—, chmn. emeritus, 1985—; dir. Piper, Jaffray, Inc., Berkley and Co., Inc.; mem. regional export expansion council Dept. Commerce, 1966-74; bd. dirs. Exec. Council Fgn. Diplomats, 1976-78. Exec. com. Minn. Hist. Soc., 1983, Minn. Orchestral Assn., United Negro Coll. Fund, 1973-75; chmn. Capitol City Renaissance Task Force, 1985; trustee Mpls. Found.; mem. sr. campaign cabinet Carlson com. U. Minn., 1985; corp. relations com. The Nature Conservancy, 1985; mem. Nat. Cambodia Crisis Com., Pres.' Pvt. Sector Dept. Transp. Task Force, 1982, Pres.' Pvt. Sector Survey on Cost Control, 1983; chmn. YWCA Tribute to Women in Internat. Industry. Served to 2d lt. inf. U.S. Army, 1943-46. Recipient Golden Plate award, Am. Acad. Achievement, Disting. Bus. Leadership award, St. Cloud State U., Miss. Valley World Trade award, Outstanding Achievement award, Dartmouth Coll., Hotatio Alger award, 1986, Medal of Merit, U.S. Savs. Bond Program; honered with William H. Spoor Dialogues on Leadership, Dartmouth Coll. Mem.Grocery Mfrs. Am. (treas., bd. dirs. 1973-84), Nat. Fgn. Trade Council (dir. 1973-75), Minn. Hist. Soc. (bd. dirs.), Minn. Bus. Partnership. Clubs: River (N.Y.C.); Woodhill, Minneapolis , Lafayette, Tower (Mpls.); Del Ray Yacht, Gulf Stream Bath & Tennis, Gulf Stream Golf (Fla.); Old Baldy (Saratoga, Wyo.). Home: 622 W Ferndale Rd Wayzata MN 55391 Office: Pillsbury Bldg 608 2d Ave S Minneapolis MN 55402

SPORTSMAN, SALLY JEAN, teacher; b. St. Louis, Oct. 26, 1948; d. Irwin and Mae Ann (Hyatt) Walpert; m. Michel Allain Sportsman, Feb. 21, 1970; children: Elise M., Gregory D. BS in Edn., U. Mo., 1970, MA in English, 1983. Cert. tchr., Mo. Tchr. J.C. Nichols Sch., Kansas City, 1972-73, Grandview (Mo.) Pub. Schs., 1973-75, Peculiar (Mo.) Elementary Sch., 1979-81; tchr. gifted program and French Raymore-Peculiar Middle Sch., 1981-85; tchr. secondary English and French Raymore-Peculiar High Sch., 1985—; mem. faculty Mo. Scholars Acad., U. Mo., Columbia, 1987—; pvt. tutor, Kansas City, 1980-86; sponsor Nat. Writing Project U. Calif., Berkeley, 1983—. Contbr. articles to profl. jours. Liason Kansas City Regional Council for Higher Edn., Leawood, Kans., 1986—. U. Mo. scholar, 1966-70, 1983. Mem. Phi Kappa Phi, Pi Lambda Theta, Delta Kappa Gamma (v.p. Mu chapt., 1987—). Avocations: tennis, piano, reader, symphony, live theater. Home: 509 N Washington St Raymore MO 64083 Office: Raymore-Peculiar High Sch 211 & School Rd Box 366 Peculiar MO 64078

SPRANDEL, DENNIS STEUART, management consulting company executive; b. Little Falls, Minn., June 1, 1941; s. George Washington and Lucille Margaret (Steuart) S.; A.B., Albion Coll., 1963; M.Ed., U. Ariz., 1965; Ph.D., Mich. State U., 1973. Grad. teaching asst. U. Ariz., Tucson, 1964-65; dir. athletics, Owen Grad. Center Mich. State U., East Lansing, 1965-68; prof., dir. student teaching Mt. St. Mary's Coll., 1968-70; exec. dir. Mich. AAU, 1974-81, mem. numerous nat. coms., 1974-81; mem. U.S. Olympic Com., 1974-77; pres., chmn. bd. Am. Sports Mgmt., Ann Arbor, 1976—, Am. SportsVision, 1981—, Am. Sports Research, 1977—, Sprandel Group, 1984—; pres. Nat. Sports & Entertainment, Inc., 1984—, Sprandel Assocs., 1984—; bd. dirs. Nat. Golden Gloves, 1980—, bd. trustees, 1986 , Port Huron TV Project, 1985—; pres. Detroit Golden Gloves Charities; pres. adminstrv. bd. Detroit Golden Gloves, 1985—; Bd. dirs. Mich. Sports Hall of Fame, 1976—; Cons. in field. Recipient Detroit Striders award, 1978; Emerald award, 1979; World TaeKwonDo award, 1979; Detroit Spl. Olympics award, 1978; Community Service award Mich. State U., 1985. Mem Am. Soc. Assn. Execs., Nat. Assn. Phys. Edn. in Higher Edn., AAHPER, Nat. Recreation and Parks Assn., Internat. Boxing Fedn., N.Am. Boxing Fedn., U.S. Boxing Assn., World Boxing Assn., World Boxing Council, Nat. Assn. for Girls and Women in Sport, Psi Chi. Contbr. articles to profl. jours. Home: 1530 Pine Valley Apt 5 Ann Arbor MI 48104 Office: 27208 Southfield Rd Suite 3 Lathrup Village MI 48076

SPRANG, MILTON LEROY, obstetrician-gynecologist; b. Chgo., Jan. 15, 1944; s. Eugene and Carmella (Bruno) S.; m. Sandra Lee Karabelas, July 16, 1966; children: David, Christina, Michael. Student, St. Mary's Coll., 1962-65; MD, Loyola U., 1969. Diplomate Am. Bd. Ob-Gyn; Nat. Bd. Med. Examiners. Intern than resident St. Francis Hosp., Evanston, Ill., 1969-70, resident, 1972-75; assoc. attending physcian Evanston Hosp., 1975-79, attending physician, 1980-84; sr. attending physician Evanston Hosp., St. Francis Hosp., 1985—; chmn. ob-gyn Cook County Grad. Sch. Medicine, Chgo., 1983—; instr. Northwestern U. Med. Sch., Chgo., 1975-78, assoc. prof. 1979-84, asst. prof. 1984—; chmn. Med. Audit Com. Evanston Hosp., 1977-85, chmn. birthing room establishment 1978-79; lectr. academic and civic groups; bd. govs. Ill. State Med. Inter-Ins. Exchange, 1987—. Editorial bd. Jour. Chgo. Medicine, 1986; contbr. articles to profl. jours. Bd. dirs. Am. Cancer Soc., chmn. profl. edn. com. North Shore unit, 1982-85; mem. Nat. Repub. Congl. Com., 1981—, Ill. Med. Polit. Action Com. Served with USN, 1970-72. Fellow ACS, Am. Coll. Ob-Gyn (chmn. Ill. sect. 1975-76), Am. Soc. Colposcopy and Cervical Pathology; mem. AMA (Physicians Recognition award 1977, 80, 83, Ill. State Med. Soc. delegation 1987—, Ill. Found. Med. Rev. (bd. dirs.), Chgo. Med. Soc. (v.p. 1984-85, adv. com. advt. standards 1978-84, counselor, physicians rev. com. 1980-85, sec., mem. exec. council north suburban br. 1981-82, trustee ins. bd. 1982-85, nominating com. 1985-86, treas. 1986—, bd. trustees 1986—), Chgo. Found. Med. Care (nominating com. 1980-84, med. care evaluation and edn. com. 1980-83, practice guidelines com. 1984). Roman Catholic. Avocations: reading, raising fish, swimming. Home: 4442 Concord Ln Skokie IL 60076 Office: AGSo 2500 Ridge Ave Evanston IL 60201

SPRECHER, JOHN WILLIAM, advertising executive; b. Milw., Aug. 2, 1955; s. Clarence Albert and Martha Mae (Schauer) S.; m. Lori Ellen Ewert, June 21, 1975; 1 child, Jeffrey John. BA in English, U. Wis., 1977, MA in Creative Writing, 1979. Editor Wis. Monthly, Brookfield, 1980-82; communications dir. Owens-Darr-Koffron, Milw., 1982-84; creative dir., v.p. Wilcox Mktg., Wauwatosa, Wis., 1984-86; pres. Ellingsen-Sprecher, Milw., 1986—. Recipient First Place Mag. award, 1984, Nat. Agri-Mktg. award 1984, Pres.'s Recognition award Wis. Art Edn. Assn., 1986. Mem. Milw. Advt. Club (editor newsletter 1985, 2d Place Direct Mail award 1983, Direct Mail Merit award 1986). Avocations: tennis, jogging, softball, fiction writing. Home: 5104 W20699 Cindy Dr Muskego WI 53150 Office: Ellingesen-Sprecher Inc 312 E Wisconsin Ave Milwaukee WI 53202

SPRECKELMEYER, KENT FITZGERALD, architect; b. St. Joseph, Mo., Oct. 27, 1950; s. William Eugene and Eleanor (Fitzgerald) S.; m. Antha Cotten, May 21, 1971. BArch, Kans. U., 1973; Diploma in Architecture, London U., Eng., 1974; DArch, U. Mich., 1981. Project designer Brunner & Brunner, St. Joseph, 1969-73; research architect U. Mich., Ann Arbor, 1978-81; assoc. prof. U. Kans., Lawrence, 1981—; prin. Kent Spreckelmeyer, AIA, Lawrence, 1981—. Co-author: Evaluating Built Environments, 1981 (Progressive Architecture award 1982); contbg. author: Environmental Programming, 1986. Chmn. Lawrence (Kans.) Arts Commn., 1983-86. Served to capt. USAF, 1974-78. Ewart fellow U. Kans., 1973-74, Seabury fellow Seabury Found., 1978-80; research grantee Nat. Endowment for Arts, 1983. Mem. AIA, Kans. Soc. Architects (exec. com. 1986—), Environ. Design Research Assn. Episcopalian. Home: 1510 Stratford Rd Lawrence KS 66044 Office: U Kans Sch Architecture and Urban Design Lawrence KS 66045

SPRENGNETHER, MICHAEL THOMAS, lawyer; b. St. Louis, Aug. 25, 1951; s. Aloysius Bernard and Hildegard (Messmer) S.; m. Mary Mildred Witzke, Aug. 18, 1973; children: Sara Margaret, Michael Thomas II. BS, St. Joseph's Coll., 1973; JD, Loyola U., Chgo., 1976. Bar: Ill. 1976. Assoc. Kralovec, Marquard, Doyle and Gibbons, Chgo., 1976-83, ptnr., 1983—. Mem. ABA, Ill. Bar Assn., Chgo. Bar Assn. (tort litigation com.). Club: Trial Lawyers Chgo. Avocations: sports, reading. Office: Kralovec Marquard Doyle & Gibbons 39 S LaSalle Chicago IL 60603

SPRICH, WILLIAM WALTERS DANIEL, neurosurgeon; b. St. Louis, June 7, 1952; s. Gene Frank and Roberta (Walters) S.; m. Gina Wiegand, May 20, 1977 (div. Oct. 1981). BA magna cum laude, Washington U., St. Louis, 1973; MD, St. Louis U., 1977. Intern U. Cin., 1977-78, resident in neurosurgery, 1978-82; fellow in neuroendocrinology Yale U., New Haven, Conn., 1979; pvt. practice specializing in neurosurgery Belleville, Ill., 1982—; fgn. house surgeon Nat. Hosp. for Nervous Diseases, London, 1982-83. Contbr. articles to profl. jours. Dep. sheriff St. Claire County Sheriffs Dept., 1986; bd. dirs. St. Clair County Med. Soc., Belleville, 1986—. Fellow Am. Assn. Neurological Surgery; mem. AMA. Presbyterian. Club: St. Louis. Avocations: fgn. travel, wines, paintings, scuba, sports cars. Office: Neurological Services Belleville 6401 W Main Belleville IL 62223

SPRIGGS, DAVID WILLIAM, physician, radiologist; b. Fremont, Ohio, June 13, 1949; s. Donald Henry and Betty Eileen (Schuster) S.; m. Jill Lynn Fagert, Sept. 22, 1973; children: Aubrey Lee, Dawn Renee, Julia Lynn. Student, Bowling Green (Ohio) State U., 1967-69; BS, Ohio State U., 1971, MD, 1974. Intern E.W. Sparrow Hosp., Lansing, Mich., 1974-75, resident, 1975-78; staff radiologist Timken Mercy Med. Ctr., Canton, Ohio, 1978—; asst. residency dir. Canton Radiology Residency, 1981—. Contbr. articles to profl. jours. Mem. AMA, Assn. Univ. Radiologists, Am. Roentgen Ray Soc., Soc. Cardiovascular and Interventional Radiology, Radiol. Soc. N.Am., Ohio State Med. Assn., Ohio State Radiol. Soc., Northeast Ohio Radiol. Soc., Stark County Med. Soc. Republican. Roman Catholic. Avocations: gardening, golf, cross country skiing. Home: 1431 Springhaven Circle NE Massillon OH 44644 Office: Timken Mercy Med Ctr Radiology Dept 1320 Timken Mercy Dr NW Canton OH 44708

SPRIGGS, ROBERT PAUL, bank executive, petroleum engineer; b. Muskogee, Okla., July 4, 1932; s. Paul Snow Spriggs and Hazel Alpha (Dawson) Binda; m. Betty Nell Culver, Dec. 12, 1954 (div. 1971); children—Paul David, Sandra Lee, Mary Sue; m. Berna Dene Vance, Aug. 31, 1973; 1 child, Lori Lynn Lessenden. B.S. in Petroleum Engring., U. Okla., 1954. Registered profl. engr., Tex., Kans. Engr. Humble Oil & Refining, Baytown, Tex., 1954-59; profl. engr. D.R. McCord & Assocs., Dallas, 1959-63, G.L. Yates & Assocs., Wichita, Kans., 1965-69; v.p. Energy Res. Group, Wichita, 1969-78; ops. mgr. Beren Corp., Wichita, 1978-79; pres. Midco Drilling, Inc., Wichita, 1979-86; v.p. , petroleum engr. Bank IV, Wichita, 1986. Patentee wireline extension hanger. Union Oil Tex. scholar, 1953. Mem. Soc. Petroleum Engrs., AIME, Am. Assn. Petroleum Geologists. Republican. Methodist. Clubs: Crestview Country, Wichita Ski (treas. 1975-76). Avocations: fishing; scuba diving; skiing; flying. Office: Bank IV Wichita 100 N Broadway Wichita KS 67201

SPRINGER, BRANCH JON, accountant; b. Ft. Wayne, Ind., June 30, 1955; s. Raymond C. and Roberta (Stella) S.; m. Jacqueline S. Spriggs, May 22, 1976; children: Ryan, Nicholas. BS in Acctg., Ind. U., Ft. Wayne, 1977—. CPA, Ohio. Acct. Arthur Young & Co., Toledo, 1977—. Mem. Am. Inst. CPA's, Ohio Soc. CPA's, Ohio Contractors Assn., Toledo Area Merchandising Execs., Health Care Fin. Mgmt. Assn. Lutheran. Avocation: sports. Office: Arthur Young & Co One Seagate Toledo OH 43604

SPRINGER, DANIEL STEPHEN, retail executive; b. La Jolla, Calif., June 26, 1957; s. John Ellison and Shirley Anne (Rudolph) S.; m. Karen Jean Roberts, June 28, 1980; children: Benjamin, Joshua. Asst. mgr. Anthony's, Sleepy Eye, Minn., 1981; mgr. Anthony's, Wabasha, Minn., 1981-83, Humboldt, Iowa, 1983-84, Mason City, Iowa, 1984-85, Lisbon, N.D., 1985-87; owner MSA, Inc., Lisbon, 1987—. Served with USMC, 1975-77. Republican. Lutheran. Home: 902 Oak St Lisbon ND 58054 Office: MSA Inc 424 Main St Box 948 Lisbon ND 58054

SPRINGER, HARRY AARON, surgeon; b. El Paso, Tex., Nov. 23, 1937; s. Moses David and Louise (Fessinger) S.; m. Nancy K. Springer, Sept. 1, 1958 (div. 1977); children—Rhonda Springer Levin, Michael R., Steven. m. Mavis Leona Springer, May 4, 1980; children: Margo Louise, David Lee. D.D.S., Northwestern U., 1960; M.D., U. Tex., 1964. Diplomate Am. Bd. Plastic Surgery. Intern Cook County Hosp., Chgo., 1964-65, resident in gen. surgery, 1964-69; resident in plastic surgery Northwestern U., 1968-71; practice medicine specializing in plastic surgery, Evanston, Ill. Contbr. articles to med. jours. Served with USAR, 1981-84. Fellow ACS; mem. Am. Soc. Plastic and Reconstructive Surgeons, AMA, Ill. State Med. Soc. (2d v.p. 1985-86, 1st v.p. 1986-87, pres. elect 1987-88), Chgo. Med. Soc. (pres. 1983-84, trustee 1983—). Office: Aesthetic Surgery Ltd 800 Austin Suite 610 Evanston IL 60202

SPRINGER, JAMES BERNE, financial consultant; b. Bloomington, Ill., Feb. 17, 1943; s. Howard B. and Edna (Ropp) S.; m. Janet J. Martin, Sept. 2, 1967. Student, U. Colo. Real estate sales person Reeder Realty, Denver, 1965-67; ptnr. Don Martin Co., Tecumseh, Mich., 1967-72; owner Gamble's of Belleville, Mich., 1972-75; franchise sales person Bostwick Braun, Toledo, 1975-79; fin. cons. Merrill Lynch, Youngstown, Ohio, 1979—; instr. investing Kent State U., Salem, 1980-85; instr. entrepreneur tng. Youngstown State U., 1986—. Club: Salem (Ohio) Golf. Lodge: Elks. Home: 703 N Union Salem OH 44460 Office: Merrill Lynch 1000 City Centre One Youngstown OH 44503

SPRINGER, MAY ENG, clinical laboratory supervisor; b. Newark, Dec. 28, 1949; d. James Seedor and Mei Tan (Lew) Eng.; m. Larry Dale Springer, June 19, 1971; 1 child, Kimberly Rae. BS, Washburn U., 1972. Head lab. dept. Meml. Hosp., Topeka, 1973-74, dept. head, 1977-80, staff technologist, 1977-85; asst. chief technologist St. Francis Hosp., Maryville, Mo., 1975-76; staff technologist Damon Labs., Topeka, 1976-77; lab. mgr. Hillcrest Med. Lab., Lawrence, Kans., 1985—. Mem. Nat. Assn. Clin. Lab. Scientists, Am. Soc. Clin. Pathologists. (cert.). Baptist. Avocations: family activities, horses, reading, needlecrafts. Office: Hillcrest Med Labs 1400 W 6th Lawrence KS 66044

SPRINGER, MICHAEL RICHARD, information consultant; b. Evanston, Ill., Oct. 23, 1942; s. Joseph Gotthold and Kathryn Dorothy (Houston) S.; m. Patricia Ann Fazio, Sept. 3, 1977; children: Michelle Ann, Mary Patricia, Maria Rene. BS in Fin., De Paul U., 1969, MBA in Fin., 1973. Systems analyst Continental Bank, Chgo., 1969-71, mgr. micrographics, 1971-72, audit mgr., 1972-73, mgr. personal banking, 1973-76; pres. Cons. for Info. Resource Mgmt. Inc., Bloomingdale, Ill., 1976—; mem. systems rev. com. Tex. Instruments Corp., 1982-83, competitive issues com., 1983-84; instr. Am. Mgmt. Assn., 1971-79, Elmhurst (Ill.) Coll., 1977-82. Copyright portfolio acctg. system. Bd. dirs. Chgo. Jaycees, 1974-76, Bloomingdale C. of C., 1983-86, Wayne (Ill.) Twp. Promising Children, 1982-84. Served as cpl. USMC, 1960-65. Recipient Wall Street Jour. Achievement award, 1969. Mem. Soc. Info. Mgmt. (bd. dirs. 1981), Inst. Mgmt. Cons. Republican. Roman Catholic. Home: 796 Pawnee Dr Carol Stream IL 60188 Office: Cons Info Resource Mgmt Inc 109 Fairfield Way Bloomingdale IL 60108

SPRINGER, NEIL ALLEN, manufacturing company executive; b. Fort Wayne, Ind, May 2, 1938; s. Roy V. and Lucille H. (Gerke) S.; m. Janet M. Grotrian, Sept. 3, 1960; children: Sheri Lynn, Kelly Jean, Mark Allen. BS, U. Ind, 1960; MBA, U. Dayton, 1966. Staff asst. acctg. Navistar Internat. Corp., Bridgeport, Conn., 1966-68; asst. comptroller Navistar Internat. Corp., Fort Wayne, Ind., 1968-70; staff asst. Navistar Internat. Corp., Chgo., 1970-75, asst. corp. comptroller, 1975-77, v.p. fin., 1977-79, v.p. gen. mgr. trucks, 1979-81, pres. truck group, 1981-84, pres., chief operating officer, 1984-87; chmn., pres., chief exec. officer Navistar Internat. Transp. Corp., Chgo., 1987—; bd. dirs. Century Life Ins. Co., Waverly, Iowa; vice chmn. Am. Trucking Assn. Found., 1985—. Bd. dirs. Lutheran Home & Services for Aged, Arlington Heights, Ill., 1980—. Mem. Ill. Soc. CPA's. Office: Navistar Internat Transp Corp 401 N Michigan Ave Chicago IL 60611

SPRINGER, RAYMOND LOUIS, lawyer, manufacturing company executive; b. Louisville, June 8, 1913; s. Byron Marcellus and Louise (Pitts) S.; m. Jane Dorsey, Sept. 4, 1953. J.D., U. Louisville, 1936. Bar: Ky. 1936. Asst. office mgr., atty. Fed. Land Bank of Louisville, 1930-41; asst. gen. mgr. H.T. Colling Co., Cin., 1949-51, v.p., gen. mgr., 1951-56; pres. Auto Sun Products Co., Cin., 1956—; metal finishers rep. Nat. Indsl. Pollution Control Council, 1971. Served to maj. AUS, 1941-46, U.S. Army, 1946-49, col. Res. ret. Mem. Fed. Bar Assn., Ret. Officers Assn., Mil. Order of World Wars, Ky. Bar Assn. (Sr. Counselor award 1986), C. of C., Nat. Assn. Metal Finishers (pres. 1967-69, Silvio C. Taormina award 1972), Metal Finishers Found. (pres. 1972-74), Sigma Delta Kappa. Clubs: Kenwood Country, Jaguar; Brit. Auto Racing; Masons, K.T. Home: 7100 Ragland Rd Cincinnati OH 45244

SPRINGER, TIMOTHY JON, ergonomic consulting company executive; b. Fort Wayne, Ind., Nov. 12, 1952; s. Daniel Christian and Mabel Ann (Fuhrman) S.; m. Joyce Eileen McAllister, Sept. 1, 1973; children—Laura Trese, Benjamin Jon. Student, U.S. Naval Acad., 1970; B.A., Augustana Coll., 1974; M.A., U. S.D., 1976, Ph.D., 1978. Research asst. Dept. Transp., Vermillion, S.D., 1974-77, S.D. Hwy. Patrol, Pierre, 1977-78; assoc. research adminstr. State Farm Ins., Bloomington, Ill., 1978-82; assoc. prof. psychology Ill. State U., Normal, 1979-80; pres. Springer Assocs., Inc., St. Charles, Ill., 1982—. Author: Improving Productivity in the Workplace: Reports from the Field, 1986; (with others) Designing for High Technology Production Environments, 1987; ergonomics editor: Internat. Facility Management Assn. newsletter; contbr. articles to profl. jours. Patentee ergonomic forearm rest. Bd. dirs. Bethlehem Presch., St. Charles. Mem. Human Factors Soc., Environ. Research and Design Assn. Office: Springer Assocs Inc 1405 W Main St PO Box 1159 Saint Charles IL 60174

SPRINGER, WILLIAM LAWRENCE, accountant; b. Carbondale, Ill., Jan. 15, 1945; s. William Norman and Sibyl Lee (Davis) S.; m. Elizabeth Jeanne Drone, June 6, 1970; 1 child: Elizabeth Ericka. BA, So. Ill. U., 1967. CPA, Ill., Mo. Field auditor IRS, East St. Louis, 1967-69; ptnr. Bert H. Allison & Co. CPAs, East St. Louis, 1969-77; mgr. Tiger, Fireside & Co. CPAs, Clayton, Mo., 1977-78, Stone, Carlie & Co. CPAs, Clayton, 1978-79; pvt. practice acctg. Carbondale and Du Quoin, Ill., 1979—; instr. Belleville (Ill.) Area Coll., 1974-80. Mem. Am. Inst. CPA's, Mo. Soc. CPA's. Republican. Club: Jackson County Bus. Boosters (Carbondale) (treas. 1981—). Avocations: photography, automobiles, travel. Home: Rt 1 Box 269A Carbondale IL 62901 Office: 1224A W Main Carbondale IL 62901

SPRINT, STEPHEN CHRISTIAN, service executive; b. Firbault, Minn., Sept. 24, 1939; s. Howard Lloyd and Eileen Ellis (Knauss) S.; m. Julienne Denise Carter, Nov. 23, 1979; children: Michelle Marie, Thomas Stephen. BA, Mankato (Minn.) State U., 1961; cert., St. Louis U., 1981. Interviewer Minn. State Employment Services, 1961-63; personnel dir. Saint Joseph's Hosp., St. Paul, 1964-81, v.p., 1982-84; v.p. Carondelet Community Hosps., MPls., 1985-87, Health East Corp., 1987—. Scoutmaster Boy Scouts Am., St. Paul, 1975-78; com. chmn. explorer div., 1974—; personnel commn. St. Paul Red Cross, 1975-82, St. Paul Rehab. Cen., 1980-84. Recipient Woodbadge award Boy Scouts Am., St. Paul, 1982, Silver Beaver award Boy Scouts Am., 1985. Mem. Health Employers, Inc. (bd. dirs. 1985-86), Twin City Hosp. Personnel Assn. (pres. 1977-78), Am. Soc. Personnel Adminstrs. Avocations: fishing, boating, wildlife art, travel. Home: 15421 Bryant Ave S Burnsville MN 55337 Office: Carondelet Community Hosps 2414 S Seventh St Minneapolis MN 55424

SPROUL, ROBERT GARDNER, JR., real estate developer; b. Washington, Sept. 19, 1941; s. Robert Gardner and F. Pauline (Sager) S.; m. T. Virginia Estes, June 21, 1969; children: Crandall E., Robert G. III. BSCE, Duke U., 1963; MBA, Columbia U., 1968. CPA, N.Y.; registered profl. engr., N.C. Civil engr. Raymond-Morrison Knudsen-Brown & Root, Jones, Vietnam, 1963-67; acct. Peat, Marwick, Mitchell & Co., N.Y.C., 1968-72; real estate developer The Pyramid Cos., Syracuse, N.Y., 1972-80, The Mall Co., Alliance, Ohio, 1980—. Recipient Key to City, Alliance, Ohio, 1983. Mem. N.C. Bd. Profl. Engrs. Republican. Baptist. Club: Birmingham (Ala.) Country. Lodge: Rotary. Avocations: skiing, sailing, church ministry. Home: 3301 E Briarcliff Rd Birmingham AL 35223 Office: The Mall Co 2500 W State St Alliance OH 44601

SPROWLS, ROBERT ALLEN, restaurant owner; b. Garden City, Kans., Mar. 10, 1952; s. Henry Allen and Betty Lou (Reppenhagen) S.; m. Kathryn Ann Fraizer, Nov. 28, 1970; children: Christopher Allen, Brett Alden. Grad., High Sch., Kans., 1970. Mgr. Denny's Restaurant, Wichita, Kans., 1973-74, Angelo's Restaurant, Wichita, 1974-80; owner, operator Kingfisher's Inn, Marion, Kans., 1980—. Mem. Marion C. of C. (bd. dirs. 1986—). Republican. Methodist. Lodge: Kiwanis (bd. dirs. 1985-86). Avocations: walking, jogging. Home: 17 Rock Rd Box 36 Marion KS 66861 Office: Kingfishers Inn Rural Rt 2 Box 73A Marion KS 66861

SPUNGIN, JOEL, manufacturing company executive; b. 1936. With United Stationers Supply Co., Des Plaines, Ill., 1957—, exec. v.p., 1972-77, pres., chief operating officer, 1977-81; pres., chief operating officer United Stationers Inc., Des Plaines, 1981—. Office: United Stationers Inc 2200 E Golf Rd Des Plaines IL 60016 *

SPUNT, S. C., manufacturing company executive. Pres. Curtis Industries Inc., Eastlake, Ohio. Office: Curtis Industries Inc 34999 Curtis Blvd Eastlake OH 44094 *

SPURGEON, GIZELLE A., neurologist; b. Chgo., Feb. 13, 1952. BA, Clarke Coll., 1974; MD, U. Iowa, 1978. Diplomate Am. Bd. Psychiatry and Neurology. Intern U. Utah Med. Ctr., Salt Lake City, 1978-79, resident in neurology, 1979-82; neurologist, active staff Wausau (Wis.) Med. Ctr., 1982—; cons. staff Holy Cross Hosp., Merrill, Wis., 1984—; cons. neurologist Alzheimer's unit Heritage Haven Care Ctr., Schofield, Wis., 1985—. Mem. Am. Acad. Neurology, Wis. Neurol. Soc., State Med. Soc. Wis., Marathon County Med. Soc., Midstate Epilepsy Assn. (bd. dirs. 1986—), Alzheimer's Disease and Related Disorders Assn. (bd. dirs. 1985—). Office: Wausau Med Ctr 2727 Plaza Dr Wausau WI 54401

SPURGEON, KAREN ELAINE, music educator; b. Ottumwa, Iowa, Nov. 14, 1942; d. John Edward and Frances Elizabeth (Schroeder) Amstutz; m. Charles Gary Spurgeon, Sept. 1, 1962; children: Shari, Scott, Stephanie. MusB with highest distinction, U. Iowa, 1964; MA in Music Edn., Northeast Mo. State U., 1975. Cert. tchr., Iowa. Tchr. music Davis County Community Schs., Bloomfield, Iowa, 1965—. Choir dir. Bloomfield Methodist Ch., 1973—, Community Choirs, Bloomfield, 1976—; mus. dir. Davis County Players Community Mus., Bloomfield, 1977—; exec. bd. Davis County Arts Council; past. sec. Am. Field Service, Bloomfield. Mem. NEA, Iowa State Edn. Assn., Davis County Community Edn. Assn. (treas., v.p. 1985), Music Educators Nat. Conf., Iowa Music Educators Assn. (county chmn. 1985—), Delta Kappa Gamma (music chmn.). Democrat. Methodist. Club: Music Boosters (pres. 1985-86). Avocations: directing choirs, reading, sewing. Home: Rural Rt 2 Bloomfield IA 52537 Office: Davis County Middle Sch 500 East North Bloomfield IA 52537

SPURGEON, WILLIAM MARION, engineer, chemist, research administrator; b. Quincy, Ill., Dec. 5, 1917; s. Samuel Marion and Winifred Aileen (Martin) S.; m. Richarda Neuberg, Dec. 9, 1941; children—William A., Richard M., Benjamin G. B.S., U. Ill.-Urbana, 1938; M.S., U. Mich., 1939, Ph.D., 1941. Research chemist Texaco, Beacon, N.Y., 1941-42, 46; asst. prof. U. Cin., 1946-48; v.p. Am. Fluresit Co., Cin., 1948-54; mgr. phys. chemistry Gen. Electric Co., Evendale, Ohio, 1954-59; mgr. materials dept. Bendix Research Labs., Southfield, Mich., 1959-73, dir. mfg. program, 1973-78, sr. research planner, 1978-80; dir. prodn. research program NSF, Washington, 1980-85; dir. mfg. systems engring. program U. Mich.-Dearborn, 1985—. Author: Product Quality Assurance, 1980; patentee Electropolishing Titanium, 1960, and others; contbr. articles to profl. jours. Served to col. USAR, 1942-73. Recipient Arch T. Colwell award Soc. Automotive Engrs., 1967. Mem. Am. Chem. Soc., Am. Soc. Metals, Soc. Mfg. Engrs. (Joseph A. Siegel Meml. award 1981), Inst. Indsl. Engrs., Sigma Xi. Republican. Clubs: Army and Navy. Home: 24799 Edgemont Rd Southfield MI 48034 Office: Sch Engring U Mich-Dearborn 4901 Evergreen Rd Dearborn MI 48128

SPURRELL, FRANCIS ARTHUR, animal disease genetics educator, researcher; b. Independence, Iowa, Apr. 13, 1919; s. John Arthur and Evangeline (Francis) S.; m. Joy Dibble, Dec. 24, 1942; 1 dau., Margaret Joy. B.S. in Animal Husbandry, U. Wis., 1941; D.V.M., Iowa State Coll., 1946; Ph.D., U. Minn., 1955. Lic. in vet. medicine, Minn. County livestock agt. U. Wis. Extension, Fond Du Lac, 1946; veterinarian Land-O-Lakes Breeders Coop., 1947; instr. in vet. anatomy U. Minn., St. Paul, 1947-49, instr. in vet. obstetrics, 1949-55, assoc. prof. vet. radiology, 1955-62, prof. vet. radiology, 1962-68, prof. theriogenology, 1968—, dir. Summer Inst. in Radiation Biology, 1960-64. Trustee Master Eye Found., Minnetonka, Minn., 1950—, treas., 1980—. Served with Vet. Service, AUS, 1941-43. Mem. Am. Coll. Vet. Radiology (charter), Minn. Vet. Med. Assn., N.Y. Acad. Sci., Minn. Pure Bred Dog Breeders Assn., Minn. Humane Soc., Sigma Xi. Lutheran. Designer livestock data base mgmt. system Systems Therio, 1974, 80, 82; research in race-track computer systems; designer equine racing mgmt. control systems, 1983, 84, 85; designer nat. animal disease reporting systems, 1986. Office: 1988 Fitch Ave PO Box 8137 Saint Paul MN 55108 Office: Master Eye Found 10709 Wayzata Blvd Minnetonka MN 55343

SPURRIER, JAMES JOSEPH, theater educator; b. Mexico, Mo., Oct. 1, 1946; s. Jack Joseph and Ruth Marilyn (Mundy) S.; m. Jean Madelon Alkire, June 5, 1976; children: Jenna, Jamie. BA, U. Mich., 1968; MA, UCLA, 1970; PhD, So. Ill. U., 1979. Tchr., dept. chmn. Alemany High Sch., Mission Hills, Calif., 1968-74; prof. speech, dir. theater Vincennes (Ind.) U., 1977—. Composer various music selections, 1974-79. Choir dir. First Christian Ch., Vincennes, 1977—. Recipient dir. best musical award Northridge (Calif.) Arts Council, 1971; fellow So. Ill. U., 1974-77. Mem. Assn. for Theater in Higher Edn. (com. chmn. 1986—), Speech Communication Assn., Ind. Theater Assn., Phi Kappa Phi. Roman Catholic. Lodge: Kiwanis. Home: 114 Seminole Dr Vincennes IN 47591 Office: Vincennes U Shircliff 15 Vincennes IN 47591

SPYERS-DURAN, PETER, educator, librarian; b. Budapest, Hungary, Jan. 26, 1932; came to U.S., 1956, naturalized, 1964; s. Alfred and Maria (Almasi-Balogh) S-D; m. Jane F. Cumber, Mar. 21, 1964; children: Kimberly, Hilary, Peter. Certificate, U. Budapest, 1955; M.A. in L.S, U. Chgo., 1960; Ed.D., Nova U., 1975. Profl. asst. library adminstrn. div. ALA, Chgo., 1961-62; assoc. dir. libraries, assoc. prof. U. Wis., 1962-67; dir. libraries, prof. Western Mich. U., 1967-70; dir. libraries, prof. library sci. Fla. Atlantic U., 1970-76; dir. library Calif. State U., Long Beach, 1976-83; prof. library sci., dir. Wayne State U., Detroit, 1983-86, dean library sci. program and libraries, 1986—; vis. prof. State U. N.Y. at Geneseo, summers 1969-70; cons. publs., library-related enterprises; chmn. bd. internat. confs., 1970—. Author: Moving Library Materials, 1965, Public Libraries-A Comparative Survey of Basic Fringe Benefits, 1967; Editor: Approval and Gathering Plans in Academic Libraries, 1969, Advances in Understanding Approval Plans in Academic Libraries, 1970, Economics of Approval Plans in Research Libraries, 1972, Management Problems in Serials Work, 1973, Prediction of Resource Needs, 1975, Requiem for the Card Catalog: Management Issues in Automated Cataloging, 1979, Shaping Library Collections for the 1980's, 1981, Austerity Management in Academic Libraries, 1984, Financing Information Systems, 1985, Issues in Academic Libraries, 1985. Mem. Kalamazoo County Library Bd., 1969-70; Bd. dirs. United Fund. Mem. ALA, Mich. Library Assn., Internat. Fed. Library Assns., Assn. Info. Sci., Fla. Library Assn., Calif. Library Assn., Fla. Assn. Community Colls., Boca Raton C. of C., U. Chgo. Grad. Library Sch. Alumni Club (pres. 1973-75), Mich. Library Consortium (bd. dirs.), DALNET (bd. dirs.), Am. Soc. Info. Sci., Assn. of Library and Info. Sci. Edn. Republican. Methodist. Home: 517 Kimberly Birmingham MI 48009 Office: Wayne State Univ Libraries Detroit MI 48202

SQUILLANTE, MARC DAVID, osteopathic physician; b. Balt., Aug. 2, 1955; s. Alphonse M. and Diana J. (Keilman) S.; m. Carol Ann Galeazzi, May 29, 1982. B.S. in Pharmacy with distinction, U. Iowa, 1978; D.O., Coll. Osteo. Medicine and Surgery, Des Moines, 1981. Diplomate Am. Bd. Emergency Med. Intern, Des Moines Gen. Osteo. Hosp., 1981-82; resident in emergency medicine St. Francis Med. Ctr., Peoria, Ill., 1982-84, also chief resident in emergency medicine U. Ill.-Peoria and St. Francis Med. Ctr., Peoria, 1983-84; mem. staff emergency dept. East Liverpool (Ohio) City Hosp., 1984-87, med. dir., 1986-87; mem. staff Grandview Hosp., Dayton, Ohio, 1987—. asst. clin. prof. Ohio U. Coll. Osteo. Medicine, 1987—. Mem. Am. Coll. Emergency Physicians, Am. Osteo. Assn., Rho Chi. Office: East Liverpool City Hosp 425 W 5th St East Liverpool OH 43920

SQUIRES, RICHARD ALMA, dentist; b. Salt Lake City, May 12, 1945; s. Marvin Almar and Elsie Marie (England) S.; m. Sharon Lee Abernathy, Feb. 17, 1974; 1 child, Richard Alma Jr. BS, U. Utah, 1968; DDS, Washington U., St. Louis, 1972. Clin. instr. Washington U., 1972-73; gen. practice dentistry St. Louis, 1973—; pres. Acacia Dental Group, St. Louis, 1975—; lectr. Acad. Dental Group Practice, 1982—. Author (radio comml., TV and newspaper mktg. ad) We Care About Your Smile, 1982 (Gold award 1982). Elder Ch. of Jesus Christ Latter-day Saints. Fellow Internat. Congress Oral Implantologists, Am. Acad. Implant Dentistry; Greater St. Louis Implant Study Club (pres. 1987—). Republican. Avocation: radio controlled land and air vehicles. Home: 300 Hereford Saint Louis MO 63135 Office: Dental North 11863 Benham Rd Saint Louis MO 63138

SQUIRES, ROBERT EUGENE, communications executive; b. Hixton, Wis., May 8, 1922; s. George Frank and Odanah Letha (Brown) S.; m. Nancy Irlene Lamkins, July 7, 1951; children: Thomas, Brian, James. Grad. high sch., Black River Falls, Wis. Owner, mgr. Movie Theatre, Manawa, Wis., 1946-60; asst. mgr. Manawa Telephone Co., 1953-67, pres., 1967—. Troop leader Boy Scouts Am., Manawa; mem. City Council, Manawa, 1975-87. Served to staff sgt. USAF, 1942-45, ETO. Recipient Silver Beaver award Boy Scouts Am., 1974. Mem. Wis. Locally Owned Telephone Assn. (bd. dirs. 1974—, pres. 1975-76), Wis. State Telephone Assn. (bd. dirs. 1983—, pres. 1986-87). Republican. Methodist. Lodges: Lions, Masons, Shriners (marshall 1985, 2d ceremonial master 1987). Office: Manawa Telephone Co Inc 131 2d St Manawa WI 54949

SQUIRES, SANDRA KAY, special educator, consultant; b. Glendive, Mont., June 3, 1944; d. Ralph E. and M. Elouise (Cabbage) S.; m. James A. Boland, June 19, 1965 (div. May 1, 1980); children: Michael F., Jennifer L. BS in Elem. Edn., Eastern Mont. Coll., 1966; MA in Mental Retardation, Colo. State Coll., 1969; EdD in Mental Retardation, U. No. Colo., 1972. Cert. elem. tchr., Mont., Okla., Colo. First grade tchr. Billings Pub. Sch., Mont., 1966-67; spl. edn. tchr. Ft. Benning Children's Schs., Ga., 1967-68, Comanche County United Cerebral Palsy Assn., Lawton, Okla., Weld Bd. Coop. Services, Ault, Colo., 1970; instr. Loretto Heights Coll., Denver, 1972; instructional materials specialist Rocky Mountain Instructional Materials Ctr., Greeley, Colo., 1971-72, asst. prof., 1973-74; dir. career edn. for Mentally Handicapped Weld Bd. Coop. Services, LaSalle, Colo., 1974-77; asst. prof. Colo. State U., Ft. Collins, 1978; sr. project assoc. Pa. State U., Bur. of Edn. for Handicapped, Washington, 1979; asst. prof. Wash. State U., Pullman, 1979-81; assoc. prof., chmn. counseling and spl. edn. U. Nebr. Omaha, 1981—; pres. Ednl. Cons. Enterprises Inc., Greeley, 1974-79; speaker, cons. univs., local, state, and federal agencies, profl. orgns. U.S. and Canada, 1972—; sec., treas. Squires, Inc., Glendive, Mont., 1980—. Co-editor, editor: (newsletter) Inservice Consultant, 1974-77; author tng. manuals, monograph, children's books; contbr. articles to profl. jours. Polit. action network coordinator Nebr. Fedn. Council for Exceptional Children, Omaha, 1982-85, 87—. Recipient Robert G. Sando award Eastern Mont. Coll., 1966. Mem. Internat. Council Exceptional Children, Internat. Div. on Career Devel. (sec. 1976-79, v.p. 1979-80, pres.-elect 1980-81, pres. 1981-82), Internat. Council of Adminstrs. in Spl. Edn. Tchr. Edn., Phi Delta Kappa. Home: 681 S 85th St Omaha NE 68114 Office: U Nebr Dept Counseling and Spl Edn Omaha NE 68182

SRINIVASAN, SAMUEL, physiatrist; b. Pasumalai, India, July 17, 1936; s. Appasrinivasan and Ruby Jemima Vethanayagam; m. Victoria Sathianathan, June 8, 1960; children: Reuben, David. MBBS, U. Madras, 1960; FRCS, Royal Coll. Surgeons, 1968. Diplomate Am. Bd. Phys. Medicine and Rehab. Registrar orthopaedic surgery Royal Lancaster (Eng.) Infirmary, 1966-68; surgeon Kalyani Hosp., Madras, 1969-70; orthopaedic surgeon Queen Victoria Hosp., Morecambe, Eng., 1970-73; resident U. Mich. Med. Ctr., Ann Arbor, 1976-79; dir. rehab. R.I. Hosp., Providence, 1979-84; practice medicine specializing in rehab. medicine Saginaw, Mich., 1984—; asst. prof. Brown U., Providence, 1979-84; chmn. Bd. Physical Therapy, State of R.I., 1981-84. Fellow Am. Acad. Physical Medicine and Rehab.; mem. AMA, Am. Acad. Thermology, Am. Soc., Clin. Evoked Potentials, Am. Assn. Electrodiagnosis and Electromyography. Republican. Episcopalian. Clubs: Saginaw Country, Centurian. Avocations: music, travel, tennis, golf. Home: 850 Kenton Dr Saginaw MI 48603 Office: 830 S Jefferson Saginaw MI 48601

SRIVASTAVA, GOPAL KRISHNA, electrical engineer, manufacturing executive; b. Lucknow, India, Oct. 13, 1940; came to U.S., 1967; s. Oudh Behari Lal and Brijesh Srivastava; m. Sarojini Srivastava, May 18, 1969; chldren: Devendra, Shefali. BS, Lucknow (India) U., 1960; BS in Engring., London U., 1965; MSEE, Rochester Inst. Tech., 1974. Engr. Magnavox, Ft. Wayne, 1967-68; sr. engr. GTE Sylvania, Batavia, N.Y., 1968-74; engring. specialist Admiral, Chgo., 1974-76; engring group leader Zenith Electronics Corp., Glenview, Ill., 1976-82, mgr. engring., 1982—crw. Holder of numerous patents in field. Hindu. Avocations: tennis, bridge. Home: 4222 Walnut Ave Arlington Heights IL 60004 Office: Zenith Electronics Corp 1000 Milwaukee Ave Glenview IL 60025

SRIVASTAVA, NARAYAN SWARUP, manufacturing engineer; b. Sitapur, India, Sept. 15, 1951; s. Bhagwan Bux and Kamni Devi Srivastava; m. Sushma Srivastava, Apr. 30, 1977; children: Amit, Sunit. B MechE with honors, U. Roorkee, India, 1972; MS in Mech. Aerospace Engring., Ill. Inst. Tech., 1974. Plant engr. Miles Labs. Inc., Lisle, Ill., 1974-77; project engr. Motorola, Comml. Div., Schaumberg, Ill., 1977-78; corp. indsl. engr. Hosp. Laundry Services, Chgo., 1978-79; mgr. mfg. engring. Evenflo Juvenile Furniture Co., Piqua, Ohio, 1979—; pres. Internat. Gift House Inc., Piqua, 1985—. Contbr. to profl. publs. Vice-chmn. Piqua Safety Council, 1982-83, chmn., 1983-84; treas. Alumni Assn. Univ. Roorkee, Chgo., 1976-77. Mem. ASME, Soc. Mfg. Engrs. (charter mem. computer and automated systems assn.), Soc. Plastics Engrs. Avocations: photography, reading. Home: 810 Branford Rd Troy OH 45373 Office: Evenflo Juvenile Furniture Co 1801 Commerce Dr Piqua OH 45356

SRIVASTAVA, PRATAP KUMAR, computer engineer; b. Basti, India, Jan. 2, 1943; s. Gopal Prasad and Vidyawati S.; m. Anita Choudhry, Jan. 22, 1967; 1 child, Sameer. BS, U. Lucknow, India, 1959; B Tech in Elec. Engring., I.I.T. Bombay, 1963; M Mgmt., Northwestern U., 1983. Elec. engr. Hindustan Steels, Durgapur, India, 1963-65; cons. IBcon Ltd., Jaipur, India, 1965-67; systems engr. IBM Corp., New Delhi, India, 1967-78; regional mktg. adminstr. IBM Corp., Rolling Meadows, Ill., 1978-82; sr. systems engr. IBM Corp., Oakbrook, Ill., 1982-84; sr. planning mgr. IBM Corp., Rochester, Minn., 1984—. Mem. Phi Beta Sigma. Avocation: bridge. Home: 2017 15 St NE Rochester MN 55904 Office: IBM Corp SPD 48N/030-3 Hwy 52 & 37 St Rochester MN 55901

STAAB, PAUL CHARLES, chemist, engineer; b. Pitts., July 1, 1958; s. Charles W. and Helen P. (Miklas) S.; m. Diane H. Matty, June 24, 1985. BS in Chemistry, Carnegie Mellon U., 1979. Product chemist BF Goodrich Co., Akron, Ohio, 1979-82, product engr., 1982-84, advanced product engr., 1984-87; sr. product engr. Uniroyal Goodrich Tire Co., Akron, 1987—.

Patentee High Performance Tire, 1987. Mem. Am. Chem. Soc., Soc. Automotive Engrs., Akron Rubber Group, Smithsonian Inst. (assoc.). Democrat. Roman Catholic. Avocations: photography, travel, sports. Home: 1433A Timber Trail Akron OH 44313

STAAS, JOHN WILLIAM, psychologist, educator; b. Freeport, Ill., July 28, 1942; s. William Franklin and Lucille Ann (Harney) S.; AA, Cerritos Jr. Coll., 1962; student Calif. State U., Fullerton, 1962-63; BS, No. Ill. U., 1964; MA, U. Mo., Kansas City, 1966; postgrad. in Psychology, Bowling Green State U., 1966-67, Wayne State U., 1969-71; m. Zee L. Kinman, children: Laura Christine, Kevin Gregory. Research asst. Kansas City Mental Health Found., 1965-66; asst. psychologist Peace Corps., U. Mo., Kansas City, 1966; research assoc. Kans. U. Med. Ctr., 1965; staff psychologist Kansas City Found. for Exceptional Children, 1965-66; asst. prof. psychology Mary Manse Coll., Toledo, 1967-70; assoc. prof. psychology Monroe County (Mich.) Community Coll., Monroe, 1970—; pvt. practice clin. psychology, Toledo, 1968—; cons. psychologist Rescue, Inc., 1968-71, Holy Spirit Sem. and Vocat. Office Toledo Cath. Charities, 1971-77, Dr. S.N. Petas, Med. Clinic, Toledo, 1972-76; cons. clin. psychologist Toledo Mental Hygiene Clinic, 1967-74; clin. psychologist, adj. med. staff St. Charles Hosp., Oregon, Ohio, 1977—; cons. psychologist Monroe County Crisis Ctr., 1983—; workshops on non-verbal communication and psychology of multiple personalities, 1968—. Named Tchr. of Year, Monroe County Community Coll., 1975-76, 78-79, 82-83; registered psychologist; lic. psychologist, Ill., Ohio; cert. hypnotist. Mem. Am. Psychol. Assn., Assn. for Advancement of Psychology, Ill. Psychol. Assn., Assn. for Advancement of Behavior Therapy, N.W. Ohio Psychol. Assn., N.W. Ohio Clin. Hypnosis Assn., NEA, Mich. Edn. Assn., Phi Theta Kappa (spl. tchr.'s award 1973, hon. mem.). Roman Catholic. Club: Heatherdowns Country (Toledo). Author script Voice of Am. Radio. Home: 4125 Greenglen Rd Toledo OH 43614 Office: Monroe County Community Coll Dept Psychology 1455 S Raisinville Rd Monroe MI 48161 Office: Briarwood Medical Center 5321 Southwyck Blvd Suite L Toledo OH 43614

STABEJ, RUDOLPH JOHN, computer consultant; b. Milw., Dec. 14, 1952; s. Rudolf and Katharina (Schaab) S. BS in Acctg., U. Ill., Chgo., 1975; MBA in Fin., De Paul U., 1981, MS in Computer Sci., 1986. Gen. acct. Field Mus. Nat. History, Chgo., 1975-77, Victor Bus. Products, Chgo., 1977-80, Northrop Def. Systems, Rolling Meadows, Ill., 1981-82; programmer Fed. Reserve Bank, Chgo., 1983-84; programmer/analyst Arthur Andersen & Co., Chgo., 1984-85; cons./programmer Sycomm Systems Corp., Chgo., 1985-86; computer cons. Cara Corp., Oakbrook Terrace, Ill., 1986—. Mem. Assn. MBA Execs. Avocations: stamp collecting. Home: 8541 W Catalpa Chicago IL 60656

STABLER, DUANE ERWIN, engineer executive; b. Mobridge, S.D., Nov. 14, 1949; s. Erwin and Helen (Schmidt) S.; m. Dorothy Ann Wangler, Dec. 30, 1972. BS in Indsl. Edn., No. State U., Aberdeen, S.D., 1973. With configuration control Tex Instruments, Dallas, 1973-75; prject mgr. Internat. Computer Products, Dallas, 1975-77; mfg. engr. Magnetic Peripherals Inc., Aberdeen, 1977-80; quality control engr. Magnetic Peripherals Inc., Burnsville, Minn., 1980-84; mgr. engring. Magnetic Peripherals Inc., Bloomington, Minn., 1984—. Mem. Twin Cities Tandy Users Group (newsletter editor, 1983-86, bd. dirs. 1983—, pres. 1986—). Lutheran. Avocations: photography, home computers. Home: 11228 Radisson Dr Burnsville MN 55337 Office: Magnetic Peripherals Inc 7801 Computer Ave Minneapolis MN 55337

STABLER, NANCY RAE, infosystems specialist; b. Elgin, Ill., June 15, 1946; d. Raymond Herman and Eleanora Marie (Gaedke) Redmer, m. Jay Stabler, Mar, 29, 1970; 1 child: Andrea Marie. AAS with honors, Elgin Community Coll., 1982, AA with Honors, 1985. Programmer, analyst Houghton-Mifflin, Geneva, Ill., 1966-77; project leader Kane County, Geneva, 1978-83; systems designer Burgess Norton, Geneva, 1983—; tutor Elgin (Ill.) Community Coll., 1983—. Home: 775 South St Elgin IL 60123 Office: Burgess-Norton 737 Peyton Geneva IL 60134

STABLER, TIMOTHY ALLEN, educator, researcher; b. Port Jerus, N.Y., Sept. 27, 1940; s. Ralph A. and Marjorie (Hoyt) S. BA, Drew U., 1962; MA, DePauw U., 1964; PhD, U. Vt., 1969. Asst. prof. Hope Coll., Holland, Mich., 1969-71; asst. prof. Ind. U. NW, Gary, 1973-76, assoc. prof., 1976—, chmn. dept., 1983-85, 87—. Mem. Ind. Coll. Biol. Tchrs. (sec. 1985—), Cen. Assn. of Advisors for Health Professions (treas. 1980—), Nat. Assn. of Advisors for Health Professions (bd. dirs. 1981-85), Tissue Culture Assn. (exec. com. Midwest br. 1985—). Home: 1901 Alice St Valparaiso IN 46383 Office: Ind U NW 3400 Broadway Gary IN 46408

STACK, PAUL FRANCIS, lawyer; b. Chgo., July 21, 1946; s. Frank Louis and Dorothy Louise Stack; m. Nea Waterman, July 8, 1972; children—Nea Elizabeth, Sera Waterman. B.S., U. Ariz., 1968; J.D., Georgetown U., 1971. Bar: Ill. 1971, U.S. Ct. Claims 1975, U.S. Tax Ct. 1974, U.S. Ct. Customs and Patent Appeals 1977, U.S. Supreme Ct. 1975. Law clk., U.S. Dist. Ct., Chgo., 1971-72; asst. U.S. atty. No. Dist. Ill., Chgo., 1972-75; ptnr. Stack & Filpi, Chgo., 1976—. Bd. dirs. Riverside Pub. Library, 1977-83, Suburban Library System, Burr Ridge, Ill., 1979-82, Suburban Health Systems Agy., Inc., Oak Park, Ill., 1983. Mem. ABA, Chgo. Bar Assn. Presbyterian. Club: Union League. Home: 238 N Delaplaine Rd Riverside IL 60546 Office: 140 S Dearborn St Suite 411 Chicago IL 60603

STACK, ROBERT J., librarian; b. Milw., Apr. 18, 1949; s. James Jerome and Ann (McIntaggart) S.; m. A. Christine Nelson, Nov. 24, 1972; children—Amanda, Matthew. B.A., Lakeland Coll., 1971; M.L.S., U. Wis.-Madison, 1974. Asst. dir. Clinton (Iowa) Pub. Library, 1975-78; dir. Granite City Pub. Library, Ill., 1978—; mem. adv. com. for LTA program Lewis & Clark Community Coll., Godfrey, Ill., 1981-83. Mem. Ill. Library Assn., ALA, Beta Phi Mu. Club: Rotary (sec. 1982-84, v.p. 1984-85, pres. 1985-86). Office: Granite City Public Library 2001 Delmar St Granite City IL 62040

STACK, STEPHEN S., manufacturing company executive; b. DuPont, Pa., Apr. 25, 1934; s. Steve and Sophie (Baranowski) Stasenko. BSME, Case Western Res. U., 1956; postgrad. Syracuse U. Registered profl. engr., Ill. Mech. engr. Kaiser Aluminum, Erie, Pa., 1956-58; instr. Gannon U., Erie, 1958-60, Syracuse (N.Y.) U., 1960-61; engring. supr. A. O. Smith Corp., Erie and Los Angeles, 1961-66; gen. mgr. Am. Elec. Fusion, Chgo., 1966-67; mgr. new products Maremont Corp., Chgo., 1967-69; dir. market planning Gulf and Western Ind., Bellwood, Ill., 1969-71; mgmt. and fin. cons. Stack & Assos., Chgo., 1971-76; pres. Seamcraft, Inc., Chgo., 1976—; mem. Ill. Legis. Small Bus. Conf., 1980, Gov.'s Small Bus. Adv. Commn., 1984—, Ill. State House Conf. on Small Bus., 1984, 85; del. White House Conf. on Small Bus., 1986. Patentee in liquid control and metering fields. Active Sem. Townhouse Assn., Lincoln Park Conservation Assn., Sheffield Neighbors Assn. Recipient Am. Legion award, 1948, Case Western Res. U. Honor key, 1956, Eagle Scout award, 1949. Mem. Ill. Mfrs. Assn. (bd. dirs. 1986—), Small Mfrs. Action Council (vice chmn. 1986-87), Mfrs. Polit. Action Com., Am. Mgmt. Assn., Pres.' Assn., Blue Key, Beta Theta Pi, Theta Tau, Pi Delta Epsilon. Clubs: Chgo. Execs., East Bank, Chgo. Corinthian Yacht, Fullerton Tennis (pres. 1971-79, treas. 1979-83, bd. dirs. 1983-86), Mid-Town Tennis, Lake Shore Ski (v.p. 1982). Office: 932 W Dakin St Chicago IL 60613

STACKHOUSE, DAVID WILLIAM, JR., furniture systems installation contractor; b. Cumberland, Ind., Aug. 29, 1926; s. David William and Dorothy Frances (Snider) S.; B.S., Lawrence Coll., Appleton, Wis., 1950; m. Shirley Pat Smith, Dec. 23, 1950; 1 son, Stefan Brent. Indsl. designer Globe Am. Co., Kokomo, Ind., 1951-53; product designer, chief engr. L.A. Darling Co., Bronson, Mich., 1954-66; contract mgr. Brass Office Products, Indpls., 1966-73; mfrs. rep., Nashville, Ind., 1973-78; mktg. exec. Brass Office Products, Inc., Indpls., 1978-80; office furniture systems installation contractor, 1980—. Precinct committeeman Republican Party. Served with USNR, 1944-46; PTO. Mem. Bldg. Owners and Mfrs. Assn. (past pres. Indpls. chpt.), Brown County Bd. Realtors, Beta Theta Pi. Anglican. Clubs: Lions, Kiwanis (past v.p.), Masons, Shriners. Patentee interior structural systems. Home: Rural Route 3 Box 324 Nashville IN 47448

STACY, BILL WAYNE, college president; b. Bristol, Va., July 26, 1938; s. Charles Frank and Louise Nelson (Altwater) S.; m. Jane Cooper, July 26, 1958; children—Mark, Sara, James. B.S.Ed., S.E. Mo. State U., 1960; M.S., So. Ill. U., 1965, Ph.D., 1968. Tchr. Malden High Sch., Mo., 1960-64; asst. prof. communication Southeast Mo. State U., Cape Girardeau, 1967-71, assoc. prof., 1971-74, prof., 1974—, asst. to pres., 1972-76, dean Grad. Sch., 1976-79, interim pres., 1979, pres., 1980—; dir. 1st Nat. Bank. Mem. Cape Girardeau C. of C. (chmn.), Am. Assn. State Colls. and Univs., Am. Assn. Higher Edn. Democrat. Am. Baptist. Club: Optimist. Home: Wildwood Cape Girardeau MO 63701 Office: SE Mo State U Cape Girardeau MO 63701

STACY, DONALD ROBERT, financial executive; b. Milw., Apr. 4, 1951; m. Mary Louise O'Hara, Apr. 8, 1978. B.A., U. Wis., 1973, M.S., 1975. C.P.A., Wis. Mgr., Arthur Andersen & Co., Milw., 1976-82; v.p. fin. Inland Diesel, Inc., Butler, Wis., 1982—. V.p., treas. maj. events Friends of Art, Milw. Art Mus., 1982-86; unit chmn. United Way, Milw., 1979-82; treas. Milw. ABC Co., 1977-78. Mem. Am. Inst. C.P.A.s, Wis. Soc. C.P.A.s, Fin. Execs. Ins., Beta Alpha Psi (v.p. 1974-75). Home: 4831 Newhall Whitefish Bay WI 53217

STADEM, PAUL DAVID, dentist; b. Ada, Minn., Sept. 12, 1953; s. Clifford Jennings and Gladys (May) S.; m. Diana Lynn Mjoen, Sept. 7, 1974; children: Nicholas Karl, Erica Lynn. BS in Biology, Moorhead State U., 1976; DDS, U. Minn., 1980. Field researcher agronomy N.D. State U., Fargo, 1976; student research fellow U. Minn. Dental Sch., Mpls., 1978-80, pre clin. instr., 1979-80; gen. practice dentistry East Grand Forks, Minn., 1980—; cons. Tri-Valley Head Start, Crookston, Minn., 1982—, Migrant Health, Crookston, 1983—. Bd. dirs. United Way Grand Forks, 1986; pres. East Grand Forks C. of C., 1985; scouting coordinator No. Lights council, Boy Scouts Am., 1984—; com. mem. Ducks Unltd., Grand Forks, 1983—. Recipient Annual Student award Am. Acad. Periodontology, U. Minn., 1980, Unit Commr. award No. Lights council Boy Scouts Am., 1983. Mem. ADA, N.W. Dist. Dental Study Club (v.p. 1980-84), Alpha Omega (award for Excellence in Scholarship 1980), Omicron Kappa Upsilon. Lodge: Rotary (pres.-elect East Grand Forks club). Avocations: hunting, fishing, camping. Home: 22 Forest Ct East Grand Forks MN 56721 Office: 418 NW 3d St East Grand Forks MN 56721

STADLEN, DIANE E., marketing professional; b. Chgo., Nov. 10, 1953; s. Harvey O. and Regina E. (Kozlowski) Nottke; m. Richard W. Stadlin, Feb. 17, 1974; 1 child, Jennifer Beth. Student, Southwest Coll., Chgo., 1971-72. Traffic mgr. WDAI-FM Radio, Chgo., 1973-81; assoc. Creswell, Munsell, Fultz & Zirbel, Inc., Cedar Rapids, Iowa, 1981—. Mem. communications com. United Way East Cen. Iowa, 1986. Mem. Nat. Assn. Farm Broadcasters (adv. bd. 1983—). Office: Creswell Munsell Fultz & Zirbel 4211 Signal Ridge Rd NE Cedar Rapids IA 52406

STADTLANDER, PETER JOHN, data communications executive; b. Ravenna, Ohio, July 27, 1951; s. Joseph Peter and Barbara Ann (Swartz) S.; m. Leann McConnaughey, Nov. 3, 1973; children: Jason, Heidi, Adam. BS in Indsl. Art Edn., Kent State U., 1973. Cert. secondary indsl. art tchr. Indsl. art tchr. Medina (Ohio) High Sch., 1973-75; sales contractor Forest City, Cleve., 1975-78; regional sales mgr. Maintenance Engring., Ltd., Fargo, N.D, 1978-79; v.p. sales Gerhard and Assocs., Columbus, Ohio, 1980-85; pres. Statcom, Inc., Columbus, 1985—; project mgr. Mead Data Cen., Dayton, Ohio, 1985—; pres., owner Stadtlander Tree Farms, Loudonville, Ohio, 1979—; bd. dirs. CLANRO, Medina. Paul J. Conley scholar Kent State U., 1970. Mem. Assn. Computing Machinery (Columbus chpt.), Data Processing Mgrs. Assn., Ohio Christmas Tree Growers, Epsilon Pi Tau. Republican. Methodist. Pioneer pvt. fiber-optic network in Midwest. Avocation: experimenting with lightwave technology. Home: 1273 Oakfield Dr N Columbus OH 43229 Office: Statcom Inc 623 D Park Meadow Dr Westerville OH 43081

STAFFORD, JOHN M., food company executive; b. Evanston, Ill., Oct. 25, 1936; s. Charles Marshall and Harriet Helen (Walker) S.; m. Ardietta Ford, June 12, 1958; children: John Marshall, Lisa, Michael. B.A., Yale U., 1958. Vice pres., account supr. Leo Burnett Co., Chgo., 1960-72; sr. v.p. mktg. KFC Corp., Louisville, 1972-75; v.p. mktg., sr. v.p. Green Giant Co., Chaska, Minn., 1975-79; chief operating officer Green Giant Co., 1979—; exec. v.p., pres. consumer foods group Pillsbury Co., 1979-84, pres., 1984—, chmn., chief exec. officer, 1985—, dir., 1983—; bd. dirs. Cooper Industries. Bd. dirs. Minnetonka, Corp. Served with USMC, 1958-60. Office: Pillsbury Co 200 S 6th St Minneapolis MN 55402

STAFFORD, THOMAS JANEWAY, ophthalmologist, educator; b. Detroit, Jan. 9, 1934; s. Frank Williams John and Bertha May (Arthur) S.; m. Jean Lois Whitten, June 21, 1958; 1 child, Alan. Student Cornell U., 1951-54; M.D., U. Mich., 1958. Diplomate Am. Bd. Ophthalmology. Intern Harper Hosp., Detroit, 1958-59; resident Kresge Eye Inst., Detroit, 1959-60, King County Hosp., Seattle, 1960-62, Children's Orthopedic Hosp., Seattle, 1960-62; fellow U. Miami Bascom Palmer Eye Inst., Fla., 1965-66; practice medicine specializing in ophthalmology, Evanston, Ill., 1966—; sr. attending surgeon Children's Meml. Hosp., Chgo., 1969—, Evanston Hosp., 1973—; researcher ind. ophthal. studies, 1966—; asst. prof. clin. ophthalmology Northwestern U., Chgo., 1974—. Commr. Zoning Amendment Com., Evanston, 1982—. Served to lt. comdr. USNR, 1962-64. Fellow Am. Acad. Ophthalmology (Honor award 1983), ACS, AMA; mem. Ill. State Med. Soc., Chgo. Med. Soc., Assn. for Research in Vision and Ophthalmology, Am. Assn. of Ophthalmology, Ill. Assn. Ophthalmology. Congregationalist. Home: 1206 Croft Ln Evanston IL 60202 Office: 636 Church St Evanston IL 60201

STAFFORD, THOMAS MICHAEL, obstetrician and gynecologist; b. Muncie, Ind., Aug. 28, 1946; s. Frank G. and Alice (Rinker) S.; m. Deborah Root, June 14, 1969; children: Jennifer, John, Joey. BS, Notre Dame U., 1968; MD, Ind. State U., 1971. Diplomate Am. Bd. Ob-Gyn. Intern, then resident Ind. U. Med. Ctr., 1971-74; gen. practice medicine ob-gyn Ft. Wayne, Ind., 1974—; asst. prof. ob-gyn Ind. U. Sch. Medicine, Indpls., 1982—. Bd. dirs. Three Rivers Neighborhood Health Clinic, Ft. Wayne, 1980-86. Fellow Am. Coll. Ob-Gyn; mem. Ind. Med. Assn. Republican. Roman Catholic. Avocations: family, running, church. Office: Duemling Clinic 2828 Fairfield Ave Fort Wayne IN 46807

STAFL, ADOLF, obstetrician, gynecologist, educator; b. Prague, Czechoslovakia, May 5, 1931; came to U.S., 1965; s. Adolf and Anna (Gabrielova) S.; children: Jan, Denny. MD, Charles U., Prague, 1951-57, PhD, 1964. Cert. Am. Bd. Ob-Gyn. Asst. prof. ob-gyn Charles U., Plzen, Czechoslovakia, 1962-68; instr. ob-gyn Johns Hopkins U., Balt., 1968-69; from asst. prof. to prof. ob-gyn Med. Coll. Wis., Milw., 1969-85, prof. ob-gyn, 1985—. Author: Atlas of Colposcopy, 1982; contbr. articles to profl. jours. Fellow Am. Coll. Obstetricians and Gynecologists; hon. mem. British Soc. Colposcopy and Cervical Pathology, Italian Soc. Colposcopy and Cervical Pathology, Obstet. and Gynecologic Soc. of Valencia, Spain, Obstet. and Gynecol. Soc. Paraguay; mem. Internat. Fedn. Cervical Pathology and Colposcopy (pres. 1975-78), Am. Soc. Colposcopy and Cervical Pathology (pres. 1982-84), Am. Assn. Obstetricians and Gynecologists. Home: 2528 W 124th St Wauwatosa WI 53226 Office: Med Coll Wis 8700 W Wisconsin Ave Milwaukee WI 53226

STAFNE, ERIC EDWARD, dentist, educator; b. Rochester, Minn., Apr. 7, 1935; s. Edward Christian and Adeline (Mittelstadt) S.; m. Dorie Jean Supplee, July 8, 1961; children: Mark Eric, Melanie Ross. Student, Carleton Coll., 1953-55; BA, U. Minn., 1958, BS, 1960, DDS, 1960, MSD, 1965. Clin. asst. prof. U. Minn. Sch. Dentistry, Mpls., 1965-70, clin. assoc. prof., 1970-82, clin. prof., 1982—; periodontal cons. 3M, St. Paul, 1972—; ins. cons. Delta Dental Ins. Co., Mpls., 1984—. Pres. Minn. div. Am. Cancer Soc., Mpls., 1984-85; bd. dirs. Ramsey County unit Am. Cancer Soc., St. Paul, 1971-77, 78-86. Served to capt. USAF, 1960-62. Mem. ADA, Am. Acad. Periodontology, Minn. Dental Soc., St. Paul Dist. Dental Soc. (pres. 1975-76), Minn. Assn. Periodontics (pres. 1972-73), U. Minn. Sch. Dentistry Century Club (pres. 1982-83). Avocations: tennis, cross-country skiing, jogging. Home: 7315 N Shore Trail Forest Lake MN 55025 Office: 706 Lowry Med Arts Saint Paul MN 55102

STAHL, CARROLL CLIFFORD, II, investment management company executive, consultant; b. Danville, Pa., Mar. 13, 1948; s. Carroll Clifford and Mildred Geneva (Yingling) S.; m. Amy F. Seesholtz, Aug. 25, 1972 (div. 1976) m. Betty Jean Green, June 21, 1980; 1 stepson, Ronald Lee. B.B.A., The Citadel, 1970. Asst. bond mgr. First Nat. Bank of East Pa., Wilkes-Barre, 1970-74; mgr. equities, v.p. investments Armco Inc., Middletown, Ohio, 1974-82; pres., chief investment officer C-S Capital Advs., Inc., Cin., 1982—. Mem. Cin. Fin. Analysts Fedn. Chpt. Mem. Assembly of God Ch. Avocations: snow skiing; autograph collecting; reading. Home: 8137 Timbertree Way West Chester OH 45069 Office: C-S Capital Advisors Inc 8150 Corporate Park Dr Suite 224 Cincinnati OH 45242

STAHL, CLAUD LAWRENCE, screen co. exec.; b. Pierceton, Ind., Feb. 4, 1928; s. Lawrence Nay and Minnie Alice (Bareham) S.; student Internat. Corr. Sch., 1948-52, Purdue U., 1967-71; grad. Ind. Coll. Auctioneering, 1975; m. Betty Rose Nichols, Oct. 23, 1948; children—Bradley Rene, Belinda Jane. With Gatke Corp., Warsaw, Ind., 1946-55, R. T. Brower Co., Pierceton, Ind., 1955-57; with Da-Lite Screen Co., Inc., Warsaw, 1957—, personnel mgr., 1976—. Interim bd. mem. Whitko Community Sch., 1966-68, treas., 1967; active Boy Scouts Am., Warsaw, 1946-49, Jr. Achievement, 1976-79; bd. dirs. Kosciusko Community Hosp., Warsaw, 1967-81; trustee Washington Twp., 1963-71. Served with Ind. N.G., 1948-52. Mem. Kosciusko County Hist. Soc. (1st pres. 1965-66), Ind. Auctioneers Assn., Ind. Personnel Mgrs. Assn., Ind. C. of C. (com. on occupational health and safety 1980—). Democrat. Methodist. Clubs: Lions, Masons, Shriners, Order Eastern Star. Inventor reversible boat oars. Home: 207 W Elm St Pierceton IN 46562

STAHL, WILLIAM FREDERICK, lawyer; b. Junction City, Kans., Mar. 4, 1925; s. Edward John and Reta Mae (Cline) S.; m. Janice Hillyard, Sept. 1946 (div. 1959); children—Jill Diane, Eric Austin; m. Mary Lou Wall, June 16, 1961; 1 child, Marsha Ann. B.A., Washburn U., 1949, J.D., 1950. Bar: Kans. 1950, U.S. Dist. Ct. Kans. 1950, U.S. Supreme Ct. 1967, U.S. Ct. Claims 1971, U.S. Ct. Appeals (10th cir.) 1968. Sole practice, Junction City, 1950—; county counselor Geary County, Junction City, Kans., 1978-81; city atty. City of Ogden, Kans., 1957-58; police judge Junction City, 1956-60; county atty. Geary County, 1954-55; Pres. March of Dimes, Junction City, 1953, Geary County Mental Health Assn., 1965; bd. dirs. Pawnee Mental Health Assn., Manhattan, Kans., 1975-80. Mem. Kans. Bar Assn., Central Kans. Bar Assn., Geary County Bar Assn. (pres. 1977), Am. Legion (Kans. 4th dist. judge advocate 1970—), La Societe des 40 Hommes et 8 (Kans. advocate 1986—). Republican. Methodist. Lodges: Lions, Masons, Shriners. Home: 115 Rimrock Junction City KS 66441 Office: 815 W 6th St Junction City KS 66441

STAHLMAN, LEROY EDWARD, pharmacist; b. Washington, Mo., Oct. 17, 1951; s. Earl Ruben and Mildred Henrietta (Bone) S.; m. Barbara Ann Knoernschild, Aug. 11, 1973; children—Jennifer Lee, Michael Leroy, Jonathan Edward. B.S. in Applied Math., U. Mo.-Rolla, 1974, B.S. in Pharmacy, Creighton U., 1977. Pharmacist Whaley East End Drugs, Jefferson City, Mo., 1977-79, Osco Drugs, Jefferson City, 1979-82; chief pharmacist Medicare Glaser, Jefferson City, 1983-84; pharmacist Super D, Jefferson City, 1984—. Active Faith Lutherans for Life, Jefferson City, 1984; elder Faith Luth. Ch., Jefferson City, 1985. Recipient Eagle Scout award Boy Scouts Am. Mem. Mo. Pharm. Assn. Avocations: softball, woodworking, fishing, hunting. Home: 2000 Meadow Ln Jefferson City MO 65101 Office: Super D 1404 Missouri Blvd Jefferson City MO 65101

STAINBROOK, JAMES RALPH, JR., educator; b. Indpls., Dec. 8, 1936; s. James Ralph, Sr., and Alta Marie (Doty) S.; m. Margaret Ann McKinley, June 21, 1959; children—Susan Ann, Steven James. A.B., Butler U., Indpls., 1959; M.A., U. Wis., Madison, 1964; Ed.D., Ind. U., Bloomington, 1970. Cert. Latin tchr., secondary sch. adminstr., counselor guidance and social studies, Ind. Tchr. Indpls. public schs., 1963-68; teaching asst. Ind. U., 1968-70; prof. edn. Ball State U., Muncie, Ind., 1970—. Served as officer USAF, 1959-62. Mem. Assn. Teacher Educators, Assn. for Supervision and Curriculum Devel., Phi Delta Kappa, Kappa Delta Pi, Phi Kappa Phi. Republican. Methodist. Clubs: Scottish Rite, Shriners. Masons. Contbr. numerous articles to profl. jours. Home: 8225 Lockwood Ln Indianapolis IN 46217 Office: Ball State U Teachers Coll 822 Muncie IN 47306

STAISCH, KLAUS JUERGEN, obstetrician-gynecologist; b. Stettin, Fed. Republic Germany, Aug. 28, 1938; came to U.S., 1968; s. Emil and Dorothea (Reck) S.; m. Christina Maria Rodriguez, Mar. 8, 1982; children: Julia, Lydia. BS, Philips U., Marburg, Germany, 1963; MD, Freie U., Berlin, 1966. Intern U. Berlin Hosp., 1966-67, Passaic (N.J.) Gen. Hosp., 1968-69; resident U. Minn., Mpls., 1969-73; fellow in perinatology U. So. Calif., Los Angeles, 1971-72; assoc. prof. U. Calif., Los Angeles, 1973-84, U. Minn., Mpls., 1984—; dir. obstetrics Hennepin County Med. Ctr., Mpls., 1984-86, dir. maternal-fetal medicine, 1986—. Fellow Am. Coll. Ob-Gyn; mem. Soc. Perinatal Obstetricians, Minn. Perinatal Orgn. (bd. dirs. 1984—), Minn. Soc. Ob-Gyn., Twin Cities Perinatal Club (pres. 1986—), Am. Acad. Pediatrics (Investigator award 1983). Avocations: hunting, photography. Office: Hennepin Faculty Assocs 825 S 8th St Minneapolis MN 55404

STALLARD, WAYNE MINOR, lawyer; b. Onaga, Kans., Aug. 23, 1927; s. Minor Regan and Lydia Faye (Randall) S.; B.S., Kans. State Tchrs. Coll., Emporia, 1949; J.D., Washburn U., 1952; m. Wanda Sue Bacon, Aug. 22, 1948; children—Deborah Sue, Carol Jean, Bruce Wayne (dec.). Admitted to Kans. bar, 1952 pvt. practice, Onaga, 1952—; atty. Community Hosp. Dist. No. 1, Pottawatomie, Jackson and Nemaha Counties, Kans., 1955—; Pottawatomie County atty., 1955-59; city atty. Onaga, 1953-79; atty. Unified School Dist. 322, Pottawatomie County, Kans., 1966-83. Bd. dirs. North Central Kans. Guidance Ctr., Manhattan, 1974-78; lawyer 2d dist. jud. nominating commn., 1980—; atty. Rural Water Dist. No. 3, Pottawatomie County, Kans., 1974—; chmn. Pottawatomie County Econ. Devel. Com., 1986—. Fund dr. chmn. Pottawatomie County chpt. Nat. Found. for Infantile Paralysis, 1953-54. Served from pvt. to sgt., 8th Army, AUS, 1946 to 47. Mem. ABA, Pottawatomie County, Kans. bar assns., Onaga Businessmen's Assn., Am. Judicature Soc., City Attys. Assn. Kan. (dir. 1963-66), Phi Gamma Mu, Kappa Delta Pi, Delta Theta Phi, Sigma Tau Gamma. Mem. United Ch. of Christ. Mason (Shriner); mem. Order Eastern Star. Home: 720 High St Onaga KS 66521 Office: Stallard & Roe 307 Leonard Onaga KS 66521

STALLARD, WAYNE REX, manufacturing company executive; b. Lawrence, Kans., Nov. 17, 1926; s. Clarence N. and Nora E. (Herd) S.; m. Florence Anne Schutte, Sept. 6, 1952; children: Rebecca Anne, Melanie Kay, Jennifer Elaine. BSBA, U. Kans., 1948. CPA, Mo., Kans. Acct., Haskins & Sells, N.Y.C. and Kansas City, Mo., 1948-55; exec. v.p., pres. Pitman Mfg. Co., Grandview, Mo., 1955-68; sr. v.p., treas. A.B. Chance Co., Centralia, Mo., 1968-71; pres. Stelco, Inc., Kansas City, Kans., 1970—; bd. dirs. Western Forms, Inc., Kansas City, Mo. Bd. dirs. Farm and Indsl. Equipment Inst., Chgo., 1980—. Served to 2d lt. USAF, 1944-46. Republican. Methodist. Clubs: Carriage, Milburn. Lodges: Masons, Shriners. Home: 6107 W 64th Terr Shawnee Mission KS 66202 Office: Stelco Inc 5500 Kansas Ave Kansas City KS 66106

STALLINGS, GENE CLIFTON, professional football coach; b. Paris, Tex., Mar. 2, 1935; s. Eugene C. and Neil (Moye) S.; m. Ruth Ann Jack, Dec. 1, 1956; children: Anna Lee, Laura Nell, John Mark, Jacklyn Ruth. B.S., Tex. A&M U., 1958. Asst. football coach U. Ala., 1958-64; head football coach, dir. athletics Tex. A&M U., 1964-72; asst. coach Dallas Cowboys, 1972-85; head football coach St. Louis Cardinals, 1986—; dir. Bank of A&M, College Station, Tex., Rolling Internat., Inc., Dallas; Spalding sports cons. Mem. Sam Houston council Boy Scouts Am. Mem. Nat. Assn. Collegiate Dirs. Athletics, Am. Football Coaches Assn., Fellowship Christian Athletes. Mem. Ch. of Christ. Office: care St Louis Football Cardinals Busch Stadium Box 888 Saint Louis MO 63188 *

STALLS, MADLYN A., developmental skills specialist, educator; b. Metropolis, Ill., Oct. 22, 1947; s. Robert Alvin and Freda Mae (Houston) S.; 1 child, Robert C. Goodwin. BA in Sociology, So. Ill. U., 1970, MS in Rehab. Adminstrn., 1976, postgrad. in ednl. adminstrn. higher edn. Social welfare worker Ill. Dept. Child and Family Services, Murphysboro, 1970-76; manpower coordinator Ill. Farmers Union, West Frankfort, 1976-77;

researcher So. Ill. U., Williamson County, 1977-78; counselor spl. services So. Ill. U., Carbondale, 1980-82, coordinator, 1982-83; devel. skills specialist Ctr. for Basic Skills Southern Ill. U., Carbondale, 1983—; cons. Jackson County Pub. Housing Initiatives Program, Carbondale, 1985; cons. headstart program So. Ill. U., Carbondale, 1985, women's studies dept., 1986—; bd. dirs. KASL. Bd. vols. Carbondale Women's Ctr., 1973-76; bd. dirs. Attuck Community Service Bd., 1973-75; mem. steering com., fellow Ill. Com. Black Concerns in Higher Edn., 1985—. Mem. Am. Assn. Counselling and Devel., Assn. Multi-Cultural Concerns, Massac County Afro Am. History Soc., Black Women's Coalition of Carbondale (founder 1982), Kappa Delta Pi (edn. hon. 1987—). Lodge: Order of Eastern Stars. Avocations: writing, reading, playing piano, dancing, exercise. Home: 407 N Barnes St Carbondale IL 62901 Office: So Ill U Woody Hall C9B Carbondale IL 62901

STALNAKER, ARMAND CARL, insurance company executive; b. Weston, W.Va., Apr. 24, 1916; s. Thomas Carl and Alta (Hinzman) S.; m. Rachel Pickett, Apr. 26, 1946; children: Timothy, Thomas. B.B.A., U. Cin., 1941; M.A., U. Pa., 1945; Ph.D., Ohio State U., 1951. Asst. prof. bus. Ohio State U., Columbus, 1946-50; with Prudential Ins. Co., 1950-63; adminstrv. v.p., exec. v.p., pres., chmn., chief exec. officer Gen. Am. Life Ins. Co., 1963-86; prof. mgmt. Washington U. Sch. Bus., St. Louis, 1982—; dir. Anheuser-Busch Cos., Inc., Gen. Am. Life Ins. Co., Edward D. Jones & Co., Civic Ctr. Corp. Bd. dirs. YMCA, St. Louis council Boy Scouts Am.; chmn. bd. dirs. Barnes Hosp. Mem. Am. Psychol. Assn., Am. Econ. Assn., AAAS, Omicron Delta Kappa. Mem. Soc. of Friends. Clubs: Noonday, Bogey, St. Louis, N.Y. Yacht. Home: 8027 Kingsbury Blvd Saint Louis MO 63105 Office: Washington Univ Sch Bus Saint Louis MO 63130

STALNAKER, SUSAN DENISE, dentist; b. Portsmouth, Ohio, June 29, 1954; d. Earl Lindsay and Helen Jean (Sanford) Fultz; m. Russell Ray Stalnaker, Mar. 20, 1976; children: Angela Lissette, Alissa Nicole. BS, U. Cin., 1976; DDS, Ohio State U., 1979. Gen. practice dentistry Columbus, Ohio, 1979—. Mem. ADA, Am. Acad. Gen. Dentistry, Ohio Dental Assn., Columbus Dental Assn., Westerville Dental Study Club (sec., treas. 1984, v.p. 1985, pres. 1986), Delta Sigma Delta (historian 1984—). Democrat. Club: Forest Hills Women's Garden (chmn. publicity 1983-84). Office: 883 Eastwind Dr Westerville OH 43081

STALOCH, JAMES EDWARD, JR., vocational educator; b. Worthington, Minn., Aug. 14, 1946; s. James Edward and Cecil Ilo (Rist) S.; m. Susan Kay Schroeder, June 8, 1968; children: Paul, Jennifer, Michael. BS, Moorhead (Minn.) State U., 1971; MEd, U. Minn., 1986. Asst. constrn. engr. Ford Motor Co., Dearborn, Mich., 1968-69; tchr. St. Paul Pub. Schs., 1971-72; mgr. Litho Shop, Mpls., 1972-74; trade and indsl. supr. Dakota County Vocat. Sch., Rosemount, Minn., 1974—. Sr. mem. Civil Air Patrol, cert. flight instr.; pres. Northview Elem. PTA, Eagan, Minn.; pres. Rosemount Youth Hoc Assn. Served with U.S. Army, 1966-68, Vietnam. Mem. Am. Legion, Dakota County Vocat. Inst. Alumni Assn. (dir.), Nat. Assn. Flight Instrs., Kapa Phi. Roman Catholic. Office: PO Box K Rosemount MN 55068

STALTER, WILLIAM, obstetrician-gynecologist; b. Cin., Sept. 26, 1941; s. Chester Clayton and Alverta Grace (Miller) S.; m. Bonnie Suellen Dieterich, June 23, 1962; children: Susan, Stephen. BS in Zoology, Ohio State U., 1963, MD, 1967. Diplomate Am. Bd. Ob-Gyn. V.p. Miami Valley Ob-Gyn., Dayton, Ohio, 1973—; ultrasonographer Miami Valley Hosp., Dayton, 1970-71, 73-75, chmn. ob-gyn dept., 1986—; assoc. clin. prof. Wright State U. Sch. Medicine, Dayton, 1973—. bd. dirs. Crisis Valley Pregancy Ctr., Dayton, 1984—; bd. dirs., vice chmn. Washington Heights Bapt. Ch., Centerville, Ohio, 1978-85; pres. Dayton Obstetrics and Gynecol. Soc., 1987-88. Served to maj. U.S. Army, 1971-73. Fellow Am. Coll. Ob-Gyn.; mem. Dayton Ob-Gyn. Soc. (program chmn. 1982). Republican. Baptist. Avocations: photography, fishing, skiing, biking, amateur radio. Office: Miami Valley Ob-Gyn Assoc Inc 30 E Apple St Dayton OH 45409

STAMBERGER, EDWIN HENRY, farmer, civic leader; b. Mendota, Ill., Feb. 16, 1916; s. Edwin Nicolaus and Emilie Anna Marie (Yost) S.; m. Mabel Edith Gordon,)ct. 6, 1937; 1 child, Larry Allan. Farmer seed corn, livestock, machinery devel. Mendota, 1939—; bd. dirs. Mendota Coop. & Supply Co., 1949-67, pres., 1958-67. Mem. Mendota Luth. Ch. council, 1958-64, chmn. 1964, treas. northwest conf., 1966-68, trustee Bible camp; mem. Mendota Watershed Com., 1966-73, 77—, rev. and comment com. subregion and region Ill. Cen. Comprehensive Health Planning Agy., 1974-76; asst. in devel. Mendota Hosp., Mendota Lake; chmn. bldg. com. Mendota Luth. Home, 1972-73; bd. dirs. LaSalle County Mental Health Bd., 1969-74, U. Ill. County Extension, 1963-67, chmn. 1966-67; bd. dirs. Soil and Water Dist., 1968-73, vice chmn., 1971-73. Recipient Future Farmers Am. award. Mem. Am. Soc. Agrl. Engrs., Soil Soc. Am., Ill. Council Watersheds (founder), Smithsonian Inst., Mental Health Assn., People to People Internat., Platform Assn., Mendota C. of C. (Honor award 1974). Club: Mendota Sportsman's. Lodge: Lions (Mendota chpt. bd. dirs. 1965-67, Honor award 1981). Home and Office: Sabine Farm Rural Rt 1 Mendota IL 61342

STAMEY, WILLIAM LEE, college dean; b. Chgo., Oct. 19, 1922; s. Kendrick C. and Ingar Miriam (de la Gardie) S.; m. Jean Raydelle Wilson, June 25, 1945; children: Robert William, Thomas Edward, Janet Susan Stamey Elliott. B.A., U. No. Colo., Greeley, 1947; M.A., U. Mo., 1949, Ph.D., 1952. Asst. prof. math. Ga. State U., 1952-53; mem. faculty Kans. State U., Manhattan, 1953—; prof. math. Kans. State U., 1962—; dean Kans. State U. (Coll. Arts and Scis.), 1969—; sec.-treas. Council Colls. Arts and Scis., 1978—; chmn. commn. arts and scis. Nat. Assn. State Univs. and Land-Grant Colls., 1979-81. Served to 1st lt. USAAF, 1943-46. Mem. AAAS, Am. Math. Soc., Math. Assn. Am., Sigma Xi. Methodist. Lodge: Rotary. Home: 416 Edgerton Ave Manhattan KS 66502 Office: Kans State U Coll Arts and Scis Eisenhower Hall Manhattan KS 66506

STAMOS, THEODORE JAMES, clinical social worker; b. Oskaloosa, Iowa, May 1, 1933; s. James Theodore and Sophia (Zaffiras) S.; m. Sally Jane Huston, Aug. 18, 1978; children: Jacqueline, Sara, James, Theodore. Student, Ball State U., 1951-52, NYU, 1952-53; BA, U. Iowa, 1957, MSW, 1959. Clin. social worker Hastings (Minn.) State Hosp., 1959-62, Mental Hygiene Clinic VA Hosp., St. Paul, 1962-63; exec. dir. Dakota County Mental Health Ctr., South St. Paul, Minn., 1963-73, 78-83; pvt. practice clin. social worker St. Paul, 1973-78; clin. social worker Children's Home Soc. Minn., St. Paul, 1983—, Family Practice Med. Assocs., St. Paul, 1983—, Harley Clinic Ramsey County, St. Paul, 1983—; clin. instr. grad. sch. social work U. Minn., Mpls., 1965-73, 78-83; appointee Gov.'s Blue Ribbon Task Force on Use of State Mental Health Facilities, 1967, Gov.'s Statewide Study Com. on Prevention of Suicide, 1966, 67; mem. Gov.'s Health Study Com. Comprehensive State Health Planning, 1967-69; guest lectr. U. Minn. Med. Sch., 1967, Ctr. for Continuation Study Bur. Family Services U. Minn., 1964, 65; cons. family therapy Red Wing State Tng. Sch., 1968, 69; mem. State Guidelines Com. for Programmatic Integrations of State Hosps., Mental Health Ctrs. and Welfare Depts., 1966-68; mem. Paramed. Careers Adv. bd. Dakota County Vocat. Ctr., 1973-76; mem. adv. bd. Dakota County Crisis Intervention Service, 1981, State Bd. Oral Examiners for Psychologists and Social Workers, 1967, 69, Twin City Agy. Liaison Com., 1966-68. Mem. Study Com. for Devel. New Minn. Committment Law, 1966; mem. profl. adv. bd. Wesleyan Meth. Ch. Counseling Ctr., 1965-68; mem. Minn. Child Welfare Planning Adv. Com., 1966-68; mem. comprehensive health planning adv. com. Twin Cities Met. Council, 1969-70. Mem. Am. Group Psychotherapy Assn., Am. Assn. Marriage and Family Therapy (clin.), Nat. Assn. Social Workers (cert., del., bd. dirs. southwestern Minn. chpt., 1963-65, 67-69, participant leadership tng. program), Acad. Cert. Social Workers, Minn. Welfare Assn. (chmn. health com.), Minn. Assn. Mental Health Ctrs. (sec. 1968-69). Mem. United Ch. of Christ. Lodge: Masons. Avocations: flying.

STAMP, WILLARD JAY, optometrist; b. Salem, Ohio, Oct. 25, 1932; s. J. Richard and Leora H. (Hoopes) S.; m. Barbara Jean Schoeder, Dec. 31, 1984; children: Joel W., Alan J., Brandi G., Rob. Student, Kent (Ohio) State U., 1950-52; OD cum laude, Ohio State U., 1955, postgrad., 1985. Gen. practice optometry Barberton, Ohio, 1955-56, Salem, Ohio, 1958—; cons. County Health Dept., Lisbon, Ohio, 1980—, USAR, Sam Houston, 1981—, U.S. Army Health Services Command. Bd. dirs. Am. Heart Assn., Columbiar County, Lisbon, Ohio, 1984—. Served to 1st lt. U.S. Army, 1956-58, col. Res. Mem. Am. Optometric Assn., Ohio Optometric Assn. (past pres.), Ohio Vision Found. (pres. 1984), Better Vision Inst., Salem C. of C. (bd. dirs. 1983-86), Mental Health Assn., Salem High Alumni Assn. (pres., bd. dirs. 1972—), Res. Officers Assn., Epsilon Psi Epsilon (past dir.), Beta Sigma Kappa. Clubs: United Comml. Travelers, Salem Golf. Lodges: Lions (past pres., bd. dirs.), Masons (sr. warden), Shriners (pres. 1978), Elks. Home: 1575 Manor Dr Salem OH 44460 Office: 389 N Ellsworth Salem OH 44460

STANBERY, ROBERT CHARLES, veterinarian; b. Conneaut, Ohio, Apr. 5, 1947; s. Robert James and Ruth Virginia Stanbery; student Miami U., Oxford, Ohio, 1965-67; D.V.M., Ohio State U., 1971; m. Constance Ann Coutts, July 24, 1971; children: Scott Andrew, Mark Donald. Veterinarian, Lexington (Mass.) Animal Hosp., 1971-74, Avon Lake Animal Clinic Inc. (Ohio), 1974-76; pres., treas. Bay Village Animal Clinic Inc. (Ohio), 1976—. Mem. AVMA, Ohio Vet. Med. Assn., Animal Hosp. Assn. Cleve. Acad. Vet. Medicine, Lorain County Vet. Assn. Internat. Platform Assn., Bay Village C. of C. (bd. dirs., pres.), U.S. Jaycees. Fundamentalist Christian. Home: 309 Timberlane Dr Avon Lake OH 44012 Office: 627 Clague Rd Bay Village OH 44140

STANDERWICK, RAYMOND EARNEST, JR., construction executive; b. Chgo., Nov. 9, 1927; s. Raymond Earnest and Anna Marie (McKenna) S.; m. Rachelle Ann Pogue, Aug. 3, 1952; 1 child, Ann Marie. BS, Grinnell Coll., 1952; postgrad., U. Iowa, 1957. High sch. basketball coach Cen. and Western Iowa, 1952-65; mktg. mgr. K&M Electronics, Inc., Mpls., 1965-71, The Durrant Group, Inc., Dubuque, Iowa, 1971-86; dir. mktg. Neumann Bros., Inc., Des Moines, 1986—; speaker, lectr. to various bus. orgns. Ordained minister Westfield Community Ch., Oak Grove Ch., Grinnell, Iowa. Served to cpl. USMC, 1944-46. Mem. AIA (assoc.), Soc. Mktg. Profl. Services, YMCA Fitness Ctr. Methodist. Lodge: Masons. Home: 1722 Spencer St Grinnell IA 50112 Office: Neumann Bros Inc 811 Grand Ave PO Box 1315 Des Moines IA 50305

STANDLEY, GILBERT DANFIELD, stockbroker, tax consultant; b. South Bend, Ind., Feb. 18, 1959; s. Gilbert Dennis and Kathleen (Klute) S.; m. Sarah Englehart, Aug. 4, 1984. BA in Liberal Arts, DePauw U., 1982; JD, Ind. U., 1985. Bar: U.S. Dist. Ct. (no. and so. dists.) Ind. 1985, Ind. 1986. Dep. prosecutor intern Marion County Prosecutors Office, Indpls., 1984-85; stockbroker Dean Witter Reynolds, Indpls., 1985—. Mem. Rep. precinct com., Indpls., 1985—. Mem. ABA, Ind. Bar Assn., Indpls. Bar Assn., Moot Ct. Soc., Sigma Delta Chi. Roman Catholic. Home: PO Box 44659 Indianapolis IN 46204 Office: Dean Witter Reynolds 11611 N Meridian Carmel IN 46204

STANFORD, MELVIN JOSEPH, university dean, management consultant; b. Logan, Utah, June 13, 1932; s. Joseph Sedley and Ida Pearl (Ivie) S.; m. Linda Barney, Sept. 2, 1960; children: Connie Stanford Tendick, Cheryl Stanford Bohn, Joseph, Theodore, Emily, Charlotte, Charles, Sarah. B.S. (First Security Found. scholar), Utah State U., 1957; M.B.A. (Donald Kirk David fellow), Harvard U., 1963; Ph.D., U. Ill., 1968. Asst. audit supr. Utah Tax Commn., 1958-61; acct. Haskins & Sells, C.P.A.s, Boston, 1961-62; acctg. staff analyst Arabian Am. Oil Co., Dhahran, Saudi Arabia, 1963-66; teaching and research asst. U. Ill., Urbana, 1966-68; mem. faculty Brigham Young U., Provo, Utah, 1968-82; dir. mgmt. devel. programs Brigham Young U., 1970-73, prof. bus. mgmt., 1974-82; dean Coll. Bus. Mankato (Minn.) State U., 1982—; vis. prof. mgmt. Boston U., Europe, 1975-76. Author: New Enterprise Management, 1975, 82, Management Policy, 1979, 83; also articles, mgmt. cases. Founder Midwestern Jour. Bus. and Econs., 1985. Served with USAF, 1951-55; also Res. Mem. N. Am. Case Research Assn. (v.p. for research 1985-86, pres. elect 1986-87), Acad. Mgmt., Strategic Mgmt. Soc., SAR (pres. Utah 1978-79, nat. trustee 1979-80, Meritorious Service medal 1981), Alpha Kappa Psi, Phi Kappa Phi. Mem. Ch. Jesus Christ Latter Day Saints. Lodge: Kiwanis. Home: 221 Crestwood Dr North Mankato MN 56001 Office: Mankato State U Coll Bus 120 MH Mankato MN 56001

STANFORD, PHYLLIS KAY, tax consultant; b. Adrian, Mich., July 20, 1941; d. Frank Olin and Lydia May (Jenkins) Mason; m. James C. Moulton, June 17, 1961 (div. Nov. 1974); children: Connie M., Jeffrey T., Kendra J., James F.; m. Gerald L. Stanford, July 4, 1976. Student, Jackson (Mich.) Jr. Coll., 1959-60. Tax. cons. Stanford Services, Maumee and Whitehouse, Ohio, 1974—; pres. Mindo, Inc., Whitehouse, 1985—; ptnr. Venture Capital Ptnrs., Whitehouse, 1986—; bd. dirs. Nu-Joint Internat., Denver. Republican. Home: 10341 Ramm Rd Whitehouse OH 43571 Office: 9410 Airport Hwy Monclava OH 43542

STANFORD, RALPH HONNELL, advertising executive; b. Columbus, Ohio, June 10, 1923; s. Carl H. and Pansy B. (Cheek) S.; m. Geraldine F. Bedal, June 4, 1944; children: Meredith A., Roberta S. Cert., Pasadena Coll., 1942; BS, John Brown U., 1947; postgrad., Northwestern U., 1947-51. Cert. bus. communicator. Advt. mgr. Aetna Plywood Co., Chgo., 1947-51, Pioneer Gen. Motor, Chgo., 1951-58, Howell Furniture Co., St. Charles, Ill., 1959-70, Equipto Mfg. Co., Aurora, Ill., 1970—. Editor 20 catalogs Equipto Mfg. Co. Storage System, 1970—, Better Idea Reports, 1970—. Elder Wheaton Evang. Free Ch., 1986—. Served to tech. sgt. U.S. Army, 1942-45, ETO. Mem. Am. Mgmt. Assn., Bus. Profl. Advt. Assn., Valley Advt. Club (pres. 1976-77). Republican. Avocations: coin and stamp collecting, photography, travel. Home: 1438 S 7th Ct Saint Charles IL 60174 Office: Equipto Mfg Co 225 S Highland Ave Aurora IL 60507

STANGE, JAMES HENRY, architect; b. Davenport, Iowa, May 25, 1930; s. Henry Claus and Norma (Ballhorn) S.; m. Mary Suanne Peterson, Dec. 12, 1954; children: Wade Weston, Drew Dayton, Grant Owen. BArch, Iowa State U., 1954. Registered architect, Iowa, Nebr., Kans., Mo., Okla. Designer Davis & Wilson, Lincoln, Nebr., 1954-62, v.p., 1962-68; v.p., sec. Davis, Fenton, Stange, Darling, Lincoln, Nebr., 1968-76, pres., 1976—, chmn., 1978—. Prin. works include Lincoln Airport Terminal, Sq. D Mfg. Plant, Lincoln, Bryan Meml. Hosp. (masterplans and additions), Lincoln, Hasting (Nebr.) YMCA, various structures U. Nebr., Lincoln, ctr. and br. offices Am. Charter Fed. Savs & Loan, Southeast High Sch. (addition), 1984, U. Nebr. Animal Sci. Bldg., 1987. Pres. Lincoln Ctr. Assn., 1979, Capitol Assn. Retarded Citizens, 1972; chmn. United Way Campaign, 1986, Bryan Hosp. Found. Endowment Com.; bd. dirs. Delta Dental, 1987—; deacon Presbyn. Ch., 1960, chmn. bd. trustees, 1968, elder, 1972. Recipient Honor award Conf. on Religious Architecture, 1969, also numerous state and nat. awards from archtl. orgns. Mem. AIA (bd. dirs. 1964-65, treas. 1965, sec. 1966, v.p. 1967, pres. Nebr. soc. 1968, mem. com. on architecture for health, Regional Design award 1976), Am. Assn. Health Planners, Interfaith Forum on Religion, Art, Architecture, Lincoln C. of C. (bd. dirs. 1982). Republican. Clubs: Exec. (pres. 1972), Crucible, 12, Hillcrest Country (pres. 1977) (Lincoln). Avocations: travel, photography, golf. Home: 3545 Calvert St Lincoln NE 68506 Office: 211 N 14th St Lincoln NE 68508

STANGELAND, ARLAN INGHART, congressman; b. Fargo, N.D., Feb. 8, 1930; s. Inghart and Pearle (Olson) S.; m. Virginia Grace Trowbridge, June 24, 1950; children: David, Beth, Brian, Jean, Todd, Jeffrey, Stuart. Student pub. schs., Moorhead, Minn. Farmer Barnesville, Minn., 1951—; mem. Minn. Ho. of Reps., St. Paul, From 1966, 95th-99th Congresses from 7th Minn. Dist.; mem. public works and transp. com., mem. agr. com. 95th-100th Congresses from 7th Minn. Dist., 1977—. Pres. Barnesville PTA, 1964; sec. Republican Party of Wilkin County, Minn., 1960-65, pres., 1965-66; mem. Barnesville Sch. Bd., 1976-77. Recipient N.D. State U. Agr. award for community service. Mem. Minn. Shorthorn Assn. (dir.). Lutheran. Office: 1526 Longworth House Office Bldg Washington DC 20515 also: 403 Center Ave Moorhead MN 56560*

STANGER, ROBERT JOHN, instrumentation company executive; b. Easton, Pa., Feb. 10, 1939; s. John and Catherine Ann (Seaman) S.; m. Marjorie Gabrella Peters, July 1, 1961; children: Theresa, Clayton, Christopher, Kevin. BSEE, Lafayette Coll., 1971; MBA, Pepperdine U., 1981. Engring. mgr. research and devel. Amerace Corp., Hackettstown, N.J., 1971-79; program mgr. Electric Power Research Inst., Palo Alto, Calif., 1979-81; pres., gen. mgr. Amerace Corp., Toronto, Ont., Can., 1981-84; gen mgr. Barber Coleman Co., Rockford, Ill., 1984—. Patentee in field. Served with USAF, 1958-62. Mem. IEEE, Am. Assn. Metals, Indsl. Heating Equipment Assn. Republican. Roman Catholic. Avocations: boating, skiing, camping, golf. Home: 1976 Shaw Roods Dr Rockford IL 61132 Office: Barber Coleman Co 1354 Clifford Ave Coves Park IL 61132

STANGER, ROY LAWRENCE, architect; b. Chgo., July 16, 1931; s. Roy Luken and Helen Jean (McCabe) S. BArch, U. Ill., 1966. Registered architect, Ill. Staff architect Constrn. Economists Collaborative, Chgo., 1973-75; comptroller Metz Train and Youngren, Inc., Chgo., 1975-77; dor. projects Charles Kober Assocs., Chgo., 1977-82; dir. architecture Horman DeHann Assocs., Chgo., 1982-83; v.p. Eckland Cons. Inc., Deerfield, Ill., 1983—. Trustee Village Bd. Riverwoods, Ill., 1985—. Mem. AIA, Am. Arbitration Assn. Republican. Roman Catholic. Club: Cliffdwellers (Chgo.). Avocations: gardening, woodworking, carpentry. Home: 2451 Riverwoods Rd Riverwoods IL 60015 Office: Eckland Cons Inc 108 Wilmot Rd Deerfield IL 60015

STANGER, VERNON JOHN, accountant; b. Ft. Wayne, Ind., July 1, 1953; s. Vincent Lee and Marie Barbara (Halley) S.; m. Deborah Kay Baumgartner, May 25, 1974; 1 child, Vincent John. BS in Business, Ind. U., 1978, MS in Business, 1984. CPA. Staff acct. Drees, Robinson & Perugini, CPA's, Ft. Wayne, 1978-79; cost analyst N.Am. Van Lines, Ft. Wayne, 1979-84; fin. analyst Gen. Electric Co., Ft. Wayne, 1984-85; acctg. supr. Navistar Internat. Transp., Ft. Wayne, 1985—. Served with USN, 1973-78. Mem. Am. Inst. CPA's. Ind. Assn. CPA's. Roman Catholic. Avocations: tennis, bowling, basketball, collecting records. Home: 7723 Tendall Ct Fort Wayne IN 46825 Office: Navistar Internat Transp 2911 Meyer Rd Fort Wayne IN 46803

STANGLER, GREG FRANK, infosystems executive; b. Melrose, Minn., July 8, 1960; s. Robert Henry and Mary Ann (Hudovernik) S. BS in Computer Sci., N.D. State U., 1982. Sci. programmer Sperry Corp., Eagan, Minn., 1982-86; mktg. systems analyst McQuay Corp., Plymouth, Minn., 1986—; cons., owner, Dawning Co., Mpls., 1986—. Tech. writer Gary Hart Campaign for Pres., St. Paul, 1984; steering com. Nat. Issues Forum Dakota County Library Systems, Eagan, 1986. Mem. Robotics Internat., Assn. Computing Machinery (chmn. 1981-82), MICOM (stock analyst 1983—). Avocations: racquetball, hiking, study in internat. relations.

STANGLEWICZ, CHRISTOPHER GERARD, computer information scientist; b. Detroit, Dec. 16, 1955; s. Raymond J. and Irene L. (Sosnowski) S.; m. Denise J. Epperson, May 19, 1979; 1 child, Kristin J. BS, Wayne State U., 1978. Programmer/analyst Fed. Mogul, Southfield, Mich., 1979-82, ANR, Detroit, 1982-83; project mgr. Mich. Consol. Gas, Detroit, 1983—. Republican. Roman Catholic. Avocation: golf. Office: Mich Consol Gas 500 Griswold Detroit MI 48226

STANIEC, MARJAN PETER, associate judge; b. Chgo., Aug. 1, 1914; s. Hipolit and Mary (Rulikowski) S.; m. Mary M. Hobbs, Oct. 21, 1977; children—Wayne P., Joyce, Carol Ann, William, Joseph G. J.D., Catholic U. Am., 1941, LL.M., 1942, J.D., 1957. Bar: D.C. 1941, U.S. Ct. Appeals (D.C. cir.) 1941, U.S. Supreme Ct. 1959, Ill. 1970, U.S. Dist. Ct. (ea. dist.) Ky., U.S. Dist. Ct. (ea. dist.) Wis., U.S. Ct. Appeals (7th cir.), U.S. Dist. Ct. (no. dist.) Ill. Adminstr., Social Security Adminstrn., various midwestern states, 1940-68; dep. regional dir. HEW, Chgo., 1968-76; assoc. judge Ill. Circuit Ct. Cook County, Chgo., 1976—; adj. prof. law Loyola U., Chgo., 1986-87; lectr. legal topics; co-producer, host TV program WCIU-TV, Chgo., 1965-68. Mem. Chgo. Adv. Council Aging, 1957—, vice chmn., 1978-82; mem. pub. edn. com. Ill. div. Am. Cancer Soc., 1966-80; active numerous civic orgns.; nat. del. to White House Conf. on Aging, 1981; mem. forum subcom. Met. Chgo. Coalition on Aging, 1981-83. Recipient meritorious service citation Fed. Govt., 1944, 49, disting. service award Back of Yards Council, 1965, citation in Congl. Record, 1967, outstanding service citation Am. Cancer Soc., 1974, 75, outstanding performance in fed. service citation Fed. Exec. Bd., 1975, cert. of merit Sec. of HEW, 1976, outstanding service award Ill. Citizens for Better Care, 1982, Humanitarian award Central Lions Club, Chgo., 1982, numerous others. Mem. Ill. Jud. Conf., Ill. Judges Assn. (bd. dirs. 1984-87), Fed. Bar Assn. (pres. Chgo. chpt. 1963-64, nat. v.p. 1964-65), Chgo. Bar Assn. (mental health and adoption coms. 1978—), N.W. Suburban Bar Assn., West Suburban Bar Assn., Advocates Soc. (award of merit 1966), Polish Nat. Alliance, Chgo. Soc., Sigma Delta Kappa. Lodges: Lions, Moose. Co-author: Are You Planning To Live the Rest of Your Life, 1965; columnist Chgo. Daily Law Bull., 1963—; bi-weekly columnist Your Social Security, Chgo. Tribune, 1965-67. Home: 5707 N New Hampshire Ave Chicago IL 60631

STANISLAO, JOSEPH, engineer, educator; b. Manchester, Conn., Nov. 21, 1928; s. Eduardo and Rose (Zaccaro) S.; m. Bettie Chloe Carter, Sept. 6, 1960. B.S., Tex. Tech. U., 1957; M.S., Pa. State U., 1959; D.Engring. Sci., Columbia U., 1970. Registered profl. engr., Mass. Asst. engr. Naval Ordnance Research, University Park, Pa., 1958-59; asst. prof. N.C. State U., Raleigh, 1959-61; dir. research Darlington Fabrics Corp., Pawtucket, R.I., 1961-62; from asst. prof. to prof. U. R.I., Kingston, 1962-71; prof., chmn. dept. Cleve. State U., 1971-75; prof., dean N.D. State U., Fargo, 1975—, acting v.p. agrl. affairs, 1983—, asst. to pres., 1983—; dir. Engring. Computer Ctr. N.D. State U., 1984—; pres. XOX Corp., 1985—. Contbr. chpts. to books, articles to profl. jours. Served to sgt. USMC, 1948-51. Recipient Sigma Xi award, 1968; recipient N.D. State U. Order of the Iron Ring, 1972, USAF Recognition award, 1979, ROTC Appreciation award, 1982. Sr. mem. Am. Inst. Indsl. Engrs. (v.p. 1964-65); mem. ASME, Am. Soc. Engring Edn. (campus coordinator 1979-81), Phi Kappa Phi, Tau Beta Pi (advisor 1978-79). Roman Catholic. Lodges: Lions; Elks. Home: 3520 Longfellow Rd Fargo ND 58102 Office: North Dakota State U Coll of Engring and Architecture Fargo ND 58105

STANISLAV, CAROL MARIE MURDOCK, dentist; b. Gowanda, N.Y., Dec. 7, 1957; d. George Albert and Mary Ann (Schaus) Murdock; m. Richard George Stanislav, July 3, 1984. BA in Biology, Canisius Coll., 1979; DDS, Creighton U., 1984. Dentist-assoc. Dr. Richard Clark, Sioux City, Iowa, 1984-85; pvt. practice gen. dentistry Blencoe, Iowa, 1985—. Com. mem. Burgess Meml. Health Found., Onawa, 1986, Blencoe Betterment Community Club, 1986. Mem. Sioux City Dental Soc. Roman Catholic. Avocations: waterskiing, classical piano, guitar, all sports. Home: RR 1 Little Sioux IA 51545 Office: 412 Main St Blencoe IA 51523

STANKEWICZ, MARY JANE, retail executive, consultant; b. Cleve., May 16, 1944; d. George John and Mary Grace (Millen) Biros; m. Ben Andrew Stankewicz, Aug. 1, 1964; children—Renee Lynn, Ben Anthony, Heather Janette. Owner, operator Cornerstone Book & Gift Shoppe, Strongsville, Ohio, 1983—. Advisor, Holy Trinity Youth Group, Bedford Heights, Ohio, 1971-75; pres. Bedford Co-op Nursery Schs., 1971; officer Citizens League of Bedford Heights, 1975; bd. dirs. Womankind, Inc., Bedford, 1976-78. Mem. Christian Booksellers Assn., Strongsville C. of C., Ohio Right to Life Soc. Roman Catholic. Office: Cornerstone Book & Gift Shoppe 14698 Pearl Rd Strongsville OH 44136

STANKO, IVAN, physician; b. Topolcany, Czechoslavakia, Mar. 28, 1939; came to U.S., 1968; s. Andrej and Gabriella (Bachnerova) S.; m. Anna Pancakova, July 24, 1965; children: Susan, Peter. MD, Komensky U., 1962. Internship County Hosp., Michalovce, Czechoslavakia, 1962-63; gen. practice medicine County Hosp., Michalovce, 1963-65, neurologist, 1965-68; neurology resident U. Ariz., Tucson, 1970-73; gen. practice medicine specializing in neurology Wausau (Wis.) Med. Ctr., 1973—. Mem. Am. Acad. Neurology, Wis. Neurol. Soc. (sec. 1984-85, v.p. 1985-86, pres. 1987—). Home: 9114 Reed Rd Rothschild WI 54474 Office: Wausau Med Ctr 2727 Plaza Dr Wausau WI 54401

STANLEY, ARTHUR JEHU, JR., judge; b. nr. Lincoln, Kans., Mar. 21, 1901; s. Arthur and Bessie (Anderson) S.; m. Ruth Willis, July 16, 1927; children—Mary Louise (Mrs. Bob Andrews), Carolyn (Mrs. Richard Lane), Constance (Mrs. Sherman Yunghans), Susan (Mrs. Paul Keith Hoffman). LL.B., Kansas City Sch. Law (U. Mo.), Kansas City, 1928. Bar: Kans. bar 1928. County atty. Wyandotte County, Kans., 1935-41; U.S. dist. judge Dist. of Kans., Leavenworth, 1958-71; chief judge Dist. of Kans., 1961-71, sr. U.S. dist. judge, 1971—; Mem. Jud. Conf. U.S., 1967-70, chmn.

com. on operation of jury system, 1973-78, mem. bicentennial com., 1975—. Mem. Kans. Senate, 1941. Served with 7th U.S. Cav. Can. Army, World War I; with USN, 1921-25; Yangtze Patrol Force 1923-25; 9th Air Force USAAF, 1941-45; disch. to Inf. Res. as lt. col. Fellow Am. Bar Found.; mem. ABA, Kans. Bar Assn., Wyandotte County Bar Assn. (past pres.), Leavenworth County Bar Assn., Am. Judicature Soc., Kans. Hist. Soc. (pres. 1974-75), Am. Legion. Anglican. Home: 501 N Esplanade Leavenworth KS 66048 Office: U S Dist Ct 235 Fed Bldg Leavenworth KS 66048

STANLEY, DAVID, retail company executive; b. Kansas City, Mo., 1935; married. Grad. U. Wis., 1955; LLB, Columbia U., 1957. Assoc. Paul, Weiss, Rifkind, Wharton & Garrison, N.Y.C., 1957-60; ptnr. Faegre & Benson, Mpls., 1960-71; exec. v.p. Piper, Jaffray & Hopwood, Mpls., 1971-80; pres. Payless Cashways, Inc., Kansas City, 1980-86, chief exec. officer, 1982—, chmn., 1985—, also bd. dirs. Office: Payless Cashways Inc PO Box 466 Kansas City MO 64141 *

STANLEY, JOHN RICHARD, school principal; b. Canton, Ohio, Oct. 1, 1955; s. Edward John and Joan Marie Stanley; m. Barbara Ellen Corrigan, June 27, 1981; 1 child, Matthew. BS, U. Dayton, 1978; MS in Adminstn., U. Akron, Ohio, 1984. Child care worker St. Joseph's Home, Dayton, 1977-78; tchr. Lake Local High Sch., Uniontown, Ohio, 1978-84; prin. Sacred Heart Sch., Louisville, Ohio, 1984-86, St. Paul's Sch., North Canton, Ohio, 1986—. Commr. Stark, Portage League, North Canton. Mem. Nat. Cath. Edn. Assn., Assn. Sch. Curriculum, Ohio Assn. Elem. Adminstrn., Ohio Edn. Assn. Democrat. Roman Catholic. Lodge: Elks. Avocations: skiing, biking, remodeling. Home: 7918 Fox Run NW North Canton OH 44720 Office: St Paul Sch 303 S Main North Canton OH 44720

STANLEY, MARGARET DURETA SEXTON, speech therapist; b. Wells County, Ind., Aug. 7, 1931; d. James Helmuth and Bertha Anna (Kizer) Roberts; m. Gale Sexton, Nov. 21, 1950; children: Cregg Alan, Donna Sue, Sheila Rene; m. 2d, Charles Stanley, Mar. 24, 1979. BS, Ball State U., 1952, MA, 1963. Speech and hearing clinician Hamilton (Ohio) City Schs., 1955-59, Kettering (Ohio) Pub. Schs., 1959-60; speech, lang. and hearing clinician Muncie (Inc.) Community Schs., 1960—; dir. Psi Iota Xi Summer Clinic, Decatur, Ind., 1964; clinician Ball State U., 1965-77; supr. clinician Tri-County Hearing Impaired Assn., 1978-81. Compiler, editor curriculum for speech, lang. and hearing clinicians of Muncie Community Schs. Mem. Am. Speech and Hearing Assn. (cert. clin. competency in speech pathology), Ind. Speech and Hearing Assn., Am. Fedn. Tchrs., Muncie Fedn. Tchrs., Ind. Edn. Assn., Ind. Council Suprs. Speech and Hearing (pres. 1982-84), Adminstrv. Women's, Speech and Hearing Area Educators Ind. (founder, 1st. pres. 1984-86)., Delta Kappa Gamma. Republican. Methodist. Lodge: Women Moose. Home: 3201 E Oaklawn Dr Muncie IN 47303 Office: 3201 S Macedonia St Munice IN 47302

STANLEY, RICHARD DALE, food products executive; b. Chgo., Nov. 17, 1930; s. Cyril Richard Stanley and Grace Irene (Musgrave) Linder; m. Lois Louise Thompson, Sept. 15, 1951; children: Randa Dale Stanley Johnson, Kimberly Ann Stanley Barstad. Student, Washington U., St. Louis, 1948-49, U. Ill., 1949-51. Sales rep. Armour & Co., National Stock Yards, Ill., 1951-59; dist. mgr. George A. Hormel, Phoenix, 1959-67; mgr. mktg. George A. Hormel, Austin, Minn., 1967-70, dir., gen. mgr., 1970—. Moderator Congl. Ch., Austin, 1985-87. Mem. Gelatin Mfr. Inst. (bd. dirs. 1970—, pres. 1979-81), Am. Spice Trade Assn. (chmn. com. 1970-85), Inst. Food Tech., Jaycees (pres. Phoenix chpt. 1965-67, pres. Ariz. chpt. 1966-67, senator nat. orgn. 1967). Republican. Clubs: Austin Country (bd. dirs.). Lodges: Masons, Elks. Avocations: golfing, fishing, fgn. travel. Home: 509 22d St NW Austin MN 55912 Office: George A Hormel Co PO Box 800 Austin MN 55912

STANLEY, RICHARD HOLT, consulting engineer; b. Muscatine, Iowa, Oct. 20, 1932; s. Claude Maxwell and Elizabeth Mabel (Holthues) S.; m. Mary Jo Kennedy, Dec. 20, 1953; children: Lynne Elizabeth, Sarah Catherine, Joseph Holt. BSEE, Iowa State U., 1955, B.S. in Mech. Engring., 1955; M.S. in San. Engring., U. Iowa, 1963. Registered profl. engr., Iowa, other states. With Stanley Cons. Inc., Muscatine, 1955—; pres. Stanley Cons. Inc., 1971-87, chmn., 1984—, also dir.; chmn., dir. Stanley/Mettee-McGill-Murphy, Inc., Stanley/Wantman Inc.; vice chmn., dir. HON Industries, Inc.; chmn. Middle West Service Co., 1981—, Nat. Constrn. Industry Council, 1978, Com. Fed. Procurement Archtl./Engring. Services, 1979; pres. Eastern Iowa Community Coll., Bettendorf, 1966-68; mem. adv. council Coll. Engring., Iowa State U., Ames, 1969—, chmn., 1979-81. Contbr. articles to profl. jours. Bd. dirs., pres. Stanley Found., Muscatine; bd. dirs. Muscatine United Way, 1969-75, Iowa State U. Meml. Union, 1968-83, U. Dubuque, Iowa, 1977—; bd. govs. Iowa State U. Achievement Found., 1982—. Served with C.E., AUS, 1955-57. Recipient Young Alumnus award Iowa State U. Alumni Assn., 1966, Disting. Service award Muscatine Jaycees, 1967; Profl. Achievement citation Coll. Engring., Iowa State U., 1977; named Sr. Engr. of Year, Joint Engring. Com. of Quint Cities, 1973. Fellow ASCE, Iowa Acad. Sci., Am. Cons. Engrs. Council (pres. 1976-77); mem. Cons. Engrs. Council Iowa (pres. 1967), Nat. Soc. Profl. Engrs., IEEE (sr.), ASME, Am. Soc. Engring. Edn., Iowa Engring. Soc. (John Dunlap-Sherman Woodward award 1967, Disting. Service award 1980, Voice of Engr. award 1987, pres. 1973-74), Muscatine C. of C. (pres. 1972-73), C. of C. of U.S. (internat. com. and econ. devel. subcom. 1975-82, constrn. action council 1976—), Tau Beta Pi, Phi Kappa Phi, Pi Tau Sigma, Eta Kappa Nu. Presbyterian (elder). Club: Rotary. Home: 601 W 3d St Muscatine IA 52761 Office: Stanley Bldg Muscatine IA 52761

STANLEY, WILLIAM ELDON, surgeon; b. Mercer, Mo., Aug. 16, 1947; s. Richard H. and Alta B. (Cox) S.; m. Lynda Akeright, May 31, 1969; children—Darrell, Patrick. Student N.E. Mo. State Tchrs. Coll., 1965-67; B.S., U. Iowa, 1969; D.O., Kirksville Coll. Osteo. Medicine, 1973. Diplomate Am. Bd. Thoracic Surgery. Intern, Des Moines Gen. Hosp., 1973-74, resident in gen. surgery, 1974-77; resident in cardiovascular and thoracic surgery Cleve. Clinic, 1977-79; practice osteo. medicine specializing in cardiac, vascular and thoracic surgery, Des Moines, 1979—; mem. staff, chmn. dept. surgery Des Moines Gen. Hosp.; adj. clin. assoc. prof. surgery U. Osteo. Medicine and Health Scis. Mem. Am. Osteo. Assn., Am. Coll. Osteo. Surgeons, Iowa Soc. Osteo. Physicians and Surgeons. Contbr. articles to profl. jours. Home: 8028 NE 46th Ave Altoona IA 50009 Office: 1440 E Grand Ave Suite 1A Des Moines IA 50316

STANTON, BLAINE WENDELL, gemologist; b. St. Joseph, Mo., Dec. 11, 1948; s. William J. and Helen H. (Hitchcock) S.; m. Leslee Ann Taylor, Nov. 23, 1970. Mktg. student, Mo. Western Coll., 1968-73; cert. gemology, European Gemological Inst., Antwerp, Belgium, 1978. Pres. Stanton & Co. Jewelers & Gemologists, St. Joseph, 1972—, Stanton Cellular Communications, St. Joseph. Lodge: Lions (pres. St. Joseph East Hills club 1980-81). Home and Office: 506 Edmond Saint Joseph MO 64501

STANTON, DONALD LEO, banker; b. Orleans, Mich., Mar. 7, 1923; s. William Otto and Sarah Caroline (Webster) S.; m. Emma Jean Kirby, Nov. 22, 1942; children: Terrel Gordon, Diana Lynn, Michael William. Grad. high sch., Belding, Mich.; cert. credit union mgmt., U. Wis., 1963. Supr. hosp. security Mich. Dept. Mental Health, Ionia and Lansing, Mich., 1945-71; treas., grn. mgr. Govtl. Employees Credit Union, Ionia, 1954—. Mayor City of Ionia, 1971-74, past city councilman; mem. 1st Meth. Ch., Ionia; charter mem. Pres. Reagan task force; active crippled children programs, Ionia. Served with USN, 1944-45. Named Mich. Credit Union Person Yr., 1986. Mem. Ionia C. of C. (pres. 1983), Am. Legion (commdr.), Credit Union Exec. Soc., Founders Club Mich. Credit Union League, Mich. Assn. State Employees Credit Unions (sec., past pres.). Methodist. Lodges: Masons (jr. warden 1983), Shriners (ambassador 1982-86). Avocation: swimming. Home: 405 N Jefferson St Ionia MI 48846 Office: Govtl Employees Credit Union 346 4th St Ionia MI 48846

STANTON, JAMES DANIEL, quality control engineer; b. Keokuk, Iowa, Oct. 9, 1936; s. James Daniel and Dorothy Marie (Swenson) S.; m. Caroline Elizabeth Lyon, Aug. 16, 1959; children: Kimberly Kay, Kevin James, Kelly Marie. Student, Simpson Coll., 1954-56, Drake U., 1959; BA, U. Iowa, 1958. Tchr. New London (Iowa) Schs., 1958-60; process engr. Silas Mason, Mason Hanger, Middletown, Iowa, 1967-68; quality control chemist Sheller Globe Corp., Keokuk, 1960-67, quality control engr., 1968—. Dist. chmn. Boy Scouts Am., Keokuk, 1983-84, dist. commr. 1985-86. Recipient Merit award Puckeshetuck dist. Boy Scouts Am., 1977; Silver Beaver award, S.E. Iowa council Boy Scouts Am., 1985; Taguchi Excellance award Am. Supplyer Inst., 1986. Mem. Am. Soc. for Quality Control (sr.) (cert., edn. chmn. 1981-82, 1986—, service award 1982), Jaycees (past pres. Keokuk, past state v.p. Newton Iowa). Republican. Presbyterian. Club: Keokuk Camera (v.p. 1986—). Avocations: wood carving, photography, camping. Home: 24 Pleasant Ln Keokuk IA 52632 Office: Sheller Globe Corp 3200 Main St Keokuk IA 51632

STANTON, JEANNE FRANCES, retired lawyer; b. Vicksburg, Miss., Jan. 22, 1920; d. John Francis and Hazel (Mitchell) S.; student George Washington U., 1938-39; B.A., U. Cin., 1940; J.D., Salmon P. Chase Coll. Law, 1954. Admitted to Ohio bar, 1954; chief clk. Selective Service Bd., Cin., 1940-43; instr. USAAF Tech. Schs., Biloxi, Miss., 1943-44; with Procter & Gamble, Cin., 1945-84, legal asst., 1952-54, head advt. services sect. legal div., trade practices dept., 1954-73, mgr. advt. services, legal div., 1973-84, ret., 1984. Team capt. Community Chest Cin., 1953; mem. ann. meeting com. Archaeol. Inst. Am., 1983. Mem. AAAS, Am., Ohio (chmn. uniform state laws com. 1968-70), Cin. (sec. law day com. 1965-66, chmn. com. on preservation hist. documents 1968-71) bar assns., Vicksburg and Warren County, Cin. hist. socs., Internat. Oceanographic Found., Otago Early Settlers Assn. (asso.), Intercontinental Biog. Assn., Cin. Lawyers (pres. 1983, exec. com. 1978—), Cin. Women Lawyers (treas. 1958-59, nominating com. 1976). Clubs: Terrace Park Country; Cincinnati. Home: 2302 Easthill Ave Cincinnati OH 45208

STANTON, JOHN PINCKEY, manufacturing executive; b. Washington, Nov. 26, 1936; s. Raleigh Alton and Thelma Havens (Tracy) S.; m. Patricia Ann St. Clair, Aug. 22, 1959; children: Elizabeth Ann, Joanna Lynn. AB, U. N.H., 1961; MBA, Dartmouth Coll., 1965. Mng. dir. Holset Engring. Co. Ltd., Haddersfield, Eng., 1976-79; v.p. components Cummins Engine Co., Columbus, Ind., 1979-82, v.p. fin., adminstrn., 1982-83, v.p. components, 1983-84; pres. Fleetguard, Columbus, Ind., 1984—. Served with U.S. Army, 1954-57. Mem. Motor Equipment Mfrs. Assn. Republican. Avocation: photography, boating. Home: 4410 N Riverside Dr Columbus OH 47203 Office: Fleetguard Inc c/o Cummins Engine Co Columbus IN 47001-3005 also: Fleetguard Inc Route 8 Cookeville TN 38501

STANTON, WILLIAM TAYLOR, manufacturing engineer; b. Detroit, Oct. 27, 1926; s. Luther Dill and Maggie Ethel (Smith) S.; m. Sue Carol Reed, Feb. 19, 1960 (div. Jan. 1983); stepchildren: Terry, Steven; 1 son, William. Grad. high sch., Cookeville, Tenn. Registered profl. engr., Calif. Contract engr. various locations, 1968—. Lodge: Eagles, Moose. Home: PO Box 1124 Connersville IN 47331

STAPLES, LAURANCE STARR, JR., manufacturing company executive; b. Kansas City, Mo., Jan. 31, 1931; s. Laurance Starr and Bertha Marie (Schaefer) S.; B.S. in Gen. Engring., U. Ill., 1956; m. Barbara Ruth Hazard, Oct. 5, 1957; children—Laurance Starr, III, Mary Ruth. Mgr. applied products Marley Co., Kansas City, Mo., 1957-69; dir. customer service Tempmaster Corp., Kansas City, 1969-71; sales rep. Kansas City Equipment Co., Kansas City, 1971; sales mgr. Havens Cooling Towers div. Havens Steel Co., Kansas City, 1971-73; with L.S. Staples Co., Kansas City, 1974-81, pres., 1974-81; v.p. mktg. projects Marley Cooling Tower Co., Mission, Kans., 1981—; cons. Butler Mfg. Co., Kansas City, 1971. Superwalk chmn. safety and communications March of Dimes, Kansas City, Mo., 1972—, mem. gen. bd., 1977, 79; bd. dirs. Heart of Am. Radio Club, Kansas City, 1978-80; Master of servers St. Paul's Episcopal Ch., Kansas City, 1959-65, vestryman, 1967-73, treas., 1975-81, jr. warden, 1982, sr. warden, 1983-84; stewardship officer Episc. Diocese W. Mo., 1980-81, mem. Pres.'s Council, U. Ill, 1985—, diocesan council, 1981-83. Served with U.S. Army, 1953-55. Mem. ASHRAE (chpt. pres. 1980-81, energy mgmt. Region IX 1981-84, regional chmn., bd. dirs. 1984, soc. nominating com. 1987—), Am. Soc. Mech. Engrs., Kansas City Engrs. Club, Refrigeration Engring. and Tech. Assn., Quarter Century Wireless Assn. (v.p. 1986-87), Tau Kappa Epsilon. Episcopalian. Clubs: Heart of America Radio, Kansas City VHF (pres. 1961-62, corp. agt., trustee). Home: 425 W 49th Terr Kansas City MO 64112 Office: 5800 Foxridge Dr Mission KS 66201

STAPLETON, ELLA MAE, educational administrator; b. Detroit, Feb. 20, 1928; d. Thomas Daniel Lee and Dilsie (Christian) Jimerson; m. James Foster Stapleton, Nov. 29, 1953; children: James, Maureen. BA, Mich. State Normal Coll., 1949; MA, U. Mich., 1963; EdS, Wayne State U., 1974, EdD, 1981. Tchr., counselor, asst. prin., prin. Detroit Pub. Schs., 1949-79; instr. Wayne State U., 1979, LaVerne Coll., 1977-80, Regis Coll., Newton, Mass., 1976, Boston State U., 1978, East Strausburg U., Allentown, Pa., 1978-79, Elizabethtown Coll., N.J., 1980; region asst. supt. Detroit Pub. Schs., 1979-83; area asst. supt., 1983—; lectr. various schs. 1971-81. Vol. ARC, United Negro Coll. Fund; active NAACP, Detroit Urban League, YWCA, Nat. Alliance Females for Urban Concerns. Mem. Am. Assn. Sch. Adminstrs. (Valiant Woman award 1981), Assn. Suprs. and Curriculum Developers, New Profl. Women's Network, Alpha Kappa Alpha. Democrat. Episcopalian. Clubs: Carrousel Women's, Bridge-A-Dears. Home: 19405 Warrington Dr Detroit MI 48221 Office: 4400 Oakman Blvd Detroit MI 48204

STAPP, DONALD MAURICE, marketing professional; b. Louisville, Ky., July 31, 1943; s. Maurice Lacy and Bernice E. (Reeser) S.; m. Louise Jo Maier, Jan. 28, 1967; children: Kristine, Joseph. BA, U. Louisville, 1970; postgrad., So. Sem., 1974-75; MS, Aurora U., 1986. Lab. Tech. Celanese, Louisville, 1964-68; plastics engr. Gen. Electric, Louisville, 1968-73, 78-79, Magnavox, Ft. Wayne, Ind., 1973-74; mgr. mktg. Velsicol Chem., Chgo., 1976-78, 79—. Served with USAF, 1962-64. Mem. Soc. Plastic Engrs. Democrat. Baptist. Avocations: golf, reading. Home: 676 Van Nortwick Batavia IL 60510

STARA, NANCY JOYCE, law educator; b. Jefferson City, Mo., Nov. 2, 1943; d. Maurice Joyce and Pearl Grace (Baker) Ayres; m. William Lee Sullivan, June 23, 1967 (dec. July 1970); m. Dennis Charles Stara, Feb. 1973. BA, Park Coll., 1964; JD, U. Nebr., 1967; LLM, U. Denver, 1985. Bar: Colo., Nebr.; CPA. Staff atty. Nebr. Dept. Revenue, Lincoln, 1967-68, sr. legal counsel, 1970-73; dep. county atty. Hall County, Grand Island, Nebr., 1968; law clk. Ray, Owens, Keil & Hirsch, Columbus, Ga., 1969, McCoy & Weaver, Fayetteville, N.C., 1969; inheritance tax analyst Colo. Dept. Law, Denver, 1970; tax mgr. Johnson, Grant & Co., CPA's, Lincoln, 1974-84; asst. prof. U. Nebr., Lincoln, 1985—; mem. planning com. Great Plains Fed. Tax Inst., Nebr., 1981—. Contbr. articles to profl. jours. Mem. Gov.'s Task Force on Investment of Pension Funds, Lincoln, 1983, Nebr. Econ. Forecasting Adv. Bd., Lincoln, 1984—; treas. Lincoln-Lancaster County YMCA, 1982-83, v.p. 1986—. Recipient Tribute to Women award Lincoln YWCA, 1986. Mem. Am. Inst. CPA's, Am. Acctg. Assn., Nebr. Bar Assn., Nebr. Soc. CPA's (vice chmn. taxation com. 1980-81, chmn. 1981-82). Office: U Nebr 131 Coll Bus Adminstrn Lincoln NE 68588

STARBIRD, L. DARRYL, producer of custom car shows, designer, builder of custom automobiles; b. Topeka, Aug. 7, 1933; s. Austin Tyler and Lucy Marie (Campbell) S.; m. Donna Mae Gray, July 5, 1953; children: Debra Marie, Clifford Dean, Cristy Mae, Rick Alan. Student, Wichita State U., 1951-54. Owner Starbird Custom Autos, Wichita, Kans., 1955-86, Starbird Prodns., Wichita, 1957-83; pres. Nat. Rod & Custom Assn., Mulvane, Kans., 1970-84, Dickens Christmas Exposition, Mulvane, 1982-83, Nat. Show Prodn., Inc., Mulvane, 1983—, Nat. Ad Agy. Inc., Mulvane, 1983—; design cons. Monogram Models, Morton Grove, Ill., 1963-67; freelance photographer leading auto mags. 1957-86. Starbird creations featured in Stern Mag. in Germany, 1986, Custom Car mags. in England and Australia, 1979, 83; L & M Custom Car tour of Europe - 6 Starbird creations over 20 major cities, 1986. Named Custom Car Builder of Yr., Nat. Hot Rod Assn., 1960, Constructer of Yr., Internat. Show Car Assn., 1986; recipient Master Builder award Grand Nat. Roadster Show, 1963; winner of 500 trophies in leading auto shows throughout US. Mem. Internat. Auto Show Producers Assn. (v.p. 1986). Roman Catholic. Home: 504 SE Louis Blvd Mulvane KS 67110 Office: Nat Show Producers Inc 504 SE Louis Blvd Mulvane KS 67110

STARCKOVICH, KAREN SUE, data processing analyst; b. Denison, Iowa, June 3, 1954; d. Walter William Otto and Edna Sophie (Mohr) Jahn; m. Robert Dean Starckovich, Jan. 27, 1979; 1 child, Sara. Student, Morningside Coll., 1972-74; BS, Iowa State U., 1977. Data processing specialist II State Farm Mut. Auto Ins., Bloomington, Ill., 1979-80, data processing specialist III, 1980-82, data processing specialist IV, 1982-85, data processing analyst, 1985—. Mem. Ins. Inst. Am. Lutheran. Office: State Farm Mut Auto Ins 1 State Farm Plaza CP Bloomington IL 61710

STARK, HARRY D., electronic company executive; b. Gregory, S.D., Apr. 21, 1908; s. Otto George and Anna Elizabeth Stark; E.E., U. Minn., 1933; m. Myrle Mae Miller, Feb. 10, 1934; children—Mary Ann, Judith Kay, Richard Miller. Partner, N.W. Radio Supply Co., Mpls., 1934-37; with Stark Electronics Supply, Inc., Mpls., 1938—, now chmn., pres. Mem. Nat. Electronics Distbrs. Assn. (nat. sec., mem. exec. bd.), Electronic Distbrs. Research Inst. (pres., dir.), Council of Ind. Mgrs. Clubs: Athletic (Mpls.); Spectators, Masons. Office: 401 Royalston Ave Minneapolis MN 55405

STARK, JAMES EWING, II, sales executive; b. Cin., Sept. 27, 1947; s. Clovis Ewing and Thelma Mae (Wellbaum) S.; m. Nancy Jean Forte, July 10, 1979 (div. Feb. 1981); 1 child, Lauren Amber. BA in Mktg. and Psychology, Parsons Coll., 1969; student, Officer's Candidate Sch., 1970-71. Cert. AMF instr., Ohio. Dept. mgr. Federated Dept. Stores, Dayton, Ohio, 1969-70; store supr. Elder-Beerman Stores, Dayton, 1970-72; v.p. Centerville Lanes Inc., Dayton, 1972-81; office mgr. GTE Sprint, Dayton, 1981-84; acct. exec. Lexitel-Allnet, Dayton, 1984-87, Litel Inc., Dayton, 1987—. Served with USAR, 1970-76. Mem. Dayton C. of C., South Metro C. of C., Pi Kappa Alpha. Republican. Methodist. Avocations: bowling, swimming, golf. Home: 5950 Mad River Rd Dayton OH 45459 Office: Litel Telecommunications 1538 First National Plaza Dayton OH 45402

STARK, MARK JOSEPH, real estate corporation executive; b. Chgo.; m. Sheila McMahon; children: Ellen M., Michael T., Sarah A. BS in Acctg., No. Ill. U., 1958. Accounts service mgr. U.S. Gypsum, Chgo., 1958-68, superintendent, 1968-73; asst. v.p. Seay & Thomas Real Estate, Chgo., 1973; gen. mgr. John Hancock Ctr., Chgo., 1974. Bd. dirs. Mayor Daley's Council on Aged, Chgo., 1977-78, New City YMCA, Chgo., 1985; chmn. Ch. Community Ctr. com., Oak Lawn, Ill., 1985-86; pres. Ch. Men's Club, Oak Lawn, 1984-85. Served with U.S. Army, 1954-56. Named Outstanding Student Del., No. Ill. Conf. Accountancy Clubs, 1958. Mem. Inst. Real Estate Mgmt., Bldg. Mgrs. Assn. Chgo. (bd. dirs. 1987), Chgo. Real Estate Bd., Digest Club Chgo. (pres. 1984-85), Am. Legion (commdr. 1960-61). Avocations: hunting, fishing, golfing, camping. Office: Coldwell Banker Real Estate 875 N Michigan Ave 3215 John Hancock Ctr Chicago IL 60611

STARK, PATRICIA ANN, psychologist; b. Ames, Iowa, Apr. 21, 1937; d. Keith C. and Mary L. (Johnston) Moore; m. Edward Milton Stark, June 13, 1959. B.S., So. Ill. U., Edwardsville, 1970, M.S., 1972; Ph.D., St. Louis U., 1976. Counselor to alcoholics Bapt. Rescue Mission, East St. Louis, 1969; researcher alcoholics Gateway Rehab. Center, East St. Louis, 1972; psychologist intern Henry-Stark Counties Spl. Edn. Dist. and Galesburg State Research Hosp., Ill., 1972-73; instr. Lewis and Clark Community Coll., Godfrey, Ill., 1973-76, asst. prof., 1976-84, assoc. prof., 1984—, coordinator child care services, 1974-84; mem. staff dept. psychiatry Meml. Hosp., St. Elizabeth's Hosp., 1979—; supr. various workshops in field, 1974—; dir. child and family services Collinsville Counseling Center, 1978-82; clin. dir., owner Empas-Complete Family Psychol. and Hypnosis Services, Collinsville, 1982—; cons. community agys., 1974—; mem. adv. bd. Madison County Council on Alcoholism and Drug Dependency, 1977-80. Mem. Am. Psychol. Assn., Ill. Psychol. Assn., Midwestern Psychol. Assn., Nat. Assn. Sch. Psychologists, Am. Soc. Clin. Hypnosis, Internat. Soc. Hypnosis. Home: 202 Bill Lou Dr Collinsville IL 62234 Office: 2802 Maryville Rd Collinsville IL 62234

STARK, STEPHEN DOUGLAS, marketing communication executive; b. Toledo, Sept. 16, 1949; s. Geller Leo and Edith May (Stephens) S.; m. Donna Jeanne Stierhoff, June 13,1970; children: Colleen Julianna, Ian Douglas. A in Mktg., U. Toledo, 1969; BA in Advt., Ohio U., 1971. Cert. bus. communicator. With retail advt. sales Dayton Newspapers, Inc., 1971-73; mgr. advt. TRW Globe, Dayton, 1973-75; mgr. advt. and sales promotion J.A. Becker Co., Dayton, 1975-76; mgr. mktg. communications Harshaw Chem., Cleve., 1976-78; account exec. Meldrum & Fewsmith, Southfield, Mich., 1978-80; mgr. mktg. communication Diversey Wyandotte (Mich.) Corp., 1980—. Author: Anthology of Poetry, 1969. Mem. Bus. and Profl. Advt. Assn. (cert. chmn. 1984-86). Republican. Unitarian. Avocations: art, photography, reading, racquetball, bicycling. Office: Diversey Wyandotte Corp 1532 Biddle Ave Wyandotte MI 43182

STARK, THOMAS FRANCIS, university president; b. Duluth, Minn., Mar. 18, 1935; s. Bernard Francis and Emma (Harris) S.; m. Judith Olsen, July 26, 1958; children: Bradley, Kathryn, Cynthia. BS, U. Minn., 1957; MS, So. Ill. U., 1959; PhD, Mich. State U., 1966; postdoctoral in edml. mgmt., Harvard U., 1985. Supt. schs. City of Grand Rapids, Minn., 1966-69; assoc. prof. U. Minn., Mpls., 1969-74; supt. schs. Mankato (Minn.) Pub. Schs., 1974-80; v.p. fiscal affairs Mankato State U., 1980-83; pres. Winona (Minn.) State U., 1983—; adv. bd. inst. ednl. mgmt. Harvard U., 1985—. Bd. dirs. Found. for Minn. Progress, 1969-74, United Way, Mankato and Winona. NDEA fellow, 1960; Bush fellow, 1985. Mem. Am. State Colls. and Univs. Assn., Winona C. of C. (bd. dirs.), Phi Delta Kappa. Lutheran. Lodge: Kiwanis (bd. dirs. Grand Rapids, Mankato and Winona chpts. 1962—). Avocations: tennis, racquetball, camping, hunting, fishing. Office: Winona State U 8th and Johnson Sts Winona MN 55987

STARKEY, EDWARD DAVID, academic librarian; b. Oswego, N.Y., Oct. 21, 1942; s. Edward Davidson and Eileen (Heaney) S.; m. Paulette Schaller, Aug. 17, 1968; children—Brendan, Elyane. B.A., Stonehill Coll., 1965; postgrad. Gregorian U., Rome, Italy, 1965-66; M.A. in Lit., SUNY-Albany, 1968; M.S. in L.S., U. Ky., 1976; M.A. in Religion, U. Dayton, 1985. Tchr., Voorheesville (N.Y.) High Sch., 1968-70, Lees Jr. Coll., Jackson, Ky., 1970-73, The Lexington (Ky.) Sch., 1973-75; coll. librarian Urbana (Ohio) Coll., 1976-79; head reference U. Dayton (Ohio) Library, 1979-85; head pub. services Ind. U.-Purdue U. at Indpls., 1985—; cons. librarian Porter, Wright, Morris & Arthur, Dayton, Ohio, 1982-85; mem. accreditation com. North Central Assn., 1979. Author: Judaism and Christianity: a Guide to the Reference Literature, 1987. Library Services and Constrn. Act grantee Urbana Coll., 1978-79. Mem. ALA, Acad. Library Assn. Ohio (pres. 1983-84), Ohio Multitype Library Coop. Com. (vice-chmn. 1980-83), Assn. Coll. and Research Libraries. Roman Catholic. Home: 4409 Grayson St Kettering OH 45429 Office: IUPUI Library Indianapolis IN 46202

STARKEY, LAWRENCE HARRY, philosophy educator, editor; b. Pa., July 10, 1919. BA in Biology with honors, U. Louisville, 1942; MDiv, So. Bapt. Theol. Sem., Louisville, 1945; MA, U. So. Calif., 1951; PhD, UCLA, 1960. Instr., registrar Los Angeles Bapt. Theol. Coll. and Sem., 1945-51; writer Moody Inst. Sci., West Los Angeles, Calif., 1955-57; assoc. prof. philosophy Bethel Coll., St. Paul, 1958-62; assoc. prof. philosophy and religion, dept. chmn. Linfield Coll., 1962-63; engring. writer Convair div. Gen. Dynamics Corp., San Diego, 1963-66; assoc. prof. philosophy, humanities Alma (Mich.) Coll., 1966-68; assoc. editor and prin. philosophy editor Ency. Britannica, Chgo., 1968-72; assoc. prof. philosophy and dept. chmn. Jamestown (N.D.) Coll., 1973-75; lectr. philosophy and religion, TV studies and field coordinator N.D. State U., Fargo, 1976-79; mech. designer Concord, Inc., Fargo, 1977-85; instr. philosophy Moorhead (Minn.) State U., 1985-86; lectr. philosophy U. Mo., Rolla, 1986—; mem. editorial bd. Jour. of Am. Sci. Affiliation, 1960-65, philosophy of sci. commn., 1960-65; freelance editor scholarly works, N.D., 1974; freelance writer and editor Harcourt Brace Jovanovich, San Diego, 1987. Co-author (TV documentaries) Mystery of Three Clocks, 1956, Red River of Life, 1957, Windows of the Soul, 1958; producer: (pub. TV series) Springboard to Sucess, 1976; contbr. articles and editor on philosophy Ency. Britannica, 1974; contbr. articles to popular mags. and profl. jours. Mem. Am. Philos. Assn., Metaphysical Soc. Am. Republican. Presbyterian. Home: 608 E 11th St Rolla MO 65401 Office: U Mo Philosophy Dept Rolla MO 65401

STARNES, JAMES WRIGHT, lawyer; b. East St. Louis, Ill., Apr. 3, 1933; s. James Adron and Nell (Short) S.; m. Helen Woods Mitchell, Mar. 29, 1958 (div. 1978); children: James Wright, Mitchell A., William B. II; m. Kathleen Israel, Jan. 26, 1985. Student St. Louis U., 1951-53; LLB, Washington U., St. Louis, 1957. Bar: Mo. 1957, Ill. 1957. Assoc. Stinson, Mag & Fizzell, Kansas City, Mo., 1957-60, ptnr., 1960—; ptnr. Mid-Continent Properties Co., 1959—, Fairview Investment Co., Kansas City, 1971-76, Monticello Land Co., 1973—; sec. Packaging Products Corp., Mission, Kans., 1972—. Bd. dirs. Mo. Assn. Mental Health, 1968-69, Kansas City Assn. Mental Health, 1966-78, pres., 1969-70; bd. dirs. Heed, 1965-73, 78-82, pres., 1966-67, fin. chmn. 1967-68; bd. dirs. Kansas City Halfway House Found., exec. com., 1966-69, pres., 1966; bd. dirs. Joan Davis Sch. for Spl. Edn., 1972—, v.p., 1972-73, 79-80, pres., 1979-82; bd. dirs. Sherwood Ctr. for Exceptional Child, 1977-79, v.p., 1978-79. Served with AUS, 1957. Mem. ABA, Mo. Bar Assn., Kansas City Bar Assn., Kansas City Lawyers Assn. Presbyterian (deacon). Mem. adv. bd. Washington U. Law Quar., 1957—. Home: 1246 Huntington Rd Kansas City MO 64113 Office: Stinson Mag & Fizzell 2100 Boatmen's Ctr Kansas City MO 64105

STAROSTOVIC, EDWARD JOSEPH, JR., engineer, engineering company executive; b. Chgo., Apr. 8, 1933; s. Edward J. and Esther Ruth (Guinee) S.; m. Marilyn Ann Mucek, June 23, 1956; children—Lynn, Ann, Karen, Susanne. B.A., Ill. Inst. Tech., Chgo., 1958. Registered profl. engr., Wis. Owner, Structural Plywood Co., Chgo., 1958-60; engr., mgr. Wausau Homes Inc., Wis., 1960-72; engr., exec. v.p. PFS Corp., Madison, Wis., 1972-78, engr., pres., 1978—; bd. dirs. Wood Heating Alliance, Washington, 1982—; del. U.S.-USSR Tech. Exchange Agreement, Washington, 1977—. Mem. editorial rev. bd. Automation in Housing, 1973—. Chmn. Wausau Area Regional Plan Commn., 1967. Served with U.S. Army, 1953-55, Korea. Recipient E. Kurtz award Nat. Assn. Bldg. Mfrs., 1972. Mem. Nat. Soc. Profl. Engrs., Nat. Inst. Bldg. Scis., Am. Soc. Quality Control, Forest Products Research Soc., Internat. Assn. Elec. Inspectors, ASTM. Office: PFS Corp 2402 Daniels St Madison WI 53704

STARR, STEVE MARSHALL, small business owner, design consultant; b. Chgo., Dec. 22, 1946; s. Samuel Morris and Gloria (Friedlander) S. Student, Columbia Coll., Chgo., 1965-67, Chgo. Acad. Fine Art, 1967-70. Owner, operator Steve Starr Studios, Chgo., 1967; curator Art Deco Exhbn., Chgo., 1973, Art Ultra Exhbn., Chgo., 1983; producer, dir., prodn. designer Vanity theatre, Chgo. 1970-74. Office: 2654 N Clark St Chicago IL 60614

STASCH, JEFFREY JOHN, dentist; b. Valentine, Nebr., Feb. 27, 1958; s. John Laverne and Delores Claire (Peterson) S.; m. Debra Lee Klinginsmith, May 30, 1981. BS in Life Scis., U. Nebr., 1980, DDS, 1984. Gen. practice dentistry Garden City, Kans., 1984—. Med. dir. Am. Cancer Soc., Garden City, 1986. Mem. ADA, Acad. Gen. Dentistry, Southwest Kans. Dental Study Club (Sec.), Garden City C. of C. (beautification com. 1984—). Methodist. Avocations: hunting, fishing, all outdoor sports. Home: 105 Cambridge Ct Garden City KS 67846 Office: 306 East Spruce Garden City KS 67846

STASSEN, JOHN HENRY, lawyer; b. Joliet, Ill., Mar. 22, 1943; s. John H. and Florence C. (McCarthy) S.; m. Sara A. Gaw, July 6, 1968; children: John C., David A. BS, Northwestern U., 1965, JD, Harvard U., 1968. Bar: Ill. 1968. Assoc. Kirkland & Ellis, Chgo., 1968, 73-76, ptnr. 1977—. Contbr. articles to legal jours. Served to lt. comdr. JAGC, USN, 1969-72. Mem. ABA (chmn. com. on futures regulation), Ill. Bar Assn., Chgo. Bar Assn., Phila. Soc. Club: Mid-America (Chgo.). Home: 1310 N Astor St Chicago IL 60610 Office: Kirkland & Ellis 200 E Randolph Dr Suite 5700 Chicago IL 60601

STATTENFIELD, MERRIE JO, computer programming consultant; b. Camus, Wash., Sept. 20, 1939; d. Howard Alton Seymour and Edna Evelyn (Dunavin) Brewer; m. David Boyce Stattenfield, June 17, 1961; children: Boyce, Ryan. BA in Math, Duke U., 1961. Cert. data processor. Programmer Ill. Water Survey, Champaign, 1961-62, Chrysler Corp., Highland Park, Mich., 1962-63, Ford Motor Credit Co., Dearborn, Mich., 1963-66; sr. programmer Cummins Engine Co., Columbus, Ind., 1966-69; pres. System Two, Inc., Columbus, 1971—. Publicizer Columbus Youth Hockey, 1986—. Mem. Assn. for System Mgmt. (treas. 1972). Avocations: water skiing, boating. Home: 5261 S Poplar Dr Columbus IN 47201 Office: System Two Inc 716 3rd St Columbus IN 47201

STAUB, JAMES RICHARD, chiropractor; b. Peoria, Ill., Apr. 22, 1938; s. John and Dorothy Christine (Benson) S.; student Bradley U., 1956-60, U. Wis., 1972; D.Chiropractic, Palmer Coll. Chiropractic, 1972; B.A., Columbia Coll., 1977; m. Sandra Lee Herman, Dec. 21, 1958 (div. July 1979); children: Gary James, Gregory Alan; m. Sheryl Ann Vander Velde, Nov. 17, 1979; 1 child Abigail Joy. Asst. to mgr. A & J Lumber Co., Peoria Hts., Ill., 1956-60; with Central Ill. Light Co., Peoria, 1961-69; pvt. practice chiropractic, Valparaiso, Ind., 1972—. Missionary to Haiti, Christian Chiropractic Assn., 1984; minister of music South Haven Ch. of Nazarene, 1985. Recipient certificate of merit Palmer Coll. Chiropractic Clinic, 1972. Mem. Valparaiso Bus. and Profl. Couples Club (chmn. 1974-75), Internat., Am., Ky., Ind., Porter County (v.p. 1975-76), N.W. Dist. Ind. (sec. 1975-76), Christian chiropractic assns., Palmer Coll. Alumni Assn. (Ind. pres. 1974-79), Internat. Acad. Preventive Medicine, N.W. Ind. Comprehensive Health Planning Council, Phi Mu Alpha. Club: Exchange. Home: 1400 E Evans Valparaiso IN 46383 Office: 1402 E Evans Ave Valparaiso IN 46383

STAUBITZ, ARTHUR FREDERICK, lawyer, pharmaceutical company executive; b. Omaha, Nebr., Mar. 14, 1939; s. Herbert Frederick Staubitz and Barbara Eileen (Dallas) Alderson; m. Linda Medora Miller, Aug. 18, 1962; children: Michael, Melissa, Peter. AB cum laude, Wesleyan U., Middletown, Conn., 1961; JD cum laude, U. Pa., 1964. Bar: Ill. 1964, U.S. Dist. Ct. Ill. (no. dist.) Ill. 1964, U.S. Ct. Appeals (7th cir.) 1964, Pa. 1972. Assoc. Sidley & Austin, Chgo., 1964-71; sr. internat. atty., asst. gen. counsel, dir. Japanese ops. Sperry Univac, Blue Bell, Pa., 1971-78; from asst. to assoc. gen. counsel Baxter Travenol Labs., Deerfield, Ill., 1978-85, v.p., dep. gen. counsel, 1985—. Mem. Planning Commn., Springfield Twp., Montgomery County, Pa., 1973-74, Zoning Hearing Bd., 1974-78; bd. dirs. Twp. High Sch. Dist. #113, Deerfield and Highland Park, Ill., 1983—. Mem. ABA, Chgo. Bar Assn. Episcopalian. Home: 1144 Walden Ln Deerfield IL 60015 Office: Baxter Travenol Labs Inc One Baxter Pkwy Deerfield IL 60015

STAUDE, PETER, resort executive; b. Gmunden, Austria, Feb. 9, 1944; came to U.S., 1958, naturalized, 1965; s. Leonard Staude and Hildegard (Steiner) Whitman; m. Wanda Fay Mosier, May 20, 1976; 1 child, Rachael. Resident mgr., gen. mgr. Tan-Tar-A Resort, Osage Beach, Mo., 1960-76; v.p., gen. mgr. Olympia Resort, Oconomowoc, Wis., 1976-78; owner, operator Staude's Trucking, Ft. Wayne, Ind., 1978-80; gen. mgr. Hilton Inn, Kansas City, 1980-83, Holiday Inn, Lake Ozark, Mo., 1983-87, Airport Hilton Plaza Inn, Kansas City, Mo., 1987—; chmn. hotel and restaurant vocat. tech. Platt County Vocat.-Tech. Sch., Mo., 1983. Served as staff sgt. USAF, 1966-70. Mem. Lake Assn. (bd. dirs. 1984-85), Mo. Hotel Assn. (bd. dirs. 1982-83, 84-85), Mo. Hotel/Motel Assn. (bd. dirs. 1987—), Mo. Travel Council (bd. dirs. 1984—, v.p. 1986—). Avocations: snow skiing, tennis, swimming. Lodge: Rotary (bd. dirs. Lake Ozark 1985-86). Home: 1514 NE 54th St Kansas City MO 64118 Office: Route 1 Box 45 Lake Ozark MO 65049

STAUFFER, CLAY WALLACE, newspaper editor; b. Denver, Jan. 23, 1954; s. Stanley Howard and Suzanne (Wallace) S.; m. Susan Lynn, Sept. 3, 1978; children: Louise, Timothy. BA, Haverford Coll., 1976. Reporter Capital-Jour., Topeka, 1977-78; bus. editor The Herald, Bellingham, Wash., 1978-79; newswriter AP, Jefferson City, Mo., 1979-80; asst. gen. mgr. Shawnee (Okla.) News-Star, 1980-82; editor Glenwood Post, Glenwood Springs, Colo., 1982-85, Holland (Mich.) Sentinel, 1985—. Bd. dirs. Garfield County United Way, Glenwood Springs, 1982-85, Holland Area Arts Council, 1985, Holland Hist. Trust, 1985. Mem. Am. Soc. Newspaper Editors, Soc. Profl. Journalists. Episcopalian. Lodge: Rotary. Avocations: painting, astronomy. Home: 2365 Sunset Bluff Dr Holland MI 49423 Office: Holland Sentinel 54 W 8th St Holland MI 49423

STAUFFER, LEE DALLAS, public health educator; b. Wisner, Nebr., Mar. 20, 1929; s. Lee Henry and Myrtle Ann (Schulz) S.; m. Donna Lois Frederickson, Aug. 27, 1952; children—Karl, Lisa, Dane, Kristian. B.S., U. Nebr., 1951; M.P.H., U. Minn., 1956. Registered sanitarian, Minn. Various teaching and sanitarian positions U. Minn., Mpls., 1952-62, asst. prof., asst. dir. sch. pub. health, 1962-66, dean sch. pub. health, 1970-82, assoc. prof., 1982—; dep. health officer City of Coon Rapids, Minn., 1960-64; exec. sec. Am. Coll. Health Assn., Coral Gables, Fla., 1966-68; exec. dir. postgrad. edn. Coll. Med. Scis., Mpls., 1968-70; mem. Met. Health Bd., St. Paul, 1970-73; trustee, pres. Northlands Regional Med. Program, St. Paul, 1970-78; counselor, v.p., pres. Council Edn. for Pub. Health, Washington, 1974-80. Contbr. articles to profl. jours. Mem., trustee, pres. North Suburban San. Sewer Dist., Spring Lake Park, Minn., 1962-66; mem., v.p., pres. sch. bd., St. Anthony, Minn., 1969-73; chmn. Am. Field Service Club, St. Anthony, 1976-78. Served with USMC, 1946-47; served as midshipman USNR, 1947-48. Recipient spl. recognition award Am. Coll. Health Assn., 1976, Sch. Pub. Health award, 1983, Gaylord W. Anderson award, 1987; named adm. Nebr. Navy, 1982. Fellow Am. Pub. Health Assn. (gov. council 1983-85); mem. Nat. Acad. Sanitarians (founder, diplomate, bd. dirs. 1970-73), Nat. Assn. Pub. Health Policy (sec., environ. health council 1984-85), Nat. Environ. Health Assn. (registered, Cert. Merit 1971), Minn. Environ. Health Assn. (chmn. registration com. 1962-66, Sanitarian of Yr. 1971), Assn. Sch. Pub. Health (sec.-treas. 1980-82). Democrat. Lutheran. Club: Campus (Mpls.). Avocation: music. Home: 3000 Croft Dr NE Minneapolis MN 55418 Office: Mayo Hospital 420 Delaware St SE Minneapolis MN 55455

STAUFFER, RICHARD LA VERGNE, art educator, sculptor, glassblower; b. New Cambria, Kans., Apr. 1, 1932; s. Kenneth L. and Mary (Bell) S.; m. Mary Hake, Aug. 23, 1953; children—Brad, Bridgett, Brendy. B.S., Kans. State Tchrs. Coll., 1955; M.S., Kans. U., 1962. Tchr. art Emporia City Schs., Kans., 1957-62; prof. art Emporia State U., 1962—; judicator Scholastic Art Awards, Wichita, Kans., 1984—. Pres. Friends of Art, Emporia, 1970; chmn., trustee Congl. Ch., 1985. Served with U.S. Army, 1955-57. Recipient HM award Kans. Designer Craftsman, 1972, Smokey Hill Art, 1976, Juror's award Art Inc., 1984; named Outstanding Art Educator, Nat. Art Edn. Assn., 1984, Govs. Artist Arts Commn., 1985. Fellow Art Glass Directory, Kans. Sculpture Assn. (regional adviser 1983-87, Group Sculpture Design prize, 1984); mem. Kans. Artist Craftsman Assn. (treas. 1973-77), Kans. Art Edn. Assn. (editor 1984-88). Democrat. Avocations: sports, archeology. Home: 2001 Lincoln St Emporia KS 66801 Office: Emporia State U 12th and Commercial Sts Emporia KS 66801

STAUFFER, STANLEY HOWARD, newspaper and broadcasting executive; b. Peabody, Kans., Sept. 11, 1920; s. Oscar S. and Ethel L. (Stone) S.; m. Suzanne R. Wallace, Feb. 16, 1945 (div. 1961); children: Peter, Clay, Charles; m. Elizabeth D. Priest, July 14, 1962; children: Elizabeth, Grant. A.B., U. Kans., 1942. Assoc. editor Topeka State Jour., 1946-47; editor, pub. Santa Maria (Calif.) Times, 1948-52; rewrite, copy editor Denver Post, 1953-54; staff mem. AP (Denver bur.), 1954-55; exec. v.p. Stauffer Publs., Inc., 1955-69; gen. mgr. Topeka Capital-Jour., 1957-69; pres. Stauffer Communications, Inc., 1969-86, chmn., 1986—; bd. dirs. Yellow Freight System, Inc., Bank IV, Topeka, Great Lakes Forest Products Ltd., Thunder Bay, Ont., Newspaper Advt. Bur. Past pres. Topeka YMCA; past chmn. adv. bd. St. Francis Hosp.; past chmn. Met. Topeka Airport Authority; trustee William Allen White Found., Menninger Found., Midwest Research Inst., Capper Crippled Children's Found. Served as officer USAAF, 1943-45. Named Chief Boss of Year Am. Bus. Women's Assn., 1976; Outstanding Kans. Pub. Kappa Tau Alpha, 1980; Legion of Honor De Molay; Topeka Phi of Year, 1971. Mem. Kans. Press Assn. (past pres.), Inland Daily Press Assn. (past dir.), Air Force Assn. (past pres. Topeka), Kans. U. Alumni Assn. (past dir.), Kans. Chamber Commerce and Industry (past chmn.), Phi Delta Theta (past chpt. pres.), Sigma Delta Chi (past chpt. pres.). Episcopalian (past sr. warden). Clubs: Topeka Country, Top of the Tower; Garden of the Gods (Colorado Springs); Learned (Lawrence, Kans.). Home: 2801 MacVicar Ave Topeka KS 66611 Office: Stauffer Communications Inc 6th & Jefferson Sts Topeka KS 66607

STAUN, PHILIP JACOB, JR., manufacturing executive; b. Carmichaels, Pa., May 20, 1948; s. Philip J. and Marian Louise (Murray) S.; m. Karen J. Renfro, May 1, 1981; 1 stepchild, Brian; 1 child, Philip J. III. BSEE, Lafayette Coll., 1970; MBA, U. Louisville, 1976. Foreman prodn. Gen. Electric, Louisville, 1972-74, quality process engr., 1974-76, unit mgr. ops., 1976-78, mgr. prodn. control, 1978-79, mgr. shop ops., 1979-84; dir. mfg. Haworth, Inc., Holland, Mich., 1984—. Mem. Am. Prodn. and Inventory Control Soc., Am. Mgmt. Assn. Democrat. Roman Catholic. Avocations: weight-lifting, jogging, photography. Home: 195 Portchester Rd Holland MI 49424 Office: Haworth Inc One Haworth Ctr Holland MI 49423

STAVROPOULOS, D(IONYSOS) JOHN, banker; b. Vicksburg, Miss., Jan. 19, 1933; s. John Dionysos and Olga (Balodemos) S.; m. Alexandra Gatzoyanni, Jan. 10, 1976; children: John, Theodore, Mark, Olga, Katerina. B.S., Miss. State U., 1955; M.B.A., Northwestern U., 1956. Chartered fin. analyst. With trust dept. First Nat. Bank of Chgo., 1956-69, internat. banking dept., 1970-76, sr. v.p. real estate dept., 1976-78, exec. v.p. comml. banking dept., 1979-80, chmn. credit strategy com., 1981—, chief credit officer, 1986—; v.p., dir. research Bache & Co., N.Y.C., 1969-70; instr. finance Northwestern U., 1962-68; dir. Central Ill. Public Service Co. Served with U.S. Army, 1951-53. Mem. Am. Bankers Assn., Assn. Res. City Bankers, Council Fgn. Relations (Chgo. com.), Robert Morris Assocs., (nat. dir.). Greek Orthodox. Clubs: Westmoreland Country; Economic (Chgo.). Office: First Chgo Corp 1 First Nat Plaza Chicago IL 60670

STAZAK, SUSAN MARIE, optical engineer; b. Chgo., Feb. 25, 1959; d. Edward Francis and Florence Frances (Kaliski) S. BS in Math. and Physics, U. Ill., Chgo., 1981; MSEE, U. Ill., 1983, MS in Physics, 1987. Microprocessor research and devel. U. Ill., Chgo., 1979-80; seismic test engr. Westinghouse Electric, Chgo., 1981; electro-optics engr. McDonnell Douglas Astronautics, St. Louis, 1984—. Mem. Am. Inst. Aeronautics and Astronautics, Optical Soc. Am., Optical Soc. Greater St. Louis. Avocations: photography, baking, swimming, drawing, volleyball. Office: McDonnell Douglas Astronautics Co E413/106/2/B10 PO Box 516 Saint Louis MO 63166

STEAD, JAMES JOSEPH, JR., securities company executive; b. Chgo., Sept. 13, 1930; s. James Joseph and Irene (Jennings) S.; B.S., DePaul U., 1955, M.B.A., 1957; m. Edith Pearson, Feb. 13, 1954; children—James, Diane, Robert, Caroline. Asst. sec. C. F. Childs & Co., Chgo., 1955-62; exec. v.p., sec. Koenig, Keating & Stead, Inc., Chgo., 1962-66; 2d v.p., mgr. midwest municipal bond dept. Hayden, Stone Inc., Chgo., 1966-69; sr. v.p., nat. sales mgr. Ill. Co. Inc., 1969-70; mgr. instl. sales dept. Reynolds and Co., Chgo., 1970-72; partner Edwards & Hanly, 1972-74; v.p., instnl. sales mgr. Paine, Webber, Jackson & Curtis, 1974-76; v.p., regional instl. sales mgr. Reynolds Securities, Inc., 1976-78; sr. v.p., regional mgr. Oppenheimer & Co., Inc., 1978—; instr. Mcpl. Bond Sch., Chgo., 1967—. Served with AUS, 1951-53. Mem. Security Traders Assn. Chgo., Nat. Security Traders Assn., Am. Mgmt. Assn., Municipal Finance Forum Washington. Clubs: Executives, Union League, Municipal Bond, Bond (Chgo.); Olympia Fields Country (Ill.); Wall Street (N.Y.C.). Home: 20721 Brookwood Dr Olympia Fields IL 60461 Office: One S Wacker Dr Chicago IL 60606

STEADMAN, JACK W., professional football team executive; b. Warrenville, Ill., Sept. 14, 1928; s. Walter Angus and Vera Ruth (Burkholder) S.; m. Martha Cudworth Steinhoff, Nov. 24, 1949; children: Thomas Edward, Barbara Ann, Donald Wayne. B.B.A., So. Methodist U., 1950. Accountant Hunt Oil Co., Dallas, 1950-54; chief accountant W.H. Hunt, Dallas, 1954-58, Penrod Drilling Co., Dallas, 1958-60; gen. mgr. Dallas Texans Football Club, 1960-63; gen. mgr. Kansas City Chiefs Football Club, 1963-76, exec. v.p., 1966-76, pres., 1976—; mem. NFL Exec. Com.; chmn. NFL Coaches and Front Office Pension Plan com.; Chmn. Hunt Midwest Enterprises, Inc. Kansas City, HME Entertainment Div. (Worlds of Fun, Oceans of Fun), Kansas City, 1972—; chmn. Full Employment Council Inc., Pvt. Industry Council; dir. Commerce Bank of Kansas City. Former bd. dirs. Children's Mercy Hosp., bd. dirs. Civic Council, C. of C. of Greater Kansas City, Kansas City, Starlight Theatre Assn., Kansas City, Am. Royal Assn.; pres. Heart of Am. United Way, 1981; adv. trustee Research Med. Ctr., Kansas City; trustee Midwest Research Inst.; mem. Kansas City Area Econ. Devel. Council; mem. Village Presbyn. Ch. Clubs: Kansas City, 711 Inner, River, Carriage, Vanguard (Kansas City). Home: 6436 Wenonga Terr Shawnee Mission KS 66208 Office: Kansas City Chiefs 1 Arrowhead Dr Kansas City MO 64129

STEAGALL, VIRGINIA ANNE, nursing educator; b. Newark, Ohio, Aug. 5, 1933; d. Forest LeDoyt and Virginia Lucas (Larason) Eagle; m. Larry Prescott, Aug. 21, 1955; children: Scott William, Mark Benjamin. BS in Nursing, U. Cin., 1955; MS in Nursing, Med. Coll. of Ohio, Toledo, 1985; doctoral student, U. Toledo, 1982—. Staff nurse Grant Hosp., Columbus, Ohio, 1956; office nurse Ft. Worth, 1956-57; staff nurse Flower Hosp., Toledo, 1974-75; instr. Owens Tech. Coll., Toledo, 1975—, course coordinator, psychiatric nursing, 1984-87, assoc. prof., 1987—. Mem. AAUW (recording sec., membership chmn. new mems. chmn., scholarship 1982), Pi Lambda Theta (hospitality chmn. 1986-87, recording sec. 1987—). Avocations: bridge, tennis, reading, traveling, meditation. Home: 3720 Monroe St Toledo OH 43606

STEC, ROBERT GERARD, high school educator, theologian; b. Cleve., Oct. 8, 1961; s. Frank J. and Rita Jane (Penn) Stec. BA in Psychology, Borromeo Coll., 1983; postgrad., St. Mary Sem., 1983—. Asst. devel. dir. Padua Franciscan High Sch., Parma, Ohio, 1983—; cons. Padua Franciscan High Sch., 1984—, Gerald Jindra Devel. Inc., Parma, 1985—; adminstrv. asst. St. Charles Ch., Parma, 1983—. Author: Adolescent Chemical Dependency: A Diocesan Perspective, 1983. Named one of Outstanding Young Men of Am., 1985. Mem. Young Reps. for Reagan, Serra, Internat. Roman Catholic. Lodge: KC. Avocations: skiing, photography, football, classical music. Home: 6319 W Ridgewood Dr Parma OH 44129 Office: Padua High Sch 6740 State Rd Parma OH 44134

STECKLER, WILLIAM ELWOOD, judge; b. Mt. Vernon, Ind., Oct. 18, 1913; s. William Herman and Lena (Menikheim) S.; m. Vitallas Alting, Oct. 15, 1938; children: William Rudolph, David Alan. LL.B., Ind. U., 1936, J.D., 1937; LL.D., Wittenberg U., Springfield, Ohio, 1958; H.H.D., Ind. Central U., 1969. Bar: Ind. 1936. Practiced in Indpls., 1937-50; mem. firm Key & Steckler; pub. counselor Ind. Pub. Service Commn., 1949-50; judge U.S. Dist. Ct. So. Dist., Ind., 1950—; chief judge U.S. Dist. Ct. So. Dist., 1954-82; faculty mem. for judges confs. Fed. Jud. Ctr., 1973-74. Mem. Ind. Election Bd., 1946-48; chmn. speakers bur. Democratic State Central Com., 1948; bd. dirs. Community Hosp., Indpls.; bd. visitors Ind. U. Sch. Law, Indpls. Served with USNR, 1943. Recipient Man of Yr. award Ind. U. Sch. Law, Indpls., 1970, Disting Alumni Service award, 1985; Disting. Alumni Service award Ind. U., 1985. Mem. Am., Fed., Ind., Indpls. bar assns., Am. Judicature Soc. Nat. Lawyers Club, Jud. Conf. U.S. (dist. judge rep. from 7th fed. circuit 1961-64, mem. study group pretrial com. 1956-60, pretrial procedure com. 1960-65, trial practice and procedure com. 1965-69, coordinating com. for multiple litigation 1966-69, operation of jury system com. 1969-75, jud. ethics com. 1985—), Am. Legion, St. Thomas More Soc., Order of Coif, Sigma Delta Kappa. Lutheran. Club: Indianapolis Athletic. Lodges: Masons (33 deg.), Shriners, Order DeMoley, Royal Order Jesters. Home: 30 Jurist Ln Lamb Lake Trafalgar IN 46181 Office: 204 US Courthouse 46 E Ohio Indianapolis IN 46204

STEELE, CLEMENT JOSEPH, computer professional; b. Waukon, Iowa, June 16, 1937; s. Burnill William and Susan Lois (Stubstad) S.; student Marquette U., 1955-56; B.A., Loras Coll., 1961; postgrad. Ill. Inst. Tech., 1964, Lawrence U., 1966, U. Wyo., 1971, U. Iowa, 1972, U. Wis., 1973-76; M.S., Rutgers U., 1968; m. Mary Jane Valley, Aug. 11, 1962; children—Maureen, Teresa, Daniel. Tchr. math. Jefferson Jr. High Sch., Dubuque, 1961-63, Lake Forest (Ill.) High Sch., 1963-67, Campion Acad., Prairie du Chien, Wis., 1968-73; math. supervisory intern Milw. public schs., 1973-74; teaching asst., research asst. U. Wis., Madison, 1974-76; research and evaluation cons. Keystone Area Edn. Agy., Dubuque, 1976-77; instructional computer cons., computer center dir. Keystone Area Edn. Agy., 1977-83, coordinator computer services, 1983—; guest lectr. in research Clarke Coll., 1978-83; instr. Loras Coll., 1979-81; adj. prof. No. Ill. U., 1983—. Served with U.S. Army, 1961. Named Outstanding Young Educator, Wis. Jaycees, 1972; NSF grantee, 1973-74. Mem. Iowa Computer Using Educators (bd. dirs. 1980-82), Nat. Council Tchrs. Math., Nat. Council Suprs. Math., Iowa Council Tchrs. Math., Tri-State Data Processing Assn., Phi Delta Kappa. Roman Catholic. Club: Lions. Contbr. articles to profl. jours. Home: 2371 Carter Rd Dubuque IA 52001 Office: 1473 Central Ave Dubuque IA 52001

STEELE, DEBRA LEAH, management develoment specialist; b. San Francisco, July 4, 1957; d. Wallace William and Theresa (Orosz) S. BA in Psychology, U. Calif., San Diego, 1979; grad. studies in Indsl. Psychology, U. Minn. Employee relations intern Honeywell Corp, Minn., 1979-81, curriculum specialist, 1981—. Research grantee U. Minn., 1982. Mem. Acad. Mgmt., Am. Soc. Tng. and Devel. Avocations: reading fiction, classical and jazz music, tennis, volley ball. Office: Honeywell A&D Mgmt Devel Ctrs 3600 W 80th St Suite 255 Bloomington MN 55431

STEELE, HILDA HODGSON, retired home economist, consultant; b. Wilmington, Ohio, Mar. 24, 1911; d. George and Mary Jane (Rolston) Hodgson; A.A., Wilmington Coll., 1931, B.S., 1935; M.A. in Home Econs. Edn., Ohio State U., 1941; postgrad. Ohio U., 1954, Miami U., 1959; m. John C. Steele (dec. Jan. 1973). Tchr., Brookville (Ohio) Elementary Sch., 1932-37; tchr. home econs. Lincoln Jr. High Sch., Dayton (Ohio) Pub. Schs., 1937-40, coordinator home econs. dept., traveling exptl. home econs. tchr., 1940-45, supr. home econs., 1945-81, cons., 1981—; program dir. Family Life Adult Disadvantaged Program, 1969-81. Mem. Ohio Farm Electrification Com., 1964-66. Mem. town and country br. career com. Miami Valley br. YMCA, 1948-59. Adv. bd. Dayton Sch. Practical Nursing, 1951—; adv. com. Dayton Miami Valley Hosp. Sch. Nursing, 1951-63; jr. adv. com. Montgomery County chpt. ARC, 1940-80; mem. com. United Appeal, 1970—; bd. dirs. (Ohio) FHA-HERO, 1979-81. Recipient Outstanding Service recognition Dayton Met. Girl Scouts U.S., 1987. Mem. Dayton area Nutrition Council, Am. Home Econs. Assn. (del. 1961), Ohio Home Econs. Assn. (chmn. elementary and secondary edn. com. 1947-51, co-chmn. ann. conv. 1961-77, mem. housing and equipment coms. 1965-68, chmn. found. com. 1979-81), Dayton Met. Home Econs. Assn. (pres. 1949-50, 60-61); Nat., Ohio edn. assns., Ohio Council Local Adminstrs., Dayton Sch. Adminstrs. Assn., Elec. Women's Round Table (pres. 1960-61), Dayton City Sch. Mgmt. Assn. (charter), Ohio Vocat. Assn. (Disting. Service award 1981), Am. Vocat. Edn. Assn., Ohio Vocat. Edn. Assn., Phi Upsilon Omicron (hon.). Mem. Ch. of Christ. Mem. Order Eastern Star. Club: Zonta (pres. Dayton 1950-52). Research in pub. sch. food habits, 1957. Home: 1443 State Route 380 Xenia OH 45385

STEELE, PATRICIA ANN, librarian; b. Columbus, Ohio, Mar. 28, 1943; s. Gerald Henry and June Eileen (McCullough) Costlow; m. Charles Nolan Steele, Aug. 31, 1963; children: Kelly Colleen, Ryan Charles. AB in English, Ind. U., 1966, MLS, 1981. Cert. tchr., Mich. Tchr. Chippewa Valley Schs., Mt. Clemens, Mich., 1966-67; br. head, extension asst. Lansing (Mich.) Pub. Library, 1967-74; head librarian, Atomic Energy Commn. plant research lab. Mich. State U., East Lansing, 1969-73; head librarian, Health, Physical Edn. and Recreation Library Ind. U., Bloomington, 1979-81, head librarian sch. of library and info. sci., 1981—; chmn. faculty council ednl. task force on pornography Ind. U., 1985—; cons., specialist conspectus Research Libraries Group, 1985-86. Editor Library Sci. Nat. Newsletter, 1984-86; columnist Library Bookshelf, 1981—, InULA Innuendo, 1984—. Mem. ALA (v. chmn. library sci. librarians discussion group 1984-86), Ind. Library Assn. (chmn. exec. com. div. on women 1983-86), Ind. U. Librarian's Assn., Stone Hills Area Library Sci. Authority. Avocations: swimming, jogging, hiking. Home: 4791 N Benton Dr Bloomington IN 47401 Office: Ind U SLIS Library 002 Bloomington IN 47405

STEELE, WASHBURN WHITING, Realtor, puppeteer; b. Mpls., Apr. 16, 1919; s. Harrison C. and Lydia Marie (Jepson) S.; m. Harriet Ann Rogers, Sept. 10, 1950; children—Lowell N., Quentin M., Miranda Lou. B.A. in Econs., Carleton Coll., 1940; postgrad. in civil enging. Iowa State Coll., 1941-42. Acctg. teller Steele State Bank, Cherokee, Iowa, 1946-51, farm mgr., agrl. loan officer, 1946-52; owner, operator Sioux River Ranch, Cherokee, 1953-69; owner, operator W.W. Steele Realty, Cherokee, 1969—; co-owner Honeybee Nutrition, Cherokee, 1978—. Mem. platform com. Republican Nat. Conv., Chgo., 1960; chmn. Cherokee County Rep. Com., Iowa, 1961; mem. Iowa Ho. of Reps., Des Moines, 1963-64. Served to lt. USNR, 1942-46; Cuba, PTO, comdr. USNR, ret. Mem. United Counties Bd. Realtors (past pres.), Am. Soc. Farm Mgrs. and Rural Appraisers, Am. Quarter

Horse Assn. Mormon. Home: PO Box 60 Cherokee IA 51012 Office: W W Steele Realty 116 E Main Cherokee IA 51012

STEEN, DONALD MARINER, agri-business executive; b. Scottsbluff, Nebr., Mar. 24, 1924; s. Clarence Guido and Jean Mabel (Whipple) S.; m. Bonnie Jeanne Jirdon, Oct. 30, 1946; children—John Robert, William Gary. Student U. Nebr., 1941-42; B.Sc., U.S. Merchant Marine Acad., 1981. Pres., Blue J. Feeds, Inc., 1970-81, Jirdon Wyoming Inc., 1970-80, Wyo. Chem., Inc., 1975-80, Chems. Internat. Ltd., 1974-79, Jirdon Livestock Co., Morrill, Nebr., 1983—; cons. Allied Chem. Corp.; chmn. bd. PAB Nebr. Natural Resources Commn., 1981. Chmn., Gov.'s Forward Nebr. Task Force, 1982; state vice chmn. Nebr. Republican Party, 1975. Served to lt. USN, 1943-46. Recipient Outstanding Community Service award Am. Feed Mfrs. Assn., 1975; Service to Handicapped, Goodwill Industries of Wyo., 1979, others. Mem. Am. Legion, Nat. Water Alliance, Nebr. Water Resources Assn. (pres. 1982), Nebr. Assn. Commerce and Industry (v.p. 1981). Presbyterian. Clubs: Rotary, Stockgrowers, Masons, Shriners, Elks. Patentee liquid protein supplement, artificial protein, liquid fire retardant. Office: PO Box 456 Morrill NE 69358

STEEN, JAN PHAFF, international financier, banker; b. Frederiksberg, Denmark, Jan. 31, 1935; s. Thomas and Else Steen; m. Rebecca Sherk; 1 child, Sara. B.A., Copenhagen State Coll., 1954; M.B.A., Copenhagen Comml. U., 1956. Trainee, East Asiatic Co., Copenhagen, 1954; adminstrv. asst. USAF Base Exchange, Sondrestrom AFB, Greenland, 1959-60; purchase/sales mgr., Royal Greenland Trade Dept., Copenhagen, 1960-63; comml. attache Royal Danish Consulate Gen., Kuwait, 1964-65; asst. v.p., mgr. Privatbanken Copenhagen, 1966-69; internat. mgr. Winters Nat. Bank & Trust Co., Dayton, Ohio, 1969-71, asst. v.p., 1971-73, v.p., div. mgr., 1973-77, sr. v.p., 1977-82; pres., internat. fin. cons. JPS Export-Import Trading, 1982-85; mgr. internat. fin. and banking Mead Corp., Dayton, 1986—. Pres., Dayton Council World Affairs, 1977-79; gov. Ohio Adv. Council Internat. Trade, 1974-78; treas. So. Ohio Dist. Export Council, 1975-84; bd. dirs. Dayton Opera Assn., 1977-83. Served to capt. Royal Danish Army, 1956-63. Danish Dept. Commerce Export fellow, 1964. Mem. Dayton C. of C. (chmn. world trade council 1974-75) Fgn. Credit Ins. Assn. (midwest adv. com. 1980-83), Res. Officers Assn. U.S. (hon.), Danish Res. Officers Assn. Clubs: Royal Danish Yacht; Dayton Racquet, Dayton Country. Contbr. articles to profl. jours. Home: 200 W Thruston Blvd Dayton OH 45419 Office: Mead Corp Courthouse Plaza NE Dayton OH 45463

STEEN, LOWELL HARRISON, physician; b. Kenosha, Wis., Nov. 27, 1923; s. Joseph Arthur and Camilla Marie (Henriksen) S.; m. Cheryl Ann Rectanus, Nov. 20, 1969; children—Linda C., Laura A., Lowell Harrison, Heather J., Kirsten M. B.S., Ind. U., 1945, M.D., 1948. Intern Mercy Hosp.-Loyola U. Clinics, Chgo., 1948-49; resident in internal medicine VA Hosp., Hines, Ill., 1950-53; practice medicine specializing in internal medicine Highland, Ind., 1953—; pres., chief exec. officer Whiting Clinic, 1960-85; mem. sr. staff St. Catherine Hosp., East Chicago, Ind.; staff Community Hosp., Munster, Ind.; bd. commrs. Joint Commn. Accreditation of Hosps. Served with M.C., AUS, 1949-50, 55-56. Recipient Disting. Alumni Service award Ind. U., 1983. Fellow ACP; mem. AMA (trustee 1975, chmn. bd. trustees 1979-81), Ind. Med. Assn. (pres. 1970, chmn. bd. 1968-70), World Med. Assn. (dir. 1978-82, chmn. 1981-82, del. world assembly), Ind. Soc. Internal Medicine (pres. 1963), Lake County Med. Soc. Presbyterian. Home: 8800 Parkway Dr Highland IN 46322 Office: 3641 Ridge Rd Highland IN 46322

STEEN, RONALD ARDIS, religious music director; b. Greenville, Tex., Sept. 12, 1954; s. Rush Ardis and Winnie Mae (Wright) S.; m. Cynthia Ann Mallory, May 1, 1983. MusB, Stephen F. Austin State U., 1977. Ordained to ministry Assemblies of God Ch., 1983. Minister fine arts Northland Cathedral, Kansas City, Mo., 1978—; clinician, workshop leader, guest conductor various chs., colls., performing groups. Producer religious music and drama presentations. Named one of Outstanding Young Men Am. U.S. Jaycees, 1981. Mem. Am. Choral Dirs. Assn., Choristers Guild. Republican. Avocations: fishing, hunting, racquetball. Home: 4608 N Kenwood Kansas City MO 64116 Office: Northland Cathedral 600 NE 46th St Kansas City MO 64119

STEENO, DAVID LAWRENCE, legal educator; b. Green Bay, Wis., June 20, 1944; s. Paul Wilbur and Grace Nina (Martell) S.; m. Mary Joanne Shea, Aug. 7, 1971; children—Karen Marie, John Paul. B.S., U. Wis., 1966; M.S., Mich. State U., 1973; J.D., Cooley Law Sch., 1976. Bar: Mich. 1976, U.S. Dist. Ct. (ea. dist.) Mich. 1977, U.S. Ct. Appeals (6th cir.) 1977, U.S. Ct. Appeals (7th cir.) 1979, U.S. Ct. Appeals (8th cir.) 1982. Instr. U. Ill. Police Tng. Inst., Champaign, 1973; dist. security mgr. Venture Stores, St. Louis, 1971-73; assoc. Schneider, Handlon & Steeno, Midland, Mich., 1976-78; assoc. prof. dept. law enforcement adminstrn. Western Ill. U., Macomb, 1978-85; Ferris State Coll., Big Rapids, Mich., 1985—; cons. in field. Contbr. articles to profl. jours., chpt. to book. Bd. dirs. Western Ill. U. Found., 1983-85. Served to capt. USAF, 1966-70, Vietnam. Mem. Nat. Dist. Attys. Assn., Midwestern Assn. Criminal Justice Educators, Security Law Inst., Am. Soc. Indsl. Security, Alpha Phi Sigma, Phi Alpha Delta. Lodge: Elks. Home: 520 Mecosta Ave Big Rapids MI 49307 Office: Ferris State Coll 501 Bishop Hall Big Rapids MI 49307

STEFAN, EDWIN S., psychology educator, minister, psychotherapist; b. Milw., Nov. 18, 1933; s. Edwin and Loraine F. Stefan; m. Katheryn J. Rouse, Aug. 30, 1959; children: Cynthia L., Deborah A., Jennifer S. BA cum laude, Carroll Coll., 1955; MDiv, Garrett Theol. Sem., 1959; MST, Boston U., 1960; D of Religion, Sch. of Theology at Claremont, 1966. Lifetime jr. coll. teaching cert., Calif.; ordained to ministry, United Meth. Ch., 1956. Minister various states, 1956-69; prof. psychology, dir. personal counseling services Findlay (Ohio) Coll., 1969—. Contbr. articles and papers on aging and coping with death. Mem. Am. Psychol. Assn., Am. Assn. Pastoral Counselors. Avocations: camping, backpacking, bicycling, music composition. Home: 132 Defiance Ave Findlay OH 45840 Office: Findlay Coll 1000 N Main St Findlay OH 45840

STEFANIK, JANET RUTH, realtor; b. Harrisville, W.Va., Apr. 25, 1938; d. John Jackson Jr. and Helen Virginia (Waller) D.; m. Robert John Stefanik, Oct. 13, 1956 (div. Apr. 1977); children: Robert Mark, Deborah Ruth, Perry Wayne, David Lee, Susan Irene. Grad. high sch., Grafton, Ohio; student, Lorain County Coll., Elyria, Ohio, 1982, 85. Salesperson Demby Real Estate, Elyria, 1970-71, Schwed Real Estate, Elyria, 1971—. Mem. Nat. Assn. Realtors, Ohio Assn. Realtors, Lorain County Bd. Realtors (telephone com. 1972-73), Womens Council Realtors (v.p. 1973, pres. 1974), Lorain County Hist. Soc. Republican. Roman Catholic. Clubs: Beaver Creek Sportsmans, Scandinavian Health Spa. Avocations: golf, travel, fishing, swimming, organ music. Home: 36301 Butternut Ridge Rd Elyria OH 44035 Office: Schwed Real Estate 38932 Butternut Ridge Elyria OH 44035

STEFFAN, MICHAEL DALE, accountant, auditor; b. Jamestown, N.D., Dec. 10, 1954; s. Fred and Esther Martha (Weidler) S.; m. Kimberly Jo Bye, Jan. 14, 1977; 1 child, Lisa Jo. BSsumma cum laude, U. N.D., 1976. CPA, N.D. Supr. Orser, Olson, and St. Peter, CPA's, Bismark, N.D., 1977-84; audit mgr., ptnr. Zine, Hoover and Voller, P.C., Williston, N.D., 1984—. Rep. treas. Dist. 1, 1985—; deacon First Union Ch., 1986—. Named one of Outstanding Young Men of Am., Jaycees, 1983. Mem. Am. Inst. CPA's, N.D. Soc. CPA's (nominations com., govtl. acct. com.). Republican. Lodges: Kiwanis (bd. dirs. 1980-84, sec., treas. 1984-85), Elks. Avocations: fishing, golfing, volleyball, hunting. Home: 2305 6th Ave E Williston ND 58801 Office: Zine Hoover and Voller PC PO Box 1387 Williston ND 58801

STEFFEL, JEFFREY JOHN, police officer; b. Chgo., May 28, 1948; s. Vern John and Adeline Terese (Safranski) S. BS, Mich. State U., 1971; JD, Thomas M. Cooley Law Sch., 1982. Bar: Mich. 1982, Fed. Dist. Ct. 1984, U.S. Supreme Ct. 1986. Trooper Mich. State Police, Erie, Brighton, and Lansing, Mich., 1972-80; sgt. Mich. State Police, Lansing, 1980-83; lt. Mich. State Police Hdqrs., East Lansing, 1983-84, first lt., 1984—. Author: Warrantless Search and Seizure, 1983, Michigan Criminal Law and Procedure, 1983, 2d edit., 1986. Recipient Donald S. Leonard award Mich. State Bar, 1985. Mem. Mich. State Bar, ABA, Mich. Trial Lawyers Assn., Am. Trial Lawyers Assn. Office: Mich State Police 714 S Harrison Rd East Lansing MI 48823

STEFFEL, RONALD VICTOR, electronics executive; b. Defiance, Ohio, Apr. 8, 1940; s. Victor B. and Anna A. (Siler) S.; m. Lynn Marie Bertolli, Apr. 12, 1969; children: Cheryl, Jeffrey, Jennifer. BEE, Ohio State U., Columbus, 1963; MBA, U. Chgo., 1975. Section mgr. Motorola, Inc., Schaumburg, Ill., 1970-73, engring. mgr., 1973-76, product mgr., 1976-79, group product mgr., 1979-85, sr. product mgr., 1985—. Patentee amplifier protection circuit, 1972. Mem. bd. St. James Sch., Glen Ellyn, 1982-85. Avocations: woodworking, personal computers. Office: Motorola Inc 1301 E Algonquin Rd Schaumburg IL 60196

STEFFKA, MARK ANDREW, reliability engineer; b. Wyandotte, Mich., June 24, 1958; s. Norman Lloyd and Diane Elizabeth (Overholt) S.; m. Rebecca Lynn Lemanski, Sept. 18, 1981; 1 child, Aaron. BEE, U. Mich., Dearborn, 1981. Engr. Sparton Corp., Jackson, Mich., 1981-82; reliability engr. Fed. Express Corp., Memphis, 1982-84; reliability project engr. Magnavox Co., Ft. Wayne, Ind., 1984—. Lutheran. Avocations: history reading, amateur radio, bicycling, canoeing. Home: 1024 Candlewood Way Fort Wayne IN 46825 Office: Magnavox 1313 Production Rd Fort Wayne IN 46808

STEFFY, GARY ROBERT, lighting design company executive; b. Lancaster, Pa., Feb. 6, 1954; s. George Robert and Ann Louise (Eshleman) S. B Archtl. Engring., Pa. State U., 1977. Research engr. Owens-Corning Fiberglas, Granville, Ohio, 1977-79; lighting designer Smith, Hinchman & Grylls, Detroit, 1979-82; pres. Gary Steffy Lighting Design, Ann Arbor, Mich., 1982—. Contbr. articles to profl. jours. Mem. Internat. Assn. Lighting Designers, Illuminating Engring. Soc. N. Am. Republican. Lutheran. Avocation: stamp collecting. Office: 315 E Eisenhower Pkwy Suite 216 Ann Arbor MI 48104

STEFOSKI, DUSAN, neurologist; b. Osijek, Yugoslavia, Feb. 25, 1947; came to U.S., 1974; s. Vladimir and Lilly (Görög) Stefoski. MD, U. Zagreb, Yugoslavia, 1970. Diplomate Am. Bd. Psychiatry and Neurology. Resident in neurology Presby.-St. Luke's Hosp., Chgo., 1974-76; resident in neuropathology Stanford U. Hosp., 1976; attending neurologist Presby.-St. Luke's Hosp., Chgo., 1977—; instr. neurology, Rush Med. Coll., Chgo., 1976-77, asst. prof., 1977—; dir. Clin. Research Lab., Rush Multiple Sclerosis Ctr., Chgo., 1984—. Contbr. numerous articles to profl. jours. Fellow Am. Acad. Neurolgy; mem. AAAS, N.Y. Acad. Sci., Sigma Xi. Office: Rush Presby St Lukes Med Ctr 1725 W Harrison St Chicago IL 60612

STEGALL, TRIPP (ELBERT S.), III, accountant, finance executive; b. Jackson, Tenn., Oct. 26, 1952; s. Elbert S. (I.O.) and Mildred (Beman) S.; m. Nancy Thorn, Nov. 24, 1979; children: Thomas Baldwin, Jonathan Hays Thorn and Martha Beman (twins). BS, Vanderbilt U., 1974; MBA, Memphis State U., 1977. Accountant Peat, Marwich, Mitchell and Co., Memphis, 1977-79; accountant, cons. Union Planters Nat. Bank, Memphis, 1980; exec. v.p. Vining Sparks Securities, Inc., Memphis, 1981-83; pres., chief exec. officer Plansmith Securities, Inc., Palatine, Ill., 1984—. Mem. Am. Inst. CPA's, Ill. Soc. CPA's, Tenn. Soc. CPA's. Republican. Mem. Community Ch. Home and Office: 767 Quail Run Inverness IL 60067

STEGER, JOHN FRANCIS, dentist; b. Waterloo, Iowa, Mar. 18, 1939; s. Gilbert T. and Bernice C. (Freymann) S.; m. Karla Jean (Krapfl), Feb. 25, 1962. BS, Loras Coll., Dubuque, Iowa, 1961, teaching cert., 1962; DDS, U. Iowa, 1966. Dentist USPHS, Cleve., 1966-68, Dubuque Dental Assocs., PC, Iowa, 1968-86. Mem. ADA, Tri-State Dentistry for Children (past pres.), Iowa Dental Assn., Dubuque County Dental Assn., Dubuque Dist. Dental Assn., Gold Wing Rd. Riders Assn. Lodge: Elks. Office: 1890 JF Kennedy Rd Dubuque IA 52001

STEGER, JOSEPH A., university president. Formerly sr. v.p. and provost U. Cin., pres., 1984—. Office: U Cin Office of Pres Cincinnati OH 45221

STEGER, PAUL A., manufacturing company executive; b. Buffalo, N.Y., May 11, 1950. Mktg. rep. B.F. Goodrich Co., Akron, Ohio, 1975-77, supr. mktg. communications, 1977-79; mktg. mgr. Acme Burgess, Grayslake, Ill., 1979-80, Estech, Inc., Chgo., 1980-83; dir. product prodn. and devel. Estech Branded Fertilizers, Fairview Heights, Ill., 1983-86; v.p. product promotion and devel. Vigoro Industries, Inc., Fairview Heights, Ill., 1986—. Dwight D. Eisenhower scholar Eisenhower Coll., 1970-72. Mem. Am. Mktg. Assn., Am. Mgmt. Assn. Lodge: Elks. Office: Vigoro Industries Inc 2007 W Hwy 50 Fairview Heights IL 62208

STEGMAN, JOSEPH ANTHONY, electronics manufacturer's representative firm executive; b. Covington, Ky., Nov. 12, 1930; s. Carl Edward and Leona Elizabeth (Schmitz) S.; m. Suzanne Terese Santel, June 18, 1955; children: Judith, Jennifer, Janet, Jill, Joseph Scott, Bradley. BEE, U. Ky., 1958. Elect. engr. City of Cin., 1958-60; sales engr. Semiconductor div. Hughes Aircraft, Cin., 1960-62; mfrs. rep., sales engr. R.O. Whitesell and Assoc., Cin., 1962-83; pres. Stegman Blaine Mktg., Cin., 1983—. Served to staff sgt. U.S. Army, 1951-53. Mem. Engring. Soc. Cin., Nat. Fedn. Ind. Bus., Electronic Representative Assn., Cin. C. of C., Eta Kappa Nu. Avocations: photography, woodworking, tennis, electronics. Office: Stegman Blaine Mktg 8444 Winton Rd Cincinnati OH 45231

STEHMAN, FREDERICK BATES, gynecologic oncologist, educator; b. Washington, July 20, 1946; s. Vernon Andrew and Elizabeth Coats (Bates) S.; m. Helen Sellinger, July 17, 1971; children—Christine Renee, Eileen Patricia, Andrea Kathleen, Lara Michelle. A.B., U. Mich., 1968, M.D., 1972. Diplomate Am. Bd. Ob-gyn. Resident in ob-gyn. U. Kans. Med. Ctr., Kansas City, 1972-75, resident in surgery, 1975-77; fellow in gynecol. oncology UCLA, 1977-79; asst. prof., attending staff Ind. U. Med. Ctr., Indpls., 1979-83, assoc. prof., 1983-87, prof., 1987—, chief gynecol. oncology, 1984—; chief ob-gyn service Wishard Meml. Hosp., Indpls., 1987—. Author: (with B.J. Masterson and R.P. Carter) Gynecologic Oncology for Medical Students, 1975; also articles. Nat. Cancer Inst. grantee, 1981—. Fellow Am. Coll. Obstetricians and Gynecologists, ACS (chpt. dir. 1984—); mem. AMA, Am. Soc. Clin. Oncology, Am. Cancer Soc., Ind. Med. Assn., Assn. Profs. Gynecology and Obstetrics, Central Assn. Obstetricians and Gynecologists, Gynecol. Oncology Group, K.E. Krantz Soc., Marion County Med. Soc., Radiation Therapy Oncology Group, Soc. Gynecol. Oncologists, Western Assn. Gynecol. Oncologists, Phi Chi. Office: Ind U Med Ctr Wishard Meml Hosp 1101 W 10th Indianapolis IN 46204

STEICHEN, JAMES MATTHEW, agricultural engineer, educator; b. Stillwater, Okla., Nov. 14, 1947; s. John Henry and Ione Elizabeth (Schroeder) S.; m. Ethel Marie Honeyman, Aug. 17, 1968; children: Christine, Laurel, Bethany. BS, Okla. State U., 1970, PhD, 1974. Registered profl. engr. State extension specialist U. Mo., Columbia, 1974-78; asst. prof. Kans. State U., Manhattan, 1978-80, assoc. prof., 1980—; speaker Ctr. Govt. Tng., Nashville, 1987—. Contbr. articles to profl. jours. Co-chmn. com. Benefit Auction for Sch., Manhattan, 1984-85; senator faculty Kans. State U., 1987—. Grantee Bur. Reclaimation, 1979-81, Kans. Water Resources Research Inst., 1982-83. Mem. Am. Soc. Agrl. Engrs. (chmn. erosion group 1985—), Soil Conservation Soc. Am. (pres. 1981-82), Kans. Engring. Soc. (pres. 1983-84), Sigma Xi. Democrat. Roman Catholic. Avocations: reading, travel. Home: 509 Valley Dr Manhattan KS 66502 Office: Kans State U Agrl Engring Dept Seaton Hall Manhattan KS 66506

STEICHMANN, KATHLEEN CAROL, teacher; b. Quincy, Ill., Dec. 25, 1942; d. Earl Washburn McCune and Elizabeth Marie (Hall) Mosley; children: Trudi, Heather. BS in Elementary Edn., Western Ill. U., 1965; MS in Elementary Edn., No. Ill. U., 1972, degree in Ednl. Adminstrn., 1983; Reading Specialist degree, Nat. Coll. Edn., 1986. Tchr. Fox Lake (Ill.) Schs., 1965-68; Title I remedial reading tchr. Grant Reading Co-op, Fox Lake, 1972-81; 3d grade tchr. Gavin Dist. #37, Ingleside, Ill., 1981—, mem. reading com., 1987. sec., treas., pres., trustee Fox Lake Library Dist.; publicity chmn. Midlothian Scottish Pipe Band, Mundelein, Ill., 1979—. Mem. Internat. Reading Assn. (area rep. Evanston 1987), AAUW, Fox Lake PTO, Gavin PTA, Scottish Cultural Soc., Elgin Scottish Soc., Pi Delta Epsilon. Republican. Episcopalian. Lodge: Order of Eastern Star (matron Grayslake chpt. 1972). Avocations: golf, sewing, cooking, reading. Home: 208 Woodlock Ingleside IL 60041 Office: Gavin Sch Dist #37 26016 W Grand Ave Ingleside IL 60041

STEIGER, FREDRIC ADAMS, child and adolescent psychiatrist; b. Cleve., Nov. 15, 1945. BA, Oberlin Coll., 1967; MD, Northwestern U., 1971. Resident in psychiatry Northwestern U. Med. Sch., Chgo., 1971-74; child psychiatry fellow Med. Coll. Wis., Milw., 1975-76, asst. prof., 1976—; pvt. practice specializing in child psychiatry Milw., 1982—. Served to maj. U.S. Army, 1977-79. Mem. Am. Acad. Child Psychiatry, Am. Psychiat. Assn., Wis. Psychiat. Assn., State Med. Soc. Wis., Med. Soc. Milw. County. Office: 2350 N Lake Dr Milwaukee WI 53211

STEIL, GORDON ELWYN, perforated materials manufacturing company executive; b. Garner, Iowa, Feb. 17, 1920; s. Jacob Nicholas and Mabel (Rasmus) S.; m. Nathalie B. Knox, Dec. 5, 1942; children—Mark, Blythe, Linda. B.S. in C.E., Iowa State U., 1942. With Curtis-Wright Aircraft Corp., Buffalo, 1942-44; with Page Engring. Co., McCook, Ill., 1946-72; pres. Harrington & King Perforating Co., Inc., Chgo., 1972 ; pres., dir. H&K South, Cleveland, Tenn.; pres., dir. H&K West, San Jose, Calif. Pres., River Forest Park Bd., 1975-78; mem. River Forest Traffic Commn., 1972-75. Served with USNR, 1944-46. Mem. ASME, Am. Mgmt. Assn. Republican. Presbyterian. Clubs: Union League, Big Foot Country. Patentee in field. Office: 5655 W Fillmore St Chicago IL 60644

STEIL, LYMAN KENT, professional speaker, communications expert; b. Albert Lea, Minn., July 23, 1938; s. Leland Kenneth and Gretchen (Johnston) S.; m. DeAnna Therese Halvorson, July 27, 1938; children: Scott Alan, Sara Ann, Stacy Leigh. AA, U. Minn., 1962, BS, 1964, MA, 1969; PhD, Wayne State U., 1977. Tchr. New Lenox (Ill.) High Sch., 1964-65; teaching asst. U. Minn., Mpls., 1965-66; instr. speech communications, dir. debate/forensics Macalaster Coll., St. Paul, 1966-71; chmn. speech communication div. dept. rhetoric U. Minn., St. Paul, 1972-82; pres. Communication Devel. Inc., St. Paul, 1979—; lectr. communication Minn. Bur. Criminal Apprehension, St. Paul, 1975-80; mem. faculty extension and continuing edn. U. Minn., St. Paul, 1973-82; chmn. bd. dirs. Internat. Listening INst., St. Paul. Author: Listening, Training and Development: Guidelines for Human Resource Professionals, 1982, Secondary Teacher's Listening Resource Unit, 1982; co-author: Listening ... It Can Change Your Life, 1983, Effective Listening: Key to Your Success, 1983; author (video servies) Effective Listening Video Series, 1980. Served with USN, 1956-59. Mem. Nat. Speakers Assn., Minn. Nat. Speakers Assn. (bd. dirs. 1983-87), Internat. Listening Assn. (founder, pres. 1979-81, exec. dir. 1983-85, named to Listening Hall of Fame 1985). Home and Office: 25 Robb Farm Rd Saint Paul MN 55110

STEIMLE, JOHN JOSEPH, manufacturing company executive; b. Little Ferry, N.J., May 13, 1923; s. John Joseph and Ida Marie (Rupprecht) S.; m. Kathryn Ida Kohring, July 24, 1948; 1 child, Robert Edward. BS in Bus. Mgmt., Rutgers U., 1956. Prodn. control supr. Aluminum Co. Am., Edgwater, N.J., 1941-66; traffic warehouse mgr. Aluminum Co. Am., New Kensington, Pa., 1966-72; production supr. Lincoln Mfg. Co. Inc., Ft. Wayne, Ind., 1972—. Served to cpl. U.S. Army, 1943-45, PTO. Mem. VFW, Am. Legion, Delta Nu Alpha. Roman Catholic. Lodge: KC. Avocation: golf. Home: 4707 Crystal Ridge Cove Fort Wayne IN 46835 Office: Lincoln Mfg Co Inc PO Box 1229 Fort Wayne IN 46801

STEIN, ADLYN ROBINSON (MRS. HERBERT ALFRED STEIN), jewelry company executive; b. Pitts., May 8, 1908; d. Robert Stewart and Pearl (Geiger) Robinson; Mus.B., Pitts. Mus. Inst., U. Pitts., 1928; m. F. J. Hollearn, Nov. 14, 1929 (dec.); children—Adlyn (Mrs. Brandon J. Hickey), Frances (Mrs. Ralph A. Gleim); m. Allen Burnett Williams, Dec. 5, 1955 (dec.); m. Herbert Alfred Stein, Nov. 28, 1963 (dec. Oct. 1980); 1 dau., Rachel Lynn (Mrs. Stephen M. Kampfer). Treas., R. S. Robinson, Inc., Pitts., 1947—. Mem. Tuesday Musical Club, Pitts.; mem. women's com. Cleve. Orch. Mem. DAR. Republican. Anglican. Clubs: Duquesne, University, South Hills Country (Pitts.); Lakewood Country, Clifton (Cleve.). Home: 22200 Lake Rd Cleveland OH 44116

STEIN, ARNOLD, retail executive; b. Bronx, N.Y., Mar. 12, 1936; s. Jacob and Jennie (Mark) S.; m. Linda Sheryl DePoy; children—Rhonda Sheryl, Kristyn Marie, Jeremy Jacob. A.S. in Bus. Adminstrn., Vincennes U., 1955; B.B.A., Ind. U., 1957. Mgmt. trainee Sears Roebuck & Co., Massillon, Ohio, 1957-63, asst. store mgr., Newark, Ohio, 1963-65, Mid-Central Zone staff field rep., Dayton, Ohio, 1966-71, store mgr., Tiffin, Ohio, 1971-73, Elkhart, Ind., 1973-76, St. Louis, 1976-84, Fox Valley Store, Chgo., 1984—; pres. Tiffin Shopping Ctr. Assn., 1972, Pierre Moran Shopping Ctr. Assn., Elkhart; 1974-75, Crestwood Plaza Shopping Ctr. Assn., Mo., 1977-82. Bd. dirs. Urban League, Elkhart, 1974, Campfire Inc., St. Louis, 1983-84, United Way, Tiffin, 1973; mem. Heidelberg U. Assocs., Tiffin, 1973. Served with U.S. Army, 1959-60. Recipient Others award Salvation Army, Tiffin, 1973. Mem. Tiffin C. of C., Elkhart C. of C., St. Louis C. of C. Lodges: Masons, Shriners, Order Eastern Star, Royal and Select Masters. Avocations: sailing; racquetball; physical fitness.

STEIN, ARTHUR JOEL, insurance agent; b. Chgo., July 10, 1941; s. Albert and Edith (Suloway) S.; m. Susan Lynn Wilensky, June 19, 1966; children: Todd, Mitchell. BA, Columbia Coll., 1966. Mgr. Fabric Mart Draperies, Chgo., 1967-74; ins. agt. State Farm Ins. Co., Matteson, Ill., 1974—. Mem. Pi Tau Pi. Republican. Jewish. Club: Millionaire. Lodge: Rotary (v.p. Matteson club 1986). Avocations: racquetball, football. Office: State Farm Ins 4331 W 211th St Matteson IL 60443

STEIN, BERNARD ALVIN, business executive; b. Winnipeg, Can., June 4, 1923; s. Herman Louis and Rebecca (Harris) S.; m. Dorothy Lock, Jan. 1, 1942; 1 dau., Marilynn Stein Lakein. Vice-pres. food drug div. Giant Food, Inc., Washington, 1951-69; v.p., gen. mgr. Read Drug Stores, Balt., 1969-70; pres. Scotty Stores div. Sav-A-Stop, Jacksonville, Fla., 1970-71; pres., gen. mgr. Liberal Markets, Dayton, Ohio, 1971-72; pres. Pueblo Supermarkets, San Juan, P.R., 1972-74, Hills Supermarkets, Brentwood, N.Y., 1974-75, Allied Supermarkets, Detroit, 1976-78, Chatham Supermarkets, Detroit, 1978-81, Network Assocs., Chgo., 1981—. Mem. Presdl. Com. for Emergency Food Controls, 1969. Served with USAAF, 1943-45. Decorated Air medal. Home: 151 N Michigan Ave Chicago IL 60601 Office: Network Assocs 180 N Wacker Dr Chicago IL 60606

STEIN, DALE F., technical university president; b. Kingston, Minn., Dec. 24, 1935; s. David Frank and Zelda Jane S.; m. Audrey Dean Bloemke, June 7, 1958; children—Pam, Derek. B.S. in Metallurgy, U. Minn., 1958; Ph.D., Rensselaer Poly. Inst., Troy, N.Y., 1963. Research metallurgist research lab. Gen. Electric Co., Schnectady, N.Y., 1958-67; asso. prof. U. Minn., 1967-71; prof. metall. engring., head dept. Mich. Tech. U., Houghton, 1971-77; head mining engring. Mich. Tech. U., 1974-77, v.p. acad. affairs, 1977-79, pres., 1979—; cons. NSF, Dept. Energy, 1972—. Contbr. articles to profl. jours. Fellow Metall. Soc. (pres. 1979, inst. Hardy Gold medal 1965), Am. Soc. Metals (Geisler award Eastern N.Y. chpt. 1967); mem. AIME, AAAS, Nat. Acad. Engring., Sigma Xi, Phi Kappa Phi, Tau Beta Pi, Alpha Sigma Nu. Mem. United Ch. Club: Houghton Rotary. Office: Mich Tech Univ Houghton MI 49931 *

STEIN, DAVID S., health care education educator; b. Bklyn., Apr. 6, 1947. BA, SUNY, Buffalo, 1969; EdM, U. Rochester, 1971; PhD, U. Mich., 1976. Research assoc. U. Mich., Ann Arbor, 1973-75; edn. dir. Children's Hosp., Columbus, Ohio, 1975-77; asst. prof. health edn. Ohio State U., Columbus, 1977-83, assoc. prof., 1983—; dir. edn. Ohio State U. Hosp., Columbus, 1978—; pres. David Stein Assocs., Columbus, 1980—. Mem. smoking cessation inst. Ohio Lung Assn., Columbus, 1985—; first aid instr. Cen. Ohio Red Cross, Columbus, 1983—. Served to 1st lt. USAF, 1972-73. Mem. Am. Soc. Health Care Edn. (chmn. 1986, dist. chmn. 1980), Am. Soc. Tng. and Devel., Am. Pub. Health Assn., Ohio Soc. Health Care Edn. (pres. 1980-82, Presdl. award 1986), Phi Kappa Psi. Avocations: stamp collecting, photography, bicycling. Home: 173 N Cassingham Rd Bexley OH 43209 Office: Ohio State U Hosps 410 W 10th B415 Columbus OH 43210

STEIN, ELEANOR BANKOFF, judge; b. N.Y.C., Jan. 24, 1923; d. Jacob and Sarah (Rashkin) Bankoff; m. Frank S. Stein, May 27, 1947; children—Robert B., Joan Jenkins, William M. Student, Barnard Coll., 1940-42; B.S. in Econs., Columbia U., 1944; LL.B., NYU, 1949. Bar: N.Y. 1950, Ind. 1976, U.S. Supreme Ct. 1980. Atty. Hillis & Button, Kokomo, Ind., 1975-76, Paul Hillis, Kokomo, 1976-78, Bayliff, Harrigan, Kokomo, 1978-80; judge Howard County Ct., Kokomo, 1980—; co-juvenile referee Howard County Juvenile Ct., 1976-78. Mem. Republicans Women's Assn. Kokomo, 1980—; bd. dirs. Howard County Legal Aid Soc., 1976-80; dir. Howard County Ct. Alcohol and Drug Services Program, 1982—; bd. advisors St. Joseph Hosp., Kokomo, 1979—; commn. mem. Kokomo Bd. Human Relations, 1967-70. Mem. law rev. bd. NYU Law Rev., 1947-48. Mem. Am. Judicature Soc., Ind. Jud. Assn., Nat. Assn. Women Judges, ABA, Ind. Bar Assn., Howard County Bar Assn. Jewish. Clubs: Kokomo Country, Altrusa. Home: 3204 Tally Ho Dr Kokomo IN 49602 Office: Howard County Ct Howard County Courthouse Kokomo IN 46901

STEIN, GERTRUDE EMILIE, educator, pianist, soprano; b. Ironton, Ohio; d. Samuel A. and Emilie M. (Pollach) S.; Mus.B., Capitol Coll. Oratory and Music, 1927; B.A., Wittenberg Coll., 1929, M.A., 1931, B.S. in Edn., 1945; Ph.D., U. Mich., 1948; piano and voice student Cin. Coll. Conservatory Music; cert. in piano Cin. Coll. Music, 1939. Music supr. Centralized County Schs. Ohio, Williamsburg, 1932-37; dir. jr. high sch. music, 1937-68, elem. music, 1968-71; mem. faculty Adult Evening Sch. Springfield (Ohio) Public Schs., 1951-68; head dept. music, asso. prof. piano and music edn. Tex. Lutheran Coll., Seguin, 1948-49. Donor, founder Rev. Dr. and Mrs. Samuel A. Stein Meml. Funds, 1955—. Mem. AAUW, Am. Symphony Orch. League, NEA, Ohio Edn. Assn., Ohio Assn. Supervision and Curriculum Devel., Council for Exceptional Children, Assn. Tchr. Educators, Ohio Assn. Adult Educators, Associated Council Arts, Met. Opera Guild, Soc. Educators and Scholars, Am. Film Inst., Ohio Music Tchrs. Assn., Nat. Story League, Music Tchrs. Nat. Assn., Music Educators Nat. Conf., Nat. Assn. Schs. Music, Nat. Fedn. Music Clubs (spl. mem. Ohio), Amateur Chamber Music Players, Women's Assn. Springfield Symphony Orch., Springfield Authors Guild, Nat. Fedn. Bus. and Profl. Women, Zonta Internat., Phi Kappa Phi (hon.), Pi Lambda Theta (hon.). Lutheran. Club: Fortnightly Musical (Springfield). Contbr. articles to profl. jours.; research in field. Home: 133 N Lowry Ave Springfield OH 45504

STEIN, JAY WOBITH, social and political sciences educator; b. Sauk Centre, Minn., June 19, 1920; s. Julius A. and Emaline (Wobith) S.; married, 1953; children: Holly Jayne, Navida Carol, April Jae, Andrew John, John Henry. BA, U. Minn., 1942; MA, Stanford U., 1949, Syracuse U., 1960; MS, Columbia U., 1950, PhD, 1952. Dir. library, asst. prof. social studies Southwestern U., Memphis, 1954-57; adminstv. assoc. to v.p. Syracuse (N.Y.) U., 1958-61; faculty Maxwell Sch., Syracuse, 1958-61; asst. to pres. Drake U., Des Moines, Iowa, 1961-64; dir. State Higher Edn. Commn., Des Moines, 1964-67; dean Coll. Arts and Scis., prof. polit. sci. Western Ill. U., Macomb, 1967-69, prof. polit. sci. and edn., 1969—; catalogue planner N.Y. Pub. Library, 1953; proposal reviewer U.S. Dept. Edn. Fund for the Improvement of Post-secondary Edn., 1982. Author: The Mind and the Sword, 1961, How Society Governs Education, 1975, Mass Media, Education and a Better Society, 1979; editor Scholar and Educator jour., 1977-85; contbr. articles to profl. jours. Mem. Council of Faculties of Bd. Govs. State Colls. and Univs., 1980-86, chmn. 1984-85; mem. Macomb 2000, 1982-83; active with church and civic groups. Served to lt. USN, 1942-46. Coolidge Foundation fellow, 1984; grantee, U. Research Council and others. Mem. AAAS, ALA, AAUP, Am. Assn. Higher Edn., Am. Polit. Sci. Assn., Am. Recorder Soc., Am. Soc. Pub. Adminstn., Nat. Soc. Study of Edn., Soc. Advancement Edn., Soc. Educators and Scholars (founder 1976, exec. dir. 1976-82, chmn. bd. dirs. 1980—), Am. Arbitration Assn, World Leisure and Recreation Assn., Phi Beta Kappa, Phi Kappa Phi, Phi Delta Kappa, Alpha Mu Gamma, Pi Sigma Alpha, Lamda Alpha Psi. Lodge: Rotary (Macomb). Avocations: books, swimming, bicycling, music. Office: Western Ill U 900 W Adams Macomb IL 61455

STEIN, J(UANITA) SUE, instructional systems specialist, educator; b. Urbana, Ill., Jan. 4, 1950; d. James Stanley and Claudine Sara (Perry) S.; m. Douglas Clyde Rose, Nov. 15, 1980. BS in Park Adminstrn., U. Ill., 1972, MS in Outdoor Edn., 1973; EdD in Adult Edn., Ind. U., 1983. Area camping specialist Ill. Coop Extension, Jacksonville, Ill., 1973-74; state camping specialist Iowa Coop Extension, Ames, 1974-79; dir. ednl. services Am. Camping Assn., Martinsville, Ind., 1979-83; edn. specialist Ft. Harrison, U.S. Army, Indpls., 1984-85; instr., systems specialist Def. Logistics Agy., Dept. Def., Columbus, Ohio, 1985—. Sr. editor numerous profl. publs., 1979-83. Named one of Outstanding Young Women Am., 1978; recipient Melvin A. Fineburg award Ind. U. Meml. Union, Bloomington, Ind., 1983. Mem. Nat. Soc. Performance and Instruction. Avocations: volksmarching, acqua aerobics, reading. Home: 74 E Patterson Columbus OH 43201

STEIN, MICHAEL JOHN, health care consultant; b. Chgo., Mar. 26, 1942; s. James R. and Helen E. (Waterhouse) S. B.A. in Math., DePaul U., 1964; M.S. in Mgmt., Northwestern U., 1976. Chief mgmt. research sect. Def. Atomic Support Agy., Albuquerque, 1966-67, dir. edn. and tng. programs, 1967-68; mgr. med. assistance program Cook County, Chgo., 1969-72; dir. med. services program No. Cook County, 1972-73; dir. med. services City of Chgo. Programs, 1973-74; spl. cons. for health care Ill. State Legislature, Markham, Ill., 1974-79, dir. health programs Ill. Legis. Adv. Com., Chgo., 1980; fin. cons. Hyatt Med. Mgmt. Services, Inc., Chgo., 1981-82; sr. cons. Mediflex Systems, Evanston, Ill., 1983—; cons. in mgmt. Recipient disting. service award for uncovering fraud in fed. med. care programs Chgo. Assn. Commerce and Industry, 1977. Mem. Assn. for Computing Machinery, Grad. Mgmt. Assn., Am. Coll. Hosp. Adminstrs., Chgo. Health Execs. Forum, Air Force Assn., Chgo. Zool. Soc., Northwestern U., DePaul U. alumni assns., Chgo. Council Fgn. Relations, Beta Alpha Psi. Club: Century. Home: 3044 W Addison St Chicago IL 60618 Office: 60 Gould Ctr Suite 900 Rolling Meadows IL 60008

STEIN, PAUL DAVID, cardiologist; b. Cin., Apr. 13, 1934; s. Simon and Sadie (Friedman) S.; m. Janet Louise Tucker, Aug. 14, 1966; children—Simon, Douglas, Rebecca. B.S., U. Cin., 1955, M.D., 1959. Intern Jewish Hosp., Cin., 1959-60, med. resident, 1961-62; med. resident Gorgas Hosp., C.Z., 1960-61; fellow in cardiology U. Cin., 1962-63, Mt. Sinai Hosp., N.Y.C., 1963-64; research fellow in medicine Harvard Med. Sch., Boston, 1964-66; asst. dir. cardiac catheterization lab. Baylor U. Med. Ctr., Dallas, 1966-67; asst. prof. medicine Creighton U., Omaha, 1967-69; assoc. prof. medicine U. Okla., Oklahoma City, 1969-73; prof. research medicine U. Okla. Coll. Medicine, Oklahoma City, 1973-76; dir. cardiovascular research Henry Ford Hosp., Detroit, 1976—. Author: A Physical and Physiological Basis for the Interpretation of Cardiac Auscultation: Evaluations Based Primarily on Second Sound and Ejection Murmurs, 1981. Contbr. articles to profl. jours. Am. Heart Assn. Council on Clin. Cardiology fellow, 1971, Council on Circulation fellow, 1972. Fellow Am. Coll. Cardiology, Am. Coll. Chest Physicians; mem. Am. Physiol. Soc., Central Soc. Clin. Research, ASME. Office: Henry Ford Hosp 2799 W Grand Blvd Detroit MI 48202

STEINBACH, ALAN HENRY, church official; b. St. Louis, Aug. 5, 1930; s. John Emil and Erna (Gieselmann) S.; m. Ruth A. Wischmeier, June 28, 1953; children—Steven, Carol. B.S., Concordia Coll., 1952; M.A., San Diego State U., 1957; M.Sci. Teaching, U. Ariz., 1964; Ph.D., U. Tex., 1968; cert. in theology Concordia Seminary, St. Louis, 1987. Sch. prin., San Diego, 1952-61; prof. chemistry St. John's Coll., Winfield, Kans., 1961-70, acad. dean, 1970-78; v.p., acad. dean Bethany Coll., Lindsborg, Kans., 1979-85; dir.student Personnel services Bd. Hgher Edn. Services, Luth. Ch.-Mo. Synod, 1985—. ednl. cons. Kans. Dist. Luth. Ch.-Mo. Synod, 1979-85. Mem. Total Community Devel., Winfield, 1970-72; bd. dirs. Kans. Dist., Lutheran Ch.-Mo. Synod, 1973-85; vice chmn. Cowley County chpt. Am. Cancer Soc., 1975-76; chmn. Kans. Corrections Ombudsman Bd., 1976-84. Named Winfield Citizen of Month, Optimist Club, 1978. Mem. Nat. Assn. Student Personnel Adminstrs., Phi Delta Kappa. Lodge: Rotary (Winfield). Contbr. chpts. to books, publs. in field. Home: 518 E Essex Saint Louis MO 63122 Office: Internat Hdqrs Luth Ch-Mo Synod 1333 S Kirkwood Saint Louis MO 63122

STEINBECK, DAVID WILLIAM, publisher; b. St. Louis; s. Elmer W. and L. Virginia (Smith) S.; m. JoAnn R. Crawford, Aug. 26, 1956; children: Daniel, Deanna, Jennifer. BA, Culver-Stockton Coll., 1952. Asst. editor Dem.-Message, Mt. Sterling, Ill., 1947-52, 54-55; pub. relations dir. Culver-Stockton Coll., Canton, Mo., 1955-64, asst. to pres., 1964-68; owner Press-News Jour., Canton, 1968—; pres. Golden Eagle Enterprises, Canton, 1978—. Served to sgt. U.S. Army, 1952-54. Author: (musicals) High and Dry, 1976, Pearl, 1982, Dixie Gray, 1983, The Prince and the Pauper, 1985. Pres. Human Rights Commn., Canton, 1968-70, Canton Library Bd., 1963-71. Mem. Northeastern Mo. Press Assn., Mo. Press Assn. (best photograph 1979), Canton C. of C. Democrat. Baptist. Home: Rt 2 Canton MO 63435 Office: Press News Jour 130 N 4th St Canton MO 63435

STEINBERG, ARNOLD DAVID, dentist; b. Warsaw, Poland, Oct. 30, 1930; s. Morris Arron and Leila Merium (Baum) S.; m. June Bender, June 14, 1953; children: Steven, Barbara, Ruth, Mark. DDS, Northwestern U., 1954; MS, U. Ill., 1964. Assoc. attending dentist Michael Reese Hosp., Chgo., 1958-79; practice gen. dentistry Evergreen Park, Ill., 1956—; prof. biochemistry and periodontics U. Ill. Med. Ctr., 1976—; dir. Lincoln Dental Caries Study, 1963-71. Contbr. articles to profl. jours. Served to capt. USAF, 1954-56. Epilepsy Found. grantee, 1967, 70; NIH grantee, 1970, Collagen Corp. grantee, 1981-83. Fellow Internat. Coll. Dentists, Am. Coll. Dentists, Acad. Gen. Dentistry, Acad. Dentistry Handicapped (pres. 1971-72),; mem. AAAS, Tay Sachs Assn. (med. chmn. 1959-75, med. adv. bd. 1969-73, Man of Yr. 1960). Republican. Jewish. Avocations: racquetball, computers. Home: 3724 Arcadia Skokie IL 60076 Office: 9825 S Pulaski Evergreen Park IL 60642

STEINBORN, LEONARD, pharmaceutical company executive; b. Chgo., Apr. 29, 1946; s. Ben and Pearl (Burrows) S.; m. Sharon Diane Feinglass, Dec. 24, 1977; 1 child, Melissa Ilene. BS, Elmhurst Coll., 1976. Quality engr. Baxter Travenol Labs., Morton Grove, Ill., 1969-73; quality assurance supr. Hollister Inc., Lincolnwood, Ill., 1973-77; quality assurance auditor Am. Critical Care, Mount Prospect, Ill., 1977-78; compliance mgr. Searle Labs., Skokie, Ill., 1978-82; quality assurance mgr. Abbott Labs., North Chicago, Ill., 1982-84; strategic projects leader Abbott Labs., North Chicago, 1984—; lectr. in field. Author: The Quality Assurance Manual for the Pharmaceutical and Medical Device Industries. Mem. Am. Soc. for Quality Control (cert. quality engr.).

STEINBRENNER, GEORGE EDWARD, marketing executive; b. Euclid, Ohio, June 7, 1947; s. Edward George and Easter L. (Sanger) S.; m. Grazyna Gockowski, July 31, 1971; children: Paul, Peter. BA, Wittenberg U., 1969; OPM, Harvard U., 1985. V.p. E.S. Advt. Services, Cleve., 1972-81, pres., 1982—; chmn. E.S. Advt. Services, 1987—; founding trustee, officer Historic Warehouse Dist. Devel. Corp., Cleve., 1977-84; Family Bus. Assn., 1978-85. Contbr. articles to profl. jour. Bd. dirs. Council Smaller Enteprises, Cleve. 1986. Mem. Bus. Profl. Advt. Assn., Mail Advt. Service Assn. Internat., N.E. Ohio Direct Mail Mktg. Assn. Home: 851 High St Bedford OH 44146 Office: ES Advt Services Inc 1890 E 40th St Cleveland OH 44103

STEINBRUCK, CHARLES ROBERT, sales executive; b. Ocheyedan, Iowa, Mar. 20, 1940; s. Otto Herman and Grace Helen (Greenfield) S.; m. Margaret Madeline Buysse, Aug. 24, 1963; children: Stephanie Ann Steinbruck Ehher, Kristine Robin. AA, Southwest Minn. State U., 1961. Gen. sales mgr. Coca Cola Co., Spirit Lake, Iowa, 1971-77; v.p. mktg. Atlantic (Iowa) Bottling Co., 1977-79; account mgr. Cornelius, Anoka, Minn., 1979-83, regional mgr., 1983-86, v.p. sales western div., 1986—. Avocations: woodworking, golf. Home: 2147 129th Ave NW Coon Rapids MN 55433 Office: Cornelius 1 Cornelius Place Anoka MN 55303

STEINER, HOWARD ABRAHAM, physician, radiologist; b. Cleve., June 11, 1913; s. Louis Eliazar and Bertha (Mahrer) S.; m. Bess Tomarkin, June 10, 1945; children: Joanne Gerson, Paul Lewis. BS, Ohio State U., 1934; MD, Washington U., St. Louis, 1938; MS, U. Colo., 1942. Diplomate Am. Bd. Radiology. Intern Jewish Hosp., St. Louis, 1938; resident St. Louis Maternity Hosp., 1939, Colo. Gen. Hosp., 1942; practice medicine specializing in radiology Huron Rd. Hosp., 1946-49; chief dept. radiology Sharon (Pa.) Gen. Hosp., 1949-57, Suburban Community Hosp., Cleve., 1957-78; asst. dir. dept. radiology VA Med. Ctr., Cleve., 1978—; Past pres. Mercer County (Pa.) Med. Soc., Mercer County Cancer Soc., Mercer County Tb Soc., Sharon Gen. Hosp. Med. Staff. Contbr. articles to profl. jours. Served to capt. Med. Service Corps, AUS, 1942-46. Mem. AMA, Radiol. Soc. Am., Cleve. Acad. Medicine, Ohio State Med. Assn., Ohio State Radiol. Soc., Suburban Community Hosp. Med. Soc. (past pres.). Democrat. Jewish. Club: Temple Men's (Cleve.) (bd. dirs., bd. trustees 1985—, past pres.). Avocation: golf. Office: VA Med Ctr 10701 East Blvd Cleveland OH 44106

STEINER, ISIDORE, podiatrist; b. Bklyn., Oct. 23, 1951; s. Solomon and Felice Steiner; m. Bracha Kahn, June 24, 1973; children: Joshua, Andrew, Eric, Lauren. BS, Bklyn. Coll., 1974; DPM, Pa. Coll. Podiatric Medicine, 1978; JD, U. Detroit, 1987. Diplomate Am. Bd. Podiatric Surgery, Internat. Coll. Podiatric Laser Surgery. Pvt. practice podiatry Southfield and Howell, Mich., 1979—; dir. state podiatric preceptorship program, Highland, 1983—; adj. prof. Scholl Coll. Podiatric Medicine, Chgo.; adj. faculty clinician Ohio Coll. Podiatric medicine. Contbr. articles to profl. jours. Fellow Acad. Ambulatory Foot Surgery; mem. Am. Podiatric Med. Assn., Am. Coll. Foot Surgeons (assoc.), Mich. Podiatric Med. Assn., Am. Soc. Law and Medicine. Office: 1221 Byron Rd Howell MI 48843

STEINER, LINDA CLAIRE, communications educator; b. Schenectady, N.Y., Mar. 1, 1950; d. Frank Charles and Helen (Edwards) S.; m. Edward Henry Salomon, June 5, 1977; children: Sarah, Paul. BA, U. Pa., 1972; PhD, U. Ill., 1979. Editorial asst. Grose Pubs., Ballston Spa, N.Y., 1972-73; teaching asst. U. Ill., Urbana, 1973-78; prof. Govs. State U., University Park, Ill., 1978—. Co-author: And Baby Makes Two, 1984; contbr. articles to profl. jours. Chmn. adv. com. Cable TV, Oak Park, Ill., 1983—; dir. YWCA Rape Hotline, Urbana, 1975-77. Home: 847 S Ridgeland Oak Park IL 60304 Office: Govs State U Stuenkel Rd University Park IL 60466

STEINER, RODNEY D., tool compny executive; b. DeWitt, Iowa, Sept. 10, 1927; s. Fay A. and Edna C. (Levsen) S.; m. Mary C. Merkel, Feb. 16, 1951; children: Craig D., Marcia L. Steiner Brown. Student, Cornell Coll., Mt. Vernon, Iowa, 1948; CLU, The Am. Coll., 1971. Prin. Steiner's IGA, Davenport, Iowa, 1953-63, Regal Laun-Dry Clean, East Moline, Ill., 1963-71; spl. agt. Prudential Life Ins. Co., Davenport, 1963-83; agt. Northwestern Nat. Life Ins. Co., Davenport, 1983-86; pres. Davenport (Iowa) Tools, 1986—. Mem. Davenport Life Underwriters Assn. (pres. 1971-72, States Best 1972), Quad City CLU's (pres. 1975-76, v.p. 1986-87). Republican. Mem. United Ch. of Christ. Avocations: needlepoint, crewel work, stamps. Home: 2521 Jersey Ridge Davenport IA 52803

STEINIGER, (IRENE) MIRIAM LARMI, child development specialist; b. Weirton, W.Va., Dec. 20, 1916; d. (Kustaa) Edward and Aune Ellen (Raitanen) Larmi; B.S. in Edn., Ohio State U., 1936; M.A., Miami U., Oxford, Ohio, 1964; Ed.D., U. Cin., 1975; m. Erich W. Steiniger, June 6, 1941; children—Erika, Fredrik, Anthony, Karsten, Theron. Tchr., Ohio Sch. for Deaf, Columbus, 1937-41, 44-46; tchr. English and lit. Mason (Ohio) High Sch., 1955-56; tchr. elementary schs., Hamilton, Ohio, 1956-59, tchr. of deaf, Hamilton Pub. Schs., 1959-63, speech and hearing therapist, 1963-70; tchr.-cons. for neurologically handicapped, Hamilton, 1970-72; cooperating tchr. Tchr. Tng. Program, Miami U., Hamilton, 1970-72; vis. asst. prof., adj. vis. prof. U. Cin., 1972-75, asst. prof., 1975-79; asst. dir. presch. programs Cin. Center for Devel. Disorders, 1975-79; dir. Children's Diagnostic Center, Inc., Butler County, Ohio, 1979-83; ret., 1983; early childhood diagnostic cons., 1983—; teaching cons. Perceptual Motor Workshops, Miami U., 1970, 71; dir., planner tchr. tng. projects and workshops Hamilton City Schs., 1965, 68, 69, 71. Vice pres. Talawanda Bd. Edn., Oxford, Ohio, 1968-72; pres., chmn. coms. LWV, Oxford; ednl. com. Butler County Mental Hygiene Assn.; leader Girl Scouts U.S.A., Dan Beard council Boy Scouts Am.; chmn. Early Childhood Edn. Task Force, SW Ohio Early Childhood Coalition Task Force on Certification; Sunday sch. tchr. Lutheran Ch.; mem. CORVA. Recipient ann. action award Action for Handicapped, 1983; ACT award ACTion for Handicapped, Inc., 1983; Martha Holden Jennings Found. grantee, 1968; grantee Ohio Dept. MR/DD and Ohio DD Planning Council, 1981-83. Mem. Butler County (pres. 1969, legis. chmn. 1964—, dir. 1964—), Ohio, Nat. councils exceptional children, Am. (cert.), Cin., Ohio, Nat. speech and hearing assns., Tri-County (certificate of appreciation 1974), Ohio, Nat. assns. for children with learning disabilities, Nat., Ohio, Cin. assns. for edn. of young children, Butler County Assn. Edn. Young Children, Day Care and Child Devel. Council Am., Inter-Univ. Council for Exceptional Children, AAUP, Delta Kappa Gamma. Democrat. Contbr. to Piagetian research book. Home: 208 Beechpoint Dr Oxford OH 45056

STEINKAMP, CAROL SUE, financial analyst; b. Evansville, Ind., Sept. 26, 1956; d. Henry Landolin and Mary Virginia (Whitehead) S.; m. Gregg D. Lauderbaugh, June 12, 1982. BS in Indsl. Mgmt., Purdue U., 1978; MBA, U. Chgo., 1987. CPA, Ill. Sr. cons. Price Waterhouse, Chgo., 1979-84; sr. fin. analyst Comdisco, Rosemont, Ill., 1984—. Mem. Am. Inst. CPA's, Ill. Soc. CPA's, U. Chgo. Women's Bus. Group. Avocations: travel, biking. Office: Comdisco Inc 6400 Shafer Ct Rosemont IL 60018

STEINKAMP, CHERYL DUNLOP, small business owner, consultant; b. Chadron, Nebr., Mar. 28, 1944; d. Ralph William and Mariana Mildred (Cunningham) Dunlop; m. Robert Theodore Steinkamp, Aug. 19, 1967; children—Theodore Bewick, Rebecca Anne. Student Stephens Coll., 1962-63; B.A., William Jewell Coll., Liberty, Mo., 1965-67. Speech therapist Headstart Program, Hutchinson, Kans., 1967; speech instr. William Chrisman Jr. High Sch., Independence Mo., 1967-69; dist. dir. Sunflower council Campfire Girls, Inc., 1969-73; dir. alumni services William Jewell Coll., Liberty, 1979-83, dir. devel. and alumni relations, 1984-85, chief devel. officer, 1985—; now owner, pres. Equus and Muse Cons. Past officer, bd. dirs. Liberty Symphony, Mo., 1982—; mem. staff. parrish relations com. United Methodist. Ch., 1983, trustee, 1986—; mem. Liberty Fall Festival Com., 1979-83; bd. dirs. Jr. Women's Philharmonic Assn., Kansas City, 1974-77; mem. exec. bd. North Suburban Swim Conf. Mem. Council Advancement and Support Edn. Republican. Meth. Clubs: Kansas City, Central Exchange; Liberty Hills Country. Avocations: writing poetry, songs; traveling.

STEINKAMP, JAMES ROBERT, photographer; b. Burlington, Iowa, July 7, 1954; s. Roland Edwin and Frances Mae (Kramer) S.; m. Maureen Catherine Gallagher, Sept. 18, 1983; 1 child, Sean Connor. BA with honors, Columbia Coll., Chgo., 1980. Photographer Murphy/Jahn Architects, Chgo., 1979-87, Steinkamp/Ballogg Photography, Chgo., 1983—. Several one-man traveling exhibits. Mem. Am. Soc. Mag. Photographers, Columbia Coll. Gallery. Roman Catholic. Home: 4944 N Kedvale Chicago IL 60630 Office: Steinkamp/Ballogg Photography 311 N Desplaines Suite 409 Chicago IL 60606

STEINLAGE, WILLIAM SCOTT, insurance company executive; b. St. Louis, Aug. 11, 1946; s. Henry J. and Rosemary L. (Pallmeier) S.; m. Elizabeth J. Byrne, Aug. 19, 1967 (div. Oct. 1982); children: Tracy, William Jr.; m. Sandy A. Parker, Mar. 31, 1984; 1 child, Michael Henry. BS, Northeastern Mo. U., 1968. CLU. Agt. Reliable Life Ins. Co., St. Louis, 1971-75, asst. mgr., 1975-78; dist. mgr. Reliable Life Ins. Co., Columbia, Mo., 1978-84; v.p. Reliable Life Ins. Co., St. Louis, 1984—, also bd. dirs.; tchr. ins. course Life Underwriters TNg. Course, 1982-83; vice chmn. Inter-Co. Mktg. Group. Served with U.S. Army, 1968-70. Mem. Mo. Life Underwriters (chmn. 1981-84), Mo. Vet. Assn. (bd. dirs.). Republican. Roman Catholic. Avocations: golf, motorcycling. Home: 6 Stonebriar Ct Ballwin MO 63011 Office: Reliable Life Ins Co 231 W Lockwood Saint Louis MO 63119

STEINMAN, CHARLES HUNTER, electrical engineer; b. Pocahontas, Ark., May 18, 1958; s. Hunter Andrew and Serena Bea (Miller) S.; m. Jane Ellen Tabor, Sept. 15, 1984; children: Valerie Clason, Kenneth Clason. ASEE, North Cen. Tech. Coll., 1984; student, Cook's Inst. Electronic Engring., 1986—. Electronics salesman Servex Electronics, Mansfield, Ohio, 1977-83; instrumentation engr. City of Mansfield, 1984-85; with service dept., engr. Universal Enterprises, Mansfield, 1985-86, research and devel. engr., 1986—; cons. engr. Comsumer Elec. Mfg., Ontario, Ohio, 1984—; instr. North Cen. Tech. Coll., Mansfield, 1987—. Author (programs) Diskfile, Disksplit, Whodos; inventor 4/8 Point Temperature Monitor. Mem. Nat. Arbor Day Found., 1987—. Mem. Cen. Ohio 6502 Users Group (pres. 1984-85), Mid-Ohio Atari Users Group, Mid-Ohio Sysops Club. Avocations: computer programming, all-terrain cycle, photography, electronic bulletin bd. Home: 3308 Park Ave W Mansfield OH 44906 Office: Universal Enterprises Inc 525 Beer Rd Mansfield OH 44906

STEINMETZ, DONALD WALTER, justice Wisconsin Supreme court; b. Milw., Sept. 19, 1924. B.A., U. Wis., 1949, J.D., 1951. Bar: Wis. bar 1951. Individual practice law Milw., 1951-58; asst. city atty. City of Milw., 1958-60; 1st asst. dist. atty. County of Milw., 1960-65; spl. asst. atty. gen. State of Wis., 1965-66; judge Milwaukee County (Wis.) Ct., 1966-80; justice Wis. Supreme Ct., 1980—; chmn. Wis. Bd. County Judges; sec.-treas. Wis. Bd. Criminal Ct. Judges; mem. State Adminstrv. Commn. Cts., Chief Judge Study Com., Study Com. for TV and Radio Coverage in Courtroom, Wis. Council on Criminal Justice. Mem. Am., Wis. bar assns., Am. Judicature Soc. Office: Wis Supreme Ct 231 E State Capitol Madison WI 53702 *

STEINMETZ, ROBERT FRANCIS, lawyer; b. Cleve., Oct. 12, 1950; s. William C. and Winifred A. (Jones) S.; m. Barbara Nan Dean, Aug. 4, 1979; children—Timothy Robert, Nan Elizabeth. B.A., Bowling Green U., 1972; postgrad. Cleve. State U., 1973; J.D., Ohio State U., 1976. Bar: Ohio, U.S. Dist. Ct. (no. dist.) Ohio. Router, Ford Motor Co., Brook Park, Ohio, 1972-73; sole practice law, Fairview Park, Ohio, 1976—; guardian ad litem Cuyahoga County Juvenile Ct., Cleve., 1980—, Cuyahoga County Domestic Relations Ct., Cleve., 1984-86; litigation counsel The Cuyahoga Savs. Assn., 1986—; mem. Legal Aid Soc. Vol. Services, Cleve., 1977—. Water safety instr. ARC, YMCA and YWCA, Cleve., 1981—; lector St. Patrick's West Park Roman Catholic Ch., Cleve., 1983—; mem. St. Patrick's Liturgical Planning Commn., Cleve., 1983-84. Recipient Recognition for Services-Guardian ad Litem Project and Legal Aid Soc., Cuyahoga County Commrs. Mem. ABA, Cleve. Bar Assn., West Shore Writers. Avocations: sailing, alpine and Nordic skiing, water skiing, writing. Office: Robert F Steinmetz & Assoc 19443 Lorain Rd Fairview Park OH 44126

STEINMEYER, NANCY LEE, artist; b. Carlinville, Ill., Feb. 12, 1956; d. Elwood E. and Nancy L. (Schmitt) S. Student Western Ill. U., 1974-78; grad. Rockland Ctr. for Internat. Studies, Colchesterm Eng., 1984. Art lectr. So. Ill. high schs., 1974-82; mem. faculty Western Ill. U. Coll. Fine Arts, Macomb, 1978; co-founder, coordinating artist Ann. Art Affair, Raymond, Ill., 1979; asst. to dir., Evanston Art Ctr., Chgo., 1987—; vis. artist Rembrandt Soc., 1982. One man shows include Kean-Mason Gallery, N.Y.C., 1982, Springboard Gallery, Springfield, Ill., 1982; exhibited in group shows at Joy Horwich Gallery, Chgo., 1981, Sioux City Art Ctr., Iowa, 1983, Winner's Circle Gallery, Van Nuys, Calif., 1983, Internat. Art Competition, Los Angeles, 1984, Evanston Art Ctr., Ill., 1985; illustrator book: The Old Town, 1977. Western Ill. U. grantee, 1974-78. Mem. Internat. Fine Arts Guild, Chgo. Artist Coalition, Women's Caucus for Art. Home and Studio: 1400 W Thorndale #3E Chicago IL 60660-3346

STEIN-ORLANDELLA, NANCY APRIL, record company executive; b. Winthrop, Mass., May 1, 1952; d. John Charles and Barbara Ann (Hilton) Montuori; m. Anthony Orlardella, Sept. 1, 1972 (div. Oct. 1974); m. David Michael Stein, Sept. 15, 1984. Mgr. Karma Records, Indpls., 1978-79; promotion and mktg. mgr. Warner Bros., Bensenville, Ill., 1979—. Named promotion/mktg. mgr. yr. Warner Bros. Records, 1986. Home: 633 Prospect Elmhurst IL 60126 Office: Warner Bros Records 222 W Silvert Ct Bensenville IL 60106

STEINWALD, OSMAR PAUL, plastic and reconstructive surgeon; b. Balt., Feb. 11, 1937; s. Osmar Paul and Minnie (Suter) S.; m. Nancy Jordan; children: Paul, Susan, George. BA, Johns Hopkins U., 1958; MD, U. Md., 1962. Diplomate Am. Bd. Plastic Surgery. Intern Presbyn. St. Lukes Hosp., Chgo., 1962-63; resident in gen. surgery Rush-Presbyn. St. Lukes Hosp., Chgo., 1963-64, 66-69; resident in plastic and reconstructive surgery Rush Presbyn. St. Luke's Hosp. and U. Ill. Hosp., Chgo., 1969-71; practice medicine specializing in plastic and reconstructive surgery Balt., 1971-74, Lake Forest, Ill., 1974—; chmn. dept. surgery Rush-Presbyn. St. Lukes Hosp., 1960-63, sec., treas. med. staff, 1965-67, pres. elect, 1967—. Served to capt. U.S. Army, 1964-69. Fellow ACS; mem. AMA, Lake County Med. Soc., Am. Soc. Plastic and Reconstructive Surgery, Chgo. Soc. Plastic Surgery (pres. 1984-85), Warren Cole Soc. Club: Knollwood (Lake Forest) (bd. govs. 1985-86). Avocation: golf. Office: 700 N Westmoreland Rd Lake Forest IL 60045

STELLA, FRANK DANTE, food service and dining equipment executive; b. Jessup, Pa., Jan. 21, 1919; s. Facondino and Chiara (Pennoni) S.; m. Martha Theresa Stella; children: Daniel, Mary Anne, William J., Philip J., Marsha, James C., Stephen P. Student, U. Detroit, 1937-41, Washington and Lee, 1944; D in Bus. and Industry (hon.), Gentium Pacem U., Rome, 1979; D in Sci. and Bus. Adminstn. (hon.), Cleary Coll., 1985. Pres. F.D. Stella Products Co., Detroit, 1946—; founding ptnr. The Fairlane Club (sold to Club Corp. Am., 1979); chmn. bd., chief exec. officer Stella Internat., N.Y.C.; mem. Mich. Higher Edn. Facilities Commn., Area-Wide Water Quality Bd., Fed. Statis. Commn., White House Fellows Commn. and others; chmn. Detroit Income Tax Rev. Bd.; instr. orgn. and mgmt. small bus. U. Detroit; vice chmn., bd. dirs. Met. Realty Corp.; bd. dirs. Fed. Home Loan Bank Indpls. Bd. dirs. March of Dimes Mich., 1976, mem. exec. com., 1984; corp. bd. dirs. Boys Club Met. Detroit., 1979; bd. dirs., exec. com. Orchestra Hall, 1974, vice chmn., 1979-82, chmn. 1982—; trustee U. Detroit, 1971-80, 82—, exec. com. 1971-77, chmn. devel. com. 1971-80, chmn. nominating com. 1971-78; chmn. Nat. Vol. Commn., Nat. Rep. Heritage Council, 1985—; trustee Sacred Heart Rehab. Ctr., 1981—, St. Gabriel Media, Inc., 1980—; group chmn. food and drug div. United Found., 1978; mem. adv. bd. dirs. Bishop Borgess High Sch., 1984—; bd. dirs. Ctr. for Ind. Living, Detroit Rehab. Inst., 1977-82, New Detroit Inc., Detroit Econ. Growth Corp., 1983, Detroit Econ. Growth Fund, 1983, Detroit Symphony, Mich. Opera; mem. St. John's Hosp. Guild, Friend of the Folger Library, Washington, 1978—; mem. divisional bd. trustees Mt. Carmel Mercy Hosp., 1979, founding chmn. 1979-82, mem. exec. com. 1979—; mem. exec. com. Nat. Rep. Com. 1985—; active Mich. Rep. Com. Recipient 28 awards from local, nat. and internat. civic and profl. orgns. Mem. Alliance for Mich. (bd. dirs. 1984—), Detroit Cen. Bus. Dist. Assn., Nat. Comml. Refrigerator Sales Assn. (bd. dirs., pres. 1953-54, adv. bd. 1954—), Nat. Assn. Wholesaler-Distbrs. (del. 1982—), Wholesale Distbrs. Assn. (bd. dirs. 1973—, v.p. 1976, pres. 1977-79), Bus. Edn. Alliance (various offices), Mich. Restaurant Assn., Food Service Executives Assn., Italian-Am. C. of C. Mich., Nat. Italian-Am. Found. (charter, bd. dirs., exec. com., pres. 1979—), Hispanos Organized to Promote Entrepreneurs (bd. dirs. 1976-81), Econ. Club Detroit (bd. dirs. 1982—), Air Force Assn. (charter), Am. Soc. Legion Merit, Greater Detroit C. of C. (chmn. 1980-81, bd. dirs.). Clubs: Detroit, Detroit Athletic, Detroit Golf, The Fairlane, Capitol Hill, Georgetown. Home: 19180 Gainsborough Rd Detroit MI 48223 Office: F D Stella Products Co 7000 Fenkell Ave Detroit MI 48238

STELLERS, THOMAS JOE, educational administrator; b. Dover, Ohio, May 22, 1940; s. Joseph A. and Jane Elizabeth (Stieber) S.; m. Carol Jean Crichton, Aug. 28, 1971. B.S. in Edn., Bowling Green State U., 1962; postgrad. U. Pitts., 1963-64, So. Ill. U., 1965; M.Ed., Kent State U., 1968, Ph.D., 1973. Cert. tchr., high sch. prin., supt., Ohio. Biology tchr., yearbook adviser Austintown-Fitch High Sch., Austintown, Ohio, 1962-71, 72-74; univ. fellow Kent (Ohio) State U., 1971-72; supr. middle schs., supr. sci., Mahoning County Schs., Youngstown, Ohio, 1974-76, dir. adminstrv. services and mgr. data processing, 1976—; instr. yearbook workshops Kent State U., 1968-71, Northwood Inst. and Delta Coll., Mich., 1971-72; chmn. beginning computer awareness Ohio Statewide Ednl. Computer Fair, 1982, 84; chmn. software adv. com. Ohio Dept. Edn., 1987—. Edn. chmn. Am. Cancer Soc., 1977, United Way, 1979, 80; cooordinator Mahoning County Health Promotion Program. Recipient No. One award Ohio's Project Leadership. Mem. Ohio Ednl. Data Systems Assn. (pres., Outstanding Mem. award 1986), Ohio Ednl. Computer Mgmt. Council (bd.), Ohio Com. for Ednl. Info. Systems, Nat. Sci. Tchrs. Assn. (task force for establishing clearinghouse for research evaluation instruments), Ohio Ednl. Assessment Program (panel mem.), Buckeye Assn. Sch. Adminstrs., Phi Delta Kappa, Sigma Phi Epsilon. Mem. Christian Ch. Home: 2405 Vollmer Dr Youngstown OH 44511-1951 Office: 2801 Market St Youngstown OH 44507-1693

STEMEN, DOUGLAS ALAN, financial consultant; b. Lima, Ohio, Apr. 2, 1955; s. Alvin Wilbur and Dorothy Ann (Britt) S.; m. Cynthia Lou Crum, Sept. 8, 1979; 1 child, Melissa. BSBA in Fin. and Mktg., Ohio State U., 1977, MA in Fin., 1985. Registered investment advisor, SEC. Ops. mgr., comptroller Zaganos World Inc., Lima, 1973-78; ter. mgr. Burroughs Corps., Lima, 1978-79; communications cons. United Telecommunications, Lima, 1979-85; fin. cons. Stemen Fin. Cons., Wapakoneta, Ohio, 1985—; inst. fin. Ohio No. U., Lima Tech. Coll., 1986—. Bd. dirs. NW Ohio Easter Seals, Lima, 1986-87. Mem. Beta Gamma Sigma, Phi Alpha Kappa. Republican. Lodge: Sertoma (sec., bd. dirs. Sunrise chpt. 1986-87). Avocations: woodworking, fishing. Home: Rt 6 Box 145 Wapakoneta OH 45895 Office: Stemen Fin Cons 18069 State Rt 65 Wapakoneta OH 45895

STEMMONS, RANDEE SMITH, lawyer; b. Springfield, Mo., July 15, 1958; d. Robert Lee and Connie (Smith) S. BA, William Woods Coll., 1980; JD, U. Mo., 1983. Bar: Mo. 1983, U.S. Dist. Ct. (we. dist.) Mo., 1983. Ptnr. Stemmons & Stemmons, Mt. Vernon, Mo., 1983—. V.p. Democratic Alliance, Springfield, 1984—; mem. adv. bd. Hospice. Recipient Profl. Responsibility award Am. Jurisprudence, 1983. Mem. ABA, Assn. Trial Lawyers Am., Mo. Assn. Trial Lawyers, 39th Judicial Cir. Bar Assn. (pres. 1984—), Student Bar Assn. (v.p. 1982-83), Mt. Vernon C. of C. (bd. dirs., v.p. 1984-87, pres. 1987), Order of the Coif, Phi Delta Phi. Democrat. Presbyterian. Home: 520 E Center Mount Vernon MO 65712 Office: Stemmons and Stemmons 101 E Dallas Mount Vernon MO 65712

STENBERG, SHELDON LEROY, accountant; b. Rapid City, S.D., Feb. 5, 1957; s. Erland LeRoy and Mary Ann (Marquess) S.; m. Lisa Marie Kuehl, Aug. 20, 1983. BBA in Acctg., U. S.D., 1979. CPA, S.D. Jr. staff acct. dept. legis. audit State of S.D., Pierre, 1979-81; sr. staff acct. Sayler Thorstenson & Co., Rapid City, S.D., 1981—. Mem. Am. Inst. CPA's, S.D. Soc. CPA's (pub. relations com. 1984—, pres. Black Hills chpt. 1986, 87). Republican. Lutheran. Club: Cosmopolitans. Lodge: Elks. Avocations: running, golf, reading, hiking. Home: 3607 Westridge Rd Rapid City SD 57702 Office: Sayler Thorstenson & Co PO Box 3140 Rapid City SD 57709

STENE, DENNIS CARTER, podiatrist; b. Elgin, Ill., Aug. 1, 1944; s. Arvin and Erna Wanda (Loechelt) S.; D.P.M., Ill. Coll. Podiatric Medicine, 1967; m. Carol Jean Gray, May 25, 1974. Pvt. practice podiatry, Bensenville, Ill., 1967-69, Rockford, Ill., 1969-70, Elgin, Ill., 1969—. Active Norwegian Lutheran Bethesda Home Assn. Mem. Am. Podiatry Assn., Ill. Podiatry Soc., Alumni Assn. Ill. Coll. Podiatric Medicine. Republican. Lutheran. Clubs: Masons (worshipful master 1973), Shriners, Scottish Rite, York Rite. Home: 1785 Joseph Ct Elgin IL 60123 Office: 100 E Chicago St Elgin IL 60120

STENEHJEM, WAYNE KEVIN, lawyer, state senator; b. Mohall, N.D., Feb. 5, 1953; s. Martin Edward and Marguerite Mae (McMaster) S.; m. Tama Lou Smith, June 16, 1978 (div. Apr. 1984); 1 child, Andrew. AA, Bismarck (N.D.) Jr. Coll., 1972; BA, U. N.D., 1974, JD, 1977. Bar: N.D. 1977. Ptnr. Kuchera, Stenehjem & Wills, Grand Forks, N.D., 1977—; spl. asst. atty. gen. State of N.D., 1983—; mem. N.D. Ho. Reps., 1976-80, N.D. State Senate, 1980—; chmn. Senate Com. on Social Services, 1985-86, Interim Legis. Judiciary Com., 1987—. Chmn. Dist. 42 Reps., Grand Forks, 1986—; bd. dirs. N.D. Spl. Olympics, 1985—, Christus Rex Luth. Ch., pres., 1985-86. Named Champion of People's Right to Know, Sigma Delta Chi, 1979, Outstanding Young Man of N.D., Grand Forks Jaycees, 1985. Mem. N.D. State Bar Assn., Grand Forks County Bar Assn. Home: 1616 1st Ave N Grand Forks ND 58206 Office: Kuchera Stenehjem & Wills 212 S 4th St PO Box 52 Grand Forks ND 58206

STENERSON, DOUGLAS C., educator; b. Barron, Wis., Aug. 29, 1920; s. Christopher P. and Maxine Miliam Ureal (Dalton) S.; m. Marjorie Barrows, Jan. 11, 1957. A.B. magna cum laude, Harvard U., 1942, I.A., 1943; M.A., U. Minn., 1947, Ph.D., 1961. Asst. prof. English, U. Miami, Coral Gables, Fla., 1955-57; asst. prof. English, Macalester Coll., St. Paul, 1958-59; asst. prof. English, Winona State (Minn.) Coll., 1959-63, assoc. prof., 1963-67, dept. head, 1966-67; assoc. prof. Roosevelt U., Chgo., 1967-68, prof. English, Am. studies, grad. adviser, 1968-84, prof. emeritus, 1984—; cons. North Central Assn. for Colls. and Secondary Schs., 1970—; cons. NEH, 1972-74. Served with U.S. Army, 1943-46. So. Fellowships grantee, 1957-58; Fulbright vis. prof., Finland, 1965-66; recipient McKnight Found. humanities award, 1961; Ill. Humanities Council grantee, 1982. Mem. Am. Studies Assn., MLA, AAUP. Democrat. Author: H.L. Mencken: Iconoclast from Baltimore, 1971; editor: Critical Essays on H.L. Mencken, 1987; contbr. chpts. to books and articles to profl. jours.

STENSBY, KENNETH NORMAN, real estate executive; b. Mpls., Aug. 19, 1939; s. Edward T. and Ann G. (Iverslie) S.; m. Darlene J. Auger, July 11, 1964; children: Robin, Heidi, Angela. BA in Econs., Carleton Coll., 1961. Mortgage analyst Conn. Gen. Life Ins. Co., Hartford, 1961-67; v.p. Northland Mortgage Co., Mpls., 1967-71; v.p. United Properties, St. Paul, 1971-75, pres., 1975—; bd. dirs. Northland Ins. Co., St. Paul, First Asset Realty Advisors, Mpls. Served to sgt. USAR. Named Minn. Real Estate Exec. of Yr. Minn. Real Estate Jour., 1985. Mem. Nat. Assn. Indsl. and Office Parks (pres. 1986), Urban Land Inst. Clubs: Edina (Minn.) Country, Decathlon Athletic. Avocations: running, golf, sailing, travel. Home: 7112 Shannon Dr Edina MN 55435 Home: United Properties 3500 W 80th St Minneapolis MN 55431

STENZEL, JOSEPH A., architect; AA, Cuyahoga Community Coll., 1971; BS in Architecture, Ohio State U., 1975. Registered architect, D.C., Ohio. Project coordinator Karlsberger & Assoc. Architects Inc., Columbus, Ohio, 1972-77; sole practice architecture Dayton, Ohio, 1977-80; project mgr. Design Group Inc., Columbus, 1980-81, 3D Group Inc., Architects (Design Build), Columbus, 1981-82; assoc., project mgr. Collins Rimer and Gordon Architects Inc., Cleve., 1982-86; prin. Fogle/Stenzel Architects, Cleve., 1986—. Office: Fogle/Stenzel Architects 2044 Euclid Ave Cleveland OH 44115

STEPAN, FRANK QUINN, chemical company executive; b. Chgo., Oct. 24, 1937; s. Alfred Charles and Mary Louise (Quinn) S.; m. Jean Finn, Aug. 23, 1958; children: Jeanne, Frank Quinn, Todd, Jennifer, Lisa, Colleen, Alfred, Richard. A.B., U. Notre Dame, 1959; M.B.A., U. Chgo., 1963. Salesman Indsl. Chems. div. Stepan Chem. Co., Northfield, Ill., 1961-63, mgr. internat. dept., 1964-66, v.p. corporate planning, 1967-69, v.p., gen. mgr., 1970-73, pres., 1974-84; pres., chmn., chief exec. officer Stepan Co., Northfield, Ill., 1984—, also bd. dirs. Mem. liberal arts council Notre Dame U., South Bend, Ind., 1972—. Served to 1st lt. AUS, 1959-61. Mem. Chem. Mfgs. Assn. (bd. dirs.). Clubs: Economic (Chgo.), Exmoor, Bob O'Link (Highland Park, Ill.), Harbour Ridge (Stuart, Fla.). Home: 200 Linden St Winnetka IL 60093 Office: Stepan Co Edens and Winnetka Sts Northfield IL 60093

STEPANIC, JAMES, metallurgist, manufacturing company executive; b. Latrobe, Pa., Apr. 7, 1952; s. Stanley Joseph and Helen Rosalia (Ulishney) S.; m. Marla Jean Janik, Sept. 9, 1978; 1 child, Daniel Wayne. BS in Metallurgy, Carnegie Mellon U., 1974; MBA, Akron (Ohio) U., 1981. Research metallurgist Latrobe Steel, 1974-78; mill metallurgist Timken Co., Akron, 1978-79, supr. melt shop, 1979-81, ops. mgr. steel project, 1981-82, exec. asst. steel ops., 1982-83, mgr. steelmaking Harrison steel plant, 1983—. Patentee in field. Mem. AIME (papers chmn. 1985—), Assn. Iron and Steel Engrs., Electric Metal Makers Guild. Office: Timken Co 1835 Dueber Ave SW Canton OH 44706

STEPHAN, DENNIS EUGENE, military, information management officer; b. Big Spring, Tex., July 8, 1949; s. Eugene Dyer Stephan and Alta Mae (Claxton) Bart; m. H. Carol Bynum, Sept. 30, 1983; 1 child, Danita Carol. BS in Indsl. Engring., U. Tex., Arlington, 1975; MS in Systems Mgmt., U. So. Calif., 1984. Commd. U.S. Army, 1975, advanced through grades to capt.; adminstrv. officer U.S. Army, Ft. Riley, Kans., 1977; mgr. database U.S. Army, Ft. Riley, 1977-80; data processing mgr. U.S. Army, Bremen, Fed. Republic Germany, 1980-83; automation mgmt. officer U.S. Army, Ft. Riley, 1983-84, info. ctr., info. services cons., 1984—; chmn. Info. Mgmt. Users Group, Kans., 1983-85; microcomputer cons. Tex. and Kans., 1983—. Mem. Assn. U.S. Army. Avocations: microcomputers, soccer, running. Home: 396 Rimrock Terrace Unit #6 Fort Riley KS 66442 Office: Directorate Info Mgmt AFZN-IM Fort Riley KS 66442

STEPHAN, KAY ELLEN, business educator; b. Wadsworth, Ohio, Oct. 26, 1946; d. John Franklin and Virginia Maye (Resseger) Kunkle; m. John Dennis Stephan, Sept. 9, 1968; children: Dennis, Scott, Joel. BS in Edn., Wittenberg U., 1968; MS in Edn., U. Akron, 1978. Instr. Northwest High Sch., Canal Fulton, Ohio, 1968-71, Barberton (Ohio) Sch. Commerce, 1971-74; real estate agt. Boebinger Realty, Canton, Ohio, 1975-78; bus. instr. U. Akron, 1979—, office adminstrn. coordinator, 1980—; state advisor Office Edn. Assn., 1983-84. Mem. Ohio Bus. Tchrs. Assn., Nat. Assn. Bus. Educators, Am. Vocat. Assn. Republican. Lutheran. Avocation: antique thimbles. Home: 264 Cherrywood Ln Canal Fulton OH 44614 Office: U Akron Wayne Gen and Tech Coll 10470 Smucker Rd Orrville OH 44667

STEPHAN, ROBERT TAFT, attorney general of Kansas; b. Wichita, Kans., Jan. 16, 1933; s. Taft and Julia S.; children: Dana, Lisa. BA, Washburn U., 1954, JD, 1957; grad., Nat. Coll. State Trial Judges, U. Pa., 1967. Bar: Kans. 1957. Sole practice 1957-63; judge Wichita (Kans.) Mcpl. Ct., 1963-65, Kans. Dist. Ct., 18th Jud. Dist., 1965-78; atty. gen. State of Kans., 1979—; chmn. Kans. Jud. Conf., 1977; mem. adv. bd. Shawnee County Ct.-Appointed Spl. Adv. Program. Hon. crusade chmn. Kans. div. Am. Cancer Soc., 1979-81; mem. adv. bd. Kans. Big Bros.-Big Sisters, Kans. Spl. Olympics, Shawnee County Ct.-Appointed Spl. Advocate Program; bd. dirs. Accent on Kids, Am. Cancer Soc., state chpt. and Sedgwick County unit, Parents Against Leukemia and Malignancies Soc., Kans. chpt. Leukemia Soc. Am. Named Kans. Trial Judge of Yr. Kans. Trial Lawyers Assn., 1977, Big Bro. of Yr., 1984, Outstanding Big Bro. Midwest, 1985. Mem. Am. Judges Assn., Am. Judicature Soc., ABA (mem. adv. commn. youth alcohol and drug problems), Nat. Assn. Attys. Gen. (past pres.). Republican. Club: Wagonmasters. Lodges: Elks; Moose; Masons; Shriners. Office: Office Atty Gen Kans Judicial Center Topeka KS 66612

STEPHANS, DANIEL JAMES, architect; b. LaCrosse, Wis., Apr. 23, 1948; s. Charles Jack and Beuhla Mae (Naas) S.; m. Lori Lynn Steffen, May 25, 1968; 1 child; m. Audrey Ann Cecka, Nov. 12, 1976. BArch, Iowa State U., 1971. Lic. architect, Wis., Minn., Ind., Wyo., Iowa, Kans., S.C., Mont., N.D., Fla.; cert. Nat. Council Architects Registration Bd. Architect trainee Larson & Darby, Architects, Rockford, Ill., 1971-72; architect, constrn. mgr. Larson & Tetzlaff, Architects, Rockford, Ill., 1972-76; architect, job capt. archtl. dept. Am. Med. Bldg., Milw., 1976; architect Studio Three Enterprises Inc., Tomah, Wis., 1976-79; pvt. practice architecture D.J. Stephans, Warrens, Wis., 1976—; constrn. mgr. RDS Inc., Madison, Wis., 1979; assoc. Sieger Architects, Madison, 1984. Developer numerous projects in field. Past pres. Village of Warrens; sponsor Girl Scouts Am. troops. Recipient Merit award Wis. Dept. Natural Resources archtl. design competition, 1983; Concrete Design award Wis. Ready-mix Concrete Assn., 1984. Mem. AIA, Wis. Soc. Architects, Nat. Rifle Assn., Wis. Rifle and Pistol Assn., Internat. Shooter Devel. Fund, Nat. Fedn. Ind. Bus., Internat. Platform Assn. Club, 3d Wheel Inc. Home and Office: 4705 Crescent Rd Madison WI 53711

STEPHEN, RICHARD JOSEPH, oral and maxillofacial surgeon; b. Joliet, Ill., Jan. 2, 1945; s. Joseph E. and Marcella M. (Pearson) S.; m. Jacqueline H. Thom, Aug. 5, 1967; children: Anne, Susan, George. Student, Lewis U., Lockport, Ill., 1962-65; DDS, Loyola U., Chgo., 1969; Cert. in Oral and Maxillofacial Surgery, Loyola U., Maywood, Ill., 1972. Practice dentistry specializing in oral and maxillofacial surgery Mt. Vernon, Ill., 1972—; cons. Ill. Cancer Council, Chgo., 1979—; Centralia (Ill.) Correctional Facility, 1980—, Vandalia (Ill.) Correctional Facility, 1980—. Fellow Am. Coll. Stomatologic Surgeons, Am. Soc. Oral and Maxillofacial Surgeons, Am. Dental Soc. of Anesthesiology, Internat. Assn. Oral Surgery, Internat. Assn. Maxillofacial Surgery. Lodges: Lions, Elks. Avocation: raising cattle. Home: Rt #5 Box 226 Mount Vernon IL 62864 Office: 2413 Broadway Box 582 Mount Vernon IL 62864

STEPHENS, ADRIENNE CONKLIN, legal administrator; b. Chgo., Sept. 26, 1933; d. Clarence R. and Ellen (Gleason) Conklin; m. Russell Francis Stephens, Aug. 16, 1955 (div. Aug. 1973); children: Jennifer S., Russell F. (dec.). BA, Wellesley Coll., 1955; MBA, George Williams Coll., 1982. Researcher, staff asst. Field Mus. Natural History, Chgo., 1971-73; field reseacher dept. epidemiology Am. Health Found., N.Y.C., 1974-80; health planner Health Systems Agy., Oak Park, Ill., 1980-83; legal adminstr. Conklin and Adler Ltd., Chgo., 1983—; cons., staff asst. Loyola Med. Ctr., Maywood, Ill., 1978-80; asst. to dir. research and devel. Ill. Hosp. Assn., Oak Brook, Ill., 1979-80. V.p. Condo J-B Lake Hinsdale Homeowners Assn., Willow Brook, Ill., 1984-87. Mem. Assn. Legal Adminstrs., Law Office Mgrs. Assn. Chgo. Club: West Suburban Wellesley (pres. 1968, alumni admissions rep. 1968-72). Home: 77 Lake Hinsdale Dr #106 Clarendon Hills IL 60514 Office: Conklin and Adler Ltd 100 W Grand Ave Chicago IL 60610

STEPHENS, CHARLES GUSTON DURBROW, physician, farmer; b. Mountainburg, Ark., July 27, 1913; s. Clive and Ida May (Renfroe) Durbrow; m. Jennie Madeline Costello, June 21, 1936; children—Joan Shirley, Diann Elizabeth, Thomas Michael; m. 2d, Millie Cjeka, Apr. 6, 1968. D.O., Univ. Health Scis., 1938; apprentice in gen. surgery Lakeside Hosp., 1943-48; resident in clin. surgery Allgemines Krankenhaus, Linz, Austria, 1954; resident in basic sic. and lab. surgery, Coll. Osteo. Physician and Surgeons, 1950; gen. chmn. Nat. Child Health Conf. and Clinic, 1941-42; gen. practice osteo. medicine, Kansas City, Mo., 1937—; chief surg. staff Cass County Meml. Hosp., Harrisonville, Mo., 1983. Pres. bd. Paseo Methodist. Ch., 1953. Mem. Nat. Wildlife Fedn., Nat. Geog. Soc., Ducks Unlimited, Mo. Prairie Found., Am. Mus. Natural History, Mo. Audubon Soc., Nat. Audubon Soc., Greater Kansas City Dahlia Soc., Am. Osteo. Assn., Mo. Osteo. Assn., Jackson County Osteo. Assn. (pres. 1943), Coll. Osteo. Surgeons (life mem.), Alumni Found. of Kansas City Coll. Osteopathy (pres. 1942). Democrat. Lodges: Lions (charter mem. Alpha Kansas City, Mo.), Westport Masons, Shriners. Home: RR 1 Clear Creek Farm Cleveland MO 64734 Office: 400 E Red Bridge Rd Kansas City MO 64131

STEPHENS, GEORGINA YVONNE, financial executive; b. Seoul, Republic of Korea, Nov. 6, 1955; came to U.S., 1960; d. George and Margaret Louise (Napue) S. BA in Econs., Cornell U., 1977; MBA in Fin., U. Mich., 1979. Staff fin. analyst IBM, East Fishkill, N.Y., 1979-82; sr. fin. analyst United Brands Co., Manhattan, N.Y., 1982-83; mgr. fin. mgmt. AT&T Info. Systems, Morristown, N.J., 1983-85; Mgr. fin. planning and analysis Dayton Hudson Corp., Mpls., 1985—; bd. dirs. Freeport West, Inc. Mem. Nat. Black MBA Assn., Assn. MBA Exec. Clubs: Women's (Mpls.); Cornell (Minn). Avocations: piano, racquetball. Home: 10705 Bush Lake Rd Cir S Bloomington MN 55438 Office: Dayton Hudson Corp 777 Nicollet Mall Minneapolis MN 55402

STEPHENS, LARRY RALPH, history educator, publisher; b. Council Bluffs, Iowa, Nov. 10, 1940; s. Ralph L. and Agnes Leona (Fitzsimmons) S.; m. Betty Jean Tally, Aug. 29, 1965; children—Tally Jill, Libby Gail, Tyler Lane. B.A. in Ministry, Nebr. Christian Coll., Norfolk, 1964, B.Theology, 1964; M.A. in History, Fort Hays Kans. State Coll., 1968. Instr. history Northeast Mo. State U., Kirksville, 1968-73, asst. prof., 1974—; pub. Lancaster Excelsior Newspapers, Mo., 1980—. Author: Long Branch Lake Historical Resources: A History, 1975. Bd. dirs. Mo. Com. Humanities, NEH, 1984—, sec. 1986—. Mem. Am. Hist. Assn., Am. Assn. State and Local History, Campus Vols. of Kirksville. Democrat. Mem. Christian Ch. Lodges: Masons, Rotary. Avocations: acting, gardening, raising Bantam chickens. Home: Route 2 Box 304A Kirksville MO 63501 Office: NE Mo State U Social Sci Dept Kirksville MO 63501

STEPHENS, PAUL ALFRED, dentist; b. Muskogee, Okla., Feb. 28, 1921; s. Lonndy and Maudie Janie (Wynn) S.; m. Lola Helena Byrd, May 7, 1950; children: Marsha Stephens Wilson, Payl Alfred, Derek M. BS cum laude, Howard U., 1942, DDS, 1945. Instr. dentistry Howard U., Washington, 1945-46; gen practice dentistry Gary, Ind., 1947—; chmn. bd. Assocs. Med. Ctr., Inc., Gary; Sec. Gary Ind. Sch. Bldg. Corp., 1967—; pres. Bd. Health, 1973—; Ind. State Bd. Dental Examiners, 1979—. Mem. adv. bd. Ind. U.-Purdue U. Calumet Campus, 1973; bd. dirs. Urban League Northwest Ind. Served with AUS, 1942-44. Fellow Internat. Coll. Dentists, Acad. Dentistry Internat., Acad. Gen. Dentistry (pres. chpt. 1973, nat. chmn. dental care com. 1977, Midwestern v.p.), Am. Coll. Dentists; mem. ADA, C. of C., Nat. Dental Assn., Northwest Ind. Dental Assn. (dir., pres. 1976-77), Am. Soc. Anesthesia in Dentistry, Am. Acad. Radiology, Alpha Phi Alpha. Baptist. Home: 1901 Taft St Gary IN 46404 Office: 2200 Grant St Gary IN 46404

STEPHENS, ROBERT ALLAN, service agency executive; b. St. Louis County, Mo., Jan. 15, 1937; s. Charles Franklin and L. Pearl (Cales) Stephens; m. Carolyn Beth Hurst, Aug. 26, 1956; children—Shari Lee, Beth Ann. B.A., Mo. Valley Coll., 1958; M.S., Nova U., 1984. Claims supr. Gen. Am. Life Ins. Co., Pitts., 1958-61; underwriting mgr. Gen. Am. Life Ins. Co., St. Louis, 1961-67; dist. sales mgr. Gen. Am. Life Ins. Co., Oklahoma City and St. Louis, 1967-69, New Eng. Life, Dallas, 1969-71; exec. dir. Goodland Presbyn. Children's Home, Hugo, Okla., 1971-74, Beech Acres, Cin., 1974—. Mem. Hamilton County Juvenile Ct. Rev. Bd., 1975-83; Hamilton County Youth Services Adv. Bd., 1981-84; bd. dirs. Pro Kids, 1987—, Presbytery of Cin. Planning com. 1984-86; chmn. Stewardship and Mission Interpretation com. 1986—; legis. bd. Southeastern Ecumenical Ministries Manor, 1976-81, bd. dirs., 1980-82; mem. Clermont County Mental Health Bd., 1980-86, vice chmn., 1981, chmn., 1982-85; mem. Clermont County Youth Service Coordinating Council, 1980-83, Clermont County Juvenile Ct. Adv. Bd., 1980-81, Hamilton County Juvenile Ct. Adv. Bd., 1982—. Named Nat. United Presbyn. Man of Mission, 1978. Mem. Nat. Assn. Homes for Children (dir. 1975-80, accreditation commn. 1983—), Ohio Assn. Child Caring Agys. (bd. dirs. 1975-80, pres. 1978-79). Presbyterian. Clubs: Exchange (pres. 1980-81, Book of Golden Deeds award 1984). Home: 1258 Maplecrest Ct Amelia OH 45102 Office: 6881 Beechmont Ave Cincinnati OH 45230

STEPHENS, THOMAS MARON, educator; b. Youngstown, Ohio, June 15, 1931; s. Thomas and Mary (Hanna) S.; m. Evelyn Kleshock, July 1, 1955. B.S., Youngstown Coll., 1955; M.Ed., Kent State U., 1957; Ed.D., U. Pitts., 1966. Lic. psychologist, Ohio. Tchr. Warren (Ohio) public schs., 1955-57, Niles (Ohio) public schs., 1957-58; psychologist Montgomery County, Ohio, 1958-60; Asso. prof. edn. U. Pitts., 1966-70; prof. edn. Ohio State U., 1970—, chmn. dept. exceptional children, 1972-82, chmn. dept. human services edn., 1982-87, assoc. dean coll. edn., 1987—, prof., 1987—; mem. Higher Edn. Consortium for Spl. Edn., chmn., 1976-77; pub., pres. Cedars Press, Inc. Author: Directive Teaching of Children with Learning and Behavioral Handicaps, 2d edit, 1976, Implementing Behavioral Approaches in Elementary and Secondary Schools, 1975, Teaching Skills to Children with Learning and Behavioral Disorders, 1977, Teaching Children Basic Skills: A Curriculum Handbook, 1978, 2d edit., 1983, Social Skills In The Classroom, 1978, Teaching Mainstreamed Students, 1982; dir.: Jour. Sch. Psychology, 1965-75, 80—; exec. editor: The Directive Tchr.; assoc. editor: Spl. Edn. and Tchr. Edn., Techniques, Behavioral Disorders, Spl. Edn. and Remedial Edn.; contbr. articles to profl. jours. U.S. Office of Edn. fellow, 1964-65. Mem. Am. Psychol. Assn., Nat. Assn. Sch. Psychologists (charter), State Dirs. for Gifted (pres. 1962-63), Council Exceptional Children (gov., Tchr. Educator of Yr. Tchr. Edn. Div. 1985), Council Children with Behavioral Disorders (pres. 1972-73). Home: 1753 Blue Ash Pl Columbus OH 43229 Office: Ohio State U 1945 N High St Columbus OH 43210

STEPHENSON, MARK RAY, audiologist, consultant; b. East St. Louis, Ill., Sept. 13, 1949; s. Richard Clark and Muriel May (Cox) S.; m. Ronna Dean Childers, Dec. 30, 1971; children: Matthew, Andrew. BS, So. Ill. U., 1972, MS, 1973; PhD, Ohio State U., 1986. Cert. audiologist, Ohio; ordained to ministry Bapt. Ch. as deacon., 1980. Grad. asst. So. Ill. U., Carbondale, 1972-73; commd. 2d lt. USAF, 1973, advanced through grades maj.; lab. biomed. audiologist Air Force Med. Research Lab., Wright-Patterson AFB, Ohio, 1973-81, research assoc., 1983-84; chief dept. audiology Air Force Regional Med. Ctr., Clark Air Base, Philippines, 1984-86; research audiologist Armstrong Aerospace Med. Research Lab., Wright-Patterson AFB, 1986—; cons. ASME, 1980-82, com. hearing bioacoustics and biomechanics Nat. Acad. Sci., 1976-80, Command Surgeon of Pacific Air Forces, 1985-86. Contbr. articles to profl. jours. Counselor merit badge Boy Scouts Am., Dayton, coordinator Tiger Cubs, 1986-87. Recipient Gold award United Way, 1977, Co. Grade Officer of Yr. award Air Force Med. Research Lab, 1978. Mem. Acoustical Soc. Am., Ohio Council Audiology, Mil. Soc. Audiologists and Speech Pathologists, Air Force Audiology Soc., Co. Grade Officers Council (pres. 1976), Alpha Delta Upsilon (pres. 1970). Republican. Avocations: astronomy, ornithology. Home: 2434 Spicer Rd

Beavercreek OH 45431 Office: Armstrong Aerospace Med Research Lab Biological Acoustics Br Wright-Patterson AFB OH 45433

STEPHENSON, MICHAEL DAVID, chemical engineer; b. Huntington, N.Y., July 8, 1957; s. Thomas Edgar and Helen Julia (Mizzoni) S. BA in Chemistry, SUNY, Potsdam, 1979; MSChemE, Iowa State U., 1982. Grad. asst. Ames Labs., 1979-82; assoc. chem. engr. Ill. State Geol. Survey, Champaign, 1983—. Contbr. articles to profl. jours. Research fellow NSF, 1978. Mem. Am. Inst. Chem. Engrs. Democrat. Home: 810 Kerr Ave #202 Urbana IL 61801 Office: Il State Geol Survey 615 E Peabody Dr Champaign IL 61820

STEPHENSON, ROBERT STORER, physiologist; b. Corpus Christi, Tex., Apr. 30, 1943; s. George S. and Natalie (Gauss) S.; m. Saadia Sabah, June 17, 1969; children: Tleytmas, Abdelkrim. AB, Princeton U., 1965; SM, MIT, 1967, PhD, 1973. Lectr. in biology U. Mohammed V, Rabat, Morocco, 1973-76; postdoctoral trainee Purdue U., West Lafayette, Ind., 1976-80, asst. research scientist, 1980-81; assoc. prof. Wayne State U., Detroit, 1981—. Contbr. articles to profl. jours. Research grantee NIH, 1980—. Mem. AAAS, Assn. for Research in Vision and Ophthalmology, Biophysical Soc., N.Y. Acad. Scis., Sigma Xi. Home: 530 W Oakridge Ferndale MI 48220 Office: Wayne State U Dept Biological Scis Detroit MI 48202

STEPHENSON, WILLIAM LEE, JR., computer systems executive; b. Birmingham, Ala., Dec. 29, 1942; s. William L. and Katherine (Mason) S.; m. Lynne Love, June 11, 1965; children: Laura L., P. David, Stephen N. BS in Forest Mgmt., U. Mo., 1965, MS in Econs., 1970. Forest mgr. Potlatch, Prescott, Ark., 1965-66; with forestry research dept. Buckeye Cellulose Corp., Perry, Fla., 1969-71, with forest mgmt. dept., 1971-73, econs. mgr., 1973-78; sr. systems analyst Procter & Gamble, Cin., 1978-84, tech. mgr. banking, fin. and decision support systems, 1984—; forestry cons., Cin. and Perry, Fla., 1970—; systems cons., Cin., 1980—. Elder Presbyn. Ch., Cin. and Perry, Fla., 1971. Served to sgt. U.S. Army, 1966-68. Mem. Soc. Am. Foresters, Cin. Woodworking Club, Xi Sigma Pi. Lodge: Elks. Avocations: woodworking, computer graphics, gardening. Office: Tech Devel 2 Procter & Gamble Plaza Cincinnati OH 45202

STEPHNEY, TYRONE, sales executive; b. Chgo., Feb. 13, 1959; s. Clarence and Georgia (Stephney) Brown; married; 1 child, Katrese Chanell. Student, Kennedy-King Coll., 1977-84. Singer, performer The Lyrics of Soul, Chgo., 1971-75; writer T.S. Corp., Chgo., 1975-85; producer, writer T.S. Music Co., Chgo., 1978—, pres., 1979—, also bd. dirs. Author: Two Chosen Harts, (music) Sugar Darling, 1983, Loving You, 1981, (musical message) Crack Down The Message, 1986. Baptist. Avocations: fishing, boating, writing, designing, computers. Office: T S Music Co 5243 Hoyne Ave Chicago IL 60609

STEPTO, ROBERT CHARLES, educator, physician; b. Chgo., Oct. 6, 1920; s. Robert Louis and Grace Elvie (Williams) S.; m. Ann Burns, Sept. 13, 1942; children: Robert Burns, Jan Kristin. B.S., Northwestern U., 1938-41; M.D., Howard U., 1944; Ph.D., U. Chgo., 1948. Intern Provident Hosp., Chgo., 1945; resident in obstetrics and gynecology Provident Hosp., 1946-48, now trustee; resident Chgo. Lying-In Hosp., 1946-48; USPHS fellow Michael Reese Hosp., Chgo., 1948-51; asst. prof. Loyola U., Chgo., 1953-56, U. Ill., Chgo., 1956-60; assoc. prof. U. Ill., 1960-69; prof., chmn. dept. obstetrics and gynecology Chgo. Med. Sch., 1970-75; prof. Rush Med. Coll., Chgo., 1975-79; prof. U. Chgo., 1979-87, prof. emeritus, 1987—; dir. obstetrics and gynecology Cook County Hosp., 1972-75, Mt. Sinai Hosp. Med. Center, 1970-79; mem. Chgo. Bd. Health, v.p., 1981—; sec. Chgo. Health Research Found., Am. Cancer Soc., Family Planning Coordinating Council Met. Chgo.; pres., bd. dirs. emeritus Nat. Med. Fellowships. Bd. dirs. Chgo. Urban League, 1960-63, Mus. Contemporary Art, Lyric Opera; trustee Ill. Children's Home and Aid Soc., 1967-71. Served to capt. AUS, 1951-53. Fellow ACS, Internat. Coll. Surgeons (pres. 1978, corr. sec. 1982, sec. N.Am. 1984-85), Am. Coll. Obstetrics and Gynecology (life), Inst. of Med.; mem. Am. Soc. Clin. Pathologists, Gynecologic Urology Soc. (bd. dirs.), Am. Soc. Colpscopy (emeritus), AMA, Nat. Med. Assn., Central Assn. Obstetrics and Gynecology (life), Chgo. Gynecol. Soc. (life, v.p. 1969, pres. 1982), Chgo. Pathol. Soc., Assn. Chgo. Gynecol. Oncologists (pres. 1982). Clubs: Quadrangle, Carlton, Wayfarers (Chgo.). Home: 5201 S Cornell Ave Chicago IL 60615 Office: U Chgo 5841 S Maryland Ave Chicago IL 60637

STER, THOMAS DALE, insurance company executive; b. Columbus, Ind., July 13, 1952; s. Peter and Ann G. (Gleason) S.; m. Susan Helen Kamenick, Nov. 10, 1973; children: David, Katherine. AB, Ind. U., 1976, MBA, 1977. CPA, Wis. Cons. Arthur Andersen, Inc., Milw., 1978-82; project mgr. MGIC Investment Corp., Milw., 1982-85, regional mgr., 1985—. Served to sgt. U.S. Army, 1971-74. Mem. Wis. Inst. CPA's, Wis. Mortgage Bankers Assn., Beta Gamma Sigma. Roman Catholic. Home: 6844 S Juniper Ct Oak Creek WI 53154 Office: MGIC Investment Corp PO Box 688 Milwaukee WI 53201

STERLE, JOSEPH JOHN, funeral home executive; b. Euclid, Ohio, Oct. 4, 1954; s. Joe R. and Marie J. (Debevec) S. AA, Cuyahoga Community Coll., 1977; student, Lakeland Community Coll., 1985; grad., Pitts. Inst. Mortuary Sci., Inc., 1986. Apprentice funeral dir., embalmer, asst. A. Grdina and Socns, Inc. Funeral Homes, Cleve., 1977-84; intern Burton L. HIrsch Funeral Home, Pitts., Mar. to Dec., 1985; intern, pvt. contractor Schellhaas Funeral Homes, Inc., Pitts., Jan. to Sept., 1986; asst. Sankovic-Johnston Funeral HOme, Cleve., 1986—. Mem. Am. Soc. Notaries, Slovenian Home Soc. Collinwood, Inc., Croation Farm, St. Mary's Holy Name Soc., Assn. Slovenian Nat. Home, Slovenian Nat. Benefit Soc., Am. Slovenian Cath. Union, Am. Mut. Life Assn. Roman Catholic. Club: Lithuanian Am. Citizens. Lodges: Eagles, Moose, Cath. Order Foresters (rec. sec. St. Mary's Ct. 1975—, Legion of Honor 3d degree 1984, Cert of Merit 1980). Avocations: bowling, golf, hunting, fishing. Home: 1284 E 168th St Cleveland OH 44110 Office: Sankovic-Johnston Funeral Home 15314 Macauley Ave Cleveland OH 44110

STERLING, JAMES CLARK, publishing executive; b. Detroit, Nov. 29, 1942; s. Kenneth Clark and Mary Elizabeth (Denison) S.; m. Charlotte Susan Butler, July 8, 1966 (div. Oct. 1975); children: Elizabeth Lee, Stephanie Diane; m. Jill Phillips, Oct. 26, 1984. AA, Southwest Bapt. Coll., Bolivar, Mo., 1962; BJ, U. Mo., 1965. Gen. mgr., assoc. pub. Bolivar Herald-Free Press, 1967-79; pub. Bolivar Herald-Free Press, Buffalo Reflex, Stockton Cedar County Rep., 1979-86; pres. Sterling Media, Ltd., Bolivar, 1985—; v.p. Bolitho-Sterling Newspaper Service, Kansas City and Bolivar, Mo., 1987—. Author: (with others) Polk County Classics, 1985. Bd. curators U. Mo., Columbia, Rolla, St. Louis and Kansas City, 1987—. Served to lt. USNR, 1972. Paul Harris fellow Rotary; recipient Trustees Medallion, Southwest Bapt. U., 1985, Silver medal Am. Advt. Fedn./Springfield (Mo.) Ad Club, 1986. Mem. Mo. Press Assn. (bd. dirs., pres. 1985). Republican. Methodist. Club: Springfield Ad. Lodge: Rotary (pres. Bolivar chpt. 1983). Home: Rt 3 Box 559 Bolivar MO 65613 Office: Bolitho-Sterling Newspaper Service 335 S Springfield PO Box 492 Bolivar MO 65613

STERN, ANDREW MICHAEL, lawyer; b. Covington, Ky., June 28, 1949; s. Joseph F. and Matilda I. (Domaschko) S.; m. Eileen Marie Beringer, Dec. 28, 1973; children: Mary Kathryn, Elyse Marie. B.A. in Biology and Psychology, Thomas More Coll., 1976; J.D., No. Ky. U., 1980. Bar: Ky. 1980, Ohio 1981, U.S. Dist. Ct. (ea. and we. dists.) Ky. 1981, U.S. Dist. Ct. (ea. dist.) Tex. 1982. Jud. clk. U.S. Dist. Ct. (ea. dist.) Ky., Covington, 1980; sole practice, Covington, 1980-83; assoc. White, Getgey & Meyer, Cin., 1983—; instr. torts, research and investigation Am. Inst. Paralegal Studies, Inc., Cin., 1981—. Served to sgt. USMC, 1968-72, Vietnam. Decorated Purple Heart; named Outstanding Young Men Am., Jaycees, 1981. Mem. Ky. Bar Assn., Ohio Bar Assn., Fed. Bar Assn., ABA (litigation sect. admiralty com.), Cin. Bar Assn., Am. Judicature Soc. Democrat. Home: 122 Highland Ave Fort Thomas KY 41075 Office: White Getgey & Meyer Co LPA Adam Riddle House 2021 Auburn Ave Cincinnati OH 45219

STERN, DONALD MARTIN, medical corporation executive; b. N.Y.C., Sept. 19, 1933; s. Harry Aaron and Sophie (Zwillinger) S.; m. Eileen Block, Feb. 6, 1966 (div. Feb. 1981); children: Michelle, Linda; m. Sharon Hope Rauch, Apr. 5, 1981; children: Tracey, Janice. BBA, NYU, 1959. V.p. Trans World Shipping, N.Y.C., 1960-64; pres. A.F. Burstrom & Son, Inc., Ferndale, Mich., 1965-84; pres. and chief exec. officer Multi-Care Med., Ferndale, 1977-84, DMS Mgmt. and Cons. Services, West Bloomfield, Mich., 1985—, O-2 Emergency Med. Care Services, West Bloomfield, 1986—; cons. in field. Mem. Nat. Assn. Med. Equipment Suppliers, Am. Assn. Respiratory Therapy. Republican. Clubs: World Trade (Detroit), Danish (Redford, Mich.), Skyline. Avocation: tennis. Home: 5950 Pinetree Dr West Bloomfield MI 48322

STERN, DOUGLAS DONALD, foundry company official, consultant, educator; b. New London, Wis., Apr. 29, 1939; s. Sylvester S. and Gretchen W. S.; divorced; children—Randal, Richard, Robert, Russell. B.S. in Bus. and Math., U. Wis.-Oshkosh, 1962. With Neenah Foundry Co. (Wis.), 1962—, indsl. engr., 1962-65, dir. indsl. engring., 1965-73, gen. supt. Plant 3, 1973-83, plant mgr. Plant 2, 1983—; cons. FMC, Lenox; instr. Fox Valley Tech. Inst., Leach; dir. Dura Products. Coach. Neenah Baseball, 1976—, treas., 1976—; pres. Our Savior's Lutheran Ch., 1971, treas. Found., 1983. Recipient Neenah Football Rocket award, 1981. Mem. Am. Foundrymen's Soc. (speaker's award 1976, pres. N.E. Wis. chpt.), Am. Inst. Indsl. Engrs. (past pres. and bd. dirs.), Nat. Foundry Assn. (indsl. engring. com.). Republican. Author student workbook: Operations Analysis, 1983. Home: 946 Hickory Ln Neenah WI 54956 Office: 2121 Brooks Ave Neenah WI 54956

STERN, ELLEN SUSAN, psychologist; b. Balt., Apr. 7, 1942; d. William and Ada (Bargrosser) Gottlieb; m. Samuel Edward Stern, Sept. 3, 1963; children: Jennifer Anne, Nathan William. BS, U. Wis., 1964; MA, U. Nebr., 1966, PhD, 1970. Lic. psychologist, Wis. Asst. prof. Hunter Coll., N.Y.C., 1970-72; dir. Ga. Learning Resource Ctr., Atlanta, 1972-75; assoc. prof. Valdosta (Ga.) State Coll., 1975-77; pvt. practice psychology Oxford, Miss., 1977-78; assoc. prof. Carthage Coll., Kenosha, Wis., 1979-86; pvt. practice psychology Milw., 1986—; cons. Rochester (Minn.) Pub. Schs., 1982-84; bd. dirs. Hillel Acad., Milw., 1981-87, Milw. Assn. for Jewish Edn., 1983—; sr. faculty Wis. Sch. of Profl. Psychology, Milw., 1981—. Active Nat. Council Jewish Women. Mem. Council for Exceptional Children, Milw. Area Psychol. Assn. (nominating com. 1983-85), Milw. Area Women in Psychology (treas. 1981-86), Wis. Educators for Learning Disabilities, Pi Lambda Theta (pres. Greater Milw. chpt. 1982-86). Club: Hadassah (Milw.). Avocations: needlework, Chinese cooking. Home: 1644 Journeys Dr Hartland WI 53029

STERN, NORISSA CYNTHIA, teacher; b. Milw., Oct. 11, 1947; s. Jack and Beatrice (Polland) S. BA, Stephens Coll., 1970; MS, U. Wis., Milw., 1977. Cert. tchr., Wis. 2d grade tchr. Grafton (Wis.) Pub. Schs., 1970—. Bd. dirs. Sisterhood Congregation Emanuel B'ne Jeshuron, 1986—; mem. steering com. Young br. Jewish Nat. Fund, 1985—. Mem. NEA, Wis. Edn. Assn., Grafton Edn. Assn. Democrat. Club: City Wide Jewish Singles (Milw.) (coordinator, pres. 1984-86). Avocations: needlepoint, travel, baking, reading. Home: 8453 N Indian Creek Pkwy Milwaukee WI 53217 Office: Woodview Elementary Sch 600 5th Ave Grafton WI 53024

STERN, PAUL GEORGE, electronic data processing company executive; b. Oct. 31, 1938; s. Franz and Irene (Arje) S.; B.S.E.E., U. Manchester, 1961, M.S., 1963, Ph.D., 1966; m. Patricia Anne Portney, July 14, 1965; children—Alexander, Andrea, Andrew. Sr. physicist E.I. duPont de Nemours & Co., Inc., Wilmington, Del., 1966-68; various sr. mgmt. positions IBM, 1968-73, asst. to chief fin. officer, exec. v.p., mem. bd., Armonk, N.Y., 1973-74, dir. orgn., 1974-75, dir. future mfg. systems, 1975-76; chief operating officer Braun, Kronberg, W. Ger., 1978, chmn. bd., chief exec., 1978-80; v.p. Gillette Corp., 1976-80; pres. electronic ops., v.p. strategic mgmt. Rockwell Internat., Pitts., 1980-81; exec. v.p. Burroughs Corp., Detroit, from 1981, chief operating officer, 1982—, now also pres.; mem. adv. bd. BHF Bank, Frankfurt, W. Ger., 1978-82, Deutschbank, Frankfurt, 1978-82; dir. Artech Corp., Fairfax, Va., Barrington, Inc., Campbell, Calif. Mem. Am. Mgmt. Assn., IEEE, Engring. Soc. Detroit. Clubs: Renaissance (Detroit); Open Hunt (Bloomfield Hills, Mich.); Union Internat. (Frankfurt). Patentee in field. Office: Burroughs Corp Burroughs Pl Detroit MI 48232 *

STERN, PETER JOSEPH, orthopaedic surgeon; b. Cin., May 16, 1944; s. Joseph Smith and Mary Stern, m. Sandra Schoening, May 28, 1970; children: Kimberly Anne, Joseph Smith, Lisa. BA, Williams Coll., 1966; MD, Washington U., St. Louis, 1970. Diplomate Am. Bd. Orthopaedic Surgery. Intern Beth Israel Hosp., Boston, 1970-71; resident Mass. Gen. Hosp., Boston, 1975-77; clin. prof. orthopaedic surgery U. Cin. Coll. Medicine, 1986—. Contbr. articles to profl. publs. Served with M.C., USAF, 1972-74. Fellow ACS; mem. Am. Soc. Surgery Hand, Am. Acad. Orthopaedic Surgeons. Jewish. Home: 5780 Drewry Farm Ln Cincinnati OH 45243 Office: 2800 Winslow Suite 401 Cincinnati OH 45206

STERN, ROY DALTON, manufacturing financial executive; b. Beulah, N.D., July 24, 1943; s. Earhart G. Stern and Eleanora (Trusskey) Moonen; m. Donna Lynne Blickenstaff, June 20, 1970; children: Heather Lynne, Courtney Mae. BSME, N.D. State U., Fargo, 1965; MSME, Colo. U., 1967; MBA, Ohio State U., Columbus, 1971. CPA, Ind.; cert. managerial acct., Ind.; lic. profl. engr, Ohio. Fin. mgr. Cummins Engine Co., Inc., Columbus, Ind., 1971-83; chief fin. officer Micro Sonics, Inc., Indpls., 1983-85; v.p. fin. Seradyn, Inc., Indpls., 1985—; trustee employee 401K plan Seragen Diagnostics, Indpls.; instr. Ind. U.-Purdue Extension, Columbus, 1975-80. Advisor Jr. Achievement, Columbus, 1981. Served to capt. USAF, 1967-71. Recipient Sylvia Farney awrad Am. Soc. Mech. Engring. 1963, Marjorie Roy Rothermal award Am. Soc. Mech. Engring, 1965. Mem. Ind. CPA's Soc., Fin. Executive Inst., Nat. Assn. Accts. Republican. Presbyterian. Avocation: jogging. Home: 3620 Waycross Dr Columbus IN 47203 Office: Seradyn Inc PO Box 1210 Indianapolis IN 46206

STERNBERG, PETER ELLIS, psychotherapist, educator; b. Chgo., Sept. 18, 1950; s. Robert Mitchell and Marilyn (Banowitz) S. BA, U. Ill., Chgo., 1972, MSW, 1975. Cert. social worker, Ill. Child care worker Maryville Acad., Des Plaines, Ill., 1972-74; psychotherapist Lake County Mental Health Ctr., Waukegan, 1975-78; pvt. practice psychotherapy Chgo., Libertyville, Ill., 1978—; tchr. U. Ill., Chgo., 1984-86, Coll. of Lake County, Grayslake, Ill., 1986—; presenter seminars, confs., throughout U.S., 1978—. Mem. Avery Brundage Scholarship Com. U. Ill., Chgo., 1972. Mem. Nat. Assn. Social Workers, Assn. Humanistic Psychology, Health and Medicine Assn., Sierra Club. Avocations: 3d degree black belt Budo Aikido, backpacking, mountaineering, skiing, photography. Home: 1313 Michele Dr Palatine IL 60067 Office: 53 W Jackson Room 1653 Chicago IL 60604

STERNBERGER, STEPHEN JEFFREY, insurance company executive; b. Indpls., May 26, 1949; s. Robert Sidney and Sandra Sue (Knoy) S.; m. Valerie Dale Garbrecht, July 31, 1971. EdB, Ind. U., 1971. CLU; registered health underwriter; chartered fin. cons. Tchr., coach, Pike Twp. (Ind.) Schs., 1971-74; agt. Mass. Mut. Ins. Co., Indpls., 1974-75; dir. adminstrn. Compensation Systems, Inc., Indpls., 1975; author, cons. Pictorial Publishers, Inc., Indpls., 1975-83; v.p. advanced underwriting and mktg. services United Presdl. Life Ins. Co., 1983-86, v.p. mktg. and advt. sales, 1986—. Author: Advanced Underwriting Training Course, 1978, Estate Planning Training Course, 1979, Pension Planning Training Course, 1981, Business Insurance Basics, 1982; contbr. articles to profl. jours. Recipient Heart Fund Solicitors award, 1979. Mem. Indpls. Assn. Life Underwriters, Indpls. Assn. Health Underwriters (v.p. 1974-75), Nat. Assns. Life and Health Underwriters, Estate Planning Council Indpls. (bd. dirs.), Am. Soc. CLU's, Indpls. Soc. CLU's (officer 1984—, pres. 1987—), Am. Soc. Chartered Fin. Cons., Assn. for Advanced Life Underwritng, Internat. Assn. Fin. Planning, Am. Mgmt. Assn. Ind. U. Alumni Assn., Pi Kappa Alpha. Republican. Unitarian. Club: Ind. U. Varsity. Home: 4343 Idlewild Ln Carmel IN 46032 Office: PO Box 9006 217 Southway Blvd E Kokomo IN 46902-9006

STERNE, MARK ELLIOT, management consultant; b. Cin., Nov. 15, 1960; s. Harold Emanuel and Judilee (Tash) S.; m. Cari Shore, Aug. 24, 1985. BS in Ops. Mgmt., Ind. U., 1982. CPA, Ill.; cert. prodn. inventory control. Sr. cons. Arthur Andersen & Co., Chgo., 1982-85, Friedman, Eisenstein, Raemer & Schwartz, Chgo., 1986—. Mem. Am. Inst. CPA's, Ill. Inst. CPA's, Am. Prodn. and Inventory Control Soc. Avocations: photography, biking, music, reading. Home: 2564 Brian Dr Northbrook IL 60062 Office: Friedman Eisenstein Raemer & Schwartz 401 N Michigan Ave Chicago IL 60611

STETZEL, MARK ROBERT, dentist; b. Ft. Wayne, Ind., Nov. 28, 1957; s. Robert M. and Leatrice Joy (McKinze) St. AB, Ind. U., Bloomington, 1980; DDS, Ind. U., Indpls., 1984. V.p. R.M. & M.R. Stetzel DDS, Inc., Ft. Wayne, Ind., 1985—. Mem. ADA, Am. Soc. Dentistry for Children, Ind. Acad. Gen. Dentistry (regional bd. dirs. 1985—). Republican. Lodge: Rotary. Home: 5716 Bayside Dr Fort Wayne IN 46815 Office: RM & MR Stetzel DDS Inc 4604-C E State Blvd Fort Wayne IN 46815

STETZEL, ROBERT M., dentist; b. Huntington, Ind., July 28, 1927; s. Arthur Daniel Stetzel and Donna L. (Zent) Levintoff; m. Leatrice Joy McKenzie, Mar. 29, 1953; children: Eric John, Mark Robert. BS, Hillsdale Coll.; DDS, Ind. U., 1953. Gen. practice dentistry Ft. Wayne, Ind., 1956—; instr. preventive dentistry Ind. U., Ft. Wayne, Ind., 1965-72. Served to comdr. USN, 1950-56, with Res. 1956-70. Fellow Internat. Coll. Dentists, Acad. Gen. Practice; mem. ADA (council on dental care programs, chmn. council on dental practice 1979-81), Ind. Dental Assn. (pres. 1976-77, Disting. Service award), Isaac Knapp Dist. Dental Soc. (pres. 1962-63). Republican. Methodist. Lodges: Rotary (local v.p. 1986), Masons. Avocations: tennis, aviation. Home: 5024 Chaucer Rd Fort Wayne IN 46835 Office: 4606C E State Blvd Fort Wayne IN 46815

STEUBINGER, RICHARD PAUL, mortgage company executive, real estate company executive; b. Peoria, Ill., Mar. 17, 1927; s. Paul L. and Edna M. (Wier) S.; m. Helen M. Roedell, Nov. 4, 1951 (div. 1968); children—Connie, Linda, Richard, Jr., Cathy; m. Jonnee M. Johnson, Feb. 18, 1978; 1 child, Shawnda. Student Bradley U., 1944-48. Lic. real estate broker, Ill. Owner, pres. Holiday Store, Peoria, 1948-57; pres. Lynnhurst Devel. Co., Peoria, 1957-80, Pioneer Realty Co., Peoria, 1959—, Tri-County Mortgage Co., Peoria, 1983—. Pres. Counseling and Family Service, Peoria, 1981; chmn. Am. Heart Assn., Peoria, 1981-82. Served with USN, 1945-46. Mem. Bradley U. Alumni Assn. (pres. 1982-83, Pres. award 1982), Nat. Assn. Realtors. Lutheran. Lodge: Kiwanis (Leadership award 1979, pres. 1979). Home: 4518 Hetherwood Peoria IL 61615 Office: Tri-County Mortgage Ltd 6816 Frostwood Peoria IL 61615

STEUER, KATHLEEN ANNE, architect; b. Bedford, Ohio, Aug. 14, 1953; d. Ralph and Evelyn May (Ryan) Steuer. BArch, Kent State U., 1978; student Rosary Coll., Florence, Italy, 1977. Registered architect, Ohio. Architect, Richard Jencen Assocs., Cleve., 1978-79, Koerper Blatchford, Cleve., 1979-82, Technicare Corp., Solon, Ohio, 1982-86; corp. architect, Deluxe Check Printers, Inc., St. Paul, 1986—. Mem. AIA (com. on architecture for health), Archtl. Soc. Ohio, Am. Bus. Women's Assn. (pres. 1985-86, mem. ways and means com. 1984, del. nat. conv. 1984), Kent State U. Alumni Assn., Kappa Omicron Phi. Avocations: traveling, dancing, theatre. Home: 5450 Douglas Dr #221 Crystal MN 55429 Office: Deluxe Check Printers Inc 1005 Gramsie Rd PO Box 64468 Saint Paul MN 55164-0468

STEVE, LINDA FLYNN, accountant; b. El Paso, Tex., Mar. 14, 1954; d. Wayne Robert and Dorothy Marion (Jensen) Flynn; m. Craig Francis Steve, May 24, 1975; 1 child, Kathryn Marie. AA in Bus. Adminstrn., Worthington (Minn.) Community Coll., 1974; BA in Acctg., Moorhead (Minn.) State U., 1976. CPA, N.D. Internal auditor Investors Diversified Service, Mpls., 1976-77; controller Park Enterprises, Fargo, N.D., 1977-78, Candee Constrn., Dickinson, N.D., 1978-79; tax mgr. Reichert, Fisher & Co., Dickinson, N.D., 1979-84; pvt. practice acctg. Dickinson, N.D., 1984-85; sr. ptnr. Steve and Hulsing, CPA's, Dickinson, N.D., 1985—; cons. pres. adv. bd. Dickinson State Coll., 1984—. Named Outstanding Young Dickinson Resident, Dickinson Jaycees, 1984, Competent Toastmaster, Toastmasters Internat., 1984. Mem. Bus. and Profl. Women (Young Career Woman of Yr. 1983), N.D. Soc. CPA's (chmn. com. 1985—), Am. Inst. CPA's, Am. Soc. Women Accts., Am. Women's Soc. CPA's, Am. Assn. Univ. Women. Home: 648 Park St PO Box 1334 Dickinson ND 58602-1334 Office: Steve & Hulsing 25 First Ave West Dickinson ND 58601

STEVENS, ANDREW LEE, editor; b. Woodstock, Ohio, Jan. 7, 1936; s. Raymond H. and Ruth M. (Penn) S.; m. Theresa A. Bell, Sept. 29, 1956; children: Terry, Brian, Michelle, Micah. BS, Ohio State U., 1958, MS, 1963. Tchr. Richwood (Ohio) High Sch., 1958-63; assoc. editor The Ohio Farmer, Columbus, Ohio, 1963-75, editor, 1975—. Contest judge Nat. Assn. Animal Breeders Publ., judge Ohio State Fair Queen; chmn. Ohio Farm City com., Columbus, 1968-72, chmn. Ohio Future Farmers Am. Found. sponsoring com., Columbus, 1982-83; com. mem. Ohio State U. Agrl. Edn. Service Adv., com. mem. Ohio Stat U. Dairy Sci. Adv. Recipient Ohio Dairy Shrine Club award, Ohio Young Farmers Outstanding Service award; named Ohio State Hall Fame. Mem. Am. Soc. Bus. Press Editors, Buckeye Agrl. Mktg. Assn., Nat. Agrl. Mktg. Forum, Ohio Ayrshire Breeders Assn., Ohio Farm and Home Safety (com. mem.), Ohio Farm Bur. Fedn., Ohio Agrl. Mktg. Forum (pres. 1986), Am. Agrl. Editors Assn. (trustee), Ohio Agrl. Council (2d v.p. 1985-86, v.p. 1987), Ohio Future Farmers Am. Alumni (pres. 1986), Agrl. Relations Council, Town and Country Coalition of Ohio Council Chs., Ohio State U. Alumni Assn., Sigma Delta Chi. Home: 20920 Pherson Pike Williamsport OH 43164 Office: The Ohio Farmer 1350 W 5th Ave Columbus OH 43212

STEVENS, BOBBIE RAY, management consultant; b. Cooksprings, Ala., May 1, 1935; d. Talley Bert and Clurcy Augusta (Masters) S.; m. Billy Ray Watson, June 6, 1953 (div. 1957); m. Dean Richard Portinga, Sept. 1, 1979. Student, U. Ala., Brimingham, 1957-59; PhD in Psychology Bus. Mgmt., Columbia Pacific U., 1981. Exec. secretary Hayes Aircraft Corp., Birmingham, 1955-60; model, tchr. Margo George Modeling Agy., Birmingham, 1959-60; flight attendant Northwest Orient Airlines, St. Paul, 1960—; office mgr. Minn. Twins, Bloomington, 1960-61; acct. Rochlin & Lurie CPA's, Mpls., 1962-64; pub. relations agt. Breezy Point Estates, Piquot Lakes, Minn., 1964; sales rep. Success Motivation Inc., 1965-66; pub. relations rep. Employers Overload Inc., Mpls., 1966-67; cons. Dolphin Employment Agy., Mpls., 1968; real estate agt. Relocation Realty, Bloomington, 1971; assoc. townhouse developer Wakely Investment Co., Bloomington, 1971-74; assoc. broker Century 21, Red Carpet Realty, Bloomington, 1974-76; broker, fin. planner Bobbie Stevens Real Estate & Fin. Planning, Bloomington, 1976-82; pvt. practice counseling 1982-86; pres., chmn. bd. dirs. Exec. Futures Inc., Excelsior, 1984. Bd. dirs. Continuum Minn., Mpls., 1983—. Avocations: writing, reading, interior design, tennis, golf. Home and Office: 400 Hwy 7 Excelsior MN 55331

STEVENS, CHARLES THOMAS, psychologist; b. Nevada, Mo., Oct. 25, 1932; s. Glenn Monroe and Edna Estelle (Thomas) S.; B.S. in Agr., S.W. Mo. State U., 1955, B.S. in Psychology, 1974, M.S. in Guidance and Counseling, 1974; Ph.D. candidate, U. Mo., Columbia; m. Helen Louise Utterback, Dec. 27, 1953; children—Mark Thomas, Diana Lynn, Eric Allen. Enlisted U.S. Army N.G., 1954-55, commd. 2d lt., 1955, advanced through grades to lt. col. inf., 1969, ret., 1971; vets. benefits counselor U. Mo. Counseling Center, Columbia, 1977-79; dir. Bur. for Blind, State of Mo., Jefferson City, 1979-84; field rep. Nat. Fedn. of Blind, 1984—; cons., counselor visually impaired coll. students, 1975-78; guest lectr. on blindness; state pres. Nat. Fedn. of the Blind, 1977-79. Editor: Blind Missourian, 1976-81, 85-87, Associate Raiser, 1985—. Decorated Legion of Merit, Bronze Star with V and 6 oak leaf clusters, Army Commendation Medal with V and 3 oak leaf clusters, 2 Purple Hearts; Cross of Gallantry with palm (Vietnam); grantee Handicapped Manpower Availability Survey. Mem. Am. Personnel and Guidance Assn. Mem. Christian Ch. Club: Lions. Home and Office: 1203 Fairview Rd Columbia MO 65203

STEVENS, CHESTER WAYNE, real estate executive; b. Milw., May 24, 1925; s. Daniel Augusta and Genevieve (Kingston) S.; m. Bernice Louise Limberg, Nov. 8, 1947; 1 child, Doreen Louise Scholtes. Student, Augustana Coll., 1944. Mgr. ops. Plankinton Bldg., Milw., 1962-72; v.p. 1st Wis. Devel. Corp., Milw., 1972-78; pres., chief exec. officer Stevens Carley Co., Milw., 1978-81, C.W. Stevens Co., Milw., 1981-85; v.p. Towne Realty Inc., Milw., 1985—; cons. Milw. Redevel., 1981-82, Milw. Ins., 1983. Served with USAAF, 1943-46. Mem. Bldg. Owners and Managers Assn. (pres. 1972-73, dir. exec. com. 1976-82), Inst. Real Estate Mgmt. (pres. 1982, Mgr. of Yr., 1981), Milw. Bd. Realtors. Democrat. Lutheran. Club: Milw. Athletic. Avocations: stamp collecting, wood working. Home: N 4439 Friedel Cambridge WI 53253 Office: Towne Realty Inc 710 N Plankinton Ave Milwaukee WI 53203

STEVENS, HAROLD RUSSELL, physician, anesthesiologist; b. Detroit, Nov. 18, 1930; s. Harold Russell and Etheleen Mae (Stone) S.; m. Karen Lee Leathers; children—Kirk Russell, Martha Lee, Kori Lynn, Kelly Lou. A.B., Albion Coll., 1952; M.D., U. Mich., 1955. Diplomate Am. Bd. Anesthesiology. Resident in anesthesiology Toledo Hosp., Ohio, 1960-62, research assoc. Inst. Med. Research, 1965-70, dir. respiratory team, 1967—, chmn. anesthesiology, 1983-86, dir. intensive care, 1975—, dir. cardiac surgery, 1981-84; health councilor Community Planning Council Northwestern Ohio, 1970-71; co-dir. respiratory therapy Mercy Hosp., Toledo, 1969-83, dir. anesthesiology, 1968-79; adj. prof. U. Toledo, 1971—; asst. clin. prof. Med. Coll. Ohio, Toledo, 1971—. Contbr. articles to Anesthesiology, Jour. Asthma Research, LANCET, Internat. Anesthesiology Clinics. Trustee Maumee Valley Found., Toledo, 1971-73; site examiner Joint Rev. Com. for Respiratory Theraphy Edn., 1977—. Served to capt. MC, USAF, 1957-59. DeVilbiss Fund grantee, 1965. Fellow Am. Coll. Anesthesiology; mem. Acad. Medicine Toledo and Lucas County (councilor 1970-71), Ohio Soc. Anesthesiology (pres. 1982-83), Ohio State Med. Assn. (del. 1983—), Am. Soc. Anesthesiologists (alt. del. 1980), AMA, Am. Heart Assn. (trustee Northwestern Ohio 1980—), Lung Assn. Northwestern Ohio (trustee 1977-80). Republican. Episcopalian. Clubs: Inverness, Toledo. Lodges: Masons, Shriners. Home: 4204 Northmoor Rd Toledo OH 43606 Office: 3939 Monroe St Suite 116 Toledo OH 43606

STEVENS, H(ARRY) LYNN, school system administrator; b. Enid, Okla., Apr. 17, 1948; s. Everett Marion and Lola Jeanne (Whiting) S.; m. Lana Cheryl Green, Aug. 1, 1968; children: Clayton, Kylee. BA, Nrthwestern Okla. U., 1970; MEd, Wichita State U., 1977; PhD, Kans. State U., 1981; cert., Nat. Acad. for Supts., 1985. Tchr. Unified Sch. Dist. 270, Plainville, Kans., 1970-74, Unified Sch. Dist. 306, Salina, Kans., 1974-75, Unified Sch. Dist. 308, Hutchinson, Kans., 1975-77; prin. Unified Sch. Dist 309, Nickerson, Kans., 1977-82; supt. Unified Sch. Dist. 394, Rose Hill, Kans., 1982—; In-service presentor Okla. and Kans. Sch. Bds., 1978—; cons. Reno County (Kans.) Child Care Assn., Hutchinson, 1979-81; labor negotiator for Okla. and Kans. Sch. Bds., 1982—; lectr. Wichita State U., 1985—. Named Outstanding Young Educator, Plainville Jaycees, 1973. Mem. Am. Assn. Sch. Adminstrs., Nat. Assn. Ednl. Negotiators, Assn. for Supervision and Curriculum Devel. Lodge: Lions. Avocation: golf. Home: 6664 Eagle Dr Derby KS 67087 Office: Unified Sch Dist 394 315 S Rose Hill Rd Rose Hill KS 67133

STEVENS, JONATHAN BUELL, health insurance executive, public health administrator; b. New Haven, June 4, 1948; s. Phillips and Sarah (Wallis) S.; m. Margaret Hiller, Oct. 9, 1971. BA, Yale U., 1971; MPH, U. N.C., 1975. Exec. dir. Coop. Health Info. Ctr. of Vt., Burlington, 1975-83; cons. Edward Hosp., Naperville, Ill., 1983; v.p. Bodimetric Health Services, Chgo., 1983-85; exec. dir. John Hancock Preferred Health Plan, Schaumburg, Ill., 1985—. Vol. Beverly Area Planning Assn., Chgo., 1985—. Recipient traineeship grant USPHS, 1972-74. Mem. Am. Pub. Health Assn., Group Health Assn. Am., Ill. Assn. Preferred Provider Orgns. (bd. dirs. 1987—). Clubs: Beverly Hills Univ., Yale of Chgo. Home: 9941 S Hoyne Ave Chicago IL 60643 Office: John Hancock Preferred Health Plan PO Box 4005 Schaumburg IL 60194

STEVENS, JOSEPH EDWARD, JR., judge; b. Kansas City, Mo., June 23, 1928; s. Joseph Edward and Mildred Christian (Smith) S.; m. Norma Jeanne Umlauf, Nov. 25, 1956; children—Jennifer Jeanne, Rebecca Jeanne. B.A., Yale U., 1949; J.D., U. Mich., 1952. Bar: Mo. 1952, U.S. Supreme Ct. 1973. Assoc. Lombardi, McLean, Slagle & Bernard, Kansas City, Mo., 1955-56; assoc. then ptnr. Lathrop, Koontz, Righter, Clagett & Norquist, Kansas City, Mo., 1956-81; judge (we. dist.) U.S. Dist. Ct. Mo., Kansas City, 1981—. Bd. govs. Citizens Assn. Kansas City, 1959-70; bd. dirs., exec. com. Truman Med. Ctr., Kansas City; trustee Central United Methodist Ch., Kansas City, 1978—, Barstow Sch., Kansas City, 1978—. Served with USNR, 1952-55. Recipient Lon O. Hocker Meml. Trial Lawyer award, 1963. Mem. ABA (ho. of dels.), Am. Judicature Soc., Kansas City Bar Assn., Lawyers Assn. Kansas City, Mo. Bar (pres. 1980-81, bd. govs. 1976-82). Clubs: University, Carriage, Mercury, Vanguard. Home: 425 W 55th St Kansas City MO 64113 Office: US Dist Ct 811 Grand Ave 404 US Courthouse Kansas City MO 64106

STEVENS, JULIE CLARK, marketing executive; b. Birmingham, Mich., Sept. 25, 1949; d. Robert Stanford and Mary Elizabeth (Caskey) Clark; m. John Robert Stevens, Dec. 11, 1971 (div. Aug. 1984); 1 child, Robert. BA, Mich. State U., 1971. Advt. mgr. Midlantic Bank, Englewood, N.J., 1973-77, Despatch Industries, Mpls., 1977-79; account exec. Donaldson Co., Inc., Bloomington, Minn., 1979-83, Red Barron, Inc., Minnetonka, Minn., 1983-84; mgr. mktg. and communications Zetaco, Inc., Eden Prairie, Minn., 1984—. Mem. Bus. and Profl. Advt. Assn. Office: Zetaco Inc 6850 Shady Oak Rd Eden Prairie MN 55344

STEVENS, KIPP KOPMEIER, industrial designer, consultant; b. Milw., May 16, 1951; s. Clifford Brooks and Alice Elizabeth (Kopmeier) S.; m. Lauren Carol Burack, Sept. 20, 1981. B of Indsl. Design, Syracuse U., 1974. Staff designer Am. Motors Corp., Detroit, 1974-75, Raymond Loewy Internat., N.Y.C., 1975-76; project mgr. Henry Dreyfuss Assocs., N.Y.C., 1976-77; account mgr. C.L. Mauro Assocs., N.Y.C., 1977-78; pres., chief exec. officer Brooks Stevens Design Assocs., Mequon, Wis., 1978—. Mem. Indsl. Designers Soc. Am., Soc. Typographic Arts, Milw. Mgmt. Support Orgn. (bd. dirs. 1983—), Milw. Artists Found. (bd. dirs. 1984—), Milw. Inst. Art & Design (bd. dirs. 1986—). Lodge: Rotary. Avocations: tennis, travel. Office: Brooks Stevens Design Assocs 1415 W Donges Bay Rd Mequon WI 53092

STEVENS, MARJORIE, librarian; b. Calhoun County, Mich., Jan. 1, 1923; d. Will Oliver and Ethel Grace (Frye) Rundle; m. Paul Andrew Stevens, Mar., 1940 (dec. Mar. 1971); children—Loraine Marie, Norman Douglas, Clare Eugene, Janice May, Sandra Kay, Garry Alan, Maynard Carl, Lynn Carol, Ronald Paul. B.A., Olivet Coll., 1982; M.S.L., Western Mich. U., 1977. Clk., Olivet (Mich.) Coll. Library, 1960-75, acquisitions technician, 1976-78, acquisitions and govt. documents librarian, 1978-80, acquisitions and fed. govt. documents librarian, 1980-85, also archivist, audio-visual instr., dir. libraries, 1985—. Mem. Mich. Archival Assn., Women's Soc. Christian Service. Methodist.

STEVENS, MARK OLIVER, superintendent of schools; b. Youngstown, Ohio, Mar. 9, 1948; s. Paul E. and Janet L. (Weisert) S.; m. Kelline Ann White, June 28, 1975. M.A. in Ednl. Adminstrn., Ohio State U., 1978, M.A. in Pub. Adminstrn., 1979, postgrad., 1979—. Tchr., coach Austintown (Ohio) Schs., 1972-74, Bexley City (Ohio) Schs., 1974-78; grad. adminstrv. asst. to assoc. dean for program devel. Ohio State U., Columbus, 1978-80; asst. prin. Groveport Madison (Ohio) Local Schs., 1980, supt., 1981—. Pres., Coll. Edn. adv. council Ohio State U., 1982—; mem. Greater Groveport Human Needs Com., 1982—, Citizens Opposing Noise, 1982—, Coalition for Local Adminstrn. Schs., 1983, Franklin County Sch. Funding Task Force, 1981—; chmn. Franklin County Ednl. Council Governing Bd., 1986—; v.p. sch. study council of Ohio, 1986-87; co-chmn. United Way Edn. Sector, 1986, 87; mem. Groveport devel. com., 1986—, YMCA outdoor services bd., 1986. Recipient Ross-Gainer award Ohio State U., 1971, Martin W. Essex award, 1980, Ednl. Achievement award, 1982, Dir.'s award Southeast Columbus Mental Health Ctr., 1983; Dan. H. Eikenbury fellow, 1980. Mem. Buckeye Assn. Sch. Adminstrs. (Ednl. Leadership award 1984), Am. Assn. Sch. Adminstrs., Ohio Local Supts. Assn., Franklin County Supts. Assn. (pres. 1983-84), Sigma Phi Epsilon (pres. 1970-71, alumni pres. 1974-80), Phi Delta Kappa (pres. 1983-84). Unitarian. Club: Bexley Celebrations. Lodge: Lions. Contbr. chpts. to books, articles to profl. pubs. Home: 377 E Cooke Rd Columbus OH 43214 Office: 5055 S Hamilton Rd Groveport OH 43125

STEVENS, MARY LOUISE, psychologist; b. Duluth, Minn., Aug. 15, 1945; d. William Harrison and Louise Margaret (Vlahovich) Tucker; m. Larry Brent Stevens, Feb. 11, 1967 (div. Oct. 1976); 1 child, Brent Maxwell. BA in Psychology, U. Minn., Duluth, 1966; MS in Sch. Psychology, Ind. U., 1969-70; PhD in Psychology, Western Mich. U., Kalamazoo, 1980. Lic. cons. psychologist; cert. sch. psychologist. Psychologist Cen. State Hosp., Indpls., 1970-72; instr. Western Mich. U., 1978-80; sch. psychologist Burnsville (Minn.) Pub. Sch., 1973-77, 80-81,; pvt. practice clin. psychology Edina, Minn., 1981—; speaker in field. Author: The Child Psychology Book, Underachievement: An Epidemic with Life Long Consequences. Vol. supr. counselors Walk In Counseling Ctr., Mpls., 1984. Mem. Minn. Psychol. Assn., Assn. for Behavior Analysis, Nat. Speakers Assn., Mensa, Phi Kappa Phi. Club: Ullr Ski. Avocations: downhill skiing, boating, swimming, triathlons. Home: 1527 Clemson Dr Eagan MN 55122 Office: 7101 York Ave S Edina MN 55435

STEVENS, ROBERT JAMES, engineer; b. Detroit, July 11, 1933; s. Joseph Aloysius and Elizabeth Rose (Buzza) Szczepanski; m. Mary Jane McFadden, Apr. 16, 1966; children: Lisa Marie, Eric Michael, Gina Lee. BS MechE, Wayne State U., 1957. Office manager Chrysler Corp., Detroit, 1957—. Office: Chrysler Corp 12800 Lynn Townsend Dr Detroit MI 48288

STEVENS, RON A., lawyer, public interest organization administrator; b. Indpls., Sept. 4, 1945; s. Granville Thomas and Charlotte May (Wheeler) S.; m. Judy Rohde, June 15, 1968. BA, Okla. State U.; JD with honors, Ill. Inst. Tech., 1976. Staff atty. Legal Assistance Found. Chgo., 1976-79; staff atty., dir. housing agenda Bus. and Profl. People for Pub. Interest, Chgo., 1979-81; chief housing div. Office of Cook County State's Atty., Chgo., 1981-82; campaign coordinator north lakefront Washington for Mayor, Chgo., 1982-83; program officer The Joyce Found., Chgo., 1983-86; pres. Citizens for a Better Environment, Chgo., 1986—; adv. bd. state support ctr. on environ. hazards Nat. Ctr. for Policy Alternatives, Washington, 1987—. Mem. bldg. code enforcement com. Mayor's Transition Team Housing Task Force, Chgo., 1983, steering com. Chgo. Ethics Project, 1986—; founder, chmn. Progressive Chgo. Area Network, 1981-83; bd. dirs. Uptown Recycling Sta., Chgo., 1987—. Mem. Chgo. Council Lawyers (chmn. housing com. 1978-81, bd. govs. 1981-83, bd. dirs. Fund for Justice, 1982—), Chgo. Area Runners Assn. (founder, v.p. 1977-81). Home: 740 Melrose Chicago IL 60657 Office: Citizens for a Better Environment 506 S Wabash Suite 523 Chicago IL 60605

STEVENS, WILLIAM E., consumer and commercial corporation executive; b. 1942; married. B.S. in Bus. Adminstrn., U. Akron, 1965; M.B.A., Ind. U., 1967. Dir. planning and bus. devel. Samsonite Corp., 1970-73; v.p., pres. consumer and comml. products div. Beatrice Foods Co., 1973-82; pres. and chief operating officer, dir. Chromalloy-Am. Corp., St. Louis, 1982-85; exec. v.p., dir. Black & Decker, Inc., Towson, Md., 1985—. Office: Black & Decker Inc 701 E Joppa Rd Towson MD 21204

STEVENS, WILLIAM LOUIS, Episcopal bishop; b. Yuba City, Calif., Jan. 12, 1932; s. Ralph Fremont and Elsie Mae (Schultz) S.; B.A., San Francisco State Coll., 1953; M.Div. Gen. Theol. Sem., 1956. Ordained priest, Episcopal Ch.; curate St. Luke's Ch., San Francisco; sr. curate St. Savior's, London, Order of the Holy Cross, N.Y.; rector St. Benedict's Ch., Plantation, Fla. to 1980; bishop Episcopal Diocese of Fond du Lac (Wis.), 1980—. Trustee, Nashotah Ho. Sem.; bishop visitor Sisterhood of the Holy Nativity; mem. Nat. Right to Life Com. Office: Diocese of Fond du Lac PO Box 149 Fond du Lac WI 54935 *

STEVENSON, JAMES DOUGLAS, advertising executive; b. Cadillac, Mich., May 18, 1956; s. Robert and Lorraine (Victor) S.; m. Susan Lynn Kuatycz; Apr. 15, 1978; children: Nathan Andrew, Brendan James. BS in Edn., Cen. Mich. U., 1978. Classified outside sales Holland (Mich.) Sentinel, 1978-79, retail outside sales, 1979-80; system mgr. Continental Cablevision, Holland, 1980-81; retail outside sales The Goshen (Ind.) News, 1982-85; mgr. retail advt. Terre Haute (Ind.) Tribune-Star, 1985-86, advt. dir., 1986—. Mem. Advt. Fedn. Republican. Roman Catholic. Lodge: KC. Avocations: umpiring, golfing, photography. Office: The Terre Haute Tribune-Star 721 Wabash Ave Terre Haute IN 47807

STEVENSON, MICHAEL RICHARD, radio communications executive; b. N.Mex., Nov. 29, 1958; s. Richard Donald and Phylis Carol (Saunders) S.; m. Connie Marie Welk, Aug. 7, 1981; 1 child, Paul Michael. BS in Bus. Adminstrn., U. N.D., 1981. Marketing rep. Xerox Corp., Sioux City, Iowa, 1981-83; sales rep. Hoechst Rousell, Sioux City, 1983-84; radio communications rep. Motorola Inc., Bismarck, N.D., 1984—. Avocations: golf, music, photography. Home: 2003 N16 #21 Bismarck ND 58501

STEVENSON, RICHARD ANDREW, finance educator, consultant; b. Utica, N.Y., Aug. 5, 1938; s. Edward D. and Doris Stevenson; m. Sheila Vaughn, Aug. 12, 1967; children—Daniel, Maura, Susan. B.B.A., St. Bonaventure U., 1961; M.B.A., Syracuse U., 1962; Ph.D., Mich. State U., 1965. Chartered fin. analyst. Research analyst Household Fin., Chgo., 1965-67; prof. fin. U. Iowa, Iowa City, 1967—, dept. chmn., 1981-86, acting treas., 1986—, bd. dirs., chmn. Univ. Credit Union. Author: (with others) Fundamentals of Investments, 1984; Asset-Liability Management for Credit Unions, 1984; Fundamentals of Finance, 1980. Contbr. articles to profl. jours. Mem. adv. bd. Iowa Sch. Banking, 1977—; treas. Bicyclists of Iowa City, 1982—. Ford Found. fellow, 1963-65. Mem. Am Fin. Assn., Des Moines Soc. Fin. Analysts, Inst. Chartered Fin. Analysts, Fin. Mgmt. Assn. (bd. dirs. 1978-80), Midwest Fin. Assn. (pres. 1983-84). Avocations: biking, reading. Office: U Iowa Coll of Bus Iowa City IA 52242

STEVENSON, ROBERT BENJAMIN, III, prosthodontist, writer; b. Topeka, Feb. 13, 1950; s. Robert Benjamin and Martha (McClelland) S.; m. Barbara Jean Sulick, June 6, 1975; children: Jody Ann, Robert Woodrow. BS, U. Miami, Coral Gables, Fla., 1972; DDS, Ohio State U., 1975, MS, MA, 1980. Cert. in prosthodontics splty. tng. Practice dentistry specializing in prosthodontics Columbus, Ohio, 1981—; clin. asst. prof. Ohio State U., Columbus, 1981-87; chmn. oral cancer com. Columbus Dental Soc., 1981-85, Am. Cancer Soc., Columbus, 1985—. Editor Columbus Dental Soc. Bulletin, 1981-87, Ohio State U. Dental Alumni Quarterly, 1982—, Am. Med. Writer's Assn. Ohio newsletter, 1983-86, Ohio State Journalism Alumni Assn. newsletter, 1986—; assoc. editor Jour. Prosthetic Dentistry, 1987—; inventor intraoral measuring device. Vol. Am. Cancer Soc., Columbus, 1982—, Lion's Club, Gahanna and Reynoldsburg, Ohio, 1983, 84; fundraiser Sertoma, Worthington, Ohio, 1983-85, Columbus council Boy Scouts of Am., 1984. Served to capt. USAF, 1975-78. Mem. Am. Coll. Prosthodontists, Ohio Dental Assn. (alt. del. 1982—), Am. Assn. Dental Schs., Am. Assn. Dental Editors, Council Biology Editors, Carl O. Boucher Prosthodontic Conf., AAAS, Procrastinator's Club of Am. Avocations: playing electric organ, music, reading. Home: 1300 Southport Circle Columbus OH 43220 Office: 3600 Olentangy River Rd Columbus OH 43214

STEVENSON, THOMAS HERBERT, management consultant, writer; b. Covington, Ohio, Oct. 16, 1951; s. Robert Louis and Dolly Eileen (Minnich) S.; m. Pamela F. Blythe, Mar. 10, 1979. BA, Wright State U., 1977. Teaching asst., research asst. Wright State U., 1975-77; teaching asst. Bowling Green State U., 1978; loan officer Western Ohio Nat. B Bank & Trust Co., 1979-80, asst. v.p. adminstrs., 1981-82, v.p. mgmt. services div., 1983-85; v.p., bank mgmt. cons. Young & Assocs., Inc., 1985-86, exec. v.p., 1987—; legis. impact analyst Community Bankers Ohio, 1985—; mem. exec. com. Owl Electronic Banking Network, 1981-85; mem. adv. bd. Upper Valley Joint Vocat. Sch. for Fin. Instns., 1981-85. Contbr. articles to profl. jours. Served to cpl. USMC, 1972-73. Recipient George Washington medal of Honor Freedom's Found., 1974. Mem. Am. Inst. Banking (adv. bd. 1982-85), Community Bankers Assn. Ohio, World Future Soc. Republican. Mem. Ch. of Brethren. Club: Eagles. Home: 9020 W U S Hwy 36 Covington OH 45318 Office: 121 E Main St Kent OH 44240

STEVENSON, THOMAS RAY, Plastic surgeon; b. Kansas City, Mo., Jan. 22, 1946; s. John Adolph and Helen Ray (Clarke) S.; m. Judith Ann Hunter, Aug. 17, 1968; children: Anne Hunter, Andrew Thomas. BA, U. Kans., 1968, MD. Diplomate Am. Bd. Plastic and Reconstructive Surgery. Resident in gen. surgery U. Va., Charlottesville, 1972-78; resident in plastic surgery Emory U., Atlanta, 1980-82; asst. prof. surgery U. Mich., 1982—; chief plastic surgery Ann Arbor VA Hosp., 1982—. Served to maj. USAR, 1978-80. Fellow ACS; mem. Am. Soc. Plastic and Reconstructive Surgery. Office: U Mich Hosps Sect Plastic Surgery 2214 Taubman Ctr Ann Arbor MI 48109

STEVOFF, AUDREY LAZNICKA, investment analyst, telecommunications specialist; b. Chgo., Dec. 13, 1934; d. Frank and Bessie (Srp) Laznicka; m. Nick Spiro Stevoff, Dec. 26, 1970; children—Nadine, Sheryl. B.S. in Acctg., U. Ill., 1956; M.B.A., Northwestern U., 1965. Acct. Arthur Andersen & Co., Chgo., 1956; statistical analyst Standard Oil (Ind.), Chgo., 1956-66; public utility analyst Harris Trust & Savs. Bank, Chgo., 1966-71; telecommunications analyst Duff & Phelps, Inc., Chgo., 1982—, asst. v.p., 1984-86, v.p., 1986— . Mem. Investment Analysts Soc. Chgo. (chmn. membership com. 1985-87), Inst. Chartered Fin. Analysts (cert.), Fin. Analysts Fedn., Pub. Utility Securities Club Chgo. (treas. 1968-69, sec. 1969-70). Club: Women's Assn. 1st Presbyterian Ch. Deerfield (treas. 1978-79, v.p. 1980-81, pres. 1981-82). Avocations: golf, travel, arts and crafts, attending concerts and theater. Office: Duff & Phelps Inc 55 E Monroe St Chicago IL 60603

STEWARD, WELDON CECIL, architecture educator, architect, consultant; b. Pampa, Tex., Apr. 7, 1934; s. Weldon C. and Lois (Maness) S.; m. Mary Jane Nedbalek, June 9, 1956; children: Karen A., W. Craig. Cert. in architecture and planning, Ecole des Beaux Arts, Fontainebleu, France, 1956; B.Arch., Tex. A&M U, 1957; M.S. in Architecture, Columbia U., 1961. Registered architect, Tex. Designer Perkins & Will, Architects, White Plains, N.Y., 1961-62; asst. prof. architecture Tex. A&M U., College Station, 1962-67, assoc. chmn. Sch. Architecture, 1966-69, assoc. dean, prof. Coll. Environ. Design, 1969-73; dean, prof. Coll. Architecture U. Nebr., Lincoln, 1973—; ednl. cons. Peoples Republic of China, 1979; project dir. Imo State U. Planning, Nigeria, 1981—; vis. prof. Tong ji U., Shanghai, 1984; co-chmn. nat. coordination com. AIA Nat. Council Archtl. Registration Bd. Intership, Washington, 1980-81. Designer, Quinnipiac Elem. Sch., New Haven, Conn., 1961 (Am Assn. Sch. Adminstrs. Exhibit 1969), J.J. Buser Residence, Bryan, Tex., 1969. Mem. Lincoln Architects, Engrs. Selection Bd., 1979—; mem. Nat. Com. for U.S., China Relations, N.Y.C., 1981—; profl. adviser, nat. design competition Wick Alumni Ctr., Lincoln, 1981. Served to capt. USAF, 1957-60. Grad. fellow Columbia U., 1960. Fellow AIA (pres. Brazos chpt. 1969, chmn. profl. devel. com. 1979); mem. Nebr. Soc. Architects (bd. dirs. 1977—), Archtl. Found. Nebr. (bd. dirs. 1981—, treas. 1981—), Assn. Collegiate Schs. Architecture (bd dirs. 1975-79), Nat. Archtl. Accrediting Bd. (bd. dirs. 1986—), Tau Sigma Delta, Phi Kappa Phi. Home: 1250 Aldrich Rd Lincoln NE 68510 Office: Coll Architecture U Nebr Lincoln NE 68588

STEWART, CHESTER ARTHUR, motel owner, rancher; b. North Platte, Nebr., Oct. 20, 1929; s. Arthur H. and Getty (Greeley) S.; m. Norine V. Bayne, Oct. 7, 1951; children: Glenn, Dale, Dianne, Carol, Peggy, Rodney. Grad., High Sch., North Platte, 1946. Rancher North Platte, 1946-51, 53-68; owner, operator Best Western Chief Motel, McCook, Nebr., 1968—. Served to cpl. U.S. Army, 1951-53. Fellow McCook C. of C. (named outstanding businessperson 1985), Best Western Internat. Republican. Home: 601 W 12th St McCook NE 69001 Office: Best Western Chief Motel 612 W B St McCook NE 69001

STEWART, CLAYTON B., food products company executive; b. 1924. Owner M.Hakes and Sons, Lorens, Iowa, 1945-65; with Hakes Foods Inc., Lorens, 1965—, now pres., also bd. dirs. Served to 2d lt. USAF, 1942-45. Office: Hakes Foods Inc 210 N 1st St Laurens IA 50554 *

STEWART, DAVID DICKSON, psychologist; b. Sharon, Pa., Aug. 19, 1949; s. Thomas Dickson and Mary Ella (Rodecker) S.; m. Jodi Anne Martin, Dec. 13, 1970. BA, Mich. State U., 1971; MS, George Williams Coll., Downers Grove, Ill., 1974; PhD, U.S. Internat. U., San Diego, 1981. Lic. cons. psychologist, Minn. Family therapist, team leader Youth in Crisis, Berwyn, Ill., 1974-75, counseling coordinator, 1975-77; program coordinator Harmonium, Inc., Poway, Calif., 1979-80; psychology intern Hennepin County Med. Ctr., Mpls., 1980-81; staff psychologist Dakota Mental Health Ctr., South St. Paul, Minn., 1981-86, dir. psychol. services, 1986, clin. dir., 1987—. Mem. Am. Psychol. Assn., Minn. Psychol. Assn. Democrat. Avocations: gardening, reading. Office: Dakota Mental Health Ctr 744 19th Ave N South Saint Paul MN 55075

STEWART, DAVID KENNETH, optometrist; b. Dayton, Ohio, June 15, 1949; s. Kenneth L. and Hilda (Long) S.; m. Rebecca Jones, Mar. 2, 1974; children: Brian Kenneth, Lori Elizabeth. OD, Ohio State U., 1973. Pvt. practice optometry Beavercreek, Ohio, 1973—. Chmn. Beavercreek Health Adv. Bd., Beavercreek Health Fair, 1981-82, Robert Doyle for State Rep., Greene County, Ohio, 1982, 84, 86. Paul Harris fellow, 1985. Fellow Am. Acad. Optometry; mem. Am. Optometric Assn., Ohio Optometric Assn., Miami Valley Soc. Optometrists (pres. 1981-82). Republican. Lodge: Rotary (Beavercreek pres. 1979-80). Home: 1900 Deerbrook Trail Beavercreek OH 45385 Office: 3351 Dayton-Xenia Rd Beavercreek OH 45432

STEWART, DAVID MACK, association administrator, author; b. St. Louis, Sept. 20, 1937; s. Harold Mack and Lora Mae (Coil) S.; m. Lee Frances Pomeroy, Sept. 10, 1986; children: Jonathan, LoraLee, Keith, Benjamin, Anthony. BS, U. Mo., Rolla, 1965, MS, 1969, PhD, 1971. Registered geophysicist, Calif.; cert. childbirth educator, Mo. Asst. prof. U. N.C., Chapel Hill, 1971-78; exec. dir. Internat. Assn. Parents and Profls. for Safe Alternatives in Childbirth, Marble Hill, Mo., 1978—; cons. Am. Coll. Nurse-Midwives, Washington, 1979-81; bd. dirs. Health Systems Agy., Poplar Bluff, Mo., 1981-83; advisor Utah Sch. Midwifery, Provo, 1984—. Author: (book) Five Standards for Safe Childbearing, (booklets) God's Existence: Can Science Prove It?, Fathering and a Career: Keeping a Healthy Balance, (pamphlet) Father to Father on Breastfeeding, numerous other articles, pamphlets and booklets; co-author (books) The Childbirth Activists' Handbook, Safe Alternatives in Childbirth, 1976 (Book of Yr. award Am. Jour. Nursing), 21st Century Obstetrics Now!, 1977, Compulsory Hospitalization or Freedom?, 1979 (Book of Yr. award Am. Jour. Nursing). Republican. Lodge: Optimists (v.p. Marble Hill 1981—). Avocations: piano, pencil drawing, singing. Home: 646 Pomeroy Rd Marble Hill MO 63764 Office: Internat Assn Parents & Profls for Safe Alternatives in Childbirth PO Box 300 Marble Hill MO 63764

STEWART, ERNEST WILLIAM, market research executive; b. Kansas City, Kans., Oct. 16, 1950; s. Ernest William Davey and Elizabeth Jeannette (Forbes) S.; m. Deborah Gayle Hofling, Dec. 8, 1979; children: Catherine Soteldo, Ernest William III. Student S.W. Mo. State U., 1968-71; B.S. in Communications, Lindenwood Coll., 1972; M.A. in Bus. Adminstrn. and Mktg., Webster U., 1982. Youth news editor St. Louis County Star, Overland, Mo., 1965-67; corr. St. Louis Post-Dispatch, 1971-72; writer/news editor Sta.-KMOX, St. Louis, 1972-73; reporter, then news editor St. Charles (Mo.) Jour., 1973-76; editorial dir. Ednl. Media Inc., St. Charles, 1976; dir. mem. relations St. Louis Tchrs. Credit Union, 1976-79; pub. relations rep. Mercantile Bancorp., St. Louis, 1979-82; dir. mktg. research Nat. Decorating Products Assn., St. Louis, 1982-86, dir market research and bus. devel., 1986—; tchr. seminars, condr. workshops in journalism, mktg.; cons. advt. agys. Recipient cert. excellence for best news story Suburban Newspapers Am., 1975, cert. appreciation Vocat. Indsl. Clubs Am., 1974, Pioneer award Mo. Credit Union League, 1978; named hon. Ky. col. Mem. Am. Mktg. Assn., Direct Mktg. Club St. Louis, Webster U. Alumni Assn. (long-range planning commn. 1982-86, bd. dirs. 1983—, pres. elect 1985). Episcopalian. Author: (SBA Publ.) Starting a Retail Decorating Products Business. Contbr. numerous articles to decorating-products industry trade publs. Home: 323 E Jefferson Ave Kirkwood MO 63122 Office: Nat Decorating Products Assn 1050 N Lindbergh Blvd Saint Louis MO 63132

STEWART, GARY MICHAEL, industrial engineer; b. Michigan City, Ind., July 14, 1951; m. Kristy L. Stewart, Mar. 3, 1973; 1 child, Courtney M. BBA, St. Joseph's Coll., Collegeville, Ind., 1973. Acct. Pullman Standard, Chgo. and Hammond (Ind.), 1973-77; gen. acct. Sealy Spring Corp., Rensselaer, Ind., 1977-79, indsl. engr., 1979—. Mem. Inst. Indsl. Engrs., Methods Time Measurement Assn. Standards and Research. Office: Sealy Spring Corp 1132 N Cullen St Rensselaer IN 47978

STEWART, GLEN JAY, minister; b. Lorain, Ohio, Nov. 12, 1949; s. Charles Leonard and Connie Rae (Jellison) S.; m. Joyce Ellen Long, May 24, 1975; 1 child, John-Paul. BA, U. Toledo, 1971; MDiv, Vanderbilt U., 1974, D in Ministry, 1975. Ordained to ministry of Christian Ch., 1974. Pastor Matlock Meml. Christian Ch., Salem, Ky., 1972; pastor 1st Christian Ch., Madison, Tenn., 1974-75, Sidney, Ohio, 1975-80; sr. minister 2d Christian Ch., Warren, Ohio, 1980-85; assoc. area minister Christian Ch. Greater

Kansas City, Mo., 1986—; bd. dirs. Christian Ch. Elyria, Ohio, 1983-85. Co-founder, pre.s, Big Bros./Big Sisters Shelby County, Sidney, 1978, 80; mem. Safety Com., Lenexa, Kans., 1986; trustee Battered Spouse Shelter, Warren, 1983-85. Mem. Amnesty Internat., Mensa. Democrat. Lodge: Rotary. Avocations: investments, sports, leading glass, geneology. Office: Christian Ch Greater Kansas City PO Box 17088 Kansas City MO 64132

STEWART, JAMES ALDEN, optometrist; b. Flint, Mich., Mar. 11, 1946; s. Joseph Stanley and Beulah Fern (Burkholder) S.; m. Nancy Lee, Dec. 27, 1969; 1 child, Andrew Lee. AS, Genesee Community Coll., 1972; BS in Visual Sci., Ill. Coll. Optometry, Chgo., 1976, OD, 1978. Gen. practice optometry Montrose, Mich., 1980—. Treas. Montrose Area Hist. Assn., 1980-84. Served to sgt. USAF, 1966-69. Named one of Outstanding Young Men Am., 1978. Mem. Am. Optometric Assn., Mich. Optometric Assn., Saginaw Valley Optometric Assn., Ill. Coll. Optometry Alumni Assn. (bd. dirs. Great Lakes chpt. 1983—, v.p. 1985-87), Montrose Area C. of C. Methodist. Avocation: photography. Office: 119 N Saginaw St Box 67 Montrose MI 48457

STEWART, JAMES HOWARD, corporate training, stategic planning executive; b. Cin., Dec. 16, 1950; s. James William and Sue Frances (Lewis) S.; m. Carol Jean Robinson, June 23, 1973; children: Elizabeth Jean, WIlliam Howard, Rebekah Sue. BA, U. Cin., 1973. Mgmt. trainee Gen. Tool Co., Reading, Ohio, 1973-78, prodn. control mgr., 1976-81, tng. mgr., 1981-85, dir. tng. and edn., 1985—; bd. dirs. Greater Cin. Tng. Corp., Cin., 1983—. Adv. Jr. Achievement of Cin., 1981—; mem. adv. com. Reading Community Schs., 1984—, Great Oaks Vocat. Sch. Dist., Cin., 1986—; mem. machine tools adv. com. Cin. Pub. Schs., Cin., 1984—; Sunday Sch. Tchr., dir. Ch. Choir. Mem. Internat. Assn. Quality Circles (bd. dir. Cin. chpt. 1981-86, v.p. 1983-84), Nat. Tooling and Machinery Assn., Cin. Tooling and Machinery Assn. (tng. coordinator, 1983-86). Republican. Baptist. Office: Gen Tool Co Inc 101 Landy Ln Cincinnati OH 45215

STEWART, JOHN ANTENEN, physician; b. Hamilton, Ohio, Sept. 1, 1920; s. James E.B. and Rose Carol (Antenen) S.; m. Marian Louise Vail, June 23, 1945; children: John Vail, Robert Vail, Barbara Vail Stewart Keating. BS, U. Cin., 1942, MD, 1945. Diplomate Am. Bd. Ob-Gyn. Intern Harper Hosp., Detroit, 1945-46; at VA Hosp., 1946-48; resident Chgo. Maternity Ctr., 1948-49, Chgo. Lying-In Hosp., 1949, Ravenswood Hosp., Chgo., 1949-51; practice medicine specializing in ob-gyn Hamilton, Ohio, 1951—. Mem. Hist. Hamilton. Served to capt. M.C., U.S. Army, 1942-48. Fellow: Am. Coll. Ob-Gyn.; mem. Ohio State Med. Soc., Butler County Med. Soc., Hamilton Acad. Medicine, AMA, Royal Soc. Medicine, Am. Inst. Ultrasound Medicine, Am. Assn. Laparoscopists and Colposcopists, Am. Soc. for Colposcopy and Cervical Pathology, Royal Soc. Medicine, Am. Instn. Nuclear Magnetic Resonance, Am. Guild Organists, Ohio Genealogy Soc., Butler County Hist. Soc. Republican. Presbyterian. Avocations: computers, woodworking, organist, photography. Home: 701 Oakwood Dr Hamilton OH 45013 Office: 240 Park Ave Hamilton OH 45013

STEWART, JOHN FRAISER, engineer, educator; b. Overland, Mo., Aug. 22, 1934; s. William Fraiser and Marion Clare (Williams) S.; m. Ilene Kate Woods, oct. 18, 1955 (div. Aug. 1966); 1 child; James Leslie; m. June Shaw, May 13, 1967. BS in Indsl. Mgmt., So. Ill. U., 1972; grad. in ednl. ministry, Sem. Extension, Nashville, 1980-86. Tool and die maker R.C. Can Co., Hazelwood, Mo., 1957-68, liaison engr., 1968-70; project engr. Boise Cascade, Hazelwood, 1970-78, ops. specialist, 1978-82, tech. assoc., 1982—; cons. Coca-Cola, Fla., 1981-82, Merico, Tex., 1985; trainee Boise Envelope Div., Allentown, Pa., 1982-83, Pillsbury, E. Greenville, Pa. & Denison, Tex., 1981-83. Editor tng. manuals 1831 Bliss Press, 1970-71, D&A 800 Liner, 1971-72, 1103 Scroll Shear, 1973-74; contbr. articles to profl. jours. Chief trainer West Overland (Mo.) Fire Dept., 1957-68; advisor Boy Scouts Am., Florissant, Mo., 1967-78; disaster specialist ARC, Franklin County, Mo., 1982—, field service chmn., Region II Territory, 1984—. Served with USMC, 1952-55, Japan. Fellow Am. Soc. Tool and Mfg. Engrs., Soc. Mfg. Engrs., Am. Soc. Quality Control, VFW (chaplain 1982-83, vice-commr. 1983-84). Democrat. Baptist. Club: Owensville Gun. Avocations: trout fisning, trapshooting, hunting. Home: R1 Box 35 Leslie MO 63056 Office: Boise Cascade 13300 Interstate Dr Hazelwood MO 63042

STEWART, KENDALL LEUOMON, psychiatrist; b. Rome, Ga., Sept. 19, 1950; s. Leuomon and Flora Mae (Miller) S.; m. J. Faye Alley, Nov. 16, 1974; children: Jonathan Brock, Timothy Brenton. BS magna cum laude, Berry Coll., 1972; MD, Med. Coll. Ga., 1976. Diplomate Nat. Bd. Med. Examiners, Am. Bd. Psychiatry and Neurology. Resident in psychiatry Med. Coll. Ga., Augusta, 1976-79; practice medicine specializing in psychiatry Mercy Hosp., Portsmouth, Ohio, 1982—, Scioto Hosp., Portsmouth, 1982—, So. Hills Hosp., Portsmouth, 1982—; cons. psychiatrist Beekman Ctr. for Mental Health Services, Greenwood, S.C., 1977-79, Comprehend, Inc., Maysville, Ky., 1982-83, Portsmouth Receiving Hosp., 1983, So. Ohio Correctional Facility, Lucasville, 1982, Pathways, Inc., Greenup, Ky., 1982-87; mem. med. staff exec. com. Mercy Hosp., Portsmouth, 1984-87, chief of staff, 1986; clin. asst. prof. psychiatry Ohio U. Coll. Osteo. Medicine, Athens, 1985—. Served as capt. USAF, 1979-81. Named one of Outstanding Young Men of Am. Mem. AMA, Am. Psychiat. Assn., Christian Med. Soc., Scioto County Med. Soc., Am. Assn. Suicidology. Republican. Avocations: reading, writing, canoeing, fishing. Office: 1725 27th St Portsmouth OH 45662

STEWART, MICHAEL OSBORNE, university administrator; b. Sacramento, Aug. 25, 1938; s. Morris Albion and Marjorie Cathryn (McFarlin) S.; m. Lucille Arnette Cooper, June 11, 1961; children—Heather, Blaine. B.A., U. Calif.-Berkeley, 1960, M.A., 1961; Ph.D. Kans. State U., 1972. Asst. dean of students San Jose State U., Calif., 1965-66; assoc. dean of students Fort Hays State U., Kans., 1966-71, asst. v.p. acad. affairs, dir. instl. research, 1971-74; v.p. adminstrn. Peru State Coll., Nebr., 1974-79, U. S.D., Vermillion, 1979-82; v.p. bus. affairs, treas. Lawrence U., Appleton, Wis., 1982—; v.p., sec., treas. Lawrence Corp. Wis., 1983—; dir. Sch. Coll., Univ. Underwriters Ltd., 1987—. Mem. editorial bd. College and University Business Administration, 4th edit., 1981-82. Contbr. articles to profl. jours. Bd. dirs., chmn. Youth Care Inc., Hays, 1969-74. Served to capt. U.S. Army, 1961-65, col. Res., 1966. Alumni scholar U. Calif.-Berkeley, 1956-57; NDEA fellow, 1967-68. Mem. Kans. Assn. Student Personnel Adminstrn. (pres. 1970-71), Am. Assn. Univ. Adminstrns. (bd. dirs. 1979-82, chmn. audit budget com. 1982-84), Nat. Assn. Coll. Bus. Officers (small coll. and minority insts. com. 1985—, chmn. 1986—, task force on bus. competition 1987—), Central Assn. Coll. Bus. Officers (exec. com., idea exchange, publs. and host coms. 1974—), Appleton Taxpayers Assn. (bd. dirs. 1986), Theta Chi (nat. chaplain, sec. 1972-80). Democrat. Episcopalian. Lodge: Kiwanis (bd. dirs. Auburn club 1974, Appleton club 1984—, pres.-elect 1987). Avocations: collecting stamps, boating. Office: Lawrence Univ 115 S Drew St PO Box 599 Appleton WI 54912

STEWART, NORINE VERYL, restaurant owner; b. North Platte, Nebr., Jan. 14, 1932; d. Louis M. and Bertha M. (William) Bayne; m. Chester A. Stewart, Oct. 7, 1951; children: Glenn, Dale, Dianne, Carol, Peggy, Rodney. Grad., High Sch., Stapleton, Nebr., 1950. Salesperson F.W. Woolworth, North Platte, 1950; dental technician Dr. Fitzpatrick, North Platte, 1951; owner, operator Chief Restaurant, McCook, Nebr., 1968—. Fellow McCook C. of C. (named outstanding businessperson 1985), Best Western Internat. Republican. Home: 601 W 12th St McCook NE 69001 Office: Chief Restaurant 606 W B St McCook NE 69001

STEWART, PAMELA JAN, biochemist; b. Kenosha, Wis., July 6, 1958; d. Jan Lee and Dora Mae (Commer) S. BS, U. Ill., Chgo., 1980, PhD, 1984. Research scientist Northwestern U., Chgo., 1984—. Contbr. articles to profl. jours. Fellow NIH. Mem. AAAS, AAUW (research fellow), Endocrine Soc., Am. Soc. Bone and Mineral Research, Sigma Delta Epsilon (Eloise Gerry fellow 1985-86). Avocations: piano, watercolors. Home: 1121 S Humphrey Oak Park IL 60304 Office: Northwestern U 303 E Chicago Ave Chicago IL 60611

STEWART, PAUL ARTHUR, pharmaceutical company executive; b. Greensburg, Ind., Sept. 28, 1955; s. John Arthur and Alberta Jeannette (Densford) S.; m. Susan Rhodes, Dec. 20, 1975. B.S., Purdue U., 1976; MBA, Harvard Bus. Sch., 1987. Grad. asst. Purdue U., West Lafayette, Ind, 1977; asst. treas. Stewart Seeds, Inc., Greensburg, Ind., 1977-82, sec., treas., 1982-84; cons. The Boston Cons. Group, Inc., Chgo., 1986; founder, owner PASCO Group, mgmt. and computer cons., aircraft leasing, 1979-87; mgr. bus. planning-agrichems. Eli Lilly & Co., Indpls., 1987—. Mem. Greensburg-Decatur County Bd. of Airport Commrs., 1980-85, pres., 1980, 81, 83; mem. Decatur County Data Processing Bd., 1982-85. Mem. Ind. Seed Trade Assn. (dir. 1982-85, v.p. 1983-84, pres. 1984-85, chmn. legis. com. 1982-83), Am. Seed Trade Assn. (legis. com. 1983-85), Alpha Gamma Rho. Republican. Presbyterian. Office: Ely Lilly & Co Lilly Corp Ctr Indianapolis IN 46285

STEWART, RAYMOND A., JR., transportation holding company executive; b. Topeka, 1935. Pres., dir. Yellow Freight System, Inc. of Del., Overland Park, Kans., 1984—. Office: Yellow Freight System Inc of Del 10990 Roe Ave Box 7563 Overland Park KS 66207 *

STEWART, RICHARD CLAIR, podiatrist, educator; b. Columbus, Ohio, Mar. 30, 1949; s. Robert C. and Mary E. (Lodge) S.; m. Sara M. Macklin, June 13, 1970 (div. Mar. 1982); children: Robert, Sheila, Emily; m. Debra Lee Schwartz, Feb. 29, 1984. Student, Ohio State U., 1967-70; D in Podiatric Medicine, Ohio Coll. Podiatric Medicine, 1974; BA, Edison State U., Clifton, N.J., 1986. Diplomate Am. Bd. Podiatric Surgery. Resident Md. State Hosps., Balt., 1973-74; pvt. practice podiatry Columbus, 1974—; clin. instr. Ohio State U., 1976—; residency dir. Doctors Hosp., Columbus, 1983—. Author: (with others) Skin Tumors of the Foot, 1976. Bd. dirs. Easter Seals Soc., Columbus, 1978—. Fellow Am. Coll. Foot Surgeons; mem. Am. Podiatric Medicine Assn. (chmn. com. 1978-83), Ohio Podiatric Medicine Assn. (pres. 1982-83, contbr. articles to jour.). Roman Catholic. Clubs: Agonis, Maenerchor. Avocations: music, boating. Home: 1489 Michigan Ave Columbus OH 43201 Office: 1208 W Fifth Ave Columbus OH 43212

STEWART, RICHARD WARREN, agricultural company executive; b. Postville, Iowa, Aug. 3, 1951; s. William Warren and Mary Helen (Merriam) S.; m. Alisa Colleen Greenhaw, Jan. 1, 1976 (div. July 1982); children: Saasha, Winlock, Coleman, Kane. Student, Coe Coll., 1987. Founder Frontier Cooperative Herbs, Inc., Norway, Iowa, 1976-80; chief fin. officer Frontier Cooperative Herbs, Inc., Norway, 1980-85, chief exec. officer, 1985—; bd. dirs., treas. New Pioneer Cooperative Soc., Iowa City, Iowa, 1985—. Contbr. to book Who Is Guru Maharaj Ji?, 1972. Mem. Nat. Cooperative Bus. Assn., Consumer Cooperative Mgmt. Assn. (instr. 1983—), Cen. States Cooperatives (bd. dirs., treas. 1985-86), Alpha Sigma Lambda. Buddhist. Avocations: travel, classical music, karate, volleyball. Home: 855 Camburn Ct SE Cedar Rapids IA 52403 Office: Frontier Cooperative Herbs Box 299 Norway IA 52318

STEWART, TRENT ANTHONY, pharmacist; b. Cin., Dec. 10, 1954; s. Philip Howard and Essie Mae (Kilgore) S. B.S., U. Cin., 1978. Registered Pharmacist. Staff pharmacist Kettering Med. Ctr., 1978-81; staff pharmacist St. Elizabeth Med. Ctr., Dayton, Ohio, 1981-83; sales rep. Eli Lilly & Co., Portland, Oreg., 1983-84; mgr. pharmacy Dunbar Pharmacy and Med. Supply, Inc., Dayton, 1984-85; intravenous admixture pharmacist Dayton VA Med Ctr., 1985—. Sponsor, Big Bros. and Big Sisters of Dayton, 1981. Mem. Dayton Area Soc. Hosp. Pharmacists (sec. 1985), Ohio Soc. Hosp. Pharmacists, Cin. Pharm. Soc., Internat. Platform Assn. Democrat Roman Catholic. Club: Dayton Indoor Tennis, Ohio River Road Runners. Home: 1769 Sheltering Tree Dr West Carrollton OH 45449 Office: Dayton VA Med Ctr 4100 W 3d St Dayton OH 45428

STEWART, VIRGINIA KAMPP (MIMI), public relations executive; b. Oak Park, Ill., Dec. 12, 1939; d. Hubert Eugene and Virginia (Dalton) Kampp; student Northwestern U., 1957-59, Rosary Coll., 1959-60; m. Henry Lawrence Stewart III, Apr. 7, 1961; children—John Hubert, Peter David, Michael Edward. Asst. editor Internat. Altrusan, 1961-64; free-lance writer, 1964-71; editor Wheaton (Ill.) Leader, 1971-73; assoc. dir. pub. relations Central DuPage Hosp., Winfield, Ill., 1973-78, dir. pub. relations, 1978-83; v.p. pub. relations Healthcorp Affiliates, Naperville, Ill., 1983-85; assoc. exec. dir. Altrusa Internat., Inc., Chgo., 1985-86; pres. Communique: Communication Concepts, Inc., 1986—. Founder The Art Fair, Pitts., 1970; chmn. judges Daily Jour. Ad Craft, 1975-82; chmn. Wheaton City Council Nominating Assembly, 1976; bd. dirs. Community Nursing Service DuPage County, 1976-83, DuPage County Bd. Health Dept., 1985—; mem. Wheaton Plan Commn., 1979—, chmn., 1983. Named Editor of Yr., Ill. Press Assn., 1972; Profl. Woman of Yr., Bank of Wheaton, 1976; recipient Ron Brinkman award Wheaton C. of C., 1982. Mem. Am. Soc. for Hosp. Pub. Relations, Acad. Hosp. Pub. Relations (sec. 1979-80, dir. 1980— pres. 1984), Am. Soc. Assn. Execs., Greater Wheaton C. of C. (dir. 1973-81, Brinkman award 1982). Republican. Clubs: Service (Chgo.). Home and Office: 1103 N President St Wheaton IL 60187

STEWART, W. RODERICK, manufacturing company executive; b. Norwood, Ohio, Mar. 22, 1916; s. Raymond Forrest and Estelle Marie (Keller) S.; m. Dolores Faye Doll, Apr. 15, 1944; 1 dau., Sharon Marie. BBA, U. Cin., 1939. Owner, dir. Music by Roderick Orch., 1934-49; v.p. Cin. Lithographing Co., 1949-63; owner, pres. Concrete Surfacing Machinery Co., Cin., 1963-71, Bossert Machine Co., Cin., 1963-71, R & C Tool & Mfg., Amelia, Ohio, 1970-71, Bourbon Copper & Brass, Cin., 1968-71; pres. Stewart Industries, Inc., Cin., 1971-80, chmn. bd., chief exec. officer, 1980—; pres. Printing Machinery Co., Cin., 1976—; chmn bd. dirs. Stewart Safety Systems, Inc., 1981—. Chmn., dir. Greater Cin. & Ky. chpt. Nat. Hemophilia Found., 1976-80; del. White House Conf. Small Bus., 1980; trustee Ohio Presbyn. Retirement Services. Served with USNR, 1942-45. Mem. Cin. C. of C. (Small Businessman of Yr. 1980), Lambda Chi Alpha. Presbyterian. Clubs: Maketewah Country, Northport Point Golf, Cin. (Man of Yr. 1979), Officers of World Wars. Lodges: Rotary, Masons, Shriners, Royal Jesters. Home and Office: 220 Linden Dr Wyoming OH 45215

STEYER, FRANCIS JAMES, food company executive; b. Fostoria, Ohio, Jan. 26, 1935; s. Francis Albert and Helen Lucille (Smith) S.; m. Marilyn Ann Thiel, June 8, 1957; children—Laura, Denise, Lisa, Brian. B.S., Ohio State U., 1957. Produce buyer, store mgr. Kroger Co., Toledo, Ohio, 1960-65, advt. mgr., Pitts., 1965-67, zone mgr., Detroit, 1967-70; exec. v.p. Cardinal Foods, Inc., Columbus, Ohio, 1970-79; pres. Dublin Food Gallery, Ohio, 1979-83; with Food Gallery Supermarkets, Columbus, 1983—; ptnr. Steyer Assocs., Worthington, Ohio, 1984—. Info. officer U.S. Naval Acad., Annapolis, Md., 1982—; bd. dirs. Dublin Arts Council, 1984—. Served with USN, 1957-60, comdr. USNR. Republican. Roman Catholic. Club: Navy League. Lodge: Rotary.

STEYER, RAYMOND JAMES, II, computer programmer; b. Downers Grove, Ill., Aug. 11, 1950; s. Raymond James and Jeane Olga (Wensch) S.; m. Karen Sue Jones, Mar. 3, 1984; children: William Christopher, Andrew Jacob. BA in Math. and Physics, Beloit (Wis.) Coll., 1972. Sr. programmer No. Trust Co., Chgo., 1972-75; v.p. software dept. Child Inc., Lawrence, Kans., 1975-77; sr. analyst/programmer Zurich Ins. Co., Chgo., 1977; programmer technician Montgomery Ward, Chgo., 1977-78; sr. systems engr. Econorex Systems, Kansas City, Mo., 1978-81; system engr. Electronic Data Systems, Kansas City, Mo., 1981-82; cons., 1980—; sr. analyst Universal Systems Am., Overland Park, Kans., 1984—. Fellow Life Mgmt. Inst.; mem. Assn. Computing Machinery. Roman Catholic. Home: 12736 Winchester Ave Grandview MO 64030 Office: 4550 W 109th St Overland Park KS 66211

STIBBE, AUSTIN JULE, accountant; b. St. Paul, Mar. 29, 1930; s. Austin Julius and Agnes Dorothea (Delaney) S.; m. Mary Elizabeth King, May 29, 1952; children: Anne Marie, Craig Jule, David King, Karen Lee. BBA in Acctg., U. Minn., 1952. CPA, Minn., Wis. Tax acct. Ernst & Ernst, Mpls., 1955-60; corp. tax mgr. Econs. Lab., Inc., St. Paul, 1960-65; audit mgr. Coopers & Lybrand, Mpls., 1965-74; v.p. Wilkerson, Guthmann & Johnson, Ltd., St. Paul, 1974—. exec. officer Twin Cities Squadron, U.S. Naval Sea Cadet Corps, Mpls., 1974-80; bd. dirs., treas. Twin Cities Council Navy League, 1970—, pres. 1979-81; mem. adv. council to U. Minn. Dept. Acctg., Mpls., 1983-86; bd. dirs., chmn. audit com. St. Paul Area Council Chs., 1985-87; mem. adv. bd. Headwaters Soc., 1987—. Served to lt. USN, 1952-55. Mem. Am. Inst. CPA's, Minn. Soc. CPA's, Nat. Assn. Accts. Republican. Presbyterian. Clubs: St. Paul Athletic, St. Paul Pool and Yacht. Lodges: Rotary (dist. 596 treas. elect 1987—), Masons (chmn. audit com. 1975—). Avocations: music, boating, history. Home: 1439 Cherry Hill Rd Mendota Heights MN 55118 Office: Wilkerson Guthmann & Johnson Ltd 1300 Norwest Ctr Saint Paul MN 55101

STICKLER, ROBERT BROWN, surgeon; b. Red Oak, Iowa, Aug. 24, 1917; s. Archie Jay and Lois (Brown) S.; m. Charlotte Hill, Nov. 23, 1920; chilren—Linda Elizabeth, Robert Hill. B.S., U. Iowa, 1941, M.D., 1941. Diplomate Am. Bd. Surgery. Intern, Iowa Methodist Hosp., Des Moines, 1941-42; resident U.S. Army, 1942-45; with Iowa Meth. Hosp., 1945-47, S.W. Iowa Hosp., Iowa City, 1947-50; pvt. practice medicine specializing in surgery, Des Moines, 1950—; mem. staff, mem. teaching staff Iowa Meth. Hosp.; mem. staff Iowa Luth. Hosp., Mercy Hosp., Broadlawn Hosp. Bd. dirs. various civic orngs.; active Tallcorn council Boy Scouts Am. Served to maj. U.S. Army, 1942-45. Fellow ACS; mem. AMA, Iowa State Med. Assn., Polk County Med. Assn., Iowa Acad. Surgery. Congregationalist. Clubs: Wakonda (Des Moines); Garden of the Gods (Colorado Springs, Colo.). Contbr. articles to med. jours. Home: 2626 Sioux Run Des Moines IA 50321 Office: 1418 Woodland Ave Des Moines IA 50309

STICKNEY, JOHN MOORE, lawyer; b. Cleve., Apr. 8, 1926; s. Isaac Moore and Alicia Margaret (Burns) S.; m. Elfriede von Rebenstock, Oct. 4, 1958; children—Michaela B., Alicia J., Thomas M. A.B., Western Res. U., 1948, L.L.B., 1951. Bar: Ohio 1952. Sole practice, Cleve., 1952-79; ptnr. Burgess, Steck, Andrews & Stickney, Cleve., 1979—; pres. Scranton-Averell, Inc., Cleve., 1979—. Trustee Cleve. Music Sch. Settlement, 1967—, Salzedo Sch. Harp, Cleve., 1962—, Bishop Brown Fund, Cleve., 1981—; co-trustee Margaret & Edwin Griffiths Trusts, Cleve., 1968—. Served with USNR, 1945-46. Mem. ABA, Ohio State Bar Assn., Cleve. Bar Assn., Republican. Episcopalian. Club: Hermit (Cleve.). Avocation: woodworking. Office: Burgess Steck Andrews & Stickney 1140 Terminal Tower Cleveland OH 44113

STICKNEY, TRUMAN MANVILLE, engineer; b. Crookston, Minn., Dec. 2, 1922; s. Truman Leander, and Thora (Hagen) S.; m. Bernice Lillian Wheeler, Apr. 14, 1951; children—George, Jeffrey, Sandra. B.S. in Aerospace Engring., U. Minn., 1944, B.E.E., 1948. Research scientist NASA, Cleve., 1948-56; engring. supr. Aero Research Instrument Co., Chgo., 1956-60; project engr. Cook Electric Co., Chgo., 1960-63; sr. design engr. Rosemount, Inc., Eden Prairie, Minn., 1963-84, prin. design engr., 1984—. Contbr. articles to sci. jours Patentee high temperature measuring probe. Chmn. U.S. Savs. Bonds campaigns Rosemount plants, 1985. Served with USN, 1944-46, PTO. Assoc. fellow Am. Inst. of Aeros. and Astronautics (chmn. twin cities chpt. 1976). Republican. Presbyterian. Club: Spartan Speakers (Richfield, Minn.) (pres. 1972). Avocations: duck hunting, classical music. Home: 2409 W 97th St Bloomington MN 55431

STIEGLITZ, JOHN FRANKLIN, automotive executive; b. Indpls., Feb. 11, 1953; s. Thomas and Jean Avis (Scheuring) S.; m. Janice Louise Bronson, Oct. 1, 1977; children: Daren Bronson, Karl William, Micah John. B in Mech. Engring., Gen. Motors Inst., 1976. Area plant engr. AC Spark Plug div. Gen. Motors Corp., Flint, 1976-78, supr. maintenance and constrn., 1978-79, area indsl. engr., 1979-82, floorspace adminstr., 1982-86, supr. plant layout, 1986-87, facilities CAD database mgr., 1987—. Mem. admnstrv. bd. Calvary United Meth. Ch., Flint, 1980—, chmn. bd. trustees, 1985—. Mem. Gen. Motors Applicon Users Group. Office: AC Spark Plug div Gen Motors Corp 1300 N Dort Hwy Flint MI 48556

STIEHL, CHARLES WILLIAM, physician, surgeon; b. South Milwaukee, Wis., Apr. 23, 1924; s. Carl Ernst and Marjorie (Simon) S.; m. Sarah D. Harding, Dec. 20, 1945 (div. 1957); children—Patti Stiehl Boris, Carl Harding, Sarah Ann; m. Edith Ann Mauer, Nov. 1967; 1 child, Edith Ann. B.S., Northwestern U., 1942, B.M., M.D., 1947. Intern Columbia Hosp., Milw., 1947-48; resident St. Mary's Hosp., Milw., 1948-49; physician and surgeon Algoma Clinic, Wis., 1950-66; chief surgery Algoma Meml. Hosp., 1964—; med. dir. Heil Co., Milw.; owner Von Stiel Wine, Inc., Algoma, 1961—; pres. S&M Real Estate Corp., Algoma, 1958—. Author emergency medicine computer dictation software program; originator Von Stiehl natural cherry wine, stabilization natural cherry wine, aging wrap. Mem. Sch. Bd., 1954-58. Served with USNR, 1942. Mem. Wis. Med. Soc., Kewaunee County Med. Soc. (past pres.), Wis. Coll. Emergency Physicians (pres.), Acad. Indsl. Medicine, Beta Theta Pi, Nu Sigma Nu. Lutheran. Home and office: 2740 W Forest Home Ave Milwaukee WI 53215

STIEHL, WILLIAM D., federal judge. Judge U.S. District Court, Southern Illinois, East Saint Louis, 1986—. Office: 212 US Courthouse East Saint Louis IL 62202 *

STIER, SERENA DEBORAH, law professor, psychologist; b. Chgo., Oct. 8, 1939; d. Morris Carren and Claire (Hadden) A.; m. Herbert Allen Stier, June 4, 1961 (dec. Oct. 1969); m. Steven Jay Burton, Aug. 7, 1977; children: Daryn, Max, Sam. BA, Stanford U., 1960; MA, Boston U., 1961; PhD, UCLA, 1967; JD, U. Iowa, 1981. USPHS Mt. Sinai Hosp., Los Angeles, 1968-70; asst. prof. med. psychology UCLA, 1970-73; policy studies officer Am. Psychol. Assn., Washington, 1974-77; pvt. practice psychology Coralville, Iowa, 1977—; founding faculty Calif. Sch. Profl. Psychology, Los Angeles, 1970-72; adj. prof. law U. Iowa, Iowa City, 1982—. bd. dirs. Iowa Civil Liberties Union, 1981-83; mem. nat. task force on committment guidelines Ctr. for State Cts., Williamsburg, Va., 1984-86. Mem. ABA, Am. Psychol. Assn., Council for Applied Social Research (founder, bd. dirs. 1974-77). Democrat. Jewish. Avocations: viewing and studying art. Home: 302 Olde Hickory Ridge Coralville IA 52241 Office: U Iowa Coll Law Iowa City IA 52241

STIFFEL, JULES NORMAN, lighting consultant; b. Chgo., June 2, 1933; s. Theophile Alphonse and Esther (Aronson) S.; m. Lisbeth Cherniack, Oct. 16, 1966; 1 child, Lisa Cherniack. BA, Duke U., 1955; advanced mgmt. program, Harvard U., 1978. Various positions leading to chmn. The Stiffel Co., Chgo., 1957-79; pres. Jules Stiffel Concepts Inc., Chgo., 1980-83; cons. Jules Stiffel Assocs., Chgo., 1985—. Bd. dirs. vis. com. Northwestern U. Sch. Music, Evanston, 1984-86, Lyric Opera Guild, Chgo., 1968-86; pres. Chgo. Sinai Congregation, Chgo., 1984-86. Served to lt. (j.g.) USNR, 1955-57. Clubs: Saddle & Cycle (Chgo.) (bd. dirs. 1985-86), Casino, Standard.

STIFFMAN, ARLENE RUBIN, social work educator; b. Bklyn., Aug. 7, 1941; d. Samuel and Rina (Gordon) Rubin; m. Jeffrey Barry Stiffman, June 26, 1960; children: Michael, Martha, Cheryl. BA, U. Cin., 1963; MSW, Washington U., St. Louis, 1975, PhD, 1980. Research dir. Washington U., 1980-84, research instr. social work, 1984-86, asst. prof. social work, 1986—. Editor: Advances in Adolescent Mental Health, 1986; contbr. articles to profl. jours. V.P. Am. Jewish Com., St. Louis, 1985—; bd. dirs. Jewish Community Relations Council, St. Louis, 1984—, Women's Div. Jewish Fedn., St. Louis, 1986—. Adminstrn. Children, Youth and Families grantee, 1982-83, Office Adolescent Pregnancy Programs grantee, 1985-86. Mem. Nat. Assn. Social Workers, Am. Orthopsychiat. Assn., Am. Assn. Behavior Therapists, Social Work Group for Study of Behavioral Methods (newsletter editor 1984-86). Democrat. Home: 21 Ramsgate Saint Louis MO 63132 Office: Washington U Box 1196 Saint Louis MO 63130

STIGEN, REED ARLIN, accountant; b. Detroit Lakes, Minn., Nov. 10, 1944; s. Manley Arlin and Helen Clarice (Johnson) S.; m. Vicki Lynn Leeman, Apr. 10, 1964; children: Brent, Matthew, Lana. AA, Fergus Falls Community Coll., 1965; BA summa cum laude, Moorhead State U., 1967. CPA, N.D., Minn. Acct. Anderson, Helgeson, Lieser & Thorsen, Mpls., 1967-74; ptnr. Adrian S. Helgeson & Co., Mpls., 1974-77, Broeker Hendrickson & Co., Mpls., 1977-78, Charles Bailly & Co., Fargo, N.D., 1978—. Chairperson profl. div. United Way, Fargo, 1983; dean of fund dr. Moorhead State U., 1984. Mem. Am. Inst. CPA's, Minn. Soc. CPA's (Outstanding Com. award 1987, chairperson mgmt. acctg. practice com. 1986-87, chmn. mgmt. adv. services com., chmn. bd. govs. Am. Group CPA Firms), N.D. Soc. CPA's. Republican. Lutheran. Avocations: fishing, hunting, reading, sailing, skiing. Home: 3118 S River Shore Dr Moorhead MN 56560 Office: Charles Bailly & Co 1100 First Interstate Ctr Fargo ND 58124

STIGLER, GEORGE JOSEPH, economist, educator; b. Renton, Wash., Jan. 17, 1911; s. Joseph and Elizabeth (Hungler) S.; m. Margaret Mack, Dec.

26, 1936 (dec. Aug. 1970); children: Stephen, David, Joseph. B.B.A., U. Wash., 1931; M.B.A., Northwestern U., 1932; Ph.D., U. Chgo., 1938; Sc.D., Carnegie Mellon U., 1973, U. Rochester, 1974, Helsinki Sch. Econs., 1976, Northwestern U., 1979; LL.D., Brown U., 1980. Asst. prof. econs. Iowa State Coll., 1936-38; asst. prof. U. Minn., 1938-41, asso. prof., 1941-44, prof., 1944-46; prof. Brown U., 1946-47; prof. econs. Columbia, 1947-58; Walgreen prof. Am. instns. U. Chgo., 1958—, dir. Center Study Economy and the State, 1977—; lectr. London Sch. Econs., 1948; vice chmn., dir. Securities Investor Protection Corp., 1971-74; dir. Chgo. Bd. Trade, 1980-83; bd. dir. Lynde and Harry Bradley Found., 1986. Author: Production and Distribution Theories, 1940, The Theory of Price, 1946, Trends in Output and Employment, 1947, Five Lectures on Economic Problems, 1949, (with K. Boulding) Readings in Price Theory, 1952, Trends in Employment in the Service Industries, 1956, (with D. Blank) Supply and Demand for Scientific Personnel, 1957, The Intellectual and the Market Place, 1964, 84, Essays in the History of Economics, 1965, The Organization of Industry, 1968, (with J.K. Kindahl) The Behavior of Industrial Prices, 1970, The Citizen and the State, 1975, The Economist as Preacher, 1982, The Essence of Stigler, 1986; Editor: Jour. Polit. Economy, 1972—; Contbr. articles to profl. jours. Mem. atty. gen.'s. com. for study anti-trust laws, 1954-55; mem. Blue Ribbon Def. Panel.; Trustee Carleton Coll. Recipient Nobel prize in econs., 1982; Guggenheim fellow, 1955; fellow Center for Advanced Study in Behavioral Scis., 1957-58; recipient Nat. Medal of Science, 1987. Fellow Am. Acad. Arts and Scis., Am. Statis. Soc., Econometric Soc., Nat. Acad. Sci.; mem. Am. Econ. Assn. (pres. 1964), Royal Econ. Soc. Am. Philos. Soc., History of Econs. Soc. (pres. 1977), Mt. Pelerin Soc. (pres. 1977-78). Office: Univ of Chgo Dept of Economics 1101 E 58th St Chicago IL 60637

STILL, KEN DOYLE, industrial marketing executive; b. Falls City, Nebr., Aug. 1, 1952; s. Thomas M. and Freda (Hanson) S.; m. Jana J. Larson, Apr. 30, 1977; children: Jamie Ryan, Colin Michael. BSEE, U. Mo., Columbia, 1974; postgrad., Coll. St. Thomas, St. Paul. Research engr. Fisher Controls, Marshalltown, Iowa, 1974-76, project mgr., 1976-78; product planner Rosemount, Mpls., 1978-82; product mgr. ADC Controls, Mpls., 1982-83; mgr. mktg. Computrol, Ridgefield, Conn., 1983-84; mgr. sales Analogic, Peabody, Mass., 1984-87; mgr. sales and mktg. Systems Assocs. Inc., Libertyville, Ill., 1987—. Mem. Instrument Soc. Am. Presbyterian. Home: 704 Hunters Way Fox River Grove IL 60021 Office: Systems Assocs Inc 205 Peterson Rd Libertyville IL 60048

STILL, TIM WAYNE, accountant; b. Chicapee Falls, Mass., Mar. 23, 1955; s. Roy William and Helen Virginia (Stillion) S.; m. Barbara Marie Roach, June 27, 1975; children: Jim, Christy, Amy, Mark. BS in Acctg., William Jewell Coll., 1976. CPA, Mo. Sr. auditor Baird, Kurtz and Dobson, Kansas City, Mo., 1976-79, Wright, Herfordt, and Sanders, Independence, Mo., 1979-81; asst. to controller Kenworth and Truck, Kansas City, 1981-82; supr. Touche Ross, Kansas City, 1982-84; treas. Mo. Nat. Life, Kansas City, 1984—. Mem. Am. Inst. CPA's, Mo. Soc. CPA's. Home: 2028 Clay Liberty MO 64068

STILLEY, WILLIAM DOUGLAS, lawyer; b. Kansas City, Mo., Feb. 21, 1957; s. Robert James and Dorothy Lee (Blue) S. BA, William Jewell Coll., 1979; JD, U. Mo., Kansas City, 1982. Bar: Mo. 1982, U.S. Dist. Ct. (we. dist.) Mo. 1982, Mo. Ct. Appeals 1983. Law clk. to cir. judge, baliff Jackson County Cir. Ct., Kansas City, 1983; asst. pros. atty. Cass County, Harrisonville, Mo., 1983-85, Platte (Mo.) County, 1985-86; ptnr. Stilley & Fowler, P.C., Raytown, Mo., 1987—. Res. firefighter Raytown Fire Protection Dist., 1978-86; Rep. candidate Jackson County Legislature, 1982; bd. dirs. SE Workshop for Handicapped, Raytown, 1982-84; deacon 1st Bapt. Ch. of Independence, Mo., 1987—. Named one of Outstanding Young Men in Am., 1983. Mem. ABA, Mo. Bar Assn., Platte County Bar Assn., Eastern Jackson County Bar Assn. Lodge: Kiwanis (sec. Harrisonville chpt. 1984-85, sec. South Platte chpt. 1985-87, Parkville chpt. 1986-87). Avocations: genealogy, antiques, old books and autographs, photography, collecting political items. Home: 5227 Blue Ridge Blvd Raytown MO 64133 Office: Stilley & Fowler PC 6240 Raytown Rd Raytown MO 64133

STILLWELL, BERMAR S., aircraft construction company executive; b. 1927. Owner B.S. Stillwell and Co.; with Gates Learjet Corp., Tucson, 1970—, sr. v.p. mktg., 1979-82, now pres., chief operating officer. Office: Grand Prix Motors 4635 E 22nd St Tuscon AZ 85711 *

STILLWELL, WILLIAM LEE, insurance executive; b. Steubenville, Ohio, Sept. 19, 1945; s. William A. and Frances M. (Nation) S.; m. Wanda Joyce Womack, Oct. 11, 1969; children: William E., W. Brian, Brittany L. BS, U. Nebr., Omaha, 1968. Supr. mfg. DuPont Corp., Chattanooga, Tenn., 1968-70; sales mgr. Safeco Ins. Co., Indpls., 1971-74; product devel. mgr. Meridian Ins., Inc., Indpls., 1974-79; pres., owner, agt. W.I. James & Sons Agys., Martinsville, Ind., 1979—. Pres. Big Brothers-Sisters Morgan County, Martinsville, 1984; mem. youth com. 1st Christian Ch., Martinsville, 1986—. Served with USAF, 1963-67, including Vietnam. Mem. Profl. Ins. Agts. Ind. (automation com. 1986—), Soc. Cert. Ins. Counselors, Ins. Mktg. Services Orgn. Republican. Lodge: Rotary (bd. dirs. 1985—). Avocations: golf, tennis, water skiing, travel. Home: 1545 West Shore Dr Martinsville IN 46151 Office: 560 E Morgan Martinsville IN 46151

STIME, MARK BOYD, farmer; b. Volga, S.D., Aug. 3, 1937; s. Osborne Burnette and Opal Viola (Boyd) S.; m. Sharon Kay Anderson, June 30, 1961; children: Todd Mark, Lisa Kay Stime Norgaard, Lori Ann. Student, Luth. Bible Inst., Mpls., 1957-58, Augustana Coll., Sioux Falls, S.D., 1959-60. Owner, operator Harmony Hills Farm, Arlington, S.D., 1960—; mem. Brookings County Conservation Bd., 1986; field rep. Land Stewarship Project, St. Paul, 1984—. Named Outstanding Young Farmer, Volga Jaycees and S.D. Bankers Assn., 1967, Wildlife Conservationist of Yr., S.D. Wildlife Fedn. and Nat. Wildlife Fedn., 1986; named to Soil Conservation Golden Honor Roll, State of S.D., 1985; recipient Soil and Moisture Conservation Achievement award Greater S.D. Assn., 1975, Tree Care award Brookings Conservation Dist., 1982, Wild Habitat award Izaak Walton league, 1983, Land and Wildlife Stewardship award Brookings Wildlife Fedn., 1985. Mem. S.D. Ridge Tillers Assn. (treas. 1985—), Sinai Luth. Ch. Council, deacon, 1970-80, pres. 1980-83. Republican. Avocations: woodworking, hunting, fishing. Home and Office: Harmony Hills Farm Route 2 Box 100 Arlington SD 57212

STIMSON, JUDITH ANN, consumer products executive; b. Gary, Ind., May 9, 1957. BS in Mgmt., Pa. State U., 1979; MBA in Fin., Xavier U., 1982. Packaging assoc. buyer Procter & Gamble Co., Cin., 1979-80, equipment buyer, 1980-82, commodities sr. buyer, 1982-84, chems. purchasing agt., 1984-86, mgr. packaging purchasing, 1987—; mem. bus. commerce adv. bd. Raymond Walters Coll. U. Cin., 1985-87, lectr. 1984-87. Corp. sponsor Jr. Achievement, Cin., 1979-87, fund raiser, 1985-86. Recipient Highest Fund Raiser award Jr. Achievement, 1985. Mem. Nat. Assn. Purchasing Mgrs. (cert.), Purchasing Mgmt. Assn. Cin., Am. Prodn. and Inventory Control Soc. Home: 163 Circle Dr Harrison OH 45030-1852

STINE, ROBERT HOWARD, pediatrician; b. Nov. 1, 1929; s. Harry Raymond and Mabel Eva (Newhard) S.; m. Lois Elaine Kihlgren, Oct. 22, 1960; children: Robert E., Karen, Jonathan. BS in Biology, Moravian Coll., 1952. Diplomate Am. Bd. Pediatrics, Am. Subbd. Pediatric Allergy, Am. Allergy and Immunology. Intern St. Luke's Hosp., Bethlehem, Pa., 1960-61, resident in surgery, 1961-62; intern Jefferson Med. Coll., Bethlehem, Pa., 1956-60; resident in pediatrics U. N.Y., Syracuse, 1962-64; resident in allergy Inst. Allergy Roosevelt Hosp., N.Y.C., 1965-66; clin. instr. pediatrics U. Ill., Chgo., 1965-71; mem. courtesy staff Proctor Community Hosp., Peoria, Ill., 1966-77, mem. active staff, 1977—; mem. teaching staff St. Francis Hosp., Peoria, 1969—; clin. instr. pediatrics Rush-Presbyn. St. Luke's Hosp., Chgo., 1971—. Served to lt. JG, USN, 1953-56. Fellow Am. Acad. Pediatrics, Am. Acad. Allergy and Immunology, Am. Coll. Allergists, Am. Assn. Cert. Allergists; mem. Ill. Soc. Allergy and Clin. Immunology. Home: 105 Hollands Grove Ln Washington IL 61571 Office: 710 E Archer Ave Peoria IL 61603

STINSON, SCOTT LINNELL, doctor of chiropractic; b. Goldsboro, N.C., Nov. 24, 1956; s. Phillip Cedric and Arlene Joan (Linnell) S.; m. Renette Mary Grandstrand, June 23, 1984. Student St. Cloud State U., 1974-78; D.Chiropractic, Northwestern Coll. Chiropractic, 1982. Lic. chiropractor, Minn. Gen. practice chiropractic medicine, cert. sports physician, Inver Grove Heights, Minn., 1982—. Pres. Chiropractic Communications Group, St. Paul, 1985; student Leadership South St. Paul, 1984-85. Mem. Am. Chiropractic Assn., Minn. Chiropractic Assn., Am. Soc. Chiropractic Orthopedists, Northwestern Coll. Chiropractic Alumni Assn. Avocations: rugby; running; reading; fishing. Office: Cahill Chiropractic Office 6115 Cahill Ave Inver Grove Heights MN 55075

STIPAK, JAMES PAUL, dentist; b. Chgo., Sept. 2, 1950; s. Emil Paul and Eleanor (Gillespie) S.; m. Mary Anne Turza, July 28, 1973; children: Michael, Jamie, Jessica. BS, Loyola U., Chgo., 1972; DDS, Loyola U., Maywood, Ill., 1975. Gen. practice dentistry Chgo., 1975—. Bd. dirs. Plum Grove Property Assn., Palatine, Ill., 1981-83, Adoptive Parents Guild, Cath. Charities, Chgo., 1985—; mem. sch. bd. St. Colette Parish, Rolling Meadows, Ill., 1982-84; mem. med. adv. com. Lincoln Park Zoo, Chgo. Fellow Acad. Gen. Dentistry (chmn. Ill. continuing edn. 1985—, Ill. bd. dirs. 1985—, pres. Chgo. chpt. 1986-87), Acad. of Dentistry Internat.; mem. ADA, Ill. State Dental Soc., Chgo. Dental Soc. (sec. n.w. br. 1986-87, v.p. 1987—), Pierre Fauchard Soc. Office: 5251 N Harlem Ave Chicago IL 60656

STIRITZ, WILLIAM P., food company executive; b. Jasper, Ark., July 1, 1934; s. Paul and Dorothy (Bradley) S.; m. Susan Ekberg, Dec. 4, 1972; children—Bradley, Charlotte, Rebecca, Nicholas. B.S., Northwestern U., 1959; M.A., St. Louis U., 1968. Mem. mktg. mgmt. staff Pillsbury Co., Mpls., 1959-62; account mgmt. staff Gardner Advt. Co., St. Louis, 1963—; with Ralston Purina Co., St. Louis, 1963—; pres., chief exec. officer, chmn. Ralston Purina Co., 1981—; Dir. Angelian Corp., Ball Corp., Johnson Wax Co., Centerre Bank, May Dept. Stores, S.C. Johnson & Son. Bd. dirs. Washington U., St. Louis. Served with USN, 1954-57. Mem. Grocery Mfrs. Assn. (dir.). Office: Ralston Purina Co Checkerboard Sq Saint Louis MO 63164

STIRTS, HUGH MICHAEL, federal government executive; b. Des Moines, Feb. 4, 1947; s. Hugh Henry and Beverly Joan (Moolick) S.; m. Catherine Mary Aiello, Feb. 7, 1970; children: Cara and Hollie (twins). BCE, U.S. Mil. Acad., 1969; MS in Biology, Fla. Inst. Tech., 1978, PhD in Biology, 1980. Cert. hazardous material mgr. Commd. 2d lt. U.S. Army, 1969, advanced through grades to capt., 1971, resigned, 1974, served in Federal Republic of Germany and Vietnam; environ. scientist Hdqrs. SAC, Omaha, 1980-82, environ. mgr., 1982-83, chief environ. quality br., 1983-84, chief environ. planning div., 1984-86, dir. environ. mgmt., 1986—; mem. adj. faculty, Fla. Inst. Tech., Melbourne, 1978-80. Contbr. chpts. to books and articles to profl. jours. Maj. USAR, 1984—. Sigma Xi research grantee, Fla. Inst. Tech., 1977, NSF grantee, 1978; named Environ. Engr. of Yr., Hdqrs. SAC, 1986. Mem. Am. Inst. Biol. Scis., Soc. Am. Mil. Engrs., Inst. Hazardous Material Mgrs., Nat. Solid Wastes Mgmt. Assn. Avocations: scuba diving, fishing. Home: 710 E Cary St Papillion NE 68046 Office: Hdqrs SAC/DEV Offutt AFB NE 68113

STITCH, MORTON, aerospace company executive; b. N.Y.C., Aug. 26, 1929; s. Milton and Gussie (Levine) S.; m. Lois Eileen Algren, Nov. 21, 1952; children—Merryl Lynn, Mark Alan, Frank Brian, Douglas Bruce. B.E.E., CCNY, 1950. Jr. engr. Cons. & Designers, Inc., 1950, Teletone TV, 1950; engr. Arma Corp., 1951; div. mgr. Hazeltine Corp., Little Neck, N.Y., 1953-61; with McDonnell Aircraft Corp., St. Louis, 1961-68, group mgr. reliability, 1964-66, sect. mgr. reliability, 1966-68; with McDonnell Astronautics Co. (became McDonnell Douglas Astronautics Co.-St. Louis div. 1968), 1966—, chief effectiveness engr., 1975-76, mgr. harpoon product assurance, 1976-77, dir. product assurance, 1977—; pres. Advanced Healthcare Systems, St. Louis, 1982—, Stitch Mgmt. Enterprises, St. Louis, 1982—, Lomor Assocs. Ltd., 1987—. Bd. dirs., sec. bd. Normandy Osteo. Hosp., St. Louis, 1974-84. Served as 1st lt. USAF, 1951-53. Assoc. fellow AIAA; mem. IEEE (sr.), Electronic Industries Assn. Avocations: computer programming; medical electronics. Home: 23 N Walling Dr Saint Louis MO 63141 Office: McDonnell Douglas Corp J S McDonnell Blvd Saint Louis MO 63134

STITELY, ROSE PATTON, psychologist; b. Bklyn., Feb. 13, 1948; d. William Robert and Rose Anna (Flynn) Patton; m. Thomas Beane Stitely, Oct. 25, 1974. AB, U. Rochester, 1970; PhD, U. Tenn., 1975. Cert. sch. psychologist; registered psychologist. Psychologist Rockford (Ill.) Pub. Schs., 1974-76, No. Suburban Spl. Edn. Dist., Highland Park, Ill., 1976—. Contbg. editor Breed and Show mag., 1985. Mem. Am. Orthopsychiatric Assn., Nat. Assn. Sch. Psychologists. Avocation: dog obedience tng. Home: 658 Sycamore Rd Buffalo Grove IL 60089

STITH, JOSEPH, computer information systems specialist; b. Ann Arbor, Mich., Sept. 1, 1962; s. Raymond Joseph and Rosemary Theresa (Babione) S.; 1 child, Charles. BS in Computer Sci., Aurora (Ill.) Coll., 1983. Computer programmer, operator Aurora Coll., 1980-83; system programmer Moline Corp., St. Charles, Ill., 1983-84; system tech. Longman Group USA, Inc., Chgo., 1984—. Mem. Digital Equipment Computer User's Soc., Alpha Chi. Roman Catholic. Avocations: running, biking, fishing, coin collecting, reading. Home: 1993 A Lilac Ln Aurora IL 60506 Office: Longman Group USA Inc 520 N Dearborn Chicago IL 60610

STITT, DAVID MOFFAT, financial planning executive; b. Middletown, Ohio, July 12, 1942; s. Arthur Brown and Dorothy Brewster (Moffat) S.; divorced; children: C. Gregory, Tracy M., Christopher M., Jonathan D. BS in Fin., Miami U., Oxford, Ohio, 1980. CLU, chartered fin. cons. Exec. dir. Jr. Achievement, Middletown, 1969-78, Hamilton, Ohio, 1977-78; v.p., gen. mgr. Security Strassberger, Inc., Middletown, 1978-81; sr. v.p. Fin. Planning Cons., Inc., Middletown, 1981-87; fin. planner GEM Fin. Corp., Dayton, Ohio, 1987—. Author: Proplan, 1985, How to Select Hardware for Financial Planning, 1987. Republican. Episcopalian. Clubs: Middletown "32", High Twelve (Middletown) (pres. 1985). Lodges: Lions (past pres., zone chmn., Guiding Lion award), Masons, KT, Shriners. Home: 215 Kenwood Drive Middleton OH 45042-3528

STIVENDER, DONALD LEWIS, mechanical engineer; b. Chgo., May 8, 1932; s. Paul Macon and Grace (Larsen) S.; m. Margaret Ann Lourim, Apr. 14, 1956; children—Anne, Robert, Carole. B.S. in Engring, U.S. Coast Guard Acad., 1954; M.S., U. Mich., 1959. Registered profl. engr. Research and devel. Research Labs., Gen. Motors Corp., Warren, Mich., 1959—, sr. research engr., 1968—; pres., dir. Sq. Lake Corp., 1974-87; owner Stivender Engring. Assos., 1980—; cons. public domain engring. disciplines. Contbr. articles tech. jours. on diesel, gas turbine and spark ignition engine combustion, emission, constrn. and control aspects. Served with USCG, 1950-58. Mem. Soc. Automotive Engrs. (Arch T. Colwell award 1968, 69, 79, governing bd. 1971-73), ASME, Combustion Inst., Sigma Xi. Invented internal combustion engines and control systems. Home: 1730 Hamilton Dr Bloomfield Hills MI 48013 Office: GM Research Labs Project Trilby 12 Mile and Round Roads Warren MI 48090

STIVER, JAMES FREDERICK, pharmacist, health physicist, administrator; b. Elkhart, Ind., Jan. 27, 1943; s. Melvin Hugh and Pauline Anna (Schrock) S.; m. Joan Louise Trindle, Aug. 14, 1965; children—Gregory James, Richard Frederick, Kristin Louise, Elizabeth Ann. B.S. in Pharmacy and Pharm. Scis., Purdue U., 1966, M.S., 1968, Ph.D., 1970. Lic. pharmacist, Ind., N.D. Asst. prof. N.D. State U., Fargo, 1969-73, assoc. prof., 1973-76, radiol. safety officer, 1969-76; radiation safety officer KMS Fusion Inc., Ann Arbor, Mich., 1976-80; mgr., pharmacist Kroger Sav-On Pharmacy Co., Elkhart, Ind., 1980-81; pharmacist Elkhart Gen. Hosp., 1981; environ. regulatory affairs adminstr. Upjohn Co., Kalamazoo, Mich., 1981—; cons., lectr. Mem. Emergency Med. Service, Jefferson Township, Elkhart County, 1981—; mem. Trinity Luth. Ch., Goshen, Ind. Mem. Am. Pharm. Assn., Ind. Pharmacists Assn., N.D. Pharm. Assn., Am. Chem. Soc., Health Physics Soc., Internat. Radiation Protection Assn., Am. Biol. Safety Assn., N.Y. Acad. Scis., AAAS, Kappa Psi, Rho Chi, Phi Lambda Upsilon, Sigma Xi. Lodge: Masons. Contbr. articles, abstracts to publs. Home: 59089 SR15 Goshen IN 46526 Office: Upjohn Co Kalamazoo MI 49001

STOBAUGH, ROBERT EARL, chemical service research executive; b. Humboldt, Tenn., June 24, 1927; s. William Howard and Mary Ellen (Stephens) S.; m. Louise Piper, Dec. 29, 1956. BS in Chemistry, Rhodes Coll., 1947; MS in Chemistry, U. Tenn., 1949, PhD, 1952. Asst. editor Chem. Abstracts Service, Columbus, Ohio, 1954-56, assoc. editor, 1957-59, sr. assoc. editor, 1959-60, asst. mgr. organic chemical, 1960-65, tech. cons. registry, 1965-67, mgr. research, 1967—. Contbr. articles to profl. jour. Mem. Am. Chem. Soc., Am. Soc. Info. Service. Office: Chem Abstracts Service PO Box 3012 2540 Olentangy River Rd Columbus OH 43210

STOBER, (MELL) JAMES, manufacturing company executive; b. Winner, S.D., Aug. 23, 1946; s. Mell James Stober and Audrey (Baker) Klemme; m. Ruth Ellen Bardenwerper, July 12, 1969; children: Herbert William, Amy Marie, Heidi Ruth, James Andrew. BS, USAF Acad., 1969; MBA, So. Ill. U., Edwardsville, 1974. Commd. 1st lt. USAF, 1969, advanced through grades to capt., 1972, resigned, 1974; cash mgr. Joseph Schlitz Brewing Co., Milw., 1974-76; asst. v.p. First Wis. Nat. Bank, Milw., 1976-78; asst. treas. A.O. Smith Corp., Milw., 1978—. Campaign worker Watts for Gov., Waukesha, Wis., 1986; bd. dirs. Boy Scouts Am., Waukesha. Decorated Air medal with bronze oak leaf cluster. Mem. Reserve Officers Assn., Assn. Grads. USAF Acad. Republican. Methodist. Club: North Hills Country (Menomonee Falls, Wis.). Avocations: flying, golf. Office: AO Smith Corp PO Box 23976 Milwaukee WI 53223-0976

STOCK, BARBARA M., psychologist; b. Pitts., May 4, 1943; d. Samuel M. and Hilda (Marmins) Morris; B.A., Chatham Coll., 1964; Ph.D., U. Mich., 1972; div.; children—Aric, Adam, Michael. Cons., Ky. Infant Presch. Project, Dept. Econ. Security, Frankfort, 1972; asst. prof. dept. spl. edn. Eastern Ky. U., Richmond, 1972-74; instr. parent courses, Lexington, Ky., London, Eng., 1972-75; stringer, feature writer Suburban Tribune, Hinsdale, Ill., 1977-81; pvt. practice clin. psychology, Wilmette, Ill., 1980—; staff psychologist One to One Learning Center, Wilmette, 1980-83; psychologist Lake County Mental Health, Round Lake Park, Ill., 1983-85, Mt. Sinai hosp., Chgo., 1985-87; psychologist Assn. Adolescent Psychiatry, Riveredge Hosp., Forest Park, Ill., 1987— . Mem. Ky. Gov.'s Ad Hoc Com. for Programs for Children with Behavioral Disorders, 1972; mem. Lake County Task Force for Sexual Abuse. Mem. Am. Psychol. Assn., Ill. Psychol. Assn., Internat. Transactional Analysis Assn., Phi Beta Kappa. Home: 930 Linden Ave Wilmette IL 60091 Office: Riveredge Hosp 8311 W Roosevelt Rd Forest Park IL 60130

STOCKERT, JEFFREY ALLEN, accountant; b. Dickinson, N.D., Nov. 12, 1959. BS in Acctg., Moorhead (Minn.) State U., 1983. CPA, N.D. Sr. acct. Reichert Fisher & Co., Dickinson, 1984-86, Eide, Helmke & Co. CPA's, Aberdeen, S.D., 1987—. Vol. United Way, Dickinson, 1986—. Mem. Am. Inst. CPA's, N.D. Soc. CPA's, Dickinson Soc. CPA's. Republican. Roman Catholic. Lodge: Optimist, Elks. Avocations: golf, fishing, softball, reading. Home: 809 S McCoy Aberdeen SD 57401 Office: Eide Helmke & Co CPA's 124 S 1st St Aberdeen SD 57401

STOCKGLAUSNER, WILLIAM GEORGE, accountant; b. St. Louis, Dec. 25, 1950; s. William George and Mary Virginia (Lopez) S.; m. Vickie Kay Mackler, Nov. 17, 1973; children: Tyson Marshall, Jacob Cameron. BS summa cum laude, Columbia (Mo.) Coll., 1985. CPA, Mo. Staff acct. Wright-Price Inc., Jefferson City, Mo., 1974-77; staff acct. Williams-Keepers CPA's, Columbia, 1977-81, supr. acctg. service, 1981-85, auditor, 1985-86; acct. Don Landers & Co. CPA's, Columbia, 1986—. Coach Daniel Boone Little League, Columbia, 1986. Served with USAR, 1971-78. Mem. Am. Inst. CPA's, Mo. Soc. CPA's. Republican. Roman Catholic. Lodge: Lions (sec. Columbia 1983-85, bd. dirs. Columbia 1986—). Avocations: fishing, photography. Office: Don Landers & Co 33 E Broadway Suite 190 Columbia MO 65203

STOCKLEY, DARLEEN J., lawyer; b. Champaign, Ill., July 14, 1943; d. John Ted and Florence Belle (Gadberry) Dixon; m. Dale Leon Stockley, June 12, 1965; children: James Dale, Robert DeLeon. Student, U. Ill.; BS in Edn., No. Ill. U., 1973, MS, 1980; JD, De Paul U., 1984. Bar: Ill. 1984, U.S. Dist. Ct. (no. dist.) Ill. 1984. Research asst. U. Ill., Champaign, 1960-62, researcher, 1962-69; tchr. Ottawa (Ill.) Pub. Schs., 1973-84; ptnr. Pool & Stockley, Ottawa, 1984—. Contbr. research articles to profl. jours. Coordinator Citizens for Stockley for (Ill. State) Senate, 1985-86. Mem. ABA, Ill. Bar Assn., LaSalle County Bar Assn., Women Bus. and Profl. Club. Club: Zonta (Ottawa). Office: Pool & Stockley 611 1/2 LaSalle St Ottawa IL 61350

STOCKMAN, RICHARD OWEN, manufacturing company executive; b. Plymouth, Ind., Oct. 9, 1930; s. Samuel Seth and Emma Gail (Amones) S.; student public schs.; children—Gary Blake, Roxanne, John Jay. Field service specialist Worthington Corp., Harrison, N.J., 1955-63; service mgr., product engr. Haskon, Inc., Warsaw, Ind., 1963-70; mgr. customer service DePuy div. Bio Dynamics Co., Warsaw, 1970-80; dir. ops. Kellogg Industries, Jackson, Mich., 1981-84, v.p. ops., 1984—; instr. Ind. Vocat. Tech. Coll. Served with USN, 1948-52. Clubs: Masons, Shriners. Home: 2842 Wooddale Ct Jackson MI 49203-3655 Office: 159 W Pearl St Jackson MI 49201

STOCKMEYER, NORMAN OTTO, JR., legal educator, consultant; b. Detroit, May 24, 1938; s. Norman O. and Lillian R. (Hitchman) S.; m. Marcia E. Rudman, Oct. 1, 1966; children: Claire, Kathleen, Mary Frances. AB, Oberlin Coll., 1960; JD, U. Mich., 1963. Bar: Mich. 1963, U.S. Ct. Appeals (6th cir.) 1964, U.S. Supreme Ct. 1974. Legis. grad. fellow Mich. State U., 1963; legal counsel Senate Judiciary Com., Mich. Legislature, 1964; law clk. Mich. Ct. Appeals, 1965, commr., 1966-68, research dir., 1969-76; assoc. prof. law Thomas M. Cooley Law Sch., 1977-78, prof., 1978—; vis. prof. Mercer U. Sch. Law, 1986. Contbr. numerous articles to state and nat. legal jours. Fellow Am. Bar Found.; mem. ABA (chmn. Mich. membership 1972-73, lectr. Appellate Judges Conf. jud. seminars 1972-76), Nat. Conf. Bar Founds. (trustee 1985—), Mich. State Bar Found. (pres. 1982-85, trustee 1971—), State Bar Mich. (chmn. Young Lawyers sect. 1971-72, bd. commrs. 1985—), Ingham County Bar Assn. (bd. dirs. 1981-85), Mich. Assn. Professions (bd. dirs. 1981-84), Thomas M. Cooley Legal Authors Soc. (pres. 1982-83), Scribes, Delta Theta Phi (dean Christiancy Senate 1962; Outstanding Prof. 1984-85). Address: PO Box 13038 Lansing MI 48901

STOCKTON, CARL REX, history educator; b. Monett, Mo., Oct. 13, 1935; s. Ira James and Edith (Turner) S.; m. Gillian Winifred Adams, Dec. 30, 1972; children: Matthew Basil, Adam Francis. BS, Southwest Mo. State U., 1957; STB, Boston U., 1960; DPhil, Oxford U., Eng., 1970. Assoc. chief-of-party Internat. Vol. Services, Vietnam, 1963-65; asst. prof. history McKendree Coll., Lebanon, Ill., 1967-70; prof. history, chmn. social sci. div. Talladega (Ala.) Coll., 1970-82; prof. history, acad. dean. U. Indpls., 1982—; cons. in field. Editor: KAIROS, 1959-60, The Origin and Development of Extra-Liturgical Worship in 18th Century Methodism, 1970; contbr. articles to profl. jours. Mem. Indiana Council World Affairs, 1984—; standing com. Diocese of Indpls.; pres. Talladega County chpt. Am. Heart Assn., 1980; judge Brain Game, Sta. WTHR-TV, Indpls., 1982; bd. dirs., v.p. The Episc. Day Sch., Ala., 1979-82; vestryman Christ Ch. Cathedral, Indpls.; chmn. Consortium for Urban Edn. Acad. Deans, 1985—; gov. bd. Ind. Office Campus Ministries, 1986—. Lester So. fellow, 1974-75, Mellon fellow, 1981. Mem. Ecclesiastical Hist. Soc. Gt. Britain, Oxford Soc., Am. Soc. Ch. History, Ch. History Soc., AAUP, English Speaking Union, Ind. Assn. Historians, Alpha Chi, Alpha Psi Omega, Phi Alpha Theta. Democrat. Episcopalian. Club: Oxford and Cambridge (London). Lodge: Kiwanis (pres. Indpls. club 1987—). Home: 6740 Yellowstone Pkwy Indianapolis IN 46217 Office: U Indpls 1400 E Hanna Ave Indianapolis IN 46227

STOCKTON, STEPHEN FINCH, insurance company executive; b. Phila., July 4, 1947; s. Richard Finch and Veronica (Myszak) S.; m. Linda Browning, Feb. 1, 1986; children: Stacey, Richard. BS, Northwestern U., 1969, JD, 1972, MBA, 1973. CPA, CLU, CPCU. Tax atty. State Farm Mut. Auto Ins. Co., Bloomington, Ill., 1973-78, adminstrv. asst. acctg., 1978-79, asst. div. mgr., 1979-80, adminstrv. asst., 1980-82, v.p. adminstrv. services, 1982—; mktg. cons., Chgo., Bloomington, 1969-82. Active various civic orgns., Bloomington. Mem. ABA, Ill. Bar Assn., McLean County Bar Assn. Club: Bloomington Country. Home: 19 Brompton Ct Bloomington IL 61701 Office: State Farm Mut Auto Ins Co 1 State Farm Plaza Bloomington IL 61710

STOCKWELL, WAYNE VERNE, transportation executive; b. Salem, Wis., May 30, 1950; s. Vernon Floyd and Ruth (Jones) S.; m. Kathleen Louise Lasco, Aug. 7, 1971; children: Mary Catherine, Aaron Thomas. BA, U. Wis., Parkside, 1973. Plant supr. John Weinert Co., Kenosha, Wis., 1973; transp. supr., inventory controller Walker Mfg., Racine, Wis. and Greenville, Tex., 1974-79; ops. mgr. Dallas Carriers, 1979-84; dir. ops. Apple Lines, Madison, S.D., 1984-86; dir. mktg. and ops. Hagen, Inc., Sioux City, Iowa, 1986—. Sec. Greenville Revitalization Orgn., 1978, pres., bd. dirs., 1979. Republican. Methodist. Avocations: hunting, coin collecting, antiques. Home: 820 N Catherine Madison SD 57042 Office: Hagen Inc 3232 Hwy 75 N PO Box 3208 Sioux City IA 51102

STODDARD, CHERRY ANN, insurance company executive; b. Chgo., June 11, 1944; d. Craig and Charlotte Mary (Lingel) S.; m. Donald Joseph Babo, Jan. 9, 1982. BS in Math., No. Ill. U., 1966. CPA, Ill. Auditor Peat Marwick Mitchell, Chgo., 1966-72; EDP auditor Kemper Group, Long Grove, Ill., 1972-79, asst. gen. auditor, 1979-81, field acctg. officer, 1981-83, gen. auditor, 1983—. Fin. sec., mem. Holy Innocents Ch., Hoffman estates, Ill, 1983—; advisor No. Ill. U. exec. adv. com. Sch. Bus., DeKalb, Ill., 1987—. Mem. Am. Inst. CPA's, Ill. CPA Soc., Inst. Internal Auditors (dist. dir. 1987—), Securities Industry Assn. Internal Audit Div. Republican. Episcopalian. Office: Kemper Group Internal Audit B-7 Long Grove IL 60049

STODDARD, DAVID JAY, dentist; b. North Platte, Nebr., June 19, 1952; s. Jay Curtis and Dorothy Jean (Hosek) S.; m. Kathleen Louise Fell; children: Jayson, Sarah, Nicholas. BA, Hastings Coll., 1974; DDS, U. Nebr., 1978. Gen. practice dentistry Grand Island, Nebr., 1978—. chmn. United Way, Grand Island, 1984; deacon Episcopal Ch. Grand Island, 1985. Republican. Avocation: sports. Home: 1607 S Harrison Grand Island NE 68803

STOECKEL, RONALD FREDERICK, chemical engineer; b. Linton, Ind., May 13, 1932; s. Edward Baranhard and Anna Fredericka (Kramer) S.; m. Betty Ann McCumber, Sept. 4, 1960; children: Ronald Frederick Jr., Clyde Edward, Anna Patrice, David Theodore. BS, Purdue U., 1953. Registered profl. engr., Ind., Ohio. Process engr. Olin Mathieson Chem. Corp., Niagara Falls, N.Y., 1953-58; project engr. Underwriter Lab., Inc., Chgo., 1958; quality control lab. supr. Tee Pak, Inc., Danville, Ill., 1958-62; sr. mfg. engr. Westinghouse Electric Co., Muncie, Ind., 1962-83; project mgr. MTS Internat., St. Louis, 1984-86; cons. Chem. Engring. Services, Middletown, Ind., 1986—. Leader Cub Scout Webelos; mem. Jr. Achievement. Mem. NSPE (vice chmn. profl. engr. industry cen. region 1977-79, Ind. chmn. 1975-77, internat. soc. pharm. engrs. 1972), Am. Chem. Soc., Soc. Mfg. Engrs. Club: Toastmasters. Lodge: Lions. Avocations: gardening, travel. Home: PO Box 153C Middletown IN 47356 Office: Chem Engring Services PO Box 164 Middletown IN 47356

STOFER, JACOB GORDON, accountant, hospital controller; b. Sacramento, May 26, 1946; s. Jacob Paul and Hilma Marie (Freeman) S.; m. Bonnie Lu Cary, June 27, 1970; children: Eric Jacob and Christopher Daniel (twins). BS, Calif. State U., Los Angeles, 1969. CPA, Calif., Kans. Acct. Haskins & Sells, Los Angeles, 1970-73; controller Pioneer Hosp., Artesia, Calif., 1973-76; controller, trustee Meml. Hosp., McPherson, Kans., 1977—. Asst. scoutmaster troop 130 Boy Scouts Am.; treas. McPherson Unified Sch. Dist., 1981—; elder First Presby. Ch., McPherson, 1986; bd. dirs. Leadership McPherson, 1985-86; trustee Meml. Hosp. Aux., 1987—. Served to sgt. Calif. Army N.G., 1965-71. Named one of Outstanding Young Men Am., 1982. Mem. Am. Inst. CPA's, Healthcare Fin. Mgmt. Assn. (bd. dirs. 1986—), McPherson C. of C. (bd. dirs. 1986). Republican. Lodges: Shriners, Optimist, Elks, Masons. Avocations: hunting, trap shooting, woodworking, antique car restoration. Home: 1471 Dover Rd McPherson KS 67460 Office: Meml Hosp Inc 1000 Hospital Dr McPherson KS 67460

STOFER, JOHN MILTON, JR., history and government educator; b. Lakewood, Ohio, Nov. 17, 1935; s. John Milton and Lillian Caroline (Tinnerman) S.; m. Anna Marie Gerig, June 10, 1974 (div. June 1984). BA in History magna cum laude, Colgate U., 1958; student, Syracuse U., 1958-59; MEdn, Kent State U., 1966; JD, U. Akron, 1976. Cert. elem. tchr., Ohio. Tchr. Greene Local Schs., Smithville, Ohio, 1960—. Served with Army NG, 1959-65. Recipient Tchr. of Yr. award Greene Local Edn. Assn., 1980; Jennings scholar, 1984. Mem. Greene Local Edn. Assn. (pres. 1970-71, 81-82, 86-87), Ohio Edn. Assn., NEA, Ohio Hist. Soc., Nat. Hist. Soc., Phi Beta Kappa. Mem. Christian Ch. (Disciples of Christ). Avocations: running, physical fitness, reading, investments, cats. Home: 2340 C Cardinal Ct Wooster OH 44691 Office: Greene Middle Sch 484 E Main St Smithville OH 44677

STOFFELS, DOUGLAS ROBERT, accountant; b. Madison, Wis., Mar. 28, 1958; s. Donald Herbert and Diane Arlene (Hupke) S.; m. Linda Lee Feuerstahler, Sept. 26, 1981; children: Daniel Robert, Jessica Lynnae; stepchildren: Donald Bradley Kippert, Richard William Kippert. BBA, U. Wis., 1980, MBA, 1981. CPA, Wis. Fin. technician Cumis Ins. Soc., Inc., Madison, 1981-83, budget, tax specialist, 1983, mgr. fin. info., 1983-84; sr. staff acct. Suby, Von Haden & Assocs., Madison, 1984—. Fellow Am. Inst. CPA's (Elijah Watt Sells award 1982), Wis. Inst. CPA's, Janesville (Wis.) Soccer Club (v.p. 1986—). Lutheran. Avocations: soccer, volleyball, softball, water skiing, swimming. Home: 2418 Whitlock Rd Madison WI 53719 Office: Suby Von Haden & Assocs 901 S Whitney Way Madison WI 53711

STOFFER, TERRY JAMES, advertising executive; b. Alexander, Iowa, May 28, 1946; s. Jacob John and Almeda Juanita (Roe) S.; m. Linda Rosburg, Apr. 14, 1966 (div. Mar. 1980); m. Catherine S. Jewell, Dec. 28, 1984; 1 child, Alan J. BS in Journalism, Iowa State U., 1968, MS in Journalism, 1970. Instr. Iowa State U. Sch. Journalism, Ames, 1969-70; publs. mgr. Express Communications, West Des Moines, Iowa, 1970-72; sr. v.p. Creswell, Munsell, Fultz and Zirbel, Des Moines, 1972—. Mem. Nat. Adv. Bd. Iowa State U. Sch. Journalism, Ames, 1985—; bd. dirs. Better Bus. Bur., Des Moines, 1983. Mem. Des Moines Advt. Club (v.p. 1974-75, Cliff DePuy award 1978), Advt. Profls. of Des Moines (pres. 1982-83, Ad Person of Yr. 1980), Am. Advt. Fedn. (nat. standards com. 1984-85). Republican. Methodist. Avocations: literature, cooking. Home: 325 34th St West Des Moines IA 50265 Office: Creswell Munsell Fultz & Zirbel 600 E Court Ave Des Moines IA 50306

STOFFLE, CARLA J., university library administrator.; b. Pueblo, Colo., June 19, 1943; d. Samuel Bernard and Virginia Irene (Berry) Hayden; m. Richard William Stoffle, June 12, 1964; children: Brent William, Kami Ann. AA, So. Colo. State Coll., Pueblo, 1963; BA, U. Colo., 1965; MLS, U. Ky., 1969; postgrad., U. Wis., 1980. Head govt. publ. dept. John G. Crabbe Library, Eastern Ky. U., Richmond, 1969-72; head. pub. services U. Wis.-Parkside Library, Kenosha, 1972-76, exec. asst. to chancellor, 1978, asst. chancellor edn. services, 1979-85; assoc. dir. U. Mich. Library, Ann Arbor, 1985—, dep. dir., 1986—; mem. adv. commn. Sch. Library Sci. U. Mich., Ann Arbor, 1986—; vol. Peace Corps, Barbados, W.I., 1965-67; bd. dirs. Bowker Library Adv. Bd., N.Y., 1985—. Co-author: Administration Government Documents Collection, 1974, Materials and Method for History Research, 1979, Materials and Methods for Political Science Research, 1979; assoc. editor Collection Building, 1986—. Mem. ALA. (exec. bd. dirs. 1985-89, councilor 1983-87), Assn. Coll. Research Libraries (pres. 1982-83). Home: 2420 Blueberry Ln Ann Arbor MI 48103 Office: U Library U U Mich 818 Hatcher S Ann Arbor MI 48109

STOGA, KATHLEEN ELIZABETH, social worker; b. Chgo., Feb. 10, 1944; d. James Thomas and Marian Elizabeth (Statham) McDermott; m. Stanley Roger Stoga, Jan. 30, 1971. BS, No. Ill. U., 1966; cert., Ctr. for Pub. Mgmt., 1984. Supr. Chgo. Foundling Home, 1967-71; exec. dir. Lafayette (Ind.) Home Hosp. div. Dept. Social Services, 1971-72; dir. Mt. Prospect (Ill.) Sr. Ctr., 1973-78; exec. dir. Proviso Council on Aging, Bellwood, Ill., 1978-84, South Madison (Wis.) Coalition of the Elderly, 1985—; dir., initiator and developer Mt. Prospect Sr. Ctr., 1976, Adult Day Care and Sr. Ctr. Proviso Twp., 1984. Recipient Cert. of Merit Village of Mt. Prospect, 1978, Cert. of Appreciation Telephone Pioneers of Am., 1980, Luth. Gen. Hosp., Park Ridge, Ill., 1976, Kiwanis of Northlake and Westchester, Ill. Mem. Nat. Council on Aging, Wis. Coalition on Aging, Dane County Com. on Aging (bd. dirs.). Home: 5017 Coney Weston Madison WI 53717 Office: South Madison Coalition Elderly 540 W Olin Room 109 Madison WI 53715

STOHLER, MICHAEL JOE, dentist; b. Anderson, Ind., Mar. 26, 1956; s. Herbert Warren and Mary Jo (Philbert) S.; m. Mary Anne Poinsette, May 16, 1981; children: James Lawrence, Maria Christine. Student, Lake-Sumter Community Coll., Leesburg, Fla., 1974-76; BS, Ball State U., 1978; DDS, Ind. U., 1982. Gen. practice dentistry Anderson, 1982—. Mem. Ind. Dental Assn., E. Cen. Dental Assn., Madison County Dental Assn., Acad. Gen. Dentistry, Acad. Dentistry for Handicapped, Anderson Personal Computer User's Group, Psi Omega. Lodge: Rotary (sgt.-at-arms Anderson chpt. 1986—). Avocations: snow and water skiing, computers, traveling. Home: Rural Rt 4 Box 223 Anderson IN 46011 Office: 2012 E 53d St Anderson IN 46013

STOHR, PAUL EDWARD, neurosurgeon; b. Terre Haute, Ind., June 7, 1934; s. Stanley Edward and Helen J. (Lee) S.; m. Suzanne Phillips (div.); children: Stanley E., Jonathan M.; m. Sue Johnson, May 2, 1971; 1 child, Paul A. Student, Ind. U., 1952-55; MD, Washington U., St. Louis, 1959. Diplomate Am. Bd. Neurological Surgeons. Intern Barnes Hosp., 1959-60, resident in gen. surgery, 1960-61, asst. resident in neurol. surgery, 1963-64; sr. resident in neurol. surgery Barnes Hosp. and VA Hosp., 1965; fellow neurol. surgery Washington U., St. Louis, 1961-62, 1966, instr. neurol. surgery, 1966-68; prcatice medicine specializing in neurosurgery St. Louis, 1970—; asst. clin. prof. neurosurgery St. Louis U., 1970-75, assoc. clin. prof. neurosurgery, 1975—; chmn. dept. neurosurgery St. Mary's Hosp., St. Louis, 1985—. Served to lt. col. U.S. Army, 1968-70. Mem. St. Louis Med. Soc., Am. Assn. Neurol. Surgeons, Congress Neurol. Surgeons, St. Louis Neurol. Soc., So. Neurol. Soc., Mo. State Neurol. Soc. (pres. elect 1986), St. Louis Soc. Neurol. Scis. (pres. elect 1985). Home: #2 Kirken Knoll Dr Saint Louis MO 63131 Office: 1035 S Bellevue Saint Louis MO 63117

STOKELY, RANDOLPH HOME, real estate executive; b. Indpls., Dec. 27, 1944; s. Alfred J. and Elizabeth (Home) S.; m. Lynn Kinsey, June 23, 1968; children: Andrew K., Alexander W. BS, DePauw U., 1967; MBA, Ind. U., 1970. V.p. Hart Develment Corp., Indpls., 1970-74; exec. v.p. Barrett & Stokely, Inc., Indpls., 1975—. v.p., bd. dirs. Penrod Soc., Indpls., 1974-86. Mem. Indpls. Bd. Realtors, Inst. Real Estate Mgmt. (cert. property mgr.). Presbyterian. Clubs: Woodstock Country (Indpls.), University (Indpls.) (bd. dirs.). Home: 9275 Hunt Club Rd Zionsville IN 46077 Office: Barrett & Stokely Inc 6502 Westfield Blvd Indianapolis IN 46220

STOKES, FRANCIS GEORGE, commodities trader; b. New Brunswick, N.J., Feb. 26, 1933; s. Elward Collier and Sophia Anna (Holzworth) S.; m. Kathlene Mosby Hill, July 26, 1969 (div. Nov. 1982); children: Francis George, Sophia Kathlene. BS, U.S. Naval Acad., 1955; MBA, U. Md., 1972. V.p. Internal Fund Mgmt., Washington, 1970-72; trader Keystone Trading Corp., Chgo., 1972—. Pres., trustee Park Ridge (Ill.) Pub. Library, 1978-83. Served to lt. USN, 1955-59, capt. Res. ret. Mem. Chgo. Merc. Exchange, Antarcticans Soc., Polar Soc. Republican. Lutheran. Club: Explorers (N.Y.C.). Avocations: exploration, travel. Home: 134 N Washington St Park Ridge IL 60068

STOKES, JAMES HAROLD, communications specialist, writer, producer; b. Britton, S.D., Oct. 24, 1938; s. Harold Aloysius and Dolores Lorraine (Harms) S.; married; 3 children. BA, U. S.D., 1960; postgrad., U. Minn., 1964-66. FCC 1st class radiotelephone lic. Dir. pub. info. Am. Lung. Assn., Mpls., 1968-71; dir. audio visual edn. Minn. Lung Assn., St. Paul, 1971-82; promotion mgr. Sta. WLOL, BFR Broadcasting, Mpls., 1972-75; salesman Johnston Printing Co., Mpls., 1975-76; pub. relations dir., announcer, technician Sta. KTWN-FM, Anoka, Minn., 1976-77; owner, mgr. Jim Stokes Communications Services, Mpls., 1977—. Writer videoscripts on paramed. tng. and diseases in women; screenwriter, dir. radio spots on respiratory diseases; dir., photographer various ednl. filmstrips; photographer several books on careers; Mpls. corr., columnist Back Stage. Mem. Am. Assn. Consumer Awareness (bd. dirs. 1986), Minn. Comml. Indsl. Photographers Assn., Soc. Broadcast Engrs., Advt. Club Minn., Sigma Delta Chi, Tau Kappa Epsilon. Roman Catholic. Avocations: collecting movie soundtracks, walking, jogging, reading. Home and Office: 453 S Cedar Lake Rd Minneapolis MN 55405

STOKES, JOSEPH POWELL, psychologist, educator; b. Hendersonville, N.C., June 8, 1946; s. William F. and Sally Moore (Pippen) S. BA, Duke U., 1968; MA, U. Ill., Chgo., 1970, PhD, 1972. Lic. psychologist, Ill. From asst. to assoc. prof. psychology U. Ill., Chgo., 1974—; therapist Assoc. Mental Health Services, Chgo., 1980—; cons. Leo Burnett Co., Chgo., 1983-84, Arthur Andersen & Co., Chgo. and St. Charles, 1985—. Contbr. articles to profl. jours. Am. Psychol. Assn. Home: 1875 N Orchard Chicago IL 60614 Office: U Ill Psychology Dept PO Box 4348 Chicago IL 60680

STOKES, JUDITH RAE, human resources manager, personnel manager, psychologist; b. Hazen, Ark., Oct. 30, 1950; s. Kenneth Marvin Stokes and Norma Jean (McGee) S.; m. Terry Lee Smith, Dec. 26, 1977; children: Shannon, Ashley, Erin. BA in Psychology and Spl. Edn., Antioch Coll., 1972; MA in Curriculum and Instrn., U. Oreg., 1975; postgrad. in behavioral psychology, U. Kans., 1977. Tchr. Sch. for Contempory Edn., Ellicott City, Md., 1971-72; dir. observation systems HEW, Eugene, Oreg., 1972-75; sr. indsl. psychologist AT&T, Greensboro, N.C., 1977-84; mgr. human resources staff AT&T, Lisle, Ill., 1984—.

STOKES, LOUIS, congressman; b. Cleve., Feb. 23, 1925; s. Charles and Louise (Stone) S.; m. Jeanette Frances, Aug. 21, 1960; children—Shelley, Louis C., Angela, Lorene. Student, Western Res. U., 1946-48; J.D., Cleve. Marshall Law Sch., 1953; LL.D. (hon.), Wilberforce U., 1969, Shaw U., Livingstone Coll., Morehouse Coll., Meharry Coll. Medicine. Bar: Ohio 1953. Since practiced in Cleve.; mem. 91st-99th congresses from 21st Ohio dist.; mem. appropriations com., chmn. ethics com., chmn. 91st-100th congresses from 21st Ohio dist. (Congl. Black Caucus), 1969—; guest lectr., 1960—. Mem. adv. council African-Am. Inst. Internat.; mem. exec. com. Cuyahoga County Democratic Party, Ohio State Dem. Party; bd. dirs. Karamu House; trustee Martin Luther King, Jr. Center for Social Change, Forest City Hosp., Cleve. State U. Served with AUS, 1943-46. Recipient numerous awards for civic activities including Distinguished Service award Cleve. br. NAACP; Certificate of Appreciation U.S. Commn. on Civil Rights. Fellow Ohio State Bar Assn.; mem. Am., Cuyahoga County, Cleve. bar assns., Nat. Assn. Def. Lawyers Criminal Cases Fair Housing (dir.), Urban League, Citizens League, John Harlan Law Club, ACLU, Am. Legion, Kappa Alpha Psi. Clubs: Masons (Cleve.), Plus (Cleve.). Home: Cleveland OH Office: US Ho of Reps 2465 Rayburn House Office Bldg Washington DC 20515 *

STOKES, THOMAS LOUIS, accountant, educator; b. Great Falls, Mont., Aug. 29, 1955; s. Tom William Stokes and Lella Lee (Shelden) Smith; m. Deborah Jo Hunt, Feb. 14, 1975; children: Rebecca Carol, Daniel Louis. BBA, U. So. Calif., 1977; MBA, U. S.D., 1984. CPA, S.D. Ptnr. Vigoren & Stokes, CPA, Spearfish, S.D., 1982—; instr. Black Hills State Coll., Spearfish, 1984-86, adv. bd. div. bus., 1986—; asst. prof. U. S.D., Rapid City, 1985—. Treas. Dale Bell for Congress Com., Spearfish, 1986. Served to capt. U.S. Army, 1977-82. Named one of Outstanding Young Men of Am., 1985. Mem. Am. Inst. CPA's, S.D. Soc. CPA's. Republican. Lutheran. Lodge: Optimist. Avocations: hunting, fishing. Home: 23 Lourie Ln Spearfish SD 57783 Office: Vigoren & Stokes CPA's 123 E Jackson Box 430 Spearfish SD 57783

STOLARSKYJ, ALEX THEODORE, radiologist; b. Strilkiw, Ukraine, USSR, Sept. 19, 1940; s. Wolodymyr and Anna (Puczkowska) S.; m. Carolyn Ann Dobbs, Nov. 10, 1962; children: Christine, Michael, Kathleen. BS, Creighton U., 1963, MD, 1967. Cert. Am Bd. Radiology. Radiologist Radiology Cons., Omaha, 1978—. Served to maj. USAFR, 1969-76. Mem. Am. Coll. Radiology, Radiol. Soc. N. Am., Nebr. Med. Assn., Met. Omaha Med. Soc. Byzantine Catholic. Avocations: golf, fishing, hunting. Home: 216 Fairacres Rd Omaha NE 68132 Office: Radiology Cons PC 13918 Gold Circle Omaha NE 68144

STOLEE, MICHAEL JOSEPH, education educator, consultant; b. Mpls., Aug. 22, 1930; s. Gullik R. and Adeline J. (Thomason) S.; m. Marilyn Sandbo, June 7, 1952; children—Margaret Kay, Anne Marie. B.A., St. Olaf Coll., 1952; M.A., U. Minn., 1959, Ph.D., 1963. Assoc. dean edn. U. Miami, Coral Gables, Fla., 1970-75, prof., 1963-75; dean Sch. Edn., U. Wis.-Milw., 1975-84, prof., 1975—; acting assoc. headmaster U. Sch. Milw., 1985-86; cons. sch. desegregation HEW, U.S. Dept. Justice, White House, NAACP, NAACP Legal Def. Fund, ACLU, states and sch. dists., Boston, Miami, Fla., Chgo., Phila., San Francisco, Mpls., Dallas, St. Louis, Pitts., Los Angeles, 1965—. Named Disting. Alumnus, St. Olaf Coll., Northfield, Minn., 1972. Mem. Am. Assn. Colls. Tchr. Edn. (govt. relations com. 1980-83), Phi Delta Kappa (area coordinator 1984—, pres. Milw. chpt. 1984-85). Democrat. Lutheran. Avocations: gardening, philately, photography. Home: 7033 N Lombardy Rd Milwaukee WI 53217 Office: U Wis-Milw PO Box 413 Milwaukee WI 53201

STOLESON, JUAN KARSTEN, architect; b. LaCrosse, Wis., Jan. 17, 1944; s. Stephen Theodore and Maxine Carmen (Dregne) S.; m. Judy Lee Brettingen, Feb. 16, 1946; children: Michelle Lynn, Erik Justin. BArch, U. Minn., 1968. Registered architect, Minn. Architect Setter, Leach, Lindstrom, Mpls., 1969-75, Hammel, Green, Abrahamson, Mpls., 1975—. Mem. Minn. Soc. AIA. Presbyterian. Avocations: photography, fishing. Office: Hammel Green Abrahamson Inc 1201 Harmon Pl Minneapolis MN 55403

STOLLER, JAMES KEVIN, pulmonary and intensive care physician; b. N.Y.C., Mar. 3, 1953; s. Alfred and Norma (Shapiro) S.; m. Terry Fox, Nov. 27, 1982. BA magna cum laude, Amherst Coll., 1975; MD cum laude, Yale U., 1979. Diplomate Am. Bd. Internal Medicine, Am. Bd. Pulmonary Medicine. Resident in internal medicine Peter Bent Brigham Hosp., Boston, 1979-82; pulmonary fellowship Brigham and Women's Hosp., Boston, 1982-83, Yale U. Sch. Medicine, New Haven, Conn., 1983-85; critical care fellowship Mass. Gen. Hosp., Boston, 1985-86; practice medicine specializing in pulmonary medicine, staff physician The Cleve. Clinic Found., 1986-87. Contbr. sci. articles to med. jours. Mem. Am. Coll. Chest Physicians, Am. Thoracic Soc., ACP. Avocations: running, scuba diving.

STOLLINGS, JAN GENE, pharmacist, dentist; b. Xenia, Ohio, Jan. 6, 1954; s. Roger Neil and Ingrid Gertrude (Odenthal) S.; m. Debra Lynn Schafer, July 16, 1977; children: Carissa, Ty Justin. BS in Pharmacy, Ohio No. U., 1977; DDS, Ohio State U., 1983. lectr. in field; provider mobile dental care for elderly and homebound. Pharmacist Kettering (Ohio) Med. Ctr., 1977-79; gen. practice dentistry Xenia, 1983—; cons. various nursing homes, Xenia, 1986—. Mem. ADA, Acad. Gen. Dentistry. Republican. Lodges: Rotary, Shriners, Masons (32d degree), Elks, Moose. Avocations: sports, reading, family. Home: 1641 Valley Heights Rd Xenia OH 45385 Office: 1237 N Monroe Dr Xenia OH 45385

STOLNITZ, GEORGE JOSEPH, economist, educator; b. N.Y.C., Apr. 4, 1920; s. Isidore and Julia (Jurman) S.; m. Monique Jeanne Delley, Aug. 26, 1976; children: Cindy, Wendy, Dia. B.A., CCNY, 1939; M.A., Princeton U., 1942, Ph.D., 1952. Statistician U.S. Bur. Census, 1940-41; research assoc. Princeton U. Office of Population Research, 1948-56; asst. prof. Princeton U., 1953-56; vis. research scholar Resources for the Future, 1965-67; prof. econs. Ind. U., Bloomington, 1956—; dir. Ind. U. Internat. Devel. Research Ctr., 1967-72, Ind. U. Population Inst. for Research and Tng., 1986—; prin. officer Population and Econ. Devel. UN, N.Y.C., 1976-78; cons. Ford Found., U.S. Congress, Rockefeller Found., UN, U.S. Dept. Commerce, Dept. Energy, Health and Human Services, U.S. Dept. State. Author books, numerous articles in field. Served to capt. USAF, 1942-46. Nat. Sci. Found. fellow, 1959-60. Mem. Population Assn. Am. (pres. 1983), Am. Econ. Assn., Am. Statis. Assn., Econometric Soc., Internat. Union Sci. Study of Population. Club: Cosmos. Home: 2636 Covenanter Ct Bloomington IN 47401 Office: Dept Econs Ind Univ Bloomington IN 47405

STOLTE, LARRY GENE, computer processing company executive; b. Cedar Rapids, Iowa, Sept. 17, 1945; s. Ed August and Emma Wilhelmena (Tank) S.; B.B.A. with highest distinction (FS Services scholar), U. Iowa, 1971; m. Rebecca Jane Tappmeyer, June 13, 1970; children—Scott Edward, Ryan Gene. Tax and auditing acct. McGladrey Hendrickson & Co., Cedar Rapids, 1971-73; sr. v.p. TLS Co., Cedar Rapids, 1973—, also dir. Served to sgt. USMC, 1964-67. C.P.A., Iowa, Ill., Mo., Minn., Mich., Wis.; cert. mgmt. acct. Mem. Nat. Assn. Computerized Tax Processors (pres.), Nat. Assn. Accts., Am. Inst. C.P.A.'s, Am. Mgmt. Assn. Republican. Methodist. Home: 2107 Linmar Dr NE Cedar Rapids IA 52402 Office: TLS Co 425 2d St Se PO Box 1686 Cedar Rapids IA 52406

STOLTZ, CHARLES EDWARD, meat packing executive; b. Dubuque, Iowa, July 31, 1936; s. Edward and Bertha (Klingenberg) S.; m. Jean Wahlert, Aug. 20, 1964; children: Jennifer, Michael, John, Charles II. B.S. in Bus. Adminstrn., U. Dubuque, 1961; M.A., U. Iowa, 1964. Salesman, Am. Can Co., 1961-62; v.p. Dubuque Packing Co., 1965, exec. v.p., to 1977, pres., 1977—, now also chief exec. officer, chmn.; dir. Dubuque Bank & Trust Co. Trustee U. Dubuque, United Fund, Boys Club. Served with USMC, 1956-58. Office: Dubuque Packing Co 7171 Mercy Rd Omaha NE 68106

STOLZ, BENJAMIN ARMOND, foreign language educator; b. Lansing, Mich., Mar. 28, 1934; s. Armond John and Mabel May (Smith) S.; m. Mona Eleanor Seelig, June 16, 1962; children: Elizabeth Mona, John Benjamin. A.B., U. Mich., Ann Arbor, 1955; certificat, U. Libre de Bruxelles, Belgium, 1956; A.M., Harvard U., 1957, Ph.D., 1965. Mem. faculty U. Mich., 1964—, prof. Slavic langs. and lits., 1972—, chmn. dept., 1971-85; cons. in field. Editor: Papers in Slavic Philology, 1977; co-editor: Oral Literature and the Formula, 1976, Cross Currents, 1982-85, Language and Literary Theory, 1984; co-editor, translator: (Konstantin Mihailovic): Memoirs of a Janissary, 1975; contbr. articles to profl. pubs. Served to lt. (j.g.) USNR, 1957-60. Recipient Orion E. Scott award humanities U. Mich., 1954; Fulbright scholar, 1955-56; Fgn. Area fellow Yugoslavia, 1963-64; Fulbright-Hays research fellow Eng. and Yugoslavia, 1970-71; grantee Am. Council Learned Socs. 1968-70, 73, Internat. Research and Exchanges Bd., 1985. Mem. Am. Assn. Advancement Slavic Studies, Am. Assn. Tchrs. Slavic and East European Langs., MLA, Midwest MLA (pres. 1976), Phi Beta Kappa, Phi Kappa Phi. Democrat. Club: Huron Valley Tennis. Home: 1060 Baldwin Ave Ann Arbor MI 48104 Office: 3040 MLB Univ Mich Ann Arbor MI 49109

STONE, ALLAN DAVID, economics educator; b. Joliet, Ill., Jan. 9, 1937; s. William E. and Leona V. (Frieh) S.; m. Peggy J. Carter, Jan. 11, 1958; children: David, Richard. BA, Beloit Coll., 1961; MA, U. Okla., 1964, PhD, 1973. Asst. prof. econs. U. Tex., El Paso, 1963-65; instr. econs. Wartburg Coll., Waverly, Iowa, 1965-66; asst. prof. econs. Oklahoma City U., 1966-72; prof. econs., dept. head S.W. Mo. State U., Springfield, 1972—. Served with U.S. Army, 1956-58. NSF grantee. Am. Econ. Assn., S.W. Social Scis. Assn., Mo. Council Econ. Edn. (bd. dirs. 1977-80), Phi Beta Kappa, Phi Kappa Phi. Home: 820 E Cherokee Springfield MO 65807

STONE, DAVID SHELTON, advertising executive; b. Detroit, May 23, 1942; s. Raymond Leslie and Nancy L. (Wilson) S.; m. Storm Ann Rossi, Apr. 5, 1963 (div. Mar. 1979); children: David, Lisa, Michelle; m. Paulette Rose Trayhnum, June 4, 1983. BBA, Wayne State U., 1974. Computer operator Campbell-Ewald, Warren, Mich., 1965-66, programmer, 1966-68, systems analyst, mgr., 1968-69, mgr. systems and programming, 1969-74, sr. v.p., dir. mgmt. info. systems, 1974-86, sr. v.p. specialized mktg. and communications, 1986—; instr. Marygrove Coll., Detroit, 1979-83. chmn. Friends of Detroit Pub. Library, 1982—; bd. dirs. Neighborhood Resource Ctr., Detroit, 1982-83, Neighborhood Info. Exchange, Detroit, 1982-83, Condominium Associated, Southfield, Mich., 1984-85. Served with USN, 1961-65. Mem. Nat. Computer Graphics Assn., Cooperating Users of Burroughs Equipment, Microcomputer Mgmt. Assn. Avocations: music, travel, record collecting, reading, dancing. Office: Campbell Ewald Co 30400 Van Dyke Warren MI 48093

STONE, DONALD EUGENE, insurance executive; b. Racine, Wis., Aug. 10, 1937; s. Hubert Charles and Margaret Ellen (Smith) S.; m. Judith Frances Hettrick, June 18, 1960; children: Michael, Matthew, Amy, Kristin,

Jennifer. Student, Marquette U., 1955; BS, U.S. Naval Acad., 1960; postgrad., Nev. So. U., 1965, Am. Coll., 1982, 86. Chartered Fin. Cons., CLU. Commd. 2d lt. USN, 1960, advanced through grades to lt., resigned, 1975; gen. plant supt. Ideal Cement Co., Denver, 1965-75; fin. planner N.Y. Life Ins. Co., Green Bay, Wis., 1975—. Recipient various company awards N.Y. Life Ins. Co., 1975-86. Mem. Nat. Assn. Life Underwriters (Nat. Sales Achievement awards 1975-86, Nat. Quality awards 1975-86), Million Dollar Round Table, U.S. Naval Acad. Alumni Assn., Green Bay Estate Planning Council. Lodge: Optimists (pres. Green Bay club 1981-82). Avocations: sailboat racing and cruising, skiing, camping. Home: 919 S Quincy St Green Bay WI 54301 Office: NY Life Ins Co 425 S Adams St Green Bay WI 54301

STONE, DONALD JAMES, retail executive; b. Cleve., Mar. 5, 1929; s. Sidney S. and Beatrice (Edelman) S.; m. Norma Fay Karchmer, Oct. 26, 1952; children—Michael, Lisa, Angela. B.B.A., U. Tex., Austin, 1949. With Foley's, Houston, 1949-75; v.p., gen. mdse. mgr. Foley's, 1960-75; chmn., chief exec. officer Sanger-Harris, Dallas, 1975-80; vice chmn. Federated Dept. Stores, Inc., Dallas and Cin., 1980—; dir. M Corp., Bloom Agy., XTEC Corp., Cin. Pres. Dallas Symphony Soc., 1980-82; chmn. exec. com. Dallas Ballet, 1979; bd. dirs. Dallas Mus. Fine Art, 1979-81; mem. adv. council Coll. Bus. Adminstrn., U. Tex., 1981—; bd. dirs. Cin. Ballet, 1982—; bd. dirs. Cin. Symphony, 1983—, pres., 1987. Mem. Dallas C. of C. (chmn. cultural com. 1979-81), Asso. Mdse. Corp . (dir., exec. com.), Hebrew Union Coll. (bd. overseers). Democrat. Jewish. Home: 2813 Ambleside Cincinnati OH 45208 Office: Federated Dept Stores Inc 7 W 7th St Cincinnati OH 45202

STONE, ESTHER GARBER, psychotherapist; b. N.Y.C., Oct. 12, 1935; d. Morris D. and Pearl (Borka) G.; m. Ira Lyons, Aug. 21, 1955 (div. 1971); children: Rhona Sue, Amy Marla; m. Walter N. Stone, Dec. 30, 1982. BA, City Coll. N.Y., 1955; MSW, Columbia U., 1958. lic. clin. social worker, N.Y., Ohio. Psychiat. social worker Westchester County Mental Health Bd., Ohio, 1958-61; sr. clinician therapist Rockland County Mental Health Clinic, Pamona, N.Y., 1962-79; sole practice psychotherapy Spring Valley, N.Y., 1968-83, Cin., 1983—; instr. Rockland Community Coll., Suffern, N.Y., 1977-78, U. Cin. Dept. Psychiatry, 1983—; cons. Mental Health Clinics, Rockland, 1959, Cin., 1983-84. Fellow Am. Orthopsychiat. Assn.; mem. Am. Group Psychotherapy Assn. (instr. 1982—, Recognition award 1982), Tri-state Group Psychotherapy Soc. (sec. 1984-85). Office: 2600 Euclid Inc Cincinnati OH 45219

STONE, GERALD L., university administrator, educator, psychologist; b. Glendale, Calif., Aug. 25, 1941; s. Jack Charles and Edith Bernice (Alexander) S.; m. Chery Ann Montgomery, Sept. 6, 1963; children: Corbin Lee, Carrie LeeAnn. BA, UCLA, 1963; BD, Princeton U., 1966; MA, Mich. State U., 1970, PhD, 1972. From asst. prof. to assoc. prof. U. Western Ont., Can., 1972-79; from assoc. prof. to prof. U. Iowa, Iowa City, 1979—, dir. counseling service, 1985—; cons. VA Med. Ctr., 1979—. Author: Cognitive/ Behavioral Approach to Counseling Psychology, 1980, Counseling Psychology: Perspectives and Functions, 1986. Fellow Am. Psychol. Assn. (sec. div. 17 1981-84); mem. Am. Ednl. Research Assn. (sec. div. E 1981-83), Am. Coll. Student Personnel Assn. Democrat. Presbyterian. Avocation: tennis. Office: U Iowa U Counseling Service 101 IMV Iowa City IA 52240

STONE, GREGORY MICHAEL, electronics company director; b. Hartford, Conn., July 31, 1959; s. George William Jr. and Patricia Gertrude (Fitton) S. BA in Polit. Sci., Loyola U., Chgo., 1982. Dir. advanced projects Sachs/Freeman Assocs. Inc., Lake Bluff, Ill., 1980—; bd. dirs. Telescis. Internat. Ltd., Mundelein, Ill., Consolidated News Service, Mundelein, RCT:SFA Joint Venture, Lake Bluff; prin. Stone Industries Inc., Mundelein, 1982—; dir. systems enging. Airfone Inc., Oak Brook, Ill., 1983-84. Contbr. articles in field to profl. jours. Mem. Lake County Rep. Fedn., Waukegan, Ill., 1985—. Fellow Radio Club Am.; mem. AAAS, IEEE (chmn. Chgo. sect. vehicular tech. soc. 1983—), John Birch Soc., Am. Def. Preparedness Assn. (chmn. ops. security working group), Am. Soc. for Indsl. Security, Armed Forces Communications and Electronics Assn., Scientist's Inst. for Pub. Info., U.S. Naval Inst., SAR, Mayflower Soc.; assoc. mem. Internat. Assn. Chiefs Police, Nat. Sheriffs Assn., Internat. Assn. Bomb Technicians and Investigators, Internat. Narcotic Enforcement Officers Assn., Inc. Avocations: physics, writing in and deciphering codes, automobile racing, flying, photography. Mailing: Box 485 Mundelein IL 60060 Office: Sachs/Freeman Assocs Inc 21 N Skokie Hwy Lake Bluff IL 60044

STONE, HARRIS BOTWINIK, architect, author; b. New Haven, Jan. 18, 1934; s. Herman Y. and Stella (Botwinik) S.; m. Joan Phillips, Aug. 28, 1963. AB, Brown U., 1955; MArch, Harvard U., 1959. Registered profl. architect, Conn. Pvt. practive architecture New Haven and Lawrence, Kans., 1966—; assoc. prof. U. Kans. Sch. Architecture, 1978—; lectr. Yale U. Sch. Architecture, 1973; asst. prof. Hampshire Coll., Amherst, Mass., 1975-78; dir. summer architecture program, Spannocchia, Italy, 1983—. Author: Workbook of an Unsuccessful Architect, 1973, Monuments and Main Streets, 1983. Active Hist. Resources Com., 1986, Nat. Trust for Hist. Preservation, 1986. Served with U.S. Army, 1959-65. Mem. AIA. Office: U Kans Sch Architecture Lawrence KS 66045

STONE, HARRY H., business executive; b. Cleve., May 21, 1917; s. Jacob and Jennie (Kantor) Sapirstein; m. Lucile Tabak, Aug. 10, 1960; children: Phillip, Allan, Laurie (Mrs. Parker), James Rose, Douglas Rose. Student, Cleve. Coll., 1935-36. With Am. Greetings Corp., Cleve., 1936—; v.p. Am. Greetings Corp., 1944-58, exec. v.p., 1958-69, vice chmn. bd. chmn. finance com., chmn audit com., 1969-78, now dir., chmn. audit com.; chmn. Barks Williams Oil, Ltd., London, 1985—, Barks Williams Trading Ltd., London, 1985—; mem. Ofcl. U.S. Mission to India and Nepal, 1965; cons. U.S. Dept. Commerce, U.S. Dept. State, adviser U.S. del. 24th session UN Econ. Commn. for Asia and Far East, Canberra, Australia, 1968; cons. Nat. Endowment for Arts, Nat. Council on Arts. Treas. Criminal Justice Coordinating Council., 1968-82; trustee emeritus Brandeis U., also univ. fellow. Jewish. Club: Rotary. Home: Bratenahl Pl No 2 Suite 9D Cleveland OH 44108 Office: The Courtland Group Inc 1540 Leader Bldg Cleveland OH 44114

STONE, IRVING I., greeting card company executive; b. Cleve., Apr. 5, 1909; s. Jacob and Jennie (Canter) Sapirstein; m. Helen K. Sill, Dec. 12, 1976; children: Hensha (Mrs. Hirsch Gansbourg), Neil, Myrna (Mrs. Harold Tatar), Judith (Mrs. Morry Weiss). Student, Case-Western Res. U., Cleve. Inst. Art. With Am. Greetings Corp., Cleve., 1923—, pres., 1960-78, chmn. bd., chief exec. officer, 1978—, also chmn. exec. com. Chmn. bd. Hebrew Acad. Cleve.; bd. dirs. Cleve. Inst. Art, Young Israel of Cleve., Yeshiva U.; trustee Simon Wiesenthal Ctr. for Holocaust Studies; 1st v.p. Telshe Yeshiva; life mem. bd. dirs. Jewish Community Fedn. of Cleve.; v.p. Am. Assn. for Jewish Edn., Bur. Jewish Edn., Cleve., Am. Friends of Boys Town Jerusalem; founder Kiryat Telshe Stone, Israel. Office: Am Greetings Corp 10500 American Rd Cleveland OH 44144 *

STONE, J. W., superintendent schools; b. Fortescue, Mo., Nov. 6, 1927; s. Perry Allen and May (Murrah) S.; B.S., NW Mo. State Coll., 1956; M.A., U. Mo., Kansas City, 1957, also postgrad. Farmer, Fortescue, Mo., 1944—; instr. Craig (Mo.) R-III High Sch., 1957-59; supt. schs., Holt County, Oregon, Mo., 1959-61, Craig R-III Sch. Dist., 1961—; del. to Hungary, USSR, Internat. Edn. Soc., 1968; mem. Mo. Adv. Council on Vocat. Edn., 1983—. Dist. dir. ARC, 1954—, bd. dirs. Midland Empire region, 1979—; bd. dirs. Heart Assn., Crippled Children's, March of Dimes, Tb Soc., 1954—; mem. Town Bd., Fortescue, Mo., 1962-78; mayor City of Fortescue, 1968-78; chmn. Holt County Citizens Council, 1979—; vice chmn. Wesley Found., NW Mo. State U., 1970—; mem. regional empire com. bd. Girl Scouts, 1973-75; mem. com. Mo. Council Public Higher Edn., 1973; regional dir. Mo. Vocat. Rehab., 1967—; chmn. bd. NW Mo. Community Services, 1980—. Mem. 6th Congressional Dist., 1960—, 6th Congressional Legis. Dist., 1960—, Mo. Republican State Com., 1960—; chmn. Holt County Rep. Central Com., 1954—; state com. del. to inauguration Pres. Reagan, 1981; mem. Balance of State Planning Council, State of Mo., 1981—. dir. OEO Corp.; sec.-treas. NW Mo. Econ. Opportunity Corp., Maryville, Mo., chmn. bd., 1969-79; v.p. Mo. Council Chs., 1948-50; dir. Camps and Conf., W. Mo. Conf., United Meth. Ch., 1965—, mem. bd. adminstrv. fin., 1972—; mem. Selective Service Bd. Mo. Region I, 1982, Appeals Bd. Western half of Mo., 1983; U.S. del. World Meth. Council Meeting, Dublin, 1976, Honolulu, 1981; Maryville dist. trustee Meth. Ch., 1960—. World del. Meth. Conf., Oslo, Norway, 1961; del. United Meth. Ch. Mo. West Conf. to World Meth. Council Evangelism, Jerusalem, 1974; world del. representing U.S. on Christian Edn., Tokyo, 1958; U.S. del. Comparative and Internat. Edn. Soc., Round-the-World, 1970, S. Am., 1971. Served with AUS, 1950-52. Mem. NEA, Nat., Mo. State assns. sch. adminstrs., Mo. State, Holt County (past pres.) tchrs. assns., Pi Omega Pi, Kappa Delta Pi, Tau Kappa Epsilon. Methodist (dist. lay leader 1968—). Clubs: Masons (32 deg., Shriner), Order Eastern Star. Home: Fortescue MO 64452 Office: Craig MO 64437

STONE, JAMES MERRILL, lawyer; b. Columbus, Ohio, Mar. 7, 1952; s. Irving Joseph and Dessie (Flauhaus) S. m. Winifred Ann Storkan, Apr. 11, 1981; 1 child, Jennifer Elizabeth. BA, Ohio State U., 1976; JD summa cum laude, Cleve. State U., 1986. Bar: Ohio 1986, U.S. Dist. Ct. (no. dist.) Ohio 1986, U.S. Ct. Appeals (6th cir.) 1986. Tech. dir. Karamu House, Cleve., 1974-77; pres. and gen. mgr. Merrill Stone Assocs., Inc., Cleve., 1977-83; assoc. Burke, Haber and Berick Co., Cleve., 1986—; adv. bd. Vincent Lighting Systems, Cleve., 1986—. Trustee First Congl. Ch., Twinsburg, Ohio, 1987—. Recipient Jaeger Award Delta Theta Phi, 1984. Mem. ABA, Ohio State Bar Assn., Cleve. Bar Assn., Cuyahoga County Bar Assn., Akron Bar Assn., U.S. Inst. Theatre Tech. (state chmn. 1977-80), Ohio State Alumni Assn. Republican. Home: 9436 Fairfield Dr Twinsburg OH 44087 Office: Burke Haber and Berick Co 300 Nat City Bank Bldg Cleveland OH 44087

STONE, JOHN MCWILLIAMS, JR., electronics executive; b. Chgo., Nov. 4, 1927; s. J. McWilliams and Marion (Jones) S.; m. Cheryl Johansen Cullison, Dec. 18, 1976; children: Jean, Lee Stone Nelson, John III, Michael, Shannon, Tammy. BA, Princeton U., 1950. Salesman A.B. Dick Co., Milw., 1950-51; prodn. supr. Dukane Corp., St. Charles, Ill., 1951-56, exec. v.p., 1956-62, pres., 1962-70, pres., chmn. bd., 1970—; bd. dirs. State Bank of St. Charles. Trustee The Elgin (Ill.) Acad., recipient Elgin medal 1984, emeritus, 1985—, Phillips Exeter (N.H.) Council, 1985—, Two Rivers Council Boy Scouts Am., St. Charles; mem. Delnor Hosp. Men's Found., St. Charles. Served with USNR, 1950-52. Named Exec. of Yr. Valley chpt. Profl. Secs. Internat., Aurora, 1981. Republican. Episcopalian. Clubs: Commonwealth, Econ., Princeton, Execs. (Chgo.); Dunham Woods Riding (Wayne, Ill.) (pres. 1967-68, 78-79). Avocation: tennis. Home: Box 18 Wayne IL 60184 Office: Dukane Corp 2900 Dukane Dr Saint Charles IL 60184

STONE, JOHN RICHARD, insurance company executive; b. Chgo., Apr. 5, 1938; s. Emil Fred and Lena Maud (Meyer) S.; divorced; children: Ruth, Rebecca, John Jr. BS, Ill. Wesleyan U., 1960; MBA, Loyola U., Chgo., 1973. CPA, Ill. Mgr. Ill. Bell, Chgo., 1960-70; sr. v.p. human resources div. AON Corp. (formerly Combined Internat. Corp.), Chgo., 1970—; instr. Lake Forest (Ill.) Grad. Sch., 1982—; vice chmn. Paysaver Credit Union, Westhral, Ill., 1982—. Served to comdr. USNR, 1960-86. Fellow Life Office Mgmt. Assn. (personnel policy com. 1987). Lodges: Kiwanis (pres. Chgo. club 1968), Masons. Home: 1366 Barclay Ln Deerfield IL 60615 Office: AON Corp 123 Wacker Dr Chicago IL 60606

STONE, JOHN TIMOTHY, JR., author; b. Denver, July 13, 1933; s. John Timothy and Marie Elizabeth (Briggs) S.; m. Judith Bosworth Stone, June 22, 1955; children: John Timothy, George William. Student Amherst Coll., 1951-52, U. Mex., 1952; BA, U. Miami, 1955. Sales mgr. Atlas Tag, Chgo., 1955-57; br. mgr. Household Fin. Corp., Chgo., 1958-62; pres. Janeff Credit Corp., Madison, Wis., 1962-72; pres. Recreation Internat., Mpls., 1972-74; pres. Continental Royal Services, N.Y.C., 1973-74; bd. dirs. Madison Credit Bur., Wis. Lenders' Exchange. Author: Mark, 1973, Going for Broke, 1976, The Minnesota Connection, 1978, Debby Boone So Far, 1980, (with John Dallas McPherson) He Calls Himself "An Ordinary Man", 1981, Satiacum, The Chief Who's Winning Back the West, 1981, The Great American Treasure Hunt, 1983-86, Runaways, 1983, (with Robert E. Gard) Where The Green Bird Flies, 1984. Served with CIC, U.S. Army, 1957-59. Mem. Sigma Alpha Epsilon. Republican. Presbyterian. Clubs: Minarani, African First Shotters. Home: 1009 Starlight Dr Madison WI 53711 Office: Pubs Adv Group PO Box 5562 Madison WI 55705

STONE, PAMELA ANN, accountant; b. Flint, Mich., Jan. 10, 1954; d. Leslie Elwood and Aloha Agusta (Wegener) S. AS in Acctg., Baker Bus. U., 1980; BS in Acctg., Detroit Coll. Bus., 1981; AS in Computer Programming, Baker Jr. Coll., 1983; MS in Profl. Accountancy, Walsh Coll., 1986. Acct., bus. mgr. Drury Bros. Inc., Durand, Mich., 1982-85; instr. Pontiac (Mich.) Bus. Inst., 1985-86; pvt. practice acctg., Flint, 1985—; instr. Baker Coll., Flint, 1986—. Avocations: piano, organ, tennis, bowling, needlepoint. Office: G3117 Corunna Rd Suite 230 Flint MI 48504

STONE, ROGER WARREN, container company executive; b. Chgo., Feb. 16, 1935; s. Marvin N. and Anita (Masover) S.; m. Susan Kesert, Dec. 24, 1955; children: Karen, Lauren, Jennifer. B.S. in Econs, U. Pa., 1957. With Stone Container Corp., Chgo., 1957—; dir. Stone Container Corp., 1968-77, v.p., gen. mgr. container div., 1970-75, pres., chief operating officer, 1975-79, pres., chief exec. officer, 1979—, chmn. bd., chief exec. officer, 1983—; bd. dirs. First Chgo., Interstate Bakeries Corp., Kans. City, Am. Appraisal Assocs., Milw. Trustee Glenwood (Ill.) Sch. for Boys, Chgo. Symphony Orch. Assn.; fellow Lake Forest (Ill.) Acad.; bd. overseers Wharton Sch., U. Pa.; pres. com. Smith Coll.; adv. council Kellog Sch. Mgmt. Northwestern U. Named Best or Top Chief Exec. Officer in firm's industry, Wall St. Transcript, 1981-86; recipient Top Chief Exec. Officer award in Forest & Paper Specialty Products Industry, Fin. World Mag., 1984. Mem. Am. Paper Inst. (chmn. bd. 1986—), Chief Execs. Orgn., Corrugated Industry Devel. Corp. (former pres.), Inst. Paper Chemistry (former trustee), The Chgo. Com., Mid-Am. Com., Chgo. Council Fgn. Relations. Republican. Clubs: Standard, Tavern, Comml., Econ. (Chgo.); Lake Shore Country (Glencoe, Ill.). Office: Stone Container Corp 150 N Michigan Ave Chicago IL 60601-7568

STONE, STEPHEN PAUL, dermatologist; b. N.Y.C., Aug. 22, 1941; s. C. Sidney and Sylvia (Alpher) S.; m. Lisa Jane Wald, Mar. 1, 1969; children: Jason Harris, Erica Lauren, Charles David. AB cum laude, Tufts U., 1963; MD, N.Y.U., 1969. Diplomate Am. Bd. Dermatology, Nat. Bd. Med. Examiners. Intern Lincoln Hosp., Bronx, N.Y., 1967-68; resident in internal medicine Mayo Clinic, Rochester, Minn., 1968-69; resident in dermatology Mayo Grad. Sch. Medicine, Rochester, Minn., 1971-74; pres. Dermatology Ctr. Ltd., Springfield, Ill., 1974—; clin. assoc. prof. medicine S. Ill. U., Springfield. Assoc. editor Dialogs in Dermatology, 1976—; contbr. articles to profl. jours. Pres. Jewish Community Relations Council, 1986—; bd. dirs. Council of Jewish Fedns., 1981-83, 85—, chmn. small cities nat. com. 1981—, nat. com. leadership devel., 1981—; bd. dirs. Springfield Jewish Fedn., 1976—, v.p. 1977-79, pres. 1980-83; bd. dirs. Springfield Zool. Soc., 1983—, Temple B'rith Sholom, 1984—, United Way of Greater Springfield, 1985—, Planned Parenthood, Springfield area, 1979-80; mem. United Jewish Appeal, Nat. Young Leadership Cabinet, 1977-82, regional chmn., 1980-81, midwest regional cabinet, 1980-82, midwest project renewal com., 1986—; sec. B'nai Israel Synagogue, Rochester, Minn., 1973-74; bd. dirs. West Cen. Ill. Health Systems Agy., 1978-84, exec. bd., 1978-84, v.p., 1982-84. Fellow Am. Coll. Physicians, Am. Soc. Dermatologic Surgery, Am. Soc. Laser Medicine and Surgery; mem. AMA, Chgo. Dermatological Soc. (plans and policy com. 1982-84), Ill. Dermatologic Soc. (sec.-treas. 1978-80, pres. 1981), Ill. State Med. Soc. (alternate del. 1984-85, council on govtl. affairs 1983-86), Internat. Soc. Tropical Dermatology, Noah Worcester Dermatological Soc. (continuing med. edn. com. 1982-83), Sangamon County Med. Soc. (chmn. liaison com. 1985), Soc. for Investigative Dermatology, N.Y. Bd. Med. Examiners (cert.), Minn. Bd. Med. Examiners, Calif. Bd. Med. Examiners, Ill. Bd. Med. Examiners, Am. Acad. Dermatology (council on communications 1980-84, chmn. council on communications 1987—). Lodge: B'nai Brith (v.p. Springfield, 1975-76, pres. 1976-77). Home: 3013 Mill Bank Ln Springfield IL 62704 Office: 630 N 1st St Springfield IL 62702

STONE, W. CLEMENT, insurance company executive, civic leader; b. Chgo., May 4, 1902; s. Louis and Anna M. (Gunn) S.; m. Jessie Verna Tarson; children: Clement (dec.), Donna Jessie (dec.), Norman Clement. Student, Detroit Coll. Law, 1920, LL.D., 1983; student, Northwestern U., 1930-32; hon. degrees; J.D., Monmouth Coll., 1963; H.H.D., Interlochen Arts Acad., 1964, Whitworth Coll., 1969, S.W. Baptist Coll., Bolivar, Mo., 1970, Lincoln (Ill.) Coll., 1971; L.H.D., De Paul U., 1970, Warner Pacific Coll., Portland, Oreg., 1978; LL.D., Whittier Coll., 1973; Litt.D., Nat. Coll. Chiropractic, Lombard, Ill., 1969; D.Public Service, Salem (W.Va.) Coll., 1974. Chmn. bd. Combined Am. Ins. Co. (formerly Am. Casualty Co.), 1939-82, Combined Internat. Corp., Chgo., 1980—; organizer Combined Mut. Casualty Co., 1940, pres., 1940-47; pres. Combined Ins. Co. Am. (formerly Pa. Casualty Co.), 1947-69, chmn. bd. dirs., 1969—, chief exec. officer, 1969-73; pres. Combined Ins. Co. Wis. (formerly 1st Nat. Casualty Co.), 1953-73, chmn. bd., chief exec. officer, 1973-82; pres., chmn. bd. Combined Life Ins. Co. N.Y., 1971-79, chmn. bd., 1979—; dir., chmn. bd. W. Clement Stone PMA Communications, Inc., 1980—; bd. dirs. Alberto-Culver Co., Hal Publs. Inc.; chmn. Walter V. Clarke & Assocs. Inc.; founding chmn. bd. Success Unlimited, Inc.; chmn. nat. bd. Congl. Award. Author: (with Napoleon Hill) Success Through a Positive Mental Attitude, 1960, The Success System that Never Fails, 1962, (with Norma L. Browning) The Other Side of the Mind, 1964. Pres., trustee Religious Heritage of Am., Inc., Washington.; Chmn. bd. W. Clement and Jessie V. Stone Found.; past bd. dirs. John Howard Assn., Chgo.; nat. exec. com. Boys Clubs Am.; life mem. bd. mgrs. Robert R. McCormick Chgo. Boys Club; hon. chmn. bd. Chgo. Boys Clubs; chmn. bd. Insts. Religion and Health; chmn. bd. trustees Internat. Council on Edn. for Teaching; mem. exec. com. Internat. Fedn. Keystone Youth Orgns.; hon. chmn. Found. for Study Cycles; chmn. bd. trustees Interlochen Arts Acad. and Nat. Music Camp. Named Chicagoan of Yr. Chgo. Boys Clubs, 1980; nominee for Nobel Peace prize, 1981. Mem. Internat. Assn. Health Underwriters, Ill. C. of C., Chgo. Assn. Commerce and Industry, Am. Mgmt. Assn., Sales Marketing Execs. Internat. Presbyterian. Clubs: Executives, Michigan Shores (Wilmette, Ill.). Lodges: Kiwanis, Masons. Office: Combined Internat Corp 123 N Wacker Dr Chicago IL 60606 also: Combined Ins Co of America 222 N Dearborn Chicago IL 60601 *

STONE, WILLIAM BRUHN, English educator; b. Milw., May 31, 1929; s. William Herbert and Martha Emily (Bruhn) S.; B.A. with gen. honors, U. Chgo., 1948, M.A., 1957; m. Jane Bergman, Mar. 13, 1953; children—David, Daniel, Joyce. Instr. English, U. Ky., Lexington, 1958-61, Wis. State U., LaCrosse, 1961-62; lectr. English, Ind. U. N.W., Gary, 1962-71, 80—; asst. dir. composition U. Ill., Chgo., 1976-80; editorial cons. various pubs. Active member Amnesty Internat. U.S.A. Served with AUS, 1952-54; Korea. Mem. AAUP, Assn. Tchrs. Advanced Composition (v.p. 1984-87), Conf. Coll. Composition and Communication, Midwest Modern Lang. Assn., MLA, Nat. Council Tchrs. of English, Rhetoric Soc. Am., Anthony Powell Soc. (sec.-treas. 1983—), U.S. Chess Fedn., ACLU. Editor: Anthony Powell Communications, 1977-79; editorial bd. Jour. Advanced Composition, 1979—, contbg. editor, 1984—. Contbr. articles, revs. and poetry to profl. jours., articles to ency. Home: 5704 S Kenwood Ave Chicago IL 60637 Office: Indiana University Northwest Gary IN 46408

STONER, PATRICIA SUE, accountant; b. Springfield, Mo., June 3, 1958; d. Homer Eugene and Dorothy Virginia (Womac) S. BS in Acctg., Southwest Mo. State U., 1982. CPA, Mo. Staff acct. Robert J. Davis, CPA, Springfield, 1977-84, Baird, Kurtz & Dobson, CPa, Springfield, 1984-86; pvt. practice acctg. Springfield, 1986—. Mem. Am. Inst. CPA's, Mo. Soc. CPA's, Am. Soc. Women Accts., Nat. Assn. Female Execs. Methodist. Avocations: water skiing, watching stock car racing. Office: 1031 E Battlefield Suite 115 B Springfield MO 65807

STONER, RALPH BOYD, small business owner; b. Mt. Pleasant, Pa., Oct. 13, 1939; s. Lyle Hunt and Mary Jane (Boyd) S.; m. Nancy Jane Hayden, Dec. 20, 1960 (div. 1971); children—Stephen H., Robert M.; m. Sharalyn Sue Durr, May 4, 1978 (div. 1987); 1 child, Kenneth Durr. B.S. in B.A., W.Va. U., 1961; M.B.A., Kent State U. Ohio, 1971. With Firestone Tire, Akron, 1961-66; sec., controller Firestone Singapore, 1966-69; corp. acct. Firestone Tire, Akron, 1969-72, adminstrv. asst. to pres., 1972-74; controller NDM Corp., Dayton, 1974-85; prin., Ralph Stoner & Assocs., 1986—. Mem. Nat. Assn. Accts., Soc. Mfg. Engrs., Miami Valley Mgmt. Assn. Republican. Avocations: computer programming; investment analysis; auto mechanics; bowling; jogging. Home: 4832 Philadelphia Dr Dayton OH 45405 Office: 4844 Philadelphia Dr Dayton OH 45414

STONER, ROBERT ALAN, orthodontist; b. Indpls., Mar. 27, 1951; s. Morris Meyer and Joan Beverly (Jackson) S.; m. Ruth Ann Darden, July 7, 1982; 1 child, Jacob William. DDS, Ind. U., 1980; MS in Orthodontics, U. Mich., 1983. Gen. practice dentistry Ann Arbor, 1980-83; gen. practice dentistry specializing in orthodontics Indpls., 1983—; Cons. Golden Rule Ins. Co., Indpls., 1983-86; judge dental div. Cen. Ind. Regional Sci. Fair, Indpls., 1983—. Co-chmn. Children's Dental Health Month, Indpls., 1987; active B'nai B'rith; bd. dirs. Jewish Community Relations Council, Indpls., 1986. Grantee U. Mich. Sch. Dentistry, 1982; Horace B. Racklam fellow U. Mich., 1982. Mem. Am. Assn. Orthodontics, ADA, Ind. Soc. Orthodontists, Great Lakes Soc. Orthodontists, Alpha Omega (pres. 1986-87). Club: Indpls. Sailing. Avocations: sailing, aquariums, photography, wilderness survival. Home: 5327 N Pennsylvania St Indianapolis IN 46220 Office: 1261 W 86th Indianapolis IN 46260

STONER, RONALD EDWARD, astrophysics educator; b. Indpls., Nov. 25, 1937; s. William I. and Freda I. (Mock) S.; m. Jeanne Anne Smith; children: Gwynne, Holly. BA, Wabash Coll., 1959; MS, Purdue U., 1961, PhD, 1966. Asst. prof. Bowling Green (Ohio) State U., 1965-70, assoc. prof., 1970-75, prof. physics, 1975—. Fulbright lectr. Univ. Sri Jayewardenepura, Sri Lanka, 1980-81; grantee NASA, 1980—. Mem. Am. Phys. Soc. (chmn. Ohio sect. 1986-87), Am. Astron. Soc., Am. Assn. Univ Profs. (pres. local chpt. 1985-86), Am. Assn. Sci., Phi Beta Kappa, Omicron Delta Kappa, Sigma Xi. Office: Bowling Green State U Dept Physics & Astronomy Bowling Green OH 43403

STOOPS, BRADLEY NEIL, engineering company executive; b. Anderson, Ind., Feb. 25, 1951; s. Joseph Neil and Deloris Mae (Oesch) S.; m. Melaney Sue Jannelli, Oct. 27, 1979; children: Elizabeth Ann, Patrick Neil. BA, DePauw U., Greencastle, Ind., 1973; M in Internat. Mktg., Am. Grad. Sch. Internat. Mgmt., Glendale, Ariz., 1975; MSMechE, Cleve. State U., 1980. Analyst, supr. Premier Industries, Cleve., 1975-76; with mktg. B.F. Goodrich, Cleve., 1976-80; product mgr. Nordson Corp., Amherst, Ohio, 1980-84; gen. mgr. Otto Engring., Carpentersville, Ill., 1984—. Contbr. articles to profl. jours. Mem. ASME, Soc. Mfg. Engrs. Avocations: athletics, art. Home: 1080 Cedar Crest Dr Crystal Lake IL 60014 Office: Otto Engring 2 E Main St Carpentersville IL 60110

STOOPS, JON WALTON, public administrator; b. Pitts., Mar. 24, 1944; s. Walton W. and Martha S. (Nietz) S.; m. Carol Mae Kelch, July 6, 1968; children: Randall A., Claire E. BA, Coll. Wooster (Ohio), 1966; postgrad., U. Mich. Sch. Law, 1966-67; M of Urban Planning, U. Mich., 1973; M of Pub. Adminstrn., U. Pitts., 1969. Sr. planner Genesee County, Mich., 1973-74; asst. dir. Ind. Assn. Cities and Towns, Indpls., 1974-76; dep. dir. acad. pub. service Georgetown U., Indpls., 1976-80; exec. dir. Ind. Acad. Pub. Service, Indpls., 1981-83; dir. acad. pub. service mgmt. office Ind. U., Indpls., 1983-85; fin. dir. City of Beavercreek, Ohio, 1986—; instr. urban planning Ind. U., Indpls., 1984-85. Mem. Am. Soc. Pub. Adminstrn. (Ind. chpt. pres. 1985-86), Am. Planning Assn., Internat. City Mgmt. Assn. (cooperating). Democrat. Unitarian. Home: 1378 New Haven Ct Beavercreek OH 45385 Office: City of Beavercreek 1368 Research Park Dr Beavercreek OH 45432

STORCH, STEPHEN FRANK, accountant; b. Milw., Apr. 16, 1954; s. Gerard M. and Charlotte T. (Liebhauser) S.; m. Dori Lynn Birnschein, June 28, 1980; children: Stephanie Lynn, Nicholas Gerard. BS in Fin. and Acctg., U. Wis., Milw., 1976. CPA, Wis. Corp. acctg. supr. Universal Mortgage Co., Milw., 1976-79, fin. reporting analyst, 1979-80, gen. account supr., 1980-84, ins. account analyst, 1984—. Mem. Wis. Inst. CPA's, Am. Inst. CPA's, Risk and Ins. Mgmt. Soc. Roman Catholic. Club: Northwest Investment (Milw.) (pres. 1984—). Avocations: sports, stock market, chess. Home: 7857 N Edgeworth Dr Milwaukee WI 53223 Office: Miller Brewing Co 3939 W Highland Blvd Milwaukee WI 53201

STORCK, JOHN ROBERT, lawyer; b. Beaver Dam, Wis., June 27, 1954; s. Robert Emil and Caroline E. (Feutz) S.; m. Paula J. Schaefer, Aug. 22, 1976; children: Eric John, Michael Schaefer. BBA, U. Wis., 1976; JD cum laude, Harvard U., 1979. Bar: Wis. 1979. Sole practice Mayville, Wis., 1979—. Pres. Mayville Community Devel. Corp., 1986. Mem. Wis. Bar Assn., Wis. Acad. Trial Lawyers, Mayville C. of C. (v.p. 1986, pres. 1987). Avocations: waterskiing, sailing. Home: 603 River Dr Mayville WI 53050 Office: Storck Law Office 116 S Main St Mayville WI 53050

STORICH, AL, accountant; b. N.Y.C., June 7, 1918; s. Charles and Goldie (Diamond) S.; m. Del Storich, Oct. 31, 1940; children: Maxine, Nikki. BBA, CCNY, 1939. CPA, Ohio. Pres. Storich CPA Corp., Mansfield, Ohio, 1960—; lectr. MOIC, Mansfield, 1967, Cuyahoga Community Coll., Palma, Ohio, 1968, Ohio State U., Mansfield, 1970-75; asst. prof. Ashland (Ohio) Coll., 1969-72. Author books on mgmt. services, 1968, tax practice, 1970; editor (report) Farmers Taxes, 1980; cons. editor Prentice-Hall, Englewood Cliffs, N.J., 1972—; guest writer Mansfield News Jour., 1986. Chmn. Mayor's Legal Justice Com., Mansfield, 1967. Served with U.S. Merchant Marine, 1943-45, MTO, PTO, ETO, CBI. Recipient Speaker's award Acctg. Edn. Found., 1980. Mem. Am. Inst. CPA's, Ohio Soc. CPA's, Nat. Accts. Assn. (Author's award 1965, 66, Speaker's award 1967), NAACP (life), Mansfield C. of C. (chmn. legis. com. 1965). Jewish. Lodges: Lions (contbr. Helping the Handicapped mag. 1986, bd. dirs. Mansfield 1985-86), Masons, Baku, Shriners, B'nai Brith. Avocations: sailing, travel, music, theater, film. Office: Storich CPA Corp 502 Richland Bank Bldg Mansfield OH 44902

STORM, WILLIAM CHARLES, metal processing company manager; b. Toledo, Oct. 9, 1953; s. William Edwin and Mary Dorothy (Toth) S.; m. Patsy Leigh Lederman, Oct. 30, 1976; children: Anna Leigh, Emily Faith, Christopher William. BBA, U. Toledo, 1975, MBA, 1976. Gen. supr. systems dept. Inland Steel Coal Co., Sesser, Ill., 1983-86; with J.T. Ryerson & Sons, Chgo., 1986—. Deacon Sub. Bible Ch., Highland, Ind., 1979-82, bd. sec., 1978; treas. Grace Alliance Ch., Carbondale, 1984-85; leader Christian Home Sch. Support Group, So. Ill., 1985-86. Named one of Outstanding Young Men Am., 1980. Mem. Data Processing Mgmt. Assn., Beta Gamma Sigma. Republican. Home: 5 S Mill St Naperville IL 60540 Office: JT Ryerson & Sons 2558 W 16th St Chicago IL 60608

STORTZUM, JAMES TIMOTHY, research architect, design and construction consultant; b. Effingham, Ill., May 19, 1955; s. Delbert Wayne and Barbra Lou (Rinehart) S. AS, Lake Land Coll., Mattoon, Ill., 1975; BS in Archtl. Studies, U. Ill., 1978, postgrad., 1985—. Solar technician Solar Design Assocs., Inc., Champaign, Ill., 1978-81; designer, builder Hillshire Constrn., Champaign, 1981-83; research architect C.E. U.S. Army, Champaign, 1983—; solar instr. Danville (Ill.) Area Community Coll., 1979-81; solar lectr. Ill. Inst. Natural Resources, Springfield, 1979-81. Avocations: hiking, canoeing, skiing. Home: 211 W Hill St Champaign IL 61820 Office: USA-CERL PO Box 4005 Champaign IL 61820

STOTTLEMYER, HERBERT LEE, retired city letter carrier; b. Anderson, Ind., May 9, 1926; s. Herbert and Alice Catherine (Seybert) S.; m. Carolyn Sue Stohler, Oct. 26, 1952. Student Gen. Motors Inst. Tech., 1944. Apprentice toolmaker Delco Remy, Anderson, 1943-45; farm machinery mechanic, Case Farm Machinery, Anderson, 1945-48; semi-skilled machinist Pierce Governor Co., Anderson, 1948-53; cable splicers helper, Gen. Telephone, Anderson, 1953-55; city carrier U.S. Postal Service, Anderson, 1955-85; nat. sec. Nat. Federated Craft, 1970—. Trustee, chmn., deacon United Ch. Christ, Anderson. Served with U.S. Army, 1950-51. Lodges: Ky. Cols., Masons (32d degree). Avocations: gardening, traveling, reading. Home and Office: 5824 S Ridge Rd Anderson IN 46011

STOTTLEMYRE, DONNA MAE, jewelry store executive; b. Mystic, Iowa, Nov. 11, 1928; d. Clarence William and Nina Alene (Millizer) Clark; m. Robert Arthur Stottlemyre, May 8, 1946; children—Roger Dale, Amber Anita, Tamra Collette. Owner, operator Donna's Dress Shop, Unionville, Mo., 1973-76, Donna's Jewelry Box and Bridal Boutique, Unionville, 1978—. Sunday sch. tchr. First Baptist Ch., Unionville, Bible sch. tchr.; 4H Club judge County Fair, Unionville. Mem. C. of C. Avocations: sewing; flower arranging. Home: 217 N 14th Unionville MO 63565 Office: Donna's Jewelry and Bridal 1610 Main Unionville MO 63565

STOUGH, CHARLES DANIEL, lawyer; b. Mound Valley, Kans., Dec. 6, 1914; s. Charles Daniel and Narka Pauline (Ice) S.; m. Mary Juliet Shipman, Feb. 13, 1936; children—Vera Rubin, Sally Randall Stough Bartlett. A.A., Kemper Mil. Sch., 1934; A.B., U. Kans., 1936, LL.B., 1938, J.D., 1968. Bar: Kans. 1938, Ill. 1938. City atty. City of Lawrence, Kans., 1947-67, City of Eudora (Kans.), 1949-85; spl. counsel, Douglas County Kans., 1951-85; sole practice, Lawrence, 1939-82; with firm Stough & Heck, 1982—; prof. local govt. law U. Kans., 1969-70. Mem. U. Kans. Spencer Mus., 1986; mem. Kans. Ho. of Reps., 1947-55, majority leader, 1951-53, speaker of house, 1953-55. Trustee, U. Kans. Endowment Assn., Nat. Parks and Conservation Assn., Washington. Served to lt. j.g. USNR, 1943-46. Recipient Ellsworth award U. Kans., 1980; named one of Outstanding Kansans U. Kans., 1986; named to Gallary of Outstanding Kansans, 1986. Trustee Hertzler Research Found., Halstead, Kans., 1983—. Mem. ABA (chmn. Local Govt. Law Sect. 1964-67), Kans. Bar Assn. (chmn. world Peace Through Law Sect. 1970—), Nat. Inst. Mcpl. Law Officers (trustee 1964-65), City Attys. Assn. (exec. com.). Republican. Congregationalist. Clubs: Kiwanis, Masons (Lawrence); Republican Vets. of Kans. (state pres. 1959-60).

STOUP, ARTHUR HARRY, lawyer; b. Kansas City, Mo., Aug. 30, 1925; s. Isadore and Dorothy (Rankle) S.; m. Kathryn Jolliff, July 30, 1948; children—David C., Daniel P., Rebecca Ann, Deborah E. Student, Kansas City Jr. Coll., Mo. 1942-43; B.A., U. Mo., 1950; J.D., 1950. Bar: Mo. 1950, D.C. 1979. Practice law Kansas City, Mo., 1950—; mem. firm Stoup & Thompson; mem. Lawyer to Lawyer Consultation Panel-Litigation, 1976—; chmn. U.S. Merit Selection Com. for Western Dist. Mo., 1981. Chmn. com. to rev. continuing edn. U. Mo., 1978-79; trustee, pres. U. Mo.-Kansas City Law Found., 1979-82; trustee U. Kansas City, 1979—. Served with USNR, 1942-45. Recipient Alumni Achievement award U. Mo.-Kansas City Alumni Assn., 1975. Fellow Internat. Soc. Barristers, Am. Bar Found. (life mem.); mem. Kansas City Bar Assn. (pres. 1966-67), Mo. Bar Assn. (bd. govs. 1967-76, v.p. 1972-73, pres. 1974-75), ABA (ho. dels. 1976-80), Lawyers Assn. Kansas City, Mo. Assn. Trial Attys., Assn. Trial Lawyers Am. (sustaining), So. Conf. Bar Pres.'s (life), Mobar Research Inc. (pres. 1978-86), Phi Alpha Delta Alumni (justice Kansas City area 1955-56). Lodges: Optimists (pres. Ward Pkwy. 1961-62, lt. gov. Mo. dist. internat. 1963-64), Sertoma, B'nai B'rith. Home: 9002 Western Hills Dr Kansas City MO 64114 Office: Home Savs Bldg Kansas City MO 64106

STOUT, DONALD EVERETT, real estate developer and appraiser; b. Dayton, Ohio, Mar. 16, 1926; s. Thorne Franklin and Lovella Marie (Sweeney) S.; B.S., Miami U., 1950; m. Gloria B. McCormick, Apr. 10, 1948; children—Holly Sue, Scott Kenneth. Mgr. comml.-indsl. div. G.P. Huffman Realty, Dayton, 1954-58; leasing agt., mgr. Forest Park Plaza, Dayton, 1959-71; developer 1st transp. center for trucking in Ohio; pres. devel. cos. Sunderland Falls Estates, Wright Gate Indsl. Mall, Edglo Land Recycle, pres. Donald E. Stout, Inc. Served with AUS, 1944-45, USN, 1945-46. Named Outstanding Real Estate Salesman in Dayton, Dayton Area Bd. Realtors, in Ohio, Ohio Bd. Realtors, 1961. Licensed real estate broker, Ohio, U.S. Virgin Islands. Mem. Dayton Area Bd. Realtors (founder; 1st pres. salesman div. 1959, dir. 1959-60), Nat. Assn. Real Estate Bds., Soc. Real Estate Appraisers (sr. real estate appraiser, dir. chpt. 1959-60, pres. chpt. 1964), Am. Inst. Real Estate Appraisers, Nat. Assn. Rev. Appraisers (charter), Soc. Indsl. Office Realtors, Res. Officers Assn., C. of C., Phi Delta Theta. Clubs: Masons (32 deg.), Shrine. Contbr. articles to profl. jours. Home: 759 Plantation Ln Dayton OH 45419 Office: 1336 Woodman Dr Dayton OH 45432

STOUT, EDWARD IRVIN, medical manufacturing company executive; b. Washington, Iowa, Mar. 2, 1939; s. George L. and M. Gladys (Gorsh) S.; divorced; children: Deborah L., Cathy A., Angela F. BS, Iowa Wesleyan Coll., 1960; Ms in Chemistry, Bradley U., 1968; PhD in Organic Chemistry, U. Ariz., 1973. Analytical chemist Laver Bros. Research, Edgewater, N.J., 1961-62; research chemist USDA, Peoria, Ill., 1962-78; dir. research Spenco Med. Corp., Waco, Tex., 1978-81; pres. S.W. Techs. Inc., Kansas City, Mo., 1981—; dir. research Chemstar Product Co., Mpls., 1982-86, cons.; cons. Stout Product Co., Ainsworth, Iowa, 1985—; instr. Bradley U., Peoria, 1970-78. Contbr. articles to profl. jours.; patentee in field. Mem. Am. Chem. Soc., Inst. Food Technologists, Am. Assn. Cereal Chemists, Am. Burn Assn. Avocation: tennis. Home: 5207 W 76th St Prairie Village KS 66208 Office: SW Techs Inc 1510 Charlotte Kansas City MO 64108

STOUT, GLENN EMANUEL, water resources center administrator; b. Fostoria, Ohio, Mar. 23, 1920. AB, Findlay Coll., 1942, DSc, 1973. Sci. coordinator NSF, 1969-71; asst. to chief Ill. State Water Survey, Champaign, 1971-74; prof. Inst. Environ. Studies, Urbana, Ill., 1973—, dir. task force, 1975-79; dir. Water Resources Ctr. U. Ill., Urbana, 1973—; mem. Gov.'s Task Force on State Water Plan, 1980—; bd. dirs. Univ. Council Water Resources, 1983-86. Contbr. articles to profl. jours. Active Salvation Army. Mem. Internat. Water Resources Assn. (sec. gen. 1985—, exec. dir. 1984—), Am. Meteorol. Soc., Am. Geophys. Union, N.Am. Lake Mgmt. Soc., Ill. Lake Mgmt. Assn. (bd. dirs. 1985—), Internat. Assn. Research Hydrology, Sigma Xi (pres. U. Ill. chpt. 1985-86). Lodge: Kiwanis (local chpt. pres. 1979-80, lt. gov. 1982-83). Home: 920 W John St Champaign IL 61821 Office: Water Resources Ctr 208 N Romine St Urbana IL 61801

STOUT, GORDON HOWARD, computer systems executive, consultant; b. Northville, Mich., Dec. 8, 1939; s. Leslie Harold Stout and Wilma Elizebeth (Bell) Stout; m. Judith Kay Sieberg, June 21, 1957 (div. Apr. 1986); children—Debra Lynn, Mark Douglas, Jeffrey Todd, Jonathan Paul. B.A., So. Ill. U., 1964; postgrad., U. Ky., 1966, Purdue U., 1966. Tchr. math., sci. Evansville Day Sch., Ind., 1964-66; sci. programmer Monsanto Research, Miamisburg, Ohio, 1966-68; sci. programmer, analysis Duriron Co., Dayton, Ohio, 1968-69, mgr. programming engring. analysis, 1969-77, mgr. programming, ops., 1977-81, asst. dir. info. systems, 1981—; mgr. process control system, 1985—; systems cons. dir. Hipple Lab.-Cancer Research, Kettering, Ohio, 1983-85; analyst, programmer Carousel Dance Studio, Dayton, 1984-85. Sec., chmn. edn. com. Dayton Christian Schs. Inc., 1972-82. NIH grantee, 1966. Mem. Assn. Systems Mgmt. Republican. Baptist. Avocations: swimming, scuba diving, ballroom dancing. Home: 1054 Park Ln Apt D Middletown OH 45042 Office: Duriron Co Inc PO Box 1145 425 N Findlay Dayton OH 45401

STOVER, JAMES R., manufacturing company executive; b. Marion, Ind., 1927; married. BSME, Cath. U. Am., 1950; LLB, George Washington U., 1955. With legal dept. Eaton Corp., Cleve., 1955-63, with corp. engring., 1963-67, with engineered fasteners div., 1973-74, group v.p. indsl. and security products, 1974-77, exec. v.p. ops., 1977-78, vice chmn. and chief operating officer transp. products, 1978-79, pres. and chief operating officer, 1979-86, chmn. and chief exec. officer, 1986—, also bd. dirs.; bd. dirs. Nat. City Corp., Nat. City Bank, Ohio Bell Telephone Co., Leaseway Transp. Corp. Bd. dirs. Greater Cleve. Growth Assn. Mem. Machinery and Allied Products Inst. (exec. com.), Nat. Electrical Mfrs. Assn. (bd. govs.), U.S. C. of C. (bd. dirs.). Office: Eaton Corp Eaton Center Cleveland OH 44114

STOVER, PHILLIP JEROME, real estate corporation officer; b. Kans. City, Mo., Dec. 29, 1938; s. Emmert George and Miriam (Gephart) S.; m. Annette Ashlock, Sept. 7, 1968; children: Stephanie Lee, Scott Jason. BA, Yale U., 1961; MBA, U. Chgo., 1971. V.p. Collaborative Devel., Chgo., 1971-74; analyst Capital Resources, Chgo., 1975-76; broker Rubloff & Co., Chgo., 1976-77; pres. Stover & Co., Chgo., 1977—. Pres. assoc. bd. trustees U. Chgo. Cancer Research Found., 1982. Mem. Inst. Real Estate Mgmt., Chgo. Real Estate Bd. Republican. Presbyterian. Avocations: skiing, swimming, dancing. Home: 903 Monroe Evanston IL 60202 Office: Stover & Co 30 N La Salle St Chicago IL 60602

STOVER, WILLIAM RUFFNER, insurance company executive; b. Washington, Aug. 31, 1922; s. Daniel I. and Carrie E. (Brubaker) S.; m. Carolyn McKean, July 19, 1947; children—Deborah Ann Stover Bowgren, Wendi Lee Stover Mirretti, Sheree Kay Stover Bloss. Student, Northwestern U., 1941-45. Sales rep. Old Republic Life Ins. Co., 1945-1949, v.p., 1949-60, sr. v.p., 1960-68, dir., 1961-68, pres., 1968-69; pres. Old Republic Internat. Corp., 1969—, chmn. bd., chief exec. officer, 1976—; dir. Old Republic Life N.Y., Old Republic Ins. Co., Internat. Bus. and Merc. Reassurance Co., Home Owners Life Ins. Co. and subs., Minn. Title Fin. Corp., Bitco Corp., Founders Title Group, Inc., Republic Mortgage Ins. Co. Republican. Home: 907 N Sheridan Rd Waukegan IL 60085 Office: Old Republic Internat Corp 307 N Michigan Ave Chicago IL 60601

STOWELL, THOMAS PATRICK, computer information scientist; b. Quincy, Ill., Apr. 18, 1951; s. Arthur Francis and Mildred Mabel (Werner) S.; m. Kim Hudson, Aug. 24, 1979. BA in Behavioral Psychology, Quincy Coll., 1973; MA in Energy Planning and Resource Mgmt., Sangamon State U., 1983. Behavioral therapist Adams County, Quincy, 1973-74; fin. mgr. Positively Front St., Quincy, 1975-78; holographer Firestone Fire & Rubber, Decatur, Ill., 1979-81, quality auditor, 1981-83, engr. computer systems, 1983—; owner, mgr. Canine Hair Design, Decatur, 1983—. Author: (book) Wind Power: Future Energy, 1981, Alternative Energy Technologies, 1983. Mem. Sierra Club, Greenpeace. Democrat. Avocations: pure-bred dogs, bicycling, sailing. Office: Canine Hair Design 345 W Prairie Decatur IL 62522

STOY, PATRICK JAMES, physician; b. Lafayette, Ind., Jan. 16, 1949; s. Robert Andrew and Doretta Nora (Lynch) S.; m. Margaret Ann Folsom, May 1, 1957; children: Heather Marie, Daniel Paul, Sean Patrcik. BS, U. Notre Dame, 1971; MD, U. Minn., 1974. Resident in internal medicine U. Minn., Mpls., 1974-77, pulmonary and allergy fellow, 1977-79; staff Fargo Clinic, Fargo, N.D., 1979—; assoc. prof. U. N.D. Med. Sch., Grand Forks, 1979—. Mem. AMA, Am. Acad. Allergy and Immunology, Am. Thoracic Soc. Roman Catholic. Avocations: tennis, skiing, golf, swimming, sailing. Home: 3437 Peterson Pkwy Fargo ND 58102 Office: Fargo Clinic 737 Broadway Fargo ND 58123

STOYE, FRED DECKERT, JR., dentist; b. Detroit, June 10, 1950; s. Frederick Deckert and Barbara Devina (James) S.; m. Deborah Ann Wood, Sept. 18, 1976; children: Emily Susanne, Grant Frederick, Jonathan Paul. Gen. practice dentistry Lathrup Village, Mich., 1976—; bd. dirs. Lamina Inc., Oak Park, Mich. Councilman City of Lathrup Village Council, 1980-83, 86; mem. Recreation com., Lathrup Village, 1979-80; chmn. Mich. Bicentennial Com., Lathrup Village, 1986—. Mem. ADA, Mich. Dental Assn., Detroit Dist. Dental Soc., Oakland County Dental Soc. Republican. Episcopalian. Avocations: hunting, radio controlled models, golfing. Home: 27852 Rainbow Circle Lathrup Village MI 48076 Office: 27445 Southfield Rd Lathrup Village MI 48076

STRACHAN, WILLIAM MERION, environmental engineer; b. Cleve., Aug. 3, 1955; s. Donald M. and Suzanne (Merion) S. BS, U. Cin., 1978, MS, 1981. Environ. engr. U.S. EPA, Cin., 1980-81, Ohio EPA, Dayton, 1982-85, R.O. Zande & Assocs., Ltd., Columbus, Ohio, 1985—; bd. dirs. Ohio Ecol. Food and Farm Assn. Contbr. articles to profl. jours. Mem. ASCE (assoc.). Office: RD Zande & Assoc Ltd 1237 Dublin Rd Columbus OH 43215

STRADAL, WALTER JOHN, real estate executive; b. St. Louis, Oct. 3, 1927; s. Walter John Sr. and Mary L. (Welsh) S.; m. Joan Weir, May 15, 1954; children: Stephen W. and David W. (twins), Ann Penfield Stradal Lanpheir. BFA, Washington U., St. Louis, 1952. Art dir. Gardner Advt., St. Louis, 1952-56, exec., 1956-63; dir. alumni fund Washington U., 1963-67; exec. v.p. Real Estate Bd. St. Louis, 1968—. Alderman. police commr. City of Creve Coeur, Mo., 1962-68; adv. bd. dirs. Deaconess Hosp., St. Louis, 1980—. Served with USN, 1945-46. Mem. St. Louis Beta Theta Pi Alumni Club. Republican. Club: Clayton. Avocations: tennis, home repair, remodeling. Home: 510 N Spoede Rd Creve Coeur MO 63141 Office: Real Estate Bd Met St Louis 12777 Olive Saint Louis MO 63141

STRADER, DAVID ALLEN, marketing professional; b. Ft. Wayne, Ind., Oct. 9, 1950; s. Wayne A. and Marjorie A. (Zink) S.; m. Janet A. Barron, Aug. 12, 1972; children: Melissa, Benjamin, Joshua. B in Polit. Sci. and History, U. Iowa, 1973. CLU; chartered fin. cons. Coll. agt. Aetna Life, Iowa City, 1972-74; spl. agt. Northwestern Mut., Iowa City, 1974-1982; dir. field devel. Mut. Security Life, Ft. Wayne, Ind., 1982-86; dir. mktg. 1 On 1 Cons. & Pub., Ft. Wayne, 1986—. Author: Principles of Management, 1984, Having Your Cake & Eating It Too, 1985, Introduction to Financial Risk Management, 1986; editor Accelerated Sales Action Plan, 1983. Sec., committeeperson Rep. Party Johnson County, Iowa City, 1972-78; chmn. bd., founder Iowa Service Project, Iowa City, 1975-82; chmn. bd. Coralville (Iowa) United Meth. Ch., 1977-79. Recipient Young Religious Leader award U.S. Jaycees. Mem. Am. Soc. CLU's, Gen. Agts. and Mgrs. Assn., Nat. Assn. Life Underwriters. Avocations: fishing, woodworking, gardening. Home: Rt 5 Columbia City IN 46725

STRADLEY, NORMAN HENRY, ceramic engineer; b. Newark, Ohio, June 28, 1924; s. Edward Foster and Catherine Leah (Keller) S.; m. Margaret Jeanne Coy, Nov. 27, 1947; children—Edward Ray, Pamela Jeanne. B.S., Ohio State U., 1949, M.S., 1949; student U. Va., 1943-44. Registered profl. engr., Tenn. Research fellow Ohio State U. Found., Columbus, 1949; research engr., group supr. Minn. Mining & Mfg. Co., St. Paul, 1950-59; tech. and supervisory research positions Am. Lava Corp., Chattanooga, 1960-75; product devel. specialist 3M Co., 1976-81; patent liaison 3M Co., St. Paul, 1982—; cons. in field. Served to maj. USAFR, to 2d lt. USAF, 1943-46. Fellow Am. Ceramic Soc., Am. Inst. Chemists; mem. Nat. Inst. Ceramic Engrs., Keramos, Sigma Xi, Tau Beta Pi, Sigma Gamma Epsilon, Sigma Nu. Club: Lions (dist. gov. 1982-83). Contbr. articles to profl. jours.; patentee in field. Home: 740 Nightingale Blvd Stillwater MN 55082 Office: 3M Co 3M Center Saint Paul MN 55101

STRADTNER, BETTY JANE, educator; b. Paris, Tenn., May 19, 1949; d. B. Frank and Edna (Rutland) Wofford; m. John William Stradtner, July 7, 1974. BS, Murray (Ky.) State U., 1971; MA, U. Evansville, Ind., 1976. Elem. tchr. Clarke Sch., Loge Sch., Boonville, Ind., 1971—; tutor, Boonville, 1977—; coordinator math, reading Loge Sch.; pub. relations rep. Loge Sch. Soloist, ch. choir mem., sec. worship com., wedding cons. Main St. United Meth. Ch., Boonville, family coordinator, 1986. Mem. Warrick County Sch. Tchrs. Assn. (dir. external pub. relations 1986—), Ind. State Tchrs. Assn., NEA, Murray State U. Coll. Edn. Alumni Assn., Kappa Kappa Kappa, Boonville Bus. and Profl. Women's Club (sec. 1982-84, historian 1984—). Democrat. Avocations: singing, tole painting, entertaining, crafts. Home: 614 Parkview Dr Boonville IN 47601 Office: Loge Sch Boonville IN 47601

STRAHLER, VIOLET RUTH, educational consultant; b. Dayton, Ohio, Sept. 30, 1918; d. Ezra F. and Bertha (Daniels) S. A.B. magna cum laude, Wittenberg U., 1944; M.A., Miami U., Ohio, 1959; Ed.D., Ind. U., 1972; L.H.D. (hon.), Wittenberg U., 1986. Cert. tchr., supt., Ohio. Tchr. Miamisburg Pub. Schs., Ohio, 1944-51; tchr., counselor Dayton Pub. Schs., 1952-66, supr. sci. and math. curriculum, 1967-72, acting asst. supt. curriculum, 1972-73, exec. dir. curriculum services, 1973-85; instr. U. Dayton, Miami U., 1959-74; ednl. cons.; supervisor student tchrs., U. Dayton, 1986—. Author and coauthor numerous textbooks, lab. guides. Editor newsletter Ohio Jr. Acad. Sci., 1950-52. Contbr. articles to profl. jours. Mem. Dayton/Montgomery County Arson Task Force; trustee Dayton Mus. Natural History. Ford Found. fellow, 1952-53. Mem. NOW, Am. Assn. Sch. Adminstrs., Buckeye Assn. Sch. Adminstrs. (life), Assn. Supervision and Curriculum Devel., Am. Chem. Soc., Nat. Sci. Tchrs. Assn. (life), Ohio Acad. Sci., Phi Delta Kappa. Methodist. Home: 5340 Brendonwood Ln Dayton OH 45415 Office: U Dayton Dept Tchr Edn Chaminade Hall 300 College Park Dayton OH 45469-0001

STRAIGHT, BONNIE JEAN, information systems engineer; b. Inglewood, Calif., Nov. 17, 1942; d. James A. and Evelyn Mae (Ash) Reeser; m. Richard Leroy Straight, Aug. 12, 1966. B.A., DePaul U., 1985; student N. Central Coll., Naperville, Ill., 1965-66, El Centro Coll., Dallas, 1970-72. Programmer analyst Assn. Logos Bookstores, Ann Arbor, Mich., 1975-78, Spring Arbor Distbrs., Ann Arbor, 1978-79; systems rep. Honeywell Info. Systems, Southfield, Mich., 1979-80; programmer analyst Mfg. Data Systems, Inc., Ann Arbor, 1980-81; data processing mgr. Callaghan & Co., Wilmette, Ill., 1981-84; dir./cons. Dunham Systems Corp., Roselle, Ill., 1984-86; pres., cons. The Alpha Group, Chgo., 1985; prin. systems engr. The Saddlebrook Corp., Oak Brook, Ill., 1986—. Vol., Peace Corps/Nat. 4-H Found., Brazil, 1963-65; elder 1st Presbyn. Ch., Evanston, Ill., 1985—; deacon Univ. Reformed Ch., Ann Arbor, 1980-81. NSF/Tex. Women's U. grantee, 1971. Mem. Women in Mgmt., Assn. Systems Mgmt. (chpt. treas. 1982, v.p. 1983), Christian Ministries Mgmt. Assn. Avocations: fiber arts, literature; Bible studies; humanitarian issues; mentor and presenter Marketplace 86th Conf., Chgo., 1986. Home: 1860 Sherman Ave #1 SE Evanston IL 60201 Office: The Saddlebrook Corp 122 W 22nd St Suite 300 Oak Brook IL 60521

STRAIN, HERBERT ARTHUR, III, plastic surgeon; b. St. Louis, Dec. 26, 1954; s. Herbert Arthur Jr. and Roberta (Heller) S.; m. Constance Ann Dziuk, Oct. 10, 1981; children: Nicholas Andrew, Ryan Arthur, Kathleen Elizabeth. BA in Biology, U. Mo., Kansas City, 1977, MD, 1979. Diplomate Am. Bd. Med. Examiners. Intern, then resident in gen. surgery St. Luke's Hosp., Kansas City, 1979-82; fellow in plastic and reconstructive surgery U. Mo., Kansas City, 1982-84; practice medicine specializing in plastic surgery Kansas City, 1984—; asst. clin. prof. plastic surgery U. Mo., 1984—; affiliated staff mem. St. Luke's Hosp., Research Med. Ctr., St. Mary's Hosp., Truman Med. Ctr. West, North Kansas City Meml. Hosp., Trinity Luth. Hosp., Menorah Med. Ctr., Bapt. Med. Ctr., Children's Mercy Hosp., St. Joseph's Hosp. Mem. AMA, Mo. Med. Assn., Jackson County Med. Soc., Am. Soc. Plastic and Reconstructive Surgeons, Kansas City Plastic Surg. Soc., Assn. Academic Chmn. Plastic Surgery. Episcopalian. Home: 421 Huntington Kansas City MO 64113 Office: 4320 Wornall #420 Kansas City MO 64111

STRALEY, DONA SUE, librarian; b. Circleville, Ohio, Jan. 7, 1952; d. Warren Gamaliel and Edith Alice (Schleich) S. BA with distinction in history, Ohio State U., 1974; PhD, Edinburgh U., 1977; MLS, Ind. U., 1981. Mid. East cataloger Ohio State U., Columbus, 1981-82, Mid. East librarian, 1984—; catalog librarian U. Ariz., Tucson, 1982-84. Recipient Gen. Motors scholarship Gen. Motors Corp., 1970-74, Vans Dunlop scholarship Edinburgh U., 1974-77. Mem. ALA, Mid. East Librarians Assn. (sec. treas. 1983-86), Mid. East Studies Assn., Assn. Coll. and Research Libraries (resources and tech. div.), Phi Alpha Theta, Beta Phi Mu. Home: 114 E California Ave Columbus OH 43202 Office: Ohio State U 1858 Neil Ave Mall Columbus OH 43210

STRALEY, THOMAS JOHN, automotive company executive; b. Hoboken, N.J., Mar. 25, 1950; s. Thomas Lincoln and Eleanor S.; m. Nancy Straley, July 7, 1975 (div. Jan. 1986). BME, Gen. Motors Inst., 1973; MBA, Xavier U., 1975. Sr. project engr. Fisher Body, Columbus, Ohio, 1980-85; supr. product design Fisher Guide div. Gen. Motors, Warren, Mi., 1986—. Mem. Nat. Soc. Profl. Engrs. (regional v.p. 1982-83), Soc. Mfg. Engrs. (sr.). Avocations: tennis, skiing, outdoor activities. Home: 5118 Galaxy Utica MI 48087 Office: Fisher Guide div Gen Motors 901 Tower Dr Troy MI 48098

STRANAHAN, ROBERT A., JR., manufacturing company executive; b. Toledo, 1915; married. With Champion Spark Plug Co., Toledo, 1935—, v.p., 1949-54, pres., 1954-85, chmn. bd., dir., 1962—, chief exec. officer, 1962-86; chmn. bd., dir. Baron Drawn Steel Corp., Anderson Co.; pres., dir. Hellertown Mfg., Iowa Industries, P B Mktg. Office: Champion Spark Plug Co Inc 900 Upton Ave PO Box 910 Toledo OH 43661 *

STRAND, GAIL CHRISTINE, pharmacist; b. Mankato, Minn., May 12, 1955; d. Stanley John and Mildred T. (Chlian) Hadac; m. Timothy John Strand, Sept. 17, 1983. B.S. in Pharmacy, S.D. State U., 1978. Registered pharmacist, Minn. Pharmacist Volness Drug Store, Lake Crystal, Minn., 1978-79, Corner Drug Store, LeSueur, Minn., 1978-79, Merwin Drug Store #4, Maple Grove, Minn., 1979-81, Erickson Valu Drug Store, St. Peter, Minn., 1981—. Vol. VFW Aux., St. Peter, 1973—, Ladies Guild St. Peter's Ch., 1984—. Mem. Am. Pharm. Assn., Minn. Pharm. Assn. Republican. Roman Catholic. Lodge: Redmen (Pochohontas 1982—). Avocations: sewing; crewel work; quilting; cooking. Home: 1413 Winona St Saint Peter MN 56082

STRANDBERG, DANIEL PAUL, financial consultant; b. Chgo., Oct. 2, 1952; s. Donald George Strandberg and Betty (Storm) Smith; m. Geri A.

Radanovich, Sept. 6, 1975; children: Kyle Paul, Scott David. Student, Eastern Ill. U., 1970-73. Cert. fin. planner. Mgr. Prudential, Olympia Fields, Ill., 1978-81; cons., planner Quinn Fin. Group, Peotone, Ill., 1981—. Served as sgt. USNG, 1971-77. Mem. Inst. Cert. Fin. Planners, Internat. Bd. Standards and Practices Cert. Fin. Planners, Lincolnshire East Assn. (fin. dir.). Republican. Roman Catholic. Avocations: tennis, golf, camping. Office: Quinn Fin Group 108 E North St Peotone IL 60468

STRANDHAGEN, ADOLF GUSTAV, engineering educator; b. Scranton, Pa., May 4, 1914; s. Daniel Peter and Theresa Ann (Lylick) S.; m. Lucile E. Perry, Aug. 22, 1941; children—Karen, Gretchen. B.S., U. Mich., 1939, M.S., 1939, Ph.D., 1942. Asst. prof., research physicist Nat. Def. Research Council, Carnegie Inst. Tech. and Princeton U., 1942-46; assoc. prof. engring. sci. U. Notre Dame, 1946-50, prof., 1950—, chmn. dept. engring. sci., 1950-68; cons. U.S. Navy Mine Def. Lab., 1961-67; temporary staff U.S. Navy David Taylor Model Basin, 1958-60. Recipient Outstanding Engr. award St. Joseph chpt. ASME, 1958. Mem. Soc. Naval Architects and Marine Engrs. (mem. panel H-10 ship maneuvering 1965-75), Soc. Engring. Sci., ASME. Assoc. editor Jour. Vehicle Dynamics, 1972-80, Bull. on Ship Maneuvering, 1975; contbr. research papers and reports on hydrodynamics, ship maneuvering, applied math., probability theory to profl. jours. Office: U Notre Dame Coll Engring Notre Dame IN 46556

STRANG, CHARLES DANIEL, marine engine manufacturing company executive; b. Bklyn., Apr. 12, 1921; s. Charles Daniel and Anna Lincoln (Endner) S. B.M.E., Poly. Inst. Bklyn., 1943. Mem. mech. engring. staff MIT, 1947-51; v.p. engring., exec. v.p. Kiekhaefer Corp. div. Brunswick Corp., Fond du Lac, Wis., 1951-64; v.p. marine engring. Outboard Marine Corp., Waukegan, Ill., 1966-68; exec. v.p. Outboard Marine Corp., 1968-74, pres., gen. mgr., 1974-80, pres., chief exec. officer, 1980-82, chmn. bd., chief exec. officer, 1982—, also dir. Contbr. research papers to sci. publs. Bd. dirs. Poly. Inst. N.Y. Served with USAAF, 1944-47. Mem. Am. Power Boat Assn. (past pres.), Soc. Automotive Engrs., Union Internat. Motorboating (v.p.), Sigma Xi. Club: Waukegan Yacht. Patentee engine design and marine propulsion equipment. Home: 25679 W Florence Ave Antioch IL 60002 Office: 100 Seahorse Dr Waukegan IL 60085

STRANG, DURWOOD STANLEY, tax commissioner; b. Marshall County, Ind., July 30, 1924; s. Dolph R. and Lila G. (Miller) S.; m. Agnes Jean Friend; 1 dau., Diane. Diploma in Gen. Acctg., South Bend (Ind.) Coll. Commerce, 1943; B.S.C., Internat. Bus. Coll., Ft. Wayne, Ind., 1948. Acct., Studebaker Corp., South Bend, 1954-64; field auditor Ind. Bd. Tax Commrs., Indpls., 1964-66, no. supr., 1966-67, commr., 1967—. Served with U.S. Army, 1943-46, 50-51. Decorated Bronze star. Mem. Internat. Assn. Assessing Officers, Am. Legion. Democrat. Methodist. Lodges: Odd Fellows, Moose. Home: 867 Golfview Terr Plainfield IN 46168 Office: 201 State Office Bldg Indianapolis IN 46204

STRANGES, JOSEPH FRANCIS, III, technical methods executive; b. Wheeling, W.Va., June 21, 1951; s. Joseph Francis Jr. and Mary Elizabeth (Kaczmarek) S.; m. Julie Lucia Lytus, Sept. 9, 1972; children: Jospeh F. IV, Jodelle N., Joshua D., Jillian R. BS in Math., Ohio State U., 1972. Programming specialist Nationwide Ins. Co., Columbus, Ohio, 1973-79, lead systems programmer, 1979-84; sr. systems programmer Gold Circle, Columbus, 1984-85; sr. capacity planner Bank One, Westerville, Ohio, 1985-86, mgr. tech. methods, 1986—. Roman Catholic. Avocation: sports. Home: 137 Waterton Ct Westerville OH 43081 Office: Bank One Westerville OH 43271-0033

STRANGWARD, W. J., manufacturing company executive; b. Cleve., Mar. 6, 1942; s. W.P. and Thelma M. (McGoogan) S.; m. Maralyn Louise Rees, June 10, 1971; children: Billy, Lisa. BA in Econs., U. Miami, Fla., 1965; Cert. Tool & Die Maker, Max Hayes, Cleve., 1969. Pres. Langenau Mfg. Co., Cleve., 1982—, World Trade Winds, Inc., Cleve., 1985—, Metal Tech. Research Co., Cleve., 1984—. Patentee in field. Recipient William O. Stillman award William O. Stillman Found., 1958. Mem. Am. Metal Stamping Assn., Am. Assn. Airport Execs., Nat. Tool and Machine Assn., Casket Mfrs. Assn. Republican. Episcopalian. Club: Cleve. Athletic. Avocations: flying, motorcycling, skiing, electronics, amateur radio. Office: Langenau Mfg Co 7306 Madison Ave Cleveland OH 44102

STRASS, CLAUDE ANTHONY, electronics executive; b. Chgo., June 17, 1945; s. Gerald H. and Bertha V. (Rechiel) S.; m. Lenore G. Wagner, June 1, 1968 (div. Sept. 1977); m. Beth G. Grayson, Apr. 13, 1985; children: Beckie, Steven, Michael, Michelle. AS, Coll. of DuPage, 1972; BBA, Elmhurst Coll., 1974; postgrad., U. Chgo., 1982-84. Controller TIRB, Chgo., 1968-69; mgr. ops. acctg. Molex Inc., Lisle, Ill., 1969-77, asst. to v.p. ops., 1977-80, dir. corp. budgets, 1980-82, dir. corp. planning, 1982-84, dir. corp. devel., 1984-87, pres. Indsl. Interfaces, 1987—; bd. dirs. Indsl. Interfaces, Batavia, Ill. Served with U.S. Army, 1966-68. Mem. Nat. Assn. Accts., Mfg. Automation Protocol Users Group of Soc. Mfg. Engrs., Electronic Computer Study Group, Am. Electroplaters Soc., Internat. Soc. Planning and Strategic Mgmt., Am. Mgmt. Assn. Republican. Roman Catholic. Avocations: golfing, softball, tennis, running. Home: 1149 Kenilworth Circle Naperville IL 60540 Office: Molex Inc 2222 Wellington St Lisle IL 60532

STRASSER, DENNIS KEITH, librarian, educator; b. Watervliet, Mich., June 27, 1951; s. Sherman Eugene and Constance (Jones) S.; m. Debra Holt, Sept. 5, 1975 (div. July 1978). BS, Western Mich. U., Kalamazoo, 1975, MS, 1978. Pub. service librarian Nat. Coll. Edn., Evanstons, 1979-81; dir. learning resource ctr. Nat. Coll. Edn., Chgo., 1981-83; asst. prof. library instructional services, coordinator online services Sangamon State U., Springfield, Ill., 1983—; cons. Evaluation Ctr. Western Mich. U., Kalamazoo, 1971. Contbr. computer software reviews to tech. publs. Mem. Ill. Library Assn., Ill. Heartland Users Group. Avocation: railroad history. Home: 10 Candlewood Dr #3 Springfield IL 62704-5606

STRASSER, DON DAVIS, automobile sales executive; b. Burnettsville, Ind., Mar. 13, 1944; s. Thomas Robert Sr. and Margaret Estelle (Regan) S.; m. Sharon Sue Smith, May 31, 1964. Grad., Burnettsville High Sch., 1962. Salesman Dave Mason Oldsmobile-Cadillac, Logansport, Ind., 1977-79, Greg Rudd Oldsmobile-Cadillac, 1979-81, Bill Timberman Motor Sales, 1981-84; owner, mgr. Don Strasser Motor Sales, Logansport, 1984—. Active Cass County Mental Health Assn., Cass County United Way, Logansport. Served with U.S. Army, 1966-68, Vietnam. Mem. Cass County C. of C., Cass County Churchmen United. Methodist. Lodges: Kiwanis (pres. 1980-82), Eagles, Avocations: electronics repair; bowling; automobile repair. Office: Don Strasser Motor Sales Inc Logansport IN 46947

STRASSER, KURT ALBERT, township official; b. Chgo., Nov. 6, 1942; s. Carl Joseph and Mary Eugena (Gifford) S.; m. Martha Etta Adams, Sept. 20, 1962; children—Dawn, Adam, Sarah; m. Sandra Emily Zimmerman, July 5, 1985; step-children: Laura, Brian, Corrie. Cert. in acctg. and bus. adminstrn. McBride Bus. Coll., Dallas, 1963. Cert. assessing officer, rev. appraiser, Ill. Dep. assessor York (Ill.) Twp., 1973-75; appraiser DuPage County (Ill.), 1975-77; chief dep. assessor Addison Twp. (Ill.), 1977-82, assessor, 1982—; tchr. Ill. Property Assessment Inst. Past pres. DuPage Young Reps. (Ill.); past treas. Ill. State Young Reps.; Rep. committeeman Addison (Ill.) Twp. Served to 2d lt. USAF, 1961-62. Mem. Internat. Assn. Assessing Officers, Am. Fed. Appraisers, Ind. Fee Appraisers, Paralyzed Vets. Am., DAV. Roman Catholic. Lodges: Wood Dale Lions; Moose; Masons (32d deg.) (Chgo. and Lombard, Ill.). Office: Township Addison 401 N Addison Rd Addison IL 60101

STRATHMAN, MICHAEL SULLIVAN, oil company executive; b. Findlay, Ohio, Nov. 3, 1948; s. Norman Robert and Jeanne Anne (Sullivan) S.; m. Jacqueline R. Dantuono, Apr. 21, 1972; children: Michelle Anne, Michael Dantuono Strathman, Anthony Robert. BS, Miami U., Oxford, Ohio, 1970; MA in Mgmt., Northwestern U., 1973. Systems analyst Marathon Oil Co., Findlay, 1970-72, mgr. planning and analysis, 1974-78, supr. internat. banking, 1979-81, dir. industry and corp. affairs, 1981-83, mgr. London fin. services, 1983-87; mgr. Gas Transp., London, 1987—; cons. Touche Ross, Chgo., 1973-74. Spl. asst. to adminstrn. on aging U.S. Govt., Washington, 1978-79; trustee Am. Sch. London Ednl. Trust, 1985—; chmn. pub. relations com. St. Michael Cath. Ch., Findlay, 1981-83, chmn. parish council, 1975-78; coach Little League Baseball, Findlay, 1974-78, London, 1985-87. Mem. Assn. MBA Execs., Exec. Exchange Alumni Assn. (pres.). Lodge: Rotary. Home: 1725 Queenswood Dr Findlay OH 45840 Office: Marathon Oil UK Ltd, 174 Marylebone Rd, London England NW1 5AT

STRATTAN, ERIC JESSE, minister; b. Cleve., July 20, 1956; s. Robert Martin and Joanne Julia (Lovejoy) S.; m. Marcia Anne Frier, July 4, 1981; children: Arianne, Valerie, Alissa. BA in Religion, Grand Rapids (Mich.) Bapt. Coll., 1981; MA in Pastoral, Faith Bapt. Coll., 1983. Ordained to ministry Bapt. Ch., 1983. Assoc. pastor Calvary Bapt. Ch., Muskegon, Mich., 1983—. Author: (evangelism manual) L.E.A.D., 1983; also articles. Active steering com. Muskegon County Crisis Pregnancy Ctr., 1985. Avocations: gourmet cooking, model rocketry, music, computer programming and use. Office: Calvary Bapt Ch 1600 Clinton St Muskegon MI 49442

STRATTEN, KRISTIN JO, auditor; b. Noblesville, Ind., Nov. 12, 1959; s. John Raymond and JoAnn (Roberts) R.; m. Gary Andrew Stratten, July 23, 1983. BS, Ind. U., 1982. CPA. Auditor Arthur Andersen & Co., Dallas, 1982-83, Arthur Young & Co., Chgo., 1983-85; sr. auditor Arthur Young & Co., Indpls., 1985; tax acct. GTE, Westfield, Ind., 1985-86; auditor GTE, Tampa, Fla., 1986—. Mem. Ind. CPA Soc., Am. Inst. CPAs. Republican. Methodist. Home: 8765 N Pennsylvania Indianapolis IN 46240 Office: GTE Service Corp One Tampa City Ctr Tampa FL 33601

STRATTON, RICHARD LEROY, optometrist; b. Springfield, Ill., Oct. 19, 1925; s. Solon Clifford Stratton and Alice Leora (Beeler) Harrison; m. Jeanette Elaine Duda, Aug. 9, 1945; children: Pamela, Richard L. II, Janna, Kenneth W., James T. OD, Ill. Coll. Optometry, 1948. Optometrist Dr. Chas R. Lenz & Assocs., Springfield, 1949-61, Drs. Irvine & Stratton, Springfield, 1961-65; gen. practice optometry Springfield, 1965—; chmn. State Bd. Optometry, Ill., 1972—. Past officer Sangamon/Menard Council on Alcohol and Drugs, Springfield; sec. Triangle Ctr., Springfield. Served to staff sgt. U.S. Army Air Corps, 1943-45, ETO. Mem. Am. Optometric Assn.(contact lens sect.), Internat. Optometric and Optical League, Ill. Optometric Assn. (Optometrist of Yr. 1983), Midstate Optometric Soc., Internat. Assn. of Bds. of Examiners in Optometry. Methodist. Lodges: Lions (pres. 1965-66), Elks (exalted ruler 1966-67). Avocations: antique cars, woodworking. Home: 100 Circle Dr Springfield IL 62703 Office: 1700 S 7th St PO Box 5033 Springfield IL 62705

STRATTON, WILLIAM GRANT, banker; b. Ingleside, Ill., Feb. 26, 1914; s. William J. and Zula (Van Wormer) S.; m. Shirley Breckenridge; B.A., U. Ariz., 1934; hon. degrees John Marshall Law Sch., North Central Coll., Shurtleff Coll., 1954, Bradley U., Lincoln Coll., 1955, Elmhurst Coll., 1956, Lincoln Meml. U., 1957, So. Ill. U., U. Ariz., 1958; Mem. U.S. Congress from Ill., 1941-43, 47-49; treas. State of Ill., 1943-45, 51-53, gov., 1953-61; livestock farmer, Cantrell, Ill., 1954-70; ins. bus., Chgo., 1965-68; asst. to pres. Canteen Corp., Chgo., 1968, v.p. corp. relations, 1968-81, dir., 1981-84; v.p. Chgo. Bank of Commerce, 1984—; dir. Dartnell Corp. Chmn., Interstate Oil Compact Commn., 1955, Nat. Gov.'s Conf., 1957; pres. Council State Govts., 1958; mem. Lincoln Sesquicentennial Commn., 1958, Fed. Adv. Commn. Intergovtl. Relations, 1959, Ill. Task Force on Higher Edn., 1970-71, Ill. Legis. Reapportionment Commn., 1971; regent Lincoln Acad. of Ill., 1966—; del. Rep. Nat. Conv., 1952, 56, 60, 76; former chmn. bd. trustees Robert Morris Coll., Carthage, Ill.; mem. adv. council U. Toledo Coll. Bus. Adminstrn., 1976-79; bd. dirs. Mundelein Coll., Chgo., 1976—, Davenport Coll., Grand Rapids, Mich., 1976—, Nat. Inst. Foodservice Industry, 1975-78, Kemper Charitable and Ednl. Found., Chgo. Better Bus. Bur., Chgo. Crime Commn., pres. USO, Chgo., 1984-85, chmn. bd., 1985—; co-chmn. Ill. Election Reform Commn., 1985; chmn. Five Hos. Home Bound Elderly Program Found., 1986—, Chgo. Salvation Army Adv. Bd., 1986—, Chgo. Citywide Coll. Bd., 1987—. Served to lt. (j.g.) USNR, 1945-46; PTO. Mem. Chgo. and Ill. Restaurant Assn. (chmn. 1977—), Ill. C. of C. (dir. 1976—), Am. Legion, Amvets, Mil. Order World Wars (comdr. Chgo. chpt. 1971-72), Nat. Inst. Foodservice Industry (pres. 1979-80), Delta Chi. Methodist. Club: Executives (Chgo.) (bd. dirs. Lodges: Masons (33 deg.), Rotary (pres. Chgo. 1979-80). Home: 3240 N Lake Shore Dr Chicago IL 60657 Office: Chgo Bank of Commerce 225 N Michigan Ave Chicago IL 60601

STRAUSS, JAMES LESTER, sales executive, accountant; b. Indpls., Aug. 24, 1944; s. Lester H. and Rosalie (Grossman) S. BS, Ind. U., 1966; MBA, Columbia U., 1968. CPA, Ohio. Acct. Deloitte Haskins & Sells, Dayton, Ohio, 1975-79, Main Hurdman, Cin., 1979-83; mng. exec. Integrated Resources, Cin., 1983—. Served with USAR, 1968-74. Mem. Am. Inst. CPA's, Ohio Soc. CPA's, Mensa. Home: One Lytle Pl #2004 Cincinnati OH 45202 Office: Integrated Resources Equity Corp 120 E Fourth St Suite 1500 Cincinnati OH 45202

STRAUSS, JUDI SCHLEIMER, human resources management educator; b. Bklyn., Nov. 17, 1943; d. Irving G. and Irene (Bober) Schleimer; m. Bruce P. Strauss, July 7, 1964 (div. Mar. 1978); children: Lori Strauss, Lisa Strauss; m. Lawrence Lipkin, Nov. 2, 1986. BA, U. Pa., 1964; MEd, Harvard U., 1967; PhD, Union Grad. Sch., 1982. Prof. mgmt. George William Coll., Downers Grove, Ill., 1968-86; prof. human resource mgmt. Ill. Benedictine Coll., Lisle, 1986—; freelance writer Today's Chgo. Woman. Contbr. articles to profl. jours. Mem. Am. Soc. Personnel Adminstrs., Acad. Mgmt., Human Resource Planning Soc., Human Resource Mgmt. Assn. Chgo., Midwest Acad. Mgmt., Nat. Assn. Tax Practitioners. Jewish. Avocations: cooking, travel, swimming. Home: 624 62d St Downers Grove IL 60516 Office: Ill Benedictine Coll 5700 College Rd Lisle IL 60532

STRAUSS, ROBERT ALLAN, oral and maxillofacial surgeon; b. Bklyn., Feb. 19, 1955; s. Alfred Leo and Janet Barbara (Geller) S.; m. Robyn Debra Oshin, Aug. 6, 1977. BS, U. Buffalo, 1975, DDS, 1979. Diplomate Am. Bd. Oral and Maxillofacial Surgery. Resident in anesthesiology Michael Reese Med. Ctr., Chgo., 1981-82, resident in oral and maxillofacial surgery, 1982-84; practice medicine specializing in oral and maxillofacial surgery U. Chgo. Med. Ctr., 1984—, clin. asst. prof. oral and maxillofacial surgery, 1984—; attending surgeon Michael Reese Med. Ctr., Chgo., 1984—. Contbr. articles to med. jours. Named Student of Yr., Am. Acad. Oral Medicine, 1979, Student of Yr., Am. Acad. Oral Pathology, 1979. Fellow Am. Assn. Oral and Maxillofacial Surgeons. Avocations: Chinese cooking, scuba diving. Home: 1700 E 56th St #3202 Chicago IL 60637 Office: U Chgo Med Ctr 5841 S Maryland PO Box 418 Chicago IL 60637

STRAW, GARY ROBERT, resort management executive; b. Springfield, Vt., Mar. 19, 1951; s. Robert Archie and Muriel Gwendolyn (Mayette) S.; m. Diane Leslie Durnall, Mar. 17, 1979; children: Gary Robert II, Megan June. Student, Deerfield Acad., 1970; BS, U. Vt., 1974. Gen. mgr. Point Sebago Resort, Casco, Maine, 1974-80; gen. mgr Meramec Valley Resort, Cuba, Mo., 1980-81; gen. mgr., dir. sales and mktg. Lost Valley Lake Resort, Owensville, Mo., 1981-86; pres. Straw and Assocs. Inc., Wash., Mo., 1986—; v.p. cons. Retreat At Lee Canyon, Las Vegas, Nev., 1985—; guest speaker Coast To Coast, Inc., Marco Isle, Fla., U. Vt., 1975-78; sales and mktg. mgmt. Jellystone Park, Milw., Trevoli Hills Resort, Clarksville, Mo., Erie Island Resort and Marina, Port Clinton, Ohio. Bd. dirs. El Vallejo Owners Assn., Wash., 1986-88. Republican. Episcopalian. Avocations: skiing, flying, racquetball, snowmobiling, boating. Home and Office: 50 Ladera Ln Washington MO 63090

STRAWHECKER, DANIEL CHARLES, manufacturing company executive; b. Cleve., June 5, 1936; s. Frederick and Lillian (Fredric) S.; m. Helga Marie Seib, June 30, 1961; 1 child, Karen Lynn. BS in Bus., The Citadel, The Mil. Coll of S.C., Charleston, 1959. Sales rep. Am. Olean, Lansdale, Pa., 1969-75; br. mgr. Dal-Tile Corp., Dallas, 1975-78, mgr. nat. accounts, 1978-80; v.p. sales Dal-Tile Corp., Cin., 1980—. Office: Dal-Tile Corp 11335 Reed Hartman Hwy Cincinnati OH 45241

STRAWHUN, LEE CHRIS, hospital administrator; b. Chgo., Oct. 19, 1944; s. Everett William and Edith H. (Papke) S.; m. Velma Louise Kirby, Aug. 31, 1974; children: Jayne Ann, Kristin Leigh. AB, Ind. U., 1969, MPA, 1974. Comml. mgr. Ill. Bell Telephone Co., Chgo., 1964-68; asst. coordinator research and devel. Ind. U., Bloomington, 1969-70; dep. dir. Northwest Ind. Comprehensive Health Planning Council, Inc., Highland, 1970-76; pres., chief exec. officer Southlake Ctr. for Mental Health, Inc., Merrillville, Ind., 1976—; adj. faculty health adminstrn. Ind. U., Gary, 1974—. Pres. bd. dirs. Calumet Region Montessori Sch., Inc., Hobart, 1984-85. Served to maj. USAR, 1965—. Named Disting. Hoosier State of Ind., 1982; recipient Disting. Alumnus award Sch. Pub. and Environ. Affairs, Gary, 1983. Mem. Am. Coll. Health Care Execs., Nat. Council Community Mental Health Ctrs., Am. Correctional Assn., Res. Officers Assn. Republican. Club: Columbia (Indpls.). Lodge: Rotary. (bd. dirs. Merrillville 1986—). Avocations: gardening, boating, fishing. Home: 702 E 77th Pl Merrillville IN 46410 Office: Southlake Ctr Mental Health Inc 8555 Taft Merrillville IN 46410

STRAWN, EARL HOWARD, city official; b. Lancaster, Ohio, Mar. 1, 1937; s. Howard H. and Florence A. Strawn; m. Julia A. Phillips, June 14, 1963. Student Columbus Tech. Inst., 1977. With Lancaster & Carroll Elevator Co., 1955-63; with Ohio Dept. Transp., Lancaster, 1963-87, service-safety dir., 1980-87; state exec. adminstr. Ohio Lions, Inc., 1987—. Bd. advisors Salvation Army; precinct committeeman Rep. Party. Served with U.S. Army, 1957. Named to Hon. Order of Ky. Cols. Mem. Ohio Assn. Pub. Safety Dirs. (trustee), Buckeye State Sheriff Assn., Fraternal Order of Police Assn., C. of C. Methodist. Lodges: Lions, Elks, Masons, Shriners. Home: 445 Hilltop Dr Lancaster OH 43130

STRAYER, ROBERT LOUIS, underwriter, financial planner; b. Piqua, Ohio, Dec. 1, 1943; s. Joseph L. and C. Fern (Brelsford) S.; m. Carol E. Simons, July 7, 1973; children: Robert II, Michael, Scott. BS, Ohio State U., 1964, 65, MBA, 1968; MS in Fin., Am. Coll., Bryn Mawr, Pa., 1979. CLU; chartered fin. cons.; cert. financial planner, 1987. Owner Strayer Fin. Services, Sidney, Ohio, 1973—; registered rep. Anchor Nat. Fin. Services, 1977—; assoc. prof. Edison State Coll., 1975—. Republican. Avocation: photography. Home and Office: 505 Karen Ave Sidney OH 45365

STRECKER, IGNATIUS J., archbishop; b. Spearville, Kans., Nov. 23, 1917; s. William J. and Mary B. (Knoeber) S. Student, St. Benedict's Coll., Atchison, Kans., 1931-37, Kenrick Sem., St. Louis, 1937-42, Cath. U. Am., 1944-45. Ordained priest Roman Cath. Ch., 1942; aux. chaplain USAAF, Great Bend, Kans., 1942-44; chancellor Diocese Wichita, 1948-62; bishop Diocese Springfield-Cape Girardeau, Mo., 1962-69; archbishop Archdiocese of Kansas City, Kans., 1969—. Office: Chancery Office PO Box 2328 2220 Central Ave Kansas City KS 66110 *

STRECKER, LOUIS FREDERICK, III, marketing company executive; b. St. Louis, Feb. 21, 1942; s. Louis F. and Helen M. (Reiser) S.; m. Carol A. Meyer, Sept. 6, 1965. B.A., U. St. Louis, 1963; postgrad. Washington U., St. Louis, 1963-65. Sales mgr. Rayfax div. Litton Industries, St. Louis, 1966-70, regional mgr., Columbus, Ohio, 1970-73; regional mgr. C. ITOH, Columbus, 1973-76; v.p. Govtl. Interiors, St. Louis, 1976-80; owner, pres. Contract Design Products, St. Louis, 1980—; cons. furniture mfg. firms, Iowa, 1983—, Ill., 1984—; guest speaker U. Mo. Sch. Design, Columbia and St. Louis, 1984. Served with N.G., 1965-69. Mem. Midwest Travelers, Nat. Office Products Assn. Avocations: golf; chess. Office: Contract Design Products 9378 Olive Blvd Saint Louis MO 63132

STREETER, DENNIS LYNN, osteopath; b. Hope, Mich., June 27, 1943; s. Wilbur and Mable (Schearer) S.; m. Jean Watson, Dec. 18, 1965; children: Elizabeth, Timothy, Suzanne, David. BS in Biology, Cen. Mich. U., 1965; DO, Chgo. Coll. Osteopathic Medicine, 1971; HHD (hon.), Hyles Anderson Coll., Crown Point, Ind., 1975. Cert. cardiovascular thoracic surgery, 1984, gen. surgery, 1984. Intern Chgo. Osteopathic Hosp., 1971-72, resident in gen. surgery, 1972-75; fellow in urology U. Chgo. Hosps. and Clinic, 1975-76, fellow in vascular and thoracic surgery, 1976-77; fellow Columbus Hosp., Chgo., 1978-79; practice osteopathic surgery Griffith, Ind., 1980—; lectr. nurse practitioner program Purdue U., West Lafayette, Ind., 1980-82; adj. prof. surgery Chgo. Osteopathic Coll. Medicine, 1981; sec. med. staff Gary (ind.) Meth. Hosp., 1981; chmn. quality care Gary Meth. Hosp., 1985. Fellow Am. Acad. Osteopathic Surgeons (bd. govs. 1986, chmn. doctoral edn. com. 1986); mem. Am. Coll. Osteopathic Surgeons (cert.), Am. Cancer Soc., Ill. Osteopathic Assn., Ind. Osteopathic Assn. Home: 1211 N Harvey St Griffith IN 46319 Office: 1212 N Broad St Griffith IN 46319

STREETT, JAMES KENNETH, small business owner; b. Balt., July 31, 1927; s. Marshall Bernard and Mabel Victoria (Hollins) S.; m. Jean Elizabeth Potter, June 6, 1952 (dec. July 1965); children: Suzanne Whitmore, Carol Nabakowski, David, Nancy Cackling; m. Shirley Anne McCraven, Aug. 20, 1966; 1 child, Matthew. BS, U.S. Naval Acad., 1952; MS in Aero. Engring., U. Mich., Ann Arbor, 1958, MS in Instrumentation Engring., 1958. Commd. 2d. lt. USAF, 1952, advanced through ranks to col., electronic engr., electronic systems div., 1966-67; asst. ops. officer 21st Helicopter Squadron USAF, Nakhon Phanom, Thailand, 1967-68; chief, office of engring. Def. Contract Adminstrv. Region USAF, N.Y.C., 1968-71; chief, aircraft engring. div. Hdqrs. SAC, Offutt AFB, Nebr., 1972-82; retired USAF, 1982; owner, mgr. Bellevue (Nebr.) Solar, 1982—. Craftsman, artist constrn. of high altar at St. Martin of Tours Episc. Ch., Omaha, Nebr., 1985. Mem. dept. missions Episc. Diocese of Nebr., 1984—; acolyte warden Episc. Ch. of the Holy Spirit, Bellvue, 1980—. Named to Legion of Merit USAF. Republican. Avocations: church activities.

STREFLING, JOHN LOUIS, psychiatrist, neurologist; b. Galien, Mich., Dec. 31, 1927; s. Michael and Pauline (Ratz) S.; m. Elizabeth M. Tadych, Mar. 27, 1954; children: Lisa Ann, John Jr. BA, Eastern Mich. U., 1950; BS, U. Mich., 1950; MD, U. Havana, 1955; spl. student, Roosevelt U., Chgo., 1950-52, George Williams Coll., Chgo., 1950-52; DO, Chgo. Coll. Osteo. Medicine, 1958; LLB, Blackstone Coll., 1970; PhD, Century U., 1986; cert. U.S. Army Health Care Adminstrn., Baylor U., 1985; cert., Command and Gen. Staff Coll. U.S. Army, 1985, Mobilization and Deployment of U.S. Army, 1985. Diplomate Am. Bd. of Psychiatry and Neurology, Am. Bd. of Quality Assessment and Utilization Rev. Physicians. Rotating intern Art Centre Hosp., Detroit, 1958-59; pvt. practice gen. medicine Michigan City, Ind., 1960-67, Stephenson, Mich., 1967-69; physician, staff psychiatrist Beatty Meml. Hosp., Westville, Ind., 1969-70; resident Winnebago (Wis.) Mental Health Inst., 1970-73; resident in forensic psychiatry Cen. State Hosp. for Criminally Insane, Waupun, Wis., 1973-74; dir. Manitowoc (Wis.) County Mental Health Ctr., 1974-75; chief forensic psychiatrist County of Manitowoc, 1974-75; pvt. practice forensic and cons. psychiatry Michigan City, 1975; dir. Milw. County Mental Health Ctr., 1975-76; chief forensic psychiatrist Milw. County, 1975-76; chief psychiatry service Ind. State Prison, Michigan City, 1976-79, VA Med. Ctr., Marion, Ind., 1979-82; chief of staff Ind. State Prison, Michigan City, 1982-83; sr. psychiat. cons. Ind. Dept. Corrections, 1982-83; chief community mental health services U.S. Army, Fort Leavenworth, Kans., 1983—; chief psychiatrist U.S. Army Disciplinary Barracks, Fort Leavenworth, Kans., 1983—; cons. in forensic psychiatry U.S. Penitentiary, Leavenworth, 1983—, VA Med. Ctr., Leavenworth, 1983—. Contbr. over 27 articles to profl. jours. and mags. Served as col. M.C., U.S. Army, 1981—. Lutheran. Home: 1219 Delaware St Leavenworth KS 66048 also: 1807 E Michigan Blvd Michigan City IN 46360 Office: US Army Med Corps Fort Leavenworth KS 66027

STREHL, FRANK EMERSON, chiropractic physician; b. Evansville, Ind., Apr. 19, 1951; s. Frank Love and Margaret (Emerson) S.; m. Nellie A. Peters, Aug. 10, 1974; 1 child, Frank Matthew. BA, Taylor U., 1973; postgrad., George Washington U., 1975-77; BS in Human Biology, Nat. Coll. Chiropractic, 1980, D of Chiropractic, 1980. Gen. practice chiropractic medicine Wheaton, Ill., 1981—. Mem. Am. Chiropractic Assn., Ill. Chiropractic Soc., Council on Diagnosis of Am. Chiropractic Assn., Parker Chiropractic Research Found. Avocation: golf. Home and Office: 2129 Driving Park Rd Wheaton IL 60187

STREIBEL, MICHAEL JOHN, education educator; b. Bezau, Austria, Mar. 22, 1945; came to U.S., 1961; s. Hans Leo and Margarete (Ludwig) S.; m. Barbara Jean Wilson, Mar. 21, 1970; 1 child, M. Theo. BS in Physics, Pa. State U., 1967, MS in Biophysics, 1973; MA in History of Sci., U. Wis., 1975, PhD in Curriculum and Instrn., 1980. Sr. physicist HRB Singer, Inc., State College, Pa., 1967-73; project asst. U. Wis., Madison, 1973-80, assoc. prof. ednl. tech., 1983—; asst. prof. Pa. State U., University Park, 1980-83. Designer videodisc system for tchrs., 1982-83. Trochos grantee U. Wis., 1984-87, U.S. Dept. Edn. grantee, 1984, Fund for the Improvement of Post-Secondary Edn. grantee, 1985-87. Mem. Assn. for Ednl. Communications and Tech. (divisional bd. 1980-86), Am. Ednl. Research Assn., Internat. Visual Literacy Assn. Home: 2327 Eton Ridge Madison WI 53705 Office: U Wis 225 N Mills St Madison WI 53706

STREICH, ARTHUR HAROLD, business exec.; b. Mpls., Apr. 22, 1925; s. Herman Henry and Rose (Anderson) S.; B.A. in Journalism, Macalester Coll., 1952; m. Arlene June Ostlund, Aug. 30, 1947; children—Jennifer Streich Hallam, Jack, Paula Jo. Partner, S&E Publs., St. Paul, 1952-55; asst. sec. Northwestern Lumbermans Assn., 1955-57; gen. mgr. Nat. Electronics Conf., 1957-59; public relations exec. Mullen & Assos., Inc., Mpls., 1959-60; investment adviser Dempsey Tegeler & Co., Inc., Mpls., 1960-63; regional sales mgr. Dreyfus Corp., 1963-68; regional v.p. Anchor Corp., Chgo., 1968-69; regional v.p. wholesale sales and mgmt. Dreyfus Sales Corp., Chgo., 1969-72; regional v.p. Crosby Corp., Chgo., 1972-73; regional sales mgr. John Nuveen & Co., Chgo., 1973-74; owner Fin. Planning Services Co., Wayzata, Minn., 1974—. Republican candidate for mayor St. Paul, 1952. Served with USN, 1942-46. Mem. Nat. Assn. Security Dealers (registered prin.), Nat. Speakers Assn. Republican. Mem. Evang. Free Ch. Club: Toastmasters (Disting. Toastmaster). Address: 14431 Wellington Rd Wayzata MN 55391

STREICHLER, JERRY, educator; b. N.Y.C., Dec. 8, 1929; s. Samuel and Mirel (Waxman) S.; m. Rosalind Fineman, Feb. 25, 1951; children: Stuart Alan, Seth Ari, Robin Cheryl. Spl. courses cert., Newark Coll. Engring., 1951; BS magna cum laude, Kean Coll. N.J., 1956; MA, Montclair State Coll., 1958; PhD, NYU, 1963. Cons. machine designer to Time Savers Inc., Montclair, N.J., 1950-63, Bristol Equipment Co., Hamilton Equipment Co., 1952-67; mem. faculty dept. indsl. edn. Montclair (N.J.) State Coll., 1958-65, Trenton (N.J.) State Coll., 1965-67; prof., chmn. dept. indsl. edn. and tech. Bowling Green (Ohio) State U., 1967-78; dir. Sch. Tech., 1978-85; dean Coll. Tech., 1985—; vis. prof. S.I. Community Coll., CCNY, 1965, Rutgers U., 1966, U. Mo., 1967, U. Mich., Saginaw, 1971; cons., tchr. Newaygo Vocat. Ctr., Saginaw Career Opportunities Ctr., 1971; cons. indsl. tng., pub. schs., colls. Asst. editor: Jour. Indsl. Tchr. Edn, 1968-70; co-editor: The Components of Teacher Education, 20th Yearbook Am. Council on Indsl. Arts Tchr. Edn; editor: Jour. Epsilon Pi Tau.; contbr. articles to profl. jours. Founding com. chmn. Ohio Council on Indsl. Arts Tchr. Edn., 1968-69; past Jewish temple trustee. Served with USAF, 1951-52. Univ. honors scholar, 1963. Mem. Internat. Tech. Edn. Assn., Am. Vocat. Assn., NEA, Am. Soc. Engring. Edn., Miss. Valley Indsl. Tchr. Edn. Conf., Epsilon Pi Tau (exec. sec. 1976—, Laureate citation 1972), Omicron Delta Kappa, Phi Delta Kappa, Kappa Delta Pi. Home: 1302 Charles St Bowling Green OH 43402 Office: Bowling Green State U Coll Tech Tech Bldg Bowling Green OH 43403

STRENGER, JAN ELIZABETH, program director; b. Lake Forest, Ill., Jan. 6, 1954; d. Donald Sell and Mona Elizabeth (Benson) S.; B.A., Yankton Coll., 1976. Supr., counselor Lewis/Clark Mental Health Center, Yankton, S.D., 1976-78, acting program adminstr., 1978; case mgr. Yankton Area Adjustment Tng. Ctr., 1978-80, program dir., 1980—; cons. S.D. Human Service Ctr., Ctr. for Devel. Disabilities, U. S.D. Sch. Medicine, 1985—. Mem. Gov.'s Task Force on Dual Diagnosis/DD Offenders. Cert. in behavior mgmt. techniques, U. S.D.; cert. mental retardation profl., S.D. State Adjustment Tng. Services; cert. trainer Mandt System. Coach, Yankton Spl. Olympics Team. Mem. Am. Assn. Mental Deficiency, Nat. Rehab. Assn., Assn. for Retarded Citizens. Republican. Presbyterian. Home: 416 E 16th St Yankton SD 57078 Office: Yankton Area Adjustment Tng Center 909 W 23d St Yankton SD 57078

STRESEN-REUTER, FREDERICK ARTHUR, II, mining company executive; b. Oak Park, Ill., July 31, 1942; s. Alfred Proctor and Carol Frances (von Pohek) S.-R.; cert. in German, Salzburg Summer Sch., 1963; B.A., Lake Forest Coll., 1967. Mgr. advt. Stresen-Reuter Internat., Bensenville, Ill., 1965-70; mgr. animal products mktg. Internat. Minerals & Chem. Corp., Mundelein, Ill., 1971-79, dir. animal products mktg., 1979—; pres. Brit. Iron Ltd., 1984—; lectr. mktg. U. Ill., 1977, Am. Mgmt. Assn., 1978; cons. mktg. to numerous agrl. cos., 1973—. lectr. Trustee, governing mem. Library Internat. Relations, 1978, Chgo. Recipient cert. of excellence Chgo. 77 Vision Show, 1977; Silver Aggy award, 1977; spl. jury gold medal V.I., N.Y. Internat. film festival awards, 1977; CINE Golden Eagle, 1980; Bronze medal N.Y. Internat. Film Festival, 1981, Silver medal, 1982; Silver Screen award U.S. Indsl. Film Festival, 1981. Mem. Nat. Feed Ingredients Assn. (chmn. publicity and publs. 1976), Nat. Agrl. Mktg. Assn. (numerous awards), Am. Feed Mfrs. Assn. (citation 1976, public relations com., conv. com.), Nat. Agrl. Mktg. Assn., Mid-Am. Commodity Exchange, USCG Aux., U.S. Naval Inst., Am. Film Inst., Bugatti Owners Club. Episcopalian. Club: Sloane (London). Contbr. articles to profl. jours. Home: Tryon Grove Farm 8914 Tryon Grove Rd Ringwood IL 60072 Office: 421 E Hawley St Mundelein IL 60060

STREY, FRED C., financial executive; b. Milw., Mar. 13, 1937; s. Walter and Louise (Genz) S.; married, 1966; children: Karen, Julie. BA, U. Wis., 1961. CPA, Wis. Internal auditor Gen. Mills, Mpls., 1961-62; acct., cons. bus. Touche, Ross & Co., Milw., 1966-69; treas. Gateway Foods, LaCrosse, Wis., 1966-69; v.p. fin. The Azco Group and Related Cos., Appleton, Wis., 1969—; also bd. dirs. The Arco Group and Related Cos., Appleton, Wis.; bd. dirs. Sanco, Ltd., Appleton, others. Mem. Am. Inst. CPA's, Wis. Inst. CPA's, Fin. Execs. of Northeastern Wis. (various offices 1981-86). Republican. Lutheran. Lodge: Rotary (local treas., bd. dirs. 1977-82). Office: Azco Hennes Inc PO Box 567 Appleton WI 54914

STRIBLING, FRANK LLEWELLYN, JR., consultant, tax service company executive; b. San Diego, June 6, 1939; s. Frank Llewellyn and Bliss May (Johnson) S.; m. Iva Mae Wright, Feb. 15, 1964; children—Alan, Darren. B.S. in Chemistry, San Diego State U., 1962; M.B.A. in Fin., U. Mo.-Kansas City, 1974. Process devel. engr. DuPont, Chattanooga, 1964-67; asst. to quality control mgr. Baxter Labs., Kingstree, S.C., 1967-68; quality control coordinator Mobay Chem. Corp., Kansas City, 1968-81; mng. asst. research and devel. West-Agro Chem. Inc., Kansas City, 1981-83; pres. Stribling Tax Service Inc., Raytown, Mo., 1979—; cons., 1983—. Served as seaman USN, 1962-64. Mem. Am. Soc. for Quality Control (cert. quality engr. 1980). Mem. Reorganized Ch. Latter Day Saints (ordained minister, elder).

STRICKLAND, FREDERICK WILLIAM, JR., osteopathic physician, educator; b. Kansas City, Mo., Aug. 24, 1944; s. Frederick William and Ardene (Graves) S.; Student Coffeyville Jr. Coll., 1962-64; B.A. in Biology, Southwestern Coll., Winfield, Kans., 1966; M.A. in Ecology, Drake U., 1976; D.O., Coll. Osteo. Medicine and Surgery, Des Moines, 1978. Diplomate Am. Bd. Osteo. Medicine, Am. Osteo. Bd. Gen. Practice. Tchr. pub. schs., Oklahoma City and Des Moines, 1967-75; instr. Area XI Community Coll., Des Moines and Ankeny, Iowa; biomed. communications technician Coll. Osteo. Medicine and Surgery, Des Moines, 1975-77; electrocardiogram technician Des Moines Gen. Hosp., 1976-78, intern, 1978-79, resident in family practice, 1979-80, mem. staff, 1980—, mem. Found., corp. bd. dirs., trustee; gen. practice osteo. medicine, Des Moines, 1980—; mem. staff Mercy Hosp. Med. Ctr.; clin. dir., student trainer Coll. Clinics East and West, U. Osteo. Medicine and Health Scis., Des Moines, 1980—, prof. family medicine, 1986—; chmn. bd. Des Moines Osteo. Employees Credit Union; mem. Iowa Physician's Asst. Adv. Com., 1985—, Iowa Pharmacy Commn., 1984—. Active NAACP, People United to Save Humanity, SCLC, Still Nat. Osteo. Mus., Des Moines Art Ctr.;; del. Dem. Nat. Conv., 1984; mem. Des Moines Plan and Zoning Commn., 1985—. Served to maj. M.C., Iowa Army N.G., 1979—. Recipient Found. Builder award Southwestern Coll., Winfield, Kans., 1978; disting. service award Corinthian Bapt. Ch., Des Moines, 1978. Mem. Am. Acad. Osteopathy, Iowa Found. for Med. Care, Osteo. Physicians and Surgeons, Iowa Physicians Asst. Assn. Mil. Surgeons of U.S., Assn. Army Flight Surgeons, Am. Coll. Gen. Practitioners Osteo. Medicine and Surgery, Arthritis Found., Assn. Retarded Citizens, Omega Psi Phi, Sigma Phi Pi. Baptist. Home: 4910 Country Club Des Moines IA 50312 Office: 1300 21st St Des Moines IA 53111

STRICKLAND, JOHN ARTHUR VAN, minister; b. Detroit, Sept. 25, 1952; s. Maurice Alexander and Irma (Surovy) S.; m. Constance Fillmore, Dec. 24, 1976 (div. Aug. 1984); m. Brenda Cecile Bunch, Nov. 23, 1985. BA cum laude, Ga. State U., 1974; ministry program, Unity Ministerial Sch., 1974-76. Ordained to Assn. Unity Chs., 1976. Minister Unity Ch. Christianity, Santa Rosa, Calif., 1976-77, Jacksonville, Fla., 1978-79; v.p. prayer ministry Unity Sch. Christianity, Unity Village, Mo., 1979—, mem. task force, 1984—; vol. chaplain, Jackson County Jail, Kansas City, 1974-75; coordinator internat. youth of unity Assn. Unity Chs., Unity Village, 1975-76. Contbr. articles to profl. jours. Vol. Unity Help Line, Unity Village, 1975-76. Named one of Outstanding Young Men Am., 1982. Republican. Lodge: Rotary (youth services com. 1984—). Avocations: running, physical fitness, golf, hiking, music. Home: 405 NE Stanton Ln Lee's Summit MO 64064 Office: Unity Sch Christianity Hwy 350 and Colbern Rd Unity Village MO 64062

STRICKLAND, ROSEMARY, physical therapist; b. Gary, Ind., Aug. 23, 1946; s. Tascho and Florence Ann (Meehan) Saems; m. Gary William Strickland, Apr. 3, 1971; children: Laura Anne, Kathryn Marie. BS, Loyola U., Chgo., 1968; cert. of phys. therapy, U. Iowa, 1969. Staff physc. therapist U. Ill. Hosp., Chgo., 1969-71; staff phys. therapist St. Joseph Mercy Hosp., Ann Arbor, Mich., 1971-77; phys. therapist Saline (Mich.) Community Hosp., 1977-78; pvt. practice phys. therapist Ypsilanti, Mich., 1978—. Roman Catholic. Avocations: gardening, reading, sewing. Home: 1441 Collegewood Ypsilanti MI 48197

STRICKLAND, STEVEN CLIFFORD, psychologist; b. Mpls., June 26, 1953; s. James Clifford and Marjorie Pauline (Brown) S.; m. Beth Marie Krussow, Aug. 11, 1979; children: Mark Clifford, Susan Marie. BA cum laude, U. Minn., 1975; MA cum laude, Trinity Evang. Div. Sch., 1977. Lic. psychologist, Minn. Psychotherapist Harley and Nelson Clinic, Mpls., 1978-82; psychotherapist, psychologist Christian Counseling Ctr., St. Louis Park, Minn., 1982-84; founder, owner, chief psychologist Christian Psychology Ctr., St. Louis Park, 1984—. Republican. Mem. Evang. Covenant Ch. Club: Apollo Men's (Mpls.). Avocations: jogging, golf, softball, choral singing. Office: Christian Psychology Ctr 7601 Wayzata Blvd Suite 220 Saint Louis Park MN 55426

STRIGENZ, ANTHONY JOSEPH, dentist; b. Milw., Nov. 25, 1931; s. Anton and Catherine (Hoffer) S.; m. Elizabeth Ann Walker, Aug. 20, 1955; children: Deborah Ann, Michael A., Mark, Andrew, Anthony K., Elizabeth, Thomas, Timothy W., Carrie M. Student, Wis. State U., 1949-51; DDS, Marquette U., 1955; postgrad., Northwestern U., 1960. Gen. practice dentistry Milw., 1957—; pres. Moraine Co., Farmington Realty. Served to capt. Dental Corps, U.S. Army, 1955-57. Mem. ADA, Wis. Dental Soc., Washington County Dental Soc., Internat. Acad. Orthodontics, Am. Dental Soc. Anesthesiology, Am. Acad. Orthodontics for Gen. Practioners, European Orthodontic Soc., Psi Omega. Roman Catholic. Home: 9409 Moraine Dr Kewaskum WI 53095

STRIKE, ANTHONY YOUNG, automotive executive, manufacturing executive; b. Salt Lake City, Dec. 1, 1955; s. George Louis and Janice Lee (Young) S.; m. Kathryn West, Dec. 30, 1980; children: Anthony Jr., Samuel, Kathryn Sloan. BA, Harvard U., 1978, MBA, 1982. Sr. cons. Bain & Co., Boston, 1982-85; v.p. Hess and Eisenhardt, Madison Heights, Mich., 1985—; mem. exec. com. Martin Franchises. Clubs: Harvard (Detroit); Harvard Bus Sch. (Eastern Mich.). Avocations: tennis, golf, skiing, reading, movies. Home: 186 Hamilton Birmingham MI 48010 Office: Hess and Eisenhardt 32501 Dequindre Madison Heights MI 48071

STRINGER, EDWARD CHARLES, lawyer, food company executive; b. St. Paul, Feb. 13, 1935; s. Philip and Anne (Driscoll) S.; m. Mary Lucille Lange, June 19, 1957; children: Philip, Lucille, Charles, Carolyn. BA, Amherst Coll., 1957; LLD, U. Minn., 1960. Bar: Minn. Ptnr. Stringer, Donnelly & Sharood, St. Paul, 1960-69, Briggs & Morgan, St. Paul, 1969-79; sr. v.p., gen. counsel Pillsbury Co., Mpls., 1980-82, exec. v.p., gen. counsel, 1982-83, exec. v.p., gen. counsel, chief adminstrv. officer, 1983—. Trustee William Mitchell Coll. Law, Macalester Coll., Minn. Pvt. Coll. Fund; bd. dirs. Mpls. United Way, 1983, Northland Coll. Mem. ABA, Minn. State Bar Assn., Ramsey County Bar Assn. (sec. 1977-80), Order of Coif. Unitarian. Clubs: Mpls.; Somerset Country; Madeline Island Yacht (La Pointe, Wis.). Home: 795 Hilltop Ct Saint Paul MN 55118 Office: Pillsbury Co 200 S 6th St Minneapolis MN 55402

STRIZEK, JAN, graphic designer; b. Berwyn, Ill., June 11, 1947; d. William J. and Rose F. (Jana) S.; B.F.A., No. Ill. U., 1969. Prin, Strizek & Assocs., Chgo., 1980—. Recipient awards for design excellence N.Y. Art Dirs. Club, Women in Design, Inst. of Bus. Designers 1st annual effective product brochure and binder competition, 1984. Mem. Women in Design (treas. Chgo. 1980-81), Soc. Typographic Arts (treas. Chgo. 1980-81, v.p. 1981-82), AIA (affiliate). Prodn. of graphics and designs for corp. image devel. Office: 213 W Institute Pl Chicago IL 60610

STROBECK, CHARLES LEROY, real estate executive; b. Chgo., June 27, 1928; s. Roy Alfred and Alice Rebecca (Stenberg) S.; m. Janet Louise Halverson, June 2, 1951; children: Carol Louise, Nancy Faith, Beth Ann, Jane Allison, Jean Marie. BA, Wheaton Coll., 1949. Mgr. Sudler & Co., Chgo., 1949-50, ptnr., 1951-63; chmn. bd. Strobeck, Reiss & Co., Chgo., 1964-82; pres. Jacanabe Mgmt. Co., Chgo., 1983—; bd. dirs. Am. Slide-Chart Corp., Carol Stream, 1971—. Bd. dirs. YMCA, Humane Soc., 1982—; pres. Chgo. Youth Ctrs., 1981-83. Mem. Inst. Real Estate Mgmt. (pres. 1970-71), Am. Soc. Real Estate Counselors, Mental Health Assocs. of Greater Chgo. (bd. dirs.), Lamda Alpha. Republican. Clubs: Chgo., Chgo. Golf (bd. dirs. 1984-86), Union League (pres. 1975-76), Mid-Am.; Clearwater Yacht. Home: 1 S 751 Hawthorne Ln Wheaton IL 60187 Office: Jacanabe Mgmt Co 104 S Michigan Ave Chicago IL 60603

STROBEL, RUDOLF GOTTFRIED KARL, biochemist; b. Kiessling Thuringia, Germany, Feb. 7, 1927; came to U.S. 1958, naturalized 1968; s. Karl M.F. and Frida L. (Weber) S.; m. Josefine M. Haunschild, Sept. 2, 1958; children: Wolfgang R., Christine B., Oliver K., Roland W. B. Sci., U. Regensburg, Bavaria, 1953; Dipl. Chem., U. Munich, Fed. Republic Germany, 1956, Ph.D., 1958. Biochemist, The Procter & Gamble Co., Cin., 1958-75, group leader, 1975-81, sect. head, 1981—. Patentee in fields of flour tech., emulsion tech., coffee aroma and flavor tech., tea and fruit juices. Mem. Am. Chem. Soc., Assn. Scientifique Internat. du Café, Internat. Apple Inst. Avocations: farming, gardening, pomology, machine design, classical music. Office: The Procter & Gamble Co 6110 Center Hill Rd Cincinnati OH 45224

STROBL, FREDERICK THOMAS, neurologist; b. Chgo., June 20, 1949; s. Frederick John and Estelle Strobl; m. Deborah Anne Smith. Student, Rensselaer Poly. Inst., 1967-68; BEE, U. Minn., 1971, MD, 1975. Cert. Am. Bd. Neurology and Electromyography. Intern Hennepin County Med. Ctr., 1975-76; engring. asst. Honeywell Research, Mpls., 1970-71; mgmt. trainee N.W. Bell Telephone, Mpls., 1971-72; resident in neurology U. Minn. Hosps., Mpls., 1975-79; EEG fellow Mayo Clinic, Rochester, Minn., 1979; neurologist, ptnr. Mpls. Clinic Neurology, 1979—; chmn., co-founder CNS Inc., Mpls., 1982—. Patentee computerized spectral analysis. Scholar Lockheed Leadership Rensselaer Poly. Inst., Troy, N.Y., 1967, Nat. Inst. Neurologic Disease, London, 1977; recipient Upjohn award 1975, Shapiro award 1978. Fellow Am. Acad. Neurology, Am. Assn. Electrophysiology and Electrodiagnosis; mem. AMA, Am. Electroencepalographic Soc., Hennepin County Med. Soc., Minn. Med. Assn., Mensa. Office: Mpls Clinic Neurology Ltd 4225 Golden Valley Rd Minneapolis MN 55422

STROBLE, FRANCIS ANTHONY, manufacturing company executive; b. St. Louis, Aug. 20, 1930; s. Frank J. and Loraine L. (Michel) S.; m. Ruth M. O'Neill, Feb. 14, 1953; children—Deborah, Mark, Susan, Matthew, Karen. B.S. in Commerce, St. Louis U., 1952, M.S. in Commerce magna cum laude, 1960; postgrad., Northwestern U., 1968. Auditor Hochschield, Bloom & Co., St. Louis, 1954-56; with Monsanto Co., St. Louis, 1956—; dir. data processing, then v.p., controller Monsanto Co., 1973-79, v.p. fin., 1979-81, sr. v.p., chief fin. officer, 1981—, adv. dir.; dir. Mercantile Trust N.A., Mercantile Bancorp. Mem. profl. adv. bd. U. Ill.; mem. council Fin. Execs. Conf. Bd.; v.p. lay adv. bd. St. Mary's Health Center, St. Louis; trustee St. Louis U.; bd. dirs. Inroads, Cath. Charities of St. Louis. Served to 1st lt. USAF, 1952-54. Mem. Am. Inst. C.P.A.s, Fin. Execs. Inst. Office: Monsanto Co 800 N Lindbergh Blvd Saint Louis MO 63167

STROCK, SHEILA ANNE, dentist; b. Yonkers, N.Y., July 12, 1954; d. Henry and Ruth Mary (Spoor) Strock.; m. Keith R. Minnich; children: Paul, Anne, Sarah. BAAS magna cum laude, U. Del., 1976; DMD, U. Pa., 1980. Dentist USPHS, Rockford, Ill., 1980-82, North Point Dental Group, Milw., Wis., 1983-85; assoc. dentist Bradley Dental Assocs., Milw., 1986—. Served to lt. commdr. USPHS, 1982. Recipient Crusaders Clinic Service award, 1982. Mem. Am. Assn. Women Dentists (co-chmn. 1985-86), ADA, Acad. Gen. Dentistry, Psi Omega. Democrat. Clubs: N. Shore Quilters Guild, Bach Chamber Orchestra (Milw.) (chmn. 1985—).

STROH, PETER WETHERILL, brewery executive; b. Detroit, Dec. 18, 1927; s. Gari Melchers and Suzanne (Suddards) S.; m. Nicole Elizabeth Fauquet-Lemaitre, June 30, 1964; children—Pierre Alexander, Frederic Charlton. B.A., Princeton U., 1951. Asst. to pres. Stroh Brewery Co., Detroit, 1952-65, v.p., 1965-66, dir. ops., 1966-68, pres., 1968-82, chmn., chief exec. officer, 1982—, also dir.; dir. NBD Bancorp., Inc. ; bd. dirs. Detroit Renaissance, Inc., The Beer Inst., Atlantic Salmon Found.; vice chmn. Detroit Econ. Growth Corp.; trustee New Detroit, Inc., Solomon Guggenheim Found., Inst. Resource Mgmt.; vice chmn. Detroit Med. Ctr. Served with USN, 1945-46. Mem. Nat. Audubon Soc. (bd. dirs.), Conservation Internat. (bd. dirs.), Econ. Alliance Mich. (bd. dirs.). Clubs: Detroit, Detroit Athletic; Country of Detroit (Grosse Pointe Farms, Mich.), Grosse Pointe; Yondotega; Anglers of N.Y.; Island of Hobe Sound (Fla.). Office: Stroh Brewery Co 100 River Place Detroit MI 48207

STROH, STEVEN EDWARD, controller; b. Des Moines, July 30, 1935; s. Edward Bernard and Yvonne Elizabeth (Scheffer) S.; m. Ottilieanne Ruth Hoppe, Aug. 4, 1962; children: Elizabeth R., Catherine A. BS, U. Ill., 1957; JD, Chgo.-Kent Coll. Law, 1964. Supr. R.R. Donnelley, Chgo., Ill., 1958-63; mgr. R.R. Donnelley, Crawfordsville, Ind., 1966-73; div. controller R.R. Donnelley, Dwight, Ill., 1974—. Chmn. Planning Commn., Dwight, 1975—. Served with U.S. Army, 1958-60. Mem. Fin. Execs. Inst., Am. Contract Bridge League (bd. dirs. 1976—), Delta Upsilon (treas. 1956-57), Phi Delta Phi (treas. 1963-64). Republican. Lutheran. Avocations: tournament bridge, reading. Home: 903 S Chicago Dwight IL 60420 Office: R R Donnelley & Sons Co Rural Rt 1 Box 118 Dwight IL 60420

STROHM, GARY THOMAS, accounting firm executive; b. Burlington, Wis., Apr. 22, 1959; s. Richard John and Joan Agnes (Scherrer) S.; m. Mary Louise Rusch, June 12, 1982; 1 child, Ryan. BBA in Acctg., U. Wis., Whitewater, 1981. CPA, Wis. Staff acct. Houghton, Taplick and Co., Madison, Wis., 1981-83, sr. staff acct., 1983-86, mgr., 1987—. Asst. treas. Mt. Olive Luth. Ch., Madison, 1986—. Mem. Am. Inst. CPA's, Wis. Inst. CPA's, Ins. Acctg. and Systems Assn. Lodge: Optimists (sec., treas. 1986—). Avocations: gardening, hunting, running, biking. Home: 2914 Greenway Trail Madison WI 53719 Office: Houghton Taplick and Co CPA's 7601 Ganser Way Madison WI 53719

STROHMAIER, THOMAS EDWARD, designer, educator; b. Cin., Aug. 26, 1943; s. Charles Edward and Margaret Mary (Meyers) S.; m. Margaret Ann Haglage, June 7, 1980; children: Paige Maura, Edward Michael, Phoebe Greer. BFA, U. Cin., 1969, MFA, 1973. Lectr. in design U. Cin., 1975-76; instr. in design U. Dayton, Ohio, 1976-80, asst. prof. design, 1980-83; pres. Strohmaier Design, Cin., 1983—; cons. City Arts Corp., Cin., 1977-78, City Beautiful Program, Dayton, 1982; adj. prof. design U. Cin., 1983—. Designer urban wall projects Ohio Arts Council, Columbus, 1974, Corbet award, Cin., 1977; patentee in field. U. Dayton grantee, 1980. Mem. Contemporary Arts Ctr., Design, Architecture, Art and Planning Alumni Com., Internat. Freelance Photographers Orgn., U. Cin. Decade Club. Republican. Roman Catholic. Club: Decade. Avocations: running, cycling. Home: 2431 Ingleside Cincinnati OH 45206 Office: Strohmaier Design 906 Main St Suite 500 Cincinnati OH 45202

STROHMEYER, WILLIAM RAYMOND, healthcare executive; b. Cleve., Nov. 13, 1949; s. Carl George and Delia Helen (Boehmer); m. Miki Lynn Adams, Nov. 23, 1984; children: Dru Christopher, Niki Lynn Adams. BS in Mgmt., Malone Coll., 1986. Mgr. mdse. ops. Higbee Co., Cleve., 1974-76, exec. placement mgr., 1976-77, exec. employment mgr., 1980-82; ops. mgr. Higbee Co., Canton, Ohio, 1977-80; dir. employee services Aultman Hosp. Assn., Canton, 1982-85, asst. v.p., 1985—. Campaign mgr. State Senator Thomas Walsh, Canton, 1977, 82, State Senator W. Scott Oelslager, Canton, 1986. Served to sgt. NG, 1969-75. Mem. Nat. Coll. Healthcare Mktg., Am. Soc. Personnel Adminstrn., Midwest Coll. Placement Assn., Coll. Placement Council, Am. Soc. Healthcare Edn. and Tng., Jackson-Belden C. of C. (pres. 1980). Republican. Avocations: politics, auto restoration, woodworking. Office: Aultman Hosp Assn 2600 6th St SW Canton OH 44646

STROM, DAVID HUGH, importer, exporter, manufacturer, marketing consultant; b. Chgo., Nov. 13, 1913; s. Max and Freda (Hechtman) S.; m. Sylvia Dorothy Abelson, Aug. 14, 1938; children: Terry B., Susan Strom Mogerman, Michael A. Student, U. Ill., 1933-34. Pres. Strom Internat., Ltd., Chgo., 1961—; appointed commnr. internat. trade State of Ill.; mem. exec. com. Bus. Friends of Mayor of Chgo. Patentee inflatable products. Hon. trustee Sky Ranch for Boys, 1978; mem. City of Hope; mem. exec. com. Chgo. Cerebral Palsy Telethon, 1978, 79; past pres. Leukemia Research Found.; active United Jewish Appeal; bd. dirs., past v.p. Hebrew U. Jerusalem, bd. dirs., dir. major donor div. United Cerebral Palsy. Mem. Internat. Exec. Club (past pres.), Nat. Acad. Mktg. Scis., Nat. Inst. Advt. and Merchandising, Internat. Acad. Mktg. Cons., Am.-Israel C. of C. and Industries, World Trade Com., Small. Bus. Council, Chgo. Assn. Commerce and Industry, Bus. Friends of Chgo. (exec. com.), Combined Jewish Appeal Trades and Industries. Office: 1474 Merchandise Mart Chicago IL 60654

STROM, JUSTIN VERNON, JR., management consultant; b. Seattle, Mar. 17, 1949; s. Justin Vernon and Adelaide (Guptill) S.; m. Barbara Vandivier, Apr. 3, 1981; 1 child, Justin Kenneth. BA in Econs., U. Wash., 1971; postgrad., U. Wis., Oshkosh, 1983—. Personnel mgr. Whitney-Fidalgo Seafoods, Seattle, 1971-77; v.p. Mendheim Co., Chgo., 1978-80; dir. staffing Kimberly-Clark Corp., Neenah, Wis., 1980-86; ptnr. Overland Group, Chgo., 1986—. Republican. Avocation: boating. Home: 1242 Saint James Pl Libertyville IL 60048 Office: Overland Group 4 Northwest Hwy Arlington Heights IL 60004

STROM, LYLE ELMER, federal judge; b. Omaha, Jan. 6, 1925; s. Elmer T. and Eda (Hanisch) S.; m. Regina Ann Kelly, July 31, 1950; children: Mary Bess, Susan Frances, Amy Claire, Cassie A., David Kelly, Margaret Mary, Bryan Thomas. Student, U. Nebr., 1946-47; AB, Creighton U., 1950, JD cum laude, 1953. Bar: Nebr. 1953. Assoc. Fitzgerald, Brown, Leahy, Strom, Schorr & Barmettler and predecessor firm, Omaha, 1953-60, ptnr., 1960-63, gen. trial ptnr., 1963-85; judge U.S. Dist. Ct. Nebr., Omaha, 1985—; bd. dirs. World of Sleep Inc., Unpainted Furniture Ctr. Inc.; adj. prof. law Creighton U., 1959—; mem. com. pattern jury instrns. and practice and proc. Nebr. Supreme Ct., 1965—; spl. legal counsel Omaha Charter Rev. Commn., 1973. Mem. exec. com. Covered Wagon council Boy Scouts Am., 1953-57; chmn. bd. trustees Marian High Sch., 1969-71. Served as ensign USNR and with U.S. Maritime Service, 1943-46. Fellow Am. Coll. Trial Lawyers, Internat. Acad. Trial Lawyers; mem. Citizens for Ednl. Freedom, ABA, Nebr. Bar Assn. (ho. of dels. 1978-81, exec. council 1981—), Omaha Bar Assn. (pres. 1980-81), Am. Judicature Soc., Midwestern Assn. Amateur Athletic Union (pres. 1976-78), Alpha Sigma Nu (pres. alumni chpt. 1970-71). Republican. Roman Catholic. Lodge: Rotary. Office: U S Dist Ct PO Box 607 Omaha NE 68101

STROMBERG, DONALD RICHARD, music educator, keyboard consultant; b. Des Moines, Jan. 23, 1940; s. Donald Laverne and Mary Elizabeth (Shultice) S.; m. Eleanor Brindle, Aug. 21, 1963; children: Daniel Richard, Emily Jane. BA, U. No. Iowa, 1963; MusM, Northwestern U., 1965, PhD, 1974; postgrad., Denver U., 1975, U. Minn., 1975, Memphis State U., 1975-77. Vocal music tchr. Reinbeck (Iowa) Community Schs., 1963-64; tchr. choral music Evanston (Ill.) Twp. High Sch., 1965-69; faculty mem. Grand View Coll., Des Moines, 1970-78, prof. music, 1970-78; prof. music U. S.D., Vermillion, 1978-85; dist. mgr. Mathews Williams, 1985-86; mgr. Baldwin Piano and Organ, Cin., 1986—. Composer: Sing, Shout and Praise, 1981, Psalm 100, 1981, Sing to the Lord of Harvest, 1981. Mem. Am. Orff-Schulwerk Assn., Sioux Valley Orff Assn. (pres. 1982-83), Music Educators Nat. Conf., NEA, S.D. Music Educators Assn., S.D. Edn. Assn.,

Orgn. Am. Kodaly Educators, Midwest Kodaly Music Educators Assn., Nat. Consortium for Computer-Based Music Instrn., Assn. for Devel. Computer-Based Instructional Systems, Phi Mu Alpha Sinfonia, Phi Delta Kappa. Baptist.

STROMBERG, GREGORY, printing ink company executive; b. Milw., Feb. 10, 1948; s. Clifford Norman and Margaret Betty (Hoover) S.; m. Gail Elizabeth Steinbach, Aug. 22, 1970; children—Christopher, Brian, Ellen. B.S., Marquette U., Milw., 1970. Office contact salesman Continental Can Co., Milw., 1970-78; sales rep. Sun Chem. Co., Milw., 1978-82; v.p., gen. mgr. Acme Printing Ink Co., Milw., 1982—; exec. v.p. Can. operation Acme Printing Ink Can. Ltd., 1985—; pres. Toobee Internat., Inc., Milw., 1981—. Author: Toobee Air Force Flight Training Manual, 1983. Advisor Milw. Jr. Achievement, 1974; sponsor Muscular Dystrophy, 1983; asst. com. mem. Toys for Tots, Children's Hosp., Milw., 1983. Mem. Sales and Mktg. Execs. of Milw., Am. Mgmt. Assn. Home: N69 W23448 Donna Dr Sussex WI 53089

STRONCEK, GREGORY GEORGE, oral and maxillofacial surgeon; b. Mpls., Oct. 9, 1952; s. Frank Stanley and Theresa Elizabeth (Kocisko) S.; m. Juliet Louise Uglem, June 22, 1973; children: Carolyn, Renee, Joanna. BA, U. Minn., 1974, DDS, 1976; MS, U. Iowa, 1980. Diplomate Am. Bd. Oral and Maxillofacial Surgeons. Resident gen. practice Denver Gen. Hosp., 1976-77; resident oral and maxillofacial surgery U. Iowa, Iowa City, 1977-80; oral and maxillofacial surgeon Madison (Wis.) Oral and Maxillofacial Surgeons, 1980—; clin. instr. dept. plastic surgery U. Hosp, Madison, 1982—. Recipient Merle L. Hale Grad. Research award U. Iowa Coll. Denistry, 1980, Henry B. Clark Meml. award Minn. Soc. Oral Surgeons, 1976. Fellow Am. Assn. Oral and Maxillofacial Surgeons; mem. ADA, Wis. Dental Assn., Wis Soc. Oral and Maxillofacial Surgeons, Dane County Dental Soc. (trustee 1984—). Lodge: Rotary. Home: 4133 Council Crest Madison WI 53711 Office: Madison Oral & Maxillofacial Surgeons 6425 Odana Rd Madison WI 53719

STRONG, DOROTHY MAE, educational administrator; b. Memphis, Feb. 3, 1934; d. John Harrison and Willie Beatrice (Hawkins) Swearengen; B.S. in Edn., Chgo. State U., 1958; M.A. in Math. Edn., 1964; Ed.D., Nova U., 1985; m. Joseph Nathaniel Strong, Mar. 19, 1953; 1 dau., Joronda Ramette. Elem. and secondary tchr. Chgo. Pub. Schs., 1958-65, dir. math., 1976—; cons. math, 1965-76; instr. Chgo. State U., 1969-71; mem. Commn. on Tchr. Edn., Task Force on Math. in Urban Centers, Ill. Basic Skills Adv. Council, Nat. Inst. Edn. Conf. on Basic Skills; mem. council acad. affairs Coll. Bd., v.p., 1983—; bd. dirs. Allendale Sch. for Boys, 1974—. Pres. youth dept. Midwest dist. United Pentecostal Council, Assemblies of God Inc., 1979—. Recipient Edn. PaceSetter award President's Nat. Adv. Council on Supplementary Centers, 1973. Mem. Assn. Supervision and Curriculum Devel., Nat. Council Tchrs. Math. (bd. dirs. 1987—), Nat. Council Suprs. Math. (sec. chpt. 1973-75, pres. chpt. 1977-79), Elem. Sch. Math. Advs. Chgo. Area, Met. Math. Club, Math. Club Chgo. and Vicinity, Nat. Alliance Black Sch. Educators, Ill. Council Tchrs. Math., Delta Sigma Theta, Kappa Delta Pi, Kappa Mu Epsilon. Author: Modern Mathematics Structure and Use-Spirit Masters, 1977; author Chgo. Public Schs. curriculum materials; contbr. articles to profl. publs.; coordinator devel. numerous curriculum guides. Home: 2820 Paris Rd Olympia Fields IL 60461 Office: 1819 W Pershing Rd 6C-SE Chicago IL 60609

STRONG, JEROME ANTON, political science consultant; b. Muskegon, Mich., Aug. 18, 1947; s. Ben and Anna Belle (Childress) S.; m. Deborah Deon, July 28, 1968; 1 dau., Simone Yvette. BS, U. Mich., 1976, MA in Polit. Sci., 1978. Research assoc. Inst. Social Research, U. Mich., Ann Arbor, 1976-80, Joint Center for Polit. Studies, Washington, 1977—; adminstrv. asst. Mich. State Senator Lana Pollack, Ann Arbor, 1983-84; exec. asst. to state budget dir. for legis. liaison Mich. Dept. Mgmt. and Budget, Lansing, 1984-86 ; dep. dir. Mich. Dept. Civil Rights, Lansing, 1986—; founder SAJ Research, Inc., 1980—; instr. polit. sci. Washtenaw Community Coll., 1980-81. Mem. state central com. Mich. Dems., 1976-83; vice chmn. Ypsilanti Dems.P, 1980-82, Washtenaw County Dems., 1984—; bd. dirs. ACLU, Washtenaw County, del. State of Mich. ACLU. Mem. Mich. Soc. Gerontology, Gerontol. Soc., Am. Polit. Sci. Assn., Am. Assn. Budget and Program Analysis, NAACP, Midwest Polit. Sci. Assn., Am. Soc. Pub. Adminstrn., Econ. Club of Detroit. Roman Catholic. Lodges: Masons, Shriners, KC. Home: 921 Pleasant Dr Ypsilanti MI 48197 Office: Mich Dept Civil Rights 303 W Kalamazoo 4th Floor Lansing MI 48933

STRONG, JOHN DAVID, insurance company executive; b. Cortland, N.Y., Apr. 12, 1936; s. Harold A. and Helen H. S.; m. Carolyn Dimmick, Oct. 26, 1957; children: John D., Suzanne. BS, Syracuse U., N.Y., 1957. With Kemper Group, 1957—, empire div. sales mgr., 1972-74, exec. v.p. Fed. Kemper Ins. Co., Decatur, Ill., 1974-79, pres., bd. dirs., 1979—; bd. dirs. Pershing Nat. Bank. Mem. adv. council Sch. Bus. Millikin U., 1975-79; bd. dirs. United Way of Decatur and Macon County, Ill., 1976-79, campaign chmn., 1978-79, pres. bd. dirs., 1979-81; pres. United Way of Ill., 1981-83; bd. dirs. Decatur-Macon County Econ. Devel. Found., 1983—, Decatur Meml. Hosp., 1986—, DMH Health Systems, 1987—, Richland Community Coll. Found.; bd. dirs. Ill. Ednl. Devel. Found., 1983—, pres., 1985—. Served to capt. USAR, 1958-69. Mem. Metro Decatur C of C. (bd. dirs. 1977-80, 2d vice chmn. 1981-82, 1st vice chmn. 1982-83, chmn. 1983-84), Alpha Kappa Psi. Club: Decatur (bd. dirs. 1980-83, pres. 1983), Country of Decatur. Office: 2001 E Mound Rd Decatur IL 62526

STRONG, MARCELLA LEE, music specialist, educator; b. East Liverpool, Ohio, Oct. 16, 1954; d. Carl and Ruth I. (White) Hinkle; m. David Lee Strong, Feb 19, 1977. BA magna cum laude, U. Toledo, 1976; MA in Early Childhood Edn., Kent State U., 1982. Cert. music, elem. tchr., Ohio. Music instr. Cardinal Local Schs., Parkman and Huntsburg, Ohio, 1977—. Choir dir. G.V. Nazarene Ch., Orwell, Ohio 1981-83; organist Huntsburg Congl. Ch., 1985-86; mem., officer Orwell Farm Bur. Mem. Cardinal Edn Assn. (negotiator 1982, 84, 87, sec. 1983-84, treas. 1984-85, pres. 1985-86), Ohio Music Educators Assn., Kappa Delta Pi, Mu Phi Epsilon. Democrat. Avocations: spectator sports, traveling, reading, chess. Home: Box 370 Orwell OH 44076

STRONG, SCOTT MARTIN, auditor; b. Saginaw, Mich., Jan. 16, 1956; s. Raymond Daniel and Dolores Helen (Tufts) S. AS in Acctng., Delta Coll., University Center, Mich., 1976; BS in Acctng., Ferris State Coll., Big Rapids, Mich., 1978. CPA, Mich.; cert. internal auditor. Auditor Blue Cross Blue Shield Mich., Holt, 1983-85; asst. auditor gen. Office of Auditor Gen., State of Mich., Lansing, 1978-83, 85—. Mem. Am. Inst. CPA's, State Assn. Accts., Auditors and Bus. Adminstrs., Delta Sigma Pi (activities chmn. 1978). Roman Catholic. Avocations: woodworking, skiing, tennis, softball, golfing. Home: 512 Dutch Hill Dr Lansing MI 48917 Office: Office of Auditor Gen 333 S Capitol Suite A Lansing MI 48913

STROSS, ROBERT MARSHALL, JR., marketing and management development executive; b. Dayton, Ohio, May 24, 1943; s. Robert Marshall and Christine (Noland) S.; m. Charlane JoAnn Colip, Aug. 20, 1966 (div.); children—Andy, Betsy; m. 2d, Ruth Ann Lenhard, Dec. 21, 1974; children—Sandy, Kelly, Kerry. B.A. in Psychology, DePauw U., 1965; M.B.A., Mich. State U., 1970. Ops. mgr. Marriott In-Flite Services, Washington, 1970-73; dir. Tng. and Planning W.T. Sistrunk & Co., Lexington, Ky., 1974-79; dir. orgn. mgmt., develop. Wetterau, Inc., St. Louis, 1979-84; dir. mktg. Wetterau, Inc., 1984, v.p., 1985-87, 1st v.p., 1987—. Supt. ch. sch. St. Timothys Episcopal Ch., Creve Coeur, Mo., vestryman, 1985-87, jr. warden, 1987—. Served to capt. USAF, 1965-69; Vietnam. Recipient Robert E. Crouch Meml. award DePauw U., 1965. Mem. Am. Soc. Tng. and Devel. (pres. chpt. 1978-79; Service award, 1982), Internat. Platform Assn. Republican. Episcopalian. Home: 11445 N Forty Dr Saint Louis MO 63131 Office: 8920 Pershall Rd Hazelwood MO 63042

STROTHER, GREGORY LYNN, quality engineer; b. St. Louis, Nov. 3, 1948; s. George Hamilton and Blanche (Wood) S.; m. Paula J. Jacobs, May 29, 1971; children: Jacob Hamilton, Martin Alexander, Benjamin Daniel. Student, U. Mo., St. Louis, 1969; BS in Engring. Mgmt., U. Mo., Rolla, 1971; postgrad., Rend Lake Coll., Ina, Ill., 1980, Frontier Community Coll., Fairfield, Ill., 1984. Surp. mgmt. trainee Brown Shoe Co., St. Louis, 1971-74; mfgr. engr. Am. Chain and Cable, Salem, Ill., 1974-75; supr. Sportline, Salem, 1975-79; quality engr., analyst General Tire, Mount Vernon, Ill., 1979—. Jr. high tchr. Sunday sch. First Bapt. Ch., 1980, deacon, 1981—. Mem. Am. Soc. Engring. Mgmt., Am. Soc. Quality Control (cert.). Baptist. Avocations: baseball card collecting, fishing, fin. studies, bowling. Home: 750 Reel Salem IL 62881 Office: Gen Tire and Rubber Co PO Box 1029 Mount Vernon IL 62881

STROUSE, ROBERT ALLEN, computer systems engineer; b. Williamsport, Pa., Jan. 11, 1948; s. William John and Catherine Ursula (Nork) S.; m. Susan June Mitstifer, Aug. 16, 1969; 1 child, Gabrielle. BS in Edn., Ind. U. of Pa., 1970; MEd, Pa. State U., 1978; MS, U. Dayton, 1982; postgrad., Wright State U., 1982-84. Cert. tchr., Pa. Tchr. maths. and computer sci. Altoona (Pa.) Area Schs., 1970-80, also coach football, track and field, dir. ski club and intramural basketball program; engring. programmer, analyst Hobart Corp., Troy, Ohio, 1980-83, mgr. engring. computer systems, 1983—; chmn. applications program SIG com. CADAM User Exchange, Torrance, Calif., 1984, chmn. software com., 1985, gen. chmn. 1986—. Bd. dirs. Easter Seals of Miami County, Troy, 1984-86, Miami County Soc. for Handicapped Children and Adults, 1986—. Served to lt. U.S. Army, 1970-72. Mem. Computer and Automated Systems Assn. of Soc. Mech. Engrs., Jaycees (treas. Troy chpt. 1981-82, pres. 1982-83, chmn. bd. dirs. 1983-84). Democrat. Roman Catholic. Lodges: Kiwanis, K.C. Avocations: golf, travel, skiing. Home: 801 Branford Rd Troy OH 45373 Office: Hobart Corp World Hdqrs Ave Troy OH 45374

STRUBBE, THOMAS R., insurance holding company executive; b. Ft. Wayne, Ind., Mar. 30, 1940; s. Rudolph C. and Maverne E. (Wagoner) S.; m. Theresa Hoog, Apr. 29, 1967; children: Tracy Lynn, Patrick Thomas, Christina Lee. B.S., Ind. U., 1962; J.D., Tulane U., 1965. Bar: Ind. 1965, Ill. 1969. Atty. Lincoln Nat. Life Ins. Co., Ft. Wayne, 1965-66; asst. counsel Lincoln Nat. Life Ins. Co., 1967-68; with Washington Nat. Corp., Evanston, Ill., 1968—; gen. counsel Washington Nat. Corp., 1973-79, sec., 1970-84, v.p., 1975-79, sr. v.p., 1979-83, exec. v.p., 1983-84, pres., 1984—, also dir., mem. exec. com.; dir. Washington Nat. Ins. Co., Washington Nat. Life Ins. Co. N.Y., United Presdl. Corp. Trustee Glencoe (Ill.) Union Ch.; v.p., bd. dirs., exec. com. Chgo. chpt. Epilepsy Found. Am., 1975-79; bd. dirs. Assn. Retarded Citizens Ill., Northlight Theater. Served to lt. USNR, 1965-71. Lincoln Found. grantee, 1964. Mem. Assn. Life Ins. Counsel, Nat. Investor Relations Inst., Am. Soc. Corp. Secs., ABA, Ind., Ill., Chgo. bar assns. Club: Skokie Country (Glencoe). Address: Washington Nat Corp 1630 Chicago Ave Evanston IL 60201

STRUBEL, RICHARD PERRY, manufacturing company executive; b. Evanston, Ill., Aug. 10, 1939; s. Arthur Raymond and Martha (Smith) S.; m. Linda Jane Freeman, Aug. 25, 1961 (div. 1974); children: Douglas Arthur, Craig Tollerton; m. Ella Doyle G'sell, Oct. 23, 1976. B.A., Williams Coll., 1962; M.B.A., Harvard U., 1964. Assoc. Fry Cons., Chgo., 1964-66, mng. prin., 1966-68; with N.W. Industries, Inc., Chgo., 1968-83, v.p. corp. devel., 1969-73, group v.p., 1973-79, exec. v.p., 1979-83, pres., 1983; chmn. bd., pres. Buckingham Corp., N.Y.C., 1972-73; pres., chief exec. officer Microdot Inc., Chgo., 1983—; trustee Benchmark Funds, Instl. Liquid Assets and Associated Funds. Trustee Marvelwood Sch., U. Chgo., Better Govt. Assn., Chgo.; bd. dirs. Children's Meml. Hosp., Children's Meml. Med. Ctr.; mem. vis. com. Divinity Sch., U. Chgo. Presbyterian. Clubs: Mid-Day, Casino, Chicago, Comml., Commonwealth (Chgo.). Office: Microdot Inc 20 S Clark St Chicago IL 60603

STRUBEL, STEPHEN JOHN, finance executive; b. St. Louis, July 1, 1940; s. Julius Christopher and Margaret (Furi) S.; m. Linda Carol Galemore, Oct. 12, 1963; children: Sherri, Michael. BS in Acctg., Washington U., 1970; MBA, Quincy Coll., 1987. Cert. mgmt. acct. Mgr. cost/budgets Moog Industries, St. Louis, 1965-72; controller ISCO Mfg. Co., Kansas City, Mo., 1972-74; v.p. fin. Knapheide Mfg. Co., Quincy, Ill., 1974-85; v.p. fin. and adminstrn. Prince Mfg. Co., Quincy, 1985—. Bd. dirs. Great River affiliate of Aplastic Anemia Found. of Am., Quincy, 1986. Served with USN, 1959-63. Mem. Fin. Execs. Inst., Inst. Cert. Mgmt. Accts. Republican. Roman Catholic. Lodge: Rotary. Avocations: fishing, sports. Home: 2911 Curved Creek Quincy IL 62301

STRUBLE, DAVID ALLEN, dentist; b. Harlingen, Tex., Nov. 17, 1957; s. Jack Gordon and Mary Ruth (Hudspeth) S.; m. Darohnn Louise Harris, Dec. 18, 1982. BA in Biology, U. Tex., 1980; DDS, Baylor Coll. Dentistry, 1983. Assoc. Dr. Richard Martin, Ft. Worth, 1983-84, Dr. Howard Hudspeth, Dallas, 1983-84; gen. practice dentistry Ozark, Mo., 1984—. Named Male Vocalist of Yr., Country Music Revue, Ft. Worth, 1982, Male Vocalist of Yr., Ozark Music Awards, Branson, Mo., 1985, 86. Mem. ADA, Springfield Dental Soc., Mo. Dental Assn. Republican. Avocations: singing, entertaining, sports. Home: Rt 4 Box 125-16 Ozark MO 65721 Office: 104 S 2d Ave Ozark MO 65721

STRUCK, ANN MARIE, dentist; b. Morris, Ill., Feb. 20, 1955; s. Walter Anthony and Victoria Helen (Such) S. BA, North Cen. Coll., Naperville, Ill., 1977; DDS, Loyola U., Maywood, Ill., 1981. Gen. practice dentistry Kankakee, Ill., 1981-82, Morris, Ill., 1982—. Sec. Morris Hosp. Aux., 1985-86, treas., 1986-87, 1st v.p., 1987—; vice chmn. Am Cancer Soc., Morris, 1986—, profl. edn. chmn., 1986—; mem. adv. com., Morris High Sch., 1983-87; treas. Philanthropic Edn. Orgn., 1987—. Mem. ADA, Ill. State Dental Soc., Ill. Valley Dental Soc., Acad. Gen. Dentistry, Chgo. Dental Soc., Grundy County Assn. Commerce and Industry, Am. Assn. Women Dentists, Bus. and Profl. Women's Club (nbwwchmn. 1986-87). Roman Catholic. Club: Invesment (Morris). Avocations: tennis, biking, photography, reading, golf. Home: 721 Spruce St Morris IL 60450 Office: 619 Wauponsee St Morris IL 60450

STRUTZ, WILLIAM CHARLES, periodontist; b. Detroit, Oct. 29, 1945; s. William Carl and Margaret Theresa (Guertz) S.; m. Patricia Stevens, Aug. 22, 1981. BS, Mich. State U., 1968; MBA, U. Kans., 1974; DDS, U. Mo., 1981. Fin. analyst Citicorp, St. Louis, 1974-77; practice dentistry Shawnee, Kans., 1981—; practice dentistry specializing in periodontics Shawnee, 1983—. Served to lt. comdr. USNR, 1969-81. Mem. Am. Dental Assn., Am. Acad. Periodontics (cert.), Kans. Dental Assn., 5th Dist. Dental Soc., Greater Kans. City Soc. Clin. Periodontists. Republican. Roman Catholic. Avocations: weight lifting, running, cooking, photography, stained glass artisan. Office: 6333 Long Ave #201 Shawnee KS 66216

STRZELECKI, LEONARD JOHN, health scince association adminstrator; b. South Bend, Ind., Sept. 4, 1956; s. Arthur Joseph and Mary Fern (Schnieder) S.; m. Amy Jo Yauch, Sept. 10, 1983. BS in Acctg., Ball State U., 1978. CPA, Ind. From staff acct. to mgr. Arthur Andersen and Co., Chgo., 1978-86; v.p. fin., chief fin. officer St. Joseph and Care Group, Inc., South Bend, 1986—. Mem. Am. Inst. CPA's, Healthcare Fin. Mgmt. Assn. Roman Catholic. Club: Knollwood Country (Granger, Ind.). Avocations: golf, bowling. Office: St Josephs Care Group Inc 707 E Cedar St Suite 200 South Bend IN 46617

STUARK, BARBARA IRENE, retail management executive; b. Chgo., Mar. 19, 1948; d. Frank R. and Irene Julia (Wojnicki) S. Ph.B., Northwestern U., 1973, cert. in computer sci., 1985; C.B.A., Keller Grad. Sch. Mgmt., Chgo., 1978. Buyer, Goldblatts, Chgo., 1974-79; outside sales rep. Raymor/Moreddi, Ridgefield, N.J., 1979-80; div. mgr. Lord & Taylor-Water Tower Place, Chgo., 1980-83; dir. pub. merchandising Field Mus. of Natural History, Chgo., 1983—. Mem. Nat. Assn. Female Execs., Am. Booksellers Assn., Assn. Am. Mus., Am. Mgmt. Assn., Internat. Platform Assn., Mus. Store Assn. Roman Catholic. Club: Northwestern of Chgo. Office: Mus Stores Field Mus Natural Hist Roosevelt Rd and Lake Shore Dr Chicago IL 60605

STUART, ANN, technical writer, educator; b. Madisonville, Ky., Dec. 22, 1935; s. Peter Frank and Laura (Hord) S.; m. Raymond R. Poliakoff, Aug. 22, 1980. BA in Edn., U. Fla., 1958; MA in English, U. Ky., 1962; PhD in English, So. Ill. U., 1976. Tchr. Maderia Beach Jr. High Sch., St. Petersburg, Fla., 1958-59, Bourbon County High Sch., Paris, Ky., 1959-60, Henry Clay High Sch., Lexington, Ky., 1960-62; prof. tech. writing U. Evansville, Ind., 1962—, asst. dean Coll. Arts and Scis., 1986—, adminstrv. coordinator writing programs, 1985—, also dir. computer div.; lectr. various regional and nat. profl. orgns.; dir. computer edn. Vanderburgh Sch. Corp., U. Evansville, Ball Communications, Inc., Evansville, 1985—; adminstrv. coordinator writing programs U. Evansville, 1985—; cons. various local bus., 1982—; vis. prof. computer tech. Purdue U., West Lafayette, Ind., 1987—. Author: Writing and Analyzing Effective Computer System Documentation, 1984, Corresponding with Customers, 1985, The Technical Writer, 1987. Bd. dirs. Evansville Arts and Edn. Council, 1972-75, Harlaxton Soc., Evansville, 1981-85. Mem. Ind. Corp. Sci. and Industry, Nat. Council Tchrs. of English, Assn. Tchrs. Tech. Writing, Modern Language Assn., Phi Kappa Phi, Delta Kappa Gamma. Club: Musicians of Evansville (pres. 1972-78). Avocations: art museums, performing arts, architecture. Home: 7200 Monroe Ave Evansville IN 47715 Office: U Evansville 1800 Lincoln Ave Evansville IN 47714

STUART, GORDON EDGAR, dentist; b. St. Louis, Feb. 7, 1951; s. Gordon Edgar and Iris (Bass) S.; m. Marcia Jane Meier, Aug. 5, 1977; children: Gordon Geoffrey, Catherine Marie. BA cum laude, St. Louis U., 1973, grad. fellow in organic chemistry, 1973; DDS magna cum laude, U. Mo., Kansas City, 1978. Gen. practice dentistry St. Louis, 1978—; dentist II St. Louis Health/Hosp., 1978-83, Michael Sch. Handicapped Children, St. Louis, 1980-81. Mem. ADA, Acad. Gen. Dentistry, Psi Omega, Am. Chem. Soc., St. Louis Dental Research Group. Republican. Lutheran. Avocations: profl. drummer, swimming, small homes project. Office: 9811 W Florissant Saint Louis MO 63136

STUART, RICK DAVID, info systems specialist; b. Lancaster, Pa., Sept. 23, 1953; s. Harold Victor and Carrie Carlotta (Loser) S. BA in History, U. Cin., 1977, postgrad., 1977-79; MEd, Xavier U., 1987. Head dept. computer sci. Southwestern Bus. Coll., Cin., 1982-83; lectr. info. sci. Xavier U., Cin., 1984, asst. dir. acad. computing, 1983—; computer researcher 3RC, Inc., Cin., 1977-82; software reviewer Edn. Tech. Publs., Englewood, N.J., 1983-84. Contbr. author: DPMA Model Curriculum, 1985, (chpt.) Computer Applications in Emerging Third World Nations, 1987. Participating judge Engrs. and Scis. of Cin. Sci. Fairs, 1984. Recipient Cert. of Recognition Data Processing Mgmt. Assn., 1984. Mem. DECUS. Avocations: writing science fiction, conflict simulations, chess. Office: Schmidt Hall Xavier Univ 3800 Victory Parkway Cincinnati OH 45207

STUART, STEVEN LEE, facilities engineer; b. Fulton, Ill., Feb. 17, 1944; s. Harold John and Ethel (Campbell) S.; m. Linda Jo Edwards, June 16, 1966; children: Bradd Michael, Laura Lynn. AA, Clinton (Iowa) Community Coll., 1966. Test technician Collins Radio Co., Cedar Rapids, Iowa, 1966-69; test engr. Gen. Elec. Co., Morrison, Ill., 1969-75; facilities engr. Case IH, East Moline, Ill., 1975—; cons. in field, Fulton, Ill. Dir. Youth Ctr., Fulton, 1971-73; treas., campaign chmn. Community Fund, Fulton, 1973-76; trustee Presbyn. Ch., Fulton, 1979-81, elder, 1981-84. Named One of Outstanding Men Am., Jaycees, 1973. Mem. Soc. Mfg. Engrs. Republican. Avocations: sailing, painting, skiing, tennis, golf. Home: 1414 9th Ave Fulton IL 61252 Office: Case IH 1100 3d St East Moline IL 61244

STUART, WILLIAM CORWIN, federal judge; b. Knoxville, Iowa, Apr. 28, 1920; s. George Corwin and Edith (Abram) S.; m. Mary Elgin Cleaver, Oct. 20, 1946; children: William Corwin II, Robert Cullen, Melanie Rae, Valerie Jo. B.A., State U. Iowa, 1941, J.D., 1942. Bar: Iowa 1942. Practice in Chariton, 1946-62, city atty., 1947-49; mem. Iowa Senate from, Lucas-Wayne Counties, 1951-61; justice Supreme Ct. Iowa, 1962-71; Judge U.S. Dist. Ct., So. Dist. of Iowa, Des Moines, 1971-76, sr. judge, 1976—. Served as aviator USNR, 1943-45. Recipient Distinguished Alumni award Iowa U. Coll. Law, 1987, Outstanding Service award Iowa Acad. Trial Lawyer, 1987. Mem. ABA, Iowa Bar Assn. (spl. award 1987), Am. Legion, All For Iowa, Order of Coif, Omicron Delta Kappa, Phi Kappa Psi, Phi Delta Phi. Presbyn. Club: Mason (Shriner). Home: 216 S Grand St Chariton IA 50049 Office: 103 US Court House 1st and Walnut Sts Des Moines IA 50309

STUBBLEFIELD, CHARLES THATCHER, gynecologist/obstetrician; b. Watertown, S.D., Apr. 28, 1932; S. Kirk Irwin and Mildred Mattie (Smith) S.; m. Bertha Anne Smith, Aug. 21, 1955; children: Jennifer L., Stephen T., John C. BA, U. Kans., 1955; MD, U. Kans., Kansas City, 1958. Cert. Am. Bd. Ob-Gyn. Intern Kansas City (Mo.)Gen. Hosp., 1958-59, resident in ob-gyn, 1961-64; practice medicine specializing in ob-gyn Kansas City, Kans., 1964—; asst. prof. medicine U. Kans. Med. Ctr., Kansas City, 1976—; staff Bethany Med. Ctr., Kansas City, 1964—, chief dept. ob-gyn, 1970-75; staff Providence-St. Margaret's Hosp., Kansas City, 1964—. Contbr. articles to profl. jours. and mags. Founding mem. Planned Parenthood, Kansas City, 1967; active Citizen's Adv. Com., Sch. Dist. 500, Kansas City; mem. adv. bd. Kansas City chpt. ARC; vol. Kansas City dist. Boy Scouts Am., 1969—; life mem. Kans. State PTA, Kansas City, 1971; active Men's Club Trinity United Meth. Ch., Kansas City. Served to capt. USAF, 1959-61. Named to Centennial Hall Fame Wyandotte High Sch., Kansas City, 1986. Fellow Am. Coll. Ob-Gyn; mem. AMA, Greater Kansas City Obstetrics/Gynecol. Soc., Wyandotte County Med. Soc., Kans. State Med. Soc. Republican. Avocations: photography, stained glassmaking, sports, music, gardening. Home: 1900 N 40th St Kansas City KS 66102 Office: Assocs for Female Care 8917 Parallel Pkwy Kansas City KS 66112

STUBBLEFIELD, JOHN WILLIAM, cosmetology schools and salon executive; b. Decatur, Ill., Oct. 20, 1940; s. John H. and Florence E. (Chrysler) S.; m. Brenda J. Hyle, June 4, 1961 (div. Dec. 1980); children: Kristi, John J., Lisa, Stacy; m. Kathy E. Farrier, Oct. 20, 1984. Student Milliken U. Dir., Decatur Sch. Cosmetology, 1963-67; pres. Mr. John's Sch. Cosmetology, Decatur, 1967-83, Mr. John's Schs. of Cosmetology Inc., Decatur and Springfield, Ill., 1983—, Champaign, Ill., 1987—; dir. lic. testing services, 1982-83. Chmn. Maroa Bicentennial Com. (Ill.), 1975-76; commr. Lincoln Trails council Boy Scouts Am., Decatur, 1979—; advisor Jr. Achievement, Decatur, 1973-75, Ill. Dept. Corrections Vast Program, Decatur, 1973-74. Recipient Silver Beaver award Boy Scouts Am., 1981, awards Ill. Jaycees, 1977, 78. Mem. Ill. Hairdresser and Cosmetology Assn. (1st v.p. 1982-84, pres. 1984-86, dir. 1980-84), Ill. Cosmetology Council (vice chmn. 1982-83). Methodist. Lodge: Kiwanis (dir. Decatur). Home: 5384 Wilcar Ct Decatur IL 62521 Office: Mr Johns Sch Cosmetology Inc 1745 E Eldorado Decatur IL 62521

STUBING, PETER ROBERT, psychiatrist; b. Ellsworth, Maine, July 6, 1930; s. Fredrick Jacob and Avis (Dennett) S.; m. Kathryn Jeanne Spahr, Sept. 10, 1986; children: Jeanne, David, Michael. BA, Yale U., 1957; MD, U. Fla., 1961. Diplomate Am. Bd. Psychiatry and Neurology. Psychiatrist U. Ill., 1965—, asst. prof., 1965-72, assoc. prof., 1972—, dir. mental health, 1980—; cons. Champaign County (Ill.) Mental Health Clinic., 1969—. Served to cpl. U.S. Army, 1949-52, Korea. Mem. Am. Psychiatric Assn., Ill. Psychiatric Soc. Roman Catholic. Avocations: cross country skiing, bicycling.

STUCKER, GILLES ALFRED EUGENE, real estate company executive; b. Paris, Mar. 21, 1947; came to U.S., 1971; s. Alfred G.E. and Suzie M. S.; m. Jan F. DeWitt, Aug. 18, 1973; children—Gilles A.E., Benjamin D. Degree in internat. affairs, Ecole Superieure de Commerce de Paris, 1970; M.B.A., Cornell U., 1973. Asst. mgr. adminstrn. Goldman Sachs, N.Y.C., 1977-78; v.p. corp. controller Cantor Fitzgerald, N.Y.C., 1978-79; v.p. corp. planning Forest City Enterprises, Cleve., 1979-80; sr. v.p. fin. Forest City Enterprises, 1980—. Fulbright scholar, 1971-73. Mem. Fin. Execs. Inst., Am. Inst. C.P.A.s, Urban Land Inst. Home: 11586 River Moss Strongsville OH 44136 Office: Forest City Enterprises Inc 10800 Brookpark Rd Cleveland OH 44130

STUCKER, WILLIAM ERVIN, dentist; b. Billings, Mont., Feb. 15, 1923; s. Albert Ervin and Mary Matilda (Birck) S.; m. Rose Mary Reddy, June 7, 1947; children: Joanne E. Stucker Beyer, Robert A., Lisa M. Stucker Johnstone. AB, Hanover Coll., 1949; DDS, Ind. U., 1955. Traffic mgr. USN, Argentia, Newfoundland, 1946-50; purchasing agt. Pinker Constrn. Co., Madison, Ind., 1950; pvt. practice dentistry Madison, 1955—. Pres. Jefferson County Parochial Sch. Bd., Madison, 1965, Phi Gamma Delta House Corp. Hanover Coll., 1982; treas. Madison Regatta; chmn. bd. Jefferson County Health Dept., Madison, 1961—; mem. Jefferson County Medicare Adv. Bd., Madison. Served to lt. USN, 1942-46, capt. res. ret. Mem. Ind. Dental Assn. (bd. trustees 1967-78, leadership award 1979, honor award 1981), Omicron Kappa Upsilon. Roman Catholic. Lodge: KC (Faithful

Navigator). Home: 402 W First St Madison IN 47250 Office: 205 W Main St Madison IN 47250

STUCKEY, RICHARD JORIAN, accounting company executive; b. Reading, Eng., Jan. 6, 1943; came to U.S., 1965; s. Derek Richard and Gladys Muriel (Saunders) S.; m. Lois Ilene Engel, July 3, 1976. BS with gen. honors, U. London, 1965; MBA, Stanford U., 1967.Cons., Arthur Andersen & Co., San Francisco, 1967-76, world hdqrs. mgr. advanced practices, Chgo., 1976-81, ptnr., 1981—; lectr. Golden Gate U., San Francisco, 1974-76; speaker mini/microcomputer systems, factory automation and computer integrated mfg. Mem. Assn. for Computing Machinery, Soc. Mfg. Engrs., Stanford Grad. Sch. Assn., King's Coll. London Assn. Clubs: Cliff Dwellers, Chgo. Yacht. Contbr. articles in field to profl. publs. Home: 2101 N Bissell St Chicago IL 60614 Office: Arthur Andersen & Co 33 W Monroe St Chicago IL 60603

STUCKI, JACOB CALVIN, pharmaceutical company executive; b. Neillsville, Wis., Nov. 30, 1926; s. Benjamin and Ella S.; m. Naomi Bersch, Nov. 24, 1948; children—Marcia, Heidi, J. Christopher. B.S., U. Wis., 1948, M.S., 1951, Ph.D., 1954. Research endocrinologist, William S. Merrell Co., 1954-57; research endocrinologist Upjohn Co., Kalamazoo, 1957-60, mgr. endocrinology research, 1960-61, mgr. pharmacology research, 1961-68, asst. dir. biochem. research, 1968-69, dir. adminstrn. and support ops., 1969-81, corp. v.p. pharm. research, 1981—; mem. acad. corp. liaison program NRC; bd. dirs. NRC Space Applications Bd. Bd. dirs., trustee, pres. Lift Found.; bd. dirs., pres., treas. Planned Parenthood Assn. Kalamazoo County, Inc.; chmn. housing task force Community Services Council/Community Chest; bd. dirs. Kalamazoo Arts Council; mem. human subjects instl. rev. bd. Western Mich. U.; bd. govs. Rackham Found., Mich. State U.; mem. econ. adv. council Mich. Democratic party. Served with USN, 1944-46. Mem. AAAS, Soc. Exptl. Biology and Medicine, Endocrine Soc., Kalamazoo Math and Sci. Ctr. (bd. advisors), Project Mgmt. Inst., Nat. Assn. Biomed. Research (bd. dirs.), Pharm. Mfrs. Assn., Indsl. Research Inst., Internat. Assn. Study of Interdisciplinary Research, Gamma Alpha, Sigma Xi. Contbr. numerous articles to profl. jours. Office: Upjohn Co Pharm Research Div 7000 Portage Rd Kalamazoo MI 49001

STUCKI, WARREN WILLIS, broadcast engineer; b. Helena, Mo., Nov. 1, 1921; s. William W. and Ella May (Thomann) S.; m. Georgia Lee Blakley, Jan. 9, 1943; children—Warren Douglas, Roger Blake. Student Northwest Mo. State Tchrs. Coll., 1939-40, U. Utah, 1943-44. Radio mechanic Am. Airlines, St. Joseph, Mo., 1946-47, St. Joseph Aviation Sales, 1947; owner Airadio Service, St. Joseph, 1947-48; engr. Sta. KFEQ, KFEQ-TV; with Sta. KFEQ, 1948-72, chief engr., 1969-72; chief engr. Sta. KXCV-FM, Northwest Mo. State U., 1972—; guest lectr. Served in U.S. Army, 1942-45. Recipient Bohlken award Northwest Mo. State U., 1980. Mem. Soc. Broadcast Engrs. (sr. charter mem.), Nat. Inst. Cert. Engring. Techs. (sr. engring technician). Baptist. Office: Sta KXCV Northwest Mo State U Maryville MO 64468

STUCKY, MARVIN WAYNE, automobile manufacturing company executive; b. Decatur, Ind., Oct. 22, 1932; s. Ivan N. and Hilda (Beeler) S.; m. Patricia Louise Lockhart, May 24, 1958; children: William Vincent, David Brian, Eric Randall. BS, Purdue U., 1954; MBA, Harvard U., 1959. Purchase analyst Ford Motor Co., Dearborn, Mich., 1959-67; v.p. numerous divs. Am. Motors Corp., Detroit and Southfield, Mich., 1967-83; v.p. civic and govtl. affairs Am. Motors Corp., Southfield, 1983—; bd. dirs. Automotive Hall of Fame, Midland, Mich. Mem. Detroit area council Boy Scouts Am.; bd. assocs. Adrian (Mich.) Coll.; bd. dirs. French Sch. Detroit, Bus. Consortium for the Arts. Served to lt. (transp. corps) U.S. Army, 1954-56. Named Outstanding Young Man of Yr. Outstanding Young Americans Found., CHgo., 1968. Mem. Soc. Automotive Engrs., Traffic Safety Now (exec. com.), Motor Vehicle Mfrs. Assn., Hwy. Users Fedn., The Am. Coalition for Traffic Safety, Greater Detroit C. of C., Econ. Club Detroit. Club: Harvard Bus. Sch. Detroit. Office: Am Motors Corp 27777 Franklin Rd Southfield MI 48034

STUDEBAKER, DAVID ALAN, data processing executive; b. South Bend, Ind., Sept. 25, 1942; s. Albert Joseph and Delores Anne (Davidson) S.; m. Karen Kay Hamersley, June 13, 1965; children: Rebecca Anne, Christopher David. BSME, Purdue U., 1965; MBA, U. Chgo., 1976. EDP mgr. Comtrac, Columbus, Ohio, 1969-71; systems cons. Zettler Software, Columbus and Chgo., 1971-72; ops. mgr. Metridata-Chgo., 1972-73; dir. systems and programming Chgo. Transit Authority, 1973-76; dir. sales, engring. Digital Systems House, Batavia, Ill., 1976-84; pres. Studebaker Tech. Inc., Glen Ellyn, Ill., 1984—. Co-author: (audio tapes) How to Use Your Computer with CP/M, 1982, 1983. Commn. mem. Glen Ellyn Recreation Commn., 1979-83; sch. bd. v.p. Dist. 41 Sch. Bd., Glen Ellyn, 1983—. Mem. Assn. Computing Machinery (chpt. pres. 1967-68), Council of Logistics Mgmt., IEEE Computer Soc., Microcomputers in Meeting Planning. Avocations: reading, stained glass work, philately. Office: Studebaker Tech Inc 346 Taft Ave Glen Ellyn IL 60137

STUDER, WILLIAM JOSEPH, library executive; b. Whiting, Ind., Oct. 1, 1936; s. Victor E. and Sarah G. (Hammersley) S.; m. Rosemary Lippie, Aug. 31, 1957; children: Joshua E., Rachel Marie. B.A., Ind. U., 1958, M.A., 1960, Ph.D. (Univ. fellow), 1968. Grad. asst. div. Library Sci., Ind. U., 1959-60, reference asst., 1960-61; spl. intern Library of Congress, 1961-62, reference librarian, sr. bibliographer, 1962-65; dir. regional campus libraries Ind. U., Bloomington, 1968-73; assoc. dean univ. libraries Ind. U., 1973-77; dir. libraries Ohio State U., Columbus, 1977—; mem. Library Services and Constrn. Act Adv. Com. of Ind., 1971-76, Adv. Council on Fed. Library Programs in Ohio, 1977-85, chmn., 1980-81; mem. ARL Office Mgmt. Studies Adv. Com., 1977-81, ARL Task Force on Nat. Library Network Devel., 1978-83, chmn., 1981-83, com. on preservation, 1985—, task force on scholarly communication, 1983-87, bd. dirs., 1981-84; mem. adv. com. Library of Congress Network, 1981—. Contbr. articles to profl. jours. Trustee OCLC, Inc., 1977-78; bd. dirs. OHIONET, 1977-87, chmn., 1980-82, 86-87, treas., 1983-86; treas. Monroe County (Ind.) Mental Health Assn., 1968-76; active Mental Health Social Club, 1971-73; budget rev. com. United Way, 1975-77; bd. dirs. Mental Health Assn. Recipient citation for participation MARC Insts., 1968-69; Louise Maxwell award Ind. U., 1978. Mem. ALA, Ohio Library Assn. (dir. 1980-83), Assn. Coll. and Research Libraries (bd. dirs. 1977-81, com. on activities model for 1990 1981-82), Am. Soc. Info. Sci., AAUP, Acad. Library Assn. Ohio, Phi Kappa Phi (pub. relations officer 1982-83, sec. 1983-85), Phi Eta Sigma, Alpha Epsilon Delta, Beta Phi Mu. Home: 724 Olde Settler Pl Columbus OH 43214 Office: Ohio State U William Oxley Thompson Meml Library 1858 Neil Ave Mall Columbus OH 43210-1286

STUDT, KURT HENRY, dentist; b. St. Louis, June 25, 1941; s. Harold Henry and Dorothy Helen (Fauth) S.; m. Janet Kay Doherty, Nov. 20, 1971; children: Gregory, Jennifer Denise, Elizabeth Kay. BA, Washington U., St. Louis, 1963, DDS, 1966; MS in Oral Diagnosis, U. Iowa, 1972. Diplomate Am. Bd. Oral Medicine. Commd. capt. USAF, 1966, advanced through grades to col., 1984; dental intern USAF, Washington, 1966-67; gen. dental officer USAF, Athens, Greece, 1967-70; dental resident USAF, Iowa City, 1970-72; gen. dental officer USAF, Riverside, Calif., 1972-76; ret. USAF, 1976; gen. practice dentistry St. Louis, 1976—; Dental cons. Faith Hosp., St. Louis, 1976—. Merit badge counsellor Boy Scouts Am., St. Louis, 1986; pres. Ascension Sch. Bd., Chesterfield, Mo. 1986. Fellow Acad. Gen. Dentistry; mem. ADA, Mo. Dental Assn., Greater St. Louis Dental Soc. (speakers. bur. dir. 1986), Acad. Oral Medicine, Xi Psi Phi. Republican. Roman Catholic. Avocations: tennis, reading, walking. Office: 1040 N Mason Rd Suite 103 Saint Louis MO 63141

STUDWELL, WILLIAM EMMETT, librarian; b. Stamford, Conn., Mar. 18, 1936; s. Alfred Theodore and Mary Alice (Baker) S.; m. Ann Marie Stroia, Aug. 28, 1965; 1 dau., Laura Ann. BA, U. Conn., 1958, MA, 1959; MLS, Cath. U. Am., 1967. Tech. abstracter Library Congress, Washington, 1963-66; asst. editor decimal classification office, 1966-68; head librarian Kirtland Community Coll., Roscommon, Mich., 1968-70; head/prin. cataloger No. Ill. U., DeKalb, 1970—; mem. U.S. Adv. Com. to Chemistry Sects., Universal Decimal Classification, 1968-72; chmn. adv. group Library Research Ctr., Urbana, Ill., 1982-84; advisor subject headings subject cataloging div., Library Congress, 1984—. Author: Chaikovskii, Delibes, Stravinski, 1977, Christmas Carols, 1985, Adolphe Adam and Leo Delibes, 1987, Ballet Plot Index, 1987; contbr. over 50 articles music history and library sci. to profl. jours. Co-founder Infertility Forum Support Group, Rockford, Ill., 1978. Mem. Ill. Assn. Coll. and Research Libraries (exec. bd. 1980-85, newsletter editor 1980-85), Ill. Library Assn. (editor 1986-87, bd. dirs. 1986-87), Librarians for Social Responsibility. Lodge: Kiwanis. Home: Rural Route 1 Box 88A Sycamore IL 60178 Office: No Ill U Univ Libraries DeKalb IL 60115

STUEBE, DAVID CHARLES, steel products manufacturing company executive; b. Racine, Wis., May 29, 1940; s. Edwin C. Stuebe and Henrietta (Dryanski) Stuebe Tunnell; m. Joy L. Laughlin, Aug. 23, 1986; children: David C., Kelly Ann, Ginger, Kelly Catherine, Jon. B.B.A., U. Notre Dame, 1962. C.P.A., Ill. Audit mgr. Arthur Andersen, Chgo., 1962-75; v.p.-fin. School Products div. Schering Plough Inc., 1975-76, 80; pres. Arno Adhesives div. Schering Plough Inc., 1976-79; v.p. fin.-adminstrn. Carpetland, Merrillville, Ind., 1980-81; v.p. fin. MSL Industries, Inc., Lincolnwood, Ill., 1981-84; chmn. MSL Industries, Inc., Oak Brook, Ill., 1982—, pres., chief exec. officer, 1984-87, also bd. dirs.; chmn., chief exec. officer Laughlin & Flynn, Inc., Barrington, Ill., 1987—. Vice pres., bd. dirs. Ill. Assn. Retarded Citizens, Chgo., 1971-75. Mem. Ill. Soc. C.P.A.s, Am. Inst. C.P.A.s. Club: Metropolitan (Chgo.); DuPage (Oak Brook). Home: 1632 Mirror Lake Dr Naperville IL 60540 Office: Laughlin & Flynn Inc 1300 Grove Ave Suite 105 Barrington IL 60010

STUHLREYER, PAUL AUGUSTUS, III, cultural organization administrator; b. Cin., Oct. 7, 1952; s. Paul Augustus Stuhlreyer Jr. and Genevieve Adams (Edwards) Hilmer; m. Janet Barbara Vidal, May 21, 1977; children: Hillary Brooke, Erica Adams, Ryan Edwards. BS, Miami U., Oxford, Ohio, 1974; MBA, U. Va., 1976. Dir. investor relations Baldwin-United Group, Cin., 1976-78; treas. Diem-Wing Paper Co., Cin., 1978-85; pvt. practice venture capitalist Cin., 1985-87; mng. dir. Cin. Opera Assn., 1987—; chmn. Uvonics Co. Inc., Columbus, Ohio, 1985—; adj. instr. Coll. of Mt. St. Joseph, Cin., 1981—. Mem. AMBA, Gyro Club Internat. Republican. Episcopalian. Club: Cin. Country. Avocations: hunting, swimming, golf. Home: 740 Crevelings Ln Cincinnati OH 45226 Office: 1241 Elm St Cincinnati OH 45210

STUKER, THOMAS ROBERT, training company executive; b. Oak Park, Ill., Dec. 20, 1953; s. Alan Arthur and Marian Jane (Osterburg) S.; m. Susan Marchese, Oct. 18, 1975; 1 child, Timothy. Student, Coll. Dupage, Glen Ellyn, Ill., 1972, Mankato (Minn.) State U., 1973-74. Salesman Hembrough Motors, Rockford, Ill., 1975-78; dist. mgr. Poorman Douglas Corp., Portland, Oreg., 1978-80; pres. Stuker & Assocs., Lombard, Ill., 1980—. Author: Motivation Through Education, 1985. Republican. Roman Catholic. Avocations: deep sea fishing, wine collecting, tennis. Home: 11702 Glen Eagles Ln Belvidere IL 61008 Office: Stuker & Assocs 1919 S Highland Ave Suite 129D Lombard IL 60148

STULBERG, BERNARD NATHAN, orthopaedic surgeon, research scientist; b. Kalamazoo, Aug. 2, 1948; s. Julius and Esther (Lieberman) S.; m. Carolyn Sue McComish, Oct. 16, 1976; children: Jonah James, Benjamin, Micah Adam. BA, U. Mich., 1970, MD, 1974. Diplomate Am. Bd. Orthopaedic Surgery. Intern U. Chgo., 1974-75, basic surg. residency, 1974-76; orthopaedic surgery residency Hosp. for Spl. Surgery, N.Y.C., 1979; fellow in orthopaedic research Hosp. for Spl. Surgery, 1980; staff surgeon in orthopaedic surgery Cleve. Clinic Found., 1980—, staff scientist dept. musculoskeletal research, 1985—; cons. Johnson & Johnson Orthopaedic Div., Inc., New Brunswick, N.J., 1983—, DePuy Corp. Devel. Core Biopsy Needle, Warsaw, Ind., 1986—. Contbr. several articles to profl. jours. Mem. AMA, Am. Acad. Orthopaedic Surgeons, Orthopaedic Research Soc., Am. Rheumatism Assn., N.Y. Acad. Scis., Mid-Am. Orthopaedic Assn., Interurban Arthritis Assn., Ohio Med. Assn., Ohio Orthopaedic Soc., Ohio Rheumatism Soc., Cleve. Orthopaedic Club, Cleve. Acad. Medicine, Cleve. Rheumatism Soc., Internat. Knee Soc., Phi Beta Kappa, Phi Kappa Phi, Pi Sigma Alpha. Jewish. Avocations: music, violins, tennis, long distance running. Home: 7470 Water Fall Trail Chagrin Falls OH 44022 Office: Cleve Clinic Found 9500 Euclid Ave Cleveland OH 44106

STULL, JAMES FREDERICK, furniture manufacturing company executive; b. Joliet, Ill., Sept. 9, 1940; s. Oland Glenn and Lucille (Poates) S.; B.S., U. Ill., 1963; M.B.A., Northwestern U., 1976; m. Victoria Howorth Butler, Feb. 26, 1977; children by previous marriage: Anna, Sally, Ashley. Adminstrv. assoc. Rodman Job Corps Center, New Bedford, Mass., 1965-67; asst. dean men Northwestern U., Evanston, Ill., 1967-69, dean of students, 1970-75; mgr. ednl. services Chgo. Bd. Trade, 1969-70; dir. market devel. Morrison-Knudson Co., Inc., Boise, Idaho, 1976-85; with Steelcase Inc., Grand Rapids, Mich., 1985—. Bd. dirs., pres. Boise Philharmonic Assn., 1977-79; bd. dirs. Idaho Park Found., 1977-85. Served with U.S. Army, 1963-69. Home: 2930 Lake Dr SE East Grand Rapids MI 49506 Office: Steelcase Inc 901 44th St SE Grand Rapids MI 49508

STULL, WALTER JOHN, marketing executive; b. Sioux City, Iowa, June 1, 1943; s. Carroll Dell and Frances Joy (Marquart) S.; m. Jane Elizabeth Oden, June 18, 1967; children: Matthew Prescott, Emily Ardelle. BA, U. Nebr., 1966; MBA, Coll. St. Thomas, 1983. Math. tchr. Fresno (Calif.) Unified Schs., 1967-69, San Francisco Unified Schs., 1969-72, Austin (Minn.) Pub. Schs., 1972-78; with mgmt. and tng. dept. Data 100/Northern Telecom, Mpls., 1978-84; sales engr. Tektronix, St. Paul, 1984-85; gen. mgr. Comtrol div. Control Systems, St. Paul, 1985—. Author: (reference manual) Display Phone PBX Handbook, 1983. Treas. PTA, Bloomington, 1984-85; fellowship com. Unitarian Universalists, Mpls., 1986—. Democrat. Unitarian Universalist. Avocations: jogging, golfing, tennis, reading, travel.

STUMP, EARL SPENCER, psychologist; b. Parkersburg, W.Va., Dec. 12, 1943; s. Amos Earl Stump and Harriet Gertrude (White) Stiff; m. Ann Chadwick, Sept. 30, 1967 (div. 1985); 1 child, Andrea Renee; m. Joan Irene Croft, Sept. 28, 1985. BA, Ohio State U., 1966; MS in Corrections, Xavier U., 1971. Lic. pyschologist, Ohio. Psychiat. aide Harding Hosp., Worthington, Ohio, 1965-67; psychology trainee Athens (Ohio) State Hosp., 1966-67; psychologist Ohio Dept. Rehab. and Correction, Columbus, 1967—; supr. psychology Chillicothe (Ohio) Correctional Inst., 1977—; pvt. practice psychology Columbus Mental Health Clinic, Columbus, 1976-77; instr. psychology Hocking Tech. Coll., Chillicothe, 1973-78; instr. diagnostics Ohio U., Athens, 1983-84. Vol. radio operator Athens Marathon, 1983-86, Red Cross Marathon, Athens, 1986, O'Blennis Charity Golf Tournament, Athens, 1983. Mem. Am. Correctional Assn., Cen. Ohio Psychol. Assn., State Assn. Psychologists and Psychology Assts., Biofeedback Soc. Ohio, Athens County Amateur Radio Assn., Antique Wireless Assn., Am. Radio Relay League, Titanic Hist. Soc. Home: 15 N May Ave Athens OH 45701 Office: Chillicothe Correctional Inst 15802 SR 104 Chillicothe OH 45601

STUMPF, LOWELL C(LINTON), artist-designer; b. Canton, Ill., Dec. 8, 1917; s. Oral Baxter and Marie (Dawson) S.; grad. Chgo. Acad. Fine Arts; student L'Ecole de Beaux Arts, Marseille, France, 1945; m. Jacqueline Jeanne Charlotte Andree Lucas, Sept. 5, 1945; children—Eric Clinton, Roderick Lowell. Staff artist Internat. Harvester Co., Chgo., 1939-42, Nugent-Graham Studios, Chgo., 1945-47; free lance artist, designer, Chgo., 1947—. Served with AUS, 1942-45; NATO USA, ETO. Mem. Artist Guild Chgo., Internat. Platform Assn. Contbr. sci. and tech. illustrations, maps to Compton's Pictured Ency., Rand McNally & Co., Macmillan Co., Scott, Foresman & Co., Ginn & Co. textbooks, World Book Year Book, Field Enterprises Sci. Yearbooks, Childcraft Ann. and Library, World Book Dictionary. Home and Office: 7N161 Medinah Rd Medinah IL 60157

STUMPF, ROBERT MARION, II, educator, cultural organization administrator; b. Portsmouth, Ohio, Jan. 5, 1947; s. Robert Marion and Constance Louise (Queen) S.; m. Janet Bates, Dec. 28, 1970 (div. Jan. 1981); children: Robert Marion III, Sarah Dawn; m. Susan Michelle Betz, Oct. 31, 1981. BS, Ohio State U., 1971; MEd, U. Toledo, 1976. Cert. profl. edn. Substitute tchr. Worthington (Ohio) City Schs., 1982-83; instr. composition Columbus (Ohio) Tech. Inst., 1983-85; pres. Leopold Stowkowski Soc. Am., Columbus, 1983—; English tchr. Dept. Youth Services, Columbus, 1985—; adj. prof. speech, Franklin U., Columbus, 1983—. Dir. recordings by Leopold Stowkowski, 1984—; editor Maestrino Mag., 1984—. Democrat. Avocations: chess, classical music. Home: 870 N Meadows Ct #E Columbus OH 43229

STURGEON, MYRON T(HOMAS), geology educator; b. Salem, Ohio, Apr. 27, 1908; s. Thomas Hendricks and Leona (Borton) S.; m. Carolyn Mae Wolter, Aug. 11, 1946; children: Lynn Carol, Sharon Leona. AB, Mount Union Coll., 1931; MA, Ohio State U., 1933, PhD, 1936. From asst. to assoc. prof. geology Mich. State Normal Coll., Ypsilanti, 1937-46; from asst. to assoc. prof. geology Ohio U., Athens, 1946-78, prof. emeritus of geology, 1978—; asst. geologist Ohio Div. Geol. Survey, Columbus, summers, 1947-58. Contbr. articles to profl. jours. Mem. Geol. Soc. Am., Ohio Acad. Scis., Paleontol. Soc., Internat. Paleontol. Soc., Internat. Oceanographic Found. Home: 13220 Robinson Ridge Rd Athens OH 45701 Office: Ohio U Dept Geol Scis Porter Hall Athens OH 45701

STURGEON, PAULINE RUTH, editor; b. Centralia, Mo., Sept. 4, 1907; d. William Arthur and Ruth Jane (Cook) Sturgeon. B.J., U. Mo.-Columbia, 1929, B.A., 1977. Staff, Centralia Fireside Guard, 1956-60; feature writer Columbia Daily Tribune (Mo.), 1960-64; editor The Russell Record, (Kans.), 1967—. Mem. Kans. Press Women, Fedn. Press Women, DAR, Sigma Delta Chi. Club: Bus. and Profl. Women's. Address: The Russell Record 802 N Maple St Russell KS 67665

STURGES, SIDNEY JAMES, pharmacist, educator, investment and development company executive; b. Kansas City, Mo., Sept. 29, 1936; s. Sidney Alexander and Lenore Caroline (Lemley) S.; m. Martha Grace Leonard, Nov. 29, 1957 (div. 1979); 1 child, Grace Caroline; m. Gloria June Kitch, Sept. 17, 1983. BS in Pharmacy, U. Mo., 1957, post grad., 1959; MBA in Pharmacy Adminstrn., U. Kans., 1980; PhD in Bus. Adminstrn., Pacific Western U., 1980; cert. in Gerentology, Avila Coll., 1986. Registered pharmacist, Mo., Kans.; registered nursing home adminstr., Mo.; cert. vocat. tchr., Mo. Pharmacist, mgr. Crown Drugs, Kansas City, Mo., 1957-60; pharmacist, owner Sav-On-Drugs and Pharmacy, Kansas City, 1960-62; ptnr. Sam's Bargain Town Drugs, Raytown, Mo., 1961-62; pharmacist, owner Sturges Drugs DBA Barnard Pharmacy, Independence, Mo., 1962—; pres., owner Sturges Med. Corp., Independence, Mo., 1967-1977, Sturgess Investment Corp., Independence, 1967-1978, Sturwood Investment Corp., Independence, 1968—, Sturges Agri-Bus. Co., Independence, 1977—, Sturges Devel. Co., 1984—; instr. pharmacology Penn Valley Community Coll., 1976-84; instr., lectr. various clubs and groups. Contbr. articles to profl. jours. Bd. dirs. Independence House, 1981-83; mem. Criminal Justice Adv. Commn., Independence, 1982—. Recipient Outstanding award Kans. City Alcohol and Drug Abuse Council, 1982. Mem. Mo. Sheriffs Assn., Mo. Pharm. Assn. (pharmacy dr. 1981), Mo. Found. Pharm. Care, U. Mo. Alumni Assn. Home: 16805 Cogan Rd Independence MO 64055 Office: Sturges Co 13701 E 35th St Independence MO 64055

STURM, DIETER HANS, publicist, special effects expert; b. Milw., Sept. 15, 1955; s. Dieter Hans and Gertrude Norma (Zielke) S.; m. Marrietta Sturm, 1986. Student U. Wis.-Milw., 1973-75, Marquette U., 1974-76. Proto-type design, prodn. engr. Venture Computer Systems, New Berlin, Wis., 1972-73; dir. promotions and pub. relations Malrite Broadcasting Co., Milw., 1973-81; pub. relations mgr. Playboy Clubs Internat., Lake Geneva, Wis., 1981-82; corp. pub. relations dir. TSR, Inc., Lake Geneva, 1982—; pres. Sturm's Spl. Effects Internat., Inc., 1987—. Author (manual): Laser Light Entertainment Optic Techniques, 1982. Mem. steering com. Toys for Tots program; judge Jr. Achievement Talent Search. Mem. Visual Music Alliance, Creative Communications Council, Spl. Effects Internat. (founder), Broadcasters Promotion Assn. Democrat. Lutheran. Home: Route 2 Box 242 Lake Geneva WI 53147 Office: PO Box 756 Lake Geneva WI 53147

STURM, MICHEL ROBERT, dentist; b. Parris Isle, S.C., Nov. 2, 1947; s. Robert Joseph and Patricia Ann (Cass) S.; m. Diana Jo Anderson, Dec. 30, 1972; children: Kelly J., Andrew R., Abbey K., Cassie R., Charles M. BS in Biology and Chemistry, Xavier U., 1969; DDS, Ind U., Indpls., 1973. Gen. practice dentistry Ft. Wayne, Ind., 1973—; mem. staff Luth. Hosp., St. Joseph's Hosp., 1977—. Contbr. Ind. Dental Jour. Bd. dirs. Am. Cancer Soc., Ft. Wayne, 1975; chmn. Harlan (Ind.) Town Fair, 1986; scoutmaster Boy Scouts Am., Anthony Wayne Council, 1984—. Mem. Acad. Operative Dentistry, ADA, Ind. Dental Assn., Isaac Knapp Dental Soc. (bd. dirs. 1981-83, 84—). Republican. Roman Catholic. Lodge: Rotary. Avocations: painting, reading, sculpturing in stone. Home: 18519 Killian Rd Spencerville IN 46788 Office: 4302 E State Fort Wayne IN 46815

STURM, ROBERT CHARLES, healthcare equipment buyer; b. Mankato, Minn., Oct. 14, 1944; s. Robert Russell and Mary Elizabeth (Berendt) S.; m. Karen Ann Dahlke, June 3, 1967; children: Megan Elizabeth, Joshua Robert. BS, St. John's U., Collegeville, Minn., 1972. Pharmacy purchasing agt. Golden Valley (Minn.) Health Ctr., 1972-74; pharm. sales rep. Organon, East Orange, N.J., 1974; mgr. equipment planning and procurement Health Cen. Inc., Mpls., 1974—. Pres. Immaculate Conception Home and Sch. Assn., Columbia Heights, 1984. Mem. Am. Hosp. Assn., Healthcare Materials Mgmt. Soc. Roman Catholic. Home: 5490 Matterhorn Dr Minneapolis MN 55432 Office: HealthOne 2810 57th Ave N Minneapolis MN 55430

STURROCK, IAN TYNDALE, university official; b. Birmingham, Ala., Dec. 22, 1943; s. Ian William and Margaret (Sloss) S.; m. Lynette Russell, Apr. 3, 1971; 1 child, Emily Margaret. B.S., Birmingham So. Coll., 1965; M.A., U. Ala., 1968, Ph.D., 1972. Cert. fund raising exec. Dir. recruitment Birmingham So. Coll., Ala., 1965-68, dean students, 1968-70; dir. inst. devel., Dickinson Coll., Carlisle, Pa., 1972-74; vice chancellor devel. U. Tenn., Chattanooga, 1974-80; v.p. devel. and univ. relations Bradley U., Peoria, Ill., 1980—. Author, producer ednl. TV series College Life, 1967. Contbr. articles to profl. publs., chpts. to books. Vice pres. fin. W.D. Boyce council Boy Scouts Am.; mem. exec. bd. First Federated Ch., Peoria; mem. Midwest Contbns. Forum. Mem. Council for Advancement and Support of Edn., Nat. Soc. Fund Raising Execs. (nat. bd. dirs. 1983—, pres. central Ill. chpt. 1982), Omicron Delta Kappa, Phi Eta Sigma, Kappa Delta Pi. Republican. Presbyterian. Clubs: Mount Hawley Country (Peoria); Creve Coeur. Lodge: Rotary. Office: Bradley U 1501 W Bradley Ave Peoria IL 61625

STURZ, JOHN EDWARD, media specialist; b. Oak Park, Ill., Mar. 18, 1949; s. Edward and Ruth Delores (Dahlberg) S.; m. Carol Lee Cottingham, Aug. 7, 1971; childred: Jill, Caryn. BS in Edn., No. Ill. U., 1971; MS in Edn., Eastern Ill. U., 1975; MLS, No. Ill. U., 1987. Asst. librarian Stephen Decatur High Sch., Decatur, Ill., 1971-73; librarian Argenta/Oreana (Ill.) High Sch., 1974; head librarian Barclay Pub. Library, Warrensburg, Ill., 1974-75; dir. audio-visual services Crown High Sch., Carpentersville, Ill., 1975-79; media specialist William Rainey Harper Coll., Palatine, Ill., 1979—. Mem. Ill. Assn. for Edn. Communications and Tech. (publs. editor 1984-86). Avocation: golf. Office: William Rainey Harper Coll Roselle and Algonguin Rds Palatine IL 60067

STUTESMAN, BARRY SCOTT, entertainment and broadcast producer; b. Flint, Mich., Nov. 18, 1953; s. Virgil Milton and Shirley Naomi (Popps) S.; m. Rhonda Marie Price, Apr. 11, 1987; children: Jessica Ann, Jason Kenneth. Grad. N.E. Mich. Acad. Broadcast Arts, 1971. Staff announcer Sta. WHSB, Alpena, Mich., 1971-72, Sta. WDBI, Tawas City, Mich., 1980-81; news dir. Sta. WBMB, West Branch, Mich., 1972-79, Sta. WKLT, Kalkaska, Mich., 1979-80, Sta. WJEB-WGMM, Gladwin, Mich., 1980; program dir. Cable Channel 13, Rose City, Mich., 1981-82, Sta. WBMB-WBMI, West Branch, 1983-84; gen. mgr. Great No. Recovery Inc., Rose City, 1982-83, v.p., 1982-83; producer B&B Prodns., Prudenville, Mich., 1982-83; co-creator, producer Mich. Record Rev., Lupton, Mich., 1984—. Producer: (half hour radio mag.) Spectrum, 1974 (honorable mention Mich. AP 1974), (daily cable TV series) Northern Michigan Horizons, 1983, (daily morning TV show) Good Morning Rose City, 1983; co-producer, writer: (daily satellite network radio series) Michigan Record Review, 1985. Campaign chmn. Ogemaw county USO, 1973-74. Recipient Outstanding Local News Coverage award Mich. AP, 1974. Home: Box 272 Rose City MI 48654 Office: Michigan Record Review 386 HIghland Pines Rose City MI 48654

STUTZ, I. HAROLD, manufacturing company executive; b. Cleve., Sept. 9, 1924; s. Maurice Edward and Hester Rachel (Sherman) S.; m. Hannah Zelda Kaufman, Apr. 12, 1951; children: Carol, Joanne, Ilene, Debra. BSME, Case Inst. Tech., 1949, MS in Indsl. Engring., 1954. Registered profl. engr., Cleve. Sr. engr. Gen. Electric Co., Cleve., 1952-65; mgr. prodn. Clevite Gould Inc., Cleve., 1965-72; pres. Bowes Mfg. Inc., Cleve., 1974—. Officer Religious Temple, Cleve., 1956—; bd. dirs. Council Smaller Enterprises,

Cleve. 1980-86; founding chmn. Ohio Small Bus. Council, Columbus, 1985-86. Mem. Case Inst. Tech. Alumni Assn. (mem. council 1986—, mem. adv. com. 1986—). Club: Case Inst. Tech. (Cleve.) (chmn. 1980-82). Avocations: golf, bridge, home remodeling. Office: Bowes Mfg Inc 28815 Aurora Rd Solon OH 44120

STWALLEY, WILLIAM CALVIN, chemistry and physics educator, science facility administrator, consultant; b. Glendale, Calif., Oct. 7, 1942; s. Calvin Murdoch and Diette Clarice (Hanson) S.; m. Mauricette Lucille Frisius, June 14, 1963; children—Kenneth William, Steven Edward. B.S., Calif. Inst. Tech., 1964; Ph.D., Harvard U., 1968. Asst. prof. U. Iowa, Iowa City, 1968-72, assoc. prof., 1972-75, prof. dept. chemistry, 1975—, prof. dept. physics and astronomy, 1977—, dir. Iowa Laser Facility, 1979—; program dir. NSF, Washington, 1975-76 (leave of absence); program chmn. Internat. Laser Sci. Conf., 1985, co-chmn., 1986, chmn., 1987; lectr. Chinese Acad. Scis., 1986. Editor books in field; contbr. more than 140 articles to profl. publs. Japan Soc. for Promotion of Sci. fellow, 1982; Sloan fellow, 1970-72; numerous grants in field, 1970—. Fellow Am. Phys. Soc. (sec.-treas. div. of chem. physics, 1984—); mem. Am. Chem. Soc., AAAS, Optical Soc. Am. Democrat. Avocations: comic books and cartoons, philately. Home: 141 Green Mountain Dr Iowa City IA 52240 Office: Univ of Iowa Dept of Chemistry Iowa City IA 52242-1294

STYBR, DENISE SWANSON, school psychologist; b. Kansas City, Mo., Dec. 25, 1956; d. Ernest William and Marie Julia (Votta) Swanson; m. David James Stybr, Jan. 26, 1980. BS, U. Ill., 1979; MA, Govs. State U., 1982. Cert. sch. psychologist. Intern psychologist Kankakee (Ill.) Sch. Dist., 1982-83; psychologist Prince George's County Pub. Schs., Upper Marlboro, Md., 1983-85, So. Will County Coop., Ill., 1986—; instr. Moraine Valley Community Coll., 1986. Mem. Nat. Assn. Sch. Psychologists, Ill. Sch. Psychologist's Assn., Alpha Sigma Alpha. Roman Catholic. Avocations: bridge, traveling, theater. Home: 190 Acorn Ridge Dr Frankfort IL 60423 Office: So Will County Coop 106 Tryon Channahon IL 60410

SUBICH, LINDA MEZYDLO, counseling psychology educator; b. Milw., Jan. 27, 1956; d. Ralph Joseph and Sylvia Lucille (Schultz) Mezydlo; m. Carl Brice Subich, Aug. 23, 1980. BS in Psychology, U. Wis., Milw., 1977; MA in Counseling Psychology, Ohio State U., 1979, PhD in Counseling Psychology, 1981. Lic. psychologist, Ohio. Asst. prof. counseling psychology U. Akron, Ohio, 1981-87, assoc. prof., 1987—. Contbr. articles to profl. jours.; ad hoc reviewer Jour. Counseling Psychology, Jour. Vocat. Behavior, 1985—. Provider workshop on stress mgmt. Wadsworth (Ohio) Fire Dept.; panel mem. Rape Awareness Program, Akron, 1986. Grantee Nat. Acad. Scis., 1986. Mem. AAUP, Am. Psychol. Assn., Phi Beta Kappa. Democrat. Roman Catholic. Avocations: cooking, cross country skiing, jogging, reading. Home: 258 S Portage Path Akron OH 44302 Office: U Akron Dept Psychology Akron OH 44325

SUBRAMANIAN, SETHURAMAN, scientist, researcher; b. Mattur, Tamilnadu, India, May 16, 1940; came to U.S., 1970, naturalized, 1978; s. P. Sethuraman and Rajalakshmi (Panchanathan) S.; m. Ananthi Gopala Krishnan, Jan. 29, 1969; children—Sumathi, Sukanya, Mekhala. B.Sc., U. Madras, India, 1960, M.Sc., 1965; Ph.D., Indian Inst. Tech., Kanpur, 1969; M.B.A., Ind. U. South Bend, 1985. Research assoc. U. Kans., Kansas City, 1970-74; research physicist Naval Med. Research Inst., Bethesda, Md., 1974-75; vis. scientist NIH, Bethesda, 1975-82; research scientist Miles Labs., Elkhart, Ind., 1982-84, sr. research scientist, 1984-86, staff scientist, 1986, supr. protein chemistry group, biotech. research and devel., 1987—. Contbr. articles to profl. jours. and chpts. to books. Fellow AEC, 1963-65, NRC, 1974-75. Mem. Am. Chem. Soc. (chmn. St. Joseph Valley sect. 1986), Am. Soc. Biol. Chemists (elected), Miles Sci. Forum (chmn. 1984). Avocations: reading, tennis, classical music. Home: 54648 Glenwood Park Dr Elkhart IN 46514 Office: Miles Labs Inc PO Box 932 Elkhart IN 46515

SUCHYTA, ROBERT PETER, accountant; b. Detroit, June 5, 1926; s. John and Rosalie (Cieslowski) S.; m. Marie Bernice Merecki; children: Mary Rose, Sharon Therese, Karen Lee, Julie Ann. BS in Acctg., U. Detroit, 1956, MBA in Acctg. and Fin., 1960. CPA, Mich. Acct. Chrysler Corp., Detroit, 1944-50, 53; dynamo operator and test engr. Gen. Motors, Detroit, 1954-56; sr. acct. Coopers & Lybrand, Detroit, 1956-63; factory acctg. supr. Walker Mfg. div. Tenneco, Jackson, Mich., 1964-68; controller Walker Mfg. div. Tenneco, Cambridge, Ont., Can., 1969-72; fin. specialist Walker Mfg. div. Tenneco, Racine, Wis., 1973—. Panel reviewer Racine area United Way, 1973—, mem. budget com., 1978—. Served with arty. U.S. Army, 1950-52. Mem. Am. Inst. CPA's, Nat.Mgmt. Assn. Republican. Roman Catholic. Lodge: KC. Avocations: photography, bowling, golf, camping. Home: 1115 Palamino Dr Racine WI 53402 Office: Walker Mfg Co div Tenneco Inc 1201 Michigan Blvd Racine WI 53402

SUCKOW, ROBERT WILLIAM, management consultant; b. Plymouth, Wis., June 26, 1919; s. William Frank and Anna (Schulz) S.; m. Mildred Lucille Thompson, Oct. 10, 1942 (dec. Jan. 1970); children: Roger Lee, Carolyn Ann, Bonnie Jean; m. Shirley Ann Bollhoefer, Jan. 1, 1972. AA, Sheboygan Bus. Coll., 1952; B Degree equivalent, Milw. Area Tech. Coll., 1985. Controller, office mgr. Plymouth Industrial Foods, Plymouth and Sheboygan, Wis., 1952-60; gen. office mgr. H.G. Weber & Co., Kiel, Wis., 1960-61; controller D.J. Peterson Co., Sheboygan, Wis., 1961-63; gen. office mgr. four plants Longview Fibre Co., Milw., 1963-78; pres., cons. R.W. Suckow & Assocs., Milw., 1978—; instr. U. Wis. Extension, Milw. and Madison, Wis., 1964-80; cons. Performax Internat. (div. Carlson Learning Co.), Mpls., 1981—; counselor, speaker Milw. Area Tech. Coll., Milw., 1963—, counselor, 1984—. Vol. speaker St. Luke's Hosp., Milw., 1978—. Served to lt. col. USAF, 1941-46, ETO. Fellow Acad. Cert. Adminstrv. Mgrs. (chmn. bd. regents 1979, life); mem. Internat. Adminstrv. Mgmt. Soc. (v.p. 1979-80, Merit award 1970, Diamond Merit award 1973, 300 Club award 1981, Ambassador award 1983), Wis. Profl. Speakers Assn., Am. Legion. Republican. Lutheran. Avocations: flying, swimming, scuba diving, camping, golf. Home and Office: 6035 N Alberta Lane Milwaukee WI 53217

SUDBRINK, JANE MARIE, sales and marketing executive; b. Sandusky, Ohio, Jan. 14, 1942; niece of Arthur and Lydia Sudbrink. B.S., Bowling Green State U., 1964; student in cytogenetics Kinderspital-Zurich, Switzerland, 1965. Field rep. Random House and Alfred A. Knopf Inc., Mpls., 1969-72, Ann Arbor, Mich., 1973, regional mgr., Midwest and Can., 1974-79, Canadian rep., mgr., 1980-81; psychology and ednl. psychology adminstrv. editor Charles E. Merrill Pub. Co. div. Bell & Howell Corp., Columbus, Ohio, 1982-84; sales and mktg. mgr. trade products Wilson Learning Corp., Eden Prairie, Minn., 1984-85; fin. cons. Merrill Lynch Pierce Fenner & Smith, Edina, 1986—. Mem. Am. Ednl. Research Assn., Nat. Assn. Female Execs. Lutheran. Home: 6730 Vernon Ave Edina MN 55436 Office: Merrill Lynch 3400 W 66th St Southdale Pl Suite 190 Edina MN 55436

SUDHEENDRA, RAO, cardio-thoracic and peripheral vascular surgeon; b. Bangalore, India, Aug. 25, 1941; came to U.S., 1965, naturalized, 1978; s. K. Ragothama and R. Nagaratnamma Rao; m. Sarala S. Krishna, Sept. 19, 1971; children—Deepak, Kiran. Diploma in Intermediate Sci., Chemistry, Botany and Zoology with honors, U. Mysore, India, 1958, B.Medicine, B.Surgery, 1964. Diplomate Am. Bd. Surgery. Houseman in medicine, surgery, pediatrics, radiology, ophthalmology, anesthesiology, obstetrics, gynecology, dermatology and dental surgery Med. Coll. Hosps., Mysore, 1964-65; sci. officer dept. surgery Atomic Energy Establishment India, Bombay, 1965; intern St. Frances Community Health Ctr., Margaret Hague Maternity Ctr., Jersey City, 1965-67; resident in surgery, clin. instr. surgery Methodist Hosp. Bklyn., SUNY-Kings County Hosp., Bklyn., 1967-71; resident in thoracic and cardiovascular surgery La. State U.-Charity Hosp. La., New Orleans, 1971-73; clin instr. surgery La. State U. Med. Ctr., New Orleans, 1972-73; assoc. attending surgeon div. cardiovascular surgery Hamot Med. Ctr., Erie, Pa., 1973-76; cons. cardiovascular surgery Shriner's Hosp. for Crippled Children, Erie, 1973-76; chief dept. thoracic and cardiovascular surgery, dir. vascular lab. Trumbull Meml. Hosp., Warren, Ohio, 1976—; active attending thoracic and cardiovascular surgery, dir. vascular lab. St. Joseph Riverside Hosp., Warren, 1976—; cons. thoracic and cardiovascular surgery Warren Gen. Hosp., 1976—; attending surgeon Youngstown Hosp. Assn., Ohio, 1982—; dir. Angiosonics Vascular Lab., Warren. Bd. dirs. Trumbull County br. Eastern Ohio chpt. Am. Heart Assn. Fellow ACS, Internat. Coll. Surgeons, Am. Coll. Angiology; mem. James D. Rives Surg. Soc., Ohio Thoracic Soc., Trumbull County Med. Soc., Ohio State Med. Assn., AMA, Am. Assn. Critical Care Medicine, Non-Invasive Vascular Technologists (adv. bd. local chpt.), World Med. Assn. (assoc.). Avocation: tennis. Office: 1216 E Market St Warren OH 44483

SUDOMA, ALBERT LOUIS, marketing professional; b. Streator, Ill., Sept. 5, 1952; s. Albert John and Joanne Frances (Sankovich) S.; m. Nancy Marie Trojan, May 19, 1979; children: Julie Marie, Jeffrey Louis (dec.), Scott Jeffrey. Research scientist Christian Hansen's Lab., Milw., 1976-77, supr. quality control, 1977-79, product specialist, 1979-80, product specialist-agriculture, 1980-82, product mgr., 1982-84, product mktg. mgr., 1984-86, mktg. mgr., 1986—; mem. chmn. Nat. Feed Ingredient Corp., Des Moines, 1984-85, sec. div. S.I. Tech. Inst., 1984-86, prof., 1981-85, chmn. subcoms., 1984—, v.p., 1987—. Inventor in field. Mem. Community council Sudden Infant Death Syndrome, Milw., 1982-83, contact parent, 1982—. Recipient award for Outstanding Achievement, Christian Hansen's Lab., Inc., 1986. Mem. Nat. Feed Ingredient Assn. (chmn. 1984—, sec. 1985-86, v.p., 1986—), Am. Feed Ingredient Assn., Am. Dairy Sci. Assn., Animal Sci. Assn. Avocations: fishing, sports. Home: W225 N2641 Alderwood Ln Waukesha WI 53186 Office: Chr Hansen's Lab Inc 9015 W Maple St Milwaukee WI 53214

SUEDHOFF, CARL JOHN, JR., lawyer; b. Ft. Wayne, Ind., Apr. 22, 1925; s. Carl John and Helen (Lau) S.; m. Carol Mulqueeney, Apr. 10, 1954; children—Thomas Lau, Robert Marshall, Mark Mulqueeney. B.S., U. Pa., 1948; J.D., U. Mich., 1951. Bar: Ind. 1951. Assoc. mem. firm Hunt & Mountz, Ft. Wayne, 1951-54; ptnr. Hunt, Suedhoff, Borrorr & Eilbacher and predecessors, Ft. Wayne, 1955—; officer, dir. Inland Chem. Corp., Ft. Wayne, 1952-81; pres., dir. Lau Bldg. Co., Ft. Wayne, 1951-78, S.H.S. Realty Corp., Toledo, 1960-78; officer, dir. Inland Chem. P.R., Inc., San Juan, 1972-81, Northeast Cogen, Inc., others. Mem. Allen County Council, 1972-76, pres., 1974-76; mem. Allen County Tax Adjustment Bd., 1973-74, N.E. Ind. Regional Coordinating Council, 1975-76; bd. dirs. Ft. Wayne YMCA, 1961-63. Served with AUS, 1943-45. Mem. VFW (comdr. 1958-59), ABA, Ind. Bar Assn., Allen County Bar Assn., Beta Gamma Sigma, Phi Delta Phi, Psi Upsilon. Republican. Lutheran. Clubs: Univ. Mich. (pres. 1965-66), Friars, Ft. Wayne Country, Mad Anthony's. Office: 900 Paine Webber Bldg Fort Wayne IN 46802

SUERTH, MICHAEL WILLIAM, insurance executive; b. Chgo., Sept. 8, 1955; s. Robert Francis and Mary Ann (Murphy) S.; m. Elizabeth Knittel, 1987. BS, No. Ill. U., 1977; student, Northwestern U., 1987—. CPA, Ill. Asst. treas. Interstate Nat. Corp., Chgo., 1980-86, asst. to chmn., 1987—. Mem. Am. Inst. CPA's, Ill. CPA Soc. Republican. Roman Catholic. Avocations: golf, running, tennis, water sports. Home: 50 Windsor Dr Lincolnshire IL 60015 Office: Interstate Nat Corp 55 E Monroe St Chicago IL 60603

SUESS, MANFRED E., manufacturing executive, engineer; b. Munich, Sept. 25, 1940; came to U.S., 1950; s. John A. and Erna K. (Mohr) S.; m. Gail F. Hoeft, June 13, 1964; children: Barbara J., Michael E., Steven J., Laura K., Jeanette M., Christopher J. BS in Metall. Engring., U. Wis., 1964, MS in Metall. Engring., 1965. Registered profl. engr., Wis. Various positions Caterpillar Tractor Co., Peoria, Ill., 1965-70; mgr. materials engring. Koehring Co., Milw., 1970-78; pres., founder Technimet Corp., New Berlin, Wis., 1978—. Mem. ASTM, Soc. Automotive Engrs. (chmn. off-hwy. material com. 1976-77), Am. Soc. Metals (dir. Milw. chpt. 1974-77), Am. Welding Soc. Avocations: raising a family, pro-life activities, golf. Office: Technimet Corp 2345 S 170th St New Berlin WI 53151

SUGDEN, RICHARD LEE, pastor; b. Compton, Calif., Apr. 13, 1959; s. L. Fred Sugden and Nancy Jane (Motherwell) Coulter; married, June 1981; children: Richard Lee II, Ryan Leon. BA, Pensacola (Fla.) Christian Coll., 1981. Ordained pastor, 1985. Assoc. pastor Chippewa Lake Bapt. Ch., Medina, Ohio, 1981-84; dir., evangelist Victory Acres Christian Camp, Warren, Ohio, 1985; asst. pastor Bible Bapt. Temple, Campbell, Ohio, 1985—; del. pastors' sch. 1st Bapt. Ch., Hammond, Ind., 1982—. Mem. Christian Law Assn., Buckeye Ind. Bapt. Fellowship. Republican. Avocations: gardening, home improvements. Home: 3208 Powersway Youngstown OH 44502 Office: Bible Bapt Temple 230 Lettie Ave Campbell OH 44405

SUGG, REED WALLER, lawyer; b. Morganfield, Ky., Dec. 1, 1952; s. Matt Waller and Iris (Omer) S. BA, Furman U., 1975; JD, Vanderbilt U., 1978. Bar: Mo. 1978, Ill. 1979, U.S. Ct. Appeals (8th, 9th and 7th cirs.), U.S. Dist. Ct. (ea. dist.) Mo., U.S. Dist. Ct. (so. dist.) Ill. Atty. Coburn, Croft, Shepherd & Herzog, St. Louis, 1978-79, Shepherd, Sandberg & Phoenix, St. Louis, 1979—. Mem. ABA, Bar Assn. Met. St. Louis, Christian Legal Soc., Lawyers Assn. St. Louis, Aviation Ins. Assn., Lawyer-Pilots Bar Assn., Phi Beta Kappa. Republican. Presbyterian. Clubs: Mo. Athletic, Westborough Country (St. Louis). Avocations: basketball, golf, tennis, reading. Home: 6 Cricket Ln Saint Louis MO 63144 Office: Shepherd Sandberg & Phoenix One City Centre Suite 1500 Saint Louis MO 63101

SUH, HWI YOL, psychiatrist; b. Chouju, Chonpuk, Rep. of Korea, Aug. 8, 1936; came to U.S., 1967; s. Sangsoon and Bokrye (Rhee) S.; m. Hehsoo, June 4, 1967; children: Jimmy, Jane, Eileen, Christine. Degree in liberal arts and scis., Seoul Nat. U., 1957, MD, 1961. Resident Ind. U. Med. Ctr., Indpls., 1968-71, staff psychiatrist, 1971—. Served to capt. Rep. of Korea Army, 1961-67, Korea. Mem. Am. Psychiat. Assn., Ind. Psychiat. Assn., Soc. Friends of Korean Study at Ind. U. (pres. 1986—). Office: Ind U Med Ctr 1001 W 10th St Indianapolis IN 46202

SUHADOLNIK, GARY C., state senator; b. Cleve., Apr. 20, 1950; s. John Frank and Eleanor (Vorthman) S.; m. Nancy Christine Davis, 1969; children: Jena, Timothy. BS, Cleve. State U., 1973. Foreman trainee Jones and Laughlin Steel Corp., 1969-71; mfg. engr. Gen. Electric, 1971-74; indsl. engr. Republic Steel Corp., 1974—; councilman City of Parma Heights, Ohio, 1978-80; state senator State of Ohio, Columbus, 1981—. Office: Office of State Senate State Capitol Bldg Columbus OH 43215 *

SUHRHEINRICH, RICHARD F., federal judge; b. 1936. B.S., Wayne State U., 1960; J.D. cum laude, Detroit Coll. Law, 1963. Bar: Mich. Assoc. Moll, Desenberg, Purdy, Glover & Bayer, 1963-67; asst. prosecutor Macomb County, 1967; ptnr. Rogensues, Richard & Suhrheinrich, 1967; assoc. Moll, Desenberg, Purdy, Glover & Bayer, 1967-68; ptnr. Kitch, Suhrheinrich, Saurbier & Drutchas, 1968-84; judge U.S. Dist. Ct. (ea. dist.) Mich., Detroit, 1984—. Office: US Dist Ct US Courthouse 231 W Lafayette Blvd Room 235 Detroit MI 48226

SÜHS, HERMANN JOSEF, restauranteur; b. Neufeld, Austria, June 22, 1947; came to U.S., 1976; s. Hermann Josef and Charlotte (Schwarzott) S.; m. Rosita Inge Welk, Aug. 6, 1980; m. Martha J. Carlson, Oct. 3, 1982; 1 child, Roman Alexander. Cert. pastry chef, Konditorei Zum Roten Apfel, 1964; cert. chef, Hotel Sacher Sch., 1966. Exec. chef Hotel Anna Purna, Kathmandu, Nepal, 1977-78; exec. sous chef Innisbrook Resort, Tarpon Springs, Fla., 1978-80; exec. chef Grand Traverse Hilton, Traverse City, Mich., 1981-84, Hawks Cay, Marathon, Fla., 1984-85; owner, chef Hermann's European Café and Chef's Deli, Cadillac, Mich., 1984—. Mem. Downtown Devel. Assn., 1985-86. Served with Austrian Army, 1964-65. Mem. NW Mich. Chef's Assn. (pres. 1982-83, chmn. apprenticeship com. 1985-86), Chaine de Rotisseur, Internat. Gourmet Club. Baptist. Avocations: tennis, scuba diving, traveling, skiing. Office: Culinary Cons Cadillac 214 N Mitchell Cadillac MI 49601

SULG, MADIS, corporation executive; b. Tallinn, Estonia, May 25, 1943; came to U.S., 1950; s. Hans Eduard and Erika (Turk) S.; m. Mary Diane Detellis, Dec. 30, 1967; children—Danielle Marie, Michaella Erika. S.B. in Indsl. Mgmt., MIT, 1965, S.M. in Mgmt., 1967. Cons. Barss, Reitzel & Assocs., Cambridge, Mass., 1970-71; mgr. planning and research Converse Rubber Co., Wilmington, Mass., 1971-75; dir. bus. planning and devel. AMF, Inc., Stamford, Conn., 1975-79; sr. v.p. planning and devel. Bandag, Inc., Muscatine, Iowa, 1978—; pres. Muscatine Natural Resources Corp., 1981—. Contbr. articles to profl. jours. Served with U.S. Army, 1968-70. Mem. Am. Inst. Decision Scis., Ops. Research Soc. Am., Planning Forum, Inst. Mgmt. Scis, Am. Mktg. Assn., Machinery and Allied Products Inst. (vice chmn. corp. planning council). Presbyterian. Club: Davenport Country (Iowa). Avocations: bridge; jogging; swimming. Home: 4855 Rambling Ct Bettendorf IA 52722 Office: Bandag Inc Bandag Center Muscatine IA 52761

SULLIVAN, ANTONY THRALL, foundation executive, consulting firm official; b. New Haven, Nov. 7, 1938; s. Francis Joseph and Hazel Mae (Thrall) S.; m. Marjory Elizabeth Kuhn, May 5, 1962; children—Sandra Lincoln, David Thrall. B.A., Yale U., 1960; M.A., Columbia U., 1961; Ph.D., U. Mich., 1976. History instr. Internat. Coll., Beirut, 1962-67; counselor U. Mich., Ann Arbor, 1968-69; program officer, corp. sec. Earhart Found., Ann Arbor, 1969—; dir. Near East Support Services, Ann Arbor, 1984—. Author: Thomas-Robert Bugeaud, France and Algeria, 1784-1849: Politics, Power and the Good Society, 1983. Contbr. articles to profl. jours. Mem. Middle East Studies Assn., Middle East Inst. Republican. Episcopalian. Club: Liberty Tennis. Home: 908 Westwood Ann Arbor MI 48103 Office: Earhart Found 2929 Plymouth Rd Suite 204 Ann Arbor MI 48105

SULLIVAN, BARBARA KATHRYN, social sciences teacher; b. Springfield, Ill., Oct. 7, 1948; d. Joseph and Sophia Ann (Yanko) Pristave; m. Richard Joseph Sullivan, June 18, 1971; children: Ryan Richard, Kristen Jane, Kevin Joseph. BS, Ill. State U, 1970; postgrad., Western Ill. U., 1978-80. Cert. social sci., English tchr., Ill. Tchr. St. Simeon Sch., Bellwood, Ill., 1970-71, St. Aloysius Sch., Springfield, 1972-76, Williamsville (Ill.) High Sch., 1980—; Dir. Youth and Govt., Williamsville, 1985—; workshop speaker Title I, Peoria, Ill., 1981, 82. Campaign vol. Ill. Rep. Mike Curran, Springfield, 1985—; sec. North Sangmon County Dems., Sherman, Ill., 1986; chmn. commn. Bicentennial Celebration U.S. Constitution City of Sherman. Mem. NEA, Ill. Edn. Assn., Williamsville Edn. Assn. (v.p. 1985-86), Taft Inst. for 2 Party Govt. (Taft Accolade 1986), Springfield Art Assn. Roman Catholic. Club: Bridge (Springfield). Avocations: golf, bridge, travel, cooking. Home: 808 Adrian Dr Sherman IL 62684 Office: Williamsville High Sch 900 S Walnut Williamsville IL 62693

SULLIVAN, BARRY, banker; b. Chgo., Mar. 7, 1939; s. J. Barry and Marta (Yokubat) S. B.S. in Bus. Adminstrn., Northwestern U., 1961. With trust dept. Continental Ill. Nat. Bank & Trust Co. of Chgo., 1961—, trust officer, 1970-80, 2d v.p., 1980—. Mem. Art Inst. Chgo. (life). Home: 15322 West Fair Ln Libertyville IL 60048 Office: Continental Ill Nat Bank & Trust Co Chgo 231 S LaSalle St Chicago IL 60697

SULLIVAN, BARRY F., banker; b. Bronx, N.Y., Dec. 21, 1930; s. John J. and Marion V. (Dwyer) S.; m. Audrey M. Villeneuve, Apr. 14, 1956; children: Barry, Gerald P., Mariellen M., Scott J., John C. Student, Georgetown U., 1949-52; B.A., Columbia U., 1955; M.B.A., U. Chgo., 1957. Exec. v.p. Chase Manhattan Bank, N.Y.C., 1957-80; chmn., chief exec. officer 1st Chgo.-1st Nat. Bank Chgo., Chgo., 1980—; dir. Am. Nat. Corp. Dir. Econ. Devel. Commn., Chgo.; mem. Chgo. Urban League, Chgo. Central Area Com.; trustee Art Inst. Chgo., U. Chgo. Served with U.S. Army, 1952-54; Korea. Mem. Assn. Res. City Bankers, Trilateral Commn. Roman Catholic. Avocations: golf; jogging. *

SULLIVAN, CAROLINE ELIZABETH, nursing educator; b. Milw., May 23, 1925; d. Chester and Agnes Walczak; m. Robert J. Sullivan, May, 13, 1950; children: Cynthia, Timothy, Michael. BS in Nursing, Marquette U., 1947; MS, U. Wis., Milw., 1980. GI asst. St. Luke's Hosp., Racine, Wis., 1972—, mem. faculty nursing, 1972-86; operating room supr. St. Joseph Hosp., Milw.; cons. Ostomy Club, Racine, 1980—; advisor student nursing Racine, 1975-86; organizer continuing edn. in nursing Marquette U., 1971; mem. study group S.E. Wis. Blood Pressure. Author textbook Nutrition for Nurses, 1983. Rep. Women's Civic Soc., Racine, 1983—; mem. Parish Council. Mem. Am. Nurses Assn. (dist. del. 1978), Nurses Found. Racine (sec.-treas. 1981-86), Marquette U. Nurses Alumni Assn. (pres. 1972). Roman Catholic. Avocations: tennis, square dance, computers, painting, needlework. Home: 5522 Willowview Rd Racine WI 53402

SULLIVAN, CLIFFORD WAYNE, architect; b. Wichita, Kans., Oct. 31, 1951; s. A. Wayne and Joylene E. (Mason) S.; m. Kathryn Lynn Boggs, Sug. 9, 1975; children: Kellie Anne, Brenton Wayne. Student, Johnson County Community Coll., 1969-72; BArch, Kans. State U., 1977. Registered architect, Kans. Pvt. practice residential design Shawnee, Kans., 1977-78; designer Ellswood-Smith-Carlson, Mission, Kans, 1978-80, Marshall and Brown, Kansas City, Mo., 1980-81; pvt. practice cons. Overland Pk., Kans.M, 1981; architect Butler Mfg. Co., Kansas City, Mo., 1981—. Mem. AIA, Nat. Muzzle Loading Rifle Assn., Kaw Valley Sportsmans Assn. (bd. dirs., chmn. black powder com.). Avocations: hunting, camping, muzzle loading competition, gun building, reading. Office: Butler Mfg Co 7400 E 13th Kansas City MO 64126

SULLIVAN, GARY WYATT, corporate communications executive; b. Panama City, Fla., Feb. 7, 1944; s. Thomas A. and Mable (Arnold) S.; m. Karin Temple, Mar. 3, 1979; 1 child, Brian E. Student, Gulf Coast Community Coll., 1962-63. Sales rep. Mead-Johnson Labs., Arlington, Va., 1969-70; nat. instr. Dare To Be Great, Inc., Orlando, Fla., 1970-72; dir. mktg. Topi Systems, Inc., Irvine, Calif., 1973-78; with project sales Elson-Alexandre, Los Angeles, 1978-80; gen. mgr. Best of Everything, Solvang, Calif., 1980-83; dir. tng. and edn. Dodson Group, Kansas City, Mo., 1983-85, dir. corp. communications, 1985—; instr. Johnson County Community Coll., Overland Park, Kans., 1985—. Co-chmn. Project L.I.F.E., Kansas City, 1985, 86; tng. coordinator United Way, Kansas City, 1985, 86, bd. dirs. for Johnson County, 1987; bd. dirs. Pan Ednl. Inst., Independence, Mo., 1986—. Served as sgt. U.S. Army, 1965-69. Mem. Internat. Platform Assn., Nat. Assn. for Corp. Speakers' Activities, Am. Soc. for Tng. and Devel. Republican. Methodist. Club: Toastmasters. Avocations: golf, fishing, spectator sports. Home: 12304 W 100 Pl Lenexa KS 66215 Office: Dodson Group 9201 Stateline Kansas City MO 64114

SULLIVAN, JAMES ALFRED, vocational educator; b. Fairmont, Wash., May 11, 1937; s. Joseph Patrick and Emily (Skiles) S.; m. Sylvia Messick, Apr. 29, 1967; children: Emily, Kathleen, Eileen Kerry. BS, Fairmont State Coll., 1959; MA, W.Va. U., 1964, DEd, 1968. Tchr. Wicomico (Md.) County Sch., 1960-64, area ctr. dir., 1964-67; from asst. prof. to assoc. prof. vocat. edn. So. Ill. U., Carbondale, 1967-74, prof., 1974—, chmn. dept. vocat. edn. studies, 1974-80. Author: Fundamentals of Fluid Mechanics, 1978, Plumbing: Installation and Design, 1980, Fluid Power, Theory and Applications, 2d edit. 1982. Mem. Am. Vocat. Assn. (life), Fluid Power Soc. (pres. St. Louis chpt. 1984). Lodge: Rotary (pres. Carbondale club 1985). Home: Rural Rt 1 Box 268 Carbondale IL 62901 Office: So Ill U Occupational Edn Carbondale IL 62901

SULLIVAN, JAMES STEPHEN, bishop; b. Kalamazoo, July 23, 1929; s. Stephen James and Dorothy Marie (Bernier) S. Student, St. Joseph Sem.; BA, Sacred Heart Sem.; postgrad., St. John Provincial Sem. Ordained priest, Roman Cath. Ch., 1955, consecrated bishop, 1972. Assoc. pastor St. Luke Ch., Flint, Mich., 1955-58; assoc. pastor St. Mary Cathedral, Lansing, Mich., 1958-60, sec. to bishop, 1960-61; assoc. pastor St. Joseph (Mich.) Ch., 1961-65, sec. to bishop, 1965-69; assoc. pastor Lansing, 1965, vice chancellor, 1969-72; aux. bishop, vicar gen. Diocese of Lansing, 1972-85, diocesan consultor, 1971-85; bishop Fargo, N.D., 1985—. Mem. Nat. Conf. Cath. Bishops (bishop's liturgical commn.). Address: Bishop's House 608 Broadway PO Box 1750 Fargo ND 58107 *

SULLIVAN, JOHN JOSEPH, bishop; b. Horton, Kans., July 5, 1920; s. Walter P. and Mary (Berney) S. Student, Kenrick Sem., St. Louis, 1941-44. Ordained priest Roman Catholic Ch., 1944; parish priest Archdiocese of Oklahoma City, 1944-61; nat. dir. extension lay vols. Extension Soc., Chgo., 1961-68; parish priest Tulsa, 1968-72; bishop Diocese of Grand Island, Nebr., 1972-77, of Kansas City-St. Joseph, Mo., 1977—. Vice pres. Extension Soc., Chgo. Office: Chancery Office PO Box 1037 Kansas City MO 64141 *

SULLIVAN, JOHN JOSEPH, animal husbandry executive; b. N.Y.C., Mar. 28, 1935; s. John and Lillian Healy S.; m. Joan U. Lackovich, June 8, 1963; children: Jude C., Mark T. BS, Rutgers U., 1957, PhD, 1964; MS, U.

Tenn., 1959. Research assoc. Am. Breeders Service, DeForest, Wis., 1963-67; assoc. dir. labs. and research Am. Breeders Service, DeForest, 1967-79, dir. labs. and research, 1979-81; v.p. prodn. Am. Breeders Service, DeForest, Wis., 1981—; v.p., bd. dirs. Cert. Semen Services, 1982—. Contbr. 41 articles to profl. jours. Mem. Am. Soc. Animal Sci., Soc. for Cryobiology, Soc. for the Study of Reproduction. Lodge: KC (Grand Knight DeForest 1977-78). Avocations: gardening, reading. Home: Rt 2 Box 294 Stevenson Dr Poynette WI 53955 Office: Am Breeders Service Box 459 DeForest WI 53532

SULLIVAN, JOHN LEONARD, public utility executive; b. Kansas City, Kans., Aug. 29, 1923; s. Leonard Riley and Katherine Bell (Singleton) S.; corr. student Internat. Accts. Soc., 1951-57; B.A., Ottawa U., 1982; m. Mary Jane Sechrest, Apr. 13, 1947; children—Kay Cheryl, Patricia Lee, John Michael. Acct., Kansas City, Suburban Water Co., Inc., 1947-57; acct. Water Dist. 1 of Johnson County, Mission, Kans., 1957-60, chief acct., office mgr., 1960-69, asst. controller, 1970, dir. fin., 1970—; acctg., fin. mgmt. cons. for small businesses, 1962—. Served with USNR, 1942-46. Mem. Adminstrv. Mgmt. Soc. (pres. Kansas City chpt. 1971-72, asst. area dir. 1972-73, Diamond Merit award 1975), Am. Water Works Assn., Nat. Assn. Accts., Overland Park (Kans.) C. of C. Presbyterian. Club: Sertoma (life, steering com. Theater in Park project 1976-78). Contbr. articles to Adminstrv. Mgmt., Public Works. Home: 9618 Nieman Pl Overland Park KS 66214 Office: Water Dist 1 Johnson County 5930 Beverly St Mission KS 66202

SULLIVAN, LORI LYNNE, artist; b. Stuttgart, Fed. Republic Germany, Mar. 8, 1958; came to U.S., 1961; d. William Eberly and Janice Ray (Walz) S. BFA, Stephens Coll., 1980. Scenic artist Chanhassen Diner, Mpls., 1982-84; resident designer Mixed Blood Theatre, Mpls., 1983-85; scenic artist Guthrie, Mpls., 1983-84; resident designer Quicksilver Stage, Mpls., 1983—; owner A Stroke of Brush, Mpls., 1986—. Illustrator: (book) Phenomena of the Belt/Pop Voice, 1985. Democrat. Avocations: music, dancing.

SULLIVAN, MARCIA WAITE, lawyer; b. Chgo., Nov. 30, 1950; d. Robert Macke and Jacqueline (Northrop) S.; m. Steven Donald Jansen, Dec. 20, 1975; children: Eric Spurlock, Laura Macke, Brian Northrop. BA, DePauw U., 1972; JD, Ind. U., 1975. Assoc. Arnstein, Gluck, Weisenfeld & Minow, Chgo., 1975-76; ptnr. Greenberger and Kaufmann, Chgo., 1976-86, Katten, Muchin & Zavis, Chgo., 1986—. Mem. ABA, Ill. Bar Assn., Chgo. Bar Assn. Avocations: bicycling, cross country skiing, gardening, camping. Office: Katten Muchen et al 525 W Monroe Chicago IL 60606

SULLIVAN, MARY JANE LEAHY, university program administrator; b. Bklyn., Mar. 11, 1939; d. George W. and Dorothy (Kane) Leahy; m. William Sullivan, Dec. 26, 1959 (div. 1982); children: Deirdre, George, Mary-Laura. BA, Hunter Coll., 1960; MA, Ball State U., 1976, EdD, 1980. Freelance writer N.Y. Daily News, N.Y.C., 1959-69; tchr. English Westfield (N.J.) Pub. Schs., 1973-75; coordinator continuing edn. So. Ill. U., Carbondale, 1978-85; dir. Ctr. for Continuing Edn. U. Wis., Superior, 1985—. Contbr. articles to profl. jours. Grantee NSF. Mem. LWV (units chairperson 1986—). Office: U Wis Ctr for Continuing Edn 1800 Grand Ave Superior WI 54880

SULLIVAN, MICHAEL ANDREW, human resource adminstrator; b. Anderson, Ind., Jan. 2, 1943; s. Arlus Garfield and Doris (Hale) S.; m. Sandra Kay Sparks, Oct. 16, 1965; children: Bradley Cullen, James Michael. BS in Indsl. Engring., Gen. Motors Inst., Flint, Mich., 1966; MBA, Ball State U., Muncie, Ind., 1985; postgrad., U. Mo., St. Louis, 1987—. Mfg. gen. supr. Delco Remy div. Gen. Motors Co., Anderson, 1970-75, mfg. gen. supt., 1975-84, maintenance supt., 1984, divisional coordinator tech. tng., 1984-85; asst. co-dir. region 3 UAW-Gen. Motors Human Resource Ctr., Indpls., 1985-86; co-dir. region 5 UAW-Gen. Motors Human Resource Ctr., St. Louis, 1986—. Mem. Anderson Area Post-Secondary Edn. Com., 1984-86; bd. chmn. East Christian Ch., Markleville, Ind., 1984, elder, 1982-85. Republican. Avocations: jogging, tennis, golf, reading. Home: 127 Dauphine Dr Lake Saint Louis MO 63367 Office: UAW-GM Human Resources Area Ctr PO Box 9603 507 S Cool Springs Rd O'Fallon MO 63366

SULLIVAN, THOMAS CHRISTOPHER, coatings company executive; b. Cleve., July 8, 1937; s. Frank Charles and Margaret Mary (Wilhelmy) S.; m. Sandra Simmons, Mar. 12, 1960; children: Frank, Sean, Tommy, Danny, Kathleen, Julie. B.S., Miami U., Oxford, Ohio, 1959. Div. sales mgr. Republic Powdered Metals, Cleve., 1961-65; exec. v.p. Republic Powdered Metals, 1965-70; pres., chmn. bd. RPM, Inc., Medina, Ohio, 1971-78; chmn. bd. RPM, Inc., 1978—; dir. Pioneer Standard Electronics, Inc., Cleve., Nat. City Bank, Cleve. Bd. dirs. Culver Ednl. Found. Served to lt. (j.g.) USNR, 1959-60. Mem. Nat. Paint and Coatings Assn. (bd. dirs., exec. com.), Young Pres. Orgn., Nat. Assn. Securities Dealers (bd. govs.). Roman Catholic. Office: 2628 Pearl Rd Medina OH 44256

SULLIVAN, THOMAS JAMES, financial services executive; b. Mpls., Dec. 25, 1946; s. Leo Patrick and Mildred Marie (Pelter) S.; m. Margaret Ann Saxton, Dec. 29, 1967 (div. May 1980); children: Robert, Sheryl. BME, U. Minn., 1967, MSME, 1974. Design engr. FMC Corp., Mpls., 1968-73, project engr., 1979-80, mgr. bus. group, 1980-86; v.p. Consolidated Design Inc., Mpls., 1973-79, Sullivan & Sullivan, Inc., Mpls., 1986—. Bd. dirs. Minn. Council on Chem. Dependency, 1986—; loaned exec. campaign, vol. allocation panel United Way Mpls., 1984—; reunion celebration co-chmn. Freedom Fest '86, Mpls., St. Paul, Minn., 1986; youth ministry parish council Parish Community St. Joseph's, New Hope, Minn., 1984-85; field advocate, marriage tribunal Archdiocese St. Paul, 1984—. Mem. U. Minn. Alumni Assn., Loaned Exec. Alumni Assn., Nat. Assn. Securities Dealers. Club: St. Mary's Teens Encounter Christ (St. Paul); Toastmasters (internat. asst. Area Gov. 1986—, Area Toastmaster of Yr. award 1984). Lodge: KC. Avocations: travel, skiing, boating, racquet sports. Home: 4180 Trenton Ln N Plymouth MN 55441 Office: Sullivan & Sullivan Inc 600 S County Rd 18 Suite 1525 Minneapolis MN 55426

SULLIVAN, WILLIAM DONALD, insurance executive; b. Monongahela, Pa., Jan. 19, 1939; s. William Donald and Esther Jane (Jones) S.; m. Beatrice Barbara Trolier, Aug. 12, 1961; children—Beth, Kelly. B.S., Pa. State U., State College, 1960; M.S. in Adminstrn., George Washington U., 1973. C.P.C.U., C.L.U. Mgmt. devel. supt. State Farm Ins. Co., Bloomington, Ill., 1972-74, div. mgr., Costa Mesa, Calif., 1974-78, exec. asst., Bloomington, 1978-80, dep. regional v.p., West Lafayette, Ind., 1980—. Pres. Jr. Achievement, Lafayette, Ind., 1984—; chmn. stewardship com. Covenent Presbyterian Ch., Lafayette, 1983-84; pres. Camelot Homeowners Assn., Lafayette, 1983-84; bd. dirs., exec. com. United Way, 1987—. Mem. Lafayette C. of C. (chmn. various coms. 1980—). Republican. Avocations: flying, golfing, fishing. Home: 1309 King Arthur Dr Lafayette IN 47905 Office: State Farm Ins Cos 2550 Northwestern Ave West Lafayette IN 47906

SULLIVAN, WILLIAM TIMOTHY (TIM), systems administrator; b. Cin., Sept. 7, 1961; s. Edward William and Frances Louise (Biddle) S.; m. Bridgett Ann Fewell, May 21, 1983. Student, Edgcliff Coll., 1979-81. Systems analyst Am. Computer Tech., Cin., 1981-82; v.p. techs. Mikal Corp., Cin., 1982-84; tech. systems analyst Optimal Decision Systems, Cin., 1985-87; group mgr. decision support ctr. Andrew Jergens Co., Cin., 1987—; cons. data processing Sullivan Assocs., Cin., 1982—. Contbr. articles to profl. jours.; inventor in field. Mem. Internat. Fidonet Assn. (system operator), Am. Mgmt. Assn., Mensa. Roman Catholic. Club: Optimal Eating Soc. Avocations: computers, science fiction, photography, reading. Home: 735 Delta Ave Cincinnati OH 45226 Office: Andrew Jergens Co 2535 Spring Grove Ave Cincinnati OH 45214

SULLY, IRA BENNETT, lawyer; b. Columbus, Ohio, June 3, 1947; s. Bernie and Helen Mildred (Koen) S.; m. Nancy Lee Pryor, Oct. 2, 1983. B.A. cum laude, Ohio State U., 1969, J.D. summa cum laude, 1974. Bar: Ohio 1974, U.S. Dist. Ct. (so. dist.) Ohio 1974. Assoc. Schottenstein, Garel, Swedlow & Zox, Columbus, 1974-78; atty. Borden Inc., Columbus, 1978-80; sole practice, Columbus, 1980—; instr. Real Estate Law Columbus Tech. Inst., 1983—; title ins. agt. Sycamore Title Agy., Columbus, 1983—. Commentator Sta. WOSU, Columbus, 1980. Treas. Leland for State Rep., Columbus, 1982, 84, Leland for City Atty., Columbus, 1985; asst. treas. Pamela Conrad for City Council, Columbus, 1979; bd. dirs. Research Franklin County Celeste for Gov., Columbus, 1978. Mem. Columbus Bar Assn., Ohio Bar Assn., ABA. Democrat. Jewish. Club: Agonis (Columbus). Avocations: running, coin collecting. Home: 305 E Sycamore Columbus OH 43206 Office: 844 S Front St Columbus OH 43206

SULSKI, JIM MICHAEL, writer; b. Chgo., Apr. 23, 1957; s. James Frank and Marian Irene (Jastrzembowski) S. BA in Journalism, Columbia Coll., Chgo., 1984; postgrad. in Communication, U. Ill., Chgo. Reporter Daily Calumet Newspaper, Chgo., 1977-82; videotex editor Keycom Electronic Pub., Chgo., 1982-86; freelance writer Chgo., 1982—. Contbr. articles to Chgo. Tribune, Crain's Chgo. Bus., others; author (short story) Hair Trigger Vol. III, 1984. Community coordinator S.E. Chgo. Hist. Project, 1982-84. Mem. Independent Writers of Chgo., Players Workshop of Second City. Roman Catholic. Avocations: running, computer scis. Home: 10643 Ave E Chicago IL 60617

SUMMERFELT, ROBERT C., animal ecology educator; b. Chgo., Aug. 2, 1935; s. Clarence Glenn and Ernestina Clara (Henschel) S; m. Deanne E. Walsh, June 25, 1960; children: Scott R., Steven T., Sloan M. BS, U. Wis., Stevens Point, 1957; MS, So. Ill. U., 1959; postgrad., Duke U., 1962; PhD, So. Ill. U., 1964. Lectr. So. Ill. U., Carbondale, 1962-64; asst. prof. Kans. State U., Manhattan, 1964-66; leader Okla. Coop. Fishery Unit, U.S. Fish and Wildlife Service, Stillwater, 1966-76; prof., dept. chmn. Iowa State U., Ames, 1976-85, prof. animal ecology, 1985—; vis. prof. So. Ill. U., 1963, Oreg. Inst. Marine Biol., Charleston, 1975, Utah State U., Logan, 1983. Contbr. articles to profl. jours, 1960-87; editor symposium proceedings, 1976, 87. Charter mem. Ill. River Conservation Council, Tulsa, 1975; active numerous environ. orgns., 1960—. Honor lectr. Mid-Am. State Univ. Assn., 1987. Fellow Am. Inst. Fishery Research Biologists; mem. Am. Fisheries Soc. (pres. edn. sect. 1981-82, Best Paper awards so. div., 1971, north-cen. div., 1981), Fisheries Soc. of Brit. Isles, Wildlife Disease Assn. Democrat. Lutheran. Avocations: fishing, hunting, canoeing, hiking, bird watching. Home: 2021 Greenbriar Circle Ames IA 50010 Office: Iowa State U Dept Animal Ecology Ames IA 50011

SUMMERS, FRANK LESLIE, psychologist, educator; b. Chgo.; s. Paul and Lillian (Ruttenberg) S.; m. Peggy Hallum, Aug. 23, 1966 (div. July 1974); 1 child, Kristen Maria; m. Renee Ann Schaffner, Aug. 15, 1981; 1 child, Nicole Ann. AB, U. Calif., Berkeley, 1966; MA, Columbia U., 1969, U. Chgo., 1972; PhD, U. Chgo., 1975. Intern psychology Michael Reese Hosp., Chgo., 1973-74; staff psychologist Cook County Hosp., Chgo., 1974-76; staff psychologist Northwestern U. Med. Ctr., Chgo., 1976-79, dir. research and tng. ext. amb. care, 1979-84, dir. ext. amb. care, 1984-86; pvt. practice psychologist Chgo., 1976—; assoc. prof. psychology Northwestern U.Med. Ctr., Chgo., Ill., 1982—. Contbr. numerous articles to profl. jours. Grantee Ill. State Dept. Mental Health, 1972. Mem. Am. Psychol. Assn., Chgo. Psychoanalytic Soc., Chgo. Assn. Psychoanalytic Psychology. Avocation: running. Office: 333 E Ontario 4509B Chicago IL 60611

SUMMERS, H. MEADE, JR., lawyer; b. St. Louis, Mar. 12, 1936; s. H. Meade and Josephine Elizabeth (Hicks) S.; m. Bonnie Barton, Sept. 2, 1960 (div. June 1987); children—H. Meade III, Elizabeth Barton. A.B., Brown U., 1958; J.D., U. Mich., 1961. Bar: Mo. 1961, U.S. Supreme Ct. Practice law St. Louis, 1961—; assoc. firm Thompson & Mitchell, St. Louis, 1960-67. Chmn. Mo. Adv. Council Hist. Preservation, 1973-78; mem. exec. com. Am. Revolution Bicentennial Commn. Mo., 1973-76; mem. Thomas Hart Benton Meml. Homestead Commn., 1976-77, co-founder, v.p., bd. dirs. Mo. Heritage Trust, Inc., 1976-79; mem. Old Post Office Landmark Com., St. Louis, 1969—; mem. exec. com. St. Louis-St. Louis County Commn. Equal Ednl. Opportunities, 1968-74; chmn. legis. com. City of Ladue, Mo., 1976—; bd. dirs. Landmarks Assn. St. Louis, 1969—, pres., 1972-73, counselor, 1973—; mem. St. Louis County Hist. Bldgs. Commn., 1971-83; bd. advisers Churchill Sch., St. Louis, 1977-87; bd. dirs. Jefferson Nat. Expansion Meml. Assn. (The Gateway Arch), 1986—; mem. Preservation Task Force East-West Gateway Coordinating Council, 1976-80, Gateway Preservation Com., 1981-83; vice chmn. Clayton Twp. Rep. Club, 1970-73; trustee Mo. Hist. Soc. 1978—, sec. 1984—. Mem. ABA, Mo. Bar Assn., St. Louis County Bar Assn., St. Louis Met. Bar Assn. (spl. com. on jud. reform 1975-76), Nat. Trust Hist. Preservation, Preservation Action, State Hist. Soc. Mo., Market Preservation Inc., Thomas Jefferson Soc.; St. Louis Met. C. of C. (bd. dirs., chmn. edn. com. 1964-74), Jefferson Nat. Expansion Meml. Assn., Beta Theta Pi, Phi Delta Phi. Lodge: Rotary. Home: 4400 Lindell Blvd Saint Louis MO 63108 Office: 7777 Bonhomme Ave Saint Louis MO 63105

SUMMERS, PHILLIP M., university official. Pres. Vincennes (Ind.) U. Office: Vincennes Univ 1002 N 1st St Vincennes IN 47591-9986 *

SUMMERS, ROBERT BRUCE, pharmacist, medical equipment company executive; b. Montclair, N.J., Feb. 7, 1954; s. Robert and Mavis (Bedwin) S.; m. Gail Paige Houser, June 21, 1980; 1 child, Christopher. BS in Pharmacy, U. Kans., 1978. Pharmacist Blaylock Drugs, Topeka, 1978, VA, Kansas City, Mo., 1978-84; sales specialist Boehringer Mannheim, Kansas City, 1984-85; assoc. product mgr. Boehringer Mannheim, Indpls., 1985-86, product mgr., 1986—. Active with First Bapt. Ch., Kansas City, 1981-83; vol. Am. Diabetes Assn., 1982-85. Mem. Am. Pharm. Assn., Am. Assn. Diabetes Educators, Midwest Pharm. Advt. Council. Democrat. Avocations: soccer, woodworking. Home: 6136 Drawbridge Ln Indianapolis IN 46250 Office: Boehringer Mannheim Diagnostics 9115 Hague Rd Indianapolis IN 46250

SUMMERSETT, KENNETH GEORGE, psychiatric social worker, educator; b. Marquette, Mich., Mar. 9, 1922; s. Frank Elger and Ruth H. (Fairbanks) S.; B.S., No. Mich. U., 1948, M.A. in Sociology, 1964; M.S.W., Wayne State U., 1951; student U. Puget Sound, 1942-43; m. Vivian M. Wampler, June 17, 1950; children—Nancy M., Kenneth R., Mark G. With Mich. Dept. Mental Health, 1950—, Marquette (Mich.) Child Guidance Clinic, 1950-52; chief psychiat. social worker Battle Creek (Mich.) Child Guidance, 1952-54; dir. social services Newberry (Mich.) State Hosp., 1954-66, dir., cons. social services, 1966-73, adminstrv. dir. community psychiatry, 1973—, mental health exec., 1975-82, dir. community services div., 1975-82; extension prof. sociology dept. No. Mich. U., 1962-70; lectr. sociology Lake Superior State Coll., 1968—; pvt. practice marriage and family counseling, 1982—; v.p. Luce County Social Services, 1985—; adv. com., bd. dirs. Mich. County Social Services, 1985—. Mem. Upper Peninsula Mental Health Planning Com., 1964-65, Mich. Task Force Com. Mentally Retarded, 1964-65, Upper Peninsula Mental Health Com. for Comprehensive Health Planning, 1972-75, Mich. Dept. Mental Health Legis. Planning Com. Release Planning, 1975—. Bd. dirs. Eastern Upper Penninsula Mental Health Clinic, v.p., 1970-72; bd. dirs. Luce County Extension Program, sec. bd., 1972-75; bd. dirs. Luce County Social Services, 1983—. Served with AUS, 1943-46. Certified marriage counselor. Mem. Nat. Assn. Social Workers (chmn. upper Peninsula chpt. 1957-59, 64-65, vice chmn. 1972-73), Acad. Cert. Social Workers, Mich. County Social Services Assn., Theta Omicron Rho. Clubs: Lions (pres. 1959-60), Elks (maj. projects chmn. 1968-70). Author various articles pub. in profl. jours. Home: PO Box 14 Newberry MI 49868

SUMMITT, GAZELLA ANN, university administrator; b. Wheatland, Ind., Feb. 27, 1941; d. John Ferrell and Rhoda Gazella (Howard) Granger; m. Paul Summitt, July 11, 1964; children: Krista, Dana. AS, Vincennes U., 1964; BS in Bus., St. Mary-of-the-Woods Coll., 1983. Sec. to pres. Vincennes (Ind.) U., 1960-63, administrv. asst. to pres., 1964-80, asst. to pres., affirmative action officer, 1980—. Mem. office occupations adv. com. Lincoln High Sch., Vincennes, 1981—, hist. rev. bd. Vincennes City Council, 1987—, fund raising com. Riley Children's Hosp.; chmn. women's div. Knox County United Fund, Vincennes, 1985-86; co-chmn. March of Dimes Walkathon, Vincennes, 1987. Recipient Woman of Yr. award Am. Bus. Women's Assn., 1974, Valiant Woman award Ch. Women United, 1982, Disting. Blue/Gold Award Vincennes U., 1982. Mem. Am. Assn. for Affirmative Action (sec. Region V 1986—). Democrat. Mem. Ch. of God. Avocations: walking, racquetball, reading, sewing. Home: 711 N 3d Vincennes IN 47591

SUMNER, BONNIE LEE, nurse; b. Wilkes-Barre, Pa., May 18, 1944; d. Allan Monroe and dorothy Louise (Young) Gregory; m. Peter William Grigas, Feb. 4, 1967 (div. Dec. 1974); children: Peter A. Grigas, Scott G. Grigas; m. Victor Dale Sumner; Dec. 10, 1982; 1 child, David Andrew Sumner. Student, Wyo. Seminary, Kingston, Pa., 1962-63; cert. lic. practical nurse, Wilkes-Barre Area Vocat. Tech. Sch., 1967; student social justice, social welfare, Olivet Nazarene Coll., 1982—. Indsl. nurse Marriner Mfg. Co., Methuen, Mass., 1967-69; obstetric nurse Bon Secour Hosp., Methuen, 1969-71, pediatric nurse, 1971-73, oncology nurse, 1973-75; mental health nurse Clarks Summit (Pa.) State Hosp., 1978-81; renal dialysis nurse St. Mary's Hosp., Kankakee, Ill., 1981—. Vol. ARC, Herscher, Ill., 1982; participant Kankakee Symphony Chorus, 1986. Mem. Internat. Soc. Peritoneal Dialysis. Republican. Baptist. Lodge: Lady of the Moose. Home: 1102 Jefferson St Apt 5 West Bend WI 53095

SUMRALL, PETER ANDREW, broadcasting executive; b. Manila, Oct. 17, 1953; s. Lester Frank and Louise (Layman) S.; m. Susan Unruh, Sept. 18, 1976; children: David, Angela, Andrew. Student pub. sch., South Bend, Ind. Announcer LeSea Broadcasting, South Bend, 1972-73, engr., 1973-74, producer, 1974-75, prodn. mgr., 1975-80, v.p., 1980-82, v.p., gen. mgr., 1982—. Republican. Avocations: jogging, photography. Office: LeSea Broadcasting Box 12 South Bend IN 46624

SUNDBERG, WILLIAM DUANE, sales engineer; b. Chgo., Sept. 10, 1952; s. Stanley W. and Alice L. (Walstad) S.; m. Diane L. Rutledge, Sept. 16, 1978; children: Erik, Brittany. BS in Phys. Sci., Northeastern Ill. U., 1975. Cert. secondary sch. tchr., Ill. Tchr. high schs. Chgo., 1976-80; sr. sales engr., asst. sales mgr. Gaertner Scientific Corp., Chgo., 1980—. Republican. Lutheran. Avocations: French horn, classical music, computer programming, jogging.

SUNDFORS, RONALD KENT, physics educator; b. Santa Monica, Calif., June 3, 1932; s. Earl Harold and Stella Marie (Silen) S.; m. Marjorie Gibson, June 9, 1963; children: Karen, Margaret, Emily. BS, Stanford U., 1954, MS, 1955; PhD, Cornell U., 1963. Teaching and research asst. Cornell U., Ithaca, N.H., 1958-63; postdoctoral appointee Washington U., St. Louis, 1963-65, asst. prof. physics, 1965-68, assoc. prof., 1968-76, prof., 1976—. Contbr. articles to profl. jours. Served to lt. (j.g.) USN, 1955-58. Mem. Am. Phys. Soc., Am. Assn. Physics Tchrs. Democrat. Episcopalian. Home: 304 N Central Ave Saint Louis MO 63105

SUNDT, THORALF MAURITZ, JR., neurosurgeon, educator; b. Wenonah, N.J., Apr. 3, 1930; s. Thoralf Mauritz and Elinor (Stout) S.; m. Lois Ethelwyn Baker, Oct. 26, 1952; children: Laura E., Thoralf Mauritz, John H. B.S., U. S. Mil. Acad., 1952; postgrad., U. Ariz., Tucson, 1955; M.D., U. Tenn.-Memphis, 1959. Diplomate: Am. Bd. Neurol. Surgery. Intern John Gaston Charity Hosp., Memphis, 1959-60; resident U. Tenn.-Memphis, 1960-63, Mayo Clinic, 1963-65; asst. prof. neurosurgery U. Tenn., Memphis, 1965-68; practice medicine specializing in neurosurgery Rochester; prof. neurosurgery Mayo Clinic, Rochester, 1976—, chmn. dept., 1980—, Vernon F. and Earline D. Dale prof. neurosurgery, 1978. Mem. editorial bd.: Jour. Neurosurgery, 1981—, chmn. editorial bd., 1986. Served to 1st lt. U.S. Army, 1952-55, Korea. Decorated Bronze Star with oak leaf cluster; NIH fellow, 1965. Fellow ACS; mem. Am. Acad. Neurol. Surgeons, Am. Assn. Neurol. Surgeons (chmn. sect. of cerebrovascular surgery), AMA (resident rev. com. for neurosurgery 1978—), Neurosurg. Soc. Australia (hon.). Republican. Episcopalian. Office: Mayo Clinic 200 1st St SW Rochester MN 55905 Home: 1406 Weatherhill Ct SW Rochester MN 55902

SUNDY, GEORGE JOSEPH, JR., refractories reliability engineer; b. Nanticoke, Pa., Apr. 22, 1936; s. George Joseph Sr. and Stella Mary (Bodurka) S.; m. Stella Pauline Miechur, May 21, 1966; children: Sharon Ann, George Joseph III. BS, Pa. State U., 1958. Research engr. Bethlehem (Pa.) Steel Corp., 1959-85; reliability engr. Flo-Con Systems, Inc., Champaign, Ill., 1985—. Patentee in field. Mem. Am. Ceramics Soc., Iron and Steel Soc. AIME, Keramos, Sigma Tau. Democrat. Roman Catholic. Home: 39 Woodfield W Rt 4 Box 5-C Mahomet IL 61853 Office: Flo-Con Systems Inc 1404 Newton Dr Champaign IL 61821

SUNKEL, ROBERT JACOB, manufacturing company executive; b. Paris, Ill., June 6, 1926; s. Jacob Roy and Mary Elizabeth (Mansfield) S.; divorced; children: Steven Ray, Debra Kay. BS in Music, Ind. U., 1950. Music tchr. Martinsville (Ill.) Schs., 1950-52; sales, owner Men's Shop, 1952-59; sales rep. Midwest Body, Paris, 1959-69, sales mgr., 1969-83, v.p. sales and mktg., 1983—. Active Paris Youth Ctr. Bd., 1965-70. Served as staff sgt. U.S. Army, 1944-46. Mem. Am. Legion, Nat. Truck Equipment Assn., (bd. dirs., trustee 1983-86). Republican. Roman Catholic. Club: Sycamore Hills Country. Lodge: Elks. Avocations: music, golf. Home: 235 W Madison St Apt 15 Paris IL 61944 Office: Midwest Body Corp 2104 S Cen Ave Paris IL 61944

SUNNE, RANDALL HENRY, computer programmer, analyst; b. Faulkton, S.D., Aug. 7, 1950; s. Carlos Grant and Justine Rita (Prisbe) A.; m. Sharon Kay Hausmann, June 14, 1980; children: Morgan Marie, Grant Robert. BS in Computer Sci., U. S.D., 1979. Programmer Farmers State Bank, Parkston, S.D., 1980-83; programmer/analyst EROS Data Ctr., Sioux Falls, S.D., 1983—. Served to 1st lt. USNG, 1979-86, with Res. 1986—. Roman Catholic. Avocations: sports, computers. Home: 509 4th Ave Brandon SD 57005 Office: TGS Inc EROS Data Ctr Sioux Falls SD 57101

SUOZZI, HENRY, social services administrator; b. N.Y.C., Mar. 28, 1928; s. Ralph and Mary (Mancini) S.; m. Carole Elaine Madson; children: Kathy, Anna. BS in Pub. Adminstrn., U. So. Calif., 1951; MSW, U. Conn., 1956. Psychiat. social worker Mental Health Ctr., Waterloo, Iowa, 1956-59; casework supr. Family Service Agy., Waterloo, 1959-60; exec. dir. Family Service Soc., Marion, Ohio, 1960-63, Mental Health Assn., Sacramento, Calif., 1963-71, Counseling & Family Service, Peoria, Ill., 1971—; cons. in field various hosps. and agys., Sacramento, 1970-71. Pres. Sacramento Econ. Opportunity Council, 1969-70. Served to cpl. U.S. Army, 1952-54. Mem. Nat. Assn. Social Workers, Acad. Cert. Social Workers, Child Care Assn. Ill. (com. 1973-78), Ill. Assn. Family Service Agys. (pres. 1974-76, Plaque 1976), Child Welfare League (Nat. Council Execs., nat. membership com. 1984—), Family Service of Am. (mem. exec. com. Midwest regional council 1981-83, evaluation strategic planning com. 1985—). Lodge: Lions, Kiwanis. Avocations: fishing, gardening, travel, sports. Office: Counseling and Family Service 1821 N Knoxville Ave Peoria IL 61603

SUPALLA, DONALD DEAN, educational administrator; b. Mankato, Minn., Mar. 9, 1948; s. Robert George and Betty Jane (Schroeder) S.; m. Stephanie Ann Walvoord, Apr. 17, 1971; children—Michelle, Kristen. A.A., Rochester Community Coll., 1968; B.S., Winona State U., 1971, M.S., 1975. Instr. bus. edn. Rochester Area Vocat. Tech. Inst., Minn., 1972-83, bus. office, tech. coordinator, 1983-87, coordinator student services, 1987—, instr. adult edn., 1975—. Instr. vocat. edn. Winona State U., Minn., 1984—. Mem. steering com. Jefferson Sch. Council, Rochester, 1982, St. Francis Edn. Com., 1987—. Mem. Minn. Bus. Educators (state treas. 1978-80), S.E.Minn. Bus. Educators (exec. bd. 1974-87, pres. 1976-78), Minn. Assn. Area Vocat. Tech. Insts. (fiscal mgr. 1984—), Nat. Bus. Edn. Assn., Am. Vocat. Assn., Minn. Vocat. Assn. Democrat. Roman Catholic. Home: 1906 NE 3d Ave Rochester MN 55904 Office: Rochester Tech Inst 1926 SE 2d St Rochester MN 55904

SUPER, WILLIAM ALAN, industrial engineering executive; b. Evergreen Park, Ill., Dec. 9, 1953; s. Peter and Adeline Marie (Gulch) S.; m. Terrie Elaine Helms, Sept. 22, 1979; children: Emilee Erin, Nicholas William. BS in Indsl. Mgmt., Purdue U., 1975; MBA, No. Ill. U., 1976; MS in Indusl. Tech., U. Wis., Platteville, 1980; postgrad. in indsl. engring., U. Iowa, 1983—. Indsl engr., analyst John Deere Dubuque (Iowa) Works, 1977-79; sr. indsl. engr., analyst Deere Co. Corp., Moline, 1979-81, advanced indsl. engr., analyst, 1981-85; mgr. indsl. engring. Sheller Globe, Iowa City, 1985—; instr. St. Ambrose Coll., Davenport, Iowa, 1983-84. Mem. Inst. Indsl. Engrs. (sec. 1978-79), Robotics Internat. Soc. Mfg. Engrs., Human Factors Soc., Soc. MBA Execs., No. Ill. U. Alumni Assn. (bd. dirs. 1981-86). Republican. Roman Catholic. Club: Sertoma (Davenport) (sec., treas. 1982-83). Lodges: Masons, Elks. Avocations: golf, model railroading, reading, music, softball. Home: 2674 Concord Circle Iowa City IA 52240 Office: Sheller Globe 2500 Hwy # 6 E Iowa City IA 52240

SUPINSKY, KATHY LEE, banking executive; b. Bellaire, Ohio, Sept. 30, 1948; d. George Frederick and Rose (Veverka) Freno; m. Anthony F. Supinsky, July 22, 1977. Student, Ohio U., 1966-72, W.Va. No. Community Coll., 1986—. Loan clk Farmers & Merchants Nat. Bank, Bellaire, 1969-73, asst. cashier, 1975-76, v.p., 1976-83, exec. v.p., 1983—; payroll clk. Rodever-Gleason Glass Co., Bellaire, 1973-74. Mem. Nat. Assn. Bank Women, Ohio Bankers Assn. (human resources div. 1984-86), Bellaire Area C. of C. Club: Big Band 200 (Wheeling, W.Va.). Lodge: Lady Elks. Avocations: traveling, dancing, gardening. Home: 3631 Lincoln Ave Shadyside OH 43947 Office: Farmers & Merchants Nat Bank 426 34th St Bellaire OH 43906

SUPPES, DONALD JAMES, architect; b. Hector, Minn., Apr. 22, 1941; s. Jacob Adam and Caroline Marie (Youngquist) S.; m. Valerie Rae Hanson, Oct. 13, 1962; children: Gwen Marie, Lynn Anne. BA, U. Minn., 1964, BArch, 1968. Registered architect, Minn., N.D., Wyo., Mo., Mich., Mass., R.I., Va., N.C., S.C., Pa. Architect Hammel, Green & Abrahamson, Mpls., 1968-72; assoc. prin. The Archtl. Alliance, Mpls., 1972-78; prin. Ritter, Suppes, Plantz Architects, Ltd., Mpls., 1978—. Mem. AIA, Minn. Soc. of AIA. Avocations: photography, scuba diving, fishing, camping, traveling. Office: Ritter Suppes Plantz Architects 120 1st Ave N Minneapolis MN 55401

SURA-THOMSON, WENDY, automotive executive; b. Detroit, Nov. 29, 1950; d. John Paton and Dorothy Ann (Sura) Thomson; m. William Edward Thomas, Sept. 1, 1979; children: Brittany Nicole (dec.), Christopher Quinn Thomas. Student Mich. State U., 1968-70; BBA, U. Miami (Fla.), 1973; postgrad. U. Chgo., 1977; MS, Fla. State U., 1977. Pension fund mgr. Centel, Chgo., 1977-79; auditor Gen. Motors Fisher Body Div., Warren and Grand Blanc, Mich., 1979-81, gen. supr. gen. acctg., Flint and Grand Blanc, 1981-82, div. staff asst., Warren, 1982-83, treas. staff, Gen. Motors, Detroit, 1983-84, comptroller's staff, 1984—. Mem. Assn. MBA Execs., Beta Gamma Sigma, Lambda Delta, Phi Kappa Phi. Club: Choral Creations (treas. 1981-83) (Oxford, Mich.). Office: Gen Motors Corp 3044 W Grand Blvd 12-102 GM Bldg Detroit MI 48202

SURESH, BINDINGANAVLE RAGHAVAN, electrical engineer; b. Bangalore, Karnataka, India, May 17, 1953; came to U.S., 1973; s. Bindinganavle and Padma Raghavan; m. Jayanti Seshadri, Oct. 11, 1981. BS with honors, Bangalore U., 1970; BE, Indian Inst. Sci., Bangalore, 1973; MEE, U. Minn., 1975, PhD, 1979. Sr. research engr. Honeywell Inc., Mpls., 1979-81, prin. research engr., 1981-83, chief research sect., 1983—; tutor Purdue U., Lafayette, Ind., 1983. Contbr. articles to profl. jours.; patentee automated inspection. Mem. IEEE (pres. local chpt. 1981-82). Avocations: photography, travel. Home: 47 15th Ave SW New Brighton MN 55112 Office: Honeywell Inc MN65-2300 PO Box 1361 Minneapolis MN 55440

SURILLO, THEODOSIA VAZQUEZ, educator; b. Yabucoa, P.R., Mar. 19, 1950; d. Rogelio and Agustina (Solis) Surillo; m. Michael T. Montgomery, July 19, 1986. B.A., John Carroll U., 1973; M.Ed., Baldwin Wallace Coll., 1979. Cert. in adminstrn. and supervision. Day care dir. Spanish Am. Com. Day Care Ctr., Cleve., 1975-77; tchr. corps intern Cleve. Pub. Schs., 1977-79, resource cons., tchr., 1980-82, tchr. Spanish, 1979-80, 82—. Recipient Secondary Bilingual Program service award, 1982. Mem. Cleve. Assn. Multicultural Educators. Democrat. Methodist. Home: 2863 Avondale Cleveland Heights OH 44118 Office: John Adams High School 3817 E 116th St Cleveland OH 44105

SURVIS, GENE FRANCIS, small business owner; b. West Bend, Wis., Mar. 29, 1950; s. Forrest and Ruth (Bandle) S.; m. Susan M. Gundrum, June 9, 1973; children: Kimberly, Amanda. Student, Moraine Park Tech. Sch., West Bend, 1968-70. Cert. tool and die maker. Tool maker Lemberg Tool Corp., Milw., 1968-73; plant mgr. Petersen Industries, Fredonia, Wis., 1974-79; tool maker Kettle Moraine Tool and Die, West Bend, 1979-80; mfg. engr. Bolens FMC Corp., Port Washington, Wis., 1980-82; pres., owner Survis Tool and Die, Inc., Kewaskum, Wis., 1982—. Mem. Soc. Mfg. Engrs. (sr.). Roman Catholic. Club: Toastmasters (master host 1982-83). Avocations: trapshooting, fishing. Home: 2197 SunnyBrook Dr Kewaskum WI 50340

SUSSMAN, GARY MARK, auditor; b. Dayton, Ohio, Mar. 1, 1954; s. Meyer Sussman and Sylvia Florence (Oltusky) Lehman; m. Carrie Lynn Chaskin, Nov. 25, 1984. BSBA cum laude, Ohio State U., 1976; MBA, U. Chgo., 1978. CPA, Tex. Assoc. auditor Armco, Inc., Middletown, Ohio, 1978-79; auditor Armco, Inc., Houston, 1980-83; sr. auditor Armco, Inc., Middletown, 1984-87; supervising auditor Northwestern Nat. Ins. Co. subs. Armco, Inc., Brookfield, Wis., 1987—. Named Outstanding Young Man Am., 1986. Mem. Tex. Soc. CPA's, Inst. Internal Auditors, Alpha Kappa Psi (treas. 1974-75). Jewish. Home: 2500 Stonefield Ct Waukesha WI 53188 Office: Northwestern Nat Ins Co 18650 W Corporate Dr Brookfield WI 53005

SUSSMAN, JASON HUGH, health care consultant; b. Balt., Mar. 7, 1957; s. Harold and Belle (Awerbuch) S.; m. Alona Weissberg, Nov. 15, 1980. BA, Johns Hopkins U., 1978; MA in Mgmt., Northwestern U., 1980. CPA, Ill. From staff cons. to sr. mgr. Ernst and Whinney, Chgo., 1981—. Bd. dirs. Temple BethEl Chgo., 1985-86, fin. v.p., 1986—; mem. steering com. health profls. div. Jewish United Fund Chgo., 1987—. Mem. Nat. Health Lawyers Assn., Am. Hosp. Assn., Am. Coll. Healthcare Execs., Am. Inst. CPA's, Ill. CPA Soc., Chgo. Health Execs. Forum. Club: Standard (Chgo.). Home: 1207 Sherwood Rd Glenview IL 60025 Office: Ernst & Whinney 150 S Wacker Dr Chicago IL 60606

SUTCLIFFE, RICHARD LEE (RICK), professional baseball player; m. Robin Ross. Profl. baseball player Los Angeles Dodgers, Nat. League, 1976-81, Cleve. Indians, Am. League, 1982-84, Chgo. Cubs, Nat. League, 1984—. Mem. Am. League All-Star Team, 1983; recipient Cy Young award Nat. League, 1984. Office: Chgo Cubs Wrigley Field Chicago IL 60613 *

SUTER, ALBERT EDWARD, manufacturing company executive; b. East Orange, N.J., Sept. 18, 1935; s. Joseph Vincent and Catherine (Clay) S.; m. Michaela Sams Suter, May 28, 1966; children: Christian C., Bradley J., Allison A. BME, Cornell U., 1957, MBA, 1959. Pres., chief exec. officer L.B. Knight & Assocs., Chgo., 1959-79; v.p. internat. Emerson Electric Co., St. Louis, 1979-80, pres. motor div., 1980-87, group v.p., 1981-83, exec. v.p., 1983-87, vice chmn., 1987; with Firestone Tire and Rubber Co., Akron, Ohio, 1987—. Bd. dirs. Jr. Achievement Miss. Valley; chmn. Torch div. St. Louis chpt. United Way, 1982—. Republican. Episcopalian. Clubs: Chgo; Glenview Country (Chgo.); St. Louis; Old Warson Country (St. Louis). Office: Firestone Tire and Rubber Co 1200 Firestone Pkwy Akron OH 44317

SUTER, SUSAN SOWLE, rehabilitation services administrator; b. Rockford, Ill., Apr. 16, 1950; d. John Thompson and Shirley Mae (Flanagan) S.; m. Carl Alexander Suter, Feb. 5, 1972; 1 child, Elan Joshua. Student, George Peabody Coll., 1968-70; BS, U. Ill., 1972; MA, Ea. Ill. U., 1975. cert. clin. psychologist. Psychologist Ill. Dept. Mental Health, Danville, 1975-76, mental health specialist, 1976-77; research analyst Div. Vocat. Rehab. State of Ill., Springfield, 1977-78, coordinator rehab. planning, 1978; specialist devel disabilities program Gov.'s Planning Council State of Ill., Springfield, 1979-80; dir. community services Ill. Devel. Disabilities Advocacy Authority, Springfield, 1980-81; coordinator Insternat. Yr. Disabled Persons for Ill. Office of Gov. State of Ill., Springfield, 1981-82; exec. assoc. dir. Ill. Dept. Rehab. Services, Springfield, 1982-84, dir., 1984—; chmn. Client Services Com. CSAVR, Washington, 1986; adv. bd. dirs. rehab. continuing edn. So. Ill. U., Carbondale, 1984—. Mem. Nat. Women's Polit. Caucus, 1985—; co-chair Springfield Women's Polit. Caucus, 1983—. Mem. Nat. Rehab. Asn., Ill. Rehab. Assn., Council State Adminstrs. of Vocat. Rehab. (exec. com.), Ill. Coalition Citizens with Disabilities, Women in Mgmt., Nat. Orgn. Women Execs. in State Govt. Republican. Home: 3221 Haviland Springfield IL 62704 Office: State of Ill Dept Rehab Services 623 E Adams St Springfield IL 62794-9429

SUTHERLAND, ALAN DOUGLAS, controller; b. Mt. Clemens, Mich., July 30, 1957; s. William Edward and Ceinwyn Dunten (Lees) S.; m. Denise Marie Kania, Aug. 1, 1982; children: Kristen Noelle, Jaclyn Danielle. BBA, Mich. State U., 1979. CPA, Ill. Asst. acct. Peat, Marwick, Mitchell, San Antonio, Tex., 1979-80; sr. acct. Peat, Marwick, Mitchell, Chgo., 1980-84, mgr., 1985—; planning dir. Nuvatec, Inc., Downers Grove, Ill., 1984, controller, 1986—. Mem. Am. Inst. CPA's, Ill. CPA Soc., Beta Gamma Sigma, Beta Alpha Psi. Roman Catholic. Avocations: music, sports.

SUTLIFF, DENNIS JAY, architect; b. Mpls., June 17, 1953; s. Elbert Anson and Jane Carol (Carson) S. BArch, B of Environ. Design, U. Minn., 1975. Registered architect, Minn. Architect Ralph Rapson & Assocs., Inc., Mpls., 1971-75; cons. Thomas & Vecchi, Architects, Duluth, Minn., 1975; v.p. B.R.W. Inc., Mpls., 1976—; lectr., critic U. Minn., Mpls., 1982-84; mem. Com. on Urban Environment; advisor Gov.'s Design Team, 1986. Mem. AIA (Minn. chpt.), Urban Land Inst., Illuminating Engrs. Soc. (Lighting Design award 1983), Precast Concrete Inst. (Archtl. Design award 1982), Alpha Rho Chi. Avocations: skiing, scuba, art collecting, sports cars. Office: BRW Inc 700 3d St S Minneapolis MN 55415

SUTTER, JOHN RICHARD, manufacturing company executive; b. St. Louis, Jan. 18, 1937; s. Richard Anthony and Elizabeth Ann (Henby) S.; m. Mary Etta Trexler, Apr. 4, 1964 (div. Nov. 1983); children: John Henby, Mary Elizabeth, Sarah Katherine; m. Madeline Ann Traugott, June 5, 1984; 1 child, William Stribling. BA, Princeton U., 1958; MBA, Columbia U., 1964. CPA, N.Y., Mo. Mgr. Price Waterhouse, N.Y.C., 1964-71; pres. John Sutter and Co., Inc., St. Louis, 1972-86, Handlan-Buck Co., St. Louis, 1975—; pres. Sutter Mgmt. Corp., St. Louis, 1972-79; bd. dirs. Inside/Outside, Inc., St. Louis; cons. Greenway Products Co., St. Louis, 1984—. Served to lt. (j.g.) USN, 1959-63. Mem. Am. Inst. CPA's, Mo. Soc. CPA's, N.Y. Soc. CPA's, Royal Hort. Soc. Republican. Episcopalian. Clubs: Carlyle Yacht (treas. 1979-80), Sugar Tree (bd. dirs. 1979-86), Clayton, Princeton (bd. dirs. 1983-87). Avocations: orchid culture, photography, sailboat racing. Home: 6317 Southwood Clayton MO 63105 Office: Handlan Buck Co 4519 Ridgewood Saint Louis MO 63116

SUTTER, LYNN ROBERT, marketing communications executive; b. Cleve., Oct. 13, 1940; s. Robert Carl and Inez Rose (Smith) S.; m. Gayle Carol Kaplan, June 18, 1966; children: Kirsten Lyn, David Reed. BA in Econs., N. Park Coll., Chgo., 1966. Salesman Del Monte Foods, Chgo., 1964-65, SCM Corp., Chgo., 1965-66; v.p. mktg. and sales Century Communications, Skokie, Ill., 1966-76; pres. Sutter/Martin, Inc., Buffalo Grove, Ill., 1976—, Pub. Mgmt. Group, Buffalo Grove, 1979—; chmn. Health Market, Inc., Buffalo Grove, 1984—. Home: 1726 Emerald Ln Palatine IL 60074 Office: Sutter/Martin Inc 165 Arlington Heights Rd Buffalo Grove IL 60084

SUTTON, CLEMENT OTIS, window company executive; b. Iowa City, Iowa, July 4, 1937; s. Arthur Donald and Marvel Elma (Deitz) S.; m. Constance Ann Little, Feb. 14, 1957; children: Mark Clement, Marla Lynn, Marlo Lynn, Layne Adam. AS in Bus., Moline (Ill.) Community Coll., 1962. Asst. mgr. Benner Tea Co., Moline, 1953-55; research and devel. assoc. Montgomery Elevator, Moline, 1955-57, engrng. records mgr., 1957-62, purchasing agt., 1962-73; corp. pres. Clement Sutton Corp., Westby, Wis., 1973—. Pres. East Moline (Ill.) Dad's Club, 1959, Y-Indian Guides YMCA, East Moline, 1960; county chmn. Dad's Club of U. Ill., Moline, 1981-82. Mem. Nat. Assn. Self Employed, Westby Bus. Assn. Republican. Methodist. Avocations: traveling, reading. Home: Main & Mill St Wauzeka WI 53826 Office: Clement Sutton Corp High Echo Ln Westby WI 54667

SUTTON, DONALD RAY, dentist; b. Dayton, Ohio, Mar. 16, 1949; s. William Lester and Mary Evelyn (Rowe) S.; m. Louanne O'Dell, Sept. 27, 1974 (div. Aug. 1983); children: Brett Alan, Bryan Michael; m. Jackie Spencer, Feb. 14, 1987. BA, Earlham Coll., 1971; DDS, Ohio State U., 1974. Gen. practice dentistry Canal Winchester, Ohio, 1975—. Mem. ADA, Hocking Valley Dental Soc. (v.p. 1982-83, pres. 1983-84). Republican. Avocations: sports car racing, aviation. Office: Tri County Med Ctr 11965 Lithopolis Rd Canal Winchester OH 43110

SUTTON, GARY SCOTT, physical therapist; b. Alliance, Ohio, Feb. 28, 1954; s. Robert Jay and Margaret Elizabeth (Raber) S.; m. Linda Leigh Fitch, Oct. 14, 1978; children: Adam Christopher, Kelley Lynne. BA, Mt. Union Coll., 1976; cert. in phys. therapy, Northwestern U., 1978; MS, Inst. Grad. Health Scis., Atlanta, 1982. Lic. phys. therapist, Ohio, Va.; cert. ambulance emergency med. technician, Va., cert. athletic trainer. Staff phys. therapist Meml. Hosp., Danville, Va., 1978-81; cons. phys. therapist Atlanta Falcons Football Club, Suwanee, Ga., 1982; phys. therapist, athletic trainer The Sports Medicine Clinic, Atlanta, 1983; dir. phys. therapy Kolczun & Kolczun Orthopaedic Assocs., Lorain, 1983-85; dir. sports phys. therapy Michael Supler and Assocs., Cleve., 1985—; faculty intern physical therapy program Cleve. State U.; trainer U.S. Olympic Tng. Ctr., Colorado Springs, Colo., 1984, Nat. Jr. Olympic Championships, Iowa City, 1985, U.S. Olympic Festival, Houston, 1986; cons. sports med. St. Joseph High Sch., Cleve., 1985—, Charles F. Brush High Sch., Lyndhurst, 1985—; cons. U.S. Taekwondo Union, East Hartford, Conn., 1986—. Contbr. articles to profl. jours. Named one of Outstanding Young Men of Am., 1980. Mem. Am. Phys. Therapy Assn. (orthopaedic sect., sports phys. therapy sect.), Am. Phys. Therapy Assn. (Ohio and Va. chpt.), Nat. Athletic Trainers Assn. (cert.), Blue Key, Sigma Nu. Republican. Methodist. Avocations: weight tng., martial arts. Home: 1188 Homestead Rd South Euclid OH 44121 Office: Univ Suburban Sports Med Ctr 1611 S Green Rd Cleveland OH 44121

SUTTON, GREGORY PAUL, obstetrician-gynecologist; b. Tokyo, Dec. 12, 1948; (parents Am. citizens); s. Vernon S. And Vonna Lou (Streeter) S.; m. Judith Craigie Holt, June 26, 1977; children: Anne Craigie, James Streeter. BS in Chemistry with honors, Ind. U., 1970; MD, U. Mich., 1976. Diplomate Am. Bd. of Ob/Gyn. Assoc. prof. ob-gyn Ind. U. Sch. Medicine, Indpls., 1983—. Cancer Clin. fellow Am. Cancer Soc., Phila., 1981-83; recipient Career Devel. award Am. Cancer Soc., Indpls., 1986. Fellow Am. Coll. Obstetrics and Gynecology; mem. Gynecologic Oncology Group (cert. Spl. Competence in Gynecologis Oncology 1985), Marion County Med. Soc., Ind. State Med. Soc., Bayard Carter Soc., Soc. of Gynecologic Oncologists. Avocations: swimming, cycling, woodworking. Office: Ind U Hosp 926 W Michigan St Indianapolis IN 46223

SUTTON, HAROLD ALAN, farmer; b. Texas City, Ill., Dec. 14, 1946; s. John Jr. and Mabel (McGhee) S.; m. Alice Ann Morris, Mar. 28, 1975; children: Amanda, Allison, Victoria. BS in Agrl. Econs., So. Ill. U., 1968. Farmer Norris City, Ill., 1968—. Assessor Indian Creek Twp, Ill. Home and Office: Rt 2 Box 77A Norris City IL 62869

SUTTON, PATRICIA MARLENE, jewelry store executive; b. Goodland, Kans., July 1, 1953; d. Richard L. and Betty D. (Wright) Roth; 1 child, Kelli M. Reinbold. Student pub. schs., Dodge City. Salesperson (part-time) Roth Jewelers, Dodge City, Kans., 1966-72, Vernon Jewelers, Salina, Kans., 1972-73; salesperson, 1973-76, mgr., 1976—. Bd. dirs. Greater Downtown Salina Inc., 1981—, 2d v.p., 1985—, promotion com., 1984—. Mem. Kans. Jewelers Assn., Nat. Platform Assn., BID (mktg. com. for Salina Downtown, Inc.), Salina C. of C. (retail activities com. 1984-85). Republican. Avocations: scuba diving; fishing; archaeology. Office: Vernon Jewelers of Salina 123 N Santa Fe Salina KS 67401

SUTTON, PETER ALFRED, archbishop; b. Chandler, Que., Can., Oct. 18, 1934. B.A., U. Ottawa, 1960; M.A. in Religious Edn, Loyola U., Chgo., 1969. Ordained priest Roman Catholic Ch., 1960, bishop, 1974; oblate of Mary Immaculate; high sch. tchr. St. Patricks, Ottawa, Ont., 1961-63, London (Ont.) Cath. Central Sch., 1963-74; bishop of Labrador-Schefferville, Que., Can., 1974—; apptd. coadjustor archbishop Missionary Diocese of Keewatin-Le Pas, Man., 1986—, archbishop, 1986—; mem. social affairs com. Can. Conf. Cath. Bishops; accompanying bishop L'Arche Internat. (homes for mentally handicapped), 1983—. Contbr. religious articles to newspapers. Office: PO Box 270 108 1st St, The Pas, MB Canada R9A 1K4

SUTTON, RICHARD RUEL, pastor; b. Mason City, Iowa, Jan. 20, 1934; s. Reuben Reul and Florence Irene (Schultz) S.; m. Florence Alice Sage, Sept. 15, 1951; children: Steven Lee, John Allen, Richard Dean, James Milton, Sharon Beth, Karen Ann. Grad. high sch., Mason City, 1952. Ordained to ministry Seventh Day Adventist Ch., 1986. Printer Arrow Printing Co., Mason City, 1951-60, M.C. Blue Print, Mason City, 1960-63; postal clk. Mason City Post Office, 1963-77; publ. mgr. Allied Purchasing, Mason City, 1980—; pastor Seventh Day Remnant Advent Ch., Nora Springs, Iowa, 1986—; pres. Am. Postal Workers Union, 1965-77. Republican. Home: 116 N Jefferson PO Box 1628 Mason City IA 50401

SUTTON, SHARON EGRETTA, architectural design educator, artist; b. Cin., Feb. 18, 1941; d. Booker and Egretta (Sutton) Johnson. Student, Manhattan Sch. Music, 1959-62; MusB, U. Hartford, Conn., 1963; postgrad., Parson's Sch. Design, N.Y.C., 1967-69; MArch, Columbia U., 1973; PhM, CUNY, 1981, MA, PhD in Psychology, 1982. Registered architect, N.Y., Mich. Visiting asst. prof. Pratt Inst., N.Y.C., 1975-81; pvt. practice architect N.Y.C. and Dexter, Mich., 1976—; architect-in-residence Nat. Endowment Arts, N.Y.C., 1978-82; adj. asst. prof. Columbia U., N.Y.C., 1981-82; asst. prof. U. Cin., 1982-84; assoc. prof. U. Mich., Ann Arbor, 1984—. One-woman shows include Nat. Urban League, N.Y.C., 1980, Your Heritage House, Detroit, 1986; exhibited in group shows at Studio Mus., N.Y.C., 1979, Fine Art Mus. L.I., Hempstead, N.Y., 1983, June Kelly Gallery, N.Y.C., 1987; represented in permanent collections Mint Mus., Charlotte, N.C., Wadsworth Atheneum, Hartford, Conn., Balt. Mus. Art; Author: Learning Through The Built Environment, 1985; editorial bd. Jour. Archtl. Edn., 1984—; contbr. articles to profl. jours. Recipient William K. Fellow Travel award Columbia U., 1971, 73, Postbaccalaureate award Danforth Found., 1977-81, Design Research award Nat. Endowment Arts, 1983; W.K. Kellogg Found. fellow, 1986—. Mem. AIA, Am. Psychol. Assn. Democrat. Home: 8071 Main St Dexter MI 48130 Office: U Mich Coll Architecture and Urban Planning Ann Arbor MI 48109

SUTZ, ROY E., industrial engineer, consultant; b. Chgo., Aug. 10, 1925; s. Ben and Bertha (Goodheart) S.; m. Rosemary Herman, Oct. 22, 1950; children: Eileen, Eric. BSME, Ill. Inst. Tech., 1958; BS, Roosevelt U., Chgo., 1970. V.p. engring. Smith Victor Corp., Griffith, Ind., 1960-66; mgr. mfg., sr. engr. Polaroid, Cambridge, Mass., 1966-75; pres. Greenwood Sutz & Assocs. Inc., Glenview, Ill., 1975—; cons. in field. Author: Quality Control for Small Businesses, 1979, Practical Time Study, 1981, Jig and Fixture Design, 1984; patentee in field. Mem. Am. Soc. Quality Control Engrs., Inst. Indsl. Engrs., Midwest Soc. Profl. Cons. Avocations: photography, video, travel, walking, painting. Office: 146 James Ct Glenview IL 60025

SUYEMATSU, KIYO, music librarian, music educator; b. Casper, Wyo., Apr. 17, 1926; d. Benjamin Tschuchio and Masa S. B.Mus., U. Colo., 1949, M.Mus., 1963; M.A., U. Denver, 1970. Sec., Bur. of Reclamation, Casper, Wyo., 1949-51; sec. Marathon Oil Co., Casper, 1951-61; accompanist, piano tchr., Casper, 1949-61; instr. music Mankato (Minn.) State U., 1963-70, music librarian, music instr., 1970—; asst. condr. Women's Choir, Casper, 1956-61; pianist Kiwanis Club, Casper, 1956-61. Mem. negotiating council faculty bargaining unit State Univs. of Minn.; mem. vestry St. John's Episc. Ch., Mankato. Mem. Music Educators Nat. Conf., Music Library Assn., Minn. Edn. Assn., Sigma Alpha Iota (faculty adviser), Delta Kappa Gamma. Office: Mankato State University Performing Arts Center Mankato MN 56001

SVADLENAK, JEAN HAYDEN, museum administrator; b. Wilmington, Del., Mar. 4, 1955; d. Marion M. and Ida Jean (Calcagni) Hayden; m. Steven R. Svadlenak, May 26, 1979. BS in Textiles and Clothing, U. Del., 1977; MA in History Mus. Studies, SUNY, Oneonta, 1982; postgrad., U. Calif., Berkeley, 1982. Curatorial asst. The Hagley Mus., Wilmington, 1976-77; curator of costumes and textiles The Kansas City (Mo.) Mus., 1978-82, chief curator, 1982-84, assoc. exec., 1984—, dir. for collection and exhibits mgmt., 1986—, interim pres., 1986-87; researcher, guest curator N.Y. State Hist. Assn., Cooperstown, 1980; grant reviewer Inst. for Mus. Services, 1985—. Mem. Am. Assn. Mus. (mus. assessment program surveyor 1986—), Am. Assn. State and Local History, Costume Soc. Am. Avocations: music, sports, photography, cooking. Office: The Kansas City Mus 3218 Gladstone Blvd Kansas City MO 64123

SVEC, SUSAN MARIE, social worker; b. Oak Park, Ill., Oct. 10, 1945; d. August Frank and Vera Agnes (Winfrey) S. AA, Morton Community Coll., 1965; BS, U. Ill., Urbana, 1968; postgrad., U. Ill., Chgo., 1985—. Caseworker Misericordia Home, Chgo., 1968-74; field exec. West Cook Girl Scouts U.S., La Grange, Ill., 1974-79; exec. dir. Cloverleaf Girl Scouts U.S., Cicero, Ill., 1979-86; social worker West Town Hospice, Berwyn, Ill., 1985—. 1st aid inst. Mid-Am. chpt., ARC, Westchester, 1977—; chmn. bd. trustees Morton Community Coll., Cicero, 1980-85; pres. Friends of Hospice, Berwyn, 1983-85; bd. dirs. Children's Ctr. of Cicero-Berwyn, 1986—. Recipient Recognition Cert. ARC, Westchester, 1985, Recognition Plaque, Morton Community Coll., 1985, Thanks Badge, Cloverleaf Girl Scouts U.S., 1986. Mem. Nat. Assn. Social Workers, Oncology Social Workers Assn., Berwyn Hist. Soc., Girl Scouts of USA.

SVEDE, GEORGE EDGAR, desgin engineer; b. Riga, Latvia, Nov. 30, 1938; came to U.S., 1949; s. Janis (John) Girts Svede and Erna Frida (Dzerve) Jakobsons; m. Patricia Ann Bedore, Sept. 5, 1959; children: Mark, Greg, Michelle. BA in Indsl. Design, Mich. State U., 1961. Designer Reo div. White Motors, Lansing, Mich., 1959-63, Duplex/Warner-Swasey, Lansing, 1963-64; project engr. Hein-Werner, Waukesha, Wis., 1964-70; product engr. Harnischfeger Corp., Cedar Rapids, Iowa, 1970-77; supr. crane devel. Galion (Ohio) Mfg./ Dresser, 1977-82; mgr. engring. Ohio Locomotive Crane, Bucyrus, 1983-87, 1987—; bd. dirs. ARLOW, Waukesha, Cedar Rapids, 1965-74; research dir. Automotive Research Library, Mansfield, Ohio, 1977—. Patentee in field. leader boy Scouts Am., Wis., Iowa, Ohio, 1967-84. Recipient Wood Badge Boy Scouts Am., 1977. Mem. Soc. Am. Value Engrs., Antique Auto Club Am., Soc. Automotive Historians. Avocations: automotive history, design and restoration, the outdoors, sports, Indian lore. Home: 543 West Straub Rd Mansfield OH 44904 Office: Ohio Locomotive Crane Co Inc 811 Hopley Ave Bucyrus OH 44820

SVEEN, MELISSA JILL, pediatric dentist; b. Canton, S.D., Sept. 9, 1957; d. Theodore Art and Margaret Doris (Westergren) Angelos; m. Jay Alan Sveen, May 19, 1979; children: Jared Michael and Stephanie Nicole (twins). AA in Nursing, U. S.D., 1977; DDS, U. Nebr., Lincoln, 1984, cert. pediatric dentistry, 1986; MS, U. Nebr., Omaha, 1986. Nurse med. surgical unit Lutheran Med. Ctr., Omaha, 1977; nurse post critical care Bergen Mercy Hosp., Omaha, 1978; nurse obstetrics Meth. Hosp., Omaha, 1979-81; clin. instr. fixed prosthodontics U. Nebr., Lincoln, 1984; clin. instr. pedodontics U. Nebr., 1986—; practice pediatric dentistry Lincoln, 1986—; dental provider Medically Handicapped Children's Program, Lincoln, 1986—. Regents fellow, U. Nebr., Lincoln, 1984. Mem. ADA, Am. Acad. Pediatric Dentistry, Am. Soc. Dentistry for Children, Nebr. Dental Assn., Lincoln Dental Assn. Presbyterian. Avocations: swimming, crewel. Office: 770 N Cotner Blvd Suite 214 Lincoln NE 68505

SVENDSEN, DANIEL L., accountant, financial executive; b. Madison, Wis., Aug. 7, 1946; s. Hoaken Carl and Astrid Christine (Wold) S.; m. Cynthia Elaine Pierce, Oct. 31, 1970; 1 child, Carl D. BS, U. Minn., 1968. CPA. Acct. Haskins & Sells, Mpls., 1968-70; mgr. Blue Cross of Minn., St. Paul, 1970-74; ptnr. Stillman, House, & Swanson, Duluth, Minn., 1974-84, McEladren, Hendrickson & Pollen, Duluth, 1984-86; chief fin. officer Miller-Dwan Med. Ctr., Duluth, 1986—. Mem. Am. Inst. CPA's, Minn. Soc. CPA's, Healthcare Fin. Mgmt. Assn. Lodge: Rotary. Home: 288 Heine Rd Choquet MN 58720 Office: Miller-Dwan Med Ctr 504 E 2d St Duluth MN 55805

SWAIMAN, KENNETH FRED, pediatric neurologist, educator; b. St. Paul, Nov. 19, 1931; s. Lester J. and Shirley (Ryan) S.; m. Phyllis Kammerman Sher, Oct. 1985; children: Lisa, Jerrold, Barbara, Dana. B.A. magna cum laude, U. Minn., 1952, B.S., 1953, M.D., 1955; postgrad., 1956-58; postgrad. (fellow pediatric neurology), Nat. Inst. Neurologic Deseases and Blindness, 1960-63. Diplomate: Am. Bd. Psychiatry and Neurology, Am. Bd. Pediatrics. Intern Mpls. Gen. Hosp., 1955-56; resident pediatrics U. Minn., 1956-58, neurology, 1960-63; asst. prof. pediatrics, neurology U. Minn. Med. Sch., Mpls., 1963-66; asso. prof. U. Minn. Med. Sch., 1966-69, prof., dir. pediatric neurology, 1969—, exec. officer, dept. neurology, 1977—, mem. internship adv. council exec. faculty, 1966-70; Cons. pediatric neurology Hennepin County Gen. Hosp., Mpls., St. Paul-Ramsey Hosp., St. Paul Children's Hosp., Mpls. Children's Hosp. Author: (with Francis S. Wright) Neuromuscular Diseases in Infancy and Childhood, 1969, Pediatric Neuromuscular Diseases, 1979, (with Stephen Ashwal) Pediatric Neurology

Case Studies, 1978, 2d edit., 1984; Editor: (with John A. Anderson) Phenylketonuria and Allied Metabolic Diseases, 1966, (with Francis S. Wright) Practice Pediatric Neurology, 1975, 2d edit., 1982; mem. editorial bd.: Annals of Neurology, 1977-83, Neurology Update, 1977-82, Pediatric Update, 1977—, Brain and Devel. (Jour. Japanese Soc. Child Neurology), 1980—, Neuropediatrics (Stuttgart), 1982—; editor-in-chief: Pediatric Neurology, 1984—; Contbr. articles to sci. jours. Chmn. Minn. Gov.'s Bd. for Handicapped, Exceptional and Gifted Children, 1972-76; mem. human devel. study sect. NIH, 1976-79, guest worker, 1978-81. Served to capt. M.C. U.S. Army, 1958-60. Fellow Am. Acad. Pediatrics, Am. Acad. Neurology (rep. to nat. council Nat. Soc. Med. Research); mem. Soc. Pediatric Research, Central Soc. Clin. Research, Central Soc. Neurol. Research, Internat. Soc. Neurochemistry, Am. Neurol. Assn., Minn. Neurol. Soc., AAAS, Midwest Pediatric Soc., Am. Soc. Neurochemistry, Child Neurology Soc. (1st pres. 1972-73, Hower award 1981), Internat. Assn. Child Neurologists (exec. com. 1975-79), Profs. of Child Neurology (1st pres. 1978-80), Phi Beta Kappa, Sigma Xi. Home: 420 Delaware St SE Minneapolis MN 55455 Office: U Minn Med Sch Dept Pediatric Neurology Minneapolis MN 55455

SWAIN, DANIEL WILBERT, psychologist; b. Milbank, S.D., Aug. 12, 1934; s. Bruce Wright and Alice Mary Ellen (Moeller) S.; m. Dorothy Joy Wubbena, Dec. 27, 1958; children: Elizabeth Ann, Amy Carolyn, William Joseph. Student, U. S.D., 1952-55, BA, 1959, MA, 1960; postgrad., U. Ky., 1961-62; MA in Religion, Va. Theol. Sem., 1970. Lic. psychologist, Iowa. Psychologist trainee VA Hosp., Lexington, Ky., 1961-62; psychologist Ft. Wayne (Ind.) State Sch., 1960-61, Minn. Home Sch., Sauk Centre, 1962-68, Pastoral Counseling and Cons. Ctr. of Washington D.C., 1968-70; psychologist, II, III and program dir. adolescent unit Mental Health Inst., Cherokee, Iowa, 1970-79, chief psychologist, 1979; cons. Boys and Girls Home and Family Service Inc., Sioux City, Iowa, 1979—; cons. commn. on ministry Episc. Diocese Iowa, 1972—; cons. Florence Crittenton Home, Sioux City, 1984—, Wholistic Health, Inc., Sioux City, 1985—. Bd. dirs. Sanford Mus. Assn., Cherokee, 1980-83, Cherokee Work Activity Ctr., 1986—. Served with U.S. Army, 1955-57. Mem. Am. Group Psychotherapy Assn., Iowa Psychol. Assn., Nat. Assn. for Prevention Child Abuse and Neglect (bd. dirs. Iowa 1980-85). Democrat. Avocations: amateur radio, beekeeping, hunting, camping, writing. Home: 471 Euclid Ave Cherokee IA 51012 Office: Cherokee Mental Health Inst 1200 W Cedar Cherokee IA 51012

SWAIN, JACQUE LEE, accountant; b. Detroit, June 6, 1950; d. Irving George and Vivian May (Stockard) Wallace; m. Dennis Michael Swain, Mar. 20, 1971; 1 child, Jason Patrick. AA, Northwestern Mich. Coll., 1980; BA, Mich. State U., 1982. CPA, Mich. Taxpayer service specialist IRS, Lansing, Mich., 1971-72, Traverse City, Mich., 1972-79; tax dept. sr. Danielson, Schultz & Co., Traverse City, 1979-82; pvt. practice acctg. Manistee, Mich., 1983-85; mgr. Merskin & Merskin, P.C., Manistee, 1985—. mem. Manistee City Planning commn., 1982—; campaign coordinator Connie Binsfeld Senate Com., Manistee County, 1985-86. Mem. Am. Inst. CPA's, Mich. Assn. CPA's, Manistee Bus. and Profl. Women's Club (v.p., treas. 1984-86). Republican. Episcopalian. Avocations: bicycling, cross country skiing. Home: 410 Pine St Manistee MI 49660 Office: 234 Aarkdale Ave Manistee MI 49660

SWAIN, NANCY JO, advertising company owner; b. Kingman, Kans., June 1, 1957; d. Melvin Lee and Betty June (Kemp) White; m. Thomas Robert Swain, Dec. 19, 1981; 1 child, Elliott Thomas. Student, Hutchinson Community Jr. Coll., 1975-76. Admissions aide Hutchinson (Kans.) Community Jr. Coll., 1975-76; nurse's aide Winfield (Kans.) State Hosp., 1976-77; bookkeeper Sedan (Kans.) Seed House, 1978, Meschkes Mens Wear, Hutchinson, 1978-79; acct. exec. Sta. KWHK, Hutchinson, 1979-85; owner Ad Man Services, Hutchinson, 1985—. Developer, organizer 30th St. St. Patrick's Day parade, Hutchinson, 1982—; organizer Hutchinsons Christmas parade, 1982-83, March of Dimes Walk-a-thon, 1986-87; Hutchinson Civitan Club, 1986—. Mem. Am. Bus. Womens Assn. (pres. 1982-83), Hutchinson C. of C. (ambassador, asst. chmn. 1987, ambassador, chmn. 1988). Republican. Avocations: skiing, singing, home decorating, golf. Home: 200 Crescent Blvd Hutchinson KS 67502 Office: Advt Mgmt Services 1120 B North Halstead PO Box 3203 Hutchinson KS 67501

SWALES, WILLIAM EDWARD, oil company executive; b. Parkersburg, W.Va., May 15, 1925; s. John Richard and Ellen (South) S.; m. Lydia Eugena Mills, Dec. 26, 1948; children: Joseph V., Susan Eugena, David Lee. BA in Geology, W.Va. U., 1949, MS in Geology, 1951; grad., advanced mgmt. program Stanford U., 1968; DSc (hon.), W.Va. U., 1986; LLD (hon.), Marietta Coll., 1986. With Marathon Oil Co. (subs. USX Corp.), Findlay, Ohio, 1954-70, 74-87, mgr. Western Hemisphere and Australia div., 1967-70, spl. asst. to sr. v.p. prodn., internat., 1974, v.p. prodn., internat., 1974-77, sr. v.p. prodn., internat., 1977-82, also bd. dirs., chmn. bd., 1983-84, sr. v.p. exploration and prodn., 1983-84, pres., 1985-87, pres. Marathon Petroleum Co., 1982-83; vice-chmn. energy USX Corp., Pittsburgh, 1987—; bd. dirs. Tex. Oil & Gas Corp, Pitts. Nat. Bank, Pitts Nat. Bank Fin. Corp.; exec. v.p. Oasis Oil Co. of Libya, Inc., Tripoli, 1970-72, pres., 1972-74; exec. dir. USX Corp. Served with USN, 1943-45. Mem. Am. Petroleum Inst. (bd. dirs.), Am. Assn. Petroleum Geologists, Soc. Petroleum Engrs., Am. Geol. Inst., Nat. Petroleum Council, 25 Yr. Club. Clubs: Findlay Country, JDM Country, Laurel Valley Golf, Rolling Rock, 25 Yr. of Petroleum Industry. Office: USX Corp 600 Grant St Pittsburgh PA 15230

SWAN, ALLEN DEAN, health facility administrator; b. Chgo., Apr. 13, 1930; s. Elvin Caleb and Freda Christine (Frederickson) S.; m. Lydia Janke, Sept. 27, 1952; children: Timothy, Phillip. BS in Indsl. Edn., U. Wis., Stout, 1952. Ops. shift foreman Gen. Mills, Inc., Belmond, Iowa, 1957-65; administr. Spring Valley (Wis.) Nursing Home, 1965-66, Hillsboro (N.D.) Community Hosp. and Nursing Home, 1966-69, Kittson Meml. Hosp. and Nursing Home, Hallock, Minn., 1969-79; chief exec. officer Jenkins Meth. Home, Watertown, S.D., 1979—; Adminstr. perceptor S.D. Nursing Home, 1981—. Served as sgt. U.S. Army, 1952-54, Korea. Fellow Am. Coll. of Health Care Administrs. Methodist. Lodge: Kiwanis (Watertown). Office: Jenkins Meth Home 12 2d Ave SE Watertown SD 57201

SWAN, HARRY DAVID, private investigator, design engineer, personnel and criminal justice consultant; b. Rochester, N.Y., Feb. 25, 1926; s. Harry and Florence (Ellison) S.; m. Pauline E. Gunnison, May 20, 1950 (div.); children—David, Lynne. A.S. in Commerce, Henry Ford Community Coll., Dearborn, Mich., 1965; B.S. in Criminal Justice, Madonna Coll., Livonia, Mich., 1977; M.A. in Criminal Justice, U. Detroit, 1980. Lic. pvt. investigator, Ky. Design checker Chrysler Corp., Highland Park, Mich., 1953-64, Hydramatic div. Gen. Motors, Ypsilanti, Mich., 1980, AC Spark Plug div. Gen. Motors, Flint, Mich., 1981, Alliance-Renault-AMC, Detroit, 1982; design engr. Corvette-Chevrolet, Gen. Motors, Warren, Mich., 1983; design checker Ford Motor Co., Dearborn, 1984-87; chief exec. officer Covert Intelligence Agy. and Covert Pvt. Police, Lexington, Ky., 1983—. Served with USAAF, 1944-45. Mem. Am. Soc. for Indsl. Security, Sports Car Club Am., Delorean Internat. Club. Democrat. Presbyterian. Designer automotive chassis innovations, 1953-83. Address: 411 S Woodward Suite 1013 Birmingham MI 48011

SWAN, MARVIN ALLEN, dentist; b. Grant, Nebr., Jan. 2, 1953; s. Robert E. and Delores A. (Stutheit) S.; m. Marcia E. Bartak, May 28, 1977; children: Daniel K., Michael R., Russel J. BA, U. Nebr., 1975, DDS, 1979. Gen. practice dentistry Grant, Mo., 1979—. Mem. ADA, Acad. Gen. Dentistry, Am. Soc. Dentistry for Children, U.S. Dental Inst., Grant C. of C. Democrat. Lutheran. Home: 115 W 3d Box 863 Grant NE 69140

SWAN, RITA RIGGIN, healthcare association executive; b. Ogden, Utah, June 27, 1943; d. Harlan Wendell and Betty Frances (Raebone) Riggin; m. Douglas Arthur Swan, Aug. 25, 1963; children: Catherine Emma, Marsha Lorraine. BA in English, Kans. State U., 1963; MA in English, U. Wis., Madison, 1965; PhD in English, Vanderbilt U., 1975. Instr. English Monticello Coll., Godfrey, Ill., 1964-66; instr. German Principia Coll., Elsah, Ill., 1966-67; editor environ. program U. Vt., Burlington, 1973-75; assoc. editor Gen. Motors, Troy, Mich., 1977-78; asst. prof. English Jamestown (N.D.) Coll., 1979-82; pres. Children's Healthcare Is a Legal Duty, Inc., Sioux City, Iowa, 1983—; speaker 3 addresses nat. confs. 5th Nat. Conf. Child Abuse and Neglect, Milw., 7th Nat. Conf. CA/N in Chgo., Com. for Sci. Investigation of Claims of Paranormal, Buffalo; 5 appearances nat. TV Donahue, PBS Latenight, Break Away, Today and Crossroads; about 20 appearances on local TV around the country. Contbr. articles to profl. jours. Sr. teaching fellow Vanderbilt U., 1967-68; recipient Scholarship awards Kans. State U.. 1960-63, U. Wis., 1963-64; Award for Excellence in Teaching Jamestown Coll., 1982. Mem. Nat. Assn. Counsel for Children, Cult Awareness Network, So. Poverty Law Ctr., Siouxland Council Child Abuse and Neglect (treas. 1983-85, sec. 1985-86), Nat. Council Against Health Fraud (affiliate). Democrat. Methodist. Avocations: horseback riding, camping. Office: CHILD Inc Box 2604 Sioux City IA 51106

SWAN, RONALD DAVID, university police chief, criminal justice educator; b. St. Louis, Mar. 2, 1943; s. David Percy and Dorothea Prudence (Myers) S.; m. Cheryl Ann Ramey, May 11, 1972; children—Ronald David II, Brendan Daniel. A.A.S., Hannibal-LaGrange Coll., 1964; B.S. in Adminstrn. Justice, U. Mo.-St. Louis, 1973; M.A., Webster U., 1974; grad. Inst. Applied Sci., 1974; B.S., SUNY-Albany, 1982; postgrad. New Scotland Yard. Maj., Hillsdale (Mo.) Police Dept., 1968-71; chief police, Beverly Hills, Mo., 1971-77, Monticello, Ill., 1977-83; chief univ. police Ill. State U., Normal, 1983—; part-time instr. criminal justice St. Louis Community Coll., 1975-77, St. Mary's Coll., O'Fallon, Mo., 1975-77, Columbia Coll., Mo., 1976-77, Parkland Coll., Champaign, Ill., 1980-84, Richland Community Coll., Decatur, Ill., 1982—, Lincoln (Ill.) Coll., 1985—, Ill. State U., 1986—. Contbr. articles to profl. jours. Recipient Medal of Distinction City of Monticello. Mem. Brit. Acad. Forensic Scis., Acad. Criminal Justice Scis., Internat. Assn. Chiefs of Police, Ill. Assn. of Chiefs of Police, Am. Soc. Criminology. Methodist. Home: 102 Sheringham Normal IL 61761 Office: Ill State U Police Dept 700 W College Normal IL 61761

SWANGER, STERLING ORVILLE, appliance manufacturing company executive; b. Battle Creek, Iowa, Jan. 5, 1922; s. Orville M. and Alma Louise (Messing) S.; m. Maxine O. Hindman, July 2, 1950; 1 son, Eric. B.S., Iowa State U., 1947; student U. Va., 1965. Registered profl. engr., Iowa. Indsl. engr. Maytag Co., Newton, Iowa, 1947-52, methods engr., 1952-54, asst. chief methods engr., 1954-57, chief methods engr., 1957-68, mgr. prodn. engring., 1968-71, mgr. engring., 1971-74, asst. v.p. mfg., 1974-75, v.p. mfg., 1975-86, sr. v.p. and chief mfg. officer, 1986-87, also dir., cons., 1987—. Mem., Newton Planning and Zoning Commn., 1966-70; trustee Newton Skiff Hosp. Served with AUS 1943-46. Mem. Nat. Soc. Profl. Engrs., Iowa Engring. Soc., Nat. Mgmt. Assn., Am. Mgmt. Assn., Am. Ordnance Assn. Republican. Presbyterian. Clubs: Newton Country, Elks.

SWANGO, MARILYN ANN, science educator; b. Vincennes, Ind., Dec. 12, 1942; d. Henry J. and Anna Marie (WIlliams) DeBuisseret; m. David M. Swango, Apr. 16, 1966; children: Stephanie, Melissa, Melinda, Jonathan. AA, Vincennes U., 1962; BA, U. Calif., Santa Barbara, 1964; MA, Ball State U., 1970; PhD, Ind. U., 1983. Middle sch. tchr. math. and sci. Indpls. Pub. Schs., 1964-66; middle sch. tchr. math. Met. Sch. Dist. of Lawrence (Ind.) Township, 1967-68; dir. religious edn. St. Thomas More, Mooresville, Ind., 1975-80; research asst. to Dr. Hans Anderson Ind. U., Indpls., 1977; grad. asst., assoc. instr. Ind. U., Inpls. and Bloomington, 1977-82; 7th grade sci. tchr. Wayne Township Schs., Indpls., 1982—; pres. Kindergarten-12th grade Teaching Doctors in Ind. Author articles in jours. and book revs. Pres. Federated Ch. Bd. Mooresville, 1985-86; chmn. Evangelical and Ecumenical Growth Commn., St. Thomas More, 1981-85; founder Ecumenical Gathering, 1982-85; active Archdiocesan Commn. on Ecumenism, Archdiocese of Indpls., 1982—; chmn. policy adv. council, South Wayne Jr. High Sch., 1983-86; cons. to Council on Christian Unity, Inpls., at-large cons. Ind. Council of Chs., Dept. of Peace and Justice. Grantee Ind. U., 1982. Mem. World Council for Curriculum and Instrn., Wayne Township Classroom Tchrs. Assn., Hoosier Assn. Sci. Tchrs., Inc., Phi Delta Kappa. Roman Catholic. Home: 2260 Old St Rd 67N Martinsville IN 46151 Office: South Wayne Jr High 4901 W Gadsden Indianapolis IN 46241

SWANSON, ALLAN FREDERICK, engineer; b. Thief River Falls, Minn., Sept. 11, 1929; s. George Gottfried and Thora (Hanson) S.; m. Betty Lou Huber, June 16, 1957; children: Susan, Mark. BSEE, U. N.D., 1956. Registered profl. engr., Minn. Supr. quality assurance 3M Co., St. Paul, 1970-77, supr. elec. design, 1977-81, mgr. product devel., 1981-83, mgr. quality assurance, 1983-85, mgr. reliability engring., 1985—. Served to sgt. U.S. Army, 1951-52, Korea. Mem. Am. Soc. for Quality Control (reliability div.). Republican. Lutheran. Avocations: photography, home computing, wood carving, cross country skiing. Home: 2456 Elm Dr White Bear Lake MN 55110

SWANSON, BEVERLY JANE, records and information management executive; b. Willmar, Minn., Jan. 27, 1949; d. Vernon Leroy and Betty Arlene (Schockley) Fullerton; m. Roger William Swanson, Mar. 21, 1970; children: Tammy Marie, Randolph William. BS in Speech, Mankato (Minn.) State U., 1971. Mgmt. analyst, records mgr. Minn. Dept. Hwys., St. Paul, 1974-76; chief records mgr. Minn. Dept. Adminstrn., St. Paul, 1977-79; records mgr. City of Mpls., 1980—. Advisory bd. Minn. Hist. Soc., 1981-83. Named Outstanding Records Mgr. of Yr. IRM mag., 1979. Mem. Assn. Records Mgrs. and Adminstrs. (cert., v.p. region IV 1982-86, membership chmn., sec., v.p., pres. Twin City chpt. 1973-79, chpt. mem. of yr. award 1980), Inst. Cert. Records Mgrs. and Adminstrs. Lutheran. Avocations: fishing, camping, reading, sewing. Home: 7003 164th Ave NW Anoka MN 55303 Office: City of Mpls 300 City Hall Minneapolis MN 55415

SWANSON, DAVID H(ENRY), economist, educator; b. Anoka, Minn., Nov. 1, 1930; s. Henry Otto and Louise Isabell (Holiday) S.; B.A., St. Cloud State Coll., 1953; M.A., U. Minn., 1955, PhD, Iowa State U., 1987; m. Suzanne Nash, Jan. 19, 1952; children—Matthew David, Christopher James. Economist area devel. dept. No. States Power Co., Mpls., 1955-56, staff asst., v.p. sales, 1956-57, economist indsl. devel. dept., 1957-63; dir. area devel. dept. Iowa So. Utilities Co., Centerville, 1963-67, dir. econ. devel. and research, 1967-70; dir. New Orleans Econ. Devel. Council, 1970-72; div. mgr. Kaiser Aetna Texas, New Orleans, 1972-73; dir. corp. research United Services Automobile Assn., San Antonio, 1973-76; pres. Lantern Corp., 1974-79; adminstr. bus. devel. State of Wis., Madison, 1976-78; dir. Center Indsl. Research and Service, Iowa State U., Ames, 1978—, mem. mktg. faculty Coll. Bus. Adminstrn., 1979-85; dir. Iowa Devel. Commn., 1982-83; mem. adv. bd. Iowa Venture Capital Fund, 1985—; dir. Applied Strategies Internat. Ltd., 1983—; chmn. Iowa Curriculum Assistance System, 1984-85. Mem. Iowa Airport Planning Council, 1968-70; mem. adv. council office Comprehensive Health Planning, 1967-70; mem. adv. council Ctr. Indsl. Research and Service, 1967-70, New Orleans Met. Area Com., 1972-73; mem. Dist. Export Council, 1978—; mem. region 7 adv. council SBA, 1978—; dir. Mid-Continent R&D Council, 1980-84; chmn. Iowa del. White House Conf. on Small Bus., 1980; chmn. Gov.'s Task Force on High Tech., 1982-83; chmn. Iowa High Tech. Council, 1983-86; adv. com. U. New Orleans, 1971-73; county finance chmn. Republican Party, 1966-67; bd. dirs. Greater New Orleans Urban League, 1970-73, Indsl. Policy Council, 1984—; mem. Iowa Gov.'s Export Council, 1984—; v.p. Iowa Sister State Friendship Com., 1985—, Fed. lab. Consortium, 1985—. Served with USAF, 1951-52. C.P.C.U. Mem. Nat. Assn. Mgmt. Tech. Assistance Ctrs. (pres. 1985, bd. dirs. 1986—), Tech. Transfer Soc. (bd. dirs. 1984—, v.p. 1987—), Nat. Univ. Continuing Edn. Assn., Internat. Council Small Bus. Republican. Episcopalian. Clubs: Rotary (bd. dirs. 1986—), Toastmasters (past pres.). Home: 1007 Kennedy Dr Ames IA 50010 Office: Iowa State U Ames IA 50011

SWANSON, DAVID LEONARD, engineer; b. Detroit, Mar. 23, 1940; s. Carl Thure and Mary Catherine (Smith) S.; m. Sally Ann Hack, Oct. 3, 1964; children: Jeffrey, Marc, Andrea. BS in Mech. Engring., Mich. Tech. U., 1962. Registered profl. engr., Mich. Engr. Chevrolet Motor div. Gen. Motors, Warren, Mich., 1962-72, Warner Electric, South Beloit, Ill., 1972-76; v.p. engring. Atwood Mobile Products div. Atwood Industries, Inc., Rockford, Ill., 1976—. Patentee in field. Moderator Product Safety and Liability Workshop, U. Wis., 1984-86. Mem. Soc. Automotive Engrs., Can. Standards Assn., Recreational Vehicle Industry Assn., Rockford C. of C. (moderator leadership community awareness program 1984-86). Home: 5438 Inverness Rockford IL 61107 Office: Atwood Mobile Products 4750 Hiawatha Rockford IL 61103

SWANSON, DAVID WENDELL, psychiatrist; b. Fort Dodge, Iowa, Aug. 28, 1930; s. David Verner and Edith Bengta (Peterson) S.; m. Lois Marie Rasmussen, Aug. 8, 1953; Children: Susan Marie, David Karl, Bruce Alan. BA, Augustana Coll., 1952; MD, U. Ill., Chgo., 1956. Diplomate Am. Bd. Psychiatry and Neurology. Intern Ill. Cen. Hosp., Chgo., 1956-57; resident in psychiatry and neurology Ill. State Psychiat. Inst., Chgo., 1959-62, service chief, 1962-63; asst. chmn., assoc. prof. Loyola Med. Sch., Chgo., 1964-70; cons., prof. Mayo Clinic, Rochester, Minn., 1970—; sect. head adult psychiatry Mayo Clinic, 1974-78, asst. chmn. psychiatry, 1978-85, dir. pain mgmt. ctr., 1974-79. Author: The Paranoid, 1970; contbr. numerous articles to profl. jours. Served to capt. U.S. Army, 1957-59. Fellow Am. Psychiat. Assn. Am. Coll. Psychiatrists; mem. AAAS, Internat. Assn. Study Pain. Lutheran. Avocations: golf, travel, gardening. Office: Dept Psychiatry 200 First St SW Rochester MN 55905

SWANSON, DONALD KNOX, electrical company executive, mechanical engineer; b. Clayton, Ga., Apr. 3, 1935; s. George Starlin and Hattie May (Brooks) S.; m. Stella Jane Christian, July 5, 1957; Kimberly, Kellye, Todd. BSME, Ga. Inst. Tech., 1959; MBA, Xavier U., 1970. Registered profl engr., Ohio. Engr. AID Corp., Clayton, 1959-60; design engr. Alcoa Corp., Maryville, Tenn., 1960-62; project engr. Def. Electronics Supply Ctr., Dayton, Ohio, 1962-68, staff engr., 1968-70, br. chief, 1970-75, div. chief, 1975—. Author papers in field. Named Engr. of Yr. Def. Logistics Agy., Alexandria, Va., 1985; recipient numerous performance awards Def. Electronics Supply Ctr. Mem. Nat. Soc. Profl. Engrs., Dayton chpt. Ohio Soc. Profl. Engrs. (mem. chmn. 1970-71, Standards Engring. Soc. (sec. 1982, 84, 85, Outstanding Sect. Mem. award 1985), Exec. Devel. Assn. (bd. dirs. 1984-85). Democrat. Baptist. Lodge: Masons. Avocations: golf, woodworking, photography. Home: 101 Pine Bluff Dr Dayton OH 45440 Office: Def Electronics Supply Ctr 1507 Wilmington Pike Dayton OH 45444

SWANSON, D'ORSEY DUANE, entrepreneur; b. Mankato, Minn., July 1, 1926; s. Carl Edward and Anna Mary (Sanger) S.; m. Virginia May Weingartz, May 8, 1948; children: Cheryl, Stephen, Francie, Kevin, Dale, Patricia, Brian. Grad., High Sch., Mankato, 1946; student, Dunwoody Inst., 1948, Mankato Area Vocat. Tech. Inst., 1977-82. Baker Johnson Bakery, Mankato, 1946-51; carpenter Carl Swanson Contractor, Mankato, 1951-53; maintenance machinist Continental Can Co., Mankato, 1953-78; owner, operator, pres. Ginny May Donuts, Mankato, 1975—; ptnr. KDS Equipment Co., Mankato. Mem. Manatoans for Good Govt., 1982-84; mem. adv. bd. Mankato Area Vocat. Tech. Inst., 1982-85. Served with U.S. Army, 1944-46. Mem. Small Bus. Adv. Assn., Am. Legion, Mankato Area C. of C. Republican. Roman Catholic. Lodges: Moose, Eagles, Elks. Avocations: woodworking, numismatics, boating, traveling. Office: Ginny May Donuts 1215 N Front St Mankato MN 56001

SWANSON, GORDON MERLE, food company executive; b. Chgo., Oct. 22, 1930; s. Carl Elmer and Edith Marie (Bergeson) S.; m. Ann Louise Johnson, July 5, 1958; children—John, Robert. B.S., Northwestern U., 1958, M.B.A., 1961. Supr. advt. services finance Quaker Oats Co., Chgo., 1958-62; controller Ansul Co., Marinette, Wis., 1962-70, Amtel, Inc., Providence, 1971-78; v.p. fin. Ravenhorst, Bellows & Assocs., Inc., Olivia, Minn., 1978-79, Marshall Foods, Inc., Minn., 1979-80; treas. Minn. Malting Co., Cannon Falls, Minn., 1981-83; v.p. fin. Minn. Grain Pearling Co., 1983—. Served with USAF, 1951-55. Mem. Am. Inst. C.P.A.'s. Home: 765 Sibley Dr Northfield MN 55057

SWANSON, HOWARD DALE, lawyer; b. Grand Forks, N.D., June 25, 1958; s. M. Dale and Anna Mae (Widner) S.; m. Debbie J. Fowler, Aug. 25, 1984. BS/BA, U. N.D., 1980; JD cum laude, Hamline U., 1983. Bar: N.D. 1983, U.S. Dist. Ct. N.D. 1983, U.S. Ct. Appeals (8th cir.) 1983, Minn. 1984, U.S. Dist. Ct. Minn. 1984. Legal intern Minn. Pub. Utilities Commn., St. Paul, 1981-83; assoc. Letnes, Marshall, Feidler & Clapp, Grand Forks, 1983—; atty. City of Grand Forks, 1984—. Named one of Outstanding Young Men in Am., 1985; Hamline U. scholar, 1980-81. Mem. ABA, Nat. Inst. Mcpl. Law Officers, Am. Trial Lawyers Assn., N.D. Bar Assn., Minn. Bar Assn. Democrat. Lutheran. Club: St. Paul Athletic. Avocations: tennis, traveling, cooking, music, skiing. Home: 38 Vail Circle Grand Forks ND 58201 Office: Letnes Marshall Fiedler & Clapp 401 DeMers Ave Suite 202 Grand Forks ND 58201

SWANSON, LAURENCE ALBERT, lawyer, magazine editor; b. Monmouth, Ill., June 29, 1941; s. Ronald Louis and Jeanne (McIntyre) S.; m. Patricia Pickens, Mar. 11, 1964. MusB, Boston U., 1963; MEd, Western Ill. U., 1967; JD magna cum laude, No. Ill. U., 1985. Bar: Ill. 1985, U.S. Dist. Ct. (no. dist.) Ill. 1985. Band dir. Colchester and Sciota (Ill.) Pub. Schs., 1967-70; yardmaster and operator Burlington No. R.R., Aurora, Ill., 1970-82; pvt. practice Aurora, Ill., 1986—. Editor Turning Wheels, 1972—, SDC, Inc., 1972—. Mem. ABA, Ill. Bar Assn., Kane County Bar Assn., Am. Agrl. Law Assn., Studebaker Drivers Club. Avocations: photography, automobiles. Home: Box 1040 Oswego IL 60543 Office: 15 N Edgelawn Dr Aurora IL 60506

SWANSON, LESLIE CHARLES, writer, photographer, publisher; b. Moline, Ill., Aug. 21, 1905; s. Victor Ansfrid and Agnes Hilda (Wyman) S.; m. Gladys C. Huddleson, Aug. 10, 1940 (div. 1958); children: Vicki Swanson Wassenhove, Wendy; m. Mildred Clara Hyler, Oct. 7, 1972; stepchildren: Gary, Gerald, Sandra. BA, Augustana Coll., 1928. State editor Davenport (Iowa) Times, 1929-45; freelance writer and photographer Moline and Rock Island, Ill., 1945-60. contbr. articles to newspapers and mags.; pub. author Americana Books, Moline, 1960-85; author: Covered Bridges in Illinois, Iowa and Wisconsin, 1986, Old Mills in the Mid-West, 1962, Canals of Mid-America, 1963, Rural One-Room Schools of Mid-America, 1976. Pianist, mem. Tri-City Musical Soc., 1926—. Home: Box 334 Moline IL 61265

SWANSON, NELS PETER, natural resources conservation officer; b. Battle Creek, Mich., Jan. 18, 1946; s. Oscar Elis and Grace Monimia (Watts) S.; m. Dorothy Elaine Hartman, Mar. 31, 1970; children: Erika Heather, Fritz Garner. BS, Mich. State U., 1968; postgrad., Cen. Mich. U., 1968-70. Cert. law enforcement officer Mich. Law Enforcement Officer Training Council; lic. social worker, Mich. Social worker State of Mich., Allegan, 1971-77; conservation officer State of Mich., Parma, 1977—. Asst. cub master Boy Scouts Am., Parma, 1985-86; breeder Golden Retriever dogs for Blind Project Jackson Lions Club, 4-H. Mem. N. Am. Wildlife Enforcement Officers Assn. Avocations: farming. Home and Office: 11501 Mackie Rd Parma MI 49269

SWANSON, NORMA C., financial executive; b. Mpls., June 4, 1933; d. John L. and Marion A. (Groschen) Theisen; m. Arthur J. Swanson, Nov. 11, 1952; children—Denise, Ken, Dave, John, Jerry, Gary. Mpls. Corp. officer Art's Superette, Inc., Fridley, Minn., 1968-70; credit clk. Unity Hosp., Fridley, 1970; office mgr. Bryant-Franklin Corp., Mpls., 1970-75; acct. Authorized Cons., Mpls., 1976; mng. ptnr. Theisen B Partnership, Mpls., 1982—; corp. officer Bossaire, Inc., Mpls., 1982—. Home: 361 Rice Creek Terr Fridley MN 55432 Office: Bossaire Inc 1321 Tyler St NE Minneapolis MN 55413

SWANSON, PAUL JOHN, JR., finance educator; b. Crawfordsville, Ind., May 10, 1934; s. Paul John and Helen (Bath) S. Student DePauw U., 1952; B.S. in Accountancy, U. Ill., 1959, B.S. in Econ. and Fin., 1960, M.S. in Fin., 1962, Ph.D., 1966. Grad. teaching asst. U. Ill., Urbana, 1960-65, grad. research asst., 1964-65; asst. prof. finance U. Cin., 1965-67, assoc. prof., 1967—, prof.-in-charge dept. quantitative analysis, 1967-68; pres. Paul Swanson and Assocs., Inc., 1983—; cons. local bus. and govt. agencies; mem. Perfect North Slope Ski Patrol, Ind. Served with AUS, 1956-58. Mem. Nat. Def. Exec. Res., Inst. Mgmt. Scis. (past pres. Miami Valley chpt.), Ops. Research Soc. Am., Am., Midwest finance assns., Fin. Analysts Soc., Inst. Chartered Fin. Analysts, Am. Statis. Assn., Delta Chi, Delta Sigma Pi. Republican. Episcopalian (treas., chmn. TV ministry com. 1983—, vestry). Home: 3441 Telford St Cincinnati OH 45220

SWANSON, PHILLIP ALAN, real estate developer; b. Urbana, Ill., Mar. 18, 1950; s. Lloyd Phillip and Virginia Ruth (Clark) S.; m. Jane Ashworth Robertson, July 8, 1978; children: Phillip, Ann, Kathryn. Student, Eastern Ill. U., 1968-69, Parkland Jr. Coll., 1969-71; BS, So. Ill. U., 1973. Owner

Swanson Properties, Rantoul, Ill., 1973—, North Am. Lodging and Devel., Rantoul, 1984—, Best Western Heritage Inn, Inc., Rantoul, 1984—. Mem. Base Community Council, Rantoul, 1982-83; pres. Maplewood Cemetery Assn., Rantoul, 1982—; bd. dirs. Meth. Day Care Ctr., Rantoul, 1986—. Mem. Nat. Assn. Realtors, Best Western Internat., Am. Hotel/Motel Assn., Champaign C. of C., Rantoul C. of C. (pres. 1982-83), Airforce Assn. Episcopalian. Avocations: sailing, glider soaring, flying, hot air ballooning, landscaping. Home: 1001 N State Monticello IL 61856 Office: North Am Lodging and Devel 301 N Century Rantoul IL 61866

SWANSON, RAYNOLD A., retired electronics executive; b. Ellsworth, Wis., Feb. 7, 1920; s. August J. and Ida M. (Hansen) S.; m. Millicent J. Wicklund, Dec. 27, 1947; children: Vern, Larry, Doug. Mech. draftsman Collins Radio, Cedar Rapids, Iowa, 1947-50, mech. engr., 1950-67; sect. head Harris Corp., Quincy, Ill., 1967-70, v.p. mfg., co-founder Quintron Corp., Quincy, 1970-82, exec. v.p., 1982-85, also bd. dirs. Patentee mech. stop. Town clk. Riverside (Ill.) Township, 1980—; bd. dirs. Chaddock Sch., Quincy, 1976—; advisor bd. dirs. Salvation Army, Quincy, 1975—. Served with U.S. Army, 1942-45, ETO. Lodge: Kiwanis (pres. Quincy 1964-65, 1984-85). Avocations: golf, bowling, snow skiing. Home: 2335 N 12th St Quincy IL 62301

SWANSON, RICHARD CARL, electronics company executive; b. Mpls., Feb. 21, 1937; s. Carl E. and Signa Alvilde (Omodt) S.; children: Michael S., Dale K., Brian R.C., Kimberly A. BEE, U. Minn., 1960. Sales engr. Honeywell, Mpls., 1958-60; engr. Am. Monarch, Mpls., 1960-62; regional mgr. Semiconductor Specialists, Bloomington, Minn., 1962-67; pres., owner Indsl. Components Inc., Edina, Minn., 1967-76, Electronic Tool Supply, Inc., Burnsville, Minn., 1976—; cons. Terado Corp., St. Paul, 1959-64. Contbg. author: Select Semiconductor Circuits, 1960. Patentee in field. Scoutmaster, Boy Scouts Am., St. Paul, 1967—, tng. chmn., 1977-79, dist. chmn., 1979-82. Served with USAFR, 1958-62. Recipient Silver Beaver award Boy Scouts Am., 1982, Dist. Award of Merit, 1979, others. Mem. Soc. Mfg. Engrs. Republican. Lutheran. Lodge: Optimists. Home: 110 Shoshoni Trail Apple Valley MN 55124 Office: Electronic Tool Supply Inc 755 E Cliff Rd Burnsville MN 55337

SWANSON, ROBERT LOUIS, treasurer; b. Perrysburg, Ohio, May 6, 1938; s. Robert Rae and Inez Marie (Finch) S.; m. Doris Kramer, Oct. 21, 1967; children: Robert E., Steven M., Katharine L. BS, Bowling Green State U., 1964. CPA, Ohio. Auditor U.S. GAO, Cleve., 1964-65; audit supr. Ernst & Ernst, Toledo, 1965-71; audit mgr. Whinney Murray Ernst & Ernst, Hamburg, Fed. Republic of Germany, 1971-76; sec., treas. Jennson-Wright Corp., Toledo, 1977-82; treas. Fulton Industries Inc., Wauseon, Ohio, 1983—. Pres. Perrysburg Youth Athletic Assn., 1980-82; treas. Perrysburg Amateur Baseball Assn., 1982-84; treas., bd. dirs. Abundant Life of Perrysburg, Inc. Served with USAF, 1956-60. Mem. Am. Inst. CPA's, Ohio Soc. CPA's, Fin. Execs. Inst. (bd. dirs. 1984-86), Automotive Industry Action Group, Ohio Mfrs. Assn., Beta Alpha Psi, Beta Gamma Sigma. Club: Am. Club Hamburg (sec.-treas. 1975-76). Home: 8 Applewood Ct E Perrysburg OH 43551 Office: Fulton Industries 135 E Linfoot St Wauseon OH 43567

SWANSON, ROBERT MARTIN, medical center administrator; b. Bell, Calif., Oct. 14, 1940; s. Harold M. and Elsie Lorraine (Allison) S.; AB, Long Beach (Calif.) State Coll., 1963; MA, U. Iowa, 1965; PhD, UCLA, 1970; m. Katharine Vivian Martin, Feb. 16, 1980. Dir., Office of Mental Health Research, U. Iowa, Iowa City, 1966-70; research dir. Health Planning Council, St. Paul, 1970-73; exec. dir. Kansas City (Mo.) Health Plan, 1973-75; asst. dir. St. Louis U. Hosps., 1975-80; asst. v.p. and chief planning officer St. Louis U. Med. Ctr., 1981—; dir. Organizational Research & Devel. Corp., Kansas City; dir., sec., chmn. awards com. Group Health Found. of Greater St. Louis, dir. alliance for community health; clin. prof. St. Louis U. Grad. Program in Health and Hosp. Adminstrn., 1980—; adj. prof. Webster Coll., St. Louis, 1975-82; spl. cons. to Kansas City (Mo.) Health Dept., 1974-75; tech. cons. Health Services Adminstrn., HEW, 1973-75; coordinator St. Louis Community-Univ. Conf., 1977-80; mem. health affairs task force Mo. Cath. Conf., 1977. Named Adm. in Nebr. Navy, 1971; State of Iowa grantee, 1969. Mem. Nat. Assn. Hosp. Devel. (cert.), Am. Mgmt. Assn., Soc. for Advancement Mgmt., N.Am. Soc. Corp. Planners, Internat. Platform Assn., Advt. Club Greater St. Louis, Zeta Beta Tau. Republican. Eastern Orthodox. Contbr. articles on health services to profl. jours. Office: 3556 Caroline St Saint Louis MO 63104

SWANSON, ROBERT S., university administrator. Chancellor U. Wis.-Stout. Office: U Wis-Stout Office of Chancellor Menomonie WI 54751 *

SWANSTROM, KATHRYN RAYMOND, conv. mgmt. exec.; b. Milw., Sept. 5, 1907; d. William Hyland and Jessie Viola (Bliss) Raymond; student Bryant and Stratton Bus. Coll., 1927-28; m. Luther D. Swanstrom, Aug. 27, 1937; 1 son, William Hyland Raymond. Caterer, Racine, Wis., 1926; field rep., asst. mgr. Master Reporting Co., 1936-52; dir., sec. Diesel-Ritter Corp., 1942-46; pres. Kay C. Raymond Assos., 1952—; v.p., treas. Kenneth G. MacKenzie Assos., 1954—. Asst. sec. nat. com. U.S.A. 3d World Petroleum Congress, 1950-51. Sec. Ridge Civic Council, 1940-60; sec. Police Traffic Safety Com.; state chmn. legislation Ill. Congress Parents and Tchrs., 1943; Rep. state central committeewoman, 1938-44, asst. ofcl. reporter Rep. Nat. Conv., 1940-48. Mem. Anti-Cruelty Soc., AIM, Soc. Mayflower Descs. (dep. gov. gen.), Soc. Sons and Daus. of Pilgrims (3d v.p.), DAR (ofcl. timekeeper), Nat. Geog. Soc., ASTM, Ladies Oriental Shrine N. Am., Founders, Patriots (nat. councillor), Aux. Ancient Honorable Arty. Co. of Boston (nat. pres. 1977-80), John Alden Kindred, Internat. Platform Assn., Nat. Hugenot Soc. (pres. gen. 1979-83), Pi Omicron (nat. pres. 1950-54), Soc. Daughters of Colonial Wars (nat. sec. 1983-86). Republican. Episcopalian. Clubs: Beverly Hills Woman's, Crescendo. Address: 9027 S Damen Ave Chicago IL 60620 also: 3 Old Hill Farms Rd Westport CT 06880

SWARTZ, JACK E., marketing executive; b. Kenosha, Wis., July 23, 1931; s. George Henry and Eleanor Mary (Schreier) S.; m. Betty Hearn, June 12, 1953 (div. 1965); children: Robert, John; m. Teresa Ann Molgaard, Mar. 20, 1982. Grad. high sch., Kenosha. V.p. sales and mktg. Frost Co., Kenosha, 1961—, also bd. dirs. Republican. Roman Catholic. Club: Kenosha Yacht (rear commadore). Lodges: Elks, Moose. Avocations: fishing, boating, hunting, reading, crafts. Home: 2008 87th Pl Kenosha WI 53140

SWARTZ, TED ALLAN, advertising executive; b. Muskegon, Mich., May 1, 1953; s. Allan E. and Wilma Jeanne (Wilson) S.; m. Christena A. Rath, Apr. 25, 1981. BA in Chemistry, Hope Coll., 1975. Tech. writer Amoco Chems. Corp., Chgo., 1975-79; account exec. Kolb/Tookey & Assocs., Chgo., 1979-81; account supr. Bozell & Jacobs, Chgo., 1981-86; elected v.p. Bozell, Jacobs, Kenyon & Eckhardt, Chgo., 1983, mgmt. supr., 1986—. Mem. Chgo. Advt. Club. Republican. Presbyterian. Home: 159 W Burton Pl Chicago IL 60610 Office: Bozell Jacobs Kenyon & Eckhardt 625 N Michigan Ave Chicago IL 60611

SWARTZ, WILLIAM JOHN, transportation resources company executive; b. Hutchinson, Kans., Nov. 6, 1934; s. George Glen and Helen Mae (Prather) S.; m. Dorothy Jean Parshall, June 5, 1956; children: John Christopher, Jeffrey Michael. BSME, Duke U., 1956; JD, George Washington U., 1961; MS in Mgmt. (Alfred P. Sloan fellow), MIT, 1967. With AT & SF Ry., 1961-78, 79—, asst. v.p. exec. dept., 1973-77, v.p. adminstrn., 1977-78, exec. v.p., 1979-83; exec. v.p. Santa Fe Industries, Chgo., 1978-79, pres., 1983—; vice chmn. Santa Fe So. Pacific, 1983—; pres. AT & SF Ry., 1983—. Served with USMC, 1956-59. Mem. Chgo. Assn. Commerce and Industry, Western Ry. Assn., Assn. Am. R.R. (bd. dirs.). Republican. Methodist. Clubs: Chgo. Athletic Assn., Mid-Am., Chgo. Home: 233 E Walton Pl Chicago IL 60611 Office: Atchison Topeka & Santa Fe Rwy Co 80 E Jackson Blvd Chicago IL 60604

SWARTZLANDER, GLENN CARROLL, osteopathic pediatrician; b. Toledo, Aug. 19, 1943; s. Glenn C. and Virginia Mae (Hartman) S.; m. Patricia A. Wenzel, Aug. 28, 1965; children—Christi A., Kurt D. A.A., Muskegon Community Coll., 1963; B.S., Central Mich. U., 1966; D.O., Kansas City Coll. Osteopathy and Surgery, 1970. Intern, Muskegon (Mich.) Gen. Hosp., 1970-71; gen. practice medicine, Ravenna, Mich., 1971-72; resident in pediatrics Grand Rapids Osteo. Hosp. (Mich.), and Butterworth Hosp., Grand Rapids, 1973-75; practice medicine specializing in pediatrics, Muskegon, 1975—; chief of staff Muskegon (Mich.) Gen. Hosp., 1984—; clin. assoc. prof. pediatrics W.Va. Sch. Osteo. Medicine. Pres. Westshore Heart Assn., 1977, 79, adviser Multicap Presch. program, 1975-82; mem. SCAN com. Protective Services Muskegon County; committeeman Boy Scouts Am., 1980—; soccer coach Tri-Cities Soccer League, 1979—. Mem. Western Mich. Pediatric Soc., Mich. Assn. Osteo. Physicians and Surgeons, Am. Osteo. Assn., Am. Coll. Osteo. Pediatricians (sr.). Republican. Mem. Ref. Ch. Am. Home: 18690 Pinecrest St Spring Lake MI 49456 Office: 1828 Oak Ave Muskegon MI 49442

SWARTZLE, CHARLES DAVID, biological and chemical company executive; b. Battle Creek, Mich., Feb. 6, 1953; s. Simon Joseph and June (Harmond) S.; m. Maryann Sophie, Sept. 13, 1986. BS in Ecosystems Analysis, Grand Valley State Coll., 1977; postgrad., Western Mich. U., 1979. Chemist Flexfab, Inc., Hastings, Mich., 1978-81; owner, pres. Besco Water Conditioning, Inc., Battle Creek, 1981—, Leland Pump Co., Battle Creek, 1983—. Mem. Water Quality Assn. (cert.), Nat. Assn. Am. Bus. Clubs, Battle Creek Assn. Home Builders. Republican. Roman Catholic. Avocations: sailing, downhill skiing, photography. Home: 1200 Arms Rd Marshall MI 49068 Office: Besco Water Conditioning Inc 1071 Capital Ave NE Battle Creek MI 49017

SWEARINGEN, JOHN ELDRED, business executive; b. Columbia, S.C., Sept. 7, 1918; s. John Eldred and Mary (Hough) S.; m. Bonnie L. Bolding, May 18, 1969; children by previous marriage: Marcia L. Swearingen Pfleeger, Sarah K. Swearingen Origer, Linda Swearingen Arnold. B.S., U. S.C., 1938, LL.D. (hon.), 1965; M.S., Carnegie-Mellon U., 1939, D.Eng. (hon.), 1981; hon. degrees from numerous colls. and univs. Chem. engr. research dept. Standard Oil Co. (Ind.), Whiting, Ind., 1939-47; various positions Amoco Prodn. Co., Tulsa, 1947-51; gen. mgr. prodn. Standard Oil Co. (Ind.), Chgo., 1951; dir. Standard Oil Co. (Ind.), 1952, v.p. prodn., 1954, exec. v.p., 1956, pres., 1958, chief exec. officer, 1960-83, chmn. bd., 1965-83; chmn., chief exec. officer Continental Ill. Corp., Chgo., 1984—; dir. Lockheed Corp., Continental Ill. Corp., Continental Ill. Bank, Sara Lee Corp., AON Corp.; chmn. Nat. Petroleum Council, 1974-76, Am. Petroleum Inst., 1978-79. Mem. adv. bd. Hoover Instn. on War, Revolution and Peace, 1967—; trustee Carnegie Mellon U., 1960—, DePauw U., 1966-81, Chgo. Orchestral Assn., 1973-79; bd. dirs. McGraw Wildlife Found., 1964-75; bd. dirs. Automotive Safety Found., 1959-69, chmn., 1962-64; bd. dirs. Hwy Users Fedn. for Safety and Mobility, 1969-75, Northwestern Meml. Hosp., 1965—. Recipient decorations from govts. of Iran, Italy, Egypt, Phillipines; recipient Washington award Western Soc. Engrs., 1981, Gold medal for disting. achievement Am. Petroleum Inst.; Laureate, Nat. Bus. Hall of Fame, Jr. Achievement. Fellow Am. Inst. Chem. Engrs.; mem. Am. Inst. Mining, Metall. and Petroleum Engrs. (Charles F. Rand Meml. gold medal 1980), Am. Chem. Soc., Nat. Acad. Engring., Phi Beta Kappa, Sigma Xi, Omicron Delta Kappa, Tau Beta Pi. Clubs: Mid-Am., Chgo., Racquet (Chgo.); Links (N.Y.C.); Bohemian (San Francisco); Eldorado Country (Palm Springs); Old Elm (Lake Forest, Ill.); Glen View (Golf, Ill.). Office: Continental Ill Corp 231 S La Salle St Chicago IL 60697

SWEARINGEN, LON STEELE, data processing executive, consultant; b. Cleve., Sept. 16, 1947; s. Glenn Steele and Cynthia (Mramer) S.; m. Bonnie Cifranic, Feb. 5, 1971; children: Bryce, Glenn. BS, Cleve. State U., 1970; postgrad., Case Western Reserve U., 1976-77. V.p. Meta Technologies, Cleve., 1978-79; program mgr. TRW, Cleve., 1980-84; mgr. info. systems TRW/PCC, Minerva, Ohio, 1984—. Pres. West Geauga Baseball Fedn., Chesterland, Ohio, 1979-84. Republican. Lodge: Masons. Avocations: history, woodworking. Home: 7870 Sandleford Ave NW North Canton OH 44720 Office: TRW/PCC 3860 Union Ave SE Minerva OH 44657

SWEARINGEN, RUSSELL LYLE, manufacturing engineer; b. Drakesville, Iowa, Apr. 7, 1926; s. Russell Lyle and Sada Mae (Paris) S.; m. Ila Patricia Robertson, June 11, 1955; children: Pamela Brackey, Patricia Jackson, Russell, Ronald. BSME, U. Iowa, 1949. Chief indsl. engr. Freuhauf Trailer Co., Cedar Rapids, Iowa, 1950-60; process engr. Rockwell-Collins, Cedar Rapids, 1960—. Master Cub Scouts Am., Marion, Iowa, 1970-71; mgr. Marion kids baseball team, 1969-77. Served with U.S. Army, 1944-46, ETO. Decorated Purple Heart, Bronze Star. Mem. SME (chpt. chmn. 1959-60, other offices), Am. Legion. Democrat. Club: Fawn Creek Country (Anamosa, Iowa). Home: 820 30th St Marion IA 52302 Office: Rockwell Collins 105-233 400 Collins Rd NE Cedar Rapids IA 52498

SWEAT, ROBERT WARREN, research and development company executive; b. Wisconsin Rapids, Wis., Dec. 21, 1946; s. Warren Harding and Ella Jane (Dewitt) S.; m. Leona Mae Capek, Sept. 2, 1968 (div. Nov. 1980); children: Michelle, Sheila; m. Patricia Ruth Smith, Nov. 7, 1981; children: David, Wendy. BS in Adminstrn. and Econs., U. Wis., Stevens Point, 1969; postgrad, life ins. mktg. inst., Purdue U., 1976-81. Gen. mgr. Golden Hanger, Stevens Point, 1967-69; rep. Met. Life Ins. Co., Wisconsin Rapids, 1969-78; pres. Sweat Ins., Inc., Wisconsin Rapids, 1975—; chief exec. officer W.I.F.C. Corp., Wisconsin Rapids, 1981—. Chmn. small bus. com. City of Wisconsin Rapids, 1987—, chmn. airport com., 1987. Recipient Citizenship award VFW, 1965. Nat. Quality award Nat. Assn. Life Underwriters, 1976, Wis. Men Achievement award Hooper Pub. Co., 1976. Mem. Wisconsin Rapids C. of C. Avocations: music, flying. Home: 2131 12th St S Wisconsin Rapids WI 54494 Office: WIFC Corp 410 Daly Suite 3 Wisconsin Rapids WI 54494

SWEATMAN, PHILLIP JAY, computer services company executive, data processing executive; b. Norfolk, Va., Sept. 23, 1955; s. Julius Caleb and Lucille (Nollet) S.; m. Lynne Denise Baltic, June 27, 1980; children: Phillip Charles Julius, Adrienne Nicole. BSBA in Econs., U. Denver, 1978; MBA in Fin., U. Pitts., 1982. Chartered fin. analyst. Asst. officer Mellon Bank Corp., Pitts., 1979-81, planning officer, 1983-84; fin. planning analyst Copperweld Corp., Pitts., 1981-83; bus. planning analyst Computer Sci. Corp., El Segundo, Calif., 1984-85, mgr. strategy, analyst, 1985-86; controller, asst. sec. CSC Comtec Inc., Farmington Hills, Mich., 1986-87; controller Franks Nursery & Crafts Inc., Detroit, 1987—; founder, pres., chmn. P$L Computer Services Ltd., Pitts., 1983—; instr. Grad. Sch. Bus., Robert Morris Coll., Pitts., 1984. Mem. World Affairs Council Pitts., 1979-80; treas. Perry Point Townhome Owner's Assn., Pitts., 1981-83, Rolling Ranchos Homeowner's Assn., Lomita, Calif., 1985. Recipient Univ. Honors Scholarship U. Denver, 1976-78. Republican. Roman Catholic. Avocations: music, arts. Home: 25612 Livingston Circle Farmington Hills MI 48018 Office: Franks Nursery and Crafts Inc 6501 E Nevada Detroit MI 48034

SWEDBACK, JAMES M., insurance company executive; b. 1935. With Pioneer Mut. Life Ins. Co., Fargo, N.D., 1962—, now pres., chief exec. officer. Office: Pioneer Mut Life Ins Co 203 10th St N Fargo ND 58102 *

SWEDLUND, HARRY ARVID, allergist, internist; b. Mpls., Apr. 13, 1929; s. Peter S. and Ellen E. (Hamberg) S.; m. Delores Luella Scholz, Aug. 1, 1953; children: Roy, Jane, Lynn, Glen, James, Robert. BA, U. Minn., 1951, MD, 1954, MS in Medicine, 1961. Diplomate Am. Bd. Internal Medicine, Am. Bd. Allergy and Immunology. Practice medicine specializing in internal medicine, allergy and immunology Mayo Clinic, Rochester, Minn., 1962—, cons., 1962—. Served with USPHS, 1954-57. Fellow ACP, Am. Acad. Allergy, Phi Beta Kappa, Alpha Omega Alpha. Lutheran. Home: 730 SW 11th St Rochester MN 55902 Office: Mayo Clinic 200 SW 1st St Rochester MN 55905

SWEDLUND, SHARI LOU, social worker; b. Boone, Iowa, Nov. 29, 1955; s. Robert Lyle and Beverly Lou (Jay) S. AA in Human Services, Des Moines Area Community Coll., 1976; BSW, U. No. Iowa, 1978. Child devel. worker Woodward (Iowa) State Hosp., 1978-79, resident treatment worker, 1981-83; social worker Welcome Inn Community Ctr., Hamilton, Ont., Can., 1979-81; child/adult protection investigator State of Iowa, Des Moines, 1983—; cons. social work Bayard (Iowa) Care Ctr., 1978-79. Evangelical. Avocations: planning and devel. holistic treatment ctr.

SWEEN, MARK GREGORY, real estate comapny executive; b. Schnectady, N.Y., June 12, 1951; s. A. Randolph and Glenyce Marie (Nolan) S. BSBA, Pa. State U., 1975. CPA, Minn. Sr. cons. Peat, Marwick, Mitchell & Co., Mpls., 1976-82; pres. Hawthorne Mgmt. Co., Mpls., 1982—. Treas. various polit. campaigns, Mpls., 1978-82; alt. del. to conv. Minn. Ind. Reps., 1980-82; treas., 2d v.p., bd. dirs. Minn. Multi Housing Assn. Served with U.S. Army, 1972-74. Named Outstanding Bd. Mem., Minn. Multi Housing Assn., 1985, 86. Mem. Am. Inst. CPA's, Minn. Soc. CPA's. Clubs: Mpls. Athletic; St. Paul Breakfast (bd. dirs. 1984-86), Commodore Squash (St. Paul). Lodge: Optimist. Home: 596 Summit Ave #3 Saint Paul MN 55102 Office: Hawthorne Mgmt Inc 1624 Harmon Pl Suite 207 Minneapolis MN 55414

SWEENEY, ASHER WILLIAM, justice Supreme Court Ohio; b. Canfield, Ohio, Dec. 11, 1920; s. Walter William and Jessie Joan (Kidd) S.; m. Bertha M. Englert, May 21, 1945; children: Randall W., Ronald R., Garland A., Karen M. Student, Youngstown U., 1939-42; LL.B., Duke U., 1948. Bar: Ohio 1949. Practiced law Youngstown, Ohio, 1949-51; judge adv. gen. Dept. Def., Washington, 1951-65; chief Fed. Contracting Agy., Cin., 1965-68; corp. law 1968-77; justice Ohio Supreme Ct., Columbus, 1977—. Democratic candidate for Sec. of State Ohio, 1958. Served with U.S. Army, 1942-46; col. Res. 1951-68. Decorated Legion of Merit, Bronze Star; named to Army Hall of Fame Ft. Benning, Ga., 1981. Mem. Ohio Bar Assn., Phi Delta Phi. Democrat. Home: 6690 Drake Rd Cincinnati OH 45243 Office: 30 E Broad Columbus OH 43215

SWEENEY, CLIFTON RANDOLPH, management consultant; b. Cleve., Mar. 16, 1949; s. Dallas Roy and Tarrah Virginia (Edwards) S.; divorced;1 child, Clifton Randolph Jr. BA, Case Western Res. U., 1971; postgrad., Columbia U. Mktg. exec. Xerox Corp., Cleve., 1972-74, IBM Corp., Cleve., 1974-75; dir. Blue Cross of N.E. Ohio, Cleve., 1975-77; pvt. practice mgmt. cons. Cleve., 1979—; pres. Grade 1 Thoroughbred Stables, Cleve., 1985—. Author: Management, Horses (Thoroughbred), Horse Racing and Handicapping, numerous poems. Fundraiser, loaned exec. United Way, Cleve., 1976. Recipient L. Edwin Brown award Case Western Res. U., 1970; grantee Columbia U., 1971. Mem. Am. Psychol. Assn., Case Western Res. U. Alumni Assn. Republican. Avocation: Thoroughbred horses and handicapping.

SWEENEY, HILDA MAE, nurse, infection control coordinator; b. Arenac County, Mich., Sept. 17, 1937; d. Edward L. and Irene M. (Yacks) Smith; m. Joseph Francis Sweeney, Nov. 7, 1959; children: Linda Sweeney Slayden, Timothy, Gary, Bryan. Diploma St. Mary's Hosp. Sch. Nursing, Saginaw, Mich., 1959. Staff nurse various depts. Huron Meml. Hosp., Bad Axe, Mich., 1960-74, infection control coordinator, 1975—, employee health coordinator, 1980—; tchr. emergency medicine. Roman Cath. parish religion tchr. and coordinator, 1975-78; 4-H leader, Elkton, Mich.; mem. Mich. Farm Bur. Mem. Mich. Nurses Assn., Huron Dist. Nurses Assn. (pres.), Mich. Soc. Infection Control, Thumb Area Infection Control Coordinators (organizer), Friends For Life, Confrat. Christian Mothers, Popple Trail Blazers Conservation Club, Home Extension Club. Home: 2165 Moore Rd Elkton MI 48731 Office: Huron Meml Hosp 100 S Van Dyke St Bad Axe MI 48413

SWEENEY, JAMES LEE, retired government defense supply center official; b. Rocky River, Ohio, Mar. 23, 1930; s. John H. and Mary J. (Walkinshaw) S.; m. Marion J. Ridley, Oct. 4, 1958; children: John A., James L. BBA, Case-Western Res. U., 1959. Cost acct. AFB, Dayton, Ohio, 1959-62; acct. Def. Electronics Supply Center, Dayton, 1962-64, budget analyst, 1964-67, budget officer, 1967-74, supervisory budget analyst, 1974-82, supervisory mgmt. analyst, 1982, supervisory program analyst, 1983—; pres. 3001 Hoover Inc.; mem. tax adv. com. Dayton-Montgomery County, 1967-70. Bd. dirs. Dayton Human Relations Commn., 1970-74, Model Cities Housing Corp., 1972-74, M & M Broadcasting Co., Ohio Valley Broadcasting Co., 1979-81; vestryman St. Margaret's Episc. Ch. Served with U.S. Army, 1952-54. Recipient Public Service award Def. Electronics Supply Cen., 1972, Meritorious Civilian Service award, 1981, Unity award in Media, Lincoln U., 1982-83, Disting. Career award Def. Electonics Supply Ctr., 1986. Mem. Alpha Phi Alpha. Producer, commentator Spl. Community Report Sta. WHIO-TV, twice weekly 1970-76, daily, 1976—, producer, commentator Spotlight; spl. cons. Sta. WHIO-TV. Home: 743 Argonne Dr Dayton OH 45408

SWEENEY, MICHAEL PATRICK, dentist; b. Omaha, June 16, 1953; s. Francis Joseph and Sylvia Russell S., m. Cinderella Marie Williams, Dec. 4, 1981; 1 child, Aubree Lee. BA, Creighton U., 1975, DDS, 1980. Assoc. Jerold Buresh DDS, Omaha, 1980-82, Family Dental Assns., Omaha, 1982-84; owner, mgr. Dental Care Ctr., Ralston, Nebr., 1984—. Mem. ADA, Nebr. Dental Assn., Omaha Dist. Dental Soc., Quality Dental Care Omaha. Republican. Roman Catholic. Avocations: tennis, piano, golf, softball. Home: 7319 S 41 Terr Bellevue NE 68127 Office: 7975 L St Ralston NE 68127

SWEENEY, PAUL RINEHART, banker; b. Knox County, Ind., Feb. 27, 1942; s. Paul Joseph and Anna Lee (Rinehart) S.; m. Shirley Virginia Steffey, Nov. 7, 1964; children: Paulette R., Chad J., Jamie R. AS, Vincennes U., 1962; BS, Ind. State U., 1964; grad., Stonier Sch. Banking, Rutgers U., 1979. Sr. bank examiner Ind. Dept. Fin., 1964-67; sr. auditor bank div. George S. Olive & Co. CPA's, Indpls., 1967-69; auditor Security Bank and Trust Co., Vincennes, Ind., 1969-75, asst. v.p., controller, 1975-79, v.p., cashier, 1980-85, sr. v.p., 1985—; sec. bd. dirs. Security Bank and Trust Co., Vincennes; sec., treas. Security Bancorp, Inc.; instr. bus. Vincennes U., 1975—. Active YMCA; pres. Knox County Hosp. Assn. Served with USAR, 1965-71. Ind. Bankers Assn., Knox County C. of C., Delta Sigma Pi. Democrat. Presbyterian. Lodge: Kiwanis (bd. dirs.). Home: Monroe City Rd Box 79-A Vincennes IN 47591 Office: 20 N 3d St Vincennes IN 47591

SWEENEY, THOMAS JOHN, education counselor, psychology educator; b. Akron, Ohio, Aug. 25, 1936; s. Thomas and Sarah Sweeney; m. Elizabeth Ann Jackson, Aug. 22, 1959; children: Elizabeth R., Ann K., Thomas P., Kathryn S., Michael J. BA, U. Akron, 1959; MS, U. Wis., 1960; PhD, Ohio State U., 1964. Cert. profl. counselor, psychologist. Commd. 2d lt. U.S. Army, 1958, advanced through grades to capt., 1958-65, resigned, 1966; tchr. Akron Pub. Schs., 1958-61; instr. Ohio State U., Columbus, 1961-63; counselor S.W. City Schs., Grove City, Ohio, 1963-64; prof. Univ. S.C., Columbia, 1964-72, Ohio U., Athens, 1972—; cons. Gen. Electric Found., Fairfield, Conn., 1969-86. Author: Adlerian Counseling, 1981; author, producer telecourse series Coping With Kids, 1978; contbr. articles to profl. jours. Mem. Am. Assn. for Counseling and Devel. (pres. 1979-82, Disting. Service award 1984, Disting. Legislature Service award 1986), Assn. for Counselor Edn. and Supervision (pres. 1976-79, Disting. Service award 1984), Am. Psychol. Assn., Chi Sigma Iota (pres., exec. dir. 1985—). Avocation: pvt. pilot.

SWEET, ARTHUR, orthopaedist; b. Chgo., Aug. 30, 1920; s. Mandel and Yetta (Spector) S.; m. Natalie Levy, Feb. 21, 1964; 1 child, Margaret H. BS, U. Ill., 1941, MD, 1944. Diplomate Am. Bd. Orthopaedic Surgery. Instr. Northwestern U., 1947-52; mem. staff Decatur (Ill.) Meml. Hosp., 1954—, St. Mary's Hosp., Decatur, 1954—; cons. Wabash Hosp. Assn., Decatur, 1954—; instr. U. Ill., 1972—; pres. med. staff St. Mary's Hosp., Decatur, Ill. Served to capt. USMC, 1953-54, Korea. Fellow Am. Bd. Orthopaedic Surgery; mem. Am. Acad. Orthopaedic Surgery. Jewish. Club: Decatur. Avocation: amateur radio operator. Home: 245 Park Pl Decatur IL 62522 Office: 250 N Water Decatur IL 62522

SWEET, JERRY JAMES, clinical psychologist; b. East Stroudsburg, Pa., Dec. 1, 1951; s. Waldo Thomas and Betty Jane (Flory) S.; m. Nancy Ann Sullivan, July 9, 1971; children: Christopher, Jamie. BS with distinction, Pa. State U., 1973; MS, Western Wash. U., 1975; PhD, U. S.D., 1979. Registered psychologist, Ill.; diplomate Am. Bd. Profl. Psychology. Sr. psychologist pain ctr., neuropsychologist dept. psychiatry Ill. Masonic Med. Ctr., Chgo., 1979-86; dir. psychol. evaluation and testing service Evanston (Ill.) Hosp., 1986—; clin. assoc. prof. psychiatry Northwestern U., adj. assoc. prof. Northwestern U., 1982—, assoc. dir. clin. tng., 1986—; neuropsychology cons. Cook County Hosp., Chgo., 1983—; lectr. psychology Loyola U., Chgo., 1983, 85; neuropsychol. seminar instr. Ill. State Psychiat. Inst., Chgo., 1986—. Cons. editor Jour. Cons. and Clin. Psychology; mem. editorial bd. Internat. Jour. Clin. Neuropsychology.; contbr. articles to profl. jours. Mem. Am. Psychol. Assn., Internat. Neuropsychol. Soc., Internat. Assn. Study of Pain, Biofeedback Soc. Am. Avocations: basketball, guitar, music. Home: 9247 Harding Ave Evanston IL 60203 Office: Evanston Hosp Dept Psychiatry 2650 Ridge Ave Evanston IL 60201

SWEET, KENNETH PATRICK, JR., accounting dir.; b. Oshkosh, Wis., Apr. 11, 1951; s. Kenneth Patrick and Dolores Elaine (Nelson) S.; m. Jeanne Marie Kautzmann, July 26, 1980; children: Kenneth III, Gina. BBA, U. Wis., Oshkosh, 1975. CPA, Wis., Pa. Sr. auditor Deloitte, Haskins & Sells, Milw., 1975-78; asst. to chief auditor Mellon Bank N.A., Pitts., 1978-79; sr. fin. policy analyst Rockwell Internat., Pitts., 1979-81; mgr. gen. and cost acctg. Rockwell Internat., Anaheim, Calif., 1981-85; mgr. product cost systems Rockwell Internat., Cedar Rapids, Iowa, 1985-86, dir. acctg., 1986—. Advisor Jr. Achievement, Pitts., 1980. Mem. Am. Inst. CPA's, Acctg. Research Assn., Beta Gamma Sigma. Republican. Methodist. Avocations: nat./internat. politics, tennis, photography. Home: 3304 Shasta Ct NE Cedar Rapids IA 52402 Office: Collins Def Communications 350 Collins Rd Cedar Rapids IA 52498

SWEETAPPLE, GARY NICHOLAS, data processing executive; b. Bradford, Pa., Apr. 3, 1948; s. Willis H. and Violet F. (Chiarenza) S.; m. Sandra Sue Wolcott, Nov. 30, 1968; children: Stephen Paul, Jessica Beth, Christopher Michael. BA, Aquinas Coll., 1971; MBA, Mich. State U., 1978; Harvard U., 1987. Assoc. buyer K-Mart Corp., Troy, Mich., 1972-78, sr. acct., 1978-81, mgr. cen. system devel., 1983-85, dir. mdse. systems, 1985-86, sr. dir. corp. systems devel., 1986—. group leader Jr. Achievement of Mich., Royal Oak, 1973-1977; leader Boy Scouts Am., Troy, 1984-86; mem. Kmart Political Action Com., 1986. Mem. Cath. Infants Soc. Oakland, Phi Kappa Phi, Beta Gamma Sigma. Home: 2157 Cumberland Troy MI 48098 Office: Kmart Corp 3100 W Big Beaver Rd Troy MI 48084

SWEETEN, GARY RAY, religious counseling educator; b. Ina, Ill., May 5, 1938; s. Thomas Jefferson and Leota Leone (Taylor) S.; m. Karen J. Sweeten, Nov. 21, 1961; children: Julie Rae, Timothy Andrew. AA, Rend Lake Coll., 1960; BS, So. Ill. U., 1965, MS, 1967; EdD, U. Cin., 1975. Tchr., coach pub. schs. Ina, Bellerive and Mt. Vernon, Ill., 1960-65; asst. dean U. Cin., 1967-69, asst. to univ. provost, 1969-73; minister of Christian edn. Coll. Hill Presbyn. Ch., Cin., 1973-76, minister of counseling and growth, 1976—; cons., founder Sweeten Creative Cons., Cin., 1970—; founder, pres. Christian Info. Com., Cin., 1978—; pres., bd dirs. Presbyn. Renewal Ministry, Oklahoma City, 1980-85. Named Outstanding Alumni Rend Lake Coll., Ina, 1986. Mem. Ohio Assn. Counselor Devel., Christian Assn. Psychol. Studies. Avocations: travel, basketball. Home: 1184 Mosswood Ct Cincinnati OH 45224 Office: Coll Hill Presbyn Ch 5742 Hamilton Cincinnati OH 45224

SWEEZY, JOHN WILLIAM, political party official; b. Indpls., Nov. 14, 1932; s. William Charles and Zuma Frances (McNew) S.; B.S. in Mech. Engring., Purdue U., 1956; M.B.A., Ind. U., 1958; student Butler U., 1953-54, U. Ga., 1954-55, Ind. Central Coll., 1959; m. Carole Suzanne Harman, July 14, 1956; children—John William, Bradley E. Design, test engr. Allison div. Gen. Motors Corp., Indpls., 1953-57; power sales engr. Indpls. Power & Light Co., 1958-69; dir. pub. works City of Indpls., 1970-72; chmn. Marion County Republican Central Com., 1972—; mng. partner MCLB Co., Indpls., 1972—; dir. Lorco Engring., Indpls. Bd. dirs. Indpls. Humane Soc.; chmn. 11th Dist. Rep. Com., 1970, 73—; chmn. Nat. Assn. Urban Rep. County Chmn.; alt. del. Rep. Nat. Conv., 1968, del., 1972, 76, 80, 84, del., mem. credentials com., 1984; mem. credentials com., 1980; mem. Rep. Nat. Com., 1984—, exec. com., 1984—; mem. Warren Schs. Citizens Screening Com., 1958-72. Served with AUS, 1953-55. Mem. AMA, Mensa, Sigma Iota Epsilon. Home: 166 N Gibson Indianapolis IN 46219 Office: 14 N Delaware St Indianapolis IN 46204

SWENSEN, CLIFFORD HENRIK, JR., psychologist, educator; b. Welch, W.Va., Nov. 25, 1926; s. Clifford Henrik and Cora Edith (Clovis) S.; m. Doris Ann Gaines, June 6, 1948; children—Betsy, Susan, Lisa, Timothy, Barbara. B.S., U. Pitts., 1949, M.S., 1950, Ph.D., 1952. Diplomate Am. Bd. Profl. Psychology. Instr. U. Pitts., 1951-52; clin. psychologist VA, 1952-54; from asst. prof. to assoc. prof. U. Tenn., Knoxville, 1954-62; assoc. prof. psychology Purdue U., West Lafayette, Ind., 1962-65, prof., 1965—; dir. clin. tng. Purdue U., 1975-85; vis. prof. U. Fla., 1968-69, U. Bergen, Norway, 1976-77, 83-84; cons. VA, 1981 White House Conf. on Aging, others; Am. Psychol. Assn.-NSF Disting. Sci. lectr., 1968-69; Fulbright-Hays lectr., Norway, 1976-77. Author: An Approach to Case Conceptualization, 1968; Introduction to Interpersonal Relations, 1973; contbr. chpts. to books, articles to profl. jours. Served with USN, 1944-46. Fellow Am. Psychol. Assn. (pres. div. cons. psychology 1976-77), Soc. Personality Assessment; mem. Midwestern Psychol. Assn., Southeastern Psychol. Assn., Ind. Psychol. Assn., Gerontol. Soc., Sigma Xi., Psi Chi. Republican. Mem. Ch. of Christ. Home: 611 Hillcrest Rd West Lafayette IN 47906 Office: Purdue U West Lafayette IN 47907

SWENSON, ELIZABETH VON FISCHER, psychologist, educator, lawyer; b. Cleve., Mar. 4, 1941; d. William and Cordelia (Thacker) von Fischer; m. Paul F. Swenson, Aug. 26, 1961; children: Karen, Connie, Kirsten. BS, Tufts U., 1963; MA, Case Western Res. U., 1972, PhD, 1974; JD, Cleve. State U., 1985. Bar: Ohio 1986, U.S. Dist. Ct. (no. dist.) Ohio 1986. Prof., chmn. dept. psychology John Carroll U., Cleve., 1979—; law clk. to justice U.S. Dist. Ct. (no. dist.) Ohio, Cleve., 1987. Contbr. articles to profl. jours. Mem. ABA, Am Psychol. Assn., Phi Beta Kappa. Office: John Carroll U Dept Psychology Cleveland OH 44118

SWENSON, MARK GREGORY, architect; b. Mpls., Nov. 29, 1949; s. Stanley S. and Linnea Marie (Anderson) S.; m. Marcy Gayle Stevenson, Apr. 6, 1974; 1 child, Gregory Peter. B in Environ. Design, U. Minn., 1971, MArch, 1973. Registered architect, Minn. Project planner Ellerbe, Inc., Bloomington, Minn., 1972-78; prin., v.p. Bennett-Ringrose-Wolsfeld-Jarvis-Gardner, Inc., Mpls., 1978—; lectr. architecture U. Minn., Mpls., 1974-82. Evans scholar Western Golf Assn., 1967-71. Mem. AIA (lectr. profl. devel. 1983—), Profl. Services Mgmt. Assn. Club: Svenska Sällskapet (Mpls.). Home: 5501 Dever Dr Edina MN 55424 Office: BRW Inc Thresher Sq 700 S 3d St Minneapolis MN 55415

SWENSON, RICHARD JOHN, dentist; b. Mpls., July 27, 1927; s. Elmer Carl Swenson and Lois Eileen Glatzmaier; m. Mary Isabella Ouellette, May 16, 1964; children: Richard, Mary, John, Catherine, Christopher. BS in Liberal Arts, U. Minn., 1953, DDS, 1953. Practice dentistry Eden Valley, Minn., 1954-86. V.p. Eden Valley Sch. Bd., 1973, pres., 1976, 77. Served to 2d lt. U.S. Army, 1946-47. Mem. ADA, Am. Endodontic Soc., West Cen. Dist. Dental Soc. (bd. dirs. 1984), 2M Dental Study Group, Minn. State Dental Soc. (Cert. 1955, 69), Tri-County Dental Soc. (program dir., 1961, pres. 1963-66), U. Minn. Alumni Assn., Am. Legion, VFW (life), Eden Valley C. of C. (pres. 1969, 85), U. Minn. Dentistry Century Club. Roman Catholic. Club: Koronis Golf (Paynesville, Minn.). Lodges: KC, Lions (pres. 1974-75). Avocations: fishing, golf. Home: 438 Brook St Eden Valley MN 55329

SWEPSTON, STEPHEN MCGEE, sales executive, sales engineer; b. Columbus, Ohio, Feb. 14, 1950; s. Dwight Carroll and Ruth (Lee) S.; m. Maryann Coffeen, Sept. 23, 1978; children: Todd Stephen, Andrew Dwight. BBA, Capital U., 1978, M in Sales Mgmt., 1980. Sales engr. F. F. Leonard Inc., Columbus, 1972-75; sales engr. Atlas Butler Inc., Columbus, 1975-79, sales mgr., 1979-86; pres. Swepston Heating and Cooling, Chillicothe, Ohio, 1986—; treas. Columbus Met. Area Community Action Orgn., 1979-83. Commr. Boy Scouts Am., Columbus, 1977-83, troop scout master, 1980; treas. community camp, cen. Ohio, 1975-80. Served with U.S. Army, 1970-72. Named Eagle Scout Cen. Ohio council, Columbus, 1964, Spark Plug of Yr., Columbus Jaycees, 1978. Mem. Am. Soc. Heating, Refrigeration and Air Conditioning Engrs., Air Conditioning Contractors Am., Air Conditioning Contractors Cen. Ohio. Republican. Lodges: Lions, Sertoma. Avocations: aviation, farming, amateur radio, church. Home: 9084 US 35 SE Washington Court House OH 43160 Office: Swepston Heating and Cooling Chillicothe OH 45601

SWETLAND, DAVID WIGHTMAN, investment company executive; b. Cleve., Apr. 13, 1916; s. Fredrick L. and Pauline (Wightman) S.; m. Mary Ann Sears, May 15, 1943 (dec. July 1969); children: David S., Ruth W., Polly M.; m. Jean Thomas, Sept. 23, 1971; stepchildren: Christine Anderson, Dane Anderson, Carol Anderson, Chace Anderson. AB, Williams Coll., 1938. Mgr. Swetland Co./Park Investment Co., Cleve., 1939-60; owner Park Investment Co., Cleve., 1960—. Trustee Univ. Circle, Inc., Cleve. Mus. Natural History, Western Res. Hist. Soc., Holden Arboretum, Vocat. Guidance Services, Cleve. Soc. for the Blind, Emeritus Western Res. Acad. Served to capt. USAF, 1942-46. Mem. Nature Conservancy (trustee Ohio chpt.), Cleve. Assn. Bldg. Owners and Mgrs. (trustee), Yosemite Nat. Inst. (trustee). Clubs: The Bath (Miami, Fla.), The Pepper Pike, Rowfant (Cleve.). Home: 3505 Main Lodge Dr Miami FL 33133 Office: Park Investment Co 907 Park Bldg 140 Public Square Cleveland OH 44114

SWETLIK, WILLIAM PHILIP, orthodontist; b. Manitowoc, Wis., Jan. 31, 1950; s. Leonard Alvin and Lillian Julia (Knipp) S.; m. Cheryl Jean Klein, June 30, 1973; children: Alison Elizabeth, Lindsey Ann. Student, Luther Coll., Decorah, Iowa, 1968-70; DDS, Marquette U., 1974; MS in Dentistry, St. Louis U., 1977. Diplomate Am. Bd. Orthodontics. Resident in gen. dentistry USPHS, Norfolk, Va., 1974-75; practice dentistry specializing in orthodontics Green Bay, Wis., 1977—; instr. oral pathology NE Wis. Tech. Inst., Green Bay, 1979-86. Author: (with others) Orthodontic Headgear, 1977. Served to lt. USPHS, 1974-75. Fellow Coll. Diplomates Am. Bd. Orthodontics; mem. ADA, Am. Assn. Orthodontists, Wis. Dental Assn. (Continuing Edn. award 1986), Wis. Soc. Orthodontists, Orthodontic Edn. and Research Found., Brown Door Kewaunee Dental Soc. (program chmn. 1985-86, sec., treas. 1986-87, v.p. 1987-88), St. Louis U. Orthodontic Alumni Assn. (pres. 19887), Violet Club of Am. Roman Catholic. Avocations: racquetball, skiing, jogging, raising violets, recording equipment. Home: 3211 Tuckaway Ct Green Bay WI 54301-2611 Office: 2626 S Oneida St Green Bay WI 54304

SWICK, HERBERT MORRIS, neurology and pediatrics educator; b. Baton Rouge, Nov. 22, 1941; s. Edgar Haight and Mary Ellen (Morris) S.; m. Mary Lynne McCluggage, June 29, 1963; children: Kristin Ann, Elizabeth May, Diane Marie. BA with honors, Johns Hopkins U., 1963, MD, 1966. Cert. Am. Bd. Psychiatry and Neurology, Am. Bd. Pediatrics. Resident in pediatrics Johns Hopkins U., Balt., 1966-69; resident in neurology U. Ky., Lexington, 1971-74, asst. prof. neurology and pediatrics, 1974-75; asst. to assoc. prof. neurology and pediatrics Med. Coll. Wis., Milw., 1975-84, prof. pediatrics and neurology, 1984—, asst. dean med. edn., 1987—; chief dept. neurology Children's Hosp. Wis., Milw., 1981-87, acting chmn. dept. neurology, 1987—; vis. prof. neurol. edn. Mayo Clinic and Found., Rochester, Minn., 1985. Contbr. numerous articles to profl. jours. Bd. dirs. Milw. Chamber Music Soc., 1982—, pres. 1986—. Served to lt. commdr., USN, 1969-71. Fulbright sr. scholar, 1978. Fellow Am. Acad. Neurology (edn. com., undergrad. edn. subcom. 1985—); mem. Am. Assn. History Medicine, Child Neurology Soc. (archives and history com. 1981—, exec. com. 1982—, sci. selection com. 1983, 84), Columbia History of Medicine Club, Found. Med. Care Evaluation, Internat. Child Neurology Assn., Profs. of Child Neurology, Wis. Neurol. Soc. (sec.-treas. 1981-82, pres.-elect 1982-84, pres. 1984-85), Assn. Univ. Profs. in Neurology (undergrad. edn. com. 1979—), Nat. Bd. Med. Examiners (test com. in neurology). Office: Med Coll Wis Office Academic Affairs 8701 Watertown Plank Rd Milwaukee WI 53226

SWICK, MYRA AGNES, accountant; b. Chgo., Dec. 5, 1945; d. Arthur T. and Marcella M. (Pankiewicz) Swick. B.B.A. cum laude, Loyola U.-Chgo., 1967. C.P.A., Ill. Mem. audit staff Ernst & Ernst, Chgo., 1967-72; controller Shorr Paper Products, Aurora, Ill., 1972-73; audit mgr. Otto Hillsman & Co., Ltd., Chgo., 1973-81; audit mgr. Walton, Joplin, Langer & Co., Chgo., 1981-82, ptnr., 1982—; mem. audit com. Loyola U., Chgo., 1977—. Contbr. articles to profl. jours. Mem. Am. Woman's Soc. C.P.A.s (hon., pres. 1976-77), Chgo. Soc. Women C.P.A.s (founder, dir. 1977-80), Am. Soc. Women Accts. (chpt. pres. 1974-75), Chgo. Fin. Exchange (dir. 1984-86), Ill. C.P.A. Soc. (com. mem. 1982-86, task force chair 1985-86, dir. 1986—), Am. Inst. C.P.A.s, Nat. Assn. Accts. (chpt. dir. 1972-74), Women's Bd. of Loyola Univ. of Chgo., Beta Alpha Psi, Beta Gamma Sigma. Avocations: travel; reading; crafts. Office: Walton Joplin Langer & Co 122 S Michigan Ave Chicago IL 60603

SWIDER, DAVID ALLEN, finance company executive; b. Highland Park, Mich., Dec. 16, 1954; s. Anthony and Lillian Louise (Balicki) S.; m. Deborah Krystek, Aug. 23, 1985. BBA, U. Mich., 1975; MBA, Wayne U., 1980. CPA, Mich. Ter. mgr. Burroughs Corp., Detroit, 1975-77; acting tax mgr. Arthur Andersen & Co., Detroit, 1977-82; asst. treas. Guardian Industries, Northville, Mich., 1982-84; v.p. Hall Fin. Group, Southfield, Mich., 1984-85, First Nat. Capital Corp., Birmingham, Mich., 1985—. Inventor, patentee candy mfg., 1979. Pres. student council U. Mich. Sch. of Bus., Ann Arbor, Mich., 1975. Mem. Am. Inst. CPA's, Mich. Assn. CPA's, Nat. Assn. Accts. (bd. dirs. 1976—), Accts. Aid Soc. (bd. dirs. 1976—), Internat. Assn. Fin. Planning, Greater Detroit C. of C. (pres. club 1978—). Republican. Roman Catholic. Club: Kingsway Assn. (pres. 1986—). Avocation: tennis. Home: 160 E Long Lake Rd Bloomfield Hills MI 48013

SWIDERSKI, ELIZABETH BACH, investment industry sales training executive; b. St. Cloud, Minn., Mar. 26, 1952; d. William Edward and Elizabeth (Jackson) Bach; m. James Walter Swiderski, June 15, 1974; children: Kristin Elizabeth, Ryan James. BS in Edn., St. Cloud State U., 1974; MEd, George Washington U., 1980. Reg. investment prin. Learning disability instr. Fairfax (Va.) County Pub. Schs., 1975-80; mng. ptnr. Learning Endeavors, St. Cloud, Minn., 1980—; v.p., dir. sales tng. Dain Bosworth, Inc., Mpls., 1981—. Vol. United Way Mpls., 1984—, Girl Scouts U.S.A., 1985. Mem. Securities Industry Assn. (Roundtable of Tng. Dirs. 1985—), Twin City Investment Women's Club (v.p. 1983-84, pres. 1984-85), Bus. and Profl. Women's Org. Avocations: running, swimming, racquetball, piano, travel. Office: Dain Bosworth Inc 800 Dain Tower Minneapolis MN 55402

SWIFT, DOLORES MONICA MARCINKEVICH (MRS. MORDEN LEIB SWIFT), public relations executive; b. Hazleton, Pa., Apr. 3, 1936; d. Adam Martin and Anna Frances (Lizbinski) Marcinkevich; student McCann Coll., 1954-56; m. Morden Leib Swift, Dec. 18, 1966. Pub. relations coordinator Internat. Council Shopping Centers, N.Y.C., 1957-59, Wendell P. Colton Advt. Agy., N.Y.C., 1959-61, Sydney S. Baron Pub. Relations Corp., N.Y.C., 1961-65, Robert S. Taplinger Pub. Relations, N.Y.C., 1965-66; prin. Dolores M. Swift, Pub. Relations, Chgo., 1966—. Bd. dirs. Welfare Pub. Relations Forum, 1971-79, treas., 1975-77; mem. pub. relations adv. com. Mid-Am. chpt. A.R.C., 1973—; mem. women's com. Mark Twain Meml., 1968-69; pub. relations dir. N.J. Symphony, Bergen County, 1969-70, mem. pub. relations/promotion com.; mem. Wadsworth Atheneum, 1968-69; bd. dirs. Youth Guidance, 1972-75; mem. NCCJ Labor, Mgmt. and Pub. Interest Conf., 1977—; mem. pub. relations com. United Way/Crusade of Mercy, 1979-80, 83, chmn. health services com., 1984, direct mail com. 1985-86. Mem. Pub. Relations Soc. Am. (accredited, chmn. subcom. Nat. Center for Vol. Action 1971-72, pub. service com. Chgo. chpt. 1971-72, dir. 1975—, chmn. counselors sect. 1976-77, assembly del. 1976, 79-81, 84-87, sec. 1977-78, v.p. 1978-79, pres.-elect 1979-80, pres. 1980-81, Midwest dist. chmn. 1984, nat. bd. dirs. 1985-87, sec. 1987, host chpt. chmn. 1981 conf., chmn. Midwest Dist. Conf. 1983). Clubs: Women's (publs. chmn. Englewood, N.J., 1970-71); Publicity (chmn. pub. info. com. 1975-76) (Chgo.). Editorial bd. Pub. Relations Jour., 1978. Address: 525 Hawthorne Pl Chicago IL 60657

SWIFT, ROBERT W., accounting manager; b. St. Louis, June 28, 1956; s. Harold and Edna Elizabeth (Thompson) S. BBA magna cum laude, U. Mo., St. Louis, 1974-77; MBA, Washington U., 1982. CPA, Mo.; cert. mgmt. acct. Consolidations acct. Wetterau, St. Louis, 1978-79; auditor Stone Carlie, CPA, St. Louis, 1979-80, Chromalloy Am., St. Louis, 1982-83; sr. auditor St. Joe Minerals, St. Louis, 1983-86, supr., 1985-86; acctg. mgr. Ralston Purina Corp., St. Louis, 1986—; tax cons., auditor, St. Louis, 1982-86. Recipient scholarship U. Mo., 1974-77. Mem. Mo. Soc. CPA's, Univ. Mo. Alumni Assn. (budget com. 1986), Washington Univ. Alumni Assn. Avocations: reading (hist. and bus.), tennis, theater. Home: 1379 Trampe Saint Louis MO 63138 Office: Ralston Purina Corp 14th Floor Equitable Bldg Saint Louis MO 63102

SWIFT, SANDRA LEE, interior designer; b. Evanston, Ill., Sept. 11, 1953; d. Robert Clarence and Patricia (Venetos) S.; m. Kenneth A. Horsey, July 7, 1979; children: Bryan Kenneth, Matthew Robert. Student, U. Wis., Oshkosh, 1971-72, Northern Ill. U., Dekalb, 1972-73; BFA, Harrington Inst. Interior Designing, 1976. Draftperson Continental Bank, Chgo., 1976-77; interior designer Lucas Design Group, Balt., 1977-78; dir. design George Vaeth Assocs., Balt., 1979-82; interior designer Allstate Ins. Co., South Barrington, Ill., 1982—. Mem. Am. Soc. Interior Designers (cert.). Roman Catholic. Avocations: racquetball, skiing, aerobics. Home: 522 Castlewood Ln Deerfield IL 60015 Office: Allstate Comml 51 W Higgins Rd South Barrington IL 60010

SWIGERT, ALICE HARROWER (MRS. JAMES MACK SWIGERT), civic worker; b. Montrose, Pa., Dec. 18, 1908; d. Lewis Titcomb and Margaret (Ayars) Harrower; student U. Tenn., 1927-29; m. James Mack Swigert, July 7, 1931; children—Oliver, David Ladd, Sally Harper (Mrs. Swigert Hamilton). Sec. to profs. Harvard Law Sch., Cambridge, Mass., 1932-35; pub. relations U. Chgo. Press, 1935-36. Mus. panoramas chmn. Cin. Symphony Orch. Women's Com., 1963-65; founder, treas. Citizens Crusade, 1967-77; vol. Children's Convalescent Hosp., 1969-75; founder, corr. sec. New Life for Girls, Inc., Cin., 1971-75, trustee, 1971-82, hon. trustee and adv. 1982—. Mem. adv. council Ohio Presbyn. Home, 1973-75; trustee emeritus Cin. Speech and Hearing Center; trustee, scholarship chmn. 3 Arts Scholarship Fund, 1972-75; Mem. DAR, Mensa, Chi Omega. Republican. Presbyterian. Clubs: Cincinnati Womans, Cincinnati Country, Queen City, Town. Home: 196 Green Hills Rd Cincinnati OH 45208

SWIMMER, JEROME, chemical company executive; b. Chgo., Nov. 11, 1915; s. Emanuel and Ida Stern S.; m. Shirley Swimmer, May 5, 1950; children: Glenn I., Mark L. BS, U. Ill., 1939; MS, Georgetown U., 1946. Registered profl. engr. in chem., Ill. Chemist chemical warfare div. U.S. Amry, 1941-44; chemist Manhattan dist. Atomic Energy Dept., 1945; owner, research dir. Nat. Biochemical Co., Chgo., 1946-79; pres., research dir. Geoliquids, Inc., Chgo., 1979—. Patentee in field. Mem. AAAS, Am. Chem Soc. Office: Geoliquids Inc 3127 W Lake St Chicago IL 60612

SWINDLE, ALBERT BRINTWOOD, JR., accountant; b. Adrian, Mich., July 20, 1949; s. Albert Brintwood and Jewel Florence (Rye) S.; m. Teresa Lynn Isaacson, Mar. 5, 1976; 1 child, Jonathan. AA in Bus. Adminstrn., Jackson Bus. U., 1970, Mich. Christian Coll., 1975; BA in Acctg., Sienna Heights Coll., 1976. Asst. acct. Goodwill Industries, Adrian, 1971-73; balance clk. 1st Nat. Bank, Birmingham, Ala., 1976-78; acct. Prentice Aircraft, Adrian, 1978-82, Tecumseh (Mich.) Country Club, 1982—. Named one of Outstanding Young Men in Am., 1982. Avocations: numismatics, reading, walking, church activities. Home: 506 Allis St Adrian MI 49221

SWIRSKI, AARON, architect; b. Mexico City, Mar. 19, 1938; came to U.S., 1967; s. Salomon Swirski and Ray Rosenthal; m. Edith Norma Roldan, Mar. 29, 1968; children: Miriam, Natania. BArch, U. N.Am.-Mex., 1967, MArch. Archtl. designer Minoru Yamasaki, Troy, Mich., 1967-70; project architect James Sudler, Denver, 1973-77, archtl. designer, 1971-72; architect coordinator Seymour Levine, Birmingham, Mich., 1978-72; architect Gunn Levine Assoc., Detroit, 1985—, Gunn Levine Assocs., Detroit, 1985—. Assoc. architect Tiergaarten Mus. Berlin, 1965, (2d prize 1965), Peugeout Bldg. 1963; architect Singer House, Mexico City, 1967, archtl. designer World Trade Ctr. Bldg., 1968. Mem. AIA (Assoc.). Avocations: painting, stage design. Home: 902 F Chestnut Hills Dr Auburn Hills MI 48057 Office: Gunn Levine Assoc 726 Lothrop Detroit MI 48202

SWISHER, CHARLES NASH, physician; b. Oxford, Eng., Mar. 4, 1940; came to U.S., 1949; s. Raymond Bernard and Margaret Mary (Dixon) S.; m. Linda Jane Peck, May 31, 1965 (div. June 1977); children: Wayne Andrew, Laura Johanna; m. Judith Hope Hartnett, Apr. 28, 1979. AB, Harvard U., 1961; MD, McGill U., 1965. Diplomate Am. Bd. Pediatrics, Am. Bd. Child Neurology. Instr. pediatrics Washington U., St. Louis, 1970-72; asst. prof. pediatrics, medicine U. N.C., Chapel Hill, 1972-75; asst. prof. pediatrics, neurology U. Chgo., 1972-85; dir. div. pediatric neurology Michael Reese Hosp., Chgo., 1975—; assoc. prof. clin. pediatrics, neurology U. Chgo., 1985—; sect. head Pediatrics div. for Disorders of Devel. and learning, Chapel Hill, 1972-75. Contbr. articles on child neurology topics to profl. jours. Served to capt. U.S. Army Med. Corps., 1967-69. Recipient Osler medal Am. Assn. Hist. Medicine, 1967; Logan Clendening Travelling fellow U. Kans., 1963-64. Fellow Am. Acad. Pediatrics; mem. Am. Acad. Neurology, Child Neurology Soc., Sierra Club, Sigma Xi. Democrat. Episcopalian. Club: Harvard. Avocations: art, music, hiking activities. Home: 3105 Park Pl Evanston IL 60201 Office: Michael Reese Hosp Dept Pediatrics 31st and Lake Shore Dr Chicago IL 60201

SWITZER, JON REX, architect; b. Shelbyville, Ill., Aug. 22, 1937; s. John Woodrow and Ida Marie (Vadalabene) S.; m. Judith Ann Heinlein, July 7, 1962; 1 child, Jeffrey Eric. Student, U. Ill., 1955-58; BS, Millikin U., 1972; MA, Sangamon State U., 1981. Registered architect, Ill., Mo., Ohio, Colo. Architect Warren & Van Praag, Inc., Decatur, Ill., 1970-72; prin. Decatur, 1972-81, Bloomington, Ill., 1981-83; architect Hilfinger, Asbury, Cufaude, Abels, Bloomington, 1983-84; ptnr. Riddle/Switzer, Ltd., Bloomington, 1984-86; withbldg., design and constrn. div. State Farm Ins. Cos., Bloomington, 1986—. Served with U.S. Army, 1958-61. Mem. AIA (pres. Bloomington chpt. 1983, pres. Decatur chpt. 1976, v.p. Ill. chpt. 1986-87, sec. Ill. chpt. 1985, treas. Ill. chpt. 1984), Am. Econ. Assn., Nat. Trust Hist. Preservation, Decatur C. of C. (Merit Citation 1974, Merit award 1979). Republican. Presbyterian. Lodge: Masons (32d degree). Avocations: swimming, hunting, fishing, reading, drawing. Home: 403 E Virginia Ave Normal IL 61761 Office: State Farm Ins Cos Bldg Design and Constrn Div One State Farm Plaza Bloomington IL 61701

SWITZKY, HARVEY NEWTON, clinical psychologist, special education educator; b. Bklyn., Oct. 19, 1942; s. Abraham Switzky and Norma (Zand) Leib; m. Lynne Carol Tanenbaum, June 13, 1965; children: Andrew, Rachel. BS, Brooklyn Coll., 1963; MS, Brown U., 1965, PhD, 1970; postgrad., George Peabody Coll., Nashville, 1971. Registered psychologist. Supr. child devel. Trudeau Ctr., Warwick, R.I., 1966-68; postdoctoral research assoc. George Peabody Coll., 1970-71, prof. psychology, 1971-73; chief psychologist No. Wis. Clinic, Chippena Falls, Wis., 1974-75; prof. spl. edn. No. Ill. U., Dekalb, Ill., 1975—. Contbr. articles to profl. jour.; cons. editor various mental health research jours. Fellow Am. Assn. Mental Deficiency; mem. Am. Acad. Mental REtardation, Am. Ednl. Research Assn., Sigma Xi. Home: 125 Stony Creek Ave Dekalb IL 60115 Office: No Ill U LDSE Dekalb IL 60115

SWOMLEY, JOHN MONTGOMERY, ethics educator; b. Harrisburg, Pa., May 13, 1915; s. John Montgomery Swomley and Florence Edna Forsyth; m. Laura Golding, 1941 (div. 1956); 1 child, Kathryn; m. Marjie L. Carpenter, Aug. 4, 1957; children: Joanna, John G., Sarah Jean. BA, Dickinson Coll., 1936; MA, Boston U., 1939, STB, 1940; PhD, U. Colo., 1958. Assoc. exec. sec. Fellowship of Reconciliation, N.Y.C., 1940-52, nat. exec. sec., 1953-60; prof. social ethics St. Paul Sch. Theology, Kansas City, Mo., 1960-84, prof. emeritus, 1985—; vis. prof. Union Theology Faculty, Buenos Aires, 1969, Union Theol. Sem., Manila, 1973; vis. lectr. United Theol. Coll., Salisbury, Zimbabwe, 1977. Author: The Military Establishment, 1964, Religion, the State and the Schools, 1967, American Empire, 1970, Liberation Ethics, 1972, The Politics of Liberation, 1984, War, Peace and Justice: The Prophetic Record, 1985, Religious Liberty and the Secular State: The Constitutional Context, 1987; editor: Facts for Action; assoc. editor: The Churchman; contbr. over 200 articles to profl. jours; chpts. to books. Exec. dir. Nat. Council Against Conscription, Washington, 1944-52; pres. Meth. Peace Fellowship, 1960-86, Ams. for Religious Liberty, Washington, 1985—, ACLU, western Mo., 1969-73, nat. chmn. ch.-state com., N.Y.C., 1979—, nat. bd. dirs. 1970—; mem. Kans. east conf. United Meth. Ch., 1970-84. Recipient Malin award ACLU, 1975, Humanist Pioneer award Am. Humanist Assn., 1985; named Kansas City's World Citizen of Yr., Mayor's UN Day Com., 1976. Mem. Am. Soc. Christian Ethics (bd. dirs. 1964-69). Home: 9203 Rocky Point Dr Kansas City MO 64152

SWONGER, CLARON WINTHROP, image processing executive; b. Dover, N.H., Dec. 2, 1935; s. Clair Woods and Mona Carol (Foulk) s.; m. Ruth Esther Anderson, June 13, 1959 (div. Oct. 1977); children: James, William, Roy, Lawrence; m. Pamela Rose Eckert, July 8, 1978. BEE, Tufts U., 1957; MEE, MIT, 1959. V.p. tech. products Calspan Corp., Buffalo, 1959-78; corp. dir. advanced devel. NCR Corp., Dayton, Ohio, 1978; dir.

distributed tech. div. Comshare Inc., Ann Arbor, Mich., 1978-81; v.p. product engring. Perceptron Corp., Farmington Hills, Mich., 1982-84; dir. Image Processing Systems div. Environ. Research Inst. Mich., Ann Arbor, 1984—; bd. dirs. Perceptron, Farmington Hills. Co-inventor, patentee in field; contbr. papers to profl. jours. Mem. IEEE, Machine Vision Assn. of Soc. Mfg. Engrs. (v.p. 1984—), Nat. Computer Graphics Assn. (bd. dirs. 1980-81). Republican. Avocations: skiing, photography, gardening. Office: Environ Research Inst Mich 3300 Plymouth Rd PO Box 8618 Ann Arbor MI 48107

SWORDS, GARY PATRICK, advertising executive; b. La Salle, Ill., Mar. 29, 1955; s. William John and Lorraine (Yerly) S.; m. Jane Marie Brown, Sept. 10, 1983. BS in Mktg., No. Ill. U., 1980. Market analyst Ottawa (Ill.) Silica Co., 1980-81, sales rep., 1981-82; sales rep. News-Tribune, La Salle, Ill., 1982-86, advt. mgr., 1986—. Mem. Illini Valley Bd. Realtors (assoc.), Ill. C. of C. (affiliate). Republican. Roman Catholic. Lodge: KC. Avocations: golf, fishing. Home: 1406 James Ct Unit B Ottawa IL 61350 Office: News-Tribune 426 2d St La Salle IL 61301

SWYGERT, LUTHER MERRITT, judge; b. Miami County, Ind., Feb. 7, 1905; s. Irven W. and Catherine (Hoover) S.; m. Mildred Kercher, Oct. 10, 1931 (dec. Jan. 1969); m. Mrs. Gari Pancoe, July 1, 1969; children—Robert L. (dec.), Michael I. LL.B. magna cum laude, Notre Dame U., 1927; LL.D., Valparaiso Sch. Law, 1964, U. Notre Dame, 1969, Stetson U., 1982. Bar: Ind. bar. In law practice 1927-31; dep. pros. atty. Lake Co., Ind., 1931-33; asst. U.S. atty.; asst. No. Dist. Ind., 1934-43, U.S. dist. judge, 1943-61, chief judge, 1954-61; judge U.S. Circuit Ct. Appeals, 1961—, chief judge, 1970-75, sr. cir. judge, 1981. Mem. ABA, Ind. Bar Assn. Office: 219 S Dearborn St Chicago IL 60604

SYDNOR, MARVIN DALE, financial executive, consultant; b. Long Beach, Calif., Dec. 17, 1952; s. Charles Richard and Ruby Louise (Mathews) S.; m. Carol Elaine Kahnwald, June 3, 1978; children: Stephanie Ann, Andrea Layne. BS, Ohio State U., 1977. CPA, Ill. Auditor Alexander Grant & Co., Chgo., 1977-79, Arthur Young & Co., Columbus, Ohio, 1979-80; various fin. positions Diebold, Inc., Hebron, Ohio, 1980-83; mgr. acctg. Advanced Robotics, Columbus, 1983-85; treas. Cranston Csuri Prodns., Columbus, 1986—. Mem. Am. Inst. CPA's. Avocations: golf, personal computers, cars. Home: 3044 Breed Dr Reynoldsburg OH 43068-3912 Office: Cranston Csuri Prodn 1501 Neil Ave Columbus OH 43201

SYED, MUHAMMAD HUMAYUN, psychiatrist; b. Swat, Pakistan, Jan. 15, 1938; Came to U.S., 1971; s. Badshah Gul and Shirin Syed; m. Zenu H. Syed, July 18, 1964; children: Rubina, Wiqar, Amjad, Samina. MD, Liaquat Med. Coll., Hyderabad, Pakistan, 1963. Staff psychiatrist Mental Health Inst., Independence, Iowa, 1974-78, asst. chief, 1978-80, clin. dir., 1980-81; chmn. psychiat. dept. Midland (Mich.) Hosp. Ctr., 1985-87, pvt. practice psychiatry, 1987—; asst. prof. Mich. State U., Lansing, 1981—. Mem. AMA, Mich. Med. Soc., Am. Psychiat. Soc., Mich. Psychiat. Soc., Am. Soc. Clin. Hypnosis. Office: Psychiat Assocs 2726 N Saginaw Midland MI 48640

SYFERT, SAMUEL RAY, librarian; b. Beecher City, Ill., July 20, 1928; s. Fred and LaVonne Mildred (High) S.; B.S. in Edn., Eastern Ill. U., 1957, M.S., 1961; M.S. in Edn., Calif. Christian U., 1979. Tchr. bus. Geneseo (Ill.) Community Unit schs., 1957-59; tchr. English, Bethany (Ill.) Community Unit schs., 1961-77, sch. librarian, 1977—; bd. dirs., treas. Marrowbone Twp. Library, Bethany, 1978-84, sec., 1984-85, pres., 1985—. Served with AUS, 1950-52. Named Tchr. of Yr. in Moultrie County (Ill.), 1975. Mem. NEA, ALA, Ill. Edn. Assn., Ill. Library Assn., Bethany C. of C. (sec. 1977-81, pres. 1982), Am. Legion. Republican. Mem. Christian Ch. (Disciples of Christ) (bd. chairperson). Home: Box 402 Bethany IL 61914 Office: Box 97 Bethany IL 61914

SYKES, PHILIP KIMBARK, retail executive; b. Berwyn, Ill., Nov. 30, 1949; s. Felix J. and Grace (Forster) S.; m. Carol Erickson, May 3, 1980; children: Brian, Jennifer. BA, St. Mary's Coll., 1971; postgrad., Northeastern Ill. U., 1973, Coll. of St. Thomas, 1984-85; MBA, Kotz Grad. Sch. Mgmt., 1987. Dir. Video Homes of Am., Buffalo Grove, Ill., 1975-77; dist. mgr. Sony Corp. of Am., Niles, Ill., 1977-81; v.p. Blackbourn Inc., Eden Prairie, Minn., 1981—; owner, mgr. Video Listing Services, Shoreview, Minn., 1981—. Patentee injection molded video cassette packaging, clear vinyl video cassette packaging. Mem., mktg. cons. Minn. Citizens Concerned For Life, Mpls., 1984—. Mem. Internat. TV Assn., Internat. Tape and Disc Assn. Roman Catholic. Home: 5865 Fernwood St Shoreview MN 55126 Office: Blackbourn Inc 10150 Crosstown Circle Eden Prairie MN 55344

SYLVESTER, TERRY LEE, business manager; b. Cin., June 12, 1949; s. Wilbert Fairbanks and Jewell S.; B.S. in Bus. Accounting, Miami U., Oxford, Ohio, 1972; M.B.A. in Fin., Xavier U., Cin., 1983; m. Janet Lynn Brigger, Nov. 29, 1975; children—Carisa, Laura, Jason, Katherine. Staff accountant Alexander Grant & Co., C.P.A.'s, Cin., 1972; treas., controller Imperial Community Developers, Inc., Cin., subs. of Chelsea Moore Devel. Corp., 1972—; controller home bldg. div. Chelsea Moore Devel. Corp., 1978—; controller, chief fin. officer Armstrong Cos., apt. mgmt., 1978-79, Dorger Investments, Cin., 1979-81, Delta Mechanical Constructors, Inc., Fairfield, Ohio, 1981-83; bus. mgr. Oak Hills Local Schs., Cin., 1983-87; treas. Lockland City Schs., Cin., 1987—. Home: 31 Woodmont Ct Fairfield OH 45014 Office: 210 N Cooper Ave Cincinnati OH 45215

SYLVESTRI, MARIO FRANK, educational administrator; b. San Francisco, Mar. 26, 1948; s. Bennie and Carolina Elizabeth (D'Amante) S.; m. Mary Catherine Gurnee, Feb. 16, 1985. A.A. in Chemistry and Biology, Coll. San Mateo, 1969; B.A. in Chemistry and Biology, Coll. Notre Dame, Belmont, Calif., 1970; B.S. in Pharmacy, Creighton U., 1973; M.S., U. Pacific, Stockton, Calif., 1976, Pharm.D. summa cum laude, 1976. Instr. dept. pharmaceutics U. Pacific, 1974-75; teaching asst. U. Nebr. Med. Ctr., Omaha, 1977; research fellow Creighton U., Omaha, 1980-82, instr. div. allied health scis., 1981-82, asst. dir., 1982-83, asst. dean, 1983-84, 84—, dir. continuing edn., 1984—; pres. bd. dirs. Nebr. Council Continuing Pharm. Edn., 1984—; chmn. com. on continuing edn. Nebr. State Bd. Pharmacy, 1984—. Contbr. articles to profl. publs. Recipient Eli Lilly Achievement award, 1973; grantee Cutter Labs., 1973-74, U. Pacific, 1974-76, U. Nebr. Med. Ctr., 1979-80, 83-84, Squibb Research and Devel., 1984-85; Nat. Achievement Rewards for Coll. Scientists scholar, 1976; Robert Lincoln McNeil Meml. fellow, 1977-80. Mem. Am. Pharm. Assn., AAAS, Am. Soc. Hosp. Pharmacists, Am. Soc. Allied Health Professions, Am. Assn. Colls. of Pharmacy, Greater Omaha Pharmacists Assn. (bd. dirs. 1984—), Rho Chi. Avocations: cooking, racquetball. Home: 15006 Cuming St Omaha NE 68154 Office: Creighton U Sch Pharmacy and Allied Health Professions California at 24th St Omaha NE 68178

SYMULESKI, RICHARD ALOYSIUS, chemical engineer; b. N.Y.C., June 21, 1947; s. Samuel Michael and Josephine Rose (Koda) S.; m. Mary Susan Sommers, Aug. 24, 1974; 1 child, Margaret Joan. BSChemE, Cath. U. Am., 1970, MSChemE, 1973, PhD in ChemE, 1977. Research engr. Nat. Bur. Standards, Washington, 1972-77; research chem. engr. Amoco Chems. Co., Naperville, Ill., 1977-78; coordinator environ. affairs Amoco Chems. Co., Chgo., 1978-80, dir. environ. affairs, 1980-83; dir. environ. planning Amoco Corp., Chgo., 1983-86, dir. product safety, 1986—; editorial advisor Chem. Processing mag., 1987—. Contbr. articles to profl. jours. Mem. Air Pollution Control Assn., Am. Chem. Soc., Am. Inst. Chem. Engrs., Chem. Mfrs. Assn. (mem. environ. mgmt. com. 1984-87), Water Pollution Control Fedn., Nat. Acad. Scis. (joint U.S.-USSR com. on civil environ. constrn. 1977—), Sierra Club, Sigma Xi. Roman Catholic. Avocations: photography, hiking, backpacking, skiing, stamp collecting. Office: Amoco Corp MC 4901 200 E Randolph Dr Chicago IL 60601

SYVERTSEN, EDWIN THOR, JR., automotive manufacturing executive; b. Cleve., Dec. 2, 1923; s. Edwin Thor and Elva Ann (Shafer) S.; m. Peggy Ann Winningham, June 20, 1952; children: Edwin Thor III, Sue Ann, Viki Lynn, Joe Allen. BS, Bowling Green State U., 1948. Salesman Accurate Parts Mfg., Cleve., 1948-55; sales mgr. Grantello Sales, Cleve., 1955-65; from sales mgr. to dir. mktg. K.D. Lamp Co., Cin., 1965-75; from sales mgr. to v.p. sales, then v.p. mktg. ROLERO, Inc., Cleve., 1975-81, pres., 1981—; pres. Truck Safety Equipment Inst., 1967-69. Pres., bd. dirs. Sherbrook Home Owners Assn., Solon, Ohio, 1978-83; track ofcl. K-C Track Meet, Cleve., 1970-85. Served to sgt. USMC, 1943-48, PTO. Named to Hon. Order Ky. Cols., 1970. Mem. Automotive Service Industry Assn. (del.), Motor Equipment Mfg. Assn. (del.), Automotive Warehouse Distbn. Assn. (del.), Automotive Booster Club (pres. 1962-64), Automotive Sales Council (treas. 1986-87). Club: Pals (Chgo.). Avocations: skiing, boating, cards. Home: 34695 Lakeview Dr Solon OH 44139 Office: ROLERO Inc 4933 E 154th St Cleveland OH 44128

SZABADOS, ERNEST DANIEL, orthopaedic surgeon; b. Bridgeport, Conn., Dec. 18, 1920; s. Daniel Ferenc Kisszabados and Mary (Tirpak) Szabados; m. Eva Katalin Erőss. BS, Fordham U., 1943; MD, Marquette U., 1946; postgrad., U. Vienna, Austria, 1948-49. Diplomate Am. Bd. Orthopaedic Surgeons, Am. Bd. Neurological Orthpaedic Surgeons. Intern St. Vincent's Hosp., Bridgeport, 1946-47; intern gen. surgery St. Luke's Hosp., Kansas City, 1952, children's orthopaedics intern, 1953; intern Dickson-Dively Group, Kansas City, 1952-56; intern adult orthpaedics Kansas City Gen. Hosp., 1954; intern Kansas City VA Hosp. and Children's Mercy Hosp., 1955; practice medicine specializing in orthopaedic surgery Independence, Mo., 1955—; courtesy staff Independence (Mo.) Sanitarium and Hosp., St. Joseph Hosp., Kansas City, St. Mary's Hosp., Kansas City; active Truman Med. Ctr. W., Kansas City, Med. Ctr. Independence; courtesy staff Trinity Luth. Hosp., Kansas City; asst. clin. prof. orthopaedics, U. Mo., Kansas City, 1971—. Contbr. articles to profl. jours. Served to maj. Med. Service Corps, U.S. Army, 1947-52. Fellow Am. Acad. Orthopaedic Surgeons; mem. AMA, Mo. State Med. Assn., So. Med. Assn., Am. Geriatric Soc., Internat. Acad. Law and Sci., N.Y. Acad. Sci., Orthopaedic Sect. of Pan-Am. Med. Soc., Jackson County Medical Soc., Semmelweiss Scientific Soc. of N.Y.C., Mid-Cen. Orthopaedic Surgeons, Mo. State Orthopaedic Soc.,Latin Am. Soc. Orthopaedic Surgeons (reciprocal member), Soc. Alumni and Friends of MEDICO. Roman Catholic. Avocations: music, photography, literature. Home: 1901 S Leslie Independence MO 64055 Office: 17221 E 23d St Independence MO 64057

SZAJNER, ROBERT MARTIN, professional jazz musician, producer, consultant; b. Detroit, Sept. 12, 1938; s. Stanley Martin and Stella (Kuciemba) S.; m. Loretta Marie Swiatkowski, Oct. 8, 1960. Student, U. Mich., 1958-59; AA in Music Composition, Berklee U., Boston, 1979. With sales dept. house appliances Admiral Corp., Detroit, 1960-67; sales and mktg. home entertainment products RCA Distbg. Corp., Taylor, Mich., 1967-77; prin. RMS Triad Prodns., West Bloomfield, Mich., 1978—; entertainment producer, consultant Grenier & Moore Prodns., Madison Heights, Mich., 1984-86. Producer and performer various jazz albums, 1978, 1982. Recipient honorable mention in jazz, Detroit Metro Times, 1981-82, Grammy award nominee, 1982, Jazz Showcase Performance award Detroit Montreux, 1981. Mem. Am. Soc. Composers, Authors and Pubs., Am. Fedn. Musicians, Nat. Acad. Recording Arts and Scis. Roman Catholic. Avocations: writing, jazz theory. Home and Office: RMS Triad Prodns 6267 Potomac Circle West Bloomfield MI 48322

SZALEWSKI, STEPHEN MICHAEL, pharmacist; b. South Bend, Ind., June 22, 1957; s. Edward and Thersa (Futa) S. BS in Pharmacy, Purdue U., 1981. Pharmacist Peoples Drug Store, Marion, Ind., 1982-83, Kroger Pharmacy, Frankfort, Ind., 1983-84, Osco Drug Store, South Bend and Mishawaka, Ind., 1984—. Mem. Am. Pharm. Assn., Tau Kappa Psi (social chmn. 1978—). Home: 1345 N Bertrand Rd Niles MI 49120 Office: Osco Drug Store 4401 W Western South Bend IN 46619

SZCZUREK, THOMAS EUGENE, marketing executive; b. Chgo., Aug. 29, 1957; s. Eugene and Anne (Potaniec) S.; m. Vickie Lynn Dodds, Oct. 20, 1984. AAS, Morton Coll., Cicero, Ill., 1977; BBA with highest honors, Western Ill. U., 1979; MBA, U. Cin., 1981. Assoc. account mgr. Burroughs Corp., Chgo., 1979-80; sr. mktg. analyst NCR Corp., Dayton, Ohio, 1982-84; mktg. and bus. mgr. Monarch Marking Systems, Dayton, 1984-86; dir. mktg. Reynolds & Reynolds, Dayton, 1986—. Jr. asst. scoutmaster Boy Scouts Am., Cicero, 1972-73; chmn. Cicero Young Adults Assn., 1979-80; big brother Big Bros. Am., Macomb, Ill., 1978-79; mem. St. Marys Holy Name Soc., 1977-80. Recipient Eagle Scout award Boy Scouts Am., 1973; named one of Outstanding Young Men of Am., U.S. Jaycees, 1986. Mem. Health Industry Bar Code Council, Am. Mktg. Assn. (chmn. promotion com. 1978-79), Dayton Sales and Mktg. Exec. Assn., Phi Beta Lambda, Phi Kappa Phi, Beta Gamma Sigma, Alpha Mu Alpha. Avocations: golf, hiking, reading, investing. Home: 4602 Burkhardt Ave Dayton OH 45431 Office: Reynolds & Reynolds 800 Germantown Dayton OH 45401

SZILAGYI, ELIZABETH MARIA, social services administrator; b. Chgo., Dec. 28, 1949; d. Bernard and Elizabeth (Szombathy) S. BS in Social Welfare, Olivet Nazarene U., 1973. Registered social worker, Ill. Social worker Proviso Council on Aging, Bellwood, Ill., 1980-84, dir. sr. citizen services, 1984—; mem. Older Adults Job Fair com. Operation Able, Oak Park, Ill., 1983-86. Mem. Proviso Coordinating Com., (sr. com., pres. 1986-87), Family Care Sr. Companion Adv. Council (v.p. 1985-86, pres. 1986-87). Avocations: bicycling, swimming, sewing. Office: Proviso Council on Aging 439 Bohland Bellwood IL 60104

SZKOTNICKI, GERALD MATEUSZ, health care administrator; b. Buffalo, Nov. 12, 1953; s. William and Josephine (Pytlak) S. BS, U. Rochester, N.Y., 1977; M in Health Adminstrn., Ohio State U., 1981. Asst. dir. Community Hosp. Bedford, Ohio, 1981—. N.Y. State Regents scholar. Mem. Health Care Adminstrs. Assn. Northeast Ohio, Am. Coll. Health Exec., Am. Hosp. Assn., Solon C. of C. Republican. Lodge: Kiwanis (program chmn. 1985). Avocations: photography, music, flying. Home: 656 Broadway Apt 2 Bedford OH 44146 Office: Community Hosp Bedford 44 Blaine Bedford OH 44146

SZOKA, EDMUND CASIMIR, archbishop; b. Grand Rapids, Mich., Sept. 14, 1927; s. Casimir and Mary (Wolgat) S. B.A., Sacred Heart Sem., 1950; J.C.B., Pontifical Lateran U., 1958, J.C.L., 1959. Ordained priest Roman Catholic Ch., 1954; asst. pastor St. Francis Parish, Manistique, Mich., 1954-55; sec. to bishop Marquette, Mich., 1955-57, 59-62; chaplain St. Mary's Hosp., Marquette, 1955-57; tribunal, notary, defender of bond Marquette, 1960-71; asst. chancellor Diocese of Marquette, 1962-69, chancellor, 1970-71; pastor St. Pius X Ch., Ishpeming, Mich., 1962-63, St. Christopher Ch., Marquette, 1963-71; bishop Diocese of Gaylord, Mich., 1971-81; archbishop of Detroit, 1981—; sec.-treas. Mich. Cath. Conf., Lansing, 1972-77, now chmn. bd. dirs.; chmn. region VI Nat. Conf. Cath. Bishops, 1972-77, treas., 1981-84; mem. adminstrv. bd. and adminstrv. com., budget and fin. com. Nat. Conf. Cath. Bishops/U.S. Cath. Conf., 1981-84. Trustee, mem. exec. com., chmn. com. for univ. relations Cath. U. Am., 1981—; trustee Nat. Shrine of the Immaculate Conception, Washington, 1981—; chmn. bd. trustees Cath. Telecommunications Network Am., 1984—. Office: Chancery Office 1234 Washington Blvd Detroit MI 48226 *

SZOKE, JOSEPH LOUIS, psychologist, mental health facility administrator; b. Rahway, N.J., May 6, 1947; s. Louis Joseph Sr. and Julia Dorothy (Jasa) S.; m. Carolyn Kay Orr, Jan. 13, 1971; children: Elizabeth, Amy. BS, U. Dayton, 1969, MA, 1973. Cert. clin. psychologist, mental health adminstr. Psychologist Dayton (Ohio) Mental Health Ctr., 1969-71; dir. psychol. and social services Dayton Bur. Drug Abuse, 1971-73; assoc. dir. Montgomery County Bd. Mental Health, Dayton, 1973-74; exec. dir. Tri-County Bd. Mental Health, Troy, Ohio, 1974—; adj. prof. U. Dayton, 1975—, Sinclair Coll., Dayton, 1973-78; cons. Applications Research Corp., Dayton, 1973-74. Treas. Hospice of Miami County, Troy, 1986—, Epilepsy Assn. Miami County, Troy, 1986—. Served to capt. U.S. Army, 1969-72. Fellow Assn. Mental Health Adminstrs. (pres. elect 1987); mem. Am. Evaluation Assn., Nat. Assn. Rural Mental Health, Ohio Assn. Community Mental Health Bds. (treas. 1987-88). Roman Catholic. Lodge: Kiwanis (pres. Troy club 1983). Avocations: running, softball, stamp collecting, woodworking. Home: 1675 Old Schoolhouse Rd Troy OH 45373

SZOTT, FRAN STANLEY, floor covering consultant and executive; b. LaSalle, Ill., Apr. 10, 1939; s. Henry Leo and Stella Esther (Witalka) S.; m. Sheila Marie Studzinski, June 27, 1959; children: Kathy Ann, Gary Lee. Student Ill. State U., 1957, Ray-Vogue Sch., 1959; cert. Chgo. Sch. Interior Design, 1960. Interior design cons. Szott's of Peru (Ill.), 1960-65, installation cons., 1965-70, buyer, sales mgr., 1970-75, adminstrv. mgr., 1975-78, personnel mgr., 1978-79, v.p., acting mgr., 1979—. Asst. mgr., mgr. Peru Youth Baseball, 1969-76; mgr. Babe Ruth League, Peru, 1976-77; mgr. com. Peru Airport Com., 1983; city rep. for state beautification, Peru, 1982; sec. Northview Parents Club, Peru. Roman Catholic. Lodges: Elks, KC. Home: 4th at Creek Bed Trail Peru IL 61354 Office: Rt 51 and Wenzel Rd Peru IL 61354

SZPREJDA, EVELYN A., international marketing executive; b. Green Bay, Wis., Nov. 30, 1944; s. John O. and Pearl (Cwiak) S.; Student U. Wis., 1962-63, 67-68, U. Minn., 1975-77; B.A., Coll. St. Thomas, 1980. Various adminstrv. positions Campbell-Mithun Advt., Mpls., 1968-71; adminstrv. asst. Internat. div. First Nat. Bank Mpls., 1971-73; ops. admintr. Far East ops. Medtronic Inc., Mpls., 1973-76, mktg. coordinator, 1976-78, market adminstrn. specialist Internat. div., 1978-79, mgr. internat. market planning and adminstrv. mgr., 1979-80, mgr. internat. market info. and research, 1980-81; dir. market research and planning Gibsongroup, Inc., Mpls., 1981-82; trade ops. devel. mgr. Control Data Commerce Internat., Mpls., 1982-83; mktg. mgr. healthcare products, 1983-84; dir. planning and new program devel. First Internat. Corp., Mpls., 1984-85; mgr. IXI World Trade Corp., 1985-87; instr. Coll. St. Thomas, 1985-88; export cons., 1981—; ptnr. Intermar Group Ltd., 1985—; gen. mgr. the LISAshop, 1986—. Mem. Minn. Gov.'s Task Force on Internat. Bus. Edn., 1983-84. Recipient Bus. Woman Leader award YMCA, 1980. Mem. Am. Mktg. Assn., Internat. Advt. Assn., Japan Am. Soc. Minn. (sec. 1981-82), Mpls. C. of C. (world trade com.), Minn. World Trade Assn. (bd. dirs. 1980, pres. 1983—). Roman Catholic. Club: Greenway Athletic. Home: 121 S Washington Ave 1310 Minneapolis MN 55401

SZYBALSKI, WACLAW, molecular geneticist, educator; b. Lwów, Poland, Sept. 9, 1921; came to U.S., 1950, naturalized, 1957; s. Stefan and Michalina (Rakowska) S.; m. Elizabeth Hunter, Feb. 5, 1955; children: Barbara A., Stefan H. BS in Chem. Engr., Poly. Inst. Lwów, 1943; DSc, Poly Inst. Gdańsk, Poland, 1949; Ph.D. (hon.), U. Marie Curie, Lublin, Poland, 1980. Asst. prof. Poly. Inst., Gdańsk, 1946-50; mem. staff Cold Spring Harbor (N.Y.) Biol. Labs., 1951-55; assoc. prof. Inst. Microbiology, Rutgers U., New Brunswick, N.J., 1955-60; prof. oncology McArdle Lab., U. Wis.-Madison, 1960—; mem. recombinant DNA adv. com. (RAC) NIH, 1974-78; Wendel H. Griffith meml. lectr. St. Louis U., 1975. Author numerous papers, revs., abstracts and books in field.; editor-in-chief: Gene; mem. editorial bd. other jours. Recipient Karl A. Forster lecture award U. Mainz, 1970, A. Jurzykowski Found. award in biology, 1977. Mem. Am. Soc. Biochemists, Genetic Soc. Am., Am. Soc. Microbiologists (chmn. virology div. 1972-74, chmn. div. IV 1974-75), AAAS, European Molecular Biology Orgns. (lectr. 1971, 76), Polish Soc. Microbiologists (hon.), Italian Soc. Exptl. Biology (hon.), Polish Med. Alliance (hon.). Home: 1124 Merrill Springs Rd Madison WI 53705 Office: U Wis McArdle Lab Madison WI 53706

SZYMANSKI, DAVID JOHN, recreation educator; b. Adams, Mass., Feb. 17, 1951; s. John Gabriel and Flora Kathryn (Nowak) S.; m. Elizabeth Ann Knotts, July 22, 1978; children—Kate Emily, Laura Elizabeth. A.A., St. Thomas Jr. Coll., 1970; B.A., Niagara U., 1972; M.A., Coll. St. Rose, 1973; student U. Iowa, 1975-77; Re.D., Ind. U., 1987. Project coordinator Spl. Project Grant, N.Y. State Edn. Dept., Albany, 1973-75; instr. U. Iowa, Iowa City, 1975-77; vis. lectr. dept. recreation and park adminstrn. U. Mo., Columbia, 1978; asst. prof. dept. health, phys. edn. and recreation U. Kans.-Lawrence, 1978-82; vis. asst. prof. dept. recreation and park adminstrn. U. Mo.-Columbia 1982-83, asst. prof., 1983-85; mgr. tng. and devel. Air Force Global WEather Cen., Offutt, AFB, Nebr., 1986—; park ranger U.S. Army Corps Engrs.; dir. Youth Conservation Corps, Lawrence, Kans. Vol., Wakarusa Twp. Vol. Fire Dept., Boone County Fire Dept., Douglas County Ambulance Service; instr. CPR, Am. Heart Assn., Kans. also Mo. Mem. Nat. Therapeutic Recreation Soc., AAHPERD, Soc. Park and Recreation Educators, State Park and Recreation Assn. Republican. Roman Catholic. Home: 1802 Sherry Dr Bellevue NE 68005-2248

TABER, MARGARET RUTH, electrical engineering technology educator, electrical engineer; b. St. Louis, Apr. 29, 1935; d. Wynn Orr and Margaret Ruth (Feldman) Gould Stevens; m. William James Taber, Sept. 6, 1958. B.Engring. Sci., Cleve. State U., 1958, B.E.E., 1958; M.S. in Engring., U. Akron, 1967; Ed.D., Nova U., 1976; postgrad., Western Res. U., 1959-64. Registered profl. engr., Ohio; cert. engring. technologist. Engring. trainee Ohio Crankshaft Co., Cleve., 1954-57, devel. engr., 1958-64, tng. dir., 1963-64; instr. elec.-electronic engring. tech. Cuyahoga Community Coll., Cleve., 1964-67, asst. prof., 1967-69, assoc. prof., 1969-72, prof., 1972-79; assoc. prof. elec. engring. tech. Purdue U., West Lafayette, Ind., 1979-83, prof., 1983—, chmn. engring. tech., 1977-79; lectr. Cleve. State U., 1963-64; mem. acad. adv. bd. Cleve. Inst. Electronics, 1981—, ednl. cons., author, 1979—. Author: (with Frank P. Tedeschi) Solid State Electronics, 1976, (with Eugene M. Silgalis) Electric Circuit Analysis, 1980, (with Jerry L. Casebeer) Registers, (with Kenneth Rosenow) Arithmetic Logic Units, Timing and Control, Memory Units, 1980, 6809 Architecture and Operation, 1984, Programming I: Straight Line, 1984; contbr. articles to profl. jours. Bd. dirs. West Blvd. Christian Ch., deaconess, 1974-77, elder, 1977-79; deacon Federated Ch., 1981-84, 86—. NSF grantee, 1970, 71, 72, 73, 78. Fellow Soc. Women Engrs. (sr. fellow, counselor Purdue chpt. 1983-88, Disting. Engring. Educator award 1987); mem. IEEE, Am. Bus. Women's Assn. (ednl. chmn. 1964-66), Nat. Rifle Assn., Am. Soc. Engring. Edn., Am. Tech. Edn. Assn., Tau Beta Pi (hon.), Phi Kappa Phi. Avocations: robotics; camping; housekeeping. Home: 3036 W State Rd 26 West Lafayette IN 47906 Office: Purdue U Elec Engring Tech Dept Knoy Hall Tech West Lafayette IN 47907

TABOR, ARTHUR RALPH, data processing executive; b. Beloit, Wis., Jan. 18, 1942; s. Ralph Arthur and Edith Adele (Wheeler) T.; m. Joan Evelyn Fredrickson, Dec. 22, 1963; children: Melissa Lynne, Gregory Arthur. Student, U. Ill., 1960-63, Ind. U., 1963-64; postgrad., Roosevelt U., 1985—. Analyst Dept. Def., Ft. Meade, Md., 1967-68; programmer CAI, Inc., Silver Springs, Md., 1968-70, G.C. Electronics, Rockford, Ill., 1970-73; sr. programmer Unisys, Elk Grove Village, Ill., 1973—. Cook County Election Judge, Schaumburg, Ill., 1984—. Served to sgt. USAF, 1963-67. Democrat. Lutheran. Club: Hoffman Estates Soccer (v.p. 1982-83). Avocations: reading, personal computers. Office: Unisys CSIS 1905 Lunt Ave Elk Grove Village IL 60007

TABOR, THEODORE EMMETT, research chemist; b. Great Falls, Mont., Dec. 28, 1940; s. John Edward and Alviva Lillian (Thorsen) T.; m. Jacqueline Lou Hart, Aug. 5, 1959; children: Lori, John, Lexi. BA, U. Mont., 1962; PhD, Kansas State U., 1967. Various research and devel. positions Dow Chem. Co., Midland, Mich., 1967-81, mgr. coop. research, 1981—; mem. governing bd. Council for Chem. Research, Bethlehem, Pa., 1985-88. Mem. Am. Chem. Soc. Mem. United Ch. Home: 2712 Mt Vernon Dr Midland MI 48640 Office: Dow Chem Co 1801 Building Midland MI 48674

TACHA, DEANELL R., federal judge; b. 1946. BA, U. Kans., 1968; JD, U. Mich., 1971. Spl. asst. to U.S. Sec. of Labor, Washington, 1971-72; assoc. prof. law U. Kans., Lawrence, 1974-77, prof., 1977-85, assoc. dean, 1977-79, assoc. vice chancellor, 1979-81, vice chancellor, 1981-85; dir. Douglas County Legal Aid Soc., Kans., 1974-77; assoc. Thomas J. Pitner Law Firm, Concordia, Kans., 1973-74; judge U.S. Ct. Appeals (10th cir.), Denver, 1985—. Office: U S Ct of Appeals 430 Fed Bldg 444 SE Quincy Topeka KS 66683 *

TACKETT, KEVIN A., health care specialist; b. Huntington, Ind., Nov. 2, 1956; s. Carl Jackson and Carolyn Sue (McClure) T.; m. Ruth Ann Moorman, Aug. 27, 1976 (div. July, 1982). BS, Ind. U., 1981. Sales rep. UARCO Inc., Toledo, Ohio, 1982-83; account rep. UARCO Inc., Toledo, 1983-84, hosp. systems specialist, 1984-85, health care specialist, 1985—; mgmt. cons. Better Bus. Bur., Muncie, Ind., 1978-79, advt. cons. 1980-81. Sponsor Save the Children. 1st place Mad Anthony Auto Cross, 1982. Mem. Am. Mktg. Assn., Data Processing Mgmt. Assn., Ind. U. Alumni Assn., Great Lakes Hist. Soc. (sustaining). Baptist. Avocations: race car driving. Office: UARCO Inc 2509 Sylvania Ave Toledo OH 43613

TACKOWIAK, EUGENE CHARLES, insurance, public relations executive; b. East Troy, Wis., June 1, 1923; s. Valentine Walter and Mary Anne (Sokolowski) T.; m. Bernadine Van Engel, June 12, 1954; children—Mary Virgine, Bruce Joseph, Janine Ann Baretta, Edith Christine, Paula Jane. B.A. in Journalism, Marquette U., 1950. Reporter, editor Milw. Sentinel, 1951-62; mng. editor Am. Sch. Bd. Jour., 1962-67; info. and publs. dir. Wis. Dept. Pub. Instrn., 1967-69; v.p. pub. relations Wis. Ins. Alliance, Madison, 1969—; lectr. colls., tech. schs., high schs.; consumer cons. Mem. Gov.'s Com. Safety 1967-69, Gov.'s Com. Ins., 1976-80; bd. dirs. Wis. Consumer League, 1979—, U. Wis. Cath. Ctr. Found., 1986—, Madison Sr. Ctr. Coalition, 1987—, Wis. Consumer Action Program 1983-85. Served with USNR, 1943-46; PTO. Recipient W.R. Hearst Reporting award, 1957; award of excellence Nation's Schs., 1964, award of distinction, 1970, cert. of excellence Sch. Mgmt., 1969, 70; Outstanding Service award Wis. Driver Tng., 1974. Mem. Madison Club, Pub. Relations Soc. Am., Nat. Assn. Ins. Info. Dirs., Milw. Press Club, Nat. Sch. Pub. Relations Assn. Roman Catholic. Home: 210 Eddy St Madison WI 53705 Office: 121 E Wisconsin St Madison WI 53703

TADWALKAR, VISHWAS DATTATREY, otolaryngologist; b. Solapur, Maharashtra, India, Dec. 18, 1948; came to U.S., 1977; s. Dattatrey Bhaskar and Pramila (Deshpande) T.; m. Pallavi Joshi, July 6, 1975; children: Rucha, Rigved. MBBS, Govt. Med. Coll., Nagpur, India, 1971, MS, 1975. Diplomate Am. Bd. Otolaryngology. Intern, then resident in surgery The Brookdale Hosp. Med. Ctr., Bklyn., 1977-78; resident in otolaryngology The L.I. Coll. Hosp., Bkyln., 1979-83; practice medicine specializing in otolaryngology Van Wert, Ohio, 1983—. Contbr. articles to profl. jours. Fellow Am. Acad. Otolaryngology, ACS, Royal Coll. Physicians and Surgeons Can.; mem. Am. Acad. Facial Plastic and Reconstructive Surgery (assoc.), Ohio Med. Assn. Lodge: Lions. Avocations: reading, travel. Office: 140 Fox Rd Van Wert OH 45891

TAECKENS, DOUGLAS RICHARD, plastics mfg. co. exec.; b. Flint, Mich., May 9, 1950; s. Richard Ernst and Shirley Joanne (Currie) T.; B.B.A., U. Mich., 1972, M.B.A., 1985. m. Pamela Kay Webb, Sept. 29, 1984; children—James, April. Mem. sales dept. Helmac Products Corp., Flint, 1972-74, Southwest regional mgr., Dallas, 1974-76, nat. sales mgr., Flint, 1976-78, v.p. sales and mktg., 1978—. Mem. Sales and Mktg. Execs. Club, Nat. Assn. Service Merchandising, Gen. Mdse. Distbrs. Council, U. Mich. Alumni Assn. Republican. Office: Helmac Products Corp PO Box 73 Flint MI 48501

TAEGE, ALAN JAY, physician; b. Norfolk, Nebr., Nov. 3, 1952; s. Virgil Roy and Marlene Joy (Heinold) T.; m. Linda Susan Mariani,)ct. 27, 1979; children: Christopher, Leslie, Nicholas. BS in Microbiology, U. Nebr., 1979; MD, St. Louis U., 1979. Diplomate Am. Bd. Internal Medicine. Family practice intern U. Nebr. Med. Ctr., Omaha, 1979-80; internal medicine resident St. Louis U., 1980-83; gen. practice medicine Neligh, Nebr., 1983—; instr. Nebr. Tech. Coll., Norfolk, 1984—, Am. Heart Ass., 1983—. Advisor Antelope Meml. Hosp. Emergency Med. Services, Norfolk, 1986—, Heritage Village, Neligh, 1986—. Mem. AMA, ACP (diplomate), Nebr. Med. Assn. Democrat. Lutheran. Lodge: Lions (v.p. Neligh 1984-85). Avocations: jogging, biking, skiing, photography, teaching. Home: 104 G St Neligh NE 68756 Office: Box 28 Neligh NE 68756

TAERBAUM, BARRY RICHARD, health care executive; b. Chgo., Oct. 17, 1954; s. Ernest Sidney and Geraldine Audrey (Spevock) T. BA cum laude, Pa. State U., 1976; MA, Western Ky. U., 1978. Lic. nursing home adminstr. Long-term care adminstr. Kenwood Terr., Chgo., 1978-79; long-term care cons. Chgo., 1979-80, 3-G Care Mgmt., Northbrook, Ill., 1980-81; long-term care adminstr. Chicago Ridge Nursing Ctr., Chicago Ridge, Ill., 1981—; cons. long-term health care, Skokie, Ill., 1982—; dir. health ops. 3-G Cove Mgmt., Skokie, 1987—. Mem. Ill. Nursing Home Adminstrs. Assn. Democrat. Jewish. Avocations: sailing, scuba diving. Home: 7831 N Kildare Skokie IL 60415 Office: Chicago Ridge Nursing Ctr 10602 SW Hwy Chicago Ridge IL 60411

TAFLIN, CHARLES OLAF, civil engineer; b. McIntosh, Minn., July 4, 1934; s. Carl E. and Selma O. (Hagen) T.; m. Marlys R. Melberg, June 14, 1958; children—Daniel, David, Mary. B.S. in Engring., U. Minn., 1956, postgrad., 1956-58. Registered profl. engr., Minn. Project engr. Mpls. Water Works, 1958-65, supt. planning and engring., 1967-75, supt. plant ops., 1975-87; project mgr. Progressive Cons. Engrs., Mpls., 1987—; environ. engr. Schoell & Madsen, Hopkins, Minn., 1965-66; mem. faculty U. Minn., 1975-76. Served to 1st lt. U.S. Army, 1958-62. Mem. Internat. Water Supply Assn., Am. Water Works Assn. (Fuller award 1976), Am. Water Resources Assn. Home: 10811 French Lake Rd Champlin MN 55316 Office: Progressive Cons Engr 6040 Earle Brown Dr Minneapolis MN 55430

TAFT, ROBERT, JR., lawyer, former U.S. senator; b. Cin., Feb. 26, 1917; s. Robert A. and Martha (Bowers) T.; m. Blanca Noel, 1939 (dec.); children: Robert A., Sarah B. Taft Jones, Deborah, Jonathan D.; m. Joan M. Warner, 1978. B.A., Yale U., 1939; LL.B., Harvard U., 1942. Bar: Ohio, D.C. Assoc. Taft, Stettinius & Hollister, Cin., 1946-51; ptnr. Taft, Stettinius & Hollister, 1951-63, 77-87, of counsel, 1987—; mem. Ohio Ho. of Reps., 1955-62, majority floor leader, 1961-62; mem. 88th Congress at-large from Ohio, 90th-91th Congresses from 1st Ohio Dist.; U.S. senator from Ohio 1971-76; practice law Washington and Cin., 1977—. Trustee Children's Home Cin., Inst. Fine Arts. Served with USNR, 1942-46. Mem. ABA, Ohio, Cin., D.C. bar assns. Republican. Clubs: Camargo, Racquet, Literary, Queen City (Cin.); Alibi. Home: 4300 Drake Rd Cincinnati OH 45243 Office: 1620 I St NW Washington DC 20006 also: 1800 First National Bank Ctr Cincinnati OH 45202

TAGATZ, GEORGE ELMO, obstetrician, gynecologist, educator; b. Milw., Sept. 21, 1935; s. George Herman and Beth Elinore (Blain) T.; m. Susan Trunnell, Oct. 28, 1967; children: Jennifer Lynn, Kirsten Susan, Kathryn Elizabeth. A.B., Oberlin Coll., 1957; M.D., U. Chgo., 1961. Diplomate: Am. Bd. Obstetricians and Gynecologists, Am. Bd. Reproductive Endocrinology (examiner, bd. reproductive endocrinology 1976-79). Rotating intern Univ. Hosps. of Cleve., 1961-62, resident in internal medicine, 1962-63; resident in ob-gyn U. Iowa, 1965-68; sr. research fellow in endocrinology U. Wash. dept. obstetrics and gynecology, 1968-70; asst. prof. ob-gyn U. Minn. Med. Sch., 1970-73, asso. prof., 1973-76, prof., 1976—, asst. prof. internal medicine, 1970-73, dir. div. reproductive endocrinology, 1974—; mem. fertility and maternal health adv. com. FDA, USPHS, HHS, 1982-86; cons. in field, 1986—. Ad hoc editor: Am. Jour. Ob-Gyn, Fertility and Sterility; contbr. articles to profl. publs. Served with M.C. U.S. Army, 1963-65. Mem. AMA, Minn., Hennepin County med. socs., Minn. Obstet. and Gynecol. Soc., Am. Coll. Ob-Gyn (subcom. on reproductive endocrinology 1979-82), Endocrine Soc., Am. Fertility Soc., Central Assn. Obstetricians and Gynecologists, U. Iowa Ob-Gyn Alumni Soc. Home: 5828 Long Brake Trail Edina MN 55435 Office: U Minn Dept Ob-Gyn PO Box 395 Mayo Minneapolis MN 55455

TAINTER, JAMES F(RANCIS), service company executive; b. St. Louis, Aug. 13, 1939; s. Thomas P. and Mary E. (McKenna) T.; m. Michele A. Christian, Dec. 20, 1980; children: James P. Teri, Mary Ellen. BS, St. Louis U., 1961. Pres. Pandjiris Inc., St Louis, 1963-84; sr. v.p. Dealers SErvice and Supply sub. C. F. Vatterott, St. Louis, 1984—. Republican. Roman Catholic. Avocations: golf, tennis, other outdoor activities. Home: 485 Hunters Hill Dr Chesterfield MO 63017 Office: C F Vatterott Inc 10449 Saint Charles Rock Rd Saint Ann MO 63074

TAIRA, FRANCES SNOW, nurse educator; b. Glasgow, Scotland, Feb. 27, 1935; came to U.S., 1959, naturalized, 1964; d. Thomas and Isabel (McDonald) Snow; m. Albert Taira, June 20, 1962; children—Albert, Deborah, Paul. B.S.N., U. Ill., 1974, M.S.N., 1976; Ed.D., No. Ill. U., 1980. Staff nurse various hosps., 1959-73; instr. nursing Triton Coll., 1976-81; asst. prof. nursing Loyola U., Chgo., 1981—. Mem. Am. Nurses Assn., Ill. Nurses Assn., U. Ill. Nursing Alumni Assn., Sigma Theta Tau, Phi Delta Kappa. Roman Catholic. Author: Aging: A Guide for the Family, 1983, Home Nursing: Basic Rehabilitation Care of Adults, 1986; contbr. articles to profl. jours. Home: 404 Atwater Ave Elmhurst IL 60126 Office: Loyola U Lake Shore Campus 6525 N Sheridan Rd Chicago IL 60626

TAIT, HAROLD ROBERT, manufacturing company executive; b. Bottineau, N.D., Sept. 26, 1912; s. Robert and Catherine M. (Thompson) T.; m. Barbara A. Schonberg, Oct. 27, 1939; children: Roberta Tait Lovell, John B., Craig Cole. BS, U. N.D., 1937. Dist. mgr. Ford Motor Co., Fargo, N.D., 1939-40; zone mgr. Pontiac Motor div. Gen. Motors Corp., Fargo, 1940-43; from sales mgr. to pres. Fargo Glass & Paint Co., 1945-81, chmn., 1981—. Mem. Fargo-Cass County Indsl. Devel. Corp., Neuropsychiat. Inst. Served to capt. U.S. Army, 1942-45, ETO. Mem. Fargo C. of C. (pres.). Republican. Baptist. Lodges: Masons, Shriners, Rotary (pres. Fargo chpt. 1962-63). Avocation: golf. Home: 1714 7th St S Fargo ND 58103 Office: Fargo Glass & Paint Co 1801 7th Ave N Fargo ND 58102

TAKACS, ANDREW JOSEPH, manufacturing executive; b. Toledo, July 20, 1933; s. Andrew Joseph and Ann Marie (Masney) T.; B.B.A. in Journalism and Bus. Adminstrn., U. Toledo, 1956, B.E. in Social Sci., 1957, M.E. in Polit. Sci., 1961; m. Anne Louise Schlicher, Nov. 10, 1956; children—Michael, David, Karen. Publicity dir. City of Toledo, 1954-56; reporter Toledo Times, 1954-56; asso. news dir. Sta. WSPD Radio-TV, Toledo; pub. relations Toledo Scale, 1957-59; with Whirlpool Corp., 1959—, mgr. community relations Clyde (Ohio) div., 1959-61, pub. relations asst., Benton Harbor, Mich., 1962-63, mgr. pub. affairs, 1963-66, mgr. legis. affairs, 1966-67, dir. govt. affairs, 1967-70, dir. govt. and urban affairs, 1970-73, dir. pub. affairs, 1973-78, v.p. govt. and pub. affairs, 1978—; chmn., dir. Whirlpool Opportunities, Inc. Mem. Washington reps. Bus. Roundtable, mem. corp. responsibility and govt. regulation task force. Trustee, Twin Cities Area Cath. Sch. Fund, Inc. Served with U.S. Army, 1957, 61-62. Mem. Assn. Home Appliance Mfrs. (chmn. fed. energy task force, trustee polit. action com.; leadership award 1980), Am. Acad. Polit. and Social Sci., NAM (govtl. issues com.), U.S. C. of C. (pub. affairs com.), Mich. Mfrs. Assn. (bd. dirs.), Pub. Relations Soc. Am., Twin Cities C. of C. (pres.), Internat. Protocol Assn. Roman Catholic. Clubs: Berrien Hills Country, Chgo. Press; Capitol Hill, City (Washington). Office: 2000 M63 Harbor MI 49022

TAKESHITA, TAKUO, metallurgist; b. Takase, Kagawa, Japan, Aug. 13, 1941; came to U.S., 1966; s. Takanosuke and Kazue (Morikawa) Hosokawa; m. Setsuko Shinohara, Nov. 24, 1970; children: Akiko, Marie, Taro, Sachiko. BS, U. Tokyo, 1965; PhD, SUNY, Stony Brook, 1970. Chemist Sumitomo Chem., Japan, 1965-72; research assoc. U. Pitts., 1972-74; research asst. prof. U. Pitts., 1974-77; vis. metallurgist Ames Lab., Iowa State U., 1977-78, assoc. metallurgist, 1978—. Contbr. articles to sci. jours.; patentee in field. Mem. Am hys. Soc., Am. Soc. for Metals, Sigma Xi.

TALARICO, MARIA THERESA, tax accountant; b. Chgo., July 11, 1960; d. Alfredo and Maria Rose (Altomari) T. BS in Commerce, DePaul U., Chgo., 1982, postgrad., 1985—. CPA, Ill. Jr. tax acct. Harris Trust and Savs. Bank, Chgo., 1982-86, tax acct., 1986—. Mem. Am. Inst. CPA's, Ill. Soc. CPA's. Office: Harris Trust and Savs Bank 111 W Monroe St Corp Tax 200/18 Chicago IL 60690

TALBOTT, JOHN WALLACE, developer, fundraiser; b. Middleport, Ohio, Aug. 22, 1937; s. John C. and Virginia A. T.; m. Marilyn J. Darnell, Aug. 24, 1963; children: John H., Michelle E. BSBA, Ohio State U., 1960; student, Ohio U., 1972-74, W.Va. U., 1974. Exec. dir. Am. Heart Assn., Columbus, Ohio, 1965-68, Wilmington, Del., 1968-70, Milw., 1970-72; regional dir. St. Jude Research Hosp., Memphis, 1972-78; sr. program dir. Campbell & Co., Chgo., 1978-82; v.p. United Ch. Homes, Upper Sandusky, Ohio, 1982—. Col. Kentucky Cols., Frankfurt, 1974—; pres. PTO, Barnesville, Ohio, 1973-74. Served as 1st sgt. U.S. Army, 1960-67. Mem. Nat. Assn. Hosp. Devel., Nat. Soc. Fund-Raising Execs., Am. Mktg. Assn., Am. Soc. Assn. Execs., Am. Pub. Health Assn. Avocation: officiating high sch. basketball. Home: 56-D Siesta Dr Tiffin OH 44883 Office: United Church Homes Inc 320 W Maple St Upper Sandusky OH 43351

TALKINGTON, ROBERT VAN, state senator; b. near Patrick, Tex., Aug. 23, 1929; s. William Henry and Nannie J. (Patrick) T.; m. Donna Jill Schmaus, Mar. 25, 1951; children—Jill Talkington McCaskill, Jacki Talkington Chase, James, Thomas, Lisa. A.A., Tyler Jr. Coll., 1949; B.S., U. Kans., 1951, LL.B., 1954, J.D., 1971. Bar: Kans. 1954. County atty. Allen County, Kans., 1957-63; city atty. Moran, Kans., 1968—; mem. Kans. Ho. of Reps. from 10th Dist., 1969-73; mem. Kans. Senate from 12th Dist., 1973—, v.p., 1977-81, majority leader, 1981-85, pres., 1985—; chmn. Republican Party, Allen County, 1964-68, state treas., 1964-66. Trustee Iola Pub. Library, 1962-70; mem. advisory bd. Greater U. Fund, U. Kans., 1967-72. Served with CIC AUS, 1954-56. Mem. Am. Legion, Sigma Alpha Epsilon, Phi Delta Phi. Clubs: Masons, Shriners, Elks. Home: 20 W Buchanan St Iola KS 66749 Office: 20 N Washington St Iola KS 66749

TALLCHIEF, MARIA, ballerina; b. Fairfax, Okla., Jan. 24, 1925; d. Alexander Joseph and Ruth Mary (Porter) T.; m. Henry Paschen, Jr., June 3, 1957; 1 child, Elise. Student pub. schs., Calif.; D.F.A. (hon.), Lake Forest Coll., Ill., Colby Coll., Maine, 1968, Ripon Coll., 1973, Boston Coll., Smith Coll., 1981, Northwestern U., 1982, Yale U., 1984, St. Mary of Woods, 1984, Dartmouth Coll., 1985. Joined Ballet Russe de Monte Carlo, 1942, prima ballerina, N.Y.C. Ballet, 1947-60, guest star, Paris Opera, 1947, Royal Danish Ballet, 1961; prima ballerina Am. Ballet Theater, 1960, with N.Y.C. Ballet Co., until 1965, formerly artistic dir. Lyric Opera Ballet Chgo.; founder, Chgo. City Ballet, 1979—,. Named Hon. Princess Osage Indian Tribe, 1953; recipient Disting. Service award U. Okla., 1972, award Dance mag., 1960; Jane Addams Humanitarian award Rockford Coll., 1973; Bravo award Rosary Coll., 1983; award Dance Educators Am., 1956; Achievement award Women's Nat. Press Club, 1953; Capezio award, 1965. Mem. Nat. Soc. Arts and Letters. Office: care Chgo City Ballet 223 W Erie St Chicago IL 60610 *

TALLEY, HAYWARD LEROY, communications executive; b. Nov. 3, 1923; s. Roy and Reta (Hayward) T.; m. Emma Mae Chandler, Sept. 2, 1950; children: Brian, Kevin. BS, U. Ill., 1948. From engr. to chief engr. Sta. WOKZ-AM-FM, Alton, Ill., 1948-50; pres., gen. mgr. Talley Broadcasting Corp., Litchfield, Ill., 1950—; pres. Talley Broadcasting Co., Ft. Madison, Iowa, 1960—, North Cen. Iowa Broadcasting Co., Mason City, 1963-83. Chmn. ofcl. bd. Meth. Ch., 1961-63, 65-66. Served with Signal Corps, U.S. Army. Mem. Nat. Assn. Broadcasters, Ill. Broadcasters Assn. Lodges: Rotary, Masons. Home: 1414 N Harrison Litchfield IL 62056 Office: Sta WSMI Box 10 Litchfield IL 62056

TALLIEU, LEO JOSEPH, music educator; b. Detroit, Aug. 18, 1937; s. Leo Michael and Marie Ella (Henn) T.; m. Carol Marie Adams, Aug. 5, 1967. MusB Edn., U. Detroit, 1959; MEd, Wayne State U., 1962. Band dir. St. Benedict Sch., Highland Park, Mich., 1957-62, St. Alphonsus Sch., Dearborn, Mich., 1962-66, Divine Child Sch., Dearborn, 1966—; dance band leader Leo Tallieu Orch., Detroit, 1955—. Travel cinematographer, lectr. amature film Sate of Mich., 1972-73, 75. Mem. Am. Fedn. Musicians, Nat. Trumpet, Mich. Band and Orch. Assn., Detroit Cinema Club (pres. 1976). Republican. Roman Catholic. Avocations: travel, cinematography, skiing. Home: 25650 Jennifer Redford MI 48239 Office: Divine Child High Sch 1001 N Silvery Ln Dearborn MI 48128

TALLON, RICHARD DALE, dentist; b. Tulsa, June 10, 1952; s. Ted Morgan and Jimmie Bell (Henry) T.; m. Patricia Ann Gentzke, July 28, 1979; 1 child, Cassie Jannel. BS in Biology, Mo. So. State Coll., 1976; DDS, U. Mo., Kansas City, 1980. Gen. practice dentistry Branson (Mo.) Ctr., Inc., 1980—; adv. bd. dirs. Security Bank & Trust, Branson, 1982—. Century mem. Ozarks council Boy Scouts Am., 1983, 84; sponsor Ducks Unlimited, Branson, 1986; bd. dirs. Am. Cancer Soc., Taney County, Mo., 1986—, Tri-lakes Christian Layman's Assn., 1984—; bd. dirs. 1st Presbyn. Ch., Boston, 1986, 87. Named one of Outstanding Young Men Am., 1981. Mem. ADA, Acad. Gen. Dentistry, Springfield Dental Soc., Mo. Dental Assn, Beta Beta Beta, Psi Omega. Republican. Lodges: Rotary (bd. dirs. Brayson-Hollister club 1987), Sertoma. Home: 603 Cherokee Branson MO 65616 Office: Branson Dental Ctr Inc 1034 W Main Branson MO 65616

TAMBORSKI, CHRIST, chemist; b. Buffalo, Nov. 12, 1926; s. Ignatius and Anna (Kwiatkowski) T.; children: Anne, Peter, John, Jean, Mark, David, Julie. BA, U. Buffalo, 1949, PhD, 1953. From research chemist to sr. scientist sr. exec. service USAF, Dayton, Ohio, 1955-86; cons. Fluidics Inc., Dayton, 1986—. Contbr. articles to profl. jours.; patentee in field. Recipient Jacobowitz Sci. award U. Buffalo, 1953, Inventors award U.S. Dept. Commerce, 1980; named Outstanding Engring. and Scientist, Dayton Engring. and Scientist Found., 1983. Mem. Am. Chem. Soc. (sec. and treas. fluorine chemistry div. 1968-70, chmn. fluorine chemistry div. 1971-72), Sigma Xi. Avocations: photography, hiking, tennis, music. Office: Fluidics Inc PO Box 1886 Dayton OH 45429

TAMBURRINO, MARIJO BERNADETTE, psychiatrist; b. Mansfield, Ohio, Jan. 10, 1952; d. Joseph David and Rosemary (Nicita) T.; m. Ronald Anthony McGinnis, Sept. 24, 1977. B.S. summa cum laude, Ohio State U., 1974; M.D., Med. Coll. Ohio, 1977. Intern, Med. Coll. Ohio, Toledo, 1978, resident, 1981, asst. prof. psychiatry, 1981—. Mem. Northwest Ohio Psychiat. Assn. (program chmn. 1981-83, pres. 1983—), Am. Med. Women's Assn. (sec. 1979-81), Ohio State Med. Assn., AMA., Phi Beta Kappa. Office: Med Coll Ohio Dept Psychiatry Arlington Ave CS #10008 Toledo OH 43699

TAMELING, GRETTA ANN, lawyer; b. Evanston, Ill., Apr. 6, 1943; d. Carl G. and Judith Ann Karna; m. Bernard J. Tameling, Nov. 8, 1963. BA with high honors, Wheaton Coll., 1967; JD with high honors, Ill. Inst. Tech., 1984. Bar: Ill. 1984, U.S. Dist. Ct. (no. dist.) Ill. 1984. Univ. teller Clyde Svgs., North Riverside, Ill., 1963-64; note teller Bank of Glen Ellyn, Ill., 1964-65; coordinator state-wide League of Women Voters, Chgo., 1979-80; mgr. Rand Rd Mobilehomes, Des Plaines, Ill., 1980-81; asst. state's atty. DuPage County, Wheaton, Ill., 1985—. Precinct committeeman Milton Twp. Rep. Cen. Com., Wheaton, 1976—; dir. Planned Parenthood Assn., Chgo., 1976-80, West Sub. Women's Polit. Caucus, LaGrange, Ill., 1976-80, B.R. Ryall YMCA, Glen Ellyn, 1980—. Recipient Rothschild Heart of Gold award, United Way, 1985; named Vol. of Yr., Ryall YMCA, 1986. Mem. ABA, Ill. Bar Assn., DuPage County Bar Assn., Assn. Trial Lawyers Am., Ill. Trial Lawyers Assn. Republican. Avocations: skiing, sailing. Home: 1303 Aurora Way Wheaton IL 60187 Office: DuPage County State's Attys Office 207 S Reber St Wheaton IL 60187

TAMISIEA, BRUCE, manufacturing executive; b. Omaha, July 27, 1955; s. Jerry and Alpha (Byers) T.; m. LuAnn Cornish, June 11, 1981; children: Tyler, Reid. BS, Iowa State U., 1977. Buyer Eaton Corp., Spencer, Iowa, 1977-81; pres. Tecton Industries, Inc., Spencer, Iowa, 1981-86. Mem. Soc. Mfg. Engrs. (sr.), Spencer Jaycees (v.p. 1978). Republican. Avocations: waterfowl hunting. Home: 1115 18th Ave W Spencer IA 51301 Office: Tecton Industries Inc 1105 E Milwaukee St Spencer IA 51301

TANCK, CATHERINE ANN, law clerk; b. Canton, S.D., Aug. 28, 1957; d. Charles H. and Betty J. (Bothe) T. BA, Augustana Coll., 1979; JD, U. S.D., 1987. CPA, S.D. Intern IRS, Sioux Falls, S.D., 1977-79; tax mgr. McGladrey, Hendrickson & Pullen, Sioux Falls, S.D., 1979-85; law clk. to presiding justice U.S. Ct. Appeals (8th cir.), Pierre, S.D., 1987—. Editor S.D. Law Rev., 1986-87. Recipient West Pub. Award West Pub. Co., 1985, 87; McKusick scholar U. S.D. Found., 1985-86, Law Found. scholar U. S.D. Found., 1986-87. Mem. ABA(student chpt.), Am. Inst. CPA's, S.D. Soc. CPA's, Sterling Honor Soc. Lutheran. Home: 1701 S West Ave Sioux Falls SD 57105

TANCULA, THOMAS NICHOLAS, labor relations specialist; b. Chgo., Mar. 14, 1956; s. Bruno Walter and Virginia (DiPrizio) T.; m. Judith Lynn La Haye, July 24, 1982; 1 child, Nicholas Thomas. B.A., Elmhurst Coll., 1981. With Chgo., Milw., St. Paul & Pacific R.R. Co., Chgo., 1978—, asst. labor relations officer, 1981, labor relations officer, 1981-82, mgr. labor relations, 1982-85; labor relations specialist NIRCRC/METRA, Chgo., 1985—; author, negotiator labor agreement Internat. Brotherhood of Firemen and Oilers, 1983. Mem. Gov.'s Com. for Future of Ill.; Ill. Ry. Mus., Union, 1977; trustee Village of Addison, Ill., 1987—, vice chmn. pub. health, safety and jud. com. Mem. Ry. Fuel and Operating Officers Assn., Chgo. R.R. Car Assn. (mem. audit com. 1984), Air Brake Assn., Car Dept. Officers Assn. Roman Catholic. Avocations: photography; railroad history. Home: 1206 Scarlet Ct Addison Il 60101 Office: NIRCRC/METRA 547 W Jackson Blvd Chicago IL 60606

TANDON, JAGDISH SINGH, pollution control co. exec.; b. New Delhi, India, Apr. 3, 1940; s. Mool C. and Vidya V. (Somra) T.; came to U.S., 1961, naturalized, 1973; B.Sc., U. Delhi, 1961; M.S., U. Minn., 1963, postgrad., 1963-67; m. Monika Dettmers, May 12, 1967; 1 son, Hans Peter. Mgr. mech. collector div. Aerodyne Corp., Hopkins, Minn., 1968-69; dir. control systems div. Environ. Research Corp. div. Dart Industries, St. Paul, 1969-70; gen. mgr. pollution control systems div. George A. Hormel & Co., Coon Rapids, Minn., 1970-77; pres. Am. Envirodyne div. Pettibone Corp., Chgo., 1977-78; dir. mktg. MMT Environ. Inc., St. Paul, 1978-80; pres. Environ. Cons., Northbrook, 1980—; pres. Am. Environ. Internat. Inc., Northbrook, 1982—; instr. U. Minn. Inst. Tech.; vis. scientist Nat. Center Atmospheric Research, Boulder, Colo. Mem. ASCE, Air Pollution Control Assn., Am. Foundry Soc. Contbr. pollution control articles to profl. lit. Home: 1344 Southwind Dr Northbrook IL 60062

TANG, HENRY, technical training specialist; b. Peoples Republic of China, Mar. 24, 1956; came to U.S., 1964; s. William and Mae Jung (Wong) T.; m. Pui King Leung, June 28, 1981; children: Kevin Edward, Jennifer Marie. BS, Ohio State U., 1980. Programmer Nationwide Ins. Co., Columbus, Ohio, 1980-81, sr. programmer, 1981-82, programmer analyst, 1982-84, sr. programmer analyst, 1984-85, tech. tng. specialist, 1985—. Avocations: personal computers, chess, bowling. Office: Nationwide Ins Co 1 Nationwide Blvd Plaza 2 17th Floor Columbus OH 43215

TANGEL, EDWARD JOHN, engineering company executive; b. Mar. 28, 1932; s. John and Theresa (Leib) T.; m. Beatrice C. deLyra, Sept. 17, 1955; children: Jeffrey J., Douglas J., Lawrence E., Colette T., Neil R. BSME, Poly. Inst. N.Y., Bklyn., 1953; MSME, N.Y.U., 1962. With Combustion Engring., Va., 1953-54; sales engr. White Motor Co., N.Y.C., 1956-61; sales engr., v.p. Republic Electric and Devel. Co., Peoria, Ill., 1961-73; pres. Enercon Engring., Inc., East Peoria, Ill., 1975—. Served to 1st lt. C.E., U.S. Army, 1954-56. Home: Rural Rt 3 Box 51 Delavan IL 61734 Office: Enercon Engring Inc #1 Altorfer Ln East Peoria IL 61611

TANIN, GARY STEVEN, songwriter, producer, electronics consultant; b. Milw., Sept. 19, 1952; s. Ananij and Natalie (Holowinsky) T. Student U. Wis., 1970-72. Recorded with Odessa Records, 1969, Vera Records, 1972, 75, 76, 81; recorded, produced numerous records, albums; pub. 29 songs; sole owner, founder Compu-Clinic Electronics Cons., Milw., 1986—. Active drug and alcohol abuse work. Recipient certs. Milw. Psychiat. Hosp. for work in drug and alcohol field, 1981, 82, 83, 84. Mem. Country Music Assn., Nat. Acad. Rec. Arts and Scis. (voting mem.), Broadcast Music Inc. Home: PO Box 10181 Milwaukee WI 53210

TANN, EDWARD MICHAEL, perfusionist; b. Columbus, Ohio, Dec. 15, 1948; s. Edward Joseph and Charlotte Frances (Snyder) T.; m. Linda Freudenthal, June 13, 1976; children: Aaron Scott, David Edward. BS, Ohio Domincan Coll., 1970; cert., Ohio State U., 1973. cert. clin. perfusionist. Perfusionist St. Vincent Hosp., Indpls., 1973—. Presenter sci. papers., 1976, 80, 81. Speaker Family Support Ctr. Speaker's Bur., Indpls., 1984; vol. Pan-Am Games/Walt Disney World Prodn., 1987. Mem. Am. Soc. Extracorporeal Tech. (region V chmn. 1975-76, region V sec. 1981-83). Roman Catholic. Home: 1040 W 72nd St Indianapolis IN 46260 Office: St Vincent Hosp 2001 W 86th St Indianapolis IN 46260

TANNAHILL, BRUCE ALLAN, computer software executive; b. Ft. Riley, Kans., June 13, 1955; s. Ralph Ellsworth and Joan (Salisbury) T.; m. Deanna Kay Houser, May 16, 1987. BSBA, U. Dayton, 1976; JD, U. Mo., Kansas City, 1979. Bar: Ohio 1980; CPA. Advanced staff acct. Ernst & Whinney, Dayton, Ohio, 1980-81, sr. acct., 1981; research analyst Dynatax, Wichita, Kans., 1981-82, 1982-84, research, design mgr., 1985—. Mem. ABA, Ks. State Bar Assn. (legis. com. 1983) Am. Inst. CPAs, Ks. Soc. CPA's (data processing com. 1985-87), Nat. Assn. Computerized Tax Processors (sec. 1986—), Dayton Bar Assn., Wichita Bar Assn. Democrat. United Methodist. Avocations: running, tennis, photography, reading. Home: 34

Lansdown Wichita KS 67220 Office: Dynatax 619 E William Wichita KS 67202

TANNENBERG, DIETER E. A., manufacturing and distributing company executive; b. Chevy Chase, Md., Nov. 24, 1932; s. E.A. Wilhelm and Margarete Elizabeth (Mundhenk) T.; m. Ruth Hansen, Feb. 6, 1956; 1 child, Diana Tannenberg Collingsworth. BSME, Northwestern U., 1959. Registered profl. engr., N.Y., Conn., Ohio, Ill., Ind., Wis., N.J. Supervising engr. Flexonics div. Calumet & Hecla, Inc., Chgo., 1959-61, chief engr., 1961-63, program mgr. advanced space systems, 1963-65, dir. mfg. services, 1965-67; dir. mfg. engring. SCM Corp., Cortland, N.Y., 1967-69; tech. dir. internat. Singer Co., N.Y.C., 1969-71; v.p. ops. internat. div. Addressograph-Multigraph Corp., Cleve., 1971-74; mng. dir. Addressograph Multigraph GmbH, Frankfurt/Main, W. Ger., 1974-78; v.p., gen. mgr. Europe, Middle East, Africa AM Internat. Inc., Chgo., 1978-79; pres. AM Bruning div., 1979-82, AM Multigraphics Div., Mt. Prospect, Ill., 1982-86; corp. v.p. AM Internat., Inc., 1981-83, corp. sr. v.p., 1983-86; chmn. bd. dirs., pres., chief exec. officer Sargent-Welch Sci. Co., Skokie, Ill., 1986—; chmn. AM Internat. GmbH, Frankfurt, 1977-86; bd. dirs. Artra Group, Inc. Contbr. chpts. to handbooks, articles to tech., trade mags.; patentee in machinery field. Served with M.I., U.S. Army, 1953-56. Named Man of Yr. Quick Print Mag., 1985. Mem. Assn. Reprodn. Materials Mfrs. (bd. dirs. 1979-82, v.p. 1980-82), Nat. Assn. Quick Printers (bd. dirs. 1982-84), Nat. Printing Equipment and Supplies Mfg. Assn. (bd. dirs. 1983-86, chmn. govt. affairs com. 1985-86), Computer and Bus. Equipment Mfg. Assn. (bd. dirs. 1983-86), Soc. Am. Value Engrs. (hon. v.p. 1985—), Value Found. (trustee 1985—), Chgo. Council Fgn. Relations, ASME, Nat. Soc. Profl. Engrs., Pi Tau Sigma. Club: Economic (Chgo.). Office: Sargent-Welch Sci Co 7300 N Linder Ave Skokie IL 60077

TANNER, BRUCE A., sales company executive; b. Wichita, Kans., Dec. 21, 1944; s. Homer Ardel and Vera (Hila) T.; m. Phyllis Marr, Sept. 9, 1966 (div. July 1981); m. Diana Kay Burns, May 9, 1984; 1 child, Bruce A. Student, Wichita (Kans.) State U., 1962-64. Sales mgr. Crowl Publs., Wichita, 1958-62; sr. salesman Victor Comptometer Corp., Wichita, 1962-65; sales mgr. Colo. Devel. Co., Wichita, 1965-67; distbr. Internat. Law Success, Wichita, 1967-72; pres. Bruce Tanner Internat., Beverly Hills, Calif., 1972—, Nat. Sales. Inst., Inc., Wichita, 1984—, Bruce Tanner Sales Inst., Inc., Springfield, Mo., 1986—; cons. various nat. cos., 1982—. Served with USN, 1962-64. Mem. Sales and Mktg. Execs., Am. Entrepreneurs Assn., Nat. Assn. Martial Artists. Republican. Baptist. Club: Salesmen With A Purpose (local pres. 1971-72). Avocations: tennis, karate, boating. Office: National Sales Inst Inc 513 S Woodlawn Suite 115 Wichita KS 67218 Office: Bruce Tanner Sales Inst Inc Suite 2-100 Corp Ctr 1949 E Sunshine Springfield MO 65804

TANNER, JOAN MARIE, lawyer; b. St. Louis, Nov. 30, 1958; d. Jerry V. and Dolores B. (Ostenfeld) T. BA in Polit. Sci., St. Louis U., 1980, JD, 1983. Bar: Mo. 1983, U.S. Dist. Ct. (we. dist.) Mo. 1983. Assoc. Fitzsimmons & Fitzsimmons, St. Louis, 1983-85, Suelthaus & Kaplan, P.C., St. Louis, 1985—. Mem. ABA, Bar Assn. Met. St. Louis, St. Louis County Bar Assn. Democrat. Roman Catholic. Avocations: camping, fishing. Office: Suelthaus & Kaplan PC 8000 Maryland 9th Floor Saint Louis MO 63105

TANPHAICHITR, KONGSAK, rheumatologist, allergist, immunologist, internist; b. Bangkok, Thailand, Feb. 22, 1946; came to U.S., 1971; s. Boonchoo and Hong (Nayakovit) T.; m. Sirirat Tareesung, June 17, 1973; children: Saksiri Marc, Marisa. Student, Mahidol U., Bangkok, Thailand, 1964-66, MD cum laude, 1970. Diplomate Am. Bd. Internal Medicine, Am. Bd. Rheumatology, Am. Bd. Allergy and Immunology; cert. Rheumatologist Royal Coll. Physicians Can. Straight med. intern Detroit Gen. Hosp.-Wayne State U., 1971-72; resident Barnes Hosp.-Washington U., St. Louis, 1972-74, fellow in rheumatology and immunology, 1974-76; instr. in medicine Washington U., St. Louis, 1976-77, asst. prof. medicine, 1977—; attending physician Barnes Hosp., St. Louis, 1976—, Jewish Hosp. of St. Louis, 1981—; dir. Allergy, Rheumatology & Immunology Specialists, St. Louis; cons. rheumatology Washington U., St. Louis, 1976—. Author: Amyloid Fibrils in Joint Fluid, 1976, Studies of Tolerance in NZB/NZW Mice, 1977, Vasculitis and Multiple Sclerosis, 1980. Bd. dirs., sec. Wat Phrasriratanaram, The Buddhist Temple, St. Louis, 1983—. Recipient Silver medal award Mahidol U., 1970, Bronze medals in medicine and physiology, 1968, 70. Fellow Am. Coll. Physicians, Am. Acad. Allergy and Immunology, Am. Rheumatism Assn., Royal Coll. Physicians of Can.; mem. Thai Assn. St. Louis. Buddhist. Club: Shorinryu (St. Louis). Avocations: karate, insight meditation, swimming. Home: 12166 Royal Valley Dr Saint Louis MO 63141 Office: Allergy Rheumatology & Immunology Specialists 11115 New Halls Ferry Rd Suite 306 Saint Louis MO 63033

TANSEK, KARIN MARYA, head and neck surgeon, researcher; b. Columbus, Ohio, Jan. 13, 1948; d. Lester Robert and Margaret Elaine (Worsham) T.; m. Michael Horwath Hoffmeister, July 4, 1970 (div. June 1977); m. Erol Tugrul Üke, July 14, 1984. BS in Zoology, Wayne State U., 1970, MS in Microbiology and Biochemistry, 1972; MD, Mich. State U., 1976. Intern UCLA Harbor Gen. Hosp., Torrance, 1976-77; resident in gen. and plastic surgery Yale U. Waterbury Hosp., New Haven, 1978-79; resident in gen. surgery UCLA Harbor Gen. Hosp., Torrance, 1979-81; resident in gen. surgery Northwestern U., Chgo., 1979-81, resident in otolaryngology, head and neck surgery, 1981-84; surgeon ENT Profl. Assocs., Mpls., 1985—. Mem. AMA, Women's Am. Med. Assn., Hennepin County Med. Soc. Avocations: photography, skiing, bicycling. Home: 4370 Thielen Ave Edina MN 55436 Office: ENT Profl Assocs 315 Med Arts Bldg Nicolet Mall Minneapolis MN 55402

TANSKY, ROBERT EUGENE, economics and business educator; b. Flint, Mich., Apr. 7, 1942; s. James E. and Dorothy M. (Drohn) T.; m. Beverly L. Baszler, Nov. 11, 1967; children: Jonathan, Autumn. BS, U. Detroit, 1964; MBA, Mich. State U., 1965; postgrad., U. Mich., 1966, Wayne State U., 1973. Prof. econs. and bus. adminstrn. St. Clair County Community Coll., Port Huron, Mich., 1966—, chmn. dept., 1971—; Pres. Econ. Research Corp., Port Huron, 1974—. Vice chmn. St. Clair County Met. Planning Commn., Port Huron, 1978—; mem. parish fin. com. St. Stephen's Ch., Port Huron, 1980—. Recipient Disting. Faculty award St. Clair County Community Coll., 1982. Mem. Nat. Assn. Bus. Economists, Detroit Assn. Bus. Economists, Am. Econs. Assn., Mich. Assn. Higher Edn., Mich. Edn. Assn. (regional assembly del. 1978—). Club: St. Francis (Detroit). Avocation: photography. Office: St Clair County Community Coll 323 Erie St Port Huron MI 48060

TANTILLO, CHARLES ROBERT, financial planning firm executive, restaurant executive; b. N.Y.C., June 30, 1936; s. Charles and Mary (Masauro) T.; m. Carol Adler, 1955; children: Charles R. II, Cynthia Ann, Christopher, Curtis Jon. Assoc. Arts and Scis., SUNY, Cobbeskill, 1956; BA cum laude, Tulsa U., 1958. CLU; chartered fin. cons. Agt., supr. Am. Nat. Inc. Co., Galveston, Tex., 1956-62; agency mgr. Woodmen A/L Co., Topeka, 1962—; pres., chief exec. officer Tantillo and Miller Inc., Topeka, 1982—; chmn. Restaurant Services Inc., Topeka, 1965—. Mem. Am. Soc. CLU's, Million Dollar Round Table (life) (Honor Role 1984). Republican. Presbyterian. Avocations: hot air ballooning, sailboat racing, formula car racing. Home: 3861 Chelmsford Rd Topeka KS 66610 Office: Capitol City Bank Plaza 3706 SW Topeka Blvd Topeka KS 66609

TANZMAN, MARY, social worker; b. Bialystok, Poland, Sept. 29, 1915; came to U.S., 1920; d. Jacob and Bertha (Cohen) Grodman; m. Jack Tanzman, Feb. 22, 1942; children: Elaine, Edward. BA in Social Work, Wayne State U., 1939; MSW, U. Chgo., 1964. Social worker, dist. supr. Jewish Family and Community Services, Chgo., 1942-49; dir. social work marital dept. Forest Hosp., Des Plaines, Ill., 1959-64; pvt. practice social work Evanston, Ill., 1955—; cons. in field. Fellow Am. Orthopsychiat. Assn.; mem. Nat. Assn. Social Work, Am. Assn. Marital and Family Therapists (clin.). Home: 1613 Seward St Evanston IL 60202

TAPLETT, LLOYD MELVIN, human resources management consultant; b. Tyndall, S.D., July 25, 1924; s. Herman Leopold and Emiley (Nedvidek) T.; B.A., Augustana Coll., 1949; M.A., U. Nebr., 1958; postgrad. S.D. State U., U. S.D., U. Iowa, Colo. State U.; m. Patricia Ann Sweeney, Aug. 21, 1958; children—Virginia Ann, Sharon Lorraine, Carla Jo, Carolyn Patricia, Catherine Marie, Colleen Elizabeth. Tchr., Sioux Falls (S.D.) public schs., 1952-69; with All-Am. Transport Co., Sioux Falls, 1969-78, Am. Freight System, Inc., Overland Park, Kans., 1978-79; dir. human resources and public relations, corp. affirmative action compliance ofcl. Chippewa Motor Freight Inc., Sioux Falls, 1979-80; human resource and mgmt. cons., 1980-81; mgr. Sioux Falls Job Services, 1981—; chmn. Chippewa Credit Union; mem. adv. bd. dirs. Nelson Labs., Sioux Falls 1981-82; evening mgmt. instr Nat. Coll., Sioux Falls, 1981—, chmn. adv. com., 1984—. Past bd. dirs. Jr. Achievement, United Way, Sioux Vocat. Sch. for Handicapped; past mem. Gov.'s Adv. Bd. for Community Adult Manpower Planning; chmn. bus. edn. adv. com. Sioux Falls Public Schs., 1982—; chmn. adv. com. South East Area Vocat. Sch., 1982—. Served to capt. USMC, 1943-46, 50-52. Recipient Liberty Bell award S.D. Bar Assn., 1967; Sch. Bd. award NEA/Thom McAn Shoe Corp., 1966; named Boss of Yr., Sioux Falls, 1977; cert. tchr. and counselor, S.D. Mem. Am. Soc. for Personnel Adminstrn. (accredited personnel mgr., S.D. dist. dir. 1980-84), Am. Trucking Assn., NEA (life mem., Pacemaker award), S.D. Edn. Assn. (life), Sioux Falls Personnel Assn. (past pres.), Sales and Mktg. Club Sioux Falls, Sioux Falls Traffic Club, VFW (life), Am. Legion. Republican. Roman Catholic. Clubs: Toastmasters (past gov. dist. 41, Disting. Toastmaster award, Outstanding Toastmaster award dist. 41, Hall of Fame 1977), Elks. Contbr. articles to nat. mags. Office: 213 W 13th St Sioux Falls SD 57102

TAPPIN, ANTHONY GERALD, marketing executive; b. London, July 17, 1925; came to U.S., 1940; naturalized, 1944; s. Edward Laurence Charles and Cecilia Mary (Seymour) T.; m. Nancy C. Harper, May 17, 1952; children: Cynthia Marie, Amy Elizabeth. AB, Cornell U., 1949; advanced mgmt. program, Harvard Bus. Sch., 1968. Asst. product mgr., chem. div. FMC Corp., N.Y.C., 1950; rep. FMC Corp., Washington, 1950-52; dist. sales mgr. FMC Corp., Cin., 1952-58, gen. sales mgr., 1958-67, dir. mktg., asst. div. mgr., 1967-70, dir. purchases, 1970-77, regional v.p., corp. exec. mktg., 1977-82, v.p. corp. exec. mktg., 1982—. Active United Fund, Crippled Children's Assn; pres., bd dirs. Saddle Brook Community Assn., 1985—. Served with inf. U.S. Army, 1944-46. Decorated Bronze star, Combat Inf. Badge. Mem. Nat. Assn. Mfrs. (dir. exec. com. 1985—), Nat. Assn. Purchasing Mgmt. (cert. purchasing mgr.), Nat. Accounts Mgrs. Assn. (dir. 1978-82), Racemics. Chem. Industries council Midwest (dir. 1982—), Phi Gamma Delta. Roman Catholic. Clubs: Cornell Fairfield County (Conn.) (pres. 1972-73), Cornell of Chgo., Harvard Bus. Sch., Chicago, Mid-America (Chgo.); Union League (Phila.); Aronimink Golf (Newtown Square, Pa.); Country Darien (Conn.); Capilano Golf and Country (Vancouver, B.C., Can.); Butterfield Country (Oak Brook, Ill.). Avocations: golf, fishing. Office: FMC Corp 200 E Randolph Dr Chicago IL 60601

TAPSCOTT, THOMAS MICHAEL, health care executive; b. Muncie, Ind., Nov. 20, 1939; s. Raymond Thomas and Dorothea L. (Lambert) T.; m. Jane A. Hocker, June 17, 1967; children: T. Kevin, Kathleen J. BBA, U. Cin., 1962. Sales rep. IBM, Indpls., 1966-69; surgical specialist Johnson & Johnson, Indpls., 1969-71; mgmt. cons. Ind. Hosp. Assn., Indpls., 1971-76; sr. mgmt. engr. Wishard Meml. Hosp., Indpls., 1976-78; dir. mgmt. systems Ind. U. Hosps., Indpls., 1978-83; dir. systems & data services La Porte (Ind.) Hosp., 1983—; Cons. in field, 1971—. Contbr. articles to profl. jours. bd. dirs. Skiles Test Baseball League, Indpls., 1979-81, Devonshire Civic Assn., Indpls., 1981-83; mem. stewardship com. La Porte Presbyn. Ch., 1985-86. Served to lt. USN, 1962-66. Mem. Hosp. Mgmt. Systems Soc., Hosp. Mgmt. Systems Soc. Ind. (pres. 1982, bd. dirs. 1981-83). Republican. Presbyterian. Avocations: bridge, reading, fishing. Home: 5570 W Lakeview Dr La Porte IN 46350 Office: La Porte Hosp 1007 Lincoln Way La Porte IN 46350

TARASZKIEWICZ, WALDEMAR, physician; b. Wilno, Poland, July 6, 1936; came to U.S., 1979; s. Michal Taraszkiewicz and Nina (Lutomska) Dylla; m. Teresa Barbara Szwarc, Oct. 15, 1966. MD, Med. Acad., Gdansk, Poland, 1961, internal medicine specialty, 1967, internal medicine specialty II, 1972; family practice specialty, Am. Bd. Family Practice, 1985. Family physician Out Patient Clinic, Sopot, Poland, 1962-64; resident doctor U. Hosp., Gdansk, 1965-71; allergist Clinic of Allergy, Gdansk, 1965-75; physician Cardiology Dept., Gdansk, 1971-75, Hôpital Civil, Telagh, Algeria, 1975-79; surg. asst. Hinsdale (Ill.) Hosp., 1979-82; resident physician St. Mary of Nazareth Hosp., Chgo., 1982-85, emergency room physician, 1984-85; family practice medicine Brookfield, Ill., 1985—; sr. asst. dept. cardiology Univ. Hosp., Gdansk, 1971-75; mem. adminstrv. com., pres. med. staff Hôpital Civil, Telagh, 1976-79. Contbr. articles to profl. jours. Recipient Bronze medal Polski Zwiazek Wodkarski, 1970; cert. 3d place Polski Zwiazek Wedkarski, 1971. Fellow Am. Acad. Family Practice; mem. AMA (continuing edn. award), Ill. Med. Soc., Chgo. Med. Soc. (practice mgmt. com.), World Med. Assn., Am. Acad. Allergy and Immunology, Am. Assn. Clin. Immunology, Polish Med. Alliance, N.Y. Acad. Sci. Avocations: art collecting, fishing. Office: Family Practice Ctr Brookfield 9211 W Ogden Ave Brookfield IL 60513

TAREN, JAMES A., physician; b. Toledo, Nov. 10, 1924; s. Joseph Clarence and Mary Frances (Walker) T. BS, U. Toledo, 1948; MD, U. Mich., 1952. Diplomate Am. Bd. Neurosurgery. Intern U. Mich., Ann Arbor, 1952-53, resident in surgery, 1953-54; research fellowneurosurgery Boston Children's Hosp.; research fellow surgery Peter Bent Brigham Hosp., Boston, 1955; resident neurosurgery U. Mich., Ann Arbor, 1955-57, faculty mem., 1957—, prof. neurosurgery, 1969—, dir. neurobehavioral scis., 1974-78, dir. brain tumor immunology, 1984; assoc. dean U. Mich., Ann Arbor, 1978—; vis. prof. Saint Anne Hosp., Paris, 1981, Karolinski Inst., Stockholm, 1981, Haukland Sykehus, Bergen, Norway, 1984, Hosp. Foch, Paris, 1966-67. Author, co-editor: Correlative Neurosurgery, 3rd edit., 1982; contbr. articles on neurosurgery to profl. jours. Dep. med. examiner Washtenaw County Dept. Health, Ann Arbor, 1962—, vol. surgeon Project Hope, Peru, 1962, Ecuador, 1963, Guinea, 1964, West Africa, 1964. Served with USMC, 1943-46, PTO. Fellow NIH, 1953. Mem. Congress of Neuro. Surgeons, ACS, Am. Assn. Neuro. Scis., Am. Assn. Med. Colls., Am. Soc. for Stereotactic and Functional Neurosurgery. Home: 2222 Fuller Rd #901A Ann Arbor MI 48105 Office: Univ Mich Hosps Sect Neurosurgery 2124 Taubman Box 0338 Ann Arbor MI 48109

TARKINGTON, ANDREW CHARLES, dentist; b. Detroit, Jan. 5, 1954; s. John Marshall and M. Joan (Keller) T.; m. Karen Marie Skiba, Jan. 9, 1982; children: Sarah Anne, Drew Marshall. DDS, U. Mich., 1979. Gen. practice dentistry Alpena, Mich., 1979—. Mem. ADA, Mich. Dental Assn. (del. 1986), Northeastern Mich. Dental Soc. (pres. 1983-84, v.p. 1982-83, sec.-treas. 1981-82). Clubs: Alpena Yacht. Avocations: sailing, hunting. Office: 234 S Second Alpena MI 49707

TARM, FELIX, internist, medical researcher; b. Tallinn, Estonia, May 22, 1939; came to U.S., 1950, naturalized, 1960; s. Feliks and Eugenia (Semyonov) T.; m. Kay A. Mallicoat, Sept. 2, 1962; children—Susan A., Michael V., Viktor F. M.D., U. Iowa, 1965. Diplomate Am. Bd. Internal Medicine. Intern Med. Coll. Va., Richmond, 1966; fellow Mayo Clinic, Rochester, Minn., 1970-73, assoc. cons., 1973; physician, researcher, cons. Internal Medicine Specialists PA, Hutchinson, Kans., 1973—; lectr. Hutchinson Hosp. Corp., 1973—. Mem. editorial bd. jour. Postgrad. Medicine, 1979. Contbr. articles to profl. jours. Served to maj. U.S. Army, 1967-70. Recipient Outstanding Achievement in Internal Medicine award Mayo Found., 1973; FDA grantee; Mem. Mayo Clinic Assn., AMA (Physician's Recognition award, 1983), Am. Soc. Internal Medicine. Libertarian. Avocations: writing poetry; racquetball. Home: 43 Linksland Hutchinson KS 67502 Office: Internal Medicine Specialists PA 2020 N Waldron Hutchinson KS 67502

TAROSKY, ROBERT EUGENE, consulting engineer; b. New Kensington, Pa., Apr. 29, 1942; s. Frank John and Mary Wanda (Bartos) T.; m. Verna May Lucci, Feb. 1, 1964 (dec. 1976); m. 2d, Diane Carol Baran, Feb. 25, 1978; children: Michele Lynn, Renata Elizabeth. BS in Mech. and Aerospace Engring., Ill. Inst. Tech., 1970. Registered profl. engr., Ill. With Tuthill Pump Co., Alsip, Ill., 1963-68; with Gen. Environments Corp., Morton Grove, Ill., 1970-75, staff engr., 1970-74, cons. engr., 1975; with Hazard Engring. Inc., Morton Grove, 1975-86 , v.p., 1979-86; pres. Omnitek Engring. Inc., Prospect Heights, Ill., 1986—. Mem. NSPE, Nat. Acad. Forensic Engrs., ASME, Nat. Soc. Mech. Engrs., Nat. Acad. Forensic Engrs., Am. Soc. Metals, Ill. Soc. Profl. Engrs., Soc. Automotive Engrs., Chgo. Curling Club. Office: Omntek Engring Inc 65 E Palatine Rd Suite 101 Prospect Heights IL 60070

TARPLEY, JAMES DOUGLAS, journalism educator, magazine editor; b. Los Angeles, May 2, 1946; s. Clement Henry and Grace Lorraine (Everson) T.; m. Patricia Jean McIntosh, June 18, 1966; children: Tamara Jean, James David, Jonathan Eric. BS in Edn., SW Mo. U., 1968, MA in English, 1972; MA in Mass Communications, Cen. Mo. U., 1976; PhD in Journalism, So. Ill. U., 1983. Cert. tchr., Mo. Tchr. Eldon (Mo.) Pub. Schs., 1968-75; prof. journalism Evangel Coll., Springfield, Mo., 1976-87, Christian Broadcasting Network U., Virgina Beach, 1987—; guest lectr. Cen. Mo. U., SW Mo. U., So. Ill. U., U. Ohio summer journalism workshops, 1976—. Youth page editor Eldon Advertiser, 1972-76, mng. editor High Adventure, 1983-87, Criminal Justice Management, 1978-81, editor Ranger News, 1979-81, design and layout editor Vision Magazine, 1984-87; free-lance writer, contbr. biographical entries to profl. publ.; free-lance photographer; graphic artist, copywriter Disco-Fair advt. dept., 1964-68. Exec. com. Eldon PTA, 1971-74; youth dir. Eldon Assembly of God, 1968-75; Sunday sch. supt. Cen. Assembly of God, Springfield, Mo., 1978-82; mem. Sch. Effectiveness Evaluation Team Springfield Pub. Schs., 1985-86, 86-87. Recipient Mo. Journalism Tchr. Yr. award, 1976, Cert. of Merit Columbia U., 1984; named Outstanding Grad., Dept. Mass Communication Cen. Mo. U. 1976; fellow U. Pa. and Freedom Found. project on press freedom, 1984, Nat. Newspaper Fund Fellow Dow Jones and U. Mo., 1975. Mem. Coll. Media Advisers (bd. dirs., chmn. various coms., pres. citation 1981, 84, 85), Soc. Coll. Journalists (exec. dir. 1983—, pres. citation 1981, 85, Gold Medal of Merit 1984), Assn. Edn. in Journalism and Mass Communication, Nat. Conf. Editorial Writers (com. scholarly research 1985—), Soc. Newspaper Design (edn. com. 1986), Broadcast Edn. Assn. (intern. com. 1984), Assn. Journalism Historians, Inst. Cert. Photographers, Mo. Tchrs. Assn., Evang. Press Assn., Pi Delta Kappa. Republican. Lodge: Kiwanis. Avocations: writing, photography, painting.

TARR, RICHARD ROBERT, biomedical engineer; b. Springfield, Ill., June 13, 1948; s. Robert William and Margaret Helen (Kobialka) T.; m. Joan Elaine Marcks, Aug. 15, 1970; children: Julianne Janell, Kevin Cody. BS in Sci. Engring., Northwestern U., Evanston, Ill., 1970; diploma, Northwestern U. Sch. Radiol. Tech., Chgo., 1975; MS in Bioengring., Tex. A&M, 1977. Clin. design engr. Northwestern U., Chgo., 1973-75; research assoc. U. Miami, Fla., 1977-78; instr., dir. U. So. Calif., Los Angeles, 1978-85; dir. product devel. DePuy, Warsaw, Ind., 1985—; cons. Hall, Tarr & Assocs., Cypress, Calif., 1981-85; lectr. U. So. Calif., Los Angeles, 1980-85. Contbr. articles on orthopedic biomechanics, total joint arthroplasty, fracture healing to profl. jours. Chmn. bd. elders St. John's Luth. Ch., Orange, Calif., 1983-84; sec. voters' assembly, elder Redeemer Luth. Ch., Warsaw, 1985-86. Served with U.S. Army, 1970-73. Mem. Am. Soc. Mech. Engrs., Orthopaedic Research Soc., Soc. Biomaterials, Vet. Orthopaedic Soc., Internat. Soc. Fracture Repair. Avocations: golf, photography, gardening, woodworking. Office: DePuy PO Box 988 Warsaw IN 46580

TARRANT, PHYLLIS ANN, school administrator, athletic director; b. Heavener, Okla., Sept. 7, 1944; d. Arlis and Emily Frances (Helton) Garner; m. Lee R. Tarrant Jr., Feb. 15, 1963; children: Kimberly Dawn, Michelle Leigh-Ann. BS in Home Econs. and Edn., Okla. State U., 1972; MS in Counseling, Kans. State U., 1979, PhD in Adminstrn., 1982. Tchr. Washington Jr. High Sch., Ottumwa, Iowa, 1973-76, Junction City (Kans.) High Sch., 1976-80; counselor/adminstr. Ell-Saline, Brookville, Kans., 1980-83; prin., curriculum dir. Russel (Kans.) USD 407, 1983-86; asst. supt. Dexter Pub. Schs., Dexter, Kans., 1986—; Presentor at numerous state and nat. educators confs. Dir., author Career Education Grant K-12 Activity Book, 1981, Career Education Computers, 1981; dir. grant repication for small schs. Mastery Learning, 1981. Bd. dirs. Cancer Soc., Russell, 1985-86. Mem. Assn. for Supervision and Curriculum Devel. (state Yr. of the Tchr. com.), Mid Am. Assn. Ednl. Data Systems, Kans. United Sch. Adminstrs. (NW chmn. 1985-86), Kans. Career Edn. Consortium, Russell C. of C. (Outstanding Educator 1985), Phi Upsilon Omicron, Kappa Delta Pi. Republican. Episcopalian. Lodge: Eastern Star. Avocations: sports, sewing, reading, horses. Home: PO Box 57 Dexter KS 67038 Office: USD 471 PO Box 97 Dexter KS 67038

TARRO, RICHARD BENJAMIN, accountant; b. Wyandotte, Mich., Sept. 25, 1947; s. James R. and Roseann A. (Florian) T.; m. Jeannette K. Wimberly, Mar. 8, 1969. BS, So. Ill. U., 1973. Agt. IRS, Decatur, Ill., 1973-79; ptnr. Keller, Disbrow, Morrison & Chamblin P.C., Decatur, 1979—. Mem. Ill. CPA Soc. (sec. 1985-86, treas. 1986—). Republican. Roman Catholic. Home: 537 Sheffield Dr Decatur IL 62526 Office: Keller Disbrow Morrison & Chamblin PO Box 1108 Decatur IL 62523

TARVER, MAE-GOODWIN, consulting company executive; b. Selma, Ala., Aug. 9, 1916; d. Hartwell Hill and R. Louise (Wilkins) T.; B.S. in Chemistry, U. Ala., 1939, M.S., 1940. Project supr. container shelflife Continental Can Co., Inc., Chgo., 1941-48, project engr. stats., 1948-54, quality control cons., research statistician, 1954-77; pres., prin. cons. Quest Assocs., Park Forest, Ill., 1978—; adj. assoc. prof. biology dept. Ill. Inst. Tech., Chgo., 1957-81. Bd. dirs. Ash Street Coop., Park Forest, Ill., 1976-85. Fellow Am. Soc. Quality Control (Joe Lisy award 1961, Edward J. Oakley award 1975, E.L. Grant award 1983); mem. Inst. Food Technologists, Soc. Women Engrs., Am. Statis. Assn., Park Forest C. of C. (pres. 1986), Sigma Xi. Home: 130 26th St Park Forest IL 60466

TASCH, ALCUIN (BUD) MARTIN, advertising and public relations agency executive; b. Oak Park, Ill., Apr. 21, 1924; s. John Leo and Anne Catherine (Smith) T.; m. Joyce Madden, Jan. 17, 1955; children—Cuin, Gail, Martin, William, Robert. Student Idaho State Tchrs. Coll., 1943, U. Okla., 1944. Ptnr., co-founder Aerial Photography, Chgo., 1946-60; pres. Alcuin Tasch & Co., River Forest, Ill., 1958—, Cuill Advt. Co., Chgo., 1963—. Served to lt. comdr. AC, USN, World War II. Decorated Air medal, 6 others. Mem. Naval Commandery, Naval Airmen of Am. (past nat. comdr. 1949-50). Republican. Roman Catholic. Clubs: Press, Germania. Home and Office: 7979 Chicago Ave River Forest IL 60305

TASKER, FRED L., physician, educator; b. Gloucester, Mass., May 13, 1931; s. Fred L. and Frances C. (Spiller) T.; m. Edna May Taylor, June 27, 1955; children—Gregory Allen, Patricia Ann, Cynthia Ann, Jennifer Sue. B.S., Calvin Coll., Grand Rapids, Mich., 1961; M.S. in Physiology and Pharmacology, U. N.D., 1963; M.D., U. Kans.-Kansas City, 1966. Intern, Wesley Med. Ctr., Wichita, 1966-67, resident in surgery, 1967-68; dir. emergency room and dept. St. Joseph Hosp., Wichita, 1969-70; resident in ophthalmology Eye & Ear Hosp., Pitts., 1970-73; practice medicine specializing in ophthalmology, Sandusky, Ohio, 1973—; chief of staff Good Samaritan Hosp., Sandusky, 1982-83; clin. asst. prof. surgery Med. Coll. Ohio, Toledo, 1975—; cons. ophthalmologist Providence Hosp., Meml. Hosp., Sandusky. Served with USAF, 1950-54. Mem. AMA, Ohio State Med. Assn., Erie County Med. Soc., Am. Acad. Ophthalmology, Internat. Assn. Ophthalmic Surgeons, Sigma Xi. Republican. Club: Nat. Wildlife Assn. Contbr. article in field. Office: 521 W Perkins Ave Sandusky OH 44870

TASSANI, SALLY MARIE, advertising and marketing company executive; b. Teaneck, N.J., Dec. 30, 1948; d. Peter R. and Marie Irene (Sorbello) T. BA, Am. U., 1970. Elem. sch. tchr., Washington, 1970-73; asst. prodn. and promotion mgr. First Nat. Bank of Chgo., 1973-74; exec. dir. Jack O'Grady Graphics, Inc., Chgo., 1974-76; creative dir. Dimensional Mktg., Inc., Chgo., 1976-78; pres., founder Tassani Communications (formerly Nexus, Inc.), Chgo., 1978—. Mem. Alliance for the Art Inst. Chgo., World Com. on Fgn. and Domestic Affairs, Landmark Preservation Council of Ill., Chgo. Council on Fgn. Relations. Mem. Internat. Assn. of Bus. Communicators, Women's Advt. Club of Chgo., Am. Mgmt. Assoc. Club: Women's Athletic. Home: 1735 N Orleans St Chicago IL 60614 Office: Tassani Communications 625 N Michigan Ave Suite 1600 Chicago IL 60611

TATE, BENJAMIN FRANKLIN, professional placement representative; b. Rockford, Ill., July 28, 1953; s. Nathan Hughes and Almer (McDaniels) T.; m. Laura Marie Knight, June 23, 1979; children: Brianna Janae, Jarron Vincent. BA in Sociology, William Jewell Coll., 1976. Social worker trainee Jackson County Juvenile Ct., Kansas City, Mo., 1976-77; service mgr. Urban Services YMCA, Kansas City, 1977-79; vol. coordinator Mo. Div. Family Services, Kansas City, 1979-80; personnel rep. Burns & McDonnell Engring., Kansas City, 1980-83; profl. placement rep. Allied/Bendix, Kansas City, 1983—; cons. William Jewell Pres.'s Adv. Com., Liberty, Mo., 1978-79.

Mem. Inner City Vol. Action Bd., Kansas City, 1980-81. Recipient cert. appreciation Urban League Greater Kansas City, 1980-85, Kansas City Sch. Bd., 1983-84; named one of the Outstanding Young Men in Am., 1985. Mem. Personnel Mgmt. Assn. (subcom. chmn. Kansas City 1985-86). Democrat. Baptist. Avocations: tennis, softball. Home: 1413 E 77th St Kansas City MO 64131

TATE, DAVID GENE, health sciences educator, psychotherapist; b. Lafayette, Ind., Feb. 9, 1946; s. Vernon Eugene and Marjorie Glenn (Powell) T.; m. Maureen Ann Krug, Mar. 11, 1972; 1 child, Ryan Churchill. B.S., Purdue U., 1970, M.S., 1980, Ph.D., 1985. Instr., Purdue U., West Lafayette, Ind., 1979-80, instr., supr. in counseling personnel services, 1980-82, instr. edn., 1982-84, grad. instr. health scis., 1984—, dir. clin. med. tech. program, dir. student services Sch. Health Scis., 1985—; dir. student services St. Joseph's Coll., Rensselaer, Ind., 1981-82; cons. Warren Co. Sheriff's Dept., Williamsport, 1984—; adj. faculty Ind. Affiliated Clin. Hosps., 1985; nat. liaison mem. Am. Personnel Guidance Assn., Washington, 1982. Pres., County Park and Recreation Bd., Williamsport, 1983—; co-founder Tippecanoe Council on Alcohol Abuse Lafayette chapt., 1983; co-founder 360 House for Alcohol Abuse, Purdue Univ., 1984; precint committeman Republican Party, Warren County, 1984—. Named hon. capt. Airborne Rangers. Mem. Menninger Found., Am. Assn. for Counseling and Devel., Am. Psychol. Assn., AMA (curriculum edn. com.), Eta Sigma Gamma, Sigma Iota, Omicron Delta Kappa, Kappa Delta Pi, Theta Xi. Clubs: Health Sci. (Purdue) (advisor 1984—), Grad. Student Orgn. (Purdue) (pres. 1984—). Avocations: weightlifting; classical music; match pistol shooting. Home: 307 E Monroe St Williamsport IN 47993 Office: Purdue Univ Sch Health Sci Pharmacy Bldg 3 156 West Lafayette IN 47906

TATE, HARRY RAY, communications executive; b. Elizabethtown, Ky., Apr. 6, 1947; s. George William and Hattie (Hall) T.; m. Jane Dixon Miner, June 17, 1972; children: Kevin Tobias, Carrie Dixon, Jordan Marshall. BA, U. Ky., 1970. With production dept. Sta. WKYT-TV, Lexington, Ky., 1971-73, producer/dir., 1973-76; producer/dir./writer Consultative Services, Lexington, 1976-77, Sta. WPGH-TV, Pitts., 1977-79; prodn. mgr. Meredith Broadcast Sta. WPGH-TV, Pitts., 1979-83; gen. mgr. Telemation Prodns., Inc., Chgo., 1983—; Speaker U. Ind., Pa., 1982, 3M Symposium, Park Rapids, Minn., 1985. Producer NHL Hockey, Pitts., 1979-81; speaker Point Park Coll. Career Day, Pitts., 1982; mem. Vernon Hills (Ill.) Cable Com., 1985—; coach, mgr. Vernon Hills Park Dist. Baseball, 1984-85. Mem. Internat. TV Soc., Chgo. Audio/Visual Producers Assn., Chgo. Coalition, Chgo. C. of C. Democrat. Baptist. Avocations: writing, swimming, tennis. Office: Telemation Prodns Inc 100 S Sangamon St Chicago IL 60607

TATIKONDA, LAKSHMI UMAVIJAYA, business educator, researcher; b. Guntur, India, Sept. 27, 1942; came to U.S., 1962; s. Ranganayakul and Sarojini Devi (Tunuguntla) Ilindra; m. Rao Jagannadha, Aug. 11, 1962; children: Mohan, Sekhar. BA, Andhra U., Waltair, India, 1960; MS, Sri Venkateswara U., Tirupati, India, 1962; PhD, U. Tex., 1966; MBA, Loyola U., New Orleans, 1976. CPA, La.; nationally cert. mgmt. acct. Asst. prof. acctg. U. Fla., Gainesville, 1966, U. New Orleans, 1966-72; assoc. prof. acctg. Ea. Ill. U., Charleston, 1976-78; assoc. prof. acctg. U. Wis., Oshkosh, 1978-84, prof. acctg., 1984—. Author: (study guide) Management Information Systems, 1985. Mem. Nat. Assn. Accts. (bd. dirs. local chpt. 1986—, Outstanding mem. 1985-86), Am. Inst. CPA's, Am. Acctg. Assn., Inst. Cert. Mgmt. Accts., Soc. for Info. Mgmt., Am. Prodn. and Inventory Control Soc. Avocations: reading, sewing. Home: 1921 Hazel St Oshkosh WI 54901 Office: U Wis Coll of Bus 800 Algoma Blvd Oshkosh WI 54901

TATOOLES, CONSTANTINE JOHN, cardiovascular and thoracic surgeon; b. Chgo., May 7, 1936; m. Betty Ann, Jan. 30, 1960; children: Julie Denise, Anton John, Jon William. BS, Albion (Mich.) Coll., 1958; MS in Physiology, Loyola U., Chgo., 1961, MD, 1961. Research asst. Loyola U., 1958-59, research assoc., 1959-60; intern U. Chgo. Hosps., 1961-62, resident in surgery, 1962-68, instr. in surgery, 1966-68; clin. assoc. surgery Nat. Heart Inst.; sr. registrar in surgery Gt. Ormond St. Hosp. for Children, London, 1968-69; practice medicine specializing in cardiovascular and thoracic surgery, Chgo., 1969—; asst. prof. surgery and physiology, Loyola U., 1969-73, attending surgeon, 1969-73; assoc. attending surgeon thoracic and cardiovascular surgery Cook County Hosp., Chgo., 1969-73, chmn. dept. cardiothoracic surgery, 1969-78, attending surgeon, 1970, lectr. in cardiac surgery, 1970; chief cardiovascular and thoracic surgery Abraham Lincoln Sch. Medicine, U. Ill., Chgo., 1973-74, assoc. prof. surgery, 1973-76, prof. surgery, 1976; attending surgeon U. Ill., 1973; chmn. dept. cardiothoracic surgery St. Francis Hosp., Evanston, Ill., 1977-78, St. Mary's of Nazareth Hosp., Chgo., 1981—; chmn. Chgo. Inst. for Heart and Lung, 1972; chmn. bd. Penda Corp., Portgage, Wis., 1981-85; mem. Chgo. Bd. Trade. Contbr. to films in field, articles to profl. publs. Fellow A.C.S., Am. Coll. Cardiology, Am. Coll. Chest Physicians (chmn. motion picture div., 1975-76); mem. Am. Assn. Thoracic Surgery, Am. Heart Assn. (council on cardiovascular surgery), AMA, Am. Thoracic Soc., Assn. for Acad. Surgery, Chgo. Heart Assn. (council on cardiovascular surgery), Chgo. Med. Soc., Chgo. Surg. Soc., Ill. State Med. Soc., Inst. of Medicine Chgo., Royal Soc. Medicine London (Eng.), Soc. Thoracic Surgeons, Chgo. Thoracic Soc. (pres. 1981), A.G. Morrow Soc. (exec. dir.), Warren J. Cole Soc. Office: 800 Austin St Evanston IL 60202

TATSUOKA, MAURICE MAKOTO, psychology educator; b. Shanghai, People's Republic of China, Feb. 1, 1922; came to U.S., 1949; s. Noboru and Yuri (Pratt) T.; m. Hisako Tanahashi, Apr. 10, 1946 (div. Mar. 1964); 1 child, Francis; m. Kikumi Kim Kanemitsu, Nov. 5, 1965; children: Kay, Curtis. BS, Nagoya U., Japan, 1945; MA, George Peabody Coll., 1951; EdD, Harvard U., 1956. Lectr. Kinjo Women's Coll., Nagoya, 1945-49; asst. prof. U. Hawaii, Hilo, 1956-61; assoc. prof. U. Ill., Urbana, 1961-64, prof. ednl. psychology, 1964—; cons. Inst. for Personality and Ability Testing, Champaign, Ill. 1965—. Author: Multivariate Analysis, 1971, 87. Mem. Am. Statis. Assn., Am. Ednl. Research Assn. Democratic. Unitarian. Office: Coll Edn U Ill 1310 S 6th St Champaign IL 61820

TAUBE, ROBERT ROY, surgeon; b. Chgo., Apr. 8, 1936; m. Donna M. Friend, Dec. 22, 1962; children: Patrick, Ann. BS, U. Ill., 1960; MD, U. Ill., Chgo., 1964. Diplomate Am. Bd. Surgery (examiner 1977). Intern Cook County Hosp., Chgo., 1964-65, resident in gen. surgery, 1965-69; fellow in gen. surgery Lahey Clinic Found., Boston, 1969-70; asst. prof. surgery U. Iowa, Iowa City, 1970-73; clin. asst. prof. surgery Ind. U., Indpls., 1974—; active staff mem. Terre Haute (Ind.) Regional Hosp., 1979—, pres.-elect med. staff; courtesy staff mem. Union Hosp., Terre Haute, 1979—, Vermillion County Hosp., Clinton, Ind., 1984—; mem. cons. staff Wishard Meml. Hosp., Indpls., 1974—; chief of surgery Fayette Meml. Hosp., Connersville, Ind., 1975-78; mem. Gov.'s Emergency Med. Service Adv. Council State of Iowa, 1971-73, facilities task force categorization emergency facilities; dir. emergency room U. Iowa Hosps., 1971-73; lectr. in surgery Ind. U. Med. Sch., 1974-80. Contbr. articles to profl. jours. Fellow ACS; mem. Ind. State Med. Soc. (med. services commn. 1973-78), Vigo County Med. Soc. (alt. del. to Ind. State Med. Assn. 1982-85), Midwest Surg. Assn. Republican. Roman Catholic. Club: Terre Haute Country. Lodge: Rotary. Avocations: golfing, fishing. Home: 185 Deming Ln Terre Haute IN 47803 Office: 501 Hospital Ln Terre Haute IN 47802

TAUBMAN, ALFRED A., food products company executive. Chmn., chief exec. officer A&W Restaurants Inc., Dearborn, Mich. Office: A & W Restaurants Inc 1 Parklane Blvd Dearborn MI 48126 *

TAUGHER, MARY PATRICIA, occupational therapy educator; b. Milw., Aug. 30, 1934; d. James Patrick and Mary Margaret (Quick) T. BS, Mt. Mary Coll., 1956; MS, U. Wis., Milw., 1969. Registered occupational therapist. Occupational therapy supr. Milw. County, 1957-69; lectr. Mt. Mary Coll., Milw., 1969-70; chief occupational therapist Luth. Hosp. Milw., Inc., 1970-83; clin. asst. prof. occupational therapy program U. Wis., Milw., 1983—; cons. Tower Assocs., Milw., 1983—. Profl. cons. Midtown Neighborhood Citizens Group, Milw. Model Cities Program, 1969-71. Mem. Am. Occupational Therapy Assn., Wis. Occupational Therapy Assn. (treas. 1969, sec. 1986—), Wis. Soc. Allied Health Profls., World Fedn. Occupational Therapists, U. Wis. at Milw. Assn. Women in Edn. (vice chair 1987—), Am. Congress Rehab. Medicine. Roman Catholic. Avocations: golf, biking, arts and crafts. Home: 10202 A W Denis Ave Hales Corners WI 53130 Office: U Wis Occupational Therapy Program PO Box 413 Milwaukee WI 53201

TAUKE, THOMAS J(OSEPH), Congressman; b. Dubuque, Iowa, Oct. 11, 1950; s. Joseph A. and Esther M. (Reicher) T. B.A. magna cum laude, Loras Coll., 1972; J.D., U. Iowa, 1974. Bar: Iowa 1974. Mem. firm Curnan, Fitzsimmons, Schilling and Tauke, Dubuque, 1976-79; mem. Iowa Gen. Assembly, 1975-79, 96th-100th Congresses from Iowa 2d Dist., 1979—; del. Republican Nat. Conv., 1976; chmn. 2d Congl. Dist. of Iowa Rep. Party, 1974-77; mem. Iowa Rep. Central Com., 1974-77; chmn. Dubuque County Rep. Party, 1972-74. Mem. pastoral council Roman Catholic Archdiocese of Dubuque, 1971-73; trustee Mt. Mercy Coll., Cedar Rapids, Iowa. Mem. Am. Bar Assn., Iowa Bar Assn., Dubuque County Bar Assn., Dubuque C. of C., Cedar Rapids Area C. of C. Clubs: Rotary, Junipera Serra. Home: 1715 Glen Oak Dubuque IA 52001 Office: 2244 Rayburn Washington DC 20515 *

TAUSCH, WILLIAM JOSEPH, advertising agency executive; b. Chgo., Sept. 22, 1930; s. Benjamin Joseph and Marian Bridget (Rowland) T.; m. Marianne Merritt, Sept. 1, 1953; children—Benjamin Joseph, William Joseph. B.Sc., DePaul U., 1959. Copywriter Marsteller, Inc., Chgo., 1966-68; copywriter Campbell-Ewald Co., Detroit, 1968-79, account supr., 1969-73, dir. retail service div., 1975-79; exec. v.p., account dir. Campbell-Ewald Co., Warren, Mich., 1979—; account supr. McCann-Erickson, Detroit, 1973-75. Served to sgt. U.S. Army, 1951-53. Republican. Clubs: Adcraft, The Recess (Detroit); Birmingham Country (Mich.). Home: 281 Nantucket Bloomfield Hills MI 48013 Office: Campbell-Ewald Co 30400 Van Dyke Warren MI 48093

TAYLOR, ANNA DIGGS, U.S. district judge; b. Washington, Dec. 9, 1932; d. Virginius Douglass and Hazel (Bramlette) Johnston; m. S. Martin Taylor, May 22, 1976; children: Douglass Johnston Diggs, Carla Cecile Diggs. B.A., Barnard Coll., 1954; LL.B., Yale U., 1957. Bar: Mich. 1961. Atty. Office Solicitor, Dept. Labor, W, 1957-60; asst. prosecutor Wayne County, Mich., 1961-62; asst. U.S. atty. Eastern Dist. of Mich., 1966; partner firm Zwerdling, Maurer, Diggs & Papp, Detroit, 1970-75; asst. corp. counsel City of Detroit, 1975-79; U.S. dist. judge Eastern Dist. Mich. Detroit, 1979—; adj. prof. labor law Wayne State U. Law Sch., Detroit, 1976. Trustee Receiving Hosp. Detroit, Episcopal Diocese Mich., Detroit Symphony, Sinai Hosp., United Found., Community Found. Southeastern Mich. Mem. Fed. Bar Assn., Nat. Lawyer's Guild, State Bar Mich., Wolverine Bar Assn., Women Lawyers Assn. Mich. Democrat. Episcopalian. Office: US District Court 231 W Lafayette Blvd Detroit MI 48226

TAYLOR, BARBARA KLINE, consultant; b. Phila., Aug. 10, 1945; d. Bernard and Mary Helen (Warren) K.; m. Robert Ellsworth Taylor, Dec. 21, 1985. BS, Temple U., 1969; MA, Mich. State U., 1977; EdD, Va. Tech. U., 1981. Adminstrv. intern Pima Community Coll., Tucson, 1979, Tex. Instruments, Dallas, 1979-80; coordinator, research specialist Nat. Ctr. for Research in Vol. Edn., Columbus, Ohio, 1981-83, asst. dir. nat. acad., 1983-84, dir. nat. acad., 1984-86; cons. Taylor and Taylor, Silver City, N.Mex., 1986—; tech. advisor U.S. Dept. Edn., Washington, 1985-86. Author: Vocational Education and Economic Development in the United States, 1985, (with Robert E. Taylor) Distance Delivery of Vocational Education, 1987. Mott Found. scholar, 1970; Edn. Professions Devel. Act fellow, 1978-81, Carl Duisberg Soc. exchange fellow, 1985. Mem. Am. Vocat. Edn. Personnel Devel. Assn. (sec., treas. 1985-86, pres.-elect 1986-87), Am. Soc. Tng. and Devel. (sec., 1985-86, v.p. for profl. devel. 1984-85), Am. Vocat. Assn., Am. Vocat. Edn. Research Assn., Phi Delta Kappa. Club: Bus. and Profl. Women (Silver City, N.Mex.). Avocations: cooking, flower arranging, antiques. Home and Office: HCR 88061 35 McMillen Rd Silver City NM 88061

TAYLOR, BILLY MAC, manufacturing company executive; b. Ferriday, La., May 4, 1951; s. Richard Elbert and Mary (Brown) T.; m. Gwen Eleanor Lyles, June 2, 1973; children: Billeta Gwenel, Carrice Maryet. BS, Grambling State U., 1973; MA, MBA, U. Toledo, 1984. Research physicist Libbey Owens Ford Co., Toledo, 1973-84, sr. prodn. planner, 1984—. Counselor Toledo Rescue Mission 1976—. NSF fellow. Mem. Am. Prodn. and Inventory Control Soc. Baptist. Avocations: jogging, weightlifting, photography. Office: Libbey Owens Ford Co 811 Madison Ave Toledo OH 43695

TAYLOR, BYRON DAVID, commercial real estate broker; b. Sangamon County, Ill., June 1, 1943; s. Byron Garfield and Ruth Isabel (Vallette) T.; m. Joan Elizabeth McPherson, Aug. 27, 1965. BS in Engring., So. Ill. U., 1965; MS in Bus. Adminstrn., U. So. Calif., 1971; MS in Engring., U. Kans., 1972. Engr. EPA, Kansas City, 1972-74, Apollo Equipment, Kansas City, 1974-78; real estate broker Cohen & Co., Kansas City, 1978-86, Taylor Co., Kansas City, 1986—; bd. dirs. Fgn. Trade Zone, Kansas City, 1985—. Editorial bd. Midwest Real Estate News, Chgo., 1985—. Chmn. com. Downtown Council of Kansas City; vets. affairs Missourians for Kit Bond, Kansas City; bd. dirs. Vietnam Meml. Found., Kansas City, 1984—. Served to lt. col. USAFR, 1965-86, Vietnam. Decorated DFC. Mem. Soc. Indsl. and Office Realtors, Internat. Council of Shopping Ctrs., Res. Officers Assn. Clubs: Kansas City, Kansas City Breakfast (pres. 1980), Nashville City. Avocations: cycling, running, skiing, water sports. Home and Office: 810 W 54th St Kansas City MO 64112

TAYLOR, CHARLES ANDREW, publisher; b. Cape Girardeau, Mo., Feb. 25, 1950; s. Ollie and Inez (Walker) T.; m. Gloria Ross, Mar. 8, 1970 (div. Dec. 1980); 1 child, Charles II. BS, Southwest Mo. State U., 1972; MS, U. Oreg., 1976; postgrad., U. Wis., 1986—. Counselor Fin. Aid Office, Madison, 1973-75; dir. Civic Ctr., Cape Girardeau, 1976-77, Multicultural Edn. Ctr., Oshkosh, Wis., 1977-80, Madison Pub. Schs., 1980-83; pub. Nat. Minority Campus Chronicle, Madison, 1982—; cons. Nat. Conf. Student Services, Madison, 1979—. Author: Effective Ways to Recruit and Retain Minority Students, 1985, Guide to Multicultural Resources, 1985. Recipient Leadership award Racine Pub. Schs., 1980, Leadership award Govs. Black Adv. Council, 1982. Mem. Wis. Assn. Black State Employees, Am. Assn. Excellence and Equality, Nat. Jaycees (Named Outstanding Man Am. 1979). Baptist. Avocations: writing, jogging. Office: Nat Minority Campus Chronicle PO Box 9869 Madison WI 53715

TAYLOR, CLARA, manufacturing executive; b. Piqua, Ohio, Dec. 23, 1934; s. Garret Arthur and Florence Belle (Niswonger) Kirby; m. Orville Taylor, Dec. 27, 1952; children: Arthur Paul, Larry J. AS in Acctg., Sinclair Community Coll., 1981. Various positions Chrysler Airtemp, Dayton, Ohio, 1952-63; supr. Duriron Co., Dayton, 1965-66; supr. Hobart Corp., Troy, Ohio, 1972-77, project mgr., 1977-86, mgr., 1986—. v.p. bd. dirs. Miami East Sch., Fletcher, Ohio, 1986—. Mem. Data Processing Mgmt. Assn. (mem. steering body bd.), ALTRUSA (v.p. 1985-86, pres. 1985—). Republican. Baptist. Lodges: Order of Eastern Star, Shriners. Avocation: spending time with grandchildren. Home: 6205 E US 36 Fletcher OH 45326

TAYLOR, DAL-MAR DEENI, pharmacist; b. Dublin, Ga., Oct. 19, 1956; s. George Washington Taylor and Susi (Bruggenschmidt) Perkins; m. Leslie Kay Myers, Nov. 21, 1976; children: Aaron Michael, Jennifer Lise. Student, Ind. U. SE, New Albany, 1974-76; BS in Pharmacy, Purdue U., 1980. Lectr., instr. biology Purdue U., West Lafayette, Ind., 1978-82; relief pharmacist Wabash Valley Hosp. Mental Health Ctr., West Lafayette, 1980-82, Hook Drugs, Indpls., 1980-82; staff pharmacist St. Joseph Hosp., Augusta, Ga., 1982-83, operating room pharmacy supr., 1983-85, dir. pharmacy, 1985—; relief pharmacist Jefferson County Hosp., Louisville, Ga., 1983-85; contract dir. pharmacy McDuffie County Hosp., Thomson, Ga., 1985—; cons. pharmacist Surgi-Ctr., Augusta, 1985-86; instr. Advanced Cardiac Life Support, Augusta, 1985—. Dist. youth coordinator Meth. Chs., Augusta, 1984-86; sec. bd. trustees Briarwood Acad., Thomson, 1986-87. Mem. Am. Soc. Hosp. Pharmacy, Ga. Pharm. Assn., Ga. Soc. Pharmacy (bd. dirs. 1986—), Soc. Ambulatory Care Profls., Purdue Alumni Assn. Democrat. Methodist. Avocations: fishing, running. Home: PO Box 15 Warrenton GA 30828 Office: St Joseph Hosp 2260 Wrightsboro Rd Augusta GA 30910

TAYLOR, DARRELL LYNN, nuclear engineer, consultant; b. Indpls., Mar. 13, 1959; s. Clarence A. and Helen C. (Mankivitz) T.; m. Teresa Dianne Hanlon, Aug. 3, 1985. BS in Nuclear Engring., Purdue U., 1981, MS in Nuclear Engring., 1982, MS in Indsl. Adminstrn., 1983. Nuclear engr. Commonwealth Edison Co, Chgo., 1983—; pres., cons. Manatec, Inc., Chgo., 1986—. Mem. Beta Gamma Sigma, Sigma Pi. Avocation: travel. Home: 532 W Belmont Apt #1-A Chicago IL 60657 Office: Commonwealth Edison 72 W Adams Suite 922 Chicago IL 60690

TAYLOR, DAVID RIDDLE, JR., advertising executive; b. Waycross, Ga., May 21, 1948; s. David Riddle and Martha Eleanor (McNary) T.; m. Carole Ann Fitzpatrick, July 11, 1970; children—Michelle, Caroline, David John. B.B.A., Kent State U., 1970; M.B.A., U. Dayton, 1977. Advt. asst. DAP, Inc., Dayton, Ohio, 1970-72, merchandising services coordinator, 1972-74, asst. product mgr., 1974-76; account exec. Parker Advt. Co., Dayton, 1976-80, v.p., 1980-82, v.p., dir., 1982-87, sr. v.p., dir., 1987—. Mem. Miami Valley Mil. Affairs Assn., Sales and Mktg. Execs. Assn. (treas., bd. dirs. 1986—), Sales and Mktg. Execs. Internat. Accreditation Inst. (founding and charter mem., cert. mktg. exec.), Dayton Advt. Club, Am. Assn. Advt. Agys. Republican. Methodist. Clubs: Patrons; Sycamore Creek Country (Springboro, Ohio); Quail Run Racquet (Kettering, Ohio); Pleasant Hill Swimming (Centerville, Ohio). Lodge: Optimists (bd. dirs. 1973-81, v.p. 1979-81). Avocations: golfing, swimming, skiing, tennis. Home: 6230 Millbank Dr Dayton OH 45459 Office: Parker Advt Co 3077 S Kettering Blvd Dayton OH 45439

TAYLOR, DONALD, manufacturing executive; b. Worcester, Mass., June 2, 1927; s. John A. B. and Alice M. (Weaver) T.; m. Ruth L. Partridge, June 24, 1950; children: Linda Taylor Robertson, Donald, Mark, John. B.S.M.E., Worcester Poly. Inst., 1949; grad., Northeastern U. Mgmt. Devel. Program, 1962, Harvard Bus. Sch. Advanced Mgmt. Program, 1979. Registered profl. engr., Mass. With George J. Meyer Mfg. Co., Milw., 1954-69; pres. mfg. div. A-T-O, Inc., 1969; exec. v.p. Nordberg div. Rex Chainbelt, Inc., Milw., 1969-73; v.p. ops. Rexnord Inc., Brookfield, Wis., pres., chief operating officer, 1978-85, chmn., chief exec. officer, 1985—; pres. Nordberg Machinery Group, Milw., 1973-78; dir. Harnischfeger Corp., Johnson Controls, Inc., Marine Corp., Marine Bank N.A., Wis. Bell. Bd. dirs. Blood Ctr. Southeastern Wis., Ethics Resource Ctr., Greater Milw. Com., Metro Milw. Assn. of Commerce, Met. Milw. YMCA; v.p., bd. dirs. Milw. Symphony Orch. Served with USNR, 1951-54. Mem. ASME. Clubs: Milw. Country, Milw. Athletic, Town, Univ., Masons. Office: Rexnord Inc 350 N Sunny Slope Rd Brookfield WI 53005

TAYLOR, DONALD ELDRIDGE, III, computer engineering executive; b. Canton, Ohio, Mar. 17, 1953; s. Donald Eldridge Jr. and Dolores Ethel (Sutcliffe) T.; m. Linda Dianne Carroll, Apr. 18, 1981; 1 child, Donald Eldridge IV. BEE, Rensselaer Poly. Inst., 1976. Electrical engring. staff Ball Corp., Muncie, Ind., 1976-78; design engr. Struthers-Dunn, Bettendorf, Iowa, 1978-83; sr. design engr. Allen-Bradley, Highland Heights, Ohio, 1983-85, project supr., 1985—. Mem. IEEE, IEEE Computer Soc. Avocations: sailing, charcoal drawing, electronics, computers. Office: Allen-Bradley 747 Alpha Dr Highland Heights OH 44143

TAYLOR, DONALD FRANCIS, manufacturing company executive; b. Milw., May 14, 1914; s. Francis Edwin and Anna L. (Gatien) T.; m. Eileen M. Weber; children: Sandra M. Taylor Annis, Richard L. Student Merrill Comml. Coll., U. Wis., Marquette U. Chmn. bd. dirs. Merrill Mfg. Corp. Mem. U.S. C. of C. (past bd. dirs.), Wis. C. of C. (past pres.), Wis. Assn. Mfrs. and Commerce (bd. dirs.). Republican. Roman Catholic. Club: Wausau (Wis.). Lodge: Rotary (past pres. Merrill chpt.). Home: N 2790 Taylor Dr Merrill WI 54452 Office: 236 S Genesee St Merrill WI 54452

TAYLOR, EDMUND EUGENE, metrologist; b. Eaton, Ind., May 30, 1924; s. Howard and Guila Beatrice (Barley) T. D.Sc. in Elec. Engring., Sussex Coll. Tech., Eng., 1983. Electronic insp. Farnsworth TV Corp., Marion, Ind., 1942-43; radio facsimile developer RCA, Indpls., 1943-44; elec. metrologist Mallory Components Group, Indpls., 1944—; owner, chief engr. Taylor Elec. Lab., Indpls., 1943—; curator, historian, archivist Ed Taylor Radio Mus., Indpls., 1973—. Author: Taylorvision, 1984. Contbr. articles to profl. jours. Patentee in field. Mem. Instrument Soc. Am., Internat. Soc. Profl. Inventors, Antique Wireless Assn., Tesla Coil Builders Assn., Ind. Hist. Radio Soc. (founder), Indpls. Radio Club, Mallory Mgmt. Club, Am. Guild Organists, Am. Theatre Organ Soc., Ind. Jaguar Club. Home: 245 N Oakland Ave Indianapolis IN 46201 Office: Mallory Components Group 3029 E Washington St Indianapolis IN 46206

TAYLOR, GARY LEE, marketing executive; b. Akron, Ohio, Mar. 28, 1953; s. Robert Eugene and Betty Jayne (Mayles) T.; m. Karen Sue Bates, Oct. 7, 1978; children: Lindsay Rose, Craig Scott. BBA in Mktg., U. Akron, 1975, MBA in Mktg., 1977. Media coordinator Rex Humbard Found., Akron, 1977-79, gen. mgr. advt., 1979-80, dir. mktg., 1980-82; pres. InfoCision Mgmt. Corp., Akron, 1982—. Editor newsletter Telephone Fundraising News, 1986. Speaker, lectr. Nat. Religious Broadcasters Conv., 1982-85. Republican. Methodist. Avocations: golf, fishing, racquetball. Office: InfoCision Mgmt Corp 1755 Merriman Rd Akron OH 44313

TAYLOR, GENE, congressman; b. Sarcoxie, Mo., Feb. 10, 1928; m. Dorothy Wooldridge, July 26, 1947; children: Linda, Larry. Ed., S.W. Mo. State Coll. Mayor Sarcoxie, 1954-60; mem. Rep. Nat. Com., 1966-72, 93d-100th Congresses from 7th Dist. Mo.; house com. on rules, ranking minority mem. com. on civil service and post office. Former trustee Mo. So. Coll., Joplin; trustee Harry S. Truman Scholarship Found.; past bd. dirs. Mo. Automobile Dealers Assn. Served with Mo. N.G., 1948-49. Mem. Mo., Sarcoxie chambers commerce. Methodist. Lodges: Masons; Shriners; Lions. Address: 2134 Rayburn House Office Bldg Washington DC 20515

TAYLOR, GREGORY LEE, manufacturing executive; b. Annapolis, Md., Apr. 21, 1951; s. Floyd McKinley and Rosalee (Randall) T.; m. Donna Lynn Brooks, Sept. 21, 1974; 1 child, Brooke. BA, Yale U., 1973; MM, Northwestern U., 1975. CPA, N.Y., Ill. Fin. analyst Zenith Radio, Melrose Park, Ill., 1975-76; supr. Zenith Radio, Glenview, Ill., 1976-77; supr., cons. Ernst & Whinney, Chgo., 1977-82; dir. internal audit Kearney Nat., N.Y.C., 1982-84; v.p. fin. Wabash Datatech, Huntley, Ill., 1984-86, v.p mfg., 1986—. Mem. Am. Inst. CPA's, Ill. CPA Soc. Club: Yale (Chgo.). Avocations: tennis, racquetball, squash, motorcycling. Home: 9016 Kilbourn Ave Skokie IL 60076

TAYLOR, HERBERT RICHARD, graphics company executive; b. Kansas City, Kans., Oct. 14, 1942; s. Harold Raymond and Mary Margaret (Hagen) T.; m. Janice Jo Phelan, June 21, 1964; children: Shawna Leigh, Tasha Renate. Grad., Turner High Sch. Apprentice typesetter, prodn. estimator, sales rep. Henry Wurst, Inc., North Kansas City, Mo., 1961-81; with sales Lehigh Press, Pennsauken, N.J., 1982-84; v.p. Nevada Web Graphics, Sparks, Nev., 1982—. Served as staff sgt. U.S. Army, 1967-69, Vietnam. Mem. Kansas City Direct Mktg. Club, Kansas City Prodn. Club. Republican. Lodge: Abdallah Shriners. Home and Office: Nevada Web Graphics 12317 W 74th Terr Shawnee KS 66216

TAYLOR, JACK PAUL, superintendant of schools; b. Wapakonata, Ohio, Jan. 27, 1931; s. George T. and Frieda (Moeller) T.; B.S., Bowling Green State U., 1953, M.S., 1954; Ph.D., Ohio State U., 1966; m. Berneda Florence Ruck, Dec. 27, 1953; children—Thomas Roberts, Carole Jane. Sr. social studies instr., guidance Perrysburg (Ohio) Schs., 1954-56; high sch. prin. Liberty Center Schs., 1956-59; supt. schs., Crestline, Ohio, 1959-62, Xenia, Ohio, 1964-67, Saginaw, Mich., 1967-76, Shaker Heights, Ohio, 1977-82, Omaha, 1982-84; exec. Cleve. Pub. Schs., 1984-85; supt. schs. City of Waukegan, Ill., 1985—; coordinator Sch. Mgmt. Inst., Columbus, Ohio; vis. prof. Central State U.; adj. prof. Cleve. State U.; cons. grad. faculty Ohio State U.; host Taylor on Edn. Show Cox Cable, Omaha. Co-author: Who Runs America's Schools. Pres., Future Tchrs. Ohio, 1952; mem. Library Bd., Crestline, 1959-62; mem. Human Relations Commn., Mayor's Com. Concern; chmn. Nat. Consortium on Ednl. Evaluation. Mem. exec. com. Young Republicans Ohio, 1950-54. Chmn. edn. div.; bd. dirs. United Way of Midlands; bd. dirs. United Fund, Jr. Achievement, YMCA; mem. exec. com. Cuyahoga Council for Handicapped Children; mem. Lt. Gov.'s Task Force on Edn.; pres. Saginaw Symphony Assn.; trustee United Appeal Crestline, Shaker Lake Regional Nature Center; bd. dirs. Ohio Adminstrs.; chmn.

YMCA Bldg. FUnd Membership Drive, Waukegan, 1987; mem. planning com. Boy Scouts Am., Omaha. Action Com. Recipient Worth McClure award Am. Assn. Sch. Adminstrs., 1964; E.E. Lewis award in edn. Ohio State U., Frontier's Internat. service award of year, 1973, also Meritorius Service award, 1986, Outstanding Educator award The Exec. Edn. Mag. Mem. Xenia Area C. of C. (dir.), Distributive Edn. Clubs Am. (past nat. v.p.), Mich. Middle Cities Edn. Assn. (pres.), Bowling Green State U. Alumni Assn. (trustee), Buckeye Assn. Sch. Adminstrs. (legis. com.), Ohio Soc. N.Y., Delta Tau Delta, Omicron Delta Kappa, Pi Sigma Alpha, Phi Delta Kappa. Mem. United Ch. Christ. Rotarian. Club: Edliners (pres.) (Ohio State U.). Home: 901 Sunset Terr Waukegan IL 60087 Office: 1201 N Sheridan Rd Waukegan IL 60085

TAYLOR, JACKSON H., songwriter, music publisher, record producer; b. Madison, Wis., Nov. 26; s. Thomas Hayhurst and Margaret Jackson (Tucker) T.; m. Louise Ann Talma, June 20, 1964. Student U. Wis.-Madison; grad. Automation Inst., Milw., 1964. Profl. singer and musician with The Stratosonics and other groups, 1961-64; automobile salesman, 1965-69; songwriter, 1970—, affiliated with Broadcast Music, Inc., 1973—; founder and owner Play Me Records, 1974—, Superjack Music, pub., 1976—. Recipient Hall of Fame award, 1969; Legion of Leaders award, 1969; winner numerous profl. songwriting competitions, 1974-83. Mem. U.S. Ski Assn., Nat. Thespian Soc. Composer more than 100 songs; author: The Professional Approach to Selling Your Songs, 1979; inventor Doggie-Sox, 1983, Advance Brake Warning System, 1986.

TAYLOR, JAMES EDWARD, insurance company executive; b. Cin., June 18, 1947; s. Victor E. and Charlotte M. (Sowers) T.; m. Martha A. Ennis, July 2, 1966 (div. 1980); children—James D., Cherie L.; m. Phyllis J. Stubbers, Aug. 8, 1981. B.S., U. Cin., 1979. Computer operator Union Central Life Ins. Co., Cin., 1965-66; mgr. data processing ops. Ohio Nat. Life Ins. Co., Cin., 1970—. Pres. Parents Anonymous of S.W. Ohio, Inc., 1986-87. Served with USAF, 1966-70. Mem. Assn. Systems Mgmt., Data Processing Mgmt. Assn. Avocations: reading; home computers. Home: 2430 Whitewood Ln Cincinnati OH 45239 Office: Ohio Nat Life Ins Co 237 William H Taft Rd Cincinnati OH 45219

TAYLOR, JOHN F., accountant; b. Cadillac, Mich., Aug. 29, 1948; s. John Ernest and Helen Marie (Ziegler) T.; m. Joyce Rennay Morrison, Sept. 7, 1974; children: John Matthew, Joshua Nathan, Erin Marie. BS, Ferris State Coll., 1970. CPA, Mich. Staff acct. Baird, Cotter & Bishop, P.C., Cadillac, 1970-74, sr. acct., 1974-76, ptnr., 1977—. Mem. Zoning Bd. of Appeals, Caddilac, 1985-87, Planning Bd., Cadillac, 1987—. Mem. Am. Inst. CPA's, Mich. Assn. CPA's, Cadillac Area C. of C. Presbyterian. Club: Exchange (Cadillac) (pres. 1986—). Avocations: winemaking, golf, hunting, fishing. Home: 412 Prospect Cadillac MI 49601 Office: Baird Cotter & Bishop PC 134 W Harris Cadillac MI 49601

TAYLOR, JOHN R., insurance company executive; b. Moscow, Idaho; m. Earlene Taylor; 5 children. B.S., U. Idaho, 1949; M.A., U. Mich., 1951. C.L.U.; chartered fin. cons. Mem. actuarial dept. Bankers Life Co., Des Moines, 1951-70; head corp. planning Bankers Life Co., 1970-72, sr. v.p., 1972-73, exec. v.p., 1973-82; pres. Bankers Life Co. (became Principal Fin. Group in 1986), 1982-86; chief exec. officer Principal Fin. Group, 1984—; chmn. BLC Investment Co., BLC Equity Mgmt. Co.; dir. Northwestern Bell Telephone Co. Bd. visitors Coll. Bus. Adminstrn., U. Iowa; pres. Des Moines Art Ctr., 1982-84, trustee; bd. dirs. Iowa Heritage Found. Fellow Soc. Actuaries; mem. Am. Acad. Actuaries, Life Office Mgmt. Assn. (bd. dirs.), Greater Des Moines C. of C. (pres. 1982), Actuaries Club, Phi Beta Kappa, Beta Gamma Sigma (hon.). Office: Principal Fin Group 711 High St Des Moines IA 50307 *

TAYLOR, JOHN WILLIAM, III, bank executive; b. Evanston, Ill., Mar. 17, 1940; s. John William and Francis Lillian (Buck) T.; m. Kaari Tobina Torstenson, Apr. 30, 1966; children—Buck Mathison, Katharine Kaari. B.A., DePauw U., 1962. Trainee to sr. v.p. No. Trust Co., Chgo., 1963-83; chmn., bd. dirs. State Nat. Bank, Evanston, Ill., 1983—, Bank & Trust Arlington Heights, Ill., 1983—; pres., bd. dirs. Thunder Mountain Ranch Co., 1980. Bd. dirs. Evanston Hosp. Corp., 1984, Evanston YMCA, 1983, Ravinia Festival, 1982, Evanston Youth Job Ctr., 1983, Am. Friends Covent Garden and Royal Ballet, N.Y.C., 1979, Northlight Theater, 1985, Chaplin Hall for Children, 1985. Clubs: Indian Hill (Winnetka, Ill.); Attic, University (bd. dirs.) (Chgo.); Fly Fishers (London). Avocations: fly fishing, golf, skiing.

TAYLOR, JOYCE GERALDINE, educator; b. Gibsland, La., June 16, 1929; d. Lonnie Howard and Beattie (Williams) Lewis; B.S., Mercy Coll., Detroit, 1968; M.Ed., Wayne State U., 1972, Ed.S., 1976; children by previous marriage—Bruce A., Joyce Annette, Gloria, Billy. Tchr. elem. schs., Detroit Public Schs., 1968—. Mem. Detroit Fedn. Tchrs. (bldg. rep. 1981—), Nat. Assn. Supervision and Curriculum Devel., Mich. Assn. Supervision and Curriculum, Am. Fedn. Tchrs. Home: 9655 Whitcomb St Detroit MI 48227 Office: 20601 W Davison St Detroit MI 48223

TAYLOR, L(ARRY) JOE, accountant; b. Springfield, Ill., Aug. 3, 1951; s. Paul Joseph Taylor and Virginia (Reynolds) Horn; m. Alora T. Anderson, Sept. 20, 1971; 1 child, Shannon Christal. AS, Lincoln Land Community Coll., 1974; BA, Sangamon State U., 1976. CPA, Ill. Audit mgr. Patterson Cameron & Londrigan CPA's, Springfield, 1976-86; pvt. practice acctg. Springfield, 1987—; audit mgr. Dept. Rehab. Services, State of Ill., Springfield, 1987—. Team leader, sr. mem. Springfield Underwater Search and Recovery Team, 1974—. Served as sgt. U.S. Army, 1969-71, Vietnam. Mem. Am. Inst. CPA's, Ill. Soc. CPA's, Springfield Jaycees, Mensa. Avocations: reading, scuba diving, computers. Home: 2661 S 9th Springfield IL 62703 Office: State of Illinois Dept Rehab Services Springfield IL 62701

TAYLOR, MARK ROBERT, hospital administrator; b. Pontiac, Mich., Jan. 10, 1952; s. Robert Vincent and Zetta Elanore (Jarrard) T.; m. Marianne Coronado, July 7, 1950; children—Benjamin, Christopher, Bethany. B.A., Hillsdale Coll., 1974; M.Health Service Adminstrn., U. Mich., 1983. Asst. dir. personnel Saginaw (Mich.) Osteo. Hosp., 1975-77; dir. personnel Chelsea (Mich.) Community Hosp., 1977-83; v.p. St. Lukes Hosp., Saginaw, 1983—; exec. v.p.; bd. dirs. St. Luke's Devel. Corp. bd. dirs. Saginaw-Mercy Ambulance Inc. Bd. dirs. Chelsea United Way, 1981-82. Recipient Share Our Savs. award Mich. Hosp. Assn., 1980; Pres.'s award Hosp. Personnel Adminstrs. Assn. S.E. Mich., 1981-82. Mem. Am. Coll. Hosp. Adminstrs., Am. Soc. Hosp. Personnel Adminstrs., Am. Hosp. Assn. Republican. Roman Catholic. Home: 714 Westchester Saginaw MI 48603 Office: St Lukes Hosp 700 Cooper St Saginaw MI 48602

TAYLOR, MARY CHRISTINE, tax coordinator, consultant; b. Buffalo, N.Y., May 1, 1950; s. Foster and Bettie (Wall) Lee; m. Winford Wilson, Apr. 29, 1977; children: Zachary Marwin, Allison Camille. BA in English, Wayne State U., 1976, MA in Speech Communications, Radio and TV Journalism, 1986. Cert. tax preparer. Collector Sears Roebuck & Co., Detroit, 1969-72; gen. acct. Excello, Detroit, 1972-74; tax coordinator Gen. Motors Corp., Detroit, 1974—; founder, owner Sunshine Products & Services, Detroit, 1985—. Advisor Explorer Post, Detroit, 1978; mem. PTO, Precious Blood Sch., pres. 1985—; fellow mem. Stansbury Forence/Grove Block Club, 1981-83. Club: Toastmasters. Avocations: reading, writing children's books, teaching. Office: Sunshine Products & Services PO Box 47175 Oak Park MI 48237

TAYLOR, MARY LOU, health science educator; b. Springfield, Mo., Sept. 19, 1931; s. Floyd Monroe and Mary Etta (James) Robards; m. Allen Gwyn Taylor, Dec. 24, 1955. B.S., Drury Coll., 1954; M.A., U. Mo-Kansas City, 1965; Ph.D., Kansas State U., 1983. Registered nurse Staff nurse Springfield Baptist Hosp., Mo., 1954-55; instr., part-time supr. nursing service Trinity Luth. Hosp. Sch. Nursing, Kansas City, Mo., 1955-60, asst. dir., 1960-64, dir. 1964-70; coordinator nursing program. Johnson County Community Coll., Overland Park, Kans., 1970-74, 75-84, dir. Nat. and Health Related Sci., 1984-86, Dean of Instrn., 1986—; program officer Pub. Health Service HEW, Kansas City, 1974-75; adv. com. nursing degree programs, Kansas, Mo., 1975—; cons., vis. com. Kans. State Bd. Nursing, Topeka, Kans., 1975—; regional vis. bd. rev. Nat. League Nursing Council Diploma Program, N.Y.C., 1964-70; mem. Council of Assoc. Degree Programs, N.Y.C., 1982-84. Contbr. articles to profl. jours. Mem. nominating credentials com. Mid-Am. Health Systems Agy., Kansas City, 1979; bd. dirs. Faith Handicap Village, Overland Park, Kans. 1981-86 , Shawnee Mission Med. Ctr., Health Net PPO, 1986—; mem. adv. panel health care Padgett-Thompson, Inc., Overland Park, 1982; mem. Press Room Presdl. Debate LWV, Kansas City, 1984. Recipient Recognition of Leadership and Service award Trinity Luth. Hosp. Med. staff, 1970; named Kans. Nurse of Month, Kans. State Nurses Assn., 1981. Mem. Am. Nurses Assn. (numerous offices 1954—), Kans. State Nurses' Assn. (numerous offices 1954—), Nat. League Nursing (nominations com. 1982-84), AAUW, Phi Delta Kappa (offices 1981—), Beta Beta Beta, Sigma Theta Tau, Phi Kappa Phi, Kappa Delta Alumni Assn. Avocations: golf, antiques. Home: 7917 Halsey St Lenexa KS 66215 Office: Johnson County Community Coll 12345 Coll at Quivira Overland Park KS 66210

TAYLOR, MICHAEL ALAN, psychiatrist; b. N.Y.C., Mar. 6, 1940; s. Edward D. and Clara D. T.; m. Ellen Schoenfield, June 28, 1963; children—Christopher, Andrew. B.A., Cornell U., 1961; M.D., N.Y. Med. Coll., 1965. Intern Lenox Hill Hosp., N.Y.C., 1965-66; resident N.Y. Med. Coll., 1966-69, asst. prof. psychiatry, 1971-73; asso. prof. SUNY Med. Sch., Stony Brook, 1973-76; prof. psychiatry, chmn. dept. Univ. Health Scis., Chgo. Med. Sch., 1976—. Author: The Neuropsychiatric Mental Status Examination, 1981; sr. author: General Hospital Psychiatry, 1985; also numerous articles. Served to lt. comdr. M.C. USNR, 1969-71. Grantee NIMH, 1971-73; Grantee Ill. Dept. Mental Health, 1976-81; VA grantee, 1985—. Fellow Am. Psychiat. Assn.; mem. Behavior Genetics Assn., Am. Psychopath. Assn., Soc. Biol. Psychiatry, AAAS, Internat. Neuropsychology Soc., Psychiat. Research Soc., Assn. Acad. Psychiatry, Behavioral Neurology Assn., Ill. Psychiat. Assn. Address: UHS Chgo Med Sch 3333 Greenbay Rd North Chicago IL 60064

TAYLOR, MORRIS, JR., insurance company executive; b. Richmond, Va., Aug. 28, 1956; s. Morris Sr. and Lillie Mae (Lipscomb) T. BA, U. Va., 1978. Program coordinator Baha'i Nat. Ctr. U.S., Wilmette, Ill., 1980-85; owner, pres. Talisman Enterprises, Evanston, Ill., 1985—; mgr. telemktg. Allstate Ins. Corp., Northbrook, Ill., 1986—. Author, illustrator: The Top of the Hill, 1987; contbr. poetry to Brilliant Star, 1983, Spiritual Mothering Jour., 1985; contbr. articles to mag. Chmn. Baha'is of Evanston, 1981-86; mem. aux. bd. Baha'is of U.S., 1986—. Mem. Soc. Am. Magicians, Japanese Cultural Ctr. Chgo. (bd. dirs. 1983-84). Avocations: magic, martial arts, composing music, graphic illustrating. Home: 718 Mulford Evanston IL 60202 Office: Allstate Ins Cos Allstate Plaza S Suite G4-B Northbrook IL 60062

TAYLOR, PATRICIA ANN, occupational therapist; b. Allegan, Mich., Sept. 15, 1922; d. John William and Grace Adele (Burnett) Exton; B.S., Milw./Downer Coll., 1944; diploma in Occupational Therapy, Lawrence U., 1945; M.S., U. Mich., 1976; m. Ernest Taylor, Mar. 19, 1954; children—Sally, Carolyn, Steven, David, John. Asst. prof. phys. medicine U. Wis., 1946-49; dir. activity therapy Menninger Found., Topeka, 1949-53; supr. occupational therapy VA, Fayetteville, N.C., 1956-66; coordinator activity therapy Mich. Dept. Mental Health, Northville, 1966-75; clin. instr. Eastern Mich. U. and Wayne State U., 1967-75; curriculum cons. Ohio State U., 1969-70, Wayne State U., 1976-77; rehab. cons. Kans. Dept. Mental Health, Topeka, 1950-54. Civilian occupational therapist U.S. Army Hosps., 1945-46, recreation cons., Korea, 1953; dir. service club Pope AFB, N.C., 1954-55; mem. Southeastern Mich. adv. council White House Conf. on Aging, 1981. Recipient Civilian Merit award Hdqrs. Korean Communications Zone, 1953, Mich. Civil Service award, 1968. Mem. Nat. Assn. Retarded Citizens, Mich. Soc. Gerontology, Am. Occupational Therapy Assn. (bd. mgmt. 1950-53), Older Women's League. Episcopalian. Contbg. editor Am. Jour. Occupational Therapy, 1950-53. Address: 2477 Sandalwood Circle Ann Arbor MI 48105

TAYLOR, PAUL EDWARD, veterinarian; b. Adrian, Mich., Mar. 5, 1949; s. Neil Ford and Naomi Arlene (Dings) T.; m. Carol Jean Leonard, June 12, 1971; children: Robert Lee, Sally Marie, Todd Joel. BS, Mich. State U., 1971, DVM, 1972. Gen. practice vet. medicine Lambertville, Mich., 1972—. Mem. AVMA, Mich. Vet. Med. Assn., Toledo Vet. Med. Assn. Republican. Methodist. Avocation: gardening. Home: 6906 Whiteford Ctr Rd Lambertville MI 48144 Office: 3277 W Sterns Rd Lambertville MI 48144

TAYLOR, RANDALL WILLIAM, quality assurance administrator; b. Paulding, Ohio, Mar. 10, 1948; s. Virgil Myron and Deloris Elizabeth (Myers) T.; m. Patricia Helen Rager, Apr. 29, 1972. AAS in Supervision, Purdue U., Ft. Wayne, 1979, student, 1986—. Broadcaster Radio Sta. WTVB-WANG, Coldwater, Mich., 1969; quality control inspector tire div. B.F. Goodrich, Woodburn, Ind., 1969-74; quality assurance supr. Uniroyal Goodrich Tire Co., Woodburn, Ind., 1974—. V.p. Big Bros./Big Sisters, Ft. Wayne, 1982-86. Mem. Ind. State Trapshooting Assn. (bd. dirs. 1984—). Republican. Methodist. Lodge: Masons. Avocations: trapshooting, golf, fishing, travel. Home: 7714 Clover Meadow Dr Fort Wayne IN 46815

TAYLOR, RAY, state senator; b. Steamboat Rock, Iowa, June 4, 1923; s. Leonard Allen and Mary Delilah (Huffman) T.; student U. No. Iowa, 1940-41, Baylor U., 1948-49; m. Mary Allen, Aug. 29, 1924; children—Gordon, Laura Rae Taylor Hansmann, Karol Ann Taylor Flora, Jean Lorraine Taylor Mahl. Farmer, Steamboat Rock, Iowa, 1943—; mem. Iowa Senate, 1973—; bd. dirs., sec. Am. Legis. Exchange Council, 1979—. Sec., Hardin County Farm Bur., 1970-72; mem. Iowa div. bds. Am. Cancer Soc.; chmn. Am. Revolution Bicentennial Com. Mem. Steamboat Rock Community Sch. Bd., 1955-70; coordinator Republican youth, 1968-72. Bd. dirs. Faith Bapt. Bible Coll.; pres. Am. Council Christian Chs.; chmn. Iowans for Responsible Govt. Mem. Wildlife Club. Baptist. Office: Box 148 Steamboat Rock IA 50672

TAYLOR, RICHARD AYLETTE, neurologist; b. Portland, Ind., June 25, 1925; s. Basil Mitchel Taylor and Cora (Bartlett) Cort; m. Melana Marta Korybutiak, Dec. 19, 1959; children: Richard Andrew, Gregory Phillip. BS, Ind. U., Bloomington, 1950; MD, Ind. U., Indpls., 1953. Diplomate Am. Bd. Psychiatry and Neurology. Intern King County Hosp., Seattle, 1953-54; resident in neurology Ind. U., Indpls., 1956-59; practice medicine specializing in neurology Detroit, 1959—; chief of neurology Mt. Carmel Hosp., Detroit, 1961-81; vice chief of neurology Harper Grace Hosp., Detroit, 1961-81; chief of neurology St. John Hosp., Detroit, 1973—. Contbr. articles to profl. jours. Served as pfc. U.S. Army, 1943-45, ETO. Fellow Am. Acad. Neurology; mem. AMA, AAAS, Mich. Neurol. Soc. (counselor 1973-81, pres. 1976-78), N.Y. Acad. Sci. Roman Catholic. Office: St John Hospital 22151 Moross #223 Detroit MI 48236

TAYLOR, RICHARD LEE, lawyer; b. Des Moines, Mar. 23, 1954; s. Glen Charles and Erma Arlene Taylor. B.S., Iowa State U., 1976; J.D., Drake U., 1979. Bar: Iowa 1979, Ill. 1980, U.S. Dist. Ct. (so. dist.) Iowa 1979. Staff atty. Am. Farm Bur. Fedn., Park Ridge, Ill., 1979-82; corp. atty. United Fed. Savs. Bank, Des Moines, 1982—. Mem. ABA, Iowa State Bar Assn., Polk County Bar Assn., Des Moines Civic Ctr. Republican. Presbyterian. Office: United Fed Savs Bank 400 Locust Des Moines IA 50308

TAYLOR, RICHARD LEE, retail executive; b. Indpls., June 25, 1948; s. Arthur Richard and Mary Loretta (Pfau) T.; m. Diane Joan Kerson, Dept. 12, 1978; children: Samuel A., Matthew K., Daniel R. BS, Ball State U., 1970; MBA, U. Denver, 1979. Regional mgr. The Edward J. DeBarrolo Corp., Youngstown, Ohio, 1972-80; v.p. First Union Mgmt. Co., Cleve., 1980-83; sr. v.p. May Ctrs. Inc., St. Louis, 1983—. Served with USAR, 1970-76. Named Citizen of Yr., Aurora, Colo., 1977. Mem. Internat. Council Shopping Ctrs. (state dir. 1981-83). Roman Catholic. Avocation: outdoor activities. Home: 508 Shadowridge Dr Ballwin MO 63011 Office: May Ctrs Inc 611 Olive St Suite 1555 Saint Louis MO 63101

TAYLOR, RICK JOSEPH, tax executive; b. Escanaba, Mich., Feb. 24, 1956; s. Harold J. and Helen T. BS in Acctg., U. Wis., Green Bay, 1979; M in Taxation, U. Wis., Milw., 1985. CPA, Wis. Fin. acct. Shopko Stores, Green Bay, 1979-81; audit sr. Grant Thornton, Appleton, Wis., 1981-83; teaching asst. U. Wis., Milw., 1983-85; tax sr. Peat Marwick Main & Co., Milw., 1985-86, tax mgr., 1986—. Author: (with others) CPA's Guide to Financial and Estate Planning After the Tax Reform Act of 1986, 1985 (Wis. Uniform Marital Property Act award), Trust and Estate Provisions, 1987; (newspaper column) Smart Money, 1986—; editor: (with others) Multistate Tax Almanac, 1986; mem. editorial bd. Jour. of State Taxation, 1983—. Fund raiser Boys and Girls Club, Milw., 1987—. Recipient Meldman Case Weine award Meldman Case Weine, 1985; taxation scholar U. Wis. Milw., 1983-84. Mem. Am. Inst. CPA's (Elijah Watts Sells award 1982), Wis. Inst. CPA's (mem. fin. planning com.),U. Wis.-Milw. Tax Assn. Roman Catholic. Home: 384 N Mill #211 Saukville WI 53080 Office: Peat Marwick Main & Co 777 E Wisconsin Ave Milwaukee WI 53202

TAYLOR, ROBERT ALLEN, dentist; b. Toledo, May 1, 1947; s. Charles Randolph and Elizabeth Maxine (Hannah) T. BA, Miami U., Oxford, Ohio, 1969; DDS, Ohio State U., 1973. Treas. Amnesty Internat., Toledo, 1978—. Mem. ADA, Ohio Dental Assn., Toledo Dental Soc., Soc. for Occlusal Studies, Mensa, Tau Kappa Epsilon Alumni. Democrat. Presbyterian. Avocations: helping polit. prisoners, historic preservation. Home: 5710 Olde Post Rd Sylvania OH 43560 Office: 3900 Sunforest Ct Suite 224 Toledo OH 43623

TAYLOR, ROBERT JAMES, bank executive, accountant; b. Clayton, Mo., Mar. 16, 1943; s. James and Vernita (Dollar) T.; married Nov. 14, 1975; children: Robert, Christopher, Bradley. BS, Washington U., St. Louis, Mo., 1966; M in Commerce, St. Louis U., 1969. CPA, Mo. Audit supr. Coopers & Lybrand, St. Louis, 1967-76; asst. controller Nat. Liberty Corp., Valley Forge, Pa., 1977-78; asst. v.p. Fed. Res. Bank of St. Louis, 1978—. Loan exec. United Way of Greater St. Louis, 1980; bd. dirs. Coll. Sch. of Webster Groves, Mo., 1982-85, treas. 1982-1985. Served with USCG, 1967-72. Mem. Am. Inst. CPA's. Republican. Roman Catholic. Home: 15660 Sugar Ridge Ct Chesterfield MO 63017

TAYLOR, ROBERT LEE, information sciences company executive, educator; b. Adrian, Mich., Jan. 9, 1944; s. Jack Raleigh and Virginia Dixon (Oakes) T.; m. Janice Grace George, Dec. 9, 1961; children—Robin, Lynne, David. A.A., Siena Heights Coll., 1974, B.A., 1976. With computer operation Gen. Parts div. Ford Motor Co., Rawsonville, Mich., 1965-66, prodn. monitoring supr. Saline Plant, Mich., 1966-75, methods and systems analyst, Ypsilanti Plant, Mich., 1975-77, data processing supr. Milan Plant, Mich., 1977-82, sr. systems analyst Plastics, Paint and Vinyl div., Wixom, Mich., 1982-85; systems engr. Electronic Data Systems, Warren, Mich., 1985-86, systems engring. mgr. Romulus (Mich.) Parts Distbn. Ctr. Plant, 1986—; instr. data processing Siena Heights Coll., Adrian, 1985-86. Commr. Tecumseh Planning Commn., Mich., 1976-80, vice-chmn., 1981-82; trustee Tecumseh Bd. Edn., 1981-82, sec., 1983-84, chmn. citizens adv. com., 1983, chmn. computer adv. com., 1984, chmn. policy com., 1983-84; chmn. Tecumseh Area Laymen's Assn., 1983; mem. exec. com. Lenawee County Republican party, 1982-85, precinct del., 1982—, chmn. computer com., 1984—; state del. State of Mich., 1983-85, 87—; founding advisor Evang. Free Ch. at Adrian-Tecumseh, 1984-85, elder, 1986—, Sunday Sch. supt., 1984-87, chmn. Christian edn., 1986—; asst. Sunday Sch. supt. Berean Baptist Ch., Adrian, 1980-83; tchr. mentally impaired, 1977-83; deacon, Sunday Sch. supt., Grace Bible Ch., Tecumseh, 1973-76; chmn. bd. deacons First Bapt. Ch., Tecumseh, 1970-71, youth advisor, 1968-71, Layman of Yr., 1970; vice chmn. Tecumseh Area Crusade for Christ, 1973, facilities chmn. Lenawee County Crusade for Christ, 1986; chmn. Life Action Crusade, 1987. Served with USAF, 1961-65. Mem. Computer and Automated Systems Assn. (sr., Manufacturing Automation Protocol), Soc. Mfg. Engrs. Republican. Avocations: golf; genealogy. Home: 603 Outer Dr Tecumseh MI 49286 Office: Electronic Data Systems 36501 Van Born Rd Romulus MI 48174

TAYLOR, SCOTT MAXFIELD, department store executive; b. Evanston, Ill., Aug. 13, 1953; s. Brett Maxfield and Gretchen Pauline (Porter) T., Jr. BA, Coe Coll., 1975; M in Mgmt., Northwestern U., 1977; MSC, New Sem., 1985. Sales mgr. Daytons, Mpls., 1977-78, asst. buyer, 1978-79; store mgr. Brett's Dept. Store, Mankato, Minn., 1979-80, buyer jr. dept., 1981-83, v.p., 1981—, div. mdse. mgr., 1984-85, gen. mdse. mgr., 1985—, also bd. dirs. Bd. dirs. Blue Earth County Hist. Soc., Mankato, 1984-87, Mankato Area Conv. and Visitors Bur., 1985—; Presbyn. deacon, 1986—, moderator 1987—. George F. Baker scholar, 1975. Mem. Omicron Delta Epsilon. Lodge: Kiwanis (bd. dirs. 1984—). Avocation: curling. Home: Box 3642 Mankato MN 56002 Office: Bretts Dept Stores Box 609 Mankato MN 56002

TAYLOR, SHARON LEE SHEETS, newspaper editor; b. Toledo, June 6, 1936; d. Jake Charles and Helen Elizabeth (Winegardner) S.; m. Ross William Taylor, Oct. 14, 1956; children: Brent Charles, Jania Ann. Student in Journalism, Northwestern U., 1954-56. Gen. reporter Archbold (Ohio) Buckeye, 1956-78, news editor and bus. mgr., 1978-86, exec. editor, bus. mgr., 1986—. Mem. Ohio Newspaper Assn. (conv. vice chmn. 1987), Buckeye Press Assn. (sec. 1981-82, treas. 1982-84, v.p. 1984-85, pres. 1985-86), Ohio Press Women, Ohio Newspaper Women. Republican. Mem. United Ch. Christ. Club: Bus. and Profl. Women (Archbold). Avocations: gardening, travel, reading. Home: 207 Church St PO Box 33 Archbold OH 43502 Office: Archbold Buckeye Inc 207 N Defiance St Archbold OH 43502

TAYLOR, STEPHEN LLOYD, food toxicology educator; b. Portland, Oreg., July 19, 1946; s. Lloyd Emerson and Frances Hattie (Hanson) T.; m. Susan Annette Kerns, June 23, 1973; children: Amanda, Andrew. BS in Food Sci. Tech., Oreg. State U., 1968, MS in Food Sci. Tech., 1969; PhD in Biochemistry, U. Calif., Davis, 1973. Research assoc. U. Calif., Davis, 1973-74, research fellow, 1974-75; chief food toxicology Letterman Army Inst., San Francisco, 1975-78; asst. prof. food toxicology U. Wis., Madison, 1978-83, assoc. prof., 1983—; cons. in field, 1978—. Contbr. articles to profl. jours. Fellow Nat. Inst. Environ. Health Sci., Inst. Food Technologists (div. chmn. 1981-82, sect. chmn. 1984—); mem. Am. Acad. Allergy, Am. Chem. Soc. Democrat. Presbyterian. Home: 9 Wintersct Circle Madison WI 53717 Office: U Nebr Dept Food Sci Technology Lincoln NE 68583-0919

TAYLOR, TERRY SKLAIR, librarian, infosystems specialist; b. Chgo., Sept. 20, 1951; d. Victor and Marilyn Gloria (Susman) Sklair; m. Mark Barry Taylor, May 19, 1985. BA in French, U. Ill., 1973, MLS, 1975; MA in French, U. Ill., Chgo., 1981. Cert. French and English tchr., Ill. Editorial asst. Commerce Clearing House, Chgo., 1975-78; teaching asst. U. Ill., Chgo., 1978-79; librarian online services McDermott, Will & Emery, Chgo., 1980—; database news columnist, U.S. Law Library Alert, Chgo., 1981-82; participant video law seminar, ABA, Chgo., 1983. Mem. Spl. Libraries Assn., Chgo. Assn. Law Libraries (membership com. 1981-82, union list com. 1983-84), Am. Soc. Info. Sci. (editorial asst. reporter newsletter 1981-82, sec.-treas. 1983-85), Pi Delta Phi, Kappa Delta Pi. Jewish. Avocations: music, photography. Office: McDermott Will & Emery 111 W Monroe St Chicago IL 60603

TAYLOR, WILLIAM MENKE, manufacturing company executive; b. Logansport, Ind., May 24, 1918; s. William Thomas and Ethel Mae (Menke) T.; m. Betty Lorraine Flory, May 8, 1945; children: William M. Jr., Alan Richard. BBA, LaSalle Coll., Chgo., 1940. Cost acct. Essex Wire Corp., Logansport, 1935-50, salesman, 1950-55; plant mgr. Essex Wire Corp., Phila., 1955-56; sales mgr. Dill Products co., Norristown, Pa., 1960-73; pres. Tay-Mor Industries, Inc., Logansport, 1973—; pres. BABB Assoc., Logansport, 1972—; v.p. I.B.D. Corp., Logansport, 1972—; pres. Taylor Industries, Inc., Logansport, 1975—. Served with USAF, 1942-46, ETO. Named Ky. Col., Hon. Order Ky. Cols., 1965. Mem. Soc. Automobile Engrs., Ind. State Police Alliance, Ind. Sheriffs Assn. Republican. Lodges: Masons, Elks. Avocations: antique and special interest cars. Home: 2825 Perrysburg Rd Logansport IN 46947

TAYLOR, WILLIAM MENKE, JR., manufacturing company executive; b. Logansport, Ind., Feb. 8, 1946; s. William M. and Betty L. (Flory) T.; m. Barbara L. Caikoski, Oct. 18, 1969; children: Todd R., W. Zachary. BBA, Temple U., 1968. Pres. Logansport Screw Products, 1972-76; v.p. Tay-Mor Industries Inc., Logansport, 1972—; pres. Taylor Industries, Logansport, 1978—; bd. dirs. F&M State Bank, Logansport, 1985—. Committeeman precinct Logansport Reps., 1983-86; bd. dirs. Cass County Family YMCA, 1984—. Served with U.S. Army, 1968-71. Mem. Soc. Automotive Engrs., Nat. Council Corvette Clubs. Clubs: Crosley of Am. Lodges: Kiwanis, Elks. Avocations: classic automobiles, skiing, boating, travel. Home: PO

Box 1 Logansport IN 46947 Office: Tay-Mor Industries Inc 800 Burlington Ave Logansport IN 46947

TAYLOR-GORMAN, DORIS JEAN, historic renovation company owner, freelance writer; b. Waynesburg, Ky., Oct. 25, 1939; d. Clinton and Agnes Hazel (Acton) Epperson; m. Edward J. Gorman, Sept. 6, 1986; children (from previous marriages): Anna, DeWayne, Jeff, Jana. BS in Vocat. Home Econs., Ind. U., 1974. Tchr. Monroe County Sch. System, Bloomington, Ind., 1974-85; owner Helpmates Constrn. Systems, Indpls. and Bloomington, 1974—; hist. renovator Eichholtz Constrn., Indpls., 1985-86, Haydens Contractors Services, 1986—, Renovation Union Station, Indpls.; counselor Singles Helpmates Teaching Systems, Bloomington and Indpls., 1975—, R; cons. hist. renovation, preservation and reproductions Helpmates, Indpls., 1983—. Author: Single's Survival Guide, 1985, Setting Up a Home, 1986, Organizing Self, 1983-86. Avocations: photography, music. Office: Helpmates Systems PO Box 55029 Indianapolis IN 46205-0001

TAYLOR-PATWARDHAN, LAURY BETH, marketing executive; b. Elgin, Ill.; d. Arthur William and Caryl Ruth (Knowles) Taylor; m. P.R. Patwardhan, Sept. 30, 1979. BA in German and Bus. Adminstrn., Ill. State U., 1976; MIM, Am. Grad. Sch. Internat. Mgmt., 1979. Office mgr. Ill. State U., 1978; sales specialist Nordson Corp., Amherst, Ohio, 1979-80; mgr. mktg. services Nordson Corp., Amherst, 1980-85, mktg. mgr., 1986—; session chairperson Liquid Coatings Conf., 1980, Finishing '81 Conf., 1981. Co-pres. Am. Field Service, Ridgeville, Ohio. Mem. Assn. Finishing Processes (vice chairperson liquid coatings div. 1982-83), Inst. for Interconnecting and Packaging Electronic Components, Structure Steel Painting Council, Thunderbird Alumni Assn., Jr. Achievement (exec. advisor 1979-85), Delta Phi Alpha, Delta Phi Epsilon. Mem. United Ch. Christ. Office: PO Box 151 Amherst OH 44001

TAZELAAR, EDWIN JOSEPH, II, insurance company executive; b. Chgo., June 16, 1947; s. Edwin Joseph and Nancy Annette (DeStevens) T.; m. Mary Anne Marnul, July 3, 1982; children: Bradley James, Marcus Thomas, Edwin Joseph III, Danielle Marie; stepchildren: Brian Thomas, Bradley Louis Siok. Grad. N.W. Police Acad., 1971; student Harper Coll., 1974-76. Police officer Village of Hoffman Estates (Ill.), 1971-77; assoc. Am. Family Life Assurance Co. of Columbus, Ga., 1977; dist. mgr., 1978, regional mgr., Palatine, Ill., 1979-83; state mgr. Capitol Am. Life Ins., Hoffmann Estates, 1983-86 ; ptnr., v.p. mktg. Am. Triad Corp., Streamwood, Ill., 1986—; store mgr. Robert Hall Clothes, Chgo., 1968-71. Served with U.S. Army, 1966-68. Recipient Patrol Achievement award Village of Hoffman Estates, 1973, cert. of Achievement Lake County Dept. Ct. Services, 1985, Fireball award Am. Family Life Assurance Co., 1977, Family Life Assurance Co. awards, 1977-78; named to President's Club, 1978. Mem. Am. Mgrs. Assn., Internat. Platform Assn. Roman Catholic. Home: 21 Kristin Dr Apt #1 Schaumburg IL 60195 Office: Am Triad Corp 1527 Bourbon Pkwy Streamwood IL 60107

TEARE, WALLACE GLEED, architect; b. Cleve., June 5, 1907; s. George Wallace and Florence Elizabeth (Gleed) T.; m. Dorothy Gabriel Schaefer, June 24, 1933; children: Richard W., Virginia Gabriel (Mrs. Albert M. Katz). B.Arch., Western Res. U., 1929, M.A., 1933; diploma, Fontainebleau (France) Sch. Fine Arts, 1930. Partner Conrad & Teare, architects, Cleve., 1931-38; Ptnr. Joseph L. Weinberg and Conrad & Teare, assoc. architects, Cleve., 1932-36; housing planner U.S. Housing Authority, Washington, 1938-39; chief planning and research Cleve. Met. Housing Authority, 1939-44; chmn. bd. Teare, Herman, & Gibans, Inc. (ptnr. predecessor firms), Cleve., 1946—; instr. Western Res. U., 1931-38, 45-47, trustee, 1948-56; housing cons. to gov., Panama Canal, 1945; archtl. cons. Cleve. City Planning Commn., 1959, vice chmn., 1971-74, chmn., 1975—; mem. Lakewood (Ohio) City Planning Commn., 1944-60, chmn., 1952-53; mem. exec. com. Regional Planning Commn. Cuyahoga County, 1951-60, 75—. Most important works of the firm include Lakeview Terrace, Cleve., 1937, O'Neil-Sheffield Shopping Center, Sheffield Twp., Ohio, 1954 (A.I.A. award of merit 1955), West Shore Unitarian Ch., Rocky River, 1962; (assoc. architect with Edward D. Stone) Jewish Community Fedn. Office Bldg, Cleve., 1965; (Charles Luckman Assocs., Cons.) Chesterfield Apts, Cleve., 1968; Lakeview Tower, Cleve., 1973, other housing for elderly in Ohio, Pa., Conn., 1954—, restoration Stouffer's Tower City Plaza Hotel (Preservation award Cleve. chpt. AIA 1979, honor award Architects Soc. Ohio 1981); author articles on housing for elderly. Trustee Regional Assn. Cleve., Friends of Cuyahoga Met. Housing Authority ; trustee W. Shore Concerts, Lakewood, Ohio, pres., 1954-56; trustee Koch Sch. Music, Rocky River, Ohio, chmn., 1970-71. Recipient Cleve. Arts prize, 1977, Silver Medal Alpha Epsilon chpt. Tau Sigma Delta, 1987; named to Cleve. Engrng. Soc. Constrn. Hall of Fame, 1985. Fellow AIA (sec. Cleve. chpt. 1944, v.p. 1948, pres. 1949, profl. adv. 1978—, mem. nat. housing com. 1972-77, chmn. 1975, HUD/AIA liaison task force 1977-78, Cleve. chpt. award honor 1983); mem. Architects Soc. Ohio (sec. Cleve. sect. 1937, v.p. 1938, Gold medal 1983), Am. Soc. Planning Ofcls. (hon. life), Am. Planning Assn., Soc. Archtl. Historians, Western Res. Archtl. Historians, Soc. for History of City and Regional Planning, Nat. Assn. Housing and Redevel. Ofcls., Internat. Assn. Housing Sci. Unitarian. Home: 16500 Edgewater Dr Lakewood OH 44107 Office: Teare Herman & Gibans Inc 1120 Terminal Tower Cleveland OH 44113

TEDESCO, PAUL A., data processing consultant; b. Omaha, Sept. 4, 1938; Michael Lewis and Georgia Elizabeth (Kabourek) T.; m. Janice Victoria Johnson, May 1, 1965; children: Joseph, Maia. BA, Creighton U., Omaha, 1960; MS, De Paul U., Chgo., 1964. Systems supr. Blue Cross Blue Shield, Chgo., 1970-77; systems engr. City of Chgo., 1977-80; pres. Tedesco and Assocs., Chgo., 1980-83; supr. Bus. Systems Corp. Am., Chgo., 1983-85; data processing cons. Cap Gemini Am., Des Plaines, Ill., 1985—; council dir. Micro Bus. System, Wheaton, Ill., 1983—, Martin Burns Assocs., Chgo., 1984—. Author: (computer programs) Fuzzy Logic, 1965, System Generation, 1972, Constructive Data Processing Implementation, 1983. Active area mktg. Edgewater Community Council, Chgo., 1981; mem. Uptown Commn., Chgo., 1981. Mem. Ind. Computer Cons. Am., Assn. Computing Machinery, Data Processing Mgmt. Assn. Democrat. Roman Catholic. Club: Chgo. Corinthian Yacht. Avocations: sailing, dancing, artificial intelligence. Home: 5221 N Wayne Chicago IL 60640 Office: Cap Gemini Am 1011 E Touhy Ave Des Plaines IL 60018

TEEPLE, HOWARD MERLE, educator; b. Salem, Oreg., Dec. 29, 1911; s. Charles and Eltruda (Branchflower) T.; m. Gladys Windedahl, Oct. 26, 1947; M.A. in L.S., U. Chgo., 1963, Ph.D., 1955. Farmer, 1938-47; research asst. Emory U., 1955-57; vis. instr. Bexley Hall, 1957-58; assoc. prof., chmn. dept. religion W.Va. Wesleyan Coll., 1958-61; ind. researcher, 1961-62; librarian order/reference depts. Deering Library, Northwestern U., Evanston, Ill., 1963-69; head reference dept. Douglas Library, Chgo. State U., 1969-77; exec. dir. Religion and Ethics Inst., Evanston, 1973—. Mem. Soc. Bibl. Lit. Democrat. Author: The Mosaic Eschatological Prophet, 1957; The Literary Origin of the Gospel of John, 1974; The Noah's Ark Nonsense, 1978; The Historical Approach to the Bible (cert. of recognition NCCJ), 1982; video producer Conflicts over the Bible, 1985, The Quest to Understand the Bible, 1986; contbr. articles to profl. jours. Home: 400 Main St Evanston IL 60202 Office: Religion and Ethics Inst PO Box 664 Evanston IL 60204

TEETZEN, MERLE LEE, neurologist; b. Shawano, Wis., Apr. 29, 1947; s. Charles A. and Elsie E. (Wendorf) T.; m. Susan Stockdale, Nov. 6, 1976; children: Christa, Charles, Lauren, David. BS, U. Wis., 1970; MD, Med. Coll. Wis., 1976. Cert. Am. Bd. Psychiatry and Neurology. Psychiatry resident Dartmouth-Hitchcock, Hanover, N.H., 1977-78; neurology resident U. Wis., Madison, 1978-81; neurologist Grand Forks (N.D.) Clinic, 1981—; clin. asst. prof. neurology U.N.D., Grand Forks, 1981—; cons. Med. Ctr. Rehab. Hosp., Grand Forks, 1981—, Grafton (N.D.) State Sch., 1984—. Examiner Social Security Disability Determining Services, St. Paul, 1983—. Mem. AMA, Am. Acad. Neurology, Am. EEG Soc., Am. Epilepsy Soc., Soc. Neuroscience. Lutheran. Home: 1911 S 38th St Grand Forks ND 58201 Office: Grand Forks Clinic 1000 S Columbia Rd Grand Forks ND 58201

TEI, TAKURI, accountant; b. Korea, Feb. 25, 1924; s. Gangen and Isun (Song) T.; came to U.S., 1952, naturalized, 1972; diploma Concordia Theol. Sem., 1959; B.D., Eden Theol. Sem., 1965; M.Ed., U. Mo., 1972; m. Maria M. Ottwaska, Dec. 1, 1969; 1 dau., Sun Kyung Lee. Partner, Madeleine Ottwaska & Assos., St. Louis, 1968—; pres. TMS Tei Enterprises Inc., Webster Groves, Mo., 1969—; instr. Forest Park Community Coll. Mem. Am. Coll. Enrolled Agts. (pres. 1976—), Am. Accounting Assn., Am. Taxation Assn., Assn. Asian Studies, NAACP. Republican. Lutheran. Home and office: 7529 Big Bend Blvd Webster Groves MO 63119

TEICHMANN, DIETRA DUFFALA, psychologist; b. Cleve., Sept. 9, 1946; d. Stephen Harold and Mary (Hrivnak) Duffala; B.A. in Math., Valparaiso U., 1969; B.S. in Psychology, Mills Coll., 1974; M.S. in Counseling and Sch. Psychology, Calif. State U., Hayward, 1976; Ph.D. in Psychology, Calif. Sch. Profl. Psychology, 1978; m. Nelson E. Teichmann, Aug. 30, 1980; 1 dau., Natalie Dyann. Staff psychologist, head injury treatment program Santa Clara Valley Med. Center, San Jose, Calif., 1976-79; psychol. asst. Behaviordyne, Inc., Palo Alto, Calif., 1978-79; supr., staff psychologist, coordinator Neuropsychol. Ctr. for Evaluation and Tng., Inst. Phys. Medicine and Rehab., Peoria, Ill., 1979—; speaker; tchr. neuropsychology Bradley U., 1979-82; resource person rehab. centers; co-founder Cen. Ill. Parkinson Support Group, 1984—, Heart of Ill. Head Injury Support Group, 1982—. Mem. Am. Psychol. Assn., Ill. Psychol. Assn., Internat. Neuropsychol. Soc., Midwest Neuropsychology Group. Lutheran. Office: Inst Phys Medicine & Rehab 6501 N Sheridan Rd Peoria IL 61614

TELANDER, JUDITH HANSEN, psychologist; b. Evanston, Ill., Apr. 24, 1949; s. Frederick Owen and Elizabeth Barnes (Griebel) Hansen; m. Richard Forster Telander, May 17, 1980; children: Lauren Hansen, Cary Hansen, Robin Hansen. BA, Wells Coll., 1971; MEd, Rutgers U., 1973; PhD, Loyola U., Chgo., 1979. Registered psychologist; cert. sch. psychologist. Intern Loyola Counseling Ctr., 1977-78; assoc. prof. Oakton Community Coll., Des Palines, Ill., 1980-82; practice psychology Lake Forest, Ill., 1977—; cons. regions 4 and 5 drug prevention program U.S. Dept. Edn., 1979-81, Rosary Coll., River forest, 1977-78, Florida Keys Community Coll., Key West, 1978. NDEA fellow Rutgers U., New Brunswick, N.J., 1971-72; Loyola U. fellow, 1978. Avocation(s) reading, running, swimming, aerobics, tennis, gardening. Home and Office: 524 Illinois Rd Lake Forest IL 60045

TELANDER, RICHARD DAVID, vocational educator; b. Milaca, Minn., Nov. 15, 1941; s. William L. and Agnes C. (Rolstad) T.; m. Sandra K. Miller, Sept. 23, 1962; children—Karen, Mark, Kaye. Student Mankato (Minn.) Vocat. Tech. Inst., 1960-62. Lic. post secondary instr., Minn. Foreman tool room Midtex Inc., Mankato, Minn., 1961-69; shop foreman Amdevco Engrng., Mankato, 1969-72; product mgr. North Star Concrete, Mankato, 1973; instr. tool and die Alexandria (Minn.) Tech. Inst., 1973—, com. chairperson profl. devel., 1983—. Named Educator of Yr., Alexandria Tech. Inst., 1982-83. Mem. Minn. Trade and Industry Assn. (pres.), Minn. Vocat. Assn. (pres. 1987-88), Am. Vocat. Assn., Minn. Edn. Assn. Lutheran.

TELL, A. CHARLES, lawyer; b. Chgo., May 9, 1937; s. William K and Virginia S (Snook) T.; m. Wendy Thomsen, June 16, 1962; children—Tracey, Melissa, A. Charles, Jr. A.B., Dartmouth Coll., 1961; J.D., Ohio State U., 1963. Ptnr. George, Greek, King & McMahon, Columbus, Ohio, 1964-78, Baker & Hostetler, Columbus, 1978—; dir. Kaplan Trucking Co., Cleve. Editor Your Letter of the Law, 1984. Contbr. articles to profl. jours. Served with U.S. Army, 1958-60. Mem. ABA, Am. Judicature Soc., Ohio State Bar Assn., Columbus Bar Assn., Transp. Lawyers Assn. (pres. 1986-87). Republican. Presbyterian. Clubs: City (pres. 1985), Columbus Country (trustee 1985—), Athletic. Office: Baker & Hostetler 65 E State St Suite 2200 Columbus OH 43215

TELLERMAN, JUDITH SIMONE, clinical psychologist. B.A., Brandeis U.; M.A.T., Harvard U.; MEd, Ph.D. in Psychology, Boston Coll. Intern, Michael Reese Hosp., Chgo., 1978-86, Roosevelt Univ., Chgo., 1978-86; cons. Gary (Ind.) Community Mental Health Ctr., 1978-86; pvt. practice psychology Chgo., 1978—; clin., research psychologist Rush-Presbyn.-St. Luke's Hosp. and Med. Ctr., Chgo., 1986—; cons. psychologist to various cos., orgns.; attending staff psychologist Michael Reese Hosp., Barclay Hosp., Chgo. Legis. chair, Ill. Assn. Suicidology; Ill. State Coordinator Nat. Com. on Youth Suicide Prevention; bd. dirs. Samaritans, Assn. for Mental Health Affiliation with Israel. Interviews on local and nat. radio programs. Home: 2020 Lincoln Park W 38J Chicago IL 60614 Office: 505 N Lake Shore Dr Suite 1318 Chicago IL 60611

TELLINGHUISEN, ROGER A., state official. Atty. gen. State of S.D., Pierre, 1987—. Office: Attorney General's Office State Capitol Pierre SD 57501

TEMIN, HOWARD MARTIN, scientist, educator; b. Phila., Dec. 10, 1934; s. Henry and Annette (Lehman) T.; m. Rayla Greenberg, May 27, 1962; children: Sarah Beth, Miriam Judith. BA, Swarthmore Coll., 1955, DSc (hon.), 1972; PhD, Calif. Inst. Tech., 1959; DSc (hon.), N.Y. Med. Coll., 1972, U. Pa., 1976, Hahnemann Med. Coll., 1976, Lawrence U., 1976, Temple U., 1979, Med. Coll. Wis., 1981, Colo. State U., 1987. Postdoctoral fellow Calif. Inst. Tech., 1959-60; asst. prof. oncology U. Wis., 1960-64, assoc. prof., 1964-69, prof., 1969—, Wis. Alumni Research Found. prof. cancer research, 1971-80, Am. Cancer Soc. prof. viral oncology and cell biology, 1974—, H.P. Rusch prof. cancer research, 1980—, Steenbock prof. biol. scis., 1982—; mem. research policy adv. com. U. Wis. Med. Sch., 1979-85; mem. Internat. Com. Virus Nomenclature Study Group for RNA Tumor Viruses, 1973-75, subcoms. HTLV and AIDS viruses, 1985; mem. virology study sect. NIH, 1971-74, mem. dir.'s adv. com., 1979-83; cons. working group on human gene therapy NIH/RAC, 1984—, mem. Nat. Cancer Adv. Bd., 1986—; mem. NAS/IOM Com. for a Nat. Strategy for AIDS, 1986; mem. Nat. Cancer Inst. (spl. virus cancer program tumor virus detection segment working group), 1972-73; sponsor Fedn. Am. Scientists, 1976—; sci. adv. Stehlin Found., Houston, 1972—; mem. Waksman award com. Nat. Acad. Sci., 1976-81; mem. U.S. Steel award Com., 1980-83, chmn., 1982. Assoc. editor: Jour. Cellular Physiology, 1966-77, Cancer Research, 1971-74; mem. editorial bd.: Jour. Virology, 1971—, Intervirology, 1972-75, Proc. Nat. Acad. Scis, 1975-80, Archives of Virology, 1975-77, Ann. Rev. Gen., 1983, Molecular Biology and Evolution, 1983—, Oncogene Research, 1987—. Co-recipient Warren Triennial prize Mass. Gen. Hosp., 1971, Gairdner Found. Internat. award, 1974, Nobel Prize in medicine, 1975; recipient Med. Soc. Wis. Spl. commendation, 1971; Papanicolaou Inst. PAP award, 1972; M.D. Anderson Hosp. and Tumor Inst. Bertner award, 1972; U.S. Steel Found. award in Molecular Biology, 1972; Theobald Smith Soc. Waksman award, 1972; Am. Chem. Soc. award in Enzyme Chemistry, 1973; Modern Medicine award for Distinguished Achievement, 1973; Harry Shay Meml. lectr. Fels Research Inst., 1973; Griffuel prize Assn. Devel. Recherche Cancer, Villejuif, 1972; New Horizons lectr. Radiol. Soc. N.Am., 1968; G.H.A. Clowes lectr. award Assn. Cancer Research, 1974; NIH Dyer lectr. award, 1974; Harvey lectr., 1974, Charlton lectr. Tufts U., 1976, Hoffman-LaRoche lectr. Rutgers U., 1979, Yoder hon. lectr. St. Joseph Hosp., Tacoma, 1983; Cetus lectr. U. Calif., Berkeley, 1984; DuPont lectr. Harvard Med. Sch., 1985; Japanese Found. for Promotion Cancer Research lectr., 1985, Herz Meml. lectr. Tel-Aviv U., 1985, Amoros. Meml. lectr. U. West Indies, 1986; Albert Lasker award in basic med. sci., 1974; Lucy Wortham James award Soc. Surg. Oncologists, 1976; Alumni Disting. Service award Calif. Inst. Tech., 1976; Gruber award Am. Acad. Dermatology, 1981; mem. Central High Sch. Hall of Fame Phila., 1976; Pub. Health Service Research Career Devel. awardee Nat. Cancer Inst., 1964-74, 1st Hilldale award in Biolog. Sci. U. Wis., 1986, Braund Disting. vis. prof. U. Tenn., 1987, Eisenstark lectr. U. Mo., 1987, 1st Wilmon vis. prof. U. Rochester, 1987. Fellow Am. Acad. Arts and Scis.; fellow Wis. Acad. Sci., Arts and Letters; mem. Nat. Acad. Scis., Am. Philos. Soc. Office: Univ of Wis McArdle Lab 450 N Randall St Madison WI 53706

TEMKIN, MIRA HYMEN, freelance advertising executive, copywriter; b. Chgo., Sept. 24, 1951; d. Harold T. and Doris (Belinkoff) Hymen; m. Darryl Owen Temkin, Mar. 20, 1976; children: Alison, Hilary, Ari. Student, Ind. U., 1969-71; BA in Advt., Mich. State U., 1973. Copywriter Martin Simmons Advt., Chgo., 1973-74, U.S. League of Savs. Assn., Chgo., 1974-76; supr. copy Frankel & Co., Chgo., 1976-79; assoc. creative dir. William A. Robinson, Inc., Chgo., 1979-81; freelance advt. and promotional copywriter Highland Park, Ill., 1981—. V.p. spl. projects Twin Acres chpt. Women's Am. ORT, Buffalo Grove, Ill., 1983-84, women,s v.p. bulletin Harmony Way chpt., Highland Park, 1986—; chmn. Lake County Region Bulletin, 1987. Jewish. Avocations: reading, travel, writing. Home and Office: 3022 Lexington Ln Highland Park IL 60035

TEMPEL, EUGENE RAYMOND, foundation administrator, speaker, researcher; b. St. Meinrad, Ind., Mar. 30, 1947; s. Charles Xavier and Bernadette Scholastica (Otto) T.; m. Mary Ekerle, May 24, 1969; children—Jonathan, Jason, Zachary. B.A. in English and Philosophy, St. Benedict Coll., 1970; M.A. in English, Ind. U., 1973, Ed.D. in Higher Edn., 1985. Asst. prof. English, Vincennes U., Ind., 1970-77, dir. Jasper Ctr., 1973-77; v.p., dean of faculty Three Rivers Community Coll., Poplar Bluff, Mo., 1977-80; dir. external affairs Ind. U., Bloomington, 1980-83; exec. dir. for Indpls. Ind. U. Found., 1983-85, v.p., 1985—; bd. dirs. devel. cons. Marian Heights Acad., Ferdinand, Ind., 1973—; devel. cons. Ind. Agrl. Inst., Indpls., 1985; asst. prof. higher edn. (part-time), 1985—. Author (study) Decline in Small Colleges, 1984. Commr. Jasper Community Arts Commn., Ind., 1975-77; mem. Mingo Community Relations Council, Poplar Bluff, bd. overseers St. Meinrad Sem., 1986—. Mem. Indpls. C. of C., Council for Advancement and Support Edn., Am. Assn. Higher Edn., Nat. Soc. Fund Raising Execs. Roman Catholic. Club: Athletic (Indpls.), Skyline. Lodge: Rotary. Avocations: soccer parents, sailing. Home: 5215 E 72d St Indianapolis IN 46250 Office: Ind U Found 355 N Lansing Indianapolis IN 46202

TEMPLAR, GEORGE, judge; b. Cowley County, Kans., Oct. 18, 1904; s. John and Carlotta E. (Linn) T.; m. Helen Marie Bishop, Mar. 29, 1924; children—Joana (Mrs. Jerry Smith), Ted. LL.B. cum laude, Washburn Coll., 1927, J.D., 1970, LL.D., 1971. Bar: Kans. bar 1927. Practiced in Arkansas City, 1927; dep. oil insp. State of Kans., 1930-32; mem. Kans. Ho. Reps., 1933-41, Kans. Jud. Council, 1941-45, Kans. Senate, 1945-53; U.S. dist. atty. 1953-54; judge U.S. Dist. Ct., Topeka, 1962—. Contbr. articles to law jours. Trustee Southwestern Coll., 1947—, pres. bd. trustees, 1959-70. Recipient award of merit Assn. Trial Lawyers of Am., 1972, medal honor D.A.R., 1973. Fellow Internat. Acad. Trial Lawyers; mem. Kans., Fed. bar assns., Kans. Hist. Soc. (trustee 1938—, v.p. 1968, pres. 1970). Methodist. Clubs: Mason (DeMolay Legion of Honor), Nat. Lawyers. Home: PO Box 32 Arkansas City KS 67005 Office: U S Dist Ct 420 Fed Bldg 444 SE Quincy St Topeka KS 66683

TEMPLE, DONALD, allergist, dermatologist; b. Chgo., May 21, 1933; s. Samuel Leonard and Matilda Eve (Riff) T.; m. Sarah Rachel Katz, Sept. 29, 1957; children: Michael A., Matthew D., Madeline B. AB in Biology cum laude, Harvard U., 1954; MD, U. Chgo., 1958. Am. Bd. Allergy and Immunology, Am. Bd. Dermatology, Nat. Bd. Med. Examiners; lic. Intern Michael Reese Hosp., Chgo., 1958-59; resident in dermatology U. Chgo. Hosps., 1959-62; preceptee in allergy Offices of Leon Under, M.D., and Donald Unger, M.D., Chgo., 1965-69; practice medicine specializing in allergy and dermatology Med. Profl. Bldg., Des Plaines, Ill., 1969-76; mem. allergy dept. Glen Ellyn (Ill.), 1972—; mem. dermatology and allergy staff, L.A. Weiss Hosp. Profl. Bldg., Chgo., 1965-73; mem. allergy sect. Loyola U. Med. Ctr., Maywood, Ill., 1977-80; clin. assoc. prof. dermatology Abraham Lincoln Sch. Medicine, U. Ill., 1972-75; clin. asst. prof. medicine sect. allergy and dermatology, Loyola U., 1977-85; mem. staff Alexian Bros. Med. Ctr., Elk Grove Village, 1978-80, Glendale Heights (Ill.) Community Hosp., 1980—; exec. staff Cen. DuPage Hosp., Winfield, Ill., 1973—. Contbr. articles to profl. jours. Bd. dirs. Am. Lung Assn., DuPage, McHenry counties, 1980—; chmn. Contract Medicine, HMO Com., Glen Ellyn Clinic, 1985—. Served to capt. U.S. Army, 1962-64. Fellow Am. Coll. Chest Physicians, Am. Assn. Cert. Allergists, Am. Coll. Allergists, Am. Acad. Allergy, Am. Acad. Dermatology, Ill. Soc. Allergy and Clin. Immunology, Chgo. Dermatol. Soc.; mem. AMA, Ill. State Med. Soc., DuPage County Med. Soc., Chgo. Med. Soc. Republican. Jewish. Avocations: sailing, investing. Home: 2819 Floral Dr Northbrook IL 60062 Office: Glen Ellyn Clinic 454 Pennsylvania Ave Glen Ellyn IL 60137

TEMPLE, GEADELIA WOLFE, data processing analysis; b. Spartanburg, S.C., Aug. 30, 1925; s. George Lee and Mary Elizabeth (Settle) W.; m. Lonnie Everette Temple, June 8, 1946 (div. Feb. 1979); children: Larry Everette, Wanda Temple Stephens, Glenn Allen. BA in Math., Winthrop Coll., Rock Hill, S.C., 1946; cert. in supervision, Florissant Valley Coll., 1979; M in Mgmt. Sci., Maryville Coll., St. Louis, 1986. Sr. sect. mgr. McDonnell Douglas, St. Louis, 1973, br. mgr., 1978-80, sr. sect. mgr., 1980-81, mgr. systems analysts, 1981-83, prin. specialist sr., 1983—. Bd. dirs. Florissant Valley Single Adults, 1979-82. Mem. Nat. Micrographics Assn., Bus. Forms Mgmt. Assn., Assn. Records Mgmt. and Adminstrs., McDonnell Douglas Mgmt. Club. Lodge: Soroptimist (sec., treas. 1973, bd. dirs. 1980-81), Eastern Star (worthy matron 1986-87). Home: Route 67 Box 91D Cullowhee NC 28723 Office: McDonnell Douglas Corp Box 516 Saint Louis MO 63166

TEMPLE, JOSEPH GEORGE, JR., chemical executive; b. Bklyn., Aug. 29, 1929; s. Joseph George and Helen Frances (Beney) T.; m. Ann Elizabeth McFerran, June 21, 1952; children: Linda Jo, James, John. BSChemE, Purdue U., 1951. With Dow Chem. Co., Midland, Mich., 1951—, v.p. mktg., 1976-78, dir., 1979—; pres. Dow Chem. Latin Am., Coral Gables, Fla., 1978-80; group v.p. human health Dow Chem. Co., Cin., 1980-83; pres. Merrell Dow Pharmaceuticals Inc., Cin., 1983—; bd. dirs. Chem. Bank and Trust Co.; trustee Com. for Economic Devel. Mem. pres.'s council Purdue U., 1978—. Recipient Disting. Engr. Alumni award Purdue U., 1978. Mem. Am. Inst. Chem. Engrs., Soc. Plastics Industry (bd. dirs.), Pharm. Mfrs. Assn. (bd. dirs.), Nat. Agmt. Assn. (Silver Knight award 1976, Gold Knight award 1982). Episcopalian. Office: Dow Chemical Co 2030 Willard H Dow Ctr Midland MI 48674

TEMPLE, STEVEN RAY, chemical company manager; b. Shirley, Mass., Oct. 1, 1955; s. Donald J. and Julie A. (Lightner) T.; m. June M. Etzold, May 16, 1982. BSME, Mont. State U., 1976. Designs engr. Chevron USA, El Segundo, Calif., 1976-78, lead engr., 1979-82; sr. engr. Chevron Chem. Co., Richmond, Calif., 1982-83, prodn. supr., 1983-84; plant mgr. Chevron Chem. Co., Ft. Madison, Iowa, 1984-85, ops. mgr., 1985—. chmn. industry div. United Way, Ft. Madison, 1985; co-chmn. industry div. partnership with youth campaign YMCA, Ft. Madison, 1985, 86.; dist. chmn. Southeast Iowa council Boy Scouts Am., 1986. Mem. Ft. Madison C. of C. (ambassador, 1986). Republican. Roman Catholic. Lodge: Rotary.

TEMPLETON, BARBARA ANN, civil engineering technologist; b. Miller, S.D., Aug. 26, 1954; s. Edward Eugene and Helen Roxanne (Siegling) Labor; m. Daivd James Templeton Jr., Aug. 7, 1976; 1 child, Brian James. AS, U. S.D., 1974. Staff asst. S.D. Dept. Water, Pierre, 1978-81; civil engring. tech. Corps of Engrs., Pierre, 1981—. Republican. Lutheran. Home: 804 Cherry Dr Pierre SD 57501

TEMPLIN, JOHANN, paralegal business owner; b. Milw., Mar. 9, 1956; m. Sandra Lee Erickson, Dec. 31, 1976; children: Thor Heidrek, Thomas Wolfgang, Teddy Horst. Student, Paralegal Inst., N.Y., 1976. Mgr. Templin & Assocs., Milw., 1976—. Author monthly column in German-Am. newspapers. Chmn. acad. com. German-Am. Nat. Congress, 1984-85, chmn. polit. action com.; chmn. German-Am. Civil Rights Orgn., 1986. Recipient Civil Rights award German-Am. Civil Rights orgn., 1986. Mem. Internat. Platform Assn. Democrat. Lutheran. Avocation: chess (U.S. Chess Fedn. Master). Home and Office: 1551 S 15th Pl Milwaukee WI 53204

TEN EYCK, ROBERT LANCASTER, JR., psychologist; b. Hartford, Conn., Nov. 13, 1944; s. Robert Lancaster Sr. and Anne Laurie (Van Hook) Ten E.; m . Hannah Jo Hofherr, Aug. 12, 1967; children: Peter, Nicholas. BA, DePauw U., 1966; MS, Fla. State U., 1968, PhD, 1970. Registered health service provider. Dir. internship program Larue Carter Meml. Hosp., Indpls., 1973-79, chief psychologist children's dept., 1970—; instr. Ind. U. Sch. Medicine, Indpls., 1970-73, asst. prof., 1973—; cons. psychologist Marion Superior and Cir. Cts., Indpls., 1976—, Raines Pastural Counseling Ctr., Indpls., 1986—. Contbr. articles to profl. jours. Pres. pres. Raines Pastural Counseling Ctr., Indpls., 1975, v.p., 1976-86; bd. dirs. Ind. Prevention of Child Abuse Assn., 1985; mem. adv. commn. State Ind Commn. for the Handicapped, 1985—. USPHS Pre Doctoral Research fellow NIMH, 1968. Mem. Am. Psychol. Assn. (council of reps. 1987, Ind. Psychol. Assn. (pres. div. profl. psychol. 1977-78, pres. 1985-86, council reps. 1987—), Sigma Xi. Home: 1749 Brewster Rd Indianapolis IN 46260 Office: Ind U

Sch Medicine Larue D Carter Meml Hosp 1315 W 10th St Indianapolis IN 46202

TENNANT, CAROLYN GAY, college administrator; b. Janesville, Wis., June 19, 1947; d. Ralph Benjamin and Beverly Jane (Hart) Jenny; m. Raymond Frank Tennant, Dec. 28, 1968. B.A., U. Colo., 1969, M.A., 1973, Ph.D. in Ednl. Adminstrn. and Supervision, 1979. Ordained to ministry Assemblies of God Ch., 1985. Tchr. Adams County Sch. Dist. 12, Denver, 1969-73, spl. programs coordinator, dir. gifted and talented, instr. staff devel., 1978-79; dir. Inst. Cognitive Devel., Denver, 1979-81, Dayton, Ohio, 1981-83; v.p. student life N. Central Bible Coll., Mpls., 1983—. Nat. Inst. Edn. grantee, 1975-78; recipient Fulbright-Hays award, 1981. Mem. Assn. Supervision and Curriculum Devel., Assn. Christians in Student Devel., Nat. Assn. Gifted Children, Colo. Lang. Arts Soc. (treas. 1973-74), Nat. Soc. Study Edn., Nat. Council Tchrs. English, Internat. Reading Assn. Republican. Author: (with H.S. Morgan and M. Gold) Elementary and Secondary Level Programs for the Gifted and Talented, 1980. Office: 910 Elliot Ave S Minneapolis MN 55404

TENNANT, STEVEN CRAIG, engineering technician; b. Ashland, Ohio, June 20, 1959; s. Myron Alfred and Betty (Smeltzer) T.; m. Barbara Sue Mattes, Aug. 31, 1985; 1 child, Jennifer Michele. AAS in Drafting and Design, N. Cen. Tech. Coll., Mansfield, Ohio, 1981, AAS in Mech. Engring., 1983. Engring. technician Wooster (Ohio) Brush Co., 1981—. Home: 9504 Zimmerman Rd Wooster OH 44691 Office: Wooster Brush Co 604 Madison Ave Wooster OH 44691

TENNER, EUGENE ARTHUR, marketing professional; b. Chgo., Dec. 5, 1947; s. Harvey O. and Evelyn (Kleinau) T.; m. Nancy Karen Pepin; 1 child, Sean C. BA in Art, Econs., Blackburn Coll., 1970; MA in Art, No. Ill. U., 1975. Salesperson Rockford (Ill.) Newspapers, 1976-78; advt. mgr. Wolfe Newspapers, Rochester, N.Y., 1979-80, Reporter Progress Newspapers, Downers Grove, Ill., 1980-82; mktg. mgr. Gorman Pub., Chgo., 1982-84; mktg. dir. MIMA The Mgmt. Assn, Westchester, Ill., 1984—. Served with Res. Recipient Citizenship award Blackburn Coll., 1970. Mem. Midwest Mfg. Mgrs. Assn., Midwest Personnel Mgrs. Assn., Blackburn Coll. Alumni Assn. (bd. dirs. 1986—). Unitarian. Avocations: art, movies. Home: 2757 Greenfield Lisle IL 60532 Office: MIMA The Mgmt Assn 2400 S Downing Westchester IL 60153

TENNEY, MARK WILLIAM, civil engineering, consultant; b. Chgo., Dec. 10, 1936; s. William and Frieda (Sanders) T.; B.S., Mass. Inst. Tech., 1958, M.S., 1959, Sc.D., 1965; m. Jane E. Morris, June 1, 1974; children Scott, Barbara. Design engr. Greeley & Hansen, Engrs., Chgo., 1959-61; asso. prof. civil engring. U. Notre Dame, 1965-73; pres. TenEch Engring., Inc., South Bend, Ind., 1973—. Served with C.E., AUS, 1959-60; brig. gen. USAR. USPHS research fellow, 1961-64. Diplomate Am. Acad. Environ. Engrs. Fellow ASCE; mem. Nat. Soc. Profl. Engrs., Am. Cons. Engrs. Council, Water Pollution Control Fedn., Am. Water Works Assn., Sigma Xi, Chi Epsilon, Phi Delta Theta. Clubs: South Bend Country, Landings Yacht and Golf, Columbia, Summit, Ill. Athletic; Lake Macatawa Yacht; Summit. Contbr. articles to profl. jours. Home: 2110 Niles-Buchanan Rd Niles MI 49120 Office: 744 W Washington St South Bend IN 46601

TENNYSON, ROBERT DUANE, education, computer science and psychology educator; b. Culver City, Calif., Aug. 19, 1945; s. Harry Langley and Alise Vivian (Lowder) T.; m. Halyna Hajovy, Sept. 19, 1978. B.S., Brigham Young U., 1967, Ph.D., 1971; M.A., Calif. State U., 1968, M.A., 1969. Tchr., Newhall (Calif.) High Sch., 1967-69; prof. Fla. State U., 1971-74; prof. edn. and psychology U. Minn., Mpls., 1974—, dir. Instructional Systems Lab., 1974—. Fulbright Research scholar, Germany, 1981-82. Fellow Am. Psychol. Assn. Editor Am. Ednl. Research Jour. Contbr. numerous articles to profl. jours. Home: 8710 Hunters Way Apple Valley MN 55124 Office: U Minn 159 Pillsbury Dr SE Minneapolis MN 55455

TENTONI, STUART CHARLES, clinical psychologist; b. Chgo., June 17, 1949; s. Robert Archibald and Vivian Anne (Ginsberg) T.; m. Priscilla Jane Diehl, Jan. 8, 1972 (div.); 1 child, Christian Todd; m. Charlotte Marie Hall, May 4, 1985. BS, Wis. State U., Oshkosh, 1970; MEd, U. Wis., Oshkosh, 1971; PhD, North Tex. State U., 1974. Registered psychologist, Ill.; lic. psychologist, Wis.; diplomate Am. Acad. Behavioral Medicine, Am. Bd. Med. Psychotherapists. Psychol. asst. Behavior and Mgmt. Cons., Inc., Milw., 1974-76; clin. psychologist Kettle Moraine Hosp., Oconomowoc, Wis., 1977-78, Waukesha (Wis.) County, 1978—; cons. psychologist Inst. Motivational Devel., Milw., 1981-85. Contbr. articles to profl. jours.; author two books. Fellow Am. Bd. Med. Psychotherapists; mem. Am. Psychol. Assn., Psi Chi, Kappa Delta Pi, Phi Delta Kappa. Lutheran. Avocations: cinema, college football, Harley-Davidson motorcycle maintenance, voice impersonations, writing. Home: 202 Linden Ct Hartland WI 53029-1308

TENUTA, FRED TAYLOR, dentist; b. Kenosha, Wis., June 13, 1954; s. Fred and Lucy Ann (Taylor) T. Student, U. Wis., Madison, 1973-74, U. Wis., Parkside, 1972-73, 74-75; DDS, Marquette U., 1980. Gen. practice dentistry Kenosha, 1981—. Active Tremper High Sch. Boosters, Kenosha, 1984—. Mem. ADA, Wis. Dental Assn., Kenosha County Dental Soc., Am. Soc. of Dentistry for Children, Chgo. Detal Soc. (assoc.). Methodist. Club: Kenosha Wheelmen (v.p. 1984). Lodge: Kiwanis. Avocations: softball, scorekeeping. Home: 9023 17th Ave Kenosha WI 53140-6806 Office: 1225 75th St Kenosha WI 53140-6039

TEPATTI, ROBERT JAMES, insurance company executive; b. Hillsboro, Ill., Apr. 17, 1951; s. Antone and Roberta Marie (Marti) T.; m. Terri Ann Clayton, July 7, 1973 (div. 1982); children: Ann Marie, Stephen James. BA, Greenville Coll., 1973; MS, Ill. State U., 1974. CLU. Teaching asst. Ill. State U. Normal, 1973-74; agt. Mut. and United of Omaha, Springfield, Ill., 1975-77; dir. advanced underwriting Horace Mann Life Ins. Co., Springfield, 1977—. Contbr. tech. articles to profl. publs. Bd. dirs. Sangamon Valley Estate Planning Council, 1986—; publicity chmn. Springfield Sangamon County CRON Walk, 1985—. Mem. Am. Soc. Pension Actuaries, Cen. Ill. CLU Soc. (bd. dirs. 1987—), Am. Soc. CLU's and Chartered Fin. Cons., Springfield Assn. Life Underwriters, Ill. Assn. Life Underwriters, Nat. Assn. Life Underwriters, Cen. Ill. Life Mgmt. Inst. Lodge: Masons. Home: 119 Exeter Ct Springfield IL 62704 Office: Horace Mann Life Ins Co 1 Horace Mann Plaza Springfield IL 62715

TEPLEY, JOHN FREDERICK, systems analyst; b. Mpls., July 29, 1952; s. James E. Tepley and Dorothy (Steuvan) Du Vall; m. Virginia C. Chin, Nov. 12, 1982; 1 stepchild, Grace. Student, U. Chgo., 1970-74. Analyst/programmer Bankers Life & Casualty Co., Chgo., 1974-78; analyst, programmer Blue Shield Assn., Chgo., 1978, U.S. Gypsum Co., Chgo., 1978-79; cons. ACI Inc., Chgo., 1979-80; systems analyst Victor Bus. Products, Chgo., 1980-81; lead system programmer Berry Bearing Co., Lyons, Ill., 1981—; cons. BTT Assocs., Lombard, 1978—. Author: (software) Peekcsa, 1985, Showtell, 1985. Presbyterian. Avocations: gardening, study of stock market and real estate. Home: 233 N Charlotte St Lombard IL 60148

TEPPER, MARC JEFFREY, corporation manager; b. Chgo., Mar. 19, 1956; s. Samuel and Grace Lael (Goldstein) T.; m. Carolyn Marie Thompson, May 29, 1983. B.S., Colo. State U., 1979. Lab. asst. Environeering, Des Plaines, Ill., 1980-81, research and devel. engr., 1981-82; sales engr. Flex-Kleen, Chgo., 1982-84, regional sales mgr., 1984-86; sales rep. P.H. White and Assocs., 1986—; cons. Mem. Air Pollution Control Assn. Republican. Jewish. Avocations: downhill skiing; golf; softball. Office: PH White and Assocs 130 W Liberty Wheaton IL 60187

TEPPER, NEAL GARY, counselor; b. Bklyn., Mar. 12, 1951; s. Leon and Bernice Rhoda (Fisher) T.; m. Nadine C. Claymore, Oct. 24, 1977; children: Beth, Wayland, David, Neal Jr.; B.A., State U. N.Y., Potsdam, 1972; M.A., U. N.D., 1973, B.S. in Edn., 1985. Group therapist St. Mike's Hosp., Grand Forks, N.D., 1972-73; tchr. courses Center Teaching and Learning, U. N.D., 1973-75, grad. teaching asst. dept. counseling and guidance, 1974-77, intern counselor Counseling Center, 1975-77; practicum guidance counselor Red River High Sch., Grand Forks, 1973-74; mental health clinician IV, Meml. Mental Health and Retardation Center, Mandan, N.D., 1977-79; dir. Children and Family Services for Standing Rock Sioux Tribe, Ft. Yates, N.D., 1978-81; dir. counseling United Tribes Ednl. Tech. Center, 1981-83; counselor Bur. Indian Affairs, Dept. Interior, Fort Totten, N.D., 1983-85; family therapist Lutheran Soc. Services of Minn., Grand Forks, N.D., 1985—; bd. dirs. Understanding the Child, Grand Forks, N.D., 1976—; supr. NW Counseling, Crookston, Minn.; counselor Cathedral Parish. Mem. Polk County Child Protection Team. Mem. Am. Personnel and Guidance Assn., North Cen. Assn. Counselor Educators Assn., Mental Health Assn., Assn. Edn. of Young Children, N.D. Conf. Social Welfare. Lodge: Lions. Home: 118 7th St S Crookston MN 56716 Office: PO Box 985 Grand Forks ND 58206

TEREBELO, HOWARD RICHARD, hematologist, oncologist, educator; b. Detroit, May 10, 1949; s. George Raymond and Ruth (Stockler) T.; m. Robin Amy Strickler, Aug. 10, 1977; children: Bradley, Joshua. BS, Mich. State U., 1971; DO, Coll. Osteo. Medicine, 1974. Commd 2d lt. U.S. Army, 1974, advanced through grades to lt. col; intern, then resident Walter Reed Army Med. Ctr., Washington, 1974-77, fellow in hematology and oncology, 1978-81; attending physician 121 evacuation hosp. Walter Reed Army Med. Ctr., Seoul, 1977-78; attending physician Walter Reed Army Med. Ctr., Washington, 1981-83; resign U.S. Army, 1983; attending physician Chgo. Coll. Osteo. Medicine, 1983-86; attending physician Chgo. Med. Sch., 1983—, assoc. prof. medicine, 1986—; assoc. prof. medicine Henry Ford Hosp., 1987—; vis. scientist Nat. Cancer Inst., Bethesda, Md., 1980-81; asst. prof. medicine Uniformed Services U. of Health Scis., Bethesda, 1981-83; assoc. prof. medicine Chgo. Coll. Osteo. Medicine, 1983-86. Contbr. articles to profl. jour. Recipient Leukemia Research award Ill. Cancer Council, Chgo, 1984, Lab. Research award Am. Osteo. Assn., Chgo., 1985. Fellow ACP (lic.); mem. AMA, Am. Soc. Clin. Oncology, Am. Soc. Hematology. Jewish. Avocation: cycling. Home: 5440 Claridge Ln West Bloomfield MI 48033

TERKEL, STUDS LOUIS, interviewer, author; b. N.Y.C., May 16, 1912; s. Samuel and Anna (Finkel) T.; m. Ida Goldberg, July 2, 1939; 1 son, Paul. Ph.B., U. Chgo., 1932, J.D., 1934. Stage appearances include Detective Story, 1950, A View From the Bridge, 1958, Light Up the Sky, 1959, The Cave Dwellers, 1960; star: TV program Studs Place, 1950-53; radio program Wax Mus, 1945—, Studs Terkel Almanac, 1952—, Studs Terkel Show, Sta. WFMT-FM, Chgo., master of ceremonies, Newport Folk Festival, 1959, 60, Ravinia Music Festival, 1959, U. Chgo. Folk Festival, 1961, others; panel moderator, lectr., narrator films. Program, Wax Museum (winner 1st award as best cultural program in regional radio category Inst. Edn. by Radio-TV, Ohio State U. 1959, recipient Prix Italia, UNESCO award for best radio program East-West Values 1962, Communicator of Year award U. Chgo. Alumni Assn. 1969); Author: book Giants of Jazz, 1956, Division Street America, 1966, Chicago, 1986; play Amazing Grace, 1959, Hard Times, 1970, Working, 1974, Talking to Myself, 1977, American Dreams: Lost and Found, 1980; The Good War: An Oral History of World War II (Pulitzer prize 1985); also short stories. Office: 303 E Wacker Chicago IL 60601 *

TERMAN, DAVID MATTHEW, psychoanalyst; b. Chgo., May 23, 1935; s. Meyer H. and Ella Libby (Morris) T.; m. Mari Jane DeCosta, June 14, 1959; children: Mark, Anne, Eric. BA, U. Chgo., 1955, BS, 1956, MD, 1959. Diplomate Am. Bd. Psychiatry and Neurology; cert. psychoanalyst, Ill. Intern Phila. Gen. Hosp., 1959-60; resident at Psychosomatic and Psychiat. Inst. Michael Reese Hosp., Chgo., 1960-63, asst. dir. outpatient psychiatry, 1963-66; practice medicine specializing in psychiatry and psychoanalysis Chgo., 1963—; tng. and supervising analyst Chgo. Inst. for Psychoanalysis, 1979—. Contbr. articles to profl. jours. Fellow Am. Psychiat. Assn.; mem. Am. Psychoanalytic Assn. Jewish. Avocations: music, mountain hiking. Office: 230 N Michigan Ave Chicago IL 60601

TERP, DANA GEORGE, architect; b. Chgo., Nov. 5, 1953; s. George and June (Hansen) T.; m. Lynn Meyers, May 17, 1975; children: Sophia, Rachel. BA in Architecture, Washington U., St. Louis, 1974; postgrad., Yale U., 1975-76; MArch, Washington U., 1977. Registered architect, Ill., Calif. Architect Frank Chapman Architects, New Haven, 1976, Skidmore Owings & Merrill, Chgo., 1976, 1978—, Terp Meyers Architects, Chgo., 1982-86; prin. Arquitectonica Chgo. Inc., 1986—. Exhibited in group shows at Moming Gallery, Chgo., 1980, Printers Row Exhibit, 1980, Frumkin Struve Gallery, Chgo., 1981, Chgo. Bar Assn., 1981, W. Hubbard Gallery, Chgo., 1981, Chgo. Art Inst., 1983. Recipient Chgo. Townhouse Competition hon. mention, 1978, Prog. Architecture archtl. design citation for Printing Press Addition, 1980. Mem. AIA (task force com. for 1992 World's Fair), Young Chgo. Architects, Chgo. Archtl. Found. Office: Arquitectonica Chgo Inc 919 N Michigan Ave Suite 2402 Chicago IL 60611

TERRELL, MABLE JEAN, association executive; b. North Little Rock, Ark., Aug. 2, 1936; d. Rudolph and Mable (Edwards) Webb; m. William Bennett Terrell, Apr. 5, 1955; children: Venita, Vickie, Camela. BA in Sociology, Roosevelt U., Chgo., 1970. Cert. info. systems specialist, 1976. Sr. rep. Honeywell, Inc., Chgo., 1972-82; sr. analyst Walter E. Heller, Chgo., 1982-84; pres., chief exec. officer Internat. Black Writers Conf., Chgo., 1984—. Author: We Want Washington, 1984; pub. The Black Writer mag., 1985. Recipient Ark. Traveler award Ark. Gov. Clinton, 1982. Mem. NAACP, Urban League, Push, Roseland Women's Council (sec. 1983-86, Service award 1985), Jones Alumni Assn. (chmn. nat. scholarship com., Cert. Merit 1986, pres.). Mem. United Ch. Christ. Avocations: reading, traveling.

TERRELL, WILLIE ANDREW, JR., educator; b. Dayton, Ohio, June 18, 1951; s. Willie A. and Hazel (Wright) T.; B.S., Central State U., Ohio, 1972; Ed.M., Miami U., Ohio, 1977, Wright State U., 1980. Youth advocate Youth Services Bur., Dayton, 1972-76; tchr. social studies Dayton Bd. Edn., 1973-76, 77—; substitute tchr. Hamilton (Ohio) Public Schs., 1977; notary public, Ohio, 1980—. Named Black Man of Yr., Roosevelt Black Awareness Council, 1974. Mem. Assn. for Supervision and Curriculum Devel., Nat. Council Social Studies, NEA, Ohio Council Social Studies, Western Ohio Edn. Assn., Dayton Edn. Assn., Central State U. Alumni Assn., Kappa Delta Pi, Alpha Kappa Mu, Phi Alpha Theta, Omega Psi Phi (Omega Man of Yr. 4th Dist. 1985). Club: Masons. Home: 1721 Radio Rd B-6 Dayton OH 45403 Office: 48 W Parkwood Dayton OH 45403

TERRILL, CHARLES MERLE, transportation executive; b. Mineral Point, Wis., Aug. 16, 1935; s. Merle Willis and Thelma Margaret (Potterton) T.; m. Marilyn Ann Sturdevant, Aug. 31, 1953; children: David, Corinne, Wanda, Kevin, Jill. AS in Bus. Adminstrn., Rockford (Ill.) Bus. Coll., 1954; A in Bus. Adminstrn. in Sales and Mktg., Am. Inst. Tech., 1961; student, Tri State U., 1979-80; cert. in safety engring., Mich. State U., 1985. Dist. sales mgr. Babson Bros. Co., Chgo., 1953-57, Internat. Mineral and Chem., Chgo., 1957-60; ops. mgr. Terrico, Mineral Point, 1960-69; road driver CW Transport, Milw., 1969-79; safety supr. CW Transport, Fond Du Lac, Wis., 1979-85; v.p. safety Flexible Transport, Milw., 1985—; bd. dirs. Wis. Decision Driving Ctr., Appleton; past chmn. Truck Driving Championship, Wis., 1983. Treas. Mineral Point Sch. Bd., 1967-68; campaign mem. Washington City Rep. Party, 1979-80. Mem. Wis. Council Safety Suprs. (chmn. 1979, Safety Driver of Yr. award 1984), Am. Trucking Assn. (safety council 1986—), Interstate Carriers Conf. (safety council 1986—), Nat. Safety Council (winter driving league 1984—), Wis. Motor Carriers Assn. (past chmn.), Fox Valley Tech. Inst. (bd. dirs. 1982—). Clubs: West Bend Toastmasters (treas. 1984-85), Long Riders (Milw.). Lodges: Shriners, Odd Fellows (past noble grand master), Masons (past master). Avocations: golf, travel, camping. Home: 6897 Glacier Dr West Bend WI 53095 Office: Flexible Transport Inc PO Box 21875 Milwaukee WI 53221

TERRILL, MARILYN JEAN, psychologist, psychotherapist; b. Champaign, Ill., Apr. 1, 1950; d. Stanley Wallace and Vivian LaVerne (Benton) T.; m. Ted Lindberg, July 17, 1978; children: Shawn Terrill Lindberg, Danielle Lindberg Terrill. BA, U. Ill., 1972, MA, 1974, PhD, 1978. Lic. psychologist, Mich., Nebr.; cert. clin. psychologist, Nebr. Dir. children and family services Great Plains Mental Health Ctr., North Platte, Nebr., 1978-80; pvt. practice psychology North Platte, 1980-81; pvt. practice psychologist Humanistic Psychotherapy Ctr., Ann Arbor and Southfield, Mich., 1981-83; psychologist Profl. Psychol. Services, Trenton, Mich., 1982-83; dir. children, adolescent family program Psychol. Ctr., Marshall and Battle Creek, Mich., 1983-85; staff psychologist Kalamazoo (Mich.) Consultation Ctr., 1985—; cons. Lincoln County Welfare Dept., North Platte, 1978-81, Outpatient Chronic Pain Clinic, Marshall and Battle Creek, 1982-83; instr. Clague Community Edn. Ctr., Ann Arbor, 1982-83, Kellogg Community Coll. Adult Edn., Marshall and Battle Creek, 1983-85. Named one of Outstanding Young Women in Am.; recipient Am. World War Vets. scholarship. Mem. Am. Psychol. Assn., Assn. Women in Psychology, Mich. Psychol. Assn., Phi Beta Kappa, Phi Kappa Phi, Alpha Lambda Delta. Avocations: reading, aerobics, music, needlework, family time. Office: Kalamazoo Consultation Ctr 3227 S Westnedge Kalamazoo MI 48108

TERRY, JAMES ANDREW, III, clinical psychologist, administrator, consultant; b. Chgo., July 7, 1935; s. James Andrew and Gussie Ola (Jones) T. B.A. in History, Roosevelt U.; M.S., Ill. Tchrs. Coll., 1966; Ph.D. in Clin. Psychology, Northwestern U., 1978. Cert. high sch. history, supervision, adminstrn., Ill. History tchr. Chgo. Bd. Edn., 1957-63; dir. and supr. jobs project YMCA, Chgo., 1964-68; dir. services Ebony Mgmt. Assocs., Chgo., 1968-69; dir. Englewood Mental Health Clinic, 1969—; cons. to indsl. cos. and agys.; condr. seminars for Ministry Edn. and Culture, Freeport Bahamas. Fellow Northwestern U. Med. Sch.; recipient Health Services award Young Execs. in Politics, 1983. Mem. Am. Psychol. Assn., Ill. Psychol. Assn., Chgo. Psychol. Assn., Musicians Union, Kappa Alpha Psi. Roman Catholic. Contbr. articles to profl. jours. Home: 1916 S Hamlin St Chicago IL 60623 Office: 641 W 63d St Chicago IL 60621

TERSCHAN, FRANK ROBERT, lawyer; b. Dec. 25, 1949; s. Frank Joseph and Margaret Anna (Heidt) T.; m. Barbara Elizabeth Keily, Dec. 28, 1974; 1 child, Frank Martin. BA, Syracuse U., 1972; JD, U. Wis., 1975. Bar: Wis. 1976, U.S. Dist. Ct. (ea. and we. dists.) Wis. 1976, U.S. Ct. Appeals (7th cir.) 1979. From assoc. to ptnr. Frisch, Dudek & Slattery Ltd., Milw., 1975—. Treas., sec. Ville du Park Homeowners Assn., Mequon, Wis., 1985-86. Served with USCG, 1972-73. Mem. ABA, Wis. Bar Assn., Assn. Trial Lawyers Am., Wis. Assn. Trial Lawyers, Ins. Trial Counsel Wis. Republican. Lutheran. Avocations: swimming, coin collecting, reading, outdoor activities. Office: Frisch Dudek & Slattery Ltd 825 N Jefferson St Milwaukee WI 53202

TERTOCHA, JEAN-PAUL RICHARD, freelance producer; b. Decatur, Ill., Feb. 18, 1955; s. Richard Wayne and Andree Marcelle (Senelle) T.; m. Jennifer Lynn Rhodes, July 7, 1974 (div. July 1984); children: Jessica, Austin, Aubrey. News reporter WOZ Radio, Decatur, 1973-76; ind. field producer WCIA TV, Champaign, Ill., 1979-86; prodn. mgr. H.T.E. Prodns., Decatur, 1979—. Producer, dir., editor (TV show) O' Glorious Queen, 1982, (TV comml.) Decorteke, 1983; producer, dir. (record) X static Troubled Heart, 1985-86. Avocations: jeep safaries, bass guitar and keyboards, swimming, hiking. Home and Office: 724 W Macon Decatur IL 62522

TERVOLA, SHARON LOUISE, nurse, educator; b. Mountain Lake, Minn., Sept. 18, 1945; d. August H. Egdorf and Louise (Carter) Egdorf Fredrich; m. Robert Steven Tervola, May 21, 1966; children: Jennifer, Shawna, Tanya. LPN, Alexandria Tech. Inst., 1963-64; student, Worthington Jr. Coll., 1966-67; RN, Northland Community Coll., 1980; BS in Health Edn., Bemidji State U., 1982. RN, Minn. Emergency room nurse Clearwater County Hosp., Bagley, Minn., 1967-68; community health nurse Bagley Nursing Services, 1971-77; charge nurse Greensview Health Care Ctr., Bagley, 1978-82; nursing educator Detroit Lakes (Minn.) Area Vocat. Tech. Inst., 1982-85; community health nurse Redlake (Minn.) Comprehensive Health, 1985—. Recipient Dedicated Service award Redlake Tribal Council, 1985. Mem. AAUW, Nat. League Nurses. Avocations: shooting sports, canoeing. Home: Rt 1 Box 168 Bagley MN 56621 Office: Redlake Comprehensive Health Redlake MN 56671

TERWILLIGER, ROBERT HOMMEL, marketing executive; b. Newark, Nov. 21, 1946; s. Robert Hommel and Margaret Christine (Wager) T.; m. Pamela Lee McCreedy, May 23, 1970 (div. Dec. 1980); m. Patricia Ann Wiltrakis, Apr. 11, 1981; children: Robert Hommel III, James Christopher Shaw, Rachael Elizabeth. BA in Psychology, Hope Coll., 1968; MDiv, Western Theology Sem., 1972. Ordained to ministry Reformed Ch. Am. Sr. pastor Bethel Reformed Ch., Harvey, Ill., 1972-77, Hope Reformed Ch., Kalamazoo, Mich., 1977-80; mktg. mgr. Kellogg Co., Battle Creek, Mich., 1980-86; dir. mktg. CRC Publs., Grand Rapids, Mich., 1986—. elder Bethany Reformed Ch., Kalamazoo, 1983-85. Mem. Classis of Southwest Mich., Southwest Mich. Spina Bifida Assn. (pres. 1985, v.p. 1986). Avocations: golf, bowling, swimming, piano, reading. Home: 1019 Northampton Kalamazoo MI 49007 Office: CRC Publs 2850 Kalamazoo SE Grand Rapids MI 49560

TERZIC, BRANKO DUSAN, international consultant, engineer; b. Diepholz, W. Ger., June 19, 1947; came to U.S., 1950; s. Dusan Branko and Olivera (Beljakovic) T.; m. Judith Ware Antonic, Oct. 7, 1978; children—Dusan-Alexander, Elizabeth Alexandra Olivera, Branko G. III. B.S. in Energy Engring., U. Wis.-Milw., 1972. With Am. Appraisal Milw., 1970-72, 73-36; engr. Wis. Electric Power Co., Milw., 1972-73; v.p. Assoc. Utility Services, Milw., 1976-79; ptnr. Terzic & Mayer, Milw., 1979-81; mem. Wis. Pub. Service Commn., Madison, 1981-86; group v.p. The Associated Consulting Group. Chmn. Fifth Congl. Republican Orgn., 1975-77. Decorated comdr. Cross of Merit, Sovereign Mil. Order of Malta, Knight Grand Officer of Crown (Yugoslavia) Knight S.O.M. Constantine and St. George, Knight Order of Saints Maurice and Lazarus. Mem. Nat. Assn. Regulatory Utility Commrs. (chmn. engring. com. 1982—). Serbian Orthodox. Club: Milwaukee Athletic. Office: Associated Consulting Group 606 E Wisconsin Ave Box 92757 Milwaukee WI 53202

TESCHENDORF, ALAN DAVID, polygraph examiner; b. Bad Axe, Mich., June 21, 1957; s. Ward James and Maxine Mary (Witherspoon) T.; m. Sharon Katherine Brandt, July 23, 1983; 1 child, Ryan David. A in Applied Sci., Delta Coll., 1977; BA, Mich. State U., 1979. Police officer City of Crest Hill, Ill., 1980-84; li polygraph examiner, Bur. Forensic Scis. Ill. Dept. State Police, Fair iew Heights, 1984—. Mem. Am. Assn. Police Polygraphists, Ill. Polygraph Soc. (bd. dirs. 1987—), Profl. Office Help. Avocations: sports, hunting. Home: 704 Ostle Dr Collinsville IL 62234 Office: Ill Dept State Police Metro East Forensic Scis Lab 10023 Bunkum Rd Fairview Heights IL 62208

TESMER, NANCY ANN STUTLER, librarian; b. Akron, Ohio, Aug. 25, 1934; d. Ernest Lynn and Sophrona Rebecca (Pepper) Stutler; student U. Akron, 1952-54; B.A., Kent State U., 1956; m. Clifford Frank Haines, Aug. 20, 1960 (div.); m. John A. Tesmer, Sept. 10, 1980. Jr. asst. librarian E. Br. Library, Akron, 1956-59; hosp. librarian VA Hosp., Northampton, Mass., 1959-61; med. librarian VA Hosp., Brecksville, Ohio, 1961-65, chief librarian, 1965-73; assoc. chief librarian Cleve. VA Hosp., 1973-75, chief librarian, 1975—; chief Regional Library Service, 1986—. Mem. Med. Library Assn., N.E. Ohio Med. Library Assn., Zeta Tau Alpha. Home: 603 Tollis Pkwy Broadview Heights OH 44147 Office: 10000 Brecksville Rd Brecksville OH 44141

TESSMER, CRAIG ROBERT, mechanical engineer; b. Detroit, Feb. 22, 1952; s. Robert George and Claudine (Waterman) T.; m. Veronica Mulay, Mar. 6, 1982; 1 child, David Craig. BSME, U. Mich., 1975; postgrad., Keller Grad. Sch. Mgmt., Chgo., 1983—. Plant engr. Gen. Foods Corp., Battle Creek, Mich., 1975-78; sr. prin. engr. Baxter Travenol Labs., Inc., Deerfield, Ill., 1978-86; staff engr. Davy McKee Corp., Chgo., 1986—. Mem. Soc. Mfg. Engrs. Republican. Avocations: coin collecting, stamp collecting, snow skiing, sailing. Home: 1233 W Hampton Pl Palatine IL 60067 Office: Davy McKee Corp 300 S Riverside Plaza Suite 1800 Chicago IL 60606

TESZLEWICZ, ROBERT SAMUEL, custody investigator; b. Lansing, Mich., Nov. 7, 1952; s. William S. and Mary Jane (LaMacchia) T. AA, Lansing (Mich.) Community Coll., 1973; B in Social Work, Lewis U., 1975. Tchr. St. Patrick High Sch., Chgo., 1976-79; social worker Muskegon (Mich.) Cath. High Sch., 1979-83; fund raising coordinator Muskegon Cath. Schs., 1983-85; custody investigator Friend of the Ct., Muskegon, 1984—; exec. dir. New Horizons, Inc. of Western Mich., 1984—. Mem. Ams. for Substance Abuse Prevention, Mich. Orgn. Human Rights. Democrat. Avocation: photography. Office: New Horizons Inc of Western Mich 1593 Peck Muskegon MI 49441

TETERYCZ, BARBARA ANN, entrepreneur, advertising executive; b. Chgo., Jan. 23, 1952; d. Sylvester and Anne (Deutsch) T.; m. Robert Nathan Estes, Oct. 13, 1984. B.A., U. Ill., 1974; postgrad. Parkland Coll., 1975-76, U. Ill., 1976-77. Teller, First Fed. of Champaign, Ill., 1974-75; cashier Korger Co., Champaign, 1975-77; merchandise rep. RustCraft Greeting Cards, Champaign, 1977-78; sales rep. Hockenberg-Rubin, Champaign, 1978, John Morrell & Co., Champaign, 1978-80; account exec. WICD TV, Champaign, 1981-86 ; owner Left-Handed Compliments, Champaign. Contbg. editor mag. Champaign County Bus. Reports, 1986. Vol. Am. Cancer Soc., 1985, U. Ill. Alumni Assn., 1985, Com. to Elect Beth Beauchamp to City Council, Champaign, 1984. Ill. State scholar, 1970-74. Mem. Ad Club of Champaign, Women's Bus. Council Urbana C. of C., Champaign C. of C. (pub. relations com.), Nat. Assn. Female Execs. (network dir.), Alpha Omega. Roman Catholic. Avocations: reading; writing; bicycling; bodybuilding. Home: 1615 Harbor Point Dr PO Box 873 Champaign IL 61820 Office: Left-Handed Compliments 723 E Neil St PO Box 873 Champaign IL 61820

TETRICK, RICHARD WILSON, mechanical engineer; b. Clarksburg, W.Va., May 29, 1957; s. Richard Frederick and Rebecca Ann (Wilson) T.; m. Kimberly Lynn Southworth, June 27, 1981; children: Andrea Rebecca, Jessica Aileen. BSME, W.Va. U., 1980. Maintenance foreman Weirton (W.Va.) Steel, 1980-83; mfg. engr. BF Goodrich, Marietta, Ohio, 1983—. Democrat. Methodist. Avocations: golf, woodworking, family activities. Home: 1039 Ann St Parkersburg WV 26101 Office: BF Goodrich Oak Grove Marietta OH 45750

TETTAMBEL, MELICIEN A(NN), osteopathic obstetrician-gynecologist; b. St. Louis, July 17, 1951; d. Michael Nicholas and Agnes (Olinski) T.; m. William John Elliott, Feb. 20, 1981. BS in Biol. Sci., Quincy Coll., 1972; DO, Kirksville Coll. Osteo. Medicine, 1978. Diplomate Am. Bd. Osteo. Medicine. Intern South Bend (Ind.) Osteo. Hosp., 1978-79; resident in ob-gyn. Normandy Hosp., St. Louis, 1979-83; practice osteopathic medicine specialing in ob-gyn. St. Louis, 1983-85; asst. clin. prof. ob-gyn., instr. osteo. manipulative medicine Chgo. Coll. Osteo. Medicine, 1986—; preceptor ob-gyn. for housestaff at Normandy Hosp., St. Louis, 1983-85, dir. resident clinics ob-gyn.; clin. instr. ob-gyn and osteo. medicine, Chgo., 1986. Recipient Electron Microscopy award NSF, 1972, Mead Johnson clin. research award, 1981. Mem. AMA, Am. Osteo. Assn., Am. Acad. Osteopathy, Am. Coll. Osteo. Obstetricians and Gynecologists, Cranial Acad. Osteopathy, Ill. Assn. Osteo. Physicians, St. Louis Gynecol. Soc. Roman Catholic.

TEWARI, RAM PRATAP, microbiology educator, researcher; b. Faizabad, India, Oct. 1, 1934; came to U.S., 1963; s. Raghubir Prasad and Ramrati (Pandey) T.; m. Gyan Mati Pandey, May 18, 1986; children: Arun, Shashi, Sheela. BS, Lucknow U., India, 1956; DVM, Agra U., India, 1960; MS, Agra U., 1962; SM in Hygiene, Harvard U., 1964; PhD, Ohio State U., 1966. Research fellow Ohio State U., Columbus, 1966-67; A.E.C. fellow Oak Ridge (Tenn.) Assoc. U., 1969; fellow Karolinska Inst., Stockholm, 1970; from asst. prof. to assoc. prof. microbiology Rutgers U., New Brunswick, N.J., 1967-75; dir. clin. microbiology Perth Amboy (N.J.) Gen. Hosp., 1971-75; prof. So. Ill. U., Springfield, 1975—; vis. scientist Kothari Ctr. for Gastroenterology, Calcutta, India, 1979—, UN TOKTEN Program, 1985—, Am. Assn. Immunologist Program, 1983—; cons. in field. Contbr. numerous articles to profl. jours. and chpts. to books. Grantee NIH, 1968-73, 73-75, 72-75, 72-73, 75-78, 79-83, 86—, Busch Found., 1972-75, Research Corp., 1973-76, U.S. Army , 1973-76; recipient research support Ill. Heart Assn., 1984-86, 85-87, So. Ill. U. Sch. Medicine Research Funds, 1985-86. Fellow Am. Acad. Microbiology, Infectious Diseases Soc. Am.; mem. Soc. Experimental Pathology, Am. Assn. Immunologists, Am. Soc. Microbiology, Internat. Soc. Human and Animal Mycology, Mycological Soc. Am., Med. Mycology Soc. Americas (chmn. com. on future direction research in fungus diseases, fin. com.), Med. Mycology Soc. N.Y., Am. Thoracic Soc., Reticuloendothelial Soc. Home: 47 Frontier Lake Dr Springfield IL 62707 Office: So Ill U Sch Medicine Dept Med Microbiology/Immunology PO Box 3926 Springfield IL 62708

THAIN, JOHN GRIFFITHS, laboratory administrator; b. Hayes, Middlesex, Eng., Sept. 27, 1937; s. Charles J. and Dilys D. (Griffiths) T.; came to U.S., 1958; student Acton Tech. Coll., 1955-58, Ind. U., 1958-63; A.S. in Bus. Adminstrn., U. New Haven, 1980; m. Jacqueline M. Hart, Nov. 3, 1962; children—Jeremy Guy, Richard Gary, Jennifer Ann. Lab. asst. Castrol Ltd., Hayes, Middlesex, U.K., 1953-58; lab. technician Miles Labs., Inc., Elkhart, Ind., 1958-61, coordinator mfg. records, 1961-67, coordinator packaging devel. and labelling, 1967-72, adminstr. regulatory affairs and inspections, 1972-74, supr. records and auditing, 1974-75, mgr. corp. quality assurance-tng. services, 1976-79, mgr. quality assurance, corp. research, 1979-86, mgr. regulary compliane corp. quality assurance, 1986—. Mem. Regulatory Affairs Profl. Soc., Am. Soc. Quality Control. Episcopalian. Home: 59527 Ridgewood Dr Goshen IN 46526 Office: 1127 Myrtle St Elkhart IN 46514

THAKORE, NARENDRA RAMANLAL, investment company executive, service executive; b. Padra, Gujrat, India, Aug. 18, 1935; came to U.S., 1981; s. Ramanlal Jivanlal and Nandgauri R. Nandgauri T.; m. Jyotsna Purnanand Bhatt, Mar. 26, 1963; children: Gnan, Jigna. BS, U. Baroda, India, 1955. Supr., head printing dept. Shree Bansidhar Textile Mills, Ahmedabad, Gujrat, India, 1955-63, Calico Mills, Bombay, 1963-67; mgr. printing dept. East India Textile Mills, Faridabad, 1967-75; supt. processing Patel Mills, Ahmedabad, 1975-81; owner, mgr. Suburbanite Motel, Medina, Ohio, 1981—; ptnr., adminstr. Murphy's Motel, Stronsville, Ohio, 1985—; pres. East Ind. Investment Corp., Medina, 1985—. Mem. Medina C. of C. Hindu. Avocation: literature. Home and Office: 2909 Medina Rd Medina OH 44256

THAR, FERDINAND AUGUST (BUD), trade company executive; b. Paw Paw, Mich., Oct. 26, 1940; s. James Ferdinand and Louise Olga (Schmidt) T.; m. Siri Ashelman, Jan. 28, 1967; Jonathan Justin, Christina Sheri, Amanda Hope. BA, Mich. State U., 1964; postgrad., Boston U., 1964-65, Am. U., 1968-72, U. Ga. Sch. Internat. Law, 1978. Exec. dir. Ctr. Internat. Transp., East Lansing, Mich., 1979-82; program officer Govtl. Affairs Inst., Washington, 1964-73; assoc. dir. Battle Creek (Mich.) Unltd., 1980-83; pres. Eagle Trade, Battle Creek, 1983—; exec. dir. Great Lakes World Trade Ctr., Detroit, 1986; U.S. del. 1st World Agrl. Fair, New Delhi, India, 1959-60, Internat. Farm Youth Exchange, Israel, 1962; mem. White House Conf. Internat. Cooperation, Washington, 1972, White House Conf. Balanced Growth, Washington, 1978; mem. NRC, Washington, 1979—, transp. research bd. Intergovtl. Relations Com., 1985—; guest govts. of France, Fed. Republic of Germany, Jamaica, Yugoslavia, Peoples Republic of China, and British R.R.s, French Nat. R.R., 1979; author devel. proposal agribus. project, 1982; cons. Great Lakes Regional Commn., Ann Arbor, Mich., 1984-85, Japanese Electronics Assn., Washington and Japan, 1984-86; instr. Ednl. Services with People's Republic China, 1987—. Author: Influence of International Travel on Vocational Choice, 1963, Rural Youth in Michigan, 1964. Leader youth vol. group, Costa Rica, 1963. Mem. Am. Assn. Polit. Sci., Nat. Govs. Assn. (staff dir. 1973-83, advisor 1980),World Trade Ctrs. Assn., Internat. Farm Youth Exchange (pres. 1963), Gideons Internat.

THAYER, CRAIG BRUCE, radiologist; b. Rockford, Ill., Apr. 17, 1949; s. Bruce Clothier and Wanda Jean (Harber) T.; m. Barbara Lee Carson, Oct. 2, 1977. BA in Biology, Northwestern U., 1971; MD, U. Ill., Chgo., 1975. Cert. diagnostic radiologist. Resident in diagnostic radiology Northwestern Meml. Hosp., Chgo., 1975-79; radiologist Meth. Med. Ctr., Peoria, Ill., 1979-80, S. Suburban Hosp., Hazel Crest, Ill., 1980-82, MacNeal Hosp., Berwyn, Ill., 1982—; adv. com. diagnostic med. sonography Triton Coll. Contbr. articles to profl. jours. Bd. dirs. Am. Cancer Soc., Orland Park, Ill., 1985-86. Mem. AMA, Radiol. Soc. N.Am., Am. Inst. Ultrasound in Medicine, Am. Assn. Weather Observers, Sand Ridge Audobon Soc. Presbyterian. Avocations: photography, meteorology, fine wines.

THEESFELD, CAROLE ANN, educator; b. Elmwood Park, Ill., Apr. 29, 1943; d. Howard Maurice and Ann (Romcoe) Kumlin; m. David Alan Theesfeld, Aug. 7, 1965; children: Michael Dean, Michelle Sue. BS in Edn., Ill. State U., 1965; MS in Math. Edn., U. Ill., 1968. Cert. tchr., Ill. Tchr. math. Fremd High Sch., Palatine, Ill., 1965-70, Harper Jr. Coll., Palatine, 1970—; tchrs. aide math. Arlington Heights (Ill.) Grade Schs. Dist. 25, 1976-82; tchr. math. Rolling Meadows (Ill.) High Sch., 1982-83, East Leyden High Sch., Franklin Park, Ill., 1983-84, Addison (Ill.) Trail High Sch., 1984—; dir. plays Addison Trail High Sch., 1984—. Author: Essentials of Algebra (TRB), 1987. Mem. Nat. Council Tchrs. Math., Ill. Council Tchrs. Math, Kappa Mu Epsilon. Lutheran. Club: Addison Trail Fishing (sponsor run 1985—). Avocations: walking, swimming, fishing, crafts, sewing. Home: 712 N Kennicott Arlington Heights IL 60004 Office: Addison Trail High Sch 213 N Lombard Addison IL 60101

THEIN, ANTHONY PETER, music educator, administrator; b. Montevideo, Minn., Dec. 28, 1938; s. John Joseph and Rose Katharine (Thissen) T. B.A., St. John's U., 1960; M.M., Ind. U., 1967; Ph.D., U. Minn., 1978. Vocal music dir. Mapleton Pub. Schs. (Minn.), 1960-61; prof. theory, history and voice Mayville (N.D.) State U., 1963—, chmn. music dept., 1980-81, chmn. div. humanities and social sci., 1981—; tenor soloist U.S., Can., Europe, 1960—; music adjudicator, N.D., Minn., Can., 1963—. Founding mem., v.p. West Winds Council Arts, Mayville, 1980-81. Bush Found. grantee, 1969-75. Mem. Music Educators Nat. Conf., NEA, Am. Choral Dirs. Assn., Nat. Assn. Tchrs. of Singing. Club: Community. Lodges: Elks, Eagles, K.C. Home: 343 3d Ave NE Mayville ND 58257 Office: Mayville State U Mayville ND 58257

THEIS, FRANK GORDON, judge, past mem. Democratic Nat. Com.; b. Yale, Kans., June 26, 1911; s. Peter F. and Maude (Cook) T.; m. Marjorie Riddle, Feb. 1, 1939 (dec. 1970); children: Franklin, Roger. A.B. cum laude, U. Kans., 1933; J.D., U. Mich., 1936. Bar: Kans. 1937. Since practiced in Arkansas City; sr. mem. firm Frank G. Theis, 1957—; atty. Kans. Tax Commn., 1937-39; chief counsel OPS for Kans., 1951-52; U.S. dist. judge Dist. Kans., 1967—; chief judge 1977-81, active sr. status, 1981—; Pres. Young Democrats Kan., 1942-46, Kans. Dem. Club, 1944-46; chmn. Kans. Dem. Com., 1955-60; mem. nat. adv. com. polit. orgn. Dem. Nat. Com., 1956-58, nat. committeeman from Kans., 1957-67; chmn. Dem. Midwest Conf., 1959-60; Dem. nominee for Kans., Supreme Ct., 1950, U.S. Senate, 1960. Mem. Kans. Jr. Bar Conf. (pres. 1942), Am., Kans. bar assns., Phi Beta Kappa, Phi Delta Phi, Sachem. Presbyn. Club: Mason. Office: U S Dist Ct 414 U S Courthouse 401 N Market St Wichita KS 67202

THELEN, J. CHRISTINE, physician, retired; b. Madison, Wis., May 15, 1913; s. Rolf and Catherine Elizabeth (Phelps) T. BS in Med. Sci., U. Wis., 1934; MD, Med. Coll. Va., 1937. Intern Mercy Hosp., Cedar Rapids, Iowa, 1937-38; coll. physician Greensboro (N.C.) Coll., 1939-41; gen. resident Deaconess Hosp., Milw., 1941-42; ob-gyn resident Lying-In Hosp., Chgo., 1942-44, Lewis Meml. Hosp., Chgo., 1944-45; staff mem. Jackson Clinic, Madison, 1945-50; practice medicine specializing in ob-gyn Wichita, 1951-80. Bd. dirs. YWCA, Wichita, Family Consultation Services, Wichita, Big Bros.-Big Sisters, Wichita, United Way of Wichita & Sedgwick County, Women's Crisis Ctr. Adv. Bd. Named Woman of Achievement, Women in Communication, 1975. Fellow Am. Coll. Ob-gyn (life); AMA, Sedgwick County Med. Soc., Kans. Med. Soc. Republican. Mem. United Ch. of Christ. Club: Town (Wichita). Lodge: Zonta (gov. dist. VII 1970-72). Avocations: travel, photography. Home: 1738 N Roosevelt Wichita KS 67208

THENO, DANIEL O'CONNELL, former state legislator; b. Ashland, Wis., May 8, 1947; s. Maurice William and Janet Nora (Humphrey) T.; B.S., U. Wis., Madison, 1969; student, Brazil, 1969; m. Sue Burnham, June 16, 1973; children—Scott Patrick, Tad William. Tchr. agr. public schs., Oregon, Wis., 1969-72; mem. Wis. State Senate, 1972-87; mayor, Ashland, 1987—; mem. Wis. Bldg. Commn. Named Superior Hon. Alumni, U. Wis., 1977; recipient Vet. Recognition award, 1978. Mem. Coll. Agr. Alumni Assn., U. Wis. Alumni Assn., Iron Cross Honor Soc. Clubs: Ashland County (Wis.) Republican, Elks, K.C.

THEODORE, GEORGE T., private investigator; b. Elmhurst, Ill., July 7, 1940; s. Ted and Alice (Nicopoulos) T. Cert. genealogy, Elmhurst Coll., 1965; cert. electronics, Triton Coll., 1967, cert. locksmithing, 1969. Pres. Tracer's, Inc., Elmhurst, 1961—. Mem. Am. Security Council, Nat. Genealogy Soc. Home: 197 Addison St Elmhurst IL 60126 Office: Tracers Inc 122 N York Rd Elmhurst IL 60126

THEODORE, WILLIAM JAMES, educational administrator; b. Chgo., Feb. 6, 1947; s. George and Winnie (Stafford) T.; m. Dana Yeargin, Mar. 1, 1980 (div. Nov. 1981). A.B., U. Mich., 1969, A.M., 1972; Ed.S., Wichita State U., 1981. Tchr. Tecumseh High Sch., Mich., 1970-72, Orleans Parish, La., 1972-76; prin. Nickerson sch. dist., Kans., 1980-82; tchr. Jefferson Parish schs., Gretna, La., 1976-80, 1982-83; asst. prin. Arch Blenk High Sch., Gretna, 1983-84; prin., supt., Hillcrest Rural Sch. Dist., Cuba, Kans., 1984—. Mem. Nat. Assn. Secondary Prins., Nat. Assn. Elem. Prins., Kans. Unified Sch. Adminstrs., Kans. Assn. Elem. Prins., Phi Kappa Phi. Avocation: sports. Home: PO Box 85 Agenda KS 66930 Office: Hillcrest Rural Schs PO Box 167 Cuba KS 66940

THEODOROU, CAROL ANN, school administrator; b. Chgo., Dec. 28, 1938; d. Speros Harry and May (Patros) Stavrakos; m. Philip C. Theodorou, Dec. 29, 1957; children: Stefanie, Anastasia, Suzanne, Kevin. BA, Govs. State U., 1974; MEd, U. Ill., 1984, postgrad., 1986—. Asst. prin. Community High Sch. Dist. 218, Oak Lawn, Ill., 1974—. Chmn. bd. trustees Pilgrim Faith United Ch. of Christ, Oak Lawn, 1985-86, bd. dirs., 1983-86. Mem. Ill. Dirs. of Student Activities (treas. 1985—), Assn. for Supervision and Curriculum Devel., Ill. Women Adminstrs., Ill. Assn. for Supervision and Curriculum Devel., Ill. Deans Assn., Chgo. Deans Assn. Democrat. Avocations: reading, singing, bicycling, walking.

THEODOSIOU, GEORGE EVANGELOS, physicist; b. Mantamados, Mytilene, Greece, Oct. 1, 1946; came to U.S., 1969; s. Evangelos Eustratios and Eleni Thelxioi (Voyiatzi) T.; m. Katerina George Skoufi, Oct. 20, 1984. BS in Physics, Athens Nat. U., Greece, 1964; MS in Physics, U. Notre Dame, 1972; PhD in Physics, Cornell U., 1977. Grad. fellow N.R.C. Demokritos, Athens, 1968-69; teaching asst. U. Notre Dame, Ind., 1969-72; research asst. Cornell U., Ithaca, N.Y., 1972-77; research assoc. Argonne (Ill.) Nat. Lab., 1977-80; research investigator U. Pa., Phila., 1980-81, resident asst. prof., 1981-87; physicist Fermilab, Batavia, Ill., 1987—. Contbr. articles to profl. jours.; inventor, patentee in field. Mem. Am. Phys. Soc., Union of Concerned Scientists, Hellenic Profl. Soc. Ill., Smithsonian Assocs. Christian Eastern Orthodox.

THEYS, FELIX LIONEL, mechanical engineer; b. Beaverdale, Pa., Sept. 18, 1938; s. Felix Joseph and Agnes Celina (Draye) T.; m. Carol Marie Harvanec, May 19, 1962; children—Deborah, Scott, Kristen, Amy. Student in mech. engring. Cleve. State U., 1967-72. Registered profl. engr., Ohio, Ky., Ind., Wis., Calif., Pa., Okla., Fla. Machinist Donn Products, Westlake, Ohio, 1960-64; project engr. Evans & Assocs., Cleve., 1964-72; assoc. Denk-Kish Assocs., 1972-78; cons. engr. F. L. Theys Assocs., 1978—. Chmn. Medina County Bd. Appeals, 1984—. Served with USAF, 1956-60. Mem. Am. Cons. Engrs. Assn., Ohio Assn. Cons. Engrs., Cleve. Cons. Engrs. Council, Smoke Control Assn., ASHRAE. Republican. Mem. United Ch. of Christ (elder). Office: F L Theys Assocs 672 E Royalton Rd Cleveland OH 44147

THIBODEAU, GARY ARTHUR, university administrator; b. Sioux City, Iowa, Sept. 26, 1938; m. Emogene J. McCarville, Aug. 1, 1964; children: Douglas James, Beth Ann. BS, Creighton U., 1962; MS, S.D. State U., 1967, S.D. State U., 1970; PhD, S.D. State U., 1971. Profl. service rep. Baxter Lab., Inc., Deerfield, Ill., 1963-65; tchr., researcher dept. biology S.D. State U., Brookings, 1965-76, asst. to v.p. for acad. affairs, 1976-80, v.p. for adminstrn., 1980-85; chancellor U. Wis., River Falls, 1985—; Mem. investment com. U. Wis., River Falls; trustee W. Cen. Wis. Consortium U. Wis. System; bd. dirs. U. Wis. at River Falls Found. Author: Textbook of Anatomy and Physiology, 1987; Author: (with others) Structure and Function of the Body, 1982, Basic Concepts in Anatomy and Physiology, 1983, Athletic Injury Assessment, 1985. Mem. AAAS. Office: U Wis Chancellors Office 116 North Hall River Falls WI 54022

THICKINS, GRAEME RICHARD, marketing consultant; b. Perth, Australia, Apr. 4, 1946; came to U.S., 1952; s. Richard Percy and Lucie Joy (McDiarmid) T.; m. Jane Elizabeth Bantle, Nov. 6, 1969; children: Jeffrey, Christopher, Sarah. AA, Austin State Jr. Coll., 1967; postgrad. U. Minn., 1967-70. Editor Data 100 Corp., Edina, Minn., 1970-72; pub. relations and promotion writer, editor MTS Systems Corp., Eden Prairie, Minn., 1972-73; dir. pub. relations services, writer, account exec. The Communication Coalition, Inc., Edina, 1973-74; free-lance writer, cons., Mpls., 1974-75; mktg. communications writer, asst. mgr. Medtronic, Inc., Mpls., 1975-77; mktg. services mgr., communications mgr., Am. Med. Systems, Inc., Mpls., 1977-78; account exec. D'Arcy-MacManus & Masius, Twin Cities, Minn., 1978; cons. editorial services, corp. communications Control Data Corp., Mpls., 1978-79, mgr. editorial services, 1979, mgr. promotion lit., 1980, mgr. creative services, 1981, mgr. advt. and promotion, systems and services co., 1982; cons. mktg., advt., direct mail, pub. relations, Mpls., 1975-82; founder, pres. GT&A, Inc., high tech. advt. and mktg., Mpls., 1982—; mem. Minn. High Tech. Council. Bd. dirs. Cystic Fibrosis Found., Minn.; co-chairperson mktg. and communications 1986 Minn. Orch. Symphony Ball. Recipient numerous awards and certs. of excellence from various profl. assns. Mem. Advt. Fedn. of Minn., Midwest Direct Mktg. Assn., Direct Mktg. Assn., Am. Inst. Graphic Arts, Med. Alley Assn., Phi Gamma Delta. Clubs: Flagship Athletic (Eden Prairie). Avocations: tennis, swimming, surfing, skiing. Home and Office: 8135 Kentucky Circle West Bloomington MN 55438

THIEBAUTH, BRUCE EDWARD, advertising executive; b. Bronxville, N.Y., Oct. 30, 1947; s. Bruce and Margaret Evelyn (Wiederhold) T.; student Colby Coll., Waterville, Maine, 1965-66, Pace Coll., 1971; B.A. magna cum laude in Bus. Adminstrn. and Sociology, Bellevue Coll., 1972; m. Sherry Ann Proplesch, Aug. 31, 1968; 1 son, Bruce Revere. Credit mgr. Gen. Electric Credit Corp., Croton Falls, N.Y., 1971; ops. mgr. Bridal Pubs., Inc., Omaha, 1972-73; regional mgr. Bridal Fair, Inc., Omaha, 1973-74, sales mgr., 1974-76, chmn. bd., pres., 1976—; dir. Multi-Media Group, Inc., Fair Communications, Inc., Bridal Fair mag. Served with USAF, 1966-70; Vietnam conflict. Recipient Nat. Def. Service medal; Somers League citizenship and pub. service award, Somers, N.Y., 1965. Mem. Nat. Small Bus. Assn., Nat. Radio Broadcasters Assn., Nat. Assn. Broadcasters, Airline Passengers Assn., Bellevue Coll. Alumni Assn. Republican. Congregationalist. Office: 8901 Indian Hills Dr Omaha NE 68114

THIEL, JOHN CHARLES, association executive; b. Chester, Pa., Mar. 18, 1945; s. August and Anne Marie (Kane) T.; m. Alethia Ann Morris, Dec. 20, 1969; children: Adam Kane, Clare Alethia. A.A., St. Charles Coll., 1965; B.A., Coll. William and Mary, 1968; M.S., U. Tenn., 1971; Ed.S., U. Colo., 1972; postgrad., Mich. State U., 1972-73. Cert. assn. exec., 1985. Tchr. public schs. Williamsburg, Va., 1968-70; Mott Found. intern Mich. State U., 1972-73; prin. Okemos (Mich.) Public Schs., 1973-77; asst. exec. dir. for edn. Am. Dietetic Assn., Chgo., 1977-79; acting exec. dir. Am. Dietetic Assn., 1980; exec. dir. Am. Dental Assts. Assn., 1981-87, Am. Dental Hygienists Assn., Chgo., 1987—. Mem. Nat. Commn. for Health Certifying Agys. (chmn., exec. council, speaker gen. assembly), Am. Soc. Allied Health Professions, Am. Soc. Assn. Execs., Chgo. Soc. Assn. Execs. (bd. dirs.). Roman Catholic. Home: 810 Fair Oaks Oak Park IL 60302 Office: Am Dental Hygienists Assn 444 N Michigan Ave Suite 3400 Chicago IL 60611

THIEL, RUTH ELEANOR, real estate broker; b. Chgo., June 11, 1930; d. Frank A. and Lucille L. (Bromm) Dell; m. Joseph Donald Thiel, Sept. 30, 1950; children—Michael F., Jeffrey D., Patti Thiel Fricks, Mary Beth Thiel Cramer, Tracy J. Thiel Carroll. A.A., Evanston Twp. Community Coll., 1950; grad. Realtors Inst., 1972. Sales assoc. Indian Hill Realty, Winnetka, Ill., 1967; v.p., mgr. Mitchell Bros. Realtors, Northbrook, Ill., 1972-75; exec. v.p., gen. mgr. Century 21 Mitchell Bros., Evanston, Ill., 1975-82; v.p. Koenig & Strey Realtors, 1982-87; sr. v.p., 1987—. Mem. State of Ill. Real Estate Examining Com., 1977—, Evanston Econ. Devel. Com., 1979; treas. North Shore Assn. Retarded, 1977-79; mem. instl. rev. com. St. Francis Hosp., 1981—; mem. Evanston Zoning Bd., 1983-85; pres. Evanston Library Friends, 1984-86; alderman 2d Ward, City of Evanston, 1985-86. Recipient Ill. Women's Council of Realtors Woman of the Year award, 1979; Service award City of Hope, North Shore Assn. for Retarded, 1977. Mem. Nat. Assn. Realtors (bd. dirs. 1978—), Ill. Assn. Realtors (exec. com. 1979, bd. dirs. 1977-85, Realtor of Yr. award 1984), North Shore Bd. Realtors (dir. 1970-80), Evanston North Shore Bd. Realtors (pres. 1978), Women's Council Realtors (state pres. 1977), Women in Real Estate (award 1980). Clubs: Woman of Evanston, Univ., YWCA, Million Dollar, Zonta Internat. Home: 1221 Greenwood St Evanston IL 60201 Office: Koenig & Strey Realtors 601 Green Bay Rd Wilmette IL 60091

THIELEN, JAMES MICHAEL, manufacturing company executive; b. Racine, Wis., May 6, 1926; s. Michael William and Margaret Mary (Groenke) T.; m. Helen Mae Ruenzel, Apr. 28, 1951; children: Michael, Claudia, Mark, Rebecca, Robert. Student, U. Wis., Racine, 1946-48; BS, Marquette U., 1950. Asst. plant mgr. Simmons Co., Munster, Ind., 1950-70; v.p. mfg. Berko Electric Co., Michigan City, Ind., 1970-77; gen. mgr., v.p. Hively Mfg. Co., Inc., Roanne, Ind., 1977-79; sr. v.p. Alsons Corp., Hillsdale, Mich., 1979—. Councilman Crown Point (Ind.) City Council, 1967-70. Served with USN, 1944-46, CBI. Republican. Roman Catholic. Club: Hillsdale Golf and Country. Lodge: Elks. Avocations: golf, fishing, boating. Home: 4 Azalea Ct Hillsdale MI 49242 Office: Alsons Corp 42 Union St Hilsdale MI 49242

THIESSEN, DAVID RAY, educator; b. Winchester, Ky., Aug. 22, 1940; s. Isaac Holzrichter and Margaret Grace (Richards) T.; m. Ximena Ann Brumitt, Aug. 1, 1965; children—Timothy David, Tamara Ximena. B.S., Wheaton Coll., 1962; M.A. in Edn., U. Chgo., 1964; M.S. in Physics, Purdue U., 1970. Cert. tchr., Ill. Tchr. pub. sch., Wheeling, Ill., 1964-84, Deerfield, Ill., 1984—; computer cons. Lake County Computer Tech. Consortium, Grayslake, Ill., 1984, Micro labs., Highland Park, Ill., 1984, Sch. Dist. 214, Mt. Prospect, Ill., 1980-84, Sch. Dist. 113, Highland Park, 1984, Micro Ideas, Glenview, Ill., 1982. Mem. Soccer Parents Com. Arlington Heights, Ill., 1979; soccer coach, 1977-84. Named Outstanding Young Educator, Mt. Prospect Jaycees, 1968, Master Tchr., Gov. Ill., 1984. Mem. NEA, Am. Assn. Physics Tchrs. Republican. Presbyterian. Clubs: Call Apple, Boats/U.S. Avocations: computers, sailing, camping, tennis, racquetball. Home: 215 W Hintz Rd Arlington Heights IL 60004 Office: Deerfield High Sch 1959 N Waukegan Rd Deerfield IL 60015

THIEWES, RONALD CHARLES, tax accountant, lawyer; b. Winona, Minn., July 14, 1946; s. Harold Frank and Marian Rose (Fisher) T.; m. Barbara Ann Erickson, Mar. 16, 1974; children—Joseph Gerard, Mary Elizabeth. B.A., St. Mary's Coll., 1968; J.D., St. Louis U., 1974; LL.M. in Tax, Washington U., St. Louis, 1975. Bar: Mo. 1974, Minn. 1975, U.S. Tax Ct. 1975, U.S. Ct. Claims 1982, U.S. Supreme Ct. 1979. Tax supr. Hurdman & Cranstoun, CPAs, Kansas City, Mo., 1978-79; asst. tax mgr. Kansas City Power & Light Co., 1979-83; tax. mgr. Troupe, Kehoe, Whiteaker & Kent, Kansas City, 1983—. Editor Mo. Taxation Law and Practice, 1981, 82, 85; contbr. articles to profl. jours. Mem. Kansas City Citizens Assn., Kansas City Consensus. Decorated Silver Star medal. Mem. ABA, Mo. Bar Assn., Kansas City Bar Assn., Kansas City Lawyers Assn., Kansas City Citizens Assn. Republican. Roman Catholic. Home: 1408 NW 67th St Kansas City MO 64118 Office: Troupe Kehoe Whiteaker & Kent 900 Penntower Office Ctr 3100 Broadway Kansas City MO 64111

THIMJON, ROBERT JEROME, controller; b. Breckenridge, Minn., Feb. 6, 1952; s. Marvin Herman and Marie (Buck) T.; m. Joan Louise Budahl, May 18, 1974; children: Lisa Marie, Sarah Jane. BA, Augustana Coll., 1974; MBA, U. S.D., 1981. CPA, S.D. Audit sr. Deloitte Haskins & Sells, Mpls., 1974-78; audit mgr. Eide Helmeke & Co., Sioux Falls, S.D., 1978-80; v.p. fin. Hegg Cos., Sioux Falls, 1980-83; developer, chief fin. officer Marathon Investments, Omaha, 1983-85; fin. cons. Sioux Falls and Omaha, 1983-85; controller Ramkota, Inc., Sioux Falls, 1985—; adj. instr. bus. Augustana Coll., Sioux Falls, 1979-84. Pres. Minnehaha County Vis. Nurses Assn., Sioux Falls, 1984. Mem. Beta Gamma Sigma. Democrat. Lutheran. Lodge: Rotary (pres. Sioux Falls 1986). Avocations: tennis, activities with children, biking, photography. Home: 2908 S Holly Sioux Falls SD 57105 Office: Ramkota Inc 2600 N Louise Sioux Falls SD 57107

THIMM, RONALD GERARD, accountant; b. Hartford, Wis., Aug. 9, 1955; s. Harold George and Mary Lou (Mueller) T.; m. Barbra Ann Ehmke,

Dec. 2, 1978; children: Andrea, Richard, Matthew. BBA in Acctg., U. Wis., Milw., 1978, MBA, 1984. CPA, Wis. Cost analyst Chrysler Outboard, Hartford, 1975-77; cost acct. Aqua-Chem, Inc., Milw., 1978, staff acct., 1979, fin. analyst, 1979-81, asst. treas., 1981—, treas. polit. action com., 1986—. Mem. Am. Inst. CPA's, Wis. Inst. CPA's, Milw. IBM Personal Computer Users Group. Roman Catholic. Avocation: golf. Office: Aqua-Chem Inc PO Box 421 Milwaukee WI 53027

THINNES, KIMBERLY ANN, nurse; b. Cin., Sept. 19, 1956; d. Robert Louis and Patricia Louise (Staehlin) T. Student Ohio State U., 1974-75; diploma in Nursing, Miami Valley Hosp. Sch. Nursing, Dayton, Ohio, 1979; student Wright State U., 1983-84, BS in Mgmt. Nursing Services, Mt. St. Joseph Coll., 1987. Registered nurse, Ohio. Primary scrub nurse U. Ala. Hosp., Birmingham, 1980-81; surg. asst. Thoracic and Cardiovascular Assocs., San Antonio, 1981; charge nurse ICU, Kimberly Nurses, San Antonio, 1981-83; nurse surgery/recovery SW Ambulatory Surg. Ctr., San Antonio, 1982-83; charge nurse ICU, Grandview Hosp., Dayton, 1983-84; radiology/spl. procedures nurse, 1984-85, dir. central distbn. and linen distbn., 1985—; lectr. in field; vol. San Antonio Marathon Med. Team, 1982. Coach, coordinator hosp. volleyball teams, 1984-85; mem. campaign com. United Way, 1986; coach, coordinator hosp. team Dayton Battle of Businesses, 1986. Mem. Miami Valley Hosp. Sch. Nursing Alumni Assn., Phi Mu. Club: Excel Investment (treas. 1984-85, Dayton). Home: 63 Glencroft Pl Centerville OH 45459 Office: Grandview Hosp 405 Grand Ave Dayton OH 45405

THOEN-PASZKIEWICZ, MARY ROSE, business educator, consultant; b. Winona, Minn., Oct. 7, 1949; d. David J. and Mary R. (Repinski) Paszkiewicz; m. Merlin A. Thoen; children: Gregory, Michael David, Heather. BS, Winona State U., 1974; MS, U. Wis., Eau Claire, 1981. Cert. vocat. tchr., secondary tchr., Minn. Instr. Hamilton Coll., Mason City, Iowa, 1974-75, Winona Area Vocat.-Tech. Inst., 1975-80, 85—; owner Profl. Ctr., Winona, 1980—; instr. Winona State U., 1983-85; cons. Staff One, Mpls., 1986—. Contbr. LaCrosse (Wis.) City Bus. Newspaper, 1984-86, Woman & Co. mag., 1985. Scheduler Re-Elect Rep. Senator, Winona, 1986. Named Tchr. of Yr., Winona Sch. Dist. 861, 1986. Mem. Minn. Edn. Assn., Winona Edn. Assn., Delta Kappa Gamma (editor 1980—),Minn. Bus. Educators, Inc., Delta Pi Epsilon (editor 1981—). Avocations: reading, traveling. Office: Profl Ctr 123 1/2 Johnson St Winona MN 55987

THOLEN, CHARLES ENGLE, real estate executive; b. Janesville, Wis., May 25, 1933; s. Bernard Henry and Sara (Engle) T.; m. Eloise Grace Finch, Sept. 14, 1957; children: David Charles, John William. Student, Trinity Coll., 1952-55; BBA, Hofstra U., 1963; postgrad., U. Mich., Dearborn, 1964-65. Lic. real estate broker, Mich. Real estate supr. Sinclair Refining Co., N.Y.C., 1958-63; real estate mgr. Ford Motor Co., Detroit, 1963—. Chmn. planning bd. City of Birmingham, Mich., 1978-82. Served with U.S. Army, 1956-58. Mem. Nat. Assn. Corp. Real Estate Execs. Episcopalian. Clubs: Woodside Athletic, Cranbrook Tennis (Bloomfield Hills, Mich.). Home: 895 Lake Park Dr Birmingham MI 48009 Office: Ford Motor Co 300 Renaissance Ctr Detroit MI 48243

THOMA, CHARLES WILLIAM, civil engineer, architect; b. Reyno, Ark., Oct. 14, 1927; s. William and Reva Lois T.; m. Barbara Lee Stephens, Apr. 24, 1951; children: Sue Ann, Barbara Jean, John Stephens. BS in Civil Engring., Tex. A&M U., 1948. Profl. engr., Kans., Tex., Okla., Ark.; registered architect, Kans., Okla., Tex., Mo.; registered land surveyor, Kans. Resident engr. Tex. Hwy. Dept., Ft. Worth, 1953-55; v.p. Scott Engring. Co., Ft. Worth and Watertown, S.D., 1955-60; ptnr. Stitzel & Thoma, P.A., Arkansas City, Kans., 1960-73; pres. Charles W. Thoma & Assocs., Arkansas City, 1973—. Served to 1st lt. U.S. Army, 1951-53, Korea. Fellow ASCE; mem. Am. Soc. Profl. Engrs. Democrat. Episcopalian. Lodge: Rotary. Avocations: hunting, fishing. Office: Charles W Thoma & Assocs 106 S Summit St Suite D Arkansas City KS 67005

THOMAN, MARK EDWARD, physician; b. Chgo., Feb. 15, 1936; s. John Charles and Tasula Mark (Petrakis) T.; A.A., Graceland Coll., 1956; B.A., U. Mo., 1958, M.D., 1962; m. Theresa Thompson, 1984; children—Marlisa Rae, Susan Kay, Edward Kim, Nancy Lynn, Janet Lea, David Mark. Intern, U. Mo. at Columbia, 1962-63; resident in pediatrics Blank Meml. Children's Hosp., Des Moines, 1963-65, chief resident, 1964-65, lt. comdr. USPHS, Washington, 1965-66, cons. in toxicology, 1966-67; chief dept. pediatrics Shiprock (N.Mex.) Navajo Indian Hosp., dir. N.D. Poison Info. Center, also practice medicine, specializing in pediatrics Quain & Ramstad Clinic, Bismarck, N.D., 1967-69; dir. Iowa Poison Info. Center, Des Moines, 1969—; pvt. practice pediatrics, Des Moines, 1969—; sr. aviation med. examiner, accident investigator FAA, 1976—; faculty Iowa State U., U. Iowa, U. Osteo. Sci. and Health; dir. Cystic Fibrosis Clinic, 1973-82; dir. Mid-Iowa Drug Abuse Program, 1972-76; mem. med. adv. bd. La Leche Leauge Internat., 1965—; pres. Medic-Air Ltd., 1976—. Bd. dirs. Polk County Pub. Health Nurses Assn., 1969-77, Des Moines Speech and Hearing Center, 1974-79. Served with USMCR, 1954-58. Recipient N.D. Gov.'s award of merit, 1969; Cystic Fibrosis Research Found. award, 1975, Am. Psychiat. Assn. Thesis award, Diplomate Am. Bd. Pediatrics, Am. Bd. Med. Toxicology (examiner). 1962. Mem. AMA (del. 1970—), Polk County Med. Soc., Iowa State Med. Assn., Aerospace Med. Assn., Soc. Adolescent Medicine, Inst. Clin. Toxicology, Internat. Soc. Pediatrics, Am. Acad. Pediatrics, Cystic Fibrosis Club, Am. Acad. Clin. Toxicology (trustee 1969—, pres. 1982-84), Am. Assn. Poison Control Centers, Nat. Rifle Assn. (life). Republican. Mem. Reorganized Latter-Day Saints Ch. Clubs: Flying Physicians, Aircraft Owners and Pilots Assn., Nat. Pilots Assn. (Safe Pilot award), Hyperion Field and Country. Editor-in-chief AACTION. Home: 6896 NW Trailridge Dr Johnston IA 50131 Office: 1426 Woodland Ave Des Moines IA 50309

THOMANN, JERRY WAYNE, accountant; b. Olney, Ill., Apr. 21, 1955; s. Jerry Dean and Peggy Arlene (Brant) T.; m. Deborah Kay Gumble, Aug. 21, 1976; children: Elissa, Alison, Lindsey. AAS, Olney Cen. Coll., 1975; BS, Eastern Ill. U., 1977. CPA, Ill. Staff acct. Kemper CPA Group, Lawrenceville, Ill., 1977-79; mgr. Kemper CPA Group, Palm Bay, Fla., 1979-82; ptnr. Kemper CPA Group, Salem, Ill., 1982—. Mem. Am. Inst. CPA's, Ill. Soc. CPA's, Fla. Inst. CPA's, Salem C. of C. (v.p. fin. 1985—). Lodge: Rotary (pres. Salem 1986—). Avocations: tennis, waterskiing. Office: Kemper CPA Group 401 W McMackin Box 388 Salem IL 62881

THOMAS, ALAN, candy company executive; b. Evansburg, Pa., Jan. 1, 1923; s. William Roberts and Letta (Garrett) T.; student Rutgers U., 1941-42, 46-47; B.S., Pa. State U., 1949; M.S., U. Minn., 1950, Ph.D., 1954; m. Marguerite Atria, July 1, 1972; children—Garrett Lee, Michael Alan, Randall Stephen, Brett Eliot. Instr., Temple U., Phila., 1950-51, U. Minn., St. Paul, 1951-54; research asst. Bowman Dairy Co., Chgo., 1954-56; research project mgr. M&M Candies div. Mars, Inc., Hackettstown, N.J., 1956-60, product devel. mgr., 1961-64, chocolate research dir. 1964; v.p. research and devel. Mars Candies, Chgo., 1964-67; v.p. research and devel. M&M/Mars Div., Hackettstown, 1967-77, v.p. sci. affairs, 1977-78; gen. mgr. Ethel M, Las Vegas, 1978-83, cons., 1985; sr. cons. Knechtel Research Scis., Inc., Skokie, Ill., 1984; v.p. tech. Ferrara Pan Candy Co., Forest Park, Ill., 1986—. Chmn. industry council of industry liaison panel Food and Nutrition Bd., Nat. Acad. Scis./NRC, 1972-73; adv. U.S. del. Codex Alimentarius Com. on Cocoa and Chocolate Products, 1967-78. Served to 1st lt. inf. AUS, 1942-46. Recipient research award Nat. Confectioners Assn. U.S., 1971. Mem. AAAS, Grocery Mfrs. Am. (chmn. tech. com. 1975-76), Chocolate Mfrs. Assn. (chmn. FDA liaison com. 1975-77), Inst. Food Technologists, Am. Assn. Candy Technologists, Gamma Sigma Delta, Phi Kappa Phi. Home: 1625 Westwood Dr Las Vegas NV 89102 Office: Ferrara Pan Candy Co 7301 W Harrison St Forest Park IL 60130

THOMAS, ARTHUR LAWRENCE, teacher, author; b. Cleve., July 8, 1952; s. Anthony Leonard and Anne Louise (Rinkus) T. BA, Baldwin-Wallace Coll., 1974; MA, Kent (Ohio) State U., 1987. Tchr. West Tech. High Sch., Cleve., 1975-80, Brooklyn (Ohio) High Sch., 1980-83, St. Ignatius High Sch., Cleve., 1983—; bus. mgr. New Mayfield Repertory Cinema, Cleve., 1974-85; cons. various theater groups, 1980—. Author: Recreational Wrestling, 1976, Merry Go Round Book, 1984, Sports for Me, 1980-84; theatre critic West Life, Westlake, Ohio, 1982—; contbr. articles to newspapers and mags. Grantee Martha Holden Jennings Found., 1978, 87, NEH, 1986. Mem. U.S. Inst. for Theatre Technology, Nat. Council Tchrs. of English, MENSA. Roman Catholic. Home: 12500 Edgewater Dr #1601 Lakewood OH 44107

THOMAS, BIDE LAKIN, utility executive; b. Mason City, Iowa, Aug. 14, 1935; s. Brice Lakin and Jane (Duffield) T.; children: Brice, Lorraine, Carolyn. BS in Indsl. Adminstrn., Yale U., 1957; MBA, Harvard U., 1959. With Commonwealth Edison Co., Chgo., 1959—, div. v.p., 1970-73, gen. div. mgr., 1973-75, v.p. div. ops., 1975-76, v.p. indsl. relations, 1976-80, exec. v.p., 1980—; bd. dirs. Commonwealth Edison Co., No. Trust Corp., No. Trust Co., R.R. Donnelley & Sons Co. Trustee Rush-Presbyn.-St. Luke's Med. Ctr., DePaul U.; bd. dirs. Ravenswood Hosp. Med. Ctr., chmn., 1973-77; bd. mgrs. YMCA Met. Chgo., chmn., 1985-86; bd. dirs. Civic Fedn., United Way/Crusade of Mercy, United Way of Ill., Chgo. Crime Commn.; assoc. Northwestern U. Mem. Electrical Assn. Clubs: Chicago, Econs. of Chgo., Commercial (Chgo.). Office: Commonwealth Edison Co PO Box 767 One First National Plaza Chicago IL 60690

THOMAS, BRENDA, bookstore executive; b. Russell, Ky., Mar. 16, 1948; d. Charles X. and Jeannette Frances (Thompson) Calia; m. Evan Thomas, July 11, 1972; children—Alexandra Logan, Jessica Theon, Erin Elizabeth. Dir. Am. Lang. Ctr., Fez, Morocco, 1968-70; proprietor The Bookshop, St. Paul, 1981—. Commr. human rights Roseville, Minn., 1979—, chmn., 1986—; bd. dirs, Quantum Theatre, St. Paul, 1984-87. Mem. NOW, ACLU, Amnesty Internat. Avocation: astrology. Office: The Bookshop 2100 N Snelling Ave Saint Paul MN 55113

THOMAS, CHRISTOPHER YANCEY, III, physician, educator; b. Kansas City, Mo., Oct. 27, 1923; s. Christopher Yancey and Dorothea Louise (Engel) T.; m. Barbara Ann Barcroft, June 27, 1946; children—Christopher, Gregg, Jeffrey, Anne. Student, U. Colo., 1942-44; M.D., U. Kans., 1948. Diplomate Am. Bd. Surgery. Intern U. Utah Hosp., Salt Lake City, 1948-49; resident in surgery Cleve. Clinic Found., 1949-52; practice medicine specializing in surgery Kansas City, Mo., 1954—; mem. staff St. Luke's Hosp., chief of surgery, 1969-70; mem. staff Children's Mercy Hosp.; assoc. prof. surgery U. Mo., Kansas City Med. Sch.; dir. Mission Hills Bank; pres. St. Luke's Hosp. Edn. Found., 1977-83, Med. Plaza Corp., 1977-79; pres. Midwest Organ Bank, 1977-82, also. dir.; v.p., dir. HealthPlan Mid-Am. Editor IMTRAC investment adv. letter, 1978—. Served to capt. M.C., U.S. Army, 1952-54. Fellow ACS; mem. AMA, Southwestern Surg. Congress, Central Surg. Assn.; Mo. State Med. Soc., Kansas City Surg. Soc. (pres. 1968), Jackson County Med. Soc. (pres. 1971). Republican. Methodist. Clubs: Kansas City Country, Homestead Country. Home: 5830 Mission Dr Shawnee Mission KS 66208 Office: 4320 Wornall Rd Suite 308 Kansas City MO 64111

THOMAS, DANIEL GLEN, energy engineer; b. Milw., May 25, 1951; s. Eugene Milton and Eva Marie (Harris) T.; m. Gloria Rose Hart, Sept. 1, 1973; children: Rebecca Lynn, Christina Marie, David Gregory. BS, U. Wis., Milw., 1973; energy mgmt. diploma, U. Wis., Madison, 1987. Registered profl. engr., Wis. Conservation and utilization engr. Wis. Nat. Gas Co., Racine, 1974-77; project engr. Donohue & Assocs., Waukesha, Wis., 1977-79, Entech Engring., Elm Grove, Wis., 1979-80; resource engr. Milw. Met. Sewerage Dist., 1980-84; energy mgmt. engr. Wis. Electric Power Co., Milw., 1984—. Mem. sign appeals bd. City of Waukesha, 1979-80. Mem. Assn. Energy Engrs., Am. Soc. Heating, Refrigeration and Air-Conditioning Engrs. (Energy Achievement award 1982). Roman Catholic. Avocations: bicycling, camping. Office: Wis Electric Power Co 3100 W North Ave Milwaukee WI 53208

THOMAS, DAVID HENRY, librarian; b. Highland Park, Mich., June 22, 1934; s. Raymond James and Ida Elizabeth (Rosemergy) T.; m. Katheleen Thomas, Oct. 4, 1958; children: Raymond James, Sharon Marie. BA, Mich. Tech. U., 1974; MA, U. Mich., 1976. Investigator, supr. Retail Credit Co., Pontiac, 1960-64; circulation librarian Mich. Tech. U., Houghton, 1964-81, head tech. services, 1981—; owner Great Lakes Bookman, Houghton, 1974; state alt. White House Conf. Libraries and Info. Services, Lansing, Mich., 1978-81. Author: Cemeteries of the Copper Country, 1973, Congressmen from the Cooper, Country, 1973. Trustee Cen. Mine (Mich.) Meth. Ch., 1964, Keweenaw County Hist. Soc., Eagle Harbor, Mich.,1984; bd. dirs. Calumet Pub. Lib., 1983, Fort Wilkins Natural History Assn., Copper Harbor, Mich., 1967. Served with USCG. Mem. ALA, Mich. Library Assn., Assn. Coll. and Research Libraries. Avocations: boating, photography, sucba diving. Home: PO Box 162 Houghton MI 49931 Office: Mich Tech U Library Houghton MI 49931

THOMAS, D(ORIS) JULIENNE, pastoral psychotherapist; b. St. Charles, Mo., June 8, 1936; d. Austin H. and Doris Mary (McQueen) T.; children: Gahlen Crawford, Lana Julienne Petersen, Thomas Glenn Crawford. BA, Park Coll., 1979; MDiv., Midwestern Bapt. Theol. Sem., 1979; DMin., San Francisco Theol. Sem., 1982. Ordained to ministry Bapt. Ch., 1977. Pastoral psychotherapist The Counseling Inst., Kansas City, Mo., 1979—, dir. resourceing div.; freelance writer; cons./speaker in field. Editor LifeBldg. Newsletter, 1984—. Republican. Avocations: travelling, reading, cooking, horticulture. Office: The Counseling Inst 411 Nichols Rd Suite 246 Kansas City MO 64112

THOMAS, EDWARD CLARE, manufacturing company executive; b. Chgo., Feb. 22, 1939; s. Clare Louis and Helen (Hunt) T.; m. Barbara DuFresne, Aug. 14, 1958; children: Debra Carol, Royce Edward. BBA, U. Oreg., 1961. Mgr. Arthur Andersen & Co., San Francisco, 1961-66, 69-70, The Hague, Netherlands, 1966-69; ptnr. Frank Rimerman & Co., Palo Alto, Calif., 1970-77, Edward Thomas & Co., Menlo Park, Calif., 1977-83; v.p., controller Econ. Data Products, Inc., Des Moines, 1986—. Co-founder Beyond War Found., Palo Alto, 1982, Des Moines, 1983, mem. nat. staff, 1983—. Mem. Am. Inst. CPA's, Calif. Soc. CPA's, Peninsula CPA Soc. (founding mem.). Republican. Avocations: travel, hiking, gardening, internat. relations. Home: 3904 Welker Ave Des Moines IA 50312 Office: Econ Data Products Inc 2134 NW 108th St Des Moines IA 50322

THOMAS, EMILY ANN, feature writer, song writer, composer; b. Warsaw, Ind., Dec. 21, 1952; d. Dester and Myrtle Joann (Bohnstedt) Bell; m. Daryl Eldon Thomas, June 12, 1976; children: Amanda Eilleen, Schaya Jennifer. Grad. high sch., Syracuse, Ind., 1971. Feature writer The Mail-Jour., Milford, Ind., 1983—, The Paper, Milford, Ind., 1983—. Writer, composer song and lyrics: Hometown Feelin', 1985 (Gov. Commn. recognition), The Circuit Rider, 1986; poet September Morn', Am. Poetry Anthology, 1986. Charter mem. Statue of Liberty Ellis Island Found., N.Y.C., 1984—; mem. Rep. Nat. Com., Washington, 1982—. Mem. ASCAP (assoc.), Gospel Music Assn. (assoc.). Avocations: guitar and piano playing, family activities.

THOMAS, FAYE EVELYN J., educator; b. Summerfield, La., Aug. 3, 1933; d. Reginald Felton and Altee (Hunter) Johnson; B.A., So. U., 1954; student Tuskegee Inst., 1958, 69, U. Detroit, summers, 1961, 62, 63, Central Mich. U., summer 1965; M.S., U. Central Ark., 1971; M.S., Cleve. State U., 1979; m. Archie Taylor Thomas, Sept. 8, 1960; 1 son, Dwayne Andre. Tchr., Cullen (La.) Elem. Sch., 1957; tchr. English and social studies Charles Brown High Sch., Springhill, La., 1957-70; tchr. English, Upward Bound Program, Grambling State U., 1968; tchr. English, Springhill (La.) High Sch., 1970; elem. intermediate tchr. Riveredge Elem. Sch., Berea, Ohio, 1971—; tchr. asst. elem. council curriculum and instrn. Berea Sch. Dist., 1984-85. Trustee, Charles Brown Soc. Orgn. EPDA grantee, 1970-71; Internat. Paper Found. grantee, summers 1958, 60; NDEA grantee, summer 1965; Martha Holden Jennings scholar, 1984-85. Mem. NEA, Ohio Edn. Assn., Berea Edn. Assn., N.E. Ohio Tchrs. Assn., Assn. for Supervision and Curriculum Devel., Charles Brown Soc. Orgn. (trustee 1984—), People United to Save Humanity, Black Caucus Nat. Edn. Assn., Ohio Motorists Assn. Democrat. Baptist. Mem. Order Eastern Star. Home: 19353 E Bagley Rd Middleburg Heights OH 44130 Office: 224 Emerson Dr Berea OH 44017

THOMAS, FRANCIS DARRELL, oil compounder executive; b. Palestine, Ill., Feb. 11, 1928; s. Odin F. and Dorothy (Carrol) T.; m. Nancy Thomas; children: Steven, Bruce, Gail. BS, Butler U., 1951. Regional mgr. Sun Oil Co., Cin., 1955-72; pres. Keenan Oil Co., Cin., 1972-74; gen. mgr. Weatherator Engring. Co., Columbus, Ohio, 1975-76; pres. Nat. Oil Products div. Concord Industries, Inc., Hamilton, Ohio, 1976—. Served with USMC, 1946-47. Mem. Ind. Lubricant Mfrs. Assn., Assn. Petroleum Re-Refiners (past mem. nat. exec. com.), Am. Soc. Lubrication Engrs. (past chmn. Cin. sect.). Republican. Club: Clovernook Country. Lodges: Masons, Shriners. Office: 1000 Forest Ave Hamilton OH 45015

THOMAS, GARY ALLEN, dentist; b. Springfield, Ohio, Feb. 7, 1956; s. Donald James and Isabelle Jean (Grau) T.; divorced; 1 child, Christopher James. BA in Fin., Ohio State U., 1978, DDS, 1981. Gen. practice dentistry Springfield, Ohio, 1981—. Mem. Zion Luth. Ch. council, Springfield, 1984—. Mem. Mad River Valley Dental Soc., Jaycees (bd. dirs. Springfield, 1982), Psi Omega. Lutheran. Clubs: Northwood Hills Country (Springfield). Avocations: golf, football, basketball, camping. Office: 1220 E Home Rd Springfield OH 45503

THOMAS, GEORGE, physician; b. Miklos, Syria, Oct. 22, 1946; came to U.S., 1947; s. Ghattas Deeb and Sameera (Haddad) T.; children: Farrah, Tiffany. B.S., U. Pitts., 1968; D.O., Kirksville Coll. Osteo. Medicine, 1972. Cert. Am. Coll. Gen. Practice. Intern, Still Osteo. Hosp., Jefferson City, Mo., 1972-73; practice medicine, Euclid, Ohio, 1973—; pres. staff Richmond Heights Gen. Hosp., Ohio, 1985—, sec.-treas. staff, 1977-80, v.p. staff, 1980-85, chief of staff, 1987—, chief of quality assurance, 1986—. Fellow Am. Coll. Gen. Practitioners; mem. Am. Osteo. Assn., Ohio Osteo. Assn. (treas. 1985, 2nd v.p. 1986—), Cleve. Acad. Osteo. Medicine (program chmn. 1982, v.p. 1981-82, pres. 1983-84), Am. Coll. Gen. Pactitioners in Osteo. Medicine and Surgery, Undersea Med. Soc. Avocations: scuba diving. Office: 26151 Euclid Ave Euclid OH 44132

THOMAS, GEORGE WILLARD (BILL), micrographics quality control company executive, consultant; b. York, Pa., Jan. 26, 1927; s. George Washington and Ruth Jeanette (Lukens) T.; m. Juanita Anne Vinson, Feb. 6, 1948; children—Lynn Anne Thomas Nelson, George Willard Jr. Student York Jr. Coll. (Pa.), 1946-47; A.B., Gettysburg Coll. (Pa.), 1949; postgrad. U. Del.-Newark, 1949-51. Physicist, U.S. Navy, Panama City, Fla., 1951-56, Corona, Calif., 1956-71; owner, mgr. MicroFilming Services, Corona, 1971-79; pres. Neoteric Arts, Inc., Corona and Burnsville, Minn., 1972—; pres. MicroD Internat., Corona and Burnsville, 1973—. Contbr. articles in field. Commr. Inland Empire council Boy Scouts Am., Corona. Served with U.S. Navy, 1945-46. Recipient Disting. Merit award Boy Scouts Am., 1974; Merit award So. Calif. Micrographics Assn., 1980. Mem. Assn. Info. and Image Mgmt., Internat. Info. Mgmt. Congress, Can. Info. and Image Mgmt. Soc., Internat. Records Mgmt. Council, Am. Nat. Standards Inst., Records Mgmt. Assn. Republican. Office: Neoteric Arts Inc 15000 County Rd 5 Burnsville MN 55337

THOMAS, HARLEY HASTINGS, III, plastics company executive; b. Poplar Bluff, Mo., June 16, 1941; s. Harley Hastings Jr. and Emily Grace (Ockenfels) T.; m. Carol Sue Clemons, Dec. 20, 1964; children: Harley IV, Jason Stuart. BS, U. Mo., 1964; MS, Ind. U., 1965; PhD, Mich. State U., 1969. Sales engr. Masonite Corp., Evansville, Ind., 1969-70; mktg. mgr. Masonite Corp., Chgo., 1970-72; nat. mktg. mgr. Plaskolite, Inc., Columbus, Ohio, 1972-73; chmn. bus. adminstrn. Columbia (Mo.) Coll., 1973-76; v.p. sales Portage (Wis.) Industries, 1976-78; v.p. and gen. mgr. Vinyl Plastics, Inc., Sheboygan, Wis., 1979—; cons. Plaskolite, Inc., 1973-76. Served with USNG, 1966-72; Mich. Army Air Guard, Mich. Army N.G., Ind. N.G., Ill. Air N.G. Mem. Soc. Plastics Industry (sheet producers div., mktg. com. chmn. 1985—). Avocations: golf, skiing, travel. Office: Vinyl Plastics Inc 3123 S 9th St Sheboygan WI 53081

THOMAS, HARVEY MONROE, psychology consultant; b. Marshall, Mo., Sept. 22, 1925; s. David Monroe and Sue E. (Eads) T.; m. Irene Simon, Dec. 28, 1947; children: Blake David, Kent Monroe, Jonathan Lee. AB, William Jewell Coll., 1947; PhD, Washington U., 1953. Lic. psychologist, Mo. Instr. Washington U., St. Louis, Mo., 1947-49; prof. William Jewell Coll., Liberty, Mo., 1949-56; staff psychologist Nordli, Ogan, Wilson, N.Y.C., 1955-58; pres. Thomas Assoc., Inc., Liberty, 1958—; cons. Marion Labs., Kansas City, Mo., 1970—, Hallmark Cards, Kansas City, 1968—, Kans. City Chiefs, 1983—, S.W. Research Internat., San Antonio, Tex, 1955—; trustee William Jewell Coll. Served to lt. USNR, 1943-46. Fellow Washington U., 1947-49. Mem. Am. Psychol. Assn., Sigma Xi (sec. 1949). Republican. Baptist. Clubs: Kans. City, Claycvest Country (sec. 1985—). Home and Office: 617 Jefferson Circle Liberty MO 64068

THOMAS, ISIAH LORD, professional basketball player; b. Chgo., Apr. 30, 1961. Student, Ind. U. Profl. basketball player Detroit Pistons, NBA, 1981—. Player, NBA All-Star Game, 1982-86, Most Valuable Player, 1984, 86. Office: Detroit Pistons Pontiac Silverdome 1200 Featherstone Pontiac MI 48057 *

THOMAS, JAMES ALLEN, publisher; b. Indpls., Dec. 12, 1943; s. William F. and Florence I. (Hansel) T.; m. Mary Lou Furnish, June 13, 1965 (div. May 1982); children: Troy Allen, Ty Ashley, Trevor Andrew. BBA, Cen. State U., Edmond, Okla., 1970. Indsl. engr. Owens Ill., Inc., Warsaw, Ind., 1970-73; owner service stations, Greenfield, Indpls., Ind., 1972-76, Hancock Delivery Service, Inc., Greenfield, Ind., 1974—; pub. Ad News, Greenfield, 1979-86, Ad News Indy East, Greenfield, Indpls., 1986—. Pres. bd. dirs. Boys Club, Greenfield, 1982-84; chmn. bd. ARC, Greenfield, 1985; chmn. Am. Cancer Soc., Greenfield, 1985-86. Served to sgt. USAF, 1966-70. Mem. Independant Free Papers of Am., cert. Independant Suburban Newspapers. Democrat. Methodist. Lodge: Sertoma (pres. Greenfield, 1981). Avocations: racquetball, tennis, camping. Home: PO Box 4 Greenfield IN 46140 Office: Hancock Ad News PO Box 602 Greenfield IN 46140-0602

THOMAS, JAMES HENRY, data processing executive; b. Rockford, Ill., Nov. 16, 1947; s. John Allen and Bernita Lucille (Peterson) T.; m. Betty Jean Steinhauser, Oct. 15, 1977; children: Jason Harold, Brian James. Cert., Programming Systems Inst., Rockford, Ill., 1970. Shipping clk. Mid-States Screw Corp., Rockford, 1965-70; computer operator Am. Nat. Bank, Rockford, 1970-80; lead computer operator Sundstrand Corp., Rockford, 1980-84, data network adminstrn., 1984-87, group leader, 1987—. Membership chmn. CMC Assn., Rockford, 1983-84. Republican. Roman Catholic. Avocations: geneology, computers, reading, gardening. Home: 5718 Moccasin Run Rockford IL 61109-6104 Office: Sundstrand Corp 4751 Harrison Ave Rockford IL 61125-7003

THOMAS, JAMES ROBERT, physician in maternal and fetal medicine, consultant; b. Lodi, Calif., Nov. 22, 1948; s. Harold Morse and Lillian Bertha (Litvin) T.; m. Mona Lee Mason, June 1, 1969; adopted children: Sarah Marie, Jesse Lee-Hwan. BS, Loma Linda U., 1970, MD, 1977; PhD, U. Calif., 1974. Cert. Am. Bd. Ob-Gyns, Nat. Bd. Med. Examiners. Resident in ob-gyn Yale U., New Haven, 1978-83; fellow maternal-fetal medicine U. Vt., Burlington, 1982-84; dir. maternal-fetal medicine U. S.D., Sioux Falls, 1984—, asst. prof. ob-gyn, 1984-87, assoc. prof., 1987—. Fellow Am. Coll. Ob-Gyn (Mead Johnson Clin. Research fellow 1984); mem. AMA, Soc. Perinatal Obstetrics, Am. Inst. Ultrasound. Club: Wine of Sioux Falls (charter pres. 1984-85). Home: 300 E 27th St Sioux Falls SD 57105

THOMAS, JAMES SAMUEL, bishop; b. Orangeburg, S.C., Apr. 8, 1919; s. James and Dessie Veronica (Mark) T.; m. Ruth Naomi Wilson, July 7, 1945; children: Claudia Thomas Williamson, Gloria Jean Thomas Randle, Margaret Yvonne Thomas Glaze, Patricia Elaine. AB, Clafin Coll., Orangeburg, 1939, DD (hon.), 1953; BD, Gammon Theol. Sem., Atlanta, 1943; MA, Drew U., 1944, LHD (hon.), 1986; PhD, Cornell U., 1953; LLD (hon.), Bethune Cookman Coll., 1963, Simpson Coll., 1965, Morningside Coll., 1966, Iowa Wesleyan Coll., Coe Coll., 1968, Westmar Coll., 1970, W.Va. Wesleyan Coll., 1980; LHD (hon.), Cornell Coll., 1965, Ohio Weslyan U., 1967, DePauw U., 1969; HHD (hon.), St. Ambrose Coll., 1970; STD (hon.), Parsons Coll., 1972, Baldwin-Wallace Coll., 1977; DH (hon.), Rust Coll., 1975; DD (hon.), Allegheny Coll., 1979, Wofford Coll., 1972, Ohio No. U., 1983, Asbury Theol. Sem., 1983, Emory U., 1985; LittD (hon.), Mt. Union Coll., 1979; LHD, Drew U., 1986. Ordained to ministry Meth. Ch., 1944; pastor Orangeburg Circuit, 1942-43, York, S.C., 1946-48; chaplain S.C. State Coll., 1944-46; prof. Gammon Theol. Sem., 1948-53; asso. sec. Meth. Bd. Edn., 1953-64; bishop Iowa area Meth. Ch., 1964-76; bishop Ohio East area United Meth. Ch., 1976—; pres. Gen. Council on Ministries; dir. Equitable of Iowa; vis. prof. Perkins Sch. Theology, So. Meth. U., summer

1958, Duke U. Div. Sch., fall 1978. Trustee Baldwin-Wallace Coll., Meth. Theol. Sch. in Ohio, Mt. Union Coll., Ohio Wesleyan U., Otterbein Coll., Copeland Oaks, Elyria Home, Berea Children's Home, St. Luke's Hosp. Address: 8800 Cleveland Ave NW North Canton OH 44720

THOMAS, JAMES WILLIAM, lawyer; b. N.Y.C., May 12, 1949; s. Howard and Alice (Brennan) T.; m. Cecilia Coleman Goad, July 7, 1973; children—James William Jr., Brennan McKinney. B.S., U. Dayton, 1971; J.D., Ohio No. U., 1974. Bar: Ohio 1974, U.S. Dist. Ct. Ohio 1976. Ptnr., Earley & Thomas, Eaton, Ohio, 1974—; village solicitor Village of Lewisburg (Ohio), 1977-81, Village of Verona (Ohio), 1979-81; asst. pros. atty. Preble County (Ohio), 1980-81. Mem. Community Improvement Corp., Eaton. Mem. Preble County Bar Assn. (pres. 1982-84). Republican. Roman Catholic. Club: Eaton Country. Lodge: Rotary (dir. 1980-87, pres. 1987—). Avocations: boating; tennis. Home: 761 Vinland Cove Eaton OH 45300 Office: Earley & Thomas 112 N Barron St Eaton OH 45320

THOMAS, JOAN WOLENS, media specialist, educator; b. St. Paul, Feb. 26, 1941; d. Anton Peter Wolens and Eunice (Belland) Long; m. James Edward Thomas, June 26, 1970; 1 child, Shawn Riley. BA, U. Minn., 1963, MA, 1974; EdS, St. Cloud State U., 1975. cert. tchr. kindergarten-12th grade, media specialist. Tchr., librarian various schs., Fed. Rep. Germany, Japan, U.S., 1963-71; librarian, media specialist Wilder Sch., Mpls., 1972-78; elem. media cons. Mpls. Pub. Schs., 1978; instr. Mankato (Minn.) State U., 1979; head librarian Cranbrook Sch., Bloomfield Hills, Mich., 1980-82; media specialist West Maple Middle Sch., Birmingham, Mich., 1982—; cons. Bayfield (Wis.) Schs., 1978; ednl. cons. Chgo., Mpls. and Richfield, Wis., 1977; keynote lectr. MEMO State Confs. Contbr. articles to profl. jours. Contbg. mem. The Peace Mus., Chgo., 1983—, Foster Parents Plan, Warwick, WIs., 1985—, U.S-China Friendship Assn., Mpls. and Detroit, 1976—, Founders Soc. Detroit Inst. Art, 1980—; founding mem. Nat. Women's Art Gallery, Washington, 1987. Recipient Photo award Detroit Free Press, 1986, Exemplary Sch. award U.S. Dept. Edn., Minn., 1978, Mich. 1987. Mem. Media Educators of Minn. Orgn. (program chmn. 1977), Mich. Assn. Media Educators (sec. 1984, 87, bd. dirs. 1984, 87, presenter at state workshops), Am. Assn. Sch. Librarians, Mich. Computer Assn. Avocations: art, travel, photography. Home: 4260 South Shore Pontiac MI 48054 Office: West Maple Middle Sch 6275 Inkster Birmingham MI 48010

THOMAS, JOHN, engineer, research and development executive; b. Tiruvalla, Kerala, India, Jan. 2, 1946; came to U.S., 1974; s. Munnencheril Varghese and Rachel (Mathai) T.; m. Mary Parapat Varghese, Apr. 28, 1975; children: Joel George, Sayana Rachel. BSME, Birla Inst. Tech., Ranchi, India, 1969; MSME, U. Waterloo, Ont., Can., 1973. Registered profl. engr., Wis. Lectr. engring. U. Kerala, India, 1970-71; design engr. Combustion Engring., Inc., Springfield, Ohio, 1974-76; mech. engr. Ingersoll-Rand Co., Painted Post, N.Y., 1977-80; engr. Allis-Chalmers Corp., Milw., 1980-82; pvt. practice engring. cons. Milw., 1982-84; sr. tech. devel. engr. div. Cross & Trecker Kearney & Trecker Corp., Milw., 1984—. Patentee in field. Avocation: photography. Home: 18330 Benington Dr Brookfield WI 53005 Office: Kearney & Trecker Corp 11000 Theodore Trecker Way Milwaukee WI 53214

THOMAS, JOHN CHARLES, retail executive; b. Mpls., Nov. 14, 1950; s. David Earl and Virginia Ann (Seidl) T.; m. Deborah Ann Smiddy, Oct. 23, 1982; children: John Charles II, Michael Lloyd. BSBA, U. Minn., 1974. V.p. Lancer Stores, Inc., Bloomington, Minn., 1974—. Williams scholar, 1971. Mem. Minn. Retail Merchants Assn. (bd. dirs. 1984—), Upper Midwest Mutual Assn. (bd. dirs. 1985—), Minn. Family Bus. Council, Twin City Personnel Assn., Am. Soc. Personnel Adminstrs., Psi Upsilon. Republican. Congregationalist. Home: 6525 Parnell Ave Edina MN 55435 Office: Lancer Stores Inc 5115 W 80th St Bloomington MN 55437

THOMAS, JOHN MARK, dentist; b. Shelbyville, Ind., Apr. 28, 1950; s. John M. and Jean (Kerr) T.; m. Karen Lynn Lewis, Aug. 22, 1970; children: Katie, Brooke, Jill. AB, Ind. U., 1972, DDS, 1980. Gen. practice dentistry Seymour, Ind., 1980—. Bd. dirs. Turning Point, Columbus, Ind., 1985-86; mem. Target 2000, Seymour, 1985-86. Named one of Outstanding Young Men of Am., 1985. Mem. ADA, Ind. Dental Soc., Greater Seymour C. of C. (chmn. pub. relations 1986). Mem. Christian Ch. Club: Seymour Sports (pres. 1984-86) Lodge: Lions (pres. Seymour 1986—). Avocations: fishing, hunting, outdoor activities, golf, spectator sports. Home: Rural Rt 6 Box 110 Seymour IN 47274 Office: 325 N Walnut St Seymour IN 47274

THOMAS, JON CAYSON, financial advisor, real estate developer; b. St. Louis, June 22, 1947; s. Jefferson C. and Edna W. Thomas; B.S., U. Mo., 1971; M.B.A., So. Ill. U., 1978; m. Alma DeBasio, Aug. 31, 1968; children—Jennifer Anne, Jon Cayson, II. Div. mgr. pensions and mut. funds Safeco Securities Co./Safeco Life Ins. Co., St. Louis, 1970-74; v.p. fin. planning dept. A.G. Edwards & Sons, Inc., St. Louis, 1974-77; pres. Intermark Assets Group Inc., St. Louis, 1978—; founder, 1980, thereafter prin. Monetary Mgmt. Group, St. Louis. Cert. fin. planner. Mem. Nat. Assn. Securities Dealers (registered investment advisor), Internat. Assn. Fin. Planners, Inst. Cert. Fin. Planners, Beta Theta Pi. Office: 120 S Hanley Rd Clayton MO 63105

THOMAS, JOSEPH ERUMAPPETTICAL, psychologist; b. Piravom, Kerala, India, Feb. 11, 1937; came to U.S., 1971; s. Iype Erumappettiyil and Kunjamma M. (Padiyil) T.; m. Chinnamma Kavatt, Nov. 23, 1964; children: Joseph Jr., Kurian, Elizabeth. BA, Kerala U., India, 1957, MA, 1960, PhD, 1969. Diplomate Am. Bd. Behavioral Medicine; lic. psychologist. Lectr. psychology U. Kerala, Trivandrum, India, 1967-70; fellow in psychology Northwestern U. Med. Sch., Chgo., 1971-72; psychologist U. Chgo., 1972-74; instr. psychiatry Northwestern U. Med. Sch., Chgo., 1972-76, asst. prof. dept. psychiatry, 1977—; psychologist Northwestern Meml. Hosp., Chgo., 1974-80; pvt. practice psychology Chgo., 1980—; cons. Michael Reese Hosp., Chgo., 1980-86. Contbr. articles to profl. jours. Mem. Dupage County Health Planning Com., Wheaton, Ill., 1984. Commonwealth fellow Govt. U.K., U. Glasgow, 1970. Mem. Am. Psychological Assn., Mental Health Assn. DuPage County (bd. dirs. 1982-84), Biofeedback Soc. Ill. (pres. 1984-85). Home: 16 W 731 89th Pl Hinsdale IL 60521 Office: 320 N Michigan Ave #602 Chicago IL 60601

THOMAS, JOSEPH WESLEY, lawyer; b. Detroit, Aug. 16, 1955; s. John Joseph and Geraldine Clare (France) T.; m. Jamie Ann MacKercher, Aug. 16, 1980. B.A., Oakland U., 1977; J.D., Thomas M. Cooley Law Sch., 1980; M.L.T., Georgetown U., 1982. Bar: D.C. 1980, Mich. 1981, U.S. Dist. Ct. D.C. 1981, U.S. Dist. Ct. (ea. dist.) Mich. 1981, U.S. Tax Ct. 1981, U.S. Ct. Appeals (D.C. cir.) 1981, U.S. Ct. Appeals (6th cir.) 1982. Assoc. Dickstein, Shapiro & Morin, Washington, 1980-81; sole practice, Troy, Mich., 1982-83; ptnr. Farhat & Thomas, P.C., Farmington Hills, Mich., 1983-86; ptnr. Driggers, Schultz, Herbst & Paterson, Troy, Mich., 1986—; panel mem. Mich. Atty. Discipline Bd. Mem. Mich. Bar Assn. (com. on unauthorized practice of law). Office: Driggers Schultz Herbst & Paterson 888 W Big Beaver Rd Suite 400 Troy MI 48084

THOMAS, LEONA MARLENE, medical records educator; b. Rock Springs, Wyo., Jan. 15, 1933; d. Leonard H. and Opal (Wright) Francis; m. Craig L. Thomas, Feb. 22, 1955; (div. Sept. 1978); children—Peter, Paul, Patrick, Alexis. B.A., Govs. State U., 1982, MHS, 1986; cert. med. records adminstrn. U. Colo., 1954. Dir. med. records dept. Meml. Hosp. Sweetwater County, Rock Springs, 1954-57; staff assoc. Am. Med. Records Assn., Chgo., 1972-77, asst. editor, 1979-81; asst. prof. Chgo. State U., 1984—; statistician Westlake Hosp., Melrose Park, Ill., 1982-84. Co. pres. Ill. Dist. 60 PTA, Westmont, Ill., 1972. Mem. Am. Med. Records Assn., Ill. Med. Records Assn., Chgo. and Vicinity Med. Records Assn. Democrat. Methodist. Home: 6340 F Americana Dr Apt 1101 Clarendon Hills IL 60514 Office: Coll Allied Health Chicago State Univ 95th at King Dr Chicago IL 60608

THOMAS, LEROY, newspaper executive editor; b. Detroit, Dec. 17, 1936; s. Leroy and Victoria (Shelton) T.; divorced; children: Sheldon L., Stephen M. AA, Wilson Jr. Coll., Chgo., 1962; student, Roosevelt U., 1962-63, Northwestern U., 1982-83. Asst. mng. editor Chgo. Defender, 1970-76, exec. editor, 1985—; pub. relations rep. midwest region Ford Motor Co., Chgo., 1976-80; sr. editor Blue Cross and Blue Shield of Ill., Chgo., 1981-82; asst. press sec. Office of Mayor, Chgo., 1982-85; adj. instr. journalism Columbia Coll., Chgo., 1973-85; lectr. and cons. various Black orgns. and civic groups. Democrat. Baptist. Club: Jackson Park Yacht (Chgo.). Avocations: sailboating, traveling, collecting antiques, creative writing. Office: Chicago Defender Robert S Abbott Pub Co 2400 S Michigan Ave Chicago IL 60616

THOMAS, LEWIS EDWARD, laboratory executive, retired petroleum company executive; b. Lima, Ohio, May 18, 1913; s. Lewis Edward and Ilma Kathryn (Siebert) T.; B.S., Ohio No. U., 1935; M.S., Purdue U., 1973; m. Elinda Patricia Grafton, Dec. 21, 1939; children—Linda Thomas Collins, Stephanie Thomas Pawuk, Kathryn Thomas Ramsey, Deborah G. Asst. prof. chemistry Va. Mil. Inst., 1940-45; devel. engr. Sun Oil Co., Toledo, 1945-49, lab. supr., 1950-69, div. supr., 1969-73, lab. mgr., 1973-78; mgr. Toledo Symphony, 1978-79; mktg. staff Jones & Henry Labs., Toledo, 1979—; dir. First Fed. Savs. & Loan Assn.; vis. scientist to area high schs. Ohio Acad. Sci., 1960-67. Lay reader Episcopal Ch., 1962; pres., treas. Harvard Elem. Sch. PTA, 1953-54; mem. Mayor's Indsl. Devel. Com., Toledo, 1963-66; mem. Gov.'s Com. Statewide Health Planning Council, 1976—; mem. Lucas County Central Com., precinct committeeman Republican Party, 1958—; trustee Toledo Public Library, 1966-70, pres., 1969-70; trustee Toledo Lucas County Public Library, 1970—, v.p., 1971-72, pres., 1972-75, 85—; trustee U. Toledo, 1967—, vice chmn. bd., 1971-75; mem. adv. bd. St. Charles Hosp.; mem. Assn. Governing Bds. Univs. and Colls., 1969—; mem. governing bd. Northwest Ohio Council Girl Scouts U.S., 1981—; chmn. Northwest Ohio Easter Seals, 1983. Named Chem. Engr. of Year, Toledo Area, 1961, 63, 76; registered profl. engr., Ohio. Mem. Nat., Ohio (chmn. state conv. 1975), Toledo (trustee 1974—) socs. profl. engrs., Am. Inst. Chem. Engrs., Am. Chem. Soc. (pres. Toledo sect. 1960), Nat. Mgmt. Assn. (trustee Toledo chpt. 1962-70, nat. dir. 1968-70), Tech. Soc. Toledo (pres. 1968-69), Explorers Club, Sigma Xi, Pi Kappa Alpha, Tau Beta Pi, Nu Theta Kappa. Club: Toastmasters. Home: 4148 Deepwood Ln Toledo OH 43614 Office: PO Box 920 Toledo OH 43693

THOMAS, LYNDON MARK, data processing executive; b. Canton, Ohio, Nov. 16, 1959; s. Larry Clifton and Janice Norine (Ragon) T.; m. Barbara Emery, Oct. 8, 1983. BA in Math., Malone Coll., Canton, 1982; postgrad., Kent State U., 1984—. Sr. programmer and analyst Timken Co., Canton, 1982—; prof. Malone Coll., 1986. Mem. Assn. Systems Mgmt., Malone Coll. Alumni Assn. (pres. 1987—). Republican. Avocations: snow skiing, water skiing. Home: 1439 Ridgeway Pl NW Canton OH 44709 Office: Timken Co 1835 Dueber Ave SW Canton OH 44706

THOMAS, LYNN, magazine executive; b. Newark, Jan. 25, 1947; d. Ruth Eileen (Graham) Massimino; m. Allen A. Vargo, July 30, 1938. Student, Miami-Dade Coll., 1968-70, U. Miami, 1970-72. Midwest mgr. Ms. mag., Chgo., 1972-76; pres. The Thomas Team Inc., Chgo. and Fla., 1978-80, George Steinbrenner Pub. Div., 1980-84; midwest mgr. Psychology Today mag., Chgo., 1984—; cons. George Steinbrenner Publ. div., Tampa, Fla., 1983-84; guest AM Chgo., 1977, NBC Talk Show, Kansas City, 1977. Named to All-Star Sales Team Madison Ave. mag., N.Y.C., 1986. Mem. Am. Mktg. Assn. (speaker), Chgo. Ad Club. Roman Catholic. Club: East Bank (Chgo.). Home: 1079 S Park Terr Chicago IL 60605 Office: Psychology Today 180 N Michigan Ave Chicago IL 60601

THOMAS, MARGARET ANN, psychologist; b. Cleve., June 2, 1945; d. Frank Robert and Marie (Prochazka) Wiesenberger; m. Charles Walter Geggie, Aug. 30, 1969 (div. 1978); 1 child, Anne Marie; m. James Blake Thomas, Sept. 14, 1978. BA, Albion Coll., 1967; MA, Mich. State U., 1969, PhD, 1981. Lic. psychologist, Mich. Head advisor Albion (Mich.) Coll., 1967-68; head advisor Mich. State U., East Lansing, 1970-72, assoc. dir. Holmes Hall, Lyman Briggs Coll., 1972-74, grad. asst. dept psychiatry, 1974-79, psychology intern, 1977-79; cons. Stress Mgmt. Inc., Okemos, Mich., 1979-80; staff psychologist James B. Thomas, M.D., P.C., Okemos, Mich., 1980—; clin. instr. Dept. Psychiatry, Mich. State U., East Lansing, 1980-86. Pres. parent adv. com., Mich. State U. Day Care Ctr., 1975-77; mem. Friends of Bob Carr for U.S. Ho. Reps., East Lansing, 1982; parent adv. com. Mason (Mich.) Middle Sch., 1985-86. Mem. Am. Psychol. Assn., Mich. Psychol. Assn., Greater Lansing Area Women Therapists (founder, chairperson 1983-84), Nat. Assn. Career Women (sec. Lansing Founding chpt. 1985-87). Democrat. Episcopalian. Home: 322 E Oak St Mason MI 48854 Office: 2946 Mt Hope Okemos MI 48864

THOMAS, MARGARET JEAN, clergywoman, religious research consultant; b. Detroit, Dec. 24, 1943; d. Robert Elcana and Purcella Margaret (Hartness) T. BS, Mich. State U., 1964; MDiv, Union Theol. Sem., Va., 1971. Ordained to ministry Presbyn. Ch., 1971. Dir. research bd. Christian edn. Presbyn. Ch. U.S., Richmond, Va., 1965-71; dir. research gen. council Presbyn. Ch. U.S., Atlanta, 1972-73; mng. dir. research div. support agy. United Presbyn. Ch. U.S.A., N.Y.C., 1974-76; dep. exec. dir. gen. assembly mission council United Presbyn. Ch. U.S.A., 1977-83; dir. N.Y. coordination Presbyn. Ch. (U.S.A.), 1983-85, also mem. permanent jud. commn.; exec. dir. Minn. Council Chs., Mpls., 1985—; sec. com. on ministry Twin Cities Area Presbyn. Ch., Mpls., 1985—; dir. joint religious legis. coalition, 1985—; bd. dirs. Franklin Nat. Bank, Mpls. Contbr. articles to profl. jours. Mem. adv. panel crime/victim services Hennepin County Atty.'s Office, Mpls., 1985-86, Police/Community Relations Task Force, St. Paul, 1986; bd. dirs. Minn. Foodshare, Mpls., 1985—, Minn. Coalition on Health, St. Paul, 1986—, Twin Cities Coalition for Affordable Health Care, 1986—. Mem. Nat. Assn. Ecumenical Staff, Religious Edn. Assn. (sec. 1974-76), People for the Am. Way, NOW (Outstanding Woman of Minn. 1986), Amnesty Internat. Democratic Farm Laborer. Avocation: archaeology. Office: Minn Council of Chs 122 W Franklin Ave #230 Minneapolis MN 55404

THOMAS, MICHAEL CRAIG, physician; b. Massillon, Ohio, July 25, 1950; s. Henry Daniel and Margaret Grace (Spangler) T.; m. Karen Raley, June 30, 1973 (div.); children—Matthew Reese, Michael Ryan. B.S. cum laude, Marietta Coll., 1972; M.D., Case Western Res. U., 1978. Diplomate Am. Bd. Emergency Physicians.Intern, Northwestern Meml. Hosps., Chgo., 1978-79; emergency medicine physician, Lakewood (Ohio) Hosp., 1979-80; dir., chmn. dept. emergency medicine Trumbull Meml. Hosp., Warren, Ohio, 1980—; asst. clin. prof. emergency medicine N.E. Ohio Coll. Medicine. Chmn. Trumbull County Paramedic Adv. Com., med. dir. EMT-Advanced Program; trustee Eastern Ohio chpt. Am. Heart Assn. Fellow Am. Coll. Emergency Physicians; mem. Ohio State Med. Soc., Trumbull County Med. Soc., Cleve. Acad. Medicine, Phi Beta Kappa, Omicron Delta Kappa. Methodist. Office: Trumbull Meml Hosp 1350 E Market St Warren OH 44482

THOMAS, NORVIN EUGENE, internist; b. Marshall, Mo., Apr. 25, 1945; s. Jesse Dale and Irene Bell (Johnson) T.; m. Eva Sue Gibbons, Jan. 22, 1967 (div. June 1979); children: Sean E., Tiffany Sue; m. Sandra Marie Rotter, June 15, 1979; 1 child, Christopher Dale. BA, U. Mo., 1973; DO, Kansas City Coll. Osteo. Medicine, 1978. Diplomat Am. Bd. Internal Medicine. Intern Kansas City Coll. Osteo. medicine, 1978-79; resident internal medicine U. Mo., Kansas City, 1979-82; fellow in pulmonary and environ. medicine Harry S. Truman VA Hosp., Columbia, 1982-84; practice osteo. medicine specializing in internal medicine Audrain Med. Ctr., Mexico, Mo., 1984—, dir. cardiopulmonary dept., 1984—; asst. prof. dept. medicine U. Mo., Columbia, 1985—. Served with USN, 1966-70. Nat. Cancer Inst. grantee, 1975. Fellow Am. Coll. Chest Physicians; mem. Am. Osteo. Assn., Am. Coll. Physicians, Sigma Sigma Phi, Mexico C. of C. Republican. Roman Catholic. Avocations: music, home recording, production and engring. Home: 2330 Southern Hills Mexico MO 65265 Office: 209 E Jackson Mexico MO 65265

THOMAS, PATRICIA GRAFTON, educator; b. Michigan City, Ind., Sept. 30, 1921; d. Robert Wadsworth and Elinda (Oppermann) Grafton; student Stephens Coll., 1936-39, Purdue U., summer 1938; B.Ed. magna cum laude, U. Toledo, 1966; postgrad. (fellow) Bowling Green U., 1968; m. Lewis Edward Thomas, Dec. 21, 1939; children—Linda L. (Mrs. John R. Collins), Stephanie A. (Mrs. Andrew M. Pawuk), I. Kathryn (Mrs. James N. Ramsey), Deborah. Tchr., Toledo Bd. Edn., 1959-81, tchr. lang. arts Byrnedale Sch., 1976-81. Dist. capt. Planned Parenthood, 1952-53, ARC, 1954-55; mem. lang. arts curriculum com. Toledo Bd. Edn., 1969, mem. grammar curriculum com., 1974; bd. dirs. Anthony Wayne Nursery Sch., 1983—; bd. dirs. Toledo Women's Symphony Orch. League, 1983—, sec., 1985—. Mem. Toledo Soc. Profl. Engrs. Aux., Helen Kreps Guild, AAUW, Toledo Artists' Club, Spectrum, Friends of Arts, Phi Kappa Phi, Phi Delta Kappa, Kappa Delta Pi, Pi Lambda Theta (chpt. pres. 1978—), Delta Kappa Gamma (chpt. pres. 1976-78, area membership chmn. 1978-80, 1st place award for exhbn. 1985). Republican. Episcopalian. Home: 4148 Deepwood Lane Toledo OH 43614

THOMAS, PEGGY LEE, special educator; b. Ross, Calif., Sept. 9, 1948; d. Albert Harold and Dolores Vivian (Hansen) Henson; m. Dan Ronald Salden, Oct. 4, 1969 (div. Oct. 1978); m. Terrance Stephen Thomas, June 14, 1986. Student, Ill. State U., 1968; BS in Edn., So. Ill. U., 1971, MS in Edn., 1974, postgrad., 1984—. Cert. elem. tchr., Ill. Spl. edn. tchr. Collinsville (Ill.) Unit 10, 1971-82, dept. head, work study coordinator, 1982-84, mgr. individual edn. plan, work study coordinator, 1984-86; regional spl. needs coordinator Sangamon Area Vocat. Edn. Region, Springfield, Ill., 1987—. Mem. staff Ill. Teenage Inst., Springfield, 1982-83; mem. staff, presenter Opn. Snowball-Drug Prevention, Springfield, 1982-85; exec. bd. dirs. Piasa Health Care, Woodriver, Ill., 1983-86. Recipient Disting. Service award Piasa Health Care, 1986. Mem. Assn. for Supervision and Curriculum Devel., Ill. Assn. for Supervision and Curriculum Devel., Nat. Assn. Vocat. Spl. Needs Personnel, Ill. Assn. Vocat. Spl. Needs Personnel. Lutheran. Avocations: crafts, needlework, volksmarching, cooking, theater. Home: 8 Jenny Ln Springfield IL 62707 Office: Sangamon Area Vocat Edn Region 2201 Toronto Rd Springfield IL 62707

THOMAS, RICHARD C., orchestra executive. Gen. mgr. Milw. Symphony Orch. Office: Milw Symphony Orch Uihlein Hall/Performing Arts Ctr 212 W Wisconsin Ave 8th Fl Milwaukee WI 53203 *

THOMAS, RICHARD L., banker; b. Marion, Ohio, Jan. 11, 1931; s. Marvin C. and Irene (Harruff) T.; m. Helen Moore, June 17, 1953; children: Richard L., David Paul, Laura Sue. B.A., Kenyon Coll., 1953; postgrad. (Fulbright scholar), U. Copenhagen, Denmark, 1954; M.B.A. (George F. Baker scholar), Harvard U., 1958. With First Nat. Bank Chgo., 1958—, asst. v.p., 1962-63, v.p., 1963-65; v.p., gen. mgr. First Nat. Bank Chgo. (London (Eng.) br.), 1965-66, v.p. term loan div., 1968, vice-chmn. bd., 1973-75, pres., dir., 1975—; sr. v.p., gen. mgr. First Chgo. Corp., 1969-72, exec. v.p., 1972-73; vice chmn. bd. 1973-74, pres., 1974—, also dir.; dir. CNA Fin. Corp., Sara Lee Corp., Chgo. Bd. Options Exchange. Trustee, past chmn. bd. trustees Kenyon Coll.; vice chmn. Rush-Presbyn.-St. Luke's Med. Ctr.; trustee Northwestern U.; chmn. bd., Orchestral Assn. Served with AUS, 1954-56. Mem. Chgo. Council Fgn. Relations (dir.), Phi Beta Kappa, Beta Theta Pi. Clubs: Sunningdale Golf (London); Economic (past pres.), Commercial, Chicago, Casino, Mid-America (Chgo.); Indian Hill (Winnetka, Ill.); Old Elm (Ft. Sheridan, Ill.). Office: First Nat Bank of Chgo 1 First National Plaza Chicago IL 60670

THOMAS, RICHARD STEPHEN, treasurer and controller; b. Mason City, Iowa, June 5, 1949; s. H. Idris and Mildred (Keen) T.; m. Pamela Jane Chipka, Sept. 11, 1982. AA, No. Iowa Community Coll., 1969; BA, U. No. Iowa, 1971. Cost acct. Boise Cascade, Mason City, Iowa, 1971-72; cost acct. mgr. Boise Cascade, Shippensburg, Pa., 1973-74; staff acct. Grumman Corp., Williamsport, Pa., 1974-76; acctg. mgr. Pullman Power Products, Williamsport, 1976-79; treas, controller Schweizer Dipple Inc., Cleve., 1979-87; controller Langenau Mfg. Co., Cleve., 1987—, chief fin. officer, 1987—; corp. sec. World Trade Wins Inc., Cleve., 1987—; bd. dirs. Dover Co., Westlake, Ohio. Mem. Nat. Assn. Accts. (controller's council, 1985—), Constrn. Fin. Mgmt. Assn., Am. Assn. Indsl. Investors, Am. Acctg. Assn. (profl. relations com. 1986-87), Westshore Businessman's Assn. (v.p.). Republican. Lodge: Masons (local treas. 1984—). Avocations: skiing, photography, traveling, investing. Home: 22597 Locust Ln Rocky River OH 44116 Office: Langenau Mfg Co 7306 Madison Ave Cleveland OH 44102

THOMAS, ROBERT JACK, electrical contracting company executive; b. St. Louis, Jan. 27, 1947; s. Eugene J. and June R. (Conklin) T.; m. Nancy J. LeMoyne, June 20, 1970; children: Robert J., Tiffany N. BSEE, Washington U., 1979. Sales expediter Gen. Elec. Co., St. Louis, 1970-71; with Internat. Brotherhood of Elec. Workers, St. Louis, 1971-85; chief exec. officer Tiffany Electric Co., St. Louis, 1982—. Served with USN, 1967-69. Mem. Internat. Assn. Elec. Inspectors, Eagle Scout Assn. Episcopalian. Club: Mo. Athletic. Home and Office: Tiffany Electric Co Inc 6488 Fairford Ct Florrissant MO 63033

THOMAS, ROSEMARY CARLIN HYDE, language professional; b. Central Falls, R.I., Jan. 4, 1939; d. Ralph Bowen and Anna Morgan (Flynn) Hyde; m. Ronald Walter Thomas, Aug. 26, 1965; 1 child, Liessa Hyde. BA magna cum laude, Salve Regina Coll., 1961; MA, Ind. U., 1966; PhD, St. Louis U., 1978. Instr. English Université de Nancy, France, 1963-64; instr. French Lindenwood Coll., St. Charles, Mo., 1967-68; prof. French St. Louis Coll. Forest Park, 1968-78; prof. English St. Louis Coll. Meramec, 1978—; dir. Great Rivers in Mo. Life Project, St. Louis, 1986—; dir. Old Mines ResearchProject, 1977-81; cons. Regional Consortium for Edn. Tech., 1986—. Author: It's Good To Tell You, 1981; editor St. Louis Heritage, 1978-86; contbr. articles on Mo. folklore to profl. jours. Leader West County 4H Club, Kirkwood, Mo., 1982—. Fullbright fellow, 1961, 62; Mo. Arts Council grantee, St. Louis, 1981. Mem. Nat. Council Tchrs. English, Mo. Folklore Soc. (pres. 1979-80, bd. dirs. 1980—, editorial bd. 1982—), Mo. Assn. Community Colls., Am. Soc. Tng. Devel. (editor Torch 1983—), Regional Consortium Edn. and Tech. Mem. Unitarian Ch. Office: St Louis Community Coll Meramec 11333 Big Bend Kirkwood MO 63122

THOMAS, RUSSELL, professional football team executive; b. Griffithsville, W.Va., July 24, 1924; m. Dorothy Thomas, Aug. 3, 1945; children: John, Jim. Student, Ohio State U., 1943-46. Formerly asst. coach St. Bonaventure Coll.; player Detroit Lions, then mem. coaching staff, scout, mem. radio broadcasting team, dir. player personnel, 1964, exec. v.p., gen. mgr., 1966—; Dir. Nat. Football League Properties. Inducted into W. Va. Sports Hall of Fame, 1983. Address: Detroit Lions 1200 Featherstone Rd Box 4200 Pontiac MI 48057

THOMAS, STEPHEN C., writer, editor, consultant; b. Paulding, Ohio, Sept. 18, 1952; s. Isaac Rily and Mabel Marie (Essex) T.; m. Marsha Elaine Nichols, Nov. 10, 1978; 1 child, Seth. BSCE, U. Dayton, Ohio, 1977. Editor The Observer, Paulding, 1970-72; photographer McJon, inc., Ft. Wayne, Ind., 1972-73, Chromalloy Photographic, Janesville (Wis.) and Indpls., 1973-74; researcher processing engring. Drackett Co. div. Bristol-Myers, Cin., 1977-79; researcher fats and oils Cen. Soya, Ft. Wayne, 1979-81; mng. editor APRAWS, Inc., Ft. Wayne, 1981—; cons. New Haven (Ind.) Star-Times, 1981-82, New Ft. Wayne mag., 1983-84; columnist Ft. Wayne News-Sentinel, 1985—; editor Waynedale News, Ft. Wayne, 1986. Author: Computer-Based Estimating, 1983, BYOB-Be Your Own Boss!, 1987, Aerobic Gardening, 1987. Mem. Ft. Wayne Writers Guild (bd. dirs. 1985—). Methodist. Club: Emerald Community (Cecil, Ohio). Home: 6010 SE Willow Rd Warren IN 46792 Office: APRAWS Inc 1417 N Anthony Fort Wayne IN 46805

THOMAS, STEVEN LYNN, oral surgeon; b. Maryville, Mo., Nov. 18, 1957; s. Bobbie Alfred and June Marie (Rose) T. BS, N.W. Mo. State U., 1978; DDS, U. Mo., Kansas City, 1982. Resident in dentistry Truman Med. Ctr., Kansas City, Mo., 1982-83; resident in oral and maxillofacial surgery Henry Ford Hosp., Detroit, 1983-86; pvt. practice oral and maxillofacial surgery Overland Park, Kans., 1986—; staff surgeon Shawnee Mission (Kans.) Med. Ctr., 1986—; chief div. dentistry and oral surgery dept. surgery Humana Hosp., Overland Park. Steward Internat. Assn. Fire Fighters, Kansas City, 1981. N.W. Mo. State U. scholar, 1975. Mem. Am. Assn. Oral and Maxillofacial Surgeons, Am. Acad. Oral Medicine (merit award 1982), Am. Coll. Oral and Maxillofacial Surgeons, ADA, Kans. Dental Assn., 5th Dist. Dental Soc., Beta Beta Beta (pres. 1977-78). Republican. Baptist. Avocations: golf, tennis. Home: 8650 W 116th Terrace Overland Park KS 66210 Office: 8005 W 110th Suite 218 Overland Park KS 66210

THOMAS, WILLIAM ANDREW, computer and marketing consultant; b. Detroit, Sept. 9, 1959; s. Eugene Victor and Mary Elizabeth (Williams) T. Student, Shaw Coll., Detroit, 1976-78, Wayne State U., 1979-83, Ea.

Mich. U., 1986. Fin. planner Fin. Services Am., Bloomfield Hills, Mich., 1976-80; mktg. dir. Attainment Enterprises, Inc., Detroit, 1980-82, v.p., pub. relations, 1982-86, pres., chief exec. officer, 1986—; cons. Mich. Dept. Edn., Detroit, 1985—; cons. and researcher United Federated Exporting Co., Detroit, 1980-82; cons. Small Bus. Retailers Assn., Detroit, 1981-82, Boys Club of Detroit. Asst. football coach Cass Tech. High Sch., Detroit, 1986—, head vollyball coach, 1986—; bd. dirs. Jr. Achievement, Detroit, 1979-80. Mem. Am. Mktg. Assn., Engring. Soc. Detroit, Entrepreneur Assn. Am., Internat. Financiers Am., Jaycees. Clubs: Booster (Detroit) (pres.). Lodge: Masons. Office: Attainment Enterprises Inc 2727 2d Ave Suite 231 Detroit MI 48201

THOMAS, WILLIAM KERNAHAN, judge; b. Columbus, Ohio, Feb. 15, 1911; m. Dorothy Good, 1936; children: John R., Richard G., Stephen G., Cynthia G. B.A., Ohio State U., 1932, LL.B., 1935. Bar: Ohio 1935. Practiced in Cleve. until 1950; judge Ct. Common Pleas, Geauga County, Ohio, 1950-53, Ct. of Common Pleas, Cuyahoga County, Cleve., 1953-66; now judge U.S. Dist. Ct., No. Dist. Ohio, Eastern div., Cleve., sr. judge, 1981—. Served with USNR, 1944-46. Mem. Common Pleas Judges Assn. (pres. 1959-60), Nat. Conf. State Trial Judges (chmn. sociopathic offender com. 1963-66), 6th Circuit Dist. Judges Assn. (pres. 1981-82), Jud. Conf. U.S. (com. on adminstrn. bankruptcy system 1968-71, com. on operation of jury system in U.S. 1971-77, subcom. on fair trial free press 1977—.). Office: U S Dist Ct 338 U S Courthouse 201 Superior Ave NE Cleveland OH 44114

THOMASON, JESSICA L., physician, ob-gyn educator; b. Gaffney, S.C., Apr. 16, 1950; d. Henry Clayton and Helen (Humphries) T. BS, U. N.C., 1971, MD, 1974. Diplomate Am. Bd. Ob-Gyn (maternal-fetal medicine). Instr. ob-gyn U. Ill., Chgo., 1979-82, asst. prof., 1982-84; asst. prof. U. Wis. Med. Sch., Madison, 1984-85, assoc. prof., 1985—. Contbr. book chpts. and articles in field. Fellow Am. Coll. Obstetricians and Gynecologists; mem. Soc. Perinatal Obstetricians, Assn. Profs. Gynecology and Obstetrics, Infectious Disease Soc. Am., Infectious Disease Soc. Obstetrics and Gynecology. Office: Mt Sinai Med Ctr Dept Ob-Gyn PO Box 342 Milwaukee WI 53201-0342

THOME, JACK MARTIN, osteopath; b. Lancaster, Pa., Aug. 23, 1949; s. Ralph G. and Minerva (Martin) T.; m. Lilian Tadena, July 22, 1981. BS in Biology, Elizabethtown Coll., 1974; DO, Phila. Coll. Osteopathy Medicine, 1978; MS, Phila. Coll. Osteo. Medicine, 1981. Intern Lancaster (Pa.) Osteo. Hosp., 1978-79; resident gen. practice Phila. Coll. Osteo. Medicine, 1979-80, fellow in gen. practice, 1980-81; asst. prof. dept. family medicine Coll. Osteo. Medicine, Ohio State U., 1981-82, also clin. coordinator physical diagnosis cours; student health physician Hudson Health Ctr., Ohio U.; assoc. dir. family practice residency Doctors Hosp., Columbus, 1983-86; mem. hypertension del. People to People Citizen Ambassador Program, Republic of China, 1983. Served as cpl. USMC, 1969-71. Mem. Pa. Osteo. Med. Assn., Am. Osteo. Assn., Ohio Osteo. Assn., Soc. Med. Assn., So. Tchrs. of Family Medicine. Republican. Presbyterian. Home: 5543 Old Pond Dr Dublin OH 43017

THOMPSEN, JOYCE ANN, manufacturing executive; b. Owatonna, Minn., Mar. 21, 1946; d. Stanley Albert and Elda Margaret Elsie (Buehring) Moeckly; m. Paul Jerome Thompsen, Jan. 21, 1967; children: James Paul, Matthew John. BS in Bus. Edn. summa cum laude, Mankato State U., 1984; postgrad., Coll. St. Thomas, St. Paul, Minn., 1984—. Exec. sec. Josten's Co., Owatonna, 1964-71; univ. relations supr. U. Minn., Waseca, 1971-72; adminstrv. asst. to pres. E.F. Johnson Co., Waseca, 1972-77, corp. sec., 1977-81, v.p. adminstrn., corp. sec., 1981-86, v.p. employee and community relations, corp. sec., 1986—; mem. adv. council U. Minn., Waseca, 1984—, adv. council Mankato (Minn.) State U., MBA program, Coll. of St. Thomas, in St. Paul, industry adv. council, 1987—; trustee E.F. Johnson Co. Found; founder, bd. dirs. P.J. Thompsen, Inc.; v.p. Thompsen Alternators, Owatonna; bd. dirs. Minn. Cooperation Office. Mem. Gov.'s Computer Edn. Council, Minn.; dir. Waseca United Way, Minn. Coop. Office; chmn. Waseca Star Cities Econ. Devel. Com.; dir. Waseca Devel. Corp.; pres. Grace Luth. Ch. Womens' Club, Waseca. Mem. Am. Electronics Assn. (chmn. mgmt. devel.), Minn. High Tech. Council , AAUW, Phi Kappa Phi. Avocations: travel abroad, classical music. Home: 26 Valleyview Waseca MN 56093 Office: E F Johnson Co 299 Johnson Ave Waseca MN 56093

THOMPSON, BILL LAWRENCE, lawyer; b. Chillicothe, Mo., May 20, 1950; s. Charles William and June Rose (Alger) T.; m. Julia Watkins, Aug. 14, 1976. BS in Bus. Adminstrn., Drake U., 1972; JD, U. Mo., 1975. Bar: Mo. 1975, U.S. Dist. Ct. (we. dist.) Mo. 1979. Research atty. Mo. Gen. Assembly, Jefferson City, 1975-78; staff counsel Supreme Ct. Mo., Jefferson City, 1978—. Mem. ABA, Assn. Trial Lawyers Am., Am. Judicature Soc., Cole County Bar Assn., Boone County Bar Assn. Methodist. Avocations: softball, gardening, traveling. Home: Rt 1 Box 94A Ashland MO 65010 Office: Supreme Ct Mo PO Box 150 Jefferson City MO 65102

THOMPSON, CHARLES EDGAR, insurance company executive; b. Kirksville, Mo., Jan. 26, 1944; s. Samuel E. and Carrie N. (Hoffman) T. Sales agt. Londen Ins. Group, Phoenix 1977-79, assoc. regional mgr., 1979-80, regional mgr., 1980, regional v.p., 1980-81, div. v.p., 1981—. Co-editor: History of Elmer, 1976. Mayor, city of Elmer, 1976-78, mem. city council, 1972-76; chmn. Bicentennial Com., 1976. Served with U.S. Army, 1965-67; Vietnam. Named Mgr. of Yr., Londen Ins. Group, 1979, Top Divisional Vice-Pres., 1982, Salesman of Yr., 1980; All Star Honor Roll, Ins. Sales Mag., 1981. Democrat. Home: 1711 S Fifth St Elmer MO 63538 Office: Lincoln Heritage Mktg Ctr 1711 S 5th St Springfield IL 62703

THOMPSON, DALE MOORE, mortgage banker; b. Kansas City, Kans., Nov. 19, 1897; s. George Curl and Ruth Anna (Moore) T.; m. Dorothy Allen Brown, July 2, 1921; 1 son, William Brown (dec. 1978). A.B. cum laude, U. Mich., 1920. With City Nat. Bank and Trust Co. (and predecessor), Kansas City, Mo., 1920-34; v.p. City Nat. Bank and Trust Co. (and predecessor), 1930-34; with City Bond & Mortgage Co. (now United Mo. Mortgage Co.), Kansas City, Mo., 1934—; exec. v.p. City Bond & Mortgage Co. (now United Mo. Mortgage Co.), 1943-48, pres., 1948-68, chmn. bd., 1968-74, hon. chmn., 1974—; chmn. emeritus Central Mortgage & Realty Trust, Kansas City, 1975—; dir. Regency Bldg. Co., Kansas City.; Lectr. schs. mortgage banking Northwestern U., Stanford. Mem. Mo. Bd. Edn., 1966-82, pres., 1968-69; pres. Kansas City Philharmonic Assn., 1944-54, bd. dirs., 1943—; bd. dirs., exec. com. Truman Med. Center (formerly Kansas City Gen. Hosp. and Med. Center), 1962—, treas., 1962-78; chmn. Kansas City campaign United Negro Coll. Fund, 1958-59; Trustee Childrens Mercy Hosp., U. Kansas City; former bd. dirs. Kansas City Art Inst., Conservatory Music Kansas City. Recipient Disting. Service citation Mayor Kansas City, 1955, Community Service citation Archbishop Kansas City, 1954, citation Kansas City C. of C., 1954, citation as Pioneer in Edn. State of Mo., 1982; Protestant honoree NCCJ, 1966; sch. named in his honor, 1982. Mem. Mortgage Bankers Assn. Am. (nat. pres. 1962-63, gov. 1956—, distinguished service award 1968), U. Mich. Alumni Assn. (past dir.), English-Speaking Union (pres. Kansas City br. 1966-67), Phi Beta Kappa (pres. Kansas City 1946-49), Phi Kappa Psi, Trigon. Mem. Christian Ch. Clubs: Monterey Peninsula Country (Pebble Beach, Calif.); River (Kansas City, Mo.), University (Kansas City, Mo.), Indian Hills Country (Kansas City, Mo.). Home: 221 W 48th St Apt 1402 Kansas City MO 64112

THOMPSON, DAVID ALLEN, health care company executive; b. Milbank, S.D., Dec. 4, 1941; s. Lester George and Henrietta Josephine (Gannon) T.; m. Marilyn Marie Selgeby, June 27, 1964; children—Dawn, Virginia, Brian. B.S. in Dairy Sci., S.D. State U., 1964. With Abbott Labs., 1964—, dir. mfg. and engring., Columbus, Ohio, 1972-75, v.p. mfg. and engring., 1975-76, v.p. ops., 1976-81, v.p. corp. materials mgmt., North Chicago, Ill., 1981-82, v.p. personnel, 1982-83, pres. Abbott Diagnostics Div., 1983—. bd. dirs. Dainabot Co., Ltd., Tokyo. Mem. C. of C. (dir. 1972). Republican. Roman Catholic. Club: Biltmore Country (Barrington, Ill.). Lodge: Rotary (dir. 1972). Office: Abbott Labs Abbott Park IL 60064

THOMPSON, DAVID DUANE, new director; b. Bismarck, N.D., Nov. 20, 1956; s. Duane Jackson and Anna Marie (Kaizer) T. Student, Mary Coll., 1975-76; BA in Speech, U. N.D., 1978. News dir. Sta. KBOM, Bismarck, 1978-80; news reporter Sta. KNOX-KYTN, Grand Forks, N.D., 1980-81; news dir. Prairie Pub. Radio, Bismarck, 1981—. Mem. Radio-TV News Dirs. Assn., Pub. Radio News Dirs. Assn., N.D. Associated Press Broadcasters (bd. dirs. 1980-82, 85—, pres. 1982-85). Club: Press (pres. 1983-84) (Bismarck). Home: 818 W Bowen Ave Bismarck ND 58501 Office: Prairie Public Radio 1814 N 15th St Bismarck ND 58501

THOMPSON, DIANE LOGAN, family psychologist, educator; b. Hackensack, N.J., Aug. 25, 1953; d. Curtis P. and Julia Ann (Ryan) L.; m. Gregory Mark Thompson, June 30, 1985; 1 child, Kaitlyn. BA, Fairfield U., 1975; MS, U. Ga., 1977, PhD, 1980. Lic. psychologist, Nebr., Iowa; cert. clin. psychologist, Nebr. Postdoctoral fellow U. Pa., Phila., 1980-82; instr. Harvard Med. Sch., Cambridge, Mass., 1983-85; asst. prof. U. Nebr. Med. Ctr., Omaha, 1983-85, U. Iowa, Iowa City, 1985—; clin. psychologist Share Health Plan, Omaha, 1985; co. dir. Marriage and Family Clinic, U. Iowa, Iowa City, 1985—. Author: (with others) Alcohol & Sexuality, 1983; contbr. articles to profl. jours. Mem. Women's Project on Alcohol, Atlanta, 1978-80, Phila. Area Task Force on Women & Addiction, Phila., 1981-82; chair N.E. Ga. Forum on Women, Athens, 1979. Named one of Outstanding Young Women Am., 1980. Mem. Nat. Council on Family Relations (award 1980), Am. Assn. Marriage & Family Therapists (clin.), Am. Assn. Sex Educators & Therapists, Am. Psychol. Assn. Roman Catholic. Avocations: reading, cooking, travel, shopping. Office: U Iowa Counselor Edn N338 Lindquist Ctr Iowa City IA 52242

THOMPSON, DOROTHY BROWN, writer; b. Springfield, Ill., May 14, 1896; d. William Joseph and Harriet (Gardner) Brown; m. Dale Moore Thompson, July 2, 1921; 1 child, William B. (dec.) AB., U. Kans., 1919. Began writing professionally, 1931; contributed verse to nat. mags. and newspapers including Saturday Rev., Saturday Evening Post, Va. Quar. Rev., Poetry, Commonweal, Good Housekeeping and others, author research articles for various hist. jours.; poems pub. in over 200 collections and textbooks; mags. and textbooks pub. in Eng., Australia, N.Z., Can., India, Sweden; 25 in Braille. Author: (poetry) Subject to Change, 1973. Leader poetry sect. Writers' Conf., U. Kans., 1953-55, McKendree Coll., 1961, 63, Creighton U., Omaha, 1966; lectr. writers' conf. U. Kans., 1965, Am. Poets Series, Kansas City, Mo., 1973; mem. staff Poets Workshop, Cen. Mo. State U., 1974; poet-in-schs. residency for Mo. State Council of Arts, 1974. Recipient Mo. Writers' Guild Award, 1941, Poetry Soc. Am., nat. and local awards. Mem. Diversifiers, Poetry Soc. Am., Nat. Soc. Colonial Dames, First Families of Va. (Burgess for Mo.). Mem. Christian Ch. Clubs: Woman's City, Filson (Louisville). Address: 221 W 48th St Apt 1402 Kansas City MO 64112

THOMPSON, DOUGLAS JAMES, farmer; b. Lincoln, Ill., July 9, 1953; s. Robert James and Kathryn Ann (Carson) T.; m. Laverne Louise Huber, Aug. 27, 1977; children: Janelle Lynn, Nathan James. BS, U. Ill., 1975; grad., Ill. Bankers Sch., 1981. Asst. trust officer Elliott State Bank, Jacksonville, Ill., 1977-80, farm mgr., 1980-83, asst. v.p., 1983-86; owner, mgr. Thompson Farms, Atlanta, Ill., 1986—. Adv. bd. dirs. Salvation Army, Jacksonville, treas. 1979-81, chmn., 1981-86; mem. WIBI Radio Mgr.'s Adv. Com., Carlinville, Ill., 1985. Mem. Ill. Soc. Profl. Farm Mgrs. and Rural Appraisers, Am. Soc. Farm Mgrs. and Rural Appraisers. Republican. Avocations: computers, fishing, swimming. Home: Rural Rt 1 Box 4 Atlanta IL 61723 Office: Thompson Farms Rural Rt 1 Box 51 Atlanta IL 61723

THOMPSON, EDWARD FRANCIS, lawyer, municipal judge; b. Yonkers, N.Y., Aug. 29, 1953; s. Edward Francis and Mary Frances (Keating) T. BA, Manhattanville Coll., 1975; JD, U. Puget Sound, 1978. Bar: Wis. 1978, U.S. Dist. Ct. (ea. and we. dists.) Wis. 1978, U.S. Ct. Claims 1980, U.S. Ct. Appeals (7th cir.) 1980, U.S. Supreme Ct. 1982. Legal intern Puget Sound Legal Assistance Found., Tacoma, Wash., 1976-78; assoc. Hammett, Williams, Riemer & Thompson and predecessor Hammett, Williams & Riemer, Delavan, Wis., 1978-80, ptnr., 1980-84; mcpl. judge Town of Delavan, 1983—; ptnr., v.p. Clair Law Offices, Delavan, 1984—; atty. chmn. Wis. Patients Compensation Panel, 1982-84. Bd. dirs. Delavan-Darien Sch. Dist. Found., 1982—, pres., 1983—. Mem. ABA, Assn. Trial Lawyers Am., Wis. Bar Assn., Walworth County Bar Assn. (v.p. 1984-85, pres. 1985-86), Wis. Acad. Trial Lawyers, Wis. Mcpl. Judges Assn., Walworth County Judges Assn. Home: 311 Holig Ln Rt 4 Box 638 Delavan WI 53115 Office: Connie Zonka & Assocs 1655 N Vine St Chicago IL 60614

THOMPSON, FRED WELDON, clergyman, administrator; b. Durant, Okla., Aug. 1, 1932; s. Fredrick Weldon and Mary Mauvolyn (Barnes) T.; m. Lois Bell Reedy, Apr. 25, 1954; children—Alicia Ann, Penny Sue. B.A., Ottawa U., 1954, D.D. (hon.), 1984; B.D., Central Bapt. Theol. Sem., 1958, Th.M., 1959. Ordained to ministry Am. Bapt. Chs. U.S.A., 1956; pastor South Broadway Bapt. Ch., Pittsburg, Kans., 1961-66; campus minister Bapt. Student Union, Pittsburg, 1962-66; area minister Am. Bapt. Ch. Central Region, Topeka, Kans., 1966-77, assoc. exec. minister, exec. minister, 1982—; assoc. gen. sec. Am. Bapt. Chs., Valley Forge, Pa., 1982—. Bd. dirs. Central Bapt. Theol. Sem., Kansas City, Kans., 1982—, Ottawa U., Kans., 1980—, Bacone Coll., Muskogee, Okla., 1974-82; bd. dirs. United Sch. Dist. 503 Sch. Bd., Parsons, Kans., 1971-77, pres., 1973-76. Recipient Ch. and Community award for Outstanding Alumni, Ottawa U., 1979. Mem. Ottawa U. Alumni Assn. (pres. 1977), Central Bapt. Sem. Alumni Assn. (pres. 1964). *

THOMPSON, GARY ARTHUR, pharmacokineticist; b. Ft. Roberts, Calif., Jan. 30, 1953; s. Marilyn A. (Westermann) T.; m. Claire E. Wiechart, June 30, 1979; 1 child, Laura Anne. BS in Pharmacy, U. Cin., 1976, PhD, 1983. Registered pharmacist. Instr. in biopharmaceutics U. Cin., 1981-83; sr. research biochemist Merrell Dow Research Inst., Cin., 1983-85, sr. research pharmacokineticist II, 1985—. Contbr. articles to profl. jours. U Cin and Inst. for Clin. Pharmacology joint fellowship. Mem. Am. Pharm. Assn., Ohio Pharm. Assn., Acad. Pharm. Scis., Am. Assn. Pharm. Scientists, Rho Chi. Avocations: golf, softball, jogging, music. Home: 5187 Hanley Rd Cincinnati OH 45247 Office: Merrell Dow Research Inst 2110 E Galbraith Rd Cincinnati OH 45215

THOMPSON, HAROLD LEE, lawyer; b. Dayton, Ohio, Feb. 17, 1945; s. Harold Edward Thompson and Johnita Dorothy (Cox) Metcalf; m. Kathryn Lynn Coleman, Aug. 3, 1968 (div. May 1983); children: Aishah T., Aliya S. BA in Econs., Cen. State U., Wilberforce, Ohio, 1967; JD, U. Conn., 1972. Bar: Ohio 1975, U.S. Dist. Ct. (so. dist.) Ohio 1975, D.C. 1976. Acct. Communication Satellite Corp., 1968-69; atty. Ohio State Legal Service, Columbus, Ohio, 1972-74; lawyer Ohio Indsl. Commn., Columbus, 1974-76; sole practice Columbus, 1976-84; ptnr. Jones & Thompson, Columbus, 1984—. Legal counsel Franklin County Rep. Club, Columbus, 1986—; mem. Ohio Rep. Council, Columbus, 1986—. Reginald Heber Smith fellow U.S. Fed. Ct., 1972; named one of Outstanding Young Men of Am., 1974. Mem. Ohio Bar Assn., Columbus Bar Assn., Assn. Trial Lawyers Am., Cen. State U. Alumni Assn. (chmn. scholarships com. 1986—), Columbus Area C. of C. Roman Catholic. Lodge: Masons. Avocations: reading, music. Office: 65 E State St Suite 306 Columbus OH 43215

THOMPSON, HOBSON, JR., librarian; b. Tuscumbia, Ala., Sept. 26, 1931; s. Hobson and Marie (BeLue) T.; m. Geneva Elaine Simon, Feb. 14, 1965; children—Michael Stewart, Sharon Marie. B.S.Ed., Ala. State U., 1952; M.S. in Library Sci., Atlanta U., 1958. Head librarian, instr. math Morris Coll., Sumter, S.C., 1954-62; asst. prof. math, head librarian Elizabeth City (N.C.) State U., 1962-74; br. head Chgo. Public Library, Chgo., 1976—. Mem. adv. council librarians Bd. Govs. U. N.C., 1968-74. Served with USN, 1955-57. Mem. ALA, Ill. Library Assn., Am. Topical Assn., Postal Commemorative Soc., Black Am. Philatelic Soc., Omega Psi Phi, Beta Kappa Chi. Democrat. Methodist. Home: 400 E 33d St Apt 212 Chicago IL 60616 Office: Chicago Public Library 115 S Pulaski Rd Chicago IL 60624

THOMPSON, JAMES CUMMINGS, JR., accountant; b. St. Louis, Mar. 12, 1936; s. James Cummings and Alice V. (Igoe) T.; m. Merilyn B. Bensinger, Sept. 10, 1960; children: Meridith Lynn, Darrett B. BBA in Fin., Boston Coll., 1958. Prin. James C. Thompson & Co., St. Louis, 1960—; bd. dirs. Whitaker Charitable Found., St. Louis, Internat. Plating Corp., St. Louis. Mem. St. Louis U. Bequest and Gift council. Mem. Am. Inst. CPA's, Mo. Soc. CPA's, Aircraft Owners and Pilots Assn., Estate Planning Council of St. Louis. Republican. Roman Catholic. Clubs: Sain Louis, Noonday (St. Louis). Home: 9 Upper Ladue Rd Saint Louis MO 63124 Office: James C. Thompson & Co 319 N 4th St Saint Louis MO 63102

THOMPSON, JAMES ROBERT, governor of Illinois; b. Chgo., May 8, 1936; s. James Robert and Agnes Josephine (Swanson) T.; m. Jayne Carr, 1976; 1 dau., Samantha Jayne. Student, U. Ill., Chgo., 1953-55, Washington U., St. Louis, 1955-56; J.D., Northwestern U., 1959. Bar: Ill. 1959, U.S. Supreme Ct. 1964. Asst. state's atty. Cook County, Ill., 1959-64; assoc. prof. law Northwestern U. Law Sch., 1964-69; asst. atty. gen. State Ill., 1969-70; chief criminal div. 1969, chief dept. law enforcement and pub. protection, 1969-70; 1st asst. U.S. atty. No. Dist. Ill., 1970-71, U.S. atty., 1971-75; counsel firm Winston & Strawn, Chgo., 1975-77; gov. Ill., 1977—; mem. joint com. to revise Ill. criminal code, mem. drafting subcom. Chgo.-Ill. bar assns., 1959-63, chmn. joint com. to draft indigent def. legis., 1966-68; mem. com. to draft handbooks for petit jurors in civil and criminal cases and for grand jurors Jud. Conf. Ill., 1959; mem. com. to draft uniform instrn. in criminal cases Ill. Supreme Ct.; co-dir. criminal law course for Chgo. Police and Indsl. Security Personnel, 1962-64; mem. Chgo. Mayor's Com. to Draft Legis. to Combat Organized Crime, 1964-67; adviser Pres.'s Commn. Law Enforcement and Adminstrn. Justice, 1966; mem. Pres.'s Task Force on Crime, 1967; lectr. Northwestern U. Law Sch., U. Calif.-Davis, Mich. State U., Nat., Ill., Ohio, N.D., Va., N.J., Ala., Md. and Ga. prosecutors' assns.; former bd. dirs. Chgo. Crime Commn.; v.p. Americans for Effective Law Enforcement, 1967-69. Co-author: Cases and Comments on Criminal Justice, 2 vols, 1968, 74, Criminal Law and Its Adminstration, 1970, 74; asst. editor-in-chief: Jour. Criminal Law, Criminology and Police Sci, 1965-69; bd. editors: Criminal Law Bull. Mem. ABA, Ill. Bar Assn. (past chmn. criminal law sect.). Republican. Address: Office of Gov 207 State House Springfield IL 62706 *

THOMPSON, JAMES S., JR., agricultural property management executive; b. Oklahoma City, May 24, 1924; s. James Scarborough and Mary (Crocker) T.; m. Inga Erickson, June 28, 1952 (div. 1982); m. Barbara Westgor, July 8, 1986; children: Eric C., James Anthony, Horace A., Mark S. Student, Yale U., 1942, St. Olaf Coll., 1942, U. Minn., 1942, 46-47, St. Thomas Coll., 1943, U. Ga., 1943. Pres., chief exec. officer Fairland Mgmt. Co., Windom, Minn., 1964—. Contbr. articles to profl. jours. Mem. steering com. Middle Des Moines Watershed Dist., 1982-86; pres. Youth Athletic Orgns., Windom, 1970's; chmn. county fin. Minn. Rep. Orgn., 1960's.Served with USN, 1943-46, PTO. Recipient Sears Roebuck Conservation award, 1956. Mem. Minn. Soc. Farm Mgrs. and Rural Appraisers, Am. Soc. Farm Mgr. and Rural Appraisers, DUcks Unltd. (county fin. chmn.). Episcopalian. Clubs: St. Paul Athletic, Pool and Yacht. Avocations: hunting, fishing, outdoor activities. Home: PO Box 128 Windom MN 56101 Office: Fairland Mgmt Co 310 11th St Windom MN 56107

THOMPSON, JANA LYNN EILERS, laboratory technician; b. Holland, Iowa, May 13, 1959; d. Wayne Laverne and Judith Dee (Heerts) Eilers; m. William Richey Thompson, Mar. 21, 1981. A in AS, U. Minn. Tech. Coll., 1979; BS in Animal Sci., U. Minn., 1982. Bookkeeper Bank of S.W., Dodge City, Kans., 1983; lab. tech Servi-Tech, Dodge City, 1983—. Mem. Bus. & Profl. Women (v.p. 1986-87), Gamma Sigma Delta Agrl. Honor Soc., Beta Sigma Phi-Alpha-Delta (treas. 1984-85, extension officer 1986-87, Woman of Yr. award 1985). Republican. Avocations: reading, computer programming, alpine skiing, needlework, volleyball. Home: Rural Rt 2 Box 511 Dodge City KS 67801 Office: Servi-Tech 1816 E Wyatt Earp Dodge City KS 67801

THOMPSON, JANICE IONE, producer, director; b. Oceanside, Calif., Aug. 10, 1957; d. Robert Earl and Fern Ione (Sebring) T.; m. Bruce Kraig, July 21, 1984. AA, Loop Coll., 1978; BA, Roosevelt U., 1982, B in Music, 1983. Radio producer Roosevelt U., Chgo., 1979-82; assoc. producer Board of Rabbis, Chgo., 1980-82; producer, dir. Cablenet Assn., Mt. Prospect, Ill., 1982-85, City of Park Ridge, Ill., 1985—; media cons. Holocaust Meml. Found., Skokie, Ill., 1981-82. Producer, dir. TV documentaries Voices, 1982, Acapulco Blues, 1981; theme music composer TV show Beyond Magic Door, 1982-84 (Emmy award 1984), radio show Interface for Sheffield Winds, 1983-84; dir. (film) The Rock That Glowed, 1987; dir. Good As Gold Prodns., 1987. Named one of Outstanding Young Women in Am., 1984. Mem. Nat. Acad. TV Arts and Scis., Am. Film Inst., Chgo. Area Film and Video Network, Ctr. for New TV. Avocations: racquetball, softball.

THOMPSON, JOE DOUGLAS, banker; b. Kansas City, Mo., Jan. 28, 1956; s. Joseph Roy and Jenny Mae (Wiesner) T.; m. Wanda Sue Franken, Mar. 4, 1983; children: Nathanael and Philip (twins). BS Acctg., SW Mo. State U., 1979. CPA, Mo.; cert. realtor. Semi-sr. auditor Mo. State Auditors Office, Jefferson City, 1979-84; sr. credit analyst Cen. Trust Bank, Jefferson City, 1984-86, comml. loan officer, 1986—. Mem. Am. Inst. CPA's, Mo. Soc. CPA's, Jefferson City C. of C., United Way. Republican. Methodist. Avocations: computers, softball, antiques. Home: 1609 Rosewood Dr Jefferson City MO 65101 Office: Cen Trust Bank 238 Madison St Jefferson City MO 65101

THOMPSON, JOHN RICHARD, psychologist; b. Mt. Morris, Ill., Sept. 19, 1929; s. John Reginald and Nell Elizabeth (Conrad) T.; m. Wynona Francis Marion Tank, Mar. 20, 1951; children: Steven John, James John, Michael John, Merri Christine. BA, U. Colo., 1952, MA, PhD, 1960. Diplomate Am. Bd. Profl. Psychology. Intern V.A. Hosp., Denver and Ft. Lyon, Colo., 1956-59; research asst. VA Hosp., Denver, 1959-60, clin. and counseling psychologist, 1960-64; prof. psychology, dir. psychol. services Oberlin (Ohio) Coll., 1964—. Editor (jour.) Rocky Mountain Psychologist, 1960-64; assoc. editor (jour.) Nursing Digest, 1973-75; contbr. articles to profl. jours. Bd. dirs. Allen Meml. Hosp., Oberlin, 1974-76, Oberlin Community Found., 1968-70, Lorain (Ohio) County Mental Health, 1969-82. Served with U.S. Army, 1952-54. Recipient Spl. Citation, Am. Coll. Health Assn., 1969; med. fellow U. N.C., 1970; grantee Oberlin Coll., 1971. Mem. Am. Psychol. Assn. Democrat. Lodge: Rotary. Avocations: sailing, photography. Home: 254 Elm St Oberlin OH 44074 Office: Oberlin Coll Peters Hall Oberlin OH 44074

THOMPSON, JOSEPH P., data processing executive; b. N.Y.C., May 20, 1937; s. Joseph J. and Susan An. (Dorman) T.; m. Carmen I. D'Amore, Aug. 29, 1959; children: Steve D., Christine A., Michael J. BBA, St. John's U., 1960; MBA, U. Chgo., 1975. Dir. systems mgmt. Kraft Inc., Glenview, Ill., 1969-84; dir. mgmt. info. systems Stone Container, Chgo., 1984—. Roman Catholic. Avocations: golf, fishing. Home: 401 Carol Ln Mount Prospect IL 60056 Office: Stone Container 150 N Michigan Ave Chicago IL 60601

THOMPSON, JOSEPH WARREN, physician, surgeon; b. Wichita Falls, Tex., June 27, 1950; s. Allen Dulaney and Norma Helen (Rinabarger) T.; m. Harriet Ann Weeks, June 19, 1976 (div.). BS, S.E. Mo. State U., 1972; DO, U. Health Scis., Coll. Osteo. Medicine, Kansas City, Mo., 1976. Diplomate Am. Coll. Gen. Practitioners, Nat. Bd. Osteo. Med. Examiners. Intern Normandy Hosp., St. Louis, 1976-77, resident in family practice, 1977-79; pvt. practice medicine, St. Louis, 1979—; program dir. family practice residency, 1982—, chief of staff, Normandy Osteo. Hosps. North and South, 1986-87. Mem. Mo. Osteo. Assn. (polit. action com.), Am. Osteo. Assn. (com. on edn. and evaluation), Nat. Library of Medicine, Region V111, (mem. adv. council), Am. Coll. Gen. Practitioners (past pres. Mo. soc.), Mo. Assn. Osteo. Physicians and Surgeons, St. Louis Dist. Assn. Osteo. Physicians and Surgeons. Democrat. Methodist. Lodges: Elks, Masons, Shriners. Office: 3301 Ashby Rd Saint Ann MO 63074

THOMPSON, JUUL HAROLD, lawyer, educator; b. Chgo., May 3, 1945; s. Jules Harold and Ruth Edith (Pudark) T.; m. Elizabeth Jean Bohler, Sept. 20, 1975; children: Michael, Erin, David, Margaret, Joseph. BA in History, U. Chgo., 1967; JD, U. Ill., 1973. Bar: Ill. 1973. Asst. states atty. Kane County, Ill., 1974-76; ptnr. Beck and Thompson, Batavia, Ill., 1976-82; sole practice, Batavia, 1983—; counsel Batavia Council on Aging, 1979—; counsel, grant chmn. Batavia Social Services Com., 1983-86; counsel Programming for Low Income and Urban Services Community Service Agy., Batavia, 1978-86; local collection counsel Alcoa Bldg. Products, Security Pacific Fin. Corp., I.C. Collection Systems St. Paul; instr. law Elgin Community Coll., Ill., 1981-84, Harper Community Coll., Palatine, Ill., 1981-83, Waubonsee Community Coll., Sugar Grove, Ill., 1982, Person Wollinsky CPA Rev. Course, Downers Grove, Ill., 1984. Mem. Holy Cross Cath. Ch. Parish Council, 1985-86; pres. A.G.S. PTO, 1986-88. Served as 1st lt. U.S.

Army, 1969-71, Vietnam. Decorated Bronze Star (2). Mem. VFW (Batavia comdr. 1979-80, trustee 1985-86), Holy Cross Players. Republican. Lodge: K.C. (4th degree). Avocations: reading, woodworking, writing. Home: 1220 S Batavia Batavia IL 60510 Office: 150 W Houston St PO Box 543 Batavia IL 60510

THOMPSON, LYLE FRANCIS, advertising agency executive; b. South Milwaukee, Wis., May 9, 1929; s. Clarence L. and Emily (Martinek) Nowack; m. Helen Marie Taberman, Apr. 6, 1963. Student, U. Wis., Madison and Milw., 1947-48. Asst. advt. mgr. Mordberg Mfg., Milw., 1958-61; mng. editor Tri Town News, Hales Corner, Wis., 1961-63; advt. mgr. Controls Co. Am., Milw., 1963-68; v.p. Andrews Advt., Milw., 1968-73; pres. Thompson Gardner Olsen, Inc., Mequon, Wis., 1973—. Mem. Bus. Profl. Advt. Assn. (chpt. pres. 1968-69, internat. dir. 1970-71), Milw. Advt. Club (bd. dirs. 1980-83), Sales Promotion Execs. Assn. (Wis. Sales Promotion Man of Yr. 1970), U.S. Ski Assn. Republican. Lutheran. Clubs: South Shore Yacht, Vagabond Ski (pres. 1965-66), Lac Du Cours Yacht (commodore 1984). Avocations: snow skiing, golfing, sailing. Home: 3517 W LeGrande Blvd Mequon WI 53092 Office: Thompson Gardner Olsen Inc 11512 N Port Washington Rd Mequon WI 53092

THOMPSON, MARC EDWARD, broker; b. Sacramento, Jan. 4, 1952; s. William Edward and Carmen Sidney (Drollet) T.; m. Collier Young, Dec. 19, 1986. BA in Econs., U. Calif., Berkeley, 1974; postgrad., Stanford U., 1975. Resident mgr. Clayton Brokerage Co., San Francisco, 1974-77, spread specialist, Chgo., 1977-78, fin. instruments specialist, 1978-80; dir., arbitrage ptnr. Tradelink Corp., Chgo., 1980-83; floor broker, ind. trader Chgo. Bd. Trade, 1983—; v.p. E.F. Hutton & Co., 1985—, Va. Trading Corp.; dir. Bd. Trade Found., mem. various coms. Sponsor, Chgo. Fgn. Affairs Council; active Chgo. Archtl. Found., Field Mus. Found. Mem. Internat. Monetary Market. Republican. Home: 79 E Elm St Chicago IL 60611 Office: PO Box 900 141 W Jackson Blvd Chicago IL 60604

THOMPSON, MARY EMMA, principal; b. Paris, Ill., Oct. 14, 1933; d. Fred Mascher and Velma (Britton) G.; m. George Elmer Thompson, Aug. 6, 1950 (dec. Aug. 1959); children—Tony, Bobbi Thompson Harris, Gary. A.A., Palm Beach Jr. Coll., 1965; B.S. in Elem. Edn., Fla. Atlantic U., 1966; student So. Ill. U., 1969-71; M.S. in Elem. Edn., Eastern Ill. U., 1975 Ed.S., 1978; student Western Ill. U., 1975-76, 78; Ph.D. in Edn. Adminstrn., Ind. State U., 1985. Elem. tchr. Monroe County Schs., Fla., 1967-68, Pittsfield Dist. 10, Ill., 1968-78; elem. prin. Westfield Dist. 105, Ill., 1978-83; fellow Ind. State U., Terre Haute, 1983-84; chpt. I dir. Westfield Schs., 1979-85, prin., 1984-85; head tchr. Westfield Elementary Sch., 1985-86, tchr. sixth grade 1986—. mem. survey and evaluation teams Ind. State U., Terra Haute, 1983-84. Sponsor Cystic Fibrosis Bike-a-thon, Westfield, 1979-82; mem. Clark County Mental Health Bd., Marshall, Ill., 1979—, treas., 1983—. Mem. Delta Kappa Gamma, Alpha Upsilon, Phi Delta Kappa. Republican. Baptist. Club: 4-H (leader 1967-73) (Pearl, Ill.). Avocations: reading, sewing, crocheting, travel. Home: Rural Route 1 Box 85 Westfield IL 62464

THOMPSON, PAUL LELAND, artist; b. Buffalo, Iowa, May 20, 1911; s. Buell and Flora Elizabeth (Steen) T.; student Calif. Sch. Fine Arts, 1932-34, Corcoran Sch. Art, 1944-45; m. Phyllis McGregor, June 15, 1953; 1 dau., Leslie Ruth. One-man shows Internat. Galleries, Washington, 1946, M. Knoedler Co. Inc., 1954, Unitarian Ch., Plainfield, N.J., 1975, Cin. Art Club, 1978, others; exhibited group shows Seattle Art Mus., 1937, Honolulu Acad. Art, 1933, Corcoran Biennial Nat. Painting Exhbn., 1945, San Francisco Palace of Legion of Honor, 1948, San Francisco Art Mus., 1948, NAD Nat. Watercolor Exhbn., 1956, Hunterdon County Art Center, Clinton, N.J., 1968; executed two murals Shiloh Baptist Ch., Plainfield, N.J.; represented in permanent collections Barry's Art Gallery, Scotch Plains, N.J., Cin. Bell Collection, The Heritage Gallery, Cin. Recipient Soc. Washington Artists prize, 1946; The Washington Times Herald award, 1947. Mem. Artists Equity N.Y., Cin. Art Club, Cin. McDowell Soc., Am. Inst. Conservation Works of Art. Home: 314 Ludlow Ave Cincinnati OH 45220 Office: 3412 Telford St Cincinnati OH 45220

THOMPSON, PETER RUSSELL, retired construction and development company executive; b. N.Y.C., Dec. 12, 1921; s. Alfred Peter and Edythe Morris (Helfenstein) Swoyer; m. Elizabeth Smith Park, Oct. 23, 1948 (dec. 1971); children—Sharon F., Peter Russell, Elizabeth Park; m. Elizabeth Ann Edwards, Jan. 28, 1973. B.E. in C.E., Yale U., 1947. Engr., Gulf Oil Corp., N.Y.C., 1947-49, Gilbane Bldg. Co., Providence, 1949-52; sales engr. Masonite Corp., Providence, 1952-53; regional sales mgr. Nat. Homes Corp., Lafayette, Ind., 1953-58; exec. v.p. Inland Homes Corp., Piqua, Ohio, 1958-61; chief exec. officer, pres. Mid-Continent Properties, Inc., Piqua, 1962-86; bd. dirs. C&H Bancorp, Citizens Heritage Bank, N.A.; chmn., Piqua Planning Commn., 1967-74; mem. Ohio Housing Devel. Bd., 1971-74; mem. adv. com. on truth in lending to Bd. Govs., FRS, 1971-76; trustee Miami Valley Health Systems Agy., 1980; trustee Upper Valley Med. Ctr., Dettmer Hosp., Piqua Meml. Med. Ctr., Stouder Hosp., Dittmer Hosp. Found.; bd. dirs.Piqua YMCA; past pres., bd. dirs. Piqua United Fund. Served to lt. AUS, 1943-46; ETO. Decorated Air medal; recipient Man of Yr. awards Piqua Jaycees, Piqua C. of C. Mem. Nat. Assn. Home Builders (dir. 1965-78), Ohio Home Builders Assn. (trustee, past pres.), Miami County Home Builders Assn. (life dir., past pres.), Piqua C. of C. (past pres., past dir.). Republican. Episcopalian. Clubs: Piqua Country (past pres., dir.), Rotary (past pres., dir.), Yale of Dayton. Office: 322 W Water St PO Box 1659 Piqua OH 45356

THOMPSON, PHEBE KIRSTEN, physician; b. Glace Bay, N.S., Can., Sept. 5, 1897; d. Peter and Catherine (McKeigan) Christianson; M.D., C.M. Dalhousie U., Halifax, N.S., 1923; m. Willard Owen Thompson, M.D., June 21, 1923 (dec. Mar. 1954); children—Willard Owen, Frederic, Nancy, Donald. Came to U.S., 1923, naturalized, 1937. Intern Children's Hosp., Halifax, N.S., 1922-23; asst. biochemistry, dept. applied physiology Harvard Sch. Pub. Health, 1924-26; asst. and research fellow in medicine, thyroid clinic, Mass. Gen. Hosp., Boston, 1926-29; asst. in metabolism dept. (endocrinology) Rush Med. Coll. of U. Chgo. and The Central Free Dispensary Chgo., 1930-46; assoc. with husband in practice medicine, Chgo., 1947-54; mng. editor Jour. Clin. Endocrinology and Metabolism, 1954-61, cons. editor, 1961-65; editor Jour. Am. Geriatrics Soc., 1954-82; cons. editor Endocrinology, 1961-65; free-lance editor and writer. Recipient Thewlis award Am. Geriatrics Soc., 1966; cert. of appreciation Am. Thyroid Assn., 1966. Fellow Am. Med. Writers' Assn. (adv. com. 1955-60, v.p. Chgo. 1962), Am. Geriatrics Soc., Gerontological Soc. Am.; mem. Endocrine Soc., AAAS, Am. Genetic Assn., Am. Pub. Health Assn., Ill. Pub. Health Assn., Ill. Acad. Scis., Art Inst. Chgo. (life), Chgo. Hist. Soc. (life). Clubs: Univ.; Harvard; Canadian (corr. sec. 1968-73; mem. bd. 1973-76). Address: 4250 N Marine Dr Chicago IL 60613

THOMPSON, R. RICKERD, automotive company executive; b. Grosse Pointe, Mich., Sept. 10, 1950; s. Jospeh Patrick and Barbara (Rickerd) T.; m. Julie Coyle, Aug. 7, 1971 (div. Jan. 1977); m. Janet Opdyke, Dec. 30, 1981; children: Kelly I., Kerry G. BS in Econs., Eastern Mich. U., 1973. Sales promotion mgr. Am. Motors, McLean, Va., 1973-76; treas. Thompson Industries, Southgate, Mich., 1976-80, pres., 1981—; pres. Metro Jobbers, Ferndale, Mich., 1985—; chmn. Thompson, Jones, Grosse Ile, 1986—. vice chmn. Grosse Ile Planning Commn., 1986. Served to lt. U.S. Army, 1972-73. Clubs: Detroit Athletic, Grosse Ile Golf and Country, Grosse Pointe (Mich.) Hunt. Office: Thompson Industries 16225 Fort Box 360 Southgate MI 48195

THOMPSON, RAYMOND LOUIS, JR., data systems executive; b. Des Moines, Nov. 8, 1946; s. Raymond Louis and Harriet (Eldred) T.; m. Deborah Jessica Eisenberg, July 5, 1970; children—Rachel, Rebekah, David. Student Kans. U., 1964-67; B.S. in Bus. Mgmt., Drake U., 1972. Cert. data processer; cert. systems profl. Mgr. data processing Funeral Security Plans, Kansas City, Mo., 1972-75, City of Olathe, Kans., 1978-84; supr. licensing Ozark Nat. Life, Kansas City, 1975-76; mgr. credit systems and procedures Western Auto, Kansas City, 1976-78; mgr. data systems fin. planning United Data Services, Inc., Overland Park, Kans., 1984—; speaker internat. confs. Served with USNR, 1967-69. Recipient Cert. Accounting Conformance, Mcpl. Fin. Officers Assn., Olathe, 1979. Mem. Data Processing Mgmt. Assn., Assn. System Mgrs., Assn. Computer Users, Urban Regional Info. Systems Assn. Republican. Lodge: Optimists. Avocations: home improving; wood working. Office: United Data Services Inc 5454 W 110th St Overland Park KS 66207

THOMPSON, RICHARD LLOYD, small business owner, education administrator; b. Custer, S.D., Oct. 9, 1941; s. Lloyd Emery and MaeJo (Duprel) T.; m. Judy Coreen Anderson, Aug. 25, 1962; children: Brian, Tamra, Kevin (dec.), Kara. BA in Edn., Creighton U., 1964; MA in Ednl. Adminstrn., U. Colo., 1977. Gen. mgr. Sylvan Lake Resort, Custer, 1968-76; chmn. bus. div. Black Hills State Coll., Spearfish, S.D., 1977-84; owner, mgr. Sluice an' Laughing Water Restaurant, Spearfish, 1978—; prin. St. Martin's Acad., Rapid City, S.D., 1984-86, fin. adminstr., 1986—; cons. Ctr. Indian Studies, Spearfish, 1976-77, RAMKOTA, Sioux Falls, 1985. Contbr. articles to profl. jours. Mem. Nat. Assn. Secondary Sch. Prins., Nat. Restaurant Assn. Roman Catholic. Avocations: writing poetry, collecting cars and watches. Home: 735 8th Spearfish SD 57783 Office: Sluice Inc Box 396 Spearfish SD 57783

THOMPSON, RUSSELL VERN, school district superintendent; b. Clarinda, Iowa, Feb. 24, 1934; s. Vern Russell and Parrie Lee (Pricer) T.; m. Ruth Ann Steeve, Apr. 1, 1956; children—Kevin Lee (dec.), Lisa Kim, Russell Vern II (dec.). B.S., N.W. Mo. State U., 1956; M.Ed., U. Mo., 1960, Ed.D., 1968; postdoctoral Columbia U., 1977. Lic. ednl. adminstr., Mo. Tchr., chmn. dept. Hickman High Sch., Columbia, Mo., 1957-62, asst. prin., 1962-63, prin., 1963-65; dir. secondary edn. Columbia pub. schs., Mo., 1965-69, asst. supt., 1969-76, supt., 1976—; vis. assoc. prof. U. Mo., Columbia, 1972—. Contbr. articles to pamphlets and profl. jours. Pres., bd. dirs. Columbia United Way, Mo., 1970—; bd. dirs. Indsl. Devel. Bd., Columbia, 1976—; chmn. Mo. Edn./Bus. Ptnrs. Program, 1984—; mem. grant adv. com. State of Mo. Edn. Block, state adv. com. on profl. devel. Mo. State Bd. Edn., 1986-87; co-chmn. Boone County Hist. Soc. Mus., 1986-87. Named Outstanding Young Man of Yr., Jaycees, Columbia, 1970; named Disting. Leader, Kiwanis Internat., 1974; One of Top 100 Exec. Educators of N.Am., The Exec. Educator, 1984. Mem. Am. Mgmt. Assn., Am. Assn. Sch. Adminstrs., Mid-Am. Assn. Supts., Mo. Assn. Sch. Adminstrs. (pres. 1983-84), Phi Delta Kappa (Gamma chpt. 1967-68). Lodges: Kiwanis (pres. 1970-71), Rotary (pres. 1986-87). Avocations: horseback riding; reading; swimming; golf. Home: Route 4 Columbia MO 65203 Office: Columbia Pub Sch District Adminstrn Bldg 1818 W Worley Columbia MO 65203

THOMPSON, SETH CHARLES, oral and maxillofacial surgeon; b. Whittemore, Mich., Aug. 12, 1927; s. Seth Charles and Annie Ernestine (Washburn) T.; m. Effie Valore Garland, Jan. 20, 1954; children: Seth Charles III, David Garland. BS, Mich. State U., 1949; DDS, U. Mich., 1952, MS, 1959. Pvt. practice oral and maxillofacial surgery Midland, Mich., 1959—. Discoverer surgical treatment for trigeminal neuralgia, 1976. Bd. dirs. Midland (Mich.) Christian Sch., 1971-72, Inst. for Achievement of Human Potential, Midland, 1970-71. Served to capt. USAF, 1953-55. Fellow Am. Assn. Oral and Maxillofacial Surgery; mem. ADA, Mich. Dental Assn., Mich. Assn. Oral and Maxillofacial Surgery, Midland County Med. Soc. Republican. Baptist. Lodge: Rotary. Avocations: hunting, fishing, travel, woodworking. Home: 2728 Parrish Rd Midland MI 48640 Office: 2706 Louanna Midland MI 48640

THOMPSON, STANLEY DEAN, radiologist; b. Fergus Falls, Minn., Apr. 8, 1933; s. Ole Orville and Gladys CHarlotte (Weiss) T.; m. Denise Myrna Lindseth, May 19, 1962; children: Brent, Jeffrey, Michelle. BA, U. N.D., 1955, BS, MS, 1957; MD, U. Pa., 1959. Diplomate Am. Bd. Radiology. Radiologist Fargo (N.D.) Clinic, 1964—; bd. dirs. Fargo Clinic Ltd., St. Luke's Hosp. Mem. AMA, N.D. State Med. Soc., N.D. State Radiologic Soc. (pres. 1970-71), Soc. Clin. Radiologists, Am. Coll. Radiology. Lutheran. Club: Fargo-Moorhead Camera (v.p. 1973-74, pres. 1974-75). Avocations: photography, gardening. Home: 143 S Woodcrest Dr Fargo ND 58102 Office: Fargo Clinic Ltd 737 Broadway Fargo ND 58123

THOMPSON, STEPHEN M., accountant; b. Vincennes, Ind., Apr. 4, 1944; s. Richard Maurice and Mary Martha (Begeman) T.; m. June Martin Zock, June 22, 1968; children: Kristin Michelle, David Andrew. AA, Vincennes U., 1964; BS, Ind. U., 1966, MBA, 1967. CPA. Mem. audit staff Peat Marwick Mitchell & Co., N.Y.C., 1967-68, Indpls., 1968-71; ptnr. Smith, Thompson, Wihebrink, Lafayette, Ind., 1971—; pres. CPA Mgmt. Systems, 1986—. Dir. Christian Radio, Leadership, Lafayette, 1986; mem. Home Hosp. Fin. Commn., Lafayette, 1986. Mem. Am. Inst. CPAs, Ind. CPA Soc., Lafayette Chpt. CPAs. Republican. Presbyterian. Home: 618 Northridge Dr West Lafayette IN 47906 Office: Smith Thompson Wihebrink & Co 427 N 6th St Lafayette IN 47902

THOMPSON, THOMAS ADRIAN, teacher; b. Sidney, Mont., Aug. 28, 1944; s. Vernon Eugene and Helen Alice (Torstenson) T.; m. M. Aileen Braun, June 7, 1968; children: Blair C., Meghann C. BA, Concordia Coll., 1966; postgrad., Mich. State U., 1968-69, Oakland U., 1970-72. Art tchr. Carman Ainsworth Sch. Cist., Flint, Mich., 1966—; chmn. Flint Art Curriculum Com., 1980. Mem. NEA, Nat. Art. Edn. Assn., Mich. Art Edn. Assn. (liaison mem.), Mich. Den. Assn. Lutheran. Avocations: painting, sculpture, golf. Home: 1120 Old Town Ct Grand Blanc MI 48439 Office: Carman Ainsworth Sch Dist Flint MI 48501

THOMPSON, THOMAS HENRY, academic dean, philosophy educator; b. Sioux City, Iowa, Jan. 10, 1924; s. Elmer Edwin and Ruth Alma (Baker) T.; m. Diane Sargent, Nov. 23, 1955; children: Brenda, Alicia, Mark, Rosemary. B.A., U. Iowa, 1948, M.A., 1950, Ph.D., 1952. Asst., instr. U. Iowa, Iowa City, 1948-52; mem. faculty U. No. Iowa, Cedar Falls, 1952—; prof. philosophy U. No. Iowa, 1969—, head dept., 1969-81, acting dean Coll. Humanities and Fine Arts, 1981-82, dean Coll. Humanities and Fine Arts, 1982—. Mem. Sigmund Freud Gesellschaft (Vienna), Am. Philosophy Assn. Home: 2122 California St Cedar Falls IA 50613 Office: U Northern Iowa Communication Arts Ctr 269 1222 W 27th St Cedar Falls IA 50614

THOMPSON, TOMMY GEORGE, state governor; b. Elroy, Wis., Nov. 19, 1941; s. Allan and Julie (Dutton) T.; m. Sue Ann Mashak, 1969; children: Kellie Sue, Tommi, Jason. BS, U. Wis., 1963, JD, 1966. Polit. intern U.S. Rep. Thomson, 1963; legis. messenger Wis. State Senate, 1964-66; sole practice Elroy and Mauston, Wis., 1966-87; mem. Dist. 87 Wis. State Assembly, 1966-87, asst. minority leader, 1972-81, floor leader, 1981-87; self-employed real estate broker Mauston, 1970—; gov. State of Wis., 1987—; alt. del. Rep. Nat. Conv., 1976. Served with USAR. Recipient med. award for Legis., Wis. Acad. Gen. Practice. Mem. ABA, Wis. Bar Assn., Phi Delta Phi. Roman Catholic. Office: Office of the Gov PO Box 7863 Madison WI 53707-7863

THOMPSON, WALTER EARL, JR., banking executive; b. Okmulgee, Okla., Oct. 15, 1946; s. Walter Earl and Thelma Grace (Horn) T.; m. Margaret Ann Gargus, Apr. 14, 1973. BSBA, George Washington U., 1972; Degree in Banking, Rutger U., 1984. Auditor Commerce Bank Kansas City, Mo., 1972-75; asst. v.p. Commerce Bank, St. Louis, 1975-77, v.p., controller, 1978-80; v.p. regional ops. Commerce Bank, Clayton, Mo., 1984—; audit mgr. Commerce Bancshares, Kansas City, 1977-78; v.p., cashier Commerce Bank St. Charles, Mo., 1980-84. Bd. dirs., treas. United Services for Handicapped, St. Charles, 1981-82, St. Peters (Mo.) Drug Abatement Council, 1981-83; mem. St. Peters Police Adv. Bd., 1981; campaign chmn. Tom Brown for Mayor Com., St. Peters, 1982. Mem. Bank Adminstrn. Inst., Am. Inst. Banking (tchr. 1983). Republican. Presbyterian. Lodge: Lions (pres. 1983-84, bd. dirs. 1984—, New Lion of Yr. 1981). Avocations: computer programming, flower gardening. Office: Commerce Bank St Louis County 4019 Chouteau Ave Saint Louis MO 63110

THOMPSON, WILLIAM EDWIN, sociology educator; b. Tulsa, Oct. 20, 1950; s. Edwin N. and Flora L. (Davis) T.; m. Marilyn R. Asbill, May 17, 1972; children: Brandon W., Mica L. BA in Edn., N.E. Okla. State U., 1972; MS in Edn., S.W. Mo. St. U., 1974; PhD, Okla. State U., 1979. Vis. instr. sociology U. Tulsa, 1979; assoc. prof. sociology Emporia State U., Kans., 1979—, chmn. div. sociology, family scis. and anthropology, 1985—; cons. Kans. Law Enforcement Officers, Emporia, 1982—, S.E. Okla. State U., Durant, 1986. Assoc. editor Midwest Am. Rev. Sociology Jour., 1985—, Quarterly Jour. Ideology, 1985—; contbr. articles to profl. jours. Vol. Big Bros., Big Sisters, Emporia, 1986; dem. precinct capt. Lyon County, Emporia, 1986; Little League coach, Emporia Recreation Commn., 1984-86. Mem. Am. Sociol. Assn., Kans. Sociol. Soc., Midwest Sociol. Soc., Acad. Criminal Justice Scis. Unitarian. Home: 2507 Apple Dr Emporia KS 66801 Office: Emporia State U Dept Sociology 1200 Commercial Emporia KS 66801

THOMPSON, WILLIAM RICHEY, nutritionist, consultant; b. Greenville, Ala., Sept. 18, 1956; s. Ralph C. and Mona B. (Richey) T.; m. Jana Lynn Eilers, Mar. 21, 1981. BS, Kans. State U., 1977, MS, 1979; PhD, U. Minn., 1981. Cons. nutritionist Farmland Industries, Inc., Dodge City, Kans., 1981-84; mgr. livestock services Servi-Tech., Inc., Dodge City, 1984—. Contbr. articles to profl. jours. Mem. Am. Dairy Sci. Assn., Am. Soc. Animal Sci., N.Y. Acad. Sci., Phi Kappa Phi, Gamma Sigma Delta. Republican. Avocations: Alpine skiing, reading. Home: Rt 2 Box 511 Dodge City KS 67801 Office: Servi-Tech Inc 1816 E Wyatt Earp Dodge City KS 67801

THOMPSON-LEEKLEY, MARCIA BRYANT, real estate broker; b. Denver, Nov. 20, 1937; d. Don R. and Marion F. (Miall) Bryant; m. Philip A. Leekley, Feb. 21, 1987; children—Richard, Kristen. B.A., U. Mich., 1959; grad. Realtors Inst., 1980. Real estate broker Koenig & Strey Inc., Wilmette, Ill., 1977-83, Baird & Warner, Winnetka, Ill., 1983—. Mem. Ill. Assn. Realtors (life; Million Dollar Club), North Shore Bd. Realtors, Nat. Assn. Realtors. Republican. Club: Michigan Shores (Wilmette). Home: 3121 Country Ln Wilmette IL 60091 Office: Baird & Warner 576 Lincoln Winnetka IL 60093

THOMS, PAUL EDWARD, educational administrator, music education consultant; b. Louisville, Apr. 16, 1936; s. B. C. and Augusta T.; m. Marion Carol Cox, Aug. 16, 1958; children—Monica, Melinda. B.M., U. Ky., 1958; M.M., Miami U., Oxford, Ohio, 1965; postgrad. Ind. U., Millikin U., Calif. State Coll., Baldwin-Wallace Conservatory, Ohio State U. Rural music supr., Brown County, Ohio, 1958-60; dist. music coordinator, choral dir. Fairfield (Ohio) City Schs., 1960-82, curriculum coordinator, 1982—. Recipient Ohio Senate Resolution, mayoral proclamation and Bd. Edn. resolution establishing Paul Thoms Day; named One of Ten Most Outstanding Sch. Music Dirs. in U.S. and Can., Sch. Musician mag. Mem. Ohio Music Edn. Assn. (pres.), Tri-M (pres. bd. dirs.). Contbr. articles to profl. jours. Home: 128 S D St Hamilton OH 45013 Office: 5050 Dixie Hwy Fairfield OH 45014

THOMSON, GEORGE RONALD, lawyer; b. Wadsworth, Ohio, Aug. 25, 1959; s. John Alan and Elizabeth (Galbraith) T. BA, Miami U., Oxford, Ohio, 1982, MA, 1983; JD, Ohio State U., 1986. Bar: Ill. 1986. Teaching fellow Miami U., 1982-83; assoc. Peterson, Ross, Schloerb & Seidel, Chgo., 1986—. Recipient Spl. Commendation Ohio Ho. of Reps., 1984, 85. Mem. ABA (tort and ins. sect. 1986—), Ill. State Bar Assn., Chgo. Bar Assn., Speech Communication Assn. Am., Amnesty Internat. (adminstr. 1978-82, 86—), Mortar Bd., Phi Beta Kappa, Phi Kappa Phi, Omicron Delta Kappa. Democrat. Presbyterian. Avocations: tennis, flute performance, antique collecting, reading, travel. Home: 450 W Briar Pl Apt 8H Chicago IL 60657 Office: Peterson Ross Schloerb & Seidl 200 E Randolph Chicago IL 60601

THOMSON, JAMES ADOLPH, medical group practice administrator; b. Kansas City, Mo., Feb. 25, 1924; s. Edward Wilkins and Gladys Lucile (Opperman) T.; m. Patricia Jane Herron, Jan. 24, 1943; children: Linda Lee Thomson Schwartz, Kenneth Leroy, James Howard. BBA, Rockhurst Coll., Kansas City, 1950. Cost acct. Standard Brands, Inc., Kansas City, 1950-52; asst. comptroller Menorah Med. Ctr., Kansas City, 1952-56; comptroller Holzer Hosp. and Clinic, Gallipolis, Ohio, 1956-63; bus. mgr. Oberlin (Ohio) Clinic, Inc., 1963-71; adminstr. and treas. Thompson, Brumm & Knepper Clinic, Inc., St. Joseph, Mo., 1971-80; bus. mgr. Cin. Neurological Assocs., Inc., 1980—; cons. med. groups, Ohio, 1968-70. V.p. St. Joseph (Mo.) Area C. of C., 1976-78; pres. Oberlin Health Commn., 1968-69; bd. dirs. St. Joseph Sheltered Workshop, 1978-80. Served with M.C. U.S. Army, 1943-46, ETO. Recipient Disting. Service award St. Joseph Area C. of C., 1979. Fellow Am. Coll. Med. Group Adminstrs.; mem. Am. Assn. Hosp. Accts. (charter, pres. 1954-56), Mo. Med. Group Mgmt. Assn. (charter, pres. 1978-79), Med. Group Mgmt. Assn., Ohio Med. Group Mgmt. Assn., Cin. Med. Group Mgmt. Assn. (pres. 1983-84). Republican. Lutheran. Lodges: Rotary (pres. Oberlin and St. Joseph clubs); LIons (Gallipolis) (pres. 1962-63), K.C., Masons, Shriners (clown). Avocations: woodworking, gardening, golf. Office: Cin Neurological Assocs Inc 111 Wellington Pl Cincinnati OH 45219

THOMSSEN, ELI LEE, pharmaceutical company executive; b. Grand Island, Nebr., Jan. 2, 1938; s. Eli L. Sr. and Evelyn I. (Grossnicklaus) T.; m. Sue Ann Burton, Nov. 26, 1960; children: Cynthia, Jeffrey, Gail, Sarah. BS, U. Nebr., 1960; MBA, Western Mich. U., 1981. With mktg. dept. Rath Packing Co., Waterloo, Iowa, 1960-61; sales rep. Upjohn Co., Des Moines, 1961-67; dist. mgr. Upjohn Co., Mpls., 1967-73; product mgr. Upjohn Co., Kalamazoo, Mich., 1973-78, dir. mktg. planning, 1978-86, dir. new product and strategic planning, 1986—. Chmn. mktg. com. Kalamazoo County Red Cross. Lodge: Elks (trustee 1984-86). Avocation: golf. Home: 6314 Trotwood Kalamazoo MI 49002 Office: The Upjohn Co Dept 9535-190-7 Kalamazoo MI 49001

THOPPIL, PAUL, computer engineer; b. Manalur, Trichur, India, Feb. 12, 1944; came to U.S., 1968; s. T.K. and Cicily Paul; m. Alice Thoppil, Dec. 26, 1972; children: Powell, Sindhu. BS, Reg. Engring. Coll., Calicut, India, 1966; MS, S.D. State U., 1970; MBA, U. Wis., Whitewater, 1978. Indsl. engr. RTE Corp., Waukesha, Wis., 1971-79, sr. computer engr., 1979—; v.p. fin. and systems The Rajan Group, Milw., 1987—; cons. IMRS, Milw., 1980—. Mem. Digital Equipment Computer Users Soc., Inst. Indsl. Engrs. (sr.). Avocations: tennis, reading. Home: 4630 S Scot Dr New Berlin WI 53151

THORESON, RICHARD MYRON, insurance company executive; b. Sioux City, Iowa, Feb. 12, 1935; m. Judith Murtagh, Feb. 3, 1957; children: Becky, David, Wendy, Mike. BA, U. Iowa, 1957. Lic. ins. agent, Iowa, Ariz. Underwriter Druggists Mutual, Algona, Iowa, 1960-67; v.p. Druggists Mut., Algona, Iowa, 1967-75, v.p., sec., 1975-87, sr. v.p., 1987—, also bd. dirs.; bd. dirs. The Pharmacists Life Ins. Co., DM Ins. Services. Mem. Algona City Council, 1975-86; commr. Algona Airport Commn., 1986; bd. dirs. Algona Indsl. Devel. Commn., 1985-87. Served to lt. col. USMCR, 1956-76. Mem. Marine Corps Res. Officers Assn., Marine Aviation Assn., Phi Delta Theta, Alpha Delta Sigma. Republican. Lodges: Masons, Shriners. Avocations: golf, aviation, writing, politics, art. Office: Druggists Mut Ins Co Box 370 Algona IA 50511

THORN, WILLIAM ELWOOD, environmental services administrator; consultant; b. Duquoin, Ill., June 27, 1936; s. Sylvan Elwood and Margaret Thorn; m. Iris Ann Cargal, Dec. 15, 1964; 1 son, Jonathon; m. 2d, Karen Dillon, Nov. 9, 1974; children—Matthew, Karen. B.A., McKendree Coll., Lebanon, Ill., 1976; M.A., Webster U., St. Louis, 1977. Joined U.S. Air Force, 1956; personnel supt. various locations, ret., 1976; asst. mgr. housekeeping MediService, Springfield, Mo., 1976-77; bus. mgr. II, Chester Mental Health Ctr. (Ill.), 1977-80; dir. environ. services Alexian Bros. Hosp., St. Louis, 1980—, also cons. Alexian Bros. Corp. Am.; instr. U. Mo., St. Louis. Decorated Bronze Star medal. Mem. Nat. Exec. Housekeepers Assn. (cert.), Mo. Hosp. Adminstrv. Housekeepers Soc., Mo. Assn. Hosp. Central Supply Personnel, VFW. Republican. Mem. Christian Ch. Lodge: Elks. Office: Alexian Bros Hosp 3933 S Broadway St Saint Louis MO 63118

THORN, WILLIAM T., accountant; b. Middletown, Ohio, Nov. 29, 1947; s. William T. and Adele E. (Goldschmidt) T.; m. Judith Ann Danner, Mar. 21, 1970; children: Elizabeth, William III, Kathryn. BS, Miami U., 1969, MBA, 1971. CPA. Staff acct. Deloitte Haskins & Sells, Dayton, Ohio, 1971-74, sr. acct., 1974-76, mgr., 1976-80, ptnr., 1980-85; pvt. practice acctg. Dayton, 1985—. Mem. Am. Inst. CPAs (tax div. 1986), Ohio Soc. CPAs, Nat. Assn. Accts. (pres. Miami Valley chpt. 1972-84). Republican. Presbyterian. Avocations: golf, camping, antique cars. Home: 3224 McGee Ave Middletown OH 45044 Office: 1183 Lyons Rd Dayton OH 45459

THORNBURG, DONALD DELWIN, banker; b. Turlock, Calif., Apr. 2, 1937; s. Vernon and Helen (Kling) T.; m. Judith Anne Dixon, Apr. 1, 1961; children: Brant Merrill, Tracy L. B.A. in Econs., Stanford U., 1959;

M.B.A., U. So. Calif., 1967. With United Calif. Bank (now First Interstate Bank of Calif.), Los Angeles, 1962-81, sr. v.p., 1978-81; pres. Unibancorp Inc. (formerly Midland Bancorp Inc.), Chgo., 1981—; chmn. bd., chief exec. officer UnibancTrust Co. (formerly Sears Bank and Trust Co.), Chgo., 1981; chmn. bd. UniBancTrust/Hawthorne (subs. Unibancorp Inc.), 1984—. Bd. govs. Met. Planning Council of Chgo., 1984—; trustee, treas. Adler Planetarium, 1982—; mem. bd. reference Deicke Ctr. for Visual Rehab., 1986—; active United Way/Crusade of Mercy. Served to 1st lt. U.S. Army, 1960-62. Clubs: Economic, Chicago, Metropolitan (Chgo.); Glen View Golf. Office: UnibancTrust Sears Tower Chicago IL 60606

THORNBURG, JERRY WAYNE, auditor; b. Lakewood, Ohio, Apr. 14, 1943; s. Paul F. and Dorthy S. (Trautman) T.; m. Betty Jane Garmen, Sept. 25, 1964; children: Kristine C., Lynn C. BSBA, Dyke Coll., 1964; postgrad., Dartmouth Coll., 1984. CPA, Ohio, Mich. Acctg. clk. Sherwin-Williams Co., Cleve., 1964-65, auditor headquarter and elect. data processing, 1970-71; staff auditor Price Waterhouse, Cleve., 1965-70; audit mgr. Main Lafrenz & Co., Canton, Ohio and Lansing, Mich., 1972-78, Clark Equipment Corp., South Bend, Ind., 1978-80; dir. internal audit AMCA Internat. Corp., Oakbrook, Ill., 1980—. Mem. Inst. Internal Auditors (founding pres. Chgo. West chpt. 1985-86, membership chmn. 1986, treas. chgo. chpt. 1984-85, gov. 1983-84, edn. com. 1983—), Am. Inst. CPA's, Nat. Assn. Accts, Ill. Found. CPA's. Home: 26W384 Durfee Rd Wheaton IL 60187 Office: AMCA Internat Corp 2311 W 22d St Suite 217 Oakbrook IL 60521

THORNE, OAKLEIGH B., publishing company executive; b. 1932. Chmn. Commerce Clearing House, Inc., Deerfield, Ill. Office: Commerce Clearing House Inc 4025 Peterson Ave Chicago IL 60646 also: Coammerce Clearing House Inc 2700 Lake Cook Rd Riverwoods IL 60015 *

THORNE, RICHARD CHARLES, television producer, writer; b. Chgo., Oct. 10, 1925; s. Theodore Charles Thorne and Alta Inez (Brown) Polley; m. Janice Ann Olsen, Apr. 29, 1948; children: Janice Adair, Alynne Lee, Richard Norman, Robin Elizabeth, Lowell Ann. BA in Speech, Columbia Coll., 1948. Writer, producer, announcer TV sta. WGN, Chgo., 1948-52; writer, producer Mut. Broadcasting Systems, Chgo., 1952-54; asst. to county judge, then gov. State of Ill., Chgo., 1955-64; dir. news program Sta. WNUS, Chgo., 1964-69; v.p. Universal Tng. Systems, Northbrook, Ill., 1969—. Author (radio series) Hall of Fantasy, 1952 (CFAC Best Series 1954), The Silver Eagle. Exec. dir. Citizens for Kerner, Ill., 1960, 64. Mem. Am. Fedn. of TV and Radio Artists, Screen Actors Guild. Episcopalian. Office: Universal Tng Systems 255 Revere Dr Northbrook IL 60062 Office: Thorne Enterprises 7925 Country Club Ln Elmwood Park IL 60635

THORNTON, ANDRE, professional baseball player. First baseman Cleve. Indians. Office: Cleve Indians Cleveland Stadium Cleveland OH 44114 *

THORNTON, ROBERT RICHARD, lawyer; b. Jersey City, Oct. 16, 1926; s. Arthur A. and Sabina V. (Williams) T.; m. Dorothy M. McGuire, Sept. 10, 1966; children: Matthew, Nicholas, Jennifer, Julia. AB, Georgetown U., 1950; LLB, Columbia U., 1953. Bar: N.Y. 1953, Ill. 1970. Assoc. Dorr, Hand & Dawson, N.Y.C., 1953-63, Mudge, Rose, Guthrie & Alexander, N.Y.C., 1963-70; gen. atty. Caterpillar Inc. (formerly Caterpillar Tractor Co.), Peoria, Ill., 1970-74, assoc. counsel, 1974-83, gen. counsel, sec., 1983—. Mem. ABA, Ill. State Bar Assn., Peoria County Bar Assn., Assn. Bar City of N.Y. Republican. Roman Catholic. Club: Country of Peoria. Home: 3715 Linden Ln Peoria IL 61614 Office: Caterpillar Inc 100 NE Adams St Peoria IL 61629-7310

THORNTON, THEODORE KEAN, diversified company executive; b. St. Louis, June 4, 1949; s. Leonard Frend and Maxine Belle (McKinley) T.; m. Colleen Bridget Purdy, June 23, 1974; children, Theodore McKinley, Alastair Griffin. B.A., Harvard U., M.B.A. Asst. treas. Chase Manhattan Bank, N.Y.C., 1975-79; asst. treas. Colgate-Palmolive Co., N.Y.C., 1979-84, Sperry Corp., N.Y.C., 1984-85; v.p., treas. Household Internat., Prospect Heights, Ill., 1985—. Mem. Am. Fin. Assn., Nat. Assn. Corp. Treasurers. Clubs: Harvard (N.Y.C.). Office: Household Internat 2700 Sanders Rd Prospect Heights IL 60070

THORNTON-LOCKWOOD, BARBARA RAE, food products company executive, food marketing consultant; b. Mpls., June 30, 1931; d. Mathew Hillard and Stella Pearl (Lien) Thornton; m. James Franklin Lockwood, May 4, 1974. BS, U. Minn., 1953. Various positions with The Pillsbury Co., Mpls., 1953-70, dir. consumer service Ann Pillsbury Consumer Service Kitchens, 1967-70; pres. Barbara Thornton Assocs., Mpls., 1970—; cons. in food mktg.; del., advisor Inst. Agriculture, Forestry and Home Econs., 1970-76. Author: (cookbook) Centennial Bread Sampler, 1981, Cooking for One, 1987. Mem. council Peace Luth. Ch., West Bloomington, Minn., 1979-82. Mem. Am. Home Econs. Assn., Inst. Food Technologists, Twin City Home Economists in Bus. (chair elect 1958-59), U. Minn. Alumni Assn. (bd. dirs., U. Minn. Nat. Alumnae Bd. Home and Office: 8001 Pennsylvania Rd Minneapolis MN 55438

THORPE, NORMAN RALPH, air force officer; b. Carlinville, Ill., Oct. 17, 1934; s. Edwin Everett and Imogene Midas (Hayes) T.; m. Elaine Frances Pritzman, Nov. 1, 1968; children: Sarah Elizabeth, Carrie Rebecca. AB in Econs., U. Ill., 1956, JD, 1958; LLM in Pub. Internat. Law, George Washington U., 1967. Bar: Ill. 1958, U.S. Supreme. Ct. 1969. Commd. 2d lt. USAF, 1956, advanced through grades to brig. gen., 1983—; legal advisor US Embassy, Manila, 1969-72; chief internat. law hdqrs. USAF, Washington, 1972-77; staff judge adv. 21st Air Force, McGuire AFB, N.J., 1977-80, U.S. Air Force Europe, Ramstein AB, Fed. Republic Germany, 1980-84; comdr. Air Force Contract Law Ctr., Wright-Patterson AFB, Ohio, 1984—; adj. prof. U. Dayton Sch. Law, 1986—. Contbr. articles to profl. jours. Staff mem. Commn. on Police Policies and Procedures, Dayton, 1986; trustee Dayton Philharm. Orch., 1987—. Mem. ABA (com. chmn. internat. law sect. 1977-80, council mem. pub. contract law sect. 1986), Air Force Assn., Dayton Council on World Affairs. Republican. Clubs: Moraine Country, Dayton Racquet. Avocations: music, piano, gardening. Home: 429 Johnson Wright-Patterson AFB OH 45433 Office: Hdqrs Air Force Contract Law Ctr/CC Wright-Patterson AFB OH 45433-5000

THORPE, SCOTT THOMAS, architect; b. St. Paul, Nov. 8, 1951; s. Walter Wyman and Dona Mae (Baab) T.; m. Lydia Kulesov, June 24, 1976 (div. 1979); m. Karen Pratt Smith, Feb. 15, 1986. BArch with distinction, U. Minn., 1975. Registered architect, Minn., Wis. Designer Radloff & Assocs. Inc., Mpls., 1975-79; v.p., design ptnr. Howell, Radloff & Thorpe Architects, Mpls., 1979-81; v.p., sr. project mgr. Ellerbe Assocs. Inc., Mpls., 1981—. Prin. works include Decio Faculty Hall U. Notre Dame (citation Am. Sch. and U. mag. 1985), Rolf's Aquatic Ctr., U. Notre Dame, Notre Dame Law Sch., St. Paul Winter Carnival Ice Palace (citation Progressive Architecture mag. 1986, Honor award Minn. Soc. Architects, 1986, Grand award Minn. Cons. Engrs. Council, 1986, Grand award Am. Cons. Engrs., 1986, 60th award Illumination Engring. Soc., 1986), U. Notre Dame All-Sports Facility. Mem. AIA (Minn. Soc.), Trout Unlimited, Lake Superior Steelhead Assn. Avocations: fly fishing, downhill skiing, upland bird hunting. Home: 1510 Dora Ln Saint Paul MN 55106 Office: Ellerbe Assocs Inc 1 Appletree Sq Minneapolis MN 55106

THORSON, MILTON ZENAS, paint and varnish company executive; b. Thorsby, Ala., Oct. 26, 1902; s. Theodore T. and Emma (Hokanson) T.; student Am. Inst. Banking, extension courses U. So. Calif.; m. 3d, Helen Lob, Aug. 31, 1978. Chief teller Tenn. Valley Bank, Decatur, Ala., 1919-28; teller Security First Nat. Bank, Los Angeles, 1928-29; with Red Spot Paint & Varnish Co., Inc., Evansville, Ind., 1929-60, chmn. exec. bd., dir., 1961-79; chmn. exec. bd. Owensboro Paint & Glass Co. (Ky.), former mem. Regional Export Expansion Council, U.S. Dept. Commerce. Mem. Audubon Soc., Nat. Paint and Coatings Assn. (hon.), Soc. Plastic Engrs. (Plastic Industry Pioneer). Republican. Club: President's of U. Evansville (life). Contbr. tech articles prof. jours. Home: Box 418 Evansville IN 47703 also: 527 Harbor Dr Key Biscayne FL 33149 Office: 110 Main St Evansville IN 47701

THOTTAM, JOHNSON JOHN, surgeon; b. Moovattupuzha, India, Mar. 18, 1947; came to U.S., 1971; s. John Paul and Annamma (Kolencheril) T. MD, U. Kerala, India, 1969. Intern in gen. surgery Med. Coll. Ohio, Toledo, 1972-76; plastic surgeon City Hosp., Akron, Ohio, 1976-78; asst. prof. plastic surgery Northeastern Ohio U., Rootstown, 1984—. Fellow ACS; mem. Am. Soc. Plastic Reconstructive Surgeons, Ohio Med. Assn. Avocations: paiting, tennis, skiing. Office: 4800 Higbee Ave Canton OH 46718

THRASHER, PHILIP CHARLES, lawyer; b. Indpls., Oct. 18, 1941; s. Winfred W. and Ruth M. (Hutchins) T.; m. Elaine L. Pees, Feb. 13, 1965; children: Jennifer Lynn, Thomas Andrew, Ann Lorraine, Jill Louise. BS, Ind. U., Bloomington, 1963, MBA, 1964; JD, Ind. U., Indpls., 1978. Bar: Ind. 1978. Real estate appraiser Ind. Nat. Bank, Indpls., 1965-69; real estate developer Coll. Park Corp., Indpls., 1969-75; real estate counsel Coll. Life Ins. Co., Indpls., 1975-79; sole practice Indpls., 1978-81; assoc. Lowe, Gray et al, Indpls., 1981; pntr. Krieg, DeVault, Alexander & Capehart, Indpls., 1982—. Editor: Ind. Law Rev., 1976-77. Mem. Ind. Bar Assn., Indpls. Bar Assn. (chmn. real property div. bus. law sect. 1983-85). Republican. Quaker. Club: Hillcrest (Indpls.). Lodge: Shriners. Avocation: golf. Office: Krieg Devault et al 1 Indiana Square Suite 2800 Indianapolis IN 46204

THROCKMORTON, TOM DUDLEY, general surgeon; b. Willows, Calif., Nov. 24, 1945; s. Robert Bentley and Frances (Turman) T.; m. Nyla Jane Postma, Apr. 14, 1973; children: Thomas Ward, Courtenay Jane. BS, U. Iowa, 1967, MD, 1970. Intern U. Oreg., Portland, 1970-71; fellow in surgery Mayo Clinic, Rochester, Minn., 1971-76; practice medicine specializing in gen. surgery Spencer, Iowa, 1978—; bd. dirs. Spencer Hosp., 1983—. Served to maj. U.S. Army, 1976-78. Mem. AMA, Am. Soc. Colposcopy and Surg. Pathology, Iowa Med. Soc. (jud. council 1984—, grievance com. 1981-84), Clay County Med. Soc., Throckmorton Surg. Soc., Mayo Clinic Priestly Surg. Soc. Republican. Congregationalist. Club: Spencer Country. Avocations: golf, tennis, flying. Office: 116 E 11th St Spencer IA 51301

THUEME, WILLIAM HAROLD, educator; b. St. Clair, Mich., Sept. 4, 1945; s. Harold Arthur and Delphine Betty (Buhl) T.; m. Nora Kathleen Koning, May 8, 1971; children—Benjamin William, Rebecca Kathleen, Jeffrey William. Student Port Huron Jr. Coll., 1963-64; B.A., Mich. State U., 1967, M.A., 1969; postgrad. Oakland U., 1971, U. Mich., 1971, San Francisco State U., 1975, U. Hawaii, 1975. Cert. tchr., Mich. Tchr. pub. schs., Charlotte, Mich., 1967-69, Ann Arbor, Mich., 1969—; fgn. travel coordinator Ambassadors Abroad Program, Amsterdam, Netherlands, 1968—; regional driver coordinator for Southeastern Mich., Avis Rent-a-Car, 1983—. Participant Skyhook II Project; elections coordinator Eaton County (Mich.) Republican Party, 1968; mem. troop com. Troop 210, Boy Scouts Am., Ypsilanti; active Mich. United Conservation Clubs, Big Brothers Am., Charlotte, Mich.; elders quorum instr., exec. sec. Ch. of Jesus Christ of Latter-day Saints, 1976-81, adult spl. interest coordinator, 1982—, Sunday Sch. sec. Ann Arbor stake, 1983—; mem. Mich. Mormon Concert Choir, 1977—, Ypsilanti Mormon Choir. Recipient Spl. Recognition award Reagan Presdl. Campaign, 1981, Am. Security Council 30th Anniversary Spl. Recognition Cert. Mem. NEA, Mich. Edn. Assn., Internat. Reading Assn., Mich. Sheriffs Assn. (assoc.), Police Marksmanship Assn., Washtenaw Reading Council, Southeastern Mich. Reading Assn., Mich. Reading Assn., Mich. Assn. for Supervision and Curriculum Devel., Ann Arbor Edn. Assn., Am. Security Council, Nat. Geog. Soc., Am. Film Inst., Nat. Rifle Assn., Tri-County Sportsman League, Sigma Alpha Eta. Club: Washtenaw Sportsmen's (Ypsilanti). Lodge: Optimist (v.p. and dir. 1975-78) (Ann Arbor). Office: 401 N Division St Ann Arbor MI 48104

THULIN, ADELAIDE ANN, design company executive, interior designer; b. Chgo., Nov. 15, 1925; d. Martin Evold and Kathleen Marie (Glennon) Peterson; m. Frederick Adolph Thulin, Jr., Aug. 18, 1945; children—Frederick, Kristin, Mary, Margaret, Francis, Peter, Andrea, Charles, Joseph, Kathleen, James, Suzanne, Patricia. Student Northwestern U., 1943-46; AA in Interior Design, Harper Coll., 1977. Asst. production mgr. Cruttenden & Eger, Chgo., 1946; editor Mt. Prospect (Ill.) Independent, 1960; real estate salesperson Homefinders, Northwest Chgo. suburbs, 1965, 69-70; asst. v.p. advt. Littelfuse, Des Plaines, Ill., 1966-67; owner, pres. Applied Design Assocs., Mt. Prospect, 1977—; career day speaker local high schs., 1982—; ambassador Pvt. Industry Council. Author, editor monthly newsletter Women's Archtl. League, 1983-85 , The Binnacle, CYC, 1979-81. Organizer, Mother's March of Dimes, Mt. Prospect, 1953-54, Vols. for Stevenson, 1952, 56, Citizens for Douglas, 1954, Citizens for Kennedy, 1960; mem. Fair Review Council, Chgo., 1983-84; mem. 13th Congl. Dist. Dem. Women's Club, publicity chmn. 1957-58; mem. Chgo. Symphony Orchestra Chorus, 1972; del. Ill. Statehouse Conf. on Small Bus., 1984, 85; dir. Arts Council of Mt. Prospect; chmn. Mt. Prospect Sign Rev. Bd.; mem. community edn. council High Sch. Dist. 214; Mem. AIA (profl. affiliate Chgo. chpt.), Ill. Devel. Council, Friends of Small Bus., Women's Archtl. League (publicity chmn. 1964-65), Mt. Prospect C. of C. Roman Catholic. Avocations: reading for print-handicapped on CRIS radio; choral singing. Home: 4 S Owen St Mount Prospect IL 60056 Office: Applied Design Assocs Ltd 200 E Evergreen Ave Mount Prospect IL 60056

THURMAN, JAMES WINSTON, children's home executive, investment and insurance consultant; b. Marshall, Mo., Sept. 22, 1943; s. Ewell S. and Katherine P. (Arend) T.; m. Gail A. Snyder, Oct. 7, 1966; children—Cynthia D., Christopher M. B.S. in Bus., S.W. Mo. State U., 1966. Registered prin. Nat. Assn. Security Dealers; lic. ins. broker, Mo. Sr. staff supr. traffic dept. Southwestern Bell Telephone Co., St. Louis, 1966-70; v.p., sec. K.W. Chambers & Co., St. Louis, 1970-77; assoc. exec. dir. fin., treas. Presbyterian Children's Services, Inc., Farmington, Mo., 1977—. Elder Richmond Heights Presbyn. Ch.; chmn. bd. Coll. Sch., Webster Groves, Mo. Mem. Nat. Soc. Fund Raising Execs. Republican. Home: 105 Turf Ct Webster Groves MO 63119 Office: 412 W Liberty St Farmington MO 63640 Office: 7339 Lindbergh Dr Richmond Heights MO 63117

THURSWELL, GERALD ELLIOTT, lawyer; b. Detroit, Feb. 4, 1944; s. Harry and Lilyan (Zeitlin) T.; m. Lynn Satovsky, Sept. 17, 1967 (div. Aug. 1978); children—Jennifer, Lawrence; m. Judith Linda Bendix, Sept. 2, 1978; 1 son, Jeremy. LL.B. with distinction, Wayne State U., 1967. Bar: Mich. 1968, N.Y. 1984, D.C. 1986, Wis. 1986, U.S. Dist. Ct. (ea. dist.) Mich. 1968, U.S. Ct. Appeals (7th cir.) 1968. Student asst. to U.S. atty. Ea. Dist. Mich., Detroit, 1966; assoc. Zwerdling, Miller, Klimist & Maurer, Detroit, 1967-68; sr. ptnr. Thurswell, Chayet & Weiner, Southfield, Mich., 1968—; arbitrator Am. Arbitration Assn., Detroit, 1969—; mediator Wayne County Cir. Ct., Mich., 1983—, Oakland County Cir. Ct. Mich., 1984—; twp. atty. Royal Oak Twp., Mich., 1982—. Pres. Powder Horn Estates Subdiv. Assn., West Bloomfield, Mich., 1975, United Fund, West Bloomfield, 1976. Arthur F. Lederle scholar Wayne State U. Law Sch., Detroit, 1964, grad. profl. scholar Wayne State U. Law Sch., 1965, 66. Mem. Mich. Trial Lawyers Assn. (legis. com. on govtl. immunit, 1984, newsletter com. editor 1984), Assn. Trial Lawyers Am. (treas. Detroit met. chpt., 1986-87), Detroit Bar Assn. (lawyer referral com., panel pub. adv. com. judicial candidates), Oakland County Bar Assn. Jewish. Clubs: Wabeek Country (Bloomfield Hills), Boca Pointe Country (Boca Raton, Fla.). Home: 1781 Golf Ridge Dr S Bloomfield Hills MI 48013 Office: Thurswell Chayet & Weiner 17117 W Nine Mile Rd Suite 500 Southfield MI 48075

THWAITS, JAMES ARTHUR, manufacturing executive; b. London, Apr. 3, 1923; came to U.S., 1958, naturalized, 1973; s. Arthur Roper and Iris Maud (Mason) T.; m. Joyce Holmes, July 26, 1947; children: Joanna, Philip, David, Steven. Grad., East-Ham Coll. Tech., London, 1939, Thames Poly., London, 1942; Cert. Higher Math., Poly. of South Bank, London, 1944. Higher nat. cert. in elec. engring. Project engr. Standard Telephones and Cables Ltd., Eng., 1945-46; plant engr. Kelvinator Ltd., Eng., 1946-49; with 3M, St. Paul, 1949—, v.p. Afro-Asian and Can. areas, 1968-71, v.p. Tape and Allied Products Group, 1972-74, v.p. Internat. Group, 1974-75, pres. internat. ops. and corp. staff services, 1975—, also bd. dirs.; bd. dirs. First Trust Co., St. Paul. Mem. London Inst. Elec. Engrs. Clubs: St. Paul Athletic; White Bear (Minn.); Yacht, North Oaks (Minn.) Golf; King Solomon's Lodge (London, Ont., Can.). Office: Minnesota Mining & Mfg Co 3M Center Saint Paul MN 55101 *

TIBBS, DENISE JOAN, law enforcement trainer; b. Detroit, Sept. 8, 1953; d. Peter Samuel and Ollie Cecelia (Roy) T.; 1 child, Demond. BA, St. Louis U., 1977. Teleprocessing operator Regional Justice Info. Service, St. Louis, 1978-79, computer operator, 1979-80, user coordinator, 1980-82, mgr. user coordination, 1982-86, sr. trainer, 1986—. Mem. Assn. St. Louis Info. Systems Trainers, Pheonix User Group (chairperson 1985-86). Democrat. Roman Catholic. Avocations: reading, writing.

TIBENSKY, JAMES WALTER, officer of U.S. court system; b. Chgo., Sept. 11, 1948; s. Joseph and Josephine (Slivak) T.; m. Gail Dee Eisenstein, May 2, 1971. AB, Washington U., St. Louis, 1971; MA, U. Ill., 1976. Correctional officer U.S. Bur. Prisons, Chgo., 1975-77; officer pretrial services U.S. Ct. System, Chgo., 1977—. Contbr. articles to Canoeing mag. Mem. Am. Canoe Assn. (nat. champion 1969, 86), Assn. Gravestone Studies, Chgo. Whitewater Assn. Avocations: kayak racing, carriage driving, carousel horse restoration, wine collecting. also: PO Box 2576 Chicago IL 60690 Office: US Pretrial Services 219 S Dearborn Room 1100 Chicago IL 60604

TICE, ROBERT GALEN, banker; b. Lincoln, Nebr., June 8, 1956; s. Wayne Kilmer and Jean Louise (Bell) T. Student, Tex. Christian U., 1976; BS in Fin., Samford U., 1978; MBA in Fin., Rockhurst Coll., 1984. Asst. debate coach Samford U., Birmingham, Ala., 1978-79; asst. mgr. Barclay's Am. Credit, Birmingham, 1978-82; credit analyst Home State Bank, Kansas City, Kans., 1982-83; asst. cashier, loan officer Landmark K.C.I. Bank, Kansas City, Mo., 1983-85; dir. bus. devel. Centerre Bank Northland, North Kansas City, Mo., 1985-87; pvt. practice loan brokerage and investment cons. Kansas City, Mo., 1987—; bd. dirs. Indsl. Devel. Com., Platte County, Mo., Clay County Indsl. Devel. Com., Ambassadors Com. Mem. race relations com. Kansas City (Mo.) Consensus, 1986, pub. improvements adv. com. City of Kansas City, 1986, issue selection com. and mail-in ballot task force, reelection campaign Bonnie Sue Cooper for State Rep.; key gifts chmn. Boy Scouts of Am., Kansas City, 1985; Platte County chmn. Friends of Margaret Kelley CPA for State Auditor, 1986; pres. North Kansas City Young Reps., 1986; bd. dirs. Kansas City Young Reps, 1986—. Mem. Suburban Bankers Assn. (bd. dirs. 1985-86), United Ostomy Assn. (bd. dirs, treas. 1984-86), Bus. and Profl. Assn. of Platte County (legis. action com., pub. relations com. 1985-86), Citizens Assn. of Kansas City, Greater Kansas City C. of C. (co-host Bus. After Hours 1985-86), Northland C. of C. (legis. com., Look North com. 1985-86). Presbyterian. Lodges: Rotary (local bd. dirs. 1986), Lions (bd. dirs. 1984-85). Home: 8272 NW Barrybrooke Kansas City MO 64151 Office: Centerre Bank Northland 2301 Burlington North Kansas City MO 64116

TIDWELL, JOHNIE LEWIS, SR., personnel specialist; b. Bernice, La., May 4, 1936; s. Lovell and Rosa (Wilson) T.; m. Ritsuko Irabu, Oct. 14, 1960; 1 child, Johnie Lewis Jr. AA, Parkland Community Coll., 1983; BA, Eastern Ill. U., 1986—. Enlisted USAF, 1955, advanced through grades to master sgt., 1976, ret., 1981; asst. personnel specialist Chanute AFB, Rantoul, Ill., 1984—; unit career advisor Duluth IAP, 1974-77; tech. advisor Air NG, USAFR Communication Flight Commdrs., Chgo., 1977-81. Mem. Blacks in Govt., Air Force Sgts. Assn. (pres. Chgo. 1980, pres. Rantoul 1986), Am. Vets., VFW (adjutant Wheeling, Ill. chpt. 1978). Democrat. Baptist. Lodge: Masons (sr. warden 1976-77). Avocations: cooking, photography, pool. Home: 317 S Tanner St Rantoul IL 61866 Office: 3345 ABG/DPCS Stop 5A Chanute AFB IL 61868

TIEDEMANN, ADOLF CARL, IV, real estate investor, property management executive; b. Elkhart, Ind., Jan. 22, 1948; s. A. Carl III and Frances (Stuckman) T.; m. Emilie C. Arbogast, Oct. 1, 1966; children: Benjamin P., Elizabeth C. Cert. property mgr.; lic. real estate broker, Ind. Dir. property mgmt. Federated Media, Elkhart, Ind., 1976—; pres., chief exec. officer FM Properties Corp., Elkhart, 1978—; bd. dirs. Elkhart Ctr., Inc., 1986—; mem. faculty Continuing Edn. div. Ind. U., South Bend, 1986—. Mem. printing and pub. sect. exec. com. Nat. Safety Council, 1973-75; chmn. long term com. Downtown Steering Com., Elkhart, 1985—. Mem. Nat. Assn. Realtors, Inst. Real Estate Mgmt. (chpt. charter mem. v.p. 1985-86, pres. 1986-87), Soc. Indsl. Office Realtors, Ind. State Bd. Realtors, Internat. Facility Mgmt. Assn. Republican. Episcopalian. Office: FM Properties Corp 421 S 2d St Elkhart IN 46516

TIEDEMANN, THOMAS ROSS, advertising executive; b. Westfield, N.Y., Jan. 21, 1948; s. Donald Charles and Jean (Welch) T.; m. Leslie Ann Burigo, May 20, 1972; children: Ross Welch, Charles Mark. Student, U. Notre Dame, 1966-69, Fordham U., 1969-71. Media buyer Compton Advt., Inc., N.Y.C., 1969-71; media planner D'Arcy, MacManus & Masius, N.Y.C., 1971-74; assoc. media dir. Keenan & McLaughlin, N.Y.C., 1974-76; dir. media services CMS&Z div. Y&R, Cedar Rapids, Iowa, 1976-78; v.p., dir. client market planning Bader Rutter & Assocs., Brookfield, Wis., 1978—; speaker Am. Mktg. Assn., Washington, 1985, Nat. AgriMktg. Assn., Washington, 1984. Contbr. articles to Marketing and Media Decisions, other mags., profl. jours. Mem. Am. Mktg. Assn. (sec. Ag-Chem mktg. research sect. 1985—), Nat. AgriMktg. Assn. Roman Catholic. Club: Notre Dame (Milw.). Avocations: piano, skiing, computers. Home: 4529 N Murray Ave Whitefish Bay WI 53211 Office: Bader-Rutter & Assocs 13555 Bishops Ct Brookfield WI 53005

TIEFENTHAL, MARGUERITE AURAND, school social worker; b. Battle Creek, Mich., July 23, 1919; d. Charles Henry and Elisabeth Dirk (Hoekstra) Aurand; m. Harlan E. Tiefenthal, Nov. 26, 1942; children: Susan Ann, Daniel E., Elisabeth Amber, Carol Aurand. BS, Western Mich. U., 1941; MSW, U. Mich., 1950. Tchr. No. High Sch., Flint, Mich., 1941-44, Cen. High Sch., Kalamazoo, 1944-45; acct. Upjohn Co., Kalamazoo, 1944-48; social worker Family Service Agy., Lansing, Mich., 1948-50, Pitts., 1950-53; sch. social worker Gower Sch. Dist., Hinsdale, Ill., 1962-70, Hinsdale (Ill.) Dist. 181, 1970—; field instr. social work interns U. Ill.; impartial due process hearing officer; mem. adv. com. sch. social work ISBE approved programs, U. Ill. and GWC; speaker Nat. Conf. Sch. Social Work, Denver, U. Tex. Joint Conf. Sch. Social Work in Ill. Co-editor The School Social Worker and the Handicapped Child: Making P.L. 94-142 Work; sect. editor: Sch. Social Work Quarterly, 1979. Sec. All Village Caucus Village of Western Springs, Ill., mem. village disaster com.; deacon Presbyn. Ch. Western Springs, Sunday sch. tchr., mem. choir; instr. Parent Effectiveness, Teacher Effectiveness, STEP; trainer Widowed Persons Service Tng. Program for Vol. Aides AARP. Mem. Nat. Assn. Social Workers (chmn. exec. council on social work in schs.), Ill. Assn. Social Workers (past pres., past conf. chmn., conf. program chmn.), Sch. Social Workers Supervisors Group (del. to Ill. Commn. on Children), Programs. for Licensure of Social Work Practice in Ill., LWV, Philanthropic Ednl. Orgn., Delta Kappa Gamma. Clubs: DKG, PEO (Western Springs). Avocation: square dancing. Home: 4544 Grand Ave Western Springs IL 60558 Office: Hinsdale Jr High Sch S Garfield Ave Hinsdale IL 60521

TIEGS, KRISTY J., accountant; b. Ellendale, N.D., Feb. 8, 1956; d. Loren L. and Betty L. (Olson) T. BBA with high distiction, U. Iowa, 1978. CPA, Ill.; chartered property casualty underwriter, Ill. Tax trainee State Farm Ins. Cos., Bloomington, 1978-79, tax specialist, 1980-81, tax analyst, 1981-82, acct. I, 1982-83, acct. II, 1983-86, sr. acct., 1986—. Treas., bd. dirs Habitat for Humanity of McLean County, Bloomington, 1986—. Mem. Am. Inst. CPA's, Ill. CPA Soc., Chartered Property Casualty Underwriters Assn. (Cen. Ill. chpt.). Club: Toastmasters (treas.). Avocations: golf, volleyball. Home: 2909 Wellington Way Bloomington IL 61701 Office: State Farm Ins Cos 1 State Farm Plaza Bloomington IL 61710

TIERNEY, EUGENE FRANCIS, lawyer, air force reserve officer; b. Hartford, Conn., Sept. 26, 1930; s. William Albert and Katherine Mary (Egan) T.; m. Cynthia Jane Palen, May 25, 1957; children—Gwyn C., Alison S. B.A., U. Conn., 1953, L.L.B., U. Conn.-Hartford, 1956, M.B.A., 1966. Bar: Conn. Claims adjuster Allstate Ins. Co., West Hartford, Conn., 1956-57, 60-63, claims examiner, 1963-65; claims atty. Nationwide Ins., Hamden, Conn., 1965-70, regional claims atty., Memphis, 1970-73, claims staff atty., Columbus, Ohio, 1973—; bd. dir. N.Y. Med. Malpractice Ins. Assn., N.Y.C., 1978-83, Air Force Logistics Command, Judge Adv. Res., Wright Patterson AFB, Dayton, Ohio, 1973-82; mem. Air Force Logistics Command Judge Adv. Res. Exec. Bd., 1979-82. Drafted first arson reporting statute for Ohio, 1976 (later became model law adopted by all 50 states). Pres. Worthington Resource Ctr., 1984-85; mem. Concerned Citizens of Worthington Sch. Dist., 1984—. Served as 1st lt. USAF, 1957-60, to lt. col. USAFR. Mem. Ohio Assn. Civil Trial Attys. (edn. chmn. 1978-84, trustee 1980—, editor 1984-86). Republican. Lutheran. Clubs: Worthington Men's (pres. 1981-82), Del.

Golf Inc. (Ohio). Avocation: golf. Home: 219 Northigh Dr Worthington OH 43085 Office: Nationwide Ins Co One Nationwide Plaza Columbus OH 43216

TIERNO, EDWARD GREGORY, insurance company executive; b. Latrobe, Pa., Oct. 9, 1948; s. Frank Albert and Mary Christine (Santarelli) T.; m. Emily Mittacos, Nov. 27, 1971. B.A., Youngstown State U., 1970; postgrad. Indiana U. Pa., 1969. Tchr., coach Youngstown (Ohio) Bd. Edn., 1970-74; liability supr., mktg. rep. Underwriters Adjusting Co., Youngstown and Southfield, Mich., 1974-78; ins. risk mgr. McNicholas Transp. Co., Youngstown, 1978-82; pres. Ins. Claim Service, Youngstown, 1982—. Pa. Higher Edn. Assn. scholar, 1966-70. Mem. Common Carrier Conf. Irregular Route Carriers, Ohio State Claims Assn., Ohio Assn. Ind. Adjusters, Youngstown Claims Assn. (pres., scholarship chmn. 1981-82), Nat. Assn. Ind. Insurance Adjusters, Youngstown C. of C., Order of Ahepa. Greek Orthodox. Lodge: Kiwanis. Author: Ohio Comparative Negligence, An Overview, 1980. Co-author: How to Collect An Insurance Claim, 1984; mem. St. John's Parish Council. Home: 3605 Hummingbird Hill Dr Poland OH 44514 Office: 1749 S Raccoon Rd Suite 3 Youngstown OH 44515

TIESZEN, LAURENCE A., accounting and business instructor, accountant; b. Sioux Falls, S.D., June 13, 1937; s. Jacob A. and Tina A. (Wiens) T.; m. Mabel Ann Voss, July 21, 1962; children—Paul, Michelle, Mark, Marissa. B.A., Sioux Falls Coll., 1959; M.A., Mankato State U., 1965; postgrad. U. Mo.-Kansas City, U. Nebr., U. Minn., Mankato State U. Tchr. bus. Hills (Minn.) Pub. Sch., 1961-63, Met. Jr. Coll., Kansas City, Mo., 1965-68; dept. chmn. bus edn. Augustana Coll., Sioux Falls, S.D., 1968-73; instr. acctg. Pipestone Area Vocat. Tech. Inst., 1973-74; dir. edn. services and asst. personnel Sioux Valley Hosp., 1974-77; instr. bus. Mankato (Minn.) Area Vocat.-Tech. Inst., 1977—. Served with USAR, 1959-65. Mem. Mankato Tchrs. Assn., Minn. Tchrs. Assn., Nat. Tchrs. Assn., Mankato Vocat. Tchrs. Assn., Minn. Vocat. Tchrs. Assn., Am. Vocat. Tchrs. Assn. Republican. Home: 1031 Orchard Rd Mankato MN 56001 Office: 1920 Lee Blvd North Mankato MN 56001

TIGGES, JOHN THOMAS, writer, musician; b. Dubuque, Iowa, May 16, 1932; s. John George and Madonna Josephine (Heiberger) T.; m. Kathryn Elizabeth Johnson, Apr. 22, 1954; children: Juliana, John, Timothy, Teresa, Jay. Student Loras Coll., 1950-52, 57, U. Dubuque, 1960. Clk. John Deere Tractor Works, Dubuque, Iowa, 1957-61; agt. Penn Mut. Life Ins. Co., Dubuque, 1961-74; bus. mgr., bd. dirs. Dubuque Symphony Orch., 1960-68, 71-74; v.p., sec. Olson Toy and Hobby Inc., 1964-66; pres. JKT Inc., 1978-82; research specialist Electronic Media Services (Scripp-Howard); violinist. Author: (novels) The Legend of Jean Marie Cardinal, 1976, Garden of the Incubus, 1982, Unto the Altar, 1985, Kiss Not the Child, 1985, Evil Dreams, 1985, The Immortal, 1986, Hands of Lucifer, 1987, As Evil Does, 1987, Pack, 1987; (plays) No More-No Less, 1979, We Who Are About to Die, 1979; radio plays: Valley of Deceit, 1978, Rockville Horror, 1979, The Timid, 1982; TV drama: An Evening with George Wallace Jones, 1982; biographies: George Wallace Jones, 1983, John Plumbe Jr., 1983; co-author history book: The Milwaukee Road Narrow Gauge: The Bellevue, Cascade & Western, Iowa's Slim Princess, 1985; co-author: They came from Dubuque, 1983; co-editor, editor: A Cup and a Half of Coffee, 1977; editorial asst. Julian Jour.; interviewer, spl. reporter Editorial Assocs., 1982-84; columnist Memory Lane; syndicated columnist Tough Trivia Tidbits; tchr. creative writing Northeast Iowa Tech. Inst.; co-founder Dubuque Symphony Orch., 1960; founder Julien Strings, 1972, Dubuque Sch. of Novel, 1978, Northeast Iowa Writers Workshop, 1981; co-host Big Broadcast Radio Program, WDBQ Radio, 1979-82; co-founder Sinipee Writers Workshop, 1985. Founder, bus. mgr. Dubuque Pops Orch., 1957. Recipient Nat. Quality award, 1966-70, Carnegie-Stout Library World of Lit. honors award, 1981. Fellow World Lit. Acad.; mem. Nat. Writers Club (profl.), Iowa Authors, Am. Fedn. Musicians, Internat. Platform Assn., Toy Train Collectors Club. Roman Catholic. Office: PO Box 902 Dubuque IA 10011

TIGGES, KENNETH EDWIN, financial executive; b. Sandusky, Ohio, Sept. 4, 1927; s. Edwin Ernest and Ruth Dorothea (Krapp) T.; m. Mary Anne Richardson, June 11, 1955. BS in Bus. Adminstrn., Bowling Green (Ohio) State U., 1950. C.P.A., Ohio. With Konopak & Dalton (C.P.A.s), Toledo, 1950-57; with Owens-Illinois, Inc., 1957-84, comptroller, 1963-71, v.p., comptroller, 1971-84; v.p. control and adminstrn. The De Vilbiss Co. div. Champion Spark Plug Co., Toledo, 1984—. Mem. fin. com. St. Vincent Hosp., Toledo, 1968—, Bowling Green State U. Bus. Adv. Council; bd. dirs. Jr. Achievement, Toledo, 1986—. Served with U.S. Army, 1946-47. Recipient Acct. of Yr.-Industry award Bowling Green State U., 1982, 83. Mem. Am. Inst. C.P.A.s, Ohio Soc. C.P.A.s, Fin. Execs. Inst. (pres. Toledo chpt. 1970-71, v.p., bd. dirs. 1972-73, mem. com. on govt. liaison), Bowling Green State U. Alumni Bd. Dirs., Sigma Chi. Episcopal. Lodge: Rotary. Avocations: golf, reading. Home: 6655 Mill Ridge Rd Maumee OH 43537 Office: The DeVilbiss Co 300 Phillips Ave Toledo OH 43612

TILLER, JAMES E(UGENE), psychologist; b. Pekin, Ill., Mar. 23, 1950; s. James E. Sr. and Barbara (Patterson) T.; m. Theresa Jane Gunnar, May 27, 1972; children: Melissa T., Jennifer L. BA magna cum laude, Bradley U., 1972, MA, 1974; PhD in Psychology, So. Ill. U., Carbondale, 1978. Registered psychologist Ill; lic. psychologist, Wis. Therapist Project Earn, Peoria, Ill., 1974; psychologist No. Wis. Ctr., Chippewa Falls, Wis., 1977-80; clin. specialist, child psychologist Spoon River Community Mental Health Ctr., Galesburg, Ill., 1980—; cons. psychologist Cottage Hosp., Galesburg, 1980—. Contbr. articles to profl. jours. Bd. dirs. Greater Peoria Rose Soc., 1985-87. Mem. Phi Kappa Phi. Avocations: electronics, mechanics. Office: Spoon River Community Mental Health Ctr PO Box 1447 Galesburg IL 61402-1447

TILLEY, C. RONALD, gas company executive; b. Welch, W.Va., Oct. 20, 1935; s. Clarence D. and Mildred R. (Carnes) T.; m. Janice E. Tilley, Aug. 24, 1956; children: Christopher R., Cory G., Beth Ann. B.S. in Acctg., Concord Coll., 1957. Clk. rate dept. United Fuel Gas Co., Charleston, W.Va., 1957-62, rate analyst, 1962-64; engr. rate dept. Columbia Gas Service Corp., N.Y.C., 1964-71; mgr. rate dept. Columbia Gas Service Corp., Columbus, Ohio, 1971-73; dir. rate dept. Columbia Gas Service Corp., Charleston, 1973-75; v.p. corp. Columbia Gas Service Corp., Washington, 1975-80; v.p. rate Columbia Gas Service Corp., Wilmington, Del., 1980-82; sr. v.p. Columbia Gas Distbn. Cos., Columbus, 1982-85, pres., 1985-87, chmn. chief exec. officer, 1987—; Bd. dirs. BancOhio Nat. Bank. Bd. dirs. United Negro Coll. Fund, 1987—. Served with U.S. Army, 1958-60. Mem. Columbus Area C. of C. (bd. dirs. 1987—). Republican. Avocations: golf; reading. Office: Columbia Gas Distbn Cos 200 Civic Ctr Dr Columbus OH 43215

TILLMAN, DAVID FREDRICK, graphic arts company executive; b. Mpls., June 29, 1953; s. Raymond Kenneth and Phyllis Marie (Gillipsie) T.; m. Paulette Ann Zelazny, Aug. 8, 1951; stepchildren: Jessica, Westley. BS in Indsl. Tech., U. Wis. Stout, Menomonie, 1975; MBA, Coll. of St. Thomas, St. Paul, 1981. Mgr. prodn. MIU Press, Livingston Manor, N.Y., 1976-77; customer service rep. McGill-Jensen, St. Paul, 1977-79, account exec., 1979-85, nat. sales mgr., 1985-87, v.p. customer services, 1987—. Mem. Twin Cities House of Printing Craftsmen. Republican. Lutheran. Club: Good O'Boys (Mpls.). Lodges: Masons, Shriners (Zuhrah Shrine Band). Avocations: water and snow skiing, traveling. Home: 1103 Pike Lake Dr Mpls MN 55112

TILLMAN, JUDY ANN, human resource development consultant and trainer; b. Bloomington, Ind., Apr. 18, 1947; d. Theodore Nelston and Dorothy Alice (Schoener) Wells: m. Brian T. MacIntosh, (div. Sept. 1971); children: Katharine, Brian; m. Marty J. Tillman, Nov. 2, 1974. Student, Ind.-Purdue U., 1978-81; cert. tng. cons., Ball State U., 1980. Instr., curriculum developer John Robert Powers Finishing Schs., Indpls., 1977-78; owner Success Devel. Cons., Indpls., 1978—, also bd. dirs., 1978—; mem. assoc. staff Ind. Cen. U., Indpls., 1984-85, Ind. U.-Purdue U., Indpls., 1984, U. So. Ind., Evansville, 1986. Author: Corporate Play, 1987; contbr. articles to profl. jours. Mem. Indpls. C. of C. (seminar presenter), Am. Soc. for Tng. and Devel. (bd. dirs. Cen. Ind. chpt. 1981—), Nat. Speakers Assn., Women's Bus. Initiative. Republican. Club: Toastmasters Internat. Avocations: fgn. travel, the arts. Office: 10401 E 30th St Indianapolis IN 46229

TILLOTSON, JOSEPH HUGH, banker; b. Marshall, Mo., Nov. 27, 1944; s. Joseph Andrew and Virginia C. (Fisher) T.; m. Carolyn Kay Coleman, Apr. 10, 1965; children: Ricky Lynn, Ronald Lynn. BBA, Southwest U. Asst. mgr. CIT Fin. Services, Lawton, Okla., 1970-72; regional supr. Avco Fin. Services, Chgo., 1972-79; div. v.p. Unity Savs Assn., Chgo., 1979-82; sr. v.p. Talman Home Savs. & Loan, Chgo., 1982-83; exec. v.p., chief operating officer USA Consumer Credit Corp., Burbank, Ill., 1983-86; sr. v.p. corp. planning United Savs. Am., Chgo., 1986—. Bd. dirs. New Horizon Center for Profoundly Handicapped and Retarded, Chgo., 1982-83. Served with AUS, 1961-70. Decorated Air medal with cluster, Bronze Star with cluster and V device. Mem. Inst. Savs. Instns., U.S. League Savs. Instns. (nat. com. on consumer lending). Republican. Baptist.

TILLSON, JOHN BRADFORD, JR., newspaper editor; b. Paris, Tex., Dec. 21, 1944; s. John Bradford Sr. and Frances (Ragland) T.; m. Patricia Hunt, June 14, 1966 (div. June 1978); children: John, Karen; m. Cynthia Wornom, Oct. 10, 1981. BA, Denison U., Granville, Ohio, 1966. Reporter Charlotte (N.C.) News, 1969-71; reporter Dayton (Ohio) Daily News, 1971-76, city editor, 1977-80, asst. mng. editor, 1980-82; mng. editor features Dayton Daily News and Jour. Herald, 1982-84, editor, 1984—; lectr. Am. Press Inst., Reston, Va., 1980-84. Exec. com. Vietnam Vets. Meml. Park Fund, Dayton, 1985—; community bd. advisors Jr. League Dayton, 1986; trustee Dayton Art Inst., 1984—, Victory Theatre, 1986. Mem. Am. Soc. Newspaper Editors, AP Mng. Editors. Episcopalian. Home: 4833 Far Hills Ave Kettering OH 45429 Office: Dayton Daily News & Jour Herald Dayton Newspapers Inc 37 S Ludlow St Dayton OH 45401

TIMBERLAKE, GEORGE WILLIAM, judge; b. Mt. Carmel, Ill., Nov. 17, 1948; s. Richard Woodrow Timberlake and Edith Helen (Beagley) Risley; m. Mary Jo Dunkel, Aug. 16, 1975. BA, U. Ill., 1970, MBA, JD, 1977. Bar: Ill. 1977. Clk. Office U.S. Magistrate, Benton, Ill., 1978; ptnr. Townsend, Townsend, Keenan & Timberlake, Mt. Carmel, 1979-81, Townsend, Timberlake, Price & Sawyer, Mt. Carmel, Ill., 1982-85; cir. ct. judge Edwards County, Albion, Ill., 1985-86; assoc. cir. judge 2d Jud. Cir. Ct., Mt. Vernon, Ill., 1987—. Pres. So. Ill. Arts, Carbondale, 1985-86. Mem. Ill. Bar Assn., Tri-County Bar Assn., Ill. Judges Assn. Democrat. Lodge: Lions. Avocations: sailing, acting. Home: 239 N 6th St Albion IL 62806 Office: Jefferson County Cir Ct Jefferson County Courthouse Mount Vernon IL 62864

TIMKEN, W. ROBERT, JR., manufacturing company executive; b. 1938; married. B.A., Stanford U., 1960; M.B.A., Harvard U., 1962. With Timken Co. (formerly The Timken Roller Bearing Co.), Canton, Ohio, 1962—, asst. v.p. sales, 1964-65, dir. corp. devel., 1965-68, v.p., 1968-73, vice-chmn. bd., chmn. fin. com., 1973-75, chmn. bd., chmn. fin. com., 1975—, chmn. exec. com., 1983—, also dir. Office: Timken Co 1835 Dueber Ave SW Canton OH 44706 *

TIMM, HENRY PAUL, JR., engineer, marketing executive; b. St. Paul, Sept. 29, 1944; s. Henry Paul and Maddlyn Helen (Sommer) T.; m. Karen Jean Eichten, June 1, 1968; children: Bridget Marie, Laura Jean, Rebecca Michelle. BS in Engring., U.S. Mil. Acad., 1967. Commd. 2d lt. U.S. Army, 1967, advanced through grades to capt., 1969, resigned, 1971; trainer Honeywell, Mpls., 1972-75; training officer U.S. Govt., Mpls., 1975-81; with mktg. Anderson Cornelius, Mpls., 1981—. Served to maj. USAR, 1975. Mem. West Point Alumni Assn., Minn. West Point Alumni Assn. (sec. 1978-84), VFW. Roman Catholic. Avocations: mil. history, personal computing.

TIMM, KENT EDWARD, exercise scientist, physical therapist; b. Wisconsin Rapids, Wis., Oct. 21, 1958; s. Reuben E.A. and Harriet B. (Schleich) T.; m. Deborah J. Cicinelli, Sept. 27, 1986. BA in Biology, BA in Sports Medicine, Ripon (Wis.) Coll., 1981; BS in Phys. Therapy, MS in Sports Medicine, U. Pitts., 1982, MS in Athletic Tng., 1983, MS in Orthopaedic Phys. Therapy, 1984; PhD in Exercise Sci., Columbia U., 1986. Cert. sports phys. therapist, athletic trainer, back specialist. Athletic trainer Pitts. Steelers, 1981-82, Carnegie-Mellon U., Pitts., 1981-83; sports phys. therapist Pitts. Penguins, 1981-83, Podiatry Hosp. Pitts., 1983-84, Ohio Inst. for Sports, Columbus, 1984; indsl. medicine coordinator St. Luke's Hosp., Saginaw, Mich., 1984—; cons. Saginaw Gens., 1985—, Ripon (Wis.) Coll., 1981—, Cybex Corp., Ronkonkoma, N.Y., 1983—; adj. instr. U. Mich., Flint, 1985—. Mem. editorial bd. Jour. Orthopaedic Sports Phys. Therapy, LaCrosse, Wis., 1986—; contbr. articles to profl. jours. Mem. Am. Coll. Sports Medicine, Am. Phys. Therapy Assn. (Mich. Northeastern dist. treas. 1984—, sports sect., orthopaedic sect.), Nat. Athlete Trainers Assn., Acad. Clin. Electrodynography, Planetary Soc., Mensa, Phi Delta Theta, Phi Beta Kappa, Beta Beta Beta. Republican. Lutheran. Club: Saginaw Bridge. Avocations: classical music, contact and duplicate bridge, hockey, chess. Home: 4809 Brook Dr Saginaw MI 48603 Office: St Luke's Hosp 700 Cooper Ave Saginaw MI 48603

TIMMINS, RICHARD HASELTINE, foundation executive, educator; b. Ottumwa, Iowa, Jan. 24, 1924; s. Isaiah Phillip and Nellie Mae (Haseltine) T.; m. Jean Ardelle Moore, Feb. 16, 1946 (dec.); 1 dau., Cynthia Lea; m. Mischelle Christene Talley Mitchell, Aug. 10, 1983. B.A., U. Iowa, 1948, M.A., 1956; Ed.D., Columbia U., 1962. Cert. jr. coll. adminstr., Iowa. Vice-pres. Tarkio (Mo.) Coll., 1962-68; pres. Huron (S.D.) Coll., 1968-74; exec. dir. Council Chiropractic Edn. and Found. Chiropractic Edn. and Research, Des Moines, 1974-76; pres. Western States Coll., Portland, Oreg., 1976-79; exec. dir. N.D. Community Found., Bismarck, 1979-81, pres., 1981; pres. S.D. Assn. Pvt. Colls., 1968-71; chmn. bd. Colls. Mid-Am. Inc., 1972-74; pres. S.D. Edn. Assn. Dept. Higher Edn., 1974. Mem. adv. com. higher edn. Midwestern Conf., Council State Govts., 1969-71. Served as capt. USAF, 1943-45, U.S. Army, 1948-54. Am. Assn. Fund Raising Councils fellow, 1960-62. Mem. Am. Legion, Sigma Delta Chi, Kappa Tau Alpha, Kappa Delta Pi, Phi Delta Kappa. Presbyterian. Clubs: Omaha, Rotary. Lodges: Masons, Shriners, Elks. Contbr. to books and profl. jours. Home: Box 2633 Bismarck ND 58502 Office: 1002 E Central Bismarck ND 58501

TIMMONS, BESS SPIVA, foundation executive, education advocate; b. Galena, Kans., Oct. 12, 1901; d. George Newton and Bess (Tamblyn) Spiva; m. Leroy Kittrell Timmons, Sept. 2, 1922 (dec. 1954); children: Robert L., George S., Judith Ann Timmons Spears. Grad. Monticello Coll., 1921. Mem. George N. Spiva scholarship com. Pittsburg State U., Kans., 1951—; pres. Bess Spiva Timmons Found., Pittsburg, 1967—; donor Univ. Scholarship Trusts in Kans., Mo., Wyo., 1967—; mem. Timmons Chapel Com., Pittsburg, 1966—; charter mem., trustee Pittsburg U. Found., 1984. Author: Yesterday, 1976. Life mem., past pres. Salvation Army Adv. Bd., Pittsburg, 1930's—; charter mem., past pres. Pittsburg State U. Endowment Assn., 1951—, Mt. Carmel Found., Pittsburg, 1984—. Mem. Altrusa Internat. (hon.). Republican. Presbyterian.

TIMMONS, GERALD DEAN, pediatric neurologist; b. Rensselaer, Ind., June 1, 1931; s. Homer Timmons and Tamma Mildred (Spall) Rodgers; m. Lynne Rita Matrisciano, May 29, 1982; 1 child, Deanna Lynne; children from previous marriage: Jane Christina Timmons Mitchell, Ann Elizabeth, Mary Catherine. AB, Ind. U., 1953, MD, 1956. Diplomate Am. Bd. Psychiatry and Neurology. Intern Lima (Ohio) Meml. Hosp., 1956-57; resident Ind. U. Hosp., Indpls., 1957-59, 61-62; instr. neurology dept. Ind. U., Indpls., 1962-64; practice medicine specializing in psychiatry and neurology Indpls., 1962-64; practice medicine specializing in pediatric neurology Akron, Ohio, 1964—; chief pediatric neurology Children's Hosp. Med. Ctr., Akron, 1964—; chmn. neurology subcouncil Coll. Medicine Northeastern Ohio Univs., Rootstown, 1978—. Contbr. articles to profl. and scholarly jours. Served to capt. USAF, 1959-61. Mem. Summit County Med. Soc., Ohio Med. Soc., AMA, Am. Acad. Pediatrics, Am. Acad. Neurology (practice com. 1980—), Child Neurology Soc. (chmn. honors and awards com. 1978—), Am. Soc. Internal Medicine, Am. Electroencephalographic Soc. Republican. Methodist. Club: Cascade. Lodge: Rotary. Office: Akron Pediatric Neurology 300 Locust St Suite 370 Akron OH 44302

TIMMONS, JEFFREY CLARK, finance executive, accountant, consultant; b. Columbus, Ohio, Nov. 14, 1959; s. Robert Lacey Timmons and Jane Anne (Dodge) Kenan. BA, BS, Otterbein Coll., 1981; MBA, Ohio State U., 1983. CPA, Ohio; cert. managerial acct. Staff acct. Dale R. Saylor, CPA, Dublin, Ohio, 1980-83; pvt. practice cons. Columbus, Ohio, 1983-84; treas., chief fin. officer Great Am. Fun Corp., Columbus, 1984—; mgmt. rep. to bd. dirs. Great Am. Fun Corp., Columbus, 1985—; cons. computer programming, Columbus, 1984—. Mem. Am. Inst. CPA's, Ohio Soc. CPA's, Nat. Assn. Accts., Phi Eta Sigma. Clubs: Columbus Ski, Sawmill Athletic (Columbus). Avocations: skiing, racquetball, tennis, golf, white-water rafting, bicycling. Home: 1461 Runaway Bay Dr Apt 1-D Columbus OH 43204 Office: Great Am Fun Corp 1361 King Ave Columbus OH 43212

TIMOSCHUK, WALTER J., III, manufacturing engineer; b. Spencer, Tenn.; s. Walter J. Jr. and Ava Nell (Bouldin) T.; m. Cynthia Suzanne; 1 child, Walter J. Timoschuk IV. BS, Tenn. Tech., 1983; MS in Adminstrn., Cen. Mich., 1986—. Registered profl. engr. Mfg. engr. Oster div. Sunbean, McMinnville, Tenn., 1983-84; mfg. engr. transmission and Chassis Ford Motor, Sterling Heights, Mich., 1984—; Served 2d lt. CAP. Mem. ASME, NSPE, Am. Welding Soc., Am. Soc. Metals, Soc. Mfg. Engrs., Welding Inst.Am. Foundryman's Soc., Soc. Automotive Engrs., Sigma Iota Epsilon. Office: Ford Engring Transmission and Chassis 39000 Mound Rd Sterling Heights MI 48310-2799

TIMPE, DAVID ANTHONY, auditor; b. Dubuque, Iowa, Feb. 20, 1948; s. Vincent A. and Rosemary C. (Pauly) T.; m. Benita M. Heston, May 23, 1970; children: Lisa, Brian, Kevin. BA, Loras Coll., 1970. Acct. Fahey & Toohey, Sioux Falls, S.D., 1970—. Treas. Interparish Presch., Sioux Falls, 1982-84, Sioux Falls Swim Team, 1984-86. Fellow Healthcare Fin. Mgmt. Assn. (pres. S.D. chpt. 1986-87); Am. Inst. CPA's, S.D. Soc. CPA's. Avocations: traveling, fishing, photography. Home: 3541 Spencer Blvd Sioux Falls SD 57103 Office: Fahey & Toohey 3708 Brooks Pl Suite 2 Sioux Falls SD 57106

TINCHER, RAY CARTHY, corrections officer; b. Bond, Ky., July 17, 1935; s. John and Zoe (Moore) T.; m. Joyce Ann Unger, Nov. 9, 1985. Student, Ball State U., 1983-84. Cert. ACA instr. From asst. mgr. to mgr. Danner Bros., Indpls., 1955-58; prin. R & J Photography Studios, Rushville and Greensburg, Ind., 1958-60; state dist. circulation mgr. Indpls. Star & News, 1960-68; correctional officer Ind. Reformatory, Pendleton, Ind., 1968—; unit team mgr. Ind. Reformatory, Pendleton, 1978, correctional capt., supr., 1982—; dir. Medaryville Youth Camp, 1970-72; coordinator offender youth program Ind. Dept. Natural Resources, 1970-72, drug abuse program Ind. State Police, 1970-72; chmn. inst. conduct adjustment bd., Ind. Reformatory, 1979; tng. officer Branchville (Ind.) Tng. Ctr., 1984-85. Served with USMA, 1953-55, to capt. Res. 1976. Mem. Ind. Correctional Assn. (bd. dirs. 1986—, Outstanding Contbn. award 1985), Ind. Jaycees (award of Honor 1970). Republican. Lodge: Elks. Avocations: golf, bowling, computers. Office: Ind Reformatory PO Box 28 Pendleton IN 46064

TINDALL, JOHN WILLIAM, chiropractic physician; b. Kansas City, Mo., Feb. 14, 1948; s. Jack Ralph and Margarete Irene (Whitten) T.; m. Junis Loveen Sipes, July 16, 1970. Doctorate, Cleve. Chiropractic Coll., 1973-78. Lectr. Individual Achievement Motivation, Kansas City, 1978; attending physician Laurel Chiropractic Ctr., Raytown, Mo., 1979-81; dir. Tindall Chiropractic Ctr., Camdenton, Mo., 1981—; cons., lectr. Bio-Tech Co., Fayetteville, Ark., 1985-86, The Key Co., St. Louis, 1986—; cons. Nutri-Health Products, Joplin, Mo., 1985—; field instr. DECA-Lake Area Vocat. Schs., Camednton, Mo., 1985. Contbr. articles to profl. jour., 1983-84. Mentor Anti Drug and Alcohol Addiction for Children, 1984—; v.p. Camden (Mo.) Rural Fire Dept., 1985; lectr. St. Anthony Ch., Camdenton, Mo., 1981-86. Mem. Mo. State Chiropractic Assn. (sub chmn. 1983—, sec. dist. 3 1983-84, pres. 1984-85, del. 1985-86), Am. Chiropractic Assn., Paker Research Found., Beta Chi Rho. Republican. Roman Catholic. Lodge: KC. Avocation: photography. Home: 2508 S Weller Springfield MO 65804 Office: Advanced Chiropractic Clinic 3170 E Sunshine Suites F and G Springfield MO 65804

TINKER, H(AROLD) BURNHAM, chemical company executive; b. St. Louis, May 16, 1939; s. H(arold) Burnham and Emily (Barnicle) T.; m. Barbara Ann Lydon, Feb. 20, 1965; children: Michael B., Mary K., Ann E. BS in Chemistry, St. Louis U., 1961; MS in Chemistry, U. Chgo., 1964, PhD in Chemistry, 1966. Sr. research chemist Monsanto, St. Louis, 1966-69, research specialist, 1969-73, research group leader, 1973-77, research mgr., 1977-81; tech. dir. Mooney Chems., Inc., Cleve., 1981—. Patentee in field; contbr. article to profl. jours. Mem. Am. Chem. Soc. (chmn. bd. St. Louis Sect. 1978-79). Roman Catholic. Avocation: computers. Home: 2889 Manchester Shaker Heights OH 44122 Office: Mooney Chems Inc 2301 Scranton Rd Cleveland OH 44113

TINNEY, JAMES VIRLET, architect; b. Pitts., Apr. 13, 1945; s. Martin Robert and Ruth Ann (Hummel) T.; m. Kathleen Ann Crotty, June 16, 1979; children: Bridget Ann, James Dugan. BArch, Kent State U., 1969. Registered architect, Ohio, Pa., S.C., Mich., Fla. V.p. Edge & Tinney, Architects, Inc., Dayton, Ohio, 1980—. Fin. chmn. Montgomery County (Ohio) Reps., 1985-86. Office: Edge & Tinney Architects Inc 2769 Orchard Run Rd Dayton OH 45449

TINSEY, FREDERICK CHARLES III, accountant; b. Detroit, Sept. 12, 1951; s. Frederick Charles Jr. and Barbara Ann (Barrett) T.; m. Diane Helen Sarsfield, June 14, 1975; children: Christina, Frederick IV, Robert. BBA, U. Mich., 1973. CPA, Mich. Staff acct. Price Waterhouse, Detroit, 1973-75, sr. acct., 1975-78; tax mgr. Price Waterhouse, Detroit, N.Y.C., 1978-80, sr. tax mgr., 1980-84; tax ptnr. Price Waterhouse, Detroit, 1984—. Contbr. articles to profl. jours. Mem. Am. Inst. CPA's, Mich. Assn. CPA's. Republican. Lutheran. Clubs: Detroit Athletic, Lochmoor Country, Renaissance. Avocations: golf, skiing. Home: 4568 Odette Ct Troy MI 48098 Office: Price Waterhouse Suite 3900 200 Renaissance Ctr Detroit MI 48243

TINSLEY, STEPHEN JAMES, real estate developer; b. Chgo., Nov. 7, 1950; s. Milton and Phylis (Silverman) T.; m. Bibi Lewison, May 21, 1978; children—Lauren, Susan. B.S., U. Ill., 1974; M.A., U. Chgo., 1976. Sales mgr. Am. Invesco, Chgo., 1976-77; v.p. Met. Structures, Chgo., 1977-80; sr. v.p. Alter Group, Wilmette, Ill., 1980—. Contbr. articles to profl. jours. Mem. Urban Land Inst., Chgo. Office Leasing Brokers Assn., Real Estate Bd., Am. Inst. Real Estate Brokers, Assn. Indsl. Real Estate Brokers, Nat. Assn. Indsl. and Office Parks (pres. 1987).

TINTARI, CARL R., dentistry; b. Chgo., Apr. 21, 1954; s. Frank N. and Mary (Pisterzi) T. AB, U. Ill., 1976; DMD, So. Ill. U., Edwardsville, 1980; postgrad., U. Ill., Chgo., 1981. Resident in gen. practice Mt. Sinai Hosp. Med. Ctr., Chgo., 1980-81; gen. practice cosmetic dentistry Chgo., 1981—. Fellow Acad. Gen. Dentistry; mem. Arcolian Dental Arts Soc., Chgo. Dental Soc. (chmn. speaker bur. s. suburban br.), Joint Civic Com. Italian Ams. (life). Roman Catholic. Avocations: golf, tennis. Home: 340 N Arquila Dr Chicago Heights IL 60411 Office: 46 E Oak St Chicago IL 60611

TIPPETT, CHARLES ALLEN, insurance executive; b. Columbus, Ohio, Nov. 3, 1929; s. Charles and Clara (Barstow) T.; m. Barbara J. Riddle, Nov. 4, 1951; children—Steve A., Sandra L. B.S., Ohio State U., 1951. C.P.A., Ohio. With Peat, Marwick, Mitchell & Co., Columbus, Ohio, 1954-62; pres. J.C. Penney Casualty, Columbus, 1962-76; sr. v.p. J.C. Penney Life, Dallas, 1976-78; v.p. CM Team, San Diego, 1978; group v.p. Nat. Revenue Corp., Columbus, 1978-81; sr. v.p. Credit Life Ins., Springfield, Ohio, 1981—. Served to 1st lt. U.S. Army, 1952-54. Mem. Am. Inst. C.P.A.s, Ohio Soc. C.P.A.s. Home: 801 Brice Rd Reynoldsburg OH 43068 Office: Credit Life Ins Co One S Limestone St Springfield OH 45502

TIPPING, HARRY ANTHONY, lawyer; b. Bainbridge, Md., Nov. 2, 1944; s. William Richard and Ann Marie (Kelly) T.; m. Kathleen Ann Palmer, July 12, 1969; 1 child, Christopher A. B.A., Gannon U., 1966; J.D., U. Akron, 1970. Bar: Ohio. Asst. law dir. City of Akron, Ohio, 1971-72, chief asst. law dir., 1972-74; ptnr. Gillen, Miller & Tipping, Akron, 1974-77, Roderick, Myers & Linton, Akron, 1977-86; sole practice, Akron, 1987—. Chmn., Bd. of Tax Appeals, City of Fairlawn, Ohio, 1979-81, mem. merger com., 1980-82. Served with USCGR, 1966-72. Mem. Akron Bar Assn., Ohio Bar Assn., ABA, Ohio Acad. Trial Lawyers, Assn. Trial Lawyers Am., Defense Research Inst., Am. Arbitration Assn. Republican. Roman Catholic. Clubs: Fairlawn Country (Ohio); Cascade (Akron). Office: 600 CitiCtr Bldg Akron OH 44308

TIPTON, CLYDE RAYMOND, JR., communications and resources development consultant; b. Cin., Nov. 13, 1921; s. Clyde Raymond and Ida Marie (Molitor) T.; m. Marian Gertrude Beushausen, Aug. 6, 1942; children: Marian Page Cuddy, Robert Bruce. BS, U. Ky., 1946, MS, 1947. Research engr. Battelle Meml. Inst., Columbus, Ohio, 1947-49, sr. tech. adviser, 1951-62, coordinator corporate communications, 1969-73, v.p. communications, 1973-75, asst. to pres., 1978-79, v.p., corp. dir. communications and pub. affairs, 1979—; staff mem. Los Alamos Sci. Lab., 1949-51; dir. research Basic, Inc., Bettsville, Ohio, 1962-64; asst. dir. Battelle Pacific N.W. Labs., Richland, Wash., 1964-69; pres., trustee Battelle Commons Co. for Community Urban Redevel., Columbus, 1975-78; secretariat U.S. del. 2d Internat. Conf. on Peaceful Uses Atomic Energy, Geneva, 1958; cons. U.S. AEC in Atoms for Peace Program, Tokyo, 1959, New Delhi, 1959-60, Rio de Janeiro, Brazil, 1961. Author: How to Change the World, 1982; editor: Jour. Soc. for Nondestructive Testing, 1953-57, The Reactor Handbook, Reactor Materials, vol. 3, 1955, vol. 1, 1960, Learning to Live on a Small Planet, 1974; patentee in field. Bd. dirs., past pres. Pilot Dogs; bd. dirs. Central Ohio United Negro Coll. Fund, Columbus Assn. for Performing Arts, Central Ohio resource bd. CARE, Pilot Guide Dog Found., Jazz Arts Group; bd. dirs., past pres. Architects Soc. Ohio Found., Greater Columbus Arts Council; chmn. bd. Battelle Scholars Program Trust Fund; mem. governing bd. Battelle Youth Sci. Program. Served with USAAF, 1943. U. Ky. Haggin fellow, 1947; Otterbein Coll. Sr. fellow, 1978. Mem. Am. Soc. Metals, NSPE (sec.), Ohio Soc. Profl. Engrs. (bd. dirs., treas., Disting. Service award), Pub. Relations Soc. Am., Sigma Xi, Alpha Chi Sigma. Episcopalian. Club: Athletic (Washington). Lodge: Lions. Home: 2354 Dorset Rd Columbus OH 43221

TIPTON, J. DAVID, newspaper marketing executive; b. Abilene, Tex., Aug. 9, 1945; s. Donald L. and Lorraine I. (Bassinger) T.; m. Barbara J. Nathan, Apr. 29, 1966; children: Jay E., Scott A. Student, Ind. U., 1963-65, U. No. Colo., 1965-66. Advt. rep. Ft. Wayne (Ind.) Newspapers, 1966-69; advt. mgr. Bluffton (Ind.) News-Banner, 1969-70, Ft. Wayne Newspapers, 1971-84; corp. mktg. dir. Nixon Newspapers Inc., Peru, Ind., 1984—. Mem. Internat. Newspaper Advt. & Mktg. Assn. (small newspaper com. 1986—), Indiana Newspaper Advt. Execs. Assn. (bd. dirs.). Lodge: Rotary. Avocation: fishing. Office: Nixon Newspapers Inc 35 W Third St Peru IN 46970

TIPTON, JON PAUL, allergist; b. Lynchburg, Ohio, Nov. 8, 1934; s. Paul Alvin and Jeanette (Palmer) T.; m. Martha J. Johnson, Dec. 29, 1968; children: Nicole Ann, Paula Michelle. BS, Ohio U., 1956; MD, Ohio State U., 1960. Resident internal medicine Ohio State U. Hosps., Columbus, 1964-66; fellow in allergy and pulmonary disease Duke U. Med. Ctr., Columbus, 1963-64, 66-67; pvt. practice medicine specializing in allergy Athens, Ohio, 1967-74, Marietta, Ohio, 1974—; cons. Ohio U. Hudson Health Ctr., 1967—, Marietta (Ohio) Coll. Health Ctr., 1974—, United Mine Workers of Am. Funds, 1984—; dir. cardio respiratory therapy Marietta Meml. Hosp., 1983—. vol. Marietta Rep. hdqrs., 1978—; mem. choir St. Luke's Luth. Ch., Marietta, 1983—. Served to capt. USAF, 1961-63. Mem. Am. Acad. Allergy, Ohio State Med. Assn., W. Va. Med. Assn., Wash. County Med. Soc., Parkersburg (W.Va.) Acad. Med. Republican. Methodist. Avocations: yardwork, piano, attending plays, football, children. Home: 101 Meadow Ln Marietta OH 45750 Office: 100 Front St Marietta OH 45750

TISDALE, THOMAS EDWARD, engineer; b. Chgo., Mar. 14, 1942; s. Eugene Ephriam Tisdale and Modena (Hess) Pulliam; m. Mary Ellen Szarowicz, July 25, 1959 (div. Apr. 1977); children—Elizabeth Marie, Julie Anne, Thomas Edward. B.S. in Mech. Engring., San Jose State U., 1963; postgrad. Ill. Inst. Tech., 1966, U. Chgo. Engr., Cook Research Co., Morton Grove, Ill., 1963-65, Dale & Assocs., Chgo., 1965-69; project engr. U.S. Army, Charlestown, Ind., 1969-74, Sundstrand Corp., Rockford, Ill., 1974-77; project mgr. FMC Corp., San Jose, Calif., 1977-79, Abbott Labs., North Chicago, Ill., 1979—; cons. Dept. Energy, Idaho Falls, Idaho, 1977-79. Contbr. articles on engring. to profl. jours. Chmn. No. Ill. Heart Assn., Rockford, 1976, 77; mem. Young Republicans of Ill., Oak Park, 1968, 69. Mem. Soc. Mfg. Engrs. (cert.), ASME, Am. Def. Preparedness Assn., Robotics Internat. (cert. robotics engr.). Roman Catholic. Lodges: Eagles, Masons. Home: 827 Chatham Elmhurst IL 60126 Office: Abbott Labs AP4A/04B North Chicago IL 60064

TISHK, ALAN JAY, podiatrist; b. St. Louis, Dec. 13, 1949; s. Walter and Libby (Jaffe) T.; m. Cecilia Hinolan, Jan. 10, 1979; 1 child, Melissa Nan. BA, U. Mo., 1971; D of Podiatric Medicine, Ill. Coll. Podiatric Medicine, Chgo., 1975. Diplomate Nat. Bd. Podiatry. Ge. practice podiatric medicine Gladstone, Mo., 1975—. Editor Current Podiatric Medicine Jour., 1984—. Fellow: Am. Soc. Podiatric Medicine, Acad. Ambulatory Foot Surgery, Am. Soc. Podiatric Dermatology, Am. Acad. Hosp. Podiatrists, Acad. Practice Adminstrn. Avocation: music. Home: 12329 Pembroke Leawood KS 66209 Office: 5601 N Antioch Suite 7 Gladstone MO 64119

TITENS, SHERMAN JAY, marketing professional; b. Cleve., July 27, 1932; s. Louis and Celia (Shafran) T.; m. Margaret Ann Glick, Aug. 16, 1959; children: Michael Corey, Stacey Ruth, Joan Beth. BA, Western Res. U., 1954, LLB, 1956, JD, 1958. Bar: Ohio 1956. Litigation atty. U.S. Dept. Labor, Cleve., 1956-58; ptnr. Dettelbach, Titens & Viola, Cleve., 1958-69; pres., chief exec. officer Edutronics, Inc., Los Angeles, 1969-73; chmn. Coleman Am. Cos., Kansas City, Mo., 1973-78; gen. mgr. McGraw-Hill Book Co., N.Y.C., 1978-80; chmn. MCS Group, Kansas City, 1980-83; pres. Fromm Inst., Kansas City, 1983—, also lectr., cons., 1983—; acad. dean Automotive Warehouse Distbrs. Assn. U., Kansas City, Mo., 1985. Developed workshop Spl. Concerns of the Family Bus., 1984; author: Stranger In The House, 1985, Applied Research at Grad. Level, 1986. Pres. Jewish Vocat. Service and Sheltered Workshop, Kansas City, 1985—, trustee, treas. Temple B'nai Jehudah, 1976-82. Titens Bus. Library named in his honor Webster U., 1985. Mem. ABA, Am. Mktg. Assn. (v.p. Kansas City 1986—), Am. Assn. Profl. Cons. (pres.), Nat. Speakers Assn. Avocations: lecturing, reading, writing, travel. Home: 9609 Linden Ave Overland Park KS 66207 Office: Fromm Inst 9140 Ward Pkwy Kansas City MO 64114

TITER, JEFFRY LEE, stock broker, financial planner; b. Springfield, Ohio, Dec. 25, 1957; s. Howard Neal Sr. and Mary Frances (Clark) T.; m. Diane Lynn Kennedy, Sept. 15, 1984. BA, Wright State U., Dayton, Ohio, 1981, postgrad., 1984—; Cert. in Fin. Planning, Coll. Fin. Planning, Denver, 1984. Asst. treas. and bd. dirs. TC Industries, Springfield, 1978—; fin. planner Benefit Communication Services, New Carlisle, Ohio, 1981-83; v.p. and fin. planner Fin. Focus, Dayton, 1983-86; broker and fin. planner Prudential-Bache, Dayton, 1986—. Mem. Internat. Assn. Fin. Planning, Inst. Cert. Fin. Planners, Wright State U. Alumni Assn. (benefits com.), Xenia (Ohio) Area C. of C. Republican. Methodist. Lodge: Optimists. Office: Prudential-Bache Securities 130 W 2d St Dayton OH 45402

TITLE, MONROE MORRIS, hospital administrator; b. Bklyn., Oct. 6, 1918; s. Joseph and Helen (Sonnenberg) T.; m. Fran Title, Jan. 7, 1942 (div. 1972); 1 child, Diane; m. Sylvia Altshuler July 10, 1983. BA, CCNY, 1939; MA, U. Mich., 1941, MSW, 1941. Adminstr. Brent Gen. Hosp., Detroit, 1953-64, Woodside Med. Ctr., Pontiac, Mich., 1964-65, Park Community Hosp., Detroit, 1965-66; adminstr. North Detroit Gen. Hosp., 1966-87 ; instr., dir. health care adminstrn. program Oakland Community Coll., Bloomfield Hills, Mich., 1979—; instr., chmn. dept. nursing home adminstrn. Applied Mgmt. and Tech. Ctr., Wayne State U., Detroit, 1969-81, field instr. Sch. Social Work, Detroit, 1978—; chmn. com. shared services Greater Detroit Area Hosp. Council, 1974-79. Pres. Westbrook Manor Neighborhood Assn., Farmington Hills, Mich., 1980-82. Fellow Am. Coll. Hosp. Adminstrs. (life); mem. Mich. Assn. Community Hosps. and Physicians (sec. 1980-82), Am. Pub. Health Assn., Am. Assn. Hosp. Planning, Am. Arbitration Assn. (arbitrator 1982—), Hamtramck C. of C. (pres. 1986-87). Lodge: Rotary (pres. 1986-87). Avocations: chess; writing. Home: 7326 Devonshire West Bloomfield MI 48033

TITUS, J. RICHARD, physician; b. Columbus, Ohio, May 5, 1926; s. Richard Mott and Elizabeth Mary Titus; m. Anne Mary Greely, Mar. 15, 1952; children: Dianne Lynn, Nancy Lee, Karen Sue, John Richard. BA, Wesleyan U., 1946; MD, Jefferson Med. Coll., 1950; M of Med. Sci., Ohio State U., 1957. Diplomate Am. Bd. Ob-Gyn. Intern Ohio State U. Hosp., 1950-51, resident ob/gyn, 1954-57; gen. practice medicine Springfield, Ohio, 1957—. Home and Office: 2121 E High St Springfield OH 45505

TITUS, LAURA WOLF, psychologist; b. Kirksville, Mo., Oct. 25, 1924; d. Roy Milton and Lee Ola (Burch) Wolf.; m. Robert A. Titus, Dec. 21, 1946 (div. 1968); children: Susan Lee, John Elliott, Robert Christopher (dec.). MusB, State U. Iowa, 1946, MA, 1972; postgrad., Ohio State U., 1972. Lic. psychologist; cert. sch. psychologist. Asst. prof. music Mansfield (Pa.) State Coll., 1968-75; psychologist Psychol. Services, Inc., Worthington, Ohio, 1975-77, Children's Mental Health Ctr., Columbus, Ohio, 1977-79; coordinator Family and Group Edn. Inst., Columbus, 1977-80; dir., psychologist Interaction, Worthington, 1980—; developer, presenter workshops; lectr., psychologist Orton Dyslexic Soc., Columbus, 1986. Contbr. articles on divorce to profl. jours. Host family Columbus Area Internat. Program, 1983, 87; mem. area women's com. Am. Friends Service Com., Dayton, Ohio, 1984-86; mem. Women's Services, Ohio State U., Columbus; vol. Ark House, Columbus, 1986. Named Scholar in Residence, Wooster (Ohio) Coll., 1985. Mem. Am. Group Psychotherapy Assn., Ohio Psychol. Assn., Cen. Ohio Cons. Psychologists, NOW, Delta Omicron. Democrat. Mem. Soc. of Friends. Avocations: photography, reading, music, nature study. Home: 585 Plymouth Worthington OH 43085 Office: Interaction 25 W New England Ave Worthington OH 43085

TIVERS, RICK ALAN, psychotherapist; b. Chgo., Dec. 19, 1956; s. William and Pauline (Zeleznick) T.; m. Robin Kane, Sept. 20, 1981; children: Jamie, Justin. BA, No. Ill. U., 1979; MSW, U. Ill., Chgo., 1981. Cert. social worker. Staff therapist Human Effectiveness, Skokie, Ill., 1980-82; pres., clin. dir. Rick Tivers & Assocs., Skokie, 1982—; trainer Searle, Skokie, Ill., 1982—, Xerox, Mundelien, Ill., 1985—, Coll. Lake County, Grayslake, Ill., 1982—; field instr. Loyola U., Chgo. Mem. Nat. Assn. Social Workers, Ill. Soc. Clin. Social Workers. Office: Rick Tivers & Assocs 9150 N Crawford Skokie IL 60076

TIWANA, NAZAR HAYAT, librarian; b. Kalra, India, Nov. 27, 1927; came to U.S., 1965; s. Khizar Hayat and Sultan (Bibi) T.; m. Sita Sarware Sahgal, Jan. 24, 1951; children—Yasmine, Omar. B.A. in Econs., Pembroke Coll., Cambridge, Eng., 1947; M.A. in L.S., U. Chgo., 1971. Reference librarian Chgo. Pub. Library, 1973-75, adminstrv. asst., 1975-76; adult services librarian Rogers Park Library, Chgo., 1976-79; dir. America's Ethnic Heritage Program, Chgo., 1979-81; head dept. Hild Regional Library, Chgo., 1981-83; reference librarian Mt. Prospect (Ill.) Library, 1985—; spl. staff asst. White House Conf. on Libraries and Info. Services, Washington, 1979; del. Ill. White House Conf. Librarian and Info. Services, 1978; del. State Dept. Adv. Conf. on Exchange of Internat. Info., Washington, 1979. Author: (with Don Schabel) Integrated Rural Information Systems, 1976. Assoc. Newberry Library, Chgo., 1981—. Recipient Spl. Service award Friends of Chgo. Pub. Library, 1979. Mem. ALA, Internat. Fedn. Library Assns., Ill. Libraries Assn., Art Inst. Chgo., Field Mus., Beta Phi Mu. Club: Chgo. Library. Home: 2620 W Pratt Blvd Chicago IL 60645

TKATCH, KENNETH MICHAEL, financial planner; b. Sewickley, Pa., Apr. 1, 1959; s. Alfred Michael and Irene Goldie (Vobrak) T. BS in Econs., Bowling Green (Ohio) State U., 1981; MBA, U. Pitts., 1982. Chartered fin. cons.; CLU. Agt. Acacia Group, Pitts., 1982-84; registered rep. WRP Investments, Youngstown, Ohio, 1984—; pres., chartered fin. cons., CLU Range One Investors, Poland, Ohio, 1984—; br. mgr., registered rep. WRP Investments, Youngstown, 1984—; mgr. Poland, 1986—. Mem. fin. com. Holy Family Sch. and Ch., Poland, 1985. Mem. Internat. Assn. for Fin. Planning, Nat. Assn. Life Underwriters. Republican. Roman Catholic. Avocations: automobiles, phys. fitness. Home: 7605 Forest Hill Ave Poland OH 44514 Office: Range One Investors 1 N Main St Suite 108 Poland OH 44514

TOBIAS, RAYMOND JULIUS, educator; b. East Chicago, Ind., Apr. 6, 1941; s. George Adalbert and Jessie Agnes (Pawenski) T.; m. Trudy Beth Rodkin, Oct. 6, 1979. BA, Christian Bros. Coll., Memphis, 1965; MA, St. Mary's Coll., Winona, Minn., 1970. Cert. secondary tchr., Ill. Tchr. Notre Dame High Sch., Niles, Ill., 1979-81; bus. cons. and tng. dir. R.T.S. Systems, Deerfield, Ill., 1981-84; tchr. A.E. Stevenson High Sch., Prairie View, Ill., 1984—; trainer, cons. Silva Method Stress Mgmt., Westchester, Ill., 1964—. Mem. NEA, Ill. Edn. Assn., Nat. Speakers Assn., Ill. Speakers Assn., Jaycees. Avocations: tennis, swimming, gardening, climbing.

TOBIAS, RICHARD CHARLES, science educator, consultant; b. Chgo., Sept. 12, 1937; s. Joseph and Genevieve (Stwora) T.; m. Marian Jeanette Johnson, June 4, 1966; children—Timothy Richard, Denise Marie. B.S. in Edn., U. Wis.-River Falls, 1959, M.S. in Edn., 1968, D.Arts, U. No. Colo., 1976. Cert. tchr., Minn., Wis. Instr. sci. Webster (Wis.) Sr. High Sch., 1962-66, Burnsville (Minn.) Sr. High Sch., 1966—, chmn. sci. dept., 1985—; cons. product devel. 3M, St. Paul, 1980-84. Mem. steering com. North Cen. Assn. Com. Schs., 1974-78, chmn., 1981-84. Contbr. articles to profl. jours. Active Indianhead council Boy Scouts Am., 1980-87. Served with U.S. Army, 1960-62. Recipient Tchr. Intern Program award St. Paul C. of C., 1980-81. Mem. Am. Soc. Parasitologists, Assn. Biology Tchrs., Minn. Sci. Tchrs. Assn., Minn. Acad. Sci., Minn. Edn. Assn., NEA (life), Sigma Xi. Democrat. Roman Catholic. Home: 4337 Onyx Dr Eagan MN 55122

TOBIN, CALVIN JAY, architect; b. Boston, Feb. 15, 1927; s. David and Bertha (Tanfield) T.; m. Joan Hope Fink, July 15, 1951; children—Michael Alan, Nancy Ann. B.Arch., U. Mich., 1949. Designer, draftsman Arlen & Lowenfish (architects), N.Y.C., 1949-51; with Samuel Arlen, N.Y.C., 1951-53, Skidmore, Owings & Merrill, N.Y.C., 1953; architect Loebl, Schlossman & Bennett (architects), Chgo., 1953-57, v.p., 1953-57; v.p. Loebl Schlossman & Hackl, 1957—; Chmn. Jewish United Fund Bldg. Trades Div., 1969; chmn. AIA and Chgo. Hosp. Council Com. of Hosp. Architecture, 1968-76. Archtl. works include Michael Reese Hosp. and Med. Center, 1954—, Prairie Shores Apt. Urban Redevel, 1957-62, Louis A. Weiss Meml. Hosp, Chgo., Chgo. State Hosp, Central Community Hosp, Chgo., Gottlieb Meml. Hosp, Melrose Park, Ill., West Suburban Hosp, Oak Park, Ill., Thorek Hosp and Med. Center, Chgo., Water Tower Pl., Chgo., Christ Hosp., Oak Lawn, Greater Balt. Med. Ctr., Shriners Hosp. for Crippled Children Chgo., also numerous apt., comml. and community bldgs. Chmn. Highland Park (Ill.) Appearance Rev. Commn., 1972-73; mem. Highland Park Plan Commn., 1973-79; mem. Highland Park City Council, 1974—, mayor pro-tem, 1979—; mem. Highland Park Environ. Control Commn., 1979-84, Highland Park Hist. Preservation Commn., 1982—; bd. dirs. Young Men's Jewish Council, 1953-67, pres., 1967; bd. dirs. Jewish Community Centers Chgo., 1973-78. Served with USNR, 1945-46. Fellow AIA (2d v.p. Chgo. chpt.), Pi Lambda Phi. Jewish. Clubs: Standard, Highland Park Country. Home: 814 Dean Ave Highland Park IL 60035 Office: 845 N Michigan Ave Chicago IL 60611

TOBIN, CRAIG DANIEL, lawyer; b. Chgo., Aug. 17, 1954; s. Thomas Arthur and Lois (O'Connor) T. BA with honors, U. Ill., 1976; JD with high honors, Ill. Inst. Tech., 1980. Bar: Ill. 1980, U.S. Dist. Ct. (no. dist.) Ill. 1980, U.S. Dist. Ct. (no. dist.) Ind. 1986, U.S. Ct. Appeals (7th cir.) 1986, U.S. Supreme Ct. 1987. Trial atty. Cook County Pub. Defender, Chgo., 1980-82; trial atty. homicide task force Pub. Defender, Chgo., 1982-84; ptnr. Craig D. Tobin and Assocs., Chgo., 1984—; lectr. Cook County Pub. Defender, Chgo., 1983, Ill. Pub. Defender Assn., 1987. Named One of Outstanding Young Men in Am., 1985. Mem. ABA, Chgo. Bar Assn., Nat. Assn. Criminal Def. Lawyers. Roman Catholic. Office: Craig D Tobin and Assocs 79 W Monroe Chicago IL 60603

TOBIN, ILONA L., psychologist, marriage/family counselor, sex educator and counselor, consultant; b. Trenton, Mich., Apr. 15, 1943; d. Frank John and Marjorie Cathalean (Lines) Kotyuk; m. Roger Lee Tobin, Aug. 20, 1966. B.A., Eastern Mich. U., 1965; M.A., 1968; M.A., Mich. State U., 1975; Ed.D., Wayne State U., 1978. Tchr., counselor Willow Run Pub. Schs., Ypsilanti, Mich., 1966-72; prof. Macomb County Community Coll., Mt. Clemens, Mich., 1974-79; psychotherapist Identity Center, Inc., Mt. Clemens, 1974-79; dir. treatment Alternative Lifestyles, Inc., Orchard Lake, Mich., 1979-80; psychologist Profl. Psychotherapy and Counseling Ctr., Farmington Hills, Mich., 1980-83; pvt. practice clin. psychology, Birmingham, Mich., 1983—; lectr. Wayne State U., Detroit, 1977—; recruitment dir. Upward Bound Eastern Mich. U., Ypsilanti, 1969-72. Creator Doc's Dolls, 1986. Pres. Hair Prep.; co-chmn. Birmingham Families in Action, 1982-83; bd. dirs. HAVEN-Oakland County's Physical and Sexual Abuse Ctr. and Oakland Area Counselors Assn., 1984-85 ; mem. exec. bd., v.p. personnel Birmingham Community Women's Ctr., 1984-85, also dir.; mem. adv. bd. Woodside Med. Ctr. for Chemically Dependent Women, 1984-86 . NIMH fellow, 1976-78; Wayne State U. scholar, 1976-78. Mem. Am. Psychol. Assn., Mich. Psychol. Assn., Am. Assn. Sex Educators, Counselors and Therapists, Am. Assn. for Counseling and Devel., Pi Lambda Theta, Phi Delta Kappa. Unitarian. Clubs: Birmingham Bus. Womens.

TOBIN, JAMES ROBERT, hospital supply company executive; b. Lima, Ohio, Aug. 12, 1944; s. J. Robert and Doris L. (Hunt) T.; m. Janet Trafton, Dec. 30, 1971; children: James Robert III, Amanda Trafton. BA in Govt., Harvard U., 1966, MBA, 1968. Fin. analyst Baxter Travenol Labs., Inc., Deerfield, Ill., 1972-73, internat. controller, 1973-75; mng. dir. Japan Baxter Travenol Labs., Inc., Tokyo, 1975-77; mng. dir. Spain Baxter Travenol Labs., Inc., Valencia, 1977-80; pres. parenteral products Baxter Travenol Labs., Inc., Deerfield, 1981-84, group v.p., 1984—. Served to lt. USN, 1968-72. Republican. Home: 53 Canterbury Ln Lincolnshire IL 60015 Office: Baxter Travenol Labs Inc 1 Baxter Pkwy Deerfield IL 60015

TOBIN, MICHAEL ALAN, architect; b. N.Y.C., Dec. 27, 1952; s. Calvin Jay and Joan Hope (Fink) T.; m. Nancy Jo Liff, Apr. 7, 1979; 1 child, Rebecca Shana. BS, U. Mich., 1974, MArch summa cum laude, 1975. Registered architect, Ill. Sr. architect Skidmore, Owings & Merrill, Chgo., 1975-79; dir. property services Harris Bank, Chgo., 1979-84; real estate exec. Met. Structures, Chgo., 1984—. Bd. dirs. Young Men's Jewish Council, Chgo., 1982-84. Mem. AIA, Ill. Council Architects. Democrat. Avocations: skiing, sailing, photography, swimming. Office: Metropolitan Structures 111 E Wacker Chicago IL 60601

TOBIN, MICHAEL E., banker; b. Newtown Square, Pa., Jan. 17, 1926; s. Michael Joseph and Emma (Roberts) T.; m. Judith Anne Brown; children: Michael E., Allegra, Corey. B.S. in Econs, U. Pa., 1948. Cons. Philco, RCA, Ebasco Services, Inc., 1950-56; sr. cons. Arthur Young & Co., N.Y.C., 1956-59; midwest dir. cons. services Arthur Young & Co., Chgo., 1959-68; pres. Midwest Stock Exchange, Chgo., 1968-78; pres. Am. Nat. Bank & Trust Co., Chgo., 1978, chmn. bd., chief exec. officer, 1979—. Trustee Orchestral Assn. (Chgo. Symphony Orch.); mem. governing bd. Lyric Opera Chgo., Ill. Council on Econ. Edn.; mem. bus. adv. council Chgo. Urban League. Served with U.S. Army, World War II, ETO. Mem. Chgo. Assn. Commerce and Industry (past dir.). Office: Am Nat Bank & Trust Co of Chgo 33 N LaSalle St Chicago IL 60690

TOBIN, RICHARD LARDNER, journalism educator; b. Chgo., Aug. 9, 1910; s. Richard Griswold and Anne (Lardner) T.; m. Sylvia Cleveland, Oct. 11, 1937; 1 child, Mark Cleveland. B.A., U. Mich., 1932. Reporter, editor, war corr., asst. to pub. N.Y. Herald Tribune, 1932-56; dir. news ABC, N.Y.C., 1945-46; asst. to pres. Campbell Soup Co., N.J., 1957-59; mng. editor, exec. editor, assoc. pub., sr. v.p. Saturday Rev. mag., N.Y.C., 1960-76; assoc. prof. Columbia U., N.Y.C., 1940-52; Riley prof. journalism Ind. U., Bloomington, 1977—. Author: Invasion Journal, 1944; Golden Opinions, 1948; The Center of the World, 1951; Decisions of Destiny, 1961; Tobin's English Usage, 1985. Nat. pub. relations chmn. Citizens for Eisenhower, 1955-56. Recipient Disting. Alumnus award U. Mich., 1964; named to Journalism Hall of Fame, U. Mo., 1968. Republican. Episcopalian. Clubs: University, Pilgrims (N.Y.C.). Avocations: gardening; music; English usage. Office: Ind U Bloomington IN 47405

TODD, ALEXANDER WILLIAM, JR., librarian; b. Vandalia, Ill., Apr. 14, 1928; s. Alexander William and Elsa Alvina (Staroske) T.; m. Claire Mathilda Garland, Apr. 9, 1955 (dec. Dec. 1984); children: Susan, Nancy, Diane, Ellen, Alaine, Alexander. BS, USN Acad., Annapolis, Md., 1951; MLS, Drexel U., 1972. Commd. ensign USN, 1951, advanced through grades to lt. comdr., supply officer, 1951-71, retired, 1971; dir. McCowan Mem. Library, Pitman, N.J., 1971-75, Fountaindale Pub. Library Dist., Bolingbrook, Ill., 1975—. Author: Standards for Public Libraries: in Trustees Fact Files, 1986. Chmn. Will County Dist. ARC, Joliet, Ill., 1985—; bd. dirs. Mid Am. Chpt. ARC, Chgo., 1985. Mem. ALA, Ill. Library Assn. (v.p. elect 1986 pub. library sect., Librarian of Yr. award 1986), Dist. Libraries Round Table (pres. 1978-79). Republican. Methodist. Lodge: Masons. Home: 354 Sword Way Bolingbrook IL 60439 Office: Fountaindale Pub Library Dist 300 W Briarcliff Rd Bolingbrook IL 60439

TODD, ARTHUR RURIC, III, state senator, aerospace manufactuing company executive; b. San Jose, Calif., July 17, 1942; s. Arthur Ruric Jr. and Cornelia (Grace) T.; m. Karine Kay Kessel, July 15, 1972; children: Arthur Ruric IV, Allison Karine, Sean Michael. BBA, U. Calif., Berkeley, 1966. Mgmt. trainee Western Gear Corp., Lynwood, Calif., 1966-67; adminstrv. asst. Western Gear Corp., Everett, Wash., 1967-69; indsl. relations mgr. Western Gear Corp., Jamestown, N.D., 1970-73, program mgr., 1974—; mem. N.D. State Senate, Bismarck, 1982—. Alderman City of Jamestown, 1974-78; advisor Nat. Trust Hist. Preservation, 1984—. Named one of Outstanding Young Men of Am., Jaycees, 1974; recipient Disting. Service award Jamestown Jaycees, 1974. Mem. N.D. Archeol. Assn. Republican. Episcopalian. Lodge: Elks. Avocations: scuba diving, soaring, archeology, homebuilt aircraft, collecting antique firearms.

TODD, GARY ALAN, mechanical engineer; b. Cin., Sept. 1, 1961; s. Estel Robert and Helen Lavern (Wathen) T.; m. Pamela Lynn Gruber, Mar. 16, 1985. BSME, U. Cin., 1984. Linear and rotary servo drives designer, analyst Cin. Milacron, 1984-85, machine tool design engr., project leader, IBM Cadam operator, 1985-86, automated composites machine design engr., analyst, 1986—. Inventor adjustable torque takeup reel, tilt crossfeed fiber placement machine. Recipient Nat. Design award Soc. Automotive Engrs., 1984; scholar Cin. Milacron, 1980, John. W. Springmeyer Found., 1980. Mem. ASME, Cin. Milacron Engring. Club, Pi Tau Sigma. Republican. Methodist. Home: 3426 Bighorn Ct Cincinnati OH 45211 Office: Cin Milacron 4701 Marburg Ave Cincinnati OH 45209

TODD, HENRY REYNOLDS, JR., director state tourism office; b. St. Paul, Mar. 26, 1951; s. Henry Reynolds Sr. and Ruth Elizabeth (Malm) T.; m. Sue Ann Rosen, Aug. 3, 1974; children: Alison Dawn, Mackenzie Reynolds. BBA, Mankato (Minn.) State U., 1973. Travel and tourism rep. Minn. Office Tourism, St. Paul, 1973-78, dir., 1978—. Bd. dirs. St. Paul Winter Carnival, 1983—; trustee U.S. Travel Data Ctr., Washington, 1985—. Mem. Nat. Council State Travel Dirs. (chmn. 1985—), Travel Industry Assn. Am. (bd. dirs. 1984—, Travel Dir. Yr. award 1982, Nat. Travel Mktg. award 1986), Nat. Tour Assn., Am. Bus. Assn. Office: Minn Office of Tourism 375 Jackson St Suite 250 Saint Paul MN 55101

TODD, JACKSON DEAN, oral surgeon, educator; b. Bedford, Ind., Sept. 23, 1929; s. Theodore Price and Iona (Cox) T.; m. Sally Katherine Tinkle, June 30, 1957; children: Kimberly Ann, Jeffrey Dean. AB in Zoology, Ind. U., 1951, DDS, 1955. Intern Ind. U. Hosps., Indpls., 1955-56, resident, 1956-58; pres. Marion (Ind.) Oral and Maxillofacial Surgeons, Inc., 1959—; asst. prof. Ind. U., Indpls., 1966—; cons. VA Hosp., Marion, 1976—. Fellow Am. Assn. Oral and Maxillofacial Surgeons, Acad. Internat. Dentistry; mem. ADA, Ind. Dental Assn., Great Lakes Soc. Oral and Maxillofacial Surgeons, Ind. Soc. Oral and Maxillofacial Surgeons. Avocation: sports. Home: 602 Berkley Dr Marion IN 46952 Office: Marion Oral and Maxillofacial Surgeons Inc 444 Wabash Ave Marion IN 46952

TODD, JOHN JOSEPH, lawyer; b. St. Paul, Mar. 16, 1927; s. John Alfred and Martha Agnes (Jagoe) T.; m. Dolores Jean Shanahan, Sept. 9, 1950; children: Richard M., Jane E., John P. Student, St. Thomas Coll., 1944, 46-47; B.Sci. and Law, U. Minn., 1949, LL.B., 1950. Bar: Minn. bar 1951. Practice in South St. Paul, Minn., 1951-72; partner Thuet and Todd, 1953-72; asso. justice Minn. Supreme Ct., St. Paul, 1972-85; sole practice West St. Paul, 1985—. Served with USNR, 1945-46. Mem. Am. Bar Assn., state bar assns., Am. Legion, VFW. Home: 6659 Argenta Trail W Inver Grove Heights MN 55075 Office: Minn Supreme Ct 1535 Livingston Ave West Saint Paul MN 55118

TODD, JOHN ODELL, ins. co. exec.; b. Mpls., Nov. 12, 1902; s. Frank Chisholm and Mary Mable (Odell) T.; A.B., Cornell U., 1924; C.L.U., Am. Coll., 1933; m. Katherine Sarah Cone, Feb. 21, 1925; children—John Odell, George Bennett. Spl. agt. Equitable Life Assurance Soc., Mpls., 1926-28; ins. broker, Mpls., 1928-31; spl. agt. Northwestern Mut. Life Ins. Co., Mpls., 1931-38, Evanston, Ill., 1938—; ptnr. H.S. Vail & Sons, Chgo., 1938-43, Vail and Todd, gen. agts. Northwestern Mut. Life Ins. Co., 1943-44; sole gen. agt., Chgo., 1944-51; pres. Todd Planning and Service Co., life ins. brokers, 1951—; founder, chmn., prin. John O. Todd Orgn. Inc., Exec. Compensation Specialists and Cons., 1970—; faculty lectr. C.L.U. Insts., U. Conn., 1952-53, U. Wis., 1955-57, U. Calif., 1956, U. Hawaii, 1966; host interviewer ednl. Films Series of the Greats, 1973-74. Pres. Evanston (Ill.) 1st. Ward Non-Partisan Civic Assn., 1956-57; trustee Evanston Hist. Soc., 1973-76; bd. dirs. First Congl Ch., Evanston, 1987. Recipient Golden Plate award Am. Acad. Achievement, 1969; Huebner Gold medal for contbn. to edn., 1978; named Ins. Field Man of Year, Ins. Field Pub. Co., 1965; Ill. Room in Hall of States dedicated to him by Am. Coll., 1981. Mem. Nat. Assn. Life Underwriters (John Newton Russell award 1969), Assn. Advanced Life Underwriters (pres. 1963-64), Am. Coll. Life Underwriters (trustee 1957-78), Chgo. Life Underwriters Assn. (dir. 1938-41, Disting. Service award 1984), Northwestern Mut. Spl. Agts. Assn. (pres. 1955-56), Life Agy. Mgrs. Assn. (dir. 1945-48), Northwestern Mut. Assn. Agts. (pres. 1957-58), Chgo. Life Trust Council, Million Dollar Round Table (pres. 1951, qualifier 52 consecutive yrs.), Psi Upsilon, Sphinx Head. Republican. Clubs: Evanston Univ.; Glen View. Author: Taxation, Inflation and Life Insurance, 1950; Ceiling Unlimited, 1965, 5th edit., 1984; contbg. author to text Huebner Foundation, 1951.

TODD, JOHN ROBERT, educational director, educator; b. Detroit, Oct. 29, 1946; s. John Lyle and Helen Avis (Leroy) T.; m. Joyce F. Whitaker, Aug. 25, 1973; children: Lacey Joy, Jessica Elizabeth. Student, Columbia U., 1973-74; AB magna cum laude, U. Mich., 1976; JD, Georgetown U., 1979. Bar: Mich., 1979; U.S. Dist. Ct. (ea. dist.) Mich., 1980. Legis. dir. Blinded Vets. Assn., Washington, 1977-79; asst. prof. Mich. Christian Coll., Rochester, 1979—, dir. legal assts. program, 1979—; chmn. Mich. Vietnam Vets. Leadership Program, Pontiac, Mich., 1983—. Author: Michigan Business Law for the Undergraduate. City charter commr. Rochester Hills, Mich. (wrote city constitution), 1983. Served as officer U.S. Army, 1967-70, Vietnam. Decorated DFC, Purple Heart, 17 Air medals; Cross of Gallantry (Republic of Vietnam). Mem. Rochester Bar Assn. (bd. dirs. 1983—), Freedoms Found. (spokesman, editorialist; George Washington award 1970, 71). Republican. Office: Mich Christian Coll 800 W Avon Rd Rochester MI 48309

TODD, KENNETH S., JR., parasitologist, educator; b. Three Forks, Mont., Aug. 25, 1936; s. Kenneth S. and Anna Louise (Seeman) T. B.S., Mont. State U., 1962, M.S., 1964; Ph.D., Utah State U., 1967. Asst. prof. U. Ill., Urbana, 1967-71; assoc. prof. U. Ill., 1971-76, prof. vet. parasitology, 1976—, chmn. div. parasitology, 1983—, asst. head vet. pathobiology, 1984—, prof. vet. programs in agr., %. Served with USAF, 1954-58. NSF grad. fellow, 1966-67. Mem. AAAS, Am. Assn. Vet. Parasitologists, Am. Heartworm Soc., Am. Micros. Soc., Am. Soc. Parasitologists, Am. Soc. Zoologists, Am. Soc. Tropical Medicine and Hygiene, Am. Soc. Tropical Vet. Medicine, Chgo. Zool. Soc., Helminthologic Soc. Washington, Midwest Conf. Parasitologists, Wildlife Disease Assn., AVMA, Soc. Protozoologists. Office: Coll Veterinary Medicine Univ Illinois 2001 S Lincoln St Urbana IL 61801

TODD, OLIVER E., retired physician, educator; b. Lamar, Colo., May 26, 1909; s. Alfred and Myrtle (Biddleman) T.; m. Olive Stouffer, Aug. 22, 1936; children: Virginia Todd Hessler, Oliver E. Jr., Christopher J. BS in Medicine, U. Mich., 1932, MD, 1934. Diplomate Am. Bd. Ob-Gyn. Mem. staff Toledo Hosp., 1938-67, chief of staff, 1967-69, former chief dept. ob-gyn., now hon. staff mem.; clin. prof. ob-gyn. Med. Coll. at Toledo, 1979—. Mem. governing bd. Sr. Ctrs. Inc., Toledo, 1986; formerly bd. dirs. Toledo area council Boy Scouts Am.; mem. Toledo Mus. Art, Toledo Zool. Soc. Served to maj. M.C., U.S. Army, 1942-45, ETO. Fellow ACS, Am. Coll. Ob-Gyn. (life); mem. Cen. Assn. Obstetricians and Gynecologists (life). Republican. Methodist. Lodges: Kiwanis (former pres. Toledo club), Masons. Address: 2726 Emmick Dr Toledo OH 43606

TODD, STEPHEN MICHAEL, financial analyst; b. Chgo., Sept. 3, 1961; s. Norbert Michael and Maxine Karen (Eltman) T. AA, William Rainey Harper Coll., 1981; BS, Quincy Coll., 1983; MBA, Roosevelt U., 1987. Auditor Donald Bark, CPA, Arlington Heights, Ill., 1983-84; program planner assoc. Northrop Def. Systems, Rolling Meadows, Ill., 1984-85; program planner Northrop Def. Systems, Rolling Meadows, 1985-86, sr. fin. analyst, 1986—. Roman Catholic. Avocations: basketball, soccer, reading. Home: 2728 College Hill Circle Schaumburg IL 60173 Office: Northrop Defense Systems Div 600 Hicks Rd Rolling Meadows IL 60008

TODD, VICTORIA L., social worker; b. Warren, Ohio, Oct. 29, 1954; d. Martin August and Marguerite Virginia (Campsey) T. BA, Kent (Ohio) State U., 1976; M in Social Service Adminstrn. summa cum laude, Case Western Res. U., 1985—. Social worker Children and Family Services, Youngstown, Ohio, 1977-78, Summit County Children Services Bd., Akron, Ohio, 1978—; mem. Ohio Child Sexual Abuse Grant Treatment Com., Akron, 1985-86. Vol. Akron Art Mus., 1983-85; chmn. pub. relations Akron Art Fest, 1984. Mem. Nat. Assn. Social Workers, Jr. League (Akron chpt. bd. dirs. 1984-85, chmn. community research 1984-85). Republican. Roman Catholic. Home: 315 Pembroke Rd Fairlawn OH 44313 Office: Summit County Children Services Bd 264 S Arlington St Akron OH 44306

TODD, ZANE GREY, utility executive; b. Hanson, Ky., Feb. 3, 1924; s. Marshall Elvin and Kate (McCormick) T.; m. Marysnow Stone, Feb. 8, 1950 (dec. 1983); m. Frances Z. Anderson, Jan. 6, 1984. Student, Evansville Coll., 1947-49; BS summa cum laude, Purdue U., 1951, D in Engring. (hon.), 1979; postgrad., U. Mich., 1965. Fingerprint classifier FBI, 1942-43; electric system planning engr. Indpls. Power & Light Co., 1951-56, spl. assignments supr., 1956-60, head elec. system planning, 1960-65, head substation design div., 1965-68, head distbn. engring. dept., 1968-70, asst. to v.p., 1970-72, v.p., 1972-74, exec. v.p., 1974-75, pres., 1975-81, chmn., 1976—, chief exec. officer, 1981—; chmn., pres. IPALCO Enterprises, Inc., Indpls., 1983—; chmn. bd., chief exec. officer Mid-Am. Capital Resources, Inc. subs. IPALCO Enterprises, Inc., Indpls., 1984—; gen. mgr. Mooreville Pub. Service Co., Inc., Ind., 1956-60; bd. dirs. Mchts. Nat. Bank, Mchts. Nat. Corp., Am. States Ins. Co., Environ. Quality Control, Inc.; sr. v.p. 500 Festival Assocs., Inc., pres., 1987. Contbr. articles to tech. jours. and mags. Mem. adv. bd. St. Vincent Hosp.; bd. dirs. Commn. for Downtown, YMCA Found., Crime Stoppers Cen. Ind.; mem. adv. council, trustee Christian Theol. Sem.; chmn. bd. trustees, dir. corp. community council Ind. Cen. U. (now U. Indpls.); bd. govs. Associated Colls. of Ind.; chmn. U.S. savs. bond program State of Ind.; mem. Nat. and Greater Indpls. adv. bds. Salvation Army. Served as sgt. AUS, 1943-47. Named Disting. Engring. Alumnus, Purdue U., 1976, Knight of Malta, Order of St. John of Jerusalem, 1986. Fellow IEEE (past chmn. power system engring. com.); mem. ASME, NSPE, NAM (bd. dirs.), Am. Mgmt. Assn. (gen. mgmt. council), Power Engring. Soc., Ind. Electric Assn. (bd. dirs., past chmn.), Assn. Edison Illuminating Cos. (bd. dirs.), Edison Electric Inst. (bd. dirs.), Ind. Fiscal Policy Inst. (bd. govs.), Indpls. Pvt. Industry Council (bd. dirs.), Ind. C. of C. (bd. dirs.), Indpls. C. of C. (bd. dirs.), Mooreville C. of C. (past pres.), Newcomen Soc. (chmn. Ind.), Eta Kappa Nu, Tau Beta Pi. Clubs: Columbia, Indpls. Athletic (past bd. dirs.), Meridian Hills Country; Skyline (bd. govs.). Lodges: Rotary, Lions (past pres.). Originator probability analysis of power system reliability. Home: 7645 Randue Ct Indianapolis IN 46278 Office: 25 Monument Circle Indianapolis IN 46206

TODOROVIC, RADMILO ANTONIJE, veterinarian, technical development executive; b. Zabojnica, Yugoslavia, Oct. 30, 1927; came to U.S., 1960; s. Antonije Ilija and Rajka (Otasevic) T. m. Lillian Djukic, June 9, 1960; children: Jovan, Ilija, Joan, Jane. DVM, U. Belgrade, Yugoslavia, 1953; MS, U. Wis., 1963; PhD, U. Ill., 1967. Diplomate Am. Coll. Vet. Medicine. Veterinarian Vetinary Hosp., Bare-Knic, Yugoslavia, 1953-55; asst. prof. U. Belgrade, 1955-60; veterinarian Am. Breeders, Madison, Wis., 1960-63; dir. Ctr. Tropical Agr., Cali, Colombia, 1968-78; assoc. prof. Tex. A&M U., College Station, 1968-80; mgr. research and devel. Internat. Minerals & Chem. Corp., Terre Haute, Ind., 1980—, research veterinarian, 1983—; research veterinarian Colombian Inst. Agr., Bogota, 1968-72; cons. U.S. Aid-Vet Dept., Lima, Peru, Micronesia, 1969-73; invited speaker World Vet. Congress, 1970, 75, Agrl. Seminar, China, 1984. Contbr. over 120 articles to profl. jours. and textbooks. Postdoctoral fellow N. Atlantic Treaty Pact. Mem. Am. Vet. Med. Assn., Ill. Soc. Med. Research, Conf. on Research Workers in Animal Diseases, Soc. Protozoologists, Assn. Univ. Profs., AAAS, Latin Am. Assn. Agrl. Scis., Colombian Vet. Med. Assn., N.Y. Acad. Sics., Soc. Tropical Vet. Medicine, Ind. State Vet. Med. Assn., Smithsonian Assocs., U.S. Animal Health Assn., Am. Assn. Indsl. Vets., Sigma Xi, Phi Sigma, Phi Zeta. Home: 1355 Winterberry Ct Terre Haute IN 47802 Office: Internat Minerals & Chem Corp PO Box 207 Terre Haute IN 47808

TOEBE, KENNETH WILBURT, resort owner; b. Woodville, Wis., Feb. 13, 1935; s. Wilburt William and Lucille Laura (Lopas) T.; m. Carol Jean Odegard, Nov. 14, 1981. B.S., U. Wis.-Oshkosh, 1958; M.A., Eastern Mich. U., 1961. Cert. tchr., Wis. English tchr. Cement City Schs., Mich., 1960-62, Kaukauna Community Schs., Wis., 1962-68, Hayward Community Schs., Wis., 1968-75; resort owner, operator Sunset Lodge, Hayward, 1966—; chmn. English dept. Hayward Community Schs., 1969-75. Pres. Northwest Territories tourism orgn., Wis., 1981—; v.p. Hayward Lakes Resort Assn., 1984—, sec., treas. 1973-79; pres. Lost Land-Teal Resort Assn., Hayward, 1978-80. Recipient Outstanding Service award Hayward Lakes Resort Assn., 1979. Mem. Am. Birkebeiner Ski Found., Fresh Water Fishing Hall of Fame (charter), Humane Soc. U.S. World Concern, Christian Blind Mission Internat., Hayward Concert Assn., Internat. Platform Assn. Lutheran. Lodge: Masons. Avocations: reading; music; travel; skiing; swimming. Home and Office: Route 7 Hayward WI 54843

TOEPP, FRANK CONRAD, podiatrist; b. South Bend, Ind., Jan. 30, 1928; s. Frank Conrad and Martha (Scanlon) T.; m. Rosemary Williams, Aug. 23, 1951; children: Kathleen, David, Stephen, Phillip, Kevin. DSc, Ill. Coll. Podiatric Medicine, 1952; D in Podiatric Medicine, William Scholl Coll. Podiatric Medicine, Chgo., 1968. Diplomate Am. Bd. Ambulatory Foot Surgery. Practice podiatric medicine South Bend, 1952—; instr. in surgery Ill. Coll. Podiatric Medicine, 1974-77; aux. clin. prof. William Scholl Coll Podiatric Medicine, 1977—; preceptor Mich. Community Hosp. and Pvt. Office, South Bend, 1975—. Served with USN, 1946-48. Recipient St. George award Cath. Com. on Scouting, South Bend, 1978. Fellow Acad. Ambulatory Foot Surgery (Service award 1977); mem. Am. Podiatric Med. Assn., Ind. State Podiatric Med. Assn. (pres. 1961-62), Am. Bd. Podiatric Surgery (bd. dirs. 1983-86), Am. Bd. Ambulatory Foot Surgery (co-founder 1975, pres. 1977-79). Republican. Roman Catholic. Club: Serra (South Bend). Lodge: Rotary. Avocation: designing podiatry offices. Home: 52762 Brookdale Dr South Bend IN 46637 Office: 727 E Jefferson Blvd South Bend IN 46617

TOERING, MYRON DEAN, lawyer; b. Hospers, Iowa, Jan. 11, 1948; s. Mince and Nellie (Steenhoven) T.; m. Marla Joy Kleinhesselink, Aug. 23, 1974; children—Mickey, Matthew. B.B.A., U. Iowa, 1975, M.A., 1976; J.D., U. Tulsa, 1979. Bar: Iowa 1979. C.P.A., Iowa. Acct. Arthur Young Co., Tulsa, 1978; clk. Dyer, Power, Marsh, Tulsa, 1978-79; trust officer Am. State Bank, Sioux Center, Iowa, 1979-80; sole practice, Sioux Center, 1980—; sec. Hospice of Sioux County Inc., Sioux Center, 1984—; mem. adv. bd. Mid-Sioux Opportunity Inc., Remsen, Iowa, 1984—. Councilman Sioux Center City Council, 1983; v.p. Sioux Center PTA, 1983—. Served as sgt. USAF, 1967-71. Chester Phillips scholar U. Iowa, 1975. Mem. Christian Legal Soc., Iowa State Bar Assn., Sioux Center C. of C. Democrat. Mem. Reformed Ch. Am. Lodge: Lions. Home: 1115 Eastside Dr Sioux Center IA 51250 Office: 128 3d St NW Sioux Center IA 51250

TOFT, RICHARD P(AUL), title insurance executive; b. St. Louis, Sept. 20, 1936; s. Paul C. and Hazel F. T.; B.S.B.A., U. Mo., 1958; m. Marietta Von Etzdorf, Oct. 5, 1963; children—Christopher P., Douglas J. With Lincoln Nat. Life Ins. Co., 1959-73, group and pension sales mgr., 1969-73; 2d v.p. Lincoln Nat. Sales Corp., Ft. Wayne, Ind., 1973-74, v.p., 1974-80, v.p., treas., 1980-81; pres. Chgo. Title Ins. Co., 1981-82, pres., chief exec. officer Chgo. Title Ins. Co. and Chgo. Title and Trust Co., 1982—, also dir. both; dir. Lincoln Nat. Devel. Corp. Trustee, Chgo. Community Trust, 1982. Served to 2d lt. U.S. Army, 1958-59. Mem. Am. Land Title Assn. Congregationalist. Club: Union League (Chgo.). Office: Chgo Title & Trust Co 111 W Washington St Chicago IL 60602 *

TOFTNER, RICHARD ORVILLE, engineering firm executive; b. Warren, Minn., Mar. 5, 1935; s. Orville Gayhart and Cora Evelyn (Anderson) T.; B.A., U. Minn., 1966; M.B.A., Xavier U., 1970; m. Jeanne Bredine, June 26, 1960; children—Douglas, Scott, Kristine, Kimberly, Brian. Sr. economist Federated Dept. Stores, Inc., Cin., 1967-68; dep. dir. EPA, Washington and Cin., 1968-73; mgmt. cons. environ. affairs, products and mktg., 1973-74; prin. PEDCo Environ., Cin., 1974-80; trustee PEDCo trusts, 1974-80; pres. ROTA Mgmt., Inc., Cin., 1980-82; gen. mgr. CECOS, 1982-85, cons., 1985—; v.p. Smith, Stevens & Young, 1985—; real estate developer, 1980—; adj. prof. U. Cin.; lectr. Grad. fellowship rev. panel Office of Edn., 1978—; advisor, cabinet-level task force Office of Gov. of P.R., 1973; subcom. Nat. Safety Council, 1972; nominee commr. PUCO, Ohio; Cin. City mgr. Waste Task Force, 1987—. Served with AUS, 1954-57. Mem. Am. Inst. Cert. Planners, Soc. Advancement Mgmt., Water Pollution Control Fedn., Engring. Soc. Cin., Cin. C. of C. Republican, Lutheran. Clubs: Columbia (Indpls.); Bankers (Cin.). Contbr. articles to mgmt. planning and environ. to periodicals, chpts. in books; developer Toxitrol. Home: 9175 Yellowwood Dr Cincinnati OH 45239 Office: 11475 Northlake Dr Cincinnati OH 45242

TOGNARELLI, RICHARD LEE, lawyer; b. Collinsville, Ill., Aug. 12, 1949; s. Albert John and Rosalie Frances (Brogliatto) T.; m. Gail Marie Culliton, June 11, 1971; children—Michael Anthony, Matthew Paul. A.B., St. Louis U., 1971, J.D., 1974. Bar: Ill. 1975, U.S. Dist. Ct. (so. dist.) Ill. 1975, U.S. Dist. Ct. (ea. dist.) Ill. 1975, U.S. Ct. Appeals (7th cir.) 1976. Clk., then assoc. firm Dunham, Boman, Leskera & Churchill, East St. Louis, Ill., 1973-78; ptnr. Cadagin, Cain & Tognarelli, Collinsville, 1978-84; ptnr. firm Tognarelli & Mattea, Collinsville, 1984—. Pres. parish council Sts. Peter and Paul Roman Cath. Ch., Collinsville, 1984-85. Named One of Outstanding Young Men of Am., Collinsville Jaycees, 1981, also recipient Disting. Service award, 1984. Mem. ABA (sect. of econs. of law practice com. on lawyer relations with pub. 1986-87), Ill. State Bar Assn. (chmn. jud. adv. polls com. 1986-87, membership and bar activities), Collinsville C. of C. (chmn. ambassadors 1984-87, v.p. orgn. affairs 1986—), Phi Beta Kappa. Democrat. Lodges: Rotary (pres. Collinsville 1983-84), K.C. Home: 303 Chesapeake Ln Collinsville IL 62234 Office: Tognarelli & Mattea 1605 Vandalia St Collinsville IL 62234

TOIG, RANDALL MARC, gynecologist/obstetrician; b. Pitts., Sept. 19, 1950; s. Harry M. and Florence (Levy) T.; m. Allison Beth Wines, June 9, 1985; 1 child, Andrew. BS, U. Mich., 1972; MD, U. Pitts., 1977. Intern Presbyn.-St. Lukes, Chgo., 1977-78; resident Northwestern Meml. Hosp., Chgo., 1978-82; practice medicine specializing in ob-gyn Chgo., 1982—; instr. medicine Northwestern U., Chgo., 1982—. Bd. dirs. Make A Wish, Chgo., 1985, Friends of Prentice Hosp., Chgo., 1986. Fellow Am. Coll. Ob-Gyn; mem. AMA, Chgo. Med. Soc. Avocations: tennis, architecture. Office: 666 N Lake Shore Dr Chicago IL 60611

TOKAR, EDWARD, architect, consultant; b. Chgo., Nov. 18, 1923; s. August and Anna (Wardzala) Tokarske; m. Maureen Tansey, June 29, 1974. BA, Northwestern U., 1961. Registered architect, Ill. Engr. Chgo. Bridge and Iron Co., Seneca, Ill., 1942-44; archtl. planner Marshall Field and Co., Chgo., 1946-54; store planner and designer Sears Roebuck and Co., Chgo., 1954-67; corp. architect Goldblatt's, Chgo., 1967-74; project architect Holabird & Root, Chgo., 1975-81; prin. Planning and Design Cons., Chgo., 1981—; sec.-treas. Program Devel. Cons., Evanston, Ill., also bd. dirs.; cons. Marshall Field and Co., Chgo. Illustrator Marine Elect. Constrn., 1943. Bd. dirs. Meth. Youth Services, Chgo., 1986—; mem. Chgo. Art Inst. Served with USN, 1944-46. Mem. AIA (corp.), Inst. Store Planners (treas., bd. dirs.), World Federalists. Roman Catholic. Club: Gen. Semantics (Chgo.) (pres. 1957).

TOKAR, MAUREEN TANSEY, architect; b. Cin., Mar. 4, 1931; d. Bernard Joseph and Cecile Marie (Sunman) Tansey; B.S. in Architecture, U. Cin., 1955; m. Edward Tokar, June 29, 1974. Job capt. Hixson, Tarter & Merkel, Cin., 1964-68; dir. interior architecture Ferry & Henderson, Springfield, Ill., 1968-72; project coordinator Skidmore, Owings & Merrill, Chgo., 1972-76; rev. architect Ill. Capital Devel. Bd., Chgo., 1977-82; v.p. Planning and Design Cons., 1975—. Active, Art Inst. Chgo. Mem. AIA, Chgo. Women in Architecture, Alpha Omicron Pi. Club: Chgo. Altrusa.

TOLBERT, HERMAN ANDRE, child psychiatrist; b. Birmingham, Ala., May 29, 1948; s. John and Ruth Juanita (Danzy) T. BS magna cum laude, Stillman Coll., 1969; MD, U. Calif. San Diego, La Jolla, 1973. Clin. instr., psychiatry resident, child psychiatry fellow Ohio State U., Columbus, 1974-78, asst. prof., child psychiatrist, 1978—. Contbr. chpts. to books. Bd. dirs. Univare Child Devel. Ctr., Urbancrest, Ohio, 1984—, Huckleberry House, Columbus, 1979-82; mem. adv. com. Ohio Dept. Mental Health, Columbus, 1985—. Fellow John Hay Whitney Found., N.Y.C., 1970, Am. Psychiat. Assn./NIMH, Washington, 1978. Fellow Am. Acad. Child Psychiatry; mem. Am. Psychiat. Assn., Assn. Acad. Psychiatry, Psychiat. Soc. Cen. Ohio (sec. 1985—), Mental Health Assn. (bd. dirs. 1978-83). Democrat. Avocations: singing, theatre, fashion design. Home: 6454 Strathaven Ct E Worthington OH 43085 Office: Ohio State U 473 W 12th Ave Columbus OH 43210

TOLCHINSKY, PAUL DEAN, organizational psychologist; b. Cleve., Sept. 30, 1946; s. Sanford M. and Frances (Klein) T.; children: Heidi E., Dana M. BABA, Bowling Green State U., 1971; PhD in Orgnl. Behavior, Purdue U., 1978. Mgmt. trainer Detroit Bank and Trust Co.; tng. and devel. mgr. Babcock & Wilcox Co., Barberton, Ohio, 1973-75; internal cons. Gen. Foods, Inc., West Lafayette, Ind., 1975-77; prof. Fla. State U., Tallahassee, 1978-79, U. Akron, Ohio, 1979-81; prin. Performance Devel. Assocs., Cleve., 1981—; adj. prof. Bowling Green State U., 1981-82. Contbr. numerous articles to profl. jours. Served in U.S. Army, 1966-69, Vietnam. Mem. Am. Psychol. Assn., Cert. Cons. Internat., Acad. Mgmt. Home: 22132 E Byron Shaker Heights OH 44122

TOLENTINO, GERARDO A., JR., small business owner; b. Tuy, Batangas, Philippines, June 1, 1931; s. Gerardo F. Sr. and Carmen (Apacible) T.; m. Rosie V. Eser, Dec. 30, 1959; children: Gerardo III, Glenda, Gilbert. BS in Commerce, Far Eastern U., Manila, Philippines, 1958; postgrad., Feati Inst. Tech., Manila, Philippines, 1949. Mgr. casualty ins. dept. Philippine Am. Gen. Ins. Cos., Manila, Philippines, 1952-69; underwriter Am. Internat. Underwrtiters Agy., Chgo., 1970-72; ins. agt. State Farm Ins. Cos., Chgo., 1972-87; prin. G.A. Tolentino, Jr. Ins. Co., Inc., Chgo., 1987—; adviser Assn. Filipino-Am. Businessmen Chgo., 1972-75. Founder, advisor Queen of Angels Filipino Fellowship, Chgo., 1975—; advisor Batangas Club of Midwest, 1984—. Mem. Philippine C. of C. (bd. dirs.), Millionaire Club. Club: Unido. Avocations: bowling, photography, video recording. home: 4435 Fitch Ave Lincolnwood IL 60646 Office: 2015 W Montrose Chicago IL 60618

TOLIN, BRUCE GEORGE, food products executive; b. Chgo., June 22, 1957; s. Stanley and Anita (Kasindorf) T.; m. Andrea Deborah Schornstein, Sept. 21, 1985. BS in Food Sci., U. Ill., 1981; MBA in Mktg., Northwestern U., 1986. Food scientist, internat. mktg. Union Carbide Corp., Chgo., 1981-84; mktg. mgr. Intek Internat. Food Products, Inc., Barrington, Ill., 1984—; pres. Rosetta Software, Ltd., Barrington, Ill., 1985—. Patentee Human Language Computer Interpretor Program. Mem. Inst. Food Technologists (editor internat. newsletter, 1981—), Am. Translators Assn., Am. Liszt Soc. Republican. Avocations: travel, piano, music composition. Fluent in 9 languages. Home: 626 Old Barn Rd Barrington IL 60010

TOLIVER, C. R., fashion coordinator; b. Chgo., Aug. 4, 1952; d. William Saunders and Amo B. (McWhorter)-Evans; m. Steve N. Toliver, July 2, 1969 (div. July 1980); 1 dau., Stephanie Monique. Telephone operator Ill. Bell Telephone Co., Chgo., 1979-82; owner, pres. Ceci, fashion coordinating, Chgo., Lacquered Images, Ltd., 1979—; chmn. Adaptations, entertainment service and cons. firm, not-for-profit, 1984—. Mem. Cosmopolitan C. of C., Notaries Assn. Ill., Am. Mus. Natural History, Am. Film Inst., Nat. Assn. Female Execs. Democrat. Roman Catholic. Office: PO Box 19161 Chicago IL 60619

TOLLESTRUP, ALVIN VIRGIL, physicist; b. Los Angeles, Mar. 22, 1924; s. Albert Virgil and Maureen (Petersen) T.; m. Alice Hatch, Feb. 26, 1945 (div. Nov. 1970); children: Kristine, Kurt, Eric, Carl. BS, U. Utah, 1944; PhD, Calif. Inst. Tech., 1950. Mem. faculty Calif. Inst. Tech., Pasadena, 1950-77, prof. physics, 1968-77; scientist Fermi Nat. Lab., Batavia, Ill., 1977—, head collider detector facility. Co-developer superconducting magnets for Tevatron, Fermi Lab. Served to lt. (j.g.) USN, 1944-46. NSF fellow. Mem. Am. Physical Soc., AAAS. Democrat. Home: 29W254 Renoud Dr Warrenville IL 60555 Office: Fermi Nat Lab Box 500 Batavia IL 60510

TOLLIVER, KEVIN PAUL, dentist; b. Ft. Wayne, Ind., Mar. 17, 1951; s. Herbert and Norma Jean (Scheele) T.; m. Melanie Beth Johnson, May 5, 1973; children: Chad, Joshua, Jordan. BA, Ind. U., 1973; DDS, Ind. U., Indpls., 1977. Lic. dentist, Ind. Gen. practice dentistry Indpls., 1977—. Pres. Williston Green Assn., Indpls., 1983, 85; vol. Pan Am. Games, Indpls., 1986-87. Named one of Outstanding Young Men of Am., 1984. Fellow Acad. Functional Prosthodontics, Acad. Physiologic Dentistry; mem. ADA, Ind. Dental Assn., Indpls. Dist. Dental Soc., Chgo. Dental Soc., Ind. U. Hoosier Hundred. Democrat. Lodge: Kiwanis. Avocation: athletics. Home: 11394 St Andrew's Ln Carmel IN 46032 Office: 3390 W 86th St Suite C-1 Indianapolis IN 46268

TOLMAN, DAN EDWARD, oral and maxillofacial surgeon; b. Silver Creek, Nebr., Aug. 9, 1931; s. Nathaniel Edward and Virginia (West) T.; m. Suzanne Nelson, June 8, 1957; 1 child, Kimberly Suzanne. BSBA, U. Nebr., 1953, BS in Dentistry, 1957, DDS, 1957; MSD, U. Minn., 1961. Diplomate Am. Bd. Oral and Maxillofacial Surgery. Resident, Mayo Grad. Sch. Medicine, Rochester, Minn., 1959-62; practice dentistry specializing in oral and maxillofacial surgery, Rochester, 1965—; cons. sect. dentistry and oral surgery Mayo Clinic, Rochester, 1965-66; instr. Mayo Grad. Sch. Medicine, U. Minn., 1966-70, asst. prof. dentistry, 1970-73, asst. prof. Mayo Med. Sch., 1973-78, assoc. prof., 1978—; mem. staff Mayo Clinic; mem. adv. group Northlands Regional Med. Program, 1969-71; mem. panel, div. ednl. resources and programs Assn. Am. Med. Colls., 1976—. Contbr. articles to profl. jours.; editor Jour. Oral Surgery, 1974-81. Mem. nominating com. Minn. Cancer Council, 1978-79, 1st vice chmn., 1980, chmn., 1981, 82, 83, Minn. Dental Assn. rep. 1978—; bd. dirs. Minn. div. Am. Cancer Soc., 1973-82, 83-84, v.p., pres. elect, 1979-80, pres. Minn. div., 1980-81, bd. dirs. Olmsted County Unit, 1972-81, chmn. standing crusade com., 1979-80; active Olmsted County Republican Party, 1968-72; pres.-elect Jefferson PTA, 1970-71, mem. scholarship com. Rochester Council, 1970-71; mem. benevolence com. 1st Presbyn. Ch., 1984—. Served with USAF, 1956-65; served to col. USAR, 1979—. Recipient cert. merit Am. Soc. Dentistry for Children, 1957; Nat. Divisional award Am. Cancer Soc., 1983; named hon. Adm., Nebr. Navy, 1953. Fellow Internat. Assn. Oral Surgeons, Am. Coll. Dentists; mem. Am. Assn. Oral and Maxillofacial Surgeons (trustee 1978-82, presdl. adv. com. 1982-83, sec.-treas. 1985—, trustee 1985—), Midwestern Soc. Oral and Maxillofacial Surgeons (sec.-treas. 1973-78, v.p. 1978-79, pres.-elect 1979-80, pres. 1980-81, 81-82, nominating com. 1981—, chmn. com. 1984—), Minn. Soc. Oral and Maxillofacial surgeons (constl. and by-laws com. 1984—), Minn. Dental Assn. (Meritorious Service citation 1978, 81, rep. to Minn. Cancer Council 1978—), Zumbro Valley Dental Soc. (Olmsted County welfare com. 1967-68, community dental health com. 1970-71), Am. Bd. Oral and Maxillofacial Surgery (adv. com. 1975-78), ADA, Southeastern Dist. Dental Soc., Am. Acad. Dental Radiology, U. Nebr. Alumni Assn., Mayo Alumni Assn., Milw. Dental Forum (hon.), Am. Assn. for Cancer Edn., Sigma Chi. Lodges: Masons (32 degree), Shriners. Home: 2709 Merrihills Dr SW Rochester MN 55901 Office: Mayo Clinic Dept Dentistry 200 1st St SW Rochester MN 55905

TOLMAN, SUZANNE NELSON, psychologist; b. Omaha, Nov. 8, 1931; d. Raymond LeRoy and Lottie (Kerns) Nelson; B.A. with distinction in Spanish, U. Nebr., Omaha, 1951; M.A., U. Nebr., Lincoln, 1952, Ph.D., 1957; m. Dan Edward Tolman, June 8, 1957; 1 dau., Kimberly Suzanne. Research asst. U. Nebr., Lincoln, 1951-52; tchr. Omaha Pub. Schs., 1952-53, counselor, high sch. instr. history and English, 1953-59; instr. psychology U. Nebr., Omaha, 1957-59; social service worker Mayo Clinic, Rochester, Minn., 1959-60; instr. psychology U. Tampa, 1962-63; sch. psychologist Sch. Dist. 535, Rochester, 1966—. Bd. dirs. Jefferson PTA, Rochester, 1966-68; bd. dirs., sec. Family Consultation Center, Rochester, 1970-76; bd. dirs. Olmsted County (Minn.) Council Coordinated Child Care, 1971-75, pres., 1973-75; bd. dirs. Olmsted County Assn. Mental Health; pres. condr.'s com. Rochester Symphony, 1977-78. Mem. Minn., Rochester edn. assns., Minn. Sch. Psychologists, Rochester Civic Music Guild (pres. 1981-82), Am. Psychol. Assn., AAUW, Zumbro Valley Dental Aux. (pres. 1970-71), Phi Delta Kappa, Alpha Lambda Delta, Alpha Delta Kappa, Psi Chi, Chi Omega. Presbyterian. Club: Order Eastern Star. Home: 2709 Merrihills Dr SW Rochester MN 55901 Office: Ind Sch Dist 535 Rochester MN 55901

TOLTZIS, ROBERT JOSHUA, cardiologist; b. Phila., May 6, 1949; s. Louis and Shirley (Weiner) T. AB, Temple U., 1970; MD, Hahnemann U., 1974. Cert. Am. Bd. Internal Medicine, Cardiovascular Diseases. Intern, resident, fellow Peter Bent Brigham Hosp., Boston, 1974-79, Children's Hosp., Boston, 1974-79; chief of service in cardiology Nat. Heart Lung and Blood Inst., Bethesda, Md., 1980-82; assoc. prof. clin. medicine and pediatrics U. Cin., 1982—; fellow in medicine Harvard U., Boston, 1974-79, instr. 1979-80; dir. coronary care U. Hosp., Cin., 1982—. Fellow Am. Coll. Cardiology, Council on Clin. Cardiology, Am. Heart Assn.; mem. Am. Soc. Echocardiography, Alpha Omega Alpha. Home: 1 Muirfield Ln Cincinnati OH 45241 Office: U Cin Med Ctr ML542 Cincinnati OH 45267-0542

TOMANEK, GERALD WAYNE, educator; b. Collyer, Kans., Sept. 16, 1921; s. John James and Hazel Marie (Orten) T.; m. Ruth Ardis Morell, Apr. 30, 1945; children—Walta, Sheila, Lisa. B.A., Ft. Hays (Kans.) State U., 1942, M.S., 1947; Ph.D., U. Nebr., 1951. Mem. faculty Ft. Hays State U., 1947-87, prof. biology, chmn. div. natural scis. and math., 1970-72, v.p. acad. affairs, 1972-75, acting pres., 1975-76, pres., 1976-87, ret. Author, editor in field. Served to capt. USMCR, 1942-46. Named Conservationist Educator of Year; recipient Alumni Achievement award Ft. Hays State U.; Kansan of Yr. award, 1979. Mem. Soc. Range Mgmt., Ecol. Soc. Am., Am. Inst. Biol. Scis., Southwestern Assn. Naturalists, Kans. Wildlife Assn., Kans. Acad. Sci., Nature Conservancy, Phi Kappa Phi, Phi Delta Kappa. Methodist. Office: Fort Hays State Univ Hays KS 67601

TOMARO, MICHAEL PAUL, psychoanalyst; b. Milw.; s. Michael Joseph and Dorothy May (Daehling) T.; m. Rita K. Wituschek, Apr. 3, 1965 (div. June 1986); children: Gina, Lisa. BS in Psychology, U. Wis., 1967; MS in Psychology, U. Wis., Milw., 1970, PhD in Clin. Psychology, 1972; cert. psychoanalysis, West Psychoanalytic Inst., 1981. Lic. psychologist, Wis. Research cons., family counselor Family Service Milw., 1967-72, dir. research, 1972-78; pvt. practice clin. psychology Milw., 1974—; staff cons. psychologist New Berlin (Wis.) Meml. Hosp., 1979-85; staff psychologist Milw. Psychiat. Hosp., 1979—, Midwest Psycholanalytic Inst., Milw., 1981—; cons. Milw. Psychiat. Services, 1972—; cons. psychologist Deaconess Hosp. and Good Samaritan Med. Complex, 1974—; asst. clin. prof. psychology U. Wis., Milw., 1974-80, assoc. clin. prof. psychology, 1980—; dir. psychology Psychoanalytoc Psychology Assocs., S.C., 1976—, Clinic of Psychology, 1986—; teaching and cons. psychologist Family Service of Waukesha, Wis., 1980-82; cons. mental health Milw. Head Start, 1986—; flight instr., aviation psychologist Mitchell Aeronautical Inst., 1987—. Contbr. articles to profl. jours. Mem. Am. Acad. Psychotherapists (clin.), Nat. Assn. for the Advancement of Psychoanalysis (cert.), Assn. Aviation Psychologists. Avocations: aviation, sports. Office: Clinic of Psychology 2040 W Wisconsin Ave Milwaukee WI 53233

TOMASEK, HANA, organization development consultant; b. Prague, Czechoslovakia, Apr. 4, 1935; came to U.S., 1972; d. Josef and Jana (Letochova) Krasna; m. Jaroslav Tomasek, Nov. 6, 1959. MEE, Tech. U. Prague, 1958, PhD in Elec. Engring., 1967; cert. tng. and devel. in industry and bus., U. Minn., 1984. Assoc. prof. Charles U. Prague, 1960-72; staff devel. specialist 916 AVTI, White Bear Lake, Minn., 1976-83; pres. Innovative Cons. Services, Mpls., 1983—. Author: (book) Basic Electronics, 1968; contbr. articles to profl. jours. Mem. Orgn. Devel. Inst., Am. Soc. Tng. and Devel. (Trainer of Trainers award 1985), Nat. Soc. Performance and Instrn. (bd. dirs. 1987—), Minn. Software Assn. (v.p. 1986). Avocations: sports, travel. Office: Innovative Cons Services 10024 S Shore Dr Minneapolis MN 55441

TOMASI, THOMAS EDWARD, biology educator; b. San Diego, Aug. 10, 1955; s. Julius F. and Grace (Frontiera) T.; m. Susan Jayne Pelletier, Aug. 4, 1978; children: Danielle, Nathaniel. BS, U. R.I., 1976, MS, 1978; PhD, U. Utah, 1984. Vis. lectr. U. Calif., Davis, 1984-86; asst. prof. biology S.W. Mo. State U., Springfield, 1986—. Contbr. articles to profl. jours. Mem. AAAS, Am. Soc. Mammalogists (Anna M. Jackson award 1983), Am. Soc. Zoologists, Internat. Soc. Crytozoology, Sigma Xi. Office: SW Mo State Univ Dept Biology Springfield MO 65804-0095

TOMASIK, THOMAS CARL, family medicine educator; b. Chgo., Dec. 13, 1933, s. Thomas Michael and Harriet (Dyker) T.; m. Patricia Ann Lejman, June 29, 1957; children: Mark, Thomas, Scott, Mary. MD, Loyola U., Maywood, Ill., 1959. Diplomate Am. Bd. Ob-gyn. Intern Resurrection Hosp., Chgo., 1959-60; ob-gyn resident St. Francis Hosp., Evanston, Ill., 1960-63; commd. 2d lt. USAF, 1960, promoted to 1st lt., 1962, advanced through grades to capt., 1965; chief surg. services USAF Res. Hosp., Chgo., 1963-66; resigned USAF, 1968; assoc. clin. prof. ob-gyn, community and family practice Loyola Med. Sch., Maywood, Ill., 1970—; chief family medicine sect. Loyola Med. Sch., Maywood, 1980—; chmn. dept. ob-gyn Resurrection Hosp., Chgo., 1974-77, dir. family practice ctr., 1976—; chmn. med. edn. com. Resurrection Hosp., 1965-66. Book reviewer Jour. Family Medicine. Mem. Am. Acad. Family Physicians, Internat. Acad. Family Physicians (Chgo. maternal and child health adv. com., chmn. commn. on edn. 1984.). Club: Maine East Boosters (Park Ridge, Ill.). Avocations: sailing, swimming, diving. Home: 1133 N Lincoln Park Ridge IL 60068 Office: Resurrection Hosp Family Practice Residency Program 7447 W Talcott Ave Chicago IL 60631

TOMASSI, RALPH VINCENT, academic administrator; b. Scranton, Pa., Aug. 19, 1954; s. Ralph and Anna Charolette (Pagnani) T.; m. Betty Jo Slotterbeck, July 18, 1981. BS, Ashland Coll., 1977; postgrad., Bowling Green State U., 1977-78. Grad. asst., hall dir. and asst. baseball coordinator Heidelberg Coll., Tiffin, Ohio, 1977-78, Bowling Green (Ohio) State U., 1977-78; project coordinator Ashland (Ohio) Coll., 1978-80, dir. transfer admissions, 1980-84, asst. dir. devel., 1984—. Vol. United Appeal Campaign, Ashland, 1984-86; team capt. Symphony Orch. Campaign, Ashland, 1984-86, Community capt. Community Stadium Campaign, 1985-86; bd. dirs. Ashland Bus. Community. Mem. Ind. Coll. Advancement Assn., Ohio Sojc. Fund Raising Execs., Council for Advancement of Support of Edn., Ashland Coll. Alumni Assn. (Disting. Service award 1984). Lodges: Kiwanis, Elks. Avocations: all sports, coin collecting, antiques. Home: 82 Vernon Ave Ashland OH 44805 Office: Ashland Coll 301 Founders Hall Ashland OH 44805

TOMAZI, GEORGE DONALD, electrical engineer; b. St. Louis, Dec. 27, 1935; s. George and Sophia (Bogovich) T.; m. Lois Marie Partenheimer, Feb. 1, 1958; children: Keith, Kent. BSEE, U. Mo., Rolla, 1958, Profl. EE (hon.), 1970; MBA, St. Louis U., 1965, MSEE, 1971. Registered profl. engr., Mo., Ill., Wash., Ohio, Calif., Va. Project engr. Union Electric Co., 1958-66; dir. corp. planning Gen. Steel Industries, 1966-70; exec. v.p. St. Louis Research Council, 1970-74; exec. v.p. Hercules Constrn. Co., St. Louis, 1974-75; dir. design and constrn. div. Mallinckrodt, Inc., St. Louis, 1975—. Author: P-Science: The Role of Science in Society, 1972, The Link of Science and Religion, 1973. Active Nat. Kidney Found.; bd. dirs. U. Mo. Devel. Council; elder Luth. Ch. Served with U.S. Army, 1959-61. Mem. NSPE, IEEE, Japan-Am. Soc., AAAS, Am. Inst. Chem. Engrs., Am. Def. Preparedness Assn., U. Mo. Alumni Assn. (bd. dirs. 1972-78), Sigma Pi Frat. Club: Engrs. (pres. 1985-86). Lodge: Rotary. Office: Mallinckrodt Inc 675 McDonnell Blvd Saint Louis MO 63134

TOMCHEFF, ERIN JEAN, film director, film writer, actress; b. Ft. Wayne, Ind., Aug. 23, 1932; d. Henry Elmer and Norma Augusta (Snyder) Webb; m. Daniel Demeter Tomcheff, Aug. 4, 1956; 1 child, Theon Daniel. BFA, Goodman Theatre, Sch. of Art Inst., Chgo., 1955; MFA, U. Ill., 1984. Staff instr. Actors and Dirs. Lab., Los Angeles, 1968-70; prin. Tomcheff Films Inc., Urbana, Ill., 1986—. Dir., cinematographer, editor and writer: (film) including The Univ. of Ill....a Portrait, Abominations are done in the forest, Architecture: Urbana to Versailles, Art & Design & Art & Design, Dispose of Property, Two Songs, Nothing is Forever; producer film He and Me; actress regional plays Los Angeles workshop productions including The Human Element, I Am A Star, The Rose Tattoo, Look Homeward Angel; Chgo. Equity productions including A Streetcar Named Desire, Measure for Measure, Electra, Macbeth; actress in films including: Chicago Story, Four Friends, Somewhere in Time, The Awakening Land. Mem. Screen Actors Guild, Actors Equity Assn., AFTRA. Avocations: reading, walking, music. Home and Office: 903 S Race St Urbana IL 61801

TOMCZYK, SHARON ANN, management consulting executive; b. Tokyo, Japan, Aug. 8, 1957; came to U.S., 1958; d. Kenneth H. and Irene A. (Baran) Schons. BA, Mundelein Coll., 1986. Cashier Nat. Tea Foods, Arlington Heights, Ill., 1972-74; sec. Allstate Ins. Co., Northbrook, Ill., 1974-81, adminstrv. trainee, 1981-82, nat. urban affairs rep., 1982-84; pres. Tomczyk & Assocs., Chgo., 1984-87; mgmt. cons. Morris Anderson Assocs., Glenview, Ill., 1987—; bd. dirs. Econ. Devel. Council, Chgo. Mem. nat. corp. adv. bd. League of Latin Am. Citizens, 1982-84, nat. amigos de SER Jobs for Progress, Dallas, 1982-84; bd. dirs. Evanston Community Devel. Corp. Recipient Nat. Hispanic Women's award Nat. League of United Latin Am. Citizens, 1983, Outstanding Buyer's award Chgo. Regional Purchasing Council, 1984; named one of Outstanding Young Women in Am., 1982. Mem. Nat. Assn. Women Bus. Owners, Midwest Women's Ctr. Avocations: tennis, scuba diving, running, reading, skiing. Office: 950 Milwaukee Ave Glenview IL 60025

TOMER, LEWIS PHILLIP, marketing executive; b. Charleroi, Pa., Feb. 19, 1936; s. Lewis Phillip and Lillian Susan (Gall) T.; m. Isabel Doreen Jarrell, Aug. 30, 1958; 1 child, Doreen Susan. BEE, Fenn Coll., 1964; MBA, Cleve. State U., 1981. Lab. tech. to test engr. Weatherhead Co., Cleve., 1958-63; design engr. Parker Hannifin, Cleve., 1963-65; project engr. to gen. sales mgr. Fluid Controls, Mentor, Ohio, 1965-84; dir. mktg. Childers Products, Beachwood, Ohio, 1984-85; gen. sales mgr. Teledyne Republic, Cleve., 1985-86; v.p. sales and mktg. B.W. Rogers Co., Akron, Ohio, 1986—. Coordinator J.C.C Project Bus. Shore jr. High, 1983. Republican. Lutheran. Lodges: Rotary, Masons, Kiwanis. Avocations: golf, camping, reading. Home: 5404 Wilson Dr Mentor OH 44060 Office: BW Rogers Co PO Box 1030 Akron OH 44309

TOMES, KENNETH JAMES, accountant, consultant; b. Granite Falls, Minn., Nov. 11, 1950; s. Ervin A. and Tena (Grussing) T.; m. Mary Margaret Nester, Aug. 2, 1975; children: Gregory, Christina, Anna, Angela. BA, Southwest State U., 1972; MBA, Coll. St. Thomas, 1984. CPA, Minn. Jr. high sch. math. tchr. Graceville (Minn.) Pub. Schs., 1974-75; high sch. math. tchr. Renville (Minn.) Pub. Schs., 1976-77; constrn. acct. PPG Industries, Marshall, Minn., 1977-78; staff acct. Bowlby, Anfinson, Crandall, Head & Co., Austin, Minn., 1978-81; related services cons. Farm Credit Services, St. Paul, 1981—; supervisory com. Farm Credit Employee's Fed. Credit Union, 1983—. Chmn. bd. Ch. St. Charles, Austin, 1981; bd. dirs., treas. St. Croix Cath. Schs., Stillwater, Minn., 1985—. Served with U.S. Army, 1972-74. Mem. Am. Inst. CPA's, Minn. Soc. CPA's. Lodge: KC. Home: 1716 Olene Ave N Stillwater MN 55082 Office: Farm Credit Services 375 Jackson St Saint Paul MN 55101

TOMHAVE, JONATHAN, artist, marketing executive; b. Hibbing, Minn., Dec. 6, 1946; s. Wesley G. and Anne (Rukavina) T.; m. Beverly Korstad, Oct. 15, 1977; children: Anna Mercedes, Dane Stefan. BS, U. Minn., 1969, BA summa cum laude, 1971; MA, U. Mich., 1972; postgrad. philosophy U. Minn. Program coordinator U. Minn., Mpls., 1970-71, 72-73; pres. Jonathan Studios, Mpls., 1974—. Editor: (mag.) Acad., 1970-71; illustrator: The Family Caregivers Manual, 1984. Mem. Am. Soc. Interior Designers, AIA, Phi Beta Kappa. Roman Catholic. Avocations: tennis, weight lifting, reading. Office: Jonathan Studios 1628 Oakways Wayzata MN 55391

TOMINS, PATTI R., accountant; b. Cleve., May 15, 1960; d. Walter Gordon and Ruth Helen (Maskoske) Buttolph; m. Andrejs Aldis Tomins, July 30, 1983. BBA, Cleve. State U., 1981. CPA, Ohio. Sr. acct. Pannell Kerr Forester, Shaker Heights, Ohio, 1982-85; acctg. supr. Mentor (Ohio) Lumber & Supply Co., 1985—. Mem. panel United Way Allocations Com., Cleve., 1984-85. Mem. Am. Inst. CPA's, Ohi Soc. CPA's. Presbyterian. Avocations: golf, home remodeling, sewing. Home: 6812 Palmerston Mentor OH 44060 Office: Mentor Lumber & Supply Co 7180 N Center St Mentor OH 44060

TOMITA, TADANORI, neurosurgeon; b. Osaka, Japan, Nov. 19, 1945; s. Tadao and Noriko (Ikeda) T.; m. Kathryn Morley, June 28, 1980; children: Tadaki M., Kenji W., Dan Y. MD, Kobe (Japan) U., 1970. Diplomate Am. Bd. Neurol. Surgery. Attending neurosurgeon Children's Meml. Hosp., Chgo., 1981—, dir. neurosurg. oncology, 1984—. Contbr. articles to profl. jours. Recipient Sherry Kallick award Northwestern Meml. Hosp., 1979, Frank Notides award Children's Meml. Hosp., Chgo., 1980. Fellow ACS, Am. Acad. Pediatrics; mem. Am. Assn. Neurol. Surgeons, Congress Neurol. Surgeons, Internat. Soc. Pediatric Neurosurgery. Office: Childrens Meml Hosp 2300 Childrens Plaza Chicago IL 60614

TOMKOWIAK, TERENCE LEE, industrial engineer; b. Stanley, Wis., Sept. 16, 1956; s. Edward Peter and Theresa Marie (Przybylski) T.; m. Gail Marie Sheard, Aug. 13, 1977; children: Anna, Michael. AS, Milw. Sch. Engring., 1977, BS in Indsl. Mgmt., 1978. Prodn. supr. Warner Electric, South Beloit, Ill., 1978-80, indsl. engring. trainee, 1980-81, indsl. engr., 1981-83, supr. indsl. engring., 1983-87, supr. mfg. engring. brake and clutch div., 1987—; mem. supervisory com. Warner Electric Credit Union (chmn. 1984, chmn. bd. dirs. 1985). advisor Jr. Achievement, Rockford, Ill., 1985; cons. Project Bus., Rockford, 1986. Named one of Outstanding Young Men of Am., 1986. Mem. Inst. Indsl. Engrs., Aimtech. Democrat. Roman Catholic. Lodge: KC. Avocations: woodworking, photography, reading, music, automobiles. Office: Warner Electric 449 Gardner St South Beloit IL 61080

TOMLIN, THOMAS ALVIN, automotive company executive; b. Muncie, Ind., Sept. 18, 1938; s. Leo C. and Lois E. (Hickman) T.; m. Anita M. Ellis, June 14, 1957; children: Deborah, Kelly, Thomas B. BS MechE, Gen. Motors Inst., 1962. Process engr., prodn. Gen. Motors Corp., Muncie, Ind., 1962-65, sr. engr., gen. supr., 1965-69, supt. prodn., 1969-80, supt. material control, 1980-81, supt.-master mechanic, 1981—. Republican. Methodist. Club: Green Hills Country (Selma, Ind.) (pres. 1972-74). Lodge: Elks. Avocations: boating, golfing. Home: 4113 Kings Row Muncie IN 47304 Office: DDA Transmission Plt 1200 W 8th St Muncie IN 47302

TOMLINSON, JAMES CHRISTOPHER, architect; b. Jefferson City, Mo., Oct. 11, 1958; s. James Neal and Judith Beatrice (Spalding) T.; m. Leslie Venable, Dec. 28, 1985. BArch, U. Kans., 1982. Registered profl. architect, land surveyor. Architect Patty Berkebile Nelson Immenschuh Architects, Inc., Kansas City, Mo., 1982—. V.P. Friends of Art Guild, Nelson-Atkins Mus. Art, Kansas City, 1983-86. Mem. AIA. Republican. Avocation: athletics, art history. Office: Patty Berkebile Nelson Immenschuh Architects Inc 120 W 12th Suite 1500 Kansas City MO 64105

TOMLINSON, JAMES WYMOND, medical electronics company executive; b. Columbus, Ohio, Oct. 28, 1949; s. Allen H. and Greta Lovada (Hartley) T.; m. Mary Jean Culler, July 21, 1973; children: James Allen, Susan Kay. Student, Ohio State U., 1967-69, USN Hosp. Corps. Sch., 1970. With Unevol, Inc., Lucas, Ohio, 1983—; instr., lectr. U. Cin., 1985—; exec. v.p. Occupational Mktg., Inc., Houston, 1987—. Served with USN, 1970-75. Avocations: flying, skiing, farming, soccer and baseball coach. Home: Rt 1 Box 345-A Lucas OH 44843 Office: Unevol Inc Lucas-Perrysville Rd Lucas OH 44843

TOMLINSON, MICHAEL JAMES, insurance company executive; b. Detroit Lakes, Minn., Feb. 4, 1958; s. Marion Delbert and Ozella (Shipley) T.; m. Michelle Marie Mikula, Apr. 30, 1977; children: Jeremy, Jesse, Jackson. Grad. high sch., Audubon, Minn. Pvt. practice musician 1976-80; dist. sales mgr. Am. Family Life Assurance Co., Columbus, Ga., 1980-85, regional sales mgr., 1985-87, mem. home office adv. council, 1987; regional sales mgr. Am. Family Life Assurance Co., Minnetonka, Minn., 1987—. Republican. Baptist. Avocation: music.

TOMLINSON, ROBERTA ANN, medical technologist; b. Beardstown, Ill., Feb. 17, 1958; d. Robert William and JoAnn (Ray) Cooper; m. David J. Tomlinson, Sept. 6, 1986. BS cum laude, Bradley U., 1980; cert. med. tech., Meth. Med. Ctr., 1981. Med. tech. Graham Hosp., Canton, Ill., 1981—. Mem. Community Chorus Bradley U., 1977-80. Mem. Am. Soc. for Med. Tech., Ill. Med. Tech. Soc. (legis. liason Canton area 1986), Alpha Lambda Delta. Avocations: collecting antiques, reading, sports.

TOMLINSON, THOMAS WILLIAM, insurance company executive; b. Keokuk, Iowa, July 5, 1946; s. William Lloyd and Ruth Ellen (Furrow) T.; m. Pauline Ann Biondahl, Mar. 5, 1983; children: Joni M., Chad J., Jaret. BA, Eureka Coll., 1968. Tchr. English Moline (Ill.) Bd. Edn., 1968-69; tchr. English and Journalism Sherrard (Ill.) Bd. Edn., 1969-71; underwriting trainee Bituminous Casualty Corp., Rock Island, Ill., 1971-72, mtkg. tech., 1972-79, sr. mktg. analyst, 1979—. Vol. fireman, sec.-treas. Blackhawk Fire Protection Dist. Milan, Ill., 1974-83; chmn. law and legis. Bettendorf (Iowa) Task Force on Adolescent Chem. Abuse, 1984-85. Mem. Ins. Inst. Am. (cert.), Nat. Rifle Assn. (life), N.Am. Hunting Club. Democrat. Avocations: softball, racquetball, hunting, fishing, boating. Home: 1318 Parkway Dr Bettendorf IA 52722 Office: Bituminous Casualty Corp 320 18th St Rock Island IL 61201

TOMPKINS, DANIEL LESTER, financial consultant; b. Defiance, Ohio, Jan. 7, 1958; s. Lester Tilden and A. Bernice (Vandemark) T. BA, Ohio State U., 1979; MBA, U. Akron, 1984; postgrad., U. Mass., 1984-85. Substitute tchr. Canton (Ohio) City Schs., 1980-82; research asst. U. Akron, Ohio, 1982-83, lectr., 1983-84, 86-87; teaching asst. U. Mass., Amherst, 1984-85; prof. Am. Internat. Coll., Springfield, Mass., 1985; fin. cons. Thurable Services, Canton, 1985—; cons. Stark Devel. Bd., Canton, 1986. Elder John Knox Presbyn. Ch., North Canton, Ohio, 1987, mem. audit com., 1986, fin. sec., 1982-83, budget com., 1982-84. Named Eagle Scout, Boy Scouts Am., 1975. Mem. Am. Fin. Assn., Fin. Mgmt. Assn., Am. Real Estate Soc., Rho Epsilon. Republican.

TOMPKINS, DOUGLAS GORDON, orthopedic surgeon; b. N.Y.C., Dec. 23, 1926; s. Sydney Edward and Katharine Elaine (Reed) T.; m. Nancy Jane Vanderbilt, Sept.. 1, 1951; children: Douglas Jr., John, William, Katharine, Charles. AB, Yale U., 1946; MD, Columbia U., 1950. Diplomate Am. Bd. Orthopaedic Surgery. Intern Presbyn. Hosp., N.Y.C., 1950-52; asst. resident Millard Fillmore, Buffalo, 1954-55, Children's Hosp., Boston, 1955-56; asst. resident Mass. Gen. Hosp., Boston, 1956-57, sr. resident, 1957-58; mem. staff orthopaedic surgery Gundersen Clinic, La Crosse, Wis., 1958—, dir., 1970-74, exec. v.p., 1971-74; chmn. dept. surgery La Crosse Luth. Hosp., 1965-70. Contbr. articles to scholarly jour. Trustee La Crosse Luth. Hosp., 1974-76; dep. Gen. Conv. Episcopal Ch., Denver, Colo., 1979; sr. warden Christ Episcopal Ch., La Crosse, 1979-81. Served to lt. USNR, 1952-54. Fellow Am. Acad. Orthopaedic Surgeons; mem. AMA, Wis. Orthopaedic Soc., State Med. Soc. of Wis., La Crosse County Med. Soc., Arthroscopy Assn. N.Am. Republican. Club: Assembly. Avocations: tennis, woodworking. Home: 122 N 16th St La Crosse WI 54601 Office: Gundersen Clinic 1836 South Ave La Crosse WI 54601

TOMPKINS, MARK ALLEN, pediatrician; b. O'Neill, Nebr., Nov. 14, 1949; s. Harvey Alfred and Lois Lenore (Caldwell) T.; m. Janice Irene Wellensiek, July 22, 1972; Marc Andrew, Jill Elizabeth. BS, Nebr. Wesleyan U., 1971; MD, U. Nebr., 1974. Cert. Am. Bd. Pediatrics. Resident in pediatrics U. Nebr. Med. Ctr., Omaha, 1974-77; pediatrician Grand Island Clinic, Inc., Nebr., 1977—; active staff St. Francis Med. Ctr., Grand Island, Nebr., 1977—, Grand Island Meml. Hosp., 1977—, mem. exec. com., chmn. infection control com.; vol. faculty U. Nebr. Med. Ctr., Omaha, 1977—. Fellow Am. Acad. Pediatrics; mem. AMA, Nebr. Med. Assn., Hall County Med. Soc., Grand Island C. of C. Republican. Presbyterian. Club: Riverside Golf (Grand Island). Avocations: reading, singing in church choir, golf, jogging. Office: Grand Island Clinic Inc 2444 W Faidley Ave Grand Island NE 68801

TOMS, MILLIAN MCKAY, accountant; b. Detroit, Jan. 27, 1942; d. Thomas Stanley and Mildred McKay (Stone) Dean; m. Richard A. Stan, July 20, 1963 (div. 1969) 1 dau., Michele Anne Stan. Grad. Internat. Accts. Soc., 1968. CPA, Mich. Sr. acct. Plante & Moran, CPA's, Southfield, Mich., 1967-76; pvt. practice acctg., Royal Oak, Mich., 1976—. Contbr. articles to profl. jours. Vol. Detroit-Renaissance Found., Detroit, 1983-87; treas. Nat. Council Alcoholism Greater Detroit. Mem. Mich. Assn. CPA's (chmn. small practitioners 1981-83, vice chmn. 1979-81, chmn. monthly meeting group Southfield 1978—, vice chmn. pvt. cos. practice div. 1985-87), Am. Women's Soc. CPA's, Am. Inst. CPA's, Royal Oak C. of C. (fin. com., bd. dirs. 1987—), Nat. Council of Alcoholism and other Dependencies (treas. 1986—). Clubs: Women's Econ., Toastmasters. Office: 521 9th St Royal Oak MI 48067

TOMSA, CHRISTINA IRENE, sales professional; b. Cleve., July 27, 1950; d. Samuel and Irene (Szabo) T. AA, Cuyahoga Community Coll., 1978; BA, Baldwin Wallace Coll., Berea, Ohio, 1980. Sales rep. mktg. dept. Northwest Airlines, Cleve., 1981—. Publicity dir. Caballares Drum and Bugle Corps, Cleve., 1981—. Democart. Roman Catholic. Avocations: tennis, swimming, theatre.

TON, L. EUGENE, church official. Dir. Ind. Bapt. Conv., Indpls. Office: Ind Bapt Conv 1350 N Delaware ST Indianapolis IN 46202 *

TONGREN, JOHN DAVID, computer security company executive, consultant; b. Erie, Pa., Dec. 1, 1942; s. John Corbin and Alice Jeanette (Jones) T.; m. Nancy Cowie, Aug. 28, 1965 (div. Dec. 1972); 1 son, Jon Eric; m. Kathleen McKay, Feb. 14, 1981. B.A., DePauw U., 1964; M.B.A., U. Mich., 1965; postgrad. Calif. Coast U., Santa Ana, 1987—. Cert. info. systems auditor; cert. systems profl., cert. mgmt. acct. Cost study coordinator U. Louisville, 1971-72; sr. internal auditor Westinghouse Co., Columbus, Ohio, 1972-74, corp. audit mgr.-audit systems, Pitts., 1974-78; mgmt. cons. Alexander Grant & Co., Chgo., 1978-79, nat. dir. computer acctg. and auditing, 1979-81; pres. Tongren & Assocs., Chgo., 1981—; dir. edn. EDP Auditors Found., Chgo., 1983-85. Vice-pres. Saddle Lake Property Owners Assn., Grand Junction, Mich., 1983. Mem. EDP Auditors Assn. (pres. Pitts. chpt. 1975-76, bd. dirs. Chgo. chpt. 1986—), Inst. Internal Auditors, Inst. Cert. Mgmt. Accts., Info. Systems Security Assn., Meeting Planners Internat., Computer Security Inst. Office: Tongren & Assocs 502 W Roscoe St Suite 3N Chicago IL 60657

TONIA, CYNTHIA F., training director; b. Bay Village, Ohio, Aug. 8, 1950; s. Frank L. and Eleanor D. (Karamus) T. BA, Kent State U., 1971; MA, Carnegie-Mellon U., 1975, PhD, 1982. Tchr. Normandy High Sch., Parma, Ohio, 1972-74; dept. head Rocky River (Ohio) High Sch., 1977-80; asst. prin. Orange High Sch., Pepper Pike, Ohio, 1980-81; dist. mgr. Am. Health, Orangeburg, N.Y., 1982-85; mktg. training dir. Blue Cross Blue Shield of Ohio, Cleve., 1985—. Louis D. Beaumont scholar, 1974; research asst. Rockefellow Found., 1976. Mem. Am. Mktg. Assn., Am. Soc. for Tng. and Devel. Office: Blue Cross Blue Shield of Ohio 2060 E 9th St Cleveland OH 44115

TOOKER, GARY LAMARR, electronics company executive; b. Shelby, Ohio, May 25, 1939; s. William Henry and Frances Ione (Melick) T.; m. Diane Rae Kreider, Aug. 4, 1962; children: Lisa, Michael. B.S.E.E., Ariz. State U., 1962. With Motorola Inc., Phoenix, 1962—, v.p., gen. mgr. internat. semicondr. div., 1980-81, v.p., gen. mgr. semicondr. products sector, 1981-82, sr. v.p., gen. mgr. semicondr. products sector, 1982-83; exec. v.p., gen. mgr. semicondr. products sector Motorola Inc., 1983-86; sr. exec. v.p., chief corp. staff officer Motorola Inc., Schaumburg, Ill., 1986—; also bd.

dirs.; mem. engring. adv. council Ariz. State U., Tempe, 1982-86. Bd. dirs. Scottsdale (Ariz.) Boys Club, maj. corp. campaign div. United Way, Chgo., 1987. Named Outstanding Alumni of Yr., Ariz. State U., 1983. Mem. IEEE, Am. Mgmt. Assn., Semicondr. Industry Assn. (dir. 1981-86, chmn. bd. 1983-86), Ariz. Assn. Industries (dir. 1981-86). Republican. Office: Motorola Inc 1303 E Algonquin Rd Schaumburg IL 60196

TOOL, BRIAN JOHN, social worker; b. Elgin, N.D., May 21, 1945; s. Everett Arthur and Edna (Henne) T.; m. Lynn Constance Brand, Sept. 12, 1970; children: Brandon, Chelsey, Tyler, Laura. BS, N.D. State U., 1971; MSW, Tulane U., 1973. Clin. social worker Minot (N.D.) Area Ctr., 1974-75, supr. children and family services, 1975-78; clin. social worker Guidance Ctr., Portage, Wis., 1978-82; dir., co-founder Pauquette Children's Services, Portage, 1982—. Bush Found. fellow, Mpls., 1977. Mem. Nat. Assn. Social Workers, Acad. Cert. Social Workers, Am. Assn. Marriage and Family Therapists (clin.). Lodge: Rotary. Avocations: golf, reading, stained glass projects, tennis. Home: 535 Winnebago Portage WI 53901 Office: Pauquette Childrens Services 304 W Cook St PO Box 301 Portage WI 53901

TOOMBS, KELLY HUNTER, orthodontist; b. Wichita, Kans., Aug. 28, 1956; s. E.H. and PollyAnn (Meeker) T.; m. Kathryn S. Lehman, May 26, 1979; children: Whitney Kathryn, Mallory Ann. BS, Wichita State U., 1978; DDS, U. Mo., 1982; cert. in orthodontics, U. Mo., Kansas City, 1984. Pres. Max R. Moore DDS and Kelly H. Toombs DDS, PA, Prairie Village, Kans., 1984—. Mem. ADA, Am. Assn. Orthodontists, Southwestern Soc. Orthodontists, Kans. Dental Assn. Soc., Greater Kansas City Soc. Orthodontists (sec.-treas. 1986, v.p. 1987). Avocations: golf, skiing, sports cars. Home: 7527 Mohawk Dr Prairie Village KS 66208 Office: 3700 W 83d St Rm 215 Prairie Village KS 66208

TOOPS, RICHARD ALAN, commodity broker, game company executive, music publisher; b. Apr. 1, 1942; s. Glynn Herbert and Mary Jane (Clampitt) Toops; m. Diane C. Kolettes; 1 son, Philip. Student Roosevelt U., Chgo., 1962-65. Pres. Flaky Crust Music Pubs., Chgo., 1968—; commodity broker Chgo. Bd. Trade, 1971-83; gen. ptnr. Total Games, Inc., Chgo., 1981—; stock index broker N.Y. Futures Exchange, 1982—; mem. Broadcast Music, Inc. Inventor board game Multinational; composer pop songs. Mem. N.Y. Futures Exchange, N.Y. Coffee, Sugar and Cocoa Exchange, Chgo. Bd. Trade.

TOOPS, TIMOTHY RAY, superintendent schools; b. Dayton, Ohio, Aug. 18, 1948; s. Warren George and Reecie Reva T.; m. Constance Kathleen Amon, Aug. 28, 1970; children—Michele, Laura. B.E., Marion Coll., 1970; M.Ed., Wright State U., 1976; Ed.S., U. Dayton, 1983. Cert. tchr., prin., supt., Ohio, 1983. Tchr., Troy (Ohio) City Schs., 1970-80; prin., Bethel Local Schs., Tipp City, Ohio, 1980-85; supt., 1985—Mem. adv. com. to supt. State of Ohio Dept. Edn.; bd. dirs. Meth. Ch. Served with AUS, 1970-77. Mem. Assn. Sch. Adminstrn., Ohio Elem. Sch. Prins. Assn., Nat. Elem. Sch. Adminstrs., Phi Delta Kappa. Lodge: Rotary Internat.

TOOT, JOSEPH F., JR., bearing manufacturing company executive; b. 1935; married. A.B., Princeton U., 1957; postgrad., Harvard U. Grad. Sch. Bus. Adminstrn., 1961. With Timken Co., Canton, Ohio, 1962—; dep. mgr. Timken (France) Co., 1965-67; v.p. internat. div. Timken Co., Canton, 1967-68, corp. v.p., then exec. v.p., 1968-79, pres., 1979—, also bd. dirs.; bd. dirs. Rockwell Internat. Office: The Timken Co 1835 Dueber Ave SW Canton OH 44706

TOOTIKIAN, LAWRENCE PETER, marketing research executive; b. Cleve., Dec. 18, 1931; s. Jack P. and Marie (Turabian) T.; B.B.S., Northwestern U., 1954; m. Christine Mink, Oct. 7, 1980. Research analyst WGN, Inc., Chgo., 1960-61; research mgr. WBBM-TV, Chgo., 1962-63, WLS-TV, Chgo., 1963-64, Fawcett Pubs., Chgo., 1967-72; pres. Research U.S.A., Inc., Chgo., 1972—. Served with U.S. Army, 1955-57. Mem. Am. Mktg. Assn., Nat. Agrl. Mktg. Assn., Soc. Nat. Assn. Pubs., Western Publs. Assn., Chgo. Assn. Commerce and Industry, Chgo. Council Fgn. Relations, Fla. Mag. Assn., Am. Soc. Assn. Execs. Clubs: Executives, Chgo. Press, Chgo. Media Research (pres. 1976-77). Contbr. articles to profl. jours. Office: 150 E Huron St Chicago IL 60611

TOPAZ, WILLIAM N., publishing company executive; b. Chgo., Apr. 12, 1947; s. Martin and Marjorie R. (Peters) T.; m. Denise L. Cohen, Aug. 17, 1968; children: Jason A., Chad M. BJ, Northwestern U., 1969. Pres., pub. Profl. Press, Inc. div. Capital Cities Communications, Inc., Chgo., 1969-83; gen. mgr. Wallace-Homestead Book Co. div. Capital Cities/ABC, Inc., Lombard, Ill., 1984—. V.p. Music Ctr. of North Shore, Winnetka, Ill., 1986—. Home: PO Box 37 Winnetka IL 60093-0037 Office: ABC/Wallace Homestead Book Co 580 Waters Edge Lombard IL 60148

TOPPER, JOSEPH RAY, housewares manufacturing company executive; b. Waynesboro, Pa., May 8, 1928; s. Clarence E. and Sarah Frances (Stahley) T.; m. Mary Helen Bromage, July 25, 1953; children: Mary Kathleen, Sarah Helen, Joseph Ray, James Michael. B.S. in Elec. Engring, Brown U., 1952. With Gen. Electric Co., Fairfield, Conn., 1952-71, gen. mgr. personal appliances dept., 1968-71; v.p. Anchor Hocking Corp., Lancaster, Ohio, 1972-76, exec. v.p., 1977-78, pres., chief operating officer, 1978-82, pres., chief exec. officer, 1982—, also bd. dirs.; bd. dirs. Towle Mfg. Co., Huntington Bancshares, Inc., Shelby Ins. Co. Past chmn. bd. trustees Lancaster-Fairfield Community Hosp.; past pres. Fairfield County Health Found. Served with USN, 1946-48. Mem. IEEE, Nat. C. of C., Am. Mgmt. Assn., Am. Glass Assn. (past chmn.). Republican. Roman Catholic. Clubs: Lancaster Country, Symposiarchs, Capital, Golf. Home: 2800 Marietta Rd Lancaster OH 43130 Office: Anchor Hocking Corp 109 N Broad St PO Box 600 Lancaster OH 43132

TOREN, BRIAN KEITH, communication systems consultant; b. St. Paul, Jan. 8, 1935; s. Clarence August and Ann (Penner) T.; divorced; children: Sean Marshall, Kisten Kaye. BBA, U. Minn., 1970. Programmer Sperry Corp., Mpls., 1957-67, sales support staff, 1968-71; site mgr. Sperry Corp., Atlantic City, 1972-76; mktg. cons. Sperry Corp., Mpls., 1976-83; communication service support cons. Sperry, Mpls., 1983-86; mgr. quality analysis and support Unisys, Mpls., 1986—; pres., cons. Internat. Robot, Mpls., 1982—; bd. dirs. Anticipatory Scis., St. Paul. Mem. Soc. Gen. Systems Research (contbr. monthly column 1981—), Minn. Futurists (pres., 1986—, contbr. monthly column 1986—), Robotic Soc. Am. Avocations: computer and history research, photography, writing, speaking. Home: 4516 Pleasant Ave S Minneapolis MN 55409 Office: Unisys 3001 Metro Dr Bloomington MN 55420

TORGERSEN, TORWALD HAROLD, architect, designer; b. Chgo., Sept. 2, 1929; s. Peder and Hansine Malene (Hansen) T.; m. Dorothy Darlene Peterson, June 22, 1963. B.S. in Archtl. Engring. with honors, U. Ill., 1951. Registered architect Nat. Council Archtl. Registration Bds. Partner Coyle & Torgersen (Architects-Engrs.), Washington, Chgo. and Joliet, Ill., 1955-56; project coordinator Skidmore, Owings & Merrill, Chgo., 1956-60; corp. architect, dir. architecture, constrn. and interiors Container Corp. Am., Chgo., 1960—; guest lectr. U. Wis. Served to capt. USNR, 1951-55. Recipient Top Ten Design award Factory mag., 1964. Fellow Am. Soc. Interior Designers; mem. AIA, Naval Res. Assn., Ill. Naval Militia, Am. Arbitration Assn., Am. Soc. Mil. Engrs., Paper Industry Mgmt. Assn. (hon.), Sports Car Club Am., Nat. Eagle Scout Assn. Club: 20 Fathoms. Home: 3750 N Lake Shore Dr Chicago IL 60613 Office: 500 E North Ave Carol Stream IL 60187

TORGERSON, LARRY KEITH, lawyer; b. Albert Lea, Minn., Aug. 25, 1935; s. Fritz G. and Lu (Hillman) T. B.A., Drake U., 1958, M.A., 1960, LL.B., 1963, J.D., 1968; M.A., Iowa U., 1962; cert. Hague (the Netherlands) Acad. Internat. Law, 1965, 69; LL.M., U. Minn., 1969; Columbia U., 1971, U. Mo., 1976; PMD, Harvard U., 1973, Ed.M., 1974. Bar: Minn. 1964, Wis. 1970, Iowa 1970, U.S. Tax Ct. 1971, U.S. Supreme Ct. 1972, U.S. Dist. Ct. Minn. 1964, U.S. Dist. Ct. (no. dist.) Iowa 1971, U.S. Dist. Ct. (ea. dist.) Wis. 1981, U.S. Ct. Appeals (8th cir.) 1981. Asst. corp. counsel First Bank Stock Corp., Mpls., 1963-67; v.p., trust officer Nat. City Bank, Mpls., 1967-69; sr. mem. Torgerson Law Firm, Northwood, Iowa, 1969—; trustee, gen. counsel Torgerson Farms, Northwood, 1977—, Redbirch Farms, Kensett, Iowa, 1987—, Sunburst Farms, Grafton, Iowa, 1987—; chmn., gen. counsel Internat. Investments, Mpls., 1983—, Transoceanic, Mpls., 1987—; pres., gen. counsel Torgerson Investments, Northwood, 1984—, Torgerson Properties, Northwood, 1987—. Mem. ABA, Am. Judicature Soc., Iowa Bar Assn., Minn. Bar Assn., Wis Bar Assn., Mensa, Psi Chi, Circle K, Phi Alpha Delta, Omicron Delta Kappa, Pi Kappa Delta, Alpha Tau Omega, Pi Delta Epsilon, Alpha Kappa Delta. Lutheran.

TORGHELE, SALLY JANE DAVIDSON, jeweler, appraiser; b. Trinidad, Colo., Apr. 14, 1947; d. Paul Benjamin and Julia Ann (Dobesh) Davidson; m. John Bradford Torghele, Mar. 19, 1977 (dec. Jan. 1983). Student, Kearney (Nebr.) State Coll., 1965-67; diploma, Kearney Vocat. Sch. Practical Nursing, 1967; cert., U. Calif., San Diego, 1972, Gemological Inst. Am., 1980. Practical nurse Good Samaritan Hosp., Kearney, 1967-70, Palomar Hosp., Escondido, Calif., 1970-72, Hastings (Nebr.) Regional Ctr., 1973-75; jeweler, appraiser Davidson's Jewelry, Kearney, 1976—. Co-founder Ft. Kearney Humane Soc., 1980—. Mem. Am. Gemological Soc. (registered jeweler), Jewelers of Am. (bd. dirs. 1981), Nebr. and S.D. Jewelers Assn. (v.p. 1985—), Gemological Inst. Am. Alumni Assn., Buffalo County Bus. and Profl. Women's Assn., Under Water Soc. Am., Gt. Plains Dive Council (sec. 1982-85). Republican. Roman Catholic. Club: Kearney Aqua Lords (treas. 1981-83). Avocations: scuba diving, competition spearfishing, skiing, camping, woodworking. Home: 3818 Ave G Kearney NE 68847 Office: Davidson's Jewelry Inc 2311 Central Ave Kearney NE 68847

TORISKY, DONALD DAVID, financial executive; b. Pitts., Aug. 20, 1938; s. Charles A. and Cecilia G. (Blahut) T.; m. Patricia A. Sucs, June 2, 1962; children: Shawn, Kristina. Grad. advanced mgmt. program, Harvard U., 1978. Salesman Sears Roebuck & Co., 1958-60, 84 Lumber Co., 1960-62; regional rep. sales securities Wadell & Reed, 1962; with Borg-Warner Acceptance Corp., Chgo., 1962—, group v.p., 1976-79, exec. v.p., 1979-80, pres. consumer div., 1980-83, pres., chief exec. officer, 1983—; v.p. Borg-Warner Corp., Chgo., 1986—; mem. vol. good govt. action com., Borg Warner Acceptance Corp.; bd. dirs. The Bank & Trust Co., Arlington Heights. Mem. Schaumburg Transp. Study Com., Schaumburg Cable TV Commn. Com., 1982, Borg-Warner Polit. Action Com., Northwest Community Hosp. Bd.; trustee, vice chmn. William Rainey Harper Coll., Palatine, Ill. Served to sgt. USMC, 1956-58. Democrat. Roman Catholic. Club: Harvard (Chgo. and N.Y.C.). Office: Borg-Warner Acceptance Corp Boulevard Towers N 225 N Michigan Ave Chicago IL 60601

TORMEY, T. NICHOLAS, psychotherapist; b. Des Moines, Sept. 19, 1938; s. Thomas Carmody and Catherine Alexandria (Reinig) T.; m. Julie Ellen Gammack, June 2, 1979; 1 child, Thomas James Gammack. BA magna cum laude, Loras Coll., 1961; MA, Mt. St. Bernard Sem., 1964; PhD, Union Grad. Sch., 1978. Assoc. pastor Christ the King Ch., Des Moines, 1965-67; instr., counselor St. Albert High Sch., Council Bluffs, Iowa, 1967-68; founding pastor Drake Newman Community Ch., Des Moines, 1968-75; pvt. practice psychotherapy West Des Moines, Iowa, 1975—; inst. dir. Siena Heights Coll., Adrian, Mich., 1976; fellow Nat. Ctr. for Campus Ministry, Cambridge, Mass., 1970; mem. staff La Jolla (Calif.) Program, 1972; adj. asst. prof. U. Osteo. Medicine and Health Sci., Des Moines, 1976—, Sch. Social Work U. Iowa, Des Moines, 1980—; dir. conf. on human sexuality Drake U., Des Moines, 1978. Dir. campus ministry Diocese of Des Moines, 1970-75; bd. dirs. Polk County Mental Health Ctr., Des Moines, 1970-80, Civic Music Assn. Des Moines, 1979—, Health Care Plus, Inc., Des Moines, 1980-83, Young Womens Resource Ctr., Des Moines, 1980—. Underwood fellow, 1976-77, NIMH fellow, 1978. Mem. Am. Bd. Med. Psychotherapists, Am. Assn Sex Educators, Counselors and Therapists, Soc. for Sci. Study of Sex, Iowa Psychol. Assn. Democrat. Avocations: classical music, detective fiction, cycling. Home: 2800 Forest Dr Des Moines IA 50312 Office: West Bank Bldg Suite 210 1601 22d St West Des Moines IA 50265

TOROK, JOHN ANTHONY, III, dentist; b. Cin., July 16, 1952; s. John Anthony Jr. and Anne Champ (Busch) T.; m. Jacquelyn Ann, Aug. 26, 1977; children: Amanda, Morgan. BS in Biology with honors, U. Cin., 1974; DDS, Ohio State U., 1977, MBA in Fin., 1986, postgrad. in law, 1986—. Gen. practice dentistry Cin., 1979—. Cardio Pulmonary Resuscitation instr. Am. Heart Assn., Lake County, Ill., 1977-79. Served to lt. USN, 1977-79. Recipient Disting. Service award Lake County Heart Assn., 1979, Disting. Service award United Appeal Assn, 1981; named one of Outstanding Young Men Am., U.S. Jaycees, Cin., 1983. Mem. ADA, Ohio Dental Assn., Cin. Dental Soc., Assn. Am. Mil. Surgeons, Ohio State U. Alumni Assn. for Dentists, Mensa. Republican. Roman Catholic. Club: U. Cin. Vets. Lodge: KC. Avocations: woodworking, mil. history, photography.

TORRES, ANTHONY IGNATIUS, educator; b. Chgo., July 5, 1929; s. Anastasio and Bivina (Garcia) T.; B.S., No. Ill. U., 1954; M.Ed., DePaul U., 1956, Ed.S., 1958; Ed.D., Loyola U., Chgo., 1973. Tchr., Chgo. Public Schs., 1954-66; adminstr. Ill. Office of Edn., 1966-72; prin. Park Ridge (Ill.) Public Schs., 1972-76; dir. personnel Prairie State Coll., Chicago Heights, Ill., 1976-77; supt. schs., River Grove, Ill., 1977-79, Sauk Village, Ill., 1979-87; dir. adminstrv. services, Bellwood, Ill., 1987—. Bd. govs. United Republican Fund; mem. Ill. Ednl. Facilities Authority, 1979—; bd. dirs. United Way Suburban Cook County, 1981—; bilingual chmn. Nat. Adv. and Coordination Council, 1984—. Recipient Those Who Excel award Ill. State Bd. Edn., 1978. Mem. Am. Assn. Sch. Adminstrs., Ill. Assn. Sch. Adminstrs., Am. Assn. U. Adminstrs., Phi Delta Kappa (Service award Loyola U. chpt.). Club: Columbia Yacht (Chgo.). Contbr. articles to profl. jours., column on edn. to local newspapers. Home: 1700 N North Park Chicago IL 60614

TORRES, EUGENIO, business official; b. San Juan, P.R., May 14, 1950; s. Eugenio and Pura (Agosto) T.; A.E.E., U. P.R., 1971; E.E.T., Wentworth Inst. Tech., Boston, 1973; B.S. in Mfg., Western Mich. U., 1985; m. Elba; children—Eugenio F., Herbert. Prodn. supr. Union Carbide, Inc., P.R.; automation specialist Honeywell, Inc., Rio Piedras, P.R.; account mgr. Mal del Caribe, Santurce, P.R.; applications engr. comml. mktg. Carrier Corp., Syracuse, N.Y.; engr. internat. group Rapistan div. Lear Seigler, Grand Rapids, Mich.; now tech. and sales support mgr. Ammeraal Conveyor Belting, Grand Rapids. Served with P.R. Air N.G., 1975-78, N.Y. Air NG, 1978-80; capt. Mich. Army NG, 1981—. Cert. mfg. engr. in robotics, engring. technician. Mem. IEEE, ASHRAE, Internat. Material Mgmt. Soc., Delta Phi Theta, Alpha Phi Omega. Roman Catholic. Clubs: Exchange, Nyang, Mich. Army N.G. Officers, Prang NCO. Home: 2050 Foxboro Ct NW Grand Rapids MI 49504 Office: PO Box 1245 Grand Rapids MI 49501-1245

TORRES, RICHARD ERICK, health sciences communications executive; b. N.Y.C., Feb. 27, 1948; m. Carol Anteau, Sept. 20, 1986; 1 child, Christine Margaret. BS, Ohio State U., Columbus, 1971, MA in Edn., 1973. Coordinator instructional media Ohio State U., Columbus, 1973-78; mgr. media services The Toledo Hosp., 1978—. Mem. Health Scis. Communications Assn. (exe. com. 1983-85). Office: The Toledo Hosp 2142 N Cove Blvd Toledo OH 43606

TORREY, GREGORY (BEEF), psychologist; b. Torrington, Wyo., Mar. 7, 1958; s. Glen Wilard Torrey and Marian (Britthouer) Hoy. BA, Doane Coll., 1980; MA, Southeastern Okla. State U., 1982; postgrad., U. Nebr., 1984—. Instr., counselor Murray State Coll., Tishomingo, Okla., 1980-84; adj. prof. Doane Coll., Lincoln, Nebr., 1985—; sch. psychologist Crete (Nebr.) Pub. Schs., 1984—; adj. prof. Doane Coll., Lincoln, 1985—. Field editor (mag.): Behavior in Our Schools, 1986—. Adv. bd. Community Intervention System on Domestic Abuse, Crete, 1985-86; adminstrv. bd. Grace United Meth. Ch., Crete, 1986—. Recipient Disting. Teaching award Murray State Coll., 1982-83, 83-84, Doane Scholar award Doane Coll., 1984; Presdl. fellow Southeastern Okla. State U., Durant, 1981-82; Regents fellow U. Nebr., Lincoln, 1985-86. Mem. Nat. Assn. Sch. Psychologist, Nebr. Sch. Psychologists Assn. (mem. ethics com. 1984—), Council for Exceptional Children, Council for Children with Behavioral Disorders, Phi Delta Kappa, Delta Kappa Pi, Beta Beta Beta, Phi Eta Sigma (v.p. 1979-80). Democrat. Home: 807 Ivy Crete NE 68333 Office: Crete Pub Schs 920 Linden Crete NE 68333

TOSTO, LOUIS FRANK, retail lumber manager; b. Chgo., Mar. 20, 1948; s. Michael Angelo and Eleanor Elizabeth (Caster) T.; student William Penn Coll., Oskaloosa, Iowa, 1966-67, North Park Coll., Chgo., 1967-68, William R. Harper Community Coll., Palatine, Ill., 1968-70. Produce mgr. Jewel Cos. Inc., Chgo., 1964-72; sales rep. Internat. Playtex Corp., N.Y.C., 1972-74; asst. field supr. Southland Corp., Chgo., 1974-75; asst. mgr. Ace Hardware, Elk Grove Village, Ill., 1975-78; asst. store mgr. Edward Hines Lumber Co., Villa Park, Ill., 1978-84, store mgr. Dundee (Ill.) br., 1984—; founder, bd. dirs. Housing and Shelter Program, Inc., 1985—. Vol. fireman Elk Grove Village Fire Dept., 1969-86; bd. dirs. Elk Grove Community Services and Mental Health Bd., 1977-81; founder Elk Grove Village Jayteens, 1977—, Elk Grove Village's Village Fair, 1977—; chmn. Elk Grove Village Youth Services Com., 1978-81; co-mem. Congregation of Alexian Bros., Roman Cath. Ch., 1982—; chaplain Alexian Bros. Med. Ctr., Elk Grove Village, 1983—. Mem. Elk Grove Village Jaycees (dir. 1976-78, pres. 1979-80, ambassador 1983—). Club: Elks. Home: 1507 Armstrong Ln Elk Grove Village IL 60007 Office: 900 E Main St Dundee IL 60118

TOTH, CHRISTINA ANN (TINA), title company executive; b. Berwyn, Ill., July 11, 1947; d. Frank Earl and Dorothy Mary Ann (Dahlfors) T. BS, U. Dubuque, 1969; MA, Northeastern Ill. U., 1974. Lic. real estate broker, Ill.; cert. elem. tchr., Ill., Fla. Educator Murphy Jr. High Sch., Wilmette, Ill., 1970-76; account mgr. Lawyers Title, Chgo., 1976-79, Ticor Title, Arlington Heights, Ill., 1979-81, Title Services, Wheaton, Ill., 1981-83; account mgr., escrow officer Safeco Title, Arlington Heights, 1983-86; exec. v.p. Americorp Title, Hoffman Estates, Ill., 1986—; educator, broker Hoeller Real Estate, Mundelein, 1976-78. Tchr. first aid ARC, Arlington Heights and Dubuque, Iowa, 1970-74. Mem. Am. Land Title Assn. (assoc.), NW Bd. Realtors (assoc.), Ill. Mortgage Bankers (assoc.), Chgo. Real Estate Bd. (assoc.), Pi Kappa Delta. Avocations: fishing, music, hiking. Office: Americorp Title Inc 2500 W Higgins Suite 370 Hoffman Estates IL 60195

TOTH, DAVID SCOTT, podiatrist; b. Cleve., Jan. 5, 1952; s. Joseph Francis and Margaret Judy (Kovacs) T.; B.A., Coll. of Wooster, 1973; D.P.M., Ohio Coll. Podiatric Medicine, 1977; m. Donna Georgene Dolch, July 19, 1975; children—David Scott, Jennifer Theresa. Resident Ohio Coll. Podiatric Medicine, 1978; asso. Dr. Marvin Z. Arnold, Maple Heights, Ohio, 1977-78; practice podiatric medicine, Brecksville, Ohio, 1978—, Chardon, Ohio, 1983—; mem. staff Geauga Community Hosp., Huron Rd. Hosp.; chmn. bd. K.T.E. Found.; lectr. profl. seminars; cons. Geauga Fitness Ctr., Chardon, Ohio, 1982—, Scandinavia Health Spa, Broadview Heights, Ohio, also various high sch. sports programs; guest appearances on local cable TV programs. Bd. dirs. Geauga County chpt. Am. Cancer Soc., 1983—. Recipient Order of Battered Boot award March of Dimes, 1975. Fellow Acad. Ambulatory Foot Surgery; mem. Am. Podiatry Assn., Ohio Podiatry Assn. (geriatrics com. 1984-85), N.E. Ohio Acad. Podiatric Medicine (sec. 1984-85, v.p. 1985-86, pres. 1987—), Am. Coll. Sports Medicine, Alumni Assn. Ohio Coll. Podiatric Medicine (dir. 1981—, trustee 1981-85, v.p. 1985-87, pres.-elect 1987—, chmn. scholarship com.), Kappa Tau Epsilon (treas. 1976-77, Outstanding Alumni award), Pi Delta (treas., 1976-77). Roman Catholic. Contbr. articles on foot surgery to profl. jours. Home: 13050 Kenyon Dr Chesterland OH 44026 Office: 7650 Chippewa Rd Suite 205 Brecksville OH 44141 Office: 100 Parker Ct Chardon OH 44024

TOTH, GEORGE ANTHONY, advertising executive; b. Dearborn, Mich., Feb. 12, 1941; s. George and Emma Mildred (Truaxe) T.; m. Andrea Eloise Stephenson, Sept. 4, 1969; children: George, Matthew, Karen. BS in Advt., U. Cin., 1964. Art dir. Darcy McManus, Bloomfield Hills, Mich., 1964-67; sr. art dir. Baker Advt., Detroit, 1967-75; creative dir. Hartman Pub., Troy, Mich., 1975-78; prin. Toth Advt., Sylvan Lake, Mich., 1978-83; sr. graphics designer Gen. Dynamics, Centerline, Mich., 1983-84; advt. sales mgr. Finite div. Parker Hannifin Corp., Oxford, Mich., 1984—. Designer Internat. Freedon Fest. logo, 1980, City of Sylvan Lake logo, 1982. Leader Boy Scouts Am., Sylvan Lake, 1977-84; councilman City of Sylvan Lake, 1986. Presbyterian. Lodge: Optimists. Avocations: sailing, photography.

TOTH, MICHAEL ANTHONY, communications sales executive; b. Detroit, May 18, 1960; s. Michael Alvin and Dorothy Ann (Brudzisz) T. BBA in Mktg., Eastern Mich. U., 1982. Account rep. Sta. WAAM-Radio, Ann Arbor, Mich., 1983-84; sales mgr. Sta. WAAM-Radio, Ann Arbor, 1984—. Mem. Detroit Adcraft, Mich. Assn. Broadcasters, Explorers, Lambda Chi Alpha. Republican. Roman Catholic. Avocations: golf, raquetball, ice hockey, softball, music. Home: 4165 Diamond Ypsilanti MI 48197 Office: Sta Radio-WAAM 4230 Packard Rd Ann Arbor MI 48104

TOUCHSTONE, FRANK VIRGIL, psychologist; b. London, Ky., July 11, 1927; s. Cary and Mabel Ellen (Thomas) T.; m. Dorothy Viola Anderson, Nov. 10, 1961; 1 child, Ellen E. BA, So. Meth. U., 1950; MS in Psychology, Purdue U., 1952, PhD in Psychology, 1957. Lic. psychologist, Ky., Nebr. Counseling psychologist VA, Marion, Ind., 1956-60; clin. and counseling psychologist VA, Shreveport, La., 1960-63; assoc. prof. psychology Centenary Coll., Shreveport, 1963-67; assoc. prof. edn. Pa. State U., State College, 1967-70; chief psychologist Mental Health Ctr., Hazard, Ky., 1970-74; dir. psychology Hastings (Nebr.) Regional Ctr., 1974—; vocat. specialist, cons. U.S. Social Security Adminstrn., 1967—. Editor Rehab. Counseling Bull., 1966-70. Served as sgt. USAF, 1946-49. Mem. Am. Psychol. Assn., Am. Assn. for Counseling and Devel. (chmn. com. 1983-84), Am. Rehab. Counseling Assn. (pres. 1978-79, Superior Service award 1976). Presbyterian. Home: 2320 W 10th St Hastings NE 68901-3536 Office: Hastings Regional Ctr W 2d St Hastings NE 68901-0579

TOUPIN, HAROLD OVID, chemical company executive; b. Hibbing, Minn., Jan. 21, 1927; s. Ovid Pascal and Ellen (Holt) T.; m. Edna F. Sallila, Feb. 8, 1948 (div. Feb. 1973); m. Colleen Beverly Lange, Apr. 18, 1981; children: James, Ronald. BS, U. Minn., 1954, MA, 1955, postgrad, 1968; PhD (hon.), Internat. Acad. Color, Las Vegas, Nev., 1982. Mgr. Firestone Tire Co., East Los Angeles, Calif., 1948-51; dir. vocat. edn. Hopkins (Minn.) Pub. Schs., 1955-75; with research and devel. Power-o-Peat Co., Gilbert, Minn., 1966-67; chief exec. officer, cons. Color Specialties Inc., Mpls., 1976—; bd. dirs. Vu-tek Inc., St. Paul, Airport Auto Sales, St. Paul, Color Specialties of nev., Las Vegas, Instant Air Inc., Mpls. Contbr. articles to profl. jours. Bd. dirs. Hopkins Jaycees, 1958-60. Served with USAAF, 1944-47. Mem. Am. Assn. Mfrs., Internat. Assn. Color, Nat. Ret. Tchrs. Assn., Am. Assn. Self Employeed, Met. Area Dist. Edn. Instrs. Assn. (pres.), Mpls. C. of C., Am. Legion, VFW. Democrat. Roman Catholic. Lodge: Lions (sec. Hopkins club 1956-76). Avocations: travelling, golfing, writing. Office: Color Specialities Inc 6405 Cedar Ave S Richfield MN 55423

TOURLENTES, THOMAS THEODORE, psychiatrist; b. Chgo., Dec. 7, 1922; s. Theodore A. and Mary (Xenostathy) T.; m. Mona Belle Land, Sept. 9, 1956; children—Theodore W., Stephen C., Elizabeth A. B.S., U. Chgo., 1945, M.D., 1947. Diplomate: Am. Bd. Psychiatry and Neurology, asst. examiner, 1964-85. Intern Cook County Hosp., Chgo., 1947-48; resident psychiatry Downey (Ill.) VA Hosp., 1948-51; practice Medicine specializing in psychiatry Chgo., 1952, Camp Atterbury, Ind., 1953, Ft. Carson, Colo., 1954, Galesburg, Ill., 1955-71; staff psychiatrist Chgo. VA Clinic, 1952; clin. instr. psychiatry Med. Sch., Northwestern U., 1952; dir. mental hygiene consultation service Camp Atterbury, 1953-54, Ft. Carson, 1953-54; asst. supt. Galesburg State Research Hosp., 1954-58, supt., 1958-71; dir. Comprehensive Community Mental Health Center Rock Island and Mercer Counties; dir. psychiat. services Franciscan Hosp., 1971-85; asso. clin. prof. psychiatry U. Ill., Chgo., 1955—; preceptor in hosp. adminstrn. State U. Iowa, Iowa City, 1958-64; Councilor, del. Ill. Psychiat. Soc.; chmn. liaison com. Am. hosp. and psychiat. assns., 1978-79. Contbr. articles profl. jours. Mem. Gov. Ill. Com. Employment Handicapped, 1962-64; zone dir. Ill. Dept. Mental Health, 1964-71; mem. Spl. Survey Joint Commn. Accreditation Hosps.; chmn. Commn. Certification Psychiat. Adminstrs., 1979-81; Pres. Knox-Galesburg Symphony Soc., 1966-68; Bd. dirs. Galesburg Civic Music Assn., pres., 1968-70. Served to capt. M.C. AUS, 1943-46, 52-54. Fellow AMA, Am. Psychiat. Assn., AAAS, Am. Coll. Psychiatrists, Am. Coll. Mental Health Adminstrs.; mem. Ill. Med. Soc. (chmn. aging com. 1968-71, council on mental health and addictions 1987—), Ill. Psychiat. Soc. (pres. 1969-70), Am. Pub. Health Assn., Soc. Biol. Psychiatry, Ill. Hosp. Assn. (trustee 1968-70), Am. Coll. Hosp. Adminstrs., Assn. for Research Nervous and Mental Diseases, Am. Assn. Psychiat. Adminstrs. (pres. 1978-79), Central Neuro-Psychiat. Assn. (pres. 1985-86). Home: Box 251 Rural Rt 2 Valley View Rd Galesburg IL 61401

TOURTILLOTT, ELEANOR ALICE, nurse, educational consultant; b. North Hampton, N.H., Mar. 28, 1909; d. Herbert Shaw and Sarah (Fife) T. Diploma Melrose Hosp. Sch. Nursing, Melrose, Mass., 1930; B.S., Tchrs. Coll., Columbia U., 1948, M.A., 1949; edn. specialist Wayne State U., 1962. Gen. pvt. duty nurse, Melrose, Mass., 1930-35; obstet. supr. Samaritan Hosp., Troy, N.Y., 1935-36, Meml. Hosp., Niagara Falls, N.Y., 1937-38, Lawrence Meml. Hosp., New London, Conn., 1939-42, New Eng. Hosp. for Women and Children, Boston, 1942-43; dir. H. W. Smith Sch. Practical Nursing, Syracuse, N.Y., 1949-53; dir., founder assoc. degree program Henry Ford Community Coll., Dearborn, Mich., 1953-74, project dir. USPHS, 1966-71; prin. cons., initial coordinator Wayne State U. Coll. Nursing, Detroit, 1975-78; cons. curriculum design, modular devel., instructional media Tourtillott Cons., Inc., Dearborn, Mich., 1974—; mem. Mich. Bd. Nursing, Lansing, 1966-73, chmn., 1970-72; condr. numerous workshops on curriculum design, instructional media at various colls., 1966—; mem. rev. com. for constrn. nurse tng. facilities, div. nursing USPHS, 1967-70, mem. nat. adv. council on nurse tng., 1972-76. Served to capt. Nurse Corps, U.S. Army, 1943-48; ETO. Recipient Disting. Alumnae award Tchrs. Coll. Columbia U., 1974, Spl. tribute 77th Legislature Mich., 1974, Disting. Alumnae award Wayne State U., 1975, Disting. Service award Henry Ford Community Coll., 1982. Mem. Melrose Hosp. Sch. Nursing Alumnae, Am. Nurses Assn., Nat. League Nursing (chmn. steering com. dept. assoc. degree programs 1965-67, bd. dirs. 1965-67, 71-73, mem. assembly constituent leagues 1971-73, council assoc. degree programs citation 1974), Mich. League for Nursing (pres. 1969-71), Tchrs. Coll. Alumnae Assn., Wayne State U. Alumnae Assn., Phi Lambda Theta, Kappa Delta Pi. Republican. Contbg. author: Patient Assessment-History and Physical Examination, 1977-81; contbr., chpts., articles, speeches to profl. publs.

TOUSLEY, BRENDA BARNES, school psychologist; b. Canastota, N.Y., Sept. 30, 1958; d. James Edward and Marjorie Louise (Barnard) B.; m. Dan Robert Tousley, Nov. 29, 1985. Student, Westmont Coll., 1978; BS in Psychology, Houghton Coll., 1980; postgrad., Cowley County Com. Coll., 1985-86; MS in Sch. Psycholgy, Emporia State U., 1986. Cert. sch. psychologist, Kans. Sch. psychologist Cowley County Spl. Service Coop., Winfield, Kans., 1982-86, Blick Clinic for Devel. Disabilites, Inc., Akron, Ohio, 1986—. Editor/chmn. publs. newsletter Kans. Assn. Sch. Psychologists, 1984-86. Sunday sch. tchr. and Pioneer Girl leader Calvary Chapel, Arkansas City, Kans., 1982-85. Named one of Outstanding Young Women in Am., 1983; recipient Appreciation award Pioneer Club, 1984-85. Fellow Kans. Assn. Sch. Psychologists (publs. chmn., editor 1984-86), Nat. Assn. Sch. Psychologists; mem. Ohio Assn. Sch. Psychologists (assoc.), AAMD (Ohio chpt.), Jaycettes (named Woman of the Quarter 1985, Sparkette 1985). Democrat. Baptist. Avocation: camping. Home: 1853 6th St Cuyahoga Falls OH 44221 Office: Blick Clinic Devel Disabilities 640 W Market Akron OH 44303

TOUSSAINT, JACK LAYTON, hospital administrator; b. Allerton, Iowa, Nov. 25, 1924; s. Harry Lorenz and Verda Leota (Layton) T.; m. Betty Lucille Eppel, Nov. 24, 1944 (dec. Mar. 1969); children—John Steven, Carol Diane; m. Diane Nadine Bernard, Mar. 18, 1978. B.S. in Commerce, State U. Iowa, 1949, M.A. in Hosp. Adminstrn., 1954. Adminstrn. intern U. Iowa, Iowa City, 1953-54, adminstrn. resident, 1954-55, dir. admitting, research assoc., 1955-62; asst. supt. St. Luke's Hosp., Cedar Rapids, Iowa, 1963-75, assoc. dir., 1975-80, sr. v.p., 1980—; bd. dirs. Iowa Statewide Family Practice Tng. Program, Iowa City, 1975-79, Family Service Agency, Cedar Rapids, 1974-79, Dental Health Clinic, Cedar Rapids, 1978—, St. Paul's United Meth. Ch., Cedar Rapids, 1984-87; active United Way, 1970; mem. Cedar Rapids Care Ctr. Rev. Com., 1978, Orthopedic Physicians Asst. Adv. Com. 1972-79; mem. adv. com. County Health Ctr. Medically Indigent, 1977. Served with U.S. Army, 1943-46. Mem. Am. Coll. Healthcare Execs., Am. Hosp. Assn. (life), Pi Omega Pi. Republican. Avocations: travel; fishing; reading. Home: 435 Memorial Dr SE Cedar Rapids IA 52403 Office: St. Luke's Hosp 1026 A Ave NE Cedar Rapids IA 52402

TOUTLOFF, BETTY JANE, social worker; b. Sheboygan, Wis., Jan. 9, 1940; s. Herman Frederick William and Hazel Marie (Ackeret) Boehm; m. John Lloyd Toutloff, Sept. 7, 1963; children: Michelle, Catherine. BA, Lakeland Coll., 1963; MA, No. Mich. U., 1977. Caseworker Dept. Social Services, Wis., 1963-67; sch. social worker Delta/Schoolcraft (Mich.) Intermediate Sch., 1974-76; family assessment specialist Child and Family Services, Delta County, 1978-79; sch. social worker Escanaba (Mich.) Area Pub. Schs., 1979; caseworker Juvenile div. Probate Ct., Escanaba, 1980—. Active Girl Scouts U.S., Escanaba, 1976—; past area chmn. United Way, Escanaba. Mem. LWV (active various coms. 1971—). Roman Catholic. Avocation: travelling. Home: 920 Fifth Ave S Escanaba MI 49829

TOUTON, DAVID FORREST, manufacturing company executive; b. Ft. Atkinson, Wis., Nov. 10, 1927; s. Forrest Cedric and Grace Redella (Hannah) T.; m. Mary Alice Zwiebel, Dec. 26, 1950; children: Cynthia Ann, Daniel David, Barbara Grace, Karen Jane. BEd, U. Wis., Whitewater, 1950. Sales mgr. Rock Paint and Chem. Co., Ft. Atkinson, 1952-55; tech. sales rep. Ill. Paint, Chgo., 1955-58; pres. Stay New Paint Corp., Lake Mills, Wis., 1958—. Served with USN, 1945-46. Mem. Am. Legion. Lodge: Elks, Masons. Home: 418 Adams St Fort Atkinson WI 53538 Office: Stay New Paint Corp 1022 Mulberry St Lake Mills WI 53551

TOW, MARK RANDALL, pharmacist; b. Rensselaer, Ind., May 21, 1952; s. Ralph F. and Gladys May (Duley) T.; m. Cathie J. White, Nov. 27, 1970 (div. 1972); 1 son, John Mark; m. Donna Jean Hayden, Dec. 30, 1972; children—Jaclyn Suzanne, Jillian Leanne. Student U.S. Coast Guard Acad., 1970; B.S. in Pharmacy, Purdue U., 1975. Registered pharmacist. Apprentice pharmacist Ribordy Drug, Knox, Ind., 1972-75; asst. mgr. Hook's Drugs, Winamac, Ind., 1975-78, mgr., 1978-85, buyer, promotions coordinator, 1985—; cons. pharmacist Winamac Nursing Home, 1978-82; extern instr. Sch. Pharmacy, Purdue U., 1980-84. Republican. Nazarene. Lodge: Rotary (past sec., treas., v.p., pres. 1984-85). Office: Hook Drug Co Inc 2800 Enterprise St Indianapolis IN 46226

TOWBIN, RICHARD BRUCE, radiologist; b. Bklyn., Jan. 4, 1948. BS, U. Cin., 1969, MD, 1974; post-graduacao Em Radiologia (hon.), Universidade Federal Do Rio De Janeiro, 1983. Diplomate Am. Bd. Radiology, Am. Bd. Pediatrics, Nat. Bd. Examiners. Resident in pediatrics Los Angeles Children's Hosp., 1974-76; resident in radiology U. Cin., 1976-77, 78-79; resident in pediatric radiology Cin. Children's Hosp. Med. Ctr., 1977-78, fellow in pediatric radiology, 1979-80; chief resident radiology dept. Children's Hosp., Cin., 1977-78, 79-80, asst. prof. radiology and pediatrics, 1980-84, assoc. prof., 1984—, staff radiology dept., 1980—, preceptor clerkship-pediatrics, 1980—, chief neuroradiology, chief special procedures radiology dept., 1985—; staff radiology dept. Univ. Hosp., Cin., 1980—; student advisor U. Cin. Coll. Medicine, 1983—. Author: Comprehensive Management of Head and Neck Tumors, 1985, Principles of Pediatric Neurosurgery, 1985, Diagnosis and Treatment of Head Injuries, Infants and Children, 1986; contbr. artcles to profl. jours. Coach Youth Basketball, 1984-85, Youth Soccer, 1985. Recipient Teaching award Children's Hosp. Med. Ctr., 1983. Fellow Am. Acad. Pediatrics; mem. Am. Soc. Neuroradiology, Am. Coll. Radiology, Soc. Pediatric Radiology, Radiol. Soc. N.Am., Ohio State Radiol. Soc., Sociedade Paulista de Radiologia. Office: Childrens Hosp Dept Radiology Elland & Bethesda Aves Cincinnati OH 45229-2899

TOWE-LESCHER, NANCY ELLEN CARPENTER, electronics manufacturing company executive; b. Kildav, Ky., July 28, 1941; d. John Henry and Nora Jenny (Snyder) Carpenter; m. Marshall Towe, Sr., Dec. 1, 1958 (div. 1981); children—Marshall, Jr., Michael Lee; m. John Edward Lescher, July 26, 1986. A.A.S. in Mktg. Mid-Mgmt., McHenry Community Coll., 1981; B.A. in Orgnl. Psychology, Nat. Coll. Edn., 1982. Switchboard operator Malibu Answering Service, Chgo., 1964-71; corr. Seaboard Life Ins. Co., Chgo., 1972-74; sales corr. Chgo. Miniature div. Gen Instrument Co., Chgo., 1975-77; product mgr. Oak Industries, Crystal Lake, Ill., 1978-82; pres., chief exec. officer Lamptronix Co., Ltd., Crystal Lake, 1982—; speaker in field. Den mother Chgo Area council Boy Scouts Am., 1970-75; active Pierce Sch. PTA, Chgo., 1973; mem. Lake in the Hills Property Owners Assn., 1978-82; founder Woodstock Ctr. for Women, Ill., 1982. Recipient Disting. Service scroll Ill. Congress PTA, 1973. Mem. Women in Electronics, Nat. Network of Women in Sales, Aerospace Lighting Inst., Crystal Lake C. of C. (bd. dirs.). Congregationalist. Home: 2412 N Orchard Beach McHenry IL 60050 Office: Lamptronix Co Ltd 81 N Williams Crystal Lake IL 60102

TOWER, RAYMOND CAMILLE, manufacturing company executive; b. N.Y.C., Feb. 20, 1925; s. Raymond C. and Elinor (Donovan) T.; m. Jaclyn Bauerline, Feb. 7, 1948; children: Raymond, Patricia, Christopher, Robert, Mary, Michael, Victoria. B.S., Yale U., 1945; postgrad., Advanced Mgmt. Program, Harvard U. Research chemist Westvaco Chlorine Products Corp., Carteret, N.J., 1946-48; v.p., gen. mgr. Organic Chem. div. Westvaco Chlorine Products Corp., 1964-67, exec. v.p., mgr. chem. group, 1967-77; pres., chief operating officer FMC Corp., Chgo., 1977—; also dir. FMC Corp.; dir. Firestone Tire and Rubber Co., Akron, Ohio, Household Internat., Inland Steel Co.; chmn. bd. dirs., chief exec. officer FMC Gold Co. Trustee Ill. Inst. Tech.; bd. govs. IIT Research Inst.; vice chmn. Evanston (Ill.) Hosp. Corp.; assoc. Northwestern U. Served to lt. USNR, 1944-46, 51-53. Mem. Chem. Mfrs. Assn., Machinery and Allied Products Inst. (exec. com.), Aerospace Industries Assn. Am., Chgo. Assn. Commerce and Industry (dir.), Nat. Safety Council (bd. govs.), Chgo. Council Fgn. Relations, Alpha Chi Sigma. Clubs: Chicago, Commercial, Economic, Mid-Am. Glen View. Office: FMC Corporation 200 E Randolph Dr Chicago IL 60601

TOWNER, RICHARD MCKINLEY, dentist; b. La Cross, Wis., Sept. 6, 1931; s. Richard M. and Evelyn Elizabeth (Peterson) T.; m. Barbara Beatrice Arndt, Sept. 8, 1953; children: Steven, Susan. BS, U. Minn., 1953, DDS, 1955. Gen. practice dentistry Mankato, Minn., 1957—. Served to capt. U.S. Army, 1955-57. Mem. ADA (alt. del. 1985, del. 1986-88), Minn. Dental Assn. (trustee 1982—), So. Dist. Dental Assn. (pres. 1976-77). Republican. Lutheran. Club: Mankato Golf (pres. 1967). Lodge: Sertoma (pres. Mankato chpt. 1961). Avocations: skiing, golf, bridge. Office: 430 S Broad St Mankato MN 56001

TOWNSEND, EARL CUNNINGHAM, JR., lawyer, author, composer; b. Indpls., Nov. 9, 1914; s. Earl Cunningham and Besse (Kuhn) T.; m. Emily Macnab, Apr. 3, 1947; children: Starr (Mrs. John R. Laughlin), Vicki M. (Mrs. Christopher Katterjohn), Julia E. (Mrs. Edward Goodrich Dunn, Jr.), Earl Cunningham III, Clyde G. Student (Rector scholar), De Pauw U., 1932-34; A.B., U. Mich., 1936, J.D., 1939. Bar: Ind. 1939, Mich. 1973, U.S. Supreme Ct. 1973, U.S. Ct. Appeals (4th, 6th, 7th cirs.), U.S. Dist. Ct. (no. and so. dists.) Ind., U.S. Dist. Ct. (ea. dist.) Va., U.S. Dist. Ct. (ea. dist.) Mich. Sr. partner firm Townsend & Townsend, Indpls., 1940-69; sr. partner Townsend, Hovde & Townsend, Indpls., 1979-84, Townsend, Yosha & Cline, Indpls., 1985-86, 1986—; individual practice Roscommon, Mich., 1973—; dep. prosecutor, Marion County, Ind., 1942-44; radio-TV announcer WIRE, WFBM, WFBM-TV, Indpls., 1940-49, 1st TV announcer Indpls. 500 mile race, 1949, 50; Big Ten basketball referee, 1940-47; lectr. trial tactics U. Notre Dame, Ind. U., U. Mich., 1968-79; chmn. faculty seminar on personal injury trials Ind. U. Sch. Law, U. Notre Dame Sch. Law, Valparaiso Sch. Law, 1981; Terney-Townsend Historic House, Roscommon, Mich.; founder, v.p., treas. Am. Underwriters, Inc., Am. Interinsurance Exchange, 1965-70; mem. Com. to Revise Ind. Supreme Ct. Pattern Jury Instructions, 1975-83; lectr. Trial Lawyers 30 Yrs. Inst., 1986. Author: Birdstones of the North American Indian, 1959, also articles in legal and archeol. fields; composer: Moon of Halloween. Founder, life fellow Roscoe Pound Am. Trial Lawyers Found., Cambridge, Mass.; co-founder, dir. Meridian St. Found.; mem. fin. and bldg. coms., bd. dirs., later life trustee Indpls. Mus. Art; life trustee Ind. State Mus.; trus judge Cale J. Holder Meml. Scholarship Fund, Ind. U. Law Sch.; trustee Cathedral High Sch., Indpls., Starlight Musicials; mem. Ind. U. Found.; mem. Dean's Council, Ind. U.; life dir. Indpls./Marion County Hist. Soc.; fellow Meth. Hosp. Found. Recipient Ind. Univ. Writers Conf. award, 1960; Hanson H. Anderson medal of honor Arsenal Tech. Schs., Indpls., 1971; named to Council Sagamores of Wabash, 1969, Hon. Ky. Col., 1986; Ind. Basketball Hall of Fame; hon. chief Black River-Swan Creek Saginaw-Chippewa Indian tribe, 1971. Fellow Ind. Coll. Trial Lawyers (pres. 1984-86), Ind. Bar Found., Indpls. Bar. Found. (disting., charter), Internat. Acad. Trial Lawyers, Internat. Soc. Barristers; mem. Ind. Trial Lawyers Assn. (pres. 1963-64, life dir. 1981—), ABA (com. trial techniques 1964-76, com. aviation and space 1977—), Ind. State Bar Assn. (del. 1977-79), Indpls. Bar Assn., 34th Dist. (Mich.) Bar Assn., State Bar Mich., Assn. Am. Trial Lawyers (v.p. Ind. 1959-60, bd. govs. 7th jud. circuit 1966-68, assoc. editor Jour. 1964—), Am. Bd. Trial Advocates (diplomate, pres. Ind. chpt. 1982-85), Bar Assn. 7th Fed. Circuit, Roscommon County Bar Assn., Lawyers Assn. Indpls., Am. Judicature Soc., Am. Arbitration Assn. (panel), ASCAP, Ind. Archaeol. Soc. (founder, pres.), Indpls. C. of C., Ind. State C. of C., Genuine Indian Relic Soc. (co-founder, chmn. frauds com.), Ind. Hist. Soc., Trowel and Brush Soc. (hon.), U. Mich. Pres.'s Club, U. Mich. Victors Club (charter), Soc. Mayflower Descs. (gov. 1947-49), Key Biscayne C. of C., Delta Kappa Epsilon, Phi Kappa Phi. Republican. Methodist. Clubs: Mason (32 deg., Shriner), Players, U. Mich. (local pres. 1950), Columbia, Indpls. Athletic, Key Biscayne Yacht. Home: 5008 N Meridian St Indianapolis IN 46208

TOWNSEND, HAROLD GUYON, JR., publishing company executive; b. Chgo., Apr. 11, 1924; s. Harold Guyon and Anne Louise (Robb) T.; A.B., Cornell U., 1948; m. Margaret Jeanne Keller, July 28, 1951; children—Jessica, Julie, Harold Guyon III. Advt. salesman Chgo. Tribune, 1948-51; gen. mgr. Keller-Heartt Co., Clarendon Hills, Ill., 1951-62; pub. Santa Clara (Calif.) Jour., 1962-64; pres., pub. Dispatch-Tribune newspaper Townsend Communications, Inc., Kansas City, Mo., 1964—; dir. United Mo. City Bank. Chmn., Suburban Newspaper Research Commn., 1974—; dir. Certified Audit Bur. of Circulation, 1968-72. del. Rep. Nat. Conv., 1960; chmn. Mission Hills Rep. Com., 1966-77; bd. dirs. Kansas City Jr. Achievement, 1966-68, Kansas City council Girl Scouts U.S.A., 1969-71, Kansas City council Boy Scouts Am., 1974, Kansas City chpt. ARC, 1973-79, Kansas City Starlight Theater, Clay County (Mo.) Indsl. Commn.; treas., trustee Park Coll., Parkville, Mo., 1970-78. Mem. adv. com. North Kansas City Hosp.; bd. dirs. Taxpayers Research of Mo., 1978—, Nelson Gallery Friends of Art, 1980-85. Served with inf. AUS, World War II. Mem. Kansas City Advt. and Sales Club, Kansas City Press Club, Suburban Press Found. (pres. 1969-71), Suburban Newspapers Am. (pres. 1976-77), Kansas City Printing Industries Assn. (pres., dir.), Printing Industries of Am. (pres. non-heatset web sect. 1980-82), North Kansas City C. of C. (dir., pres. 1964-70), Univ. Assocs. (treas. 1977-80), Sigma Delta Chi, Pi Delta Epsilon, Phi Kappa Psi. Clubs: University (treas. 1977), Indian Hills Country; Hinsdale (Ill.) Golf; Mission Valley Country, Field (Sarasota, Fla.). Home: 7435 Sanderling Rd Sarasota FL 34242 Office: 7007 NE Parvin Rd Kansas City MO 64117

TOWNSEND, J. RUSSELL, JR., insurance executive; b. Cedar Rapids, Iowa, Nov. 21, 1910; s. J. Russell and Mabel (Ferguson) T.; B.S., Butler U., 1931; M.B.A., U. Pa., 1933; m. Virginia Holt, Aug. 1, 1938; 1 son, John Holt. Registered health underwriter. Field asst. Equitable Life Ins. Co. Iowa, 1933-50, gen. agt., 1950-69, gen. agt. emeritus, 1969—; mng. asso. J. Russell Townsend & Assos., 1969—; assoc. prof. emeritus bus. adminstrn. Butler U., Indpls., 1982; cons. Ind. Dept. Ins., 1948-50; mem. Ind. Ho. of Reps., 1946-48, Ind. Senate, 1956-64; lectr., writer ins. field. Chmn. Indpls. Bicentennial Com., 1975-76; pres. Indpls. Jaycees, 1940. Served with USNR, 1942-46; lt. comdr. Res. ret. Recipient 25-year teaching award Am. Coll. C.L.U.s, 1960; Alumni Achievement award Butler U., 1979. Mem. Indpls. chpt. C.L.U.s (past pres.), Ind. Life Underwriters Assn. (past v.p.), Ret. Officers Assn. (past pres. Indpls. chpt.), Ind. Soc. Assn. Execs., Naval Res. Assn., Navy League U.S., Am. Soc. C.L.U.'s, AAUP, Am. Soc. Risk and Ins., Ind. Acad. Sci., Sales and Marketing Execs. Council, U.S. Naval Inst., Phi Delta Theta (past pres. Indpls. alumni club). Republican. Presbyterian. Clubs: Columbia, Meridian Hills Country, Indpls. Literary, Kiwanis (dir. Ind. Found., lt. gov. Ind. dist. internat. 1975-76), Indpls. Press, Ft. Harrison Officers, Masons, Sojourners (Indpls); Army and Navy (Washington); Crystal Downs Country (Frankfort, Mich.) (past pres.); U. Pa. Faculty. Contbr. articles to trade mags. Home: 8244 N Pennsylvania St Indianapolis IN 46240 Office: 906 Investors Trust Bldg 107 N Pennsylvania St Indianapolis IN 46204

TOWNSEND, LAWRENCE DE WITT, travel editor; b. Seattle, Apr. 17, 1935; s. Lawrence De Witt and Sadie Sylvia (Saloma) T.; m. Carol Jean Kimmel, Sept. 12, 1958; children: Richard Steven, Laura Diane. BA, San Diego State U., 1958; MS in Journalism, Northwestern U., 1960. Radio editor UPI, Chgo., 1959; editor Chgo. Tribune, Chgo., 1959-65, 68-86, exec. travel editor, 1986—; editor Internat. Minerals and Chem. Corp., Skokie, Ill., 1965-68. Editor: Harvey Olson's Europe, 1964. Mem. adv. com. Art Inst., Chgo., 1972—. Avocations: tennis, reading, writing. Home: 57 Salem Ln Evanston IL 60203 Office: Chgo Tribune 435 N Michigan Ave Chicago IL 60611

TOWNSEND, PAMELA GWIN, business educator; b. Dallas, Aug. 24, 1945; d. William Thomas and Doris (Gwin) T. B.A. with distinction in Econs. (Univ. scholar), U. Mo., Kansas City, 1977, M.B.A. (Outstanding Acctg. Grad.), 1980. Real estate sales assoc. KEW Realtors, Austin, Tex., 1967-70; staff mktg. asst. Lincoln Property Co., Dallas, 1970-72; dir. mktg. Commonwealth Devel. Co., Dallas, 1972-73; v.p. market analysis Fin. Corp. N.Am., Kansas City, 1973-75; asst. prof., dir. dept. acctg. Park Coll., Parkville, Mo., 1980—, on leave to Kansas U. Ph.D. program. Mem. Friends of Art, Nelson Gallery; mem. Mo. Repertory Theater Guild; underwriter Folly Theater. C.P.A., Kans.; lic. real estate broker, Tex., Mo., Kans. Mem. Am. Inst. C.P.A.s, Kans. Soc. C.P.A.s, Mo. Soc. C.P.A.s, Am. Acctg. Assn., Nat. Assn. Accts., Nat. Tax Assn., Am. Fin. Assn., Beta Alpha Psi Alumnae (pres. 1982), Beta Gamma Sigma, Phi Kappa Phi, Omicron Delta Epsilon, Alpha Chi Omega, Mortar Bd. Episcopalian. Columnist: Tax Tips, Platte County Gazette, 1981. Home: 2604 University St Lawrence KS 66044 Office: U Kans Summerfield Hall Lawrence KS 66044

TOWNSEND, RAY N., data processing executive; b. Sioux Falls, S.D., June 15, 1952; s. Lloyd V. and Irene A. (Kirchner) T.; m. Gwyneath (Chicky) Monson, Aug. 30, 1975; children: Ryan, Katie. BS in Math., U. S.D., 1974; MBA, Ind. U., 1979. Programmer, analyst U. S.D., Vermillion, 1973-76, asst. dir. computer ctr., 1980-85; sr. analyst, programmer Ind. U., Bloomington, 1976-79; info. systems officer Western Surety Co., Sioux Falls, 1985—; cons. in field, 1981—. coach Sioux Falls Soccer Assn., 1986-87. Mem. Pi Mu Epsilon. Home: 5909 W 28 St Sioux Falls SD 57106 Office: Western Surety Co 101 S Phillips Ave Sioux Falls SD 57192

TOWNSEND, WILLIE CORNELIUS, electrical engineer, manufacturing company executive; b. Brundidge, Ala., Nov. 9, 1949; s. Payton Sr. and Mary Sue (Hardwick) T.; m. Margaret Ruth Rader, Dec. 15, 1984. BSEE, U. Notre Dame, 1974. Profl. football player Los Angeles Rams, 1974; indsl. elec. engr. Corning Glass Works, State College, Pa., 1974-75, line foreman, 1975-76; application engr. Corning Glass Works, Corning, N.Y., 1976-77; design engr. Ford Motor Co., Dearborn, Mich., 1977-84; mgr. product quality Hobart Corp., Troy, Ohio, 1984—. Methodist. Avocations: softball, basketball, computers, art, paddle ball. Home: 4319 Lamont Dr Kettering OH 45429 Office: Hobart Corp 1 World Hdqrs Troy OH 45374

TOWSEND, RICHARD CRAIG, accountant; b. Lacrosse, Wis., Apr. 11, 1945; s. Roy Jr. and Ellen Jane (Affeldt) T.; m. Mary Harness, Dec. 28, 1978; children: Marcy Lynn, Michael Andrew. BS in Acctg., U. Ill., 1967, JD, 1971. CPA. Tax mgr. Touche Ross & Co., Chgo., 1971-81; regional tax ptnr., head tax dept. Grant Thornton, Mpls., 1981-86, mng. ptnr., 1986; also nat. tax adv com. Grant Thornton, Washington. Fin. Asst. Oglivie for Gov., Chgo., 1972; exec. com. Rep. Tom MacNamara, Chgo. 1974-76; mem. Gov.'s Tax Simplicity Task Force, Mpls., 1982; Frenzel Tax Adv. Commn., Mpls., 1984; Mpls. Leadership, 1983—. Mem. ABA, Minn. Bar Assn., Minn. CPA Soc., Ill. Soc. CPA's, Am. Inst. CPA's, Mpls. Tas Roundtable, Mpls. Internat. Tax Club. Republican. Methodist. Clubs: Athletic (Mpls.); U. Ill. Sch. Law Deans; Horse and Hunt (Shakopee, Minn.). Lodge: Rotary. Home: 5520 Malibu Dr Edina MN 55436

TOZER, THEODORE WILLIAM, mortgage company executive; b. Bloomington, Ind., Feb. 3, 1957; s. William Thomas and Joan Marie (Heberlein) T.; m. F. Sandra Williams, Mar. 28, 1981. BS, Ind. U., 1978. CPA, Ill., Ohio., cert. mgmt. acct. Staff acct. Borg-Warner, Chgo., 1978, Armco, Inc., Middletown, Ohio, 1979; mgr. investment ops. BancOhio Nat. Bank, Columbus, Ohio, 1979-85; controller BancOhio Mortgage Co., Columbus, Ohio, 1985-86, chief fin. officer, 1986—. Mem. Nat. Assn. Accts., Am. Inst. CPA's. Home: 3258 Palomar Ave Columbus OH 43229 Office: BancOhio Mortgage Co 51 N High St Columbus OH 43251

TOZZER, JACK CARL, civil engr., surveyor; b. Marion, Ohio, Jan. 5, 1922; s. Carl Henry and Henrietta (Schellenbaum) T.; B.C.E., Ohio No. U., 1944; children—Brent Jack, Hal Jack; m. Aleta C. Lehner, July 14, 1974. Pres. firm Tozzer & Assos. Inc., Marion, 1948—; county engr. Marion County, Ohio, 1964—; city engr. Marion, 1959, Galion, Ohio, 1960-85 . Cons. civil engr. Mem. consultants bd. Coll. Engring. Ohio No. U., 1970, recipient Order of Engr., 1971; v.p. Marion Community Improvement Corp.; mem. Marion County Regional Planning Commn. Served with USNR, 1944-46. Registered profl. engr., Ohio, Fla., registered surveyor, Ohio. Fellow ASCE; mem. Nat. Soc. Profl. Engrs., Marion C. of C., Cons. Engrs. Ohio, Profl. Land Surveyors Ohio, Ohio, Marion County (past dir.) hist. socs., Delta Sigma Phi. Lutheran (past trustee). Elk. Home: 307 Forest Lawn Blvd Marion OH 43302 Office: Room 1 Courthouse Marion OH 43302

TOZZI, MARK ANTHONY, podiatrist; b. Cleve., Dec. 17, 1951; s. Michael Angelo and Margaret Eleanor (Klimo) T.; m. Paula Jeanne, Stewart, Nov. 13, 1981; children: Tara Nicolle, Ashley Shea, Britni Jeanne. D in Podiatric Medicine, Ohio Coll. Podiatric Medicine, 1975. Cert. Am. Bd. Podiatric Surgery. Asst. prof. podiatric medicine and surgery Ohio Coll. Podiatric Medicine, Cleve., 1977-81, assoc. prof., 1982—; pvt. practice podiatry Mayfield Heights, Ohio, 1976—. Contbr. articles to profl. jours. Fellow Am. Coll. Foot Orthopedists, Am. Coll. Podopediatrics; mem. Am. Coll. Sports Medicine. Roman Catholic. Home: 32615 Wintergreen Dr Solon OH 44139

TRABANCO, RAFAEL JORGE, marketing executive; b. Holguin, Cuba, July 11, 1963; came to U.S., 1965; s. Julio Ceasar and Maria Christina (Torres) T.; m. Dinah Adrianne Gucrin, Oct. 12, 1984 (div. Sept. 1986). G rad. high sch., Manchester, Mo. Sales mgr. Am. Prestige, St. Louis, 1982-83; broadcast engr. Sta. KSTL Radio, St. Louis, 1984—; pres. Tropicana Market Inc., St. Louis, 1983—. Mem. Hispanic C. of C., Benito Juarez Mexican Soc. Republican. Roman Catholic. Avocations: music, sports. Office: Tropicana Market Inc 5001 Lindenwood Ave Saint Louis MO 63109

TRABERT, JOHN EARLE, corporate executive; b. Hastings, Nebr., Jan. 28, 1934; s. J. Earle and Fern Elizabeth (Wiar) T.; m. Mary Ann Daly, Dec. 28, 1957; children: Kathryn, William John, Anne. BS, U. Nebr., 1955. Dist. mgr. Northwestern Bell, West Des Moines, 1957-64, div. mgr., 1964-69; exec. v.p. ITA, Inc., West Des Moines, 1969-74, pres., chief exec. officer, 1974—; bd. dirs. Des Moines Devel. Corp., 1986—. Served to sgt. U.S. Army, 1955-57. Republican. Clubs: Des Moines Country (bd. dirs.), Drake Athletics, Iowa Venture Capitol. Lodge: Masons. Home: 1601 Thornwood Rd West Des Moines IA 50265 Office: ITA Inc 4800 Westown Pkwy Suite 300 Regency 3 West Des Moines IA 50265

TRACY, BRIDGET ANNE, lawyer; b. Dayton, Ohio, Nov. 26, 1957; d. Louis Edward and Estelle Mary (Purdy) T. BSBA, Ohio State U., 1980; JD, U. Dayton, 1983. Bar: Ohio 1984, U.S. Dist. Ct. (so. dist.) Ohio 1984. Ptnr. Tracy & Tracy, West Carrollton, Ohio, 1984—. Trustee United Cerebral Palsy of S.W. Cen. Ohio, chairperson pub. policy com. Mem. ABA, Ohio Bar Assn., Dayton Bar Assn., Assn. Trial Lawyers Am., Miami Valley Assn. Women Attys., Alpha Chi Omega (treas. Dayton alumni 1985—). Office: Tracy & Tracy 31 E Central Ave West Carrollton OH 45449

TRACY, EUGENE ARTHUR, utility executive; b. Oak Park, Ill., Dec. 14, 1927; s. Arthur Huntington and Emily Margaret (Groff) T.; m. Irene Walburga Kacin, June 30, 1951; children: Glen Eugene, Diane Emily Tracy Champion, Janet Freda. B.S. in Bus. Adminstrn, Northwestern U., 1951; M.B.A., DePaul U., Chgo., 1958. With Peoples Gas Light & Coke Co., Chgo., 1951—; pres. Peoples Gas Light & Coke Co., 1977-84, chmn., chief exec. officer, 1981—, also dir.; pres. North Shore Gas Co., Waukegan, Ill., 1977-84; chmn., chief exec. officer North Shore Gas Co., 1981—, also dir.; chmn., chief exec. officer Peoples Energy Corp., 1981—, pres., 1981-84, also dir.; dir. La Salle Nat. Bank, Chgo. 1986—. Trustee Taxpayers Fedn. Ill., 1973-77; bd. dirs. Civic Fedn. Chgo., 1966-77; bd. dirs. Central YMCA Community Coll., Chgo., 1971—, treas., 1972-77, chmn. bd., 1977-79; treas. St. David's Episcopal Ch., Glenview, Ill., 1970-79; bd. dirs. Jr. Achievement, Chgo., 1978—, Chgo. Assn. Commerce and Industry, 1979-84; trustee Mus. Sci. and Industry, 1981—, DePaul U., 1982—; bd. dirs. United Way of

Chgo., 1983—, vice chmn., 1986-87, chmn., 1987—; dir. Met. Crusade of Mercy, Chgo., 1986—; dir. NCCJ, Chgo., 1986—; co-chmn. Chgo. United, 1984-86 . Served with U.S. Army, 1946-47. Mem. Am. Gas Assn. (dir. 1981-85, vice chmn. 1986—), Midwest Gas Assn. (dir. 1979—, chmn. 1985-86), Inst. Gas. Tech. (trustee, chmn. 1985-86). Clubs: Econ. (Chgo.), Univ. (Chgo.), Chicago (Chgo.), Commercial (Chgo.); Sunset Ridge Country (Northbrook, Ill.). Office: Peoples Energy Corp 122 S Michigan Ave Chicago IL 60603

TRACY, MARY ELIZABETH, librarian; b. Joliet, Ill., Aug. 18, 1922; d. Charles Joseph and Catherine (Fay) Tracy; B.A. cum laude, Coll. St. Francis, 1944; M.A., Rosary Coll., 1958. Tchr., librarian Joliet pub. schs., 1944-52, 54-61, Am. schs., Bremerhaven and Frankfurt, Germany, 1952-54; librarian Cen. Campus Joliet Twp. High Sch., 1961-86; chmn. Joliet Local Archives Com., 1981-87. Sec., v.p., and mem. adv. bd. Alumnae of the Coll. of St. Francis. Mem. Am., Ill. Library Assns., Ill. Assn. for Media in Edn., Ill. Audio-Visual Assn., Will County Library/Media Assn. (pres. 1976), Joliet Jr. Cath. Woman's League (pres. 1950-51), Joliet Area Hist. Soc. (bd. advisors 1986—). Home: 1010 Glenwood Ave Joliet IL 60435

TRACY, RODNEY BRICE, mortgage company executive; b. Lancaster, Wis., Apr. 12, 1930; s. James Franklin and Nora Alice (Knox) T.; m. Mona Leola Burr (div. Feb. 1976); children: Sandra, Nancy, James, Kevin, Merri, Dawn Tracy; m. Marcia Kay McGuire, July 4, 1976; children: Meghan Gail, Laura Elizabeth. Student, U. Wis., Platteville, 1948, U. Wis., 1961, Purdue U., 1959. Lic. Minn. real estate broker. Owner Skelgas Skelly Oil, Eagle River, Wis., 1953-61, Newspaper, Ins., Cassville, Wis., 1961-65, Harvestore, Waconia, Minn., 1965-83; owner Mortgage Banking, Blair, Nebr., 1983-84, Elk River, Minn., 1985—; cons. Ericson (Nebr.) State Bank, 1983-85, Trausch Co., Carroll, Iowa, 1983-87, Harstad Cos. New Brighton, Minn., 1986-87, Nepa Pallet, Snohomish, Wash., 1986-87. Pres. Eagle River Indsl., 1958; v.p. Eagle River Hosp., 1959. Served to sgt. USAF, 1948-49. Named Wholesaler of Yr., Skelgas Skelly Oil, 1955, Man of Yr., Eagle River C. of C., 1960, Dealer of Yr., A.O. Smith, Waconia, Minn., 1970. Mem. VFW. Lodge: Eagles. Avocations: golf, fishing, hunting. Office: 544 3d St Box 361 Elk River MN 55330

TRADER, HERBERT FREDERICK, business machines company executive; b. Mpls., July 20, 1937; s. Herbert Carl and Lucille Mae Trader; m. Mary Isaac, June 20, 1966; children: Dominic, Andrew. BBA, U. Minn., 1959. With Control Data Corp., Mpls., 1961—, gen. mgr. Cybernet Services div., v.p., gen. mgr. Cybernet Services div., v.p. fin. industry mgmt. office, v.p., group exec. fin. group, sr. v.p. mktg. Comml. Credit Corp., pres. City Venture Corp., v.p. urban and rural ventures, pres. bus. devel. group, v.p. mktg. and bus. devel., tng. and edn. group; bd. dirs. Norstan, Inc., Plymouth, Minn. Co-chmn. Minn. State Emergency Energy Com., 1973; mem. nat. adv. council SBA, Washington, 1977-81; bd. dirs. Vol. Action Ctr., St. Paul. Mem. Phi Kappa Psi. Clubs: Town and Country (St. Paul); Pool and Yacht (Lilydale, Minn.). Avocations: reading, fishing. Office: Control Data Corp 8100 34th Ave S Minneapolis MN 55420

TRADER, JOSEPH EDGAR, orthopaedic surgeon; b. Milw., Nov. 2, 1946; s. Edgar Joseph and Dorothy Elizabeth (Senzig) T.; M. Janet Louise Burzycki,Sept. 23, 1972; children: James, Jonathan, Ann Elizabeth. Student, Marquette U., 1964-67; MD, Med. Coll. Wis., 1971. Diplomate Am. Bd. Orthopaedic Surgery. Emergency room dr. Columbia, St. Joseph's and St. Luke's Hosps., Milw., 1972-76; orthopaedic surgeon Orthopaedic Assn., Manitowoc, Wis., 1978—; med. dir. EMT-I Program, Manitowac, 1983—, EMT-D Program, Manitowoc, 1983—, Sports Medicine Program, Holy Family Med. Ctr., Manitowoc, 1985—; med. advisor Physical Therapy, Two Rivers, Wis., 1985—. Mem. Holy Innocents Men's Choir. Served with USN, 1976-78. Fellow Am. Acad. Orthopaedic Surgeons, ACS; mem. AMA, Wis. Med. Soc., Wis. Orthopaedic Soc., Phi Delta Epsilon, Psi Chi, Crown & Anchor. Roman Catholic. Club: Manitowoc Yacht. Avocations: singing, piano, scuba diving, tennis, skiing. Home: 2105 Rheaume Rd Manitowoc WI 54220 Office: Orthopaedic Assocs 501 N 10th St Manitowoc WI 54220

TRAEGER, BARBARA SHIELDS (MRS. JOHN E. TRAEGER), hospital executive; b. Pitts., Oct. 19, 1932; d. Marshall Charles and Margaret Helen (Ward) Shields; BA in English, Ripon (Wis.) Coll., 1954; postgrad. U. Chgo., 1971; m. John E. Traeger, Apr. 30, 1971; children by previous marriage: Cynthia, Charles R., Henry. Dir. pub. relations Am. Cancer Soc., Chgo., 1964-65; asst. bur. pub. info. Am. Hosp. Assn., Chgo., 1966-68; dir. pub. relations U. Chgo. Hosps. and Clinics, 1968-72, Evanston Hosp. Corp., Ill., 1972-84, asst. v.p. pub. relations, 1984—. Recipient Excellence award Am. Inst. Graphic Arts, 1975-76, Achievement award Nat. Publs. Assn., 1975, MacEachern award, 1972-75, 79-80, 85, Type Dirs. Club award, 1970, Excellence award Modern Publicity, 1972, Outstanding Editorial Achievement award Chgo. Assn. Bus. Communicators, 1978-83, Best Internal Publ. award Suburban Press Club, 1979, 80, 82, Best 4-color brochure awards Best mag., 1983, 84, 85. Mem. Assn. Am. Med. Colls., Am. Soc. Hosp. Pub. Relations (chmn. mktg. com., mem. accreditation com., chmn. budget com. 1981-83, Horizons com. 1983, Silver Touchstone award 1983, Gold Touchstone award 1985), Acad. Hosp. Pub. Relations (seminar chmn. 1974, dir. 1976, pres. 1978-79, dir. 1980-81, 82-83), Ill. Hosp. Assn. (ann. meeting com. 1977, 78, 79), Press Council of McGaw Med. Ctr. Northwestern U., Pub. Relations Soc. Am. (chmn. mktg. com.) Chgo. Hosp. Council, Voluntary Hosps. of Am.-Midwest (mem. mktg. com.). Clubs: Publicity (Chgo.); Suburban Press. Contbr. articles to Hosps. jour., chpt. to book; mem. editorial adv. bd. Profiles in Hosp. Mktg. Home: Box 381 Winnetka IL 60093 Office: 2650 Ridge Ave Evanston IL 60201

TRAFICANT, JAMES A., JR., congressman; b. Youngstown, Ohio, May 8, 1941; s. James A. and Agnes T. T.; m. Patricia Coppa; children—Robin, Elizabeth. B.S., U. Pitts., 1963, M.S., 1973; M.S., Youngstown State U., 1976. Exec. dir. Mahoning County Drug Program, Ohio, 1971-81; sheriff Mahoning County, Ohio, 1981-85; mem. 99th Congress from 17th Ohio dist., Washington, 1985—. Office: Ho of Reps Office House Members Washington DC 20515 *

TRAFTON, THAXTER R., professional sports team executive. m. Mona Trafton; 4 children. Grad., Husson Coll. Pres. Cleve. Cavaliers, 1985—. Office: Cleve Cavaliers The Coliseum 2923 Streetsboro Rd Richfield OH 44286 *

TRAICOFF, ELLEN BRADEN, psychologist; b. Gary, Ind.; d. Charles Leonard and Blossom (Riggin) Braden. BS, Ind. U., 1971, MS, 1974; D of Psychology, Forest Inst. Profl. Psychology, 1987. Edn. and family therapist Cath. Family Services, 1974-78; child and family specialist Porter Starke Services, Valparaiso, Ind., 1978-79; dir. family violence programming Southlake Ctr. Mental Health, Merrillville, Ind., 1979-83, dir. forensic services, 1983-84; cons. Lake County (Ind.) Dept. of Pub. Welfare, 1984-86; psychologist Walbash Valley Hosp., Lafayette, Ind., 1987—. Contbr. articles to profl. jours. Del. White House Conf. on Families, 1980. Mem. Am. Assn. Marriage and Family Therapy (clin.), Family Inst. Chgo. Alumni Assn. Avocations: archeology, anthropology. Office: Walbash Valley Hosp 2900 N River Rd West Lafayette IN 47906

TRAINOR, JOHN FELIX, educator; b. Mpls., Dec. 1, 1921; s. James Patrick and Myra Catherine (Pauly) T.; m. Margaret Dolores Pudenz, July 3, 1965 (dec. 1977); children: John Anthony, Patrick James. BA cum laude, Coll. St. Thomas, 1943; MA, U. Minn., 1950; PhD, Wash. State U., 1970. Instr. high sch. Mpls., 1946-47; v.p. Trainor Candy Co., Mpls., 1949-56; instr., asst. prof. econs. Rockhurst Coll., Kansas City, Mo., 1956-62; instr. Wash. State U., Pullman, 1966-67; asst. prof. Moorhead (Minn.) State U., 1967-70, assoc. prof. econs., 1971—, chmn. dept. econs., 1981—. Author: (with Frank J. Kottke) The Nursing Home Industry in the State of Washington, 1968. Served to lt. (j.g.) USNR, 1943-46, ETO. Mem. AAUP, NEA, Am. Econs. Assn., Minn. Econs. Assn. (pres. 1976-77), Assn. Social Econs., Minn. Acad. Sci., Interfaculty Assn., Minn. Edn. Assn., Omicron Delta Epsilon. Democrat. Roman Catholic. Home: 1333 4th Ave S Moorhead MN 56560 Office: Moorhead State U Dept Econs Moorhead MN 56560

TRAMILL, JAMES LOUIS, psychology educator; b. Clarksville, Tenn., July 25, 1945; s. Louis H. and Mable Louise (Clark) T.; m. Jeannie Klienhammer, May 19, 1982; 1 child, Lacey Taylor. B.S., Austin Peay State U., 1967, M.A., 1977; Ph.D., U. So. Miss., 1981. Tchr., Montgomery (Tenn.) County Bd. Edn., 1968-77; instr. Austin Peay State U., 1977-78; assoc. prof. ednl. psychology Wichita State U., 1980—. Mem. Am. Psychol. Assn., Am. Ednl. Research Assn., Soc. Research in Child Devel., Assn. Psychol. and Ednl. Research in Kans. (pres. 1980-82). Home: 7523 E 26th St Wichita KS 67226 Office: Wichita State U PO Box 28 Wichita KS 67208

TRAMMELL, ALAN STUART, professional baseball player; b. Garden Grove, Calif., Feb. 21, 1958; m. Barbara Leverett, Feb. 21, 1978; 1 child, Lance. Shortstop Detroit Tigers, Am. League, 1977—. Named Most Valuable Player, So. League, 1977; recipient Golden Glove award, 1980, 81; mem. Am. League All-Star Team, 1980, 84; named Most Valuable Player 1984 World Series. Office: Detroit Tigers Tiger Stadium Detroit MI 48216 *

TRAMMELL, HOMER CONRAD, business consultant; b. Laurel, Miss., Oct. 10, 1937; s. Homer Lee and Evie Louisa (Breazeale) T.; m. Gail Elaine Lacy, Feb. 14, 1960. BBA, U. Miss., 1964; postgrad., Ind. U., 1968-71, Purdue U., 1968, Ind. State U., 1969. Jr. exec. Sears, Roebuck and Co., Vicksburg, Miss., 1964-67; asst. mgr. Western Auto Co., Jackson, Miss., 1967; tchr. Northwestern Sch. Dist., Kokomo, Ind., 1967-71; bus. cons. Trammell Assocs., Kokomo, 1971—. Pres. Promised Land, Inc., Kokomo, 1974—; v.p. bd. dirs. Kokomo Rescue Mission, 1982-84, pres. 1984—. Served with USAF, 1956-60. Mem. Soc. for the Advancement of Mgmt. (v.p. 1962-63, pres. 1963-64), Ind. Gospel Music. Assn. (pres. 1976-78), Christian Motorcyclists Assn. Mem. Ch. of God. Avocation: motorcycle riding. Home: 13018 E 340 S Greentown IN 46936 Office: Trammell Assocs PO Box 388 Kokomo IN 46901

TRANKINA, LEONARD VINCENT, hotel executive, consultant; b. Chgo., June 27, 1936; s. Leonard A. and Kathryn A. (Ihm) T.; m. Virginia A. Taylor, Dec. 16, 1965; 1 child, Robin Anna. Gen mgr. Stockyard Inn-Internat. Amphitheatre, Chgo., 1971-73; food and beverage cons. Arlington Hotel, Hot Springs, Ark., 1973-79, State of Ark., Little Rock, 1974-79; gen. mgr. Pheasant Run Corp., St. Charles, Ill., 1979-81, Mackinac Hotel, Mackinac Island, Mich., 1981—; cons. in field. Author: The Way Out Plan, 1973; Welcome to the Hotel Industry, 1975; A Little to Do with Wines, 1979. Mem. Mich. C. of C., Mackinac Island C. of C., Hotel Sales Mgrs. Assn. (pres. 1969), Front Office Mgrs. Assn., Wine and Food Soc. Club: Sons of Italy. Lodge: Elks. Avocations: writing, comedy writing, commercial art, music, gourmet cooking. Office: Stonecliffe Mackinac Island MI 49757

TRANQUILLI, ROLAND ANTHONY, JR., electrical company executive; b. Springfield, Ill., May 20, 1941; s. Roland A. and Marian I. (Peters) T.; B.S. in E.E., Wayne State U., 1969; M.B.A., Ill. Benedictine Coll., 1984; m. Paulette I. Pritula, Mar. 25, 1967; children—Ronald Scott, Tammy Lyn. Engr. printing instrumentation and control Safran Printing Co., Detroit, 1966-70; with Western Electric Co., Naperville, Ill., 1970—, engr. spl. projects devel., 1970-76, sr. engr., 1979-80, project engr. mfg. communication switching systems, 1976-80, mgr. engring., 1980-82, processor product mgr., 1982-86, mgr. computing systems pricing, 1986—; microprocessor coordinator Western Electric Co., No. Ill. Works, Lisle, 1974-76, vice-chmn. X3T9 standards com. for minicomputers, 1980-84. Mktg. and exec. adv. Jr. Achievement, Lisle, 1979-81. Served with USAF, 1960-64. Recipient Spl. Achievement Engring. award Western Electric Co., 1980. Mem. IEEE, Am. Motorcycle Assn., Instrument Soc. Am. Office: AT&T 4513 Western Ave Lisle IL 60532

TRAPP, DONALD WILLIAM, computer company executive; b. Hampton, Va., Sept. 28, 1946; s. Chester Arthur and Ida Lee (Holt) T.; m. Shirley Ann Stokes, May 28, 1971; children: Rashaad, Brandon. BS, Va. State U., 1968; MBA, Ind. U., 1973. Mgr. treasury and reporting Irwin Mgmt. Co., Columbus, Ind., 1973-76; asst. treas. Cummins Engine Co., Columbus, 1976-78, dir. pricing, 1978-81, dir. internat. logistics, 1982-84; pres. Remote Equipment Corp., Indpls., 1985—. Bd. dirs. Columbus Area United Way, 1977-80, William R. Laws Found., Columbus, 1976-85, pres. 1981. Recipient Achievement award Wall St. Jour., 1968. Mem. Ind. U. Sch. Bus. Alumni Assn., Kappa Alpha (life). Baptist. Home: 3241 Beechnut Ct Columbus IN 47203 Office: Remote Equipment Corp 2502 Roosevelt Ave Indianapolis IN 46218

TRAUTH, PAUL AUGUST, health care marketing professional, consultant; b. St. Louis, June 12, 1950; s. Paul August Sr. and Lucille Clara (Purzner) T.; m. Carol Ann Vehlewald, Sept. 5, 1970; children: Dawn Marie, Jeffrey Allen, Karen Beth. BS, George Washington U., 1970; BS in Pharmacy, U. Mo., 1974; MPH, Lindenwood Coll. and U. Mo. (combined program), 1977. Surg. cons. U.S. Surg. Corp., Norwalk, Conn., 1979-82; sr. cons. ophthalmic systems Precision Cosmet, Minnetonka, Minn., 1982—; pres. Smart Solutions, Inc., St. Louis, 1980—; dir. MTF Med. Assocs., Inc., Fairview Heights, Inc., 1980-82. Served with USN, 1968-72. U.S. Surg. Corp. fellow U. Pitts., 1979. Fellow Am. Acad. Physicians Assts. (state dir. 1974-80), Greater St. Louis Soc. Health Edn. and Tng.; mem. Am. Pub. Health Assn. Democrat. Lutheran. Lodge: Lions (pres. St. Louis Harmony chpt. 1980, bd. dirs. 1981—). Avocation: swimming. Home and Office: 1024 Beso Ct Saint Louis MO 63026

TRAVELLI, RENATO, radiologist; b. Rome, Mar. 13, 1931; s. Alessandro and Adelia (Ricci) T.; m. Charlotte Dorothea Schwieger, July 20, 1968; children: Eric, Irene, Elsa, Sara. MD, U. Rome, Italy, 1956. Intern Union Meml. Hosp., Balt., 1958-59; resident in radiology Albany (N.Y.) Hosp., 1960-61; fellow Mayo Found., Rochester, Minn., 1961-64; radiologist Holy Cross Hosp., Calgary, Alta., Can., 1966-67, St. Joseph Hosp., Milw., 1970-71, Luth. Hosp., La Crosse, Hosp., 1981—. Served as commd. USNR, 1968-70. Mem. Am. Coll. Radiology, AMA, Radiological Soc. N.Am. Episcopalian. Office: Gundersen Clinic 1836 South Ave La Crosse WI 56601

TRAVIS, EUGENE CHARLES, investment banker; b. Chgo., May 2, 1920; s. Eugene Charles and Claire Patricia T.; m. Grace Elizabeth Koerner, Dec. 6, 1944; children—Richard Bruce, Diane Grace, Patricia Kay, Eugene Charles, Michael Allen. M.B.A., U. Chgo., 1953. Mcpl. bond analyst and trader Continental Ill. Nat. Bank, Chgo., 1937-49; mcpl. bond underwriting and trader Harriman Ripley, Chgo., 1949-60; dir. inst. sales and mcpl. bond dept. Hayden, Stone & Co., Chgo., 1960-62, v.p., 1962-63, div. v.p., dir., 1963-69, dir. nat. inst. sales, 1966-69; 1st v.p. Shearson, Hammill & Co., San Francisco, 1969-71; chmn., mng. dir. Travis, Weiner & Housman, San Francisco, 1972-74; mng. dir. Mesirow & Co., Chgo., 1974—; founder The Exempters, 1949; gov. Midwest Stock Exchange, Chgo., 1966-70. Served with USNR, 1944-46. Mem. Am. Fin. Assn., Newcomen Soc. Clubs: Attic, Union League, Bond of Chgo., Mcpl. Bond of Chgo. Lodges: Masons, Shriners. Home: 754 N Waukegan Rd Lake Forest IL 60045 Office: Mesirow & Co 135 S LaSalle St Chicago IL 60603

TRAVIS, J(AMES) EDWARD, III, small business owner; b. St. Charles, Mo., Mar. 20, 1934; s. J. Edward Jr. and Margaret Gray (Martin) T.; m. Irene Blanchard Cariffe, Dec. 29, 1962; children: J. Edward IV, Andrew C., Lynn I. BSBA, U. Mo., 1956. Mgr. prodn. Lynch and Hart Advtg., St. Louis, 1958-61; sales rep. Dictaphone Corp., St. Louis, 1961-66; br. mgr. Dictaphone Corp., Paterson, N.J., 1966-68; dist. mgr. Dictaphone Corp., N.Y.C., 1968-72; dir. mktg. and sales bldg. services div. ITT, Cleve., 1972-73; owner, pres. Mgmt. Recruiters West County, Inc., St. Louis, 1973—; bd. dirs. Gen. Automatic Transfer Co., St. Louis. Pres. Westchester and Nipher Sch. PTA's, Kirkwood, Mo., 1975-77. Served to 1st lt. U.S. Army, 1956-58, Korea. Mem. Mo. Assn. Personnel Cons. (bd. dirs. 1976, 79), U. Mo. Alumni Assn. (chmn. athletic com. 1981—, mem. intercollegiate athletic com. 1981—), v.p. exec. com. 1984—). Republican. Clubs: Algonquin Golf (St. Louis), Mizzou Quarterback (St. Louis) (pres. 1977-85). Office: Mgmt Recruiters West County Inc 200 Fabricator Dr Saint Louis MO 63026

TRAVIS, LAWRENCE ALLAN, accountant; b. Bloomington, Ill., Sept. 17, 1942; s. Willard Burns and Florence May (Harvey) T.; m. Katy Quinones, Apr. 4, 1965 (div. Feb. 1978); children: Lawrence A. Jr., Matthew B. BS in Bus. Edn., Ill. State U., 1968; MA in Pub. Adminstrn., Sangamon State U., Springfield, Ill., 1976. CPA, Ill. Staff acct. Alexander Grant & Co., Chgo., 1969; internal auditor State Farm Ins., Bloomington, 1969-73; dep. dir. Ill. Dept. Ins., Springfield, 1973-74; mgr. auditing Ill. Auditor Gen., Springfield, 1974-81; pres. Lawrence Travis & Co., P.C., Virden and Springfield, Ill., 1979—; v.p. Virden Broadcasting Corp., 1986—; pres., bd. dirs. Travco, Inc., Virden, 1985—; v.p., bd. dirs. Miller Communications, Inc., Virden, 1987—. County coordinator Dan Walker for Gov., Bloomington, 1971-72; bd. dirs. Ill. Common Cause, Springfield, 1975. Mem. Am. Inst. CPA's, Assn. Govt. Accts., Ill. CPA Soc. (legis. contact 1981—). Democrat. Roman Catholic. Avocation: sports. Home: 2409 Idlewild Dr Springfield IL 62704 Office: Lawrence Travis & Co P C 701 S Grand Ave W Springfield IL 62704

TRAXLER, BOB, congressman; b. Kawkawlin, Mich., July 21, 1931; children: Tamara, Bradley, Sarah. B.A. in Polit. Sci, Mich. State U., 1953; LL.B., Detroit Coll. Law, 1959. Bar: Mich. bar. Asst. prosecutor Bay County, 1960-62; individual practice; mem. Mich. Ho. of Reps., 1963-74, majority floor leader, 1965-66, chmn. judiciary com., 1969-74; mem. 93d-100th Congresses from 8th Dist. Mich., 1973—. Served with U.S. Army, 1954-56. Mem. Am., Mich., Bay County bar assns. Democrat. Episcopalian. Office: US Ho of Reps 2366 Rayburn House Office Bldg Washington DC 20515 *

TREASH, HAROLD THEODORE, fund raising executive; b. Pontiac, Ill., Feb. 14, 1918; s. Walter Alden and Nanie Rosetta (Aker) T.; m. Sally Leona Crader, Apr. 26, 1942; children—Myra Catherine, Anya Rae. B.Ed., Ill. State U., 1941. Program dir YMCA, Springfield, Ill., 1941-44, program edn. dir., Boston, 1944-51, program edn. dir., Hartford, Conn., 1951-54; field rep. Ward Dreshman & Reinhardt, Inc., N.Y.C., 1954-64, v.p., N.Y.C., Worthington, Ohio, 1964-73, pres., Worthington, 1973-81, chmn. bd., 1981—. Mem. Am. Assn. Fund Raising Counsel (bd. dirs.). Republican. Mem. United Ch. of Christ. Avocation: tennis. Office: Ward Dreshman & Reinhardt Inc 6660 N High St Worthington OH 43085

TREBBY, JAMES PAUL, accounting educator; b. Milw., May 6, 1949; s. Eugene Paul and Lois Elaine (Schuster) T.; m. Janis Gail Conrad, Sept. 19, 1981. BS, Marquette U., 1971, MBA, 1973; D of Bus. Adminstrn., U. Ky., 1982. CPA, Wis. Asst. prof. acctg. U. Ky., Lexington, 1981-83, Marquette U., Milw., 1983—. Author: State Auditor Handbook, 1984, Instructor's Resource Manual to Accompany Accounting Today, 1986; contbr. articles to profl. jours. Mem. Am. Inst. CPA's, Am. Acctg. Assn. (doctoral consortium fellow 1980), Am. Taxation Assn., Nat. Assn. Accts. (Norman A. Schley Meml. Fund Manuscript award 1985), Wis. Inst. CPA's. Republican. Roman Catholic. Avocations: golf, racquetball, jogging. Home: 1384 Harris Dr Waukesha WI 53186 Office: Marquette U Coll Bus Adminstrn Milwaukee WI 53233

TREBELHORN, THOMAS LYNN, professional baseball team manager; b. Portland, Oreg., Jan. 27, 1948; children: Robert, Jeffrey, Christopher. BA, Portland State U. Player various minor league teams, 1970-75, mgr., 1975-86; mgr. Milw. Brewers, Am. League, 1986—. Office: Milwaukee Brewers Baseball Team Milwaukee County Stadium Milwaukee WI 53214 *

TREDINNICK, KIM LEIGH, accountant; b. Dodgeville, Wis., May 24, 1952; s. Donald Francis and Cathryn Irene (Jewell) T.; m. Toni Jane Cerutti, Dec. 23, 1972; children: Christopher, Matthew. BBA in Acctg., U. Wis., Madison, 1974. CPA, Wis. Staff acct. Virchow, Krause & Co., Madison, 1972-78, ptnr., 1978—. Mem. allocations panel United Way of Dane county, Madison, 1982—. Recipient Fayette H. Elwell scholarship U. Wis., Madison, 1973. Mem. Am. Inst. CPA's (mem. peer review com. 1982-85, tech. issues com. 1986—, Elijah Watt Sells Hon. Mention, 1974), Continental Assn. CPA's (mem. acctg. and auditing com. 1981—), Wis. Inst. CPA's, Wis. Mcpl. Treas. Assn. Roman Catholic. Lodges: Rotary, Optomists (sec., treas.). Avocations: golf, skiing. Home: 7041 Bridgman Rd De Forest WI 53532

TREGENZA, WILLIAM KENNETH, retired obstretician gynecologist, executive; b. Detroit, July 2, 1908; S. William Edward and Carrie (Evans) T.; m. Helen Robertson Cree, May 11, 1935; children: Nancy L. Tregenza Little, William Kenneth Jr., Arthur Robert, Donald. BA, Wayne U., 1930, MD, 1935. Pvt. practice ob-gyn. Detroit, 1937-75; pres., chmn. bd. Can. Engring. Co., Windsor, Ontario, 1976—. Served with USNR, 1945-46, PTO. Fellow: Am. Coll. Ob-Gyns., Am. Coll. Surgeons; mem. Mich. State Med. Soc. (50 Yr. award 1985), Oakland County Med. Soc. Republican. Presbyterian. Club: Orchard Lake Country (Mich.); Tam O'Shanter (Fla.); Lodge: Masons. Avocations: photography, golf. Office: Canadian Engring & Tool Co, PO Box 7039, Windsor, ON Canada H9C3Y6

TREIBLE, JAMES CHARLES, motor manufacturing executive; b. Milw., July 1, 1932; s. James Harlow and Lauretta Otilia (Schultz) T.; m. Mary Nell Bachhuber, Feb. 11, 1956; children: Timothy, Patricia, Peter, Kathleen. BSEE, Marquette U., 1955. Sales rep. Allis-Chalmers, Pitts., 1964-65; sales mgr. large AC motors Louis Allis div. MagneTek, Inc., Milw., 1965-68, mgr. sales, 1968-71, dir. planning and devel., 1971, v.p. devel. and mktg., 1971-86, sr. v.p., gen. mgr., 1986—. Mem. Pres.' Council Marquette U., Indsl. Adv. Bd. Marquette U. Coll. Engring. Mem. Marquette U. Engring. Alumni Assn. (pres. 1979-80, service award 1986). Roman Catholic. Office: Louis Allis div MagneTek Inc 427 E Stewart St Milwaukee WI 53201

TREINAVICZ, KATHRYN MARY, programmer analyst, computer consultant; b. Brockton, Mass., Nov. 25, 1957; d. Ralph Clement and Frances Elizabeth (O'Leary) T. B.S., Salem State Coll., Mass., 1980. Tchr., Brockton Pub. Schs., 1980-81; instr. Quincy CETA Inc., Mass., 1981-82; programmer systems Architects Inc., Randolph, Mass., 1982, programmer analyst, Dayton, Ohio, 1982-84; sr. programmer analyst System Devel. Corp., Dayton, 1984-86; project mgr. Unysis Inc., Dayton, 1986— . Mem. Nat. Assn. Female Execs. Democrat. Roman Catholic. Avocations: Steven King novels; needlepoint; knitting; crocheting.

TREJBAL, HELEN VICTORIA, hospital administrator; b. St. Louis, Oct. 7, 1917; d. Victor and Theresa (Valdhans) T. Student Shurtleff Coll., 1934-36, Washington U., St. Louis, 1945-60. Legal sec., St. Louis, 1936-40; sec. to adminstr. Mo. Bapt. Hosp., St. Louis, 1940-50, adminstrv. asst., 1950-72, asst. adminstr., 1972-80, v.p., 1980-85. Mem. Literacy Council of Greater St. Louis, 1978-84, sec., 1981-82, tutor, 1979; Sunday sch. tchr., Southwest Bapt. Ch., St. Louis, 1936—, co-chmn. stewardship com., 1979-80, chmn., 1979-80, 82-85, chmn. constn. com., 1979-81, 82-86; Mo. rep. stewardship commn. So. Bapt. Conv., 1975-83, vol. missionary to Alaska, Home Mission Bd., 1982, Colo., 1985, Ariz., 1986, Shriner's Hosp. for Crippled Children, 1986—, ARC Blood Donor Program, 1986—; mem. rev. com. Mo. Bapt. Conv., 1979-82, mem. exec. bd. Woman's Missionary Union, 1958-64; pres. Mo. Bapt. Bus. Women's Fedn., 1958-61, dir. Sunday sch. tng., 1945-47; life mem. Mo. Bapt. Hosp. Aux., 1970—; mem. Mo. Bapt. Hosp. Pacesetters, 1972—. Mem. Am. Hosp. Assn. Pub. Relations Soc., Southside Bus. and Profl. Women's Club (named outstanding career woman 1982). Lodge: Soroptimists Internat.

TREJO, JOSÉ DIAZ, accountant; b. Carrizo Springs, Tex., Feb. 11, 1948; s. Elisandro Briones and Maria Trinidad (Diaz) T. AA, Coll. DuPage, 1969; BA, No. Ill. U., 1971. CPA, Ill. Revenue acctg. and banking Spector Industries, Inc., Bensenville, Ill., 1977-81; revenue auditor State of Ill., Springfield, 1982-84; pvt. practice acctg. Itasca, Ill., 1985—; cons. in field. Mem. Am. Inst. CPA's (tax div. 1986-87, personal fin. planning div. 1986-87), Ill. CPA Soc. (various coms.). Roman Catholic. Avocations: reading, writing, outdoor activities, social activities. Home: 320 N Elm St Itasca IL 60143

TREMBLEY, SUSAN JANE, science educator, paleontologist; b. Wadsworth, Ohio, Feb. 5, 1931; d. Gilbert Peter and Miley Caroline (Witchey) Glossen; m. Robert Joseph Barcus, Apr. 9, 1950 (dec. June 1967); children—Gilbert, Hugh, Paul; m. 2d, Marion Henry Trembley, Nov. 11, 1968. B.A. magna cum laude, U. Akron, 1971, M.S., 1974. Cert. tchr., Ohio. Research asst. Yoder Bros. Inc., Barberton, Ohio, 1959-65; teaching asst. paleontology Cleve. Community Coll., 1972-73; teaching asst. geology, asst. to dir. environ. studies dept. U. Akron (Ohio), 1973-77; tchr. sci. Stow (Ohio) City Schs., 1977—; environ. cons. Harrison Hills Assn., Carrollton,

Ohio, 1974-76, pres., 1976—. Named tchr. of Yr., Stow Workman High Sch., 1981-82; Martha Holden Jennings grantee, 1972; U. Akron scholar, 1969-71; Jennings Found. scholar, 1981-82. Mem. Geol. Soc. Am., Nat. Sci. Tchrs. Assn., Nat. Educators Orgn., Ohio Acad. Sci., Stow Tchrs. Assn., Sigma Xi, Phi Alpha Theta. Office: Stow City Schs 3732 Darrow Rd Stow OH 44224

TRENNEL, LAWRENCE WILLIAM, accountant; b. East Cleveland, Ohio, May 21, 1955; s. Anthony John and Jennie (Perko) T.; m. Bette Lou Witherspoon, May 12, 1984; 1 child, Lauren Ivana. BBA, Cleve. State U., 1977; MA in Human Resource Mgmt., Pepperdine U., 1981. CPA, Ohio. Commd. 2d lt. USMC, 1974, advanced through grades to capt., resigned, 1981, active Res., 1981—; internal auditor USMC, Okinawa, Japan, 1977-78; comptroller, budget officer USMC, New Orleans, 1979-81; internal auditor Med. Mutual div. Blue Shield, Cleve., 1981-82, supr. cost and budget, 1982-84; fin. analyst Cleve. Pneumatic, 1984-85; ptnr. Varner, LaCorte & Trennel, Willoughby, Ohio, 1985—; instr. Los Angeles Community Coll., Okinawa, 1978, Harding Bus. Coll., Maple Heights, Ohio, 1985-86, MTI Bus. Sch., Cleve., 1987—. Mem. Am. Soc. Mil. Comptrollers, Am. Inst. CPA's, Ohio Soc. CPA's, Am. Legion, Nat. Rifle Assn. Republican. Episcopalian. Club: Euclid Rifle and Hunting (trustee 1985—). Lodge: Slovene Nat. Benefit Soc. (sec., treas. #614 1984—). Avocations: baseball, golf, running, camping, investments. Office: Varner LaCorte & Trennel Smart Bldg #201 4145 Erie St Willoughby OH 44094

TREPPLER, IRENE ESTHER, state senator; b. St. Louis County, Mo., Oct. 13, 1926; d. Martin H. and Julia C. (Bender) Hagemann; student Meramec Community Coll., 1972; m. Walter J. Treppler, Aug. 18, 1950; children—John M., Steven A., Diane V., Walter W. Payroll chief USAF Aero. Chart Plant, 1943-51; enumerator U.S. Census Bur., St. Louis, 1960, crew leader, 1970; mem. Mo. Ho. of Reps., Jefferson City, 1972-84; mem. Mo. Senate, Jefferson City, 1985—. Mem. Oak-Le-Mehl Republican Club, Concord Twp. Rep. Club; alt. del. Rep. Nat. Conv., 1976, 84; charter mem., bd. dirs. Windsor Community Ctr. Mem. Nat. Order Women Legislators (rec. sec. 1981-82, pres. 1985), Nat. Fedn. Rep. Women. Republican. Mem. Ch. of Christ. Office: Mo State Senate State Capitol Bldg Room 424 Jefferson City MO 65101

TRESS, RUDOLPH JOSEPH, bank executive; b. Detroit, June 24, 1941; s. Camillo B. and Evelyn O. (Scarton) T.; m. Carole M. Kendziorski, Jan. 13, 1967; children: James R., Kimberly Ann, Theresa M. BBA, Detroit Inst. Tech., 1965. Mgr. Great Scott Supermarkets, Detroit, 1958-65; bank property officer City Nat. Bank, Detroit, 1965-73; 2d v.p. Nat. Bank of Southfield, Mich., 1973-80; bank property officer Mfrs. Nat. Bank Detroit, 1980—. Served to lt. col. USAFR, 1965—. Roman Catholic. Avocations: fishing, golf, woodworking crafts. Office: Mfrs Bank Detroit PO Box 659 Detroit MI 48231-0659

TRESTER, JAMES MATTHEW, accountant; b. Homestead, Fla., Jan. 17, 1961; s. Walter Carl and Janice (Kaiser) T.; m. Holly M. Mitchell, July 14, 1984. BBA, W. Wis., Eau Claire, 1983. CPA, Wis. Tax auditor U.S. Dept. Revenue, Milw., 1983-86; sr. tax acct. Seidman & Seidman, Milw., 1986—. Mem. Am. Inst. CPA's, Wis. Inst. CPA's. Lutheran. Avocations: running, skiing, golf, water skiing, coin collecting. Home: 1180 Sunnycrest Dr Waukesha WI 53186 Office: Seidman & Seidman 300 E Kilbourn Milwaukee WI 53202

TRETHEWAY, BARTON GLENN, marketing professional; b. Bakersfield, Calif., July 3, 1945; s. Raymond Lester Jr. and Ruth Elizabeth (Bowen) T. BS, Calif State U., Chico, 1968; MBA, Ind. U., 1970. Nat. mktg. mgr. Sears Roebuck, Chgo., 1970—. Mem., guide Am. Found. for Blind Skiing, Chgo., 1976; v.p., bd. dirs. Lawrence Hall Sch. for Boys, Chgo., 1979; met. bd. United Charities, Chgo., 1984; mem. Council of Fgn. and Domestic Affairs, Chgo., 1985; chmn. spl. events Mental Health Assn. Chgo., 1986. Served to 1st lt. USAR, 1970-76. Named one of Outstanding Young Men Am., 1980. Mem. Connoisseur Internat., Brotherhood Knights of the Vine (vice commdr. 1982). Republican. Presbyterian. Club: Saddle and Cycle (Chgo.). Avocations: outdoor sports, symphony, opera, theater, wine and fine food. Office: Sears Roebuck Sears Tower Chicago IL 60684

TRETTER, ANN DALY, communications and marketing counsel; b. Atlanta, July 14, 1945; d. Emmett Forrest and Dorris (Burnette) Gardner; m. Clayton Thomas Tretter, Jan. 13, 1975 (dec. Apr. 1978); 1 child, Stacey. Student, Barry Coll., 1962-63; B in Journalism, U. Mo., 1967. Reporter, editor St. Louis Globe-Democrat, 1967-69; counselor Fleishman-Hillard, Inc. Pub. Relations, St. Louis, 1969-74; pres. Tretter Communications, Venice, Fla., 1974-78; v.p., account exec. Frank Block Assocs., St. Louis, 1977-78; v.p. Aaron D. Cushman, St. Louis, 1978-81; mng. ptnr. Tretter-Gorman, Inc. Pub. Relations, St. Louis, 1981—. Author: (book) Island of the Mind, 1977. Campaign dir. St. Louis County Library tax increase, St. Louis, 1983, Chesterfield (Mo.) Fire Dist. bond issue, 1984, Hayner Pub. Library expansion vote, Alton, Ill., 1986; founding dir. State of Ill. Com., bd. dirs. St. Louis Sci. Ctr., 1986—, Vis. Nurse Assn. Greater St. Louis, 1985—. Recipient Leadership award St. Louis YWCA, 1985, Leadership award Danforth Found., 1980.; named Businessperson of Week, Sta. KEZK, St. Louis, 1986. Mem. Nat. Assn. Women Bus. Owners, Women In Communication, Inc. (pres. 1979-80, Ruth Philpott Collins award 1978, 79), Pub. Relations Soc. Am. (Silver Anvil program 1981). Avocations: skiing, sailing. Office: Tretter-Gorman Inc 711 N 11th St Saint Louis MO 63101

TRIBBEY, CHARLES LEE, optometrist; b. Peoria, Ill., Apr. 14, 1951; s. Charles L. and Mary E. (Turner) T.; m. Diana J. Michaels, Sept. 4, 1976; children: Leah Mary, Adam Charles. BS in Zoology, Loyola U., Chgo., 1973; BS in Visual Sci., So. Calif. Coll. Optometry, 1977, D of Optometry, 1979. Pvt. practice optometry Menominee, Mich., 1979080, Modesto, Calif., 1980-84; optometrist Danville (Ill.) Eye Clinic, 1985—. Mem. adv. com. Nursing Home Patient Advocacy, Modesto, 1981-84; co-chmn. adv. com. Special Edn. Planning Assn., Modesto, 1982-84; participant Leadership Danville, 1986—. Mem. Am. Optometric Assn., Ill. Optometric Assn., E. Cen. Optometric Soc. Roman Catholic. Lodge: Lions (v.p. 1985—). Avocations: tennis, racquetball, canoeing, swimming, securities analysis. Home: 217 Denvale Dr Danville IL 61832 Office: Danville Eye Clinic 1104 N Vermilion Danville IL 61832

TRIBBLE, RICHARD WALTER, oil and gas company executive, investment executive; b. San Diego, Oct. 19, 1948; s. Walter Perrin and Catherine Janet (Miller) T.; m. Joan Catherine Sliter, June 26, 1980. B.S., U. Ala.-Tuscaloosa, 1968; student Gulf Coast Sch. Drilling Practices, U. Southwestern La., 1977. Stockbroker, Shearson, Am. Express, Washington, 1971-76; ind. oil and gas investment sales, Falls Church, Va., 1976-77; pres. Monroe & Keusink, Inc., Falls Church, Columbus, Ohio, 1977—. Served to cpl. USMC, 1969-71. Mem. Va. Oil and Gas Assn. (charter), Ohio Oil and Gas Assn., Soc. Petroleum Engrs. (assoc.), Ohio Geol. Soc. Am. Republican. Methodist. Club: Columbus (Columbus).

TRICKLER, SALLY JO, technical artist; b. Burlington, Iowa, Jan. 7, 1948; d. Frank Joseph and Florence Christina (Hein) Koehler; m. James Edward Trickler, Nov. 4, 1967; children: Brenda Jo, Michael Edward. AA, Southeastern Community Coll., West Burlington, Iowa, 1976; BA, Western Ill. U., 1987. Draftsman Iowa Army Ammunition Plant, Middleton, 1967-73; tech. artist III J.I. Case Co., Burlington, 1973—. Mem. pub. relations com. United Way, Burlington, 1975, chmn. pub. relations 1976-77, art designer, 1987. Mem. Burlington Engrs. Club (v.p. 1974-75, pres. 1975-76, chmn. high sch. counseling com. on career days, 1977-80), Allegro Motor Home Club Iowa, Phi Kappa Phi. Roman Catholic. Club: Good Sam (Big River Sams, Iowa) (sec./treas. 1985-87). Avocations: architectural drawing, landscaping, photography, travel, reading. Home: Rural Rt 1 Box 121 Burlington IA 52601 Office: JI Case Co 1930 Des Moines Ave Burlington IA 52601

TRIGG, SHARI JENELL, sales account executive; b. Lawton, Okla., Sept. 21, 1957; d. Jasper Alphonso and Aurora Lou (Cooke) T. B.S., Northwestern U., 1978. Asst. mgr. The Ltd., Chgo., 1978; advt. asst. Bentley, Barnes & Lynn Advt., Chgo., 1978-79; account mgmt. trainee Leo Burnett Advt., Chgo., 1979-80; sales account exec. WMAQ-TV NBC Channel 5, Chgo., 1980—; spl. events com. mem. Broadcast Advt. Club Chgo., 1981—, also bd. dirs. Mem. Chgo. Urban League, 1982-84; mem. employer adv. bd. Project Skil-Disadvantaged Youth Employment Service, Chgo., 1982-83, chair adv. bd., 1983—, pres. employer aux. bd., 1982-86; co-chmn. Friends of the El-Commuter Group, Chgo., 1978; trustee Lawrence Hall Sch. for boys, 1985-86; pres. The Lollipop League, 1987. Recipient Outstanding Leadership award YWCA Met. Chgo., 1982, named Outstanding Achiever of Industry, 1983, One of Outstanding Young Women of Am, 1984. Mem. Nat. Assn. Female Execs., Delta Sigma Theta, Inc. (mem planning com. 75th anniversary celebration, nat. mktg. rep. 1987—) Club: NBC Variety Soc. (com. chmn. 1983). Democrat. Unitarian. Office: WMAQ-TV NBC Chgo Merchandise Mart Plaza Chicago IL 60654

TRIGGIANI, LEONARD VINCENT, corporate executive; b. Paterson, N.J., June 24, 1930; s. Mario and Theresa (Tierno) T.; m. Aldona Witko, Apr. 24, 1965; 1 son, Paul. B.A., Drew U., 1952; M.S., Catholic U. Am., 1954, Ph.D., 1958; postgrad., Duke U. Sch. Medicine, 1956. Instr. Cath. U. Am., Washington, 1958-60; with research div. W.R. Grace & Co., Columbia, Md., 1960-84; sr. research chemist, research supr. W.R. Grace & Co., 1960-66, mgr.-dir. nuclear research, 1967-72, dir. inorganic research, 1972-73, dir. indsl. research, 1973-74, pres. research div., 1974-83, v.p. co., 1978-84, v.p. for tech. ventures, 1983-84; exec. v.p., chief tech. officer B.F. Goodrich Co., Akron, Ohio, 1984—; symposium chmn. nuclear fuels, 1967, 70. Author and patentee in field. Bd. dirs. Montgomery Gen. Hosp. Recipient Alumni Achievement award Cath. U. Am., 1978, Drew U., 1978. Mem. Am. Chem. Soc. (chmn. corp. assocs. com. 1979-81), Soc. Chem. Industry, Am. Nuclear Soc., Indsl. Research Inst., Am. Inst. Chem. Engrs., Chem. Industry Inst. Toxicology (dir., finance com.), AAAS, Electrochem. Soc., Licensing Execs. Soc., Comml. Devel. Assn., Sigma Xi. Methodist. Club: Chemists (N.Y.C.). Home: 36 Pinewood Ln Hudson OH 44236 Office: 9921 Brecksville Rd Brecksville OH 44141

TRIKILIS, EMMANUEL MITCHELL, manufacturing company executive; b. Sacramento, Jan. 14, 1916; s. Michael and Maria (Coulias) T.; m. Harriet Beroth Fields, Apr. 18, 1944. BS, Youngstown Coll., 1938; postgrad., Cleve. Coll., 1952-53, U. Mich., 1963-64. Pres. Buckeye Novelty Co., Youngstown, 1938-41; metall. asst. Republic Steel corp., Youngstown, 1937-44; investigative reporter Indsl. Commn. of Ohio, Columbus, Cleve., 1944-61; pres. Gen. Nucleonics, Inc., Columbus, Cleve., 1961—, Genesec. Devel. Corp., Brunswick, Ohio, 1973—; cons. Pro-Arts, Inc., Medina, Ohio, 1976-80; bd. dirs. Bio-Graphic, Inc., Chippewa Lake, Ohio. Patentee in field (60). Recipient 1st prize design excellence award Design News, 1980, Excellence in Design award Aluminum Assn. Extrusion Council, Washington, 1980. Mem. Soc. Mfg. Engrs. (sr.). Avocations: swimming, basketball, baseball, soccer, writing. Home: PO Box 109 Hinckley OH 44233 Office: Gen Nucleonics Inc PO Box 815 1545 W 130th St Brunswick OH 44212

TRIMBLE, KAREN ILLINGWORTH, career consulting executive; b. Lafayette, Ind., June 16, 1954; d. Robert LaVerne and Betty Mae (Long) Illingworth; m. Tony L. Trimble, Aug. 30, 1975. BS in Office Adminstrn. cum laude, Ind. State U., 1975; MBA, Butler U., 1986. Sec. to dir. sales The Studio Press, Inc., Indpls., 1976-78; exec. sec. to pres. Indpls. Conv. and Visitors Bur., 1978-79, conv. services mgr., 1979-80, bus. mgr., 1980-83, dir. bus. office, 1983—; cons. Career Cons. Indpls., Inc., 1983, office mgr., 1984—; instr. Clark Coll., Indpls., 1979-82. Active United Way campaigns, 1978, 80; V.I.P. host Pan Am Games, 1987. Named one of Outstanding Young Women Am., 1986. Mem. Am. Bus. Women's Assn. (enrollment event com. 1978, rec. sec. 1979), Exec. Women Internat. (membership com., audit com.). Roman Catholic. Office: 107 N Pennsylvania Suite 400 Indianapolis IN 46204

TRIPODI, MARY ANN, physical education educator; b. Massillon, Ohio, Feb. 3, 1944; d. Domenico A. and Margaret P. (Cicchinelli) T. B.S., Kent State U., 1966, M. Ed., 1970, postgrad., 1981—. Instr. phys. edn. Canton (Ohio) South High Sch., 1966-69; instr. health and phys. edn. Notre Dame Coll., Cleve., 1969-71; instr. health and phys. edn. U. Akron (Ohio), 1971-80, coordinator women's sports clubs, 1971-79, asst. prof. health and phys. edn., 1980—, asst. to dir. athletics, 1979-85, asst. athletic dir., 1985—, head coach women's volleyball, 1971-75, head coach women's basketball, 1971-81, dir. coaching workshops, 1981—; cons. Ohio Female Athletic Found., 1982-83. Mem. AAHPER and Dance, Nat. Assn. Phys. Edn. Coll. Women, Fin. Aid and Ethics and Eligibility (chmn. 1974-80), Midwest Assn. Phys. Edn. Coll. Women, Ohio Assn. Health, Phys. Edn., Recreation and Dance, Ohio College Assn. (chmn. elect curriculum div. women's phys. edn. sect. 1971, mem.-at-large 1972), Ohio Assn. Intercollegiate Sports for Women (N.E. dist. commr. 1974-77), Ohio Female Athletic Found. (trustee, v.p.), Cleve. Women's Phys. Edn. and Recreation Assn., Pi Lambda Theta, Delta Psi Kappa. Roman Catholic. Contbr. articles to profl. jours. Clubs: University, Touchdown, Varsity A Assn. (Akron, Ohio). Home: 1303 Cedarwood Dr Kent OH 44240 Office: Jar Annex U Akron Akron OH 44325

TRIPP, CARLTON ELI, SR., architectural and marine engineer executive; b. Huntington, W.Va., Apr. 4, 1918; s. Walter Joseph and Alta May (Squire) T.; m. Frances Elaine Symons, Apr. 28, 1948; 1 child, Carlton E. Jr. BS, USN Acad., 1941; MSE, U. Mich., 1950. Commd. to 2d lt. USMC, 1941, advanced through grades to capt., 1943; engr. Ingalls Ship Bldg. Corp., Pascagoula, Miss., 1950-51; chief engr. marine Cons. and Designers Inc., Cleve., 1951-55, v.p., 1955-59, pres., 1959-85; chmn. bd. 1985—. Contbr. tech. papers to profl. publ. Recipient Sperry medal, 1985. Mem. Am. Soc. Naval Engrs., Soc. Naval Architecture and Marine Engrs. (chmn. bd. Great Lakes chpt. 1962-63). Club: Athletic (Cleve.). Home: 3321 Hilside Rd Cleveland OH 44131

TRIPP, LUCIUS CHARLES, neurosurgeon, automobile manufacturing company medical director; b. Memphis, Nov. 10, 1942; s. Luke Samuel and Dorothy Mae (Watson) T.; m. Delores Christine Whitus, July 23, 1963; 1 child, Felicia. BS in Biology, U. Detroit, 1964; MD, Wayne State U., 1968; MPH, U. Mich., 1983. Diplomate Am. Bd. Preventive Medicine. Intern Detroit Gen. Hosp., 1968-69; resident in surgery Wayne State U. Hosps., Detroit, 1969-70, resident in neurosurgery, 1970-74; asst. med. dir. gear and axel div. Gen. Motors Corp., Detroit, 1974-75; med. dir. spring and bumper div. Gen. Motors Corp., Livonia, Mich., 1975-77; med. dir. proving grounds div. Gen. Motors Corp., 1977-80, med. dir. assembly div., 1980-85; med. dir. Buick, Oldsmobile and Cadillac div. Gen. Motors Corp., Warren, Mich., 1985—; co-owner The Wells Group, Inc., 1983—; mem. Pres.' Com. on Employment of Handicapped; group med. dir. BOC Gen. Motors Corp., 1985—; med. dir. Gen. Motors Tech. Ctr., 1987—. Contbr. articles to profl. jours. Exec. bd. Detroit Hearing and Speech Ctr., 1978—; chairperson handicapped scouting Boy Scouts Am., 1985—. Served to maj. U.S. Army. Fellow Am. Occupational Med. Assn.; mem. AMA, Am. Assn. Automotive Medicine, Mich. State Med. Soc., Am. Acad. Occupational Medicine, Mich. Occupational Med. Assn., Detroit Indsl. Physician's Club, Assn. Labor-Mgmt. Adminstrs. and Cons. on Alcoholism. Avocations: boating, fishing, skiing, scuba diving, jogging. Home: 23060 Britner Birmingham MI 48010 Office: Gen Motors Corp BOC Div 30009 Van Dyke Warren MI 48093

TRIPP, THOMAS NEAL, lawyer, political consultant; b. Evanston, Ill., June 19, 1942; s. Gerald Frederick and Kathryn Ann (Siebold) T.; m. Ellen Marie Larrimer, Apr. 16, 1966; children: David Larrimer, Bradford Douglas, Corinne Catherine. BA cum laude, Mich. State U., 1964; JD, George Washington U., 1967. Bar: Ohio 1967, U.S. Ct. Mil. Appeals 1968, U.S. Supreme Ct. 1968. Sole practice, Columbus, Ohio, 1969—; real estate developer, Columbus, 1969—; chmn. bd. Black Sheep Enterprises, Columbus, 1969—; vice chmn. bd. Sun Valley-Elkhorn Assn., Idaho, 1983-85, chmn., 1986-87, chmn. 1987—; vice chmn. Sawtooth Sports, Ketchum, Idaho, 1983-85; legal counsel Wallace F. Ackley Co., Columbus, 1973—; bd. dirs. KWRP Broadcasting Corp., 1986—; presiding judge Ohio Mock Trial Competition, 1986-87. Trustee Americans for Responsible Govt., Washington, GOPAC; mem. Bob Dole for Pres. Nat. Fin. Com., 1987-88; mem. Peace Corps Adv. Council, 1981-85; mem. U.S. Commn. on Trade Policy and Negotiations, 1985—; campaign mgr., fin. chmn. Charles Rockwell Saxbe, Ohio Ho. of Reps., 1974, 76, 78, 80; campaign mgr. George Bush for Pres., 1980, nat. dep. field dir., 1980; mem. alumni admissions council Mich. State U., 1984—; regional co-chmn. Reagan-Bush, 1984, mem. nat. fin. com., 1984; mem. Victory '84 Fin. Com. Served to capt. U.S. Army, 1967-69. Fellow Pi Sigma Alpha; mem. Phi Delta Phi. Republican. Avocations: swimming, tennis, skiing, writing, politic essays. Home: 5420 Clark State Rd Gahanna OH 43230

TRISCHLER, FLOYD D., real estate executive, consultant; b. Pitts., Aug. 31, 1929; s. Edward C. and Margaret (Sirlin) T.; m. Gloria N. Fusting, June 30, 1951; children: Thomas J., John D., Annette M., Nannette L., Rene L., Denise M. BS, U. Pitts., 1951; postgrad. San Diego State U., 1953-56, postgrad. in bus. adminstrn., 1963-69. Cert. master real estate cons. Program dir. Whittaker Corp., San Diego, 1963-71; exec. v.p. Turner Devel., Indpls., 1971-73; pres. Guadalupe Developers, Inc., Indpls., 1973-78; pres. Iroquois Realty, Inc., Indpls., 1978—, also dir; cons. NASA, Huntsville, Ala., 1963-69, Rincon Indian Reservation, Escondido, Calif., 1969-71, Promotora Ritco Alpemex, Cancun, Mex., 1985. Author publs. Patentee in polymer chemistry. Vol. Central State Hosp., Indpls., 1984—; notary pub., Indpls., 1980—; mem. Scottish Rite Chorus; mem. nat. publicity com. Nat. Pow-wow VII, 1987. Mem. Nat. Assn. Home Builders, Indpls. Builders Assn., Indpls Bd. Realtors, Ind. Bd. Realtors, Nat. Assn. Real Estate Cons., Midwest Cherokee Alliance, VFW. Republican. Roman Catholic. Lodges: Masons, Tecumpseh. Home: 8249 Filly Ln Plainfield IN 46168 Office: Iroquois Realty Inc 8249 Filly Ln Plainfield IN 46168

TRIVEDI, HARISH SUMANCHANDRA, information scientist; b. Ahmedabad, Gujarat, India; came to U.S., 1968; s. Sumanchandra Manilal and Indu Bhogilal (Indu) T. BS in Econs., Statistics, U. Bombay, 1957, M in Econs., Polit. Sci., 1961, B in Law, 1962. Cert. library scientist, Bombay, 1966. Sub-editor Vyapar Fin. Newspaper, Bombay, 1962-63; research asst. The Times of India, Bombay, 1963-68, Mich. State U., East Lansing, 1968-69; dir. reference-research library Dayton (Ohio) Newspapers, Inc., 1969—. Contbr. articles to profl. jours. Chmn. India Found., Dayton, 1986—. Mem. Spl. Libraries Assn. (bd. dirs. newspaper div. 1977-78, 83-84, sec.-treas. newspaper div. 1978-80, chmn.-elect 1981-82, chmn. 1982-83, award of merit 1983), Am. Soc. Info. Sci., Assn. for Info. and Info Mgmt. Avocation: tennis. Home: 895 Kentshire Dr Centerville OH 45459 Office: Dayton Newspapers Inc 37 Ludlow St Dayton OH 45902

TRIVELLINI, BRUCE JOHN, dentist; b. Oak Park, Ill., Mar. 14, 1956; s. Spartaco and Ruth Ann (Janov) T.; m. Katherine Kubica Greene, June 23, 1979; 1 child, Scot Michael. BS, Loyola U., Chgo., 1978, DDS, 1982. Gen. practice dentistry Arlington Heights, Ill., 1982—; lectr. sci. programs ADA, San Francisco, 1985 Miami Valley Hosp., Dayton, Ohio, 1985, La. State U., New Orleans, 1986. Mem. Delta Sigma Delta (life). Office: 1614 W Central Rd #108 Arlington Heights IL 60005

TRIVERS, ANDREW JAMES, architect; b. Chattanooga, Tenn., July 22, 1946; s. Ira and Sarah Louise (Cohen) T.; children: Ian, Benjamin. BArch, Tulane U., 1968; MArch and Urban Design, Washington U., St. Louis, 1971. Registered architect, 1973. Architect Cambridge (Mass.) 7, 1969-70; project designer Hoffman Saur, St. Louis, 1972-74; pres. SRT Architects, St. Louis, 1975-82, Tivers Assocs., St. Louis, 1982—; speaker Nat. Housing World convention, St. Louis, 1985. Bd. dirs. Dance St. Louis, 1978-85, Delcrest Home for Aged, St. Louis, 1980-85; v.p., bd. dirs. Jewis Ctr. for Aged, St. Louis, 1981-85. Recipient Merit Design award Builder Mag., Louisville, 1981. Mem. AIA, Nat. Council Archtl. Registration Bds. Democrat. Jewish. Office: Trivers Assocs Architects 77 Maryland Plaza Saint Louis MO 63108

TROIANO, PAUL FRANCIS, metal company executive; b. Boston, July 31, 1937; s. Amadio and Helen (Akus) T.; m. Jeannette Marie Somma, July 2, 1960; children: Nancy, Thomas, John, Michael. BS, Northeastern U., 1960; PhD, MIT, 1964. Research chemist Cabot Corp., Cambridge, Mass., 1964-72; dir. research and devel. Cabot Corp., Billerica, Mass., 1972-78; ops. mgr. Cabot Corp., Boston, 1978-79; asst. gen. mgr. Cabot Corp., Tuscola, Ill., 1979-80, gen. mgr., 1980-85; group v.p. Cabot Corp., Kokomo, Ind., 1985-87; pres., chief exec. officer Haynes Internat., Inc., 1987—. Mem. Am. Chem. Soc., Am. Soc. Metals, Sigma Xi. Home: 5506 Four Mile Hill Dr Kokomo IN 46901

TROILO, MARK P., dentist; b. Emporia, Kans., Jan. 31, 1952; s. Lodorick P. and Irene T. (Ramanda) T.; m. Luisella M. Cole, May 16, 1981; 1 child, Zachary P. AS, Garden City Community Jr. Coll., 1972; BS in Biology, Kans. Newman Coll., 1974; DDS, Creighton U., 1978. Gen. practice dentistry Rose Hill, Kans., 1978—. Home: Box 98 Rose Hill KS 67133

TROMBLEY, ROBERT BENTHIEN, scientist; b. South Croydan, Surrey, England, Sept. 28, 1942; came to U.S., 1947; s. Roland Russel and Irene (Nielsen) T.; m. Lucille Ann Panetta, Feb. 23, 1973; 1 child, Katie Marie. BSEE, Lawrence Inst. Tech., 1965; LLB, LaSalle U., 1973; PhD, Dallas State Coll., 1974. Sr. engr. Chrysler Defense, Centerline, Mich., 1976-80; chief scientist Radiation Effects, Royal Oak, Mich., 1980-83, 85-86; sr. staff physicist Hughes Aircraft, Los Angeles, 1983-85; sr. tech. cons. Nastec Corp., Southfield, Mich., 1986—. Contbr. articles to profl. jours. Served to staff sgt. USAF, 1965-69. Mem. Nat. Model R.R. Assn. (vice chmn. 1983—), Great Lakes Maritime Inst. (bd. dirs. 1976-80, 87—). Avocation: model railroading. Home: 1227 Greenleaf Royal Oak MI 48067 Office: Nastec Corp 24681 Northwestern Hwy Southfield MI 48075

TROMBOLD, WALTER STEVENSON, supply company executive; b. Chanute, Kans., June 21, 1910; s. George John and Margaret (Stevenson) T.; m. Charlotte Elizabeth Kaufman, Dec. 28, 1941; children: Joan Kleitsch, Lynn Oliphant, Walter Steven, David George, Charles Phillip. BS in Bus., U. Kans., 1932; AA, Iola Jr. Coll., 1930; spl. degree, Balliol Coll., Oxford U., 1943. Asst. mgr. S.H. Kress & Co., 1932-38; counselor Penn Mut. Life Ins. Co., 1938-41; field mgr. Travelers Ins. Co., Kansas City, 1938-41; with Reid Supply Co., Wichita, Kans., Kansas City, Mo., Topeka, Kans. 1946-86, pres. Trombold Consultation Service, 1986—, also chmn. bd. dirs. Bd. dirs., officer YMCA, 1922—; merit badge councilor Boy Scouts Am.; bd. dirs. Camp Fire Girls; life mem. PTA, 1953—, pres., 1952; chmn. personnel adv. bd. City of Wichita (Kans.), 1956—; commr. Gen. Assembly Presbyn. Ch. USA, past deacon, elder, trustee; commr. Synods of Mid-Am., Presbytery of So. Kans.; assoc. chmn. Nat. Laymen's Bible Week, 1972-86. Served to lt. comdr. USN, 1941-45. Recipient various awards including Honor Man Wichita Swim Club, 1970, Disting. Service award to Youth YMCA, 1970, Service award to Swimmers Kansas City High Sch. Activities, 1975. Mem. Kans. U. Alumni Assn. (life), Kans. C. of C., Wichita C. of C., Sales and Mktg. Execs. (bd. dirs., v.p.), Textile Care and Allied Trades Assn., Alpha Tau Omega. Clubs: Old Timer (sec., treas. 1964-86, Honor Man of Yr. 1977), Wichita Racquet, Knife and Fork Internat. (bd. dirs., v.p.), Univ. (chmn. bd. dirs., v.p.). Lodges: Rotary, Masons (32 deg.). Republican. Home: 340 Hillsdale Wichita KS 67230

TROPP, ROBERT LLOYD, endodontist; b. Jamaica, N.Y., Mar. 24, 1947; s. Jack and Sylvia (Abrams) T.; m. Brenda Edelman, June 13, 1986; 1 child, Joanna Gabrielle. BA, Lafayette Coll., 1968; DDS, Columbia U., 1972. Diplomate Am. Bd. of Endodontics. Assoc. dentist Drs. Lerner, Symons & Schlagel, Bklyn., 1972-78; pvt. practice dentistry Buffalo Grove, N.Y., 1978—; cons. Good Shepard Hosp., Barrington, Ill., 1982—; attending staff Peninsula Hosp. Ctr., 1975-77, Maimonides Hosp., 1977-78; pres. dental staff Northwest Community Hosp., Arlington Heights, Ill., 1986—, adj. prof. Endodontists, Northwestern U. Evanston, Ill. Fellow Am. Bd. Endodontics; mem. ADA, Am. Assn. Preventive Dentistry, N.Y. Assn. Endodontists (charter), Tri-State Endodontic Soc., Ill. Dental Soc., Chgo. Dental Soc., Arlington Village Dental Group (pres. 1984-86). Jewish. Office: 1213 W Dundee Rd Buffalo Grove IL 60089

TROPPITO, CHARLES C., JR., toxic waste management-chemical manufacturing executive; b. Kansas City, Mo., Sept. 14, 1947; s. Charles C. and Philomene (Magness) T.; m. Mary A. Barthelmass, June 7, 1969; children: Christopher M., Laurie A. BA, U. Mo., Kansas City, 1970, MPA, 1975. Bond underwriter Reliance Ins. Co., Kansas City, Mo., 1969-70; title examiner trainee St. Paul Title Ins. Co., Kansas City, 1970-71; adminstrv. asst. to mayor/plan commn. City of Leawood (Kans.), 1971-75; dir. adminstrn. and budget City of Prairie Village (Kans.), 1975-78; chief adminstrv. officer, budget dir. City of Urbana (Ill.), 1978-83; pres. Cantro div. U.S. Pollution Control, Inc.; adminstr. regulatory affairs PPM, Inc. div. U.S. Pollution Control, Inc.; guest lectr. U. Ill., Urbana; mem. adj. faculty public adminstrn. Columbia Coll., Kansas City; treas., bd. dirs. Urbana Promotion Com., 1980-81; mem. planning com. Sch. Adminstrn., U. Mo., Kansas City, 1976; mem. bd. Champaign-Urbana High Tech. Devel. Group, 1980; mem. faculty adv. com. grad. program in pub. adminstrn. U. Ill., Urbana; industry mem. Kansas City (Mo.) City council's task force on toxic and hazardous materials. Author papers and reports on pub. adminstrn. and hazardous waste regulations. Recipient various certs. of appreciation. Mem. Internat. City Mgmt. Assn., Mcpl. Fin. Officers Assn., Am. Public Works Assn., Greater Kansas City C. of C. (chmn. energy and environment com.). Lutheran. Club: Rotary. Office: 2023 Washington Kansas City MO 64108

TROSMAN, HARRY, psychiatry educator, psychoanalyst; b. Toronto, Ont., Can., Dec. 9, 1924; came to U.S., 1948; s. Samuel and Esther (Sherman) T.; m. Marjorie Susan Goldman, June 22, 1952; children: Elizabeth, Michael, David. MD, U. Toronto, 1948. Diplomate Am. Bd. Psychiatry. Intern Grace Hosp., Detroit, 1948-49; resident Iowa Psychopathic Hosp., Iowa City, 1949-51; resident in psychiatry Cin. Gen. Hosp., 1951-52; from asst. instr. to asst. prof. psychiatry U. Chgo., 1952-59, assoc. prof. psychiatry, 1959-75, prof. psychiatry, 1975—; acting chmn. dept. psychiatry U. Chgo., 1986—; cons. Cen. Religion and Psychotherapy, Chgo., 1969—. Author: Freud and the Imaginative World, 1985; contbr. articles to profl. jours.; editorial bd. Internat. Jour. Psychoanalysis, Internat. Rev. Psychoanalysis, Jour. Am. Psychoanalytic Assn. Served to lt. USNR, 1954-56. Mem. Am. Psychiat. Assn., Am. Coll. Psychoanalysts, Ill. Psychiat. Soc., Chgo. Pschoanalytic Soc., Am. Psychoanalytic Assn., Internat. Psychoanalytic Assn., Ctr. for Advanced Psychoanalytic Studies (trustee 1978—), Chgo. Inst. for Psychoanalysis (cert., council mem., Franz Alexander prize, 1965). Jewish. Office: U Chgo Med Ctr 5841 S Maryland Ave Chicago IL 60637

TROTIER, BRIAN LEE, investment banker; b. Eau Claire, Wis., Apr. 18, 1955; s. Donald Leon and Audrey Priscilla (Cornwell) T.; m. Brigitte Maria Mueck, Sept. 3, 1977; 1 child, Christopher Logan. AB in Adminstrv. Sci., Yale U., 1977; JD, U. Cin., 1980. Assoc. Carlile, Patchen, Murphy & Allison, Columbus, Ohio, 1980-83; stockbroker J.C. Bradford, Columbus, 1983-85; investment advisor Prescott Ball Turben, Columbus, 1985-87; investment banker Lowe & Assocs., Columbus, 1987—. Active Big Bros., Columbus, 1981-84; corp. solicitor, mem. devel. bd. Children's Hosp., Columbus, 1983—; wish planner Spl. Wish Found., Columbus, 1986—. Mem. ABA, Ohio Bar Assn., Columbus Bar Assn (chmn. legal asst. lawyer com. 1982). Club: Yale of Cen. Ohio (Columbus) (treas. 1985—). Avocations: coaching youth sports, photography, landscaping. Home: 4150 Ashmore Rd Columbus OH 43220 Office: Lowe & Assocs 100 E Campus View Blvd #390 Columbus OH 43085

TROTTER, RICHARD DONALD, psychologist, clergyman, consultant; b. Grand Island, Nebr., June 9, 1932; s. P. Dean and Ethel Dell (Masters) T.; m. Kathleen Marie Tyler, Apr. 10, 1966; children—Terri Marie, Nancy Lee, Laurel Lynn. Student U. Wis.-Madison, 1950; B.S., U. Nebr., 1968; M.Div., Iliff Sch. Theology, Denver, 1970; Ph.D., Southwest U., Phoenix, 1974; D.H.L. (hon.), London Inst., 1973. Ordained to ministry United Meth. Ch., 1971. Sr. pastor, 1st United Meth. Ch., Miller, S.D., 1970-73; pvt. practice counseling and therapy, Rapid City, S.D., 1974-78; sr. pastor Canyon Lake United Meth. Ch., Rapid City, 1978-80; theologian in residence Collins Ctr., Portland, Oreg., 1981-83; counselor, therapist Wellspring Inc., Marion, Inc., 1983—, also dir. Author: 40,000 Pounds of Feathers, 1970; 'Til Divorce Do Us Part, 1982. Mem. council City of West Lincoln, Nebr., 1960-61, mayor, 1962; mem. Rapid City Bd. Edn., 1977-80, pres., 1979-80; bd. dirs. Marion Civic Theatre, 1984—. Served with USAF, 1949-52. Named hon. col. Cody Scouts of North Platte, 1965; recipient Service award Rapid City Bd. Edn., 1980. Mem. Nat. Council Family Relations, Sex Info. and Edn. Council, Assn. for Humanistic Psychology, Am. Assn. Marriage and Family Therapists, Nat. Assn. Social Workers, Assn. for Transpersonal Psychology, U. Nebr. Alumni Assn. Democrat. Avocations: philately, sports officiating, acting. Home: 1106 Windsor Dr Marion IN 46962

TROUB, DONALD LESLIE, osteopathic physician; b. Camden, N.J., May 7, 1944; s. Nathan Lawrence and Mildred (Goldberg) T.; m. Sarah Jane Haynes, June 23, 1968; 1 dau., Leslie Shannon. B.A. in Biology, U. Tenn., 1967; postgrad. Tenn. Tech. U., 1967-68; D.O., Chgo. Coll. Osteo. Medicine, 1974. Diplomate Nat. Bd. Examiners Osteo. Physicians and Surgeons, Am. Bd. Emergency Medicine. Intern Mt. Clemens Gen. Hosp. (Mich.), 1974-75, emergency physician, 1976-82; emergency physician Providence Hosp., Novi, Mich., 1982—, med. dir. emergency room, 1982—; former clin. instr. Mich. State U., Des Moines Coll. Osteo. Medicine. Fellow Am. Coll. Emergency Physicians; mem. Am. Osteo. Assn., Am. Coll. Emergency Medicine. Jewish. Office: 39500 W Ten Mile Rd Novi MI 48050

TROUP, WILLIAM ROGER, physician; b. Dallas, Mar. 3, 1944; s. Roger Chenot and Natalie Florene (Valkus) T.; m. Violet Marie Packard, Aug. 19, 1967; children—Cristine, Denise, Danae. Student Wheaton Coll., 1963-65; M.D., U. Colo.-Denver, 1969. Diplomate Am. Bd. Family Practice. Intern, St. Francis Hosp., Wichita, Kans., 1969-70; practice medicine specializing in family practice, Walsh, Colo., 1970-84, Johnson, Kans., 1984—; mem. staff Walsh Dist. Hosp., 1970—, chief of staff, 1976-84; mem. staff S.E. Colorado Hosp., Springfield, 1972—, chief of staff, 1976-78; chief of staff Stanton County Hosp., 1984—. Dep. coroner Baca County, Colo., 1970-84; mem. Walsh Pub. Sch. Bd. Edn., 1974-81, v.p., 1978-81. Mem. AMA, Colo. Med. Soc., Am. Acad. Family Practice, S.E. Colo. Med. Soc. (pres. 1978-80, v.p. 1980-82). Methodist. Club: Prairie Twisters Sq. Dance (Walsh). Office: 101 E Greenwood St Johnson KS 67855

TROUTMAN, BRUCE WEBER, health science facility administrator; b. Dayton, Ohio, Mar. 15, 1947; s. H. Eugene and Margaret (Weber) T.; m. Kay Stevens, May 16, 1981; 1 child, Brian H. B.S., Ohio State U., 1969; D.O., Chgo. Coll Osteo. Medicine, 1973. Intern Zieger Botsford Hosp., Detroit, 1974; osteo. physician Shelby Dale Clinic, Utica, Mich., 1974-75, Lane-Swayze Clinic, Almont, Mich., 1975-77, Knollwood Clinic, Lapeer, Mich., 1977-86, med. dir. Health Plus Mich., Flint, 1986—; physician reviewer Profl. Rev. Orgn., Genesee, Lapeer, Shiawassee counties, Mich., 1976-86 ; med. dir. two health maintenance orgns., 1984-86; cons. health maintenance orgns. Mem. Am. Osteo. Assn., Mich. Assn. Osteo. Physicians and Surgeons, Lapeer Osteo. Soc., Nat. Bd. Osteo. Examiners,,Group Health Assn. Am. (med. dirs. div.), Lapeer C. of C. (bd. dirs. 1983-84). Republican. Lutheran. Lodge: Optimists (bd. dirs. 1981-83, 85—, v.p. 1983-84). Avocations: photography, cross country skiing, raising racoons, landscaping. Home: 2033 Gray Rd Lapeer MI 48446 Office: Health Plus 2050 S Linden Rd Flint MI 48507

TROUTNER, JOANNE JOHNSON, computer resource educator, consultant; b. Muncie, Ind., Sept. 9, 1952; d. Donal Russel and Lois Vivian (Hicks) Johnson; m. Lary William Troutner, May 17, 1975. B.A. in Media and English, Purdue U., 1974, M.S. in Edn., 1976. Media specialist Lafayette Sch. Corp. (Ind.), 1974-77, 81-83, computer resource tchr., 1983-84; media specialist, Tippecanoe Sch. Corp., Lafayette, Inc., 1984-85, ednl. computer coordinator, 1985—; tchr. English, Minot Pub. Schs. (N.D.), 1978-79, media specialist, 1979-81; vis. prof. continuing edn. U. S.C., Columbia, summer 1983; instr. Purdue U., West Lafayette; vis. prof. continuing edn. U. N.D. Author: The Media Specialist, The Microcomputer and the Curriculum, 1983; contbr. materials rev. column Sch. Library Media Quar.; computer literacy columnist Jour. Computers in Math. and Sci. Teaching; pub.: Computers and the Gifted Student; editor newsletter Videodisc. Active Greater Lafayette Leadership Acad. Alumni Group, 1983—; bd. dirs. Lafayette Family Service Agy., 1987—. Mem. ALA, Assn. Media Educators (chmn. computer div. 1982-84), Am. Assn. Sch. Librarians (sec. 1983-84, 2d v.p. 1985-86), Internat. Council for Computers in Edn. (interactive video spl. interest group newsletter editor 1986—), Ind. Computer Educators (bd. dirs. 1986—), Phi Beta Kappa, Kappa Delta Gamma, Phi Delta Kappa (UP programs 1987-88). Home: 3002 Roanoke Circle Lafayette IN 47905 Office: Klondike Middle Sch 3310 N 300 W West Lafayette IN 47906

TROUTT, ARTHUR ROBERT, artist, arborist; b. Mt. Vernon, Ill., Aug. 26, 1946; s. Arthur glen and Marry Jewel (Hilt) T.; m. Karen Joice Johnston, May 21, 1976 (div. 1982); m. Leona Sue Troutt Thacker, Feb. 14, 1984; children: Sarah Ann, Travis Ryan. BS in Forestry, So. Ill. U., 1974. Arborist Timber Wolfe Tree Co., Mt. Vernon, 1975-83; artist Bold Stroke Studio, Mt. Vernon, 1983—. Author various works of art, including murals and illustrations in nat. and internat. publs. Served with Green Berets U.S. Army, 1966-69, Vietnam. Home: Rural Rt #5 Mount Vernon IL 62864

TROWBRIDGE, MARK ALAN, accountant; b. South Bend, Ind., June 9, 1959; s. Richard D. and Betty L. (Rogers) T.; m. Kathy Sue McIntyre, Aug. 29, 1981; 1 child, Melissa Ann. BA in Acctg., Manchester Coll., 1981. CPA, Ind. Audit supr. Smith, Thompson, Wihebrink & Co., Inc., Lafayette, Ind., 1981—; ptnr. Acme Investors, Lafayette, 1983—. Mem. Am. Inst. CPA's, Ind. Soc. CPA's (audit and account com.). Roman Catholic. Avocations: collecting baseball cards and sports memorabilia, jogging, sports. Home: 3617 Valdez Dr Lafayette IN 47905 Office: Smith Thompson Wiherbrink & Co Inc 427 N 6th Box 116 Lafayette IN 47902

TROWELL-HARRIS, IRENE, nurse; b. Aiken, S.C., Sept. 20, 1939; d. Frank and Irene (Battle) Trowell; m. Benoni Harris, Oct. 2, 1978 (div. May 1983). BA, Jersey City State U., 1971; RN, Columbia Hosp., 1959; MPH, Yale U., 1973; MEd, Columbia U., 1983, EdD, 1983. Staff nurse Talmadge Hosp., Augusta, Ga., 1959-60; head nurse N.Y. Hosp., N.Y.C., 1960-64; pediatric supr. Brookdale Hosp., N.Y.C., 1964-66; adminstr. HHA Maimonides Hosp., Bklyn., 1966-71; adminstr., coordinator Misericordia Hosp., Bklyn., 1974-85; policy devel. Am. Nurses Assn., Kansas City, Mo., 1985—; mem. adj. grad. faculty U. Mo., Kansas City. Contributing editor Jamaica Times Mag., 1978-85; contbr. articles to profl. jours. Mem. leadership com., chief of staff to Gov. N.Y., Latham., 1986—; AIDS advisor ARC, 1987—. Served to lt. col. N.Y. ANG, 1963—. Mem. Am. Nurses Assn. (congl. dist. coordinator 1981-85, task force on AIDS 1986—), N.Y. State Nurses Assn., Am. Pub. Health Assn., Nat. Guard Assn. U.S., Res. Officers Assn. (life), NAACP (life), Kappa Delta Pi. Democrat. Baptist. Club: Yale (N.Y.C). Avocations: tennis, racquetball, jogging, hiking. Home: 7040 N Bales Apt 235 Gladstone MO 64119-1247 Office: Am Nurses Assn 2420 Pershing Rd Kansas City MO 64108

TROXEL, JAMES PAUL, organization development executive; b. Oklahoma City, Sept. 7, 1946; s. Austin Burge and Paula LaVerne (Goad) T.; m. Karen B. Snyder, Mar. 16, 1969; 1 child, Jonathan Conrad Paul. BS, Okla. State U., 1968. Mem. research faculty Inst. Cultural Affairs, Chgo., 1968-72; regional office dir. Inst. Cultural Affairs, Washington and Los Angeles, 1972-76; resource devel. dir. Inst. Cultural Affairs, Chgo., 1976-80, econ. devel. dir., 1980-83, program dir., 1983—; cons. Fifth City Human Devel. Project, Chgo., 1968-84, City of Chgo., 1983—. Co-founder The Order: Ecumenical, Chgo., 1968—; founder, dir. Chgo. Capital Fund, 1984—. Methodist. Avocations: Chgo. sports, yoga, meditation. Office: The Inst of Cultural Affairs 4750 N Sheridan Rd Chicago IL 60640

TROY, GEORGE F., business machines company executive. Pres. computer and consumer service group Control Data Corp., Mpls. Office: Control Data Corp 8100 34th Ave S Minneapolis MN 55440 *

TROYER, MELVIN LEWIS, insurance company executive; b. Springfield, Mo., Oct. 31, 1944; s. William Lewis Troyer and Katherine (Kellogg) McKean; m. Audrey Alice Troyer, Feb. 13, 1970 (div. Feb. 1979); 1 child, Jenny Rebecca. BA in Philosophy, Drury Coll., 1968; CTS in Group Dynamics, Pacific Sch. Religion, 1970; MA in Earth Sci., Western Mich. U., 1974. Loss prevention cons. Factory Mut. Enring., Rolling Meadows, Ill., 1976-80; safety rep. Western Ins. Co., Crystal Lake, Ill., 1980-85; tng. and edn. coordinator Western Ins. Co., Ft. Scott, Kans., 1985-86; mgr. loss control div. Am. States Ins. Co., Ft. Scott, 1986—. Mem. Am. Soc. Safety Engrs., Phi Mu Alpha Sinfonia. Methodist. Lodge: Kiwanis. Office: Am States Ins Co 2801 Horton St Fort Scott KS 66701

TROZZOLO, ANTHONY MARION, chemist; b. Chgo., Jan. 11, 1930; s. Pasquale and Francesca (Vercillo) T.; m. Doris C. Stoffregen, Oct. 8, 1955; children: Thomas, Susan (Mrs. Bruce Hecklinski), Patricia, Michael, Lisa, Laura. B.S., Ill. Inst. Tech., 1950; M.S., U. Chgo., 1957, Ph.D., 1960. Asst. chemist Chgo. Midway Labs., 1952-53; asso. chemist Armour Research Found., Chgo., 1953-56; mem. tech. staff Bell Labs., Murray Hill, N.J., 1959-75; Charles L. Huisking prof. chemistry U. Notre Dame, 1975—; vis. prof. Columbia U., N.Y.C., 1971, U. Colo., 1981, Katholieke Universiteit Leuven, Belgium, 1983; vis. lectr. Academia Sinica, 1984, 85; AEC fellow, 1951, NSF fellow, 1957-59; Phillips lectr. U. Okla., 1971; P.C. Reilly lectr. U. Notre Dame, 1972; C.L. Brown lectr. Rutgers U., 1975; Sigma Xi lectr. Bowling Green U., 1976, Abbott Labs., 1978; M. Faraday lectr. No. Ill. U., 1976; F.O. Butler lectr. S.D. State U., 1978; Chevron lectr. U. Nev.-Reno, 1983; Hesburgh Alumni lectr. U. Notre Dame, South Bend, Ind., 1986, disting. lectr. sci., 1986. Assoc. editor: Jour. Am. Chem. Soc, 1975-76; editor: Chem. Reviews, 1977-84; editorial adv. bd. Accounts of Chem. Research, 1977-85; contbr. articles to profl. jours; patentee in field. Fellow N.Y. Acad. Scis. (Halpern award in Photochemistry 1980), AAAS, Am. Inst. Chemists; mem. Am. Chem. Soc. (Disting. Service award St. Joseph Valley sect. 1979, Coronado lectr. 1980), AAUP, Sigma Xi. Roman Catholic. Home: 1329 E Washington St South Bend IN 46617 Office: U Notre Dame Notre Dame IN 46556

TRUCANO, JOHN, finance company executive, consultant; b. Morris, Ill., June 9, 1950; s. Peter Joseph and Fern Margaret (Bauer) T.; m. Judy Ann Kish, Feb. 4, 1978; 1 child, Jason. BA, Carlton Coll., 1972; postgrad., U. Minn., 1972-73. Comml. loan officer Am. Nat. Bank, St. Paul, 1974-77; asst. v.p. N.W. Bank S.W., Bloomington, Minn., 1977-78; v.p. Community Investment Enterprises, Inc., Mpls., 1978-82, Cherry Tree Ventures, Bloomington, 1982-84; pres. Acorn Fin. Corp., Edina, Minn., 1984—; bd. dirs. Unisource Corp., Edina, Impact Systems Corp., Milw., Omnium Corp., Stillwater, Minn., Matrex, Inc., Maple Plain, Minn. Mem. Twin Cities Venture Club, Mpls. C. of C. (pres. small bus. council 1983-84). Clubs: Northfield (Minn.) Golf, N.W. Racquet (Mpls.). Office: Acorn Fin Corp 5200 W 73d St Edina MN 55435

TRUE, WILLIAM HERNDON, health care administrator; b. Huntsville, Ala., Nov. 15, 1938; s. William and Bernice Victoria (Herndon) T.; m. Sandra Delores Cox, Feb. 14, 1959; children: William H. Jr., Lelia Beth, Victoria Claire. BBA, Cleve. State U., 1971; postgrad., U. Minn., 1973-75. Cert. acct., Ohio. Broker Merrill Lynch, Cleve., 1971-73; research adminstr. Cleve. Clinic Found., 1973-79; exec. dir. Am. Sickle Cell Anemia Assn., Cleve., 1979-82, 1986—; dir. Project Golden-Age Outreach for Health Inc., Cleve., 1982-85; cons. fin. planning, Cleve., 1968—; cons. Chem. Rubber Co., Cleve., 1976-78, Watson-Rice CPA's, 1978-79, Alpha-Omega Chem. Co., 1982—. Contbr. articles to profl. jours. Mem. Health Com. Cleve. Urban League. Mem. Nat. Assn. Sickle Cell Disease Clinics (v.p.), Ohio Sickle Cell and Health Assn., Cleve. High Blood Pressure Coalition (sec.). Republican. Mem. United Ch. Christ. Clubs: Duplicators, Kings and Queens (both Cleve.). Home: 18800 S Woodland Shaker Heights OH 44122 Office: Am Sickle Cell Anemia Assn 10300 Carnegie Ave Cleveland OH 44106

TRUEBLOOD, JOE THOMAS, publishing executive; b. Seymour, Ind., Sept. 1, 1947; s. Francis Marion and Lavina Edith (Thralls) T.; m. Darla Jo Bechtel, July 12, 1969 (div. 1980); 1 child, Thomas Brent; m. Louanne Ward, Feb. 20, 1981; children: Lance Ward, Laura Ward. BEd, Oakland City (Ind.) Coll., 1971; postgrad., Ind. U., 1973-75; student in bus. mgmt., So. Meth. U., 1981. Coach, tchr. Washington (Ind.) Pub. Sch., 1971-74, Shelby County Sch. Dist., Waldron, Ind., 1974-76; publs. sales cons. Jostens, Inc., Mpls., 1976-79, regional sales mgr., 1979-86, dir. sales adminstrn. devel., 1986—, coordinator, facilitator, 1985—. Mem. Am. Mgmt. Assn. Home: 4902 S Safari Ct Eagan MN 55122

TRUELOVE, C. KEITH, small business owner and executive; b. French Lick, Ind., July 4, 1949; s. Woodrow Truelove and Opal R. (Chastain) Tucker; m. Becky Cornet, Apr. 29, 1977; children: Derek R., Devon R., Erica R. AS, Northwood Inst., 1969, BBA, 1971. Personnel mgr. piano div. Kimball, West Baden, Ind., 1971-74, indsl. engr. piano div., 1974-76, 1979-80; plant mgr. piano div. K. Spinet, French Lick, 1976-79; dir. corp. personnel and safety Kimball Internat., Inc., Jasper, Ind., 1980-86, v.p., 1986—; pres. Midwest Inn, Paoli, Ind., 1983—. Mem. exec. adv. com., past pres. Patoka Valley Vocat. Coop., Jasper, 1980—; mem. adv. bd. Vincennes U. Furniture Prodn. Mgmt. Curriculum, 1980-85, Ind. Employment Security Div. Job Service, 1983—; mem., past v.p. 70,001 program for disadvantaged youths, 1983-84; pres. Springs Valley Youth League, 1985—; sec. Springs Valley Regional Water Dist. Bd., 1985—. Recipient Spl. Proclamation Citation State of Ind., 1985. Mem. Am. Soc. Personnel Adminstrn., Ind. Personnel Assn., Ind. C. of C. (labor relations com.), Springs Valley C. of C. (pres. 1980-81), Am. Soc. Tng. and Devel., Ind. Mfrs. Assn. (personnel and indsl. relations com.). Republican. Home: Rural Rt 2 Box 343 West Baden IN 47469 Office: Kimball Internat Inc 1600 Royal St Jasper IN 47546

TRUEMAN, EDWARD EARL, marketing executive; b. Royal Oak, Mich., Sept. 29, 1955; s. James William and Dorothy Ione (Rice) T.; m. Margaret Ann Ashton, Aug. 25, 1979; 1 child, Clifford Edward. BS, Eastern Mich. U., 1979. Sales, market specialist U.S. Indsl. Chem., N.Y.C., 1979-82; regional dir. mktg. Georgia Pacific, Atlanta, 1982-84; automotive market mgr. Research Polymers Internat., Troy, Mich., 1984—. Mem. Soc. Plastics Engrs. Republican. Home: 4248 Lake Knolls Dr Oxford MI 48051

TRUESDELL, JAMES LESLIE, supply company executive; b. ST. Louis, Dec. 26, 1949; s. Harry James and Betty Jane (Dreier) T.; m. Gayle Gladys Brauer, Dec. 30, 1972; children: Jason, Daniel, Christina, Melinda, Adam. BA, Southeastern Mo. State U., 1972; JD, U. Mo., Kansas City, 1973, ML, 1977. Bar: Mo. V.p., sr. trust officer United Mo. City Bank, Kansas City, 1973-78; v.p., sec. Brauer Supply Co., St. Louis, 1978—. Chmn. Sch. Bd. St. Pauls Lutheran Sch., Des Peres, Mo., 1981-83; treas. Shepherd of the Hills Lutheran Ch., Ballwin, Mo., 1984-86. Mem. N.Am. Heating and Air Conditioning Wholesalers Assn. (chmn. govt. relations 1981—). Avocations: musician and performer. Office: Brauer Supply Co 4260 Forest Park Saint Louis MO 63108

TRUMBLA, MARGARET HELEN, automotive company executive; b. Port Huron, Mich., Aug. 3, 1937; d. William James and Winnifred (Phillips) Veen; m. Gary P. Trumbla, Sept. 1, 1955; children: Nikka M., Brian D., Gary P. II, Keith D., Kirt D. Grad. high sch., Marysville, Mich. Pres., gen. mgr. Dependable Parts Service, Inc., Dearborn, Mich., 1964—; gen. mgr. Mocar Automotive Inc., Dearborn, 1975—. Mem. Mich. Autoparts Assn. Mich. Autoworkers Assn. (dir.-at-large, 1982-85, treas. 1985-86, v.p. 1986—). Roman Catholic. Avocations: family activities, bowling. Office: Mocar Automotive Inc 5746 Schaefer Dearborn MI 48126

TRUMBULL, STEPHEN MICHAEL, music educator; b. Columbus, Ohio, Sept. 18, 1954; s. Clyde Austin and Patricia Ann (Ranck) T. MusB in Voice Performance and Choral Edn., DePauw U., Greencastle, Ind., 1977; postgrad., Ohio State U., 1982-85. Cert. profl. music educator, Ohio. Dir. vocal music Columbus City Schs., 1978—; pres., owner Columbus Music Studios, 1984—; pres. Trumbull Pub., Washington, 1986—, Stephen M. Trumbull, Inc., Columbus, 1986—; account exec. Goldmark Securities Corp., Columbus, 1987—; v.p. tng. Kaiser Devel. Corp., Columbus, 1987—; soloist First Community Ch., Columbus, 1982—; mktg. cons. Beckenhorst Press, Inc., Columbus, 1986—. Adv. Lambda Chi Alpha, Ohio State U., 1982—, chmn. alumni adv. bd., 1982—; pres. Friends of Neoteric Dance Theatre, Columbus, 1986—; coordinator nat. co. competition Jr. Achievement Nat. Conf., Bloomington, Ind., 1985—; bd, dirs. Neoteric Dance Theatre, 1986—. Named Outstanding Alumni, Lambda Chi Alpha, 1984. Mem. Columbus Edn. Assn. Lodge: Optimist. Avocations: swimming, traveling. Home and Office: 119 E Willow St Columbus OH 43206

TRUNNELL, EUGENE ERLE, psychiatrist; b. Novinger, Mo.; s. Eugene Erle and Mahala Livingston (Robb) T.; m. Joan Utara, Jan. 30, 1954; children: Rebecca Susan, Matthew Thomas, Nancey Robb, Paul Robert. MD, Washington U., 1952; postgrad., Western New Eng. Inst. for Psychoanalysis, 1964. Diplomate Am. Bd. Psychiatry and Neurology. Resident Topeka State Hosp., 1953-55; sr. staff Austen Riggs Ctr., Stockbridge, Mass., 1958-64; courtesy staff Jewish Hosp., St. Louis, 1964-67; tng. and supervision analyst St. Louis Psychiat. Inst., 1973—; vis. psychiatrist Smith Coll., Northampton, Mass., 1960; cons. U.S. Peace Corps, St. Louis, 1965-66, Vets. Hosp., St. Louis, 1972-81, Mo. U., Columbia, 1986; clin. asst. prof. St. Louis U., 1972—. Contbr. articles to profl. jours. Served to sgt, U.S. Army, 1944-46, ETO. Fellow Am. Psychiat. Assn.; mem. Am. Psychoanalytic Assn. (cert.), Internat. Psycho-Analytic Assn., World Psychiat. Assn., St. Louis Psychoanalytic Soc. (past pres.). Avocations: sailing, flying. Home: 4915 Pershing Pl Saint Louis MO 63108 Office: St Louis Psychoanalytic Inst 4524 Forest Park Saint Louis MO 63108

TRUNNELL, H. MARK, dentist; b. Waterloo, Iowa, Aug. 18, 1951; s. Howard Hadley and Mary Elizabeth (Barnes) T.; m. Marilyn Joyce Backerman, Aug. 21, 1971; children: James Edward, Katharine Suzanne, Tyler, Megan Elizabeth. BA, U. No. Iowa, 1973; DDS, U. Ill., 1977; cert. in orthodontics, U.S. Dental Inst., 1986. Pvt. practice dentistry Cedar Falls, Iowa, 1977—; anatomy instr. Hawkeye Inst. Tech., Waterloo, 1977-79. Editor The Probe, 1975-76. Bd. dirs. Walnut Ridge Baptist Acad., Waterloo, 1986—. Mem. ADA, Iowa Dental Assn., Black Hawk Dental Soc. Republican. Clubs: Loofalls Investors (Waterloo) (pres. 1985—); Exchange (Cedar Falls). Office: 922 Rainbow Dr Suite 201 Cedar Falls IA 50613

TRUSHEIM, H. EDWIN, insurance executive; b. Chgo., May 3, 1927; s. H. Edwin and Lucy (Genslein) T.; m. Ruth M. Campbell; children—John E., Mark R. BS in Edn., Concordia Tchrs. Coll., Chgo., 1948; MA in Polit. Sci., Northwestern U., 1955; postgrad. in polit. sci. and econs., Washington U., St. Louis, 1951-54. With Gen. Am. Life Ins. Co., St. Louis, v.p., 1966-67, sr. v.p., 1974, exec. v.p., 1974-79, pres., 1979—, also chief exec. officer, 1981—, chmn., 1986—; bd. dirs. Am. Council Life Ins., Washington. Bd. dirs. Angelica Corp., St. Louis, Civic Progress, St. Louis, United Way Greater St. Louis. Fellow Life Ins. Assn. Office: Gen Am Life Ins Co 700 Market St Saint Louis MO 63101 *

TRUSSELL, TERESA JA-TUN, university administrator; b. Chgo., May 25, 1955; d. William T. and Dorothy Mae (Kimble) T. BS in Engring., Princeton U., 1977; M in Mgmt., Northwestern U., 1982. Registered profl. engineer, Ohio. Staff engr. Amoco Oil Co., Chgo., 1977-78; project engr. Monsanto Co., Miamisburg, Ohio, 1978-85; dir. minority engring. program So. Ill. U., Carbondale, 1985—. Mem. Nat. Assn. Minority Engring. Program Adminstrs., Bus. and Profl. Women's Assn. Office: So Ill U Technology A311 Carbondale IL 62901

TRUTTER, JOHN THOMAS, consulting company executive; b. Springfield, Ill., Apr. 18, 1920; s. Frank Louis and Frances (Mischler) T.; m. Edith English Woods II, June 17, 1950; children: Edith English II, Jonathan Woods. BA, U. Ill., 1942; postgrad., Northwestern U., 1947-50, U. Chgo., 1947-50; LHD (hon.), Lincoln Coll., 1986. Various positions Ill. Bell, Chgo., 1946-58, dir. ednl. services, 1958, gen. traffic mgr., asst. v.p. pub. relations, asst. v.p. suburban ops., gen. mgr. N. suburban area, v.p. pub. relations, 1969-71, v.p. operator services, 1971-80, v.p. community affairs, 1980-85; pres. John T. Trutter Co., Inc., Chgo., 1985—; mem. personnel staff AT&T, N.Y.C., 1955-57; pres., chief exec. officer Chgo. Conv. and Visitors Bur., 1985—; bd. dirs. State Nat. Bank, Evanston; mem. adv. bd. Alford and Assocs., Chgo., 1984—. Co-author: Handling Barriers in Communication, 1957, The Governor Takes a Bride, 1977. Past pres. Hull House Assn.; chmn. United Cerebral Palsy Assn. Greater Chgo., v.p. nat. bd.; bd. dirs. Chgo. Crime Commn., Abraham Lincoln Assn., v.p. English Speaking Union, City Colls. Chgo. Found., Lyric Opera Chgo.; past pres. Childrens Home and Aid Soc.; chmn. adv. council PruCare HMO; v.p. Orch. Ill., hon. vice chmn.; bd. dirs. Upper Ill. Valley Assn.; treas. Chgo. United, 1970-85; mem. Ill. Econ. Devel. Commn., 1985, Commn. on Improvement Cook County Circuit Ct. System, 1985—, Civic Com. for Domestic Relations Ct. Div., 1986—; past presiding co-chmn. NCCJ; bd. dirs. Ill. Humane Soc. Found.; chancellor Lincoln Acad. Ill., 1985—; numerous others; bd. govs. Northwestern U. Library Council, 1984—; mem. State Ill. Assembly Sch. Problems Council, 1985—, spl. commn. on adminstrn. of justice in Cook County, 1986—. Served to lt. col. U.S. Army. Decorated Legion of Merit; recipient Outstanding Leadership award Chgo. West Project, 1985, Laureate award Lincoln Acad. Ill., 1980, Outstanding Civic Leader award Am. Soc. Fundraisers, Humanitarian of Yr. award, New Directions award SSMC, 1987. Mem. Pub. Relations Soc. Am., Sangamon County Hist. Soc. (founder, past pres.), Ill. State Hist. Soc. (pres. 1985-87), Alpha Sigma Phi,

Phi Delta Phi. Clubs: Tavern, Econ. Chgo., Mid Am., City (v.p.). Home and Office: 630 Clinton Pl Evanston IL 60201

TRYBER, THOMAS ANTHONY, JR., dairy foods company executive; b. Rapid City, S.D., May 18, 1943; s. Thomas A. and Rose Mary Tryber; student pub. schs., Racine, Wis; m. Kathleen M. Kober, May 25, 1963. Supr. cost and budgets J.I. Case, Racine, 1971-74, mgr. cost and budget control, 1974-77, fin. systems analyst, Wichita, Kans., 1977-78, mgr. systems and data processing, 1978-81; mgr. systems and data processing Steffens Dairy Foods Co., Inc., Wichita, Kans., 1982—. Mem. Data Processing Mgmt. Assn., Am. Prodn. Inventory Control Soc. Home: 2528 Milro Wichita KS 67204-2353 Office: 700 E Central Wichita KS 67202

TRYLCH, SCOTT WILLIAM, psychologist; b. Flint, Mich., Jan. 23, 1948; s. Donald Kent and Merodean Virginia (Harvie) T.; m. Darlene Sue Harris, May 12, 1973; children—Jason, Jeremy. M.A., Central Mich. U., 1972; Ed.D., Western Mich. U., 1982. Therapist, Genessee County Community Mental Health, Flint, Mich., 1972-73; clin. psychologist Cath. Family Service, Saginaw, Mich., 1973-81; intern Mott Children's Health Ctr., Flint, 1981-82; clin. supr., clin. psychologist Cath. Family Service, Saginaw, 1982—; pvt. practice psychology, 1984—. Mem. Am. Acad. Psychotherapists, Am. Psychol. Assn., Am. Soc. Clin. Hypnosis, Am. Orthopsychiat. Assn., Am. Assn. Marriage and Family Therapists (clin.), Mich. Assn. Profl. Psychologists, Soc. Personality Assessment, Mich. Soc. for Psychoanalytic Psychology, Mich. Psychol. Assn., Mich. Assn. Alcoholism and Drug Abuse Counselors, Mich. Burn Team. Office: 120 N Michigan Ave Suite 220 Saginaw MI 48602

TSAMADOS, CHRIS PETER, architect; b. Athens, Greece, Nov. 1, 1957; came to U.S., 1968; s. Peter Tsamados and Christina Antonopoulos. BArch with honors, U. Ill., Chgo., 1980. Registered architect, Ill. Sr. designer Skidmore Owings & Merrill, Chgo., 1980-85; project architect ESPO Engineering, Willowbrook, Ill., 1986—. Mem. Nat. Trust Hist. Preservation, 1985-86. Mem. AIA, U. Ill. Alumni. Avocations: drawing, travel. Home: 4310 1/2 N Keystone Apt 3C Chicago IL 60641 Office: SSA Inc 235 Anthony Trail Northbrook IL 60062

TSANG, LINDA HANSFORD, pharmacist; b. Ft. Sill, Okla., May 19, 1946; d. Gaylon R. and Frances E. (Fleming) Hansford; m. Joseph C. Tsang, June 2, 1969. BS in Pharmacy, U. Okla., 1969; cert. clown, U. Wis., LaCrosse, 1982. Staff pharmacist Brokaw Hosp. Pharmacy, Normal, Ill., 1969-70, acting dir., 1970-72, asst. dir., 1973-85, poison control clown BroMenn Health Ctr., 1978—, coordinator poison ctr. BroMenn Health Ctr., 1986—; prin. lectr. Brokaw Poison Prevention Program, Normal, 1980—; lectr. Poison Prevention Lecture Series, McLean County Speaker Bur., 1980—, Clown Skills Lecture Series, 1979—, Am. Life Lecture Series, People's Republic of China, 1981; coordinator NoSiop Poison Prevention Program, Normal, 1986—. Recognized Fgn. Profl., Guangdong Province Pharm. Assn., People's Republic of China, 1981. Mem. Sugar Creek Pharm. Assn. (pres. 1978-80), Corn Belt Pharm. Assn. (sec.-treas. 1972-79, Pharmacist of Yr. 1979), Ill. Council Hosp. Pharmacists (vote warden 1977-81), Am. Assn. Poison Control Ctrs., Corn Belt Clown Alley (sec. history 1980-84). Democrat. Baptist. Avocations: origami, juggling, balloon sculpturing, sign language. Home: 1317 E Washington Bloomington IL 61701 Office: BroMenn Health Care Ctr Brokaw Hosp Pharmacy Franklin & Virginia Normal IL 61761

TSCHANNEN-MORAN, ROBERT KEITH, minister; b. Cleve., Dec. 7, 1954; s. Robert Albert and June Ann (Uhlir) Tschannen; m. Megan Moran, Aug. 21, 1976; children: Bryn Mari, Evan Joseph. B, Northwestern U., 1975; postgrad., Garrett-Evang. Theol. Sem., 1976-78; M of Div., Yale U., 1979. Ordained to ministry United Meth. Ch. as deacon, 1976, as minister United Ch. Christ, 1980. Student pastor Middlefield (Conn.) Federated Ch., 1975-76, First Spanish United Ch. Christ, Chgo., 1976-78; organizing pastor Good News Community Ch., Chgo., 1979—; tri-dir. Interfaith Clergy, Rogers Park, Chgo., 1981—. Chmn. Peoples Housing, Chgo., 1979—, Congregations for Career Devel., Chgo., 1982-87; sec. Triangle Park Corp., Chgo., 1985—. Home: 7637 N Bosworth Ave Chicago IL 60626-1218 Office: Good News Community Ch 7649 N Paulina St Chicago IL 60626

TSCHANZ, MONICA AMELIA, small business owner, real estate broker; b. Buena Vista, Wis., Sept. 30, 1933; d. Thomas and Grace (Sankey) Peskie; m. Donald George Barber, June 21, 1952 (div. 1976); children: Nancy, Diane, Julie; m. Herman Tschanz, Mar. 25, 1984. Cert. real estate, Madison Area Tech. Coll., Madison, Wis., 1978. Owner, mgr. Country Side Inn, Stoughton, Wis., 1973-75; real estate salesperson First Realty, Madison, 1976-78, Capital City Real Estate, Madison, 1978-79; owner, mgr. Dunn Place Apartments, Madison, 1979, Monica Barber Realty, Madison, 1979-82, Farmside Supperclub, Montello, Wis., 1982—. Vol. aide campaign Moria Krueger for Judge, 1977. Fellow Montello C. of C. (bd. dirs. 1983-85), Madison Bd. of Realtors, Am. Leg. Aux., Tavern League of Wis., Nat. Tavern League. Republican. Roman Catholic. Lodge: Montello Lioness. Home: Route 2 Box 256-K Montello WI 53949

TSCHOPP, THEODORE MARTIN, aluminum company executive; b. Lausen, Basel, Switzerland, Jan. 5, 1937; came to U.S., 1980; s. Theodor M. and Ruth Margret (Schlueter) T.; m. Beatrice Irene Meyer, June 18, 1965; children: Andrew, Martin, Thomas, Daniel. Grad. in Engring., Fed. Inst. Tech., Zurich, Switzerland, 1959; Ph.D. in Econs., U. Basel, 1965. Project engr. Alusuisse, Zurich, 1965-69; chief engr. Alusaf, Empangeni, South Africa, 1969-71; plant mgr. Alu-Hutte Rheinfelden, Fed. Republic Germany, 1972-76; mng. dir. Leichtmetallgesellschaft GmbH, Essen, Fed. Republic Germany, 1977-80; v.p. primary ops. Consol. Aluminum Corp., St. Louis, 1980 83, pres., chief exec. officer, from 1984, now chmn.; chmn. bd. Ormet Corp., Hannibal, Ohio, 1983—. Patentee aluminum smelting technique, 1980. Mem. AIME, Aluminum Assn. (bd. dirs.), Schweizerischer Ingenieur- und Architektenverein, Gesellschaft Deutscher Metallhutten und Bergleute. Avocations: classical music; ocean sailing; hiking; tennis. Home: 305 Conway Lake Dr Saint Louis MO 63141 Office: Consol Aluminum Corp PO Box 14448 Saint Louis MO 63178 *

TUASON, RICARDO MAURICIO, general and hand surgeon; b. Bangued, Abra, Philippines, Nov. 27, 1938; s. Gabriel Barba and Mary (Foster) T.; m. Daisy Thiele Delgado, May 14, 1966. M.D., Univ. East, Manila, 1965. Diplomate Am. Bd. Surgery. Intern Ch. Home & Hosp., Balt., 1966-67, resident in surgery, 1967-71; fellow in hand surgery Cook County Hosp., Chgo., 1971-72; surgeon St. Joseph's Hosp., Bloomington, Ill., 1972-73; practice medicine specializing in hand surgery, Muncie, Ind., 1973—. Fellow ACS, Internat. Soc. Microsurgery, Am. Soc. Liposuction Surgery; mem. Del.-Blackford Med. Soc. Republican. Roman Catholic. Home: 4110 Riverside Ave Muncie IN 47304 Office: 420 W Washington St Muncie IN 47305

TUBBS, JERRY RONALD, university administrator; b. Reed City, Mich., Dec. 12, 1932; s. Roy Walter and Mildred Josephine (Holmquist) T.; m. Lorraine Bertha Grein, Nov. 21, 1953; children: Deborah Michelle, Michael Roy. BS in Acctg., Ferris State Coll., 1961; postgrad., Harvard U., 1973; MA in Ednl. Adminstrn., Cen. Mich. U., 1978. Bus. mgr. Ferris State Coll., Big Rapids, Mich., 1960-63; controller Louvers & Dampers, Inc., Somerset, Ky., 1963-64; internal auditor Cen. Mich. U., Mt. Pleasant, 1964-65, exec. asst. to v.p. bus. and fin., 1965-70, v.p. bus. fin., 1970—, treas., trustee, 1980—; chmn. Higher Edn. Adminstrn. Referral Service, Washington, 1977-85. Bd. dirs. Isabella County United Way, 1966-74, United Way Mich., 1982-85; mem. supervisory com., bd. dirs. Isabella County (Mich.) Govtl. Employees Credit Union, 1965-70; mem. citizens adv. com. City Mt. Pleasant, 1966-68; treas., chmn. budget com., mem. exec. com. Isabella County Commn. Aging, 1975-79; vice chmn. Isabella County Econ. Devel. Corp., 1978-83; mem. Mid Mich. Devel. Corp., 1982-86; treas., trustee Christ The King Luth. Chapel, 1967-70; mem. bldg. com. Immanuel Luth.Ch., 1982-85; treas. Beal city Bus. Assn., 1982 ; sec. Art Reach Mid Mich., 1981-85; bd. dirs. Cen. Mich. U. Devel. Fund, 1980—; Mt. Pleasant Area Vols. for Literacy, 1986—; sec., 1987—. Served with USN, 1951-54. Mem. Mich. Assn. Coll. and Univ. Bus. Officers, Nat. Assn. Coll. and Univ. Bus. Officers (bd. dirs. 1986—), Cen. Assn. Coll. and U. Bus. Officers (exec. com. 1983-86), Higher Edn. Adminstrn. Referral Services, Coll. U. Personnel Assn., Nat. Assn. Phys. Plant Adminstrs., VFW (life), Sigma Iota Epsilon. Club: President's (Mt. Pleasant). Home: 4986 W Jordan Rd Weidman MI 48893 Office: Cen Mich U 111 Warriner Hall Mount Pleasant MI 48859

TUBER, MILTON, accountant; b. Phila., May 12, 1919; s. Philip and Pauline Pearl (Plotnick) T.; m. Ruth Borowitz, June 28, 1941; children: Ann-Lois, Arnold Ira, Jack Steven. BA, City Coll. N.Y., 1939. CPA, Ohio. Staff acct. J. Mendlowitz, CPA, N.Y.C., 1935-38, A.E. Borts, CPA, N.Y.C., 1938-40, S.D. Leidesdorf, N.Y.C., 1946-47, Bennett Chirlian, N.Y.C., 1947-48; comptroller Art's Jewelry Chain, Canton, Ohio, 1948-53; staff acct. Shonk, Feller, Tuber, Canton, 1953—; bd. dirs. H&H Auto Parts, Canton, Pigott Industries, Clinton, Ohio. Author: (book) Milk Monopoly and Legislation in New York, 1939 (Henry Wollman award 1939). Served to capt. U.S. Army, 1940-46. Mem. Am. Inst. CPA's, Ohio Soc. CPA's, Beta Sigma Soc. Republican. Jewish. Club: Prestwick Country. Lodge: Mason. Avocation: tennis. Home: 4231 Frazer NW Canton OH 44709 Office: Shonk Feller Tuber CPAs 5566 Dressler Rd NW Canton OH 44720

TUCH, HELAN LOUISE, psychologist; b. Glassport, Pa., Oct. 25, 1926; d. William W. Coursin and Emma L. (Simpson) Clark; m. Harold A. Tuch (dec. 1977); children: Harold Raymond, Steven Arthur, Helan Adrienne. BA with honors, U. Cin., 1960; MEd, Xavier U., 1968. Tchr. Villa Madonna Acad., Covington, Ky., 1965-67; guidance counselor Newport (Ky.) Pub. Schs., 1967-68; sch. psychologist Cin. Pub. Schs., 1968-70; psychologist Cin. Health Dept., 1973—. Mem. Ohio Psychol. Assn., Cin. Psychol. Assn., Sierra Club (conservation chair 1978-82). Democrat. Unitarian. Avocations: camping, boating, conservation activities. Home: 2604 Eden Ave Cincinnati OH 45219 Office: Cin Health Dept Elm St Health Ctr 1525 Elm St Cincinnati OH 45210

TUCHMAN, STEVEN LESLIE, lawyer, theatre critic; b. Indpls., Sept. 3, 1946; s. Frederick and Lillian (Alper) T. BA, Ind. U., 1968, JD, 1971; cert. internat. law, City Coll. London, 1970. Bar: Ind. 1971. Advisor Den Danske Bank, Copenhagen, Denmark, 1971-73; assoc. Melvin Simon and Assoc., Inc., Indpls., 1973-81; sole practice Indpls., 1981—; critic Sta. WIAN-FM, Indpls., 1981—, Sta. WTHR-TV, Indpls., 1987—; adj. prof. real estate. low Ind. U. Sch. Bus., 1983-84. Author numerous articles on theatre criticism, 1981—. V.p. Dance Kaleidoscope, Indpls., 1980-81; pres. Festival Dance Theatre, Indpls. and N.Y.C., 1983-84; chmn. task force com. Indpls. Pub. Schs. Referendum, 1985; subcom. chmn. exec. com. Internat. Violin Competition of Indpls., 1986—; chmn. real estate com. community adv. council Jr. League of Indpls., 1987—; bd. dirs. Planned Parenthood of Cen. Ind., Inc., 1987—. Mem. Ins. State Bar Assn. (ho. dels. 1986—), Indpls. Bar Assn. (com. long range plans 1987-88), Am. Theatre Critics Assn., Phi Delta Phi. Lodge: Kiwanis.

TUCK, JOHN WAYNE, tax professional; b. Muncie, Ind., Mar. 20, 1958; s. William Chester and Helen Nadine (Christwell) T.; m. Mary Katherine Blackwood, Mar. 27, 1976; children: Dori, Brandi, John. BS in Acctg. and Econs., Ball State U., 1981. CPA, Ind. Staff acct. London Witte & Co, Indpls., 1981-85, tax mgr., 1985-87, ptnr., 1987—. Mem. Am. Inst. CPA's, Ind. State CPA Soc. Republican. Baptist. Lodges: Masons (sr. steward 1987—), Sertoma (treas., charter mem. Fortville, Ind. chpt.). Avocations: fishing, woodworking. Home: 745 Laurel Ln Fortville IN 46040 Office: London Witte & Co Merchants Plaza 901 E Tower Indianapolis IN 46204

TUCKER, BOWEN HAYWARD, lawyer; b. Providence, Apr. 13, 1938; s. Stuart Hayward and Ardelle Chase (Drabble) T.; m. Jan Louise Brown, Aug. 26, 1961; children: Stefan Kendric Slade, Catherine Kendra Gordon. A.B. in Math., Brown U., 1959; J.D., U. Mich., 1962. Bar: R.I. 1963, Ill. 1967, U.S. Supreme Ct. 1970. Assoc. Hinckley & Allen, Providence, 1962-66; sr. atty. Caterpillar Tractor Co., Peoria, Ill., 1966-72; counsel FMC Corp., Chgo., 1972-82, sr. litigation counsel, 1982—. Chmn. legal process task force Chgo. Residential Sch. Study Com., 1973-74, mem. Commn. on Children, 1983-85, Ill. Com. on Rights of Minors, 1974-77, Com. on Youth and the Law, 1977-79, Youth Employment Task Force; mem. White House Conf. on Children, ednl. services subcom., 1979-80; chairperson Youth Employment Task Force, 1982-83; mem. citizens com. on Juvenile Ct. (Cook County), 1978—, chmn. detention subcom., 1982—. Served to 1st lt. U.S. Army, 1962-69. Mem. ABA, Ill. State Bar Assn., R.I. Bar Assn., Chgo. (chmn. com. on juvenile law, 1976-77), Engine Mfrs. Assn. (chmn. legal com. 1972), Constrn. Industry Mfrs. Assn. (exec. com. of Lawyers' Council 1972, 1975-79, vice chmn. 1977, chmn. 1978-79), Machinery and Allied Product Inst. (products liability council 1974—, vice chmn. 1981-83, chmn. 1983-85), ACLU (bd. dirs. Ill. div. 1970-79, exec. com. 1973-79, sec. 1975-77), Phi Alph Delta. Club: Brown Univ. of Chgo. (nat. alunni schs. program 1973-85, v.p. 1980-81, pres. 1981-86). Home: 107 W Noyes St Arlington Heights IL 60005 Office: 200 E Randolph St Suite 6700 Chicago IL 60601

TUCKER, DENNIS CARL, library director; b. St. Louis, Oct. 17, 1945; s. Carl Ernest and Elsa Grace (Witt) T.; m. Maria Teresa Guillermina Castro, Dec. 6, 1975; children—Dennis Andrés, William Alexandro, Eric Scott, Michael Joseph. B.S., S.E. Mo. State U., 1967, M.A.T., 1974; M.L.S., U. Mo., 1983. Tchr. English, Univ. Autó. de Sinaloa, Culiacán, Mexico, 1971-73, Academia de Idiomas, 1974-76; owner, dir. Academia Logos, Mazatlán, Mexico, 1976-77; tchr. English, U. Américas, Cholula, Mexico, 1977-78; tchr. English and Spanish, Rifle (Colo.) High Sch., 1978-79; librarian Webb Jr. High Sch., East Prairie, Mo., 1980-83; dir. library Bethel Coll., Mishawaka, Ind., 1983—; reference librarian U. Notre Dame, Ind., 1986—. Sec.-treas. S.E. Mo. Dept. Sch. Librarians, Cape Girardeau, 1980-82. Author: From Here To There: Moving A Library, 1987; photographer El Periódico del Noroeste, 1975-76. Recipient Kodak Internat. Newspaper Snapshot award, 1975. Mem. ALA, Ind. Coop. Library Services Authority (dir. 1983—), Area Library Services Authority (dir. 1983—), Christian Writers Club Michiana (v.p. 1984, pres. 1985), Sigma Tau Delta. Home: 17745 Tollview South Bend IN 46635 Office: Library Bethel Coll 1001 W McKinley Mishawaka IN 46545

TUCKER, EULAN GENE, JR., accountant; b. Toledo, Ohio, May 4, 1942; s. Eulan G. and Ethel L. (Browning) T.; m. Linda A. Ingram, Nov. 11, 1961; children: Eulan G. III, Tonalee Tucker Resendez. BBA, U. Toledo, 1969; postgrad., Lay Sch. Religion, 1982-87. CPA, Ohio. Staff acct. I.R. Miller & CO., Toledo, 1965-69; controller Crow, Inc., Swanton, Ohio, 1969-71; pres. Tucker, Stein & Kissling, Inc., Toledo, 1971—. Treas. Toledo Mental Health Clinic, 1969-74, Meml. United Ch. Christ, Toledo, 1975, River East, Toledo, pres., 1972-78; del. White House Conf. Small Bus., Washington, 1986. Mem. Ohio Soc. CPA's, Toledo Chpt. CPAs (bd. dirs.). Avocations: sports, religion, gardening. Office: Tucker Stein & Kissling Inc 608 4th St Toledo OH 43605

TUCKER, FLORENCE RAY, library administrator; b. Henderson, Ky., July 11, 1921; d. Sanford Ray and Nannie Cosby (Moss) T. AB, U. Mich., 1944, ABLS, 1945. Reference librarian Detroit Pub. Library, 1945-59, asst. dept. chief, 1959-66, acting dept. chief, 1966, coordinator major library activities, 1966-77, assoc. dir. support services, 1978—; adj. instr. Wayne State U., Detroit, 1965-66. Mem. ALA, Mich. Library Assn., Spl. Library Assn., Phi Beta Kappa, Phi Kappa Phi. Home: 4909 Briarwood Ave Apt 6 Royal Oak MI 48073 Office: Detroit Pub Library 5201 Woodward Ave Detroit MI 48202

TUCKER, GEORGE LEON, surgeon; b. New York, N.Y., Dec. 30, 1931; s. Max and Sally (Feiden) T.; m. Beverly Jean Irvine, June 15, 1963; children—Melodie Jean Monroe, Jason Patrick, Jonathan Paxson. A.B., Columbia U., 1952; M.D., Harvard U., 1956. Diplomate Am Bd Surgery. Intern, then resident Barnes Hosp., St. Louis, 1956-63, asst., assoc. surgeon, 1963—; chief surgeon St. Luke's Hosp., Chesterfield, Mo., 1983—; successively instr., asst-prof., assoc. prof. clin. surgery Washington U. Sch., St. Louis, 1963—. Contbr. articles to profl. jours., 1963—. Served to lt. M.C., USNR. Fellow Am. Coll. Surgeons; mem. Mo. State Surg. Soc. (pres. 1983-84), Barnes Hosp. Soc. (pres. 1982-83), Mo. chpt. ACS (councillor 1983-86), AMA, St. Louis Surg. Soc. Episcopalian. Clubs: University, Racquet (St. Louis). Avocations: aviation; computer programming. Office: St Luke's Hosp 224 Woods Mill Rd S Chesterfield MO 63017

TUCKER, JANET LYNN, database analyst; b. Seymour, Ind., Jan. 10, 1961; d. Randall Edward and Laura (Johnson) Bowen; m. William Roger Tucker, May 25, 1985. BA, Ind. U., 1984. Database analyst Cummins Engine Co., Inc., Columbus, Ind., 1984—. Named one of Outstanding Young Women of Am., 1985. Mem. Psi Iota Xi. Republican. Baptist. Avocations: volleyball, aerobics, reading. Home: 3863 W Suburban Ct Columbus IN 47201 Office: Cummins Engine Co Inc 8th and Jackson MC=60104 Columbus IN 47201

TUCKER, ROBERT ALLEN, communications executive; b. Pitts., Mar. 14, 1926; s. Newman Wallace and Helen Virginia (Staley) T.; m. Jean Ardith Graves, Aug. 16, 1947; children—Robert Allen, Rebecca A., Douglas E., Kevin A. B.S. in Mktg., U. Pitts., 1950; LL.B., 1954; postgrad. Purdue U. Sch. Bus. Nat. sales mgr., dir. mktg. Fed. Plastics, Chgo., 1955-60; exec. v.p. Trindle Products, Ltd., Chgo., 1960-70; nat. v.p. sales Spl. Products div. Panasonic, 1971-75; internat. pres. Tele-Communications Radio, Inc., Des Plaines, Ill., 1975—. Chairman, chief exec. officer Trans-Continental Radio Inc., 1986—; nat. v.p. Young Republicans, 1961-62; pres. Young Reps., 1962-63. Served with USMC, 1942-46. Radio Club Am. fellow. Mem. Profl. Communications Dealers Assn. (pres.), Am. Police Communications Officers, Communications Mktg. Assn., Nat. Assn. Bus. and Ednl. Radio, IEEE (assoc.). Methodist. Clubs: Radio of Am., Sertoma (pres. 1961-63). Home: 98 East Ave Park Ridge IL 60068 Office: 960 Rand Rd Des Plaines IL 60016

TUCKER, SHERIDAN GREGORY, child psychiatrist, clinical psychopharmacologist; b. Bossier City, La., Feb. 26, 1950; s. William Samuel and Marie Regina (Nevarez) T.; m. Jaylene D. Lambert, Dec. 30, 1977; children—Julia Elizabeth, Elliott Thomas, Oliver Michael. B.S., U. Mo.-Kansas City, 1972; M.D., U. Kans., 1975. Diplomate Am. Bd. Psychiatry and Neurology. Resident in psychiatry U. Kans., Kansas City, 1975-78. chief dept. psychiatry U.S. Army, Ft. Polk, La., 1978-80; fellow dept. psychiatry Kans. U. Med. Ctr., Kansas City, 1980-82, clin. asst. prof., 1984—; staff dir. div. adolescent services Kans. Inst., Olathe, 1985; child psychiatrist Psychiat. and Psychol. Cons., Prairie Village, Kans., 1985—. Contbr. articles to profl. jours. Served to maj. U.S. Army, 1980-82. Decorated Army Commendation medal, 1980. Mem. Am. Acad. Child Psychiatry, Am. Acad. Clin. Psychiatrists, Am. Psychiat. Assn., N.Y. Acad. Scis., Assn. Child Psychology and Psychiatry. Republican. Episcopalian. Avocation: computing. Office: Psychiat and Psychol Cons 4121 W 83rd St Suite 150 Prairie Village KS 66208

TUCKER, THOMAS LESTAL, college official; b. Galatia, Ill., Nov. 6, 1937; s. Loren Denny and Ruth Edna (Dodd) T.; m. Patricia Sue Wheeler Parke, Feb. 22, 1958 (dec.); m. Karen Sue Kraemer, Feb. 10, 1968; children—Patricia Sue Bixby (dec.), Debra Lynn, Thomas Lestal, Christina Mae. BS, So. Ill. U., 1979; MA, Webster Coll., 1983, MBA, 1987; postgrad. in Social Work, U. Ill., 1987—. Enlisted in USN, 1956; tng. mgr. Coll. Lake County, Naval Tng. Schs., Great Lakes, Ill., 1980—. Mem. Am. Vocat. Assn., Am. Legion. Roman Catholic. Lodges: Masons, Moose. Home: 411 E Schaumburg Rd Streamwood IL 60103 Office: Bldg 236 Room 349 SSC NTC Great Lakes IL 60088

TUCKER, THOMAS RANDALL, engine company public relations executive; b. Indpls., Aug. 6, 1931; s. Ovie Allen and Oris Aleen (Robertson) T.; A.B., Franklin Coll., 1953; m. Evelyn Marie Armuth, Aug. 9, 1953; children—Grant, Roger, Richard. Grad. asst. U. Minn., 1953-54; dir. admissions, registrar Franklin Coll., 1954-57; trainee Cummins Engine Co., Inc., Columbus, Ind., 1957-58; dir. pub. relations, 1968—. Mem. Bd. Sch. Trustees Bartholomew County, Ind., 1966-72, pres., 1968-69; mem. Ind. State Bd. Edn., 1977—; treas. Bartholomew County Rep. Cen. Com., 1960-80; mem. Columbus Area Visitor Info. and Promotion Commn.; trustee, chmn. ednl. policy com. of bd. trustees Franklin Coll.; bd. dirs. The Hoosier Salon. Mem. Pub. Relations Soc. Am., Columbus Area Visitor Info. and Promotion Commn., Columbus (Ind.) C. of C. (Community Service award 1986), Kappa Tau Alpha, Phi Delta Theta, Sigma Delta Chi. Lutheran. Lodge: Rotary. Home: 4380 N Riverside Dr Columbus IN 47203 Office: Box 3005 Columbus IN 47202

TUFF, CHARLES CLIFFORD, manufacturing company executive; b. Mondovi, Wis., Jan. 30, 1943; s. Clifford A. and Helen E. (Steihl) T.; m. Sandra L. Zacho, Jan. 30, 1965; children: Rory P., Veronique R., Rhett C. BBA, U. Wis., 1970. Div. acctg. mgr. Modine Mfg. Co., Racine, Wis., 1970-72; prodn. control mgr. Modine Mfg. Co., McHenry, Ill., 1972-74; gen. mgr. Sentry Equipment Corp., Oconomowoc, Wis., 1974-79, exec. v.p., 1979-81, pres., 1981—, also bd. dirs.; bd. dirs. Sentry Offshore Enterprises, St. Thomas, V.I., 1984—, Guardian Software Corp., Oconomowoc, 1981-84. Served to capt. U.S. Army, 1964-68. Decorated Air medal plus one Oak Leaf Cluster. Mem. Am. Inst. Cert. Pub. Accts., Am. Nuclear Soc., The Exec. Com., Investment Club. Club: Oconomowoc Bridge. Home: 259 Woodland Ln Oconomowoc WI 53066

TUFF, TIMOTHY C., metal company executive. Pres. Alcan Aluminum Corp., Cleve. Office: Alcan Aluminum Corp 100 Erieview Plaza Cleveland OH 44114 *

TUFTE, FREDRIC WAYNE, mathematics educator, consultant; b. Seattle, Nov. 8, 1942; s. Oswald Oliver and Loal Ramona (Johnson) T.; m. Marilyn Jean Zanardi, Aug. 20, 1972. BS, U. N.D., 1964; MA, U. Mo., 1966; postgrad., U. Iowa, 1971-72, U. Wis., 1984-85. Instr. U. Wis., Platteville, 1966-70, asst., then assoc. prof., 1972—; instr. Iowa State U., Ames, 1970-71. Contbr. articles to profl. jours.; presenter several papers to ednl., profl. orgns., 1970—. Mem. Math. Assn. Am., Sch. Sci. and Math. Assn., Nat. Council Tchrs. of Math., Wis. Math. Council, Am. Ednl. Research Assn., Midwest Ednl. Research Assn. Avocations: history, woodworking, gardening. Home: 980 Hillcrest Circle Platteville WI 53818 Office: U Wis-Platteville Math Dept One University Plaza Platteville WI 53818

TUKIENDORF, BOGDAN, holding company executive; b. Zamosc, Lublin, Poland, Nov. 18, 1933; came to U.S., 1951; s. Edward and Genowefa (Podolak) T.; m. Theresa S. Kapustiuk, Jan. 10, 1959; children: Alexander B., Elizabeth M. Cert. real estate and fin., Wright Coll., 1977. Purchasing agent The Formfit Co., Chgo., 1952-63; asst. plant mgr. Genesco Ind., Chgo. and Nashville, 1963-66; mgr. quality control Genesco Ind., Nashville, 1966-68; restauranteur Chgo., 1968-79; owner night club The Riverside Club, Richland Ctr., Wis., 1979—; pres. Tukiendorf Enterprises Inc., Richland Ctr., 1979—; cons. in fin. Roman Catholic. Avocations: gun collecting, fishing, hunting, antique collecting.

TULCHINSKY, SANDRA BETH, marketing strategist; b. St. Paul, July 2, 1949; d. Max H. and Chernie (Warren) Berg; m. Ilya Tulchinsky. BA, Wells Coll., 1971; MA, Vanderbilt U., 1975, PhD, 1977; postgrad., U. N.C., 1979, Wharton Sch. Bus., U. Pa., 1980. Instr. Vanderbilt U., Nashville, 1975-77; asst. prof. U. North Iowa, Cedar Falls, 1977-81; mktg. rep. IBM Corp., Mpls., 1981-84; market strategist NCR Comten Inc., St. Paul, 1984—. Author: Book of Esther, 1978; editor Old Testament Rev., 1977-81; contbg. editor Jour. of Bibl. Lit., Vetus Testamentum; contbr. articles in the fields of ancient Near Ea. lit. and ancient Israelite history, theology and lit. to religious jours. Wells Coll. scholar, 1971, Hillel fellow Vanderbilt U., Nashville, 1974-77, NEH fellow, 1980. Mem. Democratic Farm Labor Party. Jewish. Office: NCR Comten Inc 2700 N Snelling Saint Paul MN 55113

TULEE, ROY CARL, science administrator; b. San Francisco, July 12, 1938; s. Charles Joseph and Ellen Johanna (Markert) T.; m. Ellen Ann Ross, Aug. 24, 1963; children: Carl Owen, Cameron Kenneth. Chem. technician Stauffer Chem. Co., Richmond, Calif., 1960-62, research chemist, 1962-65; plant chemist, prodn. supr. Stauffer Chem. Co., San Francisco, 1965-74; quality assurance supr. Stauffer Chem. Co., Oxnard, Calif., 1975-81; plant chemist Stauffer Chem. Co., San Jose, Calif., 1981-84; mgr. product quality Stauffer Chem. Co., Clawson, Mich., 1984—. Mem. AAAS, Am. Chem. Soc., Inst. Food Technologists. Lutheran. Home: 22966 Dundee Ct Birmingham MI 48010 Office: Stauffer Chem Co 1000 Crooks Rd Clawson MI 48017

TULLIS, BYRON WALTER, dentist; b. Holdrege, Nebr., Apr. 8, 1933; s. Byron Walter Sr. and Susan Flagg (Field) T.; m. Patricia Ann Canning, Apr. 7, 1962; children: michael Anthony, Stephen Alan. BS in Dentistry, U.

Nebr., 1954, DDS, 1958. Practice gen. dentistry Lincoln, Nebr., 1961—. Served to capt. USAF, 1958-61. Mem. Am. Dental Soc., Nebr. Dental Soc., Lincoln Dental Soc., Chgo. Dental Soc., Capital Study Club (sec., treas. 1970—). Republican. Avocations: vintage racing cars, boating. Home: Rt 1 Eagle NE 68347 Office: 6520 Holdrege Lincoln NE 68505

TULLMAN, HOWARD ALLEN, lawyer, entrepreneur; b. St. Louis, June 27, 1945; m. Judith K. Zindell, Apr. 18, 1983; children—Jamie B., Thea. B.A. cum laude, Northwestern U., 1967, J.D. with distinction, 1970. Bars: Ill. 1970, U.S. Dist. Ct. (no. dist.) Ill. 1970, U.S. Ct. Appeal (7th cir.) 1971, U.S. Supreme Ct. 1974. Assoc. Levy and Erens, Chgo., 1970-73, ptnr., 1974-81; pres. Hat Communications Co., Chgo., 1978-84, CCC Info. Services Inc., Chgo., 1980—, also bd. dirs.; pres. Howard Allen Graphics, Chgo., 1978—; arbitrator Am. Arbitration Assn., Chgo., 1976—; lectr. Grad. Bus. Sch., Northwestern U. Chmn.-assoc. editor Northwestern Law Rev., 1969; contbr. articles to profl. jours. Mem. men's council Mus. Contemporary Art, Chgo., 1974—. Ford Found. fellow 1968. Mem. ABA, Ill. State Bar Assn., Chgo. Bar Assn., Order of Coif. Home: 219 W Concord Ln Chicago IL 60614 Office: CCC Info Services Inc 640 N LaSalle St Chicago IL 60610

TULLY, THOMAS ALOIS, building materials executive; b. Dubuque, Iowa, Nov. 11, 1940; s. Thomas Aloysius and Marjorie Mae (Fosselman) T.; m. Joan Vonnetta Dubay, Nov. 30, 1963; children: Thomas Paul, Maureen Elizabeth. BA, Loras Coll., 1962; postgrad., Georgetown U., 1963-66; MPA, Harvard U., 1968. Mgmt. trainee Office of Sec. Def., Washington, 1962-63, fgn. affairs officer, 1963-70; v.p. Dubuque Lumber Co., 1970-84, pres., 1984—; part-time instr. Divine Word Coll., 1971, Loras Coll., 1972. Mem. Dubuque Human Rights Commn., 1974-75, chmn., 1975; city councilman, Dubuque, 1975-79; bd. dirs. League Iowa Municipalites, 1977-79; mayor City of Dubuque, 1978; vice chmn. Iowa Temporary State Land Pres. Policy Com., 1978-79; pres. N.E. Iowa Regional Coordinating Council, 1985—, East Cen. Intergovtl. Assn. Bus. Growth, Inc., 1985—; bd. dirs. Pvt. Industry Council of Dubuque and Delaware Counties, Inc., 1983-86; trustee Divine Word Coll., 1986—. Recipient Meritorious Civilian Service award Sec. of Def., 1970. Mem. Iowa Lumbermens Assn. (pres. 1984, chmn. 1985—), Northwestern Lumbermen Assn. (bd. dirs. 1984—). Democrat. Roman Catholic. Club: Thunder Hills Country. Home: 838 Stoneridge Pl Dubuque IA 52001 Office: Dubuque Lumber Co 2655 Lincoln Ave Dubuque IA 31955-6005

TULLY, TIMOTHY RAYMOND, architect, electrical engineer, university program administrator; b. Quincy, Ill., Aug. 8, 1952; s. Marion E. and Elizabeth L. (Heckenkamp) T. BArch, U. Ill., 1974; BSEE, So. Ill. U., 1984. Registered architect, Ill. Project architect Meyer, Peter & Co., Quincy, 1974-81; architect, engr. Crawford & Whiteside, Carterville, Ill., 1982; archtl. cons. Carbondale, Ill., 1983—; asst. prof. interior design So. Ill. U., Carbondale, 1984—, coordinator interior design program, 1986—, also lectr., 1983-84; cons. G.M. Corp., Carbondale, 1985. Mem. AIA, IEEE, Computer Soc. of IEEE, Cir. Soc. of IEEE, Illuminating Engring. Soc. N.Am., Ill. Vocat. Tchr. Educators Assn. Roman Catholic. Home: Rural RT 9 #77 Highlander Carbondale IL 62901 Office: So Ill U 410 Quigley Hall Carbondale IL 62901

TUMANIS, SUSAN KAY, marketing executive, consultant, writer; b. Sturgis, Mich., Mar. 10, 1949; d. Merritt W., Sr. and Marion A. (Stevens) T. B.A. in Journalism, Mich. State U., 1971; postgrad. In English Lit., Oakland U., 1979-80; completed various mgmt. courses, seminars. Gen. mgr. Orchard Mall, West Bloomfield, Mich., 1976-78, Trappers Alley Festival Market Place in Greektown, Detroit, 1985; asst. gen. mgr. Tel-Twelve Shopping Ctr., Southfield, Mich., 1978-80; mktg. dir. Wonderland Shopping Ctr., Livonia, Mich., 1980-84; account exec. Anthony M. Franco PR, Detroit, 1984-85, account supr., mgr. pub. relations Simons Michelson Zieve, Inc., 1985—; instr. in shopping ctr. mktg. and promotion Oakland Community Coll.-Orchard Ridge, Farmington Hills, Mich.; instr. advt. for small bus. Oakland Community Coll., Highland Lakes; mem. coll. bd. Mademoiselle mag., 1969-70, 70-71; reporter The Oakland Press, Pontiac, Mich., 1973-75, AP, Detroit, 1973; reporter, mag. editor, wire editor The Sandusky (Ohio) Register, 1972-73. Contbr. articles to profl. jours; editor Youth Today Page, Battle Creek Enquirer and News, 1965-71. Vol. Reuther for Congress, 1973; vol. Washtenaw County Commr. Kathleen Fojtak, 1973; co-chmn. Walled Lake Christmas Treelighting Com., 1975; mem. pub. relations com. Walled Lake Annual Waterfest Com., 1975, Mich. Artrain, Milford, 1976; pub. relations dir., treas. Roberts for State Rep. 24th Dist., 1976, co-mgr., 1980; mem. bicentennial research com. Walled Lake and Commerce Township Cemeteries, 1976; n chmn. West Bloomfield Mich. Week Parade com., 1977, 78; press coordinator High-Am.-Detroit News Balloon Festival, Rochester, Mich., 1980; bd. dirs. Miss Livonia Scholarship Pageant, 1983, West Bloomfield Symphony Orchestra, 1978, West Bloomfield High Sch. Co-operative Edn. Adv. Council, 1977, 78; mem. advt. com. March of Dimes Sweetheart Ball, 1987. Mem. Pub. Relations Soc. Am. (Detroit br.), Nat. Writers' Club (adv. bd. 1970-71), Internat. Council Shopping Ctrs. (cert. mktg. dir.), LWV (nominated state pub. relations chmn.), Greater West Bloomfield C. of C. (sec. 1977-78), Livonia C. of C. (bd. dirs. 1984), Sigma Delta Chi (recipient Mark of Excellence 1971). Democrat. Episcopalian. Avocations: gravestone rubbings, sailing. Home: 874 Village Green Ln #2083 Pontiac MI 48054

TUMEO, GEORGE JOSEPH, school system adminstrator; b. Columbus, Ohio, June 1, 1938; s. Anthony Joseph and Beatrice Eileen (Spang) T.; m. Monica Ann Dosch, Apr. 19, 1974; children: Elizabeth Ann, Miriam Eileen, Maria Grace, Deborah Joan. Student, Ohio State U., 1957; BA, St. Charles Coll., 1961; MA, Athenaeum of Ohio, 1964; postgrad., Ohio State U., 1969-84. Budget analyst Ohio Youth Commn., Columbus, 1974-75; tchr. social studies Plain Local Schs., New Albany, Ohio, 1975-79; asst. prin. Licking Heights Local Schs., Summit Sta., Ohio, 1979-80; prin. Big Walnut Local Schs., Sunbury, Ohio, 1980-83, asst. supt., 1983-87; supt. Northeastern Local, Defiance, Ohio, 1987—; chairperson Sch. Study Council Microcomputer Commn., Columbus, 1985-86. Author: (book) How to Study, 1976. Chmn. fund raising Big Walnut KIDS Com., 1983—. Recipient Disting. Service award Boy Scouts Am., 1969, Ohio Youth Commn., 1974. Mem. Assn. Supervision and Curriculum Devel., Ohio Assn. Adminstrs. Pupil Transp., Buckeye Assn. Sch. Adminstrs. (mem. ins. com. 1985—), Phi Delta Kappa, Phi Kappa Phi. Roman Catholic. Lodge: Lions (Big Walnut Bull. Editor 1986-87). Avocations: reading, stamp collecting, coin collecting, amateur radio, model trains. Home: 20453 Buckskin Rd Defiance OH 43512 Office: Northeastern Local Schs 05291 Domersville Rd Defiance OH 43512

TUNG, ROSALIE SUET-YING, educator; b. Shanghai, China, Dec. 2, 1948; came to U.S., 1975; d. Andrew Yan-Fu and Pauline Wai-Kam (Cheung) Lam; B.A. (Univ. scholar), York U., 1972; M.B.A., U. B.C., 1974, Ph.D. in Bus. Adminstrn. (Univ. fellow, Seagram Bus. fellow, H.R. MacMillan Family fellow), 1977; m. Byron Poon-Yan Tung, June 17, 1972; 1 dau., Michele Christine. Lectr., diploma div. U. B.C., 1975, lectr. exec. devel. program, 1975; prof. mgmt. Grad. Sch. Mgmt., U. Oreg., Eugene, 1977-80; vis. scholar U. Manchester (Eng.) Inst. Sci. and Tech., fall 1980; vis. prof. UCLA, spring 1981; prof. mgmt. Wharton Sch. Fin., U. Pa., Phila., 1981-86; prof. bus. adminstrn., dir. internat. bus. ctr. U. Wis., Milw., 1986—. Mem. Acad. Internat. Bus. (treas.), Acad. Mgmt. (bd. govs.),Internat. Assn. Applied Psychology, Am. Arbitration Assn. (comml. panel arbitrators). Roman Catholic. Author 7 books; contbr. articles to profl. jours. Office: U Wis-Milw Sch Business PO Box 742 Milwaukee WI 53201

TUNGATE, JAMES LESTER, lawyer; b. Columbus, Ohio, Sept. 27, 1947; s. Ernest O. Jr. and Diantha (Woltz) T.; m. Susan Sumner, Aug. 25, 1973; children: Edward Ernest, James Aaron. B.S., Ill. Wesleyan U., 1969; M.A., Northwestern U.-Ill., 1970, Ph.D., 1972; J.D., U. Ill.-Urbana, 1979; hon. D.H.L., London Sch. (Eng.), 1972. Bar: Ill. 1979, U.S. Supreme Ct. 1985. Spl. instr. Northwestern U., Evanston, Ill., 1971; prof., chmn. Loyola U., New Orleans, 1971-76; state dir. News Election Service, New Orleans, 1972-74; dir. Inst. Religious Communications, New Orleans, 1974-76; asst. to state's atty. Iroquois County, Watseka, Ill., 1978; ptnr. Tungate & Tungate, Watseka, 1979—; media cons. Inst. Politics, New Orleans, 1973-76; legal cons., lectr. Iroquois Mental Health Ctr., Watseka, 1980—; lectr. law Kankakee Community Coll., Ill., 1982. Author: Romantic Images in Popular Songs, 1972; Readings in Broadcast Law, 1975. Dir. Iroquois Mental Health Ctr., 1980—; chmn. Iroquois County chpt. ARC, 1982-84, 85—; dir. Iroquois Republican Council, 1983—. Recipient Internat. Radio and TV Found. award; Harnow scholar U. Ill., 1976. Mem. Ill. Bar Assn., Iroquois County Bar Assn. (Law Day chmn.), Chgo. Bar Assn., Assn. Trial Lawyers Am., Am. Film Inst., Pi Alpha Delta. Republican. Methodist. Lodges: Masons (master 1982-83), Elks. Home: PO Box 285 Milford IL 60953 Office: Tungate & Tungate 744 E Walnut St Watseka IL 60970

TUNIS, SANDRA SIMMONS, health services administrator; b. Fort Wayne, Ind., Mar. 18, 1948; d. Robert Walter and Martha Louise (Krueckeberg) Simmons; m. Ronald Ellis Tunis, Aug. 22, 1970; 1 child, Kristin Marie. BA in Microbiology with distinction, Ind. U., 1970; AA in Nursing with highest distinction, Ind. U., Kokomo, 1975. RN, Ind., Wis. Microbiology lab. asst. Ind. U., Bloomington, 1968-70; microbiologist Meml. Hosp., Logansport, Ind., 1970, student nurse, 1973-75, staff nurse, 1975, night charge nurse obstetrics, 1976, nurse epidemiologist, quality assurance coordinator, 1977-85; health services adminstr. HealthReach Health Maintenance Orgn., Milw., 1985-86; dir. health services Family Hosp. Physician Assocs., 1986—; lectr. at continuing edn. workshops; cons. to various infection control practitioners; mem. Ind. U., Kokomo Nursing Adv. Bd. Medicaid Subcom. Wis. Assn. Health Maintenance Orgns.; preceptor for baccalaureate nursing students Purdue U.; spl. com. on EMS/HMO issues City Milw. Health Dept. Mem. Assn. for Practitioners in Infection Control (pres. Ind. chpt. 1984), Wis. Assn. Quality Assurance Profls., Wis. Soc. for Health Care Planning and Mktg., Assn. for Continuity of Care, Ind. U. Alumni Assn. (active extern program), LWV, Wis. Handweavers, Inc. (bd. dirs.), Phi Beta Kappa, Psi Iota Xi (pres. Alpha Xi chpt.). Democrat. Lutheran. Home: 5561 N Diversey Milwaukee WI 53217-5202 Office: Family Hosp Physician Assocs 1333 N 12th St Milwaukee WI 53205

TUOMI, DONALD, scientific firm executive, materials scientist, consultant; b. Willoughby, Ohio, Sept. 12, 1920; s. August and Lempi (Kannasta) T.; m. Ruth Elaine Campbell, May 23, 1923; children—Donna Jean, Mary Ellen. B.S. in Chemistry, Ohio State U., Columbus, 1943; Ph.D. in Phys. Chemistry, 1952. Research scientist Manhattan Project, SAM Labs., Columbia U., 1943-45; staff mem. MIT Lincoln Lab., Cambridge, 1953-54; research scientist Research Lab. T.A. Edison Corp., West Orange, N.J., 1955-59, T.A. Research Lab., McGraw Edison Corp., West Orange, 1959-61; mgr. solid-state physics Borg-Warner Research Ctr., Des Plaines, Ill., 1961-78, sr. scientist, 1978-83; pres. Donald Tuomi Ph.D. and Assocs. Ltd., Arlington Heights, Ill., 1983—; vis. indsl. sci. lectr. Am. Chem. Soc., Am. Inst. Physics, Indsl. Research Inst.; lectr. in field. Lay del. United Methodist Ch. Ann. Conf.; active Nuclear Freeze, Clergy and Laity Concerned, Common Cause. Recipient award of Merit Chgo. Tech. Soc. Council, 1973. Fellow Am. Inst. Chem., AAAS; mem. Am. Phys. Soc., Am. Chem. Soc., The Electro-Chem. Soc. (Battery Div. award 1968), Am. Crystallographic Soc., Sigma Xi. Conbtr. articles in field to profl. jours. Patentee thermo electric energy conversion, batteries, polymers. Home: 221 S Illinois Dr Arlington Heights IL 60005 Office: 103 N Arlington Heights Rd Arlington Heights IL 60004

TURCOTTE, MARGARET JANE, nurse; b. Stow, Ohio, May 17, 1927; d. Edward Carlton and Florence Margaret (Hanson) McCauley; R.N., St. Thomas Hosp., Akron, Ohio, 1949; m. Rene George Joseph, Nov. 24, 1961 (div. June 1967); 1 son, Michael Lawrence. Mem. nursing staff St. Thomas Hosp., 1949-50; pvt. duty nurse, 1950-57; polio nurse Akron's Children Hosp., 1953-54; mem. nursing staff Robinson Meml. Hosp., Ravenna, Ohio, 1958-67, head central service, 1963-67; supr. central service Brentwood Hosp., Warrensville Heights, Ohio, 1967, emergency med. technician. Mem. St. Thomas Hosp. Alumni Assn. Democrat. Roman Catholic. Home: 6037 Highview St Lot 14-F Ravenna OH 44266 Office: 4110 Warrensville Center Rd Warrensville Heights OH 44122

TUREK, MARK EDWARD, automotive company executive; b. Berwyn, Ill., May 10, 1949; s. Edward Alloyce and Dorothy Lee (Witt) T.; m. Judith Sue Prinzing, June 30, 1972; children: Sandra, Amy. BEE, U. Ill., 1971; MS in Fin., Northwestern U., 1977. Application engr. Gen. Motors, LaGrange, Ill., 1977-78, supr., sales engr., 1978-79, mgr., sales engr., 1979-81; dist. mgr. Gen. Motors, Houston, 1981-84; acct. mgr. Gen. Motors, Omaha, 1984-87, sales mgr., 1987—. Mem. Assn. MBA Execs., Nat. Found. Ilietus and Colitis, Tau Beta Phi. Republican. Avocations: woodworking, golf, reading. Home: 2006 Dorset Dr Wheaton IL 60187

TUREK, MICHAEL HENRY, plastics company executive; b. New Britain, Conn., Sept. 19, 1949; s. Henry Joseph and Genevieve Irene (Urbanowicz) T.; m. Sharon Ann Wagner, June 26, 1971; 1 child, Christopher John. BSME, Worcester Poly. Inst., 1971; MBA, U. Conn., 1972. Project engr. Monsanto Co., Stonington, Conn., 1973-76; supt. mfg. Monsanto Co., Lima, Ohio, 1976-79, supt. engring., 1979-82; supt. plant services Monsanto Co., Ligonier, Ind., 1984—crw; market mgr. Fisher Controls, Marshalltown, Ohio, 1982-84. Patentee method and apparatus improvements for controlling parison length. Mem. Soc. Plastics Engrs. Office: Monsanto Co 910 Gerber St Ligonier IN 46767

TURK, ALICE ELAINE, banker; b. Cleve., June 15, 1948; d. Melton Norman and Alice Loretta (Paulus) McConnell. Student Sch. Banking, U. Wis., 1981. Acct., Soc. Nat. Bank, Cleve., 1968-78, asst. treas., 1978-79, sr. fin. systems officer, 1979-82, v.p., mgr. acctg. and fin. systems, 1982-85, v.p., mgr. fin. systems, 1985—. Recipient cert. merit YWCA, 1980, profl. excellence award, 1983. Mem. Bank Adminstrn. Inst., Am. Inst. Banking. Democrat. Roman Catholic. Office: 2025 Ontario St Cleveland OH 44115

TURKEL, RICKEY MARTIN, chemistry editor, linguist, translator; b. N.Y.C., Apr. 12, 1943; s. Sidney and Belle (Opochinsky) T.; m. Frayda Siller, Mar. 7, 1965 (dec. Feb. 1986); children: Ariela Sarah, Adina Leah. BA, Hofstra U., 1963; PhD, MIT, 1968; MA, Ohio State U., 1976. Postdoctoral fellow Hebrew U., Jerusalem, 1968-69, Tulane U., New Orleans, 1969-70; assoc. abstractor Chem. Abstracts Service, Columbus, Ohio, 1970-71, assoc. editor, 1971-76, sr. assoc. editor, 1976-82, sr. editor, 1982-87, sr. editor, document analysis, 1987—; cons. translator various orgns. Contbr. articles to profl. jours. Mem. Am. Chem. Soc., Sigma Xi. Jewish. Proficient in French, German, Hebrew, Russian, Serbocroatian, Yiddish. Home: 150 S Cassingham Rd Columbus OH 43209 Office: Chem Abstracts Service Dept 51 PO Box 3012 Columbus OH 43210

TURNBAUGH, RONALD NEAL, minister; b. Nebo, Ill., Sept. 25, 1935; s. Marvin Rudyard and Vera Maudin (Scranton) T.; m. Dorothy J. Pearson, Feb. 14, 1955; children: Ronald N. Jr., Deborah A., Jeanette L. AA, Hannibal Lagrange Coll., 1967; AB, William Jewell Coll., 1971; M in Div., Midwestern Bapt. Sem., 1974; D in Ministry, Luther Rice Sem., 1980. Enlisted USAF, 1954, advanced through ranks to staff sgt., 1960, resigned, 1963; pastor Curryville (Mo.) Bapt. Ch., 1967-70, Utica (Mo.) Bapt. Ch., 1970-74, Temple Bapt. Ch., Poplar Bluff, Mo., 1974-76; dir. missions N.W. Bapt. Mission Group, Maryville, Mo., 1976-1984; minister edn., adminstrn. Plaza Heights Bapt. Ch., Blue Springs, Mo., 1984—. Mem. Nat. Assn. Bus. Adminstrn. Avocations: golf, hunting, fishing. Office: Plaza Heights Bapt Ch 1500 Clark Rd Blue Springs MO 64015

TURNBEAUGH, TERRY DEAN, minister; b. Litchfield, Ill., Dec. 8, 1954; s. John R. and Joyce (Thomas) T.; m. Linda K. Swinney, Dec. 20, 1973; children: Aaron, Adam. BA in Theology, Clarksville (Tenn.) Bapt. Coll., 1977. Ordained to ministry Bapt. Ch., 1977. Pastor Gethsemane Bapt. Ch., Marengo, Ohio, 1977-78; assoc. pastor New Hope Bapt. Ch., Dearborn Heights, Mich., 1978-79; music minister Northside Bapt. Ch., Madison Heights, Mich., 1980-81; deckhand Valley Lines Co., St. Louis, 1981-83; pastor First Bapt. Ch., Pineville, Mo., 1983-86, Armour Heights Bapt. Ch., Kansas City, Mo., 1986—; conf. leader Mole St. Nicolas, Republic of Haiti, 1985; evangelism dir. Shoal Creek Baptist Assn., 1983-86; mem. evangelism com. Blue River/Kansas City Baptist Assn. Contbr. column to BMW Owners mag., 1985—. Organizer Home Aid Motorcycle Rally Charity event, Crosses, Ark., 1986; bd. dirs. Samll Victories, Inc., Powell, Mo., 1986. Mem. BMW Motorcycle Owners Am. Avocations: motorcycling, golf, music, hunting, photography. Office: Armour Heights Bapt Ch 7900 Jarboe Kansas City MO 64114

TURNBULL, CHARLES VINCENT, realtor; b. Mpls., May 13, 1933; s. Charles Vivien and Lucille Frances (Dallas) T.; m. Gloria Marlene Tilley, July 21, 1956; children—Charlene Kay, Charles Vincent II, Terry Lucille, Mary Marlene. B.A., U. Minn., 1960, M.S.W., 1962. Unit dir. Mental Health Treatment Service, Cambridge (Minn.) State Hosp., 1962-67, dir. rehab. therapies, 1967-68, program dir., 1973-74; program dir. Minn. Valley Social Adaptation Center, St. Peter, Minn., 1968-73; chief exec. officer Faribault (Minn.) State Hosp., 1974-84; owner Turnbull's Shady Acres Resort, 1979-85; adminstr. Minn. Vets. Homes, Mpls. and Hastings, 1984-85; owner, broker Turnbull Realty, Faribault, Minn., 1986—; Program cons. Rochester (Minn.) Social Adaptation Center, 1970-71; cons. St. Louis State Sch. and Hosp., 1973-74. Chmn. United Fund Drive, St. Peter, 1971; scoutmaster Twin Valley council Boy Scouts Am., 1973-75; co-chmn. Faribault Bi-Centennial Horizons Subcom., 1975-76; pres. River Bend Nature Center, 1981-84, bd. dirs. 1976-87; mem. Minn. Developmental Disabilities Planning Council, 1975-79, Chmn. comprehensive plan subcom., 1977-78; mem. Cannon River Adv. Council, 1978-79; Mayor, Village of Lexington, Minn., 1962-64; candidate for U.S. rep. 2d Dist. Minn., 1972, 74. Served with USMC, 1953-56. Mem. Democratic Farmer Labor party. Lutheran. Home: Box 169 Route 3 Faribault MN 55021

TURNBULL, MICHAEL GARY, architect, consultant; b. Stratford, Ont., Can., Apr. 13, 1949; s. Gordon McKinnon and Catherine Agnes (Keable) T.; m. Joan Del Powers, Aug. 28, 1982; children: Mark Geoffrey, Meghan Christine. BArch, U. Ill., Chgo., 1973. Registered architect, Ill. Draftsman Solomon, Cordwell, Buenz, Chgo., 1973-74; sr. draftsman Skidmore, Owings, Merrill, Chgo., 1974-75; staff architect Wendt, Cedarholm, Tippens, Winnetka, Ill., 1976-82; project architect O'Donnell, Wicklund, Pigozzi, Northbrook, Ill., 1982-84; mus. architect Art. Inst. Chgo., 1984—. Piper Chgo. Highlander Bagpipe Band, Elmhurst, Ill., 1977—; sec. U.S. br. Turnbull Clan Assn., Mt. Prospect, Ill., 1976—. Mem. AIA, Ill. St. Andrew Soc. Roman Catholic. Avocation: Highland bagpipes. Office: Art Inst Chgo Michigan at Adams Chicago IL 60603

TURNER, ARTHUR EDWARD, college administrator; b. Hemlock, Mich., Jan. 31, 1931; s. Alvin S. and Grace E. (Champlain) T.; m. Johann M. Jordan, May 10, 1953; children: Steven Arthur, Michael Scott, Kathryn Jo. BS, Alma (Mich.) Coll., 1952; MEd, Wayne State U., 1954; postgrad., Cen. Mich. U., U. Mich.; LLD, Ashland Coll., 1968; HUD, Colegio Americano de Quito, Ecuador, 1968. Admissions counselor Alma Coll., 1952-53, dir. admissions, alumni relations, 1953-59; co-founder Northwood Inst., Midland, Mich., 1959, 1st pres., 1959-74, chmn. bd., chief exec. officer, trustee, 1974-78, chmn. bd. trustees, 1978—. Mem.-at-large Nat. council Boy Scouts Am.; lay minister Presby. Ch., Alma, 1956-59, organizer, minister, 1956, elder Meml. Presby. Ch., Midland, 1964—; trustee Epilepsy Found. Recipient People of Peru award, 1966, Internat. Freedom of Mobility award Nat. Automobile Dealers Assn., 1986; Named one of Outstanding Young Americans, 1968. Mem. Alpha Psi Omega, Phi Phi Alpha. Lodges: Masons, Shriners, Rotary. Clubs: Detroit; Midland Country; Beach Poinciana (Palm Beach, Fla.). Home: 4608 Arbor Dr Midland MI 48640 Office: Northwood Inst Midland MI 48640

TURNER, DAVID ARTHUR, radiologist; b. Chgo., Dec. 30, 1940; s. Samuel Julius and Sarah (Barbakoff) T.; m. Bonita Chaden, Jan. 30, 1967; children: Jason Chaden, Joanna Rachel. BA, U. Chgo., 1962, MD, 1965. Diplomate Am. Bd. Radiology, Am. Bd. Nuclear Medicine. Instr. U. Chgo., 1972-73; asst. prof. Rush Med. Coll., Chgo., 1973-77, assoc. prof., 1977-82, prof., 1982—; dir. magazine resolution imaging Presbyn. St. Luke's Hosp., Chgo., 1986—; mem. research rev. com. Chgo. Heart Assn., 1979-83, radiol. spl. study sect. NIH, Bethesda, Md., 1978. Contbr. numerous articles to profl. jours. Mem. bd. dirs. Ill. Citizens for Handgun Control, Chgo., 1981-83. Served to lt. comdr. USN, 1966-69, Vietnam. Grantee Rush Presbyn. St. Luke's Med. ctr., 1975-76, 81-82. Mem. Soc. Nuclear Medicine (sci. program com. 1977, 79-81, 83-85, bd. govs. Cen. chpt. 1978-82, 83-85), Am. Coll. Radiology, Am. Coll. Nuclear Physicians, Soc. Magnetic Resonance in Medicine, Radiol. Soc. N.Am. Office: Rush Presbyn St Luke's Hosp Rush Med Coll 1753 W Congress Pkwy Chicago IL 60612

TURNER, DENISE DUNN, writer; b. Cairo, Ill., Aug. 2, 1947; d. Robert James and Helen Grace (Dunn) Watkins; m. Revis Eugene Turner, Dec. 22, 1967; children: Rebecca Jill, Stephen Robert. Buyer Stewart's Dept. Store, Louisville, 1970-73; freelance writer Middletown, Ohio, 1976—; newspaper reporter Middletown Jour., 1987—; lectr. in field. Author: Home Sweet Fishbowl, 1982, Scuff Marks on the Ceiling, 1986; co-author: (book series) Guideposts, 1985; contbr. articles to mags. Chmn. publicity Charity Ball, Middletown, 1985; leader discussion Middletown Area Sr. Citizens, 1984—. Mem. Middletown C. of C. (Cert. Recognition 1986), Middletown Fedn. Women's Clubs. Baptist. Avocations: reading, bicycling. Home: 217 Edith Dr Middletown OH 45042

TURNER, DOUGLAS KEITH, computer systems analyst; b. Galesburg, Ill., Sept. 22, 1948; s. William Raymond and Mary Jane (Harper) T.; m. Rita M. Salemme, May 14, 1970 (div. July 1984); remarried, Feb. 14, 1986; children: David Keith, Christopher M., Robin Marie. BA, Northwestern U., 1970; postgrad., W.R. Harper Coll., 1980-81, Sangamon State U., 1986—. Programmer II, programmer III Ill. Dept. Revenue, Springfield, 1982-87, sales tax analyst, 1986—, programmer IV, 1987—; EDP instr. Lincolnland Community Coll., Springfield, 1984-85. Republican. Avocations: jogging, cycling, personal computers. Home: 3349 S 4th St Springfield IL 62703 Office: Ill Dept Revenue 101 W Jefferson St Springfield IL 62708

TURNER, DOUGLAS MARK, architectural design draftsman; b. New Castle, Pa., Feb. 1, 1964; s. Donald Wayne and Deloris Marie (Hiles) T. AS, ITT Youngstown Coll. Bus. and Profl. Drafting, 1984. Draftsman Horace McLean & Assocs., Niles, Ohio, 1984—. Mem. AIA (assoc.). Home: PO Box 101 New Bedford PA 16140 Office: Horace McLean & Assocs 918 Youngstown-Warren Rd Niles OH 44446

TURNER, EVAN HOPKINS, art museum director, educator; b. Orono, Me., Nov. 8, 1927; s. Albert Morton and Percie Trowbridge (Hopkins) T.; m. Brenda Winthrop Bowman, May 12, 1956; children: John, Jennifer. A.B. cum laude, Harvard U., 1949, M.A., 1950, Ph.D., 1954. Head docent service Fogg Mus., Cambridge, Mass., 1950-51; curator Robbins Art Collection of Prints, Arlington, Mass., 1951; teaching fellow fine arts Harvard U., 1951-52; lectr., research asst. Frick Collection, N.Y.C., 1953-56; gen. curator, asst. dir. Wadsworth Atheneum, Hartford, Conn., 1956-59; dir. Montreal Mus. Fine Arts, Que., Can., 1959-64, Phila. Mus. Art, 1964-77, Ackland Art Mus., 1978-83, Cleve. Mus. Art, 1983—; adj. prof. U. N.C., Chapel Hill, 1978—; adj. prof. art history U. Pa. Mem. Assn. Art Mus. Dirs., Coll. Art Assn. Am., Am. Mus. Assn., Am. Fedn. Arts. Clubs: Union (Cleve.); Franklin Inn (Phila.); Century Assn. Home: 3071 North Park Blvd Cleveland OH 44118 Office: Cleve Mus of Art 11150 East Blvd Cleveland OH 44106

TURNER, FRED L., fast food franchiser executive; b. 1933; married. B.S., De Paul U., 1952. With McDonald's Corp., Oak Brook, Ill., 1956—, exec. v.p., 1967-68, pres., chief adminstrv. officer, 1968-77, chief exec. officer, 1977-87, chmn., 1977—, also dir. Served as 1st lt. U.S. Army, 1943-45. Office: McDonald's Corp One McDonald's Plaza Oak Brook IL 60521 •

TURNER, GLENN FORREST, office supply company executive; b. Lake Forest, Ill., Nov. 7, 1954; s. Forrest Eugene and Lottie Cathryn (Abshire) T. B.S., No. Ill. U. Instr. Ill. Inst. Diving, Glen Ellyn, Ill., 1978-83; mem. sales staff Suburban Office Supply, Crystal Lake, Ill., 1970-73, mgr., 1973-77, v.p., 1977-86, pres. 1986—; co-founder Kiss Research & Devel. Co., Marengo, Ill., 1984—. Mem. Ill. Retail Mchts. Assn., Nat. Office Products Assn., U.S. C. of C., Cousteau Soc. Avocations: flying; scuba diving; woodworking. Home: 127 N Main St Crystal Lake IL 60014 Office: Suburban Office Supply Inc 125 N Main St Crystal Lake IL 60014

TURNER, JOHN GOSNEY, insurance company executive; b. Springfield, Mass., Oct. 3, 1939; s. John William and Clarence Oma (Gosney) T.; m. Leslie Corrigan, June 23, 1962; children: John Fredric, Mary Leslie, James Gosney, Andrew William. B.A., Amherst Coll., 1961; student, Advanced Mgmt. Program, Harvard U., 1980. Asso. actuary Monarch Life Ins. Co., Springfield, Mass., 1961-67; group actuary Northwestern Nat. Life Ins. Co., Mpls., 1967-75, sr. v.p. group, 1975-79, sr. v.p., chief actuary, 1979-81, exec. v.p., chief actuary, 1981-83, pres., chief operating officer, 1983—; dir.

NWNL Reins. Co., NWNL Gen. No. Life, North Atlantic Life Ins. Co. N.Y. Trustee Abbott-Northwestern Hosps., Evans Sch. Found.; chmn. Minn. Trustees of the Evans Scholars Found. Fellow Soc. Actuaries; mem. Am. Acad. Actuaries, Western Golf Assn. (dir.), Minn. Golf Assn. Club: Minikahda (Mpls.). Office: Northwestern Nat Life Ins Co 20 Washington Ave S PO Box 20 Minneapolis MN 55440 *

TURNER, MARVIN STEVENSON, JR., admissions director; b. Zanesville, Ohio, Aug. 26, 1944; s. Marvin Stevenson Turner and Rebecca (Margaret) Stevenson. BA, Columbia Bible Coll., 1965; BS, Presbyn. Coll., Clinton, S.C., 1967; MDiv., Covenant Sem., 1971; MEd, U. Mo., St. Louis, 1975; PhD, St. Louis U., 1982. Counselor Mo. Bapt. Hosp. Sch. Nursing, St. Louis, 1973-75, Maryville Coll., St. Louis, 1975-77; prin. Conway Day Sch., St. Louis, 1977-81; instr. tng. and devel. dept. Barnes Hosp., St. Louis, 1981-85, dir. admissions sch. nursing, 1985—. Contbr. articles to profl. jours. Avocation: photography. Home: 4475 W Pine Apt 402 Saint Louis MO 63108 Office: Barnes Hosp Sch Nursing 416 S Kingshighway Saint Louis MO 63110

TURNER, PREWITT BATES, JR., insurance company executive; b. Kansas City, Mo., Oct. 12, 1932; s. Prewitt Bates and Mary Belle (Mundy) T.; m. Karen Van Voorst, Dec. 12, 1957; children: Rebecca, Jeniffer, Prewitt III. AB, Princeton U., 1954. Sr. v.p. Marsh & McLennan, Kansas City, 1980; pres. Agrl.-Risk Services, Inc., Kansas City; also bd. dirs. Agri-Risk Services, Kansas City; chmn. Bates Turner, Kansas City; also bd. dirs.; chmn. Turner Farms, Glasgow, Mo.; bd. dirs. Traders Ins. Co. Served to 1st lt. USAF, 1954-57. Republican. Episcopalian. Clubs: Kansas City Country, River (Kansas City). Home: 5835 Hill Dr Mission Hills KS 66208 Office: Argi-Risk Services Inc One Ward Pkwy Kansas City MO 64112

TURNER, RICHARD BARRY, communications executive; b. Phoenix, Nov. 18, 1940; s. John Richard and Elizabeth Ross (Barry) T.; B.S., Northwestern U., 1962; M.S., Ariz. State U., 1968. Gen. mgr. Arie Crown Theatre, Chicago, 1974; co. mgr., assoc. dir. pub. relations, editor Lyric Opera News, Lyric Opera of Chgo., 1974-81; dir. info. services and advt. Sta. WTTW-TV, Chgo., 1981-85; dir. communications Chgo. Community Trust, 1985—. Past chmn. Joseph Jefferson awards comm.; founding pres. bd. dirs. Wisdom Bridge, Travel Light Theatres; mem. Hubbard Street Dance bd.; mem. Acquired Immune Deficiency Syndrome Found. Chgo. bd. Club: Arts.

TURNER, RICHARD DOUGLAS, data processing executive; b. Greenville, Ohio, Mar. 22, 1955; s. Richard Wayne and Janet Ann (Liette) T.; m. Judy L. Wetzel, June 16, 1984. BS, USAF Acad., Colorado Springs, Colo., 1977; MBA, Rensselaer Poly. Inst., 1980. Commd. 2d lt. USAF, 1977, advanced through grades to capt., 1981; data processing prodn. mgr. USAF, Plattsburgh AFB, N.Y., 1977-78, data processing chief, 1978-80; computer staff officer USAF, Wright-Patterson AFB, Ohio, 1980-81, computer performance analyst, 1981-82, resigned, 1982; ops. support mgr. Chem. Abstracts Service, Columbus, Ohio, 1982—. Republican. Roman Catholic. Avocations: golf, guitar. Home: 7116 Winding Brook Ct Worthington OH 43085 Office: Chem Abstracts Service Dept 28 Box 3012 Columbus OH 43210

TURNER, ROBERT ELWOOD, physicist; b. Covington, Ky., Dec. 8, 1937; s. Elwood Fletcher and Margaret Belle (Gunn) T. BS in Physics, U. Cin., 1959, MS in Physics, 1960; MA in Physics, Columbia U., 1963; PhD in Physics, Washington U., St. Louis, 1970. Research physicist U. Mich., Ann Arbor, 1970-73, Environ. Research Inst. Mich., Ann Arbor, 1973-77; sr. scientist Sci. Applications Internat. Corp., Dayton, Ohio, 1977—; research asst. Inst. for Space Studies (NASA), N.Y.C., 1962, Washington U., 1964-69; astronomer McDonnell Planetarium, St. Louis, 1965-68; lectr. U. Mich., 1971-77. Contbr. articles to profl. jours. and books. Rep. precinct leader, Ann Arbor, 1972. Laws fellow, 1959; recipient Group Achievement award NASA, 1976. Mem. AAAS, Am. Assn. Physics Tchrs., Optical Soc. Am., N.Y. Acad. Scis., Sigma Xi. Methodist. Club: Toastmasters (ednl. v.p. Dayton 1986, pres. 1987). Avocations: swimming, tennis, ice skating, walking. Home: 3296 Wilmington Pike Apt 11 Kettering OH 45429 Office: Sci Applications Internat Corp 1010 Woodman Dr Suite 200 Dayton OH 45432

TURNER, STEVEN MAGNUS, printing co. exec.; b. St. Louis, Sept. 29, 1951; s. Edward Jerome and Joan (Magnus) T.; B.S. cum laude, Boston U., 1973; m. Lisa Philips, Dec. 30, 1972. Estimator, Universal Printing Co., St. Louis, 1973-75, salesman, 1975-78, v.p. sales, 1978-80; founder, pres. Creative Printing Services, Inc., 1980—. Mem. St. Louis Assn. Young Printing Execs. (past exec. v.p., dir.), Direct Mktg. Club of St. Louis, Printing Industries of St. Louis, St. Louis Sons of Bosses (past v.p., dir.), Direct Mktg. Club of St. Louis. Clubs: Frontenac Racquet, Town & Tennis, Westwood Country. Home: 830 Town and Country Estates Dr Town and Country MO 63141 Office: Creative Printing Services Inc 34 N Brentwood Clayton MO 63105

TURNER, THEODORE HOWARD, educational administrator; b. Wierton, W.Va., July 24, 1924; s. James Howard and Alice Josephine (Newsome) T.; m. Iva Mae Smithers, June 2, 1951; children—Marcia Lynn, Amy Kathleen. B.S., Ohio State U., 1950; B.Mus., 1950; M.Ed., U. Cin., 1956. Tchr. music, Lockland, Ohio, 1950-56, Cin., 1956-57, Columbus, Ohio, 1957-66; jr. high sch. prin., Columbus, 1966-69, high sch. prin., 1969-74, interim supt., Columbus, 1982, asst. supt., 1974-86; pres., chief exec. officer Creative Inst., Columbus, 1986—. Served with U.S. Army, 1943-46; ETO. Mem. Nat. Assn. Jazz Educators, Nat. Alliance Black Sch. Educators, Am. Assn. Sch. Adminstrs., Assn. Curriculum and Supervision Devel., Music Educators Nat. Conf., U.S. Tennis Assn., NAACP, Columbus Com. Mental Health, Columbus Leadership Conf., PUSH, Phi Mu Alpha, Phi Delta Kappa.

TURNER, TIMOTHY NICHOLAS, podiatrist; b. Arkansas City, Kans., Aug. 11, 1948; s. Nicholas Reid and Lena (Buzzi) T.; m. Diane B. Lake, Aug. 8, 1987. AA, Cowley County Jr. Coll., 1968; BS, Kans. U., 1971; BS, D, Ill. Coll. Podiatric Medicine, 1980. Resident VA Med. Ctr., Leavenworth, Kans., 1980-81; with Santa Fe Railroad, Wichita, Kans., 1971-76; pvt. practice podiatry Wichita, 1981—; cons. VA Med. Ctr., Wichita, 1984—. Bd. dirs. med. service bur. United Way, Wichita, 1983—, Upjohn Home Health Care, Wichita, 1982—, Kans. br. Am. Diabetes Assn., 1984—. Mem. Am. Podiatric Med. Assn., Kans. Podiatric Med. Assn. Presbyterian. Lodge: Masons, Consistory, Shriners, Order of DeMolay (Legion of Honor 1983). Avocations: golf, running. Office: West Side Foot Clinic 605 McLean Blvd NW Wichita KS 67203

TURNOY, BERNARD IVAN, insurance broker; b. Chgo., Nov. 8, 1954; s. Herbert Samuel and Jule H. (Young) T. BA in Polit. Sci., The Am. U., Washington, 1976; postgrad. in Legal Studies, Cambridge U., Eng., 1977-79. Lic. ins. agt., Ill. Field rep. The Mutual Life Ins. Co. N.Y., Chgo., 1980-85; chief exec. officer Bernard I. Turnoy & Assocs., Chgo., 1986—; mktg. cons. The Mut. Life Ins. Co. N.Y., 1984. Mem. Chgo. Council on Fgn. Relations, English Speaking Union, Chgo.; issues coordinator Congl. Campaign 10th Congrl. Dist., 1979. Mem. Nat. Assn. Life Underwriters (Nat. Sales Achievement award 1985), Chgo. Assn. Life Underwriters, Life Ins. Mktg. and Research Assn. (Nat. Quality award 1984). Clubs: United Oxford and Cambridge Club (London), Execs. of Chgo. Avocations: fishing, scuba diving, skiing. Home: 330 Diversey Pkwy #1905 Chicago IL 60657 Office: 10 S Riverside Plaza Suite 850 Chicago IL 60606

TURSSO, DENNIS JOSEPH, business executive; b. St. Paul, Apr. 13, 1939; s. Joseph Bias and Cecelia Beatrice (Solheid) T.; m. Sharon Ann Benike, June 6, 1964 (div. 1975); 1 son, Jason Bradford; m. 2d, Jacqueline Mary Hoffmann, Oct. 19, 1977; children—Shannon and Missey Michele (twins). Student U. Minn., 1959-61. Sales mgr. Sten-C-Labl Inc., St. Paul, 1958-65; salesman Dymo Industries, Berkeley, Calif., 1965-68; with Dawson Patterson, St. Paul, 1968—; pres., chief exec. officer Tursso Cos. holding co., St. Paul, 1980 ; bd. dirs. Summit Nat. Bank, St. Paul, Blackours Co. Advisor SBA, St. Paul, 1981-83; bd. dirs. Childrens' Home Soc. St. Paul. Recipient Star Club sales awards Dymo Industries, 1966, 67. Mem. Nat. Fed. Ind. Bus., Soc. Packaging Engrs., St. Paul C. of C. (cert. of merit, Outstanding Businessman 1987). Clubs: St. Paul Athletic, St. Paul, University, Minnesota, Decathlon, Pool and Yacht, Town and Country. Address: Tursso Cos 223 Plato Blvd E Saint Paul MN 55107

TUSCHMAN, JAMES MARSHALL, lawyer; b. Toledo, Nov. 28, 1941; s. Chester and Harriet (Harris) T.; m. Ina S. Cheloff, Sept. 2, 1967; children: Chad Michael, Jon Stephen, Sari Anne. BS in Bus., Miami U., Oxford, Ohio, 1963; JD, Ohio State U., 1966. Bar: Ohio 1966. Assoc. Shumaker, Loop & Kendrick, Toledo, 1966-84, ptnr. 1970-84; co-founder, sr. prin. Jacobson Maynard Tuschman & Kalur, Toledo, Cleve., Cin., Columbus and Dayton, Ohio, and Charleston, W.Va., 1984—, also mem. mgmt. com.; chmn. bd., sec. Tuschman Steel Co., Toledo, 1969-76; vice chmn. bd. Kripke Tuschman Industries, Inc., 1977-85, dir. 1977-86; chmn. bd., sec. Toledo Steel Supply Co., 1969-86; ptnr. Starr Ave. Co., Toledo, 1969-86; ptnr. Tulip Group Ltd.; asst. gen. counsel PIE Mut. Ins. Co., Cleve. Trustee, chmn. fin. com., treas. Maumee Valley Country Day Sch.; past trustee, v.p., treas. Temple B'nai Israel. Mem. ABA, Ohio Bar Assn., Toledo Bar Assn., Def. Research and Trial Lawyers Assn., Zeta Beta Tau, Phi Delta Phi. Clubs: Glengary Country, Toledo. Home: 2579 Olde Brookside Rd Toledo OH 43615 Office: 4 Sea Gate 9th Floor Toledo OH 43604

TUSZYNSKI, SHERRY LEE, medical instrumentation company executive; b. Monroe, La., Sept. 24, 1942; d. Lee Edward and Lyda Fern (Epley) Trahan; m. Jack Price, Mar., 1961; m. Robert Allen Tuszynski, Dec. 26, 1969; 1 son, Bruce Lee. B.A. in Econs., Ind. U., 1969. Sales analyst Puritan-Bennett Corp., Westmont, Ill., 1973-76, mgr. sales analysis, 1976, sales rep., 1976-82, dist. sales mgr., 1982—. Mem. Alpha Mu Gamma. Office: Puritan-Bennett 26 Plaza Dr Westmont IL 60559

TUTERA, GINO, obstetrician, gynecologist; b. Rome, Sept. 25, 1945; s. Frank and Ellena (Corizza) T.; m. Ursula Viehmann, July 5, 1969; children: Ashley, Dominic. AB, U. Mo., 1967, MD, 1971. Diplomate Am. Bd. Ob-Gyn. Intern, then resident in ob-gyn St. Luke's Hosp., Kansas City, Mo., 1971-74; practice medicine specializing in ob-gyn Kansas City, 1974—; med. dir. Kansas City PMS Clinic, 1984— Women's Resource Ctr. Bapt. Med. Ctr., Kansas City, 1986—; vice-chmn. dept. ob-gyn St. Joseph Hosp., Kansas City; bd. dirs. Women's Health Services Bapt. Med. Ctr., Kansas City, 1986—. Mem. Friends of the Zoo. Fellow Am. Coll. Ob-Gyn; mem. AMA, Mo. Med. Assn., Jackson County Med. Soc., Kansas City Ob-Gyn Soc. Republican. Roman Catholic. Avocation: tennis. Home: 610 E 45th St Kansas City KS 64110 Office: 400 E Red Bridge Rd Kansas City MO 64131

TUTEUR, WERNER, psychiatrist; b. Fed. Republic Germany, June 19, 1911; came to U.S., 1937.; s. Arthur and Gertrude (Frank) T.; m. Marjorie Nesbitt, Oct. 14, 1944 (dec. Mar. 1978); 1 child, Robert. Grad., Goettinger U., Fed. Republic Germany, 1936. Diplomate Am. Bd. Psychiatry and Neurology. Assoc. prof. Stritch Sch. Med. Loyola U., Chgo., 1952—; psychiatric cons. Fed. Ct., Chgo., 1970—. Contbr. articles to psychiat. pubis. Served to capt. USMC, 1944-46. Fellow Am. Psychiat. Assn., Am. Acad. Forensic Scis. Home and Office: 162 S State St Elgin IL 60120

TUTEWOHL, LARRY FRANCIS, school system administrator; b. Farmington, Minn., Dec. 4, 1946; s. Joseph C. and Margaret C. Tutewohl; m. Kathleen A. Clark, Aug. 3, 1968; children: Linda T., Steven J. BS, Winona (Minn.) State U., 1968; MA, U. N.M., 1974; MS, U. Wis., Milw., 1984. Cert. math and computer tchr., Wis. Tchr. math Port Washington (Wis.) Schs., 1968-78, Germantown (Wis.) Schs., 1978-85; instr. math Marquette U., Milw., 1985-86; curriculum coordinator Waukesha (Wis.) Pub. Schs., 1986—. Pres. Community Scholarship Fund, Cedarburg, Wis., 1978, chmn., 1980; v.p. Little League, Cedarburg, 1985-86. Grantee, Milw. Found., 1985. Mem. Assn. Supervision and Curriculum Devel., Assn. Staff Devel., Am. Assn. Sch. Adminstrs., Wis. Assn. Supervision and Curriculum Devel., Nat. Council Tchrs. Math, Wis. Math Council (exec. bd. 1984-86). Roman Catholic. Avocations: fishing, bowling, sports. Home: 4392 River Vista Dr Cedarburg WI 53012 Office: Waukesha Pub Schs 222 Maple Ave Waukesha WI 53186

TUTTLE, CHARLES ELLIOTT, management services company executive; b. Gainesville, Fla., Oct. 30, 1939; s. Frank W. and Vada Lee (Nelson) T.; m. Virginia Rhoda Carson, Nov. 25, 1961; children: Eileen, Franklin, Margaret, Luke. BA, Trinity Coll., Hartford, Conn., 1961; MBA, NYU, 1966; BS, Ohio State U., 1971, MS, 1973. Asst. sec., loan officer Irving Trust Co., N.Y.C., 1961-66; v.p., loan officer Merchants Nat. Bank, Manchester, N.H., 1966-69; asst. v.p. ops., loan officer Huntington Nat. Bank, Columbus, Ohio, 1969-73, v.p., loan officer, 1973-79; pres. Farm and Ranch Mgmt. Services Inc., Marysville, Ohio, 1981—; bd. dirs. VanDyne Crotty Co., Columbus. Contbr. articles to profl. jours. Mem. Am. Soc. Farm Mgrs. and Rural Appraisers (profl., chmn. summer meeting 1987), Am. Soc. Agrl. Cons. (cert.). Republican. Episcopalian. Lodge: Kiwanis (bd. dirs. Columbus club 1986-87). Avocations: flying, dog training and breeding. Office: FARMS Inc 837 Delaware Ave PO Box 434 Marysville OH 43040

TUTTLE, DAVE G., auditor; b. Elgin, Ill., Sept. 17, 1961. BS in Acctg., Ill. State U., 1982; MBA, De Paul U., 1985. CPA, cert. mgmt. acct., Ill. Fin. auditor Continental Ill. Nat. Bank & Trust Co. subs Continental Ill. Corp., Chgo., 1982-84; computer systems auditor Dart & Kraft, Inc., Northbrook, Ill., 1984-86; sr. computer system auditor Premark Internat., Northbrook, 1986—. Mem Am. Inst. CPA's. Office: Premark Internat 2211 Sanders Rd Northbrook IL 60062

TUTTLE, GREGORY DUANE, dentist; b. Marshall, Minn., Nov. 14, 1958; s. Donald Charles and Ruth Marie (Maas) T.; m. Kathryn Ann Berthelsen, June 7, 1986. Student, S.D. State U., 1977-80; DDS, U. Nebr., 1984. Assoc. J. Christiansen, DDS, Beresford, S.D., 1984-85; gen. practice dentistry Sioux Falls, S.D., 1984—; dental staff mem. Sioux Valley Hosp., Sioux Falls, 1985—. Bd. dirs. St. John Am. Luth. Ch., Sioux Falls, 1984—. Mem. ADA, S.D. Dental Assn., Southeast Dist. Dental Soc., Sioux Falls Jaycees (bd. dirs. 1984—), Sioux Falls Area C. of C. (council mem. 1986—). Avocations: water skiing, cross-country skiing, long distance running, camping, biking. Home: 6209 Coughran Ct Sioux Falls SD 57106-0443 Office: 1412 W 41st St Sioux Falls SD 57105

TUTTLE, ROBERT D., industrial products manufacturing company executive. Chmn., chief exec. officer, dir, former pres., Sealed Power Corp., Muskegon, Mich. Office: Sealed Power Corp 100 Terrace Plaza Muskegon MI 49443 *

TUZCU, ERTUGRUL, retail executive; b. Skopye, Sirbia, Yugoslavia, Mar. 8, 1953; came to U.S., 1976; s. Enver and Nigar Tuzcu; m. Karen Agnes Owen, May 17, 1986. BSME, Bosphorous U., Istanbul, Turkey, 1976; MS in Indls. Engring., U. Minn., 1978. Sr. analyst indsl. engring. Dayton Hudson Dept. Store Co., Mpls., 1978-81, mgr. indsl. engring, selling cost, 1981-83, mgr. indls. engring., selling cost, accounts payable, 1983-84, mgr. mdse. fin. services, 1984-85, mgr. inventory control, payroll, 1985-87, mgr. expense control, 1987—; adj. faculty U. Minn., Mpls, 1978-82. Recipient Energy Saver's Award of Excellence Minn. Energy Agy. and Natural Gas Council, 1980. Mem. Am. Inst. of Indsl. Engrs., Minn. Soc. Indsl. Engrs. (Young Engr. of Yr. 1980, 81), Am. Mgmt. Assn., Minn. Turkish Am. Assn. (auditor 1987). Home: 14100 38th Place N Plymouth MN 55441 Office: Dayton Hudson Dept Store Co 700 On The Mall Minneapolis MN 55402

TWADDLE, ARCHIBALD KERR, barrister, solicitor, judge; b. Glasgow, Scotland, Nov. 7, 1932; came to Can., 1961; s. Archibald Ferguson and Mary Kerr (Harris) T.; m. Susan Elizabeth Bowden, Aug. 17, 1957; children: Katherine, Iain. Barrister at Law, Inns of Ct. Sch. of Law, London, 1950-54. Barrister London, 1954-61; barrister and solicitor Winnipeg, Man., Can., 1961-85; judge Ct. of Appeal, Man., 1985—. Avocations: opera, oil painting. Office: Ct of Appeals, Law Cts Bldg, Winnipeg, MB Canada R3C 0V8

TWEED, THOMAS EDWARD, corporate executive; b. Mason City, Iowa, Aug. 11, 1942; s. Selmer Theodore and Clarissa F. (Dahl) T.; m. Rita Lorainne Johnson, Nov. 26, 1964; children—Nancy Anne, Michael Thomas. Student U. Iowa. Sales rep. CIBA Pharmaceutical, Summit, N.J., 1968-73; regional mgr. Ludlow Corp., Ware, Mass., 1973-81; pres. Heart Medical, Inc., Hanover Park, Ill., 1982—. Bd. dirs. Evangel. Retirement Homes/Friendship Village of Schaumburg, Chgo. and Schaumburg, Ill., 1982—; pres. Lord of Life Lutheran Ch., Schaumburg, 1984. Served as HM3 USN, 1960-63. Republican. Avocations: music; photography. Home: 1124 Court G Hanover Park IL 60103 Office: PO Box 241 Bloomingdale IL 60108

TWELLS, JOHN LAWRENCE, manufacturing and distributing company executive; b. Flint, Mich., Feb., 1934; s. Robert and Margaret Shaw (MacKillop) T.; m. Mary Jane Jentzen, Nov. 1961; children: Linda, John Lawrence, Robert William. BBA, U. Toledo, 1957; postgrad., Marquette U., 1975; MBA, Columbia Pacific U., 1981, DBA, 1983. Terr. mgr., nat. accounts rep. Motorcraft/Autolite div. Ford Motor Co., Dearborn, Mich., 1950-63; dist. mgr., regional sales mgr. MOPAR div. Chrysler Corp., Detroit, 1963-67; asst. gen. mgr. NAPA Genuine Parts Co., Atlanta, 1967-68; gen. mgr. John MacKillop and Co., Inc., Poland, Ohio, 1968—; parts mktg. mgr. Dresser Industries, Waukesha (Wis.) Engine div. 1973-76; mgr. replacement part and OEM profit ctr. Baker Material Handling Corp., 1976-78; gen. sales mgr. Amweld Bldg. Products Inc., Garretsville, Ohio, 1978-82, asst. gen. mgr., 1982, gen. mgr., 1983-87; v.p., gen. mgr. Mesker Door Co., St. Louis, 1987—; lectr. in field. Contbr. articles on microfiche, inventory control, personnel selection, motivation and evaluation to profl. jours. Deacon Immanuel Presbyn. Ch., Milw., 1974-76. Served with U.S. Army, 1957-59. Recipient Disting. Mktg. award Sales and Mktg. mag., 1980. Mem. Am. Prodn. and Inventory Control Soc., Constrn. Specifications Inst., Sales and Mktg. Execs. Internat., Am. Inst. Indsl. Engrs., Am. Def. Preparedness Assn., Am. Legion, VFW, Tau Kappa Epsilon. Republican. Lodge: Rotary. Home: 8996 Sherwood Dr NE Warren OH 44484 Office: PO Box 5214 Poland OH 44514

TWITCHELL, HANFORD MEAD, printing company executive; b. N.Y.C., Dec. 17, 1927; s. Hanford Mead and Virginia (Sterry) T.; m. Inge Dyring Larsen, Mar. 15, 1969; 1 son, Robert. Student Princeton U., 1948-50. Writer, corr., translator, Europe and Latin Am., 1954-61; prodn. mgr. Pace Publs., Los Angeles, 1962-69, Scott & Scott, Santa Monica, Calif., 1969-71; sales mgr. Noll Printing Co., Huntington, Ind., 1971-78, mktg. dir., 1978-80, v.p., 1980—. Served with U.S. Army, 1950-53. Episcopalian. Club: Orchard Ridge Country (Ft. Wayne, Ind.). Office: Noll Printing Co 100 Noll Plaza Huntington IN 46750

TWYFORD, ALFRED THOMAS, trucking company executive; b. Oakland, Calif., June 24, 1934; s. Alfred J. and Winifred (Reilly) T.; m. Helene M. Pieren; children: Thomas P., Karen M. BS, U. San Francisco, 1956. V.p. mktg. and sales Pacific Intermountain Express, Oakland, Calif., 1975-80; pres. Highway Transport, Knoxville, Tenn., 1980-82; exec. v.p. Schneider Tank Lines, Green Bay, Wis., 1982-84; pres. Nat. Bulk Transport, Green Bay, 1984-85; exec. v.p. Boncosky Transp., Algonquin, Ill., 1986—. Served with U.S. Army, 1956-58. Fellow Am. Soc. Transp.; mem. Nat. Tank Truck Assn. (bd. dirs. 1981—), Delta Nu (pres. 1968). Republican. Roman Catholic. Lodge: Kiwanis (pres. Walnut Creek club 1979). Home: 1091 Byron Ln #5 Elgin IL 60123 Office: Boncosky Transp 1301 Industrial Dr Algonquin IL 60102

TWYMAN, JACK, wholesale grocery company executive, management services company executive.; b. May 11, 1934; married. Ed., U. Cin. Basketball player Cin. Royals, 1955-67; announcer ABC, 1967-72; vice-chmn. Super Food Services, Inc., Dayton, Ohio, from 1972, now chmn., chief exec. officer, former pres., chief operating officer. Office: Super Food Services Inc 3185 Elbee Rd Dayton OH 45439

TYAGI, NARENDRA SINGH, surgeon; b. Nangola, India, Jan. 12, 1945; s. Tilak Ram and Jagwati (Tyagi) T.; M.D., All India Inst. Med. Scis., New Delhi, 1966; m. Shashi Tyagi, June 26, 1970; children—Rachana, Renuka, Ashutosh. Intern Ellis Hosp., Schenectady, N.Y., 1968; resident in gen. surgery St. Joseph Mercy Hosp., Pontiac, Mich., 1970-73; dir. Pontiac Med. Scis. Research Labs., 1973-74; dir. intensive care unit Oakland Med. Center, Pontiac, 1973-74; active attending physician St. Joseph Mercy Hosp., Pontiac, 1973—, chmn. dept. surgery, 1984-85; dir., v.p. Pontiac Emergency Care Group. Chmn. ad-hoc com. Bharatiya Temple, 1975, sec. bd. trustees, 1976. Recipient C. Walton Lilliehei award Pontiac Med. Sci. Research Lab., 1971, Charles G. Johnston award Detroit Surg. Assn., 1971-72; Frederick A. Coller award Mich. chpt. A.C.S., 1972. Diplomate Am. Bd. Surgery. Fellow A.C.S., Internat. Coll. Surgeons; mem. Mich. State, Oakland County med. socs., Am. Coll. Emergency Physicians. Developer sling suture technique for use in tracheal surgery. Home: 4209 Margate Ln Bloomfield Hills MI 48013 Office: 909 Woodward Ave Pontiac MI 48053

TYBOUT, ALICE MARIE, educator; b. Ann Arbor, Mich., Dec. 2, 1949; d. Richard Alton and Rita Harris (Holloway) T. B.A. in Bus. Adminstrn., Ohio State U., 1970, M.A. in Consumer Behavior, 1972; Ph.D. in Mktg., Northwestern U., 1975. Academic counselor Coll. Adminstrv. Scis. Ohio State U., 1970-72; research asst. Northwestern U., Evanston, Ill., 1972-74, asst. prof. mktg. and transp., 1975-81, asso. prof., 1981-85, prof., 1985—, J.L. Kellogg research prof. Kellogg Grad. Sch. Mgmt., 1980-81 Buchanan research prof. Kellogg Grad. Sch. Mgmt., 1983-84, Gen. Foods research prof., 1985-86, prof. mktg. J.L. Kellogg Grad. Sch. Mgmt., 1985—; instr. bus. U. Chgo., 1974-75; cons. Am. Bankers Assn., AT&T, Batus Corp. Sears Retailing scholar, 1969. Mem. Am. Mktg. Assn., Assn. Consumer Research (treas. 1982, 83, co-chmn. 1982, 85 confs.). Mem. editorial bd. Jour. Mktg., 1979-81, Jour. Bus. Research, 1980—, Jour. Mktg. Research, 1981-85, Jour. Consumer Research, 1982—; Co-editor: Advances in Consumer Research, Vol. 10, Cognitive and Affective Responses to Advertising; contbr. articles to profl. jours. Office: Northwestern Univ Dept Marketing 2001 Sheridan Rd Evanston IL 60201

TYCE, GERTRUDE MARY, neuroscientist; b. Wark, Eng.; d. Ernest and Mary Louise (Coulson) Sidebottom; m. Francis Anthony Jacob Tyce, June 21, 1952; 1 child, John Christopher. BS, U. Durham, Eng., 1948, PhD, 1952. Research asst. Mayo Clinic, Rochester, Minn., 1958-63, research assoc. in biochemistry, 1963-71, assoc. cons. in biochemistry, 1971-75, cons. in physiology, 1976—; prof. physiology Mayo Med. Sch., Rochester, 1981—. Contbr. 123 articles to profl. jours. Bd. dirs. Olmsted Citizens for a Better Community, Rochester, 1984-86, pres. 1985-86. Mem. AAAS, Am. Chem. Soc., Internat. Soc. Neurochemistry, Soc. Neuroscience, Soc. for Exptl. Biology and Medicine, Am. Soc. Exptl. Pathology, N.Y. Acad. Scis., Sigma Xi, Sierra Club. Avocations: antiquarian, naturalist, travel. Home: 929 11 St SW Rochester MN 55902 Office: Mayo Clinic Rochester MN 55905

TYLER, CHARLES ROBERT, architect; b. Noblesville, Ind., Oct. 31, 1957; s. Melvin Wesley and Victoria Mae (Roberts) T.; m. Karen Dieckamp, June 20, 1957. BArch, U. Cin., 1982. Registered architect, Ind. Staff architect Archonics Design Partnership, Indpls., 1982-84; project architect HNTB, Indpls., 1985; project mgr. Kennedy Brown McQuiston, Indpls., 1985-87, jr. ptnr., 1987—. Mem. Indpls. Mus. Art, 1985—; bd. dirs. Herron Morton Hist. Dist. Mem. AIA, Constrn. Specifiers Inst., Indpls. Jaycees. Republican. Methodist. Avocation: photography. Office: Kennedy Brown McQuiston 47 S Meridian Indianapolis IN 46204

TYLER, JUNE SMITH, lawyer; b. Evarts, Ky., Aug. 14, 1942; d. William Henry and Florene (Hembree) Smith; m. Morris Reed Tyler; children: William Smith, Kimberly Nichole, Florena Kaye. Diploma in nursing, Miner's Meml. Hosp. Assn., 1963; BA in Polit. Sci., No. Ky. U., 1981; JD, Northern Ky. U., 1985. Bar: Ky. 1985, Ohio, 1986, U.S. Dist. Ct. (ea. dist.) Ky. 1986, U.S. Dist. Ct. (so. dist.) Ohio 1986, U.S. Ct. Appeals (6th cir.) 1986; RN, Ohio, Ky. RN U. Ky. Med. Ctr., Lexington, Appalachian Regional Hosp., Harlan, Ky., State of Ky. Dept. Pub. Health, Booth Meml. Hosp., Covington, Ky., Grant County Hosp., Williamstown, Ky., Hoxworth Blood Ctr. U. Cin.; jud. law clk. U.S. Dist. Ct. (so. dist.) Ohio, Cin., 1985-86; assoc. Dinsmore & Shohl, Cin., 1986—. Contbr. articles to profl. jours. Mem. ABA, Ky. Bar Assn., Ohio State Bar Assn., No. Ky. Bar Assn., Cin. Bar Assn., Chase Alumni Assn. Office: Dinsmore & Shohl 2100 Fountain Sq Plaza 511 Walnut St Cincinnati OH 45202

TYLER, SHIRLEY KAY, clinical psychologist; b. San Antonio, June 4, 1947; d. Ned A. and Margaret A. (Payne) M.; m. John D. Tyler, Aug. 14, 1971; 1 child, Wade M. Cloud. BA, U. N.D., 1973, MA, 1975, PhD, 1980. Lic. cons. psychologist, Minn., N.D. Clin. psychologist Med. Ctr. Rehab. Hosp., Grand Forks, N.D., 1979—; cons. psychologist div. Vocat. Rehab., Grand Forks, 1981—. Contbr. articles to profl. jours. Fellow NIMH, 1974,

77-78. Mem. Am. Psychol. Assn., N.D. Psychol. Assn. (pres. 1983-84). Office: Med Ctr Rehab Hosp 1300 S Columbia Rd Grand Forks ND 58201

TYLER, THOMAS A(LBERT), architectural company executive, educator; b. Concordia, Kans., Jan. 20, 1949; s. William B. and Eleanor C. (Owens) T.; m. Suzanne G. Greenhaw, June 17, 1978. BArch, Kans. State U., 1974. Registered architect, Kans., NCARB. Architect Clyma-Keleher, Tulsa, 1976-78; instr. interiors Kans. State U., Manhattan, 1978-80; dir. archtl. interiors Pearce Corp., St. Louis, 1980-82; gen. mgr. design Color Art, St. Louis, 1982-83; pres. Answers, St. Louis, 1983—; instr. Washington U., St. Louis; apptd. bd. visitors Found. for Interior Design Edn. and Research. Recipient Furniture Design award Internat. Woodwork Inst., 1974. Mem. AIA (panel mem. Kansas City chpt. 1980, interiors com. chmn. 1983, nat. liaison 1984-87, St. Louis chpt. Service award 1984, Health Care Design award Chgo. chpt. 1984), Assn. Univ. Interior Designers (panel mem. 1986). Roman Catholic. Club: Alton Lake Sailing Assn. (commodore 1983, treas. 1985, sec. 1986). Avocation: sailing. Home: 6548 Bancroft Saint Louis MO 63109 Office: Answers Inc 310 Mansion House Ctr Saint Louis MO 63102

TYLER-SLAUGHTER, CECIL LORD, housing relocation specialist; b. Peoria, Ill., Oct. 15, 1958; s. William Albert and Verline Marie (Tyler) Scott. Student Ill. State U., 1974-78. Adminstrv. intern Ill. State U., Normal, 1974-76; child care coordinator Community Action Agency, Peoria, 1976-79; program coordinator Learning Tree Prep. Sch., Peoria, 1980-83; housing relocation specialist Salvation Army, Peoria, 1984—. Investigative reporting journalist Face to Face, 1982; interviewer radio news format, 1983. Cons. NAACP, Peoria, 1984; leader 4H Club, Peoria, 1980-83; election judge Peoria Democratic Party, 1984. Recipient 4H Silver Clover Leadership award, 1983, Save the Children Spl. Honor Mayor Office, Atlanta, 1981; White House fellow Presdl. Commn., 1983. Mem. George Washington Carver, ARC, Smithsonian Inst. Orthodox Jewish. Home: 1904 Grand View Peoria Heights IL 61614 Office: Cen Ill Eastern Iowa Salvation Army Hdqrs 413-415 Adams NE Peoria IL 61612

TYMKIW, BARBARA CATHERINE, financial analyst; b. Yonkers, N.Y., June 11, 1934; d. Nicholas and Mary (Bolinsky) Skrobala; m. Michael Myroslav Tymkiw, Aug. 19, 1961; children: Christine Annmarie, John Bohdan, Catherine Oksana. Assoc. in Applied Sci., Westchester Community Coll., 1954; student, Columbia U., 1957-58; BS summa cum laude, Dyke Coll., 1983; MBA, Baldwin-Wallace Coll., 1985. Adminstrv. asst. UN, N.Y.C., 1954-61, Am. Cyanamid, N.Y.C., 1954-61, U.S. Vitamin Corp., Yonkers, N.Y., 1954-61; adminstrv. asst., facilitator Alcan Aluminum Corp., Cleve., 1981-86; fin. analyst Roulston and Co., Cleve., 1986—. Editor: Business and Financial Cycles-A Systems Approach To Forecasting and Business Decision Making (George Dagnino), 1986. Mem. Am. Mgmt. Assn., Am. Soc. For Tng. and Devel., Cleve. Soc. Security Analysts. Mem. Ukrainian Catholic Ch. Home: 9300 Evergreen Dr Cleveland OH 44129 Office: Roulston and Co 4000 Chester Ave Cleveland OH 44103

TYO, MICHAEL ALEXANDER, biochemical engineer; b. Bloomington, Ind., Sept. 18, 1952; s. John Henry and Alexina Mary (Fernet) T.; m. Felice Patricia Meadow, Nov. 29, 1980; children: Natalie, Alexander. BSc, MIT, 1976, MSc, 1978. Dir. Beta Interferon Labs. So. Biotech., Tampa, Fla., 1981-82; sr. devel. engr. Johnson & Johnson Corp., Tampa, 1982-84; mgr. biochem. engrng. Endotronics, Inc., Coon Rapids, Minn., 1984—; cons. Flow Labs., MaClean, Va., 1979-80, Key Interferon, Tampa, 1980. Contbr. articles to profl. jours. Mem. AAAS, Soc. Indsl. Microbiology, Am. Chem. Soc., Sigma Xi. Democrat. Avocations: amateur radio, amateur astronomy, photography. Home: 7315 Ridgeway Rd Golden Valley MN 55427 Office: Endotronics Inc 8500 Evergreen Blvd Coon Rapids MN 55433

TYRRELL, KARINE, documentation analyst; b. Saarbrucken, Germany, Nov. 4, 1940; came to U.S., 1968, naturalized, 1978; d. Eduard and Charlotte (Faber) Ambrosius; B.A., McMaster U., Can., 1964; M.A., So. Ill. U., 1972, Ph.D., 1984; m. James Tyrrell, Aug. 27, 1964 (div. 1979); 1 child, Dalton. Tchr., Hamilton (Ont., Can.) Sch. Bd., 1964-65, Ottawa (Ont., Can.) Sch. Bd., 1966-68; research asst. U.S. Grant Assos., So. Ill. U., Carbondale, 1973-74, teaching asst. 1974-77, dissertation fellow, 1977-78; tech. writer Action Data Services, St. Louis, 1979-80, Boeing Computer Services, Wichita, Kans., 1980—. Home: 9459 E Skinner St Wichita KS 67207 Office: PO Box 7730 M/S K79-51 Wichita KS 67277-7730

TYSINGER, PHILIP LINDSEY, automotive executive, advertising agency executive; b. Durham, N.C., Jan. 31, 1948; s. Elmo Lindsey Tysinger and Gladys Virginia (Tysinger) Barringer; m. Linda Ilene Donahey, Aug. 7, 1970; 1 child, Erin Nichole. Student Campbell Coll., 1964-68; B.B.A., Washburn U., 1974. Advt. mgr. KTPK Radio, Topeka, 1974-84 ; ptnr. KINA Radio, 1979-85, B&T Advt., Topeka, 1985—; sr. v.p. Ed Bozarth Chevrolet, Topeka, 1985—. Served with USAF, 1968-72. Mem. Jr. Achievement of Northeastern Kans. (bd. dirs. 1979—), Profl. Advertisers Club Topeka (pres. 1978-79), Topeka Blood Bank (bd. dirs. 1984—), Sales and Mktg. Execs. of Topeka (bd. dirs. 1980-84, 86-87, Outstanding Salesman award 1978, 80, bd. dirs. 1980-84), Topeka C. of C. Republican. Methodist. Office: Ed Bozarth Chevrolet 3731 S Topeka St Topeka KS 66609

TYSL, GLORIA JEANNE, history educator, consultant, researcher; b. Chgo., Apr. 17, 1931; d. Anton Otto and Myrtle Geraldine (Voborsky) T. B.A., Mt. Marty Coll., Yankton, S.D., 1960; M.A., De Paul U., Chgo., 1967; Ph.D., Ind. U., Bloomington, 1976. Tchr., Sacred Heart Acad., Lisle, Ill., 1950-67; prof. history Ill. Benedictine Coll., 1968-74, 78—, acad. dean and dean of faculty, 1974-78; cons. to Nat. Endowment Humanities. NSF fellow, 1967, Carnegie fellow, 1976, NEH fellow, 1981-82. Mem. Am. Hist. Assn., Catholic Hist. Assn., Brit. Hist. Assn., English Hist. Assn., N.W. Suburban Arts Council, Chgo. Council on Fgn. Relations, AAUW, Am. Assn. Higher Edn., Am. Council Edn. Roman Catholic. Home: 1045 Mayfield Ln High Point Hoffman Estates IL 60195 Office: Ill Benedictine Coll Lisle IL 60532

TYSON, KIRK W. M., business consultant; b. Jackson, Mich., July 2, 1952; s. George Carlton and Wilma Marion (Barnes) T.; m. Janice Lynn Lorimer, Aug. 25, 1979 (div. Dec. 1984); m. Kathryn Margit Kennell, June 24, 1986; 1 child, Robert. BBA, Western Mich. U., 1974; MBA, DePaul U., Chgo., 1982. CPA, Ill.; cert. mgmt. cons., 1985. Bus. cons. Arthur Andersen & Co., Chgo., 1974-84; v.p. cons. First Chgo. Corp., 1984; pres. Kirk Tyson & Assocs., Oak Brook, Ill., 1984—. Author: Business Intelligence: Putting It All Together, 1986. Pres., Chgo. Jr. Assn. Commerce and Industry Found., 1977-79; active Easter Seals Soc., 1977, Am. Blind Skiing Found., 1977-78, Jr. Achievement, 1976-77, United Way Met. Chgo., 1979-80, Urban Gateways, 1975. Mem. Am. Inst. CPAs, Ill. Soc. CPAs, Planning Execs. Inst., N.Am. Soc. Corp. Planning, Inst. Mgmt. Cons., Am. Mktg. Assn., Alpha Kappa Psi (Disting. Service award 1982). Lutheran. Home: 7615-C Bristol Ct Woodridge IL 60517 Office: 2021 Midwest Rd Oak Brook IL 60521

TYSZKIEWICZ, ROBERT EDWARD, automotive company executive; b. Detroit, Oct. 3, 1948; s. Edward Stanley and Geraldine (Drope) T.; m. Susan Eleanor Caine, May 10, 1975; children: Kathryn, Elizabeth. BBA, Ea. Mich. U., 1971. Mgmt. trainee Chrysler Motors, Highland Park, Mich., 1971-73; mktg. asst. Lucas Industries Inc., Troy, Mich., 1974-77, mgr. mktg. services, 1978-82, mgr. product mktg., 1982-84, product gen. mgr., 1985—. Mem. Automotive Service Industry Assn., Motor Equipment Mfrs. Assn., Automotive Parts and Accessories Assn., Automotive Imports Assn. Republican. Roman Catholic. Club: Alahambra. Lodge: KC. Avocations: golfing, volleyball, racquetball, bowling. Home: 1202 N Pleasant Royal Oak MI 48067 Office: Lucas Industries Inc 5500 New King St Troy MI 48098

TZENG, REN-YU, software engineer; b. Taichung, Tawain, Republic of China, Sept. 12, 1954; came to U.S., 1978; d. Shao-Chou and Mei (Lin) T.; m. Li-Wei Jen, Jan. 30, 1978; children: I-Hsuan Jen, I-Shie Jen. BS in Animal Sci., Chung-Hsing U., Taiwan, 1976; MS in Animal Breeding, Wash. State U., 1979, MS in Computer Sci., 1983. Poultry disease inspector Kingdom Poultry Breeder Farm, Taiwan, 1976-77; research asst. animal breeding Wash. State U., Pullman, 1978-79, teaching asst. in stats., 1979-81; sr. software engr. ISC System Corp., Spokane, Wash., 1981-86, Detroit, 1986—. Scholar Hender, Taiwan, 1975-76, Hubbard, Pullman, 1978. Mem. Assn. Computer Machinery.

UBERT, HOWARD JOSEPH, computer company manager; b. Hays, Kans., July 21, 1941; s. Roderick and Eleanor (Sander) U.; m. Joyce Ann Michel, Feb. 1, 1964; children—Kevin Paul, Gregory Michael, Kathleen Ann. B.S. in Elec. Engrng., Kans. State U., 1964; postgrad. U. Ala.-Huntsville, 1965-66. Systems engr. Indsl. Nucleonics (now AccuRay Corp.), Columbus, Ohio, 1967-68, area sales mgr., 1969-73, regional mgr., 1973-76, mgr. internat. tire industry, 1976-78; eastern regional mgr. energy Measurex Corp., Cupertino, Calif., 1978-81; v.p. sales August Systems, Tigard, Oreg., 1981-82; regional mgr. Indsl. Data Terminals, Westerville, Ohio, 1982-83, field sales mgr., 1983-84, nat. sales mgr., 1984-85, v.p. sales, 1985—. Bd. dirs. Worthington (Ohio) Parks and Recreation Com.; v.p., sec., treas. Cardinal Boosters, Worthington; pres. Worthington High Sch. PTA. Served to capt. U.S. Army, 1964-67. Mem. Instrument Soc. Am., IEEE, Soc. Plastics Engrs., ASME, Worthington Jaycees (Outstanding Jaycee Committeeman 1973). Republican. Roman Catholic. Home: 6425 Meadowbrook Circle Worthington OH 43085 Office: 173 Heatherdown Rd Westerville OH 43081

UCHIMOTO, TADASHI TED, book binding and mailing firm exec.; b. Stockton, Calif., Feb. 3, 1918; s. Kometaro and Shitsu (Hanaoka) U.; grad. high sch., Hiroshima, Japan, Stockton; m. Hamako Oye, Feb. 11, 1943 (dec. Apr. 1966); 1 son, Dennis Den; m. 2d, Mitsu Miyazaki, Mar. 5, 1967. Founder, Gen. Mailing Service and Sales Co., Inc., Chgo., 1945—. Mem. Japanese Am. Assn. Chgo. (pres.), Chgo. Hiroshima Kenjinkai (pres.). Home: 5515 N Francisco Ave Chicago IL 60625 Office: 2620 W Washington Blvd Chicago IL 60612

UDEHN, CARLYSLE DAVID, dentist; b. Moline, Ill., Dec. 21, 1921; s. Axel David and Nellie Cecilia (Safe) U.; m. Catharine Isabelle Belding, June 4, 1949; children: David Duane, Kenneth James, Kathleen Ann. BA, U. Iowa, 1949; BS, U. Ill., 1951, DDS, 1953. Gen. practice dentistry Alexis, Ill., 1953-54, Cambridge, Ill., 1954-57, Moline, Ill., 1957—; adj. instr. oral diagnostic pathology U. Iowa, 1974-77. Sec. Rock Island (Ill.) County Bd. Health, 1975-77. Served to sgt. U.S. Army, 1942-45, PTO. Mem. ADA, Internat. Congress of Implantologists, Am. Running and Fitness Assn. Republican. Lutheran. Avocations: sports medicine, biking, hiking, camping, jogging. Home: 3111 38th St Moline IL 61265 Office: 551 18 th Ave Moline IL 61265

UDELL, JON GERALD, business educator, executive; b. Columbus, Wis., June 22, 1935; s. Roy Grant and Jessie M. (Foster) U.; m. Susan Smykla, June 12, 1960; children—Jon Jr., Roy Steven, Susan Elizabeth, Bruce Foster, Alan Joseph, Kenneth Grant. B.B.A., U. Wis., 1957, M.B.A., 1958, Ph.D., 1961. Instr., asst. prof., assoc. prof. U. Wis.-Madison, 1959-68, prof. bus., 1968—, assoc. dir. and dir. Bur. Bus. Research and Service, 1963-75, assoc. dir. Univ-Industry Research Program, 1967-77, Irwin Maier prof. bus., 1975—; dir., chmn. bd. Fed. Home Loan Bank of Chgo., 1982—; dir. Research Products Corp., Madison, Wis. Electric Power Co., Milw. Author: Successful Marketing Strategies in American Industry, 1972; The Economics of the American Newspaper, 1978; Reporting on Business and the Economy, 1981; Marketing in An Age of Change, 1981. Chmn. funding Madison Boyschoir, 1983-84; chmn. Consumer Adv. Council, State of Wis., 1972-74; mem. Gov.'s Council of Econ. Devel., Wis., 1967-73; v.p. Madison C. of C., 1976; elder, deacon Presbyn. Ch. Recipient Gov.'s citation for service, 1969, 71, Sidney S. Goldish award, 1973; named Wisconsinite of Yr. Wis. State C. of C., 1973, Mktg. Man of Yr. So. Wis. chpt. Am. Mktg. Assn., 1976, Robert A. Jerred Distng. Service award U. Wis., Madison, 1976, 86. Mem. Am. Mktg. Assn., Bus.-Edn. Coordinating Council (pres. 1979-80, bd. dirs. 1979—), Wis. for Research (bd. dirs.), Wis. Assn. Mfrs. and Commerce (trustee Bus. World 1981—), Assn. Pvt. Enterprise Edn. (bd. dirs.), Am. Newspaper Pubs. Assn., Wis. Builders Assn. Club: Faculty Roundtable (chmn. 1970-71). Lodge: Rotary. Home: 5210 Barton Rd Madison WI 53711 Office: U Wis Sch Bus 1155 Observatory Dr Madison WI 53706

UEBELHART, NASH RAY, obstetrician/gynecologist; b. Canton, Ohio, Dec. 7, 1948; s. Allen Paul and Lois Marjorie (Parsons) U.; m. Kathryn Meister, Dec. 23, 1972; children: Scott, Lora. BS in Biology, Ohio State U., 1970, MD, 1974. Diplomate Am. Bd. Ob-Gyn. Intern Hurley Med. Ctr., Flint, Mich., 1974-75, resident, 1975-78; dir. ob-gyn edn. St. Joseph Hosp., Flint, 1978-80; practice medicine specializing in ob-gyn McLaren Gen. Hosp., Flint, 1978—. Mem. AMA, Mich. State Med. Soc., Genesee County Med. Soc. Avocations: photography, astronomy, piano, scuba diving, ornithology.

UEHLING, THEODORE EDWARD, philosophy educator; b. Scranton, Pa., July 31, 1935; s. Theodore Edward and Ella Cuthbertson (MacMurray) U.; m. Anne Stewart Bevis, Aug. 10, 1957; children: Theodore Edward, Thomas August, Trent Stewart, Robert Carl. Student, Univ. Cin., 1953-54; BA, Ohio State U., 1959, PhD, 1965. Asst. prof. U. Minn., Morris, 1963-68, assoc. prof., 1968-72, asst. dean, 1968-72, prof. philosophy, 1972—; cons. U.S. Dept. Edn., Washington, 1987—. Author: The Notion of Form in Kant's Critique of Judgment, 1971; articles in field. Cons. NEH, Washington, 1986—. Served as sgt. USAF, 1954-57. Recipient Morse award for Contributions to Edn., U. Minn. Mem. N.Am. Kant Soc. (v.p. 1985—), Am. Philos. Assn., Australasian Assn. for Philosophy, Minn. Philos. Soc. Home: 902 W 4th St Morris MN 56267 Office: U Minn Coll Ave Morris MN 56267

UGENT, GEOFFREY RAYMOND, religious organization administrator; b. Milw., June 1, 1956; s. Irving Manuel and Nancy (Coppage) U.; m. Joann Vinci Lass, Jan. 3, 1976; 1 child, Timothy David. AA, N.W. Coll. Assemblies of God, 1981, BA, diploma in Christian Edn., 1982. Ordained to ministry Assemblies of God Ch., 1986. Assoc. youth pastor 1st Assembly of God Ch., Aberdeen, Wash., 1977-78, Cedar Park Assembly of God Ch., Kirkland, Wash., 1978-80; intern in pastoral ministry Christ Ch. of Bellevue, Wash., 1981-82; dir. campus life club Youth for Christ U.S.A., Mount Prospect, Ill., 1983—; producer community TV Cablenet, Inc., Mount Prospect, 1983—; area del. 1985 Youth Congress Youth for Christ U.S.A., Washington, 1984—. Served with USN, 1974-78. Mem. Evang. Tchr. Tng. Assn. (cert., tchr. 1982—), Ill. Dist. Council Assemblies of God, Guild Am. Luthiers. Lodge: Kiwanis (dir. high sch. activities Elk Grove club 1984—). Avocations: cycling, rock climbing, canoeing and canoe building, instrument building. Office: Youth for Christ USA North Division Campus Life 530 W Northwest Hwy Mount Prospect IL 60048

UGGERUD, WARD LEE, electric utility company executive; b. Drayton, N.D., Mar. 28, 1949; s. Edward Rudolph and Lila Marie (Soderfelt) U.; m. Jane Rachelle Triebold, July 28, 1970; children: Mark, Eric. BSEE, N.D. State U., 1971. Registered profl. engr., Minn. Engr. computer services Otter Tail Power Co., Fergus Falls, Minn., 1971-74, system engr., 1974-78, asst. mgr. systems ops., 1978-79, mgr. systems ops., 1979-84, dir. systems ops., 1984—; vice chmn. operating com. Mid-Continent Area Power Pool, Mpls., 1984, chmn., 1985; sec. operating com. N.Am. Electric Reliability Council, Princeton, N.J., 1986—. Com. mem. Boy Scouts Am., Fergus Falls, 1973-82, cub master, 1983-84; pres. Bethlehem Luth. Ch., Fergus Falls, 1974-75. Mem. IEEE. Lodge: Rotary. Avocations: cross country skiing, woodworking, reading, cooking. Home: 609 W Douglas Fergus Falls MN 56537 Office: Otter Tail Power Co 215 S Cascade Fergus Falls MN 56537

UHER, WILLIAM JOHN, bank trust officer; b. Chgo., Apr. 29, 1950; m. Isabelle Kocielski, June 27, 1976; 1 child, Alexander William. BM, DePaul U., 1972; MM, U. Ill., 1975; MBA, U. Chgo., 1985. Instr. Cen. Mo. State U., Warrensburg, 1975, St. Xavier Coll., Chgo., 1976-77; mgr. Tandy Corp, Chgo., 1977-82; fin. cons. Qantel Co., Palos Heights, Ill., 1982-83; mgmt. cons. Blvd. Bank, Chgo., 1983-84, fin. Service Mgr., 1984—; cons. in field, Chgo., 1975-80. Roman Catholic. Avocation: woodworking, golf. Home: 18657 Marshfield Homewood IL 60430 Office: Blvd Bank 410 N Mich Ave Chicago IL 60611

UHLEIN, GABRIELE, education administrator; b. Klingenberg, Federal Republic of Germany, Apr. 25, 1952; came to U.S., 1954; BS in Clin. Psychology, Ind. State U., 1979; MA in Spirituality/Religious Studies, Mundelein Coll., 1982. Mem. preaching staff Mount St. Francis (Ind.) Retreat Ctr., 1975-77; mental health worker DuPage Health Dept., Wheaton, Ill., 1979-81; regional coordinator Cath. Charities, Chgo., 1982-83; dir. Edn. Mission Services-Wheaton Franciscan Services, 1983-86, v.p., 1986—; cons. to parishes and religious orgns. in Midwest, 1982—; cons., trustee Hospice of DuPage, Lisle, Ill., 1980-86; trustee, mem. adv. bd. Christine Ctr. for Meditation, Willard, Wis., 1981—; trustee Francis Heights/Clare Gardens, Denver, 1983—; presenter workshops Cosmology for Peace, 1984—, Bereavement, Death and Dying, 1981—; mem. adv. bd. Advent Ctr. for Spiritual Devel., 1987—. Author: Meditation with Hildegard of Bingen. Active DuPage Pledge of Resistance Affinity Group, Ill., 1985; networker Action Linkage. Mem. Cath. Health Assn. Wis., Friends of Creation Spirituality, Wheaton Franciscan Social Justice Team. Office: Wheaton Franciscan Services Inc PO Box 667 Wheaton IL 60189

UHRICH, JOHN STANISLAUS, data processing executive; b. Lemon, S.D., June 14, 1959; s. Lawrence Joseph and Catherine Mary (McGowen) U.; m. Nyki Marie Stocco, Mar. 19, 1985; 1 child, Molly Jeanne. BA in Mgmt. Info. Systems, U. Wis., 1981. Programmer analyst Gopher News Co., Golden Valley, Minn., 1982-83; mgr. data processing Coldwell Banker, Mpls., 1983—. Republican. Roman Catholic. Avocations: golf, softball, fishing, hunting. Home: 1943 Berkshire Dr Eagan MN 55122 Office: Coldwell Banker 3800 W 80th St #1000 Minneapolis MN 55431

UHRIK, STEVEN BRIAN, psychotherapist; b. Chgo., June 30, 1949; s. George Steven and Elizabeth Gertrude Beisse (Will) U.; m. Mee Phon C. B.A., No. Ill. U., 1973; M.S.W., U. Ill., 1980. Vocat. coordinator O. H. Industries div. Opportunity House, Inc., Sycamore, Ill., 1970-79; clin. social worker, family counselor Rockford (Ill.) Meml. Hosp., 1979-81, co-dir. devel. chronic pain program, 1979-80; social worker West Suburban Kidney Center, S.C., Oak Park, Ill., 1981-87; social work cons. Continental Health Care, Ltd., Oak Park, 1981-87; dir. employee assistance Grant Hosp. of Chgo., 1987—; pres. Personal Consultation Counseling and Psychotherapy, Carol Stream, Ill., 1983—; pub. relations cons. Dekalb County Villages, Inc., 1975-76. Recipient award Dekalb-Sycamore Human Relations Commn., 1974; developed patient edn. program for dialysis patients and family members Nat. Kidney Found. of Ill. Mem. Nat. Assn. Social Workers, Acad. Cert. Social Workers, Omicron Delta Kappa, Alpha Kappa Delta. Office: Mona Kea Med Park 383 Schmale Rd Carol Stream IL 60188

UKMAN, LESA JEAN, editor, marketing company executive; b. Chgo., May 4, 1956; d. Alvin and Sheila (Wolin) U. BA, Colo. Coll., 1978. Coordinator events City of Chgo. Mayor's Office Spl. Events, 1979-81; cons. Crain Communications, Chgo., 1981; founder, editor Spl. Events Report, Chgo., 1982—; pres. Internat. Events Group Cons., 1984—; founder, dir. Event Mktg. Seminar Series, 1984—. founder, editor Internat. Directory of Spl. Events and Festivals, 1983—; editor: Banking on Leisure, 1985, (16-tape series) Making Sponsorship Work, 1986; contbr. articles to profl. jours. Office: Spl Events Report 213 W Institute Pl Room 303 Chicago IL 60610

ULAKOVICH, RONALD STEPHEN, real estate developer; b. Youngstown, Ohio, Nov. 17, 1942; s. Stephen G. and Anne (Petretich) U. B.S., Indsl. Engring. Coll., 1967; M.S., Method Engring., Ill. Inst. Tech., 1969. Methods engr. Supreme Products, Chgo., 1964-66; pres. Contract Chair, 1966-70; v.p. sales Amrep Corp., Rosemont, Ill., 1970-73; pres. Condo Assoc., Ltd., Arlington Heights, Ill., 1973—, Am. Resorts Internat. Ltd., 1983. Named Employee of Yr., 1965; recipient Nat. Home Builders Grand award, 1977, Million Dollar Circle award Chgo. Tribune, 1978, Cert. of Recognition award Congressional Com., 1982, Cert. of Merit award Pres. Reagan's Task Force, 1984; named to Ky. Col.State of Ky., 1982. Mem. Am. Assn. Investors, Apt. Owners Assn., Real Estate Soc. of Syndicators and Investors, Am. Resort and Resdl. Devel. Assn. Roman Catholic. Avocations: auto racing, golf. Home: 510 Van Buren St East Dundee IL 60118

ULBRICH, DOREEN ELISA, communications executive consultant; b. Mt. Clemens, Mich., Aug. 30, 1955; d. Guidone and Doris Camille (La Croix) Procopio; m. Wayne Ulbrich, Sept. 20, 1975 (div. July 1980). Cert. gen. bus., Macomb County Community Coll., 1982; BBA, Wayne State U., 1986. Lic. realtor, Mich. Installation order rep. Mich. Bell, Birmingham, 1974-75; service sales rep. Mich. Bell, Harper Woods, Mich., 1975-83; sales rep. AT&T, 1983-85; account support rep. AT&T Info. Systems, Birmingham, 1985; tech. cons. Gen. Motors div. AT&T, 1985-86; staff mgr. AT&T Nat. Product Scheduling Hdqrs., N.J., 1985-86; project mgr. AT&T Info. Systems, 1986-87; network communications mgr. AT&T Communications, Southfield, Mich., 1987—. Mem. Nat. Assn. Female Execs., Macomb County Bd. Realtors (assoc.). Avocations: water skiing, snow skiing, horseback riding, working out. Home: 16652 Festian Dr Fraser MI 48026 Office: AT&T Communications 27700 Northwestern Hwy Suite 303 Southfield MI 48010

ULBRICHT, ROBERT E., lawyer, savings and loan executive; b. Chgo., Dec. 1, 1930; s. Emil Albert and Vivian June (Knight) U.; m. Betty Anne Charleson, June 20, 1953; 1 dau., Christine Anne. A.B., U. Ill., 1952, M.A., 1953; J.D., U. Chgo., 1958. Bar: Ill. 1958, U.S. Dist. Ct. (no. dist.) Ill. 1959. Research atty. Am. Bar Found., Chgo., 1957-59; asst. trust counsel Continental Ill. Nat. Bank & Trust Co., Chgo., 1959-60; assoc. law firm Cummings and Wyman, Chgo., 1960-68; gen. atty., sec., sr. v.p. Bell Fed. Savs. & Loan Assn., Chgo., 1968—; instr. Aurora Coll., Coll. DuPage. Mem. nominating com. Dist. 41 Sch. Bd., 1970-71, vice chmn., 1971; chmn. dist. area fund raising Glen Ellyn council Girl Scouts Am., 1970. Bd. dirs. Glen Ellyn (Ill.) Pub. Library, 1979-85, pres., 1983-84. Served with AUS, 1953-55. Mem. Chgo. Bar Assn., Ill. Bar Assn., ABA. Clubs: Glen Oak Country, Glen Ellyn Tennis. Bd. editors Chgo. Bar Record, 1970-73; contbr. articles to legal jours. Office: 79 W Monroe St Chicago IL 60603

ULICHNY, BARBARA L., state legislator; b. Milw., June 10, 1947; d. Clarence and Karmen (Egge) Seybold. BA in Econ., Northwestern U., 1969. Tchr. Nicolet High Sch., Milw., 1969-74; adminstr. bicentennial City of Milw., 1975-76; program staff YWCA, Milw., 1976-78; mem. Wis. Assembly, Madison, 1978-84, Wis. Senate, Madison, 1984—; chmn. senate com. econ. devel., crime victim's council. Mem. Common Cause, Italian Community Ctr., Profl. Dimensions, Wis. Heritages, Watertower Landmark Trust, Milw. Task Force on Rape/Sexual Assault and Domestic Violence, Hist. Lower E. Side Neighborhood Assn.; adv. bd. ctr. study of entrepreneurship Marquette U.; bd. dirs. Milw. Ballet, Visiting Nurses Corp. Recipient Pub. Interest award Ctr. for Pub. Representation, 1977, Wis. Women's Polit. Caucus award, 1979, 81, Woman of Yr. award, NOW, 1980, Nat. Orgn. Victim Assistance award, 1981, Meritorious Service award Phi Kappa Phi, 1984. Mem. Nat. Conf. State Legislature (com. fed. taxation, trade and econ. devel.), Council State Govt. (bus. devel. task force), Wis. Women's Network, LWV. Democrat. Lutheran. Office: Wis State Senate PO Box 7882 Madison WI 53707-7882 Other Address: 3063 N Murray Ave MIlwaukee WI 53211

ULLE, LUDWIG JAMES, accountant; b. Painesville, Ohio, Aug. 5, 1951; s. Ludwig Frank and Theresa A. (Krzic) U. BBA, Cleve. State U., 1972. CPA, Ohio. Internal revenue agt. IRS, Cleve. and Painesville, 1973-79; propr. pvt. practice acctg. Mentor, Ohio, 1979—; instr. Lake Erie Coll., Painesville, 1980—. Treas. Cambridge Village Condominium Assn., Painesville, 1986—. Named one of Outstanding Young Men Am., U.S. Jaycees, 1984. Mem. Am. Inst. CPA's, Ohio Soc. CPA's, Econ. and Social Research Inst. (sec. 1983—). Roman Catholic. Lodge: Rotary (treas. Painesville chpt. 1982—). Avocations: model r.r.'s, volleyball, golf, history. Office: 9613 Jackson St Mentor OH 44060

ULLMAN, JULIAN BERNARD, obstetrician/gynecologist; b. Ottumwa, Iowa, Apr. 22, 1939; s. Robert and Sonia (Hackman) U.; m. Judith Susan Forgash, July 1, 1973; children: Stacey Reed, Meredith Robyn. BA in Gen. Sci., State U. Iowa, 1961, MD, 1964. Intern Phila. Gen. Hosp., 1964-65; resident in ob-gyn U. Ill. Med. Ctr., Chgo., 1967-70; practice medicine specializing in ob-gyn Chgo., 1970—; Mem. med. bd. Michael Reese Hosp., Chgo., 1985—, also trustee. Served to capt. USAF, 1965-67, Vietnam. Fellow Am. Coll. Obstetricians and Gynecologists; mem. AMA, Ill. State Med. Soc., Chgo. Med. Soc. Republican. Jewish. Avocations: skiing, tennis. Office: 111 N Wabash Suite 2018 Chicago IL 60602

ULLREY, RICHARD DEE, accountant; b. Allegan, Mich., Dec. 14, 1951; s. John F. and Elouise (Cederquest) U.; m. Nancy A. Gettys, Aug. 19, 1972; children: Aaron, Seth, John. BBA, Western Mich. U., 1974. CPA. Staff acct. Crowe Chizek & Co., South Bend, Ind., 1974-84; ptnr. Elkhart, Ind., 1984-85, Grand Rapids, Mich., 1985—. Bd. govs. Grand Valley Blood Program, Grand Rapids, 1985—. Mem. Am. Inst. CPA's (tax div.), Mich. Assn. CPA's (mem. ethics com. 1985—), Estate Planning Council of Grand Rapids, Econ. Club of Grand Rapids. Mem. Reformed Ch. in Am. Club: Cascade Hills Country (Grand Rapids). Avocations: woodworking, cross-country skiing, reading. Home: 3596 Tricklewood SE Grand Rapids MI 49506 Office: Crowe Chizer & Co CPA's 55 Campau NW Grand Rapids MI 49503

ULMER, ARTHUR ARNOLD, obstetrician-gynecologist; b. Detroit, June 4, 1922; s. Emil Ulmer and Clara (Elizibeth) Boehnke; m. Carolyn Louise Hock, June 22, 1946; children: Karen, Lawrence, Roger, Douglas, John, Barbara. BS, Wayne U., 1943, MD, 1947. Diplomate Am. Bd. Ob-Gyn. Practice medicine specializing in ob-gyn East Detroit, Mich.; chief of staff St. John Hosp., bd. dirs.; bd. dirs. Mich. Blue Cross. Served to lt. USN, 1950-55. Mem. Mich. State Med. Soc., Wayne County Med. Soc. Office: 121409 Kelly East Detroit MI 48021

UMANA, ROSEANN FRANCES, psychologist; b. N.Y.C., July 17, 1947; d. Salvatore and Palma Marie (Sciacca) U. B.S. in Psychology, Mich. State U., 1969; M.A. in Clin. Psychology, Ohio State U., 1971, Ph.D., 1979. Lic. psychologist, Ohio. Psychol. assoc. Central Ohio Psychiat. Hosp., Columbus, 1973-74; family crisis specialist Columbus (Ohio) Area Community Mental Health Ctr., 1974-75; exec. dir. Open Door Clinic, Columbus, 1975-83; pvt. practice clin. psychology, Columbus, 1979—; adj. instr. sch. social work Ohio State U., Columbus, 1978-84; cons. child assault prevention project Women's Action Collective, 1980-84; psychol. cons. Ohio Bur. Disability Determination, 1984—. Treas., Calico's, Women's Cultural Arts Ctr., Columbus, 1983-86. Mem. Am. Psychol. Assn., Ohio Psychol. Assn., Central Ohio Psychol. Assn. Democrat. Author: Crisis in the Family, 1980. Home: 1719 Eddystone Ave Columbus OH 43224 Office: 3840 N High St Columbus OH 43214

UMIKER-SEBEOK, JEAN, marketing researcher, consultant; b. Norfolk, Va., Oct. 1, 1946; d. William Oliver and Nora Anne (Burton) Umiker; m. Thomas Albert Sebeok, Oct. 30, 1972; children: Jessica Anne, Erica Lynn. Student, The Sorbonne, Paris, 1966-67; BA in French Lang. and Culture magna cum laude, Lake Erie Coll., 1968; PhD in Social and Cultural Anthropology, Ind. U., 1976. Research assoc. Research Ctr. Lang. and Semiotic Studies, Ind. U., Bloomington, 1971-81, assoc. chairperson, 1985—, asst. research scholar, 1987—; research assoc. Ind. U., Indpls., 1981-83; research collaborator Smithsonian Inst., Washington, 1983-84; vis. instr. to asst. prof. to assoc. prof. various univs., 1975-85; cons. various mktg. research orgns. and legal firms, 1985—. Author: You Know My Method, 1980; editor monograph series, 1980—; editor in chief Marketing Signs, 1987—. Chmn. com. to found elem. sch. Bloomington Montessori Sch., 1981-82. Grantee various orgns. Fellow Am. Anthrop. Assn.; Internat. Assn. Semiotic Studies, Assn. Consumer Research, Semiotic Soc. Am. Office: Ind U Research Ctr Lang & Semiotic Studies PO Box 10 Bloomington IN 47402

UNDERHILL, GLENN MORIS, physics educator; b. Trenton, Nebr., Oct. 30, 1925; s. George Frederick and Anna Mabel (Jackson) U.; student McCook Jr. Coll., 1942-44; B.S., Kearney State Coll., 1955; M.A. in Physics, U. Nebr., 1957, Ph.D., 1963; m. F. Susan Ann Day, Dec. 27, 1958; children—G. Mark, Rachel S. Lueck, Sterling D., Gretchen E., Cynthia A., Enoch M. Grad. asst. U. Nebr., Lincoln, 1955-59, instr., 1960-62; assoc. prof. Kearney (Nebr.) State Coll., 1963-67, planetarium dir., 1966—, prof. physics, 1967—, head dept. physics and phys. sci., 1971-77; vis. lectr. various schs.; lectr. in field. Mem. Riverdale (Nebr.) Village Bd., 1978—, chmn. bd., 1978—. Recipient Council of Deans Service award Kearney State Coll., 1983, Nebr. Admirals award. Mem. Am. Phys. Soc., Am. Assn. Physics Tchrs., Nebr. Acad. Sci., AAAS, Sigma Xi, Lambda Delta Lambda, Sigma Tau Delta, Kappa Delta Pi. Republican. Mem. Ch. of God. Contbr. articles to profl. jours. Home: PO Box 70 Riverdale NE 68870 Office: Kearney State Coll Kearney NE 68847

UNDERWOOD, DAVID WILLIAM, manufacturing executive; b. La Crosse, Wis., July 11, 1946; s. J.W. and Alice M. (Lenz) U.; m. Margo L. Mohr, 1967; children: Christina, Douglas. BS in indsl. adminstrn., Iowa State U., 1968. CPA, Iowa. Programmer Iowa State U., Ames, 1968-69; ptnr. McGladrey, Hendrickson & Pullen, Clinton, Mason City, Iowa, 1972-85; pres. N. Iowa Devel. Co., Mason City, 1986—, C.L.F.C., Inc., Clear Lake, Iowa, 1986—; treas., sec. Curries Co., Mason City, 1985—; found. pres. Fin. Mgrs. Group, Mason City, 1980-81; instr. Buena Vista Coll., Mason City, 1987. V.p., bd. dirs. United Way, Mason City, 1980-83. Served to lt. (j.g.) USNR, 1969-72, Vietnam. Mem. Clinton C. of C. (dir. exec. com. 1983-85), Mason City C. of C., Am. Inst. CPA's, Iowa Soc. CPA's. Republican. Lutheran. Lodges: Elks, Rotary. Avocations: hunting, fishing. Office: Curries Co 905 S Carolina Mason City IA 50401

UNDERWOOD, ROBERT LEIGH, venture capitalist; b. Paducah, Ky., Dec. 31, 1944; s. Robert Humphreys and Nancy Wells (Jessup) U.; B.S. with gt. distinction (Alcoa scholar), Stanford U., 1965, M.S. (NASA fellow), 1966, Ph.D. (NSF fellow), 1968; M.B.A., U. Santa Clara, 1970; m. Susan Lynn Doscher, May 22, 1976; children—Elizabeth Leigh, Dana Whitney, George Gregory. Research scientist, project leader Lockheed Missiles & Space Co., Sunnyvale, Calif., 1967-71; spl. asst. for engring. scis. Office Sec., Dept. Transp., Washington, 1971-73; sr. mgmt. assoc. Office Mgmt. and Budget, Exec. Office Pres., 1973; with TRW Inc., Los Angeles, 1973-79, dir. retail nat. accounts, 1977-78, dir. product planning and devel., 1978-79; pres., chief exec. officer OMEX, Santa Clara, Calif., 1980-82; v.p. Heizer Corp., Chgo., 1979-85; v.p. No. Trust Co., pres. No. Capital Corp., Chgo., 1985-86; mng. ptnr. ISSS Ventures, 1987—; dir. various portfolio cos.; mem. adv. com. indsl. sci. and tech. innovation NSF. Mem. AIAA, IEEE, Sigma Xi, Phi Beta Kappa, Tau Beta Pi, Beta Gamma Sigma. Elder, Presbyterian Ch., 1978-79. Clubs: Union League Chgo.; Manasquan River Yacht (Brielle, N.J.); Indian Hill (Winnetka, Ill.). Contbr. articles to profl. jours. Home: 59 Woodley Rd Winnetka IL 60093 Office: One Pierce Pl Suite 550 Itasca IL 60143

UNDLIN, CHARLES THOMAS, banker; b. Madison, Minn., Mar. 4, 1928; s. Jennings C. and Alice M. (Berg) U.; m. Lois M. Anderson, June 23, 1953; children: Sarah, Mary Lee, Margaret, Thomas. BA, St. Olaf Coll., Northfield, Minn., 1950. Asst. cashier Northwestern State Bank, Osseo, Minn., 1950-55, Northwest Bancorp., Mpls., 1955-57, Security Bank & Trust Co., Owatonna, Minn., 1957-59, Norwest Bank Black Hills, Rapid City, S.D., 1959-67; pres. and chief exec. officer Norwest Bank S.D., Rapid City, 1967-84, vice chmn., 1984-85; pres. Norwest Bank Nebr., Omaha, 1985—, also bd. dirs.; bd. dirs. Black Hills Corp., Homestake Mining Co. Mem. adv. council Salvation Army, Omaha, 1985; trustee Nebr. Weslyn Coll., Lincoln, 1985; past bd. dirs. Fed. Reserve Bank, Mpls.; bd. dirs. Children's Hosp., Omaha, 1986. Served to sgt. U.S. Army, 1951-52. Mem. S.D. Bankers Assn. (past pres.). Republican. Lutheran. Clubs: Omaha, Omaha Country. Avocations: golf, skiing, fishing. Home: 1133 S 113th Plaza Omaha NE 68144 Office: Norwest Bank Nebraska Box 3408 Omaha NE 68102

UNGAR, FRANK, biochemistry educator; b. Cleve., Apr. 30, 1922; s. Michael and Susan (Gelberger) U.; m. Shirley Ruth Katz, Sept. 26, 1948; children: Leanne, William, Barbara, Joanne. BA, Ohio State U., 1943; MS, Western Case Res. U., 1948; PhD, Tuft's U., 1952. Mem. research staff Worcester Found. Exptl. Biology, Shrewsbury, Mass., 1951-58; from assoc. prof. to prof. biochemistry U. Minn., Mpls., 1958—; vis. asst. prof. Clark U., Worcester, 1957-58. Co-author: (book) Metabolism of Steroids, 1955, 65; contbr. numerous articles to profl. jours. Fulbright fellow Univ. Coll. Cork, Ireland, 1974-75, Fogarty Sr. fellow NIH Weizmann Inst. Rehovot, Israel, 1982-83. Mem. AAAS, Am. Soc. Biol. Chemistry, Endocrine Soc. Home: 5232 Stevens Ave S Minneapolis MN 55419 Office: U Minn 435 Delaware Minneapolis MN 55455

UNGER, DAVID JAMES, engineering mechanics educator; b. East St. Louis, Ill., Feb. 1, 1952; s. Anthony and Stella (Borkowski) U.; m. Carolyn Elizabeth Stilwell, Feb. 21, 1981. B.S., St. Louis U., 1973; M.S., U. Ill., 1976, Ph.D., 1981. Researcher dept. chem. engring. U. Minn., Mpls., 1981-82; asst. prof. engring. mechanics Ohio State U., Columbus, 1982—. Contbr. articles to profl. jours. NSF grantee, 1984—. Mem. ASME, AIAA, AAAS, Am. Acad. Mechanics, Ohio Acad. Sci. Office: Ohio State U Dept Engring Mechanics 155 W Woodruff Ave Columbus OH 43210

UNNEWEHR, LEWIS EMORY, electrical engineer; b. Berea, Ohio, Sept. 27, 1925; s. Emory Carl and Ivy May (Lewis) U.; B.S.E.E., Purdue U., 1946; M.S.E.E., U. Notre Dame, 1952; m. L. Jean Affleck, Aug. 22, 1948; children—David, Laura, Janet, Chris. Assoc. prof. Valparaiso U. (Ind.), 1949-55; research engr. Franklin Inst., Phila., 1955-57; assoc. prof. Villanova (Pa.) U., 1957-61; sr. design engr. Garrett Corp., Los Angeles, 1961-66; mem. research staff Ford Motor Co., Dearborn, Mich., 1966-81; dir. research and devel. Lima Energy Products (Ohio), 1981-84; dir. advanced electronics dept. Allied Automotive Tech. Ctr., Troy, Mich., 1984—. Author: (with S.A. Nasar) Electromechanics and Electric Machines, 1979; Electric Vehicle Technology, 1982; Coauthor: Introduction to Electrical Engineering, 1986; contbr. articles to profl. jours.; patentee in field. Lay del. Central United Meth. Ch., Detroit, 1978-80. Mem. IEEE (vice-chmn. electronics transformer tech. com.), Sigma Xi. Democrat. Methodist. Lodges: Elks, Optimists. Home: 31093 Fairfax Dr Birmingham MI 48009 Office: 900 W Maple Rd Troy MI 48084

UNRUH, ROGER DUANE, osteopathic pediatrician; b. Enid, Okla., Dec. 13, 1944; s. Vernard W. and Evelyn E. (Buller) U.; m. Pamela J. Mueller, Apr. 5, 1969; children: Brandon, Doria, Ryan. BS, Bethel Coll., 1966; DO, Kirksville Coll., 1970. Pediatrician Wichita (Kans.) Osteo. Clinic., 1976—; dir. med. edn. Riverside Hosp., Wichita, 1983—. Mem. Am. Coll. Osteo. Pediatricians, Am. Osteo. Assn., Kans. Assn. Osteo. Med. Avocation: angling. Office: Wichita Osteo Clinic 2716 W Central Wichita KS 67203

UNTENER, KENNETH E., bishop; b. Detroit, Aug. 3, 1937. Ed., Sacred Heart Sem., Detroit, St. John's Provincial Sem., Plymouth, Mich., Gregorian U., Rome. Ordained priest Roman Cath. Ch., 1963; ordained bishop of Saginaw Mich., 1980—. Office: Chancery Office 5800 Weiss St Saginaw MI 48603 *

UNTERMAN, EUGENE REX, aviation sales company executive; b. Mpls., Sept. 3, 1953; Melvin and Nancy (Wolfson) U.; m. Melanie Wells Munson, July 12, 1980; children: H. Aaron, Jeffery Wells, Julie Ann. Student, Loyola U., Chgo., 1971-73, Northwestern U., 1973-75. Trader Chgo. Mercantile Exchange, 1975-76; pres. Mid-west Aircraft, Sandwich, Ill., 1976—; computer cons. Chgo. Rawhide Corp., Elgin, Ill., 1983. mem. airport adv. bd. City of Geneva, Ill., 1983. Mem. Jaycees. Jewish. Club: St. Charles (Ill.) Sportsman (treas. 1985-86, pres. 1987—). Avocations: trap shooting, camping, fishing. Home: 506 Sheila Ave Geneva IL 60134 Office: Mid-West Aircraft Rural Rt 2 Rt 34 W Sandwich IL 60548

UPCRAFT, JOHN OLIN, geologist; b. Mt. Vernon, Ill., June 10, 1958; s. Frederick James and Huram Maxfield (Turner) U.; m. Diana Carol Sampson, Sept. 1, 1979; children—Jennifer Leigh, Melissa Kay. A.A., Rend Lake Jr. Coll., 1980, BA So Ill U., 1986. Draftsman, Gen. Radiator, Mt. Vernon, 1976-78, salesman, 1978-79; geol. draftsman Brehm Oil Co., Mt. Vernon, 1979-82; petroleum Geologist Orion Energy Corp., Mt. Vernon, 1982-87, prin. John O. Upcraft, Geolgist, 1987—. Vol. Okwa Valley council Boy Scouts Am., 1980-87. Brehm Found. scholar, 1980-82. Mem. Am. Assn. Petroleum Geologists, Ill. Geol. Soc., Am. Inst. Profl. Geologists, Kans. Geol. Soc. Lodge: Optimist (Mt. Vernon). Avocations: music performance; fishing, hunting, shooting, boating. Home: 2023 College Mt Vernon IL 62864

UPHOFF, JAMES KENT, education educator; b. Hebron, Nebr., Sept. 1, 1937; s. Ernest John and Alice Marie (Dutcher) U.; m. Harriet Lucille Martin, Aug. 6, 1962; 1 child, Nicholas James. B.A., Hastings Coll., 1959; M.Ed., U. Nebr., 1962, Ed.D., 1967. Tchr., Walnut Jr. High Sch., Grand Island, Nebr., 1959-65, dept. chmn., 1962-65; instr. dept. edn. U. Nebr., Lincoln, 1965-66; curriculum intern Bellevue (Nebr.) Pub. Schs., 1966-67; asst. prof. edn. Wright State U., Dayton, Ohio, 1967-70, assoc. prof., 1970-75, prof. edn., 1975—, co-dir. pub. edn. religion studies ctr., 1972-75, dean br. campuses, 1974-79, dir. lab. experiences, 1982—; vis. prof. U. Dayton, 1968-69. Author: (with others) Summer Children: Ready or Not For School, 1986. Phi Delta Kappa scholar, 1969. Mem. adv. com. pub. edn. fund Dayton Found., 1985—; mem. Luth. Ch. council, 1987—. Mem. NEA, Ohio Edn. Assn. (devel. commn.), Western Ohio Edn. Assn. (pres. 1974-75, exec. com. 1979-85), Assn. Supervision and Curriculum Devel. (dir. 1974-79), Ohio Assn. Supervision and Curriculum Devel. (v.p. 1972-73), Nat. Council Social Studies (religion com.), Ohio Council Social Studies (profl. concerns com.), Dayton Area Council Social Studies (pres. (1970-71, 85-87), LWV Greater Dayton (edn. dir. 1981-85), Ohio Council Chs. (edn. com. 1973-75), Phi Delta Kappa (chpt. pres. 1983-84), Kappa Delta Pi. Republican. Lodges: Rotary (editor; dir. 1974-79), Optimists (pres. 1983-85). Contbr. chpts. to books and articles to profl. jours. Home: 150 Spirea Dr Dayton OH 45419 Office: Wright State U 320 Millett Edn Dayton OH 45435

UPSHAW, DEAN LEE, architect; b. Stillwater, Okla., Dec. 31, 1934; s. Alva Lyle and Helen (Gould) U.; m. Winnifred A. Cooper, Mar. 15, 1959 (div. Mar. 1979); children: Eric G., June E., Kris C.; m. Fran Marie McKeown, Nov. 20, 1985. BArch, Auburn U., 1959. Registered architect, Ind. Pvt. practice architecture Lafayette, Ind., 1970-76, 82; ptnr. Upshaw & Allen Architects, Lafayette, 1976-79, James Assocs., Lafayette, 1979-82, Upshaw Mattox Partnership, Lafayette, 1982-85; pvt. practice architecture The Upshaw Group, Lafayette, 1985 ; asst. prof. creative arts Purdue U., West Lafayette, Ind., 1970-73. Contbr. articles to profl. jours. Bd. dirs. Ind. Archtl. Found., Indpls., 1979-80, Tippecanoe County Bd. Zoning Appeals 1971-74; founding bd. dirs. Wabash Valley Trust for Hist. Preservation, Lafayette, 1975; chmn. Lafayette Civic Design com., 1971; commr. Tippecanoe County Area Plan Commn., 1974-75. Recipient Service to Profession award AIA, Ind. Soc. Architects, 1975. Mem. AIA (nat. urban planning design com. 1973-75, nat. com. design 1976-79), Ind. Soc. Architects (bd. dirs. 1976-80 pres. So. Chpt. 1980). Republican. Club: Down Town Bus. Ctr. (v.p. 1976-80). Lodge: Optimist (pres. 1981). Avocations: art, photography, computers. Home: 3005 Commanche Trail Lafayette IN 47905 Office: The Upshaw Group 303 Carr Robertson Bldg Lafayette IN 47901

UPTON, CATHERINE ANN, physician; b. Windsor, Ont., Can., June 30, 1951; came to U.S., 1954; d. John H. and Ann (Lenardon) U. BS, Mich. State U., 1973; MD, Wayne State U., 1980. Diplomate Am. Bd. Internal Medicine. Med. technologist St. Joseph Merly Hosp., Ann Arbor, Mich., 1974-76; intern Wayne State U., Detroit, 1980-81; resident William Beaumont Hosp., Royal Oak, Mich., 1981-83; clin. fellow div. geriatrics dept. internal medicine U. Mich., Ann Arbor, 1983-84; practice medicine specializing in internal medicine Troy, Mich., 1984—; mem. attending staff William Beaumont Hosp., Crittenton Hosp., Rochester, Mich. Mem. Am. Coll. Physicians, Am. Geriatrics Soc. Office: Internat Medicine Ctr PC 1787 W Big Beaver Troy MI 48084

UPTON, FREDERICK STEPHEN, congressman; b. St. Joseph, Mich., Apr. 23, 1953; s. Stephen E. and Elizabeth Brooks (Vial) U.; m. Amey Richmond Rulon-Miller, Nov. 5, 1983. BA in Journalism, U. Mich., 1975. Staff asst. to Congressman David A. Stockman, Washington, 1976-81; legis. asst. Office Mgmt. and Budget, Washington, 1981-83, dep. dir. legis. affairs, 1983-84, dir. legis. affairs, 1984-85; mem. 100th Congress from 4th Mich. dist., Washington, 1986—. Field mgr. Stockman for Congress, St. Joseph, 1975; campaign mgr. Globensky for Congress, St. Joseph, 1981. Republican. Office: US House of Reps 1607 Longworth Bldg Washington DC 20515

UPTON, KEVIN JOHN, public relations executive; b. N.Y.C., Jan. 3, 1947; s. John Joseph and Muriel Agnes (Weiss) U.; m. Theresa Ann Malone, Aug. 13, 1967; children—Kirsa, Bryn. Student, Notre Dame U., 1965-67; B.A., Ind. U., 1973; M.A., U. Wis., 1977. Instr. dept. polit. sci. Carroll Coll., Waukesha, Wis., 1975-77; dir. devel. Wis. Center for Pub. Policy, Madison, Wis., 1977-79; asst. to mayor Madison, 1979-80; pres. Upton, Boelter & Lincoln, Madison, 1980-83; v.p. mktg. Credit Union Nat. Assn. and CUNA Service Group, Inc., 1983—. Mem. Pub. Relations Soc. Am. Democrat. Club: Madison. Home: 7209 Branford Ln E Madison WI 53717 Office: 5710 Mineral Point Rd Madison WI 53701

UPTON, LAURENCE ROGER, educator, educational administrator, consultant; b. Keene, N.H., Aug. 27, 1947; s. Roger James and Fannie Helen (Seppa) U. BA summa cum laude, U. N.H., 1969; MS, Purdue U., 1973; postgrad. U. Minn. Instr. human devel. U. N.H., Durham, 1971-72; research asst. psychology Purdue U., West Lafayette, Ind., 1972-74; program evaluation specialist U. Minn., Mpls., 1974-76, student activities cons., coordinator program on human issues and values, 1976-79, asst. coordinator admissions Coll. Liberal Arts, 1980-86; researcher exptl. psychology, 1975—, psychology instr., 1986—; tech. edn. cons., assoc. dir. U. Research Consortium, Mpls., 1984—; presenter conf. papers. Dist. del. Democratic Farmer Labor Party, Mpls., 1976, 80, 84. Granite State Merit scholar, 1965-69, Ford Found. scholar, 1967-69; NSF trainee, 1969-71. Mem. Ctr. Research in Human Learning, Midwestern Psychol. Assn., Phi Beta Kappa, Phi Kappa Phi, Psi Chi, Pi Gamma Mu, Pi Mu Epsilon. Unitarian. Office: U Minn Dept Psychology 223 Elliott Hall 75 E River Rd Minneapolis MN 55455

UPTON, LUCILE MORRIS (MRS. EUGENE V. UPTON), writer; b. Dadeville, Mo., July 22, 1898; d. Albert G. and Veda (Wilson) Morris; student Drury Coll., 1915-16, S.W. Mo. State U., 1917-20; m. Eugene V. Upton, July 22, 1936 (dec. July 1947). Pub. sch. tchr., Dadeville Mo., 1917-19, Everton, Mo., 1920-22, Roswell, N.Mex., 1921-23; tchr. creative writing Adult Edn. div. Drury Coll., 1947-52; reporter Denver Express, 1923-24, El Paso (Tex.) Times, 1924-25, Springfield (Mo.) Newspapers, Inc., 1926-64, writer weekly hist. column, 1942-82. Mem. Springfield City Council, 1967-71, Springfield Hist. Sites Bd., 1972-78. Recipient Heritage award Mus. of Ozarks, 1978; named Woman of Achievement Woman's div. Springfield C. of C., 1967; named to Greater Ozark Hall of Fame, Sch. of Ozarks, Point Lookout, Mo., 1980. Mem. Mo. Writers Guild (past pres.), State Hist. Soc. Mo. (life), Greene County (Mo.), White River Valley hist. socs., Nat. Fedn. Press Women, Mo. Press Women. Congregationalist. Author: Bald Knobbers, 1939; (booklet) Battle of Wilson's Creek, 1950; co-author: Nathan Boone, the Neglected Hero, 1984; contbr. short stories, articles to mags., newspapers. Home: 1305 S Kimbrough Springfield MO 65807

URBAN, GILBERT JOHN, infosystems specialist; b. St. Louis, Sept. 11, 1951; s. John Samuel and LaVerna Marie (Schneider) U.; m. Regina Lee Cooksey, May 19, 1973; children: Zachary Gilbert, Brittany Alexandra. BSEE, Purdue U., 1973; MBA, U. Evansville, 1979. Computer engr. Whirlpool, Evansville, Ind., 1973-78, sr. tool. and process engr., 1978-79, supr. mgmt. info., 1979-84; mfg. infosystems mgr. Whirlpool, St. Joseph, Mich., 1984-87, dir. info. system div., 1987—; speaker in field. Commr. Pepsi Cola Youth Soccer League, Evansville, 1980-84; vice chmn. Lakeshore Soccer, Stevensville, Mich., 1986. Club: Foremans (Evansville). Home: 1463 Mulberry Ln Saint Joseph MI 49085 Office: Whirlpool Upton Dr Saint Joseph MI 49085

URBANI, ANTHONY, II, lawyer, real estate executive; b. Detroit, July 7, 1953; s. Gaeton Sr. and Florence (Casinelli) U. BA, U. Detroit, 1975, postgrad., 1976-77; JD, Detoirt Coll. Law, 1982. Bar: Mich. 1983, U.S. Ct. Appeals (6th cir.) 1983, U.S. Dist. Ct. (ea. dist.) Mich. 1985. Owner Look Landscaping, Grosse Pointe, Mich., 1971-75; v.p. Look Real Estate Co. Inc., East Detroit, Mich., 1972—; ptnr. Ideal Travel Agy., East Detroit, 1975—; spl. agt. Lucido's Ins. Agy., Clinton Twp., Mich., 1980—; ptnr. Urbani & Urbani, East Detroit, 1983—. Mem. ABA, Macomb County Bar Assn., Assn. Trail Lawyers Am., Mich. Trial Lawyers Assn., Italian-Am. Lawyers Mich., Delta Sigma Phi (pres. 1974-75), Sigma Nu Phi (librarian 1980-81). Roman Catholic. Avocations: chess, dancing, tennis, flying, travel. Home: 1001 Three Mile Dr Grosse Pointe Park MI 48230 Office: Urbani & Urbani 21216 Gratiot Ave East Detroit MI 48021

URBANIAK, DAVID LEE, restaurant exec., microfilm co. exec.; b. Dearborn, Mich., May 5, 1944; s. Joseph Frank and Ethel (Behnke) U.; student Western Mich. U., 1964-65; m. Sally Joanne Dexter, July 25, 1964; children—Matthew James, Bethany Lyn. Foreman, McGraw Edison, Albion, Mich., 1964-70; gen. foreman ITT Hancock, Jackson, Mich., 1970-76; owner Sal's 5th Ave. Restaurant, Michigan Center, Mich., 1976—; founder, pres. Automatic Microfilm Co., Michigan Center, 1978—. Mem. Leoni Bus. Assn. (co-founder 1977, chmn. 1977-81). Lutheran. Home: 484 Ballard St Jackson MI 49201 Office: 115 5th St Michigan Center MI 49254

URBOM, WARREN KEITH, judge; b. Atlanta, Nebr., Dec. 17, 1925; s. Clarence Andrew and Anna Myrl (Irelan) U.; m. Joyce Marie Crawford, Aug. 19, 1951; children: Kim Marie, Randall Crawford, Allison Lee, Joy Renee. AB with highest distinction, Nebr. Wesleyan U., 1950, LLD (hon.), 1984; student, Iliff Sch. Theology, Denver, 1950; JD with distinction, U. Mich., 1953. Bar: Nebr. 1953. Mem. firm Baylor, Evnen, Baylor, Urbom, & Curtiss, Lincoln, Nebr., 1953-70; judge U.S. Dist. Ct. Dist. Nebr., 1970-72, chief judge, 1972-86; mem. com. on practice and procedure Nebr. Supreme Ct., 1965—; mem. subcom. on fed. jurisdiction Jud. Conf. U.S., 1975-83; adj. instr. trial advocacy U. Nebr. Coll. Law, 1979—; bd. dirs. Fed. Jud. Ctr., 1982-86; chmn. Fed. Judiciat Ctr. Com. on Orientation Newly Appointed Dist. Judges, 1986—. Contbr. articles to profl. jours. Trustee St. Paul Sch. Theology, Kansas City, Mo., 1986—; pres. Lincoln YMCA, 1965-67, bd. dirs., 1982-86; bd. govs. Nebr. Wesleyan U., chmn., 1975-80. Served with AUS, 1944-46. Recipient Medal of Honor, Nebr. Wesleyan U. Alumni Assn., 1983. Fellow Am. Coll. Trial Lawyers; mem. ABA, Nebr. Bar Assn. (ho. of dels. 1966-70), Lincoln Bar Assn. (pres. 1968-69). United Methodist (bd. mgrs., bd. global ministries 1972-76). Club: Masons (33 deg.). Home: 4510 Van Dorn Lincoln NE 68506 Office: 586 Federal Bldg Lincoln NE 68501

URICE, JOHN KRAUS, college dean, management consultant; b. N.Y.C., June 11, 1946; s. Leonard H. Kraus and Babette Adele (Block) Rogers. BA, NYU, 1968; MA, U. Miami, 1973; PhD, Fla. State U., 1976. Program coordinator Fine Arts Council Fla., Tallahassee, 1976, dir., 1976-78; dir. MBA in Arts Program and Ctr. for Arts SUNY, Binghamton, 1978-84; dean Coll. Fine Arts Ball State U., Muncie, Ind., 1984—; mgmt. cons. Nat. Endowment for Arts, numerous other arts orgns., 1978—; panelist Nat. Endowment for Arts. Guest editor Jour. Arts Mgmt. and Law, 1984. Mem. Community Adv. Bd. Planned Parenthood NE Ind., Muncie, 1984—; Served to capt. U.S. Army, 1969-72, Vietnam. Nat. Endowment for Arts research grantee, 1983. Mem Assn. Arts Adminstrn. Educators (affiliate, pres. 1979-82), Am. Council for Arts. Presbyterian. Avocations: collectable cars, movies, racquetball, music, theater. Home: 4501 N Wheeling 6B-302 Muncie IN 47304 Office: Ball State U Dean Coll Fine Arts Muncie IN 47306

URSEM, RICHARD EDWARD, fluid power distributing company executive; b. Detroit, Nov. 3, 1932; s. William A. and Adelaide J. (Schwering) U.; m. Joanne Clare Hones, May 12, 1956; children—William R., DeLourde M., Brian E., Keith A. (dec.), Devra J., Durene J. B.S. in Engring. Adminstrn., U. Detroit, 1955. Salesman, F. & W. Ursem Co., Cleve., 1957-65, sales mgr., 1965-74; pres. Ursem Co., Cleve., 1974—; mem. adv. council C.A. Norgren Co., Denver, 1976-78. Contbr. bi-monthly article Safari mag., 1980-81. Served to 1st lt. AUS, 1955-57. Named State Conservationist of Yr., League Ohio Sportsmen, 1984. Mem. Fluid Power Distbrs. Assn. (charter), Fluid Power Soc., Safari Club Internat. (govt. affairs com. 1980—, pres. 1980-81, Outstanding Mem. 1980-81), Nat. Rifle Assn. (life), Quiet Birdmen (pres. Ohio 1977). Republican. Roman Catholic. Club: Cleveland Yachting. Avocations: aviation; boating; hunting sports. Office: Ursem Co 1548 W 117th St Cleveland OH 44107

URSHAN, NATHANIEL A., minister, church administrator; b. St. Paul, Aug. 29, 1920; s. Andrew David and Mildred (Hammergren) U.; m. Jean Louise Habig, Oct. 1, 1941; children: Sharon, Annette, Nathaniel, Andrew. Student, Columbia U., 1936-39; DTh (hon.), Gateway Coll. Evangelism, 1976. Ordained to ministry United Pentecostal Ch. Internat. Evangelist 1941-44; assoc. pastor Royal Oak, Mich., 1944-46, N.Y.C., 1947-48, Indpls., 1948-49; pastor Calvary Tabernacle, Indpls., 1949-78; presbyter Ind. Dist. United Pentecostal Chs., 1950-77; asst. gen. supt. United Pentecostal Ch. Internat., 1971-77; gen. supt. United Pentecostal Ch. Internat.,

Hazelwood, Mo., 1977—; host radio show Harvestime, 1961-78; chaplain Ind. Ho. of Reps., 1972. Author: Consider Him, 1962, Thest Men Are Not Drunk, 1964, Boof of Sermons of the Baptism of the Holy Spirit, 1968, Major Bible Prophecy, 1971. Mem. internat. com. YMCA, 1958-79, bd. dirs. Indpls. chpt. 1961-79, world service chmn. Region L., 1969-71; chmn. Heart Fund Campaign, 1968-69; mem. screening com. Marion County Reps., Ind., 1973-74; chmn. Ministerial Com. of Richard Lugar for May of Indpls., 1968, William Hudnut for Mayor, 1975; bd. dirs. Little Red Door, Cancer Soc. Indpls., 1974-77. Recipient gold and brass medallion Heart Fund., Indpls., 1968-69; Nathaniel A. Urshan Day named in his honor, Nov. 3, 1079, Mayor Hudnut, Indpls. Mem. Indpls. Ministerial Assn. Office: United Pentecostal Ch Internat 8855 Dunn Rd Hazelwood MO 63042 *

USERA, JOHN JOSEPH, dean, chemistry educator, researcher, consulting statistical analyst; b. Cleve., Mar. 18, 1941; s. Libertad Vivas and Beatrice (Ramirez) U.; m. Maria Bernadette Borszich, Sept. 6, 1969; children—Helen E., Karena M., Pamela Y. B.S., Black Hill State Coll., 1971, B.S. in Edn., 1972; M. Natural Sci., U. S.D., 1978, M.A., 1980; Ph.D., Kans. State U., 1984. Registered analytical chemist, Kans.; cert. secondary sch. chemistry tchr., S.D. Teaching asst. S.D. Sch. Mines, Rapid City, 1973-74; sci./math. instr. Shannon County Schs., Batesland, S.D., 1971-73; chemistry/physics instr. Bon Homme Sch. Dist., Tyndall, S.D., 1974-81; chemistry lectr. U. S.D., Springfield, 1979-80; lectr. in stats. Pitts. State U., 1986—, dean instructional services ans instl. research, 1987—; chemistry and stats. prof. Labette Community Coll., Parsons, Kans., 1981-87; dir. forensic lab. Labette Community Coll., 1982—. Author: Science Anxiety, 1984. Contbr. articles to profl. jours. Served to sgt. USMC, 1965-69, Viet Nam. Named S.D. Tchr. of Yr., S.D. Edn. Assn., 1980. Fellow Am. Inst. Chemists; mem. Am. Chem. Soc., Am. Chem. Soc. (analytical chemistry sect.), Two-Yr. Coll. Chemistry Conf., Nat. Sci. Tchrs. Assn., Kans. Edn. Assn., NEA, Maths. Assn. of Am., Kans. Sci. Tchr. Assn., Sigma Delta Nu, Pi Mu Epsilon. Roman Catholic. Lodge: K.C. Avocations: computers; reading; classical music. Home: 3102 Briggs Parsons KS 67357 Office: Labette Community Coll 200 S 14th St Parsons KS 67357

USHER, LINDA MARIE, engineering and manufacturing company executive; b. Chgo., May 13, 1953; d. Thomas E. and Joan Eileen (Shirey) U.; m. Malcolm D. Lambe. BS, U. Wis., 1974, MBA, 1977. CPA, Ill. Pub. acct. Pannell Kerr Forster, Chgo., 1978-80; asst. controller Lakewood Engring. and Mfg., Chgo., 1980-81, controller, 1981-86, v.p. fin. and adminstrn., 1986—. Mem. Am. Inst. CPA's, Ill. CPA Soc. Office: Lakewood Engring and Mfg 501 N Sacramento Blvd Chicago IL 60612

UTECHT, ALOISE JOSEPH, psychologist; b. Hamtramck, Mich., June 10, 1924; s. John Ignac and Agnes (Wawrzyniak) U.; m. Ederina I. DiBiaggio, Sept. 7, 1957; children: Steven Paul, Michael Jonathan. PhB, U. Detroit, 1950; MA, U. Pa., 1952; PhD., U. N.D., 1960. Assoc. dir. dept. psychology Hawthorn Ctr., Northville, Mich., 1967-84, dir. dept. psychology, 1984—. Editor Mich. Psychol. Assn. Newsletter, 1966, Hawthorn Ctr. Assn. Newsletter, 1985; contbr. articles to profl. jours. Bd. dirs., publicity chmn. Livonia (Mich.) Cultural League, 1980—. Served with U.S. Army, 1943-46. Mem. Am. Psychol. Assn., Mich. Psychol. Assn., Com. Psychologists in Pub. Service. Democrat. Roman Catholic. Office: Hawthorn Ctr 18471 Haggerty Rd Northville MI 48167

UTES, FRANK ALAN, osteopathic physician; b. Chgo., Apr. 20, 1951; s. Frank Edward and Esther (Rowoldt) U.; m. Karen Marie Younker, June 23, 1973; children: Christine, Julia, Laura. BS in Chemistry, U. Ill., 1973; DO, Chgo. Coll. Osteo. Medicine, 1978. Intern Lansing (Mich.) Gen. Hosp., 1978; gen. practice osteo. medicine, Winamac, Ind., 1979—; mem. staff Pulaski Meml. Hosp., Winamac, 1979—, chief obstetrics, 1981-85, chief medicine and pediatrics, 1985—; pres. Utes Family Practice, Inc., Winamac. Mem. Am. Osteo. Assn., Ind. Assn. Osteo. Physicians and Surgeons, Pulaski County Med. Assn. Club: Kiwanis.

UTIAN, WULF HESSEL, gynecologist, endocrinologist; b. Johannesburg, South Africa, Sept. 28, 1939; came to U.S., 1976; s. Harry and Ethel (Nay) U.; m. Moira Mervis, Oct. 4, 1964; children: Brett David, Lara Peta. MBBCh, Witwatersrand U., Johannesburg, S.Africa, 1962; PhD, U. Cape Town, S. Africa, 1970. Cons. ob-gyn Groote Schuur Hosp., Cape Town, 1967-76; dir. reprodn. endocrinology Univ. Hosps., Cleve., 1976-80; dir. ob-gyn Mt. Sinai Med. Ctr., Cleve., 1980—; dir. Cleve. Menopause Clinic, 1986—; cons. Internat. Health Found., Geneva, Switzerland, 1976—; assoc. prof. Case Western Res. U., Cleve., 1976—; exec. com. Internat. Menopause Soc., Internat. Soc. Gynecol. Endocrinology. Editor Maturitas, 1980—, Premenstral Syndrome, 1981; author: Menopause in Modern Perspective, 1980, Your Middle Years, 1980; contbr. articles to profl. jours. Fellow Royal Coll. Ob-Gyn, Am. Coll. Ob-Gyn, Internat. Coll. Surgeons (v.p. 1983—). Club: Cleve. Racquet. Avocations: sailing, tennis. Home: 150 Basswood Moreland Hills OH 44022 Office: Mt Sinai Med Ctr 1 Mt Sinai Dr Cleveland OH 44106

UTRECHT, JAMES DAVID, lawyer; b. Camp Polk, Ia., May 23, 1952; s. James C. and Susan (McDevitt) U.; m. Karen Lee Kelly, Aug. 17, 1975; children: Ann Elizabeth, Claire Susan. B.B.A., U. Cin., 1974, J.D., 1977. Ptnr., Shipman, Utrecht & Dixon, Troy, Ohio, 1977—; asst. law dir. City of Troy, 1984—. Chmn. Miami County Reagan-Bush Com. (Ohio), 1984. Mem. Miami County Bar Assn., Ohio Bar Assn., ABA, Troy Area C. of C. (bd. dirs. 1986—), 1/2 Republican. Roman Catholic. Clubs: Troy Jaycees (dir. 1983-84), Troy Rotary. Lodge: Elks. Home: 2299 Pleasantview Dr Troy OH 45373 Office: Shipman Utrecht & Dixon PA 12 S Plum St Troy OH 45373

UTRIE, JOHN WENDEL, gynecologist/obstetrician; b. Juneau, Wis., Dec. 2, 1933; s. Wendel N. and Eugenia E. (Becker) U.; m. Patricia K. Paciotti, June 8, 1957; children: John Jr., Anthony, Sara, Paul Nickolaus, Elizabeth Carla. MD, Marquette U., 1959. Diplomate Am. Bd. Ob-Gyn. Intern Miller Hosp., St. Paul, 1959-60; fellow U. Minn., Mpls., 1963-66; practice medicine specializing in ob-gyn Rhinelander, Wis., 1972-73, Green Bay, Wis., 1966-72, 73—; dept. chief ob-gyn St. Vincent Hosp., Green Bay, 1980-83, 85—. Served to comdr. USPHS, 1960-63. Fellow Am. Coll. Ob-Gyn, Gyn Urology Soc.; mem. AMA, Wis. Ob-Gyn Soc. (sec. 1981-84, pres. 1984-86), Minn. Ob-Gyn, Wis. Assn. Perinatal Care. Republican. Roman Catholic. Lodge: Kiwanis. Avocations: fishing, hunting, woodworking. Home: 160 Utrie Dr Green Bay WI 54301 Office: 1821 Webster Ave Green Bay WI 54301

UTZ, EUGENE JOSEPH, judge; b. Cin., July 27, 1923; s. Edward Joseph and Frances (Kraemer) U.; m. Gertrude Ellen Bernert, Nov. 27, 1948; children—Eugene Joseph II, Gary Lee, Marcia Ann, Marianne. B.B.A., U. Cin., 1949; J.D., Chase Coll. Law, 1953. Bar: Ohio 1953, U.S. Dist. Ct. Ohio 1955, U.S. Ct. Appeals (6th cir.) 1960, U.S. Supreme Ct. 1970. Sole practice, Ohio, 1953—; judge Hamilton 1st dist. Ct. Appeals County Ct., Ohio, 1963-68. Served with U.S. Army, 1943-45, ETO. Mem. Ohio Bar Assn., Cin. Bar Assn. Republican. Roman Catholic. Club: Maketewah (Cin.) (v.p., pres. 1980-82). Lodge: Elks. Avocation: golf. Home: 7865 Shawnee Run Rd Indian Hill OH 45243 Office: Hamilton County Courthouse Rm 300 1st Dist Ct Appeals Ohio Cincinnati OH 45202

UTZ, WALTER EARL, oil company executive; b. Cin., June 28, 1941; s. Walter Owen and Edna Earl (Eggers) U.; m. Patricia Ann Martin, Nov. 23, 1962; children: Andrew Earl, Beth Ann. BS in Chemistry, U. Cin., 1959-63. Bench chemist Emery Industries, Cin., 1963-68, market devel rep., 1968-74, bus. group mgr., 1974-77; v.p. Cin. Vulcan Co., 1977—, also bd. dirs. Patentee in field. Mem. Am. Soc. Lubrication Engrs., Soc. Automotive Engrs., Am. Chem. Soc. Republican. Roman Catholic. Avocations: jogging, golf, fishing, yard work. Home: 3439 Sherbrooke Dr Cincinnati OH 45241 Office: Cin Vulcan Co Vulcan Oil Div 5353 Spring Grove Ave Cincinnati OH 45200

UWANAKA, GABRIEL HART, computer information scientist; b. Port Harcourt, Nigeria, Dec. 18, 1949; came to U.S., 1975; s. Thamos Joshia and Abigel (Oyibo) U.; m. Bobbie Joiner, Apr. 4, 1977; children: Mike, Ed. BSBA, U. Nebr., Omaha, 1982, MS, 1983. Asst. circulator Omaha World Herald, 1979-80; rework specialist Control Data, Omaha, 1981—; v.p. Internat. Omni Tech., Omaha, 1985—; cons. FPA, N.Y.C., 1986—. Supr. YMCA, Omaha, 1986—; fellow ARC. Mem. Am. Mktg. Assn., Causa. Avocations: biking, swimming, soccer, travel. Home: 711 N 92d Ct #114 Omaha NE 68114 Office: Internat Omni Tech Box 24542 Omaha NE 68124

UZELAC, MICHAEL JOHN, dentist; b. Gary, Ind., Oct. 20, 1956; s. Milan and Amy Agnes (Anderson) U.; m. Maryann Mihalik, Aug. 4, 1978; children: Christopher, Elizabeth. BS in Chemistry and Biology, Valparasio (Ind.) U., 1978; DDs, Ind. U., 1982. Gen. practice dentistry Valparaiso, 1983—. Exec. bd. dirs. Porter County chpt. Am. Cancer Soc., Valparaiso, 1986-88. Club: YMCA (Valparaiso). Avocations: fishing, softball. Home: 510 Center St Valparaiso IN 46383 Office: 970 C Mill Pond Rd Valparaiso IN 46383

VAAL, JOSEPH JOHN, JR., psychologist; b. St. Louis, Nov. 19, 1947; s. Joseph John and Dorothy Jane (Collett) V.; B.A., Lawrence U., 1969; M.A. in Psychology, Western Mich. U., 1971; Ph.D., Columbia Pacific U., 1981; m. Patricia Gail Winkler, Apr. 24, 1982; 1 child, Lauren Elizabeth. Tchr. spl. edn. KVISD Title VI Program, Kalamazoo, 1970, Mannheim Pub. Schs., Franklin Park, Ill., 1971; sch. psychologist Wheaton (Ill.) Pub. Schs., 1971-79; dir. office continuing edn. Rush-Presbyn.-St. Luke's Med. Ctr., Chgo., 1979-81; adj. instr. Grad. Sch. Nat. Coll. Edn., Evanston, 1972—; spl. edn. due process hearing officer Ill. Bd. Edn., Springfield, 1978—; dir. ednl. services Healthcare Fin. Mgmt. Assn., Oak Brook, Ill., 1981-84; psychologist Vaal and Assocs., Evanston and Prospect Heights, Ill., 1984-87; asst. dir. Sch. Assn. for Spl. Edn. in DuPage, Addison, Ill., 1987—. Mem. Ill. Sch. Psychologists Assn., Nat. Assn. Sch. Psychologists. Office: SASED 301 S Swift Rd Addison IL 60101

VADER, LINDA ANDERSON, nurse; b. Grand Rapids, Mich., June 29, 1949; d. Stuart Edward and Margaret Sophia (Peterson) Anderson; m. Robert Elden Vader, July 10, 1970. Diploma, Butterworth Hosp. Sch. Nursing, 1970; BS, Eastern Mich. U., 1983. RN. Staff nurse Sparrow Hosp., Lansing, Mich., 1970-71, asst. head nurse, 1971-76; asst. head nurse U. Mich., Ann Arbor, 1976-77; head nurse Kellogg Eye Ctr., Ann Arbor, 1977—. Contbr. articles to profl. jours. and chpt. to book. Mem. Am. Soc. Ophthalmic RN's (pres. Great Lakes chpt. 1983—), Am. Soc. Ophthalmic RN's (sec. 1986—), Soc. for Advancement Modeling and Role Modeling, Sigma Theta Tau (Excellence in Nursing award 1987). Avocations: phtography, needlework. Home: 2624 Patricia Ct Ann Arbor MI 48103 Office: U Mich Kellogg Eye Ctr 1000 Wall St Ann Arbor MI 48105

VAGNIERES, ROBERT CHARLES, architect; b. Chgo., Oct. 2, 1932; s. Alfred and Elsa (Krueger) V.; B.Arch., U. Ill., 1955; m. Dorothy Lee Wandrey, June 13, 1953; children—Robert, Krista, Ross, Pam. Draftsman, Robert Soellner, Architect, Park Forest, Ill., 1957-59; asso. mem. firm Joel Robert Hillman, Architect, Chgo., 1959-71; partner Hillman Vagnieres & Assocs., Chgo., 1972-75; owner, prin. Robert C. Vagnieres Architect Ltd., Olympia Fields, Ill., 1975-79; cons., 1979-86; v.p. devel. and constrn. Jupiter realty Corp., 1986—; cons. hotel planning and constrn.; cons. Sheraton Naperville Hotel, 1980, Vista Internat. Hotel, N.Y.C., 1981, Embassy Suites Hotel O'Hare, 1986, Embassy Suites Hotel, Southfield, Mich., 1987. Served to lt., C.E., U.S. Army, 1955-57. Mem. AIA. Prin. works include Chgo. City Centre, 1976, Sheraton Plaza Hotel, Chgo., 1971, Homewood-Flossmoor (Ill.) High Sch., 1977. Home: 161 Chicago Ave E Chicago IL 60611

VAGNIERES, ROBERT CHARLES, JR., architect; b. Champaign, Ill., Mar. 27, 1954; s. Robert Charles Sr. and Dorothy Lee (Wandrey) V. BArch, U. Ill., 1976; MArch, Washington U., 1980. Architect Eva Maddox & Assoc., Chgo., 1982-83, Solomon Cordwell Buenz & Assoc., Chgo., 1980-82, 83-85; pvt. practice architecture Chgo., 1985—. Architect renovation of Exec. House Hotel, Chgo. Mem. AIA (vol. advisor Chgo. chpt. student liason program 1986—). ClClub: Alliance Francaise de Chgo. Avocations: trumpet, skiing. Home and Office: 1148 W School Chicago IL 60657

VAGTBORG, CHRISTIAN PETER, medical equipment service company executive; b. Los Angeles, Dec. 30, 1947; s. Christian Henning and Eleanor Blanche (Rydeen) V.; m. Connie Dilene Huffman, Feb. 6, 1970; children: Monty Allen, Christian Henning II. BA in English, Parsons Coll., 1970. Field service engr. Technicare Corp., Springfield, Mo., 1976-79; sr. field service engr. Technicare Corp., Solon, Ohio, 1979-80, supr. tech. support, 1980-82, mgr. tech support, 1982-84, mgr. edn., 1984-85, dir. service, 1985-87; pres. Synergistic Tech. Inc., Kent, Ohio, 1987—; cons. Rabbits Foot Electronics, Kent, Ohio, 1980—. Inventor microprocessor accelerator, 1982. Served with USN, 1970-76. Mem. Am. Soc. Tng. and Devel., Assn. for Computing Machinery, Mensa. Democrat. Home: 541 Silver Meadows Blvd Kent OH 44240

VAHL, RICHARD JAMES, chiropractor; b. Rochester, N.Y., May 4, 1940; s. Carl Heinrich and Matthie Valeria (Jerzak) V.; m. Karen Sue Sweeney, Sept. 3, 1966 (div. Nov. 1971); children: Ashley Lyn, James Brian; m. Denise Elizabeth Bettermann, Oct. 30, 1986. AS in Indsl. Tech., SUNY, Buffalo, 1962; BS, La. State U., 1966, MS, 1968; D of Chiropractic Medicine, Palmer Coll., Davenport, Iowa, 1982. Project engr. Xerox Corp., Rochester, N.Y., 1958-62; indsl. engr. Corning (N.Y.) Glass Works, 1962-63; program mgr. Corning Glass Works, Harrodsburg, Ky., 1967-72; corp. planning engr. Xerox Corp., 1963-67; mgr., sr. account exec. Merrill Lynch, Rochester, 1972-79; prof. clinical scis. Palmer Coll., Davenport, 1982-84, chmn. chiropractic tng. program, mem. instl. planning com., 1984—, mem. clin. sci. council, 1985—; postgrad. faculty Palmer Coll., 1986—, Northwestern Coll., Mpls., 1986—; indsl. cons. Beatrice Foods, Portland, Oreg., 1985—; sci. adv. bd. Cernitin Am. Corp., Yellow Springs, Ohio, 1985—, Southeast Back Inst., Atlanta, 1984—; various lectures, presentations on biomechanics, ergonomics, sports medicine and physical therapy. Contbr. articles on biomechanics, sports medicine, rehab. and physical fitness to profl. jours. Commerce and Industry capt. United Way Community Chest, Rochester, 1973-76; mem.youth program com. Am. Turners Assn., 1973-79; com. chmn. Boy Scouts Am., 1973-79; spl. advisor Kentuckiana Ctr. for Handicapped Children, Louisville, 1982—; bd. dirs. Young Reps., Rochester, 1975-79. Mem. Am. Registry Radiologic Tech. (trustee 1984—), Am. Chiropractic Assn., Internat. Chiropractic assn., Fla. Chiropractic Assn., Council on Orthopedics, Applied Spinal Biomech. Engrs. (bd. dirs. 1985—). Republican. Roman Catholic. Avocations: martial arts, scuba diving, swimming, tennis, running. Home: 2611 Tremont Ave Davenport IA 52803 Office: Palmer Coll 1000 Brady St Davenport IA 52803

VAIL, IRIS JENNINGS, civic worker; b. N.Y.C., July 2, 1928; d. Lawrence K. and Beatrice (Black) Jennings; grad. Miss Porters Sch., Farmington, Conn.; m. Thomas V.H. Vail, Sept. 15, 1951; children—Siri J., Thomas V.H. Jr., Lawrence J.W. Exec. com. Garden Club Cleve., 1962—; mem. women's council Western Res. Hist. Soc., 1960—; mem. jr. council Cleve. Mus. Art, 1953—; chmn. Childrens Garden Fair, 1966-75, Public Square Dinner, 1975; bd. dirs. Garden Center Greater Cleve., 1963-77; trustee Cleve. Zool. Soc., 1971—; mem. Ohio Arts Council, 1974-76, pub. sq. com. Greater Cleve. Growth Assn.; mem. endangered species com. Cleve. 200 Soc. Recipient Amy Angell Collier Montague medal Garden Club Am., 1976, Ohio Gov.'s award, 1977. Episcopalian. Clubs: Chagrin Valley Hunt, Cypress Point, Kirtland Country, Union, Colony, Women's City of Cleve. (Margaret A. Ireland award). Home: Hunting Valley Chagrin Falls OH 44022

VAIL, JOE FRANKLIN, marketing company executive; b. Indpls., Mar. 24, 1928; s. Frank Albert and Trixie May (Hawley) V.; B.S., Purdue U., 1951; m. Margaret Louise Warne, Nov. 24, 1984; 1 son, Kevin Joe. Treas., Apex Corp., Indpls., 1953-60; owner, operator Bus. Service Co., Indpls., 1961-63; partner Pulse Publs., Indpls., 1963-64; pres. Unique, Inc., Indpls., 1965-70; owner, operator Mid-Am. Advt. Co., Indpls., 1970-73; pres. Mid-Am. Mktg., Inc., Indpls., 1973—; editor, pub. Land Opportunity Rev., 1970—. Mem. Chgo. Assn. Direct Mktg., Nat. Fedn. Ind. Bus., Indpls. C. of C. Am. Bus. Club. Clubs: John Purdue, Masons. Author: Keys to Wealth, 1971; Your Fortune in Mail Order, 1972; How to Get Out of Debt and Live Like a Millionaire, 1977; Money-Where It Is and How To Get It, 1981. Home: 8228 E 13th St Indianapolis IN 46219 Office: 1150 N Shadeland Ave Indianapolis IN 46219

VAIL, ROBERT WILLIAM, consulting company executive; b. Columbus, Ohio, Oct. 29, 1921; s. Robert David Dmitri and Dorothy (Mosier) Vail; student Ohio State U., 1938-39; m. Martha Henderson, Apr. 7, 1939; children—William N., Veronica Vail Fish, David A., Ashley M., Victor H., Lorelei Hird, Hilary W. Chemist, Barnebey-Cheney Engring. Co., 1941-44; sr. chemist Pa. Coal Products Co., Petrolia, 1944-51; abrasive engr. Carborundum Co., Niagara Falls, N.Y., 1951-54; tech. sales Allied Chem. Corp., Cleve., 1954-59; head research lab. U.S. Ceramic Tile Co., Canton, Ohio, 1960-62; sales mgr. Ferro Chem. div. Ferro Corp., Walton Hills, Ohio, 1962-70; pres. R. William Vail Inc., Cleve., 1970-72; mgr. tech. services Manpower Inc., Cleve., 1972-74; owner, mgr. Vail, Shaker Heights, Ohio, 1974-78; sr. cons. Hayden, Heman, Smith & Assos., Cleve., 1978-83; owner Vail, Newbury, Ohio, 1983—. Recipient Am. Security Council Bus. Citizenship Competition Excellence award, 1967. Mem. Amateur Radio Relay League. Republican. Presbyterian. Lodges: Masons, Scottish Rite, Al Koran Shrine. Author: Teardrops Falling, 1963; contbg. author: Ency. of Basic Materials for Plastics, 1967. Home: Box 516 Newbury OH 44065 Office: 14871 Highview Newbury OH 44065

VAIL, SUZI MARY, livestock buyer; b. Hoven, S.D., June 21, 1951; d. Frank Joseph and Viola (Huber) Hoven; m. Charles Kenneth Vail, July 3, 1969 (dec.); children: Carla, Teddi, Charli. Grad. high sch., 1969. Bookeeper Lehrkamp Livestock, Lebanon, S.D., 1974-76, Dakota Boring, Lebanon, 1974-81, Sodak Pork, Lebanon, 1977-81; buyer in sale barn Pierce Packing Co., Billings, Mont., 1981-83; mgr. Lebanon Cafe, 1981-84; with fin. office Town of Lebanon, 1983-84; operator pvt. buying sta. Swift Industry, Huron, S.D., 1983—. Mem. council Town of Lebanon, 1978-82, mayor, 1982-83. Recipient Recognition and Appreciation award S.D. Office of Volunteerism, 1980-84. Democrat. Roman Catholic. Avocations: fishing, camping, dancing, refunding, biking. Home: PO Box 32 Lebanon SD 57455 Office: Old Faithful Livestock PO Box 114 Lebanon SD 57455

VAILLANCOURT, DANIEL GILBERT, philosophy educator; b. Lewiston, Maine, Mar. 5, 1947; s. Gilbert and Paquerette (Demers) V.; m. Kathleen Moore, Dec. 30, 1967; children: Michelle Monique, Shannon Robert. BA in French and Philosophy, St. Francis Coll., 1969; MA in Philosophy, DePaul U., 1971, PhD in Philosophy, 1976. Instr. DePaul U., Chgo., 1972-73; instr. Mundelein Coll., Chgo., 1972-75, asst. prof., 1975-79, assoc. prof., 1979-86, prof., 1986—, dean grad. sch. masters liberal studies, 1987—. Contbr. articles to profl. jours. NEH grantee, 1978; NEH project dir., 1984; named Tchr. Yr. Mundelein Graduating Class, 1986. Mem. Am. Philosophy Assn., Philosophy of the Unconscious, Personalist Forum, Phiosophers Concerned for Peace, Master of Liberal Studies Assn. Avocations: tennis, naturalism. Home: RR 2 Box 64A Blanchardville WI 53516 Office: Mundelein Coll 6363 N Sheridan Rd Chicago IL 60660

VAILLANT, DENNIS PETER, dentist; b. Mpls., Feb. 27, 1940; s. Hector A. and Helen (Graney) V.; m. Lynn Louise Falls, June 19, 1965; children: Peter, Matthew, Daniel. BS, U. Minn., 1961, DDS, 1965, BA, 1968; grad., L. D. Pankey Inst. Advanced Dental Edn., 1986. Intern Phila. Hosp., 1965-66; gen. practice dentistry Red Wing, Minn., 1970—. Pres. Red Wing United Way, 1976. Served with USN, 1965-70. Fellow Am. Acad. Gen. Practice; mem. Goodhue County Dental Soc. (pres. 1975-80). Republican. Roman Catholic. Lodge: Kiwanis (local pres. 1983, Disting. Pres. 1984). Home: 4336 Lookout Ln Red Wing MN 55066 Office: 316 Bush St Red Wing MN 55066

VAINISI, JEROME ROBERT, professional football executive, lawyer; b. Chgo., Oct. 7, 1941; s. Anthony A. and Marie (Delisi) V.; m. Doris Mary Lane, Nov. 14, 1964; children—Mary Terese, Jerome A., John A., Mark E., Melissa P. B.S. in Bus. Adminstrn., Georgetown U., 1963; postgrad. in law Loyola U., 1963-64; J.D., Chgo. Kent Coll. Law, 1969. Bar: Ill. 1969. News and sports dir. Sta. WRAM, Monmouth, Ill., 1964-65; tax acct., office mgr. Arthur Andersen & Co., Chgo., 1965-72; successively controller, corp. asst. sec., treas. Chgo. Bears Football Club, Inc., 1972-83, v.p., gen. mgr., 1983-87; gen. counsel Detroit Lions Football Club, Pontiac, Mich., 1987—; dir., chmn. bd. Forest Park Nat. Bank (Ill.), 1978—; v.p. NFL Ins. Ltd., 1984-87. Roman Catholic. Office: care Detroit Lions 1200 Featherstone Rd Box 4200 Pontiac MI 48057

VAJDA, JANETTE ANNE, psychiatric nursing educator; b. Cleve., May 22, 1954; d. Alex Francis and Catherine Helen (Hermann) V. B.S. in Nursing, U. Akron, 1976; postgrad. in psychiat./mental nursing Kent State U., 1984-85, MEd in Community Agy. Counseling, Cleve. State U., 1987. Case mgr., counselor West Side Community Mental Health Ctr., Cleve., 1976-81; psychosocial nursing instr. Cleve. Met. Gen. Hosp. Sch. Nursing, 1981—; psychiat. nurse, counselor Comprehensive Psychiat. Services, 1986—.

VAKIL, SADEGH MEISSAMI, electrical engineer, educator; b. Arak, Iran, Sept. 18, 1935; came to U.S., 1955; s. Hassan Meissami and Sedigheh (Ghaffari) V.; m. Simeen Mojtabai, Aug. 20, 1966 (div. 1972); 1 child, Maryam Maureen. BEE, U. Mo., 1958, MEE, 1959; MA in Physics, U. Calif., Berkeley, 1966, postgrad., 1962-69. Research assoc. Boeing Co., Seattle, 1960-63; sr. research engr. Lockheed Corp., Sunnyvale, Calif., 1963-69; assoc. prof. Arya-Mehr U. Technology, Teheran, Iran, 1969-82; lightning, nuclear protection specialist Collins div. Rockwell Internat., Cedar Rapids, Iowa, 1984—; cons. Rockwell Internat., Los Angeles, 1970. Contbr. articles to profl. jours. Welfare rep., organizer Arya-Mehr U. Technology, 1971-79. Avocations: translations of scientific books on space, travel.

VALANCE, MARSHA JEANNE, library director, story teller; b. Evanston, Ill., Aug. 2, 1946; d. Edward James, Jr. and Jeanne Lois (Skinner) Leonard; m. William George Valance, Dec. 27, 1966 (div. 1976); 1 dau., Marguerite Jeanne. Student Northwestern U., 1964-66; A.B., UCLA, 1968; M.L.S., U. R.I., 1973. Children's librarian trainee N.Y. Pub. Library, N.Y.C., 1968-69; reference librarian Action Meml. Pub. Library (Mass.), 1969-70; mgr. The Footnote, Cedar Rapids, Iowa, 1976-78; assoc. editor William C. Brown, Dubuque, Iowa, 1978-79; library dir. Dubuque County Library, Dubuque, 1979-81; library dir. G.B. Dedrick Pub. Library, Geneseo, Ill., 1981-84; library dir. Grand Rapids Pub. Library, Minn., 1984—; workshop coordinator, participant, sect. chmn. profl. confs. Co-author: Mystery, Value and Awareness, 1979; Pluralism, Similarities and Contrast, 1979; contbr. articles to publs. Troop leader Mississippi Valley Council Girl Scouts U.S.A., Cedar Rapids, 1976-78; mem. liturgy com. St. Malachy's Roman Catholic Ch., Geneseo, 1983; com. judging clinic 4-H, Moline, Ill., 1984; trustee KAXE No. Community Radio, 1986—; sec. Grand Rapids Community Services Council, 1986; coach Itasca County 4-H Horse Bowl Team, 1987; organizer Grand Rapids Storyfest, 1987. Iowa Humanities Bd. grantee, 1981, Minn. Library Found. grantee, 1985, 86, Arrowhead Regional Arts Council grantee, 1987. Mem. ALA, Minn. Library Assn., Iowa Libraries of Medium Size (sec. 1981), Northlands Storytelling Network, Alliance Info. and Referral Services, DAR (constn. chmn. 1983-84), Am. Morgan Horse Assn., Mississippi Valley Morgan Horse Club, North Central Morgan Assn., Alpha Gamma Delta. Club: Geneseo Jr. Women's (internat. chmn. 1983-84). Home: 1405 7th St SE Grand Rapids MN 55744-4083 Office: 21 NE 5th St Grand Rapids MN 55744

VALANCIUS, JAMES PETER, engineering executive; b. Chgo., Dec. 2, 1936; s. Joseph and Frances (Wilutis) V.; m. Alice M. Krezeminski, Aug. 9, 1958; children: James Jr., Joseph, Vicky Ann, David. Student, U. Ill., Chgo., Ill. Inst. Tech., U. Md. Registered profl. engr. Project engr. Addressograph Muligraph, Mount Prospect, Ill., 1972-77; system engr. Gen. Motors, Chgo., 1977-82; mgr. engring. Himmelstein Corp., Hoffman Estate, Ill., 1982-85; dir. engring. Dietzgen Corp., Des Plaines, Ill., 1985—. Patentee in field. Chmn. Engrs. for Carl Roth, Dupage County, Ill., 1984—; bd. dirs. Midwest Coll. Engring., Lombard, Ill., 1985—. Served to sgt. U.S. Army, 1951-53. Mem. IEEE, Nat. Soc. Profl. Engrs. (pres. Salt Creek chpt. 1986—), Ill. Soc. Profl. Engrs. Roman Catholic. Avocations: sailing, bicycling. Home: 162 N Hampshire Elmhurst IL 60126

VALENTE, PATRICIA LUCILLE, college counselor; b. Chgo., June 30, 1940; d. Joseph James and Mae L. (Durand) V.; m. Robert J. Maxwell, Jan. 19, 1963 (div. Feb. 1974); children: Kim Maxwell, Robert Maxwell; m. Robert W. Witzke, Aug. 4, 1977. BA, No. Ill. U., 1962, MS, 1967; MS, George Williams Coll., 1976. Cert. sex educator, sex therapist. Tchr. English Hinsdale (Ill.) High Sch., 1963-69; tchr. English Morton Coll.,

Cicero, Ill., 1969-71, counselor, sex therapist, 1971—; cons. West Chgo. (Ill.) Community High Sch., 1965-66; mem. north cen. visitation team Ill. State Dept. Edn., Springfield, 1968; presenter in field. Author: (with others) Community College Career Alternatives, 1981, The WOW Group: The New Frontier, 1984. Named Educator of Yr., Morton Coll., 1979. Mem. CWP (exec. bd. dirs. 1983—), ASSECT, IGPA, AGPA. Roman Catholic. Avocations: running, reading, photography, bridge, stained glass. Home: 17 W 507 Portsmouth Dr Westmont IL 60559 Office: Morton Coll 3801 S Central Ave Cicero IL 60650

VALENTINE, MARJORIE PARKS, psychologist, consultant; b. Chattanooga, Apr. 20, 1928; d. Leon C. and Marjorie (Atlee) Parks; m. Andrew Jackson Valentine, July 20, 1949; children—Rawson J., Atlee Ann, Sarah. B.A., U. Tenn., 1949; M.A., George Washington U., 1954; Ph.D., Am. U., 1977. Lic. psychologist, D.C., 1981, Ill., 1987. Sch. psychologist Escambia County Schs., Pensacola, Fla., 1962-65, dir. Headstart Program, 1965; sch. psychologist Arlington (Va.) Pub. Schs., 1966-79; instr. U. Va. Regional Ctr., 1975-76; research affiliate Program on Women, Northwestern U., 1979-82; assoc. Cassell, Rath and Stoyanoff, Ltd., Evanston, Ill., 1981-85 ; adj. faculty Seabury-Western Seminary, 1984—. Pres. bd. dirs., exec. com. Chicago Commons Assn., 1980—. Mem. Am. Psychol. Assn., Ill. Psychol. Assn. Republican. Episcopalian. Club: Junior League of Evanston. Address: 1091 Sheridan Rd Winnetka IL 60093

VALENTINE, RALPH JAMES, chemical engineer; b. Mahwah, N.J., May 11, 1922; s. Richard Van Sr. and Matilda (Fisher) V.; m. Irene M. Sandberg, Feb. 13, 1944; children—Ralph James, Dorothy June, Leonard Bradley, Christine Marie. B.Chem. Engring., Pratt Inst., 1943; postgrad Stevens Inst. Tech., 1948-51, Case Inst. Tech., 1952, Fairleigh Dickinson U., 1965-67. Registered corrosion specialist. Devel. engr. AT&T, 1946-49; chem. process engr. Lederle Labs. div. Am. Cyanamid Co., Pearl River, N.Y., 1949-51, asst. supt. chem. prodn., 1951-52, corrosion and materials engr., 1952-56, sr. chem. engr. design and constrn. chem. and prodn. facilities, cons. corrosion and materials engring. problems, 1956-73, sr. chem. project engring. mgr. Cyanamid Engring. and Constrn. div., Wayne, N.J., 1973-81; sr. engring. project mgr., corrosion cons. Upjohn Co., Kalamazoo, 1981—; prin. Val-Corr. Author: Fabrication of Equipment and Piping Using 254SMO Austenitic Stainless Steel, 1986; contbr. (book chpt.) Am. Soc. Metals Handbook Series. Elder, v.p. consistory, del. to gen. synod Reformed Ch. Am. Served to capt. USAAF, 1943-46. Fellow Am. Inst. Chemists; mem. Nat. Assn. Corrosion Engrs., Structural Steel Painting Council, Sea Horse Inst. Lodge: Vasa Order Am. (past N.J. dist. master). Home: 173 Parkland Terr Portage MI 49002 Office: Upjohn Co 7171 Portage Rd Kalamazoo MI 49001

VALENZUELA, JESUS, financial executive; b. Phoenix, Nov. 6, 1957; s. Jesus Felipe and Eloisa Amalia (Aguirre) V.; m. Helena Johanna Baranowski, May 28, 1982; 1 child, Veronica Baran. BS in Acctg. cum laude, Ariz. State U., 1983. Research analyst Ariz. Legis., Phoenix, 1982-83; independent contractor Venterprise Internat., Phoenix, 1979-83; staff auditor Coopers & Lybrand, Los Angeles, 1983-84; internat. auditor Gerber Products Co., Fremont, Mich., 1984-85, internat. fin. mgr., 1985—; mng. ptnr. Fremont Growth Investors, 1986—. Served with U.S. Army, 1975-78, Republic of Germany. Mem. Inst. Internal Auditors, Fremont Jaycees, Beta Gamma Sigma, Phi Kappa Phi. Republican. Roman Catholic. Club: Toastmasters (Best Speaker award 1984). Avocations: aviation, music, photography. Office: Gerber Products Co 445 State St Fremont MI 49412

VALERIUS, FREDERICK MICHAEL, special education administrator; b. Cin., Jan. 22, 1947; s. Frederick Anthony and Marian Gertrude (Gundlach) V.; m. Joyce Ann Rupp, July 12, 1974; children—Jillian Marie, Christina Ann. B.S. in Edn., U. Cin., 1969, M.Ed., 1971, EdD, 1987. Qualified mental retardation profl., Ohio. Instr., Hamilton County Bd. Mental Retardation, Cin., 1969-70; instr. Butler County Bd. Mental Retardation, Hamilton, Ohio, 1970-72, instr. supr., 1972-75, dir. ednl. services, 1976-79; asst. supt. program services Butler County Bd. Mental Retardation and Devel. Disabilities, Fairfield, Ohio, 1980—. Mem. Am. Assn. Mental Deficiency (membership chmn. Ohio chpt.), Assn. Curriculum and Supervision Devel., Profl. Assn. Retardation Ohio (pres. 1974-75). Office: 155 Donald Dr Fairfield OH 45014

VALESTIN, GARY ROBERT, obstetrician, gynecologist; b. Los Angeles, Mar. 31, 1950; s. Robert F. and Rita B. Valestin; m. Debra C. Valestin, Mar. 31, 1979. BS, U. Notre Dame, 1972; MD, Hahnemann Med. Coll., 1977. Diplomate Am. Bd. Ob-Gyn, Am. Bd. Med. Examiners. Intern Med. Coll. Wis. Hosps., Milw., 1977-78, resident in ob-gyn, 1978-81; practice medicine specializing in ob-gyn Des Moines, 1981—. Fellow Am. Coll. Ob-Gyn. Home: 3701 28th St SW Des Moines IA 50321 Office: 421 Laurel 306 Des Moines IA 50314

VALINSKY, MARK STEVEN, podiatrist; b. Chgo., May 24, 1951; s. Harry and Beckie (Baker) V.; m. Michelle Susan Morgan; children: Cara Linda, Erin Abra, Noah Allen, Hannah Rae. Student in biology and pre-medicine, Ohio State U., 1969-71, SUNY, Buffalo, 1971-72; BS, D in Podiatric Medicine, Ill. Coll. Podiatric Medicine, 1976. Diplomate Am. Bd. Foot Surgeons; lic. podiatrist, Ill., Calif., N.Y. Extern in podiatric medicine Podiatry Assocs. Ltd. and Children's Foot Clinic, Des Plaines (Ill.) and Great Falls (Mont.), Ill., 1975; practice medicine specializing in podiatric surgery Oak Park, Ill., 1977-82; active staff Northlake (Ill.) Community Hosp., 1979-81, Hugar Surg. Ctr., Elmwood Park, Ill., 1978-79; mem. 1st foot surg. team to Peoples Republic of China, 1983; cons. staff Riveredge Hosp., Forest Park, Ill.; pres., founder Biol. Scis. Research Inst., Inc.; pres. Aaron Podiatry Assos., P.C., Oak Park. Mem. Mayor's council Sr. Citizens and Handicapped, 1979. Mem. Am. Inst. Foot Medicine (cert.), Ill. Podiatry Soc. (sec. Zone I, 1980-82, pres. 1981-82, del. to bd. dirs. 1980-82), Am. Podiatry Soc., Acad. Ambulatory Foot Surgeons (pres. midwest region 1986—), Oak Park-River Forest C. of C. (bd. dirs.). Home: 251 Timber Trail Dr Oak Brook IL 60521 Office: 163 S Oak Park Ave Oak Park IL 60302

VALLEY, MARY MARGARET, secondary school teacher; b. Beaver Dam, Wis., Apr. 5, 1947; d. Abe and Mae Helen (Nitze) Maloof; m. Larry E. Valley, June 17, 1972; children: Lory, Gary, Cory, Kary. B in Music, Butler U., 1969; postgrad., U. Wis., Madison, 1972, U. Wis., Whitewater, 1985—. Cert. music tchr., Wis. Music tchr. Edgerton (Wis.) Community Sch., 1969-72; instr. home econs. Lakeshore Tech. Inst., Cleveland, Wis., 1976-84; tax preparer H&R Block Ltd., Sheboygan, Wis., 1978-83; bus. edn. tchr. Sheboygan Sch. Dist., 1982-86, coordinator gifted and talented children, 1986—; coach Olympics of the Mind, Horace Mann Middle Sch., Sheboygan, 1985—. Pres. PTA Holy Name Sch., Sheboygan, 1982-83, polit. corr. Home and Sch. Assn., 1979; treas., den mother Boy Scouts Am., 1984—. Mem. NEA, Wis. Edn. Assn., Sheboygan Edn. Assn., Wis. Council for Gifted and Talented, Delta Pi Epsilon. Roman Catholic. Avocations: sewing, crafts, fishing. Home: 3166 North Ave Sheboygan WI 53083

VALLEY, SCOTT MACDONALD, education association executive; b. Zaragoza, Spain, Jan. 25, 1959; s. William Robert and Barbara M. (Dunn) V. BS in Polit. Sci., Wash. State U., 1981. Cons. Acacia Fraternity, Inc., Indpls., 1981-83, exec. dir. and editor, 1983—; exec. dir. Acacia Edn. Found., Indpls., 1983—; bd. dirs. VWO Housing Corp., London, Can. Editor TRIAD, 1983—, Found. Reports Newsletter, 1983—, UPDATE Newsletter, 1983—. Mem. Am. Soc. Assn. Execs., Internat. Sect. Am. Soc. Assn. Execs., Fraternity Execs. Assn. (com. chmn. 1983—), Coll. Fraternity Editors Assn., Harrison Soc. (exec. com. 1985), Indpls. Ambassadors (founder, bd. dirs., v.p.). Republican. Methodist. Club: Columbia Indpls.) (membership com.). Lodge: Masons. Avocations: golf, sports cars, hunting, dogs, skiing. Office: Acacia Fraternity Inc 3901 W 86th St Suite 430 Indianapolis IN 46268

VALO, THOMAS SCOTT, dentist; b. Toledo, Dec. 13, 1952; s. Donald Alvin and Virginia Mae (LaCount) V.; m. Pamela Jamie Puglisi, July 17, 1976; children: Michael Joseph, Jamie Elizabeth, Walter Alexander. DDS, Ohio State U., 1976. Gen. practice dentistry Sylvania, Ohio, 1976—; mem. dental staff Toledo Hosp., 1978—, Lake Park Hosp., Sylvania, 1986—. Contbr. articles to profl. jours. Mem. ADA, Ohio Dental Assn., Toledo Dental Soc., Am. Equilibration Soc., TMJ Study Group of Toledo (pres. 1984-86). Lodge: Rotary (bd. dirs. 1984-85). Home: 4249 Whiteford Toledo OH 43623 Office: 6465 Monroe Sylvania OH 43560

VALORE, KENNETH JOSEPH, greeting card executive, accountant; b. Cleve., Dec. 24, 1941; s. Joseph Anthony and Agnes Elaine (Giardino) V.; m. Ursula Meier, July 25, 1964; children: Jason, Scott. BBA in Acctg., Case Western Reserve U., 1965. CPA, Ohio. Staff acct. Am. Greeting Corp., Cleve., 1965-69, asst. to controller, 1969-72, dir. specialized acctg., 1972-76, asst. controller, 1976-77, controller, 1977-82, v.p. fin., 1982—. Chmn. allocations com. Cleve. United Way, 1986—. Mem. Am. Inst. CPA's, Fin. Execs. Inst. (bd. dirs. NE Ohio chpt. 1986—). Roman Catholic. Avocations: reading, golf, tennis. Home: 27291 Santa Clara Dr Westlake OH 44145 Office: Am Greetings Corp 10500 American Rd Cleveland OH 44144

VAN AARTSEN, JACK GORDON, political science and history educator; b. Grand Rapids, Mich., Sept. 4, 1936; s. Woodrow and Loris Jean (Dykstra) Van A.; m. June Lorraine Brown, Mar. 21, 1958; children: Renee Diane, Brent Eric, Kimberly Joy, Scott Brian. BA, Mich. State U., 1958, MA, 1961. Cert. secondary tchr. Tchr. English Caledonia (Mich.) High Sch., 1958-59; tchr. English and Social Studies Cen. High Sch., Grand Rapids, 1959-62; instr. polit. sci. and history Grand Rapids Jr. Coll., 1962—; asst. prof. history Grace Bible Coll., Wyoming, Mich., 1962—; media coordinator Grand Rapids Jr. Coll., 1982—; visiting instr. Grand Valley State Coll., Allendale, Mich., 1986. Author: Study Guide: America's Democracy, 1985. Mem. Grand Rapids Jr. Coll. Faculty Assn. (past pres. and v.p.), Grand Rapids Jr. Coll. Found., Grand Rapids Hist. Soc. (program chmn. 1974-75). Republican. Avocations: reading, traveling, boating, coin collecting. Office: Grand Rapids Jr Coll 143 Bostwick NE Grand Rapids MI 49503

VANAGAS, RIMANTAS ANDRIUS (RAY), entrepreneur; b. Chgo., Jan. 10, 1958; s. Liudas and Birute A. (Bielskis) V. Student, Northwestern U., 1980-81; BA in Physics and Econs., Lake Forest (Ill.) Coll., 1982. Ski instr., capt. race team Breckenridge (Colo.) Ski Sch., 1979-80; chmn. bd. dirs. Vancher Corp., Wheeling, Ill., 1980-84; sales exec. Chgo. HMO, 1984-85; exec. dir. Physique, Inc., Highland Park, Ill., 1985; pres., chief exec. officer Sports Life, Inc., Highland Park, 1985—; cons. Nautilus Exercise Ctrs., Inc., Wheeling, 1979-83, G. Ross Communications, Lake Bluff, Ill., 1986. Leader Lithuanian Air Scouts, 1976-80; campaign asst. Ronald Reagan Re-Election Campaign, Ill., 1983; active Baltic Nations Athletic Olympaid; vol. coach basketball, baseball, 1984-87. Roman Catholic. Avocations: collecting coins and stamps, traveling, skiing, golf, tennis. Home: 603 W Burr Oak Dr Arlington Heights IL 60004

VAN ALLEN, MAURICE WRIGHT, physician; b. Mt. Pleasant, Iowa, Apr. 3, 1918; s. Alfred Maurice and Alma E. (Olney) Van A.; m. Janet Hunt, Aug. 20, 1949; children: David, Martha, Evalyn, Jonathan. B.A., Iowa Wesleyan Coll., 1939; M.D., U. Iowa, 1942. Diplomate: Am. Psychiatry and Neurology, Am. Bd. Neurol. Surgery. Intern Pa. Hosp., Phila., 1942-43; resident in neurology and neurosurgery Iowa City, Iowa, 1954—, practice medicine specializing in neurology; chief neurol. sect. VA Hosp., Iowa City, 1954-59; asso. prof. dept. neurology Coll. Medicine, U. Iowa, 1959-65, prof., 1965-86, head dept., 1974-86; dec. Iowa City, 1986; mem. council Nat. Inst. Dental Research. Author book in field; contbr. articles to profl. jours.; editor: Archives of Neurology, 1976-82. Served with M.C., U.S. Army, 1943-46. Mem. AMA, Am. Acad. Neurology, Am. Neurol. Assn., Assn. Research and Nervous and Mental Disease, Sigma Xi, Alpha Omega Alpha. Republican. Episcopalian. Home: 354 Lexington Ave Iowa City IA 52240 *dec. May 2, 1986.*

VAN AMAN, CONSTANCE SUE, data processing mgr.; b. South Bend, Ind., Oct. 5, 1953; d. Jack Vernon and Phyllis Henrietta (Smith) Hess; m. Dale Patrick Vanaman, Oct. 15, 1976; (div. 1985); children: Troy Alan, Chad James. ADP, Ind. Vocat. Tech. Coll., 1981. Programmer Triad-Utrad, Huntington, Ind., 1980-81; project mgr. K-Mart Corp., Fort Wayne, 1981—; prof. Ind. Vocat. Tech. Coll., Fort Wayne, 1981—. Bd. dirs. Stop Child Abuse and Neglect Orgn., Fort Wayne, 1985-87. Fellow Nat. Assn. Female Execs.; mem. Soc. to Advance Total User Systems (bd. dirs. 1985-86). Democrat. Methodist. Avocations: piano, music, interior decorating, tennis. Home: 123 N Indiana Ave Auburn IN 46706 Office: K-Mart Corp Ferguson Rd Box 359 Fort Wayne IN 46801

VAN ANDEL, BETTY JEAN, household products company executive; b. Mich., Dec. 14, 1921; d. Anthony and Daisy (Van Dyk) Hoekstra; A.B., Calvin Coll., 1943; m. Jay Van Andel, Aug. 16, 1952; children—Nan Elizabeth, Stephen Alan, David Lee, Barbara Ann. Elementary sch. tchr., Grand Rapids, Mich., 1943-45; service rep. and supr. Mich. Bell Telephone Co., Grand Rapids, 1945-52; bd. dirs. Amway Corp., Grand Rapids, 1972—. Treas., LWV, 1957-60; chmn. Eagle Forum, Mich., 1975—; bd. dirs. Christian Sch. Ednl. Found., Pine Rest Christian Hosp., Grand Rapids Opera, 1982, exec. com., nominating chmn. Mem. Nat. Trust Hist. Preservation, St. Cecelia Music Soc., Smithsonian Assos. Republican. Club: Women's City of Grand Rapids. Home: 7186 Windy Hill Rd SE Grand Rapids MI 49506 Office: PO Box 172 Ada MI 49301

VAN ARSDALE, KAREN CHOKA, social worker; b. Ft. Wayne, Ind., Oct. 21, 1946; d. Stas Thomas and Florence Frances (Staniszewski) Choka; m. George Bauerle Van Arsdale, May 20, 1972; 1 child, Anneliese. BA, Ind. U., Bloomington, 1971; MSW, Ind. U., Indpls., 1972. Social worker Quinco, Columbus, Ind., 1972-75, Planned Parenthood, Bloomington, 1975-87, Stonebelt Council for Retarded Citizens, Bloomington, 1987—; adj. faculty Ind. U., Bloomington, 1978—; ptnr. Iris Ctr. for Counseling and Edn., Bloomington, 1982—; cons. various health and service orgns., Ind., 1982—. mem. Human Resources Commn., Bloomington, 1979-83, chmn. 1982-83. Mem. Acad. Cert. Social Workers, Nat. Assn. Social Workers (regional rep. 1976, Social Worker of Yr. 1984), Am. Assn. Sex Educators, Counselors and Therapists (cert. therapist, cert. educator), Monroe County Assn. of Social Workers (pres. 1978). Democrat. Club: Bloomington Bicycling (sec. 1978). Home: 1204 E Wylie Bloomington IN 47401 Office: PO Box 5491 Bloomington IN 47401

VANASEK, ROBERT EDWARD, state legislator; b. New Prague, Minn., Apr. 2, 1949; s. Richard and Elsie (Kajer) V.; m. Mary Wagner, 1973; children: Robert Martin, Lora, Becky. BA, U. Minn., 1971. State rep. Minn. Dist. 25A, St. Paul, 1973—, state speaker, 1987—. Office: Office of the State Speaker Minnesota House of Representatives State Capitol Saint Paul MN 55155 *

VANASUPA, PRABHUNDHA, neurological surgeon; b. Dhonburi, Thailand, Sept. 18, 1928; came to U.S., 1953; s. Lung and Lew Vanasupa; m. Verna-lee Antonia, June 17, 1960; children: Ted K., Linda S., Diane, M. Undergrad. degree, Chulalongkorn U., Bangkok, Thailand, 1948, MD, 1952. Lic. physician, Thailand, Pa., N.Y., and Mich.; diplomate Am. Bd. Neurol. Surgery. Intern Chulalongkorn Hosp. Med. Sch., Bangkok, 1952-53, attending neurosurgeon, clin. instr. neurol. surgery, 1962-64; intern Jewish Hosp. St. Louis, 1953-54, asst. resident gen. surgery, 1954-55, 56-57; asst. resident gen. surgery Ellis Fischell State Cancer Hosp., Columbia, Mo., 1955-56; research fellow neurology and neurophysiology Washington U., St. Louis, 1957-59; asst. resident clin. neurology Barnes Hosp. Med. Ctr., St. Louis, 1959; asst. resident neurol. surgery SUNY Upstate Med. Ctr., Syracuse, 1959-60, sr. resident neurol. surgery, 1960-61, chief resident neurol. surgery, 1961-62; practice medicine specializing in neurol. surgery Saginaw, Mich., 1965—. Author: A Guide Book for Thai Medical Students In Neurology (Thai lang.), 1963; contbr. articles to profl. jours. Mem. AMA, ACS, Thai Med. Assn., Mich. Med. Soc., Bay Iosco Arenac Med. Soc., Mich. Assn. Neurol. Surgeons, Congress of Neurol. Surgeons N.Am., Am. Assn. Neurol. Surgeons, Saginaw Med. Soc., Saginaw Surgical Soc.

VAN ATTA, RALPH EDWARD, clinical psychologist, consultant in forensic psychology; b. Columbus, Ohio, July 24, 1933; s. Clarence Dell and Wilma (Davidson) V.; m. JoAnn Luce, Sept. 15, 1962; children: Katherine, Karen, Ralph Davidson, Sarah. BS, Ohio State U., 1955, MA, 1960, PhD, 1964. Lic. psychologist, Wis., Ill.; diplomate Am. Bd. of Psychotherapy. Intern, Ohio State Counseling Ctr., Columbus, 1962; clin. psychology intern Norwich (Conn.) Hosp., 1963; asst. prof., psychologist U. Tex., 1964-69; assoc. prof., psychologist, So. Ill. U., Carbondale, 1969-72; dir., prof. dept. psychol. services U. Wis.-Milw., 1972-80; exec. dir. Behavioral Medicine Assocs., Waukesha, Wis., 1978-87 ; pres. Behavioral Medicine Wis., Ltd., 1984-86; mem. Panel Forensic Experts, Counties of Waukesha and Milwaukee, Wis. Served to 1st lt. U.S. Army, 1955-57. Named Disting. Mil. Student Ohio State U., 1955. Mem. Am. Psychol. Assn., Wis. Psychol. Assn., Am. Acad. Psychotherapists, Am. Soc. Clin. Hypnosis (Clin. Research award 1987). Contbr. articles to profl. jours. Office: 2426 N Grandview Blvd Waukesha WI 53188

VAN AUKEN, RICHARD ANTHONY, architect; b. Cleve., July 16, 1934; s. Lewis Cornell and Loretta (Murphy) Van A.; m. Ann Katherine McPolin (div. Sept. 1977); children: Bradley, Jacqueline, Mark; m. Mary Susan Duffy, Nov. 25, 1977. BArch, U. Notre Dame, 1957. Commd. U.S. Army, 1957, advanced through grades to capt., 1962; architect Hays and Ruth, Cleve., 1958-59; prin. Dalton, Dalton Assoc., Cleve., 1959-68; pres. Van Auken & Bridges, Cleve., 1968-82; mng. prin. URS Co., Detroit, 1982-86; pres., chief exec. officer Jennings & Churella Constrn. Co., New London, Ohio, 1987—. Mem. adv. council Coll. Engring. U. Notre Dame, 1974-86; chmn. bd. trustees Ashland Coll., 1968—. Mem. AIA, Delta Mu Delta. Roman Catholic. Clubs: Birmingham (Mich.) Country; Shaker Heights Country (Cleve.); Hunters Creek (Metamora, Mich.); Carolina Trace Country; Fairlawn Country (Akron); Hill N Dale (Medina). Home: 3580 Sparrow Pond Circle Akron OH 44313 Office: Jennings & Churella Constrn Co 111 E Main St New London OH 44851

VAN BEEK, JAMES ARTHUR, restaurant executive, real estate executive; b. Menomonee, Mich., Jan. 23, 1957; s. Peter Joseph and Thelma Clementine (DeKeyser) Van B.; m. Maryann Ruth Miller, June 11, 1977; children: Jason Robert, David James, Tara Lynn. Grad. high sch., Peshtigo, Wis., 1975. Licensed real estate broker, Wis. Employee Colonial Cafe and Bar, Peshtigo, Wis., 1983, pres., treas., 1983—; ptnr. Our Home Realty, Peshtigo, 1985—, T.M.J. Investments, Peshtigo, 1985—, Autumn Woods Gallery, Peshtigo, 1986—. Roman Catholic. Avocations: coin collecting, growing Christmas trees, hunting and fishing, golf, football. Home: N3904 Right-of-Way Rd Peshtigo WI 54157 Office: Colonial Cafe and Bar 341 Oconto Ave Peshtigo WI 54157

VAN BODEGRAVEN, ARTHUR, management consultant; b. Hammond, Ind., Aug. 4, 1939; s. Arthur and Hilda (Boersma) V.; m. Phyllis Ann Laucis, Feb. 4, 1967; children—Julie, Elizabeth, David, Jonathan. B.S., Purdue U., 1961. Data processing mgr. Inland Steel Co., Chgo., 1964-68; data processing cons. Lybrand, Ross Bros. & Montgomery, Chgo., 1968-71; systems dir. Hirsh Co., Skokie, Ill., 1971-72; mgr. productivity cons. Coopers & Lybrand, Chgo., 1973-75, dir. productivity cons., Columbus, Ohio, 1975-83, regional dir. resource productivity cons., 1983—; speaker to various orgns., 1969—. Contbr. articles to various publs. Campaign worker various local Rep. campaigns, 1962—. Served with U.S. Army, 1961-64. Mem. Inst. Indsl. Engrs., Assn. Systems Mgmt., Data Processing Mgmt. Assn. Republican. Club: University (Columbus). Home: 7630 Ashworth St Worthington OH 43085 Office: Coopers & Lybrand 100 E Broad St Columbus OH 43215

VAN BROEKHOVEN, HAROLD, religious organization adiminstrator; b. Rutherford, N.J., Feb. 10, 1913; s. Adrian and Wilhelmina V.; m. Lois Mary Loraine Chafer, Sept. 20, 1938; children: Rollin Adrian, Cornelia Louise, Harold Jr., Lois Loraine. BA, Wheaton Coll., 1935; ThM, Dallas Theol. Sem., 1939, postgrad., 1939-41; DD (hon.), Trinity Evang. Divinity Sch., 1987. Missionary Cen. Am. Mission, Nicaragua, 1941-43; prof. C.A. Bible Inst., Guatemala, 1943-56; found., dir. Sta. TGNA, Guatemala, 1950-56; asst. to pres. W.R.M.F., Inc., Europe, 1957-64; founder, dir. Outreach, Inc., Grand Rapids, Mich., 1966—, Inst. Theol. Studies, Grand Rapids, 1969—; bd. reference Braille Circulating Library, Richmond, Va., 1973—, Internat. Aid., Spring Lake, Mich., 1981—; bd. trustees So. Bible Inst., Dallas, 1981—, W.R.M.F., USA, Inc., Miami, 1980—; founder, dir. Outreach, Inc., Grand Rapids, 1955—; bd. dirs. China Ministries Internat., Pasadena, Calif. Author: The Spirit-Filled Life, 1967. Mem. Evangelical Theol. Soc. Club: Peninsular (Grand Rapids). Avocations: philatelics. Home: 841 Knapp St NE Grand Rapids MI 49505 Office: Outreach Inc 1553 Plainfield NE Grand Rapids MI 49501

VAN BROOKER, MARGUERITE, data processing company adiminstrator; b. Lawrence, Mass., Jan. 14, 1923; d. Alvin Bernard and Mary Theresa (Donovan) Kane; m. Irving C. Van Brooker, May 19, 1945 (dec. Dec. 1981); children—Denise, Damien, Deborah, Danette, Daniel. Student Cin. Bus. Coll., 1940-41, U. Cin., 1941-43; B.A., Oxford Coll., Ohio, 1944. Profl. model, singer, dancer, Cin., 1939-45; co-owner Black Angus Prodns., Plymouth, Ill., 1945-78; owner, operator Regis Kennels, Plymouth, 1960-70; supr. Western Ill. U., Macomb, 1964-71, adminstrv. asst., 1971-83; owner, operator OMO Datamation Enterprises, Macomb, 1983—. Organizer, Mother's March of Dimes, Plymouth, 1948-50; leader Two Rivers council Girl Scouts U.S.A., 1953; ofcl. McDonough County, Ill., 1985—. Mem. Nat. Sec. Assn., Profl. Bus. Women, Am. Legion (adjutant 1982-85, adjutant 14th dist. 1983-84, adjutant 3rd div. 1985—), Am. Legion Aux. Served with USMC, 1943-45. Republican. Roman Catholic. Avocations: target shooting; antiques; interior decorating; golf; tennis. Home and Office: 210 Arlington Dr Macomb IL 61455

VAN BRUNT, MARCIA ADELE, social worker; b. Chgo., Oct. 21, 1937; d. Dean Frederick and Faye Lila (Greim) Slauson; student Moline (Ill.) Pub. Hosp. Sch. Nursing, 1955-57; B.A. with distinguished scholastic record, U. Wis., Madison, 1972, M.S.W. (Fed. tng. grantee), 1973; M.O.E. Bartholomew; children—Suzanne, Christine, David. Social worker div. community services Wis. Dept. Health Social Services, Rhinelander, 1973, regional adoption coordinator, 1973-79, chief adoption and permanent planning no. region, 1979-83, asst. chief direct services and regulation no. region, 1983-84, adminstr., clin. social worker No. Family Services, Inc.; counselor, public speaker, cons. in field of clin. social work. Home: 5264 Forest Ln Route 1 Rhinelander WI 54501 Office: Box 237 Rhinelander WI 54501

VAN BUREN, KURT EDWIN, automotive engineer; b. Lansing, Mich., June 2, 1957; s. George Richard and Barbara Ann (Brown) Van B. AA in Bus. Adminstrn., Lansing Community Coll., 1982; BS in Engring., Mich. State U., 1982. Assoc. engr. Gen. Motors, Lansing, 1982-83, project engr., 1983—. Mem. Soc. Automotive Engrs. (assoc.). Avocations: skiing, sailing, hunting, cars. Home: 2210 Hamilton Okemos MI 48864 Office: Gen Motors BOC Lansing 920 Townsend 66-08 Lansing MI 48921

VAN BUSKIRK, PETER KEITH, food products executive; b. Evanston, Ill., Oct. 28, 1954; s. Harlow Keith and Dorothy (DeLapp) VanB.; m. Margaret P. Kane, Aug. 29, 1976; children: Keith, Erik, Benjamin, Todd. BS summa cum laude, Ohio U., 1978; MBA, Cleve. State U., 1985. English dept. chmn. Ohio Youth Commn., Cleve., 1978-81; v.p. Desserts Delicious Inc., Cleve., 1981—; bd. dirs. Family Fellowship. Trustee Cleveland Heights Career Devel. Program, 1985—. Mem. Nat. Assn. for Splty. Food Trade, Retail Bakers Assn., Cedar-Lee Mchts. Assn. (trustee). Jewish. Avocations: sailing, travel, writing. Home: 867 Englewood Rd Cleveland Heights OH 44121 Office: Desserts Delicious Inc 4920 Commerce Pkwy Warrensville Heights OH 44128

VANCE, CHARLES CLARK, public relations executive; b. Streator, Ill., Mar. 18, 1918; s. Charles Clayton and Elizabeth V.; m. Mary Ellen Wheeler, Nov. 8, 1941; children: Penny Lee. BA in Art Edn., No. Ill. U. Reporter Ill. State Register, Springfield, 1946-49; dir. Ill. State Fair Publicity, Springfield, 1949-53; v.p., Mayer & O'Brien, Inc., Chgo., 1953-62, Buchen Pub. Relations, Chgo., 1962-71; dir. corp. communications Joslyn Mfg., Chgo., 1971-75; dir. news media Nat. Assn. Realtors, 1975-79; dir. pub. relations Nat. Safety Council, Chgo., 1979-85; nat. mktg. cons. Op. ABLE, Chgo., 1987—. Author: Boss Psychology, Manager Today, Executive Tomorrow, The Dragon Robe, A Grave for a Russian. Served with USAF, 1943-46. Decorated Air medal. Mem. Soc. Profl. Journalists, Am. Soc. Journalists and Authors, Chgo. Headline Club, Chgo. Press Club, Hump Pilots Assn., Pub. Relations Soc. Am., Sigma Delta Chi. Republican. Home: 207 Gold St Park Forest IL 60466

VANCE, GARY CRAIG, real estate corporation executive; b. Zanesville, Ohio, June 25, 1952; s. William Allison and Lita May (Derry) V.; m. Donna Kay Baird, Dec. 17, 1977; children: Derek Adam, Marcus Trevor, Travis William and Dustin Curtis (twins). BBA cum laude, Ohio U., 1975; postgrad., Ohio State U., 1976. Material controller Lennox Industries, Columbus, Ohio, 1975-78; automotive buyer Motor Div. TRW, Dayton, Ohio, 1978-79, sales engr., 1979-80; distbr. account mgr. Motor Div. TRW, Dayton, 1982-86, regional sales mgr., 1986—. Pres., gen. mgr., bd. dirs. Country Manor Condominium Assn., Tipp City, Ohio, 1983—. Shinnick scholar, 1970; recipient Homearama Builder award Home Builders Assn. of Dayton and Miami Valley, 1981. Mem. Am. Home Builders Assn., Am. Prodn. and Inventory Control Soc. Republican. Methodist. Lodge: Masons. Avocations: reading, jogging, oil painting, company cross county team. Home: 7530 Winding Way Tipp City OH 45371 Office: Precision Home Builders Inc PO Box 425 Vandalia OH 45377

VANCE, JOAN EMILY JACKSON (MRS. NORVAL E. VANCE), educator; b. Anderson, Ind., Feb. 25, 1925; d. Virgil S. and Hannah (Hall) Jackson; B.S., Ball State U., 1947, M.A., 1955; m. Norval E. Vance, Aug. 17, 1955; 1 son, Bill E. Tchr. art and phys. edn. Winchester (Ind.) High Sch., 1948-50, 50-52, Wheatfield (Ind.) Elem. Sch., Wheatfield High Sch., 1952-54; tchr. Eaton (Ind.) Elementary Sch. and High Sch., 1954—; tchr. elem. art, Elwood, Ind., 1954—, bilingual-bi-cultural migrant sch., summers 1969—; exhibited in group shows at Erica's Gallery, John Herron. Anderson Fine Art Ctr., state shows, street fairs. Mem. council Hoosier Salon, Indpls. Mus. Art. Recipient First prize Anderson Fine Arts Center show, 1975, 77. Mem. Nat. Art Edn. Assn., Western Art Edn. Assn., Ind Art Edn. Assn. (council), Ind. Art Tchrs. Assn. (mem. council), Anderson Art League (pres. 1967-68, 76—) Anderson Soc. Artists (v.p.), Ind. Weavers Guild, Elwood Art League (pres. 1960-70), Brown County Gallery, Brown County Guild, Ind. Artists and Craftsmen Assn., Delta Kappa Gamma, Delta Theta Tau. Home: Route 1 Box 68 Frankton IN 46044 Office: Elwood Community School State Rd 13 N Elwood IN 46036

VANCE, TERRY, interior designer; b. Cleve., Sept. 22, 1929; d. Toby and Edith (Zulli) Gesualdo; m. Edward Francis Vance, May 26, 1951; children—Victoria, Deborah, David, Rebecca, Sarah, Barbara. B.A., Case Western Res. U., 1951. Interior designer Bonhard Interiors, Cleve., 1968-80; pres., interior designer Terry Vance, Inc., Shaker Hts., Ohio, 1980—. Mem. Am. Soc. Interior Designers. Office: Terry Vance Inc 18740 Chagrin Blvd Shaker Heights OH 44122

VAN CLEAVE, PETER, underwriting and foundation consultant; b. Evanston, Ill., May 18, 1927; s. Wallace and Katherine M. (Ziesing) Van C.; m. Barbara Adams, Dec. 30, 1960; 1 dau., Claire. B.S., Northwestern U., 1949. Prodn. mgr. F.L. Jacobs Co., Traverse City, Mich., 1949-50; asst. to ambassador U.S. embassy, Rio de Janeiro, Brazil, 1953-55; with James S. Kemper & Co., Chgo., 1955-83, vice chmn., 1965-83; pres. Peter Van Cleave & Assocs., Inc., Chgo., 1983—; prin. Donor's Mgmt. Services; underwriting mem. Lloyds of London, Trustee Newberry Library, Chgo.; bd. dirs. Lyric Opera, Chgo. Served with U.S. Army, 1950-52. Mem. Nat. Assn. Security Dealers, Northwestern U. Alumni Assn. (past pres.). Republican. Clubs: Chicago; Bohemian (San Francisco); University, Glen View (Chgo.); The Casino. Home: 71 E Bellevue Pl Chicago IL 60611 Office: Suite 2336 35 E Wacker Dr Chicago IL 60601

VAN CLEVE, JOHN WOODBRIDGE, research chemist; b. Kansas City, Mo., Nov. 22, 1914; s. Horatio Phillips and Leslie Gertrude (Allen) Van C.; m. Ethel Dannenmaier, Feb. 7, 1947; children—John Walter, Julia Ann, Mark David. B.S., Antioch Coll., 1937; Ph.D., U. Minn., 1951. Research fellow C. F. Kettering Found. for Study Chlorophyll and Photosynthesis, Yellow Springs, Ohio, 1937-40; research chemist Aluminum Co. Am., East. St. Louis, Ill., 1943-48, No. Regional Research Ctr., U.S. Dept. Agr., Peoria, Ill., 1951—. Contbr. articles to various publs. Mem. Am. Chem. Soc., AAAS, N.Y. Acad. Sci., Sigma Xi. Republican. Presbyterian. Home: 903 W Meadows Pl Peoria IL 61604 Office: Northern Regional Research Center US Dept Agriculture 1815 N University St Peoria IL 61604

VAN CURA, JOYCE BENNETT, librarian, educator; b. Madison, Wis., Mar. 25, 1944; d. Ralph Eugene and Florence Marie (Cramer) Bennett; m. E. Jay Van Cura, July 5, 1986. B.A. in Liberal Arts (scholar), Bradley U., 1966; M.S. in L.S., U. Ill., 1971. Library asst. research library Caterpillar Tractor Co., Peoria, Ill., 1966-67; reference librarian, instr. library tech. Ill. Central Coll., East Peoria, 1967-73; asst. prof. Sangamon State U., Springfield, Ill., 1973-80, assoc. prof., 1980-86; head library ref. dept. Ill. Inst. Tech., 1987—; convenor Council II, Ill. Clearinghouse for Acad. Library Instrn., 1978; presentor 7th Ann. Conf. Acad. Library Instrn., 1977, Nat. Women's Studies Assn., 1983, others; participant Gt. Lakes Women's Studies Summer Inst., 1981. Democratic precinct Committeewoman, 1982—. Pres., Springfield chpt. NOW, 1978-79. Ill. state scholar, 1962-66; recipient Am. Legion citizenship award, 1962; cert. of recognition Ill. Bicentennial Commn., 1974; invited Susan B. Anthony luncheon, 1978, 79. Mem. ALA, Ill. Library Assn. (presentor 1984) Ill. Assn. Coll. and Research Libraries (bibliog. instrn. com.), Am. Fedn. Tchrs., AAUW (chmn. standing com. on women Springfield br., mem. com. on women Ill. state div.), Nat. Women's Studies Assn. (presentor 1983, 84, 85) Springfield Art Assn., Nat. Trust Historic Preservation, Women in Mgmt., Beta Phi Mu. Reviewer Library Jour., Am. Reference Books Ann. Contbr. article in field to publ. Home: 535 N Michigan #1614 Chicago IL 60611-3810 Office: Ill Inst Tech Paul Galvin Library Chicago IL 60616

VANDAGRIFF, VIRGIL L., consultant; b. Indpls., Sept. 30, 1942; s. Leland F. and Rosa L. (Simpson) V.; married, 1964; children: Dean Curtis, Deanna Marie. Cert. hypnosis technician, psychol. stress evaluator, Ind. Dep. sheriff Marion City Sheriff, Indpls.; prin., pres. Vandagriff & Assocs., Inc., Indpls.; prin. Employee Mgmt. Systems, Indpls.; Speaker in field. Mem. Assn. to Advance Ethical Hypnosis (cert., exec. bd. dirs., pres. 1980), Ind. Assn. to Advance Ethical Hypnosis (pres.), Ind. Truth Verification Assn. (chmn. bd.), Internat. Soc. Stress Analysts. Baptist. Office: Vandagriff & Assocs Inc 2346 S Lynhurst M702 Indianapolis IN 46241

VANDALL, ALLAN LEE, mining company executive; b. Braddock, Pa., Apr. 11, 1942; s. Leonard Lee and Cecilia (Sudyk) V.; m. Gail Elaine Vaughan, Aug. 27, 1966; children: Alison Lynn, Allan Vaughan. BS in Indsl. Engring., Pa. State U., 1965; MBA, Akron U., 1972. Registered profl. engr., Ohio. V.p. mfg. Sandvik, Inc., Fairlawn, N.J., 1982-84; pres., chief exec. officer U.S. Graphite, Inc., Saginaw, Mich., 1984—. Active United Way, Roxboro, N.C., 1973-77. Mem. Bus. and Devel. Inst. Saginaw Valley (Entrepreneur of Yr. 1986). Republican. Presbyterian. Club: Saginaw. Avocations: golf, racquetball, running. Home: 4600 Ashland Dr Saginaw MI 48603 Office: US Graphite Inc 1621 E Holland Saginaw MI 48603

VANDECASTEELE, JEFFREY JAMES, marketing executive; b. Moline, Ill., May 2, 1960; s. Robert Frank and Frances J. (Meersman) VanDeC.; m. Karen Sue Blomgren, Apr. 20, 1985. AA, Blackhawk Jr. Coll., 1980; BBA, BA in Acctg., Ill. State U., 1982. Asst. auditor Deere & Co., Moline, 1982-84, sr. auditor, 1984-85; administr. dealer systems John Deere Co. subs. Deere & Co., Kansas City, Mo., 1985-87, area parts mgr., 1987—. Mem. Deere & Co. Polit. Action Com., Moline, 1986. Mem. Am. Inst. CPA's, Ill. CPA Soc. Democrat. Roman Catholic. Avocations: golf, tennis. Home: 8024 Cooper Lincoln NE 68506 Office: John Deere Co 3210 E 85th St Kansas City MO 64132

VAN DE KOLK, SUE ELLEN, beautician; b. Waupun, Wis., Aug. 19, 1954; d. Lloyd Elton and Helen Mae (Rens) Hartgerink; m. Phillip Allen VandeKolk, May 17, 1974; children: Matthew Lloyd, Ann Marie. Grad. high sch., Brandon, Wis., 1972; license, Constance Sch. Cosmetology, Oshkosh, Wis., 1973. Licensed mng. beautician, Wis. Clk. Doug's Food Mart, Brandon, Wis., 1968-72; salesperson Avon Products, Ripon, Wis., 1972; beautician Kut & Kurl, Waupun, Wis., 1973-74, Joanne's Beauty Nook, Waupun, 1974-76; mgr. Head Start Hair Styling, Brandon, 1977—. Chmn. Cystic Fibrosis Bike-a-Thon, Brandon, 1985-86; dir. vacation bible sch. Bethel Reformed Ch., Brandon, 1983, 85-87. Home: 115 Woodward St Brandon WI 53919-0143

VAN DE KREEKE, GERALD RICHARD, SR., accountant; b. Sheboygan, Wis., Feb. 6, 1946; s. Marvin and Carol Jean (Toennies) Van De K.; m. Sharon Anne La Brecque, Nov. 30, 1968; children: Gerald R. Jr., Jennifer. BBA in Acctg., U. Wis., Milw., 1974. CPA, Wis. Mem. staff Joseph A. Biwan, CPA, Sheboygan, 1972-76; pres. Gerald R. Van De Kreeke, CPA, S.C., Sheboygan, 1976—; bd. dirs. Touchstone Fin., Sheboygan; bd. dirs., chief fin. officer Innovation Computer Corp., Cleve., 1986—; lectr., U. Wis., Sheboygan, 1980-82. Chmn. Citizens Adv. Com. on Community Devel., Sheboygan, 1977-83; pres. Sheboygan Bd. Water Commrs., 1980—; Trustee, treas. U. Wis. Sheboygan County Found., 1982—. Served to staff sgt. USAF, 1968-72. Mem. Am. Inst. CPA's, Wis. Inst. CPA's, Am. Water Works Assn., Sheboygan Area C. of C. (bd. dirs. and treas. 1981-83). Lutheran. Lodge: Rotary (Sheboygan) (bd. dirs. 1986—). Office: 1530 S 12th St Sheboygan WI 53081

VANDE KROL, JERRY LEE, architect; b. Oskaloosa, Iowa, Oct. 5, 1949; s. Glen Vande Krol and Nola Fern (Monsma) Emmert; m. Constance Louise Wood, May 30, 1970; children: Sarah Lynn, Rachel Ann, Molly Jayne. BArch, Iowa State U., 1972. Registered architect, Ohio. Designer City of Akron, Ohio, 1972-76; architect Brooks Borg and Skiles, Des Moines, 1976—. Recipient Merit Desigh award Ohio Chpt. Soc. Landscape Architects, 1977. Mem. AIA (Iowa chpt., Design award 1985, Ohio chpt. Design award 1984), Des Moines Architects Council. Republican. Mem. Brethren Ch. Avocations: music, reading, golf. Home: 4306 Allison Ave Des Moines IA 50310 Office: Brooks Borg and Skiles 700 Hubbell Bldg Des Moines IA 50309

VAN DELLEN, KENNETH J., geology educator, editorial and educational consultant; b. Ionia, Mich., May 24, 1937; s. Jerrian and Anna (Terpstra) Van D.; m. Pearl Kiel, Aug. 21, 1959; children—Lisa Anne, Kara Jane. B.A., Calvin Coll., 1958; M.S. in Zoology, Mich. State U., East Lansing, 1961; M.S. in Geology, U. Mich., 1978. Tchr. biology and chemistry Southwest Minn. Christian High Sch., Edgerton, Minn., 1958-59; tchr. Fitzgerald Jr.-Sr. High Sch., Warren, Mich., 1961-65; prof. Macomb Community Coll., Warren, Mich., 1965—. Mem. Geol. Soc. Am., Nat. Assn. Geology Tchrs., Mich. Basin Geol. Soc., Mich. Acad. Sci., Arts and Letters. Mem. Christian Reformed Ch. Avocation: photography. Home: 1018 Nottingham Rd Grosse Pointe Park MI 48230 Office: Macomb County Community Coll 14500 12-Mile Rd Warren MI 48093

VAN DEMARK, ROBERT EUGENE, orthopedic surgeon; b. Alexandria, S.D., Nov. 14, 1913; s. Walter Eugene and Esther Ruth (Marble) Van D.; m. Bertie Thompson, Dec. 28, 1940; children: Ruth Elaine, Robert, Richard. B.S., U. S.D., 1936; A.B., Sioux Falls (S.D.) Coll., 1937; M.B., Northwestern U., 1938, M.D., 939; M.S. in Orthopedic Surgery, U. Minn., 1943. Diplomate: Am. Bd. Orthopedic Surgery. Intern Passavant Meml. Hosp., Chgo., 1938-39; fellow in orthopedic surgery Mayo Found., 1939-43; 1st asst. orthopedic surgery Mayo Clinic, 1942-43; orthopedic surgeon Sioux Falls, 1946—; attending orthopedic surgeon McKennan Hosp., pres. med. staff, 1954, 70; attending orthopedic surgeon Sioux Valley Hosp., pres. staff 1951-52; clin. prof. orthopedic surgery U. S.D., 1953—, adj. prof orthopedic surgery, 1983—; med. dir. Crippled Children's Hosp. and Sch., 1952-84; chief hand surgery clinic VA Hosp., Sioux Falls.; dir. S.D. Blue Shield. Editor: S.D. Jour. Medicine; Contbr. articles to med. jours. Bd. dirs. S.D. Found. for Med. Care, 1976-83; hon. chmn. S.D. Lung Assn., 1982. Served from lt. to maj. U.S. Army, 1943-46. Recipient citation for outstanding service Pres.'s Commn. for Employment Physically Handicapped, 1960; Service to Mankind award Sertoma Internat., 1963; award for dedicated services to handicapped S.D. Easter Seal Soc., 1969; Robins award for outstanding community service, 1971; Humanitarian Service award United Cerebral Palsy, 1976; Alumni Achievement award U. S.D., 1977; Disting. Citizen award S.D. Press Assn., 1978; U. S.D. Med. Sch. Faculty Recognition award, 1980; outstanding contbns. to Handicapped Children award S.D. State Dept. Health, 1985. Fellow ACS (pres. S.D. chpt. 1952, 53); mem. Am. Assn. Med. Colls., Assn. Orthopaedic Chairmen, Am. Acad. Orthopedic Surgery, Clin. Orthopedic Soc., Am. Assn. Hand Surgery, Mid-Am. Orthpedic Assn., Am. Acad. Cerebral Palsy, S.D. Med. Assn. (pres. 1974-75), Sioux Falls Dist. Med. Soc., SAR, 500 1st Families Am., Sigma Xi, Alpha Omega Alpha, Phi Chi. Lutheran. Clubs: Optimist, Minnehaha Country. Home: 2803 Ridgeview Way Sioux Falls SD 57105 Office: 1301 S 9th Ave Sioux Falls SD 57105

VAN DEMARK, RUTH ELAINE, lawyer; b. Santa Fe, N. Mex., May 16, 1944; d. Robert Eugene and Bertha Marie (Thompson) Van D.; m. Leland Wilkinson, June 23, 1967; children—Anne Marie, Caroline Cook. A.B., Vassar Coll., 1966; M.T.S., Harvard U., 1969; J.D. with honors, U. Conn., 1976. Bar: Conn. 1976, U.S. Dist. Ct. Conn. 1976, Ill. 1977, U.S. Dist. Ct. (no. dist.) Ill. 1977, U.S. Supreme Ct. 1983, U.S. Ct. Appeals (7th cir.) 1984. Instr. legal research and writing Loyola U. Sch. Law, Chgo., 1976-79; assoc. Wildman, Harrold, Allen & Dixon, Chgo., 1977-84, ptnr., 1984—. bd. dirs., sec. Systat, Inc., Evanston, Ill. Assoc. editor Conn. Law Rev., 1975-76. Mem. adv. bd. Horizon Hospice, Chgo., 1978—; del.-at-large White House Conf. on Families, Los Angeles, 1980; mem. adv. bd. YWCA Battered Women's Shelter, Evanston, Ill., 1982-86; vol. atty. Pro Bono Advocates, Chgo., 1982—, bd. dirs. Friends of Pro Bono Advocates Orgn.; bd. dirs. New Voice Prodns., 1984-86, Byrne Piven Theater Workshop, 1987—; founder, bd. dirs. Friends of Battered Women and their Children, 1986-87. Mem. ABA, Ill. Bar Assn., Conn. Bar Assn., Chgo. Bar Assn., Appellate Lawyers Assn. Ill. (bd. dirs. 1985-87), Women's Bar Assn. Ill., AAUW, Jr. League Evanston (chair State Pub. Affairs Com. 1987-88, Vol. of Yr. 1983-84). Clubs: Chgo. Vassar (pres. 1979-81), Cosmopolitan (N.Y.C.). Home: 1127 Asbury Ave Evanston IL 60202 Office: Wildman Harrold Allen & Dixon 1 IBM Plaza Chicago IL 60611

VANDEMOTTER, PETER ALAN, electrical engineer; b. N.Y.C., Apr. 11, 1955; s. John Stephen and Barbara Frances (Mechling) V.; m. Linda Sue Ruesch, Apr. 24, 1977; 1 child, Scott David. BSEE, Rose-Hulman Inst., 1977. Engr., Commonwealth Edison, Chgo., 1977-78; project engr. Underwriters Lab., Northbrook, Ill., 1978-80; elec. engr. Fluor Corp., Chgo., 1980-81, HOH Engrs., Chgo., 1981-85, Hitachi-Zosom Clearing, Inc., Chgo., 1985—. Mem. IEEE, Des Plaines Area Jaycees (sec. 1984). Avocations: photography; train watching. Home: 837 Hollywood Ave Des Plaines IL 60016 Office: Hitachi-Zosom Clearing Inc 6499 W 65th St Chicago IL 60638

VAN DEN BERG, JOHN HOWARD, electrical engineer, recording engineer; b. Grand Rapids, Mich., July 26, 1956; s. Howard Clifton and Margaret (Brand) VanDenB.; m. Scheryl Ann Fink, Oct. 16, 1982. BSEE with distinction, U. Mich., 1979. Co-op. engr. Fed. Mogul Corp., Greenville, Mich., 1977, G.R. Mfg., Grand Rapids, 1977-78; elec. engr. Lear Siegler, Inc., Grand Rapids, 1980—. Coach Little League, Ft. Walton Beach, Fla., 1981-82. Mem. IEEE, Am. Assn. for Artificial Intelligence, U. Mich. Alumni Assn. Republican. Avocation: music. Office: Lear Siegler Inc MS102 4141 Eastern Ave SE Grand Rapids MI 49508-0727

VANDEN BLOOMEN, DENNIS RICHARD, international business educator; b. Kaukauna, Wis., Dec. 14, 1949; s. Gerald Louis and Marie Lillian (Schmidt) Vanden B.; m. Nancy Lou Pease, Dec. 28, 1974 (div. Aug. 1980); m. Josette Thadine Migawa, June 6, 1981; 1 child, Gretchen Marie. BS in Psychology, U. Wis., Stevens Point, 1972; MA in Social Sci., Pacific Luth. U., Tacoma, 1976; MBA in Internat. Bus., Monterey (Calif.) Inst. Internat. Studies, 1982; postgrad., U. Wis.-Stout, Menomonie, 1984-86. Commd. 2d lt. U.S. Army, 1972, advanced through grades to capt., 1976, resigned, 1980; owner, mgr. Super Tee, Inc., Panama Canal Zone, 1977-80; officer USAR, Mpls., 1982—; salesman Frito Lay, Inc., Eau Claire, Wis., 1983; asst. prof. U. Wis.-Stout, Menomonie, 1983—; cons. in field. Contbr. articles to profl. jours. Mem. Acad. Internat. Bus., Am. Mgmt. Assn., Cen Wis. World Trade Assn. (bd. dirs. 1986—), Am. Assn. Tchrs. of Spanish and Portuguese, Res. Officers Assn. Republican. Roman Catholic. Club: Hispano (Eau Claire, Wis.). Lodge: Elks. Avocations: foreign travel, scuba diving, sky diving. Home: 806 Dorbe Eau Claire WI 54702 Office: U Wis Stout 213-TW Menomonie WI 54751

VANDEN BRINK, JOHN ANTHONY, marketing consultant; b. Sioux City, Iowa, Nov. 22, 1932; s. George Earnest and Mary Lucile (Nickle) V.; m. Lynne Rae Fisher, Sept. 18, 1965 (dec. July 1976); m. Thelma Mae Fortier, Nov. 13, 1982; children: Shirley Salisbury Stern, Daniel John, Diana Sue Salisbury Fortier, Wesley James, George Graham. BS in Indsl. Engring., Iowa State U., 1955. Sales and mktg. exec. Nuclear Chgo. Corp., Des Plaines, Ill., 1957-67; mgr. planning and venture devel. G.D. Searle Co., Skokie, Ill., 1967-69; chief exec. officer Pelam Inc., Hinsdale, Ill., 1969-74; mgr. med. and indsl. markets Britt & Frerichs, Chgo., 1974-77; founder, prin. Tech. Mktg. Group, Des Plaines, Ill., 1977—. Editor newsletter Imaging Market Forum, 1984-86; contbr. articles to profl. jours. Sec. Assn. for Advancement of Med. Instrumentation, Washington, 1968; lay leader First United Meth. Ch., Park Ridge, Ill., 1972. Served to 1st lt. U.S. Army, 1955-57. Mem. Am. Mktg. Assn., Biomed. Mktg. Assn., Phi Delta Theta. Republican. Home: 520 S Crescent Park Ridge IL 60068 Office: Tech Mktg Group 950 Lee St Des Plaines IL 60016

VANDENDORPE, MARY MOORE, social scientist, educator; b. Chgo., June 2, 1947; d. Era William and Mary Desales (Dobis) M.; m. James Edward Vandendorpe, Aug. 16, 1969; 1 child, Laura Marie. AB, St. Louis U., 1969; MS, Ill. Inst. Tech., 1975, PhD, 1980. Copywriter, Spiegel Inc., Chgo., 1969-72; adj. instr. Lewis U., Romeoville, Ill., 1976-79, asst. prof., 1980-85, assoc. prof., 1985—, dept. chairperson, 1985—. Mem. Am. Psychol. Assn., Gerontol Soc., Chgo. Psychol. Assn. (dir. 1979—, pres. 1982—), Naperville Heritage Soc., Psi Chi. Office: Lewis U 213 Science Dept Romeoville IL 60441

VANDEN HEUVEL, THOMAS JOHN, social services adminstrator; b. Little Chute, Wis., Dec. 20, 1949; s. Harold Henry and Marian Martha (Hammen) Vanden H.; m. Sandra Jean Hancock, Aug. 23, 1973 (div. Jan. 1979); m. Maureen Jean Fitzsimmons, June 5, 1982; children: Fawn Crystal Marie, Emily Fitzsimmons, Nicholas Thomas. BA in Psychology, U. Wis., 1972, MS in Social Work, 1974. Dir. night hosp. Elmbrook Meml. Hosp., Brookfield, Wis., 1973-82; labor mgmt. cons. Milw. Psychiat. Hosp., 1982-86; mgr. employee assistance program Wheaton Franciscan Services, Inc.-Milw., 1986—; cons. Employee Counseling Services, Chgo., 1983-86; founder and dir. Employee Assistance Program Adminstrs. Group, Milw., 1982-86. Mem. Nat. Assn. Social Workers, Assn. Labor Mgmt. Asminstrs. and Cons. on Alcoholism, Am. Soc. Personnel Adminstrn. Democrat. Roman Catholic. Avocations: swimming, weight lifting, gardening, golf. Home: 2348 N 83d St Wauwatosa WI 53213 Office: WFSI MILW Employee Asst 2500 N Mayfair Rd Box M254 Milwaukee WI 53226

VANDER AARDE, STANLEY BERNARD, otolaryngologist; b. Orange City, Iowa, Sept. 26, 1931; s. Bernard John and Christina (Luchtenberg) Vander A.; m. Agnes Darlene De Beer, June 19, 1956; children: Paul, David, Debra, Mary. BA, Hope Coll., 1953; MD, Northwestern U., 1957. Diplomate Am. Bd. Otolaryngology. Intern Cook County Hosp., Chgo., 1957-59; resident in otolaryngology Northwestern U. Hosp., Chgo., 1966-70; mem. staff Mary Lott Lyles Hosp., Madanapalle, India, 1961-66, 71-87, Affiliated Med. Clinic, Willmar, Minn., 1987—. Served to capt., USAF, 1959-60. Fellow ACS, Am. Bd. Otolaryngology, Am. Acad. Otolaryngology. Republican. Mem. Reformed Church in America. Home: 1801 SE Becker #204 Willmar MN 56201 Office: Affiliated Med Clinic 101 Willmar Ave Willmar MN 56201

VANDERBEEK, DUANE LLOYD, construction company executive; b. Adams, Nebr., July 17, 1942; s. B. Frank and Minnie J. (Hietbrink) V.; m. Carol E. Daum, June 11, 1965; children: Todd D., Tami C. Student Nat. Bus. Inst., Lincoln, Nebr., 1959-65. Loan service mgr. H. A. Wolf Co., Inc., Lincoln, 1959-65; exec. v.p. Duane Larson Constrn. Co., Lincoln, 1965—; pres. HBAL Credit Union, Lincoln, 1979; builder, developer, council chmn. Homebuilders Assn. Lincoln, 1975—. Cubmaster Boy Scouts Am., 1977; coach team 6 City Recreation Girls Softball, Lincoln, 1979; mem. fin. com. St. Marks United Meth. Ch., Lincoln, 1982. Served with USNG, 1964-70. Recipient Outstanding Service awards Homebuilders Assn. Lincoln, 1976, 80. Mem. Am. Legion. Republican. Clubs: Bowling Team, Softball Team (Lincoln). Lodge: Elks. Home: 1140 Cobblestone Dr Lincoln NE 68510 Office: Duane Larson Constrn Co 201 S 84th St Lincoln NE 68510

VAN DER BOSCH, SUSAN HARTNETT, real estate broker; b. St. Louis, Mar. 19, 1935; d. Leo Joseph and Mary Julia (O'Neill) Hartnett; m. George Arthur Van Der Bosch, Sept. 10, 1955; children: Mary Jo Van Der Bosch Schauer, Anne, Leo, Ellen, George Jr. Student, Barat Coll., 1953-55. Lic. real estate salesperson, real estate broker, grad. Realtor's Inst., cert. residential specialist. Assoc. broker Covered Bridge Realty, Long Grove, Ill., 1980-83, McKee Real Estate, Buffalo Grove, Ill., 1983—; office mgr. McKee br. office Fields of Long Grove, 1986. Trustee Vernon Pub. Library, Prairie View, Ill, 1978-84; pres. Villagers, Long Grove, 1986—. Mem. Northwest Suburban Bd. Realtors, Barrington (Ill.) Bd. Realtors, North Shore Bd. Realtors, Realtors Inst., Realtors Mktg. Inst. Avocations: golf, bridge, travel. Home: Box 3253 RFD Long Grove IL 60047 Office: McKee Real Estate 125 Arlington Heights Rd Buffalo Grove IL 60089

VANDERBURG, ELLEN CAREY, accountant, tax specialist; b. Dallas, Sept. 12, 1955; d. Tom M. and E. Joyce (Derden) Carey; m. Joel Richard Vanderburg, Jan. 1, 1980. BBA, So. Meth. U., 1975; MBA in Taxation, Golden Gate U., 1984. CPA, Tex., Kans. Tax staff Peat, Marwick, Mitchell, San Antonio, 1976-78; tax supr. Seidman & Seidman, Dallas, 1978-80; tax mgr. Grant Thornton, Wichita, Kans., 1980—. Treas. YWCA, Wichita, 1981—, Wichita Park Found., 1986—, Krause for Congress Campaign, 1984; chmn. pub. relations Jr. League Wichita, 1986. Mem. Nat. Assn. Accts. (v.p., treas. 1982-84), Am. Inst. CPAs, Tex. Soc. CPAs, Kans. Soc. CPAs (membership com. 1986). Republican. Presbyterian. Avocations: music, reading, yard work, walking. Home: 7215 Ayesbury Wichita KS 67226 Office: Grant Thorton 800 4th Fin Ctr Wichita KS 67226

VANDER GOOT, MARY E., psychologist, educator; b. Orange City, Iowa, Feb. 5, 1947. AB, Calvin Coll., 1968; MA, PhD, Princeton U., 1971. Lic. psychologist, Mich. Psychologist Bd. Edn. for the Borough of North York, Toronto, Ont., Can., 1971-76; prof. psychology Calvin Coll., Grand Rapids, Mich., 1976—; pvt. practice psychology Psychology Assocs., P.C., Grand Rapids, 1978—. Author: A Life Planning Guide for Women, 1982, Piaget as a Visionary Thinker, 1985. Mem. Nat. Assn. Female Execs., Am. Psychol. Assn. Club: Older Women's League. Office: Calvin Coll Dept Psychology Grand Rapids MI 49506

VANDER GRIEND, HARLAN JAY, optometrist; b. Sheldon, Iowa, Nov. 12, 1951; s. Sidney and Marie A. (Alons) Vander G.; m. Diane Elaine Heikens, June 1, 1974; children: Sara Joy, Samuel Jay, Sally Marie. BS, Calvin Coll., 1974; OD, Ill. Coll. Optometry, Chgo., 1978. Assoc. Dr. R.B. Tuberty, Mt. Vernon, Iowa, 1978-79; pvt. practice optometry Sheldon, 1979—; v.p. Vol. Optometric Service to Humanity, Des Moines, 1986—. Mem. Sheldon Indsl. Devel. Corp. Mem. Am. Optometric Assn., Iowa Optometric Assn. (treas. 1982—); Western Iowa Study Group (pres. 1982-84), Sheldon C. of C. Republican. Mem. Christian Reformed Ch. Club: Sheldon Country (sec. 1983). Lodge: Lions (pres. Sheldon 1984-85). Avocations: cross country running, golf, swimming, reading. Office: 815 3d Ave Sheldon IA 51201

VANDERGRIFF, LELAND EDWARD, software engineering executive; b. Bonne Terre, Mo., Oct. 9, 1949; s. Willard C. and Alta Mae (Jarrette) V.; m. Alice Lynn Merton, Mar. 20, 1976; children: April Michelle, David Andrew. B.S.E.E. with honors, U. Mo.-Rolla., 1971; M.S.E., U. Pa., 1975. Registered profl. engr., Iowa. Mem. tech. staff RCA Corp., Adv. Tech. Labs., Camden, N.J., 1971-75; design engr. Fisher Controls, Marshalltown, Iowa, 1975-76, sr. design engr., 1976-79, engring. specialist, 1980—. Curator's scholar U. Mo., 1967. Mem. Assn. for Computing Machinery, IEEE Computer Soc., Tau Beta Pi, Eta Kappa Nu. Republican. Baptist. Office: RA Engel Tech Center PO Box 11 Marshalltown IA 50158

VANDER JAGT, GUY, congressman; b. Cadillac, Mich., Aug. 26, 1931; s. Harry and Marie (Copier) Vander J.; m. Carol Doorn, Apr. 4, 1964; 1 dau., Virginia Marie. A.B., Hope Coll., 1953; B.D., Yale U., 1957; LL.B., U. Mich., 1960; postgrad., U. Bonn, Germany, 1955-56. Bar: Mich. bar 1960. Practice in Grand Rapids; mem. firm Warner, Norcross & Judd, 1960-64; mem. Mich. Senate, 1964-66, 89th-100th Congresses from 9th Mich. Dist., 1965—; mem. ways and means com., trade and select revenue measures subcoms.; chmn. Nat. Republican Congressional Com.; keynote speaker Rep.

Nat. Conv., Detroit, 1980. Named One of Five Most Outstanding Young Men in Mich., Mich. Jr. C. of C., 1956. Mem. Hope Coll. Alumni Assn. Washington (pres.). Republican. Home: Luther MI 49656 Office: US Ho of Reps 2409 Rayburn House Office Bldg Washington DC 20515 *

VANDER KOOI, DARYL JAY, speech communication educator; b. Grandville, Mich., July 27, 1940; s. David J. and Edith (Woodwyk) Vander K.; m. Maris Elaine Hager, Dec. 16, 1960; children—Michelle Elaine, Dalaine Joy, David Shane. A.B., Calvin Coll., 1963, postgrad., 1965; postgrad. Coll. Great Falls, 1966; M.S., Mont. State U., 1971, Ed.D., 1979; postgrad. U. Iowa-Iowa City, 1973, U. S.D.-Vermillion, 1974. Tchr., Hope Protestant Christian Sch., Grandville, Mich., 1961-62; tchr., forensic coach Manhattan Christian High Sch. (Mont.), 1963-70; forensic coach, tchr. communications, chmn. dept. Dordt Coll., Sioux Center, Iowa, 1971—, chmn. lang./lit. div.; cons. communication, dir. Workshop of Leadership. NDEA grantee, 1966. Mem. Central States Speech Assn., Speech Communication Assn., Iowa Communication Assn., Assn. Ref. Communication (v.p., chmn. steering com.). Republican. Mem. Christian Ref. Ch. Contbr. articles to communication, scholastic jours. Office: Dordt Coll Sioux Center IA 51250

VANDERLAAN, RICHARD B., marketing company executive; b. Grand Rapids, Mich., Sept. 2, 1931; s. Sieger B. and Helen (Kerr) V.; cert. liberal arts Grand Rapids Jr. Coll., 1952; cert. mech. engring. U. Mich., 1955; cert. indsl. engring. Mich. State U., 1960; cert. Harvard Bus. Sch., 1970; m. Sally E. Conroy, Mar. 26, 1982; children—Sheryl Vanderlaan, Pamella Vanderlaan DeVos, Brenda Vanderlaan Thompson. Tool engr. Four Square Mfg. Co., Grand Rapids, 1950-60; sales engr. Ametek, Lansdale, Pa., 1960-63; br. mgr. J.N. Fauver Co., Grand Rapids, 1964-68; v.p. Fauver Co. subs. Sun Oil Co., Grand Rapids 1968-76, exec. v.p., 1976-80; pres. House of Printers, Inc., 1980-82, also dir.; pres. Richard Vanderlaan Assocs., 1982—. Named eagle scout Boy Scouts Am. Mem. Mfrs. Agts. Nat. Assn., Soc. Automotive Engrs. Republican. Clubs: Birmingham Country, Oakland Hills Country, Economic of Detroit, Detroit Athletic. Avocations: golf, tennis. Office: 22157 Metamora Dr Birmingham MI 48010

VAN DER MEULEN, DOUGLAS ALAN, dentist; b. Holland, Mich., May 26, 1958; s. Henry Gordon and Gladys Pearl (Bouwman) Van Der M.; m. Katherine Lee Beuker, Aug. 9, 1980; children: Matthew Douglas, Amy Katherine. BA, Hope Coll., 1980; DDS, U. Mich., 1984. Gen. practice dentistry Marshall, Mich., 1984—. Sec. bd. dirs. Marshall Civic Players, 1986. Mem. ADA, Mich. Dental Assn., Southwestern Mich. Dental Soc. (sec. bd. dirs. 1985—). Republican. Lodge: Rotary (bd. dirs.). Avocations: vocal music, civic theater, golf. Home: 549 East Dr Marshall MI 49068 Office: 213 E Michigan Marshall MI 49068

VANDERPLOEG, KENNETH PAUL, business executive; b. Grand Rapids, Mich., Oct. 26, 1941; s. Frederick and Eva Mae (Harvey) Vander P.; m. Sue Ann Tornga, Sept. 6, 1963; children—Laura E., Michele Ann. A.A.S., Grand Rapids Jr. Coll., 1962; B.B.A., Western Mich. U., 1964. Asst. controller Lawndale Industries, Aurora, Ill., 1969-72; asst. controller Cracker Jack, Chgo., 1972-74; controller IMS Internat., Ambler, Pa., 1974-76, Cummins Allison Corp., Glenview, Ill., 1976-78; chief exec. officer Quick-print, Downers Grove, Ill., 1978—. Served with U.S. Army, 1966-68. Methodist. Club: Rotary (Downers Grove) (bd. dirs. 1982-84, treas. 1985-86). Office: Quickprint 415 Ogden Ave Downers Grove IL 60515

VANDERPOOL, WARD MELVIN, management and marketing consultant; b. Oakland, Mo., Jan. 20, 1917; s. Oscar B. and Clara (McGuire) V.; M.E.E., Tulane U.; m. Lee Kendall, July 7, 1935. Vice pres. charge sales Van Lang Brokerage, Los Angeles, 1934-38; mgr. agrl. div. Dayton Rubber Co., Chgo., 1939-48; pres., gen. mgr. Vee Mac Co., Rockford, Ill., 1948—; pres., dir. Zipout, Inc., Rockford, 1951—, Wife Save Products, Inc., 1959—; chmn. bd. Zipout Internat., Kenvan Inc., 1952—, Shevan Corp., 1951—, Atlas Internat. Corp.; pres. Global Enterprises Ltd., Global Assos. Ltd.; chmn. bd. Atlas Chem. Corp., Merzart Industries Ltd.; trustee Ice Crafter Trust, 1949—; bd. dirs. Atlas Chem. Internat. Ltd., Shrimp Tool Internat. Ltd.; mem. Toronto Bd. Trade; chmn. bd. dirs. Am. Atlas Corp., Am. Packaging Corp.. Mem. adv. bd. Nat. Security Council; mem. Rep. Nat. Com., Presdl. Task Force, Congrl.Adv. Com. Honorary mem. Internat. Swimming Hall of Fame. Mem. Nat. (dir. at large), Rock River (past pres.) sales execs., Sales and Mktg. Execs. Internat. (dir.), Am. Mgmt. Assn., Rockford Engring. Soc., Am. Tool Engrs., Internat. Acad. Aquatic Art (dir.), Am. Inst. Mgmt. (pres. council), Am. Ordnance Assn., Internat. Platform Assn., Heritage Found., Ill. C. of C. Clubs: Jesters, Elks, Rockford Swim, Forest Hills Country, Exec., Elmcrest Country, Pyramid, Dolphin, Marlin, Univ. Lodges: Masons, Shriners. Home: 374 Parkland Dr SE Cedar Rapids IA 52403 Office: Box 242A Auburn St Rd Rockford IL 61103 also: 111 Richmond St W, Suite #318, Toronto, ON Canada M5H 1T1

VANDERROEST, ROBERT D., dentist; b. Kalamazoo, June 21, 1927; s. Richard and Emma (Stuut) VanderR.; m. Ruth A. Zwart, July 17, 1950; children—Lynn Carol, Karen Lee, Julie Diane, Steven Robert. D.D.S., U. Mich., 1954. Practice dentistry, Portage, Mich., 1954—; trustee Am. Nat. Bank, Portage, 1979—; mem. dental hygiene adv. bd. Kalamazoo Valley Community Coll., 1978-86; bd. dirs. Mich. Acad. Dentistry for the Handicapped, 1980-83; lectr. Pres., Portage Pub. Schs. Bd. Edn., 1956-70, Kalamazoo Valley Intermediate Sch. System Bd., 1970—, Mich. Assn. Retarded Children, 1984-86. Served with C.E., U.S. Army, 1946-48. Recipient Community Service award Assn. Retarded Children, 1979; deacon Bethany & Reformed Ch., 1961-64, elder, Southridge Reformed Ch., 1976-79. Mem. Kalamazoo Valley Dental Soc. (pres. 1962-63), ADA, Mich. Dental Assn. (Dental Citizen of Yr. 1984). Lodges: Optimists (pres. 1960), Rotary (Portage). Avocations: hunting; stamp collecting; photography; sailing; power boating. Home: 7603 Primrose Ln Portage MI 49081 Office: 200 E Centre Ave Portage MI 49081

VANDERVEEN, MICHAEL HENRY, dentist; b. Grand Rapids, Mich., July 18, 1950; s. Donald Nicholas and Eileen Rose (Cuddohy) V.; m. Gayle Ann Nydam, May 28, 1983; 1 child, Nicholas Henry. BS, U. Detroit, 1972; DDS, U. Mich., 1976. Pvt. practice dentistry Grand Rapids, 1977—. Recipient Service award Adult Dental Services Program, 1985, 86. Mem. ADA, Mich. Dental Soc., West Mich. Dental Soc. (bd. dirs. 1985-88, editor 1985-87, Service award 1986). Home: 651 Reynard SE Grand Rapids MI 49507 Office: 2865 Clyde Park SW Grand Rapids MI 49509

VANDERVEEN, THEODORE STEPHEN, otolaryngologist; b. Grand Rapids, Mich., June 22, 1941; s. Theodore Simon and Florence Teresa (Hoekstra) V.; m. Joan Annette Dirkse, Aug. 8, 1964; children: Timothy S., David E., Sara E., Jane E., Joel P., Elizabeth A. AB, Calvin Coll., 1963; MD, Wayne State U., 1967. Fellow Am. Bd. Otolaryngology. Intern Butterworth Hosp., Grand Rapids, 1967-68; resident in gen. surgery Henry Ford Hosp., Detroit, 1968-69; resident in otolaryngology Johns Hopkins Hosp., Balt., 1969-73; pvt. practice medicine specializing in otolaryngology Grand Haven, Mich., 1975—; chmn. bd. W. Mich. Health Systems Agy., Grand Rapids, 1977-85, Pine Rest Christian Hosp., Grand Rapids. Co-author: Complications of Sinusitus, 1975. Bd. dirs. Ottawa County br. Am. Cancer Soc., Holland, Mich., 1977-80, Grand Haven Christian Sch., 1981-84; elder Christian Reform Ch., 1985-86. Served to maj. USAF, 1973-75. Fellow ACS; mem. AMA, Am. Acad. Otolaryngology (chmn. alternative devel. systems com.), Tri Cities Physicians Assn. (pres. 1984-86). Republican. Avocation: sailing. Club: Spring Lake Yacht (bd. dirs. 1984-85). Home: 15974 Harbor Point Dr Spring Lake MI 49456 Office: 1310 Wisconsin Grand Haven MI 49417

VANDERWALL, GERALD LEROY, endodontist; b. Shelby, Mich., Sept. 17, 1929; s. John Peter and Gertrude (Groenink) V.; m. Jessica Anne Beets, Aug. 26, 1953; children: Valerie, Paula, Sondra, William, Susan. AB, Calvin Coll., 1951; DDS, U. Mich., 1955, MS, 1971. Practice gen. dentistry USAF, Chanute AFB, Ill., 1955-57, Grand Rapids, Mich., 1957-69; practice dentistry specializing in endodontics Grand Rapids, 1971—. Contbr. articles to dental jours. Chmn. U. Mich. Sch. Dentistry Alumni Assn., Ann Arbor, 1971; 1st v.p. U. Mich. Alumni Assn., Ann Arbor, 1978-79; deacon LaGrave Christian Reformed Ch., Grand Rapids, 1965-67, elder, 1977-80. Served to capt. USAF, 1955-57. Fellow Am. Coll. Dentists; mem. ADA, Mich. Dental Assn., West Mich. Dental Soc. (pres. 1967), Am. Assn. Endodontists, R.F. Sommer Endodontics Study Club (pres. 1977-78). Republican. Avocations: golf, tennis.

VAN DER WEELE, ROBERT ANTHONY, transportation company official; b. Kalamazoo, Jan. 18, 1931; s. Anthony and Meryl Eunice (Ellard) Van Der W.; B.S., Western Mich. U., 1958; m. Marilyn Ruth Martin, Aug. 16, 1953; children—Susan, Brian, Joel. Sta. agt. United Airlines, Toledo, 1958-59; traffic mgr., prodn. control supr. Brown Trailer div. Clark Equipment Co., Michigan City, Ind., 1959-62; truck fleet mgr. J.I. Case Co., Racine, Wis., 1962-67; br. mgr. Saunders Leasing System, Detroit, 1967-74; transp. mgr. Amway Corp., Ada, Mich., 1974-77; dir. transp. Havi Corp., Lemont, Ill., 1977-80; dist. mgr. Lend Lease Transp. Co., Columbus, Ohio, 1980—. Mem. Republican Precinct Com., 1964-67. Served with USAF, 1950-53. Mem. Pvt. Truck Council Am., Ill. Trucking Assn., Pvt. Carrier Conf. Episcopalian. Clubs: Rotary (past v.p.), Masons, Elks. Home: 1865 Lane Ave Columbus OH 43229 Office: 4079 Lyman Rd Hilliard OH 43026

VANDERWERF, STAN LEE, military officer; b. Morrison, Ill., Mar. 3, 1961; s. Nathan Hilbert and Dorothy Jean (Hesselink) V. BS in Indsl. Engring., Purdue U., 1983; MA, U. Dayton, 1986. Enlisted USAF, 1979, advanced through grades to 1st lt., 1985; served as resource mgmt. analyst USAF, Wright Patterson AFB, 1983-86, served as threat support mgr., 1986—; mem. Soviet Tech. Challenge Briefing Team, Dayton, Ohio, 1983-86. Contbr. articles to profl. jours. Registration coordinator Spl. Olympics Bikathon, Fairborn, Ohio, 1984; scoutmaster Boy Scouts Am., Dayton, 1985—. Mem. Air Force Assn. (VFW award, 1982), Am. Inst. Aeronautics and Astronautics (newsletter editor, Best Newsletter award), Inst. Indsl. Engrs. Presbyterian. Clubs: Dayton Cycling, Wright Patterson AFB Aero (Dayton). Avocations: flying, coin collecting, stamp collecting, writing. Home: 5013 C Cheswick Ct Dayton OH 45431 Office: ASD/FTD/TQIA Wright Patterson AFB OH 45433

VANDEVEER, MICHAEL D., city official; b. Evansville, Ind., Aug. 22, 1941; s. Adolphus William and Mary Lucinda (Smith) V.; m. Melissa Lois Malone; children—Lee, Emily. A.B. in Polit. Sci., Washington U., St. Louis, 1963; postgrad., Georgetown U., 1964-66. At-large rep. Evansville (Ind.) City Council, 1975-79; mayor City of Evansville, Ind., 1979—; chmn. urban hwys. com. U.S. Conf. Mayors, 1982—, Evansville Urban Transp. Study, 1986—, Vanderburgh County (Ind.) Dem. Central Com., 1982—. Chmn. Ind. Democratic Mayor's Caucus, 1980-85. Served to SP4 USAR, 1966-72. Recipient upper div. honor scholarship Washington U., 1961-63, Disting. Leadership Award Ind. Planning Assn., 1986. Mem. Nat. League Cities (transp. com.), Ind. Assn. Cities and Towns (chmn. legis. com.). Presbyterian. Avocations: reading; tennis; travel; politics; cooking. Home: 415 SE 1st St Evansville IN 47714 Office: City of Evansville Civic Ctr Room 302 Evansville IN 47708

VAN DEVENTER, LAWRENCE GLEN, architect; b. Moline, Ill., Aug. 25, 1946; s. Gale Thomas and Jean Margarette (Riggs) VanD.; m. Mary Lee Trogden, Aug. 17, 1968; children: Julie Ann, Melinda Lee. BArch, Ball State U., 1975, BS in Environ. Design, 1977. Registered architect, Ind., Tenn. S.C., Pa., Colo., Okla. Grad. architect Walter Scholer & Assocs., Lafayette, Ind., 1975-78; architect Ball Corp., Muncie, Ind., 1978-84, supr., 1984-85, sr. architect, 1985—. Prin. works include Ball Corp. Guest House, 1982, Ball Colo. Tech. Ctr., 1984. Trustee Halteman Village Bapt. Ch., Muncie, 1986. Served as sgt. U.S. Army, 1967-69. Decorated Bronze Star, Purple Heart; named One of Outstanding Young Men Am., Jaycees, 1983. Mem. AIA. Republican. Office: Ball Corp 1509 S Macedonia Muncie IN 47302

VANDEWALLE, GERALD WAYNE, justice state supreme court; b. Noonan, N.D., Aug. 15, 1933; s. Jules C. and Blanche Marie (Gits) VandeW. B.Sc., U. N.D., 1955, J.D., 1958. Bar: N.D. bar U.S. Dist. Ct. N.D 1959. Spl. asst. atty. gen. State of N.D., Bismarck, 1958-75; 1st asst. atty. gen. State of N.D., 1975-78; justice N.D. Supreme Ct., 1978—; mem. faculty Bismarck Jr. Coll., 1972-76; chmn. N.D. Jud. Conf. Editor-in-chief N.D. Law Rev, 1957-58. Active Bismarck Meals on Wheels; bd. dirs. Bismarck-Mandan Symphony. Mem. State Bar Assn. N.D., Burleigh County Bar Assn., Am. Bar Assn., Am. Contract Bridge League, Order of Coif, Phi Eta Sigma, Beta Alpha Psi, Beta Gamma Sigma, Phi Alpha Delta. Roman Catholic. Clubs: Elks, K.C. Office: Supreme Ct State Capitol Bismarck ND 58505 *

VAN DE WEGHE, RAYMOND FRANCIS, accountant; b. Ft. Morgan, Colo., July 17, 1934; s. Maurice and Marie Louise (Rogers) Van De W.; m. Joan Louise Kaszuba, Sept. 19, 1964; children: Louise, Matthew, Benjamin, David. BS in bus., U. Colo., 1956. CPA. V.p. N.C. Nat. Bank, Charlotte, 1967-72, 1st Nat. Bank Chgo., 1972-73; sr. v.p. fin. Bank N.C., Raleigh, 1973-75; exec. v.p., controller Huntington Nat. Bank, Columbus, Ohio, 1975-84; chief fin. officer Lamar Savs. Assn., Austin, Tex., 1984-86, Buckeye Fed. Savs., Columbus, 1986—. Served as pvt. U.S. Army, 1957-59. Mem. Am. Inst. CPA's, Fin. Exec. Inst. (chpt. pres. 1983). Roman Catholic. Home: 4590 Elan Ct Columbus OH 43220 Office: Buckeye Fed Savs 36 E Gay St Columbus OH 43215

VANDEWIELE, MARION CUNNINGHAM, oil company executive; b. Auchterderran, Scotland, Sept. 13, 1944; came to U.S., 1961; d. John Rolland and Marion G. (Johnson) Cunningham; m. Roy L. Shimer, June 20, 1965 (div. Jan. 1970) 1 son, Keith A.; m. 2d, Thomas R. VanDeWiele, Sept. 18, 1970; 1 dau., Jennifer J. Student Commerce Bus. Sch., Macomb Coll., Inst. for Energy Devel., Dallas, 1981. Acctg. supr. Splane Electric Co., Detroit, 1962-70; with assessors' office City of St. Clair Shores (Mich.), 1974-79; v.p. ops. Mid-Am. Oil & Gas Corp., New Baltimore, Mich., 1980—, dir. Mpls., 1981—; co-owner, v.p. 4x4 & More, Inc., St. Clair Shores, Mich. Mem. Petroleum Accts. Soc. of Mich., Mich. Oil & Gas Assn., Ind. Petroleum Assn. Am. Club: Clinton River Boat (Mt. Clemens, Mich.). Lodges: Order of Eastern Star (officer 1980), Women's Aux. Masons.

VAN DINE, HAROLD FORSTER, JR., architect; b. New Haven, Aug. 28, 1930; s. Harold Forster and Marguerite Anna (Eichstedt) Van D.; m. Maureen Kallick, Mar. 1, 1983; children by previous marriage: Rebecca Van Dine Smyntek, Stephanie Van Dine Natale, Gretchen. BA, Yale U., 1952, MArch, 1958. Registered architect. Designer Minoru Yamasaki & Assocs., Detroit, 1958-60; chief designer Gunnar Birkerts & Assocs., Detroit, 1960-67; prin. Straub, Van Dine & Assocs., Troy, Mich., 1967-80; sr. v.p. Harley Ellington, Pierce, Yee & Assocs., Southfield, Mich., 1980—; v.p. Mountain Kasch/HEPY, Denver, 1982—, Fields, Silverman/HEPY, Los Angeles, 1984—. Prin. works include: Mcpl. Library, Troy, Mich., campuses for Oakland Community Coll., Mich., North Hills Ch., Troy, Mich., First Ctr. Office Plaza, Mich., chemistry bldgs. at U. Mich. and Ind. U., G.M.F. Robotics Hdqrs., Flint Ink Research and Devel. Ctr., Comerica Bank Ops. Ctr., Environ. Research Inst. Mich., Christ the King Mausoleum, Chgo., Resurrection Mausoleum, Staten Island, Mich. Biotech. Inst. Served to lt. (j.g.) USN, 1952-55. Recipient Book award AIA, 1958, Excellence in Architecture Silver medal AIA, 1958, over 35 major design awards; William Wirt Winchester travelling fellowship, Yale U., 1958. Fellow AIA; mem. Mich. Soc. Architects (bd. dirs. 1978-82), Pewabic Soc. (bd. dirs. 1983—). Home: 544 Bates St Birmingham MI 48009 Office: Harley Ellington Pierce Yee Assocs 26111 Evergreen St Southfield MI 48076

VAN DONGEN, WILLIAM ORSON, information systems and accounting educator, consultant; b. Muskegon, Mich., Oct. 29, 1943; s. Fred J. and Edith J. (McIntyre) Van D.; m. Carol June Hall, Dec. 26, 1964; children: Kristine Ann, Bradley Adam. BS in Math., U. Mich., 1965; MBA in Acctg., MS in Computer Sci., Mich. State U., 1975; PhD in Acctg., North Tex. State U., 1981. CPA, Tex., Wis.; cert. systems profl., Wis. Staff Arthur Anderson, Dallas, 1975-76; systems rep. TRES Computers, Dallas, 1976-77; teaching fellow North Tex. State U., Denton, 1977-80; prof. systems U. Wis., Oshkosh, 1980—; cons in field, 1976—; expert witness, Wis., 1985—. Contbr. articles to profl. jours. Served to capt. USAF, 1966-71. Recipient various ednl. and research grants, 1971—. Mem. Soc. for Info. Mgmt., Assn. for System Mgmt., Decision Sci. Inst., Am. Acctg. Assn., Am. Inst. CPAs, Wis. Inst. CPAs, Nat. Assn. Accts. Club: FAST (Oshkosh) (treas. 1985—). Avocations: golf, bowling, reading. Office: U Wis Oshkosh Coll Bus Adminstrn Oshkosh WI 54901

VAN DUSEN, RICHARD CAMPBELL, lawyer; b. Jackson, Mich., July 18, 1925; s. Bruce Buick and Helen (Campbell) Van D.; m. Barbara Congdon, June 28, 1949; children: Amanda Van Dusen Blessing, Lisa, Katherine. BS cum laude, U. Minn., 1945; LLB, Harvard U., 1949. Bar: Mich. 1949. Assoc. Dickinson, Wright, Moon, Van Dusen & Freeman (and predecessor), Detroit, 1949-57, ptnr., 1958-62, 64-68, 73—, chmn., 1986—; mem. Mich. Ho. Reps., 1954-56; under sec. U.S. Dept. HUD, Washington, 1969-72; legal adviser to gov. Mich., 1963; del. Mich. Constl. Conv., 1961-62; mem. Council of Adminstrv. Conf. U.S., 1969-81, law revision com. State of Mich.; bd. dirs. Auto Club Ins. Group, chmn., 1978-79; bd. dirs. Pennwalt Corp., Phila., Primark Corp., McLean, Va., Fed. Nat. Mortgage Assn., W.S. Butterfield Theatres, Inc., CRi Insured Mortgage Investments II, Inc., Am. Automobile Assn. Trustee Deerfield (Mass.) Acad., 1975-80, Citizens Research Council of Mich., Kresge Found.; bd. govs. Wayne State U., 1979—; bd. dirs. Civic, Inc., United Found., Detroit Econs. Growth Corp. Served with USNR, 1943-46. Mem. Fed. Bar Assn., ABA, Detroit Bar Assn. (bd. dirs. 1965-69, trustee Found. 1973-82), Mich. Bar Assn., Greater Detroit C of C. (bd. dirs., chmn. 1987—). Republican. Episcopalian. Clubs: Econ. Detroit, Automobile of Mich. (bd. dirs., chmn. 1978-79). Home: 32205 Bingham Rd Birmingham MI 48010 Office: 800 1st National Bldg Detroit MI 48226

VAN DYKE, ELMER HAROLD, obstetrician-gynecologist; b. Sedalia, Mo., June 10, 1934; s. Frank Benjamin and Mary Irene (Sims) Van D.; m. Eileen Margaret Desmond, July 2, 1960 (div. 1973); children: Gerald, Debra, John, Richard; m. Linda Liane Murray, Nov. 7, 1980. MD, U. Mo., 1958. Diplomate Am. Bd. Ob-Gyn. Rotating intern D.C. Gen. Hosp., Washington, 1958-59; resident in ob-gyn U. Mo. Med. Ctr., Columbia, 1959-61, chief resident, 1961-62; chmn. dept. gynecology Bothwell Regional Health Ctr., Sedalia, Mo., 1964-68, chmn. ob-gyn dept., 1972-76, chief of staff, 1976-78, vice chmn. dept. ob-gyn., 1984—; pres. Women's Clinic, Sedalia, 1972—, LVS Med. Bldg. Corp., Sedalia, 1974—; mem. cons. staff U. Mo. Health Sci. Ctr., Columbia, 1972—. Served to capt. USAF, 1962-64. Recipient Appreciation of Service award Bothwell Regional Health Ctr., 1979, 10 Yr. Service award Am. Cancer Soc., 1982. Fellow Am. Coll. Ob-Gyn; mem. AMA, Pettic County Med. Soc. (pres. 1976-78), Mo. State Med. Assn., Mo. State Ob-Gyn Assn., Sedalia C. of C. (bd. dirs. 1984—). Republican. Methodist. Club: Sedalia Country. Avocations: cattle breeding, farming. Home: PO Box 1263 Rural Rt 4 Sedalia MO 65301 Office: Women's Clinic 1718 S Ingram Sedalia MO 65301

VAN DYKE, JOYCE VIVIEN, social worker; b. Detroit, Mar. 8, 1941; d. Bertil Nathaniel and Laura (Colburn) Lindblad; divorced; children: Audrey Lynn, Eric John. BA, Ohio State U., 1963; MSW, U. Mich., 1973. Cert. social worker, Mich. Assistance payment worker Solano County Welfare Dept., Vallejo, Calif., 1963-64; tchr. English Musashino Joshi Gakkuen, Tokyo, 1966-67; social worker Wayne County Welfare Dept., Detroit, 1973-76, Children's Hosp., Detroit, 1976-78, Detroit Pub. Schs., 1978-83, The Parenting Pl., Detroit, 1983—; cons. in field. Mem. Nat. Assn. Social Workers. Unitarian. Office: The Parenting Pl 18427 W McNichols Detroit MI 48219

VAN ECK, LINDA MARIE, accountant; b. Blue Island, Ill., July 18, 1962; d. William Allen and Diane Therese (Donovan) Van E. BBA in Acctg., St. Mary's Coll., Notre Dame, Ind., 1984, BA in English Lit., 1985. CPA, Ill. Sr. auditor KMG Main Hurdman, Chgo., 1984-87; supr. sr. auditor KPMG Peat, Marwick, Main & Co. (merger Peat Marwick and KMG Main Hurdman), Chgo., 1987—. Mem. St. Thomas More Choir, Chgo., 1985-87. Mem. Am. Inst. CPA's, Ill. Soc. CPA's, Chgo. Soc. Women CPA's. Roman Catholic.

VAN EENENAAM, JEFFREY ALAN, dentist; b. St. Joseph, Mich., Oct. 10, 1957; s. Robert Dale and Mary Catherine (Johnson) Van E.; m. Bonnie Lynn Boyer, May 17, 1986; 1 child, Abigail Irma. BA, U. Colo., 1979; DDS, U. Detroit, 1983. Pvt. practice dentistry Kalamazoo, 1983—. Asst. scoutmaster Boy Scouts Am., Portage, Mich., 1984—; campaign mgr. City Councilman Dale Shugars, Portage, 1983, 85. Named Eagle Scout Boy Scouts Am., 1969. Mem. ADA, Mich. Dental Assn., Kalamazoo Valley Dist. Dental Assn. Republican. Club: Kalamazoo Ski (pres. 1985—). Lodge: Lions (v.p. 1986). Avocations: golf, running, snowskiing. Home: 3187 Kalarama Portage MI 49002 Office: 3907 S Westnedge Kalamazoo MI 49008

VANEERDEN, WILLIAM ELLIS, psychiatrist, educator; b. Grand Rapids, Mich., Feb. 1, 1941; s. Thomas and Louise Jane (Ellis) VanE.; m. Connie Lynn VandeBunte, Aug. 16, 1963; children: Susan, Laura, Anita. AB, Calvin Coll., 1962; MD, U. Ill., 1966. Diplomate Am. Bd. Psychiatry and Neurology. Intern Butterworth Hosp., Grand Rapids, Mich., 1966-67; resident Lafayette Clinic, Detroit, 1967-70; staff psychiatrist Pine Rest Christian Hosp., Grand Rapids, 1972—; chief med. staff Pine Rest Christian Hosp., 1973-75, dir. med. edn., 1975—, dir. adult services, 1976—; cons. Pine Rest Rehab. Service, Grand Rapids, 1975-82; assoc. clin. prof. psychiatry Mich. State U. Coll. Medicine, East Lansing, Mich., 1976—; bd. dirs. Grand Rapids Area Med. Edn. Ctr., 1976—. Served to maj. U.S. Army MC, 1970-72. Fellow Am. Psychiat. Assn.; mem. AMA, Mich. Psychiat. Soc., Western Mich. Psychiat. Soc., Mich. Med. Soc., Kent County Med. Soc., Am. Assn. Dirs. Psychiat. Residency Tng. Office: Pine Rest Christian Hosp 300 68th St SE Grand Rapids MI 49508-6999

VAN ERT, MELVIN WILLIAM, electrical contracting company executive; b. Carson, Wis., Oct. 25, 1923; s. William and Nellie Van E.; m. Mary Agnes Zimmerman, July 2, 1949; children—Jo Anne, Robert, Paula, Terry, Jane, Chris, Carol, Mary, Julie, Anne. Student Indsl. Tng. Inst., Chgo., 1946-47. Co-owner, Thomas Electric Co., Marshfield, Wis., 1953-64; pres. Van Ert Electric Co. Inc., Wausau, Wis., 1964—. Mem. nat. adv. bd. Am. Security Council. Served with USAF, 1943-46. Mem. Nat. Elec. Contractors Assn. (Wis. dir. 1965—), Am. Legion. Republican. Roman Catholic. Home: 6984 Grotto Ave Rudolph WI 54475 Office: 7019 W Stewart Ave Wausau WI 54401

VAN ES, RICHARD JOHN, JR., electronics executive; b. South Bend, Ind., Aug. 3, 1957; s. Richard John Sr. and Barbara Jean (Frick) Van E.; m. Mary Elizabeth Sartini, June 6, 1982. BBA, U. Notre Dame, Ind., 1980. CPA, Ind. Staff acct. Price Waterhouse, South Bend, 1980-82; asst. controller St. Joseph Bank and Trust Co., South Bend, 1982-84; sr. acct. McGladrey, Hendrickson & Pullen, Elkhart, Ind., 1984-87; v.p. fin. and acctg. Am. Electronic Components, Elkhart, 1987—. Mem. Am. Inst. CPA's, Ind. Soc. CPA's. Avocations: tennis, music. Home: 2722 Eisenhower Dr South Bend IN 46615 Office: Am Electronic Components 1010 N Main St Elkhart IN 46515

VANGEL, PETER V., financial executive; b. Boston, Dec. 10, 1931; s. Visar Michael and Anastasia (Kosta) V.; m. Joan Marie Reilly, Aug. 5, 1962; children: Kathrn, Julie. BA in Sociology, Boston U., 1953; MS in Indsl. Mgmt., MIT, 1959. CPA. Fin. analyst USM Corp., Beverly, 1961-63; asst. to corp. v.p. ITEK Corp., Lexington, Mass., 1963-67; sr. fin. mgr. Polaroid Corp., Cambridge, Mass., 1967-76; group controller Mead Corp., Dayton, Ohio, 1976-80; asst. corp. controller Hobart Div. Dart & Kraft, Troy, Ohio, 1980-85; corp. controller Dayton Walter Corp., 1985—. Served to lt. USN, 1953-57. Mem. Am. Inst. CPAs, Ohio Soc. CPAs (Dayton chmn. 1986—), Planning Forum. Club: MIT. Home: 818 Barth Ln Kettering OH 45429 Office: Dayton Walther Corp 2800 E River Rd Dayton OH 45401

VAN GELDER, TERESA ANN, insurance agency executive; b. Eau Claire, Wis., Jan. 19, 1946; d. Fred Harrison and Geneva (Cook) King; m. Richard Allen Van Gelder, Sept. 4, 1965; children: Stacy L., R. Aric. Student, Ins. Inst. Am., 1971-75. Sec. Eau Claire Ins. Agy., 1964-74, mgr., 1974—; mem. agts. adv. com. Fireman's Fund, 1977-80, small bus. adv. com. to U.S. Congressman, Wis., 1981—. Leader 4-H, Eau Claire, 1979—; pres. Eau Claire Child Passenger Safety Com., 1981-85. Mem. Profl. Ins. Agts., Ind. Ins. Agts., Ins. Women of Eau Claire (named Ins. Woman Yr. 1982), Ind. Ins. Agts. Western Wis. (named Com. Chairperson of Yr. 1985), Nat. Assn. Ins. Women, Indianhead Bank Women. Republican. Lutheran. Home: Rt 2 Box 127 Eau Claire WI 54703 Office: Eau Claire Ins Agy 301 Water St PO Box 1188 Eau Claire WI 54702

VAN GORP, GREGORY ALAN, business analyst, accountant; b. Oskaloosa, Iowa, Nov. 11, 1958; s. David Lee and Eileen Elizabeth (Young); m. Pamela Lynn Reynolds, June 13, 1981. BS, N.E. Mo. State U., 1981. CPA, Iowa. Staff acct. McGladrey, Hendrickson & Co., Des Moines, 1981-82; bus. analyst, chief acct. for subs. cos. Grinnell (Iowa) Mut. Reins. Co., 1983—. Bd. pres. Jr. Achievement Grinnell, 1985-86; bd. dirs. Jr. Achievement Cen. Iowa, 1985-86; mem. Grinnell 2000, 1986. Named One of Outstanding Young Men in Am., 1982. Mem. Am. Inst. CPA's, Iowa Soc. CPA's. Republican. Roman Catholic. Club: Silver Hawks (Iowa City). Avocations: softball, basketball, bowling, Iowa Hawkeye athletics. Home: 1520 Prairie St Grinnell IA 50112 Office: Grinnell Mut Reins Co Interstate 80 & Hwy 146 Grinnell IA 50112

VAN HAGEY, WILLIAM, lawyer; b. Chgo., Sept. 30, 1946; s. William and Rama (Free) Van H.; m. Connie Wittenberg, Sept. 3, 1966; children: Catherine Elspeth, William Colin. AB, U. Ill., 1968, JD, 1972. Bar: Ill. 1972, U.S. Dist. Ct. (no. dist.) Ill. 1974, U.S. Ct. Appeals (7th cir.) 1976, U.S. Supreme Ct. 1978, U.S. Ct. Appeals (10th cir.) 1979, U.S. Ct. Appeals (11th cir.) 1985. Law clk. to chief justice Ill. Supreme Ct., 1972-73; assoc. Chadwell & Kayser Ltd., Chgo., 1973-79, ptnr., 1980-84; ptnr. Van Hagey & Bogan Ltd., Mundelein, Ill., 1984—; mem. Ill. Franchise Adv. Bd., 1981—, vice chmn., 1984—. Mem. U. Ill. Coll. Law Bd. Visitors, 1982—, pres.-elect, 1986—. Served with USAR, 1968-74. Mem. ABA, Ill. Bar Assn. (council sect. on intellectual property law 1986—), Chgo Bar Assn., Phi Alpha Delta. Clubs: Union League, Legal of Chgo. Office: Van Hagey & Bogan Ltd 700 N Lake St Mundelein IL 60060

VANHANDEL, RALPH ANTHONY, librarian; b. Appleton, Wis., Jan. 17, 1919; s. Frank Henry and Gertrude Mary (Schmidt) Van H.; m. Alice Catherine Hogan, Oct. 27, 1945; children: William Patrick, Karen Jean, Mary Jo. BA, U. Wis., 1946; AB, U. Mich., 1947. Head librarian Lawrence (Kans.) Free Pub. Library, 1947-51, Hibbing (Minn.) Pub. Library, 1951-54; library dir. Gary (Ind.) Pub. Library, 1954-74, Wells Meml. Pub. Library, Lafayette, Ind. (name now Tippecanoe County Pub. Library), 1974-84; mem. Ind. Library Cert. Bd., 1969-84, Ind. State Library and Hist. Bldg. Expansion Commn., 1973-81. Named Ind. Librarian of Year, 1971, Sagamore of Wabash, 1984. Mem. Anselm Forum (sec. 1964, v.p. 1965), ALA, Ind. Library Assn. (pres. 1963-64), Kans. Library Assn. (v.p. 1951). Clubs: KC, Rotary. Home: 3624 Winter St Lafayette IN 47905

VAN HOOK, DONALD WAYNE, manufacturing company official; b. Stanford, Ky., June 1, 1938; s. James Orville and Althene Jones Van H.; m. Beverly Gwinn Hennen, Oct. 26, 1963; children—Andrea Gwinn, James Carlton, Alison Lin. B.S., Ohio U., 1960. Asst. advt. mgr. Monarch Marking Systems Co., Dayton, Ohio, 1960-62; copywriter Yeck & Yeck Advt., Inc., Dayton, 1962-64, Deere & Co. Advt., Moline, Ill., 1964-71; supr. indsl. advt. Deere & Co., 1971-72; mgr. European Advt. Centre, Mannheim, W.Ger., 1972-76, mgr. overseas advt., Moline, Ill., 1976-84, mgr. agrl. advt., 1984—. Mem. exec. bd. local council Boy Scouts Am., 1967-71. Served with U.S. Army Res., 1961-67. Recipient awards for indsl. copywriting. Mem. Am. Mgmt. Assn., Assn. Nat. Advertisers, Internat. Advt. Assn., Nat. Agri-Mktg. Assn. Unitarian. Editorial bd. Agri-Mktg., 1981. Home: 1332 42d Ave Rock Island IL 61201 Office: Deere & Co John Deere Rd Moline IL 61265

VAN HOVEN, JAY, school system administrator; b. Holland, Mich., Aug. 11, 1944; s. Leonard Jay and Mary Helene (Schaap) Van Hoven; m. Nancy L. Voight, June 27, 1975; children—Joshua, Janna, Lydia. B.A., Hope Coll., 1966; student Wayne State U., 1966-68; M.A., No. Mich. U., 1971; postgrad. Mich. State U., 1973-75. Vol., Peace Corps, S.Am., 1968-69; tchr. St. Dunstans Sch., U.S. V.I., 1969-70; community sch. dir. Des Moines Schs., 1970-72; adminstr. Ctr. for Community Edn., Alma, Mich., 1973-75; asst. ombudsman Mich. State U., East Lansing, 1975; fin. mgr. Sch. Nursing, U. N.C., Chapel Hill, 1976-78; desegregation specialist Ind. U., Indpls., 1979-82; ptnr. Westlake Profl. Services, Indpls., 1982-85; asst. supr. fin. Melvindale (Mich.) Schs., 1985-86; supt. Detour (Mich.) Schs., 1986—; pres. Med. Specialty Disability Ins. Corp., Indpls., 1983-86. Rep., Interurban Coll. and Univ. Consortium, Des Moines, 1971-72; adminstr. Urban Cities, Flint, Mich., 1970; mem. Hispanic Edn., Des Moines, 1971-72; mem. Ind. Community Edn. Adv., Indpls., 1979—. Mott fellow, 1970-71, 73-75, 79-85. Mem. Mich. Assn. Sch. Adminstrs. Phi Delta Kappa. Lutheran. Office: Detour Schs Box 68 Detour MI 49725

VAN KIRK, DONALD JOHN, forensic and consulting engineer; b. Detroit, Jan. 6, 1935; s. Kenneth John and Helen Van Kirk; Asso. in Sci., Henry Ford Community Coll., 1961; B.S. in Elec. Engring., Wayne State U., 1964, M.S. in Engring. Mechanics, 1969; M.B.A., U. Mich., 1975; m. Wyva A. Moore, Apr. 28, 1956; 1 dau., Cheryl Ann. TV technician Sta. WXYZ-TV, Detroit, 1959-60, WTVS-TV, Detroit, 1960-64; product design engr. Ford Motor Co., Dearborn, Mich., 1964-66, research engr., 1969-73, sr. design engr., 1973-84; pres. D.J. Van Kirk P.E. & Assocs., P.C., 1985—; instr. Henry Ford Community Coll. and Ford continuing edn. programs; mgmt. cons. Chmn. bldg. and plans com. Dearborn Hills Home Owners Assn., 1973-75; vol. Consumer Product Safety Com., Washington, 1977; chmn. Consumer Affairs Com., Dearborn, 1977-79; vol. traffic safety com. Dearborn Police Dept., 1979. Served with USN, 1955-59. Recipient Outstanding Student award Wayne State U., 1963-64; Community Service award Ford Motor Co., 1973. Mem. Nat. Soc. Profl. Engrs., Soc. Automotive Engrs., IEEE, Oakland County Traffic Safety Assn., Mich. Soc. Profl. Engrs., Am. Assn. Automotive Medicine, Am. Acad. Forensic Scis. Presbyterian. Clubs: Dearborn Exchange (Outstanding Service award 1974, Man of Yr. award 1975), Masons, Shriners. Patentee cold weather diesel starting aid; contbr. articles to profl. jours. Home: 23917 Rockford Dearborn MI 48124

VANLANDUYT, MARYBETH SAFRANSKY, curriculum consultant, educator; b. Kenosha, Wis., Jan. 16, 1946; d. Charles Casmir and Elizabeth (Mulich) Safransky; m. Lee Dennis VanLanduyt, Aug. 24, 1968 (div. Jan. 1985); children: Kyle, Ravi. Student, U. Dallas, 1965-67; BS, U. Wis., Whitewater, 1968; MS, U. Wis., Milw., 1973; postgrad., Marquette U., 1978-81. Cert. elem. tchr., Wis. Tchr. second grade Kenosha Unified Sch. Dist., 1968-70, community liaison tchr., 1974-79, dissemination specialist, 1979-82, curriculum cons., 1982—; adj. assoc. prof. U. Wis., Kenosha, 1979—; cons. Conn. Facilitator, North Haven, 1984-86; coordinator Regional Staff Devel Ctr., Kenosha, 1986—. Author: Kenosha Model Kindergarten Manual, 1985, Kenosha Model Math. Manual, 1986; editor: Kenosha Model Language Experience, 1979. Mem. Racine (Wis.) Arts Council, 1980-86. Mem. Nat. Council Tchrs. English, Internat. Reading Assn., Parent Edn. and Childhood Assn. (exec. bd. 1976-83), Wis. State and Fed. Specialists (newsletter editor 1986—). Democrat. Roman Catholic. Avocations: reading, cross-country skiing, nature. Home: 1419 Crabapple Dr Racine WI 53405 Office: Kenosha Unified Sch Dist Office Govt Projects 3600 52d St Kenosha WI 53142

VAN LEUVEN, HOLLY GOODHUE, social scientist, consultant, researcher; b. Salem, Mass., Dec. 2, 1935; d. Nathaniel William and Elizabeth VanClowes (Crowley) Goodhue; m. John Jamison Porter, II, Oct. 16, 1954 (div. 1974); children: Donald J. II, Nathaniel G., Alison A. Dionne, Erin E.; m. Robert Joseph VanLeuven, Dec. 31, 1976. BA with honors, Western Mich. U., 1971, MA with honors, 1975. Exec. dir. Community Confrontation and Communication Assocs., Grand Rapids, Mich., 1969-73; coordinator tng., research Nat. Ctr. for Dispute Settlement, Washington, 1973; tng. dir. Forest View Psychiat. Hosp., Grand Rapids, 1974; case coordinator Libner, Van Leuven, & Kortering, P.C., Muskegon, Mich., 1982-87; pres. Genesis Cons. Group, Muskegon, Mich., Phoenix, 1987—; talk show host Sta. WTRU-TV, Muskegon, 1985; cons. U.S. Dept. Justice, Washington, 1969-73, No. Ireland Dept. Community Relations, Belfast, 1971; jury selection cons. various law firms in Midwest, 1975—. Contbr. articles to profl. jours. Bd. dirs. Planned Parenthood Western Mich., Grand Rapids, 1964-72, Jr. League Grand Rapids, 1955—, YFCA, Muskegon, 1981-83; chmn. Student Showcase, Inc., Muskegon, 1983—; candidate for Mich. State Rep. 97th Dist., Muskegon, 1978; pres. Planned Parenthood Assn., Muskegon, 1980. Mem. Am. Sociol. Assn. Clubs: Muskegon Country, Century; Women's City (Grand Rapids). Lodges: Zonta, Compass. Home: 966 Mona Brook Rd Muskegon MI 49441 Office: Libner VanLeuven & Kortering PC 400 Comerica Hackley Bank Bldg Box 450 Muskegon MI 49443

VAN LEUVEN, ROBERT JOSEPH, lawyer; b. Detroit, Apr. 17, 1931; s. Joseph Francis and Olive (Stowell) Van L.; student Albion Coll., 1949-51; B.A. with distinction Wayne State U., 1953; J.D., U. Mich., 1957; m. Holly Goodhue Porter, Dec. 31, 1976; children—Joseph Michael, Douglas Robert, Julie Margaret. Bar: Mich. 1957. Since practiced in Muskegon, Mich.; ptnr. Hathaway, Latimer, Clink & Robb, 1957-68, McCroskey, Libner & Van Leuven, 1968-81, Libner, Van Leuven & Kortering, 1982—; past mem. council negligence law sect. State Bar Mich. Bd. dirs. Muskegon Children's Home, 1965-75. Served with AUS 1953-55. Fellow Am. Coll. Trial Lawyers; mem. Assn. Trial Lawyers Am., Mich. Assn. Professions, Am. Arbitration Assn., Delta Sigma Phi. Club: Muskegon Country. Home: 966 Mona Brook Muskegon MI 49445 Office: Hackley Bank Muskegon Mall Muskegon MI 49443

VAN LIERE, DONALD WILBUR, psychologist, educator; b. Holland, Mich., Nov. 23, 1915; s. Christian Cornelius and Aafhe (Ten Have) V.; m. Carma Lee Parkhurst, Sept. 19, 1941; children: Jean, Mark, Mary, Judith, Eric, Christopher. AB, Hope Coll., 1939; MA, Ind. U., 1942, PhD, 1950. Lic. psychologist, Mich. Assoc. prof. Kalamazoo Coll., 1949-56, prof., 1956-81; electroencephalographer Bronson Hosp., Kalamazoo, 1956-77, diagnostic specialist, 1977-84; cons. in EEG Vets. Hosp., Battle Creek, Mich., 1980—. Pres. Kalamazoo chpt. Mich. Heart Assn., 1980. Served with U.S. Army, 1943-46, ETO. Fellow Am. EEG Soc.; mem. Am. Psychol. Assn., AAAS, N.Y. Acad. Sci., Am. Assn. Univ. Profs., Sigma Xi. Club: Kalamazoo Power Squadron (commdr. 1985). Avocations: sailing, photography. Home: 2011 Timberline Dr Kalamazoo MI 49008

VAN LOH, FREDERICK ALVIN, educator; b. Ashton, Iowa, Nov. 28, 1926; s. Jans and Fenna (Luitjens) Van L.; m. Rose Marie Helmers, July 28, 1950; children: Linda Killian, James. Student S.D. State U., summers 1944, 47-48; BS, Iowa State U., 1950, MS, 1964. Lic. tchr., Iowa. Youth asst. Osceola County, summer 1948; tchr. Correctionville High Sch. (Iowa), 1950-51; tchr. vocat. agr. Sheldon Community High Sch. (Iowa), 1951—; advisor Sheldon chpt. Future Farmers Am., 1951—; judge county fairs. Served with U.S. Army, 1944-46. Recipient Regional Dist. Conservation Tchr. award Iowa Soil Conservation Service, 1971, Beresford Quaife award, 1981, C.E. Bundy Agrl. Educator award 1986; hon. Iowa Farmer Degree, 1969, hon. Am. Farmer Degree, 1982. Mem. Nat. Vocat. Agr. Tchrs. Assn., Iowa Vocat. Agr. Tchrs. Assn. (voting del. conf. 1982, bd. dirs. 1982-84; Harry R. Schroeder Disting. Iowa Vocat. Agr. Tchr. award 1983), Am. Vocat. Assn., Iowa. Vocat. Assn. (voting del. conf. 1982, bd. dirs. 1982-84), O'Brien County Farm Bur., Gamma Sigma Delta. Republican. Baptist. Home: 1211 Kahler Ct Sheldon IA 51201 Office: 1700 E 4th St Sheldon IA 51201

VAN METRE, DOUGLAS COPLEY, corporate executive; b. Cedar Rapids, Iowa, Dec. 21, 1927; s. Douglas Ure and Mary (Copley) Van M.; m. Celia Lynch; children: Douglas L., Craig R., Kent J. Student, Cornell Coll., Mt. Vernon, Iowa, 1946-47; BA, Colo. Coll., 1950. Spl. rep. Atlas Cement USS, Kansas City, Mo., 1960-64; sales mgr. Atlas Cement USS, Chgo., 1966-70; pres. Rapids, Inc., Cedar Rapids, Iowa, 1970-86, Bauman & Co. Mens Clothiers, Mt. Vernon, Iowa, 1986—; Chmn. bd. dirs. Mt. Vernon Bank & Trust, 1986; bd. dirs. Mid Am. Pub. Co., Des Moines; trustee Cornell Coll., 1978. Served to capt. USMC, 1951-53, Korea. Mem. Cedar Rapids C. of C. (chmn. govt. relations 1982-86). Republican. Congregationalist. Clubs: X, Cedar Rapids Country. Home: 440 Squaw Creek Rd Cedar Rapids IA 52401 Office: Rapids Inc 1011 2d Ave SW Box 396 Cedar Rapids IA 52404

VANN, PETER JOEL, marketing executive; b. Buffalo, June 29, 1933; s. Benjamin George and Ulisse (Schneider) V.; m. Mary Bettis Quinby, June 16, 1956; children: Thomas Darrell, Mary Cathrine, Gregory Hamilton, Christopher Allan. BS in Engring., U.S. Mil. Acad., 1956. Commd. 2d lt. U.S. Army, 1956, advanced through grades to 1st lt., res., 1960; pres. Computer Acctg., Inc., Indpls., 1973-76; regional salesman UCCEL, Dallas, 1976-81; dir. mktg. ANACOMP, Indpls., 1981-84, Data-Link, South Bend, Ind., 1984-87, Pallm, Inc., Indpls., 1987—. Republican. Methodist. Avocations: growing roses, salmon fishing. Home: 7244 N Chester Indianapolis IN 46240

VANNATTA, DENNIS ROY, optometrist; b. Cherokee, Iowa, Sept. 3, 1955; s. Darrel Roy and Delores Jean (Jensen) V. Student in pre-optometry U. S.D., 1973-76; B.S. in Visual Sci., Pacific U., 1978, O.D., 1980. Lic. optometrist, Iowa, Nebr. Hosp. staff optometrist U.S. Navy, Patuxent River, Md., 1980-83; optometrist with Dr. Ralph Danner, Mapleton, Iowa, 1983; pvt. practice optometry, Sioux City, Iowa, 1984—; officer in-charge Naval Res. Med. Unit, Sioux City. Served to lt. with USN, 1980-83, lt. comdr. USNR, 1983—. Mem. Iowa Optometric Assn., Am. Optometric Assn., Nat. Assn. Professions, Armed Forces Optometric Soc., Siouxland Assn. Bus. and Industry. Republican. Methodist. Club: Siouxland Cosmopolitan. Lodges: Sertoma, Eagles. Avocations: photography; fishing; boating; skiing. Home: 430 South Lynn Dr LeMars IA 51031 Office: 4016 Morningside Ave Sioux City IA 51106

VAN NATTA, ELEANOR SUE POUNDSTONE, nurse; b. Decatur, Ill., Nov. 22, 1932; d. Herbert Lloyd and Blanche Cleo (Zink) Poundstone; Assoc. in Nursing Washington U., St. Louis, 1953, MS in Nursing, 1961; BS in Nursing, U. Mo., 1956; MEd, Purdue U., 1970; m. Charles R. Van Natta, Jr., June 12, 1971 (div. 1977); 1 child, Laura Sue. Staff nurse Barnes Hosp., St. Louis, 1953-54; staff nurse, then head nurse U. Mo. Med. Center, Columbia, 1954-58; instr. Decatur (Ill.) and Macon County Hosp. Sch. Nursing, 1958-60; instr. U. Colo., Denver, 1961-63; asst. prof. U. Mo., Columbia, 1964-66; asst. prof. Forest Park Community Coll., St. Louis, 1967-69; high sch. counselor, Decatur, 1970-71; coordinator diagnostic and evaluation project Comprehensive Devel. Centers, Monticello, Ind., 1975-77; asst. prof. Purdue U. Sch. Nursing, 1980-84; program supr. for nursing Ind. Vocat. Tech. Coll., Lafayette, 1984-86; pres. White County Registered Nurses Orgn., 1975-76. Vol., Twin Lakes Contact, crisis hotline, Monticello, 1975-76; bd. dirs. Tippecanoe County unit Am. Heart Assn., Purdue Women's Caucus, 1983-84. Mem. Am. Nurses Assn., Ind. Nurses Assn. (dist. 8 v.p. 1984), Ind. League for Nursing (bd. dirs. 1984-86), Phi Delta Kappa, Sigma Theta Tau, Kappa Kappa Kappa. Club: Order Eastern Star. Home: 1137 Hillcrest Rd West Lafayette IN 47906

VAN NORMAN, WILLIS ROGER, computer systems researcher; b. Windom, Minn., June 17, 1938; s. Ralph Peter and Thelma Pearl (Bare) Van N.; A.A., Worthington Jr. Coll., 1958; B.S., Mankato State Coll., 1960; m. Irene Anna Penner, Sept. 7, 1959; children—Eric Jon, Brian Mathew, Karin Ruth. Tchr. chemistry, St. Peter, Minn., 1961; tchr., Byron, Minn., 1962, spl. edn., Rochester, Minn., 1963-65; instr. pilots ground sch. Rochester Jr. Coll., 1968-69; with Mayo Clinic, Rochester, 1962—, developer biomed. computer systems, 1974—; instr. Gopher Aviation, 1968-71. Treas., United Methodist Ch. Mem. Mankato State Alumni Assn. (dir.), Minn., Nat. ednl. assns., Internat. Flying Farmers (dir.), Minn Flying Farmers (v.p.), Am. Radio Relay League (mgr. Minn. sect. traffic net), Rochester Amateur Radio Club (pres.). Founder, mgr. Van Norman's Flying V Ranch, 1972—, Van Norman Airport, St. Charles, 1977—. Home: Route 3 Box 25 Saint Charles MN 55972 Office: Mayo Clinic Rochester MN 55901

VANNUCCI, PASQUALE, accountant; b. Wilmington, Del., Dec. 26, 1946; s. Albert Joseph and Florence Antoinette (Barbizzi) V.; m. Yvonne Kay Yost, Jan. 4, 1969; children: Derek Anthony, Marisa Devon. Acctg. supr. Chrysler Corp., Newark, Del., 1980-84, Sterling Heights, Mich., 1984—. Served as staff sgt. USAF, 1966-70. Mem. Am. Legion. Democrat. Roman Catholic. Lodges: Lions (past pres. New Castle, Del.), Masons (32 degree), Shriners. Avocations: coin collecting, investing. Home: 41127 Justin Dr Mount Clemens MI 48044 Office: Chrysler Motors 38111 Van Dyke Sterling Heights MI 48077

VANO, JOSEPH JULIUS, architect; b. Chgo., Jan. 20, 1943; s. John and Mary Anna (Kubik) V.; m. Shirley Louis Kraetzner, June 4, 1966; children: Alicia Ann, Ariell Hittie. BArch, BA, U. Minn., 1968. Registered architect, Minn., Wis. Assoc. architect Baird Architects, Mpls., 1970-74; ptnr. Baird and Vano, Architects, Maiden Rock, Wis., 1982—. Mem. AIA, Wis. Soc. Architects, Minn. Soc. Architects (honor award 1972). Avocations: photography, flying.

VAN OSDOL, THOMAS DEAN, dentist; b. Warsaw, Ind., Apr. 10, 1940; s. Cortes Dean and Marjorie Louise (Bolinger) VanO.; m. Linda Dianne Conley, Oct. 13, 1962; children: Michael Dean, Scott Anthony, Matthew Thomas. DDS, Ind. U., Indpls., 1964. Pvt. practice dentistry Warsaw, Ind., 1966—. Inventor in field; contbr. articles to mags. and newspapers. Served as capt. U.S. Army, 1964-66. Recipient Crown and Bridge award Ind. U. Sch. Dentistry, 1964. Mem. Kosciusko County Dental Soc. (pres. 1975-76), N. Cen. Dental Soc., Ind. Dental Assn., ADA, No. Ind. Soc. Occlusal Studies. Republican. Roman Catholic. Club: Tippecanoe Lake Country (Leesburg, Ind.). Lodge: Rotary. Avocations: outdoor activities, hunting, fishing, family. Home: 521 N Harrison St Warsaw IN 46580 Office: 2259 DuBois Dr Warsaw IN 46580

VAN PELT, ROBERT, judge; b. Gosper County, Nebr., Sept. 9, 1897; s. Francis M. and Sarah (Simon) Van P.; m. Mildred Carter, June 17, 1925; children: Robert (dec.), Margery Van Pelt Irvin, Samuel. AB cum laude, Doane Coll., 1920, LLD (hon.), 1959; LLB, U. Nebr., 1922, LLD (hon.), 1985; LHD (hon.), Westmar Coll., 1960. Bar: Nebr. 1922. Practiced in Lincoln, 1922- 57; asst. U.S. atty. 1930-34; judge U.S. Dist. Ct. Nebr., Lincoln, 1957-70, sr. judge, 1970—; lectr. Nebr. Law Coll., 1946-57; mem. com. to implement Fed. Magistrates Act; mem. adv. com. jud. activities, adv. com. fed. rules of evidence U.S. Jud. Conf.; apptd. spl. master by U.S. Supreme Ct. in Original Nos. 27, 36, 81, 106 involving boundary disputes affecting the States of Tex., La., Calif., Nev., Ky., Ind., Ohio, Ill. del. Rep. Nat. Conv., 1940, 44, 48; trustee Doane Coll., 1928-68. Mem. Am. Coll. Trial Lawyers, Am. Coll. Probate Counsel, Phi Sigma Kappa, Phi Delta Phi. Congregationalist. Clubs: Lincoln Country, Lincoln Univ. Lodges: Masons (33 deg.), Rotary. Home: 2323 Woodscrest Lincoln NE 68502 Office: 566 Fed Bldg 100 Centennial Mall N Lincoln NE 68508

VAN PEURSEM, MARLIN JAY, accountant; b. Orange City, Iowa, May 15, 1960; s. Myron W. and Lenora (VerHoeven) V.; m. Jane R. Koth, June 8, 1985. BA cum laude, Northwestern Coll., 1982. CPA, S.D. Staff acct. Crayne-Parkinson and Assocs., Sioux City, Iowa, 1982-83; audit supr. Charles Bailly and Co., CPA's, Sioux Falls, S.D., 1983-86; corp. reporting acct. Citibank S.D., A Nat. Assn., Sioux Falls, 1986—; pvt. practice acct. Sioux Falls, 1986—. Mem. Am. Inst. CPA's, S.D. State Soc. CPA's. Republican. Club: Toastmasters (v.p. Sioux Falls chpt. 1986-87, pres. 1987—). Avocations: outdoor activities. Home: 5004 Havenhill Ave Sioux Falls SD 57103 Office: Citibank SD NA 701 E 60th St N Sioux Falls SD 57117

VAN RHEENEN, RICHARD STEPHEN, lawyer; b. Indpls., June 23, 1955; s. Robert N. and Katherine J. (Dawson) Van R.; m. Julie Moore. Student, U. Kent, Canterbury, Eng., 1975-76; BA, Hanover Coll., 1977; JD, Ind. U., 1984. Bar: Ind., U.S. Dist. Ct. (no. and so. dists.) Ind. Mgr. The Sitzmark, Indpls., 1978-81; lawyer Nile Stanton & Assocs., Indpls., 1984-85; lawyer, clk. Hon. V. Sue Shields, Indpls., 1985—. Mem. ABA, ACLU, Assn. Trial Lawyers of Am., Ind. Bar Assn., Indpls. Bar Assn., Ind. Civil Liberties Union (screening com. 1983).. Avocation: boat building. Home: 2301 W 61 Indianapolis IN 46208 Office: Ind Ct Appeals 155 W Washington St Suite 1188S Indianapolis IN 46204

VAN RIPER, GUERNSEY, JR., real estate and oil company executive, author; b. Indpls., July 5, 1909; s. Guernsey and Edith (Longley) Van R. AB, DePauw U., 1930; MBA, Harvard U., 1932. Advt. copywriter Sidener & Van Riper, Indpls., 1933-40; editor Bobbs-Merrill Co., Indpls. and N.Y.C., 1941-48; freelance writer children's books, 1949-74; pres. Crooked Stick Devel. Corp., Carmel, Ind., 1972—; pres. Van Riper Gallery Fine Arts, Inc., 1984—, Gallery Boutique, 1986—. Author: (children's books) Lou Gehrig, Boy of the Sandlots, 1949, Will Rogers, Young Cowboy, 1951, Knute Rockne, Young Athlete, 1952, Babe Ruth, Baseball Boy, 1954, Jim Thorpe, Indian Athlete, 1956, Richard Byrd, Boy Who Braved the Unknown, 1958, Yea Coach! Three Great Football Coaches, 1966, The Game of Basketball, 1967, World Series Highlights, 1970, The Mighty Macs, Three Famous Baseball Managers, 1972, Behind the Plate, Three Great Catchers, 1973, (with J. Newcomb and G. Sullivan) Football Replay, 1973, (with S.B. Epstein and R. Reeder) Big League Pitchers and Catchers, 1973, Golfing Greats, 1975. Mem. Authors League of Am., Phi Kappa Psi, Sigma Delta Chi, Phi Beta Kappa. Republican. Methodist. Address: PO Box 455 Carmel IN 46032

VANSELOW, NEAL ARTHUR, physician, university administrator; b. Milw., Mar. 18, 1932; s. Arthur Frederick and Mildred (Hoffman) V.; m. Mary Ellen McKenzie, June 20, 1958; children: Julie Ann, Richard Arthur. A.B., U. Mich., 1954, M.D., 1958, M.S., 1963. Diplomate: Am. Bd. Internal Medicine, Am. Bd. Allergy and Immunology. Intern Mpls. Gen. Hosp., 1958-59; resident Univ. Hosp., Ann Arbor, Mich., 1959-63; instr. medicine U. Mich., 1963-64, asst. prof., 1964-68, asso. prof., 1968-72, prof., chmn. dept. postgrad. medicine and health professions edn., 1972-74; dean Coll. Medicine U. Ariz., Tucson, 1974-77; chancellor Med. Center U. Nebr., Omaha, 1977-82; v.p. univ. Med. Center U. Nebr., 1977-82; v.p. health scis. U. Minn., 1982—, prof. internal medicine, 1982—; Chmn. Joint Bd. Osteo. and Med. Examiners Ariz., 1974-77, council on Grad. Med. Edn., Dept. Health and Human Services, 1986—; chmn.-elect Assn. Acad. Health Ctrs., 1987—. Bd. dirs. Devel. Authority for Tucson's Economy, 1975-77, Minn. Coalition on Health Care Costs, 1983-87; mem. exec. com. United Way Midlands, 1980-82, vice-chmn., 1981 campaign; bd. dirs., mem. exec. com. Health Planning Council Midlands, Omaha, 1978-82, v.p., 1981-82; bd. dirs. Minn. High Tech. Council, 1983-86. Fellow ACP, Am. Acad. Allergy, Am. Coll. Physician Execs.; mem. Assn. Acad. Health Ctrs. (bd. dirs. 1983—, chmn.-elect bd. dirs. 1987), Phi Beta Kappa, Sigma Xi, Alpha Omega Alpha, Beta Theta Pi, Nu Sigma Nu. Home: 3 Red Fox Rd Saint Paul MN 55110 Office: Box 501 Mayo Meml Bldg 420 Delaware St SE Minneapolis MN 55455

VAN SKYOCK, RICHARD KIT, engineerinf technician; b. Muncie, Ind., Jan. 19, 1947; s. Elmer and Birdie Louise (Coon) Van S.; m. Susan Kay Friddle, Mar. 9, 1968; children: Suzan Carol, Richard Scott. Student, Purdue U., 1965-66. Engineer Dacco Remy div. Gen. Motors, Anderson, Ind., 1970—. Assoc. guardian Job's Daughters, Daleville, Ind., 1986—. Served to sgt. USAF, 1966-70. Club: Anderson Rifle and Pistol (v.p. 1985—). Lodge: Masons. Avocations: radio control models, hunting, fishing, reading, computers.

VAN SLYKE, DEBORAH PHYLLIS, business executive; b. Rockford, Ill.; d. Harold Walter and Dorothy Violet (Callahan) Johnson; m. Richard Kelley Rodgers, Sept. 3, 1964 (div. Jan. 1973); 1 child, Kristen Elizabeth; m. Alan Van Slyke, May 27, 1978; children—John David, Jason Ross. B.A., Ripon Coll., 1960; M.A., U. Wis., 1961. Asst. librarian First Nat. Bank Chgo., 1963-69; head librarian Montgomery Ward & Co., Chgo., 1971-76, Real Estate Research Corp., Chgo., 1976-77; mgr. record services and word processing Chgo., Rock Island R.R., Chgo., 1977-78; supr. reprographic services Honeywell Inc., Mpls., 1981—. Elder, Westminster Presbyn. Ch., Mpls., Minn., 1981-83; pres. New Neighbors League, Omaha and Mpls., 1980-83. Mem. Assn. Info. Image Mgrs., Assn. Record Mgrs. and Adminstrs. (2d v.p., treas. 1983-84, v.p. 1984—). Club: St. Paul Athletic. Avocations: cross-country skiing, reading, needlepoint. Home: 310 Cloverleaf Dr N Minneapolis MN 55435 Office: Honeywell Inc 6400 France Ave Minneapolis MN 55432

VAN STEE, ELLEN LINDA, pharmacist; b. Hopewell, Va., Nov. 16, 1959; d. John Thomas Sr. and Kathryn Kelly (Kesler) Barton; m. Greg Alan Van Stee; 1 child, Andrew. Student, Coll. of William and Mary, 1977-79; BS in Pharmacy, Ferris State Coll., Big Rapids, Mich., 1981. Pharmacist Butterworth Hosp., Grand Rapids, Mich., 1981-83, asst. dir. pharmacy, 1985—; pharmacy dir. Belding (Mich.) Community Hosp., 1983-85; cons. in field. Mem. Am. Soc. Hosp. Pharmacists, W. Mich. Soc. Hosp. Pharmacists. Home: 1541 Seminole SE Grand Rapids MI 49506 Office: Butterworth Hosp Pharmacy 100 Michigan NE Grand Rapids MI 49506

VAN THORRE, CANDACE MERRICK, speech pathologist; b. Austin, Minn., Feb. 1, 1951; d. Robert Leslie and Margaret Elizabeth (Daigneau) Bulger; m. Douglas Michael Van Thorre; children: Ryan Douglas, Benjamin Merrick. BS, Mankato (Minn.) State U., 1973, MA, 1975. Cert. speech pathologist, Minn. Speech/lang. pathologist Mpls. Pub. Schs., 1975—. Mem. local PTAs. Mem. Am. Speech/Hearing Assn., Minn. Speech/Hearing Assn. Congregationalist. Avocations: racquetball, swimming, sports, music. Home: 5251 Humboldt Ave S Minneapolis MN 55419 Office: Bancroft Elem Sch 1315 E 38th St Minneapolis MN 55407

VAN TIEM, DARLENE MIRIAM, corporate executive, educator; b. Detroit, Jan. 18, 1942; d. Norman O. and Miriam (Scoots) Roff; m. Phillip Michael Van Tiem, Apr. 4, 1964; children: Bradford Michael, Adrienne Miriam. BA, Albion Coll., 1963; MA, Mich. State U., 1965; MEd, Marygrove Coll., Detroit, 1974; PhD, Wayne State U., 1986. Instr. various pub. schs., Lansing, St. Clair Shores, and Grosse Pointe, Mich., 1963-75, Wayne County Community Coll., Detroit, 1975-80; asst. prof., dir learning skills ctr. Marygrove Coll., Detroit, 1978-86; sr. analyst tech. group, Gen. Physics Corp., Warren, Mich., 1986-87; assoc. mgr. tech. tng. Gen. Physics Corp., Warren, 1987—; cons. MCI Telecommunications, Southfield, Mich., 1983-85. Lector, Eucharistic Minister St. Clare of Montefalco Ch., Grosse Pointe Park, 1980—, sec. five year planning commn. Mem. Am. Soc. Tng. and Devel. (treas. 1985-86, 1st v.p. 1987—, book reviewer newsletter 1983-84), Nat. Assn. Devel. Edn. (mem. adv. bd. 1984-86, research com. 1981-86, new directions task force, 1985-86), Mich. Devel. Edn. Consortium (founder, 1st pres. 1984-86), Soc. Mnfg. Engrs. (sr. mem. 1986), Soc. Automotive Engrs., Pi Lambda Theta, Alpha Lambda Delta, Pi Beta Phi.

VAN TIEM, PHILLIP MICHAEL, hospital business administrator; b. Grosse Pointe, Mich., Oct. 4, 1935; s. August Gerard and Margaret Mary (Power) Van T.; B.A., Mich. State U., 1963; postgrad. Wayne State U., 1972-73, U. Detroit, 1974-76; M.A. in Public Adminstrn., Central Mich. U., 1978, M.A. in Health Care Adminstrn., 1983; m. Darlene Miriam Roff, Apr. 4, 1964; children—Bradford, Adrienne. With Gen. Motors Acceptance Corp., 1963-68, credit mgr., 1965-68; comml. sales rep. Goodyear Tire & Rubber Co., 1968-69; mgr. accounts receivable Lansing (Mich.) Gen. Hosp., 1969-70; mgr. patient acctg. Sinai Hosp., Detroit, 1971-72, St. John Hosp., Detroit, 1972-79, asst. controller, 1979-81, dir. patient acctg., 1982-87, mgr. tech. fin. resources, 1987—; mem. healthcare conf. com. U. Mich., 1980-88. Bd. dirs. Lansing Gen. Hosp. Credit Union, 1969-70, treas., 1970; chmn. supr. com. Sinai Hosp. Credit Union, 1971-72. Vol. social worker Family to Family Movement, 1965-71; mem. vol. program Mich. Dept. Social Services, 1965-71, Grosse Pointe Hist. Soc., 1984—; chmn. publicity Grosse Pointe Park Civic Assn.; asst. commr. Boy Scouts Am., Lakeshore dist., 1982—. Served with AUS, 1958-60. Recipient hon. mention for suggestion Mich. Hosp. Assn., 1972; Cost Containment award Hosp. Fin. Mgmt., 1978. Mem. Hosp. Fin. Mgmt. Assn. (membership com. 1975-77, social chmn. 1975-77, awards chmn. 1977-78, public relations chmn. 1978-79, dir. 1979-83, chpt. del. for coordinating council 1980-83, vice chmn. 1982-83, placement chmn. 1981-82, 84—, Follmer award 1979, Reeves award 1982), Mich. Hosp. Assn. (various coms., publicity chmn. 1983-84), Grosse Pointe Alumnae Assn. (v.p. 1980-81, pres. 1981-82). Roman Catholic. Club: Lake Shore Club of Grosse Pointe (bd. dirs. 1985-88). Lodge: Optimists (bd. dirs. Lakeshore 1985—). Home: 1310 Kensington Rd Grosse Pointe MI 48230 Office: 22101 Moross Rd Detroit MI 48236

VAN TUBBERGEN, WAYNE, controller; b. Waukegan, Ill., Apr. 17, 1952; s. Harvey John and Dorothy (Holmes) Van T.; m. Susan Gorski, Apr. 1, 1978; 1 child, Michael. BA with distinction, U. Wis.-Parkside, 1975; MBA, U. Wis., Madison, 1976. Jr. acct. Sola Basic Industries, Inc. subs. Gen. Signal, Milw., 1977; auditor Gen. Signal, Stamford, Conn., 1977; acct. Sola Basic Industries, Inc. subs. Gen. Signal, Elk Grove Village, Ill., 1977-81, mgr. fin. reporting, 1981-84, controller, 1984—. Republican. Avocations: gardening, bicycling. Office: Sola Basic Industries Inc subs Gen Signal Corp 1717 Busse Rd Elk Grove Village IL 60007

VAN VOORHIS, STEVEN CHARLES, engineering manager; b. Flint, Mich., May 16, 1942; s. Herbert N. and Dorothy P. (Boudler) Van V.; m Barbara Jean Praeger, Sept. 24, 1966; children: Jeffrey, Dawn. BCE, Mich. Tech. U., 1965, BS in Engring. Adminstrn., 1965; MS in Indsl. Adminstrn., Purdue U., 1971. Licensed engr. Wis. Facilties engr. Gen. Electric Major Appliances, Columbia, Md., 1971-74; facilties engr. Gen. Electric Med. Systems, Waukesha, Wis., 1974-80, facilities mgr., 1980—. Served to capt. USAF, 1966-70. Mem. Am. Inst. Plant Engrs. (pres. chpt. 12 1986—), Am. Soc. Indsl. Security, Am. Soc. Heating, Refrigerating and Air Conditioning Engrs. Lutheran. Avocations: church activities, golf. Home: 2320 Broken Hill Rd Waukesha WI 53188 Office: Gen Electric Med Systems PO Box 414 (W-606) Milwaukee WI 53201

VAN VORST, CHARLES BRIAN, health facility administrator; b. Harvey, Ill., June 22, 1943; s. John William and Bessie (Borg) Van V.; m. June A.; children—Krista Ann, Dirk Brian. B.S., U. Evansville, 1966; M.B.A., George Washington U., 1968. Adminstrv. resident Meth. Hosp., Indpls., 1967-68, adminstrv. asst., 1968-69, asst. adminstr., 1969-71, assoc. adminstr., 1971-72, v.p. ops., 1972-79; pres., chief exec. officer Carle Found., Urbana, Ill., 1979—, Carle Found. Hosp., Urbana, 1979—; clin. asst. prof. Coll. Medicine, U. Ill., Urbana; dir. CarleCare, Inc.; former tchr. bus. adminstrn. Ind. Central U.; past dir., treas. Alpha Home Assn.; former mem. nat. adv. com. on pub. health tng. Dept. Tng., HEW, NIH. Former bd. dirs., med. adv. com., long range planning com. United Meth. Home, Franklin, Ind.; former bd. dirs. Met. Health Council, Inc.; former chmn. fin. com. Community Addiction Services Agy.; chmn. Champaign-Urbana Areawide Emergency Med. Services Council; trustee Ill. Provider Trust; mem. allocation com., chmn. Profl. Services div. United Way campaign, 1982; mem. Urbana Polit. Action Com. WHO fellow, 1973; recipient cert. of excellence Evansville Alumni Assn., 1973. Fellow Am. Coll. Healthcare Execs.; mem. Am. Hosp. Assn., Am. Assn. for Hosp. Planning (bd. dirs.), Health Issues Study Soc. (past pres.), Ill. Hosp. Assn. (teaching hosps. council, governing bd., trustee, sec. exec. com., cost containment com.), Ill. Health Care Cost Containment Council (bd. dirs., vice chmn.), George Washington U. Alumni Assn. for Health Care (chmn. curriculum adv. com.), Urbana Downtown Promotion Assn., Urbana C. of C. (long range planning com., mem. fin. and econ. devel. coms.). Republican. Methodist. Club: Champaign Country. Lodge: Rotary. Contbr. articles to med. jours. Home: 1914 Woodfield Rd Champaign IL 61821 Office: Carle Found 611 W Park St Urbana IL 61801

VAN VORST, JUNE ALICE, financial planner; b. Decatur, Ill., June 28, 1944; s. Joseph Wiser and Helen Grace (Howsmon) Pound; m. Charles Brian Van Vorst, Apr. 5, 1986. BS, U. Ill., 1966, MEd, 1967, EdD, 1980. Cert. fin. planner. Tchr. elem. schs. Champaign, Ill., 1967-74; ednl. cons. Ill. State Bd. Edn., Springfield, 1974-81; stockbroker A. G. Edwards, Champaign, 1981-85, cert. fin. planner, 1985—; lectr. fin. planning seminars, 1986. Author fin. planning newsletter, 1986. Div. leader United Way, Champaign, 1986. Mem. Internat. Assn. Fin. Planners (pres. Illini chpt. 1986—). Club: Ill. Executive (pres. 1982-83). Home: 1914 Woodfield Rd Champaign IL 61821 Office: A G Edwards 505 S Neil Champaign IL 61820

VAN WEY, ACE W., chief of police; b. Ionia, Kans., Nov. 18, 1935; s. John Milton and Pansy Grace Bowling Van W.; m. Mary Elaine Young, Aug. 26, 1956; children: Angela K. Van Wey Davis, Pamela R. Van Wey Vines. AA in Adminstrn. of Justice, Wichita State U., 1976. Cycle officer, traffic investigator, detective Wichita Police Dept., 1957-77; dir. civil service Sedgwick County Sheriff's Dept., Wichita, 1977-83; chief of police Park City (Kans.) Police Dept., 1983—. Served with U.S. Army, 1955-57. Recipient Medal of Valor award Sedgwick County Sheriff's Dept., 1984. Democrat. Methodist. Lodges: Masons, Shriners. Avocations: fishing, camping. Home: 10401 Cora Wichita KS 67205 Office: Park City Police Dept 6125 N Hydraulic Park City KS 67219

VAN WYK, PAUL H., research psychologist; b. Fond du Lac, Wis., Dec. 27, 1938; s. Herbert S. and Julia A. (Walvoord) Van W.; m. Betty V. Vicha, June 4, 1960 (div. June 1977); children: Laura, Mark; m. Pamela J. Collins, Jan. 1, 1984. BA in English, Hope Coll., 1960; student, Roosevelt U., 1966-69; MA in Human Sexuality, Goddard Coll., 1975; PhD in Psychology, Ill. Inst. Tech., 1982. Chemist Richardson Co., Melrose Park, Ill., 1972-73; therapist Family Counseling Clinic, Grayslake, Ill., 1973-74; psychotherapist Midwest Population Ctr., Chgo., 1974-81; psychologist Van Wyk Assocs., Oak Park, Ill., 1982-85, Mo. Eastern Correctional Ctr., Pacific, 1985—; lectr. psychology Chgo. State U., 1984-85; cons. stats., Oak Park, 1982-85. Contbr. articles to profl. jours; patentee in field. Campaign worker Citizens for Brown, Forest Park, Ill., 1968, Citizens for Downs, Oak Park, 1972. Mem. ACLU, Am. Psychol. Assn., Am. Assn. Sex Educators, Counselors and Therapists, Soc. Sci. Study of Sex, Delta Phi Alpha. Unitarian-Universalist. Avocations: guitar, gardening. Home: 1109 Twinbrook Dr Rock Hill MO 63119 Office: Mo Eastern Correctional Ctr 18701 Highway 66 Pacific MO 63069

VAN ZELST, THEODORE DAVID, landscape architect; b. Evanston, Ill., Feb. 6, 1963; s. Theodore W. and Louann (Hurter) VanZ. BS, Purdue U., 1985. Pres., founder Van Zelst, Inc., Wadsworth, Ill., 1979—; bd. dirs. Minann, Inc., Glenview, Ill., Testing Scis., Inc. Mem. Am. Soc. Landscape Architects, Ill. Nurserymen's Assn., Ill. Landscape Contractors' Assn. Club: North Shore Country. Home: 1213 Wagner Rd Glenview IL 60025 Office: Van Zelst Inc 39400 N Hwy 41 Box 247 Wadsworth IL 60083

VAN ZELST, THEODORE WILLIAM, civil engineer, natural resource exploration company executive; b. Chgo., May 11, 1923; s. Theodore Walter and Wilhelmina (Oomens) Van Z.; m. Louann Hurter, Dec. 29, 1951; children: Anne, Jean, David. B.S., U. Calif., Berkeley, 1944; B.A.S., Northwestern U., 1945, M.S. in Civil Engring., 1948. Registered profl. engr., Ill. Pres., Soil Testing Services, Inc., Chgo., 1948-52; pres. Soiltest, Inc., Chgo., 1948-78; chmn. bd. Soiltest, Inc., 1978-80; sec., dir. Exploration Data Cons., Inc., 1980-82; exec. v.p. Cenco Inc., Chgo., 1962-77; vice chmn. Cenco Inc., 1975-77, also dir., 1962-77; dir. Lab. Glass, Inc., 1970-78, Wilmad Glass, Inc., 1970-78, Virtis Co., Inc., 1974-78, Calumet Coach Co., 1969-78, Barber Greene Co., 1975-86, Houghton Mfg. Co., 1967-78, Minann, Inc., 1952—, Hoskin Sci. Co. Can., 1977-79, Testing Sci., Inc., 1959—, Aparatos S.A., 1978-80; chmn., dir. Envirotech Services, Inc., 1983-85; v.p., dir. Van Zelst Inc., Wadsworth, Ill., 1983—; pres., dir. Geneva-Pacific Corp., 1969-83, Geneva Resources, Inc., 1983—. Treas. Internat. Road Fedn., 1961-64, sec., 1964-79, dir., 1973—, vice chmn., 1980—; pres. Internat. Rd. Edn. Found., 1978-80; bd. dirs. Chgo. Acad. Scis., 1983-86, v.p., 1985-86, hon. dir. 1986—; bd. dirs. Pres.'s Assn., Chgo., 1985-86; mem. adv. bd. Mitchell Indian Mus., Kendall Coll., 1977—. Served to lt. (j.g.) USNR, 1942-45. Recipient Service award Northwestern U., 1970, Merit award, 1974; Service award U. Wis., 1971; La Sallian award, 1975. Mem. ASCE, Nat. Soc. Profl. Engrs., ASTM, Western Soc. Engrs., Evanston C. of C. (v.p. 1969-73), Ovid Esbach Soc. (pres. 1968-80), Tau Beta Pi. Clubs: Economic, North Shore. Inventor engring. testing equipment for soil, rock concrete and asphalt. Home: 1213 Wagner Rd Glenview IL 60025 Office: Box 126 Glenview IL 60025

VARCO, SONDRA MARIE, social support association executive; b. Chgo., July 29, 1938; d. Vincent Daniel and Nancee Marie (Pace) Fortunato; m. Ross Donald Varco, June 4, 1960; children: Sarina, Patricia, Vincent, Phillip. BSN, Northwestern U., 1959. Asst. to dir., co-founder Vietnam Vets Arts Group, Chgo., 1981-82, exec. dir., 1982—; cons. to univs., museums, publishers, Vet groups, etc., 1981—. Mem. Womens Bd. U. Chgo., 1980—, Northwestern Meml. Hosp., Chgo., 1960—. Recipient Honor and Appreciation award VA, Chicago Heights, Ill., 1983, Chmn.'s grant Ill. Arts Council, Chgo., 1984. Home and Office: 627 S Hamlin Park Ridge IL 60068

VAREJCKA, JANET FAYE, educational administrator; b. Columbus, Nebr., June 23, 1944; d. John and Blanche (Aringdale) V. BA in Edn., Wayne State Coll., 1966; MS in History, U. Nebr.-Omaha, 1976, postgrad, 1978. Tchr. history, speech, psychology Logan Community Sch., Iowa, 1967-80; prin. Bennett County High Sch., Martin, S.D., 1980—. Mem. adv. bd. FFA-FHA, Martin, 1980—, state adv. bd. to FHA, 1983-84; mem. Nursing Home Auxilary, Martin, 1984. Mem. Nat. Assn. Secondary Sch. Prins. (com. on small secondary schs., chmn. smaller sch. com. 1987—), Sch. Adminstrs. in S.D. (mem. exec. bd. 1985—, pres. 1987—), S.D. Assn. Secondary Sch. Prins. (regional rep. 1981-84, v.p. 1984-85, pres. 1987—), Beta Iota (sec. 1983-84, pres. 1985, parlimentarian 1987—). Democrat. Methodist. Avocations: reading, guitar. Office: Bennett County High Sch Box 580 Martin SD 57551

VARELA, RICK MICHAEL, management information services executive; b. Chgo., Sept. 13, 1943. BS in Acctg., Roosevelt U., 1974. Asst. mgr. personnel div. Arthur Anderson & Co., Chgo., 1974-77; sr. auditor EDP audit dept. FMC Corp., Chgo., 1977-79; mgr. EDP audit dept. Baxter Travenol, Deerfield, Ill., 1979-83, group mgmt. info. services, 1983-85; dir. mgmt. info. services lumber div. Wickes Cos., Inc., Vernon Hills, Ill., 1985—; mem. IBM-Bus. Adv. Com. to Teach Computers to Handicapped, Chgo., 1986. Chmn. fin. com. St. Augustine Coll., Chgo., 1982-86, vice chmn. bd. trustees, 1986—. Served with U.S. Army, 1968-69, Vietnam. Named Outstanding Youth Motivation Leader, City of Chgo., 1984. Mem. Data Processing Mgmt. Assn. Office: Wickes Cos Inc Lumber Div 706 Deerpath Vernon Hills IL 60061

VARGA, ROBERTA ODELL, management consultant; b. Oklahoma City, Oct. 26, 1925; d. Ira Ellsworth and Elizabeth (Brandon) Odell; m. Stephen Ivan Varga, Oct. 20, 1956; children: Patricia Ann Butowick; child from previous marriage: Diane Lyn Sancer. PhB, Northwestern U., 1980. Mgr. Velsicol Chem. Corp., Chgo., 1959-69; mgr. Borg-Warner Corp., Chgo., 1969-84, cons., 1985—; com. mem. Borg-Warner Found., Chgo., 1970—. Contbr. articles to profl. jours. Bd. dirs. Borg-Warner Found., Chgo., 1980—. Mem. ABA, Assn. Records Mgrs. and Adminstrs., Chgo. Office Automotive Roundtable (chmn. 1986). Unitarian. Avocations: sailing, skiing. Office: Borg-Warner Corp 200 S Michigan Ave Chicago IL 60604

VARGAS, DANIEL JOSEPH, interior designer, furniture company executive; b. Topeka, July 17, 1948; s. Manuel J. and Emily T. (Terrones) V. B.F.A., U. Kans., 1973. Pres., Vargas Fine Furniture, Inc., Topeka, 1985—; designer Everywoman's Resource Ctr., Designers Showhouse, Topeka, 1985-87. Served with AUS, 1971-73. Mem. Internat. Soc. Interior Designers. Democrat. Roman Catholic. Avocations: music; racquetball; softball. Home: 6847 SW Dunstan Ct Topeka KS 66610 Office: Vargas Fine Furniture Inc 4900 S Topeka Blvd Topeka KS 66609

VARGAS, MANUEL JOHN, clinical psychologist, consultant; b. Ft. Worth, Aug. 30, 1919; s. Hermenegildo and Macedonia (Toledo) V.; m. Judith Wells, Oct. 4, 1975 (div. May 1986); children: Philip, Richard, Veronica. BA, U. Chgo., 1943, MA, 1944, PhD, 1952. Lic. psychologist, Ill., Ind. Asst. prof. psychology Auburn (Ala.) U., 1952-55; chief psychologist Beatty Meml. State Hosp., Westville, Ind., 1958-63, Adult Psychiatric Ctr., Ft. Wayne, Ind., 1963-64, Lake County Mental Health Clinic, Gary, Ind., 1964-75; psychologist Psychol. Services, Merrillville, Ind., 1975—; cons. Lake County Juvenile Ct., Gary, 1964-75, Southlake Care Ctr., Merrillville, 1982-86, Wildwood Manor, Gary, 1975—; lectr. in psychology Ind. U. Northwest, Gary, 1972-75. Office: Psychol Services 1000 E 80th Pl Merrillville IN 46410

VARGUS, BRIAN STANLEY, sociologist, educator, political consultant; b. Vallejo, Calif., Aug. 2, 1938; s. Stanley John and Edna Nettie (Rabb) V.; m. Nanci Jean Reginelli, Aug. 29, 1964; children—Jilda, Rebecca, Abigail. B.A., U. Calif.-Berkeley, 1961, M.A., 1963; Ph.D., Ind. U., 1969. Instr., Bakersfield Coll., Calif., 1964-66, Ind. U., Bloomington, 1966-69; asst. prof. U. Pitts., 1969-75; prof. sociology Ind./Purdue U., Indpls., 1975—, dir. publ. opinion labs., 1975-86; pres. Opinion Research and Eval., Indpls., 1980—; cons. Bayh, Tabbert & Capehart, Indpls., 1984, Pub. Policy Cons., Bloomington, 1984, Ind. Bell, 1986—, Baker & Daniels, Indpls., 1985, Handley & Miller, Indpls, 1986; polit. analyst Sta. WISH-TV, Indpls., 1984—; polit. analyst, participant radio and TV programs; speaker in field. Author: Reading in Sociology, 3d edit., 1984, Tools for Sociology, 1985. Pres. bd. dirs. Greater Ind. Council on Alcholism, Nat. Council on Alcoholism, Indpls., 1982-84; cons. Greater Indpls. Progress Com., 1982, Children's Mus., Indpls., 1984, Gov.'s Task Force on Drunk Driving, Ind., 1984—. Fulbright fellow, 1973, Flynn fellow, 1981; recipient Disting. Service award Greater Council Alcoholism, 1984; recipient numerous research grants. Mem. Am. Sociol. Assn., Am. Assn. Pub. Opinion, Midwest Assn. Publ. Opinion Research, North Central Sociol. Assn. Methodist. Club: Indpls. Press. Avocations: racquetball, reading, swimming. Home: 4084 Rocking Chair Rd Greenwood IN 46142 Office: Ind/Purdue U 425 Anges St Indianapolis IN 46220

VARICK, ROBERT V., chemical company executive; b. Passaic, N.J., Mar. 14, 1924; s. Valois L. and Isabelle (Kittredge) V.; m. Lois Carlson, June 3, 1946; children: Steven B., James C. BS in Chemistry, Union Coll., Schnectady, N.Y., 1948. Salesman Armour Chem., Chgo., 1948-50; with Jensen-Souders and Assocs., Itasca, Ill., 1950—, pres. Mem. Soc. Plastic Engrs., Am. Chem. Soc. (vice chmn. rubber div. 1987—), Nat. Paint and Coatings Assn., Fedn. Socs. Paint Tech., Chgo. Rubber Group. Home: 3095 Blackthorn Riverwoods IL 60015 Office: Jensen Souders and Assocs 725 N Baker Dr Itasca IL 60143

VARIS, JOHN, educational administrator, educator; b. Arahovitika Patras, Greece, Oct. 26, 1942; s. William and Dina (Loukopoulos) Varis; m. Diane Carol Maezer, June 12, 1971; children—Jason William, Justin Albert B.S., Bowling Green State U., 1965, M.A., 1970, Ph.D., 1973; postgrad. U. Cin., 1974. Cert. supt., Ohio. Tchr., Anthony Wayne Schs., Whitehall, Ohio, 1969-70; tchr. Oregon City (Ohio) Schs., 1970-72; doctoral fellow Bowling Green State U., 1972-73; prin. Norwood City (Ohio) Schs., 1973-81, asst. supt., 1981-87; supt. Reading city Sch. Dist., 1987—; adj. assoc. prof. Xavier U. Active Sch. Found. Greater Cin., 1976-80, Sherwood Civic Assn., 1979. Served to capt. USAR, 1965-68. Recipient DAR Americanism Medal, 1979; Tchrs. award, Daus. Colonial Wars, 1980; PTA Educator of Yr. award Norwood, Ohio, 1977; Oelma Outstanding Adminstrs. award. 1987; Bowling Green State U. fellow, 1972; Mem. Buckeye Assn. Sch. Adminstrs., Assn. Supervision and Curriculum Devel., Ohio Assn. Elem. Sch. Adminstrs., Alpha Sigma Phi, Alpha Phi Omega, Phi Delta Kappa. Greek Orthodox. Contbr. articles to profl. publs. Office: 2132 William Ave Norwood OH 45212

VARNER, CHARLEEN LAVERNE MCCLANAHAN (MRS. ROBERT B. VARNER), educator, adminstr., nutritionist; b. Alba, Mo., Aug. 28, 1931; d. Roy Calvin and Lela Ruhama (Smith) McClanahan; student Joplin (Mo.) Jr. Coll., 1949-51; B.S. in Edn., Kans. State Coll. Pittsburg, 1953; M.S., U. Ark., 1958; Ph.D., Tex. Woman's U. 1966; postgrad. Mich. State U., summer, 1955, U. Mo., summer 1962; m. Robert Bernard Varner, July 4, 1953. Apprentice county home agt. U. Mo., summer 1952; tchr. Ferry Pass Sch., Escambia County, Fla., 1953-54; tchr. biology, home econs. Joplin Sr. High Sch., 1954-59; instr. home econs. Kans. State Coll., Pittsburg, 1959-63; lectr. foods, nutrition Coll. Household Arts and Scis., Tex. Woman's U., 1963-64, research asst. NASA grant, 1964-66; asso. prof. home econs. Central Mo. State U., Warrensburg, 1966-70, adviser to Colhecon, 1966-70, adviser to Alpha Sigma Alpha, 1967-70, 72, mem. bd. advisers Honors Group, 1967-70; prof., head dept. home econs. Kans. State Tchrs. Coll., Emporia, 1970-73; prof., chmn. dept. home econs. Benedictine Coll., Atchison, Kans., 1973-74; prof., chmn. dept. home econs. Baker U., Baldwin City, Kans., 1974-75; owner, operator Diet-Con Dietary Cons. Enterprises, cons. dietitian, 1973—. Mem. Joplin Little Theater, 1956-60. Mem. NEA, Mo., Kans. state tchrs. assns., AAUW, Am., Mo., Kans. dietetics assns., Am., Mo., Kans. home econs. assns., Mo. Acad. Scis., AAUP, U. Ark. Alumni Assn., Alumni Assn. Kans. State Coll. of Pittsburg, Am. Vocat. Assn., Assn. Edn. Young Children, Sigma Xi, Beta Sigma Phi, Beta Beta Beta, Alpha Sigma Alpha, Delta Kappa Gamma, Kappa Kappa Iota, Phi Upsilon Omicron. Methodist (organist). Home: Main PO Box 1009 Topeka KS 66601

VARNER, NELLIE MAE, real estate investment broker; b. Lake Cormorant, Miss., 1935; d. Tommie and Essie (Davis) V.; m. Louis S. Williams (div. Feb. 1964). AA, Highland Park (Mich.) Coll., 1956; BS, Wayne State U., 1958, MA, 1959; PhD, U. Mich., 1968. Tchr. pub. schs. Detroit Bd. Edn., 1959-64; spl. asst. to dean Coll. Lit., Sci. and Arts U. Mich., Ann Arbor, 1968-70, faculty assoc. Ctr. Russian and Ea. European Studies, asst. prof. polit. sci., 1968-79, dir. affirmative action programs, 1972-75, assoc. dean Grad. Sch., 1976-79; research assoc. Russian Research Ctr., research fellow Ctr. Internat. Affairs Harvard U., Cambridge, Mass., 1970-71; assoc. sales Real Estate One, Farmington, Mich., 1971-75; v.p. Strather & Varner, Inc., Southfield, Mich., 1978—, PRIMCO, Ltd., Southfield, 1985—; chmn. Mich. Real Estate Adv. Bd., Lansing, 1979-80; bd. dirs. Community Investment Adv., Washington, Am. Inst. for Bus., Detroit, New Detroit, Inc.; del. White House Conf. on Small Bus., 1980. Bd. regents U. Mich., Ann Arbor, 1980—; mem. exec. bd. Detroit chpt. NAACP, 1984-86; bd. dirs. Highland Park YMCA, 1980-82, Hartford Credit Union; chmn. bd. dirs. Hartford Head Start Agy. Mem. Nat. Assn. Women Bus. Owners (Community Leadership award 1984), Nat. Assn. Realtors, Mich. Assn. Realtors, South Oakland County Bd. Realtors, Delta Sigma Theta (bd. dirs., investment advisor 1987—). Democratic. Baptist. Office: Strather & Varner Inc 3000 Town Ctr #2460 Southfield MI 48075

VARNER, ROBERT BERNARD, educator, counselor; b. Ellsworth, Kans., May 31, 1930; s. Bernard Lafayette and Leota (Campbell) V.; B.S., Kans. State U., Pittsburg, 1952; M.S., U. Ark., 1959; postgrad. Mich. State U., summer 1955, U. Mo., summer 1962, (grantee) U. Kans., 1972-73; m. Charleen LaVerne McClanahan, July 4, 1953. Athletic coach, social sci. tchr. Joplin (Mo.) Sr. High Sch., 1956-63; head social sci. dept. R.L. Turner High Sch., Carrollton, Tex., 1963-66; asst. athletic coach, jr. high sch. social sci. tchr. Warrensburg, Mo., 1966-70; coach, social sci. tchr., Emporia, Kans., 1970-72; asst. cottage dir., counselor Topeka Youth Ctr., 1973—; substitute tchr. Topeka Pub. Schs., 1974—. Recreation dir. Carrollton-Farmers Branch (Tex.) Recreation Center, 1964-66; city recreation dir., Warrensburg, Mo., 1966-68. Served with USN, 1953-54. Mem. NEA, Kans. State U.-Pittsburg Alumni Assn., U. Ark. Alumni Assn., Phi Delta Kappa, Sigma Tau Gamma. Democrat. Methodist. Club: Elks. Address: Main PO Box 1009 Topeka KS 66601

VARRICCHIO, FREDERICK ELIA, pathologist, biochemist; b. N.Y.C., May 18, 1938; s. Elia and Anna M. Varricchio; m. Claudette Goulet, Dec. 29, 1962; children: Nicole, Erika. BS, U. Maine, 1960; MS, U. N.D., 1964; PhD, U. Md., 1966; MD, U.A. Ciudad Juarez, 1986. Assoc. in exptl. pathology Meml. Sloan Kettering Cancer Ctr., N.Y.C., 1972-77; assoc. prof., dir. grad. studies Life Sci. Ctr., Nova U., Ft. Lauderdale, Fla., 1977-79; vis. prof. Max Planck Inst. fuer Ernaehrungsphysiologie Dortmund, W. Ger., 1979; prof., chmn. dept. chemistry Nat. Coll., Lombard, Ill., 1980-83; resident assoc. Argonne (Ill.) Nat. Lab., 1980—; faculty research participant Oak Ridge Nat. Lab., 1979—; adj. instr. chemistry Coll. of Du Page, 1980—; clin. prof. biochemistry Loyola U. Dental Sch., 1983—; resident pathology Cook County Hosp., Chgo., 1986—. Contbr. articles in field to profl. jours. Am. Cancer Soc. fellow, 1966-68, Deutscher Akademischer Austauschdienst fellow, 1979. Mem. Am. Soc. Biol. Chemists, Am. Assn. Pathologists, Am. Assn. for Cancer Research, Am. Chem. Soc., Sigma Xi, Sigma Chi (sec. N.Y.C. alumni chpt. 1977). Home: 26 W285 Blackhawk Dr Wheaton IL 60187

VASILKO, SUE ANN, accountant; b. Hammond, Ind., Mar. 11, 1961; d. James Thomas and Anna May (Byrne) Dahlkamp; m. Michael James Vasilko, Aug. 2, 1980. Assoc. Acctg., Calumet Coll., 1980; BBA, Loyola U., Chgo., 1984. CPA, Ill. Acctg. asst. Planites Credit Union, Chgo., 1982-84; cost analyst Health Care Service Corp., Chgo., 1984-86; mgr. acctg. Compass Health Care Plans, Chgo., 1986—. Mem. Am. Woman's Soc. CPA's, Ill. CPA Soc. (industry com.), Chgo. Soc. Woman CPA's (bd. dirs. 1986—). Roman Catholic. Home: 337 S Maple #25 Oak Park IL 60302 Office: Compass Health Care Plans 310 S Michigan Ave Chicago IL 60604

VAUGHAN, DAVID JOHN, distribution company executive; b. Detroit, July 17, 1924; s. David Evans and Erma Mildred V.; A.B., U. Ill., 1950; postgrad. U. Chgo., U. Mo.; m. Anne McKeown Miles, Aug. 21, 1975; children by previous marriage—David John, Melissa Ann, Julia Crawford McLaughlin. Chemist, Midland Electric Colleries, 1950-52; pres. Varrco Distbg. Co., Peoria, Ill., 1953—; prin. David J. Vaughan, investment adv., Peoria, 1970—; investment adviser Fundamentalist Fund; instr. Carl Sandburg Coll., Peoria, 1968—; advisor Leelanau Found., Leelanau Meml. Found. Served to lt. USAAF, 1942-46, USAF, 1951-52; Korea. Registered investment adv. Mem. Alpha Tau Omega, Phi Eta Sigma, Phi Alpha Delta. Republican. Presbyterian. Clubs: Peoria Country, Northport Point (Mich.); Peoria Skeet, Racquet, Naples (Fla.). Lodges: Masons, Shriners, Jesters. Home: 4510 N Miller Ave Peoria IL 61614 Home: 4617 N Prospect Rd Peoria Heights IL 61614

VAUGHAN, ROBERT DUANE, retail company executive; b. St. Paul, Mar. 30, 1953; s. Virgil C. and Helen A. (Sipple) V.; m. Cheri A. Brunkow, Oct. 9, 1976. AS in Occupational Sci., Culinary Inst. Am., 1974; chefs cert., Mankato (Minn.) Area Vocat. Tech., 1972, bakers cert., 1973. Chef Cubs Restaurant, Mankato, 1971-73, Soloman Catering, Hyde Park, N.Y., 1973-74; food mgr. trainee Robin Hood Restaurant, Duluth, Minn., 1974-76, mgr., 1977-80; kitchen steward Kahler Hotel, Rochester, Minn., 1976; dist. mgr. food Walgreens, Milw., 1980—; instr. Food Mgr.'s Sch. Walgreen Co., Deerfield, Ill., 1984—. Mem. adv. com. Waukesha (Wis.) Area Tech. Coll., 1983—, Milw. Pub. Sch. System, 1984—. Recipient Best Performance Sales and Profit award Walgreen Co., 1981, 82, 83. Mem. Culinary Alumni Assn. Home: W225N2779 Fernwood Ct Waukesha WI 53186 Office: Walgreen/ Wags Dist Office 11601 W North Ave Wauwatosa WI 53226

VAUGHN, JACKIE, III, state legislator. BA, Hillsdale (Mich.) Coll.; MA, Oberlin (Ohio) Coll.; LittB, Oxford U.; LLD (hon.), Marygrove Coll., Detroit, Shaw Coll., Detroit, U. Windsor, Can.; HHD (hon.), Highland Park (Mich.) Community Coll. Tchr. U. Detroit, Wayne State U., Detroit; mem. Mich. Ho. Reps, Lansing; mem. Mich. Senate, Lansing, asst. pres. pro tem, pres. pro tem, assoc. pres. pro tem. Past pres. Mich. Young Dems.; chmn. Mich. Dr. Martin Luther King Jr. Hiliday commn.; exec. bd. dirs. Detroit NAACP. Served with USN. Fulbright fellow; recipient Frank J. Wieting Meml. Service award, 1977, Focus and Impact award Cotillion Club, 1980, Outstanding Achievement award Booker T. Washington Bus. Assn., Outstanding Community Service award Charles Stewart Mott Community Coll. and Urban Coalition of Greater Flint, Mich., 1981; named Outstanding State Senator of Yr., Detroit Urban League Guild, 1983, Most Outstanding Legislator of Yr., Washburn-Ilene Block Club, 1983, numerous others. Mem. Am. Oxonian Assn., Fulbright Alumni Assn. Baptist. Home: 19930 Roslyn Rd Detroit MI 48221 Office: Mich Senate PO Box 30036 Lansing MI 48909

VAUGHN, NOEL WYANDT, lawyer; b. Chgo., Dec. 15, 1937; d. Owen Heaton and Harriet Christy (Smith) Wyandt; m. David Victor Koch, July 18, 1959 (div.); 1 child, John David; m. Charles George Vaughn, July 9, 1971. BA, DePauw U., 1959; MA, So. Ill. U., 1963; JD, U. Dayton, 1979. Bar: Ohio 1979, U.S. Dist. Ct. (so. dist.) Ohio 1979, U.S. Cir. Ct. (6th cir.) 1987. Communications specialist Charles F. Kettering Found., Dayton, 1968-71; tchr. English Miami Valley Sch., Dayton, 1971-76; law clk. to judge Dayton Mcpl. Ct., 1978-79; coordinator Montgomery County Fair Housing Ctr., Dayton, 1979-81, 85—; atty. Henley Vaughn Becker & Wald, Dayton, 1981—; lectr. Wright State U., Dayton, 1965-67. Chmn. Dayton Playhouse, Inc., 1981—; pres. Freedom of Choice Miami Valley, Dayton, 1980-83, 86-87; bd. dirs. ACLU, Dayton, 1982-86; com. mem. Battered Woman Project-YWCA, Dayton, 1983-84; pres. Legal Aid Soc. Dayton, 1983-84; chmn. Artemis House, Inc., 1985—; bd. dirs. Miami Valley Arts Council, 1985-86. Recipient Order of Barristers award U. Dayton, 1979. Mem. ABA, Dayton Bar Assn. (chmn. delivery legal services com. 1983-84). Home: 3700 Wales Dr Dayton OH 45405

VAYDIK, FRANK WILLIAM, real estate investor; b. Detroit, Oct. 21, 1939; s. Frank and Anne Hunter (MacDonald) V.; m. Mary Ellen Knake, Apr. 20, 1968; children: Amy Megan, Mari Beth. BA in Econs., Wayne State U., 1965. Owner Valley Mgmt. Services, Saginaw, Mich., 1972—; trustee chpt. 11 U.S. Bankruptcy Ct., Flint, Mich., 1980—. Mem. Am. Arbitration Assn. (arbitrator), Inst. Real Estate Mgmt., Real Estate Syndication Inst., Cert. Fin. Planners. Home: 7320 Shattuck Saginaw MI 48603 Office: Valley Mgmt Services 141 Harrow Ln Saginaw MI 48603

VAZQUEZ, JOHN D., photographer, writer; b. Columbus, Ohio, May 6, 1955; s. Joseph Francis and Angela (Reydel) V. BA in Photography, Ohio State U., 1978. Photographer Olan Mills, Columbus, 1979-81; copy writer Media Enterprises, Columbus, 1981-83; camera operator Sta. WOSU-TV, Columbus, 1983-84; dir. Sta. WCMH-TV, Columbus, 1984—. Author: Vortex Voyage, 1985. Democrat. Avocations: backpacking, swimming, sailing, photography.

VECCHIO, BARRY CHARLES, manufacturing company executive; b. Elgin, Ill., Sept. 10, 1941; s. Tony and Leona May (Kruse) V.; m. Sandra Jean Christenson, Apr. 4, 1964; children: Matthew A.C., Sarah C. Student, Ellis Bus. Sch., 1961. Pres., chmn. bd. dirs. Visual Media Industries, Ltd., Elgin, 1960—, Rimar Industries Corp., Elgin, 1985—, Furniture Art Studio, Elgin, 1986—; pres., bd. dirs. Vicor Corp., Elgin, 1978—; chief exec. officer, bd. dirs. Walnut Enterprises, Elgin, 1985—. Mem. adv. bd. Hemmens Civic Bldg., 1987. Republican. Episcopalian. Avocations: archaelogy, microbiology, astronomy, religion, history. Home: 226 Wing Park Blvd Elgin IL 60123 Office: Visual Media Industries Ltd 166 North St Elgin IL 60120

VECCHIO, ROBERT PETER, organizational educator; b. Chgo., June 29, 1950; s. Dominick C. and Angeline V.; m. Betty Ann Vecchio; Aug. 21, 1974; children: Julie, Mark. BS summa cum laude, DePaul U., 1972; MA, U. Ill., 1974, PhD, 1976. Instr. U. Ill., Urbana, 1973-76; mem. faculty dept. mgmt. U. Notre Dame, 1976-86, dept. chmn., 1983—, Franklin D. Schurz Prof. Mgmt., 1986—. Mem. Acad. Mgmt., Am. Psychol. Assn., Assn. Consumer Research, Inst. Mgmt. Scis., Am. Statis. Assn., Am. Inst. Decision Scis., Midwest Acad. Mgmt., Midwest Psychol. Assn., Phi Kappa Phi, Delta Epsilon Sigma, Phi Eta Sigma, Psi Chi. Home: 16856 Hampton Dr Granger IN 46530 Office: Dept Mgmt U Notre Dame Notre Dame IN 46556

VEDDER, BYRON CHARLES, newspaper executive; b. Adrian, Mich., Feb. 9, 1910; s. Adelbert and Adah (Dibble) V.; m. Kathleen Fry, June 20, 1936 (dec. 1960); children: Richard Kent, Robert Allen; m. Helen Cochrane, Dec. 16, 1976. A.B., U. Mich., 1933. Grad. mgr. student publs. U. Mich., Ann Arbor, 1933-34; with Champaign-Urbana (Ill.) Courier, 1934-64, pub., 1960-64; v.p. ops. Lindsay-Schaub Newspapers, Inc., 1964-75, v.p. planning, 1975-79; v.p. Sun Coast Media Inc., 1979—; sec. Pasco Pub. Inc., 1981—; dir. Comml. Savs. & Loan Assn., Urbana, v.p., 1975-76, Mut. Home and Savs., dir. 1983-86. Mem. Arrowhead council exec. bd. Boy Scouts Am., 1951—, pres., 1960-64; mem. Pres.'s Com. Traffic Safety, 1954-58. Recipient Silver Beaver award Boy Scouts Am., 1959; named Boss of Year Champaign-Urbana chpt. Nat. Secs. Assn., 1958; Disting. Service to Journalism award U. Minn., 1979. Mem. Inland Daily Press Assn. (dir. 1950-53, pres. 1954, chmn. 1955), Central States Circulation Mgrs. Assn. (pres. 1944-46), Ill. Daily Newspaper Markets Assn. (pres. 1962-63, chmn. 1963-64), Am. Newspaper Pub. Assn. (com. chmn.), Urbana Assn. Commerce (v.p. 1946), Campus Bus. Men's Assn. (dir.), Champaign C. of C. (dir. 1955-57), Internat. Circulation Mgrs. Assn. (hon.). Presbyterian (trustee). Club: Urbana Country, Champaign Country. Lodge: Kiwanis (pres. 1948, lt. gov. 1951, dir., Kiwanian of Year 1971). Home: 3 Stanford Pl Champaign IL 61820

VEEMAN, FRANK CHARLES, college administrator; b. Chgo., May 12, 1946; s. Frank W.E. and Mary E. (Steokle) V.; m. Diana Loy Fry, July 15, 1967; children: Dawn Marie, Todd Stacey. AA, Iowa Western Community Coll., 1966; BS, Emporia State U., Kans., 1968, MS, 1972; EdD, U. Kans., 1979. Tchr. sci. Holton (Kans.) USD, 1968-70, USD 512, Shawnee Mission, Kans., 1971-79; McConnell coordinator Butler County Community Coll., El Dorado, Kans., 1979-81, dir. adult and community edn., 1981—; cons. sci. Prentice Hall, Shawnee Mission, Kans., 1976-79. Contbr. articles to profl. jours. coach Little League basketball, Augusta, Kans., 1975-78, treas., 1976-78. Served to 2d lt. U.S. Army , 1970-76. Mem. Am. Assn. Adult and Continuing Edn., Kans. Assn. Community Colls., Kans. Dir. Community Services, Nat. Academic Advising Assn., Am. Soc. Tng. and Devel. (sunflower chpt.). Lodge: Optimists. Avocations: hunting, fishing. Office: Butler County Community Coll 901 S Haverhill Rd El Dorado KS 67042

VEEN, JAMES CORNELIUS, III, manufacturing executive; b. East Grand Rapids, Mich., Sept. 24, 1951; s. James Cornelius Jr. and Bette Jean (Haan) V.; m. R. Jayne Keck, Aug. 21, 1981; children: Andrew Jameson, Thomas Matthew. BA in Bus. Mgmt., Albion Coll., 1973. Controller Klise Mfg. Co., Grand Rapids, 1973-86, div. mgr., 1980-86; v.p., treas. Progressive Plastics, Inc., Grand Rapids, 1987—. Bd. dirs. Brook Trails Neighborhood Assn., Grand Rapids, 1986; instr. U.S. Power Squadrons, Grand Rapids, 1974—. Mem. Grand Rapids Furniture Designers Assn., US Yacht Racing Union. Republican. Episcopalian. Clubs: Little Traverse Yacht (Harbor Springs, Mich.). Home: 3272 Brook Trails Grand Rapids MI 49508 Office: Progressive Plastics Inc 605 Maryland NE Grand Rapids MI 49505

VEENHUIS, PHILIP EDWARD, psychiatrist, educator, administrator; b. Kalamazoo, Mich., Aug. 4, 1935; s. Claude Albert and Placide Mary (Steger) V.; m. Joanne Elizabeth Williams, Aug. 8, 1959; children: Mark Edward, Suzanne Marie. BA, Kalamazoo Coll., 1957; MD, U. Mich., 1961. Diplomate Am. Bd. Psychiatry. Intern James Decker Munson Hosp., Traverse City, Mich., 1961-62; resident Lafayette Clinic Wayne State U., Detroit, 1962-65; dir. psychiat. edn. Med. Coll. Wis., Milw., 1970-73, acting chmn. dept. psychiatry, 1973-75, 82-86, dir. continuing edn. dept. psychiatry, 1975-86, dir. psychiat. tng., 1984-86; chmn. dept. psychiatry Providence Hosp., Southfield, Mich., 1986—. Contbr. articles to profl. jours. Served to lt. comdr. USNR, 1965-67. NIMH grantee, 1982-86. Fellow Am. Psychiat. Assn.; mem. AMA, AAAS, Mich. Psychiat. Soc., N.Y. Acad. Sci., Wis. Psychiat. Assn., Wis. Psychoanalytic Assn., Am. Assn. Sex Educators, Counselors, Therapists, N.Y. Acad. Sci. Office: Providence Hospital 16001 W Nine Mile Rd Detroit MI 48037

VEENSTRA, H. ROBERT, cons. engr.; b. Leighton, Iowa, Oct. 21, 1921; s. Henry and Gretta (Vandehaar) V.; B.S. in Civil Engring., Iowa State U., 1947; m. Norena D. Grandia, Sept. 9, 1944; children—Henry Robert, Cynthia L., John N., Mark A. Design engr. Stanley Engring. Co., Muscatine, Iowa, 1947-49, sect. head, 1949-51, project engr., 1951-57, supervising engr., 1957-61; ptnr. Veenstra & Kimm, Engrs. & Planners, West Des Moines, 1961-80; chmn. bd. Veenstra & Kimm, Inc., Engrs. & Planners, West Des Moines, 1980—. Served to capt. AUS, 1942-46. Fellow ASCE, Am. Council Cons. Engrs.; mem. Nat. Soc. Profl. Engrs. (past nat. dir.), Iowa Engring. Soc. (Anson Marston award 1962, Disting. Service award 1984-85), Am. Congress on Surveying and Mapping, Cons. Engrs. Council Iowa (past pres.), ASTM, Am. Water Works Assn., Water Pollution Control Fedn., Theta Xi. United Methodist. Club: Masons. Contbr. articles to profl. jours. Office: 300 West Bank Bldg 1601 22nd St West Des Moines IA 50265

VEGA, FRANCISCO MIGUEL, cemetery consultant; b. San Antonio, Tex., Feb. 28, 1922; s. Lazaro Nava and Sara Lopez (Tapia) V.; m. Phyllis Jean Lackland, May 10, 1946; children: Susan Louise, Margaret Katherine, Elizabeth Ann. Student, La. State U., 1943, Okla. A&M U., 1943, Bradley U., 1943-44, U. Mich., 1948; BA, Aquinas Coll., 1950. Clk. typist VA Regional Office, San Antonio, 1946; salesman Resurrection Cemetery, Grand Rapids, Mich., 1950-51, gen. sales mgr., 1953-55; sr. ptnr. Ninfa and Co., San Antonio, 1951-52; gen. sales mgr. Olivet Cemetry, Kansas City, Mo., 1952-53; pvt. practice cemetery consulting Grand Rapids, 1954—; pres., treas. Sunset Meml. Gardens, Inc., Ionia Mich., 1956-70; owner, pres. Kent Meml. Garden-Shrines, Inc., Grand Rapids, 1971—; pres. FaBCo., Inc., Grand Rapids, 1977—, Vega Industries Corp., 1981—. Pres. Mich. Hispanic Devel. Corp., 1973-74; active numerous civic orgns. Served with Signal Corps USAF, 1942-45. Decorated EAME Campaign medal with 5 bronze stars; recipient Spl. Tribute for Leadership and service Stat of Mich., 1977. Republican. Roman Catholic. Club: Am. GI Forum. Home: 1317 Giddings Ave SE Grand Rapids MI 49506 Office: 7101 Clyde Park Ave SW Grand Rapids MI 49509

VEGTER, ALBERT JAN, architect; b. Holland, Mich., Apr. 2, 1943; s. Alvin James and Margaret Marian (Laman) V.; m. Dorothy Jean Feenstra, Sept. 2, 1966; children: Christopher, Suzanne, Katrina. BArch, U. Mich., 1966, MBA, 1967. Registered architect, Mich., Ariz. Project mgr. Smith, Hinchman & Grylis, Detroit, 1968-73; v.p. Daniels and Zermack Assocs., Inc., Ann Arbor, Mich., 1973—; pres. Albert J. Vegter, P.C., Ann Arbor, 1985—; prin. State Valley Assocs., Ann Arbor, 1985—. Booth Traveling fellow, 1973. Mem. AIA (treas. Huron Valley chpt. 1975, sec. Huron Valley chpt. 1976-77, v.p. Huron Valley chpt. 1982, pres. Huron Valley chpt. 1983), Mich. Soc. Architects, Tau Sigma Delta. Mem. Christian Reformed Ch. Home: 2581 Esch Ann Arbor MI 48104 Office: Daniels and Zermack Assocs Inc 2080 S State St Ann Arbor MI 48104

VELAER, CHARLES ALFRED, ret. educator; b. Kansas City, Mo., Jan. 25, 1932; s. Charles Alfred and Edna (Bothwell) V.; B.S., Roosevelt U., 1957; M.S., Ill. Inst. Tech., 1960; m. Caryl Ruth Sonnenburg, Nov. 17, 1962; children—Ruth Anne, Charles Alfred. Instr., asst. prof. Roosevelt U., Chgo., 1957-68, asso. prof. physics, 1968-74, ret., 1974; cons. New Horizons Pub., Inc., Chgo. Served with Signal Corps, AUS, 1950-54. Mem. Am. (cons. rosarian 1971—), English, Chgo. Regional (dist. pres. 1966-67, dir. 1968—) rose socs., Am. Inst. Physics. Home: 9636 S Brandt Ave Oak Lawn IL 60453

VELARDO, JOSEPH THOMAS, molecular biology and endocrinology educator, scientist; b. Newark, Jan. 27, 1923; s. Michael Arthur and Antoinette (Iacullo) V.; m. Forresta M. Monica Power, Aug. 12, 1948 (dec. July 1976). A.B., No. Colo. U., 1948; S.M., Miami U., 1949; Ph.D., Harvard U., 1952. Research fellow in biology and endocrinology Harvard U., Cambridge, Mass., 1952-53, research assoc. in pathology, ob-gyn and surgery sch. medicine, 1953-54; asst. in surgery Peter Bent Brigham Hosp., Boston, 1954-55; asst. prof. anatomy and endocrinology sch. medicine Yale U., New Haven, 1955-61; prof. anatomy, chmn. dept. N.Y. Med. Coll., N.Y.C., 1961-62; cons. N.Y. Fertility Inst., 1961-62; dir. Inst. for Study Human Reprodn., Cleve., 1962-67; prof. biology John Carroll U., Cleve., 1962-67; mem. research and edn. divs. St. Ann Obstetric and Gynecologic Hosp., Cleve., 1962-67; head dept. research St. Ann Hosp., Cleve., 1964-67; prof. anatomy Stritch Sch. Medicine Loyola U., Chgo., 1967—, chmn. dept. anatomy, 1967-73; cons. Internat. Basic and Biol.-Biomed. Curricula, Lombard, Ill., 1979—. Author: (with others) Histochemistry of Enzymes in the Female Genital System, 1963, The Ovary, 1963, The Ureter, 1967, rev. edit., 1981; editor, contbr. Endocrinology of Reproduction, 1958, Essentials of Human Reproduction, 1958; cons. editor, co-author: The Uterus, 1959, Hormonal Steroids, Biochemistry, Pharmacology and Therapeutics, 1964; co-editor, contbr.: Biology of Reproduction, Basic and Clinical Studies, 1973; contbr. articles to profl. jours. Served with USAAF, 1943-45. Decorated Bronze star with 2 oak leaf clusters; recipient award Lederle Med. Fac. Awards Com., 1955-58; named hon. citizen of Sao Paulo Brazil, 1972. Fellow AAAS, N.Y. Acad. Scis., Gerontol. Soc., Pacific Coast Fertility Soc. (hon.); mem. Am. Assn. Anatomists, Am. Soc. Zoologists, Am. Physiol. Soc., Endocrine Soc., Soc. Endocrinology (Gt. Britain), Soc. Exptl. Biology and Medicine, Am. Soc. Study Sterility (Rubin award 1954), Internat. Fertility Assn., Pan Am. Assn. Anatomy, Midwestern Soc. Anatomists (pres. 1973-74), Mexican Soc. Anatomy (hon.), Sigma Xi, Kappa Delta Pi, Phi Sigma, Gamma Alpha, Alpha Epsilon Delta. Club: Harvard (Chgo.). Home: SW Corner Wilson & Cherry Ln Old Grove E Lombard IL 60148 Office: 607 E Wilson Rd Lombard IL 60148-4062

VELASQUEZ, KRISTIN RAE, personnel executive; b. Hinsdale, Ill., Apr. 8, 1955; d. Edwin F. Gottschalk and Lucy T. (Tjeerdema) Dvorak, m. Rick Velasquez, Sept. 6, 1981. BS, Coll. St. Francis, Joliet, Ill., 1973-76; postgrad, Nat. Coll. Edn. Conselor Northwest Youth Outreach, Chgo., 1976-78; teller Gt. Am. Fed., Oak Park, Ill., 1978; tng. coordinator Citicorp Savs. and Telegraph Savs., Chgo., 1978-80; dir. career devel. and tng. Cragin Fed. Savs., Chgo., 1980—, also asst. sec., 1986—; pres., founder Chgo.-Area Fin. Tng. Network, Chgo., 1983-86. Mem. Am. Soc. Tng. and Devel., Ill. Tng. and Devel. Assn., Inst. Fin. Edn. (dir. mktg., chmn. bd. Chgo. chpt. 1985—). Office: Cragin Fed Savs 5200 W Fullerton Ave Chicago IL 60639

VELDT, JOEL GERBEN, college budget director; b. Ganado, Ariz., Jan. 30, 1958; s. Gerben and Beverly Jean (Sager) V.; m. Tonya Joy Anderson, June 21, 1980; children: JoEllen, James, Mordecai. BA, Cedarville Coll., 1982. CPA, Ohio. Jr. acct. J. Marion Hoffman, CPA, Dayton, Ohio, 1981-83, sr. acct., 1983-87; budget dir. Cedarville (Ohio) Coll., 1987—. fin. sec. Shawnee Hills Bapt. Ch., Jamestown, Ohio, 1982-84, treas., deacon, 1984-86. Mem. Am. Inst. CPA's, Ohio Soc. CPA's. Avocations: philately, children's lit. Home: 261 Walnut St PO Box 372 Cedarville OH 45314 Office: Cedarville Coll PO Box 601 Cedarville OH 45314

VENARD, DAVID, banker, consultant, educator; b. Hinsdale, Ill., Nov. 27, 1955; m. Diane L. Levy, Aug. 5, 1979. B.S. in Acctg. summa cum laude, Bradley U., 1977. C.P.A., Ill. Supr. Ernst & Whinney, Chgo., 1977-84; sr. v.p. and chief fin. officer Parkway Bank & Trust Co. and First State Bank Chgo., Harwood Heights, Ill., 1984-86; v.p. fin. 1st State Corp., Harwood Heights, Ill., 1986—. pres. Dane Assocs., Inc., Buffalo Grove, Ill., 1982—, Horizon Systems, 1983—; dir., treas. The Perfect Nut Co., Chgo. Editor, author course manual Bank Operations, Accounting and Auditing, and Bank Profitability, 1983-85. Bd. dirs., treas. Horwitz-Slavin Meml. Cancer Research Found., Northbrook, Ill., 1978-84. Mem. Am. Inst. C.P.A.s (tech. adv. 1984-86), Ill. C.P.A. Soc. (instr. 1982-85, specialized com. banking 1981—), Chgo. Fin. Microcomputer Users Group (dir. 1985-86), Delta Upsilon Internatl. (bd. dirs., asst. treas. 1983-85, treas. 85-86), Bradley Delta Upsilon (bd. dirs., pres. 1977-84, treas. 1984—). Republican. Jewish. Club: River (Chgo.). Office: Parkway Bank & Trust Co 4800 N Harlem Ave Harwood Heights IL 60656

VENDER, CARL STANLEY, mining and civil engineer; b. Great Falls, Mont., Jan. 26, 1948; s. Fred and Zelma (Cunnington) V.; m. Mildred Ann Wickstrom, May 26, 1970; children—Charles, Bradley, Michael. A.A. No. Mont. Coll., 1969. Registered profl. surveyor, Mont., N.D. Rodman Mont. Hwy. Dept., Helena, 1969-70; engr. Knife River Coal, Bismarck, N.D., 1971—. Mem. N.D. Soc. Profl. Surveyors (state officer 1979-84), Nat. Soc. Profl. Surveyors (chmn. com. 1983—), N.D. Soc. Profl. Surveyors (newsletter editor 1979—), Am. Congress Surveying and Mapping (chmn. com. 1983—), Soc. Mining Engrs., Mont. Assn. Profl. Surveyors. Club: Toastmasters Internat. Office: Knife River Coal 1915 N Kavaney Dr Bismarck ND 58501

VENEMA, WILLIAM JOHN, pediatrician; b. Grand Rapids, Mich., Feb. 24, 1937; s. Charles J. and Amy Ruth (Van Peenan) V.; m. Carol Ann Duerr, Aug. 19, 1961; children—Charles William, Amy Margaret. B.A., Kalamazoo Coll., 1959; M.D., U. Mich., 1963. Diplomate Am. Bd. Pediatrics. Pediatric intern U. Mich., Ann Arbor, 1963-64, redisent in pediatrics, 1964-66; mem. faculty So. Mich. Area Health Edn. Corp., Kalamazoo, 1968—; pvt. practice medicine specializing in pediatrics, Kalamazoo, 1968—; chief pediatric sect. Bronson Methodist Hosp., Kalamazoo, 1979-81; vol. missionary M.L. Lyles Hosp., Madanapalle, India, 1984. Bd. dirs. Constance Brown Hearing and Speech Ctr., Kalamazoo, 1968-72, Family and Children's Service, Kalamazoo, 1969-74; pres. Kalamazoo chpt. Physicians for Social Responsibility, 1986. Served to capt. USAF, 1966-68. Mem. Am. Acad. Pediatrics, West Mich. Pediatric Soc. (pres. 1976-77), Kalamazoo Acad. Medicine (chmn. legis. com. 1982-83), Mich. State Med. Soc. (legis. com. 1981—). Democrat. Contbr. articles to profl. publs. Home: 2125 Sheffield Dr Kalamazoo MI 49008 Office: 517 Pleasant Ave Kalamazoo MI 49008

VENINGA, ROBERT LOUIS, public health educator; b. Milw., Dec. 10, 1941; s. Frank and Otila (Mauch) V.; m. Karen Smit, Dec. 27, 1967; 1 child, Brent Karl. BA, U. Minn., 1963, MA, 1969, PhD, 1972; B Div., N.Am. Bapt. Sem., 1966. Asst. dean Sch. Pub. Health U. Minn., Mpls., 1972-76, assoc. dean, 1976-80, assoc. prof., 1976-85, prof., 1985—. Author: (book) The Human Side of Health Administration, 1982, A Gift of Hope: How We Survive, 1985, The Work, Stress Connection: How To Cope With Job Burnout, 1981; contbr. articles to profl. jours. Recipient Edgar C. Hayhow award Am. Coll. Hosp. Adminstr., 1980. Office: U Minn Sch Pub Health 420 Delaware St SE Box 197 Minneapolis MN 55455

VENIT, STEVEN LOUIS, lawyer; b. Chgo., Jan. 22, 1958; s. William Bennett and Nancy Jean (Carlson) V. BA, Valparaiso U., 1980; JD, John Marshall Coll. Law, 1983. Bar: Ill. 1983. Ptnr. Quam & Venit, Chgo., 1984—; pub. defender County of Cook, Chgo., 1984—. Mem. Regular Dems., Chgo., 1980. Mem. ABA, Ill. Bar Assn., Chgo. Bar Assn., Assn. Trial Lawyers Am., Phi Delta Theta. Jewish. Home: 4850 N Monticello Chicago IL 60625 Office: Quam & Venit 4654 W Lawrence Chicago IL 60630

VENIT, WILLIAM BENNETT, electrical products company executive, consultant; b. Chgo., May 28, 1931; s. George Bernard and Ida (Schaffel) V.; m. Nancy Jean Carlson, Jan. 28, 1956; children: Steven Louis, Aprilann. Student U. Ill., Champaign, 1949. Sales mgr. Coronet, Inc., Chgo., 1952-63, pres., chmn. bd. dirs., 1963-74; pres., chmn. bd. dirs. Roma Wire Inc., Chgo., 1971-74; pres. bd. dirs. Swing Time, Inc., Chgo., 1985—, chmn. bd. dirs., 1986—; pres. Wm. Allen Inc., Chgo., 1972-74; pres., chmn. bd. dirs. William Lamp Co., Inc., William Wire Co., Inc., 1974-76; pres., chmn. bd. dirs. MSWV, Inc., 1981—, pres. bd. dirs. 1985—; pres. Trio Steel Inc., Chgo.; spl. cons. MacKinney Co.; cons. Nu Style Lamp Shade, Seth Thomas, Athens, Ga. Served with Q.M.C., AUS, 1949-52. Mem. Mfr. Agt. Club, Chgo. Lamp and Shade Inst. (bd. dirs.). Home: 4850 N Monticello Ave Chicago IL 60625 Office: 5512 W Lawrence Ave Chicago IL 60630 also: 323 Suwanee Ave Sarasota FL 33508

VENO, GLEN COREY, management consultant; b. Montreal, Que., Can., Sept. 5, 1951; came to U.S., 1953; s. Corey Elroy and Elsie Milly (Munro) V. BS in Aviation Tech. and Mgmt., Western Mich. U., 1986. Cert. mgmt. cons. Project mgr. The ASIST Corp., Oak Park, Mich., 1978-83; mgr. tech. support J.B. Systems, Inc., Woodland Hills, Calif., 1984-85; mgr. cons. services Mgmt. Tech., Inc., Troy, Mich., 1985—. Served with U.S. Army, 1969-72, Vietnam. Recipient Cert. Appreciation U. Wis.-Extension Dept. Engring. and Applied Sci., 1984. Mem. Inst. Mgmt. Cons., Soc. Mfg. Engrs. (sr.), Am. Prodn. and Inventory Control Soc., Inst. Indsl. Engrs., Am. Mgmt. Assn., VFW (life). Avocations: flying, boating, golfing, house design, scuba diving. Home: 6345 Oakella Dr Brighton MI 48116 Office: Mgmt Techs Inc 3221 W Big Beaver Rd Suite 103 Troy MI 48084

VENTO, BRUCE FRANK, congressman; b. St. Paul, Oct. 7, 1940; s. Frank A. and Ann V. (Sauer) V.; m. Mary Jean Moore; children—Michael, Peter, John. A.A., U. Minn., 1961; B.A., Wis. State U., River Falls, 1965. Tchr. sci., social studies Mpls. Pub. Schs.; mem. Minn. Ho. of Reps., 1971-76; asst. majority leader, chmn. jud. com., chmn. interior subcom. on nat. parks and pub. lands; mem. 95th-100th Congress from 4th Minn. Dist. Mem. legis. rev. com. Minn. Commn. on Future Del.; Democratic Farm Labor party Central Com., 1972; chmn. Ramsey County Com., 1972. NSF grantee, 1967-68. Mem. Minn. Fedn. Tchrs., Beta Beta Beta, Kappa Delta Phi. Office: 2304 Rayburn House Office Bldg Washington DC 20515

VERCLER, BETTY JO, accountant; b. Pontiac, Ill., Feb. 9, 1959; d. John Edwin and Josephine (Kinsinger) V. BS in Acctg., U. Ill., 1981. CPA, Ill., Mo. Mem. audit staff Laventhol & Horwath, Carbondale, Ill., 1981-84; audit sr. Laventhol & Horwath, St. Louis, 1984-86, audit supr., 1986—. Mem. Am. Inst. CPA's, Ill. Soc. CPA's, Mo. Soc. CPA's, Nat. Assn. Accts., Hosp. Fin. Mgmt. Assn. Republican. Methodist. Office: Laventhol & Horwath 10 S Broadway Saint Louis MO 63102

VERDIER, QUENTIN ROOSEVELT, personnel consultant; b. Mancelona, Mich., Mar. 19, 1921; s. John Walter and Louise (Hills) V.; m. Margaret Elizabeth Wells, Nov. 13, 1943; children: Margaret Louise, Quentin Wells, Nanette Marie Bloom. AB in Pub. Adminstrn., Kalamazoo Coll., 1943, MA in Pub. Adminstrn., 1947; postgrad., Am. U., 1948-51; PhD in Human Resource Devel., Columbia Pacific U., 1985. Cert. employment cons., personnel cons., forensic vocat. expert; lic. employment agt., Wis. Asst. personnel officer U.S. Savs. Bonds div. U.S. Treasury Dept., Washington, 1951-58; div. chief office of personnel Internat. Coop. Adminstrn./Agy. for Internat. Devel., Washington State Dept., 1959-63; dep. chief pub. adminstrn. div. U.S. Ops. Mission/Agy. for Internat. Devel., Saigon, South Vietnam, 1963-65; asst. dir. tng. Inst. Govt. Affairs U. Wis. Extension, Madison, 1966-67; pres., chief ops. officer AvailAbility of Madison, Inc., 1967—, also chmn. bd. dirs.; mem. adv. panel Nat. Forensic Ctr., Princeton, 1983—. Author City Employee Handbook-Better Pub. Service, 1947; editor hist. pamphlet series Understanding Backgrounds, 1964; contbr. articles to profl. jours. Bd. dirs. Capital Community Citizen's Assn., Madison, 1967; pres. Country Heights Homeowners Assn., Oregon, 1969. Served with U.S. Air Corps, 1943-46. Recipient Wm G. Howard prize, 1946; Upjohn fellow Kalamazoo

Coll., 1946-47. Mem. Nat. Assn. Personnel Cons., Am. Soc. Personnel Adminstrn., Wis. Assn. Personnel Cons., Am. Arbitration Assn. (arbitrator, mem. panel Chgo. regional office), U.S.A. Tug-of-War Assn. (sec., parliamentarian 1978), Am. Assn. Ret. Persons. Club: Toastmasters (dist. 36 gov.). Lodge: Masons (32 degree), Rotary. Avocations: choral singing, genealogy.

VEREBELYI, ERNEST RAYMOND, manufacturing company executive; b. Northampton, Pa., Nov. 17, 1947; s. Julius Ernest and Hermina Carolyn (Simon) V.; m. Linda Ann Million, Dec. 19, 1970; children: Michael, David, Jenny. BS in Engring., U. Mo., Rolla, 1969; grad. gen. electric mfg. mgmt. program, U. Louisville, 1972. Registered profl. engr., Mo. Various managerial positions Gen. Electric, Louisville (Ky.) and Columbia (Md.), 1969-83; v.p. mfg. Goodman Mfg., Houston, 1983-84; dir. strategic planning Hussmann Corp., St. Louis, 1984-85, group v.p. mfg., 1985—; VIP chmn. Gen. Electric, Columbia, 1975-76; also jr. achievement advisor. Tutor Dyslexic Children De Paul Sch., Louisville, 1980; coach Holy Trinity Basketball, Louisville, 1982, Ascension Baseball, St. Louis, 1986. Mem. Am. Ceramic Soc., Keramos (treas. 1968-69), Sigma Nu. Republican. Roman Catholic. Lodge: KC. Avocations: golf, tennis, guitar, bridge. Home: 15875 Lymington Common Chesterfield MO 63017 Office: Hussmann Corp 12999 Saint Charles Rock Rd Bridgeton MO 63044

VERGERONT, THOMAS ALLAN, food company executive; b. Rice Lake, Wis., Feb. 7, 1955; s. Robert J. and Elve (Virwink) V.; m. Jean Ellen Zastrow, June 7, 1980. BS, U. Wis., 1977, MS, 1978; MB, Marquette U., 1983. Plant supt. Universal Foods, Milw., 1978-83, mgr. prodn. planning, 1983-85; dir. sales and mktg. Blue Moon Cheese, Thorp, Wis., 1985-87; sales mgr. Tolibia Cheese, Fond du Lac, Wis., 1987—. Mem. Inst. of Food Technologists, Alpha Zeta, Beta Gamma Sigma. Avocations: fishing, camping, reading, swimming. Home: Rte 4 Box 270M Chippewa Falls WI 54729 Office: Tolibia Cheese PO Box 1418 Eau Claire WI 54702

VERMEULEN, GERALD DONALD, pathologist; b. Geneseo, Ill., Oct. 3, 1939; s. Lawrence Felix and Esther Margaret (Cummings) V.; student U. Ill., Champaign, 1957-60; M.D., U. Ill., Chgo., 1964. Intern, San Francisco Gen. Hosp., 1964-65; resident in gen. surgery U. Calif., San Francisco, 1965-66; resident in pathology U. Ill. Hosp., Chgo., 1973-77, asst. prof. pathology, 1977-78; dir. labs. Silver Cross Hosp., Joliet, Ill., 1979—. Served with USPHS, 1966-73. Fellow Am. Soc. Clin. Pathologists, Coll. Am. Pathology; mem. Am. Soc. Microbiology, AMA, Ill. State Med. Soc. Contbr. articles to profl. jours. Office: Silver Cross Hospital 1200 Maple Rd Joliet IL 60432

VERMILION, NEWTON LELAND, dentist; b. Newark, Ohio, Apr. 19, 1930; s. Newton Dillon and Julia May (Varner) V.; m. Shirley Rhea Dangerfield, Sept. 30, 1961; children: Cara Lynn, Emilee Rhea. BA, Ohio State U., 1952, DDS, 1955. Gen. practice dentistry Newark, 1959-62, Columbus, Ohio, 1962—. Served to lt. comdr. USN, 1955-59. Mem. ADA, Ohio Dental Soc., Cen. Ohio Acad. Dental Practice Adminstrns. (pres. 1980-82), Columbus Dental Soc. (pres. 1977-78), Omicron Kappa Upsilon. Republican. Avocations: golf, fishing, photography. Home: 3593 Hythe Ct Columbus OH 43220 Office: 3360 Tremont Rd Columbus OH 43221

VERMILLION, CHARLES ALLEN, accountant; b. Urbana, Ill., July 25, 1961; s. Joe Bernard and Mary Grace (Hughes) V.; m. Laurie Marie Ferrere, June 23, 1984. BS in Acctg., U. Ill., 1984. CPA, Mo. Sr. cons. Ernst & Whinney, St. Louis, 1984—. Mem. Am. Inst. CPA's, Mo. Soc. CPA's, Samll Bus. Assn. Republican. Home: 2216 St Clair Brentwood MO 63144 Office: Ernst & Whinney Gateway 1 701 N Market Saint Louis MO 63101

VERNASCO, CAROL JEAN, accountant; b. Ft. Wayne, Ind., June 30, 1957; d. Joseph P. and Barbara J. (Zimmerman). BS in Acctg., Ind. U., 1980. CPA, Ind. Mgr. Prall and Co., Bloomington, Ind., 1979-86; pvt. practice acctg. Bloomington, 1986—; pres. Customized Data Processing, Bloomington, 1982—. Rep. city council candidate, Bloomington, 1987. Mem. Am. Inst. CPA's, Ind. CPA Soc., Bloomington C. of C. Roman Catholic. Club: Hoosier Amatuer Athletic Corp. Avocations: golfing, swimming, gardening, snow and water skiing, running. Home: 210 N Washington #3 Bloomington IN 47401 Office: 302 Fountain Square Bloomington IN 47401

VERNELL, ROSE MARIE, school system administrator; b. Asbury Park, N.J., Aug. 11, 1941; d. Frank D. and Marietta Elizabeth (Butler) Booker; m. Jacob A. Vernell, Dec. 23, 1972 (dec. Sept. 1986); children: Jacob Alan III, Melissa Marie. AA, Mt. Providence Jr. Coll., Balt., 1962; BS in Edn., Notre Dame of Md., 1964; student in urban curriculum, Coll. of St. Catherine, 1970-73; student in non-pub. adminstrn., Coll. of St. Thomas, 1981—. Tchr. elem. sch. Our Lady of Consolation, Charlotte, N.C., 1961-63, St. Nicholas Sch., Buffalo, 1963-64; tchr. jr. high sch. Our Lady of Victory, Detroit, 1964-67, St. Peter Claver, St. Paul, 1967-71; prin., adminstr. Urban Cath. Community, St. Paul, 1971-81; exec. dir. Greater Lake County Food Bank, Mpls., 1982-85; edn. and employment specialist Cath. Charities of Archdioces of St. Paul and Mpls., 1986—; mem. founder's circle Cambridge Plan Internat., Monterey, Calif., 1981-84; founder, chief exec. officer Inmate Resources, Inc., St. Paul, Minn., 1986. Mem. Minority Econ. Devel. Assn., St. Paul; chmn. Cath. Charities Support Network for Females in Crisis, Mpls.; mem. exec. com. INFO/Nat. Assn. for Human Devel., Washington. Recipient Citation of Honor, Hennepin County Bd. Commrs., Mpls., 1984. Republican. Avocations: poetry, theater, music. Home: 185 Valleyside Dr Saint Paul MN 55119 Office: Cath Charities of the Archdiocese of St Paul and Mpls 404 S 8th St Minneapolis MN 55402

VERNI, ERNEST A., JR., electronics executive; b. Utica, N.Y., Aug. 31, 1949; s. Ernest A. Sr. and MaryAnn (Scambelluri) V.; m. Mary K. Halfmann, Jan. 6, 1971(div. Apr. 1982); children: Michael Paul, Matthew Frederick; m. Debra Ann Underhill, Oct. 6, 1984. Student, Long Island U.; BS in Physics, BSEE, Utica (N.Y.) Coll. of Syracuse U.; MBA, U. N.H. Pres., chief exec. officer Interplex Techs. Corp., N.Y.C., 1985-86; dir. interconnection systems Litton Industries, Watertown, Conn., 1986—. Patentee modular electrical connector. Mem. Southbury, Conn. Jaycees. Lodge: KC.

VERNON, ARTHUR E., pharmacist; b. Ashland, Ohio, Sept. 21, 1944; m. Susan Elberty, 1967; children: Elizabeth Anne, Andrew Elberty. BS in Pharmacy, Ohio No. U., 1967, postgrad., 1967-84. Registered pharmacist, Ohio. Co-owner Reynolds Drugs, Orrville, Ohio, 1967—. Com. mem. Trinity United Meth. Ch., 1967-84; active Orrville United Way, 1970-84; pres. Orrville Hist. Mus., 1974-85; bd. dirs. Orrville C. of C., 1970—, Orrville YMCA; active Orrville Revitalization Campaign; mem. Orrville Shade Tree Commn. Mem. Am. Pharm. Assn., Ohio State Pharm. Assn., Wayne Pharm. Assn. (pres.), Nat. Woodcarvers Club. Lodge: Internat. Orgn. Odd Fellows. Avocations: conservation, reforestation for wildlife, ecology, art, carving. Home: 1185 N Crownhill Rd Orrville OH 44667 Office: 120 N Main St Orrville OH 44667

VERNON, CHRISTOPHER MURRAY, advertising agency executive; b. Chgo., May 20, 1945; s. David T. and Ruth (Bond) V.; m. Melinda Jane Risius, June 18, 1966; children: Jennifer J., Daniel M. AB in History, Lawrence U., 1967; postgrad. in history, U. Wis., 1968-70. Tchr., coach Dowagiac (Mich.) Union High Sch., 1967-68, Grafton (Wis.) High Sch., 1968-70; advt. coordinator Walker Mfg. Co., Racine, Wis., 1970-73; acct. exec. Franklin, Mautner Advt., Milw., 1973-77; from v.p. to pres. Andrews Mautner, Inc., Milw., 1977—, also bd. dirs.; bd. dirs. Uniplan, Inc., Milw., 1985—. Active Boy Scouts Am., Milw., 1980—. Mem. Bus. Profl. Advt. Assn. (bd. dirs. 1983-85), Milw. Assn. Advt. Agys. (bd. dirs.), Lawrence U. Alumni Assn. (bd. dirs. 1982—). Unitarian. Club: Milw. Athletic. Avocations: book collecting, reading, fly fishing, antiques, travel. Home: 4065 N Prospect Ave Shorewood WI 53211 Office: Andrews Mautner Inc 324 E Wisconsin Ave Milwaukee WI 53211

VERNON, HENRY BERNARD, investment and development company executive; b. Belize City, Belize, Oct. 21, 1947; came to U.S., 1969; s. Henry Bouxclax and Thelma Cathrine (Hesuner) V. BA, St. John's Coll., Belize, 1968. Cert. wastewater treatment plant operator. Corr. credit reporter Dunn and Bradstreet, Indpls., 1973-78; cons. engr. Dearborn Chem., Indpls., 1978-84; pres., chief exec. officer Xanadu Investment & Devel. Inc., Indpls., 1984—. Scout master Boy Scouts Am., Indpls., 1982—. Served to sgt. U.S. Army, 1970-72. Fellow Mapelton Fallcreek Assn.; mem. Internat. Assn. Bus. and Fin. Cons. (cert.1985). Democrat. Baptist. Lodges: Optimist, Meridian (steward Indpls. chpt. 1984—). Avocations: Boy Scouts, reading, basketball. Office: Xanadu Investment & Devel Inc 3969 Meadows Dr Suite 204 Indianapolis IN 46205

VERONA, DAVID ALAN, lawyer, health services administrator; b. Hartford City, Ind., Aug. 24, 1954; s. Gus Osborne and Jean Louise (Meek) V.; m. Mary R. Thomsen, Nov. 26, 1977. BS, Ball State U., 1976; MBA, George Washington U., 1980; JD, Ill. Inst. Tech., 1985. Bar: Ill. Research asst. Dept. HHS, Health Care Fin. Adminstrn., Washington, 1979-80; planning coordinator Hinsdale (Ill.) Hosp., 1980-82; staff atty. Adv. Health System North, Hinsdale, 1985-86; assoc. Hinshaw, Culbertson, Moelmenn, Hoban & Fuller, Chgo., 1986—. Mem. Am. Acad. Hosp. Attys., Ill. Soc. Hosp. Attys., Nat. Health Lawyers Assn., Am. Coll. Health Care Execs. Home: 560 N Grant St Hinsdale IL 60521

VEROSTKO, ROMAN JOSEPH, art educator; b. Tarrs, Pa., Sept. 12, 1929; s. John Frank and Mary (Balcek) V.; m. Alice Wagstaff, Aug. 11, 1968. BA, St. Vincent Coll., Latrobe, Pa., 1955; MFA, Pratt Inst., 1960. Mem. faculty St. Vincent Coll., 1963-68; staff editor, art and architecture New Cath. Ency. Cath. U., Washington, 1964-68; faculty Mpls. Coll. Art Design, 1968—, acad. dean, 1975-78; vis. prof. Zhejiang Acad Fine Arts, Hangzhou, Republic of China, 1985. Contbr. articles on art and religion to various publs.; developed computer graphics software, 1985-86. Leadership fellow Bush Found., 1970; faculty grantee Assn. Ind. Colls. of Art, 1984, Devel. grantee U. Ind. Coll. Art, 1974. Home: 5535 Clinton Ave S Minneapolis MN 55419 Office: Mpls Coll Art and Design 200 E 25th St Minneapolis MN 55404

VERSCHOOR, CURTIS CARL, business educator; b. Grand Rapids, Mich., June 7, 1931; s. Peter and Leonene (Dahlstrom) V.; m. Marie Emilie Kritschgau, June 18, 1952; children—Katherine Anne, Carolyn Marie, John Peter, Carla Michelle. B.B.A. with distinction, U. Mich., 1951, M.B.A., 1952; Ed.D., No. Ill. U., 1977. Pub. accountant Touche, Ross, Bailey & Smart (C.P.A.'s), 1955-63; with Singer Co., 1963-68, asst. controller, 1965-68; controller Colgate-Palmolive Co., 1968-69; asst. controller bus. products group Xerox Corp., 1969-72; controller Baxter Labs., Inc., 1972-73; v.p. finance Altair Corp., Chgo., 1973-74; prof. DePaul U., Chgo., 1974—; pres. C.C. Verschoor & Assocs., Inc., 1981—; part-time instr. Wayne State U., 1955-60. Contbg. editor: Jour. Accountancy, 1961-62, Jour. Internal Auditing, 1985—. Served with AUS, 1953-55. Recipient Elijah Watts Sells award Am. Inst. C.P.A.'s, 1953. Mem. Financial Execs. Inst., Am. Inst. CPA's, Ill. Soc. CPA's, Am. Accounting Assn., Nat. Assn. Accountants, Inst. Internal Auditors, Internat. Assn. for Fin. Planning, Beta Gamma Sigma, Beta Alpha Psi, Delta Pi Epsilon, Phi Kappa Phi, Phi Eta Sigma. Home: 231 Wyngate Dr Barrington IL 60010 Office: DePaul Univ Suite 1262 25 E Jackson Blvd Chicago IL 60604-2287

VERSEY, JOHN PETER, architect; b. Sheboygan, Wis., Oct. 24, 1949; s. John Frank and Albina (Francis) V.; m. Kendra Jane Reichert, June 17, 1972; children: Brian John, Scott Michael, Chad Christopher. BS, U. Wis., Milw., 1973. Architect The Stubenrauch Assocs., Inc., Sheboygan, 1972—. Mem. AIA, Sheboygan Archtl. Rev. Bd., Ducks Unltd. (local chmn. 1978-86). Roman Catholic. Club: Y's Men (bd. dirs. 1984-86, v.p. 1986-87). Lodge: Elks. Avocations: tennis, golf, hunting, fishing, cross-country skiing. Home: 3124 N 8th St Sheboygan WI 53083 Office: The Stubenrauch Assocs Inc 708 Erie Ave Sheboygan WI 53081

VERSIC, LINDA JOAN, nurse educator, research company executive; b. Grove City, Pa., Aug. 27, 1944; d. Robert and Kathryn I. (Fagird) Davies; m. Ronald James Versic, June 11, 1966; children—Kathryn Clara, Paul Joseph. R.N., Johns Hopkins Sch. of Nursing, 1965; B.S. in Health Edn., Central State U., 1980. Asst. head nurse, Johns Hopkins Hosp., Balt., 1965-67; staff Nurse Registry Miami Valley Hosp., Dayton, Ohio, 1973—; instr. Miami Jacobs Jr. Coll. Bus., Dayton, 1977-79; pres. Ronald T. Dodge Co., Dayton, 1979-86, chmn. bd., 1987—; instr. Warren County (Ohio) Career Center, 1980-84, coordinator diversified health occupations, 1984—. Coordinator youth activities, mem. steering com. Queen of Apostles Community. Active Miami Valley Mil. Affairs Assn.; Oakwood Hist. Soc., Cox Arboretum, Friends of Smith Gardens. Mem. Ohio Vocat. Assn., Am. Vocat. Assn., Vocat. Indsl. Clubs Am. (chpt. advisor 1982-86). Roman Catholic. Club: Johns Hopkins, Yugoslav of Greater Dayton. Home: 1601 Shafor Blvd Dayton OH 45419 Office: Ronald T Dodge Co PO Box 9488 Dayton OH 45409

VER STRAATE, TERRY BRENT, accountant; b. Sheboygan, Wis., Apr. 26, 1955; s. Burton Roy and Mary Ann (Luteyn) Ver S.; m. Marlene Beth Van Bruggen, Jan. 3, 1976; children: Samantha Joy, Martina Ann. BBA, Trinity Christian Coll., 1977. CPA, Wis. Sign erecter Van Bruggen Signs, Orland Park, Ill., 1976-77; acct. Flint Kote Mfg., Chicago Heights, Ill., 1977-79; cost acct. Gilson Bros., Plymouth, Wis., 1979-80; jr. acct. K.W. Muth Co., Inc., Sheboygan, 1980-82, mgr. acctg., 1982-84, corp. controller, 1982—; vice chmn., bd. dirs. Superior First Credit Union, Sheboygan, 1984—; cons. taxes and bookkeeping, Sheboygan, 1980—. Ofcl. basketball Wis. Inter-sch. Athletic Assn., 1980, varsity coach Sheboygan County Christian High Sch., 1984-85; treas. First Christian Reformed Ch., Sheboygan, 1983-85. Mem. Am. Inst. CPA's, Wis. Inst. CPA's, Sheboygan Area CPA's. Avocation: sports. Home: Route 2 Box 658 Oostburg WI 53070 Office: K W Muth Co Inc 2021 North Ave Sheboygan WI 53081

VESELITS, CHARLES FRANCIS, manufacturing company executive; b. Chgo., Sept. 23, 1930; s. Joseph and Bertha (Wiesler) V.; m. Carroll J. Landeck, June 9, 1986; children: Catherine, Charles, Cynthia, Craig, Colleen. BS, DePaul U., 1952, MBA, 1958. CPA, Ill. Controller Schneider Metal, Cicero, Ill., 1960-63; controller, treas. O&Y Dry Corp., Elk Grove Village, Ill., 1963-79; v.p., controller Selfix, Inc., Chgo., 1979—. Served to sgt. U.S. Army, 1952-54, Korea. Mem. Ill. Soc. CPA's, Am. Inst. CPA's, Athletic Officials Assn. Roman Catholic. Home: 1010 N Drury Ln Arlington Heights IL 60004 Office: Selfix Inc 4501 W 47th St Chicago IL 60632

VESSENES, PETER, marketing executive; b. Oak Park, Ill., Oct. 16, 1950; s. Daniel John and Theodora (Karedis) V.; m. Katherine Louise Kammerzell, July 28, 1974; children: Peter Joseph, Theodore Jason, Sarah Katherine. BA, U. Denver, 1972. System cons. Comprehensive Health Planning So. Ill., Carbondale, 1975; pres. PKV Assocs., Madison, Wis., 1976-87; pres. Polygon, Inc., Black River Falls, Wis., 1981-82; sr. mktg. exec. Computerland, Inc., Madison, 1983-85; product devel. cons. Tex. Instruments, 1983-86; product mgr. Control Data Corp., Mpls., 1987—. Republican. Office: Control Data Corp 8800 Queens Ave Bloomington MN 55431

VETO, STEPHEN EDWARD, data processing executive; b. Belleville, Ill., June 17, 1951; s. Charles Edward and Carol Jean (Gass) V.; m. Barbara Ann Waldram, May 28, 1976; 1 child, Rebecca Lynne. AS in Computer Sci., Belleville (Ill.) Area Coll., 1972. Programmer NCR, St. Louis, 1972-73; programmer/analyst Deaconess Hosp., St. Louis, 1973-77; systems mgr. Belleville Nat. Bank, 1977-82; data processing mgr. Our Lady of the Snows, Belleville, 1982—. Scoutmaster Boy Scouts Am., Belleville, 1973-82. Recipient Pelican award Cath. Scouting Com., 1980. Avocations: camping, boating, waterskiing. Office: Our Lady of the Snows 15 S 59th St Belleville IL 62221

VETORT, HERMAN JOSEPH, defense company manager, retired military officer; b. Cedar River, Mich., Sept. 30, 1927; s. Edward S. and Scholastica (Lutkevicz) V. m. Alice Marie Lesperance, June 8, 1957; children: Kathryn, Barbara, Edward, John. Student, No. Mich. U., 1946 47; BS in Engring., U.S. Mil. Acad., 1951; MA, Columbia U., 1965; postgrad., U.S. Army War Coll., 1970. Commd. 2d lt. U.S. Army, 1951, advanced through grades to col., ret., 1981; program mgr. Textron Inc. (formerly Cadillac Gage Co.), Warren, Mich., 1981—. Mem. U.S. Armor Assn., Assn. U.S. Army, Am. Def. Preparedness Assn., VFW. Roman Catholic. Avocations: racquetball, handball. Home: 1229 Blairmoor Ct Grosse Pointe Woods MI 48236

VETSCH, GORDON JOSEPH, accountant; b. Princeton, Minn., May 17, 1954; s. Ammon William and Mary Cecilia (Kasper) V.; m. Laurie Marie Scharber, May 8, 1976; children: Anthony Robert, Joseph Leo, Andrea Rose, Alyssa Marie. BS in Acctg., St. John's U., Collegeville, Minn., 1976, BBA in Econs., 1976. CPA, Minn. Staff asst. to sr. mgr. Larson, Allen, Weishair and Co., Mpls., 1976-83, ptnr., 1983—. Mem. Am. Inst. CPA's, Minn. Soc. CPA's (chmn. health care industry com. 1983-84), Healthcare Fin. Mgmt. Assn. Roman Catholic. Lodge: KC. Avocations: reading, softball, gardening. Home: 10433 105th Ave N Maple Grove MN 55369 Office: Larson Allen Weishair & Co 1200 Shelard Tower Minneapolis MN 55426

VETTER, DALE BENJAMIN, educator; b. Henry County, Ill., Aug. 11, 1908; s. John and Esther (Soliday) V.; A.B., North Central Coll., 1930; A.M., Northwestern U., 1935, Ph.D., 1946; m. Frona A. Tonkinson, Mar. 28, 1932; children—Sharon, Ione, Judith, Rebecca. Prin. Hooppole High Sch., 1932-35; tchr. Harrison Pub. Sch., 1936-37; teacher-librarian Riverside-Brookfield High Sch., 1937-41; prof. English, Ill. State U., 1941-76, prof. emeritus, 1976—. Exec. com. Midwest English Conf., 1962-76. Mem. Am. Assn. U. Profs., Mod. Lang. Assn. Am., Northwestern U. Alumni Assn., Ill. Am. Soc. 18th Century Studies, Newberry Library Assos. Augustan Reprint Soc., Friends of Milner Library, Newberry Library (fellow). Unitarian. Author articles, Bull. of Friends of Milner Library, Ill. State Normal Bull., Modern Language Notes. Home: 214 W Willow St Normal IL 61761

VETTER, LINDA MARIE, tax analyst, accountant; b. Chgo.; d. Donald J. and Norma J. (Hay) Raymond; m. William P. Vetter Jr., May 15, 1982. BS in Acctg., DePaul U., 1981, MS in Taxation, 1986. CPA, Ill. Sr. tax acct. Ernst & Whinney, Chgo., 1981-85; sr. tax analyst Sara Lee Corp., Chgo., 1985—. Mem. Am. Inst. CPA's, Ill. CPA Soc. Avocations: travel, reading, arts, crafts, gardening. Office: Sara Lee Corp 3 First National Plaza Chicago IL 60602

VEURINK, GARY LEE, lawyer; b. Muskegon, Mich., Feb. 17, 1954; s. Gordon Kay and Sally Louise (Grimm) V.; m. Helena Eileen Dykstra, Aug. 21, 1976; children: Crystal Lynn, Grant William. BA, Calvin Coll., 1976; JD, Ohio No. U., 1978. Bar: Mich. 1979. Assoc. VanderPloeg, Marietti, Mullally & Grimm, Muskegon, 1979-82; ptnr. Justian & Veurink, Muskegon, 1982-86; sole practice Muskegon, 1986—. Deacon E. Muskegon Christian Reformed Ch., 1980-83; bd. dirs. Great Lakes Co-ed Soccer League, Muskegon, 1980-84, Melody Missions, Inc., Muskegon, 1983—, Bridge to Life Ministries, Muskegon, 1984—, Western Mich. Christian High Sch., Muskegon, 1985—. Mem. ABA, Fed. Bar Assn., Mich. Bar Assn., Christian Legal Soc. Republican. Mem. Christian Reformed Ch. Clubs: Christian Businessmen's (Muskegon) (sec. 1986—); Safari Internat. (Ariz.). Avocations: hunting, fishing, skiing, chess, cutting wood. Home: 18665 Fruitport Rd Spring Lake MI 49456

VIAR, CAROL RANDLES, savings and loan executive; b. Beloit, Kans., Jan. 20, 1952; d. Verdon L. and Bonnie J. (Ahlvers) Peckham; m. George Edward Viar, Nov. 8, 1985; children: Todd, Lance. BA in Edn., Wichita (Kans.) State U., 1974; BS in Acctg., Marymount Coll., Salina, Kans., 1986. Tchr. Nickerson (Kans.) Unified Sch. Dist., 1974-76; head teller 1st Nat. Bank, Ithaca, N.Y., 1976-78; acct. Nat. Bank Am., Salina, 1978-84; asst. ops. officer Peoples Heritage Fed. Savs., Salina, 1984-87, asst. v.p., 1987—. Mem. fin. com. YWCA, Salina, 1986; trustee Salina Pub. Library, 1986; treas. Domestic Violence Assn. Cen. Kans., 19887-89. Republican. Presbyterian. Avocations: gardening, sewing, tennis. Office: Peoples Heritage Fed Savs 2070 S Ohio Salina KS 67401

VICARY, DUANE S., chamber of commerce executive. Pres. Lincoln C. of C., Lincoln, Neb. Office: Lincoln C of C 1221 N St Suite 606 Lincoln NE 68508

VICKERS, JIMMY, areospace manufacturing executive; b. Lorain, Ohio, Jan. 5, 1960; s. Jimmy Sr. and Pauline (Payne) V.; m. Robin Lee Scott, Mar. 19, 1983; 1 child, Winston Alexander James. BBA in Mktg., U. Cin., 1983; postgrad, Xavier U., Cin. Customer relations rep. Cin. Water Works, 1980-83; order entry specialist Aircraft Engine Bus. Group div. Gen. Electric, Cin., 1983-84, contract adminstrn., 1984-85, specialist materials adminstrn., 1985—; bd. dirs. Gen. Electric Employees Community Services Fund, Cin., 1985—; pres. Blue Chip Cons., Cin., 1984—. Chmn. planning com. Lincoln Heights Health Ctr., 1985-86. Named one of Outstanding Young Men Am., 1986. Mem. Alpha Phi Alpha, Delta Sigma Theta (recipent Martin Luther King Speech award 1983). Baptist. Avocations: basketball, racquetball, social problems discussions, travel. Home: 269 McCormick Pl Cincinnati OH 45219 Office: Aircraft Engine Bus Group Gen Electric 1 Newmann Way Cincinnati OH 45215

VICKERY, MILLIE MARGARET, photographer, journalist; b. Clinton County, Ind., Apr. 29, 1920; d. Walter L. and Opal M. (Small) Cox; m. Eugene Livingstone Vickery, Dec. 21, 1941; children—Douglas Eugene, Constance Michelle Suski, Anita Sue Ramsey, Jon Livingstone. Student Ind. U., 1938-42, U. Toledo, 1944. Writer, Sheridan News (Ind.), 1937-38; floor mgr. Lamsons Dept. Store, Toledo, 1943-45; receptionist, bookkeeper Office E.L. Vickery, M.D., Lena, Ill., 1946-85; freelance writer-photographer, Lena, 1964—. Author: P.S. I Love You, 1983; editor Pulse of the Doctor's Wife mag., 1966-78; contbg. editor MD's Wife mag., 1964-74; contbr. articles and photographs to various newspapers and mags. Bd. dirs. Highland Coll. Found., Freeport, Ill., 1970—. Recipient Pacesetter award Highland Community Coll., Freeport, 1978; Sweepstake award, several 1st trophies Rockford Cooking Contests (Ill.), 1979-81; Disting. Alumnae award Marion-Adams High Sch., Sheridan, Ind., 1981. Mem. Ill. Woman's Press Assn. (pres. 1971-73, over 40 writing awards, Woman of Achievement award 1984), Nat. Fedn. Press Women (dir. 1971-73, Nat. Woman of Achievement nominee 1984), Ill. State Med. Soc. Aux. (state pres. 1975-76, Ill. Humanitarian of the Yr. award 1984), Ill. Acad. Family Physicians Aux. (state pres. 1976-77), Ill. Press Photographers Assn., Women in Communications, Mortar Board, Delta Delta Delta, Beta Sigma Phi (pres. chpt. 1950, 72, Order of Rose award 1981, internat. award of Distinction 1982, photography award 1982-84). Republican. Mem. Evangel. Free Church. Clubs: Lena Women's, Lena Golf. Lodges: Order Eastern Star, PEO. Home: 602 Oak St Lena IL 61048

VICKREY, ROBERT FISCHER, newspaper/broadcasting executive; b. Mendota, Ill., May 21, 1944; s. Gail Sabin and Marie Augusta (Fischer) V.; m. Barbara Ann Harmon, May 30, 1970; 1 son, Robert James. Student Ill. Valley Community Coll., 1963-64, Dana Coll., 1964. Account exec. Daily News Tribune, La Salle, Ill., 1968-71; account exec. La Salle County Broadcasting Corp., La Salle, 1971-72, sales mgr., 1972-84, v.p., 1984—; v.p. Daily News-Tribune, 1985—. Bd. dirs. United Way of Illinois Valley, 1973-75, mem. pub. relations com., 1980-82; v.p. No. Ill. Indsl. Devel. Corp., 1985-86; mem. pub. relations com. Starved Rock Area council Boy Scouts Am., 1972-76. Served with U.S. Army, 1966-68. Mem. Nat. Assn. Broadcasters, Radio Advt. Bur., Internat. Newspaper Advt. and Mktg. Execs. Assn., Nat. Radio Broadcasters Assn., Newspaper Advt. Bur., Ill. Valley Area C. of C. (past pres.). Clubs: Wide Waters Yacht (Ottawa, Ill.), Governor's (Ill.). Lodge: Elks. Home: 902 16th St Peru IL 61354 Office: 426 2d St La Salle IL 61301

VICTOR, MICHAEL GARY, physician, lawyer; b. Detroit, Sept. 20, 1945; s. Simon H. and Helen (Litsky) V.; m. Karen Sue Hutson, June 20, 1975; children—Elise Nicole, Sara Lisabeth. Bars: Ill. 1980, U.S. Dist. Ct. (no. dist.) Ill. 1980, U.S. Ct. Appeals (7th cir.) 1981; diplomate Am. Bd. Law in Medicine. Pres., Advocate Adv. Assocs., Chgo., 1982—; assoc. in medicine Northwestern U. Med. Sch., Chgo., 1982—; sole practice law, Barrington, Ill., 1982—; dir. emergency medicine Loretto Hosp., Chgo., 1980-85, chief. sect. of emergency medicine St. Josephs Hosp., Chgo., 1985—; v.p. Med. Emergency Services Assocs., Buffalo Grove, Ill; v.p. MESA Mgmt. Corp.; sec., treas. MESA Edn. and Research Found.; sec., treas. Mgmt. and Care Services Inc.; sec., treas., bd. dirs., Vital Med. Labs. Inc. Author: Informed Consent, 1980; Brain Death, 1980; (with others) Due Process for Physicians, 1984, A Physicians Guide to the Illinois Living Will Act. Recipient Service awards Am. Coll. Emergency Medicine, 1973-83. Fellow Am. Coll. Legal Medicine, Chgo. Acad. Legal Medicine; mem. Am. Coll. Emergency Physicians (pres. 1980, med.-legal-ins. council 1980-81, 83-84), ABA, Ill. State Bar Assn., Am. Soc. Law and Medicine, Assn. Trial Lawyers Am.,

Chgo. Bar Assn. (med.-legal council 1981-83), AMA, Ill. State Med. Soc. (med.-legal council 1980-86), Chgo. Med. Soc. Jewish. Home and Office: 1609 Guthrie Circle Barrington IL 60010

VICTORIN (VICTORIN URSACHE), archbishop; b. Manastioara-Siret, Dist. of Suceava, Romania, July 0, 1912. Grad., State Lyceum of Siret; L.Th., U. Cernauti, Romania; postgrad., Bibl. Inst. Jerusalem. Ordained deacon Romanian Orthodox Ch., 1937, priest, 1937, consecrated bishop, 1966, elevated to archbishop, 1973; prof. religion Orthodox Lyceum of the Romanian Orthodox Metropolis of Cernautsi, 1936-37; prof. theology Seminary of Neamtzu Monastery, 1937-46, asst. dir. sem., 1937-40, dir. sem., superior of monastery, 1940-44; rep. Romanian Orthodox Ch. at Holy Places in, Jerusalem, 1946-56; bishop Romanian Orthodox Missionary Episcopate in, Am., 1966-73; archbishop Romanian Orthodox Missionary Archdiocese in, Am., 1973—; Mem. Holy Synod, Romanian Orthodox Ch. of Romania; bd. dirs. U.S. Conf., World Council Chs.; mem. central com.; mem. Standing Conf. Canonical Orthodox Bishops in, Ams. Editor: Locurile Sfinte. Address: Romanian Orthodox Ch 19959 Riopelle St Detroit MI 48203

VIELHABER, WILLIAM EDWARD, accountant; b. Akron, Ohio, Oct. 19, 1947; s. Albert Joseph and Elizabeth Rose (Curry) V.; m. Kathleen Therese Ritty; children: Jonathon, Janice. BBA, Kent State U., 1970. CPA, Ohio. Accountant E. Ohio Gas, Cleve., 1970-74; ptnr. Sorkin Thayer & Co., Akron, 1974-82, Vielhaber Speck & Co., Akron, 1982—. Treas. Akron Zool. Park, 1977-86; pres. Akron Civic Theatre, 1982-84. Named one of Five Outstanding Young Men of Ohio, Ohio Jaycees, 1980. Mem. Am. Inst. CPAs, Ohio Soc. CPAs, Ohio Mutual Assistance Group CPAs, Akron Jaycees (pres. 1975, Disting. Service award 1979). Republican. Roman Catholic. Lodge: Kiwanis (local treas. 1982—). Home: 3496 Dollar Dr Akron OH 44319 Office: 567 E Turkeyfoot Lake Rd Akron OH 44319

VIENE, LAWRENCE EDWARD, facilities manager, architect; b. Hinsdale, Ill., Apr. 11, 1948; s. John Gerald and Loretta Marcella (Barber) V.; m. Sue Ann Bloemer, May 27, 1972 (div. 1984); children: Justin Troy, Erica Sue, Alexis Ann. BA in Polit. Sci., St. Louis U., 1971; B in Environ. Design, U. Kans., 1976. Registered architect, Mo.; cert. Nat. Council Archtl. Registration Bds. Tchr. Rosary High Sch., St. Louis, 1970-71; dir. housing Rockhurst Coll., Kansas City, Mo., 1971-73; staff architect N. Kans. City (Mo.) Hosp., 1976-77, Marshall-Waters, Springfield, Mo., 1977-78; project architect Southwestern Bell Telephone Co., Kansas City, Mo., 1978-84; facilities mgr., architect Southwestern Bell Telephone Co., St. Louis, 1984—; restoration cons. St. Elizabeth's Ch., Kansas City, Mo., 1983-84. Mem. West Pine Laclede Neighborhood Assn. Mem. AIA, Mo. Council Architects, Nat. Trust for Hist. Preservation. Roman Catholic. Avocations: inland sailing, rose gardening. Home: 4155 Laclede Saint Louis MO 63108 Office: Southwestern Bell Telephone Co 100 N Tucker Rm 801 Saint Louis MO 63101

VIETOR, HAROLD DUANE, judge; b. Parkersburg, Iowa, Dec. 29, 1931; s. Harold Howard and Alma Johanna (Kreimeyer) V.; m. Dalia Artemisa Zamarripa Cadena, Mar. 24, 1973; children: Christine Elizabeth, John Richard, Greta Maria. BA, U. Iowa, 1955, JD, 1958. Bar: Iowa. Law clk. U.S. Ct. Appeals 8th Circuit, 1958-59; ptnr. Bleakley Law Offices, Cedar Rapids, Iowa, 1959-65; judge Iowa Dist. Ct., Cedar Rapids, 1965-79, chief judge, 1970-79; U.S. dist. judge So. Dist. Iowa, Des Moines, 1979—, chief judge, 1985—. Contbr. articles to profl. jours. Served with USN, 1952-54. Mem. ABA, Iowa Bar Assn. (pres. jr. sect. 1966-67), Am. Judicature Soc., Iowa Judges Assn. (pres. 1975-76), 8th Cir. Dist. Judges Assn. (pres. 1986—). Office: 211 US Courthouse Des Moines IA 50309

VIGLIOTTI, CAROLE ANN, publishing executive; b. Cleve., July 25, 1939; d. Gabriel and Edna Frances (Hoffer) Madasz; m. Joseph John Vigliotti, Sept. 1, 1958; 1 child, Sherry Ann. Grad. high sch., Cleve. Sec. Addressograph-Multigraph, Euclid, Ohio, 1957-59; classified mgr. Chagrin Valley Pub. Co., Chagrin Falls, Ohio, 1974, office mgr., 1974-78, bus. mgr., 1978-86, gen. mgr., 1986—; cons. Shopper's Choice Inc., Medina, Ohio, 1983-84; advt. agt. Arra Hair Design, Chagrin Falls, 1974—, Gifted Gourmet Inc., Cleve., 1985—. Contbr. articles to profl. jours. V.p. PTA, John Dewey Elem. Sch., Warrensville Heights, Ohio, 1968-69; co-chmn. St. Jude Adult Edn., Warrensville Heights, 1970-72; active Warrensville Heights Commn. Coordinating Com., 1968-69, Chagrin Valley Nuclear Freeze Group, 1986-87. Mem. Women's Internat. League for Peace and Freedom/Women Speak Out. Democrat. Roman Catholic. Avocation: reading. Office: Chagrin Valley Pub Co 34 S Main St Chagrin Falls OH 44022

VIGNERI, JOSEPH W., lawyer; b. Decatur, Ill., July 28, 1956; s. Joseph Paul and Thelma Lucille (Pettus) V.; m. Martha Suzanne Smith, May 9, 1984; children: Craig Ashley Wilson, Emily Carmela. BA in Polit. Sci., Millikin U., 1980; JD cum laude, St. Louis U., 1983. Bar: Ill. 1983, U.S. Dist. Ct. (cen. dist.) Ill. 1983. Assoc. Rosenberg, Rosenberg, Bickes, Johnson & Richardson, Decatur, 1983-86; ptnr. Brilley & Vigneri, Decatur, 1986—. Mem. ABA, Ill. State Bar Assn. (sec. council on individual rights and responsibilities), Decatur Bar Assn. Republican. Roman Catholic. Club: Decatur. Avocation: karate. Home: 285 Dover Dr Decatur IL 62521 Office: Brilley & Vigneri 730 S Main St Decatur IL 62525-1549

VIGOREN, REX PAUL, accountant; b. Belle Fourche, S.D., Nov. 23, 1954; s. Maxwell Andrew and Lorraine Inez (Voyles) V.; m. Joanne Irene Roth, July 24, 1977; children: Jenny Rhaye, Andrew Maxwell. BS, U. S.D., 1977. CPA, S.D. Staff acct. Coopers & Lybrand, CPAs, Omaha, 1976-78, Ivan Bjerke, P.A., Spearfish, S.D., 1978-79; ptnr. Bjerke & Vigoren, Spearfish, 1979-82, Vigoren & Stokes, CPAs, Spearfish, 1982—. Adult supr. Jr. Achievement, Omaha, 1976-78; sustaining mem. Rep. Nat. Com., Spearfish, 1984—; chmn. adminstrv. bd. United Meth. Ch., Spearfish, 1985—. Mem. Am. Inst. CPA's, S.D. Soc. CPA's (vice chmn. tax com. 1985—), Spearfish C. of C., Phi Eta Sigma. Lodge: Kiwanis (bd. dirs. 1984—, Spiritual Aims award 1985). Avocations: running, photography. Home: 824 Harding Box 467 Spearfish SD 57783-0467 Office: Vigoren & Stokes CPAs 123 E Jackson St #2 Box 430 Spearfish SD 57783-0430

VILLAUME, PHILIP GORDON, lawyer; b. St. Paul, Sept. 9, 1949; s. Paul Eugene and Katherine Agnes (Kielty) V.; m. Kay Ann Hanratty, Sept. 30, 1979; children—Cory Philip, Allie Katharine. B.A. magna cum laude, Macalaster Coll., 1972, postgrad., 1972; M. Criminal Justice Program, Mankato State Coll., 1972; J.D., Hamline U., 1979. Bar: Minn. 1979, U.S. Dist. Ct. Minn. 1979, Wis. 1984, U.S. Supreme Ct. 1984. Probation and parole officer 2d jud. dist., Ramsey County Dept. Ct. Services, St. Paul, 1972-76; pres., owner Villaume Investigative Services, St. Paul, 1977-81; prin. Philip G. Villaume and Assocs., St. Paul and Mpls.; tchr. course Sibley Sr. High Sch., West St. Paul, 1972; instr. course Macalaster Coll., St. Paul, 1974, Maplewood Community Edn. Program, Minn., 1975; instr. legal asst. program Inver Hills Community Coll., Inver Grove Heights, Minn., 1980-82; lectr., vol. atty. Chrysalis Ctr. for Women; bd. mem. Ramsey County Atty. Referral System; bd. dirs. Families in Crisis, Lawyers Concerned for Lawyers, 1985—; apptd. Civil Commitment Def. Project, Fed. Pub. Def. Panel, Ramsey County Criminal Def. Project, Hennepin County Juvenile Def. Project. Named one of Outstanding Young Men in Am., 1985. Mem. ABA, Assn. Trial Lawyers Am., Minn. Trial Lawyers Assn. (ednl. coordinator criminal law sect. 1984—, lectr. affirmative bus. communication, continuing legal edn. 1983), Hennepin County Bar Assn., Ramsey County Bar Assn., Nat. Assn. Criminal Def. Lawyers, Hamline U. Sch. Law Alumni Assn. (pres.), Alpha Kappa Delta, Sigma Nu Phi. Home: 446 Mount Curve Blvd Saint Paul MN 55105 Office: Shepard Park Office Ctr Suite 180 2177 Youngman Ave Saint Paul MN 55116 Office: United Lbr Ctr Suite 592 312 Central Ave SE Minneapolis MN 55414

VILLEGAS, ROBERTO REGINO, JR., publishing executive; b. Weslaco, Tex., Jan. 25, 1947; s. Roberto Regino and Dominga (Arevalo) V.; m. Judith Ellen Fortner, Dec. 8, 1979 (div. Dec. 1986); children: Adriane, Dagny, Roberto Regino. Assoc. degree in Humanities, SUNY-Albany, 1978. Pub., Lion Enterprises, Walkerton, Ind., 1974—; customer service rep. United Parcel Service, 1978—. Served with U.S. Army, 1966-68. Author: Credo for Future Man-Poems and Poetic Prose, 1981; The Resurrection-A Short Play, 1977. Office: 8608 Old Dominion Ct Indianapolis IN 46231

VILONA-LABONNE, IRENE MARIE, financial planner; b. Searcy, Ark., Jan. 17, 1946; d. Samuel E. and Mary Nell (Allen) Ellis; m. Frederick J. Vilona, Sept. 29, 1969 (div. Dec. 1982); m. Daniel Paul LaBonne, June 29, 1985; children: Christopher, Scott. BS, U. Wis., Kenosha, 1983; postgrad., Coll. Fin. Planning, Denver, 1984-86. Cert. fin. planner; registered investment advisor. Office auditor E.J. Korvette, Morton Grove, Ill., 1969-72; ins. assoc. All State Tax Service, Walworth, Wis., 1973-79; tax ptnr. Hughes & Assocs., Elkhorn, Wis., 1980-82; pvt. practice tax specialist Delaven, Wis., 1982—, pvt. practice cert. fin. planner, 1984—; pres., cert. fin. planner Many Happy Returns, Inc., Delaven, 1986—; registered rep. Mut. Service Corp.; mem. Securities Investor Protection Corp. Mem. Internat. Assn. Fin. Planner, Inst. Cert. Fin. Planner, Nat. Assn. Securities Dealers. Republican. Roman Catholic. Lodge: Lioness. Avocations: swimming, sailing, reading. Home: PO Box 224 Fontana WI 53125 Office: Many Happy Returns Inc 51 E Walworth PO Box 407 DeLaven WI 53115

VINCENT, ADELE JUDITH, foundation adminstrator; b. Ashton-Under-Lyne, Lancashire, Eng., May 10, 1935; d. Ian MacDonald and Marian (Leech) Bagnall; m. Charles Geoffrey Vincent, Apr. 24, 1965; children: Wendy Anne, Christopher Loy, Mary Jane. BA with honors, Oxford (Eng.) U., 1957, MA, 1961. Staff writer The Observer, London, 1957-64, The N.Y. Times, N.Y.C., 1964-65; edit. writer The Courier-Jour., Louisville, Ky., 1971-78; program officer, assoc. dir. Cummins Engine Found., Columbus, Ind., 1981—; mem. adv. council PreCollegiate Edn. Group, Council on Founds., Washington, 1983-85. Contbr. numerous articles to profl. jours. Mem. bd. women Founds./Corp. Philanthropy, 1985—. Mem. LWV (pres. Columbus chpt. 1983-85. Democrat. Episcopalian. Home: 4873 E Windsor Ln Columbus IN 47201 Office: Cummins Engine Found PO Box 3005 Columbus IN 47202

VINCENT, DIANE MARIE, nurse; b. Rugby, N.D., June 14, 1954; d. Harold Frank and Pearl H. (Jacobson) Mueller; m. John William Vincent, Aug. 17, 1976; children: John William Jr., Heather Marie, April Joy, Rachael Elizabeth. Student, Minot (N.D.) State Coll., 1972-74, 75-77, BS in Nursing, 1982; postgrad., U. N.D, 1984. Co-owner B&S Enterprises, Minot, 1977—; RN in orthopedics Trinity Med. Ctr., Minot, 1982-83, RN in neonatal care, 1983—; mem. NICU policy and procedure com., inservice edn. com., Trinity Med. Ctr., 1984, also quality assurance com., 1987—. Counselor Pacific Garden Mission, Chgo., 1974. NSF grantee, 1976. Mem. Nat. Assn. Neonatal Nurses, Nat. Nurses Assn. Republican. Roman Catholic. Club: Inter-Varsity Christian Fellowship (asst. mission dir. 1973). Avocations: guitar, piano, painting, crafts, writing. Office: B & S Enterprises 3420 SE 47th St Minot ND 58701

VINCENT, FREDERICK MICHAEL, neurologist, educational administrator; b. Detroit, Nov. 19, 1948; s. George S. and Alyce M. (Borkowski) V.; m. Patricia Lucille Cordes, Oct. 7, 1972; children: Frederick Michael, Joshua Peter, Melissa Anne. BS in Biology, Aquinas Coll., 1970; MD, Mich. State U., 1973. Diplomate Am. Bd. Psychiatry and Neurology. Intern St. Luke's Hosp., Duluth, Minn., 1974-75; resident in neurology Dartmouth Med. Sch., Hanover, N.H., 1975-77, instr. dept. medicine, chief resident neurology, 1977-78; chief, neurology sect. Munson Med. Ctr., Traverse City, Mich., 1978-84; asst. clin. prof. medicine and pathology Mich. State U., East Lansing, 1978-84, chief sect. neurology Coll. Human Medicine, 1984—; clin. and research fellow neuro-oncology Mass. Gen. Hosp., Boston, 1985; Clin. Fellow in neurology Harvard Med. Sch., Boston, 1985; cons. med. asst. program Northwestern Mich. Coll., Traverse City, 1983-84; neurology cons. radio call-in show Sta. WKAR, East Lansing, 1984—, WCMU TV, 1987. Author: Neurology: Problems in Primary Care, 1987. Contbr. articles to profl. jours. Fellow NSF, 1969, Nat. Multiple Sclerosis Soc., 1971. Fellow Am. Acad. Neurology, ACP; mem. Am. Heart Assn., Am. Soc. Clin. Oncology, Am. Soc. Neurol. Investigation, Am. EEG Soc., Am. Fedn. Clin. Research, Am. Soc. Neurol. Investigation, N.Y. Acad. Scis. Democrat. Roman Catholic. Club: University. (East Lansing). Office: Dept Medicine Neurology Sect B-220 Life Scis East Lansing MI 48824

VINCENT, JAMES RAYMOND, accountant; b. Russell, Kans., Apr. 6, 1936; m. Jane E. Drennen, Nov. 27, 1957 (div. Dec. 1977); children: Mark A., Connie C. Williamson, William J.; m. Marilyn L. Curt, Feb. 24, 1979. BS, Anderson (Ind.) Coll., 1958. CPA, Ind. V.p. fin. and adminstrn. Payless Supermarkets, Anderson, 1961-79; pvt. practice acctg. Anderson, 1981—. Contbr. articles on computers in supermarkets to bus. jour. Mem. Am. Inst. CPA's, Ind. Soc. CPA's, Anderson C. of C. Home: 2304 Bryden Rd Muncie IN 47304 Office: 1000 First Savings Tower Anderson IN 46016

VINCENT, ROBERT KELLER, geophysicist, geological consulting company executive; b. Bunkie, La., Feb. 6, 1941; s. Edward and Frances L. (Keller) V.; B.A. cum laude, La. Tech. U., 1963, B.S. cum laude in Physics, 1963; M.S. in Physics, U. Md., 1966; postgrad. M.I.T., 1968; Ph.D. in Geology, U. Mich., 1973; m. Dinah Kay Mannerud, June 19, 1978; 1 child, Robert Anthony; stepchildren—Kimberley Jane, Hilary Beth, Cory Erwin; children by previous marriage—Derek Andrew, Heather Louise, David Christopher. Engr., Tex. Instruments, Inc., summers, 1963-65; research assoc. Willow Run Labs., U. Mich., Ann Arbor, 1970-72; research geophysicist Environ. Research Inst. Mich. (formerly Willow Run Labs.), 1972-74; founder, pres. Geospectra Corp., Ann Arbor, 1974—, chmn. bd., 1974—, cons. to oil and mining cos., 1974—; founder BioImage Corp.; pres., dir. Promethean Technologies, Inc., 1986—; cons. to NASA Planetary Radar Working Group, 1977-79, U.S. Army Expert Working Group, 1978-80. Contbr. over 60 tech. pubs. to profl. jours. Served to capt. USAF, 1966-70. Mem. Am. Geophys. Union, Am. Inst. Physics, Optical Soc. Am., AAAS, Am. Soc. Photogrammetry (chmn. geol. scis. com. 1981-82), Am. Assn. Petroleum Geologists, Mich. Tech. Council (chmn. 1984-85), Nat. Acad. Scis. (com. practical applications of remote sensing from space), Sigma Xi, Omicron Delta Kappa, Phi Kappa Phi. Methodist. Club: Masons. Contbr. articles to sci. jours. Home: 1645 Morehead Dr Ann Arbor MI 48103 Office: 333 Parkland Plaza PO Box 1387 Ann Arbor MI 48106

VINCK, WILLIAM CHARLES, data processing executive; b. Chgo., July 27, 1947; s. Charles Ferdinand and Jean (Revell) V.; m. Mary Rita Cannon, June 18, 1977; children: Jennifer Noreen, Sean Charles, Patrick William. BA, U. Ill., Chgo., 1974; MA, DePaul U., Chgo., 1977, PhD, 1984; MBA, U. Chgo., 1980. Systems analyst Inland Steel, Chgo., 1978-80; systems coordinator Nat. Steel, Pitts., 1981-82, mgr. infosystems, 1982-84; dir. infosystems Midwest Steel, Portage, Ind., 1984-85; dir. tech. Midwest Steel, Portage, 1985-87; mgr. systems and tech. planning Chrysler Motors, Detroit, 1987—. Served to cpl. USMC, 1965-69. Mem. Steel Industry Systems Assn., Assn. Systems Mgrs., Phi Kappa Phi. Roman Catholic. Home: 2001 Fairway Birmingham MI 48009 Office: Chrysler Motors CIMS 429-26-00 Auburn Hills MI 48057

VINELLA, FRANK PETER, manufacturing executive; b. Mpls., Sept. 14, 1919; s. Peter and Angela (Russo) V.; m. Irene E. Vlasak, Sept. 4, 1948; children: Joann, Patricia, James, Peter, Mary, Linda, Deborah, Teresa. BS MechE, U. Minn., 1948. Registered profl. engr., Minn. Inspection engr. Standard Oil of Ind., Whiting, Ind., 1948-50; prodn. engr. Terrazzo Machine, Mpls., 1950-53, pres., 1953—. Commr. Richfield Planning Commn., Richfield, Minn., 1962-65. Mem. ASME (chmn. local chpt. 1960, outstanding engr. award 1980). Republican. Roman Catholic. Club: Downtown Exchange (Mpls.) (pres. 1964-65), Southtown Exchange (pres. 1982-83). Avocations: hunting, golf, fishing. Home: 6732 Pillsbury S Richfield MN 55423 Office: Terrazzo Machine 2843 S 26th Ave Minneapolis MN 55406

VINGELEN, ALLAN DUANE, financial executive; b. Grand Forks, N.D., Jan. 17, 1942; s. Elmer Kenneth and Blanche Jeanette (Thorson) V.; m. Linda Jane Howard, June 7, 1964; children: John Allan, William Scott, Robert Ryan. BBA in Acctg., U. N.D., 1964; postgrad., Am. U., 1966-67; MBA with honors, Boston U., 1970. CPA, N.D. Mgr. corp. acctg. Whirlpool Corp., Benton Harbor, Mich., 1973-78, dir. corp. acctg., 1978-83; div. controller Whirlpool Corp., Ft. Smith, Ark., 1983-84; group controller Whirlpool Corp., Evansville, Ind., 1984-85; dir. mfg. acctg. Whirlpool Corp., St. Joseph, Mich., 1985-86; asst. controller Whirlpool Corp., Benton Harbor, 1986—. Served to capt. U.S. Army, 1965-70. Mem. Am. Inst. CPA's, Mich. Assn. CPA's, Econ. Club Southwestern Mich., Blue Key. Republican. Methodist. Home: 2220 Lake Shore Dr Saint Joseph MI 49085 Office: Whirlpool Corp 2000 M 63 North Benton Harbor MI 49022

VINJE, THOMAS SYVER, orthopedist; b. Bismarck, N.D., June 19, 1946; s. Ralph and Evangeline Esther (Kelley) V.; m. Laura Jean Myster, May 31, 1968; children: Pamela, Gina. BA in Zoology, U. Hawaii, 1969; MD, Autonomous U. Guadalajara, Mexico, 1975. Diplomate Am. Bd. Orthopaedic Surgery. Intern St. Francis Hosp. Med. Ctr., Peoria, Ill., 1977-78, resident, 1978-81; practice medicine specializing in orthopedic surgery Sterling (Ill.) Rock Falls Clinic, 1981—; bd. dirs. Community Gen. Hosp., Sterling. Served to 1st lt. U.S. Army, 1970-72, Vietnam. Fellow Am. Acad. Orthopaedic Surgeons; mem. AMA, Ill. Orthopaedic Assn., Ill. State Med. Soc., Whiteside County Med. Soc. (pres. 1983-84). Republican. Lutheran. Avocations: skiing, water skiing, scuba diving, miniature models. Home: 508 Walnut St Sterling IL 61081 Office: Sterling Rock Falls Clinic 101 E Miller Rd Sterling IL 61081

VINNEDGE, CHARLOTTE ALYCE, musician, publisher; b. Niles, Mich., Mar. 1, 1943; d. Robert Abner and Norma Cicelia (Frizzo) V. Grad., Niles High Sch. Leader, founder musical groups U.S., 1964-71; mem. musical group Nitro-Function, Europe, 1971; founder Electric Lady Music Co., Dowagiac, Mich., 1972—; pvt. practice music instr., Dowagiac, 1964—. Composer music and lyrics, 1964—; composer album Billy Cox's Nitro-Function, 1971. Mem. Nat. Assn. Female Execs., Broadcast Music Inc. Republican. Episcopalian. Avocations: medicine, water color, literature. Home: PO Box 261 M-51-N Dowagiac MI 49047 Office: Electric Lady Music PO Box 261 Dowagiac MI 49047-0261

VINZANT, LARRY MAX, insurance company executive; b. Davenport, Iowa, June 30, 1943; s. Wendell Ivan and Elane (Dale) V.; m. Cheryl A. Strunk, Nov. 14, 1984; children: Jill Marie, Tammy Lynn. BS, Northeast Mo. State U., 1968. CPA, Iowa. Steelworker Pittsburgh-Des Moines Steel Corp., Des Moines, 1964-65; sr. acct. Peat, Marwick, Mitchell, Des Moines, 1968-71; asst. controller Farmland Ins. Services, Des Moines, 1971-73; sec., treas. Mid-Am. Food Inc., Humboldt, Iowa, 1973-74; controller Trans-World Inns, Ltd., West Des Moines, Iowa, 1974-75; v.p., controller Gen. United Life Ins. Co., Des Moines, 1975-77; treas., dir. fin. Harco Holdings, Inc., Milw., 1977-79; agt. Equitable Life Ins. N.Y., Des Moines, 1979-80; asst. comptroller State Automobile and Casualty Underwriters, Des Moines, 1980-81; dir. acctg. Grinnell (Iowa) Mut. Reinsurance Co., 1981-85; asst. dir. life adminstrn., asst. sec. Grinnell Mut. Life Ins. Co., 1983-85, controller, 1985, v.p. adminstrn., controller, 1985—; controller Grinnell Mut. Reinsurance, 1985—; treas. Big M Agy., Inc., Grinnell, 1985—; v.p., treas. Grinnell Infosystems, Inc., 1985—. Served to cpl. USMC, 1961-64. Mem. Am. Inst. CPA's, Iowa Soc. CPA's. Republican. Avocations: reading, fishing, sports. Office: Grinnell Mut Reins Co Interstate 80 and Hwy 146 Grinnell IA 50112

VINZANT, ROBERT DAVID, dentist; b. Gary, Ind., Sept. 23, 1927; s. Robert Dean and Erma Christine (Martinson) V.; m. Marjorie Lynn Vinzant, Apr. 30, 1953; children: David Rea, John Edward, Jeannine Lynn. BS, Ind. U., Bloomington, 1950; DDS, Ind. U., Indpls., 1953. Gen. practice dentistry Hobart, Ind., 1956—; prin. oboeist N.W. Ind. Symphony, Gary, Ind., 1960-78, N.W. Ind. Chamber Winds, La Porte, Ind., 1984—, La Porte Symphony, 1985—. Served with USN, 1945-46, to 1st lt. U.S. Army, 1953-55. Fellow Internat. Coll. Dentists; mem. ADA, N.W. Ind. Dental Soc. (bd. dirs. 1956-60, pres. 1962-63), Ind. Dental Assn. (trustee 1963-64), Psi Omega. Presbyterian. Lodges: Rotary (pres. 1975-76), Elks. Home: 602 Lakeside La Porte IN 46350 Office: 295 S Wisconsin Hobart IN 46342

VIOLAND, LAWRENCE JOHN, marketing professional, media representative; b. Phila., Sept. 20, 1952; s. John Herbert and Ann Elizabeth (Rumsey) V.; m. Carol Ann DiRuscio, July 31, 1976; children: Matthew Alan, Carly Elizabeth. BS in Journalism, Bowling Green U., 1974. Cert. bus. communicator. Dist. mgr. Tech. Publ. Co., Cleve., 1983-85; mgr. Cleve. Irving Cloud Publ. Co., Cleve., 1985-87; research and devel. mag. Cahners Pub. Co., Cleve., 1987—. Childlife vol. Southwest Gen. Hosp., Middlebrug Heights, Ohio, 1986. Mem. Bus. and Profl. Advt. Assn. (gov., advisor, bd. dirs. 1984—, contbr. photos and articles to jour.), Falcon Club Bowling Green State U. Club: TF of Cleve. (historian 1986—), Falcon. Avocations: bicycling, skiing, tennis, weightlifting, music, photography. Office: Cahners Publishing Co 1621 Euclid Ave Cleveland OH 44115

VIOLETTE, AURELE JOSEPH, JR., history educator; b. Augusta, Maine, July 11, 1941; s. Aurele Joseph Violette Sr. and Juliette (DuBois) Pelletier; m. Judith Lynne Clark, July 8, 1967; children: Andrew Joel, Stephanie Christine. BA, Bowdoin Coll., Brunswick, Maine, 1963; MA, Ohio State U., 1964, PhD, 1971. Lectr. in history Ind. U.-Purdue U., Ft. Wayne, 1970-72, asst. prof., 1972-83, chmn. dept. history, 1978-82, assoc. prof., 1983—; mem. hist. preservation rev. bd. City of Ft. Wayne, 1980-85; coordinator History Day N.E. Ind., Ft. Wayne, 1980-84; reader advanced placement Ednl. Testing Service, Princeton, N.J., 1980—; cons. Cathedral Mus., Ft. Wayne, 1981—. Contbr. articles to profl. jours. Election ofcl. Allen County Election Bd., Ft. Wayne, 1974—; bd. dirs. Ind. Consortium Internat. Programs, 1973-76. Served to capt. U.S. Army, 1967-69, Vietnam. Decorated Bronze Star. Mem. Am. Hist. Assn., Am. Assn. Advancement Slavic Studies, Am. Cath. Hist. Assn., Ind. Hist. Soc., Allen County Hist. Soc., Ind. Assn. Historians. Democrat. Roman Catholic. Avocations: reading, gardening, genealogy. Home: 8414 Fawncrest Pl Fort Wayne IN 46835 Office: Ind U-Purdue U Dept History 2101 Coliseum Blvd E Fort Wayne IN 46805

VIRGILIO, SUSAN MARY, personnel administrator; b. Chgo., Oct. 25, 1957; s. Joseph Marion and Dorothy Ann (Gerut) Bernal; m. Theodore Mark Virgilio, May 23, 1982; 1 child, Daniel Mark. BS in Acctg., U. Ill., 1979; MBA, Lewis U., 1986. Various positions No. Ill. Gas Co., Naperville, Ill., 1979-83, corp. acct. div. acctg. personnel, 1983-86, tng. and employment adminstr., 1986—. Mem. Am. Soc. Tng. and Devel., Coll. Placement Council, Midwest Coll. Placement Assn. (co-chairperson utility group). Roman Catholic. Avocations: jigsaw puzzles, swimming, crafts. Home: 26W 265 Kiowa Ln Wheaton IL 60187 Office: No Ill Gas Co 1700 W Ferry Rd Naperville IL 60540

VIRGO, JOHN MICHAEL, economist, researcher, educator; b. Pressburry, Eng., Mar. 11, 1943; s. John Joseph and Muriel Agnes (Franks) V.; m. Katherine Sue Ulmrich, Sept. 6, 1980 (div. 1979); 1 child, Debra Marie. BA, Calif. State U., Fullerton, 1967, MA, 1969; MA, Claremont Grad. Sch., 1971, PhD, 1972. Instr. econs. Whittier (Calif.) Coll., 1970-71, Calif. State U., Fullerton and Long Beach, 1971-72, Claremont (Calif.) Grad. Sch., 1971-72; asst. prof. econs. Va. Commonwealth U., Richmond, 1972-74; assoc. prof. mgmt. So. Ill. U., Edwardsville, 1975-83, prof., 1984—; chief exec. officer, founder Internat. Health Econ. & Mgmt. Inst., Edwardsville, 1983—. Author: Legal & Illegal California Farmworkers, 1974; author, editor: Health Care: An International Perspective, 1984, Exploring New Vistas in Health Care, 1985, Restructuring Health Policy, 1986. Served with USN, 1965-68. Mem. Internat. Hosp Fedn., Am. Econ. Assn., Am. Hosp. Assn., Am. Soc. Assn. Execs., Royal Econ. Soc., Atlantic Econ. Soc. (founder, exec. v.p., mng. editor jour. 1973—), Allied Social Scis. Assn. (chmn. exec. confs. 1982—). Democrat. Roman Catholic. Club: Sunset Hills (Edwardsville). Avocations: tennis, skiing. Home: 315 Edwards Dr Edwardsville IL 62025 Office: So Ill U PO Box 1101 Edwardsville IL 62026-1101

VIRKHAUS, TAAVO, symphony orchestra conductor; b. Tartu, Estonia, June 29, 1934; came to U.S., 1949; s. Adalbert August and Helene Marie (Sild) V.; m. Nancy Ellen Herman, Mar. 29, 1969. B.M., U. Miami, 1955; M.M., Eastman Sch. of Music, Rochester, 1957, D.M.A., 1967. Dir. music U. Rochester (N.Y.), also assoc. prof. Eastman Sch., Rochester, 1967-77; music dir., condr. Duluth Superior Symphony Orch. (Minn.), 1977—; guest condr. Rochester Philharmo. and others, 1972—; guest condr. at Tallinn, Estonia SSR, 1978; lectr. U. Minn.-Duluth, U. of Wis.-Superior. Served with U.S. Army, 1957-58, USAR, 1957-61. Recipient Howard Hanson composition award, 1966; Am. Heritage award, JFK Library for Minorities, 1974; Fulbright Scholar, Musickhochschule, Cologne, 1963. Mem. Am. Symphony Orch. League, Condrs. Guild, Am. Fedn. of Musicians. Composer: Violin Concerto, 1966, Symphony No. 1, 1976, Symphony No. 2, 1979, Symphony No. 3, 1984. Home: 321 High St Duluth MN 55811 Office: Duluth-Superior Symphony Orch 506 W Michigan St Duluth MN 55802

VIRTUE, JACK DOWN, consulting engineer; b. Sioux City, Iowa, July 23, 1930; s. William Wayne and Ariel M. (Moore). B.S.E., Iowa State U., 1952.

Registered profl. engr., Iowa. Ptnr., Virtue & Virtue, Onawa, Iowa, 1960-74; pres. Virtue Engr. P.C., Onawa, 1974—; dir. Pioneer Valley Savs. Bank. Pres. Prairie Gold council Boy Scouts Am., 1976-79; mem. North Central Regional Bd., 1982—. Mem. Monona County Planning and Zoning Com., 1972—; trustee Onawa Pub. Library, 1969. Mem. Iowa Engring. Soc. (N.W. chpt. pres. 1974), Nat. Soc. Profl. Engrs., Soc. Land Surveyors Iowa (dir. 1972-80), Am. Congress Surveying and Mapping. Congregationalist. Lodge: Masons (33 degree). Home: 1004 15th St Onawa IA 51040 Office: Virtue Engr PC Box 99 Onawa IA 51040

VISCLOSKY, PETER JOHN, congressman, lawyer; b. Gary, Ind., Aug. 13, 1949; s. John and Helen (Kauzlaric) V. B.S. in Acctg., Ind. U.-Indpls., 1970; J.D., U. Notre Dame, 1973; LL.M. in Internat. and Comparative Law, Georgetown U., 1983. Bar: Ind., D.C., U.S. Supreme Court. Legal asst. Dist. Atty.'s Office, N.Y.C., 1972; assoc. Benjamin, Greco & Gouveia, Merrillville, Ind., 1973-76, Greco, Gouveia, Miller, Pera & Bishop, Merrillville, Ind., 1982-84; assoc. staff appropriations com. U.S. Ho. of Reps., Washington, 1976-80, assoc. staff budget com., 1980-82; mem. 99th-100th Congresses from 1st dist. Ind., 1985—. Democrat. Roman Catholic. Office: US House of Reps 1632 Longworth Bldg Washington DC 20515 *

VISNAPUU, HERK, architect; b. Tartu, Estonia, Apr. 26, 1920; s. Eduard and Lilli (Tarri) Y.; student Nomme Jr. Coll., Estonia, 1938-40, Tech. U., Tallinn, Estonia, 1942-43, Tech. Inst., Stockholm, 1947-48; A.B., Oberlin Coll., 1950; B.Arch., Western Res. U., 1953; children—Lilli, Andres; came to U.S., 1948; Architect, City Stockholm, 1945; with Ernst Gronwal, Stockholm, 1946, Ancher, Gate & Lindgren, Stockholm, 1947, H.K. Ferguson Co., Cleve., 1950-54, Garfield, Harris, Robinson, Schafer, Cleve., 1954-56; ptnr. Visnapuu & Gaede Architects & Planners, Cleve., 1956-74; chmn. bd. Visnapuu Assocs., Inc., Architects and Planners, 1974-86, chmn. bd. Visnapuu Liebig, Inc. Architects, Engrs., Planners, 1986—. Mem. fine arts adv. com. City of Cleve.; active Cleve. Mus. Art, YMCA. Bd. dirs. Estonian Nat. Com. U.S.A., Estonian Relief Com., Henrik Visnapuu Lit. Found. Recipient nat. award Ch. Archtl. Guild Am., 1962; merit certificate Ohio Prestressed Concrete Inst., 1963; Honor award Architects Soc. Ohio, 1965; Honor award Greater Cleve. Growth Assn., 1971. Registered architect, Ohio, Pa., Ill., Mass., Ind., N.Y., Mich., Fla., Man., Can. Mem. AIA, Royal Archtl. Inst. Can., Korp Sakala (Estonian frat.), Epsilon Delta Rho. Lutheran. Rotarian. Archtl. work exhibited locally and nationally and pub. in nat. archtl. and trade mags. Home: Rosseau PO Box, Rosseau, ON Canada POC 170 Office: 452 Hanna Bldg Cleveland OH 44115

VISSER, AUDRAE EUGENIE, educator, poet; b. Hurley, S.D., June 3, 1919; d. Harry John and Adeline Mae (Perryman) V.; B.S., S.D. State U., 1948; M.A., U. Denver, 1954; 1 son, Harry Gerritt. Tchr. 27 yrs. in S.D., 16 yrs. in Minn. and Japan; tchr. Verdi (Minn.) High Sch., 1974-87; apptd. poet laureate of S.D. by Gov. Richard F. Kneip, 1974. Mem. United Poets Laureate Internat., Nat. League Am. Pen Women, S.D. State Poetry Soc., Nat. Fedn. Press Women, NEA, S.D. Edn. Assn., Minn. Edn. Assn., Bus. and Profl. Women's Clubs, Gen. Fedn. Women's Clubs, AAUW, League of Minn. Poets, Western Women in the Arts, Delta Kappa Gamma. Democrat. Presbyterian. Author: Rustic Roads, 1961; Poems for Brother Donald, 1974; Meter for Momma, 1974; Poems for Pop, 1976; South Dakota, 1980; Honyocker Stories, 1981, Country Cousin, 1986. Home: Elkton SD 57026

VISTE, ARLEN ELLARD, chemistry educator; b. Austin, Minn., Aug. 13, 1936; s. Arthur E. and Edith L. (Kehret) V.; m. Elizabeth Ann Lindbeck, June 14, 1959; children—Solveig, David, Mark. B.A., St. Olaf Coll., 1958; Ph.D., U. Chgo., 1962. Asst. prof. chemistry St. Olaf Coll., Northfield, Minn., 1962-63; NSF fellow Columbia U., N.Y.C., 1963-64; asst. prof. Augustana Coll., Sioux Falls, S.D., 1964-68, assoc. prof., 1968-73, prof., 1973—. Mem. Am. Chem. Soc., Royal Soc. Chemistry (London), S.D. Acad. Sci., Midwest Assn. Chemistry Tchrs. in Liberal Arts Colls., Phi Beta Kappa, Sigma Xi. Contbr. articles to profl. jours. Home: 1500 W 30th St Sioux Falls SD 57105 Office: Augustana Coll Chemistry Dept Sioux Falls SD 57197

VITALE, GERALD LEE, credit union executive; b. Chgo., Apr. 3, 1950; s. Le Roy Allen and Gilda Leanora (Rasori) V. BS in Psychology, Loyola U., Chgo., 1972. Credit mgr. Mellon Fin., Chgo., 1973-76, Kemper Ins. Co., Chgo., 1976-78; pres. Tribune Employees Credit Union, Chgo., 1978—; pres. NCR Credit Union User Group, Dayton, Ohio, 1984—. Counselor Youth Motivation Chgo. Commerce and Industry, 1980—; active Rep. Nat. Com. Republican. Roman Catholic. Club: Press (Chgo.). Avocations: boating, hiking, running. Home: 1636 N Wells #2410 Chicago IL 60614 Office: Tribune Credit Union 435 N Michigan Chicago IL 60605

VITALLO, NUGENT JAMES, computer company executive; b. Chgo., Nov. 10, 1938; s. Angelo Joseph and Anna (Aurrichio) V.; m. Josephine DeJoy, Jan. 25, 1970; children: Michelle, Victoria, Valerie. BS, No. Ill. U., 1963; MA, U. Ill., 1965. CPA, Ill. Sr. acct. Haskins and Sells, Chgo., 1959-63; asst. controller James Beam Dist., Chgo., 1965-67; fin. asst. chmn. Arthur Rubloff, Chgo., 1967-69; v.p., midwest dir. Programmed Tax Service, Chgo., 1969-73; pvt. practice acct. Oak Brook, Ill., 1973-82; treas. Nat. Computer Services, Chgo., 1982-85, pres., 1985—, also bd. dirs.; Treas., bd. dirs. TuKaiz Litho, Inc., Franklin Park, KDA Indsl. Design, Addison, Ill., Microware, Inc., Chgo., Skyware, Inc., Chgo., KMV, Inc., St. Louis, CKMV, Inc., Chgo. Author: (book) The Best Gin, 1973, Bimetamorphisis, 1982; inventor automatic car starter, 1965. Pres. York Woods Community, Oak Brook, 1985-86; treas. York Woods Assn., Oak Brook, 1980-84. Mem. Am. Inst. CPA's, Ill. Soc. CPA's, Mensa. Home: 31 Sheffield Ln Oak Brook IL 60521

VITE, FRANK ANTHONY, realtor; b. Aurora, Ill., Feb. 9, 1930; s. Frank A. and Rose (Cosentino) V.; grad. Marmion Mil. Acad., 1948; student Sch. Mgmt., U. Notre Dame, 1958; D.B.A. (hon.), Hillsdale Coll., 1972; m. Barbara Ann Decio, Oct. 23, 1954; children—Bradley Scott, Mark Steven, Michael Lee, Leslie Ann, Lisa Ann. Plant engr. Lyon Metal Products, Aurora, 1951-52, purchasing agt., 1953-54; became sales mgr., exec. v.p., owner, dir. Skyline Homes, Inc., Elkhart, Ind., 1954; pres., owner B&F Realty, Inc., No. Ind. Appraisal Co., Golden Falcon Homes, Inc.; real estate broker; dir. 1st Nat. Bank, Elkhart, Ind. Trustee Hillsdale (Mich.) Coll.; bd. dirs. Ind. Commn. Higher Edn. Served with AUS, 1952-53, Korea. Mem. Elkhart Bd. Realtors, Nat. Sales Execs. Assn., Ind. Real Estate Assn., Nat. Inst. Real Estate Brokers, Holy Name Soc. Republican. Clubs: K.C. (4 deg.), Knight of Malta, Elks. Home: 23236 Shorelane Elkhart IN 46514 Office: 1300 Cassopolis St Elkhart IN 46514

VITEK, FRANK JOHN, association executive; b. Oak Park, Ill., Aug. 12, 1948; s. Frank John and Marian (Lamberti) V.; m. Bonnie Sue Harmon, July 13, 1970; children: Colin, Stacia. A.S. in Aviation, U. Ill., 1968, B.S. in Communications, 1970; cert. in assn. mgmt. U. Notre Dame, 1982. Mgr. Western Electric, Cicero, Ill., 1970-75; communications dir. Nat. Automatic Laundry and Cleaning Council, Chgo., 1975-79; asst. exec. dir. Nat. Carwash Council, Chgo., 1977-79; pres. Coin Laundry Assn., Downers Grove, Ill., 1979—; cons. to assns., Chgo., 1978-82. Contbr. articles to profl. mags., jours., 1977—. Press sec. Gray for Ill. Treas., 1979; com. mem. Nat. Fire Protection Assn., 1982-88. Served to lt. USMC, 1967-69. Recipient awards of appreciation U.S. Jaycees, Chgo., 1974-75. Fellow World Ednl. Congress for Laundering and Drycleaning (exec. dir. 1981-87, Meritorious Service award 1977); mem. Am. Soc. Assn. Execs., Chgo. Soc. Assn. Execs., Meeting Planners Internat., Found. Internat. Meetings, Chgo. Area Planners, Laundry Cleaning Council (treas. 1980-85), Chgo. Jr. Assn. Commerce and Industry (bd. dirs. 1972-75), Chgo. Jaycees (v.p. 1973-75). Avocations: sports (skiing, tennis, golf, racketball, and others); reading. Office: Coin Laundry Assn 1315 Butterfield Rd Suite 212 Downers Grove IL 60515

VITITOE, WILLIAM PAUL, telephone company executive; b. Evansville, Ind., Sept. 19, 1938; s. Paul Revere and Mariam Elizabeth V.; m. Susan Hoover, July 16, 1960; children: Laura, Stephanie. B.S., Ind. U., 1960. With Ind. Bell Telephone Co., 1961-71, 73-77, 82-83, gen. mgr. North area, 1977, pres., 1982-83; traffic ops. mgr. AT&T, N.Y.C., 1971-73; asst. v.p. bus. services transmission implementation AT&T, 1981-82; v.p. fin., comptroller Mich. Bell Telephone Co., Detroit, 1977-80; v.p. bus. Mich. Bell Telephone Co., 1980-81, pres., 1983—; bd. dirs. Amerisure, Inc., Comerica Inc., Comerica Bank-Detroit, Cross & Trecker Corp., Mich. Bell; mem. Conf. Bd. Bd. dirs. Detroit Symphony Orch., 1983—, Econ. Alliance for Mich., 1983—, Detroit Econ. Growth Corp., St. John Hosp., Detroit, 1983—, Mich. High Tech. Task Force, United Found., Detroit Renaissance, Inc., 1983—, Mich. Thanksgiving Parade Found.; trustee Interlochen Ctr. for Arts, New Detroit, Inc., Safety Council S.E. Mich., Traffic Safety Assn. Mich.; mem.-at-large Detroit Area council Boy Scouts Am.; chmn. Gov.'s Exec. Corps., Mich. Strategic Fund; mem. Gov.'s Commn. on Jobs and Econ. Devel., Mich. Opera Theatre, Partnerships for Edn. Task Force. Served with USAR, 1960-61. Mem. Fin. Execs. Inst., Detroit Econ. Club (chmn. bd. 1985—), NAACP (life mem.), Founders Soc. Detroit Inst. Arts, Detroit Artists Market. Clubs: Country of Detroit, Detroit Athletic, Detroit, Renaissance, Lochmoor, Grosse Pointe. Office: Mich Bell Telephone Co 444 Michigan Ave Detroit MI 48226

VITTON, PATRICIA EVA, personnel executive; b. Milw., Dec. 19, 1953; d. Robert Arthur and Frances Marie (Mainville) Gussert; m. Robert Paul Vitton, Apr. 17, 1977; children: Catherine Anne, Robert Peter. Student, Mich. Tech. U., 1972-85. Child care worker Goodwill Farm, Houghton, Mich.; employment interviewer Mich. Employment Security Commn., Houghton, 1976-81; br. mgr. Mich. Employment Security Commn., Ironwood, Mich., 1981-82; employee relations asst. Mich. Tech. U., Houghton, 1982-84, office mgr., 1984-86, asst. dir. employee relations, 1986—; mem. adv. bd. Univ. Safety Bd., Houghton, 1985. Vol. VISTA, Hancock, Mich., 1975. Nat. Merit scholar, 1971. Mem. Am. Mgmt. Assn., Coll. And Univ. Personnel Assn., Mich. Coll. and Univ. Personnel Assn. (mem. compensation com. adv. bd. 1985—, chair-elect 1987—), Mich. Women Assn., Upper Peninsula Personnel Assn. (sec.-treas.). Home: 911 Poplar St Hancock MI 49930 Office: Mich Tech U Houghton MI 49931

VITULLI, CLARK JOSEPH, auto manufacturing company executive; b. Bklyn., Apr. 2, 1946; s. William and Rosaria (Stallone) V. B.S., U. Fla., 1968. With Chrysler Corp., various locations, 1969—, zone mgr., Los Angeles, 1980-84, nat. mdse. mgr. Dodge div., Detroit, 1984-86, regional mgr., Anaheim, Calif., 1986—; mem. dealer licensing div. Fla. Dept. Motor Vehicles, 1978-79. Mem. Am. Mgmt. Assn., Sales and Mktg. Execs. Los Angeles, Adcraft Club of Detroit, Internat. Platform Assn., Mensa, Beta Theta Pi.

VIVONA, DANIEL NICHOLAS, chemist; b. Chgo., Apr. 13, 1924; s. Daniel and Mary Rose (Lamonico) V.; student Chgo. City Coll., 1941-42, 46; B.A., U. Maine, 1951; M.S., Pa. State U., 1953; postgrad. Purdue U., 1953-56; m. Helen Mary Belanger, Sept. 14, 1950; 1 son, Daniel Maurice. Instr. chemistry Purdue U., Lafayette, Ind., 1955-56; with Minn. Mining and Mfg. Co., St. Paul, 1956-86, sr. chemist, 1969-79, info. scientist, 1979-81, quality assurance sr. chemist, 1981-86; cons., 1986—. Served with USAAF, 1942-45. Decorated Air medal with oak leaf clusters, DFC. Dow Corning fellow, 1952-53. Mem. Am. Chem. Soc., Phi Beta Kappa. Roman Catholic. Club: Toastmasters. Home: 3253 Kraft Circle North Lake Elmo MN 55042 Office: Minn Mining and Mfg Co 235-1E-14 Saint Paul MN 55144

VLAHOPOULOS, BASIL ALEX, counselor; b. Jersey City, Dec. 26, 1950; s. Constantine Basil Vlahopoulos and Christina (Antos) Stratos. BA in Psychology, Deree Coll., Athens, 1973; MA in Counseling, Ball State U., 1976; EdD, U. Cin., 1986. Lic. profl. counselor, disability issues consultant. Instr. U. Cin., 1977-80; rehab. counselor Stepping Stones, Cin., 1981-82; coordinator peer counseling Total Living Concepts, Cin., 1983-84; pvt. practice as counselor to handicapped, physically disabled and multiple sclerosis patients Cin., 1984—; adviser Multiple Sclerosis Soc. Cin., 1983-85. Mem. Greater Cin. Coalition for People with Disabilities, 1980—, Law Enforcement Task Force, Cin., 1986—, Fed. Transp. Task Force, Cin., 1986—; co-chmn. Specialized Transp. Adv. Com., Cin., 1980—; bd. dirs. Project Amos, Cin., 1985—. Mem. Nat. Assn. Physically Handicapped, Nat. Rehab. Assn., Southwestern Ohio Rehabilitation Assn. (bd. dirs. 1986—). Democrat. Greek Orthodox. Avocation: reading. Home: 21 W McMillan St #403 Cincinnati OH 45219

VLAISAVLJEVICH, MICHAEL, tax research director; b. Chgo., Feb. 15, 1946; s. George and Ann (Cubra) V.; m. Laureen Jarek, July 20, 1968. BA, Knox Coll., 1967; MA in Govt., Ind. U., 1972. Cert. level II fin. analyst. Asst. prof. U. Evansville, Ind., 1969-72; instr. U. Mo., St. Louis, 1972-73; tax policy supr. Wis. Legis. Fiscal Bur., Madison, 1974-79; research dir. Wis. Dept. Revenue, Madison, 1979—; cons. Nat. Assn. State Budget Officers, Washington, 1984-86. Dir. Legislation State Tax Reform, 1985. bd. dirs. YMCA, Madison, 1976-79. Mem. Nat. Assn. Tax Adminstrs. Avocations: investment analysis, racquetball, golf. Home: 511 Sheldon St Madison WI 53711 Office: Wis Dept Revenue 129 S Webster Madison WI 53702

VLEISIDES, GREGORY WILLIAM, lawyer; b. Kansas City, Mo., June 17, 1950; s. William Chris and Irene Helen (Karos) V. B.A., U. Kans., 1972; J.D., U. Mo.-Kansas City, 1976. Bar: Mo. 1977, U.S. Dist. Ct. (we. dist.) Mo. 1977, U.S. Ct. Appeals (8th cir.) 1977. Law clk. Cir. Ct. Jackson County, Mo., Kansas City, 1977-78; assoc. Tierney & Ernst, Kansas City, 1978-84; sr. ptnr. Gregory W. Vleisides, P.C., Kansas City, 1984—; of counsel F. Lee Bailey Law Offices, Boston, 1984-85, ptnr. Turner & Boisseau, Kansas City, Mo., Overland Park, Wichita and Great Bend, Kans. 1985—; cons. Telecom Corp., Overland Park, Kans., 1978—; guest lectr. Avila Coll., Kansas City, 1984; regional counsel Video Software Dealers Assn., 1985-87. Co-author: Challenges to Court Action in Child Abuse and Neglect Cases, 1976; contbg. author: Opening Statements, 1984; Closing Arguments, 1984. Host com. Republican Nat. Conv., Kansas City, Mo., 1976. Mem. ABA, Mo. Bar Assn., Kansas City Bar Assn. (bar-media com. 1978-84), Kansas City Met. Bar Assn. (press and pub. relations adv. bd. 1985—), Phi Beta Kappa, Delta Theta Pi. Greek Orthodox. Home: 3008 W 84th Pl Leawood KS 66206 Office: Law Offices Gregory W Vleisides PC 1001 E 101st Terr Kansas City MO 64131

VLK, CHARLES ROBERT, architect, manager; b. Oak Park, Ill., Oct. 12, 1945; s. Robert Frank and Doris June (Horak) V.; m. Barbara Veronica Grodek, Dec. 30, 1967; children: Jennifer Leigh, Michael Adam. BS in Archtl. Engring., Chgo. Tech. Coll., 1969; MS in Mgmt. and Devel., Nat. Coll. Edn., 1987. Registered architect, Ill. Draftsman Holabird & Root, Chgo., 1965-66, job capt., 1967-69; draftsman Milton S. Carstens, Chgo., 1966-67; engr. Ill. Bell, Chgo., 1969-77, mgr., 1979-85; mgr. Gen. Depts. AT&T, Basking Ridge, N.J., 1977-79, Ameritech Services, Schaumburg, Ill., 1985—. architect St. Dominic's Parish Ctr., Bolingbrook, Ill., 1976. Mem. AIA (corp., registration task force Ill. council 1982—, Disting. Service award Ill. council 1984), Internat. Facility Mgmt. Assn., Soc. Am. Value Engrs., Burlington Route Hist. Soc. (tech. advisor 1984—). Roman Catholic. Club: Racine (Wis.) Yacht. Avocations: sailing, railroad history. Home: 1012 N Chestnut Ave Arlington Heights IL 60004 Office: Ameritech Services Inc 1900 E Golf Rd Schaumburg IL 60173

VOBACH, WILLIAM H., state senator. Mem. Ind. State Senate from Dist. 31, 1983—; practice law, Indpls. Republican. Office: One Indiana Sq Suite 2120 Indianapolis IN 46204

VOCK, JOY MARIE, academic administrator; b. Dixon, Ill., Mar. 5, 1959; d. Carl Joseph and Anne Louise (Rock) V. BA, Augustana Coll., 1981; MS, Western Ill. U., 1983. Dir. residence Rockford (Ill.) Coll., 1983-84, dir. career services, 1984-87, assoc. dean students, acting dean students, 1987—. Mem. Am. Assn. Counseling and Devel., Am. Coll. Personnel Assn., Midwest Coll. Personnel Assn., Assn. Schs. Coll. and Univ. Staffing. Avocations: biking, dancing, swimming, reading. Office: Rockford Coll 5050 E State St Rockford IL 61108-2393

VODERBERG, KURT ERNEST, machinery sales company executive; b. Rendsburg, Germany, Apr. 8, 1921; s. Max Henry and Margarethe (Siedel) V.; m. Louise Collier, May 21, 1948 (div. 1969); children—Paul, John, Mary Beth, Jill; m. 2d, Sophie Dufft, Sept. 5, 1969. B.S. in M.E., Ill. Inst. Tech., 1943; postgrad. Northwestern U., 1944-45. Registered profl. engr., Ill. Asst. master mechanic Danly Machine Co., Cicero, Ill., 1943-47; pres. Dynamic Machine Co., Chgo., 1947-75, pres. Dynamic Machinery Sales, Inc., Chgo., 1975—, pres. Paramount Machinery Sales Co., Chgo., 1982-85. Mem. Ill. Soc. Profl. Engrs., Soc. Mfg. Engrs., Tool and Die Inst., Chgo. Assn. Commerce and Industry (mem. com.). Lutheran. Clubs: Michigan Shores, American Turners, Glenbrook Shrine. Lodge: Masons. Patentee in field. Home: 1440 Sheridan Rd Apt 706 Wilmette IL 60091 Office: 1800 N Rockwell St Chicago IL 60647

VOEDISCH, LYNN ANDREA, reporter; b. Evanston, Ill., June 20, 1954; d. Robert William and Elaine Theresa (Strand) V.; m. Kent Van Meter, June 21, 1981 (div. 1987); 1 child, Erik Kyle. BA, Grinnell Coll., 1976. Reporter Pioneer Press, Wilmette, Ill., 1977-79, Los Angeles Times, 1979, Chgo. Sun-Times, 1980—. Recipient Stick O'Type award Chgo. Newspaper Guild, 1984. Democrat. Episcopalian. Avocations: singing, theater, baroque music, sewing. Office: Chgo Sun-Times 401 N Wabash Ave Chicago IL 60611

VOEGE, JANIS MACKEY, home economics educator, consultant, researcher, administrator; b. Carbondale, Ill., May 26, 1942; d. Paul Fairless and Lois Violet (Mallory) Mackey; m. Herbert Walter Voege, June 12, 1972; children: Jana R., Mark S., Amy J. BS, So. Ill. U., 1963, MA, 1968; PhD, Mich. State U., 1977. With Coop. Extension Service, U. Ill., Champaign-Urbana, 1963-66; prof. Adrian (Mich.) Coll., 1968-72; prof. home econs. Cen. Mich. U., Mt. Pleasant, 1972—, chmn. dept., 1980-83; owner, pres. Theory and Practice, Inc. Mem. joint council on econ. edn. programs for elderly consumers and high sch. students. Shell Oil grantee, 1969; Coll. Human Ecology grantee, 1976; Am. Home Econs. Assn. fellow, 1975; Kellogg Found. grantee, 1971. Mem. Am. Home Econs. Assn. (Premier Class of Leaders 1984), Mich. Home Econs. Assn., Nat. Council on Family Relations, Mich. Council on Family Relations, Am. Council on Consumer Interests, Consumer Educators of Mich., Assn. Consumer Research, Soc. Study Social Problems, World Future Soc., Kappa Omicron Phi, Omicron Nu. Contbr. articles to publs. in field. Office: Cen Mich U 209 Wightman Hall Mount Pleasant MI 48859

VOELKER, GERALD MILTON, dentist; b. Appleton, Wis., Aug. 24, 1955; s. Milton Harold and Margherita (DeBerry) V.; m. Teri Lynn Mensching, June 24, 1978; children: Jillian, Nicholas. Student, U. Wis., 1973-76; DDS cum laude, Marquette U., 1981. Pvt. practice dentistry Wisconsin Rapids, Wis., 1981—. Pres. United Way of Southwood County, Wisconsin Rapids, 1984; v.p. Am. Cancer Soc. Southwood Unit, Wisconsin Rapids, 1985; bd. dirs. Midstate Epilepsy Assn., Stevens Point, Wis., 1981—. U. Wis. scholar, 1976. Mem. ADA, Acad. Gen. Dentistry, Am. Acad. Orthodontics for Gen. Practitioner, Wis. Dental Assn., Omicron Kappa Upsilon, Phi Kappa Phi, Phi Eta Sigma. Avocations: woodworking, fishing, racquetball, musician. Home: 5620 Big Timber Circle Wisconsin Rapids WI 54494 Office: 1980 7th St S Wisconsin Rapids WI 54494

VOGEL, ARTHUR ANTON, clergyman; b. Milw., Feb. 24, 1924; s. Arthur Louis and Gladys Eirene (Larson) V.; m. Katharine Louise Nunn, Dec. 29, 1947; children: John Nunn, Arthur Anton, Katharine Ann. Student, U. of South, 1942-43, Carroll Coll., 1943-44; B.D., Nashotah House Theol. Sem., 1946; M.A., U. Chgo., 1948; Ph.D., Harvard, 1952; S.T.D., Gen. Theol. Sem., 1969; D.C.L., Nashotah House, 1969; D.D., U. of South, 1971. Ordained deacon Episcopal Ch., 1946, priest, 1948; teaching asst. philosophy Harvard, Cambridge, Mass., 1949-50; instr. Trinity Coll., Hartford, Conn., 1950-52; mem. faculty Nashotah House Theol. Sem., Nashotah, Wis., 1952-71; asso. prof. Nashotah House Theol. Sem., 1954-56, William Adams prof. philosophical and systematic theology, 1956-71, sub-dean Sem., 1964-71; bishop coadjutor Diocese of West Mo., Kansas City, 1971-72; bishop Diocese of West Mo., 1972—; Rector Ch. St. John Chrysostom, Delafield, Wis., 1952-56; dir. Anglican Theol. Rev., Evanston, Ill., 1964-69; mem. Internat. Anglican-Roman Cath. Consultation, 1970—; mem. Nat. Anglican-Roman Catholic Consultation, 1965-84, Anglican chmn., 1973-84; mem. Standing Commn. on Ecumenical Relations of Episcopal Ch., 1957-79; mem. gen. bd. examining chaplains Episcopal Ch., 1971-72; del. Episcopal Ch., 4th Assembly World Council Chruches, Uppsala, Sweden, 1968, and others. Author: Reality, Reason and Religion, 1957, The Gift of Grace, 1958, The Christian Person, 1963, The Next Christian Epoch, 1966, Is the Last Supper Finished?, 1968, Body Theology, 1973, The Power of His Resurrection, 1976, Proclamation 2: Easter, 1980, The Jesus Prayer for Today, 1982; editor: Theology in Anglicanism, 1985; contbr. to profl. jours. Vice chmn. bd. dirs. St. Luke's Hosp., Kansas City, Mo., 1971, chmn., 1973—. Research fellow Harvard, 1950. Mem. Am. Philos. Assn., Metaphys. Soc. Am., Soc. Existential and Phenomenological Philosophy, Catholic Theol. Soc. Am. Home: 524 W 119th Terr Kansas City MO 64145 Office: The Diocese of West Mo 420 W 14th St PO Box 423216 Kansas City MO 64141 *

VOGEL, CARL EDWARD, property administration executive; b. Chgo., Oct. 21, 1919; s. Eugene E. and Madeline (Keim) V.; student Wilson Jr. Coll., Chgo., 1937-39, Northwestern U., 1940-41; m. Frances Stevens Terrell, Mar. 17, 1945; children—Cynthia, Susan, Meredith, Kirkland. With Nat. Bur. Property Adminstrn., Inc., Chgo., 1939—, chmn. bd., exec. v.p., 1958-63, chmn. bd., pres., 1963—; chmn. bd., pres. Kirkland Corp., Chgo., 1969—. Active in local fund-raising drives. Served to 1st lt. USAAF, 1942-46. Mem. Chgo. Assn. Commerce and Industry, Nat. Assn. Rev. Appraisers, Internat. Assn. Assessing Officers, Nat. Tax Assn., Inst. Property Taxation. Clubs: Mid-America (Chgo.); North Shore Country (Glenview). Home: 720 Glenayre Dr Glenview IL 60025 Office: 1824 Prudential Plaza Chicago IL 60601

VOGEL, DAVID JOHN, financial executive, consultant; b. Clinton, Iowa, Dec. 2, 1946; s. Marion Jacob and Ruth Lorraine (Hoogheem) V.; m. Mary Katherine Armstrong, June 10, 1967; children: Christine, Thomas. BBA in Acctg. with honors, Western Ill. U., 1969. CPA, Iowa. Staff acct. McCladrey Hendrickson & Pullen CPA's, Davenport, Iowa, 1969-73; ptnr. McCladrey Hendrickson & Pullen CPA's, Clinton, 1973-79; fin. mgr. Drives, Inc., Fulton, Ill., 1979-81; exec. v.p. Agri-King, Inc., Fulton, 1981—, also bd. dirs. Founding bd. dirs. Fulton Community Fund, Inc. 1974-83. Mem. Ill. CPA Soc., Am. Inst. CPA's. Presbyterian. Avocation: sports.

VOGEL, GERALD LEON, insurance company executive; b. Dodge City, Kans., Oct. 8, 1952; s. M. Leon and Agnes P. (Tematt) V.; m. Candace F. McGrew, Mar. 26, 1977; children: Alicia D., Adrian L., Adam R. AS, Dodge City Community Coll., 1972; BS in Acctg., Ft. Hays State U., 1974. Acct. Plains Ins. Co., Cimarron, Kans., 1974-75; treas. Plains Ins. Co., Cimarron, 1975—; acct. Cimarron Ins. Co., 1974-75, treas., 1975—; acct. Cimarron Investment Co., 1974-75, treas., 1975—. Scoutmaster Troop 148 Boy Scouts Am., Cimarron, 1980-83; mem. audit com. Santa Fe council Boy Scouts Am., Garden City, Kans., 1986—; pres. Gray County Am. Cancer Soc., Cimarron, 1983—; bd. dirs. Cimarron Library, 1986—. Mem. Am. Inst. CPA's, Kans Soc. CPA's. Democrat. Roman Catholic. Lodge: Rotary (treas., sec., v.p and pres. Cimarron 1977-80). Avocations: skiing, fishing, working with kids, woodworking. Home: Box 4 Cimarron KS 67835 Office: Cimarron Insurance Co Inc Main St Cimarron KS 67835

VOGEL, RICHARD DWIGHT, funeral home director, mortician, grief counselor; b. Hampton, Iowa, Sept. 27, 1956; s. Trent Henry and Judith (Davis) V. Student, N. Iowa Area Community Coll., 1975-76, Wartburg Coll., 1977-78; grad. in mortuary sci. with honors, Dallas Inst. Funeral Services, 1980. Funeral dir. Smith Funeral Home, Grinnel, Iowa, 1980-82, Oppold Funeral Home, Waterloo, Iowa, 1982-85; ptnr. Surls Funeral Homes, Iowa Falls, Alden, Williams, Iowa, 1985—; mem. adv. bd. mortuary sci. N. Iowa Area Community Coll., 1985-86. Mem. Nat. Funeral Dirs. Assn., Iowa Funeral Dirs. Assn. (dist. lt. gov. 1984—, young funeral dirs. com. 1984—, membership com. 1985—), Iowa Ducks Unltd. (chpt. com.), Iowa Pheasants Forever. Republican. Methodist. Lodges: Rotary (fundraising chair Iowa Falls club 1986—), Elks, Moose. Avocations: skiing, swimming, golfing, raquetball, hunting. Home: 1207 Alden Alden IA 50006 Office: Surls Funeral Home 505 Stevens Iowa Falls IA 50126

VOGELSANG, WILLIAM R., utilities company executive; b. 1925. BS, Kent State U., 1949; student, Case-Western Res. U., 1971. Corp. sec. Cleve. Electric Illuminating Co., 1949-74; v.p. fin. services San Diego Gas & Electric Co., 1974-77; with Cen. Ill. Lighting Co., Peoria, 1977—, treas., asst. v.p. fin., 1977-78, v.p., treas., 1978-80, v.p. fin., 1980-81, sr. v.p. fin., 1981-82, exec. v.p. fin., 1982-84, pres., chief operating officer, 1984-85, pres., chief exec. officer, 1985—. Served with USAAF, 1943-46. Office: Cen Ill Lights Co 300 Liberty St Peoria IL 61602 *

VOGES, HENRY BYRD, JR., real estate executive; b. St. Louis, Aug. 30, 1959; s. Henry B. and Charlotte Dee (Wetteroth) V.; m. Nancy A. Minney, June 30, 1979; 1 child, Richard H. BBA, Washington U., St. Louis, 1981; postgrad., St. Louis U., 1986—. Cert. property mgr., Mo. Area mgr. Cen. Parking System, St. Louis, 1979-81; property mgr. Nooney Mgmt. Co., St. Louis, 1981-83, sr. property mgr., 1983—. Mem. Inst. Real Estate Mgmt. Republican. Methodist. Avocation: tennis. Office: Nooney Mgmt Co 7701 Forsyth Saint Louis MO 63105

VOGLER, DENNIS JOSEPH, accountant, tax consultant; b. St. Louis, Sept. 30, 1950; s. William August and Margaret Ann (Bohn) V.; m. Patricia Ann McComy, May 26, 1973; children: Michael, Karen, Kelly. BS in Acctg., St. Louis U., 1973; MA in Acctg., U. Mo., 1974. CPA, Ill., Mo. Tax mgr. Deloitte, Haskins & Sells, St. Louis, 1974-81; ptnr. Brandvein, Shapiro & Kossmeyer, St. Louis, 1981-86; pvt. practice acctg. Columbia, Ill., 1986—; adj. instr. St. Louis U., 1983—. Mem. Am. Inst. CPA's, Mo. Soc. CPA's, Ill. CPA Soc. (instr. 1985—). Avocations: racquetball, coaching soccer. Home: 5365 Gloucester High Ridge MO 63049 Office: 1020 N Main Columbia IL 63226

VOGNAR, GEORGE WILLIAM, family therapist, consultant; b. Chgo., July 25, 1937; s. George Washington and Estelle Bartyska V.; m. Joanne Ryan, July 1, 1963 (div. Aug. 1971); m. Helga Christine Midelfort, July 5, 1981; 1 child, Helga Anastasia. BA, Roosevelt U., 1965; MA, U. Chgo., 1977. Supr. Attleboro (Mass.) Mental Health Clinic, 1980-82, Northland Mental Health Clinic, Grand Rapids, 1982-83; social worker Wilder Child Guidance, Mpls., 1983-84; supr. Family Service, Milw., 1984-85; sr. psychotherapist Mt. Sinai Outpatient Clinic, Milw., 1985-86; sr. family therapy trainer Family Service Milw., 1984-86; psychotherapist Group Health, Mpls., 1986—; sr. family therapy trainer Family Service, Milw., 1984—; cons. 16th St. Health Ctr., Milw., 1985—, St. Amealans, Milw., 1985, Walkers Pt., Milw., 1985. Served with U.S. Army, 1960-62. Mem. Assn. Cert. Social Workers, Assn. Health Care Profls. in Clin. Social Work, Am. Family Therapy Assn. (charter), Am. Assn. for Marriage and Family Therapy (clin.). Democrat. Lutheran. Home: 2160 Carter Ave Saint Paul MN 55108 Office: Group Health 2500 Como Ave Saint Paul MN 55108

VOGT, DAVID RUSSELL, software company executive; b. Dayton, Ohio, Feb. 13, 1941; s. Russell Howard and Wilma Lorain (Kinsey) V.; m. Kathryn Lois Yurk, Aug. 29, 1964; children: James David, Erik Jon. BSEE, U. Wis., 1965; MS in Mgmt. Sci., U. Wis., Milw., 1979. Procedures analyst Univ. Facilities Research Ctr., Madison, Wis., 1965-67; facilities mgr. Cen. Adminstrn. U. Wis., Madison, 1967-69; registrar U. Wis. Parkside, Kenosha, 1969-80; forecast analyst Shade Info. Systems, Green Bay, Wis., 1980-86; dir. devel. WISARD Software Co., De Pere, Wis., 1986—; facilities specialist U.S. Agy. for Internat. Devel., Medillian, Columbia, 1967. Mem. Internat. Inst. Forecasters, Inst. Mgmt. Scis., Beta Gamma Sigma. Club: Trout Unltd. (bd. dirs. 1982—) (Green Bay). Avocations: fishing, cross-country skiing.

VOGT, STEPHEN HENRY, metal processing executive; b. Valparaiso, Ind., June 30, 1944; s. George H. and Kathryn T. (Liming) V.; m. Carol Ann Kontor, Jan. 13, 1968; children: Christopher A., Matthew E., Jason F. BSBA, Valparaiso U., 1966; MBA, Ind. U., 1973. Asst. div. controller U.S. Steel, Chgo., 1966-77; dir. fin. Atcor Inc., Harvey, Ill., 1977-85; exec. v.p., chief fin. officer Nat. Castings Inc., Oak Brook, Ill., 1985—, also bd. dirs. Served with USAR. Mem. Nat. Assn. Accts., Fin. Execs. Inst. Republican. Roman Catholic. Avocations: physical fitness, travel, reading, sports. Office: Nat Castings Inc 1400 S Laramie Ave Cicero IL 60650

VOGT, THOMAS ROBERT, architect; b. Spencer, Iowa, Jan. 16, 1957; s. Gaylord Lyle and Donna Jean (Valdahl) V.; m. Melanie Louise Polking, June 8, 1984; 1 child, Lindsay Ann. BArch, Iowa State U., 1980. Intern architect Griffith Co., PC, Ft. Dodge, Iowa, 1980—. Mem. AIA (assoc.). Roman Catholic. Avocations: photography, running, tennis, hunting. Home: 3140 13th Ave N Fort Dodge IA 50501 Office: Griffith Co PC Architects 709 Kenyon Rd Fort Dodge IA 50501

VOGTMANN, TERRENCE KENNETH, computer software company executive; b. Pasa Robles, Calif., Aug. 8, 1955; s. Kenneth Harry and Phyllis Elsie (Koch) V.; m. Frances Jean Williams, May 9, 1981; children: Emily Jean, Nicholas Terrence. BS, Western Mich. U., 1978. Account exec. Automatic Data Processing, Kalamazoo, 1978-80, Gen. Electric, Grand Rapids, Mich., 1980-81; mktg. mgr. computer strategies Cullinet Software Inc., Grand Rapids, 1981-84, regional mgr. computer strategies, 1984-85, v.p. sales and mktg. computer strategies, 1985—. Deacon John Knox Presbyn. Ch., Grand Rapids, 1983-86. Mem. Am. Prodn. and Inventory Control Soc. Republican. Lodge: Elks. Avocations: golf, skiing, raquetball. Home: 7639 Candlewood SE Ada MI 49301 Office: Cullinet Software Inc 3940 Peninsular Dr Suite 100 Grand Rapids MI 49506

VOICA, JOSEPH ANDREW, marketing professional; b. Sheboygan, Wis., Aug. 29, 1960; s. Rudolph and Mary Rita (Dusthimer) V. BS, U. Wis., Stevens Point, 1982; MBA, U. Wis., Oshkosh, 1984. Sales support IBM, Green Bay, Wis., 1982-83; staff mgr. mktg. Wis. Bell, Inc., Milw., 1984—; mem. exec. bd. Spl. Olympics, Milw., 1984—. Instr. Jr. Achievement, Milw., 1986. Mem. Am. Mktg. Assn. Republican. Roman Catholic. Office: Wis Bell Inc 2600 N Mayfair Rd Suite 1100 Wauwatosa WI 53226

VOICA, RUDOLPH, psychologist, educator; b. East Chicago, Ind., Aug. 6, 1923; s. Jordan and Anna V.; M.S., Inst. State U., Terre Haute, 1952; postgrad. U. Denver, 1956, Ind. U., Bloomington, 1957, Marquette U., 1959, State U. Iowa, 1962; m. Mary Rita Dusthimer, Sept. 22, 1951; children—Michael, Robert, Joseph. Tchr., counselor Roosevelt High Sch., East Chicago Public Schs., 1952-56; dir. guidance South High Sch., Sheboygan Public Schs., 1957-64; dir. student services U. Wis. Center System, Sheboygan, 1964-70; sr. sch. psychologist Stevens Point Area (Wis.) Public Sch. Dist., 1970—; dist. trainer, resource cons. child abuse and neglect, 1977—. Exec. dir. Portage County chpt. Big Bros. Am., 1972, Sheboygan chpt., 1966-69; instr. evening adult edn. program Hammond (Ind.) Vocat. Tech. High Sch., 1953-56, Sheboygan (Wis.) Vocat.-Tech. Inst., 1959-62; pres. Portage County Assn. Mental Health, 1971-72, exec. com. chmn., 1972-73; v.p. Portage County Council Alcohol and Drug Abuse, 1974-75; bd. dirs. Halfway House, Sheboygan, 1967-68, Head Start Program, Sheboygan, 1967-68. Served with U.S. Army, 1943-46, 50-51. Recipient Wis. Gov.'s Spl. award, 1968. Mem. Am. Psychol. Assn., Am. Assn. for Counseling and Devel., Phi Delta Kappa. Roman Catholic. Home: 714 Maplewood Dr Plover WI 54467 Office: 1900 Polk St Stevens Point WI 54481

VOIGHT, JERRY SAM, retired pharmacist, graphic arts company executive; b. Owosso, Mich., Oct. 27, 1935; s. Sam H. and Opal E. (Stuphen) V.; m. Carolyn Sue Osmer, June 19, 1960; children: Sheryl, Jeffrey, Laura. BS, Ferris State Coll., Mich., 1958. Owner Voights Pharmacies, Owosso, Durano and Chesaning, Mich., to 1985; pres. Owosso Graphic Arts, 1965—. Mem. Owosso C. of C. Republican. Club: Owosso Country. Lodges: Kiwanis, Masons. Avocations: running, books, music, trees. Home: 1233 Ada Owosso MI 48867

VOIGHT, NANCY LEE (MRS. JAY VAN HOVEN), counseling psychologist; b. Kansas City, Mo., Nov. 24, 1945; d. Paul and Leona Alvina (Schultz) V.; B.A., Wittenberg U., 1967; M.A., Ball State U., 1971; Ph.D., Mich. State U., 1975; m. Jay Van Hoven, June 27, 1975; children—Joshua, Janna, Lydia. Tchr. lang. arts Ashland (Ohio) City Schs., 1967-68; tchr. English, Speedway (Ind.) City Schs., 1969; basic literacy instr. Army Edn. Center, Gelnhausen, W. Ger., 1969-70; individual assistance Bethel Home for Boys, Gaston, Ind., 1970-71; counselor Wittenberg U. Ohio, 1971-72; staff psychologist Ingham County Probate Ct., Lansing, Mich., 1972-74; asst. prof. U. N.C., Chapel Hill, 1975-79, counseling psychologist, 1976-79; psychologist for employee devel. Gen. Telephone Electronics, No. Region Hdqrs., Indpls., 1979-80; behavioral sci. coordinator Family Practice Center, Community Hosp., Indpls., 1980-82; media psychologist Sta. WIFE, Indpls., 1981-82; asst. dir. Chapel Hill Counseling Center, 1980-86; dir. Behavior Therapy Ctr., Indpls., 1982-86; treas. Med. Specialty Disability Ins. Corp., Indpls., 1982-86; psychologist Alternatives to Boys Sch., 1983-85; staff psychologist Meth. Hosp. Ind., 1985-86; psychologist Dept. Corrections State of Mich., Kincheloe, 1986—; advisor Sex Info. and Counseling Center, Chapel Hill, 1977-79. Chmn. housing bd. U. N.C., 1976-79. Office Edn. grantee, 1977-78, 78-80; Spencer Found. young scholars grantee. Mem. Am. Psychol. Assn., Ind. Psychol. Assn., Mich. Psychol. Assn., Assn. Advancement Behavior Therapy, Inst. Rational Living, Soc. Behavioral Medicine, Am. Assn. Marriage and Family Therapists. Lutheran. Author: Becoming, 1978; Becoming: Leader's Guide, 1978; Becoming Aware, 1979; Becoming Informed, 1979; Becoming Strong, 1979; also articles. Home: Box 326 DeTour Village MI 49725 Office: Kinross Corrections Facility Health Services Kincheloe AFB MI 49788

VOINOVICH, GEORGE V., city official; b. Cleve., July 15, 1936; m. Janet Voinovich; 3 children. B.A., Ohio U., 1958; J.D., Ohio State U., 1961; LL.D. (hon.), Ohio U., 1981. Bar: Ohio 1961, U.S. Supreme Ct. 1968. Asst. atty. gen. State of Ohio, 1963-64; mem. Ohio Ho. of Reps., 1967-71; auditor Cuyahoga County, Ohio, 1971-76; commr. 1976-78; lt. gov. State of Ohio, 1979; mayor City of Cleve., 1979—; 1st v.p. Nat. League Cities, 1984-85, pres., 1985; trustee U.S. Conf. Mayors. Recipient cert. of Merit award Ohio U., Humanitarian award NCCJ, 1986; named one of Outstanding Young Men in Ohio Ohio Jaycees, 1970; one of Outstanding Young Men in Greater Cleve. Cleve. Jaycees. Mem. Omicron Delta Kappa, Phi Alpha Theta, Phi Delta Phi. Republican. Office: City Hall 601 Lakeside Ave E Cleveland OH 44114

VOJTUSH, DELCIA PAULINE, nurse; b. Warfordsburg, Pa., Apr. 10, 1932; d. Lester Joseph and Martha Elizabeth (Parnell) Mann; m. John Stephen Vojtush, Aug. 2, 1956; children: John Jr., Janice, Gary, Gayle, Dean, Daryl, Lisa. Diploma, Sch. Nursing Uniontown (Pa.) Hosp., 1952, Anesthesia Sch. St. Francis Hosp., 1956. Registered nurse anesthetist. Nurse Uniontown Hosp., 1952-55; nurse anesthetist Children's Hosp., Pitts., 1956, Doctors Hosp., Cleve., 1957-68, Suburban Commn. Hosp., Warrensville Heights, Ohio, 1968—. Mem. Am. Assn. Nurse Anesthetists. Democrat. Roman Catholic. Avocations: camping, reading, sewing, traveling. Home: 45 Oviatt Dr Northfield OH 44067

VOLFSON, BORIS, sanitation products company executive; b. Leningrad, USSR, Oct. 19, 1951; came to U.S., 1978; s. Naum and Eugenia (Goldenberg) V.; m. Karen Elaine Overbey, Mar. 1, 1986. MSME, MA in Indsl. Design, Leningrad Mukhina Inst. Indsl. Arts, Leningrad, 1975. Engr. research bur. Dobrovol'noe Obshchestvo Sodeistviia Armii, Aviatsii, iFlotu, Leningrad, 1972-78, Kayson Lighting, Woodside, N.Y., 1978-79, Van Wyck Internat., Mineola, N.Y., 1979-80; project engr. Graber Industries, Middleton, Wis., 1980-83; sr. project engr. Kenner Toys, Cin., 1983-86; sr. project mgr. Thetford Corp., Ann Arbor, Mich., 1986—. Patentee in field. Avocation: oil painting. Home: 8699 Spinnaker Way #C-2 Ypsilanti MI 48197 Office: Thetford Corp 7101 Jackson Rd Ann Arbor MI 48103

VOLK, DAVID LAWRENCE, state official; b. Mitchell, S.D., Apr. 12, 1947; s. Erwin John and Joan (Nieses) V. B.S., No. State Coll., Aberdeen, S.D., 1969. Treas. State of S.D., Pierre, 1972—. Mem. adv. com. U.S. Commn. on Civil Rights; mem. exec. com. Boy Scouts Am. Served with U.S. Army, 1969-71, Vietnam. Decorated Bronze Star. Republican. Roman Catholic. Clubs: Elks, Am. Legion, VFW. Home: St Charles Hotel #301 Pierre SD 57501 Office: State Treas's Office Capitol Bldg Pierre SD 57501 *

VOLKERS, BURTON JAY, electrical engineer; b. Brookings, S.D., Mar. 16, 1957; s. Barteld and Johanna Dorothy (Walburg) V.; m. June Lynn Dahl, Aug. 8, 1981; children: Mischele, Justine. BEE, S. Dakota State U., 1981. Lic. Profl. Engr. Facilities elec. engr. Hercules Inc., Radford, Va., 1981-84; sr. elec. engr. Hercules Inc., Desoto, Kans., 1984—. Mem. Instrument Soc. Am., Profl. Engrs. Soc. Kans. Republican. Methodist. Club: Sunflower Toastmasters (Desoto); Radford (Va.) Toastmaster (treas. 1982-83). Lodge: Elks. Avocations: bowling, softball. Home: 3408 Oxford Ct Lawrence KS 66044 Office: Hercules Inc SFAAP Box 549 Desoto KS 66018

VOLKMER, HAROLD L., congressman; b. Jefferson City, Mo., Apr. 4, 1931; m. Shirley Ruth Braskett; children: Jerry Wayne, John Paul, Elizabeth Ann. Student, Jefferson City Jr. Coll., 1949-51, St. Louis U. Sch. Commerce and Finance, 1951-52; LL.B., U. Mo., 1955. Bar: Mo. 1955. Individual practice law Hannibal, 1958—; asst. atty. gen. Mo., 1955; pros. atty. Marion County, 1960-66; mem. Mo. Ho. of Reps., 1966-76; chmn. judiciary com., mem. revenue and econs. com.; mem. 95th-100th Congresses from 9th Mo. Dist., 1977—; mem. agr. and sci. coms. 95th-99th Congresses from 9th Mo. Dist. Served with U.S. Army, 1955-57. Recipient award for meritorious pub. service in Gen. Assembly St. Louis Globe-Democrat, 1972-74. Mem. Mo., 10th Jud. Circuit bar assns. Roman Catholic. Clubs: KC, Hannibal Lions. Office: US Ho of Reps 2411 Rayburn House Office Bldg Washington DC 20515 *

VOLL, WILLIAM HOLLAND, manufacturing company executive; b. South Bend, Ind., Nov. 11, 1925; s. Bernard John and Helen (Holland) V.; m. Virginia McIntyre, Feb. 7, 1948; children: Nancy Ann Voll Pietrangeli, William Holland Jr., John Duncan, Susan Elizabeth Voll Galbraith, Virginia Ann Voll Prochaska, Mary Jane Voll Fisher, Patricia Lynn Voll McBride, Bernard John II, Michael McIntyre, Sally Ann Voll Lochmondy, Thomas Christopher. Student, U. Mich., 1943-45; BS in Mech. Engring., U. Notre Dame, 1948; cert. smaller co. mgmt., Harvard U. Sch. Bus., 1975. Treas. Sibley Machine & Foundry Corp., South Bend, 1955-57, sec., treas, 1957-69, exec. v.p., 1969-72, pres., 1972-85, chmn. bd., 1986—; bd. dirs. First Source Bank, South Bend, First Source Corp., South Bend. Pres. Michiana Health Care Coalition, South Bend, 1985—. Served to lt. (JG) USN, 1943-46. Mem. Am. Mgmt. Assn., Castings Research Inst. (trustee), Iron Castings Soc. (bd. dirs. 1983—), Gray Iron Founders Assn. (past pres.). Roman Catholic. Office: Sibley Machine & Foundry Corp 206 E Tutt St South Bend IN 46618

VOLLING, E(LDEN) LEON, manufacturing company executive; b. Elgin, Ill., July 22, 1938; s. Edward A. and Loretta C. (Umbdenstock) Grever; m. Judith E. Frerichs, Mar. 23, 1963; children: Douglas K., Jeffrey S., Pamela L., Cynthia A. BS in Engring., U. Ill., 1964. Engr. Shell Oil Co., Wood River, Ill., 1964-67; pres. O'Brien Corp., St. Louis, 1967—. Patentee in field. Served with USNG, 1959, 62. Mem. Instrument Soc. Am. Republican. Lutheran. Avocations: automobiles, volleyball. Home: 1111 Cardinal Dr East Alton IL 62024 Office: O'Brien Corp 1919 Hampton Ave Saint Louis MO 63139

VOLLMER, STEPHEN ARTHUR, accountant; b. Madison, Wis., Apr. 7, 1951; s. Arthur Neill and Joanne Ely (Fleming) V.; m. Nancy Ann Galloway, Apr. 24, 1976; children: David Anderson, Elizabeth Ann. BSBA, Bowling Green State U., 1973. CPA, Ohio. Jr. acct. Touche Ross & Co., Columbus, Ohio, 1974-75; sr. acct. Ralph Dickson & Co., Columbus, 1975-78, Stephen Kayati & Co., Worthington, Ohio, 1978-80; controller Banc One Leasing, Columbus, 1980-82; supr., acct. Hall, Kistler & Co., Canton, Ohio, 1982-84; v.p. Rabe & Ruder CPA's, Canton, 1984—. Mem. Am. Inst. CPA's, Ohio Soc. CPA's (auditing com. 1975-76, programs com. 1980-81), Ohio Jaycees (asst. treas. 1980, treas. 1981, regional dir. 1982, adminstrv. v.p. 1983, Clint Dunalan Meml. award 1981-82). Avocations: golf, racquetball, swimming. Home: 7602 Wellesley St NW Massillon OH 44646 Office: Rabe & Rudner CPA's Inc 2719 Cleveland Ave NW Canton OH 44709

VOLTMER, MICHAEL DALE, electric company executive; b. Des Moines, July 26, 1952; s. Robert D. and Kathy A. (Miller) V.; m. Joann H. Hove, Sept. 9, 1978; children: Gerad Frank, Anna Christine. B.S., Luther Coll., 1974. Founder, pres. Voltmer Electric Co., Decorah, Iowa, 1974—; ptnr. Brown and Assocs., Decorah, 1984—; pres. Decorah Spirits Inc. Chmn. Winneshiek County Rep. Party, Decorah, 1982-83, fin. chmn., 1984—; pres. Sunflower Child Care Ctr. Inc., Decorah, 1979-80; mem. Sec. Planning and Zoning Commn., City of Decorah, 1983—; v.p. Good Shephard Luth. Ch. Mem. Illuminating Engring. Soc., Nat. Fire Protection Assn. Club: Silvercrest Golf and Country (pres. 1985). Lodge: Elks. Avocations: golf; racquetball. Home: Rural Route 6 Decorah IA 52101 Office: Voltmer Electric Inc 507 W Water St Decorah IA 52101

VOLTZ, MARY HAMILTON, accountant; b. Bklyn., May 9, 1939; s. Nils S. and Jane C. (Thomson) Samuelson; m. Clyde D. Voltz, Nov. 24, 1962; children: Charles Douglas, Jennifer Elaine, John Frederick. AA in Acctg., Wooster Bus. Coll., 1978. CPA. Staff acct. Turpin, Long and Wilson, Wooster, Ohio, 1983-86; pvt. practice acctg. Loudonville, Ohio, 1986—. Mem. Am. Inst. CPA's., Ohio Soc. CPA's. Republican. Adventist. Avocation: bridge. Home: 1679 Woodcrest Dr Wooster OH 44691 Office: 136 E Main St Loudonville OH 44842

VOLUSE, CHARLES RODGER, III, education educator; b. Balt., Oct. 14, 1943; s. Charles Rodger Jr. and Beulah (Gisriel) V.; children: Steven Michael, Andrew Craig. BS in Edn., Southwestern U., Georgetown, Tex., 1965; MEd, Boston U., 1968; EdD, U. Va., 1973. Prof. grad. reading edn. SUNY, Potsdam, 1973-77, Xavier U., Cin., 1977-80; cons. Hamilton County Office Edn., Cin., 1980—; assoc. dir. grad. reading program Xavier U., Cin., 1976-83; cons. Hamilton County Bd. of Mental Retardation, Cin., 1983-85, gifted and talented programs Hamilton County Office Edn., 1985—; dir. Curriculum Devel. Assocs., Cin., 1982—. Author: Adult Subvocalization Behaviors, 1973, Experiences in Language for the Learning Handicapped, 1985; creator ednl. programs. Mem. Internat. Reading Assn., Nat. Council Tchrs. of English, Nat. Council Tchrs. of Math, Ohio Valley Assn for the Talented and Gifted. Home: 6573 Rollymeade Cincinnati OH 45243 Office: Hamilton County Office Edn 11083 Hamilton Ave Cincinnati OH 45231

VOLZ, BERNETA KAY, social service administrator; b. Toledo, Mar. 12, 1955; s. Raymond B. and Genevieve Elleine (Clifton) Gleckler; m. Douglas Paul Volz, Aug. 4, 1984. BS with high honors, Grand Valley State Coll., 1978. Lic. social worker. Dir. therapeutic recreation Grand Valley Nursing Ctr., Grand Rapids, Mich., 1978-80; mgr. client services North Cen. Community Mental Health, Houghton Lake, Mich., 1980-85; adminstr. Luth. Social Services Mich., Roscommon, 1985—. Mem. Regional Interagy. Coordinating Council (chmn. 1984—), Mem. Council Regional Chairs (sec. 1985—). Republican. Methodist. Club: Zonta (Roscommon). Avocations: volleyball, reading, swimming, cross country skiing, snowmobiling. Home: 2208 W Lake James PO Box 498 Prudenville MI 48651 Office: Luth Social Services Mich 11675 Spink Rd Roscommon MI 48653

VOLZ, WILLIAM HARRY, educator, administrator; b. Sandusky, Mich., Dec. 28, 1946; s. Harry Bender and Belva Geneva (Riehl) V. B.A., Mich. State U., 1968; A.M., U. Mich., 1972; J.D., Wayne State U., 1975; M.B.A., Harvard U., 1978. Bar: Mich. 1975. Sole practice, Detroit, 1975-77; mgmt. analyst Office of Gen. Counsel, HEW, Woodlawn, Md., 1977; asst., then assoc. prof. bus. law Wayne State U., Detroit, 1978-85, interim dean sch. Bus. Adminstrn., 1985, now prof. bus law, dean; cons. Merrill, Lynch, Pierce, Fenner & Smith, N.Y.C., 1980—, City of Detroit law dept., 1982, Mich. Supreme Ct., Detroit, 1981; ptnr. Mich. C.P.A. Rev., Southfield, 1983-85. Author: Managing a Trial, 1982; contbr. articles to legal jours. Legal counsel Free Legal Aid Clinic, Inc., Detroit, 1976—, Shared Ministries, Detroit, 1981, Sino-Am. Tech. Exchange Council, People's Republic of China, 1982; participant Better Bus. Bur. Arbitration Program, Southfield, 1981—. Recipient Disting. Faculty award Wayne State Sch. Bus. Adminstrn., 1982. Mem. ABA, Am. Bus. Law Assn., Amateur Mendicant Soc. (commissionaire 1981-85), Golden Key, Alpha Kappa Psi, Beta Alpha Psi. Mem. Reorganized Ch. Latter Day Saints. Clubs: Econ. of Detroit, Harvard Bus. Sch. of Detroit. Home: 3846 Wedgewood Dr Birmingham MI 48010 Office: Wayne State U Sch Bus Adminstrn Cass Ave Detroit MI 48202

VON BAUER, ERIC ERNST, business consulting firm executive; b. LaHabra Heights, Calif., Apr. 12, 1942; s. Kurt Ernst and Margaret Ross (Porter) V.; m. Joyce Ruth Schmidt, Dec. 29, 1973; children—Suzanne Lynn, Katherine Jean. Student Occidental Coll., Los Angeles, 1960-63; M.B.A., U. Chgo., 1973; postgrad. U. Chgo. Law Sch., 1973. Registered rep. Piedmont Internat. Ltd. subs. Piedmont Capital Corp., Frankfurt, W.Ger., 1968-71; fin. adv. trust dept. 1st Nat. Bank Chgo., 1971-72; sec.-treas., controller, Am. Med. Bldgs. Inc., Milw., 1973-75; sr. managing cons. Mgmt. Analysis Ctr., Inc., Chgo., 1975-79; v.p., gen. mgr. corp. fin. adv. services div. Continental Ill. Nat. Bank, Trust Co., Chgo., 1979-82; pres., chief exec. officer The Capital Strategy Group, Inc., Chgo., 1982—; dir., pres. Chgo. chpt. N.Am. Soc. Corp. Planning, 1981-84; faculty mem. Keller Grad. Sch. Mgmt., Chgo., 1987—; guest lectr. U. Chgo. Grad Sch. Bus. Bd. dirs. Chgo. chpt. Reading is Fundamental, 1972-73; dist. adv. com. Fremont (Ill.) Unified Sch. Dist. Served to 1st lt. C.E. U.S. Army, 1964-67. Decorated Army Commendation award. Mem. Assn. Corp. Growth, Midwest Planning Assn., Friends of Small Bus., Am. Mgmt. Assn. C. of C. (dir. Chgo. jr. chpt. 1971-73). Presbyn. Club: Rotary (Chgo.) Author: Knowing Your Product Line Profitability: Key to Greater Strategic Success, 1984; co-author: Zero Base Planning, Budgeting, 1977; contbr. articles to profl. publs. Home: 28 Carlisle Rd Hawthorn Woods IL 60047 Office: Capital Strategy Group 20 N Wacker Dr Chicago IL 60606

VON DER EMBSE, MARIE ANNETTE, lawyer; b. Lima, Ohio, Jan. 3, 1947; d. James Vincent and Marie Catherine (Niese) Von der Embse; m. Clyde M. Simon, June 29, 1974 (div. 1975). B.Ed., Ohio State U., Columbus, 1968; M.Ed., U. Dayton, 1979; J.D., Ohio No. U., 1982. Bar: Ohio 1983. Vol., Peace Corps, Mukah, Sarawak, Malaysia, 1968-71; tchr. Lima and Ft. Jennings Schs. (Ohio), 1971-74; tchr.-librarian U. Mindanao, Philippines, 1974-75; tchr. Mizpah Community Ctr., Lima, 1975-76, Lima City Schs., 1976-80; assoc. Lawson & Smith, Lima, 1983-86; assoc. Gooding, Huffman & Kelley, Lima, 1986—. Mem. Lima City Council, 1982-84, chmn. tree com. 1982-87; solicitor Village of Spencerville, Ohio, 1987—; alt. mem. Regional Planning Commn., Lima, 1981-85, Joint Planning Commn., Delphos, Ohio, 1981-85; chmn. citizen adv. bd. Oakwood Forensic Ctr., Lima, 1985. Mem. Ohio State Bar Assn., Allen County Bar Assn., Lima Edn. Assn., Jennings Edn. Assn. Democrat. Roman Catholic. Home: 1091 N Main St Lima OH 45801 Office: Gooding Huffman & Kelley 127 N Pierce St Box 546 Lima OH 45802

VON DOHNANYI, CHRISTOPH, musician, conductor; b. Berlin, Sept. 8, 1929; s. Hans and Christina (Bonhoeffer) D.; m. Anja Silja, Apr. 21, 1979; children: Julia, Benedikt, Olga. Student, Sch. law, Munich, Ger., Musikhochschule, Ger., Fla. State U., Berkshire Music Ctr. Coach, conductor Frankfort Opera, Ger.; gen. music dir. Lubeck, Kassel, Ger.; dir. West German Radio Symphony Cologne; gen. music dir., artistic dir. Frankfort Opera, Ger.; artistic dir., prin. condr. Hamburg State Opera, Ger., 1978-84; music dir. designate Cleve. Orch., 1982-84, music dir., 1984—; guest condr. in U.S. and Europe. Numerous recs. including 5 symphonies of Mendelssohn with Vienna Philharm., opera Lulu, Petrouchka Suite, Woxxeck. Recipient Richard Strauss prize, Munich; Bartok prize, Hungary; Goethe-Plaket award City of Frankfort. Office: Cleve Orchestra 11001 Euclid Ave Cleveland OH 44106 Home: Grosse-Theater-Strasse 34,, D-2000 Hamburg 36 Federal Republic of Germany *

VON DRASHEK, STANLEY CARL, radiologist; b. Bismarck, N.D., Dec. 18, 1925; s. Stanley Augustine and Myrtle Mary (Parker) Von D.; m. Barbara Mae Samuelson, Aug. 29, 1949; children: Thomas, Nancy, Gail, Bruce. BS, U Minn., 1946, MB, 1947, MD, 1949. Diplomate Am. Bd. Radiology. Staff Cons. Radiologists, Ltd., Abbott Northwestern Hosp., Mpls., 1956, chief radiologist Cons. Radiologists, Ltd., 1963-77, pres., 1980-85; clin. instr. U. Minn. Med. Sch., Mpls., 1956—. Served to capt. USAF, 1952-54. Mem. AMA, Radiol. Soc. N.Am., Am. Coll. Radiology, Soc. Nuclear Med., Minn. Radiol. Soc. Congregationalist. Home: 6705 Southcrest Dr Edina MN 55435 Office: Cons Radiologists Ltd 453 Med Arts Bldg Minneapolis MN 55402

VONDRELL, JAMES HENRY, SR., educational administrator, criminal justice educator; b. Dayton, Ohio, Jan. 28, 1950; s. Urban J. and Louise L. (Kinninger) V.; m. Starleyne Test, July 7, 1973; children: James H. Jr., Abigail, Lisa, Lindsey, Christopher. BBA, U. Cin., 1972, MEd, 1974, EdD, 1987. Asst. to dean U. Cin., 1974-76, program dir. continuing edn., 1976-78, asst. dir. continuing edn., 1978-82, assoc. dean continuing edn., 1982—. Co-author: (book) Score with Memory Power, 1977. Bd. dirs. Health Careers Assn., Cin., 1975-82. Mem. Nat. Univ. Continuing Edn. Assn., Assn. for Continuing Higher Edn., Ohio Continuing Edn. Assn., Imprint Memory Inst. (assoc. dir. 1977—). Roman Catholic. Avocations: sports, antiques, carpentry. Home: 1214 W Seymour Cincinnati OH 45216 Office: U Cin ML #146 Continuing Edn Cincinnati OH 45221

VON FISCHER, DAVID WILLIAM, wholesale wine and imported beer company executive; b. Cleve., July 18, 1950; s. William Erhard Carl and Cordelia (Thacker) Von F.; m. Carolyn Bradford Nelson, Apr. 13, 1974; children: Nathaniel David, Sarah Louise, Rebecca Lyn. Student Ohio State U., 1968-70; BA in Psychology, Ohio U., 1972. With warehouse dept. Excello Wine Co., Columbus, Ohio, 1973-74, with outside sales dept., 1974-83, dir. sales and mktg., 1983—; tchr. creative arts Ohio State U., Columbus, 1983-84; cons. wine merchandising, Columbus, 1974—; lectr. in field, 1974—. Mem. First Community Ch. Club: Marine City Yacht (Marblehead). Avocations: reading, tennis, gardening, sport fishing, boating. Home: 1893 Bedford Rd Columbus OH 43212 Office: Excello Wine Co 1401 E 17th Ave Columbus OH 43211

VON HEIMBURG, ROGER LYLE, surgeon; b. Chgo., Feb. 5, 1931; s. Franklin Dederick and Alice Julia (Zebuhr) von H.; m. Mary Ellen Janson, July 12, 1952; children: Mary Deborah, Donald Franklin. AB, Johns Hopkins U., 1951, MD, 1955; MS in Surgery, U. Minn., Rochester, 1964. Diplomate Am. Bd. Surgery. Intern Johns Hopkins Hosp., Balt., 1955-56; resident in surgery Mayo Clinic, Rochester, 1958-62, chief resident in surgery, 1962, asst. to staff in surgery, 1962-64; practice medicine specializing in surgery Green Bay, Wis., 1964—; staff St. Vincent Hosp., Green Bay, 1964—, Bellin Meml. Hosp., Green Bay, 1964—. Contbr. articles to profl. jours. Served to lt. USNR. Fellow ACS; mem. State Med. Soc. Wis. (bd. dirs. 1980—, vice chmn. 1983-87, chmn. bd. dirs. 1987), Wis. Chpt. ACS (v.p. 1985-87, pres.-elect 1987-88), Brown County Med. Soc. (pres. 1986), Wis. Surgical Soc. (council mem. 1987—). Republican. Methodist. Avocations: piano, auto repair. Home: 344 Terraview Dr Green Bay WI 54301 Office: Webster Clinic 900 S Webster Green Bay WI 54301

VON LANG, FREDERICK WILLIAM, librarian, genealogist; b. Scranton, Pa., May 6, 1929; s. Frederick William and Carrie Della (Brundage) von L.; m. Ilsabe von Wackerbarth, July 12, 1960; children: Christoph, Karl Philipp. B.S., Kutztown U., 1951; M.L.S., Syracuse U., 1955. Librarian Broughal Jr. High Sch., Bethlehem, Pa., 1951-52; asst. librarian Bethlehem Pub. Library, 1952-55, Enoch Pratt Free Library, Balt., 1956-66; library dir. Lehigh County Community Coll. Library, Allentown, Pa., 1966-73, Auburn (Maine) Public Library, 1973-77; dir. St. Joseph (Mo.) Public Library, 1977-79, Hibbing (Minn.) Public Library, 1980—. Assoc. editor: Genealogisches Handbuch des in Bayern immatrikulierten Adels, Vol. 4, 1954. Treas., mem. exec. bd. Friends of Bethlehem Pub. Library; treas., mem. steering com. Auburn City Bicentennial Com.; mem. exec. bd. Northampton County Assn. for Blind, Pa.; ofcl. del. Mo. Gov.'s Conf. on Libraries and Info. Scis. Mem. ALA (councilor from Maine Library Assn. 1974-77), Maine Library Assn. (fed. coordinator A.L.A.), S.A.R., Maine Soc. Mayflower Descendents, Soc. Colonial Wars in Maine, Huguenot Soc. Maine, Bradford Family Compact., Beta Phi Mu. Lutheran. Clubs: Masons (32 deg.), KT, Shriners, Order Eastern Star, Elks, Rotary. Home: 2129 W 3d Ave Hibbing MN 55746 Office: 2020 E 5th Ave Hibbing MN 55746

VON ROENN, KELVIN ALEXANDER, neurosurgeon; b. Louisville, Ky., Dec. 5, 1949; s. Warren George and Catherine Jean (Bauer) Von R.; m. Jamie Hayden, June 24, 1979; 1 child, Erika Marie. BS, Xavier U., 1971; MD, U. Ky., 1975. Diplomate Am. Bd. Neurol. Surgery. Instr. neurosurgery Rush-Presbyn. St. Luke's Med. Ctr., Chgo., 1980-83, asst. prof. neurosurgery, 1983—. Fellow Am. Coll. Surgeons; mem. Congress Neurologic Surgeons, Am. Assn. of Neurol. Surgeons, Alpha Sigma Nu, Alpha Omega Alpha. Avocations: opera, golf. Office: Assocs in Neurolog Surgery 1725 W Harrison #446 Chicago IL 60612

VONRUEDEN, JOHN EDWARD, television station executive; b. Grand Forks, N.D., Jan. 4, 1934; s. John Lawrence and Teresa Margaret (Ackerman) VonR.; m. Joan Alice Schulz, Sept. 15, 1962; children—Jody Lynn, Kurt Michael, Karen Elizabeth. Ph.B., U. N.D., 1955. Sales mgr. Sta. KRYR-AM-FM, Bismarck, N.D., 1966-68, Sta. KFYR-TV, Bismarck, 1968-71; sta. mgr. Sta. KXMB-TV, Bismarck, 1971-87, gen. sales mgr., 1971—; regional sales mgr. 4X TV Network, Bismarck, 1979—; pres. Trans Dakota Advt., Bismarck, 1975—; dir. Audio Visual, Inc., Bismarck; cons., speaker in field. Author: (monthly column) Von on Vin, 1974-83. Commr., Bismarck Park Bd., 1972-76, Bismarck City Commn., 1976-84; nat. committeeman Republican Nat. Com., 1984—; bd. dirs. Young Rep. Nat. Fedn., Fargo, N.D., 1960-66. Served to 1st lt. U.S. Army, 1955-57. Mem. Advt. and Mktg. Club of Bismarck (pres. 1973-74, Ad Person of Yr. 1971, 72, 73), N.D. Broadcasters Assn. (pres. 1976), Nat. Assn. Broadcasters, TV Bur. Advt., Am. Soc. Profl. Cons., Giant Club Meyer Broadcasting Co., (life), Big K Club 4X TV Network (life), Am. Legion. Club: Apple Creek Country (Bismarck) (pres. 1976-77). Lodges: Rotary, KC, Elks. Avocations: banquet speaking, emcee; reading; wine lore. Office: Sta KXMB-TV 1811 N 15th St Box 1617 Bismarck ND 58502

VONTOBEL, PAUL, hardware company executive. Chmn. Hardware Wholesaler Inc., Ft. Wayne, Ind. Office: Hardware Wholesalers Inc PO Box 868 Fort Wayne IN 46801 *

VORHIES, JACK MCKIM, orthodontist; b. Indpls., Feb. 19, 1923; s. Bacil Jacob and Irene M. (Arbuckle) V.; m. Georgia Thelma Reese, Nov. 2, 1943; children: Lawrence, Brent Carl, Scott, Mark, Joyce, Rhonda. DDS with honors, Ind. U., Indpls., 1950; student, Muskingum Coll., 1943; MS, Ind. U., Indpls., 1953. Diplomate Am. Bd. Orthondontic. Gen. practice dentistry specializing in orthodontics Greenwood, Ind., 1952—; instr. Ind. U., 1949-53; dental cons. Conn. Gen., Indpls., 1983-84. Bd. dirs. Am. Internat. Charolais Assn., 1965-72, treas. 1969-71. Served to cpl. U.S. Army, 1943-45, ETO. Decorated Bronze Star. Mem. ADA, Am. Assn. Orthodontics, Ind. Soc. Orthodontics (past pres.), Acad. Internat. Dentistry, Orthodontic Edn. and Research Found., Tweed Found. Orthodontic Research, Edward H. Angle Soc. Orthodontists, Omicron Kappa Upsilon. Republican. Methodist. Lodge: Rotary, Shriners. Avocations: syngraphics, geneology. Office: 399 N Madison Ave Greenwood IN 46142

VORNBROCK, RICHARD PAGE, social worker; b. St. Louis, July 11, 1921; s. Walter Guerdan and Ruth (Page) V.; B.A., U. Mo., 1942; M.S.W., Washington U., St. Louis, 1949; m. Betty Jo Jamieson, Sept. 6, 1947; children—Judith Ann, Richard Page, Betty Marie. Caseworker II, St. Louis city office Mo. Dept. Welfare, 1946-48; psychiat. social worker VA Hosp., Topeka, 1948-53, Minnehaha County Mental Health Center, Sioux Falls, S.D., 1953-58; pvt. practice psychiat. social work, Sioux Falls, 1953-58; instr. sociology Augustana Coll., Sioux Falls, 1955-58; assoc. dir. psychiat. Social Services U. Iowa Hosps and Clinic, Iowa City, 1958-85; pvt. practice psychiat. social work, 1985—; lectr. Sch. Social Work, U. Iowa, 1960-65, instr., 1965—. Served with inf. U.S. Army, 1943-46. Decorated Bronze Star with oak leaf cluster; recipient cert. of appreciation VA, 1953. Mem. Nat. Assn. Social Workers (Social Worker of Yr. 1969), Acad. Cert. Social Workers, Am. Group Psychotherapy Assn., Council Social Work Edn., Nat. Conf. Social Welfare, Register clin. Social Workers, Internat. Assn. Group Psychotherapy, Mental Health Assn., Iowa Human Resources Assn., Social Workers in Health Facilities, Iowa Hosp. Assn. Democrat. Episcopalian. Club: Lions (Iowa City). Home: 1612 Derwen Dr Iowa City IA 52240 Office: 1612 Derwen Dr Iowa City IA 52240

VOROVKA, DAVID RICHARD, accountant; b. Alliance, Nebr., Feb. 13, 1954; s. George and Evelyn Lucielle (Lange) V. BS with distinction, U. Nebr., 1976. CPA, Nebr. Acct. Ernst & Ernst, Omaha, 1977-79; acct. Lincoln (Nebr.) Industries, 1979-80, asst. sec., 1980-85, asst. treas., 1985—. Mem. Am. Inst. CPA's, Nebr. Soc. CPA's (Gold Key award). Avocation: classic automobiles. Home: 3521 N 74 Lincoln NE 68507 Office: Lincoln Industries Inc 6400 Cornhusker Lincoln NE 68507

VORYS, ARTHUR ISAIAH, lawyer; b. Columbus, Ohio, June 16, 1923; s. Webb Isaiah and Adeline (Werner) V.; m. Lucia Rogers, July 16, 1949 (div. 1980); children: Caroline S., Adeline Vorys Cranson, Lucy Vorys Noll, Webb I.; m. Ann Harris, Dec. 13, 1980. BA, Williams Coll., 1945; JD, Ohio State U., 1949. Bar: Ohio 1949. From assoc. to ptnr. Vorys, Sater, Seymour & Pease, Columbus, 1949—; sr. ptnr. Vorys, Sater, Seymour & Pease, 1982—; bd. dirs. Corroon & Black Corp., First Equity Life Ins. Co., N.Am. Nat. Corp., Ohio Casualty Corp., Ohio Casualty Ins. Co., Ohio Life Ins. Co., Ohio Security Ins. Co., Pan-Western Life Ins. Co., Shelby Ins. Co., Vorys Bros., Inc., Wendy's Internat., Inc., other corps.; supt. of ins., Ohio, 1957-59. Trustee, past pres. Children's Hosp., Greenlawn Cemetery Assn., Griffith Found. for Ins. Edn., Internat. Ins. Soc.; trustee, chmn. Ohio State U. Hosps.; del. Rep. Nat. Conv., 1968, 72. Served as lt. USMCR, World War II. Decorated Purple Heart. Fellow Ohio State Bar, Columbus Bar Assns.; mem. ABA, Am. Judicature Soc., Phi Delta Phi., Chi Psi. Clubs: Rocky Fork Headley Hunt, Rocky Fork Hunt and Country (Gahanna); Columbus Athletic, Capital. Home: 5826 Havens Corners Rd Gahanna OH 43230 Office: 52 E Gay St PO Box 1008 Columbus OH 43216

VOS, DONALD KRYN, accountant; b. Kalamazoo, July 22, 1961; s. Kryn Adrian and Phyllis Harriet (Cramer) V.; m. Joyce Ann Haggard, Sept. 17, 1983; 1 child, Stephanie. BBA, Western Mich. U., 1983. CPA, Mich. Sr. acct. Siegfried, Crandall, Vos & Lewis, P.C., Kalamazoo, 1983—. Mem. Am. Inst. CPA's, Mich. Assn. CPA's. Republican. Avocations: basketball, running, golf. Home: 1541 Cedarbrook Kalamazoo MI 49004 Office: Siegfried Crandall Vos & Lewis PC 246 E Kilgore Kalamazoo MI 49001

VOS, MORRIS, foreign languages educator; b. Mahaska County, Iowa, Dec. 10, 1944; s. Peter G. and Edith (De Vries) V.; m. Mary Elizabeth Posthuma, Aug. 16, 1966; children: Jeremy, Allison. AB in English and German, Calvin Coll., Grand Rapids, Mich., 1962-66; MA in German, Calvin Coll., 1968; PhD in German, Ind. U., 1975. Cert. oral proficiency tester in German. Assoc. instr. Ind. U., Bloomington, 1970-71; asst. prof. Western Ill. U., Macomb, 1971-79, assoc. prof., 1979—, grad. faculty, 1981—, assoc. edn. for fgn. lits. Essays in Lit., 1986—; cons. Ill. State Bd. Edn., Springfield, 1984-87, chmn. Citizens Panel on lang. and internat. studies, 1984; mem. adv. council Cen. States Conf. on Teaching Fgn. Langs., 1980-87, co-editor 1988 proceedings. Adult leader Boy Scouts Am., Macomb, 1985-87. NEH grantee, 1977; also recipient various awards and scholarships. Mem. Am. Assn. Teachers of German (treas. So. Ill. chpt. 1979—), Am. Council on the Teaching Fgn. Languages, Presbytery No. Ill. (treas. 1985—). Presbyterian. Avocation: aerobic fitness activities. Home: 456 S Edwards St Macomb IL 61455-1396 Office: Western Ill U Fgn Langs and Lits Macomb IL 61455-1396

VOS, PIETER ARIE, marketing executive; b. Dordrecht, The Netherlands, Sept. 17, 1934; came to U.S., 1955; s. Jacobus Cornelis and Maaike (Bol) V.; m. Harriet Madge Meyers, Aug. 25, 1957; children: Susan Marguerite, John Pieter. Cert., The Netherlands Sch. Bus., Breukélen, 1955; BBA, U. Oreg., 1957; B in Internat. Mgmt. with honors, Am. Grad. Sch. for Internat. Mgmt., 1961. Area mgr. Cen. Am. Ralston Purina Co., St. Louis, 1958-61; mktg. mgr. Belgium Kraft Foods Co., Chgo. and Frankfurt, Fed. Republic of Germany, 1961-64; internat. sales mgr. Scott Paper Co., Phila., 1964-70; dir. mktg. Thai Scott Paper Co., Bangkok, 1970-71, Union Spl. Corp., Chgo. and Stuttgart, Fed. Republic of Germany, 1973-80; mgr. Allied Amphenol Products, The Netherlands and Hong Kong, 1980-87; dir. Vidco Jet Internat., Elk Grove, Ill., 1987—. Fullbright scholar, 1955, 56, Monsanto Chem. Co. scholar, 1958. Mem. Am. Soc. Internat. Execs. (bd. dirs. 1966-72), Fgn. Trade Assn. Phila. (v.p., pres. elect 1965-72), Am. C. of C./The Netherlands, Am. C. of C./Hong Kong, U.S.-Thai C. of C. Republican. Avocations: travel, skiing, music, reading. Home: 160 Dean Dr Palatine IL 60067 Office: Vidco Jet Internat 2200 Arthur Ave Elk Grove IL 60007

VOSBURGH, LEE FREDERICK, obstetrician-gynecologist, educator; b. Passaic, N.J., Jan. 18, 1923; s. Fred and Florence (Ingals) V.; married; children: Frederick, Lisa, Brooke, Evan, Tracy, Lee. BS in Biology, Rutgers U., 1944; MD, Albany U., 1948. From instr. to asst. prof. gynecology NYU Med. Sch., 1954-62; from asst. to assoc. prof. gynecology Cornell U., N.Y.C., 1962-82; assoc. clin. prof. Ohio State Med. Sch., Columbus, 1983—; attending ob-gyn. Northshore U. Hosp., Manhasset, N.Y., 1954-82; chief gynecology Ohio State U. Student Health Ctr., Columbus, 1983—. Mem. Am. Bd. Ob-Gyns., Am. Coll. Health Assn., Columbus Obstetrics Soc. Episcopalian. Home: 404 W 7th Ave Columbus OH 43201 Office: Ohio State U Health Ctr 1875 Millikin Rd Columbus OH 43210

VOSS, JULIAN AUGUST, electrical contracting company executive, tax consultant; b. Aurora, Ill., Nov. 14, 1925; s. Julian Albert and Irene C. (Osterland) V.; m. Maxine J. Welsh, June 25, 1949; children: Julian, Ted, Daniel, Diane. BS with honors, North Cen. Coll., 1949; postgrad., Northwestern U., 1962-63. CPA, Ill. Asst. to treas. Kroehler Mfg. Co., Naperville, Ill., 1960-64, asst. controller, 1964-70, asst. treas., 1970-78, controller, 1978-82; controller Gregory Electric Inc., Naperville, 1982-84, v.p. fin., treas., 1984—, also vice chmn. bd. dirs.; bd. dirs. Kroehler Found., Naperville; pvt. practice acctg. services, Naperville, 1942—. Contbr. articles to the Jour. of Accountancy. Vice chmn., sec. Naperville Real Estate Transaction Com., Naperville, 1968-75; fin. sec. Grace United Meth. Ch., Naperville, 1950-74, treas., 1974-83, spl. funds treas., 1984—. Served to sgt. U.S. Army, 1944-46, ETO. Mem. Am. Inst. CPA's, Naperville C. of C., Ch. Adminstrv. Bd. Home: 430 W Douglas Ave Naperville IL 60540

VOSS, KELLEE ANN, accountant; b. Washington, Mo., Feb. 26, 1958; d. David H. and Starlyn A. (Reinsch) V. BS in Acctg., S.W. Mo. State U., 1980. CPA, Mo. Asst. controller Mo. Pacific Employees' Hosp. Assn., St. Louis, 1980-82; acct. Dome Mgmt., St. Louis, 1983, Ross Burlemann, St. Louis, 1983-85, Tin Man Enterprises, St. Louis, 1986; pvt. practice acctg. St. Louis, 1987—. Mem. Am. Inst. CPA's, Mo. Soc. CPA's. Home and Office: 154A Forest Pkwy Saint Louis MO 63088

VOSS, LAWRENCE RICHARD, orthodontist; b. Chgo., Dec. 3, 1953; s. Frederick Henry and Lorraine Marie (Moravec) V.; m. Marie Meade Corbett, Oct. 9, 1982. Student, Northwestern U., 1971-74; B in Dental Sci., U. Ill., Chgo., 1976, DDS, 1978; cert. specialty in orthodontics, Loyola U., Maywood, Ill., 1982. Lic. dentist, orthodontist, Ill. Resident dentist VA Hosp., Gainesville, Fla., 1978-79; assoc. dentist Nils Sandstrom DDS, Palos Heights, Ill., 1979-80; orthodontist Graber and Assoc., Kenilworth, Ill., 1982—; research asst., cons. ADA, Chgo., 1974—. Mem. ADA, Am. Assn. Orthodontists, Omicron Kappa Upsilon. Roman Catholic. Avocations: golf, bowling, photography, reading. Home: 514 NA-WA-TA Evanston IL 60201 Office: Graber & Assocs 450 Greenbay Rd Kenilworth IL 60043

VOSS, VERNE E., accountant; b. Newcastle, Nebr., Nov. 12, 1936; s. Eldoe H. and Nellie J. (Sherman) V. Jr. acctg. cert., Comml. Extension, 1956. Enrolled to practice before IRS. Acct. Ralston Purina Co., Omaha, 1963-66; carpenter Champion Home Builders, York, Nebr., 1966; bookkeeper, acct. Stortvedt Acctg., Norfolk, Nebr., 1969-75; owner Bookkeeping Service, Pierce, Nebr., 1975—. Served with USAF, 1958-62. Republican. Lutheran. Lodge: Lions (sec. Pierce club 1977). Home and Office: 919 H&N Blvd Pierce NE 68767

VOSS, WALTER A., printing company executive. Pres. Meredith/Burda Corp., Des Moines. Office: Meredith/Burda Corp 17th & Locust St Des Moines IA 50336 *

VOSTRAK, ANNETTE STEPHANIE, advertising and public relations executive; b. Cleve., Apr. 19, 1952; s. Ruth Stephanie (Dlouhy) V. AA, Dyke Coll., 1974. Sec. Dyke Coll., Cleve., 1972-74; exec. sec. Bearings Inc., Cleve., 1974-80, adminstrv. asst., 1980-82, advt. mgr., 1982-85, mgr. advt. and pub. relations, 1985, dir. advt. and pub. relations, 1985—. Mem. adv. bd. Make-a-Wish Found. of N.E. Ohio, Cleve., 1986; lector/eucharistic minister St. Paul's Shrine, Cleve., 1983-86; leadership devel. program Fed. Cath. Community Services, 1986. Named one of Outstanding Young Women in Am, 1986. Mem. Exec. Women Internat., Bus. Profl. Advertisers Assn. Roman Catholic. Club: Cleve. City. Avocations: interior designing, travelling, ballet. Home: 5207 E Sprague Rd Independence OH 44131 Office: Bearings Advt Ctr 3600 Euclid Ave Cleveland OH 44115

VOVSI, EDGAR A., health association executive; b. Riga, Latvia, Jan. 21, 1933; s. Boris and Lea Lucy (Mischkinsky) V.; m. Mary Jane Wilmsen, Dec. 21, 1957; children: Cheryl Lynne, Susan Leslie, Scott Andrew. BS, Bradley U., 1959; MA, Holy Names Coll., 1973; cert., U. So. Calif., Los Angeles, 1978. Dir. publ. info. Ill. Heart Assn., Springfield, 1959-64; exec. dir. Alameda County Heart Assn., Oakland, Calif., 1964-68; assoc. dir. Calif. Heart Assn., San Francisco, 1968-74; dir. adminstrv. services Am. Heart Assn., Los Angeles, 1974-80; exec. v.p. Am. Heart Assn., Springfield, Ill., 1980—. Contbr. articles to profl. jours. Councilman City of Pinole, Calif., 1972-75, mayor, 1973-74. Served to sgt. USAF, 1952-56. Recipient Excellence award Staff Soc., 1973, 75. Mem. Am. Heart Assn. (pres. soc. profl. staff 1984-85), Ill. Council Vol. Health Agys. (sec. 1983—), Ill. Soc. Assn. Execs. (pres. 1987—), U.S. Jaycees (pres. 1967-68). Democrat. Club: Springfield Tennis (treas. 1984—). Lodge: Elks. Avocations: tennis, travel, collecting polit. campaign buttons. Home: 2117 Westview Dr Springfield IL 62704 Office: Am Heart Assn 1181 N Dirksen Pkwy Springfield IL 62708

VOYCHECK, GERALD LOUIS, social worker; b. Wilkes-Barre, Pa., Mar. 10, 1944; s. Martin Vojcik and Lottie (Lukashefska) V. BA, Quincy Coll., 1968; MA, Sangamon State U., 1981; postgrad., So. Ill. U., 1981-82. Tchr. St. James Trade Sch., Springfield, Ill., 1968-71; asst. adminstr. Bro. James Ct., Springfield, 1975-76, adminstr., 1976-79, social worker, 1979—; exec. dir. Springfield Devel., 1985-86; instr. Lincoln Land Community Coll., Springfield, 1981—; interpreter Ill. Dept. Mental Health, Springfield, 1986—. Mem. Nat. Assn. Social Workers (registered), Franciscan Bros. Holy Cross (sec. 1973-76, bd. dirs. 1985—). Republican. Roman Catholic. Avocations: fgn. langs., bodybuilding. Home: Rural Rt 1 Springfield IL 62707 Office: Brother James Ct Sangamon Ave Rd Springfield IL 62707

VOZAK, FRANK REDIN, III, social worker, educator; b. Alton, Ill., May 12, 1952; s. Frank Henry and Margarita (Redin) V.; m. Terrie Adrienne Rymer, June 30, 1985. B.S. in Social Work, St. Louis U., 1974, cert. environ. studies, 1974, cert. peace studies, 1975, M.S.W., 1975. Cert. assoc. addictions counselor, Ill., Clin. social work Edward J. Hines Jr. VA Hosp., Hines, Ill., 1977—; social work officer U.S. Army Med. Dept., 1975-77; instr. field work Jane Addams Sch. Social Work, U. Ill., Chgo., 1980—; social work cons. R.D. Traffic Sch., Inc., Aurora, Ill., 1984-85 . adult leader Order of Arrow, Boy Scouts Am. Capt. USAR, 1977—; vol. psychotraumatologist disaster services Mid Am. chpt. ARC, 1985—. Mem. Nat. Assn. Social Workers, Acad. Cert. Social Workers, Social Workers in Emergency Medicine (rec. sec. 1983—), Nat. Eagle Scout Assn., Psychosocial Clinicians in Emergency Medicine, Ill. Terminal R.R. Hist. Soc., Nat. Model R.R. Assn., Ill. Ry. Mus., Elmhurst Model R.R. Club, Gulf Mobile & Ohio Hist. Soc., Oak Park Soc. Model Engrs. (sec. 1983—), Am. Youth Hostels, St. Louis U. Alumni Assn., Alton, Hines & Pacific R.R. Hist. Soc., Alpha Sigma Nu. Unitarian. Office: Social Work Service VA Edward J Hines Hospital Hines IL 60141

VRABLIK, EDWARD ROBERT, export/import company executive; b. Chgo., June 8, 1932; s. Steven Martin and Meri (Korbel) V.; m. Bernice G. Germer, Jan. 25, 1958; children: Edward Robert, II, Scott S. B.S. in Chem. Engring, Northwestern U., 1956; M.B.A., U. Chgo., 1961; postgrad., MIT, 1970. Registered profl. engr., Ill. Dir. indsl. mktg. Eimco Corp., 1956-61; dir. indsl. mktg. and planning Swift & Co., Chgo., 1961-68; v.p., gen. mgr. Swift Chem. Co., Chgo., 1968-73; pres., chief exec. officer Estech Gen. Chems. Corp., Chgo., 1973-86; pres. Kare Internat. Inc., Chgo., 1986—; pres. Julius and Assocs., Inc., Kare Internat., Inc.; bd dirs. Potash Phosphate Inst., Consol. Fertilizers, Ltd.; mem. mgmt. com. Esmark Inc.; chmn. Konig, Inc., Korbel, Inc., Mister Lawn Care, Inc. Author. Bd. dirs., v.p. Northwestern U. Tech. Inst.; trustee Future Farmers Am. Mem. Internat. Superphosphate Mfrs. Assn. (dir.), Am. Inst. Chem. Engrs., Fertilizer Inst. (dir.). Lutheran. Clubs: Butler Nat. (Oak Brook, Ill.). Patentee in field. Home: 631 Thompson's Way Inverness IL 60067 Office: Bd of Trade Bldg 141 W Jackson Blvd Suite 2172 Chicago IL 60604

VRANICH, MICHAEL GEORGE, osteopath, surgeon; b. York, Pa., Apr. 3, 1949; s. John Joseph and Mary Catherine (Conjar) V.; m. Diane Patricia Dingwall, Aug. 8, 1970; children: Michael George Jr., Christopher John. BS in Zoology, Northeast Mo. State U., 1972; DO, Kirksville (Mo.) Coll. Osteo. Medicine, 1974. Diplomate Am. Bd. Med. Examiners, Am. Bd. Osteo. Surgery. Intern Normandy Osteo. Hosp., St. Louis, 1974-75, resident in surgery, 1975-79, attending surgeon, 1979—, resident trainer in surgery, 1983-84, chmn. dept. gen. surgery, 1986—; practice osteo. medicine specializing in surgery St. Louis, 1979—; attending surgeon St. Peter's (Mo.) Community Hosp., 1981-83; adj. clin. faculty New Eng. Coll. Osteo. Medicine, 1985—. Contbr. articles to profl. jours. Bd. dirs. Parents Group Retarded Children, St. Louis State Hosp., 1986—. Mem. Am. Osteo. Assn., Am. Coll. Osteo. Surgeons, Mo. Osteo. Assn., St. Louis Dist. Osteo. Physicians. Republican. Roman Catholic. Clubs: Mo. Athletic, Norwood Hills Country (St. Louis). Avocations: golf, model trains. Home: 11255 Ladue Rd Saint Louis MO 63141 Office: 11245 St Charles Rock Rd Saint Louis MO 63044

VREDENBURG, DWIGHT CHARLES, supermarket chain executive; b. Lamoni, Iowa, Jan. 17, 1914; s. David Milton and Kate Emelyn (Putnam) V.; m. Ruth Irene Taylor, Apr. 25, 1937; children: John, Maria Vredenburg Wibe, Charles. Student, Graceland Coll., 1931-34; B.S. in Commerce, U. Iowa, 1935. Store mgr. Hy-Vee Food Stores Inc., Chariton, Iowa, 1935-38, pres., 1938—, chief exec. officer, 1978—; chmn. Hy- Vee Food Stores Inc., Chariton, Iowa, 1978—; dir. Hy-Vee Food Stores Inc., Chariton, Iowa, Iowa So. Utilities Co., Centerville, Nat. Bank and Trust Co., Chariton; pres. Chariton Storage Co., Chariton; pres., dir. Iamo Realty Co. Served with USCGR, 1942-44. Named Citizen of Yr., 1965-66. Mem. Food Mktg. Inst. (sec. 1965-68, dir.). Club: Des Moines. Lodges: Masons; Shriners. Home: Rural Route 5 Box 217 Chariton IA 50049 Office: Hy-Vee Food Stores Inc 1801 Osceola Ave Chariton IA 50049 *

VREELAND, DAVID LINDEN, endodontist; b. St. Louis, June 24, 1954; s. Joseph Henry and Dorothy Ruth (Cayse) V.; m. Beverly Gail Caldwell, May 19, 1978; children: Katie Marie, Rebecca Linn. BA, U. Mo., St. Louis, 1975; DDS, U. Mo., Kansas City, 1979; MS, Ohio State U., 1984. Practice dentistry specializing in endodontics Manchester, Mo., 1984—. Served to lt. USN, 1979-82. Home: 811 Rotherham Ballwin MO 63011 Office: 14397 Manchester Rd Manchester MO 63011

VUCKOVICH, DRAGOMIR MICHAEL, neurologist, educator; b. Bileca, Herzegovina, Yugoslavia, Oct. 27, 1927; came to U.S., 1957; s. Alexander John and Anka Mia (Ivanisevich) V.; m. Brenda Mary Luther, Aug. 23, 1958; children: John, Nicholas, Adrian. M.D., U. Birmingham, Eng., 1953. Diplomate Am. Bd. Psychiatry and Neurology, Am. Bd. Pediatrics. Intern United Birmingham Hosps., Eng., 1953-54, resident in pediatrics, 1954-55; resident med. officer Princess Beatrice Hosp., London, 1955; sr. resident Hosp. for Sick Children, London, 1955; sr. resident in neurology Atkinson Morley br. St. George's Hosp., London, 1955-56; resident in neurology Nat. Hosp. Queens Sq., London, 1956-57, VA Hosp., Chgo., 1958-59; resident in psychiatry Wesley Meml. Hosp., Chgo., 1959-60; fellow in neurology Northwestern U. Med. Sch., Chgo., 1960; resident in pediatrics Children's Meml. Hosp., Chgo., 1961; asst. prof. neurology, psychiatry and pediatrics Northwestern U. Med. Ctr., Chgo., 1967-70; assoc. clin. prof. neurology and pediatrics Stritch Sch. Medicine, Chgo., 1970-77, clin. prof. neurology and pediatrics, 1977—; chmn. Columbus Hosp., Chgo., 1981—; dir. EEG Lab. Columbus Hosp., Chgo., 1969—, chief neurology and psychiatry, 1971-81; chief of child neurology Loyola U., Maywood, Ill., 1970-79. Co-author: Psychoanalysis and the Two Cerebral Hemispheres, 1983; contbr., co-contbr. articles in field to profl. jours. Served to lt. col. MC, USAR, 1983—. Decorated Army Achievement medal, Army Commendation medal, 1986; recipient Physician Recognition award AMA, 1971; named Best Attending Physician Med. House Staff, Columbus Hosp., 1979. Fellow Am. Acad. Pediatrics, Am. Acad. Neurology; mem. Am. Med. Electroencephalographic Assn., Profs. of Child Neurology, Cen. Neuropsychiat. Assn. Republican. Serbian Orthodox. Clubs: Beefeaters (N.Y.C.); Athletic, Les Gourmet's (Chgo.). Avocations: music, reading, writing, tennis, swimming. Office: Neurosci Ctr 720 Osterman Ave Deerfield IL 60015

VUKITS, JAMES STEPHEN, controller; b. Muskegon, Mich., Mar. 17, 1954; s. Ernest and Dorothy Vukits; m. Theresa J. Powers; children: Elizabeth, Matthew. BA in Acctg., Mich. State U., 1976. CPA, Mich. Auditor Grant Thornton, Muskegon, 1976-81; asst. controller Western Foundry, Holland, Mich., 1981-82; acctg. mgr. Ermanco, Spring Lake, Mich., 1982-86; controller Fitzpatrick Electric, Muskegon, 1986—. Mem. Am. Inst. CPA's, Mich. Inst. CPA's. Roman Catholic. Avocations: golf, baseball. Home: 986 Cheboygan Muskegon MI 49445

VYDELINGUM, NADARAJEN AMEERDANADEN, cell biologist, educator, researcher; b. Curepipe, Mauritius, June 1, 1945; came to U.S., 1977; s. Vythilingum Francis Vydelingum and Mareeaye Vadelingum Paratian; m.

rosemary Dowland, Nov. 6, 1971; children: Naomi, Eric. BS in Cell Biology with honors, Birkbeck London U., Eng., 1972, MS in Biochemistry, 1974; PhD in Clin. Biochemistry, St. Mary's Med. Sch., London, 1979. Adj. asst. prof. cell biology U. Wis., Milw., 1979; asst. prof. medicine and pharmacology Med. Coll. Wis., Milw., 1979—; reviewer Health Sci. Consortium Peer Rev. Bd., Carrboro, N.C., 1984—. Contbr. articles to profl. jours. Am. heart Assn. fellow, 1979-81; NIH grantee, 1985—. Mem. Am. Fedn. Clin. Research, Am. Diabetes Assn. (grantee 1982-84). Democrat. Unitarian. Avocations: Arabic, African and Indian drum. Home: 1415 N 67th St Wauwatosa WI 53213 Office: Med Coll Wis Froedtert Meml Luth Hosp 9200 W Wisconsin Ave Milwaukee WI 53226

VYVERBERG, ROBERT WILLIAM, mental health superintendent; b. Dubuque, Iowa, Dec. 23, 1940; s. William Pifer and Virginia Thelma (Rutger) V.; m. Mari Ann Jacobs, Nov. 6, 1982; children by previous marriage: Robert William, Benjamin Rutger. BEd, Ill. Wesleyan U., 1963; MS, Ill. State U., 1964; EdD, No. Ill. U., 1972. Dir. counseling services Crown High Sch., Carpentersville, Ill., 1964-67; dir. outcare services, children and adolescent unit H. Douglas Singer Mental Health Center, Rockford, Ill., 1969-72, dir. psychiat. rehab. and extended care services, 1972-82; region coordinator Services to Elderly, 1978-83; clin. dir. Children's and Adolescent Services, 1982-84, adminstrv. dir., 1982-84; supt. Zeller Mental Health Ctr., 1984—; lectr. crisis theory and crisis intervention No. Ill. U., 1970-84, instr. group counseling and psychotherapy, 1973; cons. Juvenile Justice Personnel Devel. Center, U. Wis., 1977. Mem. Nat. Rehab. Assn., Am. Assn. Counseling and Devel., Am. Rehab. Counselors Assn., Am. Mental Health Counselors Assn., Internat. Assn. Psycho-Social Rehab. Services, Assn. Mental Health Adminstrs. Methodist. Home: 4420 Lynnhurst Dr Peoria IL 61615 Office: Zeller Mental Health Ctr 5407 N University Peoria IL 61614

WAAGE, DONALD LANGSTON, public relations executive, banker; b. Minn., Jan. 30, 1925; s. John A. and Amanda O. (Andreas) W.; m. Lori deBrossoit, Sept. 8, 1946; children—Donn, Suzanne Friedman, Bruce, Eric. B.S., St. Cloud U., 1949; M.A., Am. U., 1962. Reporter, St. Cloud Daily Times, Minn., 1951-54; asst. mgr. fin. and taxation dept., sec. fin. com. C. of C. of U.S., Washington, 1954-60; asst. to bd. dirs., dir. congl. and pub. relations FDIC, Washington, 1960-62; sr. editor fin. reports and pub. Investors Diversified Services, Inc., Mpls., 1962-67; v.p. advertising and pub. relations North Am. Life and Casualty Co., Mpls., 1967-69; dir. fin. and pub. relations Josten's Inc., Mpls., 1969-72; v.p. Am. Survey Research Corp., Mpls., 1972-77; regional dir. Hwy. Users Fedn., Washington, 1977-83; exec. v.p., ptnr. Coughlan, Trepanier, Waage Assocs., Minnetonka, Minn., 1983—; cons. World Bank, Washington, 1965-70, Republican Nat. Com., Washington, 1974-77; dir. Summit Bank, Bloomington, Minn., 1968-80. Author Mil. history monograph, 1952; contbr. articles on banking to profl. jours. Vice chmn. Mpls. Symphony Orch. fund drive, 1964; chmn. Minnetonka Rep. fund drive, 1970-74; deacon Westminster Presbyn. Ch.; trustee Am. Univ., Washington, 1966-72. Served to maj. with U.S. Army, 1950-53. Mem. Minn. Press Club, French-Am. C. of C. Club: Wayzata Country; Twin City Polo; Exchequer (first chancellor, founder) (Washington).

WAALKES, JAY WENDELL, restaurateur; b. Cleve., Sept. 23, 1947; s. Robert Jay and Naomi Genevieve (Conant) W.; m. Monica M. Tuttle, Sept. 1968 (div. Nov. 1973); children: Carmen Lee, Robert Jay; m. Jerry Kay Lloyd, Oct. 26, 1974. BS, Western Mich. U., 1971. Mgr. Burger Chef, Kalamazoo, 1968-71, South Haven, Mich., 1971-74; mgr. Wendy's of Mich., Kalamazoo, 1974-76, v.p., 1979-85, pres., 1985—; supr. Wendy's of Mich., Grand Rapids, 1976-79. Fin. officer CAP, Kalamazoo, 1984-85. Republican. Avocations: pvt. pilot and aircraft owner, olympic weightlifter, runner, bicycling, mountain climbing. Office: Wendys of Mich 4613 W Main Kalamazoo MI 49007

WACHOWSKI, THEODORE JOHN, radiologist; b. Chgo., Nov. 20, 1907; s. Albert and Constance (Korzeniewski) W.; B.S., U. Ill., 1929, M.D., 1932; m. Barbara F. Benda, June 1, 1931; 1 son, Ted J. Waller. Intern, resident in radiology, asso. radiologist U. Ill. Hosps., 1931-67; clin. prof. radiology U. Ill., 1949-67; radiologist Copley Meml. Hosp., Aurora, Ill., 1935-77, Loretto Hosp., Chgo., 1941-48; practice medicine specializing in radiology, Wheaton, Ill., 1975-83; ret., 1983. Mem. Radiol. Soc. N.Am. (pres. 1960, Gold medal 1969), Am. Coll. Radiology (pres. 1963, Gold medal 1969), Ill., Kane County med. socs., AMA, Am. Roentgen Ray Soc., Chgo. Radiol. Soc. (past pres., Gold medal 1982). Republican. Club: Glen Oak Country. Contbr. articles to profl. jours. Home: 101 Tennyson Dr Wheaton IL 60187

WACHS, KATE MARY, psychologist; b. Chgo., Aug. 27, 1951; s. Charles Herbert and Rose Ann W. BA magna cum laude, Rosary Coll., 1974; MA, U. S.D., 1976, PhD, 1980. Licensed psychologist, Ill., Mich. Asst. clin. psychologist Lewis & Clark Mental Health Ctr., Yankton, S.D., 1977-78; intern clin. psychology Rush Presbyn. St. Luke's Med. Ctr., Chgo., 1978-79, house staff in psychology, 1979-80; psychologist Bay Med. Ctr., Bay City, Mich., 1980-83; pvt. practice psychology Chgo.; pres. IntiMate Introduction Service, Inc., Advanced Degrees Introductions, Inc.; columnist Chgo. Life Mag., 1984—, Women In Mgmt. Newsletter, 1984-86, Amplifier, 1986—; editor articles for local and nat. pubs. Mem. Assn. for Media Psychology (bd. dirs. 1985—), Am. Psychol. Assn. (bd. dirs. div. 46 1986—, chmn. ethics/guidelines com. 1986—), Am. Pain Soc., Women in Mgmt. (Women Achievement award 1987,. Avocations: travel, piano, dancing, white river rafting, working out. Office: 1030 N State Suite 7C Chicago IL 60610

WACHSNICHT, GALE ANNETTE, advertising executive; b. Tampa, Fla., Oct. 10, 1946; s. Henry F.and Mable (Joyner) W. Student, Chelsea Art Inst., London, 1967-69, St. Louis Community Coll., 1972, 80, Washington U., St. Louis. Account exec., food broker Halls-Fanger-Leeker, St. Louis, 1979-82; account exec., wine cons. Allied Wine and Spirits, St. Louis, 1982-84; account exec. nat. advt. St. Louis Globe Dem., 1984-86, nat. advt. mgr., 1986; v.p., ptnr. Bates Advt. & Assocs., St. Louis, 1987—. Contbr. articles to profl. jours. Bd. dirs. Soulard Restoration Group, St. Louis, 1977-84. Mem. Press Club, Sierra Club, Landmarks Assn., Allied Food Club. Avocations: renovating houses, community activities, antiques. Home: 2351 S 13th St Saint Louis MO 63104 Office: Bates Advt & Assocs 2351 S 13th St Saint Louis MO 63104

WACKER, DOUGLAS LEE, controller; b. McCook, Nebr., Nov. 24, 1958; s. Gary R. and Shirley An. (Alberts) W.; m. Jolena M. Holthas, Feb. 1, 1976 (div. Mar. 1981); m. Jana J. Fry, Apr. 3, 1981; children: Heather Ann, Timothy Paul, Christopher Lee, Catherine Kay. BA in Bus. Adminstrn. and Econs., Hastings Coll., 1981. CPA, Nebr. Staff acct. Johnson, Grant & Co., Hastings, Nebr., 1981-82; audit supr. State Auditor's Office, Lincoln, Nebr., 1982-86; controller Friend's Motor Supply, Hastings, 1986—. Mem. Am. Inst. CPA's, Nebr. Soc. CPA's. Republican. Methodist. Avocations: running, karate, cycling, swimming, reading. Home: 1148 Renue Ln Hastings NE 68901 Office: Friends Motor Supply Inc 1045 S Franklin Hastings NE 68901

WACKER, FREDERICK GLADE, JR., manufacturing company executive; b. Chgo., July 10, 1918; s. Frederick Glade and Grace Cook (Jennings) W.; m. Ursula Comandatore, Apr. 26, 1958; children: Frederick Glade III, Wendy, Joseph Comandatore. B.A., Yale U., 1940; student, Gen. Motors Inst. Tech., 1940-42. With AC Spark Plug div. Gen. Motors Corp., 1940-43; efficiency engr. 1941-43; with Ammco Tools, Inc., North Chicago, Ill., 1947-87; pres. Ammco Tools, Inc., 1948-87, chmn. bd., 1948—; founder 1954; since pres., chmn. bd. Liquid Controls Corp., North Chicago; chmn. bd. Liquid Controls Europe, Zurich, Switzerland, 1985—; ltd. ptnr. Francis I. DuPont & Co., N.Y.C., 1954-70; dir. Hydro-Air Engring., Inc., Moehlenpah Industries Inc., MiTec Industries, Inc.; mem. exec. council Conf. Bd., 1971—. Condr. Freddie Wacker and His Orch., 1955-69, orch. has appeared on TV and radio, recs. for Dolphin and Cadet records. Bd. govs. United Republican Fund Ill.; trustee Lake Forest Acad., 1956-71, Warren Wilson Coll., 1973-81, Chgo. chpt. Multiple Sclerosis Soc.; bd. govs. Lyric Opera Chgo., 1963-66; bd. advisers Nat. Schs. Com., 1966—; mem. adv. council Trinity Evang. Div. Sch., 1977—; bd. dirs., vice chmn. Rockford Inst., 1983-87, bd. govs. GMI Engring. and Mgmt. Inst., 1983—; bd. regents Milw. Sch. Engring., 1981—. Served to lt. (j.g.) USNR, 1943-45. Mem. NAM, Chief Execs. Forum, Young Pres. Orgn. (chmn. Chgo. chpt. 1965-66), Sports Car Club Am. (pres. 1952-53), Ill. Mfrs. Assn. (bd. dirs. 1966—, chmn. bd. 1975—), Chgo. Presidents Orgn. (pres. 1972-73), Automotive Hall of Fame (life, dir. 1976—), Soc. Automotive Engrs., World Bus. Council, Waukegan C. of C. (dir. 1965-68), Chgo. Fedn. Musicians (life). Presbyterian. Clubs: Chgo. (Chgo.), Racquet (Chgo.) (pres. 1960-61), Casino (Chgo.), Mid-Am. (Chgo.); Shoreacres, N.Y. Yacht; Onwentsia (Lake Forest). Home: 1600 Green Bay Rd Lake Bluff IL 60044 Office: Wacker Park North Chicago IL 60064

WACKER, RICHARD D., bank executive. Pres., chief exec. officer Lake View Trust & Savs. Bank, Chgo. Office: Lake View Trust & Savs Bank 3201N Ashland Ave Chicago IL 60657 *

WACKERLE, FREDRICK WILLIAM, management consultant; b. Chgo., June 25, 1939; s. Fred and Babette (Buck) W.; m. Elaine Gatley, Apr. 28, 1962 (div.); children: Jennifer, Ruth; m. Barbara L. Provus, Mar. 29, 1985. BA, Monmouth (Ill.) Coll., 1961. Prin. A.T. Kearney & Co., Chgo., 1964-66; v.p. Berry Henderson & Aberlin, Chgo., 1966-68, R.M. Schmitz & Co., Chgo., 1968-70; ptnr. McFeely-Wackerle-Jett, Chgo., 1970—; bd. dirs. Uccel Corp. Served with USAF, 1957-62. Mem. Assn. Exec. Search Cons. (bd. dirs., exec v.p.), Monmouth Coll. Alumni Assn. (pres., senate dir.), Tau Kappa Epsilon. Home: 3750 N Lake Shore Dr Apt #17-F Chicago IL 60613 Office: McFeely-Wackerle-Jett 20 N Wacker Dr Chicago IL 60606

WADAS, JOHN JOSEPH, JR., dentist; b. Hammond, Ind., May 22, 1939; s. John Joseph and Lottie Stella (Kula) W.; m. Geraldine Ann Kielbasa, Oct. 6, 1962; children: John J. III, Debra Marie, Christopher John, Amy Joelle, Theresa Annette, Joel Matthew. Student, Marquette U., 1957-59, DDS, 1963. Gen. practice dentistry East Chgo., 1963—; bd. dirs. Peoples Fed. Savs. & Loan Assn., Munster, Ind., 1984—. Fellow Am. Endodontic Soc.; mem. ADA, Ind. Dental Soc., NW Ind. Dental Soc. Office: Wadas Dental Ctr 4614 Baring Ave East Chicago IN 46312 also: 9307 Calumet Ave Munster IN 46321

WADDELL, OLIVER W., banker; b. Covington, Ky., Dec. 27, 1930; s. Frank and Ida Mae Waddell; m. Virgilee Casey; children—Jeffrey, Gregory, Michelle. B.A., Duke U., 1954; J.D., U. Ky., 1957; grad., Stonier Grad. Sch. Banking, Rutgers U., 1969. Mgmt. trainee First Nat. Bank of Cin., 1957-64, asst. cashier, 1964-65, asst. v.p., 1965-71, v.p., 1971-76, sr. v.p., 1976-80, pres., dir., 1980-82, pres., chief exec. officer, 1982-83, chmn., chief exec. officer, 1983—; dir. Myers Y. Cooper Co., Cin., 1981—, Ohio Nat. Life Ins. Co.; trustee Christ Hosp. Trustee Berea (Ky.) Coll., Cin. Family Services, Cin., 1983, Coll. of Mt. St. Joseph, Cin., 1984; active Cin. Bus. Com. Mem. Greater Cin. C. of C. (chmn.). Republican. Methodist. Clubs: Bankers, Comml., Cin. Country, Queen City. Office: First Nat Bank of Cin 425 Walnut St Cincinnati OH 45201

WADDELL, RICHARD JAMES, sheet metal company executive; b. Ft. Dodge, Iowa, Dec. 30, 1948; s. Richard Arvin and Shirley (Webb) W.; m. Stephanie Ann Lingreen, Sept. 8, 1972; children: Kristin Ann, Eric James. Grad. high sch., Ft. Dodge, 1967. Pres. Waddell Heating & Sheet Metal Inc., Sprit Lake, Iowa, 1983—. Mem. Air Condition Contractors Am., Nat. Fedn. Ind. Bus., Nat. Assn. Plumbing, Heating and Cooling Contractors. Office: Waddell Sheet Metal Inc Highway 9 E Spirit Lake IA 51360 Home: Rural Rt 8707 Spirit Lake IA 51360

WADDELL, WILLIAM WAYNE, II, real estate corporation executive; b. Beatrice, Nebr., Apr. 14, 1941; s. W. Wayne and Jean (Rathbun) W.; m. Marie Dickason, Apr. 21, 1973. BA, U. Nebr., 1963. Pres. Waddell Farms, Inc., Virginia, Nebr., 1965-86, Bear Creek Devel., Beatrice, 1970-81; mgr. Arapahoe (Colo.) Land and Cattle Co., 1981—; project dir. Broe Cos., Inc., Lincoln, Nebr., 1985—; pres. Clipper Am. Corp., Beatrice, 1986—. Mem. Beatrice City Council, 1964-66; trustee John J. Pershing Coll., Beatrice; mgr. Nebr. Scranton for Pres. com., McCollister for Senate com., Johnson County, Nebr., Rogers for Gov. com., Johnson County. Served with USMC, 1965-69. Named one of Outstanding Young Men of Nebr., 1972. Mem. Am. Legion. Republican. Episcopalian. Lodge: Elks. Avocations: reading, hiking. Home: Rt 1 Virginia NE 68458 Office: Broe Cos Inc 941 O St Terminal Bldg B-2 Lincoln NE 68508

WADE, DALE BROOKINS, dentist, educator; b. Columbus, Ohio, July 25, 1940; s. Robert Edward and Louise (Roby) W.; m. Jan Schwiebert, June 22, 1963; children: Goeffrey Edward, Andrew Brookins. MS, Ohio State U., 1969, DDS, 1965. Diplomate Am. Bd. Orthodontics. Asst. clin. prof. Ohio State U., Columbus, 1969—; practice orthodontics, Columbus, 1969—. Editor Great Lakes Orthodontic Soc., 1980-86, Found. for Orthodontic Research; contbr. articles to profl. jours. Life mem. Upper Arlington Civic Assn., Columbus, 1980; scoutmaster Troop 180, Cen. Ohio council Boy Scouts Am., 1984—; mem. Pierre Fauchard Acad. Served as lt. USN, 1965-67. Fellow Acad. Internat. Dental Studies, Internat. Coll. Dentists; mem. Am. Bd. Orthodontics (Coll. of Diplomates), Edward Angle Soc., Columbus Dental Soc. (pres. 1981), Ohio State U. Orthodontic Alumni Found. (pres. 1972), Omicron Kappa Upsilon. Lodge: Sertoma (N.W. chpt. pres. 1976). Avocations: camping, skiing, photography, jogging, golf. Home: 3120 S Dorchester Rd Columbus OH 43221 Office: 3220 Riverside Dr Columbus OH 43221

WADE, JOHN CORNELIUS, information systems executive; b. Somerville, Mass., Apr. 13, 1941; s. Edward Joseph and Margaret Mary (O'Callahan) W.; m. Madeline Ann Buckley, Sept. 8, 1962 (div. May 1970); children: John Cornelius II, Madelaine Marie; m. Cheri Ann Macleod, June 11, 1971; children: Amy Katherine, Daniel Lewis. Student, Northeastern U., Boston, 1960-62; BA cum laude, Boston Coll., 1969, postgrad., 1973-78. Mgr. mgmt. info. system Polaroid Corp., Waltham, Mass., 1960-75, Children's Hosp., Boston, 1975-78; dir. info. systems Northwestern Meml. Hosp., Chgo., 1979—; cons. in field; mem. faculty Ill. Sch. Communications, Chgo., 1984—. Mem. nominating com. Wheaton (Ill.) Sch. Com., 1983-85. Mem. Am. Mgmt. Assn., Healthcare Fin. Mgmt. Assn. (chmn. data processing com. 1982-83, audit com. 1985-86, chmn. membership com. 1983-84), Electronic Computing Health Oriented. Roman Catholic. Club: Indian Guide (Glen Ellyn, Ill.) (chief 1983-85). Avocations: reading, gradening, world travel. Home: 1453 Gainseboro Ct Wheaton IL 60187

WADE, JOSEPH FRANCIS, accountant; b. Charleston, W.Va., Aug. 6, 1935; s. Frank George and Mary Frances (Gootee) W.; m. Virginia Rose Mauch, June 1, 1963; children: Lori M., Mark E., Sharon A. BS, U. Dayton, 1958, MBA, 1970. CPA, Ohio. Ptnr. William S. Fry & Co., Dayton, Ohio, 1958-85; pres. Joseph F. Wade CPA Inc., Dayton, 1985—; instr. acctg. various orgns.; speaker various seminars. Contbr. numerous articles to profl. jours. Active Boy Scouts Am., 1947—; group leader Inventors Council Dayton; mem. fin. com., bd. dirs. Advancing the Developmentally Disabled; past. pres., bd. dirs. Fin. Forum; various other civic activities. Served with U.S. Army, 1958-65. Mem. Am. Inst. CPA's, Ohio Soc. CPA's, Nat. Assn. Accts. (editorial com.), Dayton Estate Planning Council, Dayton MBA Club, Inventors Council Dayton, Jr. C. of C. (treas., trustee, chmn. audit and fin. coms.), Miami Valley Mgmt. Assn. (treas., bd. dirs. exec. com.). Republican. Roman Catholic. Club: Engineers (treas., bd. govs., chmn. fin. com.), Exchange (treas., v.p., pres. 1985-86). Home: 417 Chatham Dr Kettering OH 45429-1411 Office: Joseph F Wade CPA Inc 2621 Dryden Rd Suite 103A Dayton OH 45439-1612

WADE, ORMAND JOSEPH, utility company executive; b. Key West, Fla., Apr. 12, 1939; s. Charles H. and Jean (Calhoun) W.; m. Miriam Knapp, June 11, 1960; children: Charles S., Valerie A. BS, U. Maine, 1961; MS, MIT, 1973. With AT&T Long Lines, 1961-81; staff supr., asst. v.p. personnel dept. AT&T Long Lines, N.Y.C., 1964-66, network service mgr. ops. staff dept., 1970-71; dist. plant supr. AT&T Long Lines, Balt., 1966-68; engring. mgr. engring. dept. AT&T Long Lines, White Plains, N.Y., 1968-70; div. ops. mgr. ops. staff dept. AT&T Long Lines, Washington, 1971-73, area chief engr. engirng. dept., 1973-78; v.p. staff AT&T Long Lines, Bedminster, N.J., 1978-79; v.p. central region network ops. AT&T Long lines, Chgo., 1979-81; exec. v.p. Ill. Bell Telephone Co., Chgo., 1981-82, pres., 1982—, also bd. dirs.; bd. dirs. Harris Bankcorp., Inc., Chgo., Harris Trust & Savs. Bank, Chgo., Dearborn Park Corp., Chgo. Bd. dirs. United Way-Crusade of Mercy, Chgo., 1982—; bd. mgrs. YMCA Met. Chgo., 1982—; trustee Ill. Inst. Tech., 1982—, Northwestern Meml. Hosp., Chgo., 1983—; mem. Ill. Gov.'s Task Force on Pvt. Sector Initiatives, 1983, Ill. Savs. Bond Com., 1983. Sloan fellow, 1972. Clubs: Econ. (Chgo.), Chgo. Office: Ill Bell Telephone Co 225 W Randolph St Chicago IL 60606 *

WADE, RICHARD ARNOLD, music educator, musician; b. Memphis, Apr. 28, 1948; s. Arthur and Willie Mae (Neal) W.; m. Diane Delece Perry, Aug. 2, 1969; children: Kenya, Rishaad. AS, State Community Coll., 1974; BS in Music Edn., So. Ill. U., 1980. Tchr. music Ford Middle Sch., St. Louis, 1981-83; choral dir. Lansdowne Jr. High Sch., East St. Louis, Ill., 1983-84; elem. music specialist feeder program Elem. Sch., East St. Louis, 1984—; pres. Family Prodns., East St. Louis, 1980—. Composer: Keep Breaking, 1985, Give Me One More Chance, 1985. Served with U.S. Army, 1965-68, Vietnam. Mem. Am. Fedn. Musicians, Black Music Soc. of Mo. (v.p. 1987—). Democrat. Home: 501 Green Haven Dr Belleville IL 62221

WADE, ROYCE ALLEN, real estate broker, consultant; b. Medford, Wis., Apr. 30, 1932; s. Charles L. and Mildred H. (Clarin) W.; m. Corinne Mae Weber, June 30, 1956; children: Suzanne Mae, Debra Ann. BS (acad. scholar), U. Wis., Stevens Point, 1954; MDiv, Garrett Theol. Sem., Evanston, Ill., 1960; MS in Adult Edn., U. Wis., Milw., 1968; postgrad. U. Wis., Madison, 1970-75; grad. Realtors Inst. Ordained to ministry Meth. Ch., 1960; cert. pastoral counseling and interpersonal relations. Pastor Richmond (Wis.) Meth. Ch., 1956-58, Asbury United Meth. Ch., Janesville, Wis., 1958-61; tchr., guidance counselor Edgerton (Wis.) High Sch., 1961-62; assoc. pastor Community United Meth. Ch., Whitefish Bay, Wis., 1962-66; pastor Simpson and Gardner United Meth. Chs., Milw., 1966-68; assoc. pastor St. Luke United Meth. Ch., Sheboygan, Wis., 1968-69; pastor Poynette and Inch United Meth. Chs., 1969-74; dir. Adult Study Ctr., Portage, Wis., 1974-75; dir. growth and devel. Profl. Products & Services, Inc., Sauk City, Wis., 1976-83; realtor Dick Marquardt Agy., Poynette, 1983-86, Don Lee Realty, Inc., Portage, Wis., 1986-87, Noble Properties, Poynette, 1987—; HRD cons., 1983—; curriculum cons. U. Wis. Sch. Nursing, 1974-76, instr. small group seminar, 1974-76, supr. behavioral disabilities student tchrs., 1974-76; adult edn. instr. Wis. Conf. United Meth. Ch., 1964-69. Village trustee, Poynette, 1977-81; mem. Police Aux., Whitefish Bay; bd. dirs. North Shore Council Human Relations, Milw., Inter Faith Council, Milw., Poynette Area Community Devel. Orgn., 1983—. Served with C.I.C., AUS., 1954-56. Mem. Adult Edn. Assn., Am. Soc. Tng. and Devel., Nat. Assn. Realtors, Wis. Realtors Assn., Phi Delta Kappa. Lodge: Optimists. Research on participation in adult intructional groups using Eriksonian ego-stage theory. Home: 131 N Cleveland St Poynette WI 53955 Office: 540 N Hwy 51 Poynette WI 53955

WADHWA, YASH PAL, environmental engineer; b. Delhi, India, Oct. 4, 1946; came to U.S., 1969, naturalized, 1982; s. Rikhi Ram and Ram Devi (Grover) W.; m. Usha Rani Chugh, Jan. 25, 1972; children: Ajay Raj, Ravi Kumar. BSCE, U. Delhi, 1969; MSCE, U. Pitts., 1971. Registered profl. engr., Wis., Ill., N.Y. Project engr., mgr. Larsen Engrs./Architects, Rochester, N.Y., 1971-79; pres. Larsen Engrs., S.C., Milw., 1983—; sr. project mgr. DKI Group Engr., Milw., 1979-83; bd. dirs. Larsen Engrs./ Architects, Rochester; mgmt. del. to Republic of China, 1983. Account exec. United Way of Greater Milw., 1984-86; project bus. cons. Jr. Achievement, Inc., Milw., 1985—. Mem. ASCE (chmn. mgmt. tech. com. Wis. sect. 1986—), Wis. Soc. Profl. Engrs. (pres. Milw. South chpt. 1987—), Project Mgmt. Inst. (pres. midwest chpt. 1987—). Democrat. Hindu.Club: Toastmasters. Avocations: pub. speaking, sports, reading. Home: 920 W Brentwood Ln Glendale WI 53217 Office: Larsen Engrs SC 735 W Wisconsin Ave Milwaukee WI 53233

WADINA, GILBERT STEPHEN, radiologist; b. Milw., July 29, 1935; s. Stephen Anthony and Helen Ann (Drinka) W.; m. Judith Mary Szyba, July 9, 1960; children: Suzanne Mary, Mark Stephen, Paul Thomas. MD, Marquette U., 1961. Intern Milw. Luth. Hosp., 1961-62; resident Deaconess Hosp., Milw., 1962-65; radiologist St. Catherine's Hosp., Kenosha, Wis., 1965—, Burlington (Wis.) Hosp., 1965—; radiologist, pres. Dr. Armstrong, Wadina, Huberty, Clark & Swoboda, Kenosha, 1975—; chief of staff St. Catherine's Hosp., 1984. Served to capt. U.S. Army, 1960-67. Mem. Am. Coll. Radiology. Republican. Roman Catholic. Lodge: Elks. Avocations: golf, racquetball, tennis. Home: 6827 Pershing Blvd Kenosha WI 53142 Office: 6530 Sheridan Rd Kenosha WI 53140

WADLIN, MARTHA STEDMAN, social services administrator; b. Chgo., Jan. 21, 1937; d. John Stedman and Mary Jane (Laughlin) Denslow; m. Calvin H. Van O'Linda, June 1956 (dec. Sept. 1965); 1 child: Christopher Allen; m. James Edmund Wadlin, June 1976. Student, Northeast Mo. State U., 1959-60. Student wives advisor Kirksville (Mo.) Coll. Osteopathic Medicine, 1962-64; newswoman Sta. KTVO, Kirksville, 1967-68; sales rep. Leiter Designer Fabrics, Kansas City, Mo., 1969-71; office mgr. Ruby Green Seed House, Kirksville, 1971-72; coordinator, asst. dir. Northeast Mo. Comprehensive Health, Kirksville, 1972-74; asst. dir. Northeast Mo. Area Agy. on Aging, Kirksville, 1974-80, exec. dir., 1980—. Editor: (jour.) Leisure Activities for Mature Persons, 1974-80. Mem. Mo. Alliance of Area Agys. on Aging (pres. 1984, 85), Nat. Assn. Area Agys. on Aging (bd. dirs. 1985—, pvt. sector com., membership com.), Soc. Nonprofit Orgns. (charter), Mid-Am. Council on Aging (publicity com. 1978, 79), Nat. Council on Aging. Democrat. Episcopalian. Avocations: reading, sewing, gardening. Office: NE Mo Area Agy on Aging 705 E LaHarpe PO Box 1067 Kirksville MO 63501

WAETJEN, WALTER BERNHARD, university president; b. Phila., Oct. 16, 1920; s. Walter E. and Marguerite D. (Dettmann) W.; m. Betty Walls, Sept. 28, 1945; children: Walter Bernhard, Kristi Waetjen Jenkins, Daniel G. B.S., U. Pa., Millersville, 1942; M.S., U. Pa., 1947; Ed.D., U. Md., 1951; Litt.D. (hon.), Hanyang U., Seoul, Korea; LL.D. (hon.), Gama Filho U., Brazil. Profl. football player with Detroit Lions and Phila. Eagles, 1942-45; tchr. Sch. Dist. Phila., 1945-48; research fellow U. Md., 1948-50, mem. faculty, 1950-73, prof. ednl. psychology, 1957-65; dir. Bur. Ednl. Research and Field Services, 1962-65; gen. dir. Interprofl. Research Commn. Pupil Personnel Services, 1963-65, v.p. adminstrv. affairs, 1965-70, v.p. gen. adminstrn., 1970-73; pres. Cleve. State U., 1973—; Patty Hill Smith meml. lectr. U. Louisville, 1964; psychol. cons. to sch. systems, 1951—; dir. Overseas Capital Corp.; chmn. governing bd. St. Vincent Quadrangle, Inc. Coauthor sourcebooks in field.; Contbr. ednl. jours. Trustee Woodruff Found., Conv. and Visitors Bur. Greater Cleve.; mem. governing bd. St. Vincent Charity Hosp. and Health Ctr. Corp.; bd. dirs. Clean-Land, Ohio, Greater Cleve. Literacy Coalition. Recipient Disting. Alumni award Pa. State Coll., 1972, Commdr's. Cross of Order of Merit award, Fed. Republic Germany, 1986. Mem. Assn. Mid-Continent Univs. (pres. 1983), NEA, Assn. Supervision and Curriculum Devel., Soc. Research Child Devel., AAAS, Assn. Urban Univs. (chmn. 1984—), Nat. Collegiate Athletic Assn. (mem. Pres.'s Commn. 1984-87), Am. Edn. Research Assn., Aesculapian Soc., Blue Key, Iota Lambda Sigma, Phi Delta Kappa, Phi Kappa Phi. Clubs: 50, Union, Masons (33 deg.). Home: 14706 Larchmere Blvd Shaker Heights OH 44120 Office: Cleve State Univ Cleveland OH 44115

WAFFLE, DAVID ROSS, city administrator; b. Jackson, Mich., June 29, 1950; s. Robert G. and Jean Louise (Gunther) W.; m. Pamela Ruth Roberts, May 22, 1976; children: Sarah, Katy. BS, Mich. State U., 1972; MA in Pub. Affairs, U. Oreg., 1977. Intern City of Greenbelt, Md., spring 1971; adminstrn. asst., planning City of Lansing, Mich., 1972-75; adminstrv. aide pub. works City of Springfield, Oreg., summer 1976; city adminstr. City of Oakridge, Oreg., 1977-82, City of Winston, Oreg., 1982-87, City of Platteville, Wis., 1987—. Officer, newspaper editor Whiteaker Community Council, Eugene, Oreg., 1976-77. Recipient Student Service award U. Oreg., 1977. Mem. Internat. City Mgmt. Assn., Winston-Dillard area C. of C. (treas. 1984-87). Democrat. Home: 990 N 4th Platteville WI 53818 Office: City of Platteville PO Box 252 Platteville WI 53818

WAGAMAN, JEFFREY SCOTT, disability insurance examiner; b. Topeka, Mar. 30, 1963; s. William Durrie and Marianne Jean (Chance) W. BA, Washburn U., 1984; postgrad., Kans. U., 1986—. Corrections officer State of Kans., Topeka, 1983-84, social service worker, 1984-85, disability examiner, 1985—. Fin. dir. Kans. Young Reps., Topeka, 1985—. Named one of Outstanding Young Men Am., 1985. Mem. Pub. Adminstn. Soc., Kans. Assn. Pub. Employees, Topeka Jaycees,. Methodist. Avocations: tennis, raquetball, weight training, hang gliding. Home: 1940 SW Moundview Topeka KS 66604

WAGENAAR, JOHN, educator, psychologist; b. Heerhugowaard, The Netherlands, Dec. 28, 1844; came to U.S., 1951, naturalized, 1962; s. Henry and Alice (Bouwens) W.; m. Jan Eunice LaForge, Sept. 3, 1977. BA, Calvin Coll., 1967; student, Free U., Amsterdam, The Netherlands, 1967-68; MA, U. Chgo., 1971, PhD, 1973. Lectr. Catonsville Community Coll., Balt., 1972; asst. prof. Northwestern Coll., Iowa, 1973-75, asst. prof., Villa Maria Coll., Erie, Pa., 1975-77; postdoctoral fellow McGill U., Montreal, Que., Can., 1977-78; psychologist Douglas Hosp., Montreal, 1978; faculty research assoc. Wayne State U., Detroit, 1978-79; health psychologist Ann Arbor (Mich.) Family Practice, 1978-82; pvt. practice health educator Berea, Ky., 1983-85; adj. assoc. prof. Wright State U., Ohio, 1985—; adj. lectr. numerous univs., 1978—; vis. scholar U. Mich., Ass Arbor, 1976. Mem. Am. Psychol. Assn., Am. Acad. Religion, Dutch Immigrant Soc. Home and Office: 123 W North College Ann Arbor OH 45387

WAGENAAR, LARRY JOHN, historian; b. Grand Rapids, Mich., June 11, 1962; s. Cornelius and Mary (Blom) W. BA in History and Religion with honors, Hope Coll., 1987. With customer service dept. Eberhard Foods Inc., Grand Rapids, 1978-81; ops. mgr. Video Today Inc., Holland, Mich., 1981-85; hist. researcher Kent State U., 1987—. Mem. Assn. for Advancement of Dutch-Am. Studies, Am. Assn. of State and Local History, Phi Alpha Theta. Home: O-3892 Lake Ridge Dr Holland MI 49423 Office: Kent State U Dept History Kent OH 44244

WAGENER, THOMAS KEISTER, automotive service owner, educator; b. Chicago Heights, Ill., July 11, 1955; s. Anthony Pelzer and Lucille May (Haynes) W.; m. Gloria Fay Bolling, Apr. 19, 1980; children: Christopher A., Anthony H. BS, U. Wis.-Stout, Menomonie, 1977. Cert. high sch. tchr., Wis., Va. Instr. Broad Run High Sch., Leesburg, Va., 1977-78, Cen. High Sch., Strum, Wis., 1978-86; owner, mgr. Wagener Auto Service, Independence, Wis., 1985—; instr. adult edn. Dist. 1 Tech. Inst., Eau Claire, Wis., 1979—. V.p. Immanuel Luth. Ch., Strum, 1982-83, trustee, 1983—. Wis. Bus. World grantee, 1983. Mem. Nat. Edn. Assn., Wis. Ednl. Assn., Wis. Tech. Edn. Assn., Trempeleau County Snowmobile Alliance. Democrat. Club: Strum Commercial (pres. 1983-84). Avocations: cabinet making, skiing, snowmobiling, gardening, water skiing. Home: 151 Hawthorn St Strum WI 54770 Office: 335 Greene St Independence WI 54747

WAGENHAUSER, THOMAS KENNETH, II, accountant; b. Toledo, Dec. 23, 1957; s. Thomas Kenneth Wagenhauser Sr. and Nancy Darlene (Drake) Greenwood; m. Kathleen Yvette Hooper, July 21, 1976; children: Thomas Kenneth III, Adam David. Student, U. Toledo, 1981-83; BS, Ohio State U., 1983-85. Process controller Hoover Universal, Adrian, Mich., 1980-82; asst. to commr. Pub. Utilities Commn. of Ohio, Columbus, 1983-85; acct. Arthur Young & Co., Columbus, 1985—. Editor (book) Careers in Accounting, 1984. Chmn. organizing com. Westerville (Ohio) cub scout pack, Boy Scouts Am., 1986. Served to sgt. USAF, 1976-80. Mem. Ohio Soc. CPA's (student). Republican. Lutheran. Avocations: reading, basketball, scouting. Home: 477 E Schrock Rd Westerville OH 43081 Office: Arthur Young and Co 100 E Broad St Columbus OH 43215

WAGLE, RAJ P., computer systems engineer; b. Bombay, India, Dec. 15, 1945; came to U.S., 1978; m. Shobha J. Wagh, May 1, 1974; 1 child, Supriya R. BSME, Coll. Engring., Aurangabad, India, 1967; diploma in Ops. Mgmt., Bombay U., 1975; MS in Info. Systems, Eastern Mich. U., 1986. Sr. mfg. engr. Internat. Harvester of India, Bombay, 1968-78; sr. mktg. engr. Applicon/MDSI div. Schlumberger Co., Ann Arbor, Mich., 1978-85; sr. systems engr. Electronic Data Systems, Detroit, 1985—. Mem. Soc. Mfg. Engrs. (cert.). Office: Electronic Data Systems PO Box 7019 2555 Crooks Rd Troy MI 48007

WAGNER, ALAN RAY, English and Spanish educator; b. Creston, Iowa, Mar. 22, 1949; s. Harold Emmet and Lois Ellen (Lindeman) W. BA, BS in Secondary Edn., Northwest Mo. State U., 1971, MA in English, 1973; MA in Spanish, U. Iowa, 1982. Registrar Mid-Am. Council Boy Scouts Am., Omaha, 1973-75; from tchr. to assoc. prof. English and Spanish Iowa Western Community Coll., Council Bluffs, 1975—. Mem. Nat. Council Tchrs. English, Iowa Western Community Coll. Higher Edn. Assn. (bd. dirs. 1983-85), Iowa Western Community Coll. Profl. Senate (sec. 1980-81). Avocations: barbershop quartet music, community theater. Home: 503 1/2 S 11th St Omaha NE 68102 Office: Iowa Western Community Coll 2700 College Rd Council Bluffs IA 51501

WAGNER, ALVIN LOUIS, JR., profl. real estate appraiser, cons.; b. Chgo., Dec. 19, 1939; s. Alvin Louis and Esther Jane (Wheeler) W.; student U. Ill., 1958-59; B.A., Drake U., 1962; postgrad. Real Estate Inst., Chgo., 1960-65; m. Susan Carole Fahey, Aug. 14, 1965; children—Alvin Louis III, Robert Percy. Asst. appraiser Oak Park (Ill.) Fed. Savings & Loan Co., 1955-60; v.p. real estate sales A. L. Wagner & Co., Flossmoor, Ill., 1961-63; real estate loan officer, chief appraiser Beverly Bank, Chgo., 1963-67; asso. real estate appraiser C. A. Bruckner & Assos., Chgo., 1967-70; founder, profl. real estate appraiser and cons. A. L. Wagner & Co., Flossmoor, 1970—. Mem. faculty Am. Inst. Real Estate Appraisers, Chgo., 1974—; instr. real estate appraising Prairie State Coll., Chicago Heights, Ill., 1970—; mem. adv. com. Real Estate Sch., 1972—; community prof. Gov.'s State U., 1977—, founding mem. real estate adv. bd. Mem. Rich Township (Ill.) Personal Services Commn., 1973—; v.p., drive chmn. Flossmoor Community Chest, Crusade of Mercy, 1974-75, pres., 1975-76. Auditor, Rich Township, 1973-77. Governing bd. Glenwood (Ill.) Sch. for Boys, 1973—; chmn. bus. edn. occupational adv. com. Homewood-Flossmoor High Sch., 1977; pres. South Suburban Focus Council; mem. South Suburban Mayors and Mgrs. Bus. and Industry Adv. Council, Flossmore Econ. Devel. Commn.; bd. dirs. Prairie State Coll. Found., 1985—; treas. U.S. Dept. Housing & Urban Devel. South Suburban Community Housing Resources BD., 1981—; assoc. mem. Employee Relocation Council. Mem. Am. Inst. Real Estate Appraisers (mem. governing council 1974-75, Profl. Recognition award 1977), Soc. Real Estate Appraisers (nat. pub. relations com., vice chmn. 1985—), Real Estate Educators Assn., South Suburban Assn. Commerce and Industry, Chgo. Assn. Commerce and Industry, Chgo., Homewood-Flossmoor real estate bds., Nat., Ill. assns. realtors, Homewood-Flossmoor Jaycees, Phi Delta Theta (pres. chpt. 1960), Chgo. Phi Delta Theta Alumni Club (pres.), Omega Tau Rho, Lambda Alpha. Clubs: Flossmoor Country, Variety, Rotary, Masons. Mem. editorial bd. Appraisal Jour., 1975—; contbr. articles to real estate jours., also Mobility mag., Mcpl. Econ. Devel. Home: 927 Park Dr Flossmoor IL 60422 Office: 2709 Flossmoor Rd Flossmoor IL 60422

WAGNER, ANNE MARIE, nurse; b. Mpls., Dec. 29, 1951; d. Victor Leo and Mary Bernadette (Gray) Steinbauer; m. Charles Peter Wagner, Dec. 2, 1972; children: Chad, Kristina. BA, Coll. St. Catherine, 1986. Lic. practical nurse Meth. Hosp., St. Louis Park, Minn., 1970-72, Southdale Hosp., Edina, Minn., 1974-79; registered nurse Staffbuilders Health Care Services, Mpls., 1985—. Mem. Sigma Theta Tau. Roman Catholic. Avocations: camping, swimming, fishing, sewing, bicycling. Home: 16921 Creek Ridge Pl Minnetonka MN 55345

WAGNER, BLAKE DOUGLAS, clergyman; b. Akron, Ohio, Oct. 27, 1931; s. John Ernest and Ruth Etta (Daniel) W.; m. Gere Caryl Fulmer, Aug. 6, 1954; children—Lynn Ann Wagner Wood, Blake Douglas, Jr. B.A., U. Akron, 1953; M.Div., Oberlin Grad. Sch. Theology, 1957; D.Ministry, Vanderbilt U., 1974. Ordained to ministry Methodist Ch., 1957. Pastor Zion Evang. United Brethren, Cuyahoga Falls, Ohio, 1951-53, Montrose Zion Evang. United Brethren Ch., Akron, 1953-59, The Emmanuel Ch., Evang. United Brethren, Lorain, Ohio, 1959-67, The Master's Ch., United Meth. Ch., Euclid, Ohio, 1967-74; sr. pastor Main St. United Meth. Ch., Mansfield, Ohio, 1974—; field rep. The Robert H. Schuller Inst. for Successful Church Leadership, Garden Grove, Calif., 1980—. Pres. Richland County Hospice Assn., Mansfield, 1980—; trustee Make-a-Way Center, Inc., Mansfield, 1984—; mem. exec. bd. Johnny Appleseed council Boy Scouts Am., Mansfield, 1983—; on interpropl. Ohio State U. Commn. on interprofl. edn. and practice, Columbus. Named life mem. Ohio Pastor's Convocation Ohio Council of Chs., 1973; recipient Dean Thomas Graham award Oberlin Coll. Grad. Sch., Theology, 1957, St. Martin DePorres award Lorain County Catholic Council, 1966, Founders award Ohio Wesleyan U., 1980; Pixley scholar U. Akron, 1952-53. Mem. Inter-Church Council (pres. 1984-85), The Mansfield Ministerial Assn., (pres. 1978-79), East Ohio Conf. United Meth. Ch. (bd. ministry 1984—), Mansfield Dist. Com. on Ministry (chmn. 1983—), Dist. Council on Ministries. Republican. Lodges: Optimist (pres. 1978-79), Masons. Avocations: travel, camping, photography. Home: 516 Fairoaks Blvd Mansfield OH 44907 Office: 230 S Main St Mansfield OH 44903

WAGNER, BRIAN ALLEN, distributing company executive; b. Moline, Ill., Nov. 7, 1958; s. Norbert Herbert and Mary Jane (Carden) W. A.A., Black Hawk Coll., 1976. Gen. mgr. Warren Radio Co., Davenport, Iowa, 1978—. Republican precinct committeeman, Rock Island County, Moline, Ill., 1984. Mem. Tri-City Assn. of Purchasing Mgmt. Presbyterian. Avocations: gardening; collecting political memorabilia. Home: 119 17th Ave East Moline IL 61244 Office: Warren Radio Co 1205 East River Dr Davenport IA 52803

WAGNER, CHARLES ALAN, librarian; b. Elkhart, Ind., Apr. 27, 1948; s. C. Arthur and Lydia M. (Stump) W.; B.A., Manchester (Ind.) Coll., 1970; M.L.S., Ind. U., 1973; m. Marilynn B. Dray, Aug. 17, 1971; children—Sarah, Wendy. Library dir. Peru Public Library, 1973—. Mem. Ind. Library Assn., Plymouth Club Am. Lodge: Rotary. Author articles field. Cartoons appear in comic books, newspapers, mags. Address: 102 E Main St Peru IN 46970-2338

WAGNER, CHARLES ARTHUR, oil company executive; b. Balt., Oct. 30, 1927; s. Michael Joseph and Margaret (Ryan) W.; m. Jane Josephine Kearns, Sept. 26, 1959; children: Charles A. Jr., Michael J., Mary C., Sally P. BS, Loyola Coll., Balt., 1953; Assoc. in Acctg., Loyola Coll., 1963. Supr. tax acctg. Am. Oil Co., Balt., 1955-60, supr. gen. acctg., 1961-63, auditing cons., 1964, supr. inventory control, 1965-69, supr. systems and methods, 1969-73; supr. systems and methods Am. Oil Co., Atlanta, 1973-75; analyst EDP hardware Standard Oil Co., Chgo., 1975-84; tech. cons. Amoco Corp., Chgo., 1985-86; regional sales manager CMI Corp., Chgo., 1986—. Head coach Loch Raven Lacrosse Assn. Baltimore County, Md., 1962-73; asst. coachLoch Raven Football Assn., Baltimore County, 1968-73; v.p. Waubonsie Valley High Sch. Booster Club, Naperville, Ill., 1975-84; election auditor Wheatland South, Naperville, Ill., 1979. Republican. Roman Catholic. Club: Regis (Towson, Md.) (pres. 1966-67). Lodge: KC. Home: 28 W 744 Grommon Rd Naperville IL 60565

WAGNER, CHARLES RUSSELL, accountant, educator, consultant; b. Delong, Ind., Aug. 14, 1922; s. Jacob George Wagner and Iona Elizabeth (Long) Steeb; m. Rutheda Meyer, Aug. 17, 1947; children: Skip, Barbara, Mary, William, David. BS in Acctg., U. Notre Dame, 1949; MBA in Mgmt., Creighton U., 1967; PhD in Acctg., U. Nebr., 1976. Cert. data processor, internal auditor, mgmt. acct., CPA, Ind., Minn. Commd. 2d lt. USAF, 1951, advanced through grades to lt. col., 1966, ret., 1969; asst. prof. acctg. Creighton U., Omaha, 1969-76; assoc. prof. U. S.D., Vermillion, 1976-78, Gustavus Adolphus Coll., St. Peter, Minn., 1978-83, St. Cloud State U., Minn., 1983-84; prof. Mankato (Minn.) State U., 1984-87; cons. in field, 1973-87. Author: (book) CPA and Fraud, 1979. Mem. Am. Acctg. Assn., Am. Inst. CPA's, Nat. Assn. Accts., Inst. for Cert. Computer Profls., Inst. Internal Auditors, Beta Gamma Sigma. Home: 810 Ronell St Saint Peter MN 56082 Office: Mankato State U Mankato MN 56001

WAGNER, DIANE NATALIE, psychologist; b. Chgo., Nov. 8, 1940; s. Frank Paul and Natalie Victoria (Gazdik) Dite.; m. David Leslie Wagner, June 23, 1963 (div. Aug. 1979). BS in Edn., Northern Ill. U., 1967; MA, 1968. Dir. DeKalb County Children's Services, DeKalb, Ill., 1964-67; psychologist Elgin (Ill.) State Psychiat. Hosp., 1967-69, Ben Gordon Mental Health Ctr., DeKalb, Ill., 1970-79; regional tng. mgr. Legal Services Corp., Chgo., 1979-81; tng. and devel. cons. IBM Corp., Chgo., 1982—; bd. dirs. Counseling Ctr. of Lakeview, Chgo., 1985—. Mem. Chgo. Nat. Soc. for Performance and Instruction, Indsl. Psychologists of Chgo., Orgnl. Devel. Network, Women for Peace, SERVAS. Avocation: language study. Home: 339 Barry Ave Chicago IL 60657 Office: IBM Corp One IBM Plaza 15/836 Chicago IL 60611

WAGNER, DOROTHY MARIE, court reporting service executive; b. Milw., June 8, 1924; d. Theodore Anthony and Leona Helen (Ullrich) Wagner; grad. Milw. Bus. U., 1944; student Marquette U., U. Wis., Milw. Stenographer, legal sec., Milw., 1942-44; hearing reporter Wis. Workmen's Compensation Dept., 1944-48; ofcl. reporter to judge Circuit Ct., Milw., 1952-53; owner, operator ct. reporting service Dorothy M. Wagner & Assocs., Milw., 1948—; guest lectr. ct. reporting Madison Area Tech. Coll., 1981—. Recipient Gregg Diamond medal Gregg Pub. Co., 1950. Mem. Nat. (registered profl. reporter, certificate of proficiency), Wis. shorthand reporters assns., Am. Legion Aux., Met. Milw. Assn. Commerce. Roman Catholic. Home: 214 Williamsburg Dr Thiensville WI 53092 Office: 135 Wells St Suite 400 Milwaukee WI 53203

WAGNER, DOUGLAS EDWARD, educator; b. Chgo., Aug. 14, 1952; s. Edward James and June Anne (Bork) W.; m. Sandra Lee Riddell, Nov. 18, 1978; 1 child, Jennifer Anne. B in Music Edn., Butler U., 1974, M in Music Edn., 1977. Mem. faculty North Cen. High Sch., Indpls., 1973—; church musician all denominations; leader clinics and workshops nationwide. Composer, arranger over 700 published choral, handbell, instrumental and keyboard works. Named one of Outstanding Young Men Am., 1982. Mem. ASCAP, Internat. Choristers Guild, Am. Guild Organists, Am. Choral Dirs. Assn. Republican. Episcopalian. Club: Riviera (Indpls.). Home and Office: 7210 N Pennsylvania St Indianapolis IN 46240-3038

WAGNER, ELIZABETH DOUGLAS, personnel administrator; b. Toledo, Ohio, June 17, 1928; d. Andrew and Elizabeth (Maier) Douglas; m. John A. Wagner, Dec. 17, 1948 (div. Feb. 1976); 1 child, Christopher; m. Charles Lowell Bleckner, May 1, 1986. BEd, U. Toledo, 1949, MEd, 1868, DEd, 1981. Lic. psychologist, Ohio. Pub. relations dir. Storer Broadcasting, Toledo, 1952-59; copy chief Cole Advt. Agy., Toledo, 1960-67; psychologist Toledo Pub. Schs., 1968-82, employee assistance dir., 1982—. Active exec. com. United Way, Toledo, 1985—. Recipient Sylvania TV award, 1955. Mem. Employee Assistance Soc., U. Toledo Alumni Assn., Phi Kappa Phi. Republican. Presbyterian. Avocations: golf, tennis, reading. Home: 2450 Amara Dr Toledo OH 43615 Office: Toledo Pub Schs Manhatten and Elm Sts Toledo OH 43608

WAGNER, ERIC ARMIN, sociology educator; b. Cleve., May 31, 1941; s. Armin Erich and Florence (Edwards) W. A.B., Ohio State U., 1964; M.A., U. Fla., 1968, Ph.D., 1973. Instr. sociology Ohio U., Athens, 1968-73, asst. prof., 1973-75, assoc. prof., 1975-83, prof., 1983—, chmn. sociology and anthropology, 1974-78, 86—, vice chmn. faculty senate, 1982-84. Mem. Am. Sociol. Assn., Internat. Sociol. Assn., Latin Am. Studies Assn., North Cen. Sociol. Assn., Midwest Assn. for Latin Am. Studies (pres. 1979-80), U.S. Orienteering Fedn. (dir. 1976-82, sec.-treas. 1976-78, v.p. 1979-80, sec. 1980-82), Delta Sigma Phi. Presbyterian. Contbr. articles on Latin Am. sport and society to various publs. Home: 10030 Oxley Rd Athens OH 45701 Office: Ohio U Dept Sociology Athens OH 45701

WAGNER, JEROME PETER, clinical psychologist; b. Cin., Oct. 11, 1941; s. Herbert Peter and Bertha Clara (Gossman) W.; m. Bernadette M. Veeneman, July 20, 1984. AB, Loyola U., Chgo., 1965, MA in Clinical Psychology, 1968, MDiv, 1974, PhD in Clinical Psychology, 1981. Registered psychologist, Ill. Tchr., counselor Loyola Acad., Wilmette, Ill., 1966-69; tchr., counselor Xavier High Sch., Cin., 1973-76, assoc. dir. psychol. services, 1973-76; asst. prof. Loyola U., Chgo., 1980-83, clinical asst. prof., 1983—; staff psychologist Loyola Counseling Ctr., Chgo., 1985—; pvt. practice psychotherapy, Chgo., 1980—. Contbr. articles to profl. jours. Mem. Am. Psychol. Assn., Ill. Psychol. Assn. Roman Catholic. Avocations: music. Home: 2755 Lincolnwood Dr Evanston IL 60201 Office: Loyola Univ 6525 N Sheridan Chicago IL 60626

WAGNER, KARL W., printing company executive; b. Davenport, Iowa, Nov. 11, 1925; s. Karl H. and Edith L. (Cameron) W.; m. Thelma G. Smith, Aug. 30, 1952; children: Christine E., Karl F. BA, Augustana Coll., Rock Island, Ill., 1950. Pres. Wagners Printers, Inc., Davenport, 1969-84, chmn. bd., 1984—. Served to 1st sgt. U.S. Army, 1944-46, ETO. Recipient Elmer Voigt Edn. award Printing Industries Am., 1982. Mem. Master Printers Am. (vice chmn. 1986), Nat. Assn. Printers and Lithographers (bd. dirs.), Graphic Arts Tech. Fedn. (bd. dirs.). Republican. Lutheran. Clubs: Davenport, Davenport Country, Bear's Paw Country (Naples, Fla.). Home: 10 Forest Rd Davenport IA 52803 Office: Wagners Printers Inc 1515 E Kimberly Rd Davenport IA 52808

WAGNER, NORMAN PAUL, utility company executive; b. Newark, Mar. 25, 1924; s. Julius and Gertrude (Burke) W.; m. Gwendolyn Marshall, June 3, 1950; children: Norman Paul, Neil, Carol, Elizabeth, Lisa. B.S.M.E., Clemson U., 1949. Prodn. control engr. Babcock & Wilcox, Barberton, Ohio, 1951-62; works and project mgr. Babcock & Wilcox, Mount Vernon, Ind., 1962-68; mem. staff ops. and mktg. So. Ind. Gas & Electric Co., Evansville, 1968-77, exec. v.p., 1977-79, pres., chief operating officer, 1980-81, pres., chief exec. officer, dir., chmn. exec. com., 1982—, chmn. bd., 1986—; dir. Citizens Nat. Bancshares, Evansville, Ohio Valley Electric Corp.-Ind.-Ky. Electric Corp., Columbus, Deaconess Hosp. Service Corp., Evansville, Community Natural Gas, Mt. Carmel, Ill., Internat. Steel Co., Evansville; dir., past pres. East Cen. Nuclear Group; exec. bd. East Cen. Area Reliability Council. Campaign chmn. United Way of Southwestern Ind., Evansville, 1983-84; co-chmn. Hossiers for Econ. Devel. Com., Indpls.; dir., past pres. Evansville Indsl. Found., past pres. Tri-State Health Planning, Evansville. Served as flight engr. USAF, 1943-46. Mem. ASME, Ind. Gas Assn. (bd. dirs., vice chmn.), Ind. Electric Assn. (bd. dirs., past chmn.), Edison Electric Inst. (bd. dirs.), Met. Evansville C. of C. (chmn. 1984-85), Ind. C. of C. (bd. dirs.). Clubs: Evansville Country; Petroleum (Evansville); Columbia (Indpls.). Home: 315 Charmwood Ct Evansville IN 47715 Office: So Ind Gas & Electric Co 20-24 NW 4th St Evansville IN 47741

WAGNER, PAUL DEAN, oral and maxillofacial surgeon; b. Mankato, Kans., Dec. 24, 1937; s. Oral Harlan and Mary Belle (Amis) W.; m. Sharon Kay, July 17, 1960; children: Anne, Mary Beth, Paul Jr. BS in Pharmacy, Kans. U., 1961; DDS, U. Tenn., 1968. Diplomate Am. Bd. Oral and Maxillofacial Surgery. Resident in oral and maxillofacial surgery Harrisburg (Pa.) Hosp., 1968-71; practice dentistry specializing in oral and maxillofacial surgery Hershey, Pa., 1971-75, Hays, Kans., 1975—. Pres. Hays Area Rd. Runners, 1975—. Mem. ADA, Kans. Dental Assn., Am. Soc. Oral and Maxillofacial Surgery, Kans Soc. Oral and Maxillofacial Surgery (pres. 1984-85), Oil Belt Dental Soc. (pres. 1977-78), Kans. Dental Specialty Bd. (examiner), Hays Area C. of C., Kans. C.of C., Sierra Club, Hays Area Rd. Runners (pres. 1975—). Republican. Unitarian. Avocations: running, biking, hiking. Home: 2746 Thunderbird Circle Hays KS 67601 Office: 2501 Canterbury Rd Hays KS 67601

WAGNER, PHILLIP ANTHONY, chemical researcher; b. Bay City, Mich., Nov. 9, 1937; s. Ronald Walter and Leona (Ryers) widowed; children: Connie Lynn, Kelly Jo. Student, Bay City (Mich.) Jr. Coll., 1956-57, Delta Coll., 1959-60. Electrician Gen. Motors Corp., Bay City, Mich., 1959-60; lab. tech. Dow Chem. Co., Midland, Mich., 1960-73; engr. Dow Chem. Co., Midland, 1973-80, project leader, 1980-84, research leader, 1984—. Trustee Hampton Township Bd., Essexville, Mich., 1980-84. Served to maj. U.S. Army, 1956. Mem. Soc. Plastics Engrs. (sr.). Republican. Roman Catholic. Home: 860 Center Ave Rd Essexville MI 48732

WAGNER, RICHARD, baseball club executive; b. Central City, Nebr., Oct. 19, 1927; s. John Howard and Esther Marie (Wolken) W.; m. Gloria Jean Larsen, May 10, 1950; children—Randolph G., Cynthia Kaye. Student, pub. schs., Central City. Gen. mgr. Lincoln Baseball Club, Nebr., 1955-58; mgr. Pershing Mcpl. Auditorium, Lincoln, 1958-61; exec. staff Ice Capades, Inc., Hollywood, Calif., 1961-63; gen. mgr. Sta. KSAL, Salina, Kans., 1963-65; dir. promotion and sales St. Louis Nat. Baseball Club, 1965-66; gen. mgr. Forum, Inglewood, Calif., 1966-67; asst. to exec. v.p. Cin. Reds, 1967-70, asst. to pres., 1970-74, v.p. adminstrn., 1975, exec. v.p., 1975-78, gen. mgr., 1977-83, pres., 1978-83; pres. Houston Astros Baseball Club, 1985—; pres. RGW Enterprises, Inc., Houston, 1978—. Served with USNR, 1945-47, 50-52. Named Exec. of Yr., Minor League Baseball, Sporting News, 1958. Mem. Internat. Assn. Auditorium Mgrs. Republican. Methodist. Office: care Houston Astros Astrodome PO Box 288 Houston TX 77001

WAGNER, ROBERT TODD, university president, sociology educator; b. Sioux Falls, S.D., Oct. 30, 1932; s. Hans Herman and Helen Emilie (Castle) W.; m. Mary Kay Mumford, June 23, 1954; children: Christopher, Andrea. BA, Augustana Coll., Sioux Falls, 1954; MDiv, Seabury Western Theol. Sem., 1957, STM, 1970; PhD, S.D. State U., 1972. Ordained to ministry Episc. Ch., 1957. Staff analyst AMA, Chgo., 1954-57; vicar Ch. of Holy Apostles, Sioux Falls, 1957-64; chaplain All Saints Sch., Sioux Falls, 1962-64; rector Trinity Episcopal Ch., Watertown, S.D., 1964-69; prof. sociology S.D. State U., Brookings, 1971—, acting head dept. sociology, 1978, asst. to v.p. for acad. affairs, 1980-84, pres., 1985—; v.p. Dakota State Coll., Madison, S.D., 1984-85; cons. sociologist Devel. Planning and Research, Manhattan, Kans., 1976-85; bd. dirs. Deuel County Nat. Bank, Clear Lake, S.D., Found. Seed Stock. Bd. dirs. Karl Mundt Found., Prairie Repertory Theatre, REACH, S.D. 4-H Found., S.D. State U. Found., Christian Edn. Camp and Conf. of Episcopal Dioceses of S.D. Arthur Vinning Davis Found. fellow, 1969-70, Episcopal Ch. Found. fellow, 1969-71, Augustana Coll. fellow, 1977. Mem. Nat. Assn. State Univs. and Land Grant Colls., Brookings C. of C., Phi Kappa Phi, Phi Kappa Delta, Pi Gamma Mu, Alpha Kappa Delta, Alpha Lambda Delta, Sigma Gamma Delta. Republican. Lodges: Elks, Rotary. Avocations: railroading, gardening, cooking. Home: 929 Harvey Dunn St Brookings SD 57006 Office: SD State U Office of Pres Adminstrn Bldg 222 Brookings SD 57007-2298

WAGNER, ROBERT WALTER, photography, cinema and communications educator, media producer, consultant; b. Newport News, Va., Nov. 16, 1918; s. Walter George and Barbara Anna W.; m. Betty Jane Wiles, Nov. 21, 1948; children—Jonathan R., Jeffrey A., Jennifer J. B.Sc., Ohio State U., 1940, M.A., 1941, Ph.D., 1953. Motion picture writer-dir. Office War Info., N.Y.C. and Washington, 1942-43; writer-dir. Office Coordinator Interam. Affairs for South and Central Am., 1943-44; chief info. Div. Mental Hygiene, Ohio Dept. Pub. Welfare, 1944-46; dir. div. motion pictures Ohio State U., 1946-58, prof. communications, photography and cinema, 1960—; pres. Univ. Film Found., 1979-85; internat. cons. communications; bd. dirs. Am. Film Inst., 1974-81; mem. faculty U. So. Calif., 1958-59, U. P.R., 1961, 66, 68, San Jose State U., 1967, Ariz. State U., 1971, Concordia U., Montreal, Que., Can., 1980, 81, Danish Nat. Film Sch., 1983, 84, Emerson Coll., Boston, 1987. Ency. Brit. fellow, 1953; Sr. Fulbright fellow, Peru, 1976; recipient Disting. Service award Columbus Community Film Council, 1986. Fellow Soc. Motion Picture and TV Engrs. (Eastman Gold Medal award 1981); mem. Acad. TV Arts and Scis. (Disting. Service award 1967, Ohioana Pegasus award 1985), Univ. Film/Video Assn. (bd. editors jour. 1975-85, editor jour. 1956-75), Internat. Congress Schs. Cinema and TV (v.p. 1964-82), Assn. Ednl. Communication and Tech. (bd. editors jour. 1976—). Club: Torch (Columbus, Ohio). Author film series: Series of Motion Picture Documents on Communication Theory and New Educational Media, 1966; editor: Education of Film Maker, 1975. Home: 1353 Zollinger Rd Upper Arlington OH 43221 Office: Ohio State U 156 W 19th Ave Columbus OH 43210

WAGNER, ROMAN FRANK, insurance agency executive; b. Sheboygan, Wis., Mar. 16, 1927; s. Roman N. and Clara C. (Ott) W.; m. Jacqueline Anne Randall, Aug. 13, 1949; children: Kenneth, Katherine, Julie, Lisa, Janine, Jodi, Randall. BBA, Marquette U., 1950; MS in Fin. Services, Am. Coll., 1983. With Bankers Life Co. (now Prin. Mut. Life), Sheboygan, 1950—; spl. agt. Sheboygan Falls (Wis.) Mut. Ins. Co., 1953-54; treas. Sheboygan Town & Country, Inc., 1963-87 ; pres. Roman Wagner Agy., Inc. (now United Wis. Ins. Agy., Inc.), Sheboygan, 1964—, Scorpio, Inc., Sheboygan, 1979-87 ; instr. Ins. Inst. Am., Lakeshore Tech. Inst., 1966—; condr. workshops in field; mem. Wis. Ins. Agts. Adv. Council, 1974-80. Active, United Fund drs., Sheboygan, 1963-68; mem. City of Sheboygan Police and Fire Commn., 1968-75, sec., 1970-75. Served with USN, 1945-47. Named Jaycees Key Man, 1960. Mem. Sheboygan County Ind. Ins. Agts., CLU Soc., Soc. CPCU, Am. Inst. Property and Liability Underwriters (mem. ethical inquiry bd. 1982—), Ind. Ins. Agts. of Wis (Agt. of Yr. award 1978), Wis. Assn. Life Underwriters, Wis. Found. for Ins. Edn. (Disting. Service award 1975), Sheboygan C. of C., Alpha Kappa Psi, Beta Gamma Sigma, Alpha Phi Omega. Republican. Roman Catholic. Club: Econ. (pres. 1980). Lodges: KC (4th degree), Rotary (dist. chmn. Belgium Youth Exchange

1981-82). Home: 1120A Aspen Ct Kohler WI 53044 Office: 611 New York Ave Sheboygan WI 53081

WAGNER, STEVEN EUGENE, advertising executive; b. Charles City, Iowa, May 27, 1955; s. Gerald E. and Emma L. (Landers) W.; m. Chris Marie Marmon, Nov. 5, 1982 (div. June 1986). BS in Journalism, Iowa State U., 1978. Tech. writer Fisher Controls, Marshalltown, Iowa, 1978-80, advt. writer, 1980-81; advt. writer Alexander Mktg. Services, Grand Rapids, Mich., 1981-86, advt. acct. mgr., 1986—; pub. relations writer Iowa DOT, Ames, 1977-78. Contbr. articles to profl. jours.; chpts. to ref. books. Mem. Mensa. Avocations: scuba diving, model planes, architecture, woodworking. Office: Alexander Mktg Services Inc 277 Crahen Ave NE Grand Rapids MI 49506

WAGNER, WILLIAM JOHN, physician; b. Milw., June 26, 1948; s. Alois Louis Wagner and Jeanne Wheeler (Corbett) Petermann; m. Helen Ann Friedl, Aug. 5, 1972 (div. Nov. 1978); 1 child, Ann Marie; m. Susan Marie Brennan, Sept. 27, 1986. BS, St. Norbert Coll., 1970; DO, Chgo. Coll. Osteo. Medicine, 1976. Diplomate Nat. Bd. Examiners. Intern Lakeview Hosp., Milw., 1976-77; gen. practice osteo. medicine Plymouth (Wis.) Clinic Family Med. Ctr., 1977—. Served to lt. U.S. Army, 1971. Mem. Am. Osteo. Assn., Wis. Assn. Osteo. Physicians and Surgeons (pres.-elect 1986, pres. 1987), Am. Coll. Gen. Practitioners in Osteo. Medicine (pres. Wis. soc. 1982). Roman Catholic. Avocations: skiing, sailing, horseback riding. Home: 204 Crystal Lake Dr Plymouth WI 53073 Office: Plymouth Clinic Family Med Ctr 2323 Eastern Ave Plymouth WI 53073

WAHL, BRUCE AUGUST, real estate investor; b. Breckenridge, Minn., Nov. 30, 1947; s. Ervin August and Donna Lou (Lehman) W.; m. Linda Dianne Roberts, Oct. 14, 1970; children: Timothy August, Daniel Keith. AA, U. Wash., 1971. Lic. real estate broker. Enlisted USAF, 1968, resigned, 1976; burlap bag cleaner Breckenridge, 1962-65; press operator Boeing Co., Seattle, 1966-68; prin. Wahl to Wahl Real Estate Brockerage, Independence, Mo., 1977—; pvt. practice mortgage banking, tax acctg., plumbing, elec. work, Oak Grove, Mo., 1977—; owner, mgr. duplexes, complexes, Independence, Kansas City, Mo. Republican. Baptist. Club: Landlord (Kansas City). Avocations: motorcycling, hunting. Office: 8500-B E 47th St Kansas City MO 64129

WAHL, RICHARD MICHAEL, real estate corporation executive; b. Saginaw, Mich., Jan. 29, 1955; s. Benjamin Charles and Florence Ann (Czolgosz) W.; m. Bonny Lou Tuck, Apr. 1, 1978; children: Laura Elizabeth, Carrie Lynn, Katherine Marie. AS, Delta Coll., 1975; BS, Lawrence Inst. Tech., 1978, BArch, 1979. Registered architect. Archtl. designer T. Rogvoy & Assocs., Southfield, Mich., 1977-78; archtl. draftsman Chrysler Realty, Troy, Mich., 1978-79; staff architect ABKO Properties, Troy, Mich., 1979-80; asst. real estate mgr. Mich. Bell Telephone, Southfield, 1980-82; real estate mgr. AT&T, Schaumburg, Ill., 1982-86; pres., chief exec. officer Wahl, Inc., Palatine, Ill., 1985—. Republican. Lutheran. Avocations: carpentry, scuba diving, water skiing, fishing. Home and Office: 1465 Peppertree Dr Palatine IL 60067

WAHL, ROSALIE E., judge; b. Gordon, Kans., Aug. 27, 1924; children: Christopher Roswell, Sara Emilie, Timothy Eldon, Mark Patterson, Jenny Caroline. B.A., U. Kans., 1946; J.D., William Mitchell Coll. Law, 1967. Bar: Minn. 1967. Asst. state pub. defender Mpls., 1967-73; clin. prof. law William Mitchell Coll. Law, 1973-77; assoc. justice Minn. Supreme Ct., St. Paul, 1977—; adj. prof. law U. Minn., 1972-73. Fellow Am. Bar Found; mem. ABA (chmn. sect. legal edn. and bar admissions, accreditation com., criminal justice sect., individual rights and responsibility sect.), Minn. State Bar Assn. (com. legal assistance to disadvantaged), Am. Judicature Soc., Nat. Assn. Women Judges, Nat. Assn. Woman Lawyers, Minn. Women Lawyers Assn. Office: State Capitol Supreme Ct Saint Paul MN 55155

WAHLE, JOANN GERMAN, dentist; b. Norfolk, Nebr., Mar. 19, 1958; d. Aloys Theodore and Bertha Gertrude (Rollman) German; m. Steven Mark Wahle, June 2, 1984. BA in Psychology, Creighton U., 1980, DDS, 1984. Resident in dentistry Ind. U., Indpls., 1984-85; gen. practice dentistry North Liberty, Iowa, 1985—; mem. hosp. staff St. Luke's Hosp., Cedar Rapids, Iowa, 1985—. Mem. ADA, Acad. Gen. Dentistry, Am. Assn. Hosp. Dentists, Am. Coll. Dentistry, Internat. Coll. Dentistry. Democrat. Roman Catholic. Avocations: downhill skiing, hiking, aerobic exercise, travel. Home and Office: 205 S Chestnut North Liberty IA 52317

WAHLIN, MICHAEL GLEN, accountant; b. Red Wing, Minn., July 24, 1960; s. Robert Norman and Mary Lee (Ness) W. BS magna cum laude, St. Cloud (Minn.) State U., 1982. CPA, Minn. Staff auditor Fox & Co., Bloomington, Minn., 1982-85; supr. Grant Thornton, Mpls., 1985—. St. Cloud State U. scholar, 1978, Gen. Acctg. scholar St. Cloud State U., 1981. Mem. Am. Inst. CPA's, Minn. Soc. CPA's, Phi Kappa Phi, Beta Gamma Sigma. Lutheran. Avocations: softball, golf, tennis, bowling, reading. Home: 3140 Chowen Ave S #313 Minneapolis MN 55416 Office: Grant Thornton 500 Pillsbury Ctr Minneapolis MN 55402

WAINSCOTT, JAMES LAWRENCE, accountant; b. LaPorte, Ind., Mar. 31, 1957; s. James J. and Frances J. (Cunningham) W. BS magna cum laude, Ball State U., 1979; postgrad. U. Notre Dame, 1987. CPA, Ind.; cert. mgmt. acct.; cert. internal auditor; cert. info. systems auditor. Sr. auditor Geo. S. Olive & Co., C.P.A.s, Indpls. and Valparaiso, Ind., 1979-82; fin. mgr. Midwest div. Nat. Steel Corp., Portage, Ind., 1982—; cons. Edward J. Wainscott, CPA, LaPorte, Ind., 1982—; instr. acctg. Purdue U.-Westville, 1980-82, Valparaiso U., 1980-84. Advisor Jr. Achievement, 1984; vol. Am. Cancer Soc., Valparaiso Income Tax Assistance Program, Valparaiso Community/Univ. Campaign; treas. Midwest Steel Employees Fed. Credit Union; pres. Midwest Steel Employees Assn.; mem. Intertel, Ball State U. Cardinal Connection; mem. N.W. Ind. Open Housing Council; chmn. dean's adv. council Valparaiso U. Mem. Ind. CPA Soc. (chmn. chpt. activities com. 1985-86, chpt. ed. 1983-86, chpt. pres. 1984-85, state bd. dirs. 1987—), Nat. Assn. Accts. (chpt. bd. dirs. 1982-86, chpt. pres. 1983-84; Past Pres. award 1984), Am. Inst. CPA's, Acctg. Research Assn., Am. Acctg. Assn., Inst. Mgmt. Acctg., Inst. Internal Auditors, Soc. Profl. Mgmt. Cons., Assn. MBA Execs., U. Notre Dame Exec. MBA Alumni Club, Inst. for Certification of Computer Profls., Midwest Steel Employees' Assn., Ducks Unlimited, Mensa, Blue Key, Golden Key, Delta Sigma Pi. Roman Catholic. Avocations: music, chess, coin collecting, sports, travel. Home: 554 Sheffield Dr Valparaiso IN 46383

WAIT, TYNAN ARTHUR, computer systems executive; b. N.Y.C., Feb. 24, 1949; s. Gale Pepper and Louise Arizia (Kriek) W.; m. Jutta Gertrud Lerch, Dec. 27, 1969; children: Christopher Tynan, Tara Adele, Philip Paul. BS in Computer Sci., Ohio State U., 1970; MS in Computer Sci., U. N.C., 1972. Systems programmer Chem. Abstracts Service, Columbus, Ohio, 1972-77; systems software mgr. Compuserve, Inc., Columbus, 1977-82; dir. systems devel. Matryx Corp., Columbus, 1982-83; sr. v.p., cons. PC One Devel., Columbus, 1983-85; dir. systems research and devel. Discovery Systems, Dublin, Ohio, 1985—; cons. in field, Columbus, 1983. Mem. Assn. for Computing Machinery. Avocations: computer programming, bridge, reading, photography. Office: Discovery Systems 7001 Discovery Ctr Dublin OH 43017

WAITE, DARVIN DANNY, accountant; b. Holdenville, Okla.; s. Delmer Charles and Lorraine (Young) W. BSBA, U. Ark., 1954. CPA, Ill. Auditor USDA, N.Y.C., New Orleans, 1963-69; auditor commodity exchange authority USDA, Chgo., 1969-75; auditor U.S. Commodity Futures Trading Commn., Chgo., 1975—. Mem. Am. Inst. CPA's, Assn. Govt. Accts. (Chgo. chpt.), Ill. CPA Soc., Chgo. Met. CPA. Chpt. Republican. Lutheran. Avocations: personal computers, datacommunications, bridge, chess, pinochle. Home: 101 Wallace St Bartlett IL 60103 Office: US Commodity Futures Trading Commn Sears Tower Chicago IL 60606

WAITE, ELLEN JANE, library director; b. Oshkosh, Wis., Feb. 17, 1951; d. Earl Vincent and Margaret (Luft) W.; m. Thomas H. Dollar, Aug. 19, 1977 (div. July 1984). BA, U. Wis., Oshkosh, 1973; MLS, U. Wis., Milw., 1977. Head of cataloging Marquette U., Milw., 1977-82; head catalog librarian U. Ariz., Tucson, 1983-85; assoc. dir. libraries Loyola U., Chgo., 1985-86, acting dir. libraries, 1986-87, dir. libraries, 1987—; cons. Loyola U., Chgo., 1984, Boston Coll., 1986. Contbg. author: Research Libraries and Their Implementation of AACR2, 1985. Mem. ALA. Avocation: photography. Office: Loyola U Cudahy Library 6525 N Sheridan Rd Chicago IL 60626-5385

WAITE, LAWRENCE WESLEY, physician; b. Chgo., June 27, 1951; s. Paul J. and Margaret E. (Cresson) W.; m. Courtnay M. Snyder, Nov. 1, 1974; children: Colleen Alexis, Rebecca Maureen, Alexander Quin. BA, Drake U., 1972; DO, Coll. Osteo. Medicine and Surgery, Des Moines, 1975; MPH, U. Mich., 1981. Diplomate Nat. Bd. Osteo. Examiners. Intern Garden City Osteo. Hosp., Mich., 1975-76; practice gen. osteo. medicine, Garden City, 1979-82, Battle Creek, 1982—; assoc. clin. prof. Mich. State U. Coll. Osteo. Medicine, East Lansing, 1979—; dir. med. edn. Lakeview Gen. Osteo. Hosp., Battle Creek, Mich., 1983—; cons. Nat. Bd. Examiners Osteo. Physicians and Surgeons, 1981—. Writer TV program Cross Currents Ecology, 1971; editor radio series Friendship Hour, 1971-72. Bd. dirs., instr. Hospice Support Services, Inc., Westland, Mich., 1981-86; mem. profl. adv. council Good Samaritan Hosp., Battle Creek, 1982-83; bd. dirs. Neighborhood Planning Council 11, Battle Creek, 1982—; mem. population action council Population Inst., 1984—. Served to lt. comdr. USN, 1976-79. State of Iowa scholar, 1969. Mem. Aerospace Med. Assn., AMA, Am. Osteo. Assn., Am. Pub. Health Assn., Am. Acad. Osteopathy, Bermuda Hist. Soc. (life). Episcopalian. Avocations: geography, medieval history, genealogy. Home: 140 S Lincoln Blvd Battle Creek MI 49015 Office: 3164 Capital Ave SW Battle Creek MI 49015

WAITE, PAUL J., climatologist, educator; b. New Salem, Ill., June 21, 1918; s. Wesley Philip and Edna Viola (Bartlett) W.; m. Margaret Elizabeth Cresson, June 13, 1943; children: Carolyn, Lawrence. BE, Western Ill. State U., 1940; MS, U. Mich., 1966. State climatologist Nat. Weather Service, Des Moines, Madison, 1956-73; meteorologist Nat. Weather Service, 1973-74, 1948-51, 1952-56; dep. project mgr. NOAA, Houston, 1974-76; state climatologist Iowa Dept. Agr., Des Moines, 1976—; adj. prof. geography, geology Drake U., Des Moines, 1970-74, 1976—; asst. dir. Iowa Weather Service, Des Moines, 1959-70, dir. 1970-73; U.S. Dept. Commerce collaborator Iowa State U., Ames, 1959-73. Contbr. articles to profl. jours. and chpts. to bks. Served to 1st lt. USAF, 1942-46, 1951-52, Korea. Recipient NASA Group Achievement Award, 1979. Fellow Iowa Acad. Scis. (Disting. Service award 1983, pres. 1986-87); mem. Am. Assn. State Climatologist (pres. 1977-78), Am. Meteorol. Soc., Nat. Weather Assn. Republican. Club: Toastmasters (Des Moines) (pres. 1980). Lodge: Masons. Avocations: hiking; gardening; photography. Home: 6657 NW Timberline Dr Des Moines IA 50313 Office: IA Dept Agr State Climatologist Internat Airport Room 10 Terminal Bldg Des Moines IA 50321

WAITES, ELIZABETH ANGELINE, psychologist; b. Rockmart, Ga., Oct. 20, 1939; d. Oscar Louis and Willie (Phillips) W.; children: Nicholas Graham, Emily Diane. AB, Ala. Coll., 1961; PhD, U. Mich., 1965. Lic. psychologist, Mich. Lectr. psychology dept. U. Mich., Ann Arbor, 1966; psychology counselor U. Mich., Flint, 1970-73; psychologist Cath. Charities, N.Y.C., 1968-69; pvt. practice psychology Ann Arbor, 1976—; chmn. bd. Octagon House, Ann Arbor, 1975. Contbr. articles to psychol. jours. Research assoc. Mich. House Dem. Research Staff, Lansing, 1975; mem. adv. com. Mich. Women's Commn., Lansing, 1978. Fellow USPHS; mem. Am. Psychol. Assn., Am. Orthopsychiat. Assn., Mich. Soc. Psychoanalytic Psychology. Avocations: piano, needlework. Home: 1069 Barton #109 Ann Arbor MI 48105 Office: 206 S Main Suite 200 Ann Arbor MI 48104

WAITES, WILLIAM ERNEST, advertising executive; b. Detroit, Dec. 14, 1934; s. William Ernest and Jean (Bryant) W.; m. Susanne Pinkett, Jan. 5, 1957; children: Bryant Andrew, Randel Schumann. BA, Mich. State U., 1956. Sr. v.p., creative dir. Young & Rubicam, Detroit, 1973-77; mng. dir. Young & Rubicam, Adelaide, Australia, 1977-79; sr. v.p., dir. creative services Young & Rubicam, Chgo., 1979-81; vice chmn., chief creative officer Stone & Adler, Chgo., 1981-83; sr. v.p., group creative dir. Ogilvy & Mather, Chgo., 1983—. Served to capt. USAF, 1957-60. Mem. Lambda Chi Alpha. Club: East Bank (Chgo.). Office: Ogilvy & Mather 676 St Clair Chicago IL 60611

WAKS, DENNIS STANFORD, lawyer, educator; b. Decatur, Ill., Apr. 2, 1949; s. Paul and Regina (Geisler) W.; m. Jaclyn Hoyle, Nov. 29, 1985; 1 child, Kelly. BA, U. Wis., 1971; JD, U. Miss., 1973; LLM, U. Mo., Kansas City, 1975. Bar: Miss., 1973, Ill. 1975, U.S. Dist. Ct. (no. dist.) Miaa. 1973, U.S. Dist. Ct. (so. dist.) Ill. 1975. Dir. prison legal services project So. Ill. U. Sch. Law, Carbondale, Ill., 1976-77; asst. pub. defender Jackson County Pub. Defenders Office, Murphysboro, Ill., 1977-80, chief pub. defender, 1980-85; spl. prosecutor Perry County States Atty. Office, Pinckneyville, Ill., 1985; prof. dept. law enforcement So. Ill. U., Carbondale, 1978—; sole practice Murphysboro, 1985—; faculty Ill. Defender Program, Chgo., 1982—, bd. dirs.; faculty masters thesis and doctoral com. So. Ill. U., Carbondale, 1985—. Editor Miss. Law Rev., 1973. Organizer Paul Simon for Senator, Carbondale, 1984; bd. dirs. Hill Ho. Resdl. Ctr. for Substance Abuse, Carbondale, 1981—, v.p. 1984—. Named Outstanding Young Man of Am., 1985. Mem. Nat. Assn. Criminal Def. Attys., Ill. Pub. Defender Project, Ill. Pub. Defenders Assn. Democrat. Jewish. Avocations: reading, weight-lifting, politics. Home: 2041 Edith St Murphysboro IL 62966 Office: So Ill U STC Bldg Carbondale IL 62901

WALCHER, DWAIN NEWTON, pediatrician; b. Ill., Apr. 7, 1915; s. Jesse Leroy and Lucile Agnes (Newton) W.; m. Emily Jane Jones, Dec. 31, 1939; children—Susan Dair Walcher Reed, David Newton. Student Blackburn Coll., 1933-35; B.S., U. Chgo., 1938, M.D., 1940. Diplomate Am. Bd. Pediatrics. Intern, Ind. U. Med. Ctr., Indpls., 1940-41; intern, asst. resident, then resident in pediatrics Yale U. Sch. Medicine, New Haven Hosp., 1941-44; instr. pediatrics Yale U. Sch. Medicine, 1943-46; asst. prof. pediatrics Ind. U., 1946-52, assoc. prof., 1952-62, prof., 1962-63, clin. prof. health adminstrn. and pediatrics, 1980-82, clin. prof. pediatrics, 1982-85, clin. prof. emeritus, 1985—; dir. growth and devel. program Nat. Inst. Child Health and Human Devel., NIH, Bethesda, Md., 1963-66, assoc. dir. program planning and evaluation, 1966-69, dir. Inst. Study Human Devel., 1969-78; spl. asst. to provost Pa. State U., 1971-74, sr. adv. for coll. devel. and relations, 1978-80, prof. human devel. emeritus, 1969-80; spl. asst. for med. ops. Ind. State Bd. Health, Indpls., 1980-85 ; mem. program com. Nat. Easter Seal Soc., 1969-71; cons. Nat. Inst. Child Health and Human Devel., 1969-74; trustee Nat. Easter Seal Research Found., 1968-76, chmn. bd. trustees, 1971-75. Recipient Disting. Service medal Université Rene Descartes, Academie de Paris, 1977; Disting. Alumnus award Blackburn Coll., 1982. Emeritus mem. numerous profl. assns., including Internat. Orgn. for Study Human Devel. (exec. sec.-treas. 1969-82). Presbyterian. Contbr. articles to profl. jours.; co-editor books, including: Mutations: Biology and Society, 1978; Food, Nutrition and Evolution, 1981.

WALD, MARKUS STANLEY, utility company executive; b. Bismarck, N.D., Jan. 2, 1950; s. Stanley Markus and Helen Elizabeth (Bosch) W.; m. Rebecca Ann Boehm, Oct. 14, 1977; children: Stanley Markus, Theodore James. AS, Nat. Coll. Bus., Rapid City, S.D., 1969; AS in Bus. Adminstrn., Bismarck Jr. Coll., 1976; BS in Mgmt., N.D. State U., 1978. Dataprocessing mgr. Lystad's Inc., Grand Forks, N.D., 1972-74; asst. v.p. Patterson Land Co., Bismarck, N.D., 1974-75; coordinator data processing State N.D., Bismarck, 1975-80; coordinator bus. system Basin Electric Power Cooperative, Bismarck, 1980—. Served with U.S. Army, 1970-72. Mem. N.D. Auctioneer Assn. Republican. Roman Catholic. Club: Toastmasters (pres. 1985-86). Lodge: Elks. Avocations: auctioneering, hunting, fishing. Office: Basin Electric Power Coop 1717 East Interstate Ave Bismarck ND 58501

WALDECK, JOHN WALTER, JR., lawyer; b. Cleve., May 3, 1949; s. John Walter Sr. and Marjorie Ruth (Palenschat) W.; m. Cheryl Gene Cutter, Sept. 10, 1977; children: John III, Matthew. BS, John Carroll U., 1973; JD, Cleve. State U., 1977. Product applications chemist Synthetic Products Co., Cleve., 1969-76; assoc. Arter & Hadden, Cleve., 1977-85, ptnr., 1986—. Chmn. Bainbridge Twp. Bd. Zoning Appeals, Chagrin Falls, Ohio, 1983—; sec., trustee. Greater Cleve. chpt. Lupus Found. Am., Cleve., 1978—. Mem. ABA (real property sect.), Ohio State Bar Assn. (real property sect.), Greater Cleve. Bar Assn. (real property sect.). Democrat. Roman Catholic. Club: 13th St. Racquet. Avocations: beekeeping, gardening, jogging. Home: 18814 Rivers Edge Dr W Chagrin Falls OH 44022 Office: Arter & Hadden 1100 Huntington Bldg Cleveland OH 44115

WALDECKER, THOMAS RAYMOND, social worker; b. Monroe, Mich., Sept. 4, 1950; s. Henry Stephen and Martha Louise (Skinner) W.; m. Lilian Marlene Ames, Nov. 19, 1983; 1 child, Sean. AA, Monroe County Community Coll., 1970; BS, Eastern Mich. U., 1973; MSW, U. Mich., 1977. Cert. social worker. Tng. and vol. coordinator Monroe County (Mich.) Helpline, 1970-74; substance abuse and employee assistance services coordinator Monroe County, Monroe, 1978-81; employee counselor Kelsey Hayes Co., Romulus, Mich., 1981-82; outreach counselor Flower Meml. Hosp., Sylvania, Ohio, 1983-86; health counselor Brownlee, Dolan, Stein & Assocs., Inc., Dearborn, Mich., 1986—; mem. adv. bd. Southeastern Mich. Substance Abuse, 1981—; mktg. cons. Counseling Assocs., Southfield, 1985—. Trustee Monroe County Community Coll.; bd. dirs. Monroe County Bd. Health, 1981—. Mem. Nat. Assn. Social Workers, Employee Assistance Soc. Toledo (pres. 1985-86), Assn. Labor and Mgmt. Adminstrs. and Cons. on Alcoholism, Employee Assistance Soc. N.Am., Nat. Council on Alcoholism, Comprehensive Health Planning Council of Southeastern Mich., Southfield C. of C. Democrat. Avocations: volleyball, tennis, gardening, record collecting. Home: 634 W 9th St Monroe MI 48161 Office: Brownlee Dolan Stein Assocs Inc 23400 Michigan Ave Dearborn MI 48124

WALDEN, JAMES WILLIAM, accountant, educator; b. Jellico, Tenn., Mar. 5, 1936; s. William Evert and Bertha L. (Faulkner) W.; B.S., Miami U., Oxford, Ohio, 1963; M.B.A., Xavier U., Cin., 1966; m. Eva June Selvia, Jan. 16, 1957; 1 son, James William. Tchr. math. Middletown (Ohio) City Sch. Dist., 1963-67, Fairfield (Ohio) High Sch., 1967-69; instr. accounting Sinclair Community Coll., Dayton, Ohio, 1969-72, asst. prof., 1972-75, asso. prof., 1975-78, prof., 1978—; cons., public acct. Active CAP. Served with USAF, 1954-59. Mem. Butler County Torch Club, Pub. Accountants Soc. Ohio (pres. S.W. chpt. 1985-86), Nat. Assn. Accts., Nat. Soc. Pub. Accountants, Greater Hamilton Estate Planning Council, Beta Alpha Psi. Home: 187 Westbrook Dr Hamilton OH 45013 Office: Sinclair Community Coll 444 W 3d St Dayton OH 45402

WALDEN, MARILYN HARLENE, mental health administrator; b. Winfield, Kans., June 18, 1939; d. Harley Goff and Callie Libera (Henderson) Parsons; m. J.B. Walden, June 15, 1957 (div. June 1977); children: Kristopher Kirk, Troy Todd. BA, Ft. Hays State U., 1965; MS, Mont. State U., 1971; postgrad., Colo. State U., 1966-67, Mich. State U., 1975. Mental health specialist Mich. Dept. Mental Health, Lansing, 1972-81, dept. mgr., 1981-85, dir. fed. entitlements, 1985—; instr. Mont. State U., Bozeman, 1971; mem. Mich. Devel. Disabilities Council, Lansing, 1982—; chmn. Mich. Interagy. Task Force on Disability, Lansing, 1985—. Mem. Ingham County Dems., East Lansing, Mich., 1984—, ACLU, East Lansing, 1984—. Named Mich. Vol. of Yr., Nat. Assn. Devel. Disability Coucils, 1986. Mem. LWV. Avocations: golf, skiing, piano. Home: 6141 Coach House Dr East Lansing MI 48823

WALDEN, MICKEY JOE, information system auditor, consultant; b. Wichita, Kans., June 18, 1953; s. Leonard Lerone and Blanche Virginia (White) W.; m. Debra Ann Burton, Mar. 25, 1973; 1 child, Jeremy Todd. BBA, Wichita State U., 1978. CPA, Kans., Ind.; cert. info. systems auditor, Kans., Ind. Audit sr. Regier, Carr et al, Wichita, 1979-82; audit mgr. G. Wiley & Co. CPAs, Bloomington, Ind., 1982-83; info. system auditor First Ind. Fed. Savs. Bank, Indpls., 1983-86, dir. internal auditing, 1986—; cons. R. Hawkins & Assocs., Monterey, Calif., 1985-86. Served to sgt. USAF, 1971-76. Mem. Am. Inst. CPA's, Ind. CPA's Soc., EDP Auditors Assn., Cen. Ind. EDP Auditors Assn. (bd. dirs. 1984-86), Non-Commd. Officers Assn. Avocations: automobile restoration, cart racing, racquetball, softball. Office: Walden Cons Services PO Box 441097 Indianapolis IN 46204-1097

WALDERA, GERALD JOSEPH, political science educator; b. Britton, S.D., June 18, 1931; s. Roman Lawrence and Rosalie Virginia (Jagodzinski) W.; m. Jean Anne Bigelow, Jan. 17, 1959; children—Mark, Michael, Gerald II. B.S., N.D. State U., 1958, M.S., 1960; postgrad. U. Denver, 1960-62. Grad. asst. N.D. State U., 1959-60; teaching fellow U. Denver, 1961-62; asst. prof. social sci. Millikin U., Decatur, Ill., 1962-67; assoc. prof. polit. sci. Dickinson State Coll. (N.D.), 1967—, chmn. social-behavioral sci. div., 1969—. Mem. N.D. Senate, 1982—. Served to 1st lt. USMC, 1952-58; Korea. Mem. Orgn. Am. Historians, Am. Acad. Polit. Sci., N.D. Council Social Sci., VFW, Am. Legion. Democrat. Lodges: Rotary, Century, Elks, Masons, Shriners, German-Hungarian, Eagles (Dickinson). Home: 942 9th Ave W Dickinson ND 58601 Office: Dickinson State Coll Dickinson ND 58601

WALDINGER, VIRGINIA KATHLEEN, office automation consulting company executive; b. Newark, Ohio, June 5, 1931; d. Harold and Lucille Kathleen (Gilmore) Boase; 1 son, Scott J. student U. Mich., 1975-78; grad. in engring. Wayne State U., 1980. Sec., Ford Motor Co., Dearborn, Mich., 1975-81; tchr. Dearborn Pub. Schs., 1969-81; pres. Electronic Info. Systems, Dearborn, 1980—; cons. Hewlett Parkard, Pinewood, Eng., 1983—; EDS/Systems engr., 1985—; tchr. Oakland Community Coll., 1980-83. Mem. Am. Mgmt. Assn., Am. Bus. Women's Assn., Assn. Info. Systems Profls.

WALDMAN, SIDNEY HERMAN, bookstore executive; b. Albany, N.Y., Oct. 23, 1934; s. Philip Samuel and Jennie (Samuelson) W.; m. Audrey Gail Smith, June 6, 1959; children—Karen Lynn, Eric Joseph. B.S., N.Y. U., 1957. Cert. store profl. Clk. to asst. dir. N.Y. U. Bookstore, N.Y.C., 1951-61; asst. dir. Syracuse U. Bookstores, N.Y., 1961-65, dir., 1965-74; mgr. Barnes & Noble at Cleve. State U., 1974-79, pres., chief exec. officer, 1979—. Contbr. articles to profl. jours. Mem. Cleve. Exec. Assn., Nat. Assn. Coll. Stores (past trustee), N.Y. State Assn. Coll. Stores (past pres.), Ohio Assn. Coll. Stores (past pres.). Republican. Unitarian. Office: B & N Inc 2400 Euclid Ave Cleveland OH 44115-2490

WALDON, STANLEY HOWELL, guidance counselor; b. Detroit, Sept. 9, 1943; s. Silas Hercules and Bernice Irene (Cole) W.; m. Gail E. Flood, June 3, 1972 (div. Apr. 1980); 1 child, Alycia Michelle. BS, Wayne State U., 1966, MS, 1970, edn. specialist cert., 1976, postgrad., 1987—. Tchr. vocal music Detroit Pub. Schs., 1966-70, counselor, 1970-77, dept. head counselor, 1977-84, supr. city wide, 1984—; organist Tabernacle Ch., Detroit, 1973—; asst. dir., accompanist Rackham Symphony Choir, Detroit, 1973—; accompanist for various concert artists USA, Europe, Arica. Support group mem. Mus. of Afro-Am. History, Detroit, 1980; mem. Detroit Inst. of Arts, 1982; bd. dirs. Detroit Community Music Sch., 1987; bd. dirs. Art Ctr. Mus. Sch., 1987—. Fulbright-Hayes Teaching fellow, 1982; recipient City-wide Appreciation Service award "Friends of Waldon Com.", 1983, recognition awards Detroit City Council and Mich. Senate, 1983. Mem. Mich. Assn. Multi-Cultural Counseling and Devel. (pres.-elect 1987), Am. Assn. Counseling and Devel., Guidance Assn. Met. Detroit (sec. 1975-78), NAACP, Alpha Phi Alpha (chmn. 1976-78). Democrat. Baptist. Avocation: travel. Home: 2236 Glynn Detroit MI 48206 Office: Detroit Bd Edn 5057 Woodward Ave #644 Detroit MI 48206

WALDRON, CHARLES M., retail company executive; b. 1920. Student, U. Pa., 1942. With Elder-Beerman Stores Corp., Dayton, Ohio, 1963—, v.p., gen. mdse. mgr., 1963-71, exec. v.p., gen. mdse. mgr., 1971-74, pres., chief operating officer, 1974—, also vice chmn. bd. Served to lt. USN, 1942-45. Office: The Elder-Beerman Stores Corp 3155 El-Bee Rd Dayton OH 45401 *

WALDRON, JOSEPH A., psychologist, educator; b. Batavia, N.Y., Oct. 3, 1943; s. Elsworth T. and Dolores A. (Kanaley) W.; m. Irene M.G. Montgomery, Oct. 31, 1966; children—Wendy, Joelle, Elizabeth. B.A. in Psychology, SUNY-Buffalo, 1972; M.A., Ohio State U., 1973, Ph.D., 1975. Lic. psychologist, Ohio. Head dept. psychology Buckeye Youth Ctr., Ohio Youth Commn., Columbus, 1973-76; chief psychologist Mahoning County Diagnostic and Evaluation Clinic, Youngstown, Ohio, 1976-77; owner Towne Square Psychol. Services, Youngstown, 1976—; assoc. prof. and dir. forensic research lab. Youngstown State U., 1977—; founder Integrated Profl. Systems Inc., Youngstown, 1981, Polymetrics Lab., Youngstown, 1982—. Served with USMC, 1961-65. Recipient numerous research grants. Mem. AAAS, Acad. Criminal Justice Sci., Mahoning Valley Acad. of

Psychologists (pres. 1981-82), Sigma Xi, Kappa Delta Pi. Contbr. numerous articles to profl. jours; developer computer programs in field. Home: 266 Bradford Dr Canfield OH 44406 Office: Polymetrics Lab PO Box 367 Canfield OH 44406

WALDROP, HOWARD LEON, dentist; b. Pampa, Tex., June 10, 1948; s. J. B. and Wanda Virginia (Carr) W.; m. Shelley Kay Sydnor, Dec. 29, 1973; 1 child, Robert Leon. BS, West Tex. State U., 1970; DDS, Baylor U., 1974. Instr. West Tex. State U., Canyon, 1970; gen. practice dentistry Peoria, 1974-78, 78—; advisor Meth. Hosp. Bd. Wholistic Health, Peoria, 1974-78; prof. Ill. Cen. Coll., Peoria, 1976; lectr. Ill. U. Coll. Medicine, Peoria, 1978; dir. dental services Brimfield (Ill.) Area Health Services, 1982-83; cons. Sumerford Assocs., Peoria, 1985-86. Editor: dental newsletter informer, 1985—; author ednl./dentistry software, dental info. radio show, 1986. Leadership Young Life Cen. Ill., Peoria, 1976-81; adv. bd. Ill. Cen. Coll., Peoria, 1983-84; coach Peoria Soccer League, 1986. Mem. ADA, ADA Journalists, Ill. State Dental Assn., Tex. State Dental Assn., Chgo. Dental Soc., Peoria Dist. Dental Soc. (officer 1985—; Editorial award 1986), Beta Beta Beta, Xi Psi Phi. Lodges: Order of Eastern Star, Masons, Shriners. Avocations: music, art, jewelry, hunting, fishing. Home: 600 Knollcrest Dr Peoria IL 61614 Office: 6500 N University Suite 1B Peoria IL 61614

WALEGA, DOUGLAS RAYMOND, architect; b. Chgo., Aug. 25, 1955; s. Raymond Henry and Dorothy Anne (Lorenz) W.; m. Carolyn Sue Peterson, May 4, 1980, Julie Corin, Kevin Scott. BArch, Ill. Inst. Tech., 1978. Registered architect, Ill. Draftsman Anderzhon/Diehl & Assoc., Schaumberg, Ill., 1978-80; archtl. designer Tilton & Lewis Assoc., Chgo., 1980-83; project mgr. Powell/Kleiwschmidt, Chgo., 1983-84; job capt. Mekus-Johnson, Inc., Chgo., 1984-86; project supt. CSE Constrn., Chgo., 1986-87; estimator Interior Alterations, Inc., Chgo., 1987—. Bd. dirs., sec. Berwyn (Ill.) Hist. Soc. 1980—. Mem AIA. Roman Catholic. Home: 2532 Wesley Ave Berwyn IL 60402 Office: Interior Alterations Inc 550 W Jackson Chicago IL 60606

WALENTIK, CORINNE ANNE, pediatrician; b. Rockville Centre, N.Y., Nov. 24, 1949; d. Edward Robert and Evelyn Mary (Brinskele) Finno; m. David Stephen Walentik, June 24, 1972; children: Anne, Stephen, Kristine. AB with honors, St. Louis U., 1970, MD, 1974. Diplomate Am. Bd. Pediatrics, Am. Bd. Neonatal and Perinatal Medicine. Resident in pediatrics St. Louis U. Group Hosps., 1974-76, fellow in neonatalogy, 1976-78; neonatalogist St. Mary's Health Ctr., St. Louis, 1978-79; co-dir. neonatal unit St. Louis City Hosps., 1979-84, dir. neonatal unit, 1984-86; dir. neonatalogy St. Louis Regional Med. Ctr., 1986—; asst. prof. pediatrics St. Louis U., 1980—; supr. nursery follow up program Cardinal Glennon Children's Hosp., 1979—. Contbr. articles to profl. jours. Mem. adv. com. Mo. Perinatal Program., 1983-86. Fellow Am. Acad. Pediatrics; mem. Mo. Perinatal Assn. (pres. 1983), Nat. Perinatal Assn. (council 1984—), Mo. State Med. Assn., St. Louis Met. Med. Soc. Roman Catholic. Avocations: bridge, baseball, sports. Home: 7234 Princeton Ave University City MO 63130 Office: St Louis Regional Med Ctr 5535 Delmar Blvd Saint Louis MO 63112

WALES, STEPHEN HENRY, SR., accounting educator; b. Northampton, Mass., Aug. 12, 1932; s. Earl Edward and Doris Rita (Jay) W.; m. Charlotte Beatrice Orner, 1955 (div. 1959); children—Donna Lee, Jay Stephen; m. 2d Patsy Lou Blackwell, Oct. 17, 1960; children—Cynthia Marie, Stephen H., II. Student, U. Conn., 1951-52; B.B.A., U. Mass., 1959; M.B.A., Ind. U., 1960; postgrad. Purdue U., 1963-68, Earlham Coll., 1963-68, Ferris State Coll., 1968-83. C.P.A., Ind., Mich. Faculty, Ind. U., Bloomington, 1960-68; faculty Ferris State U., Big Rapids, Mich., 1968—, prof. accountancy, 1984—; pvt. practice acctg., Big Rapids, 1965—. Author: Embezzlement and Its Control, 1965. Served with USAF, 1951-55. Mem. Am. Inst. C.P.A.s, Nat-Assn. Accts., Am. Acctg. Assn., Mich. Assn. C.P.A.s. Republican. Congregationalist. Avocations: fishing, traveling. Home: Box 313-21061-19 Mile Rd Rural Rt 1 Big Rapids MI 49307 Office: B338 Ferris State Coll Big Rapids MI 49307

WALGREEN, CHARLES RUDOLPH, III, retail store executive; b. Chgo., Nov. 11, 1935; s. Charles Rudolph and Mary Ann (Leslie) W.; m. Kathleen Bonsignore Allen, Jan. 23, 1977; children: Charles Richard, Tad Alexander, Kevin Patrick, Leslie Ray, Chris Patrick; stepchildren—Carleton A. Allen Jr., Jorie L. Allen. B.S. in Pharmacy, U. Mich., 1958. With Walgreen Co., Chgo., 1952—; adminstrv. asst. to v.p. store ops. Walgreen Co., 1965-66, dist. mgr., 1967-68, regional dir., 1968-69, v.p., 1969, pres., 1969-75, chmn., 1976—, also dir. Mem. bus. adv. council Chgo. Urban League.; bd. dirs. Jr. Achievement Chgo. Mem. Am. Found. Pharm. Edn. (bd. dirs.), Nat. Assn. Chain Drug Stores (bd. dirs.), Ill. Retail Mchts. Assn. (bd. dirs. 1966—), Am. Pharm. Assn., Ill. Pharm. Assn., Delta Sigma Phi. Clubs: Economic, Commercial (Chgo.); Great Lakes Cruising; Yacht and Country (Stuart, Fla.); Exmoor Country (Highland Park, Ill.); Key Largo Anglers (Fla.). Office: Walgreen Co 200 Wilmot Rd Deerfield IL 60015

WALINSKI, NICHOLAS JOSEPH, federal judge; b. Toledo, Nov. 29, 1920; s. Nicholas Joseph and Helen Barbara (Morkowski) W.; m. Vivian Melotti, June 26, 1954; children: Marcianne, Barbara, Deanna and Donna (twins), Nicholas Joseph III (dec.). B.S. in Engring, U. Toledo, 1949, LL.B., 1951. Bar: Ohio 1951. Law dir. Toledo, 1953; police prosecutor 1953-58, mcpl. ct. judge, 1958-64, common pleas ct. judge, 1964-70; judge No. dist. Ohio Western div. U.S. Dist. Ct., Toledo, 1970—. Served to capt. USNR, 1942-48. Mem. Am., Toledo, Lucas County bar assns., Am. Legion, VFW, Cath. War Vets, Toledo Jr. Bar Assn. (Order of Heel 1970). Office: 1716 Speilbusch St 203 US Courthouse Toledo OH 43624

WALKENSHAW, DONNADENE WOODFORD, school psychologist; b. Caldwell, Ohio, Sept. 24, 1922; d. Walter and Hazel (McKee) Woodford; m. George Walkenshaw, Jan. 15, 1944 (dec. Apr. 1984); children: Barry, Philip. BS in Edn., Ind. U., 1973; MA in Edn., Ohio State U., 1976. Lic. sch. psychologist, Ohio. Intern sch. psychologist Franklin County Schs., Columbus, Ohio, 1976-77; sch. psychologist Marion (Ohio) County Schs., 1977-84, Ohio State U., Columbus, 1985—. Mem. Nat. Assn. Sch. Pyschologists, Ohio Sch. Psychologists Assn., Assn. of Handicapped Student Services Programs in Post Secondary Edn. Club: Ohio State U. Faculty Women's. Avocation: raising Arabian horses. Office: Ohio State U Office Disability Services 1960 Neil Ave Columbus OH 43210

WALKER, CARRIE RAMSEY, special educaiton educator; b. Kingman, Ariz., Sept. 2, 1948; d. Jay O'Dell and Evelyn Rose (Elicker) Ramsey; m. Charles Thomas Walker, Sept. 14, 1973. BA in Elem Edn., Ariz. State U., 1973, MA in Early Childhood Edn., 1978. Cert. tchr. Ariz., Wis., Minn. Spl. edn. aide Tempe (Ariz.) Pub. Schs., 1974-79; substitute tchr. Dept. Def. Schs., Stuttgart, Fed. Republic Germany, 1978-79; cross-categorical tchr. Sacaton (Ariz.) Pub. Schs, 1979-81; Laveen (Ariz.) Pub. Schs., 1981-85; tchr. for emotionally disturbed New Richmond (Wis.) Dist., 1985—; cons. Sci. Research Assn., Phoenix, 1984, Laveen Sch. Dist., 1984-85. Author: (curriculum) Sci. Curriculum, 1984. Mem. Pi Lambda Theta. Avocations: amateur athletics, gourmet cooking, traveling, observing ednl. insts. Home: Rt 2 Box 124A Hudson WI 54016 Office: New Richmond Pub Schs 152 E 4th St New Richmond WI 54017

WALKER, CLIFFORD MILTON, JR., pharmacist, student; b. Poterdale, Ga., June 14, 1944; s. Clifford M. and Letitia (Hollingsworth) W.; m. Jill Gray, Aug. 8, 1965; children—E. Wade, John S., James M. B.S. in Pharmacy, U. Ga., 1966; postgrad. U. N.C., 1986—. Registered pharmacist, Va., N.Y., Ga. Pharmacist Patterson Drug Co., Lynchburg, Va., 1966-68; pharmacist U.S. Air Force, Niagara Falls, N.Y., 1969-70, Ramstein, Fed. Republic Germany, 1970-71; chief pharmacy services U.S. Air Force, Upper Heyford, Eng., 1971-74, Moody AFB, Ga., 1974-80, Wurtsmith AFB, Mich., 1981-86. Mem. Am. Soc. Hosp. Pharmacy, Am. Pharm. Assn., Assn. Mil. Surgeons, Air Force Assn. Republican. Baptist. Avocations: reading, agriculture.

WALKER, DANIEL EUGENE, health care industry executive; b. San Diego, Nov. 24, 1952; s. Russell Eugene and Jerry Mae (Hamilton) W.; m. Jennifer Anne Walker, Aug. 2, 1975 (div. 1982); 1 child, Paul Daniel; m. Sharon Elaine Jackson, July 23, 1983 (div. 1987). AB cum laude, Humboldt State U., 1974; postgrad., U. S.C., 1975; Ind. Cen. U., 1979; PhD, Purdue U., 1978. Sr. quality control chemist Dow Chem. Co., Indpls., 1979-81; mgr. quality control Dow Instruments and Reagents, Indpls., 1981-82; dir. quality assurance Seragen Diagnostics, Indpls., 1983-84, mgr. internat. sales amd mktg., 1984-85; mktg. mgr. Tech Am., Inc., 1985-86; mgr. Telemarketing Ops. Synbiotics Corp., 1986-87; mgr. sales and mktg. Neogen Corp., Lansing, Mich., 1987—. Author: Proc. Health Industry Mfrs. Assn. Meeting, 1980; contbr. articles to profl. jours. Mem. Am. Assn. Clin. Chemists, Am. Chem. Soc. Republican. Avocations: water skiing, sports. Office: Neogen Corp 620 Lesher Pl Lansing MI 48912

WALKER, DAVID NEIL, psychologist, human services administrator; b. Flint, Mich., Feb. 16, 1944; s. Charles Scott and Jean Calvert (Pierson) W.; m. Anne Mathews Bridgman, June 11, 1966; children: Christine, Mark, Matthew. BA, Albion Coll., 1966; PhD in Clin. Psychology, U. Conn., 1970. Lic. psychologist, Mich. Asst. prof. psychology Moravian Coll., Bethlehem, Pa., 1970-72, chmn. dept. psychology, 1973-75; asst. dir. Bay Area (Mich.) Guidance Ctr., 1975-79, Northwestern Guidance Ctr., Garden City, Mich., 1979-82; clin. psychologist Davis Counseling Ctr., Farmington Hills, Mich., 1981—; dep. dir. Children's Ctr., Detroit, 1982—; psychologist Northampton (Pa.) County Prison, 1972-75. Contbr. articles to profl. jours. Moderator Ch. of Good Shepard, Ann Arbor, Mich., 1985-86. Lehigh Valley Exchange Scholar, 1975. Mem. Am. Psychol. Assn., Phi Beta Kappa. Democrat. Avocations: water sports, reading, remodeling older homes. Home: 3244 Bluett Ann Arbor MI 48105 Office: Childrens Ctr 101 Alexandrine Detroit MI 48201

WALKER, DAVID WILLIAM, trade association administrator; b. Libertyville, Ill., Feb. 16, 1959; s. Edward Allen and Beverly Jean (Nehmer) W.; m. Catherine Marie Thys, Oct. 15, 1983; 1 child, Amy Lauren. BA in Govt., Notre Dame U., 1981; postgrad. in bus. adminstrn., Lake Forest Grad. Sch. Mgmt. Asst. mng. ptnr. Eagle Constrn., Ingleside, Ill., 1973-80; maj. house whip Congressman John Brademas, South Bend, Ind., 1980; asst. rep. govt. affairs Amoco Corp., Chgo., 1981-84; rep. pub. affairs Nat. Assn. Mfrs., Park Ridge, Ill., 1984-87, sr. dist. mgr., 1987—; lectr. Coll. Lake County, Grayslake, Ill., 1982; bd. dirs. Chgo. Cheesecake Co., Palatine, Ill. Editor, programmer election coverage, 1982. Coordinator youth Betty Lou Reed for state rep., Deerfield, Ill., 1976-80; social caseworker South Bend Juvenile Diagnostic Facility, 1979-80; vice chmn. Notre Dame Coll. Rep. Party, South Bend, 1979-80; bd. dirs. Project LEAP, Chgo., 1982-84, treas., 1983; group leader United-Way Crusade of Mercy, Chgo., 1983; lay minister youth Edison Park Luth. Ch., Chgo., 1984-85, pres. parish bd. edn., 1986—. Named one of Outstanding Young Men in Am., Jaycees, 1983. Mem. Phi Theta Kappa. Avocations: tennis, golf, volunteer services, reading, travel. Home: 2711 W Oakton Park Ridge IL 60068 Office: Nat Assn Mfrs 315 S NW Hwy Park Ridge IL 60068

WALKER, DUARD LEE, medical educator; b. Bishop, Calif., June 2, 1921; s. Fred H. and Anna Lee (Shumate) W.; m. Dorothea Virginia McHenry, Aug. 11, 1945; children: Douglas Keith, Donna Judith, David Cameron, Diane Susan. A.B., U. Calif. - Berkeley, 1943, M.A., 1947; M.D., U. Calif. - San Francisco, 1945. Diplomate Am. Bd. Microbiology. Intern, U.S. Naval Hosp., Shoemaker, Cal., 1945-46; asst. resident Stanford U. Service San Francisco Hosp., 1950-52; asso. prof. med. microbiology and preventive medicine U. Wis., Madison, 1952-59; prof. med. microbiology U. Wis., 1959—, prof., chmn. med. microbiology, 1970-76, 81—, Paul F. Clark prof. med. microbiology, 1977—; cons. Naval Med. Research Unit, Gt. Lakes, Ill., 1958-74; mem. microbiology tng. com. Nat. Inst. Gen. Med. Scis., 1966-70; mem. nat. adv. Allergy and Infectious Diseases Council, 1970-74; mem. adv. com. on blood program research ARC, 1978-79; mem. study group on papovaviridae Internat. Com. on Taxonomy of Viruses, 1976—; mem. vaccines and related biol. products adv. com. FDA, 1985—. Mem. editorial bd.: Infection and Immunity, 1975-83, Archives of Virology, 1981-83, Microbial Pathogenesis, 1985-88. Served to lt. comdr. USNR, 1943-46, 53-55. NRC postdoctoral fellow virology Rockefeller Inst. Med. Research, N.Y.C., 1947-49; USPHS fellow immunology George Williams Hooper Found., U. Calif. - San Francisco, 1949-50. Fellow Am. Pub. Health Assn., Am. Acad. Microbiology, Infectious Diseases Soc. Am.; mem. Am. Assn. Immunologists, Am. Soc. Microbiology, AAAS, Soc. Exptl. Biology and Medicine (editorial bd. Procs.), Reticulendothelial Soc. AAUP, Am. Soc. Virology, Wis. Acad. Scis., Arts and Letters. Home: 618 Odell St Madison WI 53711 Office: U Wis Med Sch 1300 University Ave Madison WI 53706

WALKER, EARL VICTOR, special education educator; b. Ventura, Calif., Feb. 17, 1935; s. John Victor and Ruby Lee (Mack) W.; m. Carol JoAnne Earle, May 2, 1959; children: Scott L., Eric C., John H., Joel V. BA in History, Calif. State U., Northridge, 1964; MS in Edn., Ind. U., 1980. Pvt. investigator Retail Credit Co., Torrance, Calif., 1962-65; prodn. control analyst J.I. Case, Rock Island, Ill., 1966-67; tchr. Rock Island (Ill.) Sch. Dist. 41, 1967—; counselor monitor JTPA, Rock Island, 1986. Cons. Venice (Calif.) Teen Post, 1964, Ice Skating rink Com., Rock Island, 1984;mem. Old Rock Island Devel. Corp., 1987; bd. dirs. Iowa-Ill Boy Scouts, 1975-76. Served to sgt. USMC, 1952-55. Named Master Tchr. State of Ill., 1984. Mem. NEA, Ill. Edn. Assn., Ill. Alt. Edn. Assn. (pres. 1986), Assn. Supervision and Curriculum Devel., Rock Island Edn. Assn. (rep., negotiation bd.. exec. bd.), Phi Delta Kappa, Gamma Alpha Beta, Am. Legion. Club: Toastmasters. Avocations: water sports, coin collecting, woodwork, gardening. Home: 2812 35th St Rock Island IL 61201 Office: Rock Island High Sch Spl Edn Dept Room 34 Rock Island IL 61201

WALKER, ELVA MAE DAWSON, cons. health, hosps., aging; b. Everett, Mass., June 29, 1914; d. Charles Edward and Mary Elizabeth (Livingston) Dawson; R.N., Peter Bent Brigham Hosp., Boston, 1937; student Simmons Coll., 1935, U. Minn., 1945-48; m. Walter Willard Walker, Dec. 16, 1939 (div. 1969). Supr. nursery Wesson Maternity Hosp., Springfield, Mass., 1937-38; asst. supr. out-patient dept. Peter Bent Brigham Hosp., Boston, 1938-40, supr. surgery and out-patient dept. Univ. Hosps., Mpls., 1945. Chmn. Gov.'s Citizens Council on Aging, Minn., 1960-68, acting dir., 1962-66, Econ. Opportunity Com. Hennepin County, 1964-69; v.p., treas. Nat. Purity Soap & Chem. Co., 1968-69, pres., 1969-76, chmn. bd., 1976—; cons. on aging to Minn. Dept. Pub. Welfare, 1962-67; mem. nat. adv. Council for Nurse Tng. Act, 1965-69, Com. Status on Women in Armed Services, 1967-70; dir. Nat. Council on the Aging, 1963-67, sec., 1965-67, 1986—; dir. Planning Agy. for Hosps. of Met. Mpls., 1963—, United Hosp. Fund of Hennepin County, 1955—, Nat. Council Social Work Edn., 1966-68; vice chmn. Henr pin County Gen. Hosp. Adv. Bd., 1965-68; sec. Hennepin County Health C ·li- tion, 1973; chmn. bd. dirs. Am. Rehab. Found, 1962-68, vice chmn., 1968-70, Minn. Bd. On Aging, 1986—, Sr. Resources, 1985-87, Nat. Retiree Vol. Council, 1986—; pres. bd. trustees Northwestern Hosp., 1956-59, Children's Hosp. Mpls., 1961-65; dir. Twin Cities Internat. Program for Youth Leaders and Social Workers, Inc., 1965-67; mem. community adv. council United Community Funds and Council Am., Inc., 1968, Nat. Assembly Social Policy and Devel., Inc., 1968—; mem. priorities determination com. United Fund Mpls., 1971; vice chmn. govt. specifications com. Soap and Detergent Assn., 1972-76, vice-chmn. indsl. and instn. com., 1974-76, chmn., 1976-78, bd. dirs., 1974—; candidate for Congress, 3d Minn. Dist., 1966; trustee Macalester Coll., Archie D. and Bertha H. Walker Found.; chmn. St. Mary's Jr. Coll. Bd., 1970-74, 78-80; pres. U. Minn. Sch. Nursing Found., 1958-70. Mem. Am. Pub. Welfare Assn., Mpls. Med. Research Found., Minn. League Nursing (pres. 1971-73), Jr. League Mpls. Democrat. Presbyterian. Home: 3655 Northome Rd Wayzata MN 55391 Office: Nat Purity Soap & Chem Co 110 SE 5th Ave Minneapolis MN 55414

WALKER, FRANK BANGHART, pathologist; b. Detroit, June 14, 1931; s. Roger Venning and Helen Frances (Reade) W.; m. Virginia Elinor Granse, June 18, 1955; children—Nancy Anne, David Carl, Roger Osborne, Mark Andrew. B.S., Union Coll., N.Y., 1951; M.D., Wayne State U., 1955, M.S., 1962. Diplomate Am. Bd. Pathology (trustee bd. 1982—, treas. 1984—). Intern Detroit Meml. Hosp., 1955-56; resident Wayne State U. and affiliated hosps., Detroit, 1958-62; pathologist 1962—; dir. labs. Detroit Meml. Hosp., Grosse Pointe, Mich., 1984-87, Cottage Hosp., Grosse Pointe, Mich., 1984—; pathologist, dir. labs. Macomb Hosp Ctr. (formerly South Macomb Hosp.), Warren, Mich., 1966—, Jennings Meml. Hosp., Detroit, 1971-79, Alexander Blain Hosp., Detroit, 1971-85; ptnr. Langston, Walker & Assocs., profl. corp., Grosse Pointe, 1968—; instr. pathology Wayne State U. Med. Sch., Detroit, 1962-72, asst. clin. prof., 1972—. Pres. Mich. Assn. Blood Banks, 1969-70; mem. med. adv. com. ARC, 1972-83; mem. Mich. Higher Edn. Assistance Authority, 1975-77; trustee Alexander Blain Meml. Hosp., Detroit, 1974-83, Detroit-Macomb Hosp. Assn., 1975—; bd. dirs. Wayne State Fund, 1971-83. Served to capt. M.C., AUS, 1956-58. Fellow Detroit Acad. Medicine; mem. Wayne State U. Alumni Assn. (bd. govs. 1968-71), Wayne State U. Med. Alumni Assn. (pres. 1969, trustee 1970-85, disting. alumni award 1974) Coll. Am. Pathologists, Am. Soc. Clin. Pathologists (sec. 1971-77, pres. 1979-80), Mich. Soc. Pathologists (pres. 1980-81), Econ. Club Detroit, AMA (council on long range planning and devel. 1982—, vice chmn. 1985-87, chmn. 1987—), Wayne County Med. Soc. (pres. 1984-85), Mich. Med. Soc. (bd. dirs. 1981—, vice chmn. 1986—), Am. Assn. Blood Banks, Mich. Assn. Blood Banks, Phi Gamma Delta, Nu Sigma Nu, Alpha Omega Alpha. Republican. Episcopalian. Clubs: Detroit Athletic, Lochmoor; Mid-America (Chgo.). Home and Office: 47 DePetris Way Grosse Pointe Farms MI 48236

WALKER, GORDON DELBERT, manufacturing executive; b. Eureka, S.D., Apr. 30, 1933; s. Samuel and Ida (Brandner) W.; m. Adeline Jane Volness, Nov. 6, 1954; children: Stanley, Patricia Walker Bacon, Dale. Grad. pub. sch., Ashley, N.D. Equipment operator City of Moorhead, Minn., 1960-66; heavy equipment op. FM Asphalt, Inc., Moorhead, 1966-73; foreman Ehrichs Mfg., Fargo, N.D., 1973-78; plant supr. PK Mfg., Fargo, 1978-83; corp. pres. Curbwalker, Inc., Fargo, 1983—. Democrat. Lutheran. Avocations: hunting, fishing, golf, travel. Home: Rural Rt 4 Box 107 Moorhead MN 56560 Office: Curbwalker Inc 4301 12th Ave NW Fargo ND 58102

WALKER, IRMA JEAN, educational administrator; b. Fayette, Ala., Jan. 13, 1942; d. Willie Harris and Lucy Mae (Gay) Hudson; m. Charlie Palmer, Oct. 4, 1958 (div. May 1971); children: Lee, Charlie, Constance, Martin, L'Tanya Jemison; m. Aubrey Walker, Jr., July 29, 1972; 1 child, Aubrey Walker III. BS in Community Edn. cum laude, U. Wis., Milwaukee, 1980. Office mgr. Northcott Nbhhd., Milw., 1977-78; program supr. U. Wis.-Extension, Milw., 1978-81, adminstrv. asst., 1981-85, extension assoc., 1985—; adminstrv. sec. Walker's Janitorial, Milw., 1978—. Editor, author: Shoots N Roots Cookbook, 1982. Chmn. Mayor's Beautification Arbor Day Com., Milw., 1984-86; adult Sunday sch. tchr. Recipient Human Relations award Milw. Commn. on Community Relations,1987. Mem. U. Wis.-Extension Community Devel. Assn., Wis. Assn. for Adult and Continuing Edn., Nat. Assn. Housing and Redevel. Ofcls., Urban Family Camping Assn. (founder), Black Women Network, Milw. Council for Adult Learning, Met. Milw. Fair Housing, Wis. Assn. Equal Opportunity, Women of Color Career Action Network. Club: Urban Family Camping (advisor 1985—). Avocations: reading, Bible study, camping. Home: 3726 W Capitol Dr Milwaukee WI 53216 Office: Univ Wis Extension 929 N 6th St Milwaukee WI 53203

WALKER, JACK D., state official. Lt. governor Kansas, Topeka, 1987—. Office: Office of the Lieutenant Governor State Capitol Topeka KS 66620 *

WALKER, JAMES ARTHUR, insurance company executive; b. Marshalltown, Iowa, Apr. 16, 1948; s. Arthur Caroll and Helen L. (Severson) W.; m. Sharon Sue Anderson, June 8, 1969. BA, Morningside Coll., 1970. Registered health underwriter, Minn. With admissions dept. Morningside Coll., Sioux City, Iowa, 1969-71, dir. devel., 1970-74; dist. mgr. Old N.W. Co., Mpls., 1974-76, v.p., 1976-85, exec. v.p., 1985—, also bd. dirs., 1986—; bd. dirs. Morningside Coll. Contbr. articles to profl. jours. Served to 1st lt. USNG, 1966-74. Mem. Nat. Assn. Health Underwriters (charter). Republican. Methodist. Avocations: boating, swimming, running, travel. Office: Old NW Co 4901 W 77th St Suite 154 Minneapolis MN 55435

WALKER, JAMES CHARLES, quality assurance executive; b. Kansas City, Mo., Dec. 28, 1949; s. Kenneth Morris and Shirley (Kinzel) W.; m. Karen Sue Coverstone, Oct. 26, 1974; children—Andrea, Melissa, Stephen. B.S. in Indsl. Mgmt., Purdue U., 1972; postgrad. U. Tenn., 1983. Quality control supr. Copeland Corp., Sidney, Ohio, 1972-73, quality engr., 1973-76, sr. quality engr., 1976-77, quality control mgr., West Union, Ohio, 1977-78; quality assurance mgr. Oster div. Sunbeam Corp., Milw., 1978-79; mgr. quality control Fram div. Allied-Signal Corp., Greenville, Ohio, 1979-85, dir. quality assurance Prestolite Motor and Ignition div., Toledo, 1985-86, dir. quality assurance Prestolite Electric Inc., Toledo, 1986—. Mem. Am. Soc. Quality Control (sr., cert. quality engr.), Am. Statis. Assn., Soc. Mfg. Engrs., Soc. Automotive Engrs. (assoc.), U. Tenn. Inst. for Productivity Through Quality Alumni Assn. Republican. Roman Catholic. Home: 935 Bexley Dr Perrysburg OH 43551 Office: Prestolite Electric Inc Four Seagate Toledo OH 43691

WALKER, JESSIE, writer, photographer; b. Milw.; d. Stuart Richard and Loraine (Freuler) Walker; m. Arthur W. Griggs, Feb. 5, 1984; B.S., Medill Sch. Journalism, Northwestern U., also M.S. First major feature article appeared in The Am. Home mag.; contbr. numerous articles to nat. mags. including Am. Heritage's Americana, Better Homes and Gardens, McCall's, House and Garden, Good Housekeeping, others; midwest editor Am. Home mag.; contbg. editor Better Homes & Gardens; cover photographer Country Living, 1984, 85. Recipient Dorothy Dawes award for distinguished journalistic coverage in home furnishing, 1976, 77. Mem. Am. Soc. Interior Designers (press mem.), Women in Communications. Author: How to Plan a Trend Setting Kitchen, 1962; How to Make Window Decorating Easy, 1969; Shaker Design-150-year-old Modern, 1972; Good Design—What Makes It Last?, 1973; Junking Made Easy, 1974; Poster Power, 1976; For Collectors Only, 1977; Bishop Hill-Utopian Community 1978; also articles. Photographer cover photo Better Homes & Gardens, Sept. 1982, Oct. 1980, House Beautiful, Dec. 1981, Country Living, Jan., Feb., Sept., Nov., 1983, Jan., 1984, Dec., 1985, May, 1986, Jan., Feb., May, 1987. Address: 241 Fairview Rd Glencoe IL 60022

WALKER, JONATHAN LEE, lawyer; b. Kalamazoo, Mar. 8, 1948; s. Harvey E. and Olivia M. (Estrada) W. B.A., U. Mich., 1969; J.D., Wayne State U., 1977. Bar: Mich. 1977, U.S. Dist. Ct. (ea. dist.) Mich. 1982. Assoc. firm Moore, Barr & Kerwin, Detroit, 1977-79; ptnr. firm Barr & Walker, Detroit, 1979-82; assoc. firm Richard M. Goodman, P.C., Detroit, 1983—; hearing officer Mich. Civil Rights Commn., Detroit, 1983—; participant Detroit Bar Assn. Vol. Lawyer Program. Bd. dirs. Community Treatment Ctr.-Project Rehab., Detroit, 1983—; mem. scholarship com. Latino en Marcha Scholarship Fund, Detroit, 1984. Mem. State Bar Mich. Found., Wayne County Mediation Tribunal, Inc. (mediator), Am. Arbitration Assn. (arbitrator), Nat. Lawyers Guild, Mich. Trial Lawyers Assn., Assn. Trial Lawyers Am., State Bar Mich. (chmn. com. on underrepresented groups in law 1983-85, com. judicial qualifications 1985-86 , council mem. Latin-Am. sect. 1978—), Trial Lawyers for Pub. Justice (founder 1981, Amicus com. 1985-86), Ctr. for Auto Safety. Office: Richard M Goodman PC 1394 E Jefferson St Detroit MI 48207

WALKER, JOSEPH PATRICK, dentist; b. Indpls., Nov. 28, 1953; s. Louis Augustus and Sylvia Olene (McGuire) W.; m. Sally Lynn Scott, June 26, 1976; 1 child, Erin Lynn. BS in Chemistry, Tenn. Tech. U., 1976; DDS, U. Tenn., 1979. Gen. practice dentistry Birdseye, Ind., 1980-83, Cannelton, Ind., 1983—. Vice chmn. St. Michael's Ch. Council, Cannelton, 1985—, chmn. bd., 1986—. Served to capt. USAR, 1980—. Mem. Cannelton Jaycees (sec. 1984-85, pres. 1985—). Roman Catholic. Lodge: Kiwanis. Avocations: golf, target shooting, painting, modeling, woodworking. Home: Rt 1 Box 125 Cannelton IN 47520 Office: 607 Washington St Cannelton IN 47520

WALKER, KAY L., insurance agent; b. Rigby, Idaho, Dec. 4, 1942; s. Allen H. and Lora (Taylor) W.; B.S., Brigham Young U., 1967; student So. Ill. U., 1967-68, U. Mo., St. Louis, 1968-69; m. Angela Galloway, Jan. 27, 1966; children—Kara, Kindra, Karsten, Kimber, Kenton, Kayla, Kyle. Agt., N.Y. Life, St. Louis, 1970-77; pres. Walker, Morris & Walker, Inc., St. Louis, 1973—; pres. Nauvoo Devel. Inc., 1977—; pres. Halcyon Travel Ltd., 1980—; mng. ptnr. Walker, McElliott & Wilkinson, 1984—. State coordinator Mo. Citizens Council, 1980—; mem. St. Louis Commn. on Human Relations 1981—. Mem. Life Underwriters Assn., Million Dollar Round Table. Republican. Mormon. Office: PO Box A 7001 Howdershell Rd Hazelwood MO 63042

WALKER, NANCY ANN, women's studies and English educator; b. Shreveport, La., Sept. 5, 1942; d. Kirkby Alexander and Phyllis (Pettegrew) W.; m. John Thomas Hand, Nov. 23, 1965 (div. Aug. 1974); m. Burton Michael Augst, Jan. 24, 1976. BA, La. State U., 1964; MA, Tulane U., 1966; PhD, Kent State U., 1971. Instr. Kent State U., East Liverpool, Ohio, 1966-68; teaching fellow Kent State U., Kent, 1968-71; faculty mem. Stephens Coll., Columbia, Mo., 1971—, exec. asst. to pres., 1984-85; bd. dirs. James M. Wood Inst. for Study of Women's Edn., Columbia, 1981-87. Author: The Tradition of Women's Humor in America, 1984; editor Humor in America: The View from Open Places, 1985; mem. edit. bd. American Studies, Tulsa Studies in Women's Lit., Feminist Inquiry. Woodrow Wilson fellow, 1964, NEH fellow. Mem. Modern Lang. Assn., Am. Studies Assn., Nat. Women's Studies Assn. Avocations: gardening, cooking, jogging. Home: 807 Maupin Rd Columbia MO 65203 Office: Stephens Coll Columbia MO 65215

WALKER, NEAL FRANCIS, pharmacist, consultant; b. Crosby, Minn., May 12, 1955; s. Neal Edward and Mary Grace (Lee) W.; m. Kim Kathleen Krier, June 19, 1976; children—Christina Ann, Matthew Neal, Eric Robert. B.S. in Pharmacy, N.D. State U., 1978. Registered pharmacist. Pharmacist Prescription Shoppe Co., Detroit Lakes, Minn., 1978-79; sr. pharmacist White Drug Co., East Grand Forks, Minn., 1979; staff pharmacist Central Mesabi Med. Ctr., Hibbing, Minn., 1979—; cons. Adams Clinic, Hibbing, 1983—; instr. Minn. Inst. Health, 1983-85. Contbr. articles to profl. jours. Chmn. Hibbing Commn. on Alcohol and Drug Awareness, 1983—; v.p. Hibbing Mcpl. Band, 1984. Recipient Pvt. Enterprise award Minn. Power, 1984, Disting. Service award 1986, Outstanding Alumnus award Hibbing Community Coll., 1987. Mem. Range Area Pharmacists, Minn. Soc. Hosp. Pharmacists, Am. Fed. Musicians, Jaycees (v.p. Hibbing 1983-85; C. William Brownfield award Detroit Lakes chpt. 1979, Outstanding Community Project award Hibbing chpt. 1984, Statesman award 1986). Roman Catholic. Lodge: K.C. Avocations: basketball; cross country skiing; camping. Home: 4111 4th Avenue E Hibbing MN 55746 Office: Central Mesabi Med Ctr 750 E 34th St Hibbing MN 55746

WALKER, ROBERT COLEMAN, jewelry store executive, watchmaker; b. Hoxie, Ark., Apr. 28, 1925; s. Robert Tony and Ailsie Ann (Coleman) W.; m. Pauline Hudson, Jan. 15, 1944; children—Carrol Jean Walker Fisher, Susan Lee Walker Cox. Student pub. schs. Watchmaker, Gift Chest Jewelers, Poplar Bluff, Mo., 1940-43; watchmaker, mgr. Lane's Jewelry, Malden, Mo., 1945-49; instr. Lane's Sch. Watchmaking, Malden, 1949-51; watchmaker Dale's Jewelry, Carmi, Ill., 1951-53; watchmaker, mgr. Saliba's Jewelry, Charleston, Mo., 1953-80; owner, jeweler Walker's Jewelry, Charleston, 1980—. Served with AUS, 1943-45, ETO. Mem. Am. Watchmaker Inst., Jewelers of Am., Mo. Jewelers and Watchmakers Assn. (bd. dirs., pres. 1973-74), Horological Assn. Mo. (pres. 1961-62). Democrat. Baptist. Avocations: photography; woodworking. Home: 803 S Main St PO Box 253 Charleston MO 63834

WALKER, RONALD F., diversified financial services, telecommunications, and food company executive; b. Cin., Apr. 9, 1938; married. BBA, U. Cin., 1961. Vice pres. Kroger Co., Cin., 1962-72; with Am. Fin. Corp., Cin., 1972—, exec. v.p., 1978-84, pres., chief operating officer, dir., 1984—; exec. v.p. Gt. Am. Ins., Cin., 1972-80, pres., 1980—, vice chmn., 1986—; pres., chief operating officer, dir. United Brands Co., N.Y.C.; pres., chief exec. officer Penn Cen. Corp., 1987—; also bd. dirs.; dir. United Brands, Cin., Fisher Foods, Cleve., Mission Ins. Co., Los Angeles, Am. Fin. Enterprises, Cin. Office: Gt Am Ins Co PO Box 2575 Cincinnati OH 45201 Other Address: American Financial Corp 1 E Fourth St Cincinnati OH 45202 *

WALKER, WALTER WILLARD, real estate and investments executive; b. Mpls., Dec. 4, 1911; s. Archie Dean and Bertha Willard (Hudson) W.; B.A., Princeton U., 1935; M.D., Harvard U., 1940; postgrad. U. Minn., 1942-48; m. Elva Mae Dawson, Dec. 16, 1939 (div. Oct. 1969); m. Elaine Barbatsis, Mar. 17, 1972. Teaching fellow pathology U. Minn., 1942-48; left medicine, went into bus., 1948; dir. Shasta Forest Co., Redding, Calif., 1951-71, treas., 1954-66, v.p., 1966-71; sec., dir. Barlow Realty Co., Mpls., 1954-67, pres., 1967-77, chmn., 1977-80, sec., 1980-83, v.p., 1983—; sec., dir. Walker Pence Co., 1950-72; sec. Penwalk Investment Co., 1958-72, dir., 1943-72; dir. Craig-Hallum Corp., Mpls., 1954—; adv. bd. Lincoln office Northwestern Nat. Bank, Mpls., 1957-74. Bd. dirs. T.B. Walker Found., 1953-76, v.p., 1954-76; bd. dirs. Minn. Opera Co., 1968-73, Archie D. and Bertha H. Walker Found., 1953—, Mpls. Found., 1962-79, Walker Art Center, 1954-76, United Fund, 1966-72; trustee Abbott-Northwestern Hosp., 1969-77; trustee Children's Health Center, Inc., 1968-73, treas., 1969-73; pres. Found. Services, 1967-73; bd. dirs., exec. com. Minn. Charities Review Council, 1965-74; mem. Hennepin County Capital Budgeting Task Force, 1973-74. Mem. Sigma Xi, Nu Sigma Nu. Methodist. Clubs: Minneapolis; Woodhill Country; Princeton (N.Y.C.); U. Minn. Alumni. Home: 1900 Knox Ave S Minneapolis MN 55403 Home: 4143 Gulf Dr Sanibel FL 33957 Office: 1121 Hennepin Ave Minneapolis MN 55403

WALKER, WILLIAM DERRICK, financial consultant; b. Detroit, May 23, 1961; s. Willie Allen and Minnie Lee (Green) W. BS in Computer Sci., Wayne State U., 1982. Supr. data processing Henry Ford Hosp., Detroit, 1982-84; fin. broker Attainment Enterprises, Detroit, 1983-85; pvt. data processing cons. Detroit, 1984—, pvt. fin. cons., 1985—; bd. dirs. Three Dimensional Unity, Inc., Detroit. Pub. relations mgr. William A. Thomas, Rep. for Congress, Detroit, 1982. Lodge: Roscrucians.

WALKER, WILLIE MARK, electronics engineering executive; b. Bessemer, Ala., Aug. 18, 1929; s. Johnnie and Annie Maimie (Thompson) W.; m. Mae Ruth Fulton, Apr. 28, 1952; children—Patricia Ann, Mark William, Karen Marie. B.E.E., Marquette U., 1958; M.S. in Elec. Engring., U. Wis., 1965. Registered profl. engr., Wis. Devel. technician AC Spark Plug, Milw., 1953-56, project engr., 1956-60, engring. supr., 1960-65; sr. devel. engr. AC Electronics, Milw., 1965-71; sr. prodn. engr. Delco Electronics, Oak Creek, Wis., 1971—; mem. occupational adv. bd. on computer sci. Milw. Area Tech. Coll., 1983—. Author various proprietary reports. Pres., Potawatomi Area council Boy Scouts Am., Waukesha, Wis., 1982-84; chief camp inspector area 1, east central region, 1987; loaned exec. United Way of Greater Milw., 1983; usher, minister of communion St. Mary Catholic Ch., Menomonee Falls, Wis., 1967—. Served with USAF, 1949-53. Elected to Black Achievers in Bus. and Industry, Milw. Met. YMCA, 1984; recipient Civic Service award Rotary Club, 1983; Gen. Motors award for Excellence, 1980; St. George award Milw. Archidiocese, 1975; Silver Beaver award Boy Scouts Am., 1973, Silver Antelope award Boy Scouts Am., 1987; Black Achiever in Bus. and Industry award YMCA Greater Milw., 1984. Mem. Wis. Soc. Profl. Engrs., Computer Soc. of IEEE, NAACP. Lodges: Lions (chpt. pres. 1979-80, sec. 1974-75); K.C. (recorder 1966-67, advocate 1975-76). Office: Delco Electronics Div Gen Motors Corp 7929 S Howell Ave Oak Creek WI 53154

WALKUP, THOMAS B., telecommunications company executive. Pres. Gen. Telephone Co. of Ind. Inc., Westfield. Office: Gen Telephone Co of Ill 1312 E Empire Bloomington IL 61701 also: Gen Telephone Co of Indiana 8001 W Jefferson Fort Wayne IN 46801 also: Gen Telephone Co of Michigan 455 E Ellis Rd Muskegon MI 49443 also: Gen Telephone of Ohio 100 Executive Dr Marion OH 43302 also: Gen Telephone Co of Pennsylvania 150 W Tenth St Erie PA 16512 also: Gen Telphone Co of Wisconsin 100 Communications Dr Sun Prairie WI 53590 *

WALL, ARTHUR FREDERIK, building contracting company executive; b. Cedar Rapids, Iowa, July 2, 1927; s. Arthur John and Randi Aletta (Bruas) W.; m. Ulla Viola Simonsen, May 29, 1973. B.A., U. Iowa, 1951. Treas., Wall & Co., Cedar Rapids, 1949-55, v.p., 1955-61, pres., 1961—. Served with USAF, 1945-46. Lutheran. Lodge: Cedar Rapids Danish Brotherhood (pres. 1978-82), Danish Brotherhood (pres. Iowa-Minn. dist. 1984-85). Avocations: fraternal lodges; organizing; building. Home: 362 E Post Rd SE Cedar Rapids IA 52403 Office: Wall & Co 1220 6th St SW Cedar Rapids IA 52404

WALL, CONSTANCE MARY, marketing executive; b. Detroit, May 13, 1945; d. Joseph and Grace (Craig) Mulholland; m. Allen Joseph Wall, Aug. 3, 1968; children: Craig Peter, Robert Patrick. BA, Mich. State U., 1967; MBA, Wayne State U. Cert. bus. communicator. Fin. analyst Mobile Oil Corp., Detroit, 1967-70; mktg. analyst Gen. Motors, Detroit, 1970-72; pub. relations supr. G.E. Craft, Southfield, Mich., 1972-76; gen. mgr. Halbert Co., Birmingham, Mich., 1976-80; pres. Alcon Mktg. Inc., Bloomfields Hills, Mich., 1980—. Editor advt. newsletter, 1983—. Founder Orchards Com. Theatre, Auburn Hills, Mich., 1972; mem. Auburn Hills Arts Council, 1973-76. William F. Uhl scholar Mich. State U., 1965. Mem. Bus. Profl. Advt. Assn., Mich. Advt. Assn. Council, Adcraft Club Detroit. Republican. Roman Catholic. Avocations: music, art, aerobics, yoga. Office: Alcon Mktg Inc 25 W Long Lake Suite 200 Bloomfield Hills MI 48013

WALL, JAMES MCKENDREE, minister, editor; b. Monroe, Ga., Oct. 27, 1928; s. Louie David and Lida (Day) W.; m. Mary Eleanor Kidder, Sept. 11, 1953; children: David McKendree, Robert Kidder, Richard James. Student, Ga. Inst. Tech., 1945-47; BA, Emory U., 1949, BD, 1955, LHD (hon.), 1985; MA, U. Chgo., 1960; LittD (hon.), Ohio No. U., 1969; DHL (hon.), Willamette Coll., 1978; DD (hon.), MacMurray, 1981; DHL (hon.), Coe Coll., 1987. Ordained to ministry United Meth. Ch., 1954. Asst. minister East Lake Meth. Ch., Atlanta, 1953; asst. to dean students Emory U., Atlanta, 1954-55; pastor North Ga. Conf. Moreland, Luthersville Meth. Chs., Ga., 1955-57, Bethel United Meth. Ch., Chgo., 1957-59; mng. editor Christian Adv. mag., Park Ridge, Ill., 1959-63, editor, 1963-72; editor Christian Century mag., Chgo., 1972—. Author: Church and Cinema, 1971, Three Eurpoean Directors, 1973. Del. Dem. Nat. Conv., 1972, 76, 80; mem. Dem. Nat. Com., 1976-80, Dem. State Cen. Com., 1974-86, Pres. Commn. White House Fellowships, 1976-80. Served to 1st lt. USAF, 1950-52. Mem. Alpha Tau Omega, Omicron Delta Chi, Sigma Delta Chi. Home: 451 S Kenilworth Elmhurst IL 60126 Office: Christian Century 407 S Dearborn St Suite 1405 Chicago IL 60605

WALL, NORMAN RAY, plastic surgeon; b. Thayer, Mo., Nov. 25, 1934; s. F. Harry and Helen (Eder) W.; m. Beverly Briggs, Aug. 11, 1957; children: Deborah Ann, John Kevin, Judith Kay. AB, U. Mo., 1956, MD, 1960. Commd. ensign USN, 1956, advanced through grades to capt., 1977; intern gen. rotating Naval Hosp., San Diego, 1960-61; resident in gen. surgery Naval Hosp., Chelsea, Mass., 1964-68; resident in plastic surgery Naval Hosp., Bethesda, Md., 1968-70; staff physician Naval Air Sta., Pensacola, Fla., 1961-63; med. officer USS Francis Marion, 1963-64, Amphibious Squadron 12, 1963-64; chief plastic surgery Naval Hosp., St. Albans, N.Y., 1970-72; head plastic surgery div. dept. surgery Naval Regional Med. Ctr., Portsmouth, Va., 1972-74, chief plastic surgery dept., 1974-79, dir. residency program plastic surgery, 1977-79; cons. to surgeon gen. plastic surgery code 31J USN, Washington, 1977-79; ret. USN, 1979; practice medicine specializing in plastic surgery Springfield, Mo., 1979—; asst. prof. plastic surgery Ea. Va. Med. Sch., Norfolk, 1974-79, assoc. prof. 1979; assoc. prof. plastic surgery U. Mo., Columbia, 1984—. Contbr. articles to profl. jours. Fellow ACS; mem. AMA, Am. Soc. Plastic and Reconstructive Surgeons, Mo. State Med. Assn., Assn. Mil. Surgeons U.S., Am. Cleft Palate Assn., Greene County Med. Soc., Assn. Mil. Plastic Surgeons (ret., exec. com. 1974-75, exec. chmn. 1978-79). Baptist. Office: Plastic Surgery Clinic Springfield 1443 N Robberson Suite 901 Springfield MO 65802

WALL, ROBERT EVANS, dentist; b. Linton, Ind., Feb. 29, 1948; s. George Arthur and Rosalie Elaine (Francis) W.; m. Christine Lois Huber, May 15, 1982; 1 child, Morgan Sage. B.A., DePauw U., 1970; D.D.S., Ind. U., 1974. Resident VA Hosp., Indpls., 1974-75; staff VA Hosp., North Chicago, Ill., 1975-77; gen. practice dentistry, Madison, Ind., 1977—; on staff King's Daughter's Hosp., Madison, 1977—, Madison State Hosp., 1984—. Pres. Jefferson County Labor/Mgmt. Commn., Madison, 1984—; bd. dirs. Lide White Boys Club, Madison, 1978—, Girls Club Jefferson County, Madison, 1977-83; mem. Madison Riverfront Commn. Mem. ADA, Ind. Dental Assn., Southeastern Ind. Dental Soc., Madison C. of C. Republican. Methodist. Club: Madison Country (v.p. 1985, bd. dirs.). Lodge: Elks. Avocations: fishing; golf; travel. Home: 312 Cragmont St Madison IN 47250 Office: 753 W Main St Madison IN 47250

WALL, WILLIAM E., utility executive; b. 1928. BS, U. Wash., 1951, LLB, 1954. Asst. atty. gen. State of Wash., 1956-59; chief examiner Pub. Service Commn., 1959; sec., house counsel Cascade Natural Gas Corp., 1959-64; pres. United Cities Gas Co., 1964-65; exec. v.p. Cascade Natural Gas Corp., 1965-67; spl. asst. to chmn. bd. Consol. Edison Co., N.Y.C., 1967-68, v.p., 1968-70, sr. v.p. gas ops., 1970-71, exec. v.p. div. ops., 1971-73; gen. mgr. pub. affairs Standard Oil Co., 1973-74; exec. v.p. Kans. Power and Light Co., Topeka, 1974-75, pres., 1975-85, chief exec. officer, 1976—, chmn., 1979—. Served with AUS, 1954-56. Office: KPL Gas Service 818 Kansas Ave PO Box 889 Topeka KS 66601 *

WALLACE, CHARLES LESLIE, bank executive; b. Monmouth, Ill., Dec. 26, 1945; s. Leslie and Harriet Elizabeth (Weathers) W.; m. Marie Elizabeth Lancaster, June 24, 1967; children: Allison Marie, Bryan Charles. BS, No. Ill. U., 1967; MBA, U. Chgo., 1973. CPA, Ill. Sr. accountant Arthur Andersen & Co., Chgo., 1967-74; fin. analyst Joseph Schlitz Brewing Co., Milw., 1974-76; corp. treas. Universal Foods Corp., Milw., 1976-80, Pabst Brewing Co., Milw., 1980-85, Norrell Corp., Atlanta, 1985-87; pres., chief exec. officer North Milw. State Bank, 1987—. Mem. adv. com. United Negro Coll. Fund, Univ. Wis. at Milw.; bd. dirs. Milw. Art Mus. Served to 1st lt. USMCR, 1967-72. Arthur J. Mellinger Found. scholar, 1963-67; Chase Manhattan Bank Careers for Blacks in Mgmt. fellow, 1971-73. Mem. Am. Inst. C.P.A.s, Fin. Execs. Inst., Kappa Alpha Psi. Club: Bank Execs. Office: North Milw State Bank 5630 W Fond Du Lac Ave Milwaukee WI 53216

WALLACE, ELAINE MARIA, osteopath; b. Newark, May 15, 1954; d. Clarence Rufus and Camille (Mobilia) W. BS, U. Miss., 1976; DO, U. Health Scis., 1980. Intern Lakeside Hosp., Kansas City, Mo., 1980-81; research asst. sch. pharmacology U. Miss., Oxford, 1979-80; practice medicine specializing in osteopathic medicine Kansas City, Mo., 1980—; physician well baby clinics Kansas City Pub. Health Dept., 1980-83, emergency room Lakeside Hosp., Kansas City, 1980-82; physician, dir. Rape Crisis Ctr. Lakeside Hosp., 1980—; lectr. U. Health Scis., Kansas City, 1982—; chmn. osteopathic medicine dept. U. Health Sci. Med. Sch., 1987—. Recipient Golden Poet award World Poetry Assn., 1987. Mem. AMA, Am. Osteopathic Acad., Am. Osteopathic Assn., Mo. Osteopathic Assn., Am. Womens Assn., Sigma Sigma Phi, Delta Omega. Avocations: pub. speaking, poetry. Office: 6724 Troost #600 Kansas City MO 64131

WALLACE, FRANKLIN SHERWOOD, lawyer; b. Bklyn., Nov. 24, 1927; s. Abraham Charles and Jennie (Etkin) Wolowitz; student U. Wis., 1943-45; B.S. cum laude, U.S. Mcht. Marine Acad., 1950; LL.B., J.D., U. Mich., 1953; m. Eleanor Ruth Pope, Aug. 23, 1953; children—Julia Diane, Charles Andrew. Admitted to Ill. bar, 1954, since practiced in Rock Island; ptnr. firm Winstein, Kavensky, Wallace & Doughty; asst. state's atty. Rock Island County, 1967-68; local counsel UAW at John Deere-Internat. Harvester Plants. Bd. dirs. Tri City Jewish Center; trustee United Jewish Charities of Quad Cities. Mem. ABA Ill. (chmn. jud. adv. polls com. 1979-84), Rock Island County bar assns., Am., Ill. trial lawyers assns., Nat. Assn. Criminal Def. Lawyers, Am. Orthopsychiat. Assn., Am. Judicature Soc., Blackhawk Coll. Found. Democrat. Jewish. Home: 3405 20th St Ct Rock Island IL 61201 Office: Rock Island Bank Bldg Rock Island IL 61201

WALLACE, ISAAC, JR., teacher; b. Delray Beach, Fla., May 16, 1948. BA in History, Barber-Scotia Coll., 1971; postgrad., Hamline U., 1970, Washington U., St. Louis, 1973-80; MBA, Lindenwood Coll., 1985. Tchr. St. Louis Bd. Edn., 1972, 86—; gen. transp. clk. Chgo. and Rock Island Ry., St. Louis, 1972-73; asst. supr. ops., mech. engring. records Union Pacific R.R., St. Louis, 1973-86. Mem. Big Bros. and Big Sisters of Am., 1979; mem. program com. for downtown YMCA, St. Louis, 1986—; vol. Contact St. Louis. Mem. Assn. Records Mgrs. and Adminstrs. (treas. 1979-82, bd. dirs. 1981-82, Chpt. Mem. of Yr. 1982), St. Louis Gateway Alumni Chpt. Barber-Scotia Coll. (pres. 1984—), Alpha Phi Alpha. Avocations: traveling, aerobics, jogging. Home: 4883 Farlin Ave Apt A Saint Louis MO 63115 Office: St Louis Bd Edn 911 Locust St Saint Louis MO 63103

WALLACE, JACK HAROLD, employee development specialist; b. Pleasant Ridge, Mich., Dec. 3, 1950; s. Jack Alfred and Mary Hilda (Hemming) W.; m. Laura Jeannine Placer, May 20, 1978. AA, Oakland Community Coll., 1972; BA, Oakland U., 1974; postgrad., Cen. Mich. U., 1984; MeD, Wayne State U., 1986. Cert. secondary tchr., Mich. Supply systems analyst TACOM, Warren, Mich., 1979-84; employee devel. specialist Army Tank Automobile Command, Tng. and Dev. Div., Warren, 1985—; instr. Ferndale (Mich.) Bd. of Edn., 1976-86; instr., cons. Jordan Coll., Detroit, 1986—, Detroit Coll. Bus., Dearborn, Mich., 1986—; trainer, instr. govt. agys. Coauthor: Balancing the Scales of Justice, 1986. Mem. Am. Soc. for Tng. and Devel., Assn. for Ednl. Communications and Tech., Mich. Soc. Instructional Tech., Phi Delta Kappa. Lutheran. Avocations: reading, camping, fishing, public speaking, travel. Home: 3005 Kenmore Berkley MI 48072 Office: TACOM 11 Mile Rd Warren MI 48397-5000

WALLACE, LAWRENCE REECE, optometrist; b. Stapleton, Nebr., July 25, 1924; s. Charles Wesley and Martha Idoma (Newton) W.; m. Thelma A. Cook, Jan. 14, 1944; children: Lisa Anne, Linda Kay. BS in Occular Sci., O.D., No. Ill. Coll. of Optometry, 1951. Practice medicine specializing in optometry Broken Bow, Nebr., 1951—. Incorporator Broken Bow Community Hosp., 1957. Served with USN, 1943-46. Mem. Nebr. Optometric Assn., Am. Optometric Assn., Am. Optometric Found., Broken Bow C. of C., Jaycees (life), Nebr. Bowling Assn. Republican. Methodist. Lodge: Elks (Exalted Ruler Broken Bow club 1960-61, trustee 1961-66, Elk of Yr. 1964, All State Exalted Ruler 1961). Avocations: golfing, bowling, fishing, waterskiing. Office: 411 S 9th St PO Box 547 Broken Bow NE 68822

WALLACE, MICHAEL ARTHUR, manufacturing executive; b. Wichita, Kans., Nov. 22, 1951; m. Christine Campbell, May 30, 1981; 1 child, Morgan Elizabeth. BS, U. Kans., 1973; MBA, Wichita State U., 1986. Acct. exec. Merrill Lynch, Wichita, Kans., 1976-77; mgr. sci. systems devel. Boeing Mil. Airplane Co., Wichita, 1979—. Competitor World Bobsled Championships, Cervinia, Italy, 1975. Mem. Wichita Area C. of C., Mensa.

WALLACE, THOMAS PATRICK, university administrator; b. Washington, Apr. 11, 1935; 4 children. BS, SUNY, Potsdam, 1958; MS, Syracuse U., 1961, St. Lawrence U., 1964; PhD in Physics and Chemistry, Clarkson Coll. Tech., 1968. Asst. prof. chemistry SUNY, Potsdam, 1961-67; Mellon Inst. fellow Carnegie-Mellon Inst., 1967-68; mem. faculty Rochester (N.Y.) Inst. Tech., 1968-78, assoc. prof., 1970-78, head dept. chemistry, 1970-72, assoc. dean, 1972-73, dean, 1973-78; prof. chem. scis. Old Dominion U., Norfolk, Va., 1978-86, dean sci. and health professions, 1978-83, v.p. acad. affairs, 1983-86; chancellor Ind. U.-Purdue U., Ft. Wayne, 1986—. Contbr. articles to profl. jours. Mem. Am. Chem. Soc. Office: Ind Univ-Purdue Univ 2101 Coliseum Blvd E Fort Wayne IN 46805

WALLACE, VICTOR LEW, computer science educator; b. Bklyn., Mar. 20, 1933; s. Frank Hobart and Victoria (Schwerthoffer) W.; m. Mary E. Jamieson, June 23, 1962; children: Robert Joseph, Andrew Gilbert. BEE, Poly. Inst. N.Y., 1955, MEE, 1957; PhD in Elec. Engring., Computer Sci., U. Mich., 1967. Mem. tech. staff Bell Telephone Labs., N.Y.C., 1954-55; mathematician-programmer IBM Corp., N.Y.C., 1955-57; instr. elec. engring. U. Mich., Ann Arbor, 1957-69, research scientist, 1959-69; assoc. prof. computer sci. U. N.C., Chapel Hill, 1969-76; prof. computer sci. U. Kans., Lawrence, 1976—, chmn. dept. comuter sci, 1976-84; acad. vis. U. London, Eng., 1970; cons. Los Alamos (N.Mex.) Nat. Lab., 1975-78, Honeywell Corp., Phoenix, 1982—; cons. in field., 1962—. Co-author: To Compute Numerically--Concepts and Strategies, 1983; contbr. articles to profl. jours. Mem. IEEE (sr.), AAUP, Assn. Computing Machinery, Inst. Mgmt. Scis., Sigma Xi. Democrat. Congregationalist. Home: 1509 Massachusetts St Lawrence KS 66044 Office: U Kans Dept Computer Sci Lawrence KS 66045-2192

WALLACE, WILLIAM BERT, management consultant, accountant; b. Detroit, Sept. 17, 1944; s. William and Betty Jean (Naylor) W.; m. Sandi Jean DiBasio, July 1, 1977; children: Jennifer, Amy, Daniel, Lindsey. BSBA, Wayne State U., 1967. CPA, Mich. Ptnr. in charge of cons. Ernst & Whinney, Detroit, 1967—. Mem. Am. Inst. CPA's, Mich. Assn. CPA's (chmn. met. Detroit chpt. 1981-82). Presbyterian. Clubs: Detroit Athletic, Econ. of Detroit (membership com.), Forest Lake Country (treas. 1979-80, 83). Avocations: golf, cross-country skiing. Office: Ernst & Whinney 200 Renaissance Ctr Suite 2300 Detroit MI 48243

WALLACH, JOHN S(IDNEY), library administrator; b. Toronto, Ohio, Jan. 6, 1939; s. Arthur M. and Alice I. (Smith) W.; children: John Michael, Wendy Anne, Bethany Lynne, Kristen Michele. B.S. in Edn, Kent State U., 1963; M.L.S., U. R.I., 1968; M.P.A., U. Dayton, 1977. Dir. Mercer County (Ohio) Library, 1968-70, Greene County (Ohio) Library, 1970-77; asso. dir. Dayton and Montgomery County (Ohio) Library, 1978, dir., 1979—. Vice-chmn. Community and Agy. Rev. Com.; bd. dirs. United Way, Dayton, Dayton Mus. Natural History, Family Service Assn., Dayton, Miami Valley Literacy Council. Served with USN, 1963-68, capt. Res. Mem. ALA, Ohio Library Assn. (dir.), Naval Res. Assn. Office: 215 E Third St Dayton OH 45402

WALLE, JAMES PAUL, lawyer; b. Detroit, Sept. 4, 1956; s. Leonard Julius and Mary Frances (Baigent) W.; m. Joanne Marie Albert, Aug. 23, 1986; 1 child, Patrick Joseph. Honors BA summa cum laude, U. Detroit, 1977, JD- MBA cum laude, 1979; LLM, Wayne State U., 1986. Bar: Mich. 1980, U.S. Dist. Ct. (ea. and we. dists.) Mich. 1980, U.S. Ct. Appeals (6th cir.) 1980, U.S. Ct. Appeals (D.C. cir.) 1982, U.S. Supreme Ct. 1983. Law clk. to assoc. justice Mich. Supreme Ct., Detroit, 1980-82; atty. environ. law Gen. Motors Corp., Detroit, 1982—; teaching fellow Detroit Coll. Law, 1980-81; adj. prof. law U. Detroit, 1981-82. Case and comment editor U. Detroit Law Rev., 1979-80; mem. editorial bd. Mich. Corp. Fin. and Bus. Law Jour. Vol. 3. Vol. legal services St. Benedict Cath. Ch., Highland Park, Mich., 1983-85. Mem. ABA, Mich. Bar Assn. (environ. and energy law sect., subcom. 1983-85, speaker young lawyers sect. 1983-86), Detroit Bar Assn. (pro bono atty. 1985—). Avocations: classical music, sci. fiction, sci., travel. Office: Gen Motors Legal Staff 7-101 New Center One Bldg Detroit MI 48232

WALLENBROCK, ANGELA BELL, psychiatrist; b. Oklahoma City, May 16, 1947; d. Richard Wray and Jean Catherine (Graham) Bell; m. Terry David Wallenbrock, Jan. 22, 1969; 1 child, Eric Dale. MD, Med. Coll. S.C., 1973. Cert. psychiatrist, Mich., Ohio. Resident in psychiatry Cen. State Hosp., Norman, Okla., 1973-75; child psychiatry fellow U. Mich., Ann Arbor, 1975-77; attending psychiatrist Mercywood Hosp., Ann Arbor, 1977-85; attending psychiatrist Marion (Ohio) Gen. Hosp., 1985—, co-dir. psychiat. unit, 1986—. Mem. AMA, Am. Psychiat. Assn. Home: 552 Grant Rd Delaware OH 43015 Office: Marion Gen Hosp 1271 Crescent Heights Marion OH 43302

WALLER, JONATHAN MICHAEL, telecommunications company executive; b. Cleve., May 3, 1953; s. John and Phyllis Estelle (Sizemore) W. Student, Control Data Inst., 1971-72, Cuyahoga Community Coll., 1973-74. Systems technician and computer operator Ohio Bell Telephone Co., Cleve., 1971-82; prin. Cleve. Telecommunications Corp., 1983—. Mem. NAACP, Minority Bus. Enterprise, Black Profls. Assn., Minority Contractor's Assn. of Northeast Ohio, Nat. Telecommunication Assn. Club: Toastmasters Lodge: Rosicrucian Order Amorc (Patron award 1985). Avocations: chess, metaphysics, basketball. Office: Cleve Telecommunications Corp 12000 Shaker Blvd #27 & 19 Cleveland OH 44120

WALLER, LARRY JAMES, chamber of commerce executive; b. Mason City, Iowa, Feb. 27, 1940; s. Franklin James and Bernadine Grace (Van Blair) Kaiser W.; m. Kim Davenport, Nov. 20, 1964; children—Jeffrey Waller, Jennifer Waller. B.Acad. of Orgn. Mgmt., U. Notre Dame, 1976; B.S., Nat. Coll., Rapid City, S.D., 1977. Cert. chamber exec. Iowa. Mgr., SM Fin. Co., Jefferson, Iowa, 1965-67; exec. v.p. Marion C. of C., Iowa, 1967-70; gen. mgr. Billings C. of C., Mont., 1970-71; pres. Rapid City C. of C., S.D., 1971-81, Cedar Rapids Area C. of C., Iowa, 1981—; Colo. bd. regents U.S. C. of C., 1977—; bd. dirs., vice chair Am. C. of C. Execs., 1978-83; pres. Mid-Am. Chamber Execs., 1978; pres. bd. dirs. Iowa C. of C., 1982—. Mem. task force Cedar Rapids Pub. Schs.; bd. dirs. All-Iowa Fair Assn., 1981—;

treas. Five Seasons Leadership, Cedar Rapids, 1982—; v.p. Jr. Achievement, Cedar Rapids, 1985. Served with U.S. Army, 1959-62. Recipient numerous speaking awards Toastmasters, Jr. C. of C., Air Force Assn. medal of merit, 1980. Republican. Presbyterian (elder). Club: Rotary (Cedar Rapids). Avocations: golf; reading; youth sports. Home: 3951 Sally Dr NE Cedar Rapids IA 52402 Office: Cedar Rapids Area C of C 424 1st Ave NE Cedar Rapids IA 52401

WALLER, LOU A., advertising executive, creative director; b. Oklahoma City, Nov. 21, 1938; d. Paul Travis and Deborah Frances (Heep) Lower; m. John H. Waller, Mar. 1, 1961; children: Jennifer L., David A. BS, U. Okla., 1960; Assoc. Applied Arts, Ind. Tech. Coll., 1980. Cert. practitioner neuro-linguistic programming; registered nurse. Operating room nurse various hosps., Ind., Ohio, Okla., 1961-78; acct. exec. Ash Advt., Elkhart, Ind., 1980; v.p., creative mgr. NPC Printing Co., Niles, Mich., 1981-84; owner, pres., creative dir. NPC Communications of Ind., Inc., South Bend, 1984—; adj. assoc. prof. advt. art design U. Notre Dame, Ind., 1985-86. Mgr. county fair campaign Gretick for Pros., Bryan, Ohio, 1976. Featured in Success Story ann. report, Ind. Tech. Coll., South Bend, 1986. Mem. Am. Mktg. Assn. (dir. Michiana chpt. 1982-86), Nat. Assn. Neuro-Linguistic Programming, Women Bus. Owners Michiana (steering com. 1986, logo design 1987). Republican. Clubs: Knollwood Country (Granger, Ind.); The Pickwick (Niles, Mich.). Avocations: horseback riding, mountain camping, sailing, snorkeling, dancing. Office: NPC Communications of Ind Inc 300 N Michigan South Bend IN 46601

WALLER, ROBERT MORRIS, health care services company executive, international trade consultant; b. Flint, Mich., Jan. 3, 1944; s. Ashton Carr and Nell Kathryn (Morris) W.; m. Sharon L. Spratt, July 24, 1965; children—Robert M., Jennifer Anne. B.S. in Bus. Adminstrn., Northwestern U., 1966; M.B.A. with high honors, Hotchkiss scholar, Lake Forest Sch. Mgmt., 1984. Area ops. mgr. Am. Hosp. Supply Corp., Evanston, Ill., 1970-72, dir. distbn., 1972-74, v.p. ops., 1974-77, v.p. hosp. services, 1977-82; pres. AH-SECO internat. sub., Am. Hosp. Supply Corp., Evanston, 1982-85, Baxter-Travenol Labs., Inc., 1985—. Contbr. articles to profl. jours. Mem. Internat. Mgmt. and Devel. Inst., Washington, 1984—; apptd. by Sec. Commerce to Ill. Dist. Export Council, 1985, exec. commn. India, U. S. Bus. Council, 1985—; deacon Presbyn. Ch., Deerfield, Ill., 1974; guest lectr. Northwestern U., 1980-82. Home: 1365 Elm Tree Rd Lake Forest IL 60045 Office: Baxter Inc One Baxter Pkwy Deerfield IL 60015

WALLESTAD, PHILIP WESTON, physician; b. Madison, Wis., May 14, 1922; s. John Oscar and Dorothy Francis (White) W.; B.A., U. Wis., 1947, M.D., 1954; m. Edith Stolle, Jan. 15, 1949 (div. Mar. 1967); children—Kristin Eve, Ingrid Birgitta, Erika Ann; m. 2d, Muriel Annette Moen, June 22, 1968; children—Thomas John, Scott Philip. Intern, Calif. Lutheran Hosp., Los Angeles, 1954, resident in surgery, 1955-56; gen. practice medicine, Fredonia and Port Washington Wis., 1957-72, Libby, Mont., 1972-74; staff physician VA Hosp., Fort Harrison, Mont., 1974-77, Tomah, Wis., 1977-78, VA Hosp., Iron Mountain, Mich., 1978-87. Served with AUS, 1943-46; ETO; lt. col. USAF Res., 1979-82. Mem. Exptl. Aviation Assn., Am. Legion, DAV, Assn. Mil. Surgeons U.S., Air Force Assn., Am. Security Council, Conservative Caucus, Am. Def. Preparedness Assn., U. Wis. Alumni Assn., Nat. W Club, NRA. Republican. Presbyterian Ch. (elder). Club: Rotary. Home: 1005 Bluff St Kingsford MI 49801 Office: VA Hosp Center H Iron Mountain MI 49801

WALLGREN, RAYMOND ERIC, steel toy manufacturing company executive; b. Chgo., June 14, 1927; s. Eric Matthew and Elvira Martha (Johnson) W.; m. Frances Sere Nelson; children: Scott, John, Julie. BS in Mktg., Northwestern U., 1950. Sales mgr. Radio Steel and Mfg. Co., Chgo., 1950-71, exec. v.p., 1971—; bd. dirs. Hardware Mktg. Council. Served with USN, 1945-46. Republican. Office: Radio Steel and Mfg Co 6515 W Grand Ave Chicago IL 60635

WALLICK, JACK L., real estate developer; b. New Orleans, July 18, 1928; s. Harry and Fannie (Pailet) W.; m. Muriel Norman, Mar. 27, 1955 (dec. 1979); children: Howard Neal, Julie Wallick Rubin; m. Joan Plaine, Sept. 22, 1980. B in Engring., Tulane U., 1948. Cert. property mgr.; lic. gen. contractor, Fla. Cementer Haliburton Oil Co., Houma, La., 1948-49; from superintendent to v.p. Chipley Realty & Devel. Co., Columbus, Ohio, 1956-59; pres. Hali Constrn. Co., Columbus, 1959-66; chmn. bd. The Wallick Cos., Columbus, 1966—, The Bradley Cos., Clearwater, Fla., 1974—. Bd. dirs. Ctr. Sci. and Industry, Columbus, 1981—; bd. dirs. Columbus Jewish Fedn., 1976—, pres., 1984-85. Served to lt. U.S. Army, 1950-53. Recipient Builder of Yr. award Builders Exchange Cen. Ohio, 1987, Community Achievement award Orgn. Rehab. and Tng., 1987. Mem. Nat. Assn. Home Builders, Columbus Apt. Assn., Nat. Assn. Sr. Living Industries, Columbus Bd. Realtors, Inst. Real Estate Mgmt., Urban Land Inst., Ohio Oil and Gas Assn, Associated Builders and Contractors. Home: 2532 Fair Ave Columbus OH 43209 Office: The Wallick Cos 6880 Tussing Rd PO Box 1023 Columbus OH 43216

WALLIN, WINSTON ROGER, manufacturing company executive; b. Mpls., Mar. 6, 1926; s. Carl A. and Theresa (Hegge) W.; m. Maxine Houghton, Sept. 10, 1949; children: Rebecca, Brooks, Lance, Bradford. BBA, U. Minn., 1948. With Pillsbury Co., Mpls., 1948-85, v.p. commodity ops., 1971-76, exec. v.p., 1976, pres., chief operating officer, 1977-84, vice chmn. bd., 1984-85; chmn. bd., pres., chief exec. officer Medtronic, Inc., Mpls., 1985—, also bd. dirs.; bd. dirs. Soo Line Corp., Bemis Co. Bd. dirs. Sci. Mus., Abbot Northwestern Hosp.; trustee Carleton Coll. Served with USN, 1944-46. Mem. Mpls. Grain Exchange (bd. dirs. 1977—). Clubs: Minneapolis, Minikahda, Interlachen. Home: 7022 Tupa Circle Edina MN 55435 Office: Medtronic Inc 7000 Central Ave NE Minneapolis MN 55432

WALLING, MYRON BLISS, JR., real estate appraiser, consultant; b. Chgo., Dec. 10, 1928; s. Myron B. Sr. and Marie (Hedrick) W.; m. R. Audrey Baker, June 9, 1954; 1 child, Alison A. BS in Edn., No. Ill. State Tchrs. Coll., 1953. V.p. Mid Am. Fed. Savs. and Loan, Cicero, Ill., 1962-74; owner Walling & Assocs., Elmhurst, Ill., 1974—. Served with USN, 1946-48. Mem. Am. Inst. Real Estate Appraisers, Soc. Real Estate Appraisers. Lodge: Masons. Avocation: piloting airplanes. Home: 735 Killarney Ct Elmhurst IL 60126 Office: Walling & Assocs 110 Schiller St Elmhurst IL 60126

WALLMAN, CHARLES JAMES, former money handling products exec., author; b. Kiel, Wis., Feb. 19, 1924; s. Charles A. and Mary Ann (Loftus) W.; student Marquette U., 1942-43, Tex. Coll. Mines, 1943-44; B.B.A., U. Wis., 1949; m. Charline Marie Moore, June 14, 1952; children—Stephen, Jeffrey, Susan, Patricia, Andrew. Sales promotion mgr. Brandt, Inc., Watertown, Wis., 1949-65, v.p., 1960-70, exec. v.p., 1970-80, v.p. corp. devel., 1980-83, past dir.; written formal paper to the inst. "The 48ers of Watertown", presented orally at Symposium U. Wis.-Madison (Inst. for German-Am. Studies), 1986; guest speaker dept. German, U. Wis.-Madison, 1987. Mem. exec. bd. Potawatomi council Boy Scouts Am., also former v.p. council; former bd. dirs., pres. Earl and Eugenia Quirk Found., Inc. Trustee, Joe Davies Scholarship Found.; bd. dirs. Watertown Meml. Hosp. Served with armored inf. AUS, 1943-45; ETO. Decorated Bronze Star. Mem. Am. Legion, E. Central Golf Assn. (past pres.), Wis. Alumni Assn. (local past pres.), 12th Armored Div. Assn., Watertown Hist. Soc. (bd. dirs.), Am. Ex-Prisoners of War, Inc., Phi Delta Theta. Republican. Roman Catholic. Clubs: Rotary (bd. dirs.), Elk (past officer), Watertown Country (past dir.). Author: Edward J. Brandt, Inventor, 1984. Home: 700 Clyman St Watertown WI 53094

WALLNER, ADRIEN DIANE, public relations executive; b. Lakewood, Ohio, June 17, 1959; s. Lewis Ellis and Jean Emy (Berger) W. BS, U. Cin., 1983; post grad. in bus. adminstrn., Baldwin Wallace Coll., 1986—. Prodn. mgr. Tony Chase Ltd, N.Y.C, 1983; prin. Markadrien, N.Y.C., 1983-85; pub. relations exec. King James Group, Westlake, Ohio, 1985—. Mem. Nat. Assn. Indsl. and Office Parks. Republican. Roman Catholic. Avocations: horseback riding, the arts, various sports. Home: 700 Brick Mill Run #102 Westlake OH 44145 Office: King James Group 24650 Center Ridge #165 Westlake OH 44145

WALLWORK, W. W., JR., auto retail executive. Pres. W.W. Wallwork Inc., Fargo, N.D. Office: W W Wallwork Inc 4001 W Main Fargo ND 58103 *

WALNER, ROBERT JOEL, lawyer; b. Chgo., Dec. 22, 1946; s. Wallace and Elsie W.; m. Charlene Walner; children: Marci, Lisa. BA, U. Ill., 1968; JD, DePaul U., 1972. Bar: Ill. 1972, U.S. Dist. Ct. (no. dist.) Ill. 1972, U.S. Ct. Appeals (7th cir.) 1972, Fla. 1973. Atty. SEC, Chgo., 1972-73; sole practice Chgo., 1973—; adminstrv. law judge Ill. Commerce Commn., Chgo., 1973-76; atty. Allied Van Lines, Inc., Broadview, Ill., 1976-79; sr. v.p., gen. counsel, sec. The Balcor Co., Skokie, Ill., 1979—; prin. fin. ops. Balcor Securities div. The Balcor Co., Skokie, 1984—; mem. securities adv. com. to Ill. Sec. of State. Mem. editorial bd. Real Estate Securities Jour. and Real Estate Syndicator; program chmn. Regulators and You seminar, Washington, 1983—; contbr. chpts. to books, articles on real estate and securities law to profl. jours. Served with USAR, 1968-73. Mem. ABA, Ill. Bar Assn., Chgo. Bar Assn., Am. Real Estate Com. (pres. com. 1985—), Real Estate Syndication (chmn. Ill. com.), Ill. Inst. Continuing Legal Edn., N.Am. Securities Adminstrs. Assn. Inc. (industry adv. com. to real estate com.), Real Estate Securities and Syndication Inst. of Nat. Assn. Realtors (chmn. regulatory and legis. com., specialist real estate securities, group v.p. exec. com.), Nat. Real Estate Investment Forum (chmn.). Office: The Balcor Co 4849 Golf Rd Skokie IL 60077

WALSH, EDWARD FRANCIS, business consultant, accountant; b. Chgo., July 11, 1944; s. Patrick J. and Mary J. Walsh; B.B.A., Loyola U., 1967; M.B.A., No. Ill. U., 1969; M.A. in Bus. Adminstrn., Govs. State U., 1976; m. Joan Elizabeth Ambrose, June 26, 1971; children—Erin Ann, Daniel Edward. Teaching asst. No. Ill. U., DeKalb, Ill., 1967-69; mem. faculty dept. bus. Prairie State Coll., Chicago Heights, Ill., 1969-80, prof., 1972-80; owner Walsh Bus. Ops. Cons., Homewood, Ill., 1981—; gen. mgr. Assn. for Health Care, Ltd., Chgo., 1980-82; cons. Allied Tube and Conduit Corp., Harvey, Ill., 1973; acct. Wilkes Besterfield, C.P.A.'s, Olympia Fields, Ill., 1979-80; vis. prof. Govs. State U.; prof. Keller Grad. Sch. Mgmt. Vice chmn. sch. bd. Infant Jesus of Prague Sch., 1985—. C.P.A., Ill. Mem. Ill. C.P.A. Soc., Illiana C.P.A. Soc., Midwest Bus. Adminstrn. Assn., Blue Key, Sigma Iota Epsilon (pres.), Alpha Beta Gamma (nat. pres. 1979-80), Delta Sigma Pi (life, Man of Yr.). Office: 18161 Morris Homewood IL 60430

WALSH, JAMES AARON, mortician; b. Columbus, Ohio, Aug. 13, 1943; s. Lloyd W. Walsh and Betsy Fae (Hard) W.; m. Bette J. (Sherman) W., Aug. 29, 1964; children: H. Reneé, Joshua Aaron, Sara F. AA, Lansing Community Coll., 1963; profl. degree, Wayne State U., 1965. Cert. State Bd., Mortuary Sci., Nat. Bd. Examiners. Mgr. Santeiu Funeral Home, Inkster, Mich., 1971-74; gen. mgr. Voran Funeral Homes, Allen Park, Mich., 1974-77; mgr. Temrowski Funeral Home, Warren, Mich., 1977; sales, pub. relations Am. Vault & Concrete, Detroit, 1977-79; owner, dir. Faulmann & Walsh Funeral Home, Fraser, Mich., 1979—. Bd. dirs. Downtown Devel. Authority, Fraser, 1985; bd. dirs. St. John Luth. Ch., Fraser, edn. elders, pub. relations, fellowship; bd. edn. St. John Luth. Sch. Named Kiwanian of Yr. Dearborn Heights Kiwanis Club, 1974. Fellow Order of Golden Rule, Nat. Funeral Dirs. Assn., Mich. Funeral Dirs., Classic Car Club Am., Auburn, Cord, Deusenburg Club. Republican. Lodge: Rotary (pres. 1986-87), Lions. Avocations: antique autos, antique furniture, hunting, fishing. Office: Faulmann & Walsh Golden Rule Funeral Home 32814 Utica Fraser MI 48026

WALSH, JAMES PATRICK, JR., insurance consultant, enrolled actuary; b. Ft. Thomas, Ky., Mar. 7, 1910; s. James Patrick and Minnie Louise (Cooper) W.; m. Evelyn Mary Sullivan, May 20, 1939. Comml. engr. degree, U. Cin., 1933. Acct. Firestone Tire & Rubber Co., also Gen. Motors Corp., 1933-36; rep. ARC, 1937, A.F.L., 1938-39; dir. Ohio Div. Minimum Wages, Columbus, 1939-42; asst. sec.-treas. union label trades dept. A.F.L., Washington, 1946-53; v.p. Pension and Group Cons., Inc., Cin., 1953—; Mem. Pres.'s Commn. Jud. and Congl. Salaries, 1953, Ohio Gov.'s Commn. Employment of Negro, 1940, Hamilton (O.) County Welfare Bd., 1955—, council long term illness and rehab. Cin. Pub. Health Fedn., 1957-68. Bd. dirs. U. Cin., 1959-67; bd. govs. St. Xavier High Sch., Cin.; trustee Brown Found., Newman Cath. Center, Cin. Served to lt. col. AUS, 1942-46; col. Res. ret. Decorated Legion of Merit, Commendation ribbon with two oak leaf clusters; named Ky. col., 1958, Ky. adm., 1968, Ohio commodore, 1985; recipient Disting. Alumni award U. Cin., 1969, Disting. Alumni award Covington Latin Sch., 1983, Insignis award St. Xavier High Sch., 1973, Americanism award Am. Legion, Kevin Barry award Ancient Order of Hiberians. Fellow Am. Soc. Pension Actuaries; mem. Am. Arbitration Assn. (nat. community disputes panel, employee benefit claims panel), Marine Corps Res. Officers Assn., Naval Res. Assn., Res. Officers Assn., Am. Legion, Q.M. Assn., VFW, Am. Mil. Retiree Assn., Nat. Assn. Uniform Services, English Speaking Union, Ohio Ret. Officers Assn. (past pres. council), Ret. Officers Assn. (past pres. Cin. chpt. 1973-74), Amvets, Air Force Assn., Ret. Officers Assn. (nat. bd. dirs. 1983—), Marine Corps League, Nat. Football Found. and Hall of Fame, Am. Fedn. State, County and Employees Union, Internat. Alliance Theatrical Stage Employees (past sgt. at arms), Internat. Hodcarriers, Bldg. and Common Laborers Union, Ins. Workers Internat. Union, Office Employees Internat. Union, Cooks and Pastry Cooks Local, Friendly Sons St. Patrick (past pres.), Covington Latin Sch. Alumni Assn. (past pres.), Soc. for Advancement Mgmt., Defense Supply Assn., Ancient Order Hibernians (past pres.), Assn. U.S. Army (trustee), Am. Ordnance Assn., Soc. Am. Mil. Engrs., Order of Alhambra, Internat. Assn. Health Underwriters, Allied Constrn. Industries, Navy League, Scabbard and Blade, Nat. Council of Cath. Men, Indsl. Relations Research Assn., Zoo Soc. of Cin., Millcreek Valley Assn., Alpha Kappa Psi. Republican. Roman Catholic. Clubs: C. Cin. (past pres.), Queen City, American Irish, Insiders, Touchdown, Blue Liners, Roundtable, Scuttlebuts, Newman, Bankers, Mil. (Cin.). Lodges: K.C. (4 deg.), Elks. Home: 5563 Julmar Dr Cincinnati OH 45238 Office: 309 Vine St Room 200 Cincinnati OH 45202

WALSH, JOHN JOSEPH, advertising company executive; b. Chgo., Apr. 16, 1943; s. Patrick Joseph and Mary Jane (Duigan) W.; m. Mary Beth Sexton, July 6, 1968; children: Elizabeth Anne, Patrick Michael, Margaret Mary. BA, Mich. State U., 1965; MBA, No. Ill. U., 1968; grad., AT&T Advanced Mgmt. Sch., Cooperstown, N.Y., 1970. Data systems mgr. AT&T, Chgo., 1968-71, ops. mgr., 1971-73, mktg. mgr., 1973-76, industry mgr., 1976-78, mktg. cons., 1978-79; nat. sales mgr. Fed. Sign Co., Burr Ridge, Ill., 1979-83, gen. mgr., 1983-85, v.p., gen. mgr., 1985—; bd. dirs., asst. treas., chmn. supervisory com. Chgo. Comml. Credit Union, 1973-79; mem. faculty mid. mgmt. program Aurora (Ill.) Coll., 1973-76; vis. prof. Keller Grad. Sch. Mgmt., Chgo., 1979—; mgmt. advisor Jr. Achievement, Chgo., 1969-71. Mem. parish council, exec. com., vice chmn., youth minister dir. St. John of the Cross Ch., Western Springs, Ill., 1982—. Served with USMC, 1965-71. Mem. Sign Industry Employers Assn. (treas. 1983-86, bd. dirs.), Alpha Beta Gamma, Sigma Iota Epsilon. Roman Catholic. Club: Executive (Chgo.). Home: 4369 Woodland Western Springs IL 60558 Office: Fed Signal Corp Fed Sign Div 140 E Tower Dr Burr Ridge IL 60521

WALSH, JOHN PATRICK, accounting company executive; b. Evergreen Park, Ill., July 27, 1947; s. James Francis and Nora Marie (Stanton) W.; m. Joyce Lorraine Ernd, Jan. 24, 1981; children: Dawn Marie, Cheryl Lynn, John Patrick Jr., Joseph James, Bridget Ann. BS of Acctg., Walton Sch. Commerce, 1976; BA, De Paul U., 1979. CPA, Ill. Acct. Walsh & Assocs., Chgo., 1976-79; ptnr. Fischer, Walsh & Co., CPA's, Oak Brook, Ill., 1979—; Treas., bd. dirs. Doyle, O'Brien and Fahey, Meml., Inc., Chgo., 1982—. Mem. Am. Inst. CPA's, Ill. CPA Soc. Roman Catholic. Avocations: hunting, racquetball, trap shooting, exercise. Office: Fischer Walsh & Co 600 Enterprise Dr Suite 120 Oak Brook IL 60521

WALSH, JOSEPH PATRICK, JR., investment advisor, small business owner; b. Lawrence, Mass., May 8, 1952; s. Joseph Patrick and Eileen Catherine (Hannagan) W.; m. Michele La Roche, Dec. 18, 1976; children: Joseph Patrick III, Katherine, Michael. BS in Mgmt., No. Ill. U., 1974, MBA in Fin., 1986. Registered real estate broker, investment advisor, ins. agt.; cert. fin. planner. Owner J.P. Hannagan's Restaurant, DeKalb, Ill., 1975—, Midwest Bus. Assocs., DeKalb, 1984-85; pres. J.P. Walsh & Assocs., DeKalb, 1985—; mem. adj. faculty Coll. Fin. Planning, 1986. Mem. Inst. Cert. Fin. Planners, Internat. Assn. Cert. Fin. Planners, Nat. Assn. Securities Dealers, Mutual Service Corp., Inst. Chartered Fin. Analysts, Am. Bus. Clubs, Sycamore (Ill.) Jaycees. Office: JP Walsh & Assocs 1215 Blackhawk DeKalb IL 60115

WALSH, KENNETH ALBERT, chemist; b. Yankton, S.D., May 23, 1922; s. Albert Lawrence and Edna (Slear) W.; B.A., Yankton Coll., 1942; Ph.D., Iowa State U., 1950; m. Dorothy Jeanne Thompson, Dec. 22, 1944; children—Jeanne K., Kenneth Albert, David Bruce, Rhonda Jean, Leslie Gay. Asst. prof. chemistry Iowa State U., Ames, 1950-51; staff mem. Los Alamos Sci. Lab., 1951-57; supr. Internat. Minerals & Chem. Corp., Mulberry, Fla., 1957-60; mgr. Brush Beryllium Co., Elmore, Ohio, 1960-72; assoc. dir. tech. Brush Wellman Inc., Elmore, 1972-86. Democratic precinct chmn., Los Alamos, 1956, Fremont, Ohio, 1980. Mem. Am. Chem. Soc. (sect. treas. 1956), Am. Soc. for Metals, AIME, Theta Xi, Phi Lambda Upsilon. Methodist. Club: Toastmasters Internat. Patentee in field. Home: 2624 Fangboner Rd Fremont OH 43420

WALSH, MICHAEL PATRICK, accountant; b. St. Louis, Apr. 2, 1954; s. John George and Rose (Cooke) W.; m. Judith Marie Chappie, May 26, 1978; children: Kevin Anthony, Brian Patrick. BSBA, Southeast Mo. State U., 1977; postgrad., Lindenwood Coll., 1986—. CPA, Mo. Staff acct. Kerber, Eck and Braeckel, CPA's, St. Louis, 1977-79, Mueller and Herring, CPA's, St. Louis, 1980-82; tax acct. Emerson Electric Co., St. Louis, 1982-84; staff supr. taxes Contel Service Corp., Wentzville, Mo., 1984—, also pub. affairs coordinator. Advisor jr. achievement program with Wentzville High Sch., 1985; trustee Steve Sheldon Officer Recognition fund, 1985—; mem. St. Lawrence lunch com., 1980—. Mem. Am. Inst. CPA's, Mo. Soc. CPA's. Roman Catholic. Club: Anglers of Mo. (Gerald). Home: 14821 Parlier Dr Bridgeton MO 63044 Office: Contel Service Corp PO Box 307 Wentzville MO 63385

WALSH, PATRICK ROBERT, neurosurgeon; b. St. Paul, May 29, 1948; m. Patricia Ann Kane, Dec. 23, 1968; children: Brian Patrick, Monica Lee. Student, St. Mary's Coll., 1969; MD, Med. Coll. Wis., 1973, PhD, 1984. Diplomate Am. Bd. Neurol. Surgery, Am. Bd. Med. Examiners. Intern in surgery Milwaukee County Med. Complex, 1973-74; resident in neurol. surgery Med. Coll. Wis., Milwaukee, 1974-78, asst. prof., 1978-84, assoc. prof. dept. neurosurgery, 1984—; attending neurosurgeon VA Med. Ctr., Milwaukee, 1978—, Froedtert Luth. Meml. Hosp., 1980—; assoc. attending neurosurgeon Milwaukee County Med. Complex, 1978—. Contbr. over 30 articles to profl. jours. Paralyzed VA Postdoctoral fellow, 1978-80; recipient Outstanding Clin. Achievement award Upjohn Pharms., 1973. Fellow Am. Coll. Surgeons; mem. AMA, Am. Assn. Neurol. Surgeons (spinal disorders joint sect.), Am. Soc. Stereotactic and Functional Neurosurgery, Biophys. Soc., Congress of Neurol. Surgeons, Neuroelectric Soc. (nat. adv. bd.), Soc. Neurosci., Soc. Neurosurgical Anasthesia and Neurologic Supportive Care, Midwest Pain Soc., Wis. Neurosurgical Soc. (sec.-treas. 1986), Alpha Omega Alpha. Roman Catholic. Avocations: music, auto restoration. Office: Med Coll Wis 8700 W Wisconsin Ave Milwaukee WI 53226

WALSH, SUSAN FRANCES, psychiatric social worker; b. Fostoria, Ohio, Apr. 5, 1943; d. Edward Doty and Frances Elizabeth (Storey) W.; B.S., Ind. U., 1965; A.M., U. Chgo., 1968, Ph.D., 1984. Instr. social work Northwestern U. Med. Sch., also staff social worker Northwestern Meml. Hosp., Chgo., 1968-75; pvt. practice psychotherapy, Chgo., 1974—; asso. dept. psychiatry Northwestern U., also coordinator outpatient services Inst. Psychiatry, Northwestern Meml. Hosp., 1975-84, asst. to dir. Inst. Psychiatry, 1984-85; lectr. U. Chgo., 1984-86 ; field instr. U. Chgo., U. Ill., Chgo. Circle; pres. Susan F. Walsh, Ph.D. Ltd. Mem. Nat. Assn. Social Workers. Research on alternative to psychiat. hospitalization. Home: 3150 N Lake Shore Dr Chicago IL 60657 Office: 333 E Ontario St Chicago IL 60611

WALSH, THOMAS J(OSEPH), chemical engineer, educator; b. Troy, N.Y., July 17, 1917; s. Thomas Joseph and Anna (Sharp) W.; m. Beatrice Metcalfe Passage, July 12, 1941; 1 child, Joan Beatrice Waltz. BS, Rensselaer Poly. Inst., 1939, MS, 1941; PhD, Case Inst. Tech., 1949. Chem. engr. Standard Oil Co. Ohio, 1941-47; prof. Case Inst. Tech., 1947-61; engr. Lewis Flight Propulsion Lab. NACA, 1951-55; cons. Thompson Ramo Wooldridge, 1955-61, sr. staff specialist, requirements mgr. research applications equipment labs. division, 1961-66; process specialist corp. engring. dept. Glidden-Durkee div. SCM Corp., Cleve., 1966-68, mgr. process engring., from 1968, mgr. environ. conservation, energy coordinator, to 1979, mgr. corp. energy conservation, 1979-80; v.p. Consultex, Inc., 1980—; cons. Glascote Products Co., 1954-61, Hukill Chem., Booth Oil Co., ECA, Inc., Argonne Nat. Lab.; adj. prof. chem. engring. Case Western Res. U., 1980—; adj. prof. chem. engring., spl. lectr. Cleve. State U., 1980-85, prof. chem. engring., 1983-86. Pres. Northeastern Ohio Sci. Fair, Inc. Recipient Jr. Tech. award Cleve. Tech. Soc. Council, Merit award Cleve. Chem. Profession; named Engr. of Yr., Cleve. Engring. Profession, 1985. Fellow Am. Inst. Chem. Engrs.; mem. AAAS, Am. Chem. Soc. (trustee), ASCE, AAUP, Cleve. Tech. Socs. Council (past pres.), AIAA, Cleve. Engring. Soc. (gov.), Order of Engr. Home: 32555 Creekside Dr Pepper Pike OH 44124 Office: Case Western Res U AJ Smith Bldg Cleveland OH 44106

WALSTON, LOLA INGE, dietitian; b. Chgo., Jan. 26, 1943; d. Willy and Ingeborg (Smith) Neumann; m. Steven Ward Walston, Aug. 5, 1967; children—Bradley, Scott. B.S., No. Ill. U., 1965; M.S., U. Iowa, 1967. Registered dietitian. Asst. dietary dir. Alaska Hosp. Med. Ctr., Anchorage, 1975-78; cons. dietitian Mercer County Hosp., Coldwater, Ohio, 1979; profl. service cons. Health Care and Retirement Corp. Am., Lima, Ohio, 1981-84; dietary dir. Estes Health Care Ctr., Montgomery, Ala., 1979-80, Mercy Meml. Hosp., Urbana, Ohio, 1984-86, Dairy & Nutrition Council Mid East, Dayton, Ohio, 1987—, Sharonview Nursing Home, South Vienna, Ohio, 1987—. Mem. com. Tecumseh council Boy Scouts Am., 1984, Tri-County Community Action Commn./CLS Nutrition, Bellefontaine, Ohio, 1987—. Mem. Am. Dietetic Assn., Ohio Dietetic Assn., Ohio Cons. Dietitians Health Care Facilities (chmn. 1982-84), Dayton Dietetic Assn., AAUW. Club: Hilltoppers (Fairborn, Ohio) (pres. 1982-83). Avocations: camping; sewing; knitting; crocheting; cooking. Office: Dairy & Nutrition Council Mid East 135 S Perry St Dayton OH 45402-1804

WALSWORTH, JAMES FRANK, financial executive; b. Manitowoc, Wis., Oct. 15, 1927; s. George Revilo and Marjorie (Kutil) W.; m. Caroline Sylvia Weber, Dec. 31, 1951; children: Daniel George, Frank James, John Weber, Robert Edward. BS, U. Wis., 1952; MBA, Northwestern U., 1972. Unit supr. Assocs. Investment Co., Chgo., 1952-59; gen. acct. Sloan Valve Co., Franklin Park, Ill., 1959-62, fin. acctg. mgr., 1963-74, dir. fin. and acctg., 1974-77, chief fin. officer, 1977—, also bd. dirs. Treas., bd. dirs. Parents and Friends of Ludeman Ctr., Park Forest, Ill., 1984-86, Dixon (Ill.) Assocs. Retarded Citizens, 1982-83. Served with U.S. Army, 1946-48, Korea. Mem. Fin. Execs. Inst. (bd. dirs.), Ill. Mfrs. Assn., Midwest Mgmt. Assn., Ill. State C. of C. Republican. Roman Catholic. Clubs: Rolling Green Country, Club Internat., Union League of Chgo. Avocations: tennis, golf. Office: Sloan Valve Co 10500 Seymour Ave Franklin Park IL 60131

WALTER, DWIGHT DANIEL, professional society administrator; b. Ellwood City, Pa., Sept. 7, 1945; s. Daniel A. and Ruth I. (Marsh) W.; m. Deborah S. Barker, June 10, 1967; children: Angela, Matthew. BSBA, Youngstown (Ohio) State U., 1968; MBA, Nat. Exec. Inst., Mendham, N.J., 1969. Dist. exec. Boy Scouts Am., Cleve., 1968-70; dir. devel. Nat. Arthritis Found., Cleve., 1970-73; regional dir. Nat. Multiple Sclerosis Soc., N.Y.C., 1973-76; mgr. membership devel. Am. Soc. for Metals, Metals Park, Ohio, 1976-79, asst. dir. chpt. and membership devel., 1979—; cons. various non-profit groups, Northeast Ohio, 1976—. Author: (with others) How Book, 1969, Dare to Think Big, 1972. Mem. bd. zoning appeals, Burton Twp., Ohio, 1986—. Mem. Am. Soc. for Metals Internat. (editor chpt. newsletter, 1983-85), Am. Welding Soc., Am. Soc. for Non Destructive Testing, Burton C. of C., Alpha Sigma Mu (bd. dirs. 1980—). Republican. Lutheran. Avocations: personal computing, field sports, hunting, fishing. Home: 14826 Rider Rd Burton OH 44021

WALTER, JAMES KENT, educational administrator, consultant; b. Kokomo, Ind., Jan. 26, 1948; s. Jack Gibson and Marie (Kaplan) W.; m. Deborah Marie Crouch, Jan. 29, 1968; children—Zachary Fitzgerald, Andrea Marie. B.S., Ind. U., 1970; M.A., Ball State U., 1972, EdD, 1986. Tchr. English, Sycamore Middle Sch., Kokomo, 1970-72, dept. head, Right to

Read coordinator, 1972-80; head trade and tech. div. Ind. Vocat. Tech. Coll., Kokomo, 1980-81; tchr. English, Haworth High Sch., Kokomo, 1981-84; asst. prin. Kokomo High Sch., 1984-86, Maple Crest Sch., Kokomo, 1986—; lectr. in field, 1983—. Author: (with others) School Fiscal Management: How to Keep Out of Trouble, 1987. Contbr. articles to profl. jours. Named Outstanding Educator and Adminstr., Ind. Vocat. Tech. Coll. Student Body, 1981. Mem. NEA, Nat. Council Tchrs. English, Ind. Council Tchrs. English, Ind. State Tchrs. Assn., Kokomo Tchrs. Assn., Nat. Orgn. Legal Problems in Edn., Nat. Assn. Secondary Sch. Prins., Ind. Secondary Sch. Adminstrs., Kokomo Prins. Assn., Assn. for Supervision and Curriculum Devel., Phi Delta Kappa. Democrat. Roman Catholic. Club: Elks. Developer programs and curriculum materials for academically and culturally disadvantaged. Home: 200 S Western Ave Kokomo IN 46901 Office: Maple Crest School 300 W Lincoln Rd Kokomo IN 46902

WALTER, JOSEPH DAVID, tire company research executive, educator; b. Merchantville, N.J., July 6, 1939; s. Joseph and Dorothy Madeline (Schenck) W.; m. Virginia Catherine Burke, July 14, 1962; children—Joseph, Michael, Martin. B.S. with honors, Va. Poly. Inst., 1962, M.S., 1964, Ph.D., 1966; M.B.A., U Akron, 1985. Naval architect Phila. Naval Base, 1962; mech. engr. Litton, Blacksburg, Va., 1963; adj. prof. engring. U. Akron (Ohio), 1975—; research scientist Firestone Co., Akron, 1966-69, research mgr., 1969-74, asst. dir. research, 1974—; instr. Va. Poly. Inst., 1964-66. NSF summer fellow, 1964, 66; NDEA fellow, 1962-65. Mem. ASME, Fiber Soc., AIAA (best paper awards), Tire Soc., Soc. for Exptl. Mechanics, Am. Acad. Mechanics, Am. Chem. Soc. (rubber div.), Phi Kappa Phi, Tau Beta Pi, Pi Tau Sigma, Sigma Pi Sigma, Beta Gamma Sigma. Roman Catholic. Clubs: Torch, Franklin (Akron). Contbr. articles to profl. jours. Home: 343 Barnstable Ave Akron OH 44313 Office: Firestone Tire & Rubber Co 1200 Firestone Pkwy Akron OH 44317

WALTER, RALPH COLLINS, III, business executive; b. Hinsdale, Ill., Nov. 25, 1946; s. Ralph Collins and Ethel Marie (Eustice) W.; B.A., Knox Coll., 1969; M.A., Ind. U., 1972; m. Sharon L. Maretta Koop, Aug. 9, 1980. Chartered fin. analyst. Instr., Ind. U. Bloomington, 1971-72; with A.G. Becker, Inc., Chgo., 1973-81, v.p., 1976-81; v.p. Dean Witter Reynolds Co., 1981-82; prof. fin. Northeastern Ill. U., Chgo., 1982-86, chmn. dept. fin., acctg. and law, 1983-86; v.p. The Chgo. Corp., 1986—.Trustee Northeastern Ill. U. Found., 1987—. Served to capt. U.S. Army, 1973. Woodrow Wilson fellow, 1969, Alfred P. Sloan scholar, 1966-69. Mem. Am. Econ. Assn., Am. Fin. Assn., Fin. Mgmt. Assn., Investment Analyst Soc. Chgo., Phi Beta Kappa. Home: 10501 5th Ave Cutoff LaGrange IL 60525 Office: The Chgo Corp 208 S LaSalle Chicago IL 60604

WALTER, ROBERT D., wholesale food company executive; b. 1945. BMechE, Ohio U., 1967; MBA, Harvard U., 1970. With Cardinal Foods Inc., Dublin, Ohio, 1971—; chief exec. officer, chmn. bd. Cardinal Distbn. Inc., Dublin, 1979—. Office: Cardinal Distbn Inc 655 Metro Pl S Dublin OH 43017 *

WALTER, U(LRIC) WILLIAM, construction contracting executive; b. Lima, Ohio, May 3, 1937; s. William Henry and Hildegard Louise (Zoellner) W.; m. Charlene Marguerite Piana, Aug. 22, 1959; children: Steven, Lisa, Brian, Julie. BSME, U. Notre Dame, 1959. Sales rep. Trisco System, Inc., Lima, 1959-61, mgr. prodn. and engring., 1961-63, gen. mgr., 1966-75, owner, chief exec. officer, 1975—; gen. mgr. engring. Trisco Plastics, Inc. div. Trisco System, Inc., Toledo, 1963-66; bd. dirs. Metbank Corp., Lima, Met. Bank, Lima; cons. Restoration Cons. Services, LIma; founder, adv. dir. Comax, Inc., Phila., 1985—. Co-author: Sealants: Professional's Guide, 1984, Sealant Guide Specifications, 1984. Council mem. Lima Econ. Devel. Council. Mem. Assn. Gen. Contractors, Constrn. Specifications Inst., Sealant and Waterproofers Inst. (past pres., bd. dirs. 1986—). Republican. Club: Shawnee Country. Lodge: Elks. Avocations: tennis, boating, fishing.

WALTERMEYER, NANCY ELIZABETH, draftsman; b. Jasper, Ohio, Feb. 9, 1953; d. Harry Edmond and Annie (Sloas) Harris; m. Richard Paul Waltermeyer Jr., Aug. 23, 1980. AArch, Columbus (Ohio) Tech. Inst., 1974. Draftsman R.S. Fling & Ptnrs., Columbus, 1974-78; drafter II Goodyear Atomic Corp., Piketon, Ohio, 1978-85; technician III Dennis E. Roby & Assoc., Decatur, Ill., 1986—. Democrat. Baptist. Clubs: Goodyear Atomic (sec. 1982-84, pres. 1984-85). Avocations: church librarian, singing, reading, crocheting. Home: 111 Heather Hills Dr Decatur IL 62522 Office: Dennis E Roby & Assocs 1900 E Eldorado Decatur IL 62525

WALTERS, BRUCE ALLEN, real estate director; b. Carmel, Calif., Apr. 3, 1957; s. Bruce Hanley and Inna (Koval) W.; m. Linda Ann Caramazza, July 21, 1979; children: Jennifer Marie, Cory James. BA in Econs., Stanford U., 1979. Real estate rep. Southland Corp., San Jose, Calif., 1979-80, Carl Karcher Internat., Fremont, Calif., 1980-81; real estate rep. McDonalds Corp., San Jose, 1981-83, real estate mgr., 1983-85; real estate dir. McDonalds Corp., Oak Brook, Ill., 1985—. Avocations: golf, racquetball. Home: 817 Amherst Ct Naperville IL 60565 Office: McDonalds Corp One McDonald's Plaza Oak Brook IL 60565

WALTERS, GARY DEAN, record manager administrator; b. Cin., June 11, 1959; s. Cecil McKinnley and Mila Jean (Tobergte) W. BA in Mgmt., Xavier U., Cin., 1981. Adminstrv. analyst Bethesda Hosp. Inc., Cin., 1983—. Active Big Bros., Big Sisters Am., Cin., 1985; affiliate Robert Kelly for Judge Campaign, Cin., 1986. Mem. Assn. Records Mgrs. and Adminstrs. Democrat. Roman Catholic. Club: Cin. Horsemans. Lodges: Norwood, Faternal Order Eagles. Avocation: horseback reiding. Home: 5227 Carthage Ave Cincinnati OH 45212 Office: Bethesda Hosp Inc 619 Oak St Cincinnati OH 45206

WALTERS, GEORGE KAUFFMAN, business educator; b. Abilene, Kans., Oct. 10, 1929; s. Harry Elmer and Stella (Kauffman) W.; m. Martha Flo Kissell, June 27, 1954; 1 child, Jon K. BS, Ft. Hays State U., 1955; MA, U. No. Colo., 1958, EdD, 1968. Tchr. bus. Ashland (Kans.) High Sch., 1955-57, Norton (Kans.) High Sch., 1957-60; v.p. western div. Suttle Directory Co., Norton, 1960-62; asst. prof. No. State Coll., Aberdeen, S.D., 1962-64; prof. Emporia (Kans.) State U., 1964—, assoc dean sch. bus. Contbr. articles to profl. jours. Served with USN, 1947-48, 52-54. Recipient Leadership award Boy Scouts Am., Emporia, 1974. Mem. Nat. Assn. for Bus. Tchr. Edn. Inst. (pres.), Nat. Bus. Edn. Assn., Kans. Bus. Edn. Assn., Mountain-Plains Bus. Edn. Assn., Am. Vocat. Assn., Nat. Council for Consumer Interests, Am. Legion, Pi Omega Pi (past nat. pres.), Delta Pi Epsilon, Phi Delta Kappa, Kappa Delta Pi. Club: Emporia Camera (pres. 1985—). Lodge: Lions (bd. dirs. 1986—). Avocations: travel, hiking, hunting, civic activity, photography. Home: 1029 West St Emporia KS 66801 Office: Emporia State U Sch Bus 1200 Commercial Emporia KS 66801

WALTERS, JEFFERSON BROOKS, musician, real estate broker; b. Dayton, Ohio, Jan. 20, 1922; s. Jefferson Brooks and Mildred Frances (Smith) W.; student U. Dayton, 1947; m. Mary Elizabeth Espey, Apr. 6, 1963 (dec. July 22, 1983); children—Dinah Christine Basson, Jefferson Brooks; m. 2d, Carol Elaine Clayton Gillette, Feb. 19, 1984. Composer, cornetist Dayton, 1934—; real estate broker, Dayton, 1948—; founder Am. Psalm Choir, 1965; apptd. deferred giving officer Kettering (Ohio) Med. Ctr., 1982—. Served with USCGR, 1942-45; PTO, ETO. Mem. SAR, Greater Dayton Antique Study Club (past pres.), Dayton Art Inst., Montgomery County Hist. Soc., Dayton Area Bd. Realtors. Presbyterian. Club: Masons (32 deg.). Condr., composer choral, solo voice settings of psalms and poetry Alfred Lord Tennyson; composer Crossing the Bar (meml. performances U.S. Navy band), 1961. Home: 4113 Roman Dr Dayton OH 45415 Office: Classics Realty 53 Park Ave Dayton OH 45419

WALTERS, JEFFREY PAUL, accountant; b. Menominee, Mich., July 25, 1955; s. Robert Henry and Mildred Agnes (Francour) W.; m. Diane Marie Boivin, May 20, 1978; children: Sarah Louise, Jessica Lynn, Kayla Marie. BBA in Acctg., St. Norbert Coll., 1977. CPA, Wis. Acct. Schumaker, Romenesko & Assocs., Appleton, Wis., 1977—. Campaign com. div. chmn. United Way, Appleton, 1985—. Recipient Vol. of Yr. award Big Bros./Sisters of Fox Valley Region, 1979, 80. Mem. Am. Inst. CPA's, Wis. Inst. CPA's (com. mem. acctg. and auditing conf. 1984—). Roman Catholic. Lodge: Kiwanis (pres. Appleton Fox Cities chpt. 1983, treas. 1984—, Kiwanian of Yr. 1982). Avocations: hunting, fishing, home renovation projects. Home: 133 Ellen Ln Appleton WI 54915 Office: Schumaker Romenesko & Assocs 555 N Lynndale Appleton WI 54915

WALTERS, RONALD JEFFREY, savings and loan executive; b. Chgo., Aug. 14, 1949; s. James John and Wanda Bertha (Sinclair) W.; m. Patricia Ann Tell, Nov. 22, 1974; children: Elizabeth, Kathleen, Kimberly, Christy. BS in Acctg., U. Ill., Chgo., 1972. CPA, Ill. Auditor Ernst & Ernst, Chgo., 1973-76; mgr. corp. acctg. First Fed. of Chgo., 1976-78; chief fin. officer Am. Heritage Savs., Bloomingdale, Ill., 1978-84; v.p. Household Bank, Fed. Savs. Bank, Bloomingdale, 1984; chief fin. officer Kankakee (Ill.) Fed. Savs., 1984—. Mem. St. Alexander's Parish Fin. Com., Villa Park, Ill., 1982-84; mem. Maternity Blessed Virgin Mary Parish Fin. Com., Bourbannais, Ill., 1985—; dir., officer Briarcliff Estates Community Assn., Bourbannais, 1985—; mem. fin. adv. com. City of Kankakee, 1986. Mem. Am. Inst. CPA's, Ill. CPA Soc., Fin. Mgrs. Soc. Roman Catholic. Lodge: Rotary. Home: 1387 Sommerset Way Bourbonnais IL 60914 Office: Kankakee Fed Savs 310 S Schuyler Kankakee IL 60901

WALTERS, SUMNER JUNIOR, judge; b. Van Wert, Ohio, Oct. 4, 1916; s. Sumner E. and Kittie (Allen) W.; m. Marjorie Acheson, May 22, 1948; 1 son, Sumner E. JD, Ohio No. U., 1940. Bar: Ohio 1940. Ptnr. Walters & Koch, 1941-42, Stroup & Walters, 1946-68; sole practice, Van Wert, 1969-71; ptnr. Walters, Young & Walters, 1971-80; judge Van Wert Mcpl. Ct., 1980-87; asst. pros. atty. Van Wert County, 1946-48, pros. atty., 1948-60; acting judge Van Wert Mcpl. Ct., also asst. city solicitor City of Van Wert, 1962; village solicitor Middle Point, 1960-80; pres. Van Wert Indsl. Devel. Corp., 1966-76. Pres. Humane Soc., 1963—, YMCA, 1962-63; mem. council Camp Fire Girls, 1965-72; pres. bd. trustees Van Wert County United Fund, 1959-60; trustee United Health Found., Van Wert County Hosp., Van Wert County Found., Marsh Found., Van Wert; chmn. ofcl. bd. Meth. ch., 1963-64, lay del. Ohio West Conf., 1967-79, conf. sec., 1970-71, mem. bd. hosps. and homes, trustee, 1983-86. Served with Mil. Police, C.I.C., AUS, 1942-45, ETO. Named Outstanding Citizen of Yr., Van Wert Jr. C. of C., 1965. Mem. Ohio Bar Assn., Northwestern Ohio Bar Assn. (pres. 1957-58), Van Wert County Bar Assn. (pres. 1953-55), Am. Legion, V.F.W., Sigma Phi Epsilon. Lodge: Masons (32 deg.), Shriners, K.T., Rotary (pres. 1966-67). Home: Rt 2 Ohio City OH 45874 Office: Rt 2 Box 40 Ohio City OH 45874

WALTERS, TOM FREDERICK, manufacturing company official; b. Des Moines, Oct. 18, 1931; s. Basil Leon and Reah E. (Handy) W.; m. Mary Katherine Russell, Dec. 8, 1956; children—Karen E., Juliet M., Thomas R., Alexandra K., Suzanne C. B.A., Beloit Coll., 1953; M.B.A. candidate Northwestern U., 1962-66. Sales and advt. staff Eaton, Yale & Towne, Chgo., 1956-62, prodn. mgr., 1962-65; sr. cons. Cresap, McCormick & Paget, Chgo., 1965-67; materials mgr. Joy Mfg. Co., Michigan City, Ind. 1967-73, gen. mgr., Elk Grove Village, Ill., 1973—; lectr. Contbr. articles to profl. jours. Pres., LaPorte County Young Republicans, Ind., 1970-71; dist. chmn. Boy Scouts Am., 1972; elder, trustee 1st Presbyterian Ch., Libertyville, Ill., 1980-83; mem. village bd. Village of Long Beach, Ind., 1969. Served to lt. (j.g.) USNR, 1953-56; Far East. Mem. Indsl. Compressor Distbrs. Assn. (chmn. com. 1979-84), Constrn. Industry Mfrs. Assn. (bd. dirs., com. chmn. 1975-82), Am. Prodn. and Inventory Control Soc. (chpt. pres. 1970-71), Greater O'Hare Assn. Commerce and Industry, Omicron Delta Kappa, U.S. Power Squadrons. Republican. Presbyterian. Clubs: Abbey Yacht (Lake Geneva, Wis.); Michigan City Yacht (Ind.). Avocations: boating; fishing; skiing; swimming. Home: 766 Kenwood Ave Libertyville IL 60048 Office: Joy Mfg Co 2300 W Devon Ave Elk Grove Village IL 60007

WALTHOUR, BRUCE SHUEY, minister; b. Jeannette, Pa., Jan. 7, 1949; s. Murry Caldwell and Alice Jean (Shuey) W.; m. Joanna Darlene Patrick, Aug. 15, 1982; children: Bruce Elliott, Heather Marie. BA, Catawba Coll., 1970; M Div., Lancaster (Pa.) Seminary, 1973. Ordained to ministry United Ch. of Christ, 1973. Correctional specialist Md. State Dept. Corrections, Balt., 1974-78; minister 1st United Ch. Christ, Warren, Ohio, 1978-81; minister edn. 2d Christian Ch., Warren, Ohio, 1982-85; minister First Congregational Ch., Pontiac, Mich., 1985—; cons. First Congl. Ch., Pontiac, 1987—. dist. exec. Clinton Valley Council Boy Scouts of Am., Pontiac, 1987—. Mem. Pontiac Clergy Assn., Warren Area Clergy Assn. Republican. Home: 6291 Church St Clarkston MI 48016 Office: First Congregational Ch PO Box 3012 Pontiac MI 40859

WALTON, BARBARA GAYLE, nurse, consultant; b. Detroit, Jan. 6, 1955; d. Calvin Arthur and Harriet Jane (Best) Lepien; m. Larry Austin Walton, Oct. 11, 1980. Student, Mich. State U., 1973-76; diploma, Henry Ford Hosp. Sch. Nursing, 1978; BA, Columbia Pacific U., 1987, MA, 1987. Staff nurse Univ. Hosp., Ann Arbor, Mich., 1978-79, nurse clinician, 1979-81; charge nurse Vet.'s Adminstrn. Med. Ctr., Ann Arbor, 1981-82; instr. edn. Saline (Mich.) Community Hosp., 1982-84, asst. dir. edn., 1984-87; Co-founder NurseWise Inc., Ann Arbor, 1986—. Mem. Am. Assn. Critical Care Nurses (cert., bd. dirs. and Washtenaw County chpt. 1987—), Mich. Soc. Health Edn. and Tng., Soc. Pub. Health Educators, Mich. Nurses Assn., Am. Assn. Neurosurgical Nurses. Avocations: computers, scuba diving, gardening, needlework, stenciling. Home: 800 E Forest Ypsilanti MI 48198 Office: Nurse Wise Inc 1495 Cobblestone Ann Arbor MI 48108

WALTON, JOHN RICHARD, health care company executive, health educator; b. Chgo., Apr. 6, 1951; s. Charles Chandler and Dolores Barbara (Oehmen) W.; children—Scott, Michael, Tracey. B.S. in Chemistry, Loyola U., 1973; M.H.A., Chgo. Med. Sch., 1979; M.B.A., U. Chgo., 1985. Registered respiratory therapist, cert. respiratory technician, Ill. Various positions respiratory therapy dept. Northwestern Meml. Hosp., Chgo., 1971-76, adminstrv. dir. respiratory therapy dept., 1976-83; pres. John Walton & Assocs., Chgo., 1983-86; pres. IPA Mgmt. Corp., Oak Park, Ill., 1986—, Respiratory Care Seminars, Chgo., 1983-84; prin. Health Care Mgmt., Oak Park, 1985—; instr. respiratory therapy program Northwestern U. Med. Sch. Recipient Outstanding Young Man of Am. award, 1980; Literary award Am. Respiratory Therapy Found., 1983. Mem. Am. Assn. Respiratory Therapy (pres., chmn. bd. dirs. 1982, Recognition Plaque award 1982), Ill. Soc. Respiratory Therapy (pres. 1976-77). Author: Clinical Application of Blood Gases, 3d edit., 1983; contbr. chpts. to books, articles to profl. jours. Office: IPA Mgmt Corp 1515 N Harlem Suite 400 Oak Park IL 60302

WALTON, LAURENCE ROLAND, information scientist, librarian; b. Coffeyville, Kans., Mar. 27, 1939; s. Orvile Mac and Zora Laverne W.; B.A. in Chemistry, Okla. State U., 1965; B.S. in L.S., Washington U., St. Louis, 1972; m. Lucretia Jane Mize, June 1, 1963; 1 son, Laurence Roland. Library asst. Stillwater (Okla.) Public Library, 1957-65; tech. librarian Research and Devel. Center, Pet, Inc., Greenville, Ill., 1965-73, mgr. corp. info. center, 1973—. Mem. Spl. Libraries Assn., Am. Soc. Info. Sci., Inst. Food Technologists, Am. Assn. Cereal Chemists, Am. Soc. Microbiologists. Editor: Food Publication Roundup: A Bibliographic Guide, 1977-83. Home: 1516 Marbella Dr Saint Louis MO 63138 Office: Pet Inc 400 S 4th St Saint Louis MO 63102

WALTON, ROBERT KIM, psychological and neurological consultant; b. Battle Creek, Mich., Mar. 2, 1945; s. Robert Edward Walton and Mary Alice (Phelps) Antonelli; m. Martha Wilson, Apr. 10, 1964; 1 child, Timothy Lee. AB, John Carroll U., 1968, M in Soviet Studies, 1970; MEd, Cleve. State U., 1971; postgrad., Northwestern U., 1973; ThD (hon.), Fla. Inst. Bibl. Studies, 1975. Cert. tchr., adminstr., Ohio. Cons. Western Res. Edn. System, Cleve., 1969—, Learning Ctr. Forum, Inc., Cleve., 1971—; dir. Univ. Forum Acad., Cleve., 1974—; cons. Capital Edn. Services, Columbus, Ohio, 1980—, Ohio Council on Disabled, Columbus, 1980—, Manna House Bible Sch., Columbus, 1980—, Sociopaths Anonymous, Lima, Ohio, 1984—. Author: Light Side of Argument & Debate, 1969, Deviant Personality Dysfunctions, 1974. Mem. local exec. bd. ARC, 1984—, cons., vol., 1984; chmn. Cath. Interfaith Council, Allen County, 1984. Recipient Commendation, Sacred Congregation for Cath. Insts., 1974; NDEA fellow, 1970. Fellow Phi Alpha Theta, Delta Sigma Rho, Tau Kappa Alpha. Republican. Club: Phoenix One (Lima) (chair 1984—). Avocations: chess, Shakespeare, stamps, reading, Latin. Home and Office: PO Box 4571-175-999 Lima OH 45802-4571

WALTON, STEVEN CRAIG, dentist; b. Columbus, Ohio, Nov. 1, 1955; s. Craig Carlton and Gwen (Norton) W.; m. Nancy Lynn Biederman, Sept. 6, 1980; children: Adam Craig, Paige Elizabeth. BA, Ohio Wesleyan U., 1977; DDS, Ohio State U., 1980. Gen. practice dentistry Columbus, 1980—; dental cons. E&E Benefit Ins., Columbus, 1981—; clin. instr. Ohio State U., Columbus, 1982—. Mem. ADA, Ohio Dental Soc., Columbus Dental Soc., Upper Arlington Civic Assn., Ohio State U. Alumni Assn., Dental Vets. Assn. (bd. dirs.). Republican. Lutheran. Avocations: tennis, golf, skiing. Office: 3600 Olentangy River Rd Columbus OH 43214

WAMBLES, LYNDA ENGLAND, academic administrator, consultant; b. Nashville, Dec. 30, 1937; d. Henry Russell and Doris Olivia (Stuart) England; m. Byron Adolph Wambles, Sept. 3, 1965; 1 child, Teri Leigh Moore Wambles Taylor. Student, U. Tenn., 1964-65, 73-74, Washington U., St. Louis, 1984-86. Cert. profl. sec. Exec. sec. Gen. Truck Sales, Knoxville, Tenn., 1972-74; asst. to dean Coll. Law U. Tenn., Knoxville, 1974-76; office mgr. Washington U. Sch. Bus., St. Louis, 1977-78, registrar, dir. info. systems, 1978-83, asst. dean for faculty and adminstrn. services, 1983-86; cons. in field St. Louis, 1978-86, Overland Park, Kans., 1986—; cons. in field, St. Louis, 1978—; lectr. div. continuing edn. Washington U., St. Louis, 1978-80. Active United Way of Greater Knoxville, 1973-74; leader lunch participant YWCA, St. Louis, 1981-83. Fellow Acad. Cert. Profl. Secs.; mem. Profl. Secs. Internat., Nat. Secs. Assn. (Tenn. div. Sec. of Yr. 1975), Assn. Info. Systems Profls. Republican. Presbyterian. Avocations: fishing, gardening, cooking. Home and Office: 8425 W 113th St Overland Park KS 66210

WAMBSGANSS, JACOB ROY, accounting educator; b. Hillsboro, Kans., Nov. 9, 1950; s. Eldor Jacob and Betty Maxine (Wait) W.; m. Dona Kay Koby, May 22, 1971; children: Warren Jacob, Jay Roy. BA in History, Wichita (Kans.) State U., 1973; MBA, Emporia (Kans.) State U., 1981; PhD in Bus., Acctg., U. Nebr., 1985. CPA, N.D. Owner Wagon Wheel Restaurant, Strong City, Kans., 1975-76; mgmt. instr. Minot (N.D.) State U., 1981-83; asst. prof. U. S.D., Vermillion, 1985—; bd. dirs. Campus Bookstore, Vermillion. Contbr. articles to profl. jours. Treas. council Pleasant Valley Ch., 1986—. Bush Found. grantee, 1987. Mem. Am. Inst. CPA's, Am. Acctg. Assn., N.D. Soc. CPA's, Decision Sci. Inst. Republican. Lutheran. Avocations: reading, walking, camping, gardening. Home: Rt 1 Box 168A Volin SD 57072 Office: U SD 414 E Clark Vermillion SD 57069

WAMPLER, LLOYD CHARLES, lawyer; b. Spencer, Ind., Nov. 4, 1920; s. Charles and Vivian (Hawkins) W.; m. Joyce Ann Hoppenrath, Sept. 28, 1950 (dec. 1954); 1 child, Natalie Gay; m. Mary E. Shumaker, Sept. 16, 1982. A.B., Ind. U., 1942, J.D., 1947. Bar: Ind. 1947, U.S. Supreme Ct. 1971. Instr. bus. law U. Kans., 1947-49; dep. atty. gen. Ind., 1949-50; mem. legal com. Interstate Oil Compact Commn., 1950; asst. pub. counselor Ind., 1950-53; mem. Stevens, Wampler, Travis & Fortin, Plymouth, 1953-76; claim counsel Am. Family Ins. Group, Indpls., 1983—. Mem. Ind. Rehab. Services Bd., 1978-86; Democratic nominee for judge Ind. Supreme Ct., 1956. Served with USNR, 1942-46. Mem. Am. Judicature Soc., ABA, Ind. Bar Assn. (bd. mgrs. 1975-77), Indpls. Bar Assn., Ind. Acad. Sci., Ind. Def. Lawyers Assn. (bd. dirs. 1967-72, v.p. 1970, pres. 1971-72), Ind. Hist. Soc., Marshall County Hist. Soc. (dir. 1969-75), Assn. Ins. Attys. U.S. and Can., Sagamore of the Wabash, Am. Legion, Phi Delta Phi, Delta Sigma Pi. Lodge: Moose. Home: 4000 N Meridian St Indianapolis IN 46208 Office: 1625 N Post Rd Indianapolis IN 46219

WANAMAKER, RICHARD EDWARD, marketing executive, writer; b. Findlay, Ohio, Apr. 8, 1923; s. Fred P. and Marion L. (Sites) W.; m. Juanita R. Raborn, Mar. 11, 1946; children: Richard E. Jr., Cheri Lynn (dec.). BS in Commerce, U. Cin., 1958. Copywriter Wm. Powell Co., Cin., 1947-52, asst. advt. mgr., 1952-62, advt. mgr., 1962-73, dir. mktg. services, 1973—; advisor Cin. Tech. Coll., 1982—; mem. awards rev. com. Am. Advt. Fedn., Washington, 1978-80. Author: Cincinnati Industrial Advertising-60 Years, 1986. Pres. North College Hill (Ohio) High Sch. Band Boosters, 1965; asst. scoutmaster North College Hill Boy Scouts Am., 1964. Served to sgt. U.S. Army, 1943-46. Recipient Scouters award Boy Scouts Am., 1964; named to Hon. Order Ky. Cols., 1970. Mem. Cin. Indsl. Advertisers (pres. 1977-78, Person of Distinction 1979, Cert. Bus. Communicator 1981, Bus. Advt. Person of Yr. 1987), Am. Legion (comdr. North College Hill chpt. 1971-73). Avocations: golf, reading, traveling, music. Home: 7701 Cella Dr Cincinnati OH 45239 Office: The Wm Powell Co 2503 Spring Grove Ave Cincinnati OH 45214

WANATICK, MARY ANN, foundation administrator; b. Detroit, June 12, 1929; d. Samuel Tilden and Cilenore Catherine (Smith) Steedman; m. Michael D. Wanatick, Oct. 30, 1958; 1 child, Robert Michael. BA, U. Toledo, 1951, BEd, 1964. Instr. computer and related systems Remington Rand, Inc., Toledo, 1951-54; city dir. New Neighbors League, Toledo, 1954-58; area dir. Relax-a-Cizor, Inc., Toledo, 1966-68; elementary tchr. Toledo Pub. Schs., 1962-65; exec. dir. Arthritis Found., Northwestern Ohio chpt., Toledo, 1968-84; exec. dir. Easter Seal Soc. Northwestern Ohio, 1986-87; mem. arthritis adv. com. Ohio Dept. Health. Active Toledo Symphony Orch. League; bd. dirs. Toledo Opera Guild. Mem. Easter Seal Soc., Barrier Free Toledo Com. (adv. com.), N.W. Ohio Rehab. Assn., Nat. Rehab. Assn., Ohio Rehab. Assn., Ohio Pub. Health Assn., Toledo Execs. Forum, Ohio Rheumatism Soc., Fund Raising Exec. of N.W. Ohio, Alpha Omicron Pi. Club: Zonta, Toledo One (Toledo). Home and Office: 4857 Rudgate Blvd Toledo OH 43623

WANDEL, JOSEPH FRANK, account executive; b. Buffalo, Nov. 28, 1942; s. Joseph Frank and Florence Mary (Gluszkowski) W.; B.S. in Chemistry, Alliance Coll., 1964; postgrad. St. John's U., N.Y.C., 1964-65; M.B.A., Kent State U.; m. Sally Ann Jessen, Feb. 14, 1976; 1 son, Stephen. Chem. sales rep. Emery Industries, Inc., Cin., 1966-79; tech. rep. Glyco Chem. Co., Greenwich, Conn., 1979—; tech. sales engr. Henkel Corp., chem. spltys. div., Maywood, N.J., 1980-84; account exec. Loxiol Lubricants, 1984—. Adv. merit badges Boy Scouts Am. Served with USAR, 1965-72. Mem. Soc. Plastics Engrs., Vinyl Siding Inst., Soc. Plastics Industry, Chem. Mktg. Research Assn., Am. Chem. Soc., Cleve. Chem. Assn., Akron Rubber Group. Republican. Roman Catholic. Clubs: Bishop's Century, Hudson Montessori Parents, Polish Nat. Alliance. Address: 270 Kennedy Blvd Northfield OH 44067

WANDLING, RAYMOND LEWIS, graphic designer; b. St. Louis, Mar. 30, 1951; s. Grover Edmond and Lucille Elizabeth (Neumann) W.; m. Lesley Ann Leader, Mar. 19, 1983. BFA, Washington U., St. Louis, 1974. Graphic designer McGraw-Hill, St. Louis, 1974, McDonnell-Douglas, St. Louis, 1974; graphic designer The Robert Falk Group, St. Louis, 1974-77, sr. designer, 1977-79, design dir., 1979-81, v.p., 1981—. Recipient awards Printing Industries Am., Am. Advt. Fedn., Bus. and Profl. Advt. Assn., Advt. Fedn. St. Louis, Internat. Assn. Bus. Communicators. Club: Art Directors of St. Louis. Avocations: music, photography, racquetball. Home: 604 Atalanta Saint Louis MO 63119

WANDOR, MARY ANN, real estate officer; b. Mason, Mich., Dec. 17, 1961; d. Robert Neil and Mary Jean (Miner) Clark; m. David Gordon Wandor, Oct. 6, 1984. BS in Bus. Adminstrn., Bowling Green (Ohio) State U., 1983. Sales assoc. DeVries Realty, Inc., Midland, Mich., 1984—, closing officer, 1985—. Mem. Midland Bd. Realtors. Roman Catholic. Avocations: skiing, sewing, quilting, piano. Home: 5406 Bloomfield Dr Midland MI 48640 Office: DeVries Realty Inc 509 S Saginaw Midland MI 48640

WANDTKE, EDWARD THOMAS, chemical company executive; b. Rochester, N.Y., Dec. 12, 1942; s. Edward and Florence (Herman) W.; m. Dolores Mary Zemaitis, Aug. 14, 1965; children: Scott, Todd, Aaron. BS in Acctg., U. Rochester, 1965; MBA, Rochester Inst. Tech., 1973. CPA, N.Y. Acct. Price Waterhouse Co., Rochester, N.Y., 1965-68; mgr. acctg. Schlegel Mfg. Co., Rochester, 1968-70; gen. mgr. Rochester Truck Rental, 1970-73; controller Erie Sci. Co., Buffalo, 1973-74; v.p. adminstrn. Arvin Industries, Lancaster, Ohio, 1974-78; corp. fin. mgr. Chemlawn, Columbus, Ohio, 1978-83; pres. All-Green Mgmt. Assocs., Columbus, 1985—; bd. dirs. Driveseal, Columbus, 1986—. Co-contbr. monthly columns on landscape mgmt., lawn care and pest control to profl. jours. Bd. dirs. Columbus chpt. Jr. Achievement, 1979—, exec. com., 1984—. Mem. Am. Inst. CPA's, N.Y. State Soc. CPA's, Ohio Soc. CPA's. Roman Catholic. Home: 1550 Windrush Ct Blacklick OH 43004 Office: AGMA Inc 1033 Dublin Rd Columbus OH 43215

WANEK, RONALD MELVIN, orthodontist; b. Richland Center, Wis., Nov. 3, 1938; s. Melvin Leo and Mary Esther (Picha) W.; m. Janet Eleanor Lundquist, June 22, 1974; children: Lynn Ann, Mark Ronald. Student, U. Wis., 1956-60; DDS, Marquette U., 1964, MS, 1969. Practice dentistry specializing in orthodontics Madison, Wis., 1969—. Served to lt. USNR, 1964-67, Vietnam. Mem. ADA, Wis. Dental Assn., Dane County Dental Assn., Am. Assn. Orthodontists, Wis. Soc. Orthodontists, Midwest Soc. Orthodontists, Omicron Kappa Upsilon. Republican. Methodist. Avocations: organ, piano, directing handbell choir. Office: 4915 Monona Dr Madison WI 53716

WANETIK, ANN SARA DENGROVE, social worker; b. Newark, Apr. 16, 1948; d. Irving Genderovsky and Esther (Wexler) Dengrove; m. Leonard Ira Wanetik, Dec. 27, 1969; children: Ezra Samuel, Devra Naomi. BA in Psychology, Carnegie-Mellon U., 1970; MEd, Wheelock Coll., 1976; MSW, U. Mich., 1985. Cert. elementary tchr., Mass.; cert. social worker, Mich. Caseworker Allegheny County Dept. Pub. Assistance, Pitts., 1970-71, Lycoming County Children's Services, Williamsport, Pa., 1971-73; head tchr. day care Lesley Coll. Children's House, Cambridge, Mass., 1973-74; youth worker, crisis counselor City of Salem (Mass.) Youth Commn., 1975; family life specialist Multi-Edn. Learning and Devel. Ctr., Inc., Stoneham, Mass., 1975-79; head tchr. Jewish Community Ctr. of Met. Detroit, West Bloomfield, Mich., 1981; social worker Cath. Social Services of Wayne County, Detroit, 1981-84; coordinator perinatal coaching program Oakland Family Services, Pontiac, Mich., 1985—. Mem. Nat. Assn. Social Workers, Mich. Soc. for Clin. Social Work. Democrat. Jewish. Avocations: crocheting, kite flying. Office: Oakland Family Services 132 Franklin Blvd Pontiac MI 48053

WANG, CHIH, educator; b. Changsha, Hunan, Republic of China, Oct. 15, 1906; s. Ta Wang; m. Tso-fang, Feb. 2, 1937; children: Chang-Yi, Hui-Tze. BA, Norwich U., 1928; BS, US Mil. Acad., 1932. Commd. Chinese Army, Republic of China, 1932, advanced through grades to MG; Chinese liaison officer USAFFE, SCAP, Philippines and S.W. Pacific, 1941-46; mil. counselor to The President Republic of China, 1932-65; ret. Chinese Army, 1965; prof., dean Soochow U., Taipei, Taiwan, 1960-83; adj. prof. Mich. State U., East Lansing, 1983—. Author: Mao Tse-tung's Thought of Military Insurrection, 1963, Mao Tse-tung's Military Thought from Guerrilla Warfare to Mobile Warfare, 1977. Decorated Freedom medal with oak leaf cluster; recipient Disting. Service medal, Govt. Republic of China, 1965. United Methodist. Office: Asian Studies Mich State U East Lansing MI 48823

WANG, JOHN JENGSHYONG, steel company executive; b. Taichung, Republic of China, Dec. 10, 1938; came to U.S., 1963; s. Yu-Te and Julie (Lee) W.; m. Suzy Shaw, Sept. 16, 1967; children: Amy, Jason. BS in Indsl. Engring., Nat. Cheng Kung U., Republic China, 1962; MS in Indsl. Engring., W.Va. U., 1966. Quality control engr. Lear Siegler, Grand Rapids, Mich., 1966-68, Gen. Electric Corp., Johnson City, N.Y., 1968-69; advanced mgr. engring. Gen. Electric Corp., Morrison, Ill., 1969-75; process control supr. Northwestern Steel, Sterling, Ill., 1975—; v.p. House of Wong Chinese Restaurant, Rock Falls, Ill., 1977-82, pres. 1982—. Served to 2d lt. R.O.C., USAF, 1962-63. Mem. Ill. Food Service (cert.). Republican. Mem. First Christian Ch. Avocation: classical guitar. Office: Northwestern Steel and Wire 121 Wallace St Sterling IL 61081

WANG, JOSEPH HOW-JYH, oral and maxillofacial surgeon; b. Shanghai, China, June 21, 1939; s. Kim and Y.L. (Mau) Wong; m. Tan-Wei Chou Wang, Jan. 31, 1971; children: Eric M., Teresa S. DDS, Nat. Def. Med. Ctr., Taipei, Republic of China, 1964; PhD, U. Minn., 1971. Intern Army 801 Gen. Hosp., Taipei, 1963-64; gen. practice dentistry Taipei, 1964-65; dental fellow Guggenheim Dental Clinic, N.Y.C., 1965-66; resident in gen. anesthesia Hennepin County Gen. Hosp., Mpls., 1971-72; instr. oral and maxillofacial surgery U. Minn., Mpls., 1973-74, asst. prof., 1974-76; practice dentistry specializing in oral and maxillofacial surgery Willmar, Minn., 1976—; mem. dental staff Hennepin County Gen. Hosp., Mpls., 1975-76, Divine Redeemer Hosp., St. Paul, Minn., 1975-77, Hutchinson (Minn.) Community Hosp., Chippewa County Hosp., Montevideo, Minn., Douglas County Hosp., Alexandria, Minn., Renville County Hosp., Olivia, Minn.; mem. dental staff Rice Memorial Hosp., chief of dentistry, 1982—. Contbr. articles to profl. jours. Del. Independent Reps., Willmar, 1980-86. Roman Catholic. Home and Office: PO Box 550 Willmar MN 56201

WANG, VINCENT TSAN-LEUN, food service executive; b. Taipei, Republic of China, Oct. 18, 1953; came to U.S., 1978.; s. Chen-Tong and Chen Chin-Lien Wang. BS, Fu Jen Cath. U., Republic of China, 1976; MS, U. Fla., 1980. Pres., chief exec. officer Dr. Wang Restaurant, Inc., Mankato, Minn., 1982—, also chmn. bd. dirs.; cons. Tien Hsiang Co., Republic of China, 1974-78. Author: Kitchen Manuel of Chinese Restaurants, 1985, Service Manuel of Chinese Restaurants, 1986. Mem. Restaurant Bus. Assn. (research adv. panel), Inst. Food Technologists. Republican. Lodges: Lions, Sertoma. Avocations: inventing, horticulture, Chinese cooking. Home: 106 Hinckley St Mankato MN 56001 Office: 230 S Front St Mankato MN 56001

WANGEN, ROBERT CLARK, jeweler; b. Duluth, Minn., July 22, 1925; s. Elmer Morris and Edna May (Clark) W.; m. Shirley Ann Robert, Jan. 10, 1947; children: Stephen Robert, Laurie Ann, Cynthia Sue, David Jay. BA, U. Minn., 1950. Acct. DM&IR Co., Duluth, 1946-50; auditor State of Minn., St. Paul, 1950-52; dept. mgr. W.P. & R.S. Mars Co., Duluth, 1952-58; v.p. Mayflower Co., Duluth, 1959-69; editor Fin. Record, Duluth, 1970-81; owner Wangen's Gifts & Jewelry, Moose Lake, Minn., 1972—. Author: Introduction to Hockey, 1973, (short stories) Wildlife, 1984. Vol. goodwill Duluth Ambassadors, 1956-58; pres. Campfire, Inc., Duluth, 1965-68; area capt. United Fund, Duluth, 1955. Served to lt. col. USAF, 1943-45. Mem. Gift Buyers Assn., Minn. Jewelers Assn., Nat. Jewelers Assn., Amateur Hockey Assn. (coach 1971-82), Nat. Writers Club, Retired Officers Assn.. Avocations: music, singing, swimming, walking, reading. Home: Rt 2 PO Box 340 Sturgeon Lake MN 55783 Office: Wangen's House Gifts & Jewelery 321 Elm Ave Moose Lake MN 55767

WANGLER, GARY WILLIAM, financial executive; b. Celina, Ohio, Nov. 1, 1946; s. William Henry and Rita Frances (Vielkind) W.; m. Pamela J. Thompson, Aug. 31, 1968; 1 child, Douglas G. BS, Ball State U., 1969. CPA, Ind. Internal auditor NCR Corp., Dayton, Ohio, 1969-71; audit mgr. George S. Olive & Co., Muncie, Ind., 1971-82; fin. mgr. Pathologists Associated, Muncie, 1982—; fin. mgr. BWTB & K Profl. Corp., Muncie, 1982—. Treas. Delaware County Mental Health Assn., Muncie, 1978-83; deacon Westminster Presbyn. Ch., Muncie, 1981—. Mem. Am. Inst. CPA's, Ind. CPA Soc. Avocations: reading, running, hiking, photography. Home: 5201 N Grass Way Muncie IN 47304 Office: Pathologists Associated 407 W Main St Muncie IN 47305

WANGLER, JOHN EDWARD, JR., sales executive; b. Chgo., Jan. 27, 1962; s. John Edward and Wilma Irene (Webb) W. BA in Communications and Journalism, Eastern Ill. U., 1984. Asst. editor Dana Chase Pubs., Oak Brook, Ill., 1984-85, dist. sales mgr., 1985—. Mem. Bus. Profl. Advt. Assn. Republican. Roman Catholic. Avocations: racquetball, golf. Office: Dana Chase Pubs 1110 Jorie Blvd Oak Brook IL 60522-9019 Office: Dana Chase Pubs 1000 Jorie Blvd Suite 312 Oak Brook IL 60521

WANNEMACHER, THOMAS LEE, systems programmer; b. Delphos, Ohio, July 5, 1947; s. Orville E. and Mary M. (Finlay) W.; m. Yali Wang, Dec. 30, 1979; children: David, Daniel. BA, St. Meinrad Coll., 1969; MA, U. Hawaii, 1974. Computer programmer civil service Wright-Patterson AFB, Ohio, 1977-81, database analyst, systems programmer, 1981—; freelance software designer. Served with U.S. Army, 1969-72, Vietnam. U.S. Govt. grantee, U. Hawaii, 1973-74. Mem. Assn. for Computing Machinery, IEEE, Am. Assn. for Artificial Intelligence. Democrat. Roman Catholic. Home: 2706 Rockledge Trail Dayton OH 45430

WANNEN, HERBERT RICHMOND, mental health administrator, psychotherapist; b. Balt., Aug. 24, 1946; s. Herbert Keidel and Mildred Joy (Holden) W.; m. Marieta Mae Showalter, July 12, 1980. BA, Washington U., 1968, MSW, 1974. Welfare caseworker St. Louis County Welfare, Brentwood, Mo., 1968-69; social work specialist U.S. Army, Heidelberg, Fed. Republic Germany, 1971-73; psychiat. social worker Western Mo. Mental Health Ctr., Kansas City, 1975-76; psychotherapist Wyandot Mental Health, Kansas City, Mo., 1976-84, coordinator admissions, 1980-82; clin. services mgr. Matrix Inc., Kansas City, Mo., 1982—; freelance cons., instr. psychodiagnosis, Kansas City, Mo. area, 1982—. Author articles on motion pictures, 1982—. Served with U.S. Army, 1970-73. Avocations: motion picture history, sci. fiction and fantasy, collecting film memorabilia, religious history, natural sciences. Office: Matrix Inc 7447 Holmes Rd Kansas City MO 64131

WANSING, ALVIN DANIEL, civil engineer; b. Waynesville, Mo., Feb. 3, 1947; s. Karl Joseph and Margaret Elizabeth (Fitzpatrick) W.; m. Sheila M. Smith, Sept. 16, 1972; children: Daniel, Lee Anne. BSCE, U. Mo., Rolla, 1969. Registered profl. engr., Ohio; lic. water supply operator, water distbn. operator, Ohio. Resident engr. Black & Veatch, Various locations, 1969-73; asst. water dir. City of Springfield, Ohio, 1973-75, water dir., 1975-83, service dir., 1983-87, utilities dir., 1987—. Mem. Nat. Am. Water Works Assn. (asst. rep. for Ohio sect. com on leak detection 1984—) Am. Water Works Assn. (dist. chmn. 1981-82, water utility council Ohio sect. 1987—, M.W. Tatlock Meml. Citation award 1982), Water Pollution Control Fedn., St. Maintenance Sanitation Officials (1st vice chmn. 1986-87, pres. 1987—), Am. Pub. Works Assn., Gov. Refuse Collect and Disposal Assn., Mo. Sch. Mines-U. Mo. Rolla Alumni Assn. (chairperson 1985—), George Rogers Clark Heritage Assn. (trustee 1980-84), Tau Beta Pi, Chi Epsilon. Avocation: deltiology. Office: City of Springfield 1515 Mitchell Blvd Springfield OH 45503

WANTLAND, WILLIAM CHARLES, lawyer, bishop; b. Edmond, Okla., Apr. 14, 1934; s. William Lindsay and Edna Louise (Yost) W. BA, U. Hawaii, 1957; JD, Okla. City U., 1967; D in Religion, Geneva Theol. Coll., Knoxville, Tenn., 1976; DD (hon.), Nashotah House, Wis., 1983, Seabury-Western Sem., Evanston, Ill., 1983. With FBI, various locations, 1954-59, Ins. Co. of N.Am., Oklahoma City, 1960-62; law clk.-atty. Bishop & Wantland, Seminole, Okla., 1962-77; vicar St. Mark's Ch., Seminole, 1963-77, St. Paul's Ch., Holdenville, Okla., 1974-77; presiding judge Seminole Mcpl. Ct., 1970-77; atty. gen. Seminole Nation of Okla., 1969-72, 75-77; exec. dir. Okla. Indian Rights Assn., Norman, 1972-73; rector St. John's Ch., Oklahoma City, 1977-80; bishop Episcopal Diocese of Eau Caire (Wis.), 1980—; adj. prof. U. Okla. Law Sch., Norman, 1970-78; mem. nat. council Evang. & Cath. Mission, Chgo., 1977—. Author: Foundations of the Faith, 1983, Canon Law of the Episcopal Church, 1984; co-author: Okla. Probate Forms, 1971; contbr. articles to profl. jours. Pres. Okla. Conf. Mcpl. Judges, 1973, Wis. Conf. Chs., 1984-86; trustee Nashotah House, Wis., 1981—; bd. dirs. SPEAK, Eureka Springs, Ark., 1983—, MORE, Eureka Springs, 1984—. Recipient Most Outstanding Contbn. to Law and Order award Okla. Supreme Ct., 1975, Outstanding Alumnus award Okla. City U., 1980, Wis. Equal Rights Council award, 1986. Mem. Okla. Bar Assn., Living Ch. Found., Oklahoma City Law Sch. Alumni Assn. (pres. 1968), Wis. Conf. Chs. (pres. 1983-86). Democrat. Episcopalian. Avocations: canoeing, skindiving. Home: 145 Marston Ave Eau Claire WI 54701 Office: Diocese of Eau Claire 510 S Farwell Eau Claire WI 54701

WANZEK, JOSEPH M., JR., insurance company executive; b. Clinton, Iowa, Feb. 12, 1951; s. Joseph Anthony and Mildred (Boehmer) W.; m. Joan Maureen Daly, July 21, 1973; 1 child, Joseph Matthew. BS, Iowa State U., 1973. Programmer Hawkeye-Security Ins., Des Moines, 1973-76, lead programmer, 1976-80, sr. programmer, 1980-81, data base adminstr., 1981-84, asst. programming supr., 1984-86, programming mgr. and asst. v.p., 1986—. Automation advisor fin. com. St. Pius X Ch., Urbandale, Iowa, 1983-85. Mem. Assn. Systems Mgmt. (student advisor 1984-85), Assn. Inst. for Cert. Computer Profls. Roman Catholic. Home: 8805 Hammontree Circle Des Moines IA 50322-1410 Office: Hawkeye-Security Ins 1017 Walnut Des Moines IA 50309

WAPP, MICHAEL ARTHUR, insurance executive; b. Seneca, Kans., July 12, 1951; s. Arthur Aloysious and Mary Elizabeth (Gose) W.; m. Sally Jo Koehn, June 14, 1980; children: Kimberly Jo, Christine Marie. BBA, Washburn U., Topeka, 1973. Staff Kans. Ins. Dept., Topeka, 1973-76; mgr. A&H div. Nebr. Ins. Dept., Lincoln, 1976-79; compliance coordinator Life Investors Ins. Co., Cedar Rapids, Iowa, 1979-81; adminstrv. mgr. annuities Life Investors Ins. Co., Cedar Rapids, 1981-86, v.p. adminstrn. annuity div., 1986—. Mem. Bldg. Com. King Of Kings Luth. Ch., Cedar Rapids, 1986. Fellow Life Mgmt. Inst.; mem. Am. Soc. CLU's, Cedar Rapids CLU, Nat. Mgmt. Assn. (v.p. planning Cedar Rapids Met. chpt. 1986-87, pres. elect. 1987-88). Republican. Lutheran. Avocations: sports, hunting, fishing, collecting baseball cards. Office: Life Investors Ins Co Am 4333 Edgewood Rd NE Cedar Rapids IA 52499

WARD, ALICE MARIE, civic worker; b. New London, Ohio; d. Clyde Eugene and Daiwy (White) W. BA, Ohio Wesleyan U., 1932. Sec., asst. treas. C.E. Ward Co., New London, 1937-72. Composer songs In the Swim, 1959, Tennis for Everyone, 1963, I Hear a Bird Singing, 1963. Recipient Rotary Community Service award, 1975; named to Ohio Wesleyan Sports Hall of Fame, 1977. Mem. New London Bus. and Profl. Women's Club (pres. 1967-68, 72—), U.S. Lawn Tennis Assn., Mortar Board, Alpha Xi Delta. Republican. Methodist. Clubs: Medalist, Southwood Tennis. Home: 139 E Main St New London OH 44851

WARD, ANTHONY GILES, futures and options exchange executive; b. Bloomington, Ill., July 16, 1938; s. William V. and Leone J. (Costigan) W.; B.S. in Polit. Sci., Loyola U., Chgo., 1961; postgrad. Sch. Bus., U. Chgo., 1967-68; m. Diane J. Anstett, Jan. 9, 1965; children—Joseph M., Daniel S., Kevin P., Christopher B. Mgmt. asst., sales asst., sales mgr., group sales mgr., mktg. mgr. data communications, Ill. Bell, Chgo., 1965-69; cons. Fry Cons., Chgo., 1969-72; cons., assoc., mng. assoc. Booz, Allen & Hamilton, Chgo., 1972-78; v.p. Space/Mgmt. Programs, Chgo., 1978-83; sr. v.p. ops. Chgo. Merc. Exchange, 1983—. Mem. Businessmen for Loyola U. Served with U.S. Army, 1962-64. Mem. Futures Industry Assn. (bd. dirs. ops. div. Chgo. chpt.). Roman Catholic. Clubs: River, Univ. (Chgo.). Home: 1231 Lake St Libertyville IL 60048 Office: Chgo Merc Exchange Center 30 S Wacker Dr Chicago IL 60606

WARD, CARL DONALD, management consultant, educator; b. Louisa, Ky., Feb. 18, 1950; s. Tansy Bud and Juanita Maye (Ferguson) W. BS in Social Work, Rio Grande (Ohio) Coll., 1974. Cert. in sociology and visual art edn. Dir. Greater Lima (Ohio) Bus. Assn., 1979-80; founder Exec. 200, Inc., Lima, 1982-83; instr. Lima Edn. Ctr., 1983—; cons. CETA, Lima and Columbus, Ohio, 1974. Author catalog Always in Good Taste for Exec. 200 Inc., 1982. Courthouse named in his honor Hancock County Hist. Soc., 1975. Mem. Ohio Edn. Assn. Home: 1613 Patton Dr Lima OH 45805

WARD, CHESTER VIRGIL, banker; b. Wood River, Ill., Dec. 2, 1949; s. Martin Wesley and Bernadine Fay (Behrer) W.; m. Melinda Jo Temperly, Oct. 6, 1973; 1 child, Meredith. Student Bradley U., 1968-69; AA, Columbia Coll., 1984; BA magna cum laude, Columbia Coll., 1986. Mgr., Household Internat., Kansas City, Mo., 1971-76; asst. v.p. So. Ill. Bank, Fairview Heights, Ill., 1976-78; v.p. Bethalto Nat. Bank (Ill.) 1978-84; exec. v.p., chief exec. officer Cen. Bank of Glen Carbon, Ill., 1984—, dir., 1985—; pres., chief exec. officer, bd. dirs. Landmark Bank, Alton, Ill., 1987— . Bd. dirs. Piasa Bird council Boy Scouts Am., 1980-83, Bethalto Hist. Soc., 1980-83, Easter Seal Soc., Alton, Ill., 1983; mem. Glen Carbon Econ. Commn., 1985-86. Named Outstanding Young Man in Ill., Ill. Jaycees, 1982, Outstanding Young Man Am., U.S. Jaycees, 1983. Mem. Am. Inst. Banking (cert. 1979, 80), Ill. bankers Assn. (cert. 1980, 81, 83), So. Ill. Bank Officers, Bethalto C. of C. (dir. 1978-79, pres. 1979), Wood River C. of C. (dir. 1980-83, pres. 1982), Metro East C. of C. (dir. 1981-82), Edwardsville C. of C. (bd. dirs. 1985), Phi Theta Kappa. Methodist. Lodge: Rotary (bd. dirs. 1978-83, pres. 1982-83, gov's aide 1986, Bethalto). Home: 704 Euclid Pl Alton IL 62002 Office: Landmark Bank 2850 Adams Pkwy Alton IL 62002

WARD, DANIEL EDWARD, business executive; b. Kansas City, Mo., July 29, 1956; s. Edward Byrd and Dolores Mary (Dreier) W.; m. Leslie Marie Pruitt, Oct. 11, 1980; 1 child, Nicholas Robert. BA, U. Mo., 1978; MBA, Rockhurst Coll., 1984. With personnel dept. Western Forms, Inc., Kansas City, 1978-79, prodn. supr., 1979-80, cost acct., 1980, adminstrv. mgr., 1980-83, v.p. fin., 1983—. Bd. mgrs. YMCA, Kansas City, 1985-88. Roman Catholic. Club: Kansas City.

WARD, DANIEL P., justice Ill. Supreme Ct.; b. Chgo., Aug. 30, 1918; s. Patrick and Jane (Convery) W.; m. Marilyn Corleto, June 23, 1951; children—Mary Jane, John, Susan, Elizabeth. Student, St. Viator Coll., 1936-38; J.D., DePaul U., 1941, L.H.D., 1976; LL.D., John Marshall Law Sch., 1972. Bar: Ill. bar 1941. Asst. prof. law Southeastern U., 1941-42; pvt. practice law 1945-48; asst. U.S. atty. No. Dist. Ill., 1948- 54, chief criminal div., 1951-54; with Eardley & Ward, Chgo., 1954-55; dean DePaul U. Coll. Law, 1955-60, adj. prof. law, 1979—; states atty. Cook County, Ill., 1960-66; judge Supreme Ct. Ill., 1966—, chief justice, 1975-78; chmn. Ill. Cts. Commn., 1969-73. Served with AUS, 1942-45. Mem. Am. Fed., Ill., Chgo. bar assns. Roman Catholic. Office: Supreme Ct Ill Richard J Daley Center Chicago IL 60602

WARD, DAVID ALLISON, lawyer; b. Charleston, S.C., Sept. 28, 1951; s. Leslie A. and Leola J. (Erickson) W. BA in Math., So. Ill. U., 1973; MA in Econs., Western Ill. U., 1975; JD, Ill. Inst. Tech., Chgo.-Kent Coll. Law, 1983. Bar: Ill. 1983, U.S. Dist. Ct. (no. dist.) Ill. 1983, U.S. Tax Ct., U.S. Ct. Appeals (5th and 7th cirs.) 1986. Economist Office of Gov., Bur. of Budget, Springfield, Ill., 1975-79; exec. asst. to dir. Ill. Dept. Revenue, Springfield, 1979-80; dir. Ill. Local Govt. Fin. Study Commn., Chgo., 1980-81; assoc. Silets & Martin, Ltd., Chgo., 1983-87; ptnr. Ward & Metti, P.C., Chgo., 1987—; summer intern Office of Ill. Atty. Gen., Chgo., 1981; mem. of various govtl. coms., 1978-80. Contbr. articles to profl. jours. Mem. com. Oak Park Rep. Orgn., 1983-85. Pres.'s scholar So. Ill. U., 1969-73. Mem. ABA, Ill. State Bar Assn., Chgo. Bar Assn., Moot Court Soc., Omicron Delta Epsilon. Office: Ward & Metti PC 6571 N Avondale Chicago IL 60631

WARD, JACK DONALD, lawyer; b. Blue Island, Ill., Aug. 14, 1952; s. Sylvan Donald and Beatrice Dorrell (Stackhouse) W.; m. Sharmon Oaks, Nov. 21, 1973; children—Spencer, Julianna, Christopher, Brent, Stefani. B.S. summa cum laude in Acctg., Brigham Young U., 1975, J.D. cum laude, 1978. Bars: Ill. 1978, U.S. Dist. Ct. (no. dist.) Ill. 1979, U.S. Ct. Appeals (7th cir.) 1982, U.S. Supreme Ct. 1983. Assoc. Reno Zahm Law Firm, Rockford, Ill., 1978-82, ptnr., 1982—; speaker, chmn. Fed. Trial Bar seminars, N.D., Ill. Research asst.: Bogert on Trusts, 5th edit., 1978. Vol. missionary Ch. of Jesus Christ of Latter-Day Saints, Italy, 1971-73; mem. com. for today and tomorrow Rockford Meml. Hosp., 1980—; vice chmn. Bicentennial of Constitution com., N.D., Ill. Mem. ABA, Ill. Bar Assn., Winnebago County Bar Assn. (continuing legal edn. com.), Assn. Trial Lawyers Am., Fed. Trial Bar, Beta Gamma Sigma. Republican. Club: City of Rockford. Office: Reno Zahm Law Firm 1415 E State St Rockford IL 61108

WARD, JERRY WAYNE, health care systems manager; b. Mankato, Minn., Sept. 18, 1947; s. William Everett and Fern E. (Tyrell); m. Laura Marie Carpenter, May 11, 1968; children: Jennifer, John. BA, Mankato State U., 1975. CPA, Minn. Mgr. McGladrey Hendrickson & Co., Mpls., 1975-83; supr. regional health care Vol. Hosps. of Am., Irving, Tex., 1983—; sr. v.p. Intercare, Inc., Minnetonka, Minn., 1983—, Intercare Ventures, Minnetonka, 1984—, Vol. Hosps. Am. North Cen., Inc., Minnetonka, 1985—; bd. dirs. InterHome Care, Inc., Mankato, 1984—. Mem. Sci. Mus. Minn., St. Paul, 1986. Served with U.S. Army, 1969-71. Mem. Am. Soc. CPA's, Minn. Soc. CPA's, Health Care Fin. Mgrs., Acctg. Research Assn., Minn. Deer Hunters Assn., Am. Legion. Republican. Lutheran. Lodge: Eagles. Avocations: fishing, camping, gardening. Home: Rural Rt 2 Box 61 Harris MN 55032 Office: Vol Hosps Am North Cen Inc 9800 Bren Rd E Suite 444 Minnetonka MN 55343

WARD, JONATHAN THATCHER, engineer; b. Kansas City, Mo., July 21, 1953; s. Gerald Leslie and Sarah Elizabeth (Houck) W.; m. Mary Lou Brown, Mar. 15, 1981. BA in History, U. Kans., 1977, BS in Engring., 1983. Engr. AT&T, Kansas City, 1984—. Mem. Pi Tau Sigma. Democrat. Office: AT&T 777 N Blue Pkwy Lee's Summit MO 64063

WARD, LARRY S., audio systems company executive; b. Pittsfield, Ill., Aug. 9, 1955; s. E. Wayne and Carol Ann (Sutton) W.; m. Nancy Lynn Kearns; children: Amber, Alesha, Alex. Diploma, Pittsfield High Sch. Tech. dir. Sta. WSOY, Decatur, Ill., 1973-85; pres., owner Ward Sound, Inc., Decatur, 1977—; pres. Crosspoint, Inc., Decatur, Ward Devel. Co., Decatur; bd. dirs. Sta. WFRL, Inc., Decatur. Chmn. bd. United Bapt. Ch., Decatur. Named one of Outstanding Young Men of Am., 1984. Home: 2940 S Twin Bridge Rd Decatur IL 62521 Office: Ward Sound 5565 Rt 36 E Decatur IL 62521

WARD, MARILYNN ITALIANO, Spanish language educator; b. N.J., Oct. 2, 1942; d. Felix M. and Philomena (Verderosa) Italiano; m. Richard J. Ward, June 25, 1965; children: Christopher L., Craig R. BA, Mich. State U., 1963, MA, 1964; PhD, U. Colo., 1969. Cert. Spanish, English and remedial reading tchr., Ohio. Migrant tchr. Eastwood Schs., Pemberville, Ohio, 1979-84; Spanish and reading tchr. Woodmore Local Schs., Elmore, Ohio, 1984-86; asst. prof. Spanish Findlay (Ohio) Coll., 1986—; instr. Bowling Green (Ohio) State U., 1980. Mem. NEA, Tchrs. of English to Speakers of Other Languages, AAUW (edn. chmn. 1981-82, membership v.p. 1982-83), Delta Kappa Gamma, Sigma Delta Pi. Avocations: travel, yoga. Office: Findlay Coll BLMC 1000 N Main St Findlay OH 45840

WARD, PAUL HERBERT, JR., real estate executive; b. Niles, Mich., Oct. 13, 1948; s. Paul H. Sr. and Anna M. (Rossow) W.; m. Lynnette J. Farris, Dec. 31, 1971; children: Paul H. III, Charles Robert. BS, Ind. U., 1975; postgrad., Marion Coll., 1987—. Prin. Ward Realty, Kokomo, Ind., 1976. Mem. Nat. Assn. Realtors, Indiana Assn. Realtors (Honor Soc. 1982), Internat. Orgn. Real Estate Appraisers (Community Service award 1983). Home: 824 W Sycamore Kokomo IN 46901 Office: 1355 S Locke Kokomo IN 46902

WARD, RICHARD HURLEY, university administrator; b. N.Y.C., Sept. 2, 1939; s. Hurley and Anna C. (Mittasch) W.; children from a previous marriage: Jeanne M., Jonathan B.; m. Michelle Ward, June 19, 1987. BS, John Jay Coll. Criminal Justice, 1968; M in Crim., U. Calif.-Berkeley, 1969, D in Crim., 1971. Detective, N.Y.C. Police Dept., 1962-70; coordinator student activities John Jay Coll., N.Y.C., 1970-71, dean students, 1971-75, v.p., 1975-77; vice chancellor, prof. criminology U. Ill., Chgo., 1977—; U.S. del. People to People Citizen Ambassador Program in China, 1983; del. to China, Eisenhower Found., 1985; English lang. coordinator Internat. Course Higher Specialization Police Forces, Messina, Italy, 1981, 83, Madrid, 1984, course dir., 1982, 85; chmn. Joint Commn. on Criminology and Criminal Justice Edn. and Standards, 1975-80; vis. prof. Zagazig U., Egypt, Egyptian Police Acad., 1986; host, coordinator for Terrorism and Organized Crime Conf., U. Ill., 1986, 87; U.S. del., co-leader for police specialization Crime Prevention and Criminal Justice Deln. to China, 1984; team leader del. to Taiwan, 1985. Author: (with others) Police Robbery Control Manual, 1975; Introduction to Criminal Investigation, 1975, An Anti-Corruption Manual for Administrators in Law Enforcement, 1979; (with Robert McCormack) Quest for Quality, 1984; gen. editor Foundations of Criminal Justice, 46 vols., 1972-75; editor: (with Austin Fowler) Police and Law Enforcement, Vol. I, 1972; Police and Law Enforcement, Vol. II, 1975; The Terrorist Connection: A Pervasive Network; (newsletter) CJ Internat., 1985—; (with Harold Smith) International Terrorism: The Domestic Response.. Mem. Near West Side Community Conservation Council, 1982—; varsity baseball coach U. Ill., Chgo., 1980-82; varsity baseball coach John Jay Coll. Criminal Justice, N.Y.C., 1971-72. Served to cpl. USMC, 1957-61. Recipient Leonard Reisman award John Jay Coll. Criminal Justice, 1968, Alumni Achievement award, 1978; Richard McGee award U. Calif.-Berkeley Sch. Criminology, 1971; Justice Dept. fellow U. Calif.-Berkeley, 1968-69; Danforth Found. fellow, 1971. Mem. Acad. Criminal Justice Scis. (pres. 1977-78, Founder's award 1985), Am. Soc. Pub. Adminstrn., Internat. Assn. Chiefs of Police (chmn. edn. and tng. sect. 1974-75), Am. Assn. for Higher Edn., Am. Acad. for Profl. Law Enforcement (nat. bd. dirs. 1978-84), Sigma Delta Chi. Home: 918 S Bishop Chicago IL 60607 Office: U Ill at Chicago Box 6998 Chicago IL 60680

WARD, ROBERT VINCENT, advertising an public relations executive; b. Kansas City, Mo., May 30, 1931; s. Robert Lynn and Mary Christina (Bock) W.; m. Mary Susan Shaffer, Dec. 12, 1953; children: Robert Joseph, Timothy David, Michelle Suzanne, Thomas Vincent. AB in Polit. Sci. cum laude, Benedictine Coll., Atchison, Kans., 1953; postgrad., U. Mo., 1958; MBA with honors, Rockhurst Coll., 1980. Sales promotion mgr. Western Auto

Supply Co., Kansas City, 1955-67; dir. mktg. Burstein-Applebee, Inc., Kansas City, 1967-68; dir. circulation, mktg. Intertec Pub. Co., Kansas City, 1968-70; pub. relations, advt. dir. United Bus. Communications, Inc., Kansas City, 1970-73, United Telecommunications, Inc., Kansas City, 1973—; ptnr. Ward & Ward Mktg. Cons., Kansas City, 1962—; bd. dirs. Scott's Custom Frames; adj. faculty Sch. Mgmt. Rockhurst Coll., 1983—. Contbr. articles to profl. jours. Bd. dirs. Kansas City Ballet, 1980; mem. com. Kansas City Cultural Mall, 1980—. Served with U.S. Army, 1953-55. Named Hon. Fellow Truman Library, Independence, Mo., Nat. Direct Mktg. Writer of Yr., 1973, Pub. Relations Profl. of Yr., Kansas City, Mo., 1981. Mem. Am. Mgmt. Assn., Bus. and Profl. Advt. Assn. (internat. v.p. 1978), Kansas City Advt. Fedn., Accredited Pub. Relations Soc. Am. (pres. Kansas City chpt. 1978, nat. utilities sect. exec. com. 1980, 81), Direct Mktg. Writers Guild N.Y.C., Nat. Hist. Soc., Kansas City Conv. and Visitors Bur., Greater Kansas City C. of C. (com. nat. affairs 1977-78, sub.-com. chmn. edn. 1975). Roman Catholic. Club: Advt. and Mktg. Club of Kansas City. Lodge: KC. Avocations: classical music, flowers, model airplanes, woodworking. Home: 3861 Blue Ridge Blvd Independence MO 64052 Office: United Telecom 2330 Shawnee Mission Pkwy Westwood KS 66205

WARD, STEPHEN R(OSBOROUGH), manufacturers' representative; b. St. Louis, Mar. 1, 1948; s. Gershon Albert and Ruth Juanita (Rosborough) W.; m. Susan Lee Charlesworth, June 12, 1970; children—Adam Whitehall, Kathryn Lindsay. B.A., Hope Coll., 1970; M.B.A., Mich. State U., 1973. Mgr. Steak and Ale Restaurants Am. Inc., Atlanta, 1973-75; ptnr. Charlesworth-Imre Assocs., St. Louis, 1975-76, Charlesworth-Ward Assocs., St. Louis, 1977-78, Charlesworth-Ward-Rafferty Assocs., St. Louis, 1978-79; v.p. Charlesworth-Ward-Rafferty, Inc., St. Louis, 1979-82, pres., 1983-85, chmn. bd., 1983-85; pres., chmn. bd. Ward, Raffery & Jacobs, Inc., 1985—; dir. W, R & J Profit Sharing Plan and Trust. Served to capt. Air N.G., 1970-76. Mem. Illuminating Engring. Soc. N.Am., St. Louis Elec. Bd. Trade. Republican. Presbyterian. Club: Town and Country Racquet. Home: 1633 View Woods Dr Kirkwood MO 63122 Office: 130 W Monroe Ave Saint Louis MO 63122

WARD, WILLIAM EDWARD, museum exhibition designer; b. Cleve., Apr. 4, 1922; s. Edward and Lura Dell (Eckelberry) W.; B.S., Western Res. U., 1947, M.A., 1948; diploma Cleve. Inst. Art, 1947; postgrad. Columbia U., 1950; m. Evelyn Svec, Nov. 12, 1952; 1 dau., Pamela. Mem. staff edn., Oriental depts. Cleve. Mus. Art, 1947—, designer, 1957—, now chief designer; prof. calligraphy and watercolor Cleve. Inst. Art, 1960—, after 1960, now prof. cons. graphic and installation exhbn. Exhibited in numerous exhbns. including (with Evelyn Svec Ward) Oaxacan Inspirations: An Exhbn. of Collage and Watercolor, 1986; Cleve. Playhouse Gallery, 1984; designer George Gund Collection of Western Art Mus., 1972; Firemen's Meml., Cleve., sculpture design, 1968; designer ofcl. seals Case Western Res. U., also Sch. Medicine, 1969; curator Culcon exhbn. Masterpieces of World Art from Am. Museums, Tokyo and Kyoto, Japan, 1976; co-author (catalogue, exhibition) Folk Art of Oaxaca: The Ward Collection, Cleve. Inst. Art, 1987. Mem. Internat. Design Conf., Aspen, 1959—; mem. Fine Arts Adv. Com. City Cleve., 1966—; mem. mayor's com. for selection of ofcl. seal City of Cleve., 1973. Served with Terrain Intelligence, AUS, 1942-45; CBI. Recipient commn. award City Canvas competition Cleve. Area Arts Council, 1975. Mem. Cleve. Soc. Contemporary Art, Print Club Cleve. Club: Rowfant (Cleve.). Home: 27045 Solon Rd Solon OH 44139 Office: Cleve Mus Art 11150 E Boulevard Cleveland OH 44106

WARD, WILLIAM LESLIE, JR., insurance company executive; b. Kansas City, Mo., Jan. 23, 1936; s. William Leslie Sr. and Frances Helen (Johnson) W. AB, Harvard U., 1958. Stock broker Kansas City, 1960-64; various mgmt. positions Universal Underwriters Ins. Co., Kansas City, 1964-76, v.p., 1976—, also bd. dirs. Served to lt. USNR, 1958-60. Mem. Am. Soc. Personnel Adminstrn. Clubs: Harvard (Kansas City)(pres. 1968-70). Avocation: sailing, golf. Home: 9807 Woodland Ln Kansas City MO 64131 Office: Universal Underwriters Ins Co 5115 Oak St Kansas City MO 64112

WARD, WINDSOR EARL, marketing professional; b. Ionia, Mich., Dec. 30, 1939; s. Mason Somerville and Ida Virginia (Mulholland) W.; m. Barbara Louise Fusco, Sept. 26, 1964; children: Lisa Marie, Jennifer Lynn. BS, U.S. Mil. Acad., 1962. Commd. 2d lt. U.S. Army, 1962, advanced through grades to maj., 1968, resigned, 1970; internat. mktg. exec. def. contractor Cadillac Gage Co., Warren, Mich., 1973—. Mem. Assn. U.S. Army, Am. Def. Preparedness Assn., U.S. Armor Assn. Avocations: golf, sailing, skiing. Office: Cadillac Gage Textron PO Box 1027 Warren MI 48090

WARDEN, BRUCE LELAND, music publishing company executive; b. Beloit, Wis., July 14, 1939; s. Jack Leland and Violet Matelda (Sampson) W.; m. Judith Ann Guetschow, Sept. 10, 1960; children—Lea Ann, Wendy, Gina, Gary. Student U. Ill., 1957-59; B.S. in Tech., So. Ill. U., 1965; M.S. in Tech./Mgmt., No. Ill. U., 1970; postgrad. U. Ill., 1969-70. Cert. tchr., Ill. Tchr. Rockford (Ill.) pub. schs., 1965-70; with D.R. Johnson Cons. Engring. Co., 1966-67; pres. WGE Prodns., Rockford, 1968-82; v.p. Mark Allen Corp., Rockford, 1970-73; pres. Leland Investment Corp., Rockford, 1972-76; pres. Leland Constrn. Corp., Rockford, 1976—, Forest Hills Investment, Inc., Rockford, 1981—, WGE Record Co., 1967—, WGE Music Pub. Co., Rockford, 1979—, W.L. Bruce Engring. & Assoc. Inc., 1986 . Mem. ASCAP, Am. Fedn. Musicians, Iota Lambda Sigma. Mem. Evangelical Free Ch. Lodge: Lions (Rockford). Office: WGE Music Pub Corp 3311 Carefree St Rockford IL 61111

WARE, BEVERLY GISS, public health educator; b. Chelsea, Mass., June 30, 1933; d. Benjamin and Ruth (Taylor) Giss; m. Robert E. Mytinger, Feb. 19, 1961 (div. 1970); m. 2d, Richard Anderson Ware, Dec. 22, 1972; stepchildren—Alexander, Bradley, Patricia. Student Forsyth Sch. for Dental Hygiene, Boston, 1951-53; B.Ed., Boston U., 1955; M.P.H., U. Mich., 1957; Dr.P.H., UCLA, 1969. Registered dental hygienist, Mass., N.Y. Health educator Grand Rapids-Kent County (Mich.) Health Dept., 1957-59, Denver Dept. Health and Hosps., 1959, Santa Clara County Health Dept., San Jose, Calif., 1960-62; asst. in pub. health U. Hawaii, Honolulu, 1966-68; asst. prof. Calif. State U.-Northridge, 1969-70; asst. prof. U. Mich., Ann Arbor, 1970-76; cardiovascular risk intervention coordinator Ford Motor Co., Dearborn, Mich., 1976-77, corp. health edn. programs coordinator, 1977-87; pvt. practice cons., 1982—; cons. Nat. Cancer Inst., Nat. Heart Lung and Blood Inst.; trainer Am. Occupational Med. Assn., Nurse's Assn. Bd. dirs. Washtenaw County League for Planned Parenthood, 1973-76; bd. dirs., chmn. com. on environ. health Am. Lung Assn. Southeastern Mich., 1982-87; trustee Am. Heart Assn. Mich., 1986-87; med. adv. bd. Mich. Parkinson Found. Mem. Am. Pub. Health Assn., Soc. Pub. Health Edn., Pi Lambda Theta, Delta Omega. Democrat. Jewish. Club: Women's Economic. Contbr. articles to profl. jours. Home: 16 Haverhill Ct Ann Arbor MI 48105 Office: 900 Parklane Towers W Suite 900 Dearborn MI 48126

WARE, GEORGE HENRY, botanist; b. Avery, Okla., Apr. 27, 1924; s. Charles and Mildred (Eshelman) W.; B.S., U. Okla., 1945, M.S., 1948; Ph.D., U. Wis., 1955; m. June Marie Gleason, Dec. 21, 1955; children—David, Daniel, Patrick, John. Asst. prof. Northwestern State U. of La., Natchitoches, 1948-56, asso. prof., 1956-62, prof., 1962-67; dir. Conservation Sect., No. La. Supplementary Edn. Center, Natchitoches, 1967-68; dendrologist Morton Arboretum, Lisle, Ill., 1968—, adminstr. research group, 1976—, dir. Urban Vegetation Lab., 1986—; vis. prof. U. Okla., Norman, summers, 1957, 61, 63, 64; adj. prof. Western Ill. U., 1972—; mem. extension faculty George Williams Coll., Downers Grove, Ill., 1969-76, Nat. Coll. Edn., Evanston, Ill., 1972-76. Trustee nomination caucus Coll. of DuPage, Glen Ellyn, Ill., 1974-78; bd. dirs. Kane-DuPage Soil and Water Conservation Dist., 1969-81; pres. La. Acad. Scis., 1966-67; dir. La. State Sci. Fair, 1966. Served with USN, 1942-46. Mem. Ecol. Soc. Am., Soil Conservation Soc. Am., Southwestern Assn. Naturalists (treas. 1963-69), Internat. Soc. Arboriculture, Ill. Arborist Assn. (pres. 1987-88). Home: 23W 176 Indian Hill Dr Lisle IL 60532 Office: Morton Arboretum Lisle IL 60532

WARE, LUCILE MAHIEU, child psychiatrist, educator, researcher; b. Kansas City, Mo., Feb. 23, 1929; d. Robert Georges and Lucile (Bailey) Mahieu; m. Jean Andre Demonchaux, Sept. 4, 1958; children: Elisabeth (dec.), Catherine, Theodore. AB cum laude, Bryn Mawr Coll., 1949; MD, Columbia U., 1953. Diplomate Am. Bd. Psychiatry and Neurology, Am. Bd. Child Psychiatry. Staff psychiatrist, Children's Div. Menninger Found., Topeka, 1968—, dir. Presch. Day Treatment Ctr., 1972—; dir. admissions and diagnosis Children's Div. Menninger Found., 1974-75,77,78; cons. CMF Hosp., Topeka, 1975—, No. Topeka Head Start, 1976—, co-principle investigator, DHHS-NIMH (CPR) MH#39895, 1982-87; mem. faculty Karl Menninger Sch. of Psychiatry, Topeka, 1969—, Topeka Inst. for Psychoanalysis, 1974—; cons. C.F. Menninger Hosp. and Children's Hosp., Topeka, 1975—. Contbr. articles to profl. jours. Assoc. leader Campfire Girls, Topeka, 1968-72; bd. dirs. Dance Arts of Topeka, 1974-77; bd. dirs., founder Ballet Midwest, 1977—. Fellow Albert Einstein Coll. Med. N.Y.C., 1957-58, Seeley Fellow Menninger Found. Children's Div.; named Kenworthy Prof., Menninger Found., 1983-84. Fellow Am. Assn. Child and Adolescent Psychiatry; mem. Am. Psychiatric Assn., AMA. Club: Alliance Francaise (Topeka). Home: 1925 Wayne Topeka KS 66604 Office: Menninger Found Children's Div PO Box 829 Topeka KS 66601

WARKOCZESKI, LARRY STANLEY, lawyer, health care executive, consultant; b. Battle Creek, Mich., Dec. 17, 1951; s. Harold Stanley and Beverly Ann (Gorham) W.; m. Vicki Carol Mandernach, Aug. 31, 1979. B.S. summa cum laude, Western Mich. U., 1974; J.D., Valparaiso U., 1977; M.H.S.A., U. Mich., 1984. Bar: Mich. Adminstrv. asst. to chmn. bd. Alliance Foods, Inc., Coldwater, Mich., 1976-78, gen. counsel, dir. research and devel., 1978-80, v.p., 1979-80; asst. prof. law Eastern Ill. U., Charleston, 1980-82; strategic planner Sarah Bush Lincoln Health Ctr., Mattoon, Ill., 1981-82; atty., health care cons., Ypsilanti, Mich., 1982-84; assoc. Office of Bus. Devel., Catherine McAuley Health Ctr., 1984-85; v.p. corp. devel. Health Mgmt. Co., 1985-86; pres. and chief exec. officer Tech-Share, Inc., Ann Arbor, Mich., 1986—. Bd. dirs. Mich. Internat. Council, East Lansing, 1978-80; spl. agrl. policy advisor Am. Freedom from Hunger Found., Washington, 1978-79; chmn. Union City (Mich.) Village Police Commn., 1978-79, Democratic party, Branch City, Mich., 1980. Recipient Mich. Ho. of Reps. cert. Outstanding Citizenship, 1971. Mem. ABA, Mich. Bar Assn., Midwest Bus. Adminstrn. Assn., Health Care Forum. Address: 5159 Christine Dr Ann Arbor MI 48103

WARMS, LEON JAMES, retail executive; b. Phila., Dec. 6, 1920; s. Leon and Viola Regina (Ullman) W.; B.A. in Edn., Washington and Lee U., 1942; postgrad. U. Pa., 1942; m. Ruth Hanstein, Jan. 4, 1947. Jr. exec. trainee, buyer M.E. Blatt Co., Atlantic City, N.J., 1946-48; asst. to gen. mdse. mgr. Strouss, Youngstown, Ohio, 1948-49, div. mdse. mgr., 1949-58; div. mdse. mgr. Charles Livingstons, Youngstown, 1958-61; pres. The Clothes Tree, Youngstown, 1961—, also 3 other stores; instr. mktg. Rutgers U., 1946-47; instr. bus. adminstrn. Youngstown U., 1949-54. Served with USCGR, 1942-46. Mem. Better Bus. Bur., Youngstown C. of C., Kappa Phi Kappa, Zeta Beta Tau. Republican. Jewish. Club: Rotary. Home: 207 Gypsy Ln Youngstown OH 44504 Office: 570 Gypsy Ln Youngstown OH 44505

WARNE, RICHARD ARTHUR, pharmaceutical executive; b. Indpls., May 22, 1932; s. Allan Henderson and Esther Luvonne (Forkner) W.; m. Jane Leahy, Aug. 15, 1954; children: John, Kathy. BA, DePauw U., 1954; MBA, Indiana U., 1956. CPA, Ind. Asst. corp. controller Eli Lilly & Co., Indpls., 1972-79, corp. controller, 1979-82, v.p., controller, 1982-86, v.p. acctg. devel., gen. auditor, 1986—. Mem. Govt. Fiscal Policy Adv. Council, Indpls., 1983-86; chmn. adv. bd. Salvation Army of Indpls., 1986; chmn. YMCA of Greater Indpls., 1979. Recipient Outstanding Beta Alpha Psi Alumnus Award Ind. U., 1987, Others Award Salvation Army, 1987; named DePauw/Wabash Man of Yr., Indpls. Assn. Wabash Men, 1986. Mem. Am. Inst. CPA's, Ind. CPA Soc., Fin. Execs. Inst. (com. corp. reporting 1985—), Nat. Assn. Accts., Inst. Internal Auditors, Ind. U. Sch. Bus. Alumni Assn. (pres. exec. council 1986), DePauw U. Alumni Assn. (nat. pres. 1977), Beta Gamma Sigma, Beta Alpha Psi, Phi Beta Kappa. Republican. Episcopalian. Office: Eli Lilly and Co Lilly Corporate Ctr Indianapolis IN 46285

WARNECKER, WILLIAM JOSEPH, JR., personnel company owner; b. Balt., Apr. 26, 1942; s. William Joseph Sr. and Madeline Ruby (Elliott) W.; m. Marilynn L. Stanfield, Aug. 6, 1980 (div. Oct. 1982); 1 child, William Joseph III. Student, U. Wis., 1962-64. Mgr. dept. A & P Food Stores, Kansas City, Mo., 1965-69; exec. recruiter Sales Cons., Kansas City, 1969-71; salesman Foremost Foods, Kansas City, 1971-72; pres., owner, operator Sales Recruiters, Inc., Kansas City, 1972—. Author manual Sales Recruiters Inc. Consultant Training, 1976, producer, dir. video, 1978. Mem. Kansas City Assn. Employment Agys. (pres. 1976-77, 86—), Mo. Assn. Personnel Consultants (pres. 1978-79, 82-83, v.p. 1980-81, bd. dirs. 1984-85, lobbiest 1977, disting. service award 1985), Kansas City Assn. Personnel Consultants (chmn. 1984, pres. 1985-86, disting. service award 1983), Nat. Assn. Personnel Consultants (chmn. 1978-79, recipient service award 1978), Cert. Personnel Cons. Sorority, Kansas City C. of C. (pres.'s club 1976). Club: Hillcrest Country (Kansas City). Avocations: golf, tennis, bowling, pool, boating. Office: Sales Recruiters Inc 9229 Ward Pkwy Suite 265 Kansas City MO 64114

WARNER, ANDREW JAMES, controller; b. N.Y.C., July 25, 1948; s. Fred James and Natalie (Wolfensohn) W.; m. Mary Louise Bartlett, Aug. 5, 1972; children: Matthew, Stephen. BS in Acctg., NYU, 1970. CPA, Mich. Audit mgr. Troupe Kehoe Whitaeker, Kansas City, Mo., 1972-76; with Ford Motor Credit Co., Dearborn, Mich., 1976—, asst. controller, 1986—. Active Ward Presbyn. Ch., Livonia, Mich., 1980—. Mem. Am. Inst. CPA's. Home: 16834 Golfview Livonia MI 48154 Office: Ford Motor Credit Co American Rd Dearborn MI 48121

WARNER, BARRY ALLEN, osteopathic physician, endocrinologist; b. Wilkes-Barre, Pa., Mar. 27, 1952; s. John Robert and Elizabeth Caroline (Keller) W.; m. Evelyn Gladys Spruce, Sept. 16, 1978; children: Christina Lynn, David Allen, Elizabeth Joy. BS in Biology cum laude, Wilkes Coll., Wilkes-Barre, 1974; DO, Phila. Coll. Osteo. Medicine, 1978. Resident in internal medicine Harrisburg (Pa.) Hosp., 1978-80; fellow in endocrinology Milton S. Hershey Med. Ctr., Hershey, Pa., 1980-82; chief med. resident Pa. State U. Coll. Medicine, Hershey, 1982-83, instr. in medicine, 1982-83; asst. prof. medicine U. N.Mex. Coll. Medicine, Albuquerque, 1983-84; asst. prof. medicine Sch. Medicine Wright State U., Dayton, Ohio, 1984—; clin. asst. prof. endocrinology Coll. Osteo. Medicine, Ohio U., Athens, 1986—; cons. in diabetes VA Med. Ctr., Lebanon, Pa., 1980-81; dir. life support room VA Med. Ctr., Albuquerque, 1983-84; staff endocrinologist VA Med. Ctr., Dayton, 1984—; cons. endocrinology Wright Patterson AFB Med. Ctr., Dayton, 1984—. Contbr. articles to profl. jours. Mem. ACP, Christian Med. Soc., Endocrine Soc., Am. Fedn. Clin. Research, Am. Diabetes Assn. (bd. dirs. 1986), Ohio River Rd. Runners Assn., Ultra Marathon Cycling Assn. Republican. Avocations: cycling, running, basketball. Home: 8904 Deep Forest Ln Centerville OH 45459 Office: VA Med Ctr Med Service 111 4100 W 3d St Dayton OH 45428

WARNER, CHARLES WILLIAM, JR., real estate broker, developer; b. Columbus, Ohio, Apr. 11, 1928; s. Charles William and Elsie (Burns) W.; m. Marjorie Lucille Dillin, July 20, 1952; children—Belinda Mae, Charles William III. B.Mus., Ohio State U., 1951. With Don M. Casto Orgn., Columbus, Ohio, 1951-69; pres. Chuck Warner & Assocs., Columbus, 1969—. Chancel choir dir. Northwest United Meth. Ch., Columbus, 1963-75, Northwest Evang. Christian Ch., 1975—. Mem. Nat. Assn. Realtors, Ohio Assn. Realtors, Columbus Bd. Realtors, Mansfield Bd. Realtors, Am. Fedn. Musicians. Evangelical Christian. Office: Chuck Warner & Assocs 236 E Town St Columbus OH 43215

WARNER, DALE BRYAN, construction executive; b. St. Louis, Apr. 12, 1955; s. Gilbert and Anita L. (Greespoon) W. BA in Polit. Sci. and History, U. Kans., 1978; postgrad., U. Mo. Sch. Law, 1978-80. Contract adminstr. Brooks Erection & Constrn. Co., St. Louis, 1980-84, contract mgr., 1984-85; cons. St. Louis, 1985-86; contract specialist Sverdrup Corp., St. Louis, 1986—; cons. Continental Boiler Works, Inc., St. Louis, 1985—, Strange & Coleman, Inc., Granite City, Ill., 1985—. Mem. Campaign for Space Polit. Action Com., Bainbridge, Ga., 1980—, friends of scouting St. Louis Area Council Boy Scouts Am., 1986—. Mem. Nat. Assn. Purchasing Mgmt., Purchasing Mgmt. Assn. St. Louis, Planetary Soc., Pi Sigma Alpha. Republican. Office: Sverdrup Corp 801 N 11th Saint Louis MO 63101

WARNER, JAMES DANIEL, clergyman; b. Sheridan, Wyo., May 1, 1924; s. Stephan Daniel and Grace Margaret (Caple) W.; m. Barbara A. Wallgren, Sept. 6, 1952 (dec. 1957); m. Marcy Walk Swan, Feb. 8, 1960; children—Stephen, David, Cheryl, Mark, Kathryn, James, Tammy. B.S., Northwestern U., 1950; M.Div., Seabury Western Theol. Sem., 1953, D.D., 1977. Vicar St. James Ch., Mosinee, Wis., 1953-56; rector St. Paul's Ch., Marmette, Wis., 1956-60; asst. chaplain St. James Ch., U. Wichita, Kans., 1960-62; rector St. Stephen's Ch., Wichita, 1962-70, Trinity Ch., Oshkosh, Wis., 1970-77; bishop Diocese of Nebr., Omaha, 1977—; pres. St. Com., Diocese of Kans., 1966-68. Pres. Community Planning Council, Wichita, 1965-66, police chaplain several community social agencies. Served in USN, 1942-46, PTO. Episcopalian. Home: 64 Ginger Cove Valley NE 68064 Office: Episc Ch 200 North 62d Omaha NE 68132 *

WARNER, JOHN ANDREW, III, communications company executive; b. New Haven, Apr. 16, 1946; s. John A. Jr. and Josephine (Esposito) W.; m. Joyce Ellen Van Wagner, Jan. 30, 1971; children: Anita Grace, Andrew Martin. BS in Engring., Princeton U., 1968; MS, Northwestern U., 1971. Mgr. strategic planning Conrail, Phila., 1978-79, asst. to pres., 1979-81, dir. financing, 1981-82, asst. treas., 1982-86; treas. Mich. Bell. Telephone, Detroit, 1986—; cons., Phila., 1972-78. Served with U.S. Army, 1970-71. Mem. Fin. Execs. Inst. Home: 254 Lothrop Rd Grosse Pointe MI 48236 Office: Mich Bell Telephone Detroit MI 48226

WARNER, ROBERT MARK, archivist, historian, university dean; b. Montrose, Colo., June 28, 1927; s. Mark Thomas and Bertha Margaret (Rich) W.; m. Eleanor Jane Bullock, Aug. 21, 1954; children: Mark Steven, Jennifer Jane. Student, U. Denver, 1945; B.A., Muskingum Coll., 1949, LL.D. (hon.), 1981; M.A., U. Mich., 1953, Ph.D., 1958; H.H.D. (hon.), Westminster (Pa.) Coll., 1981; L.H.D. (hon.), DePaul U., 1983. Tchr. high sch. Montrose, Colo., 1949-50; lectr. dept. history U. Mich., 1958-66, asso. prof., 1966-71, prof., 1971—, prof. Sch. Library Sci., 1974—, dean Sch. Library Sci., 1985—; asst. in research Mich. Hist. Collections, 1953-57, asst. curator, 1957-61, asst. dir., 1961-66, dir., 1966-80; archivist of U.S. 1980-85; Mem. bd. visitors Sch. of Library Sci., Case Western Res. U., 1976-80, chmn., 1980-84; bd. visitors Maxwell Sch. Govt., Syracuse U., 1982—; chmn. Gerald R. Ford Presdl. Library Bldg. Com., 1977-79; bd. dirs., sec. Gerald R. Ford Found., 1987—; trustee Woodrow Wilson Internat. Center for Scholars, 1980-85, chmn. fellowship com., 1983-85; chmn. Nat. Hist. Publs. and Records Commn., 1980-85; mem. exec. com. Internat. Council on Archives, 1984—. Author: Chase S. Osborn, 1860-1949, 1960, Profile of a Profession, 1964, (with R. Bordin) The Modern Manuscript Library, 1966, (with C.W. Vanderhill) A Michigan Reader: 1865 to the Present, 1974, (with F. Blouin) Sources for the Study of Migration and Ethnicity, 1979. Served with U.S. Army, 1950-52. Fellow Soc. Am. Archivists; mem. Am. Hist. Assn. (council 1981-85), Orgn. Am. Historians, Am. Assn. State and Local History, Hist. Soc. Mich. (trustee 1960-66, v.p. 1972-73, pres. 1973-74), Soc. Am. Archivists (mem. council 1967-71, sec., exec. dir. 1971-73, v.p. 1974-75, pres. 1976-77), Am. Antiquarian Soc., Phi Alpha Theta. Presbyterian. Club: U. Mich. Research. Lodge: Rotary. Home: 1821 Coronada Dr Ann Arbor MI 48103 Office: U Mich Sch Library Sic Ann Arbor MI 48109

WARNER, SALLY, social services administrator; b. Tulsa, Dec. 26, 1939; d. John William Edward and Ina Mae (Tomlin) W. BA, Rollins Coll., 1960; diploma in Spanish Studies, Madrid, 1961. Lic. social worker, real estate agt. Teaching asst. Emory U., Atlanta, 1961-62; mgr. Fred E. Dick Corp., Winter Park, Fla., 1962-63; owner, mgr. Afortunada Farm, DeLand, Fla., 1962-68; social worker State of Mich., 1968-72; supr. Dept. Social Services State of Mich., Detroit, 1972—. Avocations: oil painting, sculpting.

WARNER, THOMAS PAUL, dentist, engineer; b. Detroit, Aug. 9, 1959; s. Byron Lloyd and Patricia Anne (Higgins) W.; m. Carol Diane Turansky, Aug. 9, 1985. BSEE, Mich. State U., 1982; DDS, U. Mich., 1986. Design engr. Engring. Tech., Troy, Mich., 1982-83; design engr. Pontiac Motor div. Gen. Motors Corp., 1983-84; gen. practice dentistry Rochester Hills, Mich., 1986—. Organizer swim for cancer Am. Cancer Soc., East Lansing, Mich., 1979. Mem. ADA, Mich. Dental Assn., Oakland County Dental Soc., Acad. Gen. Dentistry, Eta Kappa Nu. Republican. Roman Catholic. Avocations: skiing, waterskiing, scuba diving, golf, fishing. Home: 475 Baldwin Dr #209 Rochester MI 48063 Office: 930 W Avon Rd Suite 14 Rochester Hills MI 48063

WARNICK, TERRY LEE, marketing professional; b. Indpls., May 17, 1947; s. James William and Iona Mae (Hadley) W.; m. Virginia Lane Morrow, Mar. 2, 1974; 1 child, Heather Marie. BS in Mktg. with honors, Ind. U., Indpls., 1973, MBA, 1977. Sales rep. Cordage Paper Co., Indpls., 1967-71; sr. account exec. Walker Research Inc., Indpls., 1973-76; account exec. Ind. Bell Telephone, Indpls., 1976-81; dist. staff mgr. AT&T hdqrs., Morristown, N.J., 1981-86; dist. tech. mgr. AT&T, Southfield, Mich., 1986—. Served as sgt. USMC, 1967-71. Named one of Outstanding Young Men Am., 1980. Republican. Home: 4217 Gaylord Troy MI 48098 Office: AT&T 26957 Northwestern Hwy Southfield MI 48034

WARNKE, GLEN ALVIN, material management executive, consultant; b. St. Paul, Mar. 27, 1942; s. Alvin Gottlieb and Lucille Lydia (Mahle) W.; m. Susan Frieda Kottke, June 28, 1968; children—Dunoon, Lucy, Michael. Student U. Minn., 1962-70; B.A. in Bus. Adminstrn., Columbia Coll., 1976. Cert. practitioner inventory mgmt. Prodn. control analyst visual products 3M, St. Paul, 1968-70, prodn. control supr., Columbia, Mo., 1970-76, material control mgr. electronic products, Columbia, 1976-84, material control specialist staff mfg., St. Paul, 1984-87, material control mgr., SARNS, Inc./ 3M, Ann Arbor, Mich., 1987— ; cons. speaker Sch. Indsl. Engring., U. Mo., Columbia, 1975-77. Vice chmn. better bridges com. Boone County Ct., Columbia, 1979; dir., treas., v.p., pres. Boone County R-IV Sch. Bd., Hallsville, Mo., 1976-82; vice-chmn. Commn. on Role and Status of Women, Mo. East Conf., United Meth. Ch., St. Louis, 1980-84; pres., dir. central region Mo. Sch. Bds. Assn., Columbia, 1979-82. Served with USNR, 1963-68. Mem. Am. Prodn. and Inventory Control Soc. (pres. Mid-Mo. chpt. 1975-76). Republican. Methodist. Avocations: tennis; swimming; skiing; travel; home improvement. Office: SARNS Inc/3M 6200 Jackson Rd PO Box 1247 Ann Arbor MI 48106-1247

WARNKEN, PAULA NEUMAN, university library director, educator; b. La Crosse, Wis., Mar. 11, 1948; d. David M. and Gladys F. (Glickman) Neuman; m. Clifford H. Warnken, Sept. 12, 1970; children: Devin A., Jonathan D. BA, U. Wis., 1970; MLS, Kent (Ohio) State U., 1980; M of Edn. and Personnel Tng. and Devel., Xavier U., 1985. Pub. service librarian Ohio U., Zanesville, 1976-80; head reader services Xavier U., Cin., 1980-84, dir. univ. libraries, 1984—, adj. instr. English, 1983—. Mem. ALA, Acad. Library Assn. Ohio (pres. 1985-86). Office: Xavier Univ McDonald Meml Library 3800 Victory Pkwy Cincinnati OH 45207

WARNOCK, STEPHEN RICHARD, manufacturing engineer; b. Richmond, Ind., June 6, 1953; s. Donald Harry and Phyllis Jean (Upchurch) W.; m. Carol Ann Bosmeny, Mar. 11, 1978 (div. May 1983); m. Darlene Mary Heinemann, Sept. 27, 1985. BS in Indsl. Tech., U. Wis., 1972; student, U. Wis. Stout, Menomonie, 1972-76. Mfg. mgmt. program trainee Gen. Electric Co., Syracuse, N.Y., 1977-79, Chgo., 1977-79; vendor quality engr. Gen. Electric Med. Systems, Waukesha, Wis., 1979-80, supr. final test, receiving inspection, 1980-86, mfg. engr., 1986—. Mem. Am. Power Boat Assn. (nat. champion 25 Super Stock Hydro award 1985, 1986, nat. hipoint champion 25 Super Stock Hydro award 1986, world champion 25 Super Stock Hydro award 1986), Badger State Outboard Assn. (sgt. at arms 1979-83, vice commodore 1983-84, commodore 1984-88). Avocations: power boat racing, skiing. Home and Office: Badger State Outboard Assn N49 W27721 S Courtland Circle Pewaukee WI 53072

WARREN, CLARENCE JAMES, oil company executive; b. Princeton, Ind., Nov. 12, 1946; s. Marvin James and Lydia Theresa (Judice) W. BA with honors, Western Ky. U., 1969. Sales exec. DuPont Glore Forgan, N.Y.C., 1971-72; supr. So. Triangle Oil Co., Mt. Carmel, Ill., 1972-76; pres. C.J. Warren Oil Co., Inc., Mt. Carmel, 1976—, also bd. dirs. Contbr. articles to profl. publs. Mem. zoning bd. City of Mt. Carmel, 1983—; mem. Rep. Presdl. Task Force, 1980—. Served to capt. USAR, 1969-71. Football scholar Western Ky. U., 1964-68. Mem. Ohio Oil and Gas Assn., Ill. Oil and Gas Assn., Ind. Oil and Gas Producers Assn. Methodist. Lodge: Elks. Home: 11 Skiles Dr Mount Carmel IL 62863 Office: 319 Market St Mount Carmel IL 62863

WARREN, JAMES CALDWELL, educator, physician; b. Oklahoma City, May 13, 1930; s. William Bl and Geraldyn (Caldwell) W.; m. Mary Ann Carpenter, Dec. 27, 1951 (div.); children—Richard Bruce, Jamie Ann, James Douglas, Allison Jean; m. Margaret Christian Dullum, Jan. 18, 1986. A.B., Wichita U., 1950; M.D., U. Kans., 1954; Ph.D., U. Neb., 1961. Intern U. Kans. Hosp., 1954-55; resident U. Nebr. Hosp., 1957-60; practice medicine specializing in obstetrics and gynecology Kansas City, Kans., 1961-71, St. Louis, 1971—; from asst. prof. to prof. obstetrics, gynecology and biochemistry U. Kans. Sch. Medicine, 1961-71; prof., head obstetrics and gynecology, prof. biochemistry Washington U. Sch. Medicine, St. Louis, 1971—; cons. NIH. Contbr. articles to profl. jours. Served to lt. M.C. USNR, 1955-57. Markle scholar med. sci., 1961. Fellow Am. Coll. Obstetricians and Gynecologists; mem. Am. Soc. Biol. Chemists, Soc. Gynecol. Investigation, Sigma Xi, Alpha Omega Alpha. Office: Washington U Sch Medicine Dept Ob-Gyn 4911 Barnes Hosp Plaza Saint Louis MO 63110

WARREN, JAMES EDWARD, information systems specialist; b. Detroit, Aug. 19, 1933; s. Frank Edward and Olive Hazel (Walker) W.; m. Helen Edna Hendricks, Dec. 30, 1961; 1 child, Charles. BS in Math., Roosevelt U., 1956. Programer Western Electric Co., Boston, Syracuse (N.Y.) and Montgomery (Ala.), 1956; systems analyst, programmer Western Electric Co., Cicero, Ill., 1959-72, 1977-78, Warrensville, Ill., 1972-77; applications planner Western Electric Co., Warrensville, 1978-79, data adminstr., 1979-80; data base adminstr. Western Electric (name changed to AT&T), Warrensville, 1980-87; also cons. various brs. Western Electric (name changed to AT&T). Contbr. articles to profl. jours. Mem. Assn. Computing Machinery. Democrat. Baptist. Clubs: Am. Postal Chess (Western Springs, Ill) (bus. mgr. 1969-87); Ill. Chess Assn. (Chgo.) (treas. 1980-84). Avocations: table tennis, music, mathematics. Home: PO Box 147 Western Springs IL 60558 Office: AT&T Network Systems PO Box 450 Warrenville IL 60555

WARREN, JANE ELIZABETH, clinical psychologist; b. Fargo, N.D., Oct. 16, 1948; d. Frederick Wallace and Lois Mae (Partenheimer) Quam; m. Daniel Craig Warren, May 24, 1975; children: Emily, Katherine. BA, N.D. State U., 1970; MA, U. Kans., 1973, PhD, 1976, M in Pub. Adminstrn., 1983. Lic. psychologist, Kans. Program dir. Youth Ctr. at Topeka, 1976-83; sr. psychologist Hennepin County Mental Health Ctr., Mpls., 1983-84; clin. psychologist St. Francis Med. Ctr., Wichita, Kans., 1984—; cons., lectr. Wichita div. Health Care Outreach, U. Kans. Sch. Medicine, 1985—. Sec. bd. dirs. Wichita Children's Theater, 1985-87. Mem. Am. Psychol. Assn., Kans. Psychol. Assn., Wichita Area Psychol. Assn., Kans. Correctional Assn. (pres. 1983-84), Phi Kappa Phi, Pi Sigma Alpha. Democrat. Lutheran. Office: St Francis Regional Med Ctr 929 N St Francis St Wichita KS 67214

WARREN, JANET ELAINE, librarian; b. Lindsborg, Kans., Sept. 19, 1951; d. Jack Edward and Mildred Louise (Ahlstedt) Beebe; m. Perry DeLong Warren, July 6, 1974; children—Emily Louise, Britta Elizabeth. Student Stephens Women's Coll., 1969-70; B.S. in Edn., Kans. U., 1973; M.L.S., Emporia State U., 1974. Asst. dir. Goodland Pub. Library (Kans.), 1974-75, library dir., 1975—. Sec., Sherman County Day Care Bd., Goodland, 1983; bd. dirs. Sherman County Jr. Miss Program, 1979. Mem. ALA, Kans. Library Assn., Mountain Plains Library Assn., AAUW. Republican. Club: Thalia Women's (pres. 1982-83). Home: Rt 1 PO Box 185 Goodland KS 67735 Office: Goodland Pub Library 8th & Broadway Goodland KS 67735

WARREN, KENNETH JOHN, transit system executive; b. Milw., Nov. 19, 1948; s. Robert Francis Warren and Marion Irene (Heyer) Simmons; m. Irene Ann Guthrie, Aug. 26, 1972; children: Nathan, Michael. BA in Math., Ripon Coll., 1969; MS in Urban and Regional Planning, U. Wis., 1973. Transportation planner Dane County Regional Planning Commn., Madison, Wis., 1971-73; exec. asst. Milw. Transp. Services, 1976-81; asst. mgr. ops. Milw. Transport Services, 1981-83, v.p., dir. ops., 1983—, also bd. dirs. Mem. design rev. bd. City of Wauwatosa, Wis. Mem. Inst. Transp. Engrs. (assoc.), Transp. Research Bd., Transp. Devel. Assn. (bd. dirs. 1984—), Transp. Employees Mut. Benefit Assn., Wis. Urban Transit Assn. (past chmn.). Office: Milw Transport Services Inc 1942 N 17th St Milwaukee WI 53205

WARREN, ROBERT WILLIS, judge; b. Raton, N.M., Aug. 30, 1925; s. George R. and Clara (Jolliffe) W.; m. Laverne D. Voagen, Aug. 23, 1947; children: Cheryl Lynn, Iver Eric, Gregg Alan, Treiva Mae, Lyle David, Tara Rae. B.A. magna cum laude, Macalester Coll., 1950; M.A., U. Minn., 1951; J.D., U. Wis., 1956; postgrad., Fgn. Service Inst., 1951-52. Bar: Wis. 1956. Fgn. affairs officer U.S. Dept. State, 1951-53; mem. firm Godfrey, Godfrey & Warren, Elkhorn, 1956-57; ptnr. firm Warren & Boltz, Attys., Green Bay, 1957-59, Smith, Will & Warren, 1965-69; asst. dist. atty. Brown County, Wis., 1959-61; dist. atty. 1961-65; mem. Wis. Senate, 1965-69; atty. gen. Wis., 1969-74; U.S. dist. judge Milw., 1974—; Mem. Gt. Lakes Commn., Wis. Council on Criminal Justice, Wis. Bd. Commrs. Pub. Lands, Four Lakes council Boy Scouts Am., Wis. Controlled Substances Bd., Wis. Council on Drug Abuse, Wis. State Urban Affairs. Served with AUS, 1943-46, ETO. Decorated Purple Heart. Mem. ABA, Wis. Bar Assn., Nat. Assn. Attys. Gen. (pres. 1973-74), Midwestern Conf. Attys. Gen., Wis. Dist. Attys. Assn., VFW, DAV. Republican. Methodist. Club: Optimist. Office: U S Dist Ct 364 U S Courthouse 517 E Wisconsin Ave Milwaukee WI 53202 *

WARRING, DOUGLAS FRANKLIN, education educator, program director; b. Braham, Minn., Aug. 16, 1949; s. Herbert Franklin and Maxine (Anderson) W.; m. Sally Winifred Latimer, July 25, 1981; children: Jana, Leah, Andrew. BA, Bethel Coll., 1971; MA in Teaching, Coll. St. Thomas, 1975; PhD, U. Minn., 1983. Lic. social studies tchr., secondary sch. prin., Minn. Instr. bus. Inver Hills Community Coll., Inver Grove Heights, Minn., 1980-83; instr. psychology Concordia Coll., St. Paul, 1983; asst. prof. psychology U. Minn., Waseca, 1982-84; asst. prof. edn. Coll. St. Thomas, St. Paul, 1984—, dir. tchr. edn., 1985—; bd. dirs. Project Fresh Start, Mpls., 1986—. Mem. Curriculum Com., Bloomington, Minn., 1985—, Planning, Evaluation and Reporting Com., Bloomington, 1985—. Served with USAR. Named one of Outstanding Young Men of Am., 1985. Mem. NEA, Am. Psychol. Assn., Am. Assn. Tchr. Edn. (exec. bd. Minn. chpt. 1985—), Minn. Edn. Assn., Minn. Community Edn. Assn., Am. Ednl. Research Assn., Minn. Human Relations Assn., Am. Legion., Met. Wrestling Officials Assn.(v.p. 1982-86). Home: 9625 13th Ave S Bloomington MN 55420 Office: Coll St Thomas 2115 Summit Ave Saint Paul MN 55105

WARRUM, RICHARD LINDAMOOD, neon design company executive, designer; b. Rushville, Ind., Sept. 18, 1942; s. Robert Paul and Mary Evelyn (Lindamood) W. B.F.A. cum laude, Sch. Chgo. Art Inst., 1965; M.A. in Art History, Ind. U., 1968. Installation designer and asst. registrar Ind. U. Art Mus., Bloomington, 1965-68; asst. to dir. Indianapolis Mus. Art, 1968-70, asst. dir., 1970-75, graphic designer, 1975-78; pres., chief exec. officer Neonics Inc/Light & Space Design, Chgo., 1978—. Editor and graphic designer mus. publs., 1970-75. Mem. Soc. of Friends. Office: Light & Space Design 3050 N Lincoln Chicago IL 60657

WARSCHEFSKY, THOMAS LEE, sales executive; b. Lansing, Mich., May 10, 1951; s. Leland A. and Joyce A. (Rumble) W.; m. Susan L. Linenger, June 19, 1976; 1 child, Thomas L. II. BS, Mich. State U., 1973. Asst. to pres. Ruminant Nitrogen, Okemos, Mich., 1973-76; regional sales dir. Conklin Co. Inc., Mpls., 1976—; mem. bldg. products com. Conklin Co., Mpls., 1986. Ch. dir. Billy Graham movie promotion, Lansing, 1985. Mem. Urethane Foam Contractors Assn. Republican. Avocations: running, cross country skiing, tennis, hunting, fishing. Home and Office: 2100 Noble Williamston MI 48895

WARSHAY, MARVIN, chemical engineer, educator; b. Tel Aviv, Jan. 12, 1934; s. Isaac and Miriam (Lepon) W.; m. Ieda Wilkof Bernstein, Feb. 11, 1962; children—Daniel, Susan, Alisa. B.Ch.E., Rensselaer Poly. Inst., 1955; M.S.Ch.E., Ill. Inst. Tech., Chgo., 1957, Ph.D.Ch.E., 1960. Research and devel. Esso Research & Engring. Co., Linden, N.J., 1960-62; basic researcher NASA Lewis Research Ctr., Cleve., 1962-75, mgr. fuel cell project office, 1975—; adj. prof. chem. engring. Cleve. State U., 1967—. Rep. NASA to Nat. Fuel Cell Coordination Group, 1982—. Mem. Cleve. Council on Soviet Anti-Semitism, Police Athletic League of Cleve., Zionist Orgn. Am. Recipient Tech. Utilization award NASA, 1976, dirs. recognition, 1978, 1980, Group Achievement award, 1984. Mem. Am. Inst. Chem. Engrs., Am. Chem. Soc., AAAS, Electrochem. Soc., Jewish Engrs. and Scientists Club, Sigma Xi, Tau Beta Pi, Phi Lambda Upsilon, Alpha Epsilon Pi. Democrat. Jewish. Lodge: B'nai B'rith. Editor: Progress in Batteries and Solar Cells, 1984, 87. Contbr. articles to profl. jours. Home: 3652 Latimore Rd Cleveland OH 44122 Office: 21000 Brookpark Rd Cleveland OH 44135

WARTH, CHARLES JOSEPH, executive trustee; b. Lexington, Ky., Sept. 3, 1922; s. Charles Joseph and Lorraine (Greene) W.; m. Jossphine Dockery, Oct. 10, 1951. Student, Air Force U., U. Ariz. lectr. in field. Enlisted U.S. Army Air Corps, 1942, advanced through grades to sgt., 1971; prisoner of war Germany, 1943; escape; retired USAF, 1971; governing trustee USAF Hist. Found., Washington, 1980—; exec. trustee 44th Heritage Meml. Group, Ellsworth AFB, S.D., 1986—. Reviewer of aviation and mil. books. Mem. Rep. Nat. Com. Mem. Air Force Assn. (pres. Ohio chpt.), 8th Air Force Hist. Soc. (pres.), RAF Escape Soc. Republican. Lodges: Toastmasters (pres.), Elks (exalted ruler 1982-83). Home: 5709 Walkerton Dr Clarendon Hills Cincinnati OH 45238

WARYJAS, RONALD JOSEPH, orthodontist, researcher; b. Chgo., June 12, 1951; s. Walter S. and Rose M. (Kajmowicz) W.; m. MaryAnn A. Kaminski, June 15, 1974; children: Julie Noelle, Bryan Ronald. BS magna cum laude, Loyola U., Chgo., 1973; DDS with honors, U. Ill., Chgo., 1977, MS in Orthodontics, 1985. Gen. practice dentistry Calumet City, Ill., 1977-85; practice dentistry specializing in orthodontics Calumet City, Hoffman Estates and Arlington Heights, Ill., 1985—. Editor, host (TV show) Health Mag., 1986—. Loyola scholar, 1969-73, J.A. Morrissey scholar, 1972-73, U. of I. Grad. Coll. fellow. Mem. ADA, Am. Assn. Orthodontists, Ill. Dental Soc., Chgo. Dental Soc. (com. chmn., br. corr. 1982-83), Ill. Soc. Orthodontics, Midwest Soc. Orthodontists (speakers bur. 1980-86). Avocations: cooking, carpentry, sports. Office: 552 Torrence Calumet City IL 60409

WASCHER, MICHAEL KONRAD, electrical engineer; b. Wuerzburg, Fed. Rep. Germany, Jan. 7, 1954; came to U.S., 1956; s. Konrad and Gisela Albine (Kempf) W.; m. Jean Margaret Pergola, May 10, 1986. BSEE, U. Akron, Ohio, 1977. Sr. engr. undersea systems Loral Systems Group (formerly Goodyear Areospace Corp.), Akron, 1977—. Office: Loral Systems Group Def Systems Div 1210 Massilon Rd Akron OH 44315

WASHBURN, HARRY L., coal company executive; b. Carlisle County, Ky., June 4, 1920; s. Arthur Stevens and Ruby (Biggs) W.; m. Gay Everman, Sept. 12, 1946; children—Kent L., Shannon, Lynn. B.S.E.M., U. Ky., 1950, M.S., 1951. Registered profl. engr., Ky., Ohio, Pa., W.Va., N.D. Project engr. Consolidation Coal Co., Library, Pa., 1951-55; preparation engr. Mountaineer Coal Co., Fairmont, W.Va., 1955-59, chief engr., 1959-63; preparation mgr. Clinchfield Coal Co., Dante, Va., 1963-66; v.p. N. Am. Coal Corp., Cleve., 1966-74, sr. v.p., 1974-83, pres., 1983—. Office: N Am Coal Corp 12800 Shaker Blvd Cleveland OH 44120 *

WASHBURN, WILLIAM OTHO, dentist; b. Gravois Mills, Mo., Sept. 14, 1920; s. William S. and Lottie C. (Webster) W.; m. Mary Jean Kilby, Oct. 1, 1944; children: Colon O., William R., John T., Jean L. Student, Cen. Meth. U., 1938-39; DDS, U. Mo., Kansas City, 1943. Gen. practice dentistry Versailles, Mo., 1946—. Served to lt. USN, 1943-46, PTO. Republican. Presbyterian. Avocations: golf, fishing. Home: 312 N Fisher Versailles MO 65084 Office: 201 S Monroe Versailles MO 65084

WASHBURNE, PETER JAMES, restaurateur; b. Bklyn., May 15, 1940; s. James Mortamer and Betty Louise (Ziegler) W.; married; children: Jeffrey, Paula. Student, Culinary Inst. Am., 1960-61. Chef mgr. Turtle Point Yacht Club, Florence, Ala., 1961-65; gen. mgr. Dividson Catering, Dearborn, Mich., 1965-66; exec. mgr. Szabo, Ara & Grayhound & Profet Co., 1965-68; chef., gen. mgr. Back 40 Restaurant, Decatur, Ind., 1975-78; owner Redwood Prime Rib and Crab Chalet, Angola, Ind., 1978—, Pepper Chip and Prime Restaurant, Angola, 1986—; with exec. sales div. Target Directories, Addison, Mich., 1987—. Inventor pepper chip, 1981; patentee portable work and display case. Served with U.S. Army, 1961-63. Mem. Wabash Jaycees (pres. 1976-77). Home: 412 Hilltop Dr Angola IN 46703 Office: Redwood Prime Rib & Crab Chalet Angola IN 46703

WASHER, ROBERT PAUL, construction company executive; b. Watertown, N.Y., Sept. 18, 1950; s. Robert Chapman and Alice (Bradshaw) W.; m. Deborah Marie Duerr, June 9, 1973; children: Jill Marie, Timothy Robert, Kyle David. BSCE, Clarkson Coll. Tech., 1972. Chief engr. Foreman Industries, Dayton, Ohio, 1976-81; various positions Turner Constrn. Co., Columbus, Ohio and Dayton, 1972-76; project engr. Columbus, 1981-84; chief purchasing agt. 1984-85; bus. devel. engr. Detroit, 1985-86; mgr. bus. devel. 1986—. Group chmn. sustaining membership drive Detroit council Boy Scouts Am., 1986. Mem. Constrn. Mgmt. Assn. Am. (Great Lakes chpt. v.p., pres. elect, membership chmn. 1987, pres. 1988), Engring. Soc. Detroit. Club: Farmington Soccer (bus. mgr. 1986—). Lodge: Optimists (sgt. at arms, membership chmn. 1987, v.p. 1987—, pres.-elect). Avocations: coaching, golf. Office: Turner Constrn Co 1800 Fisher Bldg Detroit MI 48202

WASHINGTON, HAROLD, mayor; b. Chgo., Apr. 15, 1922; s. Roy L. and Bertha (Jones) W. B.A., Roosevelt U., Chgo., 1949; J.D., Northwestern U., 1952. Bar: Ill. 1953. Asst. city prosecutor City of Chgo., 1954-58; arbitrator Ill. Indsl. Commn., 1960-64; mem. Ill. Ho. of Reps., Springfield, 1965-76, Ill. Senate, Springfield, 1976-80, 97th-98th Congresses from 1st Ill. Dist., 1981-83; mayor City of Chgo., 1983—. Vice pres. Ams. for Democratic Action; bd. dirs. Suburban So. Christian Leadership Conf.; founder, pres. Washington Youth and Community Orgn.; bd. dirs. Mid-South Mental Health Assn. Served with USAAF, 1942-46, PTO. Recipient numerous awards. Mem. Am. Vets. Assn., Cook County Bar Assn., Ill. Bar Assn., Nat. Bar Assn., NAACP, Urban League, Nu Beta Epsilon. Office: City Hall 5th Floor 121 N LaSalle St Chicago IL 60602 *

WASHINGTON, JOHN WILLIAM, obstetrician, gynecologist; b. Boston, Oct. 3, 1921; s. Lawrence Mitchell and Marion Louise (Underwood) W.; m. Glynn Lott, June 29, 1957; children: John, Byron. Student, Northeastern U., W.Va. State Coll., Yale U.; MD, Meharry Med. Sch., 1948. Diplomate Am. Bd. Ob-Gyn. Intern Harlem Hosp., N.Y.C., 1948-49; resident in ob-gyn Good Samaritan Hosp., Dayton, Ohio, 1954-56; resident in surgery VA Hosp., Pitts., 1956-57; obstetrician/gynecologist Reug, Herman & Kiefer, Detroit, 1957-58; practice medicine specializing in ob-gyn Dayton, 1958—; asst. clin. prof. ob-gyn Wright State U. Sch. Medicine, Dayton. Served to capt. Med. Service Corps, U.S. Army, 1952-54, Korea. Fellow: Am. Coll. Ob-Gyn. Episcopalian. Home: 849 Olympian Circle Dayton OH 45427 Office: 30 Apple St Dayton OH 45409

WASHINGTON, SONDRA KAYE, medical social worker; b. Omaha, Oct. 14, 1942; d. George Jackson and Mildred (Downs) McCain; m. Robert Frank Washington, Sept. 6, 1964; children: Salina Entoile, Coretta Patrice, Robert Frank. BA, Bishop Coll., 1964; MSW, Loyola U., Chgo., 1970. Case worker II Cook County Dept. Pub. Aid, Chgo., 1965-68; social worker Evang. Child Welfare Agy., Chgo., 1969-73; site dir., social worker New World Christian Ministries, Chgo., 1978-79; med. social worker Home Health Service Chgo. North, Inc., Chgo., 1979-86; pvt. practice as med. social worker Chgo., 1986—. Mem. Operation People United to Save Humanity, Chgo., 1986, NAACP, 1984-85. Mem. Nat. Assn. Social Workers (cert.), Ill. Social Workers in Home Health Care. Avocations: Sacred Concert singing, composing, Christian educating, sewing, reading. Home: 518 S 2d Ave Maywood IL 60153 Office: Home Health Service Chgo North Inc 33 W Grand Ave Chicago IL 60610

WASIK, ROBERT ANTHONY, manufacturing and retail executive; b. Detroit, Sept. 6, 1938; s. Edward and Alice (Prowicka) W.; m. Valerie Ann Sergi, July 5, 1958 (div. Aug. 1985); children: Robert Todd, Greg Scott, Laura Rene. BSME, Lawrence Sch. Tech., 1968. Engring. mgr. Hayes Albion Corp., Jackson, Mich., 1969-72; gen. mgr. OEM Maremont Corp., Chgo., 1972-79; pres., chief exec. officer Formed Tubes, Sturgis, Mich., 1979-80; pres. Grand Exhaust Systems Inc. div. Armada, Detroit, 1980—; bd. dirs. Armada, Grand Exhaust Systems, Grand Tubes Inc., Merlin Muffler & Brakes, Ring & Pinion Sales Inc. Chmn. March of Dimes, Jackson, 1970. Republican. Avocations: skiing, tennis, boating, fishing. Office: Armada 600 Buhl Bldg Detroit MI 48226

WASMUND, WILLIAM PATRICK, financial executive; b. Chgo., Nov. 14, 1947; s. William E. and Mary A. (Battaglia) W.; m. Joan E. Vana, Sept. 5, 1976; 1 child, William P. II. BS in Acctg., So. Ill. U., 1975; MS in Acctg., Roosevelt U., 1978. CPA, Ill. Controller Hertz Corp., Chgo., 1976-79; budget mgr. DePaul U., Chgo., 1979-82; controller Bell & Howell, Lincolnwood, Ill., 1982-83, TLK Advt., Chgo., 1984-86; pres. AFS & Assocs., Libertyville, Ill., 1987—. Treas. Police and Fire Review Bd., Addison, Ill., 1973-75. Served with USAF, 1965-69. Mem. Am. Inst. CPA's, Ill. CPA Soc., Ill. CPA Loop Forum Group. Republican. Home: 107 Fairfield Lindenhurst IL 60046

WASMUS, ROBERT THEODORE, minister; b. Columbus, Ohio, Oct. 3, 1933; s. Robert Brannon and Jean McMath (Rust) W.; m. Patricia Annette McCleany, May 25, 1962; children: William, Richard, Francis, Victoria and Vincent (twins). Student, Drake Bus. Coll., 1957-59. Ordained to ministry Ch. of Living Savior. Minister Ch. of the Living Savior, Grove City, Ohio, 1973—; active TV ministry, Columbus, Ohio, 1973—. Active Columbus Reps. Served as sgt. USAF, 1953-57. Republican. Avocations: boating, camping, swimming, skiing. Home and Office: 1586 Dyer Rd Grove City OH 43132

WASSELL, LOREN W., editorial administrator, writer; b. Chgo., July 15, 1948; s. H. W. and Bernice (Kramer) W.; m. Rhonda Rothballer, Sept. 29, 1979; 1 child, Courtney C. BA, Lakeland Coll., 1969; postgrad., Ill. Cen. Coll., 1981-83. Reporter, anchorman Stas. WXCL and WZRO, Peoria, Ill., 1970-73; reporter Journal Star, Peoria, Ill., 1973-82; publs. editor Cen. Ill. Light co., Peoria, Ill., 1982-84; exec. communications writer Caterpillar Tractor Co., Peoria, Ill., 1984-85; mgr. editorial services Monsanto Chem. Co., St. Louis, 1985—. Commr. Peoria Pub. Bldg. Commn., 1982-85; mem. communications com. St. Louis Council Girl Scouts U.S., 1986—, pub. relations com. Theatre Project Co., St. Louis, 1986—; guest lectr. Community Leadership Sch., 1981. Recipient Enterprise Reporting award Ill. Valley Press Club, 1974, Spot News Reporting award Ill. Valley Press Club, 1974. Mem. Internat. Assn. Bus. Communicators, Pub. Relations Soc. Am., Peoria Area C. of C. (sec., community improvement com., bus. expansion subcommittee 1984.). Avocations: reading, computer programming.

WASSENAR, CATHERINE LYNN, social worker; b. Hartford, Ind., June 13, 1957; d. Philip and Marietta (Elgersma) Van Wynen; m. Ronald Keith Wassenar, May 2, 1981; 1 child, Rachel Lynn, David Peter. BA in Sociology, Calvin Coll., 1980. Social service designee Carestoel Rehab. and Nursing Ctr., McHenry, Ill., 1980-81; med. social worker Oak Park (Ill.) Hosp., 1981-84; admissions rep. Calvin Coll., Grand Rapids, Mich., 1984—; utilization reviewer Quality Care Home Health Care Orgn., North Riverside, Ill., 1982—. Mem. bazaar com. Timothy Christian Sch., Elmhurst, Ill., 1986—. Mem. Myasthenia Gravis Found. Mem. Christian Ch. Club: Lily of the Valley (Elmhurst) (bd. dirs. 1983-85). Home and Office: 129 W Monroe Villa Park IL 60181

WASSERMAN, FREDERICK LOUIS, controller; b. Paterson, N.J., Nov. 24, 1939; s. Philip and Iris (Nankas) W.; m. Alisa Nan Glass, June 27, 1976; children: Alana, David. BS, Fairleigh Dickinson U., 1961. CPA, N.J., Ohio. Supervising sr. acct. Peat Marwick Mitchell and Co., N.Y.C., 1961-69; internal audit supr. J.C. Penney Co., Inc., N.Y.C., 1969-76, ins. acctg. mgr., 1976-81, acctg. mgr., 1981-86; v.p., controller J.C. Penney Casualty Ins. Co., Westerville, Ohio, 1986—. Mem. Am. Inst. CPA's, N.J. Soc. CPA's, N.Y. Soc. CPA's, Ohio Soc. CPA's. Home: 6912 Bonnie Brae Ln Worthington OH 43085

WASSERMAN, MARVIN, sales and marketing company executive; b. Bklyn., Feb. 16, 1931; s. William and Mary (Moskowitz) W.; m. Anita Strain, Jan. 1, 1956 (div. Aug. 1972); children: Steven, Neil, Mark; m. Mary M. McColgan, Aug. 7, 1981. AA, Glendale (Calif.) Coll., 1955; student, U. Calif. Los Angeles, 1964. Resident engr., sr. designer Pacific div. Bendix Corp., North Hollywood, Calif., 1955-62, sr. engr. systems div., Ann Arbor, Mich., 1962-64; configuration control coordinator Mich. div. Ling-Temco-Vought, Warren, 1964; sr. gen. engr. liaison Brown Engring. Co., Inc., Huntsville, Ala., 1964-66; sr. tech. asst. IBM Fed. Systems div. Space Systems Center, Huntsville, 1966-67; sr. engring. specialist ARINC Research Corp., Ridgecrest, Calif., 1967-68; prin. devel. engr. Honeywell, Inc., Marine Systems Center, West Covina, Calif., 1968-69; sr. value engr. Aerojet ElecTroSystems Co., Azusa, Calif., 1969-74; mgr. value engring. Byron Jackson Pump div. Borg Warner Corp., Vernon Calif., 1974-75; valve engr. Ingersoll Rand Co. Proto Tool Div., Fullerton, Calif., 1975-77; v.p. Orosico, Inc., 1976-77; account mgr. McGraw-Hill Pub. Co., Westminster, Calif., 1977-78, regional mgr. Mid-West/Can. region, Chgo., 1978-80; mktg. mgr. aerospace Pyle-Nat., Chgo., 1980; owner, chief exec. officer The Listening Post, 1981—; instr. Grad. Sch. Mgmt., UCLA Extension. Com. chmn.Tennessee Valley council Boy Scouts Am., 1966-67, mem. awards com., Ridgecrest, 1967-68, mem. spl. projects com., Cypress, Calif., 1969-71. Loaned exec. Jr. Achievement fund raising campaign, 1975. Served with USAF, 1951-52. Mem. Soc. Am. Value Engrs. (Editorial award 1966-67, Value Engr. of Yr. award 1967, nat. dir. 1967-71, pres. Orange County chpt. 1970-71, nat. v.p. S.W. region 1971-74), Am. Soc. Performance Improvement (gen. chmn. nat. conf. 1976, v.p. So. Calif. chpt.). Jewish.Contbr. articles to profl. jours. Home: 4555 El Monte Dr Saginaw MI 48603 Office: The Listening Post 716 Washington Ave Bay City MI 48708

WASYLYCIA-LEIS, (KLAZINA) JUDITH, provincial cabinet minister; b. Kitchener, Ont., Can., Aug. 10, 1951; d. Harry and Klazina (Nielsen) Wasylycia; m. Ronald Wayne Leis, Aug. 26, 1972; 1 child, Nicholas Henry. BA in Polit. Sci. and French with honors, U. Waterloo, Ont., Can., 1974; MA in Polit. Sci., Carlton U., Ottawa, Ont., 1976. Parliamentary intern House of Commons, Ottawa, Ont., Can., 1976-77; women's organizer Fed. New Dems., Ottawa, 1977-80; exec. asst. to leader New Dems., Ottawa, 1980-81; policy advisor Premier of Man., Winnipeg, Can., 1981-85; exec. dir. Man. Women's Directorate, Winnipeg, 1985-86; minister Man. Culture, Heritage and Recreation, Winnipeg, 1986—. Pres. Fed. New Dems., Ottawa, 1981-83. Home: 59 Bannerman Ave, Winnipeg, MB Canada R2W 0T1 Office: Ministry of Culture Heritage & Recreation, Legis Bldg Broadway Ave Room 141, Winnipeg, MB Canada R3C 0V8

WASZAK, EDWARD FRANK, chemical engineer, chemical company executive; b. East Chicago, Ill., Nov. 18, 1924; s. Frank Vincent and Clara Mary (Przystas) W.; m. Therese Frances Krysinski, Sept. 4, 1954; children: Mary Ellen, Michael Edward, Daniel Anthony. BS in Chem. Engring., Purdue U., 1949. Registered profl. engr., Ind. Research engr. Nalco Chem., Chgo., 1950-51; process engr. Am. Maize Products, Hammond, Ind., 1951-62; plant mgr. Morton Chem. div. Morton Thiokol, Inc., Chgo., 1962-75, dir. engring. Morton Chem. div., 1975-85, v.p. Morton Chem. div., 1985—. Served as cpl. U.S. Army, 1943-45, ETO. Mem. Am. Inst. Chem. Engrs., Nat. Assn. Profl. Engrs., Ill. Assn. Profl. Engrs., Western Soc. Engrs. Republican. Roman Catholic. Office: Morton Thiokol, Inc Morton Chem Div 333 W Wacker Dr Chicago IL 60606

WATERBURY, JACKSON DEWITT, marketing executive; b. Evanston, Ill., Feb. 4, 1937; s. Jackson D. and Eleanor (Barrows) W.; m. Suzanne Butler, Aug. 27, 1958 (div. Jan. 1970); children: Jackson D. III, Arthur Barrows; m. Lynn Hardin, Mar. 17, 1971 (div. July 1984); 1 child, Timothy Bradford; m. Carolyn Jenkins, Sept. 20, 1986. AB, Brown U., 1959. Account exec. D'Arcy Advt. Co., St. Louis, 1958-63, Batz-Hodgson-Neuwoehner, Inc., St. Louis, 1963-66; exec. v.p., sec. Lynch, Phillips & Waterbury, Inc., St. Louis, 1966-68; pres. Jackson Waterbury & Co., St. Louis, 1968-73; v.p., ptnr. Vinyard & Lee & Ptnrs., 1973-74; pres. Waterbury Inc., 1975-80, Bright Ideas, Inc., 1977-80; v.p./group supr. Batz-Hodgson-Neuwoehner, St. Louis, 1980-81; sr. v.p. Fawcett McDermott Cavanagh, Honolulu, 1981-82; pres. Waterbury Cons., 1982—; sr. v.p. planning & research Kenrick Advt., Inc., St. Louis, 1984-86; chmn. Pocket Guide Publs., Inc., Denver, 1986—; chmn. Mountain Sports Sales, Inc., Denver, 1987—; chmn. publicity U.S. Golf Assn. Open Championship, 1964; bd. dirs. River Cities Broadcasting Corp., Belleville, Ill., Mo. Motorcycle Assn., Strathalbyn Farms Club, Alice Blake Realtors, Arimo Distbrs., Children's Christmas. Football coach Mo. High Sch. All-Stars, 1966-67, St. Louis U., 1968-70; vice chmn. bd. dirs. Hawaii Soccer Assn., 1981-83. Mem. Ducks Unltd., Am. Motorcycle Assn., St. Louis Advt. Producers Assn. (steering com., negotiating com. 1977-80), Nat. Rifle Assn., Beta Theta Pi. Episcopalian. Clubs: Racquet, Strathalbyn Farms (bd. dirs.). Home: 118 N Bemiston Saint Louis MO 63105 Office: 7711 Carondelet #200 Saint Louis MO 63105

WATERFIELD, RICHARD DALLAS, bank executive, mortgage company executive; b. Ft. Wayne, Ind., Nov. 15, 1944; s. Richard Hobbs and Anne Kendrick (McGill) W.; m. Julie Ruth Rhinehart, July 6, 1968; children: Richard R., John R., Jill L. BA, Denison U., 1966; MBA, Northwestern U., 1968. V.p. Waterfield Mortgage, Ft. Wayne, 1972-76, exec. v.p., 1976-80, chmn., 1980—; chmn. Union Fed. Savs. Bank, Indpls., 1984—; bd. dirs. Ft. Wayne Nat. Bank, MSKTD Architects, Ft. Wayne. Bd. dirs. Ft. Wayne Downtown Coalition, 1980-83, Community Devel. Corp., 1978-84; mem. Mayors Task Force on Downtown Area, Ft. Wayne, 1985. Served as sgt. U.S. Army, 1968-74. Mem. Nat. Assn. Realtors, Young Pres. Orgn., Mortgage Bankers Assn., Ft. Wayne C. of C. (bd. dirs. 1985—). Presbyterian. Clubs: Ft. Wayne Country, Bus. Forum (dir. 1980, pres. 1981). Avocations: sports, travel. Office: Waterfield Mortgage Co 333 E Washington Blvd Fort Wayne IN 46802

WATERS, JAMES JOSEPH, accountant; b. Janesville, Wis., July 29, 1954; s. Donald S. and Dorris E. Waters. BBA, U. Wis., Eau Claire, 1976. CPA, Wis. Mem. staff, tax mgr. Williams, Young & Assocs., Madison, Wis., 1976-87; assoc. Friedman, Eisenstein, Raemer & Schwartz, Chgo., 1987—. Author, editor newsletter, 1981-86, newpaper column, 1986. Mem. Friends of WHA-TV, Madison, 1984, Friends of Civic Ctr., Madison, 1986. Mem. Am. Inst. CPA's, Wis. Inst. CPA's, CPA Assocs. Avocations: music, sports, theater, travel. Office: Friedman Eisenstein Raemer & Schwartz 401 N Michigan Ave Chicago IL 60611

WATERS, RICHARD, publishing company executive; b. Sterling, Mass., May 13, 1926; s. Sherman Hoar and Viola (Arnold) W.; m. June Hollweg Dorer, Aug. 27, 1949; children: Karl, Kurt, Kris. B.A., Hobart Coll., 1950, LL.D. hon., 1970; M.B.A., Harvard U., 1951. Assoc. acct. Hunter & Weldon, N.Y.C., 1953-55; exec. v.p., chief fin. officer Reader's Digest Assn., Pleasantville, N.Y., 1955-77; assoc. dean Harvard U. Bus. Sch., Boston, 1977-81; pres., chief exec. officer Sporting News, St. Louis, 1981—; trustee Manhattan Savs. Bank, N.Y.C. Trustee Hobart Coll., 1971—; trustee William Smith Coll., 1971—; regional v.p. Associated Industries N.Y. State, Albany, 1965-79; chmn. bd. Westchester Heart Assn., Port Chester, N.Y., 1975-76. Served as 1st lt. USN, 1944-46, PTO; served to 1st lt. USAF, 1951-53. Mem. Nat. Assn. Pub. Accts; mem Baseball Writers Assn. Am. Republican. Clubs: Old Warson Country; University (St. Louis); Sky (N.Y.C.); Ponte Vedra (Fla.). Home: 20 Somerset Downs Ladue MO 63124 Office: Sporting News Pub Co 1212 N Lindbergh Blvd Saint Louis MO 63132

WATERS, WAYNE ARTHUR, conference and travel service agency executive; b. Ft. Wayne, Ind., Mar. 9, 1929; s. Roy Edwin and Mary Catherine (Housel) W. m. Helen Marie Gump, Nov. 18, 1950; children: Bradley Wayne, Jeffry Scott, Ann Kathryn. Owner, mgr. Grain and Dairy Farm, Ft. Wayne, 1947-54; auto salesman Haynes & Potter, Auburn, Ind., 1956-58; asst. v.p. Lincoln Nat. Life, Ft. Wayne, 1958-83; pres. Conf. and Travel Services Inc., Ft. Wayne, 1983—; bd. dirs. Meeting World, 1979-81, 87. Contbr. articles to profl. jours. and mags. Named Boss of Yr., Am. Bus. Women. Assn., 1972. Mem. Soc. Co. Meeting Planners (bd. dirs. 1973-74, pres. 1975-76, Leadership award 1974), Ins. Conf. Planners (bd. dirs. 1979-81, pres. 1982), Am. Soc. Travel Agts., Soc. Incentive Travel Execs., Cruise Line Internat. Assn., Meeting Planners Internat., Ft. Wayne C. of C. (air service council 1984—, Small Bus. Person of Month 1984). Republican. Mem. Ch. of the Brethren. Clubs: Orchard Ridge Country (Ft. Wayne), Summit. Avocations: bowling, golf, tennis. Office: Conf and Travel Services Inc 1300 S Clinton Suite One Fort Wayne IN 46802

WATHAN, JOHN DAVID, professional baseball team manager; b. Cedar Rapids, Iowa, Oct. 4, 1949. Profl. baseball player Kansas City (Mo.) Royals, Am. League, 1976-84, mgr., 1987—. Office: Kansas City Royals PO Box 1969 Kansas City MO 64141 *

WATKINS, CURTIS WINTHROP, artist; b. Pontiac, Mich., Apr. 9, 1946; s. Robert James and Arvella Marquitta (Chenoweth) W.; student Ann Arbor Art Center, 1964-66, Kendall Sch. Design, 1966-68, Kraus Hypnosis Center, 1966, 70, Arons Ethical Hypnosis Tng. Center, 1977; m. Gayle Lynn Blom, Dec. 19, 1975; 1 dau., Darcy Ann. Illustrator, instr. Ann Arbor Art Center, 1969-71; owner, dir. Hypno-Art Research Center and Studio, Howell, Mich., 1971—; research on visualization process of subconscious by doing art work under hypnosis; lectr. hypnosis convs. and schs.; one-man shows include: LeVern's Gallery, 1969, Rackham Gallery, 1973, Hartland Gallery, 1974, Platt Gallery, 1975, Detroit Artists Guild Gallery, 1975, Golden Gallery, 1977, Cromaine Gallery, 1982, Driggett Gallery, 1982, Mill Gallery, 1983, Walnut Street Gallery, 1983, Merrill Gallery, 1986, Corbino Gallery, 1986; group shows include Mich. All-State Show, 1980, Mich. State Fine Arts Exhibit, 1980, Washington Internat., 1981, Lansing Art Gallery (Mich.), 1981, Capitol City Arts Show, 1981, Mich. Ann., 1981, Mich. Ann., 1982-83; bd. dirs. 9th Ann. Hartland Art Show, 1975, Livingston Arts and Crafts Assn., 1977-79, Hartland Art Council, 1974-78. Recipient numerous awards of excellence in art. Mem. Internat. Soc. Artists, Assn. Advance Ethical Hypnosis, Am. Assn. Profl. Hypnologists, Internat. Soc. Profl. Hypnosis, Internat. Platform Assn. Presbyterian. Home and Studio: 1749 Pinckney Rd Howell MI 48843

WATKINS, JANE AILEEN, music educator; b. Kirksville, Mo., Jan. 9, 1948; d. Eugene Wilson and Vera Faye (White) W. MusB, NE Mo. State U., 1970, MA in Aesthetics, 1975; EdS in Adult Edn., U. Mo., 1985. Jr. high vocal Lenihan Jr. High Sch., Marshalltown, Iowa, 1970-73; music and humanities instr. Marshalltown, Iowa, 1973-76; jr. highvocal Cen. Jr. High Sch., St. Louis, 1976-79; music instr. Riverview Gardens Sch. Dist., St. Louis, 1979—; pvt. piano tchr. various locations, 1959—. Mem. Nat. Assn. Humanities Edn., Music Educators Nat. Conf., Mo. Assn. Adult and Continuing Edn., Phi Delta Kappan, Sigma Alpha Iota. Democrat. Mem. Christian Ch. Lodge: Order of Eastern Star (organist 1976—). Avocation: piano and organ. Home: PO Box 425 Lancaster MO 63548

WATKINS, JOAN MARIE, osteopath, emergency physician; b. Anderson, Ind., Mar. 9, 1943; d. Curtis David and Dorothy Ruth (Beckett) W.; m. Stanley G. Nodvik, Dec. 25, 1969 (div. Apr. 1974). BS, West Liberty State Coll., 1965; Cert. of Grad. Phy. Therapy, Ohio State U., 1966; DO, Phila. Coll. Osteo., 1972; M of Health Professions Edn., U. Ill., Chgo., 1986. Diplomate Am. Bd. Emergency Medicine, Osteo. Nat. Bds. Emergency osteo. physician Cooper Med. Ctr., Camden, N.J., 1974-79, Shore Meml. Hosp., Somers Point, N.J., 1979-81, St. Francis Hosp., Blue Island, Ill., 1981-82; emergency osteo. physician Mercy Hosp. and Med. Ctr., Chgo., 1982—, dir. emergency ctr., 1984—. Fellow Am. Coll. Emergency Physicians. Avocations: sailing, needlework, swimming. Home: 505 N Lake Shore Dr #1509 Chicago IL 60611 Office: Mercy Hosp and Med Ctr 26th and King Dr Chicago IL 60616

WATKINS, JOHN BARR, III, pharmacologist, toxicologist, educator; b. Jacksonville, Fla., Apr. 25, 1953; s. John Barr and Ella Weems (Hawkins) W.; m. Jayne E. Schumacher. B.A. cum laude, Wake Forest U., 1975; M.S., U. Wis., 1977, Ph.D., 1979. Lab. asst. Methodist Hosp., Jacksonville, Fla., summers 1972-75; NIH trainee U. Wis. Sch. Pharmacy, Madison, 1975-79, U. Kasn. Med. Ctr., Kansas City, 1979-82; asst. prof. pharmacology and toxicology Ind. U. Sch. Medicine, Bloomington, 1982—. Marie Christine Kohler fellow U. Wis., 1978-79; Biomed. Research Support grantee, 1982-83; PMA Found. grantee, 1984-86; Am. Diabetes Assn. grantee 1985-86; diplomate Am. Bd. Toxicology. Mem. Am. Chem. Soc., Soc. Toxicology, Am. Soc. Pharmacology and Exptl. Therapeutics, Sigma Xi, Rho Chi. Republican. Presbyterian. Contbr. articles to profl. publs. Office: Ind Univ Med Scis Program Bloomington IN 47405

WATKINS, LLOYD IRION, university president; b. Cape Girardeau, Mo., Aug. 29, 1928; s. Herman Lloyd and Lydia Mina (Irion) W.; m. Mary Ellen Caudle, Aug. 14, 1949; children: John Lloyd, Joseph William, Robert Lawrence. B.Ed., Southeast Mo. State U., 1949; M.S., U. Wis., 1951, Ph.D., 1954; D.H., U. Dubuque, 1974; EdD (hon.), Srinakharinwirot U., Thailand, 1986. Tchr. Jackson (Mo.) High Sch., 1948-50; asst. prof. Moorhead State Coll., 1954-56; asso. prof., asst. to academic v.p. Ohio U., 1956-66; exec. v.p. Ida. State U., 1966-69; pres. Ia. Assn. Pvt. Colls. and Univs. Des Moines, 1969-73, West Tex. State U., 1973-77, Ill. State U., Normal, 1977—; dir. Champion Fed. Savs. and Loan Assn. Contbr. articles to profl. jours. Bd. dirs. Ill. State U. Found., Stevenson Lectr. Series; trustee Lincoln Acad., Mennonite Hosp. Coll. of Nursing. Recipient Baker grant for Research Ohio U., 1963, Alumni Merit award S.E. Mo. State U., 1978. Mem. McLean County C. of C. (dir.), Am. Assn. State Colls. and Univs., Internat. Assn. Univ. Pres. (chmn. N.Am. council), Kappa Delta Pi, Phi Delta Kappa, Phi Alpha Theta, Alpha Kappa Psi. Presbyterian. Lodge: Rotary. Home: 1000 W Gregory St Normal IL 61761 Office: Office of Pres Ill State U Normal IL 61761

WATKINS, PAUL BARNETT, transportation company executive; b. Kansas City, Mo., May 3, 1949; s. Barnett Turner and Kathryn Irene (Bremer) W.; m. Judy Jean Horn, June 15, 1971; children: Heather, Nathan, Zachary. BS, U.S. Mil. Acad., 1971; MBA, U. Wis., Oshkosh, 1982. Commd. 2d lt. U.S. Army, 1971, advanced through grades to capt., resigned, 1976; mgr. ops. Schnieder Transport Co., Green Bay, Wis., 1976-78, div. mgr. ops., 1978-79, area mgr. mktg., 1979-80, dir. mktg. staff, 1980-83; pres. Tran-Star, Inc., Waupaca, Wis., 1983—. Republican. Methodist. Avocations: flying, racquetball, reading. Home: PO Box 128 Iola WI 54945 Office: Tran-Star Inc PO Box 47 Waupaca WI 54981

WATKINS, RAY A., design engineer; b. Danville, Ill., Apr. 6, 1925; s. Harry Edwin and India Dale (MacMillan) W.; m. Jo Ann Beyer, Feb. 20, 1948; children: Warren, Edris, Paul, Patricia, Mark, Winifred, Chris Ellen, Matthew. BSME, Rose Hulman Inst. Tech., Terre Haute, Ind., 1950. Registered profl. engr., Ill. Sr. design engr. Pines Engring. Co., Inc., Aurora, Ill., 1951-60, tab dept. supr., 1960-63; mgr. engring. services Teledyne Pines, Aurora, 1963-68; product engr. Western Electric, Montgomery, Ill., 1968-71; design engr. AT&T Technologies, Inc., Lisle, Ill., 1971—; instr. Aurora U., 1965-67; tutor Joliet (Ill.) Pub. Schs., 1977—, cons. on handicapped, 1983—. Patentee in field. Hon. life mem. Ill. Congress PTA, Joliet, 1984—. Served with USN, 1943-46, PTO. Mem. Western Soc. Engrs., Ill. Soc. Profl. Engrs. Avocations: woodworking, photography. Home: 117 S Westlawn Ave Aurora IL 60506 Office: AT&T Technologies Dept 11NW501221 2600 Warrenville Rd Lisle IL 60532

WATNEY, WILLARD LYNN, geologist, researcher, administrator; b. Mason City, Iowa, Mar. 6, 1948; s. Willard Vincent and Lucille Mae (Radloff) W.; m. Karen Louise Amundson, Dec. 28, 1970; 1 child, Chris. A.A., No. Iowa Area Community Coll., 1968; B.S. with distinction, Iowa State U.-Ames, 1970, M.S., 1972; Ph.D., U. Kans., 1985. Petroleum geologist Chevron, U.S.A., New Orleans, 1972-76; research assoc. Kans. Geol. Survey, Lawrence, 1976-81, chief geologic investigations, 1981—, chief petroleum research section, 1987—; cons. petroleum geologist, Lawrence, 1981—; cons. Univs. Field Staff Internat., AID. lectr. Daqing Inst., People's Republic China; participant NATO Advanced Study Inst., Lucca, Italy, 1986. Contbr. articles to sci. jours. Mem. Am. Assn. Petroleum Geologists, Soc. Econ. Paleontologists and Mineralogists, Soc. Profl. Well Log Analysts, Soc. Petroleum Engrs., Kans. Geol. Soc., Phi Kappa Phi, Sigma Chi. Avocations: reading, water skiing; computer programming. Office: Kans Geol Survey 1930 Constant Ave Campus W Lawrence KS 66046

WATSON, ALBERT JOHN, podiatrist; b. Saginaw, Mich., Feb. 9, 1911; s. John Alexander Watson and Laura Bertha (Rainke) Shilling; m. Isabelle Louise Wilcox, May 19, 1934; children: Hallie Louise, Albert J.M. Student, Ferris State Coll., Big Rapid, Mich., 1930; D Surg. Chiropody cum laude, Ill. Coll. Chgo., 1932; D in Podiatric Medicine, Ill. Coll. of Podiatry, Chgo., 1962. Pvt. practice podiatry Saginaw, 1932-86; with Allied Health St. Mary Hosp., Saginaw, 1980—. Vice chmn. City Planning Commn., Saginaw, 1961; chmn. Pit and Balcony Theater, Saginaw, 1972, Salvation Army, Saginaw, 1982, Point Lookout Assocs., Au Gres., Mich., 1962; bd. dirs. First Congregational Ch., Saginaw, 1984; chmn. bd. and adminstr. St. Francis Home, Saginaw, 1984. Mem. Am. Podiatric Med. Assn., Mich. Podiatric Medicine Soc. (also northeastern Mich. div.), Kappa Phi, Alpha Gamma Kappa. Republican. Lodge: Elks. Avocations: photography, writing, gardening, home maintenance.

WATSON, ANDREW SAMUEL, physician, law educator; b. Highland Park, Mich., May 2, 1920; s. Andrew Nicol and Eva Arvel (Barnes) W.; m. Catherine Mary Osborne, Sept. 1942; children: Andrew Nicol, John Lewis, David Winfield, Steven; m. Joyce Lyne Goldstein, July 21, 1967. BS in Zoology, U. Mich., 1942; MD, Temple U., 1950, M in Med. Sci., 1954. Intern, U. Pa. Grad. Hosp., 1950-51; resident in psychiatry Temple U., Phila., 1951-54; spl. lectr. Sch. Social Work, Bryn Mawr Coll., 1955-59; mem. med. faculty U. Pa., 1954-59, law faculty, 1955-59; prof. psychiatry U. Mich., Ann Arbor, 1959-80, mem. law faculty, 1959—; pvt. practice medicine, specializing in psychiatry, Ann Arbor, 1959—. Mem. Mich. Law Enforcement and Criminal Justice Commn., 1968-72. Served to capt. Med. Service Corps, AUS, 1942-46. Recipient Issac Ray award Am. Psychiat. Assn., 1978. Mem. Am. Psychiat. Assn., Am. Coll. Psychiatry, ABA (assoc.). Democrat. Unitarian. Author: Psychiatry for Lawyers, rev. edit., 1978; The Lawyer in the Interviewing and Counseling Process, 1976; others. Home: 21 Ridgeway Ann Arbor MI 48104 Office: U Mich Law Sch 304 Hutchins Hall 621 S State St Ann Arbor MI 48109

WATSON, DALE ALAN, computer company executive, educator, consultant; b. DeKalb, Ill., Aug. 27, 1955; s. Wilferd Arthur and Faye Esther (Pillischafske) W.; m. Katherine Lillian Clyborne, May 14, 1977; 1 child, Scot Anthony. AS, Kishwaukee Coll., 1975; BS, No. Ill. U., 1977. Maintenance programmer DeKalb Agrl. Assn., 1976-77; systems programmer Ill. Bell Telephone Co., Chgo., 1977-78; specialist software Cincom Systems, Inc., Cin., 1978—; cons. Watson Cons., Cin., 1981—; instr. U. Cin., 1983-85. Mem. Mensa. Republican. Club: Apple-Siders (SIG coordinator 1984) (Cin.). Avocations: Apple computer programming, chess. Home: 3987 Bainbridge Dr Sharonville OH 45241 Office: Cincom Systems Inc 11499 Chester Rd Cincinnati OH 45246

WATSON, EVERETT DONALD, real estate developer, management consultant; b. Elgin, Ill., Jan. 26, 1931; s. Everett Glen and Helen (Knop) W.; m. Barbara Catlin, June 13, 1953; children: Barbara Lynn, Mark Everett. PhB, Ill. Wesleyan U., 1953; MBA, Ind. U., 1956. Chief quality control engr. Louis Allis Co. div. Litton Industries, Milw., 1956-59, mfg. supt., 1959-62, mgr. mfg. small motor div., 1962-65, mgr. mfg. medium motor div., 1965-66; plant mgr. Milw. Works, 1967-70; exec. v.p. House of Harmony, Inc., Reedsburg, Wis., 1970-71; pres. Everett D. Watson and Assocs., Milw., 1971—; mem. plant mgmt. adv. com. U. Wis., Milw., 1969, conf. leader exec. devel. program, 1968—. Assoc. campaign chmn. United fund of Greater Milw., 1965—; chmn. speakers bureau United Way, 1959—; pres. bd. dirs. Family Services Agy. Waukesha County; bd. dirs. Milw. County Health Assn.; chmn. troop com. Boy Scouts Am., 1976—, Ad Hoc Com. Prevention Mental Health Problems in Industry; listener Dial Now, Parents Help Line, Family Service Hot Line; pres. local Luth. Ch., 1959, chmn. bd. edn., 1969-75, chmn. bd. trustees, 1980-83, asst. exec. dir. 1983-85, chmn. bd. elders, 1985—. Served with AUS, 1953-55. Mem. Mental Health Assn. Wis. (bd. dirs., v.p. 1983—), Meta Found. (bd. dirs. 1970-73), Am. Soc. Tng. and Devel., Wis. Profl. Speakers Assn., Reach for Stars Agy. (bd. dirs. 1987). Home: 5952 Kurtz Rd Hales Corners WI 53130 Office: 1840 N Farwell Ave Suite 205 Milwaukee WI 53202

WATSON, IRA BENJAMIN, III, utilities executive; b. Winchester, Va., Jan. 17, 1949; s. Ira Benjamin Jr. and Nellie (Park) W.; m. Kathryn Jean, June 20, 1970; children: Louise Reames, Emily Kathryn, Tracy Lynn. BS Hampden-Sydney (Va.) Coll., 1971; postgrad. in acctg., U. Va., 1973-75. CPA. Dist. mgr. Blue Cross Blue Shield Va., Charlottesville, 1971-74; staff acct. Arthur Andersen & Co., Washington, 1975-77; mgr. settlements Continental Telephone, Dulles, Va., 1977-78; gen. acctg. mgr. Contel, Dulles, Va., 1978-80; asst. v.p. settlements Contel, Bakersfield, Calif., 1980-83; v.p. adminstrn. United Telephone, Overland Park, Kans., 1983-87. Mem. Am. Inst. CPA's, Va. Soc. CPA's, Kansas City C. of C. (state affairs com. 1986). Republican. Presbyterian. Club: Blue Hills Country. Avocations: golf, skiing, tennis. Office: United Telephone 6666 W 110 St Overland Park KS 66211

WATSON, JAMES RITZ, physician; b. Indpls., Aug. 29, 1950; s. Harry John and Josephine Elizabeth (Mangold) W.; m. Judith Ann Ford, Aug. 10, 1973; children: James R. Jr., Jennifer, Jill, Joan. BS summa cum laude, U. Notre Dame, 1968-72; MD, Ind. U., 1976. Diplomate Am. Bd. Family Practice. Resident in family practice F. Wayne, 1976-79; ptnr. Family Practice Ctr., Lafayette, Ind., 1982—. Served to maj. USAF, 1979-82. Mem. AMA, Am. Acad. Family Practice, Phi Beta Kappa. Roman Catholic. Lodge: KC. Avocations: racquetball, wood crafts. Office: Family Practice Ctr 2323 Ferry St Lafayette IN 47904

WATSON, LARRY GORDON, school psychologist; b. Amherst, Ohio, Aug. 7, 1957; s. Denver F. and Catherine M. (Wehrle) W.; m. Antoinette Marie Mihalic, Aug. 20, 1983. BS in Elem. Edn., Bowling Green (Ohio) State U., 1980; EdM in Sch. Counseling, Kent (Ohio) State U., 1984, EdS in Sch. Psychology, 1985. Tchr. Keystone Schs., LaGrange, Ohio, 1980-84; sch. psychologist Copley (Ohio)-Fairlawn Schs., 1985—. Mem. Nat. Assn. Sch. Psychologists, Ohio Sch. Psychologist Assn., Kent Akron Area Sch. Psychologists. Republican. Roman Catholic. Avocations: running, travel, boating, wood working. Home: 86 Ravenna St Hudson OH 44236 Office: Copley Fairlawn Schs 3797 Ridgewood Rd Copley OH 44321

WATSON, LELAND (LEE) HALE, theatrical lighting designer, educator, critic; b. Charleston, Ill., Feb. 18, 1926; s. Dallas V. and Hazel Emma (Dooley) W. B.A., State U. Iowa, 1948; M.F.A., Yale U., 1951. Instr. Utah State Agrl. Coll., Logan, 1948-49, Bklyn. Coll., 1952- 54; with CBS-TV, N.Y.C., 1951-55, Polakov Studio Design, N.Y.C., 1957-62; mem. faculty U. Houston, 1968-71; asst. prof. C.W. Post Coll., L.I.U., 1971-75; guest lectr. Syracuse (N.Y.) U., 1974-75; assoc. prof. Purdue U., 1975-81, prof., 1981—; guest lectr. Butler U., Indpls. Lighting designer, Cin. Ballet, 1977-80; lighting designer Broadway Productions, Diary of Anne Frank, View From the Bridge; off-Broadway prodns., The Blacks, Suddenly Last Summer; operas, N.Y.C., Houston, Phila., Balt., Vancouver, Wash., Milw., dance cos.; Seattle's World's Fair, 1962; 26 Broadway prodns., indsl. shows, Washington Arena.; co-author: Theatrical Lighting Practice, 1954; former columnist, sr. contbg. editor: Lighting Dimensions mag.; columnist Lighting Design and Application mag.; contbr. articles to mags. Served with AUS, 1944-45. Decorated Purple Heart; recipient Obie award for Machinal; rcipient Show Bus. award, 1959. Mem. United Scenic Artists, Internat. Alliance Theatrical and Stage Employees, U.S. Inst. Theatre Tech. (pres. 1980-82, Fellows award, Founders award 1982, Career Achievement award 1986), Soc. Brit. Theatre Designers, Internat. Assn. Lighting Designers, Am. Soc. Lighting Dirs., Illuminating Engring. Soc., Assn. Brit. Theatre Technicians, Canadian Soc. TV Lighting Dirs., Phi Beta Kappa. Methodist. Address: 2400 State St Lafayette IN 47905

WATSON, RALPH EDWARD, physician, educator; b. Cin., Apr. 4, 1948; s. John Sherman and Evelyn (Moore) W.; m. Demetra Rencher, Sept. 9, 1972; children: Ralph, Jr., Monifa. BS, Xavier U., 1970; MD, Mich. State U., 1976. Diplomate Am. Bd. Internal Medicine. Intern, U. Cin. Med. Ctr., 1976-77; resident in internal medicine U. Cin. Med. Ctr., 1977-79, asst. clin. prof., internal medicine, 1980—. Bd. dirs. Cin. chpt. Am. Cancer Soc. Mem. Nat. Med. Assn., Cin. Acad. Medicine, Ohio State Med. Assn., ACP, Am. Soc. Internal Medicine, Xavier U. Alumni Assn. Home: 684 Clinton Springs Ave Cincinnati OH 45229 Office: Bethesda Oak Profl Ctr 629 Oak St #606 Cincinnati OH 45206

WATSON, STEVEN PETER, candy and tobacco company executive; b. St. Paul, June 24, 1947; s. James Robert and Jeanne Elizabeth (Carson) W.; m. Jane Ellen McMahon, June 22, 1986. 1 child, Amanda Jane. Grad. high sch., Cambridge, Minn., 1965. V.p. sales Watson Candy and Tobacco Co., Cambridge, 1967—. Served with USAR, 1967-72. Methodist. Avocations: collecting antique firearms, hunting, fishing, scuba diving. Home: Rt 3 Box 253 Coldeswood Cambridge MN 55008 Office: Watson Candy Tobacco Co Inc South Hwy 65 Cambridge MN 55008

WATSON, W. MARK, accounting firm executive; b. Rochester, N.Y., July 23, 1950; s. Harvey Duane Watson and Eileen (Klos) Riordan; m. Lori Jean Henderson, Jan. 5, 1980; children: Lindsey, Lucy, Lorin. BS in Acctg., Marquette U., 1972. Staff acct. Deloitte Haskins & Sells, Rochester, N.Y., 1973-77; sr. cons. Deloitte Haskins & Sells, Cin., 1977-79, mgr., 1979-86, ptnr., 1986—. Chmn. bd. dirs. Hamilton County Spl. Olympics, 1986—; bd. dirs., mem. fin. com. Cerebral Palsy Services Ctr., Inc., Cin., 1987—. Mem. Am. Inst. CPA's, Healthcare Fin. Mgmt. Assn. (chmn. May Inst. program 1987—), Ohio Soc. CPA's, N.Y. State Soc. CPA's. Republican. Roman Catholic. Avocations: golf, outdoor activities, family. Home: 316 Harvard Ave Terrace Park OH 45174 Office: Deloitte Haskins & Sells 250 E 5th St Cincinnati OH 45202

WATSON, WILLIAM VERITY, orthopedic surgeon; b. Balt., May 17, 1946; s. Dennis W. and Alicemay (Whittier) W.; m. Vickie Kennedy, Sept. 4, 1971; 1 child, Ben. BA, Hamline U., 1969; MD, U. Minn., 1974. Intern Northwestern U., Chgo., 1974-75; surgeon Orthpaedic Clinic, Grank Forks, N.D., 1979-80; resident in orthopedics Mayo Clinic, Rochester, Minn., 1975-79; surgeon Orthopaedic Ctr., Sioux Falls, S.D., 1980-81; mem. staff McKenna Hosp., Sioux Falls, 1980—, Sioux Valley Hosp., Sioux Falls, 1980—; surgeon Orthopaedic & Sports Medicine Clinic, Sioux Falls, 1981—; mem. staff Sioux Ctr. (Iowa) Hosp., 1987—; cons. St. Mary's Hosp., Pierre, S.D., 1980-81, Brookings (S.D.) Hosp., 1981-86, Dell Rapids Hosp., S.D., 1986, Madison (S.D.) Hosp., 1987—. Fellow Am. Acad. Orthopaedic Surgeons; mem. AMA, Am. Coll. Sports Medicine, S.D. State Med. Assn. Office: Orthopaedic & Sports Medicine Clinic PC 301 S 9th Ave Suite 600 Sioux Falls SD 57105

WATT, WILLIAM JOHN, business consultant; b. Berwyn, Ill., Nov. 20, 1943; s. Lester John and Lorraine Jeanette (Shammo) W. Student, Ind. U., 1961-65. Writer, editor AP, Indpls., 1966-69; adminstrv. asst. Lt. Gov's Office, Ind., 1969-73; exec. asst. Gov. Otis Bowen, Ind., 1973-81; pres. Watt & Assocs., Indpls., 1981—; bd. dirs. Northeast-Midwest Inst., Washington; chmn. Ind. Toll Fin. Authority, Inpls., 1983—, White River Park Devel. Commn., 1982—; Ind. Econ. Devel. Council, Indpls., 1985—. Author: Bowen: The Years as Governor, 1981; editor: Indiana's Citizen Soldiers, 1980. Bd. dirs. Commn. for Downtown, Indpls., 1982—; treas. White River Park Found., Indpls., 1982—. Served to lt. col. USNG, 1966—. Mem. Co. Mil. Historians, Soc. Profl. Journalists, Am. Forestry Assn., The Nature Conservancy, Nat. Guard Assn. of the U.S. Republican. Methodist. Avocations: writing, reading, hiking. Office: Watt & Assocs 150 W Market St Indianapolis IN 46204

WATTENBERG, SHIRLEY HIER, social worker, educator; b. N.Y.C., June 24, 1922; d. Phillip and Ida Hier; m. Albert Wattenberg, Sept. 5, 1943; children: Beth, Jill, Nina. AB, Hunter Coll., 1942; MA, U. Chgo., 1945. Med. social worker Cook County Hosp., Chgo., 1945-47; instr., clin. researcher Harvard Sch. Pub. Health, Boston, 1954-58; caseworker, supr., acting dir. Family Service of Champaign (Ill.), 1959-66; asst. prof. Sch. Social Work, U. Ill., Champaign, 1966-72; assoc. prof. Coll. Medicine U. Ill., Champaign, 1973—; bd. dirs. East Cen. Ill. Health Systems Agy.; speaker numerous workshops and seminars. Contbr. numerous articles and book revs. to major publs. Active Family Service of Champaign, 1979—, bd. dirs. 1982—. Mem. Nat. Assn. Social Workers (local chairperson 1975-77, nat. bd. dirs. 1977-79, 1st v.p., 1981-82, chairperson program com. Ill. dist. 1981-82, state bd. dirs. 1982-83), Am. Assn. Marriage and Family Therapists, Council Social Work Edn., Am. Pub. Health Assn., Acad. Cert. Social Workers (chairperson competency cert. bd. 1984-85), LWV. Avocations: tennis, swimming. Home: 701 W Delaware Ave Urbana IL 61801 Office: Sch Social Sork U Ill Urbana IL 61801

WATTENBERG, WILLIAM WOLFF, psychologist, educator; b. N.Y.C., Jan. 5, 1911; s. Louis and Bella (Wolff) W.; m. Jean Arvey, July 25, 1942; children: Franklin A., David A. BS, CCNY, 1930; AM, Columbia U., 1932, PhD, 1936. Lic. psychologist, Mich. Instr. Northwestern U., Evanston, Ill., 1936-38; tchr. Chgo. Tchrs. Coll., 1938-46; assoc. supt. Detroit Pub. Schs., 1964-68; prof. Wayne State U., Detroit, 1946-79. Author: The Adolescent

Years, 1973; (with others) Mental Hygiene in Teaching, 1959. Chmn. monitoring commn. Detroit schs. desegregation case U.S. Dist. Ct., 1975-78; pres. Student Aid Found. Mich., Detroit, 1980-84. Served to maj. U.S. Army, 1942-45, ETO. Recipient Liberty Bell award Mich. Bar Assn., Detroit, 1964, faculty recognition award Bd. Govs. Wayne State U., 1977. Mem. Am. Psychol. Assn., Mich. Psychol. Assn., Retirees Assn. Wayne State U. Democrat. Jewish. Clubs: Torch (Detroit), Probus (award 1964). Avocations: fishing, stamp collecting. Home: 5861 Burnham Rd Bloomfield Hills MI 48013 Office: Wayne State U Retirees Assn 71-A E Ferry Detroit MI 48013

WATTS, GLENN HARVEY, university administrator; b. Racine, Wis., Mar. 18, 1943; s. Harvey Howard and Lillian (Chernick) W.; m. Jane Kundmann, July 31, 1965; children: Michael A., Carolyn L. BS, U. Wis., 1966, MA, 1969. Budget analyst Wis. Budget Office, Madison, 1966-68, chief edn. analyst, 1969-72; budget coordinator U. Wis., Madison, 1972-78, dir. budget and planning, 1978—; sec. Cable Communications Commn., Fitchburg, Wis., 1987. Mem. Nat. Assn. Coll. and Univ. Bus. Officers, Nat. Assn. State Budget Officers, Assn. Instl. Research. Home: 1849 Briarwood Ln Oregon WI 53575-2001 Office: U Wis Office Budget and Planning 171 Bascom Hall Madison WI 53706

WATTS, GORDON EDWARD, associate dean, consultant; b. Buffalo, Apr. 13, 1945; s. Albert Louis and Ella Elizabeth (Jeffrey) W.; m. Louise Marion Brown, July 29, 1967 (div. 1985); children: Keith, Kathleen. BA, U. Fla., 1967, MEd, 1968; PhD, U. Tex., 1976. Counselor SE Community Coll., Whiteville, N.C., 1968-71, dir. admissions, 1971-73; social sci. research assoc. U. Tex., Austin, 1973-75; dir. staff devel. Westark Community Coll., Ft. Smith, Ark., 1976-84, div. chairperson devel. edn., 1984-85; assoc. dean instruction Inver Hills Community Coll., Inver Grove Heights, Minn., 1985—; staff assoc. ACCTion Consortium, Pendleton, S.C., 1980—; adj. faculty mem. U. Ark., Fayetteville, 1979—; cons. Watts Enterprises, Ft. Smith, 1983—. Co-author: Staff Development in the Community College, 1978; contbr. articles to profl. jours. and chpts. in books. Bd. dirs. Mental Health Assn. Western Ark., Ft. Smith, 1977-83, pres., 1982; bd. dirs. Sebastian Count Aquatic Assn., Ft. Smith, 1983-84. Mem. Am. Soc. Tng. and Devel., Nat. Council Instruction Adminstrs., Nat. Assn. Devel. Edn., Nat. Council for Staff, Program and Orgn. Devel. (pres. 1982-83, v.p. 1981-82), Phi Delta Kappa. Lodge: Kiwanis. Avocations: running, writing, stamp collecting. Home: 405 10th Ave N Apt 305 South Saint Paul MN 55075 Office: Inver Hills Community Coll 8445 College Trail Inver Grove Heights MN 55075

WATTS, JOHN RANSFORD, university administrator; b. Boston, Feb. 9, 1930; s. Henry Fowler Ransford and Mary Marion (Macdonald) W.; m. Joyce Lannon, Dec. 2, 1975; 1 child, David Allister. AB, Boston Coll., 1950, MEd, 1965; MFA, Yale U., 1953; PhD, Union Grad. Sch., 1978.Prof., asst. dean Boston U., 1958-74; prof., dean of fine arts Calif. State U., Long Beach, 1974-79; dean and artistic dir. The Theatre Sch. (Goodman Sch. of Drama), DePaul U., Chgo., 1979—; gen. mgr. Boston Arts Festivals, 1955-64; adminstr. Arts Programs at Tanglewood, 1966-69; producing dir. Theatre Co. of Boston, 1973-75. Chmn., Mass. Council on Arts and Humanities, 1968-72; dir., v.p. Long Beach (Calif.) Pub. Corp. for the Arts, 1975-79; mem. theatre panel, Ill. Arts Council, 1981—. Served with U.S. Army, 1953-55. Mem. Mass. Ednl. Communications Commn., Am. Theatre Assn., Nat. Council on Arts in Edn., Met. Cultural Alliance, League Chgo. Theatres, Chgo. Internat. Theatre Festival, Phi Beta Kappa. Club: St. Botolph (Boston), Cliffdwellers (Chgo.). Office: De Paul U The Theatre Sch Goodman Sch of Drama 2135 N Kenmore Chicago IL 60614

WATTS, MICHAEL WAYNE, economist; b. Medicine Lodge, Ks., Nov. 3, 1950; s. Victor Wayne and Lois Melba (Anthony) W.; m. Julie Ann Bolotte, May 17, 1974; children: Jonathan Wayne, Matthew Michael. BA, La. State U., 1972, MA, 1974, PhD, 1978. Assoc. prof., dir. ctr. econ. edn. Krannert Ctr. Purdue U., West Lafayette, Ind., 1981—; cons. Joint Council on Econ. Edn., N.Y.C., 1978—, Agy. Instrnl. Tech., 1984-86; assoc. dir. Ind. Council for Econ. Edn., Purdue U., West Lafayette, 1981—. Mem. Nat. Assn. Econ. Educators (pres. 1986-87), Am. Econ. Assn., Nat. Council for Social Studies, Am. Ednl. Research Assn., So. Econ. Assn., Midwest Econ. Assn. Democrat. Home: 30 Merlin Ct Lafayette IN 47905 Office: Purdue U Krannert Ctr West Lafayette IN 47907

WATTS, ROBERT ALLAN, publisher, lawyer; b. Adrain, Mich., July 4, 1936; s. Richard P. and Florence (Hooker) W.; m. Emily Stipes, Aug. 30, 1958; children—Benjamin H., Edward S., Thomas J. Student DePauw U., 1954-55; B.A., U. Ill., 1959, J.D., 1961. Bar: Ill. 1961. Assoc. Stipes Publishing Co., Champaign, Ill., 1962-67, ptnr., editor, 1967—. Treas., Planned Parenthood, 1976-80; mem. Pres.'s Council, U. Ill.; pres. Friends of Library, U. Ill., 1980-82; bd. dirs. local United Way, 1972-81. Mem. Ill. Bar Assn., U. Ill. Found., Nat. Acad. Arts (bd. dirs. 1983—). Republican. Clubs: Champaign Country; Saugatuck Yacht (Douglas, Mich.); Lake Shore Bath & Tennis (pres. 1983-85). Home: 1009 W University St Champaign IL 61821 Office: Stipes Publishing Co 10-12 Chester St Champaign IL 61820

WATTS, WADE RILEY PATRICK, dentist; b. Kansas City, Mo., Mar. 12, 1932; s. John Lonly Watts and Frances Gail (Riley) Wickizer; m. Dorothy Mae Skelton, June 18, 1955; children: Marc Brian, Cynthia Ann Lyons, Brent Skelton. AB, Culver-Stockton Coll., 1954; DMD, Washington U., 1961. Practice dentistry St. Louis, 1961—; faculty Washington U. Sch. Dental Medicine, St. Louis, 1961-70, Sch. Medicine, 1965-71; ptnr. RW Investment Co., Frontenac, Mo., 1974—. Mem. ADA, Mo. Dental Assn., Greater St. Louis Dental Soc., U.S. Fencing Assn., U.S. Fencing Coaches Assn., SAR (sec., editor 1986—, pres. 1987), Am. Legion, U.S. Naval Inst. Served to sgt. U.S. Army, 1954-56. Republican. Presbyterian. Clubs: Westborough; Washington U. (St. Louis). Avocations: aviation history, fencing, militaria collector. Office: 717 N Lindbergh Frontenac MO 63131

WATZMAN, BARRY ALAN, software publisher; b. Steubenville, Ohio, May 26, 1949; s. Milton Irving and Betty Jane (Denmark) W.; m. Debra Jo Hayward, Aug. 14, 1985; 1 child, Jeffrey. BS in Elec. Engring., Rensselaer Poly. Inst., 1971; MBA, Emory U., 1973. Cert. computer programming and data processing. Staff cons. Kurt Salmon Assoc., Atlanta, 1973-75; sr. fin. analyst M. Lowenstein & Sons, Rock Hill, S.C., 1975-77; sr. systems analyst Boeing Computer Services, McLean, Va., 1977-78; product line dir. Zenith Data Systems, Benton Harbor, Mich., 1978-83; propr. Software Publ. Bus., Benton Harbor, 1983—. Patent Zenith Z-100 Series computer system, 1984; author computer software. Avocations: flying, electronics. Home and Office: 560 Sunset Rd Benton Harbor MI 49022-7142

WAWSZKIEWICZ, EDWARD JOHN, microbiology educator; b. North Smithfield, R.I., Feb. 10, 1933; s. Joseph Albert and Sophie Helen (Banas) W. AB, Harvard U., 1954; postgrad., Stanford U., 1954-55; PhD, U. Calif., Berkeley, 1961. Research asst. U. Calif., Berkeley, 1955-61; postdoctoral fellow Max-Planck Inst. fuer Zellchemie, Munich, 1961-63; resident research assoc. Argonne Nat. Lab., 1964-66; asst. mem. AMA Inst. Biomed. Research, 1967-70; assoc. prof. microbiology U. Ill. at Chgo., 1970—; cons. enologist Mt. Eden Vineyards, Saratoga, Calif., 1972-73; first plaintiff Wawszkiewicz et al. vs. U.S. Treasury Dept. et al. challenging adequacy of Bur. Alcohol, Tobacco and Firearms regulations on wine labelling; activist for accurate labeling of alcoholic beverages. Contbr. 12 sci. papers to prof. jours.; discovered compound, 1969; (with other researchers) chem. structure of water soluble anti-salmonellosis pacifarin, methyl pacifarinic acid, 1984; producer first Pinot noir vin gris in Am., 1972; producer, condr. winetasting program A Matter of Taste, Sta. KPFA-FM, 1959-60. Westinghouse Sci. Talent Search winner, 1950; Lilly predoctoral fellow, Stanford U., 1954-55; USPHS fellowship, 1961-63; NIH research grant, 1973-75. Fellow Am. Inst. Chemists; mem. AAAS, Am. Chem. Soc., Am. Inst. Biol. Scis., Am. Soc. Microbiology, N.Y. Acad. Scis., Soc. Wine Educators, Sigma Xi. Club: Chgo. Literary. Home: 1960 Lincoln Park W Apt 1809 Chicago IL 60614 Office: U Ill at Chgo Dept Microbiology PO Box 6998 Chicago IL 60614

WAX, DAVID M., orchestra executive. Gen. mgr. Minn. Symphony Orch. Office: Minnesota Orchestra 1111 Nicollet Mall Minneapolis MN 55403 *

WAY, CAROLYN STEHR, dentist; b. Pitts., May 14, 1954; d. Franz Josef and Dolores Carolyn (Knauss) Stehr; m. Richard Henry Way, Apr. 27, 1979. AS in Radiology Tech. summa cum laude, Robert Morris Coll., 1975; grad., U. Pitts., 1979; DDS, U. Detroit, 1983. Radiol. tech. Presbyn. U. Hosp., Pitts., 1975-79; gen. practice dentistry Douglas Faber Dental Ctr., Wayne, Mich., 1983-84, Pontiac (Mich.) Family Dental Ctr., 1984—; instr. radiology Doug Fraser Dental Ctr., 1984, Pontiac Family Dental Ctr., 1986. Recipient Russel F. Bunting award, 1983, Francis Vedder Soc. award, 1983. Mem. ADA, Am. Registry Radiol. Techs., Mich Dental Assn., Macomb County Dental Soc., Mich. Humane Soc. Avocations: weight-lifting, aerobics, sewing, golf, skiing. Home: 4965 Bruner Dr Sterling Heights MI 48310 also: 2161 Willow Leaf Dr Rochester Hills MI 48063

WAY, SCOTT ALAN, accountant; b. Wichita, Kans., July 15, 1950; s. Sheldon Luther and Corinne Elizabeth (Pierce) W.; m. Laura Elizabeth Oswald, Aug. 14, 1971 (div. Apr. 1986); children: Karen Marie, David Scott. BSBA, Kans. State U., 1973. CPA, Mo. Acct. Ernst & Whinney CPA's, Kansas City, Mo., 1973-77, McMullen & Co. CPA's, Kansas City, 1977-84; ptnr., owner Guttery & Way CPA's, Overland Park, Kans., 1985-86; mgr. bus. cons. Donnelly, Meiners & Jordan CPA's, Kansas City, Mo., 1986—. Treas. City of Countryside, Kans., 1985—. Mem. Am. Inst. CPA's, Mo. Soc. CPA's. Avocations: handball, fishing, boating, golf, skiing. Office: Donnelly Meiners & Jordan 9215 Ward Pkwy Kansas City MO 64114

WAYMAN, DAVID ANTHONY, publishing executive; b. Feb. 8, 1950. BA in Psychology, Sangamon State U., 1980; MA in Psychology, U. Tex., 1983. Devel. dir. Travis Assn., Austin, Tex., 1980-83; market researcher Support Services, Springfield, Ill., 1983-85; devel. dir. Illinois Issues mag., Springfield, 1985—; cons. Ill. Alcoholism and Drug Dependence Assn., 1976; Evaluator, expert witness various Springfield law firms., 1983-84. Organizer Pres. campaigns of Eugene McCarthy, Springfield, 1964, George McGovern, Chgo., 1968, John Anderson, Springfield, 1980; coach, organizer Ill. Spl. Olympics, Springfield and Chgo., 1971-73. Democrat. Avocations: tennis, racquetball, swimming. Office: Ill Issues Mag care of Sangamon State U Springfield IL 62794-9243

WAYNE, LISLE, II, plastic surgeon; b. N.Y.C., Feb. 9, 1936; s. Ernest Lisle and Teresa (Garcia) W.; m. Martha Weatherford, Jan. 4, 1964 (div. July 1977); children: Teresa, Lisle III; m. Sheila Ann Adkins, Sept. 10, 1977; children: Todd, Kyle. BS, Tex. A&M U., 1957; MD, U. Tenn., 1962. Diplomate Am. Bd. Plastic Surgery. Intern Jackson Meml. Hosp., Miami, Fla., 1962-63; resident in gen. surgery VA Hosp., Memphis, 1963-68; resident in plastic surgery Duke U. Med. Ctr., Durham, N.C., 1970-73; practice medicine specializing in plastic surgery Evansville, Ind., 1977—; chief plastic surgery Trover Clinic, Madisonville, Ky., 1973-77; clin. instr. U. Louisville Med. Sch., Ky., 1976-77; mem. staff St. Mary's Med. Ctr., Evansville, 1977—; deaconess Welborn Bapt. Hosp., Evansville, 1977—. Contbr. articles to profl. jours. Deaconess Welborn Bapt. Hosp., Evansville, 1977—. Served to maj. USAF, 1968-70. Fellow ACS; mem. AMA, Ind. Med. Soc., Vanderburgh County Med. Soc., Am. Soc. Plastic and Reconstructive Surgeons, Am. Soc. for Aesthetic Plastic Surgery, Southeastern Soc. for Plastic and Reconstructive Surgeons, Ohio Valley Soc. Plastic and Reconstructive Surgeons, Bowers Surgical Soc. Republican. Methodist. Club: Petroleum (Evansville). Avocations: stamp collecting, scuba diving. Home: 811 Blue Ridge Rd Evansville IN 47715 Office: Evansville Plastic Surgery Assoc 3700 Bellemeade Ave Suite 105 Evansville IN 47715

WAYNE, MARK, plastics manufacturing company executive; b. Detroit, Feb. 19, 1942; s. Harry and Helen (Bush) W.; m. Carolyn L. Clynick, May 23, 1964. Cert. in mech. engring., Lawrence Tech., 1971. Cert. profl. engr., Mich. Pres. Armax Robotics, Farmington Hills, Mich., 1979-82; v.p. mfg. and engring. Durakon Industries, Lapeer, Mich., 1982-85; pres. Zefflamb Industries, Fenton, Mich., 1982-85, Beaverton Plastics, Clare, Mich., 1983-85; pres., chief exec. officer Martec Plastics Inc., Fenton, 1985—; assoc. prof. robotics Mich. State U., Lansing, 1980. Patentee in field. Mem. exec. com. Gov.'s office State of Mich., 1986, dir. high tech. task force, 1984. Recipient Appreciation award Office Civil Def. State of Mich., 1979. Mem. Soc. Mech. Engrs. (sr.), Robotics Inst. Am. (bd. dirs. 1979-81), Sales and Mktg. Execs. Internat., Amateur Radio Club. Club: Cardinal Flying. Avocations: flying, amateur radio. Office: Martec Plastics Inc 3201 W Thompson Rd Fenton MI 48430

WAYTULONIS, ROBERT WILLIAM, federal agency supervisor; b. Almont, Mich., May 7, 1945; s. William Joseph and Sally Elvira (Rysberg) W.; m. Lisa Ellen Gutzmann, July 27, 1984; 1 child, Siri Ellen. Assoc. in Indsl. Tech., Port Huron (Mich.) Jr. Coll., 1965; BSME, Western Mich. U., 1972. Truck design engr. Clark Equipment Co., Battle Creek, Mich., 1972-75; mech. engr. Bur. of Mines, U.S. Dept. Interior, Mpls., 1976-80, supr. research, 1981—. Author publs. for Bur. of Mines (Publ. of Yr. 1984). Served with USN, 1967-71. Mem. Soc. Automotive Engrs. (author tech. series, 1979—), Soc. Mining Engrs. of AIME. Avocations: sailing, guitar, gardening.

WEAKLAND, REMBERT G., archbishop; b. Patton, Pa., Apr. 2, 1927; s. Basil and Mary (Kane) W. A.B., St. Vincent Coll., 1948; M.S. in Piano, Juilliard Sch. Music, N.Y.C.; grad. studies, Sch. Music, Columbia U., 1954-56; L.H.D., Duquesne U., 1964, Belmont Coll., 1964, Cath. U. Am., 1975, Cardinal Stritch Coll., Milw., 1978, St. Joseph's Coll., Rensselaer, Ind., 1979, Marquette U. Joined Benedictines, Roman Catholic Ch., 1945; ordained priest 1951; mem. faculty music dept. St. Vincent Coll., 1957-63, chmn., 1961-63, chancellor chmn. of bd. of Coll., 1963-67; elected co-adjutor archabbot 1963; abbot primate Benedictine Confederation, 1967-77; archbishop of Milw., 1977—. Mem. Ch. Music Assn. Am. (pres. 1964-66), Am. Guild Organists. Office: Archbishop Cousins Cath Ctr 3501 S Lake Dr PO Box 2018 Milwaukee WI 53201 *

WEAR, GARY DOUGLAS, public health official; b. Sycamore, Ill., Sept. 26, 1942; s. Marvin Walter Wear and Norma Eileen (Behler) Riske; m. Susan Kathleen Carlson, Mar. 17, 1967 (div.); 1 dau., Jennifer Sue; m. Patricia Anne Crawford, July 14, 1984. Student U.S. Naval Acad., 1963-66; A.S., Rock Valley Coll., 1968; B.A., Judson Coll., 1969; M.A., Western Mich. U., 1974. Quality control engr. Automatic Electric Co., Genoa, Ill., 1966-67; personnel mgr. Flexfab, Inc., Hastings, Mich., 1969-72; dir. Occupational Health Center, Kalamazoo, 1972-74; tng. dir. Mead Corp., Dayton, 1975-76; personnel and labor relations mgr. Office of Substance Abuse Services-Mich. Dept. Pub. Health, Lansing, 1976—; instr. Davenport Coll., Grand Rapids, 1977-79. Instr., ARC, Lansing, 1981-83. Served with USN, USMC, 1961-66. Alumni Assn. scholar, 1973; grantee: Nat. Inst. on Alcohol Abuse and Alcoholism, 1972-74, HHS, 1981. Mem. Profl. Assn. Diving Instrs. (master scuba diver trainer 1983), Internat. Personnel Mgmt. Assn., Mich. Pub. Employee Labor Relations Assn., Nat. Fresh Water Fishing Hall of Fame, Am. Legion, Mensa. Club: Capitol City Dive (Lansing). Home: 135 W Walnut St Hastings MI 49058 Office: Office Substance Abuse Services Mich Dept Pub Health 3 500 N Logan St Lansing MI 48909

WEATHERHEAD, ALBERT JOHN, III, business executive; b. Cleve., Feb. 17, 1925; s. Albert J. and Dorothy (Jones) W.; m. Celia Scott, Jan. 1, 1975; children: Dwight S., Michael H., Mary H. AB, Harvard U., 1950, postgrad., 1951. Prodn. mgr. Yale & Towne, Stamford, Conn., 1951-54, Blaw-Knox, Pitts., 1954-56; plant mgr. Weatherhead Co., Cleve., 1957-59, gen. mgr., 1959-61, v.p., gen. mgr., 1962-66, gen. sales mgr., 1962-63, v.p. mfg., 1964-66; v.p., dir. Weatherhead Co. of Can., Ltd. 1960-63, pres., chief exec. officer, dir., 1964-66; treas. Weatherchem Corp., 1971-82, pres., dir., 1971—; pres. Weatherhead Industries, 1987—, also bd. dirs., 1987—; bd. dirs. Weatherhead Co., Protane Corp., L.P.G. Leasing Corp., Leasepac Corp., Leasepac Can., Ltd., Creative Resources, Inc. Author: The New Age of Business, 1965. Mem. Harvard U. com. on univ. resources; trustee Case Western Res. U., mem. resources com., council on research involving human subjects, trustee Michelson-Morley Centennial Celebration, mem. Univ. Sch. alumni council, trustee Univ. Sch.; mem. vis. com. Ohio U., Athens, v.p. nat. adv. com. Rollins Coll., Winter Park, Fla.; adv. trustee Pinecrest Sch., Ft. Lauderdale, Fla.; mem. capital campaign steering com. Laurel Sch.; trustee Vocat. Guidance and Rehab. Services, Hwy. Safety Found., Arthritis Found.; v.p. Weatherhead Found.; bd. dirs. New Directions Inc., Glenwillow, Ohio; col. CAF. Served with USAAF, 1943-46. Mem. Am. Newcomen Soc., Beta Gamma Sigma (hon.). Clubs: Union (Cleve.); Country (Shaker Heights, Ohio); Ottawa Shooting (Freemont, Ohio); Ocean (Delray, Fla.); Everglades (Palm Beach, Fla.); Codrington (Oxford, Eng.). Home: 19601 Shelburne Rd Shaker Heights OH 44118 Office: 25700 Science Park Dr Beachwood OH 44122

WEATHERMAN, CHERYL LOUISE, school counselor; b. Danville, Ill., July 25, 1942; d. Elwood R. and Clara Louise (Cook) Endicott; m. William E. Weatherman, Aug. 16, 1964; 1 child, Lisa Dawn. BS, Indiana State U., 1964, MS, 1967. Lic. guidance counselor. Physical edn., social studies tchr. North Vermillion High Sch., Cayuga, Ind., 1964-66; physical edn., health tchr. Granville Wells High Sch., Jamestown, Ind., 1968-69; counselor, coach Franklin (Ind.) Community High Sch., 1974-85; guidance counselor Triton Cen. High School, Fairland, Ind., 1986—; college basketball officiating Ind. Bd. Women's Sports Officials, 1971-85; head basketball official Nat. Women's Jr. Coll. Tournament, 1976, 77. Editor: Ind. Coaches of Girl's Sports Assn. Newsletter, 1984-85. Mem. Ind. Adv. Council on Vocational Edn., Indpls., 1981-86. Selected to coach Ind. girl's all-star team, 1979, 82, Ind. All-Star Com., Vincennes, 1976; named Sagamore of the Wabash, Gov. of Ind., 1986. Mem. NEA, Ind. Assn. Coll. Admissions Counselors, Classroom Tchrs. Assn., Nat. Sports Officials Assn., Ind. Bd. Women Sports Officials (basketball chmn. 1971-87), Ind. Basketball Coaches Assn. (bd. dirs. 1980-85), Ind. High Sch. Athletics Assn. (girl's adv. bd. 1984-85), Ind. Coaches Girl's Sports Assn. (v.p. 1983-84, pres. 1984-85, editor newsletter 1984-85), Shelby County Relief Soc. (tchr.). Mormon. Avocations: reading, boating, handicrafts, woodworking. Home: 2105 W Jefferson St Franklin IN 46131

WEATHERSBY, JOSEPH BREWSTER, civil rights administration executive; b. Cin., Nov. 23, 1925; s. Albert and Gertrude (Renfro) W.; m. Louberta Gray, Oct. 28, 1950 (div. Oct. 13, 1980). B.B.A., Salmon P. Chase Coll., 1950; M.Div., Berkley Div. Sch., 1960. Ordained priest Episcopal Ch. Rector St. Mary's Episcopal Ch., Detroit, 1961-68, St. Clement's Episcopal Ch., Inkster, Mich., 1973-74; dir. Saginaw Urban Ministry, Mich., 1969-72, 74-75; dist. exec. Mich. Dept. Civil Rights, Saginaw, 1976-83; exec. recipient rights Mich. Dept. Mental Health, 1986—. Served with USMC, 1944-46, PTO. Mem. Alpha Phi Alpha. Democrat. Home: 48641-1-94 Service Dr Apt 310 Bldg 44 Belleville MI 48111

WEAVER, ARTHUR LAWRENCE, physician; b. Lincoln, Nebr., Sept. 3, 1936; s. Arthur J. and Harriet Elizabeth (Walt) W.; B.S. (Regents scholar) with distinction, U. Nebr., 1958; M.D., Northwestern U., 1962; M.S. in Medicine, U. Minn., 1966; m. JoAnn Versemann, July 6, 1980; children—Arthur Jensen, Anne Christine. Intern U. Mich. Hosps., Ann Arbor, 1962-63; resident Mayo Grad. Sch. Medicine, Rochester, Minn., 1963-66; practice medicine specializing in rheumatology and internal medicine, Lincoln, 1968—; mem. staff Bryan Meml. Hosp., chmn. dept. rheumatology, 1976-78, 82-85, vice-chief staff, 1984—; mem. courtesy staff St. Elizabeths Hosp., Lincoln Gen. Hosp.; mem. cons. staff VA Hosp.; chmn. Juvenile Rheumatoid Arthritis Clinic, 1970—; assoc. prof. dept. internal medicine U. Nebr., Omaha, 1976—; med. dir. Lincoln Benefit Life Ins. Co., Nebr., 1972—; mem. exam. bd. Nat. Assn. Retail Druggists; mem. adv. com. Coop. Systematic Studies in Rheumatic Diseases III. Bd. dirs. Nebr. chpt. Arthritis Found., 1969—; trustee U. Nebr. Found., 1974—. Served to capt., M.C., U.S. Army, 1966-68. Recipient Outstanding Nebraskan award U. Nebr., 1958, also C.W. Boucher award; Philip S. Hench award Rheumatology, Mayo Grad. Sch. Medicine, 1966; diplomate Am. Bd. Internal Medicine, Am. Bd. Rheumatology. Fellow A.C.P. (Nebr. council 1983—); mem. Am., Nebr. socs. of internal medicine, Am. Rheumatism Assn. (com. on rheumatologic practice 1983—, pres.-elect Central region 1983-84, pres. Central region 1984-85; exec. com. 1985—), Nebraska Rheumatism Assn., AMA, Nebr. Med. Assn., Lancaster County Med. Soc., Mayo Grad. Sch. Medicine Alumni Assn., Arthritis Health Professions Assn. (com. on practice 1984—), Nat. Soc. Clin. Rheumatology. Phi Beta Kappa, Sigma Xi, Alpha Omega Alpha, Pi Kappa Epsilon, Phi Rho Sigma. Republican. Presbyterian. Editorial bd. Nebr. Med. Jour., 1982—; contbr. articles to med. jours. Home: 4239 Calvert Pl Lincoln NE 68506 Office: 2121 S 56th St Lincoln NE 68506

WEAVER, BETTY MARIA, health science facility administrator; b. Ellisville, Ill., July 15, 1922; d. Ross Mitchell and Lola Anna (Jacobus) W. BEd, Western Ill. U., 1943; MBA, Ind. U., 1951. Sec. to chief Ill. State Water Survey, Urbana, 1949-50; asst. prof. mgmt. Ohio U., Athens, 1951-68; bus. mgr. Peoria (Ill.) Assn. for Retarded Citizens, 1970-77; dir. bus. services Graham Hosp., Canton, Ill., 1977—. Served with USNR, 1944-46. Methodist. Office: Graham Hosp Assn 210 W Walnut Canton IL 61520

WEAVER, CHARLES LYNDELL, JR., architect, consultant, hat company executive; b. Canonsburg, Pa., July 5, 1945; s. Charles Lyndell and Georgia Lavelle (Gardner) W.; m. Ruth Marguerite Uxa, Feb. 27, 1982; children: Charles Lyndell III, John Francis. B.Arch., Pa. State U., 1969; cert. in assoc. studies U. Florence (Italy), 1968. Registered architect, Pa., Md., Mo. With Celento & Edson, Canonsburg, Pa., part-time 1966-71; project architect Meyers & D'Aleo, Balt., 1971-76, corp. dir., v.p., 1974-76; ptnr. Borrow Assocs.-Developers, Balt., 1976-79, Crowley/Weaver Constrn. Mgmt., Balt., 1976-79; pvt. practice architecture, Balt., 1976-79; cons., project mgr. U. Md., college Park, 1979-80; corp. cons. architect Bank Bldg. & Equipment Corp., Am., St. Louis, 1980-83; dir. archtl. and engring. services Ladue Bldg. & Engring. Inc., St. Louis, 1983-84; v.p., sec. Graphic Products Corp.; vis. Alpha Rho Chi lectr. Pa. State U., 1983; panel mem. Assn. Univ. Architects Conv., 1983. Project bus. cons. Jr. Achievement, 1982-85; mem. cluster com., advisor Explorer Program, 1982-85. Recipient 5 brochure and graphic awards Nat. Assn. Indsl. Artists, 1973; 1st award Profl. Builder/Am. Plywood Assn., 1974; Honor award Balt. chpt. AIA, 1974; Better Homes and Gardens award Sensible Growth, Nat. Assn. Home Builders, 1975; winner Ridgely's Delight Competition, Balt., 1976. Mem. BBC Credit Union (bd. dirs. 1983-85), Vitruvius Alumni Assn., Penn State Alumni Assn., Alpha Rho Chi (nat. treas. 1980-82). Home and Office: 1318 Shenandoah Saint Louis MO 63104

WEAVER, DANIEL ROBERT, architect; b. Rochester, N.Y., Feb. 19, 1951; s. Robert Musser and Berneice (Sanders) W.; m. Elizabeth Katz, Aug. 3, 1974; children: Aaron Seth, Jenna Beth. BArch with honors, Kent State U., 1974. Registered architect, Ohio. Drafter, designer Page & Steele Architects, Toronto, Ont., Can., 1974-76; designer Cole Sherman Assocs., Toronto, 1976-77, Richard Jensen Assocs., Cleve., 1977-79; designer Clark & Post Architechts, Lorain, Ohio, 1979—, also bd. dirs. Mem. AIA, Architects' Soc. Ohio, Commerce & Industry Assn. of Elyria, Alpha Rho Chi. Avocations: wildlife conservation, photography. Home: 475 Whitman Blvd Elyria OH 44035 Office: Clark & Post Architects Inc 6125 S Broadway Lorain OH 44053

WEAVER, JAMES ELMER, accountant; b. Troy, Ind., May 31, 1947; s. Carl Adam and Loretta Martina (Maffenbeier) W.; m. Virlee Rose, Sept. 5, 1970; children: Chris, Matt, Scott. BS, Ind. State U., 1973. Staff acct. Whipple & Co., Indpls., 1973-76, mgr., 1976-78, ptnr., 1978-84, pres., 1984—, also bd. dirs.; bd. dirs. The Criterion, Indpls., 1986—. Served with USAF, 1966-70. Mem. Am. Inst. CPA's, Ind. CPA Soc., Hoosier CPA Group. Roman Catholic. Club: Athletic (Indpls.). Lodge: Rotary (bd. dirs. 1983-85, sec. 1987). Avocations: woodworking, gardening. Office: Whipple & Co 9302 N Meridian St Indianapolis IN 46260

WEAVER, JAMES RICHARD, surgeon; b. Columbus, Ohio, Mar. 31, 1953; s. Richard Irvin and Rubie Jane (Miller) W.; m. Susan Elaine Boldys, Aug. 19, 1978; children: Erin Elizabeth, Nathan James, Ashleigh Mary. DDS, Ohio State U., 1976. Diplomate Am. Bd. Oral and Maxillofacial Surgery. Resident in gen. practice St. Vincent's Hosp., Toledo, 1976-77; resident in oral and maxillofacial surgery Detroit Gen. Hosp., 1977-80; practice dentistry specializing in oral and maxillofacial surgery Toledo, 1980—; asst. prof., chief div. oral and maxillofacial surgery Med. Coll. Ohio, Toledo, 1980—. Trustee Dental Dispensary Northwest Ohio, 1984—. Presdl. scholar U. Dayton, 1971-73. Fellow: Am. Dental Soc. Anesthesiology, Am. Assn. Oral and Maxillofacial Surgery, Ohio Soc. Oral and Maxillofacial Surgery; mem. ADA, Ohio Dental Assn., Toledo Dental Soc (bd. dirs. 1986—). Republican. Methodist. Lodge: Masons (32 degrees), Shriners, Elks. Avocations: golf, fishing, family outings. Home: 26010 W River Rd Perrysburg OH 43551 Office: 136 Michigan St Toledo OH 43624

WEAVER, JOHN ALBERT, chemical company executive; b. Sandusky, Ohio, Oct. 12, 1942; s. John A. and Margaret L. (Hast) W.; m. Ann E. Palmer, Aug. 29, 1970; children: Amy, Bryan. BChemE, Ohio State U., 1965. Process devel. engr. B.F. Goodrich, Avon Lake, Ohio, 1965-70; sr. computer engr. B.F. Goodrich, Orange, Tex., 1970-74; mfg. engr. B.F. Goodrich, Orange, 1978-80; sr. process control engr. B.F. Goodrich, Cleve., 1974-78, gen. mgr., 1980-85, v.p., gen mgr. polymer chemicals, 1985—. Mem. Plastic Pipe and Fitting Assn. (bd. dirs. 1983—, treas. 1984-86, pres. 1987), Am. Chem. Soc. (rubber div.). Republican. Methodist. Club: Weymouth Country (Medina, Ohio). Avocation: sports. Home: 13276 Tradewinds Strongsville OH 44136

WEAVER, KIT TANYON, health physicist; b. Moline, Ill., Sept. 4, 1953; s. Rue Alvin and Roselyn (Betcher) W. BS in Engring. Physics, U. Ill., 1975, MS in Nuclear Engring., 1976. Health physicist Commonwealth Edison, Marseilles, Ill., 1976-79; lead health physicist Commonwealth Edison, Braceville, Ill., 1979; emergency planner Commonwealth Edison, Chgo., 1980, physicist corp. health, 1986—; lead health physicist Commonwealth Edison, Byron, Ill., 1981-86, corp. health physicist, 1986—. Author, editor: (corp. document) Generating Stations Emergency Plan, 1980; author, tech. reviewer: Byron Radiation Protection Procedures, 1981-85. Mem. Am. Nuclear Soc., Health Physics Soc. (sec. Midwest chpt. 1980-81, chmn. memberships 1981-82, pres. 1983-84), Phi Kappa Phi, Tau Beta Pi. Presbyterian. Avocations: photography, Lionel train collector, bicycling, computers. Office: Commonwealth Edison 72 W Adams Room 1248 Chicago IL 60690

WEAVER, MELISSA ELLEN, personnel manager, accountant; b. Greenfield, Iowa, Aug. 29, 1961; d. Mervin D. Weaver and Delores E. Kirk. BSBA cum laude, U. Nebr., Omaha, 1984. CPA, Nebr. Supr. staff acct. Bland, Datesman & Assocs, P.C., CPA's (formerly Bland & Co., CPA's), Omaha, 1984-87; customer support rep. Word and Data Processing Products, Inc., Omaha, 1987—. Mem. Am. Inst. CPA's, Nebr. Soc. CPA's, Internat. Thespian Soc. (life, various offices). Republican. Methodist. Avocations: dancing, piano, singing, cats, Star Trek aficianado. Home: 10664 Lafayette Plaza #202 Omaha NE 68114-2080 Office: Word and Data Processing Products Inc 7262 Mercy Rd Omaha NE 68124

WEAVER, MURIEL MARGARET, music educator; b. Dayton, Ohio, Apr. 22, 1943; d. Robert Flower and Dixie Faye (Wakeman) McKibben; m. Fredrick Daniel Weaver, June 5, 1965; children: Meva Anne, Kelly Marie, Christopher Ryan, Melissa Faye. BA cum laude, Miami U., Oxford, 1965; MEd, Mt. St. Joseph, Cin., 1986. Music tchr. Trotwood-Madison (Ohio) Pub. Sch., 1965-73, Worthington Pub. Sch., Chillicother, Ohio, 1975-76, Chillicothe Pub. Sch., 1983—; pvt. practice tchr. music, Dayton and Chillicothe, 1960—. Violinist, Dayton Symphony Orch., 1962-73, Columbus Symphony Orch., 1973-75; dir. Agapé Handbell Choir, Chillicothe, 1976—; co-dir. Chillicothe Community Chorus, 1981—. Fellow NEA, Chillicothe Educator's Assn., Ohio Music Educator's Assn., Am. Guild English Handbell Ringers, Am. String Tchrs. Assn., Phi Beta Kappa, Delta Omicron. Republican. Methodist. Clubs: Chillicothe Raquet, Miriam-Rebekah Circle. Avocations: family camping, tennis, raquetball.

WEAVER, RICHARD L., II, speech communication educator; b. Hanover, N.H., Dec. 5, 1941; s. Richard L. and Florence B. (Grow) W.; m. Andrea A. Willis; children: R. Scott, Jacquelynn Michelle, Anthony Keith, Joanna Corinne. A.B., U. Mich., 1964, M.A., 1965; Ph.D., Ind. U., 1969. Asst. prof. U. Mass., 1968-74; assoc. prof. speech communication Bowling Green State U., 1974-79, prof., 1979—; dir. Basic Speech Communication Course, 1974—; vis. prof. U. Hawaii-Manoa, 1981-82. Author: (with Saundra Hybels) Speech/Communication, 1974, 2d edit., 1979, Speech/Communication: A Reader, 1975, 2d edit., 1979, Speech/Communication: A Student Manual, 1976, 2d edit., 1979, Understanding Interpersonal Communication, 1978, 4th edit., 1987, (with Raymond K. Tucker, Cynthia Berryman-Fink) Research in Speech Communication, 1981, Foundations of Speech Communications: Perspectives of a Discipline, 1982, Speech Communication Skills, 1982, Understanding Public Communication, 1983, Understanding Business Communication, 1985, Understanding Speech Communication Skills, 1985, Readings in Speech Communication, 1985, (with Saundra Hybels) Communicating Effectively, 1986, 2d edit., 1987, Skills for Communicating Effectively, 1987; contbr. articles to profl. jours. Mem. Internat. Communication Assn., Internat. Soc. Gen. Semantics, Speech Communication Assn., Cen. States Speech Assn., Ohio Speech Assn., Midwest Basic Course Dirs. Conf., Golden Key, Phi Kappa Phi (Scholar award). Home: 9583 Woodleigh Ct Perrysburg OH 43551 Office: Bowling Green State U Dept Interpersonal and Pub Communication Bowling Green OH 43403

WEAVER, TERRY ROYCE, electronics executive; b. Greensburg, Kans., Aug. 5, 1951; s. Eldon R. and Mildred M. (Crandall) W.; m. Pamela J. McCanon, Mar. 26, 1972; children: Janelle, Scott. BSEE, Kans. State U., 1973. Registerd profl. engr., Mo. Sales engr. Johnson Controls, St. Louis, 1973-79, br. mgr., 1979-84; regional mgr. S.E. Johnson Controls, Atlanta, 1984-86; v.p. electronic systems unit Johnson Controls, Milw., 1986—. Recipient Outstanding Br. Mgr. award S.W. Region Johnson Controls, Dallas, 1980-82. Lodge: Rotary. Avocations: music, piano, organ. Home: 2370 Woodmoor Ln Brookfield WI 53005 Office: Johnson Controls Inc 507 E Michigan St Milwaukee WI 53202

WEAVER, WARREN W., bank executive. Pres. Commerce Bank of Kansas City, Mo. Office: Commerce Bancshares Inc 1000 Walnut St 18th Floor Kansas City MO 64106 *

WEAVER, WILLIAM CLAIR, JR., human resources development executive; b. Indiana, Pa., Apr. 11, 1936; s. William Clair and Zaida (Bley) W.; m. Janet Marcelle Boyd, Sept. 18, 1963 (div. 1976); 1 child, William Michael; m. Donna June Hubbuch, Feb. 10, 1984. B Aero Engring., Rensselaer Politechnic Inst., 1959; MBA, Washington U., ST. Louis, 1971; postgrad., Rutgers U. Registered profl. engr. Engr. aerodynamics N.Am. Aviation, Los Angeles, 1959-60; engr. flight test ops. Boeing/Vertol, Phila., 1963-66; engr. flight test project Lockhead Electronics, Plainfield, N.J., 1966-69; project engr. advanced systems, sr. staff engr. Emerson Electric Co., St. Louis, 1969-72; pres. Acievement Assocs., Inc., St. Louis, 1972—; founder, charter mem. Catalyst, 1978—. Contbr. articles to profl. jours. 1965-71; author: Winning Selling, 1983. Mem. adv. com. Boy Scouts Am., Bridgeton, Mo., 1974. Served to capt. USAF, 1960-63. Mem. Nat. Soc. Profl. Engrs., Am. Soc. Bus. and Mgmt. Cons., Am. Ordnance Soc., Am. Inst. Aeronoutics and Astrounautics, Assn. MBA Execs., Air Force Assn., Am. Helicopter Soc., St. Louis C. of C., Mensa, Beta Gamma Sigma. Republican. Lutheran. Avocations: photography, music, sports. Home and Office: 13018 Ray Trog Ct Saint Louis MO 63146

WEBB, CHARLES RAY, cardiologist; b. Detroit, Dec. 22, 1948; s. Charles Ray and Eva Jeanette (Love) W.; m. Barbara Sokolowski, Sept. 17, 1983. BS in Chemistry, U. Mich., 1974, MD, 1975. Diplomate Am. Bd. Internal Medicine, Am. Bd. Cardiovascular Diseases. Intern Case Western Res. U., Cleve., 1975-76; resident in internal medicine Univ. Hosps. Cleve., 1976-78; fellow in cardiology Wayne State U. Med. Ctr., Detroit, 1978-79, Henry Ford Hosp., Detroit, 1979-81; asst. prof. medicine U. Mo., Kansas City, 1981-82; cardiologist Truman Med. Ctr., Kansas City, 1981-82; fellow in electrophysiology Hahnemann U., Phila., 1982-83, asst. prof. medicine, 1983-85; asst. prof. medicine U. Mich., Ann Arbor, 1985—; dir. electrophysiology Henry Ford Hosp., Detroit, 1985—, mem. project research and human rights com.; cons., lectr. numerous presentations on heart rhythm abnormalities to univs., med. ctrs. and profl. confs. Contbr. 20 articles on cardiology to med. jours. Fellow Am. Coll. Cardiology, Am. Coll. Chest Physicians (council on critical care), Am. Heart Assn. (clin. council); mem. ACP, AMA, Am. Heart Assn. (Laenec Soc.), Heart Assn. Mich. (Healthsite com., profl. edn. com., research peer rev. com.), Henry Ford Hosp. Alumni Assn., N.Y. Acad. Scis., N.Am. Soc. for Pacing and Electrophysiology (cert.), U. Mich. Alumni Assn., Wayne County Med. Soc., U.S. Tennis Assn. Episcopalian. Clubs: Sq. Lake Racquet, Somerset Tennis. Avocations: tennis, symphonic and chamber music, violin, computers. Home: 4610 Charing Cross Rd Bloomfield Hills MI 48013 Office: Henry Ford Hosp Dir Clin Cardiac Electrophysiology Lab 2799 W Grand Blvd Room WC-567 Detroit MI 48202

WEBB, HERBERT GERALD, railroad engineer; b. Ash Grove, Kans., Apr. 25, 1934; s. Harley H. and Mildred (Herman) W.; m. Marilyn J. Pankratz, July 11, 1954; children: Stephen D., Michael J. BSCE, Kans. State U., 1957; MS in Bus. Mgmt., MIT, 1973. Div. engr. Santa Fe Rwy., La Junta, Colo., 1968-69, Ft. Madison, Iowa, 1969-71; dist. engr. Santa Fe Rwy., Los Angeles, 1971-74; asst. chief engr. Santa Fe Rwy., Chgo., 1974-83, chief engr., 1983—; bd. dirs. Roadmaster 8 Maintenance of Way Assn., 1982-85; pres. Chgo. Maintenance of Way Club, 1985-86. Served to capt. U.S. Army, 1957-60. Mem. NSPE, Am. Rwy. Engrs. Assn. (pres. 1986-87), Am. Bridge and Bldg. Assn., ASCE. Republican. Presbyterian. Club: Cress Creek Country (Naperville, Ill.). Avocations: golf, woodworking. Home: 1628 Fox Bend Naperville IL 60540 Office: 4100 S Kedzie Chicago IL 60632

WEBB, JAMES THURMAN, psychologist, educator; b. Memphis, Sept. 14, 1939; s. Bunyan Munroe and Cleo Anez (Miller) W.; children: Amy, Mary, Patty. AB, Rhodes U., 1960; PhD, U. Ala., 1967. Program coordinator Roche Psychol. Inst., Nutley, N.J., 1968-70; asst. prof. Ohio U., Athens, 1970-73, assoc. prof., 1973-75; dir. psychology Children's Med. Ctr., Dayton, Ohio, 1975-77; prof. psychology, asst. dean Sch. Profl. Psychology Wright State U., Dayton, 1977—. Author: Configunal Interpretations of MMPI, 1975, Guiding the Gifted Child, 1982 (Am. Psych. Assn. award 1983); contbr. articles to profl. jours. Fellow Am. Psychol. Assn., Ohio Psychol. Assn., Soc. Personality Assessment; mem. Nat. Assn. for Gifted Children (bd. dirs. 1984—), Am. Assn. for Gifted Children (pres. 1985—). Home: 423 Volusia Dayton OH 45409 Office: Wright State U Sch Profl Psychology Dayton OH 45429

WEBB, JERVIS B., manufacturing company executive; b. 1915. BMechE, MIT, 1937. Pres. Jervis B. Webb Co., Farmington, Mich., 1952—, also bd. dirs. Office: Jervis B Webb Co 1 Webb Dr Farmington MI 48018 *

WEBB, MARVIN LEROY, architect; b. Nampa, Idaho, May 29, 1946; s. Ernest LeRoy and Ruth Louisa (Pollard) W.; m. Jeanne Masson, Nov. 23, 1974; children: Emily Nicole, Justin Ross. Student, Kearney State Coll., 1967; BArch, U. Nebr., 1971. Registered architect, Nebr. Grad. architect Henningson, Durham, Richardson, Omaha, 1971-72, Wilscam, Birge Assocs., Omaha, 1972, Thomas Bachtold & Assocs., Lincoln, Nebr., 1972-77; architect Findley & Assocs., Lincoln, 1979-81, James L. Cannon & Assocs., Architects, Grand Island, Nebr., 1981—. Cons. architect Mayor's Com. on Disability Issues, Grand Island, 1981—; pres., bd. dirs. Jefferson Sch. PTA, Grand Island, 1982—. Mem. AIA (v.p. western chpt.), Nebr. Soc. Architects (sec., treas. Western chpt. 1985, 2d v.p. 1986), Nat. Trust Historic Preservation, Grand Island C. of C. (Project 2M Priorities com. 1984-85), Sierra Club (Lincoln coordinator Nebraskans for Returnable Containers 1976-78, rep. Citizens for Environ. Improvement 1976-80, Bluestem Nebr. conservation com. 1979-81, Cottonwood treas. 1983—). Democrat. Roman Catholic. Avocations: camping, photography, bicycling, computers. Office: James L Cannon & Assocs 231 S Locust Grand Island NE 68801

WEBB, MARVIN R., state agency director; b. Dodge City, Kans., Sept. 15, 1918; s. Loris Everett and Clara Mae (Crotinger) W.; m. Dorothy Daugherty, Feb. 15, 1948 (div. Mar. 1963); m. Betty Louise McDonald, (div. Apr. 1983); m. Georgina M. Haydon, June 5, 1983; 1 child, Walter Loris. Student, U. Nebr., 1937-39, U. Mo., 1964. Warehouse examiner Kans. State Grain Inspection Dept., Topeka, 1959-61, dir., 1981—; warehouse examiner agr. stabilization and conservation service USDA, Kansas City, Mo., 1962-66; warehouse cert. examiner agr. stabilization and conservation service USDA, Camphill, Pa., 1966-73; conservation specialist Fed. Energy Dept., Kansas City, 1973-79. Pres. St. John's Mil. Sch., Salina, Kans., 1974-78, trustee, 1978-84. Mem. Am. Legion (chmn. state energy commn. 1976—), U.S. Army Assn. Democrat. Methodist. Home: 4240 Wisconsin Topeka KS 66609 Office: Kans Grain Inspection Dept 235 S Topeka Ave Topeka KS 66603

WEBB, O. GLENN, farm supplies company executive; b. 1936; married. B.S., U. Ill., 1957; Ph.D., So. Ill. U., 1973. With Growmark, Inc., Bloomington, Ill., 1965—, sec., 1968-72, v.p., 1972-80, pres., from 1980, chmn., 1980—, also dir.; trustee, chmn. Am. Inst. Coop.; dir. St. Louis Farm Credit Banks, Farmers Export Co., Nat. Coop. Refinery Assn., Ill. Agr. Leadership Found.; trustee Grad. Inst. Coop. Leadership. Office: Growmark Inc 1701 Towanda Ave Bloomington IL 61701 *

WEBB, O(RVILLE) LYNN, physician, pharmacologist, educator; b. Tulsa, Aug. 29, 1931; s. Rufus Aclen and Berla Ophelia (Caudle) W.; m. Joan Liebenheim, June 1, 1954 (div. Jan. 1980); children—Kathryn, Gilbert, Benjamin. B.S., Okla. State U., 1953; M.S., U. Okla., 1961; Ph.D. in Pharmacology, U. Mo., 1966, M.D., 1968. Diplomate Nat. Bd. Med. Examiners, Am. Bd. Family Practice. Research assoc. in pharmacology U. Okla., 1959-61; research fellow NIH, 1962-66; instr. pharmacology U. Mo., Columbia, 1966-68, asst. prof., 1968-69; intern, U. Mo. Med. Center, 1968-69; family practice, New Castle, Ind., 1969—; mem. staff Henry County Meml. Hosp., New Castle, 1969—; guest prof. pharmacy and pharmacology Butler U. Coll. Pharmacy, Indpls., 1970-75; owner, dir. Carthage Clinic, 1975—; clin. assoc. prof. family medicine Ind. U., 1986—; county physician, jail med. dir. Henry County, Ind., 1976—. Recipient Cert. of merit in Pharmacol. and Clin. Med. Research, 1970; Med. Student Research Essay award Am. Acad. Neurology, 1968. Fellow Am. Acad. Family Physicians; mem. AMA (ann. award recognition 1975—), Ind. State Med. Assn., Am. Coll. Sports Medicine, AAAS, N.Y. Acad. Sci., Am. Soc. Contemporary Medicine and Surgery, Festival Chamber Music Soc. (bd. dirs. Indpls. 1981—), Mensa, Sigma Xi. Clubs: Columbia, Skyline (Indpls.). Lodge: Elks. Author: (with Blissitt and Stanaszek, Lea and Febiger) Clinical Pharmacy Practice, 1972; contbr. articles to profl. jours. Home and Office: 420 S Main New Castle IN 47362

WEBB, ROBERT DONALD, JR., financial executive; b. Chgo., Apr. 23, 1943; s. Robert D. and Marjorie (Hoffman) W.; m. Linda Dale Wasserman, June 25, 1967; children: Lauren, Robyn. B.S.A., No. Ill. U., 1965. C.P.A., Ill. From auditor to audit mgr. Arthur Andersen & Co., Chgo., 1965-78; dir. corp. fin. CF Industries, Inc., Long Grove, Ill., 1978-79, corp. controller, 1980-87, v.p. planning and control, 1987—; v.p. fin. Valley Nitrogen Producers, Fresno, Calif., 1979-80. Served as staff sgt. USAFR, 1965-71. Named Outstanding Acctg. Alumnus, No. Ill. U., 1982. Mem. Fin. Execs. Inst., Fertilizer Inst. (fin. mgmt. com.), Am. Inst. C.P.A.s, Ill. Soc. C.P.A.s, Nat. Soc. Accts. for Coops., Beta Alpha Psi (Gamma Pi chpt.). Lutheran. Office: CF Industries Inc Salem Lake Dr Long Grove IL 60047

WEBB, RONALD MICHAEL, real estate developer; b. St. Joseph, Mo., Sept. 16, 1944; s. Earl Andrew and Willa Mae (Gerhart) W.; m. Susan Jean Unger, Sept. 3, 1966; children: Scott S., Amy E. BS, Cen. Mo. State U., 1967. Asst. v.p. trust mktg. Mercantile Trust Co., St. Louis, 1967-83; v.p. trust dept. Pioneer Bank & Trust, St. Louis, 1979-83; treas. and v.p. fin. Barberg & Assoc., Inc., Eau Claire, Wis., 1982—; v.p. Hotel Operators Co., Eau Claire, 1983—; pres. Regency Broadcasting Co., Green Bay, Wis., 1985—, Webb Aviation, Inc., Eau Claire, 1985—, Zimmani's Licensing Corp., Green Bay, 1986—, C&I Realty Group, Green Bay, 1986—. Pres. Sigma Tau Gamma Found., Warrensburg, Mo., 1977-81, Cen. Mo. State U. Found., Warrensburg, 1981-83; elder Christ United Presby. Ch., St. Louis, 1981-83. Fellow Wilson C. Morris Fellowship; mem. bd. Realtors. Club: Eau Claire Country. Avocations: flying, sailing. Office: Webe Devel Co 306 S Barstow St Suite 204 Eau Claire WI 54701

WEBB, ROSAMOND LYDIA, controller; b. Stevensville, Ont., Can., Oct. 5, 1936; d. James Clarence and Lydia Mabel (Sider) Milne; m. Barry Henry John Webb, June 9, 1956; children: Gregory, Randall. Cert. in secretarial acctg., Bryant and Stratton Bus. Inst., 1955; AA with high honors, Coll. of DuPage, 1983; student, No. Ill. U., 1983—. CPA, Ill. Acct. Victor D. Naples, Acct., Buffalo, 1962-66, F.A. Hinrichs & Co., Wheaton, Ill., 1967-79; controller Domain Communications, Inc., Carol Stream, Ill., 1979-86; staff acct. Dugan & Lopatka CPA's P.C., Wheaton, 1986—. Treas. Wheaton Wesleyan Ch., 1968-71. Mem. Met. Chgo. Assn. Sq. Dancers (dir., 1st and 2d v.p. 1975-79, pres. 1980-81), Nat. Sq. Dance Conv. (vice chmn. sq. dance program 1978-79), Legacy (trustee 1981—). Republican. Club: Widar Sqs. (Berkley, Ill.). Avocations: sq. dancing, travel. Home: 804 S President St Wheaton IL 60187

WEBB, THOMAS HARLAN, minister; b. Springfield, Ohio, Mar. 31, 1944; s. Eugene Mumpher and Mary Marvalee (Powell) W.; m. Linda Suue Moore, June 6, 1964; children: Lori Ann, Jennifer Christine, Thomas Patrick. Student, St. Louis Christian Coll., 1982-83, Cin. Bible Coll., 1978-81. Pub. relation rep. CWBA, St. Louis, 1979-83; minister Marion Christian Ch., West Salem, 1983-85, Pleasant Christian Ch., Murphys Boro, Ill., 1985—. Served with USAF, 1963-67. Lodge: Masons. Avocations: fishing, woodworking. Home: Route 4 Murphysboro IL 62966 Office: Pleasant Hill Christian Ch Rt 4 Murphys Boro IL 62966

WEBB, THOMAS IRWIN, JR., lawyer; b. Toledo, Sept. 16, 1948; s. Thomas Irwin and Marcia Davis (Winters) W.; m. Polly S. DeWitt, Oct. 11, 1986; 1 child, Elisabeth Hurst. BA, Williams Coll., 1970; postgrad. Boston U., 1970-71; JD, Case Western Res. U., 1973. Bar: Ohio. Assoc. Shumaker, Loop & Kendrick, Toledo, 1973-79, ptnr., 1979—; dir. Comml. Aluminum Cookware Co., Yark Oldsmobile, Inc. Council mem. Village of Ottawa Hills, Ohio, 1978-85, planning commn., 1978-85; adv. bd. Ohio Div. Securities, 1979—; bd. dirs. Kiwanis Youth Found. of Toledo, Inc. Mem. ABA, Ohio Bar Assn., Toledo Bar Assn., Northwestern Ohio Alumni Assn. of Williams Coll. (pres. 1974-83), Nat. Assn. Bond Lawyers, Toledo-Rowing Found. (trustee 1985—), Order of Coif. Republican. Methodist. Clubs: Crystal Downs Country, Toledo Country, The Toledo (trustee 1984—); Williams Club of N.Y. Office: Shumaker Loop & Kendrick 1000 Jackson Toledo OH 43624

WEBBER, LAWRENCE JOSEPH, infosystems specialist; b. Dayton, Ohio, June 3, 1954. AS in Data Processing, Albany Jr. Coll., 1980; BBA, Rockhurst Coll., 1983, MBA, 1985. Enlisted USMC, Albany, Ga., 1972; advanced through ranks to sgt. USMC, 1977, resigned, 1980; sgt. USAFR, Kansas City, KS, 1980-83, USAR, Kansas City, 1983—; analyst Waddell & Reed, Kansas City, Mo., 1980-81, Temperature Industries, Kansas City, 1981-82; coordinator mktg. data applications United Telephone, Overland Park, Kans., 1982-84, cons. info. ctr., 1984-85, mgr. info. ctr., 1985-87; applications mgr. Shook, Hardy & Bacon, Kansas City, Mo., 1987—. Mem. Data Processing Mgrs. Assn., Armed Forces Communication and Electronic Assn., USAF Assn. Home: 20001 Travis Ln Stilwell KS 66085 Office: 1101 Walnut Kansas City MO 64106

WEBER, ALBAN, association executive, lawyer; b. Chgo., Jan. 29, 1915; s. Joseph A. and Anna (von Plachecki) W.; AB, Harvard U., 1935, LLB, 1937; m. Margaret Kenny, Dec. 29, 1951; children: Alban III, Peggy Ann, Gloria, Brian. Bar: Ill. 1938, Mich. 1985. Ptnr. Weber & Weber, 1937-41; gen. counsel Fgn. Liquidation Commn., State Dept., 1946; trust officer Lake Shore Nat. Bank, Chgo., 1952-55; univ. counsel Northwestern U., Evanston, Ill., 1955-70; pres. Fedn. Ind. Ill. Colls. and Univs., Evanston, 1971-84; of counsel Schuyler, Roche & Zwirner, Evanston, 1984—. Bd. dirs. Benjamin Franklin Fund, Inc., 1965-75, Northwestern U. Press, Inc., 1965-70, pres., 1961-70; chmn. State Assn. Execs. Council, 1981. Pres. Northeast Ill. council Boy Scouts Am., 1970-71. Alderman, City of Chgo., 1947-51. Served to comdr. USNR, 1941-45, rear adm., 1974. Recipient Silver Beaver award Boy Scouts Am.; Meritorious Service award Loyola U., 1978; Edn. for Freedom award Roosevelt U., 1984. Mem. Nat. Assn. Coll. and Univ. Attys. (pres. 1962), Harvard Law Soc. Ill. (pres. 1984), Navy League (pres. Evanston council 1967-70, Univ. Risk Mgmt. Assn. (pres. 1965), Univ. Ins. Mgrs. (pres.). Clubs: Law, Economics, Harvard, Executives, Chicago Yacht; White Lake Golf, White Lake Yacht. Lodge: Kiwanis (lt. gov.). Home: 1555 SE Sunshine Ave Port Sainte Lucie FL 33452 Office: Schuyler Roche & Zwirner State Bank Bldg Evanston IL 60201

WEBER, ANDREW JAMES, JR., publishing company executive; b. Waukesha, Wis., Sept. 3, 1953; s. Andrew James and Katherine Louise (Hoelz) W.; m. Susan Andrea Hausman, Jan. 23, 1982; children: Lesly Hope, Marissa Gail. BS, U. Wis., 1977. Salesman Century Communications, Skokie, Ill., 1977-79, Vance Pub., Chgo., 1979-81; sales mgr. Vance Pub., Kansas City, Mo., 1981-83, assoc. pub., 1983-84; pres. Vet. Medicine Pub. Co., Lenexa, Kans., 1985—. Mem. Midwest Pharm. Advt. Club, Nat. Agrl. Mktg. Assn., Ducks Unlimited, NRA. Republican. Roman Catholic. Club: Leawood South Country. Avocations: golf, hunting, fishing, wine collecting. Office: Vet Medicine Pub Co 9073 Lenexa Dr Lenexa KS 66215

WEBER, ARNOLD R., university president; b. N.Y.C., Sept. 20, 1929; s. Jack and Lena (Smith) W.; m. Edna M. Files, Feb. 7, 1954; children: David, Paul, Robert. B.A., U. Ill., 1951; M.A., MIT, 1958, Ph.D. in Econs., 1958. Instr., then asst. prof. econs. MIT, 1955-58; faculty U. Chgo. Grad. Sch. Bus., 1958-69, prof. indsl. relations, 1963-69; asst. sec. for manpower Dept. Labor, 1969-70; exec. dir. Cost of Living Council; also spl. asst. to Pres. Nixon, 1971; Gladys C. and Isidore Brown prof. urban and labor econs. U. Chgo., 1971-73; provost Carnegie-Mellon U.; dean Carnegie-Mellon U. (Grad. Sch. Indsl. Adminstrn.), prof. labor econs. and pub. policy, 1973-80; pres. U. Colo., Boulder, 1980-85, Northwestern U., Evanston, Ill., 1985—; vis. prof. Stanford U., 1966; cons. union, mgmt. and govt. agys., 1960—, Dept. Labor, 1965; mem. Pres.'s Adv. Com. Labor Mgmt. Policy, 1964, Orgn. Econ. Coop. and Devel., 1964, Exec. Com. of Council on Competitiveness; vice chmn. sec. labor task force improving employment services, 1965; chmn. research adv. com. U.S. Employment Service, 1966; assoc. dir. Office Mgmt. and Budget, Exec. Office of Pres., 1970-71; chmn. Presdl. Railroad Emergency Bd., 1982; trustee Com. for Econ. Devel., Joint Council on Econ. Edn.; bd. dirs. Chgo. Council Fgn. Relations, Burlington Northern, Inc., Inland Steel Co., Pepsico Inc., Super Valu Stores, Inc. Author: (with G.P. Shultz) Strategies for the Displaced Worker, 1966; Contbr. (with G.P. Shultz) articles to profl. jours. Served to lt. (j.g.) USCGR, 1952-54, PTO. Ford Found. Faculty Research fellow, 1964-65. Mem. Indsl. Relations Research Assn. (bus.-higher edn. forum), Am. Econ. Assn., Nat. Acad. Pub. Adminstrn., Consortium of Social Scis. Assns. (bd. dirs.), Comml. Club Chgo., Econ. Club Chgo., Phi Beta Kappa. Jewish. Office: Northwestern University Office of the President 633 Clark St Evanston IL 60201

WEBER, CALVIN ADOLPH, dentist; b. Omaha, Feb. 18, 1958; s. George Calvin and Velma Ann (Myers) W.; m. Laura Lee Milligan, Sept. 12, 1981. BS, U. Iowa, 1985; DDS, Northwestern U., 1983. Gen. practice dentistry Glenwood, Iowa, 1983—; staff mem. Grape Community Hosp., Hamburg, Iowa, 1983—. Recipient Eagle Scout award, Boy Scouts Am., 1974. Mem. Iowa Dental Assn. of Am. Dental Assn. (sec., treas. SW Iowa dist. 1985—), Acad. Gen. Dentistry. Republican. Methodist. Club: Glenwood Golf. Avocations: softball, golf, farming, motorcycles, driving semi-trucks. Home: 146 Glenbrook Dr Glenwood IA 51534 Office: Weber Dental 208 N Walnut Glenwood IA 51534

WEBER, D(AVID) M(ALCOLM), controller, accountant; b. Zanesville, Ohio, Nov. 19, 1948; s. Philip T. and Bernice L. (Harmon) W.; m. Deborah R. Thompson, May 18, 1974; children: Dustin, Kyle, Amber. BS in Math., Ohio U., 1971. Tax agt. Ohio Dept. Taxation, Columbus, 1972-81; corp. treas. The Roekel Co., Zanesville, 1981—, also bd. dirs. Fin. chmn. Boy Scouts Am., Zanesville, 1986-87. Mem. Nat. Assn. Accts. Presbyterian. Lodge: Kiwanis. Office: The Roekel Co 36 S 2d St Zanesville OH 43701

WEBER, DEBRA ROSE, medical assistant; b. Savannah, Ga., Jan. 10, 1952; d. William Howard and Margaret Emma (Neumeister) Geiger; m. Gary Henry Weber, Jan. 2, 1970; children: Tonia, Tricia. Cert. med. asst. with honors, Inst. Med. Dental Tech., 1979. Cert. med. asst., Ohio; cert. phebotomist; cert. notary pub. Med. asst., phlebotomist Nat. Health Lab., Cin., 1979—; instr. med. assistance Met. Coll., Cin., 1986—. Avocations: softball, camping, fishing.

WEBER, DELBERT D., university administrator; b. Columbus, Nebr., July 23, 1932; s. Charles and Ella M. (Hueschen) W.; m. Lou Ann Ross, Dec. 29, 1954; children: William, Bethany, Kelly. BA, Midland Coll., Fremont, Nebr., 1954; MEd, U. Nebr., 1958, EdD, 1962; LittD (hon.), Shizuoka (Japan) U., 1982; LLD (hon.), U. City of Manila, 1984. Tchr. social studies and English, prin. Creston (Nebr.) High Sch., 1956-58; instr. edni. founds. U. Nebr., Lincoln, 1958-60, instr. and coordinator jr. high lab. sch., 1960-62; chancellor U. Nebr., Omaha, 1977—; from asst. to assoc. prof. edn. Ariz. State U., Tempe, 1962-65, dean and prof. edn., 1969-77; asst. to pres. and sec. to trustees Cleve. State U., 1965-69; chmn. commn. on culture and edn. to Pakistan, U.S. Dept. of State, 1984; bd. dirs. Norwest Bank, Omaha. Author: (with N.L. Haggerson, L.H. Griffith) Secondary Education Today,

1968; contbr. articles to profl. jours. Mem. exec. bd. Mid-Am. council Boy Scouts Am., Sister Cities Internat., 1987; trustee Nebr. Meth. Hosp., Luth. Ch. of the Master, Omaha, Omaha Home for Boys; bd. dirs. Omaha Telecasters Ednl. Found., Met. YMCA, Great Plains council Girl Scouts U.S., Midlands region NCCJ, Omaha Community Playhouse; gen. campaign chmn. United Way of Midlands, 1983. Served with U.S. Army, 1954-56. Named Citizen of Yr., United Way of Midlands, 1984; recipient Centennial Medallion of Merit, Ariz. State U., 1985, Univ. Nebr. Lincoln Tchrs. Coll. Alumni Assn. award of excellence, 1987. Mem. Am. Assn. Colls. for Tchr. Edn. (bd. dirs. 1976-79, chmn. ann. conv. 1975, appeals bd. 1984-85, task force 1984-85), Am. Assn. State Colls. and Univs. (task force on excellence in edn. 1982-84, bd. dirs., exec. com. 1983—, com. communications tech. 1984-86, resource ctr. bd. liaison 1985, com. acad. affairs, com. on internat. programs 1987, com. on urban affairs 1987), Assn. Urban Univs. (bd. dirs. 1980-85), Nat. Assn. State Univs. and Land Grant Colls. (mem. exec. com. 1982-83, chmn. urban affairs div. 1982-83), Nat. Assn. Colls. and Schs. of Edn. in State Univs. and Land Grant Colls. (bd. dirs. 1974-77, pres. 1977-78), Nat. Collegiate Athletic Assn. (pres. commn. 1984—), Nat. Council for Accreditation of Tchr. Edn. (appeals bd. 1983), Omaha C. of C. (bd. dirs.). Lutheran. Avocation: golf. Home: 6445 Prairie Ave Omaha NE 68132 Office: Univ Nebr at Omaha Eppley 201 60th and Dodge St Omaha NE 68182

WEBER, DONALD JOHN, retired military officer; b. Cumberland, Iowa, May 3, 1932; s. Wesley Horatio and Helen Mae (Hopkins) W.; m. Marilyn June Cook, Dec. 26, 1954; children: Donald (dec.), Richard. Student, Iowa Western Community Coll., 1977-79. Enlisted USAF, 1952, commd. 2d lt., 1959, advanced through ranks to maj., 1969, retired, 1972; archtl. draftsman Midway Distbg., Atlantic, Iowa, 1972-74; structural draftsman Atlantic Steel Corp., 1974-78; corp. pilot Burk Erectors, Griswold, Iowa, 1978-80; pvt. practice tech. draftsman Atlantic, 1980—. Decorated Bronze Star. Mem. Retired Officers Assn., Exptl. Aircraft Assn. Club: Atlantic (Iowa) Aero (sec., treas. 1979-81, pres. 1981-82). Lodge: Elks. Home: 1202 Birch St Atlantic IA 50022

WEBER, DWIGHT EDWARD, press relations executive; b. Cin., June 3, 1951; s. Edward Harry and Elizabeth Mae (Koch) W.; m. Susan Alice Galvin, July 14, 1973; children: Molly Elizabeth, Megan Susan. BA in English, Ohio State U., 1973; MA in English, SUNY, Binghamton, 1975; postgrad., Miami U., Oxford, Ohio, 1975-79. Mgr. media relations The Icon Group, Dayton, Ohio, 1979; communications program rep. Gen. Electric Co., Cin., 1980-81, mgr. press relations, 1981—. Teaching fellow, Miami U., 1975-79. Mem. Aviation and Space Writers Assn., Phi Beta Kappa. Republican. Club: Wings. Avocations: reading, writing, music, sports. Office: Gen Electric Co 1 Neumann Way Mail Drop F87 Cincinnati OH 45215-6301

WEBER, EDWARD, food products company executive; b. Chgo., Feb. 17, 1931; s. Philip and Mary (Arlinsky) W.; m. Barbara Taradash, Jan. 12, 1958; children: Michele Leslie, Ronald Lee, Joseph Bradley. Grad., Herzyl Coll., 1952. Pres. Lincoln State Ins. Co., Chgo., 1960-77, Master Brew Beverage, Inc., Northbrook, Ill., 1966—; adv. Coffee Devel. Group, Washington, 1986. Mem. safety commn. Village of Northbrook, 1986; bd. dirs. Homeowners Assn. Wildebrook, 1986. Served with USCG, 1952-54. Mem. Nat. Coffee Service Assn. (founder, bd. dirs. 1971), Nat. Auto Mdse. Assn., No. Ill. Indsl. Assn. Jewish. Clubs: Boca West Country (Boca Raton, Fla.), NSCI Mens (Glencoe, Ill.), Great Lakes Yacht, Multiplex. Avocations: flying, power boating, managing Little League team. Office: Master Brew Beverages Inc 3160 Commercial Ave Northbrook IL 60062

WEBER, FRANK EARL, periodontist; b. New Albany, Ind., Aug. 30, 1932; s. Frank H. and Elizabeth W.; divorced; children—Gregory K., Frank H. B.A., U. Louisville, 1954, D.D.S., 1962; M.S., U. Ky., 1955; postdoctoral specialty Ind. U., 1962-64. Grad. asst. U. Ky., Lexington, 1954-55; ins. underwriter Am. States Ins. Co., Indpls., 1958-60; grad. asst. Ind. U. Sch. Dentistry, 1962-64; practice dentistry specializing in periodontics, Indpls., 1964—; faculty practitioner Ind. U. Sch. Dentistry, 1978—. Contbr. articles to profl. jours. Served with USAF, 1956-58. USPHS scholar, 1959-62; Daman Runyon Cancer Research grantee, 1959-62. Fellow Royal Soc. Health, Acad. Dentistry Internat., Acad. Gen. Dentistry; mem. ADA, Ind. Dental Assn., Indpls. Dist. Dental Soc., Internat. Platform Assn., Nat. Fedn. Ind. Bus., Am. Endodontic Soc., Westside Dental Study Club, Chgo. Dental Soc., Fedn. Advanced Ethical Hypnosis, Acad. Oral Medicine (Merit award 1962), Am. Legion, Omicron Kappa Upsilon, Phi Kappa Phi, Phi Delta (pres. 1961-62) Beta Delta, Omicron Delta Kappa, Delta Sigma Delta (life), Sigma Phi Epsilon (life). Avocations: piloting; golfing; fishing; hunting. Office: Northwest Medical Center 3500 Lafayette Rd Indianapolis IN 46222

WEBER, GEORGE RUSSELL, microbiologist; b. Novinger, Mo., Dec. 29, 1911; s. William and Celia Iciphene (Helton) W.; B.S., U. Mo., 1935; Ph.D., Iowa State Coll., 1940; D.Sc. (hon.) in Pub. Health, Internat. Univ. Found., Malta, 1986; spl. evening student George Washington U., 1944-45, U. Cin., 1948-49; m. Margaret Carrington Cable, Apr. 19, 1947; children—Jeanine Marie, Michael Elwin. Asst. chemist, expt. sta. U. Mo., 1935-36; teaching fellow in bacteriology Iowa State Coll., 1936-38, asst., 1938-39, teaching asst., 1939-40, instr., 1940-42; bacteriologist USPHS, 1946, sr. asst. scientist, 1947, scientist, 1949, chief sanitizing agents unit, 1949-53; research microbiologist Nat. Distillers & Chem. Corp., 1953-63, research project leader, 1963-73, sr. research microbiologist, 1973-75, research asso., 1975, ret., 1977; lectr. in biology U. Cin., 1969-70. Dir. Ky. br. Nat. Chinchilla Breeders of Am., 1955-57, research chmn., 1958-64; pres. Greater Cin. Chinchilla Breeders Assn., 1957-58, 63-64. Served from 1st lt. to maj. AUS, 1942-46; lt. col. AUS (ret.). Recipient War Dept. citation for control of food poisoning and infection, 1946, Albert Einstein Acad. Bronze Medal for Peace, 1987. Fellow Am. Public Health Assn., Royal Soc. Health (Eng.); mem. AAAS, Am. Soc. Microbiology, Am. Inst. Biol. Scis., Ohio Acad. Sci., N.Y. Acad. Scis., Am. Soc. Profl. Biologists (v.p. 1957-58), Smithsonian Assos., Inst. Food Technologists, Research Soc. Am., Res. Officers Assn. U.S. (exec. council Cin. chpt. 1963-65, chpt. pres. 1966-67), Ret. Officers Assn., Mil. Order World Wars, others, Sigma Xi, Phi Kappa Phi. Patentee animal feed, biol. metal corrosion control. Home: 1525 Burney Ln Cincinnati OH 45230

WEBER, HANNO, architect; b. Barranquilla, Colombia, Sept. 24, 1937; came to U.S., 1952; s. Hans and Ester (Oks) W. BA magna cum laude, Princeton U., 1959, MArch, 1961. Registered architect, Ill., Fla., Mo., Pa., N.J. Urban designer, research assoc. Guayana project MIT and Harvard U., Caracas, Venezuela, 1961-63; project architect Paul Schweikher Assocs., Pitts., 1963-67; asst. prof. architecture Princeton U., 1967-73; assoc. prof. architecture Washington U., St. Louis, 1973-80; sr. design architect, studio head, assoc. Skidmore, Owings & Merrill, Chgo., 1980-83; prin. Hanno Weber & Assocs., Chgo., 1984—; vis. lectr. Escuela Nacional de Arquitectura Universidad Nacional de Mex., 1975; research assoc. Research Ctr. Urban and Environ. Planning, Princeton, N.J., 1967-70; project dir. The Community Design Workshop, Washington U. Sch. Architecture, St. Louis, 1973-78; assoc. prof. architecture U. Wis., Milw., 1983—. Contbr. articles to profl. jours. Mem. Pres.'s Commn. on Education of Women Princeton U., 1968-69. Fellow NEH, 1970, Graham Found., 1973; 1st prize winner Flagler Dr. Waterfront Master Plan design competition, West Palm Beach, Fla., 1984, 1st prize winner Mcpl. Ctr. design competition, Leesburg, Va., 1987. Mem. AIA, The Arch. Assn., Phi Beta Kappa. Office: Hanno Weber & Assocs 417 S Dearborn Chicago IL 60605

WEBER, HERMAN JACOB, federal judge; b. Lima, Ohio, May 20, 1927; s. Herman Joacb and Ada Minola (Esterly) W.; m. Barbara L. Rice, May 22, 1948; children: Clayton, Deborah. BA, Otterbein Coll., 1949; JD summa cum laude, Ohio State U., 1951. Bar: Ohio 1952. Assoc. Weber & Hogue, Fairborn, Ohio, 1952-61; judge Fairborn Mayor's Ct., 1956-58; acting judge Fairborn Mcpl. Ct., 1958-60; judge Greene County Common Pleas Ct., Xenia, Ohio, 1961-82, Ohio Ct. Appeals (2d dist.), Dayton, 1982-85, U.S. Dist. Ct. (so. dist.) Ohio, Cin., 1985—; chmn. Ohio Jud. Conf., Columbus, 1980-82; pres. Ohio Common Pleas Judges Assn., Columbus, 1975. Vice mayor City of Fairborn, 1955-57, council mem., 1955-59. Served with USNR, 1945-46. Mem. ABA, Fed. Bar Assn., Ohio Bar Assn., Cin. Bar Assn., Dayton Bar Assn., Greene County Bar Assn. (pres. 1961-62), Fed. Judges Assn., Am. Judicature Soc. Office: US Dist Ct 808 US Courthouse & PO Bldg 5th & Walnut Sts Cincinnati OH 45202

WEBER, LYNN KATHLEEN, occupational therapist; b. Fond du Lac, Wis., June 9, 1961; d. Eugene Walter and Marion D. (Faubel) Eggert; m. Michael James Weber, Sept. 14, 1985. BS, U. Wis., Milw., 1983. Main desk clk. U. Wis. Housing Dept., Milw., 1981-83; occupational therapist Eau Clair (Wis.) County Human Services, 1983-86, Sacred Heart Hosp., Eau Claire, 1986—; instr. evening sch. Dist. 1 Tech. Sch., Eau Claire, 1984-85. Mem. Am. Occupational Therapy Assn., Wis. Occupational Therapy Assn. (sec.-treas. 1984-86), Chippewa Valley Theatre Guild. Democrat. Lutheran. Home: 3637 River Dr Eau Claire WI 54703 Office: Sacred Heart Hosp 900 W Clairemont Ave Eau Claire WI 54701

WEBER, MARK ALAN, property assessor, city councilman; b. Fond du Lac, Wis., Aug. 11, 1953; s. Lawrence F. and Esther M. W.; m. Debra Jean Kletzine, Nov. 2, 1974; children: Jennifer Lynn, Jason Thomas, John Alan. AA in Acctg., Moraine Park Tech. Coll., 1973. Cert. assessment specialist, Wis. Assessment technicain Wis. Dept. Revenue, Fond du Lac, 1974-78, property assessment specialist, 1978-83, field supr. property assessment, 1983—; real estate broker, Wis., 1976—; instr. appraisal courses, 1984—. chmn. cost reduction com. Forward to Basics Com., Fond du Lac, 1985; mem. Fon du Lac City Council, 1986—; council rep. Area Econ. Authority, 1987—. Mem. Soc. Real Estate Appraisers (bd. dirs. Fox Valley Chpt., sec.-treas. 1985-86, pres. 1986—, sr. real property appraiser). Lutheran. Club: Lutheran Pioneer Boy (Fond du Lac)(group leader 1982-83). Avocations: golf, pheasant and deer hunting. Home: 264 Gillet St Fond du Lac WI 54935 Office: Wis Dept Revenue 131 S Mian St Fond du Lac WI 54935

WEBER, MILAN GEORGE, ret. army officer, mgmt. cons.; b. Milw., Oct. 15, 1908; s. Adam George and Frances (Lehrbaumer) W.; B.S., U.S. Mil. Acad., 1931; grad. Coast Arty. and Air Def. Sch., 1938, Nat. War Coll., 1952; m. Mary Agnes Keller, Sept. 2, 1931; 1 son, Milan George. Commd. 2d lt. U.S. Army, 1931, advanced through grades to col., 1944; various army command and staff exec. positions, Philippine Islands, 1932-36, Hawaii, 1938-41, Ft. Monroe, Va., 1936-38; anti-aircraft exec., hdqrs. 3d and 9th armies, U.S., Europe, 1943-45; mem. Gen. Patton's staff, 1944, War Dept. Gen. Staff, 1945-48; mil. adviser to Argentine govt., 1949-51; global strategic planner Joint Chiefs of Staff, 1952-54; comdr. Missile Defense of Norfolk and Hampton Roads, 1954-55; chief of staff advisory group, Japan, 1955-58; dept. comdr. Air Def. Region, Ft. Meade, Md., 1958-60, ret., 1960; mgr. electronic counter measures Loral Electronics Corp., N.Y.C., 1960-62; product mgr. electronic counter measures Hallicrafters Corp. (name changed to Northrop Corp.), Chgo., 1962-64; partner Weber Assos., Mgmt. Cons., Deerfield, Ill., 1964-69; pres. dir. Milan G. Weber Associates, Inc., Deerfield, 1969—; mgmt. cons. to various bus. firms, 1964—; acquisitions and mergers cons. to various corps., 1969—. Chmn. Great Lakes Ecology Assn. Ill., 1974—; chmn. Citizens Com. Honesty in Govt., 1969—; mem. Ill. Drivers Safety Adv. Com., 1975—, Deerfield Library Bd., 1976—, Deerfield Caucus Com., 1978—, Deerfield Energy Adv. Council, 1981—. Decorated Legion of Merit, Bronze Star, Commendation medal with oak leaf cluster. Mem. Assn. Old Crows, West Point Soc. Chgo., Internat. Platform Assn., Assn. Grads. U.S. Mil. Acad., Electronic Counter Measures Assn., Great Lakes Ecology Assn. of the Mil. Clubs: Army Navy, Army Navy Country. Contbr. articles on anti-aircraft arty., air def. and mil. strategy to profl. publs. author of joint strategic capabilities plan; author weekly column on environment, 1977—. Home: 611 Colwyn Terr Deerfield IL 60015 Office: PO Box 81 Deerfield IL 60015

WEBER, NEIL WALTER, architect; b. Appleton, Wis., Dec. 13, 1946; s. Walter C. and Verdane (Meltz) W.; m. Patti Bell, June 26, 1982. BArch, U. Minn., 1971. Architect Schwartz/Weber, Mpls., 1971-83; ptnr., v.p. Richard Schwarz/Neil Weber Architects, Inc., Mpls., 1979—; instr. N. Hennepin Community Coll., Inver Hills Community Coll. Commr. Suburban Hennepin Regional Park Dist. Recipient Manufactured Housing Program award U.S. Dept. Energy, 1981, others. Mem. AIA. Clubs: Wayzata Yacht, Minnetonka Yacht. Home: 5111 Windsor Rd Mound MN 55364-9275 Office: Richard Schwarz/Neil Weber Architects Inc 1500 Excelsior Ave E Hopkins MN 55343

WEBER, PAUL ANTHONY, dentist; b. New Albany, Ind., Mar. 8, 1950; s. George Edward and Laurina Cathrine (Libs) W., m. Pamela Dee Wise, June 9, 1972; children: John Michael, Mark Edward, Beth Anne. Student, Ind. U. S.E., 1968-71; DDS, Ind. U., 1975. Gen. practice dentistry Batesville, Ind., 1975—. Mem. Ind. Council on Dental Edn., Indpls., 1977—. Mem. ADA, Ind. Dental Assn., Southeastern Ind. Dental Assn. (pres. elect 1985-87, pres. 1987—), Ind. U. Sch. Dentistry Alumni Assn. (bd. dirs. 1976-79). Roman Catholic. Lodge: Eagles. Avocation: photography. Home: 32 Village Rd Batesville IN 47006

WEBER, RAYMOND WILLIAM, accountant; b. Mendota, Ill., May 12, 1949; s. Edmund Andrew and Loretta Rose (Sondgeroth) W.; m. Patricia Ann Scholle, Aug. 3, 1973; 1 child, Chad Michael. BS, Ill. State U., 1975. CPA, Ill. Staff acct. Hofmann, Imig & Gemberling, LaSalle, Ill., 1975-82; controller Pvt. Industry, Ottawa, Ill., 1982-86; pvt. practice acctg. Raymond W. Weber, CPA, LaSalle, 1986—. Served with U.S. Army, 1969-71, Vietnam. Mem. Am. Inst. CPA's, Ill. State Soc. CPA's, Ill. Valley Area C. of C. Roman Catholic. Club: St. John Bosco (Spring Valley, Ill.). Avocations: golf, reading. Home: 318 Marquette Rd Spring Valley IL 61362 Office: 2999 E 350th Rd PO Box 1206 LaSalle IL 61301

WEBER, ROY EDWIN, savings and loan association executive; b. Ann Arbor, Mich., Aug. 17, 1928; s. Edwin J. and Ruth E. (Nichols) W.; m. Carol Warren, Oct. 29, 1948; children—Michael R., Douglas J. Student, Mich. State U., 1946-48. With Great Lakes Fed. Savs. & Loan Assn., 1948—, v.p., treas., 1959-68, exec. v.p., treas., 1968-69, pres., 1969—, chmn. bd., 1973—; past dir. Fed. Home Loan Bank, Indpls.; 6th Dist. rep. to adv. council Fed. Home Loan Bank Bd., 1980-81; trustee Fin. Instns. Retirement Fund. Mem. city council, Ann Arbor, 1969-71, exec. com. Catherine McAuley Health Ctr. Devel. Council; trustee Ann Arbor Found. Mem. Mich. Savs. and Loan League (dir. 1970, pres. 1976), U.S. Savs. and Loan League (legis. com. 1969—), Ann Arbor C. of C. (past dir.). Republican. Lutheran. Club: Barton Hills Country. Office: Gt Lakes Fed Savs & Loan Assn 401 E Liberty St Ann Arbor MI 48107 Home: 3332 Riverbend Dr Ann Arbor MI 48103 *

WEBER, VIN, congressman; b. Slayton, Minn., July 24, 1952. Student, U. Minn., 1970-74. Former pres. Weber Publ. Co.; co-pub. Murray County Herald, 1976-78; press sec. to Congressman Tom Hagedorn, 1974-76; campaign mgr. for Rudy Boschwitz 1978; sr. Minn. aide to Senator Rudy Boschwitz, 1979-80; mem. 97th from 6th Dist. Minn., 98th-100th Congress from 2d Dist. Minn.; asst. minority whi, chaired election com., 1984, from budget com. to appropriations com., 1987—; mem. 98th, 99th and 100th congresses from 2d dist. Republican. Office: 106 Cannon House Office Bldg Washington DC 20515

WEBER, WILLIAM MULLER, tooling company executive; b. South Bend, Ind., Apr. 22, 1941; s. William O. and Ruth L. (Muller) W.; m. Janet Anne McCandlish, June 11, 1964; children: Anne Louise, William Roy. Cert. electronics technician, South Ea. Signal Sch., Ft. Gordon, Ga., 1961; cert. pneumatics technician, Miller Fluid Power Sch., Bridgman, Mich., 1968, cert. hydraulic technician, 1969. Journeyman tool and die maker Buchanan Trade Sch., Three Oaks, Mich., 1964-68; journeyman machine builder Weldun Internat., Bridgman, 1963-73, Capitol Tooling, South Bend, 1973-74; sr. prototype technician Bendix Automotive Control Systems Group, South Bend, 1974-79; journeyman machine builder Adams Engrng., South Bend, 1979-81; pres. Weber Quality Tool, Michawaka, Ind., 1981—. Fire Fighter second class Penn South Fire Dept., Mishawaka, 1977-85, capt., 1978-82, cert. first responder, 1983-86. Served with U.S. Army, 1959-62. Baptist. Lodges: Masons (master 1972), KT. Home: 15280 Kelly Rd Mishawaka IN 46544 Office: Weber Quality Tooling Inc 421 N Cedar Mishawaka IN 46544

WEBSTER, ALICE MAE, museum administrator; b. Youngstown, Ohio, Aug. 14, 1948; d. Alexander and Martha Miller; m. Lawrence E. Webster, Dec. 27, 1975; children: John, Charles. AAB in Bus. with high honors, Youngstown State U., 1982, BSBA magna cum laude, 1985. Bus. mgr. The Butler Inst. of Am. Art, Youngstown, 1984—. Active Poland (Ohio) PTA, 1984, Poland Band Boosters, 1984. Mem. Williamson Soc. Office: The Butler Inst of Am Art 524 Wick Ave Youngstown OH 44502

WEBSTER, DAVID LOGAN, physician; b. Mpls., Feb. 19, 1951; s. David Dyer and Lucy Christeen (Furman) W.; m. Dianne Susan Wolf, Oct. 25, 1975; children: Michael Aaron, Matthew Jullian. BS, U. Minn., 1973, MD, 1977. Diplomate Am. Bd. Psychiatry and Neurology. Resident in neurology U. Minn., Mpls., 1977-81; fellow in neurology, instr. Vanderbilt U., Nashville, 1981-82; physician, neurologist Group Health Inc., Mpls., 1983—; clin. instr. U. Minn., 1985—. Contbr. articles to profl. jours. Fellow AMA, Am. Acad. Neurology, Am. EEG Soc.; mem. Minn. Med. Soc., Minn. Transp. Mus., Tenn. Valley R.R. Mus. Avocations: railroad history, locomotive restoration. Office: Group Health Inc 606 24th Ave S Minneapolis MN 55454

WEBSTER, JEFFREY LEON, graphic designer; b. Idaho Falls, Idaho, Nov. 23, 1941; s. Leon A. and Marjory M. (McAllister) W.; student Sch. Associated Arts, St. Paul, 1962; m. Judith Kess, Apr. 17, 1965; children—Eric J., Marjorie P. Sci. illustrator Mayo Clinic, Rochester, Minn., 1963-66; layout artist Brown & Bigelow, St. Paul, 1966; graphic designer U. Minn., Mpls., 1966-67, U. Calgary (Alta., Can.), 1967-68; sr. artist Control Data Corp., St. Paul, 1968-70; mem. Idaho State U. Meml. Lectureship Com.; graphic designer Idaho State U., 1970-78; owner, operator studio, Harmony, Minn.; design, advt. and mktg. cons. Mem. Idaho Civic Symphony Bd. Recipient Profl. citation Library Congress, 1976. Artist pub. ednl. exhibits. Home and Office: Route 1 Harmony MN 55939

WEBSTER, ROBERT FRANKLIN, retail executive; b. Canton, Ohio, July 7, 1943; s. Lee Wilson and Frankie Catherine (Titus) W.; m. Kathleen Crum (div. 1973); 1 child, Robin; m. Karen Marie Vereshack, Mar. 3, 1977; children: Whitney, Morgan. BS in Bus., Miami U., Oxford, Ohio, 1965. Trainee, asst. buyer O'Neil's Dept. Store, Akron, Ohio, 1965-69, dress buyer, 1969-72, store mgr. Summit Mall, 1972-74, DDM sportswear, jrs., 1974-75, v.p., gen. mdse. mgr., 1975-80, sr. v.p., gen. mdse. mgr., 1980—; RTW steering com. May Dept. Stores, N.Y.C., 1983-86; bd. dirs. Smyth Bus. Systems, Canton. Adv. com. YMCA, Akron, 1976-86. Republican. Methodist. Club: N.Y. Athletic. Avocations: handball, tennis, running. Home: 8810 Blossom Circle Massillon OH 44646 Office: O'Neils Dept Store 226 S Main St Akron OH 44308

WEBSTER, WILLIAM LAWRENCE, state attorney general; b. Carthage, Mo., Sept. 17, 1953; s. Richard Melton and Janet Posten (Whitehead) W.; m. Susan Kaye Tiemann, May 17, 1980; children: Jonathan Noel, Mark Andrew. Ed., U. Kans., 1975; J.D., U. Mo.-Kansas City, 1978. Bar: Mo. 1978. Assoc. Collins, Webster, Rouse, Joplin, Mo., 1978-84; mem. Mo. Ho. of Reps., Jefferson City, 1981-84; atty. gen. State of Mo., Jefferson City, 1985—. Office: Office Atty Gen PO Box 899 Jefferson City MO 65102 *

WECHTER, LARRY SCOT, retail food executive; b. South Bend, Ind., July 22, 1955; s. Monte and Betty May (Freeze) W.; m. Janis Marie Havens, Mar. 3, 1984; children: Jourdan Marie, Logan Scot. BS, Ball State U., 1976. CPA, Ill., Ind. Pub. acct. Fowler, Suttles & Co., CPA, Indpls., 1976-79; v.p. O'Malia Food Mkts., Noblesville, Ind., 1979—. Mem. Food Mktg. Inst. (electronic funds transfer com. 1985—), Nat. Assn. Accts., Am. Mgmt. Assn., Indpls. Soc. CPA's, Indpls. C. of C. (tax subcom., govtl. affairs com. 1985—, retail task force), Sigma Alpha Epsilon. Republican. Methodist. Avocations: tennis, working out, reading. Office: O'Malia Food Mkts 1555 Westfield Rd Noblesville IN 46060

WECHTER, MARILYN R., psychotherapist; b. N.Y.C., Aug. 25, 1952; d. William H. and Dorothy (Tannenbaum) W. BA, Washington U., St. Louis, 1973; MSW, Washington U., 1975. Cert. social worker. Psychotherapist Quad City Mental Health Ctr., Granite City, Ill., 1975-76, Growth Ctr., St. Louis, 1976-80; pvt. practice psychotherapy St. Louis, 1980—; adj. faculty Washington U., 1984-85; faculty child develop. project St. Louis Psychoanalytic Inst., 1981-84; mem. St. Louis Study Group for Applied Psychoanalysis, 1983—. Mem. Mo. Psychol. Assn., Nat. Assn. Social Workers, Soc. Advancement Self Psychology, St. Louis Women's Commerce Assn. Home: 7460 Stratford Saint Louis MO 63130 Office: 141 N Meramec #205 Saint Louis MO 63105

WECHTER, NORMAN ROBERT, paint manufacturing executive; b. Chgo., Apr. 12, 1926; s. Charles S. and Emily (Miller) W.; m. Harriet Golub, Oct. 10, 1948; children: Robin, Clari. BSBA, Northwestern U., Chgo., 1950. Pres. Federated Paint Mfg. Co., Chgo., 1950—. Served with USN, 1944-46. Republican. Jewish. Avocation: mining. Home: 180 E Pearson Chicago IL 60611 Office: Federated Paint Mfg Co 1882 S Normal Ave Chicago IL 60616

WEDELSTAEDT, CATHERINE ANN, chemist; b. Oak Park, Ill., May 15, 1957; d. Howard Nichols and Margaret Catherine (Sable) W. BS in Chemistry, U. Notre Dame, 1979; MS in Chemistry, Cen. Mich. U., 1986. Lab asst. U. Notre Dame, 1978-79; sr. research chemist Dow Chem. Co. Analytical Labs., Midland, Mich., 1979—. Mem. Am. Chem. Soc., Notre Dame Alumni Club. Clubs: Midland Adult Soccer (capt. 1979—), Midland Tennis Ctr. Avocations: skiing, golf, biking, stitchery. Home: 1412 Carolina St Midland MI 48640 Office: Dow Chem Co Analytical Labs 574 Bldg Midland MI 48667

WEDER, DONALD ERWIN, manufacturing executive; b. Highland, Ill., Aug. 18, 1947; s. Erwin Henry and Florence Louise (Graham) W.; student U. Ill., 1965-66; B.S. summa cum laude, Bradley U., 1969; m. Phyllis Ann Styron; children—Erwin Michael, Andrew Styron, David August, Ann Marie. Pres. Highland Supply Corp., 1977—, also dir.; pres. Seven W Enterprises, 1977—, also dir.; pres. LEXCO, 1977—, IMUTEK, 1977—, Pullex, 1977—; dir. 1st Nat. Bank Highland, Ill. Served to capt., inf. AUS, 1969-71. Mem. Zeta Phi, Phi Kappa Phi. Republican. Lodge: Kiwanis. Home: 621 Main St Highland IL 62249 Office: 1111 6th St Highland IL 62249

WEDGE, MARGARET ALICE, social worker; b. Ningpo, People's Republic of China, May 17, 1930; (parents Am. citizens); s. Augustus Inglesbe and Alice (Carter) Nasmith; m. George Francis Wedge III, Aug. 29, 1953; Philip, Louise, Alberta. BA in Am. Studies, George Washington U., 1953; postgrad., Washburn U.; MSW, U. Kans., 1979. Social worker Jefferson County Welfare, Oskaloosa, Kans., 1969-77; social worker Kans. Social & Rehab. Services, Lawrence, 1979-86, social worker supr., 1986—; coordinator Breakthrough, Lawrence, 1980-86; practicum field instr. Kans. Sch. Social Welfare, Lawrence, 1981-86. Mem. Domestic Violence Task Force, Lawrence, 1984-86. Mem. Douglas County Mental Health Assn. (bd. dirs. 1979-83), Kans. Sch. of Social Welfare Alumni Soc. (sec. 1985—). Avocations: singing, birdwatching. Home: 1645 Louisiana St Lawrence KS 66044 Office: Lawrence SRS Office PO Box 590 Lawrence KS 66044

WEE, LARRY EING, dentist; b. Dearborn, Mich., Mar. 17, 1952; s. Edward Eing and Vivian (Chow) W. BA in Biology, U. Louisville, 1974, DMD, 1978. Practice dentistry Saginaw, Mich., 1978—; Cons. to nursing homes in Saginaw area, 1980-86. Commr. Bridgeport (Mich.) Charter Twp., 1985—. Honarary capt. Belle of Louisville; named one of Outstanding Young Men of Am., 1985. Mem. ADA, Saginaw County Dental Soc., Trout Unlimited, Ducks Unltd. (sponser). Republican. Lodge: Optimist. Avocations: fishing, hunting, snow skiing, tennis, skeet shooting. Office: 5303 Dixie Hwy Saginaw MI 48601

WEED, BRENDA CAROL, pharmacist; b. Indpls., May 21, 1956; d. Gene Vinton and Barbara Jacqueline (Boyd) Black; m. Stanley Eugene Weed, Dec. 29, 1979; 1 child, Burton Gene. B.S. in Pharmacy, Butler U., 1980, M.S. in Pharmacology, 1985. Registered pharmacist, Ind. Pharmacist Am. Assn. Retired Persons, Indpls., 1980-82, Kroger Co., Frankfort, Ind., 1982-83; pharmacist, clin. services MetroHealth, Indpls., 1983—. Contbg. author. Maxicure Pharmacy Newsletter. Mem. Ind. Pharm. Assn., Tri Kappa, Kappa Kappa Gamma. Republican. Avocation: equestrian competition. Home: 8210 E 725 N Brownsburg IN 46112

WEED, EDWARD REILLY, marketing executive; b. Chgo., Jan. 25, 1940; s. Cornelius Cahill and Adelaide E. (Reilly) W.; student Fordham U., 1959-

61, Loyola U., 1961-62; m. Lawrie Irving Bowes, Feb. 2, 1969. Account exec. Leo Burnett Co., Chgo., 1961-71; pres. GDC Ad Inc., corporate officer advt. and sales promotion Gen. Devel. Corp., Miami, Fla., 1971-74; v.p., account supr. D'Arcy Mac Manus & Masius, Chgo., 1975; group v.p. mktg. Hart Schaffner & Marx (Hartmarx), Chgo.; pres. Hart Services, Inc., 1975-82; v.p. mktg. Tishman, 1983-86; v.p. mktg. Hannah Marine, 1986—; dir. First Nat. Bank So. Miami. Trustee, Latin Sch. Found., 1976—; bd. dirs. North Ave. Day Nursery, 1969-73, Santa for Poor, 1975—, Off-the-Street, 1982—, Chgo. Boys' and Girls' Clubs, 1983—. Served with Ill. N.G. Republican. Roman Catholic. Clubs: Tavern, Cliff Dwellers, Saddle and Cycle. Office: 361 Frontage Rd Suite 101 Burr Ridge IL 60521

WEED, LOIS LORRAINE HORA, teacher; b. Three Rivers, Mich., Jan. 9, 1949; d. Raymond Francis and Marjorie Ruth (Ream) Hora; m. Steven Bryant Weed, Jan. 4, 1969; 1 child, David Brian. BS, Western Mich. U., 1972, MA, 1981. Cert. elem. tchr., Mich. Tchr. remedial reading and math Cetreville (Mich.) Pub. Schs., 1972-76, elem. tchr., 1976-80, tchr. kindergarten and devel. kindergarten, 1984—; grad. asst. dir. summer program for gifted children Western Mich. U., Kalamazoo, 1981; mem. Devel. Kindergarten Support Group, Portage, Mich., 1984-86. Organist then asst. organist Trinity Episcopal Ch., Three Rivers, 1964—, vestry mem., 1982-84; vol. Three Rivers Sports Boosters, 1982—, Fred Upton Campaign, Three Rivers, 1986. Mem. NEA, PTA, AAUW (program v.p. 1983—), Nat. Assn. Gifted Children, Nat. Sci. Tchrs. Assn., Mich. Edn. Assn., Centreville Edn. Assn. (PAC chair 1986—). Avocations: biking, reading, sewing, swimming, music, needlework. Home: 11170 Corey Lake Rd Three Rivers MI 49093 Office: Centreville Pub Schs PO Box 158 Centreville MI 49032

WEED, MARY THEOPHILOS, psychology educator; b. Miami, Fla., Nov. 11, 1928; d. John George and Elizabeth (Sodergrer) Theophilos; m. Perry L. Weed, Mar. 29, 1963 (div. 1969); 1 child, Heather. BA, U. Miami, 1953; MA, U. Chgo., 1960. Sch. psychologist Chgo. Bd. Edn., 1960-62; asst. prof. psychology Chgo. City Colls., 1962—; pvt. practice clin. psychology, Chgo., 1963—. Mem. Am. Psychol. Assn. (assoc.), Ill. Psychol. Assn. Home and Office: 5534 S Harper Chicago IL 60637

WEEDA, VITO PHILIP, food service executive; b. Follansbee, W.Va., Feb. 27, 1938; s. Phillip Peter and Margaret Ceclia (Good) W.; m. Anita Rae Couch, May 14, 1960; children: Kimberly, Karri, Phillip, Dewey. Student, Ohio U., 1955-56, Coll. Steubenville, 1956-57, U. Cin., 1972-73. Asst. supr. agys. Western Southern Life Ins. Co., Cin., 1961-75; v.p., dir. southern region Harte Hanks Communications, Cin., 1975-80; pres., chmn. bd. Presto "America's Favorite Foods and Bakery Products", Dayton, Ohio, 1980—. Mem. Rep. Presdl. Task Force, Washington, 1982—. Served with U.S. Army, 1958-60, 61-62. Mem. Dayton C. of C., Dayton Ad Club. Republican. Roman Catholic. Lodge: KC (Grand Knight 1963-64). Avocations: golf, boating, reading. Home: 820 Oakwood Ave Dayton OH 45419 Office: Presto 1522 Manchester Rd West Carrolton OH 45449

WEEKLY, JOHN WILLIAM, insurance company executive; b. Sioux City, Iowa, June 21, 1931; s. John E. Weekly and Alyce Beatrice (Preble) Nichols; m. Bette Lou Thomas, Dec. 31, 1949; children: John William Jr., Thomas Patrick, Michael Craig, James Mathew, Daniel Kevin. Grad. high sch., Omaha. V.p. First Data Resources, Inc., Omaha, 1969-74; v.p. Mut. United Omaha Ins. Co., Omaha, 1974-81, sr. exec. v.p., 1981-87; officer Mut. United Omaha Ins. Co., 1986—; pres. Mut. United Omaha Ins. Co., Omaha, 1987—, bd. dirs.; bd. dirs. United of Omaha Ins. Co., Companion Life Ins. Co., Kirkpatrick, Pettis, Smith, Polian, Inc., Conservative Savs. Bank. Mem. chancellor's adv. council U. Nebr., Omaha, 1984—; pres. bd. dirs. Madonna Sch., Omaha, 1984—; bd. dirs. Salvation Army, Omaha, 1984—, United Way of Midlands, 1987—, Bellevue (Nebr.) Coll., 1986—. Club: Omaha Country (treas. 1986—). Avocations: hunting, fishing, golf. Office: Mut Omaha Ins Co Mutual of Omaha Plaza Omaha NE 68175

WEEKS, CHARLES R., bank executive; b. 1934. Pres., chief exec. officer Citizens Comml. & Savs. Bank, Flint, Mich., 1982—. Office: Citizens Comml & Savs Bank One Citizens Banking Center Flint MI 48502 *

WEEKS, M. J., academic administrator; b. N.Y.C., June 12, 1942; d. Kenneth James and Annette Jude (Williams) Altman; m. Robert S. Weeks, June 15, 1960; children: Sean Robert, Megan Elizabeth. BA cum laude, U. S.D., 1967, MA, 1969. Tchr. high sch. Orono Schs., Long Lake, Minn., 1970-74; mem. faculty Winona (Minn.) State U., 1976-82; mem. faculty Sioux Falls (S.D.) Coll., 1982—, dir. Ctr. Mgmt., 1985—; communications cons., Sioux Falls, 1982—. Author communications tng. manuals. Bd. dirs. League of Women Voters, Sioux Falls, 1983-85; mem. Women's Network, S.D., 1984-86, Peace and Justice Ctr., 1984-86. Mem. AAUW (bd. dirs. 1983-84), Am. Soc. Tng. and Devel., Nat. Council Tchrs. of English, Nat. Am. Soc. Tng., Sioux Falls Personnel Assn. Avocations: reading, writing, tennis, traveling, gourmet cooking. Home: 3505 Spencer Blvd Sioux Falls SD 57103 Office: Ctr Mgmt 1505 S Prairie Sioux Falls SD 57105

WEEKS, PAUL MARTIN, plastic surgeon, educator; b. Clinton, N.C., June 11, 1932; m. Doris Hill, Apr. 28, 1956; children: Christopher, Heather, Paul, Thomas, Susan, Phillip. AB, Duke U., 1954; MD, U. N.C., 1958. Diplomate Am. Bd. Surgery, Am. Bd. Plastic Surgery. Intern N.C. Meml. Hosp., 1959-62, asst. resident in surgery, 1962-63, chief resident in gen. surgery, 1962-63, chief resident in plastic surgery, 1963-64; from instr. to asst. prof. surgery U. Ky., 1964-68, assoc. prof. surgery, 1968-70; prof. surgery, plastic and reconstructive surgery, head of div. Washington U. Sch. Medicine, St. Louis, 1971—; plastic surgeon-in-chief Barnes Hosp., St. Louis, 1971—, St. Louis Children's Hosp., 1971—. Assoc. editor Jour. Hand Surgery, 1976—, Plastic and Reconstructive Surgery, 1978-84; contbr. articles to profl. jours. Mem. AMA, ACS, Soc. Univ. Surgeons, So. Med. Assn., Assn. Academic Surgeons, Am. Cleft Palate Assn., Am. Soc. Plastic and Reconstructive Surgeons, Am. Soc. Surgery of the Hand, Plastic Surgery Research Council, Am. Burn Assn., Am. Assn. Plastic and Reconstructive Surgeons, Mo. State Med. Assn., St. Louis Med. Soc., Canadian Soc. Plastic and Reconstructive Surgeons, Nathan Womack Soc. Republican. Avocations: golf, sailing. Home: 6470 Ellenwood Clayton MO 63105 Office: Washington U Sch Medicine 4949 Barnes Hosp Plaza Saint Louis MO 63110

WEEKS, ROBERT EARL, advertising executive; b. Yazoo City, Miss., Sept. 17, 1925; s. Dennis H. and Mamie O. (Randolph) W.; children: Suzanne Lynn, Robin Denise, Linda, Robert Earl II, Lisa Ann. Student, Wilson Jr. Coll., 1947, Latin Am. Inst. Pub. Relations, 1950, DePaul U., 1952. Br. mgr. King Records Inc., Chgo., 1948-50; assoc. Pursell Pub. Relations, Chgo., 1950-65; insp. Chgo. Bd. Health, 1965-66; adminstrv. asst. to Alderman Robert H. Miller, Chgo., 1966-69; coordinator task force for community broadcasting Chgo. Digest mag., 1969-76; pres. Troubadour & Assocs., Ltd., Chgo., 1969—; pub. Troubadour Digest mag., 1976—; writer Cablecommunications Resource Ctr., Washington, 1972—. Author: Cable TV in Chicago, 1976; editor Chgo. Radio Guide, 1985. Active with South Side Community Art Ctr., Hyde Park Improvement Assn. Served with USAAF, 1944-46. Mem. Black Media Reps. (v.p. 1976), Ill. Arts Assn., Am. Soc. Profl. Cons., Pub. Relations Soc. Am. Democrat. Roman Catholic. Clubs: Clef Social, Publicity of Chgo. Home: 5325 S Cottage Grove Ave Chicago IL 60615

WEERTS, RICHARD KENNETH, music educator; b. Peoria, Ill., Oct. 7, 1928; s. Gerhard Nicholas and Ellen Marie (Lindeburg) W. BS, U. Ill., 1951; MA, Columbia U., 1956, EdD, 1960; MA, N.E. Mo. State U., 1973. Tchr. Lyndhurst (N.J.) Pub. Schs., 1956-57; dir. instrumental music Scotch Plains (N.J.) Pub. Schs., 1957-61; prof. music N.E. Mo. State U., Kirksville, 1961—. Author: Handbook for Woodwinds, 1965, Developing Individual Skills for the High School Band, 1969, How to Develop and Maintain a Successful Woodwind Section, 1972, Original Manuscript Music, 1973, Handbook of Rehearsal Techniques for Band, 1976. Dir. music First United Meth. Ch., Kirksville, 1970—. Served with U.S. Army, 1951-55. Mem. Nat. Assn. Coll. Wind and Percussion Instrs. (nat. exec. sec./treas. 1971—, editor jour. 1968—), Music Educators Nat. Conf., Phi Delta Kappa. Office: care Northeast Mo State U Div Fine Arts Kirksville MO 63501

WEESE, CYNTHIA ROGERS, architect, educator; b. Des Moines, June 23, 1940; d. Gilbert Taylor and Catharine (Wingard) Rogers; m. Benjamin H. Weese, July 5, 1963; children: Daniel Peter, Catharine Mohr. B.S.A.S., Washington U., St. Louis, 1962; B.Arch., Washington U., 1965. Registered architect, Ill. Pvt. practice architecture Chgo., 1965-72, 1974-77; draftsperson, designer Harry Weese & Assocs., Chgo., 1972-74; prin. Weese Hickey Weese Ltd., Chgo., 1977—; design critic Ball State U., Muncie, Ind., Miami U., Oxford, Ohio, 1979, U. Wis.-Milw., 1980, U. Ill.-Chgo., 1981, 85, Iowa State U., Ames, 1982, Washington U., St. Louis, 1985. Mem. AIA (dir. Chgo. chpt. 1980-83, v.p. 1983-85, 1st v.p., pres. 1987—, disting. building awards 1977, 81, 82, 83, 86, interior architecture award 1981, disting. service award 1978), Chgo. Women in Architecture, Chgo. Network, Chgo. Archtl. Assistance Ctr. (bd. dirs.), Alpha Rho Chi. Democrat. Club: Arts (Chgo.). Office: Weese Hickey Weese 9 W Hubbard St Chicago IL 60610

WEESE, HARRY M., architect; b. Evanston, Ill., June 30, 1915; s. Harry E. and Marjorie (Mohr) W.; m. Kate Baldwin, Feb. 8, 1945; children: Shirley, Kate, Marcia. Student, Yale U., 1936-37; B.Arch., Mass. Inst. Tech., 1938. Fellow Cranbrook Acad. Art, 1938-39; prin. firm Baldwin & Weese, Kenilworth, Ill., 1940-42; with firm Skidmore, Owings & Merrill, Chgo., 1946-47; ind. practice as Harry Weese & Assos., Chgo., 1947—. Principal projects include Am. Embassy, Ghana, New Town Riyadh Internat. Airport, Saudi Arabia, Crown Center Hotel, Kansas City, Master Plan and Archtl. Design, Chinatown, Chgo.; restoration of Adler-Sullivan Auditorium, Chgo., 1st Bapt. Ch, Columbus, Ind., metro transit systems, Washington, Los Angeles, Miami, Buffalo, Dallas. Fed. Correctional Center, Chgo., Arena Stage, Washington, Performing Arts Ctr., Milw., Grand Rapids, Mich., Wolf Point Landings, Chgo.; 200 S. Wacker Bldg, Chgo., Time and Life Bldg, Chgo., Am. Embassy Housing, Tokyo, Fed. Triangle Master Plan, Washington, Tech. Ctr. Cummins Engine Co., Columbus, Ind., campus project U. Wis.-Madison, Terman Engrng. Ctr. Stanford U., renovation Field Mus. Chgo., South Cove Marina and Condominiums, New Buffalo, Mich., renovation and master plan Henry Cobb Ives Bldg. Newberry Library, Chgo., Oak Park (Ill.) Village Hall, Harwick Bldg. Mayo Clinic, Rochester, Minn., corp. hdqtrs. Union Underwear Co., Bowling Green, Ky., Printing House Row, Chgo., Navy Pier Marina, Chgo., U.S. Custom House Post Office restoration, St. Louis, numerous others; pub. Inland Architect mag. Mem. Pres.'s Citizens' Adv. Com. Recreation and Natural Beauty, 1966-69, Pres.'s Citizens' Adv. Com. Environ. Quality, 1969-71, Gov. Ill. Commn. on Orgn. Ill. Dept. Transp., 1972-74, Urban Design Rev. Bd. San Jose (Calif.) Redevel. Agy., 1984—; co-chair Mayor Jane Byrne's Archtl. Adv. Com., Chgo., 1979-82; archtl. cons. fgn. bldgs. program Dept. State, 1973-76; mem. Nat. Council on Arts, 1974-80; trustee Latin Sch., Chgo. Served as lt. USNR, 1941-45. Recipient Chgo. Architecture award Archtl. Record Mag. and Ill. Council AIA, 1987, Diplome de Lauret, Biennale Mondale de l'Architecture, Union of Architects, Bulgaria, 1983, Disting. Service award Chgo. chpt. AIA, 1981, Firm of Yr. award AIA, 1978, Total Design award Ill. chpt. AIA, 1975; named Chicagoan Yr., Chgo. Press Club, 1978. Fellow AIA (pres. Chgo. chpt. 1975); mem. NAD (academician), Nat. Assn. Housing and Redevel. Ofcls. (adv. bd. 1985—), Nat. Council Arts (design arts com. 1984—). Clubs: Arts, Comml., Yacht, Tavern (Chgo.). Home: 314 W Willow St Chicago IL 60610 Office: Harry Weese & Assocs 10 W Hubbard St Chicago IL 60610

WEFALD, JON, university president; b. Nov. 24, 1937; s. Olav and Walma (Ovrum) W.; m. Ruth Ann; children—Skipp, Andy. B.A., Pacific Lutheran U., Tacoma, 1959; M.A., Wash. State U., Pullman, 1961; Ph.D., U. Mich., Ann Arbor, 1965. Teaching asst. Wash. State U., Pullman, 1959-61; teaching fellow U. Mich., Ann Arbor, 1961-64; assoc. prof. Gustavus Adolphus Coll., St. Peter, Minn., 1965-70; commnr. agr. State of Minn., St. Paul, 1971-77; pres. Southwest State U., Marshall, Minn., 1977-82; chancellor Minn. State Univ. System, St. Paul, 1982-86; pres. Kans. State U., 1986—. Author: A Voice of Protest: Norwegians in American Politics 1890-1917, 1971. Mem. Mid-Am. Internat. Agri-Trade Council (pres. 1974-75), Midwest Assn. State Depts. of Agr. (sec.treas. 1976-77), U.S. Dept. Agr. Joint Council on Food and Agrl. Scis. Office: Kans State U Manhattan KS 66506

WEGMAN, STEVEN MICHAEL, energy engineer; b. Sioux Falls, S.D., Apr. 29, 1953; s. Herbert S. and Iva M. (Voss) W.; m. Donna R. Endahl, Sept. 30, 1978; children: Rachel Von, Adriane Kay. BSCE, S.D. State U., 1973. Cert. infared thermography operator. Engr. State of S.D. Dept. Transp., Pierre, 1976-78; staff asst. State of S.D. Energy Office, Pierre, 1978-79, dir. solar program, 1979-81, dir. R.H. energy program, 1981—, dir. alternate energy project, 1981—; bd. dirs. Pilot Plant Corp., Rapid City, S.D.; cons. S. D. Cement Plant, Rapid City, 1980—, Energy Efficient Building Group, Pine Island, Minn., 1982—. Author: Energy Efficient Building, 1980, Infared Thermography for Residential Building, 1985, Thermography for Utilities, 1986. Novel Use of Solar Energy award U.S Dept. Energy, 1979; recipient Supervisor Control and Data Acquisition award Western Area Power Adminstrn., 1985, Outstanding Energy Engr. award S.D. Energy Office. Fellow S.D. Renewable Energy Assn. (bd. dirs., exec. sec., outstanding researcher award 1980), S.D. Thermography Soc.; mem. ASHRAE, Sioux Falls Homebuilders Assn. Republican. Lutheran. Lodge: Elks. Avocations: camping, photography, chess, woodworking. Office: SD Energy Office PO Box 491 Pierre SD 57501

WEGMILLER, DONALD CHARLES, health care corporation executive, health care consultant; b. Cloquet, Minn., Sept. 25, 1938; m. Janet A. Listerud, Apr. 27, 1957; children: Katherine, Mark, Dean. BA, U. Minn., 1960, MHA, 1962. Adminstrv. asst. Fairview Hosp., Mpls., 1962-65; asst. adminstr. Fairview-Southdale Hosp., Mpls., 1965-66, adminstr., 1966-76; sr. v.p. Health Central System, Mpls., 1976-78, pres., chief exec. officer, 1978-84; pres. Health Central Corp., 1984-87; pres., chief exec. officer HealthOne Corp., 1987—; preceptor, faculty U. Minn., 1974—, U. Colo., 1974—, U. Mich., 1974—, Duke U., 1974—, U. Ariz., 1977—; cons. div. med. services U.S. Dept. State, Washington, 1975; bd. dirs. Am. Healthcare Systems, Internat. Clin. Labs., Minn. Bus. Ptnrship., Council of Community Hosps., Healthcare Minn.; U.S. del. King's Fund Internat. Invitational Conf., 1983-85, nat. coordinator, 1985; U.S. Internat. Hosp. Fed., 1987—. Contbr. articles to profl. jours. Chmn. Bd. Edn., Richfield, Minn., 1970-74; staff asst. to Presidents Nixon, Ford and Reagan, 1972—; adv. com. Sen. Durenberger's Health Care, Mpls., 1979—. Named Outstanding Young Man of Yr. Mpls. Jaycees, 1971; recipient Nat. Healthcare award B'nai B'rith, 1987. Fellow Am. Coll. Health Care Execs. (Robert S. Hudgen's award 1969), Am. Hosp. Assn. (chmn. bd. trustees 1987), Minn. Hosp. Assn., Mpls. Jaycees (pres. 1968-69). Republican. Methodist. Lodge: Rotary. Home: 7871 Cheshire Ln Maple Grove MN 55369 Office: HealthOne Corp 2810 57th Ave N Minneapolis MN 55430

WEHLACZ, JOSEPH THEODORE, toxicologist; b. Chgo., May 29, 1946; s. Theodore and Marjorie (Dunaj) W.; m. Cherilyn Beth Anderson, June 2, 1972; children: Jennifer, Amy. BS in Sci., Memphis State U., 1968; MS in Organic Chemistry, Ind. U., 1970, MLS, 1972. Sci. cataloguer Ind. U., Bloomington, 1972; engrng. librarian Memphis State U., 1972-73; sr. librarian Eli Lilly & Co., Greenfield, Ind., 1973-79, toxicologist, info. specialist, 1980-86. Mem. Am. Chem. Soc., Spl. Library Assn., Ind. Online User Group. Presbyterian. Avocations: sports, reading, collecting mugs, travel. Office: Eli Lilly & Co Toxicology Div Lilly Research Labs PO Box 708 Greenfield IN 46140

WEHR, KENNETH LEWIS, internist; b. Hamilton, Ohio, May 11, 1943; s. Charles Herman Jr. and Betty Jane (Lotz) W.; m. Marcia Lee Grimm, Aug. 7, 1965; children: Jennifer Katherine, Erin Elizabeth, Jason Kenneth. BS, Wake Forest Coll., 1965, MD, 1968. Intern then resident Wake Forest Coll. Hosp., Winston-Salem, N.C., 1968-71; pulmonary fellow U. Tex. Southwest Med. Sch., Dallas, 1971-73; practice medicine specializing in internal & pulmonary medicine Hamilton, Ohio, 1975—. Contbr. articles to profl. jours. Pres. bd. dirs. Hamilton (Ohio) City Schs., 1978-82. Served to maj. USAF, 1973-75. Fellow ACP, Am. Coll. Chest Physicians; mem. AMA, Ohio Med. Assn., Am. Soc. Internal Medicine. Home: 510 S D St Hamilton OH 45013 Office: Taft Place Med Ctr 1380 NW Washington Blvd Hamilton OH 45013

WEHRKAMP, JEFFREY ALLEN, dentist; b. Sioux Falls, S.D., Aug. 12, 1955; s. Dale Richard and Geraldine (Fischer) W.; m. Sandra Mae Fredrickson, July 25, 1981; children: Jeremy John, Jessica Marie. BS, S.D. State U., 1977; DDS, Loyola U., Maywood, Ill., 1981. Gen. practice dentistry Brandon, S.D., 1981—; cons. Palisades Nursing Home, Garretson, S.D., 1981—, Prince of Peace Retirement Ctr., Sioux Falls, S.D., 1986—. Mem. ADA, S.D. Dental Assn. (SELECT coordinator, mem. peer rev. com. 1987—, dental advisor to the dental asst. tng. program Vo-Tech 1985—), Brandon Jaycees (pres. 1983-84), S.E. Dist. Dental Soc. (del.). Republican. Roman Catholic. Club: Comml. (pres. 1985-87). Lodge: Optimists. Avocations: hunting, fishing, skiing, jogging, golf, taxidermy. Home: 104 Oakridge Rd Brandon SD 57005 Office: 117 Holly Blvd Brandon SD 57005

WEICHMAN, TERESA LYNN, school social work counselor; b. Columbus, Ind., Jan. 28, 1956; d. John Carlton Dutro and Shirley Ann (Devers) Park; m. Carl E. Weichman, Dec. 1, 1979; 1 child, Kylie Ann. BSW, Ind. U., Indpls. and Bloomington, 1978. Cert. vocat. tchr., Ind. Program coordinator mgr. Devel. Services Inc., Columbus, 1978-81; teller Irwin Union Bank & Trust, Columbus, 1982-84; mgr., employment counselor Employment Asst. Services, Columbus, 1984-85; coordinator, support and pupil services Bartholomew Consol. Sch. Corp., Columbus, 1985—; pvt. practice resume cons., Columbus, 1985—. Author brochures and tng. manuals. Coach Columbus Spl. Olympics, 1978—, treas. 1978-81; youth leader First Bapt. Ch., Columbus, 1978-84; chmn. Ride-A-Bike for Cystic Fibrosis, Columbus, 1983; vice chmn. County Auditor's Campaign, Columbus, 1986. Named Outstanding Young Woman of Columbus, Local Optimists, 1974. Mem. Am. Bus. Women's Assn. (chmn. ways and means 1985—), Am. Vocat. Assn., Ind. Edn. and Tng. Assn., Ind. Vocat. Assn., Ind. U. Sch. Social Work Alumni Assn. Avocations: playing guitar, singing, volleyball, softball, swimming. Home: 2303 Maple St Columbus IN 47201

WEICKER, JACK EDWARD, educational administrator; b. Woodburn, Ind., June 23, 1924; s. Monald Henry and Helen Mae (Miller) W.; A.B., Ind. U., 1947, M.A. (James Albert Woodburn fellow, All-Univ. fellow), 1951; m. Janet Kathryn Thompson, May 29, 1946; children—John H., Kathryn Ann, Jane Elizabeth, Emily Jo. Tchr. history and English, Harrison Hill Sch., Ft. Wayne, Ind., 1947-48, South Side High Sch., Ft. Wayne, 1951-61; counselor, asst. prin. South Side High Sch., 1961-63, prin., 1963—. Mem. Ind. State Scholarship Commn., 1969-77; mem. exec. com. Midwest regional assembly Coll. Entrance Exam. Bd., 1974-77, chmn. nominating com., 1976-77, mem. nat. nominating com., 1979; mem. Midwest Regional Coll. Access Services Com., 1982-84. Chmn., Easter Seal Telethon, Allen County Soc. Crippled Children and Adults, 1982, 83. Recipient award for meritorious service Ball State U., 1980; Outstanding Prin. of Yr. award Ind. Secondary Sch. Adminstrs. Assn., 1981, Ind. Prin. Yr., Ind. Assn. Ednl. Secs., 1986, Disting. Service award Midwestern Regional Assembly of Coll. Entrance Examination Bd., 1987; Rotary Paul Harris fellow, 1985. Mem. Ft. Wayne Prins. Assn., Nat. Assn. Secondary Sch. Prins. (conf. speaker New Orleans 1985), Ind. Secondary Sch. Adminstrs., PTA (life), Phi Beta Kappa, Phi Delta Kappa, Phi Alpha Theta. Mem. Christian Ch. (Disciples of Christ) (moderator of bd. trustees 1975-79). Clubs: Ft. Wayne Rotary (dir. 1973-76, 79-82, pres.-elect 1981-82, pres. 1982-83), Quest (dir. 1979-81), Fortnightly (v.p. 1984-85, pres. 1985-86). Author: (with others) Indiana: The Hoosier State, 1959, 63; (monographs) Due Process and Student Rights/Responsibilities: Two Points of View, 1975; Back to Basics: Language Arts, 1976; College Entrance Exams—Friend or Foe?, 1981; How the Effective Principal Communicates, 1983; Readin', Writin', and Other Stuff, 1984. Home: 5200 N Washington Rd Fort Wayne IN 46804 Office: 3601 S Calhoun St Fort Wayne IN 46807

WEIDLER, RALPH A., computer science executive; b. Presque Isle, Maine, Mar. 13, 1954; s. Robert William and Irene (Munro) W.; m. Gertrude Kay Westphal, May 7, 1976; children: Rachel, Christopher, Steven, Rebecca, Nathanael. BS in Biology and Chemistry, Marquette U., 1976. Programmer First Bank, Milw., 1976-78; dir. computer services Foley & Lardner, Milw., 1978—. Scout master Boy Scouts Am., Milw., 1984—. Mem. ABA, Assn. Legal Adminstrs., Assn. Computing Machinery. Republican. Mormon. Avocations: reading, cycling. Home: 4606 W Woodale Ave Brown Deer WI 53223 Office: Foley and Lardner 777 E Wisconsin Ave Suite 3800 Milwaukee WI 53202

WEIDNER, EDWARD WILLIAM, university chancellor, political scientist; b. Mpls., July 7, 1921; s. Peter Clifford and Lillian (Halbe) W.; m. Jean Elizabeth Blomquist, Mar. 23, 1944; children: Nancy Louise, Gary Richard, Karen, William. BA magna cum laude, U. Minn., 1942, MA, 1943, PhD, 1946; postgrad., U. Wis., 1943-45; LHD (hon.), No. Mich. U., 1969; PhD (hon.), Linköping U., Sweden, 1975. Staff mem. Nat. Mcpl. League, 1944, research assoc., 1944-45; cons. govts. div. U.S. Bur. Census, 1945; statistician U.S. Bur. Census, Washington, 1946; lectr. U. Wis., Madison, 1945; instr. U. Minn., Mpls., 1945-47, asst. prof., 1947-49, asst. dir. research in inter-govtl. relations, 1946-53; asst. prof. UCLA, 1949-50; faculty Mich. State U., East Lansing, 1950-62, from assoc. prof., dir. govtl. research bur., to prof. polit. sci., 1952-62, chmn. polit. sci. dept., 1952-57; coordinator, chief adviser Vietnam Project, 1955-57; dir. Inst. Research on Overseas Programs, 1957-61; vice chancellor E.W. Ctr., 1962-65; prof. polit. sci., dir. ctr. for devel. change U. Ky., Lexington, 1965-67; chancellor U. Wis., Green Bay, 1966-86, prof. polit. sci., 1966—, dir. Cofrin Arboretum, 1986—; dir. Univ. Bank, Green Bay; cons. Fgn. Ops. Adminstrn., Vietnam, 1954-55, Baltimore County (Md.) Reorgn. Commn., 1953-54, Ford Found., Pakistan, 1956, Nat. Assn. Fgn. Student Advisers, 1959-60, Pres.'s Task Force Fgn. Econ. Assistance, 1961, Dept. State, 1962-63, AID, 1964-65, Lees Coll., 1971-72; mem. Gov. Mich. Commn. Inter-Govtl. Relations, 1954-55, UN Univ. Council, 1974-80. Author: (with William Anderson) American Government, 1951, State and Local Government, 1951, (with others) The International Programs of American Universities, 1958, Intergovernmental Relations as Seen by Public Officials, 1960, (with William Anderson, Clara Penniman) Government for the Fifty States, 1960, The World Role of Universities, 1962, Technical Assistance in Public Administration Overseas, 1964; editor: Development Administration in Asia, 1970. Mem. Wis. Gov.'s Commn. on UN, 1975-81; trustee Prairie Sch., 1969—; bd. dirs., adv. bd. Inst. for Shipboard Edn., 1976—; chmn. adv. bd. ARC Lakeland chpt., 1981-84; mem. N.Am. adv. group UN Environ. Programme, 1983—; bd. advisers Nature Conservancy of Wis., 1984—. Recipient Outstanding Achievement award U. Minn., 1975. Mem. Am. Polit. Sci. Assn. (nat. council 1950-52), Eastern Regional Orgn. Pub. Adminstrn., Comparative Edn. Soc., Am. Soc. Pub. Adminstrn. (nat. council 1947-50), Am. Council on Edn. (sec. 1971-72, mem. commn. on acad. affairs 1971-74), Assn. Am. Colls. (bd. dirs. 1978-81), Nat. Mcpl. League, Nature Conservancy, Audubon Soc., Am. Birding Assn., Phi Beta Kappa, Pi Sigma Alpha. Home: Rt 1 Box 348 New Franken WI 54229-9758

WEIDNER, JEAN E(LIZABETH) B(LOMQUIST), psychotherapist; b. Mpls., Apr. 23, 1923; d. Wallace V. and Gertrude (Ryan) Blomquist; m. Edward W. Weidner, Mar. 23, 1944; children: Nancy, Gary, Karen, William. BA, U. Minn., 1945; MSW, U. Wis., Milw., 1977. Social worker Child and Family Service, Honolulu, 1964-66, Family Service, Green Bay, Wis., 1968-83; psychotherapist Psychiat. Services, Green Bay, 1983—; cons. Community Service Ctr., Green Bay, 1974-84, Jefferson Manor, Green Bay, 1984—. Contbr. articles to profl. jours. Mem. Nat. Assn. Social Workers, Am. Assn. Marriage and Family Therapy, Green Bay Antiquarian Soc., Brown County Hist. Soc. Home: Rt 1 PO Box 348 New Franken WI 54229-9758 Office: Psychiat Services Bellin Bldg 130 E Walnut St Green Bay WI 54301

WEIGEL, OLLIE J., dentist, mayor; b. Ankeny, Iowa, Sept. 29, 1922; s. Verne Noble and Ethel Rebecca (Johnson) W.; m. Mary Kathryn Finnegan, June 3, 1944; children: John, Marilyn, Larry, Susan. DDS, U. Iowa, 1951. Practice dentistry Ankeny, 1951—; mayor City of Ankeny, 1974—. Mem. Ankeny City Council, 1966-73; chmn. Cen. Iowa Regional Govt., 1978. Served to 2d lt. USAAF, 1943-45, ETO. Mem. ADA, Iowa Dental Assn., Des Moines Dist. Dental Soc., Ankeny C. of C. (Outstanding Citizen 1976), Mid Iowa Assn. Local Govts., League of Iowa Municipalities (pres. 1976-77), Am. Legion. Republican. Methodist. Lodge: Lions. Avocation: fishing. Home: 2506 NW 4th Ankeny IA 50021 Office: 306 SW Walnut Ankeny IA 50021

WEIL, DAVID MAXWELL, packaging company executive; b. Chgo., Apr. 21, 1912; s. Joseph and Blanch (Falter) W.; m. Aase Pedersen, Feb. 28, 1950; children: Lise, Greta, Kari. BA magna cum laude, Harvard U., 1933.

Chmn. bd. dirs., treas. Cromwell Paper Co., Chgo., 1949—; fgn. editor Chgo. Jour. Commerce, 1939-42; book reviewer Chgo. Sun, 1946-48; hon. consul El Salvador, 1940-42, 46—; fin. adviser Yugoslavian embassy. Governing mem. Library Internat. Relations; sponsor Chgo. Council Fgn. Relations. Served with AUS, 1942-45. Decorated comdr. Order St. Sava (Yugoslavia); officer Order Homayoun (Iran), Order Merit 1st class (Iran). Mem. Alliance Francaise, Pan Am. Soc., Phi Beta Kappa. Clubs: Arts, Standard (Chgo.); Harvard (N.Y.C.). Home: 1540 N Lake Shore Dr Chicago IL 60610 Office: Cromwell Paper Co 4801 S Whipple St Chicago IL 60632

WEIL, ROMAN LEE, accountant, educator; b. Montgomery, Ala., May 22, 1940; s. Roman L. and Charlotte (Alexander) W.; children: Alexis Cherie, Charles Alexander Roman, Lacey Lorraine. B.A., Yale U., 1962; M.S. in Indsl. Adminstrn, Carnegie-Mellon U., 1965, Ph.D. in Econs., 1966. C.P.A.; cert. mgmt. acct. From instr. to assoc. prof. U. Chgo., 1965-74, prof. acctg., 1976—; Mills B. Lane prof. indsl. mgmt. Ga. Inst. Tech., 1974-76; adv. com. replacement cost implementation SEC, 1976-77; prof. acctg. Stanford U., 1984, prof. econs., 1985; prof. acctg. and law NYU Sch. of Law, 1985. Author: Fundamentals of Accounting, 1975, Financial Accounting, 5th edit, 1988, Accounting: The Language of Business, 7th edit, 1987, Inflation Accounting, 1976, Replacement Cost Accounting, 1976, Managerial Accounting, 1979, 3d edit., 1988; editor: Handbook of Modern Accounting, 1977, 3d edit., 1983, Handbook of Cost Accounting, 1978, Intermediate Accounting, 1980, 4th edit., 1985, Accounting Rev, 1974-79, Fin. Analysts Jour, 1980—. NSF grantee, 1967-81. Mem. Am. Inst. C.P.A.s, Ill. Soc. C.P.A.s, Am. Econ. Assn., Inst. Mgmt. Scis., Nat. Assn. Accts. (cert. mgmt. accounting), Am. Acctg. Assn., Inst. Managerial Acctg. Home: 175 E Delaware Pl Apt 8302 Chicago IL 60611-1732 Office: U Chgo Grad Sch Bus 1101 E 58th St Chicago IL 60637

WEILAND, DONALD GERARD, lawyer, educator; b. Evanston, Ill., Jan. 29, 1954; s. Francis John and Frances Rita (Summers) W.; m. Sonia I. Rodriguez, Sept. 17, 1983. Student Am. U., 1974; B.A., Ill. Wesleyan U., 1976; postgrad. comparative law study Coll. William and Mary, Exeter, Eng., 1979; J.D., John Marshall Law Sch., 1980. Bar: Ill. 1980, U.S. Dist. Ct. (no. dist.) Ill. 1980, U.S. Ct. Appeals (7th cir.) 1980. Law clk. Ill. Supreme Ct., Bloomington, 1980-81; instr. law John Marshall Law Sch., Chgo., 1981—; sole practice, Chgo., 1981—; hearing officer Ill. Bd. Edn., 1984; staff atty. Holiday Project, Chgo., 1982; lectr. in continuing legal edn. problems. Contbr. numerous articles to law jours. Mem. ABA, Ill. State Bar Assn., Chgo. Bar Assn. (co-chmn. nat. moot ct. competition 1984), Assn. Trial Lawyers Am., John Marshall Law Sch. Alumni Assn. Democrat. Roman Catholic. Office: 135 S LaSalle Chicago IL 60603

WEILAND, EDMOND LLOYD, health care administrator; b. Sioux Falls, S.D., Dec. 2, 1953; s. Lester E. and Delores J. (Wilcox) W.; m. Susan J. Gustman, Sept. 22, 1979; 1 child, Joshua. BA, Augustana Coll., Sioux Falls, 1977; MA in Hosp. Adminstrn., U. Minn., 1985. Adminstr. Plainview (Nebr.) Hosp., 1978-82; assoc. adminstr. Meml. Med. Ctr., Watertown, S.D., 1982-85; adminstr. Prairie Lakes Health Care Ctr., Watertown, 1986—. Council Luth. Ch. of Our Redeemer, 1985; div. dir. United Way, 1986. Recipient Health Care Leader for 21st Century award Hosp. mag., Chgo., 1986. Mem. Am. Coll. Health Care Execs. Republican. Lodges: Rotary, Elks. Office: Prarie Lakes Health Care Ctr 400 10th Ave Watertown SD 57201

WEILER, JOHN M., physician; b. Erie, Pa., Mar. 9, 1945; s. Ad R. and Ruth (Schlosser) W.; m. Kay Lynn Boese, Dec. 23, 1971; children: Rebecca Lynn, James Michael. BS, U. Mich., Ann Arbor, 1967; MD, Temple U., Phila., 1971. Research fellow Harvard U., Boston, 1975-77; asst. prof. U. Iowa, Iowa City, 1978-83, assoc. prof., 1983—; visiting investigator Scripps Clinic and Research Found., La Jolla, Calif., 1986; program specialist immunology VA Cen. Office, Washington, 1985—. Served as surgeon Pub. Health Service, 1972-74. Recipient Research Career Devel. award Nat. Inst. Health, 1983, Clin. Investigator award VA, 1983-85, Research Assoc. award, 1980-83. Mem. Am. Acad. Allergy, Am. Assn. Immunologists, Am. Coll. Physicians, Am. Rheumatism Assn. Avocations: amateur radio, computer software design. Office: Univ of Iowa Hosp SW34E GH Iowa City IA 52242

WEILER, PATRICK JOHN, engineer; b. Remsen, Iowa, Nov. 1, 1957; s. Allan A. and Doris (Lenertz) W.; m. Sharon Sue Harpenau, June 5, 1981; children: Megan, Marlene. BS in Agrl. Engring., Iowa State U., 1980. Designer Vermeer Mfg., Pella, Iowa, 1980-81, project engr., 1981-83, dir. engring., 1983—. Home: 814 Sunset Ave Pella IA 50219 Office: Vermeer Mfg PO Box 200 Pella IA 50219

WEIMER, FERNE LAURAINE, librarian; b. Valparaiso, Ind., May 28, 1950; d. John Junior and Helen Lorraine (Dillingham) W. A.B. in History, Wheaton Coll., 1972; M.A. in L.S., No. Ill. U., 1974. Cataloger, Lake County Pub. Library, Merrillville, Ind., 1974-77. Cataloger Billy Graham Ctr. Library, Wheaton (Ill.) Coll., 1977-79, dir., 1979—. Mem. ALA, Am. Theol. Library Assn., Assn. Christian Librarians, Chgo. Area Theol. Library Assn. (v.p. 1985-86, pres. 1986-87), DuPage Librarians Assn. (sec. 1981-82, pres. 1982-83). Office: Billy Graham Ctr Library Wheaton Coll Wheaton IL 60187

WEIMER, JEAN ELAINE, nursing educator; b. Denver, June 8, 1932; d. John and Marquerite Christina (Friehauf) Jacoby; m. James David Weimer, Aug. 5, 1956; 1 dau., Lisa Marie. Diploma in nursing Children's Hosp. Sch. Nursing, Denver, 1953; B.S.N., U. Denver, 1954; M.A., N.Y. U., 1962. R.N., Colo., S.D., N.Y., Ill. Staff nurse Children's Hosp., Denver, 1953-54, head nurse, 1954-56; dir. nursing edn. Yankton (S.D.) State Hosp., 1956-60; instr. Mt. Sinai Hosp. Sch. Nursing, N.Y.C., 1962-63, curriculum coordinator, 1964-67; asst. prof. nursing City Colls. Chgo., 1968-78, assoc. prof., 1978-85, prof., 1985—; co-chmn. nursing dept. Truman Coll., 1984—. NIMH grantee, 1960-62. Mem. Am. Nurses' Assn., Council Advanced Practioners Psychiat. Nursing (dir. R.N. tutoring project), Truman Coll. Faculty Council, City Coll. Faculty Council, Kappa Delta Pi, Pi Lambda Theta. Mem. United Ch. of Christ. Home: 6171 N Sheridan Rd Apt 2811 Chicago IL 60660 Office: Truman Coll 1145 W Wilson Ave #2824 Chicago IL 60640

WEIMER, RITA JOYCE, reading educator; b. Boricourt, Kans., Aug. 25, 1933; d. Lovell Frank and Leona B. (McCoach) Click; m. Gerald Wayne Sullivan, Aug. 9, 1953 (div. June 1977); children—Lovell Wayne, Laura Beth; m. Robert J. Weimer, Dec. 2, 1977; children—Robyn, Scott, Sandra, Jody. B.S.Ed., Kans. State Tchrs. Coll., 1956; M.S.Ed., U. Kans., 1964, Ed.D., 1974. Instr. Army Edn. Ctr., Fed. Republic Germany, 1956-58; elem. tchr., pub. schs., Kans., 1959-60; tchr. bus. and English, pub. high sch., Topeka, 1960-66; instr. Kans. State U., Manhattan, 1966-74, asst. prof. reading, 1974—. Mem. Internat. Reading Assn., Internat. Reading Assn. (Kans. chpt.), Nat. Council Tchrs. English, Phi Delta Kappa. Episcopalian. Avocation: swimming. Home: 3001 Amherst Ave Manhatten KS 66502 Office: Kans State U Coll Edn 211 Bluemont Hall Manhattan KS 66506

WEINACHT, KEVIN SCOTT, manufacturers representative executive; b. East St. Louis, Ill., June 7, 1955; s. Laverne George and Shirley Mae (Sipole) W. Student, Belleville (Ill.) Area Coll., 1973-74. Salesman, dist. mgr. Frontier Ins. Co., Jefferson City, Mo., 1975-76; sales rep. Barry and Sewall, Mpls., 1976-78; nat. sales rep. Emerson Electric Co., St. Louis, 1978-80; ptnr. Curt & Weinacht and Assocs., St. Louis, 1978-80; pres. Weinacht and Assocs., St. Louis, 19805—. Mem. Soc. Mfrs. and Engring., Mfrs. Agents Nat. Assn. Republican. Avocations: softball, basketball, bicycling. Home: 701 Illinois Collinsville IL 62234 Office: Weinacht & Assocs Inc 25 A S Florissant Rd Suite 210 Saint Louis MO 63135

WEINBERG, HOWARD JAY, plastic and reconstructive surgeon; b. Chgo., Nov. 28, 1947; s. Benjamin A. and Jean M. Weinberg; m. Ruth Guttstein, June 21, 1970; children: Sara, Aaron. Student Northwestern U., 1965-1968; MD, Ind. U., 1972. Diplomate Am. Bd. Plastic Surgery. Intern, resident in gen. surgery Presbyn. St. Luke's Hosp., Chgo., 1972-76; resident in plastic surgery U. N.Mex. Hosps., Albuquerque, 1976-78; fellow in hand surgery U. N.Mex., 1978-79; pvt. practice medicine specializing in plastic and reconstructive surgery, Munster, Ind., 1979—. Mem. Am. Soc. Plastic and Reconstructive Surgeons, AMA. Avocations: golf, tennis, travel, sports cars. Office: 9337 Calumet Ave Munster IN 46321

WEINBERG, RICHARD ALAN, psychologist, educator; b. Chgo., Jan. 28, 1943; s. Meyer and Mollie I. (Soell) W.; m. Gail E. Blumberg Aug. 25, 1964; children: Eric, Brett. BS, U. Wis., 1964; MAT, Northwestern U., 1965; PhD, U. Minn., 1968. Lic. cons. psychologist, Minn. Asst. prof. Tchrs. Coll., Columbia U., N.Y.C., 1968-70; prof. ednl. psychology, psychology and child psychology U. Minn., Mpls., 1970—, assoc. dir. Inst. Child Devel., dir. Ctr. for Early Edn. and Devel.; cons. EPA; reviewer Office of Edn., NSF; guest speaker TV and radio shows. Mem. adv. com. Children's Mus. Minn.; pres. Am. Assn. State Psychol. Bds.; liaison Nat. Register for Health Care Providers in Psychology. Grantee Bush Found.; NSF; NIH. Fellow Am. Psychol. Assn.; mem. Soc. for Research in Child Devel., Behavior Genetics Soc., Am. Edn. Research Assn., Phi Beta Kappa, Phi Kappa Phi. Author: (with A. Boehm) The Classroom Observer: A Guide for Developing Observation Skills, 1977; (with Scarr and Levine) Understanding Development, 1986; assoc. editor Contemporary Psychology. Office: U Minn N 548 Elliott St Minneapolis MN 55455

WEINBERG, STEVEN JEFFREY, sales executive, accountant; b. Chgo., Mar. 30, 1947; s. Lawrence and Ruth D. Weinberg; m. Phyllis J. Klor, Mar. 16, 1969; children: Genevieve, Joel. BA, North Park Coll., 1970; MBA, Loyola U., Chgo., 1977. CPA, Ariz., Ill. Mgr. acctg. Ramada Inns, Inc., Phoenix, 1972-76; from salesperson to v.p. sales dept. McCormack & Dodge subs. Dun & Bradstreet, Schaumburg, Ill., 1976—. Mem. Am. Inst. CPA's, Ill. Inst. CPA's, Nat. Assn. Accts. Avocations: sports, sports collectibles. Home: Box 1225 RFD Long Grove IL 60047 Office: McCormack & Dodge 1100 Woodfield #430 Schaumburg IL 60194

WEINER, CARL PHILLIP, obstetrician, gynecologist, educator; b. Paterson, N.J., July 2, 1951; s. Harold and Lynn (Rich) W.; m. Earline Pendley, Sept. 4, 1976; children: Kimberly Anne, Colin Wolf. BS, Lehigh U., 1972; MD, Med. Coll. Ga., 1977. Resident Ohio State U. Hosp., Columbus, 1978-81; fellow Northwestern U., Chgo., 1981-83; asst. prof. U. Iowa, Iowa City, 1983-87, assoc. prof., 1987—. Guest editor Clinical Obstetrics and Gynecology, 1985; reviewer Am. Jour. Ob-Gyn, 1980—, Obstetrics and Gynecology, 1982—; contbr. articles to profl. jours. March of Dimes Basil O'Connor Research fellow, 1984-87. Fellow Am. Coll. Ob-Gyn; mem. AMA, Am. Inst. Ultrasound in Medicine (sr.), Soc. Perinatal Obstetricians, Great Plains Genetic Service Network (chmn. 1984-87), Soc. Gynecologic Investigation, Fetal Medicine and Surgery Soc., Am Diabetes Assn. Home: 1829 Kathlin Dr Iowa City IA 52240 Office: U Iowa Sch Medicine Dept Ob-Gyn Iowa City IA 52242

WEINER, DAVID MERRILL, real estate developer; b. Rock Island, Ill., June 29, 1936; s. Morris and Lillian (Eisenberg) W.; m. Marlyne Feldman, Nov. 28, 1965; 1 child, Steven L. BA in Econs., Princeton (N.J.) U., 1958. Pres., owner Car City, Inc., Moline, Ill., 1962-67; exec. v.p. Franchise Growth Corp., Rock Island, Ill., 1968-71; pres., owner David M. Weiner & Assocs. Inc., Moline, 1972—. Bd. dirs. Rock Island (Ill.) Econ. Growth Corp., 1982—; mem. Quad City Devel. Group, Rock Island, 1978—. Served to lt. USN, 1958-61, PTO. Mem. Soc. Indsl. Office Realtors (various coms.), Rock Island County Bd. Realtors (pres. 1976-77, Realtor of Yr. 1978), Greater Davenport Bd. Realtors. Avocations: fishing, reading, tennis, jogging. Home: 3511 15th St Ct Rock Island IL 61201 Office: 1570 Blackhawk Rd Moline IL 61265

WEINER, GERALD ARNE, stockbroker; b. Chgo., Dec. 20, 1941; s. Irwin S. and Lilyan (Stock) W.; m. Barbara I. Allen, June 18, 1967; children—Rachel Anne, Sara Naomi. B.S.S., Loyola U., Chgo., 1964; student U. Vienna, Austria, 1962-63; M.S., Georgetown U., 1966; postgrad. Ind. U., 1966-72, S.E. Asian Areas cert., 1967. Pacification specialist AID, Laos, 1965; instr. polit. sci. Loyola U.-Chgo., 1970-72; asst. v.p. A.G. Becker & Co., Chgo., 1973-78; sr. v.p. Oppenheimer & Co., Chgo., 1978-83; sr. v.p. J. David Securities, Inc., Chgo., 1983-84; sr. v.p. Dean Witter Reynolds, Chgo., 1984—; fin. v.p. Data Dog Corp. Bd. dirs. Travelers Aid and Immigrant League. Mucia fellow, 1969. Mem. Midwest Bonsai Soc. Republican. Jewish. Club: East Bank (Chgo.). Office: Dean Witter Reynolds 70 W Madison Chicago IL 60602

WEINER, GERSHON RALPH, physician; b. Detroit, Apr. 12, 1935; s. Morris and Phyllis (Lemberg) W.; m. Myra H. Levenson, July 1956 (div. May 1962); children: Bruce J., Sandra C., Stuart J. (dec.); m. M. Jean (Jeannie) Mann, Dec. 31, 1975; 1 child, Joel Edward Jackson. BS, Wayne State U., 1955; DO, Coll. Osteopathic Medicine and Surgery, 1963. Diplomate Nat. Bd. Examiners, Am. Bd. Osteo. Rehab. Medicine. Intern Mt. Clemens (Mich.) Gen. Hosp., 1963-64; family practice Detroit and Warren, Mich., 1964-71; practice in emergency medicine Macomb (Mich.) County hosps., 1964-73; dep. med. examiner Macomb County, 1965-74; resident, fellow in physical medicine and rehab. Wayne State U. Sch. Medicine, Detroit, 1971-74; practice medicine specializing in physical medicine and rehab. Wayne and Macomb Counties, 1974—; team physician Detroit Sparks, 1971-72; rehab. med. cons. Detroit League Handicapped Goodwill Industries, 1972-76; lectr. phys. therapy Wayne State U., 1972-74; postgrad. trainer, lectr., cons., staff physiatrist Detroit Osteopathic Hosp., Highland Park, Mich., BiCounty Community Hosp., Warren, Riverside Osteopathic Hosp., Trenton, Mich., 1974—; speaker in field. Contbr. articles to profl. jours. Served to capt. USAF, 1955-58. Fellow Am. Osteopathic Coll. Rehab. Medicine (trustee 1982—, pres. 1984-85); mem. Am. Osteopathic Assn., Mich. Assn. Osteopathic Physicians and Surgeons, Am. Congress Rehab. Medicine, Macomb County Osteo. Assn. Jewish. Avocations: photography, reading, community service.

WEINER, JOEL DAVID, food products executive; b. Chgo., Aug. 27, 1936; m. Judith L. Metzger; children: Beth, David. BBA, Northwestern U. Dir. new products and household div. Alberto-Culver Co., Melrose Park, Ill., 1963-66; group mktg. mgr. Bristol Myers Co., N.Y.C., 1966-74; v.p. new products Carter Wallace Co., N.Y.C., 1974-78; exec. v.p. Joseph E. Seagram Corp., N.Y.C., 1979-84; exec. v.p. corp. mktg. Kraft, Inc., Glenview, Ill., 1984—. Office: Kraft Inc Kraft Ct Glenview IL 60025

WEINER, MICHAEL A., financial executive; b. Evanston, Ill., Oct. 21, 1956; s. Allen N. and Marilyn (Shull) W. BS in Acctg., U. Ill., 1978. CPA, Ill.; chartered fin. cons. Acct. Price Waterhouse, Chgo., 1978-82, Goldstein, Maller & Pierce, Chgo., 1982-84; pres. Michael A. Weiner & Assocs., Des Plaines, Ill., 1984—. Mem. Internat. Assn. Fin. Planning, Am. Inst. CPA's, Ill. CPA Soc., Nat. Assn. Life Underwiters, Chgo. Assn. Life Underwriters. Office: Michael A Weiner & Assocs Ltd 2340 River Rd #115 Des Plaines IL 60018

WEINER-DAVIS, MICHELE, therapist, consultant; b. N.Y.C., May 27, 1952; d. Harry and Beth (Wolff) W.; m. James Davis, Mar. 19, 1977; children: Danielle, Zachary. BA, Grinnell Coll., 1973; MSW, U. Kans., 1977. Cert. Brief family therapist, Wis. Sch. social worker Woodstock, Ill., 1977-79; family therapist, coordinator tng. and research McHenry County Youth Service Bur., Woodstock, 1979—; pvt. practice family therapy Woodstock, 1980—; research assoc. Brief Family Therapy Ctr., Milw., 1983—. Contbr. articles to profl. jours. Mem. Am. Assn. Marriage and Family Therapy (clin.). Office: McHenry County Youth Service Bur 14124 South St Woodstock IL 60098

WEINERT, CARL R., banking executive; b. East Detroit, Mich., June 27, 1923; s. Albert Gustav and Caroline W. (Moldenhauer) W.; m. Doreen A. Kann, June 19, 1948; children: Allyn, Carla, Bryan, Daryl. AS, Walsh Coll., 1949; grad. cert., Am Inst. Banking, 1952, U. Wis., 1957. Bank trainee Bank of the Commonwealth, Detroit, 1941-42; bank teller United Savings Bank, Detroit, 1942-43; pres. Bank of Commerce, Hamtramck, Mich., 1946-86, vice chmn., 1987, also bd. dirs.; pres. Commerce Bancorp, Inc., Hamtramck, Mich., 1985—, also bd. dirs.; bd. dirs. State Bank of Fraser (Mich.), 1985—, Security Bancorp, Inc., Southgate, Mich., 1986-87. Served as sgt. U.S. Army, 1943-46. Named Luth. Layman of Yr. Luth. Luncheon Club, 1983. Mem. Detroit Athletic Club, Robert Morris Assocs., Luth. Frats. of Am. (asst. treas. 1952-80). Republican. Home: 15658 Mok Ave East Detroit MI 48021 Office: Commerce Bancorp Inc 11300 Joseph Campau Ave Hamtramck MI 48212

WEINHOLD, JOHN DONALD, educator; b. Kansas City, Mo., Jan. 21, 1935; s. Theophil A. and Magdelene (Spilker) W.; m. Esther Jens, June 8, 1957; children—Kim D., Karmin F., Nathan R. B.S. in Edn., Concordia Tchrs. Coll., Seward, Nebr., 1957; M.A. in Sci., Ball State U., 1962, Ed.D., 1970. Cert. elem. and secondary tchrs., Nebr. Tchr. elem. sch. St. John's Luth. Sch., Arnold, Mo., 1954-55; instr. Concordia High Sch., Seward, 1957, Concordia Luth. High Sch., Fort Wayne, Ind., 1957-62; asst. prof. Concordia Coll., River Forest, Ill., 1962-68; prof. edn., Concordia Coll., Seward, 1968—; cons. in edn. to Luth. Sch. Tchrs.' Confs., N.Y., N.J., Iowa, Miss., Nebr. Aid Assn. for Lutherans fellow, 1966-67. Mem. Luth. Edn. Assn. (nat. dir. 1972-76), Nat. Sci. Tchrs. Assn., Phi Delta Kappa. Lutheran. Contbr. articles on edn. to profl. jours. Home: 604 N Fifth St Seward NE 68434 Office: 800 N Columbia Seward NE 68434

WEINHOLD, MARK DONALD, dentist; b. Joliet, Ill., Mar. 2, 1955; s. Donald Goodson and Yolanda Rose (Denault) W.; m. Jeanette Lynn Hanneken, Oct. 18, 1980; 1 child, Jeffrey Mark. BA in Psychology, Creighton U., 1977, DDS, 1981. Gen. practice dentistry Sandwich, Ill., 1981—. V.p. St. Paul's Parish Council, Sandwich, 1985-86. Mem. ADA, Ill. Dental Assn., Fox River Valley Dental Assn., DeKalb Dental Soc., Indian Valley Theater. Roman Catholic. Lodge: Rotary (pres. local chpt. 1985-86). Avocations: golf, running, astronomy.

WEINHOLD, VIRGINIA BEAMER, interior designer; b. Elizabeth, N.J., June 21, 1932; d. Clayton Mitchell and Rosemary (Behrend) Beamer; B.A., Cornell U., 1955; B.F.A. summa cum laude, Ohio State U., 1969; M.A. in Design Mgmt., Ohio State U., 1982; divorced; children—Thomas Craig, Robert Scott, Amy Linette. Freelance interior designer, 1969-72; interior designer, dir. interior design Karlsberger and Assos. Inc., Columbus, Ohio, 1972-82; assoc. prof. dept. indsl. design Ohio State U., 1982—; lectr. indsl. design Ohio State U., 1972, 79-80. Bd. visitors Found. for Interior Design Edn. and Research. Mem. Inst. Bus. Designers (chpt. treas. 1977-79, nat. trustee 1979-81, nat. chmn. contract documents com. 1979-84, chpt. pres. 1981-83), Constrn. Specifications Inst., Interior Design Educator's Council, Illuminating Engring. Soc., asso. mem. AIA. Prin. works include Grands Rapids (Mich.) Osteo. Hosp., Melrose (Mass.) Wakefield Hosp., Christopher Inn, Columbus, John W. Galbreath Hdqrs., Columbus, Guernsey Meml. Hosp., Cambridge, Ohio, Trinity Epis. Ch. and Parish House, Columbus, Hale Hosp., Haverhill, Mass., others. Author: IBO Forms and Documents Manual. Home: 112 Glen Dr Worthington OH 43085 Office: 128 N Oval Mall Columbus OH 43210

WEINKAUF, WILLIAM CARL, instructional media company executive; b. Fond du Lac, Wis., Apr. 7, 1934; s. Carl Alfred and Erma Gertrude (Lueck) W.; m. Carole Jean Hill, May 3, 1958; children: Carl William, Mary Gretchen, Donald Hill. BA, Ripon (Wis.) Coll., 1955; postgrad. U. Wis., 1954, 57-58. Dir. Wis. Cen. Lumber Co., 1959-63; with Carlton Films, Beloit, Wis., 1965-68; founder, pres. IMCO Inc., Green Lake, Wis., 1968—, IMCO Pub. Co., 1978—; bd. dirs. The Peterson System, Inc.; cons. bd. Holy Cross Coll., 1972—. Chmn. council Cub Scouts Am., 1968-69; mem. exec. com. county Reps., 1970-71. Served to maj. AUS, 1955-57. Mem. Nat. Audio Visual Assn. (chmn. legis. com. Wis. 1975—), Nat. Sch. Supply and Equipment Assn. (bd. dirs. 1986-87), U.S. Res. Officers Assn. (chpt. pres. 1966-70), Green Lake C. of C., Sigma Nu. Mem. United Ch. Christ (bd. trustees 1965-66). Lodges: Mason (32 degree), KT. Home: 596 Illinois Ave Green Lake WI 54941 Office: 506-510 Mill St Green Lake WI 54941

WEINLANDER, MAX MARTIN, retired psychologist; b. Ann Arbor, Mich., Sept. 9, 1917; s. Paul and Emma Carol (Lindemann) W.; B.A., Eastern Mich. Coll., 1940; M.A., U. Mich., 1942, Ph.D., 1955; M.A., Wayne U., 1951; m. Albertina Adelheit Abrams, June 4, 1946; children—Bruce, Annette. Psychometrist, VA Hosp., Dearborn, Mich., 1947-51; sr. staff psychologist Ohio Div. Corrections, London, 1954-55; lectr. Dayton and Piqua Centers, Miami U., Oxford, Ohio, 1955-62; chief clin. psychologist Child Guidance Clinic, Springfield, Ohio, 1956-61, acting dir., 1961-65; clin. psychologist VA Center, Dayton, Ohio, 1964-79; cons. Ohio Div. Mental Hygiene; summer guest prof. Miami U., 1957, 58, Wittenberg U., 1958; adj. prof. Wright State U., Dayton, 1975-76; cons. State Ohio Bur. Vocat. Rehab., Oesterlen Home Emotionally Disturbed Children. Pres. Clark County Mental Health Assn., 1960, Clark County Health and Welfare Club, 1961; mem. Community Welfare Council Clark County, 1964; chmn. Comprehensive Mental Health Planning Com. Clark County, 1964; trustee United Appeals Fund, 1960. Mem. citizens adv. council Columbus Psychiat. Inst., Ohio State U. Served as sgt. AUS, 1942-46. Fellow Ohio Psychol. Assn. (chmn. com. on utilization of pscyhologists; treas., exec. bd. 1968-71); mem. Am. Psychol. Assn., Ohio Psychol Assn., Mich. Psychol. Assn., DAV, U. Mich. Pres. Club, Pi Kappa Delta, Pi Gamma Mu, Phi Delta Kappa. Lutheran. Lodge: Kiwanis. Contbr. articles to psychology jours. Home: 17185 Valley Dr Big Rapids MI 49307

WEINSTEIN, BARRY ALAN, architect; b. Chgo., Oct. 31, 1943; s. Reuben and Dorothy (Weiss) W.; m. Margery Gail Spector, June 12, 1966; children: Scott Howard, Allison Beth. BArch, U. Ill., 1967. Architect-in-tng. C.F. Murphy Assocs., Chgo., 1967-69, Norman A. Koglin Assocs., Chgo., 1969-71; project mgr., tech. dir. R.M.M. Inc., Chgo., 1971-74; ptnr. Berger-Weinstein Assocs., Chgo., 1974-81; owner B. Weinstein Assocs., Chgo., 1981—; instr. Harrington Inst. of Interior Design, Chgo., 1972-74. Recipient Hon. award Am. Architecture State of the Art in the '80s, 1985. Mem. Nat. Council Archtl. Registration Bds., AIA. Home: 500 Green Bay Rd Highland Park IL 60035 Office: B Weinstein Assocs 153 W Ohio Chicago IL 60610

WEINSTEIN, GEORGE, accountant, management consultant; b. N.Y.C., Mar. 20, 1924; s. Morris J. and Sara (Broder) W.; m. Shirley Beatrice Greenberg, Sept. 1, 1945; children—Stanley Howard, Jerrald, Sara Belle. B.S., U. Ill., 1944, postgrad. Law Sch., 1944-55; M.B.A., NYU, 1947. Joined Morris J. Weinstein, Groothuis & Co., N.Y.C., 1944, ptnr., 1945-72; ptnr. Weinstein Assocs., N.Y.C. and Milw., 1973—; chmn. Weinstein Assocs. Ltd.; pres. dir. REIT Property Mgrs. Ltd., Milw.; pres. Hudson Valley Corp., WAL Ltd.; bd. dirs. Brit. Land of Am., chmn. exec. com.; bd. dirs. Regency Investors, Axminster U.S.A. Active United Jewish Appeal, Fedn. Jewish Philanthropies; bd. dirs., founder North Shore Hebrew Acad.; founder, past pres. Gt. Neck (N.Y.) Synagogue; chmn. Lake Park Synagogue; trustee M. Rainville trust; bd. dirs. Milw. Jewish Home, Jewish Nat. Fund, Milw. Hillel Acad. Mem. Am. Inst. Accts., N.Y. Soc. C.P.A.s, Hebrew Immigrant Soc., Tau Delta Phi (nat. treas.), Delta Sigma Phi. Clubs: President's of U. Ill., Westmoreland, Ambassadors of Yeshiva U., Milw. Athletic, Wisconsin of Milw.; Citrus (Orlando, Fla.). Lodge: Masons (past master). Address: 3900 N Lake Dr Milwaukee WI 53202 also: 1211 Gulf of Mexico Dr Longboat Key FL 34228

WEINSTEIN, JEREMY SAUL, manufacturing executive; b. Bklyn., Apr. 9, 1944; s. Max and Lillian (Levy) W.; m. Edith Back, June 18, 1967; children: Deborah, Marjorie, Laura. BSME, CCNY, 1966; MS in Indsl. Engring., Purdue U., 1968, PhD, 1970. Research engr. Whirlpool Corp., Benton Harbor, Mich., 1970-72; mgr. bus. planning Whirlpool Corp., St. Joseph, Mich., 1972-76; mgr. prodn. scheduling Whirlpool Corp., Marion, Ohio, 1976-79, mgr. indsl. engrs., 1979-82; dir. mfg. engrs. Whirlpool Corp., Findlay, Ohio, 1982—. Author: Computers in Manufacturing, 1974; contbr. articles to profl. jours. Mem. adv. com. U. toledo, 1985—. Mem. Inst. Indsl. Engrs. (sr.). Lodge: Kiwanis. Office: Whirlpool Corp 4901 N Main St Findlay OH 45840

WEINSTEIN, MARTIN PAUL, educator, psychotherapist; b. N.Y.C., Aug. 10, 1952; s. Fred and Phyllis (Wood) W. BA, Clark U., 1974; MA, U. Ill., Chgo., 1976; PhD, U. Ill., 1982. Registered psychologist, Ill. Asst. coordinator emergency psychiatry Northwestern Meml. Hosp., Chgo., 1982; psychotherapist Proviso Family Services, Westchester, Ill., 1982-84; asst. prof. psychology Roosevelt U., Chgo., 1984-87, chmn. psychology dept., 1987—; cons. Proviso Family Services, Westchester, 1984—. Mem. Am. Psychol. Assn. Avocation: piano. Office: Roosevelt U 430 S Michigan Ave Chicago IL 60605

WEINSTEIN, RUSSELL DEAN, acquisition analyst; b. Chgo., July 12, 1961; s. Harold Noah and Gloria (Morgan) W. BS with distinction, U. Ill., 1983; MBA, U. Mich., 1985. Analyst Pillsbury Co., Mpls., 1984, fin. analyst, 1985-86, acquisition analyst, 1986—. Cons. Jr. Achievement of Twin Cities, Bloomington, Minn., 1986. Mem. Beta Gamma Sigma. Home: 3540 S Hennepin #206 Minneapolis MN 55408 Office: Pillsbury Co 3906 Pillsbury Ctr Minneapolis MN 55402

WEINSTOCK, FRANK JOSEPH, ophthalmalogist; b. Newark, Apr. 21, 1933; m. Saragale Reinglass Weinstock, May 20, 1962; children: Michael, Jill, Jeffrey. BSc, Allegheny Coll., 1955; MD, SUNY, Syracuse, 1960. Cert. Am. Bd. Ophthalmology. Intern Mt. Sinai Hosp., Cleve., 1960-61; resident in ophthalmology Western Res. U. Hosps., Cleve., 1961-64; practice ophthalmology Canton (Ohio) Ophthalmology Assocs. Inc., 1965—; assoc. prof. ophthalmology Northeastern Ohio U. Coll. Medicine, Rootstown, 1984—; clin. asst. prof. Ohio State U. Coll. Medicine, Columbus, 1974—; pres. Soc. Geriatric Ophthalmology, Southfield, Mich., 1982—; chmn. med. adv. com. Nat. Assn. for Visually Handicapped, N.Y., 1978—. Editor: (with others) The Ophthalmologist's Office: Planning & Practice, 1975; (with M. Kuitko) Geriatric Ophthalmology, 1985; contbr. chpts. to books in field. Mem. Plain Local Bd. Edn., Canton, 1978—, pres., 1982. Served as surgeon USPHS, 1964-66. Recipient Honor award Am. Acad. Ophthalmology & Otolaryngology, 1977. Fellow ACS; mem. AMA, Soc. Geriatric Ophthalmology (charter mem., pres.), Am. Intraocular Implant Soc. (founding), Contact Lens Assn. Ophthalmologists., Keratorefractive Soc., Ohio Med. Assn. (mem. editorial bd. jour.), Stark County Med. Soc. Home: 4668 Yale Ave NW Canton OH 44709 Office: Canton Ophthalmology Assocs Inc 2912 W Tuscarawas Canton OH 44708

WEINSTOCK, ROBERT, physics educator; b. Phila., Feb. 2, 1919; s. Morris and Lillian (Hirsch) W.; m. Elizabeth Winch Brownell, Apr. 22, 1950; children—Frank Morse, Robert Brownell. A.B., U. Pa., 1940; Ph.D., Stanford U., 1943. Instr. physics Stanford U., Calif., 1943-44, instr. math., 1946-50, acting asst. prof. math., 1950-54; research assoc. in radar countermeasures Radio Research Lab., Harvard U., Cambridge, Mass., 1944-45; asst. prof. U. Notre Dame, Ind., 1954-58, assoc. prof. math., 1958-59; vis. assoc. prof. math. Oberlin Coll., Ohio, 1959-60, assoc. prof., 1960-66, prof. physics, 1966-83, emeritus prof., 1983—. Author: Calculus of Variations, 1952. Contbr. numerous tech. articles to profl. jours. Fellow Ohio Acad. Sci.; mem. Am. Assn. Physics Tchrs., Am. Phys. Soc., History of Sci. Soc., AAAS, Sigma Xi. Avocations: concert going; reading; walking; travel. Home: 171 E College St Oberlin OH 44074 Office: Oberlin Coll Dept Physics Oberlin OH 44074

WEINTRAUB, HERSCHEL J.R., chemist, educator, consultant; b. Cin., Aug. 19, 1948; s. Josef David and Eva (Felander) W.; m. Carol Kay Bell, July 25, 1981. BS in Biomed. Engring., Case Inst. Tech., 1970; MS, Case Western Res. U., 1973, PhD in Macromolecular Sci., 1975. Dir. computer based edn. Purdue U. Sch. of Pharmacy, West Lafayette, Ind., 1976-77, asst. prof., 1977-81; sr. physical chemist Lilly Research Labs., Indpls., 1981-82; sr. theoretical chemist Abbott Labs., Abbott Park, Ill., 1983-86; group leader chem. scis. Merrell Dow Research Inst., Cin., 1986—; cons. various pharmaceutical cos., 1977-81. Contbr. articles to chem. jours. Research grantee NIH, 1979. Mem. IEEE, Am. Chem. Soc., Biophysical Soc., Chemometric Soc., Internat. Soc. Quantum Biology. Office: Merrell Dow Research Inst 2110 E Galbraith Rd Cincinnati OH 45215

WEINTRAUB, JANE ANN, dentist, educator; b. N.Y.C., Nov. 17, 1954; d. Milton I. and Eleanor (Friedman) W. BS, U. Rochester, 1975; DDS, SUNY, Stony Brook, 1979; MPH, Harvard U., 1980, postdoct. cert., 1982. Diplomate Am. Bd. Dental Pub. Health. Resident in dental pub. health Harvard Sch. Dental Medicine, Boston; clin. instr. Harvard U., Boston, 1982-83, N.Y. State Dept. Health, Albany, 1980-81; program analyst Mass. Dept. Pub. Health, Boston, 1982-84; asst. prof. U. Mich., Ann Arbor, 1984—; mem. dental adv. bd. Blue Cross/Blue Shield Mich., Detroit, 1984—; supr. dentist Mass. Dept. Pub. Health, Boston, 1983-84; instr. Harvard U., 1983-84. Author: Biostats: Data Analysis for Dental Health Care Professionals; edit. bd., reviewer Jour. Pub. Health Dentistry; reviewer Jour. Dental Edn.; contbr. articles to profl. jours. Mem. ADA, Am. Assn. Dental Schs., Am. Assn. Pub. Health Dentistry, Am. Assn. Women Dentists (Colgate-Palmolive Research award com., chair mercury exposure com.), Am. Pub. Health Assn. (sect. council 1985—), Internat. Assn. for Dental Research (bd. dirs. behavioral sci. group 1986—), Mich. Dental Assn., Mich. Pub. Health Assn., SUNY at Stony Brook Sch. Dental Medicine Alumni Assn. (pres. 1983-85). Office: U Mich Sch Pub Health Program in Dental Pub Health Ann Arbor MI 48109-2029

WEINZIERL, THOMAS ALLEN, data processing specialist; b. Pitts., Sept. 5, 1951; s. George William and Genevieve Blanche (Nyga) W.; m. Elizabeth Katherine Yost, Dec. 16, 1972; children—Cynthia Ann, Cheryl Lynn, Thomas Michael. B.S. in Engring., U. Ill., Chgo., 1972; M.B.A., DePaul U., 1975. Cert. data processor. Data processing specialist Internat. Harvester, Chgo., 1972-77; supr. data communications, Milw., 1978-79, planning mgr., Chgo., 1980; cons. Blue Cross Blue Shield Milw., 1981-85; contingency planning and data security officer, Marine Bank Services Corp., Milw., 1986—. James scholar U. Ill., 1969-72. Mem. Soc. Mfg. Engrs., Phi Kappa Phi, Delta Mu Delta. Roman Catholic. Home: 3004 Fairwood Ct Wauwatosa WI 53222 Office: Marine Bank Services Corp 1000 N Market St PO Box 2071 Milwaukee WI 53201

WEINZWEIG, AURUM ISRAEL, mathematician; b. Toronto, Ont., Can., Apr. 22, 1926; s. David Zvi and Sarah (Godfrey) W.; m. Marjorie Smolensky, Aug. 23, 1953 (div. Dec. 1962); children: Meira Karen, Michael Lawrence; m. Lila Janice Perlis, Aug. 4, 1963; children: Ari Gordon, Lauren Sari, Carmi Alan. BA, U. Toronto, 1950; AM, Harvard U., 1953, PhD, 1957. Research physicist Weizmann Inst., Rehovoth, Israel, 1948-49; asst. chief geophysicist Weiss Geophys., Calgary, Alta., Can., 1957-60; asst. prof. Northwestern U., Evanston, Ill., 1960-65; prof. U. Ill., Chgo., 1965—; pres. Ill. Council on Math. Edn., 1973-78; cons. 2d Internat. Study of Math., 1976—; v.p. Internat. Commn. Study and Improvement of Teaching of Math., 1980-83; dir. Inst. for Learning and Teaching of Math., 1984—. Author: Space and Geometry, 1978, Language and Language Acquisition, 1982; contbr. articles in field to sci. jours. Governing council Am. Jewish Congress, Chog., 1964; bd. dirs. Chgo. Bd. Jewish Edn., 1980—; bd. dirs. Midwest Regions United Synagogue of Am., 1980—. Mem. Ill. Council Tchrs. of Math., Nat. Council Tchrs. of Math., Assn. Tchrs. Math., Am. Math. Soc., Math. Assn. Am., Math. Assn. Jewish. Home: 9711 N Kildare Ave Skokie IL 60076 Office: U Ill at Chgo PO Box 4348 Chicago IL 60680

WEIR, WILLIAM H., lawyer, educator; b. East Orange, N.J., Mar. 16, 1947; s. William F. and Nela (Stinnett) W.; m. Marilyn Fowler, Dec. 6, 1969; 1 child, William Bradley. B.S., Eastern Ill. U., 1969; J.D., John Marshall Law Sch., 1977. Bar: Ill. 1977, U.S. Dist. Ct. (no. dist.) Ill. 1977. Field rep. Aetna Casualty, Chgo., 1972-76; assoc. Tomlinson & Thomas, Arlington Heights, Ill., 1976-77; ptnr. Brittain, Ketcham, Strass, Terlizzi, Flanagan, Weir & Johnson, P.C., Elgin, Ill., 1977—; prof. bus. law Elgin Community Coll., 1980—. Author Tort Law Newsletter, 1981. Pres., Elgin YMCA, 1982-84. Served to capt. USMC, 1967-72. Mem. Assn. Trial Lawyers Am., Ill. Trial Lawyers Assn., ABA, Ill. State Bar Assn. (speaker, co-editor tort laws newsletter 1981-83), Kane County Bar Assn. (treas., civil practice com., speaker), Navy League, Am. Legion. Lodge: Kiwanis (Elgin). Home: 41W058 Kingston Ct Saint Charles IL 60174 Office: Brittain Ketcham et al 1695 Larkin Ave Elgin IL 60123

WEIS, JOANNE, marketing executive; b. Evergreen Park, Il., Aug. 5, 1960; d. William G. and Maureen C. W. BS, St. Joseph's Coll., Renssalaer, Ind., 1982. Sales rep. Dannon Co., N.Y.C., 1982-85; mktg. adminstr. Daubert Coated Products, Westchester, Ill., 1985—. Home: 236 S Maple Oak Park IL 60302 Office: Daubert Coated Products One Westbrook Corp Ctr Westchester IL 60153

WEIS, MARGARET EDITH, writer, editor; b. Independence, Mo., Mar. 16, 1948; d. George Edward and Francis Irene (Reed) W.; m. Robert William Baldwin, Aug. 22, 1970 (div. 1981); children: David William, Elizabeth Lynn. BA in Creative Writing, U. Mo., 1966-70. Proofreader Herald Pub. House, Independence, Mo., 1970-73, advt. dir., 1973-82; dir. div. Independence (Mo.) Press, 1977-82; editor TSR Inc, Lake Geneva, Wis., 1982-86; freelance writer. Author: (short story) The Test of the Twins, 1984, (books) The Endless Catacombs, 1984, Tower of Midnight Dreams, 1984, (with Tracy Hickman) The Dragonlance Chronicles, 1984, 85, Dragonlance Legends, 1985, 86, The Darksword Trilogy, 1988, (under Susan Lawson) (with Roger Moore) Riddle of The Griffon, 1985, (under Margaret Baldwin) The Boys Who Saved The Children, 1982, Kisses of Death, 1983, (with Pat O'Brien) Wanted: Frank and Jesse James, The Real Story, 1981, (with Janet Pack) Children of The Holocaust, 1986, My First Thanksgiving, 1983, (with Gary Pack) Computer Graphics, 1984, Robots and Robotics, 1984, (short story) The Thirty Nine Buttons, 1987, (novella) (with Tracy Hickman) The Legacy, 1987, Wanna Bet?, 1987; editor: The Art of Dungeons and Dragons, 1985, Leaves of the Inn of the Last Home, 1987, The Art of Dragonlance, 1987, Dragonlance Tales, vol. 1, 2, 3, 1987. Avocations: role-playing games, roller skating, opera.

WEIS, THOMAS BERNARD, adhesives company executive; b. Geneva, Nebr., June 7, 1942; s. Sylvester J. and Doris (Hobbs) W.; m. Patricia J. Schinoski, Aug. 8, 1964; children: Susan A., Thomas C. BS, Marquette U., 1964; MBA, U. Wis., Milw., 1967. CPA, Wis.; cert. mgmt. acct., Wis. Auditor Deloitte, Haskins & Sells, Milw., 1964-66; with Allis-Chalmers, Milw., 1967-85; v.p. fin. and adminstrn., sec., treas. Findley Adhesives, Wauwatosa, Wis., 1985—. Mem. Am. Inst. CPA's, Wis. Inst. CPA's, Inst. Mgmt. Accts., Nat. Assn. Accts., Delta Sigma Pi. Republican. Roman Catholic. Home: 9827 N Melrose Ct 99W Mequon WI 53092 Office: Findley Adhesives Inc 11320 Watertown Plank Rd Wauwatosa WI 53226

WEISBERG, BERNARD, supermarket company executive. Chmn., pres., chief exec. officer Chatham Supermarkets Inc., Warren, Mich. Office: Chatham Supermarkets Inc 2300 E Ten Mile Rd Warren MI 48091 *

WEISBERG, HERBERT F., political science educator; b. Mpls., Dec. 8, 1941; s. Nathan R. and Jean (Schlessinger) W.; m. Judith Ann Robinson, Dec. 16, 1979; 1 child, Bryan Bowen. BA, U. Minn., 1963; PhD, U. Mich., 1968. Asst. prof. polit. sci. U. Mich., Ann Arbor, 1967-73, assoc. prof. polit. sci., 1973-74; assoc. prof. polit. sci. Ohio State U., Columbus, 1974-77, prof. polit. sci., 1977—. Co-author: Introduction to Survey Research, 1977; co-editor: Theory Building and Data Analysis, 1984, Controversies in Voting Behavior, 1984; editor: Political Science: Science of Politics, 1985; co-editor Am. Jour. Polit. Sci., 1979-82. Mem. Midwest Polit. Sci. Assn. (v.p. 1983-85), Am. Polit. Sci. Assn. (program chmn. 1983), Phi Beta Kappa, Pi Sigma Alpha, Phi Kappa Phi. Home: 506 Whitney Ave Worthington OH 43085 Office: Ohio State U Dept Polit Sci Columbus OH 43210

WEISBERG, SEYMOUR WILLIAM, physician; b. Chgo., Aug. 5, 1910; s. Isaac and Eda (Provus) W.; B.S., U. Chgo., 1932; M.D., Rush Med. Coll., 1936; m. Ella Sperling, Oct. 16, 1949; children—Gerald, Louise. Intern Michael Reese Hosp.; resident Cook County Hosp., Chgo.; practice medicine specializing in internal medicine, Chgo., 1940—; asso. prof. medicine U. Ill. Coll. Medicine, Chgo.; asso. attending physician Cook County Hosp., 1940-44; chief resident tng. unit Chgo. Regional Office VA; mem. attending staffs Michael Reese Hosp., Chgo., Louis A. Weiss Meml. Hosp., Chgo., St. Joseph Hosp. Served with AUS, 1944-47. Diplomate Am. Bd. Internal Medicine. Mem. AMA, Ill. Med. Soc., Phi Beta Kappa, Alpha Omega Alpha. Office: 2800 N Sheridan Rd Chicago IL 60657

WEISENBACH-JOHNSON, SUSAN MARGARET, aerospace engineer; b. Cleve., Jan. 20, 1952; m. Eric Eugene Johnson, Sept. 7, 1974. BS in Aerospace Engring. Tech., Kent State U., 1974; MS in Mech. Engring., U. Toledo, 1980. Aerospace engr. Lewis Research Ctr. NASA, Cleve., 1974—. Author pub. reports. Acad. Model Aeronautics scholar, 1970, Cleve. chpt. Nat. Aeronautics Assn. scholar, 1970; NASA Middle Mgmt. fellow, 1984; recipient Fed. Women of Achievement award Clev. Fed. Exec. Bd. and Fed. Women's Council, 1982. Mem. NASA Lewis Bus. and Profl. Women's Club (Young Career Woman award 1982, pres. 1985-87), Am. Inst. Aeronautics and Astronautics (pres./chmn. No. Ohio sect. 1984-85), Cleve. Tech. Socs. Council (pres./bd. govs. 1983-84, Tech. Achievement award 1985), Soc. Women Engrs. (sr., charter v.p. Northeastern Ohio 1977-78, sect. rep. to nat. 1982-84), Nat. Free Flight Soc. (pres. No. Ohio chpt. 1980-82, 87—), Experimental Aircraft Assn. Avocations: flying, flying model airplanes, sewing, biathlons. Home: 6290 Olive Ave North Ridgeville OH 44039 Office: NASA Lewis Research Ctr MS 77-10 21000 Brookpark Rd Cleveland OH 44135

WEISMAN, DANIEL OTTO, computer programmer; b. South Bend, Ind., Jan. 25, 1956; s. Richard Otto and Ruth Margaret (Hoham) W.; m. Doris Ann Binkley, Apr. 6, 1985. AAS, Purdue U., 1978, BS, 1987. Computer programmer Reilly Tar and Chemical, Indpls., 1978-79, Dura-Container, Indpls., 1979-80; programmer/analyst Ind. Nat. Bank, Indpls., 1980-85, PALLM, Inc., Indpls., 1985-87, MID Inc., Noblesville, Ind., 1987—. Club: DRAFT (Indpls.). Office: MID Inc 408 S 9th St Noblesville IN 46060

WEISMANTEL, GREGORY NELSON, food products company executive; b. Houston, Sept. 8, 1940; s. Leo Joseph and Ellen Elizabeth (Zudis) W.; m. Marilyn ann Fanger, June 18, 1966; children: Guy Gregory, Christopher Gregory, Andrea Rose. BA, U. Notre Dame, 1962; MBA, Loyola U., Chgo., 1979. Dist. mgr. Gen. Foods Corp., White Plains, N.Y., 1975-80; pres., chief exec. officer Manor House Foods, Inc., Addison, Ill., 1980-82, Weismantel & Assocs., Downers Grove, Ill., 1982-84; v.p. perishable div. Profl. Marketers, Inc., Lombard, Ill., 1984-85, group v.p. sales and mktg. services, dir. corporate strategy, 1986-87; v.p. mng. prin. Louis A. Allen Assoc. Inc., Palo Alto, Calif., 1987; bd. dirs. Epicurean Foods, Ltd., Chgo.; cons. in field. Chmn. fin. St. Edward's High Sch. Jubilee, Elgin, Ill., 1982-85; bd. dirs. Dist. 301 Sch. Bd., Burlington, Ill., 1980-84, St. Edward's Found., Elgin, 1982—. Served to capt. U.S. Army, 1962-66. Mem. Grocery Mfg. Sales Execs., Chgo. C. of C. (small bus. com.). Roman Catholic. Clubs: Merchandising Execs. (bd. dirs. 1980-86); Food Products, Am. Mktg. (Chgo.).

WEISS, DONALD HERBERT, training consultant; b. Chgo., Feb. 26, 1936; s. Joseph Weiss and Ruth Lillian (Pollack) Gross; m. Dorothy Steiner, June 10, 1962 (div. May 28, 1974); children: Tobin, James. Student, Jullian Sch. Music, 1953-54; BA, U. Ariz., 1961; MA, U. Mo., 1963; PhD, Tulane U., 1964. Dir. Youth Services Bur., Tarrant County, Tex., 1971-74; cons. in field Dallas, 1974-78; mgr. mgmt. tng. Equitable Gen. Ins., Ft. Worth, 1978-80; v.p., dir. tng. Dial Agy. Group, Dallas, 1980-82; prin. Self Mgmt. Assocs., Dallas, 1982-85; mgr. spl. projects Psychol. Assocs., St. Louis, 1984—. Author: (9 booklet series) Successful Office Skills Series, 1985-86); also articles and video tapes in field. Served with U.S. Army, 1953-57. Grantee North Cen. Tex. Council Govts., 1971-74, Hogg Found., 1970. Mem. Am. Soc. Tng. and Devel., Metroplex Assn., Personnel Cons. (v.p. 1983), Nat. Assn. Sales and Mktg. Execs. Democrat. Jewish. Club: Tex. Exec. Avocations: music, theater, reading.

WEISS, FREDERIC STERLING, psychiatric nurse; b. Los Angeles, Dec. 18, 1953; s. Robert Nelson and Esther Donna (Malkin) W.; children: Yael, Gabriel, Shimon, Josiah, Rivka. Assoc. Applied Sci. magna cum laude, U. Cin., 1982. Registered nurse, Ohio. Asst. to v.p. mdse. Hale-Justis Drug Co., Cin., 1973-82; clin. nurse Univ. Hosp., Cin., 1982-83; charge nurse St. Elizabeth Hosp., Covington, Ky., 1983; psychiat. nurse supr. Rollman Psychiat. Inst., Cin., 1984-86; supr. nursing Pauline Warfield Lewis Ctr., Cin., 1986—; union activist Rollman Psychiat. Inst., 1984—. Contbr. articles to The Chabad Times, 1979-82, articles on Jewish mysticism and annotated Hebrew translation to The Cin. Jour. Cerimonial Magick, 1987; editor-in-chief (newspaper) The Catalyst, 1981-82, Heartsounds literary mag., 1982. Mem. Human Rights Com. for Area Group Homes, Cin., 1985; del. Ohio State Hosp. Employees Group on Medicaiton Policy, Cin., 1985; adminstr. family shelter div. Chabad House, Cin., 1986; del. Homeless Coalition, Cin., 1986. Mem. Mensa. Avocations: writing, reading, drawing, metaphysical study, crafts. Office: Pauline Warfield Lewis Ctr 1101 Summit Rd Cincinnati OH 45237

WEISS, HOWARD ALLEN, lawyer; b. Chgo., July 30, 1924; s. Louis A. and Goldie (Molner) W.; m. Molly Hilton, Apr. 8, 1959; children: Jeffery, Jody, Stephanie, Rebecca, Jennifer. Student, Harvard U., 1941-43, LLB, 1952; BSEE, U.S. Naval Acad., 1946. Bar: Mass. 1952, Fla. 1955, Ill. 1958. Commd. ensign USN, 1943, advanced through grades to lt., 1949, resigned, 1949; atty. Voluntary Defenders Commn., Boston, 1952-54; assoc. Kovner & Mandeimer, Miami Beach, Fla., 1954-58, David Altman Law Offices, Chgo., 1959-63; ptnr. Altman, Kurlander & Weiss, Chgo., 1964-72; of counsel Katten, Muchin et al, Chgo., 1973-80; bd. dirs. Illini Precast Co., Plano. Bd. dirs. Louis A. Weiss Meml. Hosp., Chgo., 1964—; chmn. bd. dirs. Ill. Sch. Profl. Psychology, Chgo., 1976—. Mem. Ill. Bar Assn., Fla. Bar Assn., Mass. Bar Assn., Chgo. Bar Assn. Democrat. Jewish. Clubs: Standard, Bryn Mawr Country (Chgo.). Home: 180 E Pearson St Apt 4507 Chicago IL 60611

WEISS, JAMES MOSES AARON, educator, psychiatrist; b. St. Paul, Oct. 22, 1921; s. Louis Robert and Gertrude (Simon) W.; m. Bette Shapera, Apr. 7, 1946; children: Jenny Anne Weiss Ford, Jonathan James. AB summa cum laude, U. Minn., 1941, ScB, 1947, MB, 1949, MD, 1950; MPH with high honors, Yale U., 1951. Diplomate: Am. Bd. Psychiatry and Neurology (examiner 1963-83). Teaching asst. psychology St. Thomas Coll., St. Paul, 1941-42; intern USPHS Hosp., Seattle, 1949-50; resident, fellow psychiatry Yale Med. Sch., 1950-53; from instr. to asst. prof. psychiatry Washington U., St. Louis, 1954-60; mem. faculty U. Mo., 1959—, prof. psychiatry, 1961—, founding chmn. dept., 1960—, prof. community medicine, 1971—; vis. prof. Inst. Criminology, Cambridge (Eng.) U., 1968-69, All-India Inst. Med. Scis. and U. Malaya, 1984; internat. cons., 1958—; founding co-chmn. Asian-Am. Consortium on Psychiat. Disorders, 1986—. Author numerous articles in field; editor, co-author: Nurses, Patients, and Social Systems, 1968; corr. editor: Jour. Geriatric Psychiatry, 1967—; founding editor, chmn. bd. Jour. Operational Psychiatry, 1970—; editorial advisor Community Mental Health Jour., 1979—; trustee Mo. Rev., 1982-83. Served with M.C., AUS, 1942-46, PTO; to capt. M.C., AUS, 1953-54. Decorated Philippine Liberation medal, 1945; recipient Sir Henry Wellcome award, 1955, Israeli bronze medal, 1963, Basic Books award, 1974, Disting. Service commendation Nat. Council Community Mental Health Ctrs., 1982, 83, 86, Guhleman award for Clin. Excellence U. Mo., 1987; named Chancellor's Emissary U. Mo., 1979; faculty fellow Inter-Univ. Council, 1958, sr. research fellow Am. Council Edn. and NSF, 1984. Found. fellow Royal Coll. Psychiatrists; fellow Royal Soc. Medicine, Am. Psychiat. Assn. (life), Am. Pub. Health Assn., Am. Coll. Preventive Medicine, Royal Soc. Health, AAAS, Am. Coll. Psychiatrists, Am. Assn. Psychoanalytic Physicians (hon.); mem. Assn. Mil. Surgeons U.S. (hon. life), Assn. Acad. Psychiatry, Assn. Western Profs. Psychiatry (chmn. 1970-71), Mo. Acad. Psychiatry (1st pres. 1966-67), Mo. Psychiat. Assn. (pres. 1987-88), N.Y. Acad. Scis., Mil. Order World Wars, Phi Beta Kappa, Sigma Xi, Psi Chi, Alpha Omega Alpha, Alpha Epsilon Sigma, Gamma Alpha. Clubs: Scholars (Cantab.); Wine Label (London); Yale (St. Louis); Mo. Country (Columbia). Research on suicide, homicide, antisocial behavior, aging, social psychiatry. Home: Crow Wing Farm Rt 2 Box 2 Columbia MO 65201 Office: U Mo Dept Psychiatry Columbia MO 65212

WEISS, MARTIN E., communications and marketing specialist; b. Cleve., Nov. 22, 1926; s. Samuel B. and Margaret (Freedman) W.; B.A., Columbia U., 1947; m. Regina Melville Martyn, Jan. 16, 1983; children—Jack Martyn, Kevin Martyn, Michelle Martyn, Dawn Martyn, Lorraine Frame; children from previous marriage—James L. Weiss, Andrew R. Weiss. Dir. advt. and public relations Del. Floor Products, 1948-52; promotion dir. Street & Smith Publs., 1952-56; editor, publisher Westbury (N.Y.) Times, 1956-73; publisher Edn.-Tng. Market Report, Washington, 1973-75; dir. public relations and publs. AAU/USA, Indpls., 1976-79; dir. communications, mktg. Athletics Congress/USA, Indpls., 1979—; bd. dirs. Nat. Track and Field Hall of Fame, Indpls. Served with AUS, 1944-46. Home: 11654 Buttonwood Dr Carmel IN 46032 Office: 200 S Capitol Ave Suite 140 Indianapolis IN 46225

WEISS, MORRY, greeting card company executive; b. Czechoslovakia, 1940. BS, Case Western Res. U., 1963. Salesman, field mgr. Am. Greetings Corp., Cleve., 1961-66, advt. mgr., 1966-68, v.p., 1969-73, group v.p. mktg. and sales, 1973-78, pres., 1978—, also bd. dirs. Office: Am Greetings Corp 10500 American Rd Cleveland OH 44144 *

WEISS, RICHARD EDWARD, JR., realtor; b. Chgo., July 6, 1942; s. Richard E. and Lois May (Schlesinger) W.; m. Donelle Bokich, June 14, 1969; 1 child, Cory. BA, Wabash Coll., 1965; BS, Purdue Columet, Hammond, 1972. Cert. soc. indsl. and office realtors; cert. Realtors Nat. Mktg. Inst. Indsl. broker R. E. Weiss, Realtor, Munster, Ind., 1978-82, Cyrus-Weiss Co., Munster, 1982—. Served to 1st lt. U.S. Army, 1966-70. Decorated Bronze Star. Mem. Soc. Indsl. Realtors, Realtors Nat. Mktg. Inst. Avocations: skiing, board sailing, fishing, hiking. Home: 6949 Knickerbocker Pkwy Hammond IN 46323 Office: Cyrus Weiss Co 533 Ridge Rd Munster IN 46321

WEISS, ROBIN TOD, chemical company executive; b. Dallas, Oct. 20, 1951; s. Charles A. and Clara Dora (Weiss) W.; m. Judith Ellen, July 8, 1978; children: Jaclyn Carol, Traci Danielle. BBA in Mktg., N. Tex. State U., 1974. Salesman Savin Corp., Dallas, 1974-76, Litton Industries, Dallas, 1976-77; sales mgr. Carnation Co., Los Angeles, 1977-79; div. mgr. John Crane-Houdaille, Inc., Morton Grove, Ill., 1979-84; pres, chief exec. officer RTW Internat. Corp., Skokie, Ill., 1984—, also bd. dirs. Mem. Am. Mktg. Assn., Am. Mgmt. Assn., Am. Supply and Machinery Mfgs. Assn., Chem. Spltys. Mfgs. Assn., Nat. Assn. Elec. Distbrs. Republican. Lodge: B'nai Brith. Avocations: golf, painting, consulting, coach semi-professional baseball and tennis. Home: 135 Lilac Ln Buffalo Grove IL 60089 Office: RTW Internat Corp 7200 McCormick Blvd Skokie IL 60076

WEISS, SAMUAL, hotel and restaurant company executive; b. Rock Springs, Wyo., Dec. 25, 1924; s. Morris and Alta Weiss; m. Barbara R. Coggan; children—Cathy, Marcy, Karen. B.A. cum laude, U. Mich., 1948; LL.B., Harvard U., 1951. Asst. v.p. Cuneo Press, Inc., Chgo., 1951-68; exec. v.p., treas., dir. Holly's Inc., Grand Rapids, Mich., 1968—; exec. v.p., dir. Holly Enterprises, Inc., Grand Rapids, 1969—, Holly Grills of Ind., South Bend, 1970—, Fare Devel. Corp., Grand Rapids, 1974—. Co-chmn. U.S. Olympic com. Mich., 1976-80; bd. control Intercollegiate Athletics U. Mich., 1982—. Served to 2d lt. USAAF, 1942-46. Mem. Nat. Assn. Corp. Real Estate Execs. (founding), Nat. Restaurant Assn., U. Mich. Alumni Assn. (dir.). Republican. Clubs: Peninsular (Grand Rapids). Home: 3645 Oak Terrace Ct SE Grand Rapids MI 49508 Office: PO Box 9260 255 Colrain St SW Grand Rapids MI 49509

WEISS, SANFORD ROBERT, radiologist; b. Canonsburg, Pa., Jan. 3, 1929; s. Edward and Beulah (Berman) W.; m. Blanche Lukin, June 20, 1953; children: Bradley, Bedonna, Ronald. BA, Ohio State U., 1949, MD, 1953. Intern, then resident in radiology Phila. Gen. Hosp., 1953-59; radiologist Western Res. Care System, Youngstown, Ohio, 1959—; chmn. dept. radiology Western Res. Care System, Youngstown, 1974—; assoc. prof. radiology Northeastern Ohio U., Rootstown, 1976—, vice chmn. radiol. council, 1976-86; pres. Youngstown Radiol. Assn., Inc., 1975—. Served to lt. USN, 1955-57. Mem. AMA, Am. Coll. Radiologists, Radiol. Soc. of N.Am., Ohio State Med. Assn. Republican. Jewish. Club: Squaw Creek Country (Vienna, Ohio) (golf chmn. 1968-70). Avocations: golf, sports, traveling. Home: 1179 Academy Dr Youngstown OH 44505 Office: Youngstown Radiology Assn Inc 25 N Canfield-Niles Rd Youngstown OH 44515

WEISS, WILLIAM LEE, communications executive; b. Big Run, Pa., May 21, 1929; s. Harry W. and Dorothy Jane (McKee) W.; m. Josephine Elizabeth Berry, June 3, 1951; children—Susan Leigh Weiss Miller, David William, Steven Paul. B.S. in Indsl. Engring, Pa. State U., 1951. With Bell Telephone Co. of Pa., 1951, 1953-76; v.p. staff Bell Telephone Co. of Pa., Phila., 1973-74; v.p., gen. mgr. Bell Telephone Co. of Pa. (western area), 1974-76; v.p. ops. Wis. Telephone Co., Milw., 1976-78; pres. Ind. Bell Telephone Co., Indpls., 1978-81; also dir. Ind. Bell Telephone Co.; pres. Ill. Bell Telephone Co., Chgo., 1981, chmn., 1982-83; chmn., chief exec. officer Ameritech, Chgo., 1983—, also bd. dirs.; bd. dirs. Abbott Labs., Chgo., Continental Ill. Nat. Bank, Chgo., Continental Ill. Corp., The Quaker Oats Co., Chgo., USG Corp., Chgo.; chmn. Info. Industry Council. Bd. dirs. Chgo. Council on Fgn. Relations, Lyric Opera of Chgo.; trustee Mus. Sci. and Industry, 1982, Northwestern U., 1982, Orchestral Assn., Chgo., 1982, Com. for Econ. Devel.; chmn. Info. Industry Council; mem. adv. council J.L. Kellogg Grad. Sch. Mgmt., Northwestern U.; mem. nat. adv. bd. Ill. Math. and Sci. Acad.; mem. Ctr. for Performing Arts. Served with USAF, 1951-53. Mem. Western Soc. Engrs., The Bus. Roundtable, Tau Beta Pi, Phi Delta

Theta. Clubs: Commercial, Chicago, Economic, Mid-America (Chgo.); Glen View (Ill.); Old Elm; Country of N.C. (Pinehurst). Avocations: civic work, golf, travel, family activities. Home: 1500 N Lake Shore Dr Chicago IL 60610

WEISSFELD, MICHAEL ALLYN, entertainment coordinator; b. Akron, Ohio, Apr. 3, 1958; s. Edward Marvin and Yetta (Metz) W. BS, Miami U., Oxford, Ohio, 1980; postgrad., U. Akron Sch. Bus., 1981. Electronics technician Funtime, Inc., Aurora, Ohio, 1981; mechanic Funtime, Inc., Aurora, 1981-84, mgr. live entertainment, audio-visual coordinator, 1984—; audio-visual cons. L&M Prodns., Cleve., 1985—. Firemedic Fairlawn (Ohio) Fire Dept., 1981-85; organizer Grateful Acres, Hiram, Ohio, 1986—. Mem. Ohio Forestry Assn. Club: Ohio Blues Soc. Avocations: forestry, music, film, sports, mechanics. Home: 12210 Abbott Rd Hiram OH 44234 Office: Funtime Inc.-Geauga Lake Park 1060 Aurora Rd Aurora OH 44202

WEISZ, CAREN LYNN, pediatric optometrist; b. Chgo., Dec. 20, 1953; d. Charles and Ruth (Gordon) W.; m. Steven B. Greenspan, Sept. 11, 1977; children: Neil, Joshua. BS, Ill. Coll. of Optometry, Chgo., 1975; MEd, Loyola U., Chgo., 1976; OD, Ill. Coll. Optometry, Chgo., 1977. Pediatric optometrist Pediatric Optometry Assocs., Harvey and Joliet, Ill., 1977—; asst. clinical prof. optometry Ill. Coll. Optometry, Chgo., 1981-86. Mem. med. adv. bd. Easter Seals of Will and Grundy Counties, Joliet, 1983—. Recipient Faculty Meml. award Ill. Coll. Optometry, 1977, Tomb and Key award, 1977. Fellow Am. Acad. Optometry. Office: 1520 Rock Run Dr Suite 2 Crest Hill IL 60435

WEITMAN, CARL U., clinical psychologist; b. N.Y.C., Apr. 3, 1944; s. Allan and Frances (Green) W.; m. Jeanne M., July 16, 1977; children: Lindsay A., Bradley A.U. BA, CUNY, N.Y.C., 1966; MA, Case Western Res. U., 1970, PhD, 1974. Lic. clin. psychologist, Ohio, fellow and diplomate Am. Bd. Med. Psychotherapy. Intern clin. psychology VA Hosps., Brecksville, Ohio and Cleve., 1969-72; intern Bellefaire Residential Treatment Ctr. Children, Cleve., 1972-73; clin. psychologist Hillcrest Assocs., Cleve., 1974—; cons. U. Sch., Gilmour Acad., Catholic Service Bur.; mem. clin. staff St. Vincent Charity Hosp., Euclid Gen. Hosp., Windsor Hosp., Mt. Sinai Hosp. Trustee Cleve. Children's Mus., 1985—, Listening Devel. Ctr., 1985—; mem. men's com. Cleve. Playhouse. Mem. Am. Psychol. Assn., Am. Soc. Clin. Hypnosis, Acad. Family Psychology, Ohio Psychol. Assn., Cleve. Psychol. Assn. (chmn. profl. affairs.), Cleve. Acad. Cons. Psychologists, Nat. Register Health Service Providers in Psychology, Cleve. Hypnosis Soc., No. Ohio Pediatric Soc., Psychologists Associated with Addictive Disorders, Cleve. Assn. Children and Adults with Learning Disabilities (bd. advs.). Office: 6801 Mayfield Mayfield Heights OH 44126

WEITZEL, JOHN A., insurance executive; b. Springfield, Ohio, Dec. 1, 1945; s. Paul J. and Marie S. (Eifert) W.; m. Pamela Jean Messer, Sept. 7, 1970; children: Gretchen Marie, Nicholas Todd. BSBA, Ohio State U., 1967. CPA, Wis., Ohio. Sr. acct. Peat Marwick Mitchell and Co., Columbus, Ohio, 1967-75; dir. internal auditing Armco Ins. Group, Inc., Milw., 1975-82; chief fin. officer Universal Reins. Corp., Milw., 1982-85, Milw. Ins. Group, Inc., 1985—; bd. dirs. Milw. Fin. Corp., 1986—, Milw. Equity Services, 1987—. Treas. Camp Five Found., Laona, 1986. Served to sgt. U.S. Army, 1968-70, Korea. Mem. Am. Inst. CPA's, Wis. Soc. CPA's (chmn. ins. com. 1985—), Fin. Execs. Inst. Roman Catholic. Office: Milw Ins Group Inc 803 W Michigan St Milwaukee WI 53233

WEIZMAN, SAVINE GROSS, psychologist; b. Cleve., Oct. 28, 1929; d. Isadore and Zelda (Rubenstein) Gross; m. Alvin A. Weizman, Feb. 11, 1951 (dec.); children: Elissa, David, Robert. BS in Edn., Case Western Res. U., 1951, MS, 1968, PhD, 1975. Lic. psychologist. Sch. psychologist, Ohio Elem. sch. tchr., 1951-54; psychol. staff Cleve. Pub. Schs., 1968-77; child and family therapist Beechbrook Residential Treatment Center for Children, Pepper Pike, Ohio, 1977-79; pvt. practice psychology and psychotherapy specializing in coping with loss, Beachwood, Ohio, 1975—; psychologist orthopedically handicapped program Lake-Geauga Counties, 1972-73; lectr. John Carroll U., 1970-73; asst. prof. psychology Cleve. Inst. Art, 1975-81; lectr. in field of mental health, mourning and bereavement. Author: Understanding the Mourning Process, When Your Mate Dies, 1977; About Mourning: Support and Guidance for the Bereaved, 1984; also articles. Mem. behavioral scientists com. Fairmount Temple. Mem. Am. Psychol. Assn., Ohio Psychol. Assn., Cleve. Psychol. Assn. Office: 3659 Green Rd Suite 325 Beachwood OH 44122

WELCH, L. DEAN, manufacturing executive; b. Emmett, Idaho, July 24, 1928; s. Roy W. and Luella (Bader) W.; m. Elizabeth Gay, Apr. 27, 1958; 1 child, Caroline Gay. BS, U. Idaho, 1950. Sales rep. Idaho Power Co., 1950-52; purchasing supr. Boeing Airplane Co., 1952-57; mgr. purchasing HITCO subs. Armco Inc., 1957-63, v.p. materials, 1963-66; v.p., gen. mgr. HITCO Def. Products Div., 1966-72, group v.p., 1972-79; v.p. stainless, advanced materials div. Armco Inc., 1979-80, pres. stainless steel div., 1980-81; pres., chief operating officer Ladish Co. Inc., Cudahy, Wis., 1981-85, pres., chief exec. officer, 1985-87, pres., chief exec. officer, chmn., 1987—, also bd. dirs.; bd. dirs. Oreg. Metall. Corp., Albany. Mem. adv. com. U. Wis.-Whitewater, U. Wis.-Milw.; mem. corp. com. Milw. Sch. Engring. Mem. Soc. for Advancement of Materials and Process Engring., Am. Def. Preparedness Assn., Am. Security Council (nat. adv. bd.), Beta Gamma Sigma (hon.). Office: Ladish Co Inc 5481 S Packard Ave Cudahy WI 53110

WELCH, MARK STEVEN, manufacturing company executive; b. Racine, Wis., Aug. 8, 1952; s. Fern T. and Georgine G. (Boulard) W. AS, Kenosha Tech. Inst., 1972; B in Mgmt. Sci., U. Wis., Kenosha, 1978, MBA, 1985. Lic. real estate broker, Wis. With acctg. and personnel depts. Welch Elec. Industries Inc., Racine, 1972-74, mgr. prodn. control dept., 1974-76, dir. mfg., 1976-79, v.p. mfg., 1979-81, exec. v.p., 1981-84, pres., 1984—; pres. Hazen, Welch & Assocs., Racine, Wis. and Schaumburg, Ill., 1986—; bd. dirs. Gateway Tech. Inst. Found., Racine. Republican. Office: Welch Elec Industries Inc 1515 16th St Racine WI 53403

WELCH, MARY BETHANIA, psychotherapist, social worker; b. Port Washington, Wis., July 6, 1962; d. Wayne Willard and Dorothy Geraldine (Dunlap) W.; m. David Mark DeVriendt, Jluy 11, 1987. BSW cum laude, St. Cloud State U., 1984; MSSW, U. Wis., 1986. Mental health counselor Multi-Resource Ctrs., Mpls., 1984-85; psychotherapist, dir. supportive home care program Luth. Social Services, Madison, Wis., 1985—. vol. educator Family Planning Ctr., St. Cloud, 1983-84. Mem. Nat. Assn. Social Workers, Nat. Assn. Mental Health (grant 1985-86). Lutheran. Avocations: traveling, reading, refinishing furniture, camping, cats.

WELCH, MARY ROSE DWYER, educator; b. Sparta, Wis., Feb. 5, 1946; d. Robert Edward and Margaret Ann (Gregor) Dwyer; m. Theodore William Welch, June 29, 1968. Student, U. Wis., 1967; BS, U. Wis., La Crosse, 1968, MEd in Profl. Devel., 1986. Cert. English tchr., Wis. Secondary tchr. English Sparta Area Schs., 1968—; sr. class play dir. Sparta Sr. High Sch., 1968-71, forensic coach, 1968—; ednl. cons. McDougal, Littell & Co., Evanston, Ill., 1985; forensic judge La Crosse dist. Wis. High Sch. Forensic Assn., Arcadia, 1986—. Active Friends of Terry Musser for Assembly and Senate, Melrose, Wis., 1983-84, Friends of Tommy Thompson for Gov., Mauston, Wis., 1985-86, Friends of Terry Madden for Assembly, Elroy, Wis., 1986; bd. dirs. Wilton (Wis.) Fun Fest Com., 1985—; mem. Wilton Swimming Pool Fund Com., 1985—; mem. Tax Incremental Dist. Com., Wilton, 1987. Mem. NEA, Wis. Edn. Assn., Western Wis. Edn. Assn., Sparta Edn. Assn., Parish Council Cath. Women. Avocations: walking, card playing, cycling, sewing, reading. Home: 701 Walker St Box 271 Wilton WI 54670 Office: Sparta Sr High Sch 506 N Black River St Sparta WI 54656

WELCH, MARY THERESE, assistant controller; b. Bippus, Ind., Dec. 31, 1958; d. Herman Richard and Josephine E. (Urschel) W. BA, Ball State U., 1981. CPA, Ind. Sr. acct. Ernst & Whinney, Indpls., 1981-84; asst. controller Master-Fit Corp., Indpls., 1984—. Chmn. awards White River Park State Games, Indpls., 1985, 86, 87; flag mgr. Pan Am. Games, Indpls., 1987. Mem. Am. Inst. CPA's, Ind. Soc. CPA's. Avocations: photography, painting. Home: 5806 Rosslyn Ave Indianapolis IN 46220 Office: Master-Fit Corp 1853 Ludlow Ave Indianapolis IN 46201

WELCH, MICHAEL CRAIG, orthopedic surgeon; b. Cin., Jan. 7, 1947; m. Ann; children: Matthew, Jamison. Ba, Wittenberg U., Springfield, Ohio, 1969; MD, Ohio State U., 1973. Diplomate Am. Bd. Orthopedic Surgery. Rotating intern Riverside Meth. Hosp., Columbus, Ohio, 1973-74; jr. resident orthopedic surgery Ohio State Coll., Columbus, 1974-77; chief resident orthopedic surgery Ohio State Coll. Medicine, Columbus, 1977-78; orthopedic surgeon Orthopedic Cons. of Cin., Inc., 1981—; chmn. pub. relations com. The Christ Hosp., Cin., New Generation com., mem. exec. com. Internat. scholar Swiss Soc. for Internal Fixation, 1977. Fellow Am. Acad. Orthopedic Surgeons; mem. OIho State Med. Assn., Ohio Orthopaedic Soc., Mid-Am. Orthopedic Assn. Avocation: photography. Office: 6 Dexter Place Cincinnati OH 45206 Office: Orthopedic Cons of Cin Inc 111 Wellington Pl Cincinnati OH 45219

WELCH, ROBERT ALAN, obstetrician-gynecologist; b. Perrysburg, Ohio, Aug. 1, 1951; s. Robert Chester and Dorothy Jean (Hamilton) W.; m. Sally Elizabeth Straits, June 24, 1972; children: Olivia, Robert Jr., Kathryn. BS, U. Toledo, 1973; MD, La. State U., 1980. Resident in ob-gyn. Wayne State U., Detroit, 1980-84, fellow in perinatal dept., 1984-86, asst. prof., 1986—; clin. instr. Wayne State U., Detroit, 1984-86, dir. antenatal diagnosis unit Hutzel Hosp., Detroit, 1986. Patentee modified surgical gloves; contbr. articles to books. Fellow Am. Coll. Ob-Gyn (Searle Donald F. Richardson Meml. Prize, 1986, Ephraigm McDowell award 1985); mem. Soc. Perinatal Obstetrics (assoc.), Am. Soc. Gynecologic Laparoscopists, Am. Inst. Ultrasound in Medicine, Am. Fertility Soc. Avocations: mini and microcomputing. Office: Hutzel Hosp Wayne State U 4707 St Antoine Blvd Detroit MI 48201

WELCH, ROBERT C., lawyer; b. Independence, Mo., Aug. 14, 1933; s. Arthur and Ova (Trimble) W.; m. Ellen Duncan, Sept. 2, 1955; children—Denise Louise Welch Masters, Andrea Marie. B.S., Kansas City Jr. Coll., 1955; J.D., U. Mo.-Kansas City, 1965. Bar: Mo. 1965. Ptnr. Paden, Welch, Martin, Albano & Graeff, P.C., Independence, 1965—; pros. atty. City of Blue Springs (Mo.), 1973—; pros. atty. City of Sugar Creek (Mo.), 1967—, city atty., 1981—. Author: Missouri Criminal Practice, 1977, 2d. edit., 1984. Mem. Kansas City Met. Bar Assn. (sec. 1981, 82, pres.-elect 1983, pres. 1984), Jackson County Legal Aid and Defenders Soc. (exec. bd. 1971-73, trustee 1975-77), U. Mo.-Kansas City Law Found. (sec. 1977-82, v.p. 1982-85 , pres. 1986-87), Eastern Jackson County Bar Assn. (pres. 1974-75 chmn. jud. recommendations com. 1983-84), Mo. Bar. Assn. (chmn. criminal law sect. 1975-76), Mo. Assn. Criminal Def. Lawyers (pres. 1980-81), Kansas City Bar Found. (v.p. 1985-86), Mo. Lawyers Trust Found. (bd. dirs. 1986—, 16th cir. judicial commn. 1986—) Sugar Creek Bus. and Profl. Club (past pres.). Club: Optimists (past pres.). Home: 10703 Anderson Ct Sugar Creek MO 64054 Office: Paden Welch Martin Albano et al 311 W Kansas St Independence MO 64050

WELCH, ROBERT THOMAS, state representative; b. Berlin, Wis., June 8, 1958; s. William and Betty (Baudhuin) W.; m. Jeanne M. Piechowski, Dec. 30, 1978; children: Adam, Sarah, Peter. AAS, Madison Area Tech. Coll., 1980; student, U. Wis., Stevens Point, Lawrence U., 1976-78, U. Wis., Stevens Point, 1978. Surveyor Kiedrowski Engring., Stevens Point, Wis., 1981, Welch Land Surveying, Redgranite, Wis., 1982—; state rep. Wis. 41st Assembly, 1985—; chmn. Council on Migrant Labor, Assembly Rep. Caucus; mem. assembly coms. on employment and tng., rules, elections, adminstrv. rules, orgn. Treas. Waushara County Rep., 1983-84, active State Rep. Platform Co., 1984; 4-H leader. Named one of Outstanding Young Men Am., Montgomery, Ala., 1985, 86, 87. mem. Green Lake Ripon Area Bd. Realtors. Roman Catholic. Home: Rt 124th Rd Redgranite WI 54970 Office: State Capitol Room 307 N Madison WI 54970

WELCH, THOMAS C., manufacturing executive; b. Glendale, Calif., Aug. 23, 1926; s. Thomas Perry and Martha (Abraham) W.; m. R. Virginia, Aug. 6, 1949; children: Michael, Stephen, Dennis, Tom, Patrick, Kevin. BS, UCLA, 1949. V.p., gen. mgr. clock div. Sunbeam Appliances, Chgo., 1969-74, v.p. clock and home care div., 1974; pres. Hanson Scale Co., Chgo., 1974-77, Sunbeam Leisure Products Co., Neosho, Mo., 1975—; bd. dirs. Glenview (Ill.) State Bank, 1968-74. Bd. pres. United Fund, Neosho, 1979-80; bd. dirs. Neosho Industries Inc., 1980—. Served with USN, 1944-46. Republican. Roman Catholic. Lodge: Rotary. Avocations: golf, outdoor activities, reading. Home: 58 Swanage Circle Bella Vista AR 72714 Office: Sunbeam Leisure Products Co 4101 Howard Bush Dr Neosho MO 64850

WELDON, RAMON NATHANIEL, city official; b. Keokuk, Iowa, July 26, 1932; s. Clarence and Virginia H. (White) W.; m. Betty Jean Watkins, July 24, 1955; 1 child, Ramon N., Jr. Student pub. schs., Keokuk. Patrolman, Keokuk Police Dept., Iowa, 1962-74, detective, 1974-80, capt., 1980-82, chief of police, 1982—. Mem. Keokuk Humane Soc., 1982, Lee County Juvenile Restitution Bd., Ft. Madison, Iowa, 1982, Lee County Health Care Coalition, Ft. Madison, Iowa, 1983; trustee Library Bd., Keokuk; Keokuk YMCA, 1986-87. Served with U.S. Army, 1952-54. Mem. Iowa Chief's Assn., Nat. Chief's Assn., Internat. Chief's Assn. Methodist. Lodge: Masons (master 1955). Avocations: racquetball; hunting; basketball; swimming. Home: 2510 Decatur St Keokuk IA 52632 Office: Keokuk Police Dept 1222 Johnson St Keokuk IA 52632

WELDON, VIRGINIA V., medical school administrator, pediatric endocrinologist; b. Toronto, Sept. 8, 1935; came to U.S., 1937; s. John Edward and Carolyn Edith (Swift) Verral; children: Ann Stuart, Susan Shaeffer. A.B. cum laude, Smith Coll., 1957; M.D., SUNY-Buffalo, 1962; L.H.D. (hon.), Rush U., 1985. Diplomate Am. Bd. Pediatrics in pediatric endocrinology and metabolism. Intern Johns Hopkins Hosp., Balt., 1962-63, resident in pediatrics, 1963-64; fellow pediatric endocrinology Johns Hopkins U., Balt., 1964-67, instr. pediatrics, 1967-68; asst. prof. Washington U., St. Louis, 1968-73, assoc. prof. pediatrics, 1973-79, prof. pediatrics, 1979—; v.p. Med. Ctr. Washington U., 1981—, dep. vice chancellor med. affairs, 1983—; gen. clin. research ctrs. adv. com. NIH, Bethesda, Md., 1976-80, research resources adv. council, 1980-84; dir. Centerre Trust Co., St. Louis, Southwestern Bell Corp., Gen. Am. Life Ins. Co. Contbr. articles to sci. jours. Commr. St. Louis Zool. Park, 1983; bd. dirs. United Way Greater St. Louis, 1978—, St. Louis Regional Health Care Corp. Fellow Am. Acad. Pediatrics, AAAS; mem. Inst. Medicine, Assn. Am. Med. Colls. (del., chmn. council acad. socs. 1984-85, chmn. assembly 1985-86), Am. Pediatric Soc., Nat. Bd. Med. Examiners (bd. dirs. 1987—), Endocrine Soc., Soc. Pediatric Research, AAU (joint com. health policy), Nat. Assn. Biomed. Research (bd. dirs.), St. Louis Med. Soc., Sigma Xi, Alpha Omega Alpha. Roman Catholic. Home: 4444 Lindell Blvd Suite 8 Saint Louis MO 63108 Office: Washington U Sch Medicine Box 8106 660 S Euclid Ave Saint Louis MO 63110

WELIVER, EVELYN RUTH, academic librarian; b. Meadville, Pa., June 30, 1944; s. H.D.L. and Phyllis A. (Irons) VanBockern; m. E. Delmer Weliver, Sept. 6, 1964; children: Phyllis, Wraight. BS, Cen. Mich. U., 1977, MA, 1981. High sch. librarian St. Francis High Sch., Traverse City, Mich., 1978-79; jr., sr. high sch. librarian Benzie Cen., Benzonia, Mich., 1979-81; acad. librarian Interlochen (Mich.) Ctr. for the Arts, 1984—; mem. adv. bd. Regional Ednl. Media Ctr., Traverse City, 1978-81, 84—. Mem. Assn. Supervision and Curriculum Devel., Mich. Assn. Media in Edn. Republican. Avocations: weaving, walking. Office: Interlochen Ctr for Arts Interlochen MI 49643

WELKER, HENRY ALBERT, II, personnel consulting company executive; b. Detroit, July 22, 1940; s. Henry Albert and Helen Marie (Zindler) W.; m. Teuta Bego, June 11, 1972. B.B.A., U. Detroit, 1970. Cert. personnel cons. Acct. Gen. Motors, Livonia, Mich., 1961-70; account exec. Mgmt. Recruiters, Southfield, Mich., 1971-72; placement dir. Honeywell Inst., Southfield, 1972-73; placement mgr. R. Half Personnel, Southfield, 1973-76; chief exec. officer H. Welker Personnel, Southfield, 1976—; advisor electronic data processing curriculum Oakland Community Coll., Farmington Hills, Mich., 1982—. Served with U.S. Army, 1963-64. Mem. Mich. Assn. Personnel Cons. (chmn. ethics com.). Office: Henry Welker Personnel Inc 24901 Northwestern St Suite 304 Southfield MI 48075

WELKER, JEROME LANCE, banker; b. Indianola, Iowa, Sept. 18, 1933; s. Frank Leslie and Ruth O. (Cambron) W.; m. Nancy Anne Ainsworth, Aug. 1, 1956; children: Mark D., Kirk S. BS, Drake U., 1955. V.p., co-owner Gen. Mortgage Corp., Des Moines, 1956-74; nat. accounts rep. Minn. Title Co., Des Moines, 1974-78; sr. v.p. Bankers Trust Co., Des Moines, 1978—; chmn. bd. dirs. Iowa Bankers Mortgage Corp., Des Moines, First Fed. Savs. and Loan Assn., Des Moines, First Equity Corp., West Des Moines. Bd. dirs., exec. com., chmn. spl. projects com. Polk Des Moines Taxpayers Assn., 1978—; bd. dirs., chmn. loan com. Neighborhood Housing Services, Inc., Des Moines, 1980—; past sr. warden St. Andrews, Des Moines. Mem. Mortgage Bankers Assn. of Am., Iowa Mortgage Bankers Assn. (pres. 1976-77), Des Moines Mortgage Bankers Assn. (pres.). Republican. Episcopalian. Club: Embassy. Avocations: photography, travel, hiking. Home: 2604 69th St Urbandale IA 50322 Office: Bankers Trust Co 665 Locust St Des Moines IA 50309

WELL, DON, theological college president; b. Haifa, Israel, July 15, 1937; came to U.S., 1938, naturalized, 1955; s. Ben Zion and Esther (Hill) W.; m. Hedi Esther Friedman, Oct. 5, 1975; children—Avraham B., Shira, Yishai, David S., Tamar L., Hillel, Sarah Meryl. B.A., Roosevelt U., 1959; postgrad. U. Chgo., 1961-66; B.H.L., Hebrew Theol. Coll., 1961, D.H.L., 1977. Ordained rabbi, 1960. Lectr., U. Chgo., 1964-66; research assoc. Nat. Inst. Research in Behavioral Scis., Szold Inst., Jerusalem, Israel, 1966-71, sr. research psychologist, 1966-71; prof. ednl. adminstr. U. Tel Aviv, Ramat Aviv, Israel, 1966-71; assoc. dean Hebrew Theol. Coll., Skokie, Ill., 1971-79, pres., 1981—; exec. asst. to pres. Car-X Mufflers, Chgo., 1979-81. Advisor, Minister of Edn., Govt. Israel, 1968-71. Vice-pres. Religious Zionists of Am., 1978-82. Served with Israeli Def. Forces, 1970-71. NDEA fellow, 1961-64. Mem. Chgo. Rabbinical Council, Rabbinical Council Am., Assn. Profs. Jewish Studies. Jewish Orthodox. Author: Case Book in Educational Administration, 1970; co-editor: Megamot, 1967-70; mem. editorial staff Halachah U'Refuah, 1981, 82, 83; sculptor bronze Jerusalem, 1982. Office: 7135 N Carpenter St Skokie IL 60077

WELLES, DAVID KEITH, JR., manufacturing company executive; b. New Haven, May 24, 1952; s. David Keith and Georgia (Elmes) W.; m. Hope Jones, May 7, 1977; children: David, Hope, Berkley. BA cum laude, Yale U., 1974. Ter. sales rep. Owens-Corning Fiberglas, St. Louis, 1975-77; materials mgr. Therma-Tru Corp., Van Buren, Ark., Colorado Springs, Colo., Toledo, 1977-80; dir. mktg., planning Therma-Tru Corp., Toledo, 1980-83, v.p. planning, 1984-85, v.p. sales, mktg., 1985-86, exec. v.p., 1987—, also bd. dirs.; mng. dir. Therma-Tru Doors, Ltd., Cwmbren, Wales, 1983-84. Trustee Maumee Valley Country Day Sch., Toledo, 1984—; assoc. trustee Boys and Girls Club of Toledo, 1985; mem. allocation com. United Way, Toledo, 1985-86; pres. Planned Parenthood of N.W. Ohio, Toledo, 1986—. Mem. Am. Mgmt. Assn., Am. Mktg. Assn. (1984 Marketer award N.W. Ohio chpt.), Toledo Orgn. for Mgmt., Yale Alumni Assn. (pres. N.W. Ohio chpt. 1983—). Republican. Episcopalian. Avocations: tennis, golf, sailing, skiing. Office: Therma-Tru Corp 2806 N Reynolds Rd Toledo OH 43615

WELLES, GEORGE WILLIAM, III, audio video specialist; b. Duluth, Minn., July 9, 1940; s. George William Jr. and Leslie Elizabeth (Griggs) W.; m. Maren Keith Kinney, July 27, 1963. Student, Macalester Coll., 1958-60, U. Minn., Duluth, 1961-63; BA in Journalism, U. Minn., Mpls., 1972. News KDAL TV, Duluth, 1962-63; news, documentary Hubbard Broadcasting, St. Paul, 1963-74; mgr. audio visual and employee information Northwestern Bell, Mpls., 1974—. Dir., editor (film) Who's Responsible (award of Merit Chgo. Internat. Film and Video Festival, 1984); co-dir., spl. effects (video) Escape from Ubadistan, 1985 (Silver Screen award U.S. Indsl. Film Festival, 1986, Best Interactive Video of 1985 Videotape Prodn. Assn.), producer, dir. (video) Techno-Shock! (Gold medal Internat. Film and Video Festival N.Y., 1986, gold hugo ITERCOM '86 Chgo. Film Fest., 1986). Vol. Minn. Dept. Nat. Resources, Tower, 1980—. Served with ANG, 1962-68. Mem. Audio Visual Mgmt. Assn. (pres. 1983-85), Soc. Profl. Journalists. Congregationalist. Avocations: sailing, flying, photography. Office: Northwestern Bell 200 S 5th St #395 Minneapolis MN 55402

WELLES, NYDIA LELIA CÁNOVAS, psychologist; b. Buenos Aires, Argentina, Mar. 30, 1935; came to U.S., 1968, naturalized, 1977; d. Artemio Tomás and Pura (Martínez) Cánovas; B.A. in Elem. Edn., Nat. Coll. Edn., Evanston, Ill., 1976; M.A. in Counseling Psychology, Northwestern U., 1977, PhD in Counseling Psychology, 1986; m. Lorant Welles, Oct. 21, 1967; 1 son, Lorant Esteban. Tchr. in Argentina, 1954-64; pvt. practice psychology, Argentina, 1964-67; social worker Cath. Charities, Chgo., 1971-75; translator SRA, Chgo., 1975; test adminstr. Ednl. Testing Service, 1975-76; Latin Am. Services supr. Edgewater Uptown Community Mental Health Council, Chgo., 1978-80 ; research asst. Center Family Studies, 1978-79; mem. allocation com. campaing for human devel. Archdiocess of Chgo., 1985—. Mem. Ill. Assn. for Hispanic Mental Health (co-founder), Phi Delta Kappa. Roman Catholic. Author papers in field. Home: 3110 Hill Ln Wilmette IL 60091

WELLINGTON, ROBERT HALL, manufacturing company executive; b. Atlanta, July 4, 1922; s. Robert H. and Ernestine V. (Vossbrinck) W.; m. Marjorie Jarchow, Nov. 15, 1947; children: Charles R., Robert H., Christian J., Jeanne L. B.S., Northwestern Tech. Inst., 1943; M.S. in Bus. Adminstrn, MBA, U. Chgo., 1958. With Griffin Wheel Co., 1946-61; v.p. parent co. AMSTED Industries, Inc., Chgo., 1961-74, exec. v.p., 1974-80, pres., chief exec. officer, 1981—, also dir.; bd. dirs. L.E. Myers Co., Chgo., DeSoto Inc., Chgo., Centel, Money Market Assets, Time Target Trust. Served to lt. USN, 1943-46. Clubs: Chicago, Chgo. Athletic, Economic, Mid-America, Comml. Office: Amsted Industries Inc 205 N Michigan Ave Chicago IL 60601

WELLIVER, WARREN DEE, lawyer, state supreme court justice; b. Butler, Mo., Feb. 24, 1920; s. Carl Winfield and Burdee Marie (Wolfe) W.; m. Ruth Rose Galey, Dec. 25, 1942; children: Gale Dee (Mrs. William B. Stone), Carla Camile (Mrs. Dayton Stone), Christy Marie (Mrs. Norman Sullivan). BA, U. Mo., 1945; JD, U. Mo., 1948. Bar: Mo. 1948. Asst. pros. atty. Boone County, Columbia, 1948-54; sr. ptnr. Welliver, Atkinson and Eng, Columbia, 1960-79; tchr. law U. Mo. Law Sch., 1948-49; mem. Mo. Senate, 1977-79; justice Supreme Ct. Mo., Jefferson City, 1979—; mem. Gov. Mo. Adv. Council Alcoholism and Drug Abuse, chmn. drug council, 1970-72; chmn. Task Force Revision Mo. Drug Laws, 1970-71; liaison mem. council Nat. Inst. Alcoholism and Alcohol Abuse, 1972—. Bd. dirs. Nat. Assn. Mental Health, 1970—, regional v.p., 1973-75; pres. Mo. Assn. Mental Health, 1968-69, Stephens Coll. Assocs., 1965—, Friends of Library, U. Mo., 1979; bd. dirs. Gateway Area chpt. Multiple Sclerosis Soc., St. Louis, 1986—; bd. curators Stephens Coll., 1980—; Dem. county chmn., 1954-64; hon. fellow Harry S. Truman Library Inst., 1979—. Served with USNR, 1941-45. Fellow Am. Coll. Trial Lawyers, Am. Bar Found.; mem. ABA, Mo. Bar Assn. (pres. 1967-68), Boone County Bar Assn. (pres. 1970), Am. Judicature Soc., Am. Legion (past post comdr.), Multiple Sclerosis Soc. (Gateway chpt. bd. dirs. 1986—), Order of Coif. Clubs: Country of Mo, Columbia Country (past pres.). Home: 3430 Woodrail Terr Columbia MO 65203 Office: Supreme Ct Bldg Jefferson City MO 65101

WELLMAN, W. A., window manufacturing executive; b. 1918. With Andersen Corp., Bayport, Minn., 1937—, pres., from 1975, now chmn. bd., chief exec. officer, dir. Office: Andersen Corp Foot N 5th Ave Bayport MN 55003 *

WELLNITZ, CRAIG OTTO, lawyer, English educator; b. Elwood, Ind., Dec. 5, 1946; s. Frank Otto and Jeanne (Albright) W.; m. Karen Sue Thomas, Apr. 13, 1974; children—Jennifer Suzanne, Anne Katherine. B.A., Purdue U., 1969; M.A., Ind. U., 1972; J.D., Ind. U.-Indpls., 1978. Bar: Ind. 1978, U.S. Dist. Ct. (so. dist.) Ind. 1978, U.S. Supreme Ct. 1983, U.S. Ct. Appeals (7th and Fed. cirs.) 1984. Instr. Danville Jr. Coll., Ill., 1972-74, S.W. Mo. State U., Springfield, Mo., 1974-75; ptnr. Coates, Hatfield & Calkins, Indpls., 1978—; pub. defender Marion County, Ind., 1979—; instr. U. Indpls., 1981-82; mem. adj. faculty dept. English, Butler U., Indpls., 1983—; instr. Ind. U./Purdue U., Indpls., 1985—; pres. Ind. Account Mgmt., Indpls., 1985—. Columnist: A Jury of Your Peers, 1984—; lectr. I'm Being Sued for What?, 1982, The American Legal Justice System, 1984—; The Written Word: The Power of Effective Writing, 1985, A Way With Words, 1987. Vice committeeman Indpls. Rep. precinct, 1978; chmn. fin. com. St. Luke's United Meth. Ch., 1985-87. Postgrad. study grantee S.W. Mo. State U., Springfield, 1975. Mem. Indpls. Bar Assn., Ind. Bar Assn., ABA, Assn. Trial Lawyers Am., Ind. Trial Lawyers Assn. Club: Riviera

(Indpls.). Lodge: Elks. Home: PO Box 44162 Indianapolis IN 46204 Office: Coates Hatfield & Calkins 107 N Pennsylvania Suite 902 Indianapolis IN 46204

WELLS, BEN FREDERICK, lawyer; b. Cin., Sept. 28, 1958; s. William Ben and Louise Rose (Zimmerman) W.; m. Judith Marie Wildermuth, Nov. 24, 1984; 1 child, Ben F. Jr. BBA, U. Cin., 1980, JD, 1983. Bar: Ohio 1983, U.S. Dist. Ct. (so. dist.) Ohio 1984, U.S. Tax Ct. 1987. Assoc. Santen, Shaffer & Hughes, Cin., 1983-86, Dinsmore & Shohl, Cin., 1986—. Trustee Jesuit Program for Living and Learning, Cin., 1986; bd. dirs. Cin. Community Chest Allocations Bd., 1983-86; bd. dirs., treas. Fêtes de Jeunesse, Cin., 1984-86. Named one of Outstanding Young Men of Am., 1985. Mem. ABA (taxation sect.), Ohio Bar Assn., Cin. Bar Assn. (taxation and estate planning sect.). Republican. Roman Catholic. Club: Cin. Athletic. Avocations: skiing, tennis, gardening. Home: 9005 Bordeaux Ct Cincinnati OH 45242 Office: Dinsmore and Shohl 511 Walnut St Cincinnati OH 45202

WELLS, DONNA ANN, computer sales and marketing executive; b. Lexington, Ky., July 8, 1955; d. Donald Criswell and Ann Katherine (Isaac) W.; m. Kenneth Herbert Hoffman, June 6, 1976 (div. Sept. 1980); m. Brian Dale Lieffers, Dec. 23, 1982. BS, Eastern Ky. U., 1977. Advt. artist C&H Rauch Jewelers, Lexington, 1977; graphic designer East Ky. Power Co., Winchester, 1977-78; art dir. Advance Corp., St. Paul, 1979-80; advt. coordinator PBS Computing, St. Paul, 1980-81; communications mgr. Control Data Corp., Mpls., 1982-86, mktg. and sales support mgr., 1986—. Recipient Great Performer award, Control Data Corp., 1984, Oliver Direct Mail award, Bus. & Profl. Advt. Assn., Mpls, 1984. Avocations: reading, boating, fishing. Home: 4538 Quantico Ln Plymouth MN 55446 Office: Control Data Corp 5720 Smetana Rd Minneapolis MN 55343

WELLS, HAROLD F., manufacturers representative; b. Lincoln, Nebr., Sept. 3, 1939; s. Harold F. and Jane (Wilson) W.; m. Karen Kay Klamert, July 1, 1961; children: Kevin H., Kurt D. Student, U. Nebr., 1958-59; grad., Lincoln Sch. Commerce, 1960. Fireman med. support Kansas City (Kans.) Fire Dept., 1972-75; staff adminstr. ARC, Cansas City, 1972-76; sales rep. Pieroth Wine Co. of Germany, Kansas City, 1976-77; area mgr. Curtis Industries, 1977-80; owner mgr. Sonny Wells Supply Co., Liberty, Mo., 1978—. Mem. Civil War Round Table Kansas City, Clay County Hist. Soc., Clay County Mus. Assn.; hon. mem. Wyandotte County (Kans.) Hist. Soc., Westport (Mo.) Hist. Soc., Union Cemetery Hist. Soc., Kansas City, Soc. Civil War Neocrolithologists, Mo. Civil War Re-enactors Assn., Clay County Assn. Living Historians. Mem. Sons of Union Vets. of Civil War, Confederate Hist. Inst., Medal Honor Hist. Soc. Mem. Christian Ch. Avocations: model trains, civil war, memoriabilia, gardening. Home and Office: 1209 Skyline Dr Liberty MO 64008

WELLS, JOEL WILLIAM, human development and family relationships educator; b. N.Y.C., May 20, 1941; s. Alonza James and Eleanor Marie (Schaeffer) W.; m. Catherine Margaret Cicirello, Aug. 24, 1968; children: Brett, Karen, Brian. BS, Ohio U., 1963; MA, Western Carolina U., 1968; PhD, U. Conn., 1978. Prof. Utah State U., Logan, 1978-81, U. No. Iowa, Cedar Falls, 1981—; counselor-therapist Utah State U., 1979-81, U. No. Iowa, 1981—. Contbr. articles to profl. jours. Bd. dirs. Family Service League, Waterloo, Iowa, 1981—; educator Sexual Abuse Com., Waterloo, 1983—. Mem. Am. Assn. Marriage and Family Therapy (clin.). Democrat. Unitarian. Avocations: bel canto opera, exercise physiology, backpacking. Home: 4525 Coronado Ct Cedar Falls IA 50613 Office: U No Iowa 216 Wright Cedar Falls IA 50614

WELLS, LARRY WESLEY, information services executive, consultant; b. Island Falls, Maine, Feb. 3, 1950; s. Stanley Wesley and Roxie (Bailey) W.; m. Ruth Ann Hutcheson, Oct. 25, 1969; children: John Wesley, Deborah Michelle. Grad. high sch., Ohio, 1968. Inventory clk., then billing clk. Southwestern Ohio Steel, Hamilton, 1967-74, programmer, 1971-74, mgr. data processing devel., 1979-84, mgr. data processing, 1984-85, dir. info. services, 1986—; cons. SOS Transport, Middletown, Ohio, 1984—, SOS Leveling, Middletown, Ohio. Edn. advisor cooperative office edn. Hamilton High Sch., 1984—. Mem. Data Processing Mgmt. Assn., Common Data Processing Assn. Republican. Avocations: trumpet, golf, travel. Home: 135 Littlebrook Fairfield OH 45014 Office: Southwestern Ohio Steel PO Box 148 Hamilton OH 45012

WELLS, LIONELLE DUDLEY, pathologist, consultant; b. Winston-Salem, N.C., Feb. 27, 1951; s. Lionelle D. and Mildred W. (Wohltmann) W.; m. Sara Mayes Lively, May 24, 1973 (div. Jan. 1984); children: Chris, Linda, Lionelle, Valerie; m. Mary Ellen Schroeder, June 9, 1984. BA, U. Pa., 1973; MD, Washington U., St. Louis, 1977. Diplomate Am. Bd. Pathology. Intern Yale New Haven Hosp., 1977-78, resident, 1978-80; resident UCLA Ctr. for Health Scis., Los Angeles, 1980-82; pathologist Riverside (Calif.) Community Hosp., 1982-84; dir. labs. El Centro (Calif.) Community Hosp., 1984-85, Nat. Health Labs., Evansville, Ind., 1985—, Wabash Gen. Hosp., Mt. Carmel, Ill., 1985—, Wirth Hosp., Oakland City, Ind., 1985—; cons. pathologist Carmi (Ill.) Hosp., 1985—, Ferrell Hosp., El Dorado, Ill., 1985—, Pearce Hosp., El Dorado, 1985—, Fairfield (Ill.) Meml Hosp., 1985—. Fellow Coll. Am. Pathologists, Am. Soc. Clin. Pathologists; mem. Am. Acad. Med. Dirs., Am. Assn. Blood Banks. Avocations: theatre, film, design, computing. Home: 4213 Spring Valley Rd Evansville IN 47715 Office: Nat Health Labs 3700 Bellemeade Evansville IN 47715

WELLS, STANLEY DALE, radiologist; b. Hutchinson, Ky., Dec. 14, 1944; s. Willard Dale and Helen Louise (Shores) W.; m. Mary Herndon, Dec. 29, 1967; children: Steven Michael, Shelby Lynn. BA cum laude, Sterling Coll., 1965; MD, U. Kans., 1969. Diplomate Am. Bd. Radiology. Surgery intern Rush Presbyn. St. Luke's Hosp., Chgo., 1969-70; resident in diagnostic radiology St. Luke's Hosp., Kansas City, Mo., 1972-75; instr. radiology U. Tenn., Memphis, 1975-76; asst. prof. U. Mo., Kansas City, 1976-77; attending staff Research Radiology Group Inc., Kansas City, 1977—; cons. VA Hosp., Memphis, 1975-76. Contbr. articles to profl. jours. Served to lt. USNR. Mem. AMA, Am. Coll. Radiology, Am. Roentgen Ray Soc., Radiol. Soc. N.Am. Presbyterian. Avocations: scuba diving. Office: Research Radiology Group Inc T209 6420 Prospect Kansas City MO 64132

WELLS, STEVEN ALLEN, oil company financial officer; b. Torrance, Calif., Apr. 16, 1952; s. Jack Dale Wells and Patricia (Jensen) Hawk; m. Marcy Ann Vernon, June 8, 1974; children: Abby, Allison. BS, Ohio State U., 1974. CPA, Ohio. Tax compiler Cole, Layer, Tramble, Dayton, Ohio, 1975-77; acct., mgr. V.A. Hetzel, Pub. Accts., Dayton, 1977-82; chief fin. officer Duncan Oil Co., Xenia, Ohio, 1982—. vol. Dayton Art Inst., 1982-85, Dayton Performing Arts Assoc. Bd., 1985—. Mem. Nutt Road Estates Home Owners Assn. (treas. 1985—). Republican. Avocations: golf, volleyball, racquetball. Home: 10077 Settlement House Rd Spring Valley OH 45370 Office: Duncan Oil Co 849 Factory Rd Xenia OH 45385

WELLS, THOMAS HENRY, composer, music educator; b. Austin, Tex., Jan. 8, 1945; s. Merle E. and Helen M. Wells; m. Barbara Gail Stadelman, Sept. 4, 1981; children: Thomas A., Sybil A. MusD, U. Tex., 1969. Instr. music U. Tex., 1969-76; prof. Ohio State U. Sch. of Music, Columbus, 1976—. Mem. Am. Soc. U. Campus (chmn. electronic music consortium 1981—, region 5 co-chmn. 1982). Avocation: amateur radio. Office: Ohio State U 1866 College Park Columbus OH 43210

WELLS, WILLIAM LEROY, clergyman; b. Bion Orville and Pauline (Brashler) W.; m. Mary Jesse Apolinar, June 5, 1965; children: Jeffrey Grant, William LeRoy, Mark Andrew. B.A., Seattle Pacific Coll., 1956; M.Div., Berkeley Bapt. Div. Sch., 1959; D.Min., Pitts. Theol. Sem., 1978. Ordained to ministry, Baptist Ch., 1959; pastor First Bapt. Ch., Hay, Wash., 1959-62, Delta Community Bapt. Ch., Everett, Wash., 1962-66; minister Leadership Devel. program Pitts. Bapt. Assn., 1973-80; exec. minister Wis. Bapt. State Conv., 1980—. Served with AUS, 1966-73. Decorated Bronze Star medal. Democrat. Club: Milwaukee Athletic. Author: Planning for Evangelism in the Local Church, 1978. Office: Wis Bapt State Conv 15330 W Watertown Plank Rd Elm Grove WI 53122 *

WELLS, WILLIAM LOCHRIDGE, chemical engineer; b. Mayfield, Ky., Oct. 12, 1939; s. Kenneth Morgan and Sarah Elizabeth (Lochridge) W. BS in Chem. Engring., U. Ky., 1962, MS, 1964; PhD in Physical Chemistry, U. Ill., 1967; MS in Chem. Engring., U. S.C., 1974; MBA, U. Tenn., Chattanooga, 1982. Registered profl. engr., Ky., S.C. Asst. prof. chemistry Murray State U., 1967-69; postdoctoral research assoc. Wayne State U., 1969-71; asst. prof. SW Bapt. Coll., 1971-72; prof. Midlands Tech. Coll., 1972-74; mgr. program in air pollution research TVA, Chattanooga, Tenn., 1975-83; dir. Ctr. for Research on Sulfur in Coal, Champaign, Ill., 1983—; lectr. in field. Contbr. articles to profl. jours. NSF grantee, 1968-69. Mem. Am. Chem. Soc., Royal Soc. Chemistry, Am. Inst. Indsl. Engrs., Am. Inst. Chem. Engrs. (past chmn. Chattanooga sect.), Nat. Soc. Profl. Engrs., Alpha Chi Sigma, Tau Beta Pi, Phi Lambda Upsilon, Sigma Chi, Sigma Iota Epsilon. Home: PO Box 3926 Champaign IL 61821 Office: 201 W Springfield Suite 202 Champaign IL 61820-4834

WELLS, WILLIAM STEVEN, marketing communications consultant, syndicated cartoonist; b. Detroit, Aug. 19, 1945; s. Ronald and Eleanor (Vancea) W.; m. Mary Rudolph, Nov. 27, 1969; children: Adam, David. AB, Hamilton Coll., 1967. Journalist New Haven Register, Providence Jour., Detroit Free Press, 1968-75; exec. asst. to Mich. Gov. William Milliken, Lansing, 1975-76; account exec. Fleishman-Hillard, Inc., St. Louis, 1976-78; v.p., mgr. Doremus & Co., Mpls., 1978-80; sr. v.p., mng. dir. Hill & Knowlton, Inc., Mpls., 1980-84; pres. Wells and Co., 1984—; co-author syndicated bus. cartoon strip Executive Suite, United Features Syndicate. Contbr. articles to profl. jours. Served with USNR, 1968-69. Mem. Nat. Investor Relations Inst., Issues Mgmt. Assn. Republican. Clubs: Mpls., Edina Country, Minn. Squash Raquets Assn. Office: Wells and Co Exposition Hall at River Pl Suite 504 Minneapolis MN 55414

WELNHOFER, ROBERT WILLIAM, distribution company executive; b. Chgo., Apr. 27, 1933; s. George Albert and Lillian Mary (Boscamp) W.; 1 child, William George. BBA, Northwestern U., 1955; cert. grad. sch. exec. program, Stanford U., 1967; MBA, U. Chgo., 1973. CPA, Ill. Mgr. Arthur Andersen & Co., Chgo., 1955-61; v.p. Boise Cascade Corp., Chgo., 1961-77; v.p. fin. and adminstrn. Safety-Kleen Corp., Elgin, Ill., 1977-81; sr. v.p. strategic planning United Stationers Inc., Des Plaines, Ill., 1981—. Treas. Christ Luth. Ch., Palatine, Ill., 1984—; past mem. alumni adv. council Kellogg Grad. Sch. Mgmt. Northwestern U., Evanston, Ill. Mem. Am. Inst. CPA's, Ill. Soc. CPA's, Beta Alpha Psi. Club: Rolling Green Country (Arlington Heights, Ill.). Avocations: golf, bowling, music, sports. Office: United Stationers Inc 2200 E Golf Rd Des Plaines IL 60016

WELSH, ARTHUR CRAIG (KEVIN MCCARTHY), radio station commentator; b. Alton, Ill., Apr. 21, 1947; s. Ralph Hunter and Joyce (Hanks) W.; m. Gudrun Schwenn, Sept. 3, 1979. Student, So. Ill. U., Edwardsville, 1965-66, U. Md., 1968. Mgmt. exec. Household Internat. Fin. Corp., St. Louis, 1970-82; commentator Sta. KMOX-KHTR Radio, div. CBS, St. Louis, 1982—; mgr. tng. Household Internat. Fin. Co., Stl. Louis, 1975-82; music and promotions dir. Sta. KHTR radio, St. Louis, 1984-86; pub. relations dir. Operation Liftoff, St. Louis, 1984—. Acted as Santa Claus for St. Louis chpt. USMC Toys for Tots campaign, 1985—. Served with U.S. Army, 1966-69. Mem. Am. Fedn. TV and Radio Artists. Lodge: Masons. Avocations: photography, gourmet cooking, music, sports cars, travel. Office: Sta KMOX/KHTR Radio div CBS 1 Memorial Dr Saint Louis MO 63102

WELSH, STEPHEN RICHARD, dentist; b. Mason City, Iowa, May 5, 1953; s. Richard Glen and Helen Jean (Dory) W.; m. Ann Marie Smith, Aug. 16, 1973; children: Kevin, Daniel, Matthew, Katie. AA, North Iowa Community Coll., 1973; BS, U. Iowa, 1975, DDS, 1978. Gen. practice dentistry Manly, Iowa, 1978—; cons. Manly Care Ctr., 1978—. Mem. Manly Devel. Com. Mem. ADA, North Iowa Dist. of Iowa Dental Assn. (v.p., pres.-elect 1984—). Democrat. Roman Catholic. Avocations: scuba diving, fishing, boating, golfing. Home: 23 Circle Terr Manly IA 50456 Office: 128 E Main St Manly IA 50456

WELSH, WILLIAM, II, manufacturing company executive. Pres., chief operating officer Valmont Industries Inc., Valley, Nebr. Office: Valmont Industries Inc Valley NE 68064 *

WELTE, TERRENCE LYNN, teacher; b. Sioux City, Iowa, Sept. 17, 1949; s. Francis Claire and Roberta Mae (Siefert) W.; m. Rebecca Lynn Holmstedt, May 15, 1972; children: Eric Christian, Michael Edward. BA Edn., Wayne (Nebr.) State Coll., 1972; MA Edn., U. Nebr., Omaha, 1978. Tchr. Meriden- Cleghorn (Iowa) High Sch., 1972-75, Millard Schs., Omaha, 1975—; cons. Nebr. Dept. Edn., Lincoln, 1979-80. Editor: Nebraska Anthology, 1982. Wayne County del. Nebr. Rep. Conv., Omaha, 1972; presenter Mo. Valley Hist. Conf., 1982. Recipient Outstanding Educator award Cooper Found.,1983, Hall of Fame award Wayne State 2d Guessers, 1985. Mem. Phi Delta Kappa (initiation chmn. 1987—). Lutheran. Home: 15227 T Omaha NE 68137 Office: Millard North Jr High 2828 S 139th Pl Omaha NE 68144

WELTER, HAROLD AUGUSTINE, insurance agency executive; b. La Porte, Ind., Mar. 12, 1945; s. Joseph Leo and Lou Ellen (Atchison) W.; m. Becky Jane Green, Aug. 18, 1973; children—Susan Elizabeth, Laura Jane, Cheryl Lyn, Nathan Joseph. Student, U. Ky.-Fort Knox, 1963-65; diploma Midwestern Broadcasting Sch., 1965. Staff announcer Sta. WRIN, Rensselaer, Ind., 1965-66; program dir. Sta. WLOI, La Porte, 1966-69; gen. mgr. Sta. WKVI, Knox, Ind., 1969-73; press sec. to U.S. Congressman E.F. Landgrebe, Washington, 1973-75; owner, mgr. Harold Welter & Assocs., Knox, 1975—. Trustee Knox Community Sch. Corp., 1978-86, pres., 1980-81, 82-83, 84-85; Founder, pres. Holy Family Found. for Cath. Edn., Inc.; precinct committeeman Starke County Republican Central Com., Knox, 1982-87; del. Rep. State Conv., 1978, 80, 82, 84. Served with U.S. Army, 1963-65. Recipient Prodn. Growth award Equitable Life N.Y., 1977; named to Nat. Leaders Corps, Equitable Life N.Y., 1977. Mem. Million Dollar Round Table, Nat. Assn. Life Underwriters (Nat. Quality award 1980, 81, 82, 84, 85, 86, Nat. Sales Achievement award 1978, 80, 81, 82, 84, 85, 86). Roman Catholic. Avocations: sportscasting, travel. Home: Route #3 Box 85 Knox IN 46534 Office: Harold Welter & Assocs PO Box 195 Knox IN 46534

WELTER, WILLIAM MICHAEL, marketing and advertising executive; b. Evanston, Ill., Nov. 18, 1944; s. Roy Michael and Frances (DeShields) W.; m. Pamela Bassett, June 11, 1971; children: Barclay, Robert Michael. BS, Mo. Valley Coll., 1966. Account exec. Leo Burnett Co., Inc., Chgo., 1966-74; v.p., account supr. Needham Harper Worldwide, Chgo., 1974-80; v.p. mktg. Wendy's Internat., Inc., Dublin, Ohio, 1981, sr. v.p. mktg., 1981-84, exec. v.p., 1984-87; founder Haunty & Welter, Worthington, Ohio, 1987—. Founder Santa's Silent Helpers, Columbus, Ohio, 1985. Mem. Ad Fedn. Columbus. Clubs: Scioto Country (Columbus); Muirfield Country (Dublin). Avocations: golf; fishing; tennis. Home: 4311 Woodhall Rd Columbus OH 43220 Office: Haunty & Welter 7700 Rivers Edge Dr Worthington OH 43085

WELTON, JAMES ARTHUR, transportation broker and consultant; b. Portland, Oreg., Jan. 1, 1921; s. Raymond Patrick and Birdie Vernette (Larson) W.; m. Maverette Lavonne Ness, Aug. 22, 1942 (dec. Nov. 1963); children: Richard, Timothy, Nancy; m. Marjorie Elaine Page, May 31, 1964; children: Kathleen, William. Student Am. U., 1968. Instr. Inver Hills Jr. Coll., 1975, Normandale Jr. Coll., 1977; with Soo Line R.R., 1938-78, div. supt., Enderlin, N.D., 1962-72, dir. intermodal service, Mpls., 1972-77, dir. labor relations, 1977-78; pres. Welco Driver Leasing, Burnsville, Minn., 1982; pres. Welco Cons., 1981—; transp. and safety cons. United Van Bus Delivery, Mpls., Midwest Truck Leasing, Assoc. Delivery Service, Loeffel-Engstrand Co., Network Transportation Service; sr. reservist ICC, Washington, 1961-62. Pres. Enderlin (N.D.) City Park Bd., 1962; bd. dirs. Greater N.D. Assn., Bismarck, 1961-62; pres. Big Bros., Shrine Hosp. Crippled Children, Mpls., 1983. Republican. Presbyterian. Home: 2717 Dalridge Circle Burnsville MN 55337 Office: Welco Cons One Appletree Sq Suite 1145 Minneapolis MN 55420

WELTY, TIMOTHY EDWARD, clinical pharmacist, medical educator; b. Indpls., Nov. 28, 1953; s. Willis Edward and Catherine Louise (Hatfield) W.; m. Connie Lydia Haberstroh, June 27, 1980; children: Elizabeth Anna, Nathan Edward, Luke David. Student Taylor U., 1972-73; B.S. in Pharmacy, Butler U., 1977; M.A. in Religion, Trinity Evang. Div. Sch., 1980; Pharm.D., U. Minn., 1982. Registered pharmacist, Ind., Ill. Staff pharmacist Parkview Meml. Hosp. Ft. Wayne, Ind., 1977-78, Highland Park (Ill.) Hosp., 1978-80; staff pharmacist St. Paul Ramsey Med. Ctr., 1982-83, research fellow, 1982-83; asst. prof. clin. pharmacy Purdue U., West Lafayette, Ind., 1983-85; clin. pharmacist for neurology/cardiology Meth. Hosp., Indpls., 1985—; co-investigator, asst. clin. research, 1983—. Mem. Am. Soc. Hosp. Pharmacists, Am. Coll. Clin. Pharmacists, Epilepsy Found. Am., Am. Assn. of Colls. of Pharmacy, Ind. Soc. of Hosp. Pharmacists. Mem. Christian and Missionary Alliance Ch. Avocation: photography. Office: Pharmacy Dept Meth Hosp 1701 N Senate Blvd Indianapolis IN 46202

WENDEL, LENY EMMERZAEL, marketing executive; b. Rockanje, Netherlands, May 25, 1945; came to U.S., 1972; d. Hugo and Johanna (Briggeman) Emmerzael; m. Don Wendel, Dec. 17, 1971. Diplome, Sorbonne, Paris, 1965; BA magna cum laude, U. Minn., 1980, MA, 1982. Mktg. dir. Theatre de la Jeune Lune, Mpls., 1982-83; sales rep. Xerox, Mpls., 1983-85; mktg. specialist Carlson Cos., Mpls., 1985-86, mktg. account mgr., 1986—. Mem. Minn. Women's Network (assignment editor 1985—, recognition award 1986-87), Phi Kappa Phi. Avocations: theatre, sailing, skiing, bicycling. Office: Carlson Mktg Group 12755 State Hwy 55 Minneapolis MN 55441

WENDELBERGER, JAMES GEORGE, statistician, consultant; b. Milw., Mar. 13, 1953; s. Joseph Martin and Elizabeth (Neimon) W.; m. Joanne Marie Roth. B.S. with distinction in Math. and Physics, U. Wis.-Madison, 1976, M.S. in Stats, 1978, Ph.D., 1982. Research assoc. Space Sci. and Engring. Ctr., U. Wis.-Madison, 1982-83; sr. research scientist Gen. Motors Research Lab., 1983-87, quantitative analysis mgr. Urban Sci. Applications, Inc., 1987—. Mem. Inst. Math. Stats., Soc. Indsl. and Applied Math., Am. Statis. Assn., AAAS, Sigma Xi. Subspecialties: Statistics; Mathematical software. Current work: Consulting research statistician; multiple time series analysis, multidimentional spline smoothing. Home: 5000 West Utica Rd Utica MI 48087 Office: Urban Sci Applications 200 Renaissance Ctr Suite 1230 Detroit MI 48243

WENDELBERGER, JOANNE ROTH, statistical consultant; b. Milw., June 22, 1959; d. Donald Alfred and Marie Louise (Mercury) Roth; m. James George Wendelberger, Jan. 21, 1984. AB in Maths., Econs., Oberlin Coll., 1981; MS in Stats., U. Wis., 1983. Sci. coordinator Upward Bound, Oberlin, Ohio, 1980; teaching asst. Oberlin Coll., 1980-81; research asst. U. Wis., Madison, 1982-83, stat. cons., 1983; stat. cons. Gen. Motors, Warren, Mich., 1984—. Mem. new student orientation com. Oberlin Coll., 1977-81, pres. women's sports ocom., 1981; mem. Caucus for Women in Stats., 1985—; counselor Girl Scouts Milw. area, West Bend, Wis., 1978; rep. alumnaie admissions Oberlin Coll., Madison, 1981-83. Fellow Wis. Alumnae Research Found., 1981-82; scholar Nat. Merit Corp., 1977. Mem. Am. Stat. Assn., Inst. Math. Stats., Soc. Indsl. and Applied Maths., Math. Assn. Am., Phi Beta Kappa. Roman Catholic. Avocations: travel, swimming, hiking, reading. Home: 5000 W Utica Rd Utica MI 48087 Office: Gen Motors Research Labs Computer Sci Dept GM Technical Center Warren MI 48090

WENDELBURG, NORMA RUTH, composer, pianist, educator; b. Stafford, Kans.; d. Henry and Anna (Moeckel) Wendelburg; Mus.B., Bethany Coll., 1943; Mus.M., U. Mich., 1947; Mus.M., Eastman Sch. Music, 1951, postgrad., 1964-65, 66-67, Ph.D. in Composition, 1969; postgrad. Mozarteum, 1953-54, Vienna Acad. Music, 1955. Asst. prof. music edn., piano Wayne (Nebr.) State Coll., 1947-50, Bethany Coll., Lindsborg, Kan., 1952-53, State Coll., Cedar Falls, Ia., 1956-58; asst. prof. composition, theory, piano Hardin-Simmons U., Abilene, Tex., 1958-66, chmn. grad. com. Sch. Music, 1960-66, founder ann. univ. festival contemporary music, 1959, chmn., 1959—; asso. prof. music Dallas Bapt. Coll., 1973-75; research asst. to dir. grad. studies Eastman Sch. Music, 1966-67; former asso. prof., chmn. dept. theory, composition Southwest Tex. State U.; mem. faculty Friends Bible Coll., Haviland, Kans., 1977-83; guest composer several colls. including U. Ottawa, 1984; appeared as pianist Minn. Pub. Radio (2 performances) 1986, Pub. Broadcasting Station (1 performance), Hutchinson, Kans., 1986, various solo recitals, festivals. Recipient Meet the Composer award N.Y. State Council of Arts, 1979; Composition scholar Composers' Conf. Middlebury (Vt.), 1950, Berkshire Center, 1953; Fulbright award, 1953-55; Residence fellow Huntington Hartford Found., 1955-56, 58, 61; MacDowell Colony, 1958, 60, 70. Mem. Music Tchrs. Nat. Conf., Am. Music Center, MacDowell Colonists, ASCAP, Am. Soc. Univ. Composers, Minn. Composers Forum, Am. Women Composers, Sigma Alpha Iota. Composer numerous works including Symphony, 1967, Suite for Violin and Piano, 1965, Song Cycle for Soprano, Flutes, Piano, 1974, Music for Two Pianos, 1985, Affirmation, 1982, Interlacings (organ), 1983, others. Address: 2206 N Van Buren Hutchinson KS 67052

WENDLANDT, CRAIG MICHAEL, engineer; b. Waukesha, Wis., July 12, 1954; s. Melvin and Judith Rose (Merath) W.; m. Debra Sue Hardrath, Aug. 17, 1974; children: Kerri, Kelly, Bryan. Journeymen Trade Diploma, Milw. Area Tech. Coll., 1978; A in Indsl. Engring., Milw. Sch. Engring., 1983, B in Indsl. Mgmt., 1986; postgrad. in bus. adminstrn., Marquette U., 1986—. Tool chaser Falk Corp., Milw., 1975, apprentice gear cutter, 1975-78, gear technologist, 1978-79, supr., 1979-86, engr., 1986—. Loaned exec. United Way, Milw., 1978. Mem. Falk Mgmt. Club (bd. dirs. 1984-86). Roman Catholic. Club: Hwy. G Gun (Wind Lake, Wis.) (sec. 1980-86). Avocations: hunting, fishing, softball, bowling. Home: 8135 S 57 St Franklin WI 53132 Office: Falk Corp 3001 W Canal St Box 492 Milwaukee WI 53201

WENDORF, MELVIN JAMES, municipal government controller; b. Schofield, Wis., June 1, 1929; s. Herman Frederick and Martha Augusta (Falk) W.; m. Ruth Margaret Newbauer, Feb. 7, 1959; children: Christine Ann, Laura Lynn. BBA, U. Wis., 1958. CPA, Wis., Minn. Asst. state auditor State of Wis., Madison, 1958-67; special agent IRS, St. Paul, 1967-73, group mgr., 1973-74; ptnr. Acctg. Partnership, Anoka, Minn., 1974-76; controller City of Mpls., 1976—. Bd. dirs. Bethesda Luth. Home Found., Watertown, Wis., 1981—, Travelers Protective Assn., St. Louis, 1984-86. Served with U.S. Army, 1951-54. Mem. Am. Inst. CPA's, Minn. Soc. CPA's, Acctg. Research Assn., Govt. Fin. Officers Assn. (Fin. Reporting Achievement award 1981, 84, Profl. Achievement Recognition award 1985), Mcpl. Treas.'s Assn., Am. Legion. Lutheran. Avocations: golf, fishing, boating. Home: 3162 Shorewood Dr Arden Hills MN 55112 Office: City of Mpls 350 South 4th St Minneapolis MN 55415

WENDORFF, BRUCE EDWARD, manufacturing manager; b. Tecumseh, Nebr., June 15, 1939; s. Urban Edward and Gertrude Jane (Heikes) W.; m. Judy Sue Hanneman, Nov. 22, 1960; children: Lissi Lynn, Ingrid Anna, Ilse Ann. BSEE, U. Nebr., 1957-62. Plant engr. Am. Stores, Lincoln, Nebr., 1967-72, beef supt., 1972-79, asst. plant mgr., 1979-85; plant manager Cook Family Foods, Lincoln, 1985—; cons. Dept. Agr., State of Nebr., Lincoln, 1982. Mem. Photographic Soc. Am. (assoc.). Republican. Presbyterian. Avocations: photography, outdoor sports. Home: 2244 Harrison Ave Lincoln NE 68502

WENDT, ELIZABETH WARCZAK, insurance company executive; b. Chgo., Aug. 27, 1931; d. John George and Elizabeth Marion (Jankowski) Warczak; m. John Edward Wendt, Oct. 31, 1953 (div.); children—John Alan, Brian Arthur, James Michael. Student Loyola U.-Chgo., 1951-52; B.S.B.A., St. Mary-of-the-Woods Coll., 1980; postgrad. Chgo. Kent Coll. Law, 1981-82. Asst. to actuary Globe Life Ins. Co., Chgo., 1970-74; asst. compliance officer Globe Life/Ryan Ins. Group, Chgo., 1974-86; mgr. credit product devel., 1986—; mem. FLMI Soc. Chgo., 1983—; mem. Life A&H Legis. Com. Consumer Credit Ins. Assn., Chgo., 1983—; co. rep., mem. Handout Com. Life & Health Compliance Assn., 1979—. Election judge, 1984. Mem. United Farm Workers Support Com., Chgo. Fellow Life Mgmt. Inst.; mem. Inst. Distaff Execs. Assn., Nat. Assn. Ins. Women (dir. 1981-82) (Chgo.). Democrat. Roman Catholic. Home: 5506 S Madison 11 Hinsdale IL 60521

WENDT, FRANKIE, lawyer; b. Trenton, Mo., Jan. 23, 1958; s. Henry Eckley and Audrey Eilene (Baird) W. BA magna cum laude, Northeast Mo. State U., 1980; JD, Drake U., 1983. Bar: Mo., 1984, Iowa 1983. Law clk. to presiding justice Iowa Ct. Appeals, Des Moines, 1983-84; assoc. Slagle & Bernard, Kansas City, Mo., 1984—. Mem. ABA, Iowa Bar Assn., Order of

Coif, Pi Sigma Alpha, Delta Theta Phi. Democrat. Home: 4542 Jarboe Apt 3 Kansas City MO 64111 Office: Slagle & Bernard PC 127 W 10th St Suite 500 Kansas City MO 64105

WENDT, GARY FREDERICK, architect; b. Elgin, Ill., June 10, 1951; s. Frederick G. and Esther (Reuter) W.; m. Lynn Boodnick, Nov. 7, 1976; children: Andrew, Stephanie. BArch, U. Ill., 1976, MArch, 1978. Registered architect, Ill. Architect Unteed Assocs., Palatine, Ill., 1975-76, Karson & Assocs., Northbrook, Ill., 1976-78, O'Donnell, Wicklund, Pigozzi Architects, Inc., Northbrook, Ill., 1978-84; architect, v.p., assoc. prin. O'Donnell, Wicklund, Pigozzi and Peterson Architects, Inc., Northbrook, Ill., 1984—. Home: 428 Cherry Ln Glenview IL 60025 Office: O'Donnell Wicklund Pigozzi & Peterson 570 Lake-Cook Rd Deerfield IL 60015

WENDT, THOMAS GENE, controller; b. Watertown, Wis., May 14, 1951; s. Walter Harry and Gladys Florence (Munzel) W. BBA, U. Wis., Whitewater, 1973. CPA, Wis. Auditor Coopers & Lybrand, Milw., 1973-75; supr. Conley, McDonald, Sprague & Co., Milw., 1975-80; dir. fin. E. Cen./Select Sires, Waupun, Wis., 1981—, also rec. sec., bd. dirs. Bd. dirs. Marquardt Meml. Manor, Inc., Watertown, Wis., 1985—, sec. bd. dirs., 1986—; pres. bd. trustees Watertown Moravian Ch., 1981-84; adv. del. Western Dist. Synod, Wis., 1982, 86. Mem. Am. Inst. CPA's, Wis. Inst. CPA's, Milw. Art Mus. Avocations: athletics, music, art. Office: E Central/Select Sires PO Box 191 Waupun WI 53963

WENGER, GAIL DELAP, biochemist; b. Newark, July 16, 1951; d. George Robert and Edna Marie (Hopko) Delap; m. Robert Clifford Wenger, June 15, 1974; children: Scott, Michael. BS, U. Dayton, 1973; MS, Rutgers U., 1975; PhD, Ohio State U., 1983. Research assoc. dept. medicine Ohio State U., Columbus, 1974-83, postdoctoral fellow hematology and oncology, 1983-84, research assoc. biochemistry, 1984—. Mem. AAAS, Am. Soc. Human Genetics, Nat. Soc. Genetic Counselors. Roman Catholic. Home: 1589 Austin Dr Columbus OH 43220 Office: Ohio State U Dept Medicine Hematology 410 W 10th Ave Columbus OH 43210

WENGER, STEVEN KENNETH, psychology educator, researcher; b. Horton, Kans., June 11, 1945; s. Kenneth Leo and Thelma Elizabeth (Sernes) W.; m. Barbara Jane Youmans, Dec. 23, 1972; 1 child, Noah Christopher. AS in Electronic Engring., Central Tech. Inst., 1967; BA in Psychology, Washburn U., 1975; MS in Psychology, Kans. State U., 1977, PhD in Psychology, 1980. Instr. Kans. State U., Manhattan, 1977-79; asst. prof. psychology MacMurray Coll., Jacksonville, Ill., 1979-86, assoc. prof., 1986—, chmn. Dept. Psychology, 1982—. Contbr. articles to profl. jours. Served as staff sgt. U.S. Air Force, 1967-71. Mem. Midwestern Psychol. Assn. (local rep. 1984—), AAUP (v.p. 1984-85, pres. 1985—), Psi Chi, Phi Kappa Phi. Avocation: amateur radio. Home: 803 S Church Jacksonville IL 62650 Office: Mac Murray Coll Psychology Dept Jacksonville IL 62650

WENK, DENNIS CHARLES, insurance company executive; b. Evergreen Park, Ill., Apr. 6, 1952; s. Charles Martin and Barbara Jean (Timmons) W.; m. Manette Jean McReynolds, May 14, 1978; 1 child, Marissa Ann. Student Coe Coll., 1970-72; A.A. in Bus. and data processing, Moraine Valley Community Coll., 1974; B.S. in Computer Sci., No. Ill. U., 1977, M.B.A., 1985. Cert. systems profl.; cert. data processor; cert. info. systems auditor. Programmer, analyst Allied Mills, Inc., Chgo., 1977-78; sr. cons. Consumer Systems, Oakbrook, Ill., 1978-79; acct. mgr. C.B.M., Schaumburg, Ill., 1979-80; EDP audit cons. Beatrice Cos., Chgo., 1980-82; mgr. data ctr. Zurich-Am. Inst. Co., Schaumburg, Ill., 1982-86; v.p. info. processing Heller Fin., Chgo., 1986—; Author: Management Accounting for MIS; contbr. articles to profl. jours. Mem. Assn. Computing Machinery, Computer Measurement Group. Avocations: tennis; racketball; volleyball; golf. Home: 201 Bryant Ave Glen Ellyn IL 60137

WENNDT, VERLYN RAY, social services administrator; b. Cedar Rapids, Iowa, July 22, 1941; s. Ezra Louie and Leona Louise (Brunscheen) W.; m. Janice Lee Schutte, Jan. 29, 1966; children: Blair Anthony, Noelle Simone. BSW, Wartburg Coll., 1965; MSW, U. Ill., 1967. Social worker Brenwood Children's Home, Waverly, Iowa, 1967-70; social worker, team leader Bar-None Residential Treatment Services, Anoka, Minn., 1970-73, dir. social services, 1973-75, dir., 1975—. Mem. Nat. Assn. Social Workers, Minn. Mental Health Assn. (bd. dirs. Anoka chpt. 1975-77), Minn. Council Residential Treatment Ctrs. (pres. 1977-79, bd. dirs.), Minn. Assn. Social Service Agys. (bd. dirs.). Lodge: Optimists (Anoka-Coon Rapids chpt. 1st and 2d v.p. 1978-79, sec.-treas. 1980-81, bd. dirs.). Avocations: golf, tennis, reading. Home: 5230 156th Ln NW Anoka MN 55303 Office: Bar None Residential Services 22426 St Francis Blvd Anoka MN 55303

WENNER, BRUCE RICHARD, mathematics educator; b. Lancaster, Penn., Apr. 25, 1938; s. Jerome Arthur and Mary Pauline (Albertson) W.; m. Frances Clark, Nov. 6, 1965; children: Kathleen Mary, Brian Edward, Thomas Jerome. BA, Coll. of Wooster, Ohio, 1960; PhD, Duke U., 1964. Asst. prof. math. U. Vermont, Bulington, 1964-68; from asst. prof. to prof. U. Mo., Kansas City, 1968—. Contbr. research articles to profl. jours. Mem. Math. Assn. of Am., Am. Math. Soc., Soc. for Preservation and Encouragement Barber Shop Quartet Singing in Am. (chmn. music com. 1974-75, 77—, chpt. pres. 1976). Mem. United Ch. Christ. Home: 9135 Lee Blvd Leawood KS 66206 Office: U Mo Dept Math 5100 Rockhill Rd Kansas City MO 64110

WENSTRAND, THOMAS, agribusiness executive; b. Shenandoah, Iowa, Nov. 25, 1947; s. William Sherwood and Bernice (Liljedahl) W. BS, Iowa State U., 1970; MBA, Harvard U., 1972. Seed mktg. trainee Dekalb AgResearch Inc., Red Oak, Iowa, 1970, mgr. mergers and acquisitions, DeKalb, Ill., 1977-78, mgr. animal ops., 1978-79, mgr. internat. ops., 1979-80; faculty Harvard U. Bus. Sch., 1972-73; asst. to pres. Ariz.-Colo. Land & Cattle Co., Phoenix, 1973-77; pres., owner Hawkeye Steel Products, Houghton, Iowa, 1981—. mem. editorial bd. Century Communications, 1986—. Mem. Ariz. Trade Council, 1975-77; mem. Iowa Dist. Export Council, 1981—, Farm and Indsl. Equipment Inst. (bd. dirs. 1986—). Mem. Young Pres.'s Orgn., Livestock Conservation Inst. (bd. dirs. 1984—), Phi Eta Sigma, Alpha Zeta, Gamma Sigma Delta, Gamma Gamma. Address: Soaring Hawk Pl Mount Pleasant IA 52641

WENSTROM, FRANK AUGUSTUS, state senator, city and county official; b. Dover, N.D., July 27, 1903; s. James August and Anna Petra (Kringstad) W.; student public schs., Carrington, N.D.; m. Mary Esther Pickett, June 10, 1938. In oil bus., Carrington, 1932-38, Williston, N.D., 1938-45; mgr. Williston C. of C., 1945-51; public relations officer 1st Nat. Bank, Williston, 1951-53, mng. officer real estate mortgage dept., 1953-60; exec. officer Northwestern Fed. Savs. and Loan Assn. Williston, 1964-68; spl. cons. Am. State Bank Williston, 1968-73; mem. N.D. Senate, 1957-60, 67—, pres. pro tem, 1973-74; lt. gov. State of N.D., 1963-64; dir., sec. Williston Community Hotel Co., 1950—; chmn. subscriber's com. N.W. dist. N.D. Blue Cross-Blue Shield, 1972—. Mem. Williston Public Housing Authority, 1951—, Williams County Park Bd., 1951—, N.D. Yellowstone-Ft. Union Commn., 1957-64, Legis. Research Council, 1957-60, Legis. Council, 1969-70; del. N.D. 2d Constl. Conv., 1970, pres., 1971-72; Williams County chmn. U.S. Savs. Bonds Com., 1958-69; bd. dirs. N.D. Easter Seals Soc., 1960-75, state pres., 1970-71; bd. advisors Salvation Army, 1960-75; bd. dirs. Univ. Found., U. N.D., Williston Center, 1965—; mem. joint legis. com. Nat. Assn. Ret. Tchrs.-Am. Assn. Ret. Persons, 1975—, chmn., 1979-80. Recipient Liberty Bell award N.D. Bar Assn., 1977, Disting. Service award Bismarck Jr. Coll., 1981; award Nature Conservancy, 1982; Service award Greater N.D. Assn., 1983, C.P. Lura award Disting. Service to Edn. Minot State Coll., 1986, Award of Excellence Com. of Gov.'s Council on Human Resources, 1986. Mem. Upper Missouri Purebred Cattle Breeders Assn. (sec.-treas. 1947-62), N.D. Wildlife Fedn. (state pres. 1947-48), Greater N.D. Assn. (dir. 1955-56, mem. Roosevelt Nat. Meml. Park com. 1957-63), U.S. Savs. and Loan League (legis. com. 1965-67). Republican. Congregationalist. Clubs: Rotary, Elks, Masons, Shriners, Order Eastern Star. Office: PO Box 187 Williston ND 58801

WENZEL, FRED WILLIAM, apparel manufacturing executive; b. St. Louis, Jan. 14, 1916; s. Frederick H. and Ella M. (Heuerman) W.; m. Mary Edna Cruzen; 1 child, Robert F. Grad., U. Wis., 1937. Chmn. H. Wenzel Tent & Duck Co. St. Louis, 1937-52; pres. Hawthorn Co., New Haven, Mo., 1952-64; v.p. Kellwood Co., Chgo., 1961-64; chmn. bd. Kellwood Co., St. Louis, 1964, pres., chmn., 1965-76, chmn., chief exec. officer, 1976-84, chmn., 1984—. Home: 13315 Fairfield Sq Dr Chesterfield MO 63017 Office: Kellwood Co PO Box 14374 Saint Louis MO 63178

WENZEL, RICHARD FRANK, educator, consultant; b. Milw., Sept. 10, 1930; s. Theodore Elmer and Corrinne Gladys (Collins) W.; m. Marguerite Patty Lu Anderson, July 12, 1958; children—Peter, Jeremy. B.S., Marquette U., 1952, M.A., 1958. Classroom tchr. Milw. Pub. Schs., 1954-57, speech therapist, 1952-57, supr. community relations, 1957-64, coordinator mass media services, 1964-66, dir. student transp., 1967—; dir. pub. relations Wis. Edn. Assn., 1966-67; cons. pub. relations and transp. Pres. Boesel Scholarship Found., 1967—; chmn. Milwaukee County unit Am. Heart Assn., 1970-72; mem. Milw. Presbytery Commn. on Race and Religion, 1964-67; drama dir. Red Arrow Boys Camp, 1953—. Recipient Disting. Service award Milw. Jaycees, 1964; Outstanding Transp. Supr. award Wis. AAA, 1979; Valuable Vol. award WMVS-TV, 1967. Mem. Wis. Assn. Pupil Transp. (pres. 1975), Wis. Edn. Assn. (pres. nat. pub. relations council 1966), Schoolmasters of Wis. (pres. 1969), Milw. Radio and TV Council (pres. 1966), Friends of Channel 10 (pres. 1967), Wis. Congress Parents and Tchrs. (dir. 1966-69), Wis. Assn. of the Professions (dir. 1967-70), Nat. Safety Council (com. mem. 1979—), Wis. Sch. Pub. Relations Assn. (pres. 1968-70), Nat Assn. Pupil Transp. Lodge: Masons. Producer ednl. series Wis. Ednl. TV Network, 1973; producer-dir. Bicentennial pageant Free and Equal, Milw. Pub. Schs., 1976; producer-dir. radio series High Hopes, 1966-67. Home: 17780 Royalcrest Dr Brookfield WI 53005 Office: 5225 W Vliet St Milwaukee WI 53208

WENZLER, EDWARD WILLIAM, architect; b. Milw., Feb. 17, 1954; s. William Paul and Dolores Ann (Rahn) W.; m. Georgine Marie Eggert, Apr. 3, 1976; children: Christopher E., Michael E. BArch, U. Milw., 1978. Registered architect Wis., 1981. Architect Gordon Sibeck, Dallas, 1978-79; assoc. Wenzler and Assocs., Milw., 1979-84, ptnr., 1984—. Mem. AIA, Nat. Council Archtl. Registration Bds., Constrn. Specification Inst., Old World 3d St. Assn. Club: BMW (bd. dirs. 1980-82). Home: 19600 Gebhardt Rd Brookfield WI 53005 Office: 205 W Highland Ave MIlwaukee WI 53203

WENZLER, WILLIAM PAUL, architect; b. Milw., Feb. 9, 1929; s. Paul C. and Bertha R. (Froemming) W.; m. Dolores A. Rahn, June 17, 1950; children: Edward, Deborah, John, Joan. Student, U. Wis., 1947-48; B.S. in Archtl. Engring, U. Ill., 1952. Registered architect, Wis., Ill., Iowa, Mo., Mass., Calif., Tex., Mich., Pa., others. Draftsman H.C. Haeuser (architect), Milw., 1952, A.H. Siewert (architect), Milw., 1952-54; designer Brust and Brust (architects), Milw., 1954-55; pvt. practice Milw., 1955—; pres. William Wenzler & Assos. (Architects, Inc.), 1966—. Prin. works include Germantown (Wis.) Elementary Sch., 1956, St. Edmunds Episcopal Ch., Elm Grove, Wis., 1957, Zion Evangel. and Reformed Ch., Milw., 1958, 1st Conglist. Ch., Mukwonago, Wis., 1959, Goldendale (Wis.) Elementary Sch., 1959, Bradford Terr., Milw. Protestant Home for Aged, 1962, Our Shepherd Luth. Ch., Greendale, Wis., 1963, Gerald H. Nickoll residence, Fox Point, Wis., 1963, Inland Steel Co. factory and office bldg., Milw., 1966, Brookfield (Wis.) Evangel. Luth. Ch., 1966, Luth. Social Services Wis. and Upper Mich. hdqrs., Milw., 1967, Lloyd A. Gerlach residence, Elm Grove, 1967, Eden Theol. Sem. Library, Webster Groves, Mo., 1968, Luth. Ch. Living Christ, Germantown, 1969, Grace Episcopal Ch., Galesburg, Ill., 1970, Calvary Bapt. Ch., Milw., 1970, Fine Arts Complex, Wis. State U., Stevens Point, 1971, Northridge Lakes Community Devel., Milw., 1971, phys. edn. bldg., Wis. U.-Parkside, 1972, Jewish Vocat. Services Milw., renovation, 1974, theater and anthropology bldg., Beloit Coll., 1975, Elm-Brook Ch, Brookfield, Wis., 1975, Dubuque (Iowa) Theol. Library, 1976, Portage County Human Services Ctr., Stevens Point, 1979, Henry Reuss Interpretive Ctr., Dundee, Wis., 1981, Golda Meir House, Milw., 1981, Ctr. for Arts, U. Wis. Platteville, 1983, Cen. United Meth. Ch., Milw., 1983—, Greek Orthodox Manor, Wauwatosa, 1984, River House Condominiums, Milw., 1985, Usinger Factory addition, Milw., 1985, Oak Hill Terr., Waukesha, 1986, also numerous exhbns. of works. Francis J. Plym fellow U. Ill., 1958; Ford Found. grantee U. Wis., 1961; named one of Wis. 5 Outstanding Young Men Wis. Jr. C. of C., 1961; recipient Gov. Wis. award for creativity in arts, 1967; various awards for archtl. works. Fellow AIA; mem. Am. Concrete Inst., Interfaith Forum on Religion, Art and Architecture, Gargoyle, Tau Beta Pi. Mem. East Brook Ch. Home: 2823 N Shepard Ave Milwaukee WI 53211 Office: William Wenzler & Assocs 205 W Highland Ave Milwaukee WI 53203

WEPRIN, STUART ALAN, obstetrician, gynecologist; b. Dayton, Ohio, May 24, 1949; s. Charles and Corrine (Weinstein) W.; m. Gail B. Greenblatt, July 15, 1979; children: Katherine, Matthew, Molly, Abby. BA, Case Western Res. U., 1971; MD, Ohio State U., 1974. Practice medicine specializing in ob-gyn. Davue Ob-Gyn Assocs., Dayton, 1979—; asst. clin. prof. Wright State U. Sch. Medicine, Dayton, 1980-86, assoc. clin prof., 1986—. Contbr. articles to profl. jours. Bd. dirs. Temple Israel, Dayton. Fellow Am. Coll. Ob-Gyn, Gynecologic Urology Soc., Am. Fertility Soc.; mem. AMA, Ohio State Med. Assn., Montgomery County Med. Soc., Dayton Ob-Gyn Soc. Club: Meadowbrook Country (Dayton). Home: 1424 Westwicke Pl Dayton OH 45459 Office: Davue Ob-Gyn Assocs Inc 2200 Philadelphia Dr #447 Dayton OH 45406

WERBA, BARRIE CELIA, foundation executive; b. Bklyn., Sept. 26, 1930; d. Saul and Anna (Rosen) Sakolsky; m. Gabriel Werba, June 1, 1952; children: Dean Steffen, Annmarie Alexandra. Student, Hunter Coll., 1958-62, CCNY, 1959-60, Oakland U., 1977-79. Ptnr. Stone/Werba Assocs., Franklin, Mich., 1977-80; adminstrv. asst. to ptnrs. Lenihan & Plese, Birmingham, Mich., 1980-82; exec. dir. Mich. Found. for Arts, Detroit, 1982-86; dir. devel. Attic Theatre, Detroit, 1986—. Chmn. pub. relations, dir. Chamber Music Soc. Detroit, 1981, Temple Kol Ami, West Bloomfield, Mich., 1984; treas. Lafayette Park Dems., Detroit, 1964; v.p., bd. dirs. Detroit Film Soc., 1982—, pres. 1986; bd. dirs. Detroit Pub. Library, 1982-85, Holly Hill Farms, Farmington Hills, Mich., 1984-85. Mem. Nat. Soc. Fund Raising Execs. (long range planning com., Inst. 1987). Avocations: art collecting, painting, reading, gardening, attending chamber music concerts. Home: 29770 Highmeadow Rd Farmington Hills MI 48018 Office: Attic Theater 2990 W Grand Blvd Detroit MI 48202

WERGER, PAUL MYRON, bishop; b. Greenville, Pa., June 13, 1931; s. Jacob Paul and Laura Annetta (Greenwalt) W.; m. Dianne Mae Ellisen, July 26, 1957; children: Paul Myron, Jonathan David, Matthew James, Mary Dianne. BA, Thiel Coll., 1954; MDiv, Northwestern Theol. Sem., Mpls., 1957, DD (hon.), 1976. Ordained to ministry, Luth. Ch. Am., 1957. Pastor Apostles Luth. Ch., St. Paul, 1957-61, St. Luke's Luth. Ch., Bloomington, Minn., 1961-78; bishop Iowa Synon Luth. Ch. Am., Des Moines, 1978—; chmn. stewardship and evangelism com. NW Synod, 1959-62; mem. bd. social ministry Minn. Synod, 1963-70, mem. exec. bd., dean south suburban dist.; pres., bd. dirs. Luth. Social Services in Minn.; mem. mgmt. com. dir. mission N.Am. Luth. Ch. Am., 1983—; del. Luth. Ch. Am. convs.; pastor evangelist Evangelical Outreach. Contbr. articles to profl. jours. Mem. Bloomington Human Rights Commn.; mem. citizens adv. com. Bloomington Sch. Dist. 271; bd. dirs. Luth. Ch. Am. Found., Grand View Coll.; bd. fellows Sch. Religion U. Iowa. Recipient Thiel Coll. Alumni award for profl. achievement, 1979. Mem. Assn. Bloomington Clergy. Office: Luth Ch Ctr 3125 Cottage Grove Ave Des Moines IA 50311 *

WERGOWSKE, WILLIAM GARY, accountant; b. Cin., Sept. 6, 1941; s. William Leslie and Thelma Leah (Clemons) W.; B.B.A., U. Cin., 1963; M.B.A., Xavier U., 1971; m. Mary Helen Kemper, June 7, 1975. Mem. staff Pension Group Cons.'s, Inc., Cin., 1957-63; methods analyst Western and So. Life Ins. Co., Cin., 1965-73; mgr. mgmt. services and accounting services Main Lafrentz and Co., Cin., 1973-77; pvt. practice accounting, Cin., 1977-79; pres. William G. Wergowske & Co., Inc., CPA's, Cin., 1979—; mem. faculty Coll. Mt. St. Joseph, 1979-80; chmn. bd., pres. Midwest Software, Inc., 1978—; treas. Oil Pit Shop, Inc., 1979-80; bd. dirs., treas. Nursing Staff of Louisville, Inc., 1979-80, Simon Winds, Inc., 1981—, Tri-Ax Communications, Inc., 1982-83, Country Wide Communications, Inc., 1982-83, Star-Burst Concepts, Inc., 1982—. Treas., trustee Home Aid Service of Cin./Community Chest, 1974-77, Down Syndrome Assn. of Greater Cin., 1981-83; treas. Tri-State Organized Coalition for Persons with Disabilities (Southwestern Ohio Coalition for Persons with Disabilities), 1982-85, pres., 1985-86; bd. dirs., sec./treas. Midwest Systems, Inc., 1984—; bd. dirs, treas. Dotterman, Inc., 1984-86, Harley Davidson of Hamilton, Inc., 1984-86, Consumer Graphics Corp., 1984—, TBS, Inc., 1985—; area rep. Ohio chpt. "L" Gold Wing Road Riders Assn., 1985-87. Served to 1st lt. Signal Corps, U.S. Army, 1963-65. C.P.A., Ohio. Mem. Nat. Assn. Accountants (v.p. 1976-78), Ohio Soc. CPA's (cons. systems and EDP), Am. Inst. CPA's. Roman Catholic. Club: Cincinnati (trustee 1977-79, 2d v.p. 1979). Home and Office: 5519 Lucenna Dr Cincinnati OH 45238

WERICK, PAUL, lawyer; b. Cin., May 19, 1948; m. Sharon Miller; June 22, 1972; children: John and Jennifer (twins). BA, Harvard U., 1969, JD, 1971. Bar: Mich. 1972, Ind. 1980. Assoc. Smith, Lieberman & Jones, Flint, Mich., 1972-80, ptnr., 1980-82; sole practice Indpls., 1982—; bd. dirs. North Light Repertory Co. Contbr. articles to profl. jours. Mem. ABA, Ind. Bar Assn. Republican. Office: 230 E Ohio Suite 200 Indianapolis IN 46204

WERLING, DONN PAUL, environmental educator; b. Ft. Wayne, Ind., Oct. 14, 1945; s. Paul Henry and Lydia Sophia (Rebber) W.; m. Diane Mueller, July 11, 1970; 1 child, Benjamin Paul. B.S., Valparaiso U., 1967; M.S., Mich. State U., 1968; M.Ed., Loyola U., 1970; Ph.D., U. Mich., 1979. Dir. nature project Raymond Sch., Chgo. Bd. Edn., 1969-72; dir. Evanston Environ. Assn., Ill., 1973-81; dir. Henry Ford Estate, U. Mich.-Dearborn, 1983—, adj. asst. prof. edn., 1984—; founder N.Am. Voyageur Conf., 1977. Author: Environmental Education and Your School Site, 1973; A School-Community Stewardship Model, 1979; Lake Michigan and Its Lighthouses, 1982. Mem. state master plan com. on environ. edn. State of Ill., Springfield, 1970; mem. adv. com. Ill. Coastal Zone, Chgo., 1978; bd. dirs. Ill. Shore council Girl Scouts U.S., 1978-82, Chgo. Maritime Soc., 1982. Recipient Mayor's award City of Evanston, 1976, Russell E. Wilson award U. Mich. Sch. Edn., 1979, Service award Ill. Shore council Girl Scouts U.S., 1978, J. Lee Barrett award Met. Detroit Tourist & Conv. Bur., 1986; named to Outstanding Young Men Am., Jaycees, 1975. Mem. Assn. Interpretive Naturalists, Am. Assn. Mus., Great Lakes Lighthouse Keepers Assn. (founder, pres. 1982—), Tourist and Travel Assn. Southeast Mich. (chmn. 1984-86). Club: Prairie (Chgo). Lodge: Kiwanis. Avocations: canoeing, writing, singing bluewater music. Address: Henry Ford Estate Lair Ln U Mich Dearborn MI 48128

WERMUND, STEVEN ALLEN, educator; b. Chippewa Falls, Wis., Nov. 15, 1957; s. Warren Allen and Virginia Dolores (Schemenauer) W.; m. Marcie Ellen Becker, July 13, 1985. BS, U. Wis., Eau Claire, 1980; MEd, U. Wis., Stevens Point, 1986. Cert. elem. tchr., Wis. Tchr. Wausau (Wis.) Sch. Dist., 1981—. Appeared in Wausau Community Theatre, 1984—. Songleader choir 1982— local ch., tchr. religious edn. 1983-85; active United Cerebral Palsy Telethon, 1983-85. Mem. NEA, Wis. Edn. Assn., Wausau Edn. Assn. (rep. 1983—), Am. Legion (Am. Legion award 1975), 4-H (Wis. state chorus 1973, citizenship short course 1974). Roman Catholic. Lodges: KC (Badger Boys State award 1974), Optimists. Home: 301 Arnold St Rothschild WI 54474 Office: Lincoln Elem Sch 720 S 6th Ave Wausau WI 54401

WERNER, ARNOLD, psychiatrist; b. Bklyn., June 8, 1938; m. Elizabeth A. Rederer; 2 children. BS cum laude, Bklyn. Coll., 1959; MD, U. Rochester, 1963. Diplomate Am. Bd. Psychiatry and Neurology in Psychiatry. Intern Vanderbilt U., Nashville, 1964; resident in psychiatry U. Rochester, N.Y., 1964-67, instr. psychiatry, 1966-67; instr. psychiatry Temple U., Phila., 1967-69; asst. prof. Mich. State U., East Lansing, Mich., 1969-72, assoc. prof., 1972-78, prof., 1978—; cons. Mid-Mich. Mental Health Ctr., Alma, 1972—, Health Cen., Lansing, 1976—; dir. residency tng. Mich. State U., East Lansing, 1986—, coordinator Psychosocial Curriculum, 1986—; gen. practice psychiatry Temple U., 1967-69, Mich. State U., 1969—; dir. home visiting service Temple U., 1967-69, psychiat. services Mich. State U. Health Ctr., 1969-78; dir., consultation liaison psychiatry Ingham Med. Ctr., Lansing, 1983-85. Contbr. numerous articles and book reviews to profl. jours., syndicated newspaper columnist, 1969-76. Research grantee NIMH, 1970-71, undergrad. grant, 1980, psychiat. edn. grants, 1982-85; recipient Outstanding Faculty award Sr. Class Council Mich. State U., 1971. Fellow Am. Psychiat. Assn. (com. on pub. info. 1972-75, chmn. 1974-75, peer review com. 1975-76, joint commn. on pub. affairs 1976-82, com. on med. student edn. 1982—); mem. Am. Psychosomatic Soc., Assn. for Acad. Psychiatry. Avocations: photography, woodworking, bicycling. Office: Mich State U A228 E Fee Hall East Lansing MI 48824-1316

WERNER, BERNARD, data processing manager; b. Ludwigsburg, Germany, June 17, 1949; came to U.S., 1951; s. Julius Mathew and Bella Lanka (Toth) W.; m. Renata Bohdonna Wolynec, June 1, 1974; children: Ariana Katyrina Wolynec-Werner. BA, U. N.Mex., 1967-71; student, Edinboro U., 1975, Pa. State U., 1975, U. Calif., Santa Barbara, 1971-72. Computer lab. dir. Northwestern U., Evanston, Ill., 1972-73; analyst, programmer STSC, Inc., Chgo. and Pitts., 1974-74; propr. Applied Bus. Systems, Edinboro, Pa., 1975-78; dir. data processing N.W. Inst. Research, Erie, Pa., 1977-78; mgr. data processing Premix, Inc., North Kingsville, Ohio, 1978—. Co-author Final Report on Secondary Study, 1977, Cultural Resouce Overview, 1978. Ednl. Assistance grantee Calif., 1971. Mem. Data Processing Mgmt. Assn. (bd. dirs 1984-85), Digital Equipment Users Soc. Republican. Lodge: Rotary. Avocations: skiing, antique tractors, golf, cutting firewood. Home: PO Box 21 Edinboro PA 16412 Office: Premix Inc Rt 20 North Kingsville OH 44068

WERNER, DONALD, municipal official. Fire chief City of Columbus, Ohio. Office: City of Columbus Div of Fire 200 Greenlawn Ave Columbus OH 43223

WERNER, GLENN ALLEN, psychologist; b. Mpls., June 11, 1955; s. James Allen Werner and Barbara Jean (Prigmeier) Risdall. AA in Psychology, Normandale Community Coll., 1975; BA in Psychology and Speech with honors, St. Cloud (Minn.) State U., 1977, MA in Counseling Psychology and Vocat. Rehab., 1979, B in Elective Studies, 1982; cert. adult psychiatry, U. Minn., 1984. Lic. psychologist, Minn. Counselor M&R Inc., Mpls., 1974-79; employment placement specialist St. Paul Rehab. Ctr., 1979; sr. vocat. rehab. counselor Minn. Correctional Facility, St. Cloud, 1979-81; psychologist Minn. Security Hosp., St. Peter, 1981-83; clin. psychologist Anoka (Minn.)-Metro Regional Treatment Ctr., 1983—. Author, illustrator: How to Land A Job- A Guide for Ex-Offenders, 1979. Recipient Exceptional Performance award State of Minn., 1982, 83, 85, 86, 87. Mem. Minn. Psychol. Assn., Minn. Lic. Psychologists Assn., Psi Chi. Avocations: triathlons, marathons, freestyle skiing competitions. Home: 10451 Greenbrier Rd #317 Minnetonka MN 55343 Office: Anoka Metro Regional Treatment Ctr Anoka MN 55303

WERNER, WILLIAM HOWARD, savings and loan executive; b. Granite City, Ill., Sept. 4, 1948; s. Raymond H. and Lucille I. (Moehle) W.; m. Dona K. Bruder, Sept. 21, 1948; children: Michelle, Eric. BSBA, So. Ill. U., 1970; grad. with distinction, Inst. Fin. Edn., Chgo., 1985. Jr. devel. program SS Kresge/K Mart, Pagedale, Mo., 1970-71; v.p. personnel and security Bohemian Savs. & Loan, St. Louis, 1971-76; asst. v.p. personnel officer Blue Valley Fed. Savs. and Loan Assn., Independence, Mo., 1976-85, v.p. dir. human resources, 1985, exec. v.p. adminstrv. services, 1985—; bd. dirs., treas. Inst. Fin. Edn., Kansas City, Mo., 1986-87. Past mem. occupation adv. com. Ft. Osage Area Vocat. Tech. Ctr., Buckner, Mo., 1984. Mem. Independence C. of C. Lutheran. Lodge: Rotary (treas., bd. dirs. Independence club 1985). Office: Blue Valley Fed Savs & Loan Assn 300 N Osage Independence MO 64050

WERNKE, DANIEL EDWARD, accountant; b. Cin., Jan. 14, 1959; s. Paul B. and Marian (Merk) W. BSBA, Xavier U., 1984. Staff acct. J.D. Cloud and Co., Cin., 1984—. Mem. Nat. Assn. Accts. (bd. dirs. 1985—), Am. Inst. CPA's, Ohio Soc. CPA's. Roman Catholic. Avocations: snow skiing, water skiing, reading, golf. Home: 6794 Harrison Ave Apt #56 Cincinnati OH 45247 Office: JD Cloud and Co 6 E 4th St Cincinnati OH 45202

WERREMEYER, GORDON DALE, educational administrator; b. Holland, Ind., July 28, 1941; s. Roy William and Mary Norena (Hesson) W. B in Music Edn., U. Evansville, 1963; MS, Ind. State U., 1974, EdB in Edn. Adminstrn., 1977. Cert. sch. superintendant, principal. Tchr. E. Gibson

Schs., Oakland City, Ind., 1963-68, Covington (Ind.) Community Sch., 1968-71; tchr., adminstr. Bloomfield (Ind.) Sch. Dist., 1971-84; adminstr. Whitko Community Schs., South Whitley, Ind., 1984—. Mem. Bloomfield Library Bd., Ind., 1983-84. Mem. Nat. Assn. Secondary Sch. Principals, Ind. Sec. Sch. Adminstrs., Whitley-Huntington County Group Home, Inc., Ind. Secondary Sch. Administrators, Phi Mu Alpha, Phi Delta Kappa. Lodge: Lions. Avocations: travel, antiques, reading, physical fitness, photography. Home: PO Box 444 South Whitley IN 46787 Office: Whitko High Sch One Big Blue Ave South Whitley IN 46878

WERT, HAL ELLIOTT, JR., history educator, college administrator; b. Detroit, Apr. 17, 1940; s. Hal Elliott and Frances Mary (Shadle) W.; m. Tinsley Jane Lowe, Nov. 25, 1978; children—Andrew Elliott, Allison East, Sarah Shadle. B.A., U. Iowa, 1966, MA, U. Kans., 1974, MPH, 1975. Asst. instr. U. Kans., Lawrence, 1967-71; instr. Kansas City Art Inst., Mo., 1971-74; asst. prof. Kansas City Art Inst., 1975-78, assoc. prof. history, 1979—, dir. Japan Study Abroad, 1977—, dir. Japanese studies program, 1975—, acting dean, 1986, v.p. acad. affairs and dean, 1987—. Contbr. articles to profl. jours. Served with U.S. Army, 1960-63. Recipient Andrew W. Mellon Faculty Devel. grant, 1982-87; Nat. Def. Fgn. Lang. grantee, 1969; Nat. Teaching fellow, 1972; Alliance of Ind. Colls. of Art grantee, 1984; Hoover Presdl. Library Assn. fellow, 1985. Mem. Soc. Historians of Am. Fgn. Relations, Am. Com. History of Second World War, Internat. Council Fgn. Relations, Internat. Churchill Soc., Am. Hist. Assn. Democrat. Avocations: campaign buttons; political memorabelia. Home: Rt 2 Box 181 Baldwin City KS 66006 Office: Kansas City Art Inst 4415 Warwick Blvd Kansas City MO 64111

WERTH, RICHARD GEORGE, chemistry educator; b. Markesan, Wis., Feb. 5, 1920; s. George William and Lillie (Luethe) W.; B.A., Wartburg Coll., 1942; M.S., U. Wis., 1948, Ph.D., 1950; m. Wilma Margaret Lauer, June 2, 1943; 1 son, Gerald Richard, Jr. chemist E.I. duPont de Nemours & Co., Niagara Falls, N.Y., 1942-44, 46; prof. chemistry Concordia Coll., Moorhead, Minn., 1950—, chmn. dept., 1961-69, 74-77; vis. fellow Cornell U., Ithaca, N.Y., 1970-71; vis. scientist Univ. Hygienic Lab., U. Iowa, 1983. Served with USNR, 1944-46. Fellow AAAS, Am. Inst. Chemists; mem. Am. Chem. Soc. (councilor 1964-78, com. on chem. edn. 1971-76), Midwest Assn. Chemistry Tchrs. in Liberal Arts Colls., Soc. Applied Spectroscopy, Minn., N.D. acads. sci., Am. Radio Relay League, Sigma Xi, Phi Lambda Upsilon. Home: 1207 S 7th St Moorhead MN 56560-3440

WERTHEIM, SIDNEY BEN, corporate restaurant owner; b. Bklyn., Feb. 20, 1934; s. Abraham and Rose (Kaplan) W.; m. Barbara Ann Sorbin, Feb. 16, 1958 (dec. Jan. 1983); children: Geoffrey, Robert, Lauren; m. Barbara Jean Avery Cutchall, Oct. 2, 1986. AA in Bus., CCNY, 1954. Pres. Little King Restaurant Corp., Omaha, 1968—, also bd. dirs.; pres. Barco Mcpl. Products, Omaha, 1970—, also bd. dirs.; pres. Nat. Sign Co., Ottawa, Kans., 1972—, also bd. dirs. Vol. United Way, Omaha, Jewish Fedn. Omaha, Creighton Prep High Sch., Creighton U., Omaha. Served with U.S. Army, 1954-56. Recipient Leadership award Boy Scouts Am., Omaha, Outstanding Vol. award, Creighton U. Mem. Am. Pres. Assn., Nat. Restaurant Assn., Am. Pub. Works Assn., Omaha C. of C. (Leadership award, Outstanding Vol. award), Ak-Sar-Ben. Club: Highland Country. Lodge: Henry Monsky, Ak-Sar-Ben. Avocations: racquetball, golf, reading, travel. Office: Little King Restaurant Corp 11811 I St Omaha NE 68137

WERTS, MERRILL HARMON, management consultant; b. Smith Center, Kans., Nov. 17, 1922; s. Mack Allen and Ruth Martha (Badger) W.; B.S., Kans. State U., 1947; M.S., Cornell U., 1948; m. Dorothy Wilson, Mar. 22, 1946; children—Stephen M., Riley J., Todd J., Kelly M. Beef sales mgr. John Morrell & Co., Topeka and Memphis, 1948-53; dir. mktg. Kans. Dept. Agr., Topeka, 1953-55; sec.-treas. Falley's Markets, Inc., Topeka, 1955-58; v.p. S.W. State Bank, Topeka, 1958-65; pres. First Nat. Bank, Junction City, Kans., 1965-78; individual practice mgmt. cons., Junction City, 1978—; mem. Kans. Senate, 1978—; dir. Mid Am. Machine Corp., Stockgrowers State Bank, Maple Hill, Kans., J.C. Housing & Devel., Inc. Mem. Kans. Bank Mgmt. Commn., 1967-71; mem. adv. com. U.S. Comptroller of Currency, 1971-72. Mem. Topeka Bd. Edn., 1957-61; pres. Junction City-Geary County United Fund, 1967-68; pres. Junction City Indsl. Devel., Inc., 1966-72. Trustee Kans. State U. Endowment Assn., Kans. Synod Presbyn. Westminster Found., 1965-72. Served to 1st lt., inf., AUS, 1943-46. Decorated Bronze Star medal, Purple Heart, Combat Inf. badge. Mem. Kans. State U. Alumni Assn. (pres. 1957), Am. Legion, VFW, Kans. Bankers Assn., Assn. U.S. Army, U.S., Kans. (bd. dirs., v.p. 1979-84), Junction City (pres. 1975-76) chambers commerce, Kans. Farm Bur., Kans. Livestock Assn., DAV, Sigma Phi Epsilon. Republican. Presbyterian. Clubs: Masons, Shriners, Rotary (dist. gov. 1973-74). Club: Junction City Country (past pres.). Address: 1228 Miller Dr Junction City KS 66441

WESELI, ROGER WILLIAM, hospital administrator; b. Cin., Dec. 23, 1932; s. William Henry and Margaret Antoinette (Hoffman) W.; m. Sue Ann Daggett, Sept. 1, 1956; children: Erin, Stacey, Vincent. BA in Polit. Sci, U. Cin., 1955; MS in Hosp. Adminstrn, Northwestern U., 1959; D Tech. Letters (hon.), Cin. Tech. Coll., 1985. Adminstrv. asst. Good Samaritan Hosp., Cin., 1959-61, asst. adminstr., 1961-70, assoc. adminstr., 1970-75, v.p., adminstr., 1975-78, exec. v.p., adminstr., 1978-79, pres., 1979—; sec. Greater Cin. Hosp. Council, 1978-80, chmn. bd., 1983-84. Chmn. legislation com. health dept. Ohio Cath. Conf., 1978-83, 86; bd. dirs. Friars Boys Club, 1978—. Recipient Alpha Mu Sigma award, 1975, Laura Jackson award, 1987; cert. of appreciation Ohio League for Nursing, 1978. Fellow Am. Coll. Healthcare Execs. (regent for Ohio 1983—), Am. Mgmt. Assn., Am. Hosp. Assn. (council on fed. relations 1983-84, council on patient services 1984-86), Greater Cin. C. of C., Ohio League for Nursing (v.p. 1977-79), Ohio Hosp. Assn. (chmn. govt. liaison com. 1978-83, 86, trustee 1981-83, sec., treas. 1987—), Cath. Health Assn. (trustee 1983-86). Democrat. Roman Catholic. Home: 3615 Clifton Ave Cincinnati OH 45220 Office: Good Samaritan Hosp 3217 Clifton Ave Cincinnati OH 45220

WESELY, DONALD RAYMOND, state senator; b. David City, Nebr., Mar. 30, 1954; s. Raymond Ely and Irene (Sabata) W.; m. Geri Williams, 1982; 1 child, Sarah. B.A., U. Nebr., 1977. Mem. Nebr. Legislature, Lincoln, 1978—; exec. assoc. Selection Research, Inc., Lincoln, 1984-86; sr. research assoc. Lincoln Telephone Co., 1985—. Del., Democratic Nat. Conv., San Francisco, 1984. Recipient Friend of Edn. award Nebr. State Edn. Assn., 1982, Disting. Service award Nebr. Pub. Health Assn., 1984; named Mental Health Citizen of Yr., Nebr. Mental Health Assn., 1984, Outstanding Young Man, Nebr. Jaycees, 1985. Roman Catholic. Office: State Capitol Lincoln NE 68509

WESLEY, PHILIP ALAN, marketing and advertising executive; b. Cin., Apr. 25, 1945; s. Vester Clay and Mary Theresa (Catanzaro) W.; m. Mary Kathleen Redmond, Apr. 18, 1969; children: Christopher, Jodi, Todd. BSBA, Xavier U., CIn., 1967. Advt. mgr. Wilson Freight Co., Cin., 1967-75, dir. advt. and pub. relations, 1975-80; account supr. Hogan, Nolan and Stites, Cin., 1980-84, v.p., 1984—, also bd. dirs. chmn. com. Kenwood Civic Assn., Cin., 1985-86. Recipient award for Advt. Excellence, Am. Trucking Assn., 1974. Mem. Cin. Indsl. Advertisers, Cin. C. of C. Roman Catholic. Avocation: coaching little league sports. Home: 5973 Trowbridge Dr Cincinnati OH 45241 Office: Hogan Nolan & Stites 910 Plum St Cincinnati OH 45202

WESMAN, VERNE ALVIN, mechanical engineer; b. Ewen, Mich., Apr. 20, 1934; s. Victor John and Rose Helen (Nippa) W.; m. Jean Eleanor Everette, Apr. 10, 1953; children: Karen Lynn, Debra Alison. Grad. in engring., Ford Community Coll., 1960; grad. in salesmanship, Sales Tng. Inst., Detroit, 1968. Ptnr. Pyramid Engring., Detroit, 1965-70; design engr. RCA Corp., Plymouth, Mich., 1970-73; mgr. prodn. control Ingersoll Rand, Farmington Hills, Mich., 1973-76; sr. prodn. engr. Ford Motor Co., Livonia, Mich., 1976-79; dir. engring. Agnew Machine, Highland, Mich., 1979-81; owner, operator Automa-Ton Corp., Livonia, 1981—; instr. indsl. drafting adult edn. Livonia Pub. Sch., 1983; cons. engr. Indsl. Tech. Inst., Ann Arbor, Mich., 1986—. Patentee in field. Served to sgt. U.S. Army, 1954-56. Recipient Hon. Mention award James Lincoln Arc Welding Found., Cleve., 1972. Mem. Soc. Mfg. Engrs. (cert. 1975), Robotics Internat., of Soc. Mfg. Engrs. (sr., cert. 1981). Republican. Lutheran. Lodge: Lions. Avocations: creative designing and bldg., reading, hunting, gardening, fishing. Home and Office: Automa-Ton Corp 34277 Hathaway Livonia MI 48150

WESSE, DAVID JOSEPH, university official; b. Chgo., May 5, 1951; s. Herman Theodore and Lorraine Joan (Holland) W.; m. Deborah Lynn Smith, Oct. 11, 1975; children: Jason David, Eric Joseph. AA, Thornton Coll., 1971; student Purdue U., 1971-72; BS, Ill. State U., 1973; MS, Loyola U., 1983. Cert. adminstrv. mgr. Adminstrv. mgr. Reuben H. Donnelley, Chgo., 1974-76, Loyola U., Chgo., 1976-79, Joint Commn. on Accreditation Hosps., Chgo., 1979-81; adminstrv. dir., asst. sec. Northwestern U., Evanston, Ill., 1981—. Pres., bd. dirs. Riverdale Library Dist., 1975, Riverdale Youth Commn., 1975. Recipient Service Recognition award Riverdale Library Dist., 1975. Mem. Adminstrv. Mgmt. Soc. (bd. dirs. Chgo. chpt. 1983—, pres. 1986—), Nat. Assn. Coll. and Univ. Bus. Officers (com. mem. 1986—), Lambda Epsilon. Democrat. Lutheran. Home: 207 S Washington St Wheaton IL 60187 Office: Northwestern U 633 Clark St Evanston IL 60201

WESSEL, FREDERICK PETER, television and film director, cameraman, producer, writer, editor; b. St. Louis, Dec. 27, 1941; s. Peter John and Frieda Frances (Buss) W.; m. Lois Diane Sokol, June 15, 1968; children: Jason AAron, Erik Jordan. Student, Marquette U., Milw., 1959-61; BA in Psychology, U. Colo., 1964; MA in Film Prodn., Columbia Coll., Chgo., 1971. Cert. high sch. tchr., Ill. Tchr. Barrington (Ill.) High Sch., 1966-69; freelance cinematographer Chgo., 1970-71; TV dir., producer U. Wis., Green Bay, 1972-85, Gary, Goltz & Jansen, Green Bay, 1985-86; freelance dir., cameraman DePere, Wis., 1986; ptnr. Schmidlin, Wessel Prodns., Milw., 1987—. Dir., producer pub. TV series Inside Story with Slim Goodbody, 1980-81 (Corp. for Pub. Broadcasting award 1981). Mem. grant awards panel Wis. Arts Bd., Madison, 1978-79. Recipient Gold award Chgo. Internat. Film Festival, 1973, 77, 80, Silver, Bronze awards N.Y. Internat. Film and TV Festival, 1976, 79, 80, 85, Ohio State award Inst. for Edn. by TV, 1977, 82, 86, Addy awards, 1983, 85, 86, 87. Mem. Advt. Fedn. (Addy award 1983, 85, 86). Avocations: boardsailing, running, skiing, camping, reading. Home: 940 Oakdale Ave DePere WI 54115 Office: Schmidlin Wessel Prodns 115 W Silver Spring Dr Milwaukee WI 53217

WESSEL, M. SUZANNE, corporate administrative assistant; b. Elmhurst, Ill., Oct. 23, 1937; d. Richard Henry and Meta Louise (Morgan) Irving; m. Thomas Otto Wessel, Sept. 13, 1958 (div. Dec. 1980); children: Thomas Arthur, Jane Meta, Kurt Richard. Student, No. Ill. U., 1955-57. Exec. sec. to v.p. Santa Fe RR, Chgo., 1957-60; exec. sec. to regional mgr. Am. Cyanamid, Chgo., 1974-78; adminstrn. asst. to chmn. and chief exec. officer Coca-Cola Bottling Co., Chgo., 1978—. Mem. Internat. Profl. Secs. Republican. Lutheran.

WESSEL, RANDALL CHARLES, computer company executive; b. Chgo., Oct. 18, 1954; s. Charles Henry and Alice Helen (Gill) W. BA, Marquette U., 1976; MA, U. Tenn., 1980. Research assoc. Inst. Juvenile Research, Chgo., 1980-83; mgr., sales dir. MicroAge Computer Store, Madison, Wis., 1983-85, Racine, Wis., 1985-86; owner, pres. Wessel Computer Resources, Racine, 1986—. Avocations: running, riding motorcycles.

WESSELS, BURDELL RENSEN, insurance management executive; b. Ellsworth, Minn., Dec. 3, 1939; s. Ralph and Bernadine (Mulder) W.; m. Eileen M. Binzen, Sept. 16, 1961; children—Gail Carmon, Brian Burdell. A.A., U. Minn., 1959. Adminstrv. asst. Cargill Inc., Mpls., 1960-69; dir. ins. Internat. Multifoods, Mpls., 1969-74; pres., founder Corp. Risk Mgrs., Inc., Eden Prairie, Minn., 1974—. Mem. bldg. com. Eden Prairie Presbyn. Ch., 1982-84. Mem. Eden Prairie C. of C. (transp. com. 1982-84, accreditation com. 1984, chmn. small bus. awareness com. 1986-87, bd. dirs. 1986-87), Risk Ins. Mgmt. Soc. (chpt. bd. dirs. 1973-76), Mpls. Jaycees (treas. 1973-74). Lodge: Lions (sec. 1977-79, pres. 1981-82; Lion of Yr. 1978-79, 81-82) (Eden Prairie). Avocations: travel; spectator football and hockey. Home: 9980 Dell Rd Eden Prairie MN 55344 Office: 7525 Mitchell Rd Eden Prairie MN 55344

WESSNER, KENNETH THOMAS, management services executive; b. Sinking Springs, Pa., May 1, 1922; s. Thomas Benjamin and Carrie Eva (Whitmoyer) W.; m. Norma Elaine Cook, Jan. 25, 1945; children—Barbara Wessner Anderson, David Kenneth. B.S., Wheaton (Ill.) Coll., 1947. Dist. mgr., then sales promotion mgr. Club Aluminum Products Co., 1947-54; with Servicemaster Industries Inc., 1954—, v.p., 1961, pres. Servicemaster Hosp. Corp. div., 1962-72, chief operating officer Servicemaster Hosp. Corp. div., 1962-72; exec. v.p. parent co. Servicemaster Industries Inc., Downers Grove, Ill., 1972-75; chief operating officer Servicemaster Industries Inc., Downers Grove, 1973-74; pres. Servicemaster Industries Inc., Downers Grove, Ill., 1973-81, chief exec. officer, 1975-83, chmn. bd., 1981—, also bd. dirs.; dir. Bell Fed. Savs. & Loan Assn., Chgo., Health Providers Ins. Co. Chmn. bd. trustees Wheaton Coll., Ill.; mem. adv. council U. Chgo. Grad. Sch. Bus.; trustee Chgo. Sunday Evening Club, Am. Hosp. Assn. Research and Ednl. Trust. Served with USAAF, 1942-44. Named Profl. and Bus. Leader of Yr., Religious Heritage Am., 1981; recipient Outstanding Chief Exec. Officer in Services Industry award Fin. World mag., 1980; Top Chief Exec. Officer in Indsl. Services Industry award Wall St. Transcript, 1979, 80, 81, 82, 83. Mem. Am. Mgmt. Assn., Am. Hosp. Assn., Beta Gamma Sigma. Clubs: Chgo. Golf (Wheaton); Economics (Chgo.); Imperial Golf, Naples (Fla.) Yacht. Home: 102 E Farnham Ln Wheaton IL 60187 Office: The Servicemaster Co 2300 Warrenville Rd Downers Grove IL 60515

WEST, ANNE HARDMAN, business educator; b. Grantsville, W.Va.; d. Fredrick Clark and Bessie G. (Stalnaker) Hardman; m. Paul E. West, June 1, 1943 (dec. 1961); children: Paula Anne West Warren, Kenna Clark, Paul E. II. BS, Salem Coll., 1961; MS, Madison U., 1965; post-grad., U. Akron, 1972—. Asst. prof. Salem (W. Va.) Coll., 1965-70; assoc. prof bus., coordinator office adminstrn. U. Akron, Ohio, 1971-82; prof. bus. U. Akron, 1982—; cons. in field. Mem. Bus. and Profl. Women (pres. 1983-84, Mem. of Yr. 1983-84), AAUW, Assn. Info. Specialists Profls. (bd. dirs.), Ohio Bus. Tchrs. Assn., Akron Area Bus. Tchrs. Assn., Akron Assn. Univ. Profs., Delta Kappa Gamma (fin. chmn.). Club: Altrusa (Clarksburg, W.Va.)(pres.). Avocations: oil painting, bridge, reading. Office: Univ Akron Schrank North 152E Akron OH 44325

WEST, BYRON KENNETH, banker; b. Denver, Sept. 18, 1933; s. Willis Byron and Cecil Bernice (Leathers) W.; m. Barbara Huth, June 25, 1955. A.B., U. Ill., 1955; M.B.A., U. Chgo., 1960. With Harris Bank, Chgo., 1957—; investment analyst Harris Bank, 1957-62, v.p., 1966-76; group exec. Harris Bank Internat. Banking Group, 1974-76, head banking dept., exec. v.p., 1976-80, pres., 1980—; chmn. bd., chief exec. officer Harris Bankcorp, Inc., 1984—, also dir.; chmn., chief exec. officer Harris Trust & Savs. Bank, 1985—; dir. Motorola, Inc.; bd. govs. Midwest Stock Exchange; chmn. Chgo. Clearing House. Trustee U. Chgo., Rush-Presbyn.-St. Luke's Med Center; bd. dirs. U. Ill. Found.; governing bd. Chgo. Orchestral Assn. Served with U.S. Navy, 1955-57. Mem. Res. City Bankers Assn., Christian Laymen of Chgo., Phi Beta Kappa. Republican. Clubs: Skokie Country (Glencoe, Ill.); Pine Valley (N.J.); Univ., Chicago, Commonwealth, Commercial, Economic. Home: 200 Forest St Winnetka IL 60093 Office: Harris Trust & Savs Bank PO Box 755 Chicago IL 60690 *

WEST, CHARLES CARL, radiologist; b. Detroit, July 5, 1925; s. Sam and Helen (Naftaly) W.; m. Julia Niedelson, June 21, 1951 (div. 1984); children: Lynn, David, Margo; m. Nancy Milan, July 31, 1984; children: Jeff, Mark, Sara. BA, U. Mich., 1949; MD, Wayne State U., 1955. Cert. radiologist, Mich. Intern Detroit Meml. Hosp., 1955-56; resident in radiology Wayne State U., 1957-60; practice medicine specializing in radiology Lansing, Mich., 1960—; radiologist Ingham Radiology Assocs., Lansing, 1960—, pres., 1987—; chief dept. radiology Ingham Med. Ctr., Lansing, Mich., 1985—. Active Boy Scouts Am., 1970-80. Served to cpl. USAF, 1943-46. Mem. Am. Coll. Radiology, N.Am. Coll. Radiology, Mich. Radiol. Soc. Republican. Jewish. Avocations: salmon fishing, boating, racquet sports. Home: PO Box 491 Okemos MI 48864 Office: Ingham Radiology Assocs PC 2909 E Grand River Suite 102 Lansing MI 48912

WEST, DAVID CARL, marketing manager; b. Grand Island, Nebr., Nov. 13, 1959; s. Carl James and Mary Lou (Winfrey) W.; m. Barbara Louise Loving, May 5, 1984. AS, Des Moines Area Community Coll., 1981; BA, Grand View Coll., 1983. Mgr. Lutz-Snyders Pharmacies, Altoona, Iowa, 1980-83; sr. buyer Ardan Internat., Des Moines, 1984; asst. mktg. mgr. Microware Systems Corp., Des Moines, 1984-85, software support mgr., 1985—. Republican. Mem. Evang. Covenant Ch. Avocations: computer programming, auto and motorcycle restoration, target shooting. Home: 1106 E 36th Ct Des Moines IA 50317 Office: Micrware Systems Corp Customer Support 1866 NW 114th St Des Moines IA 50322

WEST, DEREK RAYMOND, metal company executive, industrial engineer; b. London, Sept. 27, 1942; came to U.S., 1977; s. Reginald Kenneth and Marjorie Alice (Brooker) W.; m. Anita Joyce Spellerberg, May 1, 1967; children: Raymond Lee, Douglas James. Diploma in metallurgy, City of London Poly., 1972; degree in metallurgy with honors, U. Aston, Birmingham, Eng., 1973; MBA, Ohio State U., 1986. Research technician Battelle, Columbus, Ohio, 1964-67; sr. indsl. engr. Mettoy Co., Swansea, South Wales, 1973-77; divisional indsl. engr. Shunk Blade, Bucyrus, Ohio, 1977-79; sr. indsl. engr. Ohio Brass Co., Mansfield, 1983-86, project mgr., 1986—. Contbr. articles to profl. jours. Cubmaster Boy Scouts Am., Mansfield, 1978-82. Weidler scholar Ohio State U., 1986. Mem. Inst. Indsl. Engrs., Am. Prodn. and Inventory Control Soc., North Cen. Ohio Numerical Control Users Soc. Club: Sailing (Mansfield)(trustee). Avocation: camping. Home: 3335 Stephanie Dr Bucyrus OH 44820 Office: Ohio Brass Co 380 N Main St Mansfield OH 44903

WEST, JACKIE LORRAINE, analyst, computer services consultant; b. Kansas City, Mo., Oct. 14, 1957; d. Everett Raymond and Donna Corraine (Cunningham) Lauderdale; m. Charles Richard West, Dec. 18, 1976; children: Raina Marie, Joshua Thomas. Cert. in EDP, Kansas City Vocat. Tech. Edn. Ctr., 1975; AAS degree, Longview Community Coll., 1980. Sr. analyst Hallmark Cards, Kansas City, 1985—; v.p. Bits, Bytes & Prototypes, Kansas City, 1980—. Chmn. adv. bd. Kansas City Vocat. Tech. Edn. Ctr., 1985—; mem. Hallpack polit. group, 1984—. Mem. Nat. Assn. Female Execs., Commodore User Group of Kansas City. Democrat. Baptist. Home: 12201 E 61st Kansas City MO 64133 Office: Hallmark Cards 25th and McGee Srs Kansas City MO 64141

WEST, MICHAEL EUGENE, obstetrician/gynecologist; b. Charleston, S.C., Aug. 12, 1953; s. Ralph E. and Patricia J. West; m. Gloria Anne Gwost, Jan. 2, 1976; children: Jeremy, Benjamine, Elliot. BS, St. John's U., 1975; MD, Med. Coll. of Wis., 1979. Intern St. Joseph's Hosp., Milw., 1979-80, resident in ob-gyn, 1980-83; practice medicine specializing in ob-gyn Appleton, Wis., 1983—; med. dir. Life Span Ctr. for Women, Appleton, 1985—; asst. med. dir. Family Fertility Ctr., Appleton, 1986—; bd. dirs. Doctors' Park, Appleton. Bd. dirs. Resolve Northeastern Wis., Appleton, 1985—; pres. Pastoral Council, Holy Name of Jesus, Kimberly, Wis., 1986—; sponsor Holy Name of Jesus Run, 1986—. Fellow Am. Coll. Ob-Gyn; mem., AMA, Am. Fertility Soc., Wis. Med. Assn., Outagamie County Med. Soc., Appleton Jaycees. Roman Catholic. Avocations: exercising, biking, boating. Home: 1112 Fernmeadow Appleton WI 54915 Office: 1611 S Madison Appleton WI 54915

WEST, MOLLIE LOUISE, journalist; b. Detroit, Oct. 24, 1953; d. Frank Samuel and Mary Elizabeth (McKissick) W. B.A., U. Mich., 1976. Prodn. asst. NBC-WDIV-TV, Detroit, 1977-79; account exec. Daniel J. Edelman Pub. Relations, Chgo., 1980; intern reporter Detroit Free Press, 1979; gen. assignment reporter Ypsilanti Press (Mich.), 1979-80; free-lance writer Chgo. Tribune, also pub. relations div. Smith, Jones & Assocs., Chgo., also Inter-Service Mag., Washington, 1982—; dir. pub. affairs Chgo. State U., 1986—. Author: Stubborn Heart, 1984. Mem. Women in Communications (co-chmn. minority high sch. career conf. 1981, 82, rep. Ill. women's agenda 1983-84), Nat. Assn. Media Women. Home: 3427 N Elaine Pl Chicago IL 60657

WEST, ROBERT CRAWLEY, engineering company executive; b. Keytesville, Mo., Apr. 26, 1920; s. George and Bertie (Taylor) W.; m. Willie Mae Burgess, June 12, 1946; children: Robert Crawley, Susan. B.C.E., Ga. Inst. Tech., 1949. Registered profl. engr., Mo., 13 other states. Project mgr. H. K. Ferguson Co., 1950-53; with Sverdrup Corp., St. Louis, 1953—, exec. v.p., 1969-75, chief operating officer, 1973-75, pres., chief exec. officer, 1975-77, chmn. bd., pres., 1977-85; chmn. Sverdrup Corp., 1985—; dir. Centerre Bank in St. Louis, Angelica Corp.; mem. nat. adv. bd. Ga. Inst. Tech. Mem. pres.'s council St. Louis U.; mem. exec. bd. St. Louis area council Boy Scouts Am.; bd. dirs. YMCA Greater St. Louis, Ranken Tech. Inst., Jr. Achievement Mississippi Valley, Inc., St. Louis Symphony Soc., United Way Greater St. Louis, Barnes Hosp., Mo. Bot. Garden; bd. dirs. Mo. Goodwill Industries Am., 1971-83, pres., 1974-78, emeritus, 1983; chmn. bd. Mo. Corp. for Sci. and Tech.; trustee Webster Coll., St. Louis. Served with AUS, 1942-46. Recipient Engring. Achievement award Engrs. Club St. Louis, 1977, Disting. Service in Engring. award U. Mo., 1981, Silver Beaver award Boy Scouts Am., 1985, Sales Exec. of Yr. award Sales and Mktg. Execs. St. Louis, 1985; named Constrn. Industry Man of Yr., PRIDE/St. Louis, 1978. Mem. ASCE (pres. St. Louis chpt. 1974-75, Profl. Recognition award 1981, Herbert Hoover medal 1985), Am. Cons. Engrs. Council, Nat. Soc. Profl. Engrs., Mo. Soc. Profl. Engrs. (Engr. of Yr. 1976), Soc. Am. Mil. Engrs., ASTM, Brit. Tunnelling Soc., Internat. Assn. Bridge and Structural Engring., Internat. Bridge, Tunnel and Turnpike Assn., Beavers, Moles, Transp. Research Bd., St. Louis Regional Commerce and Growth Assn. (chmn. bd.), Civic Progress, Mcpl. Theatre Assn. Clubs: Engineers, Mo. Athletic, Media, St. Louis, Ambassadors, Old Warson Country (St. Louis) (bd. dirs.); Round Table, Bogey Country (bd. dirs.). Home: 11 Exmoor Dr Saint Louis MO 63124 Office: Sverdrup Corp 801 N 11th Saint Louis MO 63101 *

WEST, ROBERT H., manufacturing company executive; b. 1938. A.B., Princeton U., 1960. V.p. First Nat. Bank of Kansas City, 1962-68; asst. treas. Butler Mfg. Co., Inc., Kansas City, Mo., 1968-70, controller bldg. div., 1970-73, corp. v.p., controller bldgs. div., 1973-74, sr. v.p. adminstrn., 1974-76, exec. v.p., 1976-78, pres., chief operating officer, 1978-86, chmn., chief exec. officer, 1986—, also dir.; bd. dirs. Commerce Bancshares, Inc., Kansas City Power & Light Co., Nat. Assn. Mfrs., Santa Fe So. Pacific Corp., Commerce Bancshares Inc. Bd. dirs. St. Lukes Hosp. Served to 1st lt. U.S. Army, 1960-62. Office: Butler Manufacturing Co Inc BMA Tower Penn Valley Park Kansas City MO 64141

WEST, ROBERT LEWIS, financial planner; b. Springfield, Ohio, Aug. 18, 1951; s. Robert Leslie and Julia Belle (Early) W.; m. Helen Marie Isreal, July 24, 1982. Student Ohio State U., 1969-70, Wright State U., 1971-73; grad. Coll. for Fin. Planning, 1982. Cert. fin. planner. Ind. ins. broker and agt., 1973-79; founder Green & West Agy., Columbus, Ohio, from 1977; area sales mgr. Fireman's Fund Am. Life, San Rafael, Calif., from 1979; founder, owner West R L Fin. Planning, Columbus, from 1980; founder, owner Capital Research Services, from 1983; now investment broker, cert. planner, assoc. v.p. Prudential Bache Securities, Inc., Cin.; adj. faculty Coll. Fin. Planning, Denver; cons. in field. Organizer, pres. Children's Christian Research Found. Mem. Internat. Assn. Registered Fin. Planners (bd. govs. 1986). Republican. Lutheran. Home: 2141 Old Vienna Dr Dayton OH 45459 Office: 525 Vine St Suite 1900 Cincinnati OH 45202

WEST, ROBERT PATRICK, judge; b. Cleve., Aug. 18, 1918; s. Thomas and Helen (Pelka) W.; m. Virginia Hinterschied, June 13, 1940; children—Patrick A., Ginger, Joan M. Krueger, Michael J. Student Ohio State U., 1935-39; B.S., Franklin U., 1948, L.L.B., 1948; J.D., Capital U., 1966. Asst. mgr. Ohio Hotels Protective Assn., Columbus, 1936-40; mem. credit dept. Gen. Motors Acceptance Corp., Columbus, 1940-42; mem. claims dept. Travelers Ins. Co., Columbus, 1942-44; claims mgr. Am. States Ins. Co., Columbus, 1947-55; sr. asst. city atty. City of Columbus, 1955-57; ptnr. West & Holmes, Columbus, 1957-69, Teaford, Bernard, West & Brothers, Columbus, 1969-70; judge Franklin County Mcpl. Ct., Columbus, 1970-80, Franklin County Common Pleas Ct., 1980—; asst. sec., counsel Lake Central Airlines, Indpls., 1957-68; Ohio counsel Allegheny Airlines, Washington, 1968-70. Contbr. articles to profl. jours. Chmn. Ohio Aviation Bd., Columbus, 1962, Ohio Jud. Coll., Columbus, 1976—; mem. Columbus Urban Renewal Commn., 1957, Ohio Bldg. Authority, 1968. Served with armed forces, World War II. Recipient 12 awards for superior, excellent and outstanding jud. service Ohio Supreme Ct., 1971-85. Faculty award Ohio Jud. Coll., 1978. Mem. ABA, Am. Judges Assn. (Judge Bob Jones Meml. award for significant contbrns. to jud. edn.), Ohio State Bar Assn. (25-yr.

service award aviation law com. 1980), Columbus Bar Assn., Lawyer-Pilots Assn. Republican. Roman Catholic. Club: Athletic (Columbus). Lodge: K.C. Avocation: flying. Home: 345 E Longview Ave Columbus OH 43202 Office: Common Pleas Ct 369 S High St Columbus OH 43215

WEST, ROYAL JACKLIN, physical therapist; b. America Fork, Utah, Feb. 16, 1944; s. Ross Charles and Edith Martha (Jacklin) W.; m. Annette Black, Jan. 3, 1964; children: Shaun, Chad, Brandon, Jaime. AS, Snow Coll., Ephraim, Utah, 1964; BS, Weber State U., Ogden, Utah, 1966; Cert. in Physical Therapy, U. Iowa, 1967. Lic. physical therapist, Wis., Tex., Tenn., Utah, Ky., W.Va. Pres. Omni Services, Inc., Lake Geneva, Wis., 1972—, also bd. dirs.; pres. Maitre-D Corp., Racine, Wis., 1976-79, Omni Transp., Inc., Racine, 1977-81; pres. Omni Fitness Ctrs., Inc., Burlington, Wis., 1981—, also bd. dirs.; v.p. Physical Therapy Ctr., Inc., Appleton, Wis., 1985—; bd. dirs. Royal J. West Martial Arts Acads., Inc; instr. Gateway Tech. Inst., Kenosha, Wis., 1985-86. Author: Police Karate, 1983. Named Black Belt of Yr., Am. Kyuki-Do Fedn., 1982. Mem. Am. Physical Therapy Assn. (self-employed, orthoepedic, sports therapy sects.), Am. Kyuki Do Fedn., Inc. (Most Outstanding Martial Artist award 1984, v.p. chpt. 1985—). Mormon. Avocations: martial arts, tae kwon do. Home: 1732 Fairview Dr Lake Geneva WI 53147 Office: Omni Rehab and Sports Ctr 115 Commerce Burlington WI 53105

WEST, SUSAN DIANE, pharmacist; b. Hopkinsville, Ky., Aug. 19, 1951; d. Lowry Lewis and Jane Ailene (Underwood) W. BS, U. Ky., 1973. Pharmacist Taylor Drug Co., Louisville, 1973-76, People's Drug Co., Bloomington, Ind., 1976-77; asst. dir. pharmacy Hosp., Bedford, Ind., 1977-78; pharmacist Hosp., Evansville, Ind., 1978-80, Osco Drug Co., Evansville, 1981—. NSF fellow, 1971; recipient Sloan award for Achievement, 1973; named Top Pharmacy of Yr., Jewell-Osco Drug Co., 1984. Mem. Evansville Astron. Soc., Irish Club of Evansville, Assn. Research and Enlightenment, Mensa (treas. 1983-85), Evansville Zool. Soc., League of Women Voters, Nat. Geographic Soc., Cousteau Soc. (charter mem.), Smithsonian Soc., Am. Pharmacist Assn., Ky. Pharmacist Assn., Ind. Pharmacist Assn., Southwest Ind. Pharmacist Assn., Lambda Kappa Sigma (named outstanding pledge 1971). Republican. Baptist. Avocations: piano, painting, writing, ice skating, horseback riding.

WEST, TERENCE DOUGLAS, furniture company design executive; b. Twin Falls, Idaho, Sept. 12, 1948; s. Clark Ernest and Elsie Erma (Kulm) W. B.S., San Jose State U., 1971. Indsl. designer Clement Labs., Palo Alto, Calif., 1970-74, U.S. Govt., Washington, 1974-78; dir. design Steelcase, Inc., Grand Rapids, Mich., 1978—. Com. mem. San Jose Urban Coalition, 1971-72; Fulbright commn. on Design and Design Edn. in Great Britain. Mem. Archtl. League of N.Y., Nat. Trust for Hist. Preservation, Inst. Bus. Designers, Am. Soc. Interior Designers Industry Found. Interior Edn. and Research, Indsl. Designers Soc. Am., Design Mgmt. Inst. Democrat. Lutheran. Home: 3536 Whispering Brook SE Grand Rapids MI 49508 Office: Steelcase Inc PO Box 1967 Grand Rapids MI 49501

WESTBAY, CHARLES DUANE, farm equipment retail and service company executive; b. Yates City, Ill., Dec. 8, 1930; s. Charles Bond and Beatrice Elizabeth (Bates) W.; m. Bonnie Jean Gravitt, Sept. 30, 1950; children—Charles Grant, Shirley Jo, Steven Larry, Bette Jean. Student U. Ill., 1949. Lic. pvt. pilot. With Internat. Harvester Co., Peoria Ill. and Madison, Wis., 1949-59, zone sales mgr., 1951-56, store mgr., 1957-58, nat. del. Dealer Council, 1971-72; pres. Westbay Equipment Co., Galesburg, Ill., 1959—; pres. N.Am. dealer adv. council Versatile Mfg. Co.; owner Westbay Leasing Co., Galesburg; owner, operator Westbay Farms. Chmn. Knox County chpt. Ill. Future Farmers Am. Found., 1977-78. Recipient Hon. Chpt. Farmer's award Future Farmers Am., 1977, 78. Mem. Knox County YMCA, Galesburg Pilots Assn., Aircraft Owners and Pilots Assn. Ill. Retail Farm Equipment Assn. Republican. Methodist. Lodge: Masons. Home: 206 Division Knoxville IL 61448

WESTBROCK, DAVID ANTHONY, endocrinologist; b. Dayton, Ohio, Mar. 27, 1946; s. Raymond John and Mary (Gaier) W.; m. Judy Day; children—Jennifer Elizabeth, David. B.S., U. Dayton, 1968; M.D., Ohio State U., 1972 Diplomate Am. Bd. Internal Medicine, Am. Bd. Endocrinology and Metabolism. Intern Ohio State U. Hosps., Columbus, 1972-73, resident in internal medicine, 1973-75; fellow in endocrinology and metabolism U. Cin. Hosps., 1975-77; practice medicine specializing in endocrinology and metabolism, Dayton, 1977—; mem. staffs Miami Valley Hosp., Kettering Med. Ctr., St. Elizabeth Med. Ctr.; clin. assoc. prof. medicine Wright State U.; Trustee Am. Dayton, Western Ohio Found. Fellow ACP; mem. Greater Dayton Hormone Soc. (convener), Montgomery County Med. Soc. (bd. dirs.). Office: 60 Wyoming St Dayton OH 45409

WESTCOTT, WILLIAM WARREN, JR., utility consultant; b. Cleve., July 8, 1930; s. William Warren Sr. and Anne (Maus) W.; m. Cynthia Lall, May 29, 1967; 1 child, William Warren III. BS in Econs., U. Pa., 1957; postgrad. in mgmt. devel., Harvard U., 1971. Indsl. economist Govt. of P.R., San Juan, 1957-59; owner, mgr. P.R. Electric Constrn. Co., San Juan, 1959-70; cons. Utility Cons. Group, Cleve., 1973—; cons. in field. Mem. Ohio Rep. Com., Cleve., 1985, Cleve. Mus. Art, 1985. Club: Harvard Bus. Sch. (Cleve.). Avocations: sailing, horticulture. Home and Office: 2351 N Park Blvd Cleveland Heights OH 44106

WESTENFELDER, GRANT ORVILLE, physician, educator; b. Chgo., Jan. 12, 1940; s. Orville L. and Eleanor Jean (Langley) W.; student U. Mich., 1957-60; B.S., Northwestern U. 1961, M.D., 1964; m. Sharon L. Zelesnik, June 22, 1981; children—Mark, Bruce, Natalie; 1 stepdau., Shari. Intern, Evanston (Ill.) Hosp., 1964-65, now sr. attending physician, resident in internal medicine Northwestern U. McGaw Med. Center, 1965-68, fellow in infectious diseases, 1968-70, mem. infectious diseases sect. Med. Sch., 1970—, asst. prof. clin. medicine Northwestern U., 1974-81, asso. prof. clin. medicine, 1981—; asso. chmn. dept. medicine, head div. infectious diseases Evanston Hosp. Corp.; head dept. medicine Glenbrook Hosp., Glenview, Ill. Bd. deacons Trinity Luth. Ch., Evanston, 1970-71. Diplomate Am. Bd. Internal Medicine. Fellow A.C.P., Am. Coll. Chest Physicians; mem. Am. Soc. Microbiology, Am. Fedn. Clin. Research, Infectious Disease Soc. Am., AMA, Chgo. Soc. Internal Medicine, Assn. Practitioners in Infection Control, Am. Soc. Epidemiologists, Surg. Infection Soc., Alpha Kappa Kappa. Office: 2100 Pfingsten Rd Glenview IL 60025 also: 2050 Pfingsten Rd Glenview IL 60025

WESTER, MARK WILLIAM, controller; b. Cleve., Dec. 11, 1954; s. William Alfred and Sara Ann (Nicklos) W.; m. Lynn Annette Poznako, Apr. 16, 1977; children: Matthew, Gregory. BBA, John Carroll U., 1976. CPA, Ohio. Staff auditor Coopers & Lybrand, Cleve., 1976-78; gen. acct. Banner Industries Inc., Cleve., 1978-79, asst. corp. controller, 1979—. Mem. Am. Inst. CPA's, Ohio Soc. CPA's. Avocations: athletics, fitness. Home: 8335 Ridge Rd North Royalton OH 44133 Office: Banner Industries 25700 Sci Park Blvd Cleveland OH 44122

WESTERN, WILLIAM HANS, food service executive; b. Waterfliet, Mich., Jan. 21, 1937; s. Hans and Mary (White) W.; m. Sandra Sue Montague, June 15, 1962; children: Deane, Steven. BA, Kalamazoo Coll., 1959; postgrad. mgmt. devel., Harvard U., 1976. Area v.p. Saga Corp., Menlo Park, Calif., 1955-80; pres. Western Food Enterprises, Inc., Byron Center, Mich., 1980—; pres., owner Hol-Hi Classics, Kalamazoo. Served with U.S. Army, 1959-60. Mem. PGA, Nat. Restaurant Assn., U.S. Golf Assn. Republican. Presbyterian. Clubs: Kalamazoo Country (bd. govs. 1985—), Econ. of Grand Rapids, Mich. (com.), Harvard of Grand Rapids. Home: 1030 Hol-Hi Dr Kalamazoo MI 49008 Office: Western Food Enterprises Inc 2950 84th St Byron Center MI 49315

WESTIN, HAROLD JOSEPH, architectural engineering and construction executive; b. St. Paul, May 6, 1920; s. Joseph Anders and Elsie Karen (Hagstrom) W.; m. Dolores Marion Swanson, May 15, 1943; children: Dee Anne, Cynthia, Rosemary, Amy. BCE, U. Minn.; BS in Law, St. Paul Coll. Law. Registered profl. civil/structural engr. 13 states. Chief field engr. Dravo Corp., Pitts., 1943-44; exec. v.p. Hagstrom Constrn. Co., St. Paul, 1946-56; pres. Harold J. Westin Constructors, Inc., St. Paul, 1957—, Harold J. Westin Architects and Engrs., P.A., St. Paul, 1963—; lectr. inst. tech. U. Minn., Mpls., 1950-77; bd. dirs. Hillcrest State Bank, St. Paul, 1964-79; cons. foresic engring. for various counties, municipalities, ednl. and religious insts., 1950—. Author: An Engineer Looks at the Law, 1973, An Engineer Applies the Law, 1972, also series of articles on design responsibilities of architects and engrs., 1975. Bd. dirs. Soc. Profl. Engrs. Found., 1973-75. Served to lt. (j.g.) USNR, 1944-46, PTO. Fellow ASCE (life); mem. Minn. Soc. Profl. Engrs. (chmn. bldg. com. 1975-77), Minn. Soc. Profl. Engrs. (Engr. of Yr. 1973), Nat. Soc. Profl. Engrs. Clubs: U. Minn. Campus, St. Paul Athletic. Home: 2504 Manitou Island White Bear Lake MN 55110

WESTINGHOUSE, ANNA MARIE, nursing service administrator; b. Cin., Mar. 21, 1931; s. Aaron Fleming Johnson and Violet Naomi (Lee) Venator; m. Edwin Arnold Westinghouse, Sept. 3, 1976 (div. 1982); 1 child, Lynn Ellen. Grad. high sch., Hammond, Ind. Radio interviewer Sta. WYCA-FM, Hammond, 1970-77, Sta. WLNR-FM, Lansing, Ill., 1977-85; dir. Meals-on-Wheels, Home Nursing Service, Hammond, 1983-84, dir. mktg. and pub. relations, 1983-85, asst. exec. dir., 1985-87; adminstr. Dorchester Sr. Retirement Home, Harper Dolton, Ill., 1987—. Contbr. articles on aging, women's rights and minority rights to local newspapers; producer radio programs on women's rights and minority rights, 1983. Mem. Lake County Womens Council, exec. bd., 1976-85. Mem. N.W. Ind. Womens Bur. (exec. bd. 1976-78). Democrat. Club: Toastmasters. Avocations: chairing self-help groups, working on hot lines or rap lines. Home: 511 Conkey St Hammond IN 46324 Office: Home Nursing Service 111 Sibley St Hammond IN 46320

WESTLAND, JAMES CHRISTOPHER, educator, accountant; b. Indpls., Nov. 17, 1949; s. John Joseph and Mary (Elliott) W.; m. Randa Assad Al-Awar, Apr. 28, 1984; 1 child, Michelle Summar. BA, Ind. U., 1971, MBA, 1973; postgrad., U. Mich., 1980—. CPA, Tex. Auditor Touche Ross, Chgo., 1973-75; accounts payable mgr. Federated Dept. Stores, Dallas, 1975-76; EDP audit mgr. Republic Life, Dallas, 1976; data base adminstr. Rockwell Internat., Dallas, 1977-80; asst. prof. acctg. and fin. Eastern Mich. U., Ypsilanti, 1980—. Contbr. articles to profl. jours. Paton fellow, 1980-81, 83; Arthur Andersen fellow, 1985; Dykstra fellow, 1986-87. Mem. Am. Inst. CPA's, Am. Acctg. Assn., Am. Statis. Assn. Republican. Episcopalian. Club: Gran Fraternidad Universal (Ann Arbor) (treas. 1986-87). Avocations: piano, skiing, tennis, yoga, karate. Home: 1658 McIntyre Ann Arbor MI 48104 Office: Eastern Mich U 515j Pray-Harold Ypsilanti MI 48197

WESTMAN, JACK CONRAD, child psychiatrist, educator; b. Cadillac, Mich., Oct. 28, 1927; s. Conrad A. and Alice (Pedersen) W.; m. Nancy K. Baehre, July 17, 1953; children—Daniel P., John C., Eric C. M.D., U. Mich., 1952. Diplomate: Am. Bd. Psychiatry and Neurology. Intern Duke Hosp., Durham, N.C., 1952-53; resident U. Mich. Med. Center, 1955-59; dir. Outpatient Services, Children's Psychiatric Hosp., Ann Arbor, Mich., 1961-65; assoc. prof. U. Mich. Med. Sch., 1964-65; coordinator Diagnostic and Treatment Unit, Waisman Center, U. Wis., Madison, 1966-74; prof. psychiatry Diagnostic and Treatment Unit, Waisman Center, U. Wis., 1965—; cons. Joint Commn. on Mental Health of Children, 1967-69, Madison (Wis.) Pub. Schs., 1965-74, Children's Treatment Center, Mendota Mental Health Inst., 1965-69. Author: Individual Differences in Children, 1973, Child Advocacy, 1979; editor: Child Psychiatry and Human Devel.; contbr. articles to profl. jours. Vice-pres. Big Bros. of Dane County, 1970-73; v.p. Wis. Assn. Mental Health, 1968-72; co-chmn. Project Understanding, 1968-75. Served with USNR, 1953-55. Fellow Am. Psychiat. Assn., Am. Coll. Psychiatrists, Am. Acad. Child Psychiatry, Am. Orthopsychiat. Assn. (dir. 1973-76); mem. Am. Assn. Psychiat. Services for Children (pres. 1976-80). Home: 1234 Dartmouth Rd Madison WI 53705 Office: 600 Highland Ave Madison WI 53792

WESTMAN, JAMES FREDERICK, dentist; b. Duluth, Minn., Mar. 2, 1949; s. John Richard B. and Margaret Lorraine (Wickstrom) W.; m. Nancy Mildred Gunderson, June 26, 1971; children: Kate Ann, Lindsey Leigh. BS with honors, U. Minn., Duluth, 1971, DDS, 1973. Gen. practice dentistry Duluth, 1973—. Contbr. numerous articles to profl. jour. Bd. dirs. Am. Cancer Soc., United Way., Duluth; com. chmn. Western Area Bus. and Civic Club, West Duluth, 1975—; mem. Spirit Valley Citizens Neighborhood Devel. Assn., Duluth, 1985—, v.p. 1986-87; mem. steering com. West Duluth Planning Project, 1986.; trustee Sta. WDSE-TV. Fellow Acad. Gen. Dentistry, Am. Coll. Dentists; mem. ADA (alternate del.), Minn. Dental Assn. (chmn. MDA membership com. 1980-82, chmn. reference com 1985), Northeastern Dist. Dental Soc. (pres. 1984-85, 1st, 2d v.p. , sec., treas. and chmn. privately funded programs com.). Methodist. Avocations: music, photography, swimming, biking, antique cars.

WESTMAN, ROBERT ALLAN, management consultant; b. Marbleton, Quebec, Can., Feb. 22, 1926; s. James Amon and Flora Gladys (Gilbert) W.; m. Esther Florence Renshaw, July 2, 1949; children: Michael, Joel, Robin, Andrew. Student Chemistry, Physics, U. Bishop's Coll., Province of Quebec, Can., 1942-43; BS, U. Toronto, 1949; postgrad. Bus. Adminstrn., U. Pa., 1955-56. V.p. spl. projects Ogden Metals, Inc., Cleve., 1970-74; chmn. Warren (Ohio) Fabricating Corp., 1974-78; v.p., gen. mgr. C-L Metals, Niles (Ohio), Inc., 1978-79; pres. Inred Iron, Inc., Roseland, N.J., 1981-85, R.A. Westman & Assoc., Warren, 1979—; bd. dirs., cons. Felber Studios, Inc., Ardmore, Pa., 1984—. Patentee cast clad steel plate. Rep. ward leader, Sunnyvale, Ca., 1961-62. Served with RCAF, 1943-45. Mem. Assn. Iron and Steel Engrs. (assoc.). Presbyterian. Clubs: Duquesne (Pitts.); Ft. Henry (Wheeling, W.V.). Home and Office: 359 Quarry Ln Warren OH 44483

WESTON, DAWN THOMPSON, artist, researcher; b. Joliet, Ill., Apr. 15, 1919; d. Cyril C. and Vivian Grace Thompson; student (scholar) Penn Hall Jr. Coll., Chambersburg, Pa., 1937-38; B.S., Northwestern U., 1942, postgrad. in reading and speech pathology, 1960-61, M.A. in Ednl. Adminstrn., 1970; postgrad. U. Ill., 1964; student Art Inst. Chgo., 1954, Pestalozzi-Froebel, Chgo., 1955, Phila. Inst. for Achievement Human Potential, 1963; m. Arthur Walter Weston, Sept. 10, 1940; children—Roger Lance, Randall Kent, Cynthia Brooke. Therapist, USN Hosp., Gt. Lakes, Ill., 1940-45; tchr. Holy Child and Waukegan (Ill.) High Schs., 1946-54; elem. and jr. high art dir. Lake Bluff (Ill.) Schs., 1954-58; pioneer ednl. dir. Grove Sch. for Brain-Injured, Lake Forest, Ill., 1958-66, now life mem. corp., chmn. bd., 1984-87; one-woman shows: Evanston Woman's Club, Northwestern U., Deerpath Gallery, Lake Forest; The Hein Co., Waukegan; numerous group shows, 1939-76. Represented in permanent collections: ARC, Victory Meml. Hosp., Waukegan, Sierra Assos., Chgo., numerous pvt. collections U.S., Can., Japan, Africa; works include: Poisonous Plants of Midwest set of etchings for Country Gentleman mag., 1956, Clouds mural, 1981; ind. researcher on shifting visual imagery due to trauma, 1982—. Mem. Presdl. Gold Chain, Trinity Coll., 1979. Named Citizen of Yr., Grove Sch., 1978, room at sch. named in her honor, 1982; cert. tchr., Ill. Mem. Art Inst. Chgo., Deerpath Art League, Pi Lambda Theta. Methodist (del. Ann. Conf. 1982-87). Research on uneven growth, 1969-70. Home and Office: 349 E Hilldale Pl Lake Forest IL 60045

WESTOVER, BECKY HOSFORD, nutrition consultant; b. Keokuk, Iowa, Mar. 19, 1939; s. Harlow N. and R. Louise (Buss) Hosford; m. John P. Westover, July 1, 1961; children: Robert S., Mark H., Lynne L. BS, U. Ill., 1961; postgrad., Nat. Coll. Edn. Dir. fed. grant #44 Elementary Sch., Lombard, Ill., 1979-80; cons. Dairy Nutritionist Council, Westmont, Ill., 1977—; instr. Coll. of Dupage, Evanston, 1981—; instr., mem. adv. bd. Coll. DuPage, Glen Ellyn, Ill., 1983—. Recipient Service award ARC, Lombard, 1985-87. Mem. Ill. Soc. Profl. Trainers, Women In Mgmt. (Mktg. com. 1986—), Am. Home Econ. Assn., Consortium of Health Edn. (pres. 1981-82), Assn. for Young Children (advisor DuPage unit 1983—). Republican. Club: Sch. Booster (Glen Ellyn). Home: 548 Stafford Ln Glen Ellyn IL 60187 Office: 999 Oakmont Plaza Westmont IL 60559

WESTPHAL, EDWARD EUGENE, police officer; b. Chgo., Jan. 11, 1951; s. Vernon Charles and Helen (McGowan) W.; m. Mary Louise Meli, Oct. 25, 1980 (div. Nov. 1986); children: Eric Edward, Brett Joseph. BA, U. Ill., Chgo., 1973; MA, Roosevelt U., 1981; postgrad., Ill. SCh. Profl. Psychology, Chgo., 1980-81, John Marshall Law Sch., Chgo., 1984—. Computer operator J.C. Penny Co., Chgo., 1973-75; clin. therapist Bur. Mental Health, Chgo., 1975-85; police officer City of Chgo. Police Dept., 1985—; cons. Bur. Mental Health, 1985—; adv. bd. Lakeview Mental Health Ctr., Chgo., 1985—. open house organizer, 1985. Mem. ABA, Aviation Law Soc. (v.p. 1984—), Am. Psychol. Assn., Ill. Psychol. Assn., Aircraft Owner and Pilot's Assn. Democrat. Roman Catholic. Avocations: flying, sports, reading. Home: 6810 S Artesian Chicago IL 60629 Office: Chgo Police Dept 2255 E 103d St Chicago IL 60617

WESTPHAL, MICHAEL BRIAN, feed company executive; b. Mankato, Minn., Nov. 23, 1961; s. Bernard Lee and Myrtle Olga (Krause) W.; m. Marilyn Jean Hoechst, June 9, 1984. BS, S.D. State U., 1984. Terr. mgr. Cargill-Nutrena Feeds, Sioux City, 1984—. Mem. Jaycees. Republican. Lutheran. LodgeL Lions. Avocation: sports. Home: 1405 Redwood Dr Atlantic IA 50022 Office: Cargill Nutrena Feeds Box 356 Sioux City IA 51102

WESTRAN, ROY ALVIN, insurance company executive; b. Taft, Oreg., Apr. 30, 1925; s. Carl A. and Mae E. (Barnhart) W.; m. Dawn M. Oeschger, Oct. 18, 1952; children: Denise, Thomas, Michael, Dawna. B.B.A., Golden Gate Coll., 1955, M.B.A., 1957. Mem. sales staff C.A. Westran Agy., Taft, 1946-49; underwriter Fireman's Fund Group, San Francisco, 1949-52; ins. mgr. Kaiser Aluminum Chem. Co., Oakland, 1952-66; pres., dir. Citizens Ins. Co., Howell, Mich., 1967—; chmn. bd. 1st Nat. Bank, Howell; pres. Am. Select Ins. Co., Columbus, Ohio, 1967-85, dir., 1967—; pres. Beacon Ins. Co. Am., Westerville, Ohio, 1967-85, dir., 1967—; pres., dir. Citizens' Man, Inc.; v.p., dir. Hanover Ins. Co., Massachusetts Bay Ins. Co.; bd. dirs. Oakland Kaiser Fed. Credit Union, 1957-60, Calif. Compensation Fire Co. Mem. ins. adv. council Salvation Army, San Francisco, 1957-60; chmn. drive United Way, Livingston County, 1980; bd. dirs., mem. exec. com. Portage Trails council Boy Scouts Am., 1970-72; trustee, mem. exec. com. Child and Family Services Mich., 1972-75; past bd. dirs. McPherson Health Ctr., Howell; bd. dirs. Cleary Coll., 1984-85; mem. adv. council Olivet Coll., 1984—. Served with U.S. Army, 1943-46. Mem. Ins. Inst. Am., Mich. C. of C. (past dir.), Am. Soc. Ins. Mgmt. (past pres.), Soc. CPCU's (nat. pres. 1968-69), Traffic Safety Assn. Detroit (trustee 1967—), Traffic Safety for Mich. Assn. Office: Citizens Ins Co of America 645 W Grand River Howell MI 48834

WESTROM, RONALD LYLE, personnel manager; b. Aurora, Ill., Nov. 8, 1940; s. Lyle A. and Louise E. (Zander) W.; m. Leona R. Lance, April 23, 1966; children—Janet Caras, Jeffrey, Susan. A.A., Kemper Sch., 1960; B.S. in Bus. Adminstrn., Elmhurst Coll., 1963. Personnel specialist Continental Bank, Chgo., 1965-68; prodn. supr. Johnson & Johnson Corp., Chgo., 1968-72; asst. personnel dir. Capitol Packaging Co., Melrose Park, Ill., 1972-73; personnel dir. Glenview State Bank, Ill., 1973-76; asst. personnel dir. Dr. Scholl, Inc., Chgo., 1976-82; personnel mgr. ITW Spiroid, Chgo., 1982—. Pres., Robbie Fund of Children's Meml. Hosp. Served to 1st lt. USA, 1963-65, Korea. Mem. Am. Soc. Personnel Adminstrs., Midwest Personnel Mgmt. Assn., Midwest Indsl. Mgmt. Assn., No. Ill. Indsl. Assn., Jr. C. of C. (chmn. Spark Club com. 1967). Republican. Episcopalian. Lodge: Elks. Home: 216 N Maple St Mount Prospect IL 60056 Office: ITW Spiroid 2601 North Keeler Ave Chicago IL 60639

WETHERALD, ROBERT FRANK, facility manager, architect; b. Chgo., Feb. 2, 1954; s. William Mills and Jean Arlyce (Klimek) W. BArch, U. Ill., Chgo., 1977. Lic. architect, Ill. Designer, job capt. Sargent & Lundy Engrs., Chgo., 1977-79; project mgr. Continental Bank, Chgo., 1980-84; mgr. facilities ops. Kemper Fin. Services, Inc., Chgo., 1984—. Recipient Design Distinction award U. Ill., Chgo., 1977, Ill. State scholarship, 1972; named Eagle Scout Boy Scouts Am., 1969. Mem. Internat. Facility Mgmt. Assn. (sec. Chgo. chpt. 1986—), AIA (mem. corp. architecture commn. 1984—). Club: Sportsclub (Chgo.). Avocations: running, backpacking, theatre, art. Office: Kemper Fin Services Inc 120 S LaSalle St Chicago IL 60603

WETHERBEE, ROBERT SOLON, accountant; b. Marshall, Minn., Aug. 21, 1959; s. James Nelson and Mary Ann (Henry) W.; m. Cynthia Kay Dingman, Aug. 23, 1980; 1 child, Erin Elizabeth. BS in Acctg., Iowa State U., 1981. CPA, Iowa. Fin. trainee Aluminum Co. Am. (ALCOA), Davenport, Iowa, 1981-83; product acct. Aluminum Co. Am. (ALCOA), Davenport, 1983-85, divisional product acct., 1985, plant product acct., 1985-87, product acctg. supr., 1987—; mem. Davenport Alcoans Polit. Action Com., 1983-87. Mem. Am. Inst. CPA's, Jr. Achievement (advisor 1982-83), Triangle Fraternity Corp. Bd. (bd. dirs. 1985-87). Republican. Episcopalian. Avocations: sailing, skiing. Office: ALCOA PO Box 3567 Davenport IA 52808

WETHERINGTON, C. BARRY, lawyer; b. Ft. Lauderdale, Sept. 5, 1940; s. Lawton Levon and F. Josephine (Barlitt) W.; m. Sharon E. Seeman, June 8, 1963; children: Trevor, Christopher, Derek, Jared. BS, USAF Acad., 1963; JD, Columbia, 1973. Bar: N.Y. 1974, Fla. 1974, U.S. Dist. Ct. (ea. and so. dists.) N.Y. 1974, U.S. Ct. Appeals (2d cir.) 1974, Mich. 1976, U.S. Dist. Ct. (ea. dist.) Mich. 1976, U.S. Ct. Appeals (6th cir.) 1982. Commd. 2d lt. USAF, 1963, advanced through grades to capt.; pilot USAF, U.S., Vietnam, Canal Zone, 1963-70; resigned USAF, 1970; assoc. Mendes & Mount, N.Y.C., 1973-76; assoc. Plunkett, Cooney, Rutt, Watters, Stanczyk & Pedersen, Detroit, 1976-82, ptnr., 1982—. Coach, pres. Little League baseball, Beverly Hills, Mich., 1976-82; coach Birmingham (Mich.) Soccer, 1984-85, Our Lady Queen of Martyrs Jr. High Sch., Beverly Hills, 1980. Decorated 4 Air medals. Avocations: chess, soccer, computers. Home: 18921 Saxon Beverly Hills MI 48009 Office: Plunkett Cooney Rutt et al 900 Marquette Bldg Detroit MI 48226

WETHINGTON, NORBERT ANTHONY, college administrator; b. Dayton, Ohio, Sept. 14, 1943; s. Norbert and Sophie Lillian W.; B.A., U. Dayton, 1965; M.A., John Carroll U., 1967; postgrad. Baldwin Wallace Coll., 1968-70; m. Martha M. Vannice, Aug. 13, 1966; children—Paula, Mark, Eric, Kristen, Rebecca, Lisa, Bethany. Grad. asst., teaching asso. John Carroll U., Cleve., 1965-67; English tchr. Padua Franciscan High Sch., Parma, Ohio, 1967-70; instr., chmn. dept. tech. writing and speech N. Central Tech. Coll., Mansfield, Ohio, 1970-74; dir. evening div. Terra Tech. Coll., Fremont, Ohio, 1974-80, dir. public and community service technologies, 1980—; cons. several profl. assns. and non-profit groups. Vice pres. Sandusky County Bd. Health, 1979-80. Recipient Disting. Service award, 1987. Mem. Am. Vocat. Assn., Ohio Vocat. Assn. (pres. tech. edn. div. 1985-86), Nat. Council Tchrs. English. Democrat. Roman Catholic. Contbr. articles to profl. jours. Home: 1036 Hazel St Fremont OH 43420 Office: Terra Tech Coll 1220 Cedar St Fremont OH 43420

WETTERAU, THEODORE C., diversified food wholesaler; b. St. Louis, Nov. 13, 1927; s. Theodore C. and Edna (Ehrlich) W.; m. Helen Elizabeth Killion, Feb. 20, 1954; children: T. Conrad, Mark Stephen, Elizabeth Killion. BA, Westminster Coll., Fulton, Mo., 1952, LLD (hon.), 1977. With Wetterau, Inc., Hazelwood, Mo., 1952—, v.p. mktg., 1960-63, exec. v.p., 1963-70, pres., from 1970, chief exec. officer, 1970—, chmn. bd. dirs., 1974—, also bd. dirs.; bd. dirs. Centerre Bank of St. Louis, Godfrey Co., Waukesha, Wis. Bd. dirs. Mark Twain Inst., Boy Scouts Am., St. Louis Symphony Soc., Operation Rearch (all St. Louis); trustee Westminster Coll.; adv. bd. St. Louis Salvation Army; mem. Pres.'s Council of Community Assn. Schs. for the Arts, St. Louis. Served with U.S. Army, 1946-47, Korea. Named Man of Month, Progressive Grocer mag., 1966, Sales Exec. of Yr., Sales and Mktg. Execs. St. Louis, 1977; recipient Aggus Disting. Pub. Skrvice award, 1980, Nat. Disting. Service award Am. Jewish Com., 1980, Bus. and Profl. award Religious Heritage of Am., 1980. Mem. Nat. Wholesale Grocers Assn. (gov., past chmn. bd.), Ind. Grocers Alliance (past chmn.), Food Mktg. Inst., U.S. C. of C., Knights of Round Table, Knights of the Cauliflower Ear. Clubs: Univ., Old Warson Country, St. Louis. Office: Wetterau Inc 8920 Pershall Rd Hazelwood MO 63042 •

WETZ, GLENN WILLIAM, data processing systems analyst; b. Keokuk, Iowa, Mar. 20, 1953; s. William Waldo and June Louise (Pollack) W.; m. Barbara Ann Berry, Dec. 27, 1978; 1 child, Zachari Layne. BA in Comuter Sci., U. Iowa, 1975, MBA, 1977. Music dir., box office mgr. Old Creamery Theater, Garrison, Iowa, 1978-79; inventory control mgr. Thorac Co., Cedar Rapids, Iowa, 1979-80; programmer, analyst Crown Zellerbach Co., Greensburg, Ind., 1980-84; computer analyst 3M Corp., St. Paul, 1984-86, advanced computer analyst, 1986—. Mem. United Ch. Christ. Avocations: theater, music, jogging. Home: 94 Battle Creek Pl Saint Paul MN 55119 Office: 3M Corp Bldgs 224-3S-02 3M Ctr Saint Paul MN 55144

WEXLER, JERROLD, diversified investments executive; b. 1924. With Russell Electric, Hingham, Mass., 1948-49, Allied Rdio Corp., 1949-50, George S. Lurie Corp., 1951-60; v.p., treas. Milw. Chair Co., 1968-71; chmn. bd. Jupiter Industries Inc., Chgo., 1970—. Office: Jupiter Industries Inc 400 E Randolph St Chicago IL 60601 *

WEXLER, R. MICHAEL, financial manager; b. N.Y.C., Feb. 15, 1947; s. Elmer Wexler and Mae (Hillman) Daub; m. Sherry L. DeWeese, Nov. 28, 1970; children: Kimberley Michelle, Geoffrey Michael. BA in Econs., Muskingum Coll., New Concord, Ohio, 1969; MBA in Fin. and Acctg., U. Hartford, Conn., 1976. CPA, Fla. Sr. acct. Uniroyal, Inc., N.Y.C., 1970-71; supr. fund controls Uniroyal, Inc., Middlebury, Conn., 1971-74; controller, ops. mgr. Uniroyal, Inc., Ft. Lauderdale, Fla., 1974-81; mgr. budgets and forecasts Uniroyal, Inc., Mishawaka, Ind., 1981-82, bus. controller, 1982-86; mgr. govt. acct. Argo-Tech Corp., Cleve., 1986—. Mem. Am. Inst. CPA's, Port Everglades Fgn. Trade Zone User's Assn.(v.p. 1979-80), Aero. Industries Assn., Nat. Indsl. Security Assn. Avocations: tennis, racquetball. Office: Argo-Tech Corp 23555 Euclid Ave Cleveland OH 44117

WEXLER, STEPHEN ALAN, ophthalmologist; b. Flint, Mich., July 30, 1956; s. Max and Reva (Frumkin) W.; m. Michelle Guttenberg, Mar. 3, 1984. BS, U. Mich., 1977, MD, 1982. Diplomate Nat. Bd. Med. Examiners. Intern Henry Ford Hosp., Detroit, 1982-83; residency U. Wis., Madison, 1983-86; staff physician Barnes Hosp., St. Louis, 1986—; instr. clin. ophthalmology Washington U., St. Louis, 1986—. Contbr. articles to profl. jours. Ophthalmology scholar Taylor Lions Club, 1980-81. Mem. AMA, Am. Acad. Ophthalmology, Contact Lens Assn. Opthalmologists, Am. Bd. Ophthalmology, Physicians for Social Responsibility. Democrat. Jewish. Avocations: tennis, jazz guitar, piano. Office: Alvis Kayes Knopf & Wexler 211 N Meramec Saint Louis MO 63105

WEXLER, VERNON ROBERT, building industry executive; b. Mpls., Feb. 14, 1922; m. Lois Joyce Yager, May 5, 1945; children: Robert, Carol, Connie. Various mgmt. pos. Derickson Co., Inc., Mpls., 1946-62, pres., 1962—; Chmn. Minn. Trade Mission, 1963; commr. Minn. Small Bus. Commn., 1982, 83; Minn. SEC rep. Govt. Bus. Forum on Small Bus. Capital Formation, 1986; bd. dirs. Bank of Minn. and Trust Co. Bd. dirs. Sch. Architecture U. Minn. Recipient Disting. Service award Greater Minn. C. of C. and Mpls. Home Builders Assn., Small Bus. Person of Yr. award Greater Mpls. C. of C., 1985, Entrepreneurial award Minn. Bus. Hall Fame. Avocations: tennis, golf, handball, skiing, photography. Office: Derickson Co Inc 1100 Linden Ave Minneapolis MN 55403

WEXNER, LESLIE HERBERT, retail apparel chain executive; b. Dayton, Ohio, 1937. BS, Ohio State U., Columbus, 1959; HHD (hon.), Ohio State U., 1986; LLD (hon.), Hofstra U., 1987; LHD honoris causa, Ohio State U., 1986; DL, Hofstra U., 1987. Founder, pres., chmn. bd. The Limited, Inc., fashion chain, Columbus, 1963—; dir., mem. exec. com. Banc One Corp., Sotheby's Holdings Inc.; mem. bus. adminstrn. adv. council Ohio State U. Bd. dirs. Columbus Urban League, 1982-84, Hebrew Immigrant Aid Soc., N.Y.C., 1982—; trustee Columbus Symphony Orch.; co-chmn. Internat. United Jewish Appeal Com.; nat. vice chmn. United Jewish Appeal; bd. dirs., mem. exec. com. Am. Jewish Joint Distbn. Com., Inc.; trustee Columbus Jewish Fedn., 1972, Capitol South Community Urban Redevel. Corp., Columbus Mus. Art; chmn. Columbus Capital Corp. for Civic Improvement. Named Man of Yr. Am. Mktg. Assn., 1974. Mem. Young Presidents Orgn., Sigma Alpha Mu. Club: B'nai B'rith. Office: The Limited Inc 2 Limited Pkwy Box 16000 Columbus OH 43216

WEYAND, CINDY LOU, economic development corporation administrative assistant; b. Logansport, Ind., Dec. 20, 1957; d. Robert F. and Barbara L. (Kasch) Eisert; m. Erich S. Weyand, Oct. 9, 1981 (div. June 1985). BA in Journalism and English, Valparaiso U., 1980. Editor-in-chief Porter County Herald and The Kouts Times, Hebron and Kouts, Ind., 1980-84; reporter, photographer Vidette-Messenger, Valparaiso, Ind., 1984; copy editor Gary (Ind.) Post-Tribune, 1984; mktg. coordinator Kankakee Valley Job Tng. Corp., LaPorte, Ind., 1985; adminstrv. asst. Valparaiso Econ. Devel. Corp., 1986—; corr. Vidette-Messenger, Valparaiso, 1984-86; pvt. practice pub. relations and mktg. cons., free-lance writer Creative Concepts, Valparaiso, 1985—. Contbr. numerous articles to Ind. newspapers; author, designer, editor corp. newsletters, brochures, billboards, other publs. Mem. Valparaiso Community Theatre Guild, 1985—, NW Ind. Fed. Mktg. Task Force, 1986—, NW Ind. Area Devel. Com., 1986, Ind. State Farm Bur., 1986—. Mem. Valparaiso C. of C. Republican. Lutheran. Home and Office: 2455 Marshall Dr Valparaiso IN 46383 also: Valparaiso Econ Devel Corp 601 E Lincolnway Valparaiso IN 46383

WEYHENMEYER, JAMES ALAN, neuroscientist; b. Hazleton, Pa., Feb. 12, 1951; s. Charles Howard and Gertrude Emma (Ritter) W.; m. Janis Ann Vanthournout, Dec. 29, 1973; 1 child, James A. BA, Knox Coll., 1973; PhD, Ind. U., 1977; postdoctoral, U. Iowa, 1979. Postdoctoral fellow U. Iowa, Iowa City, 1977-79; assoc. prof. U. Ill., Urbana, 1979—, coordinator med. neurosci., 1985—. Author: Monograph Neural Sci., 1984; contbr. articles to profl. jours. Research grantee NSF, Am. Heart Assn. Fellow Pharmaceutical Mfg. Assn.; mem. Soc. for Neurosci., Am. Chem. Soc., AAAS. Home: 2406 Provine Circle Urbana IL 61801 Office: U Ill Coll Medicine 506 S Mathews Urbana IL 61801

WEYMON, ELLA LAMPKIN, accountant, computer consultant; b. Auburn, Ala., Oct. 30, 1949; d. David Lee Lampkin and Nellie Beatrice (Donner) Combs; m. Willis Marshall, Dec. 23, 1972; children: Tara Michele, Trina Denise. BS, Purdue U., 1972; MBA, Eastern Mich. U., 1981. Acct. Gen. Motors, Flint, Mich., 1972-77; instr. Baker Coll., Flint, 1978-80; cost acct. Hart and Cooley Mfg., Holland, Mich., 1980-82; cost analyst Westinghouse, Grand Rapids, Mich., 1981-82; pres. Weymon and Assocs., Inc., Holland, 1982—. Mem. Nat. Soc. Pub. Accts., Nat. Soc. Tax Profls., Ind. Accts. Assn. of Mich. Home: 2344 Sunset Bluff Dr Holland MI 49424 Office: Weymon & Assocs Inc 285 James St Suite D PO Box 8245 Holland MI 49422

WEYMOUTH, DANIEL GEORGE, small business owner; b. Chgo., Feb. 19, 1938; s. Robert George Weymouth and Ethel Mae (Mathison) Anderson; m. Ann Mary Henke, Oct. 15, 1966 (div. Aug. 1981); children: Julia Ann, Daniel George Jr. Salesman Sabin Robbins Paper, Chgo., 1958-60; dist. mgr. Roosevelt Paper Co., Chgo., 1960-67; sales mgr. Case Paper Co., Chgo., 1967-70; nat. account exec. Imperial Printing Co., Des Plaines, Ill., 1970-76; pres. TechWeb, Inc., Wheeling, Ill., 1976—. Served with U.S. Army, 1955-58. Republican. Clubs: Bob-o-link Golf (Highland Park, Ill.); East Bank (Chgo.). Avocations: golf, running, squash, tennis, sailing. Home: 5434 RFD Long Grove IL 60047 Office: TechWeb Inc 301 Alice St Wheeling IL 60090

WEYRAUCH, HERBERT EMIL, management consultant; b. Waverly, Iowa, Jan. 10, 1919; s. Emil Maximilian and Esther Emma (Guetzlaff) W.; m. Anne Burroughs Beebe, Apr. 9, 1942; children: Arthur H., Theodore H., Walter E., Carol Anne, Gerald B. BEE, U.S. Naval Acad., 1941; MEE, U.S. Naval Postgrad. Sch., 1947. Midshipman USN, 1937, commd. ensign, 1941, advanced through grades to comdr., 1951, resigned, 1954; chief field engr. Dahlberg Inc., Mpls., 1954-55; mgr. contract sales Maico Electronics Inc., Mpls., 1955-60; corp sec., div. mgr. Flotronics Inc., Mpls., 1960-63; pres. Am. Monarch Corp., Mpls., 1963-65; pvt. practice mgmt. cons. Mpls., 1965—. Mem. adv. bd., dist. commr. Boy Scouts Am., Mpls., 1958-62, pres. dir. Nokomis Council, 1978-79; mem. Mpls. Citizens Com. on Pub. Edn., Citizens League, Mpls; chmn. com. Mpls. Aquatennial, 1960. Mem. IEEE, Engrs. Club Mpls. (pres. 1983-84, Engr. of Yr. 1986), Council Ind. Profl. Cons. (pres. 1982-83). Club: Greenway Athletic. Avocations: swimming, hiking, camping, fishing, travelling. Home and Office: One Ten Grant Suite 10-B Minneapolis MN 55403

WHALEN, BRIAN B., manufacturing company executive; b. Chgo., Oct. 7, 1939; s. Donald James and Mary (Ennis) W.; m. Sheila Ann Nolan, June 9, 1967. B.S. in Social Sci., Loyola U., Chgo., 1962. Mem. staff Sen. Everett Dirksen, 1961-62; adminstrv. asst. to Sheriff Cook County, Chgo., 1963-66, to pres. Cook County Bd., 1967-68; exec. asst. to Gov. Ill., Springfield, 1969-73; dir. pub. affairs Internat. Harvester, Chgo., 1973-83, staff v.p. pub. affairs, 1983—. Chmn. Ill. Youth for Goldwater, 1964; campaign mgr. Ogilvie for Cook County Bd. Pres., 1966; deacon Chgo. United, 1979—; bd. dirs. TRUST, Inc., 1981-84; mem. adv. council Local Initiatives Support Corp., 1982—; mem. Midwest panel Pres.'s Commn. on White House Fellows, 1982-87, Ill. Gov.'s Transition Team, 1986, Ill. Gov.'s Med. Malpractice Task Force, 1984—. Mem. Associated Employers Ill. (chmn. 1984). Office: Navistar Internat 401 N Michigan Ave Chicago IL 60611

WHALEY, THOMAS PATRICK, chemical research executive, consultant; b. Atchison, Kans., Jan. 13, 1923; s. George A. and Anna Theresa (Mueller) W.; m. Betty Maxine McLaughlin, Apr. 22, 1946 (dec. 1968); children—Laura Kathleen, Michael Patrick; m. Jane Esther Wilkinson, Apr. 12, 1969; stepchildren—Charles, Conrad, Christopher, Donna Jane Pioli. B.S. in Chemistry, St. Benedict's Coll., 1943; Ph.D. in Chemistry, U. Kans., 1950. Sr. research assoc. Ethyl Corp., Detroit and Baton Rouge, 1950-62; mgr. inorganic and phys. chemistry Internat. Minerals and Chem. Corp., Libertyville, Ill., 1962-69, dir. analytical and tech. services, 1969-74; tech. dir. Sipi Metals Corp., Chgo., 1974-76; assoc. dir. solar energy Inst. Gas Tech., Chgo., 1976-81, sr. advisor, 1981—; pres. Consanal Corp., Ltd., Deerfield, Ill., 1974—. Co-author 8 tech. books and encys.; editor Chem. Bulletin, 1977-81; contbr. articles to profl. jours.; patentee. Chmn. dist. advancement Northwest Suburban council Boy Scouts Am., 1963-66; chmn. plan commn. Village Govt., Deerfield, 1973-80, chmn. energy council, 1981-83, chmn. Village Ctr. Devel. Commn., 1975—. Served to capt. USAAF, 1943-46. Recipient Key Scouter award Boy Scouts Am., 1967. Mem. Am. Chem. Soc. (dir. Chgo. sect. 1980—, chmn. 1983-84, abstractor 1966—), AAAS, Sigma Xi, Alpha Chi Sigma, Phi Lambda Upsilon. Republican. Roman Catholic. Club: Lions (bd. dirs. Baton Rouge 1962). Avocations: golf; tennis; skiing; piano; civic affairs; bridge. Home: 912 Westcliff Ln Deerfield IL 60015 Office: Inst Gas Tech 3424 S State St Chicago IL 60616

WHALLEY, RICHARD EARL, furniture manufacturing executive; b. Kalamazoo, Mich., Aug. 16, 1934; s. Vincent Luke and Ruth (Jacobsen) W.; m. Dorothy Tiffany, Aug. 29, 1959; children: Scott, Sharon. BS, Ind. U., 1955. Asst. buyer Rike-Kumler Co., Dayton, Ohio, 1955-57; buyer furniture div. Montgomery Ward & Co., Chgo., 1959-63; div. mdse. mgr. Kroehler Mfg. Co., Naperville, Ill., 1964-69, div. v.p., 1969-70; pres. parent co. Shannon Chair Co., Cleveland, Tenn., 1974—; bd. dirs. Cleve. Chair Co., Jackson Mfg. Co. Served with AUS, 1957-59. Mem. Nat. Wholesale Furniture Assn. Republican. Presbyterian. Club: Met. (Chgo.). Home: 225 E Onwentsia Rd Lake Forest IL 60045 Office: Shannon Chair Co PO Box 220 1448 Old Skokie Rd Highland Park IL 60035

WHARTON, KENNETH EUGENE, manufacturing engineer; b. Hannibal, Mo., Sept. 13, 1943; s. William Robert and Mary Margaret (Gardhouse) W.; m. Floyce Jean Dooley, Feb. 15, 1964; children: Jeanne Beth, Kenneth Eugene II. BS in Math., Quincy Coll., 1968. Work measurement analyst Motorola, Inc., Quincy, Ill., 1968-76; quality control technician Diemakers, Inc., Monroe City, Mo., 1976-79; advanced mfg. engr. Gardner-Denver Co., Quincy, 1979-85; mgr. mfg. engring. Speedrack, Inc., Quincy, 1985—. Mem. Soc. Mfg. Engrs. (sr.). Methodist. Home: 1008 S Spring St Palmyra MO 63461 Office: Speedrack Inc 1701 N 16th Quincy IL 62301

WHEAT, ALAN DUPREE, congressman, economist; b. San Antonio, Oct. 16, 1951; s. James Weldon and Emogene W. B.A., Grinnell Coll., 1972. Economist HUD, Kansas City, Mo., 1972-73, Mid.-Am. Regional Council, Kansas City, 1973-75; aide County Exec.'s Office, Kansas City, 1975-76; mem. Mo. Ho. of Reps., Jefferson City, 1977-82; mem. 98th Congress from 5th No. Dist., Washington, 1983—, mem. rules com., select com. on children, youth and families, 1983—; Dem. whip 100th Congress, Washington, 1987—, mem. exec. com. Dem. study group, congl. caucus for women's issue's, environ. and energy study conf., fed. govt. service task force, congl. human rights caucus; vice chmn. congl. balck caucus, 1987—. Named Best Freshman Legislator St. Louisan Mag., 1977-78; 1 of 10 Best Legislators Jefferson City News Tribune, 1979-80; 1 of 10 Best Legislators Mo. Times Newspaper, 1979-80. Mem. NAACP, Democratic Study Group (exec. com.), Dem. Caucus Com. on Party Effectiveness, Congl. Woman's Caucus, Environ. and Energy Study Conf., Dem. New Member Caucus (v.p.). Office: US House of Reps 1204 Longworth Washington DC 20515

WHEAT, CHRISTOPHER JOHN, SR., broadcast executive; b. Boston, Dec. 22, 1950; s. Robert Haase Wheat and Florence Edith (Potter) Wiley; m. Becky Ann Renshaw, June 3, 1972; children: Christopher John Jr., Colan Michael. BE, U. Cin., 1972; postgrad., U. Pa., 1978. Account exec. Sta. WKRQ-FM, Cin., 1972-76; account exec. Sta. WKRC-AM, Cin., 1976-78, local sales mgr., 1978-80, gen. sales mgr., 1980-82; v.p., gen. mgr. Sta. WYNF-FM, Tampa, Fla., 1982-83, Sta. WFBQ-FM, Indpls., 1983—. Named one of Outstanding Young Men of Am., 1982. Mem. Radio Broadcasters of Indpls., U. Cin. Alumni Club, Beta Theta Pi Alumni Club, Indpls. C. of C. (ptnrs. in edn. com., Ambassadors sect.). Republican. Methodist. Club: Indpls. Athletic. Avocation: racquetball. Home: 10809 Courageous Dr Indianapolis IN 46236 Office: Sta WFBQ-FM 6161 Fall Creek Rd Indianapolis IN 46220

WHEATLEY, GREGORY LEE, engineer; b. Casper, Wyo., Feb. 14, 1962; s. Stanley Harold and Mildren Jean (George) W.; m. Therese Marie Burback, Dec. 28, 1984. BS in Chem. Engring., S.D. Sch. of Mines and Tech., 1984. Process engr. Hutchinson (Minn.) Tech. Inc., 1984-85, mfg. engr., 1986—. Republican. Presbyterian. Avocations: hunting, fishing, athletics. Home: 235 Echo Circle #316 Hutchinson MN 55350 Office: Hutchinson Tech Inc 40 W Highland Park Hutchinson MN 55350

WHEELER, BARBARA MONICA, lawyer; b. Chgo., Mar. 20, 1947; d. John Benjamin and Elizabeth (Keife) Wheeler. BA, St. Dominic Coll., 1969; cert. Lewis U. Sch. Paraprofl. Studies, 1976; JD, DePaul U., 1980. Bar: Ill. 1980. Gen. supt. Md. Manor Devel. Co., Chgo., 1970-74; v.p. Omega Constrn. Co., Chgo., 1974-78; asst. state's atty. Cook County, Ill. Mem. Bd. Edn., Community High Sch. Dist. 99, DuPage County, 1974-76, pres., 1976—; mem. Ill. Assn. Sch. Bds., dir.-at-large Tri County div., 1976-77, dir. DuPage div., 1977-78, state dir., 1982-85, v.p., 1985-87, mem. exec. com., 1984-87; bd. dirs. Sch. Mgmt. Found. Ill., 1983; mem. task force on purposes of edn. in eighties Nat. Sch. Bds. Assn. Mem. ABA, Ill. Bar Assn., Chgo. Bar Assn., Am. Mgmt. Assn., Phi Alpha Delta. Roman Catholic. Office: 6301 S Cass Ave Suite 300 Westmont IL 60559

WHEELER, CAROL ESTELLE, educational administrator; b. Mobile, Ala., Sept. 9, 1936; d. Frederick G. and A. Estelle (Ryan) W. AB, Maryville Coll., St. Louis, 1958; MA in Philosophy, Georgetown U., 1971; MA in Edn., U. Chgo., 1976. Joined Sisters of Mercy, Roman Cath. Ch., 1959. Tchr. Mercy High Sch., Balt., 1961-68, asst. prin., 1971-72, advisor to beginning tchrs., 1976-77, pres., prin., 1977—; tchr. Bishop Toolen High Sch., Mobile, 1968-69; supr. student tchrs. U. Chgo., 1974-75, adminstrv. asst. MST program, 1975-76; mem. profl. standards and tchr. edn. adv. bd. Md. Dept. Edn., 1984-86. Trustee Loyola Coll., Balt., 1982—, Mercy Hosp., Balt., 1985—, Cathedral Found. Bd., Archdiocese Balt., 1983—; del. provincial chpt. Sisters of Mercy, Balt., gen. chpt. Sisters of Mercy of the Union. Mem. Mercy Secondary Edn. Assn. (pres. 1983-87), Assocs. Research in Pvt. Edn., Assn. Supervision and Curriculum Devel., Nat. Assn. Secondary Sch. Prins., Nat. Cath. Edn. Assn.

WHEELER, CLARENCE, educational administrator; b. St. Petersburg, Fla., Oct. 17, 1939; s. Mack and Eliza (Crockett) W.; B.A., Morehouse Coll., 1962; M.Ed., DePaul U., 1970; m. Lillie M. Edwards, June 8, 1963; children—Clarence, Andrea Michelle. Recreation therapist children's ward Chgo. State Hosp., 1963-64; tchr. Chgo. Bd. Edn., 1964-72, asst. prin., 1972-86; bd. dirs. DARE Disabled Residential Enterprises. Counselor, YMCA, 1968—, Boys Club, 1964; coach Little League; v.p. Wabash-104th St Block Club, 1972-74; treas. Leisure Time Council, 1979-80. Recipient Coach Forbes award Morehouse Coll. Mem. DePaul U. Alumni Assn., Morehouse Coll. Alumni Assn., Nat. Muliple Sclerosis Soc., Nat. Middle Sch. Assn., Phi Delta Kappa. Club: Chgo. Morehouse Alumni. Episcopalian.

WHEELER, DAVID MICHAEL, landscape architect; b. Rome, N.Y., Apr. 2, 1953; s. Hubert F. and H. Margaret (Crane) W.; m. Patricia Davidson Roland, Sept. 12, 1981; 1 child, Daniel. BS, SUNY, Syracuse, 1976, B in Landscape Architect, 1977. Registered landscape architect, N.Y. Mem. profl. staff Landplan Partnership, Southport, Conn., 1977-78; job capt. Saratoga Assocs., Saratoga Springs, N.Y., 1978-79; project mgr. LA Partnership, Saratoga Springs, 1979-80; prin. David Wheeler, L.A., Peoria, Ill., 1980—; devel. coordinator Peoria (Ill.) Park Dist., 1981—. Committeeman Greenway Com., Peoria, 1986—; project mgr. planning and design 1980 Winter Olympics, Lake Placid, N.Y., 1980; project mgr. landscape design Southside Manor, 1985; project adminstr. River Front Park Design, Peoria, 1987—. Recipient Critics Council award, Ill. Garden Clubs, 1983, Orchid award, Southside Manor, 1985. Mem. Am. Soc. Landscape Architects, Am. Planning Assn., Peoria C. of C. (leadership sch.). Methodist. Home: 2318 W Sherman Ave Peoria IL 61604 Office: Peoria Park Dist 2218 N Prospect Rd Peoria IL 61603

WHEELER, JAMES RUSSELL, product executive; b. Sidney, Ohio, Oct. 15, 1949; s. Donald William and Joan (Dormire) W.; m. Mary Kathryn Semler, Sept. 16, 1972; children: Jay Christopher, Andrew John. BA, Ohio No. U., 1972. Service expediter Hobart Bros. Co., Troy, Ohio, 1973-79, nat. service mgr., 1979-85, product mgr., 1985—. Pres. Troy Jr. Baseball Bd. dirs., 1986-87. Mem. Troy Jr. Bus. Bd. (pres. 1986-87), Troy C. of C. Democrat. Mem. Soc. of Friends. Lodge: Optimists (pres. 1976, lt. gov. 1977). Home: 1236 Northbrook Ln Troy OH 45373 Office: Hobart Bros Co 600 W Main St Troy OH 45373

WHEELER, JENNIFER HOPKINS, advertising executive; b. Iwakuni, Japan, Sept. 27, 1961; d. George E. and Elaine B. (Bridges) Hopkins; m. Paul R. Wheeler, May 10, 1986. BS, U. Ill., 1983. Advt. sales rep. Lerner Newspapers, Skokie, Ill., 1983-85; account exec. Alexander Communications, Chgo., 1985—. Mem. Chgo. Advt. Club (fund raising com. 1983). Democrat. Methodist. Avocations: decorating, rehabbing, sports. Office: Alexander Communications Inc 212 W Superior St Suite 400 Chicago IL 60610

WHEELER, JOHN ALLEN, educator; b. Humansville, Mo., Aug. 14, 1950; s. James Allen and Lois N. (Jones) W.; m. Gloria Joanna Pierson, June 15, 1974; children: Adam, Andrew, Aaron. BS, Southwest Bapt. U., 1972; MS, Pittsburg State U., Kans., 1977; EdS, Southwest Mo. State U., 1983. Cert. sch. supt., Mo. Tchr. Cabool (Mo.) High Sch., 1972-74, Sarcoxie (Mo.) High Sch., 1974-77, Bolivar (Mo.) High Sch., 1977-80, Springfield (Mo.) Pub. Schs., 1980-83; prof., chmn. dept. edn. Southwest Bapt. U., Bolivar, 1983-86, dir. tchr. edn., 1986—. Deacon First Bapt. Ch., Bolivar, 1986. Mem. Mo. Assn. Tchr. Educators. Home: Rt 2 Box 294 Bolivar MO 65613

WHEELER, OTIS V., JR., public school principal; b. Silex, Mo., Oct. 1, 1925; s. Otis V. and Pearla F. (Howell) W.; m. Virginia Rogers, June 7, 1947; children: Jan Leigh, Mark Patrick. BBA, U. Mo., 1948, MEd, 1965, EdD, 1971. Bus. mgr. USN, 1952-61; sci. tchr. Columbia (Mo.) Pub. Schs., 1961-63, principal, 1963—; supt. Boone County Sch. Dist., Mo., 1971; instr. U. Mo., Columbia, 1970-72, asst. prof. 1972-75, 78-79; cons. Midwest Ctr for Equal Ednl. Opportunities, 1972-75. Served to lt. USNR, 1943-85, Korea. Mem. Nat. Assn. Elem. Sch. Prins. (U.S. Dept. Edn., Nat. Disting. Prin. award 1985, Excellence in Edn. award 1986), Mo. Assn. Elem. Sch. Prins. (Disting. Service award 1984, editor jours. 1967—), Mo. State Tchrs. Assn., Retired Officers Assn., U. Mo. Columbia Coll. Edn. Alumni (Citation of Merit award 1987), Phi Delta Kappa, Phi Delta Theta, Kappa Delta Pi. Methodist. Club: Lake Ozark Yachting Assn. (Mo.). Avocations: boating, dancing, travel, scuba diving. Home: 916 West Ash St Columbia MO 65203 Office: Ridgeway IGE Sch 107 E Sexton Rd Columbia MO 65203

WHEELER, PATRICIA WELLMAN, law librarian; b. Irvine, Ky., Aug. 21, 1943; s. Linville Columbus and Ogal (Meek) Wellman; m. Erlan E. Wheeler, July 2, 1965; children: Erlan E. II, Michelle Lynn. BA in History and Polit. Sci., Eastern Ky. U., 1965. Tchr. Butler County Schs., Hamilton, Ohio, 1966-67; tchr. substitute Marietta (Ohio) City Schs., 1979-83; law librarian Washington County Law Library, Marietta, 1983—. Co-chmn. Campus Marietta Girl Scouts U.S., Marietta, 1982, trainer, 1982-86. Mem. Ohio Regional Assn. Law Librarians (chmn. com. 1986—, com. mem. 1986—). Republican. Presbyterian. Club: Hill and Dale Garden (Marietta) (pres. 1983-85). Avocations: handcrafts, travel. Home: 110 Seneca Dr Marietta OH 45750 Office: Washington County Law Library County Courthouse Marietta OH 45750

WHEELER, PAUL LEONARD, transportation executive; b. Ashland, Ky., Apr. 23, 1926; s. Ora Y. and Norma L. (Murry) W.; m. Alice Kathryn Ritchie, June 8, 1947; children: Paul Allison, David Ritchie. Student, U. Ky. Designer Refinery Engring. Co., 1943; asst. signalman C&O Rwy. Co., 1944-46; various positions leading to signal engr. C&O/B&O R.R., 1948-73; various mgmt. positions leading to pres. and chief exec. officer Safetran Systems Corp., Mpls., 1973—, also bd. dirs. Served to 2d lt. U.S. Army, 1944-46. Mem. Assn. Am. R.R.'s (communication and signals sect.), Rwy. Progress Inst. (bd. govs.). Republican. Baptist. Office: Safetran Systems Corp 4650 Main St NE Minneapolis MN 55416

WHEELER, RONALD ALLAN, optometrist; b. Conneaut, Ohio, Sept. 25, 1957; s. Howard Payne and Esther Mary (Molzon) W.; m. Corinne Dee Button, June 21, 1980; children: Brian Allan, Kevin Michael. BS, Harding U., 1979; OD, Ohio State U., 1983. Pvt. practice optometry North Kingsville, Ohio, 1983—. Mem. Am. Optometric Assn., Ohio Optometric Assn. Republican. Mem. Ch. of Christ. Home: 3256 Forest Dr Conneaut OH 44030 Office: 6427 S Main St PO Box 509 North Kingsville OH 44068

WHEELER, STEVEN MITCHELL, graphic arts executive, insurance salesman; b. Kokomo, Ind., Dec. 6, 1944; s. Stanley Wayne and Mabel Lucille (Gano) W.; m. Pamela Sue Rubow, Sept. 4, 1965; 1 child, Mitchell Wayne. Grad. high sch., Kokomo. Various mgmt. positions Cuneo Press of Ind., Kokomo, 1963-78; plant mgr. Sun Chem. Corp., Kokomo, 1978; tech. sales/service person Ridgeway (Pa.) Color Co., 1978-83; plant mgr. Rexart Ink Corp., Kokomo, 1983-84; dept. mgr. Chem. Process and Supply, Dunkirk, N.Y., 1984-86; life. ins. salesperson Am. Gen. Life and Accident, Kokomo, 1986—. Mem. Life Underwriters Club. Democrat. Club: Cin. Ink Makers. Clubs: 1st Ward Falcon (N.Y.), Dunkirk (N.Y.) Monizucko. Lodge: Eagles. Home: 917 Cornell Rd E Kokomo IN 46901

WHEELOCK, ROBERT DEAN, priest, director; b. Cherokee, Iowa, Sept. 27, 1936; s. Leslie Cyril and Cecilia Mary (Meyers) W. AB, St. Mary Sem., 1960; MA, St. Anthony Sem., 1965; D in Ministry, Aguinas Inst. Theol., 1976; MS in Edn., U. Wis., Oshkosh, 1987. Chaplain Archdiocese of Detroit, 1966-69, St. Mary Hosp., Marquette, Mich., 1969-71; dir. pastoral care services Cath. Hosp. Assn. USA, St. Louis, 1971-77; asst. prof. medicine and religion St. Louis U., 1977-79; dir. counseling St. Lawrence Sem., Mt. Calvary, Wis., 1981—. Author/editor 5 books; contbr. articles to profl. jours. Mem. com. rehab. Am. Cancer Soc., N.Y.C., 1975-79; moderator Pax Christi of St. Lawrence, Mt. Calvary, 1986—, Right to Life Club, Mt. Calvary, 1986—. Mem. Am. Assn. Counseling and Devel., Educators for Socail Responsibility, nat. Assn. Cath. Chaplains (pres. 1978-79, Prestigious award 1978), Kappa Delta Pi. Lodge: Kiwanis. Avocations: photography, classical music. Home and Office: St Lawrence Sem 301 Church St Mount Calvary WI 53057-0500

WHELAN, DONALD JOSEPH, fundraising executive; b. Omaha, Nov. 8, 1934; s. Edward Charles and Mary Margaret (Weppner) W.; m. Patricia Jean McCabe, Oct. 1, 1960; children—Donald Joseph, Jr., Timothy, Michael, Mary, Kathryn, Theresa, Joseph. B.S. in Journalism, Creighton U., 1957; L.H.D., Duchesne Coll., 1968. Dir. devel. Duchesne Coll. and Acad., Omaha, 1965-68, John Burroughs Sch., St. Louis, 1968—; cons. The Latin Sch. of Chgo., 1986—, others; workshop leader. Author, editor: Handbook for Development Officers at Independent Schools, 1979, 2d edit., 1982. Pres. sch. bd. St. Joseph Cath. Ch., Manchester, Mo., 1970-71; pres. parish council St. Clare Cath. Ch., Mo., 1973-75; bd. dirs. Campbell House Found., 1987. Served to 1st lt., U.S. Army, 1957-59. Mem. Council Advancement and Support of Edn. (nat. chmn. ind. sch. sect. 1978-81, trustee 1978-81; recipient Steel award 1974, 83, Exceptional Achievement award 1980, Disting. Service award 1980, Robert Bell Crow award 1982). Republican. Lodge: Rotary. Home: 907 Clayworth Dr Manchester MO 63011 Office: John Burroughs Sch 755 S Price Rd Saint Louis MO 63124

WHELAN, FRANCIS DANIEL, II, mortgage banking company executive; b. Grand Rapids, Mich., July 20, 1938; s. Francis Daniel and Margaret Mary (Federspill) W.; m. Jane Isabelle Erhart, Mar. 3, 1962 (dec. Oct. 1986); children: Amy Marie, Patricia Ann, Francis Daniel III. BS in Indsl. Engring., U. Mich., 1960, MBA, 1961. V.p. Citibank, San Juan, P.R., 1976-79; sr. v.p. Citibank Homeowners Services Inc., St. Louis, 1980-86, pres., 1986-87; pres. western div. Travelers Mortgage Services, St. Louis, 1987—. Bd. dirs. Life Crisis Services Inc., St. Louis, 1982—, St. Louis Repertory Theatre, 1985—, Mo. Higher Edn. Loan Authority, St. Louis, 1985—, West County YMCA, St. Louis, 1986—. Mem. Mortgage Bankers Assn. (nat. internal mgmt. com. 1981—, bd. govs. 1985—). Republican. Roman Catholic. Avocations: racquetball, sailing. Home: 15965 Sewell Ct Chesterfield MO 63017 Office: Travelers Mortgage Services 16301 Fontaine Rd Suite 200 Chesterfield MO 63017

WHELAN, JOSEPH L., neurologist; b. Chisholm, Minn., Aug. 13, 1917; s. James Gorman and Johanna (Quilty) W.; m. Gloria Ann Rewoldt, June 12, 1948; children: Joe, Jennifer Whelan Connolly. Student, Hibbing Jr. Coll., 1935-38; BS, U. Minn., 1940, MB, 1942, MD, 1943. Diplomate Am. Bd. Psychiatry and Neurology. Intern Detroit Receiving Hosp., 1942-43; fellow neurology U. Pa. Hosp., Phila., 1946-47; resident neurology U. Minn. Hosps., Mpls., 1947-49; chief neurology service VA Hosp., Mpls., 1949; spl. fellow electroencephalography Mayo Clinic, Rochester, Minn., 1951; practice medicine specializing in neurology Detroit, 1949-73, Petoskey and Gaylord, Mich., 1973—; asst. prof. Wayne State U., 1957-63; chief neurology services Grace Hosp., St. John's Hosp., Bon Secour Hosp., Detroit; cons. neurologist No. Mich. Hosps., Charlevoix Area Hosp., Community Meml. Hosp., Cheboygan, Ostego Meml. hosp., Gaylord; instr. U. Minn. Med. Sch., 1949; cons. USPHS, Detroit Bd. Edn. Contbr. articles to profl. jours. Founder, mem. ad hoc Com. to Force Lawyers Out of Govt.; chmn. Reagan-Bush Campaign, Kalkaska County, Mich., 1980. Served to capt. AUS, 1943-46. Fellow Am. Acad. Neurology (treas. 1955-57), Am. Electroencephalography Soc.; mem. Assn. Research Nervous and Mental Diseases, Soc. Clin. Neurologists, Mich. Neurol. Assn. (sec.-treas. 1967-76), AMA. Mich. Med. Assn., No. Mich. Med. Soc., AAAS, N.Y. Acad. Sci. Republican. Roman Catholic. Club: Grosse Pointe (Mich.). Home: Oxbow 9797 N Twin Lake Rd NE Mancelona MI 49659

WHELCHEL, CHARLES JOSEPH, research engineer; b. St. Charles, Ill., Aug. 2, 1947; s. Joseph Jasper and Helen Francis (Byrne) W.; m. Debra Ann Kassner, Aug. 11, 1976; 1 child, Brook Hunter Kassner. Student, U. Ill., 1965-66, 72-75, Parkland Coll., 1972-79. Research asst. U. Ill. Coordinated Sci. Lab., Urbana, 1972-73; application engr. Lafayette Radio, Urbana, 1973-79; research engr. Lucitron Inc., Northbrook, Ill., 1979-84; project engr. Cherry Elec. Products, Waukegan, Ill., 1984-85, sales engr., 1985—. Inventor flat display panel. Served as staff sgt. USAF, 1967-71. Home: 1564 Cove Dr Prospect Heights IL 60070 Office: Cherry Elec Products 3600 Sunset Ave Waukegan IL 60087

WHETSTONE, MAYNARD LEE, osteopath; b. Seiling, Okla., Oct. 9, 1916; s. James Earl and Bertha May (Steel) W.; m. Eupha Jane smith, Oct. 6, 1940; children: Patricia Jane, Charles robert, Michael Maynard, Jeffrey Aaron. DO, U. Health Sci., Kansas City, Mo., 1941. Diplomate Am. Osteo. Bd. Gen. Practice. Gen. practice osteo. medicine Independence, Mo.; intern in surgery Northeast Hosp., Kansas City, Mo., 1946-47; pres. staff U. Hosp., Kansas City, Park Lane Hosp., Kansas City, Hosp. Med. Ctr. of Independence, Mo. Mem. Am. Coll. Gen. Practitioners Osteo. Medicine and Surgery (life, Gen. Practicioners of Yr. award 1985), Mo. Soc. Gen. Practitioners (life), Jackson county Osteo. Assn. (life), Am. Coll. Osteo. Obstetricians and Gynecologists (life). Avocations: antique and classic automobiles. Home: 2909 Trenchard Independence MO 64057 Office: 1811 Harvard Independence MO 64052

WHIPPS, EDWARD FRANKLIN, lawyer; b. Columbus, Ohio, Dec. 17, 1936; s. Rusk Henry and Agnes Lucille (Green) W.; children: Edward Scott, Rusk Huot, Sylvia Louise, Rudyard Christian. B.A., Ohio Wesleyan U., 1958; J.D., Ohio State U., 1961. Bar: Ohio 1961, U.S. Dist. Ct. (so. dist.) Ohio 1962, U.S. Dist. Ct. (no. dist.) Ohio 1964, U.S. Ct. Claims 1963, U.S. Supreme Ct. 1963, Miss. 1965, U.S. Ct. Appeals (6th cir.) 1980. Assoc. George, Greek, King & McMahon, Columbus, 1961-66; ptnr. George, Greek, King, McMahon & McConnaughey, Columbus, 1966-79, McConnaughey, Stradley, Mone & Moul, Columbus, 1979-81, Thompson, Hine & Flory, Columbus, 1981—. Host: TV programs Upper Arlington Plain Talk, 1979-82; TV program Briding Disability, 1981-82, Lawyers on Call, 1982—, U.A. Today, 1982-86, The Ohio Wesleyan Experience, 1984—. Mem. Upper Arlington (Ohio) Bd. Edn., 1971-80, pres., 1978-79; mem. bd. alumni dirs. Ohio Wesleyan U., 1975-79. Mem. Columbus Bar Assn., Ohio State Bar Assn., ABA, Assn. Trial Lawyers Am., Ohio Acad. Trial Lawyers, Franklin County Trial Lawyers Assn., Am. Judicature Soc., Columbus Bar Found., Columbus C. of C., Upper Arlington Area C. of C. (trustee 1978—), Creative Living Inc. (founder, trustee 1969—), Delta Tau Delta (nat. v.p. 1976-78). Republican. Clubs: Lawyers, Barristers, Columbus Athletic, Columbus Touchdown, Ohio State U. Faculty (Columbus). Home: 3771 Lyon Dr Columbus OH 43220 Office: Thompson Hine & Flory 100 E Broad St Suite 1700 Columbus OH 43215

WHITAKER, ANTHONY JOSEPH, hotel owner; b. Toledo, Iowa, Apr. 27, 1916; s. Jon Baker and Stacie Rose (Kobliska) W.; m. Ruth Marie Allen, Oct. 1948; 1 child, Stacie Rose. BA, BS, Northwest Mo. U., 1947, 49; MS, Drake U., 1951; postgrad., Nebr. U., 1961. Cert. high sch. tchr., Iowa. Prin., tchr. Taylor County Sch., Bedford, Iowa, 1947-51; supt., tchr. Pickering (Mo.) Ind. Sch., 1951-54; county supt. of schs. Southwest County Sch. Bds., Iowa, 1954-75; owner, operator Hotel Garland, Bedford, 1975—; sec./treas. Iowa State Edn. Assn., Bedford, 1954-65, Schoolmasters Club, Bedford and Corning, Iowa, 1954-62; sec. Area 14 Supts. Group, Creston, Iowa, 1965-75. City tennis champion, Bedford, 1938-48, 50-63, 65-66; Served to sgt. inf., U.S. Army, 1941-45. Decorated Bronze Star. Mem. Am. Legion, DAV, VFW (quartermaster 1946-84), Classic Car Club Am., U.S. Sports Writers Orgn. (author). Roman Catholic. Garland Hotel named Fed. and State Landmark, Iowa History Bd., 1977. Home and Office: Hotel Garland 306 Main St Bedford IA 50833

WHITAKER, CARL ALANSON, psychiatrist; b. Norfolk, N.Y., Feb. 20, 1912; s. Calvin Alanson and Grace (Barnett) W.; m. Muriel VanderVeer Schram, Sept. 11, 1937; children: Nancy, Elaine, Bruce, Anita, Lynn Holly. MD, Syracuse (N.Y.) U., 1936, MA, 1941. Resident in ob-gyn N.Y. Hosp., N.Y.C., 1936-38; resident in psychiatry N.Y. Hosp., Syracuse, 1938-40; fellow U. Louisville, 1940-44; chmn. dept. psychiatry Emory U., Atlanta, 1946-55; prof. psychiatry U. Wis. Med. Coll., Madison, 1965-82; practice medicine specializing in psychiatry Madison, 1965—; cons. VA Hosp., Atlanta, 1946-55, Ga. State Dept. Health, Atlanta, 1948-52, Atlanta City Hosp., 1946-55. Author: Family Crucible, 1978, Roots of Psychotherapy, 1982, From Psyche to System, 1983; contbr. articles to profl. jours. Fellow Am. Psychiat. Assn. (life). Home: 5636 Pheasant Dr Nashotah WI 53058

WHITAKER, LOUIS RODMAN, professional baseball player. Second baseman Detroit Tigers, Am. League, 1977—. Mem. World Series Champion Team, 1984; player Am. League All-Star Team, 1983-86. Office: Detroit Tigers Tiger Stadium Detroit MI 48216 *

WHITAKER, MARK ALLEN, lawyer, professional sports association representative; b. Alliance, Ohio, Jan. 10, 1954; s. Walter and Maxine Belva (Reynolds) W.; m. Jill Elaine Hipkins, Oct. 11, 1980 (div. Jan. 1985); m. Karen Lynn Titak, June 29, 1985. BA, Mt. Union Coll., 1976; JD, U. Toledo, 1979. Bar: Ohio 1979. Assoc. Bair & Stone Co., P.A., Alliance, 1979-83; ptnr. Bair, Stone & Whitaker, P.A. (formerly Bair & Stone Co.), Alliance, 1983-85, Poitinger & Whitaker Sports Mgmt., Akron, Ohio, 1985—; instr. Stark Tech. Coll., North Canton, Ohio, 1984—; cons. Turner & May, Warren, Ohio, 1987—. Pres. Alliance Booster Club, 1983-85; bd. dirs. Alliance Waste Water Treatment Appeals Bd., 1983-84, bd. dirs. Children's Internat. Summer Villages, Youngstown, Ohio, 1985—. Mem. ABA, Ohio State Bar Assn., Stark County Bar Assn., Alliance Bar Assn., NFL Players Assn. Democrat. Methodist. Lodge: Elks. Office: Poitinger & Whitaker Sports Mgmt 3500 W Market St Akron OH 44313

WHITAKER, RONALD MARTIN, engineer; b. Fullerton, Nebr., Jan. 30, 1933; s. Leonard Bert and Margaret Mary (Seely) W.; student Central Tech. Community Coll., Hastings, Nebr., 1977, Franklin U., Columbus, Ohio, 1981 Ohio U., Lancaster; m. Janet Louise Spitz, Apr. 12, 1955; children—Mark David, Jeffrey Keith, Wendy Elaine. Mgr. Spitz Foundry Inc., Hastings, Nebr., 1965-78, Crosier Monastery, 1978; plant engr. Lattimer Stevens Co., Columbus, Ohio, 1978-80, v.p. engring., 1980-85, methods engr., 1985-86; facilities engr. Winters Industries div. Whittaker Corp., Canton, Ohio, 1986—; instr. Engr. Ctr., Ft. Belvoir, Va., 1953. Scoutmaster Overland Trails council Boy Scouts Am., Grand Island, Nebr., 1970-78, dist. camping dir., 1975-78, Order of Arrow advisor, 1976-78; extraordinary minister Roman Cath. Ch. Served with C.E. U.S. Army, 1953-55. Decorated Combat Infantryman's Badge, others; cert. mfg. engr.; registered profl. engr. Mem. Soc. Mfg. Engrs. (chmn. sr. mem.), Am. Foundrymen's Soc. (sr.), Nat. Rifle Assn. (endowment mem., cert. firearms instr.), Nebr. Rifle and Pistol Assn. (life mem.), Nat. Reloaders Assn., Central Ohio Council Internat. Visitors, Am Legion, Nat. Eagle Scout Assn., Am. Photog. Soc. Republican. Editorial cons. Plant Engineering mag. Home: 3042 Chaucer Dr NE North Canton OH 44721-3611 Office: Winters Industries 4125 Mahoning Rd NE Canton OH 44721

WHITCOMB, J. HARRISON, clinical social worker, mental health center administrator; b. Yorktown, Va., Aug. 9, 1946; s. James Lewis and Marjorie (Porter) W.; m. Leona Irene Miller, Aug. 29, 1969; children: Kirsten Joy, Dennis Porter. BA, So. Meth. U., 1968; MSW, Mich. State U., 1972. Lic. social worker, Ohio. Psychiatric social worker Verde Valley Guidance Ctr., Cottonwood, Ariz., 1972-81; clin. social worker Rim Guidance Ctr., Payson, Ariz., 1981-84; assoc. dir. Shawnee Mental Health Ctr., West Union, Ohio, 1984—; hosp. social worker Adams County Hosp., West Union, 1984—; cons. Eagle Creek Nursing Home, West Union, 1984—. Contbr. series of articles on teenage suicide to newspaper. Com. mem. Am. Heart Assn., West Union, 1985-86. Mem. Nat. Acad. Social Workers, Assn. Cert. Social Workers. Democrat. Methodist. Avocations: karate, piano, organ, weightlifting, bicycling. Home: 121 S 2d St West Union OH 45693 Office: Shawnee Mental Health Ctr 192 Chestnut Ridge Rd West Union OH 45697

WHITCOMB, MICHAEL E., internist, medical school administrator; b. Nov. 6, 1940. BS, Ohio State U., 1961; MD, U. Cin., 1965. Diplomate Am. Bd. Internal Medicine, Pulmonary Disease Subspecialty Bd. Commd. U.S. Army, 1964, advanced through grades to lt. col.; intern Brooke Army Med. Ctr. U.S. Army, San Antonio, 1965-66; resident in internal medicine Walter Reed Army Med. Ctr. U.S. Army, Washington, 1966-69, chief resident, 1968-69, chief pulmonary disease service, 1971-74; chief pulmonary disease div. Tripler Gen. Hosp. U.S. Army, Honolulu, 1970-71; resigned U.S. Army, 1974; assoc. dir. pulmonary disease Boston City Hosp., 1974-76; chief pulmonary disease service Univ. Hosp., Boston, 1976-77; dir. pulmonary disease div. Ohio State U. Hosps., Columbus, 1977-82, assoc. chmn. dept. medicine, asst. med. dir., 1980-81, med. dir., assoc. dean clin. affairs, 1981-85; asst. v.p. health services Coll. Medicine Ohio State U., Columbus, 1985-86; dean Sch. Medicine U. Mo., Columbia, 1986—; dir. clin. services U. Hosp., Columbia, 1986—; asst. clin. prof. medicine U. Hawaii, Honolulu, 1970-71, Georgetown U., Washington, 1971-74. Author: The Lung: Normal and Diseased, 1982; contbr. chpts. to books and numerous articles to profl. jours. Recipient Meritorious Service award Walter Reed Army Med. Ctr., 1974, Young Investigators award NIH, 1975, 77; Robert Wood Johnson fellow, 1984-85. Fellow ACP, Am. Coll. Chest Physicians; mem. Am. Fedn. for Clin. Research, Am. Thoracic Soc. (Edward Livingston Trudeau fellow 1975-79), Ohio Thoracic Soc. Office: U Mo Sch Medicine Office of Dean MA204 Med Sci Bldg Columbia MO 65211

WHITCRAFT, JAMES RICHARD, JR., accountant; b. Muncie, Ind., Jan. 27, 1947; s. James R. and Hazel V. (Garner) W.; m. Pamela D. Imel, July 29, 1977; children: Christopher K., Kelle D. BS, Ball State U., 1969, MBA, 1972. CPA, Ind., Mich. Sr. staff acct. Arthur Andersen & Co., Indpls., 1969-77; audit mgr. Holdeman, Fulmer, Elkhart, Ind., 1977-81; owner Dick Whitcraft, CPA, Elkhart, 1981-84; mng. ptnr. Whitcraft & Thomas, CPA's, Elkhart, 1984—. Treas. Life Recovery Ctr., Inc., 1985—, Presbyn. ch., 1985—. Served with U.S. Army, 1969-71. Mem. Am. Inst. CPA's, Ind. Assn. CPA's, Mich. Assn. CPA's, Blue Key, Sigma Chi (life). Republican. Lodges: Elks, Optimists (pres. Elkhart chpt. 1981-82, 84). Home: 20348 US 12 E Edwardsburg MI 49112 Office: Whitcraft & Thomas CPA's 524 S Second St Elkhart IN 46516

WHITE, BOB MCKNIGHT, grain and transportation company executive; b. Bristow, Okla., Nov. 5, 1949; s. Charles McKnight and Gladys Fern (Allee) White; m. Patricia Sue Avery, Dec. 20, 1969; children: Christopher, Julie. BBA, Wichita State U., 1971; AA, Cowley County Community Coll., 1969, MBA, Wichita State U., 1976. CPA, Ill. Asst. controller Garvey Internat. Inc., Bloomingdale, Ill., 1975-77, controller, 1977-79, v.p. fin., 1979-81, exec. v.p., 1981-82, pres., 1982—, also bd. dir.; bd. dirs. Garvey Commodities Corp., Chgo., Interail Inc., Bloomingdale, N.W. Okla. R.R., Woodward, Okla., Pacific Coast Transp. Inc., Bloomingdale. Mem. Nat. Assn. Accts. (various offices 1976-83, pres. Chgo. chpt. 1983-84, nat. bd. dirs.), Ill. Soc. CPA's, Kans. Soc. CPA's, Wichita State U. Alumni Assn. (bd. dirs. Chgo. Area chpt.). Republican. Clubs: Union League (Chgo.); St. Charles (Ill.) Country.

WHITE, C. THOMAS, justice Nebraska Supreme Court; b. Humphrey, Nebr., Oct. 5, 1928; s. John Ambrose and Margaret Elizabeth (Costello) W.; m. Joan White, Oct. 9, 1971; children: Michaela, Thomas, Patrick. J.D., Creighton U., 1952. Bar: Nebr. County atty. Platte County (Nebr.), Columbus, 1955-65; judge 21st Dist. Ct. Nebr., Columbus, 1965-77; justice Nebr. Supreme Ct., Lincoln, 1977—. Served with U.S. Army, 1946-47. Roman Catholic. Clubs: Elks, KC. Office: Capitol Bldg Lincoln NE 68509 *

WHITE, CAROLYN NEWELL PITT, museum coordinator; b. Bklyn., Oct. 13, 1943; d. Frank Rylands and Winifred Gladys (Nagel) P.; m. John James White II, Aug. 28, 1965; children—Allison Newell, Kevin Brandon. Cert. Evanston Bus. Coll., 1964; B.A., Northwestern U., 1965, M.A., 1967. Showroom rep. Am. Standard, Chgo., 1966; sec. Med. Group of Evanston (Ill.), 1967; instr. Harford Jr. Coll., Bel Aire, Md., 1968; sec. Ayres, Lewis, Norris & May, Ann Arbor, Mich., 1970-71; unit coordinator Am. Cancer Soc., Columbus, Ind., 1979-80; broker assoc. Tipton Lakes Co., Columbus, 1981-84. Bd. dirs. Mayor's Task Force on Status of Women, 1973-74; archtl. tour guide Columbus Vis.'s Center 1973-75, bd. dirs.; chmn. voters service LWV, 1974-75; vol. in pub. and pvt. schs., 1976-81; vol. instr. Columbus Girls Club, 1977; bd. dirs. Indpls. Museum of Art, Columbus, 1981-85, v.p., 1983-84, pres., 1984-85; pres. Mt. Healthy PTA, 1982-83; vol. United Way, 1983; freelance writer Arts Insight; mem. gen. com.unCommon Cause; mem. Leadership Bartholomew County, 1985-86; bd. dirs. Columbus Art League, sec., 1986-87; mem. Columbus Art & Architecture Festival Com. Recipient award Indpls. Museum of Art, 1976. Mem. Am. Assn. Mus., Am. Assn. Mus. Vols., Assn. Ind. Mus., Ind. Advocates for Arts, First Tuesday Forum, Delta Zeta. Unitarian-Universalist. Home: 3701 S Poplar Dr Columbus IN 47201 Office: Indpls Mus Art 506 5th St Columbus IN 47201

WHITE, CYNTHIA A., psychologist; b. Boston, Jan. 17, 1944; d. Sebastian Anthony and Olga (Rizzo) Adamo; m. Michael Dale White, Aug. 26, 1972. BA, Atlantic U., 1966; MS, U. Miami, 1970, PhD, 1973. Diplomate Am. Bd. Med. Psychotherapy. Asst. prof. Xavier U., Cin., 1975-76; psychologist Longview State Hosp., Cin., 1975-76, VA Med. Ctr., Cin., 1976—; adj. assoc. prof. U. Cin., 1976—; field asst. prof. dept. internal medicine U. Cin. Med. Sch., 1986—; psychol. cons. Eating Disorders Clinic, Cin., 1976-80. Mem. Am. Psychol. Assn., Ohio Psychol. Assn., Cin. Psychol. Assn. (bd. dirs. 1985—), Soc. Behavioral Medicine, Sigma Xi. Clubs: Clifton Track (Cin.), Dayton Cycle. Office: VA Med Ctr 3200 Vine St 116B Cincinnati OH 45220

WHITE, DAVID P., business machines company executive. Pres. bus. service group Control Data Corp., Mpls. Office: Control Data Corp 8100 34th Ave S Minneapolis MN 55440 *

WHITE, DONALD JERRY, English educator; b. Anderson, Ind., June 5, 1946; s. Calvin Earl and Mary Ruth White; m. Karen Luanne Johnson, June 24, 1967; children: William Wallace Eugene. AB summa cum laude, Atlantic Christian Coll., 1968; AM, U. Ill., 1972, PhD, 1977. Asst. prof., dir. drama Coll. Idaho, Caldwell, 1975-78; asst. prof. Eureka (Ill.) Coll., 1978-80; from asst. prof. to assoc. prfo. English Cen. Mo. State U., Warrensburg, 1980—. Editor: Damon and Pithias: A Critical Old-Spelling Edition (Richard Edwards), 1980; compiler Early English Drama: Everyman to 1580, 1986; contbr. articles to profl. jours. Served with U.S. Army, 1969-70. Hon. Woodrow Wilson fellow, 1968. Mem. Modern Lang. Assn. Am., Shakespeare Assn. Am., Bibliog. Soc., Bibliog. Assn. Am., Mo. Philological Assn. (exec. sec. 1984-87), Phi Kappa Phi. Home: Rt 7 Box 394 Warrensburg MO 64093 Office: Cen Mo State U Dept English and Philosophy Warrensburg MO 64093

WHITE, EUGENE M., product development executive; b. Laud, Ind., Aug. 2, 1937; s. Robert Herold and Margaret Bell (Ward) W.; A.B. in Philosophy, Ind. U., 1963; children—Michelle, Michael. Gen. ptnr. Foam Glass Insulation Devel., Ft. Wayne, Ind., 1979—. Dir. conservation caucus Ind. 4th Congl. Dist., 1977-79; alt. del. to Republican Nat. Conv., 1976; pres. Ft. Wayne chpt. Parents without Partners, 1980-81; founder Single/Single Again, 1982. Dept. Energy research grantee, 1979-80. Mem. AAAS, Soc. Mfg. Engrs., Ft. Wayne Astron. Soc., Coptic Fellowship. Republican. Methodist. Patentee in field of mechanics and chem. process. Home: 1624 Franklin Ave Fort Wayne IN 46808

WHITE, FRANKLIN MORSE, elec. co. exec.; b. Fairbury, Nebr., Dec. 6, 1920; s. Chesley Franklin and Nellie Blanch (Smith) W.; B.S.E.E., U. Nebr., 1943; m. Lydia Worster, Oct. 8, 1949; 1 dau., Janet Louise. Partner, gen. mgr. White Electric Supply Co., Lincoln, Nebr., 1946-65, pres., gen. mgr., 1965—; pres. Four Way Investments, Inc., 1978—. Pres., Lincoln Family Service Assn., 1962-65; mem. Lincoln Lancaster County Planning Commn., 1962-68, civil def. commn., 1959-71. Served with Signal Corps, U.S. Army, 1943-46; served to col. USAR. Mem. Nat. Assn. Elec. Distbrs. (bd. govs. 1966-71), Nebr.-Iowa Elec. Council (pres. 1980-81), Lincoln C. of C., Nebr. Assn. Commerce and Industry, Res. Officers Assn., Newcomen Soc., U. Nebr. Alumni Assn. Republican. Mem. Christian Ch. Clubs: Nebr., Mo. River (pres. 1969-70). Lodges: Elks, Sertoma. Home: 2701 Bonacum Dr Lincoln NE 68502 Office: White Electric Supply Co 427 S 10th Lincoln NE 68508

WHITE, GEORGE W., federal judge; b. 1931. Student, Baldwin-Wallace Coll., 1948-51; J.D., Cleveland-Marshall Coll. Law, 1955. Sole practice law Cleve., 1956-68; judge Ct. Common Pleas, Ohio, 1968-80, U.S. Dist. Ct. (no. dist.) Ohio, 1980—. Mem. ABA, Fed. Bar Assn. Office: U S Dist Ct 135 US Courthouse 201 Superior Ave NE Cleveland OH 44114

WHITE, HENRY PAUL, chemist; b. Chgo., Sept. 30, 1921; s. Millard Earl and Juliette Zoe (Kieffer) w.; m. Rhea Mae Parnock, June 4, 1948 (div. Feb. 1958); m. Dolores Esther Carlson, Mar. 1, 1958. A.A., U. Fla., 1943; B.A., Roosevelt U., 1953. Lab. technician Catalin Corp. Am., Calumet City, Ill., Fords, N.J., 1954-55, Chgo. Extruded Metals Corp., Cicero, Ill., 1955-56; chemist quality control Taylor Forge Inc., Cicero, Memphis, 1956-64, 1967-72, Burlington No. R.R., Aurora, Ill., St. Paul, 1964-66, chemist research and devel. Kester Solder Co., Chgo., 1966-67; chemist, fuels analyst No. Ind. Pub. Service Co., Chesterton and Hammond, 1979—. Mem. horn sect. N.W. Ind. Symphony Orch., 1970-73. Served with U.S. Army, 1944-46, ETO. Mem. Am. Chem. Soc., Am. Soc. Metals, Lake County Poetry Club (pres. 1980-82), Hoosier Pens Crown Point, 1st Friday Poets NW Ind. Lodge: Masons (marshall 1966-67). Avocations: music; art; writing. Home: 117 Las Olas Dr Crown Point IN 46307 Office: No Ind Pub Service Co 501 Bailly Rd Chesterton IN 46304

WHITE, HUGH ERWIN, farmer; b. Hutchinson, Kans., Mar. 8, 1905; s. David C. and Sadie Belle (Doles) W.; m. Gladys L. Black, Aug. 25, 1929 (dec. Oct. 1978); children: David, Myrea, Janis, Sharon; m. Jessie S. Bolinger, Mar. 1, 1980; 1 child, Fred Hiss. BS in Agrl. Engring., Kans. State U., 1929, MS Agrl. Engring., 1940. Republican. Presbyterian. Lodge: Lions (pres. 1978). Home: 409 Nebraska Bucklin KS 67834

WHITE, JAMES JUSTIN, JR., investment banker; b. Evanston, Ill., Nov. 10, 1959; s. James Justin and Mary Jeanne (Jacobs) W.; m. Rebecca Ballard, July 7, 1986. BA, BFA, So. Meth. U., 1982; MBA, Northwestern U., 1986. Account exec. Dean Witter Reynolds, Dallas, 1982-83; acquistion analyst James J. White & Assocs., Chgo., 1983-84; analyst Citicorp, Chgo., 1985-86; investment banker Morgan Stanley & Co., Inc., Chgo., 1986—. Commentator TV and radio fin. programs, 1982-83. Fundraiser Multiple Sclerosis, Dallas and Chgo., 1979-85, So. Meth. U. Mustang Club, 1982—, N-Club, 1984—, Rep. Conv., 1983. Roman Catholic. Club: University Chgo. Avocations: skiing, traveling, preserving nature. Home: 1085 Hill Rd Winnetka IL 60093

WHITE, JEFFREY PAUL, lawyer; b. Farmington, Maine, Apr. 5, 1955; s. Calvin Coolidge and Dorothy Louise (Barker) W.; m. Cynthia June Daugherty, May, 24, 1986; 1 child, McKenzie Sara. BA, U. Maine, Orono, 1977; JD, Suffolk U., 1981. Bar: Mass., Ill., Wis., U.S. Dist. Ct. (no. dist.) Ill., U.S. Dist. Ct. (no. dist.) N.Y., U.S. Dist. Ct. (ea. dist.) Wis., U.S. Dist. Ct. (we. dist.) Wis., U.S. Dist. Ct. Nebr. Assoc. William L. Needler & Assocs., Chgo., 1981-83; sole practice Chgo., 1983—; pres. Jeffrey White, P.C., Chgo., 1985—; real estate broker Hopscotch Realty, Chgo., 1985—; ptnr. Bosworth Real Estate Assocs., Chgo., 1985—. Mem. Ill. Bar Assn., Mass. Bar Assn., Wis. Bar Assn., Chgo. Bar Assn. (mem. bankruptcy com. 1982—, chmn. agrl. law com. 1987—), Am. Agrl. Law Assn. Avocations: golf, woodworking, skiing. Office: 20 E Jackson Suite 350 Chicago IL 60604

WHITE, JODY MARY, mortgage banking executive; b. Dubuque, Iowa, Dec. 20, 1952; d. John William and Patricia Mary (Cullen) Smith; m. Kent Alan White, Aug. 13, 1971; children: Tracey, Christopher, Matthew. Grad. high sch., Dubuque, 1971. Loan closer Norwest Mortgage Co., Waterloo, Iowa, 1974-81, mgr. tech. supt., 1981-83, mgr. data processing relocation div., 1983-85; mgr. computer ops. Prudential Home Mortgage, Mpls., 1985-86, mgr. new techs. dept., 1986—. Mem. Assn. Info. Ctr. Profls. Roman Catholic. Avocations: skiing, gardening. Home: 3509 Robinwood Ter Minnetonka MN 55343 Office: Prudential Home Mortgage PO Box 1629 100 S 5th Minneapolis MN 55440

WHITE, JOE, JR., financial executive, controller; b. Union City, Ind., Oct. 12, 1930; s. Joe Ira and Ruby G. (Ralston) W.; m. Ruth Anne Lininger, Aug. 19, 1956; children: Terry D., Jeffrey S., Melody J. And. Ind. Bus. Coll., 1950. CPA, Ind. Time keeper Anchor Hocking Co., Winchester, Ind., 1951-52; bookkeeper Stock Yards Co., Winchester, 1952-57; controller Overmyer Corp., Winchester, 1957-82; controller, treas. Randolph County Hosp., Winchester, 1982—. Pres. Lynn (Ind.) Town Bd., 1983—. Mem. Am. Inst. CPA's, Ind. Soc. CPA's, Healthcare Fin. Mgmt. Assn. Home: Rural Rt 1 Box 20 Lynn IN 47355 Office: Randolph County Hosp South Oak St Winchester IN 47394

WHITE, JOSEPH PATRICK, accountant; b. Stillwater, Minn., Oct. 19, 1958; s. Patrick Eugene and Virginia May (Casperson) W.; m. Jeanne Ann Hannah, Nov. 3, 1984. BS in Bus., U. Minn., 1982. CPA, Minn. Staff acct. Sands, Wienberg & Co., St. Paul, 1982-84; tax specialist Peat Marwick

Mitchell & Co., St. Paul, 1984-85; supr. Sands, Rust & Co., CPA's, St. Paul, 1985-87, mgr., 1987—. Treas. City of Lakeland, Minn., 1987. Mem. Am. Inst. CPA's, Minn. Soc. CPA's (mem. pub. relations com. 1982). Republican. Roman Catholic. Club: Men With A Future (St. Croix Valley, Minn.) (treas. 1986—). Avocations: golf, reading, tax matters. Office: Sands Rust & Co CPA's 1808 Am Nat Bank Saint Paul MN 55101

WHITE, JUDITH ANN O'RADNIK, social worker; b. St. Paul, Oct. 27, 1943; d. Clarence Edwin and Marcella Ann (Cappelle) O'Radnik; B.A., Quincy Coll., 1965; M.S.W., Ohio State U., 1970; m. Dean H. White, May 22, 1981. Dep. juvenile officer St. Louis Circuit Ct. Juvenile Div., 1965-68; caseworker Ohio Div. Youth Services, Powell, Ohio, 1968-69; supr. intake delinquency juvenile div. St. Louis Circuit Ct., 1970-76, supr. child abuse and neglect unit, 1976—; liaison mem. project for coordination legal and protective services for sexually abused children St. Louis Circuit Atty.'s Office, 1985—. Bd. dirs. Council on Child Abuse and Neglect of Met. St. Louis, 1979-82; mem. St. Louis Task Force on Child Abuse, St. Louis Network on Child Abuse and Neglect. Fed. grantee, 1985—. Mem. Nat. Council Crime and Delinquency, Ohio State U. Sch. Social Work Alumni Assn. Home: 138 Manlyn Dr Kirkwood MO 63122 Office: 920 N Vandeventer Ave Saint Louis MO 63108

WHITE, LARRY CURTIS, osteo. physician; b. Decatur, Ill., May 1, 1941; s. Gerald Curtis and Elizabeth Jane (Moore) W.; B.S., U. Ill., 1963; D.O., Kirksville Coll. Osteo. Medicine, 1970; m. Mary Ann Savage, Aug. 21, 1965; children—Mark, Michelle, Gerald, Barbara. Intern, Riverside Osteo. Hosp., Trenton, Mich., 1970-71; practice osteo. medicine, pres. Romeo (Mich.) Clinic, 1971—; mem. staff, mem. med. exec. com. Crittenton Hosp., 1977—, chmn. med. records com., 1977, vice chmn. dept. family practice, 1977-79, chmn., 1979—. Diplomate Am. Bd. Family Practice. Mem. Am. Osteo. Assn., Mich. Assn. Osteo. Physicians and Surgeons, Am. Acad. Family Physicians, Am. Assn. Family Practice, U. Ill. Alumni Assn., Psi Sigma Alpha, Alpha Phi Omega, Sigma Sigma Phi, Theta Psi, Alpha Kappa Lambda. Methodist. Clubs: Masons, Shriners, K.T. Home: 2250 E Gunn Rd Rochester MI 48063 Office: 241 N Main St Romeo MI 48065

WHITE, LAURIE BETH, optometrist; b. Dodge City, Kans., Apr. 2, 1958; d. Herbert C. and Rowena G. (Taylor) W.; m. Stephen R. Stephens, Nov. 23, 1985. AS, Dodge City Community Coll., 1978; BS in Gen. Biology, Emporia (Kans.) State Coll., 1979; OD, U. Houston, 1983. Lic. optometrist, Tex., Kans. Optometrist Conard Moore, MD, Houston, 1983-84; optometrist White and White, Dodge City, 1984-86, Cimarron, Kans., 1986—; vision cons. 4-H Groups, Dodge City, 1984-86. Mem. Am. Optometric Assn., Kans. Optometric Assn. (sec. Save Your Vision Week 1986—), Am. Vol. Optometric Soc. for Humanity, Kans. Vol. Optometric Soc. for Humanity (sec., treas. 1986—), Am. Aux. of Univ. Women (v.p. membership com. 1986—). Methodist. Club: Stephens Ministry. Avocations: running, bicycle, swimming, sewing, tennis. Office: White and White ODs 2010 Central Dodge City KS 67801

WHITE, MARTIN DEE, data communications executive; b. Indianola, Iowa, Oct. 11, 1944; s. Elmer Edwin and Beatrice Bertha (Howard) W.; m. Kathleen Lorraine Delaney, Feb. 25, 1967; children: Erin Michele, Kevin Michael, Amy Kathleen, Patrick Sean. Cert. computer repairman, USAF, 1966, cert. telecommunications specialist, 1967; cert. electronics tech., CIE, 1969. Mgr. data communications and tech. control Norwest Fin. Info. Systems Group, Des Moines, 1969—; cons. data communication services, Des Moines, 1979-82. Served with USAF, 1965-69, Japan. Republican. Avocations: shooting sports, fishing, raising horses, antique collecting, history. Office: Norwest Fin Info 206 8th St Des Moines IA 50309

WHITE, MICHAEL REED, state senator; b. Cleve., Aug. 13, 1951; s. Robert and Audrey (Silver) W. BA, Ohio State U., 1973, MPA, 1974. Spl. asst. Columbus (Ohio) Mayor's Office, 1974-76; adminstrv. asst. Cleve. City Council, 1976-77; sales mgr. Burks Electric Co., Cleve., 1978-84; state senator Ohio Senate, Columbus, 1984—; asst. minority whip Ohio Senate Dems., 1987—. City councilman City of Cleve., 1978-84; bd. dirs. Glenville Devel. Corp., Cleve., 1978—, Glenville Festival Found., Cleve., 1978—, United Black Fund, Cleve., 1986, Greater Cleve. Dome Corp., 1986. Named one of Outstanding Young Men Am., 1985, Outstanding Young Leader of Cleve.; recipient Outstanding Service award Cleve. chpt. Nat. Assn. Black Vets., 1985, Community Services award East Side Jaycees. Democrat. Home: 1057 East Blvd Cleveland OH 44108 Office: Ohio Senate Statehouse Columbus OH 43216

WHITE, MICHAEL SHADDWICK, accountant; b. Coldwater, Kans., Aug. 11, 1954; s. Joe Patrick and Frances Arlene (Ewy) W. BSBA, Northwestern Okla. State U., 1976; BS in Acctg., Kans. U., 1978. CPA, Kans. Staff acct. Ernst & Whinney, Kansas City, Mo., 1978-80; sr. acct. Francis, Poore & Dammeron, Wichita, Kans., 1980-83; sr. analyst Contract Surety Consultants, Wichita, 1983-85; private practice acctg. Wichita, 1985—; bd. dirs. White's King Co., Kingman, Kans., 1980—, White's Cim Co., Cimerron, 1980—. Mem. Am. Inst. CPA's, Kans. Soc. CPA's. Republican. Presbyterian. Avocations: skiing, stock market analysis. Home: 844 N Waco #A-303 Wichita KS 67203 Office: 914 Century Plaza Wichita KS 67202

WHITE, R. QUINCY, lawyer; b. Chgo., Jan. 16, 1933; s. Roger Q. and Carolyn Jane (Everett) W.; m. Joyce Caldwell, Aug. 4, 1962; children: Cleaver Dorothea, Annelia Everett. B.A., Yale U., 1954; J.D., Harvard U., 1960. Bar: Ill. 1960, U.S. Dist. Ct. (no. dist.) Ill. 1960. Assoc. Leibman, Williams, Bennett, Baird & Minow, Chgo., 1960-67, ptnr., 1967-73; ptnr. Sidley & Austin, Chgo., 1973—; hon. consul. gen. Islamic Rep. Pakistan, Chgo., 1978—; sec., dir. W.F. McLaughlin Co., Chgo., 1964-68; designated mem. U.S. Trademark Assn., 1985—. Dir., counsel Off The Street Club, Chgo., 1974-84; sec. nat. governing bd. The Ripon Soc., 1971-72; mem. exec. com. 43d-44th ward regional Republican orgn., 1970-73; mem. Council Fgn. and Domestic Affaris, 1970-76; v.p., bd. dirs. Juvenile Protective Assn., 1965-87. Recipient Sitara-i-Quaid-i-Azam Pakistan, 1982. Mem. Chgo. Council Lawyers, Chgo. Bar Assn., ABA. Home: 316 W Willow St Chicago IL 60614 Office: Sidley & Austin 1 First National Plaza Chicago IL 60603

WHITE, RAYMOND GENE, veterinarian, educational administrator; b. Elana, W.Va., Oct. 10, 1930; s. Curtis Roy and Ora Mae (Cohen) W.; m. Donna Jean Wilmoth, Mar. 21, 1952; children—Janice Leah White Richert, Keith Alan. Student U. W.Va., 1954-56; B.S., Okla. State U. Coll. Vet. Medicine, 1958, D.V.M., 1960; M.S., Coll. Agr., U. Nebr., 1971. Veterinarian, Springfield, Mo., 1960-65; research veterinarian Chemagro Corp., Kansas City, Mo., 1965-69; research extension veterinarian U. Nebr.-North Platte, 1969-76, dir. North Platte Sta., 1976-79; dir. animal health program Coll. Vet. Medicine Miss. State U., Mississippi State, 1979-82, mem. coll. devel. program, 1975-78; coordinator Coll. Vet. Medicine U. Nebr., Lincoln, 1982—; cons. Norden Labs., Lincoln, Nebr., 1971-78, Hoechst-Roussel Agri-Vet, 1984. Author 4 book chpts. Contbr. numerous articles to sci. jours. Developer Roto and Corona Calf Scour Vaccine, 1971, 79. Leader in vet. sci. 4H Clubs, North Platte, 1971-76; adviser merit badge program, Boy Scouts Am., North Platte, 1971-76; mem. adv. council U. Nebr. Sch. Tech. Agr., Curtis, 1969-84. Recipient Dean McElroy award Okla. State U. Coll. Vet. Medicine, 1960, Dedicated Service to Nebr. Livestock award Nebr. Cattleman's Assn., 1979. Mem. AVMA, Nebr. Vet. Med. Assn. (dist. pres. 1972-73, Meriterous award 1979), Am. Soc. Animal Sci., Am. Assn. Bovine Practitioners, Am. Nat. Cattleman's Assn., Am. Legion. Republican. Baptist. Lodges: Rotary (bd. dirs. 1975-76), Masons, Kiwanis. Home: 1320 Twinridge Lincoln NE 68510 Office: Univ Nebr Lab Animal Care Program Office of Director Lincoln NE 68583-0905

WHITE, RICHARD REED, real estate appraiser; b. Fairfax, Mo., Nov. 1, 1931; s. Richard Denny and Esther Margaret (Sharp) W.; m. Iona Ann Gomel, Sept. 2, 1951; children: Roxanne White Bodwell, Joseph Richard. BAgr, U. Mo., 1953. Farm mgr., appraiser Doane Agriculture Services, Chillicothe, Mo., 1953-61; appraiser C.E. U.S. Army, Kansas City, Mo., 1961-69, Burrell Hayes Inc., Knoxville, Iowa, 1969-72; co-owner, appraiser Burrell & Assocs., Inc., Knoxville, 1972-80, Burrell, White & Assocs., Knoxville, 1980-86; owner, appraiser White & Assocs., Inc., Knoxville, 1986—. Deacon United Presby. Ch., Knoxville, 1972—. Served to 1st lt. U.S. Army, 1953-55. Mem. Am. Inst. Real Estate Appraisers (elective examination subcom. 1973—, sec., treas. 1981, v.p. 1982, pres. 1983 Iowa chpt. number 34), Am. Soc. Farm Mgrs. Rural Appraisers. Office: White & Assocs Inc 110 S 1st St Knoxville IA 50138

WHITE, RICHARD THOMAS, radiology educator; b. Binghamton, N.Y., May 10, 1941; s. William Joseph and Winifred (Murphy) W.; divorced; 1 son, Kevin Michael. B.S., SUNY-Binghamton, 1967; D.O., Chgo. Coll. Osteo. Medicine, 1972. Intern, Bi County Hosp., Warren, Mich.; resident Detroit Hosp., Children's Hosp., Detroit, 1973-76; fellow Johns Hopkins Hosp., Balt., 1976; staff radiologist Bi-County Hosp., 1977-79; asst. prof. radiology Mich. State U., East Lansing, 1980-84, cons. ultra-sound research, 1980-83, cons. nuclear magnetic research, 1982-83; asst. prof. radiology U. Tex., Houston, 1984-85, U. Ill., Chgo., 1985—; physician cons. varsity sports, 1980-84; cons. handicapped athletes Spl. Olympics, Washington, 1978-84 . Med. dir. Mich. Spl. Olympics Central Mich. U., Mt. Pleasant, 1977-84; bd. dirs. Spl. Olympics, Mt. Pleasant, 1980-84; med. advisor Amateur Hockey Assn. USA, Colorado Springs, Colo., 1980-84; cons. Detroit Red Wings hockey team, 1977-84. Served with U.S. Army, 1959-64. Recipient Outstanding Contbn. award Spl. Olympics, 1980; named Team Physician U.S. Nat. Hockey Team, Mich. Amateur Hockey Assn., 1979, 81, 83. Mem. Am. Coll. Radiology, Am. Coll. Med. Imaging, Am. Coll. Sports Medicine, Am. Inst. Ultrasound in Medicine, Am. Acad. Sci. Clubs: Detroit Red Wing Hockey, Econ. (Detroit).

WHITE, ROBERT FRANKLIN, computer systems development analyst; b. Indpls., Aug. 18, 1928; s. Walter Otis and Golda Margaret (Ray) W.; m. Vernie Irene Bennett, Mar. 10, 1974; children: Dennis, Claudia, Richard, Steffani. BBA magna cum laude, Indpls. U., 1969; MBA, Butler U., 1972. Systems analyst Navistar, Indpls., 1959-75, supr. material scheduling, 1975-79, supr. systems div., 1979—. Served as cpl. U.S. Army, 1950-52, Korea. Recipient Wall St. Jour. Achievement award Dow Jones, 1969. Mem. Am. Legion, Alpha Sigma Lambda, Epsilon Sigma Alpha. Home: 485 Green Meadow Dr Greenwood IN 46142 Office: Navistar 5565 Brookville Rd Indianapolis IN 46119

WHITE, ROBERT M., II, newspaperman; b. Mexico, Mo., Apr. 6, 1915; s. L. Mitchell and Maude (See) W.; m. Barbara Whitney Spurgeon, Aug. 19, 1948 (dec. Feb. 1983); children: Barbara Whitney, Jane See, Laura L., Robert M. White III.; m. Peggy Lee Dean, Dec. 14, 1983. Grad., Mo. Mil. Acad., 1933; A.B., Washington and Lee U., 1938, LL.B. (hon.), 1972. Writer of newspaper articles Australia, Africa, S.Am., Europe, USSR, 1966—, People's Republic China, 1972, 77; reporter Mexico (Mo.) Eve. Ledger, 1938-39, editor, pub., 1945—; vis. prof. Sch. Journalism, Mo. U., 1968-69; reporter UP Bur., Kansas City, 1939-40; v.p., sec., treas. Ledger Newspapers, Inc., Mexico, Mo., 1947-61; pres. Ledger Newspapers, Inc., 1961—; spl. cons. to pub. Chgo. Sun-Times, 1956-58; pres. Mark Land Co., Mexico, 1956-82, See TV Co., Mexico, 1966-81; editor pres., dir. N.Y. Herald Tribune, 1959-61; juror Pulitzer prize journalism, 1964-65; dir. Commerce Bank of Mexico, 1971-85, Commerce Bancshares, Inc., 1971-85. Co-author: A Study of the Printing and Publishing Business in the Soviet Union. Bd. dirs. AP, 1971-80, Mo. State Hist. Soc., Mo. Mil. Acad., Stephens Coll., 1966-85, Midwest Research Inst., Washington Journalism Center, 1972-83; bd. dirs. World Press Freedom Com., 1984—; pres. MacArthur Meml. Found., 1981—. Served to lt. col. AUS, 1940-45. Decorated Bronze Star; recipient nat. disting. service award for editorials Sigma Delta Chi, 1952, 68; editorial award N.Y. Silurians, 1959; Disting. Service to Journalism award U. Mo., 1967; Pres. award of merit Nat. Newspapers Assn., 1967; Ralph D. Casey Minn. award disting. service in journalism, 1983; named hon. col., Mo.; finalist Journalist in Space 1986. Mem. Nat. Conf. Editorial Writers (past exec. council), Am. Soc. Newspaper Editors (dir. 1968-69, chmn. freedom of info. com. 1970-72), Am. Newspaper Pubs. Assn. (nat. treas. 1963, dir. 1955-63, past dir. research inst., chmn. internat. issues group 1982-86), Inland Daily Press Assn. (chmn. bd. 1958-59, pres., past sec., v.p.), Mo. Press Assn. (dir., v.p. 1981-83, pres. 1983-84), Mo. Press-Bar Commn. (chmn. 1972-74), Internat. Press Inst. (chmn. Am. Com. 1982-85), Sigma Delta Chi (nat. pres. 1967, pres. found. 1968), Beta Theta Pi. Democrat. Methodist. Clubs: Masons, Nat. Press, Rotary; Bohemian (San Francisco); Dutch Treat (N.Y.C.); Burning Tree, Chevy Chase. Office: Ledger Newspapers Ledger Plaza Mexico MO 65265

WHITE, ROGER J., bishop. Bishop Episcopal Ch., Milw. Office: Episc Ch 804 Juneau Ave Milwaukee WI 53202 *

WHITE, STANTON MCCONNELL, SR., newspaper publisher; b. Oklahoma City, Dec. 7, 1923; s. Stephen S. and Mary M. (McConnell) W.; student public schs., Kankakee, Ill.; m. Marcella M. Girard, Sept. 27, 1945; children—Stanton M., Stephen, Jackie, Rick, Shari. Salesman, Daily Jour., Kankakee, Ill., 1950-53, promotion mgr., 1953-54, asst. ad mgr., 1954-56, advt. mgr., 1956-67, advt. dir., asst. gen. mgr., 1967; with Ottawa (Ill.) Daily Times, 1967—, gen. mgr., 1968-69, pub., 1969—, pres., 1979—; dir. Ottawa Pub. Co.; pres., pub. Streator (Ill.) Times-Press, also dir. Bd. dirs. Greater Ottawa United Fund, Ottawa Downtown Devel. Corp. Served with USN, 1940-46; ETO. Mem. Am. Newspaper Pubs. Assn., Internat. Newspaper Advt. Execs., Inland Press Assn., Ill. Press Assn., Chgo. Press Club, C. of C. and Industry (bd. dirs.). Republican. Clubs: Ottawa Boat, Deer Park Country. Lodge: Elks. Office: Ottawa Daily Times 110 W Jefferson St Ottawa IL 61350 Office: Streator Times Press 115 Oak St Streator IL 61364

WHITE, TERENCE D., pastor, church administrator; b. Kittanning, Pa., Dec. 3, 1942; s. Elzie M. and Helen (Hooks) w.; m. Sharon Auxt, Apr. 16, 1965; children: Jamie Lynn, Jonathan Andrew. BME, Grace Coll., 1964; MME, Ind. U., 1967; postgrad., U. Iowa, 1969-72. Band tchr. Goshen (Ind.) Pub. Schs., 1965-66; dir. pub. relations Grace Schs., Winona Lake, Ind., 1966-69; self-study coordinator Grace Coll. and Sem., Winona Lake, 1971-72; assoc. prof. journalism Grace Coll., Winona Lake, 1972-77, St. Paul Bible Coll., Mpls., 1977-81; assoc. pastor of adminstr. and music Wooddale Ch., Eden Prairie, Minn., 1981—. Photo editor Today's Handbook of Bible Times and Customs, 1985; founder Twin Cities Christian Newspaper; co-founder, editor Business Life Mag. Sec. Winona Lake Planning Commn., 1975; Rep. del. conv., precinct leader. Mem. Nat. Assn. Ch. Bus. Adminstrn. (pres. no. cen. chpt. 1985-86), Evang. Press Assn. (gen. conv. chmn. 1983, chmn. nominating com. 85-86), Minn. Christian Writers Guild (pres. 1985-86). Avocations: photography, free-lance writing, publishing consultant, music. Home: 6812 Sugar Hill Circle Eden Prairie MN 55344 Office: Wooddale Ch 6630 Shady Oak Rd Eden Prairie MN 55344

WHITE, THOMAS ALLAN, real estate executive; b. Glendale, Calif., May 13, 1942; s. Kenneth Gould and Josephine Marion (Keltie) W.; m. Virginia Lee Lockner, July 16, 1966 (div. 1977); children: Kevin Frederick, Brian Kenneth; m. Kathryn Elizabeth White, Mar. 31, 1979; 1 child, Amy Elisabeth. BS, Calif. State U., Northridge, 1965. Dir. forward plan K&B So. Calif., Los Angeles, 1971-72, asst. div. mgr., 1972, pres., 1972-74; v.p. Kaufman & Broad Asset Mgmt., Los Angeles, 1973-74; pres. owner TAW Corp., Newport BEach, Calif., 1974-82; sr. v.p. Homart Devel. Co., Chgo., 1982—; bd. dirs. Pacific States Transport, Westminster, 1980-81. dist. dir. Orange County Explorere Scouts, 1979-81. Served to capt. U.S. Army, 1966-70. Mem. Nat. Assn. Indsl. and Office Parks, Urban Land Inst., Union League (Chgo). Club: 552 (bd. dirs. 1979-82, pres. 1981-82); Center (Costa Mesa). Avocations: tennis, golf, skiing.

WHITE, THOMAS GREGG, air force officer; b. Fort Worth, July 26, 1955; s. Thomas Arthur and Evelyn Estelle (Nichols) W.; m. Roxanne Marie Josephson, Aug. 28, 1976; children—Jason Thomas, Christina Heather. A.A., Chapman Coll., 1979, B.A. in Psychology, 1980; A.S. in Electronics Tech. Community Coll. of Air Force, 1983. Enlisted as airman basic U.S. Air Force, 1973; advanced through grades to 1st lt., 1986; radar technician 756 radar squadron Finland AFB, Minn., 1974-77, 714 radar squadron, Cold Bay, Alaska, 1977; radar technician 756 radar squadron, Finland AFB, Minn., 1977-80; space systems technician 1970 communications squadron, Woomera, South Australia, 1980-82, 1000 satellite ops. group, Loring AFB, Maine, 1982-84; munitions officer 379 munitions maintenance squadron, Wurtsmith AFB, Mich., 1984-86, munitions officer 384 munition maintenance squadron, McConnell AFB, Kans., 1986—. Mem. Air Force Assn. Lutheran. Avocations: microcomputing; shortwave radio. Home: 8600 Ent Dr Wichita KS 67210 Office: 384 MMS McConnell AFB KS 67211

WHITE, THOMAS LESTER, consulting engineer; b. Youngstown, Ohio, May 30, 1903; s. William Lester and Ethel Mary (Jackson) W.; m. Marion Elizabeth Evans, Sept. 24, 1930 (dec. July 1983); 1 dau., Harrietellen White McKendrick; m. Doris E. Zerella, Oct. 6, 1984. Tool designer, engr. Comml. Shearing Inc., Youngstown, 1924-26, chief engr., 1926-51, cons. engr., 1951-68, 68—; cons. engr. coal mines, metal mines, hwy., railroad and subway tunnels, Belgium, Portugal, India, Australia, S.Am., Can., others; lectr. various univs. and tech. orgns. Registered profl. engr., Ohio. Fellow ASME (past chmn. petroleum div.); mem. Am. Ry. Engring. Assn., Mahoning Valley Tech. Soc. (named outstanding person 1973). Baptist. Clubs: Kiwanis, Shriners, Masons. Author: (with R.V. Proctor and Karl Terzaghi) Rock Tunneling with Steel Supports, 1946; Earth Tunneling with Steel Supports, 1977. Contbr. articles to profl. jours. Address: 721 W Warren Ave Youngstown OH 44511

WHITE, TIMOTHY PETER, physical education educator; b. Buenos Aires, July 9, 1949; came to U.S., 1957; s. Anthony Robert and Mary (Weston) W.; m. Nina Marie Kasper, Oct. 11, 1981; children: Randall Patrick, Timothy Anthony, Alexander John. Student, Diablo Valley Community Coll., 1966-67; BA magna cum laude, Fresno State U., 1970; MS, Calif. State U., Hayward, 1972; PhD, U. Calif., Berkeley, 1977. Asst. prof. phys. edn. U. Mich., Ann Arbor, 1978-82, assoc. prof., 1982-84, assoc. prof., chmn. dept. kinesiology, 1985—. Editor: (with others) Frontiers of Exercise Biology, 1983; contbr. articles to profl. jours. and chpts. to books on exercise and muscle. Fellow Am. Coll. Sports Medicine (New Investigator award 1981); mem. AAAS, AAHPERD, Gerontol. Soc. Am., Am. Physiol. Soc., Phi Kappa Phi. Avocations: woodworking, nordic skiing, sailing, swimming, running. Home: 4711 Whitman Circle Ann Arbor MI 48103 Office: U Mich Dept Kinesiology 401 Washtenaw Ave Ann Arbor MI 48109-2214

WHITE, VICKI LEE, bank file executive; b. Steubenville, Ohio, Feb. 18, 1960; d. Paul W.H. and Norma Jean (Thomas) Oxier; m. John Robert White, Apr. 12, 1980. Student, Jefferson County Tech. Coll. Teller Miners and Mechs. Savings and Trust Co., Steubenville, 1979-85, mgr. cen. reference files, 1985—. Active Foster Parents Plan, Steubenville Urban Mission, People for the Ethical Treatment Animals. Mem. Am. Inst. Banking (sec. Steubenville chpt. 1985—), Steubenville Art Assn. Republican. Methodist. Lodges: Order Eastern Star, Rosicrucians. Avocations: choir, photography, stamp collecting, reading, songwriting. Home: Sugar St Richmond OH 43944-0051 Office: Miner & Mechs Savings & Trust Co N 4th St Steubenville OH 43952

WHITE, VIRGINIA LOU, township official; b. Barberton, Ohio, Oct. 23, 1932; d. Lucius F. and Edith M. (Carlton) Converse; m. Neil Mason White, Sept. 8, 1956; children:William Neil, David Converse, Holly Susanne. BA, Baldwin-Wallace Coll., 1954. Sec. to exec. sec. Adult Edn. Found. (now Inst. for Civic Edn.) U. Akron, 1954-55, office mgr., 1955-57; tchr. bus. edn. Kenmore High Sch., Akron, 1957-59, Elyria (Ohio) Pub. high Sch., 1959-60; charter twp. clk Meridian Twp., Okemos, Mich., 1972—; del., alternate Mich. Rep. Conv., 1972—. Mem. Mid-Mich. Mother's Against Drunk Driving; sec. Mich. Rep. Issues Com., 1979-80, vice chmn., 1981-87, corresponding sec., 1987—; mem. Ingham County Rep. Exec. Com., 1972—; mem. exec. com. Rep. 6th Congl. Dist., 1980—; co-chmn. Ingham County Reagan/Bush Com., 1980-84; active com. Ruppe for Senate, 1982; chmn. Com to Support Police and Fire Mileage, Meridian Twp., 1982; co-chmn. Friends of CATA, 1983. Mem. Internat. Inst. Mcpl. Clks., Mich. Mcpl. Clks. Mem. Christian Ch. (former elder). Clubs: Zonta Internat. (local pres. 1981-83), Mich. State U. Women's Sports Booster, Okemos No Name Book. Home: 1641 Birchwood Dr Okemos MI 48864 Office: 5151 Marsh Rd Okemos MI 48864

WHITE, WILFRED WALTER, dentist; b. St. Paul, Aug. 9, 1911; s. William Henry and Mae Florence (Young) W.; m. Harriet Adams, Nov. 15, 1935; children: John, Philip, Richard, Lenore. DDS, U. Minn., 1935. Gen. practice dentistry Hutchinson, Minn., 1961—. Lutheran. Lodges: KC (pres. Hutchinson 1968), Masons (master 1968—). Home: 235 Lake St Hutchinson MN 55350

WHITE, WILLIAM A., steel company executive; b. Port Huron, Mich., Aug. 26, 1952; s. William A. and Grace Elizabeth (Parker) W.; m. Alice Linda Drobat, Dec. 22, 1973; 1 child, Christopher Bruce. BA, Wabash Coll., 1974. With sales, estimating dept. Ferguson Steel, Inc., Port Huron, Mich., 1975-79, pres., 1979—. Mem. Great Lakes Fabricators and Erectors Assn., Port Huron Bus. Assn. (pres. 1979), Port Huron-Marysville C. of C. (v.p. 1983). Republican. Episcopalian. Clubs: Port Huron Yacht (commodore 1985—), Port Huron Golf. Avocation: sailing. Home: 5218 Lakeshore Rd Port Huron MI 48060 Office: Ferguson Steel Inc 2935 Howard St Port Huron MI 48060

WHITE, W(ILLIE) GLENN, counseling psychology educator, counseling psychologist, consultant, researcher; b. Dumas, Ark., Jan. 15, 1933; s. Eugene Lee and Ernestine Cornelius (Jordan) W.; m. Gloria Waters, Jan. 1, 1955; 1 dau., Terry Finister. B.A. in Edn., Harris-Stowe Tchrs. Coll., 1959; M.A., Washington U., St. Louis, 1964; Ph.D., U. Mo., 1974. Lic. psychologist, cert. counselor and tchr., Mo. Tchr., counselor St. Louis Pub. Sch. System, 1959-65; dir. research coordinating unit Mo. Dept. Elem. and Secondary Edn., Jefferson City, 1965-77; asst. prof. edn. U. Mo.-St. Louis, 1977-83, assoc. prof., 1983—; cons. to program devel. and tng. instns. Bd. dirs. Life Crisis Suicide Prevention, 1983-85. Served with U.S. Army, 1953-56. Recipient Career Achievement award Urban League, 1978, Achievement award St. Louis Assn. Counseling and Devel., 1985. Mem. Am. Personnel and Guidance Assn., Am. Psychol. Assn., Assn. Measurement and Evauation, Omega Psi Phi. Baptist.

WHITE, WILLIS SHERIDAN, JR., utilities executive; b. nr. Portsmouth, Va., Dec. 17, 1926; s. Willis Sheridan and Carrie (Culpepper) W.; m. LaVerne Behrends, Oct. 8, 1949; children—Willis Sheridan III, Marguerite Louise White Spangler, Cynthia Diane. B.S., Va. Poly. Inst., 1948; M.S., Mass. Inst. Tech., 1958. With Am. Electric Power Co. System, 1948—; asst. engr. Am. Electric Power Service Corp., N.Y.C., 1948-52; asst. to pres. Am. Electric Power Service Corp., 1952-54, office mgr., 1954-57, adminstrv. asst. to operating v.p., 1958-61; div. mgr. Am. Electric Power Service Corp. (Appalachian Power Co.), Lynchburg, Va., 1962-66; asst. gen. mgr. Am. Electric Power Service Corp. (Appalachian Power Co.), Roanoke, Va., 1966-67; asst. v.p. Am. Electric Power Service Corp. (Appalachian Power Co.), 1967-69, v.p., 1969, exec. v.p., dir., 1969-73; sr. exec. v.p. ops., dir. Am. Electric Power Service Corp., N.Y.C., 1973-75; vice chmn. ops., dir. Am. Electric Power Service Corp., 1975—; dir. Am. Electric Power Co., N.Y.C., 1972—, chmn. bd., chief exec. officer, 1976—; chmn., dir. AEP Energy Services, Inc., AEP Generating Co., Appalachian Power Columbus and So. Ohio Electric Co., Inc. & Mich. Electric Co., Ky. Power Co., Kingsport Power Co., Mich. Power Co., Ohio Power Co., Wheeling Electric Co.; pres., dir. Ohio Valley Electric Corp., Ind.-Ky. Electric Corp., 1977—, Beech Bottom Power Co., Blackhawk Coal Co., Cedar Coal Co., Cardinal Operating Co., Castlegate Coal Co., Cedar Coal Co., Central Appalachian Coal Co., Central Coal Co., Central Ohio Coal Co., Central Operating Co., Franklin Real Estate Co., Ind. Franklin Realty Co., Central Operating Co., Colomet, Inc., Franklin Real Estate Co., Kanawha Valley Power Co., Mich. Gas Exploration Co., Ind. Franklin Realty, Price River Coal Co., Simco, Inc., So. Appalachian Coal Co., So. Ohio Coal Co., Twin Br. R.R. Co., W.Va. Power Co., Wheeling Electric Co., Windsor Power House Coal Co.; pres. Internat. Conf. on Large High Voltage Elec. Systems (CIGRE). Trustee, Battelle Meml. Inst.; bd. visitors Va. Poly. Inst. and State U. Served with USNR, 1945-46. Sloan fellow, 1957-58. Mem. IEEE, Nat. Coal Assn. (dir.), Nat. Coal Council (bd. dirs.), Assn. Edison Illuminating Cos. (exec. com.), NAM (dir.), Nat. Acad. Engring., Eta Kappa Nu. Methodist. Office: AEP Service Corp 1 Riverside Plaza Box 16631 Columbus OH 43216-6631

WHITE, WOODIE W., clergyman Bishop Central Ill. and So. Ill. confs. United Methodist Ch. Office: PO Box 2050 Bloomington IL 61701 *

WHITE, ZENOBIA MAXINE, educator; b. Cotton Plant, Ark., Feb. 16, 1933; d. Willie Joe and Johnnie (Jones) Reid; B.S., Drake U., 1951; postgrad. Drake U., 1971-75; m. Harold White, Nov. 3, 1959; children—Claire, William, June Carol, Harold, Robin, Cris Jon, Grace Angela. Exec. sec. Forest Ave Mission, Des Moines, 1960-76; social worker Polk County Dept. Social

Services, Des Moines, 1976-77; tchr. public schs. Des Moines Ind. Sch. Dist., 1976—; exec. dir., founder OSACS Inc. Self Actualizing Ctr. for Women, 1979—. Mem. adv. com. State Birth Defects Inst., 1970-81; mem. older worker com. Iowa Commn. on Aging, 1985—. Mem. Assn. Childhood Edn. Am. Office: 2110 Carpenter Ave Des Moines IA 50311

WHITED, WAYNE, food service company executive; b. Richlands, Va., Oct. 31, 1953; s. Cecil Paul and Loretta Eunice (Sizemore) W.; m. Lidia Jaremenko, Aug. 2, 1980; 1 child, Jennifer Ann. Student, Fla. State U., 1972-73; AS in Bus., Lorain County (Ohio) Community Coll., 1982; BS, U. Charleston, 1984, MS, 1986. Owner, operator Rasnake & Whited Welding, Cleveland, Va., 1975; miner operator Jewell Ridge (Va.) Coal Corp., 1975-78; insp. Ford Motor Co., Brook Park, Ohio, 1978-79; owner, operator Carolina Food Systems, Grafton, Ohio, 1979—; advisor Am. Entrepreneurs, Los Angeles, 1980—; bd. dirs. Tri-Co. Quarter Horse, Wellington, Ohio; cons. Small Bus. Seminars, Elyria, Ohio, 1984-86, UAW-Ford, Lorain, Ohio. Sports editor (newspaper) The Airlift Dispatch, 1972 (Guild award 1973). Served to maj. USAF, 1971-75. Mem. Nat. Restaurant Assn., Am. Mgmt. Assn., U. Charleston Alumni Assn. (pres. 1984-86). Avocations: softball, golf, football, old movies, family activities. Home: 9311 Behrwald Brooklyn OH 44144-2631

WHITEMAN, RICHARD FRANK, architect; b. Mankato, Minn., Mar. 24, 1925; s. Lester Raymond and Mary Grace (Dawald) W.; m. Jean Frances Waite, June 20, 1948 (dec. May 1980); children: David, Sarah, Lynn, Ann, Carol, Frank, Marie, Steven; m. Mavis Patricia Knutsen, May 30, 1982. BArch, U. Minn., 1945; MArch, Harvard U., 1948. Registered architect, Minn., Wis., Ga. Designer Ellerbe Co., St. Paul, Minn., 1946; architect Thorsov and Cerny, Mpls., 1948-53; ptnr. Jyring and Whiteman, Hibbing, Minn., 1953-62; pres. AJWM Inc., Hibbing and Duluth, Minn., 1963-72, Architects Four, Duluth, 1972-83; owner Richard Whiteman, Duluth, 1983—; chmn. Architect Sect. Registration Bd., Minn., 1972-80. Prin. works include Washington Sch., Hibbing, 1957 (Minn. Soc. Architects Design award 1957), Whiteman Summer Home, Pengilly, Minn. (Minn. Soc. Architects Design award 1959), Bemidji State Coll. Phys. Edn. Bldg. (Minn. Soc. Architects Design award 1960). Served with USN, 1943-46, PTO. Mem. Minn. Soc. Architects (pres. 1972), Northeast Minn. Architects (pres. 1962), Service Corps Retired Execs. (chmn. Northeast Minn. chpt. 1986), Minn. Designer Selection Bd. (chmn. 1986). Mem. Democratic Farm Labor Party. Roman Catholic. Club: Kitchi Gammi (Duluth). Lodge: Kiwanis. Avocations: photography, fishing, cross-country skiing, travel. Home: 3500 E 3d St Duluth MN 55804

WHITESIDE, ELIZABETH AYRES, lawyer; b. Columbus, Ohio, Feb. 24, 1960; d. ALba Lea and Virginia (Ayres) W. Student, Ind. U., 1978-80; BFA, U. Wis., Milw., 1982; JD, Ohio State U., 1985. Bar: Ohio, 1985, D.C., 1986, U.S. Dist. Ct. (no. and so. dists.) Ohio, 1986, U.S. Ct. Appeals (6th and D.C. cirs.), 1986, U.S. Tax Ct., 1986. Dep. clk. Franklin County Mcpl. Ct, Columbus, 1981; law clk. Chester, Hoffman & Willcox, Columbus, 1983-84, Porter, Wright, Morris & Arthur, Columbus, 1984; assoc. Squire, Sanders & Dempsey, Columbus, 1985—. Mng. editor Ohio State U. Law Jour., 1984-85. Mem. ABA, D.C. Bar Assn., Ohio Bar Assn., Columbus Bar Assn., Am. Judicature Soc., Women Lawyers of Franklin County, Phi Delta Phi. Republican. Methodist. Avoction: playing violin. Home: 46 S Remington Rd Bexley OH 43209 Office: Squire Sanders & Dempsey 155 E Broad St Columbus OH 43215

WHITESIDE, PHILIP ELRAY, manufacturing company executive; b. Weldon, Ill., Nov. 10, 1935; s. William Rice and Hazel (Parr) W.; m. Nancy Jane Seal, Dec. 28, 1957; children: Cynthia Lea, Craig Alan. BS in Indsl. Adminstrn., U. Ill., 1959; MBA, U. Minn., 1971. Indsl engr. McCulloch Corp., Mpls., 1959-61; mfg. cost analyst Collins Radio, Cedar Rapids, Iowa, 1962-63; prodn. and inventory control Control Data, Mpls., 1963-70; mfg. engr. Josten's Inc., Owatonna, Minn., 1971-80; mfg. engr. mgr. Owatonna Tool Co., 1980—; Chmn. DClass Users Group, 1987. Served to sgt. U.S. Army, 1957-61, 62. Mem. Am. Inst. Indsl. Engr. (pres. 1969-70), Soc. Mfg. Engrs., Roseville (Minn.) Jaycees (Boss of the Yr.). Republican. Methodist. Avocations: bicycling, snow skiing. Home: 1031 Rolling Green Dr Owatonna MN 55060 Office: Owatonna Tool Co 655 Eisenhower Dr Owatonna MN 55060

WHITFIELD, DAVID LEWIS, architect; b. Vincennes, Ind., Mar. 17, 1937; s. Joseph Lewis and Verna Irene (Allen) W.; m. Rosalie Ann Boyer, Nov. 19, 1960; children: Mark, Scott, Kathleen, Patrick. Student, Vincennes U., U. Ill., Washington U., St. Louis. Registered profl. architect, Mo., Ill., Ind., Ga., N.C., Va., W.Va., Md., D.C. Architect L.W. Routt & Assocs., Vincennes, 1958, J.H. Kolbrook, Louisville, 1959; v.p. Bank Bldg. Corp., St. Louis, 1960-84; pres. DLW Inc., Chesterfield, Mo., 1984—. Served with U.S. Army, 1960-64. Mem. AIA (com. mem. 1980—). Office: DLW Inc 14266 Dinsmoor Dr Chesterfield MO 63017-2910

WHITFIELD, DAVID RICHARD, model management executive; b. Pontiac, Mich., May 24, 1928; s. Awbery and Ruth Elizabeth (Mattison) W.; m. Lee Kusiak, Mar. 22, 1958; children: Pamela, Robin, Richard, Noelle. AA, Chgo. Acad. Fine Arts, 1950. Dir. Patricia Stevens, N.Y.C., 1956-57; pres. Patricia Stevens, Cleve., 1957-70; pres. David & Lee, Inc., Cleve., 1970-75, Chgo., 1976—. Pub. (mag.) Model's Life, 1987. Served to USN, 1946-48, PTO. Mem. Am. Model Mgrs. Assn. (pres. 1986—), DuPage Power Squadron. Republican. Methodist. Clubs: Burnham Park Yacht, Lake Michigan Yachting Assn. (Chgo.). Avocations: power boating, painting, writing. Office: David & Lee Model Mgmt 70 W Hubbard St Chicago IL 60610

WHITFIELD, RUSSELL LEE, health care company execuitve; b. Detroit, May 2, 1931; s. Emerson Laurie and Ivy Evelyn (Hopps) W.; m. Rosemary Keller, May 21, 1952; children: Jeff, John, Chris, Terra. MBA, U. Mich., 1957; postgrad., Wayne State U., 1958. CPA, Mich.; cert. data processor. V.p. communications and info. systems Am. Nat. Resources Co., Detroit, 1979-82, v.p., gen. auditor, 1983-85; pres. Health Mgmt. Systems, Southfield, Mich., 1986—. Chmn. Eastwood Community Clinics, Detroit, 1980-86. Mem. Am. Inst. CPA's, Mich. Assn. CPA's, ALMACA, ICCP, Acctg. Aid Soc. (chmn. 1979). Club: Detroit Athletic. Lodge: Rotary (chmn. children's services com. 1986-87). Aovcations: photography, gardening, golf. Office: Health Mgmt Systems 26250 Northwestern Southfield MI 48067

WHITICAN, FREDERICK LEE, marketing professional; b. Port Huron, Mich., July 8, 1952; s. Kenneth Leroy and Elaine Isla (Reichard) W.; m. Beverly M. Ladd, June 28, 1975 (div. July 1986); children: Andrea Lynne, Michael Frederick. BS in Gen. Engring., USAF Acad., 1975; MBA in Mgmt., Rensselaer Poly. Inst., 1981. Commd. 2d lt. USAF, 1975, advanced through grades to capt.; instr. navigator 416th Bomb Wing, Griffiss AFB, Rome, N.Y., 1977-80; program mgr. advanced research and devel. programs Rome Air Devel. Ctr., Griffiss AFB, 1980-82; F-16 operational flight trainer and avionics familiarization trainer program mgr. Aero. Systems Div., Wright Patterson AFB, Dayton, Ohio, 1982-85, F-16 simulator dep. program mgr., 1985-86; mktg. rep. Dynamics Research Corp., Fairborn, Ohio, 1986—. Mem. Assn. Air Force Acad. Grads., Air Force Assn., Electronic Equipment Mfrs. Corp., Tech. Mktg. Soc. Am. Republican. Methodist. Avocation: sports. Home: 4418 Woodpoint Ct Dayton OH 45424 Office: Dynamics Research Corp 2900 Presidential Dr Suite 385 Fariborn OH 45324

WHITING, JOHN, manufacturing company executive; b. 1928. With Hayes-Albion Corp., Jackson, Mich., 1950—, v.p. planning, 1972-78, v.p., sec., 1978-79, sr. v.p. fabricated products group, 1979-82, pres., chief operating officer, 1982-83, pres., chief exec. officer, 1983—. Office: Hayes-Albion Corp 2701 N Dettman Rd Jackson MI 49201 *

WHITLA, F. E., psychiatrist; b. Butte, Nebr., Oct. 20, 1930; s. William Kenneth and Flora (Fleming) W.; m. carol Kinderkencht, Nov. 17, 1976 (dec. Feb. 1987); children: Beth, Scott, Barbara, Steven. BS, U. Nebr., 1952; MD, U. Nebr., Omaha, 1960. Diplomate Am. Bd. Psychiatry and Neurology. Intern Neb. Meth. Hosp., Omaha, 1960-61; resident Neb. Psychiatrist Inst., Omaha, 1965-68; chief psychiatry services Lincoln (Nebr.) VA Med. Ctr., 1981—. Served to cpl. U.S. Army, 1952-54. Mem. AMA, Nebr. Med. Assn., Nebr. Psychiat. Assn., Am. Psychiat. Assn. Home: 4201 Calvert Lincoln NE 68506 Office: 600 S 70 Lincoln NE 68510

WHITLATCH, CRAIG EUGENE, minister; b. Cedar Rapids, Iowa, July 29, 1957; s. Forrest Eugene and Margret Doris (Trosen) W.; m. Faith Edith Hald, Oct. 17, 1981. Student, Mid-Am. Nazarene Coll., 1976-78, Vennard Coll., 1979-81, 1985. Ordained minister Ch. of the Nazarene, 1986. Evangelist Ch. Nazarene, Oskaloosa, Iowa, 1978-82; assoc. minister Ch. Nazarene, Sioux City, Iowa, 1982-83; minister Ch. Nazarene, Albia, Iowa, 1983-85, Grinnell, Iowa, 1985—; dir. early youth Ch. Nazarene, Des Moines, 1985—, zone Nazarene Youth Internat. pres., 1985—. Named one of Outstanding Young Men of Am., 1985. Republican. Home: 1215 Bliss St Grinnell IA 50112 Office: Ch Nazarene 1232 Bliss St Grinnell IA 50112

WHITLOCK, BRIAN THOMAS, lawyer; b. Chgo., Oct. 5, 1954; s. James Joseph Jr. and Marjorie (Riordan) W.; m. Nancy Ellen Prendergast, May 16, 1981; 1 child, Mallory. BA, Northwestern U., 1976; JD with honors, Ill. Inst. Tech., 1979. Bar: Ill. 1979, U.S. Tax Ct. 1982, U.S. Dist. Ct. (no. dist.) Ill. 1983; CPA, Ill. Tax mgr. Stein, Larmon & Co., CPAs, Oak Brook, Ill., 1979-84; assoc. Bellows and Bellows, P.C., Chgo., 1984—. Mem. ABA, Ill. Bar Assn. (young lawyers div. sect. council), Am. Inst. CPA's, Ill. Soc. CPA's (fed. income tax com.). Office: Bellows and Bellows 79 W Monroe St Suite 800 Chicago IL 60603

WHITLOCK, RICHARD BARNES, accounting company executive; b. Springfield, Mo., Jan. 8, 1940; s. Herbert Hadley and Mary C. (McGarvey) W.; m. Jackie Louise Jorgensen, Dec. 28, 1960; children—Cary J., R. Gregory, Christopher B. B.S.B.A., U. Mo., 1963. C.P.A., Mo. With Roper & Richardson, Springfield, 1963-66, ptnr., 1966-71; ptnr. Fox & Co., Springfield, 1971-75, ptnr. in charge, 1975-85; mng. ptnr., Whitlock, Selim and Keehn, Springfield, 1985—. Bd. dirs. St. John's Regional Health Ctr., Springfield, 1975—, Make a Wish Found., Springfield, 1983-85, Springfield Family YMCA, 1975-80, United Way of Ozarks, 1986—; bd. dirs. United Way of Ozarks, 1987—. Mem. Am. Inst. C.P.A.s, Mo. Soc. C.P.A.s (pres. southwest chpt. 1977-78). Republican. Presbyterian. Club: Hickory Hills Country (pres., bd. dirs. 1983-84). Home: 2830 Covington St Springfield MO 65804 Office: Whitlock Selim and Keehn 2-300 Corp Ctr Springfield MO 65804

WHITLOW, MARION VIRGINIA, educator, nurse; b. Johnstown, Pa., May 17, 1929; d. William Sercy and Mary Thelma (Hill) Holton; m. Emery Whitlow, June 28, 1969; children: Cecily Patterson, Gary Patterson, Carol Patterson Upshur. Diploma in nursing St. Francis Hosp., Pitts. 1950; BS in Nursing, U. Pitts. 1966; MS, U. Ind.-Purdue U., Indpls., 1977. Staff nurse St. Francis Hosp., 1950-52; staff nurse Mercy Hosp., Johnstown, 1956-58, 60-65, instr. pediatrics, 1966-69; assoc. prof. nursing Purdue U., Westville, Ind., 1980—. Producer, writer: (musical production) A Peoples' Music; coordinator, presenter exhibit Odyssey of A.M.E. Ch.: 1787-1987, Quinn Historic Chapel, Chgo., 1987. Mem. AAUW, Am. Nurses Assn., (intercultural council), Am. Nurses Found., Am. Black Nurses Assn., Harriet Tubman Nurse Assn. Michigan City (organizer), NAACP (sec. Michigan City 1971-73), Ind. Com. for Blacks in Higher Edn. (charter mem., sec.), Sigma Theta Tau. Democrat. Mem. A.M.E. Ch. Office: Purdue U North Cen Campus Westville IN 46390

WHITMAN, WAYNE EARL, electronics company executive; b. Maryville, Tenn., May 8, 1944; s. Philip Henry and Mary Otis (Fisher) W.; m. Anne Bennet Lebeck, Apr. 19, 1974; children: Charles David, Jennifer McCrae. BSEE, Milw. Sch. Engring., 1971; M in Mgmt., Northwestern U., 1985. Appilcation engr. Louis Allis, New Berlin, Wis., 1973-75; design engr. Astronautics Corps., Milw., 1975-77, Digital Instruments, Watertown, Wis., 1977-80; group mgr. Ohmeda, Madison, Wis., 1980-85; v.p. Zetaco, Inc., Eden Prairie, Minn., 1985—. Mem. Computer Automation Soc. Am. (sr.), Soc. Mfg. Engrs. (sr.), Nat. Computer Graphics Assn., Beta Gamma Sigma. Republican. Home: 4620 Drexel Edina MN 55424 Office: Zetaco Inc 6850 Shady Oak Rd Eden Prairie MN 55344

WHITMARSH, WAYNE BOYD, architect; b. Burlington, Iowa, May 27, 1937; s. Glen Jonathan and Thelma (Boyd) W.; divorced; children: Phillip Wayne, Karen Elizabeth. BArch, Iowa State U., 1961. Lic. architect, Iowa, Nebr., Kans. Draftsman pvt. architects, Omaha and Cedar Falls, Iowa, 1961-67; asst. to univ. architect U. No. Iowa, Cedar Falls, 1967-72; architect pvt. firms, Iowa and Nebr., 1972-81; mgr. facility planning and space mgmt. U. Nebr., Omaha, 1981-86, campus architect, 1986—. Served to sgt. USAR. Mem. Soc. Coll. and Univ. Planning, Nat. Council Archtl. Registration Bds., Nat. Peace Inst. Found., Presbyn. Met. Ministries of Omaha (bd. dirs. 1983-86), Amnesty Internat. Republican. Presbyterian. Home: 4801 Seward Omaha NE 68104

WHITNEY, BARBARA THIELE, foundation administrator; b. Chgo., Aug. 27, 1942; d. Edward Morton and Pleasant (Williams) Thiele; m. John Alden, June 27, 1964 (div.); children: Brooks Elizabeth, Edward Alder, Amanda Colvin Whitney. BA in Writing, Denison U., 1964. Researcher Book div. Time, Inc., N.Y.C., 1964-66; freelance writer Chgo., 1966-75; exec. dir. Lincoln Park Zool. Soc., Chgo., 1975—; reviewer Inst. Mus. Services, Washington, 1982, panelist, 1984-86. Contbr. articles to profl. jours. Formerly mem. Jr. League of Chgo., Hull House Assn. Aux. Bd., Extension Bd. Chgo. Maternity Ctr., Chgo. Jr. Bd. Travelers Aid Soc., Exec. Bd. Parent's Assn. of Francis Parker Sch., Ch. of Our Savior; mem. women's bd. Rush Presbyn. St. Luke's Med. Hosp., Chgo., 1975-86, Parents Council of Latin Sch. of Chgo., Mary Meyer Sch., Northfield Community Nursery Sch. Recipient Servian award U. Chgo. Cancer Research Found., 1971, Leadership award Direct Mail Mktg. Assn., 1978, Golden Pyramid award Internat. Specialty Advt. Assn., 1980, Chgo. Industry Colleagues award Women's Advt. Club Chgo., 1980. Fellow Am. Assn. Zool. Parks and Aquariums (profl., various coms., rep. 1981); mem. Econ. Club of Chgo. (membership com. 1979-82, chmn. membership subcommittee 1982), Am. Assn. Fund Raising Execs., Publicity Club of Chgo. Office: The Lincoln Park Zool Soc 2200 N Cannon Dr Chicago IL 60614

WHITNEY, C. R., manufacturing company executive. Chmn. Allen-Bradley Co., Milw. Office: Allen-Bradley Co 1201 S 2nd St Milwaukee WI 53204 *

WHITNEY, KENT RALPH NELSON, accountant; b. Chgo., Nov. 25, 1954; s. Emerson Calhoun and Eileen (Holmberg) W.; B.B.A., Loyola U., Chgo., 1977; m. Arlene Mary Delpino, Apr. 29, 1978; 1 son, Kent Ralph Emerson. C.P.A., Arthur Andersen and Co., Chgo., 1977, Deloitte, Haskins and Sells, Chgo., 1981; stock exchange specialist Rockwell Internat. Corp. Securities, Chgo., 1976-81; exec. dir. Corpus Christi Corp., Chgo., 1978—. Internal auditor Community Coll. Dist. 508, 1984—; gov. United Rep. Fund, treas., 1987—. Mem. Ill. C.P.A. Soc., Midwest Stock Exchange, Chgo. Bd. Options Exchange, Chgo. Merc. Exchange. Home: 201 E Walton Pl Chicago IL 60611 Office: Corpus Christi Corp 320 N Michigan Ave Chicago IL 60601

WHITNEY, RICHARD GRIER, dentist; b. Ann Arbor, Mich., Nov. 22, 1924; s. Frank Thomas Sr. and Edna Grace (Wonderlic) W.; m. Loretta Marie Sulenski, Sept. 29, 1951 (div. Nov. 1981); children: Carol Tumbas, Grier Whitney; m. Suzanne Trick Winkler, Dec. 23, 1981; 1 child, Wendy Stuart. Student, U. Mich., 1942-43, DDS, 1951; student, Kenyon Coll., 1946-47. Gen. practice dentistry Saginaw, Mich., 1951-81, Ann Arbor, 1981-87. Bd. dirs. Saginaw County Red Cross, 1956-57. Served to cpl. USAC, 1943-46. Mem. ADA, Mich. Dental. Soc., Washtenaw Dist. Dental Soc., Saginaw County Dental Soc. (pres. 1957, sec.-treas. 1974-75). Republican. Avocations: golf, travel, astronomy. Home: 22 Haverhill Ct Ann Arbor MI 48105 Office: 700 Tappan Ann Arbor MI 48104

WHITNEY, SCOTT RICHARD, real estate executive, accountant; b. Chgo., July 7, 1952; s. Albert Gayle and Elaine Shirley (Van Kampen) W.; m. Robin Miller, Mar. 10, 1973; children: Bryan Miller, Kimberly May. BS, No. Ill. U., 1975. CPA, Ill. Staff acct. David A. Gotch, CPA's, Chgo., 1975-76; controller Realty & Mortgage Co., Chgo., 1976-79; prin. Scott R. Whitney & Assocs., CPA's, Cary, Ill., 1979-83; v.p. Balcor/Am. Express Inc., Skokie, Ill., 1983-84, First Capital Fin. Corp., Chgo., 1984—. Active N.W. Suburban council Boy Scouts Am. Mem. Am. Inst. CPA's, Ill. CPA Soc. Republican. Christian Scientist. Avocations: scuba diving, golf. Office: First Capital Fin Corp 2 N Riverside Plaza Suite 2200 Chicago IL 60606

WHITSEL, ROBERT MALCOLM, insurance company executive; b. Lafayette, Ind., Dec. 30, 1929; s. Earl Newton and Elizabeth (Bader) W.; m. Marilyn Katherine House, Oct. 15, 1955; children—Rebecca Sue, Cynthia Ann. B.S., Ind. U., 1951, M.B.A., 1954. With Lafayette Life Ins. Co., 1954—, dir., 1966—, mem. exec. com., 1968—, exec. v.p., 1973, pres., 1973—; dir. Lafayette Nat. Bank; chmn. N. Cen. Health Services, Inc., Purdue Research Found. Elder, trustee, deacon Presbyterian Ch., 1965-74; pres. Jr. Achievement Greater Lafayette, Inc., 1976—, Central Presbyn. Found., Edgelea PTA; past pres., bd. dirs., past campaign chmn. United Way of Greater Lafayette; past v.p., bd. dirs. Wabash Sch. for Mentally Retarded; mem. adv. bd. Purdue Ctr. for Econ. Edn.; bd. dirs. Purdue Research Found.; past treas., bd. dirs. Capital Funds Found. Greater Lafayette; bd. dirs. Lafayette Home Hosp., 1972—, mem. finance com., 1976—, past pres.; trustee YWCA Found.; chmn. Greater Lafayette Progress Inc., Westminster Village Retirement Ctr.; pres. Greater Lafayette Community Found. Served to 1st lt. USAF, 1951-53. Recipient Nat. Bus. Leadership award, 1977. Mem. Soc. Residential Appraisers, Ind. Mortgage Bankers Assn. (past pres.), Am. Council Life Ins. (com. on econ. policy, exec. round table com.), Soc. Fin. Analysts, Assn. Ind. Life Ins. Cos. (pres.), Ind. C. of C. (dir.), Greater Lafayette C. of C. (dir., past pres.), Ind. Soc. of Chgo., Beta Gamma Sigma. Republican. Clubs: Lafayette Country (past pres., dir.), Town and Gown. Lodge: Masons. Home: 541 Old Farm Rd Lafayette IN 47905 Office: Lafayette Life Ins Co 1905 Teal Road PO Box 7007 Lafayette IN 47903

WHITSITT, STEPHEN DONALD, real estate appraiser; b. Ft. Knox, Ky., Dec. 1, 1954; s. Donald L. and Wanda I. (Bash) W.; m. Ruby Jean Racicky, Feb. 10, 1979; children: Mark Stephen, Clayton Edward. BA, Hanover (Ind.) Coll., 1976. Loan officer, appraiser Champaign (Ill.) Loan and Bldg., 1976-83; appraiser Mid-State Appraising, Champaign, Ill., 1983—. Mem. Soc. Real Estate Appraisers (sec.-treas. 1984—), Champaign County Bd. Realtors. Republican. Presbyterian. Lodge: Rotary. Avocations: golf, investments, coll. atheltics. Home: Rural Rt 1 Box 107 Seymour IL 61875-9738 Office: Mid-State Appraising 210 W Springfield Suite 410 Champaign IL 61820

WHITSON-SCHMIDT, FRANCES GALE, chief financial officer; b. Balt., Oct. 31, 1946; d. Frank Gilson and Frances Elizabeth (Moore) Whitson; B.A., Towson State U., 1967; M.B.A., Northwestern U., 1981; m. Donald Eugene Schmidt. Programmer-analyst Monumental Life Ins., Balt., 1967-72; programmer-analyst United Meth. Bd. of Pensions, Evanston, Ill., 1973-77, sr. systems analyst, 1977-82, asst. gen. sec., 1982-84, asst. treas., 1984-86, chief fin. officer, 1987—. Democrat. United Methodist. Office: 1200 Davis St Evanston IL 60201

WHITTAKER, BOB, congressman; b. Eureka, Kans., Sept. 18, 1939; m. Marlene Faye Arnold, 1963; children: Steven, Stephanie, Susan. Student, Kans. U., 1957-59; grad., Ill. Coll. Optometry, 1962. Practice optometry; clinic dir. Kans. Low Vision Clinic, 1973; mem. Kans. Ho. of Reps., 1974-77, 96th-99th Congresses from 5th Kans. Dist. Mem. City Planning Commn., Augusta, Kans., 1970-74; past pres. Augusta United Fund; past chmn., elder, lay minister Christian Ch. Fellow Am. Acad. Optometry; mem. Heart of Am. Contact Lens Soc. (past pres.). Republican. Lodge: Lions (past pres.). Office: US Ho of Reps Room 332 Cannon House Office Bldg Washington DC 20515 *

WHITTEN, BONNIE LEE, property manager; b. Council Grove, Kans., June 3, 1924; d. Charles Vaughn Lloyd and Faye Alice (Bryan) Branic; m. Donald David Whitten, Apr. 18, 1947. Student George Washington U., 1943-45. Mgr. distbn. of recs. War Fin. div. U.S. Treasury, Washington, 1945-46; dental technician Drs. Paul Swanson and Curtis Babcock, Oak Park, Ill., 1947-51; tng. supr. United Airlines, Chgo., 1951-61; dir. consumer services Sperry & Hutchinson Co., N.Y.C., 1961-71; dir. apt. mgmt. Harts Co., Indpls., 1971-77; property adminstr. Basic Am. Industries, Inc., Indpls., 1977-81; dir. condominium mgmt. Barrett & Stokely, Indpls., 1981—. Mem. Pub. Relations Soc. Am., Apt. Assn. Ind., Community Assn. Central Ind., Inc., Community Assn. Inst. Republican. Mem. Christian Ch. Club: Plus Investment.

WHITTEN, STANLEY BURT, federal agency official; b. Washington, Feb. 2, 1935; s. Leslie Hunter and Linnora (Harvey) W.; m. Rose Marie McNerney, June 29, 1963; children: Cosmas Anne, Stanley Burt Jr., Mary Catherine, Lewis Edward. BME, Cornell U., 1957; postgrad., George Washington U., 1964-66. Stockbroker W.E. Hutton & Co., Washington, 1966-70, Reynolds Securities Co., Washington, 1970-74; fin. analyst SEC, Washington, 1974-78; investigator SEC, Chgo., 1978-81, chief investigator, 1981—. Contbr. crossword puzzles to mags. and newspapers. Served to lt. (j.g.) USNR, 1957-60. Club: Cornell of Chgo. Avocation: crossword puzzle construction. Home: 2324 Maple Ave Northbrook IL 60062 Office: SEC 219 S Dearborn Chicago IL 60604

WHITTENBERG, GLENN BRUCE, advertising executive; b. Carbondale, Ill., Oct. 23, 1953; s. Glenn Henry and Carolyn Joan (Schrodt) W.; m. Gayle Lynn Nesemeyer, Aug. 14, 1976; 1 child, Jacob Bruce. BS in Speech Communication, So. Ill. U., 1975. Promotion mgr. advt. sales/circulation Marion (Ill.) Pub. Co., 1975-80; advt. sales So. Illinoisan Newspaper, Carbondale, 1980-82; advt. sales mgr. So. Ill. U., Carbondale, 1982-86, advt. mgr., 1986—; asst. instr. journalism So. Ill. U., Carbondale, 1984-85. Mem. Ill. Press Assn. Advt. Mgrs. (tng. com. 1986—), Internat. Newspaper Advt. and Mktg. Execs., Assn. Newspaper Classified Advt. Mgrs., Am. Newspaper Pubs. Assn. (chmn. so. Ill. projects with industry bus. adv. com.). Avocations: reading, music, outdoor activities. Home: Rural Route 1 Box 37 Goreville IL 62939 Office: So Illinoisan Newspaper 710 N Illinois Carbondale IL 62901

WHITTERS, MICHAEL, osteopathic physician; b. Cedar Rapids, Iowa, Dec. 29, 1952; s. Thomas Steven Whitters; m. Pamella Rae Whitters, Mar. 4, 1972; children: Alison Rebecca, Amanda Rachel, Abigail Renee. AS, Kirkwood Community Coll., 1975; BS, U.Iowa, 1978; DO, Coll. Osteo. Med. and Surgery, 1981. Licensed osteopath, Iowa. Osteopath Community Family Practice Clinic, P.C., Clarion, Iowa, 1982—; Pres. med. staff Community Meml. Hosp., Clarion, 1984—. Mem. AMA, Am. Osteo. Assn., Am. Coll. Gen. Practioners, Am. Acad. Family Physicians, Wright County Med. Soc. (pres. 1985-86). Roman Catholic. Avocations: music, skiing, biking, swimming. Home: 119 4th Ave NW Clarion IA 50525 Office: Community Family Practice Clinic 215 13th Ave SW PO Box 271 Clarion IA 50525

WHITTING, ELLEN GAIL, social worker; b. Detroit, Aug. 4, 1946; d. Milton and Anita Sarah (Miller) Hecker; m. Raymond Whitting, Oct. 20, 1979; children: Jenniffer, Danny. BA, Western Mich. U., 1975, MA with honors, 1976. Lic. social worker, Mich. Psychotherapist Planning for Living, Bay City, Mich., 1976-77; social worker, case mgr. Aging Services div. Dept. Pub. Health, Saginaw, Mich., 1979—; cons. Dept. Social Services, Bay City, 1976-77, Dept. Mental Health, Saginaw, 1983; pvt. practice counselor mental health, Essexville, Mich., 1979. Contbr. articles to newspapers and mags. Mem. Assn. Retarded Citizens, Humane Soc. U.S., Greenpeace, People for the Am. Way, ASPCA. Jewish. Lodge: Rosicrucians. Avocations: reading, writing, knitting, gardening. Home: 12175 Wahl Rd Saint Charles MI 48655 Office: Sr Citizen Ctr Saint Charles MI 48655

WHITTINGTON, RICHARD OREN, biochemist; b. South Bend, Ind., Nov. 28, 1929; s. Oren Leslie and Edna Caroline (Schlundt) W.; m. Mary Eloise Vargas, Sept. 5, 1959; children—Bruce William, David Richard, Daniel Patrick. B.S., Lake Forest Coll., Ill., 1959; postgrad. Northwestern U., 1960. Research biochemist Abbott Labs., North Chicago, Ill., 1962-86; advisor to Rep. Robert W. Churchill, 62d Ill. State Dist., 1986—. Rep. Asst. scoutmaster NE council Boy Scouts Am., 1973-80; recycling coordinator Village of Grayslake, Ill., 1986—. Served with U.S. Army, 1951-53. Decorated Bronze Star, UN Service medal; recipient Presdl. award Abbott Labs., 1980, 85, Entrepreneurial award, 1982, Disting. Service award, 1982.

Mem. Sigma Xi. Lutheran. Club: Fraternal Order Police. Contbr. articles in field to profl. jours. Home: 297 Westerfield Pl Grayslake IL 60030 Office: 14th St and Sheridan Rd North Chicago IL 60064

WHITTY, LAWRENCE JOSEPH, retail executive; b. Minot, N.D., Sept. 10, 1937; s. Lawrence and Roberta (Schaffer) W.; m. Sandra Whitty, Nov. 8, 1958 (dec. Nov. 1974); children: Larry J., Juliann, Timothy, Kristel; m. Nancy Jean Vogel, May 8, 1976; stepchildren: Robert, Susan, Carolyn, Dennis, Michael. Cert., Cox Baker's and Decorating Sch., Grand Forks, N.D., 1957; hon. degree, St. Ambrose Coll., Davenport, Iowa. Owner Keg Drive Inn, Minot, 1958-60; prin. Cox's Bakery, Grand Forks, 1960-65; bakery supr. Murray's Super Value, Davenport, Iowa, 1965-66; dietary dir. Mercy Hosp., Davenport, 1966-68; supr., mgr. Shakey's Pizza Parlors, Iowa and N.Mex., 1968-72; pres., chmn. bd. dirs. Happy Joe's Pizza & Ice Cream Parlor, Inc., Davenport, 1972—; bd. dirs. Happy Joe's Nat. Franchise Bd. Mem. St. Patrick's Soc. of Quad Cities, Davenport Council of Parents and Tchrs. Recipient Friend of Edn. award Davenport Edn. Assn., 1985, Corp. Citizen award Iowa Soc. to Prevent Blindness, 1980. Mem. Retail Bakers of Am. (cert. master baker), Nat. Restaurant Assn., Mississippi Valley Restaurant Assn., Scott County Retarded Assn., Iowa Head Injury Assn. (bd. dirs. 1986—), Village of East Davenport Assn., Mississippi Valley Fair Assn. (bd. dirs. 1986), Davenport C. of C., Bettendorf (Iowa) C. of C. Roman Catholic. Clubs: Davenport, Crow Valley Golf (Bettendorf). Lodges: Elks, KC, Rotary. Avocations: golf, horses. Office: Happy Joe's Pizza & Ice Cream Parlor Inc 1875 Middle Rd Bettendorf IA 52722

WHITTY, MARY JANE, counselor; b. Baraboo, Wis., June 26, 1947; d. Robert Peter and Virginia (Marron) W. B.S. in Edn., U. Wis.-LaCrosse, 1970; M.Counseling, U. Wis.-Whitewater, 1979, M.Sch. Adminstrn., 1980. Cert. tchr., counselor, Wis. Tchr., New Berlin Schs. (Wis.), 1970-78, counselor elem., 1978-80, counselor secondary, 1980—, curriculum chmn. guidance dept., 1982—, chairperson dist. wide curriculum research, 1983. Pvt. counselor parents of terminally ill children, Greendale, Wis., 1980—. Recipient Outstanding Tchr. award Zerox Corp., 1974. Mem. Wis. Guidance Profl. Assn., Nat. Guidance Profl. Assn. Democrat. Roman Catholic. Clubs: Ski, Track (New Berlin) (dir. 1980—), Health.

WHOLF, BEVERLY DEAN, real estate broker; b. Omaha, Mar. 14, 1937; d. Everett Lee and Veronica Dean (Wakefield) Gardner; student U. Kans., 1955; cert. residential specialist; m. Emmett Clark Wholf, Oct. 12, 1956; children—Gordon Dean, Stuart Clark, Alan Ray. Broker, owner E.C. Wholf & Assos., Inc., Realtors, Lee's Summit, Mo., 1976—; pres., dir. Multiple Listing Service Kansas City. Mem. Met. Kansas City Mo. Bd. Realtors (Realtor of Yr. award 1980). Home: 338 SW Marsh Wren Lee's Summit MO 64063 Office: 116 W 3rd St Lee's Summit MO 64063

WIANS, DAVID ALAN, insurance agent; b. Chgo., Apr. 29, 1952; s. Warren and Thelma (Swedland) W.; m. Demetria Kanelos, June 10, 1978; children: Natalie, William, Anastasia. BS in Edn., No. Ill. U., 1975. Agt. State Mutual Am., Chgo., 1976-81, State Farm Ins., Chgo., 1981—. Mem. Jaycees (bd. dirs. Elk Grove Village, chmn. bd. dirs. 1986—, dir Ill. chpt., treas. 1983-84, v.p. 1984-85, pres. 1985-86, various awards); Nat. Assn. Life Underwriters (Nat. Quality award 1980), Nat. Assn. Health Underwriters (leading producers round table, 1982-84). Avocations: handball, woodworking, golf. Office: State Farm Ins 5872 N Milwaukee Ave Chicago IL 60646

WIANT, KURT DEVERE, psychologist; b. Lakewood, Ohio, Feb. 24, 1946; s. Lloyd Devere and Martha Louise W.; m. Rita Ellen Krupar, Apr. 8, 1972; children—Kyle, Ethan, Sara. B.S., Kent State U., 1968, M.Ed., 1973, Ed.S., 1975. Tchr. math. Parma (Ohio) Pub. Schs., 1969, Lakewood (Ohio) Pub. Schs., 1969-72; psychologist, adminstr. Berea (Ohio) Pub. Schs., 1972—; pvt. practice psychologist, 1979—. Mem. Nat. Assn. Sch. Psychologists, Ohio Sch. Psychologists Assn., Cleve. Area Sch. Psychologists Assn., Phi Delta Kappa, Kappa Delta Pi. Presbyterian. Home: 3097 Creekside Dr Westlake OH 44145

WIBERG, RICHARD LEE, public relations executive; b. Chgo., May 29, 1930; s. Leroy Wiberg and Lucille M. (Norcott) Furth; m. Mary Ann Nora Baer, Jan. 25, 1959; children: Kim, Lisa, Holly, Joy, Dana. BS in Journalism, Bradley U., 1960. Editor Tazwell Courier, East Peoria, Ill., 1960-61; advt. mgr. Schwinn Bicycle Co., Chgo., 1961-69; account supr. Daniel J. Edelman, Chgo., 1969-73; dir. communications services Trans Union Corp., Lincolnshire, Ill., 1973-80; mgr. pub. relations Fisher Controls, Marshalltown, Iowa, 1980—. Served with USN, 1951-55. Mem. Pub. Relations Soc. Am. (Silver Anvil award 1973). Republican. Club: Cen. Iowa Camera (MArshalltown). Avocations: photography, tennis, golf, bowling, bridge. Home: 206 Thomas Dr Marshalltown IA 50158 Office: Fisher Controls 205 S Center St Marshalltown IA 50158

WIBLE, JAMES ORAM, plastics company executive; b. Pitts., June 30, 1949; s. Lewis Alfred and Wilda (Boa) W.; m. Norma Joan Klaus, Sept. 20, 1975; children: Judson F., Jerald L., Leslie K. BA, Allegheny Coll., 1971; MBA, Xavier U., 1974. Sales rep. Pitts. Paint & Glass Indust=ries, Cin., 1971-72, Detroit, 1973-75; pres. Am. Colors, Inc., Sandusky, Ohio, 1975—. Pres. Montessori Parents Assn., Huron, Ohio, 1986; pres. bd. trustees 1st Presbyn. Ch. Sandusky, 1981. Mem. Soc. Plastics Industry. Republican. Club: Plum Brook Country (Sandusky). Avocation: golf. Home: 2509 Fairway Ln Sandusky OH 44870 Office: Am Colors Inc 1321 1st St Sandusky OH 44870

WICK, CHAD PHILIP, banker; b. Dayton, Ohio, Aug. 17, 1942; s. Daniel Martin and Louella Elizabeth (Greer) W.; student Gen. Motors Inst. Tech., 1960-62; B.B.A., U. Cin., 1965; M.Internat. Mgmt. with honors, Thunderbird Grad. Sch., 1972; m. Gail Elaine Stichweh, Sept. 19, 1964; children—Christine, Aubrey. With Frigidaire div. Gen. Motors Corp., Dayton, 1960-66; asst. v.p. Winters Nat. Bank, Dayton, 1972-75, v.p., Cin., 1975-79; pres. AmeriTrust of Cin., sr. v.p. AmeriTrust Co., 1979-81; exec. v.p., dir. So. Ohio Bank, Cin., 1981-82, pres., chief exec. officer, 1982-85; exec. v.p. Cen. Trust Co., Cin., 1985—. Served to capt. USAF, 1966-71. Trustee, Coll. Mt. St. Joseph, 1980—, Cin., Seven Hills Neighborhood Houses, Inc.; chmn. Leadership Cin., 1986; bd. dirs. Cin. Council World Affairs, 1978-87, Contemporary Arts Ctr., Downtown Council; chmn. bd. dirs. World Affairs Inst.; chmn. bd. trustees Program for Cin. Unitarian. Clubs: Bankers (bd. dirs.), Coldstream Country, Queen City. Office: Cen Bancorporation Inc Central Trust Center 201 E 5th St Cincinnati OH 45202-4117 *

WICK, JOHN F., construction company executive; b. 1926. MBA, U. Wis. Research and teaching asst. U. Wis., Madison, 1949-52; with Wick Bldg. Systems Inc., Madison, 1954—, now chmn. bd., pres., dir. Office: Wick Bldg Systems Inc 403 Walter Rd Box 490 Mazomanie WI 53560 *

WICKARD, SAMUEL EUGENE, minister, school administrator; b. Albion, Mich., Dec. 8, 1950; s. Glenn Eugene and Barbara Ruth (Stephenson) W.; m. Dawn Joy Seiple, July 26, 1969; children: Chad Eugene, Wesley Andrew, Nathan Scott. BTh, Clarksville Sch. Theology, 1976, ThM, 1980; ThD, Internat. Bible Sem., 1981, DD (hon.), 1981; PhD, Bapt. U., 1984. Ordained to ministry Bible Meth. Ch., 1974. Pastor Wesleyan Missionary Ch., Fayette, Ohio, 1970-73, pastor, sch. adminstr., 1976-82; pastor Bible Meth. Ch., Anniston, Ala., 1973-76; pastor, sch. adminstr. Wesleyan Meth. Ch., Titusville, Pa., 1982-84, Bible Missionary Ch., Fayette, 1984—. Mem. United Assn. Christian Counselors (cert. counselor, 1983, life), Am. Assn. Christian Counselors, U.S. Chaplaincy Assn. Home and Office: 307 Irene Ct Fayette OH 43521

WICKENHAUSER, THOMAS COURTNEY, writer; b. Bloomington, Ill., Apr. 12, 1949; s. George Thomas and Elizabeth Ellen (Crum) W.; m. Crystal Ann Reckling, Aug. 15, 1969; children: Nicole Ann, Aaron Thomas. AA, Winston Churchill Coll., 1969; BS, Ill. State U., 1972. With Caterpillar Inc., Peoria, Ill., 1972-74, tech. writer, 1974-78, writer, 1978—; freelance writer TWriting, El Paso, Ill., 1978—. Republican. Avocations: sports, gardening.

WICKRAMANAYAKE, SANDHYA RUKMAL(KARUNARATNE), accountant; b. Colombo, Western, Sri Lanka, Apr. 27, 1958; d. Kankanamalage Mahinda and Dolly Winifred (Wettasinghe) Karunaratne; m. Godage Bandula Wickramanayake, Dec. 1, 1983. ACA, Inst. Chartered Accts., Colombo, Sri Lanka, 1983. CPA, Ohio. Staff acct. Ernst & Whinney, Colombo, Sri Lanka, 1978-79, sr. acct., 1980-83, supr., 1983; sr. acct. Parms, Smith & Co., Columbus, Ohio, 1986—. Mem. Am. Inst. CPA's, Ohio Soc. CPA's, Inst. Chartered Accts. Sri Lanka (assoc.). Buddhist. Avocation: handicrafts. Home: 1936 Stockwell Dr Columbus OH 43220 Office: Parms Smith & Co 398 Grant Ave Suite 212 Columbus OH 43215

WICKRE, PAUL MERRILL, broadcast executive; b. Huron, S.D., Sept. 2, 1936; s. Palmer S. and Leona Nellie (Osborne) W.; m. Dorothy Jeanne Christensen, Aug. 14, 1955; children: Reneé Ann Rose, Celeste Christo Eide. Grad. high sch., S.D. Program dir. sta. KTWO, Casper, Wyoming, 1958-61; ops. mgr. sta. KROC-TV, Rochester, Minn., 1961-69; acct. exec. sta. KXLY-TV, Spokane, Wash., 1969-72; gen. sales and sta. mgr. sta. KTHI-TV, Fargo, N.D., 1972-79, sta. KXJB-TV, Fargo, 1979—. Mem. N.D. Broadcast Assn. (pres. 1985-86), Broadcast Pioneers. Republican. Lutheran. Club: Exchange (Fargo). Home: 2580 Atlantic Dr Fargo ND 58103 Office: KXJB-TV 4302 13th Ave S Fargo ND 58103

WICKSTRA, H. E., medical company executive. Pres. Sherwood Med. Co., St. Louis. Office: Sherwood Med Co 1831 Olive St Saint Louis MO 63103 *

WIDDRINGTON, PETER NIGEL TINLING, brewery, food company executive; b. Toronto, Ont., Can., June 2, 1930; s. Gerard and Margery (MacDonald) W.; m. Betty Ann Lawrence, Oct. 12, 1956; children: Lucinda Ann, Andrea Stacy. Student, Pickering Coll., Newmarket, Ont., 1935-49; B.A. with honors, Queen's U., Kingston, Ont., 1953; M.B.A., Harvard, 1955. Salesman Labatt's Co., London, Ont., 1955-57; asst. regional mgr. So. Ont. region Labatt's Ont. Breweries Ltd., 1957-58; gen. mgr. Kiewel & Pelissiers, Winnipeg, 1961-62; regional mgr. Labatt's Ont. Breweries Ltd., 1958-61; gen. mgr. Labatt's Man. Breweries Ltd., Winnipeg, Man., 1962-65, Labatt's B.C. Breweries Ltd., Vancouver, B.C., 1965-68; pres. Lucky Breweries Inc., San Francisco, 1968-71; v.p. corp. devel. John Labatt Ltd., 1971-73, sr. v.p., 1973, pres., chief exec. officer, 1973—; bd. dirs. BP Can. Ltd., Toronto Blue Jays Baseball Club, Brascan Ltd., John Labatt Ltd., Can. Imperial Bank of Commerce, Ellis-Don Ltd., Laidlaw Transp. Ltd. Bd. dirs. The Fraser Inst., Vancouver; bd. govs. Olympic Trust Fund of Can. Home: Doncaster Ave, London, ON Canada N6G 2A4 Office: John Labatt Ltd, 451 Ridout StN, London, ON Canada N6A 5L3

WIDHAM, SCOTT ROBERT, cable television executive; b. Manchester, Conn., Dec. 22, 1957; s. Robert Gordon W.; m. Susan Pierce, Aug. 5, 1957. BBA in Mktg., U. Tex., 1979. Regional sales mgr. Warner Amex, Chgo., 1979-82, regional dir., 1982-83; v.p. mktg. Cencom Cable Assn., St. Louis, 1983-85; v.p., gen. mgr. Cencom of Mo., St. Louis, 1985—; chmn. St. Louis Interconnect Co. Bd. dirs. St. Louis County Edn. Com., 1986-87. Mem. Nat. Acad. of TV Arts and Sci., C-Tam, Mo. Cable TV Assn. (bd. dirs.), Olivette C. of C. (treas. 1986-87). Republican. Club: Variety, St. Louis Advt. Avocations: skiing, basketball, tennis. Home: 21 Woodcrest Dr Saint Louis MO 63124 Office: Cencom of Mo 9358 Dielmon Dr Saint Louis MO 63132

WIDING, LAWRENCE CARL, systems programmer; b. Ill., Sept. 22, 1964; s. Richard Kenneth and Diane Caroline (Goranson) W.; m. Mary Ann Bitz, June 7, 1986. Student, U. Ill., 1982-85. Ednl. programmer Rush U., Chgo., 1983-85; systems programmer Supersoft, Inc., Champaign, Ill., 1985-86, Computer Teaching Corp., Champaign, 1986—. Mem. Am. Assn. Computing Machinery (spl. interest group programming languages, spl. interest group personal computers, spl. interest group computer graphics). Roman Catholic. Avocations: golf, skiing. Home: 16 W 518 Honeysuckle Rose Bldg 5 Apt 107 Hinsdale IL 60521 Office: Computer Teaching Corp 1713 S Neil Champaign IL 61820

WIDMER, HARRIS WAYNE, accountant; b. Fredonia, N.D., Aug. 2, 1934; s. Jacob and Bertha J. (George) W.; m. Arlyce Joan Gall, June 16, 1958; 1 child, Keith W. BSBA, Jamestown (N.D.) Coll., 1958; postgrad., U. N.D., 1959-60. CPA,. Prin. LaMoure (N.D.) High Sch., 1958-62; field agt. IRS, Fargo, N.D., 1962-63; ptnr. Broeker, Hendrickson and Co., Fargo, 1963-73, Widmer, Roel and Co., Ltd., Fargo, 1973—; bd. dirs. Cen. Minn. TV Co., N.A. Communications Co., 1st Dakota Bancorp., Crane Johnson Co., Inc. Bd. dirs. Teammakers fund raising orgn. N.D. State U., 1983—; bd. of trustees Jamestown (N.D.) Coll., 1983—, mem. exec. com., fin. com., 1985—. Served to sgt. U.S. Army, 1954-55, PTO. Mem. Am. Inst. CPA's (mem. council 1979-82, fed. taxation com. 1980-83), Red River Valley CPA's, Red River Valley Estate Planning Council (bd. dirs., pres. 1980-81), Nat. Acctg. Assn., N.D. State Bd. Accountancy, N.D. Soc. CPA's (chmn. pub. relations com., chmn. taxation com., chmn. long range planning com. 1981-84, chmn. nominating com. 1980-81, 87—, bd. dirs. 1972-78, 2d v.p. 1975-76, pres. elect 1976-77, pres. 1977-78), Am. Legion. Congregationalist. Lodges: Kiwanis, Elks. Avocations: fishing, hunting. Office: Widmer Roel and Co Ltd 317 S University Dr Fargo ND 59103

WIDMER, THOMAS GILBERT, health science facility administrator; b. Schenectdy, N.Y., June 27, 1951; s. J. William and Mary Gilbert Widmer; m. Kathleen Mary Bielawski, May 8, 1976; children: Corey Jackson, Kyle Mary. Student, Transylvania U., 1973. Mgr. mktg. communications Gen. Electric Co., Stamford, Conn., 1977-79; asst. dir. advt. Stauffer Chem. Co., Westport, Conn., 1979-81, mktg. mgr., 1981-83; v.p. community affairs Marianjoy Rehab. Hosp., Wheaton, Ill., 1983—. Mem. Soc. Hosp. Planning and Mktg., Chgo Area Hosp. Planning and Mktg. Assn (dir. 1986—), Greater Wheaton C. of C. (dir. 1987). Republican. Methodist. Club: Exchange (Wheaton) (pres.-elect). Avocations: woodworking, racquetball. Home: 110 Vernon Ave Wheaton IL 60187 Office: Marianjoy Rehab Ctr PO Box 795 Wheaton IL 60189

WIDTFELDT, JAMES ALBERT, lawyer; b. O'Neill, Nebr., Nov. 18, 1947; s. Albert Theodore and Gusteva Emma (Peterson) W. B.S., MIT, 1970, M.S., 1970; postgrad. Rensselaer Poly. Inst., 1970-75, Ph.D., 1977; J.D., U. Nebr.-Lincoln, 1978. Bar: Nebr. 1978, U.S. Dist. Ct. Nebr. 1978. Civilian employee Office Naval Research, Troy, N.Y., 1973-75; assoc. Cronin & Hannon, O'Neill, Nebr., 1978-79; sole practice law, Atkinson, Nebr., 1979—. Coauthor articles in Jour. Acoustical Soc., 1973-75. Mem. Nebr. Bar Assn., Sigma Xi, Delta Theta Phi, Sigma Pi Sigma. Republican. Methodist. Club: Toastmasters. Lodges: Masons, Shriners. Home: Anncar Rt O'Neill NE 68763 Office: 103 State St Atkinson NE 68713

WIECHERS, JAMES DAVID, data processing executive, electronic data processing auditor; b. Racine, Wis., Apr. 23, 1937; s. James Leonard and Edna May (Davidson) W.; m. Carol Jean Hlavka, July 16, 1959; children: James, Susan, Matthew. BA in Philosophy, U. Wis., 1960. Cert. data processing auditor. Systems analyst Walker Mfg. Co., Racine, Wis., 1962-71; mgr. data processing Hamlin, Inc., Lake Mills, Wis., 1971-74; v.p. Menco Corp., Springfield, Ill., 1974-77; EDP audit mgr. Western Pub. Co., Racine, 1978-81; EDP sr. auditor JI Case Co., Racine, 1981-84; pres. Logical Technologies, Racine, 1984—, also chmn. bd. V.p. Council-Trinity Luth. Ch., Lake Mills, Wis., 1972-74, pres. Racine, 1981-85. Mem. Data Processing Auditors Assn., Data Processing Mgrs. Assn., Gideons Internat. Republican. Lutheran. Club: US Senatorial (Washington). Lodge: Lions. Avocations: golf, baseball, running, biking. Home: 3826 N Bay Dr Racine WI 53402 Office: JI Case Co 700 State St Racine WI 53403

WIECHERT, ALLEN LEROY, university official; b. Independence, Kans., Oct. 25, 1938; s. Norman Henry and Serena Johanna (Steinke) W.; B.Arch., Kans. State U., 1962; m. Sandra Swanson, Aug. 19, 1961; children—Kirstin Nan, Brendan Swanson, Megan Ann. Architect in tng. McVey, Peddie, Schmidt & Allen, Wichita, Kans., 1962-63; architect Kivett & Myers, Kansas City, Mo., 1963-68; asst. to vice chancellor plant planning and devel. U. Kans., Lawrence, 1968-74, asso. dir. facilities planning, 1974-78, univ. dir. facilities planning, 1978—; mem. long range phys. planning com. Kans. Bd. Regents, 1971—; designer, archtl. programmer of ednl. facilities; bd. dirs. Kans. U. Fed. Credit Union, 1972-81, pres. bd., 1974. Chmn. horizons com. Lawrence Bicentennial Commn.; designer Kaw River Trail, 1976; mem. Action 80 Com., 1980-81; mem. standing com. Kans. Episcopal Diocese, 1976-80, pres. com., 1981, mem. diocesan council, 1982-84, chmn. coll. work com., 1982-84, commn. on ch. architecture and allied arts, 1986—; sr. warden Trinity Episc. Ch., Lawrence, 1978-80; trustee Kans. Sch. Religion, 1973-80, 82-85, v.p., 1984-85, pres., 1986-88; bd. dirs. Trinity Group Care Home, 1973-79; advancement chmn. troop com. Boy Scouts Am., 1981—, vice chmn. Pelathe dist., 1984, chmn., 1985—, exec. bd. Heart of Am. council, 1985—; sec. exec. com. Hist. Mt. Oread Fund, Kans. U. Endowment Assn., 1982-83. Served to 1st lt. Kans. Air N.G., 1961-67. Lic. architect, Kans.; cert. Nat. Council Archtl. Registration Bds. Mem. AIA, Assn. Univ. Architects (sec./treas. 1986-87, v.p. 1987-88), Nat. Hist. Trust. Editor, contbr. to Physical Development Planning Work Book, 1973. Home: 813 Highland Dr Lawrence KS 66044 Office: U Kans Office Facilities Planning Lawrence KS 66045

WIECZOREK, GERALD MICHAEL, financial executive; b. Ionia, Mich., Apr. 17, 1948; s. Michael J. C. and Betty Lou (Wheeler) W. Investigating security supr. Borman Div., Detroit, 1964-68; dir., chief investigator Counselors Advocate Internat. Inc., Lansing, Mich., 1968-78; pres., legis. agt. Fed. Legis. Cons., Inc., Washington, 1972-75; pvt. investment cons., 1978; cert. diamond broker Internat. Gems, Ltd., Boston, 1978-79; indsl. and comml. investment real estate specialist, realtor and investment instr., 1978-81; life underwriter, Newark, 1979-81; dir., researcher, computer game theorist Questor Group Unltd., 1980-83; stockbroker, coordinator tax and retirement planning Dean Witter Reynolds, Inc., Lansing, Mich., 1983—. Statistician, cons., trainer Listening Ear Crisis Intervention Ctr., East Lansing, Mich., 1974-76, chmn. bd. dirs., dir., 1976-78. Mem. Internat. Commn. of Jurists (Geneva, Switzerland), Council of Internat. Investigators (London), Fin. Analysts Fedn., Investment Analysis Soc., Am. Econ. Assn., Am. Petroleum Inst., Internat. Chess Fedn. Republican. Author: Questron; contbr. articles to mags., newspapers and profl. jours. Office: Dean Witter Reynolds Inc 6105 W St Joseph St Lansing MI 48917

WIEDEMANN, THOMAS ROBERT, dentist; b. St. Louis, Feb. 26, 1954; s. Frank Robert and Lorraine Mary (Weber) W.; m. Sherre Lynn Tokarczyk; 1 child, Robert Andrew. BA in Biology magna cum laude, St. Louis U., 1975; DDS with distinction, U. Mo., Kansas City, 1979. Gen. practice dentistry St. Louis, 1979—. bd. dirs. MoPac Credit Union, St. Louis, 1984. Mem. ADA, Mo. Dental Assn., Greater St. Louis Dental Assn., Phi Kappa Phi, Omicron Kappa Upsilon. Roman Catholic. Avocation: tennis. Home: 8205 Mackenzie Rd Saint Louis MO 63123 Office: 3707 Watson Saint Louis MO 63109

WIEDMAN, MARY ELIZABETH, occupational therapist; b. Bonne Terre, Mo., Sept. 12, 1932; d. Edward Carl and Elva (Vinetta) Johnson; student N.W. Okla. State U., 1972-75, postgrad. 1979—; B.S. in Occupational Therapy, U. Okla. Health Sci. Center, 1978; m. Bill B. Wiedman, May 23, 1977; children—Michael Pinkley, Deborah Pinkley Lewis, Mark Pinkley, Susan Pinkley Schneider; stepchildren—Michael Wiedman, Jan Wiedman Schrock, Jill Wiedman Howard. Asst. for tng. Occupational Therapy in Ednl. Mgmt., Oklahoma City and Tulsa, 1981—; pvt. practice pediatric and rehab. therapy, Kiowa, Kans., 1979—; occupational therapy cons. Achenbach Rehab. Center, Hardtner, Kans., 1979—, Cedar Crest Nursing Home, Kiowa; occupational therapist Northwestern Okla. Regional Edn. Service Center, Alva, 1978—; guest lectr. N.W. Okla. State U., 1978-79. Okla. rep. Nat. Rep. Assemble Conf., 1987. Mem. World Fedn. Occupational Therapists, Am. Occupational Therapy Assn., Okla. Occupational Therapy Assn., Kans. Occupational Therapy Assn., Am. Occupational Therapy Found., Council Exceptional Children (charter mem. chpt.), Center Study Sensory Integration Dysfunction, AAUW. Republican. Baptist. Home: 1011 Coats Kiowa KS 67070

WIEDMANN, JEROME LEE, analytical chemist; b. Midland, S.D., Aug. 25, 1945; s. Tony Harvey and Doris Mae (Becker) W.; m. Barbara Joyce Snoozy, Sept. 3, 1966; children: Fred Alan, Jenny Lin, Susan Elaine, Andy Fay. BA, U. S.D., 1966; PhD, Iowa State U., 1970. Sr. research chemist PPG Inc., Barberton, Ohio, 1970-77; supr. PPG, Barberton, Ohio, 1977-80, sr. supr., 1980-83, sr. research assoc., 1983—. Treas. troop 103 Boy Scouts Am., Doylestown, Ohio, 1986. Mem. Akron sect. Am. Chem. Soc. (nat. and Akron sects.; analytical chem. div., agrochem. div., chromatography subdiv.), Am. Inst. Chemists, Ohio Lepidopterists Soc., Analytical Lab. Mgrs. Assn. Lutheran. Club: Rubber City Stamp (Montrose, Ohio) (publicity chmn. 1983, 86). Avocations: entomology, reading, philately, gardening, square dancing. Home: 1571 S Portage St Easton Rittman OH 44270 Office: Barberton Tech Ctr Box 31 Barberton OH 44203

WIEGAND, JACK DICK, family counselor; b. Green Bay, Wis., May 4, 1934; s. Herman Leonard and Eva (Shimandl) W.; m. Vivian Beatrice Raine, Sept. 7, 1963. BA, U. Mich., 1966; MA, Oakland U., 1982. Diplomate paralegal; cert. social worker. Counselor Oakland County Friend of the Ct., Pontiac, Mich., 1969—. Served with USAF, 1955-59. Mem. Nat. Assn. Social Workers, Nat. Soc. Profls. in Dispute Resolution, Nat. Acad. Family Mediators, Mich. Psychoanalytic Soc., Mich. Assn. Family and Divorce Mediation, U. Mich. Alumni Assn., Oakland U. Alumni Assn., Am. Legion. Republican. Congregationalist. Avocation: reading. Home: 44441 Newburyport Dr Canton MI 48187-2508 Office: Friend of the Ct 1200 N Telegraph Pontiac MI 48053-1058

WIELAND, R. RICHARD, II, pharmaceutical company executive; b. Portsmouth, Ohio, Dec. 25, 1944; s. R. Richard and Helen (McClure) W.; m. Ann Newton, June 20, 1970; children: Lauren, Melissa. BA, Monmouth Coll., 1968; MBA, Washington U., St. Louis, 1970. Fin. mgr. Procter & Gamble, Cin., 1970-78; chief fin. officer Acoustiflex Co., Chgo., 1978-80; v.p. controller Oak Tech., Chgo., 1980-84; sr. v.p. fin., chief fin. officer Lyphomed Inc., Chgo., 1984—. Bd. dirs. sr. citizens program, Cin., 1976-78, Monmouth (Ill.) Coll. Alumni Group, 1982—; fund raiser United Appeal, Chgo. Mem. Fin. Ex. Inst., Nat. Investor Relations Inst., N.Am. Fin. Planning Assn. Republican. Presbyterian. Avocations: tennis, golf, sports, travel, reading. Home: 888 Georgetown Ln Barrington IL 60010 Office: LyphoMed Inc 10401 W Touhy Ave Rosemont IL 60018

WIEMANN, MARION RUSSELL, JR., biologist, microscopist; b. Chesterton, Ind., Sept. 7, 1929; s. Marion Russell and Verda (Peek) W.; B.S., Ind. U., 1959; 1 dau., Tamara Lee. Histo-research techician U. Chgo., 1959, research asst., 1959-62, research technician, 1962-64; tchr. sci. Westchester Twp. Sch., Chesterton, Ind., 1964-66; with U. Chgo., 1965-79, sr. research technician, 1967-70, research technologist, 1970-79; prin. Marion Wiemann & Assos., cons. research and devel., Chesterton, Ind., 1979—. Served with USN, 1951-53. Recipient Disting. Tech. Communicator award Soc. for Tech. Communication, 1974; named Sagamore of the Wabash Gov. Ind., 1985; McCrone Research Inst. scholar, 1968. Fellow World Literary Acad.; mem. Internat. Platform Assn., Field Mus. Natural History (assoc.), AAAS, Soil Sci. Soc. Am., Am. Soc. Agronomy, Crop Sci. Soc. Am., Internat. Soc. Soil Sci., VFW (charter mem., bd. dirs., post judge adv. 1986, apptd. post adj. 1986, Cross of Malta 1986). Club: Governors. Author: Tooth Decay, Its Cause and Prevention Through Controlled Soil Composition, 1985; contbr. articles to profl. jours. Address: PO Box E Chesterton IN 46304

WIEMER, BRENDA JANE, educator; b. St. Louis, Sept. 29, 1956; d. Herbert William and Jane Edalia (Beattie) Wandersee; m. Alloyd John Wiemer Jr., Aug. 9, 1980; children: Sarah Jane, Rachael Marie. BS in Elem. and Spl. Edn., Vanderbilt U., 1977; MEd in Counseling, U. Mo., 1984. Cert. elem. and spl. edn. tchr., Mo. Remedial reading tchr. Ritenour Schs., Overland, Mo., 1977-79; tchr. learning disabilities, behavior disorders Spl. Sch. Dist., St. Louis, 1979—; coop. tchr. U. Mo. Schs., 1985—. Mem. Young Reps., St. Louis; tchr. Sunday Sch. Kirk of the Hills Presbyn. Ch. Recipient Disting. Service award Council for Exceptional Children U. Mo., 1986. Assn. for Children Learning Disabilities (treas., bd. dirs., parent adv.), Nat. Edn. Assn. (dist. rep. 1983-84), Mo. Assn. for Children Learning Disorders (chairperson resource room), Nat. Soc. Autistic Children, Nat. Youth Assn. Retarded Citizens (bd. dirs. 1972-77). Republican. Avocations: reading, crafts, swimming, gardening, decorating. Home: 815 Big Bend Woods Dr Ballwin MO 63021 Office: Spl Sch Dist St Louis County 12110 Clayton Rd Town and Country MO 63131

WIEMERS, EUGENE LEE, psychiatrist; b. Sequin, Tex., Nov. 2, 1910; s. William Dietrick and Marie (Karbach) W.; m. Ortis Pettingill, Feb. 6, 1938 (dec. July 1954); children: Rae, Ann, Eugene, John; m. Irene Holliangsworth, Aug. 10, 1955; children: Amy, Holly. BA, Southwestern U., 1933; MD, U. Tex., Galveston, 1937. Diplomate Am. Bd. Psychiatry and Neurology. Intern Thomas D. Leo Meml. Hosp., Ogden, Utah, 1937-38; resident in psychiatry Eloise (Mich.) Hosp., 1938-40, N.H. State Hosp., Concord, 1940; psychiatrist, asst. supt. Utah State Hosp., Provo, 1946-60; psychiatrist, supt. Mental Health Inst., Cherokee, Iowa, 1960-78; cons. in psychiatry Vera French Mental Health Ctr., Davenport, Iowa, 1978—, Community Health Ctr., Davenport, 1979—; asst. prof. U. Utah Med. Sch. Served to maj. USMC, 1940-46. Mem. AMA, Am. Psychiatrists Assn. Democrat. Unitarian. Lodge: Rotary. Avocations: gardening, golf, travel. Home: 1423 W 46th St Davenport IA 52806

WIENER, DANIEL NORMAN, psychologist; b. Duluth, Minn., Feb. 6, 1921; s. Joseph Baxter and Fannie (Winer) W.; m. Phyllis Eileen Zager, Dec. 9, 1972; children: Jonathan Marc, Paul Aaron, Sara Ruth Wiener Pearson. BA, U. Minn., 1941, MA, 1942, PhD, 1950. Licensed cons. psychologist, Minn.; diplomate Am. Bd. Profl. Psychology. Psychologist State of Conn., Hartford, 1943-44; chief psychologist VA Hosp., St. Paul and Mpls., 1944-76; pvt. practice psychology Mpls., 1952—; clin. prof. psychiatry and psychology U. Minn., Mpls., 1952—; cons. Hennepin County Dist. Ct., Mpls., 1982—. Author: Discipline, Achievement and Mental Health, 1960, Dimensions of Psychotherapy, 1965, Short-Term Psychotherapy, 1966, Training Children, 1968, Classroom Management, 1972, Consumers Guide to Psychotherapy, 1975. Served with USAF, 1942-43. Fellow Am. Psychol. Assn.; mem. Minn. Psychol. Assn. (life). Avocations: writing, tennis, squash. Home and Office: 1225 LaSalle Ave Minneapolis MN 55403

WIENS, DANIEL LESLIE, accountant; b. Calgary, Alta., Can., Jan. 21, 1962; came to U.S., 1963; s. Allan Leslie and Elva Merle (Peterson) W.; m. Julie Ann Hindmand, Mar. 21, 1987. BS in Acctg., Olivet Nazarene U., 1983; postgrad., U. Chgo., 1987. CPA, Ill. Staff acct. HealthCor, Kankakee, Ill., 1983-84; fin. mgr. ServantCor, Kankakee, 1985—. treas. St. Anne Ctr., Rockford, Ill., 1987—; asst. treas. Our Lady of Victory, Kankakee, 1987—. Mem. Health Care Fin. Mgmt. Assn., Ill. CPA Soc., Am. Inst. CPA's. Republican. Avocations: basketball, raquetball, tennis, golf. Home: 376 Municipal Ctr Rd Apt 3 Bourbonnais IL 60914 Office: ServantCor 175 S Wall Kankakee IL 60901

WIERS, BRANDON HELMHOLZ, research and development executive; b. San Francisco, July 31, 1934; s. Walter Benjamin Wiers and Grace Elizabeth (Pleune) MacNaughton; m. Patricia Joan Hollingsworth, May 14, 1960; children: Matthew Dirk, Suesann Elizabeth, Carl John. BA, Calvin Coll., Grand Rapids, Mich., 1957; PhD., U. Minn., 1964. Staff chemist research and devel dept. Procter & Gamble, Cin., 1964-69, staff chemist, sect. head internat. div., 1969-74, group leader packaged soap and detergent div., 1974-78, sect. head research and devel. services and research adminstrn., 1979—; instr. phys. chemistry Colo. State Coll., Greeley, 1961, Xavier U., Cin., 1966-67. Contbr. articles to profl. jours.; patentee in field. Mem. city council, mayor City of Forest Park, Ohio, 1976-85; bd. dirs. Community Housing Resources Bd., Cin., 1982-85, Greater Cin. Charter Com., 1985—, Parkdale Home for Youth, 1986— mem. Leadership Cin., 1984—, Community Adv. to Magnet Schs. Recipient Fair Housing award Community Housing Resources Bd., 1984, Service award Troop 56 Boy Scouts Am., 1985, Pub. Service award City of Forest Park, 1985, Bus. Recognition award City of Forest Park, 1986. Mem. Am. Chem. Soc., Am. Statis. Assn., AAAS. Presbyterian. Home: 11261 Hanover Rd Forest Park OH 45240 Office: Procter & Gamble Co Miami Valley Labs PO Box 39175 Cincinnati OH 45247

WIERSMA, RUSTAN JOHN, otolaryngologist; b. Syracuse, N.Y., Mar. 12, 1950; s. Alvin Frederick and Charlotte May (Peterson) W.; m. Beth Ann Mathews, Aug. 9, 1975; children: Kurt Rustan, Michelle Lynn, Carrie Ann, Todd Jeffrey. BA, St. Olaf Coll., 1972; MD, Loyola U., Maywood, Ill., 1975. Intern Ill. Masonic Hosp., Chgo., 1975-76; resident in surgery Cook County Hosp., Chgo., 1976-77; resident in otolaryngology Northwestern U., Chgo., 1977-80; staff physician Skemp-Grandview Clinic, LaCrosse, Wis., 1980—. Bd. dirs. Congl. Nursery Sch., LaCrosse, 1984—. Fellow ACS, Am. Acad. Otolaryngology; mem. AMA, Wis. Med. Soc., Wis. Otolaryngology Soc. Avocations: tennis, flying, model ship building, skiing. Home: W6190 Bluff Pass LaCrosse WI 54601 Office: Skemp Grandview LaCrosse Clinic 815 S 10th St LaCrosse WI 54601

WIERWILL, BRYAN LINUS, dentist; b. Lafayette, Ind., Feb. 21, 1953; s. Linus Lee and Virginia Ann (Engelking) W.; m. Rose Mary Schmidt, June 28, 1981; 1 child, Benjamin Francis. DDS, Marquette U., 1978. Pres. Capitol Square Dental Assocs., Madison, Wis., 1978-85; assoc. dentist Assoc. Dentists, Madison, 1985—, pres. Macrodontics Internat., Madison, 1983—; dir. provider evaluation Oral Health Internat., Madison, 1985—. Mem. ADA, Acad. Gen. Dentistry, Chgo. Dental Soc., Internat. Coll. Oral Implantology, Am. Coll. Oral Implantology, Mendota Dental Study Club (founder, pres. 1980-83), Wis. Acad. Gen. Dentistry (nominee bd. dirs. 1986). Republican. Presbyterian. Club: Blackhawk Country (Madison). Avocations: outdoor sports, photography. Home: 709 Dearholt Rd Madison WI 53711 Office: Assoc Dentists 4506 Regent Madison WI 53705

WIERZBOWSKI, STEPHEN JOHN, architect; b. Greensburg, Pa., Mar. 16, 1953; s. Walter and Agnes (Kolano) W.; m. Deborah Rose Newmark, Dec. 8, 1985. BArch, Carnegie Mellon U., 1975; MArch, U. Ill., Chgo., 1982. Registered architect, Ill. Computer programmer Skidmore Owings & Merrill, Chgo., 1975-77, architect, designer, 1977-81; adj. asst. prof. architecture U. Ill. Sch. Architecture, Chgo., 1981-86,; ptnr. Florian Wierzbowski, Chgo., 1983—; adj. asst. prof. U. Ill., Versailles, France, 1982-83. Mem. AIA, Chgo. Archtl. Club. Office: Florian-Wierzbowski 432 N Clark Chicago IL 60610

WIESE, DAVID JOHN, retail company executive; b. St. Louis, Feb. 12, 1953; s. Fredrick William Wiese and Judith Ann (De Priest) Kaeser; m. Mary Ann Clarke, July 13, 1985. BBA, So. Mo. State U., 1975. Mgr. trainee Colonel Day's, St. Louis, 1975-76; store mgr. Colonel Day's, St. Louis and Peoria, Ill., 1976-77; supr. dist. store Colonel Day's, Kansas City, Mo., 1977-79; supr. regional store Colonel Day's, Chgo., 1980-85; v.p. Colonel Day's, St. Louis, 1986—; chmn. Colonel Day's United Fund Drive, 1986. Roman Catholic. Lodge: Rotary. Avocations: running, golf, reading. Home: 82 Heatherbrook Kirkwood MO 63122

WIESE, HOWARD HENRY, real estate executive; b. Elgin, Ill., June 6, 1943; s. Marcus Henry and Ella Helena (price) W.; m. Sharon Kay Hobart, Sept. 4, 1965; children: David, Laura. BSEE, U. Ill., 1966, MBA, 1968. Indsl. broker Cushman & Wakefield, Chgo., 1973-75, CMD Realty, Oak Brook, Ill., 1975-76; leasing mgr. Mfgrs. Real Estate, Oak Brook, 1976-77; br. mgr. Mfgrs. Real Estate, Los Angeles, 1977-81; mgr. region Mfgrs. Real Estate, Chgo., 1981—. Commr. Village of Schaumburg Bus. Devel. Commn., Ill., 1986—. Mem. Nat. Assn. Office and Indsl. Parks (v.p. 1987), Bldg. Owners and Mgrs. Assn., Inst. Real Estate Mgmt., Chgo. Real Estate Bd., Chgo. OfficeLeasing Brokers Assn., Chgo. Council Foreign Relations, U. Ill. MBA Alumni Assn. (bd. dirs. 1986—), U. Ill. Alumni Assn. Republican. Lutheran. Avocation: snow skiing. Home: 422 May St Elmhurst IL 60126 Office: Mfgrs Life Ins Co 1515 Woodfield Rd #850 Schaumburg IL 60173

WIESE, MICHAEL CLARK, real estate development corporation officer, city agency adminstrator; b. Council Bluffs, Iowa, Aug. 17, 1946; s. Clark Winston and Kristine Elizabeth (Gaskill) W.; m. Kathleen Marie Martin, Aug. 4, 1972; children: Stephanie Marie, Megan Elizabeth. BS, U. Nebr., Omaha, 1971. Cert. real estate broker. Planner City of Omaha, 1969-82; dir. devel. projects Omaha C. of C., 1982-85; exec. dir. Omaha Devel. Council, 1985—, also bd. dirs., mem. exec. com.; exec. dir. Omaha Indsl. Found., 1985—, also bd. dirs., mem. exec. com.; v.p. Metro Ctr. Realvest, Omaha, 1985—; also bd. dirs., exec. com. Metro Ctr. Realvest; bd. dirs. Land Use Authority, Omaha, 1980-82. Bd. dirs. Downtown Omaha, Inc., 1986, Summer Arts Festival, Omaha, 1986; mem. Omaha Skywalk Commn., Omaha, 1986. Served to lt. USAF, 1971-73. Mem. Am. Planning Assn., Internat. Council Shopping Ctrs., Indsl. Devel. Assn., Urban Land Inst. (assoc.). Republican. Office: Omaha Devel Council 1301 Harney St Omaha NE 68102

WIESEN, ROBERT J., real estate executive; b. Toledo, Sept. 21, 1943; s. James Douglas and Dorothy J. (Korreck) W.; m. Ruzica Marionovic, June 10, 1972; 1 child, Sasha James. B.S., Ind. U., 1965. Salesman Continental Can Co., Chgo., 1965-72; dir. sales and mktg. First Am. Realty, Chgo., 1974-75; v.p. sales Seay & Thomas, Chgo., 1975-78; v.p. investments Golub & Co., Chgo., 1986—; pres. First Am. Equities Inc., Chgo., 1972—; chmn. bd. dirs. Combined Health Appeal of Am., Alexandria, Va., 1987, also dir. Contbr. articles to publs. Bd. dirs. Cystic Fibrosis Found., 1978—. Served with Air N.G., 1966-71. Avocations: Sailing; photography. Home: 325 W Belden Ave Chicago IL 60614

WIESER, JOSEPH ALPHONSUS, educational adminstrator, alcohol and drug abuse consultant; b. Plymouth, Wis., May 29, 1943; s. Alfred A. and Anna Mae (Braun) W.; m. Wendy Mae Brandt, June 30, 1979; children: Adam, Mark; m. Doris Ann Rommelfanger, Jan. 8, 1966 (dec. Nov. 1977). BS in Elem. Edn., Lakeland Coll., 1966; MA in Elem. Sch. Adminstrn., No. Mich. U., 1971. Tchr. Milw. Pub. Schs., 1966; tchr. New Holstein Pub. Schs., Wis., 1966-74, asst. prin., 1974-77, elem. sch. prin., 1977—; cons. alcohol and other drug abuse, Wis., 1981—; speaker/trainer ETC Trainers, Campbellsport, Wis., 1985—; trainer Community Tng. Assn., Oshkosh, Wis., 1985—; coordinator SPIN Network, New Holstein, Wis., 1984—. chmn. Calumet County Rep. party, 1983—. Mem. Nat. Elem. Sch. Prins. Assn., Assn. Wis. Sch. Adminstrs. (Disting. Service and Outstanding Contributions to Sch. and Community award 1986), Wis. PTA (pres. 1975-76), Sch. Prevention Intervention Network (coordinator 1984—). Roman Catholic. Avocations: computers, jogging. Home: 1704 Mayflower St New Holstein WI 53061 Office: New Holstein Elem Sch 2226 Park Ave New Holstein WI 53061

WIESERT, KENNETH NIEL, psychiatrist; b. Cleve., Aug. 13, 1950; s. Kenneth N. Wiesert and Lois L. (Lindsay) Kinnaman; m. Loy A. Kline, July 27, 1974; children: Gregory K., Christine L. AB, Ind. U., 1972, MD, 1975. Diplomate Am. Bd. Psychiatry and Neurology. Staff psychiatrist Larue Carter Hosp., Indpls., 1978-81; practice medicine specializing in psychiatry Indpls., 1981—; asst. prof. Ind. U. Sch. Med., Indpls., 1978-81, clin. asst. prof. 1981—; assoc. dir. Winona Sleep Disorders Ctr., Indpls., 1984—. Mem. Am. Psychiat. Assn., Ind. Psychiat. Soc., Clin. Sleep Soc., So. Sleep Soc., Phi Beta Kappa. Avocations: music, photography. Office: Winona Meml Hosp 3232 N Meridian St Indianapolis IN 46208

WIFF, MARGARET EMMA, dentist; b. Mpls., Apr. 13, 1954; d. John Edward and Lavona Marie (Klecker) W.; m. Hugh William Whipple, Aug. 30, 1986. BA in Biology with honors, Ripon Coll., 1976; DDS, Loyola U., Maywood, Ill., 1980. Pvt. practice dentistry Geneva, Ill., 1980—. Creator, producer videotape, The Wizard of Floss, 1984 (Excellence in Programming, Community Preventive Dentistry award Fox River Valley Dental Soc. 1984). Recipient Arthur Duxler Humanitarian award Scholarships to Women Med. Students, Chgo., 1979. Mem. ADA, Ill. State Dental Soc., Chgo. Dental Soc. (assoc.), Fox River Valley Dental Soc. (chmn. Nat. Childrens Dental Health 1983-85, editor newsletter 1984-86, pub. relations liaison), Am. Soc. Dentistry for Children (state treas. 1983-86, sec. 1986-87, v.p. 1987—), Acad. Gen. Dentistry, AAUW, Beta Beta Beta, Delta Sigma Delta. Methodist. Club: Geneva-Batavia (Ill.) Newcomers (pres. 1983-84). Home: 465 Persimmon Dr Saint Charles IL 60174 Office: 22 James St Geneva IL 60134

WIGHT, LES D., II, lawyer; b. Independence, Mo., July 11, 1951; s. Les D. and Darlene (Van Biber) W.; 1 child, Les D. III. BA, Graceland Coll., Lamoni, Iowa, 1973; JD, U. Mo., Kansas City, 1976. Bar: Mo. 1977. Sole practice Independence, 1977-86; prin. Les D. Wight, P.C., Independence, 1986—. Fundraiser Independence YMCA, 1986. Mem. ABA, Mo. Bar Assn., Kansas City Bar Assn., Eastern Jackson County Bar Assn., Independence C. of C. (com. chmn. 1984-86). Office: 530 E 23d St Independence MO 64055

WIGLEY, MICHAEL ROBERT, management consultant; b. Mankato, Minn., Jan. 19, 1954; s. Robert John and Jean Marie (Christianson) W.; m. Barbara Ann Younghans, Sept. 6, 1974; 1 child, Kathryn Karyn. BS in Geology, U. Minn., 1978, BCE, 1978; MCE, Stanford U., 1979; MBA, Harvard U., 1986. Houseparent Group Homes, Inc., St. Paul, 1975-77; research asst. Stanford (Calif.) U., 1978-79; group mgr. Battelle Meml. Inst., Columbus, Ohio, 1979-82; ptnr. The Wigley Partnership, Wilmette, Ill., 1982—; pres., chmn. Hot Rock, Inc., Woburn, Mass., 1983-85; ind. bus. cons. Boston, 1985-86; cons. McKinsey and Co., Chgo., 1986—; mem. tech. com. on nuclear effects ASCE, 1979-82, ptnr. WDW Devel. Co., Wilmette, 1980—; bd. dirs. Terrapin, Inc., Cambridge, Mass., Fla. Sunshine Cards, Inc., Mpls. Contbr. articles to profl. jours. Del. Minn. Rep. Party, 1972. Named one of Outstanding Young Men of Am., 1983; recipient Field Camp Scholarship Geology Dept. U. Minn., 1978; EPA fellow, 1978-79. Lutheran. Avocations: sports, strategy games, reading, old movies, computers. Home: 1518 Forest Ave Wilmette IL 60091 Office: McKinsey and Co Inc 2 First National Plaza Chicago IL 60603

WIGTON, PAUL NORTON, steel company executive; b. Linesville, Pa., Aug. 13, 1932; s. Charles and Viola Grace (Dennis) W.; m. Janet Ohl, July 11, 1953; children: Bruce, Douglas. B.S. in Chemistry, Youngstown State U., 1957a; student exec. mgmt. program, MIT, 1974; hon. doctorate, Youngstown State U., 1980. Gen. supt. metal services Republic Steel Corp., Warren, Ohio, 1971-73, asst. to dist. mgr., 1973-75, dist. mgr., 1975-78; asst. v.p. ops. Republic Steel Corp., Cleve., 1978-80, v.p. steel ops., 1980-83, v.p., gen. mgr. flat rolled product group, 1983-84; pres. tubular products LTV Steel, 1984—. Served to cpl. U.S. Army, 1952-54. Scholar Henry Roemer Found., 1957; scholar Am. Soc. Chemistry, 1957; named Industrialist of Yr. Mahoning Valley Econ. Devel. Corp., 1981. Mem. Am. Iron and Steel Inst., Assn. Iron and Steel Engrs. (v.p. 1987), Am. Inst. Metall. Engrs. Presbyterian. Clubs: Chagrin Valley Country (Chagrin Falls, Ohio); Tournament Players (Prestancia-Sarasota, Fla.). Home: 6489 Creekside Trail Solon OH 44139 Office: LTV Steel 1315 Albert St Youngstown OH 44501

WIKSTROM, LORETTA WERMERSKIRCHEN, artist; b. Willow River, Minn., Mar. 2, 1938; d. Jacob Joseph and Anna Bertha (Doege) Wermerskirchen; m. Donovan Carl Wikstrom, Aug. 16, 1958; children: Bradley Donovan, Kendra Kay, Brock Karl. Student, St. Paul Sch. of Art, 1956-57, U. Minn., 1957-58, Honolulu Acad. of Art, 1963-66, Dayton Art Inst., 1985. Exhibited in group shows Sinclair Coll., 1985, Arts Venture, 1985; one woman shows Beavercreek Library, 1986, City of Englewood, 1986. Vol. artist Boy Scouts Am., Charleston, S.C. and Minn., 1967-74; vol. artist, tchr. Girl Scouts Am., O'Fallon, Ill., 1975-76; vol. art judge Pub. elem., Jr. and Sr. High Sch., Charleston and Mascoutah, Ill., 1969-78, Ill. State Hist. Library, Belleville, Ill., 1979. Recipient 2d place and hon. mention Nat. Nature and Wildfowl Show, 1987, hon. mention Wyoming (Ohio) Pub. Arts Commn. show, 1987. Mem. Guild S.C. Artists, Charleston Artists Guild, Minn. Artists Assn., Gateway East Artists Guild, St. Louis Artists Guild, Beavercreek Creative Artists Assn. (sec. 1987—), Dayton Soc. Painters and Sculptors. Home: 45 Hawthorne Glen Trail Beavercreek OH 45440

WILBANKS, GEORGE DEWEY, JR., medical educator; b. Gainsville, Ga., Feb. 24, 1931; s. George Dewey Sr. and Ruth Chamblee Wilbanks; m. Evelyn Rivers; children: George Rivers, Wayne Freeman. AB, Duke U., 1953, MD, 1956. Clin. instr. U. Okla., Oklahoma City, 1963-64; asst. prof. Duke U. Med. Ctr., Durham, N.C., 1965-69, dir. gynecol. oncology, 1967-70, assoc. prof., 1970; prof., chmn. ob-gyn Rush Med. Ctr., Chgo., 1970—; pres. Women's Health Cons., 1972.

WILBER, RONALD GEOFFREY, orthopedic spine surgeon; b. Cleve., Nov. 21, 1949; s. John Vernon and Jane Fiske (Griffin) W.; m. Elizabeth Anita Feick, Aug. 28, 1971; children: Amy Elizabeth, Charles Geoffrey. AA in Liberal Arts, Valley Forge Mil. Jr. Coll., 1969; BS in Chemistry, Muskingum Coll., 1971; MD, Case Western Res. U., 1977. Diplomate Am. Bd. Orthopaedic Surgery. Intern Case Western Res. U. Hosp., Cleve., 1977-78, resident in orthopaedic surgery, 1978-83, orthopaedic spine surgeon, 1984—; fellow in orthopaedic spine surgery Buffalo Gen. Hosp., 1983-84; head orthopaedic spine services Cleve. Met. Gen. Hosp., 1984—. Contbr. articles to profl. and scholarly jours. Am. Orthopaedic Assn. traveling fellow, 1984. Mem. AMA, Simmons Surg. Soc., Cleve. Orthopaedic Club, C.H. Herndon Alumni Assn. (Resident's Paper award 1983), Alpha Omega Alpha. Home: 115 Hunting Trail Moreland Hills OH 44022 Office: 3395 Scranton Rd Cleveland OH 44109

WILBERT, BRIAN KURT, clergyman; b. Elyria, Ohio, May 2, 1960; s. Richard Paul and Linda Lee (Sheldon) W. BA, Kenyon Coll., 1982; MDiv, Bexley Hall, 1985. Ordained to ministry Episcopal Ch. as deacon, 1985, as priest, 1986. Sem. asst. Calvary/St. Andrew's, Rochester, N.Y., 1983-85; curate St. Michael's in the Hills, Toldeo, 1985—; Mem. of the diocesan Christian Edn. Dept. Ohio, 1985—, Youth Council Ohio, 1986—; pres. Bexley Soc., Rochester, 1984-85. Named one of Outstanding Young Men of Am., 1985. Mem. Bexley Alumni Assn. (v.p. 1986—), Kenyon Toledo Alumni Admissions Program (chmn. 1985—). Democrat. Home: 4304 W Bancroft St #2 Toldeo OH 43615 Office: St Michael's in the Hills 4718 Brittany Rd Toledo OH 43615

WILBRECHT, JON KEEHN, electronics company executive; b. Apr. 11, 1942. BA, Wesleyan U., Middletown, Conn., 1964; MBA, Stanford (Calif.) U., 1967. Pres. Wilbrecht Electronics, Inc., St. Paul, 1984—. Office: Wilbrecht Electronics Inc 346 Chester St Saint Paul MN 55107

WILBURN, MARY NELSON, lawyer, writer; b. Balt., Feb. 18, 1932; d. David Alfred and Phoebe Blanche (Novotny) Nelson; A.B. cum laude, Howard U., 1952; M.A., U. Wis., 1955, J.D., 1975; m. Adolph Yarbrough Wilburn, Mar. 5, 1957; children—Adolph II, Jason David. Bar: Wis. 1975, U.S. Supreme Ct 1981. Lectr. U. Wis. Law Sch., 1975-77, 83, 84, 85; atty. adv. Bur. Prisons, Dept. Justice, 1977-82; chmn. Wis. State Parole Bd., Madison, 1986—; mem. steering com. Network Women Offenders, Women's Bur., Dept. Labor, 1981-82; mem. Wis. Sentencing Commn. Mem. Madison Met. Sch. Dist. Bd. Edn., 1975-77; assoc. mem. Schutz Am. Sch. Bd., Alexandria, Egypt, 1983-85. Mem. Fed. Bar. Assn. (nat. council 1981-82), Women's Bar Assn., Nat. Bar Assn., ABA, Dane County Bar Assn., Legal Assn. of Women, The Links, Inc., Am. Correctional Assn., Nat. Assn. Blacks in Criminal Justice, Howard U. Alumni Assn., Alpha Kappa Alpha. Clubs: Nat. Lawyers (Washington); University (Madison). Contbr. to Cairo Today, 1983-84. Office: Wis Parole Bd 1 W Wilson St PO Box 7850 Madison WI 53707

WILCH, ROBERT SAMUEL, bishop; b. Jenera, Ohio, May 20, 1923; s. Cora Wilch; m. Sandra Qua, Nov. 23, 1974. BA, Lawrence U., 1947; MDiv, Northwestern Luth. Theol. Sem., St. Paul, 1952; DD (hon.), Northwestern Luth. Theol. Sem., 1975. Asst. to pres. Lawrence U., Appleton, Wis., 1947-49; pastor St. Paul Luth. Ch., Spokane, Wash., 1952-57, St. Peter Luth. Ch., Janesville, Wis., 1957-63; asst. to pres. Wis.-Upper Mich. Synod, Milw., 1963-74, pres., bishop, 1974—; exec. bd. dirs. Pacific Northwest Synod, Seattle, 1954-59; shared staff div. for mission in N.Am. Luth. Ch. in Am. N.Y.C., 1972-74, cons. com. on women in ch. and soc., 1980-84. Trustee Carthage Coll., Kenosha, Wis., 1968—, Suomi Coll., Hancock, Mich., 1974—; bd. dirs. Luth. Social Services, Milw., 1974—, St. Luke's Hosp., Milw., 1978-82. Served to lt. (j.g.) USN, 1943-46. Recipient Disting. Service award Project Equality, 1981. Home: N61 W29799 Stoney Hill Ct Hartland WI 53029 Office: Wis-Upper Mich Synod 1933 W Wisconsin Ave Milwaukee WI 53233

WILCOCK, KEITH DICKSON, industrial psychologist, author, artist; b. Cowley, Wyo., Mar. 25, 1937; s. Vernile Eyre and Ola (Dickson) W.; m. Judith Carter, Oct. 30, 1957; children: Scott Carter, Samuel Corey, Joseph Keith. BS, Brigham Young U., 1960; MS, U. Utah, 1962. Registered psychologist, Ill.; lic. cons. psychologist, Minn. Security officer Utah State Prison, Draper, Utah, 1957-62; psychologist N.D. State Hosp., Jamestown, N.D., 1962-64; cons. Ernst & Whinney, Cleve., 1964-66, Booz, Allen, Hamilton, Chgo., 1966-68; mgr., cons. Peat, Marwick, Mitchell, Chgo., 1968-72; dir. compensation and mgmt. devel. Internat. Multifoods, Mpls., 1972-75; pres. Wilcock Assocs. (now subs. Personnel Decisions, Inc.), Wayzata, Minn., 1975—; editor The Wyer-Pearce Press, Wayzata, 1981-86. Author: The Corporate Tribe, 1984; artist numerous paintings. Served to sgt. USAR, 1960-68. Mem. Am. Psychol. Assn. (assoc.), Twin Cities Personnel Assn. Avocations: tennis, racquetball, chess. Office: Wilcock Assoc 641 E Lake St #200 Wayzata MN 55391

WILCOX, DONALD ALAN, lawyer; b. Grantsburg, Wis., July 18, 1951; s. John Charles and Lois Margaret (Finch) W.; m. Rachel Ann Johnson, Dec. 28, 1973; children: Benjamin Ray, Joseph Charles, Sara Johanna. BS, USAF Acad., 1973; JD, Georgetown U., 1979. Bar: Minn. 1979. Commd. 2d lt. USAF, 1973, advanced through grades to capt., resigned, 1979; assoc Holmquist & Holmquist, Benson, Minn., 1979-81; ptnr. Holmquist & Wilcox, 1981—; gen. counsel Swift County-Benson Hosp., 1981—, Farmer's Mut. Coop., Bellingham, Minn., 1986—, Agralite Coop., Benson, 1986—; atty. City of Benson, 1985—; examiner of titles, Swift County, Benson, 1986—. Mem. Benson Planning Commn., 1979-85; pres. Our Redeemer's Luth. Ch., Benson, 1985-86; pres., bd. dirs. Swift County Homes, Inc., Benson, 1984—. Recipient Lawyers Coop. Pub. award Lawyers Coop. Pub. Co., 1979. Mem. ABA, Minn. Bar Assn., Minn. Assn. Hosp. Attys., Benson C. of C. (bd. dirs. 1981-84). Lodge: Kiwanis (treas. Benson 1982-84). Avocations: reading, golf, skiing. Home: 604 13th St S Benson MN 56215 Office: Holmquist & Wilcox PA 1150 Wisconsin Ave Benson MN 56215

WILCOX, LAIRD MAURICE, investigator, writer; b. San Francisco, Nov. 28, 1942; s. Laird and AuDeene Helen (Stromer) W.; student Washburn U., 1961-62, U. Kans., 1963-65; m. Eileen Maddocks, 1962 (div. 1967); children—Laird Anthony IV, Elizabeth Leone; m. 2d, Diana Brown, 1978; 1 dau., Carrie Lynn. With Fluor Corp., Ltd., 1960-62; mgr. office supply store U. Kans., 1963; editor Kans. Free Press, 1963-66; owner, operator Maury Wilcox Constrn. Co., Kansas City, Mo., 1967-70; carpenter foreman various employers, 1974—; semi-profl. genealogist, 1975-78; chief investigator Editorial Research Service, Kansas City, Mo., 1977—; assoc. faculty Baker U., 1986—; lectr. various fields. Dep. sheriff Wyandotte County, Kans., 1971-75. Fellow Augustan Soc., Acad. Police Sci.; mem. Internat. Brotherhood of Carpenters and Joiners of Am. (officer 1975-82, condr. carpenter's local 61 1977-82), Nat. Rifle Assn., Mensa, ACLU, Internat. Legion of Intelligence, Nat. Coalition Against Censorship, Free Press Assn., SAR, Soc. Mayflower Descs., Mil. Order Loyal Legion of U.S., Nat. Soc. Old Plymouth Colony Descs., St. Andrew Soc. Author: Guide To The American Left, 1970; Guide to the American Right, 1970; Psychological Uses of Genealogy, 1976; Astrology, Mysticism and The Occult, 1978; Directory of the American Right, 1981; Directory of the American Left, 1981; Directory of the Occult and Paranormal, 1981; Guide to the American Right, 1984; Guide to the American Left, 1984; editor Wilcox Report, 1979—, Civil Liberties Rev., 1986—. Founder Wilcox Collection on Contemporary Polit. Movements, U. Kans. Libraries. Home and Office: PO Box 2047 Olathe KS 66061

WILD, STEPHEN KENT, insurance marketing company executive; b. Omaha, Nov. 18, 1948; s. Roger Charles and Marguerite Mae W.; m. Cheryl Katherine Sparano, June 5, 1971; children—Deric Justin, Drew Ian. Student Ottawa U., 1967-68, U. Nebr.-Omaha, 1968-71. Internal auditor Kirkpatrick, Pettis, Smith and Polian, Omaha, 1971-75; fin. planner First Fin. Planning Group, Omaha, 1975-80; mng. gen. agt. E.F. Hutton Life Ins. Co., Omaha, 1980-81; chmn. bd. Fin. Dynamics, Omaha, 1981—, Securities Am., Inc., 1984—; life ins. cons. Mem. Nat. Assn. Life Underwriters, Internat. Assn. Fin. Planners. Baptist. Home: 16561 Nina Circle Omaha NE 68130 Office: 7100 W Center Rd Suite 500 Omaha NE 68106-2798

WILD, STEVEN DAGGETT, vidoe production company executive. s. Lauren Daggett and Eleanor (Churchman) W.; m. Terri Lobdell, Apr. 26, 1980. BS in Communications, Eastern Mich. U., 1974, MA in Communications, 1983. Program mgr. WIID Radio, Garden City, Mich., 1973-76; sr. videotape editor Magnetic Video Corp., Farmington Hills, Mich., 1976-79; dir. studio ops. div. CBS/Fox Video, Farmington Hills, 1979-84; pres., chief operating officer Grace & Wild Studios, Inc., Farmington Hills, 1984—, Hollywood, 1987—; advisor communications tech. Eastern Mich. U., Ypsilanti, 1984—. Co-chmn. Grace & Wild Charity Ann. Golf Invitational, 1985. Mem. Internat. Interaction Communications Soc., Internat. Teleprodn. Soc., Internat. TV Assn., Soc. Motion Picture and TV Engrs., Detroit Adcraft Club, Detroit Producers Assn. (pres. 1986-87). Office: Grace & Wild Studios Inc 23689 Industrial Park Dr Farmington Hills MI 48024

WILDE, ALAN HUGH, orthopedist; b. Phila., Sept. 7, 1933; s. Norman T. Sr. and Elizabeth (Duthie) W.; m. Marilyn Meyer, June 13, 1958; children: Alan Jr., Douglas, Laurie. AB, U. Penn., 1955; MD, Hannemann U., 1959. Diplomate Am. Bd. Orthopaedic Surgeons. Intern Martin Army Hosp., Ft. Benning, Ga., 1959-60; resident in orthopaedic surgery U. Pitts., 1962-65; fellowship in orthopaedic surgery Edinburgh U., Scotland, 1965; staff dept. orthopaedic surgery Cleve. Clinic, 1966—, chmn. dept. orthopaedic surgery, 1976—; bd. gov's. Cleve. Clinic, 1976-80, trustee 1978-80; trustee Orthopaedic Researchand Edn. Found, 1984—. Pres. bd. deacons Presby. Ch., Cleve. Heights, 1972. Served to capt. M.C. U.S. Army, 1959-62. Fellow Am. Acad. Orthopaedic Surgeons (chmn. ednl. programming 1984-86), ACS; mem. Am. Orthopaedic Assn. (chmn. N.Am. traveling fellowship com. 1980-86), Am. Shoulder and Elbow Surgeons, Knee Soc., Hip Soc. Republican. Club: Cleve. Skating. Home: 2764 Fairmount Blvd Cleveland Heights OH 44118 Office: Cleve Clin 9500 Euclid Ave Cleveland OH 44106

WILDE, DAWN LEE, computer analyst; b. Pitts., Oct. 26, 1959; d. Chong Wan and Yong Soon (Chung) Lee; m. Nicholas Paul Wilde. BA, Cornell U., 1981, M in Engring., 1982. Cert. data processing. Commd. USAF, 1982, advanced through grades to capt.; computer systems analyst AF Data Service Ctr., Washington, 1982-84; cruise missile analyst Hdqr. Strategic Communications Div. WPFAC, Offutt AFB, Neb., 1984—. Mem. Assn. for Computing Machinery. Methodist. Home: 3515 Comstock Ave Omaha NE 68123 Office: Hdqrs SCD/WPFAC Offutt AFB NE 68113

WILDER, JOHN GARDNER, investment banking executive; b. Columbus, Ohio, Aug. 7, 1940; s. John Gardner Wilder; m. Anne Kirsten, May 28, 1966; children: Anne G., Nicolson G. BA in History, U. Va., 1962. Asst. v.p. Merrill Lynch, Columbus, 1966-84; v.p. Blunt, Ellis & Loewi, Columbus, 1981-84, E.F. Hutton, Columbus, 1984—; mem. Columbus Stock & Bond Club, 1966—. Bd. dirs., pres. condrs. com. Columbus Symphony Orch., 1974-75; pres., bd. dirs. Columbus Cancer Clinic, 1985-86. Republican. Clubs: Rocky Fork Hunts Country; Athletic of Columbus, Capital. Avocations: sailing, skiing, travel. Home: 3488 La Rochelle Dr Columbus OH 43221 Office: 88 E Broad Suite 700 Columbus OH 43209

WILDER, LEROY JOSEPH, JR., environmental engineer, hygiene technologist; b. La Crosse, Wis., Aug. 25, 1954; s. LeRoy Joseph and Bertha Pauline (Benson) W. Assoc. in Applied Sci., Western Wis. Tech Inst.; BS, U. Wis.-La Crosse, 1977, postgrad., 1980-81. Environ. engr. Rayovac Corp., Madison, Wis., 1981-85; co-ordinator environ. activities No. States Power Co., Eau Claire, Wis., 1985—; diver-biologist Environ. Impact Survey for Wis. Dept. of Natural Resources and Wis. Dept. Transp., La Crosse, 1977. Mem. Air Pollution Control Assn., Fedn. Environ. Technologists, Nat. Elec. Mfrs. Assn., Inst. Profl. Assn. Diving Instrs. (rev. com. 1982—), Wis. Utilities Assn., Wis. Mfrs. and Commerce Assn. Lodge: Eagles. Avocations: scuba diving, flying, water skiing, camping; golf. Home: 1619 LaCrescent St La Crosse WI 54603 Office: No States Power Co PO Box 8 Eau Claire WI 54702

WILDER, THOMAS RAYMOND, accountant; b. St. Louis, May 23, 1948; s. Peter Joseph Jr. and Margaret Virginia (Wiegers) W.; m. Judy Dawn Puckett, May 17, 1975; children: Jeremy John, Katherine Anne. BS in Commerce, St. Louis U., 1970. CPA, Ill., Mo. Acct. Ernst & Whinney, St. Louis, 1970-75; auditor May Dept. Stores Co., St. Louis, 1975-77; controller Worthington Service Corp., St. Louis, 1977-79; treas. Superior Insulating Tape Co., St. Louis, 1979-81, Intrav, Inc., Clayton, Mo., 1981-83; pvt. practice acctg. Wood River, Ill., 1983-85; acct. Scheffel & co., Edwardsville, Ill., 1985—. City councilman City of Wood River, 1983-87; bd. dirs. Greater Alton-Twin Rivers Growth Assn., East Alton, Ill., 1985—. Named one of Outstanding Young Men of Am., 1983. Mem. Am. Inst. CPA's, Nat. Assn. Accts., Ill. CPA Soc., Mo. Soc. CPA's, Twin Rivers C. of C. (outstanding profl. 1984). Lodges: Lions, Moose. Home: 235 8th St Wood River IL 62095-2303 Office: Scheffel & Co PC CPA's 143 N Kansas St Edwardsville IL 62025

WILDES, LINDA KATHLEEN, computer analyst; b. Quincy, Ill., June 2, 1949; s. Harold Clifford and Ella Kathleen (Spivey) Ellis; m. James Martin Peterson, Aug. 23, 1969 (div. Nov. 1977); m. Bradley Eugene Wildes, Aug. 22, 1980; 1 child, Tanner Winton. BS, U. Ill., 1970; MS in Engring. Mgmt., Milw. Sch. Engring., 1978. Internal auditor Wis. Electric Power Co., Milw., 1970-72, methods analyst, 1972-74, supr. material control, 1974-79, sr. computer analyst, 1979—. V.p. Cedarburg (Wis.) Community Scholarship fund., 1977. Named Outstanding Young Woman, YWCA, Milw., 1978. Mem. Cedarburg Jaycettes (treas. 1973, state dir. 1975). Republican. Roman Catholic. Avocations: bridge, crocheting. Home: N99 W6564 Lexington St Cedarburg WI 53012 Office: Wis Electric Power Co 231 W Michigan Milwaukee WI 53201

WILDI, JOSEPH ANTHONY, dentist; b. Columbus, Ohio, Feb. 15, 1947; s. Charles Joseph and Rosemary Rita (Miller) W.; m. Deborah Ann Stypinski, Apr. 29, 1978; children: Joseph, Michael. BS cum laude, Ohio State U., 1974, DDS, 1977. Gen. practice dentistry Columbus, 1977—. Served to sgt. USMC, 1965-69, Vietnam. Republican. Roman Catholic. Avocations: model railroading, fishing, music. Home: 8486 Nuthatch Way Worthington OH 43085 Office: Canyon Dental Ctr 6113 E Broad St Columbus OH 43213

WILDI, MARGARET ANN, word processing manager; b. Columbus, Ohio, Mar. 1, 1952; d. Charles Joseph and Rosemary Rita (Miller) W. Student, Ohio Dominican Coll., 1985—. Various positions Grange Ins. Co., Columbus, 1970-78, systems analyst, 1978-82, word processing mgr., 1982—. Mem. Assn. Info. Systems Profls. (asst. treas. 1982-83, treas. 1982-84, v.p. membership, 1984-85, pres. 1985-86, pub. relations dir. 1986—, Honor Soc. 1984, Meritorious Service award 1985). Roman Catholic. Avocations: counted cross-stitch, piano, organ. Home: 1827 Woodcrest Rd Columbus OH 43232 Office: Grange Mut Cos 650 S Front St Columbus OH 43216

WILEMAN, DOUGLAS BRIAN, computer consultant; b. South Bend, Ind., Sept. 13, 1958; s. Walter H. and Mary Ruth (Hazelip) W.; m. Jill Diane Hanna, May 23, 1981. BBA cum laude, Ohio State U., 1981. CPA, Ind.; cert. in data processing. Systems analyst, cons. Whalen & Assocs., CPA, Columbus, Ohio, 1980-81; computer cons. Crowe, Chizek & Co., CPA, South Bend, 1981-85; co-founder, ptnr. Orion Group, South Bend, 1985—. Com. chmn. Pub. TV, Elkhart, Ind., 1983-85. Mem. Am. Inst. CPA's, Inst. for Cert. Computer Profls., Ind. CPA Soc. Avocations: basketball, softball, pocket billiards. Home: 19330 Strawberry Hill South Bend IN 46614 Office: Orion Group 300 N Michigan St South Bend IN 46601

WILEMAN, JILL DIANE, controller; b. South Bend, Ind., July 20, 1959; d. David Earl and Jolene Kay (Emmons) Hanna; m. Douglas Brian Wileman, May 23, 1981. BS in Acctg., Mgmt., Ind. U., South Bend, 1981. CPA, Ind. Auditor Crowe, Chizek & Co., South Bend, 1981-84; controller Data-Link Systems Inc., South Bend, 1984—. Mem. Am. Inst. CPA's, Am. Woman's Soc. CPA's, Ind. CPA Soc. Presbyterian. Avocations: folk art painting, aerobics, water skiing. Home: 19330 Strawberry Hill South Bend IN 46614 Office: Data-Link Systems Inc 1818 Commerce Dr South Bend IN 46628

WILEY, ALBERT LEE, JR., physician, engineer, educator; b. Forest City, N.C., June 9, 1936; s. Albert Lee and Mary Louise (Davis) W.; m. Janet Lee Pratt, June 18, 1960; children: Allison Lee, Susan Caroline, Mary Catherine, Heather Elizabeth. B of Nuclear Engring., N.C. State U., 1958, postgrad., 1958-59; MD, U. Rochester, N.Y., 1963; PhD, U. Wis., 1972. Diplomate Am. Bd. Nuclear Medicine, Am. Bd. Radiology. Nuclear engr. Lockheed Corp., Marietta, Ga., 1958; intern in surgery U. Va. Med. Sch., Charlottesville, 1963-64; resident in radiation therapy Sanford U., Palo Alto, Calif., 1964-65; resident and postdoctoral fellow U. Wis. Hosp., Madison, 1965-68; med. dir. USN Radiol. Def. Lab., San Francisco, 1968-69; staff physician Balboa Hosp., USN, San Diego, 1969-70; asst. prof. radiotherapy M.D. Anderson Hosp. U. Tex., Houston, 1972-73; prof. radiology, human oncology, med. physics U. Wis., Madison, 1970—; cons. U.S. Nuclear Regulatory Commn., 1981-82, Nat. Cancer Inst.; advisor, cons. numerous univs. and govt. agys.; mem. Wis. Radioactive Waste Bd., Wis. Com. on U.N. Contbr. over 100 articles and abstracts on med. physics, nuclear medicine, biology and cancer to profl. jours. Rep. candidate for U.S. Congress from 2d Wis. dist., 1982, 1984; Rep. candidate for gov. State of Wis., 1986. Served to lt. comdr. USNR, 1968-70. Fellow Oak Ridge Inst. Nuclear Studies, N.C. State U., 1958-59. Fellow Am. Coll. Preventive Medicine; mem. IEEE, AMA, Am. Assn. Physicists in Medicine, Am. Soc. Therapeutic Radiation Oncologists, Health Physics Soc., Soc. Nuclear Medicine, VFW, Am. Legion, USN Ret. Res. Officers Assn., Tau Beta Pi. Lutheran. Avocations: fishing, skiing, scuba diving, hiking. Home: 3235 Hwy 138 Stoughton WI 53589 Office: Univ Wis 600 Highland K4B100 CSC Madison WI 53792

WILEY, GREGORY ROBERT, sales executive; b. Mpls., Sept. 21, 1951; s. William Joseph and Terese (Kunz) W.; m. Sheila Francis, May 25, 1979; children—Kathleen, Mary Glennon. B.A. in Personnel Adminstrn., U. Kans., 1972-74. Dist. sales mgr. Reader's Digest, St. Louis, 1976-80, regional sales dir., Chgo., 1980-82; nat. sales mgr. retail div. Rand McNally & Co., Chgo., 1982-83, nat. sales mgr. premium and incentive div., 1983-86, nat. slaes mgr. bookstore and mass market sales, 1986—. Mem. Nat. Premium Sales Execs., Promotional Mktg. Assn. Am. Roman Catholic. Avocations: historic restoration, golfing. Home: 2214 Linneman St Glenview IL 60025 Office: Rand McNally & Co 8255 N Central Park Ave Skokie IL 60076

WILGARDE, RALPH L., hospital administrator; b. Phila., Jan. 8, 1928; B.A., U. Pa., 1949, M.B.A., 1954; M.Pub. Adminstrn., Cornell U., 1960. Adminstrv. asst. Jefferson Hosp., Phila., 1956-58; asst. adminstr. Frankford Hosp., 1960-64; dir. Irvington (N.J.) Gen. Hosp., 1964-66, Cottage Hosp., Grosse Pointe, Mich., 1966—. Served with AUS, 1950-52. Mem. Am. Hosp. Assn., Am. Coll. Hosp. Adminstrn. Home: 1217 Bishop Rd Grosse Pointe MI 48230 Office: 159 Kercheval Ave Grosse Pointe MI 48236

WILGERS, KATHERINE HUEFTLE, librarian; b. Russell, Kans., May 10, 1938; d. Albert Frederick and B. Magdalene (Ebel) Hueftle; m. Billy Jack Hickman, Aug. 31, 1958 (dec. Sept. 2, 1982); children: Melanie, Melinda, Michelle; m. Larry Martin Wilgers, Jan. 1, 1986. Student, Kans. State, 1956-58; BA, Southwestern Coll., 1976; postgrad., Oklahoma State, 1984, Emporia State U., 1987—. Acquisitions officer Southwestern Coll., Winfield, Kans., 1972-76, asst. to librarian, 1976-85, acting library dir., 1985—. Mem. ALA, Kans. Library Assn., Cowley County Librarians. Republican. Methodist. Avocations: gardening, sewing, reading, travelling. Home: Rt 2 Box 197 Belle Plaine KS 67013 Office: Southwestern Coll Meml Library 100 College Winfield KS 67156

WILGOCKI, MARILYN ELKINS, teacher; b. Phila., Jan. 6, 1936; d. Samuel Edward and Magdalene Gene (Brennecke) Elkins; m. Edward Frank Wilgocki Jr., June 13, 1959 (dec. July 1986); children: Jennifer Lynne, Victoria Leigh. B of Music Edn., Westminster Coll., 1957; MEd, Pa. State U., 1959. Music tchr. Abington (Pa.) Sch. Dist., 1959-63, Hatboro (Pa.) Horsham High Sch., 1963-65, Sch. Dist. #69, Downers Grove, Ill., 1976-79; dir. ch. music First Congl. Ch., Downers Grove, 1976—; fine arts tchr. Sch. Dist. 41, Glen Ellyn, Ill., 1979—; dir. Quarter Notes, Downers Grove, 1969-82. Composer: (one act musicals) Magic Kazoo, Mother Goose Goes Berserk, Subject to Change, 1970-73; arranger choral music. Mem. NEA, Am. Choral Dirs. Assn., Music Educators Nat. Conf., Am. Guild English Handbell Ringers, Choristers Guild. Republican. Club: Music (Downers Grove) (com. chairperson 1969—). Avocations: travel, reading, handcrafts, gardening. Home: 62 Tower Rd Downers Grove IL 60515 Office: Hadley Jr High Sch 240 Hawthorne Ave Glen Ellyn IL 60137

WILHELMSEN, BREDT JOHN, data processing executive; b. Racine, Wis., June 14, 1944; s. Russell Nels and Karma Lydia (Hansen) W.; m. Kathleen Louise Angerman, Jan. 6, 1966; children: Robert John, Jennifer Lyn. Student, U. Wis., Racine, 1968-69. Computer operator Rainfair Inc., Racine, 1969-70, supr. data processing, 1970-71; programmer Quality Carrier Inc., Bristol, Wis., 1971-72, mgr. data processing, 1972-74; mgr. data processing Sargento Cheese Co. Inc., Plymouth, Wis., 1974—. Served with USN, 1963-67. Mem. Cooperating Users of Burroughs Equipment, Muskies Inc. (treas. 1985—). Avocations: fishing, camping, bicycling, bowling, cross country skiing. Home: 60 Moraine Dr Elkhart Lake WI 53020 Office: Sargento Cheese Co Inc PO Box 360 Plymouth WI 53073

WILHIDE, DOUGLAS GRAY, advertising industry; b. Columbus, Ohio, Oct. 15, 1946; s. Charles Ross and Helen Louise (Gray) W.; m. Jean Elliot Matthews, Nov. 1, 1970; children: Samuel Strider, Anduin Parker. BA, Miami U., 1968; MA, U. Iowa, 1974, postgrad., 1975. Advt. mgr. Honeywell, Mpls., 1977-80; assoc. creative dir. Colle & McVoy, Mpls., 1980-83, Bozell & Jacobs, Mpls., 1983-84; creative dir. Maclachlan & Assocs., Mpls., 1984-85; prin. Wilhide & Co., Mpls., 1986—; Adj. lectr. U. Minn., Mpls., 1981-84; adj. instr. Coll. St. Thomas, St. Paul, 1986. Contbr. articles to profl. jours. Served with USN, 1968-72. Recipient Sawyer award Bus. Mktg. Mag., 1985, ANDY award, N.Y. Ad Club, Caples award. Mem. Bus. and Profl. Advt. Assn. (reviewer Minn. 1980, Pro-Comm award N.Y.). Home and Office: 3019 W 43d St Minneapolis MN 55410

WILHITE, MARC ALLEN, herpetologist; b. Evansville, Ind., Dec. 3, 1956; s. Edward Lee and Ruth Lavahn (Davis) W. Grad., Ind. State U., Evansville, 1978. Zookeeper Mesker Park Zoo, Evansville, 1975-76; animal technician Houston Zool. Garden, 1981-82; satellite technician Suburban Satellite, Evansville, 1983—; herpetologist/aide Internat. Soc. on Toxinology, Rosans, France, 1981—, Herpetologist League, N.Y.C., 1981—. Contbr. articles to profl. jours. Fellow Am. Soc. Icthyologists and Herpetologists, Herpetologists League; mem. Am. Assn. Zool. Parks and Aquariums, Internat. Soc. Toxinology. Democrat. Baptist. Avocation: sports.

WILHITE, ROBERT KEITH, educational administrator; b. Alton, Ill., Aug. 9, 1947; s. Bob Lee and Carmen M. (Owens) W.; m. Carol Ann Skupien, Aug. 14, 1976. B.A., So. Ill. U., 1969; M.Ed., Loyola U., Chgo., 1976, Ed.D., 1982. Cert. tchr., sch. supr. and adminstr., Ill. English tchr. Edwardsville (Ill.) Jr. High Sch., 1969-70; lang. arts tchr. Mannheim Jr. High Sch., Melrose Park, Ill., 1972-78; reading specialist Wheaton (Ill.) Pub. Schs. 1978-82; curriculum supr. reading, lang. arts, kindergarten and career edn. Waukegan (Ill.) Pub. Schs. 1982-84, prin. Greenwood Sch., 1984-86; prin. Wayne Thomas Sch., Highland Park, Ill., 1986—; chmn. select curriculum com., Wheaton, 1979-82. Author: Techniques of Creative Writing, 1976, The Role of the Principal in Reading, 1982. Served with C.E., U.S. Army, 1970-72. Decorated Army Commendation medal. Mem. Internat. Reading Assn., Nat. Council Tchrs. of English, Assn. Supervision and Curriculum Devel., Ill. Reading Council, Secondary Reading League, Ill. Assn. Sch. Prins., Prins. Roundtable of No. Ill., Ill. Assn. Sch. Adminstrs., Nat. Assn. Elem. Sch. Prins. Office: Wayne Thomas Sch 2939 Summit Ave Highland Park IL 60035

WILHOITE, MARCIA CAROL, accountant; b. Lebanon, Ind., May 5, 1958; d. John Thomas and Julia Belle (Corbly) Cunningham; m. Alan Eugene Wilhoite, Aug. 19, 1978; children: Andrew Nathan, Aaron Lee, Monica Elaine. BBA, U. Notre Dame, 1980. CPA, Ind. Acct. Lind & Scott, P.C., Lebanon, 1980—. Mem. Am. Soc. CPA's, Ind. Soc. CPA's, Am. Woman's Soc. CPA's, Psi Iota Xi (asst. treas. 1984-85, treas. 1985-86, corr. sec. 1986—). Methodist. Club: Ulen Country. Lodge: Zonta. Avocation: golf. Home: 1025 E 375 N Lebanon IN 46052 Office: Lind & Scott PC PO Box 604 Lebanon IN 46052

WILK, DENNIS KEITH, controller; b. Milw., Dec. 3, 1952; s. Chester Peter and Margaret Florence (Kosrog) W.; m. Deborah Ann Roan, July 28, 1979. BBA in Acctg., U. Wis., Milw., 1978. CPA, Milw. Office mgr., acct. Walther & Halling, Milw., 1975-78; fin. controller, office mgr. Astromedia Corp., Milw., 1978-84; fin. controller, chief fin. exec. Kubin-Nicholson Corp., Milw., 1984—. Mem. Am. Inst. CPA's, Wis. Inst. CPA's. Avocations: golf, fishing. Home: 8513 W Hillview Dr Mequon WI 53092 Office: Kubin-Nicholson Corp 5880 N 60th St Milwaukee WI 53218

WILKE, OWEN CHARLES, optometrist; b. St. Cloud, Minn., June 26, 1920; s. Carl F. and Lillian Eleanor (Knoblaugh) W.; m. Lotty M. James, Dec. 12, 1942; 1 child, Sharon Jean. O.D., Ill. Coll. Optometry, Chgo., 1947. Gen. practice optometry, Marshall, Minn., 1947—. Past chmn. Marshall Police Commn.; chmn. Am. Legion Boy Scouts of Am. office. Served with USN, 1942-45, PTO. Fellow Am. Acad. Optometry; mem. Am. Optometric Assn., Inc., Mo. Valley Optometric Soc. (bd. dirs. 1950-60), Minn. Optometric Assn., Inc. (pres. 1958-59), Minn. State Bd. Optometry (pres. 1961-72), Southwest Minn. Optometric Soc., Marshall C. of C., Am. Legion, Tomb and Key, Beta Sigma Kappa, Omega Delta. Lutheran. Lodge: Lions. Avocations: biking, dancing. Office: 127 N 3d St Marshall MN 56258

WILKEN, PAUL WILLIAM, optometrist; b. Sandusky, Ohio, Nov. 14, 1951; s. Carl Anthony and Mary Ellen (Gentry) W.; m. Linda Irene Nierstheimer, Sept. 1, 1973; children: Jennifer, Carl, Michelle, Benjamin. BS, Ohio State U., 1973, OD, 1977. Optometrist John Wasylik, Sandusky, 1977-79; owner, v.p. John E. Wellman OD, Inc., Celina and St. Marys, Ohio, 1979—, Wellman, Wilken, Fanning & Assocs., Wapakoneta, Ohio, 1983—, Piqua, Ohio, 1984—, Lima, Ohio, 1985—, Van Wert, Ohio, 1985. Author: (newspaper column) Vision Care, 1980-81. Mem. Sch. Curriculum Council, Celina, 1982-84; speaker, cons. Mercer County Council on Aging, Mercer County Diabetic Support Group, Celina, 1980—, Joint Twp. Dist. Meml. Hosp. Diabetic Support Group, 1986—, Van Wert County Diabetic Support Group, 1987—. Mem. Am. Optometric Assn., Ohio Optometric Assn., N.W. Ohio Optemetric Assn., Ohio State U. Alumni Assn. (life), Epsilon Psi Epsilon (Pledge of Yr. award 1976). Republican. Roman Catholic. Lodge: Rotary (sec. 1979-84, pres. 1985-86). Avocations: flying, motivational speaking. Home: 616 N Main St Celina OH 45822 Office: Wellman Wilken 119 W Summit St Celina OH 45822

WILKENS, LEONARD RANDOLPH, JR. (LENNY WILKENS), professional basketball coach; b. Bklyn., Oct. 28, 1937; s. Leonard Randolph Sr. and Henrietta (Cross) W.; m. Marilyn J. Reed, July 28, 1962; children: Leesha Marie, Leonard Randolph III, Jamée McGregor. BS in Econs, Providence Coll., 1960, HHD (hon.), 1980. Counselor Jewish Employment Vocat. Services, 1962-63; salesman packaging div. Monsanto Co., 1966; profl. basketball player 1960-69; player-coach Portland (Oreg.) Trail Blazers, 1974-76; player-coach Seattle SuperSonics, 1969-72, coach, 1977-85, gen. mgr., 1985-86; head coach Cleve. Cavaliers, 1986—. Author: The Lenny Wilkens Story, 1974. Bd. regents Gonzaga U., Spokane; bd. dirs. Seattle Ctr., Big Bros. Seattle, Bellevue (Wash.) Boys Club, Seattle Opportunities Industrialization Ctr., Seattle U.; co-chmn. UN Internat. Yr. of Child program, 1979; organizer Lenny Wilkens Celebrity Golf Tournament for Spl. Olympics. Named Most Valuable Player in NBA All-Star Game, 1971, Man of Yr. Boys High Alumni chpt. Los Angeles, 1979, Man of Yr. Seattle chpt. City of Hope; recipient Whitney Young, Jr. award N.Y. Urban League, 1979, Disting. Citizens award Boy Scouts Am., 1980, Sports Star of Yr. award Seattle Post-Intelligencer, 1979, Coach of Yr. award CBS, 1979, Sports Star of Yr. award Black Pubs. Assn., 1979. Player 9 NBA All-Star Games; coach World Championship Basketball Team, 1979. Address: care of Cleve Cavaliers The Coliseum 2923 Streetsboro Rd Richfield OH 44286

WILKENS, ROBERT ALLEN, utilities executive, electrical engineer; b. Esmond, S.D., Jan. 3, 1929; s. William J. and Hazel C. (Girch) W.; m. Barbara M. Davis, Apr. 15, 1952; childrren—Bradley Alan, Beth Ann, Bonnie Sue, William Frank. B.S.E.E., S.D. State U., 1951. Dispatcher, engr. G.O., Northwestern Pub. Service Co., Huron, 1953-55, div. engr., Huron 1955-58, div. elec. supt., 1958-59, div. mgr., 1959-66, asst. to pres., 1966-69, vice pres. ops., G.O., 1969-80, pres., chief operating officer, 1980—, also dir.; v.p., past pres. N. Cen. Electric Assn., past dir. Midwest Gas Assn.; dir. Farmers & Mchts. Bank Huron; past adminstrv. chmn. Mid-Continent Area Power Pool. Mem. Salvation Army Adv. Bd., 1962; S.D. State R.R. Bd., 1982-87; past pres. Huron United Way. Served to capt. USAF, 1951-53. Named Disting. Engr., S.D. State U., 1977. Mem. North Central Elec. Assn., Midwest Gas Assn., S.D. Engring. Soc., Huron C. of C. (pres. 1963). Republican. Methodist. Lodges: Kiwanis, Masons, Shriners. Office: Northwestern Pub Service Co 3rd St & Dakota Ave S Huron SD 57350

WILKERSON, FLOYD MONROE, manufacturing company executive; b. Polo, Mo., Oct. 31, 1932; s. Floyd M. Sr. and Sarah P. (Couch) W.; m. Ruby Daralene Cooper, June 20, 1952; children: Mark William, Sherri Lynn. BBA, Rockhurst Coll., 1962. V.p. systems and data services Trans World Airlines, Kansas City, Mo., 1971-75, v.p. computer and communication services, 1975-81; v.p. info. services Eaton Corp., Cleve., 1981-83, v.p. adminstrn., 1983—. bd. dirs. United Way, Kansas City, 1978, Jr. Achievement, Kansas City, 1977-79; mem. adv. bd. Salvation Army, Cleve., 1985—. Mem. MIS Council (conf. bd.), Research Bd., Computer Execs. Group, Kansas City C. of C. (bd. dirs. 1979). Office: Eaton Corp Eaton Ctr Cleveland OH 44114

WILKERSON, KEN, retail department stores executive. Chmn. Famous-Barr Co., St. Louis. Office: Famous-Barr Co 601 Olive St Saint Louis MO 63101 *

WILKERSON, LYNN DANETTE, accountant; b. Ottumwa, Iowa, Mar. 22, 1962; d. Raymond James and Wanda Lee (Boeyink) Wonderlich; m. David James Wilkerson, June 23, 1984. BA, U No. Iowa, 1984. CPA. Staff acct. McGladrey Hendrickson & Pullen, Mason City, Iowa, 1984—. Mem. Am Inst. CPAs, Iowa Soc. CPAs. Office: McGladrey Hendrickson & Pullen 25 2d St NE Mason City IA 50401

WILKES, DELANO ANGUS, architect; b. Panama City, Fla., Jan. 25, 1935; s. Burnice Angus and Flora Mae (Scott) W.; m. Dona Jean Murren, June 25, 1960. B.Arch., U. Fla., 1958. Cert. Nat. Council Archtl. Registration Bds. Designer, Perkins & Will Partnership, Chgo., 1960-63; designer, job capt. Harry Weese, Ltd., Chgo., 1963-66; project architect Fitch Larocca Carrington, Chgo., 1967-69; architect Mittelbusher & Tourtelot, Chgo., 1970-71; assoc. Bank Bldg. Corp., Chgo., 1972-75; sr. assoc. Charles Edward Stade & Assocs., Park Ridge, Ill., 1975-77; sr. architect Consoer Morgan Architect, Chgo., 1977-83, mktg. coordinator, 1980-83; design cons. Chamlin & Assocs., Peru and Morris, Ill., 1969-82, dir. architecture, 1983-86, v.p. architecture, 1986—; archtl. cons. Sweet's div. McGraw Hill., Inc., Chgo. Mem. coordinating com. Dune Acres Plan Commn. (Ind.), 1983—; bldg.commr. City of Dune Acres, 1984—; cons. Inst. of Crippled and Disabled, N.Y.C., 1978-83; guest lectr., field trip guide Coll. DuPage, Glen Ellyn, Ill., 1968-76; guest architect med. adv. com. to Pres.'s Com. for Handicapped, 1977, 78. Vice chmn. Westchester County Dem. Precinct, Porter County, Ind., 1986; chmn. selection com. Dem. Hdqrs., Porter County, 1986; mem. Dem. Cen. Com., Porter County, 1986; treas. Com. to elect Kovach to Council, Porter County, 1986. Mem. Businessmen for Pub. Interest, Folsom Family Assn. Am. (pres. 1978-82, v.p. 1982—, nominating chmn. 1983, host ann. meeting, Chgo. 1981), AIA, Chgo AIA (chmn. design awards display com. 1978-79, producer New Mem. Show 1979, chmn. pub. relations com. 1980), Art Inst. Chgo., Chgo. Lyric Opera Guild, Chgo. Assn. Commerce and Industry (display dir. 1979 meeting), Am. Soc. Interior Design (coordinator Info. Fair 1979), N.C. Geneal. Soc., New Eng. Hist. Geneal. Soc., Putnam County Hist. Soc., Soc. Colonial Wars, Gargoyle. Democrat. Unitarian. Author: Colonel Ebenezer Folsom, 1778-1789, North Carolina Patriot and Tory Scourge, 1975; editor Folsom Bull., 1977-80; producer documentary film The Angry Minority, Menninger Found., 1978. Home: 23 Circle Dr Dune Acres IN 46304 Office: Sweets div McGraw-Hill 230 W Monroe St Chicago IL 60606

WILKES HULL, MARY LOU, publisher, author; b. Columbus, Nebr., June 21, 1939; d. Elon W. and ERma R. (Crowe) Brewer; m. Bryce Wilkes, June 7, 1959 (div. Dec. 1981); children: Brad Wilkes, Bryan Wilkes, Brent Wilkes. BS in English, Black Hills State U., 1972, MEd, 1976. Coll. instr. Nat. Coll., Rapid City, S.D., 1972-81, placement dir., 1981-83; pres. Marimac Pub., Columbus, Nebr., 1985—; seminar leader Nat. Pubs., Rapid City, 1981-83; ednl. cons. Rapid City Jour., Rapid City, 1978-79. Author: They Said It Couldn't Be Done, 1976, Professional Development: Dynamics of Success, 1981, Women's Edge, 1985. Bd. dirs. Columbus Area Arts Council, 1983-86. Mem. Am. Soc. Tng. and Devel. Avocations: biking, skiing. Home: 105 Pershing Rd Columbus NE 68601 Office: Marimac Pub 3022 14th St Columbus NE 68601

WILKINS, ARTHUR NORMAN, college administrator; b. Kansas City, Mo., Sept. 24, 1925; s. Arthur Miller and Jean (DeWitt) W.; A.A., Jr. Coll. of Kansas City, 1947; M.A., U. Chgo., 1950; Ph.D., Washington U., 1953. Grad. asst. Washington U., St. Louis, 1950-52; instr. English, La. State U., Baton Rouge, 1953-56; instr. English, Jr. Coll. of Kansas City, 1956-64, chmn. Dept. English, 1961-64; instr. English, Met. Jr. Coll., Kansas City,

Mo., 1964-69, chmn. Dept. English, 1964-68, chmn. Div. Humanities, 1968-69; instr. English, Longview Community Coll., Lee's Summit, Mo., 1969-70, chmn. dept. humanities, 1969-70, dean instrn., 1970-84; dir. acad. affairs Met. Community Colls., Kansas City, Mo., 1984—. Mem. Mo. State Library planning com., 1980-83. Served with U.S. Army, 1943-46. Washington U. fellow, 1952-53. Mem. Bookmark Soc., U. Chgo. Library Soc. Author: Mortal Taste, 1965; High Seriousness, 1971; The Leonore Overtures, 1975; Attic Salt, 1984; contbr. articles to profl. jours. Home: 5724 Virginia Ave Kansas City MO 64110 Office: 3200 Broadway Kansas City MO 64111

WILKINS, DON REED, endodontist; b. Shreveport, La., Aug. 27, 1947; s. Julius Felix and Mary Elizabeth (Johnson) W.; m. Susan Kay Adams, Aug. 18, 1979. Student, La. State U., Baton Rouge, 1965-67, Centenary Coll., 1967-68; DDS, La. State U., New Orleans, 1972; MS, Ohio State U., 1978. Commd. 2d lt. USAF, 1973, advanced through grades to maj., 1973-79, resigned, 1981; gen. practice dentistry Columbus, Ohio, 1981—. Mem. ADA, Ohio Dental Assn., Columbus Dental Assn., Am. Assn. Endodontists, Ohio Assn. Endodontists, C. Edmund Kells Honor Soc. Republican. Avocations: sailing, waterskiing, woodworking. Office: 6501 E Livingston Ave Reynoldsburg OH 43068

WILKINS, LARRY LEON, personnel executive; b. Elgin, Ill., Jan. 22, 1940; s. Walter Henry and Rose Theresa (Grupp) W.; m. Mary Beth Gough, Dec. 29, 1962; children: John Eric, Jennifer Elizabeth. BA, Rockford Coll., 1962, MA, 1969; adminstrv. cert., No. Ill. U., 1975. Cert. K-14 and secondary educator, Ill., vocat. tech. adult educator, Wis. Tchr. Rockford (Ill.) Pub. Schs., 1963-77; curriculum coordinator Kennedy Middle Sch., Rockford, 1978-79; mfg. suprv. Eclipse, Inc., Rockford, 1979-81, facilitator, 1981-83; trainer Energy Adaptive Grinding, Rockford, 1983-84; tng. supr. and facilitator Twin Disc, Inc., Racine, Wis., 1984-87; instr., coordinator productivity improvement Human Resource Services Ctr. Gateway Tech. Inst., Racine, 1987—; instr. Gateway Tech. Inst., Racine, 1985—. Pres. Edgewater Neighborhood Assn., Rockford, 1981. Mem. Internat. Assn. Quality Circles, Am. Soc. Tng. and Devel., Racine Mfrs. and Commerce. Episcopalian. Home: 3345 N Main St Racine WI 53402 Office: Gateway Tech Inst 1001 S Main St Racine WI 53403

WILKINSON, CHARLES ALLAN, radiologist; b. Bay City, Mich., Apr. 27, 1930; s. Charles Henry and Marie Elizabeth (Jacques) W.; m. Patricia Deane Steel, June 27, 1953; children: David Allan, C. Michael, James B., John P., Daniel S., Thomas M. AB, U. Mich., 1951, MD, 1955. Diplomate Am. Bd. Radiology. Intern gen. rotating St. Mary's Hosp., Grand Rapids, Mich., 1955-56; gen. practice medicine Sparta, Mich., 1956, Grand Rapids, Mich., 1959-69; radiology residency Butterworth Hosp., Grand Rapids, 1969-72; radiologist Big Rapids, Reed City, Freemont, Mich., 1972-76, St. Mary's Hosp., Grand Rapids, 1976—; asst. prof. Mich. State U. Sch. Human Medicine, Grand Rapids, 1977—. Served with U.S. Army, 1956-59. Mem. AMA, Mich. State Med. Soc., Radiol. Soc. N.Am., Mich. Radiol. Soc., Western Mich. Acad. Gen. Practice (pres. 1965-66), Kent County Med. Soc. (sec. 1966-69), Western Mich. Radiol. Soc. (pres. 1984-85), Mich. Assn. Professions. Republican. Presbyterian. Avocations: sailing, skiing, tennis, hiking, camping. Home: 1745 Vesta Ln SE Grand Rapids MI 49506 Office: Kent Radiology PC 721 Kenmoor SE Grand Rapids MI 49506

WILKINSON, JEFFREY DAVID, engineer; b. Washington, Nov. 28, 1958; s. William Mckain and Marlis Phyllis (Osnes) W.; m. Wendy Carpenter, May 31, 1980; 1 child, Rebecca Lynne. BA, St. Olaf Coll., 1980. Systems mgr. St. Olaf Coll., Northfield, Minn., 1977-80; project engr. GCA/ParSystems, St.Paul, 1980-83; sr. engr. Medtronic, Inc., Mpls., 1983—. Mem. Assn. Computing Machinery. Home: 459 Collen Dr Vadnais Heights MN 55110 Office: Medtronic Inc 7000 Central Ave NE Minneapolis MN 55432

WILKINSON, WILLIAM JAMES, educator, school administrator; b. Findlay, Ohio, Nov. 20, 1937; s. George Wayne and Gerelene Alice (Dick) W.; m. Janice May Krochot, June 11, 1960; children—William Jeffrey, Brant Wayne. B.S. Miami U., Oxford, Ohio, 1959, M.A., 1962, postgrad., 1969; postgrad., Wright State U., 1975—. Cert. secondary teacher, secondary principal, superintendant. Tchr. Versailles Schs., Ohio, 1959-60, Eaton City Schs., Ohio, 1960-63; prin. Eaton City Schs., 1963-70, Oakwood City Schs. Dayton, Ohio, 1970—; lectr. state and regional confs., instr. adult edn. classes computer utilization, chmn. visitation team North Central Assn. Schs. Colls., Sch. Edn. Adv. Com. U. Dayton, 1981-86. Author: Educational Management Computer Software, 1983; contbr. articles to profl. jours. Chmn. United Appeals Campaign, Eaton, 1968; adv. bd. Metro Dayton Ednl. Computer Assn.; bd. dirs. Jr. Achievement of Dayton and Miami Area; Fellow Inst. Devel. Edn. Activities. Mem. Zoning Appeals Bd., Citizens Fiscal Adv. Com., Western Ohio Edn. Assn. (pres. 1968), Ohio Assn. Secondary Sch. Adminstrs. (project leadership), Nat. Assn. Staff Devel., Nat. Assn. Secondary Sch. Prins., Assn. Supervision and Curriculum Devel., Phi Delta Kappa. Democrat. Methodist. Avocations: stained glass art work; sailing; internat. travel. Office: Oakwood Jr High Sch 1200 Far Hills Ave Dayton OH 45419

WILKOF, ERVIN, manufacturing company executive; b. Canton, Ohio, Sept. 10, 1918; s. Louis and Eva (Freidman) W.; m. Marie Viverette, July 21, 1945; children: Jo Anne, Ronald Shawn, Vicki Lynn. Student, Ohio State U., 1936-38. Pres., ptnr. Wilkof Steel & Supply Co., Canton, 1945—, Wilkof Indsl. Supply Co., Canton, 1955—; v.p. Wilkof Structural Steel, Canton, 1954-65; pres. Wallick Coal, Inc., Strasburg, Ohio, 1968-72; sec. Wallick Mining Co., Strasburg, 1968-72; v.p. Jerved Realty Corp., Canton, 1972—; ptnr. Turner Suspensions, Canton, 1972—; sec. Wilkof-Morris Steel Corp., 1965-77, Wilkof Indsl. Devel., Canton, 1972—. Served to 1st lt. U.S. Army, 1942-45, PTO. Recipient Small Bus. Person's award Canton C. of C., 1986. Mem. Retired Army Officers Assn., Jewish War Vets. Assn., Sigma Alpha Mu. Lodge: B'nai Brith. Home: 1507-08 Maisons-sur-Mer 9650 Shore Dr Myrtle Beach SC 29577 Office: 314 Cherry Ave SE Canton OH 44702

WILKOW, MARC R., real estate executive; b. Chgo., Jan. 18, 1950; s. William W. and Tamara (Hirschfeld) W.; m. Brenda Mary Donnelly, Aug. 21, 1975; children: Jordan, Gregg, Brett. BA magna cum laude, UCLA, 1971; JD, U. Chgo., 1974. Bar: Ill.; lic. real estate broker; lic. gen. securities broker. Assoc. atty. Friedman & Koven, Chgo., 1974-77; v.p. M & J Wilkow, Ltd., Chgo., 1977-83, pres., 1983—. Trustee Jewish Family and Community Service, Chgo., 1985—, Mt. Sinai Hosp., 1986. Mem. ABA, Ill. Bar Assn., Chgo. Bar Assn., Real Estate Securities, Nat. Assn. Securities Dealers; Phi Beta Kappa. Clubs: Standard (Chgo.), Northmoor (Highland Park, Ill.). Avocations: skiing, tennis. Home: 1047 Ridgewood Dr Highland Park IL 60035 Office: M & J Wilkow Ltd 180 N Michigan Ave Chicago IL 60601

WILKUS, FRANK JEROME, health care administrator; b. St. Paul, Apr. 20, 1923; s. Anthony and Edna (Johnson) W.; m. Theresa Borsch, May 4, 1946; children—Mary Lynn, Paul, James, Mark, Louann, Annette. B.B.A., Coll. St. Thomas, 1949; postgrad. U. Minn., 1949-51, St. Paul Coll. Law, 1952. Advt. mgr. Water Power Equipment Co., St. Paul, 1948-49; with Emporium Dept. Store, St. Paul, 1949; auditor First Grand Ave. State Bank, 1949-51; examiner Minn. Dept. Taxation, 1952-55, asst. officer mgr., 1952-55, office mgr., 1955-56; exec. dir. Olmsted Med. & Surg. Group, P.A., Rochester, Minn., 1956—. Mem. Common Council of Rochester, 1958-64, Park Bd. Rochester, 1970—. Served with USMC, 1941-45. Decorated Purple Heart. Fellow Am. Coll. Med. Group Adminstrs.; mem. So. Minn. Clinic Mgrs. Assn. (sec.), Minn. Med. Group Mgmt. Assn. (pres.). Clubs: Kiwanis, Rochester Growth. Home: 1018 10th Ave NW Rochester MN 55901 Office: 1018 10th Ave NW Rochester MN 55901

WILL, HUBERT LOUIS, U.S. district judge; b. Milw., Apr. 23, 1914; s. Louis E. and Erna (Barthman) W.; m. Phyllis Nicholson, July 23, 1938; children: Jon Nicholson, Wendy (dec.), Nikki, Ami Louise; m. Jane R. Greene, Dec. 20, 1969. A.B., U. Chgo., 1935, J.D., 1937; L.L.D. (hon.), John Marshall Law Sch., 1973. Bar: Wis. 1937, U.S. Supreme Ct 1941, Ill. 1946. Mem. gen. counsel's staff SEC, Washington, 1937-38; sec. U.S. Senator Robert F. Wagner, 1939; spl. asst. to atty. gen. U.S. 1940-41; asst. to gen. counsel OPA, 1942; tax counsel Alien Property Custodian, 1943; atty. firm Pope & Ballard, Chgo., 1946-48, Nelson, Boodell & Will, Chgo., 1949-61; U.S. dist. judge No. Dist. Ill., 1961—; Mem. Commn. on Bankruptcy Laws of U.S., 1971-73; mem. com. to consider standards for admission to practice in fed. cts. U.S. Jud. Conf., 1976-80. Contbr. articles legal publs. Chmn. Chgo. Com. Youth Welfare, 1957-61. Served as capt. OSS AUS, 1944-45, chief counter espionage br., ETO. Decorated Bronze Star. Mem. Am., Chgo. bar assns., Am. Judicature Soc., Am. Vets Com., World Vets. Fedn. (council U.S.A.). Office: US Dist Ct 219 S Dearborn St Chicago IL 60604

WILL, ROBERT ARTHUR, II, graphic designer; b. Janesville, Wis., May 20, 1956; s. Robert Arthur and Clarice Joan (Nelson); m. Carmen Guillermina Rollin, Sept. 14, 1985. BFA, U. Wis., Oskosh, 1979. Graphic designer Candee/Saueressict, Bismarck, N.D., 1980-82; sr. art dir. Meyer Assocs., St. Cloud, Minn., 1982-84, Communications Group, Mpls., 1984-85; creative dir. Adpros Design, Mpls., 1985-86; sr. art dir. Arnold Design Group, Mpls., 1986—; freelance illustration and design, 1979—; teaching asst. watercolor Bismarck Jr. Coll., 1982. Prin. designs include Sinclair Lewis Centennial Sauk Ctr. Logo, 1984 (1st cash prize); exhibited various watercolor shows (Personal prize 1981). Lutheran. Avocations: reading, history, tennis, basketball, classical music. Office: Arnold Design Group 716 N 1st St Suite 341 Minneapolis MN 55401

WILL, THOMAS RUSSELL, broadcasting executive; b. Chgo., Jan. 1, 1942; s. Albert John and Sylvia Violet (Schultz) W.; m. Erika Olson, Feb. 13, 1965; children: Kelly, Courtney. BA in Journalism, Drake U., 1964. Exec. v.p. Peters, Griffin & Woodward Inc., N.Y.C., 1971-80; sr. v.p. Seltel Corp., Chgo., 1981-85; mgr. cen. region Westinghouse Broadcasting Corp., Chgo., 1986—; bd. dirs. Am. Heritage Savs. & Loan Assn., Bloomingdale, Ill. Served as lt. USNR, 1964-68. Mem. Chgo. Broadcast Rep. Assn. (pres. 1975-76). Republican. Clubs: Broadcast Advt. (pres. 1978-79), Mid-America (Chgo.); LaGrange (Ill.) Country. Avocations: golf, skiing. Office: Group W Prodns 625 N Michigan Ave Suite 1515 Chicago IL 60611

WILLACY, HAZEL MARTIN, lawyer; b. Utica, Miss., Apr. 20, 1946; d. Julious and Willie Thelma (Barnes) Martin; m. Aubrey Barrington Willacy, Mar. 18, 1967; children: Austin Keith, Louis Samuel. Student Tougaloo Coll., 1963-64; BA in Econs., Smith Coll., 1967; JD, Case Western Res. U., 1976. Bar: Ohio 1976. Labor economist Bur. Labor Stats., U.S. Dept. Labor, 1967-70; assoc. Baker, Hostetler, Cleve., 1976-80; labor relations atty. Sherwin Williams Co., Cleve., 1980-82, asst. dir. labor relations, 1983-87, dir. labor relations, 1987—. Contbr. articles to profl. jours. Bd. dirs. YWCA, 1972, mem. fin. devel. com., 1976-80; bd. dirs., mem. recreation planning com. Shaker Heights Youth Ctr.; vis. com. bd. overseers student affairs Case Western Res. U. Mem. ABA (labor law com.), Ohio Bar Assn. (labor law com.), Cleve. Bar Assn., Order of Coif. Club: Law Wives. Office: 101 Prospect Ave Cleveland OH 44115

WILLARD, ERIC JOSEPH, data processing training executive; b. Stoneham, Mass., Feb. 17, 1948; s. Theodore E. and Linda Ann (Petris) W.; m. Elizabeth Susan Raab, Nov. 16, 1968; children: Stacey N., Terri L. AS in Computer Sci., N.H. Tech. Inst., 1973; BA in Bus., U. N.H., 1976; MBA in Mktg., Roosevelt U., 1985. Data processing supr. Associated Grocers, Manchester, N.H., 1972-76; mktg. mgr. Reliance Electric, Cleve., 1976-78, indsl. tng. mgr., 1978-80; mktg. mgr. Digital Equipment, Bedford, Mass., 1980-81; edn. mgr. Digital Equipment Corp., Chgo., 1981-83; dir. edn. Walker Interactive Products, Chgo., 1983—; prin. WriteWare, Inc., Lake Zurich, 1985—; cons. Wahg Labs., Rolling Meadows, 1985-86, GTE Data Services, Tampa, Fla., 1986. Mem. Planning Commn., Madison, Ohio, 1982-83. Served with U.S. Army, 1967-70, Vietnam. Mem. Am. Soc. Tng. and Devel., Am. Mktg. Assn., Ill. Tng. and Devel. Assn., Chgo. Orgn. Data Processing Educators. Roman Catholic. Avocations: traveling, reading, jogging. Home: 859 Windemere Ln Lake Zurich IL 60047 Office: WriteWare Inc 859 Windemere Ln Lake Zurich IL 60047

WILLE, CRAIG DONALD, school psychologist; b. Burlington, Wis., Aug. 13, 1948; s. Donald Herman and Romona Ethel (Schneider) W.; m. Christine Maria Tetting, July 17, 1976; children: Alexander, Stephanie. BA, U. Wis., Madison, 1970; BS, U. Wis., Whitewater, 1974, MS, 1977. Lic. pvt. practice of sch. psychology, Wis. Sch. psychologist Johnson Creek (Wis.) Schs., 1977-81, Waunakee (Wis.) Schs., 1981—. Mem. Nat. Assn. Sch. Psychologists, Wis. Sch. Psychologists Assn. Avocations: running, playing recorder, wellness activities. Home: 5310 Tolman Terr Madison WI 53711 Office: Waunakee Schs School Dr Waunakee WI 53597

WILLE, WARREN STANLEY, psychiatrist; b. Durand, Mich., Jan. 3, 1924; s. Glenn A. and Eathel M. (Baker) W.; m. Catherine Edwina Traphagan, Aug. 5, 1945 (div. June 1982); children: Roice, Brent, Stan; m. Barbara J. Dryer, July 16, 1982. BS, Alma (Mich.) Coll., 1943; MD, U. Mich., 1946. Diplomate Am. Bd. Psychiatry. Instr. psychiatry U. Mich., 1953; dir. psychiat. services Mich. Dept. Corrections, 1953-60; chief psychiat. service W.A. Foote Hosp., Jackson, Mich., 1960-66, 1968-72; dir. Jackson-Hillsdale (Mich.) Community Mental Health Services, 1972-77, cons., 1977—; practice medicine specializing in psychiatry Jackson, 1953—; cons. psychiat. service State Prison, Jackson, 1960-84, VA Hosp., Battle Creek, Mich., 1972-75, 84-86, Albion (Mich.) Community Health Ctr., 1983-86. Author: Citizens Who Commit Murder, 1974; also articles. Served to capt. USMC, 1951-53. Recipient Pawlowski Peace Found. prize, 1974. Fellow Am. Psychiat. Assn. (life). Office: 1615 Carlton Blvd Jackson MI 49203

WILLENBRING, MARK LEON, psychiatrist; b. Virginia, Minn., Aug. 15, 1949; s. Raymond Hilary and Margaret Leona (Quaas) W.; m. Katherine Alice Meyers, Apr. 14, 1979; children: Jesse, Morgan. BS, U. Minn., 1970, MD, 1974. Cert. Am. Bd. Psychiatry and Neurology. Intern St. Paul Ramsey Med. Ctr., 1974-75; resident psychiatry U. Calif., Davis, 1977-80; med. dir. Dane Co. Detox Ctr., Madison, Wis., 1980-82; staff psychiatrist Dane County Mental Health Ctr., Madison, 1980-82; asst. prof. U. Minn. VA Med. Ctr., Mpls., 1982—, research dir. drug dependency treatment program, 1982—. Contbr. articles to profl. jours. Mem. Govs. task force CD in Elderly, St. Paul, 1983-85, MAyor's Adv. Com. Alcohol-Drug Problems, Mpls., 1982—. U. Minn. grantee, 1983, VA grantee, 1984-86. Mem. Am. Psychiat. Assn., AAAS, Am. Med. Soc. on Alcohol and Other Drug Abuse, Research Soc. on Alcoholism. Democrat. Unitarian. Avocations: jazz, scuba diving, handball. Office: 116 A VA Med Ctr 4801 S 54th St Minneapolis MN 55417

WILLER, THOMAS FRANK, pharmaceutical company executive; b. Chgo., Sept. 30, 1946; s. Frank W. and Ann Willer; m. Jane E. Groy, Sept. 13, 1946. BA, No. Ill. U., 1968; MA, Ohio U., 1970; PhD, U. Mich., 1975. Instr. Southwestern Mich. Coll., Dowagiac, 1976-79; assoc. prof. Western Mich. U., Kalamazoo, 1977-79; mfg. supr. Beecham Labs., Bristol, Tenn., 1979-82; regulatory compliance mgr. SoloPak Labs., Franklin Park, Ill., 1982—; instr. in bus. adminstrn. Ill. Benedictine Coll., Lisle, 1984—. Author: S.E. Asian References in British Parliamentary Papers, 1977; contbr. articles to Enclyclopaedia Britanica. Co-chmn. United Way, Bristol, 1982; pres. Hunters Woods Home Owners Assn., Naperville, Ill. 1986—. Mem. Regulatory Affairs Assn. Roman Catholic. Avocations: tennis, reading, stamp collecting, golf. Home: 2008 Dichtl Ct Naperville IL 60565

WILLES, MARK HINCKLEY, food industry executive; b. Salt Lake City, July 16, 1941; s. Joseph Simmons and Ruth (Hinckley) W.; m. Laura Fayone, June 7, 1961; children: Wendy Anne, Susan Kay, Keith Mark, Stephen Joseph, Matthew Bryant. AB, Columbia U., 1963, PhD, 1967. Mem. staff banking and currency com. Ho. of Reps., Washington, 1966-67; asst. prof. fin. U. Pa., Pitts., 1967-69; economist Fed. Res. Bank, Phila., 1967; sr. economist Fed. Res. Bank, 1969-70, dir. research, 1970-71, v.p., dir. research, 1971, 1st v.p., 1971-77; pres. Fed. Res. Bank of Mpls., 1977-80; exec. v.p., chief fin. officer Gen. Mills, Inc., Mpls., 1980-85, pres., 1985—. Office: Gen Mills Inc 9200 Wayzata Blvd Minneapolis MN 55426

WILLETT, REX CORY, manufacturing executive; b. Waterloo, Iowa, July 16, 1962; s. Robert Charles and Ethel Marie (Davis) W. High sch. diploma, West High Sch., 1986. Road sales mgr. Texson Campers, Waterloo, Iowa, 1981—, sales mgr., 1983-84, v.p., 1984-85; exec. v.p. Texson Campers, Waterloo, 1985—; Republican. Mem. Recreational Vehicle Ind. Council, Recreational Vehicle Industry Assn. Office: RC Willett Co Inc 3040 Leversee Rd Cedar Falls IA 30404

WILLETT, ROBERT LEE, health care administrator; b. Takoma Park, Md., Aug. 28, 1935; s. Edward Farrand and Fern Leona (Hawkins) W.; m. Crystal May Wery, June 28, 1959; children: Jesse Allen, Gregory Dean. B.S., Columbia Union Coll., Washington, 1957; M.B.A., George Washington U., 1964. Acct. Hadley Meml. Hosp., Washington, 1960-62; dir. patient service Kettering Med. Ctr., Dayton, Ohio, 1963-66, asst. adminstr., 1966-69, assoc. adminstrn., 1969-72, v.p., 1972-79, pres., 1979—; regional v.p. Adventist Health System-Eastern and Middle Am., 1980-83. Developer: system for healthcare outpatient services Verticare. Mem. Greater Dayton Area Hosp. Assn. (chmn. 1982-83), Seventh-day Adventist Hosp. Assn. (pres. 1982), Am. Coll. Hosp. Adminstrs., Am. Hosp. Assn., Montgomery County Med. Soc. (assoc.), Kettering C. of C. (dir. 1983—), Dayton C. of C. Adventist. Lodge: Rotary (Dayton). Home: 3050 Winding Way Kettering OH 45419 Office: Kettering Med Ctr 3535 Southern Blvd Kettering OH 45429

WILLEY, JAMES LEE, dentist; b. Colorado Springs, Colo., Oct. 26, 1953; s. Elwood James and Dorothy Jean (Norton) W.; m. Catherine Margaret Whitmer, Aug. 23, 1975; children: Andrew James and David Lee (twins). BA, So. Ill. U., 1975; BS in Dentistry, U. Ill., Chgo., 1977, DDS, 1979; MBA, No. Ill. U., 1986. Pvt. practice dentistry Elburn, Ill., 1979—; lectr. Dental Arts Labs., Peoria, Ill., 1981—. Recipient Certificate of Merit, Swissedent Found., Glendale, Calif., 1983. Fellow Am. Endodontic Soc.; mem. ADA, Ill. State Dental Soc., Fox River Valley Dental Soc. Lodge: Lions (bd. dirs. Elburn, Ill. club 1984—). Avocations: fishing, photography. Home: 425 S 1st St Box 7G Elburn IL 60119 Office: 135 S Main St Box 7G Elburn IL 60119

WILLHOIT, JIM, minister; b. Springfield, Ill., June 25, 1943; s. Richard and Virginia (Hampton) W.; m. Karen Huddleston, June 19, 1966; children: Amy Lynn, Todd Christopher. BA, Lincoln Christian Coll., 1969; MDiv., Lincoln Christian Sem., 1974, MA, 1975. Ordained to ministry Ch. of Christ, 1971. Minister Salisbury (Ill.) Christian Ch., 1964-72, Walnut Grove Christian Ch., Arcola, Ill., 1972-81; sr. minister First Ch. Christ, Highland, Ind., 1981—; mem. site com. Project 300, Lincoln, Ill., 1979-81; bd. dirs. Onesimus Ministries, 1978-81; chaplain Lake County Police Dept., Crown Point, Ind., 1986—, Glenwood (Ill.) Police Dept., 1986—. Mem. sch. bd. Unit Dist. 306, Arcola, 1978-81. Mem. Soc. Bibl. Lit., Am. Sci. Affiliation (assoc.), Chgo. Dist. Minister's Assn. (sec.-treas. 1982-87). Home: 8936 Schneider Dr Highland IN 46322 Office: First Ch Christ 2420 Lincoln St Highland IN 46322

WILLIAMS, ANN C., federal judge; b. 1949; M. David J. Stewart. BS, Wayne State U., 1970; MA, U. Mich., 1972; JD, U. Notre Dame, 1975. Asst. U.S. atty. U.S. Dist. Ct. (no. dist.) Ill., Chgo., 1976-85, judge, 1985—; adj. prof., lectr. Northwestern U. Law Sch., Chgo., 1979—. Mem. Fed. Bar Assn. Office: U S Dist Ct 219 S Dearborn St Chicago IL 60604

WILLIAMS, BERNARD T., dentist; b. Mc Leansboro, Ill., Apr. 12, 1943; s. Bernard Taft and Jerry (Dungy) W.; m. Cheryl Susan Foster; 1 son, Ryan Trent. D.D.S., Wash. U., 1969. Practice dentistry specializing in occlusion, reconstructive dentistry, diagnosis and treatment facial pain and dysfunction, Kansas City, Mo., 1971—; mem. staff St. Joseph Hosp., Kansas City, 1980—; cons., lectr. Sch. Dentistry, U. Mo.-Kansas City, 1981—; lectr. in field. Served with U.S. Army, 1969-71. Mem. Mid-Continent Stomatognathic Soc. (founder 1975; pres. 1975-77), Am. Equilibration Soc. (chmn. biology of occlusion 1983), ADA, Am. Coll. Dentists, Acad. Gen. Dentistry, Soc. Occlusal Studies (trustee 1981—, instr. 1978). Author: Therapeutic Exercises for Cranio facial Pain and Dysfunction; Manual for Dentists Diagnosing. and Treating Facial Pain and Dysfunction; contbr. articles to profl. publs. Office: 1010 Carondelet Dr Suite 410 Kansas City MO 64114

WILLIAMS, BETSY LYNN, sales executive; b. Covington, Ky., Aug. 15, 1950; d. John Orwin and Eleanor Margretta (Readle) W.; m. Jeffrey Lynn Goode, May 16, 1977; children: Joshua Langston, Brittany Green. BA, U. Ky., 1972. Sales project engr. Cin. Milacron Mktg. Co., 1976-80, tech. writer, 1974-76; sales engr. Cin. Milacron Mktg. Co., Batavia, Ohio, 1980-85, mktg. commn. coordinator, 1985-86; field sales engr. Cin. Milacron Mktg. Co., Batavia, 1986—. Schmidd Lapp Found. scholar, Cin., 1968-72. Men. Cin. Area Profl. Saleswomen, Soc. Plastics Engrs. Presbyterian. Office: Cin Milacron Mktg Co 4165 Half Acre Rd Batavia OH 45103

WILLIAMS, BRENDA PAULETTE, entrepreneur, consultant; b. St. Louis, July 7, 1946; d. Herman and Hattie Williams; B.J., Ohio U., Athens, 1969; postgrad. U. Mo., Columbia. Newscaster, Sta. KATZ, St. Louis, 1969-70; reporter, talk show producer/host Sta. KPLR-TV, St. Louis, 1973-74, Stas. KSD-TV and Radio, St. Louis, 1974-77; weekend anchor-reporter Sta. KMBC-TV, Kansas City, Mo., 1977-81, weekday anchor-reporter, 1981-85; pres. H. Pearl Investments, Inc., 1986—, Kansas City Skywave, Inc., 1986—. Recipient Cert. of Appreciation St. Louis Urban League-St. Louis Sentinel, 1975, Human Relations award Nat. Assn. Colored Women's Clubs, 1975, Documentary Reporting award Mo. Radio and TV Assn., 1979, Consumer Reporting award Mo. Dept. Consumer Affairs, 1979, Outstanding Achievement in Journalism award Mo. Black Leadership Assn., 1981, Headliner award, 1982; selected for Am. journalists tour of Israel, Israeli Journalist Assn., 1980; Black Achiever award SCLC, 1981. Mem. Alpha Kappa Alpha (Women of Involvement award 1974), Sigma Delta Chi.

WILLIAMS, CALVIN, librarian, consultant; b. Hogansville, Ga., Jan. 29, 1946; s. Azell and Lella (Mullins) W.; m. Delores Hayes, June 23, 1973; children: Sheniqua LaToya, Calvin Mikkel. BA, Morris Brown Coll., 1969; MS in Library Sci., Atlanta U., 1973; MSA, Cen. Mich. U., 1979. Librarian assoc. Atlanta Pub. Library, 1972-73, community analyst, 1973; head librarian Morris Brown Coll., Atlanta, 1971-73; br. librarian Saginaw (Mich.) Pub. Library, 1973-75; acad. librarian Saginaw Valley State Coll., University Center, Mich., 1975-87; librarian Oakland Community Coll., Auburn Hills, Mich., 1987—; Mem. Bridgeport (Mich.) Library Commn., 1981—, pres. 1985-86; library cons. Saginaw County Mental Health Ctr., 1984-86. Editor (newsletter) Great Lakes and Finger Lakes, 1981—. pres. Bridgeport (Mich.) Library Commn., 1985—. Served to U.S. Army, 1969-71. Atlanta U. fellow, 1971-73; recipient Community Service awards Saginaw Pub. Schs., 1975-85. Mem. ALA, Mich. Acad. Sci. and Arts (GODORT), Mich. Library Assn. (docus chmn. 1981-82, Cert. 1980—), Acad. Polit. Sci., NAACP, Alanta U. Alumni Assn., Cen. Mich. U. Alumni Assn. (life), Saginaw Alumni Chpt. (treas. 1984—), Kappa Alpha Psi (life, Outstanding Alumni, 1982). Democrat. Methodist. Avocations: reading, bicycling, drawing, sports, writing basic programs. Home: 3286 Southfield Dr Saginaw MI 48601 Office: Oakland Community Coll 2900 Featherstone Rd Auburn Hills MI 48057

WILLIAMS, CALVIN EVEREST, anesthesiologist; b. Detroit, Jan. 25, 1955; s. Sidney Jr. Williams and Magdalene (Cawthon) Ricks; m. Michele Henderson, June 14, 1980; children: Dana Michele, Calvin Eric. BA, U. Mich., 1977, MD, 1979. Diplomate Am. Bd. Anesthesiology. Resident U. Mich. Hosps., Ann Arbor, 1979-82; staff anesthesiologist Christian Hosp., St. Louis, 1982—; asst. chief dept. anesthesiology Christian Hosp., 1985—. Bd. dirs. Petra Boradcasting Co., St. Charles, Mo., 1984—; v.p. expansion chpt. Full Gospel Businessmen's Fellowship, St. Louis, 1985-87, pres., 1987—. Named one of Outstanding Young Men Am., 1985. Mem. Am. Soc. Anesthesiology, St. Louis Soc. Anesthesiology. Republican. Avocations: swimming, singing. Home: 1488 Gettysburg Landing Saint Charles MO 63303

WILLIAMS, CARLESA IRENE, art director, television producer; b. Detroit, Dec. 30, 1951; d. Willie and Irene Macell (Blackman) Ponder; children: Ricky, Octavia, LeRoya, James, John, Anthony. Student, Wayne State U., 1969-75, Ctr. For Creative Studies, Detroit, 1983-84. Art designer Hudson's, Detroit, 1975-78; sr. art dir. Robert Solomon & Assocs., Detroit, 1978-79; creative dir. Crowley's, Detroit, 1979-80; sr. art dir. Young & Rubicam, Detroit, 1980-86; v.p., sr. art dir. Campbell-Ewald, Warren, Mich., 1986—. Art dir., producer "Keep the Doors Open", 1984, "Kinship", 1985 (Addy award 1985). Mem. Spaulding for Children Parent Group, Detroit. Recipient Creativity '83 award Art Direction Mag., 1982. Mem. Am. Film Inst., Creative Advt. Club (Caddy award 1982-85), Radio and TV (Internat. Broadcasting award 1982), Art Dirs. Club (Merit award 1982), Detroit Producers Assn. Avocations: cinematography, videography, rollerskating, fishing. Home: 206 Eliot Detroit MI 48201 Office: Campbell-Ewald Advt 30400 Van Dyke Warren MI 48093

WILLIAMS, CAROLYN LILLIAN, psychology educator; b. Coral Gables, Fla., Jan. 21, 1951; s. Robert L. and Irene (Kasa) W.; m. James Neal Butcher, Dec. 8, 1979; 1 child, Holly Krista. BA, U. Ga., 1973, MS, 1977, PhD, 1979. Lic. consulting psychologist, Minn. Asst. prof. U. Minn. Sch. Pub. Health, Mpls., 1981—. Editor: Refugee Mental Health in Resettlement Countries, 1986; contbr. articles to profl. jours. Bd. dirs. Walk-in Counseling Ctr., Mpls. Grantee NIH. Mem. Am. Psychol. Assn., Am. Pub. Health Assn., Soc. Pub. Health Edn., Soc. Pediatric Psychology. Home: 9800 Edgewood Rd S Bloomington MN 55438 Office: U Minn Div Epidemology Stadium Gate 27 Minneapolis MN 55455

WILLIAMS, CHARLES M., insurance company executive. Chmn. exec. com. Western & Southern Life Ins. Co., Cin. Office: Western & So Life Ins Co 400 Broadway Cincinnati OH 45202 *

WILLIAMS, CHARLES PAUL, pastor; b. Morgantown, W.Va., Jan. 7, 1953; s. Ralph and Mary Catherine (McCoy) W.; m. Jane Alice Cowger, Aug. 2, 1975; children: Cori Jean, Brandon Charles, Alicen Charis. AA, Anne Arundel Community Coll., 1972; BA in Bus., Marshall U., 1974; M Div., Nazarene Theol. Sem., 1974-78. Ordained to ministry, 1980. Sr. pastor. Vermilion Ch. of The Nazarene, Ohio, 1978-85; assoc. pastor First Ch. The Nazarene, Highland Heights, Ohio, 1985—; presch. tchr. Hillcrest Kiddie Kollege, Highland Heights, 1986-87; sr. pastor Somerset Ch. of Nazarene, 1987—. Sports dir. NCO Jr. Camp, Bellvue, Ohio, 1984, camp dir., 1986, 87. Mem. Vermilion Ministeral Assn. (v.p. 1980, mem. fight against pornography com. 1985). Republican. Avocations: team sports, singing, fishing, hunting, golf. Home: 1378 Eastwood Ave Mayfield Heights OH 44124

WILLIAMS, CHRISTOPHER ALAN, manufacturing company executive; b. Jackson, Miss., Jan. 10, 1961; s. Jonathan Fred and Doris Elaine (Vermulen) W. BS in Chemistry, U. Louisville, 1986. Asst. chemist Devoe & Raynolds Co., Louisville, 1980-84; v.p., gen. mgr. A.F. Wolke Co., Inc., New Albany, Ind., 1984—. Mem. Louisville Paint and Coating Assn. Republican. Roman Catholic. Clubs: Walts, WBD Lifters (Louisville). Avocations: weightlifting, baseball. Office: AF Wolke Co Inc PO Box 199 New Albany IN 47150

WILLIAMS, CLIFFORD BAUMANN, insurance company executive; b. Ft. Wayne, Ind., Aug. 7, 1952; s. Park D. and Lois Jean (Baumann) W.; m. Molly Hamilton Hinton, Sept. 1970 (div. Feb. 1974); 1 child, Matthew Park Williams. BA, U. Ariz., 1979. Regional v.p. mktg. United Presdl. Life Ins. Co., Kokomo, Ind., 1979—. Fellow Life Ins. Inst.; mem. Nat. Assn. Life Ins. Underwriters, Am. Coll. Underwriters (charter), Am. Coll. Fin. Cons. (charter). Avocations: music, sports. Home: 606 Harbourtown Ct Noblesville IN 46060 Office: United Presdl Life Ins Co 217 Southway Blvd Kokomo IN 46902

WILLIAMS, CLYDE E., JR., lawyer; b. Niagara Falls, N.Y., Dec. 17, 1919; s. Clyde E. and Martha (Barlow) W.; m. Ruth Van Aken, Oct. 16, 1948; children—Clyde E. III, Mark Van Aken, Sara. A.B., Denison U., Granville, Ohio, 1942; LL.B., Harvard U., 1945. Bar: Ohio 1945. Practice corp. and real estate law 1945—; with Spieth, Bell, McCurdy & Newell Co., Cleve, v.p., dir., 1964—; gen. counsel Growth Cos., Inc., Phila., 1950-55; pres., dir. Williams Investment Co., Cleve., 1954—; sec., dir. Williams Internat. Corp., Walled Lake, Mich., 1954—; dir., gen. counsel Techno-Fund, Inc., Columbus, Ohio, 1960-67; dir. Radio Seaway, Inc.; mem. faculty Fenn Coll. and Cleve. Coll. div. Western Res. U., 1945-50. Trustee, mem. exec. com., v.p. Cleve. Soc. for Blind, 1979—, pres., 1985-87, mem. adv. council, 1987—. Mem. ABA, Ohio Bar Assn., Cleve. Bar Assn., Sigma Chi. Clubs: Union, Skating. Lodge: Rotary. Office: Spieth Bell McCurdy & Newell Co LPA 2000 Huntington Bldg Cleveland OH 44115

WILLIAMS, CRAIG FOSTER, osteopathic emergency physician; b. Akron, Ohio, July 23, 1949; s. Robert Daniel and Jeanne Marie (Schulte) W.; m. Carol Giglia, May 6, 1978; children—Joy Caroline, Cara Jeanne, Eric James. B.A., Notre Dame U., 1971; D.O., Kansas City Coll. Osteo. Medicine, 1977. Diplomate Am. Bd. Emergency Medicine. Intern, Doctor's Hosp., Columbus, Ohio, 1977-78; resident in emergency medicine Wright State U., Dayton, Ohio, 1978-80, mem. faculty, 1982—, asst. clin. prof. emergency medicine, 1983—; commd. officer USPHS Indian Health Service, Phoenix, 1980-82; staff emergency physician St. Elizabeth Med. Ctr., Dayton, 1982—. Fellow Am. Coll. Emergency Physicians; mem. Univ. Assn. Emergency Medicine, Am. Coll. Osteo. Emergency Physicians, Am. Osteo. Assn., AMA, Notre Dame Alumni Assn. Roman Catholic. Home: 6649 Stamford Pl Dayton OH 45459 Office: Saint Elizabeth Med Ctr Dept Emergency Medicine Dayton OH 45408

WILLIAMS, DAVID ALLAN, dentist, educator; b. Dayton, Ohio, June 30, 1949; s. Robert Eugene and Mary Ellen (Moore) W.; m. Christine Diane Hofmeister, Aug. 29, 1971. BS, Mich. State U., 1971; DDS, Case Western Reserve U., 1975. Clin. assoc. prof. Northwestern U. Dental Sch., Chgo., 1978—; gen. practice dentistry Northbrook, Ill., 1979—, Chgo., 1980—. Served with USN, 1975-78. Armed Forces Health Profls. Scholar, 1972-75. Fellow Acad. Gen. Dentistry; mem. ADA (commn. on dental accreditation), Ill. Dental Soc., Chgo. Dental Soc., Acad. Operative Dentistry, Northbrook Jaycees (pres. 1983). Lutheran. Lodge: Rotary. Avocations: sailing, skiing, cycling. Office: 666 Dundee Rd Suite 801 Northbrook IL 60062

WILLIAMS, DAVID JAMES, plant science educator; b. Glendora, N.J.; s. David James and Elizabeth Helen (Weber) W.; m. Kathleen Dolores McGough, July 11, 1970; children—David, Christine, Jennifer. B.S., Delaware Valley Coll., 1969; M.S., Rutgers U., 1972, Ph.D., 1974. Research asst. Rutgers U., New Brunswick, N.J., 1969-74; asst. prof. U. Ill., Urbana, 1974-80, assoc. prof., 1980—; contbr. articles to profl. jours. Chmn. Shade Tree Commn., Savoy, Ill., 1980—; pres. Unit 4 Bd. of Edn., Champaign, Ill., 1982-83, sec., 1984—; bd. dirs. Savoy United Meth. Ch., Savoy, 1984. Pesticide Impact Assessment Regulating Office grantee, 1981, 82, IR-4 Regional Office grantee, East Lansing, Mich., 1974—. Mem. Internat. Plant Propagation Soc., Am. Soc. Hort. Sci., Am. Assn. Hort. Sci. (chmn. nursery research, 1979), Weed Sci. Soc. Am. (chmn. ornamentals and turf sect. 1980), Ill. State Nurserymen's Assn. (cons. 1974—). Republican. Episcopalian. Club: Glendora Buck. Lodge: Kiwanis. Avocations: scouting; fishing; hunting. Home: 45 Lange St Savoy IL 61874 Office: U Ill 1107 W Dorner Dr Urbana IL 61801

WILLIAMS, DAVID PHILLIPS, psychologist; b. Freeland, Pa., May 27, 1947; s. Ivor and Kathryn Lenore (Phillips) W.; m. Mele Jeanne Howland, May 23, 1981. Student, U. S.C., 1965-67; BA in Sociology, Ohio State U., 1969; MSW, U. Ga., 1975, PhDEd, 1981; PhD in Psychology, Ind. State U., Terre Haute, 1984. Lic. psychologist, Ill., Ind., Nebr. Psychiat. social worker Trenton (N.J.) State Hosp., 1971-73; research assoc. U. Pa. Sch. Social Work, Phila., 1975-77; med. psychologist VA Med. Ctr., Danville, Ill., 1984—. Co-author: Child Neglect, 1981; contbr. articles to profl. jours. Served with Air N.G., 1969-70. Mem. Nat. Assn. Social Workers (cert.), Am. Psychol. Assn., Am. Soc. Clin. Hypnosis. Avocations: auto mechanics and restoration, stock car racing. Home: 911 Timberline Dr Danville IL 61832 Office: VA Med Ctr Psychology Service 116B Danville IL 61832

WILLIAMS, DAVID PRESTON, petroleum geologist, consultant; b. Montrose, Colo., Apr. 23, 1951; s. Norville Preston and Bonnie June (Meyers) W.; m. Connie Rae Richmond, Feb. 2, 1973 (div. June 1987); children—Robert, Christy, Casey, Michael. B.S., Fort Hays State U., 1974. Jr. field engr. Dresser Atlas-Dresser Industries, Great Bend, Kans., 1973-74; exploration/prodn. geologist Benson Minerals Group, Ind., Denver, 1977-79; ind. cons. petroleum geologist, Great Bend, Kans., 1979—. Mem. Kans. Geol. Soc., Am. Assn. Petroleum Geologists, Soc. Profl. Well-log Analysts, Am. Petroleum Inst. Avocations: paleontology; paleobotany; record collecting; fishing.

WILLIAMS, DUANE ALWIN, chemical engineer; b. Marshfield, Wis., Apr. 6, 1935; s. Alwin W. and Edith L. (Young) W.; m. Judith Carol Bean, Aug. 24, 1957; children—Gary Douglas, Jeffrey Scott. B.S., U. Wis.-Madison, 1956, M.S., 1957, Ph.D. in Chem. Engring 1961. Tech. service engr. Enjay Labs., Linden, N.J., 1957-58; research chem. engr. Kimberly-Clark Corp., Neenah, Wis., 1962-64; with Rockor, Inc., Redmond, Wash., 1964-71; with Kimberly Clark Corp., Neenah, Wis., 1971—, dir. infant care products research and devel., 1983-84, dir. feminine care product devel., 1984—. Author tech. articles. Mem. Am. Inst. Chem. Engrs., Tau Beta Pi, Phi Lambda Upsilon, Theta Tau. Lutheran Home: 1976 Marathon Ave Neenah WI 54956-4046

WILLIAMS, EARL GLYNN, secondary school administrator; b. Hazard, Ky., July 12, 1949; s. James Clayton and Corrina (Schenkel) W.; m. Linda Day Davis, Aug. 15, 1970; children: Matthew, Shane, Angie. BS, Ball State U., 1973, MA, 1976; EdS, Ind. U., 1984, postgrad., 1984—. Cert. teaching adminstr., Ind. Tchr., coach Connersville (Ind.) High Sch., 1974-76; asst. prin. West Middle Sch., Martinsville, Ind., 1976-86, prin., 1986—. Bd. dirs. local YMCA, Big Bros. and Big Sisters, Morgan County Task Force for Youth. Mem. N.Cen. Assn. Colls. and Univs. (program evaluator), Assn. Curriculum and Supervision Devel., Nat. Assn. Seondary Sch. Prins., State Athletic Dirs. Assn., Phi Alpha Theta. Republican. Lodges: Lions, Elks. Office: 109 E Garfield St Martinsville IN 46151

WILLIAMS, EDWARD JOSEPH, bank executive; b. Chgo., May 5, 1942; s. Joseph and Lillian (Watkins) W.; m. Johnnita E. Daniel, June 29, 1967; children: Elaine, Paul. BBA, Roosevelt U., 1973. Owner Mut. Home Delivery, Chgo., 1961-63; sr. v.p. Harris Trust and Savs. Bank, Chgo., 1964—; mem. Consumer Adv. Council, Washington, 1986—. Trustee Adler Planetarium, Chgo., 1982; chmn. Provident Med. Ctr., Chgo., 1986. Recipient Disting. Alumni award Clark Coll., Atlanta, 1985. Mem. Nat. Bankers Assn., Urban Bankers Forum (Pioneer award 1986), Econ. Club. Chgo. Methodist. Clubs: Metropolitan, Union League (Chgo.). Office: Harris Trust and Savs Bank 111 W Monroe St Chicago IL 60690

WILLIAMS, FLORA LEONA, economics educator; b. Talahassee, Jan. 21, 1937; d. Noble J. and Dorothy (Rohrer) Rouch; m. Leiw K. Williams, June 26, 1960; children: Chadwick, Lora Lu, Matthew. BS, Manchester Coll., 1959; MS, Purdue U., 1964, PhD, 1969. Tchr., Mishawaka, Ind., 1959-64, West Lafayette, Ind., 1964-68; research asst. Purdue U., West Lafayette, 1968-69, asst. prof., 1969-75, assoc. prof. home econs., 1975—; vis. prof. U. Calif., Davis, 1976; cons. in field. Author: The Family Economy, 1973, Guidelines to Financial Counseling, 1980; contbr. articles to profl. jours. HEW grantee. Mem. Assn. Consumer Research, Am. Econs. Assn., Am. Home Econs. Assn., Am. Council on Consumer Interest, Family and Consumer Research. Home: 3815 Gate Rd Lafayette IN 47905 Office: Purdue U MTHW Hall CSR Dept West Lafayette IN 47907

WILLIAMS, FRANK NORVILLE, corporate executive; b. Ogden, Utah, Feb. 23, 1925; s. Thomas Francis and Grace (Dean) W.; m. Barbara Raymond, Aug. 15, 1946 (div. Apr. 1970); children: Susan, Frank Jr., David, James, Richard; m. Joanna Pa, May 15, 1970; 1 child, Nicole. Student, Weber State Coll., 1942, St. Olaf Coll., 1944, Columbia U., 1944. Asst. to pres. Fed. Huber, Plano, Ill., 1947-62, pres., 1962-79; pres. Imperial Marble, Somonauk, Ill., 1980—. Patentee in field. Served with USN, 1943-47. Republican. Mormon. Avocations: fishing, boating, golf. Home: 1564 Holiday Dr Sandwich IL 60548 Office: Imperial Marble 327 E LaSalle Somonauk IL 60552

WILLIAMS, GARY L., infosystems specialist; b. Cin., May 5, 1943; s. Frank W. Williams and Elizabeth D. (Ellis) W.; m. Betty J. Jenkins, Aug. 29, 1964; children: Tamatha, Stacey. AS, U. Cin., 1972, BS, 1976. Systems analyst Mac Gregor Sports, Cin., 1966-72, U. Cin., 1972-76; asst. dir. Children's Hosp., Cin., 1976-77; cons. NCR, Dayton, 1978, Stokely-Van Camp, Indpls., 1979-83; dir. VA Med. Ctr., Indpls., 1983—. Mem. Mumps User Group, Delta Mu Delta, U. Cin. Alumni Assn. (v.p. 1986—). Home: 101 Leaning Tree rd Greenwood IN 46142 Office: VA Med Ctr 1481 W 10th St Indianapolis IN 46202

WILLIAMS, G(ERHARD) MENNEN, SR., state chief justice, former governor Michigan; b. Detroit, Feb. 23, 1911; s. Henry Phillips and Elma Christina (Mennen) W.; m. Nancy Lace Quirk, June 26, 1937; children: Gerhard Mennen Jr., Nancy Williams Ketterer, Wendy Williams Burns. AB cum laude, Princeton U., 1933; JD cum laude, U. Mich., 1936, LLD (hon.); LLD (hon.), Mich. State U., Wilberforce U., Cleary Coll., Aquinas Coll., St. Augustine's Coll., Ferris Inst., 1961, Western Mich. U., Lincoln U., World U., P.R., Morris Brown Coll.; HHD (hon.), Lawrence Inst. Tech. Bar: Mich. 1936. Atty. Social Security Bd., 1936-38; asst. atty. gen. State of Mich., 1938-39; exec. asst. to atty. gen. U.S. Dept. Justice, Washington, 1939-40; with criminal div. U.S. Dept. Justice, 1940-41; dep. dir. Mich. Office of Price Adminstrn., 1946-47; assoc. Griffiths, Williams & Griffiths, Detroit, 1947-48; gov. State of Mich., 1949-60; asst. sec. state for African affairs U.S. Dept. State, 1961-66; ambassador to Philippines Manila, 1968-69; justice Mich. Supreme Ct., 1971—, now chief justice. Author: A Governor's Notes, 1961, (with others) Africa for the Africans, 1969. Mem. Mich. Liquor Control Commn., 1947-48; vestryman St. Paul's Cathedral, Detroit. Served to lt. comdr. USN, 1942-46. Decorated Legion of Merit with combat V; grand officer Order of Orange Nassau (Netherlands); grand comdr. Royal Order of Phoenix (Greece); humane band of African Redemption (Liberia); grand officer Order of Niger (Niger); comdr. Order Ivory Coast (Ivory Coast); pro merito (Latvia); Polonia Restituta (Polish Govt. in Exile); datu Order of Sikatuna (Philippines). Mem. Nat. Grange, Amvets, Am. Legion, VFW, Res. Officers Assn., SAR, Abepa, Steuben Soc., Edelweiss, Order of Coif, Phi Beta Kappa, Phi Gamma Delta, Phi Delta Phi. Democrat. Episcopalian. Clubs: Navy, University (Detroit), Detroit Country. Lodges: Masons (33 degree), Eagles, Elks, Moose, Odd Fellows. Office: Mich Supreme Ct Law Bldg Lansing MI 48933 also: Mich Supreme Ct 1425 Lafayette Bldg Detroit MI 48226

WILLIAMS, HERBERT HOOVER, social worker; b. Detroit, July 20, 1929; s. Mervin Boyd and Mabel Vane (Beelman) W.; m. Shirley Loraine Bruns Hayes, Aug. 20, 1950 (div. Sept. 1963); children: Deborah Johnson, George Hayes, Dennis Hayes; m. Grace Elaine Kibler, Dec. 21, 1980; children: Debra Boehm, Larry Litke. BS, Manchester Coll., 1953; MDiv, Bethany Sem., 1956; MSW, U. Ill., 1962. Lic. ind. social worker, Ohio, diplomate clin. social work. Chief social services Ill. Youth Commn., Geneva, Ill., 1962-64; dir. social services Masonic Med. Ctr., Chgo., 1964-74; cons. numerous agencies, Chgo., 1974-77; exec. dir. Uptown Chgo. Commn., Chgo., 1977-80; pvt. practice Austinburg, Ohio, 1980-82; exec. dir. Ashtabula (Ohio) County Family Services Agy., 1982-86; pvt. practice Ashtabula Counseling Services, Austinburg, 1986—. Chmn. bd. Old Town Players, Chgo., 1964-73, Greene Sr. Ctr., Chgo., 1966-67; pres. Jane Addams Sch. Social Work Alumni Assn., Chgo., 1966-68, Winona-Foster-Carmen-Winnemac Block Club, Chgo., 1975-76; bd. dirs. Metro-Help, Inc., Chgo., 1974-78. Mem. Nat. Assn. Social Workers, Acad. Cert. Social Workers. Democrat. Mem. Ch. of the Brethren. Lodges: Kiwanis (pres. North Shore, Chgo., 1979-80, Ashtabula, 1985-86). Avocations: camping. Home and Office: 2474 Rt 307 Austinburg OH 44010

WILLIAMS, HOMER LEE, architect; b. Craig, Mo., Oct. 11, 1938; s. Homer and Mabel L. Williams; m. Linda L. Ervin, Aug. 21, 1961 (div. 1976); children: Charles Blake, Gwendolyn Ann. Student, Northwest Mo. State U., 1957, 58; BArch, Kans. State U., 1962. Registered architect. Ptnr. Ervin & Williams, Junction City, Kans., 1963-68; prin. H.L. Williams & Assocs., Kansas City, Mo., 1968-73; pres. Archtl. Design Collaborative, Inc., Kansas City, 1973—; chmn. Mo. bd. archtl. engrs., 1984—. Principal works include B.D. Owens Library, Maryville, Mo. (Am. Inst. Steel Constrn. Archtl. Award Excellence, 1983, named in Univ. Archtl. Portfolio of Award Winning and Other Outstanding Sch. and Univ. Bldgs., 1984), Northland Fountain, Kansas City, Mo. (Elec. Assn. of Mo. and Kans. Comml. Lighting award, 1984, Mcpl. Art Commn. Cert. Merit, 1984), Warrensburg, Mo. High Sch. Chmn. Mo. Licensing and Examining Bd. for Architects, Engrs and Land Surveyors, 1982, 84, Mo. Bd. Zoning Adjustments, Mayor's Corps. Progress. Mem. AIA (corp. mem. Kansas City chpt.), Mo. Council Architects, Architects Council Mo. Sch. Bd. Assn., Nat. Council Archtl. Registration Bds. (chmn. mid cen. region), Platte County Bus. and Profl. Assn., Mo. Assn. State Troopers Emergency Relief Soc., Tau Sigma Delta, Delta Phi Delta, Sigma Phi Epsilon. Lodge: Rotary. Avocations: boating, water sports, snow skiing, photography, jazz musician. Home: 5433 Foxhill Rd Parkville MO 64152 Office: Architects Design Collaborative Inc 5205 NW Crooked Rd Kansas City MO 64152

WILLIAMS, HOPE DENISE, marketing service company executive, business consultant; b. Chgo., Dec. 24, 1952; d. Welmon and Mary Ann (Brefford) Walker; children—Albert Lee, Ebony Emani Denise. Student Ill. State U., 1971-72; B.A. in Psychology, St. Ambrose Coll., 1975, postgrad. bus. adminstrn. 1985—; postgrad. Harvard U. Grad. Sch. Design, summer 1981. Social service dir. Friendly House, Davenport, Iowa, 1977-78; data collector, cons., 1978; supr. CETA/Summer Youth Employment Program, Davenport, 1978; lead organizer Central and Western Neighborhood Devel. Corp., Davenport, 1978-79; exec. dir. Inner City Devel. Corp., Davenport, 1980-83; owner Midwestern Internat. Mktg. Assocs., San Francisco, 1983-86; counselor Marycrest Coll., 1986-87; adminstrv. asst. Parker Ross Assocs., 1984-85, asst. dean Marycrest Coll., Davenport, 1986—; bus. cons. Incorporator, sec. bd. dirs. United Neighbors Inc., 1980; ops. mgr. Dramatic Mktg. Assn., San Francisco, 1983-85; bd. dirs. Community Health Care, 1978-80; v.p., treas. Athletes Say More Edn., 1980; treas., exec. com. F&A Community Warehouse, 1982—; bd. dirs. HELP Legal Aid, 1987—, allocations panel United Way, 1987—. Recipient cert. of appreciation Palmer Jr. Coll., Davenport, 1979; cert. of merit Ch. Women United, 1983; NEH grantee, 1979; presdl. grantee Palmer Jr. Coll., 1978. Mem. Quad Cities Career Womens Network (treas., exec. com.), Nat. Assn. Female Execs. Author narrative and final report for oral history project, 1979. Home: PO Box 2741 Davenport IA 52809

WILLIAMS, HUGH ALEXANDER, JR., mechanical engineer; b. Spencer, N.C., Aug. 18, 1926; s. Hugh Alexander and Mattie Blanche (Megginson) W.; B.S. in Mech. Engring., N.C. State U., 1948, M.S. in Diesel Engring. (Norfolk So. R.R. fellow), 1950; postgrad. Ill. Benedictine Coll. Inst. Mgmt., 1980; m. Ruth Ann Gray, Feb. 21, 1950; children—David Gray, Martha Blanche. Jr. engr.-field service engr. Baldwin-Lima Hamilton Corp., Hamilton, Ohio, 1950-52, project engr., 1953-55; project engr. Electro-Motive div. Gen. Motors Corp., La Grange, Ill., 1955-58, sr. project engr., 1958-63, supr. product devel. engine design sect., 1963-86, staff engr., advanced mech. tech., 1986— . Trustee Downers Grove (Ill.) San. Dist., 1965—, pres., 1974—; pres. Ill. Assn. San. Dists., 1976-77, bd. dirs., 1977—; mem. statewide policy adv. com. Ill. EPA, 1977-79; ruling elder 1st United Presbyn. Ch., Downers Grove. Served with USAAC, 1945. Registered profl. engr., Ill. Fellow ASME (Diesel and Gas Engine Power Div. Speaker awards 1968, 84, Div. citation 1977, exec. com. Internal Combustion Engine div. 1981-87, chmn. 1985-86); mem. Soc. Automotive Engrs. Republican. Club: Masons (32 deg.). Editor: So. Engr., 1947-48; contbr. articles to profl. jours. Patentee in field. Home: 1119 Blanchard St Downers Grove IL 60516

WILLIAMS, IMA JO, home economist, civic worker; b. Bowie, Tex., Feb. 23, 1942; d. Herman Wayne and Clarice (Bilbrey) Tompkins; m. Robert Melvin Williams, Jan. 27, 1963; children—Stacy, Angie, Mark. BS in Home Econs., North Tex. State U., 1963. Home economist Lone Star Gas Co., Dallas, 1963-64, Mich. Consol. Gas Co., Ann Arbor, 1964-65; home econs. tchr. Milan High Sch., Mich., 1965-69; nutrition coordinator Shay Elem. Sch., Harbor Springs, Mich., 1979—; pres. Crooked Tree Arts Council, Petoskey, Mich., 1982-83, v.p. vols., 1983-84, fin. v.p., 1984-85; bd. dirs. Concerned Citizens for Arts, Detroit, 1983-87. Author (fairy tale): Petal, 1978. Performer local theatrical prodns., 1982—. Mem. AAUW (chmn. Mich. Ednl. Found. Program com. 1981-83, mem. nat. devel. com. 1983-85, Mich. cultural com. chmn. 1985-87, nat. sub-com. chmn. immigration reform). Republican. Methodist. Clubs: Garden (pres. 1979-81) (Harbor Springs); Antiques (program v.p. 1987—) (Petoskey). Home: 6546 Lower Shore Dr Harbor Springs MI 49740

WILLIAMS, JACK RAYMOND, civil engr.; b. Barberton, Ohio, Mar. 14, 1923; s. Charles Baird and Mary (Dean) W.; student Colo. Sch. Mines, 1942-43, Purdue U., 1944-45; B.S., U. Colo., 1946; m. Mary Berneice Jones, Mar. 5, 1947 (dec.); children—Jacqueline Rae, Drew Alan. Gravity and seismograph engr. Carter Oil Co., Western U.S. and Venezuela, 1946-50; with Rock Island R.R., Chgo., 1950-80, structural designer, asst. to engr. bridges, asst. engr. bridges, 1950-63, engr. bridges system, 1963-80; sr. bridge engr. Thomas K. Dyer Inc., 1980-82, Alfred Benesch & Co., 1982—. Served with USMCR, 1943-45. Fellow ASCE; mem. Am. Concrete Inst., Am. Ry. Bridge and Bldg. Assn. (past pres.), Am. Ry. Engring. Assn. Home: 293 Minocqua St Park Forest IL 60466 Office: 233 N Michigan Ave Chicago IL 60604

WILLIAMS, JAMES M., director college program; b. Middletown, Mo., Apr. 8, 1943; married; children: Heather, Jason. AA, Ind. Community Coll., 1963; BS, Emporia (Kans.) State U., 1965, MA, 1968; EdD, U. Kans., 1985. Tchr. English, coordinator humanities program Emporia (Kans.) High Sch., 1965-67; instr. English, dept. chmn. Highland (Kans.) Jr. Coll., 1967-69; instr. English, supr. student tchrs. Cen. Mo. State U., Warrensburg, 1969-71; instr., coordinator English program Johnson County Community Coll., Overland Park, Kans., 1971-74, acting dir. communications div., 1974-76, dir. communications/arts div., 1976-80, dir. communications div., 1980—; chmn. dean's search com. Johnson County Coomunity Coll., chmn. publs. bd., chmn. writing ctr. planning com.; mem. adv. bd. Greater Kans. City Nat. Writing Project; mem. adv. bd. Johnson County Library. Contbr. articles to profl. jours. Mem. Am. Assn. Community and Jr. Colls., Assn. Depts. English, Kans. Assn. Community Colls., Kans. City Regional Council Higher Edn., Midwest Modern Lang. Assn., Nat. Council Staff, Program and Orgnl. Devel., Nat. Council Tchrs. English, Phi Delta Kappa. Avocations: tennis, jogging, traveling, gardening. Home: 8117 W 101st Terr Overland Park KS 66212

WILLIAMS, JAMES MERRILL, microbiologist; b. Grand Forks, N.D., Aug. 6, 1928; s. Merrill Leroy and Bertha M. (Zintel) W.; B.S., U. N.D., 1950, M.S., N.D. State U., 1952; m. Ruth A. Kirby, June 20, 1954; children—Peter J., Todd K. Bacteriologist, Rocky Mountain Lab., Hamilton, Mont., 1952-54, Mont. State Bd. Health, Helena, 1954-56, Anchor Serum Co., St. Joseph, Mo., 1956-58, St. Mary's Hosp., Rhinelander, Wis., 1958-60, Ancker Hosp., St. Paul, 1960-62; dir. biol. control Philips Roxane, 1962-68; dir. bacteriol. research Boehringer Ingelheim Animal Health, Inc., St. Joseph, 1968-78, dir. biol. research, 1978—; affiliate prof. U. Idaho, 1974—. Served with M.C., AUS, 1946-48. Mem. Am. Soc. Microbiology, U.S. Animal Health Assn., Am. Mgmt. Assn. Republican. Methodist. Clubs: Masons, Shriners. Research on staphylococcal mastitis, vibriosis, reproductive, respiratory disease. Patentee brucella canis vaccine. Office: 2621 N Belt St Saint Joseph MO 64502

WILLIAMS, JIM RAY, trade association executive; b. Magic City, Tex., Oct. 24, 1934; s. Talmadge Monroe and Hattie E. Lois (Montgomery) W.; m. Ann I. Jennings, Aug. 2, 1972; children: Ronald, Denny, Stephen, Jason, Tiffini. B.B.A. in Economics, W. Tex. State U., M.B.A., 1959. With SBA, 1959-60; mgr. Amarillo (Tex.) AFB Credit Union, 1960-63, Govt. Employees Credit Union, San Antonio, 1963-66; asst. mgr. Tex. Central Credit Union, Dallas, 1966-68; pres., chief exec. officer Govt. Employees Credit Union, San Antonio, 1968-79; pres. Credit Union Nat. Assn., Madison, Wis., 1979-87, GECU Services Corp., San Antonio Area Central Credit Union, 1968-79, CUNA Service Group, Inc., Madison, 1979-87, CUNA Found., Madison, 1981-87; chmn. Financial Data Services Corp.; vice chmn. Tex. Share Guaranty Credit Union; dir. CU Bank Shares, Inc., CU Trust Co., CUNA Mortgage Corp.; ex-officio dir. CUNA Mut. Ins. Group; mem. Tex. Credit Union Commn., 1971-77; pres. U.S. Central Credit Union, 1980-87. Bd. dirs. Beautify San Antonio Assn., 1974-76, Cooperative League of U.S., 1983-85; trustee Nat. Found. Consumer Credit. Served with AUS, 1953-55. Recipient letter appreciation Office Sec. Def., 1974. Mem. Am. Mgmt. Assn (pres.' assn.), Adminstrv. Mgmt. Soc. (chpt. dir.), Credit Union Execs. Mgrs. Soc. (charter), Credit Union Nat. Assn. and Affiliates (chmn. 1976-78), Tex. Credit Union League (chmn. 1974-75), Nat. Coop. Bus. Assn. (treas. 1985-87), Air Force Assn. (exec. com., v.p. awards com. San Antonio chpt. 1974, Orgn. of Year award Alamo chpt. 1973, 77), Am. Soc. Assn. Execs., Conf. Bd., Madison C. of C. (civic progress group), Greater San Antonio C. of C. (chmn. sub-com., mil. affairs council 1972-75), Assn. U.S. Army (chpt. dir. 1976-77). Home: 7776 Westman Way Route 12 Middleton WI 53562 Office: 7776 Westman Way Rt 12 Middleton WI 53562

WILLIAMS, JIMMIE LEE, criminal justice educator, security consultant; b. Joplin, Mo., July 8, 1943; s. Marion Thad and Lefa Ione (Busse) W.; m. Sharon Irene Kendrick, Aug. 1, 1961 (div. Sept. 1974); children—Christine Diane, Barbara Jean; m. Peggy Sue Callahan, Oct. 1, 1975; children—Jimmie Lee II, Patrick Sean, Jennifer Nicole. A.S. in Law Enforcement, Mo. So. State Coll., 1970, B.S., 1974; M.S. in Criminal Justice Adminstrn., Central Mo. State U., 1976. Juvenile officer Joplin Police Dept., 1967-75, 29th Jud. Dist., Joplin, 1975-76; asst. prof. criminal justice Mo. So. State Coll., Joplin, 1976; owner, mgr. Williams Cons. Co., Seneca, Mo., 1982—. Author: (with others) Transportation Security Personnel Training Manual, 3 vols., 1978. Mem. subcom. Handbook for Law Enforcement Officers (Mo. Criminal Code), 1979. Sec.-treas. Seneca Recreation Bd., 1979-84. Served with U.S. Army, 1965-67, Vietnam. Republican. Mem. Reorganized Ch. of Jesus Christ of Latter Day Saints. Club: Seneca Athletic (pres. 1977-78). Home: Route 2 Box 270 Seneca MO 64865 Office: Mo So State Coll Newman and Duquesne Rds Joplin MO 64801

WILLIAMS, JOHN DALE, business and marketing consultant; b. Carrollton, Mo., Oct. 13, 1943; s. Dale C. and Mary (Weinhold) W.; m. Lana L. Elgin, Mar. 22, 1962 (div. 1971); 1 child, Jeffrey D. BA, U. Mo., 1970, MA, 1976. Disc jockey, newswriter Sta. KAOL-FM, Carrollton, 1959-61; quality assurance engr. Gen. Dynamics/Astronautics, San Diego, 1962-64; prodn. controller solar div. Internat. Harvester Co., San Diego, 1965-67; polit. cons. Mayor Charles B. Wheeler, Kansas City, Mo., 1970-71; clinic dir. Greater Kansas City Mental Health Clinic, 1971-81, Kansas City Drug Abuse Program, 1981-84; bus. and mktg. cons., 1984—; cons. Jackson County Legislature, Kansas City, 1981-87; controller, gen. mgr., KCCIM, 1985—; programs, systems cons., Softhaus Ltd., 1986—; dir. Jackson County Mental Health Levy Bd., Kansas City, 1982-83. Bd. dirs. Com. for County Progress, Kansas City, 1982—; mem. Kansas City Jazz Commn., 1982—; pres. Com. of Ind. Young Dems., 1971-73; v.p. Jackson County Dem. Alliance, 1978-79; Dem. committeeman, Kansas City, 1979-81. Mem. Phi Kappa Phi, Phi Alpha Theta. Office: Kansas City Center 917 McGee St Kansas City MO 64106

WILLIAMS, JOHN HOYT, history educator; b. Darien, Conn., Oct. 26, 1940; s. Cecil Edward and Florence Monica (Hoyt) W.; m. Martha Nielsen, Jan. 27, 1963; children: Elisabeth Keating, Owen Christopher. BA in History and English, U. Conn., 1963, MA in History, 1965; PhD, U. Fla., 1969. Asst. prof. Ind. State U., Terre Haute, 1969-73, assoc. prof., 1974-78, prof., 1978—; program dir. USAID, Asuncion, Paraguay, 1973-74. Author: Rise and Fall of the Paraguayan Republic, 1979, The First Transcontinental, 1987; area editor: The Americas, 1976—, Handbook of Latin Am. Studies, 1976-84; cons. editor Mil. History, 1983—; contbr. articles to profl. jours. Ford Found. fellow 1967-69, Fulbright Commn. fellow 1978; NEH grantee 1972, Am. Philos. Soc. grantee 1971, 76, 80, 85. Mem. Conf. Latin Am. History, U.S. Naval Inst., AF Assn., Midwest Assn. Latin Am. Studies. Episcopalian. Avocations: collecting rare books and rare maps of S.A. Office: Ind State U History Dept Terre Haute IN 47809

WILLIAMS, JOHN PATTISON, JR., association executive, lawyer; b. Cin., Feb. 14, 1941; s. John P. Williams and Anne (Sawyer) Greene; m. Janie Pepper, Nov. 20, 1971. B.A. in Religion, Princeton U., 1963; J.D., U. Cin., 1966; postgrad. Naval Justice, Newport, R.I., 1967. Bar: Ohio 1966, U.S. Dist. Ct. (so. dist.) Ohio 1966. Assoc., Taft, Stettinius & Hollister, Cin., 1966, 71-77, ptnr., 1977—; pres. Greater Cin. C. of C., 1984—; bd. dir. Kennedy Mfg. Co., Van Wert, Ohio, Portman Equipment Co. Served to capt. USMC, 1966-69; Viet Nam. Mem. ABA, Cin. Bar Assn., Ohio Bar Assn. Episcopalian. Clubs: Queen City, Cin. Country (Cin.), Bankers. Avocations: jogging; travel; social golf; canoeing; motorcycles. Home: 3 Resor Pl Cincinnati OH 45220 Office: Cincinnati Chamber of Commerce 120 W Fifth St Cincinnati OH 45202

WILLIAMS, JOHN RICHARD, dentist; b. Moline, Ill., Apr. 12, 1950; s. Richard Carroll and Phyllis (Martin) W.; m. Sherry Graville, Feb. 26, 1972; 1 child, Kari Leigh. BS in Zoology, BS in Psychology, Iowa State U., 1972; BS in Dentistry with honors, DDS, U. Ill., Chgo., 1979. Gen. practice dentistry Moline, 1980—; faculty Blackhawk Coll., Moline, 1981-84, mem. dental adv. com., 1981-83; mem. Dental Dept. Moline Pub. Hosp., 1980—, past chmn., mem. exec. com., 1982-83;. Coordinator dental vol. program Arrowhead Boy's Home, Coal Valley, Ill. 1982—; mem., negotiator Rock Island County (Ill.) Bd. Health, 1984—; mem. Pierre Fouchard Acad. Dentistry, 1985—, Quad-City Arts Council, Davenport, Iowa, 1986—; cabinet mem. Boy Scouts Am., Moline, 1986—; bd. dirs. Arrowhead Ranch Boys Home, 1986—. Mem. Ill. Dental Soc. (vice chmn. ins. com., spokesman tng. designate 1984, W.J. Greek Meml. award 1984), Rock Island Dist. Dental Soc. (various offices 1982—). Club: 99 Legislative. Lodge: Kiwanis (v.p., bd. mem., pres. Moline 1979—). Avocations: golf, travel, running, skiing, photography. Home: 5016 34th Ave B Moline IL 61265 Office: 2132 6th Ave Moline IL 61265

WILLIAMS, JOHN RODERIC, neurosurgeon; b. Buffalo, July 2, 1920; s. John and Elizabeth Ruby (Bray) W.; m. Jean Mildred Greenlund, Nov. 25, 1944; children: John R. Jr., Douglas, Thomas, Kathryn. BA, U. Rochester, 1941; MD, U. Buffalo, 1943. Diplomate Am. Bd. Neurological Surgery. Assoc. prof. surgery Mich. State U., 1970-85; pvt. practice neurosurgery Grand Rapids, Mich., 1944—. Bd. dirs. Goodwill Industries, Grand Rapids, 1965—. Served with U.S. Army, 1946-48. Fellow Am. Coll. Surgeons; mem. Mich. Soc. Neurosurgeons (pres. 1970), Assn. Neurological Surgeons, Congress of Neurological Surgeons. Republican. Lodge: Rotary. Avocation: photography. Home: 1122 Conlon St Grand Rapids MI 49506 Office: 833 Lake Dr Grand Rapids MI 49506

WILLIAMS, JOHN TROY, librarian, educator; b. Oak Park, Ill., Mar. 11, 1924; s. Michael Daniel and Donna Marie (Shaffer) W.; B.A., Central Mich. U., 1949; M.A. in Library Science, U. Mich., 1951, M.A., 1954; Ph.D., Mich. State U., 1973. Reference librarian U. Mich., Ann Arbor, 1955-59; instr. Bowling Green (Ohio) State U., 1959-60; reference librarian Mich. State U., East Lansing, 1960-62; 1st asst. reference dept. Flint (Mich.) Pub. Library, 1962-65; head reference services, Purdue U., West Lafayette, Ind., 1965-72; head pub. services No. Ill. U., Dekalb, 1972-75; asst. dean, asst. univ. librarian Wright State U., Dayton, Ohio, 1975-80; vis. scholar U. Mich., Ann Arbor, 1980—; cons. in field. Served with U.S. Army, 1943-46. Mich. State fellow, 1963-64; HEW fellow, 1971-72. Mem. Am. Library Assn., Spl. Libraries Assn., Genessee County Hist. Soc. (dir.), Am. Soc. for Info. Sciences, Am. Sociol. Assn., AAUP, Council on Fgn. Relations. Contbr. articles to profl. jours. Home: 1473 Wisteria Ann Arbor MI 48104

WILLIAMS, JULIE BELLE, psychiatric social worker; b. Algona, Iowa, July 29, 1950; d. George Howard and Leta Maribelle (Durschmidt) W.; BA, U. Iowa, 1972, MSW, 1973. Lic. psychologist, Iowa; lic. social worker. Social worker Psychopathic Hosp., Iowa City, 1971-72, Child Devel. Clinic, Iowa City, 1973; OEO counselor YOUR, Webster City, Iowa, 1972; group therapist Cedar Manor Nursing Home, Tipton, Iowa, 1973; therapist Mid-Eastern Iowa Community Mental Health Ctr., Iowa City, 1973; psychiat. social worker Mental Health Ctr. N. Iowa, Mason City, 1974-79, chief psychiat. social worker, 1979-80; asst. dir. Community Counseling Ctr., White Bear Lake, Minn., 1980-85, dir., 1985—; lectr., cons. in field. NIMH grantee, 1972-73. Mem. Nat. Assn. Social Workers (cert., pres. local chpt.), NOW, Am. Orthopsychiat. Assn., Am. Assn. Sex Educators, Counselors and Therapists, Minn. Women Psychologists, Minn. Lic. Psychologists, Phi Beta Kappa. Democrat. Office: 4739 Division Ave White Bear Lake MN 55110

WILLIAMS, LORRAINE STEWART, accountant; b. Birmingham, Ala., Jan. 27, 1948; d. Smith and Hattie (Rutledge) Stewart; m. Eddie Lee Williams, Jan. 19, 1969; children: Stephanie Alaine, Damon Edward. BS, Tuskegee Inst., 1969; postgrad., U. Ill., 1969-70. CPA, Ohio. Paraprofl. Deloitte, Haskins & Sells, Dayton, Ohio, 1976-77, staff acct., 1977-79; trust auditor Third Nat. Bank, Dayton, 1979-81, audit officer, 1981-82; pvt. practice acctg. Dayton, 1982—; Mem. adv. com. Auditor of State, Columbus, Ohio, 1985—, co-chmn. contracting and minority participation subcom., 1985—. V.p. Northwood Elem. PTO, Dayton, 1982-83, pres. 1983-84; treas. Youth Guidance Program, Dayton, 1983-84; chmn. bd. Ptnrs. in Success, Dayton, 1983-84. Mem. Am. Inst. CPA's, Ohio Soc. CPA's. Methodist. Lodge: Altrusa (treas. Dayton chpt. 1984-85). Office: 2590 Shiloh Springs Rd Dayton OH 45426

WILLIAMS, LOUIS CLAIR, JR., public relations agency executive; b. Huntington, Ind., Nov. 7, 1940; s. Louis Clair and Marian Eileen (Bowers) W.; m. Pamela Grace Waller, July 28, 1973 (div.); children—Terri Lynn, L. Bradley, Lisa C. B.A., Eastern Mich. U., 1963. Copywriter, Rochester (N.Y.) Gas and Electric Co., 1963-65, editor RG&E News, 1965-66; employee info. specialist Gen. Ry. Signal Co., Rochester, 1966-67, supr. employment and employee relations, 1967-69; supr. pub. relations Heublein, Inc., Hartford, Conn., 1969-70; dir. corp. communications Jewel Cos., Inc., Chgo., 1970-71; account exec. Ruder & Finn of Mid-Am., Chgo., 1971-73, v.p., 1973-76, sr. v.p., 1976-78; cons. Towers, Perrin, Forster & Crosby, Los Angeles, 1978-79; exec. v.p., gen. mgr. Harshe-Rotman & Druck, Inc., Chgo., 1979, pres. midwest region, 1979-80; v.p. Hill & Knowlton, Inc., Chgo., 1980-81, sr. v.p., 1981-83; pres. Savlin Williams Assocs., Evanston, Ill., 1983-85, L.C. Williams & Assocs., Chgo., 1985—. Recipient Clarion award Women in Communications, 1978, award of Excellence, Internat. Council Indsl. Editors, 1969, Bronze Oscar-of-Ind., Fin. World, 1974. Mem. Internat. Assn. Bus. Communicators (pres. 1979-80), Chgo. Assn. Bus. Communicators (pres.), Publicity Club Chgo., Pub. Relations Soc. Am.

WILLIAMS, LOYAL DEAN, social service agency executive; b. Lamar, Ark., May 14, 1935; s. Lester Lee and Lean Rookh (Overton) W.; m. Beverly Jane Grossman, Dec. 23, 1973; children—Loyal Dean II, Christopher Henry. B.A., Memphis State U., 1958; M.S.W., U. Denver, 1963. Social service dir. Tulsa Boys' Home, 1970-74; dir. social service St. Francis Hosp., Tulsa, 1974-77; exec. dir. Woodland Hills, Duluth, Minn., 1977-81; pres., chief exec. officer Family and Children's Ctr., Mishawaka, Ind., 1981—. Coalition. Mem. adv. bd. Child Welfare League Am., N.Y.C., 1984—; bd. dirs. Residential Assn., Indpls., 1983—, Ind. Coalition for Human Services, Indpls. Mem. Nat. Assn. Social Workers (Spl. Recognition award 1974, treas. 1984-86), Acad. Cert. Social Workers. Democrat. Mem. Ch. of Christ. Lodge: Rotary. Avocations: golf; gardening; camping. Office: Family and Children's Ctr 1411 Lincoln Way W Mishawaka IN 46544

WILLIAMS, MARY G. (TRUDI), insurance executive; b. Columbus, Ohio, May 3, 1946; d. Harold E. and Mary J. (McShane) W.; m. Thomas N. Adolph, Apr. 28, 1969 (div. 1973). Student Ohio State U., 1964-65. Various mktg. and underwriting positions Western Casualty & Surety Co., Columbus, 1966-73; mgr. agy. services Motorists Mut. Ins. Co., Columbus, 1973-75; mktg. rep. Beacon Ins. Co., Columbus, 1975-77; sr. mktg. rep. CG/Aetna Ins. Co., Columbus, 1977-79, mktg. mgr., 1979-82; territorial mgr. INA/Aetna, Cleve., 1982-85; mktg. v.p. INA/Aetna-CIGNA, Cleve., 1985-86; pres. INA of Ohio, Cleve., 1985-86; br. mgr. CNA Ins., Kansas City, Kans., 1986—. Mem. Exec. Women's Roundtable (sec. 1985, pres. 1986). Home: 10263 Cody Overland Park KS 66214 Office: 7900 College Blvd Overland Park KS 66210

WILLIAMS, MARYBETH ELIZABETH, interior designer, voice teacher; b. Glendale, Calif., Jan. 2, 1928; d. Leo Palmer and Eva Margaret (Norberg) Curtis; m. E. Donald Williams, Mar. 24, 1951; children: Carol Lee, Mark Curtis, Jane Elizabeth Kelso, David Donald. BA, U. No. Colo. (formerly Colo. State Coll. Edn.), 1949; pvt. voice student, Northwestern U., 1965-74; postgrad., William Rainey Harper Coll., 1980-83. Tchr. music Denver Pub. Schs., 1950-51; pvt. piano tchr. Denver, 1951-55; pvt. voice tchr. Deerfield, Ill., 1964—; tchr. voice Music Inst. of Lake Forest, Ill., 1976-87, Niles West High Sch., Skokie, Ill., 1979-87; interior designer, owner Williams Interiors, Highland Park, Ill., 1982—; profl. mem. Chgo. Symphony Chorus, 1971-79; pres. bd. dirs. Westminster Chamber Orch., Deerfield, 1983-85; profl. singer, recitalist. Soloist, ruling elder First Presbyn. Ch. Deerfield. Mem. Harper Interior Design Assn. Republican. Presbyterian. Home and Office: 1431 Sunnyside Ave Highland Park IL 60035

WILLIAMS, MICHAEL ALAN, psychologist; b. Cin., May 20, 1948; s. Chester and Gentry Mae (Canada) W.; m. Linda Ann Presswood, Aug. 8, 1970; children: Michael Alan II, Derrick Alexander. BA, U. Cin., 1970, MA, 1971, EdD, 1980. Instr. U. Cin., 1972-75; sch. psychologist Dayton Bd. Edn., Ohio, 1975-78; assoc. prof. Wright State U., Dayton, 1978—; clin. psychologist Profl. Psychol. Services, Dayton, 1981—; psychol. services coordinator Montgomery County Children's Services, Dayton, 1983—; program mgr. Head Start Supplementary Tng. Program, Cin., 1973-74; cons. Ohio Luth. Synod, Dayton, 1981-83, Blacks in Govt., Dayton, 1982-85, Montgomery County, Stillwater Health Ctr., Dayton, 1982-86. Co-editor (book): Teaching in a Multicultural Pluralistic Society, 1982, 2d edit., 1987. Treas. Dayton Free Clinic and Counseling Ctr., Dayton, 1983; bd. dirs. Planned Parenthood Assn., Dayton, 1983. Named Outstanding Young Man Am., Jaycees, 1984; McCall Scholarship, McCall's mag., 1966-70. Mem. Am. Psychol. Assn., Nat. Assn. Black Psychologists, Nat. Assn. Sch. Psychologists, Dayton Assn. Black Psychologists (v.p. 1986—), Mental Health Assn. (bd. dirs. 1985), Assn. Tchr. Educators. Avocations: bible student, music, handiwork, writing. Home: 4830 Old Hickory Pl Trotwood OH 45426 Office: Wright State U 373 Millett Hall Dayton OH 45435

WILLIAMS, MICHAEL DALE, insurance company executive; b. Sioux Falls, S.D., July 5, 1947; s. Loren Elmer and Delight Marie (Bluhm) W.; m. Carla Jean Ageton, Jan. 31, 1970; children: Brian, Maren. BA in Math., U. S.D., 1969. Computer programmer A.C. Nielson, Green Bay, Wis., 1969-72; programming supr. West Bend (Wis.) Co., 1972-76; chief info. systems officer Western Surety Co., Sioux Falls, 1976—. Leader Boy Scouts Am., Green Bay, 1969-72, Sioux Falls, 1983—; mem. Sch. Dist. Facilities Planning Com., Sioux Falls, 1985-86; classroom aide Irving Alternative Sch., Sioux Falls, 1981-86. Mem. Data Processing Mgmt. Assn. (v.p. 1981-83). Democrat. Avocations: sailing, hiking. Office: Western Surety Co 101 S Phillips Ave Sioux Falls SD 57192

WILLIAMS, MICHAEL JOHN, city official; b. Madison, Wis., Dec. 6, 1949; s. Robert Michael and Irene Ann (Washa) W.; m. Pamela Ann Morgan, Oct. 11, 1975; children: Megan, Matthew. BA in Landscape Architecture, U. Wis., Madison, 1972. Park supr. City of Janesville, Wis., 1973-75, asst. park supt., 1975-76, park supt., 1976-83, dir. leisure services, 1983—. Editor Jour. Park and Recreation Adminstrn., 1987. Trustee Boy Scouts Am., 1984—, Cubmaster, 1987—; trustee Janesville Credit Union, 1975—; treas. United Presbyn. Ch., Janesville, 1987. Served to major U.S. Army NG, 1972—. Mem. Nat. Park and Recreation Assn., Wis. Park and Recreation Assn., Wis. Guard Assn. (trustee 1985—), Rock County Hist. Soc. (trustee 1985—), Jaycees (Outstanding Young Person of the Yr., 1985, Cert. Appreciation, 1979). Republican. Presbyterian. Club: YMCA Men's (pres. 1977). Avocations: gardening, photography, bicycling, clock restoration. Home: Rt 3 1325 Bittersweet Milton WI 53563 Office: Janesville Leisure Services 17 N Franklin St Janesville WI 53545

WILLIAMS, MICHAEL SEWARD, manufacturing compay executive; b. Detroit, May 2, 1960; s. Robert Hull and Bonnie Lou (Brown) W.; m. Kathryn Elizabeth New, Aug. 28, 1982; children: Sara Vitaline, Adam Seward. BS in Engring., U. Mich., 1982, MBA, 1984. Assoc. ops. research analyst Whirlpool Corp., Benton Harbor, Mich., 1984-86, inventory control adminstr., 1986—. Club: Whirlpool Mgmt. (Benton Harbor). Home: 6090 DeMorrow Rd Stevensville MI 49127 Office: Whirlpool Corp 2000 M 63 N Benton Harbor MI 49022

WILLIAMS, MURRAY EDWIN, educator; b. Redfield, Iowa, Mar. 16, 1948; s. Floyd Edwin and Gladys Marion (McCabe) W.; m. Marla Kay Dowden, Mar. 30, 1973; children: Jeremy, Melissa. Grad., Panora-Linden Community Coll., 1966; cert. emergency med. tech., Des Moines Area Community Coll., 1976. Sr. instr. Lincoln Tech. Inst., West Des Moines, Iowa, 1974—. Firefighter, past exec. bd. mem. Ankeny Vol. Fire Dept., 1976—. Served with U.S. Army, 1968-69. Recipient Certificate Appreciation City of Ankeny, 1985. Mem. Nat. Inst. Automotive Service Excellence, Am. Legion (commdr. 1979). Democrat. Avocation: private pilot. Home: 325 NW Stratford Ln Ankeny IA 50021-2351

WILLIAMS, NANETTE MARIE, legal administrator, computer company executive; b. Flint, Mich., May 22, 1957; d. Charles Kenneth and Suzanne Mary (Sayan) Stevens; m. Patrick Jon Williams, May 22, 1980. BS summa cum laude, Western Mich. U., 1980. Cert. seconday tchr., Mich. Edn. dir. Tandy Corp., Kalamazoo, Mich., 1980-84; co-owner Exec. Computer Services, Kalamazoo, 1980—; dir. adminstrn. Learning Pub., Kalamazoo, 1984-85; legal adminstr. Deming, Hughey et al, Kalamazoo, 1985—; instr. Kalamazoo Valley Community Coll., 1983-85. Mem. ABA, Assn. Legal Adminstrs. Republican. Roman Catholic. Lodge: Zonta. Avocations: reading, sailing, running. Home: 3719 Old Colony Kalamazoo MI 49008 Office: Deming Hughey et al 800 Old Kent Bank Bldg Kalamazoo MI 49007

WILLIAMS, NORMAN WEEKS, broadcast executive; b. St. Paul, Aug. 10, 1922; s. William Wallace and Bertha Esther (Patton) W.; m. Lois T. Losen, May 8, 1946; children: Thomas W., John B. BA, Luther Coll., 1951. Producer, dir. Sta. KMTV-TV, Omaha, 1951-56, prodn. mgr., 1957-64; station mgr. Sta. KMA-TV, Shenandoah, Iowa, 1965-71; asst. gen. mgr. May Broadcasting Co., Omaha, 1971-80, exec. v.p., gen. mgr., 1980—; mem. adv. sales com. TV Broadcasting, N.Y., 1972-75. Served to 1st lt. U.S. Army, 1941-48, ETO. Republican. Lutheran. Avocations: photography, golf. Home: 6049 Oak Hills Dr Omaha NE 68137 Office: May Broadcasting Co 10714 Mockingbird Dr Omaha NE 68127

WILLIAMS, PATRICK TIMOTHY, dentist; b. South Bend, Ind., May 2, 1954; s. Robert Joseph and Mary Ann (Greczyczk) W.; m. Susan Mary Towner, July 26, 1975; children: Joseph, Matthew, Lindsay. BS, Creighton U., 1976, DDS, 1980. Gen. practice dentistry Granger, Ind., 1980—. Mem. ADA, Ind. Dental Assn., Acad. Gen. Dentistry, Am. Assn. Functional Orthodontics (charter), Ducks Unltd. Democrat. Roman Catholic. Avocations: fishing, hunting, family activities. Home: 51611 Shaker Ln Granger IN 46530 Office: 12545 State Rd 23 Granger IN 46530

WILLIAMS, PAUL ROBERT, school system administrator; b. Portsmouth, Ohio, Aug. 30, 1937; s. Jesse Clinton and Lola Ethel (Harden) W.; m. Catherine Wilson, Sept. 4, 1959; children: Jacqueline Joy, John Scott. BS, Taylor U., 1961; MA, Mich. State U., 1969, PhD, 1980. Tchr. Chesaning (Mich.) Union Schs., 1961-70, curriculum coordinator, 1970-74; asst. supt. Durand (Mich.) Area Schs., 1974-75; supt. Caledonia (Mich.) Pub. Schs., 1975-80, Lakeview Sch. Dist., Battle Creek, Mich., 1980—. Contbr. articles to profl. jours. Chmn. Lakeview Downtown Devel. Authority, Battle Creek, Mich., 1983—; mem. exec. bd. Battle Creek Unltd., 1986; pres. Battle Creek Symphony, 1987—, United Way of Greater Battle Creek, 1986; v.p. PTA, 1980-87; trustee Winshop Found., Battlecreek, 1986—. Recipient Ednl. Div. award Kent County United Way, 1979, Disting. Service award Mich. PTA, 1985, Campaign Chairperson award United Way of Greater Battle Creek, 1986, Econ. Fund. Devel. award Battle Creek Unltd., 1986. Mem. Mich. Assn. Sch. Adminstrs. (pres. regions 3 and 7 1980-86, governing council 1985—, chmn. interorganization com. 1985—, Service award 1986), Kent County Supt. Assn. (Disting. Service award 1980), Battle Creek C. of C. (bd. dirs. 1984—), Mich. State U. Coll. Edn. Alumni Assn. (pres. 1986—). Republican. Methodist. Lodge: Rotary (exec. bd. Battle Creek 1983—). Avocations: golf, jogging, reading. Home: 256 E Hamilton Ln Battle Creek MI 49015 Office: Lakeview Sch Dist 15 Arbor St Battle Creek MI 49015

WILLIAMS, PHILIP COPELAIN, physician; b. Vicksburg, Miss., Dec. 9, 1917; s. John Oliver and Eva (Copelain) W.; B.S. magna cum laude, Morehouse Coll., 1937; M.D., U. Ill., 1941; m. Constance Shielda Rhetta, May 29, 1943; children—Philip, Susan Carol, Paul Rhetta. Intern, Cook County Hosp., Chgo., 1942-43, resident in ob-gyn, 1946-48; resident in gynecology U. Ill., 1948-49; practice medicine specializing in ob-gyn, Chgo., 1949—; mem. staff St. Joseph Hosp., Augustana Hosp., Cook County Hosp., McGaw Hosp.; clin. prof. Med. Sch. Northwestern U., Chgo. Bd. dirs. Am. Cancer Soc. Chgo. unit and Ill. div. Served with U.S. Army, 1943-45. Recipient Civic award Loyola U., 1970; Edwin S. Hamilton Interstate Teaching award, 1984; diplomate Am. Bd. Ob-Gyn, Fellow ACS, Internat. Coll. Surgeons; mem. AMA, Chgo., Ill. med. socs., AMA, Chgo. Gynecol. Soc. (treas. 1975-78, pres. 1980-81), Am. Fertility Soc., Inst. Medicine, N.Y. Acad. Scis., AAAS. Presbyn. Clubs: Barclay, Carlton, Plaza. Contbr. articles to profl. jours. Home: 1040 N Lake Shore Dr Chicago IL 60611 Office: 200 E 75th St Chicago IL 60619

WILLIAMS, PRESTON PRINN, obstetrician-gynecologist; b. Ellensburg, Wash., Aug. 14, 1940; s. George Prinn and Vera Ethel (DeWees) W.; m. Sharon Raye Simons, July 8, 1967; children: Michelle Raye, Heather Prinn. BS, Cen. Wash. State Coll., 1961; MD, U. Wash., 1966. Diplomate div. maternal-fetal medicine Am. Bd. Ob-gyn, Nat. Bd. Med. Examiners. Intern St. Paul-Ramsey Hosp., 1966-67; resident in ob-gyn U. Minn. Hosps., Mpls., 1967-70; med. fellow ob-gyn U. Minn., Mpls., 1967-70, asst. prof. ob-gyn, 1971-75, assoc. prof., 1975—, acting dir. then dir. div. Maternal-Fetal Medicine, 1976—, on faculty staff grad. sch. Dept. Ob-gyn, 1977-83, assoc. mem. grad. faculty, 1986—; speaker, moderator, faculty 170 profl. meetings, symposia, continuing edn. courses; spl. study Harris Birthright Research Ctr. for Foetal Medicine, Dept. Ob-gyn, King's Coll. Hosp., U. London, 1984; attending physician Ob-gyn, U. Minn. Hosps., 1970—, outpatient clinic dir., 1971-79; adj. faculty Sch. Nursing, U. Minn., Mpls., 1980—; attending physician Hennepin County Med. Ctr., Mpls. , 1970—; staff physician St. Mary's Hosp, Mpls., 1970—, Met. Med. Ctr., Mpls., 1985—; staff physician St. Jospeh's Hosp., St. Paul, 1973—, coordinator ob-gyn edn., 1973-74, edn. com. 1973-74; cons. VA Hosp, Mpls., 1971—; courtesy staff mem. United and Children's Hosp., St. Paul, 1985—; assoc. staff mem. North Meml. Med. Ctr., Robbinsdale, Minn., 1986—; active numerous coms. U. Minn. Hosps. 1971-84; med. adv. bd. Childbirth Edn. Assn. Minn.-St. Paul, 1976; med. adv. com. Planned Parenthood of Minn., 1976; human genetics coordinating com. Med. Sch. U. Minn., 1979-81. Author Specialty Board Review: Obstetrics and Gynecology, 1975, 2d edit. 1978, (with T.M. Julian) 3d edit. 1986, (with M.S. Joseph) Differential Diagnosis in Obstetrics, 1978; contbr. numerous papers to profl. jours.; author chpts. in books. Grantee Am. Cancer Soc., 1972, Minn. Med. Found., 1971-72, Grad. Sch. U. Minn., 1974-75, 78-79, 85, 86; recipient Certificates of Recognition for Teaching, Am. Acad. Family Physicians, 1978, 79; Certificate of Recognition for Community Services Programs U. Minn. Hosps. and Clinics, 1985. Fellow Am. Coll. Ob-gyn, Am. Fertility Soc. (devel. and pub. relations com. 1975-77); mem. Am. Soc. Coloscopy and Colpomicroscopy, Am. Assn. Gynecologic Laparoscopists (adv. bd. 1972-81, Flying Physicians Teaching Team 1972-75, complications com. 1975), Minn. Ob-gyn Soc. (program com., local arrangements chmn. 1976, perinatal mortality sub-com. 1978—)), Minn. Council Obstetricians and Gynecologists, Gt. Plains Orgn. for Perinatal Health Care, Assn. for Voluntary Sterilization, Assn. Profs. Ob-gyn (assoc.), Hennepin County Med. Soc., Minn. State Med. Assn., Soc. Perinatal Obstetricians, North Cen. Critical Care Soc., Minn. Perinatal Orgn., Phi Chi. Office: Box 395 U Minn Health Ctr 420 Delaware St SE Minneapolis MN 55455

WILLIAMS, RALPH LEE, JR., engineering company executive; b. St. Louis, Apr. 2, 1951; s. Ralph Lee and Mary Anna (Levy) W.; m. Anita Suzzanne Hooker, Aug. 1, 1971 (div. Mar. 1984); children: Bryan Lee, Brandi Carter; m. Kimberly Joan Ueltzen, Apr. 28, 1984. Student, Cen. Mo. U., 1969-70, U. Mo., 1970-71. 1st class nuclear machinist mate USN, 1971, resigned, 1979; pres. Lectro Engring., St. Louis, 1979—. Mem. Soc. Plastics Engrs. Republican. Lutheran. Avocations: fishing, camping, reading, photography. Home: 9124 Brownridge Dr Overland MO 63114 Office: Lectro Engring Co 4243 W Dr M L King Dr Saint Louis MO 63113

WILLIAMS, RICHARD DAVID, dentist; b. Detroit, Oct. 5, 1932; s. Benjamin and Mildred (Prady) W.; m. Marian Ruskin, July 16, 1959 (dec. Sept. 1982); children: Judy, Marjorie, Janet; m. Anne Cooperstein, June 25, 1983. BS, Wayne State U., 1953; DDS, U. Detroit, 1957. Gen. practice dentistry Madison Heights, Mich., 1958—. bd. dirs. Sci. Fair, Detroit. Recipient Pub. Service award Engring. Soc. Detroit. Mem. ADA, Detroit Dist. Dental Soc., Wolverine Dental Soc. (Pub. Service award), Alpha Omega (internat. pres. 1987). Jewish. Home: 7484 Deep Run #922 Birmingham MI 48101 Office: 28119 John R Madison Heights MI 48071

WILLIAMS, RICHARD JAMES, food service executive; b. Goliad, Tex., Aug. 19, 1942; s. L. D. and Freida Irene (Watkins) W.; m. Shirley Ann Mihalik, July 11, 1967; children—Kenneth F., Dawn L. A.A., Santa Ana Jr. Coll. (Calif.), 1965. Area mgr. Jack in the Box Restaurant, San Diego, 1972-80; v.p. ops. Franchise Dirs., Inc., Bradley, Ill., 1980-81; area supr. Pizza Hut of Am., Inc., Lombard, Ill., 1981-83; regional dir. of food service Montgomery Ward Co., Chgo., 1983-84, v.p. ops. Golden Bear Restaurants, Mt. Prospect, Ill., 1983-84; franchise area dir. Wendy's Internat., Oakbrook Terrace, Ill., 1984-86; regional mgr. franchise ops. Godfather's Pizza, Inc., 1986—. Author: Anthology of American High School Poetry, 1959. Served with USMC, 1960-72. Decorated Silver Star, Bronze Star. Republican. Mem. Chs. of Christ. Home: 221 Wianno Ln Schaumburg IL 60194 Office: Godfather's Pizza Inc 9140 W Dodge Rd Omaha NE 68114

WILLIAMS, ROBERT VANCE, accountant; b. Sioux City, Iowa, July 7, 1922; s. Charles Albert and Pearl Emile (Rogers) W.; m. Helenanne Ryan, June 17, 1946; children: Jane, John, Anne, Marilou, James, Thomas. BS in Bus. and Engring. Adminstrn., U. S.D., 1944. CPA, Iowa. Indsl. engr. Wincharger Corp., Sioux City, 1944-45; acct. C.A. Williams, CPA, Sioux City, 1945-50; ptnr. Williams & Co., Sioux City, 1950—; bd. dirs. Midwest Energy Co., Sioux City, Iowa Pub. Service Co., Sioux City, Midwest Energy Mgmt., Inc., Sioux City, Warren Electric Co., Houston, Donovan Cos., Inc., St. Paul. Chmn. bd. Marian Health Ctr., Sioux City, 1977-83; chmn. Iowa Higher Edn. Loan Authority Bd., Des Moines, 1982-86; bd. dirs. U. S.D. Found., Vermillion, S.D., 1975—. Recipient Albert Gallatin award, 1974, Community Service to Mankind award Briar Cliff Coll., 1984; named Outstanding Grad. of Yr. U. S.D., 1978. Mem. Am. Inst. CPA's (Nat. Pub. Service award 1983), Iowa Soc. CPA's (Outstanding Service to Community award 1983), Associated Acctg. Firms Internat. (bd. dirs. 1980-83), Sioux City C. of C. (pres. 1966-71). Republican. Roman Catholic. Clubs: Sioux City Country (pres. 1965-66), Greater Sioux Land, Inc. (sec.-treas. 1982—). Home: 3707 S Briar Path Sioux City IA 51104 Office: Williams & Co 814 Pierce St Sioux City IA 51102

WILLIAMS, RONALD EUGENE, manufacturing company executive; b. Sioux City, Iowa, May 7, 1941; s. David E. Williams and Joyce Elizabeth (Williams) Whitaker; m. Judith Ellen Pratt, Dec. 30, 1960 (div. Apr. 1970); children—Stephen Eugene, Katherine Elizabeth; m. Doreen Elizabeth Aeilts, Feb. 26, 1977. B.A., U. S.D., 1965; M.A., U. Wyo., 1966; A.B.D., Ariz. State U., 1970. Instr., Iowa State U., Ames, 1966-69; dredging ops. Hess Oil Co., St. Croix, V.I., 1972; asst. prof. Ferris State Coll., Big Rapids, Mich., 1970-73; supr. mgmt. devel. and tng. 3M Co., St. Paul, 1973-73, human resources devel.. 1973—. Fellow: NDEA, 1969, Alta., 1969; Iowa Merit scholar, 1959. Mem. Standards Engring. Soc. (vice chmn. Minn. sect.). Lutheran. Office: Human Resources Devel 3M Bldg 225-1N-103M Ctr Saint Paul MN 55144-1000

WILLIAMS, ROSS ARNOLD, computer systems analyst; b. Canton, Ohio, Feb. 28, 1953; s. Nick P. Williams and Dolores M. (Gilson) Kobzowicz; m. Kimberly Ann Werner, June 25, 1983; 1 child, Michael. Student, Ohio State U., 1970-73; BA, U. Akron, 1977, MS, 1980. Computer systems analyst Goodyear Tire and Rubber Co., Akron, Ohio, 1979—; lectr. U. Akron, 1979-84. Mem. Kappa Kappa Psi, Pi Mu Epsilon. Lutheran. Avocations: reading, sports, chess, music.

WILLIAMS, SCOTT ROBERT, real estate appraiser; b. Milw., Aug. 6, 1949; s. Jack Robert and Florence Elizabeth (Jewell) W.; m. Janet Billington, Apr. 19, 1986; stepchildren: Roy, Cherie. BA, New Sch. Coll., N.Y.C., 1971. Pres. Scott Williams Appraisal, Inc., Wausau, Wis., 1972—. Mem. Am. Inst. Real Estate Appraisers (chmn. No. Wis. chpt. 1983), Soc. Real Estate Appraisers (sec. Wis. Valley chpt. 1973-75, pres. 1976-77), Wausau Bd. Realtors. Unitarian. Home: 1020 Sturgeon Eddy Rd Wausau WI 54401 Office: 1816 Grand Ave Wausau WI 54401

WILLIAMS, SHARON TAYLOR, interior designer; b. Waukegan, Ill., Aug. 23, 1948; d. John Issac and Ruth (Robertson) Williams; B.S. in Bus. Edn. and Interior Design, Western Ill. U., 1970; postgrad. U. Minn., 1975, 79. Interior designer masterplan sales and interior design studio Dayton's Dept. Store, St. Paul, 1973-77; owner, pres., dir. interior design The S. Williams Design Group, Mpls., 1977—; mem. faculty dept. applied arts U. Wis.-Stout; mfrs. rep. contract and furnishings for instns. Recipient design and sales achievement award Dayton's Dept. Store, 1974. Fellow Internat. Biog. Assn.; mem. Am. Soc. Interior Designers, Mpls. Soc. Fine Arts, Mpls. Inst. Arts, Nat. Assn. Women Bus. Owners, Nat. Assn. Female Execs., Minn. Soc. AIA (interiors com.), Greater Mpls. C. of C., North Suburban C. of C. Alpha Omicron Phi. Methodist. Office: Williams/Ricks Inter 235 Mackubin St Saint Paul MN 55102-1732

WILLIAMS, SUSAN JAN, nurse, consultant; b. Flint, Mich., Nov. 29, 1939; d. Arnold Raymond and Dorothy Francis (Howell) Hinterman; m. Frank Earl Williams, Jr., June 23, 1975 (dec.); 1 son, Stephen. R.N., St. Joseph Sch. Nursing, 1961; B.S. in Human Services and Edn., U. Detroit, 1983. Nurse various depts. including pediatrics, emergency room, operating room, intensive care, med. and surg. units, obstetrics St. Joseph Hosp., Flint, Mich., 1961—, infection control coordinator, 1972—; vol. cons. and tchr.; speaker confs. Active Holy Redeemer Catholic Ch.; leader local Boy Scouts Am., 1972-74. Recipient Florence Nightingale Nursing award trophy, St. Joseph Sch. Nursing, 1961. Mem. Mich. Soc. for Infection Control (founding pres. 1972-74, award 1974). Clubs: Golf, Ski. Contbr. article to profl. publ.; planner workshops and confs. hosps. and nursing homes. Home: 1490 Williamsburg Rd Flint MI 48507 Office: 302 Kensington Ave Flint MI 48502

WILLIAMS, TERENCE HEATON, neuroanatomy educator, researcher; b. Oldham, Lancashire, Eng., Jan. 5, 1929; came to U.S., 1964; s. Joseph William Edward and Mona (Heaton) W.; m. Glenys Owen Parry, June 16, 1956; children: Ruth, Jonathan, Jeremy. MB, ChB, Manchester U., Eng., 1953; DSc, Manchester U., 1977; PhD, U. Wales, 1960. Med. diplomate, Eng., Scotland, Wales, Channel Islands, Isle of Man, No. Ireland. Surgeon with various hosps., Eng., 1953-57; instr. anatomy Dublin U., Ireland, 1957-64, U. Wales, 1957-64, Manchester U., 1957-64, Harvard U., Boston, 1964-68; prof. neuroanatomy Tulane Med. Sch., New Orleans, 1968-73; head dept. anatomy U. Iowa, Iowa City, 1973-83, prof. anatomy, 1973—; dir. neuroanatomy core Gastrointestinal Ctr. U. Iowa, 1984—. Author: The Human Brain: A Photographic Guide, 1980; contbr. numerous articles to profl. jours. and chpts. to books. Travelling fellow Med. Research Council, 1964-65; research grantee NIH, 1969—; recipient Interstate Research award Interstate Postgrad. Med. Assn., 1971. Mem. Anatomical Soc. Great Britain and Ireland, Am. Assn. Anatomists (nominating com. 1977), Assn. Anatomy Chmn., Soc. Neurosci. (organizer, 1st pres. New Orleans chpt. 1970). Home: 342 Lexington Ave Iowa City IA 52240 Office: U Iowa Dept Anatomy Iowa City IA 52240

WILLIAMS, THOM ALBERT, insurance company executive; b. St. Louis, Dec. 31, 1941; s. Thom Reid and Martha Ann (Ruth) W.; m. Susan M. Raemdonck, Nov. 26, 1966 (div. Feb. 1980); children: Thom Raemdonck, Kenneth Reid; m. Mary V. Thomas, Mar. 4, 1981; 1 child, Priety Thomas. BBA, Washington U., St. Louis, 1962, postgrad., 1963-64. With Crane Co., St. Louis and Chgo., 1961-63, VW Mid Am. and VW Ins. Co., St. Louis, 1964-67; sr. ptnr. Williams Group Cons., St. Louis, 1967-68; pres. Williams Group Cos., Wood River, Ill., 1969-76; pres., dir. Reese-Wood River Drug Stores, 1972-76; div. mgr. adminstrn. and devel. Marsh & McLennan Ins., 1969-75, mgr. fin. and adminstrn., 1976, v.p., 1976-77; pres., dir. Washington Connection Investment Syndicate, St. Louis, 1970-71; v.p., dir. Remy Distbrs. Co., Highland, Ill., 1971-76; chmn. bd. dirs. Bryant Group Cos., St. Louis, 1979—. Rep. primary candidate Mo. Ho. Reps., 1968. Mem. Am. Mgmt. Assn., Pres.' Assn., C. of C. (bd. dirs.). Club: Mo. Athletic (St. Louis). Home: 7420 Saleen Ct Saint Louis MO 63130 Office: 700 Office Pkwy Saint Louis MO 63141

WILLIAMS, THOMAS HEWETT, orthodontist; b. Chickasha, Okla., Sept. 1, 1936; s. Thurman Herd and Clara Adams (Kramer) W.; m. Darilyn Sue Dutton, Jan. 13, 1979; children: Susan Kay, Tamara Ann, Edward Hewett, Michael Lambert. BS, Okla. U., 1958; DDS, Northwestern U., 1961, MS, 1965. Diplomate Am. Bd. Orthodontists. Practice dentistry specializing in orthodontics Chgo., 1965—; asst. prof. Northwestern U., Chgo., 1965-83, assoc. prof., 1986—. Served to capt. U.S. Army, 1961-63. Mem. Am. Assn. Orthodontics, Midwestern Soc. Orthodontists, Ill. Soc. Orthodontist. Republican. Episcopalian. Clubs: Exmoor Country (Highland Park, Ill.), Kenilworth (Ill.) Country, Wewoka (Okla.) Country. Avocations: golf, curling, tennis, cross country skiing. Home: 9558 Gross Point Rd Skokie IL 60076 Office: 4753 Broadway Chicago IL 60640

WILLIAMS, TIFFANY JOHNS, JR., gynecologist/obstetrician, educator; b. Iowa City, Iowa, Apr. 7, 1929; s. Tiffany Johns and Azelia T. (Kirkly) W.; m. Dohna Jean Duehr, Dec. 21, 1957; children: Tori Jo, tracy Jay, Tiffany Johns. BA, U. Va., 1948; MD, Johns Hopkins U., 1952. Diplomate Am. Bd. Ob-Gyn. Intern Duke U. Hosp., Durham, N.C., 1952-53; resident in ob-gyn Johns Hopkins U., Balt., 1953-60, from instr. to asst. prof., 1958-63; from asst. to assoc. to prof. Mayo Med. Sch., Rochester, Minn., 1963—. Contbr. numerous articles to profl. jours. Served to maj. USAF, 1954-56. Fellow Am. Coll. Obstetricians and Gynecologists, ACS; mem. Am. Gynecological and Obstetrical Soc., Cen. Assn. Obstetricians and Gynecologists, Am. Rose Soc., Zumbro Valley Rose Soc. (pres.), Phi Beta Kappa. Home: 3845 Meadowridge Dr SW Rochester MN 55902 Office: Mayo Clinic 200 1st St SW Rochester MN 55905

WILLIAMS, VIRGINIA JOYCE, controller; b. Coal City, Ind., Mar. 29, 1932; d. Warren G. and Grace (Joyce) Fulk; m. Harold E. Williams, May 20, 1951; children: Charles Robert, Janice Kay, Cheryl Ann. Grad., Vincennes U., 1968, Ind. U., 1976. CPA, Ind. Budget mgr. Am. States Ins. Co., Indpls., 1973-81; controller Baker & Daniels, Indpls., 1981—. Pres., bd. dirs. YWCA, Indpls., 1985-86; adv. bd. Ivy Tech., Indpls., 1979-84. Mem. Am. Inst. CPA's, Ind. Soc. CPA's, Nat. Assn. Accts. (pres. local chpt. 1984-85, nat. bd. dirs. 1986-88), Ind. Legal Adminstrs. (treas. 1984-87). Republican. Baptist. Office: Baker & Daniels 810 Fletcher Trust Bldg Indianapolis IN 46204

WILLIAMS, VIRGINIA WALKER, journalist; b. Walker County, Ala., June 5, 1915; married; 1 child. BA in Elem. Edn., Ala. State U., 1945; MA in Journalism, Marquette U., 1979; postgrad., U. Wis., Milw. Cert. remedial reading specialist, Wis. Tchr. various elem. schs., Ala., 1933-56; reading specialist Milw. Pub. Schs., 1956-69, journalist, editor, 1969-79; journalist Milw. Fire and Police Commn., 1980-85; founder, dir. Echo Writer's Workshop, Milw.; pub. Echo mag.; freelance writer. Contbr. articles to Milw. Jour., Milw. Sentinel, Milw. Star, Milw. Courier, Milw. Community Jour., Wis. Rep. Newspaper, Westside News, An Anthology of Black Writing, New Voices in Am. Poetry, 1985, Quill Book Anthology, 1987. Mem. Conservation Work Project Bd., Milw. Recipient Headliner award, Jack and Jill award, NAACP award, Service Club award, Advt. Club Milw. award. Mem. Nat. Press Women, Wis. Council Writers, Women in Communications, Soc. Profl. Journalists, Adminstrs. Suprs. Council, Phi Delta Kappa, Lambda Kappa Mu. Methodist. Club: Milw. Press. Lodges: Zonta, Tempo. Home: PO Box 2107 Milwaukee WI 53201

WILLIAMS, WARREN STEPHEN, educational psychology educator; b. Bklyn., Mar. 4, 1943; s. Herbert and Rosalie (Baum) W.; m. Judith Sheila Honigstock, June 29, 1968; 1 child, Lisa Sheila. BA in English, Hobart Coll., 1964; MA in Ednl. Psychology, U. Rochester, 1967, EdD in Ednl. Psychology, 1969. From asst. prof. to assoc. prof. ednl. psychology Eastern Mich. U., Ypsilanti, 1969-81, prof. ednl. psychology, 1981—; evaluation specialist primary curriculum unit U.S. Agy. for Internat. Devel., Manzini, Swaziland, 1977, Basic Edn. Devel. Project, Yemen Arab Republic, 1982; dir. testing Wayne County (Mich.) Intermediate Sch. Dist., 1978-79; cons. various Mich. sch. dists. Editor Research and the Classroom Tchr., 1965; contbr. articles to profl. jours.; text reviewer Rand McNally Pub. Co., 1980, Houghton Mifflin Co., 1981. Grantee Agy. for Internat. Devel, 1976, 1981, Mich. Dept. Edn., 1985. Mem. AAUP, Am. Ednl. Research Research Assn., Assn. Edn. Data Systems, Mich. Assn. Computer Users in Learning, Mich. Assn. Ednl. Data Systems, Nat. Council on Measurement in Edn., Nat. Appleworks Users Group (pres.). Office: Eastern Mich U Dept Tchr Edn Ypsilanti MI 48197

WILLIAMS, WILLIAM JOSEPH, insurance company executive; b. Cin., Dec. 19, 1915; s. Charles Finn and Elizabeth (Ryan) W.; m. Helen DeCourcy, May 26, 1941; children—Mary Frances Williams Clauder, William Joseph, Richard Francis, Carol Ann Williams Jodar, Sharon Mary Williams Frisbie, Thomas Luke. A.B., Georgetown U., 1937; postgrad., Sch. Bus., Harvard U., 1938. With Western-So. Life Ins. Co., Cin., 1939-54; chmn. bd. Western-So. Life Ins. Co., 1979-84, pres., 1984—; pres. N.Am. Mgmt. & Devel. Co., Cin., 1954-84; chmn. Cin. Reds Baseball Club, 1966-85; dir. Cin. Bengals, Columbus Mut. Ins., Ohio. Chmn. bd. Good Samaritan Hosp., Cin., 1984-86, Taft Mus., Cin., 1984-87; trustee, v.p. Cin. Art Mus.; trustee Cin. Inst. Fine Arts, Children's Home Cin.; bd. dirs. Georgetown U. Served to capt. U.S. Army, 1941-45. Decorated knight Order Knights of Malta, knight comdr. Holy Sepulchre; honored by NCCJ, 1979. Roman Catholic. Clubs: Queen City (pres. 1982-84), Commercial (pres. 1983), Cin. Country (Cin.); Camargo; Royal Poinciana Golf (Naples, Fla.). Home: 7801 Ayres Rd Cincinnati OH 45230 Office: Western So Life Ins Co 400 Broadway Cincinnati OH 45202

WILLIAMS-HENDERSON, IRIS MARIE, medical administrator; b. Laurel, Miss., June 15, 1942; d. Reuben Watson and Birdie Mae (Payton) W.; divorced; 1 child, Carmen Marie Henderson. Student, Rust Coll., Holly Springs, Miss., 1960-62, U. Calif., San Francisco, 1976, Sinclair Community Coll., Dayton, Ohio, 1981. Cert. tumor registrar; accredited record technician. Supr. tumor registry Miami Valley Hosp., Dayton, 1977—; cons. med. records Hill Top Nursing Home, Dayton, 1977-78, Friendship Village Nursing Home, Dayton, 1977-78. Editor OTRASCOPE newsletter, 1981—. Mem. Nat. Tumor Registrar Assn. (cert.), Ohio Tumor Registrar Assn. (pres., program chmn. 1981-82), Am. Med. Record Assn., Ohio Med. Record Assn. (cert.). Home: 1874 Rutland Dr Dayton OH 45406 Office: Miami Valley Hosp 1 Wyoming St Dayton OH 45409-2719

WILLIAMSON, D(ONALD) HUGH, adhesive manufacuring executive; b. Evanston, Ill., Jan. 6, 1948; s. D.G. and M.S. (Sailbury) W. BS, Menlo Sch. Bus. Adminstrn., Menlo Park, Calif., 1971. Pres. Williamson Adhesives, Inc., Skokie, Ill., 1980—, Williamson Export and Import, Skokie, 1980—. Mem. Adhesive Mfg. Assn. (bd. dirs. Chgo. 1985-89), Adhesive and Sealant Council (bd. dirs Washington, 1980-84). Home: 1625 Sheridan Rd Wilmette IL 60091 Office: Williamson Adhesives Inc 8220 N Kimball Ave Skokie IL 60076

WILLIAMSON, DONALD RAY, military officer; b. Amarillo, Tex., Oct. 13, 1943; s. Floy Edwin and Dorothy Lorene (Orr) W.; m. Beverly Ann Howard, Aug. 31, 1963; children: Rebecca Ann, Catherine Paige. BS in Econs., W. Tex. State U., 1966; MA in Bus., Cen. Mich. U., 1977; degree, Dept. Def. Program Mgrs., 1982; Disting. Mil. Grad., U.S. Army Command and Gen. Staff Coll., 1980. Commd. 2d lt. U.S. Army, 1966, advanced through grades to lt. col., 1982, retired, 1986; comdg. officer combat support co. U.S. Army, Ft. Hood, Tex., 1973-74; comdg. officer 2d aviation co. U.S. Army, Ft. Hood, 1974-75; dep. insp. gen. U.S. Army, Ft. Leavenworth, Kans., 1975-78; comdg. officer 213th aviation co. U.S. Army, Rep. of Korea, 1978-79; asst. program mgr. advanced scout helicopter program U.S. Army, 1981-86; owner Witan Group, Chesterfield, Mo., 1986—. Contbr. articles to profl. jours. Decorated Bronze Star, Air medal with "V" device, DFC with oak leaf cluster. Mem. Army Aviation Assn. Am., Assn. U.S. Army, Lansing Jaycees (pres.), Mensa. Avocations: flying, reading, tennis. Home: 50 Orange Hills Chesterfield MO 63017

WILLIAMSON, EVANGELINE FLOANN, vocational rehabilitation corporate executive; b. Ft. Wayne, Ind., Nov. 29, 1934; d. David Samuel and Anna Florence (Baker) McNelly; m. Clark Murray Williamson, Dec. 20, 1957 (div. 1964); 1 child, Dawn Valerie (dec.). BA with distinction Transylvania U., 1956. Asst. dir. publs. ABA, Chgo., 1958-66; pres., owner Herringshaw-Smith, Inc., Chgo., 1966-77; internal cons. Monarch Printing Corp., Chgo., 1978-80, Callaghan & Co., Wilmette, Ill., 1980-82; v.p., co-owner Career Evaluation Systems, Inc., Niles, Ill., 1983—; bd. dirs. MarTech Enterprises, Chgo. Author: From Typist to Typesetter, 1978; editor: Transylvania: Tutor to the West (John Wright), 1975; editor, designer: Silversmiths, Jewelers, Clock and Watchmakers of Kentucky, 1785-1900 (Marquis Boultinghouse), 1980. Bd. dirs., treas. West Central Assn., Chgo., 1976-77; bd. dirs. Martha Washington Hosp., Chgo., 1975-76, Mary Thompson Hosp., Chgo., 1977. Mem. Am. Voc. Assn., Nat. Rehab. Assn., Am. Assn. for Counseling and Devel., Niles C. of C. Republican. Mem. Christian Ch. Avocations: antique clock and furniture collecting; writing. Office: Career Evaluation Systems Inc 7788 Milwaukee Ave Niles IL 60648

WILLIAMSON, JERRY ROBERT, chemistry educator; b. Danville, Ill., Feb. 14, 1938; s. Jerome and Edna Marie (Walters) W.; m. Karen Gayle Horner, Jan. 30, 1965; 1 child, Stacy Anna. Student, Lawrence U., 1956-58; BA, U. Ill, 1960; MS in Chemistry, U. Iowa, 1963, PhD, 1964. Acting chmn. sci. div. Jarvis Christian Coll., Hawkins, Tex., 1964-66; post doctoral fellow Tex. Christian U., Ft. Worth, 1966-67; assoc. prof. chemistry Ea. Mich. U., Ypsilanti, Mich., 1967—; cons. safety tng. J.T. Baker Chem. Co., Phillipsburg, N.J., 1981—. Author: Improving Laboratory Safety, 1987. Mem. Am. Chem. Soc., Phi Lambda Upsilon, Sigma Xi, Alpha Chi Sigma. Avocations: travel, skiing, photography. Home: 1020 Louise Ypsilanti MI 48197 Office: Eastern Mich U Chemistry Dept Ypsilanti MI 48197

WILLIAMSON, JOHN MAURICE, accountant; b. Maroa, Ill., July 23, 1938; s. Richard and Margaret Alice (Thrift) W.; m. Donna I. Smith, Dec. 28, 1957; children: Robert, Susan, Sally, John II. BSBA in Accountancy, Bradley U., 1965. CPA, Ill. Systems analyst P & PU RY Co., Peoria, Ill., 1963-65; staff acct. Clifton Gunderson & Co., Peoria, 1965-68; controller C. Iber & Sons, Inc., Peoria, 1968-72; ptnr. John Dobson & Co., South Bend, Ind., 1973-79; controller E.H. Tepe Co., Inc., South Bend, 1979-82; dir. gift adminstrn. U. Ill. Found., Urbana, 1982—. Mem. Am. Inst. CPA's, Ill. CPA Soc. Home: No 17 Meadow Lake Rural Rt 3 Champaign IL 61821 Office: Univ Illinois Foundation 224 Illini Union 1401 W Green St Urbana IL 61801

WILLIAMSON, JOHN PRITCHARD, utility executive; b. Cleve., Feb. 22, 1922; s. John and Jane (Pritchard) W.; m. Helen Morgan, Aug. 3, 1945; children: John Morgan, James Russell, Wayne Arthur. BBA, Kent State U., 1945; postgrad., U. Toledo, 1953-56, U. Mich., 1956. C.P.A., Ohio. Sr. accountant Arthur Andersen & Co., Detroit and Cleve., 1945-51; dir. methods and procs. Toledo Edison Co., 1951-59, asst. treas., 1959-60, sec., 1960-62, sec.-treas., 1962-65, v.p. finance, 1965-68, sr. v.p., 1968-72, pres., chief exec. officer, 1972-79, chmn., chief exec. officer, 1979-86; chmn. emeritus Toledo Edison Co., Centerior Energy Corp., 1986—; dir. emeritus 1st Nat. Bank, Toledo, chmn., 1975-76; dir. Toledo Trust Co., Nuclear Electric Ins. Ltd., 1982-86, Ohio Valley Electric Co., 1982-86; chmn. N.Am. Electric Reliability Council, 1984-87. Pres. Ohio Electric Utility Inst., 1972, Toledo Hosp., 1984-86; chmn. East Central Area Power Coordination Pool, 1971-72, mem. exec. com. Edison Electric Inst., 1981-85; trustee Assn. Edison Illuminating Cos., 1982-84, pres. Toledo Orch., 1985-86 Toledo Mus. Art.; vice chmn. Greater Toledo Corp., 1984-86; elder Presbyn. Ch.;. Mem. Fin. Analysts Soc. Toledo (pres. 1968-69), Systems and Procs. Assn. (internat. treas. 1960), Inst. Pub. Utilities (chmn. exec. com. 1969-70), Toledo C. of C. (pres. 1970), Ohio C. of C. (chmn. 1979-81, Toledo's Outstanding Citizen 1976), Toledo Boys Club (Echo award 1974), Kent State U. Alumni Assn. (pres. 1971-72, outstanding alumnus 1974), Blue Key, Delta Sigma Pi, Beta Alpha Psi, Beta Gamma Sigma (hon.), Delta Upsilon. Republican. Clubs: Toledo, Inverness, Belmont Country. Lodge: Kiwanis (past pres. Toledo, Disting. Service award 1977). Home: 10661 Cardiff Rd Perrysburg OH 43551 Office: Centerior Energy Corp and Toledo Edison Co PO Box 2222 Toledo OH 43653

WILLIAMSON, JOSEPH HENRY, restaurant executive; b. Dayton, Ohio, Nov. 22, 1931; s. Joseph Henry and Dorothy Ann (Rost) W.; m. Frances Ann Keehn, Nov. 8, 1952; children: Dorothy Marie Crusoe, Gerard Joseph, Mary Jo Buckley, Karl Francis. Student, U. Dayton, 1949-50, 56-62, U. Ga., Columbus, 1953-54, U. N.C., Fort Bragg, 1954-55. Mgr. warehouse Rice-Kumler Co., Dayton, 1950-51, 55-63; supr. Cassano's, Inc., Dayton, 1963-68; corp. pres. J.H. Williamsons, Inc., Piqua, Ohio, 1968—. Pres. bd. Lehman High Sch., Sidney, Ohio, 1983-85, Piqua C. of C., 1980-81. Served with USAF, 1951-55. Mem. Ohio Restaurant Assn. (pres. bd. 1986—), Miami Valley Restaurant Assn. (pres. bd. 1984-85). Democrat. Roman Catholic. Lodge: KC. Avocations: golf, travel. Home: 402 N Parkway Dr Piqua OH 45356 Office: 414 W Water St Piqua OH 45356

WILLIAMSON, MALCOLM EDWARD, osteopath; b. Lisbon Falls, Maine, Aug. 18, 1936; s. Stewart and Virginia (Clarenbach) W.; m. Patricia Ruth Anne Holden, Oct. 25, 1961; children: Stewart, Malcolm, Anne. BS, Springfield Coll., 1958; postgrad., U. Mass., 1962-63; DO, Kirksville Coll. Osteo. Medicine, 1967. Cert. Am. Bd. Nuclear Medicine. Intern Osteo. Hosp. Maine, Portland, 1967-68; resident in internal medicine Detroit Osteo. Hosp., 1968-70; resident in endocrine nuclear medicine Wayne State U., Detroit, 1970-72; practice osteo. medicine specializing in nuclear and endocrine medicine Trenton, Mich., 1972—; dir. nuclear medicine, chmn. dept. internal medicine, dir. internal medicine residency Riverside Osteo. Hosp., Trenton, Mich., 1974—; assoc. prof. medicine Mich. State U., East Lansing, 1972—. Contbr. articles to profl. jours. Founder Troy Youth Soccer League, 1970; mem. Grosse Ile (Mich.) Drug Awareness, 1981—. Served to lt. USN, 1958-62. Nat. Osteo. Found. fellow, 1965. Mem. Mich. Coll. Nuclear Medicine Physicians (pres. 1985-86), Psi Sigma Alpha, Sigma Sigma Phi. Republican. Baptist. Club: Grosse Ile Golf and Country. Avocations: over 30 hockey, skiing, golf, Bible study. Office: 2171 W Jefferson Trenton MI 48183

WILLIAMSON, PAUL ALAN, cost analyst; b. Pitts., Sept. 4, 1947; s. Charles A. and Ora Mae (Holland) W.; m. Sharon Ann Pitlock, Oct. 16, 1982; 1 child, Nicholas Edward. AA, Prairie State Coll., 1976; BS in Acctg., Ind. U., 1982. Postal systems examiner U.S. Postal Service, Chgo., 1977-82; budget and cost analyst U.S. Postal Service, Rockford, Ill., 1982—; tax cons. H&R Block, Lansing, Ill., 1977-81. Served with USN, 1968-72. Mem. Ind. U. Alumni Assn. Home: 2120 Cortez Circle Rockford IL 61108 Office: US Postal Service 5225 Harrison Ave Rockford IL 61125

WILLIAMSON, STANLEY PAUL, orthodontist, pediatric dentist; b. Davenport, Iowa, Aug. 20, 1948; s. Philip Herald and Dorothy Florence (Wolfram) W.; m. Catharine Elizabeth Parr, Aug. 19, 1972; children: Sarah Elizabeth, Catharine Ann, Elizabeth Rebecca Parr. BS, U. Iowa, 1972, DDS, 1973; cert. in pediatric dentistry, Children's Hosp., Cin., 1975; cert. in orthodontics, Loyola U., Chgo., 1986. Diplomate Am. Bd. Pedodontics. Practice dentistry specializing in pediatric dentistry Wausau, Wis., 1975-84; practice dentistry specializing in orthodontics Edina, Minn., 1986—; cons. Wausau Hosp. Med. Ctr. Neurodevel. Clinic, 1977-84; chmn. dental dept. Wausau Hosp., 1979-83, chmn. bylaws com., 1983-84; assoc. clin. prof. U. Minn. Dept. Pediatric Dentistry, Mpls., 1986—; bd. dirs. McVay Jojoba Co., San Luis Obispo, Calif. Fellow Am. Acad. Pediatric Dentistry; mem. Am. Assn. Orthodontists, Marathon County Dental Soc. (pres. 1981). Republican. Unitarian Universalist. Office: 662 Southdale Med Bldg 6545 France Ave S Edina MN 55435

WILLIAMSON, VIKKI LYN, finance executive; b. Huntington, W.Va., June 30, 1956; d. Ernest E. and Wanda C. (Cole) W. BA in Secondary Edn., English, Temple U., 1978; postgrad. in Acctg. and Fin., U. Cin., 1984—. CPA, Ohio; cert. tchr., Tenn., Ohio. Tchr. Springfield Christian Acad., Tenn., 1978-79; acctg. asst. Children's Hosp. Med. Ctr., Cin., 1979-84; asst. dir. fin. services U. Cin. Med. Ctr., 1984-85, dir. fin. services, 1985—; instr. Miami U., Oxford, Ohio, 1984—; bd. dirs. Contemporary Dance Theatre, 1987—. Mem. Healthcare Fin. Mgmt. Assn., Am. Assn. Blood Banks, Ohio Assn. Blood Banks (fin. com. mem. 1986—), Assn. Women Adminstrs. (fin. com. mem. 1987—), U. Cin. Assn. Mid-Level Adminstrs. (bd. dirs. 1987—), Am. Inst. CPA's, Alpha Epsilon Theta, Beta Gamma Sigma, Delta Mu Delta. Office: Hoxworth Blood Ctr U Cin Med Ctr 3231 Burnet Ave ML #55 Cincinnati OH 45267

WILLIAMSON-STOUTENBURG, JANE SUE, health and safety training executive; b. Davenport, Iowa, Mar. 10, 1949; d. George Baker and Hazel Elaine (Kline) Williamson; m. Noel Wayne Stoutenburg, Aug. 25, 1979; 1 dau., Karen Elaine. Assoc. with honors, Black Hawk Coll., Moline, Ill., 1970; B.A. with honors in Med. Tech., Augustana Coll., Rock Island, Ill., 1973, B.S., 1974; cert. in fire sci., Harper Coll., Palatine, Ill., 1983. Cert. emergency med. technician. Pvt. investigator and security cons., Per Mar Security, Davenport, Iowa, 1975-76; pre-trial release investigator, 7th Judicial Dist., Scott County, Davenport, 1975-76; pharmal. rep. and territory mgr. Bristol Labs. Div., Bristol-Myers, Iowa and Ill., 1976-80; dir. tng. Zee Medical, Addison, Ill., 1981-82; founder and dir. Lake County Rescue, 1982—; asst. EMS coordinator Robbins (Ill.) Fire Dept.; tng. specialist ARC, Chgo., 1983—87; chmn. first aid program Barrington Area Devel. Council. Recipient Grand award Quint Cities Sci. Fair, 1967; Navy Sci. award, 1967; Future Scientists Am. award Ford Found., 1967; award for Outstanding Sci. Achievement in the Field of Physics, AUS, 1964-67; Nat. Sci. Tchrs. Assn. award, 1964-67; Am. Acad. Scis. award, 1967; Service award ARC. Mem. Internat. Assn. Fire Service Instrs., Am. Soc. Safety

Engrs., Am. Soc. Tng. and Devel., Am. Soc. Med. Technologists, Rescue and Emergency Specialists Assn., Am. Acad. Sci., Ill. Acad. Sci., Prehosp. Care Providers Ill. (charter), Crystal Lake Jaycees, Illiana Club Traditional Jazz, Ill. Soc. Microbiologists, Phi Theta Kappa, Alpha Phi Omega (life). Republican. Episcopalian. Club: PEO. Author poetry and profl. articles. Home: 203 S Glendale Barrington IL 60010 Office: PO Box 85 Barrington IL 60010

WILLIAMS-SCHROEDER, MARY LOU, nurse, community education specialist; b. Scranton, Pa., Feb. 6, 1937; d. John Frank and Helen Ann (Gruener) Williams; m. Stephen Gregory Schroeder, May 20, 1978; 1 child, Allen Gregory. Diploma in nursing, U. Pa., 1958; BS cum laude, Syracuse U., 1963; MEd, Columbia U., 1968. Registered nurse. Pub. health coordinator Vis. Nurse Assn., Scranton, Pa., 1959-61, asst. supr., 1963-66; instr. Northhampton County Community Coll., Bethlehem, Pa., 1968-69; asst. prof. U. Wis., 1969-77; lectr., instr. Milton (Wis.) Coll., 1979-80; community edn. specialist Rock County Bd. Alcohol, Drug, and Mental Health Services, Janesville, Wis., 1979—; organizer, cons. Alliance for Mentally Ill, Janesville, 1981-84. Lectr. Rusk County Positive Youth Outlook Workshop, Ladysmith, Wis., 1984, Mercy Hosp., Janesville, 1985; interviews with WCLO Radio, Janesville Gazette, Beloit Daily News, 1980-85; bd. dirs. Teenage Self Help Support Group, Janesville, 1983-85; organizer, cons. Rock County Sch. Dist. student assistance programs alcohol and drugs, Janesville, 1980—. Mem. Mental Health Assn. (bd. dirs. 1979-84, edn. chmn. 1982-83, Annual award 1982), Alzheimer's Disease and Related Disorders Assn., Alzheimers Disease Family Support Group (bd. dirs. local chpt. 1980—), Wis. Prevention Network, Am. Mental Health Fund, Wis. Assn. Community Human Services Programs. Democrat. Methodist. Avocations: knitting, gardening, biking, photography, reading. Home: 4929 N River Rd Janesville WI 53545 Office: Rock County Health Care Ctr Community Outreach Unit N Parker Dr PO Box 351 Janesville WI 53547-0351

WILLIFORD, CLIFFORD FREDRICK, electrical engineer; b. Norfolk, Va., July 12, 1950; s. Clifford and Frances Josephia (Rest) W.; m. Lorraine Ann Prytulak, July 18, 1970; children: Clifford Frederick Jr., Brandon Peter. BSEE, Va. Poly. Inst. and State U., 1976; MSEE, Air Force Inst. Tech., 1985. Enlisted USAF, 1970, commd. 2d lt., 1976, advanced through grades to maj., 1986; undergrad. pilot tng. Air Tng. Command, Williams AFB, Ariz., 1976-77; aircraft comdr. 492d Tactical Fighter Squadron, RAF Lakenheath, Eng., 1978-81; flight examiner standardization and evaluation 27th Tactical Fighter Wing, Cannon AFB, N.Mex., 1981-84; lead electronic warfare engr. Aeronautical System Div., Air Force Systems Command, Wright-Patterson AFB, Ohio, 1986—; adj. asst. prof. Wright State U., Dayton, Ohio, 1986. Asst. scoutmaster Boy Scouts Am., Bellbrook, Ohio, 1986-87. Mem. Assn. Old Crows, Order Daedalians, VFW, Etta Kappa Nu. Avocations: boating, water skiing, running, flying, home improvements.

WILLIG, LESLIE AUGUST, photography equipment manufacturing company executive; b. Ft. Wayne, Ind., Jan. 29, 1926; s. August Aloysius and Laura Elizabeth Willig; children: Constance J. Willig Roberts, Diana K. Willig Brummer, Larry A., Rosanne M. WIllig Johnson, Laura L. BS, Purdue U., 1947; MA, U. Louisville, 1951; PhD, U. Iowa, 1956. Asst. dean of men U. Iowa, Iowa City, 1954-56; asst. dir., assoc. prof. Purdue U., Ft. Wayne, 1956-60; exec. v.p. Tri-State U., Angola, Ind., 1960-70; v.p., bd. dirs. Bankers Investment Corp., Ft. Wayne, 1966-75; chmn. bd. dirs., chief exec. officer, pres. Photo Control Corp., Mpls., 1974—; bus. broker and cons. mgmt., Ft. Wayne, 1970—; sec., bd. dirs. North Snow Bay, Inc. Chmn. Internat. Sci. Fair Council, 1967; co-founder, bd. dirs. Sci. Edn. Found. Ind., 1963—, chmn., 1986—. Served to capt. USNR, 1944-47, 51-53. Recipient Disting. Pub. Service award Navy Dept., 1973. Mem. Am. Psychol. Assn., Midwest Psychol. Assn., Naval Res. Assn. (nat. pres. 1971-73, Merit award 1974). Roman Catholic. Club: Summit (Ft. Wayne). Home: Rural Rt 1 Box 791 Fremont IN 46737 Office: Photo Control Corp 4800 Quebec Ave N Minneapolis MN 55428

WILLIS, DONNA LAVERNE, physician; b. Oberlin, Ohio, Nov. 7, 1953; d. Robert Leslie and Bettye LaRue (Palmer) W. Student Oakwood Coll., 1971-74; B.S., M.D., Loma Linda U., 1977; MPH in Health Services and Policy, U. Mich., 1986. Diplomate Nat. Bd. Examiners. Intern, resident in internal medicine Mayo Grad. Sch. Edn., Rochester, Minn., 1977-80; med. dir. West Dayton Health Ctr., Dayton, Ohio, 1980-82; assoc. program dir. internal medicine residency Kettering Med. Ctr. (Ohio), 1982—; practice medicine specializing in internal and preventive medicine, Comprehensive Health Med. Cons., 1986—; clin. instr. Wright State U. Sch. Medicine, Dayton, 1980—; moderator radio talk show, Dayton, 1984; cons., lectr. Health Issues, Services and Policies, 1986—. Author newsletter Caring Family; columnist Ask the Doctor in Caring mag.; med. news editor NBC affiliate Sta. WKEF. Trustee, West Dayton Health Ctr., 1980-82, Kettering Coll. Med. Arts; trustee United Way/United Health Services, 1982—, chairperson nutrition com., 1983—, vice chairperson Health-O-Rama, 1984—, chairperson, 1985. Recipient Appreciation award Nat. Alliance Bus., 1982-83; YWCA Career Women award, 1984. Seventh-Day Adventist. Office: Kettering Med Ctr 3535 Southern Blvd Kettering OH 45429

WILLIS, ERNEST W., savings and loan association executive; b. Chgo., Oct. 22, 1934; s. Ernest W. and Eleanore P. (Kaiser) W.; m. Jone Leslie, Nov. 2, 1963 (dec. Nov. 1985); m. Sunday S. Willis, Dec. 28, 1986. Student, Ill. Inst. Tech., 1952-55, Northwestern U., 1955-58. Exec. v.p. Crawford Savs. and Loan Assn., Chgo., 1961-68, pres., 1968-71, co-bd., pres., 1971-82; pres. Pathway Fin. Fed. Savs. and Loan Assn., Chgo., 1982-86, chmn. bd. dirs., 1986—. Bd. dirs. Better Bus. Bur. Chgo., 1985—, Greater State St. Council, Chgo., 1985—. Mem. Ill. Savs. and Loan League (bd. dirs. 1978-81). Lutheran. Lodge: Masons. Office: Pathway Fin and Fed Assn 100 N State Chicago IL 60602

WILLIS, KEITH ALLAN, psychologist; b. Ainsworth, Nebr., Jan. 20, 1947; s. Merrill Raymond and Marvel Irene (Shambaugh) W.; m. Carole Ann Bogus, June 15, 1974; children: Katie, Amy, Andrew, Anne, Matthew. BA, U. Nebr., Lincoln, 1969; MA, U. Nebr., 1974, PhD, 1976. Lic. psychologist; cert. clin. psychologist. Psychologist Willmar (Minn.) State Hosp., 1976-79, Nebr. Regional Treatment Ctr., Lincoln, 1979-80; clin. dir. Valley Hope Alcoholism Treatment Ctr., O'Neill, Nebr., 1980—. family minister St. Mary's Cath. Ch., O'Neill, 1982—. Nebr. Bd. Regents scholar, 1965. Mem. Nebr. Psychol. Assn. Democrat. Roman Catholic. Lodge: KC. Office: Valley Hope Alcoholism Box 918 O'Neill NE 68763

WILLMAN, SISTER VINCENT MARIE, nun; b. Cin., Sept. 29, 1932; d. Vincent Leo and Bertha Cecelia (Werle) W. BS in Elem. Edn., Mount St. Joseph Coll., 1962; MA in Religion, Aquinas Coll., 1970; MA in Religious Studies, St. Charles Sem., Phila., 1987. Joined Sisters of Charity, Roman Cath. Ch., 1950. Dir. religion St. Michael's Ch., Findlay, Ohio, 1970-77, St. Gabriel Parish, Glendale, Ohio, 1979—. Avocations: classical music, walking, gardening.

WILLMANN, WENDEL EDGAR, lawyer; b. Greenville, Ohio, Feb. 25, 1935; s. R. Wayne and Twila I. (DeWalt) W.; m. Doris M. Meister, July 1, 1961; children: Diane L., Jeffrey S. Student, U. Mich., 1955-56; BA, Capital U., 1957; MEd, Kent State U., 1964; JD, Cleve. Marshall Law Sch., 1969. Bar: Ohio, 1969, U.S. Dist. Ct. (no. dist.) Ohio, 1972, U.S. Supreme Ct. 1981, U.S. Ct. Appeals (6th cir.) 1983. Tchr. Parma High Sch., Ohio, 1959-66; salesman Conn. Gen. Life., Cleve., 1966-67; tchr. Fairview (Ohio) High Sch., 1968-71; ptnr. Willmann, James & Mille, Cleve., 1969—. V.p. Parma Sch. Bd., 1980-81; bd. regents Capital U., Columbus, Ohio, 1975; bd. dirs. Luth. Children's Aid Soc., Cleve., 1972-75. Served wih U.S. Army, 1958. Named to Parma Schs. Hall of Fame, 1983. Mem. Assn. Trial Lawyers Am., Fairview Park Tchrs. Assn. (pres. 1971), ABA, Ohio State Bar Assn., Ohio Assn. Trial Lawyers, Cleve. Bar Assn., Parma C. of C., Delta Theta Phi. Lutheran. Lodge: Kiwanis (pres. 1975-76). Avocations: softball, golf, investing. Home: 2118 Oaklawn Dr Parma OH 44134 Office: Willmann James & Mille 6837 Pearl Rd Cleveland OH 44130

WILLMERING, JAMES THEODORE, manufacturing executive; b. St. Louis, July 25, 1933; s. Theodore Joseph and Marcella Willmering; m. Martha Jane Calverley, Jan. 18, 1958; children: Kathleen, Mark, Louise, Marie, Sarah, Gregory, Helen, Paul, John. BS in Indsl. Mgmt., Washington U., St. Louis, 1963. Cert. in material handling. Mgr. packaging Rexall Drug Co., St. Louis, 1959-64; mgr. distbn. Jos. Schlitz Brewery, Milw., 1964-71; plant mgr. Am. Motors Corp., Milw., 1972-75, mgr. indsl. engring., 1975-77; dir. distbn. Broan Mfg., Inc., Hartford, Wis., 1977—. Scoutmaster Milw. County Council Boy Scouts Am., 1974-86. Served as pvt. U.S. Army, 1954-56. Mem. Council Logistics Mgmt. (pres. Milw. roundtable 1984-85), Am. Mgmt. Assn. Republican. Roman Catholic. Avocations: camping, hunting. Home: 198 N 90th St Milwaukee WI 53226 Office: Broan Mfg Co Inc 926 W State St Hartford WI 53027

WILLMOTT, PETER SHERMAN, retail executive; b. Glens Falls, N.Y., 1937. B.A., Williams Coll., 1959; M.B.A., Harvard U., 1961. Sr. fin. analyst Am. Airlines, N.Y.C., 1961-63; mgr. cons. Booz Allen & Hamilton, N.Y.C., 1964-66; treas. Continental Baking Co., Rye, N.Y., 1966-69, v.p., 1969-74; sr. v.p. fin. Fed. Express Corp., Memphis, 1974-77, exec. v.p. fin. and adminstrn., 1977-80, pres., chief operating officer, 1980-83, dir., 1980—; dir. Carson Pirie Scott & Co., Chgo., 1981—, pres., chief exec. officer, 1983—, chmn., 1984—. Office: Carson Pirie Scott & Co 36 S Wabash Ave Chicago IL 60603 *

WILLOUGHBY, DAVID CHARLES, biological photographer; b. Indpls., Nov. 16, 1940; s. Charles C. and Mabelle L. (Haller) W.; student Ind. U., 1958-62, Butler U., 1962-64; m. Victoria LaMarre, Mar. 6, 1971; children—Brian D., Kara L. Med. photographer Ind. U. Sch. Medicine, Indpls., 1962-68; dir. med. media prodns. Meth. Hosp. of Indpls., 1968-85; owner, operator BioMed. Photography, Indpls., 1985— ; forensic illustrator Indpls.-Marion County Forensic Services Agy., Indpl., 1986—. Registered biol. photographer. Fellow Biol. Photog. Assn. (dir. 1978-80, exec. sec. bd. of registry 1981-85); mem. Profl. Photographers Am., Hosp. Audiovisual Dirs. Assn., Midwestern Assn. Forensic Scientists, Inc., Ind. Ofcls. Assn., Internat. Assn. Approved Basketball Ofcls. Republican. Methodist. Lodges: Masons, Shriners (Indpls.); Order of Eastern Star. Home: 6711 Studebaker Ct Indianapolis IN 46224 Office: 40 S Alabama St Indianapolis IN 46204

WILLOUGHBY, ROBERT ALLEN, manufacturing company executive; b. Denville, N.J., Dec. 7, 1936; s. George P. and Anna M. (Brogeler) W.; m. Judith A. Milby, Oct. 22, 1976; children: Chris, J. Michael Gaugler, Mary Gaugler, Glenn. BSME, Newark Coll. Engring., 1958, MSME, 1964. Devel. engr. Wallace & Tiernan, Belleville, N.J., 1958-64; research engr. Ingersoll-Rand Co., Princeton, N.J., 1964-71; mgr. engring. Ingersoll-Rand Co., Athens, Pa., 1971-80; dir. engring. The Aro Corp., Bryan, Ohio, 1980-87; tech. dir. Senco Products, Inc., Cin., 1987—; tech. rep. Pneurop, London, 1985-87. Contbr. articles to profl. jours.; patentee in field. Conv. del. Ch. of the Redeemer, Sayre, Pa., 1977-79, vestryman, 1979; mem. grant com. Diocese of Bethlehem, Pa., 1979-80. Mem. Compressed Air and Gas Inst. (engring. com. 1972-87, chmn. 1983-87), Pi Tau Sigma. Episcopalian. Avocations: cooking, camping, writing, fishing, geneology. Home: 5259 Adena Trail Cincinnati OH 45230 Office: Senco Products Inc 8485 Broadwell Rd Cincinnati OH 45244

WILLS, CHARLES BATES, JR., dentist; b. Flint, Mich., May 5, 1934; s. Charles Bates and Grace Margaret (Mercer) W.; m. Barbara Ann Romnes, Aug. 16, 1958 (div. June 1976); children: Laura, Richard, Mary; m. Catherine Rita Sweeney, July 1, 1977; stepchildren: Laura, Daphne, Elizabeth, Michael. BA, Albion (Mich.) Coll., 1956; DDS, Northwestern U., 1960. Gen. practice dentistry Petoskey, Mich., 1962—; cons. No. Mich. Health Systems, Petoskey, 1981-83, 85—. Bd. dirs. Midshipmen Drum & Bugle Corps, Petoskey, 1976-78. Served to lt. USNR, 1960-62. Mem. ADA, Mich. Dental Assn. (chmn. dental edn. com. 1986—, trustee 1987), Vacationland Dist. Dental Soc. (pres. 1983-86), Am. Endodontics Soc., Acad. Gen. Dentistry, Acad. Sports Dentistry (founding mem.), Am. Equilibration Soc. Home: 700 Hillside #15 Petoskey MI 49770 Office: 2202 Mitchell Park Ctr PO Box 805 Petoskey MI 49770

WILLS, ROBERT HAMILTON, editor; b. Colfax, Ill., June 21, 1926; s. Robert Orson and Ressie Mae (Hamilton) W.; m. Sherilyn Lou Nierstheimer, Jan. 16, 1949; children: Robert L., Michael H., Kendall J. B.S., M.S., Northwestern U., 1950. Reporter Duluth (Minn.) Herald & News-Tribune, 1950-51; reporter Milw. Jour., 1951-59, asst. city editor, 1959-62; city editor Milw. Sentinel, 1962-75, editor, 1975—; v.p., dir. Jour. Communications; sr. v.p., dir. Jour./Sentinel, Inc. Pres., Wis. Freedom of Info. Council, 1979-86; Pulitzer Prize juror, 1982, 83; mem. journalism adv. com. U. Wis., Milw., 1982-87. Mem. media-law relations com. State Bar Wis.; bd. dirs. Medill Sch. Journalism Northwestern U. Alumni Assn. Served with USNR, 1944-46. Named Wis. Newsman of Yr. Milw. chpt. Sigma Delta Chi, 1973. Mem. Wis. Newspaper Assn. (pres. 1985-86). Wis. AP (pres. 1975-76), Am. Soc. Newspaper Editors, Internat. Press Inst., Milw. Press Club, Sigma Delta Chi (pres. Milw. chpt. 1979-80, nat. pres. 1987). Unitarian. Home: 17965 Maple Tree Ln Brookfield WI 53005 Office: Milw Sentinel Div of the Journal Co 918 N 4th St PO Box 371 Milwaukee WI 53201

WILMARTH, CHARLES BURTON, radiologist; b. Ocheyedan, Iowa, June 8, 1938; s. Curtis Merle and Dorothy (Bellows) W.; m. Karen Ann Landhuis, Dec. 19, 1959; children: Steven Ray, Linda Kay, Susan Renee. BS, Morningside Coll., 1960; MD, U. Iowa, 1964. Diplomate Am. Bd. Radiology. Intern Los Angeles County Hosp., 1964-65; health dir. USPHS, Toppenish, Wash., 1965-66; resident radiology U. Iowa Hosps., Iowa City, 1967-70; radiologist Mercy Hosp., Mason City, Iowa, 1970—. Mem. AMA, Radiol. Soc. N.Am., Am. Coll. Radiology. Republican. Club: Clear Lake City Yacht. Avocation: sailing. Home: 336 Meadow Ln Mason City IA 50401 Office: Forest Pk Med Bldg 1023 Second SW Mason City IA 50401

WILMHOFF, ROY CHARLES, computer engineer; b. Covington, Ky., Sept. 12, 1948; s. Russell Lewis and Esther Shirley (Hood) W.; m. Robin Lee Tewell, June 6, 1973; children: Virginia Lee, Russell Henry. BA, No. Ky. State U., 1973, MEd, 1977; MSEE, U. Cin., 1981. Registered profl. engr., Ohio. Tchr. Boone County Bd. Edn., Florence, Ky., 1975-79; mem. tech. staff Cin. Electric Co., 1980-83; sr. asst. programer Cin. Milacron, 1983-85, group leader APC software engr., 1985—. Served with USN, 1969-71. Mem. IEEE, NEMA. Democrat. Roman Catholic. Avocations: photography, reading. Office: Cin Milacron ESD Rt 489 Mason Morrow Rd Lebanon OH 45036

WILMOTH, LOIS GERTRUDE, psychologist; b. Sydney, W.Va., Aug. 24, 1934; d. Walter and Adaline (Riggs) Ball; m. Robert Francis Wilmoth, June 27, 1953 (div. May 1968); children: Gregory Robert, Diane Elayne, Susan Lynn Wilmoth Wyatt. BS in Elem. Edn., Kent State U., 1968, MEd in Sch. Psychology, 1970, EdS in Counseling, 1972, postgrad., 1984—. Tchr. Brunswick (Ohio) Schs., 1966-70; psychologist Fairless Schs., Navarre, Ohio, 1971-76, Winter Haven (Fla.) Hosp., 1978-79; psychologist, dir. Rittman (Ohio) Schs., 1977-78, 79—; pvt. practice psychology Psychol. Counseling Ctr., Akron, Ohio, 1986—. Contbr. articles to newspapers and profl. jours. Bd. dirs. Wayne Info. and Referral Exchange, 1981-85; pres. Christian Singles Together, 1985-86. Mem. Nat. Assn. Sch. Psychologists, Ohio Sch. Psychologists Assn. (bd. dirs. 1981-84), Phi Delta Kappa. Lodge: Order Eastern Star. Avocations: creative writing, dancing. Home: 372 N Lyman St Wadsworth OH 44281 Office: Psychol Counseling Ctr 150 N Miller Rd #500 Akron OH 44313

WILMOUTH, ROBERT K., commodities executive; b. Worcester, Mass., Nov. 9, 1928; s. Alfred F. and Aileen E. (Kearney) W.; m. Ellen M. Boyle, Sept. 10, 1955; children: Robert J., John J., James P., Thomas G., Anne Marie. B.A., Holy Cross Coll., 1949; M.A., U. Notre Dame, 1950. Exec. v.p., dir. 1st Nat. Bank Chgo., 1972-75; pres., chief adminstrv. officer Crocker Nat. Bank, San Francisco, 1975-77; pres., chief exec. officer Chgo. Bd. Trade, 1977-82; chmn. LaSalle Nat. Bank, 1982—; pres., chief exec. officer Nat. Futures Assn., 1982—; dir. Pvt. Export Funding Corp.; bd. dirs. Southern Pacific Transp. Co. Trustee U. Notre Dame; mem. adv. council Kellogg Grad. Sch. Mgmt., Northwestern U. Served to 2d lt. USAF, 1951-53. Clubs: Chgo, Barrington Hill Country, Economic (dir.). Home: Rural Route 5 Caesar Dr Barrington IL 60010 Office: 200 W Madison St Chicago IL 60606

WILSHIRE, THOMAS E., financial company executive; b. 1931; married. With Equibank Corp., 1952-74; with ITT Fin. Corp., St. Louis, from 1974; former exec. v.p. ops., dir. ITT Fin. Corp.; now pres. ITT Consumer Fin. Corp. ITT Fin. Corp., Mpls.; also dir. ITT Fin. Corp. Office: ITT Consumer Fin Corp 400 S County Rd 18 Minneapolis MN 55426 *

WILSON, ARLIE JAMES, manufacturing executive; b. Wilmington, N.C., May 4, 1943; s. James Walter and Margaret (Powell) W.; m. Linda Ennis, June 21, 1969; children: Amanda, Ashley. BA in Math., Physics, U. N.C., Wilmington, 1969. Plant mgr. Wright Chem. Co., Acme, N.C., Malvern, Ark., 1969-71; plant engr. Internat. Technovation, Malvern, 1971-73; plant engr. Clear Shield Nat. Inc., Wheeling, Ill., 1973-75, v.p., 1975—. Served with USAF, 1961-65. Mem. Soc. Plastic Engrs. Republican. Baptist. Home: 3481 Regent Dr Palatine IL 60067 Office: Clear Shield Nat Inc 1175 S Wheeling Rd Wheeling IL 60090

WILSON, ARNAUD JOSEPH, management consultant; b. St. Louis, Oct. 13, 1952; s. Arnaud Joseph and Esther (Moran) W.; m. Betty McLinden, Apr. 20, 1974; children: Arnaud Christian, Brigetta Anne. BA in East Asian History, U. Tex., 1974; MA in Oriental Lang., U. Kans., 1977; M in Internat. Mgmt., Ariz. Grad. Sch. Internat. Mgmt., 1978. Analyst Barber Steamship, N.Y.C., 1979-79, mgr., 1979-81; mgr. Barber Steamship, Chgo., 1981-84, ScanBarber AS, Oslo, 1984-86, A.T. Kearney, Inc., Chgo., 1986—. Mem. Inst. Mgmt. Cons. Home: 701 W Hawthorne Blvd Wheaton IL 60187 Office: AT Kearney Inc 222 S Riverside Plaza Chicago IL 60606

WILSON, BARBARA JEAN, marketing professional; b. Mansfield, Ohio, July 9, 1948; d. Woodrow and Mary Jane (Bellore) W.; m. Richard A. Wagner, July 27, 1974; children: Elisabeth Anne, Heather Jane. Student, Albert Ludwig Universitat, Freiburg, Fed. Republic of Germany, 1968-69; BA, U. Mich., 1970, MA, 1974. Mktg. adminstrn. mgr. Univ. Microfilms, Ann Arbor, Mich., 1970-79; mktg. mgr. Comshare, Ann Arbor, 1979—; adj. lectr. U. Mich., Ann Arbor, 1978-79. Newsletter editor: Profiles Spectrum, 1980-82. Troop services dir. Huron Valley Girl Scouts U.S., Washtenaw County, Mich., 1982-83; mem. Ypsilanti council St. Philips Luth. Ch., 1986—. Mem. Human Resource Systems Profls. (bd. dirs. 1986—), Am. Mktg. Assn., Am. Soc. for Tng. and Devel. Avocations: piano, organ, music, reading. Office: Comshare 3001 S State St Ann Arbor MI 48104

WILSON, BARRY ANTHONY, financial consulting company executive; b. Bay City, Mich., June 4, 1952; s. Ardon Anthony and Betty Jane (Defoe) W.; m. MaryKay Wiergowski, Aug. 8, 1981; children: Rachael, Lisa. AA, Ferris State Coll., 1972; BA, Mich. State U., 1982; JD, Thomas M. Cooley Sch. Law, 1987. Bar: Mich. Loan officer Peoples Nat. Bank, Bay City, 1977-80; pres. East Mich. Investment, Bay City, 1980-81; bus. cons. Mich. Dept. Commerce, Lansing, 1982-83; sr. investment analyst Mich. Dept. Treasury, Lansing, 1983-86; pres. Quest Cons., Lansing, 1986—; chief fin. officer Amprotech, Grand Rapids, Mich., 1986—; regional rep. Newtek Ventures, San Francisco, 1986—. Mem. ABA, Mich. Bar Assn. Roman Catholic. Avocation: tennis. Home: 7840 W Willow Hwy Grand Ledge MI 48837 Office: Newtek Ventures 4660 S Hagadorn Rd East Lansing MI 48823

WILSON, BETTY-RUTH, librarian; b. Brownsville, Tenn., July 10, 1934; d. John Robert and Jessie Florence (Hastings) W.; m. Carlos Enrique Marrero, Aug. 14, 1965 (div. June 1981). BA, Union U., 1955; MA in Library Sci., George Peabody Coll., 1957. Loans librarian Randolph-Macon Women's Coll., Lynchburg, Va., 1957-60; extramural loans librarian U. Ill., Urbana, 1960-63; reference librarian No. Ill. U., DeKalb, 1963-65; cataloging librarian So. Ill. U., Carbondale, 1965—. Contbr. articles to profl. jours. Parlimentarian nominating com. Partnership for Disbabled, Carbondale, 1982—; acting chair So. Ill. M.S. Support Group, Carbondale, 1985—; bd. dirs. Comprehensive Health Planning for So. Ill., Carbondale, 1984-86. Mem. Am. Library Assn., Academic Librarians Assisting Disabled, Ill. Library Assn., Resources and Technical Services Sect. (past pres., various coms.), Ill. Assn. Coll. Research Libraries (various coms.). Baptist. Avocations: collecting Am. Art pottery, traveling. Home: 104B N Violet Ln Carbondale IL 62901 Office: So Ill U Carbondale Morris Library Carbondale IL 62901

WILSON, CHARLES JAMES, mechanical engineer; b. Cleve., Aug. 14, 1934; s. William Henry and Esther May (Junkey) W.; m. Mary Anna Kozma, Sept. 5, 1959; children: Suzanne Mary, Carolyn Esther. BS in Mech. Engring., Case Inst., 1957; MS in Mech. Engring., Bucknell U., 1963. Registered profl. engr., Ohio. Instr. mech. engring. Fenn Coll., Cleve., 1958-62; sec., treas. Indsl. Fasteners Inst., Cleve., 1963—, dir. engring., mgmt. services, 1984—; dir. Bolting Tech. council, N.Y.C., 1985—. Chmn. Heights Choir Scholarship fund, Cleve., 1985—; del. Internat. Orgn. for Standardization, Geneva, 1983, 84, 87. Mem. Am. Soc. for Testing and Materials, ASME, Soc. Automotive Engrs., Standards Engr. Soc., Soc. Assoc. Execs. Home: 2644 Shaker Rd Cleveland Heights OH 44118 Office: Indsl Fasteners Inst 1505 E Ohio Bldg Cleveland OH 44114

WILSON, CHARLES KEITH, pharmacist; b. Mt. Vernon, Ill., May 24, 1959; s. Charles V. and Nadine (Launius) W. BS, St. Louis Coll. Pharmacy, 1983. Pharmacist Hook Drug Co., Indpls., 1983—. Mem. Am. Pharm. Assn., Ill. Pharm. Assn., Nat. Rifle Assn., Kenilworth Pharm. Assn. Democrat. Home: 611 George St Fairfield IL 62837

WILSON, CHARLES STEPHEN, cardiologist; b. Geneva, Nebr., June 14, 1938; s. Robert Butler and Naoma Luella (Norgren) W.; B.A. cum laude, U. Nebr., 1960; M.D., Northwestern U., 1964; m. Linda Stern Walt, Aug. 21, 1960; children—Michael Scott, Amy Lynn, Cynthia Lee. Intern, Fitzsimons Gen. Hosp., Denver, 1964-65; fellow in internal medicine and cardiology Mayo Grad. Sch. Medicine, Rochester, Minn., 1968-72; practice medicine specializing in cardiology, Lincoln, Nebr., 1972—; attending staff Bryan Meml. Hosp., Lincoln, 1972—, chmn. cardiology, 1976-79; attending staff Lincoln Gen. Hosp., 1978—; assoc. prof. medicine and cardiology U. Nebr. Med. Center, Omaha; mem. Mayor's Council on Emergency Med. Services, Lincoln, 1974-78; founder, chmn. Nebr. State Hypertension Screening Program; med. dir. Lincoln Mobile Heart Team, 1977-80, Lincoln Cardiac Rehab. Program, 1978-79. Trustee U. Nebr. Found., 1983—, chmn. Nebr. Coordinating Commn. for Postsecondary Edn., 1984—; mem. Gov.'s Exec. Council, 1983-87. Served as maj., M.C., USAR, 1963-68. Diplomate Am. Bd. Internal Medicine subsplty. bd. cardiovascular disease, Nat. Bd. Med. Examiners; Gen. Motors Nat. scholar, 1956-60, Nat. Found. Med. scholar, 1960-64, Mead Johnson scholar ACP, 1968-71. Fellow ACP, Am. Coll. Cardiology, Am. Coll. Chest Physicians, Am. Heart Assn.; mem. Am. Soc. Echocardiography, Mayo Cardiovascular Soc., Nebr. Cardiovascular Soc., Nebr. Heart Assn. (dir. 1973-80, pres. 1976-77), Lincoln Heart Assn. (dir. 1972-75, pres. 1974-75), AMA, Nebr. Med. Assn., Lancaster County Med. Soc., Am. Soc. Internal Medicine, Lincoln Found., Phi Beta Kappa, Sigma Xi, Alpha Omega Alpha, Phi Delta Theta (pres. Nebr. Alpha chpt. 1959-60). Congregationalist. Clubs: U. Nebr. Chancellor's, Lincoln U. (dir. 1981-84). Lodge: Elks. Contbr. articles to profl. jours.; editorial cons. Chest, 1975-76; assoc. editor Nebr. Med. Jour., 1981—. Home: 7430 N Hampton Rd Lincoln NE 68506 Office: 1919 S 40th St Suite 300 Lincoln NE 68506

WILSON, D. C., restauranteur; b. Beech Grove, Inc., Feb. 6, 1931; s. Carl William and Lorraine (Achill) W.; m. Jacqueline L. Allen, Sept. 14, 1957; children: Scott, Faith. Student, Purdue U., 1949, U. Okla., 1958. Airtraffic controller FAA, Indpls., 1958-60; photographer Letureau Westinghouse, Indpls., 1960-62; exec. dir. Boys Scouts Am., Indpls., 1962-76; pres. Allis Chalmers Dealership, Sidney, Ill., 1976-80; mgr. Burger king, Champaign, Ill., 1980-81; owner Good Ole Days Restaurant, St. Joseph, Ill., 1982—. Served to staff sgt. USAF, 1951-55. Mem. Nat, Restaurant Assn., St. Joseph C. of C., (chmn. committee 1982—). Republican. Baptist. Club: American. Lodge: Masons. Avocations: fishing, flying, traveling.

WILSON, DELBERT RAY, newspaper publisher; b. Riverdale, Calif., Jan. 16, 1926; s. Elmer Ray and Hanna Marie (Pelto) W.; m. Beatrice Joy Daffer, Oct. 5, 1947; children: Jeri Rae, Vicky Joy, Julianne, Margaret Erin. A.A., A.S., Elgin (Ill.) Community Coll., 1975; B.S., No. Ill. U., 1980; Litt.D. (hon.), Judson Coll., 1985. Editor The Reporter, McCook, Nebr., 1949-50; co-pub. The Reporter, Times-Republican (Hayes Center, Nebr.), Pioneer-Press (Palisade, Nebr.), News (Haigler, Nebr.), 1951-52; advt. mgr. Daily Telegram, Norton, Kans., 1952-53; mgr. The Star, Dos Palos, Calif., 1953-54; gen. mgr. Tribune, Holtville, Calif., 1954-57; bus. mgr. Desert Newspapers, Glendale, Ariz., 1957-59; advt. sales rep. Union Tribune Pub. Co.,

San Diego, 1959-60, Merchandising mgr., 1961-65; gen. advt. mgr. Union Tribune Pub. Co., 1966; editor, pub. Evening Star-News, Culver City, Calif., 1966-70, Daily Courier-News, Elgin, Ill., also; Daily Jour., Wheaton, Ill., 1970—; v.p., sr. mgmt. bd. Copley Press, Inc., La Jolla, Calif. Author: The Folks, 1974, Fort Kearny on the Platte, 1980, Episode on Hill 616, 1981, Nebraska Historical Guide, 1983, Wyoming Historical Guide, 1984, Iowa Historical Tour Guide, 1985, Kansas Historical Guide, 1987, Missouri Historical Tour Guide, 1987. Founder, chmn. bd. VIP Friendship Council, Inc. of Ill., 1972—, DuPage County Heritage Gallery, Wheaton, 1976—; bd. govs. State Colls. and Univs., Ill., 1981—; trustee Judson Coll., Elgin, 1971—, Elgin Acad., 1973—; chmn. bd. Elgin Sesquicentennial Inc.; bd. mgrs. Sherman Hosp., Elgin, 1971—; active Boy Scouts Am. (Silver Beaver award 1977); chmn. bd. Christian Coll. So. Africa, Harare, Zimbabwe, 1983-87; bd. govs. Luth. Social Services of Ill., 1983—; mem. Ill. Vets. Adv. Council, 1983—; bd. dirs. Cornerstone Found., 1984—, Wheaton Eye Found., 1985—, Elgin Community Coll. Found., 1986—, Summit Sch. Found., 1987—; pres. Council on America's Mil. Past, Dept. Ill. Served with USN, 1943-45; Served with USAF, 1946-49. Mem. Am. Newspaper Pubs. Assn., Inland, Ill. daily press assns., Nebr. Hist. Soc. (life mem.), DAV (Man of Year 1978, comdr. Ill. 1980-82, editor and pub. Ill. DAV News 1977-87), Am. Legion, Sigma Delta Chi. Republican. Lutheran. Clubs: Rotary, Elks, Elgin Country. Home: 1507 Laurel Ct Dundee IL 60118 Office: 300 Lake St Elgin IL 60120 *

WILSON, DONALD PORTER, architect; b. St. Louis, Jan. 5, 1940; s. James Penfield and Elizabeth Porter (Stocking) W.; m. Carol Ann Johnson, Sept. 8, 1962; children: Jeffrey Crossen, Kathryn Porter. BS in Archtl. Scis., Washington U., 1962, BArch, 1966. Designer Fruco & Assocs., St. Louis, 1966-67; designer, project mgr. Peckham Guyton Inc., St. Louis, 1967-68; prin. Donald Porter Wilson Architects, St. Louis, 1968-73, Wilson Jones Architects Inc., Clayton, Mo., 1973-86; pres. Wilson Architects, Inc., Clayton, Mo., 1986—. Mem. AIA, Soc. for Mktg. Profl. Services. Republican. Presbyterian. Avocations: hunting, fishing, sailing. Home: 111 N Ballas Saint Louis MO 63122 Office: Wilson Architects Inc 8025 Forsyth Clayton MO 63105

WILSON, DOUGLAS FREDERICK, professional hockey player; b. Ottawa, Ont., Can., July 5, 1957; s. Douglas and Verna Wilson; m. Katherine Ann Kivisto, July 11, 1981; children—Lacey Anne. Defenseman Chgo. Black Hawks Hockey Team, 1985—; account exec. Coca-Cola, Chgo. Recipient James Norris Meml. Trophy for best NHL defenseman, 1981-82. Avocations: golf; travel. Office: Chicago Black Hawks 1800 Madison St Chicago IL 60612

WILSON, EDWARD CHURCHILL, lawyer; b. Chgo., Oct. 15, 1940; s. Max Elroy and Margaret (Tufts) W.; m. Patricia Daley, Sept. 2, 1961; children—Edward Wallace, David Maxwell. B.S. with honors, Lewis U., 1974, J.D., 1978. Bars: Ill. 1978, U.S. Dist. Ct. (no. dist.) Ill. 1978, U.S. Ct. Appeals (7th cir.) 1978, U.S. Supreme Ct. 1982. Assoc. Conklin and Adler, Chgo., 1978-81; sole practice, LaGrange, Ill., 1981—; pres. Edward C. Wilson & Assocs., Aviation Accident Investigators. Named mem. Barional Order of Magna Charta, 1970. Mem. Chgo. Bar Assn., Ill. State Bar Assn., ABA, Lawyer/Pilots Bar Assn., Internat. Soc. Air Safety Investigators, Aircraft Owners and Pilots Assn. (legis. liaison com. 1980—). Home: 724 N LaGrange Rd LaGrange Park IL 60525 Office: 521 S LaGrange Rd LaGrange IL 60525

WILSON, HARRY HOWARD, JR., educational products company executive; b. Blue Island, Ill., Dec. 30, 1926; s. Harry H. and Kathryn Anne (Nicola) W.; m. Doris Ann Flanary, July 6, 1948; children: Kimberly, Kyle Ann, Kacy. BS, Western Ill. U., 1950. With Container Corp. Am., Chgo., 1950-52; sales mgr. audio-visual and photog. products Radiant Mfg. Corp., Chgo., 1952-59; pres. H. Wilson Corp., South Holland, Ill., 1959—, Wilcom, Inc., South Holland, 1977—; bd. dirs. James Metal Products, Chgo. Patentee in field. Served with U.S. Army, 1946-47. Mem. Dept. Audio-Visual Instrn., Nat. Audio-Visual Assn. (bd. dirs. 1966, chmn. S/S/mgmt. inst.), Nat. Sch. Supply Assn. (bd. dirs. 1966-68, exec. com. 1967-68), Am. Soc. Curriculum Dirs., Kappa Delta Pi, Sigma Tau Gamma. Club: Chicago Heights (Ill.) Country. Home: 23001 Shagbark Ln Chicago Heights IL 60411 Office: 513 Taft St South Holland IL 60473

WILSON, JAMES ABBOTT, architect; b. Livonia, Mich., Jan. 31, 1961; s. Abbott Eldridge and Sarah Luella (Kratochvil) W. BArch, U. Minn., 1984. Project architect Smiley Glotter Assocs., Mpls., 1983—. Mem. AIA (assoc.), Minn. Soc. AIA (assoc.). Roman Catholic. Avocations: skiing (Nat. Ski Patrol), soccer, travel. Home: 2529 29th Ave S Minneapolis MN 55406 Office: Smiley Glotter Assoc 1021 LaSalle Ave Minneapolis MN 55403

WILSON, JAMES EDWARD, judge, barrister; b. Winnipeg, Man., Can., May 29, 1914; s. James and Catherine (Price) W.; m. Florence Margaret Sadler, Jan. 5, 1940; children: Wendy, Peter, Jennifer. BA, Man. U., 1936, LLB, 1946, LLD, 1987. Sole practice Winnipeg, 1946-65; judge Ct. of Queen's Bench Province of Man., Winnipeg, 1965—. Sec. Man. Med. Sci. Found.; v.p. Def. Found.; mem. Can. Pension Appeals Bd., 1987—; pres. Man. Paraplegia Found.; hon. council Misericordia Gen. Hosp.; chmn. Westminster Found., Man. div. Can. Corpsof Commrs.; sec. bd. trustees Westminster Ch. Served to lt. col. Can. Army. Decorated Can. Forces decoration, Order of British Empire. Mem. Can. Bar Assn., Man. Bar Assn., Can. Judge's Council, Can. Assn. Adminstrn. of Justice. Home: 91 Westgate, Winnipeg, MB Canada R3C 2C9 Office: Ct of Queen's Bench, Law Cts Bldg, 408 York Ave, Winnipeg, MB Canada R3C 0V8

WILSON, JAMES GRIFFIN, data processing executive; b. Victoria, Tex., Dec. 6, 1944; s; Herbert William and Laura Christine (Griffin) W.; m. Sharon Ann Heen, June 29, 1968; children: Keith, Beth, Ryan, Sara. BS in Math. and Phys. Edn., Minot State Coll., 1967. Computer programmer Gen. Telephone and Electronics Corp., Madison, Wis., 1969-70; programmer, analyst Morrison-Knudson, Langdon, N.D., 1970-73; data processing mgr. No. Nat. Life Ins., Bismarck, N.D., 1973-76; programming supr. Basin Electric Power Coop., Bismarck, 1976-78, asst. chief computer services, 1978-85, mgr. system devel., 1985—; mem. computer sci. adv. bd. U. of Mary Coll., 1982—, instr. mgmt., 1982-83; mgmt. info. system adv. bd. CAPCARE, Bismarck, 1981. Contbg. editor infosystems articles to mags. and profl. jours. Pres. sch. bd. St. Annes Sch., Bismarck, 1980-82; sec. treas. St. Mary's Pride Parents, Bismarck, 1985—; mem. parish council, St. Annes Cath. Ch., Bismarck, 1979; team couple Western Dakota Marriage Encounter, Bismarck, 1975-77. Mem. Stradis Users Group Liasion (pres. 1984-85, v.p. 1983-84). Avocations: hunting, racquetball, softball, woodworking, building and restoring furniture. Home: 1401 Crestview Ln Bismarck ND 58501 Office: Basin Electric Power Coop 1717 E Interstate Ave Bismarck ND 58501

WILSON, JANET LOUISE DOHERTY, social worker; b. Wichita, Kans., Jan. 14, 1951; d. Charles Henry and Alma Lucille (Schwarm) Doherty; m. Thomas Colin Wilson II, June 23, 1979; 1 child, Colin Charles. BA in Social Work, Washburn U., 1974; MSW, U. Kans., 1980. Lic. mental health technician Kans. Neurol. Inst., Topeka, 1969-75, activity therapy aide, 1975-76, qualified mental retardation profl., 1985-87; social worker Kans. Dept. Social and Rehab. Services, Topeka, 1976-85; clin. social worker Topeka State Hosp., 1987—; spl. trainer Foster Parents of Shawnee County, Topeka, 1985—. Mem. Washburn Alumni Assn. Democrat. Avocations: sewing, cooking, needlework. Home: 333 Courtland Topeka KS 66606 Office: Topeka State Hosp 2700 W 6th St Topeka KS 66606

WILSON, JAY SCOTT, cultural organization administrator; b. Waterloo, Iowa, Sept. 30, 1951; s. Walton William and Rebecca (Corine) W. BFA, Kans. City Art Inst., 1976. Mgr. Bijou Westport Theatre, Kansas City, Mo., 1977-80; studio mgr., producer sta. KCPT-TV, Kansas City, 1981-86; dir. Parks and Recreation, Kansas City, 1986—; lighting designer and stage mgr. Actor's Ensemble, Kansas City, 1983—; video cons. Mo. Repertory Theatre, Kansas City, 1985—; asst. dir. Dix & Assocs., Kansas City, 1986. 1st Place Pub. Service Comml. N.Y. Film Festival, 1975. Mem. Equity (stagemanager). Democrat. Avocations: still photography, reading. Home: 3734 Gillham Rd Kansas City MO 64111 Office: Parks and Recreation 5605 E 63d Kansas City MO 64105

WILSON, JOANNA BOHN, lawyer; b. Ft. Dodge, Iowa, July 30, 1954; d. Francis and Marlene June (White) Bohn; m. Edward Miller Wilson, Aug. 21, 1976; children: Joanna Lynn, Emily Katherine. BA, U. No. Iowa, 1976; JD, U. Iowa, 1981. Bar: Iowa 1980, U.S. Dist. Ct. (no. dist.) Iowa 1983. Asst. county atty. Clinton County, Iowa, 1982; assoc. Wilson Law Office, Manson, Iowa, 1983-87. Pres. Manson chpt. Am. Field Service, 1983-85. Mem. Iowa Bar Assn., Calhoun County Bar Assn., Iowa Dist. 2B Bar Assn. Republican. Mennonite. Home: 1636 11th St Manson IA 50563 Office: 1110 10th Ave Manson IA 50563-0632

WILSON, JOHN GEORGE, manufacturing company executive; b. Toronto, Ont., Can., July 21, 1925; s. Thomas Gibson and Edith (Freshwater) W.; m. Vivian Caroline Harrison, May 24, 1946 (dec.); children—Randy, David, Judy; m. Audrey Doreen Warner, Oct. 25, 1957; 1 dau., Shari Lee. Tool and die maker Pedlar People Ltd., Oshawa, Ont., 1947-53; owner, pres. John G. Wilson Machine Ltd., Cathcart, Ont., 1953—; mfg. cons.; chmn. Brantford Indsl. Tng. Adv. com. Served with Can. Army, 1944-45. Mem. Soc. Mfg. Engrs., Brantford Regional C. of C.

WILSON, JONATHAN CARL, lawyer; b. Montezuma, Iowa, Feb. 4, 1945; s. Carl Edwin and Miriam Josephine (Erhardt) W.; m. Joanne King, July 15, 1967; children: Matthew Carl, Elizabeth Ann. BA cum laude, Morningside Coll., 1967; JD with distinction, U. Iowa, 1971. Clk. to judge U.S. Ct. Appeals (8th cir.), 1971-72; lectr. Australian Nat. U., Canberra, 1972-74; instr. Drake U., Des Moines, 1974; sr. ptnr. Davis, Hockenberg, Wine, Brown, Koehn & Shors, Des Moines, 1974—. bd. dirs. Des Moines Independent Community Sch. Dist.; chmn. bd. govs. Greater Des Moines Leadership Inst., Council Urban Bds. Edn. Served with U.S. Army, 1968-69. Mem. ABA, Iowa Bar Assn., Polk County Bar Assn., Des Moines C. of C. (bd. dirs.), Order of the Coif. Democrat. United Methodist. Home: 2924 Druid Hill Dr Des Moines IA 50315 Office: Davis Hockenberg 2300 Financial Ctr Des Moines IA 50309

WILSON, KARLA RAE, accountant; b. Minot, N.D., May 7, 1960; d. Doran Kay and Juanita Joyce (Olson) Hanson; m. Steven Richard Wilson, Oct. 15, 1983. BSBA in Acctg., U. N.D., 1982. CPA, N.D. Acct. Brady, Martz & Assocs., P.C., Minot, 1982-85, 1986—; acct. Curtis Brekke & Co., Devils Lake, N.D., 1985-86. Mem. Am. Inst. CPA's, N.D. State Soc. CPA's (report rev. com.), Minot Chpt. CPA's. Lutheran. Club: Zonta. Home: 719 28th Ave SW Minot ND 58701 Office: Brady Martz & Assocs PC 24 W Central Minot ND 58701

WILSON, KENT SHANNON, surgery educator; b. Bemidji, Minn., Sept. 11, 1941; s. Kenneth Eugene and Ruth (Shannon) W.; m. Ann burtis Mears, Apr. 30, 1966; children: Christopher, ann. BS, U. Minn., 1964, MD, 1966, MA in Otolaryngology, 1974. Lic. surgeon Minn., Wis.; diplamate Am. Bd. Otolaryngology. Intern Denver Gen. Hosp., 1966-67; research fellow U. Minn., Mpls., 1969-70, med. fellow Dept. Otolaryngology, 1970-74, clin. asst. prof. otolaryngology, 1974—; mem. staff St. Joseph's Hosp., St. Paul; mem. staff Children's Hosp., St. Paul, chief surgery, 1983-87, chief staff, 1987—; mem. courtesy staff St. John's Hosp., St. Paul, Midway Hosp., St. Paul, United Hosp., St. Paul, Divine Redeemer Hosp., St. Paul, Samaritan Hosp., St. Paul, Lakeview Meml. Hosp., Stillwater, Minn., River Falls (Wis.) Area Hosp.; course dir. U. Minn. Dept. Otolaryngology, Am. Acad. Facil Plastic and Reconstructive Surgery, 1980, 84; mem. search com. U. Minn. Dept. Otolaryngology, 1984-85; dir. labs. Internat. Symposium Maxillofacial Trauma, Am. Acad. Facial Plastic and Reconstructive Surgery, Wayne State U. Sch. Medicine. Assoc. editor Jour. History of Medicine and Allied Scis., 1975-80; contbr. articles to profl. jours. Deacon House of Hope Presbyn. Ch., 1976-79, elder, 1982-85. Fellow ACS, Am. Acad. Facial Plastic and Reconstructive Surgery; mem. Minn. Acad. Otolaryngology (sec./treas. 1982-87, mem. council 1976-79, Honor award Head and Neck Surgery 1982), Minn. Med. Assn. (1st Pl. Honor award 1977), Ramsey County Med. Soc., James Moore Surg. Soc. Office: 393 N Dunlap 6A Cen Med Bldg Saint Paul MN 55104

WILSON, LARRY TERRIL, landscape architect, campus planner; b. Chanute, Kans., July 29, 1938; s. Lawrence Sevier and Dorothy Letha (Terril) W.; m. Nancy Jean Oyler, Apr. 17, 1962 (div. July 1974); children: Tracy Ann, Michael Barret. AA, Chanute Jr. Coll., 1958; BArch in Landscape Design, Kans. State U., 1962. Registered landscape architect, Ky., Mo. Landscape architect Miller, Winry & Brooks, Louisville, 1963-65, The Lantz Co., Louisville, 1965-66; city planner Louisville and Jefferson County Planning Commn., Ky., 1966-69, urban designer, 1974-78; landscape architect, assoc. Miller, Wihry & Lee, Inc., Louisville, 1969-74; dir. landscape and campus planning Kans. State U., Manhattan, 1978-85; landscape architect and campus planner U. Mo., Columbia, 1985-87, mgr. project architecture, 1987—; part-time pvt. practice landscape architect, Columbia, 1963—. Mem. Columbia Bicycle Commn., 1985—. Mem. Am. Soc. Landscape Architects (chmn. design awards com. St. Louis chpt. 1979-83), Gamma Sigma Delta. Democrat. Methodist. Clubs: Great Plains Balloon (Topeka), Columbia Ski. Avocations: running, sailing, volleyball, hot air ballooning, music. Home: 3001 S Providence Rd Apt 11C Columbia MO 65203 Office: Univ Mo Campus Facilities Gen Services Bldg Columbia MO 65211

WILSON, LAUREN ROSS, univ. dean; b. Yates Center, Kans., May 4, 1936; s. Roscoe C. and Margaret D. W.; m. Janie Haskin, Jan. 25, 1959; children—Lance Kevin, Keela Lynn. B.S., Baker U., Baldwin, Kans., 1958; Ph.D., U. Kans., 1963. Mem. faculty Ohio Wesleyan U., Delaware, 1963—; prof. chemistry Ohio Wesleyan U., 1971-86, Homer Lucas prof. of chemistry, dean acad. affairs, 1978-86, acting provost, 1985-86; vice chancellor for acad. affaris U. N.C., Asheville, 1987—; vis. prof. Ohio State U., asst.to the pres. 1968, 74; vis; research asso. Oak Ridge Nat. Lab., 1972-73. Recipient Outstanding Tchr. award Ohio Wesleyan U., 1968. Mem. Am. Chem. Soc., AAAS, AAUP, Chem. Soc. London, Ohio Acad. Sci., Sigma Xi. Office: Ohio Wesleyan Univ S Sandusky St Delaware OH 43015

WILSON, LESLIE JEAN, educator; b. Bedford, Ind., June 26, 1943; d. Don Bernell and Rose E. (Bridwell) Armstrong; m. M. Duane Wilson, June 17, 1965 (dec. Aug. 1986); children: Douglas Troy, Marisa Lynn. BS, Ind. U., 1965, MS, 1971; EdS, Ind.-Purdue U., Indpls., 1984. Cert. tchr. and prin., Ind. Elem. tchr. Fontana, Calif., 1965-67, Churubusco, Ind., 1967-69; dir. presch., Goshen, Ind., 1977-87; prin. Pittsboro Elem. Sch. (Ind.), 1980—; dir. summer library. Co-author: Energy Play, 1982, operettas for local schs. Mem. Internat. Reading Assn., Mortar Bd., Enomone, Pleiades, Phi Delta Kappa, Delta Kappa Gamma, Alpha Delta Kappa. Republican. Mem. Christian Ch. (Disciples of Christ). Office: Pittsboro Elem Sch North Meridian Pittsboro IN 46167

WILSON, LORENA ELIZABETH, advertising executive; b. Kansas City, Mo., Aug. 27, 1961; d. W. Kenneth Hirst and Linda L. (Kropf) Brooks; m. Roy Gregory Wilson, Mar. 7, 1987. BA in English, Mo. Western State Coll., 1983. Jr. copywriter Fletcher, Mayo Assocs., St. Joseph, Mo., 1983-84; asst. account exec. Everett, Brandt & Bernauer, Inc., Kansas City, 1984—; free lance copywriter Dave's Roe Body Shop, Lee's Summit, Mo., 1986—, Wicklund's Collision Repair Ctr., Liberty, Mo., 1986—. Editor Contemporary Christian Scene mag., 1985. Publicist music group, Kansas City, 1986—. Named one of Outstanding Young Women Am., 1984-86. Mem. Nat. Assn. Female Execs., Kansas City Media Fellowship (hostess), Sigma Tau Delta. Reorganized Ch. Jesus Christ of Latter Day Saints.

WILSON, MARC F., art museum administrator and curator. Dir., curator Oriental art Nelson-Atkins Mus. Art, Kansas City, Mo. Office: Nelson-Atkins Museum Art 4525 Oak St Kansas City MO 64111 *

WILSON, MICHAEL B(RUCE), lawyer; b. Boise, Idaho, Aug. 5, 1943; s. George E. and Helen E. (Hughes) W.; m. Sarah J. Copeland, June 18, 1966; children: David B., Janet L. BS in Math., Oreg. State U., 1965, MS in Gen. Sci., 1966; JD, Northwestern U., 1978. Bar: Oreg. 1978, U.S. Ct. Mil. Appeals 1978. Commd. 2d lt. USAF, 1966, advanced through grades to maj., 1978, served in Vietnam, 1968; chief of logistics 3d Weather Wing, Offut AFB, Nebr., 1969-71; chief maintenance 2d Weather Wing, Wiesbaden AFB, Fed. Republic Germany, 1971-75; chief civil law HQ Chanute TTC, Chanute AFB, Ill., 1978-80; chief civil and mil. affairs HQ 17th Air Force, Sembach AFB, Fed. Republic Germany, 1980-83; dir. communications and computer systems law Air Force Communications Command, Scott AFB, Ill., 1983—; chmn. Joint Services Telephone Working Group, 1983—, Air Force Comml. Communications Working Group, Scott AFB, 1985—, AFCC Comml. Communications Working Group, Scott AFB, 1985—, DOD Comml. Telecommunications Com. Liason Officer Boy Scouts Am., Sembach AFB, 1981-83. Recipient Mgmt./Adminstrv. Excellence award Interagy. Com. on Info. Resources Mgmt., 1987. Mem. ABA, Fed. Communications Bar Assn., Armed Forces Communications Electronics Assn. Home: 808 W Lakeshore Dr OFallon IL 62269 Office: HQ AFCC/JAS Scott AFB IL 62225

WILSON, MICHAEL DUANE, management educator; b. Olney, Ill., Feb. 2, 1959; s. Duane Edward and Alberta (Cole) W.; m. Nancy Ann Smith, Aug. 9, 1986. AS, Olney Community Coll., 1979; BS in Bus., Eastern Ill. U., 1981, MBA, 1982. Mgmt. educator Eastern Ill. U., Charleston, 1983—; co-owner Coles County Offfice Products, Charleston. Named one of Outstanding Young Men in Am., 1985. Mem. Soc. for Advancement of Mgmt., Ill. Jaycees (outstanding local sec. 1985), Charleston Jaycees (sec. 1984-85, treas. 1985-86). Methodist. Home: Rural Rt 4 Box 83A Charleston IL 61920 Office: Eastern Ill U Dept Mgmt Charleston IL 61920

WILSON, MICHAEL PAGE, financial analyst; b. Kirksville, Mo., Dec. 9, 1955; s. Patrick Hanley and Adena Carolyn (Page) W.; m. Pamela Suzanne Borgmeyer, June 16, 1984; 1 child, Jeffrey Michael. BS in Acctg. and Bus. Adminstrn., Northeast Mo. State U., 1978. CPA, Mo. Audit asst. Mo. State U., Jefferson City, 1978-80, semi-sr. auditor, 1981-82, sr. auditor, 1983-86; supr. sch. fin. Mo. Dept. Elem. Secondary Edn., Jefferson City, 1986—. Mem. Am. Inst. CPA's, Mo. Soc. CPA's, Assn. Govtl. Accts. Lodges: Lions (Jefferson City Tail Twister 1986-87, chmn. ham and bean dinner 1987), Elks. Avocations: fishing, prof. and coll. sports, gardening. Home: 1611 Payne Dr Jefferson City MO 65101 Office: Dept Elem & Secondary Edn PO Box 480 Jefferson City MO 65102

WILSON, MICHELE LOUISE, lawyer; b. Newport Beach, Calif., Aug. 19, 1959; d. Jerry Wayne and Colleen Roberta (Hulland) W. BS, Sch. of the Ozarks, 1981; JD, U. Mo., 1984. Bar: Mo. 1984, U.S. Dist. Ct. (we. dist. 1986) Mo., 1986. Assoc. Bussell, Hough, O'Neal, Crouch & Hall, Springfield, Mo., 1984-86; sole practice Branson, Mo., 1986—. Mem. ABA, Greene County Bar Assn., Taney County Bar Assn. Home: Rt 1 Box 100 Nixa MO 65714 Office: 104 E Main Branson MO 65616

WILSON, MURRAY P., chemical company executive. Chmn. Thompson Hayward Chem. Co., Kansas City, Kans. Office: Thompson Hayward Chem Co 5200 Speaker Rd Kansas City KS 66108 *

WILSON, MYRON FRANK, electronics company executive; b. Cleve., Oct. 18, 1924; s. Maransus Frank and Nettie Mae (Bean) W.; m. Esther June Secor, Aug. 5, 1950; children—M. Frank, Eric L., Joyce A., Rebecca J. B.S. in Mech. Engring., Case Inst. Tech., 1947, B.S.E.E., 1951, B.S. in Engring. Adminstrn., 1951. Registered profl. engr., Iowa, Ohio; cert. mfg. engr., quality engr. Various prodn. and engring. positions Collins Radio Co., Cedar Rapids, Iowa, 1951-73, v.p. mfg., 1973-75; dir. quality assurance Rockwell Internat., Dallas, 1975-77, dir. product assurance, Cedar Rapids, 1977-81, dir. group ops. Avionics Group, 1981—. Served with USN, 1944-46. Fellow Am. Soc. Quality Control (chmn. electronics div. 1983-85 , bd. dirs. 1970-72); mem. Inst. Indsl. Engrs. (v.p. region 11 1983-85, exec. v.p. chpt. ops. 1985-87, trustee 1983-87, sr. mem.), IEEE (sr. mem.). Congregationalist. Club: Collins Mgmt. (pres. 1984-85). Lodge: Kiwanis (bd. dirs. 1983-85). Home: 4221 Trailridge Rd SE Cedar Rapids IA 52403 Office: Rockwell Internat Avionics Group 400 Collins Rd NE Cedar Rapids IA 52498

WILSON, RICHARD DARREL, manufacturing executive; b. Ft. Wayne, May 12, 1924; s. Darrel Frederick and Lillian Erica (Gustafson) W.; m. Jill Pritchard, Oct. 23, 1948; children: Stuart, Jennifer, Scott, Kristin. BSAE, Purdue U. Sales engr. Johnson Controls, Indpls., 1948-50; sales engr. Johnson Controls, Cleve., 1950-57, br. mgr., 1957-61, regional mgr., 1961-67, v.p. sales, 1967-79; v.p., gen. mgr. Johnson Controls, Milw., 1979-84, v.p. controls group, 1984—. Bd. dirs. Goodwill Industries, Milw., Am. Cancer Soc., Milw. Served as ensign USNR, 1943-46. Mem. ASHRAE (pres. Cleve. chpt. 1960-61). Republican. Congregationalist. Club: Town (Milw.) (bd. dirs.). Lodges: Masons, Shriners. Avocations: tennis, golf, skiing, fishing. Home: 801 E Ravine Ln Bayside WI 53217 Office: Johnson Controls Inc 1701 W Civic Dr Glendale WI 53209

WILSON, RICHARD EVERETT, biology educator; b. N.Y.C., Dec. 28, 1939; s. Harold Lynn and Alma Louisa (Schmidt) W.; m. Faith Louise Pountney, Jan. 28, 1967; children: Richard E. Jr., Geoffrey H., Robyn L., Brittan A. Asst. to assoc. prof. biology Rockhurst Coll., Kansas City, Mo., 1971-86, prof., 1986—, chmn. div. sci., 1973—, asst. dean, 1976-78. Served with U.S. Army, 1959-62. Mem. AAAS, Assn. Midwest Colls. Biology Tchrs. (sec. 1982—). Roman Catholic. Office: Rockhurst Coll Biology Dept 5225 Troost Ave Kansas City KS 64110

WILSON, ROBERT ALLEN, religious educator; b. Geff, Ill., Oct. 7, 1936; s. Perry Arthur and Eva Mae (Dye) W.; m. Patsy Ann Jarrett, June 1, 1957; children: Elizabeth Ann, Angela Dawn, Christine Joy. AB, Lincoln (Ill.) Christian Coll., 1958, Hanover Coll., 1961; MRE, So. Bapt. Seminary, 1965, D. in Edn., 1972. Ordained to ministry Ch. Christ, 1958. Minister Fowler (Ind.) Christian Ch., 1955-59, Zoah Christian Ch., Scottsburg, Ind., 1959-64; minister of edn. and youth Shively Christian Ch., Louisville, 1964-69; prof. Christian edn. and family life Lincoln (Ill.) Christian Seminary, 1969—; pres. Christian Marriage and Family Enrichment Services, Lincoln, 1980—. Contbr. articles to profl. jours. Mem. Nat. Assn. Profs. Christian Edn. (editor newsletter 1975-79, pres. 1979-80). Lodge: Rotary. Home: 330 Campus View Dr Lincoln IL 62656 Office: Lincoln Christian Coll and Seminary 100 Campus View Dr Box 178 Lincoln IL 62656

WILSON, ROBERT FOSTER, lawyer; b. Windsor, Colo., Apr. 6, 1926; s. Foster W. and Anne Lucille (Svedman) W.; m. Mary Elizabeth Clark, Mar. 4, 1951 (div. Feb. 1972); children—Robert F., Katharine A.; m. Sally Anne Nemec, June 8, 1982. B.A. in Econs., U. Iowa, 1950, J.D., 1951. Bar: Iowa 1951, U.S. Dist. Ct. (no. and so. dists.) Iowa 1956, U.S. Ct. Appeals (8th cir.) 1967. Atty., FTC, Chgo., 1951-55; sole practice, Cedar Rapids, Iowa, 1955—; dir. Appollo Computer Tech., Veterans Pub. Safety. Democratic state rep. Iowa Legislature, Linn County, 1959-60; mem. Iowa Reapportionment Com., 1968; pres. Linn County Day Care, Cedar Rapids, 1968-70. Served to sgt. U.S. Army, 1944-46. Mem. Am. Legion (judge advocate 1970-75), Iowa Trial Lawyers Assn., Assn. Trial Lawyers Am., Iowa Bar Assn., Linn County Bar Assn., Delta Theta Phi. Club: Cedar View Country. Lodges: Elks, Eagles. Home: 100-1st Ave NE Cedar Rapids IA 52401 Office: 810 Dows Bldg Cedar Rapids IA 52401

WILSON, ROBERT M., accountant, lawyer; b. St. Louis, Aug. 10, 1952; s. William H. and Mary E. (Sacksteder) W.; m. Joli Schneeberger, Oct. 7, 1978. B.S., Miami U. Oxford, Ohio, 1974; J.D. magna cum laude, Cleve. State U., 1977. Bar: Ohio 1977; C.P.A., Ohio. With Touche Ross & Co., Dayton, Ohio, 1972—, tax ptnr., 1983—; sec., treas. Inst. for Study of Corp. Responsibility. Past pres. Friends of Dayton Ballet Inc.; treas. Dayton Ballet Assn.; treas. Downtown Dayton Assn., Leadership Dayton; Montgomery County Rep. Party. Mem. ABA (chmn. com.), Ohio Bar Assn., Dayton Bar Assn., Ohio Soc. CPA's (past pres.). Republican. Clubs: Dayton Racquet, Dayton Country. Home: 6 Lookout Dr Dayton OH 45409 Office: Touche Ross & Co 1700 Courthouse Plaza NE Dayton OH 45402

WILSON, ROGER DEAN, insurance executive; b. Des Moines, May 26, 1956; s. Robert Eugene and Maxine Patricia (Paulsen) W.; m. Mary Kay Caparelli, June 15, 1985. BA, Knox Coll., 1978. Systems programmer Job Service of Iowa, Des Moines, 1978-82; sr. tech. support analyst Hawkeye Bank Corp. Computer Services, Inc., Des Moines, 1982-86; sr. tech. software specialist Fin. Info. Trust, Des Moines, 1986-87; first v.p., tech. services Integrated Resources Life Ins. Co., Des Moines, 1987—. Democrat. Avocations: volleyball, softball, jogging. Home: 1200 21 St West Des Moines IA 50265 Office: Integrated Resources Life Ins 3737 Westown Pkwy West Des Moines IA 50265

WILSON, RUBY LEE, nurse; b. Chgo., Sept. 3, 1935; d. Henry Lee Jernigan and Ruby Nettie Frances (Willborn) Chavis; m. Franklin Tyson (div.); children: Franklin Delanor, Anthony DeWayne, Derek Alan; m. Alonzo Wilson, July 31, 1959. AA, Amundsen-Mayfair, Chgo., 1967; BS, Coll. of St. Francis, Joliet, Ill., 1976; MEd, U. Ill., 1980. Registered psychiat. and mental health nurse. Lic. practical nurse Rush Presbyn.-St. Luke's Hosp. Med. Ctr., Chgo., 1962-65, staff nurse, 1969-70, head nurse, 1970-81, program coordinator, 1981—; health coordinator Project Upgrade, Chgo., 1967-69; mem. adv. bd. Issac Ray Ctr. Rush U., Chgo., 1986—, bd. dirs., 1987; dir. nursing bd. St. Stephen A.M.E. Ch., 1986—; presenter numerous workshops psychiatry, forensic and stress issues. Recipient Merit cert. Chgo. Merit Employment of Assn. of Commerce and Industry and Vice-Presdl. Task Force on Youth Motivation, 1967-68, Cert. of Appreciation George Williams Coll., plaque for Outstanding Performance Amundsen Nursing Class. Mem. Am. Nursing Assn. (cert.), Ill. Nursing Assn. (first chairperson commn. on human rights), Peer Assistance Network For Nurses, Nat. Black Nurses Assn., Chgo. Black Nurses Assn. Orthopsychiatric Assn., Am. Assn. Suicidology, Ill. Assn. Suicidology, Lambda Pi Alpha (pres. bd. dirs. 1982—, Was Basileus 1979-81, Outstanding Contbr. plaque 1986). African Methodist Episcopalian. Avocation: church choir singing. Home: 2319 W 80th Pl Chicago IL 60620 Office: Issac Ray Ctr Rush Presbyn-St Luke's Med Ctr 1720 W Polk St Chicago IL 60612

WILSON, SANDRA JEANNE, social worker; b. Jackson, Mich., Apr. 1, 1950; d. Woodrow Vernon and Cecile May (Wright) W. AA, U. Cin., 1970, BA, 1972; MSW, Ohio State U., 1980. Lic. social worker, Mich., Ohio, Ky. Social worker Hamilton Co. Welfare, Cin., 1973-78; med. social worker Vis. Nurse Assn., Cin., 1980-83; social work Mgr. United Home Care, Cin., 1984-85; client services mgr. Community Action Agy., Cin., 1985-86; social work supr. Mich. Cancer Found., Detroit, 1986—. Com. chmn. Alzheimer's Disease Assn., Cin., 1984-85; sec. Social Workers' Oncology Group, Cin., 1984; vol. disaster services ARC, Cin., 1985. Mem. Acad. Cert. Social Workers, Nat. Assn. Social Workers, Social Workers in Home Health Care, Inc. (program chmn.), Nat. Assn. Oncology Social Workers, Mich. Assn. Onology Social Workers, Children's Leukemia Found. Mich. Methodist.

WILSON, THEODORE HALBERT, III, child care facility director; b. Balt., July 31, 1946; s. Theodore Halbert and Carolyn Sewell (Bell) W.; m. Margaret Lynn Cooper, July 12, 1969; 1 child, Colby Franklyn. AB, Yale U., 1968; MEd, U. Md., 1973, PhD, 1979. Crisis counselor Christ Child Inst., Rockville, Md., 1973-75, childcare dir., 1975-77; activities coordinator Bapt. Home for Children, Bethesda, Md., 1977-78, coordinator spl. services, 1978-79, dir. resources, 1979-80; exec. dir. VFW Nat. Home, Eaton Rapids, Mich., 1980—. Pres. Eaton Rapids Bd. Edn., 1983—; chmn. Alliance for Community Devel., Eaton Rapids, 1986. Served to lt. (j.g.) USNR, 1969-71. Fellow Am. Orthopsychiat. Assn. Democrat. Methodist. Lodge: Kiwanis. Avocation: coaching soccer. Home and Office: VFW Nat Home 3573 Waverly Rd Eaton Rapids MI 48827

WILSON, THOMAS EDWARD, environmental engineer; b. Chgo., Feb. 20, 1942; s. David and Annabelle Pauline (Thompson) W.; m. Cheryl Ann Wegener, June 11, 1966; children—Christopher, Scott. B.S. in Chem. Engring., Northwestern U., 1964, M.S. in Environ. Engring., 1967; Ph.D., Ill. Inst. Tech., 1969. Registered profl. engr., Ill., Ind. diplomate Am. Acad. Environ. Engring. Asst. prof. Rutgers U., New Brunswick, N.J., 1967-70; prin. process engr. Greeley and Hansen, Chgo., 1970—, assoc., 1976—. Contbr. articles to profl. jours. Mem. Water Pollution Control Fedn., Am. Water Works Assn., Internat. Assn. for Water Pollution Research, Am. Inst. Chem. Engrs., ASCE. Episcopalian. Home: 1527 E Fleming Dr S Arlington Heights IL 60004 Office: Greeley and Hansen 222 S Riverside Plaza Chicago IL 60606

WILSON, THOMAS MILTON, osteopathic surgeon, educator; b. Hinsdale, Ill., Aug. 17, 1937; s. Thomas Homer and Opal Onita (Schelegel) W.; m. Marlene Ann Moyer, Sept. 8, 1957: children: Tracy Jo, Tammy Sue. Student, Emmanuel Missionary Coll., 1955-56, 58-61; DO, Kansas City (Mo.) Coll. Osteo. Medicine, 1965. Intern Flint (Mich.) Osteo. Hosp., 1965-66, resident in gen. surgery, 1966-69; fellow Jervis St. Hosp., Dublin, Ireland, 1969-70; practice medicine specializing in gen. and urol. surgery Kirksville, Mo., 1982—; chmn. dept. surgery Lapeer County (Mich.) Gen. Hosp., 1973-77, Ormond Beach and Daytona Beach (Fla.) Osteo. Hosp., 1980; sect. chief gen. and urol. surgery, Kirksville Coll. Osteo. Medicine, 1982—, assoc. prof. gen. surgery, 1982—. Contbr. articles to profl. jours. Treas. Seventh-Day Adventists Profl. Club, Kansas City, 1963, pres. 1964-65. Served with U.S. Army, 1956-58. Fellow Am. Coll. Osteo. Surgeons; mem. Am. Osteo. Assn. (research grant 1983). Lodge: Rotary. Avocations: fishing, tennis, racquetball, raising beef cattle. Home: Rt 2 Millan Rd Kirksville MO 63501 Office: Kirksville Coll Osteo Medicine 700 W Jefferson Kirksville MO 63501

WILSON, THOMAS WILFORD CARMAN, marketing and management executive; b. Montgomery, Ala., Sept. 20, 1939; s. Thomas Edward and Lucy Pace (Chambless) W.; m. Judith Ann Hadrath, June 17, 1961; children: Thomas Reuben, Tamalyn Lee, Todd Edward. BS, USAF Acad., 1961; MBA, U. So. Calif., 1971. Commd. 2d lt. USAF, 1961, advanced through grades to lt. col., pilot, 1961-81, ret. Col., 1981; dir. store devel. CUB Foods Inc., Stillwater, Minn., 1981-85; pres. T. Wilson Enterprises, Stillwater, 1985—; dir. mktg. George W. Olsen Constrn., Stillwater, 1985-87; bus. devel. mgr. Roanoke Bldg. Co., Mpls., 1987—; cons. mktg. Pro-Mist Co., Woodbury, Minn., 1986—. Bd. dirs. Stillwater Area Baseball Boosters Inc., 1985—, pres., 1987—, St. Croix Valley Athletic Assn., Stillwater, 1986-87; bd. dirs. America's Best Athletes, Inc., 1987—. Mem. Sales and Mktg. Execs. Assn., Order Daedalions. Republican. Roman Catholic. Lodge: Lions. Home: 1010 Nightingale Blvd Stillwater MN 55082

WILSON, WALTER LEROY, architect; b. Pitts., Aug. 2, 1942; s. Walter Clarence and Marie Zella (Wilcox) W.; m. Maxine Davis, June 4, 1968 (div. 1970); m. Lois Mary McCollum, Mar. 24, 1984. Student, Altus (Okla.) Jr. Coll., 1961, Cen. State U., 1964-67; BArch, B Archtl. Engring., Okla. State U., 1971. Registered architect, Ohio, Tex., Ark., Wis. Architect, intern Trott & Bean Assocs., Columbus, Ohio, 1971-73; mgr. architecture Southwestern Bell, Little Rock, Houston and St. Louis, 1973-80; prin., ptrn. Caradine & Wilson Assocs., North Little Rock, Ark., 1980-82; office mgr., div. mgr. Polytech Inc., Milw., 1982-85; prin., owner The Wilson Firm, Milw., 1985—; bd. dirs. Milw. Area Tech. Ctr. Archtl. Program. Mem. Coalition for Econ. Devel. and Justice, Milw., 1986, State Capitol and Exec. Res. Bd., State of Wis., 1986; del. state Dem. conv., Milw., 1986. Served with USAF, 1960-64. Mem. AIA, Am. Solar Energy Soc., Wis. Soc. Architecture, Constrn. Specifications Inst. (pub. relations chmn. 1986). Democrat. Presbyterian. Clubs: Caddies Ltd. (Milw.) (program officer), CAD User's Group. Avocations: silk scrren printing, basketball, racquetball, computer programming, flying. Home: 7211 W Wabash Ave Milwaukee WI 53223 Office: care of The Wilson Firm 7915 W Appleton Ave Milwaukee WI 53218

WILSON, WILLIAM GILES, hospital administrator; b. Miller, S.D., Mar. 8, 1948; s. Cecil Warren and Betty June (Culey) W.; m. Dolores Marie Schley, Dec. 6, 1974; children: Matthew William, Jenni Leigh. Diploma in Nursing, St. John's Hosp., Huron, S.D., 1976; BA in Bus., Columbia (Mo.) Coll., 1977; MA in Health Services Mgmt., Webster U., 1985. R.N., Mo. Staff nurse Boone Hosp., Columbia, 1976-77, head nurse gen. surgery, 1977-78; adminstr. Schmidt Meml. Hosp., Westbrook, Minn., 1978-79, Springfield (Minn.) Community Hosp., 1979-83, Hermann (Mo.) Area Dist. Hosp., 1983—; advisory bd. Washington (Mo.) Sch. Nursing, 1983—; chmn. Mo. Health Coordinating Council, Jefferson City, Mo., 1986—. Coach Hermann Little League Assn., 1985-86; weblos leader Boy Scouts Am., Hermann, 1986. Served to sgt. USAF, 1966-69. Mem. Am. Coll. Healthcare Execs. Republican. Methodist. Avocations: sports, hunting, fishing, camping. Home: 514 E 6th St Hermann MO 65041 Office: Hermann Area Dist Hosp Rt 1 Box 30 Hermann MO 65041

WILSON, WILLIS A., JR., state appraiser; b. Cimarron, Kans., May 1, 1934; s. Willis A. and Iva Irene (Sells) W.; m. Mary Jo Crick, June 6, 1954; children—Terry Dwane, Meredith Sue. B.S., Okla. State U., 1956. Cert. assessor evaluator. Engring. draftsman Douglas Aircraft Tulsa, 1956, Chance Vaught Aircraft, Dallas, 1957; v.p., gen. mgr. Wilson Lumber Co. Inc., Cimarron, Kans., 1957-67; project mgr. Roy C. Houston Appraisal Co., Dodge City, Kans., 1967-69; property appraiser Div. Property Valuation, Kans. Dept. Revenue, Topeka, 1969-72, edn. coordinator, 1977—; supr. Kans. Assessed Public Utilities, 1972-77; treas. Indsl. Problem Solvers, Inc.; pres. Wilson Real Estate Mgmt. Co., Wilson Investment Co., Nat. Appraisal Service. Served with U.S. Army Res., 1955-57. Mem. Am. Soc. Appraisers (sr. mem., state dir., past pres. Topeka chpt.), Kans. County Appraisers Assn. (assoc.), Cert. Kans. Assessors (dir. 1972-77), Internat. Assoc. Assessing Officers, Am. Inst. Real Estate Appraisers (residential mem.). Mem. Christ's Church. Clubs: Rotary; Odd Fellow. Home: 3031 S E Starlite Topeka KS 66605 Office: 526 S State Office Bldg 10th and Topeka Topeka KS 66625

WILSON-REED, JUANITA K., auditor; b. Charleston, Ill., July 27, 1944; s. Charles Edward Gregory and Lois Juanita (Taylor) Gregory-McInturff-Wood; m. Clyde Wilson, Feb. 14, 1976 (div. mar. 1978); 1 child, April Lyn. Student, Eastern Ill. U., Cen. Fla. Community Coll., Lincolnland Community Coll.; degree in mgmt., Sangamon State U. Supr. fiscal mgmt. Ill. Dept. Cen. Mgmt. Services, Springfield, 1976-79; supr. gen. acctg. systems Ill. Dept. Commerce and Community Affairs, Springfield, 1979-80; supr. support services Ill. Dept. Pub. Health, Springfield, 1980-84; EDP auditor Ill. Dept. Corrections, Springfield, 1984-85; mgr. external auditing Ill. Dept. Pub. Aid, Springfield, 1985—; cons. in mgmt., Springfield, 1976—, in real estate, Crystal River, Fla., 1969-75. Mem. Data Processing Mgmt. Assn. (regional bd. dirs. 1979—, pres. local chpt. 1985—, sec. 1979-85), Inst. Internal Auditors (sec. 1984—), Nat. Assn. Female Execs., Ill. Pub. Health Assn. (chmn. 1986). Baptist. Lodge: Order of Eastern Star. Avocations: running, golfing, bowling, sailing. Home: 1008 N Third St Springfield IL 62702 Office: State of Ill Dept Pub Aid 100 S Grand East Springfield IL 62704

WILT, JAMES KEVIN, office systems technical analyst, researcher; b. Peoria, Ill., Aug. 15, 1960; s. William M. and Sheila M. (Byrns) W.; m. Margaret A. MacGrayne, June 26, 1982. BS, Cen. Mich. U., Mt. Pleasant, 1982. Systems programmer UpJohn, Kalamazoo, 1981-82; sr. systems engr. Burroughs, Pasadena, Calif., 1982-84; office systems tech. analyst Sundstrand Corp., Rockford, Ill., 1984—. Author computer program, 1985 (Achievement award for Excellence). Mem. Chgo. Computer Soc., Chgo. Area Microcomputer Profls. Club: Blackhawk Bicycle (Rockford). Home: 4269 Towhee Trail Loves Park IL 61111 Office: Sundstrand Corp 2504 S Alpine Rockford IL 61108

WILTON, DOUGLAS HUGHES, real estate investor; b. East St. Louis, Ill., June 30, 1941; s. William Everett and Ruth Jean (Campbell) W.; m. Barbara Ann Branch, Aug. 17, 1963; children: Scott Douglas, Deborah Ann, Elizabeth Jean. BSME, Purdue U., 1963; MBA, U. Mich., 1965. CPA, Mo. With Touche Ross & Co., St. Louis and Cleve., 1967-77, ptnr., 1977-79; v.p. May Dept. Stores Co., St. Louis, 1979-82; v.p. Nooney Co., St. Louis, 1982-83, sr. v.p., 1983—, also bd. dirs.; bd. dirs. Nooney Realty Trust Inc., St. Louis. Contbr. articles to profl. jours. Bd. dirs., treas. Alumni Vespers Choral Soc., St. Louis, 1982—; elder, trustee The Ladue Chapel, St. Louis, 1985—; dir., chmn. fund drives KWMU Studio Set, St. Louis, 1985—, dir. Kammergild Orch., 1987—. Served to capt. U.S. Army, 1965-67. Mem. Am. Inst. CPA's, Fin. Execs. Inst., Inst. Mgmt. Cons., Real Estate Bd. Met. St. Louis. Presbyterian. Clubs: Univ. (bd. dirs. 1984—), Bellerive Country (St. Louis). Avocations: reading, music, golfing, photography. Home: 52 Clermont Ln Saint Louis MO 63124 Office: Nooney Co 7701 Forsyth Blvd Saint Louis MO 63105

WILTSE, DORR NORMAN, insurance executive; b. Caro, Mich., Sept. 20, 1911; s. Norman Anson and Evie Markham (McCartney) W.; student Eastern Mich. U., 1931-33; teaching cert. Central Mich. U., 1933-37; m. Gladys May Garner, Nov. 11, 1932; children—Dorr Norman, Saire Christina. Tchr., Tuscola County (Mich.) Public Schs., 1931-42; br. mgr. Mich. Mut. Ins. Co., Caro, 1942-75; city assessor, Caro, 1964—, also casualty ins. cons., Caro, 1975-79. Vice pres. Caro Devel. Corp., 1975-79, pres., 1983—; adv. bd. DeMolay Found. of Mich., 1965-67; founder, pres. Watrousville-Caro Area Hist. Soc., 1972-75, 78; pres. Caro Hist. Commn., 1975-79; chmn. bd. Caro Community Hosp. Endowment Found., 1982—; chmn. Caro Bicentennial Commn., 1975-76; mem. Com. to Elect Pres. Gerald R. Ford, 1975-76; mem. Indianfields-Caro-Almer Planning Commn., 1972-79; co-chmn. Mich. Sesquicentennial for Tuscola County, 1986-87. Named Citizen of Yr., Caro C. of C., 1975. Mem. Mich. Assessors Assn., Caro Masonic Bldg. Assn., Inc. (pres. 1974-79), Nat. Trust Hist. Preservation, Nat. Hist. Soc., Hist. Soc. Mich., Huguenot Soc. Mich., Saginaw Geneal. Soc., Mich. Archaeol. Soc. Democrat. Presbyterian (elder). Clubs: Caro Lions (pres. 1946), Mich. Mut. Quarter Century, Masons (past master), Shriners. Author: The First Hundred Years, 1978; The Hidden Years of the Master, 1976; The Wiltse Saga, 1980; A Look in Your Own Backyard, 1983. Home: 708 W Sherman St Box 143 Caro MI 48723 Office: 247 S State St Caro MI 48723

WIMER, CONNIE, publisher; b. Merrill, Iowa, Oct. 28, 1932; d. Horace Allen and Irene (Carey) Horton; m. William Wimer, Nov. 3, 1954; children: Amy, Carey, Annabel. Student, Morningside Coll., 1951. Pres. Iowa Title Co., Des Moines, 1976—; pub. Bus. Record, Des Moines, 1981—, Skywalker, Des Moines, 1983—; bd. dirs. West Des Moines State Bank. Mem. Tax Study Com. Iowa, Des Moines, 1984; mem. adv. council Region VII SBA, Des Moines, 1983—; bd. dirs. Conv. Bur., Des Moines, 1981—; bd. dirs., exec. com. YWCA. Named Woman of Achievement, YWCA, 1983, Person of Yr., Beta Sigma, 1982, Media Adviser of Yr., SBA, 1984, Small Bus. Adviser of Yr., 1980; recipient Employers Golden Key award Bus. and Profl. Women, 1984. Mem. Greater Des Moines C. of C. (chairperson fedn. 1987). Office: The Depot at 4th St 100 4th St Des Moines IA 50309

WINAKOR, BESS RUTH, public relations executive; b. Springfield, Ill., Mar. 17, 1942; d. Arthur Harry and Annette (Wright) W. BA, Northwestern U., 1963, MS in Journalism, 1964. Contbg. editor Archtl. Digest mag., Chgo.; writer, personality Sta. WFLD-TV, Chgo.; corr. Women's Wear Daily and W mag., Chgo.; feature writer, columnist Chgo. Sun Times; now pres. Bess Winakor Communications, Ltd., Chgo., 1981—. Mem. assoc. bd. Chgo. Internat. Film Festival. Mem. Chgo. Hist. Soc. (costume com.), Chgo. Concierge Assn. (hon.). Office: Bess Winakor Communications Ltd 919 N Michigan Ave #2835 Chicago IL 60611

WINBLAD, JAMES KENT, physician; b. Kansas City, Mo., Oct. 8, 1951; s. James Norman and Gloria (Danielson) W.; m. Rebecca Lynn Barbour, June 9, 1973; children: Krista Marie, James Bret, Erik Cole. BA in Chemistry, U. Kans., Lawrence, 1973; MD, U. Kans., Kansas City, 1976. Diplomate Am. Bd. Ob-Gyn. Intern Good Samaritan Med. Ctr., Phoenix, 1976-77, resident in ob-gyn, 1978-81; diagnostic radiologist U. Kansas Med. Ctr., Kansas City, 1977-78; gen. practice medicine specializing in ob-gyn Winfield (Kans.) Med. Arts, 1981-87; staff William Newton Meml. Hosp., Winfield, 1981—; chmn. dept. ob-gyn William Newton Meml. Hosp., Winfield, 1983; mem. exec. com. dept. ob-gyn, 1983-87,sec. 1985—, pres. elect., 1986—, chief of staff, 1987—. Fellow Am. Coll. Ob-Gyn; mem. AMA, Kans. Med. Soc., Am. Assn. Gynecol. Laparoscopists, Internat. Corr. Soc. Obstetricians and Gynecologists, Cowley County Med. Soc. (v.p. 1983-84, pres. 1984-85). Avocations: water and snow skiing, tennis, family, gardening. Home: 15 Fleetwood Dr Winfield KS 67156 Office: Winfield Med Arts 1211 E 5th St Winfield KS 67156

WINBLAD, JAMES NORMAN, surgeon. m. Gloria Danielson, Mar. 30, 1969; children: J. Kent, Kristin Frahm, John M., Ingrid Culver, Sonja. Student, Bethany Coll., 1942-45, U.S. Mil. Acad., 1945-46; AB in Chemistry, U. Kans., 1948; MA in Anatomy, Kans. U., 1951, MD, 1953. Diplomate Am. Bd. Surgery. Commd. USPHS, 1946, advanced through grades to gen. surgeon; intern USPHS, San Francisco; ward surgeon USPHS, Detroit, Phoenix; gen. surgeon USPHS, New Orleans; resigned USPHS; asst. instr. , then instr. anatomy Kansas U.; instr. anatomy Kansas City Western Dental Sch.; asst. instr., then instr. surgery Tulane U., New Orleans, 1957-61; full assoc. Snyder Clinic, 1962-71; with Winfield Med. Arts, 1971—; pres. staff, mem. exec. com. William Newton Meml. Hosp. Mem. steering com. Winfield C. of C.; bd. dirs. Blue Cross Blue Shield. Fellow ACS, Southwestern Surg. Assn., Pan Am. Surg. Assn.; mem. AMA, Kans. Med. Soc., Cowley County Med. Soc. (steering com.), Sigma Xi, Phi Rho Sigma, Phi Chi. Home: 1604 E 12th St Winfield KS 67156 Office: 1211 E 5th St Winfield KS 67156

WINCKLER, WILLIAM EDWARD, pharmaceutical company executive; b. Davenport, Iowa, July 23, 1932; s. Edward Henry and Pearl Margaret (Lindstrom) W.; m. Shirley Ann Albrecht, Dec. 29, 1954; children: Catherine, James, Susan, Thomas. BS in Pharmacy, U. Iowa, 1954. Lic. pharmacist, Iowa. Pharmacist Schlegel Drug Stores, Davenport, 1954-55, Rennebohm Drug Stores, Madison, Wis., 1955, Toller Drug Co., Sioux City, Iowa, 1957-58; pharmacist U. Iowa Hosp., Iowa City, 1958-59, cir. buying, asst. mfg. Drug Service Dept., 1959-62; pharmacist Lloyd & Myers Pharmacy, Sioux City, 1962-75; exec. v.p. Medco Lab. Inc., Sioux City, 1963-82, pres., 1982—. Served with U.S. Army, 1955-57. Mem. Am. Pharm. Assn., Iowa Pharmacists Assn., Rho Chi. Lutheran. Avocation: investing. Home: 3645 Summit Sioux City IA 51104 Office: Medco Lab Inc PO Box 864 Sioux City IA 51102-0864

WIND, JOSEPH LEON, radiologist; b. Bklyn., Sept. 29, 1931; s. Bernard A. and Lena (Friedman) W.; m. Glenda F. Lucas, May 30, 1958 (div. May 1979); children: Deborah, Todd, Lisa, John; m. Barbara Lou Cox, Oct. 20, 1984. BA, Brooklyn Coll., 1953; MD, SUNY, Bklyn., 1957. Intern Ohio State U. Med. Ctrs., Columbus, 1957-58; resident internal medicine VA Hosp., Los Angeles, 1960-61; resident radiology U. Minn. Hosps., Mpls., 1961-64; staff radiologist West Allis (Wis.) Meml. Hosp., 1964-65; radiologist Radiology, Inc., South Bend, Ind., 1966—, chmn., 1984—; chmn. radiology dept. Meml. Hosp. South Bend, 1986-87. Chmn. Jewish Community Relations Council South Bend, 1984—; v.p. Jewish Fedn. St. Joseph Valley, South Bend, 1985—. Served to capt. U.S. Army, 1958-60. Mem. AMA, Am. Coll. Radiology, Radiol. Soc. N.Am. Home: 50838 Old Dover Ln Granger IN 46530 Office: 707 N Michigan St South Bend IN 46601

WINDER, CLARENCE LELAND, educator, psychologist; b. Osborne County, Kans., June 16, 1921; s. Clarence McKinley and Edna (Ikenberry) W.; m. Elizabeth Jane Jacobs, Aug. 14, 1943; children—David William, Christina Louise. Student, Santa Barbara State Coll., 1941; A.B. with honors, U. Calif. at Los Angeles, 1943; M.A., Stanford U., 1946, Ph.D., 1949. From instr. to asso. prof. Stanford, 1949-61; dir. Psychol. Clinic, 1953-61; prof., dir. Psychol. Clinic, Mich. State U., 1961-62, prof. psychology, 1961—, chmn. dept., 1963-67; dean Coll. Social Sci. Mich. State U., 1967-74, asso. provost, 1974-77; provost Psychol. Clinic, Mich. State U. (Coll. Social Sci.), 1977-86; prof., dir. Psychol. Services Center, U. So. Calif., 1962-63; cons. V.A., Mich. Dept. Mental Health; spl. research psychol. aspects schizophrenia, parent-child relations and personality devel. Served to 1st lt. USAAF, 1943-45. Decorated Air medal with 7 clusters, D.F.C. Fellow Am. Psychol. Assn.; mem. Mich. Psychol. Assn., AAAS, Sigma Xi. Home: 1776 Hitching Post Rd East Lansing MI 48823

WINDSOR, HUGH MACDONALD, data processing executive; b. Malden, Mass., Oct. 19, 1929; s. Manly McDonald and Muriel Earl (MacDonald) W.; m. Elly Nisch, Jan. 26, 1956. Mgr. computer ops. Sherwin William, Cleve., 1956-68; mgr. ops. support SCM, Cleve., 1968-82; chief exec. officer, pres. Elvenwork Specialists Inc., Sheffield Lake, Ohio, 1980—; mgr. tech. support Gen. Electric Co., Cleve., 1982—; cons. in field, Sheffield Lake, 1979—; bd. dirs. AGRI, Vestal, N.Y.; lectr. in field. Served with USAF, 1950-54. Mem. Data Processing Mgmt. Assn. (bd. dirs. 1974-78, Individual Performance award 1974), Air Force Assn., Nat. Rifle Assn. Republican. Home: 5579 E Lake Rd Sheffield Lake OH 44054

WINDSOR, ROBERT DENNIS, dentist; b. Elkhart, Ind., Dec. 22, 1951; s. Richard L. and Esther J. (Emmons) W.; m. Gayle Marie Flamion, Jan. 5, 1974; children: Robert, Michael, David. DDS, Ind. U., 1978. Gen. practice dentistry Middlebury, Ind., 1978—. Mem. ADA, Ind. Dental Assn. Avocation: basketball. Home and Office: 105 W Brown PO Box 907 Middlebury IN 46540

WINE, RAYMOND LISLE, hospital administrator; b. Oelwein, Iowa, Feb. 26, 1925; s. George A. and Gladys E. (Lisle) W.; m. Winnifred L. Anderson, Apr. 14, 1946; children—Pamela Rae, David Allan. B.S. in Acctg., Drake U., 1950. Bus. mgr. Freeport Meml. Hosp., Ill., 1950-55, asst. adminstr., 1955, acting adminstr., 1955-56, chief exec. officer, 1956-86; pres. Freeport Health Care Found., 1984—. Served with USN, 1943-46. Recipient Young Man of Yr. award Jr. C. of C., 1959. Mem. Am. Coll. Hosp. Adminstrs., Ill. Hosp. Assn. (council legis. affairs 1984-85, council on nursing 1978, council on human resources 1978-81, council on shared services 1982-83), Freeport C. of C. (past pres., past bd. dirs.), Stephenson County Mental Health Assn. (bd. dirs.). Club: Freeport Country. Lodges: Masons (consistory), Rotary (past pres., past bd. dirs.). Avocations: golf; bowling. Home: 1452 S Demeter Dr Freeport IL 61032 Office: Freeport Meml Hosp 1045 W Stephenson St Freeport IL 61032

WINE, SHERWIN THEODORE, rabbi; b. Detroit, Jan. 25, 1928; s. William Harry and Tillie (Israel) W. B.A., U. Mich., 1950, A.M., 1952; B.H.L., Hebrew Union Coll., Cin., M.H.L., 1956, rabbi, 1956. Rabbi Temple Beth El, Detroit, 1956-60, Windsor, Ont., Can., 1960-64; Rabbi Birmingham (Mich.) Temple, 1964—; cons. editor Humanistic Judaism, 1966—. Author: A Philosophy of Humanistic Judaism, 1965, Meditation Services for Humanistic Judaism, 1977, Humanistic Judaism-What Is It?, 1977, Humanist Haggadah, 1980, High Holidays for Humanists, 1980, Judaism Beyond God, 1985. Bd. dirs. Center for New Thinking, Birmingham, 1977—; founder Soc. Humanistic Judaism, 1969; pres. N.Am. Com. for Humanism, 1982—. Served as chaplain AUS, 1956-58. Mem. Conf. Liberal Religion (chmn. 1985—), Leadership Conf. Secular and Humanistic Jews (chmn. 1983—), Internat. Inst. Secular Humanistic Judaism (co-chmn. 1985—). Home: 555 S Woodward Birmingham MI 48011 Office: 28611 W Twelve Mile Rd Farmington Hills MI 48018

WINEGARDEN, TIMOTHY VAN, orthodontist; b. Fairfield, Iowa, Jan. 30, 1945; s. Virgil Lee and Opal Arlene (Bair) W.; m. Diane Louise Stover, Aug. 2, 1969; children: Anne Michelle, Jill Renee. BA in Chemistry, State Coll. Iowa, Cedar Falls, 1967; DDS, U. Iowa, 1971; MS in Dentistry, St. Louis U., 1976. Diplomate Am. Bd. Orthodontics. Gen. practice dentistry San Antonio, 1973-74, practice dentistry specializing in orthodontics, 1976-77; practice dentistry specializing in orthodontics Cedar Rapids, Iowa, 1977—. Served to capt. Dental Corps, USAF, 1971-73; maj. USAR. Mem. ADA, Am. Assn. Orthodontists, Midwest Soc. Orthodontists, Iowa Soc. Orthodontists, Orthodontic Edn. and Research Found., Am. Bd. Orthodontists (Coll. Diplomates), Iowa Dental Soc., U. Dist. Dental Soc., Linn County Dental soc., Delta Sigma Delta. Methodist. Club: Cedar Rapids Exchange. Lodge: High Noon Optimist (v.p. 1981-82). Avocations: travel, reading, sports. Home: 3522 Heatheridge Dr NE Cedar Rapids IA 52402 Office: 222 Edgewood Rd NW Cedar Rapids IA 52405

WINEINGER, DAVID MARVIN, otolaryngologist; b. Carydon, Iowa, Aug. 3, 1935. BS in Pharmacy, Drake U., 1957; MD, Iowa U., 1962. Intern Ill. Research and Edn. Hosp., 1962-63; resident in otolargyngology U. Ill., Chgo., 1963-67; practice medicine specializing in otolaryngology Eye and Ear Assocs., Green Bay, Wis., 1969—; asst. prof. surgery, U. Wis., Madison, 1971—; chmn. Ear, Nose and Throat Dept., Travis AFB, Calif., 1967-69. Served to capt. USAF, 1967-69. Fellow Am. Acad. Otolaryngology (ethics com. 1986); mem. AMA, Wis. Med. Sco., Brown County Med. Sco., Wis. Otologic Soc. (pres.), Green Bay C. of C. Republican. Lutheran. Avocations: golf, sailing, water sports. Home: 600 Terraview Dr Green Bay WI 54301 Office: Eye & Ear Assocs 923 Eliza Green Bay WI 54301

WINEMAN, JOHN HENRY, clinical psychologist; b. Detroit, Aug. 4, 1941; s. Henry Cameron and Betty Sue (Cockrall) W.; m. Sharon Kay Miller, June 9, 1979; 1 child, Mari Fox. BA, Calif. State U., Long Beach, 1967, MA, 1970; PhD, U. Utah, 1973. Sch. psychologist Granite Sch. Dist., Salt Lake City, 1971-74; dir. Miami Children's Ctr., Maumee, Ohio, 1974-79; dir. intensive teaching program Father Flanagan's Boy's Home, Boy Town, Nebr., 1979-83; dir. Woodhaven Counseling Assocs., Omaha, 1983—; cons. Richard Young Hosp., Omaha, 1984—, Youth Emergency Services, Bellevue, Nebr., 1984—, Family Support Ctr., Omaha, 1984-85. Mem. human rights com. Martin Luther Home, Omaha, 1985-86, instl. rev. bd. Magentic Imaging Ctr., Omaha, 1985-86. Served with USAF, 1960-63. Fellow Am. Orthopsychiat. Assn.; mem. Am. Psychol. Assn., Nebr. Psychol. Assn. Lutheran. Home: 5729 N 115 Plaza Omaha NE 68164 Office: Woodhaven Counseling Assocs 2612 S 158 Plaza Omaha NE 68130

WINEMILLER, JAMES D., accountant; b. Sullivan, Ind., July 22, 1944; s. Floyd Maurice and Doris Marie (Lone) W.; A.S., Vincennes U., 1964; B.S., Ind. U., 1966, M.B.A., 1967; m. Nancy Kay Walters, Aug. 10, 1963; 1 dau., Nancy Marie. Accountant, Peat, Marwick, Mitchell & Co., C.P.A.s, Honolulu, 1967-71; with Blue & Co., C.P.A.s, Indpls., 1971—, partner-in-charge, 1974-76, mng. partner, 1977—. Grad. teaching asst. dept. accounting Ind. U., Bloomington, 1966-67; instr. accounting Coll. Gen. Studies, U. Hawaii, Honolulu, 1968-69; dir. Poland State Bank (Ind.), 1974-75. Mem. state adv. com. Vincennes U. Recipient Gold Medal for highest grades in state on C.P.A. examination, State Ind., 1966; Elizah Watt Sells Nat. Honorable Mention award, 1966. C.P.A., Ind., Hawaii; Vincennes U. Found. fellow. Mem. Am. Inst. C.P.A.'s (council mem. 1987—), Ind. C.P.A. Soc. (dir. 1980-86, treas. 1981-82, exec. com. 1983-86, pres.-elect 1984-85, pres. 1985-86), Ind. C.P.A. Ednl. Found. (life), Hawaii Soc. C.P.A.s, Continental Assn. C.P.A. Firms (dir. 1978—, v.p. 1982-83, pres. 1983-84), Nat. Assn. Accountants, Am. Acctg. Assn., Ind. U. Well House Soc., Ind. U. Bus. Sch. Deans Assoc. (sr), Ind. U. Alumni Assn. (life), Ind. U. Varsity-Hoosier Hundred, Vincennes U. Alumni Assn. (life). Methodist. Clubs: Rotary (dir. 1973-75, 84—, v.p. 1984-86, pres. 1974-75, 87-88, Paul Harris fellow), Indpls. Columbia, Econ. of Indpls., Hillcrest Country, Venture of Ind. Inc., Indpls. Mus. Art. Home: 9242 Whitehall Ct Indianapolis IN 46256 Office: 9100 Keystone Crossing #500 PO Box 80069 Indianapolis IN 46280-0069

WINER, WARREN JAMES, insurance executive; b. Wichita, Kans., June 16, 1946; s. Henry Charles and Isabel (Ginsburg) W.; m. Mary Jean Kovacs, June 23, 1968 (div. Feb. 1973); m. Jo Lynn Sondag, May 3, 1975; children: Adam, Lauren. BS in Math., Stanford U., 1968. With Gen. Am. Life Ins. Co., St. Louis, 1968-73, dir. retirement plans, 1973-76, 2d v.p., 1976-80; v.p., sr. actuary Powers, Carpenter & Hall, St. Louis, 1980-84, sr. v.p., dir. pension div., 1984-85, pres., chief operating officer, 1985-86, lobbyist, commentator, 1985—, pres., chief exec. officer, 1986—; mem. Actuarial Exam. Com., Chgo.), 1973-74. Contbr. articles to profl. jours. Bd. dirs. Lucky Lane Nursery Sch. Assn., St. Louis, 1978-83; co-v.p. PTA, Conway Sch., St. Louis, 1986-87, co-pres., 1987—; bd. dirs. pilot div. United Way, 1986-87. Fellow Soc. Actuaries; mem. Am. Acad. Actuaries, Enrollment of Actuaries (joint bd.), Am. Life Ins. Assn. (small case task force 1979-80), Life Office Mgmt. Assn. (ICPAC com. 1975-80), St. Louis Actuaries Club. Jewish. Clubs: St. Louis, Clayton (St. Louis). Avocations: bridge, wine tasting, swimming, weight tng. Office: Corroon & Black Cons Group PCH Div 231 S Bemiston Suite 400 Saint Louis MO 63105

WINES, MARY ANN, dentist; b. Chgo., June 28, 1952; d. William Louis and Lauretta (Zwierowitz) Spalding; m. William John Wines, June 9, 1973. BS in Nursing magna cum laude, No. Ill. U., 1974; DDS, Loyola U., Maywood, Ill., 1982. Staff nurse Delnor Hosp., St. Charles, Ill., 1974-75; pub. health nurse DeKalb (Ill.) County Health Dept., 1975-78; dentist Dr. Frasco & Assocs., Oak Park, Ill., 1982-84, DeKalb Dental Clinic, 1982—. Bd. dirs. DeKalb County Bd. Health, 1985—. Mem. ADA, Ill. State Dental Soc., Chgo. Dental Soc., DeKalb Dental Soc. (sec./treas. 1986—), Fox River Valley Dental Soc., Kishwaukee Dental Study Club, Psi Omega (treas. 1980-82), Omicron Kappa Upsilon. Roman Catholic. Avocations: aerobics, hiking, travel, reading. Home: 1512 Kennicott Ct Sycamore IL 60178 Office: DeKalb Dental Clinic 129 S 4th St DeKalb IL 60115

WINGERT, ROBERT IRVIN, obstetrician, gynecologist; b. Canistota, S.D., Jan. 31, 1950; s. Mathias Jacob and Lyda Adelaide (Doeden) W.; m. Karen Frances Bollinger, July 16, 1960; children: Robert, Scott, Mark, Jon. BA, U. S.D., 1957; MD, Marquette U., 1959. Commd. capt. USAF, 1960, advanced through grades to col., 1981, ret., 1981; prof. ob-gyn. U. S.D. Sch. Medicine, Vermillion, 1982—; cons. ob-gyn Pub. Health Service/Indsl. Health Service Pine Ridge, Sioux San and Eagle Butte, S.D., 1982—. Fellow Am. Coll. Ob-Gyn; mem. S.D. Med. Soc., Black Hills Med. Soc., The Retired Officers Assn. (pres. 1982—). Roman Catholic. Lodge: Elks. Avocations: skiing, hiking, waterskiing, motorcycle riding, camping. Home: 4607 Ridgewood St Rapid City SD 57702 Office: U SD Sch Medicine 1011 11th St Rapid City SD 57701

WINGERTER, CAROL ANN, school system administrator; b. Cape Girardeau, Mo., Sept. 7, 1944; d. Hubert Arthur L'Hote and Cecelia Mae (Moore) Buchheit; m. Lester Edward Wingerter, July 7, 1962; children: Lisa Ann Lopez, Lynn Edward. Grad. high sch., Perryville, Mo. Sec. Perry County Sch. Dist. #32, Perryville, 1962-74. Mem. Perry County Sch. Bd., 1978-87, v.p. 1981-83, pres. 1983-87; mem. Booster Club, Perryville. Mem. Nat. Sch. Bds. Assn., Mo. Sch. Bds. Assn. (telephone network 1981-87, constitution and policies com. 1982-85, legisl. liason 1983-87, planning and devel. 1983-87), Mo. State Tchrs. Assn., Am. Assn. Sch. Adminstrs., SE Mo. Regional Sch. Bds. Assn., Mo. Vocat. Assn., Am. Legion Aux. Lodge: KC Aux. Club: Sportsman Aux. (Perryville). Home: 301 S Feltz St Perryville MO 63775 Office: 2200 Plattin Rd Perryville MO 63775

WINGET, WALTER WINFIELD, lawyer; b. Peoria, Ill., Sept. 12, 1936; s. Walter W. Winget and Arabella (Robinson) Richardson; m. Ann Robert, July 12, 1969; children: Marie, Marshall. AB cum laude, Princeton U., 1958; JD, U. Mich., 1961. Bar: R.I. 1962, Ill. 1962, U.S. Supreme Ct. 1971. Assoc. Edwards & Angell, Providence, 1961-64; sole practice Peoria, 1964-77; ptnr. Winget & Kane, Peoria, 1977—; asst. pub. defender Peoria, 1969-70; bd. dirs. various corps. Atty., bd. dirs. Better Bus. Bur. Cen. Ill., Inc. 1973—, chmn., 1979-81. Served to sgt. U.S. Army, 1961-62. Mem. ABA, Assn. Trial Lawyers Am., Ill. Bar Assn., Ill. Trial Lawyers Assn., Peoria County Bar Assn. Republican. Episcopalian. Club: Peoria Country. Avocations: competetive target shooting, big game and duck hunting. Home: 135 W Forrest Hill Peoria IL 61604 Office: Winget & Kane 416 Main St Peoria IL 61602

WINING, WILLIAM HENRY, real estate developer; b. Columbiana, Ohio, July 19, 1951; s. Henry Thomas and Virginia Louise (Steffy) W. Grad. high sch., Columbiana. Sales mgr. Pubs. Reader Services, Youngstown and Indpls., Ohio, 1970-76; mgr. Mansion, Inc., Youngstown, 1976-80; pres. Chateau Agapé, Inc., Leetonia, Ohio, 1980—. Dep. registrar Columbiana County Bd. Elections, 1980. Democrat. Home and Office: 351 Pearl St Leetonia OH 44431

WINKE, JEFFREY JAMES, communications executive, writer, editor, educator; b. Milw., Mar. 20, 1954; s. Noel Joseph and Lorraine Anne (Lucic) W.; m. Carol Jeanne Schulze, Aug. 10, 1978; 1 child, Jillian Noelle. BA with honors, U. Wis., Milw., 1976, MA, 1978. Acad. advisor U. Wis., Milw., 1978-79; asst. editor Trade Press Pub. Co., Milw., 1979-80; corp. communications editor Snap-on Tools Corp., Kenosha, Wis., 1980-81; editor, writer Mortgage Guaranty Ins. Co., Milw., 1981-84; mgr. corp. communications Verex Assurance, Inc., Madison, Wis., 1984-86; dir. mktg. Phill Thill Design, 1986; sr. assoc. Wood Communications Group, Madison, 1987—; instr. U. Wis. Extension, Milw., 1978, Milw. Area Tech. Coll., 1979, Marquette U., Milw., 1982-84; cons. Wis. Police, Wis. Sheriff, Milw., 1983-84; ptnr. Gullveig Enterprises, Madison, 1979—; pres. J. Winke & Assocs., Madison, 1986—. Author: An Opus to the Likes of All, 1980, (with others) Thirds, 1985; editor, co-founder (literary mags.) Third Coast Archives, 1976-78, (with others) Modern Haiku, 1985—; (with others) Third Coast Haiku Anthology, 1978. Recipient Merit cert. for pub. design Printing Industries Am., 1981. Mem. Internat. Assn. Bus. Communicators, Madison Advt. Fedn., Haiku Soc. Am., Wis. Acad. Scis., Arts and Letters, Madison Area Writers Assn. Avocations: real estate investing, rehabbing. Home: 301 Racine Rd Madison WI 53705

WINKEL, RAYMOND NORMAN, avionics manufacturing executive, retired naval officer; b. Flint, Mich., Dec. 8, 1928; s. Norman Martin and Evelyn Matilda (Hylen) W.; m. Ellen Stefula, Dec. 29, 1955; children: Raymond Norman, Ann, Maryellen. B.S., U.S. Naval Postgrad. Sch., Monterey, Calif., 1964; M.S., Villanova (Pa.) U., 1967; grad., Advanced Mgmt. Program, Harvard U., 1973. Enlisted in U.S. Navy, 1948, commd. ensign, designated naval aviator, 1951, advanced through grades to rear adm., 1979; service in Far East; comdg. officer Naval Electronics Systems Test and Evaluation Facility St. Inigoes, MD, 1969-71; dir. avionics U.S. Navy, 1973-76; project mgr. Navy/Marine Corps heavy lift helicopter, 1976-78; gen. mgr. Navy/industry team to develop new ship/aircraft weapon system for anti-submarine warfare LAMPS Mark III, 1978-81; ret. U.S. Navy, 1981; v.p. Washington ops. Telephonics Corp., Huntington, N.Y., 1981-82; dir. program mgmt. Astronautics Corp. Am., Milw., 1982—; cons. to aerospace industry. Decorated Legion of Merit, Meritorious Service medal, Air medal, Navy Achievement medal. Mem. Am. Helicopter Soc. (dir.), Armed Forces Communications and Electronics Assn., Navy Helicopter Assn. (trustee), Exptl. Aircraft Assn., U.S. Naval Inst., Assn. Naval Aviation. Republican. Roman Catholic. Club: Milw. Yacht, Harvard Bus. Sch. (Milw.). Home: 4401 N Lake Dr Milwaukee WI 53211 Office: 4115 N Teutonia Ave Milwaukee WI 53209

WINKELMAN, ROBERT LOUIS, retail executive; b. Petoskey, Mich., Dec. 24, 1951; s. Marvin Russell and Doris June (Steinberg) W.; m. Kathy Ann Carmean, Feb. 11, 1971; children: Scott Douglass, Andrew Gene, Mamie Rose. BA in Acctg., Mich. State U., 1974. CPA, Mich. Staff acctg. Danielson Schults & Co., Lansing, 1974-77; owner Winkelman Dept. Store, St. Ignance, Mich., 1977—. Chmn. St. Ignace Downtown Devel. Authority, 1985—. Mem. St. Ignace C. of C. (pres. 1981, Citizen of Yr. award 1986). Lodge: Kiwanis (pres. St. Ignace chpt. 1985-86). Home: 1017 Medora Saint Igance MI 49781 Office: Winkelman's Dept Store 40 N State St Saint Ignace MI 49781

WINKLE, CHARLES EDWARD, educator; b. Cin., Dec. 19, 1949; s. Gerald N. and Lorena Belle (Carrington) W.; m. Donna Jean Crawford, Dec. 3, 1971; children—Matthew Jared, Mark Edward, Rebecca Mae. B.Sc., Ohio State U., 1971, M.Sc., 1978. Tchr. vocat. agr. Blanchester (Ohio) High Sch., 1971-87, agr. edn. coordinator; county agr. extension agt., Warren County, 1987—; salesman Donald E. Fender Realtors, Hillsboro, Ohio, 1978-81, Ray Houk Realty, 1981—; cons. agr. mgmt., agronomy and integrated pest mgmt.; mem. del. People to People Citizen Ambassadors of Agr. to China, 1985. Named Outstanding Young Tchr. of Ohio, 1977. Mem. Ohio Vocat. Agr. Tchrs. Assn. (Tchr. of Tchrs. 1984, life mem.), Nat. Vocat. Agr. Tchrs. Assn. (life mem., legis. liaison), Am. Vocat. Assn., Ohio Vocat. Assn., Ohio State U. Alumni Assn., Am. Farm Bur. Fedn., Nat. Corn Growers Assn., Am. Soc. Agronomy, Am. Soybean Assn., Ohio Seed Improvement Assn. (cons.), Ohio Young Farmers Assn. (advisor), Nat. Future Farmers Assn. Alumni (advisor), Ohio State Tractor Pullers Assn., Nat. Tractor Pullers Assn. Contbr. articles to profl. jours.

WINKLER, JOSEPH MARK, aeronautical engineer; b. Bklyn., Nov. 15, 1952; s. Leonard Charles and Ann (Zucker) W.; m. Debra Jo Staub, May 21, 1983; children: Jamie Suzanne, Brandon Edward. AAS in Aerospace Design, Acad. Aeronautics, 1973; BSCE, U. New Orleans, 1979; postgrad. in mech. engr., U. Cin., 1985—. Reg. profl. engr., Ohio, Conn. Sr. engr. Martin Marietta, New Orleans, 1973-82; task mgr. structures Perkin Elmer, Danbury, Conn., 1982-84; engr., CAE rep. Gen. Electric, Cin., 1984—; pvt. practice engring. Cin., 1984—. Mem. Am. Inst. Aero. Astronautics (officer student chpt. 1971-73, photographer New Orleans chpt. 1980-82), Acad. Aeronautics Alumni Assn. (founders award 1973). Democrat. Jewish. Avocations: baseball, racquetball, skiing, bowling, photography. Home: 7231 Prince Wilbert Way West Chester OH 45069

WINN, HUNG NGUYEN, obstetrician/gynecologist, perinatologist; b. Thanh Hoa, Vietnam, Feb. 11, 1953; came to U.S., 1975; s. Su Cong Nguyen and Diep Thi Truong; m. Lee Nguyen Winn, Aug. 8, 1975; children: John, Jessica, Justin. BA in Biology and Chemistry, Greenville Coll., 1977; MD, U. Ill., Chgo., 1982. Resident in ob-gyn. U. Ill. Peoria, 1982-86, teaching assoc. coll. medicine, 1983-86; fellow in maternal-fetal medicine Yale U. Sch. Medicine, New Haven, 1986—, clin. instr., 1986—. Contbr. articles to profl. jours. and chpts. to med. textbook. Mem. AMA, Am. Coll. Obstetricians and Gynecologists, Soc. Perinatologists and Obstetricians. Roman Catholic. Avocations: tennis, swimming, reading, golf, traveling.

WINNE, M. G., clothing company executive. Pres. Lee Apparel Co., Inc., Merriam, Kans. Office: The Lee Apparel Co Inc 9001 W 67th St Merriam KS 66202 *

WINSBERG, GWYNNE ROESELER, health care executive; b. Chgo., Nov. 28, 1930; d. Berthold Ernst and Ruth Pearl (Wondrack) Roeseler; m. David Melvin Winsberg, Dec. 1, 1950 (div. Apr. 1984); children: Jeri Lynne, William Franklin. MS, U. Chgo., 1962, PhD, 1967. Asst. prof. Northwestern U., Chgo., 1967-75; assoc. dean Stritch Sch. Medicine, Loyola U., Maywood, Ill., 1975-81; sr. analyst U.S. DHHS, Washington, 1979-81; pres. GRW Assocs., Chgo., 1981-87; v.p. Efficient Health Systems, Inc., Skokie, Ill., 1987—; sec., trustee NorthCare, Evanston, Ill., 1975-81. Contbr. articles to profl. jours. Adv. Suburban Health Systems Agy., Oak Park, Ill., 1977-81; cons. Met. Chgo. Labor Council, 1983; v.p. New Music Chgo., 1983—. Recipient NEH award, U. Pa., 1974; research fellow USPHS, U. Chgo., 1962-65. Mem. Am. Pub. Health Assn., Ill. Pub. Health Assn. Democrat. Methodist. Avocations: backpacking, bicycling, avant garde music, theatre. Home: 5533 N Glenwood Chicago IL 60640 Office: Efficient Health Systems Inc 5215 Old Orchard Rd Skokie IL 60077

WINSLOW, ALFRED AKERS, retired government official; b. Gary, Ind., June 16, 1923; s. Harry Wendell and Lenora (Allen) W.; A.A., Wilson Jr. Coll., 1964; B.B.A., Northwestern U., 1969; m. Maud Esther Franklin, Jan. 15, 1954. With Chgo. Post Office, 1947-66; with U.S. Postal Service, Chgo. Central Region, 1967-83, dir. Office Employee Relations, 1973-83. Ptnr., Winslow's Apparel Shop, Chgo., 1954-66, v.p., bd. dirs. Univ. Park Condominiums. Mem. adv. com. on human relations City of Chgo., 1969-73; pres. Cheryl Condominium, Chgo., 1965-67, Evans-Langley Neighborhood Club, Chgo., 1960-64; chmn. Post Office Bd. U.S. Civil Service Examiners Ill., Mich., 1967-71. Served with USCGR, 1943-46. Recipient Outstanding Achievement award, Chgo. Assn. Commerce and Industry, 1969, 70, 68; Great Guy award, Radio Sta. WGRT, 1969. Mem. Northwestern U. Bus. Honor Soc., NAACP bd. dirs. 1968-83), Soc. Personnel Adminstrn., Indsl. Relations Assn. Chgo., Am. Legion, Field Mus. Natural History, Chgo. Art Inst., Lyric Opera, Chgo. Ednl. TV Assn., Northwestern U. Alumni Assn.

WINSTEIN, STEWART ROBERT, lawyer; b. Viola, Ill., May 28, 1914; s. Abraham and Esther (Meyer) W.; m. Dorothy Shock, Nov. 2, 1961; 1 son, Arthur R. A.B., Augustana Coll., 1935; J.D., U. Chgo., 1938. Bar: Ill. Ptnr. Winstein, Kavensky, Wallace & Doughty, Rock Island, Ill., 1939—. Trustee Marycrest Coll., Davenport, Iowa, 1980—; fin. officer State of Ill., 1963-70; del. Democratic Nat. Conv., 1968, 72 and mid-term conf., 1974, 78; 17th Dist. Dem. State Central committeeman, 1970—; vice chmn. State of Ill. Dem. State Central Com., 1970-82; pub. adminstr. Rock Island County, 1974-78; commr. Met. Airport Authority, 1972—, chmn. bd., 1986—. Mem. ABA, Ill. Bar Assn., Rock Island County Bar Assn., Chgo. Bar Assn., Assn. Trial Lawyers of Am. Jewish. Contbr. articles to profl. jours.

WINSTON, HAROLD RONALD, b. Atlantic, Iowa, Feb. 7, 1932; s. Louis D. and Leta B. (Carter) W.; m. Carol J. Sundeen, June 11, 1955 (divorced); children—Leslie Winston Yannetti, Laura L.; m. Lisa Winston Barbour. B.A., U. Iowa, 1954, J.D., 1958. Bar: Iowa 1958, U.S. District Ct. (no. and so. dists.) Iowa 1962, U.S. Tax Ct. 1962, U.S. Ct. Appeals (8th cir.) 1970, U.S. Supreme Ct. 1969. Trust Officer United Home Bank & Trust Co., Mason City, Iowa, 1958-59; mem. Breese & Cornwell, 1960-62, Breese Cornwell Winston & Reuber, 1963-73, Winston Schroeder & Reuber, 1974-79, Winston, Reuber & Swanson, P.C., Mason City, 1980—. police judge, Mason City, 1961-73. Author profl. publs. Past pres. Family YMCA, Mason City, Cerro Gordo County Estate Planning Council; other acitive local charitable orgns. Served to capt. USAF, 1955-57. Fellow Am. Coll. Probate Counsel; mem. ABA, Iowa Bar Assn. (gov., lectr. ann. meeting 1977, 78, 79), 2d Jud. Dist. Ba r Assn. (lectr. meeting 1981, 82), Cerro Gordo County Bar Assn. (past pres.), Am. Judicature Soc., Assn. Trial Lawyers Am. Republican. Presbyterian (elder). Clubs: Euchre and Cycle, Mason City Country, Masons, Kiwanis.

WINSTON, YVETTE MICHELE, healthcare administrator; b. Chgo., June 5, 1955; d. Claude Evans and Naomi L. (Roberts) Driskell; divorced; children: Tasleem Azeeza, Dhaviella Nichelle. BA, Roosevelt U., 1976, MPA, 1981, B Gen. Studies, 1982; MPH, Yale U., 1984. Research asst. South Chgo. Community Hosp., Chgo., 1981; counselor 5th Ward Aldermanic Office, Chgo., 1981-82; research asst. Argonne (Ill.) Nat. Lab., 1982-83, Rehab. Inst. of Chgo., 1983, U. Ill. Sch. Pub. Health, Chgo., 1984-85; network mgr. Infant Mortality Reduction Initiative Cook County Dept. Pub. Health, Markham, Ill., 1986—. Mem. Am. Hosp. Assn., Ill. Pub. Health Assn. Avocations: playing piano, animal rights. Office: Cook County Dept Public Health 16501 S Kedzie Pkwy Markham IL 60426

WINTER, ELMER LOUIS, business executive; b. Milw., Mar. 6, 1912; s. Sigmund and Mae (Kraus) W.; m. Nanette Rosenberg, 1936; children—Susan, Lynn, Martha. B.A., U. Wis.-Madison, 1933, LL.B., Milw., 1935, LL.D. (hon.), 1970. Bar: Wis. 1935. Ptnr. Winter & Scheinfeld, Milw., 1936-48; co-founder, pres. Manpower, Inc., Milw., 1948-76; dir. Jack Winter, Inc., Milw. Author 12 Books. Painter, sculptor. Chmn. Operation 4000, Milw., 1979; chmn. Com. for Econ. Growth of Israel, Milw.; chmn. met. Milw. div. Nat. Alliance of Businessmen, 1968-69; co-founder, chmn. Milw. Voluntary EEO Council; organizer Youthpower, Milw.; del. White House Conf. on Youth; mem. exec. com. Nat. Alliance to Save Energy; del. White House Econ. Summit, 1974; hon. pres. Am. Jewish Com. Recipient Leadership award Met. Milw. Assn. Commerce. Mem. Wis. Bar Assn., Milw. Bar Assn., Internat. Franchise Assn. (past pres.), Internat. Soc. Advancement Mgmt. (past v.p., Human Relations award). Home: 8014 N Lake Dr Milwaukee WI 53217 Office: Manpower Inc 5301 N Ironwood Rd Milwaukee WI 53217

WINTER, JOHN ALEXANDER, realtor, real estate appraiser; b. Cin., July 2, 1935; s. George Edward and Mary Alma (McAuliffe) W. B.S., Georgetown U., 1957. Ptnr. Winter & Winter, Cleve., 1957-76; residential salesman Moreland Hills Co., Chagrin Falls, Ohio, 1976-77; residential appraiser Kiebler, Smith & Co., Chardon, Ohio, 1977—; v.p., dir. The Gas Pipe Co., Chagrin Falls, 1973—. Contbr. articles to profl. jours. Pres. New Eng. Soc. of Cleve. and Western Res., 1976-77, 83-84, Shaker Heights Republican Club, 1977-84; v.p., trustee Shaker Hist. Soc., 1985—; founder, pres. Cert. Appraisal Service Co., Shaker Heights, 1985—. Recipient Service award Pres. Ronald Reagan, 1984, New Eng. Heritage award New Eng. Soc., 1984. Mem. Cleve. Independance Day Assn. (v.p., trustee 1957—, Treharne award 1984), Am. Assn. Cert. Appraisers, Ohio Assn. Realtors, Nat. Assn. Realtors (Ben Franklin award 1983), Cathedral Latin Sch. Alumni Assn. (trustee 1965—). Roman Catholic. Clubs: Georgetown (pres. 1966-67); Cleve. of Washington (trustee 1984—). Avocations: tennis; sailing; coin collecting. Home: 19271 Shaker Blvd Shaker Heights OH 44122 Office: Cert Appraisal Service Co 19271 Shaker Blvd Shaker Heights OH 44122

WINTER, MAX, profl. football team exec.; b. Ostrava, Austria, June 29, 1904; came to U.S., 1913, naturalized, 1920; s. Jacob and Bertha (Kuker) W.; m. Helen Horovitz, Dec. 5, 1939; children: Susan (Mrs. Robert Diamond), Nancy (Mrs. Dennis Ditlove), Diane (Mrs. Richard Cohen). Student, Hamline U., 1925-26, U. Chgo., 1927. Co-owner, gen. mgr. Mpls. Lakers Basketball Team, 1947-56; originator Minn. Vikings (Nat. Football League), Mpls., 1960; pres. Minn. Vikings (Nat. Football League), 1960—; pres. Max Winter Enterprises, Hawaii; v.p. Income Guarantee, Aloha C.A.T.V.; dir. Downtown Bank of St. Paul, Bank of Mpls., Viking Enterprise Mpls., Mpls. Bank and Trust Co., Gambles Continental Bank. Author: Sports Books for Children, 1957. Mem. County Park Bd., 1959-64; chmn. Muscular Dystrophy, 1961; mem. Gov.'s Bus. Adv. Com., 1965; chmn. Nat. Govs. Conf., 1965. Recipient Hon. Scout award, 1946, 47, 48. Mem. Mpls. C. of C. (pres. 1969). Jewish. Clubs: Rotary, Optimist, Mpls. Athletic, Oak Ridge Country; Waialae Country (Honolulu), Outrigger (Honolulu). Office: Minnesota Vikings 9520 Viking Dr Eden Prairie MN 55344 *

WINTER, RICHARD LAWRENCE, financial and health care consulting company executive; b. St. Louis, Dec. 17, 1945; s. Melvin Lawrence and Kathleen Jane (O'Leary) W.; B.S. in Math., St. Louis U., 1967, M.S. in Math. (fellow), 1969; M.B.A., U. Mo., St. Louis, 1976; m. Pauline Alma Pardee, Nov. 10, 1984; children from previous marriage—Leigh Ellen, Jessica Marie. Research analyst Mo. Pacific R.R., St. Louis, 1971-73; dir. fin. relations Linclay Corp., St. Louis, 1973-74; asst. v.p. 1st Nat. Bank in St. Louis (name now Centerre Bank, N.A.), 1974-79; v.p. fin. UDE Corp., St. Louis, 1979-81; pres. Health Care Investments, Ltd., St. Louis, 1981—, Fin. & Investment Cons., Ltd., St. Louis, 1981; lectr. math. U. Mo.-St. Louis, 1972-74, St. Louis U., 1982—. Active various fund raising activities including St. Louis Symphony, Jr. Achievement, United Way St. Louis, Arts and Edn. Fund, St. Louis, 1974-79. Served with U.S. Army, 1969-71. Mem. Pi Mu Epsilon. Roman Catholic. Club: Mo. Athletic (St. Louis). Home: 1321 Green Tree Ln Saint Louis MO 63122 Office: PO Box 11586 Saint Louis MO 63105

WINTER, WILLIAM BERGFORD, manufacturing company executive; b. LaCrosse, Wis., July 16, 1928; s. Gustav J. and Bergliot H. W.; m. Marie Ann; children: Jonathan, Jennifer. BSCE, U. Wis., Madison, 1951. With Becor Western Inc. (formerly Bucyrus-Erie Co.), South Milwaukee, Wis., 1953—, gen. mgr. constrn. machinery div., 1963-65, v.p. mfg. and fgn. ops., 1965-71, pres., 1978—, also bd. dirs.; mng. dir. Ruston-Bucyrus Ltd., Lincoln, Eng., 1971-77, also bd. dirs.; chmn. bd. Ruston-Bucyrus Ltd., 1978—; bd. dirs. WICOR, Wis. Gas Co. Mem. exec. bd. dirs. YMCA, Met. Milw. Served with C.E. U.S. Army, 1951-53. Clubs: Western Racquet, Univ, Milw. Country. Office: Becor Western Inc 1100 Milwaukee Ave South Milwaukee WI 53172

WINTER, WINTON ALLEN, JR., lawyer, state senator; b. Ft. Knox, Ky., Apr. 19, 1953; s. Winton A. and Nancy (Morsbach) W.; m. Mary Boyd, July 28, 1978; children—Katie, Molly, Elizabeth. B.A., U. Kans., 1975, J.D., 1978. Bar: Kans. 1978. Ptnr. law firm Stevens, Brand, Lungstrum, Golden & Winter, Lawrence, Kans., 1978—; mem. Kans. Senate, 1982—. Bd. dirs. Lawrence United Fund, Boys Club of Lawrence. Mem. ABA, Am. Judicature Soc., Kans. Bar Assn., Douglas County Bar Assn. Kans. U. Law Soc. Republican. Roman Catholic. Club: Rotary. Note and comment editor Kans. Law Rev., 1977-78. Office: 502 First Nat Bank Tower PO Box 1200 Lawrence KS 66044

WINTERER, KERRY T., corporate executive, lawyer; b. Scottsbluff, Nebr., Jan. 7, 1950; s. I. Leo and Stella (Outson) W.; m. Norma J. Hansen, Aug. 20, 1977. BA, U. Nebr., 1972; JD, Columbia U., 1975. Bar: Nebr. Atty. Baird, Holm et al, Omaha, 1975-78; trust officer Omaha Nat. Bank, 1978-81; v.p. ABACUS, Inc., Omaha, 1981-84, pres., 1984-87; from regional dir. internat. ops. to mgr. cons. services Applied Communications, Inc., Omaha, 1987—. Bd. dirs. Family Service, Omaha, 1980—, pres., 1983-85; active Leadership Omaha, 1978-79. Mem. Nebr. Bar Assn. Avocations: running, backpacking. Office: Applied Communications Inc 68154 S 108th Ave Omaha NE 68154

WINTERS, DAVID A., restaurant company executive; b. Marion, Ohio, June 22, 1942; s. Garland Eugene and Mildred Virginia (Beverly) W.; m. Judy Louise Maddox, Feb. 2, 1968 (div. Jan. 1980); children: Laurie Louise, David Ross. BS Commerce and Administrn., Ohio State U., 1966, M Acctg., 1967. CPA. Mgr. Arthur Andersen & Co., Columbus, Ohio, 1967-76; treas. United States Am., Columbus, Ohio, 1976-83; chmn. Restec Systems, Inc., Columbus, Ohio, 1983—. Mem. Am. Inst. CPA's, Nat. Assn. Accts., Ohio Soc. CPA's. Home: 18180 Pine Ln Marysville OH 43040 Office: Restec Systems Inc 1317 E Broad St Columbus OH 43205

WINTERS, DOUGLAS E., manufacturing company executive; b. 1935. BSEE, Ohio State U., 1957. With Ohio Brass Co., Mansfield, 1957—, sales engr., 1958-59, dist. mgr., 1959-63, asst. to v.p. sales, 1963-66, chief engr., 1966-68, v.p. engring., 1968-79, now pres., also bd. dirs. Served to lt. AUS, 1951-53. Office: The Ohio Brass Co 380 N Main St Mansfield OH 44902 *

WINTERS, STEVEN PAUL, accountant; b. New Castle, Ind., Jan. 10, 1945; s. Paul Henry and Marguerite (Harcourt) W.; cert. in acctg. Ind. U., 1969; B.S., Ball State U., 1972; m. Roberta L. Rahn, 1981; children: Karen, Luke. Audit supr. Coopers & Lybrand, Indpls. and Ft. Wayne, Ind., 1972-77; corp. controller Oxford Devel. Corp., Indpls., 1977-80; real estate tax specialist Kern, Hall, Ford & Co., C.P.A.s, Indpls., 1980-81; founder Steven P. Winters, C.P.A., Inc., 1981—; co-founder Genesis Group, Inc., 1982—; co-developer Indpls. Downtown Heliport, 1985—. C.P.A., Ind. Mem. Am. Inst. C.P.A.s, Ind. C.P.A. Soc., Nat. Council Corvette Clubs. Republican. Mem. The Way Internat. Club: Toastmasters (past corr. sec.). Home: 8702

Cheltenham Rd Indianapolis IN 46256 Office: 51 S New Jersey St Indianapolis IN 46204

WINTERS, THOMAS BERNARR, mechanical engineer, campground director; b. Ironton, Ohio, Sept. 18, 1931; s. Raymond Franklin and Adryenne Beryl (Lynd) W.; m. Dolores Jean Leis, Aug. 30, 1953. Attended Franklin U. With Westinghouse Electric Co., Columbus, Ohio, 1956-69; with Westreco, Marysville, Ohio, 1969—, design engr., 1969—; pres., chief exec. officer Winters Recreational Area, Raymond, Ohio, 1981—, also bd. dirs. Patentee icemaker, water delivery, defrost timer, others. Served with USNR, 1949-59. Methodist. Office: 20267 SR 347 Raymond OH 43067

WINTERSTEEN, BRUCE CHARLES, dentist, researcher; b. Canton, Ill., Oct. 2, 1954; s. Caroll Vincent and Phyllis Ann (Cowell) W. BS, U. Ill., 1977; DDS with honors, U. Ill., Chgo., 1981; postgrad., U. Chgo., 1980—. Gen. practice dentistry Chgo., 1981—. Mem. Student Clinicians of ADA, Chgo. Assn. Immunologists, Omicron Kappa Upsilon. Roman Catholic. Club: Cath. Alumni. Avocations: athletics, photography, choir. Home: 111 1/2 Bell Ave Monticello IL 61856

WINZENBURG, STEPHEN MARK (WINTERS), radio station executive; b. Mankato, Minn., Dec. 18, 1954; s. Frank Edward and Kathryn Helen (Trier) W.; m. Patricia Ann Liffrig, Dec. 20, 1981; children—Kathryn Frances, Mary Collette. B.A., U. S.D.; M.A. in Journalism, U. Minn. News dir. Sta. WCIE, Lakeland, Fla., 1977-80; prof. Fla. So. Coll., Lakeland, 1982-84, Marycrest Coll., Davenport, Iowa, 1984; dir. syndication Second Thoughts, Belleville, Ill., 1984-85; gen. mgr. Sta. KNDR, Bismarck, N.D., 1985, Sta. WRFW, River Falls, Wis., 1985—; asst. prof. journalism U. Wis., River Falls, 1985—; corr. Internat. Media Service, Washington, 1977-80. Author: The Happy Homemaker Cookbook, 1978. Recipient Commendation award Am. Women in Radio and TV, 1985, Fla. News award AP, 1980, Enterprise award Enterprise Radio Network, 1978; named Citizen of Yr., Women for Responsible Legislation, 1980. Republican. Lodges: Kiwanis, Rotary. Office: Univ of Wisconsin 310 N Hall River Falls WI 54022

WIOT, JEROME FRANCIS, radiologist; b. Cin., Aug. 24, 1927; s. Daniel and Elvera (Weisgerber) W.; m. Andrea Kockritz, July 29, 1972; children—J. Geoffrey, Jason. M.D., U. Cin., 1953. Diplomate: Am. Bd. Radiology (trustee, pres.). Intern Cin. Gen. Hosp., 1953-54, resident, 1954-55, 58-59; gen. practice medicine Wyoming, Ohio, 1955-57; mem. faculty U. Cin., 1959-67, 68—, prof., chmn. radiology, 1973—, acting sr. v.p., provost for med. affairs, 1985-86; practice medicine specializing in radiology Tampa, Fla., 1967-68. Contbr. articles to med. jours. Served with USN, 1945-46. Fellow Am. Coll. Radiology (pres. 1983-84, chmn. commn. on diagnostic radiology); mem. Radiol. Soc. N.Am., Am. Roentgen Ray Soc. (pres. 1986-87), Am. Bd. Radiology (pres. 1982-84), Ohio Med. Assn., Cin. Acad. Medicine, Radiol. Soc. Greater Cin., Ohio Radiol. Soc., Ohio Thoracic Soc., Fleischner Soc., Soc. Gastrointestinal Radiologists. Office: U Cin 234 Goodman St Cincinnati OH 45267

WIPPER, JAMES MARK, stockbroker; b. Cleve., Apr. 26, 1960; s. Michael Alan and Mary Carolyn (Finney) W. BA in History, St. Lawrence U., 1982; MBA, Case Western Res., 1986. Stockborker McDonald and Co., Cleve., 1986—; trust officer Soc. Bank, Cleve. Mem. Estate Planning Council Cleve., The Bond Club of Cleve. Republican. Episcopalian. Club: The Cleve. Skating. Avocation: historic automobile preservation. Home: 19614 Winslow Rd Shaker Heights OH 44122 Office: McDonald & Co Securities Inc 2100 Society Bldg Cleveland OH 44114

WIRKUS, THOMAS EDWARD, speech and theatre educator; b. Marshfield, Wis., May 31, 1933; s. Joseph Albert and Jamina Sylvia (Hansen) W.; m. Lois Ann Langfeldt, July 28, 1956; children: Terrance, Sheila, Mary, Timothy. BS in Secondary Edn., U. Wis., Stevens Point, 1956; MS in Speech, U. Wis., 1959; PhD in Speech Edn., Northwestern U., 1966. Tchr. high sch. Iola, Wis., 1956, Wautoma, Wis., 1956-57, Wausau, Wis., 1957-58; teaching asst. speech U. Wis., Madison, 1958-59; prof. speech and theatre U. Wis., La Crosse, 1959—, supr. student teaching, 1966—, chmn. dept., 1970-79, cons. listening, 1980—. Co-author: Communication and the Technical Man, 1972; contbr. articles to profl. jours. Bd. dirs. La Crosse Concert Band, 1981—. Mem. Speech Communications Assn., Cen. States Speech Assn., Wis. Communication Assn. (chmn. Weaver award com. 1976, chmn. nominations com. 1987—), Crest Investment Club (sec. 1984-85), Internat. Listening Assn., Phi Delta Kappa (pres. 1986-87, Pres.'s award 1986). Roman Catholic. Avocations: concert and dance band drumming, orchestra leader, camping, travel. Home: 1620 State St La Crosse WI 54601 Office: U Wis La Crosse 348 Fine Arts Bldg 1725 State St La Crosse WI 54601

WIRSCHING, CHARLES PHILIPP, JR., brokerage house executive; b. Chgo., Oct. 26, 1935; s. Charles Philipp and Mamie Ethel (York) W.; m. Beverly Ann Bryan, May 28, 1966. BA, U. N.C., 1957. Sales rep. Adams-Millis Corp., Chgo., 1963-67; ptnr. Schwartz-Wirsching, Chgo., 1968-70; sec., dir. Edwin H. Mann, Inc., Chgo., 1971-74; stockbroker Paine Webber, Inc., Chgo., 1975-85, account v.p., 1986—. Republican. Episcopalian. Avocation: fgn. travel. Home: 434 Clinton Pl River Forest IL 60305 Office: Paine Webber Inc 55 W Monroe Chicago IL 60603

WIRTH, RICHARD MARVIN, educator; b. Grosse Pointe, Mich., Aug. 26, 1929; s. Marvin Oscar and Marion (Maxfield) W.; B.Sc., Wayne State U., 1950, M.A., 1952; postgrad. U. Wis., Western State Coll. Colo., Ball State U. Tchrs. Coll. Tchr. drama and debate Warren (Mich.) Consol. Schs., 1951-87. Former organist and choir dir. St. John's Evang. United Ch. of Christ, lay minister, 1979; ordained minister of worship, 1982; former kapellmeister St. John-St. Luke United Ch. Christ; former master Co. of Lay Ministries. Mem. scholastic writing awards adv. com. SE Mich. Named Vol. of Week, United Found., 1963; recipient Silver Beaver award Boy Scouts Am., 1962; Disting. Educator award Mich. State Fair, 1964; Disting. Tchr. award Mich. Assn. Classroom Tchrs., 1969. Mem. Mich. (pres. dept. classroom tchrs., Tchr. of Yr. 1962, dir. area 6, parliamentarian 1972-80, dir.), Ky. (parliamentarian 1974), Kans., Okla. (parliamentarian 1979-80) Warren (editor Harbinger, past pres., sr. trustee) edn. assns., Mich. Student Congress (parliamentarian), Southfield Public Employees, Speech Assn. Am., Nat. Cath. Forensic League (parliamentarian 1979, 82), Nat. Council Tchrs. of English, Mich. League Credit Unions, Mich. League Practical Nurses (parliamentarian), Delta Sigma Rho. Editor of ednl. publs. Contbr. articles to profl. jours. Home: Box 283 Algonac MI 48001 Office: 2120 Russell Detroit MI 48207

WIRTH, STEWART WALTER, accountant; b. St. Louis, Aug. 16, 1961; s. Walter R. and Marie M. (Kramer) W. BS in Accountancy, U. Mo., 1983. CPA, Mo. Acct. Mueller & Herring, CPA, St. Louis, 1983-85; internal auditor Interco Inc., St. Louis, 1986—. Mem. Am. Inst. CPA's, Mo. Soc. CPA's. Lutheran. Avocation: softball. Home: 3901 Jacinto Dr Saint Louis MO 63125 Office: Interco Inc 101 S Hanley Saint Louis MO 63105

WIRTZ, ARTHUR MICHAEL, JR., professional sports team executive. m. Sunny Wirtz; children: Laura, Arthur III, Jimmy. BS, U. Pa. V.p. Chgo. Black Hawks, 1958—. Office: Chgo Black Hawks 1800 W Madison St Chicago IL 60612 *

WIRTZ, GERALD PAUL, engineering educator, consultant, researcher; b. Wisconsin Rapids, Wis., Dec. 22, 1937; s. Theodore Anton and Grace (Vincent) W.; m. Darlene Yvonne Haupt, June 3, 1961; children: Cynthia, Melissa, Lauralee. BS, St. Norbert Coll., 1959; BME, Marquette U., 1961; PhD in Materials Sci., Northwestern U., 1966. Materials research scientist Airco Inc., Niagara Falls, N.Y., 1966-68; asst. prof. ceramic engring. U. Ill.-Urbana, 1968-73, asst. dean engring., 1973-74, assoc. prof. ceramic engring., 1973—, assoc. head. ceramic engring., 1986—; cons. Brookhaven Nat. Lab., L.I., N.Y., U.S. Army C.E., Mil. Inst. Engring., Rio de Janeiro. OAS fellow, 1977; Fulbright Hays lectr. U. Aveiro (Portugal), 1980; Fulbright lectr. U. Coimbra (Portugal), 1985. Mem. Am. Ceramic Soc., Keramos, Sigma Xi, Tau Beta Pi, Pi Tau Sigma. Roman Catholic. Patentee in field; contbr. articles to tech. jours. Home: Rural Route 2 Box 159 Urbana IL 61801 Office: 105 S Goodwin Ave Urbana IL 61801

WIRTZ, JUANITA MARIE, auditor; b. Wisconsin Rapids, Wis., Mar. 7, 1952; d. George Anthony and Betty Jane (Larsen) W. AS in acctg., VTAE, 1981; student, Bank Adminstrn. Inst., 1981; BA in English, U. Wis., Superior, 1981. Chartered bank auditor. Mgr. audit dept. First Nat. Bank, Wisconsin Rapids, 1978-81, acting auditor, 1981-84, auditor, 1984—; instr. Vocat. Sch., Wisconsin Rapids, 1985. Bd. dirs., treas. Woodland Council Girl Scouts U.S., Wisconsin Rapids, 1980—; loaned exec. United Way South Wood County, Wisconsin Rapids, 1986. Mem. Inst. Internal Auditors. Roman Catholic. Office: First Nat Bank 311 W Grand Ave Wisconsin Rapids WI 54494

WIRTZ, WILLIAM WADSWORTH, real estate and sports executive; b. Chgo., Oct. 5, 1929; s. Arthur Michael and Virginia (Wadsworth) W.; m. Joan Roney, Dec. 15, 1950; children: William R., Gail W., Karen K., Peter R., Alison M. A.B., Brown U., 1950. Pres. Chgo. Blackhawk Hockey Team, Inc., 1966—, Chgo. Stadium Corp., 1966—, Consol. Enterprises, Inc., Chgo., 1966—, Forman Realty Corp., Chgo., 1965—, 333 Building Corp., Chgo., 1966—, Wirtz Corp., Chgo., 1964—. Clubs: Saddle and Cycle (Chgo.), Racquet (Chgo.), Mid-America (Chgo.); Fin and Feather (Elgin, Ill.); Sunset Ridge Country (Northbrook, Ill.). Home: Winnetka IL Office: Wirtz Corp 666 Lake Shore Dr Chicago IL 60611 *

WISCHNER, GEORGE JOSEPH, psychologist, educator; b. N.Y.C., Apr. 14, 1914; s. Morris L. and Esther (Goldfarb) W.; m. Sary Kadis, Sept. 16, 1947 (div. 1965); children: Cathy Evian, Claudia March; m. Mary Ellen Gerlach-Carder, 1972. BA cum laude, Bklyn. Coll., 1938; MA, U. Iowa (formerly State U. Iowa), 1941, PhD, 1947. Area supr., state supr. Iowa Remedial Edn Survey, 1940-42; asst. prof. psychologist student health service U. Mo., 1947-48; asst. prof. child psychology Iowa Child Welfare Research Sta. State U. Iowa, 1948-49; asst. prof. psychology and speech U. Ill., Urbana, 1949-52; project leader tng. methods div. Human Resources Research Office George Washington U., 1952-53, dir. research Human Resources Research Office, 1953-55; prof. psychology U. Pitts., 1955-72; prof., chmn. Cleve. State U., 1972-79, prof. emeritus, 1979—, interim dir. Office Research Services, 1979-80; cons. VA, 1955-72. Assoc. editorial bd. Jour. Cons. Psychology, 1955-58, Perceptual Motor Skills, 1959—; editorial cons. Jour. Speech and Hearing Disorders, 1962-81; contbr. to books and profl. jours. Served with USAAF, 1942-46. Fellow Am. Speech and Hearing Assn. (councilor 1966-69, exec. com. 1968), Am Psychol. Assn. (council of reps. 1967-70), Pa. Psychol. Assn. (pres. 1964-65), AAAS; mem. Midwestern Psychol. Assn., Eastern Psychol. Assn., Psychomonic Soc., Sigma Xi (pres. U. Pitts. chpt. 1971). Home: 6280-301 Greenwood Pkwy Sagamore Hills OH 44067 Office: Cleve State U Dept Psychology Cleveland OH 44115

WISDEN, RAYMOND FREDERICK, computer systems executive; b. Springfield, Ohio, May 4, 1946; s. George Frederick and Margaret Ruth (Currie) W.; divorced; 1 child, Raymond Paul. AA in Edu., Oscar Rose Jr. Coll., 1976; BS in Computer Sci., Cen. State. U., Edmond, Okla., 1977. Cert. system profl., Inst. for Cert. Computer Profls. Enlisted USAF, 1966, advanced through ranks to staff sgt., resigned, 1975; system coordinator Credit Life Ins., Springfield, Ohio, 1983; project mgr. Credit Life Ins., Springfield, 1981-83, system cons., 1979-81; analyst, programmer E.F. MadDonald, Dayton, 1978-79, State of Okla., Oklahoma City, 1977-78; bus. producedure cons. Commn. for Tech., City Sch. System, Springfield, 1982-85. Mem. Rep. Presdl. Task Force, 1982. Mem. Life Office Mgmt. Assn. (fellow Life Mgmt. Inst.), Assn. System Mgmt. (v.p. seminars 1984, v.p. membership 1985, pres. elect 1986). Presbyterian. Club: Toastmaster (Springfield) (pres. 1986—). Avocations: tennis, golf, swimming. Home: 2247 N Fountain Springfield OH 45504 Office: Credit Life Ins One S Limestone Springfield OH 45501

WISDOM, GUYRENA KNIGHT, psychologist, educator; b. St. Louis, July 27, 1923; d. Gladys Margaret (Hankins) McCullin; AB, Stowe Tchrs. Coll., 1945; AM, U. Ill., 1951; postgrad. St. Louis U., 1952-53, 58, 62; Washington U., St. Louis, 1959-61; U. Chgo., 1966-67; Drury Coll., 1968; U. Mo., 1971-72; Fontbonne Coll., 1973; Harris-Stowe StateColl., 1974, 81-82. Tchr. elementary sch. St. Louis Pub. Sch. System, 1945-63, psychol. examiner, 1963-68, sch. psychologist, 1968-74, cons. spl. edn., 1974-77, supr. spl. edn. dept., 1977-79, coordinator staff devel. div., 1979-81; pvt. tutor, 1971-72; sch. psychologist, 1984-85; pvt. practice psychologist, St. Louis, 1985—; instr. Harris Tchrs. Coll., St. Louis, 1973-74, Harris-Stowe Coll., 1979. Contbr. articles to profl. jours. Mem. Nat. Assn. Sch. Psychologists, Mo. Assn. Children With Learning Disabilities, Council for Exceptional Children, Mo. Tchrs. Assn., Assn. Supervision and Curriculum Devel., Pi Lambda Theta, Kappa Delta Pi. Roman Catholic. Home: 5046 Wabada St Saint Louis MO 63113

WISE, HENRY ALEXANDER, II, urologist; b. N.Y.C., Feb. 17, 1937; s. John Sargeant and Elizabeth (Thompson) W.; m. Joshan Backus, June 26, 1965; 1 child, Joshan Ridgely. BA, U. Va., 1959, MD, 1964. Intern Vanderbilt U. Hosp., Nashville, 1964-65, resident in surgery, 1967-68; resident in urology Johns Hopkins U. Hosp., Balt., 1968-72; faculty surgery Ohio State U., Columbus, 1972-86, chmn. dept. urology, 1978-85; practice medicine specializing in urology Columbus, 1978—; pres. Allied Realty, Ltd., Charlottesville, Va., 1974-86. Ohio Kidney Stone Mgmt., Inc., Columbus, 1984-86, Ohio Kidney Stone Ctr., columbus, 1985-86, Ohio Kidney Stone Equipment and Realty Co., 1985-86. Contbr. articles to profl. jours. Mem. AMA, Am. Urology Assn.(n. cen. sect.), Soc. Pediatric Urology, Ohio Urology Soc. (pres. 1986), Cen. Ohio Urology Soc. (sec., treas. 1978-82, pres. 1982), Univ. Urologist Soc. Republican. Episcopalian. Club: Brookide Country (Worthington, Ohio). Avocations: golf, tennis, work. Office: 3555 Olentangy River Rd Columbus OH 43214

WISE, JAY ALLAN, minister, real estate consultant; b. Mpls., Sept. 26, 1946; s. Howard Van and Shirley (Pomerantz) W.; m. Evelyne Annie Michelle Menet, Aug. 28, 1968; children: Myriam, Rachael. BA, U. Minn., 1968; MA, U. Madrid, Spain, 1972; DDiv, Cen. Sem., Mpls., 1981. Ordained to ministry Ind. Pentecostal Ch. Am., 1968. Pres. Allstate, Inc., Mpls., 1982—; minister Cen. Ch., Mpls., 1983—; bd. dirs. Service Investments, Inc., Mpls. Pub. (jour.) Luth. Courier, 1985. Mem. bd. Human Rights Commn., Robbinsdale, Minn., 1975-77. Mem. Am. Soc. Religious Freedom, Assn. Real Estate Cons., Minn. Real Estate Assn. (v.p.), Christian-Jewish Assn. (chmn. Mpls. 1984—). Avocations: pilot, race car driver, golf, tennis. Office: 8000 Town Line Ave #203 Minneapolis MN 55438

WISE, JON ARTHUR, accountant; b. Greenville, Mich., July 1, 1947; m. Joyce A. Bowerman, Sept. 24, 1982; children: David, Robin, Jay. BS, Ferris State Coll., 1969; MBA, U. Toledo, 1970. CPA, Mich.; cert assessor, Mich. Acct. Vannatter, Howell and Co., Hillsdale, Mich., 1970-72; asst. auditor gen. State of Mich., Lansing, 1972—; property tax adv. com. Lansing Community Coll., 1980—. Contbr. articles to profl. jours. Mem. bd. rev. Delta Twp., Lansing, 1980—. Mem. Am. Inst. CPA's, State Assn. Accts., Auditors, Bus. Adminstrs. Lodges: Masons, Elks. Avocations: baseball card collecting, golf, gardening.

WISE, LELAND JOHN, JR., educational administrator; b. Geneva, N.Y., Sept. 26, 1944; s. Leland John and Julia Marie (Lancia) W.; m. Helen Wanneta Dahlen, Jan. 6, 1954; children—Shannon Marie, Lee Jackson, Zachary Dahlen. B.A., State Coll. Iowa, 1967; M.A., U. No. Iowa, 1970; Ph.D., U. Iowa, 1978. Cert. tchr., Iowa. Tchr., Decorah (Iowa) Jr. High Sch., 1967-68; tchr. LaSalle High Sch., Cedar Rapids, Iowa, 1968-69; grad. asst. dept. phys. edn. U. No. Iowa, Cedar Falls, 1969-70; instr. Muscatine (Iowa) Community Coll., 1970-71; tchr. Cedar Rapids Community Sch., 1971-75; cons. No. Trails A.E.A., Clear Lake, Iowa, 1975-76; prin. Latimer (Iowa) Elem./Middle Sch., 1976-79; prin. Marion (Iowa) High Sch., 1979-83; supt. Benton Community Schs., Van Horne, Iowa, 1983—; ednl. cons. Active YMCA. Iowa Dept. Pub. Instrn. Title IV grantee, 1979. Mem. Assn. Supervision and Curriculum Devel., Am. Assn. Sch. Adminstrs., Rural Edn. Assn., Assn. Sch. Bus. Ofcls., Assn. Negotiators and Contract Adminstrs., Iowa Assn. Sch. Adminstrs. Iowa High Sch. Athletic Assn., Phi Delta Kappa. Roman Catholic. Clubs: Lions Internat., Optimists. Author book; contbr. article to profl. jour. Office: Central Adminstrn Bldg Van Horne IA 52346

WISE, MARK L., computer services company executive; b. Lima, Ohio, June 26, 1955; s. Calvin Cole and Marilyn (Baird) W.; m. Janet Lynn Schlosser, Jan. 21, 1977; children: Mindy Jonelle, Jeffrey Scott, Erin Nicole. BA in Computer Sci., Mt. Vernon (Ohio) Nazarene Coll., 1977. Pres. Alpha II Systems, Inc., Columbus, Ohio, 1977—. Mem. Am. Prodn. and Inventory Control Soc. Avocations: railfan, aviation. Office: Alpha II Systems Inc 5330 E Main St Columbus OH 43213

WISE, RODNEY GLEN, construction company executive; b. Mineral City, Ohio, Feb. 2, 1949; s. Glenn Albert and Donna Elizabeth (Blasenhauer) W.; m. Dolores Marie Cinson, July 18, 1970; 1 child, Brian Jon. Grad. high sch., Zorville, Ohio, 1967. Sales Reliable Auto & Indsl. Parts, Dover, Ohio, 1968-73; sales, billing Edwards Slaes & Service, Strasburg, Ohio, 1973-77; heavy equipment operator A&J Cinson Constrn., Inc., Malvern, Ohio, 1977-82, gen. supr., 1982-87, pres., 1987—. Served with Res. Mem. Ohio Oil and Gas Assn., Malvern Area Bus. and Profl. Assn., Buckeye State Sheriff Assn. Roman Catholic. Lodge: Eagles, Catholic Order Forresters. Avocations: camping, ATV riding.

WISE, STEPHEN CHARLES, nursing home administrator; b. Mt. Vernon, Ohio, Nov. 29, 1957; s. Charles F. and Neva (Edman) W.; m. Julie Faiella, Sept. 27, 1980; children: Philip Charles, Vincent Edward. BS, Ohio State U., 1980. Data processor St. Anthony's Hosp., Columbus, Ohio, 1980-81; acctg. cons. Convalescent Mgmt., Columbus, 1981-84; adminstr. Winchester (Ohio) Pl. Canal, 1984-86; area adminstr. The Hillhaven Corp., 1986—. Bd. fin. sub-com. Groveport Sch. Bd. Mem. Am. Coll. Nursing Home Adminstrs., Am. Health Care Assn., Ohio Health Care Assn., Cen. Ohio Geriatric Nurses Assn., Ohio State Alumni Assn., Alzheimer's Disease Assn., Canal Winchester C. of C. Club: Groveport Country. Avocations: golfing, traveling. Office: Winchester Pl 36 Lehman Dr Canal Winchester OH 43110

WISE, WILMA MARK, credit bureau and employment agency executive; b. Frankfort, Ill., Mar. 13, 1926; d. Paul and Louise (Staedke) Mark; m. Perry Kenneth Wise, Sept. 5, 1948; children: Douglas Kent, Dennis Mark. Student Met. Bus. Coll., 1943-44; grad. exec. devel. program Ind. U. Grad. Sch. Bus., 1975. Owner, ptnr. Naperville Credit Bur. (Ill.), 1958-70; gen. mgr., v.p. First Suburban Services, Naperville, 1970-75; pres., gen. mgr. Wise Surburban Services, Inc., divs. Snelling and Snelling, Wise Credit Bur., Wise/TempForce, Naperville, Ill., 1975—. Mem., pres. Naperville Dist. No. 203 Career Edn. Adv. Council, 1971—; mem. exec. com. North Cen. Coll. Community Fund Drive, 1980—, chmn., 1984-85; mem. exec. com. DuPage County Pvt. Industry Council, 1983—; 1st pres. Ill. Bus. Week, 1984. Named Boss of Year, Am. Bus. Women's Assn., 1979. Mem. Ill. Assn. Personnel Cons. (bd. dirs. 1976-81) Ill. Collector's Assn. (bd. dirs. 1982—, v.p. 1983-84, pres. 1985-86), Am. Collector's Assn., Internat. Fellowship Cert. Collectors, Associated Credit Burs. Inc. (Internat. Key Leadership award 1979, Excellence award 1984), Associated Credit Burs. Ill. (bd. dirs. 1975—, pres. 1979-80), Women in Mgmt. (Woman of Achievement award 1982), Naperville C. of C. (bd. dirs.), Downers Grove C. of C. (bd. dirs. 1972-75), Naperville Organ Soc. Luth. (mem. council 1978-84). Club: Cosmopolitan Dance (Naperville). Home: 7S410 Arbor Dr Naperville IL 60540 Office: 638-40 E Ogden Ave Twin Center Naperville IL 60540

WISEMAN, DANA, family physician; b. Syracuse, N.Y., Mar. 12, 1954; s. Richard D. Wiseman and Ruthann (Belloff) Newman; m. Amy Louise Post, June 14, 1980; children: Benjamin Alan, Shari Lenore. BA, Hamilton Coll., 1976; MD, SUNY, Syracuse, 1980. Diplomate Am. Acad. Family Practice. Resident in family practice Ravenswood Hosp., Chgo., 1981-83; family practitioner USAF Hosp., Chanute AFB, Ill., 1983-86; staff physician Northwestern U., Evanston, Ill., 1986—; part-time faculty family practice residency Ravenswood Hosp., 1986—; dir.Men's Health Clinic Northwestern U. Served to maj. USAF, 1983-86. Mem. Am. Acad. Family Physicians. Home: 7524 N Kedvale Skokie IL 60076 Office: Northwestern U Student Health Services 633 Emerson Evanston IL 60208

WISEMAN, MICHAEL JOSEPH, retail executive; b. St. Louis, Nov. 21, 1959; s. Cornelius Gerard and Shirley Marie (Wolfslau) W.; m. Deborah Ann Toney, Mar. 21, 1987. BS in Bus., Drake U., 1981, MBA, 1983. Customer service clk. Montgomery Ward, Des Moines, 1982-83, asst. group merchandiser, 1983-84, personnel mgr., 1984-86; personnel mgr. Montgomery Ward, Berkeley, Ill., 1986—. Mem. Assn. MBA Execs., Delta Sigma Pi (bd. dirs. 1985-86). Democrat. Roman Catholic. Avocations: model railroading, baseball. Home: 5550 Abbey Dr #4A Lisle IL 60532 Office: Montgomery Ward Nat Parts Ctr 1111 Taft Ave Berkeley IL 60163

WISER, RALPH, architect; b. Chgo., June 29, 1955; s. Heinz Helmut and Kaete Johanna (Molzahn) W.; m. Elizabeth Ann Ruppert, 1986. BArch, U. Ill., Chgo., 1978. Model builder, draftsman Harry Weese & Assocs., Chgo., 1976-82, job capt., 1982-86; chief draftsman, mgr. Anderson-Mikos Architects, Chgo., 1986—. Mem. AIA (assoc.), Constrn. Specifications Inst., Chgo. Fedn. Musicians. Democrat. Lutheran. Avocations: fishing, canoeing, handball, archery, photography.

WISHON, GORDON DUANE, military officer, computer specialist; b. Balt., Nov. 10, 1952; s. Gordon Lee Wishon and Elva June (McKinney) Morel; m. Susan Alice Logue, June 23, 1973; 1 child, Allison Ashley. BS in Computer Sci., W.Va. U., 1977. Enlisted USAF, 1971, advanced through ranks to capt., 1982; computer technician foreign tech. div. USAF, Wright-Patterson AFB, Ohio, 1971-75; navigator weapons systems officer USAF, Mountain Home AFB, Idaho, 1979-81; chief fighter support br. embedded systems div. USAF, Langley AFB, Va., 1981-85; chief ops. div. USAF Inst. Tech., Wright-Patterson AFB, 1985—. Avocations: automobile racing, electronics. Home: 386 Towncrest Dr Beavercreek OH 45385 Office: AFIT/SIO Wright Patterson AFB OH 45433

WISNIEWSKI, JOSEPH MICHAEL, engineering executive; b. Grand Rapids, Mich., Sept. 7, 1954; s. Victor Chester Sr. and Clara (Wiewiora) W.; m. Barbara Alice Berry, May 4, 1974; children: Michele, Michael. BS in Mech. Engring., Western Mich. U., 1980. Product engr. Steelcase, Grand Rapids, 1973-80; sr. project engr. Haworth, Holland, Mich., 1980-82, dir. engring., 1982-85; v.p. engring. Shaw-Walker, Muskegon, Mich., 1985—. Patentee in field. Recipient Welded Steel Tubing Inst. Design award 1980. Mem. Soc. Plastic Engrs., Soc. Mfg. Engrs. Avocations: small game and waterfowl hunting, archery hunting, fishing, golf. Home: 14093 12th Ave Marne MI 49435 Office: Shaw Walker PO Box 209 Muskegon MI 49443

WISSEL, GEORGE L., manufacturing company executive; b. Cin., Oct. 22, 1942; s. George H. and Anna M. (Weber) W.; m. Sharon M. Kammann, May 20, 1967; children: Susan M., Sondra L. BEE, U. Cin., 1965; MEE, U. Dayton, 1983. Registered profl. engr., Ohio. Project engr. Cin. Milacron, 1970-75, engring. mgr., 1975-79, mfg. mgr., 1979-80, product mgr., 1980-82, chief engr., 1982-85, div. mgr., 1985—. Com. chmn. Warren County (Ohio) United Way, 1986; elder Pleasant Ridge Presbyn. Ch., 1982-85, deacon, 1976-82. Mem. IEEE, Electronic Industries Assn., Internat. Standards Orgn., Cin. Engring. Soc. Avocations: bicycling, camping. Home: 10315 Fields Ertel Rd Loveland OH 45140 Office: Cin Milacron Mason Rd & Rt 48 Lebanon OH 45036

WISWALL, FRED HERBERT, dentist; b. Brookings, S.D., June 7, 1948; s. Fred A. and Lois Marie (Johnson) W.; m. Sandra Sue Jenson, June 8, 1970; children: Jeffrey Herbert, Steven Frederick. DDS, U. Nebr., 1972. Gen. practice dentistry Watertown, S.D., 1974—. Mem. council Luth. Ch. of Our Redeemer, Watertown, 1985—. Served as dental officer USPHS, 1972-74. Mem. ADA, Am. Orthodontic Soc., Acad. Gen. Dentistry, S.D. Dental Assn. Republican. Club: K-10 Investment (Watertown). Lodge: Rotary (bd. dirs. Watertown club). Avocations: water skiing, snow skiing, hunting, fishing, sailing. Home: 1476 S Lake Dr Watertown SD 57201 Office: 600 4th St NE Watertown SD 57201

WITCHER, DANIEL DOUGHERTY, pharmaceutical company executive; b. Atlanta, May 17, 1924; s. Julius Gordon and Myrtice Eleanor (Daniel) W.; children: Beth S., Daniel Dougherty, J. Wright, Benjamin G.; m. Betty Lou Middaugh, Oct. 30, 1982. Student, Mercer U., 1946-47, Am. Grad. Sch. Internat. Mgmt., 1949-50. Regional dir. Sterling Drug Co., Rio de Janeiro and Sao Paulo, Brazil, 1951-56; gen. mgr. Mead Johnson & Co., Sao Paulo, 1956-60; area mgr. Upjohn Internat., Inc., Sao Paulo, 1960-64; v.p. Upjohn Internat., Inc., Kalamazoo, 1964-70, group v.p., 1970-73; pres., gen. mgr. Upjohn Internat., 1973-86; v.p. Upjohn Co., 1973-86; corp. v.p.

Worldwide Human Health Bus., 1985-86, corp. sr. v.p., 1986—, also bd. dirs.; chmn. Upjohn Health Care Services, 1982—. Trustee Am. Grad. Sch. Internat. Mgmt., 1981—. Served with USN, 1943-46. Mem. Pharm. Mfrs. Assn. (chmn. internat. sect. 1981-82, 85-86). Republican. Episcopalian. Office: The Upjohn Co 7000 Portage Rd Kalamazoo MI 49002

WITCZAK, BOB ANTON, computer science and business educator; b. Manitowoc, Wis., Jan. 14, 1941; s. Felix Andrew and Lucille Laura (Klosinski) W.; m. Jane Ann Collier, June 21, 1969; children: Eric James, Wendy Jane, Amy Jo. BE, U. Wis., Whitewater, 1963; MA, U. No. Colo., 1967. Tchr. bus. and computers New London (Wis.) Pub. Schs., 1963—, Fox Valley Tech. Sch., Appleton, Wis., 1963—; Mem. and writer data processing curriculum Wis. Dept. Pub. Instrn., Eau Claire, 1980; coordinator Bus. World, New London, 1981—. Author: (booklet) Computers in the Class, 1986. Mem. NEA, Nat. Bus. Edn. Assn., Northeastern Edn. Assn. (life mem., past pres. 1982), Wis. Bus. Edn. Assn. (life mem., v.p. 1970-72, bd. dirs.), New London Edn. Assn. (pres., sec., treas., bd. dirs.), Phi Delta Kappa. Roman Catholic. Club: Wolf River Mens. Lodge: Lions (sec. New London chpt., 1970-81, pres. 1983-84). Avocations: computer programming, reading, bridge. Home: 1608 Oshkosh St New London WI 54961 Office: New London Pub Schs 1000 W Washington St New London WI 54961

WITHEROW, JUDITH KAY, educator; b. Marion, Ind., Jan. 17, 1943; d. Ivan Brazilla and Bertha Mae (Comer) Seward; B.S. in Edn., Ball State U., 1965, M.A., 1971, Reading Specialist, 1979; m. William David Witherow, Aug. 23, 1964; children—Stephen William, Terri Lyn, Brian David. Elem. tchr. South Madison Community Sch. Corp., Markleville, Ind., 1967-73; tchr. grade 5 No. Community Schs. Tipton County, Windfall, Ind., 1973-79; reading specialist, 1979-83; reading specialist No. Community Sch. Tipton County, Sharpsville, Ind., 1983—. Leader Methodist Youth Fellowship, Vanlue, Ohio. Recipient Tchr. of Yr. award No. Community Schs., 1980, 81. Mem. Internat. Reading Assn., Mid-Central Reading Council (pres. 1982-83), Assn. Supervision and Curriculum Devel., Am. Fedn. Tchrs. Democrat. Home: Rural Route 1 Box 36 Sharpsville IN 46068 Office: No Community Schs Tipton County Rural Rt 2 Sharpsville IN 46068

WITHERSPOON, FREDDA LILLY, educator; b. Houston; d. Fred D. and Vanita E. (Meredith) Lilly; A.B., Bishop Coll.; M.S.W., Washington U., St. Louis, M.A. in Guidance and Counseling, M.A. in Ednl. Psychology, Ph.D., St. Louis U., 1965; m. Robert L. Witherspoon; children—Robert L., Vanita. Social worker, supr. St. Louis City Welfare Office, Homer G. Phillips Hosp.; tchr. English, guidance counselor St. Louis Pub. Schs., 1950-65; prof. student personnel services Forest Park Community Coll., St. Louis, 1965—; cons. Ednl. Testing Service, Princeton, N.J., Head Start program, 1965-68; counseling cons. St. Louis Job Corps Center for Women, 1966-68. Organizer teenage service guild Annie Malone Children's Home, 1964; v.p. St. Louis chpt. NAACP, 1969-83, pres. Mo. Conf., 1973-84, also organizer Forest Park young adult council, also bd. dirs.; mem. Challenge of 70's Crime Commn., 1970-75; mem. adv. council Central Inst. for Deaf, 1970-78; mem. exec. bd. Mayor's St. Louis Ambassadors; mem. Mayor's Council Youth, 1970-75; dir. teens fund drive March of Dimes, 1960-72, Lily Day drive for Crippled Children, 1966-72; founder Met. St. Louis chpt. Coalition of 100 Black Women, Inc., 1984; mem. speakers bur. United Way, 1969-82; bd. dirs. children's services City of St. Louis, Mo. Heart Assn.; bd. dirs., also founder Met. St. Louis inter-alumni council United Negro Coll. Fund; bd. dirs. Social Health Assn., Conservatory Assn. Schs. for Arts, St. Louis Heart Assn., Girl Scouts; pres. St. Louis Met. YWCA, 1978-79, bd. dirs.; bd. dirs. St. Louis Urban League, vice chmn., 1977-81; organizer Jr. Annie Malone Service Guild. Named Woman of Year, Greyhound Bus Corp., 1967, St. Louis Argus, 1968, Nat. Outstanding Woman, Iota Phi Lambda, 1970; named Outstanding Woman of Achievement, Globe Dem., 1970, Outstanding Educator of Am., 1971, Nat. Top Lady Distinction, 1974; recipient Negro History award, 1971; George Washington Carver award, 1976; Health and Welfare Council award, 1975; Vol. of Yr. award United Negro Coll. Fund.; Continental Socs. award, 1984. Mem. NAACP (life; Nat. Outstanding Youth Adv. 1977, numerous awards 1977-84), Am. Personnel and Guidance Assn., AAUP (pres. 1975-81), AAUW, Nat. Assn. Women Deans and Counselors, Am. Sch. Counselors Assn., Am. Vocational Guidance Assn., Assn. Measurement and Evaluation in Guidance, Nat. Assn. Jr. Colls., Nat. Faculty Assn. Jr. Colls., LWV, Nat. Council Negro Women (life), Mo. Assn. Social Welfare, Jack and Jill, Mound City (pres. 1946-49), Nat. Assn. Women Lawyers, Nat. Bar Assn., Nat. Barristers Wives (founder), Mound City Bar Aux. (founder, pres. 1946-49), Top Ladies of Distinction (organizer Met. St. Louis chpt.), Metro St. Louis Inter-Alumni Council of UNCF, Continental Socs. (founder Met. St. Louis chpt.), Kappa Delta Pi, Iota Phi Lambda (nat. pres. 1977-81), Sigma Gamma Rho, Pi Lambda Theta, Phi Delta Kappa. Research on high sch. drop outs with police records, uses of group guidance techniques in jr. colls., community resources for jr. coll. students. Home: 20 Lewis Pl Saint Louis MO 63113

WITHERSPOON, WILLIAM, investment economist; b. St. Louis, Nov. 21, 1909; s. William Conner and Mary Louise (Houston) W.; student Washington U. Evening Sch., 1928-47; m. Margaret Telford Johanson, June 25, 1938; children—James Tomlin, Jane Witherspoon Peltz, Elizabeth Witherspoon Vodra. Research dept. A. G. Edwards & Sons, 1928-31; pres. Witherspoon Investment Co., 1931-34; head research dept. Newhard Cook & Co., 1934-43; chief price analysis St. Louis Ordnance Dist., 1943-45; head research dept. Newhard Cook & Co., 1945-53; owner Witherspoon Investment Counsel, 1953-64; ltd. partner Newhard Cook & Co., economist, investment analyst, 1965-68; v.p. research Stifel, Nicolaus & Co., 1968-81; lectr. on investments Washington U., 1948-67. Mem. Clayton Bd. of Edn., 1955-68, treas., 1956-68, pres., 1966-67; mem. Clayton Park and Recreation Commn., 1959-60; trustee Ednl. TV, KETC, 1963-64; mem. investment com. Gen. Assembly Mission Bd. Presbyterian Ch. U.S., Atlanta, 1976-79, mem. permanent com. ordination exams, 1979-85. Served as civilian Ordnance Dept., AUS, 1943-45. Chartered fin. analyst. Mem. St. Louis Soc. Fin. Analysts (pres. 1949-50). Club: Mo. Athletic (St. Louis). Home: 6401 Ellenwood Clayton MO 63105

WITHROW, MARY ELLEN, state treasurer; b. Marion, Ohio, Oct. 2, 1930; d. Clyde Welsh and Mildred (Stump) Hinamon; m. Norman David Withrow, Sept. 4, 1948; children: Linda Rizzo, Leslie Legge, Norma, Rebecca. Student, pub. schs., Marion, Ohio. With Elgin County Bd. Edn., Marion, Ohio, 1969-72; safety programs dir. ARC, Marion, 1968-72; dep. registrar State of Ohio, Marion, 1972-75; dep. county auditor Marion County (Ohio), 1975-77, county treas., 1977-83; treas. State of Ohio, Columbus, 1983—; chmn. Ohio State Bd. Deposits, from 1983. Mem. Democratic Nat. Com., co-chair farm crisis task force; mem. Met. Women's Ctr.; pres. Marion County Dem. Club, 1976; bd. advisors Ohio State U. Coll. Home Econs.; trustee Columbus Zool. Park. Inducted Ohio Women's Hall of Fame, 1986. Mem. State Assn. County Treas. (legis. chmn. 1979-83, treas. 1982), Nat. Assn. State Treas. (v.p. M.W. region 1983), Nat. Assn. State Auditors Comptrollers and Treas. (treas.), Council of State Govts. (state and fed. affairs com.), Delta Kappa Gamma Internat. (hon. Ohio mem.). Club: Bus. and Profl. Women's. Office: State of Ohio Treasury Dept 30 E Broad St 9th Floor Columbus OH 43215

WITKOWSKI, DANIEL DAVID, magician; b. Mpls., Apr. 23, 1956; s. Joseph Thomas and Olga Mary (Chas) W. BA in Communications, U. Minn., 1978. Promotion assoc. Sta. WCCO-TV, Mpls., 1974-76; ind. TV producer Mpls., 1976-78; pres., chief exec. officer MagicCom Inc., Mpls., 1978—; bd. dirs. Cath. Eldercare Inc., Mpls., 1986; cons. in field; lectr. various orgns.; exec. producer various magical programs. Author: Making Someone Disappear, 1986; producer: TV specials Houdini, The Man From Beyond, 1976, Abracadabra; command performances at The White House, 1982, 84, 86. Mem. Soc. Am. Magicians (honoree 1985), Internat. Brotherhood Magicians. Roman Catholic. Home: 1304 Boardwalk Ave N Minneapolis MN 55411 Office: MagicCom Inc 2801 Wayzata Blvd Suite 2 Minneapolis MN 55405

WITMER, PAUL LEROY, JR., auditor; b. Chambersburg, Pa., Nov. 9, 1954; s. Paul Leroy Sr. and Catherine Elizabeth (Shoemaker) W. BS, U. Wis., Platteville, 1976. CPA, Wis. Auditor 1st and 2d grade State of Wis., Madison, 1976-79; auditor 3d grade, spl. agt. State of Wis., Milw., 1984—; acct. Gould Inc. and Imperial Clevite Inc., Manitowoc, Wis., 1979-82; income tax return preparer part-time, Greenfield, Wis., 1985—. Fellow Wis. Inst. CPA's; mem. Am. Inst. CPA's. Avocations: travel, sports, amusement parks, people watching. Home: 10828 W Morgan Ave Apt 110 Greenfield WI 53228 Office: State of Wis Dept Health & Social Services 819 N 6th St #840 Milwaukee WI 53203

WITT, FRED THEODORE, jeweler; b. Downs, Kans., Jan. 28, 1916; s. Edward Henry and Barbara Elena (Brock) W.; m. Norma Lee Patten, June 6, 1937 (div. Jan. 1985); children—Sharon Lee Witt Dunham, George Clinton, Fred T. Grad. Downs High Sch., 1933. Owner, operator Fred T. Witt Jewelers Inc., Lincoln, Nebr., 1984—. Served with AUS, 1945-46. Mem. Nebr.-S.D. Jewelers Assn., Retail Jewelers Am. Am Legion. Republican. Presbyterian. Club: Nebraska. Lodges: Kiwanis, Masons, Elks. Home: 4110 Fiene St Lincoln NE 68502 Office: Fred T Witt Jewelers Inc 1033 O St Lincoln NE 68508

WITT, RICHARD ALLEN, insurance company executive; b. Milw., Nov. 29, 1951; s. Thomas Edward and Arleene Harriet (Fabrykowski) W.; m. Pamela J. Swenson, July 17, 1987. BS in Bus. Adminstrn. summa cum laude, Creighton U., 1974. Chartered fin. analyst. Jr. securities analyst United Benefit Life Ins., Omaha, 1974-76, securities analyst, 1976-78, sr. securities analyst, 1978, asst. v.p., 1978-83; second v.p. Mut. of Omaha Ins. Co., Omaha, 1983-86, v.p., 1986—. Fellow Fin. Analysts Fedn., Omaha-Lincoln Soc. Fin. Analysts (treas. 1982-83, sec. 1983-84, v.p. 1984-85, pres. 1985-86); mem. Inst. Chartered Fin. Analysts (grader 1986—). Office: Mutual of Omaha 3301 Dodge St Omaha NE 68175

WITTE, CRAIG HESS, optometrist; b. Chgo., June 25, 1943; s. William Barr and Caroline (Hess) W.; m. Dorothy Mae Blackwell, June 18, 1966; children: Christopher Scott, Adam Douglas. BS, U. Miss., 1966; OD, Ill. Coll. Optometry, 1972. Optometrist State of Ill., Springfield, 1972—. Mem. Ill. Whitehouse Commn. Children, 1980. Served with U.S Army, 1966-68. Mem. Am. Optometrists Assn., Ill. Optometrists Assn., Coll. Optometrists in Vision Devel. (assoc.), Optometric Extension Program (assoc. state dir.). Home and Office: 314 N Main St Bloomington IL 61701

WITTE, DENNIS ERWIN, computer scientist; b. Ft. Wayne, Ind., Aug. 26, 1951; s. Erwin F. and Eileen R. (Bieberich) W.; m. Marcia K. Wachtel, Aug. 26, 1972; children: Mark, David. BS, Concordia Coll., 1973; MS in Computer Sci., Ill. Inst. Tech., 1977, PhD in Computer Sci., 1983. From instr. to asst. prof. computer sci. Concordia Coll., River Forest, Ill., 1974-85, assoc. prof. computer sci., 1985—, dir. computer services, 1980—; computer sci. cons. Valparaiso U., Ind., 1981, Nat. Roofing Contractors Assn., 1984—, Luth. Layman's League, St. Louis, 1985, Luth. Ch., Mo. Synod, 1985. Mem. IEEE, Assn. for Computing Machinery, Luth. Ednl. Assn. Avocations: private pilot, snow skiing. Home: 1833 S Elizabeth Lombard IL 60148 Office: Concordia Coll 7400 Augusta Coll River Forest IL 60305

WITTEBORT, ROBERT JOHN, JR., lawyer; b. Chgo., Dec. 29, 1947; s. Robert John and Marguerite (Shaughnessy) W. B.A., Yale U., 1969; J.D., Notre Dame U., 1974. Bar: Ill. 1974, U.S. Dist. Ct. (no. dist.) Ill. 1974, U.S. Ct. Appeals (7th cir.) 1975, U.S. Tax Ct. 1977, U.S. Ct. Mil. Appeals 1982. Assoc. Hopkins & Sutter, Chgo., 1974-77; gen. counsel, asst. dir. Ill. Housing Devel. Authority, Chgo., 1977-82; ptnr. Chapman and Cutler, Chgo., 1982—. Contbg. editor: Business Law, 4th edit., 1977. Contbr. Notre Dame Lawyer, 1974. Bd. dirs. Orch. Ill. Assn., Chgo. Served to comdr. USNR, 1969—. Mem. Nat. Assn. Bond Lawyers, Naval Order U.S. (vice comdr.-gen.), Ill. Commandery Naval Order U.S. (comdr. 1987), Lambda Alpha. Republican. Clubs: Chicago, Saddle & Cycle (Chgo.).

WITTEN, BEROLD ISRAEL, reproductive endocrinologist; b. Kroonstad, Republic of S. Africa, June 21, 1949; came to U.S., 1976; s. Woolf and Esther (Krost) W.; m. Evelyn Aviva Abrahams, Nov. 30, 1975; children: Michelle, David, Jonathan. BS, U. Pretoria, Republic of S. Africa, 1970, MD, 1975. Resident St. John's Mercy Med. Ctr., St. Louis, 1977-80, reproductive endocrinologist, dept. dir., 1982—; reproductive endocrinology fellow U. Miami, Fla., 1980-82. Fellow Am. Coll. Ob-Gyn; mem. Am. Fertility Soc. Jewish. Avocations: tennis, golf, chess. Home: 14219 Kinderhook Dr Chesterfield MO 63017 Office: St John's Mercy Med Ctr 615 S New Ballas Rd Saint Louis MO 63141

WITTENBERG, JON ALBERT, accountant; b. Valparaiso, Ind., Mar. 22, 1939; s. Fred E. and Elizabeth (DeWaal) W.; m. Joann S. Zachwieja, May 13, 1967; children: Brad, Glen, Pam. BS, Ind. U., 1961. CPA, Ill. Auditor Ernst & Whinney, Chgo., 1961-66; fin. analyst Amoco Chems., Chgo., 1966-69; controller Nat. Van Lines, Broadview, Ill., 1969-76, Consolidated Millimerey, Chgo., 1976—. Mem. Am. Inst. CPA's, Ill. Soc. CPA's, Nat. Assn. Accts. Home: 1297 W New Britton Dr Hoffman Estates IL 60195 Office: Consolidated Millimerey Chicago IL 60600

WITTENBERG, SANDRA KAY, educational administrator; b. Toledo, Jan. 20, 1948; d. Robert Deery and Orpha Irene (Burton) Lloyd; m. Craig Lee Wittenberg, Aug. 28, 1967; children—Claudia Lee, Clark Lloyd. B.A., U. Toledo, 1976, M.Ed., 1980, Ph.D., 1984. Cert. tchr., ednl. adminstr., prin., supt., Ohio. With Toledo Pub. Schs., 1976—, coordinator Alt. Learning Center, 1982-83, supr. occupational work experience program, 1983—; staff devel. cons. adult edn. Mem. Northwestern Ohio Family Health Planning Council, 1972-74; sec. adv. council Adult and Continuing Edn., 1981—; pres. bd. trustees Apple Tree Cooperative Nursery Sch., U. Toledo, 1974-78; ednl. cons. Daedalus Co. Recipient U. Toledo Bd. Trustees Scholarship award, 1979-83; recipient Cert. Significant Profl. Contbn. as Tchr.-Educator, U. Toledo, 1981-82. Mem. Adult Edn. Assn., Assn. Supervision and Curriculum Devel., Phi Delta Kappa, Phi Kappa Phi, Pi Lambda Theta, Delta Kappa Gamma, Beta Sigma Phi. Mem. Ch. of Christ. Contbr. articles to profl. jours. Home: 2458 Sterns Rd Temperance MI 48182 Office: Manhattan and Elm Sts Toledo OH 43608

WITTER, JASPER CURTIS, educator, public relations executive; b. Salem, Ind., May 6, 1907; s. Edgar Curtis and Maggie May (Baynes) W.; m. Thelma Fern Monzingo, Nov. 21, 1931; children: William Curtis, Maridene Joan Witter Akin. BS, Fort Hays State U., 1936, MS, 1937; EdD, U. Kans., 1952. Prin. elem. sch. Jetmore (Kans.) Sch. Dist., 1929-35; prin. high sch. Kismet (Kans.) Sch. Dist., 1936-45; supt. of schs. Fowler (Kans.) Sch. Dist., 1945-51, Caney (Kans.) Sch. Dist., 1952-56; assoc. prof. edn. Northeastern Okla. U., Tahlequah, 1956-57; dean, dir. of admissions Southwestern Coll., Winfield, Kans., 1957-79; pub. relations cons. U. Meth. Youthville, Newton, Kans., 1978-85. Author: From Then Till Now, 1985, Pioneer Children, 1986. Vol. Meals on Wheels. Recipient Cert. of Appreciation Youthville Bd., Newton, 1984, Outstanding Citizen award Winfield City Council, 1974. Mem. Southwestern Coll. Alumni Assn. (Moundbuilder award 1974, Outstanding Alumni award 1976), Phi Delta Kappa. Republican. Methodist. Lodge: Lions (pres. 1963-64). Avocations: raising quarter horses, lecturing. Home: 330 SW 12th St Newton KS 67114

WITTIG, GREGORY JAY, dentist; b. Berwyn, Ill., Apr. 11, 1954; s. William J. and Thelma Estelle (Rogers) W.; m. Karen Ann Dempsey, May 4, 1974; children: Ryan Jay, Christopher Lee. AB, Ind. U., Kokomo, 1976; DDS, Ind. U., Indpls., 1980. Practice dentistry, pres. Badell Dental Clinic, Knox, Ind., 1980—; forum doctor, Quest, Dallas, 1985-86. Bd. dirs. Starke County (Ind.) Devel. Found., 1986. Cabot Corp. scholar, Kokomo, 1972; named Outstanding Male scholar, Ind. U., Kokomo, 1975-76. Mem. Am. Dental Assn., Ind. Dental Assn., Chgo. Dental Assn. (assoc.), Acad. Gen. Dentistry, Psi Omega Dental Frat. (v.p. Omega chpt, 1979-80). Republican. Avocations: skiing, bicycling, swimming, windsurfing, hunting. Home: 1/2 Mile S Hwy 35 PO Box 152 Knox IN 46534 Office: Badell Dental Clinic PC 1/2 Mile S Hwy 35 PO Box 152 Knox IN 46534

WITTLINGER, TIMOTHY DAVID, lawyer; b. Dayton, Ohio, Oct. 12, 1940; s. Charles Frederick and Dorothy Elizabeth (Golden) W.; m. Diane Cleo Dominy, May 20, 1967; children—Kristine Elizabeth, David Matthew. B.S. in Math., Purdue U., 1962; J.D. with distinction, U. Mich., 1965. Bar: Mich. 1966, U.S. Dist. Ct. (ea. dist.) Mich. 1966, U.S. Ct. Appeals (6th cir.) 1968, U.S. Supreme Ct. 1971. Assoc. Hill, Lewis, Adams, Goodrich & Tait, Detroit, 1965-72, ptnr., 1973—, head litigation dept., 1976—; mem. profl. assistance com. U.S. Dist. Ct. (ea. dist.) Mich., 1981-82. Mem. house of deps. Episcopal Ch., N.Y.C., 1979—; vice chmn. Robert Whitaker Sch. Theology; sec. bd. trustees Episcopal Ch., Diocese of Mich., Detroit, 1983—; bd. dirs., sec. Grubb Inst. Behavioral Studies Ltd., Washington. Mem. State Bar Mich., ABA, Nat. Bd. Trial Advocacy (cert.), Engring. Soc. Detroit. Home: 736 N Glenhurst Birmingham MI 48009 Office: Hill Lewis Adams Goodrich & Tait 100 Renaissance Ctr 32d Floor Detroit MI 48243

WITTMER, DALE EDWARD, engineering educator; b. Peoria, Ill., Jan. 26, 1949; s. Lester K. and Beulah Ann (Hoffman) W.; m. Susan M. McKibben, Dec. 23, 1979; 1 child, Dale E. Jr. BS in Ceramic Engring., U. Ill., 1973, MS in Ceramic Engring., 1975, PhD in Ceramic Engring., 1980. Research engr. Army Corp. Engrs., Champaign, Ill., 1975-76, U.S. Bur. Mines, Tuscaloosa, Ala., 1979-84; research engr. GTE Products Corp. subs. GTE Corp., Towanda, Pa., 1984-85, mgr. research and devel. ceramics, 1985-86; prof. engring. So. Ill. U., Carbondale, 1986—; pres. Wittner Cons., Inc., Carbondale, 1986—. Contbr. articles to profl. jours.; patentee in field. Served with U.S. Army, 1968-70, Vietnam. Mem. Nat. Inst. Ceramic Engrs., Am. Ceramic Soc., Am. Inst. Metall. Engrs., Am. Powder Metall. Inst., Keramos. Lodge: Elks. Avocations: bass fishing, lure making, sci. fiction, computers. Home: 622 Terrace Dr PO Box 3381 Carbondale IL 62901 Office: So Ill U Engring and Tech Carbondale IL 62901

WITTNER, LOREN ANTONOW, public relations executive, lawyer; b. N.Y.C., May 2, 1938; s. Henry Warren and Miriam Margo (Antonow) W.; m. Judith Ginsberg, June 21, 1959 (div. Sept. 1972); children: Jennifer Leslie, Elizabeth Anne; m. Dianna Marks, Apr. 2, 1975. AB, Columbia U., 1958; JD, Harvard U., 1961. Bar: N.Y. 1961, Ill. 1966. Assoc. O'Dwyer & Bernstein, N.Y.C., 1961-62, Emil & Kobrin, N.Y.C., 1962-66; assoc. Antonow & Fink, Chgo., 1966-70, ptnr., 1970-77; rep. of Sec. U.S. Dept. Commerce, Chgo. and Washington, 1977-81; exec. v.p. Daniel J. Edelman, Inc., Chgo., 1981—; chmn. Midwest region Fed. Regional Council, 1978-79. Served with USAR, 1861-65. Mem. ABA. Club: Union League (Chgo.). Avocation: classical music.

WITWER, DAVID JAMES, national sales manager; b. Detroit, Sept. 21, 1954; s. John Cyrus and Rosanna (Ayotte) W.; m. Anne Rita Langhorst, July 14, 1979 (div.); 1 child, Daniel John. BSME, U. Dayton, 1976. Sales engr. Duriron Co., Dayton, Ohio, 1977-79; ind. sales mgr. Gilbert and Bennett, Georgetown, Conn., 1979-80; field sales engr. Barry Controls, Watertown, Mass., 1980-82; nat. sales engr. Schmidt Couplings, Cin., 1982-84; nat. sales mgr. Zero-Max, Mpls., 1984—. Advisor Jr. Achievement, 1976-77. Mem. ASME, Am. Mgmt. Assn., ASTM. Republican. Roman Catholic. Avocations: golf, racquetball, camping, hunting, fishing, softball. Office: Zero-Max 2845 Harriet Ave S Minneapolis MN 55408

WITWER, SAMUEL WEILER, JR., lawyer; b. Chgo., Aug. 5, 1941; s. Samuel Weiler and Ethyl Loraine (Wilkins) W.; m. Susan P. Stewart, Sept. 18, 1971; children—Samuel Stewart, Michael Douglas. A.B. with honors, Dickinson Coll., 1963; J.D.; U. Mich., 1966. Bar: Ill. 1967, U.S. Dist. Ct. (no. dist.) Ill. 1967, U.S. Ct. Appeals (7th cir.) 1972, U.S. Supreme Ct. 1973, U.S. Ct. Appeals (6th cir.) 1985, U.S. Dist. Ct. (ea. dist.) Mich., 1987. Assoc. Witwer, Moran, Burlage & Atkinson, Chgo., 1967-74, ptnr., 1974—; mem. Fed. Trial Bar Admissions Com. No. Dist. Ill., 1982—. Governing mem. Chgo. Zool. Soc., 1986—; trustee United Meth. Homes and Services, Chgo., 1974—, Dickinson Coll., Carlisle, Pa., 1976—; mem. Cook County Home Rule Commn., Chgo., 1974-75; chmn. Agy. Appeals Com. Chgo., 1975—; gov. United Republican Fund of Ill., Chgo., 1982—; atty. Glenview Park Dist., 1982—; spl. asst. atty. gen. Auditor Gen. Ill., 1984— . Mem. Meth. Bar Assn. (pres. 1972-73), ABA, Chgo. Bar Assn., Ill. Bar Assn., Law Club of Chgo., Sigma Chi, Phi Delta Phi. Republican. Methodist. Club: Union League. Home: 1330 Overlook Dr Glenview IL 60025 Office: Witwer Moran Burlage & Witwer 125 S Wacker Dr Chicago IL 60606

WIVIOTT, WILBERT W., plastic surgeon; b. Milw., May 5, 1927. BS, U. Wis., 1954, MD, 1957, MS, 1961; DDS, Marquette U., 1953. Cert. Am. Bd. Plastic Surgery. Intern Mt. Sinai Hosp., Milw., 1957-58; resident U.S. Vet. Hosp. Wood, Wis., 1958-61; resident in plastic surgery U. Hosps., Madison, 1961-63; pvt. practice dentistry Milw., 1963—; assoc. clin. prof. dept. plastic surgery Med. Coll. Wis., Milw.; mem. Milw. Children's Hosp., Milw. County Hosps., Good Samaritan Med. Ctr., St. Michael Hosp., Mt. Sinai Hosp. Served with USNR, 1945-46. Fellow Am. Coll. Surgeons; mem. AMA, Wis. Med. Soc., Milw. County Med. Soc., Wis. Soc. Plastic Surgeons (pres.), Mid-Western Assn. Plastic Surgeons, Am. Soc. Plastic and Reconstructive Surgeons, Am. Soc. Maxillo-Facial Surgeons (editors com., treas. 1981-83, v.p. 1983-84, pres. 1985-86), Am. Cleft Palate Assn., Am. Soc. for Aesthetic Plastic Surgeons., Am. Soc. Plastic Surgeons, Wis. Med. Alumni Assn. (past pres.), Phi Delta Epsilon, Alpha Omega. Office: 1218 W Kilbourn Ave Milwaukee WI 53233

WIXOM, THEODORE MERSHON, linen rental company official; b. Galesburg, Ill., June 15, 1937; s. Robert Nelson and Doris (Cox) W.; B.S. in Indsl. Mgmt., Miami U., Oxford, Ohio, 1960; children—Elizabeth Kay, Margaret Marie. Plant mgr. F.W. Means & Co., Lexington, Ky., 1964-66, South Bend, Ind., 1966-68; staff plant mgr. Asso. Linen Services, Utica, N.Y., 1968-70, gen. mgr., 1970-74; v.p. ops. Community Linen Rental Services, Los Angeles, 1974-76; v.p., dir. Spalding's Services Ltd., Louisville, 1976-78; gen. mgr. N.Y. area Morgan Services, Inc., Buffalo, 1978-84; dir. health care services Faultless Health Care Services, Inc., Kansas City, Mo., 1984-85; gen. mgr. Faultless Uniform & Rental Services, Overland Park, 1985—. Instr. driving course Nat. Safety Council, Utica, 1972-73. Served to lt. (j.g.) USNR, 1960-62. Named Engr. of Yr., Joint Engrs. Council Mohawk Valley, 1971; cert. mfg. engr. Mem. Am. Inst. Indsl. Engrs. (v.p. region 5; sr. mem.; nat. bd. dirs.), Mohawk Valley Joint Engrs. Council (chmn. pub. relations com.), Soc. Mfg. Engrs., Linen Supply Assn. Am. (mem. nat. ops. com.), Alpha Kappa Psi, Theta Chi. Clubs: Masons, Rotary. Contbr. articles to profl. jours. Home: 10233 Outlook Overland Park KS 66207 Office: Faultless Uniform & Linen Rental Services 330 W 19th Terr Kansas City MO 64108

WIXTROM, DONALD JOSEPH, translator; b. Republic, Mich., Oct. 14, 1928; s. Joseph Albert and Edith (Johnson) W.; m. Marilyn Jean Sjoquist, Oct. 14, 1961; children: Joe Alan, Lorna Jean, Aaron Matthew. Free lance translator Republic, 1966—. Mem. Am. Translators Assn. Baptist. Home and Office: Rt 1 Box 98 Republic MI 49879-9726

WLOSZEK, EDWARD JOSEPH, JR., architectural estimator; b. Southgate, Mich., Oct. 16, 1955; s. Edward Joseph and Dorothy A. (Sturwold) W.; m. Jean MacShane, Nov. 18, 1977; children: Edward Joseph III, Steven Andrew, Paul Robert. BS in Architecture, Lawrence Inst. Tech., 1978, BArch, 1980. Registered architect, Mich. Architect R. Sherman, Dearborn, Mich., 1979-81; sr. estimator P.B. Brodak Roofing and Sheet Metal, Wixon, Mich., 1982—. Mem. AIA, Constrn. Specifications Int., Detroit Engring. Soc. Republican. Roman Catholic. Avocations: hunting, fishing, family activities, business development. Home: 2342 Phillips Berkley MI 48072 Office: PB Brodak Roofing 28850 Hass Wixon MI 48694

WOBST, FRANK GEORG, banker; b. Dresden, Germany, Nov. 14, 1933; came to U.S., 1958, naturalized, 1963; s. Robert Georg and Marianne (Salewsky) W.; m. Joan Shuey Firkins, Aug. 24, 1957; children: Franck Georg, Ingrid, Andrea. Student, U. Erlangen, 1952-54, U. Goettingen, 1954-58, Rutgers U., 1964. With Fidelity American Bankshares, Inc., Lynchburg, Va., 1958-74; exec. v.p., dir. Fidelity American Bankshares, Inc., 1973-74; chmn., chief exec. officer, dir. Huntington Nat. Bank, 1974-86, chmn. exec. com., 1986—; chief exec. officer dir. Huntington Bancshares, Inc., 1974—. Mem. Greater Columbus C. of C., Am. Inst. Banking, Assn. Res. City Bankers, Robert Morris Assos., Newcomen Soc. Club: Scioto Country. Home: 129 N Columbia Ave Columbus OH 43209 Office: Huntington Bancshares Inc 41 S High St PO Box 1558 Columbus OH 43260 *

WOCHELE, CARL DALE, advertising executive; b. Cleve., July 18, 1952; s. Clarence Friederich and Ruth (Orr) W.; m. Ann Elizabeth Farney, Oct. 29, 1977; 1 child, Abby Ann. BBA, Bowling Green State U., 1974. Copy/contact MSM Advt., Chgo., 1975-77; account exec. William A. Robinson, Inc., Chgo., 1977-79, N.W. Ayer, Inc., Chgo., 1979-81; office mgr., acctount supr. Ayer Ltd., London, Eng., 1981-83, account supr., 1983-84, v.p., account supr., 1984-86; mgr. mktg. communications Carrier Corp. div. United

Tech., Indpls., 1986—. Mem. Bus. Profl. Advt. Assn., Internat. Advt. Assn. Republican. Mem. United Ch. Christ. Avocations: golf, bowling, tennis. Home: 1609 Cool Creek Dr Carmel IN 46032 Office: Carrier NOA PO Box 70 Indianapolis IN 46206

WOECKEL, ALLAN JOHN, library administrator; b. LaSalle, Ill., Oct. 3, 1944; s. August and Victoria Harriet (Grochowski) W.; m. Vicki Lynn Flori, Oct. 3, 1964 (div. 1978); children—Renee Lynn, Scott Allan. B.A. in History, No. Ill. U., 1966, Cert. Edn., 1967, M.A. In Library Sci., 1969. Asst. dir. Plum Meml. Library, Lombard, Ill., 1969-71; ref. librarian Coll. of DuPage, Glen Ellyn, Ill., 1970-72; instr. Ill. Valley Community Coll., Oglesby, Ill., 1971-72; dir. Reddick Library, Ottawa, Ill., 1971—. Mem. regional conf. com. Ill. White House Conf. on Library and Info. Services, 1978-79; library automation rev. group Starved Rock Library System, Ottawa, 1983-84, system adv. com., 1971—; program and edn. dir. Parents Without Ptnrs., Inc., 1979-81, LaSalle, Ill., 1978-79, newsletter dir., 1979-80, pres., 1981-82, treas., 1982—. Recipient Disting. Service Award, Ottawa Lions, 1976. Mem. DuPage County Librarians Assn., ALA, Ottawa Area C. of C. and Industry, Ill. Library Assn. Lodges: Lions (pres. 1975-76), Moose. Home: 420 Park Ave Ottawa IL 61350 Office: Reddick Library 1010 Canal St Ottawa IL 61350

WOEHRLEN, ARTHUR EDWARD, JR., dentist; b. Detroit, Dec. 9, 1947; s. Arthur Edward and Olga (Hewka) W.; m. Sara Elizabeth Heikoff, Aug. 13, 1972; 1 child, Tess Helena. DDS, U. Mich., 1973. Resident in dentistry USAF, 1973-74; gen. practice dentistry Redwood Dental Group, Warren, Mich., 1976—; instr. Sinai Hosp., Detroit, 1977—; chief of dentistry Harrison Community Hosp., Mt. Clemens, Mich., 1982—; mem. dentistry staff Hutzel Hosp., Warren; reviewer Chubb Ins. Co. (malpractice claims); bd. mem. Mich. Acad. Gen. Dentistry (chmn. State of Mich. Continuing Dental Edn. Accreditation). Contbr. articles on dentistry to profl. jours. Served to capt. USAF, 1973-76. Fellow Am. Acad. Gen. Dentistry (master), Internat. Congress of Oral Implantologists; mem. ADA, Mich. Dental Assn., Acad. Gen. Dentistry, Am. Acad. Oral Medicine, Fedn. Dentaire Internationale, Acad. Dentistry for the Handicapped, Am. Acad. Oral Implantologists, Internat. Coll. Oral Implantologists, Macomb Dist. Dental Soc.; panel mem. Am. Arbitration Assn. Republican. Home: 25460 Dundee Huntington Woods MI 48070 Office: Redwood Dental Group 13403 E 13 Mile Rd Warren MI 48070

WOESTE, EARL LOUIS, construction executive; b. Ft. Thomas, Ky., Jan. 14, 1962; s. Donald Louis and Rose Lee (Meyer) W. A in Architecture, U. Cin., 1985. Constrn. mgr. Charles V. Maescher & Co., Inc., Cin., 1981—. Assoc. Gen. Contractors grantee, 1985. Mem. Am. Inst. Contractors. Office: Chas V Maescher & Co Inc 2106 Florence Ave PO Box 6098 Cincinnati OH 45206

WOFFINDEN, DUARD STEPHEN, military officer; b. Albuquerque, Jan. 31, 1949; s. Duard Sims and Rose Marie (Moscon) W.; m. SHirley Ann Tagavilla, June 12, 1976; children: John David, Marissa Lehuanani. BSEE, Utah State U., 1974; MS in Computer Sci., Naval Postgrad. Sch., 1984. Commd. U.S. Army, 1974, advanced through grades to maj.; asst. prof. AFIT/Eng, Wright Patterson AFB, Ohio, 1984—. Mem. Tau Beta Pi. Republican. Mormon. Avocations: lapidary, jewelry making, sports. Home: 2520 Kewanna Ln Beavercreek OH 45385 Office: AFIT/Eng Wright-Patterson AFB OH 45433-6583

WOFFORD, ARLENE, nurse; b. Detroit, Dec. 28, 1949; d. William Joseph and Janina (Huczek) Wojkiewicz; m. James Coogan Wofford, Jan. 24, 1969 (div. May 1978); children—James William, Steven Jarett, Jeffrey Adam. R.N., Mercy Sch. of Nursing, Detroit, 1969; B.S. in Nursing, Mercy Coll., Detroit, 1982; postgrad. Madonna Coll., Livonia, Mich., 1984—. Registered nurse, Mich. Staff nurse St. Joseph Mercy Hosp., Detroit, 1969-77; nurse practitioner Hodari, M.D. and Assocs., Detroit, 1979-81; head nurse St. Joseph Mercy Hosp., also Samaritan Health Ctr., Detroit, 1977-85; nursing adminstrv. asst. Samaritan Health Ctr., Detroit, 1985—; nurse Profl. Care, Southfield, Mich., 1985—; head nurse Sinai Hosp., Detroit, 1985—; nurse cons. Borning Corp., Spokane, Wash., 1984—. Mem. Nat. League Nursing (Mich. chpt.), Nurse Assn. of Am. Coll. Obstetricians and Gynecologists, Mich. Assn. Concerned with Sch. Age Parents, Perinatal Assn. Mich. Democrat. Roman Catholic. Avocations: ceramics; needlework. Home: 8867 Sarasota St Redford MI 48239 Office: Sinai Hosp 6767 W Outer Dr Detroit MI 48235

WOGAMAN, GEORGE ELSWORTH, insurance executive; b. Mikado, Mich., May 29, 1937; s. Edgar R. and Leah Katherine (McGuire) W.; grad. various ins. courses; m. Sandra Lee Jensen, Apr. 10, 1965; children—Jennifer, Christopher. With Blair Transit Co., Dun & Bradstreet, Chrysler Engring. Co., 1955-61; exec. chef Westward Ho!, 1961-68; owner, mgr. George Wogaman Ins. Agy., Grand Forks, N.D., 1969—; alderman East Grand Forks (Minn.) City Council, 1979—, v.p., 1982—. Corp. mem. United Hosp., Grand Forks, 1982—; mem. East Grand Forks Area Emergency Med. Services adv. com., Grand Forks- East Grand Forks Bus Com., Met. Planning Council; chmn. adminstrv. com. City of East Grand Forks; mem. Nat. Rep. Congl. Com., Rep. Presdl. Task Force; mem. Wesley United Meth. Ch., Grand Forks. Recipient Pub. Service award East Grand Forks City Council, 1979; C.L.U.; chartered fin. cons. Mem. North Valley Life Underwriters Assn., Am. Soc. C.L.U.s. Club: Elks. Home: 1703 20th St NW East Grand Forks MN 56721 Office: 2612 Gateway Dr Grand Forks ND 58201

WOHLERS, NORMA JEAN, publishing clearing agency executive; b. Charleston, W.Va., Dec. 1, 1935; d. Sterling Patrick and Rosalie Pebble (Anderson) Brown; grad. airline sch. TWA, 1954; m. Gerhard Andrew Wohlers, Mar. 5, 1960 (dec. 1977); children—Gerhard Andrew III, Shannon Diane. Sec., Ohio Nat. Bank, Columbus, 1955-57; mgr. Slenderama, Columbus and Cin., 1957-59; mgr. Civic Reading Club, Look mag., Grand Rapids, Mich., 1959-70, gen. mgr., 1972-77, v.p., 1972; pres., owner Am. Guild Circulation Corp., Detroit, 1972—, chmn. bd., 1977—; pres. Am. Guild Corp., Detroit, 1980—; founder, pres. G.N.S. Publs. Sch. Plan, 1982—, Nationwide Mag. Network. Recipient Presdl. Sports award for tennis, 1973. Mem. Audit Bur. Circulations. Republican. Office: Am Guild Circulation Corp 29200 Vassar Suite 500 Livonia MI 48152

WOHLFAHRT, BARBARA ROBBINS, manufacturing company executive; b. Chgo., Oct. 30, 1947; d. Frederick Arthur and Dorothy (Roper) Robbins; m. Timothy Harry Wohlfahrt, Aug. 23, 1969; children: Patricia, Rick, Melinda, Matthew. BSME, U. Wis., 1969. Tech. writer Gilman Engring., Janesville, Wis., 1969-70; sales person Wausau (Wis.) Metals Corp., 1970-71; exec. v.p. Modu-Line Windows, Wausau, 1972-85, Major Industries, Wausau, 1983—; exec. v.p. Prime Cons., Wausau, 1983—. Author: (with E. Jablonski) The Art of Tipping: Customs & Controversies, 1984. Bd. dirs. Luth. Social Services, Wausau, 1975-78, Tippers Internat., Wausau, 1983—. Republican. Lutheran. Home: 3012 Hubbill Ave Wausau WI 54401 Office: Major Industries Inc 7111 Stewart Ave Wausau WI 54401

WOIWODE, JOHN GREGORY, fisheries scientist, research company executive; b. L.I., N.Y., Aug. 16, 1951; s. Louis Henry and Kathryn Madeline (Uht) W. B.S. in Fish and Wildlife Resources U. Idaho, 1973, M.S. in Fisheries Resources, 1980; PhD in Fisheries U. Minn., 1987. Vol. Peace Corps, Philippines, 1975-77, fisheries tech. tng. dir., 1977; research assoc. U. Idaho and Dept. Energy, Moscow, Idaho and Raft River, Idaho, 1978-80; assoc. fisheries scientist U. Minn., St. Paul, 1980-87; pres. AquaMatrix, Inc.; cons. fish culture system design. Mem. AAAS, Am. Fisheries Soc., Wildlife Soc., World Aquaculture Soc., Nat. Audubon Soc., Sigma Xi. Contbr. articles to profl. publs. Office: Univ Minn Dept Fisheries 119 Hodson 1980 Folwell Ave Saint Paul MN 55108

WOJCICKI, ANDREW ADALBERT, chemist and educator; b. Warsaw, Poland, May 5, 1935; s. Franciszek Wojcicki and Janina (Kozlowa) Hoskins; m. Marba L. Hart, Dec. 21, 1968; children: Katherine, Christina. BS, Brown U., 1956; PhD, Northwestern U., 1960; postdoctoral fellow, U. Nottingham, Eng., 1960-61. Asst. prof. chemistry Ohio State U., Columbus, 1961-66, assoc. prof., 1966-69, prof., 1969—, acting chmn., 1981-82; assoc. chmn. Ohio State U., 1982-83, 84-86; cons. Owens-Ill., 1967; vis. prof. Case Western Reserve U., 1967; vis. researcher Univ. Coll. London, 1969; sr. U.S. scientist Alexander von Humboldt Found., Mülheim/Ruhr, West Germany, 1975-76; vis. scholar U. Calif.-Berkeley, 1984. Contbr. numerous articles to profl. and scholarly jours. Guggenheim fellow U. Cambridge (Eng.), 1976; recipient Disting. Teaching award Ohio State U., 1968, Humboldt Sr. award Humboldt Found., 1975, 76. Mem. Am. Chem. Soc., Royal Chem. Soc., Sigma Xi, Phi Lambda Upsilon. Home: 825 Greenridge Rd Worthington OH 43085 Office: Ohio State U 120 W 18th Ave Columbus OH 43210

WOJCIK, LAWRENCE FRANCIS, marketing executive; b. Pulaski, Wis., Oct. 6, 1941; s. Stanley and Margret (Maternoski) W.; m. Joanne Jeannette, Jan. 29, 1966; children: Lynn, Don. BS in Electrical Engring. Technology, Milw. Sch. Engring., 1971. Lab technician Allen Bradley, Milw., 1962-66; customer engr. Sorbus Inc., Milw., 1966-72; application engr. AMF/Paragon Electric Co., Two Rivers, Wis., 1972-79, product mgr., 1979-81, product mktg. mgr., 1981—. Contbr. articles to profl. jours. Coach YMCA and Athletic Assn., Manitowoc, Wis., 1976-82; mem. sch. bd. Holy Innocents Sch., Manitowoc, 1980-83, religion tchr. Parish, 1972—, sec., pres. Athletic Assn., 1978-81. Mem. Assn. Energy Engrs. (charter), Roncollli Athletic Assn. (sec., v.p. 1981-85), Trout Unlimited. Roman Catholic. Lodge: Kiwanis (chmn. spiritual aims Manitowoc and Two Rivers 1980—). Home: 13227 Jambro Creek Rd Two Rivers WI 54241

WOJTKOWSKI, ANDREW MICHAEL, dentist; b. Muhldorf, Germany, Aug. 5, 1948; came to U.S., 1949; s. Thaddeus G. and Charlotte (Topfer) W.; m. Sarah Patrick, 1970; children: Caroline, Todd. BS, Miami U., Oxford, Ohio, 1970; DMD, U. Louisville, 1978. Gen. practice dentistry Canfield, Ohio, 1978—; program coordinator dental edn. St. Elizabeth Hosp., Youngstown, Ohio, 1978—, asst. dir. gen. practice residency program, 1979—. Mem. ADA, Acad. Gen. Dentistry, Ohio Dental Assn., Ohio Acad. Gen. Dentistry, Corydon Palmer Dental Soc. Republican. Roman Catholic. Clubs: Cambium, Youngstown Country. Lodge: Rotary. Office: 3711 Stars Ctr Dr Canfield OH 44406

WOJTKOWSKI, WITOLD ANDRZEJ, engineer; b. Ostrow Wkp, Kalisz, Poland, Jan. 29, 1948; came to U.S., 1976; s. Stefan and Barbara (Sobis) W. m. Alicja Szlegier, Aug. 18, 1978; children: Catherine, Margaret, Elizabeth. Diploma in tech., Tech. Sch., Ostrow WKP, 1969; diploma in engring., U. Politechnik, Gdansk, Poland, 1976. Welding engr. Gdansk Shipyard; machine operator Eutectic Engring., Detroit; design engr. Q&H Metal Products, Troy, Mich.; project engr. Gentz Industries Inc., Warren, Mich. Mem. Soc. Mfg. Engrs. (sr.). Home: 12280 Myles Ct Sterling Heights MI 48078 Office: 23600 Schoenherr Rd Warren MI 48089

WOJTON, GARY WAYNE, educator; b. Chgo., Apr. 7, 1951; s. Matthew C. and Anne Marie (Roemer) W.; m. Mary Virginia O'Connell, July 10, 1976. AA, Mayfair Coll., 1970; BS, No. Ill. U., 1973; MS, U. Ill., Chgo., 1979. Cert. phys. edn. tchr., Ill. Elem. sch. phys. edn. tchr. Chgo. Bd. Edn., 1973—. Named one of Educators of the Yr., S. Cen. Community Services, Inc., Chgo., 1984. Avocations: tennis, bicycling, gardening. Home: 1420 Willow Des Plaines IL 60016 Office: Ruggles Elem Sch 7831 S Prairie Chicago IL 60619

WOLAK, MARK ANTHONY, special education director, consultant; b. Saint Cloud, Minn., Jan. 17, 1953; s. Alexander Peter and Beata (Brand) W.; m. Phyllis Ann Perish, Nov. 22, 1975; 1 child, Anthony Perish. BS, St. Cloud (Minn.) State U., 1975, MS, 1980. Tchr. spl. edn. Pima County, Topawa, Ariz., 1975-76, Galloway Boys Ranch, Onamia, Minn., 1976-79; research asst. St. Cloud State U., 1979-80; regional project dir. Benton Stearns Co-op, St. Cloud, 1980-82; spl. edn. coordinator Benton Stearns Co-op, Saint Cloud, 1982-84; dir. spl. edn Rum River Interdist. Coop., Cambridge, Minn., 1984—; cons., trainer in organizational planning, Mpls., 1984—. Author: (tng. manuals) Administrative Leadership, 1982-83. Pres. Minn. Educators for Emotionally Disturbed, 1983-85; chmn. Rum River Interdist. 10-Yr. Strategic Plan, Cambridge, 1984—. Wabasha County scholar St. Cloud State U., 1973, Alliance for Renewal in Edn. grantee State of Minn., 1985. Mem. Minn. Educators for Emotionally Disturbed, (pres. 1983-85), Phi Delta Kappa. Roman Catholic. Avocations: sailing, carpentry, flying, trave. Office: Rum River Interdist Spl Edn Coop 430 NW 8th St Cambridge MN 55008

WOLANIN, SOPHIE MAE, tutor, lecturer, civic worker; b. Alton, Ill., June 11, 1915; d. Stephen and Mary (Fijalka) W. Student Pa. State Coll., 1943-44; certificate secretarial sci. U. S.C., 1946, B.S. in Bus. Adminstrn. cum laude, 1948. Clk., stenographer, sec. Mercer County (Pa.) Tax Collector's Office, Sharon, 1932-34; receptionist, social sec., nurse-technician to doctor, N.Y.C., 1934-37; coil winder, assembler Westinghouse Electric Corp., Sharon, 1937-39, duplicator operator, typist, stenographer, 1939-44, confidential sec., Pitts., 1949-54; exec. sec., charter mem. Westinghouse Credit Corp., Pitts., 1954-72, hdqrs. sr. sec., 1972-80, reporter WCC News, 1967-68, asst. editor, 1968-71, asso. editor, 1971-76; student office sec. to dean U. S.C. Sch. Commerce, 1944-46, instr. math., bus. adminstrn., secretarial sci., 1946-48. Publicity and pub. relations chmn., corr. sec. South Oakland Rehab. Council, 1967-69; U. S.C. official del. Univ. Pitts. 200th Anniversary Bicentennial Convocation, 1986; mem. nat. adv. bd. Am. Security Council; mem. Friends Winston Churchill Meml. and Library, Westminster Coll., Fulton, Mo.; active U. S.C. Ednl. Found.; charter mem. Presdl. Task Force; patron Inst. Community Service (life), Ednl. Found. (Pa. state fund chmn. 1967-68, pres. council 1972-76, ofcl. del. rep. inauguration Bethany Coll. pres. 1973); mem. Allegheny County Scholarship Assn. (life), Allegheny County League Women voters, AAUW (life), Internat. Fedn. U. Women, N.E. Historic Geneal. Soc. (life), U. S.C. Alumni Assn., Hypatian Lit. Soc. (hon.), Acad. Polit. Sci. (Columbia) (life), Bus. and Profl. Women's Club Pitts. (bd. dirs. 1963-80, editor Bull. 1963-65, treas. 1965-66, historian 1969-70, pub. relations 1971-76, Woman of Year 1972); supporting mem. Nat. Woman's Hall of Fame; recipient numerous prizes Allegheny County Fair, 1951-56; citation Congl. Record, 1969; medal of Merit, Pres. Reagan, 1982; others. Mem. Liturgical Conf. N. Am. (life), Westinghouse Vet. Employees Assn., Nat. Soc. Lit. and Arts, Early Am. Soc., Am. Acad. Social and Polit. Sci., Societe Commemorative de Femmes Celebres, Nat. Trust Historic Preservation, Am. Counselors Soc. (life), Am. Mus. Natural History (asso.), Nat. Hist. Soc. (founding mem.), Anglo-Am. Hist. Soc. (charter), Nat. Assn. Exec. Secs., Internat. Platform Assn., Smithsonian Assos., Asso. Nat. Archives, Nat., Pa., Fed. bus. and profl. women's clubs, Mercer County Hist. Soc. (life), Am. Bible Soc., Polish Am. Numismatic Assn., Polonus Philatelic Soc. UN Assn. U.S. Republican. Roman Catholic (mem. St. Paul Cathedral Altar Soc., patron organ recitals). Clubs: Jonathan Maxcy of U. S.C. (charter); Univ. Catholic of Pitts.; Key of Pa., Fedn. Bus. and Profl. Women (hon.); Coll. (hon.) (Sharon). Contbr. articles to newspapers; Am. corr. Polish radio and TV. Home: 5223 Smith-Stewart Rd SE Girard OH 44420

WOLCOTT, HENRY WALBRIDGE, IV, tax consultant; b. Detroit, Feb. 3, 1947; s. Henry Walbridge III and Rosemary (Burman) W.; m. Nell Hurley Prince, Aug. 22, 1969; children: Kristin, Jeffrey, Matthew, Elizabeth. AA, Lansing Community Coll., 1967; BA, Mich. State U., 1970. CPA. Pvt. practice acctg. Maner, Costerisan & Ellis, Lansing, Mich., 1969-82; chief fin. officer L & G Drilling Co., Mt. Pleasant, Mich., 1982-84; tax cons., tax dir. Prof. Cons. Inc., Lansing, 1982—; bd. dirs. Union Fed. Savs., Lansing; treas., bd. dirs. PM Group, Brighton, Mich. Mem. Lansing Cath. Cen. High Sch. Bd., 1984—. Mem. Mich. Assn. CPA's, Am. Inst. CPA's. Roman Catholic. Avocation: golf. Office: Profl Cons Inc 2510 Lake Lansing Rd Lansing MI 48910

WOLCOTT, NORMAN GEORGE, chemical company executive; b. Cortland, N.Y., July 15, 1944; s. Norman G. and Lucille (Hulbert) W.; m. Valorie Irene Vickers, Aug. 29, 1964 (div. April 1977); children: Christopher, Douglas; m. Dixie Sue Purcell, June 6, 1983; children: Mark, Diana, Mathew. BS in Ceramic Engring., U. Ill., 1969. Engr. Westinghouse Electric CO., Pitts., 1967-70; dir. research Harshaw Chem. Co., Cleve., 1970-76; pres. Nor-Cote Chem. Co., Crawfordsville, Ind., 1976—, also bd. dirs.; bd. dirs. Holiday Inn, Crawfordsville, Blocks & Marbles Co., Crawfordsville, U.S. Tap Co., Frankfort, Ind.; cons. in field. Patentee in field. Mem. Mayor's Loan Rev. Bd., Crawfordsville, 1987—. Mem. Soc. Mfg. Engrs., Rad Tech Internat., Screen Printing Assn. Internat., Ind. Inst. for New Bus. Ventures, Crawfordsville C. of C. Republican. Methodist. Home: 33 Ridge Rd Crawfordsville IN 47933 Office: Nor-Cote Chem Co Inc PO Box 668 Crawfordsville IN 47933

WOLCYN, THOMAS ANTHONY, tree farmer, nurseryman; b. St. Paul, Apr. 26, 1953; s. Bernard Anthony and Deloris Vinita (McCabe) W.; m. Adrienne Mary Bohlman, Jan. 15, 1981; children: Nicholas and Benjamin (twins), Clinton. BS in Forestry, U. Minn., 1975. Owner, mgr. Wolcyn Tree Farms and Nursery, Cambridge, Minn., 1975—. Del. Ind.-Rep. State Com., Mpls., 1984; baseball coach Bethel Coll., St. Paul, 1980-81. Mem. Minn. Christmas Tree Growers Assn. (bd. dirs. 1981—), Nat. Christmas Tree Growers Assn., Am. Assn. Nurserymen, Minn. Nurserymen's Assn., Wis. Christmas Tree Producer's Assn. Baptist. Club: "M". Avocations: baseball, hunting, fishing. Home and Office: Wolcyn Tree Farms and Nursery Rural Rt 2 Box 470 Cambridge MN 55008

WOLD, JEFFREY LYNN, physical therapist; b. Fosston, Minn., Aug. 3, 1947; s. Lloyd Elmer and Carol Sylvina (Lee) W.; m. Joyce Winnifred Brakke, June 12, 1971; children: Eric Ethan, Andrea Lee. BA in Biology, Concordia Coll., 1969; BS in Physical Therapy, U. Minn., 1973. Registered physical therapist. Staff physical therapist NW Hosp., Thief River Falls, Minn., 1973-74; chief physical therapist Melrose (Minn.) Hosp./Nursing Home, 1974-78, Paynesville (Minn.) Hosp./Nursing Home, 1974-80, Albany (Minn.) Hosp., 1976-80; ptnr., co-dir., physical therapist Physical Therapy/Occupational Therapy Clinic, Fargo, N.D., 1980—; cons. Belgrade (Minn.) Nursing Home, 1975-80. Mem. Atonement Luth. Ch., Fargo, 1980—, Hospice of Red River Valley, Fargo, 1980—; founder physical therapy depts. rural hosps., Minn., N.D., 1974—. Served to U.S. Army, 1969-71. Grantee U. Minn., 1970. Mem. Am. Physical Therapy Assn., Orthopaedic and Sports Physical Therapy, Pvt. Practice Sect. Am. Physical Therapy Assn., N.D. Physical Therapy Assn., SE N.D. Dist. Physical Therapy Assn. (counsel 1981-82), Arthritis Found. Lutheran. Avocations: reading, yard work, fishing, skiing, travel. Home: 3531 S 10th St Fargo ND 58103 Office: Physical Therapy/Occupational Therapy 100 S 10th St Fargo ND 58103

WOLF, ANDREW, food manufacturing company executive; b. Budapest, Hungary, May 20, 1927; came to U.S., 1947, naturalized, 1952; s. Alfred and Magda Farkas. Diploma, Baking Inst. Tech., Budapest, 1942-45; B.S. in Mech. Engring., CCNY, 1955-62; postgrad. Ill. Inst. Tech., Chgo., 1962-64; M.B.A., U. Chgo., 1973. Pres., owner, Mignon Pastry Shops, N.Y.C., 1948-51, 1952-54; dir. new products Arnold Bakers, N.Y. and Conn., 1955-60; dir. new products research and devel. Kitchens of Sara Lee, Deerfield, Ill., 1960-71, v.p. research and devel., 1971—; cons. Hanscom Bakeries, N.Y.C., 1954-55; rep. Consol. Foods Corp., Grocery Mfrs. Am. Tech. Com. for Food Protection, 1975—; spokesman Frozen Food Action Communications Team, Inc., radio and TV, 1982—. Contbr. articles to profl. jours. Patentee bakery equipment and methods. Served with U.S. Army, 1947-48, 1951-52. Recipient Hon. Tex. Citizenship award State of Tex., 1969; Bishop award Tex. Dept. Mental Health, 1972. Mem. White House Conf. on Food and Nutrition, 1969, Pres. Reagan's Task Force on Phys. Fitness and Nutrition, 1983. Mem. Am. Frozen Food Inst. (research and tech. services council, quality maintenance task force council), Am. Bakers Assn. (liaison com. U.S. Dept. Agr.), Inst. Food Technologists, Am. Soc. Bakery Engrs., Tau Beta Pi, Pi Tau Sigma. Home: 2785 Daiquiri Dr Deerfield IL 60015

WOLF, CARY STEVEN, podiatrist; b. Detroit, Nov. 19, 1954; s. Jack and Edith Wolf; m. Sherry Lynn Seldes, Dec. 23, 1979; 1 child, Stacey. BA in Biology, Oakland U., Rochester, Mich., 1978; D of Podiatric Medicine, Ohio Coll. Podiatric Medicine, Cleve., 1982. Pvt. practice podiatric medicine Southfield, Mich., 1982—. Mem. Arthritis Found., 1983—. Fellow Acad. Ambulatory Foot Surgery. Office: Foot Care Clinics 1600 W 9 Mile Rd #107 Southfield MI 48075

WOLF, CONSTANCE B., chemical company executive; b. Wilmington, Del., Dec. 10, 1944; d. Arthur A. and Beatrice (Forman) Brace; m. Arnold Alfred Wolf, Oct. 20, 1974. B.S., Pa. State U., 1966, MS in Orgn. Devel., Pepperdine U., 1987 . Sr. media buyer Compton Advt., N.Y.C., 1966-68; sr. media planner Grey Advt., 1969-73; account exec. N.C.K. Advt., 1974-78; market mgr. Dow Corning, Midland, Mich., 1978-83, mgr. planning and devel., 1984—. Mem. Am. Soc. Tng. and Devel. Avocations: painting; reading; dancing. Home: 4204 Arlington St Midland MI 48640 Office: Dow Corning Co PO Box 994 C01134 Midland MI 48640

WOLF, DON ALLEN, hardware wholesaler exec.; b. Allen County, Ind., June 18, 1929; s. Ellis Adolphus and Bessie Ruth (Fortman) W.; m. Virginia Ann Lunz, Oct. 8, 1949; children—Rebecca, Donna, Richard, Lisa. Student exec. course, Ind. U., 1969. With Hardware Wholesalers Inc., Fort Wayne, Ind., 1947—; purchasing mgr. Hardware Wholesalers Inc., 1957—, v.p., gen. mgr., 1967-80, pres., 1980—; dir. Lyal Electric Co., Fort Wayne Nat. Bank. Pres., bd. dirs. Big Brothers, Fort Wayne, 1973-74; nat. pres. Big Brothers Soc. Am., 1977-80; bd. dirs. Russell Mueller Research Found., 1970—. Mem. Nat. Wholesale Hardware Assn. (dir. 1977—, pres. 1984-85, named Hardware Wholesaler of Year 1973, 85), Ind. State C. of C. (dir.), Fort Wayne C. of C. (dir. 1973-74, 78). Republican. Lutheran. Office: Hardware Wholesalers Inc PO Box 868 Fort Wayne IN 46801

WOLF, E(DWARD) JOSEPH, coating company executive; b. Shawano, Wis., Sept. 12, 1936; s. Edward Joseph Wolf and Bernice Marie (McCabe) W.; m. Sharon R. Herlache, June 30, 1956 (div. 1976); children: Barth, Brenda, Brian, Barry; m. Denise J. Ruprecht. BS, Marquette U., 1960. Photographer FBI, Milw., 1954-60; buyer Fort Howard Paper Co., Green Bay, Wis., 1960-66; purchasing agt. Ansul Co., Marinette, Wis., 1966-70; pres. Trowelon Inc., Green Bay, 1970-80; regional mgr. Wis. Protective Coating Corp., Green Bay, 1980—; instr. corrosion seminar U. Wis., Madison, 1975. Contbr. articles to profl. articles. Mem. Rep. Nat. Com., Washington, 1983. Mem. Nat. Assn. Corrosion Engrs., Tech. Assn. Pulp & Paper (chmn. 1978-80, corrosion and materials engring. com.), Steel Structures Painting Council. Republican. Roman Catholic. Avocations: golf, reading. Office: Wis Protective Coating Corp PO Box 216 Green Bay WI 54305

WOLF, FREDRIC M., educational psychologist; b. Canton, Ohio, Aug. 7, 1945; s. Wayne S. and Anita (Manheim) W.; m. Leora DeLelyes Lucas, Sept. 29, 1985; 1 child, Jacob M. B.S., U. Wis., 1967; postgrad. Law Sch. Georgetown U., 1967-68; M.Ed., Kent State U., 1977, PH.D., 1980. Instr. math. Cuyahoga Community Coll., Cleve., 1978-79; research assoc. behavioral scis. Northeastern Ohio U. Med. Coll., Rootstown, 1979-80; research assoc. med. edn. Ohio State U. Coll. Medicine, Columbus 1980-82, clin. asst. prof. pediatrics, 1981-82; asst. prof. postgrad. medicine U. Mich. Med. Sch., Ann Arbor, 1982-87; assoc. prof. 1987—. assoc. dir. edn. Mich. Diabetes Research and Tng. Ctr., Ann Arbor, 1982-84; acting dir. 1984-85; cons. Office Technology Assessment, U.S. Congress, 1987—; cons. Office Research U.S. Dept. Edn., 1986—; cons. Nat. Heart Lung and Blood Inst. NIH, Bethesda, Md., 1985; cons. NSF, Nat. Research Council, Nat. Acad. Scis . Author: Meta-analysis: Quantitative Methods for Research Synthesis, 1986; contbr. articles to profl. jours. Vol., Peace Corps, Latin Am., 1969-72. Grantee Mich. Dept. Pub. Health, 1984-86, Spencer Found., 1983-84, NIH, 1985—. Mem. AAAS, Am. Diabetes Assn., Am. Psychol. Assn., Am. Statis. Assn., Midwestern Ednl. Research Assn. (v.p. 1984-85, pres. 1986-87), Soc. Behavioral Medicine, Soc. Med. Decision Making, Sigma Xi. Avocations: bird watching, canoeing, tennis, squash, skiing. Office: U Mich Dept Postgrad Medicine Ann Arbor MI 48109

WOLF, GARY RICHARD, orthodontist; b. Tiffin, Ohio, Sept. 4, 1955; s. Kenneth William and Helen Mae (Shaferly) W.; m. Christine Marsha Wagner, Sept. 7, 1980. BS, Case Western Res. U., 1977, DDS, 1979; MS in Dentistry, U. Wash., 1981. Practice dentistry specializing in orthodontics Sandusky, Ohio, 1982, Norwalk, Ohio, 1983—; clin. instr. orthodontics Case Western Res. U., Cleve., 1983—. Mem. ADA, Ohio Dental Assn., North Cen. Ohio Dental Soc. (sec., editor jour.), Am. Assn. Orthodontists, Cleve. Soc. Orthodontists, Great Lakes Soc. Otrhodontists, Norwalk C. of C., Omicron Kappa Upsilon, Alpha Omega (Excellence in Scholarship award). Republican. Methodist. Avocations: photography, golfing, cross country skiing. Home: 204 S Main St Milan OH 44846 Office: 85 E Main St Norwalk OH 44857

WOLF, HOWARD M., business equipment company executive; b. 1925. With United Stationers Supply Co., Des Plaines, Ill., 1946—, pres., 1963-77, chmn. bd., chief exec. officer, 1981—. Office: United Stationers Inc 2200 E Golf Rd Des Plaines IL 60016 *

WOLF, JOANNE MARIE, sales manager; b. Akron, Ohio, July 1, 1960; d. Paul Charles Darlington and Margaret Stephanie (Kraft) Harmon; m. Joseph Anthony Wolf Jr., May 29, 1982. BA in Radio and TV, Ashland Coll., 1981. Acct. exec. Sta. WLIT, Steubenville, Ohio, 1982-83, Sta. WKWK, Wheeling, W.Va., 1983-84; acct. exec. Sta. WTOV-TV, Steubenville, Ohio, 1984-85, local sales mgr., 1985-86, gen. sales mgr., 1986—. Vol. Ohio County Spl. Olympics, West Liberty State Coll., 1986, 87, United Cerebral Palsy, Wheeling, 1986, 87. Republican. Club: Pilot (bd. dir. 1986—). Home: 430 N 7th St Martins Ferry OH 43935 Office: WTOV-TV Altamont Rd PO Box 9999 Steubenville OH 43952

WOLF, JOHN WILLIAM, pediatrician, allergist, immunologist; b. Jamaica, N.Y., June 12, 1944; s. Gerard F. and Mary R. W.; m. Mary Elizabeth Groves, Apr. 23, 1983. BS, Ohio State U., 1966, MD, 1970. Diplomate Am. Bd. Pediatrics, Am. Bd. Allergy and Immunology. From intern to resident in pediatrics Columbus (Ohio) Children's Hosp., 1970-73; gen. practice medicinespecializing in allergy and clinical immunology Henry Ford Hosp., Detroit, 1973-77, Ann Harbor, Mich., 1977—. Served to maj. U.S. Army, 1973-75. Fellow AM. Acad. Pediatrics, Am. Acad. Allergy; mem. Mich. Allergy Soc., Mich. State Med. Soc., Washtenaw County Med. Soc. Avocations: antiques, bottle collecting, reading. Office: 2350 Washtenaw Ave Suite #10 Ann Arbor MI 48104

WOLF, KARL EVERETT, aerospace and communications corporation executive; b. Hartford, Conn., Aug. 19, 1921; s. Carl Fred and Anna (Voss) W.; m. Lola Sue Stoner, Aug. 1, 1948; children: Paula R., Gloria J., Glenn K. B.S., U.S. Mil. Acad., 1943; J.D., U. Pa., 1953; S.J.D., George Washington U., 1963. Bar: D.C. 1953, Conn. 1953, U.S. Supreme Ct. 1960, Calif. 1971, Mich. 1975. Commd. 2d lt. U.S. Army, 1943, advanced through grades to lt. col., 1959, ret., 1963; assoc. counsel Philo. Corp., Phila., 1963-73; v.p., gen. counsel Ford Aerospace and Communications Corp., Detroit, 1973—; mem. adv. bd. Bur. Nat. Affairs, Fed. Contract Reports, Washington, 1963-73. Author: State Taxation of Government Contractors, 1964. Decorated Silver Star, Bronze Star; Croix de Guerre (Belgium). Mem. ABA, Fed. Bar Assn., Calif. Bar Assn. Clubs: Lawyers (Washington); Fairlane (Dearborn, Mich.). Home: 8 Brookwood Ln Dearborn MI 48120 Office: Ford Aerospace & Communications Corp 300 Renaissance Center PO Box 43342 Detroit MI 48243

WOLF, LAURENCE GRAMBOW, geography educator; b. N.Y.C., Sept. 4, 1921; s. Edward Andrew and Anna Charlotte (Grambow) W.; m. Norma Roberts Reinhardt; children: Steve, Allen, Eric. BS in Social Sci., CCNY, 1943; MA, Columbia U., 1947; PhD, Syracuse U., 1966. Instr. geography U. Cin., 1952-57, asst. prof., 1957-69, assoc. prof., 1969—; dir. Miami Valley Basemap Project, 1974-77; mem. Cin. Census Tract Com., 1959—. Contbr. articles to profl. jours. Bd. dirs. Independent Voters of Ohio, Cin., 1972-82, sec. 1973-75. Served to sgt. U.S. Army, 1943-46, PTO. Mem. Assn. Am. Geographers, Am. Assn. Univ. Profs., Internat. Soc. for Comparative Study of Civilization, Socially and Ecol. Responsible Geographers (treas., editor Transition, 1974—). Unitarian. Office: U Cin Dept Geography Cincinnati OH 45221

WOLF, MARTIN FREDERICK, architect; b. Marion, Ohio, Sept. 26, 1951; s. Paul Edward and Grace Emma (Nehring) W.; m. Julie Ann Fritz, June 23, 1979; children: Sarah Katherine, Daniel Frederick. BArch, Cornell U., 1975. Registered architect, Ill. Project architect William Downing Assoc., Ithaca, N.Y., 1975, Perkins & Will, Chgo., 1976-78; project architect Murphy Jahn, Chgo., 1978-82, v.p., 1983—; guest critic U. Wis., Milw., 1983-86, guest lectr. 1986. Exhibited works 100 Yrs. Chgo. Architecture, Mus. Sci. and Industry, Chgo., 1985, Chgo. Archtl. Club, Betsy Rosenfeld Gallery, Chgo., 1986. Recipient Matthew A. Gaudio Meml. award, Cornell U., 1975; Cornell U. fellow, 1975. Mem. AIA (guest lectr. Chgo. chpt. 1986), N.Y. Soc. Architects (hon.), Chgo. Archtl. Club. Club: Cornell (Chgo.). Avocations: sailing, skiing, sketching. Home: 1202 Lake Wilmette IL 60091 Office: Murphy Jahn 35 E Wacker Chicago IL 60601

WOLF, SISTER MARY WILMA, nun, home economics educator; b. Little Cedar, Iowa, Apr. 2, 1918; d. William Michael and Sophia Emma (Miller) W. B.A., State U. Iowa, 1943, M.A., 1944. Joined Sisters of Mercy, Roman Catholic Ch., 1936. Tchr. St. Berchman's Sch., Marion, Iowa, 1937-38, Immaculate Conception Sch., Charles City, Iowa, 1939-40, St. John's Sch., Waterloo, Iowa, 1940-41; asst. prof. home econs. Mount Mercy Coll., Cedar Rapids, Iowa, 1945—. Demonstrator, Gazette Cook-Off, Cedar Rapids, 1984, 85; speaker Mount Mercy Speaker's Bur., 1960-76. Avocations: cooking; sewing; crafts. Home and Office: Mount Mercy Coll 1330 Elmhurst Dr NE Cedar Rapids IA 52402

WOLF, MOLLIE GAMBLE, accountant, tax consultant; b. Hudson, Mich., Nov. 3, 1930; d. Edward Harmon and Mary Grace (Keasel) Gamble; m. David Graham Knox Sr., Dec. 2, 1950 (div. Dec. 1968); children: David Jr., Patrick Sr., Timothy, Jonathan; m. Edward Phillip Wolf, Aug. 2, 1972. Grad. high sch., Hudson. Exec. sec. M & S Mfg. Co., Hudson, 1948-55; receptionist Purpose Ext. Aluminum, Hudson, 1958-60; exec. sec. Rima Mfg. Co., Hudson, 1956-68; tax cons. H & R Block, Hudson, 1970—; v.p. Klee Pharmacy, Hudson, 1975—; vis. fellow MIT, Cambridge, Mass.; vis. scholar Columbia U., N.Y.C., 1967-68, Wiener Institut fur Internationale Wirtschaftsvergleiche, 1975; vis. sr. scholar Birckbeck Coll U. London, 1982; mem. Nat. Tax Orgn., Mpls., 1980-83. Helper Boy Scouts Am., Hudson, 1966-72. Mem. Am. Bus. Women's Assn. (treas. 1983-84, 85—, pres. 1984-85, Woman of Yr. award 1986). Episcopalian. Clubs: Child Study (pres. 1959-60), Friday (Hudson) (various positions 1958-65). Avocations: travel, sewing, enjoying grandchildren. Home: 14031 Harper Rd Cement City MI 49233 Office: 301 W Main St Hudson MI 49247

WOLF, ROBERT MICHAEL, lawyer; b. Evansville, Ind., June 5, 1953; s. Thomas Joseph and Margaret Gertrude (Horn) W. B.B.A., U. Notre Dame, 1975; J.D., So. Ill. U., 1978; LL.M., Emory U., 1979. Bar: Ill. 1980, U.S. Dist. Ct. (so. dist.) Ill. 1984, U.S. Ct. Appeals (7th cir.) 1985. Pub. defender Saline County, Ill., 1980-84; sole practice, Harrisburg, Ill., 1980—. Mem. ABA, Assn. Trial Lawyers Am., Ill. State Bar Assn., Saline County Bar Assn. Harrisburg Jaycees. Roman Catholic. Home: Route 4 Harrisburg IL 62946

WOLFE, CARL DEAN, electrical engineer; b. La Salle, Ill., May 13, 1957; s. Jerry Lee and Rose Marie (Geraci) W.; m. Ruth Christine Hoelzer, Sept. 13, 1980; children: Kyle Ryan, Kristin Bryce. AS, Ill. Valley Community Coll., 1977; BSEE, U. Ill., 1979. Applications engr. Harris Semicondr., Melbourne, Fla., 1979-84; mgr. component engring. Rockwell Telecommunications, Downers Grove, Ill., 1984—. Avocations: model aviation, competitive sports. Office: Rockwell Telecommunications 1431 Opus Pl Downers Grove IL 60515

WOLFE, F. D., health care construction company. Chmn. Health Care & Retirement Corp., Lima, Ohio. Office: Health Care & Retirement Corp of Am 1885 McCullogh St Lima OH 45802 *

WOLFE, GOLDIE BRANDELSTEIN, real estate company executive; b. Linz, Austria, Dec. 20, 1945; d. Albert and Regina (Sandman) Brandelstein; student U. Ill., 1963-64; B.S. with honors in Bus. Adminstrn., Roosevelt U., 1967; postgrad. U. Chgo. Grad. Sch. Bus., 1968-69; 1 dau., Alicia Danielle Schuyler. Account research mgr. J. Walter Thompson Advt., Chgo., 1967-71, assoc. account exec., 1971-72; account exec. Needham, Harper & Steers, Advt., Chgo., 1972; real estate broker office leasing dept. Arthur Rubloff & Co., Chgo., 1972—, asst. v.p., 1975-77, v.p. office leasing, 1977-80, sr. v.p., 1980—. Bd. dirs. realty div. Jewish United Fund, 1976-77, chmn., 1986-87; bd. dirs. Michael Reese Hosp. Med. Research Inst. Council, 1979—, United Charities, Met. Planning Council; chmn. services group Chgo. Public TV, 1974-75; chmn. realty div. United Jewish Fund, 1986-87. Named Top Producer of Yr., Authur Rubloff & Co., 1981-84; recipient Disting. Communal Service award B'nai B'rith Internat., 1985. Mem. Chgo. Real Estate Bd. (sales council, Salesman of Yr. award 1981, 82, 83), Chgo. Council Fgn. Relations, Roosevelt U. Alumni Assn. (bd. govs.), Urban Land Inst., Ill. Assn. Realtors, Nat. Assn. Realtors, Young Execs. Club (program v.p. 1980-81), Chgo. Network, Lambda Alpha Internat. Clubs: Chgo. Econ., East Bank, Standard. Home: 1332 Sutton Pl Chicago IL 60610 Office: Rubloff Inc 111 W Washington St Chicago IL 60602

WOLFE, JAMES RICHARD, lawyer, business executive; b. Hannibal, Mo., Nov. 7, 1929; s. James Edward and Grace (Kirn) W.; m. Helene Lorraine Rosedale, Dec. 29, 1951; children: Yvonne Bazar, Mary Viano, Theresa Henderson, James E., Michaela, Kathleen, Lorraine. Student, Georgetown U., 1947-49; B.S., Loyola U., 1951; J.D., DePaul U., 1953; LHD (honoris causa), Huron Coll., 1981. Bar: Ill. 1953, U.S. Supreme Ct. 1961. Atty. Burlington R.R., Chgo., 1953-55, 58-59; mem. Nat. R.R. Adjustment Bd., Chgo., 1959-63; counsel Southeastern Carriers Conf. Com., 1959-65; gen. atty. Nat. Ry. Labor Conf., 1965-67, gen. counsel, 1967-68; v.p. labor relations Chgo. and Northwestern Transp. Co., 1968-73, v.p. ops., 1973-76, pres., chief exec. officer, 1976-85; chmn., chief exec. officer CNW Corp., Chgo., 1985—; dir. NICOR, No. Ill. Gas Co., NALCO Chem., Continental Ill. Holding Corp., ES-II Corp. Fin. chmn. Rep. Party, State of Ill., 1987; trustee De Paul U., Chgo., Fenwick High Sch., Oak Park, Ill., Rush-Presbyn.-St. Luke's Med. Ctr., Chgo., Lyric Opera Chgo.; fin. chmn. Reps. State Ill. Served to capt. U.S. Army, 1955-58. Mem. Am. R.R.s Assn. (dir.), Western Ry. Assn. (dir.), Nat. Ry. Labor Conf. (dir.). Clubs: Hinsdale (Ill.) Golf; Commercial, Mid-Am (bd. govs.), Chicago, Carlton, Economic (bd. dirs.) (Chgo.); Old Elm (Ft. Sheridan, Ill.); Turtle Creek (Tequesta, Fla.). Lodge: Knights of Malta. Home: 30 Breakenridge Farm Oak Brook IL 60521 also: 215 W Seaview Drive Duck Key FL 33050 Office: CNW Corp One Northwestern Center Chicago IL 60606

WOLFE, JOHN WALTON, investment banker; b. Columbus, Ohio, Sept. 4, 1928; s. Edgar T. and Alice (Alcorn) W.; m. Norina Vannucci, July 20, 1978; children by previous marriage—Ann M., Robert F., Victoria G., Douglas B. Student, Miami U., Oxford, Ohio, 1946-47. With Ohio Nat. Bank of Columbus, 1948-57; v.p. BancOhio Corp. (bank holding co.), Columbus, 1957-74, also dir.; chmn. bd. Ohio Co., Columbus, 1974—, also dir.; chmn. bd. Dispatch Printing Co., 1975—; chmn. Shepherd Hill Corp.; dir. RadiOhio Inc., AgLands, Brodhead Garrett Co., WBNS-TV, Inc., VideoIndiana, Inc., Ohio Equities, Inc. Bd. govs. Aviation Safety Inst., Columbus; trustee More Bus. for Columbus Inc.; pres. Wolfe Assos. Inc., charitable found., Columbus; sec.-treas. Columbus Capital Corp. for Civic Improvements; pres. Ohio Cancer Found.; chmn. Coalition for Cost Effective Health Services. Mem. Nat. Assn. Security Dealers. Clubs: Athletic of Columbus, Buckeye Lake Yacht, Columbus, Columbus Country, Columbus Maennerchor, Muirfield Village Golf, Nat. Press, Press of Columbus. Lodges: Masons, Shriners. Office: 155 E Broad St Columbus OH 43215

WOLFE, LINDA D., entrepeneur, consultant; b. Des Moines, July 28, 1944; s. Lewell F. and Katherine A. (Ryser) Gunter; m. Thomas J. Wolfe, Apr. 22, 1967; children: Anne Marie, Rachel Lynn. BA in Internat. Relations, U. Wis., 1966. Bus. mgmt. specialist SBA, Indpls., 1975-83; pres. Wolfe Bus. Resource Corp., Indpls., 1983—; instr. Ind.-Purdue U., Indpls., 1978—. Co-editor, publisher IndyWomen, Indpls., 1983-85; contributing editor Ind. Bus. Mag., Indpls., 1984—; contbr. articles to profl. jours. Bd. dirs. Pvt. Industry Council, Indpls., 1983-85; del. White House Conference on Small Bus., Washington, 1986; dir. entrepreneurial adv. bd. Ball State U., 1986—. Mem. Nat. Assn. of Women Bus. Owners (bd. dirs. Cen. Ind. 1983-86, pres. 1985-86), Women's Bus. Initiative, Inc. (bd. dirs. 1984-86). Republican. Avocations: travel. Office: Abbott Labs Dept 45A Abbott Park IL 60064

WOLFE, PATRICIA ROBERTS, educator, curriculum consultant; b. Kings Mt., N.C., July 1, 1942; d. Garland Miller and Pearl (Webb) Roberts; m. Thomas M. Wolfe, Aug. 23, 1963 (div. Jan. 1980); 1 dau., Mary Alice. B.A., U. N.C., 1964; postgrad. U. Philippines, 1965-66, Portland State U., 1969-70; M.Ed., U. Mass., 1972; postgrad. U. Cin., 1980. Cert. tchr., prin., Ohio, Mass. Instr., Clark AFB Edn. Center, Philippines, 1964-67; tchr. Klamath Falls (Oreg.) Schs., 1967-70, Gastonia (N.C.) Schs., 1970-71; reading specialist Chicopee (Mass.) Schs., 1971-74, Greene Joint Vocat. Sch., Xenia, Ohio, 1975—; cons. in curriculum and mgmt. Mem. exec. com. Greene County (Ohio) Democratic Party; past exec. treas. Greene County Mental Health Bd., pres., 1987—. Mem. Am. Vocat. Assn., Ohio Vocat. Assn., Ohio Assn. Vocat. Edn. Spl. Needs Orgn. (pres.), NEA, Western Ohio Edn. Assn., Ohio Spl. Needs Assn., DAR, Bus. and Profl. Women, AAUW, Jamestown Grange, Internat. Platform Assn., Phi Delta Kappa. Democrat. Methodist. Author: The You Need to Read Book; contbr. poetry to mags. Home: 6565 US 35 E Jamestown OH 45335 Office: Greene Joint Vocat Sch 2960 W Enon Rd Xenia OH 45385

WOLFE, SHEEMON AARON, podiatrist; b. Dayton, Ohio, Oct. 27, 1923; s. Jacob and Fannie (Froug) W.; student U. Dayton, 1942; D.P.M., Ohio Coll. Podiatric Medicine, 1951; m. Rachell Goldrich, Jan. 2, 1960; 1 dau., Andrea Nicole. Surgical staff affiliate Good Samaritan Hosp., Dayton, 1955-83, chmn. podiatry sect., 1965-72; podiatric surgeon, active staff, podiatry residency dir. Greene Meml. Hosp., Xenia, Ohio, 1975—; podiatric surgeon assoc. attending staff St. Elizabeth Med. Center, Dayton, 1981—; asst. prof. clin. services Ohio Coll. Podiatric Medicine, 1972-76, adj. clin. instr., 1977; adj. asst. prof. Scholl Sch. Podiatric Medicine, Chgo., 1983—. Served with 217th F.A., 44th Inf. Div., U.S. Army, 1943-46; ETO. Decorated Bronze Star medal. Diplomate Am. Bd. Podiatric Surgery; lic. gen. class amateur radio operator, pvt. pilot. Fellow Am. Coll. Foot Surgeons (asso.); mem. Ohio Podiatry Assn. (chmn. bd. trustees, 1978-79, pres., 1979-80, Silver Gavel Club 1980), Am. Podiatry Assn., Am. Acad. Podiatry Sports Medicine, Am. Assn. Hosp. Podiatrists, Am. Radio Relay League (life), Dayton Amateur Radio Assn., Quarter Century Wireless Assn., Jewish War Vets. Jewish. Club: Masons. Patentee in field. Home: 180 Burgess Ave Dayton OH 45415 Office: 2422 Salem Ave Dayton OH 45406

WOLFE, WARREN DWIGHT, lawyer; b. Boston, July 30, 1926; s. Louis Julius and Rose (Daniels) W.; m. Caroline M. DuMont, Dec. 29, 1973. B.S. in Journalism, Northwestern U., 1949; M. Internat. Affairs, Columbia U., 1951; J.D. with high honors, U. Toledo, 1959. Bar: Ohio 1959, Mich. 1960. Reporter Wilmington Record, Del., 1951-52; Sunday editor, asst. news editor Middletown Jour., Ohio, 1952-55; copy reader, sect. editor Toledo Blade, 1955-60; assoc. Bugbee & Conkle, Toledo, 1960-64; ptnr. 1964—. Pres., Health Planning Assn. Northwest Ohio, 1970-73; mem. Comprehensive Health Planning Adv. Council to Ohio Dept. Health, 1972-75; mem. Ohio Gov.'s Task Force on Health, 1973-74; mem. Lucas County Health Planning Study Com., 1984—; trustee Toledo Legal Aid Soc., 1968—, pres., 1973-75; trustee Toledo Animal Shelter Assn., 1962-75; trustee Lucas County unit Am. Cancer Soc., 1964—, v.p., 1976-81, pres., 1981-83; trustee Ohio div., 1969-70, 85—. Served with USNR, 1944-46. Mem. Am. Trial Lawyers Assn., ABA, Ohio Bar Assn., Lucas County Bar Assn. (pres. 1966), Toledo Bar Assn. (exec. com. 1969-75), State Bar Mich., Law Alumni Assn. U. Toledo Coll. Law (pres. 1965), Sigma Delta Chi. Club: Toledo Ski (treas. 1972-75, pres. 1975-76). Lodge: Masons. Home: 5617 Dianne Ct Toledo OH 43623 Office: Bugbee & Conkle 1301 Toledo Trust Bldg Toledo OH 43604

WOLFF, BRUNO BERNHARD, JR., museum director; b. Chgo., June 15, 1934; s. Bruno Bernhard and Florence Mary (Renk) W.; m. Margaret P. Kelly, Aug. 25, 1956 (div. Aug. 1969); children: Bruno, Margaret, Timothy; m. Maureen Anne McMahon, Aug. 13, 1970; stepchildren: Gerald Berenson, Linda Berenson, Paul Berenson. AB in Classical Languages & Lit. with honors, Xavier U., 1956; MA, Marquette U., 1959. Editor Bruce Pub., Milw., 1958-67; dir. publs. U. Wis., Milw., 1967-70, asst. to asst. chancellor, 1971-74, sr. staff assoc., 1974-84; dep. dir. Milw. Pub. Mus., 1984—. Author: (book) Modular Programming Routines for Apple II, 1985; contbr. articles to profl. jours. Pres. Shorewood Specific Learning Disabilities Assn., 1971-72; den leader Shorewood Cub Scouts, 1970-72; mgr. Shorewood Little League, 1973-76. Served to capt. U.S. Army, 1957-58. Mem. Am. Soc. Personnel Adminstrn. Avocations: computer programming, contract bridge. Home: 2004 E Kensington Blvd Shorewood WI 53211 Office: Milw Pub Mus 800 W Wells Milwaukee WI 53233

WOLFF, DARREL EUGENE, civil engineer; b. Vandalia, Ill., Oct. 25, 1951; s. Paul Carl and Lorraine Louise (Kirchhoff) W.; m. Patricia Louise Bergstrom, Oct. 11, 1975; children: Megan Teresa, Kayla Marie. BS in Civil Engring., U. Ill., 1973; MS Civil Engring., Iowa State U., 1978. Registered profl. engr., Ill., Mo. Engr. Peace Corps, Huaraz, Peru, 1973-74, Thermogas, Inc., Des Moines, 1974-76; engr. John Mathes & Assocs., Inc., Columbia, Ill., 1978-83, br. mgr., 1983-85, div. mgr., 1985—. Mem. ASCE, Ill. Soc. Profl. Engrs. (Young Engr. of Yr. 1983), Soc. Am. Mil. Engrs., Nat. Waterwell Assn. Republican. Lutheran. Avocations: golf, weight-lifting. Home: 2607 Storm Lake Dr Saint Louis MO 63129 Office: John Mathes and Assocs Inc 210 W Sandbank Columbia IL 62236

WOLFF, GEORGE THOMAS, atmospheric scientist, educator; b. Irvington, N.J., Nov. 29, 1947; s. George C. and Margaret M. (Leroy) W.; m. Carol Ann Wirth, Aug. 12, 1972; children: Elaine, Meg, Kristen. BSChemE, N.J. Inst. Tech., 1969; MS, NYU, 1970; PhD, Rutgers U., 1974. Assoc. engr. Interstate Sanitation Commn., N.Y.C., 1973-77; sr. staff scientist Gen. Motors Research Labs., Warren, Mich., 1977-87, prin. resident scientist and section mgr., 1987—; cons. U.S. EPA, Research Triangle Park, N.C., 1975—; cons. EPA Sci. Adv. Bd., Washington, 1984-87, mem., 1987—; adj. prof. atmospheric sci. U. Mich., Ann Arbor, 1984—. Editor: Carbonaceous Particles in the Atmosphere, 1981; contbr. articles to profl. jours. Chmn. Environ. Commn., Caldwell, N.J., 1974-77. Recipient Environ. Achievement award Gen. Motors Corp., Detroit, 1983; John Campbell award, G.M. Research Labs., Warren, Mich., 1984. Russel fellow, Rutgers U., New Brunswick, N.J., 1972-73. Mem. Air Pollution Control Assn. (tech. chmn. 1984-85, bd. dirs. 1986—, editorial rev. bd. 1984—), Am. Meteorol. Soc. (atmospheric chemistry chmn. 1982-85), Sigma Xi. Roman Catholic. Office: Gen Motors Research Labs Environ Sci Dept Warren MI 48090

WOLFF, GUNTHER ARTHUR, physical chemist; b. Essen, Germany, Mar. 31, 1918; came to U.S., 1953; s. Joseph and Anna (Breidecker) W.; m. Gertrude Anna Stolte, Feb. 27, 1945; children—Christine, Francis. B.S., Berlin U., 1944, M.S., 1945; Sc.D., Berlin Tech. U., 1948. Research assoc. Fritz Haber Inst., Berlin, 1944-50, sci. head, dep. chief crystal kinetics dept., 1950-53; cons. sr. scientist, team leader Signal Corps Research and Devel. Lab. U.S. Army, Fort Monmouth, N.J., 1953-60; sr. group leader material research Harshaw Chem. Co., Cleve., 1960-63; dir. material research Erie Tech. Products Co., Pa., 1963-64; prin. scientist Tyco Labs., Inc., Waltham, Mass., 1964-70; cons. chemist Lamp Phenomena Research Lab., Lamp Envelope Materials Research Lab. Gen. Electric Co., Cleve., 1970-77; sr. staff engr. Nat. Semicondr. Corp., Hawthorne, Calif., 1977-81, indsl. cons., 1981-83; indsl. cons. G.A. Cons. NPO, 1983—; chmn. Gordon Research Conf. on Chemistry and Metallurgy of Semicondrs., 1965; mem. crystal growth com. Internat. Union Crystallography, 1967-75; mem. Am. com. for crystal growth, 1967-72. Fellow Am. Inst. Chemists, Mineral Soc. Am.; mem. N.Y. Acad. Sci., Am. Chem. Soc., Electrochem. Soc., Am. Crystallographic Assn., Am. Ceramic Soc., Am. Assn. for Crystal Growth. Home and Office: 3776 Northampton Rd Cleveland OH 44121

WOLFF, LINDA M., personnel executive; b. Chgo., June 30, 1953; d. Calvin and Marian Wolff. BA in Psychology and Speech Communications, Northeastern Ill. U., 1976. Recruiter Trans Union Corp., Chgo., 1977-78; compensation adminstr. Am. Res. Corp., Chgo., 1978-79; sr. compensation specialist Bankers Life and Casualty Co., Chgo., 1979-80; dir. human resources and devel. IDC Services, Inc., Chgo., 1980-84; v.p. regional dir. human resources Burson-Marsteller, pub. relations, Chgo., 1984—. Mem. Am. Soc. Personnel Adminstrn., Am. Compensation Assn., Soc. Human Resources Profls., Am. Soc. Tng. and Devel., Am. Mgmt. Assn.

WOLFSON, GARY MAREMONT, executive search company executive; b. Chgo., June 27, 1950; s. J. Theodore and Natalie B. (Brandwein) W.; m. Linda Mark, Nov. 5, 1978; 1 child, Jeffrey Mark. BBA, U. Denver, 1972. Dir. mktg. Bus. Builders Internat., Chgo., 1973-78; v.p. Sales and Mgmt. Search, Chgo., 1978-80; pres. The Search Group, Inc., Northfield, Ill., 1980—; cons., bd. dirs. Career Link Corp., Chgo., 1982-83. Vice chmn. jr. bd. Michael Reese Hosp., Chgo., 1976-77; chmn. jr. bd. Highland Park (Ill.) Hosp., 1986—. Mem. Nat. Assn. Personnel Cons. Republican. Avocations: running, fine wines. Office: The Search Group Inc 300 S Riverside Plaza Suite 660 Chicago IL 60606

WOLFSON, LESTER MARVIN, former university chancellor; b. Evansville, Ind., Sept. 13, 1923; s. William and Bess (Silverman) W.; m. Esther Evans, July 3, 1949; children: Alice Jeanette, Margaret Gail, George Stephen. AB, U. Mich., 1945, AM., 1946, PhD, 1954. Instr. English Wayne State U., Detroit, 1950-53; asst. prof. English and speech U. Houston, 1953-55; asst. prof. English Ind. U. N.W., Gary, 1955-61, assoc. prof., 1961-64; assoc. prof. Ind. U., South Bend, 1964-67, prof., 1967—, dir., asst. dean, 1964-66, dean, 1966-68, dean, acting chancellor, 1968-69, chancellor, 1969-87; vis. asst. prof. English U. Calif., Santa Barbara, 1958-59. Contbr. articles to profl. jours. Bd. dirs. Michiana Pub. Broadcasting Corp., Michiana Arts and Scis. Council, Studebaker Nat. Mus., Inc., South Bend Civic Found.; United Nations Assn. of St. Joseph County, South Bend Symphony Orch. Assn. Horace H. Rackham fellow, 1954. Mem. Nat. Council Tchrs. English, Coll. English Assn., MLA, AAUP, Phi Beta Kappa, Phi Kappa Phi, Phi Eta Sigma. Home: 17350 Darden Rd South Bend IN 46635 Office: Ind U 1700 Mishawaka Ave South Bend IN 46634

WOLGIN, FRANCIE JEAN, nursing administrator; b. Cin., Dec. 10, 1947; d. Francis Joseph and Betty Jane (Brauns) Sullivan; m. Paul Jonathan Wolgin, Dec. 15, 1969 (div. June 1984); 1 child, Rebecca. BS in Nursing, U. Cin., 1969; postgrad., Ohio State U., 1971-72; MS in Nursing, U. Cin., 1983. Staff nurse U. Cin. Hosp., 1969-71, head nurse, 1972-74, instr. staff devel., 1974-80, dir. nursing, 1984—; acting dir. clin. and house staff affairs Univ. Hosp., Cin., 1984-85; program cons. Greater Cin. Nurse Execs., 1984-87. Producer (video tape) Physical Crisis Management, 1984; contbr. numerous articles to profl. jours. Vol. Am. Diabetes Assn., Cin., 1977-79, Juvenile Diabetes Assn., Cin., 1982—. Recipient Leadership award, KC. Mem. Am. Nursing Assn. (chairperson continuing edn. nominating com. 1985-86), Ohio Nursing Assn. (chairperson staff devel. assembly 1983-87), South Western Ohio Nurses Assn. (pres. 1984-86, nominating com. 1986-87), Sigma Theta Tau (Community Leader award 1982). Democrat. Roman Catholic. Avocations: swimming, sailing, painting. Home: 6350 Glengariff Ct Cincinnati OH 45230

WOLK, ALAN MURRAY, lawyer, labor arbitrator; b. Cleve., Mar. 17, 1932; s. Samuel Louis and Jean (Mintz) W.; m. Phyllis Grossberg, Dec. 1, 1957; children—Martin, Jeff, Scott. B.B.A., Cleve. State Coll., 1953; J.D., Ohio State U., 1955; postgrad. Case Western Res. Sch. Law, 1959-62; postgrad. student Ohio State Bar Assn. Coll., 1983-84, 86-87. Bar: Ohio 1955, U.S. Supreme Ct., 1965. Asst. atty. gen. State of Ohio, 1958-62, 70-81; acting judge Mcpl. Ct., Shaker Heights, Ohio, 1969-77; dir. of law City of University Heights, Ohio, 1980—; seminar chmn., program chmn. Cuyahoga County Law Dirs., Cleve., 1981—, labor panel mem. Am. Arbitration Assn., Cleve., 1974—, Fed. Mediation and Conciliation Service, Washington, 1979—; mem. panel Ohio State Employment Relations Bd., 1985—. del. 8th Jud. Conf., Ohio. Editor mag. Cuyahoga County Bar Bull., 1958-63. Contbr. articles to profl. jours. Pres. University Heights Democratic Club, Ohio, 1968-74; jud. scanning com. Citizens League Cleve., 1977; bd. dirs. Temple Emanu El, University Heights, 1982-84; trustee Handgun Fedn. Ohio, 1985—. Fellow Cleve. Acad. Trial Lawyers; mem. Cuyahoga County Bar Assn. (sec. 1963-70, pres. 1984-85, exec. dir. 1963-70) (award of Special Merit 1970), ABA, Ohio Assn. Civil Trial Attys., Ohio State Bar Assn. (ho. of dels. 1974—), Ohio Jud. Conf. of 8th Jud. Dist., Tau Epsilon Rho (chancellor, 1963). Lodges: Masons (master 1974-75), B'nai B'rith (fin. sec. 1958-63). Office: 1525 Leader Bldg Cleveland OH 44114

WOLK, YALE M., health care executive, service company executive; b. Mpls., Apr. 11, 1945; s. Arnold D. and Marcia (Moorvitz) W.; m. Roberta Lynn Goldman, Mar. 4, 1967; children—Sonya, Erin. B.A., Mich. State U., 1966; M.H.A., U. Minn., 1971. Adminstrv. asst. Dekalb Gen. Hosp., Smithville, Tenn., 1971-73; asst. adminstr. Saginaw Osteo. Hosp., Mich., 1973; asst. adminstr. Community Hosp. Ottawa, Ill., 1973-74, chief exec. officer, pres., 1974—, North Central Service Corp., Ottawa, 1984—; dir. Community Hosp. Ottawa, North Central Service Corp.; mem. council on pub. relations Ill. Hosp. Assn., Naperville, 1984—. Advisor: A Guide to Stategic Planning for Hospitals, 1979. Bd. dirs., sec., treas. Camp Fire Council, Ottawa, 1980-83; bd. dirs. LaSalle County Council on Alcoholism, Ottawa, 1982—; task force mem. LaSalle County State Atty., Ottawa, 1984.

Served to 1st lt. U.S. Army, 1967-69. Named Outstanding Young Person Ottawa Jaycees, 1979. Mem. Am. Coll. Healthcare Execs., Minn. Program Alumni Assn., C. of C. (bd. dirs. 1984—). Lodge: Rotary. Avocations: handball, racketball, golf, cycling. Office: Community Hosp Ottawa 1100 E Norris Dr Ottawa IL 61350

WOLKE, N. LAWRENCE, city administrator; b. Cin., June 8, 1945; s. Lawrence George and Ruth Argretta (Smith) W.; m. Margaret Eleanore Deye, Apr. 22, 1972; children: William, Amy, Joseph. BA, U. Cin., 1967, MA, 1971. Mgmt. analyst City of Cin., 1971-72; adminstrv. asst. City of Saginaw, Mich., 1972-76, asst. city mgr., 1976; city mgr. City of Ironton, Ohio, 1976-79; adminstr. City of Urbana, Ohio, 1980—. Served to capt. U.S. Army, 1967-70, Vietnam. Decorated Bronze Star. Mem. Internat. City Mgmt. Assn. Lodge: Rotary (pres. Urbana club 1986-87). Home: 928 Bon Air Dr Urbana OH 43078 Office: Mcpl Bldg 205 S Main Urbana OH 43078

WOLKEN, RICHARD JOHN, dentist, farmer; b. Montecillo, Iowa, Apr. 28, 1951; s. Carl Henry and Betty Thais (Adams) W.; m. Cora LuAnn Husmann, Aug. 19, 1972; children: Michael, Mathew, Melissa, Brian. DDS, U. Iowa, 1976. Gen. practice dentistry Richard J. Wolken, DDS, P.C., Montecillo, 1976—. Coordinator Monticello Little League, 1985-86; mem. Ch. Trust Fund, Montecillo, 1984-86. Served with USNG, 1970-76. Mem. ADA, Iowa Dental Assn., Univ. Dist. Dental, Farm Bur., Montecillo C. of C. Republican. Lutheran. Lodge: Lions (pres. (1987—). Avocations: skiing, golf. Home: RRZ Monticello IA 52310 Office: 202 N Main St Monticello IA 52310

WOLKEN, STEPHEN HENRY, ophthalmologist; b. Monticello, Iowa, 1943. MD, U. Iowa, 1968. Diplomate Am. Bd. Ophthalmology. Intern USPHS Hosp., Seattle, 1968-69; resident in ophthalmology Iowa Hosps., 1972-75; unit dir. USPHS Indian Hosp., Sisseton, S.D., 1969-71; staff Mercy Hosp., Iowa City, 1975—; instr. ophthalmology U. Iowa, Iowa City, 1975—. Served to surgeon USPHS, 1969-71. Mem. AMA, Am. Acad. Ophthalmology. Home: 416 Monroe St Iowa City IA 52240 Office: 2409 Towncrest Dr Iowa City IA 52240

WOLL, DAVID LAWRENCE, corporate professional; b. Olney, Ill., Oct. 25, 1948; m. Rita Woll; children: Martin Bradley, Julian Reid. BA, Wash. U., St. Louis, 1970; M in Urban Planning, Columbia U., 1972; M in Pub. Adminstrn., Indiana U.-Purdue U., Indpls., 1975; JD, Ind. U., 1979. Various temporary positions govt. and polit. agys., 1967-84; sec. Woll Enterprises, Inc., Evansville, Ind., 1984—. Vol. dept. Human Resources City of University City, Mo., 1969-70; social action com. Adath B'nai Israel Temple, 1984, by-laws and Rabbi search com., 1984-85, bd. dirs., 1985-88, chmn. social action com., 1986—; bd. dirs. Am. Jewish com., 1977, program chmn., sec., 1978-80, treas., 1980-83; mem. screening com. 1980-81; bd. dirs. Boy Scouts Am., 1985—, finance com. 1984—, exec. council, v.p. membership com. 1985, chmn. ticket sales recognition dinner, 1985; active Dawn Line Drug Abuse Program, 1975-76; bd. dirs. Evansville Jewish Community Relations Council, 1984—; chmn. precinct fins. Greater Indpls. Rep. Fin. com., 1975-77; bd. dirs. Indpls. Jewish Community Relations Council, 1976-80, chmn. legis. com. 1978-79, energy com. 1979-81; bd. dirs. Outreach Ministries, 1984—, chmn. personnel, 1986—; bd. dirs. Raintree Council Girl Scouts Am., 1984—; mem. Allocations com. United Way Southwestern Ind., 1984—; advisor study group Leadership of Evansville, 1985; mem. Indpls. Hebrew Congregation Brotherhood, 1974-83; bd. dirs. Evansville Dance Theatre, Southwestern Ind. Found. on Aging. Mem. Am. Soc. Pub. Adminstrn. (exec. council Ind. chpt. 1974-76), Ind. Soc. Pub. Adminstrn. (editor newsletter 1974-76), Ill. Oil Gas Assn., Ind. State Bar Assn., Ind. Soc. Chgo., Ind. U. Alumni Assn. (life), Ky. Oil Gas Assn., Vanderburgh County Bar Assn., ACLU, ABA. Clubs: Oak Meadow Country, Broadmoor Country (mem. com. 1977-78), Columbia, Evansville Coin, Evansville Petroleum. Lodges: B'nai Brith (bd. dirs. regional anti-defamation league 1975—, chmn. 1979-81, reorganization investigation com. 1977-78, nat. new leadership council 1977-79), B'nai Brith Sol Silver (bd. dirs., 3d v.p. 1984-85, pres. 1985-86), Optimists Internat. (bd. dirs. state house chpt. 1974-75, chmn. oratorical contest 1975-76, v.p. 1976-77). Home: 7600 Newburgh Rd Evansville IN 47715 Office: PO Box 2345 Station D Evansville IN 47714

WOLL, MARGO YELLIN, dentist; b. Mt. Clemens, Mich., May 18, 1953; d. George G. and Elsie (Schwartz) Yellin; m. Douglas Robert Woll, June 22, 1975; children: Samantha Heather, Monica Leslie. DDS, U. Mich., 1978. Gen. practice dentistry Southgate, Mich., 1978—. Mem. ADA, Mich. Dental Assn., Detroit Dist. Dental Assn., Am. Assn. Women Dentists, Mortar Bd. Lodge: Hadassah. Office: 15830 Fort St Southgate MI 48195

WOLLE, CHARLES ROBERT, U.S. district court judge; b. Sioux City, Iowa, Oct. 16, 1935; s. William Carl and Vivian (Down) W.; m. Kerstin Birgitta Wennerstrom, June 20, 1961; children: Karl Johan Knut, Erik Vernon, Thomas Dag, Aaron Charles. AB, Harvard U., 1959; JD, Iowa Law Sch., 1961. Bar: Iowa 1961. Assoc. Shull, Marshall & Marks, Sioux City, 1961-67, ptnr., 1968-80; judge U.S. Dist. Ct. Iowa, Sioux City, 1981-83; justice Iowa Supreme Ct., Sioux City, 1983-87; judge U.S. Dist. Ct. (so. dist.) Iowa, Des Moines, 1987—; faculty Nat. Jud. Coll., Reno, 1983—. Editor Iowa Law Rev., 1960-61. Vice pres. bd. dirs. Sioux City Symphony, 1972-77; sec., bd. dirs. Morningside Coll., Sioux City, 1977-81. Fellow Am. Coll. Trial Lawyers; mem. ABA, Iowa Bar Assn., Sioux City C. of C. (bd. dirs. 1977-78). Methodist. Avocations: sports; music. Home: 2727 Glenwood Dr Des Moines IA 50321 Office: US Dist Ct 103 Fed Courthouse Des Moines IA 50309

WOLLER, JACK EMIL, manufacturing company executive; b. Champaign, Ill., Oct. 19, 1925; s. Emil Albert and Melita Marie (Davis) W.; m. Phyllis Carson, Nov. 27, 1947; children—Jack, Jill, Timothy, Kim, Amy. B.S., U. Ill., 1950. Mem. sales staff Internat. Silver Co., Meriden, Conn., 1952-64; with Bissell, Inc., Grand Rapids, Mich., 1964—, now nat. incentive sales mgr. Served with USN, 1943-45, 50-52; PTO. Mem. Nat. Premium Sales Execs. (pres. 1978), Assn. Retail Mkgt. Services (dir.). Republican. Methodist. Office: Bissell Inc 2345 Walker Ave Grand Rapids MI 49504

WOLLMAN, ROGER LELAND, federal judge; b. Frankfort, S.D., May 29, 1934; s. Edwin and Katherine Wollman; m. Diane Marie Schroeder, June 21, 1959; children: Steven James, John Mark, Thomas Roger. BA, Tabor Coll., Hillsboro, Kans., 1957; JD magna cum laude, U. S.D., 1962; LLM, Harvard U., 1964. Bar: S.D. 1964. Sole practice, Aberdeen, 1964-71; justice S.D. Supreme Ct., 1971-85, chief justice, 1978-82; judge U.S. Ct. Appeals (8th cir.), 1985—; states atty. Brown County, Aberdeen, 1967-71. Served with AUS, 1957-59. Office: 212 Federal Bldg Pierre SD 57501

WOLLNER, MARTIN S., computer engineer; b. Detroit, Jan. 16, 1953; s. Max and Helen (Gross) W. AS in Math, Oakland Community Coll., 1975; BS in Physiology, Mich. State U., 1977; postgrad., Lansing Community Coll. Respiratory therapy technician various hosps., Mich., 1971-81; computer physiology researcher Mich. State U., East Lansing, 1981-82; software specialist Digital Equipment Co., Farmington, Mich., 1982-84; control systems analyst Analytical Tech., Southfield, Mich., 1984—; cons. in physiology Mich. State U., East Lansing, 1981—; mem. standards com. Gen. Motors, Troy, Mich., 1984—. designer computer programs, 1982-86. Mem. Am. Soc. Engrs., Am. Soc. Respiratory Therapy, Digital Equipment Users Soc. (controller 1984—), Ultimate Players Assn. Jewish. Club: Lansing Ultimate (league organizer 1984-86), Knot Hole (sgt. 1980). Avocations: pool, billiards, fishing, camping, frisbee. Home: 6061 Orchard Lake Rd Orchard Lake MI 48033 Office: Analytical Techs 30300 Telegraph Suite 184 Birmingham MI 48050

WOLNERMAN, ALLEN PHILIP, pharmacist; b. Cleve., Sept. 1, 1953; s. David and Jennie W.; m. Amy Hollander, July 2, 1978; children: Daniel Gary, Sheri Ilene. B.S., Ind. U., 1975; B.S., Drake U., 1980. Registered pharmacist, Iowa, Fla., Ex. Pres., Graw Inc., Des Moines, 1983—; pres. 20/20 Optical, Inc., Des Moines, 1982—; cons., 1980—. Fellow Am. Soc. Cons. Pharmacists; mem. Nat. Assn. Retail Druggists, Am. Pharm. Assn., Iowa Pharmacists Assn., Ind. U. Alumni Assn., Fla. Pharmacists Assn. Jewish. Home: 5792 Linden Ct Johnston IA 50131 Office: 70th & Douglas Sts Urbandale IA 50322

WOLOSCHAK, MICHAEL JOHN, optometrist, educator; b. Youngstown, Ohio, Dec. 1, 1953; s. Metro and Shirley Ann (Breen) W. BS, Mt. Union Coll., 1976; OD, Ohio State U., 1981, MS, 1983. Lic. optometrist, Ohio. Gen. practice optometry Youngstown, Ohio, 1983—; part-time clin. instr. Coll. Optometry Ohio State U.; research cons. in field. Contbr. articles to profl. jours. Chmn. membership Mahoning Valley council Boy Scouts Am., 1984, dist. chmn., 1985, v.p. dist. operations, 1986-87. Ohio Lions fellow, 1982, Am. Optometric Found. fellow, 1982; named one of Outstanding Young Men Am., Young Ams., 1982. Mem. Am. Optometric Assn., Ohio Optometric Assn. (zone 4 sec.), Epsilon Psi Epsilon, Beta Sigma Kappa. Epsicopalian. Lodge: Kiwanis (interclub chmn. Austin club 1984-85). Avocations: model railroading, skiing, whitewater rafting, racquetball, running. Office: 3155 Canfield Rd Youngstown OH 44511

WOLOSEWICZ, RONALD MITCHELL, mechanical engineer; b. Chgo., Dec. 27, 1937; s. Frank E. and Olga (Kaminski) W.; m. Christine Maria Borawska, June 19, 1974; children: Isabella, Andrzej. BSME, Northwestern U., 1960, MSME, 1962, PhD in Mech. Engring., 1966. Registered profl. engr., Ill. Sr. devel. engr. Anocut Engring., Elk Grove Village, Ill., 1966-69; research engr. Whirlpool Corp., Benton Harbor, Mich., 1969-74, sr. research engr., 1974-77; mech. engr. Argonne (Ill.) Nat. Lab., 1977-82; mgr. engring. and mfg. TRAK Microcomputer, Downers Grove, Ill., 1982-84; prin. engr. graphic systems div. Rockwell Internat., Cicero, Ill., 1984—; instr. Mich. Soc. Profl. Engrs. Refresher, Benton Harbor, 1970-76, Mich. State U., Benton Harbor, 1973-76. Contbr. articles to profl. jours. Fulbright-Hayes fellow, 1966-67. Mem. Am. Soc. Mech. Engrs., Polish Am. Engrs. Assn. (pres. Chgo. chpt. 1970-73), Sigma Xi (pres. Whirlpool chpt. 1976-77), Pi Tau Sigma. Avocations: sailing, coin collecting. Home: 5410 Country Club Dr LaGrange IL 60525 Office: Rockwell Internat Graphic Systems Div 3100 S Central Chicago IL 60650

WOLPE, HOWARD ELIOT, congressman; b. Los Angeles, Nov. 2, 1939; s. Leon Zacharias and Zelda Harriet (Shapiro) W.; 1 son, Michael Stevenson. B.A., Reed Coll., 1960; Ph.D., MIT, 1967. Cons. Peace Corps, 1966-67, Fgn. Service Inst., Dept. State, 1967-72; assoc. prof. polit. sci. Western Mich. U., Kalamazoo, 1967-72; mem. Kalamazoo City Commn., 1969-72, Mich. State Legislature, 1973-76; regional rep. of U.S. Senator Donald Riegle of Mich., 1977-78; mem. 96th-100th Congresses from 3d dist. Mich.; mem. House budget com., fgn. affairs com.; chmn. Community and Natural Resources Task Force, Africa subcom.; co-chmn. Northeast-Midwest Congl. Coalition. Author: Urban Politics in Nigeria: A Study of Port Harcourt, 1974, (with Robert Melson) Nigeria: Modernization and the Politics of Communalism, 1974. Office: 1535 Longworth Bldg Washington DC 20515

WOLPERT, KATHERINE BLOCK, nursing home administrator; b. Sergeant Bluff, Iowa, Apr. 12, 1915; d. William Carroll and Ellen Isabel (Harder) Block; m. Paul L. Wolpert, Feb. 10, 1938 (dec.); children: Mary DeFilippes, Paul W., John A., Regina Ratino, Michael, Patricia Charles, Margaret Parra, Stephen, James. RN, St. Joseph Mercy Hosp., Sioux City, Iowa, 1935, cert. in med. tech., 1936; BA, Morningside Coll., 1971. Registered nurse, Iowa. Med. technologist St. Joseph Mercy Hosp., 1936-39; nursing home exec. Elmwood Nursing Home, Onawa, Iowa, 1960—, pres. bd. dirs., 1981-86; bd. dirs., sec. I&W Farm Corp., Onawa. Tchr. catechism St. John's Ch., Onawa, 1964-80; trustee Onawa Pub. Library, Onawa, 1977-86. Mem. Iowa State Library Assn., N.Y. Geneal. Assn., Monona County Geneal. Assn., Woodbury County Geneal. Assn., St. Joseph Mercy Nursing Sch. Alumni Assn. Republican. Roman Catholic. Avocations: reading, travel, gardening, walking, genealogy. Home: 906 15th Onawa IA 51040

WOLSKI, ARTHUR J., dentist; b. Chgo., June 7, 1921; s. John and Julia (Sitkiewicz) W.; m. Virginia Biss; children: Susan Wolski Schuman, Sharon Wolski Dunkin, Sandra Wolski Hubbard, Shiela Wolski Polansky, Sylvia, Stephanie, Sena, Thomas, Timothy. Student, Roosevelt U., 1939; AS, Wright Jr. Coll., Chgo., 1941; DDS, Northwestern U., 1944. Gen. practice dentistry Chgo., 1944—; clin. instr. dentistry Northwestern U., Evanston, Ill., Forkosh Hosp., Chgo., Northwest Hosp., Chgo.; co-chmn. med. commn. Drugs for Poland; past v.p. North Shore Memory Gardens. Instl. rep. Boy Scouts Am., scout master; coach St. George High Sch. Football, Portage Park Football Assn.; past pres. Our Lady of Victory Parish Club, sch. bd.; bd. dirs. Copernicus Ctr. Served to lt. U.S. Army. Fellow Am. Coll. Dentists, Acad. Dentistry Internat.; mem. ADA (chmn. sci. program), Ill. Dental Soc., Chgo. Dental Soc. (membership chmn. fgn. exhibitor chmn., product control chmn., sec. com. peer rev., northwest br. corr., membership chmn., program chmn., treas., sec., pres.-elect, pres., chmn. peer rev.), Acad. Gen. Dentistry, Pierre Fauchard Acad. (state chmn.), Dental Arts Club (librarian, treas., sec., v.p., pres., scholarship chmn., bd. dirs.) , Nat. Med. and Dental Assn. (treas., sec., v.p., pres., bd. dirs., chmn. scholarship com.), Acad. Continuing Edn., Northwestern U. Dental Alumni Assn. (bd. dirs.), Am. Legion, DAV (Man of Yr. award 1957), Nat. Underwater Scuba Assn. Club: Polish Am. Comml. (v.p.). Lodges: Lions, Elks. Avocations: golf, scuba, sailing, skiing, travel. Home: 5450 W Sunnyside Ave Chicago IL 60630 Office: 5450 Milwaukee Ave Chicago IL 60630

WOLSKY, ALAN MARTIN, physicist; b. Bklyn., May 17, 1943; s. Lorenz Albert and Roselyn (Casper) W.; m. Mary-Jo Bryan, Dec. 31, 1969; 1 child, Rebecca Jeannette. A.B., Columbia U., 1964; M.S., U. Pa., 1965, Ph.D., 1969. Vis. fellow Courant Inst. Math. Scis., N.Y.C., 1970-71; asst. prof. Temple U., Phila., 1971-75; scientist Argonne Nat. Lab., Ill., 1975-86, sr. scientist, 1986—; sect. leader, 1980-85; dir. tech. evaluations in EES Div., 1986—; mem. com. on data for sci. and tech. Internat. Council Sci. Unions, 1984—. Contbr. articles to profl. jours.; reviewer Rev. Econs. and Statistics, 1982—, Resources & Energy, 1982—, Internat. Jour. Hydrogen Energy, 1984—, NSF, 1984—. Photographer, exhibited in group shows, 1975, 80. Vice pres. Maple Hill Improvement Assn., Downers Grove, Ill., 1980-81; v.p. Congregation Etz Chaim, Lombard, Ill., 1982-85, pres., 1985-87. Post-doctoral fellow NRC-Air Force Office Sci. Research, 1970. Mem. Internat. Assn. Energy Economists, Am. Physics Soc. Avocations: camping, reading. Home: 5461 Hillcrest Ave Downers Grove IL 60515 Office: Argonne Nat Lab 9700 S Cass Ave Argonne IL 60439

WOLTERS, PHILLIP JOHN, JR., information specialist, consultant; b. Grand Rapids, Mich., Oct. 31, 1943; s. Phillip John Sr. and Emogene (Lynn) W.; m. Mary Ann Grandy, June 4, 1966; children: Phillip John III, Theresa Lynn. BSBA, Aquinas Coll., 1967. Systems analyst Wolverine World Wide, Rockford, Mich., 1969-72; lead implementation analyst Foremost Ins., Grand Rapids, Mich., 1972-78; sr. systems analyst Interstate Motor Freight, Grand Rapids, 1978-79; systems analyst Rapistan div. Lear Siegler, Grand Rapids, 1979-81; info. specialist Amway Corp., Ada, Mich., 1982-85; lead systems analyst Foremost Ins. Co., Grand Rapids, 1985—. Mem. West Michigan Water Ski Assn. (ski jump champion, 1980), Assn. Systems Mgmt. (treas. 1982-83), Rockford Jaycees (sec.-treas. 1969-72). Club: Chess (Grandville, Mich.) (pres. 1961-62). Lodge: Masons. Avocations: camping, tennis, water skiing, snow skiing. Home: 197 Gaylord Dr Rockford MI 49341 Office: Foremost Service Center 5251 36th St SE Grand Rapids MI 49501

WOLTERSOM, RICHARD JOHN, radiologist; b. Detroit, Sept. 24, 1943; s. John Albert and Sylvia Elizabeth (Dykstra) W. AB, Calvin Coll., 1961-65; MD, U. Mich. Med. Sch., 1969. Diplomate Am. Bd. Radiology. Internship Butterworth Hosp., Grand Rapids, Mich., 1969-70, resident in radiology, 1974-77; instr. in radiology Mich. State U., East Lansing, 1977-78; radiologist Paul Oliver Meml. Hosp., Frankfort, Mich., 1978—; cons. radiologist Westshore Hosp., Manistee, Mich., 1985—. Served to maj. USAF, 1970-74. Mem. Am. Coll. Radiology, Mich. Radiol. Soc., Intertel, Mensa. Avocations: oil painting, sailing, singing. Home: 7707 Surrey Ln Traverse City MI 49684 Office: Paul Oliver Meml Hosp 224 Park Ave Frankfort MI 49635

WOLTHAUSEN, JUDITH ANN, data processing executive; b. Highland Park, Ill., Mar. 16, 1947; d. Lewis Eugene and Bessie Rose (Sievers) W. Student, Wash. U., St. Louis, Mo., 1965-67; cert. in data processing, Bryant & Stratton, Chgo., 1968. Programmer Sears Roebuck & Co., Chgo., 1969-72, sr. systems programmer, 1973-76, systems cons., 1977-82, programming recruiting coordinator, 1983-84, data processing instr., 1984-85, mgr. computer ops., 1985—; adv. council Purdue U. Calumet, Hammond, Ind., 1985—. Sr. choir Christ Luth. Ch. of Clarendon Hills (Ill.), 1980—, ch. council mut. ministry chairperson, 1980-83, counting team, 1984—, lay reader, 1984—, mut. ministry com., 1986—. Mem. GUIDE. Republican. Lutheran. Club: Nat. Assn. Female Execs., Farmingdale, N.Y. Avocations: fishing, cooking, reading, traveling. Home: 106 S Bruner Hinsdale IL 60521 Office: Sears Roebuck & Co Sears Tower D/764 Chicago IL 60684

WOLTZ, KENNETH ALLEN, infosystems consulting executive; b. Phila., Mar. 2, 1943; s. Herman and Florence (Varell) M.; m. Barbara Hand, June 18, 1966; children: Karyn, Diane, Kenneth. BS, U.S. Mil. Acad., 1966; MBA, Xavier U., 1971. Commd. 2d lt. U.S. Army, 1966, advanced through grades to capt., 1968, resigned, 1968; various mgmt. positions Gen. Electric, Evansdale, Ohio and Bethesda, Md., 1968-73; mgr. systems Xerox Corp., Rochester, N.Y., 1973-75; dir. info. services McGraw Edison, Des Plaines, Ill., 1975-77; mng. dir., mgmt. cons. Peat, Marwick, Mitchell, Chgo., 1977-80; mgmt. cons., chief exec. officer human resources Woltz/Duffy Group, Wood Dale, Ill., 1980—. Speaker at various Univs. Mem. Soc. Mgmt. Info. Systems, Chgo. Info. Systems Exchange, West Point Soc. (treas. 1975), Assn. Corp. Growth, Assn. Mgmt. Consulting Firms, Ind. Computer Cons. Assn. Club: Crystal Lake (Ill.) Country. Home: Rural Rt 2 Bow Ln Barrington Hills IL 60010 Office: Woltz & Assocs Inc 199 S Addison Rd Wood Dale IL 60191

WOLYNES, PETER GUY, chemistry researcher, educator; b. Chgo., Apr. 21, 1953; s. Peter and Evelyn Eleanor (Etter) W.; m. Jane Lee Fox, Nov. 26, 1976 (div. 1980); m. Kathleen Cull Bucher, Dec. 22, 1984. A.B. with highest distinction, Ind. U., 1971; A.M., Harvard U., 1972, Ph.D. in Chem. Physics, 1976. Research assoc. MIT, Cambridge, 1975-76; asst. prof., assoc. prof. Harvard U., Cambridge, 1976-80; vis. scientist Max Planck Inst. für Biophysikalische Chemie, Gottingen, Fed. Republic Germany, 1977; assoc. prof. chemistry U. Ill., Urbana, 1980-83, prof., 1983—, prof. physics, 1985—; vis. prof. Inst. for Molecular Sci., Okazaki, Japan, 1982; vis. scientist Inst. for Theoretical Physics, Santa Barbara, Calif., 1987. Contbr. numerous articles to profl. jours. Mem. Ill. Alliance To Prevent Nuclear War, Champaign, 1981—. Sloan fellow, 1981-83, J.S. Guggenheim fellow, 1986-87; Beckman assoc. Ctr. for Advanced Study, Urbana, 1984-85. Mem. Am. Chem. Soc. (Pure Chemistry award 1986), Am. Phys. Soc., AAAS, N.Y. Acad. Scis., Phi Beta Kappa, Sigma Xi, Phi Lambda Upsilon, Sigma Pi Sigma. Home: 311 W Oregon Urbana IL 61801 Office: Univ of Illinois Sch of Chem Scis 505 S Mathews Urbana IL 61801

WOMACK, WILLIAM LLOYD, JR., osteopath; b. Ironton, Mo., Sept. 21, 1950; s. William Lloyd Sr. and Elba (Walker) W.; m. Trudy Gale Ervie, Sept. 1, 1984. AB, William Jewell Coll., Liberty, Mo., 1972; DO, Kirksville (Mo.) Coll. Osteo. Medicine, 1976. Intern Carson City (Mich.) Hosp., 1976-77; gen. practice osteo. medicine Trenton, Mo., 1977-82; emergency medicine physician, dir. emergency services Hedrick Med. Ctr., Chillicothe, Mo., 1982—; gen. practice osteo. medicine Meadville, Mo., 1983—. Mem. Am. Osteo. Assn., Am. Coll. Gen. Practitioners, Am. Coll. Emergency Physicians. Democrat. Lodge: Lions. Avocations: golf, farming. Home: 2509 Country Club Dr Chillicothe MO 64601 Office: Hedrick Med Ctr 100 Central Chillicothe MO 64601

WOMMACK, JOSEPH BENNO, dentist; b. Kansas City, Mo., Mar. 28, 1954; s. Bert M. and M. Virginia W.; m. Virginia A. Burress; children: Emily, Andrew. BS in Biology, Kans. U., 1976; DDS, U. Mo., Kansas City, 1982. Practice gen. dentistry Medicine Lodge, Kans., 1982—; dental dir. Cedar Crest Nursing Home, Cedar Crest Tng. Ctr., Medicine Lodge, 1984—. Mem. Rep. Nat. Com. Mem. ADA, Acad. Gen. Dentistry, Am. Assn. Functional Orthodontists, So. Dist. Dental Soc., Kans. Dental Soc., Ducks Unlimited, Omicron Kappa Upsilon. Lodge: Lions. Avocations: hunting, gardening, woodworking, distance running, bicycling. Home: 112 Lisa Circle Medicine Lodge KS 67104 Office: 102 S Main Medicine Lodge KS 67104

WONG, KENNETH FONG, computer information scientist; b. Salinas, Calif., Oct. 25, 1946; s. Kim Y. and Yat H. (Gee) W. BSEE, MIT, 1968; MS in Computer Sci., Washington U., St. Louis, 1974, DSc inComputer Sci., 1985. Research assoc. Washington U., 1980—. Author: High Performance Racquetball, 1985; contbr. numerous articles to profl. jours. Served as 1st lt. U.S. Army, 1969-71. Mem. Assn. Computing Machinery, IEEE. Avocations: racquetball, tennis, squash, skiing. Home: 1601 E Swan Circle Saint Louis MO 63144 Office: Washington U Campus Box 1045 Saint Louis MO 63130

WONG, SHARON ANN, accountant; b. Cleve., Nov. 24, 1956; s. Jack Don and Fung Suey (Chow) W. BS in Acctg. summa cum lauae, Case Western Res. U., 1978, MBA in Internat. Mgmt., 1987. CPA, Ohio. Acct. Price Waterhouse, Cleve., 1978-81, sr. acct., 1981-84; acctg. research and planning analyst Standard Oil Co., Cleve., 1984-85, sr. fin. analyst, 1985—. Bus. advisor Inroads Cleve., Inc., 1982-84. Mem. Am. Inst. CPA's, Nat. Assn. Accts., Am. Woman's Soc. CPA's (Northeastern Ohio affiliate pres. 1985-86, v.p. 1984-85, sec. 1983-84), Ohio Soc. CPA's (sec. Cleve. chpt. 1987—, chpt. bd. dirs. 1986-87, state bd. dirs. 1985-86), Young Profls. Cleve. (trustee 1984-85). Avocations: travel, outdoor activities, exercise, music, theatre. Office: Standard Oil Co 200 Public Square Cleveland OH 44114

WONG, STEPHEN RYAN, restaurant operator; b. Albert Lea, Minn., Aug. 10, 1948; s. Benjamin C.S. and Mae Sherill (Mah) W. B.A., U. Minn., 1973; B.Laws, U. B.C., 1978. Bar: B.C., 1980. Clerk, assoc. Griffiths & Co., Vancouver, B.C., 1978-80; assoc., lawyer Burnet & Fenton, Vancouver, 1980-81; barrister-at-law Wong & Co., Vancouver, 1981-82; co-owner, ptnr. Wong's Cafe, Rochester, Minn., 1982—. Served to sgt. USMC, 1968-70. Recipient Meritorious Mast Base Material Batalion U.S. Marine Corps, 1970. Mem. Soc. Wine Educators, Am. Inst. Wine and Food, Quill and Scroll. Democrat. Methodist. Avocations: wine collecting; tennis; golf; jazz and swing record collecting; reading. Home: 2452 Northern Hills Ct NE Rochester MN 55904 Office: Wong's Cafe 4 Third St SW Rochester MN 55902

WONG, YANIC, accountant; b. Hongkong, Dec. 14, 1954; came to U.S, 1976; m. Maria See, Jan. 25, 1981; 1 child, Calvin. BS in Acctg., U. Ill., Chgo., 1980. CPA, Ill. Field acct. Turner Constrn., Chgo., 1980-84, acctg. supr., 1984—. Sen. On-leung Assn., Chgo., 1985. Mem. Am. Inst. CPA's, Ill. Soc. CPA's, Chinatown C. of C. (bd. dirs.). Home: 931 Dunlop Ave Forest Park IL 60130

WOOD, ALLEN WESLEY, real estate appraiser; b. Minot, N.D., Jan. 11, 1953; s. Thomas B. and Esther (Brostrom) W.; m. Wendy M. Ringdal, Aug. 25, 1973; children: Michael, Brian, Lindsey, Jason. BBA, Minot State Coll., 1975. Appraiser Appraisal Cons., Inc., Minot, 1973-84; prin. appraiser Appraisal Assocs., Inc., Minot, 1984-86; sr. appraiser Farm Credit Services, Grand Forks, N.D., 1986—. Mem. Am. Inst. of Real Estate Appraisers, Nat. Assn. Realtors, ND Chpt. Am. Soc. Farm Mgrs. and Rural Appraisers. Avocations: hunting, sports. Home: 3302 Cherry Lynn Dr Grand Forks ND 58201 Office: Farm Credit Services 2424 32nd Ave S Grand Forks ND 58201

WOOD, BRENT RICHARD, accountant; b. Harrisburg, Pa., Nov. 21, 1961; s. William Huffman and Mary Lou (Chapple) W.; m. Donna Jean Rakers, Aug. 25, 1984. BS summa cum laude, Southeast Mo. State U., 1983. CPA, Mo. Pub. acctg. staff Conner, Ash & Co., Clayton, Mo., 1983-86; fin. acct. Zeigler Coal Co., Fairview Heights, Ill., 1986—. Treas. Lebanon Community Sch. Dist., Ill., 1985—; fin. sec. St. Paul United Ch. Christ Ch., Lebanon, 1984-86. Named Outstanding Pres., Ill. Jaycees, 1984-86. Mem. Am. Inst. CPA's, Mo. Soc. CPA's, Lebanon Jaycees (pres., sec. 1984-86). Avocations: baseball, fishing. Office: Zeigler Coal Co 331 Salem Pl Fairview Heights IL 62208

WOOD, CHARLES EARL, obstetrician, gynecologist; b. Sterling, Colo., Oct. 4, 1930; s. Walter Earl and Dorothy Nancy (Long) W.; m. Patricia Taylor, Nov. 1, 1960; children—Lecia, Spencer, Christine. B.A., Phillips U., 1959; M.D., U. Colo. 1963. Diplomate Am. Bd. Obstetrics and Gynecology. Intern, Denver Gen. Hosp., 1963-64, resident in ob-gyn, 1964-67, mem. staff, 1967-73; practice medicine specializing in ob-gyn, Casper, Wyo., 1967-86; mem. staff Skaggs Community Hosp., Branson, Mo., 1986—; mem. staff

Natrona County Meml. Hosp., Casper, 1967-84, chief of obstetrics, 1975, chmn. staff, 1981-83; mem. staff Converse County Hosp., Douglas, Wyo. 1967-85, Carbon County Hosp., Rawline, Wyo., 1968-75; mem. Wyo. Family Practice Residency program, 1978-83; clin. assoc. prof. family practice (ob-gyn) Univ. Hosp. of Wyo. Coll. Human Medicine, 1982-83. Mem. Natrona County Sch. Bd., 1974-80, vice chmn., 1976-77, chmn., 1978-79; pres. Casper YMCA, 1974-76, gen. chmn. fundraising campaign, 1976-77, mem. bldg. com. 1976-78; mem. Blue Envelope, 1970-84 ; pres., charter mem. Wyo. Right to Life, 1970-75; T-Bird booster Casper Coll., 1970-82; assoc. Sch. of the Ozarks, Pt. Lookout, Mo., 1985—. Served with USN, 1949-50, 52-53. Mem. Am. Coll. Obstetricians and Gynecologists, Am. Fertility Soc. (charter), Wyo. Med. Soc., Denver Med. Soc., Natrona County Med. Soc. (pres. 1979-80), Audubon Soc., Casper Air Modelers Assn. (charter, pres. 1969-76), Wyo. Handball Assn., Wyo. Arabian Horse Assn., Am. Hereford Assn., Irish Wolfhound Club Am., Wyo. Farm Bur. Club: Elks. Home: Route 2 Box 1096 Kirbyville MO 65679 Office: HCR 1 Box 169 Hollister MO 65672

WOOD, DONALD GENE, architect; b. Castleton, Ind., Feb. 3, 1937; s. Donald and Dora Marie (Sowers) W.; m. Carolyn Sue Wood-Stewart, Sept. 20, 1957; children—Deborah Ann, Donald Gene. B.S. in Arch., U. Cin., 1961. Ptnr., Taylor & Wood Architects, Columbus, Ind., 1961-69; owner Wood & Burd Assocs., Columbus, 1969-74; pres. Wood & Burd, Inc., Columbus, 1974-85; pres. Architect Group, Inc., 1985—; sec.-treas. Creative Devel. Corp., 1973—; ptnr. Tipton Devel. Co., K&W Co., 1978—, AGI Co., 1985—; mng. ptnr. Wood Enterprises, 1981—; mem. Ind. State Bd. Registration for Architects, 1982—. Served with Ind. N.G., 1954-55, USAR, 1955-61. Mem. AIA, Columbus C. of C., Ind. Soc. Architects, Constrn. Specifications Inst. Clubs: Hoosier Assocs., Harrison Lake Country. Office: PO Box 730 Columbus IN 47202

WOOD, HARLINGTON, JR., judge; b. Springfield, Ill., Apr. 17, 1920; s. Harlington and Marie (Green) W. A.B., U. Ill., 1942, J.D., 1948. Bar: Ill. 1948. Practiced in Springfield, 1948-69; U.S. atty. So. Dist. Ill., 1958-61; partner firm Wood & Wood, 1961-69; asso. dep. atty. gen. for U.S. attys. U.S. dept. Justice, 1969-70; asso. dep. atty. gen. Justice Dept., Washington, 1970-72; asst. atty. gen. civil div. Justice Dept., 1972-73; U.S. dist. judge So. Dist. Ill., Springfield, 1973-76; judge U.S. Ct. Appeals for 7th Circuit, 1976—. Office: U S Ct of Appeals 600 E Monroe St PO Box 299 Springfield IL 62705-0299

WOOD, JACALYN KAY, educational consultant; b. Columbus, Ohio, May 25, 1949; d. Carleston John and Grace Anna (Schumacher) W. B.A., Georgetown Coll., 1971; M.S., Ohio State U., 1976; Ph.D., Miami U., 1981. Elem. tchr. Bethel-Tate Schs., Ohio, 1971-73, Columbus (Ohio) Christian Sch., 1973-74, Franklin (Ohio) Schs., 1974-79; teaching fellow Miami U., Oxford, Ohio, 1979-81; cons. intermediate grades Erie County Schs., Sandusky, Ohio, 1981— presenter tchr. inservice tng. Mem. council Sta. WVIZ-TV, 1981—; mem. exec. com. Perkins Community Schs., 1981-85; mem. community adv. bd. Sandusky Vols. Am., Sandusky Soc. Bank, vol. Firelands Community Hosp. Mem. Am. Businesswomen's Assn. (local pres. 1985), Assn. Supervision and Curriculum Devel., Internat. Reading Assn., Ohio Sch. Suprs. Assn. (regional pres. 1986, state pres. 1986-87), Phi Delta Kappa (local sec. 1985, 86). Baptist. Home: 4512 7 Venice Heights Blvd Sandusky OH 44870 Office: 2902 Columbus Ave Sandusky OH 44870

WOOD, JAMES FRANCIS, marketing professional, engineer; b. Salem, Mass., Mar. 13, 1942; s. Murray Henderson and Helen Louise (Coleman) W.; m. Nancy Eileen Morgan, Feb. 25, 1968; children: James, Mary Elizabeth, Kathleen Ann. BS in Chem. Engring., Clarkson U., 1964; MBA in Internat. Fin., Kent (Ohio) State U., 1975. Mgr. power systems Babcock & Wilcox, Barberton, Ohio, 1975—; engring. cons. Ente Nazionale Per L'Energia Electrica, La Spezia, Italy, 1969-71. Inventor power boiler seal, 1971. Mem. ASME. Avocation: sailing. Office: Babcock & Wilcox Co PO Box 351 Barberton OH 44203

WOOD, JAMES ROBERT, printing company executive; b. Bridgeport, Ill., Apr. 17, 1922; s. George Earl and Fannie Ruth Wood; m. Frances Vivian Fleshman, Sept. 2, 1943; 1 child, David Allan. M.E., Purdue U., 1945. Litho supr. Am. Book-Stratford Press, Saddlebrook, N.J., 1975-76; plant supr. Intercollegiate Press, Kansas City, Kans., 1976-78; plant tech. rep. Hearst Publs., Salem, Ill., 1978-80; sr. project engr. World Color Press, Effingham, Ill., 1980-85; dir. research and engring. St. Dennis Mfg. Co., 1985—. Patentee flexible sheet stacking machine. Served to capt. USAF, 1951-53. Mem. Graphic Arts Tech. Found. Republican. Lodge: Rotary (Salem). Avocation: music. Home: 240 Oak Tree Dr Salem IL 62881 Office: St Dennis Mfg Co 1204 W Wabash St Effingham IL 62401

WOOD, JOHN BENSON, mathematics and statistics educator, researcher; b. Ames, Iowa, Oct. 11, 1934; s. Lyman Wench and Alice Mae (Benson) W.; children—Judith L., Elizabeth A., James S. B.S., U. Wis., 1956; M.A., U. Minn., 1962, Ph.D., 1968. Asst. prof. math. Hampton Inst., Va., 1967-70; asst. prof. elem. edn. U. N.D., Grand Forks, 1970-74; elem. tchr., math. specialist New City Sch., St. Louis, 1974-75; research psychologist II, St. Louis State Hosp., 1975-81; adj. asst. prof. Mo. Inst. Psychiatry, St. Louis, 1981-82; asst. prof. U. Wis.-Marathon County Ctr., Wausau, 1982—. Author: (with others) Computers in Mental Health, 1981. Contbr. articles to profl. jours. Mem. Am. Statis. Assn., Nat. Council Tchrs. Math., AAAS. Democrat. Avocations: Design Geometric furniture. Office: U Wis Ctr Marathon County 518 S 7th Ave Wausau WI 54401

WOOD, JOSEPH ROBERTS, music educator, composer; b. Pitts., May 12, 1915; s. Joseph Roberts and Eliza (Bell) W.; Carol Streater, Sept. 4, 1940 (div.); 1 dau., Lynne Roberts Wood Dimopoulos; m. 2d, Wendy Elizabeth Bradley, Nov. 10, 1961 (div.); 1 dau., Lorna Elizabeth. Student Bucknell U., 1932-34, Inst. Musical Art, 1934-36; piano diploma Juilliard Grad. Sch., 1940, B.S., diploma composition, 1949; M.A., Columbia U., 1949, 1950. Composer, Chekhov Theater, 1939-41; free-lance composer/arranger, N.Y., 1941-50; tchr. Oberlin Conservatory, Ohio, 1950-85; resident composer Villa Montalvo, Calif., 1957. musician. Served with U.S. Army, 1943-46. Juilliard fellow, 1936-40; MacDowell Colony fellow, 1953—; Huntington Hartford fellow, 1960; Ditson award Columbia U., 1946; Mem. Am. Composers Alliance, Ohio Tchrs. Composition and Theory (past pres.). Club: Oberlin City. Composer 4 symphonies; 4 string quartets, orchestral, choral, chamberworks; book reviewer.

WOOD, KATHLEEN OLIVER, writer and editor; b. Mt. Kisco, N.Y., Sept. 17, 1921; d. Eli Leslie and Melba Antoinette (Gislason) Oliver; student Swarthmore Coll., 1938-39, Antioch Coll., 1940-41, U. N.Mex., 1949, Cleve. Coll., 1960-61; m. John Thornton Wood, June, 1941 (div. 1947); children—Mark Thornton, Jonna Grim; m. 2d, Clifford Emanuel Huff, June, 1948 (div. 1955); 1 child, Karen Weston. Tech. sec. Gray Iron Founders Soc., Cleve., 1955-57; tchr. Whiting Bus. Coll., Cleve., 1957-62; editorial asst. Chem. Rubber Co., Cleve., 1966; editor, writer Jefferson Ency., World Pub. Co., Cleve., 1967-68; disc jockey, announcer Sta. WCLV-FM, Cleve., 1968-69; communications coordinator, writer, editor Highlights newsletter University Circle, Inc., Cleve., 1971-81; talk-show hostess, announcer Sta. WERE-AM, Cleve., 1972-73; free-lance writer, editor, cons., 1981—; tchr. Project LEARN; tutor VIP program. Hostess weekly radio show, CRRS, Cleve. Soc. for Blind; taper books for Library of Congress Service for Visually Handicapped; treas. Cleve. Beautiful Com., 1980, sec., 1982; v.p. Cleve. Cultural Garden Fedn.; trustee E. Cleve. Community Theatre. Mem. Pub. Relations Soc. Am., Internat. Assn. Bus. Communicators, Women's Advt. Club Cleve. (past pres., editor Weathervane 1982-83), Women in Communication, World Assn. Women Journalists and Writers (congress coordinator), MENSA, Early Settlers. Quaker. Clubs: Zonta Internat. (past pres. Cleve., dir. Area 3 Dist. V, 1984-86), Women's City, Esperanto League of North Am., Universal Esperanto Assn. Author: Greenwood, 1967; editor, pub. Frog in the Milk Pan (Marie Wallace), 1963; editor Graffiti Mag., 1967, Office Gal Mag., 1962-63, Smorgasbrain Mag., 1968. Home: 3118 E Overlook Rd Cleveland Heights OH 44118 Office: PO Box 5612 Cleveland OH 44101

WOOD, LEONARD CLAIR, history educator, writer; b. Utica, Pa., Jan. 1, 1923; s. John Barnard and Ethel Leota (Boughner) W.; m. Tanya Bogoslovsky, July 19, 1952; children—Stephen (dec.), Anthony, John, Sarah. B.S., Pa. State Coll., 1943; M.A. in History, U. Pa., 1948, Ph.D., 1960; postgrad. U. London. Writer, editor McGraw-Hill, 1951-55; chief social studies editor Henry Holt and Co., N.Y.C., 1955-58; sr. editor Macmillan and Co., N.Y.C., 1958-60; prof. history, dir. coop. edn. Eastern Ill. U., Charleston, 1960-82, prof. history, 1982—; cons. to ednl. pubs. Served with USN, 1943-46. Harrison fellow, 1948-50; Fulbright scholar, 1951-52. Mem. Am. Hist. Assn., Nat. Coop. Edn. Assn. Democrat. Author: The Soviet Army, 1953; The Satellite Armies, 1953; Sir Edmond Monson, 1960; American Civics, 1967, 74; America: Its People and Values, 1971, 75, 79, 83; Land of Promise, 1983. Home: RR 2 PO Box 153 Charleston IL 61920 Office: History Dept Eastern Ill Univ Charleston IL 61920

WOOD, RICHARD DONALD, pharmaceutical company executive; b. Brazil, Ind., Oct. 22, 1926; s. Howard T. and Dorothy F. (Norfolk) W.; B.S., Purdue U., 1948, LL.D., 1973; M.B.A., U. Pa., 1950; D.Sc., Butler U., 1974; LL.D., DePauw U., 1972, Phila. Coll. Pharmacy and Sci., 1975, Ind. State U., 1978; m. Billie Lou Carpenter, Dec. 29, 1951; children—Catherine Ann Wood Lawson, Marjorie Elizabeth. Gen. mgr. ops. in Argentina, Eli Lilly & Co., 1961, dir. ops., Mex. and Central Am., 1962-70, pres. Eli Lilly Internat. Corp., 1970-72, now dir.; pres. Eli Lilly & Co., Indpls., 1972-73, pres., chmn. bd., chief exec. officer, dir., 1973—, also dir.; dir. Chem. N.Y. Corp., Amoco Corp., Dow Jones & Co. Bd. dirs. Lilly Endowment, Inc.; trustee Indpls. Mus. of Art, DePauw U., Am. Enterprise Inst. for Public Policy Research, Com. Econ. Devel.; bd. govs. The Ronald Reagan Presdl. Found. Mem. Council on Fgn. Relations, Bus. Roundtable, The Conf. Bd. Presbyterian. Clubs: Links (N.Y.C.); Meridian Hills Country, Woodstock (Indpls.). Office: Eli Lilly & Co Lilly Corporate Ctr Indianapolis IN 46285

WOOD, SALLY ANN, high school teacher, counselor; b. Aurora, Mo., Mar. 6, 1949; d. Hilda Julia Bennage; m. Floyd Ray Wood, Aug. 6, 1971. BE magna cum laude, Southwest Mo. State U., 1971, MS, 1980. Cert. elem. and secondary tchr., Mo. Language tchr. Aurora High Sch., 1971—, counselor, 1980—; served numerous vis. coms. North Cen. Assn. Edn., representing Southwest Mo. Schs., 1979—. Contbr. articles to profl. jours. Mem. Mo. Guidance Assn. (Research award 1980), Mo. State Tchrs. Assn., Aurora Edn. Assn., Fgn. Language Assn Mo., Phi Delta Kappa. Baptist. Avocations: reading, writing. Home: 100 S Westview Dr Marionville MO 65705-0194 Office: Aurora High Sch West End of Locust Ave Aurora MO 65605

WOOD, SAMUEL EUGENE, college administrator, psychology educator; b. Brotherton, Tenn., Aug. 16, 1934; s. Samuel Ernest and Daisy J. (Jernigan) W.; m. Helen J. Walker, June 2, 1956; children: Liane Wood Kelly, Susan Wood Benson, Alan Richard; m. Ellen Rosenthal Green, Sept. 8, 1977; stepchildren: Bart M. Green, Julie Alice Green. BS in English and Music, Tenn. Tech. U., 1961; M in Edn. Adminstrn., U. Fla., 1967, D in Edn., 1969. Asst. prof. edn. W. Va. U., 1968-70; asst. prof. edn. U. Mo., St. Louis, 1970-75, mem. doctoral faculty, 1973-75; dir. research Ednl. Devel. Ctr., Belleville, Ill., 1976-81; prof. psychology Meramec Coll., St. Louis, 1981—; pres. Higher Edn. Ctr., St. Louis, 1985—; exec. dir. Edn. Oppurtunity Ctrs., St. Louis, 1985—; bd. commrs. Pub. TV Com., St. Louis, 1985—; planning com. St. Louis Schs., 1985—. Served with USN, 1955-59. US Office Edn. grantee 1976-81, 85. Mem. Internat. Edn. Consortium (bd. dirs. 1985—), Phi Kappa Phi. Democrat. Baptist. Avocations: writing, reading, music composition and performance. Home: 5 Sona Ln Saint Louis MO 63141 Office: Higher Edn Ctr 928A N McKnight Rd Saint Louis MO 63132

WOODALL, W. DALLAS, lawyer; b. Youngstown, Ohio, June 8, 1937; s. William L. and Roberta (Gibson) W.; m. Velma H. Szakacs, June 7, 1958; children—John M., Laura Love, Christine L. Woodall Scarmuzzi. B.S. in Edn., Youngstown State U., 1964; J.D., Ohio State U., 1967. Bar: Ohio 1967. Sole practice law, Warren, Ohio, 1967-68; assoc. Letson, Letson, Griffith and Kightlinger, Warren, 1968-71; ptnr. Letson, Griffith, Woodall and Lavelle, Warren, 1971—. Vice pres. Western Reserve council Boy Scouts Am., 1978, exec. bd.; chmn. bd. trustees First Presbyterian Ch., Warren 1980, 84, elder, 1959—, trustee, 1975-77, 78-80; trustee Warren Library Assn., 1980-86, pres., 1987—; mem. Trumbull County Met. Parks Bd., 1987—. Mem. Ohio State Bar Assn. (bd. govs. probate and trust law sect. 1987—), Trumbull County Bar Assn. (pres. 1985-86). Republican. Club: Buckeye (Warren). Lodge: Rotary (bd. dirs. 1982-84). Home: 3204 Crescent Dr NE Warren OH 44483 Office: Letson Griffith Woodall and Lavelle 155 S Park Ave Warren OH 44482

WOODARD, GERALD WALTER, insurance company executive; b. Dayton, Ohio, May 18, 1932; s. Walter M. and Harriet Lynn (Curran) W.; m. Edna Ann Wuertz, Aug. 8, 1954; children: Brian, James, Linda, Phyllis. B.S. in Bus. Adminstrn, Ohio State U., 1959; postgrad., LaSalle U., Phila. With Coopers & Lybrand (C.P.A.s), Columbus, Ohio, 1959-61; with Nationwide Ins. Co.'s, Columbus, 1961—; dir. banking and cash adminstrn. Nationwide Ins. Co.'s, 1967-75, asst. treas., 2d v.p., 1975-78, v.p., treas., 1978—; v.p., treas. Nationwide Ins. Co.'s subs. and affiliations including Employers of Wausau, 1975—; treas. Nationwide Polit. Participation Com., 1976—. Author articles in field. Pres. bd. trustees Cen. Ohio Symphony Orch. Served with AUS, 1954-56. Mem. Nat. Mut. Ins. Assn. (mem. tax task force), Ind. Insurers, Am. Council Life Insurers, Life Ins. Treasurers Roundtable, Life Office Mgmt. Assn. (chmn. debt utilization com. 1980—), Nat. Assn. Corp. Treas., Newcomen Soc., Treasurers Club Franklin County, Internat. Fin. Mgmt. Club. Republican. Lutheran. Club: Shriners. Address: 520 Braumiller Rd Delaware OH 43015

WOODARD, KATHRYN DELORIS, social services administrator; b. Kearney, Nebr., Jan. 10, 1951; d. Bernard Brunson and Deloris Mae (Hiner); m. Ronnie Duwayne Adams, Dec. 23, 1966 (div. June 1968); 1 child, Kevin Glenn; m. Otis David Woodard, Feb. 19, 1983; 1 child, Otishe Andrew; stepchildren: Otishe Analdo, Otis LeAntoni, Otishe Andre. Student, Kearney State Coll.; AA in Bus. Adminstrn., Cen. Community Coll. Community devel. dir. City of Harvard, Nebr., 1977-79; dir. food stamp ctr. H.D.C., Kansas City, 1981-83; grant cons. Luth. Family and Children's Services, St. Louis, 1984-85; dir. Contact Helpline, St. Louis, 1984—; v.p. Luth. North St. Louis Outreach, 1987—; founding mem. Nebr. State Task Force on Domestic Violence Intervention, 1976-78; founder, facilitator Clay County (Nebr.) Domestic Violence Intervention Project, 1978-79; adj. coordinator Clay County Domestice Violence Project, 1978-79. Active Freedom Inc. Black Polit. Orgn., Kansas City, 1980-83; bd. dirs. So. Christian Leadership Conf., Kansas City, 1980-83. Mem. NOW (pres. Kearny chpt. 1972-75, sec. Hastings, Nebr. chpt. 1977-79), Phi Beta Lambda. Democrat. Lutheran. Avocations: reading, hist. fiction, swimming, biking. Home: 2023 Bissell Saint Louis MO 63107 Office: Luth North St Louis Outreach 2023 Bissell Saint Louis MO 63107

WOODBRIDGE, ANNIE SMITH, emerita librarian, foreign language educator; b. Wingo, Ky., July 7, 1915; d. Ernest Herbert and Flora Susan (Parrish) Smith; B.A., Murray State Coll., 1935; M.A., Peabody Coll., 1936; postgrad. U. Wis., Tex. State Coll. for Women, U. Ky., Sorbonne, Universidad Interamericana; m. Hensley C. Woodbridge, Aug. 28, 1953; 1 dau., Ruby Susan Woodbridge Jung. Tchr. Cadiz High Sch., 1936-37, David Lipscomb Coll., 1937-43, Bethel Coll., 1943-46, Murray State Coll., 1946-54, 59-65; instr. So. Ill. U., Carbondale, 1966-74, researcher Morris Library, 1974-85. Mem. NOW, Midwest Latin Am. Studies Assn., Ellen Glasgow Soc., Soc. Study of Midwestern Lit. Democrat. Mem. Ch. of Christ. Editor: (with others) Collected Short Stories of Mary Johnston; contbr. articles jours. and newsletters. Home: 1804 W Freeman St Carbondale IL 62901

WOODBRIDGE, FREDERICK, lawyer, educator; b. Sidnaw, Mich., Apr. 10, 1904; s. James and Florence Rosina W.; m. Marian Wilson, Sept. 7, 1934; children—Frederick, Jr., Ann. A.B., Ohio No. U., 1935; LL.B., U. Cin., 1933; LL.M., Harvard U., 1938; S.J.D., U. Mich., 1940. Bar: Ohio 1933, U.S. Dist. Ct. (so. and no. dists.) Ohio 1936, 54, U.S. Ct. Appeals (6th cir.) 1936, U.S. Supreme Ct. 1944. Instr. law Ohio No. U., Ada, 1933-35, U. Cin., 1935-37, asst. prof. law, 1940-45, faculty editor Law Rev., 1940-43; research fellow Harvard Law Sch., Cambridge, Mass., 1937-38; teaching fellow Law Sch. U. Mich., Ann Arbor, 1938-39, vis. asst. prof. law, 1939-40; legal assoc. Jones, Day, Cockley & Reavis (now Jones, Day, Reavis & Pogue), Cleve., 1943-47, ptnr., 1948-76, ret. 1976; prof. law Case Western Res. U., Cleve., 1944-46; research cons. Household Fin. Corp., Chgo., 1940-41. Author study: Wage Earners' Receiverships, 1939; contbr. articles to legal publs. and travel mag. Trustee Cin. Legal Aid Soc., 1941-43. Mem. ABA (life), Ohio State Bar Assn. (life, various coms.), Order of Coif. Republican. Episcopalian. Lodge: Masons. Avocations: legal research, writing, world travel and study.

WOODBURN, CLYDE DELORM, III, hospital director; b. Waco, Tex., Dec. 22, 1945; s. Clyde Delorm Jr. and Leona Meyer (Schankai) W.; m. Rhoda Lain Marshall; children: Jocelyn, Ann, Katie Mariea. BBA, U. Syracuse, 1970, M in Psychology, 1973. Asst. mgr. cen. supply St. Luke's Hosp., Kansas City, Mo., 1980-83; mgr. cen. supply Menorah Med. Ctr., Kansas City, 1983-84, dir. materials mgmt., 1984-86. Served to capt. U.S. Army, 1963-68, Vietnam. Mem. Am. Soc. Hosp. Materials Mgrs. (pres 1985), Am. Hosp. Assn., Mo. Hosp. Assn. for Cen. Supply (bd. dirs. 1983-84), Kansas City Cen. Supply Orgn. (pres. 1982-84).

WOODBURN, WILLIAM DELL, transportation executive; b. Pratt, Kans., Nov. 27, 1940; s. Woodrow Wilson and Velva May (Brown) W.; m. Alice Jane Stone, Aug. 25, 1962; children: Mary Jane, William Dell Jr. BS, U. Kans., 1963. Advt. rep. Star-Times, Kansas City, Mo., 1963-65; asst. advt. mgr. Santa Fe Railway, Topeka, 1965-73; prodn. mgr. Santa Fe Railway, Chgo., 1973-76; regional advt. mgr. Santa Fe Railway, Los Angeles, 1976-78; gen. mgr. advt. Santa Fe Railway, Chgo., 1978-83; dir. creative service Santa Fe Southern Pacific Corp., Chgo., 1983—. bd. dirs. Cystic Fibrosis Found., Chgo., 1985. Mem. Assn. Railroad Advt. and Mktg. (v.p. 1986—), Meeting Planners Internat. Republican. Methodist. Club: Old Wayne (West Chgo.). Avocations: scuba diving, underwater photography. Office: Santa Fe So Pacific Corp 224 S Michigan Ave Chicago IL 60604

WOODBURY, MARIE SPENCER, lawyer; b. Washington, Aug. 3, 1951; d. Richard Aloysius Jr. and Helen Theresa (O'Conor) Spencer; m. David P. Woodbury, Aug. 10, 1974 (div. Apr. 1985); children: Brendan Spencer, Christopher Padfield. BS in Fgn. Studies, Georgetown U., 1973; JD, Kans. U., 1979. Bar: Kans. 1979, U.S. Dist. Ct. Kans. 1979, Mo. 1981. Assoc. Payne & Jones, Olathe, Kans., 1979-81; assoc. Shook, Hardy & Bacon, Kansas City, Mo., 1981-85, ptnr., 1986—. Mem. ABA, Mo. Bar Assn., Kans. Bar Assn., Def. Research Inst., Order of Coif. Office: Shook Hardy & Bacon 1101 Walnut Kansas City MO 64106

WOODFORD, DUANE HUGH, electrical equipment manufacturing company executive, electrical engineer; b. Dunseith, N.D., Jan. 1, 1939; s. Harold George and Edna Evelyn (Lagerquist) W.; m. Grace Carol Vandal, July 18, 1962; children—Robert Kent, Kim Ann. B.S. in Elec. Engring., U. N.D., 1961; student Western Electric grad. engring. tng. program, 1962; Mini M.B.A., Coll. St. Thomas, 1977, postgrad., 1978. Sr. sales engr. Electric Machinery Steam Turbine Motor and Generator div. Dresser-Rand Co., Hartford, Conn., 1969-76, product mktg. mgr., Mpls., 1976-79, mgr. parts and service, 1979-80, commercial ops. mgr., 1980-83, gen. mgr., 1983—; power engr. Western Electric, Chgo., 1961-63; application engr. Electric Machinery, Steam Turbine, Motor and Generator div. Dresser-Rand Co., Mpls., 1963-65, sales engr., N.Y.C., Pitts., 1965-68. Scoutmaster Boy Scouts U.S., Aurora, Ill., 1962-63; coach, Babe Ruth Baseball, Plymouth, Minn., 1978-80; treas. PTA, Wayzata (Minn.) Sch. Dist. 284, 1978-79; . Served with USMC, 1960-66. Mem. ASME (sec. gas turbine div. electric utility com. 1972-74), TAPPI. Republican. Methodist. Home: 1630 Shadyview Ln Plymouth MN 55447 Office: Electric Machinery Steam Turbine Dresser-Rand Co 800 Central Ave Minneapolis MN 55413

WOODHALL, JOHN ALEXANDER, JR., construction company executive; b. Peoria, Ill., Oct. 10, 1929; s. John Alexander and Marion Ellen (Solstad) W.; B.B.A., U. Minn., 1952; m. Donna Irene Simmons, Aug. 21, 1948; children—John Alexander, Susan, Cheryl, Douglas, Robert. Project supt. Central States Constrn. Co., Willmar, Minn., 1953-57, v.p., project mgr., 1957-60; v.p., area mgr. Allied Enterprises, Willmar, 1960-69; exec. v.p. Central Allied Enterprises, Inc., Canton, Ohio, 1969-74, chmn., chief exec. officer, 1974—. Vice chmn. Minn. Gov.'s Occupational Safety Health Adv. Council; bd. dirs., chmn. Minn. Safety Council, chmn., 1983; pres. W. Central Safety Council, 1979; bd. dirs. Nat. Safety Council, 1984—; dist. commr. Viking council Boy Scouts Am., 1969-71. Mem. Am. Mgmt. Assn., Am. Arbitration Assn., Associated Gen. Contractors Am. (dir.), Associated Gen. Contractors Minn. (pres. 1977), Pres.'s Assn. Lutheran. Clubs: Kiwanis (Willmar); Masons, Shriners, Mpls. Athletic. Home: 3201 Croydon Dr NW Canton OH 44718 also: 4 Belleview Blvd Apt 404 Belleair FL 34616 Office: Cen Allied Enterprises PO Box 1317 Willmar MN 56201 also: PO Box 80449 Canton OH 44708

WOODMAN, GREY MUSGRAVE, psychiatrist; b. Birmingham, Eng., Jan. 26, 1922; came to U.S., 1959, naturalized, 1963; s. Edward Musgrave and Ida (Cullen) W.; children—Sheila, Shonagh. B.A., U. Oxford (Eng.), 1943, M.A., B.M., B.Ch., 1945. Ship's surgeon, 1946-48; intern Whipps Cross Hosp., London, 1948-49, med. registrar, 1951-54, also Newcastle-on-Tyne, Eng., 1951-54; resident in Psychiatry U. Okla., 1959-62; staff psychiatrist Western Mo. Mental Health Ctr., Kansas City, 1962-76; med. dir. Mental Health Ctr. Clinton County, Clinton, Iowa, 1976-87; practice medicine specializing in psychiatry, Clinton, 1976—; mem. staff Lincolnshire Clinic, Jane Lamb Health Ctr., Mercy Hosp.; cons. Mufon. Served with Brit. Merc. Marines, 1946-48. Mem. AMA, Am. Psychiat. Assn., Brit. Med. Assn., Royal Soc. Medicine (London), World Fedn. Mental Health, Internat. Assn. Social Psychiatry. Republican. Episcopalian. Home: 1334 7th St NW Clinton IA 52732 Office: Lincolnshire Clinic 318 Howes Bldg Clinton IA 52732

WOODRING, DEWAYNE STANLEY, association executive; b. Gary, Ind., Nov. 10, 1931; s. J. Stanley and Vera Luella (Brown) W.; m. Donna Jean Wishart, June 15, 1957; children: Judith Lynn (Mrs. Richard Bigelow), Beth Ellen. B.S. in Speech with distinction, Northwestern U., 1954, postgrad. studies in radio and TV broadcasting, 1954-57; M.Div., Garrett Theol. Sem., 1957; L.H.D., Mt. Union Coll., Alliance, Ohio, 1967; D.D., Salem (W.Va.) Coll., 1970. Asso. youth dir. Gary YMCA, 1950-55; ordained to ministry United Methodist Ch., 1955; minister of edn. Griffith (Ind.) Meth. Ch., 1955-57; minister adminstrn. and program 1st Meth. Ch., Eugene, Oreg., 1957-59; dir. pub. relations Dakotas area Meth. Ch., 1959-60, dir. pub. relations Ohio area, 1960-64; adminstrv. exec. to bishop Ohio East area United Meth. Ch., Canton, 1964-77; asst. gen. sec. Gen. Council on Fin. and Adminstrn., United Meth. Ch., Evanston, Ill., 1977-79; assoc. gen. sec. Gen. Council on Fin. and Adminstrn., 1979-84; exec. dir. Religious Conf. Mgmt. Assn., 1982—; mem. staff, dept. radio services 2d assembly World Council Chs., Evanston, 1954; mem. commn. on entertainment and program North Central Jurisdictional Conf., 1968-76, chmn., 1972-76; mem. commn. on gen. conf. United Meth. Ch., 1972—, bus. mgr., exec. dir., 1976—, mem. div. interpretation, 1969-72; chmn. communications commn. Ohio Council Chs., 1961-65; mem. exec. com. Nat. Assn. United Meth. Founds., 1968-72; del. World Meth. Conf., London, Eng., 1966, Dublin, Ireland, 1976, Honolulu, 1981, Nairobi, 1986, World Meth. Council, 1986—; bd. dirs. Ohio East Area United Meth. Found., 1967-78, v.p., 1967-76; chmn. bd. mgrs. United Meth. Bldg., Evanston, 1977-84; lectr., cons. on fgn. travel. Creator: nationally distbd. radio series The Word and Music; writer, dir.: television series Parables in Miniature, 1957-59. Adviser East Ohio Conf. Communications Commn., 1968-76; pres. Guild Assos., 1971—; Trustee, 1st v.p. Copeland Oaks Retirement Center, Sebring, Ohio, 1969-76. Recipient Cert. Meeting Profl. award, 1985. Mem. Am. Soc. Assn. Execs., Meeting Planners Internat., Conv. Liaison Council (bd. dirs.), Def. Orientation Conf. Assn. (dir.), Cert. Meeting Profls. (bd. dirs.), Nat. Assn. Exposition Mgrs. Home: 7224 Chablis Ct Indianapolis IN 46278 Office: One Hoosier Dome Suite 120 Indianapolis IN 46225

WOODROW, JANE ZARTMAN, clinical psychologist; b. Hartville, Ohio, June 8, 1938; d. Edwin Jay and Mary Evelyn (Kile) Zartman; m. John A. Woodrow, Feb. 3, 1962. AB, Heidelberg Coll., Tiffin, Ohio, 1960; MS, Ohio U., 1966, PhD, 1973. Lic. psychologist, Ohio, W.Va. Staff psychologist Athens (Ohio) Mental Health Ctr., 1966-69, dir. psychology dept., 1970-71; dir. psychology Gallia-Meigs-Jackson Community Mental Health Ctr., Gallipolis, Ohio, 1972-76, cons., 1976-77; cons. Western Dist. Guidance Ctr., Parkersburg, W.Va., 1972-78; asst. prof. psychology Ohio U., Athens, 1976-77, 86; pvt. practice psychology Athens and Parkersburg, 1977-84, Athens, 1984—; chmn. psychology staff O'Bleness Meml. Hosp., Athens, 1981-82.

Fellow Am. Orthopsychiat. Assn.; mem. Am. Psychol. Assn., Midwest Psychol. Assn., Ohio Psychol. Assn. (bd. dirs. 1976-77), Southeastern Ohio Psychol. Assn. (pres. 1976-77), Ohio Women In Psychology (communications officer 1986—), LWV (pres. Athens chpt. 1977-79, chmn. fin. com. 1982; bd. dirs. Ohio chpt. 1981-83, v.p. 1983—; nat. long range planning com. 1982-84), Athens Area C. of C. (exec. com. 1984—, chmn. pub. affairs com. 1984—). Presbyterian. Office: 122 E State PO Box 277 Athens OH 45701

WOODRUFF, DAVID OLIVER, insurance executive; b. San Diego, June 6, 1958; s. James Fredrick and Ann (Thomas) W.; m. Nancy Wills Dooley, Oct. 2, 1982. BBA in Risk Mgmt. and Ins., U. Ga., 1981. Account supr. Great West Life Ins. Co., Atlanta, 1981-84; sr. account exec. Great Western Life Ins. Co., Chgo., 1985—. Mem. Life Underwriters Assn. Republican. Roman Catholic. Avocations: skiing, woodworking, scuba diving. Home: 472 Le Parc Circle Buffalo Grove IL 60090

WOODRUFF, JANE, sales executive; b. Derby, Eng., July 20, 1945; d. George John Schwaegerman and Joyce (Robinson) Turnock; m. Charles Walter Woodruff, Aug. 1, 1964 (div. 1976); 1 child, Jon Bradley. BA, Purdue U., 1967, MS, 1968, MA, 1970. Tchr. Kansas City (Mo.) Schs., 1970-73; asst. dir. communicatons Skyline Corp., Elkart, Ind., 1974-77; market analyst Motor Wheel Corp. subs. Goodyear Tire and Rubber Co., Lansing, Mich., 1977-80, mgr. planning and research, 1980-82, mgr. car and light truck mktg., 1982-84; account exec. Motor Wheel Corp. subs. Goodyear Tire and Rubber Co., Southfield, Mich., 1984—. Chmn. Motor Wheel Savs. Bond Drive, Lansing, 1980; fundraiser Capital Area United Way, Lansing, 1981; cons. bus. projects Jr. Achievement, Lansing, 1981-82. NDEA scholar U.S. Dept. Edn., 1967-68; teaching fellow Purdue U., 1968-70; recipient Cert. Achievement YWCA, Lansing, 1980. Mem. Indsl. Mktg. Group Am. Mktg. Assn., Automotive Market Research Council, Soc. Automotive Engrs. Office: Motor Wheel Corp 27655 Middlebelt Rd Farmington Hills MI 48018

WOODS, CHARLES HARRISON, chemist; b. Kirwan Heights, Pa., Dec. 10, 1934; s. Leroy Homer and Julia (Voinovich) W.; student Carnegie Inst. Tech., 1952, Muskingum Coll., 1957, Muskingum Area Tech. Coll., 1979-80; m. Ruth Ann Gildea, Oct. 20, 1956; children—Tamara Sue Woods Border, Charles K., Crystal Williamson, David. Chief chemist John M. Sherry Labs., Muncie, Ind., 1961-64; chief spectroscopist Vanadium Corp. Am., Cambridge, Ohio, 1965-68; analytical chemist, lab. supr. Foote Mineral Co., Exton, Pa., 1968-70; corp. dir. analytical chemistry Ohio Ferro-Alloys Corp., Philo, Ohio, 1970-85, mgr. quality control, 1982-85; supr. chem. lab. Dept. Indsl. Relations, State of Ohio, Cambridge, 1985—. Mem. citizens adv. com. Ohio EPA Muskingum River Basin; mem. data processing tech. adv. com. Muskingum Area Tech. Coll., 1979-84; loaned exec. United Way, 1978, 79; judge sci. fairs, high sch. Mem. Am. Chem. Soc., Am. Soc. Metals, Nat. Mgmt. Assn. (pres. Zanesville area 1982-83). Democrat. Lutheran. Home: 3655 Sunset Circle Zanesville OH 43701 Office: PO Box 1469 Cambridge OH 43725

WOODS, (WILLIAM) DENNIS, corporate safety professional; b. Wichita, Kans., Feb. 20, 1955; s. William Floyd and Judith Ann (McLaughlin) W.; m. Cindy Marie Snow, Aug. 7, 1976; 1 child, William Bryce. BS, Kans. State U., 1977. Sanitation supr. Oscar Mayer Foods Corp., Nashville, 1977-79; safety mgr. Oscar Mayer Foods Corp., Madison, Wis., 1980-81; corp. ops. tng. mgr. Oscar Mayer Foods Corp., Madison, 1981-84; night supt. Oscar Mayer Foods Corp., Nashville, 1984-85, 85-86, slice pak group supr., 1985; corp. safety mgr. Oscar Mayer Foods Corp., Madison, 1986—. Named one of Outstanding Young Men of Am., 1980. Mem. Nat. Safety Council (bd. dirs. meat and leather div. 1980), Wis. Safety Council, Madison Area Safety Council (bd. dirs., com. chmn. 1980). Republican. Methodist. Avocations: hunting, fishing, running, softball, volleyball. Home: 4514 Meadow Wood Circle DeForest WI 53532 Office: Oscar Mayer Foods Corp 910 Mayer Ave Madison WI 53707

WOODS, GEORGE E., federal judge; m. Janice Smith. Student, Ohio No. U., 1941-43, 46, Tex. A&M Coll., 1943, Ill. Inst. Tech., 1943; JD, Detroit Coll. Law, 1949. Sole practice, Pontiac, Mich., 1949-51, 53; atty. Oakland County, Mich., 1951-52; chief asst. U.S. atty., Ea. Dist. Mich., 1953-60, U.S. atty., 1960-61; assoc., Honigman, Miller, Schwartz and Cohn, Detroit, 1961-62; sole practice, Detroit, 1962-81; judge, U.S. Dist. Ct. (ea. dist.) Mich., Detroit, 1981-83, 83—. Served with AUS, 1943-46. Mem. ABA, Detroit Bar Assn., Oakland County Bar Assn. Office: US Courthouse 277 Federal Bldg Detroit MI 48226 *

WOODS, HARLIE DALTON, JR., architect; b. Lubbock, Tex., Dec. 11, 1924; s. Harlie Dalton and Irene (Maxwell) W.; m. Margaret Ellen Johnson, Sept. 12, 1947; children: Richard Crisman, Patti Faye Woods Revel. BArch, Tex. Tech U., 1950. Registered architect Kans., Tex., Colo., Wyo., Nebr., Mo. Architect Schefer & Merrill, Clovis, N.Mex., 1950-53; architect Woods & Starr, Hays, Kans., 1953—. Served with USAAF, 1943-45. Mem. AIA (bd. dirs. Kans. chpt. 1964-67). Republican. Presbyterian. Lodge: Rotary (pres. Hays 1964). Home: 311-W23 Hays KS 67601 Office: PO Box #780 718 Main Suite 201 Hays KS 67601

WOODS, HARRIETT RUTH, state official; b. Cleve., June 2, 1927; d. Armin and Ruth (Wise) Friedman; student U. Chgo., 1945; B.A., U. Mich., 1949; m. James B. Woods, Jan. 2, 1953; children—Christopher, Peter, Andrew. Reporter, Chgo. Herald-Am., 1948, St. Louis Globe-Democrat, 1949-51; producer Star. KPLR-TV, St. Louis, 1964-74; moderator, writer Sta. KETC-TV, St. Louis, 1962-64; council mem. University City, Mo., 1967-74; mem. Mo. Hwy. Commn., 1974, Mo. Transp. Commn., 1974-76; mem. Mo. Senate, 1976-84, lt. gov. State of Mo., 1985—. Bd. dirs. LWV of Mo., 1963; Democratic nominee for U.S. Senate, 1982, 86. Jewish. Office: PO Box 563 Jefferson City MO 65102

WOODS, JOHN DOWS, banker; b. Oak Park, Ill., Dec. 6, 1929; s. Donald Carmel and Helen (Dows) W.; m. Marion Heidenreich, May 6, 1953; children—John, Donald, Susan, Charles, Lisen. B.A., U. Colo., 1956; grad., Sch. Banking U. Wis., 1967. Asst. cashier No. Trust Co., Chgo., 1956-63; with Winters Nat. Bank & Trust Co., Dayton, Ohio, 1963-75; sr. v.p. Winters Nat. Bank & Trust Co., 1969-71, exec. v.p., 1971-72, pres., chief operating officer, dir., 1972-75; pres., chief exec. officer FirsTier Inc. (formerly Omaha Nat. Bank), 1975-78, chmn., chief exec. officer, 1978—; bd. dirs. United of Omaha. Trustee USAF Mus., Dayton, Creighton U., Omaha; bd. dirs. Bishop Clarkson Meml. Hosp.; mem. consultation staff SAC Hdqrs., Omaha. Served with USAF, 1949-54. Mem. Res. City Bankers. Clubs: Omaha (Omaha), Omaha Country (Omaha), Ak Sar Ben (Omaha) (bd. govs.); Univ. (N.Y.C.). Office: Firstier Inc 17th Farnam St Omaha NE 68102

WOODS, JOHN ELMER, plastic surgeon; b. Battle Creek, Mich., July 5, 1929; m. Janet Ruth; children: Sheryl, Mark, Jeffrey, Jennifer, Judson. BA, Asbury Coll., 1949; MD, Western Res. U., 1955; PhD, U. Minn., 1966. Intern Gorgas Hosp., Panama Canal Zone, 1955-56, resident in gen. surgery, 1956-57; resident in gen. surgery Mayo Grad. Sch., Rochester, Minn., 1960-65, resident in plastic surgery, 1966-67; resident in plastic surgery Brigham Hosp., Boston, Mass., 1968; fellow, transplant cons. Harvard Med. Sch., Cambridge, Mass., 1969; cons. in gen. and plastic surgery Mayo Clinic, Rochester, 1969—, vice chmn. Dept. Surgery; asst. prof. Mayo Med. Sch., Rochester, 1973-76, assoc. prof., 1976-80, prof. plastic surgery, 1980—; vis. prof. Yale Sch. Medicine, New Haven, 1984, Harvard Sch. Medicine, Cambridge, 1984. Contbr. 185 articles to profl. jours.; also book chpts. and 1 film. Mem. AMA (council on sci. affairs 1985—), ACS (grad edn. com. 1985—), Am. Bd. Med. Specialties, Am. Bd. Plastic Surgery (sec.-treas. 1985—), Am. Soc. Plastic Surgeons Ednl. Fedn. (pres. 1984-85). Avocations: skiing, sailing, reading, the arts. Office: Mayo Clinic 200 First St SW Rochester MN 55905

WOODS, JOHN LARUE, university administrator; b. Butler, Ill., Oct. 16, 1937; s. John Scott and Eva Marie (Zueck) W.; m. Charlotte M. Souder, Feb. 11, 1968; children: Van John, Sheri Marie. BS in Agrl. Communications, U. Ill., 1960, MS in Mass Communications, 1965, PhD in Adult Edn. Adminstrn., 1974. TV coordinator U. Ill., Urbana, 1960-68, internat. program devel. specialist, 1971-74, dir. INTERPAKS, 1985—; chief of party U.S. Agy. Internat. Devel./U. Mo., Zomba, Malawi, 1969-70; communication cons. State of Victoria, Melbourne, Australia, 1970-71; dir. Asia and Pacific program for devel. tng. and communication planning UN Devel. Program, Bangkok, 1974-85; cons. Kellogg Found., Bogota, Columbia, 1968, USAID/U. Ill., Pant Nagar, India, 1970. Author cinematography reference book, 1968; monograph, 1986; also more than 50 articles. Mem. Assn. U.S. Univ. Dirs. of Internat. Agrl. Programs, Agrl. Communicators in Edn. (Internat. Affairs award 1987). Avocations: news and current affairs, microcomputer applications. Home: 1905 Trout Valley Rd Champaign IL 61821 Office: Univ Illinois INTERPAKS 1301 W Gregory Dr Urbana IL 61801

WOODS, MARY JOAN, pediatric nurse practitioner; b. Vincennes, Ind., July 11, 1928; d. John Arthur and Maud Claribel (Davidson) Caniff; m. John Thomas Woods, Sept. 17, 1949; children—John Thomas, William Patrick, Richard, Michael, Elizabeth, Stephen, Jennifer, Cynthia. Diploma, Deaconess Hosp., 1949; cert. Sch. Nurse Practitioner, U. Evansville, 1974; cert. Pediatric Nurse Practitioner, Ind. U., 1976. Supr., Well Baby Clinic, Pub. Health Nursing Assn., Evansville, Ind., 1972; supr. Sweetser Clinic, Evansville, 1973; pediatric nurse practitioner, Evansville-Vanderburgh Health Dept., Evansville, Ind., 1973—; tchr. parenting class Welborn Clinic, Evansville State Hosp., Prevention Crisis Nursery, Friendship Ministries; instr. parenting class and CPR, ARC; lectr. U. Evansville, also Deaconess Hosp. Tchr. St. James Ch.; taskforce mem. Latchkey Program. Fellow Nat. Assn. Pediatric Nurse Assocs. and Practitioners; mem. Ind. State Nurses Assn. (former state officer), DAR (vice regent Mary Anthony McGary chpt.). Republican. Roman Catholic. Home: Rural Route 6 Baseline Rd Box 339 Evansville IN 47711 Office: Civic Center Complex Health Dept Nursing Div Evansville IN 47708

WOODS, M(ICHAEL) KEVIN, health science facility administrator; b. Chgo., Jan. 28, 1949; s. Michael Joseph and Elizabeth F. (Wright) W.; m. Patricia Lynn Funk, Mar. 8, 1974; children: Colleen Patricia, Molly Kathleen. BCE, U. Detroit, 1971; M in Regional Planning, Cornell U., 1973; postgrad., Western Mich. U., 1976-77; postgrad. exec. program, Ohio State U., 1984—. Environ. planner Genesee County, Batavia, N.Y., 1973-75; dir. planning City of Springfield, Mich., 1975-78; v.p. Leach Constrn., Grand Rapids, Mich., 1978-81; dir. planning Western Mich. Hosp. Council, Grand Rapids, 1981-83, Blodgett Meml. Med. Ctr., Grand Rapids, 1983-84; dir. wellness services St. Mary's Hosp., Grand Rapids, 1984-87; mktg. mgr. Hackley Hosp., Muskegon, Mich., 1987—. Chmn. Barry County Parks Commn., Hastings, Mich., Barry County Planning Commn. Mem. Am. Planning Assn., Nat. Wellness Assn., Am. Mgmt. Assn. Roman Catholic. Avocations: competitive running, triathlons, cross country skiing, sailing. Home: 702 Coleman SE Grand Rapids MI 49508 Office: Hackley Hosp 1700 Clinton St Muskegon MI 49442

WOODS, RICHARD JOHN FRANCIS, priest, writer, educator; b. Albuquerque, July 30, 1941; s. James Everett and Margaret Louise (Corcoran) W. BA in Philosophy, Aquinas Inst., River Forest, Ill., 1964, MA in Philosophy, 1966; MA in Theology, Aquinas Inst., Dubuque, Iowa, 1970; PhD, Loyola U., Chgo., 1978. Ordained priest Dominican Order, 1969—; grad. faculty Inst. Pastoral Studies Loyola U., Chgo., 1978—, adj. prof. Stritch Sch. Medicine, 1981—; pres. Ctr. for Religion and Soc., Chgo., 1985—, also bd. dirs.; lectr. Loyola U., 1971—; vis. prof. Grad. Theol. Union, Berkeley, Calif., 1977-78; therapist Sexual Dysfunction Clinic, Loyola U., 1981—. Author: Mysterion, 1980; Symbion, 1983; Eckhart's Way, 1986; also articles; exec. editor Spirituality Today, 1986—. Richard John F. Woods endowed chair Coll. of St. Thomas, St. Paul, 1984-85. Mem. Am. Cath. Philos. Assn., Am. Acad. Religion, Cath. Theol. Soc. Am., Authors Guild, Am. Soc. for Psychical Research, Dragon Soc. Avocations: music, harp making, photography. Home: 7200 W Division St River Forest IL 60305 Office: Inst Pastoral Studies 6525 N Sheridan Rd Chicago IL 60626

WOODS, ROBERT KENNETH, protective services official; b. Alpena, Mich., Dec. 22, 1950; s. Orville Joseph and Anna Mary (Lenhart) W.; m. M. Elizabeth Brown, Sept. 10, 1977; children: Christopher Ryan, Kelli Ann. AS, Kirtland Community Coll., 1972; student, No. Mich. U., 1973. Chief of police Leland (Mich.) Twp., 1972-75; patrol officer Grand Traverse County Sheriff's Dept., Traverse City, Mich., 1975-78, detective, 1978-82, sgt., patrol supr., 1982—. Bd. dirs. Camp Roy-El, Grand Traverse Camping for the Promotion of Physically Handicapped, Traverse City, 1975—. Lodge: Fraternal Order of Police. Home: 3149 Panorama Ln Traverse City MI 49684 Office: Grand Traverse Sheriff's Dept 320 Washington Traverse City MI 49684

WOODS, THOMAS COCHRANE, JR., communications company executive; b. Lincoln, Nebr., May 4, 1920; s. Thomas Cochrane and Sarah (Ladd) W.; m. Marjorie Jane Jones, June 1, 1943; children: Thomas Cochrane III, Avery Ladd. BA, U. Nebr., 1943. Asst. advt. mgr. Addressograph-Multigraph Corp., Cleve., 1947-58; chmn. bd., chief exec. officer Lincoln Telecommunicaitons Co., Nebr., 1958—; pres. Nellewood Corp., Lincoln, 1961-85, T-V Transmission, Inc., Lincoln, 1966-75; chmn. Lincoln Telecommunications Co., 1980—, Lincoln Telephone Co.; v.p. Lincoln Devel. Co., 1958-80, W.K. Realty Co., Lincoln, 1958-80; chmn. bd., dir. Sahara Coal Co., Chgo.; dir. Woodmen Accident & Life Co., Lincoln; dir., mem. exec. and trust coms. FirsTier Bank, Lincoln. Pres. Woods Charitable Fund, Inc., Lincoln and Chgo., 1968—; mem. State Bldg. Commn., Lincoln, 1966-80; mem. exec. com. Bryan Meml. Hosp., 1962-66; mem. Lincoln City Park and Recreation Adv. Bd., 1962-72, Lincoln Center Devel. Assn., 1967—; trustee Nebr. Human Resources Research Found., 1968—, U. Nebr. Found., 1961—, Joslyn Liberal Arts Soc., Omaha, 1964—, Nebr. Ind. Coll. Found., 1965-73. Served to 1st lt. AUS, 1943-46. Mem. U.S. C. of C., Lincoln C. of C., SAR. Congregationalist. Clubs: Lincoln Univ., Lincoln Country, Nebr. (Lincoln); Chicago. Office: Lincoln Telecommunications Co 1440 M St PO Box 81309 Lincoln NE 68501

WOODS, TIMOTHY DALE, dentist; b. Hiawatha, Kans., Oct. 2, 1953; s. Philip and Verna Ruth (Wilson) W.; m. Susan Gwen Wood, May 28, 1977; children: Joseph Timothy, Adam Christopher. BS, U. Nebr., 1975, DDS, 1982. Research asst. U. Nebr., Lincoln, 1976-78; gen. practice dentistry Hillsboro, Kans., 1982—, Goessel, Kans., 1984—; dental cons. Parkside Nursing Home, Hillsboro, 1982—, Bethesda Home for Aged, Goessel, 1983—; mem. dental staff Salem Hosp., Hillsboro, 1982—, St. Luke's Hosp., Marion, Kans., 1982—, Bethel Hosp., Newton, Kans., 1986—. Chamber rep. Hillsboro Devel. Corp., 1985. Recipient Excellence in Sci. Research award, U. Nebr. Coll. Dentistry, Lincoln, 1981. Mem. ADA, Am. Soc. Dentistry for Children, Kans. Dental Assn. (peer rev. com. 1985-87), Hillsboro C. of C. (v.p. 1986). Republican. Methodist. Avocations: tennis, travel, golf. Home: 213 S Floral Dr Hillsboro KS 67063 Office: 104 N Washington St Hillsboro KS 67063

WOODSIDE, BERTAM JOHN, engineer; b. Danville, Pa., Apr. 20, 1946; s. Cyrus G. and Almerta T. (Kitchen) W.; m. Doreen Knowles; 1 child, Russell. BS, USAF Acad., 1968. Cert. purchasing mgr. Commissioned 2d lt. USAF, 1968, advanced through grades to capt., 1971, resigned, 1976; plant engr. Linde div. Union Carbide Corp., Pitts., 1976, distribution supt., 1977-78; region purchasing mgr. Linde div. Union Carbide Corp., Cleve., 1979-82, region tech. supr., 1983; process analyst Linde div. Union Carbide Corp., Lorain, Ohio, 1984—. Club: Bay Boat (Bay Village, Ohio) (sec. 1984-87). Avocations: golf, fishing, sailing. Office: Union Carbide Corp Box 1153 Lorain OH 44055

WOODWARD, JOSIAH HERMAN, college administrator; b. Hastings, Nebr., June 22, 1948; s. Orvel E. and L. Agnes (Skelton) W.; m. Marcile M. Hensel, Dec. 23, 1969; children: Robert, Anita, Joel. BA, Kearney (Nebr.) State Coll., 1969, MS, 1979; EdS, U. No. Colo., 1981; PhD, Colo. State U., 1985. Indsl. engr. Rockwell Internat., Kearney, 1967-77; area mgr. Ideal Truck Lines, Kearney, 1977-79; tchr. Pleasanton (Nebr.) High Sch., 1980-82; assoc. prof. Kearney State Coll., 1982-83; chairperson Cen. Community Coll., Hastings, 1983—; cons. Moody Toottrup Internat., Pitts., 1980—. Recipient Cert. of Appreciation Nebr. Dept. Edn., 1984, 86. Mem. Am. Tech. Edn. Assn., Hastings C. of C. (edn. com. 1983—). Republican. Lodge: Rotary. Home: 1515 N Webster Hastings NE 68901 Office: Cen Community Coll PO Box 1024 Hastings NE 68901

WOODWARD, KIRK PATRICK, office and facilities manager; b. Kansas City, Mo., Dec. 1, 1953; s. Harry Delbert and Margaret Frances (Cheatham) W.; m. Karla Ann Wilber, June 30, 1975; children: Kelly, Kimberly, Christopher. BSBA, Kans. State U., 1975; MBA, U. Kans., 1985. Purchasing agt. Black & Veatch Engrs., Kansas City, 1975-76, mgr. bldg. services, 1976-79, dept. head bldg. services, 1979—; pres. Overland Park (Kans.) Maintenance Mgmt., 1979—. Mem. Bldg. Owners and Mgrs. Assn., Mid-Am. Telecommunications Assn. Republican. Roman Catholic. Avocations: hunting, fishing, skeet shooting, golf. Home: 10705 W 123d Terr Overland Park KS 66213 Office: Black & Veatch Engrs 1500 Meadowlake Pkwy Kansas City MO 64114

WOODWARD, PAMELA ROSE, nurse and school administrator, nurse; b. Canton, Ohio, Sept. 18, 1943; d. Wallace Ralph and Ruth Lucille (Hershberger) Hutchison; children: Angela Kay, Alison Rae. Grad. Aultman Hosp. Sch. Nursing, 1965; BS in Edn., Kent State U., 1973; MS in Edn., U. Akron, 1978. RN, cert. tchr., Ohio. Staff nurse Aultman Hosp., Canton, 1965-66; mem. faculty, supr. Aultman Hosp. and Aultman Hosp. Sch. Nursing, 1966-70, mem. faculty sch. nursing, 1970-79, adminstrv. coordinator research, 1979-81, asst. dir. curriculum, 1981-84, dir. nursing quality assurance and nursing research, 1984—; instr. CPR. Mem. Am. Nursing Assn., Ohio Nursing Assn., Am. Assn. Critical Care Nurses, Emergency Dept. Nurses Assn., Assn. Supervision and Curriculum Devel., Aultman Hosp. Nurses Alumni Assn., Minerva Area Nurses Assn., Sigma Theta Tau, Phi Delta Kappa, Pi Lambda Tau. Presbyterian. Home: 901 Lynnwood Dr Minerva OH 44657 Office: 2600 6th St SW Canton OH 44710

WOODWARD, ROBERT SIMPSON, IV, economics educator; b. Easton, Pa., May 7, 1943; s. Robert Simpson and Esther Evans (Thomas) W.; B.A., Haverford Coll., 1965; Ph.D., Washington U., St. Louis, 1972; m. Mary P. Hutton, Feb. 15, 1969; children—Christopher Thomas, Rebecca Marie. Brookings Econ. Policy fellow Dept. HEW, Washington, 1975-76; asst. prof. U. Western Ont. (Can.), London, 1972-77; asst. prof. Sch. Medicine, Washington U., St. Louis, 1978-86, assoc. prof., 1986—; pres. Tchr. Works Software, Inc., 1987—. Mem. adv. council Mo. Kidney Program, 1980-86, vice-chmn., 1983, chmn. 1984-85; coop. mem. Haverford Coll., 1968—. NDEA fellow, 1968-71; Kellogg Nat. fellow, 1981-84. Mem. Am. Econs. Assn., Am. Statis. Assn. Contbr. articles to profl. jours. Home: 7050 Westmoreland St University City MO 63130 Office: 4547 Clayton Ave Saint Louis MO 63110

WOOL, ELLIOT NEIL, obstetrician-gynecologist; b. St. Louis, Oct. 21, 1953; s. Samuel Fallek and Helen (Matusofsky) W.; m. Kimberly Dale Clements, Jan. 5, 1980; children: Phillip, Joshua. BA in Biology, Northwestern U., 1975; MD, St. Louis U., 1979. Intern Jewish Hosp., St. Louis, 1979-80, resident in ob-gyn, 1980-83. Fellow Am. Coll. Ob-Gyn; mem. AMA, Ill. Med. Soc. Jewish. Avocation: golf. Office: 7210 W Main Belleville IL 62223

WOOLDRIDGE, PATRICE MARIE, marketing professional, dance educator; b. Chgo., June 3, 1954; d. Charles E. and Marlys E. (Kuehn) Reardon; m. Patrick Wooldridge, June 27, 1981. AS, Moraine Valley Coll., 1974; BA, Govs. State U., 1976, MA, 1977; MBA, Loyola U., Chgo., 1983. Community prof. Govs. State U., University Park, Ill., 1977-78; counselor, social worker Bloom Twp. High Sch., Chicago Heights, Ill., 1977-78; market analyst Dr. Scholl Footcare, Chgo., 1978-79; supr. consumer research Unocal, Schaumburg, Ill., 1979-84; group research dir. Tatham-Laird & Kudner, Chgo., 1984—; instr. dancing, 1969—, T'ai Chi the Sch. of T'ai Chi Chuan, N.Y.C., 1986—, Arica the Arica Inst., N.Y.C., 1978—. Performer the Anawim Players, Chgo., 1985—; treas. Karma Thegsum Choling, Chgo., 1987; bd. dirs. Illustrated Theatre Co., Chgo., 1987; adv. bd. N.W. Suburban Boy Scouts, Schaumburg, 1984. Mem. Am. Mktg. Assn. Home: 2 East Oak Apt #1110 Chicago IL 60611 Office: Tatham-Laird & Kunder 980 N Michigan Ave Chicago IL 60611

WOOLEY, DONALD ALAN, manufacturing company executive; b. Coloma, Mich., July 7, 1926; s. Roscoe Norris and Ruth (Grahn) W.; m. Frances Edna Bowersox, Jan. 1, 1950 (dec. 1974); children: Kathryn Ann, Charles Alan; m. Claire Louise Franzen, Jan. 18, 1978; stepchildren: Marc Phillip, Arn David, Jil Lisa. B.S.M.E., U. Mich., 1949. Div. mgr. Allis-Chalmers Gt. Brit., London, 1958-66; mng. dir. Allis-Chalmers Gt. Brit., Stamford, Eng., 1966-69, Allis-Chalmers Australia, Sydney, 1969-73; v.p. Stansteel Co., Los Angeles, 1973-76; gen. mgr. compressor div. Allis-Chalmers Corp., Milw., 1976-80, v.p., 1980-87; pres. Marsh Hill Ltd., 1987—. Served to lt. j.g. USNR, 1944-47. Republican. Home: 456 N Waterville Rd Oconomowoc WI 53066 Office: Marsh Hill Ltd 456 N Waterville Rd Oconomowoc WI 53066

WOOLF, HOWARD L., obstetrician-gynecologist; b. Chgo., Nov. 28, 1922; s. Harry and Jeannette (Singer) W.; m. Honette Fidelman, Dec. 24, 1944; children: Jay S., Robert H., Mark G. Pre-med. student, Loyola U., Chgo., 1940-43; MD, Loyola U., 1946. Diplomate Am Bd. Ob-Gyn. Intern Mt. Sinai Hosp., Chgo., 1946-47, resident in ob-gyn, 1949-51; resident in ob-gyn Cook County Hosp., Chgo., 1951-52; pvt. practice ob-gyn Skokie, Ill., 1952—; sec. dept. ob-gyn Rush North Shore Med. Ctr. (formerly Skokie Valley Hosp.), 1970-71, chmn. dept. ob-gyn, 1972-73, 86—, sec. med. staff, 1975-78, v.p. med. staff, 1983-84, pres. med. staff, 1985-86; trustee Skokie Valley Hosp., 1985-87. Served to capt. U.S Army, 1947-49, Korea. Fellow Am. Coll. Ob-gyn. Home: 8425 Lawndale Ave Skokie IL 60076 Office: 9669 Kenton Ave Skokie IL 60076

WOOLSEY, WILLIAM STOVER, printing company executive; b. Chgo., Dec. 22, 1917; s. William Robert and Grace (Peck) W.; B.S. in Mech. Engring., U. Mich., 1939, M.S., 1940; m. Doris Marie Neely, Jan. 5, 1946; children—Robert, Mary Woolsey Porter, Carolyn Woolsey Sandberg. Engr., Commonwealth Edison Co., Chgo., 1940-55; exec. Neely Printing Co., Chgo., 1955-60, pres., dir., 1960—; pres., dir. Dayanite Corp., Chgo., 1957—, Franklin Offset Litho Co., Chgo., 1960—, N.B.L. Corp., Chgo., 1960—, 917 Bldg. Corp., Chgo., 1960—. Trustee Pressman Sch. Fund; chmn. Lithographer Health and Welfare Fund. Served to lt. col. USAAF, 1940-45. Decorated Bronze Star. Mem. Western Soc. Engrs., Printing Industry of Ill. (dir.), Union Employers Assn. (exec. bd.), Chgo. Lithographers Bd. (dir.), Franklin Assn. (dir.), Printing Industry Am. (exec. bd. union employers sect., chmn. budget com., mem. Ash Kahn Crew). Club: Westmoreland Country. Home: 1500 Sheridan Rd Wilmette IL 60091 Office: 871 N Franklin St Chicago IL 60610

WOOLSTON, RITA ALTA, probation officer; b. Ionia, Mich., Dec. 26, 1942; s. Smith Raymond and Eulah Elvira (Griswold) Rowley; m. Thoms Clinton Woolston, Oct. 5, 1963; 1 child, Tamara Lin. Student, Montcalm Community Coll., 1967—, Cen. Mich. U., 1961-63, Western Mich. U., 1963-75. Caseworker Ionia County Juvenile Ct., 1971-75, probation officer, 1975—; co-owner Action Awards, Ionia, 1986—; interviewer, counselor-therapist, investigator, cons. Ionia County Juvenile Ct., 1971—. Mem. Mich. Juvenile Justice Assn., Mich. Jud. Inst., Mich. Interscholastic Horseman Assn. (coach), English Western Horse Assn. Republican. Clubs: Blazing Trails Saddle (Ionia), Portland (Mich.) Riding, Ionia County Saddle Devel. Avocations: raising quarter horses, show horses, reading, counted crosstitch. Home: 645 Belding Rd Orleans MI 48865 Office: Ionia County Juvenile Ct Courthouse Washington St Ionia MI 48846

WOOSLEY, HOWARD R(OWAN), dentist; b. Kansas City, Mo., Dec. 3, 1929; s. Harold C. and Hettie Lee (Rowan) W.; m. Mary Gay Bagby, Dec. 21, 1955; children: David, Kenneth, Thomas. AA, Kemper Mil. Sch., 1949; AB, U. Mo., Columbia, 1955; DDS, U. Mo., Kansas City, 1959. Gen. practice dentistry Kansas City, 1959—; cons. Research Psychiat. Clinic, Kansas City, 1984—, Anesthesia Assn., Kansas City, 1982—. Served to capt. U.S. Army, 1951-53. Fellow Pierre Fauchard Acad. Mem. ADA (del. 1973—), Mo. Dental Assn. (trustee 1980-86), Greater Kansas City Dental Soc. (sec./treas. 1969-80). Republican. Club: Dental Vet. Study (Kansas City). Lodges: Masons, Shriners. Avocations: hunting, fishing, bowling. Home: 2403 W 69 Terr Mission Hills KS 66208 Office: 6400 Prospect Kansas City MO 64132

WOOTEN, BILLY MACK, health care centers adminstr.; b. San Angelo, Tex., Feb. 25, 1947; s. Billy S. and Maxine C. (Watson) W.; B.A. in Psychology, N.Mex. State U., 1969, M.A., 1976; B.A. in Social Work, St. Cloud (Minn.) State U., 1974; M.S. in Mental Retardation, Mankato (Minn.) State U., 1980; Ph.D. in Psychology, Columbia Pacific U., 1981; m. Linda Ruth Lundgren, Apr. 7, 1973; children—Joshua S., Joseph A. Mental health counselor Southwest Mental Health Center, Alamogordo, N.Mex., 1972-73; exec. dir. REM, Inc., Marshall, Minn., 1975-85; state adminstr. REM-Ind. Inc., 1985—; pres. Prairie Systems, Inc., 1983—; adj. prof. spl. edn., Mankato State U.; chmn. Services Industries, Inc.; cons. REM Cons. & Services, Inc., Mpls., Ind. Dept. Mental Health. Served with USAF, 1969-73; pvt. practice Behavior Analysts, 1978—. Served with USAF, 1969-73. Mem. Am. Assn. Mental Deficiency (vice chairperson psychology 1977-79, editor Region VIII Newsletter 1979—, Minn. sec.-treas.), Assn. Advancement of Behavior Therapy, Assn. Behavior Analysis, Minn. Assn. Behavior Analysis (membership chmn., pres. 1982-83). Democrat. Unitarian. Club: Kiwanis. Author: (with David C. Pfriem) An Introduction to Behavioral Techniques, 1979; A Rational Approach to Counseling the Mentally Retarded, 1981; contbr. articles to profl. jours. Home: 1121 Fairbanks Dr Carmel IN 46032 Office: 11711 N Meridian Suite 750 Carmel IN 46032

WORDEN, LARRY THOMAS, insurance company executive, pilot; b. Goshen, Ind., June 21, 1945; s. Wendell Thomas and Velma Darlene (Barrett) W.; m. Sherilyn Ann Frazier, Mar. 29, 1969; 1 child, Melissa Jo. BA, Olivet Coll., 1969. Commd. 2d lt. USAF, 1969, advanced through grades to capt., 1972, retired, 1979; chief pilot Niles (Mich.) Airways, 1979; capt. Britt Airlines, Terre Haute, Ind., 1979-80; corp. services analyst, corp. pilot Varlen Corp., Rolling Meadows, Ill., 1980-82; loss control account exec. spl. risk div. Zurich-Am. Ins. Co., Schaumburg, Ill., 1982-87; corp. risk mgr. R&D Thiel, Inc., Palatine, Ill., 1987—. Chmn. safety bd. Residential Constrn. Employers Council,. Decorated Air medal with two leaf clusters, Disting. Flying Cross; named Outstanding Aircraft Comdr. of Yr., 1972. Mem. Risk and Ins. Mgmt. Soc., Soc. Casualty Safety Engrs. (bd. dirs. Chgo. chpt.), Aircraft Owners and Pilots Assn., Chgo. Flight Instrs. Assn., Am. Soc. Safety Engrs., Air Force Assn., Air Safety Found. Republican. Presbyterian. Lodges: Masons (past master), Shriners, Kiwanis, KT. Home: 920 Oxford Rd Glen Ellyn IL 60137 Office: R&D Thiel Inc 1700 Rand Rd Palatine IL 60074

WORKLEY, JOHN I.L., holding company auditor; b. San Jose, Calif., May 9, 1952; s. Richard Allen Workley and Florence Mildred (Joos) Roth; m. Bobbie Rae Stewart, July 17, 1976; children: Joanna Lynn, Jessica Nichole, Jennifer Dawn, Jocelyn Renee. BS in Psychology, Ill. State U., 1974; AA in Acctg., Ill. Cen. Coll., 1981. CPA, Ill.; cert. info. systems auditor. Crisis interventionist Human Service Ctr., Peoria, Ill., 1977-82; EDP auditor Bloomington (Ill.) Fed. Savs. & Loan, Inc., 1982-85; info. systems audit mgr. Midwest Fin. Group, Inc., Peoria, 1985—. Served with U.S. Army, 1974-77. Mem. EDP Auditors Assn. (sec. 1984-85, pres. 1985-86), Inst. Internal Auditors. Methodist. Home: 634 Simon Dr East Peoria IL 61611 Office: Midwest Financial Group Inc 301 SW Adams Peoria IL 61631

WORKMAN, ROBERT PETER, artist, cartoonist; b. Chgo., Jan. 27, 1961; s. Tom Okko and Virginia (Martin) W. Freelance artist Chgo.; instr. St. Xavier Coll., Chgo., 1985; cartoonist Bridge View News, Oak Lawn, Ill., 1983—, Village View Pubs., Oak Lawn, 1983—; TV art dir. Media-In-Action, Oak Lawn. Author (cartoon strip) Cypher, 1983—; Sesqui Squirrel Coloring Book, 1982, Sesqui Squirrel History of Chicago, 1983; artworks and books in collections of 18 mus. and libraries, including Smithsonian, Art Inst. Chgo. Mem. nat. adv. bd. Am. Security Council, Boston, Va. Mem. Am. Watercolor Soc., No. Ill. Newspaper Assn., Artists' Resource Trust Ft. Wayne Mus. Art, Ridge Art Assn. Roman Catholic. Home: 2215 W 111th St Apt #307 Chicago IL 60643 Office: Village View Publications 5518 W 95th St Oak Lawn IL 60453

WORKS, ALEC RAYMOND, rate analyst; b. New Castle, Pa., Oct. 5, 1952; s. Alec and Julia (Raymond) W.; m. Margo Ellen Maire, June 21, 1986. BS in Math. cum laude, Grove City Coll., 1974; BS in Acctg., U. Akron, 1979. Technician Ohio Edison Co., Akron, 1974-80, assoc. rate analyst, 1980-83, rate analyst, 1983—. Advisor Jr. Achievement, Akron, 1975-76; deacon Westminster Presbyn. Ch., Akron, 1979-81, elder, 1986—. Mem. Nat. Assn. Accts. (bd. dirs. 1985—), Inst. Cert. Mgmt. Accts., Am. Sci. Affiliation. Club: Westminster Young Adults (Akron) (coordinator 1980-82, 86). Avocations: golf, skiing, classical music. Office: Ohio Edison Co 76 S Main St Akron OH 44308

WORLEY, MARVIN GEORGE, JR., architect; b. Oak Park, Ill., Oct. 10, 1934; s. Marvin George and Marie Hyancinth (Donahue) W.; B.Arch., U. Ill., 1958; m. Maryalice Ryan, July 11, 1959; children—Michael Craig, Carrie Ann, Alissa Maria. Project engr. St. Louis area Nike missile bases U.S. Army C.E., Granite City, Ill., 1958-59, architect N.Cen. div. U.S. Army C.E., Chgo., 1960; architect Yerkes & Grunsfeld, architects, Chgo., 1961-65, asso., 1965; asso. Grunsfeld & Assos., architects, Chgo., 1966-85.; prin. Marvin Worley Architects, Oak Park, Ill., 1985—. Dist. architect Oak Park Elementary Schs., Dist. 97, 1973-80. Mem. Oak Park Community Improvement Commn., 1973-75; mem. exec. bd. Oak Park Council PTA, 1970-73, pres., 1971-72. Served with AUS, 1959. Mem. AIA (corporate), Chgo. Assn. Commerce and Industry. Office: 37 South Boulevard Oak Park IL 60302

WORLOW, CATHY, human resource executive; b. Peoria, Ill., Sept. 27, 1949; d. Thomas William and W. LaVonne (Deavers) Endres; m. Andy Lee Worlow, May 31, 1975; 1 child, Leah Danielle. AA, Ill. Cen. Coll., East Peoria, 1970; BA, Sangamon State U., 1980. Acctg. Ruppman Adminstrv. Services, Peoria, 1971-72; sec. Ruppman Mktg. Services, Inc., Peoria, 1972-74, asst. to v.p., 1974-76, dir. purchasing, 1976-80, dept. head/mgr. bldg. services, 1980—. Mem. Am.Assn. Univ. Women (mem. publicity com. 1985—), Cen. Ill. Employee Assn. (v.p. personnel club 1987), Nat. Assn. for Female Execs. Lutheran. Lodges: Order Eastern Star, Internat. Order Job's Daus. Home: 209 S Indiana Morton IL 61550 Office: Ruppman Mktg Services 1909 E Cornell Peoria IL 61614

WORMINGTON, BARRY LEE, medical supply company marketing executive; b. Denver, Aug. 5, 1942; s. Everett Glendon Wormington and Berniece Lucille (Foster) Van Scoy; m. Regina Louise Rollo, Jan. 10, 1964; children—Christine, Aric, Amanda. B.A. in Bus. Adminstrn., U. Colo., 1971; ops. mgr. McKesson & Robbins, Denver, 1967-70; ops. mgr. Foremost-McKesson, Portland, Oreg., 1970-74, div. mgr., 1974-76; div. mgr. Gentec Hosp. Supply Co., Milw., 1976-79; regional v.p. Gentec Health Care, Milw., 1979-81; v.p. mktg. R & J Med. Supply Co., Milw., 1981—. Served with USN, 1960-63. Republican. Roman Catholic. Lodge: Rotary (bd. dirs. West Allis, Wis. 1981). Home: 8421 Kenyon Ave Wauwatosa WI 53226 Office: 7940 N 81st St Milwaukee WI 53223

WORNY, CHRISTINE MAY, psychotherapist; b. Chgo., May 3, 1941; d. Arthur B. and Helene I. (Kiefer) W.; m. William B. Merrill, Aug. 4, 1962 (div. 1979); children: Jennifer, Rebecca, Alissa, Amanda; m. Marvin R. Cohen, Oct. 27, 1984. BA in Psychology, Mundelein Coll., 1972; MA in Clin. Psychology, Roosevelt U., Chgo., 1974. Psychotherapist Centrum Counseling and Phobia Clinic, Oak Park, Ill., 1974—, dir. community edn., 1980—; also bd. dirs. Centrum Counseling and Phobia Clinic, Oak Park; psychologist Madden Mental Health Ctr., Hines, Ill., 1974-77, psychologist, team leader, 1977-83; lectr. profl. and community groups. Mem. Phobia Soc. Am. Avocations: films, theater, travel. Office: Centrum Counseling & Phobia Clinic 461 N Harlem Ave Oak Park IL 60302 Office: 25 E Medical Ctr 25 E Washington Chicago IL 60602

WORTH, BARBARA FERN KEETON, sales executive; b. Hazard, Ky., Mar. 15, 1938; d. Greenville P. and Rieta Kathleen (Patrick) K.; m. John L. Worth, Mar. 16, 1957 (widowed 1973); 1 child, Gregory L. Ed. pvt. schs., Hazel Green, Ky. Supr. Ernst & Ernst, Dayton, Ohio, 1956-61; head stenography pool Lau Blower/Conaire div. Philips Industries, Dayton, 1962; sales adminstr. Conaire div. Philips Industries, Dayton, asst. sales mgr., sales promotion mgr., nat. sales mgr. Republican. Avocations: golf, racquetball, music, piano. Home: 2326 Candlewood Dr Kettering OH 45419 Office: Philips Ind-Conaire Div PO Box 943 Dayton OH 45401

WORTHAM, JAMES CALVIN, educator; b. Oconee County, Ga., Sept. 12, 1928; s. James Notley and Effie (Cross) W.; B.A., U. Akron, 1957; M.A. (NSF Scholar), Ohio State U., 1969; m. Mary Helena Shelley, Dec. 23, 1953; children—Sharon Elaine, Marilyn Kay, Deborah Louise, James Donald. Tchr. high sch. Akron Pub. Schs., 1956-62, tchr. sr. high sch., 1962-66; math. curriculum specialist Akron (Ohio) Pub. Schs., 1966—; instr. math. U. Akron, 1966—. Served with USAF, 1951-55. Mem. NEA, Ohio Edn. Assn., Math. Assn. Am., Nat., Ohio councils tchrs. of math., Nat. Council Suprs. of Math., Greater Akron Math. Educators Soc. (pres. 1984-86), Pi Mu Epsilon. Republican. Mem. Ch. of Nazarene. Home: 1665 Wiltshire Rd Akron OH 44313 Office: 70 N Broadway Akron OH 44308

WORTHEN, JOHN EDWARD, university president; b. Carbondale, Ill., July 15, 1933; s. Dewey and Annis Burr (Williams) W.; m. Sandra Damewood, Feb. 27, 1960; children: Samantha Jane, Bradley Edward. B.S. in Psychology (Univ. acad. scholar), Northwestern U., 1954; M.A. in Student Personnel Adminstrn., Columbia U., 1955; Ed.D. in Adminstrn. in Higher Edn. (Coll. Entrance Exam. Bd. fellow), Harvard U., 1964; PhD (hon.), Yeungnam U., Daegu, Korea, 1986. Dean of men Am. U., 1959-61; dir. counseling and testing and asst. prof. edn. 1963-66, asst. to provost and asst. prof., 1966-68, acting provost and v.p. acad. affairs, 1968, asso. provost for instrn., 1969, v.p. student affairs, 1970-75, v.p. student affairs and adminstrn., 1976-79; pres. Indiana U. of Pa., 1979-84, Ball State U., Muncie, Ind., 1984—; cons. to public schs. Served with USN, 1955-59. Mem. Am. Assn. Counseling and Devel., Phi Delta Kappa, Kappa Delta Pi. Office: Ball State U Adminstrn Bldg Muncie IN 47306

WORTHINGTON, DENNIS, perinatologist; b. Palestine, Aug. 16, 1941; came to U.S., 1980; s. John Frank and Fay Zipora (Silberg) W.; m. Francine Cimo, 1965; children: Mark Dennis, Michael John, Ilana Anne. Baccalaureus Medicinae/Chirurgiae Magister, U. Edinburgh, Scotland, 1966. Diplomate Am. Bd. Ob-Gyn. Intern Rose Med. Ctr., Denver, 1966-67; resident Queen's U. Affiliated Hosps., Kingston, Ont., Can., 1967-72; fellow Nuffield Inst. for Med. Research Oxford U., Eng., 1972-73; asst. prof. Queen's U., Kingston, Ont., Can., 1973-78; assoc. prof. Queen's U., Kingston, 1978-79; chief obstetrics Maricopa County Hosp., Phoenix, 1979-80; assoc. prof. Med. Coll. Wis., Milw., 1980-84, clin. assoc. prof., 1984—; chief maternal-fetal dept. St. Joseph's Hosp., Milw., 1984—; cons. Internat. Childbirth Edn. Assn., Mpls., 1985-86, Dept. Health and Social Services, Madison, Wis., 1985—, region V Fed. Dept. Health and Human Services, Chgo., 1986—. Contbr. articles to profl. and scholarly jours. Bd. dirs. Perinatal Found., Madison, 1985-87. Grantee Ont. Ministry Health, 1974-79, Med. Research Council Can., 1975-79, March of Dimes, 1980, Med. Coll. Wis., 1982. Fellow Royal Coll. Surgeons, Am. Coll. Obstetricians and Gynecologists; mem. Soc. Perinatal Obstetricians, Wis. Assn. for Perinatal Care (pres. 1985-86), Wis. Soc. Ob-Gyn, Cen. Assn. Obstetricians and Gynecologists, Milw. Gynecol. Soc. Avocations: gardening, reading, flying, philately. Home: 939 W Green Tree Rd River Hills WI 53217 Office: 3070 N 51st St Milwaukee WI 53210

WORTHINGTON, MAX MONROE, architect; b. Beckley, W.Va., Mar. 8, 1941; s. Monroe and Lena Edith (Martin) W.; m. Jawn Frances Dumont, Aug. 28, 1967; children: Eric Morgan, Marc Aaron, Virginia Elizabeth. BArch, U. Cin., 1968; MArch, Va. Polytechnic Inst. and State U., 1972. Asst. prof. U. Cin., 1972-80; ptnr. A.M. Kinney Assocs., Cin., 1980—. Pres. Clifton Heights, University Heights, Fairview Community Council, Cin., 1975-76; mem. bd. Cin. Better Housing League, 1977-79, Clifton Heights, University Heights, Fairview Devel. Corp., Cin., 1976-80. Served with USAF, 1958-62. Recipient Mayor's award for community service, Cin. City Council, 1976. Mem. AIA, Architects Soc. of Ohio. Republican. Mem. Religious Soc. Friends. Home: 519 Howell Ave Cincinnati OH 45220 Office: A M Kinney Assocs 2900 Vernon Pl Cincinnati OH 45219

WORTHINGTON, ROBERT ALBERT, electrical engineering consultant, real estate developer; b. St. Louis, June 25, 1951; s. Richard Benjamin and Julia Carmen (Avila) W.; m. Dora Jane Byers, Feb. 1, 1985; children: Melissa, Bradley, Jessica. BSEE, U. Mo., 1974. Registered profl. engr.; lic. real estate broker. Elec. engr. Power and Light Co., El Salvador, 1974-75; project engr. Lemco Engrs., St. Louis, 1976-79; chief engr. Phelps & Phillips, Raytown, Mo., 1979-82; prin. engr. Worthington & Assocs., Blue Springs, Mo., 1983—, pres., 1986—. Mem. Mo. Assn. Mcpl. Utilities, K.C. Bd. Realtors, Nat. Fedn. Ind. Bus., U.S. C. of C., Blue Springs C. of C. Republican. Lodge: Elks. Avocation: real estate investment. Home: 3509 Lake Shore Dr Blue Springs MO 64015 Office: Worthington & Assocs 807 Vesper Blue Springs MO 64015

WORTHY, FRANCIS DURANT, data processing executive; b. Chester, S.C., Nov. 23, 1940; s. William Thomas Worthy and Johnnie Moore; m. Ridgely Renwick, Dec. 6, 1942; children: Francis Jr., Danielle, Brandon. BS in Math., Morehouse Coll., 1964; hon. degree, Internat. Coll. Copenhagen, Denmark, 1963; postgrad., Purdue U., 1964-65, Case Western Res. U., 1968-72. Programmer analyst Republic Steel Research Ctr., Cleve., 1965-70, coordinator computer ops., 1971-76; supr. computer ops. LTV Steel Research Ctr. div. Republic Steel, Cleve., 1977—. Woodrow Wilson fellow, 1964. Mem. IEEE, Honeywell Large Users Assn., Black Data Processors Assn. Club: Scandinavian. Avocations: racquetball, weight lifting, aerobics, reading. Office: LTV Steel Research Ctr 6801 Brecksville Rd Independence OH 44131

WORTLEY, NEIL C., emeritus hospital administrator; b. Lake Odessa, Mich., Dec. 3, 1921; s. Howard H. and Alma Augusta (Vietzke) W.; m. Mary Virginia Orr, Mar. 1, 1945; children: Christopher, Carolyn, David. B.S., S.W. Mo. State U.; M.H.A., Washington U. Surg. technician, instr. U.S. Army Hosp., Springfield, Mo., 1943-46; asst. adminstr., adminstr. Burge Hosp., Springfield, 1951-54, adminstr., 1954-56; dir. Hosp. constrn. Licensing, Mo. Div. Health, Jefferson City, 1956-65; adminstr. L.E. Cox Med. Ctr., Springfield, from 1965; now emeritus L.E. Cox Med. Ctr.; chmn. bd.-elect. Midwest Health Congress, Kansas City, Mo., 1983—; faculty mem. Washington U. Sch. Health Care Adminstrn., St. Louis, 1966—. Bd. dirs. Am. Cancer Soc., Springfield, 1970—; bd. dirs. Springfield Area C. of C., 1976—, ARC, Springfield, 1970-80. Served with M.C. U.S. Army, 1942-48. Recipient Disting. Service award Mo. Hosp. Assn., 1981; recipient Outstanding Service award in communit planning Community Planning Council Springfield, 1970, Pioneer award N. Springfield Betterment Assn., 1980. Mem. Am. Assn. Hosp. Planning (dir.), Am. Coll. Hosp. Adminstrs., Am. Hosp. Assn., Am. Protestant Hosp. Assn., Mo. Hosp. Assn. (chmn. bd. 1976-77). Presbyterian. Club: Hickory Hills. Lodges: Masons; Shriners; Rotary. Home: 1701 S Kimbrough Springfield MO 65807 Office: Lester E Cox Med Center 1423 N Jefferson St Springfield MO 65802

WORTMAN, ALLEN L., lay worker, music educator; b. Le Claire, Iowa, Jan. 7, 1935; s. Verne Victor and Lenore M. (Coulter) W.; m. Bette Arlene Outland, June 17, 1961; children: Joel Allen, Michelle Marie. BA, Cen. Coll., Pella, iowa, 1957; MA, U. No. Colo., 1962, EdD, 1967. Dir. choir Meth. Ch., Colo, Iowa, 1957-61; dir. music Presbyn. Ch., Pocatello, Idaho, 1963-64, United Ch. Can. St. Andrews, Regina, Sask., 1964-66; dir. music, lay leader 1st Presbyn. Ch., Mankato, Minn., 1966—; prof. music Mankato State U., 1966—; mem. ministerial relations com. Mankaty Presbytery, 1968-70. Commr. Presbyn. Gen. Assembly, Phoenix, 1984; mem. vocations com. Presbytery of Minn. Valleys, Willmor, 1984—. Mem. Am. Guild English Handbell Ringers (chmn. area VII 1984-86), Music Educators Nat. Conf., Am. Choral Dirs. Assn. Democrat. Lodges: Kiwanis (bd. dirs. Mankato club 1984-86). Avocations: tennis, golfing, photography. Home: 24 Southview Dr Mankato MN 56001 Office: Mankato State U Music Dept Manakto MN 56001

WOSKOFF, SCOTT DAVID, software systems engineer; b. Omaha, Oct. 30, 1957; s. Walter Paul amd Sara Rose (Kadis) W.; m. Sara Ann Shutkin, Sept. 14, 1986. BS in Biochemistry, U. Iowa, 1980, MS in Elec. and Computer Engring., 1982. Software systems engr. Gen. Electric Med. Systems, Milw., 1982—. Author: Texture Analysis in Two-Dimensional Echocardiography, 1982. Mem. Assn. Computing Machines. Avocations: amateur radio, cross country skiing, hiking. Office: Gen Elec Med Systems PO Box 414 W-824 Milwaukee WI 53201

WOYTHAL, CONSTANCE LEE, psychologist, consultant; b. Milw., Nov. 6, 1954; d. Gerald Clarence and Shirley Estelle (Gross) W.; m. John Francis Neisius, Mar. 20, 1982; 1 child, Adam. BS, U. Wis., Milw., 1976; MS in Edn., U. Wis., River Falls, 1978; postgrad., Alfred Adler Inst., Chgo., 1980, George Williams Coll., 1984, Marquette U., 1984, Cardinal Stritch Coll., 1987. Cert. sch. psychologist, Wis. Psychologist Sch. Dist. of Marshfield, Wis., 1978-81; psychologist Sheboygan County Handicapped Children's Edn. Bd., Sheboygan Falls, Wis., 1981—, devel. and coordinator wellness program, 1984—; workshop facilitator Marshfield Clinic, 1981; cons. wellness lifestyle program Schs. of Sheboygan County, 1985—; lectr. profl. groups. Mem. Nat. Assn. Sch. Psychologists, Nat. Wellness Assn., N.Am. Soc. Adlerian Psychologists, Wis. Sch. Psychology Assn., Sheboygan Wellness Assn. (bd. dirs. 1984—), Mental Health Assn. Avocations: swimming, singing, hiking, cross country skiing, stereophile. Home: 2239 N 27th Pl Sheboygan WI 53083 Office: Sheboygan County Handicapped Edn Bd 111 1st St Sheboygan Falls WI 53085 also: Riverview Sch Smith St Plymouth WI 53073

WOZNAK, GEORGE BRIAN, information resource management consultant; b. Cleve., Dec. 13, 1949; s. Walter George and Eva (Popick) W.; m. Diana Victoria Lesniak, Nov. 18, 1978; 1 child, Jonathan George. B.S. in Bus. Adminstrn., Ohio State U., 1971; M.B.A., Baldwin Wallace Coll., 1977; cert. Case Western Res. U., 1984. Cert. industry cons., AT&T. Industry cons. Ohio Bell Telephone Co., Cleve., 1980-83; mktg. mgr. AT&T Info. Systems, Cleve., 1983-84; mgmt. cons. Price Waterhouse, 1984—; cons. various orgns. and corps. Developer and leader seminar: Control of Operating Expenses in Mfg. Facilities: A Corporate Focus for the 1980's. Mem. Pres.'s Club Ohio Bell Telephone Co., 1982, Regional Leaders' Club, AT&T Info Systems, 1983. Mem. Am. Mktg. Assn., Soc. Telecommunications Profls., Greater Cleve. Growth Assn. Club: Univ. (Cleve.). Home: 8661 Dunbar Ln Brecksville OH 44141 Office: Price Waterhouse 1900 Society Bank Bldg Cleveland OH 44114

WOZNIAK, JOHN ANTHONY, accountant; b. Stevens Point, Wis., Apr. 7, 1952; s. John Casimir and Bernardine C. (Prais) W.; m. Cheryl Lynn Wulff, June 28, 1980; children: Thaddeus John, Nathan William. BBA in Acctg., U. Wis., 1977. CPA, Wis. Ops. auditor Mobil Oil Corp., Chgo., 1977-79; ops. controller hose and couplings div. Imp-Clevite, Manitowoc, Wis., 1979-84; pvt. practice acctg. Mequon, Wis., 1984—. Served with U.S. Army, 1972-74. Mem. Am. Inst. CPA's, Wis. Inst. CPA's, Am. Legion. Roman Catholic. Avocations: reading, travel, computers. Office: 11512 N Port Washington Rd Mequon WI 53092

WOZNY, CAROL ANN, computer programmer, consultant; b. Chgo., July 13, 1952; d. Eugene Alexander and Sophie V. (Kicmal) W. BA in Art, Northeastern Ill. U., 1977, BS in Computer Sci., 1984. Night auditor League Club of Chgo., 1984-86, programmer, 1986—; cons., software trainer. Turnkey Bus. Computers, Chgo., 1984—. zoo parent Brookfield (Ill.) Zool. Soc., 1980-86; material collector Battered Women's Shelter, Glen Ellyn, Ill., 1985-86. Mem. Catholic Alumni Club (bd. dirs. 1985), Vietnam Vets. Club (bd. dirs. 1976). Avocations: volleyball, furniture refinishing, Hawaiian dancing.

WRIGHT, BARBARA ANN, pharmacist; b. Wichita, Kans., Mar. 12, 1948; d. Kenneth Eugene and Agnes Arlene (Meade) Boyle; m. Joseph Phillip Wright; children: Kendra Anne, Joseph Kevin. BS in Pharmacy, U. Kans., 1972. Registered pharmacist, Kans., Mo. Lab. tech. Chemagro Corp., Kansas City, Mo., 1968-69, Alza Corp., Lawrence, Kans., 1962-72; retail pharmacist Russell Pharmacies, Leavenworth, Kans., 1972-73; hosp. pharmacist Cushing Hosp., Leavenworth, 1973-78; dir. pharmacy Springfield (Mo.) Park Cen., 1978-79; pharmacist St. John's Regional Hosp., Springfield, 1979—. Mem. house mgmt. com. Helping Parents Cope, Springfield, 1985—. Mem. Ozark Soc. Hosp. Pharmacists (membership del., bd. dirs.), Mo. Soc. Hosp. Pharmacists (affiliate bd. dirs.), Am. Soc. Hosp. Pharmacist, Springfield Dist. Pharm. Assn. Republican. Presbyterian. Avocation: reading. Office: St John's Regional Health Ctr 1235 E Cherokee Springfield MO 65804

WRIGHT, BARBARA ANNE, county official; b. Cedar Rapids, Iowa, Dec. 11, 1941; d. Daniel Dean and Shirley Ann (O'Rourke) Lemon; m. Kenneth E. Wright; children—Kip, Kevin, Anne. B.S., Mt. Mercy Coll., 1966. Mem. Maquoketa (Iowa) City Council, 1972-76; mayor pro-tem, Maquoketa, 1974-76; mem. Jackson County (Iowa) Bd. Adjustment, 1976-82; Jackson County supr., 1982—. Mem. Sacred Heart Sch. Bd., Maquoketa. Democrat. Roman Catholic. Club: Univ. Women. Office: Court House Maquoketa IA 52060

WRIGHT, BENJAMIN DRAKE, education and behavioral sciences educator; b. Wilkes Barre, Pa., Mar. 30, 1926; s. Harold St. Clair and Dorothy Lynde (Wadhams) W.; m. Claire Marie Engelmann, sept. 9, 1948; children: Amy Engelmann, Sara Dobbs, Christopher Edward, Andrew Wadhams. BS, Cornell U., 1947; cert., Chgo. Inst. Psychoanalysis, 1953; PhD, U. Chgo., 1957. Lic. psychologist, Ill. Physics researcher Bell Telephone Laboratory, Murray Hill, N.J., 1947; physics researcher U. Chgo., 1947-50, therapist Orthogenic Sch., 1950-56, prof. edn., 1956—, prof. behavioral sci., 1960—; cons. Nat. Bd. Med. Examiners, Phila., 1975—, Hines VA Hosp., Chgo., 1980-85, Nat. Council State Bds. Nursing, Chgo., 1985—. Author: Best Test Design, 1979, Rating Scale Analysis, 1982, Conversational Statistics, 1984; editor: Learning Environment, 1974, Sch. Rev., 1969-78. Served with USN, 1944-46. Mem. Am. Ednl. Research Assn. Club: Quadrangle. Home: 5721 Harper Ave Chicago IL 60637 Office: U Chgo 5835 Kimbark Ave Chicago IL 60637

WRIGHT, CHARLES FREDERICK, manufacturing company executive; b. Milw., July 22, 1950; s. William Charles and Jean (Warren) W.; m. Linda Christine Ritchie, Nov. 17, 1984; 1 child, Charles Frederick Jr. BA, U. S. Fla., 1973; MBA, Harvard U., 1977. Gen. mgr. Lemco Plastics, Inc., Milw., 1973-75; exec. v.p. Fall River (Wis.) Foundry Co., Inc., 1977-79; pres. Fall River Group, Mequon, Wis., 1979—; bd. dirs. U-Line Corp, Milw.; mem. Chgo. Mercantile Exchange. Treas. Goodwill Industries Milw. Area, Inc., 1981—; bd. dirs. Second Harvesters Wis., Milw., 1984—. Mem. Pvt. Industry Council Milw.. Club: Harvard Bus. Sch. Milw. Avocations: flying, tae kwon do. Office: Fall River Group Inc PO Box 40 Mequon WI 53092

WRIGHT, CLIFFORD DEAN, immunologist, researcher; b. Chgo., June 30, 1954; s. Kenneth Dean and Florence (Percival) W.; m. Diane Maria Van Haren, Aug. 20, 1976; children: Christian Corbett, David Eaton, John Halliday, Elizabeth Anne. BS, Brigham Young U., 1977, MS, 1979; PhD, U. Minn., 1983. Research assoc. Parke-Davis Pharm. Research div. Warner-Lambert Co., Ann Arbor, Mich., 1983—. Contbr. articles to sci. jours. Eli Lilly predoctoral fellow, Eli Lilly Co., 1981-83. Mem. Am. Soc. Microbiology, Am. Soc. Cell Biology. Mormon. Office: Warner-Lambert Co 2800 Plymouth Rd Ann Arbor MI 48105

WRIGHT, CRAIG, state justice; b. Chillicothe, Ohio, June 21, 1929; s. Harry and Marjorie (Riddle) W.; m. Jane LaFollette, Nov. 3, 1951; children: Marjorie Jane, Alice Ann. B.A., U. Ky., 1951; LL.B., Yale U., 1954. Ptnr. Wright, Gilbert & Jones, Columbus, 1957-70; judge Franklin County Common Pleas Ct., 1971-83; assoc. justice Ohio Supreme Ct., Columbus, 1985—. Trustee Columbus Area Council on Alcoholism, 1959-83; chmn. bd. House of Hope-Halfway House, Columbus, 1960-68; trustee Gray Brethren Ch., Columbus, 1966-81, Worthington Christian Sch., Ohio, 1974-78, St. Anthony's Med. Ctr. Served with CIC, U.S. Army, 1955-56. Recipient cert. of excellence Ohio Supreme Ct., 1972-83. Mem. ABA (state rep. jud. div. 1975-83), Ohio Bar Assn. (chmn. lawyers assistance com. 1977-84), Ohio Common Pleas Judges Assn. (exec. bd. 1972-83), Columbus Bar Assn., Am. Judicature Soc. Republican. Clubs: Columbus Country, Athletic of Columbus. Avocations: golf; duplicate bridge. Home: 443 Country Club Rd Columbus OH 43213 Office: Ohio Supreme Ct 30 E Broad St Columbus OH 43215 *

WRIGHT, CREIGHTON BOLTER, cardiovascular surgeon, educator; b. Washington, Jan. 29, 1939; s. Benjamin Washington and Catherine Adele (Bolter) W.; m. Carolyn Eleanor Craver, Jan. 29, 1966; children—Creighton Bolter, Benson, Kathryn, Elizabeth. B.A., Duke U., 1961, M.D., 1965. Diplomate Am. Bd. Thoracic Surgery, Am. Bd. Surgery, subbd. Gen. Vascular Surgery. Intern, Duke U., Durham, N.C., 1965-66; resident in surgery U. Va., Charlottesville, 1966-71; from asst. prof. to assoc. prof. George Washington U., 1974-76; assoc. prof., then prof. surgery U. Iowa, 1976-81; prof. clin. surgery U. Cin., also clin. prof. surgery Uniformed Services U., 1981—. Served to col. USAR, 1966—. Decorated Meritorious Service medal; recipient Kindred Resident Teaching award, 1967, Golden Apple Teaching award, 1975. Mem. Assn. Acad. Surgery (pres. 1980), Central Surg. Assn., Soc. Univ. Surgeons, Soc. Vascular Surgery, Internat. Soc. Cardiovascular Surgery, Muller Surg. Soc. (pres. 1985-87), Am. Assn. Thoracic Surgery, Soc. Thoracic Surg, So. Thoracic Surg. Assn., Midwestern Vascular Surg. Soc., Alpha Omega Alpha, Sigma Chi. Editor: Vascular Grafting, 1983; (with others) Venous Trauma, 1983; contbr. articles to profl. jours., chpts. to books. Home: 1242 Edwards Rd Cincinnati OH 45208 Office: Services U 2139 Auburn Ave Cincinnati OH 45219

WRIGHT, DIANNE ELAINE, employee assistance program manager; b. Saginaw, Mich., Jan. 30, 1940; s. Donald Harvey McLaren and Leota Anna (Honold) Reed; m. Leo Cowan, June 13, 1958 (div. July 1967); children: Julie L., Mark R. BA in Mgmt. of Human Resources, Spring Arbor Coll., 1984. Lic. social worker, Mich.; cert. addictions counselor, 1982. Psychiat. adminstr. Inst. for Mental Health, Flint, Mich., 1967-77; employee assistance coordinator Gen. Motors Corp., Flint, 1977—; Bd. dirs. Soc. to Overcome Drug Abuse Among Teens, Inc., Flint, 1978-80, PACE, Inc., Owosso, Mich., 1983-84, Intake & Assessment Ctr., Flint, 1978-80. Author: Reaching Out, 1982. Bd. dirs. Clayton Stroup Found., 1986; mem. adv. bd. Mbr-Koala Ctr., Flint, 1987—. Mem. Assn. Labor and Mgmt. Cons. on Alcoholism (pres. Flint chpt. 1982-83), Assn. for Substance Abuse Prevention (com. chairperson Flint chpt. 1982—), Mich. Assn. Alcoholism and Drug Abuse Counselors. Avocations: golf, gardening, reading, travel, vol. work. Home: 1002 Fremont St Flint MI 48504 Office: Buick Olds Cadillac Flint Product Team 902 E Hamilton Flint MI 48550

WRIGHT, DONALD RAYMOND, gynecologist, obstetrician; b. Indpls., June 15, 1948; s. Donald Eugene Wright and Linda Jane (Pollard) Johnson; m. Julia Ann Donner, Aug. 15, 1970; children: Jeffrey Scott, Chad Andrew. AB, Ind. U., 1971; MS, Ind. U. Med. Sch., Indpls., 1973, MD, 1977. Diplomate Am. Bd. Ob-Gyn. Intern Meth. Hosp. Grad. Ctr., Indpls., 1977-78, resident in ob-gyn, 1978-81; practice medicine specializing in ob-gyn Indpls., 1981—; resident physician rep. AMA, Saint Louis, 1980; bd. dirs. antenatal testing St. Vincent's Hosp., Indpls., 1984-86. Coach Youth Soccer League, Zionsville, Ind., 1984-86, Youth Baseball League, Zionsville, 1984-86. Fellow Am. Coll. Ob-Gyn. Republican. Clubs: Greenbriar Racquet (Indpls.); Traders Point Hunt (Zionsville). Avocations: sailing, racquetball, horseback riding, fishing, fox hunting. Home: 9599 Huntclub Zionsville IN 46077 Office: 2010 W 86th St Indianapolis IN 46260

WRIGHT, FELIX E., manufacturing company executive; b. 1936. Student, East Tex. State U., 1959. With Leggett & Platt, Inc., Carthage, Mo., 1959—, sr. v.p., from 1976, now chief operating officer, exec. v.p., dir. Office: Leggett & Platt Inc 1 Leggett Rd Carthage MO 64836 *

WRIGHT, FLORA LOU, social worker, psychotherapist; b. Eagle Butte, S.D., July 29, 1938; d. Carroll Edward and Elsie Fay (Ruffcorn) W. BA in Sociology and Psychology magna cum laude, Yankton Coll., 1966; MSW, U. Ill., 1968. Cert. social worker, Ill. Caseworker I Family Care Services, Chgo., 1968-82, dir. Foster Care, Adoption, 1982—; therapist Child Psychiatry Assn., Chgo., 1975-78; presenter various workshops, 1973-83. Poll watcher local Dem. precinct, Chgo., 1970; fundraiser State Rep. Candidate, 1974; Sunday sch. tchr. United Ch. of Christ, 1972-76. U.S. Children's Bur. grantee, 1966. Mem. Nat. Assn. Social Workers, Child Care Assn. Ill. Presbyterian. Avocations: photography, decorating, skiing, sailing, hiking. Home: 400 E Randolph Apt 3011 Chicago IL 60601 Office: Family Care Services Met Chgo 234 S Wabash Chicago IL 60604

WRIGHT, GEORGE WILLIAM, computer systems designer; b. Akron, Ohio, Jan. 24, 1940; s. Joseph Wesley and Betty Jane (Jones) W.; m. Sandra Elsie Bush, Aug. 28, 1964 (div. Feb. 1985); children: Joseph E., Matthew J., Michael W.; m. Linda Lou Kietzman, Aug. 10, 1985. Grad., Tabor Acad., Marion, Mass., 1958; student, Cornell U., 1958, Coll. DuPage, 1970, Rook Valley Coll., 1978; cert. in data processing, Inst. for Cert. of Computer Profls., Des Plaines, Ill., 1986. Programmer Aerovox Corp., New Bedford, Mass., 1959-61; programmer, analyst Arlans Dept. Stores, New Bedford, 1961-62; systems analyst Montgomery Ward & Co., Chgo., 1964-76; sr. analyst Barber-Colman Co., Rockford, Ill., 1977—; pres. Belvidere (Ill.) Parachute Ctr. Inc., 1974-76. treas. North Boone United Meth. Parish, Poplar Grove, Ill., 1981-83. Served with U.S. Army, 1963-64. Mem. Data Processing Mgmt. Assn. Republican. Methodist. Avocations: sport, history, the arts. Home: 910 Windsor Rd Loves Park IL 61111 Office: Barber-Colman Co Environ Controls Div 1354 Clifford Ave Loves Park IL 61132

WRIGHT, GORDON LEE, oil company executive; b. New Martinsville, W.Va., Sept. 11, 1942; s. Irvin Russell and Iris Justina (Kincaid) W.; m. Mary Susan Akers, June 25, 1966; children: Rebecca, Roberta. BS in Petroleum Engring., W.Va. U., 1965. Petroleum engr. Gulf Oil Corp., Evansville, Ind., 1968-69; gen. engr. Consumer's Power Co., Jackson, Mich., 1969-73, gas contract supr., 1973-77; div. mgr. Reef Petroleum Corp., St. Clair, Mich., 1977-78; ops. mgr. NOMECO, Jackson, 1978-81, v.p. ops., 1981—; mem. adv. com. petroleum program Jackson Community Coll., 1982. Mem. Rep. Nat. Com., Washington, 1981—. Served to 1st. lt. U.S. Army, 1966-68, Vietnam. Mem. Soc. Petroleum Engrs. (bd. dirs. 1974-77), Ind. Petroleum Assn. Am., Mich. Oil and Gas Assn. (chmn. gen. practices com. 1977-81, chmn. special ad hoc com. 1981-83, bd. dirs. 1984—), Tulsa Petroleum Club. Republican. Clubs: Town (Jackson), Devils Lake Yacht (Manitou Beach, Mich.). Lodge: Masons. Home: 4381 Scott Carpenter Jackson MI 49201 Office: NOMECO 1 Jackson Sq Jackson MI 49204

WRIGHT, HAROLD DALE, minister; b. Hackberry, La., Jan. 16, 1935; s. Cecil Earl and Lucette (Lejeune) W.; m. Barbara Jean Cockrell, Sept. 26, 1955. BA, La. Coll., 1955; BD, New Orleans Bapt. Theol. Sem., 1959, ThD, 1964. Pastor Harmony Bapt. Ch., Deville, La., 1953-54, Lakeshore (Miss.) Bapt. Ch., 1959-65; assoc. dir. dept. pastoral care So. Bapt. Hosp., New Orleans, 1965-74; dir. dept. pastoral care Bapt. Med. Ctr., Kansas City, Mo., 1975—; mem. supplementary faculty Notre Dame Sem., New Orleans, 1971-75; contract tchr. William Carey Coll., Hattiesburg, Miss., 1971-75; supr. pastoral and ednl. ministry Midwestern Bapt. Theol. Sem., Kansas City, 1975-85. Contbr. articles to profl. jours. Mem. instl. rev. bd. Kansas City Clin. Oncology Program, 1985—. Recipient Cert. Merit, Greater New Orleans Fedn. Chs., 1970. Fellow Coll. of Chaplains Am. Protestant Health Assn. (pres. 1982); mem. Protestant Health and Welfare Assembly (chmn. 1985-86), Assn. Clin. Pastoral Edn., Inc. (cert. supr.), Mo. Chaplains Assn., La. Chaplains Assn. (hon. life) (pres. 1972-74, Outstanding Service award, commendation, 1975). Democrat. Lodges: Kiwanis, Masons. Avocations: photography, flower gardening. Home: 201 W 70 St Kansas City MO 64113 Office: Bapt Med Ctr 6601 Rockhill Rd Kansas City MO 64131

WRIGHT, HELEN KENNEDY, editor, librarian; b. Indpls., Sept. 23, 1927; d. William Henry and Ida Louise (Crosby) Kennedy; m. Samuel A. Wright, Sept. 5, 1970; 1 child, Carl F. Prince (dec.). BA, Butler U., 1945, MS, 1950; MS, Columbia U., 1952. Prince II. Reference librarian N.Y. Pub. Library, N.Y.C., 1952-53, Bklyn. Pub. Library, 1953-54; cataloger U. Utah, 1954-57; librarian Chgo. Pub. Library; asst. dir. pub. dept. ALA, Chgo., 1958-62, editor Reference Books Bull., 1962-85; asst. dir. for new product planning, pub. services, 1985—. Contbr. to Ency. of Careers, Ency. of Library and Info. Sci., New Book of Knowledge Ency., Bulletin of Bibliography. Mem. Phi Kappa Phi, Kappa Delta Pi, Sigma Gamma Rho. Roman Catholic. Home: 1138 W 111th St Chicago IL 60643 Office: Am Library Assn 50 E Huron Chicago IL 60611

WRIGHT, JAMES EDWARD, sports physiologist, military officer; b. Little Rock, Sept. 6, 1946; s. Lois Ormand and Elizabeth Angeline (Kaczka) W.; m. Loraine P. Gaylord, July 28, 1966; children: James Edward II, Jesse Geylord. Student, Tulane U., 1964-66; BS, Fairleigh Dickinson U., 1969; PhD, Miss. State U., 1973. Asst. prof. Simon's Rock Early Coll., Great Barrington, Mass., 1973-75; NIH postdoctoral fellow, asst. research physiologist Inst. Environ. Stress, U. Calif., Santa Barbara, 1975-77; commd. capt. U.S. Army, 1977; advanced through grades to maj. 1985; research physiologist Army Research Inst. Environ. Medicine, Natick, Mass., 1977-82; comdg. officer B Co., 48th Med. Bn., 2d Armored Div., Ft. Hood, Tex., 1983-84; exec. officer, chief exercise sch. br. health fitness ctr. Hawley Army Hosp. and Soldier Phy. Fitness Sch., Ft. Harrison, Ind., 1985—; cons. in field. Author: Anabolic Steroids in Sports, vol. I, 1978, vol. II, 1982; contbr. numerous articles, abstracts, reports on exercise and environ. physiology and numerous trade jour. articles on athletic tng. Mem. Am. Coll. Sports Medicine, Internat. Council Phys. Fitness Research (corr.), Nat. Strength and Conditioning Assn. (research com. 1982ú, assoc. editor jour., 1982—), U.S. Power Lifting Fedn. (sports medicine com. 1982—). Republican. Jewish. Home: 7146 Hawks Hill Rd Indianapolis IN 46236-3117 Office: Health Fitness Ctr HACH Fort Harrison IN 46216-0007

WRIGHT, JAMES HOUSTON, evangelist, marriage and family counselor; b. Oak Ridge, Tenn., Oct. 10, 1954; s. Olney Houston and Nora Ann (Waters) W.; m. Deborah Gail Foote, Dec. 29, 1973; children: Daniel, Elizabeth, Richard. BA, David Lipscomb Coll., Nashville, 1976; MA, Middle Tenn. State U., Murfreesboro, 1981. Intern minister Mayfair Ch. of Christ, Huntsville, Ala., 1974, Ch. of Christ, Williston, S.D., 1975; evangelist Sycamore Chapel Ch. of Christ, Ashland City, Tenn., 1975-81; pvt. practice marriage and family counseling Ashland City, Tenn., 1981, Indpls., 1982—; evangelist N. Cen. Ch. of Christ, Indpls., 1982—; psychol. cons. Cheatham County Bd. Edn., Ashland City, 1979-81; dir. Wabashi Valley Youth Camp, Terre Haute, Ind., 1982—; co-dir. Mid-Am. Evang. Workshop, Indpls., 1984, dir., 1985. Chaplain Ashland City Civitan, 1980, pres. 1981. Recipient Best Sermon award Cheatham Soil Conservation Dist., 1976; named one of Outstanding Young Men of Am., U.S. Jaycees, 1980, 83, 85. Mem. Ch. of Christ. Lodge: Lions (chaplain Indpls. club 1983-84). Avocations: reading, woodworking, writing, camping. Home: 2440 E 91st St Indianapolis IN 46240 Office: N Cen Ch of Christ 9015 Westfield Blvd Indianapolis IN 46240

WRIGHT, JAMES RUSSELL, veterinarian; b. Pontiac, Mich., Aug. 13, 1946; s. Alvin and Alice (Forbes) W.; m. Janice Mae Bales, Sept. 8, 1967. B.S., Mich. State U., 1968; D.V.M., 1969. Staff orthopedic and neurosurgeon Gasow Vet. Hosp., Birmingham, Mich., 1969—. Evans Scholars scholar 1966-68. Contbr. numerous articles to various publs. Mem. Southeastern Vet. Med. Assn. (pres. 1981-82), Veterinary Orthopedic Soc. (bd. dirs. 1981-83), Am. Vet. Med. Assn., Mich. Vet. Med. Assn., Southeastern Mich. Vet. Med. Assn. (Outstanding Contbn. to Clin. Practice award 1984), Oakland County Vet. Med. Assn., Mich. State U. Alumni Assn. (council mem. 1985-89), Evans Scholars Alumni Assn. Republican. Lutheran. Home: 2540 Yorkshire St Birmingham MI 48008 Office: 1521 N Woodward Birmingham MI 48008

WRIGHT, JAMES WILLIAM, data processing executive, educator; b. Decatur, Ill., Mar. 21, 1946; s. James William Wright and Irene (Slaughter) Guthrie; m. Treva Clarice Jackson, June 17, 1967; children: James W. III, Cyrus B., Eric J., Linda J., Kimberly M., Melba I., Stacy L. BS in Indsl. Engring., Millikin U., 1969. Systems analyst Caterpillar Inc., East Peoria, Ill., 1969-74; instr. systems sci. Caterpillar Inc., East Peoria, 1974-76, applications analyst, 1976-78, sr. analyst, 1978-79, project leader, 1979—; instr. programming Ill. Cen. Coll., East Peoria, 1975-76; cons. Urban League, Peoria, Ill, 1985—. Bd. dirs., treas. Counseling and Family Services, Peoria, 1979; decon, treas. Zion Bapt. Ch., Peoria, 1980; dir. Christian Edn., 1986. Mem. Am. Inst. Indsl. Engrs., Alpha Kappa Psi. Avocations: camping, karate, racquetball. Home: 3111 W Forsythe Rd Peoria IL 61614 Office: Caterpillar Inc 600 W Washington East Peoria IL 61630

WRIGHT, JEFFREY CHAPMAN, manufacturing company executive; b. Toledo, Aug. 28, 1939; s. Benjamin S. and Ione J. (Chapman) W.; m. Judith Ann Allred, June 5, 1965. BA, Yale U., 1962. Dir. internat. sales Am. Motors Corp., Southfield, Mich., 1976-77, gen. mgr. European and African divs., 1978-79; v.p. internat. div. Am. Gen. Corp., Detroit, 1979-83; v.p. mktg. Am. Gen. Corp., Livonia, Mich., 1983-85, v.p. bus. devel., 1985—; pres. Arab Am. Vehicles, Cairo, 1977-78. Republican. Home: 494 Aspen Birmingham MI 48009

WRIGHT, JERRY DUANE, architect; b. Flint, Mich., Jan. 1, 1942; s. Merle James and Bernadine Marie (Usher) W.; m. Jacqueline Joyce Jaster, July 31, 1965; children: Teri Ann, Jon David. BArch, U. Mich., 1965. Registered architect, Mich., Ind., Okla., Calif. Field adminstr. Giffels Assocs., Detroit, 1970-75; owner, architect Jerry D. Wright and Assocs., Kalamazoo, 1975-80; project architect James Foug and Assocs., Redwood City, Calif., 1980-82; specification writer Hansen Lind Meyer, Iowa City, Iowa, 1982-84; head specification dept. The Kling Partnership, Phila., 1984-86, Tomblinson and Harburn, Flint, 1986—. Author or editor specification master construction manuals, 1982-87. Dir. Am. Youth Soccer Orgn., Kalamazoo, 1975-80, head ofcl., San Mateo, Calif., 1980-82; planning commr. Portage (Mich.) Planning Commn., 1978; worker, coach Spl. Olympics, Tex. and Mich., 1985—. Mem. AIA, Constrn. Specifiations Inst. (bd. dirs. 1987, charter organizer, 1982-84). Lodge: Elks. Avocations: abstract painting, soccer, tennis, sailing, carpentry. Office: Tomblinson Harburn & Assocs 705 Kelso St Flint MI 48506

WRIGHT, JOHN EDWARD, marketing executive; b. Columbus, Ohio, July 30, 1935; s. Merrill J. and Lucille Marie (Lawyer) W.; m. Betty Jane Evans, Feb. 16, 1961 (dec. Mar. 1979); m. Nancy Ann Deaton, Aug. 16, 1980. Grad., North High Sch., Columbus, 1953. Cert. form cons. Store mgr. Albers Super Markets, Columbus and Hillsboro (Ohio), 1953-64; order entry clk. Rotary Forms Press., Inc., Hillsboro, 1965-79, corp. mktg. mgr., 1979—. Me. Am. Mktg. Assn., Nat. Bus. Forms Assn. (from state to nat. membership chmn. 1982—, Mem. of Yr. award 1986). Republican. Lodge: KT, Knights of York Cross of Honor, Masons, Order Eastern Star. Avocation: camping. Home: 10421 US Rt 50 Hillsboro OH 45133 Office: Rotary Forms Press Inc 835 S High St Hillsboro OH 45133

WRIGHT, MARVIN GENE, dentist; b. Greenburg, Ind., Oct. 21, 1941; s. Sheldon R. and Opal F. (Clapp) W.; m. Lucretia Jean Beck, July 21, 1962; children: Nancy Joann, Josef Marvin, Jill Marie. BS in Chemistry, Butler U., 1963; DDS, Ind. U., Indpls., 1966. Assoc. R.N. Greer, DDS, Greenfield, Ind., 1966; gen. practice dentistry Wabash, Ind., 1966-74, 81—; sr. practitioner Wabash Dental Group, 1974-81; dental staff Wabash County Hosp., 1967—, chmn. dental staff, 1986. Tchr. Wabash Christian Ch., 1971—, chmn. bd. dirs., 1976-77; bd. dirs. Wabash County United Fund, 1969-70. Mem. ADA, Ind. Dental Assn., Grant County Dental Soc., Wabash Valley Dental Soc. (pres. 1972), Acad. Gen. Dentistry, No. Ind. Soc. Occlusal Studies (pres. 1985—). Republican. Lodge: Optimist (pres. Wabash cpht. 1970, 86, lt. gov. state dist. 1978). Avocations: golf, hunting, fishing, photography, greenhouse work. Home: 250 Hale Dr Wabash IN 46992 Office: 900 Manchester Ave Wabash IN 46992

WRIGHT, MICHAEL WAYNE, architect; b. Marshall, Mo., May 31, 1956; s. Fred L. and Ann R. (Smith) Wright. B in Environ. Design, U. Kans., 1978, BArch, 1979. Lic. profl. architect, Ill., Mo. Architect Wedemeyer, Cernik, and Cornbia, St. Louis, 1979; project architect Mackey and Assocs., St. Louis, 1979-84; project mgr., mgr. br. office Mackey and Assocs., Kansas City, Mo., 1984—; mgr. ednl. renovation N.W. Mo. State U., 1986. Prin. works include: (interior design) Seven-Up Corp. Hdqrs., 1982, Masters & Johnson Inst., 1983, DeBaliviere Pl., 1983, Student Loan Mktg. Assn. (SALLIE MAE) 1986-87, USDA, 1987—. Com. mem. Riverfront Task Force, Kansas City, 1986, Midtown 2000, Kansas City, 1986. Mem. AIA. Democrat. Club: Kansas City. Home: 643 E 70th Terr Kansas City MO 64131 Office: Mackey and Assocs 101 E Armour Blvd Kansas City MO 64111

WRIGHT, MICHAEL WILLIAM, wholesale food company executive; b. Mpls., June 13, 1938; s. Thomas W. and Winifred M. Wright; m. Susan Marie Guzy. B.A., U. Minn., 1961, J.D. with honors, 1963. Ptnr. Dorsey & Whitney, Mpls., 1966-77; sr. v.p. Super Valu Stores, Inc., Mpls., 1977-78, pres., chief operating officer, 1978—, chief exec. officer, 1981—, chmn., 1982—; bd. dirs., dep. chmn. Fed. Res. Bank, Mpls.; bd. dirs. Deluxe Check Printers Mpls., Honeywell, Inc., Uniform Code Council, Food Mktg. Inst., Nat. Am. Wholesale Grocers Assn.; pres. Minn. Bus. Partnership; trustee U. Minn. Found. Trustee U. Minn. Found. Served as 1st lt. U.S. Army, 1964-66. Mem. Nat.-Am. Wholesale Grocers Assn. (bd. dirs.), Food Mktg. Inst. (bd. dirs.), Minn. Bus. Ptnrship (pres.). Office: Super Valu Stores Inc 11840 Valley View PO Box 990 Minneapolis MN 55440

WRIGHT, PATRICIA DONOVAN, communications executive; b. Rhinelander, Wis., Mar. 10, 1952; s. Stanley Timothy and Evelyn Mae (Smith) Donovan; m. Larry James Wright, May 17, 1980; 1 child, Lindsay Mae. BS, U. Wis., 1974. Writer Amoco Corp., Chgo., 1974-77; rep. pub., community relations Tex. Refining Co. Amoco Corp., Texas City, 1977-81; sr. pub. affairs advisor Amoco Corp., Kansas City, Mo., 1981-84; supr. media relations Amoco Corp., Chgo., 1984-86, dir. pub., govt. affairs, 1986—. Mem. Women In Communication (bd. dirs. Chgo. chpt., chmn. 1985-86, regional meeting chmn.; Clarion award 1977, Cub's Cup award 1977), Publicity Club Chgo. Avocations: golf, biking, tennis. Home: 1818 Glencoe Wheaton IL 60187 Office: Amoco Corp 200 E Randolph Dr MC 3707 Chicago IL 60601

WRIGHT, PAUL NATHAN, health care facility administrator; b. Greenville, Mich., Dec. 16, 1950; s. Roger Johnson and Mildred Ruth (Cottrell) W. A.S., Davenport Coll., Grand Rapids, Mich., 1971; hon. degree nursing home adminstrn. George Washington U., 1974. Custodian, Belding Christian Nursing Home, (Mich.), 1966-73, asst. adminstr., 1973, adminstr., 1973-76; adminstr. Maccabee Gardens, Saginaw, Mich., 1976-78, Beverly Manor, Grand Blanc, Mich., 1978-80; adminstr., chief exec. officer Grand Blanc Convalescent Ctr., 1980—. Past charter mem. Rep. Presdl. Task Force; past mem. Rep. Nat. Com., U.S. Senatorial Club; mem. Holy Redeemer Choir. Mem. Health Care Assn. of Mich. (regional dir., legal services com., nominations com. 1985-86, conv. chmn. 1987), Genesee, Lapeer, Shiawasee Adminstrs. Council, Am. Coll. Health Care Adminstrs. (treas., fin. com., pres. Mich. chpt. 1987—), Flint Area Health Found. (edn. com.), Social Work Discharge Planning Com. (nursing home rep., ECF grant adv. com.), Am. Security Council (nat. adv. bd.). Roman Catholic. Lodge: Rotary (pres. Grand Blanc chpt. 1987). Home: 6042 Westknoll Dr A550 Grand Blanc MI 48439 Office: Grand Blanc Convalescent Center 8481 Holly Rd Grand Blanc MI 48439

WRIGHT, PETER ANTHONY, accountant; b. Kingston, Jamaica, Aug. 24, 1953; came to U.S., 1976; s. Brian Garnet O'Brien and Ethline Mary (Reid) W.; m. Vicki Louise Heichel, June 15, 1974; children: Matthew O'Brien, Tiffany Deanne. BBA, U. Wis., Whitewater, 1979. CPA, Wis. Asst. ops. officer Bank Am./Mcht. Bank, Kingston, 1976; sr. audit staff Williams, Young & Hebert, Madison, 1979-81; mgr. factory acctg. and inventory control APV Crepaco Inc., Lake Mills, Wis., 1981—; bd. dirs. Caribake Inc., Ft. Atkinson, Wis. Mem. Am. Inst. CPA's, Wis. Inst. CPA's. Episcopalian. Club: Badger Bimmers (bd. dirs. Milw. chpt. 1984-87). Avocations: auto racing, woodworking. Office: APV Crepaco Inc 100 S CP Ave Lake Mills WI 53551

WRIGHT, PHILLIP J., engineering company executive; b. Danville, Ill., Feb. 28, 1948; s. John B. and Edith L. (Grubbs) W. AS in Electronic Engrng. Tech., Ill. Inst. Tech., 1968; BS in Electronic Engring. Tech., Ind. No. U., 1970. Asst. station engr. Pub. Service Ind., Indpls., 1970-71; pres. Elinco Engring. Inc., Cayuga, Ind., 1971—; instr. Nat. Burglary and Fire Alarm Assn., 1986—. Inventor in field. Mem. Nat. Speakers Assn. Ind. Baptist. Home: 353 Wright Pl Cayuga IN 47928 Office: Elinco Engring Hwy 63 Cayuga IN 47928

WRIGHT, RAYMOND EUGENE, JR., computer science educator, consultant; b. Harlingen, Tex., Aug. 13, 1943; s. Raymond Eugene Sr. and Guadalupe (Soulas) W.; m. Margaret Mary Walsh, Feb. 10, 1962 (div. Nov. 1984); children: Rita, Ray III, Roger, Richard, Randy, Robin, Roxann, Russell; m. Barbara Rosamunda Siena, Dec. 29, 1984; stepchildren: Craig, Laura, Lisa. BS, Loyola U., Chgo., 1968, MBA, 1980. Cert. data processor. Pres. Suburban Computer Services, Palatine, Ill., 1970-72; systems analyst CPC Internat., Argo, Ill., 1973-77; mgmt. info. systems exec. Stone Container Corp., Chgo., 1977-81; prof., chmn. computer sci. dept. Roosevelt U., Chgo., 1981—; pres. Ray-Bar Enterprises, 1985—, R.E. Wright & Assocs., 1982—. Author: COBOL I for Business, 1983, COBOL II for Business, 1984, Small Business Application on IBM PC/XT, 1986. Mem. Data Processing Mgmt. Assn., Chgo. Indsl. Communications Assn., No. Officials Assn. Roman Catholic. Clubs: Northwest Classic Golf League (Palatine) (pres. 1983—), Twinbrook Golf League (Hoffman Estates) (sec. 1985—), Stonehenge Country. Avocations: golf, bridge, sports officiating, auctioneering. Home: 43 N Hale Palatine IL 60067 Office: Roosevelt U 430 S Michigan Chicago IL 60605

WRIGHT, RICHARD GEORGE, educator; b. Buffalo, Oct. 27, 1945; s. James Donald and Ethel Antonette (Denz) W.; m. Mary Carolyn Mills, Aug. 3, 1968; children: Rebecca Mary, Susana Mary. BA in Liberal Arts, SUNY, Buffalo, 1967; MS in Personnel Mgmt., SUNY, Albany, 1969; EdD in Higher Adult Edn. Adminstrn., Columbia U., 1976. Vis. prof. edn. Fed. U. Rio Grande do Sul, Brazil, 1976-80; dir. internat. admissions Bell & Howell Ednl. Group, Evanston, Ill., 1981-82; asst. prof. adult edn. Nat. Coll. Edn., Lombard, Ill., 1983—, chmn. dept. adult edn., 1985-86, chmn. Coll. Arts and Scis., 1986-87; chmn. Coll. Arts and Scis. Nat. Coll. Edn., Evanston, 1985—, chmn. Dept. Adult Edn., 1985—. Bd. dirs. ARC, North Cook County, 1984; project coordinator Experimental in Internat. Living, Chgo., 1985—; mem. Ptnrs. of the Ams., 1980—. Kellogg Found. fellow, 1974; recipient Latin Am. Teaching fellowship, 1976. Mem. Ill. Community Edn. Assn. (regional coordinator 1985-86), Am. Assn. for Continuing Edn., Am. Assn. Adult Continuing Edn. Home: 705 Lincoln St Glenview IL 60025 Office: Nat Coll Edn ABS Grad 2S361 Glenpark Rd Lombard IL 60148

WRIGHT, RODNEY H., architect; b. Valparaiso, Ind., June 2, 1931; s. George and Lena May (Cahoon) W.; m. Sydney Sullivan Goelitz, Feb. 16, 1966; children by previous marriage—Weston, Julie-An stepchildren—Louise Goelitz, Ann Goelitz, Thomas Goelitz. Grad. high sch. With various archtl. firms 1953-60, pvt. practice architecture, 1960—; former architect Hawkweed Group Ltd., Chgo.; sole propr. Rodney Wright & Assoc., Architecture & Planning; lectr Northwestern U., 1971; keynote speaker, First Solar Symposium, Sao Paulo, Brasil, 1976; presenter 1987 European Conference on Architecture, Munich, 1st/2d conf. How Successful Directors Manage, 1986-87. Bd. dirs. Lake County Urban League, 1961-69, chmn., 1961-65; bd. dirs. Uptown Devel. Ctr., Chgo., 1969-73 Served with U.S. Army, 1950-53. Design fellow Nat. Endowment for Arts, 1975. Fellow AIA (chpt. dir. 1971, co-chmn. task force 1 1969-72, mem. nat. com. community devel. ctrs. 1970-72). Pioneer in design of passive solar and superinsulated bldgs. Address: Route 4 Box 176B Osseo WI 54758

WRIGHT, ROGER WILLIAM, communications executive; b. Highland Park, Ill., July 14, 1954; s. George Nixon and Barbara (Dowd) w.; m. Julianne Lapczynski, June 14, 1986. BA in Psychology, Beloit Coll., 1976. Cert. secondary tchr., Ill. Counselor Northwestern Hosp., Chgo., 1976-77; tchr. Southern Sch., Chgo., 1978-79; dir. tng. Jobs for Youth, Inc., Chgo., 1979-82; mgmt. tng. cons. Walgreens Co., Deerfield, Ill., 1982-85; tng. project mgr. MCI Telecom, Chgo., 1985—; cons. Northern Trust, Chgo., 1979, Montgomery Wards, Chgo., 1980, McDonalds, Oakbrook, Ill., 1980. Mem. Nat. Soc. Performance and Instruction, Ill. Tng. and Devel. Office: MCI Telecom 205 N Michigan Ave Chicago IL 60601

WRIGHT, SARA ELIZABETH, psychologist; b. Aiken, S.C., May 4, 1950; d. Maurice Earl and Lily Ann (Winter) W.; m. Paul Conrad Rosenblatt, June 9, 1984; 1 child, Emily Carol Wright-Rosenblatt; 1 stepchild, Ira Rosenblatt. BS, U. Tex., 1972, MEd, 1975; PhD, U. Minn., 1985. Lic. psychologist, Minn. Coordinator Mid. Earth Drug Crisis Ctr., Austin, Tex., 1971-72; psychotherapist Austin-Travis County Mental Health-Mental Retardation, Austin, 1972-75; dir. emergency services Trinity Valley MHMR, Ft. Worth, 1975-78; program dir. Andrew, Inc., Mpls., 1978-79; family psychologist Dakota Ctr., South St. Paul, 1979—; Contbr. articles to profl. jours. Mem. Am. Assn. Marriage and Family Therapy (editor regional newsletter), Minn. Women Psychologists (steering com.), Nat. Council on Family Relations, Phi Kappa Phi, Kappa Delta Pi. Avocations: parenting, writing. Home: 1712 W Eldridge Roseville MN 55113 Office: Dakota Ctr 744 19th Ave N South Saint Paul MN 55075

WRIGHT, SCOTT KENNETH, historian, educator, author; b. St. Paul, Oct. 12, 1942; s. Orville Kenneth and Leona Clara (Lawrson) W.; m. Betty

Joan Tschida, Jan. 7, 1967; children: Rebecca, Rachel, Joseph, Adam. BA, U. Minn., 1963, MA, 1968, PhD, 1973. Acquisitions librarian Coll St. Thomas, St. Paul, 1968-71, assoc. dir. and reference librarian, 1971-74, library dir., 1974-80, asst. prof. history, 1980—; Fulbright lectr. Kyushu U. and Seinan Gakuin U., Fukuoka, Japan, 1979-80. Author: The Lynching of John Hanson, 1986; contbr. short stories to various literary mags. Mem. Am. Studies Assn., Orgn. Am. Historians, Popular Culture Assn. Democrat. Roman Catholic. Home: 2136 Dayton Av Saint Paul MN 55104 Office: Coll St Thomas 2115 Summit Ave Saint Paul MN 55105

WRIGHT, SCOTT OLIN, federal judge; b. Haigler, Nebr., Jan. 15, 1923; s. Jesse H. and Martha I. W.; m. Shirley Frances Young, Aug. 25, 1972. Student, Central Coll., Fayette, Mo., 1940-42; LL.B., U. Mo., Columbia, 1950. Bar: Mo. 1950. City atty. Columbia, 1951-53; pros. atty. Boone County, Mo., 1954-58; practice of law Columbia, 1958-79; U.S. dist. judge Western Dist. Mo., Kansas City, 1979—. Pres. Young Democrats Boone County, 1950, United Fund Columbia, 1965. Served with USN, 1942-43; as aviator USMC, 1943-46. Decorated Air medal. Mem. ABA, Am. Trial Lawyers Assn., Mo. Bar Assn., Mo. Trial Lawyers Assn., Boone County Bar Assn. Unitarian. Clubs: Rockhill Tennis, Woodside Racquet. Lodge: Rotary (pres. Columbia 1965). Office: U S Dist Ct U S Courthouse 811 Grand Ave Room 613 Kansas City MO 64106 *

WRIGHT, SUZANNE KAY, dentist; b. Great Bend, Kans., Nov. 29, 1956; d. James Lynn and Margaret Louise (Lee) W.; m. Kevin Blane Johnson, Aug. 29, 1981. A in Applied Sci., Wichita State U., 1977, B in Gen. Studies, 1979; DDS, U. Mo., 1984. Dentist Wesley Med. Ctr., Wichita, Kans., 1984-85; practice gen. dentistry Wichita, 1985—. Served to 1st lt. USAR, 1982—. Mem. Acad. Gen. Dentistry, ADA, South Cen. Kans. Dental Study Club (sec. treas. 1985-86, pres. 1986—). Democrat. Avocations: jogging, travel, needlework. Home: 1612 Brendon Wood Derby KS 67037 Office: 2821 S Hydraulic Wichita KS 67216

WRIGHT, VERNON D., hotel company executive; b. Columbus, Ohio, Mar. 14, 1943; s. Vernon H. and Ruthann (Curfman) W.; m. Shirlene Bottjen, Oct. 14, 1972; children: Mark, Beth, Jennifer. Student, U. Cin., Ohio State U. V.p. ops. Pickett Hotel Co., Dublin, Ohio. Office: Pickett Hotel Co 555 N Metro Pl Suite 600 Dublin OH 43017

WRIGHT, W. S., provincial judge. Judge Ct. of Queen's Bench, Winnipeg, Man., Can. Office: Court of Queen's Bench, Law Courts Bldg, Winnipeg, MB Canada R3C 0V8 *

WRIGHT, WILLIAM THOMAS, psychologist; b. Winfield, Kans., Dec. 27, 1923; s. William Thomas and Sarah Gladys (Hatfield) W.; m. Betty Lou Weekly, Sept. 18, 1947; children: Claudia Ann, Thomas Brian, Alison Lynn. AB, Southwestern Coll., 1946; MS, Kans. State U., 1948; PhD, U. Denver, 1958. Lic. clin. psychologist, Kans. Staff psychologist Winfield (Kans.) State Hosp., 1950-51, Larned (Kans.) State Hosp., 1951-53; chief psychologist Hertzler Clinic, Halstead, Kans., 1953-56, 58-61; pvt. practice psychology Denver, 1956-58; chief clin. psychologist Prairie View, Inc., Newton, Kans., 1962—; asst. clin. prof. psychology med. sch. U. Kans. Wichita, 1984-86. Served with M.C. U.S. Army, 1942-46. Mem. Am. Psychol. Assn., Kans. Psychol. Assn., Sigma Xi. Lodge: Elks, Masons. Avocations: oil painting, boating, travel. Home: 1205 Parkwood Ln Newton KS 67114 Office: Prairie View Inc Box Hosp 356 Newton KS 67114

WRIGLEY, WILLIAM, corporation executive; b. Chgo., Jan. 21, 1933; s. Philip Knight and Helen Blanche (Atwater) W.; m. Alison Hunter, June 1, 1957 (div. 1969); children: Alison Elizabeth, Philip Knight, William.; m. Julie Burns, Nov. 28, 1981. Grad., Deerfield Acad., 1950; B.A., Yale, 1954. With Wm. Wrigley Jr. Co., Chgo., 1956—, v.p., 1960-61, pres., chief exec. officer, 1961—; dir. Wm. Wrigley Jr. Co., 1960—, Wrigley Philippines, Inc., Wrigley Co., Ltd. (U.K.), Wrigley N.V. (The Netherlands), Wrigley Co. (N.Z.), Ltd., Wrigley Co. Pty., Ltd. (Australia), The Wrigley Co. (H.K.) Ltd. (Hong Kong), Wrigley Co. (E. Africa) Ltd. (Kenya), Wrigley Co. S.A. (Spain), Wrigley & Co. Ltd., Japan; dir., mem. audit and exec. com., mem. com. non-mgmt. dirs., chmn. nominating com. Texaco Inc.; dir., mem. compensation com. Nat. Blvd. Bank of Chgo.; dir., mem. compensation com. Am. Home Products Corp.; dir., chmn. exec. com. Santa Catalina Island Co.; dir. Grocery Mfrs. Am., Inc. Bd. dirs. Wrigley Meml. Garden Found.; bd. dirs., mem. personnel com. Northwestern Meml. Hosp.; benefactor, mem. Santa Catalina Island Conservancy; mem. adv. bd. Center for Sports Medicine, Northwestern U. Med. Sch., 1976—; trustee Chgo. Latin Sch. Found., 1975—; dir. Geneva Lake Water Safety Com., 1966—, mem. exec. com., 1968—. Served from ensign to lt. (j.g.) USNR, 1954-56; now lt. comdr. Res. Mem. Navy League U.S., Chgo. Hist. Soc., Field Mus., Wolf's Head Soc., U. So. Calif. Oceanographic Assos., Catalina Island Museum Soc., Delta Kappa Epsilon. Clubs: Saddle and Cycle, Racquet, Chicago Yacht, Tavern (Chgo.), Commercial (Chgo.); Catalina Island Yacht, Calif.), Catalina Island Gun (Catalina Island, Calif.); Los Angeles Yacht, Lake Geneva (Wis.) Country, Lake Geneva Yacht; The Brook (N.Y.C.). Office: Wm Wrigley Jr Co 410 N Michigan Ave Chicago IL 60611 *

WROBLOWA, HALINA STEFANIA, electrochemist; b. Gdansk, Poland, July 5, 1925; came to U.S., 1960, naturalized, 1970; M.Sc., U. Lodz (Poland), 1949; Ph.D., Warsaw Inst. Tech., 1958; 1 dau., Krystyna Wrobel-Knight. Chmn. dept. prep. studies U. Lodz, 1950-53; adj. Inst. for Phys. Chemistry, Acad. Scis., Warsaw, Poland, 1958-60; dep. dir. electrochemistry lab. Energy Inst., U. Pa., Phila., 1960-67, dir. electrochemistry lab., 1968-75; prin. research scientist Ford Motor Co., Dearborn, Mich., 1978—. Served with Polish Underground Army, 1943-45. Decorated Silver Cross of Merit with Swords. Mem. Electrochem. Soc., Internat. Electrochem. Soc., Mensa, Sigma Xi. Contbr. chpts. to books, articles to profl. jours., patent lit. Office: Ford Motor Co SRL S-2079 PO Box 2053 Dearborn MI 48121

WRONSKI, STEPHANIE, educator; b. Oak Park, Ill., Oct. 9, 1916; d. Romuald August and Lillian (Romanowicz) Wronski. B.S. in Edn., Clarke Coll., 1957; Th. B., St. Joseph's Coll., 1966. Cert. tchr., Iowa, Ill. Joined Sisters of Charity, Roman Catholic Ch., 1935; tchr. Mary Queen of Heaven, Cicero, Ill., 1937-38, Holy Cross Sch., Chgo., 1938-53, 57-58, St. Anthony, Davenport, Iowa, 1953-57, St. Tarcissus, Chgo., 1958—, past coordinator for reading, sci., audio-visual dept.; local coordinator Cath. TV Network of Chgo.; past mem. math. com. Archdiocese of Chgo.; past mem. TV com. Chgo. Area Schs. Archdiocese of Chgo. grantee, 1967, 69, 82, 83. Mem. Nat. Cath. Edn. Assn. Developer Math. Progress Record Chart.

WU, HARRY PAO-TUNG, librarian; b. Chinan, Shantung, China, May 1, 1932; s. James Ching-Mei and Elizabeth Hsiao (Lu) W.; B.A., Nat. Taiwan U., Taipei, 1959; student Ohio State U., 1962; M.L.S., Kent State U., 1966; m. Irene I-Len Sun, June 23, 1961; children—Eva Pei-Chen, Walter Pei-Liang. Came to U.S., 1960. Archive and library asst. Taiwan Handicraft Promotion Center, Taipei, 1959-60; student asst. Kent State U. Library, 1960-61; reference librarian Massillon (Ohio) Pub. Library, 1964-65, acting asst. dir., 1965, asst. dir., head adult services, 1966; dir. Flesh Pub. Library, Piqua, Ohio, 1966-68; dir. St. Clair County Library System, Port Huron, Mich., 1968—; founder and dir. Blue Water Library Fedn., Port Huron, 1974—; pres. Mich. Library Film Circuit, Lansing, 1977-79; bd. dirs. Mich. Waterways council Girl Scouts U.S.A., Port Huron, 1985-86. Mem. Am., Mich. (chmn. library systems roundtable 1974-75) library assns., Am. Mgmt. Assn., Assn. Ednl. Communications and Tech., Detroit Suburban Librarians Roundtable. Clubs: Port Huron Internat., Rotary (dir. 1972-74). Home: 1518 Holland Ave Port Huron MI 48060 Office: 210 McMorran Blvd Port Huron MI 48060

WU, JUNG, physician; b. Taipei, Republic of China, Oct. 12, 1943. MD, China Med. Coll., 1969. Diplomate Am. Bd. Ob-Gyn. Intern Christ Community Hosp., Oak Lawn, Ill., 1972-73; resident in ob-gyn Harper Grace Hosp., Detroit, 1973-77, physician, 1977—; physician Mcpherson Community Health Ctr., Howell, Mich., 1977—; chmn. ob-gyn Mcpherson Community Health Ctr., 1986—. Fellow Am. Coll. Ob-Gyn. Home: 968 Devonshire Ct Brighton MI 48116 Office: 1325 Byron Rd Howell MI 48843

WU, KENT K., orthopaedic surgeon; b. Nov. 11, 1937; m. Judith Nelson, 1963; children: Jonathan, Richard, Kimberly Nelson. BS magna cum laude, U. Mich., 1962, MD, 1965. Diplomate Am. Bd. Orthopaedic Surgery. Intern Harper Hosp., 1965-67; resident Henry Ford Hosp., Detroit, 1967-69, practice medicine specializing in orthopaedics, 1971—; adj. faculty pathology and sci. U. Mich. and Wayne State U. Author: Diagnosis and Treatment of Polyostotic Spinal Tumors, 1982, Diagnosis and Treatment of Benign and Malignant Monostotic Tumors of the Spine, 1985, Surgery of The Foot, 1986, Diagnosis and Treatment of Soft Tissue Sarcomas, 1987, Techniques in Surgical Casting and Splinting, 1987; contbr. numerous articles to profl. jours.; editorial bd. Orthopaedics Today, Jour. of Neurol. and Orthopaedic Surgery, Jour. Foot Surgery; inventor medical apparatus. Served to maj. MC, U.S. Army, 1969-71, Vietnam. Mem. Am. Acad. Orthopaedic Surgeons, Am. Orthopaedic Research Soc., C. L. Mitchell Orthopaedic Soc., Detroit Acad. Orthopaedic Surgery, Mich. Orthopaedic Soc., Am. Acad. Neurol. and Orthopaedic Surgeons, The Musculoskeletal Tumor Soc., Phi Beta Kappa, Phi Kappa Phi, Phi Eta Sigma. Office: Henry Ford Hosp Dept Orthopaedic Surgery Detroit MI 48202

WUCHTER, MICHAEL DAVID, pastor; b. Atlantic City, Feb. 16, 1946; s. Robert Zimmerman and Eleanor Joyce (Freed) W.; m. Shirley Ann Dyer, Aug. 16, 1969; children: Andrew, J. Kirsten. BA, Wittenberg U., 1968; M of Div., The Luth. Theol. Sem., 1972; D of Ministry, Princeton Theol. Sem., 1983. Ordained to ministry Luth. Ch., 1972. Pastor Resurrection Luth. Ch., Hamilton Sq., N.J., 1972-79; pastor to the univ. Wittenberg U., Springfield, Ohio, 1979—; pres. Trenton (N.J.) Campus Ministry, 1974-79; chaplain Lakeside (Ohio) Luth. Conf., 1980; chaplain to 75th anniversary conf. Luth. Ednl. Conf. N.Am., Washington, 1985; participant summer seminar Fulbright-Hays Faculty Devel., New Delhi, 1984. Author: (study guide) Disarmament in a Nuclear Age, 1983, (contbg.) In Praise of Preaching, 1984, Religions of India and Human Values, 1985; author numerous book revs. Pres., co-founder The Nottingham Recreation Ctr. for the Physically Ltd., Mercer County, N.J., 1979; bd. dirs. Springfield Pastoral Counseling Ctr., 1983, Specialized Ministries Council, Springfield, 1985, community adv. bd. Teen Suicide Prevention Project, Springfield, 1985. Fulbright-Hay Faculty Devel. Program grantee, 1984. Mem. Am. Acad. Religion, Nat. Assn. Coll. and Univ. Chaplains, Luth. Coll. Chaplains Assn. Democrat. Home: 710 Riverside Dr Springfield OH 45504 Office: Wittenberg U Springfield OH 45501

WUEST, GEORGE W., state judge; b. Lake Andes, S.D., Feb. 3, 1925; m. Sandra Wuest, June 25, 1956; children: Linda, Douglas. LLB, U. S.D., 1949. Atty. State of S.D., Lake Andes; asst. atty. gen. State of S.D.; judge U.S. Ct. Appeals (4th cir.), S.D., 1965-87, S.D. Supreme Ct., Pierre, 1987—. Office: Supreme Court Office Capitol Building Pierre SD 57501

WUJEK, JOHN ANTHONY, bank executive; b. Bay City, Mich., Jan. 18, 1961; s. Stanley Sylvester and Camille (Zann) W.; m. Joy Lynn Frank, June 21, 1985. BBA in Acctg., Saginaw Valley State Coll., 1983. Sales rep. Monroe Systems for Bus., Grand Rapids, Mich., 1983-84; auditor New Century Bank Corp., Bay City, 1984-85; credit analyst New Century Bank-Lapeer (Mich.), N.A., 1985-86, sr. credit analyst, 1986-87; loan examiner First of Am. Bank Corp., Kalamazoo, 1987; asst. banking officer comml. credit dept. First Am. Bank, Bay City, Mich., 1987—. Fund raiser Am. Cancer Soc., Lapeer, 1986. Home: 940 Flint St #B7 Frankenmuth MI 48734 Office: First of Am Bank 300 Center Ave Bay City MI 48708

WULFECK, JAMES ANDREW, JR., management and training consultant; b. Covington, Ky., Nov. 8, 1946; s. James Andrew and Della Mae (Testerman) W.; B.E.S., Thomas More Coll., 1975; postgrad. Xavier U., 1976-77; m. Kathleen Kordenbrock, Oct. 16, 1971; children—Christopher, Daniel. Sales promotion and tng. mgr. Merrell-Nat. Labs., Cin., 1973-76; coporate tng. officer Richardson-Merrell, Inc., Wilton, Conn., 1976-77; exec. v.p. Instructional Techniques Ltd., Manhasset, N.Y., 1977-78; pres. GMP Inst., Cin., 1979—; dir. Rocket Supply, Cin., Jet Machine & Mfg. Co., Inc. Served with U.S. Army, 1970-71. Mem. Am. Soc. Tng. and Devel., Am. Soc. Quality Control. Republican. Roman Catholic. Office: 3823 Pacific Ave Cincinnati OH 45212

WULFING, JAMES JOSEPH, machine components manufacturing company executive; b. St. Paul, Nov. 24, 1939; s. William F. and Evelyn (Waldorf) W.; m. Karen S. Riemenschneider, June 24, 1961; children: Christopher, David, Michael. Cert., St. Paul Vocat., 1960, Dunwoody Inst., Mpls., 1962. Designer Appliance Mfg., St. Paul, 1960-64; contract engr. Contract Engring. Co., St. Paul, 1964-70; mech. engr. ABM, Langdon, N.D., 1970-71; chief engr. Pneumatic Conveyance, St. Paul, 1971-73; product devel. specialist Large Multi Product Co., St. Paul, 1973-83; pres. 5W Enterprises Inc., Afton, Minn., 1983—; mem. Material Handling Council, Tape Converting Task Force. Patentee in field. Mem. Ch. Bd. Edn., Afton, 1981-84. Office: 5W Enterprises Inc 14715 30th St N Stillwater MN 55082

WUNDER, GENE CARROLL, marketing educator, business consultant; b. Waterloo, Iowa, Feb. 11, 1939; s. Lloyd Carl and Alice Marie (Reed) W.; B.B.A., U. Iowa, 1969; postgrad. U. Mo. Sch. Law, 1968-70; M.B.A., U. Mo., 1971; postgrad. U. Mo., 1972-75; grad. assoc. in Econs., U. Ark., 1977-78, Ph.D., U. Ark.; m. Judy Kay Stone, Dec. 16, 1966; children—Lara Anne, Sara Elizabeth. Underwriter Security Mut. Life, 1964-69, State Farm Mut. Ins., 1969-71; instr. bus. adminstrn. N.E. Mo. State U., Kirksville, 1972-75, asst. prof. bus. adminstrn., 1976-82; asst. prof. mktg. Ball State U., Muncie, Ind., 1982—; cons. in field. Chmn. supervisory com. N.E. Mo. Credit Union, 1976-82. Recipient Alpha Kappa Psi Outstanding Alumni award, 1968. Mem. S.W. Fin. Assn., Midwest Fin. Assn., Am. Mktg. Assn., Am. Risk Mgmt. Assn., So. Regional Bus. Law Assn., So. Mktg. Assn., S.W. Mktg. Assn., Midwest Mktg. Assn., AAUP, Alpha Kappa Psi, Phi Alpha Delta, Phi Delta Kappa, Gamma Iota Sigma. Republican. Methodist. Clubs: Masons (32 deg.), Shriners, Kiwanis, Pachyderms, Elks Country. Contbr. articles to profl. jours. Home: 9101 W Redbud Ln Muncie IN 47304 Office: Coll Bus Ball State U Muncie IN 47306

WUNDERMAN, LORNA ELLEN, medical association administrator, biostatistician; b. Hollywood, Calif., Mar. 23, 1954; d. Irwin and Gilda Shirley (Margulies) Wunderman; m. Kenneth E. Monroe, Feb. 27, 1987. AA, Foothill Coll., 1972; BS, U. Calif., Berkeley, 1976, MPH, 1978. Cert. Community Coll. tchr., Calif. Research asst. AMA, Chgo., 1978-79, research assoc., 1978-81, dir. dept., cons., 1981-86, exec. asst. to v.p., 1986—. Editor: Characteristics of Physicians, 1979, Contbr. articles to med. jours. Grantee Dept. Health and Human Services, Washington, 1979-80, 82, scholar Washington, 1976-78. Mem. Am. Soc. Assn. Execs. (com. mem. 1982—), Am. Statis. Assn., Am. Mktg. Assn., Am. Pub. Health Assn. Avocations: tennis, swimming, traveling. Home: 432 W Oakdale Chicago IL 60657 Office: Joint Commn on Accreditation 875 N Michigan Ave Chicago IL 60611

WURDEMAN, LEW EDWARD, data processing corporation consultant; b. Colorado Springs, Colo., Oct. 31, 1949; s. Robert Martin and Shirley Gladys (Reetz) W. Student U. Tex., El Paso, 1967-69, U. Minn., 1969-72. Adminstr. Control Data Corp., Bloomington, Minn., 1969-81, product specialist, 1981-83, systems mgr., 1983-84, cons., 1984—. Republican. Lutheran. Clubs: German Shepherd Dog of Mpls., German Shepherd Dog of Am. Avocations: dog breeding, training, computers, photography. Home: 13204 Ferris Ave Apple Valley MN 55124 Office: Control Data Corp PO Box 1305 BLCW1X Minneapolis MN 55440

WURFEL, DAVID GLENN, advertising executive; b. Louisville, May 5, 1952; s. Paul Glenn and Edith Kelly Wurfel; m. Barbara Jean Scott, May 15, 1976. BA in Communications, U. Ky., 1975, BS in Mktg., 1976; MBA in Mktg., Roosevelt U., 1980. Media supr. Needham, Harper & Steers, Chgo., 1978-81; media adminstr. Miller Brewing Co., Milw., 1981-84; v.p., assoc. media dir. D'Arcy, Masius, Benton & Bowles, Chgo., 1984—. Mem. Am. Mktg. Assn. Avocations: cycle touring, woodworking. Home: 231 Gillick Park Ridge IL 60068 Office: D'Arcy, Masius, Benton & Bowles 200 E Randolph Chicago IL 60601

WURMAN, LEONARD HOWARD, physician; b. N.Y.C., Aug. 14, 1941; s. Joseph Joel and Rebecca (Rubinstein) W.; m. Arleen Claire Edelman, June 9, 1963; children: Peter Richard, Nancy Lynn, Scott Eric. AB, Columbia U., 1963; MD, Tufts U., 1967; MS, U. Minn., 1975. Surgical intern Bronx (N.Y.) Mcpl. Hosp.Ctr., N.Y., 1967-68; resident in surgery Bronx (N.Y.) Mcpl. Hosp.Ctr., 1968-69; resident in otolaryngology U. Minn., Mpls., 1971-75; staff Wausau (Wis.) Hosp. Ctr., Sacred Heart Hosp., Rhinelander, Good Samaritan Hosp., Merrill; practice medicine specializing in otolaryngology Ear, Nose and Throat Assn., Wausau. Contbr. articles to profl. jours. Pres. Mt. Sinai Congregation, Wausau, 1979-80. Served to lt. comdr. USN, 1969-71. Fellow Am. Acad. Ortolaryngology, ACS, Am. Acad. of Facial Plastic and Reconstructive Surgery; mem. Med. Soc. Wis. (com. chmn. Madison 1983-84), Wis. Waterfowlers Assn. (Wausau area regional dir. 1984-87). Jewish. Avocations: hunting, dog training, soccer referee, bicycling, jogging. Home: T5942 N Troy St Wausau WI 54401 Office: Ear Nose and Throat Assn 425 Pine Ridge Blvd Wausau WI 54401

WURSTER, THELMA PAULINE, nurse; b. Celina, Ohio, June 9, 1932; d. Francis Q. and Mary Lee (Kindel) Wade; R.N., Miami Valley Hosp., Dayton, Ohio, 1953; B.S. in Nursing, Marquette U., Milw., 1961; M.Ed. in Profl. Devel., U. Wis., Whitewater, 1982; postgrad. Coll. St. Joseph, Joliet, Ill.; m. Charles Wayne Wurster, Aug. 18, 1952. Staff and head nurse hosps. in Ohio and Wis., 1953-80; dir. operating rm. Milw. Children's Hosp., 1966-78, asst. dir. nursing, 1979-80; supr. operating room Eye Inst., Milw. County Med. Complex, Wauwatosa, Wis., 1980-87. R.N., Ohio, Wis. Mem. Assn. Operating Room Nurses, AAUW, Phi Delta Kappa. Republican. Club: Kettle Moraine Curling (Hartland, Wis.). Contbr. articles to profl. jours. Office: 8700 W Wisconsin Ave Wauwatosa WI 53226

WURSTER, THOMAS BITTEL, publishing executive; b. Ashland, Ohio, Jan. 4, 1942; s. Albert Edward and Louise Ann (Morr) W.; m. Ann Marie McDonald, Feb. 27, 1972; children: David, Michael, Mathew. BS in Bus. Adminstrn. and Psychology, Ashland Coll., 1964. With customer service R.R. Donnelley & Son, Willard, Ohio, 1964-68; with sales Printing Corp. Am., San Francisco, 1968-71; pres. BookMasters, Los Altos, Calif. and Ashland, 1972—. Mem. Athletic Hall of Fame Ashland Coll. Mem. Nat. Assn. Printers. Republican. Lutheran. Home: 255 S Countryside Dr Ashland OH 44805 Office: BookMasters 638 Jefferson Ashland OH 44805

WURTZ, RICHARD JOSEPH, contract supervisor; b. Mound City, Kans., Jan. 11, 1940; s. Wesley W. and Ruth (Merriman) W.; m. Janice Elizabeth Holt, Aug. 12, 1961; children: Melissa, Joseph, Christopher. BA, U. Kans., 1961, MA, 1967; student, St. Louis U., 1966-68. Lic. abstractor, Kans. Instr. Jr. Coll. Dist., St. Louis, 1963-66, So. Ill. U., Edwardsville, 1966-73; owner George W. Huff & Co., Mound City, 1973-79; right of way agt. Coates Field Service and Wilcrest Engring., 1981-83; right of way supr. Finley Engring., Lamar, Mo., 1984—. chmn. Linn County Dem. Party, Mound City, 1984—. Mem. Internat. Right of Way Assn. (asst. sec., treas. chpt. 5 1985-86, v. chmn. chpt. region III 1986). Avocations: reading, writing, gardening. Home: Rt 2 Box 161A Mound City KS 66056

WUTHRICH, VIRGIL EUGENE, appliance manufacturing company executive; b. Milford, Ind., Sept. 12, 1934; s. Walter and Martha Jane (Rassi) W.; m. Nancy Ann, Sept. 18, 1955; children: Scott, Susan, Donna, Steven, Diane. B.Sc. in Acctg, Internat. Coll., 1953; postgrad., DePaul U., 1957-59; grad., Inst. Mgmt. program Ill. Benedictine Coll., 1976. C.P.A., Ill. Inventory control clk. Burroughs Corp., Chgo., 1953-56; sub-office adminstr. Burroughs Corp., 1956; staff acct. B.F. Kearney & Co., C.P.A.s, Chgo., 1957-63; with Sunbeam Corp., 1963—; mgr. domestic corp. acctg. Sunbeam Corp., Chgo., 1969-75; v.p. fin., treas. Oster div. Sunbeam Corp., Milw., 1975-87. Recipient Silver medal Ill. C.P.A. Exam., 1959. Baptist. Club: Kiwanis (treas. North Shore Milw. club). Home: N85W 15796 Menomonee River Pkwy Menomonee Falls WI 53051 Office: 5055 N Lydell Ave Milwaukee WI 53217

WYANDT, JOHN OWEN, manufacturer's representative; b. Chgo., May 10, 1932; s. Owen Heaton and Harriet Christy (Smith) W.; m. Dorothy Marie Johnson, Aug. 28, 1954; children: Christy Marie, Susan Leone, Elizabeth Rowe, Katherine Marguerite. BA, DePauw U., 1954; postgrad. in acctg. and fin., Northwestern U., 1954-58. With LaSalle Nat. Bank, Chgo., 1954-60; mgr. Armour Estate, Chgo., 1960-68; with McCormick & Co., 1968-70; investment mgr. dept. pvt. placement Allstate Ins. Co., 1970-74; exec. v.p. Nat. Bank of N. Evanston, Ill., 1974-76; mgr. corp. fin. Daniels and Bell, Chgo., 1977-78; pres. Dainty Maid Candy Co., Chgo., 1977-78; v.p. br. mgr. Telegraph Savs., Chgo., 1978-80; mfg. rep. Bradford Systems, Chgo., 1980—. Bd. dirs. St. Leonard's House, Chgo.; alderman 6th ward City of Evanston, 1971-83; chmn. Evanston Bicentennial Celebration 1974-76; property chmn. Evanston Vis. Nurses, 1983—. Recipient Bicentennial Chmn. Performance award State of Ill., 1976, Speech award Assn. Records Mgrs. and Adminstrs., 1984. Republican. Episcopalian. Lodge: Rotary (pres. Evanston Lighthouse 1986). Avocations: model making, photography. Office: Bradford Systems 804 Merchandise Mart Chicago IL 60201

WYANT, JOSEPH ANDREW, cablevision company executive, photographer; b. Weston, W.Va., Jan. 23, 1949; s. John Frederick and Evelyn Isabel (Mount) W.; m. Deborah Ann De Ring, Jan. 28, 1978; 3 children. BA in Geography, W.Va. U., 1971; postgrad. Ohio State U., 1975—. CCTV prodn. coordinator Columbus (Ohio) State Inst., 1972-77; mgr. Ponderosa System, Inc., Lancaster, Ohio, 1978; media specialist Cleveland Heights-University Heights (Ohio) Bd. Edn., 1979-81; dir. programming Viacom Cablevision, Cleve., 1981-84, dir. mktg. Viacom Cablevision, Dayton, Ohio, 1984—; freelance photographer, Cleve., 1979—; speaker in field. Author: Viacom Is..., 1983; contbr. photog. studies to profl. publs. Mem. dist. communications com. United Meth. Ch., Cleve., 1982-83; cons. lay pub. relations adv. com. Cleveland Heights-University Heights Bd. Edn., 1983; mem. citizens adv. com. Kettering Bd. Edn., 1985. Recipient cert. of Honor Radio-TV Council Greater Cleve., Inc., 1982; cited by Ohio Senate for Outstanding Contbn. to Community Relations, 1984. Mem. Ohio Cable TV Assn. (cablecasting com. 1982-84), Dayton Advt. Club, Nat. Fedn. Local Cable Programmers, Cable TV Adminstrn. and Mktg. Soc. Home: 3021 Mirimar St Kettering OH 45409 Office: PO Box 213 North Dayton Station Dayton OH 45404

WYATT, GLENN THOMAS, chemical company executive; b. Springfield, Ill., Jan. 31, 1939; s. Glenn Eason and Elsie May (Crouse) W.; m. Barbara Kay Miller, Mar. 18, 1960; children—Diane Michelle, Cheryl Lynn. B.S. in Acctg., Bradley U., 1960. C.P.A., Ill., Ohio. Supr. audit Ernst & Whinney, Chgo., 1960-66; mgr. audit Price Waterhouse & Co., Peoria, Ill., 1966-72; fin. analyst Borden, Inc., Columbus, Ohio, 1972-74, group controller, 1974-77, controller foods div., 1977-79; v.p. fin. and treas. Sherex Chem. Co., Inc., Dublin, Ohio, 1979—. Trustee, Knolls Civic Assn., Columbus, 1977-82. Mem. Am. Inst. C.P.A.s, Ohio Soc. C.P.A.s, Fin. Execs. Inst., Columbus C. of C., Treasurers Club (dir. 1982-86). Office: Sherex Chem Co Inc 5777 Frantz Rd PO Box 646 Dublin OH 43017

WYATT, ROSE MARIE, psychiatric and medical social worker, financial planner; b. San Angelo, Tex., Feb. 16; d. James Odis and Annie LaVernia (Lott) W.; B.A. (Ford Found. scholar, 1953-57), Fisk U., 1957; M.S., U. So. Calif., 1963; M.A., M.S.W. (univ. scholar 1970-72, United Charities scholar 1970-72), U. Chgo., 1972; postgrad. in indsl. psychology Ill. Inst. Tech., 1976—. Elem. tchr. Chgo. Bd. Edn., 1959-63, clin. social worker, 1979—; adult program dir. Chgo. YWCA, 1963-64; youth counselor Chgo. Commn. on Youth Welfare, 1964-66; supervising social worker for Head Start, Chgo. Com. on Urban Opportunity, 1966; social worker Chgo. Commn. on Youth Welfare, 1966-68, Jewish Vocat. Service, 1968; social worker Sch. Community Relations, Detroit Public Schs., 1968-70; social worker United Charities, 1972-74; clin. social worker Rosman-Wyatt and Assos., Chgo., 1980—, pres., 1981—; instr. dept. corrections Chgo. State U., 1972—. Adv. bd. United Charities, Calumet Area, program com. chmn., 1974-80; vol. Assn. of Community Agts. 1968-70, Southside Sr. Citizens Coalition, Chgo., 1963-66, Roseland Health Planning Com., 1974-76, Teen Pregnancy Caucus, 1978-82; mem. social work adv. council Chgo. Bd. Edn., 1976. Recipient Outstanding Employee award for med.-social work services Maternal and Child Health Services div. HEW; 1971. Mem. Nat. Assn. Social Workers, Acad. Cert. Social Workers, Ill. Cert. Social Workers, Chgo. Psychol. Club, Ill Acad. Criminology, NEA, Ill. Assn. Sch. Social Workers, Am. Assn. Mental Deficiency, Qualified Mental Retardation Profls., Fisk U. Alumni Assn., Alpha Kappa Alpha. Roman Catholic. Clubs: Am. Bridge Assn., Civenos Bridge.

WYCHE, SAMUEL DAVID, professional football coach; b. Atlanta, Jan. 5, 1945; m. Jane Wyche; children—Zak, Kerry. B.A., Furman U., 1966; Masters degree, U. S.C. Profl. football player Continental Football League, Wheeling Ironmen, 1966; profl. football player NFL, Cin. Bengals, 1968-70, Washington Redskins, 1971-72, Detroit Lions, 1974, St. Louis Cardinals, 1976; owner sporting goods store, Greenville, S.C., 1976-79; asst. coach San Francisco 49'ers, 1979-82; head coach Ind. U., 1983, Cin. Bengals, 1984—. Address: care Cin Bengals 200 Riverfront Stadium Cincinnati OH 45202

WYDMAN, PERRY B., bank holding company executive. Previously chmn. Interstate Fin. Corp., Dayton, Ohio; now sr. vice chmn. Society Corp., Cleve., also bd. dirs. Office: Society Corp 800 Superior Ave Cleveland OH 44114 *

WYDRA, RALPH EDWARD, offset printing executive; b. Chgo., Dec. 4, 1939; s. Edward J. and Bernice A. (Darge) W.; m. Helen Margaret Bartu, July 7, 1962 (div. Feb. 1974); children—Paul Edward, Steven Peter; m. 2d, Maureen Ann Neenan, June 15, 1974; children—Laura Lynn, Jennifer Ann, Michael Patrick. B.B.A., Northwestern U., 1972. Asst. controller I.S. Berlin Press, Chgo., 1959-75; controller Collins, Miller & Hutchings, Chgo., 1975-85; controller, v.p. fin., corp. sec. Tempo Graphics Inc., Carol Stream, Ill., 1983—; cons. to various printing corps., 1975—. Mgmt. advisor Jr. Achievement, Chgo., 1970-75. Mem. Pres.s Honor Club, Beatrice Foods Co., 1982. Mem. Alpha Sigma Phi (pres. 1962-63). Roman Catholic. Home: 500 N Rohlwing Rd Palatine IL 60067 Office: Tempo Graphics Inc 455 E North Ave Carol Stream IL 60188

WYGANT, EDGAR GERARD, allergist; b. Grand Rapids, Mich., Apr. 27, 1923; s. Edgar Hall and Sarah (O'Grady) W.; m. Dorothy Virginia Fahrenbach, Aug. 16, 1947; children: Jerry, Jimmy, Jackie, Patty, Tommy, Maureen, Mary Ellen, Robbie. MD, Loyola U., Chgo., 1948. Diplomate Am. Bd. Allergy and Immunology. Allergist Suburban Heights Med. Ctr., Chicago Heights, Ill., 1956—; med. dir. Suburban Heights Med. Ctr., Chicago Heights, 1986—; Active Chicago Heights Bd. Health, 1965—; med. dir. Applewood Living Ctr., Matteson, Ill., 1971—. Fellow Am. Coll. Allergy; mem. Am. Acad. Allergy, Am. Assn. Clinival Allergy and Immunology, Am. Soc. Internal Medicine, Interasma. Republican. Roman Catholic. Avocation: photography. Office: Suburban Heights Med Ctr 333 Dixie Hwy Chicago Heights IL 60411

WYKOFF, JOHN ROBERT, lawyer; b. Erie, Pa., Sept. 17, 1951; s. Robert George and Dorothy Jean (Conrad) W.; m. Jean Marie Vincent, Aug. 17, 1973; children—Bradford Conrad, Juli Marie, Brett William. Student in bus. Ohio U., 1970-73; B.B.A. cum laude, U. Cin., 1974; J.D. cum laude, U. Dayton, 1979. Bar: Ohio 1979, U.S. Dist. ct. (so. dist.) Ohio 1979. Assoc. Brannon & Cox, Dayton, 1979-80, Lang, Horenstein & Dunlevey, Dayton, 1980-84, White, Getgey & Meyer, Cin., 1984—; law dir. Village of New Lebanon, Ohio, 1982—, city of Forest Park, Ohio, 1987—; legal adviser KDI, Inc., handicapped workshop, Dayton, 1983-84; legal counsel, trustee Miami Valley Golf Club, Dayton, 1984. Mem. Madeira Schs. Planning Commn., 1986—, central com. and jud. screening com. Montgomery County Republican Party, Dayton, 1983-84; bd. dirs. Montgomery County unit Am. Cancer Soc., 1983-84, Daybreak, Inc., Dayton, 1984. Mem. ABA, Ohio State Bar Assn. (aviation law com.), Cin. Bar Assn. (negligence law com.), Dayton Bar Assn., Assn. Trial Lawyers Am., Ohio Assn. Trial Lawyers. Roman Catholic. Clubs: Miami Valley Golf (trustee); Kenwood Country. Home: 6552 Madeira Hills Dr Madeira OH 45243 Office: White Getgey & Meyer Co LPA 2021 Auburn Ave Adam Riddle House Cincinnati OH 45219

WYLIE, CHALMERS PANGBURN, congressman; b. Norwich, Ohio, Nov. 23, 1920; m. Marjorie Ann Siebold; children—Jacquelyn, Bradley. Student, Otterbein Coll., Ohio State U.; grad., Law Sch. Harvard; LL.D. (hon.), Otterbein Coll. Asst. atty. gen. Ohio, 1948, 51-54; asst. city atty. Columbus, Ohio, 1949-50; city atty. 1953-56; adminstr. Bur. Workmen's Compensation for State Ohio, 1957; apptd. first asst. to Gov. Ohio, 1957; formerly partner law firm Gingher & Christensen; mem. 90th-100th Congresses 15th Ohio Dist., 1967—. Pres. Ohio Municipal League, 1957; Mem. Ohio Legislature, 1961-66; past pres. Buckeye Republican Club. Served as 1st lt. AUS; col. Res. Decorated Silver Star, Bronze Star, Purple Heart, Legion of Merit; recipient Distinguished Service award as Outstanding Young Man of Year Columbus Nat. Jr. C. of C., 1955, Columbus area C. of C. award, 1983; named One of Ten Men of Year Columbus Citizen Jour., 1954. Mem. Ohio Bar Assn., Columbus Bar Assn., Am. Legion (Southway post). Republican. Methodist. Clubs: Masons (33 deg.), Kiwanis. Office: Room 2310 Rayburn Office Bldg Washington DC 20515

WYLIE, MARK EMERSON, marketing executive; b. Cambridge, Ohio, Nov. 2, 1952; s. Frank Emerson and Mary Janice (Foreman) W.; m. Donna Jean Dolson, July 28, 1973; children: Steven, Marcia. BS, U. Akron, 1975, MBA, 1980. Design engr. Diebold, Inc., North Canton, Ohio, 1976-79, project leader, 1979-81; engring. project adminstr. Allen-Bradley, Cleve., 1981-82, product supr., 1983-84, product mgr., 1984-86, mgr. product line mktg., 1986—. Mem. Am. Mgmt. Assn., IEEE, Instrument Soc. Am. Republican. Roman Catholic. Home: 2364 Silver Springs Dr Stow OH 44224 Office: Allen-Bradley Co 747 Alpha Dr Highland Heights OH 44143

WYLIE, PATSY LYNN, respiratory therapist; b. Springfield, Mo., June 12, 1950; d. Lawrence Eugene and Mae Etta (Allen) Correll. BS in Health Services Mgmt., Ind. U., 1982. Registered respiratory therapist. Respiratory tech. Ind. U. Hosps., Indpls., 1971-73, supr. third shift, 1973-75, coordinator pulmonary team, 1975-80, continuing care specialist, 1980—. Contbr. articles to profl. jours.; co-author, prodn. asst. tng. film for Ind. State Bd. Health, 1986. Mem. Am. Assn. for Respiratory Care, Am. Lung Assn. Cen. Ind. (sec. 1986-87, co-organizer Camp SuperKids and Family Asthma Programs 1976—, bd. dirs. 1979—), Ind. Soc. for Respiratory Care (chmn. com. 1982-84), Ind. Thoracic Soc. Avocations: travel, needlework. Office: Ind Univ Hosp Riley Hosp for Children 702 Barnhill Room 278 Indianapolis IN 46223

WYMAN, WILLIAM ARTHUR, music educator; b. Pitts., May 19, 1942; s. William Harper and Marian Kathryn (Bode) W.; m. Tamara Kay Riley, Sept. 14, 1984. BA, Bethany Coll., 1964; M of Music, W.Va. U., 1967, D of Music Arts, 1971; postgrad., Westminster Choir Coll., 1973-74, Ohio State U., 1982. Vocal music tchr. North Hills Sch. Dist., Pitts., 1967-68; mem. summer opera theater W.Va. U., Morgantown, 1969-71; asst. prof. music Otterbein Coll., Westerville, Ohio, 1971-75; prof. Nebr. Wesleyan U., Lincoln, 1975—; adminstv. dir. Rocky Ridge Music Ctr., Estes Park, Colo., 1976—; dir. music St. Paul United Meth. Ch., Lincoln, 1981—. Author: Songs of Guiseppe Verdi, 1971. Bd. dirs. Lincoln Community Concerts, 1978-83; program com. mem. Lied Ctr. Performing Arts, 1986—. NDEA fellow, 1966; Fulbright scholar, 1983-84. Mem. Am. Choral Dirs. Assn. (nat. com. chair 1971—), Nat. Assn. Tchrs. of Singing, Music Educators Nat. Conf. Republican. Presbyterian. Club: Prairie Life Center (Lincoln). Avocations: mountain climbing, boating. Home: 3941 Bel-Ridge Dr Lincoln NE 68521 Office: Nebr Wesleyan U 5000 St Paul Lincoln NE 68504

WYMOR, LARRY L., textile executive; b. Cleve., Jan. 14, 1936; s. Emanuel and Marie P. (Blank) W.; m. Elinor M. Fox; children: Marcia G., Steven J. BBA, Case Western Res.U., 1958, LLB, 1961. Ptnr. Burke, Haber & Berick, Cleve., 1961-81; pres. Cleve. Cotton Products Co., 1981—; sr. v.p. The Tranzonic Cos., Cleveland, 1981—; exec. com., bd. dirs. Internat. Assn. of Wiping Cloth Mfrs., Washington; bd. dirs. U.S. Carbide, Cleve. Mem. exec. com. Park Synagogue, Cleve., 1981—; bd. dirs. Mayfield Ednl. Excellence Found., Cleve., 1986—; bd. dirs. Menorah Park Ctr., Cleve., 1984—. Named Man of Yr., Park Synagogue Men's Club, 1978, named Centerite of Yr., Park Synagogue, 1981. Lodge: B'nai B'rith (pres. dist. 2 Cin. 1986-87, vice chmn. internat. youth orgn., chmn. nat. leadership cabinet, Gold Key award Youth Commn. 1985). Avocations: photography, computers. Office: Cleve Cotton Products Co PO Box 6500 Cleveland OH 44101

WYMORE, MAXINE DANNER, child welfare administrator,educator; b. What Cheer, Iowa, Aug. 26, 1924; d. Leroy Charles and Lavera Alice (Hartwig) Danner; m. Norman Edward Wymore, Aug. 29, 1942 (dec. 1974); children: Robert Dean, Norman Eugene. BS in Edn., Northern Ill. U., 1969, MS, 1974. Cert. tchr, Ill.; cert. social worker, Ill. Announcer sta. WRMN, Elgin, Ill., 1960-63; mem. 6th Ill. Constitutional Convention, Springfield, 1969-70; tchr. sch. dist. 300, Dundee, Ill., 1970-71; county superintendent Ill. Dept. Pub. Aid, Woodstock, Ill., 1972-79; child welfare adminstr. Ill. Dept. Children and Family Services, Rockford, 1980—; lectr. various orgns.; conference chmn. various locations. Vol. Boy Scouts Am., various ch. camps, 4-H clubs, 1954-82, Elgin State Mental Hosp., 1961-66; mem. adv. com Sch. Dist 300, Dundee, 1951-53; candidate 33rd dist. Ill. Ho. Reps., 1980. Mem. Ill. Welfare Assn. (Silver Bell award 1976), Am. Assn. U. Women (legis. chmn. 1976, Salute-Publication award 1974), Northern Ill. U. Alumni Assn. (bd. dirs. 1974-84, treas. 1975-76, Outstanding Alumnus 1970), Northern Ill. U. Found. Bd. (treas. 1984—), Hampshire Parent-Tchr. Assn. (pres. 1957-58), Am. Legion Aux. (pres. 1956-58, 1958-60). Republican. Methodist. Avocations: travel, slide shows, writing short stories and poetry, tailoring, camping. Home: 528 W Kimball Woodstock IL 60098 Office: Ill Dept Children & Family Services 4302 N Main St Rockford IL 61105

WYNDEWICKE, KIONNE ANNETTE, educator; b. Preston, Miss.; d. Clifton Thomas and Missouria (Jackson) Johnson; student Columbia Coll., Chgo., 1972; B.S., Ill. State Normal U., 1961; postgrad. Williams Coll., Williamstown, Mass., 1972; M.Ed., Nat. Coll. Edn., 1982; m. Eugene C. Moorer, Sept. 23, 1961 (div.). Social worker Cook County Dept. Pub. Aid, 1961; tchr. reading Chgo. Bd. Edn., 1961—; asst. to news dir. WCIU-TV, 1972-74; asst. women's editor Chgo. Defender, 1970-72; social sec. Dr. William R. Clarke, 1972—; part-time photog. model, fashion commentator, pub. relations cons., pub. speaker. Co-chmn. installation Profl. Womens Aux., Provident Hosp., 1961, corr. sec., 1969, publicity chmn., 1969-72, 74-77. Selected one of 13 persons in U.S. to attend Innovative Tchr. Tng. Seminar, funded by Henry Luce Found. at Williams Coll., 1972; one of 25 Black women of Chgo. to receive Kizzy award, 1977; recipient Outstanding Community Service award Beatrice Caffrey Youth Service, Inc., 1978, 83, 85. Mem. Ill. Speech and Theatre Assn., WTTW Channel 11 Ednl. TV, Mus. Contemporary Art, Speech Communication Assn. Am., YWCA. Lutheran. Contbr. articles to local newspapers. Office: 707 E 37th St Chicago IL 60653

WYNKOOP, ROGER DUDLEY, railcar leasing executive; b. Oakland, Calif., Mar. 3, 1948; s. Robert E. and Betty (Brown) W.; m. Mary Katharine Kline, Aug. 28, 1971; children: Karen, Jennifer. BA in Polit. Sci., West Md. Coll., 1970; postgrad., Harvard U., 1986. Various sales positions ACF Industries, Inc., St. Louis, 1970—, now v.p. sales and leasing; bd. dirs. ACFA, SA, Mexico City. Served to capt. USAR, 1971-77. Mem. Nat. Freight Traffic Assn., Nat. Indsl. Traffic League. Clubs: Glen Echo Country, Mo. Athletic (St. Louis). Avocation: golf.

WYRSCH, JAMES ROBERT, lawyer, educator; b. Springfield, Mo., Feb. 23, 1942; s. Louis Joseph and Jane Elizabeth (Welsh) W.; m. B. Darlene Wyrsch, Oct. 18, 1975; children—Scott, Keith, Mark, Brian, Marcia. B.A., U. Notre Dame, 1963; J.D., Georgetown U., 1966; LL.M., U. Mo., Kansas City, 1972. Bar: Mo. 1966, U.S. Ct. Appeals (8th cir.) 1971, U.S. Supreme Ct. 1972, U.S. Ct. Appeals (10th cir.) 1974, U.S. Ct. Appeals (5th cir.) 1974, U.S. Ct. Mil. & Appeals 1978, U.S. Ct. Appeals (6th cir.) 1982, U.S. Ct. Appeals (11th cir.) 1984, U.S. Ct. Appeals (7th cir.) 1986. Assoc., Koenigsdorf, Kusnetzky Wyrsch, and predecessors, Kansas City, Mo., 1970-71, of counsel, 1972-77, ptnr., 1978—; adj. prof. U. Mo., 1981—; mem. com. instrns. Mo. Supreme Ct., 1983—. Served as capt. U.S. Army, 1966-69. Mem. Am. Arbitration Assn. (panel arbitrators), ABA, Mo. Bar Assn. (vice chmn. criminal law com. 1978-79), Kansas City Bar Assn. (chmn. anti-trust com. 1981), Assn. Trial Lawyers Am., Nat. Assn. Criminal Def. Attys., Mo. Assn. Criminal Def. Attys. (sec. 1982), Phi Delta Phi. Democrat. Roman Catholic. Contbr. in field. Home: 811 Hearnes St Blue Springs MO 64015 Office: Koenigsdorf Kusnetzky & Wyrsch 1006 Grand Ave Suite 1050 Kansas City MO 64106

WYSE, LAMAR LARAY, hospital executive, musician; b. Manistee, Mich., Oct. 21, 1946; s. Lester A. and Miriam (Johns) W.; m. Karon Eve Swanson, Nov. 2, 1968; children—Adam Christopher, Jason LaMar. B.A., Malone Coll., 1968; M.H.A., Ohio State U., 1980. Chief technician respiratory therapy Ind. U. Med. Ctr., Indpls., 1968-71; dir. cardio-pulmonary dept. Riverview Hosp., Noblesville, Ind., 1971-74; dir. cardio-pulmonary dept. Mary Rutan Hosp., Bellefontaine, Ohio, 1974-76, adminstrv. asst., 1976-80, assoc. adminstr., 1980-81; adminstr. Bluffton Community Hosp., Ohio, 1981-85; pres. Hardin Meml. Hosp., Kenton, Ohio, 1985—; pres. Hardin Health Services, Kenton, 1986—; pres. Western Ohio Hosp. Council, Lima, 1983-85; vice-chmn. New Century Health Alliance, Findlay, Ohio, 1983-85; mem. statewide health coordinating com., 1985-87; adv. council Nursing Registration and Edn. Bd. Ohio, 1987—. Composer, arranger instrumental and choral music. Bd. dirs. Adriel Sch., West Liberty, Ohio, 1980-85, Mennonite Meml. Home, Bluffton, 1985—; mem. awards com. Ohio Lung Assn., Columbus, 1978—; pres. United Way of Bluffton Richland Twp., 1984; mem. ch. council First Mennonite Ch., Bluffton, 1984-85. USPHS traineeship grantee, 1978, 79. Mem. Am. Coll. Hosp. Adminstrs., Am. Acad. Med. Adminstrs., Mennonite Health Assn., Ohio Hosp. Assn. (mem. various coms. 1982—), Kenton C. of C. (bd. dirs. 1987—). Avocations: music (choral conducting, organ), carpentry, gardening, travel. Home: 110 Clover Ln Kenton OH 43326 Office: Hardin Meml Hosp 921 E Franklin St Kenton OH 43326

WYSOCKI, LOUIS EDWARD, agricultural executive; b. Portage County, Wis., Jan. 4, 1935; s. Francis Xavier and Clara (Grenier) W.; m. Avis Marie Steffanus, July 27, 1957; children: Jacqueline Clare Wille, Gary Joseph, James Edward, Therese Marie, Russell Martin. Grad. high sch., Stevens Point, Wis. Sec., treas. Wysocki Farms, Inc., Custer, Wis., 1963—; pres. Wysocki Sales, Inc., Custer, Wis., 1974—; sec. Paragon Potato Farms, Inc., Custer, Wis., 1978—; dir. chmn. loan commn. Bank of Park Ridge, Stevens Point, Wis., 1979—; chmn. Wis. Dept. Agriculture Bd., Madison, 1981—. Contbr. articles in field.; lectr. in field. Chmn. Wis. Dept. Agriculture Trade Consumer Protection, Madison, 1981—; active Stevens Point Area Found., 1982; conceiver, organizer Wis. Agri-Bus. Found., Madison, 1981. Recipient Outstanding Young Farmer award Wis. Jaycees, 1966, Outstanding Farmers award Future Farmers of Am., 1976, Outstanding Contbn. to Agriculture award, Cen. Wis. C. of C., 1981; named Potato Man of All Seasons, Packer Pub. Co., 1985, Master Agriculturist, Wis. Agriculturist, 1985. Mem. Wis. Potato and Vegetable Growers Assn. (pres. 1969), Wis. Potato Industry Bd. (chmn. 1974), Nat. Potato Council (pres. 1978), Wis. Agri-Bus. Council (pres. 1985). Roman Catholic. Lodge: Elks. Avocations: hunting, fishing, golfing, travel, antique autos. Home: 2041 County J Custer WI 54423 Office: Wysocki Farms Inc 6857 Hwy 66 Custer WI 54423

WYSOCKI, SHARON ANN, publisher, visual artist; b. Detroit, Feb. 20, 1955; d. Arthur Leonard and Casmira (Suchorab) W. Student, Warwick U., 1975; BS, Eastern Mich. U., 1977; postgrad., U. Mich., Mich. State U., 1977—. Cert. addiction counselor, social worker. Psychotherapist Insight, Inc., Flint, Mich., 1979—; pub. Progressive Press, Dearborn Heights, Mich., 1981—; pub. The Wire, 1981—; artist mem. Buckham Fine Arts Project. Co-author: Ariadne's Thread, 1982; editor The Art of the Journal: Journal Art, 1984; represented in Mus. Modern Art, N.Y.C. Mem. Mus. Women in Arts, King Stephen Mus. Democrat. Avocations: show jumping, English gardens and castles, ballet, art therapy. Office: Progressive Press 7320 Colonial Dearborn Heights MI 48127

WYSONG, DAVID CLARK, advertising executive; b. Kansas City, Kans., Mar. 8, 1949; s. Donald C. and Nancy (Peairs) W.; m. Kathryn O'Shaughnessy Lyman, Dec. 29, 1973; children: Erin, Elizabeth. BS in Journalism, U. Kans., 1972. Regional mgr. Strout Realty, Whitefish, Mont., 1972-74; project mgr. Corral De Tierra, Inc., Carmel, Calif., 1974-76; pres. Wysong, Quimby & Jones, Kansas City, 1976—. Corp. chmn. Easter Seals Soc. Kansas City, 1985; past v.p., bd. dirs. Marillac Ctr. for Children, Kansas City, 1984; fellow Nelson Atkins Mus., 1986. Mem. Kansas City Media Profls. (Advt. Hall of Fame 1985, 86). Presbyterian. Clubs: Kansas City (fin. com. 1986—); Mission Hills (Kans.) Country (bd. dirs. 1986—); The Dregs (treas. 1984—); Advt. of Kansas City (pres. 1986—). Avocations: skiing, golf, scuba diving, enology, astronomy. Office: Wysong Quimby & Jones 112 W 9th Kansas City MO 64105

WYSONG, RANDY LEE, medical products executive; b. Midland, Mich., May 21, 1943; s. Donald Vernon and Elizabeth Jeannette (Hagley) W.; m. Betty Jo Jablonski, Feb. 4, 1964 (div. 1979); children: Stephen, Carrie, Tyler, Leah, Deidre; m. Julie Jean Gillis, Apr. 24, 1981; children: Lucas, Logan. Assoc., Delta Coll., 1963; BS, Mich. State U., 1965, DVM, 1968. Gen. practice vet. medicine Colo. and Mich., 1968-85; prin., researcher Wysong Med. Corp., Midland, 1979—; prof. Lansing (Mich.) Coll., 1972-75. Author: The Creation-Evolution Controversy, 1975; inventor in field. Recipient Entrepreneur of Yr. award Saginaw Valley State Coll., 1986. Mem. AVMA, Nat. Health Fedn., Am. Assn. Chemists. Avocations: sports, weight lifting, banjo, woodworking. Home: 2210 El Rancho Midland MI 48640 Office: Wysong Med Corp 1880 N Eastman Midland MI 48640

WYSS, ALAN G., construction products executive; b. Ft. Wayne, Ind., Apr. 1, 1920; s. George T. and Florence (Smith) W.; m. Anne W. Winicker, Apr. 1, 1943; children: David, J. Michael, Patricia. BA, Marquette U., 1942. CPA, Ind. Auditor Gen. Electric, Ft. Wayne, 1946-48; pres., owner Old Ft. Supply Co., Ft. Wayne, 1948—; chmn. bd. Standard Alloys Corp., Hammond, Ind.; pres. Knolls Corp., Ft. Wayne, 1976—, Haciend Place Properties, Ft. Wayne, 1978—, OFM, Inc.,1987—; chmn. Ind. del. White House Conf. Small Bus., Ft. Wayne, 1980, 86. Pres. Horizons Council Econ. Devel., Ft. Wayne, 1980-81, Holy Cross Luth. Ch., Ft. Wayne, 1975-76, Concordia High Sch., Ft. Wayne, 1973-74; pres. Ft. Wayne PTA, 1970-71; bd. dirs. St. Francis Coll., Ft. Wayne. Mem. U.S. C. of C., Ft. Wayne C. of C. (pres. 1978-79, Small Bus. Person of Yr. 1986). Republican. Avocations: golf, little league baseball, restoration of historic projects. Home: 1735 Brandywine Trail Fort Wayne IN 46825 Office: Old Ft Supply Co Inc PO Box 11308 Fort Wayne IN 46857

WYSZYNSKI, RICHARD CHESTER, organization executive, musician, educator; b. Chgo., Feb. 15, 1933; s. Ignatius John and Victoria (Gerlich) W. MusB, B Music Edn., Northwestern U., 1955; Cert. in Music Criticism, U. So. Calif., 1967; pvt. study with Marcel Moyse, Brattleboro, Vt., 1961-65. Exec. dir. Consolidated Athletic Commn., Chgo., 1948—; musical dir. Interguild, Chgo., 1952-54; instr. flute DeLaSalle Inst., Chgo., 1952-56; chmn. music dept. Adult Edn. Ctrs., Chgo., 1957-60; prin. flute N.C. Symphony Orch., 1960, Shreveport (La.) Symphony Orch., 1960-61; conductor Cardinal Chamber Orch., Chgo., 1967—; asst. conductor, flutist "Man of La Mancha" Nat. Touring Companies, 1967-70; instr. music Exptl. Coll. U. So. Calif., Los Angeles, 1972, Cen. YMCA Community Coll., Chgo., 1976; conductor Lincolnwood (Ill.) Community Musical Theater, 1976, Monnacep-Oakton Coll., Des Plaines, Ill., 1977—, De Paul U., Chgo., 1978-80, Northwestern U., Evanston, Ill., 1979-81; lectr. Newberry Library, Chgo., 1979; instr. music Loyola U., Chgo., 1980-84; co-prin. flute Chgo. Symphonic Wind Ensemble, 1982; dir. Singleforum, Chgo., 1985—; lectr. music Chgo. Office Fine Arts, 1985-86. Editor Interplay mag., 1951-54; music critic Old Town Voice, Chgo., 1962-65; scriptwriter several documentary films (N.Y. Film Festival Cine award), 1965-66; producer, announcer Sta. WHPK-FM, 1973-76. Rockefeller Found. grantee, 1965-67. Mem. Am. Fedn. Musicians. Roman Catholic. Avocations: tennis, discussions. Home: 851 N Leavitt St Chicago IL 60622

WYSZYNSKI, VALENTINE ANTHONY, sound design engineer, producer, graphics consultant; b. Chgo., Dec. 24, 1941; s. Anthony Marion and Genevieve Ann (Stabosz) W.; m. Joy Anne Halverson, Oct. 5, 1966 (div. July 1976); children: April Suzanne, Brian Matthew, Charlotte Lillian. Student U.S. Air Force Inst., 1965-68, Nat. Tech Schs., 1968-70; BSEE, N.Mex. State U., 1980, BS in Music Engring. and Drama Tech., 1981. With U.S. Post Office, Lyons, Ill., 1959-64, Circle News, Joliet, Ill., 1971-73; mgr. So. N.Mex. region Combined Ins. Co. of Am., Chgo., 1973-76; sound design engr. drama dept. N.Mex. State U., University Park, 1977-81; ptnr., gen. mgr. Desert Distbg., Las Cruces, N.Mex., 1978-84; editor, photographer Coomes Advt./Entertainment Guide, Las Cruces, 1981-84; gen. mgr. Heartline Prodns., Wood Dale, Ill., 1984—; sound design engr. Candlelight Dinner Playhouse, Summit, Ill., 1985; sales engring. cons. Kayak Mfg. Corp., Westmont, Ill., 1985-86; mgr.. advt. dept. Star-Sentinel Pub., Melrose Pk., Ill., 1987—; mgr., lead guitarist The Majextics, 1959-64, The 1st Nat. Bank, 1968-73. Composer original music for original prodn. Equus, 1977, Children of a Lesser God, 1979 (Tony award 1980). Served to staff sgt.USAF, 1964-70. Mem. Soc. Broadcast Engrs., Soc. Electronic Musicians, U.S. Inst. Theatre Tech., Satellite Antenna Specialists Am., Jaycees (life Romeoville, Ill. chpt., editor Monitor mag. 1969-71, Spoke of Yr. award 1970, Editor of Yr. award 1971). Democrat. Roman Catholic. Avocations: music, photography, creative writing, crafts design. Office: Heartline Prodns PO Box 613 Wood Dale IL 60191

XAGAS, STEVEN GEORGE JAMES, executive search firm executive, consultant, researcher; b. St. Charles, Ill., May 9, 1951; s. Gus and Carolyn Ann (Schneider) X.; m. Yvonne Schafer, Oct. 19, 1985. B.S. in Psychology, Guilford Coll., 1974; postgrad. George Williams Coll., 1975. Homebound detention supr., sr. counselor 16th Judicial Ct. Dist., Geneva, Ill., 1974-77; project coordinator, family counselor Tri City Family Project and Kane County Sch. Office, Geneva, 1977-80; exec. recruiter Search Dynamics, Chgo., 1980-82, CPS, Inc., Westchester, 1982-83; owner, pres. Xagas & Assocs., Geneva, Ill., 1983—; owner, exec. v.p. Quality Research Internat., Inc., Geneva, 1987—. conducts job search seminars., employment cons., met. area Chgo., 1980—. Fundraiser Cancer Soc., Kane County, Ill., 1975—, Heart Assn., Kane County, 1982—; community vol. numerous mental health orgns., Kane County, 1974—. Recipient Community Service Recognition, Tri City Family Project, Geneva, 1980; Exemplary status Law Enforcement Assistance Adminstrn., 1980. Cert. personnel cons. Mem. Am. Soc. Quality Control, Ill. Mgmt. and Exec. Search Cons. Employment Mgmt. Assn. (affiliate), Soc. Mfg. Engrs. (sr.). Lutheran. Office: Xagas & Assocs 701 E State St Suite 1 Geneva IL 60134

YACKLEY, ROBERT FREDERICK, rancher; b. Pierre, S.D., Mar. 6, 1946; s. Beno Walter and Viola (May) Y.; m. Elaine Glee Peterson, May 4, 1961; children: Steve, Todd, Mike. BS in Agr. Edn., S.D. State U., 1962. cert. agr. edn. tchr., S.D. Vocat. agr. tchr. Clark (S.D.) High Sch., Willow Lake (S.D.) High Sch., 1962-65; ranch mgr., owner Onida, S.D., 1965—. 4-H leader, Onida; pres. parish council Cath. Ch., Onida. Named Outstanding Young Farmer Sully County, Onida, 1970, Outstanding Limousin Breeder S.D., 1975. Mem. Nat. Cattleman's Assn., S.D. Stockgrowers, N.Am. Limousin Found. (pres. 1985-86, bd. dirs.), S.D. Limousin Assn. (pres., bd. dirs.), S.D. Jaycees (state dist. v.p. 1968), Onida Jaycees (pres., bd. dirs. 1964-75), S.D. C. of C. (Soil and Moisture award 1970, 85). Democrat. Avocations: softball, boating, playing with grandson, cattle events. Home and Office: Rural Rt 1 Box 705 Onida SD 57564

YAEGER, KAREN ELIZABETH, advertising account executive; b. Wheeling, W.Va., Apr. 27, 1959; d. Louis John Jr. and Kathleen (O'Brien) Y. BBA in Sociology, BA in Mktg., U. Notre Dame, 1981; MSc in Advt., Northwestern U., 1983. Account exec. Campbell Mithum Adv., Mpls., 1984—; lectr. local colls., speaker on careers in mktg. and advt., Mpls., 1986—. Advt. vol. Minn. div. Am. Cancer Soc. Republican. Roman Catholic. Office: Campbell-Mithum Adv Inc 222 S 9th St Minneapolis MN 55402

YAEGER, WILLIAM DUBOIS, graphic design company executive; b. Columbus, Ohio, June 10, 1943; s. Dwight Dubois and Nola Marie (Craft) Y.; m. Annette Susan Richards, Sept. 4, 1964; children: Tyra, Tera, Vince, Nick. Student, Ohio State U., 1961-62, Columbus Coll. Art and Design, 1962-65. Salesman Monarch Printing, Columbus, 1966-68; mgr. sales Perlmuter Printing, Cleve., 1968-70, West-Camp Press, Westerville, Ohio, 1970-75; owner Milenthal & Yaeger, Columbus, 1975-81, Dwight Yaeger Typographer, Columbus, 1981-84; owner, ptnr. Sunset Colour Prodns., Columbus, 1984—; bd. dirs. Craftsmans Club, Columbus, 1983-84. Author: Sales Management, 1982. Recipient top honors state of Ohio, Nat. Soc. of Painters in Casein, 1982. Mem. Printing Industry of Cen. Ohio, Columbus Soc. Communicating Arts, Columbus Area C. of C. Republican. Presbyterian. Home: 7046 Doran Dr New Albany OH 43054 Office: Sunset Colour Prodns 6507 Doubletree Ave Columbus OH 43229

YAGER, GEOFFREY GILBERT, psychologist, educator; b. Schenectady, N.Y., Oct. 30, 1944; s. Jackson Tiffany and Charity Elizabeth (Dibble) Y.; m. Margaret Lee MacAskie, Aug. 23, 1969; children: Scott Thomas, Charity Allison. BA, SUNY, Binghamton, 1966; MA, SUNY, Albany, 1967; PhD, Mich. State U., 1973. Lic. psychologist, profl. counselor, Ohio; nat. cert. counselor. Instr. Mich. State U., East Lansing, 1972-73; asst. prof. U. N.D.,

Grand Forks, 1973-75; asst. prof. U. Cin., 1975-79, assoc. prof., coordinator of counseling, 1979-84, assoc. prof., head Dept. Sch. Psychology and Counseling, 1985—; visiting assoc. prof. U. Pa., Shippensburg, 1984-85; substance abuse counselor Wright State U. Med. Sch. Weekend Intervention Program, Dayton, Ohio, 1982—; coordinator Educators in Industry Program, Evendale, Ohio, 1979—. Contbr. articles to profl. jours. Mem. AAUP, Am. Psychol. Assn., Am. Ednl. Research Assn., Am. Assn. for Counseling & Devel., Assn. for Advancement Behavior Therapy. Democrat. Club: Torch (Cin.) (sec., treas. 1986—). Avocations: tent camping. Home: 11378 Kenshire Dr Cincinnati OH 45240-2238 Office: Dept Sch Psychology & Counseling U Cin Cincinnati OH 45221-0002

YAGER, JOHN WARREN, lawyer, banker; b. Toledo, Sept. 16, 1920; s. Joseph A. and Edna Gertrude (Pratt) Y.; m. Dorothy W. Merki, July 25, 1942; children: Julie M., John M. AB, U. Mich., 1942, JD, 1948. Bar: Ohio 1948. Sole practice Toledo, 1948-64; trust officer Toledo Trust Co., 1964-69; v.p., trust officer First Nat. Bank, Toledo, 1969—; sec. First Ohio Bancshares, Inc., 1980-85. Pres. Toledo Met. Park Dist., 1971-85, Neighborhood Health Assn., 1974-75, councilman, Toledo, 1955-57, 60-61, mayor, 1958-59; bd. dirs. Toledo-Lucas County Library, 1968-70, Riverside Hosp., Downtown Toledo Assn.; past pres. Toledo Legal Aid Soc., Toledo Council Chs., Toledo Mcpl. League, Econ. Opportunity Planning Assn., Toledo, Com. on Relations with Toledo, Spain. Served to maj. USMC, 1942-46, 50-52. Decorated Bronze Star; named one of 10 outstanding young men Toledo, 1952, 54, 55. Mem. Ohio Bar Assn., Toledo Bar Assn., Toledo Estate Planning Council, Delta Tau Delta. Club: Belmont Country (Toledo). Home: 29301 Bates Rd Perrysburg OH 43551-3808 Office: First Nat Bank Toledo 606 Madison Ave Toledo OH 43604

YAHRMATTER, JEROME RONALD, computer operations executive; b. Detroit, Apr. 16, 1958; s. Ronald Jerome and Maureen Elizabeth (O'Connell) Y.; m. Tracy Anne Kellstrom, Oct. 14, 1983. AAS, Macomb Community Coll., Warren, Mich., 1983. Computer operator KMart Corp., Troy, Mich., 1976-79, ops. tech. specialist, 1979-82, lead ops. analyst, 1982-84, mgr. ops. tech. support, 1984—. Avocations: radio controlled aircraft, hunting, fishing, softball. Office: K Mart Corp 3100 W Big Beaver Troy MI 48084

YAKTUS, MICHAEL ROLAND, investment broker; b. Beaver Dam, Wis., Sept. 28, 1961; s. Roland J. Yaktus and Sandra J. (Helbing) Reinke; m. Jennifer L. Helbing, June 16, 1984. BB, U. Wis., Oshkosh, 1983. CPA, Wis.; cert. fin. planner. Acct. Grant Thornton, Madison, Wis., 1983-86; investment broker Blunt, Ellis & Loewi, Madison, 1986—. Mem. Am. Inst. CPA's, Wis. Inst. CPA's, Inst. Cert. Fin. Planners. Republican. Roman Catholic. Avocations: golf, tennis, summer sports. Home: 2656 Chesapeake Dr Madison WI 53719 Office: Blunt Ellis & Loewi 426 S Yellowstone Dr Madison WI 53719

YALE, DONALD ARTHUR, accountant; b. Chgo., May 23, 1944; s. Charles and Eleanor (Gorden) Y.; m. Janis Friedman, June 12, 1968; children—Adam, Alexander, Andrew, Jason, Laura. B.S.B.A., U. Denver, 1968. C.P.A., Colo. Mgr. Stone, Gray & Co., Denver, 1967-74; pres. Yale & Seffinger, Denver, 1974-85; exec. v.p., treas. Borsheim Jewelry Co. Inc., Omaha, 1985—; chmn. Fee Arbitration Com., Denver, 1983. Bd. dirs. Allied Jewish Fedn., Denver, 1980-85; exec. com. Com. for 18, Denver, 1982-85; bd. dirs. Jewish Fedn. Omaha; adv. bd. Children's Meml. Hosp., Omaha. Recipient Adolph Kiesler Young Leadership award, 1983. Mem. Colo. Soc. C.P.A.s (bd. dirs. 1984-85). Democrat. Home: 1108 South 113 Plaza Omaha NE 68144

YALE, RUSSELL STEVEN, physician, surgeon; b. Chgo., Aug. 2, 1947; s. Seymour and Muriel Jane (Cohen) Y.; m. Susan Konik, June 14, 1973; children: Erin, Matthew. BS, U. Ill., Chgo., 1969; MD, Chgo. Med. Sch., 1973. Diplomate Nat. Bd. Med. Examiners, Am. Bd. Otolaryngology. Intern in gen. surgery Northwestern Meml. Hosp., Chgo., 1973-75; resident otolaryngolist, maxillofacial surgeon U. Iowa Hosps., Iowa City, 1975-79; practice medicine specializing in head and neck surgery Milw., 1979—; clin. asst. prof. Med. Coll. Wis.; pvt. practice otolaryngology Milw. Ear, Nose and Throat Clinic. Recipient Roche award, 1973. Mem. AMA, Centurians. Jewish. Home: 7150 W Barnett Fox Point WI 53217 Office: 10520 N Port Washington Rd Mequon WI 53092

YALOWITZ, JEROME MYER, clinical psychologist; b. Chgo., Oct. 24, 1922; s. Joseph and Mary (Shure) Y.; B.S., U. Ill., 1948, M.S., 1949; divorced; children—Rhoda L., Kenneth G., Jean B. Clin. psychologist Manteno (Ill.) State Hosp., 1949-51; chief psychologist E. Moline (Ill.) State Hosp., 1952-54, Peoria (Ill.) State Hosp., 1954-73; coordinator services for elderly Region 1B, Ill. Dept. Mental Health, also dir. Comprehensive Geriatric Treatment Service, Zeller Mental Health Center, Peoria, 1973-86; chief psychologist Painway Program Pekin (Ill.) Meml. Hosp., 1986— . Served with AUS, 1943-46. Recipient Francis J. Gerty award State of Ill., 1969, 74, 79, 82. Mem. Am. Psychol. Assn., Midwestern Psychol. Assn., Ill. Psychol. Assn. (council 1966-74), Central Ill. Soc. Health Service Providers in Psychology (v.p. 1980-82), Peoria Area Assn. Psychologists (pres. 1956-57, 75-76). Jewish. Editor, Ill. Psychologist, 1966-71. Home: 419 Clybourn Ct Peoria IL 61614 Office: Pekin Meml Hosp Court and 14th St Pekin IL 61554

YALVAC, SELIM, chemical engineer; b. Ankara, Turkey, Jan. 27, 1953; s. Mustafa Resid and Kadriye Refia (Tansug) Y.; m. Engin Deniz Tekkanat, Dec. 19, 1976; 1 child, Arda. BS, Middle East Tech. U., Ankara, 1975, MS, 1976; PhD in Chemical Engring., U. Mich., 1982. Engr. Dow Chem. Co., Midland, Mich., 1982—. Patentee in field. U. Mich. fellow 1977; Fulbright scholar 1976-80. Mem. Am. Soc. for Composites, Soc. for the Advancement of Materials and Process Engring. (v.p. Tri-City chpt.), Soc. Mfg. Engrs. (composites group). Avocations: playing flute, 8mm movie making, compact disks. Home: 2005 Candlestick Ln Midland MI 48640 Office: Dow Chem USA Central Research 1712 Bldg Midland MI 48674

YAMADA, THOMAS GORDON, advertising executive; b. Pepeekeo, Hawaii, July 2, 1923; s. Joseph Tomokichi and Momoyo (Mizuire) Y.; m. Betty Sachiko, June 24, 1951; children: David Charles, Jeffery Paul. Student, U. Hawaii, 1940-42, 46-47, Ray Coll. Comml. Art, 1947-50. Prodn. mgr. J.J. Gordon Advt., Chgo., 1951-55; account exec. Sorensen Studios, Chgo., 1955-57; owner Yamada Advt., Chgo., 1957-73, Highland, Ind., 1973—. Chmn. parks and recreation Hammond (Ind.) PTA Council, 1980-85, by-laws chmn. 1986—; chmn. N.W. Ind. ARC, 1981-83; mem. adv. council Midwest Ops. Hdqrs. ARC, St. Louis, 1983-86; 1st v.p. Calumet Goodwill Industries, 1987. Served to sgt. U.S. Army, 1943-45, CBI. Named Outstanding Vol. of Yr., Lake County Red Cross, Hammond, 1985; recipient Medal of Merit, Schererville (Ind.) Rotary Club, 1983. Republican. Lodge: Rotary (pres. Highland club 1977-78, pres. elect Hammond club 1987—). Avocation: music. Office: Yamada Advt 9219 Indianapolis Blvd Highland IN 46322

YAMIN, JOSEPH FRANCIS, lawyer, counselor; b. Detroit, Mar. 12, 1956; s. Raymond Samuel and Sadie Ann (John) Y. B.A., Oakland U., 1975; B.A., U. Mich., 1978; J.D., London Sch. Econs., 1981; J.D., Detroit Coll. Law, 1982. Bar: U.S. Ct. Appeals (6th cir.) 1982, U.S. Dist. Ct. (ea. dist.) Mich. 1982. Assoc. Alan R. Miller, P.C., Birmingham, Mich., 1981—; dir., Am. Wash Systems, Birmingham, 1979—; instr. Detroit Coll. Law, 1984—. Contbr. to publs. Recipient Am. Jurisprudence Book award Am. Jurisprudence Soc., 1981. Mem. Oakland County Bar Assn., State of Mich. Bar Assn., ABA, Chi Phi. Roman Catholic. Office: Alan R Miller PC 300 E Maple Suite 200 Birmingham MI 48011

YAMMINE, RIAD NASSIF, oil company executive; b. Hammana, Lebanon, Apr. 12, 1934; s. Nassib Nassif and Emilie (Daou) Y.; came to U.S., 1952, naturalized, 1963; m. Beverly Ann Hosack, Sept. 14, 1954; children: Kathleen Yammine Griffiths, Cynthia Yammine Rotman, Michael. BS in Petroleum Engring., Pa. State U., 1956; postgrad. Advanced Mgmt. Program, Harvard U., 1977. Registered profl. engr., Ohio. Engr. Trans-Arabian Pipe Line Co., Saudi Arabia, 1956-61; with Marathon Pipe Line Co., 1961-75, mgr. Western div., Casper, Wyo., 1971-74, mgr. Eastern div., Martinsville, Ill., 1974-75; mktg. ops. mgr. Marathon Oil Co., 1975-83; pres. Marathon Pipeline Co., 1983-84; v.p. supply and transp., dir. Marathon Petroleum Co., 1984—; also officer, bd. dirs. various subs. Patentee in field. Mem. ch. council, chmn. finance com. First Luth. Ch., Findlay; past trustee, Fisk U. Mem. ASME, Am. Petroleum Inst. Republican. Club: Findlay Country. Home: 624 Winterhaven Dr Findlay OH 45840 Office: 539 S Main St Findlay OH 45840

YAMOOR, MOHAMMED YOUNIS, animal nutritionist; b. Mosul, Iraq, July 7, 1941; s. Younis Yousif and Sabiha Ziyada (Husein) Y.; m. Catherine Marie Hagen, Sept. 11, 1965; children—Nadia Marie, Omar Wayne. B.S., U. Baghdad, 1962; M.S., U. Minn., 1967, Ph.D., 1971. Prof., head dept. animal prodn. U. Tripoli, Libya, 1972-78; expert FAO, Rome, 1978-79; Mid-East cons. agrl. devel. projects, 1979-83; expert animal prodn. FAO, Rome, Saudi Arabia, 1983—; lectr., cons. agrl. devel. specialist. Mem. U. Minn. Alumni Assn., Sigma Chi.

YANA, DAVID VARDA, pathologist; b. Paris, Sept. 22, 1937; came to U.S., 1962; s. Nemrud Beblis and Regina (David-Jean) Y.; m. M. Dawn Coffman, Mar. 27, 1968; children: Jennifer E., Jason N. MD, Tehran (Iran) Med. Sch., 1962. Diplomate Am. Bd. Pathology. Intern Episcopal Hosp., Phila., 1963; resident in pathology Albert Einstein Med. Ctr., Phila., 1964-65, Phila. Gen. Hosp., 1965-67, Wadsworth (Va.) and UCLA Hosps., Los Angeles, 1967-68; chief pathologist Suburban Gen. Hosp., Norristown, Pa., 1972-75, North Penn Hosp., Lansdale, 1975-76; assoc. pathologist Holy Family Hosp., Des Plaines, Ill., 1976—; cons. pathologist Forest Hops., Des Plaines, 1976—, Fahey Med. Ctr., Des Plaines, 1976—. Mem. Chgo. Med. Soc., Ill. State Med. Soc., AMA, Coll. Am. Pathologists, Am. Soc. Clinical Pathologists. Home: 7 Kingswood Ct Riverwoods IL 60015 Office: Holy Family Hosp 100 N River Rd Des Plaines IL 60016

YANDL, GEORGE ANTHONY, sporting goods executive; b. South Bend, Ind., Mar. 9, 1947; s. George Michael and Pauline (Helling) Y.; m. Cheryl Diane True, Aug. 24, 1968; children: Emily, Geoffrey, Michael, David. Student in elec. engring. tech., Lake Mich. Coll., Benton Harbor, Mich., 1968; BSEE with high honors, Mich. Tech. U., 1973. Sr. technician Reed Comml. Electronics, Benton Harbor, 1968-70; design engr. No. Tech. Services, Laurium, Mich., 1973-75; pres., chief exec. officer Firearms and Supplies, Inc., Hancock, Mich., 1975—. Exhibited various wilderness nature photographs, 1982-86. Mem. Phi Kappa Phi, Phi Eta Sigma. Republican. Roman Catholic. Avocations: programming micro computers in assembly lang., hunting. Office: Firearms and Supplies Inc 514 Quincy St Hancock MI 49930

YANEY, WILLIAM ALLEN, music industry executive, music educator, concert organist; b. Decatur, Ala., Mar. 27, 1945; s. Wayne Allen and Jessie Louise (Holben) Y.; m. Monica Lynne Haydu, Sept. 10, 1982. Student U. Toledo, 1963-65. Sales mgr. Brenner Music Co., Toledo, Ohio, 1965-68; v.p. Howards Organs and Pianos, Inc., Toledo, 1968-81; cons., product specialist, tchr. Gt. Lakes Pianos and Organs, Toledo, 1981—; profl. performer radio and TV, concert artist, 1959—; resident organist Ohio Theatre, Toledo, 1986—. Records include Front Row Center: Bill Yaney at the Mighty Wurlitzer Theatre Pipe Organ, 1986. Mem. Am. Fedn. Musicians, Am. Theater Organ Soc., Toledo Area Theater Organ Soc., Detroit Theater Organ Club. Home: 6537 Abbey Run Sylvania OH 43560 Office: 5212 Monroe St Toledo OH 43623

YANG, HENRY KELL, ophthalmologist; b. Phila., Oct. 27, 1951; s. Stephen Y.H. and Stella (Koo) Y. B.A., U. Pa., 1972; M.D., N.Y. Med. Coll., 1975. Diplomate Am. Bd. Ophthalmology. Intern Hosp. U. Pa., Phila., 1975-76; resident in ophthalmology U. Md., Balt., 1976-79; fellow Oram R. Kline, Jr., Woodbury, N.J., 1979-80; asst. prof. ophthalmology U. Mo., Columbia, 1980-82; courtesy med. staff Wills Eye Hosp., Phila., 1980—; active staff Boone Hosp. Ctr., Columbia, 1982—. Author: (with others) Posterior Chamber Implant Surgery, 1983. Contbr. articles to profl. jours. Vice-pres. Mus. Assocs. Mus. Art and Archaeology, U. Mo., Columbia, 1983-84. Fellow Am. Acad. Ophthalmology. Republican. Avocations: tennis; art history. Home: Cedar Grove Blvd Columbia MO 65201 Office: Doctors Park 203 W Broadway Columbia MO 65203

YANG, PHILIP YUNG-CHIN, chemist; b. Pin-ton, Taiwan, Republic of China, Nov. 20, 1954; came to U.S., 1976, naturalized, 1985; s. Tien-Ho and Shong (Lee) Y. BE, Feng Chia U., Taiwan, 1976; MS, Cleve. State U., 1978; PhD, U. Ill., 1982. Advanced chemist researh and devel. B.F. Goodrich, Avon Lake, Ohio, 1982-85, sr. chemist research and devel., 1985—, advanced chemist researh and devel., 1982-85, sr. chemist research and devel., 1985—. Mem. Am. Chem. Soc., Am. Physical Soc., Am. Inst. Chem. Engrs., Soc. Plastics Engrs. Home: 401 Hurst Dr Bay Village OH 44140 Office: BF Goodrich Chem Co Avon Lake OH 44012

YANG, WILOX, physicist; b. Canton, China, May 25, 1922; s. Shaw Hong and Ah Han (Lee) Y.; m. Constance Lee Bycofski, Jan. 20, 1960 (dec. June 1964); m. Janet D. Smith, Mar. 23, 1966; children—Eleanor, Lisa, Lori. B.Sc., Huachung U., Wuchang, China, 1947; M.Sc., Poly. Inst. N.Y., 1963, Ph.D., 1974. Mem. staff Princeton-Penn Accelerator, Princeton (N.J.) U., 1962-69; mem. staff high energy physics research U. Pa., Phila., 1969-75; engring. physicist Fermilab, Batavia, Ill., 1975—. Mem. Am. Phys. Soc., N.Y. Acad. Sci., Sigma Xi. Democrat. Club: Sigma Xi. Contbr. articles to profl. jours. Home: 30 W 113 Lindenwood Ct Warrenville IL 60555 Office: Fermi Nat Accelerator Lab PO Box 500 Batavia IL 60510

YANICKE, GEORGIA ANN, educational administrator; b. Milw., July 10, 1945; d. George Elmer and Lucille Sylvia (Schroeder) Y. Student Goethe Inst., Murnau,-W.Ger., 1966, U. Innsbruck (Austria), 1966; B.A., Cornell Coll., 1967; M.S., U. Wis. Milw., 1970; Ph.D., U. Wis., Madison, 1975. Cert. spl. edn. supr., tchr., Wis. Tchr. mentally retarded McKinley Sch., West Allis, Wis., 1967-69; lectr. U. Wis.-Milw., 1970-74, 77-79, 84-85; practicum supr. U. Wis.-Madison, 1974-75; asst. prof. Creighton U., Omaha, 1975-77; supr. programs for emotionally disturbed and generic early childhood Milw. Pub. Schs., 1977-85, early childhood: exceptional edn. needs, 1985—; cons. Sitters for Handicapped Children Project, Milw. area Girl Scouts U.S., 1973-74, Milw. Pub. Schs., 1976, Creighton U. Inst. for Bus., Law and Social Research, 1976-77; inservice coordinator for Blessed Sacrament St. Richards and St. Philip Neri Catholic Schs., Omaha, Nebr., 1975-76; developer, adminstr. pre-kindergarten screening instrument, 1976-77; mem. child care adv. com. Milw. Area Tech. Coll., 1979-80; mem. edn. study group Wis. Dept. Pub. Instrn., Madison, 1981; condr. workshops in field; speaker profl. meetings. Active Greater Milw. Girl Scouts U.S., 1961-77, bd. dirs., 1971-75; mem. ad hoc study com. Children's Day Services, Planning Council for Mental Health and Social Services, Inc., Milw., 1981-82; mem. ad hoc early childhood aquatics Greater Milw. chpt. ARC, mem. adaptive aquatics com., 1983-85; mem. vol. day care com. for ednl. programming, Milw. County Zoo, 1984. U.S. Office Edn. fellow, 1969-70; U. Wis.-Madison Grad. Sch. fellow, 1974. Mem. Council for Exceptional Children (div. children with learning disabilities state and province com. 1976-77), Am. Assn. on Mental Deficiency, Internat. Reading Assn., Wis. State Reading Assn. (emergent reading com. 1986—), Nat. Soc. for Autistic Children (bd. dirs. Milw. Assn. 1983—), Nat. Council Tchrs. of English, Wis. Assn. for Children with Behavior Disorders (adv. bd. 1977-82, 84—, pres. 1983-84), Wis. Assn. Infant/Toddler Devel. (sec. 1982—), Phi Delta Kappa, Pi Lambda Theta, Delta Kappa Gamma (sec. 1985-86). Home: 9085 N 85th St Milwaukee WI 53224 Office: Elem Zone Milw Pub Schs 3620 N 18th St Milwaukee WI 53206

YANITY, JOSEPH BLAIR, JR., lawyer; b. Homer City, Pa., Nov. 11, 1925; s. Joseph Blair and Perina Maria (Carcelli) Y.; m. Joyce Ann Gilham, Jan. 9, 1954; children: Joseph B., John M., Jennifer A. AB with honors, Eastern Ky. U., 1949; JD, Washington and Lee U., 1952. Bar: Ohio 1953, U.S. Dist. Ct. (so. dist.) Ohio 1966. Ptnr. Lavelle & Yanity, Athens, Ohio, 1953-78, Yanity & De Veau, Athens, 1978-85; pros. atty. County of Athens, 1958-61; dir. Bank One of Athens; gen. counsel O'Bleness Meml. Hosp., Athens, 1970—. Mem. Vets. Commn. Athens County, 1961—; v.p., trustee Ohio Valley Health Services Found., Athens, 1965—; pres., trustee Auto Club of Southeastern Ohio, Portsmouth, 1970—. Served to 1st lt. U.S. Army, 1943-53, ETO. Recipient Outstanding Alumnus prize Eastern Ky. U., 1976, E.E. Davis award Ohio Valley Health Services Found., 1981. Mem. Athens County Bar Assn. (pres. 1971), Ohio State Bar Assn., ABA, Am. Legion. Republican. Roman Catholic. Club: Synposiarchs (pres. 1979). Lodges: K.C. (grand Knight 1965), Elks (exalted ruler 1961). Avocation: football officiating. Home: 42 Utah Pl Athens OH 45701 Office: PO Drawer 748 Athens OH 45701

YANKEE, STEPHEN PAUL, writer, producer, director; b. Iron Mountain, Mich., July 28, 1945; s. Herbert Herman and A. Catherine (Engstrom) Y.; m. Luana Lynne Baxter, Sept. 28, 1968 (div. 1974); children: Nicole, Chay; m. Kim Kendall Kircher, Aug. 26, 1978; children: Demian, Anna, Laura. Student, Northwestern Mich. U., 1963-66. Pres. The Yankee Group, Grand Rapids, Mich., 1978-82; v.p., creative dir. J.I. Scott Co., Grand Rapids, 1982-84; exec. v.p., creative dir. Martin, Windsor & Assocs., Grand Rapids, 1984—; cons. in field, 1980—. Contbr. articles to profl. jours. Served as sgt. USARNG, 1965-71. Named Soldier of Yr., Detroit Free Press, 1969, All-Star, A/V Communications, 1981. Mem. Mensa. Lutheran. Office: Martin Windsor & Assocs 234 Federal Sq Bldg Grand Rapids MI 49503

YANKER, MARY MARGARET, management consultant; b. Henderson, Ky., Mar. 3, 1936; s. Roy Sackfield and Mary Frances (Robinson) Crawley; m. Robert Henry Yanker Sr., Sept. 1, 1956; children: Mary Anne, Robert Henry Jr., Rodney Steven, Randall Stuart, Holly Marita. Student, Vanderbilt U., 1953-55; AB in Anthropology, U. Pitts., 1960, postgrad., 1962, 63, 66; MS in Edn., No. Ill. U., 1969, EdD, 1973. Assoc. prof. Aurora (Ill.) U., 1973-79, dean grad. studies, 1979-81; dir., officer Chgo. Cons. Group, 1981-83; pres. Yanker Assocs, Ltd., Crown Point, Ind., 1983—; chairperson social and behavioral scis., Aurora, 1973-81. Contbr. articles to profl. jours. Alderwoman City Aurora, 1980; bd. dirs. Aurora Drug Abuse Council, Family Support Ctr., YWCA, United Way; mem. Instl. Rev. Com. Mercy Ctr. Danforth assoc., 1976; Kellogg fellow, 1977. Mem. Ill. Commn. Status Women, Chgo. Assn. Women Bus. Owners. Avocation: travel. Home and Office: 2529 E Lake Shore Dr Crown Point IN 46307

YANKUNAS, MICHAEL STANLEY, accountant; b. Port Washington, Wis., Apr. 26, 1950; s. Stanley Gregory and Marion Adella (Lohmann) Y.; m. Elaine Marie Dorsey, Mar. 28, 1981; children: Brian Michael, Aubrie Lynn. BBA in Fin., U. Wis., Whitewater, 1972, BBA in Acctg., 1977. CPA, Wis. Sales and service rep. Deluxe Check Printers, Milw., 1974-75; staff acct. Virchow, Krause & Co., Madison, Wis., 1976-77; acctg. mgr. Virchow, Krause & Co., Madison, 1979-85; staff acct. Peat Marwick Mitchell/W.O. Daley, Orlando, Fla., 1978-79; pvt. practice acctg. Racine, Wis., 1986—. Com. mem. Racine County Econ. Devel. Corp., 1987—; dir. Salvation Army Racine, 1983-85. Mem. Am. Inst. CPA's, Wis. Inst. CPA's (com. mem. 1987). Republican. Club: Racine Country. Lodge: Rotary (sec.-treas. downtown Racine club 1986-87, bd. dirs. 1987). Avocations: restoring old sports cars, tennis, golf. Home: 301 Elizabeth St Waterford WI 53185 Office: 601 Lake Ave Racine WI 53403

YANNELLO, MARK HUBERT, auditor, federal agency administrator; b. Streator, Ill., Sept. 21, 1950; s. Thomas Mark and Gabrielle Susan (Boeynaems) Y.; m. Judith Odegard, Dec. 5, 1981; 1 child, Ashley. BA, St. Ambrose Coll., 1972; MBA, Western Ill. U., 1974. CPA, Ill. Govt. auditor U.S. Gen. Acctg. Office, Chgo., 1980-83, U.S. Dept. Transp., Chgo., 1983-86, U.S. Defense Contract Audit Agy., Chgo., 1986—. Mem. Am. Inst. CPA's, Ill. Soc. CPA's. Roman Catholic. Avocations: golf, jogging. Home: 16 N Prospect Ave Clarendon Hills IL 60514 Office: US Defense Contract Audit Agy 527 S LaSalle St Chicago IL 60605

YANTIS, JOSEPH EDWARD, corporate communications executive, public relations counselor; b. Tipp City, Ohio, Aug. 25, 1938; s. Roy A. and Marjorie (LeVan) Y.; m. Sharon J. Ridge, Aug. 25, 1963; children: Sheryl, Jennifer, Michael. BS, Ohio State U., 1962; MA, Mich. State U., 1966. Asst. dir. pub. affairs Adrian (Mich.) Coll., 1962-65; communications coordinator Whirlpool Corp., LaPorte, Ind., 1966-67; communications mgr. Whirlpool Corp., Marion, Ohio, 1967-72; mgr. pub. relations Whirlpool Corp., Benton Harbor, Mich., 1972-75; dir. pub. relations Biggs/Gilmore Assocs., Kalamazoo, 1977-85; corp. communications dir. Prab Robots, Inc., Kalamazoo, 1985—. Mem. Portage (Mich.) No. Choir Parents, 1982—. Recipient Aid to Edn. award, Western Mich. U. Ad Club, Kalamazoo, 1986. Mem. Pub. Relations Soc. Am. (accredited, counselor's acad., pres. Western Mich. chpt. 1977). Mem. Disciples of Christ Ch. Avocations: woodworking, golf, gardening. Home: 6306 Cherrywood Portage MI 49002 Office: Prab Robots Inc PO Box 2121 Kalamazoo MI 49003

YANTIS, RICHARD PERRY, mathematics educator, consultant; b. Westerville, Ohio, July 1, 1932; s. Samuel Perry and Mabel Martha (Snook) Yantis; m. Jane McAllister, Oct. 10, 1959; children: John Perry, James Theodore. BS, U.S. Naval Acad., 1954; MS, U. N.C., 1962; PhD, Ohio State U., 1966. Commd. 2d lt. USAF, 1954, advanced thorugh grades to lt. col., 1969, served as transport navigator military air transp. service, 1956-57; instr. navigator USAF, McGuire AFB, N.J., 1957-60; instr. maths. USAF Acad., Colorado Springs, Colo., 1962-64, asst. to assoc. prof. maths., 1966-68, enrichment br., dept math., 1968-69, chief advanced br. dept. math., 1969-70; reconnaissance navigator 553 Recon Squad USAF, Korat, Thailand, 1970-71; assoc. prof. ops. research AFIT USAF, Wright-Patterson AFB, Ohio, 1971-74; retired USAF, 1974; prin. systems analyst Battelle Research, Columbus, Ohio, 1974-75; instr. math. Columbus Acad., 1975-76; assoc. prof. Otterbein Coll., Westerville, Ohio, 1976-87, prof., 1987—; cons. actuarial dept. Nationwide Ins. Co., Columbus, 1965-66, asst. chief staff Studies and Analysis, Pentagon, 1967, USAF dir. Personnel Plans, Pentagon, 1972-73, OSD Manpower and Res. Affairs, Pentagon, 1973-74, Chas E Merrill Publ. Co., Westerville, Ohio, 1985-86. Co-author: Elementary Matrix Algebra with Linear Programming, 1971, Matrix Algebra with Applications, 1977; co-editor Westerville, Ohio 1910 Census and Genealogical Data, 1985. Trustee Westerville Hist. Soc., 1985-86; mem. Westerville Hist. Soc., Franklin County Geneal. Soc., Ohio Hist. Soc., Md. Hist. Soc., Palatines to Am. Mem. Inst. Mgmt. Scis., Nat. Council Tchrs. Maths., Retired Officers Assn., Sigma Xi. Presbyterian. Lodges: Sertoma, Optimists. Avocations: general. research, fgn. travel, athletics. Home: 265 Storington Rd Westerville OH 43081 Office: Otterbein Coll Westerville OH 43081

YAO, ALBERT REN-FENG, mechanical engineer; b. Taiwan, Nov. 11, 1947; s. Wen-Chin W. and Shang-Ju C. Yao; m. Judy Y. Hsiao, Nov. 21, 1949; children—Alice Y., Lisa Y. B.S., Chunhsing U., Taiwan, 1970; M.S., U. Iowa, 1974, Ph.D. in Mech. Engring., 1976. Cert. mfg. technologist. Teaching asst. Chunghsing U., Taiwan, 1971-72; researcher asst. U. Iowa, 1972-76; mfg. engr. Internat. Harvester Co., Rock Island, Ill., 1976-83; mech. engr. for computer application Rock Island Arsenal, 1983—. Mem. Computer and Automated Systems Assn., Soc. Mfg. Engrs., ASME, Sigma Xi. Home: 3885 Tanglefoot Ct Bettendorf IA 52722 Office: SMCRI-ENE 110 Rock Island Arsenal Rock Island IL 61299

YAO, TITO GO, physician; b. Manila, May 30, 1943; came to U.S., 1970, naturalized, 1984; s. Vicente and Sin Keng (Go) Y.; M.D., Far Eastern U., Manila, 1969; m. Lilia Ytem, July 3, 1976; children—Robert James, Richard. Diplomate Am. Bd. Pediatrics, Am. Bd. Quality Assurance. Intern, Evang. Deaconess Hosp., Milw., 1970-71; resident in pediatrics T.C. Thompson Children's Hosp., Chattanooga, 1971-72, Methodist Hosp., Bklyn., 1972-73; fellow St. Christopher Hosp. Children, Phila., 1973-74, Cook County Children's Hosp., Chgo., 1974-75; dir. GSK Med. Center, Chgo., 1976—, chmn. St. Anne's Hosp. dept. pediatrics, 1986—; RJ Med. Center, Chgo.; mem. staff St. Anne's Hosp., Loretto Hosp., Mary Thompson Hosp. Fellow Am. Acad. Pediatrics, Am. Coll. Utilization Rev. Physicians; mem. AMA (Physician Recognition award 1973—), Assn. Philippine Physicians Practicing in Am., Ill. Med. Assn., Am. Assn. Individual Investors, Chgo. Med. Soc., Chgo. Pediatric Soc. Office: 5352 W North Ave Chicago IL 60639

YAP, HING, auditor; b. Seremban, Malaysia, Apr. 16, 1954; s. Hung Yap and Moi (Hon) Tai, m. Jeanne Elizabeth Ritchie, June 11, 1982; 1 child, Rachel Elizabeth. BBA, Concordia U., Montreal, Can., 1978; MBA, U. Wis., 1979. CPA, Wis., Ill. Fin. dir. Jackson Lumber Harvester Co., Mondovi, Wis., 1980-82; auditor Alexander Grant and Co., Madison, Wis., 1982-84; fin. planning mgr. Conagra, Inc., Eau Claire, Wis., 1984-85; internal auditor Wickes Co., Wheeling, Ill., 1985—; cons. Red Horse Mfg. Co., Ltd., Kuala Lampur, Malaysia, 1979—; bd. dirs. Soong Lim Credit Enterprise & Co., Malaysia. Campaign asst. Conservative Party, Ont., Can., 1975; evangel. com. Immanuel Luth. Ch., Madison, 1984. Fellow Am. Inst.

CPA's; mem. Wis. Soc. CPA's (small bus. com. 1984). Home: 1080 W Glenn Trail Elk Grove Village IL 60007

YAPOUJIAN, NERSES NICK, manufacturing executive; b. Yerevan, Armenia, USSR, June 19, 1950; came to U.S., 1975; s. John and Sandought (Chekijian) Y. BSEE, BS in Physics, Yerevan Poly. Inst., Armenia, 1973; B in English, Harvard U., 1976; postgrad. in engring., Northeastern U., Mass., 1978, Marquette U., 1980. Instr. physics Electrotech Coll., Yerevan, 1973-74; chief engr. Electric Light Corp., Yerevan, 1974-75; quality control specialist E.G. & G. Corp., Waltham, Mass., 1975-78; project leader Gen. Instrument Corp., Chgo., 1978-83; v.p. engring. General Protection Corp., Chgo., 1983—; internat. engring. cons. Protel, Paris, France, 1986—. Sr. contbg. editor NBC Defense & Technolgy, 1986—; contbr. articles to profl. jours.; patentee in field. Served to lt. Armenian Army, 1973. Avocations: tennis, golf, polo, chess. Office: Gen Protection Corp PO Box 597631 Chicago IL 60659

YARBROUGH, LARRY NATHAN, comptroller; b. Eads, Colo., Nov. 6, 1942; s. Charles Leroy and Florene Halcy (Cook) Y.; m. Helen Katherine Verhoek, Sept. 17, 1972; 1 child, Gwendolyn Leigh. BA, U. Colo., 1965; MA, U. Denver, 1969; M Mgmt., Northwestern U., 1976. CPA, Ill. Reference librarian Northwestern U., Evanston, Ill., 1970-77; sr. auditor Thomas Havey & Co CPA's, Chgo., 1977-84; comptroller Laborers' and Retirement Bd. Employees' Annuity and Benefit Fund of Chgo., 1985—. Council on Library Resources fellow, 1974. Mem. Am. Inst. CPA's, Ill. CPA Soc. Democrat. Lutheran. Avocations: microcomputers, music. Office: Laborers' and Retirement Bd Employees' Annuity and Benefit Fund 221 N LaSalle St #748 Chicago IL 60601

YARKONY, GARY MICHAEL, physician, researcher; b. N.Y.C., May 22, 1953; s. Stanley H. and Ann (Kiken) Y.; m. Janice Hollander, June, 1975; children: Judith, Rachel. BA in Biology, SUNY, Buffalo, 1974; MD, SUNY, Syracuse, 1978. Diplomate Am. Bd. Phys. Medicine and Rehab. Intern, then resident in physical medicine, rehab. Northwestern U., Chgo., 1978-81, chief resident dept. rehab. medicine, 1980; asst. dir. head trauma program Rehab. Inc. Chgo., 1981-84, attending staff, 1981—; assoc. attending staff Northwestern Meml. Hosp., Chgo., 1984—; dir. rehab. Midwest Regional Spinal Cord Injury Care System, Chgo., 1984—. Contbr. articles to profl. jours, and chpt. to book. Fellow Am. Acad. Physical Medicine and Rehab.; mem. Assn. Academic Physiatrists, Am. Spinal Injury Assn., Internat. Med. Soc. Paraplegia, Internal Rehab. Medicine Assn., Phi Beta Kappa, Phi Eta Sigma. Office: Rehab Inst of Chgo 345 E Superior Chicago IL 60004

YAROS, RONALD ANTHONY, meteorologist; b. Bay City, Mich., Jan. 9, 1957; s. Anthony Paul and Stella Alice (Kandrow) Y.; m. Carey Fosher, May 25, 1985. BA in Communications, U. Wis., 1980; student in Metereology, St. Louis U., 1982—. Weather reporter Sta. WXOX, Bay City, Mich., 1970-75; news reporter Sta. WSGW, Sta. WIOG-FM, Saginaw, Mich., 1976-78, Sta. WISM-AM-FM, Madison, Wis., 1978-80; chief metereologist Sta. WMTV-TV, Madison, 1979-82, Sta. KTVI-TV, St. Louis, 1982—; host, producer Sta. WUCM-TV (PBS), Saginaw, 1975-77; tchr. metereology St. Louis Community Coll., 1983—. Producer, author: For Spacious Skies (ednl. program), St. Louis, 1985, 86; producer Greenhouse Effect (TV edn. series), St. Louis, 1983, 84. Announcer Wis. Radio Service for Blind, Madison, 1978-80; host Children's Miracle Network Telethon, St. Louis, 1983, 84; hon. chmn. March of Dimes Walkamerica, St. Louis, 1985, 86; bd. dirs. Make A Wish, Mo. Energy Care, St. Louis Ctr. Assocs. Recipient Emmy for Best Weathercaster, St. Louis, Nat. Assn. TV, Arts and Scis., 1983, 85, Emmy for Best Ednl. Series, St. Louis, Nat. Assn. TV, Arts and Scis., 1986; named Best TV Personality Toastmasters Internat., 1986. Mem. Am. Metereol. Soc. (profl., TV Seal of Approval), Nat. Weather Assn. (profl., TV Seal of Approval), Alpha Epsilon Rho. Roman Catholic. Avocations: biking, swimming, photography, playing drums. Office: KTVI-TV 5915 Berthold Ave Saint Louis MO 63110

YATES, SANDRA ANN, corporate professional; b. Lincoln, Nebr., Sept. 27, 1948; d. Robert Eugene and Ruth Adele (May) Rohn; m. Terry Dean Lineman, Oct. 3, 1969 (div.); m. Thomas A. Yates, May 15, 1975. Grad., High Sch., Lincoln, 1966. Pub. relations asst. Bankers Life Nebr., Lincoln, 1966-75; adminstrv. v.p. Yates & Assocs., Lincoln, 1982—. V.p. Lincoln Welcome Wagon, 1985, Lincoln NuComers, 1986. Republican. Presbyterian. Avocations: golf, tennis, bridge. Office: Yates & Assocs 6447 Boxelder Dr Lincoln NE 68506

YATES, SIDNEY RICHARD, congressman, lawyer; b. Chgo., Aug. 27, 1909; s. Louis and Ida (Siegel) Y.; m. Adeline Holleb, June 24, 1935; 1 child, Stephen R. Ph.B., U. Chgo., 1931, J.D., 1933. Bar: Ill. bar 1933. Practiced as sr. mem. Yates & Holleb; asst. atty. Ill. State Bank Receiver, 1935-37; asst. atty. gen. attached as traction atty. Ill. Commerce Commn., 1937-40; mem. 80th-87th, also 89th-100th congresses from 9th Ill. Dist.; U.S. del. UN Trusteeship Council with rank of ambassador. Served to lt. USN, 1944-46. Mem. Am., Ill. State, Chgo. bar assns., Am. Vets. Com., Chgo. Council Fgn. Relations, Decalogue Soc. Lawyers. Democrat. Jewish. Clubs: City, Bryn Mawr Country. Office: US House of Reps 2234 Rayburn House Office Bldg Washington DC 20515

YEAGER, ANSON ANDERS, columnist, former newspaper editor; b. Salt Lake City, June 5, 1919; s. Charles Franklin and Elise Marie (Thingelstad) Y.; m. Ada May Bidwell, Sept. 10, 1944; children—Karen Ann, Anson Anders, Harry H., Terry Douglas, Ellen Elise. B.S., S.D. State U.-Brookings, 1947; LL.D., Dakota State Coll., Madison, S.D., 1972. Printer's devil, linotype operator Faith Ind. and Gazette (S.D.), 1935-38; printer S.D. State U., 1940-41; staff writer Argus Leader, Sioux Falls, S.D., 1947-55, Sunday editor, 1955-60, exec. editor, 1961-77, assoc. editor, 1978-84, editor editorial page, 1961-84, columnist, 1984—, author editorials and column of commentary; lectr. dept. journalism U. S.D., 1953-55. Contbr. World Book Ency., 1966—. Bd. dirs. Sioux Falls Devel. Found., 1967; dir. Sioux council Boy Scouts Am., Sioux Falls, 1967-72, v.p., 1970-72; bd. dirs. Boys' Club of Sioux Falls, 1966-68. Served to capt. U.S. Army, 1942-46, 50-52; lt. col. Res. (ret.). Decorated Army Commendation medal; recipient Editorial Excellence award William Allen White Found., 1976; Disting. Alumni award S.D. State U., 1980; Ralph D. Casey Minn. award for Disting. Service in Journalism U. Minn., 1981, Eminent Service award East River Elec. Power Coop., 1984, Mass Communications award S.D. State U., 1985. Mem. Sioux Falls Area C. of C. (dir. 1967-70), Am. Soc. Newspaper Editors, S.D. AP Mng. Editors (Newsman of Yr. award 1978, Les Helgeland Community Service award 1985), Sigma Delta Chi. Republican. Methodist. Lodge: Rotary.

YEAGLEY, MICHAEL DAVID, architect; b. Port Clinton, Ohio, Mar. 3, 1943; s. Daun Albert and Katherine Louisa (Koch) Y.; m. Cynthia Susan Leedy, Sep. 4, 1965; children—David Michael, Jennifer Susan. B.Arch., Kent State U., 1969. Registered architect, Ohio. Assoc. architect Dansizen Architects, North Canton, Ohio, 1969-73; design supr. Ohio Power Co., Canton, 1973—; archtl. cons., Louisville, 1973—. Cons., Louisville School System, Canton Area YMCA; chmn. bd. mgrs. Louisville YMCA, 1985; bd. dirs. Stark County Blood Donor Program; mem. Louisville Planning Commn., Louisville Zoning Bd. Appeals, 1984—. Rotary Internat. Found. grantee for Group Study Exchange to Austria, 1972. Mem. AIA (corp. mem.), Architects Soc. Ohio, Constrn. Specification Inst., Nat. Council Archtl. Registration Bds. Clubs: Rotary of Louisville (past pres.), Canton YMCA Athletic, North Canton YMCA Health. Mem. United Ch. of Christ. Home: 234 Dogwood Ave Louisville OH 44641 Office: 301 Cleveland Ave Canton OH 44702

YEAMANS, GEORGE THOMAS, library science educator, consultant; b. Richmond, Va., Nov. 7, 1929; s. James Norman and Dolphine Sophia (Manhart) Y.; m. Mary Ann Seng, Feb. 1, 1958; children—Debra, Susan, Julia. A.B., U. Va., 1950; M.S.L.S., U. Ky., 1955; Ed.D., Ind. U., 1965. Asst. audio-visual dir. Ind. State U., Terre Haute, 1957-58; asst. film librarian Ball State U., Muncie, Ind., 1958-61, film librarian, 1961-69, assoc. prof. library sci., 1969-72, prof., 1972—; cons. Pendleton (Ind.) Sch. Corp., 1962, 67, Captioned Films for the Deaf Workshop, Muncie, Ind., 1963, 64, 65, Decatur (Ind.) Sch. System, 1978; adjudicator Ind. Media Fair, 1979-86. Author: Projectionists' Programmed Primer, 1969, rev. edit., 1982; Mounting and Preserving Pictorial Materials, 1976; Tape Recording, 1978; Transparency Making, 1977; Photographic Principles, 1981; Computer Literacy—A Programmed Primer, 1985; contbr. articles to profl. jours. Campaign worker Wilson for Mayor, Muncie, Ind., 1979. Served with USMC, 1950-52. Recipient Citations of Achievement, Internat. Biog. Assn., Cambridge, Eng., 1973, Am. Biog. Assn., 1976. Mem. NEA (del. assembly dept. audiovisual instrn. 1967), Am. Film Inst., ALA, Audio-Visual Instrn. Dirs. Ind. (exec. bd. 1962-68, pres. 1966-67), Ind. Assn. Ednl. Communications and Tech. (dist. dir. 1972-75), Assn. Ind. Media Educators (chmn. auditing com. 1979-81), Internat. TV Assn., Am. Film Inst., Phi Delta Kappa. Republican. Unitarian. Club: Catalina (Muncie). Home: 4507 W Burton Dr Muncie IN 47304 Office: Ball State U Muncie IN 47306

YEAROUS, LOIS MARLENE, registered nurse, psychotherapist; b. Linden, Wis., Aug. 29, 1935; d. John and Blanche (Reger) Womack; m. Richard Henry Anderson, Sept. 27, 1951 (div. 1957); children—LeRoy, Mark, Karen; m. 2d, Loren Francis Yearous, Jan. 30, 1960; 1 son, Loren. B.S. in Nursing with honors, 1973, M.S. in Psychiat. Mental Health Nursing, 1978. R.N., Wis. Nurse, William S. Middleton VA Hosp., Madison, Wis., 1973—; psychotherapist in pvt. practice, Madison, 1981—; speaker, trainer in field of psychotherapy. Recipient Outstanding sr. award U. Wis. Nurses Alumni. Mem. Madison Dist. Nurses Assn. (mem. legis. com.), Wis. Nurses Assn., Phi Kappa Phi, Sigma Theta Tau. Methodist. Home: 818 Woodlawn Dr Madison WI 53716

YEAROUT, ANITA LAVERNE, dentist; b. Ypsilanti, Mich., July 25, 1953; s. Vernon Wilson and Estelle Evelyn (Hatcher) Y.; m. Gary Daniel Kier, Dec. 29, 1979. Student, Eastern Mich. U., 1971-80, 86—; DDS, U. Mich., 1984. Lab. tech. Milk Proteins Inc., Troy, Mich., 1974-75; surg. tech. Providence Hosp., Southfield, Mich., 1976-77, David D. Hawfof, MD, Southfield, 1977; gen. practice dentistry Burton, Mich., 1984—; cons. dentist Riverbend Nursing Home, Grand Blanc, Mich., 1985—, Briarwood Nursing Home, Flint, Mich., 1986—, Chateau Gardens Nursing Home, Flint, 1986—, Grand Blanc Convalescent Ctr., 1987—; speaker Continuing Edn. Ctr. for Women, Ann Arbor, Mich., 1982. Mem. ADA, Mich. Dental. Assn., Genesee Dist. Dental Soc., Kappa Delta Pi, Phi Kappa Phi. Avocations: tae kwon do (black belt), fine arts, travel. Office: 3276 S Grand Traverse Burton MI 48524

YEARWOOD, DAVID MONROE, communications executive; b. Cane Garden, St. Andrews, Barbados, Nov. 15, 1945; came to U.S., 1956; s. David M. and Una Ursula (Holder) Y.; m. Cristina Luisa Dale de Rollox, Feb. 29, 1972; children: Edward, David III. BBA in Acctg. and Fin., Pace U., 1979; MBA in Mgmt., Keller Grad. Sch., 1982, MBA in Human Resources, 1983. Supr. accounts payable Litton Industries, Plainfield, N.J., 1969-70; fin. analyst NBC Corp., N.Y.C., 1970-74; mgr. acctg. Sta. NBC-TV, N.Y.C., 1974-76, mgr. budgets, 1976-77; mgr. acctg. Sta. WMAQ-TV subs. NBC, Chgo., 1977-80, dir. fin. and adminstrn, 1980—. Served with USN, 1966-67, with Res. 1964-66, 67-70. Mem. Ill. Broadcasters' Assn. (bd. dirs., pres. elect 1987—), Keller Grad. Sch. Alumni Council. Avocations: soccer, cartography, collecting books. Office: NBC Sta WMAQ-TV Merchandise Mart Bldg Chicago IL 60654

YEARY, TERRI LYN, insurance company executive; b. LaFayette, Ind., Jan. 2, 1953; d. Robert Eugene and Betty Lou (Truman) Strader; m. Jack Yeary, Sept. 18, 1982; 1 dau., Tiffani Leigh. Grad. high sch., Claims sec. Am. States Ins. Co., Cleve., 1972-75; with group dept. Reliance Ins. Co., Cleve., administrv. asst. PIE Mut. Ins. Co., Cleve., 1975-79, underwriting mgr., 1979-85, asst. v.p. underwriting, 1985— ; treas. Rogers Ins. Consultants, Cleve., 1976-79. Office: PIE Mut Ins Co 100 Erieview Plaza 15th Floor Cleveland OH 44114

YEE, VICTOR JAMTOON, dentist; b. Detroit, July 17, 1947; s. Suey and Fay (Gin) Y.; m. Marcella Ann Yee, July 31, 1971. BS in Chemistry, Wayne State U., 1968; DDS, U. Detroit, 1974. Dentist Troy (Mich.) Dental Assocs., 1978—; asst. dir. Dental Aux. Utilization, U. Detroit, 1979-81, asst. dir. dental service, 1981, dir. dental outreach program, 1986—. Served with U.S. Army, 1969-71, Vietnam. Home: 1685 Lakewood Dr Troy MI 48083 Office: Troy Dental Assocs 1069 E Long Lake Rd Troy MI 48098

YEE, WILMING FAY, restaurant owner; b. Cleve., Nov. 29, 1949; s. Jong Pock and Pearl (Gin) Y. BA, Kent State U., 1973, M in Pub. Adminstrn., 1975. Part owner, operator Olentangy Village Tavern, Columbus, Ohio, 1975—. Mem. leadership program, Columbus, 1982—, Clintonville Commn., Columbus, 1985—. Home: 53 W Tulane Columbus OH 43202 Office: Olentangy Village Tavern 2931 N High St Columbus OH 43202

YEN, DAVID CHI-CHUNG, management information systems educator; b. Tai-Chung, Taiwan, Republic of China, Nov. 15, 1953; s. I-King and Chi-Ann (Ro) Y.; m. Wendy Wen-Yawn Ding, Aug. 2, 1981; children: Keeley Ju, Caspar Lung. MBA in Gen. Bus., Cen. State U., Edmund, Okla., 1981, BS in Computer Sci., 1982; MS in Computer Sci., U. Nebr., Lincoln, 1985, postgrad in MIS, 1985—. Asst. prof. Miami U., Oxford, Ohio, 1985—, MIS adv., computer study com., 1986—. Served to 2d lt., Rep. China Army. Mem. Data Processing Mgmt. Assn., Internat. Sch. Bus. Computer User Group, Assn. Computing Machinery, Ohio Mgmt. Info. System Assn., Decision Sci. Inst. Office: Miami U 223 Culler Hall Oxford OH 45056

YENTIS, JAY MARTIN, economist; b. Bklyn., Dec. 21, 1948; s. Jacob and Muriel (Hindin) Y. B.A. in Econs., Hofstra U., 1970; M.A. in Econs., Mich. State U., 1972, M.B.A. in Fin., 1973; m. Jacqueline Elizabeth Orsagh, Jan. 12, 1986; 1 child, Danielle Katharine Orsagh-Yentis. Instr. Lansing Community Coll., Mich., 1972-74; pricing analyst Foremost Ins., Grand Rapids, Mich., 1974-77; planning coordinator GTE of Ind., Fort Wayne, 1977-82; forecasting adminstr. Midwestern Telephone Ops. Westfield, Ind., 1982-83; pricing/econ. mgr. N.Am. Van Lines, Fort Wayne, 1983-85; mgr. market research Lincoln Nat. Pension, Fort Wayne, 1985—; instr. project bus. Jr. Achievement, Fort Wayne, 1979-80; v.p. Gen. Telephone Employees Credit U., Fort Wayne, 1979, pres., 1980. Capt. for N.Am. Van Lines, U.S. Savs. Bond Drive, Fort Wayne, 1984. Mem. Nat. Assn. Bus. Economists, Am. Mktg. Assn., Pi Gamma Mu, Omicron Delta Epsilon. Jewish. Avocations: camping; world travel; theatre; tennis; softball. Home: 10523 Haverford Pl Fort Wayne IN 46825 Office: Lincoln Nat Pension 1300 S clinton St PO Box 1110 Fort Wayne IN 46801

YEO, ROBERT VINCENT, JR., investment company executive; b. Pitts., Apr. 10, 1952; s. Robert Vincent Sr. and Virginia Mae (Guerri) Y.; Mary Kay Stanski, Mar. 4, 1975. BBA, Western Mich. U., 1978. CCPA. Acct. Plante & Morgan, Southfield, Mich., 1978-79, Peat, Marwick, Detroit, 1979-81; chief exec. officer First Continental Group, Inc., Detroit, 1981—; bd. dirs. Consolidated Fin. Group, Calif., 1984-85; cons. Worldco Services Group, N.Y.C., 1982-84, Amerigroup Fin. Services, Stamford, Conn., 1986. Mem. Am. Inst. CPA's, Mich. Assn. CPA's, Internat. Assn. Fin. Planners, Coll. Fin. Planning, Nat. Assn. Accts. (bd. dirs. 1981). Republican. Clubs: Detroit Athletic, Oakland Hills Country (Birmingham). Lodge: Optimists. Avocations: swimming, reading.

YEOH, JOSEPHINE WHITE, medical librarian; b. Moscow, USSR, July 22, 1938; d. John Edward and Helen Marie (Magnuson) W.; m. Vincent Yeoh, July 14, 1962 (div. Feb. 1975); children—Stacy, Jeffrey and Jennifer (twins). B.S., Cornell U., 1960; M.S.L.S., Case Western Res. U., 1972. Info. specialist John Hopkins Med. Inst., Balt., 1972-73; med. library dir. Riverside Meth. Hosp., Columbus, Ohio, 1973—; cons. in field. Bd. dirs. local PTA, 1976-80. Mem. Med. Library Assn., Central Ohio Hosp. Library Consortium, Ohio Health Info. Orgn., ALA, NOW, SANE, Columbus Women's Round Table (chmn. directory com. 1986—) Beta Phi Mu. Democrat. Quaker. Contbr. articles to profl. jours. Office: Riverside Methodist Hosp Medical Library Columbus OH 43214

YEP, BARBARA ANN, radiologic technologist; b. Berwyn, Ill., Dec. 27, 1958; d. Robert William and Shelby Ann (Meyers) Elslager; m. John Joseph Yep, June 22, 1985. BS, Millikin U., 1983; cert. in radiologic tech., Coll. DuPage, 1983. Tech. asst., transporter Cen. DuPage Hosp., Winfield, Ill., 1982-83, radiologic technologist, 1983—. Club: 4-H (Winfield), DuPage Youth Symphony (Wheaton Coll.). Avocations: violin, knitting, crocheting, reading. Home: 1359 Caribou Trail Carol Stream IL 60188 Office: Cen DuPage Hosp ON 025 Winfield Rd Winfield IL 60190

YERIAN, MICHAEL ALEXANDER, dentist; b. Springfield, Ohio, Feb. 18, 1949; s. Marcus Dale and Mary Katherine (Kotsanos) Y. B.S. in Biology, Ohio State U., 1971, D.D.S., 1974. Dental officer U.S. Naval Dental Corp., 1974-77; dental intern, La. State Med. Ctr., New Orleans, 1978-80; dentist USPHS, State of Ohio, 1980-81; gen. practice dentistry, Springfield, Ohio, 1981—; mem. med. staff Community Hosp., 1981-85. assoc. dir. clin. services Loncon Correctional Inst., Ohio Bur. Corrections, 1984—. Mem. Am. Security Council, Washington, 1980-84, Republican Nat. Com., Washington, 1980-84. Health Professions scholar, 1973-74. Mem. ADA, Ohio Dental Assn. Republican. Lutheran. Clubs: Gen. Dentistry Study, Springfield Racquet. Home: 2024 Providence Ave Springfield OH 45503

YERXA, CHARLES TUTTLE, agriculturist; b. Colusa, Calif., Nov. 29, 1918; s. Max N. and Charlotte (Tuttle) Y.; m. Virginia Wilson, Mar. 8, 1947; children—Woodford, Alison, Dorothy, Charles Tuttle. B.S., U. Calif., Berkeley, 1941. Pres. Charles T. Yerxa Farms Inc., Colusa, 1960—, Colusa-Glenn Prodn. Credit Assn., 1965-79; chmn. bd. Sunsweet Inc., Stockton, Calif., 1975—, Calif. Tomato Processing Bd., 1970-78; dir. Fed. Land Bank, 1962-75; bd. dirs. Prune Adminstrn. Com. Vice pres. Woodland Meml. Hosp., 1960-70; trustee Colusa Mosquito Abatement Com., 1965—. Served to lt. comdr. USNR, 1941-46. Republican. Episcopalian.

YESKIS, DOUGLAS JEROME, geologist; b. Chgo., June 22, 1958; s. Jerome Phillip and Mary (Carmody) Y.; m. Nina Louise Larsen, Mar. 21, 1981; children: Victoria, Kristin. BS, U. Ill., Chgo., 1980, MS, 1983. Teaching asst., research asst. U. Ill., Chgo., 1980-83; environ. scientist U.S. EPA, Chgo., 1983-86, geologist, 1986—. Mem. East Beverly Assn., Chgo., 1984-85, Beverly Area Planning Assn., Chgo., 1984-85. Research fellow Argonne Nat. Lab., 1981; grantee Am. Assn. Petroleum Geologists, 1981. Mem. Am. Assn. Petroleum Geologists, Nat. Water Well Assn., U. Ill. Alumni Assn., Ill. Groundwater Assn. Democrat. Roman Catholic. Avocation: stamp collecting. Home: 1739 W Beverly Glen Pkwy Chicago IL 60643 Office: US EPA 230 S Dearborn Chicago IL 60604

YETKA, LAWRENCE ROBERT, state supreme court justice; b. Cloquet, Minn., Oct. 1, 1924; s. Frank and Martha (Norkowski) Y.; m. Ellen Marie Fuller, Nov. 11, 1950; children: Frank Barry, Lawrence George, Christopher Hubert. B.S., U. Minn., 1947, J.D., 1948. Bar: Minn. bar 1949. Founder, partner firm Yetka & Newby, Cloquet, 1949-73; spl. municipal judge 1960-64; city atty. Cloquet, 1964-73; atty. Duluth Port Authority, 1957-60, Western Lake Superior San. Dist., 1970-73; asso. justice Minn. Supreme Ct., St. Paul, 1973—; atty., dir. Carlton County Fed. Savs. & Loan Assn., 1958-73; chmn. State Jud. Council, 1974-82, Select Com. on State Jud. System, 1974-77, State Jud. Planning Agy., 1976-84; Del., 12 state Democratic convs., 1948-72, Dem. Nat. Conv., 1956, 64, 68; chmn. Students for Humphrey for Mayor, 1947; Democratic Farmer Labor county officer, 1948-72, (8th Dist.), 1962-66; state Dem. vice chmn., 1966-70; mem. Minn. Ho. of Reps., 1951-61; chmn. Ho. Jud. Com., 1955-61, asst. majority leader, 1959-61; Grad. Appellate Judges Seminar sponsored by Inst. Jud. Adminstrn. at N.Y. U. Law Sch., 1976. Mem. ABA, Minn. Bar Assn., Carlton County Bar Assn. (pres. 1963-73), Am. Judicature Soc., Inst. Jud. Adminstrn. Lutheran. Office: Minn Supreme Ct State Capitol Saint Paul MN 55155 *

YETKEN, CENGIZ, architect; b. Ceyhan, Turkey, Mar. 21, 1940; came to U.S., 1965; s. Ahmet Kemal and Munevver (Hidayet) Y.; m. Gul Kayaman, Apr. 1970 (div. Jan. 1973); m. Carol Jane Hanenkratt, Aug. 20, 1977; children: Tarik Aslan, Melike Ann. BArch, Metu, Ankara, Turkey, 1963, MArch, 1964; MArch, U. Pa., 1966. Registered architect. Designer Office Louis Kahn, Phila., 1966-68; design instr. U. Pa., Phila., 1967-68; sr. lectr. Metu, 1964-75; assoc. prof. Ball State U., Muncie, Ind., 1975-77, U. Va., Charlottesville, 1977-81; sr. designer Skidmore, Owings & Merrill, Chgo., 1981-86; cons. architect Baha'i Nat. Assembly, Chgo., 1983-85, Louis Kahn Collection, Phila., 1985; mem. Baha'i Temple Restoration Com., Chgo., 1983-85. Mem. Friends of Downtown, Chgo., 1983. Served to 2d lt. Turkish Army, 1969-71. Travel grantee Fulbright Commn., 1964-68; scholar Salzburg Seminar, Austria, 1973. Mem. AIA, N.Y. Filmmakers Cinemateque, Chgo. Chpt. AIA, Chamber Architects Turkey, Union Internat. Architects, U. Pa. Alumni Assn. Mem. Baha'i Faith. Avocations: photography, film making, sailing, travel. Home: 706 N Lombard Ave Oak Park IL 60302 Office: Cengiz Yetken Assoc 412 Madison St Oak Park IL 60302

YIN, RAYMOND WAH, radiologist; b. Canton, Republic of China, July 2, 1938; came to U.S., 1972; m. Jean Youe Mok, Jan. 29, 1967; children: Linda, Dany, Judy. MD, Sun Yat Sen U., Canton, 1961, Nat. Taiwan U., 1965. Diplomate Am. Bd. Radiology, Am. Bd. Nuclear Medicine. Intern Victoria Gen. Hosp., Dalhausie U., Halifax, Nova Scotia, Can., 1967-68; resident Royal Victoria Hosp., McGill U., Montreal, Ont., Can., 1968-72; staff radiologist St. Francis Hosp., Hartford, 1972-75; radiologist St. Joseph Hosp., Bloomington, Ill., 1975—, Menonnite Brakaw Hosp., Normal, Ill., 1975—; practice medicine specializing in radiology Bloomington, 1975—; asst. prof. radiology U. Ill., Peoria, 1980—. Fellow Royal Coll. Physicians of Can. Home: 2110 Oakwood Bloomington IL 61701 Office: 703 N East St Bloomington IL 61701

YINGST, DOUGLAS ROY, physiologist; b. Chgo., Nov. 1, 1946; s. Kenneth Harry and Sylvia LaVonne (Vannorsdel) Y.; children—Rebecca Ann, Stuart Michael. A.B., McPherson Coll., 1969; Ph.D., U. So. Calif., 1976. Postdoctoral fellow Yale U., 1976-78, postdoctoral assoc., 1979; asst. prof. dept. physiology Sch. Medicine, Wayne State U., 1980-85, assoc. prof., 1985—. NIH research service awardee, 1976-78; NIH research career devel. award, 1984-89. Mem. Am. Heart Assn., Mich. Heart Assn., N.Y. Acad. Scis., Detroit Physiol. Soc., Soc. Gen. Physiologists, Biophys. Soc., Sierra Club, Sigma Xi. Mem. Ch. Brethren. Contbr. articles to sci. jours. Home: 18295 Birchcrest Dr Detroit MI 48221 Office: Wayne State U Dept Physiology 540 E Canfield Ave Detroit MI 48201

YOAKUM, MARK STEPHEN, state agency administrator; b. Cairo, Ill., May 30, 1953; s. Mark and Alberta (Stroud) Y.; m. Catherine Louise Cook, Aug. 19, 1972; children: Julie, Jeffrey. BS in Pub. Adminstrn., U. Mo., 1976. Mgr. Tyree Hardware, Columbia, Mo., 1973-78; asst. exec. sec. employees retirement system Mo. local govt., Jefferson City, 1978-85; exec. dir. Mo. Joint Com. on Pub. Employee Retirement, Jefferson City, 1985—. Editor LAGERS Newsletter, 1975-85. Named one of Outstanding Young Men of Am., 1984. Mem. Govt. Fin. Officers Assn. (seminar instr. retirement adminstrn.), Mo. Inst. Pub. Adminstrn. (bd. dirs. 1979-80), Mo. City Mgmt. Assn., Mid-Mo. Pub. Pension Forum (sec. 1978-85). Methodist. Club: Mid-Mo. Civil War Round Table (Jefferson City) (founder 1983, v.p. 1986—). Lodge: Lions. Avocations: sports, hunting, boating. Home: 729 Idlewood Ct Columbia MO 65203 Office: Joint Com on Pub Employee Retirement B-42 Capitol Bldg Senate PO Jefferson City MO 65101

YOCK, JOSEPH P(OWELL), JR., paper manufacturing company executive; b. Battle Creek, Mich., July 5, 1946; s. Joseph P. and Agnes K. (Miller) Y.; m. Joyce S. Rogosz, June 20, 1970; children: Angela, Kristopher, Gregory. Student, Kellogg Community Coll., 1964-66; BS, Western Mich. U., 1969, MBA, 1976. Tech. asst. printing Gen. Foods Corp., Battle Creek, 1968-70, gravure inks supr., 1970-72, graphic arts and engraving mgr., 1972-77; ops. tech. mgr. Am. Can Co., Neenah, Wis., 1977-79, plant supt., 1979-82; plant mgr. James River Corp., Neenah, 1982-85, dir. mfg., Kalamoazoo, 1985—; instr. Lakeland Coll., Sheboygan, Wis., 1981-84, Fox Valley Tech. Inst., Appleton, Wis., 1977-85, Kellogg Community Coll., Battle Creek, 1976-77. Served with USAR, 1969-75. Kalamazoo Valley Craftsman Club scholar, 1965-69. Mem. Gravure Tech. Assn. (chmn. 1969-85), Appleton C. of C. (bd. dirs. 1983-85). Republican. Roman Catholic. Lodge: Rotary (bd. dirs. Neenah chpt. 1981-83). Home: 8455 Phoebe Portage MI 49002 Office: James River Corp 243 E Paterson Kalamazoo MI 49007

YODER, RUSSELL WILLIAM, purchasing executive; b. Canton, Ohio, July 26, 1954; s. Forest Russell and Ruth Jane (Frase) Y.; m. Rebecca Suzanne Hawkins, Aug. 29, 1981; 1 child, Tyler Russell. AA, U. Md., 1975;

BA, Cedarville Coll., 1978. Mgmt. trainee LUK, Inc., Wooster, Ohio, 1978, personnel mgr., 1979-80, maintenance, repair and ops. purchasing, 1980—; TV host Sta. WCTV, Wooster, 1984-85. Co-author: (booklet) How Shall We Escape...?, 1974; gospel recording artist Upward Prodns., Okla. City, 1987. Vol. Rep. campaign Wayne County, 1984, 86; speaker, singer Grace Brthren Ch., Wooster, 1979—; cons. Project Bus., Jr. Achievement, Wayne County, 1982-87. Served with U.S. Army, 1972-75. Named one of Outstanding Young Men Am., Jaycees, 1981; recipient Letter of Commendation U.S. Army Security Agy., 1975, Chmn.'s award Wooster Area C. of C., 1987. Club: Oldsmobile of Am. Avocations: theology, music and the arts, travel, spl. interest autos, linguistics. Home: 1100 Summerset Dr Wooster OH 44691 Office: LUK Inc 3401 Old Airport Rd Wooster OH 44691

YOEST, DONALD DEANE, real estate and insurance executive; b. California, Mo., Jan. 17, 1941; s. Andrew John and Agnes Elizabeth (Hartman) Y.; m. Marilyn Kay Null, Sept. 18, 1965; children: Scott, Kent, Joel, Neal. BS, U. Mo., 1965. Field editor Rural Electric Missourian, Jefferson City, Mo., 1965-68, asso. editor, 1968-69, mng. editor, 1969-72, editor, 1972-77; br. mgr. Strout Realty, Inc., Tipton, Mo., 1977-85; broker/owner Don Yoest Realty & Ins. Agy., 1985—. Mem. Mid-Mo. Comprehensive Health Care Com., 1972-74. Recipient George W. Haggard Meml. Journalism award Nat. Rural Elec. Co-op Assn., 1972; various sales awards, 1979-84. Mem. Nat. Electric Co-op. Editorial Assn. (pres. 1974-75), Co-op. Editorial Assn. (pres. 1973-74). Home: Route 2 Tipton MO 65081 Office: Don Yoest Realty & Ins Agy PO Box 909 Hwy 5S Tipton MO 65081

YOFFIE, ROBERT MARK, banker; b. St. Louis, July 13, 1949; s. Robert Marshall and Evelyn Louise (Hoops) Y.; m. Vernita Roxy Carroll, Oct. 30, 1982. BA, U. Mo., 1975. Sr. tech. recruiter Mgmt. Recruiters, Bridgeton, Mo., 1975-77; account exec. Merrill Lynch, Clayton, Mo., 1977-80, E.F. Hutton, St. Charles, Mo., 1980-82; v.p., fin. cons. MidAm. Trust Co., Carbondale, Ill., 1983-85; v.p., trust officer City Nat. Bank, Murphysboro, Ill., 1986—. Pres. St. Charles County Reps., 1982, Jackson County Bus. Boosters, Carbondale, , 1985; capt. fund raising com. John A. Logan Coll. Found., 1986—. Served to staff sgt. USAF, 1969-72. Republican. Roman Catholic. Avocation: golf. Home: Rural Rt 6 Box 354 Murphysboro IL 62966 Office: City Nat Bank 1301 Walnut Murphysboro IL 62966

YOGGERST, JAMES PAUL, educator, journalist, public relations consultant; b. Springfield, Ill., Oct. 9, 1924; s. Paul Anthony and Helen (Ford) Yoggerst; m. Norma Jean White, Nov. 25, 1948 (dec. Aug. 1976); children—Maureen, Karen, Dianne, Patricia, Paul, Steven. B.S. in Journalism, U. Ill., 1949; M.A. in English, 1950, postgrad. Reporter, Ill. State Register, Springfield, 1950-51; asst. editor Austin News, Chgo., 1951-55; tchr. journalism and English, Waukegan East High Sch., 1956-85; part-time lectr. Roosevelt U., Chgo., 1971-85; instr. Coll. of Lake County, Grayslake, 1965-72; part-time reporter News-Sun, Waukegan, Ill., 1956-70; contbg. editor La Montage Mag., Lake Bluff, Ill., 1977; dir. J. P. Yoggerst and Assoc., Pub. Relations and Writing Cons., Waukegan; lectr. in field, leader seminars; writing cons. Cherry Electric Co., Waukegan, 1971-72; pub. relations dir. Lake County Contractors Assn., Waukegan, 1973-74; pub. affairs cons. Social Security Adminstrn., Chgo., 1973-74. Author weekly column "Our Prairie States", Waukegan News-Sun, 1977-79, Copley News Service, 1985—; contbr. articles and short stories to newspapers and mags. Pub. relations dir. Ray Bradbury Soc., Waukegan, 1978, Stonebridge Priory, Servite Fathers, Lake Bluff, Ill., 1971. Served with AUS, 1943-46; PTO. Democrat. Roman Catholic. Home: 2528 N Jackson St Waukegan IL 60087 Office: J P Yoggerst and Assocs 19 N Genesse St Waukegan IL 60085

YOHE, RUTH MCCHESNEY, physician; b. Elgin, Ill., Apr. 19, 1926; d. Oswald Belmont and Emma Amelia (Halsey) McChesney; m. Robert B. Yohe, Sept. 8, 1956; children: Virginia, Cynthia, Steven, Catherine. BA, State U. Iowa, 1948; MD, Med. Coll. Pa., 1954. Diplomate Am. Bd. Pediatrics, Am. Bd. Allergy and Immunology. Intern Broadlawns Polk County Hosp., Des Moines, 1954-55; resident Raymond Blank Meml. Hosp. for Children, Des Moines, 1955-57; fellow in allergy and immunology Kans. U., U. Mo., Kansas City, 1970-72; practice medicine specializing in allergy and immunology Overland Park, Kans., 1972—; asst. clin. prof. pediatrics Kans. U. Med. Ctr., Kansas City, 1958—, U. Mo., Kansas City, 1958—. Mem. Am. Acad. Allergy and Immunology, Am. Coll. Allergy, Greater Kansas City Allergy Soc. (sec., treas., v.p., pres. 1985-87). Republican. Lutheran. Address: 8600 W 95th St Overland Park KS 66212

YOHN, DAVID STEWART, virologist, science administrator; b. Shelby, Ohio, June 7, 1929; s. Joseph Van and Agnes (Tryon) Y.; m. Olivetta Kathleen McCoy, June 11, 1950; children: Linda Jean, Kathleen Ann, Joseph John, David McCoy, Kristine Renee. B.S., Otterbein Coll., 1951; M.S., Ohio State U., 1953, Ph.D., 1957; M.P.H., U. Pitts., 1960. Research fellow, scholar in microbiology Ohio State U., 1952-56, prof. virology Coll. Veterinary Medicine, 1969—, dir. Comprehensive Cancer Center, 1973—; research assoc., asst. prof. microbiology U. Pitts., 1956-62; assoc. cancer research scientist Roswell Park Meml. Inst., Buffalo, 1962-69; mem. nat. med. and sci. adv. com. Leukemia Soc. Am., 1970—, trustee, 1971—; pres. Ohio Cancer Research Assocs., 1982—; mem. cancer research centers rev. com. Nat. Cancer Inst., 1972-77. Pres. bd. deacons North Presbyn. Ch., Williamsburg, N.Y., 1967-68. Recipient Pub. Service award Lions, 1968. Mem. Am. Assn. Cancer Research, Am. Soc. Microbiology, Am. Assn. Immunologists, Internat. Assn. Comparative Research on Leukemia and Related Diseases (sec.-gen. 1974—), Ohio Valley-Lake Erie Assn. Cancer Ctrs. (sec. 1978—). Club: Sertoma (Columbus, Ohio). Home: 1237 Norwell Dr Columbus OH 43220 Office: Ohio State U Comprehensive Cancer Center Suite 302 410 W 12th Ave Columbus OH 43210

YOHN, RICHARD VAN, clergyman; b. Lancaster, Pa., Apr. 16, 1937; s. Henry Martin and Ada (Dommel) Y.; m. Linda Harriet Anderson, June 18, 1960; children—Richard Van, Steven Eric. Student Franklin and Marshall Coll., 1956; B.S., Phila. Coll. Bible, 1960; Th.M., Dallas Theol. Sem., 1964; D.Min., Talbot Theol. Sem., 1980. Ordained to ministry Evangelical Free Ch., 1971; dir. Christian edn. Oliver Presbyn. Ch., Mpls., 1964-67; pastor Windsor Park Evang. Free Ch., Winnipeg, Man., Can. 1967-71, Evang. Free Ch. Fresno, Calif., 1971-84, Grace Ch., Edina, Minn., 1984-87, Evang. Free Ch., Orange, Calif., 1987—; orginator radio program Living Word, 1980; pres. Contact Ministries Inc., 1980—; mem. faculty Winnipeg Bible Coll., 1969-70. Recipient Mark of Excellence award Campus Life Mag., 1975. Mem. Nat. Assn. Evangelicals. Author: Discover Your Spiritual Gift and Use It, 1974; Now That I'm A Disciple, 1976; What Every Christian Should Know About God, 1976; God's Answers to Life's Problems, 1976; God's Holy Spirit for Christian Living, 1977; Getting Control of Your Life, 1978; God's Answer to Financial Problems, 1978; Getting Control of Your Inner Self, 1981; What Every Christian Should Know About Bible Prophecy, 1982; Explore the Bible Yourself, 1982; Finding Time, 1984; Overcoming, 1985; Living Securely in an Unstable World, 1985. Home: 6612 Hillside Ln Edina MN 55435 Office: 5300 France Ave S Edina MN 55410

YOHO, EARL RAY, JR., construction company executive, adhesives and sealers manufacturing company executive; b. Hammond, Ind., Sept. 24, 1935; s. Earl Ray and Laura Ida (Hoeckelberg) Y.; m. Elaine Margie Hatfield, Oct. 13, 1956; children—Sharon Kay, Linda Jean, Donna Lynn, Janice Sue, Brenda Ann. Grad., Ind. Mil. Acad., Indpls., 1961, U.S. Army Engr. Sch., Ft. Belvoir, Va., 1966, U.S. Army Comd. and Gen. Staff Coll., Kans., 1972, U.S. Army Mil. Police Sch., Ark., 1976; cert. metallurgy Purdue U., 1962. Cert. Profl. Mgr., 1976. Mgr. quality control Youngstown Steel, East Chicago, Ind., 1959-61, gen. foreman ops., 1961-70, asst. supt. ops., 1970-75; mgr. ops. Nat. Steel, Houston, 1975-76; pres. Concrete Maintenance Engrng. Inc., Highland, Ind., 1978—; pres. Specialty Compounds, Inc., Merrillville, Ind., 1976—. Patentee thickness gage pipe threading. Served with AUS, 1961-64. Mem. Soc. Am. Mil. Engrs., Calumet Purchasing Assn., Ind. Sheriff's Assn., Am. Concrete Inst., Midwest Coke Plant Blast Furnace Assn., Engr. Officers Assn. (pres. 1966-67), Am. Legion, Nat. Rifle Assn. Club: Smetlake Tennis. Lodge: Masons, Shriners. Home: 3630 44th St Highland IN 46322 Office: Specialty Compounds Inc 3300 E 84th Pl Merrillville IN 46410

YOON, JONG SIK, geneticist, educator; b. Suwon, Korea, Jan. 25, 1937; came to U.S., 1962, naturalized, 1976; s. Ki and Pil (Kang) Y.; m. Kyung-Soon Ahn, Sept. 10, 1962; children—Edward, Mimi, Sunny. B.S., Yonsei U., Seoul, Korea, 1961; M.A., U. Tex.-Austin, 1964, Ph.D., 1965. Research scientist U. Tex.-Austin also Houston, 1965-68; asst. prof. Yonsei U., 1968-71; research scientist U. Tex.-Austin, 1971-78; assoc. prof. Bowling Green State U., 1978-83, prof. genetics, 1983—, dir. Nat. Drosophila Species Resource Ctr., 1982—. Presbyterian. Contbr. articles to profl. jours. Home: 4 Picardie Ct Bowling Green OH 43402 Office: Bowling Green State U Dept Biol Scis Bowling Green OH 43403

YORK, CARL DENNIS, property manager; b. Marion, Ind., May 4, 1952; s. Carl Dee and Ruth Ann (Foster) Y.; m. Marcia Ann Reynolds, Aug. 25, 1973; 1 child, Carey Donovan. Grad., Ind. U. Cert. property mgr.; cert. apt. mgr. Ops. mgr. Atkinson & Co., Indpls., 1973-74; mgr. site property Capital Bus. Systems, Indpls., 1974-75; property mgr. IN Mgmt. Corp., Indpls., 1975-81, Triangle Assocs., Inc., Indpls., 1981-84; dist. property mgr. SCC Mgmt. Corp., N.Y.C., 1984—; vice chmn. Metro Indpls. Bd. Realtors, 1984—. Inspector, judge, sheriff Marion County Election Bd., Indpls., 1972—. Named to Hon. Order Ky. Cols., 1982; named one of Outstanding Young Men Am., U.S. Jaycees, 1982; recipient Outstanding Achievement award St. Jude's Children's Hosp., 1971. Mem. Nat. Apt. Assn., Apt. Assn. Ind. (com. mem.), Metro. Indpls. Bd. Realtors (vice chmn. 1984—, equal housing com., Com. Leadership award 1985), Inst. Real Estate Mgmt. (chmn. edn. com., v.p. local chpt. #26 1986—, Chmn. award 1985), Gatling Gun Club. Republican. Methodist. Lodges: Masons, Shriners (bd. dirs. Murat Under 40 club 1981-84). Home: 3627 Ivory Way Indianapolis IN 46227

YORK, CAROLYN HOPE, social worker; b. Saleburg, Austria, Jan. 1, 1955; d. Paul Edward and Beaulah Hope (Blalock) Cox; m. Mark Alan York, Aug. 14, 1976. BA, Olivet Nazarene Coll., 1976; MSW, U. Kans., 1982; MA in Family Counseling, U. Mo., 1987. Adminstrv. asst. Burns and McDonnell, Kansas City, Mo., 1976-78; caseworker div. family services Mo. Dept. Social Services, Kansas City, 1978-80; teaching house parent Temporary Lodging for Children, Olathe, Kans., 1979-81; sch. social worker Sch. Dist. 500, Kansas City, 1982—; field instr. U. Kans., 1986—. Mem. Nat. Assn. Social Workers, Kans. Assn. Sch. Social Workers. Mem. Ch. of Nazarene. Avocations: cooking, swimming. Home: 11209 E 61st Terr Raytown MO 64133

YORK, JOHN C., lawyer, investment banker; b. Evansville, Ind., Apr. 27, 1946; s. James Edward and Madge (Weas) Y.; m. Judith Anne Carmack, Aug. 24, 1968; children—George Edward Carmack, Charlotte Bayley, Alice Mercer. B.A., Vanderbilt U., 1968; J.D., Harvard U., 1971. Bar: Ill. 1971, U.S. Dist. Ct. (no. dist.) Ill. 1971. Assoc. firm Mayer Brown & Platt, Chgo., 1971-74; sr. v.p., sec., prin. JMB Realty Corp., Chgo., 1974-84; pres. Robert E. Lend Co. Inc., 1984—, Packard Properties Inc., 1984—; counsel Bell, Boyd & Lloyd, Chgo., 1986—; bd. dirs. Riverside Corp., Chgo., McKeever Electric Supply Co., Columbus, Ohio. Bd. dirs. Landmarks Preservation Council of Ill., 1972—, Streeterville Corp., 1986—, Washington Sq. Health Found., 1985—, Henrotin Hosp., 1976—; mem. vestry St. Chrysostom's Ch., 1980—. Mem. ABA, Chgo. Bar Assn., Lambda Alpha Internat. Republican. Episcopalian. Clubs: Chgo., Casino, Racquet, Saddle and Cycle. Home: 1242 Lake Shore Dr Chicago IL 60610 Office: One N LaSalle Chicago IL 60602

YORK, JOSEPH RUSSELL, media production technician; b. Royal Center, Ind., Oct. 19, 1940; s. William Russell and Naomi (Wellman) Y.; Student Olivet Nazarene Coll., until 1965; B.S., Ball State U. student, 1980, M.S., 1982; m. Teresa Luanne Ping, June 15, 1963; children—Sherra JoAnn, Kerra SuzAnn, Darren Joseph, Terra LeAnn. Photojournalist, Danville (Ill.) Comml. News, 1961-62, Kankakee (Ill.) Daily Jour., 1963; motion picture dir.,editor Calvin Prodns., Inc., Kansas City, Mo., 1965-71, Communico, Inc., St. Louis, 1971-73; editing supr. Premier Film & Rec. Co., Inc., St. Louis, 1973—; producer, dir. TV programming Kans. Fish and Game Commn., 1983—; owner, operator Trinity Prodns., St. Louis, 1963-83; pres. York's Foto Express, Inc., 1986—. Pastor, Ch. of the Nazarene, Selma, Ind. Recipient 1st Pl. award U.S. Indsl. Film Festival, 1972; 2d Pl. award Festival of Ams.-V.I., 1977. Mem. Profl. Photographers Am., Photomarketing Assn. Internat.; Golden Key Nat. Honor Soc. Home: 506 Stout St Pratt KS 67124 Office: 611 E 1st Pratt KS 67124

YORK, RICHARD WAYNE, optometrist; b. Detroit, Nov. 10, 1950; s. Bill and Roxie Myrtle (Gambrell) Y.; m. Teresa Marie Foster, Aug. 12, 1972; 1 child, Megan. BS, Olivet Nazarene Coll., Kankakee, Ill., 1972; OD, Ohio State U., 1979. Cert. optometrist, Ohio. Secondary tchr. Mt. Vernon (Ohio) City Schs., 1972-74; pvt. practice optometry Mt. Vernon, 1979—; clin. instr. optometry Ohio State U., Columbus, Ohio, 1979—. Named one of Outstanding Young Men of Am., 1984. Mem. Am. Optometric Assn. Republican. Mem. Ch. of the Nazarene. Lodge: Kiwanis (pres. Mt. Vernon 1985—). Home: 111 N Concord St Mount Vernon OH 43050 Office: 723 Coshocton Ave Mount Vernon OH 43050

YORTY, ROLLIN DALE, bookstore executive; b. Lebanon, Pa., Feb. 12, 1924; s. Clayton Amos and Helen Louise (Wealand) Y.; m. Ethel Belle Yorty, Sept. 15, 1948; children—Bonnie, Heather, Tami, Melodie. B.S., Central Mich. U., 1951, M.A., 1962. Tchr. Gerrish-Higgins Schs., Roscommon, Mich., 1951-59, Saginaw Twp. Schs., Mich., 1959-60, Merritt Pub. Schs., Mich., 1960-62, Grayling Pub. Schs., Mich., 1962-66, Gerrish-Higgins Schs., Roscommon, 1966-83; owner Yorty's Antiques & Books, 1951—. Served with USAAF, 1943-46. Republican. Avocations: stamps, photography, swimming, rare books, piano, organ. Home and Office: 103 Yorty Dr Roscommon MI 48653

YOST, CARLEEN KAY, biologist, researcher; b. Kalamazoo, Mich., Mar. 27, 1958; d. Richard Merle Everett and Alice Mae (Minarik) Stieber; m. Hal Richard Yost, July, 25, 1981. BA in Biology and Sociogy, Olivet Coll., 1980. Lic. social worker. Social work asst. Ingham County Med. Care Facility, Okemos, Mich., 1980-83; research asst. Mich. Cancer Found., Detroit, 1983, Wayne State U., Detroit, 1983—. Mem. Sociology Club of Majs. and Minors (co-chair 1974-76, mem. of yr. 1976), Omicron Delta Kappa, Sigma Zeta. Avocations: camping, sailing, dog shows. Home: 4335 Bishop Detroit MI 48224 Office: Wayne State U Lande Bldg Rm 56 Detroit MI 48201-1497

YOUKER, BRUCE WAYNE, court administrator; b. Fremont, Mich., May 14, 1947; s. Deronda Dorn and Wynonda Marie (Dipple) Y.; m. Christine Ann Meeuwenberg, Sept. 17, 1971; children: Brandon Won, Bethany Christine, Caleb Dorn, Joilyn Renae Jee. BS, Western Mich. U., 1969, postgrad., 1971; postgrad., Utah State U., 1969. Cert. social worker, Mich. Probation officer Newaygo County Ct., White Cloud, Minn., 1971-78; ct. adminstr. Newaygo County Probate Ct., White Cloud, 1978—. Contbr. articles to profl. jours. Vol. Boys Club Am., Kalamazoo, Mich., 1965-69; mem. Peace Corps, Bolivia, 1969-70; treas. First Christian Ref. Ch., Fremont, 1979; chmn. Chief of Police Orgn., Newaygo County, 1980; mem. Multi-Agy. Approach to Human Services Consortium, Newaygo County, 1984—; bd. edn. Fremont Christian Schs., 1984—. Mem. Nat. Juvenile Justice Assn., Mich. Juvenile Ct. Adminstrs. Assn., Juvenile Justice Assn., Children's Charter. Republican. Mem. Christian Reformed Ch. Lodge: Rotary (cross cultural exchange person, Australia). Avocations: own small business, camping, outdoor sports. Office: County Courthouse 1084 Willox White Cloud MI 49349

YOUNG, ALAN CLARE, accountant; b. Inkster, Mich., Jan. 16, 1953; s. Anderson C. and Sarah (Daniels) Y.; m. Colette M. Brooks, May 2, 1982; children: Aaron, Adam. BA, Mich. State U., 1976; M in Taxation, Walsh Coll., 1985. CPA, Mich. Sr. acct. Deloitte Haskins & Sells, Detroit, 1977-81; tax mgr. Keith Warlick & Co., Detroit, 1981-83; owner, founder Alan C. Young & Assocs., Detroit and Flint, Mich., 1983—. Com. chairperson Alma Stallworth state legislature campaign, Detroit; mem. United Negro Coll. Fund Com.; dir. Harmonie Park Playhouse Theater Prodns. Mem. Am. Inst. CPA's, Mich. Assn. CPA's, Nat. Assn. Black Accts. (past v.p., achievement award 1987, scholarship ball chmn.), Booker T. Washington Bus. Assn. (bd. dirs.), Kappa Alpha Psi (past treas.). Club: Detroit Econ. Avocations: singing, basketball, studying history. Office: Alan C Young & Assocs PC 1311 E Jefferson Suite 110 Detroit MI 48207

YOUNG, COLEMAN ALEXANDER, mayor; b. Tuscaloosa, Ala., May 24, 1918; s. Coleman and Ida Reese (Jones) Y. Hon. degrees, Eastern Mich. U., Wayne State U., U. Detroit, Stillman Coll., U. Mich. Del. Mich. Constl. Conv., 1961-62; mem. Mich. Senate, 1964-73; also Dem. floor leader Mich. Senate, Detroit; mayor City of Detroit, 1974—; Del. to Dem. Nat. Conv., 1968, 72, 76, 80; Dem. nat. committeeman from, Mich.; vice chmn. Nat. Dem. Party, 1977-81; pres. U.S. Conf. of Mayors, 1982-83; also mem. tech. adv. panel on adminstrn. of programs on aging; mem. nat. adv. com. White House Conf. on Aging, 1981; mem. Nat. Adv. Commn. on Resource Conservation and Recovery. Bd. dirs. Ferndale Coop., Credit Union, Kirwood Hosp., Detroit, Detroit Renaissance, Detroit Econ. Growth Corp. Served to 2d lt. USAAF, World War II. Mem. NAACP (Spingarn medal 1981), Booker T. Washington Bus. Men's Assn., Trade Union Leadership Council, Assn. for Study Negro Life and History, AFL-CIO Council (spl. rep.). Baptist. Office: Office of Mayor 2 Woodward Ave Detroit MI 48226

YOUNG, DON J., federal judge; b. Norwalk, Ohio, July 13, 1910; s. Don J. and Elaine (Dennis) Y.; m. Seville Beatrice Shagrin, June 27, 1936; children—Don J., Patricia C. A.B. cum laude, Western Res. U., 1932, LL.B., 1934; student, Cleve. Art Sch., 1932-34. Bar: Ohio bar 1934. Pvt. practice Norwalk, 1934-52; judge Common Ct. Pleas, Huron County, Ohio, 1952-53, Probate and Juvenile Ct., Huron County, 1953-65; U.S. judge No. Dist. Ohio for Western Div., 1965—; instr., lectr. juvenile ct. laws at seminars and insts. for judges, 1959—; v.p. Ohio Assn. Probate Ct. Judges, 1958-60; pres. Ohio Assn. Juvenile Ct. Judges, 1960-62; law reporter Nat. Juvenile Ct. Found., 1959-73, sec.-treas., 1960-61, sec., 1961-62; sec. Nat. Council Juvenile Ct. Judges, 1962-65, exec. com., 1966-69. Contbr. articles to profl. jours.; exhibited jewelry, Cleve. Mus. Art, Butler Art Inst., Nat. Ceramic Exhbn. Exec. dir. Norwalk CD Corps, 1942-46; pres. Firelands Hist. Soc., 1945-46, Norwalk Cemetery Assn., 1951-57; sec. Norwalk Recreation Com., 1946-53; trustee Young Men's Library and Reading Room Assn., 1955-65, 86—, Whittlesey Acad. Arts and Scis., 1955-65. Mem. ABA, Ohio Bar Assn., Order of Coif, Phi Beta Kappa, Pi Epsilon Delta. Episcopalian. Office: U S Dist Ct 220 U S Courthouse 1716 Spielbusch Ave Toledo OH 43624

YOUNG, EUGENE SAMUEL, educational administrator, photographer; b. N.Y.C., Oct. 6, 1941; s. Martin and Fannie (Bogorad) Y.; m. Barbara Whyne, June 16, 1962; children: David, Paul. BA, CCNY, 1962; MusM, Ind. U., 1966; EdD, Columbia U., 1973. Chmn. music and drama dept. Garden Sch., Jackson Heights, N.Y., 1965-71; researcher, cons. Columbia U., N.Y.C., 1971-73; prin. Chippewa Jr. High Sch. Mounds View Pub. Schs., St. Paul, 1973—; adj. prof. Coll. of St. Thomas, St. Paul, 1976-77; organizer, cons. com. to create a high sch. for the arts in Minn., St. Paul, 1977—. Author: Kurt Weill: The Man and His Music, 1966. Photographer nature, landscapes and cityscapes. Fed. govt. scholar Tchrs. Coll., N.Y.C., 1971-73, N.Y. State scholar CCNY, 1959-62; research grantee Kurt Weill Found. for Music, N.Y.C., 1966. Mem. Nat. Assn. Secondary Sch. Prins., Nat. Assn. Supervision and Curriculum Devel., Minn. Assn. Supervision and Curriculum Devel. (exec. bd. 1980—, pres. 1987—). Avocations: music; theatre; travel; antique collecting, speaker on edn. issues. Home: 5317 84th Ave N Brooklyn Park MN 55443 Office: Chippewa Jr High Sch Mounds View Pub Schs 5000 Hodgson Rd Saint Paul MN 55126

YOUNG, FRANK NELSON, JR., biology educator, entomologist; b. Oneonta, Ala., Nov. 2, 1915; s. Frank Nelson and Mary (Loe) Y.; m. Frances Norman, July 2, 1943; children—Elizabeth Von Herrmann, Frank Nelson III. B.S., U. Fla., 1938, M.S., 1940, Ph.D., 1942. Asst. prof. biology U. Fla., Gainesville, 1946-49; asst. prof. Ind. U., Bloomington, 1949-51; assoc. prof. Ind. U., 1951-62, prof., 1963-86, prof. emeritus, 1986—. Author: Water Beetles of Florida, 1954; contbr. articles on aquatic insects to profl. jours. Served to capt. U.S. Army, 1942-46. Recipient Phi Sigma medal, 1940; Guggenheim fellow, 1960-61; La. State U. fellow, 1963. Fellow Ind. Acad. Sci., Royal Entomol. Soc.; mem. AAAS, Am. Inst. Biol. Scis. Baptist. Home: 405 S Mitchell St Bloomington IN 47401 Office: 201 Morrison Hall Ind Univ Bloomington IN 47405

YOUNG, IRVING JAMES, neurologist; b. Chgo., Apr. 2, 1929; s. James L. and Virginia Dorthea (Jourdan) Y.; m. Helen Marie Bennett, June 27, 1953; children: Mary Diane, Ann Elizabeth, Jeffrey Steven, James John. AB, DePauw U., 1950; BS, U. Ill., Chgo., 1952, MD, 1954, MS in Pharmacology, 1955, PhD in Physiology, 1960. Diplomate Am. Bd. Neurology and Psychiatry. Clin. neurology investigator VA Lakeside Hosp., Chgo., 1962-64; chief neurology service VA Hosp., Downey, Ill., 1964-72; attending neurologist, electroencephalographer and electromyographer Northwest Community Hosp., Arlington Heights, Ill., 1968—; chief neurosciences research and tng. program VA Hosp., Hines, Ill., 1972-73; cons. State of Ill., 1963—, State of Wis., 1972—, Med. Coll. Wis., Milw., 1969—. Contbr. numerous articles to profl. jours. mem. Long Grove (Ill.) Sch. Bd., 1972-75, Long Grove Planning Comm., 1975—; deacon Roman Cath. Ch., Buffalo Grove, Ill., 1979—. NIH fellow, 1959-62; NIH grantee, 1964-67. Fellow Am. Acad. Neurology; mem. Soc. Neurosciences, Soc. Biol. Psychiatry, Intern. Soc. Neurochemistry, Wis. Neurol. Soc. (pres. 1984-85), Biofeedback Soc. Am., Am. Soc. Neuroimaging. Avocations: lapidary arts, woodworking, photography, poetry, gardening. Office: Northwest Neurol Assn 2010 S Arlington Heights Rd Arlington Heights IL 60005

YOUNG, JACK ALLISON, financial executive; b. Aurora, Ill., Dec. 31, 1931; s. Neal A. and Gladys W. Young; m. Virginia Dawson, Jan. 24, 1959; children—Amy D., Andrew A. B.S. in Journalism, U. Ill., 1954. CLU; Chartered fin. cons.; registered security rep.; chartered fin. cons. Advt. writer Caterpillar Tractor Co., 1956-58; ins. agent Equitable Life Assurance Soc., St. Charles, Ill., 1958—, ins. broker, 1972—; pres. Jack A. Young and Assocs., 1978—, Tax Sav Inc., 1983—; pres. Creative Brokerage, Inc., 1982—; pres., gen. securities prin. Chartered Planning, Ltd., 1985—; v.p. Old Mill Leasing Co., 1985—; past trustee Equitable CLU Assn.; past chmn. Equitable Nat. Agents Forum. Bd. dirs. Tri-City Family Services, 1975-83, pres., 1979-81; trustee Delnor Community Health System, 1985—; chmn., pres. Delnor Community Health Care Found., 1986—. Served to lt. (j.g.), USN, 1954-56. Named to Equitable Hall of Fame, 1978. Mem. Million Dollar Round Table (life), Am. Soc. C.L.U.s, Am. Coll. C.L.U. Golden Key Soc., Fox Valley Estate Planning Council, Internat. Assn. for Fin. Planning, Inc., Aurora Assn. Life Underwriters (past pres., nat. committeeman), Nat. Assn. Securities Dealers (registered prin.). Club: Geneva Golf. Home: 18 Campbell St Geneva IL 60134 Office: 28 N Bennett St Geneva IL 60134

YOUNG, JACK I., II, management consultant; b. Iowa City, Feb. 26, 1949; s. Jack I. and Miriam J. (Stevenson) Y.; m. Pamela S. Mascher, Oct. 18, 1969; children: Leah D., Rachel N., Zachary D., Nicholas A. BS, Mankato State U., 1971. Revenue auditor Iowa Dept. of Revenue, Des Moines, Iowa, 1972-81; mgmt. cons. Profl. Mgmt. Midwest, Overland Park, Kans., 1981—; enrolled agt. U.S. Treas., 1984—. Mem. Iowa City Jaycees (bd. dirs. 1976-81), N. Liberty Jaycees. Methodist. Lodge: Elks. Avocations: golfing, tennis, boating. Home: 825 N Dodge St Iowa City IA 52240

YOUNG, JAMES JOSEPH, data processing executive; b. Canton, Ohio, Aug. 1, 1936; s. James and Annie (Thompson) Y.; m. Rita Marie Bernard, June 1, 1957; children: Linda Kay, Pamela Ann, Barbara Jean, James Joseph Jr., Patricia Louise. Programmer Timken Co., Canton, 1963-65, lead programmer, 1965-69, asst. to mgr. data processing, 1969-81, software specialist, 1981-82, sr. technical analyst, 1982—. Trustee Stark County Am. Softball Assn., Canton, 1983—. Served with U.S. Army, 1959-62. Mem. Data Processing Mgmt. Assn. (treas. 1975-76, pres. 1977-78, Individual Performance award 1977, 81, 84). Lodge: Elks. Home: 6329 Chesham Dr NE North Canton OH 44721 Office: The Timken Co 1835 Dueber SW Canton OH 44706

YOUNG, JANICE KAY, teacher; b. Terre Haute, Ind., June 13, 1943; s. Harold Dale and Bertha T. (Clark) Reed; m. Clarence H. Young Jr., June 20, 1965; children: Susan Elaine, Jonathan Thomas. BS, Ind. State U., 1965, MS, 1968; grad. studies, Ind.-Purdue U., 1982-84, U. Indpls., 1982-84. Lic. spl. edn. and music edn. tchr. (life). Tchr. physically handicapped Indpls. Pub. Sch., 1965-69, 74-83, tchr. mildly mentally handicapped, 1984-85, resource tchr., 1985—; pvt. tutor spl. needs students Greenwood, Indpls., 1980—. contbr. Curriculum Guide, 1978. Catechist Archdiocese of Indpls., 1984—. Mem. Indpls. Edn. Assn., Nat. Edn. Assn., Delta Kappa Gamma, Phi Delta Kappa. Republican. Roman Catholic. Home: 8444 S East St

Indianapolis IN 46227 Office: Indpls Pub Schs 120 E Walnut Indianapolis IN 46204

YOUNG, JOHN BURTON, otolaryngologist; b. Waterloo, Iowa, May 9, 1939; s. John B. and Margorie V.M. (Klersey) Y.; m. Cleo Ann Clementson, June 16, 1962; children: J. Craig, Erika C., Gretchen A. BS, Iowa State U., 1961; MD, U. Chgo., 1966. Diplomate Am. Bd. Otolaryngology. Intern St. Paul-Ramsey Hosp., 1966-67; post doctoral resident U. Minn., Mpls., 1967-71; chief otolaryngology USAF, Chanute AFB, Rantoul, Ill., 1971-73; pvt. practice Ear, Nose and Throat Clinic of Eau Claire, Wis., 1973—. Bd. dirs. ARC, Eau Claire, 1980-85. Served as maj. USAF, 1971-73. Recipient Bausch and Lomb award, 1957. Mem. Am. Acad. Otolaryngology. Lutheran. Avocations: distance running, sailing. Home: 391 Heather Ct Eau Claire WI 59701 Office: Ear Nose and Throat Clinic 714 W Hamilton Eau Claire WI 54701

YOUNG, KEVIN DUANE, accountant; b. St. Clair, Mich., May 10, 1961; s. Duane Roland and Mary Jayne (Cottrell) Y.; m. Heather Lynn Dunsmore, Aug. 20, 1983. BBA, Adrian Coll., 1983. CPA, Ohio. Acct. Price Waterhouse, Toledo, 1984—. Mem. Am. Inst. CPA's, Nat. Assn. Accts., Ohio Soc. CPA's, Jaycees. Avocations: sports, music, collecting baseball cards.

YOUNG, KEVIN MICHAEL, accountant; b. St. Joseph, Sept. 23, 1954; s. Floyd Kenny and Dorothy Lea (Smith) Y.; m. Cheryl Ann Elliott, July 20, 1974; children: Tiffany Ann, Michele Maelea. BS, Mo. Western State Coll., 1981. CPA, Mo. Staff acct. Gasper and Co., St. Joseph, 1982-84; ptnr. Sumner, Carter, Hardy & Simpson, St. Joseph, 1984—. Served with U.S. Army, 1973-76. Mem. Am. Inst. CPA's (tax dv), Nat. Assn. Accts. (v.p. 1985—), Mo. Soc. CPA's. Democrat. Roman Catholic. Club: St. Joseph Motor and yacht (pres., chmn. bd. dirs. 1986—). Lodges: Shriners, Sertoma (treas. East Hills chpt. 1986—). Avocations: boating, camping, golf. Home: 6102 N 26th St Terr Country Club Village MO 64505 Office: Sumner Carter Hardy & Simpson 3110 Karnes Rd Saint Joseph MO 64506

YOUNG, LAURENS DOLAN, psychiatrist; b. Chgo., Dec. 15, 1942; s. John Laurens and Viola Ann (Dolan) Y.; m. Joanne Mary Trimble, June 22, 1968; children—Jennifer, Elisabeth, Christina. A.B., Harvard U., 1965; M.D., U. Chgo., 1969. Diplomate Am. Bd. Psychiatry and Neurology. Intern, U. Ill.-Chgo., 1969-70; resident in psychiatry U. Wis.-Madison, 1970-74; asst. prof. Med. U. S.C., Charleston, 1974-76; asst. prof. Med. Coll. Wis., Milw., 1976-80, assoc. prof., 1980—; practice medicine specializing in psychiatry, Milw., Milw., 1982—; dir. dept. psychiatry Milw. County Med. Ctr., 1982—; head Div. Gen. Hosp. Psychiatry, Milw., 1982—. Contbr. articles to profl. jours. Fellow NSF, 1960, NIMH, 1967; recipient Research award in Alcoholism, Sumner Found., 1975. Mem. Wis. Psychiat. Assn. (councillor 1984-86, treas. Milw. chpt. 1983-84, pres. Milw. chpt. 1985-86). Clubs: Milw. Athletic; Union League (Chgo.). Avocations: squash, tennis, fishing, photography. Office: Milw County Med Complex PO Box 175 8700 W Wisconsin Ave Wauwatosa WI 53226

YOUNG, MARC BENJAMIN, mechanical engineer, owner scientific products distribution company; b. Painesville, Ohio, Aug. 3, 1955; s. Frank Benjamin and Ramona (Milford) Y.; m. Karen Anne Pedersen, June 12, 1982; children: Katharine Anne, Michael Benjamin, Margaret Rose. BSME, MIT, 1980; postgrad., Case Western Res. U., 1984—. Draftsman Stock Equipment, Chagrin Falls, Ohio, 1975-76, Byers, Urban, Klug & Smith, Cleve., 1977; project leader MIT, Cambridge, Mass., 1978-80; sr. engr. Standard Oil, Cleve., 1980—; pres., owner Bainbridge Sci., Cleve., 1986—. Contbr. articles to profl. jour. Pres. Mentor (Ohio) Bapt. Ch. Youth Group, 1972-73; deacon Euclid Ave. Christian Ch., Cleve., 1985—. Mem. Soc. Mech. Engrs. (treas. 1982-83, v.p. internal affairs 1983-84), Soc. Mfg. Engrs. Republican. Avocations: golf, skiing, basketball. Home: 3323 Altamont Cleveland Heights OH 44118 Office: Standard Oil Research Ctr 4440 Warrensville Rd Cleveland OH 44128

YOUNG, MAXINE KATHERINE, accountant; b. Grand Rapids, Mich., Aug. 11, 1934; d. Peter and Gladys (Saltness) Vander Veen; m. Gerald Young, July 3, 1954; children—Kathleen Jo, Derk Alan, Daryl Evan. B.S. in Acctg., Ind. U., 1975. C.P.A., Ind. Data processor Grand Rapids Wholesale Grocers, 1951-54; staff acct. Deloitte, Haskins & Sells, C.P.A.s, Ft. Wayne, Ind., 1975-76; ptnr. Young & Co., CPAs, Ft. Wayne, 1976—. Democratic precinct vice-committeeman, 1971-72; treas. Carol Angel campaign, 1978; mem. audit rev. com. and ad hoc audit subcom. Ft. Wayne United Way, 1980. Recipient Dir.'s award SBA, 1977. Mem. Am. Inst. C.P.A.s, Ind. Soc. C.P.A.s, Am. Women's Soc. C.P.A.s, Am. Soc. Women Accts., Nat. Assn. Accts. (pres. Ft. Wayne chpt. 1984-85), Nat. Conf. C.P.A. Practitioners (vice chmn. 1985-86, bd. dirs. 1986-87). Lutheran. Office: Young & Co 8026 Manor Dr Fort Wayne IN 46825

YOUNG, MICHAEL DAVID, health care company executive; b. Ames, Iowa, Oct. 20, 1952; s. Donald Frederick and Ann (Cooper) Y.; m. Krisann Jo Vasey, Nov. 14, 1978; 1 child, Nicole. BS, Iowa State U., 1974, MS, 1978; MS in Healthcare Adminstrn., Trinity U., 1986. Dept. head Mary Greeley Med. Ctr., Ames, 1973-81, dir. quality assurance, 1981-82; exec. dir. ASC, Inc., Des Moines, 1982-83, Emergency Physicians Service, Des Moines, 1983-86; pres., chief exec. officer Michael D. Young, Inc., Des Moines, 1986—; pres. Cen. Iowa Emergency Med. Services, Inc., Indianola; cons. Iowa chpt. Am. Coll. Emergency Physicians, Des Moines, 1985—. Pres. bd. Ames Community Pre-Sch., 1985, 86, 87; mem. advanced cardiac life support affiliated faculty Iowa Heart Assn., 1975—, basic cardiac life support affiliated faculty, 1973-75. Mem. Am. Coll. Healthcare Execs., Med. Group Mgmt. Assn. Lutheran. Home: 3312 Eisenhower Ave Ames IA 50010 Office: PO Box 1753 Des Moines IA 50301

YOUNG, MICHAEL ROBERT, pharmacist; b. Springfield, Mo., Apr. 18, 1956; s. Robert Floyd and Martha (Schmideskamp) Y. B.S. in Pharmacy, U. Okla., 1981; B.S. in Chemistry, So. Mo. State U., 1985; m. Ann Young, 1986. Registered pharmacist, Mo. Researcher, Drug Analysis Lab., Oklahoma City, 1979-80; student pharmacist Windham Pharmacy, Springfield, Mo., summer 1980, Bethany Gen. Hosp., Okla., 1980-81, Choctaw Pharmacy, Okla., 1980-81; pharmacy mgr. Wal-Mart Stores, Springfield, Mo., 1981-82; pharmacist St. John's Hosp., Springfield, 1982—; pharmacist Drug Info. Ctr. at St. John's Reg. Health Ctr.; pharmacy cons. Mercy Villa Nursing Home, Springfield, 1983—. Recipient Music award Regional Music Contest, 1972; Logic Probability award So. Mo. State U., 1974. Mem. Ozark Soc. Hosp. Pharmacists, Am. Pharm. Assn., Mo. Pharm. Assn. (polit. action com. 1982—). Democrat. Methodist. Avocations: flying (instrument rated pilot 1987); photography; tennis; woodworking; fishing. Home: 1120 W McGee Springfield MO 65807

YOUNG, PAUL F., real estate executive; b. Shelbyville, Ind., Sept. 18, 1946; s. S. Maurice and Pauline (Clouse) Y.; m. Sandra M. Tracy, Feb. 12, 1977; children—Carolyn Christine, Alexandra Marie, Victoria Ann. A.B. in Econs., Muhlenberg Coll., 1971; M.B.A. in Fin., Pa. State U., 1973. Asst. regional dir. Mass. Mut. Life Ins. Co., Chgo., 1972-78; v.p. fin., Am. Invsco Corp., Chgo., 1978-79; exec. v.p. Kafka, Inc., Downers Grove, Ill., 1979-81; v.p. William G. Ceas & Co., Rolling Meadows, Ill., 1981-82; pres. Prime Realty, Inc., Chgo., 1983-84; pres. Focus Real Estate Securities Corp., Chgo., 1984-87, Southpoint Corp., Chgo., 1987—. Bd. dirs. United Way of Glen Ellyn, 1982-85. Served to sgt. USMC, 1966-72. Mem. Mortgage Bankers Assn. Am., Real Estate Securities and Syndication Inst., Chgo. Real Estate Bd., Young Mortgage Bankers Chgo. (vice chmn. 1975-78). Office: Southpoint Corp 345 N Canal St Suite 700 Chicago IL 60606

YOUNG, PHILIP HOWARD, library director; b. Ithaca, N.Y., Oct. 7, 1953; s. Charles Robert and Betty Irene (Osborne) Y.; m. Nancy Ann Stutsman, Aug. 18, 1980. BA, U. Va., 1975; PhD, U. Pa., 1980, MLS, Ind. U., 1983. Asst. prof. history Appalachian State U., Boone, N.C., 1980-82; reference asst. Lilly Library, Ind. U., Bloomington, 1982-83; adminstr., info. specialist Ind. Corp. for Sci. & Tech., Indpls., 1983-85; dir. Krannert Meml. Library, U. Indpls., 1985—. Mem. Am. Library Assn., Ind. Library Assn., Archaeological Inst. Am., Phi Beta Kappa, Phi Alpha Theta, Beta Phi Mu. Democrat. Methodist. Home: 1944 Patton Dr Speedway IN 46224 Office: Univ Indpls Krannert Memorial Library 1400 E Hanna Ave Indianapolis IN 46227

YOUNG, RANDY MAURICE, psychologist, educator; b. Maryville, Mo., Aug. 6, 1952; s. Jack Maurice and Twyla Lee (Wolverton) Y.; m. Marjorie Louise Lasley, Aug. 22, 1975; children—James Allen, Timothy Lee. A.A., Iowa Western Community Coll., 1975; B.A., N.W. Mo. State U., 1977, M.S. in Counseling Psychology, 1979. Mental health worker Clarinda (Iowa) Treatment Complex, 1973-77, social work assoc., 1977-78, social worker, 1978-80, psychologist, 1980—, adminstrv. dir. alcohol and drug treatment unit, 1979—, also pres. clin. staff orgn.; instr. Iowa Western Community Coll.; outpatient therapist Waubonsie Mental Health Service, 1982-83. Bd. dirs. S.W. Iowa Family Systems Project, 1978-80. Mem. Am. Psychol. Assn. (assoc.). Baptist. Home: 609 W Nishna Clarinda IA 51632 Office: Clarinda Treatment Complex PO Box 338 Clarinda IA 51632

YOUNG, RICHARD FOGG, JR., nuclear engineer; b. Salem, N.J., Nov. 25, 1949; s. Richard Fogg Sr. and Alice Elizabeth (Shafer) Y.; m. Mayanna Ruth Van Meter, Apr. 22, 1976; children: Jordan Winthrop, William David. A in Tech. EE, U. Dayton, 1971; BS in Tech. EE, Spring Garden Coll., Chestnut Hill, Pa., 1975. Start-up engr. Bvell div. Envirotech, Lebanon, Pa., 1975; asst. plant engr. Ga. Power Co., Cartersville, 1976-79; asst. constrn. mgr. Research Cottrell, Boundbrook, N.J., 1979-81; field constrn. engr. Hope Creek Nuclear Sta. div. Bechtel Power Co., Hancock's Bridge, N.J., 1981-86; sr. plant/sched engr. Davis-Besse Nuclear Power div. Toledo Edison Co., Oak Harbor, Ohio, 1986—. Mem. Instrument Soc. Am. (sr.), Gideons Internat. (sec. 1984-85), U.S. Chess Fedn. Baptist. Avocations: pocket billiards, golf, musical instruments. Home: 725 N Streeter Rd Port Clinton OH 43452 Office: Toledo Edison Co Davis Besse Nuclear Power Sta Oak Arbor OH 43449

YOUNG, ROBERT ALLEN, communications executive; b. Chgo., Dec. 21, 1946; s. Willard Foulks and Elizabeth (Ingraffia) Y. AA, DeVry Tech. Coll., 1969. Group leader Enfermi Lab., Batavia, Ill., 1972-77; field engr. Scan Data, Hillside, Ill., 1977-79; regional support AM/ECRM, Elk Grove, Ill., 1979-82; nat. support RACAL Telesystems, Chgo., 1982-85; service mgr. Access Telecom, Downers Grove, Ill., 1985-86; pres. Mobile Services Cons., Des Plaines, Ill., 1986—. mem. adv. bd. Am. Security Council, Washington, 1986. Served with U.S. Army, 1969-71. Mem. Armed Forces Communications Assn., NRA (life), ISRA (life), Sports Car Club Am. (nat. lic. holder). Address: 2993 Curtis St #C45 Des Plaines IL 60018

YOUNG, ROBERT EUGENE, educator, university dean; b. Davenport, Iowa, Apr. 12, 1948; s. Herman and Ruth (Hanson) Y.; m. Marjorie Miller, Dec. 19, 1970; 1 child, Katherine. BA in Sociology, Drake U., 1970; MA in Edn., Mich. State U., 1973, PhD in Edn., 1976. Assoc. dir., asst. prof. Va. Commonwealth U., Richmond, 1976-80; dir., assoc. prof. U. N.D., Grand Forks, 1980-87; dean, prof. U. Wis.-Fox Valley, Menasha, 1987—; cons. 60 Colls. and Univs. Editor: Fostering Critical Thinking, 1980; cons. editor: College Teaching, 1984—; series editor New Directions for Teaching and Learning, 1987—; contbr. articles to profl. jours. Bd. dirs. KFJM Pub. Radio, Grand Forks, 1981—, United Hosp., Grand Forks, 1983—. Grantee Bush Found.m 1980, 83, Fund for Improvement Postsecondary Edn., U.S. Dept. Edn., 1983. Mem. Am. Edn. Research Found. (exec. com., chmn. program), Profl. Devel. Network (bd. dirs. 1979-82), Nat. Ctr. to Improve Postsecondary Edn. (scholar 1986—), Nat. Faculty Exchange (founder, bd. dirs. 1984—), Omicron Delta Kappa, Phi Delta Kappa (pres. 1983, recipient Brietwiser-Cushman award 1984). Lutheran. Avocations: sailing, boat building, skiing. Home: 2625 Harmon St Appleton WI 54951 Office: Univ Wis Ctr 1478 Midway Rd Menasha WI 54952

YOUNG, ROBERT LAWRENCE, ophthalmologist, educator; b. Harlem, Mont., Oct. 25, 1918; s. Morris David and Esther Rae (Urkov) Yampolsky; B.S., U. Ill., 1940, M.D., 1943; m. Roberta Sternberg, Oct. 10, 1943; children—Fredric, Barbara, James, Michael. Intern, Michael Reese Hosp., Chgo., 1944, resident, 1949-50; resident U. Ill. Hosp., 1948-49, Aspinwall VA Hosp., Pitts., 1950; practice medicine specializing in ophthalmology, Gary, Ind., 1951-74, Munster, Ind., 1974—; mem. staff, pres. St. Mary of Mercy Hosp., Gary; sr. staff Meth. Hosp., Ind. U. Hosp., both Gary, Community Hosp., Munster, Ind.; mem. adv. com. Ind. U. N.W. br. Med. Sch.; asst. prof. ophthalmology Ind. U. Bd. dirs. Munster Community Hosp. Served to capt. M.C., AUS, 1946-48. Diplomate Am. Bd. Ophthalmology. Fellow Internat. Coll. Surgeons; mem. AMA, Assn. Research in Ophthalmology, World Med. Assn., Am. Acad. Ophthalmology, Ind., N.W. Ind., Chgo. ophthalmology socs., AAAS, Ind., Munster chambers commerce, Tau Delta Phi, Phi Delta Epsilon. Democrat. Jewish (temple mens' club). Clubs: B'nai B'rith. Home: 8809 Crestwood Munster IN 46321 Office: 1646 45th Ave Munster IN 46321

YOUNG, ROBERT LERTON, insurance brokerage company executive; b. Columbus, Ohio, Feb. 21, 1936; s. Robert Lerton and Ada Beatrice (Aderholt) Y.; m. Caroline Page Dickey, May 10, 1980. Student, U. Ill., 1953-55, Ohio State U., 1958-60. Mgr. actuarial dept. Gates McDonald & Co., Columbus, 1959-66; dist. mgr. Gates McDonald & Co., Oakland, Calif., 1966-70; v.p., founder Nat. Compensation Services, Inc., Pleasant Hill, Calif., 1970-71; v.p. Fred S. James & Co., Inc., Pleasant Hill and San Francisco, 1971-76; v.p. Fred S. James & Co., Inc., Chgo., 1976—, pres. Claims Mgmt. Services div., 1985; cons. Los Angeles County Self Ins. Program; mem. adv. com. Calif. Dept. Indsl. Relations; tchr. Calif. Extension, 1970; lectr. Am. Mgmt. Assn. Contbr. articles in field to profl. jours. Mem. Pleasant Hill Youth Commn. Served with U.S. Army, 1955-58. Recipient Service award Chartered Property and Casualty Underwriters, 1971, 75. Mem. Ins. Inst. Am. (risk mgmt. diploma), Am. Soc. Safety Engrs. (indsl. safety diploma), Nat. Council Self-Insurers, Internat. Assn. Indsl. Accident Bds. and Commns., Calif., Ariz., Wash., Pa., Mass., Ga., Fla. self-insurers assns. Club: Metropolitan (Chgo.). Office: Fred S James & Co 230 W Monroe St Chicago IL 60606

YOUNG, SAMUEL MILTON, JR., neurologist; b. Kirksville, Mo., June 23, 1944; s. Samuel Milton and Mavis Lorene (Simler) Y.; m. Hoa Thi Nguyen, Dec. 4, 1972; 1 child, Kim Lorene. Student, Northeast Coll., Kirksville, 1962-63; AB, U. Mo., 1966, MD, 1970. Diplomate Am. Bd. Psychiatry and Neurology. Intern U. Kans., Kansas City, 1970-71; resident U. Iowa, Iowa City, 1973-76; neurologist Christie Clinic, Champaign, Ill., 1977—, also bd. dirs., 1986—; bd. dirs. Christie Clinic, Personal Care, Inc. Served to capt. U.S. Army, 1971-73, Vietnam. Decorated Bronze Star. Mem. AMA, Ill. Med. Soc., Champaign County Med. Soc., Am. Acad. Neurology, Am. Electroencephalographic Soc., Am. Soc. Neuroimaging. Republican. Home: 2303 Valley Brook Champaign IL 61821 Office: Christie Clinic 101 W University Champaign IL 61820

YOUNG, TERESA LYNN, exercise physiologist; b. Eureka, Kans., Aug. 30, 1959; d. Alva Leroy and Trenna Ovine (Puckett) Watts; m. Thomas B. Young, Aug. 15, 1981. BS, Baker U., Baldwin, Kans., 1981; MS, U. Kans., 1983. Exercise physiologist Maupintour, Lawrence, Kans., 1982-83; owner Young at Heart Lifetime Fitness, Lansing, Kans., 1983—, Young and Gilman, Lansing, 1985—, The Fitness Studio, Lansing, 1985—; program dir. HealthPlus, Overland Park, Kans., 1984—; cons. Health Plus Fitness, Ft. Scott, 1985—; bd. dirs. Mary Mayta Life Internat., Wichita, 1986—. Author (book) Eldercize, 1986, (videos) Young at Heart, 1985-86. Mem. Am. Coll. Sports Medicine (cert.), Assn. Fitness in Bus., Am. Assn. Health, Physical Edn., Recreation and Dance, Internat. Dance Exercise Assn., Nat. Strength Assn. Republican. Methodist. Avocation: running, aerobic dance, computers. Home: 107 N Main Lansing KS 66043

YOUNG, THOMAS LEE, lawyer; b. Los Angeles, Feb. 21, 1944; s. J. Donald and Nancy M. Young; m. Kathleen Grace Jacob, Sept. 10, 1967; children: Barbara, Deborah, Amy. Student Marquette U., 1963; BA, St. John's Coll., 1966; JD, Notre Dame U., 1972; postgrad. Harvard U., 1984-83. Bar: Ohio, 1972. Assoc. Fuller, Henry, Hodge & Snyder, Toledo, 1972-75; assoc. counsel Scott Paper Co., Phila., 1975-76; asst. gen counsel Owens-Ill., Inc., Toledo, 1976—; bd. dirs. Prudent Supply, Inc., Mpls., Health Group, Inc., Nashville, Cajas Corrugadas de Mex., Mexico City. Asst. sec. Greater Toledo Corp. Served to 1st lt. U.S. Army, 1966-69, Vietnam. Mem. ABA, Ohio State Bar Assn., Toledo Bar Assn. Roman Catholic. Avocations: tennis. Office: Owens-Illinois Inc One SeaGate Toledo OH 43666

YOUNG, TIMOTHY PETER, accountant; b. Chgo., May 30, 1962; s. Eugene R. and Phyllis Jean (Prince) Y. BS in Acctg., DePaul U., Chgo., 1984; postgrad., Northwestern U., 1986—. CPA, Ill. Acct. Peat Marwick, Mitchell & Co., Chgo., 1984—. Mem. Am. Inst. CPA's, Ill. CPA Soc. Roman Catholic. Avocations: boating, skiing, raquetball, golf. Home: 9600 S Kenneth Oak Lawn IL 60453 Office: Peat Marwick Mitchell & Co 303 E Wacker Dr Chicago IL 60601

YOUNG, VERNON LEWIS, lawyer; b. Seaman, Ohio, Oct. 13, 1919; s. Ezra S. and Anna (Bloom) Y.; m. Eileen Humble, Sept. 20, 1941; children—Robert, Loretta, Bettie Jo., Jon W., Denise L. Student Alfred Holbrook Coll., 1938-39; J.D., Ohio No. U., 1942. Bar: Ohio 1942. Sole practice, West Union, Ohio, 1942-50, 78-81; ptnr. Young & Young, West Union, 1959-78, Young & Caldwell (now called Young-Caldwell & BUBP), West Union, 1981—; spl. councel Office of Atty. Gen., State of Ohio, West Union, solicitor Cities of Jamestown, Seaman, Winchester, Manchester, Ohio; pros. atty. Adams County, Ohio, 1952-56, acting county judge, 1968-79. Mayor City of Seaman, 1944-46; mem. Adams County Health Bd., West Union, 1968-75; chmn. membership com. Eastern Shore Inst. Lifelong Learning, Fairhope, Ala., 1983-84; mem. Republican Presdl. Task Force, 1980—. Mem. Ohio State Bar Assn., Adams County Bar Assn. (former pres.), Sigma Delta Kappa (chancellor 1940). Lodges: Masons, Lions (pres. 1950-51, dist. gov. 1951-52). Avocations: fishing; hunting; gardening. Home: 10 Hickory Dr Seaman OH 45679

YOUNGBLOOD, JAMES PETER, physician, educator.; b. Detroit, May 8, 1932; s. Francis John and Cathleen Sophia (Boes) Y.; m. Bernadette Y., Aug. 8, 1953; children—Jeremy J., Kathleen A., Margaret M., Mary L., Laura A., Matthew J., Daniel B. Student U. Mich. Sch. Lit., Ann Arbor, 1950-53; M.D., U. Mich., Ann Arbor, 1957. Diplomate Am. Bd. Ob-Gyn. Intern U. Mich. Med. Ctr., Ann Arbor, 1958-62, resident in ob-gyn, 1962; physician group practice Kansas City, Mo., 1964-84; prof., chmn. dept. ob-gyn Truman Med. Ctr., Kansas City, Mo., 1984—; clin. asst. prof. U. Mo., Kansas City, 1979-84; prof. U. Mo. Sch. Medicine, Kansas City, 1984—. Contbr. articles to profl. jours. Served to capt. USAF, 1962-64. Fellow Am. Coll. Ob-Gyn (dist. sec.-treas. 1984—); mem. Central Assn. Ob-Gyn (nominating com. 1984—), Mo. State Med. Assn., AMA, Jackson County Med. Soc., Kansas City Gynecol. Soc. (pres. 1975-76). Republican. Roman Catholic. Club: Vanguard (Kansas City, pres. 1986). Avocations: hunting; fishing; golf. Office: Truman Med Ctr Dept Ob-Gyn 2301 Holmes Kansas City MO 64108

YOUNGBLOOD, JAMES ROBERT, information systems executive; b. Avon, Ohio, Oct. 20, 1939; s. Irving George Youngblood and Regina (Schneider) Dea; m. Barbara Ann Hoover, Oct. 21, 1961; children: Craig, Lynne. Student, Am. U., Washington, 1963, 64. Cert. systems profl. Programmer Nat. Security Agy., Ft. Mead, Md., 1962-68; programmer/analyst Cuyahoga County Data Ctr., Cleve., 1968-69, mgr. systems, 1969-71; assoc. dir., cons. Cuyhoga County Welfare Dept., Cleve., 1971-78; asst. v.p. systems Cuyahoga County Hosp., Cleve., 1978-83; v.p. systems, cons. Iowa Meth. Med. Ctr., Des Moines, 1983—. Advisor Boy Scouts Am., Avon Lake, Ohio, 1983. Served with U.S. Army, 1958-61. Mem. Ohio Info. Systems Soc. (pres. 1981-82), Assn. Systems Mgmt., Iowa Hosp. Assn., ECHO. Roman Catholic. Avocations: boating, hunting, fishing, hiking. Home: 7009 Coburn Ln Johnston IA 50131 Office: Iowa Meth Med Ctr 1200 Pleasant St Des Moines IA 50309

YOUNGDAHL, CARL KERR, mathematician, researcher; b. Chgo., Aug. 14, 1934; s. Carl Edward and Anne Mabel (Kerr) Y.; m. Marilyn Christina LaPalio, June 22, 1963; children: Carl, Andrew, David. AB, U. Chgo., 1953; BSME, Ill. Inst. Tech., 1956, MSME, 1957; PhD in Applied Math., Brown U., 1960. Assoc. mathematician Argonne (Ill.) Nat. Labs., 1960-74; sr. mathematician Argonne (Ill.) Nat. Lab., 1974—. Contbr. articles to profl. jours. Mem. Am. Soc. Mech. Engrs., Am. Acad. Mechanics, Sigma Xi. Office: Argonne Nat Lab Bldg 335 Argonne IL 60439

YOUNGER, KENNETH WAYNE, human resources and management consultant; b. Jacksonville, Fla., Oct. 26, 1951; s. Ralph B. Jr. and Henrietta (Wingate) Y.; m. Nancy Lynn Ford, June 5, 1971; children: Kenan, Lynden. BA, Carson-Newman Coll., 1972; MS, Okla. State U., 1974, PhD, 1975. Asst. prof. psychology and computer sci. Calumet Coll., Whiting, Ind., 1975-76; asst. prof. psychology Carson-Newman Coll., Jefferson City, Tenn., 1976-79; project mgr. mgmt. devel. Arthur Andersen & Co., Chgo., 1979-80; v.p. Drake Beam Morin Inc., Chgo., 1980-82; mng. ptnr. Savard Younger Cons. Group, Chgo., 1982—; adj. prof.; guest lectr. Recipient Outstanding Sci. Achievement award U.S. Navy, 1969, Meritorious Research award Okla. Psychol. Assn., 1973, Outstanding Faculty Service award Carson-Newman Student Found., 1977; NSF scholar, 1967, Regents scholar State of Fla., 1969. Mem. Greater O'Hare Assn. Industry and Commerce, U.S. Jaycees (Outstanding Young Am. 1981), Tenn. Squires, Phi Kappa Phi. Baptist. Office: 8700 W Bryn Mawr Suite 7405 Chicago IL 60631

YOUNGER, ROBERT JOSEPH, training and development specialist; b. Brunswick, Md., June 29, 1943; s. Harry Leonard and Elizabeth Marguerite (Potter) Y.; m. Elsibeth Semone Heimlid, Mar. 3, 1966 (div. May 1984); children; Marlena, Harry Gregory, Robert Viking, Heidi Beth, Benita Renee, Trixy Marie; m. Marjorie Lee Boettcher, Apr. 2, 1985. BSBA, Southwest Mo. State U., 1978. Enlisted U.S. Army, 1965, commd. 2d lt. adj. gen. corps, 1969, advanced through grades to maj., 1980, retired, 1985; mgr. staff tng. and devel. Kans. State U., Manhattan, 1985—, coordinator employee asst. program, 1986—. commdr. Royal Rangers Assemblies of God, Junction City, Kans., 1982-84; solicitor United Way Campaign, Manhattan, Kans., 1985-86. Mem. Am. Soc. Tng. and Devel. Republican. Mem. Ch. of the Brethern. Avocations: tennis, racquetball, crafts. Home: 825 Dondee Dr Manhattan KS 66502 Office: Kans State U Personnel Services 228 Anderson Hall Manhattan KS 66506

YOUNGHOUSE, ROBERT HARRY, JR., academic administrator, educator; b. Hutchinson, Kans., Oct. 22, 1944; s. Robert Harry Sr. and Evelyn (Prinz) Y.; m. Annette Kendall, May 5, 1966 (div. June 1976); children: RobertIII, Jeffery; m. Patricia Ann McCahren, june 24, 1984. BS, Miami U., Oxford, Ohio, 1975; MA, Ball State U., 1976; D of Edn., U. Ill., 1983. Dist. sales mgr. United Brands Co., Boston, 1966-73; staff assoc. coll. medicine U. Ill., Peoria, 1976-78, dir. coll. medicine, 1978-84; assoc. dir. U. Ill., Chgo., 1984—, acting dir., 1985—; cons. Ill. Council Continuing Med. Edn., Chgo., 1980-85, Ill. State Med. Soc., Chgo., 1986—; asst. prof. U. Ill., Chgo., 1984—. Contbr. articles to profl. jours. Mem. Nat. Found. March of Dimes, Peoria, 1977-79; v.p. Ill. Valley Lung Assn., Peoria, 1979-84; del. Am. Lung Assn., Springfield, Ill., 1981-83; mem. Am. Heart Assn., Springfield, 1983—. Served with U.S. Army, 1967-70, Korea. Recipient Cert. Appreciation, Ill. Valley Lung Assn., 1982, Excellance Seminar Mgmt. award Ill. Acad. Dental Practice Adminstrn., 1984. Mem. NAt. Univ. Continuing Edn. Assn., Am. Assn. Adult and Continuing Edn., Assn. Continuing Higher Edn., Soc. Med. Coll. Dirs. Continuing Med. Edn. (Cert. Recognition 1986, 87). Republican. Lodge: Masons. Avocations: stamp collecting, youth sports coaching. Home: 511 S Ridgeland Ave Oak Park IL 60304 Office: U Ill 912 S Wood St Chicago IL 60612

YOUNGMAN, JAMES LEONARD, psychologist; b. Duluth, Minn., Mar. 15, 1948; s. Leonard John and Mathilda Dolores (Hillesheim) Y.; m. Christine Ruth Halverson, Oct. 23, 1971; 1 child, Adam. BA, U. Minn., 1970; MA, U. N.D., 1974. Lic. psychologist, Minn. Case worker County Social Services, Grand Forks, N.D., 1971-74; psychologist Grand Forks Pub. Schs., 1974-78; psychology pvt. practice East Grand Forks, Minn., 1978-86; psychologist Upper Valley Spl. Edn., Grafton, N.D., 1978-86; dir. Harley Clinic, Long Prairie, Minn., 1986—. Contbr. articles to profl. jours. Bd. dirs. Alvarado (Minn.) Sch. Bd., 1985-86. Mem. Nat. Assn. Sch. Psychologists, Am. Inst. Indsl. Engrs. (assoc.). Lutheran. Avocations: sailing, karate, building ships in bottles. Office: Harley Clinic 917 1st Ave SE Long Prairie MN 56347

YOUNGQUIST, KEITH EUGENE, architect; b. Waverly, Iowa, July 19, 1954; s. Henry W. and Virginia J. (Norstrom) Y.; m. Laury Ellen Stuart, Feb. 19, 1977. BS, U. Ill., 1976. Registered architect, Ill., Ga., Colo., Ohio, Minn., S.D. Assoc. Cerny Architects, Glenview, Ill., 1976-80; prin., v.p. Aumiller Youngquist Architects, Mount Prospect, Ill., 1980—. Prin. works include Ed Debevic's Short Order's Deluxe, Chgo., Los Angeles, Cafe Ba-Ba-Reba, Chgo., Timbers, Highland Park, Ill., Shaws Crab House, Deerfield, Ill., Rims Corp. Headquarters Bldg., Naperville, Ill., The Eyeworks, Cleve., Scoozi., Chgo. Mem. AIA. Lutheran. Lodge: Kiwanis. Office: 800 E Northwest Hwy Mount Prospect IL 60056

YOUNGREN, RALPH PARK, architect; b. Cloquet, Minn., Dec. 26, 1924; s. Andrew Frederick and Eunice (Park) Y.; m. Ann Henderson, June 28, 1962; children: Todd Park, Malcolm Park. AB, Harvard U., 1948, BArch, MArch, 1950. Assoc. ptnr. Skidmore, Owings & Merrill, Chgo., 1950-67; pres. Metz, Train, Youngren, Chgo., 1967-84; exec. v.p. Smith, Hinchman & Grylls, Detroit, 1985—; archtl. advisor Chgo. Dept. Urban Renewal, 1962. Designer Regenstein Library, Chgo., Rush Med. Coll., Chgo., Beckman Inst., Urbana, Ill. Served to staff sgt. U.S. Army, 1943-45, ETO. Fellow AIA (bd. dirs. Chgo. chpt. 1976-78, R.J. Reynolds award 1964), Chgo. Archtl. Found. (trustee 1969-85), Thomas Jefferson Found. (trustee 1972-74). Clubs: Detroit; Cliff Dwellers (bd. dirs. 1975), Racquet (Chgo.). Home: 13 Oaks Ct Bloomfield Hills MI 48013 Office: Smith Hinchman & Grylls Assoc Inc 455 W Fort St Detroit MI 48226

YOUNKIN, GREGORY WAYNE, data processing executive; b. Buffalo, N.Y., May 28, 1953; s. George W. and Nancy L. (Greenwald) Y. Student, U. Wis. Ctr., Fond du Lac, 1973-75; BS in Secondary Edn. with high honors, U. Wis., Oshkosh, 1977; A in Programming, MPTI, 1982. Data processing mgr. PCA of Juneau, Wis., 1982-85; programmer, analyst dept. health and social services State of Wis., Madison, 1986—. Lodge: Lions (sec. Juneau 1986—). Avocations: computers, travel. Home: PO Box 152 Juneau WI 53039

YOUNT, KIM ALLEN, dentist; b. Leavenworth, Kans., Apr. 30, 1954; s. Robert Eugene and Barbara Jean (Gee) Y.; m. Janet Lee Cahill, Aug. 2, 1975; children: Jacob Allen, Lucas Arthur, Kimberly Ann. AA, Johnson County Community Coll., 1974; BS in Biology, U. Mo., 1976; DDS, &, 1981. Lic. Practitioner Dental Bd., Kans., Mo. Landscape designer Rieke Nursery, Shawnee, Kans., 1974-80; clin. dentistry instr. U. Mo., Kansas City, 1981; gen. practice dentistry Rolling Fork, Miss., 1982-83, Liberal, Kans., 1983—. Mem. sch. bd. Unified Sch. Dist. 480, Liberal, 1985, Profl. Devel. Council, Liberal, 1985. Mem. ADA, SW Dental Study Club, Miss. Dental Assn., Ducks Unltd., Psi Omega. Republican. Lodge: Kiwanis. Avocations: pvt. pilot, skiing, scuba diving. Home: 2132 Sierra Liberal KS 67901 Office: 1411 W 15th Suite 301 Liberal KS 67901

YOUSE, CYNTHIA HARLAN, restaurant owner; b. Inpls., Aug. 16, 1948; d. Kenneth Charles and Wilma (Woody) Harlan; m. Lawrence Neal Youse, Dec. 20, 1969. BS in Design, U. Cin., 1971; postgrad., Miami U., Ohio, 1980-82. Art dir. Tempo, Inc., Cin., 1970-72, Northligh-Stolley, Cin., 1972-75; co-owner Grand Finale, Cin., 1975—, also bd. dirs. Mem. Kappa Kappa Gamma. Republican. Club: Glendale Centennial Garden. Avocations: painting, travel, skiing, antique autos. Office: Grand Finale 3 E Sharon Ave Cincinnati OH 45246

YOXALL, GEORGE JARMAN, consulting firm executive; b. Bklyn., July 14, 1924; s. Henry Charles and Anna (Ogden) Y.; m. June Evelyn McPherson, Apr. 8, 1950; 1 child, Patricia Ann. AB in Psychology magna cum laude, U. Miami, Coral Gables, Fla., 1948; MS in Psychology, Purdue U., 1949; postgrad., U. Chgo., 1950-53. Asst. to adminstrv. mgr. Sinclair Research Labs., Inc., Harvey, Ill., 1949-56; personnel mgr. gen. office Inland Steel Co., Chgo., 1956-59, mgr. personnel and tng., 1959-82, mgr. personnel and orgn. devel., 1982-85; v.p., cons. Jannotta, Bray & Assocs., Chgo., 1985—; exec. com. Tng., Inc., Chgo., 1979—. Co-author: (book) The Campus Connection, 1979; contbr. articles to profl. jours. Pres. Chgo. Fedn. Settlements, 1972-75; chmn. Chgo. Alliance Bus. Employment and Tng., Inc., 1978-80; vice chmn. Govs. Manpower Adv. Council, Chgo., 1967-69. Served with USAF, 1943-45. Fellow Am. Psychol. Assn.; mem. Human Resources Mgmt. Assn. Chgo. (pres. 1965-66), Midwest Coll. Placement Assn. (various coms. 1962-68). Home: 3116 Sprucewood Rd Wilmette IL 60091 Office: Jannotta Bray & Assocs 20 N Wacker Dr Chicago IL 60606

YSSELDYKE, JAMES EDWARD, psychology educator, institute administrator; b. Grand Rapids, Mich., Jan. 1, 1944; 2 children. Student in psychology, Calvin Coll., 1962-65; B.A. in Psychology, Biology, Western Mich. U., 1966; M.A. in Sch. Psychology, U. Ill., 1968, Ph.D., 1971. Lic. consulting psychologist, Minn. Tchr. spl. edn Kent County Juvenile Ct. Ctr., Grand Rapids, 1966-67; research asst. U. Ill. Inst. Research on Exceptional Children, 1969-70, teaching asst. dept. ednl. psychology, 1970; sch. psychology intern Oakland County Schs., Pontiac, Mich., 1970-71; asst. prof. sch. psychology Pa. State U., 1971-75, assoc. prof., 1975; assoc. prof. U. Minn., Mpls., 1975-79, prof., 1979—, dir. Inst. Research on Learning Disabilities, 1977-83, dir. Nat. Sch. Psychology Inservice Tng. Network, 1977-83; advisor, cons. and researcher in field. Author: (with J. Salvia) Assessment in Special and Remedial Education, 1985, (with B. Algozzine) Critical Issues in Special and Remedial Education, 1982, Introduction to Special Education, 1984, (with J.A. Salvia) Evaluación en la Educación Especial, 1981; editor: Exceptional Children, 1984—; assoc. editor: The School Psychologist, 1972-75; mem. editorial bd. and cons. editor numerous jours.; contbr. chpts. to books and articles to profl. jours. Fellow NIMH, 1967-69; recipient Lightner Witmer award Am. Psychol. Assn., 1973; grantee in field. Fellow Am. Psychol. Assn.; mem. Am. Ednl. Research Assn., Council for Exceptional Children, Nat. Assn. Sch. Psychologists, Council for Learning Disabilities, Council for Ednl. Diagnostic Services, Nat. Council on Measurement in Edn. Office: Inst for Research on Learning Disabilities 350 Elliott Hall 75 E River Rd Minneapolis MN 55455

YU, ANNE RAMONA WING-MUI, psychologist; b. Hong Kong, Apr. 9, 1948; came to U.S., 1968, naturalized, 1974; d. Hing-wan and Sin-wah (Yau) Yu; B.A. with honors in Psychology, Ohio U., 1971; M.A., So. Ill. U., 1975. Psychol. examiner Delta Counseling and Guidance Center, Monticello, Ark., 1975-76; psychologist Mid-Nebr. Community Mental Health Center, Grand Island, Nebr., 1977—; supr. satellite clinic Loup Valley Mental Health Center, Loup City, Nebr., 1978-79; project dir. Protection from Domestic Abuse, 1978-79; pres. Taskforce on Domestic Violence and Sexual Assault, Grand Island, 1980-82. Mem. mem. Mental Health Bd. Hall County, 1979; mem. fellows Menninger Found., 1983-84; bd. dirs. YWCA, 1984—. Ohio U. Psi Chi scholar, 1968-71. Mem. Nebr. Assn. Profl. Psychologists (membership chmn. 1977-78), Am. Psychol. Assn., Nebr. Assn. for Marriage and Family Therapy (v.p. 1981-84, pres. elect 1984-85, pres. 1985-87), Am. Assn. Sex Educators, Counselors, and Therapists, Am. Assn. Univ. Women (pres. Grand Island chpt. 1984-86, v.p. Nebr. div. 1986—), Internat. Platform Assn., Asian-Am. Psychol. Assn. Home: Apt 101 1524 Coventry Ln Grand Island NE 68801 Office: Mid-Plains Ctr Profl Services 914 Baumann Dr Grand Island NE 68801

YUE, BEATRICE YUAN JIH TAN, biochemist; b. Li, Hunan, Republic of China, Feb. 4, 1948; came to U.S., 1969; d. Yuen-Kai and Bing-Ru (Yang) Tan; m. Vincent T. Yue; children: Patrick, Jenny. BS, Nat. Taiwan U., Taipei, 1968; MS, Yale U., 1972; PhD, Washington U., St. Louis, 1974. Research assoc. Tufts-New Eng. Med. Ctr. Hosp., Boston, 1974-77, asst. prof., 1977-80; research asst. prof. U. Ill., Chgo., 1980-85, research assoc. prof., 1985—. Grantee Nat. Eye Inst., 1981—, Research to Prevent Blindness Assn., 1986. Mem. AAAS, Am. Chem. Soc., Internat. Soc. Eye Research, Assn. Research in Vision and Ophthalmology. Office: U Ill 1855 W Taylor St Chicago IL 60612

YUFIT, ROBERT ISAAC, psychologist; b. Chgo., Aug. 26, 1930; s. Samuel and Ida (Mutchnik) Y.; m. Gloria Lillian Krinn, July 7, 1957; children: Lisa, David, Aveva. PhD, U. Chgo., 1956. Lic. psychologist, Ill. Research dir. Ill. Masonic Med. Ctr., Chgo., 1975-80; dir. suicide assessment project Northwestern U. Med. Sch., Chgo., 1980—; sr. cons. Ctr. Suicide Research, Rush-Presbyn. St. Lukes Med. Ctr.; bd. dirs. Am. Assn. Suicidology. Cons. editor Jour. Suicide and Life Threatening Behavior, 1982—; contbr. articles to profl. jours. Fellow Am Psychol. Assn.; mem. Am. Bd. Profl. Psychology (bd. dirs. 1982—). Home: 1458 E Park Pl Chicago IL 60637 Office: Northwestern U Med Sch 303 E Chicago Ave Chicago IL 60611

YUNG, CHEUK WO, dermatologist; b. Hong Kong, Jan. 17, 1949; came to U.S., 1969; s. Hau S. and Bun C. (Mui) Y.; m. Betsy K. Poon, May 30, 1977; children: Sophia, Steve. BS, Columbia U., 1972; MD, NYU, 1977. Diplomate Am. Bd. Dermatology. Intern Maimonides Med. Ctr., Bklyn., 1977-78; resident Cin. Med. Ctr., 1978-79; resident U. Chgo. Med. Ctr., 1979-80; chief resident, 1980-81, instr., 1981-82, clin. asst. prof., 1985—; practice medicine specializing in dermatology, Orland Park, Ill., 1982-86, Chgo., 1986—; cons. Oak Forest Hosp., Ill., Palos Community Hosp., Holy Cross Hosp., Chgo. Contbr. articles to profl. jours. Bd. dirs. Chinatown Planning Council, N.Y.C., 1971. Fellow Am. Acad. Dermatology; mem. AMA, Ill. Med Soc., Chgo. Med. Soc. Home: 13629 Idlewild Dr Orland Park IL 60462 Office: 7123 W Archer Ave Chicago IL 60638

YUSKEWICH, J. MATTHEW, accountant; b. Columbus, Ohio, Sept. 20, 1952; s. Vincent Joseph and Margaret Jean (Watson) Y.; m. Susan Ellen Essman, Aug. 14, 1976; children: J. Matthew, Sarah Elizabeth, David Arthur. BA, Ohio Dominican Coll., 1974; MBA, Xavier U., 1977. CPA, Ohio. Sr. auditor Ohio Med. Indemnity, Worthington, 1978-79; cons. William Spooner Assocs., Columbus, 1979-81; tax ptnr. Jacoby, Yuskewich & Bigley Co. CPA's, Columbus, 1981—. Fin. chmn. St. agatha Ch. Parish Council, Columbus, sec. men's club. Mem. Am. Inst. CPA's, Ohio Soc. CPA's (tech. tax matters), Ohio Dominican Coll. Alumni, Ohio State U. Alumni Assn. Roman Catholic. Home: 2296 Abington Rd Columbus OH 43221 Office: Jacoby Yuskewich & Bigley Inc 1080 Fishinger Rd Columbus OH 43221

YUSKO, EDWARD MICHAEL, JR., automotive test engineer; b. Cleve., May 27, 1957; s. Edward Michael and Rosemarie (Follina) Y.; m. June E. Nenadal; 1 child, Melissa. Cert., Cuyahoga Community Coll., 1980-84. Dynamometer technician Ford Motor Co., Brookpark, Ohio, 1975-80; asst. mgr. research and devel. Hi-Ro Industries, Cleve., 1980-81; test engr. The Whitey Co., Highland Heights, Ohio, 1981—. Patentee in field. Avocations: car racing, golf, bowling. Home: 2681 St Rt 167 Jefferson OH 44047 Office: The Whitey Co 318 Bishop Rd Highland Heights OH 44143

ZABEL, JERRY, manufacturing company executive; b. Feldafing, Fed. Republic Germany, Jan. 5, 1947, came to U.S., 1949, naturalized, 1955; s. Sam and Sara (Turetz) Z.; m. Diane L. Silverman, Feb. 16, 1969; children—Steven, Rachel, Brian, Tracy. B.B.A., Roosevelt U., 1974, M.B.A., 1978. Cert. in prodn. and inventory mgmt. Factory mgr. Hart Schaffner & Marx, Chgo., 1969-74; planner Abbott Labs., North Chicago, Ill., 1974-79; mgr. Addressograph Multigraph, Mt. Prospect, Ill., 1979-80; dir. Internat. Jensen, Schiller Park, Ill., 1980-85; mgr. mfg. FelPro, Skokie, Ill., 1985—; instr. Webster Coll., Fort Sheridan, Ill., 1981, Columbia Coll., Fort Sheridan, 1978-81. Served with U.S. Army, 1965-68, Vietnam. Decorated. Mem. Am. Prodn. and Inventory Control Soc. (profl. cert. materials mgmt. 1982), Internat. Material Mgmt. Soc., Cosmopolitan C. of C. (Cert. of Appreciation 1974). Home: 1203 Devonshire Buffalo Grove IL 60089

ZABRISKIE, WILLIAM LUM, medical association executive; b. Ridgewood, N.J., Mar. 2, 1931; s. William Lum and Eva (Kievit) Z.; m. Nancy Jean Kahler, (Nov. 26, 1953; children: Clifford, William, Kenneth, Thomas. B in Mech. Engring., Rensselaer Poly. Inst., 1952, MS in Mgmt. Engring., 1960; MSME, Ohio State U., 1953. Profl. engr., N.Y. Mgr. mech. devel. Gen. Electric, Schenectady, N.Y., 1957-66; mgr. engring. and mktg. Gen. Electric, Shelbyville, Ind., 1966-74; mgr. x-ray products engring. Gen. Electric, Waukesha, Wis., 1974-85; chmn., chief exec. officer Med. Advance, Inc., Wauwatosa, Wis., 1985—; program dir. U. Wis., Milw., 1985-86. Patentee Vortex Incinerator. Served with U.S. Army, 1955-57. Republican. Presbyterian. Avocations: jogging, cross country skiing, home remodeling. Home: 1404 N 121 St Wauwatosa WI 53226 Office: Med Advances Inc 9722 Watertown Plank Rd Wauwatosa WI 53226

ZACCONE, SUZANNE MARIA, sales executive; b. Chgo., Oct. 23, 1957; d. Dominic Robert and Lorretta F. (Urban) Z. Grad. high sch., Downers Grove, Ill. Sales sec. Brookeridge Realty, Downers Grove, 1975-76; sales cons. Kafka Estates Inc., Downers Grove, 1975-76; adminstrv. asst. Chem. Dist., Inc., Oakbrook, Ill., 1976-77; sales rep., mgr. Anographics Corp., Burr Ridge, Ill., 1977—; pres., owner Graphic Solutions, Inc., Downers Grove, 1985—. Mem. Women in Mgmt., Nat. Assn. Female Execs., Sales and Mktg. Execs. of Chgo., Women Entrepreneurs of DuPage County. Avocations: reading, sailing, cooking, needlepoint, scuba diving. Office: Graphic Solutions Inc 5117 Main St Downers Grove IL 60515

ZACHAR, KAREL ALOIS, international trade executive; b. Pardubice, June 2, 1926; s. Jan and Karolina (Slavikova) Zachar; m. Dagmar Urbankova, June 15, 1955; children—Charles K., Lenka. Comml. Engr., Coll. Fgn. Trade, U. Charles IV, 1950. Second comml. attaché The Caribbean, 1961-65, dir. Far East div., 1965-67, comml. attaché Permanent Trade Mission, Quito, Ecuador, 1967-70; export mgr. Nat. Oats Co., Inc., Cedar Rapids, Iowa, 1971-77, dir. export ops., 1977-78, v.p. internat. div., 1978—, dir., 1980—. Contbr. articles to profl. jours. Mem. Internat. Trade Bur., Am. Mgmt. Assn., Am. Soc. Internat. Execs. Roman Catholic. Lodge: Lions. Avocations: chess; volleyball; tennis; oil painting. Home: 4103 Falbrook Dr NE Cedar Rapids IA 52402 Office: National Oats Co Inc 1515 H Ave NE Cedar Rapids IA 52402

ZACHARY, ANDREA ANNE, geneticist; b. Cleve., Sept. 25, 1946; d. Anthony A. and Audrey J. (Klaus) Z. BS, Ohio State U., 1967, MS, 1969; PhD, Case Western Res. U., 1982. Research asst. Ohio State U., Columbus, 1969-70; technologist Cleve. Clinic Found., 1970-74, supr. lab., 1974-81, project scientist, 1981-82, staff, 82-84, assoc. lab. dir., 1984-86, co-dir. lab., 1986—; faculty histocompatibility specialist course South-Eastern Organ Procurement Found., 1983, 84, 86; ad hoc cons. NIH, 1985-86. Co-editor: AACHT Lab. Manual, 1981. Author audio-visual program on immunogenetics, 1983. Contbr. articles to profl. jours. and chpts. to scholarly texts. Grantee Kidney Found. of Ohio, 1984, Cleve. Clinic Found., 1985-87. Mem. United Network for Organ Sharing (bd. govs. 1987—), Am. Soc. for Histocompatibility and Immunogenetics (councillor 1977-78, 83-86, edn. program faculty 1971-83, 85, invited speaker sci. symposium 1986, chairperson tech. affairs com. 1982-84, chairperson accreditation com. 1986—, editor Lab. Manual 1987), Am. Soc. Human Genetics, Am. Soc. Transplant Physicists, Transplant Soc. of Northeast Ohio, Audobon Soc., Nat. Wildlife Fedn. Avocations: nature photography, cross-country skiing, music, leather carving. Office: Cleve Clinic Found 9500 Euclid Ave Cleveland OH 44106

ZACHARY, LOUIS GEORGE, manufacturer, chemical consultant; b. Cambridge, Mass., Aug. 14, 1927; s. George E. and Angelike (Hantsis) Zacharakis; A.B. in Chemistry, Harvard U., 1950; M.B.A., Columbia U., 1951; m. Lillie Vletas, Apr. 20, 1955; children—Leslie A., Louis George. Prodn. supr. Dewey & Almy Co., Acton, Mass., 1951-52; salesman chem. div. Union Camp Corp., Wayne, N.J., 1952-59, sales mgr. chem. div., 1959-62, gen. mgr. chem. ops., 1962-66, gen. mgr. chem. div., 1970-78, v.p., 1974-78; v.p. Drake Mgmt Co., N.Y.C., 1966-70; sr. v.p. GAF Corp., N.Y.C., 1978-82, mem. office of chmn., 1981-82; cons., 1983-84; chmn., chief exec. officer Universal Die Casting, Inc., Saline, Mich., 1984—. Mem. vis. com. chem. engring. dept. Johns Hopkins U., Balt., 1981-83. Served with USN, 1945-46. Mem. Chem. Mfrs. Assn. (dir. 1979-83), Synthetic Organic Chem. Mfrs. Assn., Soc. Chem. Industry. Clubs: Baltusrol Golf; Harvard (N.Y.C.). Co-editor: Tall Oil and Its Uses, 1965. Office: Universal Die Casting Inc 1240 Wisteria B323 Ann Arbor MI 48104

ZACHE, ROBERT ROLAND, computer company executive; b. Milw., Jan. 17, 1926; s. Robert Roland Zache and Helen L. (Heimke) Lorch; m. Jean Ann Brandner, Feb. 16, 1952; children: James R., Richard C., Jody J., Robert W. Grad. high sch., Wauwatosa, Wis. Acct. Garfield Chevrolet Inc., Milw., 1952-68; with sales and data processing dept. Reynolds & Reynolds Co., Dayton, Ohio, 1968-73, ADP Dealer Services, Portland, Oreg., 1974-75; dir. data processing Berndt Buick/Mercedes Benz/Nissan, Milw., 1980—; prin. Zac-Com. Inc., Glendale, Wis., 1983—. Treas. Nile Soik for Assembly, Madison, Wis. Served with USN, 1944-46, PTO. Recipient Letter of Appreciation, Nicolet High Sch. Dept. Fine Arts, 1985, Golden Achievement award Viacom Cablevision, 1986. Mem. Am. Assn. Profl. Cons. (cert. instr.). Avocation: tennis. Home: 2556 W Dunwood Rd Glendale WI 53209

ZACHER, ALLAN NORMAN, JR., clergyman, psychologist, lawyer; b. Decatur, Ill., May 23, 1928; s. Allan Norman and Eleanor (Shaw) Z.; student Washington U. Sch. Bus. and Pub. Adminstrn., St. Louis, 1946, 48-50; J.D., Washington U., 1952, Ph.D., 1971; M.Div., Va. Theol. Sem., 1955; S.T.M., Eden Theol. Sem., 1966; m. Deborah Bradley, July 19, 1952 (dec. Mar. 1982); children—Allan Norman III, Mark, John. Admitted to Mo. bar, 1952; asso. firm Fred B. Whalen, St. Louis, 1950-52; ordained to ministry Episcopal Ch., 1955; asst. rector Truro Episcopal Ch., Fairfax, Va., 1955-58; canon counselor Christ Ch. Cathedral, St. Louis, 1958-64; dir. Pastoral Counseling Inst., St. Louis, 1958—; vicar Grace Episcopal Ch., St. Louis, 1958-63; vis. lectr. Eden Sem., St. Louis, Washington U. Sch. Law; chmn. dept. Christian social relations Diocese of Mo., 1959-63, mem. council, 1969-63; cons. to family life, asso. joint family life com. Nat. Council Episcopal Ch., 1962-65; labor arbitrator Fed. Mediation and Conciliation Service, 1959—. Pres. mem. steering com. St. Louis Group Psychotherapy Forum, 1962-65; mem. St. Louis Bd. Edn., 1963-69; pres. Northside Neighborhood Council, St. Louis, 1959-61; treas. Mo. Council Family Relations. Chmn. psychodrama and religion round table, 1st Internat. Congress of Psychodrama, Milan, Italy, 1964, 2d Internat. Congress, Barcelona, Spain, 1966. Bd. dirs. Grace Hill House, St. Louis, chaplain, 1958-63. Served with AUS, 1946-48, Kent fellow, 1968; Community Mental Health Research fellow, 1968; cert. trainer and practitioner in psychodrama and group psychotherapy Am. Bd. Examiners; lic. clin. psychologist, Mo., Ill.; mem. Nat. Register Health Service Providers in Psychology. Fellow Am. Acad. Matrimonial lawyers; mem. St. Louis (family law com.), Am. (family law com. on marriage and family counseling conciliation), Mo. (family law com.), Fed. bar, assns., Am. Soc. Group Psychotherapy and Psychodrama, Episcopal Soc. for Racial Unity (nat. bd.), Am. Assn. Pastoral Counselors (diplomate; mem. funding bd. 1963-65), Am. Assn. Marriage Counselors, Mo. Psychol. Assn., Soc. St. Louis Psychologists (past pres.), Assn. for Clin. Pastoral Edn., Soc. for Religion in Higher Edn. Contbr. articles to religious, psychol. and legal publs. Home: 16 Hortense Pl Saint Louis MO 63108 Office: 8420 Delmar Blvd Saint Louis MO 63124

ZACHER, CANDACE MARIE, university training coordinator; b. Milw., Mar. 8, 1950; d. Harry J. and Viola (Mueller) Naumowicz; m. James Alan Zacher, Oct. 25, 1980, 1 child. BA, Northwestern U., 1971; MS, Syracuse U., 1975; PhD, Purdue U., 1984. Cert. tchr., Wis., Ill., Ind., N.Y. Tng. coordinator Milw. County Med. Complex, 1979-80, Ind. Dept. Hwys., West Lafayette, 1981-83, Purdue U., West Lafayette, 1985—; coordinator Lafayette (Ind.) Sch. Corp., 1980-81; instructional devel. cons. Lafayette, 1984-85; instructional developer Purdue U., West Lafayette, 1983-84, coordinator, 1985-87; art instr., various schs., Wis., 1971-73, 76-78; lectr. Marquette U., Milw., 1978-79; instructional devel. cons. Creative Tng. Techs., Lafayette/Medinah, 1984—. Producer, dir. (multi-media) US, 1972, Project VUE, 1980. Mem. Nat. Soc. Performance and Instrn. (v.p. Ind. 1986—), Assn. Ednl. Communications and Tech. (tng. and devel. div.), Northwestern U. Alumna Assn., Phi Kappa Delta, Pi Lambda Theta. Roman Catholic. Avocations: ballet, watercolor painting, reading, travel. Office: AT&T SB-125 Tech Pubs Bell Labs Naperville IL 60566

ZACKHEIM, MARC ALLEN, child psychologist, editor; b. N.Y.C., Oct. 12, 1950; s. Seymour David and Blanche (Kalt) Z.; m. Elisa Freiden, Mar. 14, 1978 (div.). AA, U. Fla., 1970, BA with high honors, 1972; MS, Fla. State U., 1974, PhD, 1977. Lic. psychologist, Fla., Ill., Ala. Intern, Duke U. Med. Ctr., Durham, N.C., 1976; postdoctoral fellow in psychology Fla. State U., 1978; resident in psychology Rush-Presbyn. St. Luke's Med. Ctr., Chgo., 1979; attending child psychologist Assocs. in Adolescent Psychiatry, Chgo., 1979-85, dir. tng., 1981-85; v.p. Assocs. in Clin. Psychology, 1985—; faculty Auburn (Ala.) U.; attending child psychologist Riveredge Hosp., Forest Park, Ill., 1979—; cons. editor Ednl. and Psychol. Research. Contbr. articles to profl. jours. USPHS fellow, 1973-76. Mem. Am. Psychol. Assn., Ill. Psychol. Assn., Midwest Psychol. Assn., Fla. Psychol. Assn., S.E. Psychol. Assn., Chgo. Assn. for Psychoanalytic Psychology, Acad. Psychosomatic Medicine. Home: 1322 W Chase Ave Chicago IL 60626 Office: Riveredge Hospital 8311 W Roosevelt Rd Forest Park IL 60130 Office: 1107 N Mannheim Rd #104 Westchester IL 60153

ZADROZNY, MITCHELL GEORGE, geography educator; b. Chgo., Dec. 23, 1923; s. John and Jeanette (Ulick) Z. B.S., Ill. State U., 1947; S.M., U. Chgo., 1949, Ph.D., 1956. Geog. analyst Dept. Army, Tokyo, 1950-52; lectr. geography U. Chgo., 1953-55, dir. research Cambodia Laos project, 1954-55; vis. assoc. prof. econ. geography NYU, 1958; research assoc. Mississippi Valley Investigations, So. Ill. U., Carbondale, 1955-61; tchr. geography Wright City Coll., Chgo., 1955-63, asst. prof., 1963-66, assoc. prof., 1963-69, prof., 1969—; prof. geography Chgo. WTTW-TV Coll., 1961. Bd. dirs. Uptown Chgo. Com., 1963-73; comptroller Nat. Republican Heritage Groups Council, 1970-74; treas. Ill. State Republican Nationalities Council, 1974—; treas. Great Lakes Naval Mus., Chgo., 1980—; dir. Pres. Water Pollution Adv. Bd., 1970-74. Served to lt. USAAF, 1942-45. Mem. Assn. Am. Geographers, Chgo. Geog. Soc., Ill. Geog. Soc., Ill. Edn. Assn., Soc. des Etudes Indochinoise, Royal Asiatic Soc. Japan, Hist. Naval Ships N.Am., Explorers Club. Republican. Roman Catholic. Club: Capital Hill (Washington). Author: Cambodia Handbook, 1955; Laos Handbook, 1956; Water Utilization in the Middle Mississippi Valley, 1956; World Geography TV Handbook and Map Supplement, 1961. Home: 4158 N McVicker Ave Chicago IL 60634 Office: 3400 N Austin Ave Chicago IL 60634

ZAGEL, JAMES B., lawyer, state agency administrator; b. Chgo., Mar. 4, 1941; s. Samuel and Ethel (Samuels) Z.; m. Margaret Maxwell, May 27, 1979. BA, U. Chgo., 1962, MA in Philosophy, 1962; JD, Harvard U., 1965. Asst. atty. gen. criminal justice div. State of Ill., Springfield, 1970-77; chief prosecuting atty. Ill. Jud. Inquiry Bd., Springfield, 1973-75; exec. dir. Ill. Law Enforcement Commn., Springfield, 1977-79; dir. Ill. Dept. Revenue, Springfield, 1979-80, Ill. Dept. State Police, Springfield, 1980—. Co-author: Criminal Law and Its Administration, 1974, Cases and Comments on Criminal Procedure, 1974. Named Outstanding Young Citizen, Chgo. Jaycees, 1977, Police Chief of Yr., Nat. We Turn in Pushers Orgn., 1984; recipient Disting. Service Merit award Assn. Commerce and Industry, 1983. Mem. ABA, Ill. Bar Assn. (vice chmn. criminal justice council), Chgo. Bar Assn., Ill. Assn. Chiefs of Police (exec. bd.). Office: Ill Dept State Police 103 Armory Bldg Springfield IL 62706

ZAGOREN, ALLEN, surgeon; b. Bklyn., May 17, 1947; s. Max and Harriett (Feldman) Z.; m. Gail Marie Sarcinella, Feb. 20, 1977. BA in Biology, Hofstra U., 1969; DO, Phila. Coll. Osteo. Medicine, 1975. Diplomate Am. Bd. Osteo. Surgery, Nat. Bd. Examiners Osteo.-Med. Surgery. Intern Stratford (N.J.) div. John F. Kennedy Meml. Hosp., 1975-76; resident Cherry Hill (N.J.) Med. Ctr., 1976-80; asst. prof. surgery U. Medicine and Dentistry, Piscataway, N.J., 1980-82; practice osteo. medicine specializing in surgery Rose Surg. Clinic, Des Moines, 1982—; mem. staff Mercy Hosp. Med. Ctr., Des Moines, bd. dirs. metabolic support services, 1982—; mem. staff Community Hosp., Des Moines; chmn. dept. surgery Des Moines Gen. Hosp., 1985—, also various coms.; chmn. dept. surgery Madison County Meml. Hosp., Winterset, Iowa; adj. assoc. prof. surgery and nutrition, U. Osteo. Medicine and Health Scis., Des Moines, 1982—; midwest regional physician coordinator Nat. Med. Care.; lectr. in field. Contbr. articles to profl. jours.; creator videotapes (with others). Bd. dirs. Des Moines Gen. Hosp. Found., sec. 1986—; active Iowa Found. for Med. Care, Nutritional Council Iowa. Grantee SKF Labs., Phila., 1986, Norwich (N.Y.) Eaton Labs., 1986. Fellow Am. Coll. Osteo. Surgeons (research, nutritional support, visual aids coms., 1st Prize awards 1982, 83), Am. Coll. Nutrition, Am. Coll. Abdominal Surgeons; mem. Am. Osteo. Soc., Iowa Osteo. Med. Assn. (chmn. constn. and bylaws com., chmn. polit. action com. 1984, trustee), Am. Soc. Parenteral and Enteral Nutrition (bd. dirs. 1986, mem. and chmn. various coms.), Am. Soc. Nutritional Support Services, Midwest Osteo. Surg. Soc., Midwestern Osteo. Surg. Assn. (chmn.), Am. Soc. Parenteral and Enteral Nutrition (bd. dirs. 1984-86), Nat. Wildlife Fedn., Smithsonian Inst., Airplane Owners and Pilots Assn. Jewish. Avocations: flying, golf, swimming, skiing, writing. Office: Rose Surg Clinic 1440 E Grand Ave Des Moines IA 50316

ZAHARNA, MIKE N., engineering company executive; b. Nablus, West Bank, Jordan, Nov. 6, 1941; came to U.S., 1960; naturalized; s. Nazmi and Tuhfa Z.; m. Samia Muhtadi, July 14, 1971; children: Deena, Leiha, Mia. BSEE, Ind. Inst. Tech., 1963; postgrad. in bus. law, Cleve. State U., 1972.

Registered profl. engr., Calif. Elec. engr. Air Cond & Refrigator Inst., Arlington, Va., 1963-65, Motch & Merry Wether Machines, Euclid, Ohio, 1965-66; sr. engr. Bailey Controls Co., Wickliffe, Ohio, 1966-69; mgr. software services Bailey Controls Co., Wickliffe, 1969-71, mgr. computer engring., 1971-74, mgr. indsl. process project offices, 1974-77, mgr. internat. mktg. and sales, 1977-81, v.p. internat. ops., 1981—. Mem. Greater Cleve. Growth Assn., Cleve. World Trade Assn. Mem. NSPE, IEEE, Instrumentation Soc. Am. (sr.), Ohio Soc. Profl. Engrs. Moslem. Home: 37250 Harlow Dr Willoughby OH 44094 Office: Bailey Controls Co 29801 Euclid Ave Wickliffe OH 44092

ZAHN, CLIFFORD JAMES, accountant; b. Wausau, Wis., June 1, 1932; s. Harry D. and Elsie L. (Krueger) Z.; m. Victoria M. Tewes, Aug. 23, 1958; children: Jonathan C., Christopher J., Tonja V. BBA, Marquette U., 1959; MBA, U. Wis., Milw., 1966. CPA, Wis. Ptnr. Peat, Marwick, Mitchell & Co., Milw., 1959-82; pvt. practice small bus. investment, mgmt. cons., acctg. Milw., 1982—; cons. in field; bd. dirs. Allied Computer Group, Milw., Badger Case, Inc., Milw. Chmn. bd. fin. St. John's Luth. Ch., 1980-84. Served with U.S. Army, 1952-54. Mem. Nat. Assn. CPA's (local pres. 1977-78), Am. Inst. CPA's, Wis. Inst. CPA's, Inst. of Internal Auditors. Republican. Lutheran. Clubs: Wisconsin, North Shore Athletic, Concordia Coll. Century (Milw.) (bd. dirs. treas. 1985—). Home: 7300 N Beach Dr Milwaukee WI 53217

ZAHN, JOHN JOSEPH, research engineer; b. Beaver Dam, Wis., May 8, 1932; s. George Anton and Veronica (Neihoff) Z.; m. Nancy Josephine Turgeson, Nov. 9, 1955 (div.); children—Margaret Emily, Elizabeth Ann, Rebecca Marie; m. 2d, Carol Marie Walsh, Oct. 9, 1978. B.S. in Mech. Engring. (Morse Meml. scholar), U. Wis., 1954, M.S. in Mech. Engring. (fellow), 1959, Ph.D. in Mech. Engring., 1964. Instr. mechanics U. Wis.-Madison, 1958-64, lectr. in forest products, 1964—; research engr. Forest Products Lab. U.S. Dept. Agr., Madison, 1964—. Contbr. tech. articles in field to profl. jours. Served with S.C., U.S. Army, 1954-56. Mem. Am. Soc. Civil Engrs., Am. Acad. Mechanics, Fedn. Am. Scientists, Sigma Xi, Tau Beta Pi. Democrat. Unitarian. Home: 2648 Van Hise Ave Madison WI 53705 Office: Forest Products Lab 1 Gifford Pinchot Dr Madison WI 53705

ZAHNOW, MELVIN JOHN, foundation executive; b. Saginaw, Mich., Sept. 21, 1911; s. August Christian and Caroline Wilhemena (Kuble) Z.; m. Lillian Ruth O'Brien, Sept. 29, 1935; children—Ruth Ann, Beth Jean. B.A. in Bus. Adminstrn., Albion Coll., 1934; LL.D., Saginaw Valley State Coll., 1982. Sec., dir. Wickes Boiler Co. and Wickes Bros., Saginaw, 1940-47; sec., treas., dir. Wickes Corp., Saginaw, 1947-54; v.p. fin., dir, 1954-64, sr. v.p., dir., 1964-67; pres., trustee Wickes Found., Saginaw, 1967-84, chmn., trustee, 1985—. Trustee Albion Coll., Mich., 1967-71, Saginaw Gen. Hosp., 1975-79, Citizens Research Council Mich., Detroit, 1977-86; trustee, treas. Delta Coll., University Center, Mich., 1961-64; incorporator Saginaw Valley State Coll., 1963, trustee, treas., 1963-82; trustee, vice chmn. St. Luke's Hosp., Saginaw, 1956-83; trustee, chmn. Saginaw Med. Ctr., 1977-80; bd. dirs., pres. Neighborhood House community ctr., Saginaw, 1943-50. Recreation Bldg. at Neighborhood House named in his honor, 1976, also Library at Saginaw Valley State Coll., 1985; recipient Community Service award Saginaw C. of C., 1985. Republican. Lutheran. Clubs: Saginaw, Germania (Saginaw). Avocations: Abraham Lincoln history. Office: Harvey Randall Wickes Found 4800 Fashion Square Blvd Saginaw MI 48604

ZAHRAWI, FAISSAL BAHJAT, orthopaedic surgeon; b. Homs, Syria, May 12, 1949; came to U.S., 1972; s. Bahjat and Hind (Atassi) Z.; m. Rabab Zahrawi, Aug. 10, 1972; children: Rolla, Mohanad, Razan. MD, U. Damascus, Syria, 1972. Intern Huron Rd. Hosp., Cleve., 1972-74; resident St. Luke's Hosp., Cleve., 1974-78; fellow A.I. duPont Inst., Wilmington, Del., 1978-79; orthopaedic surgeon Lake West Hosp., Willoughby, Ohio, 1979—. Fellow ACS, Am. Acad. Orthopaedic Surgeons; mem. AMA, N.Am. Spine Soc. Republican. Muslim. Club: Cleve. Racquet. Avocations: skiing, tennis. Office: Lake West Med Bldg 36100 Euclid Ave #360 Willoughby OH 44094

ZAIMAN, K. ROBERT, dentist; b. Cin., Oct. 19, 1944; s. Noboru gary and Toshiko (Matsuyama) Z.; m. Kimberly Ann Sass, Nov. 6, 1976; children: Kara Jean, Matthew Robert. Student, Craighton U., Omaha, Nebr., 1962-64, DDS, 1968. Asst. prof. Creighton U. Sch. Dentistry, Omaha, 1971-73, assoc. prof., 1973-75; pvt. practice dentistry Omaha, 1971—. Past v.p., bd. dirs. Japanese-Am. Citizens League, Omaha, 1977-86. Served with USN, 1964-71. Fellow Acad. Gen. Dentistry (pres. 1976-77, nat. del. 1971-76), Acad. Continuing Edn., Omaha Dist. Dental Soc. (treas. 1980-85, bd. dirs. 1968—), Nebr. Dental Assn. (del. 1971-86), ADA, Delta Sigma Delta. Office: 10841 Q St Suite 109 Omaha NE 68137

ZAIS, EDITH MOREIN, college administrator; b. Providence, Apr. 8, 1931; d. Samuel Joshua and Sona Morein; m. Robert S. Zais, Sept. 14, 1952; children: Louis Scott, Roberta Susan. AB, Brown U., 1952; MA in Teaching, R.I. Coll., 1964; 6th year diploma edn. U. Conn., 1968. Tchr. English E. Providence (R.I.) Sr. High Sch., 1964-66; staff writer Willimantic (Conn.) Chronicle, 1966-67; tchr. reading Crestwood Schs., Mantua, Ohio, 1969-70; coordinator learning devel. program Kent (Ohio) State U., 1970—, instr. Exptl. Coll., 1973—; mem. admissions com. Northeastern Ohio Univs. Coll. Medicine, 1979-81; project co-dir. spl. services disadvantaged students Dept. Edn., 1978—. Mem. Nat. Assn. Women Deans, Adminstrs. and Counselors, Internat. Reading Assn., Assn. Children and Adults with Learning Disabilities, LWV (chmn. edn. com. Kent chpt. 1976-78), Omicron Delta Kappa. Home: 431 Wilson Ave Kent OH 44240 Office: Kent State U Kent OH 44242

ZALESKI, ALAN JOSEPH, state legislator; b. Lorain, Ohio, Aug. 12, 1942; s. Matthew Joseph and Virginia Stella (Swiderski) Z.; m. Deborah Ann Phillips, Dec. 5, 1986. BBA, Ohio U., 1965. Stockbroker Elyria, Ohio, 1970—; councilman City of Elyria, 1974-77; commr. Lorain County, Ohio, 1977-83; mem. Ohio State Senate, Columbus, 1983—; mem. econ. devel. and small bus. com., fin. institutions and ins. com., hwys. and transp. com., Lake Erie Interstate com. 1984—; chmn. fin. com. City of Elyria, 1976-77; pres. bd. commrs. Lorain County, 1978-79. Pres. Lorian County Econ. and Indsl. Devel Corp., 1980-81; vice chmn. Lorain County Cancer Soc., 1980-81. Served to capt. USMC, 1965-70, Vietnam. Decorated Bronze Star, Purple Heart, Air medal with twenty-seven gold stars. Mem. VFW (Legislator of Yr. 1983-84), Am. Legion. Democrat. Roman Catholic. Club: United Polish. Lodge: Elks. Avocations: aviation, golf, chess. Office: Ohio Statehouse Columbus OH 43216

ZALESKI, THADDEUS B., accounting administrator; b. Penley, Eng., May 10, 1947; came to U.S., 1951; s. Wilhelm S. Zaleski and Halina B. (Baldyk) Rybinski; m. Elizabeth Berenice Nowak, June 16, 1973; children: Jacalyn, Kathryn, Nicholas. BS in Acctg., De Paul U., 1970. CPA, Ill. Asst. auditor S. D. Leidesdorf & Co., Chgo., 1969-72, tax sr., 1972-76; tax supr. Laventhol & Horwath, Chgo., 1976-79, tax mgr., 1979-84; dir. tax services Indpls., 1984—. Author: (with others) Hospital Tax Management, 1983, health care taxation course; contbr. articles to profl. jours. Mem. Am. Inst. CPA's, Ill. CPA Soc. (chmn. taxation spl. projects com. 1979-80), Ind. CPA Soc. (vice chmn. pub. relations com. 1986—), Carmel (Ind.) C. of C. Roman Catholic. Lodge: Lions (treas. Carmel chpt. 1987—). Avocations: cycling, photography, sports. Home: 15134 Goodtime Ct Carmel IN 46032 Office: Laventhol & Horwath One American Sq Suite 2210 Box 82051 Indianapolis IN 46282

ZALEWSKI, WITOLD THEODORE, energy engineering executive; b. Poznan, Poland, Oct. 22, 1949; came to U.S., 1965; s. Witold Adolf and Cecylia (Kozera) Z.; m. Darlene Fimiano, Nov. 3, 1977 (div. May 1978); m. Penelope Wiley, Dec. 29, 1981 (div. 1987). Assoc. Engr., Sch. Energetics, Poznan, 1965; diploma engr. Poly. Inst. (W. Ger.), 1971; M.S., U. Wis.-Milw., 1972. Registered profl. engr., Wis. Mfrs. rep. Contract Design Assocs., Denver, 1973-75, D. H. Baldwin, Cin., 1975-77; zone mgr. Memorex Corp., Santa Clara, Calif., 1977-80; pres. Intex, Mequon, Wis., 1980—; cons. Wis. Vocat. Colls., Madison, 1982—, Wis. Electric Co., Milw., 1981—, Kenosha Pub. Schs. (Wis.), 1981—, Johnson Controls, Erie Mfg. Patentee in field. Named Memorex Zone Mgr. of Yr., 1979; recipient Gov.'s award for Energy Innovation, 1986, 1986, U.S. Dept. Energy Spl. award for Energy Innovation, Nat. Lighting Bur. award for excellence in Design. Mem. ASHRAE Assn. Energy Engrs. (industrial energy conservation award 1985). Roman Catholic. Office: 11563 N Spring Ave -65W Mequon WI 53092

ZALIOUK, YUVAL NATHAN, conductor; b. Haifa, Israel, Feb. 10, 1939; s. Israel Nahum and Ahuda (Nathanson) Z.; m. Susan Marlys Davies, May 5, 1972; children: Eyal, Adam, Tamar. LL.B., Hebrew U., Jerusalem, 1964; student, Rubin Acad. Music, Jerusalem, 1960-63, Guildhall Sch. Music, London, 1965-67. Condr.: Royal Ballet of London, 1966-70; music dir., Opera Studio, Paris, 1973-74, Haifa Symphony, 1975-77; interim chief condr.: Edmonton (Alta., Can.) Symphony Orch, 1980-81; music dir., condr.: Toledo (Ohio) Symphony Orch, 1980—. Recipient 1st prize Am.-Israel Cultural Found. Competition, 1965; 2d prize Internat. Condrs. Competition, Besancon, France, 1966; 1st prize Internat. Condrs. Competition, Besancon, France, 1967; 1st prize for progressive programming ASCAP, 1984; winner Mitropoulos Condrs. Competition N.Y.C., 1970. Jewish. Club: Rotary. Office: The Toledo Symphony 1 Stranahan Sq Toledo OH 43604

ZAMBA, LAWRENCE CHARLES, communication executive; b. Erie, Pa., July 17, 1957; s. Lawrence Alexis and Elisa Maria (Burner) Z. BA in Mass Communications, U. Wis., 1974-79. Ind. photographer, portrait artist Zam/ba, Kenosha, Wis., 1975—; pres. Wam Bam Singing Telegram!, Inc., Kenosha, Milw., and Chgo., 1981—. Creator (TV program) Manhunt Pageant, 1983-84. Leader Boy Scouts Am., Kenosha, 1975-79. Mem. U. Wis. Alumni Assn. Avocations: photography, drawing, scuba diving, bicycling, horse riding. Home and Office: 1831-16 Ave Kenosha WI 53140

ZAMIEROWSKI, DAVID STEPHEN, plastic surgeon; b. Grand Rapids, Mich., July 19, 1942; s. Stephen J. and Eleanor T. (Gorecki) Z.; m. Marilyn M. Moffitt, May 8, 1968; children: Amy Elizabeth, Nancy Ellen. BA, Holy Cross Coll., 1964; BS in Med. Sci., Dartmouth U., 1966; MD, Johns Hopkins U., 1968. Diplomate Am. Bd. Plastic Surgery, Am. Bd. Surgery. Intern U. Pitts., 1968-69; resident in surgery Vanderbilt U. Hosp., Nashville, 1971-73; chief surg. resident Mid State Bapt. Hosp., Nashville, 1973-76; practice medicine specializing in surgery and plastic surgery Shawnee Mission, Kans., 1978—; clin. instr. Kans. U. Med. Ctr., Overland Park, 1986; chief of surgery Bethany Med. Ctr., 1986; active staff mem. Shawnee Mission Med. Ctr., Overland Park, 1986. Served to capt. USMC, 1969-71. Fellow Am. Coll. Surgeons; mem. AMA., Am. Soc. Plastic & Reconstructive Surgeons. Roman Catholic. Office: 8800 W 75th St Shawnee Mission KS 66204

ZAMIR, JAN ROSHAN, linguist, educator; b. Caspian Sea area, Persia, Nov. 13, 1941; came to U.S., 1961, naturalized, 1974; s. Hedayat Roshan and Mohtram (Naji) Z.; m. Sonia LuAnn Nelson, Aug. 8, 1964; children—Brett, Nicole. B.A., Huron Coll., 1966; M.A. Northeastern Ill. U., 1972; A.M., U. Ill., 1979, Ph.D., 1981. Dept. chmn. fgn. lang. St. George High Sch., Evanston, Ill., 1966-69; instr. German and Spanish, John Hersey High Sch., Arlington Heights, Ill., 1969—; Fulbright scholar, tchr. exchange with Germany, 1986-87. Contbr. articles to profl. jours. Fulbright scholar Mem. Linguistic Soc. Am., Am. Assn. Tchrs. German, Am. Assn. Tchrs. Spanish, Phi Kappa Phi. Home: 1402 Lama Ln Mount Prospect IL 60056 Office: John Hersey High Sch 1900 E Thomas Arlington Heights IL 60004

ZAMMAR, NORMAN ROOSEVELT, advertising and marketing executive; b. Kansas City, Mo., Oct. 28, 1932; s. Norman S. and Sophia Marie (Boulos) Z.; m. Vickie Sue Campbell, July 2, 1983; 1 child, Suzanne. B in Advt. and Graphics, U. Mo., 1960. Advt. mgr. Katz Drug Co., Kansas City, Mo., 1959-69; sr. account exec. Townsend Communications, Inc., Kansas City, 1970-84; dir. advt. Unique Supermarket Inc., Kansas City, 1984—. Creator display advertisements, Price, 1982 (2d place award 1983 Mo. Advt. Mgrs. Assn.), A Rose, 1983 (1st place award 1984 Mo. Advt. Mgrs. Assn.), Proud, 1985 (1st place award 1985 Nat. Grocers Assn.); author: (poetry) A Tragedy, 1981 (1st place award 1982 Mo. Creative Writers Assn.). Served with USN, 1952-56. Mem. Tau Kappa Epsilon (ednl. found.). Democrat. Roman Catholic. Lodge: Kiwanis (pres. N. Kansas City 1981-82, Disting. Pres. award Mo./ Ark. Dist. 1982). Avocations: oil portraits, creative advt., writing poetry, skiing, skating. Home: 16404 Crackerneck Rd Independence MO 64055 Office: Unique Supermarket Inc 1333 NE Barry Rd Kansas City MO 64155

ZANDER, GAILLIENNE GLASHOW, psychologist; b. Bklyn., Apr. 7, 1932; s. Saul and Anna (Karasik) G.; m. A.J. Zander, Aug. 5, 1952; children: Elizabeth L., Caroline M., Catherine A. MusB, U. Wis., 1953, MS, 1970; PhD, Marquette U., 1984. Music tchr. Wis. Sch. Systems, 1953-65; psychol. asst. Vernon Psychol. Labs., Chgo., 1965-70; psychologist Milw. Pub. Schs., 1970—, CESA 19, Kenosha, Wis., 1977-78; pvt. practice psychology Milw., 1980—. Mem. Am. Psychol. Assn., Psychologists Assn. in Milw. Pub. Schs. (rep., v.p., pres. 1980—), Am. Orthopsychiat. Assn. Home: 7217 Enfield Ave Greendale WI 53129 Office: Milw Pub Schs PO Box 10K Milwaukee WI 53201

ZANDER, JANET ADELE, psychiatrist; b. Miles City, Mont., Feb. 19, 1950; d. Adelbert William and Valborg Constance (Buckneberg) Z.; m. Mark Richard Ellenberger, Sept. 16, 1979; 1 child, Evan David Zander Ellenberger. BA, St. Olaf Coll., 1972; MD, U. Minn., 1976. Diplomate Am. Bd. Psychiatry and Neurology. Resident in psychiatry U. Minn., Mpls., 1976-79, fellow in psychiatry, 1979-80, asst. prof. psychiatry, 1981—; staff psychiatrist St. Paul (Minn.) Ramsey Med. Ctr., 1980—, dir. edn. in psychiatry, 1980—, dir. inpatient psychiatry, 1986—. Contbr. research articles to sci. jours. Sec. Concentus Musicus Bd. Dirs., St. Paul, 1981—; mem. property com. St. Clement's Episcopal Ch., St. Paul, 1985. Developer Assessment Life Events in Elderly Scale award Med. Edn. Research Found., 1985. Mem. Am. Psychiat. Assn., Minn. Psychiat. Soc. (ethics com. 1985—, women's com. 1985—), Minn. Med. Assn., Ramsey County Med. Soc., Am. Med. Women's Assn. Democrat. Avocations: singing, skiing. Home: 1396 Sargent Ave Saint Paul MN 55105 Office: St Paul Ramsey Med Ctr 640 Jackson St Saint Paul MN 55101

ZANGARA, PETER PAUL, neurologist; b. Hackensack, N.J., June 9, 1949; s. Bernard Herman and Anastasia (Lo Biondo) Z.; m. Marilyn Patricia Zall, May 28, 1977; children: Daniel, Jennifer, Michael. BA, Johns Hopkins U., 1971; postgrad., U. Rome, 1972-75; MD, U. Medicine and Dentistry, Newark, 1977. Diplomate Am. Bd. Psychiatry and Neurology, Am. Bd. Clin. Neurophysiology. Intern Med. Coll. of S.C., Charleston, 1977-78; resident, then chief resident in neurology Baylor Coll. Medicine, Houston, 1978-81; practice medicine specializing in neurology Toledo, 1981—; bd. dirs. neurology intensive care unit Mercy Hosp., Toledo, 1984, exec. com., 1987—; bd. dirs. neurophysiology lab. St. Luke's Hosp., Maumee, Ohio, 1986. Johns Hopkins U. scholar, 1967. Mem. AMA, Am. Acad. Neurology (assoc.), Am. Acad. Clin. Neurophysiology, Ohio State Med. Soc., Lucas County Acad. Medicine. Avocations: lacrosse, mandolin. Home: 3536 Brookside Rd Toledo OH 43606 Office: Toledo Neurol Assocs Inc 3949 Sunforest Ct Toledo OH 43623

ZAPP, DAVID EDWIN, computer programmer, analyst; b. Columbus, Ohio, Dec. 6, 1950; s. Robert Louis and Harriet (Miller) Z.; divorced; 1 child, Heather; m. Grace Lynn Spidell, Apr. 28, 1978. Road freight conductor N&W Ry., Columbus, 1971-77; with Franklin County Welfare, Columbus, 1977-78; income tax preparer J.E. Wiggins Co., Columbus, 1978-81; pub. inquiry asst. Ohio Bur. Workers Compensation, Columbus, 1978-80, auditor, 1980-82, programmer, analyst, 1982—. Council mem. Southside Orgns., Columbus, 1985-86; mem. Gates Street Block Watch, Columbus, 1986. Mem. Ohio Jaycees (program mgr. 1984-85, #1 individual devel. v.p. 1983-84, dist. dir. 1986—, named Outstanding Dist. Dir. 1986), Southside Columbus Jaycees (mgmt. v.p. 1984-85, pres. 1985-86), Employee Mgmt. Participation (chmn. 1985-86). Club: Commodore of Cen. Ohio. Avocations: running, bicycling, personal computers. Home: 299 E Gates St Columbus OH 43206 Office: Ohio Bur Workers Compensation 78 E Chestnut Columbus OH 43215

ZAPPA, LEO JOHN, JR., lawyer; b. Springfield, Ill., Sept. 27, 1957; s. Leo John and Mary Jane (Gobble) Z.; m. Antoinette Diane Dilello, Aug. 20, 1983. BA, Eastern Ill. U., 1979; JD, Tulsa U., 1982. Bar: Ill. 1983. Tech. advisor State of Ill., Springfield, 1982-83; asst. states atty. Sangamon County States Atty., Springfield, 1983-86; ptnr. Taylor and Zappa, Springfield, 1986; asst. felony prosecutor Sangamon County States Atty.'s Office, Springfield, 1986—; instr. Inst. for Paralegal Studies, Springfield, 1986—. Mem. Roman Cultural Soc., Springfield, 1983, Am. Bus. Club, Springfield, 1986; pres. Fairview Sandy Koufax League, Springfield, 1983—. Mem. ABA, Ill. Bar Assn., Sangamon County Bar Assn. Republican. Roman Catholic. Avocations: coaching boys' baseball, golf, reading. Home: 2804 Huron Springfield IL 62707

ZARANDY, SOHILA, research gynecologist/reproductive endocrinologist. m. M.H. Naheedy; children: John, Sara, Cyrus. MD, Tehran (Iran) U., 1972. Diplomate Am. Bd. Ob-Gyn. Clins. instr. Harvard U., Boston, 1978-81; asst. prof. ob-gyn Loyola U., Chgo., 1981-83, asst. prof. reproductive endocrinology and infertility, 1983-85; asst. prof., fellow in reproductive endocrinology and fertility U. Ill., Chgo., 1983-85; gynecol. endocrinology researcher Loyola U. Hosp., Maywood, Ill., 1985—. Fellow Am. Coll. Ob-Gyn; mem. AMA, Am. Fertility Soc. Home: 1610 Laurel Ln Darien IL 60559 Office: Loyola U Hosp 2160 S 1st Ave Maywood IL 60153

ZAREMBA, THOMAS EDMUND MICHAEL BARRY, educator; b. Detroit, May 6; s. Edmund Julius Thiel and Ethel Grace (Barry) Z. Ed. Oakland U., Rochester, Mich., U. Detroit, Wayne State U. Tchr., Center Line (Mich.) Public Schs., Livonia (Mich.) Public Schs.; instr. biol. scis. Wayne State U., Detroit. Mem. Mich. Eye Bank, Internat. Friends Van Cliburn, Met. Opera Guild, Friends of Detroit Symphony Orch., Founders Soc., Detroit Inst. Arts, Internat. Platform Assn., Detroit Sci. Ctr., Friends for Orch. Hall, Orch. Hall Assocs.; bd. dirs. Van. Cliburn Found, Inc., Detroit Grand Oprea Assn. Mem. AAAS, Nat. Funeral Dirs. Assn., Mich. Funeral Dirs. Assn., Am. Film Inst. (sponsor), Wayne State U. Alumni Assn., Oakland U. Alumni Assn. Roman Catholic. Club: Scarab (life), Players (Detroit). Office: 217 Farnsworth St Detroit MI 48202 Office: 5980 Cass Ave Detroit MI 48202

ZARLEY, CHARLES DAVID, molecular biologist; b. Zanesville, Ohio, June 27, 1956; s. Theodore Vivian and Isabelle (McCutcheon) Z.; m. Velva Rose Eby, Aug. 13, 1977. BS in Microbiology, Ohio State U., 1977, MS in Microbiology, 1979; PhD in Molecular Cell Devel., Ind. U., 1985. Postdoctoral fellow Battelle Meml. Inst., Columbus, Ohio, 1984-85, research scientist, 1985—; mem. Columbus Zoo Research Council, Powell, Ohio, 1986—. Vol. Columbus Zoo Edn. Dept., Powell, 1985—. Mem. Am. Soc. Microbiology, Am. Soc. Virology, AAAS, Smokey Ridge Civic Assn. Democrat. Methodist. Avocations: tae kwon do, scuba diving, weight lifting. Home: 2350 Benning Dr Powell OH 43065 Office: Battelle Meml Inst 505 King Ave Columbus OH 43201

ZARR, MICHAEL LESTER, psychiatrist; b. Bklyn., Nov. 2, 1949; s. Max and Sarah Zarr; m. Sandra Carol Sarner, Aug. 10, 1975. BS cum laude, CUNY, 1971; postgrad., U. Liège, Belgium, 1975; MD, Albany (N.Y.) Med. Coll., 1979. Diplomate Am. Bd. Psychiatry and Neurology; Nat. Bd. Med. Examiners. Resident in psychiatry Albany Med. Ctr., 1979-82, chief resident in psychiatry, 1982-83, fellow in psychiatry, 1983-84; staff psychiatrist Capital Dist. Psychiat. Ctr., Albany, 1984-85; clin. dir. Community Mental Health Ctr. of Fulton-McDonough County, Macomb and Canton, Ill., 1985-87; dir. of cons., liaison psychiatry Hurley Med. Ctr., Flint, Mich., 1987—, active various coms., 1987; adj. staff dept. psychiatry Samaritan Hosp., Troy, N.Y., 1982-83; psychiatrist Albany VA Med. Ctr., 1982-83; psychiat. cons. McDonough Dist. Hosp., Macomb, 1985-86, Graham Hosp. Assn., Canton, 1985-86. Contbr. articles to profl. jours. Mem. AMA, Am. Psychiat. Assn., Am. Assn. Community Mental Health Ctr. Psychiatrists, Assn. Advancement Psychotherapy, Am. Soc. Clin. Hypnosis. Avocation: computers. Office: Hurley Med Ctr 1 Hurley Plaza Flint MI 48502

ZARVELL, RAYMOND KENNETH, university administrator; b. Kewanee, Ill., May 12, 1938; s. Raymond William and Lillian (Odey) Z.; m. Georgia Lu Watkins, Sept. 30, 1972; children—Douglas Lee, Paul Eric. B.S., Bradley U., 1962, M.A., 1968; L.H.D. (hon.), Inst. Tech., Morrison, Ill., 1980. Cert. tchr., Ill., nat. cert. counselor. Tchr. Williamsfield Sch. Dist., Ill., 1962-67, Limestone High Sch., Bartonville, Ill., 1968-69; counselor Bradley U., Peoria, Ill., 1969-72, dir. orientation, advisement and retention, 1972-81, exec. dir. Centers for Ednl. Devel., 1982—; cons. in field. Author: (manual) Taxonomic Key for Academic Exploration Students, 1984, Nat. Orientation Directors' Manual (1st and 2d edits.); co-author: A Sequential, Narrative Guide for Acad. Advisors, 1985. Coach Christian Ctr., Peoria, 1978; bd. dirs. YMCA, Peoria, 1978; founder Nat. Peer Counseling Found., Henry County (Ill.) Mental Health Service, bd. dirs. Recipient Tchr. of Yr. award State of Ill., 1968, Outstanding Acad. Advisement Program award; named hon. mayor City of Peoria, 1983. Mem. Nat. Orientation Dirs. Assn. (editor, publs. coordinator 1984), Am. Assn. Counseling and Devel., Am. Coll. Personnel Assn., Nat. Acad. Advising Assn., Nat. Peer Counselor Assn., Little John Conservation Club (editor 1977—), Ill. Assn for Counseling and Devel., Phi Delta Kappa (advisor 1979-81). Avocations: photography; music; conservation projects; botany. Home: 5506 N Graceland Dr Peoria IL 61614 Office: Bradley U 1501 Bradley Ave Peoria IL 61625

ZASLOW, WILLIAM OWEN, health consultant; b. Washington, July 13, 1948; s. Milton Samuel and Elinor (Levy) Z.; m. Christine Boyd, Jan. 27, 1973 (div. May 1976). BA, Monmouth Coll., 1970; MA, Webster U., 1980. Cert. substance abuse counselor, Mo. Probation officer State of Md., Hyattville, 1970-75; dep. dir. Office of Drug Abuse Prevention, St. Louis, 1975-79; exec. dir. Community Orgn. for Devel. of Adult and Child Inc., Springfield, Mo., 1979-82; pres. Resource Devel. Cons. Group Inc., Springfield, 1982—; cons. Mo. Dept. Mental Health, Jefferson City, 1983-85, Nat. Drug Abuse Tng. Ctr., Washington, 1972-73. Named one of Outstanding Young Men of Am., U.S. Jaycees, 1977, 83. Mem. Nat. Assn. Prevention Profls. (bd. dirs. 1976), Community Justice Assn. (award chmn. 1983). Avocations: running, bicycling, skiing, camping. Home: 1424 S Roanoke Springfield MO 65807 Office: RDC Group Inc 333 St Louis St #1023 Springfield MO 65807

ZATKOFF, LAWRENCE P., federal judge. Judge U.S. District Court, Chicago, 1986—. Office: 211 U S Courthouse Detroit MI 48226 *

ZAVELSON, LESTER SANFORD, business management consultant; b. Cleve., July 10, 1915; s. Abraham Phillip and Sophia (Miller) Z.; m. Maxine Lois Abrams, Dec. 26, 1938; children—Thomas M., Daniel Lee. B.B.A., Ohio State U., 1937. Exec. v.p. Ind. Towel Supply Co., Mansfield, Ohio, 1938-78; pres., chmn. bd. Reed Road, Inc., Mansfield, 1978—; ptnr. Mansfield Assocs., 1960—; columnist Laundry Digest, Chgo., 1980—. Bd. dirs. Hospice, Score, ARC, Mansfield Cancer Found.; mem. Richland County Recreation Bd.; mem. local Democratic exec. com., 1960-83; pres. Temple Emanuel, 1980-87; bd. dirs. Ohio Penal Insts. Recipient Ty award Mktg. Club, 1976. Mem. Mktg. Club N. Central Ohio (past pres., dir.), Ohio State U. Alumni Assn. (past pres.), Clubs: Exchange (past pres., dir.), University, International Trade of Ohio. Lodges: Shriners, Masons, Elks. Home: 666 W Andover Rd Mansfield OH 44907 Office: PO Box 1562 210 W Longview Ave Mansfield OH 44901

ZAVISLAK, HENRY CRAIG, county law enforcement official, educator; b. Detroit, Sept. 26, 1948; s. Henry Eugene and Irene M. (Polchowski) Z.; m. Nancy Carol Griffiths, Oct. 2, 1971; children—Jonathon, Adam. B.S. in Police Adminstrn., Wayne State U., 1970, M.P.A., 1976. Officer pub. safety, investigator Wayne State U., Detroit, 1969-73; asst. adminstr. Jackson City Police Dept., Mich., 1973-76; dir. criminal justice program Jackson Community Coll., Mich., 1978-80; adj. faculty, 1981-84; sheriff Jackson County Sheriff's Dept., Mich., 1980—; v.p. Police Mgmt. Assn., Inc., Saginaw, Mich., 1973-76; presenter U.S. Dept. Justice Community Relations Forum, Dallas, 1979; chmn. administrv. bd. Jackson Emergency Dispatch, 1983; apptd. by Gov. to Mich. Law Enforcement Officers Tng. Council, Lansing, 1983, chmn., 1985; vice chmn. Region II Criminal Justice Planning Commn., Jackson, 1984; chmn. Substance Abuse Commn. Criminal Justice Task Force, Jackson, 1984. Bd. dirs. Council for Prevention of Child Abuse and Neglect, Jackson, 1984; div. chmn. United Way of Jackson, 1981; bd. dirs. Jackson Unit, Am. Heart Assn., 1982; mem. Jackson County Republic Party, 1981; chmn. Redeemer Lutheran Ch. Council, Jackson, 1978. Recipient County Achievement award Nat. Assn. of Counties, 1983, 84. Recipient numerous grants for criminal justice and hwy. safety planning. Mem. Nat. Sheriffs Assn., Mich. Sheriffs Assn. (chmn. corrections com.

1984), Internat. Assn. Chiefs of Police, Mich. Criminal Justice Educators Assn. (pres. 1979, 1980), Am. Correctional Assn. Lodge: Lions. Office: Jackson County Sheriff's Dept 212 W Wesley St Jackson MI 49201

ZAWADA, EDWARD THADDEUS, JR., physician, educator; b. Chgo., Oct. 3, 1947; s. Edward Thaddeus and Evelyn Mary (Kovarek) Z.; m. Nancy Ann Stephen, Mar. 26, 1977; children—Elizabeth, Nicholas. B.S. summa cum laude, Loyola U., Chgo., 1969; M.D. summa cum laude, Loyola-Stritch Sch. Medicine, 1973. Diplomate Am. Bd. Internal Medicine, Am. Bd. Nephrology, Am. Bd. Nutrition. Intern UCLA Hosp., 1973, resident, 1974-76; asst. prof. medicine UCLA, 1978-79, U. Utah, Salt Lake City, 1979-81; assoc. prof. medicine Med. Coll. Va., Richmond, 1981-83; assoc. prof. medicine, physiology, pharmacology U. S.D. Sch. Medicine, Sioux Falls, 1983-86, prof., 1987—, also chief div. nephrology and hypertension, 1981—; chief renal sect. Salt Lake VA Med. Ctr., 1980-81; asst. chief med. service McGuire VA Med. Ctr., Richmond, 1981-83. Contbr. articles to profl. publs. Editor: Geriatric Nephrology and Urology, 1984. Pres. Minnehaha div. Am. Heart Assn., 1984-87, pres.-elect Dakota affiliate, 1987—. VA Hosp System grantee, 1981-85, 85—. Fellow ACP, Am. Coll. Chest Physicians, Am. Coll. Nutrition; mem. Internat. Soc. Nephrology, Am. Soc. Nephrology, Am. Soc. Pharmacology and Exptl. Therapeutics. Democrat. Roman Catholic. Club: Westward Ho Country (Sioux Falls). Avocations: golf; tennis; skiing; cinema; music. Home: 1608 Cedar Lane Sioux Falls SD 57103 Office: U SD Sch Medicine 2501 W 22d St Sioux Falls SD 57105

ZAWALSKI, SANDRA JEAN, nurse; b. Elyria, Ohio, Apr. 29, 1959; d. Peter Paul and Elizabeth Ann (Rottari) Galanic; m. Michael J. Zawalski, Nov. 9, 1985. ADN in Nursing, Lorain (Ohio) County Community Coll., 1983. Asst. head nurse Lakewood (Ohio) Hosp., 1983-85; coordinator brain-injured unit Grand Valley Nursing Ctr., Grand Rapids, Mich., 1985-86; rehab. med. cons. Crawford Rehab., Grand Rapids, 1986-87; staff nurse neonatal intensive care unit Metro Gen. Hosp., Cleve., 1987. Republican. Roman Catholic. Avocations: water skiing, Tae Kwon Do.

ZBORNIK, JOSEPH JOHN, educator, accounting consultant; b. Chgo., May 30, 1912; s. Joseph and Marie (Skerik) Z.; m. Evelynne Marie Waldon, Aug. 14, 1935; children: Joseph John (dec.), Gail Patricia Frank. BS, U. Ill., 1933, MS in Acctg., 1938; EdD, Loyola U., Chgo., 1961. CPA, Ill.; cert. elem. and secondary tchr., Ill. Tchr. bus. edn. various high schs., Chgo., 1933-1940; sr. field auditor Ill. Dept. Fin., Chgo., 1940-42; tchr. bus. edn. Marshall High Sch., Chgo., 1942-44; instr. Wright Coll., Chgo., 1944-53, chmn. bus. dept., 1949-53; supr. bus. edn. Chgo. Bd. Edn., 1953-58; prin. Goodrich Elem. Sch., Chgo., 1958-61, Austin Evening Sch., Chgo., 1960-65, Brown Elem. Sch., Chgo., 1961-63, Manley Upper Grade Ctr., Chgo., 1963-65, Marshall High Sch., Chgo., 1965-67; supt. dist. 12 Chgo. Pub. Schs., 1967-77; adj. prof. Roosevelt U., Chgo., 1977—; sec. E.F. Felber Co., Maywood, Ill., 1942-83; ptnr. Brook, Zbornik & Assocs., Chgo., 1946-75; Chgo. rep. Ill. State Com., N. Cen. Assn. Schs., 1962-67; treas., bd. dirs. Rolling Lanes, Countryside, Ill., 1965-84; evaluator CSA scholarships, Berwyn, Ill., 1966—; pres. Dist. Supts. Assn., Chgo., 1971; owner J.J. Zbornik & Assocs., 1975—. Author: (with others) Public Accounting, 1953, Development of American Business, 1954, Clerical Bookkeeping, 1957; mem. editorial staff LaSalle Extension U., Chgo., 1949-53. Mem. Czechoslavak Soc. Am. Recipient Chicagoland Healthorama Community Service award, 1974, Chgo. Commn. on Human Relations plaque, 1977, Sr. Citizens award mayor City of Chgo., 1985, Man of Yr. Trophy, Archer Brighton Community Conservation Council, 1971, Spl. Appreciation Trophy, Archer Brighton Community Conservation Council, 1977; Zbornik Hall auditorium named in his honor Curie High Sch., 1975. Mem. Nat. Soc. for Study of Edn., Ret. Tchrs. Assn. Chgo. (treas. 1977—). Roman Catholic. Lodge: Kiwanis (pres. 1985-86). Avocations: performing arts, sports, reading. Home: 3219 Clarence Ave Berwyn IL 60402

ZBOROWSKI, BEVERLY JEAN, school district administrator, educator; b. Gary, Ind., Apr. 23, 1948; d. Stephen Joseph and Mary Helen (Petrovich) Soohey; m. Joseph Richard Zborowski, Aug. 10, 1968; children—Annemarie Nicole, Natalie Joelle, Nicholas Joseph. B.S., Ind. U., Gary, 1970; M.S., Purdue U., 1975. Life lic. elem. edn. Elem. tchr. Portage Twp. Sch. Corp., Portage, Ind., 1970-73, pres. Portage Twp. Sch. Corp. Bd. Edn., Hebron, Ind., sec. Porter County Vocat. Edn. Com., Valparaiso, Ind., 1984-85. Pres. Porter County Extension Homemakers, 1981-83; mem. assn. County Neighbors Group, Hebron. Mem. Sigma Beta (chpt. sec. 1982-84). Republican. Roman Catholic. Avocations: gourmet cooking; creative needlework; photography; reading. Office: Porter Twp Sch Corp 208 S 725 W Hebron IN 46341

ZDEBLICK, WILLIAM JOSEPH, manufacturing research engineer; b. Chgo., Sept. 3, 1953; s. William Thomas and Mary Denise (Demko) Z.; m. Joy Elizabeth Bodine, June 7, 1975; children: Nicholas, Anna. BSIndlE, U. Ill., 1975, MSIndlE, 1977, PhD in Mech. Engring., 1979. Pvt. practice cons. Urbana, Ill., 1977-79; sr. project engr. Metcut Research, Cin., 1979-81, mgr. mfg. systems, 1981-84, tech. dir., 1985—, dir. product devel., 1986—; lectr. in field. Contbr. articles to profl. jours. Named Outstanding Young Mfg. Engr., Soc. Mfg. Engrs., 1984. Mem. N.Am. Mfg. Research Inst. (bd. dirs. 1985—), Internat. Inst. for Prodn. Engr. Research (corr.). Roman Catholic. Avocations: golf, soccer (coach), auto mechanics. Home: 917 Poplar Ave Terrace Park OH 45174-1234 Office: Metcut Research Assocs 11240 Cornell Park Dr Cincinnati OH 45242-1812

ZECHMAN, NEIL RALPH, lawyer; b. Detroit, Aug. 26, 1947; s. Manuel and Bess (Isberg) Z. BA, U. Mich., 1969, MA, 1970; JD, Wayne State U., 1973, LLM, 1976. Bar: Mich., 1973; cert. secondary tchr. Chief appeals and interpretive standards sect. Mich. Employment Security Commn., Detroit, 1977—. Jewish. Office: Mich Employment Security Commn 7310 Woodward Ave Detroit MI 48202

ZECK, RICHARD MICHAEL, computer company executive, educator; b. Chgo., Apr. 13, 1955; s. Richard Charles and Gloria Eileen (DiMuzio) Z.; m. Jane Ann Budilovsky, Sept. 23, 1979; children—Richard John, Rebecca Ann. B.S. in Computer Sci., Ill. Inst. Tech., 1977, M.S., 1979. Instr., Sperry-UNIVAC, Chgo., 1978-79; owner, mgr. Profl. Computing, Lombard, Ill., 1978—; research engring. programmer Rockwell Graphic Systems, 1979-81; cons. Analysts Internat. Corp., Schaumburg, Ill., 1981-82; asst. prof. computer sci. DeVry Inst. Tech., Lombard, 1983-85; part-time instr. Ill. Inst. Tech. Mem. IEEE, AAAS, Assn. Computing Machinery, (mem. various spl. interest groups). Libertarian. Roman Catholic. Author: High-Level Language for Process Control, 1980; Use of Outside Data Processing Consultants, 1981; Meta-Game Theory in Design Engineering, 1981; Computer Programming for Human Beings, 1983. Home: 405 E Maple St Lombard IL 60148 Office: 2000 Finley Rd Lombard IL 60148

ZECK, ROBERT THADDEUS, physician; b. Chgo., Mar. 28, 1946; s. Herbert Charles and Lauretta Dolores (Hickok) Z.; m. Barbara Jean Voller, June 12, 1971; children: Karen, Laura, Amanda. BS, Loyola U., Chgo., 1968; MD, Loyola Stritch Sch. Medicine, 1972. Dir. pulmonary services La Grange (Ill.) Meml. Hosp., 1977-81; dir. pulmonary services Hinsdale (Ill.) Hosp., 1981—, chmn. dept. medicine, 1985—; pres. Suburban Pulmonary Assocs., Hinsdale, 1978—. Contbr. articles to profl. jours. Fellow Am. Coll. Chest Physicians; mem. Am. Thoracic Soc., Alpha Omega Alpha. Avocations: computer programming, computer design. Office: Suburban Pulmonary Assocs Ltd 211 W Chicago Ave Hinsdale IL 60521

ZEE-CHENG, ROBERT K.-Y., organic chemist; b. Kashan, Chekiang, China, Sept. 2, 1925; came to U.S., 1956, naturalized, 1973; s. Kan-Yi and Fu-Chen Zee-Cheng; m. Yu-Lan Lan Yu Oct. 10, 1949; children—Chi-Lui, Chi-Sung, Chi-Feng, Chi-Wa. B.S. in Ch. E., China Tech. Inst., Shanghai, 1945; M.S. in Organic Phys. Chemistry, N.M. Highland U.-Las Vegas, 1957; Ph.D. in Organic Chemistry, U. Tex.-Austin, 1963. Teaching asst. U. Tex.-Austin, 1957-59; sr. chemist Celanese Chem. Co. Tech. Ctr., Corpus Christi, Tex., 1962-65; prin. chemist Midwest Research Inst., Kansas City, Mo., 1965-78; asst. research prof. St. Louis U., 1978-80; prin. chemist U. Kans. Med. Ctr., Kansas City, 1980-82, research prof. pharmacology, 1982—; medicinal chemist U. Kans. Cancer Ctr., 1980—; assoc. dir. Drug Devel. Lab., 1980—. Inventor of DHAQ (mitoxantrone); contbg. editor: Drugs of the Future; c ontbr. numerous articles to sci. jours. Patentee anticancer agts, anticancer methods, antileukemic compounds, antineoplastic compounds. Recipient Council Prin. Scientists Sci. award, 1973. Mem. Am. Chem. Soc., Sci. Research Soc. North Am., AAAS. Club: Chinese. Home: 9570A W 86th St Overland Park KS 66212 Office: U Kans Med Ctr Rainbow Blvd & 39th St Kansas City KS 66103

ZEFFREN, EUGENE, toiletries company executive; b. St. Louis, Nov. 21, 1941; s. Harry Morris and Bess (Dennis) Z.; m. Steccia Leigh Stern, Feb. 2, 1964; children: Maryl Renee, Bradley Cruvant. AB, Washington U., 1963; MS, U. Chgo., 1965, PhD, 1967. Research chemist Procter & Gamble Co., Cin., 1967-75, sect. head, 1975-77, assoc. dir., 1977-79; v.p. research and devel. Helene Curtis, Inc., Chgo., 1979—. Co-author: The Study of Enzyme Mechanisms, 1973; contbr. articles to profl. jours.; patentee in field of enzymes and hair care. Mem. AAAS, Am. Chem. Soc., Soc. Cosmetic Chemists, Cosmetic Toiletry and Fragrance Assn. (mem. sci. adv. com. 1979—, vice chmn. sci. adv. com. 1984—), Omicron Delta Kappa. Republican. Jewish. Avocations: tennis, swimming, reading adventure and espionage novels. Office: Helene Curtis Inc 4401 W North Ave Chicago IL 60639

ZEGIOB-DEVEREAUX, LESLIE ELAINE, clinical psychologist; b. Cleve., Oct. 17, 1948; d. Charles G. and Elinore Lois (Jones) Zegiob; m. James Michael Devereaux, July 11, 1981. Student Allegheny Coll., 1966-68; BA, Am. U., 1971; MS, U. Ga., 1976, PhD, 1976. Lic. psychologist, Ariz., Ind. Asst. prof. dept. psychology Ariz. State U., Tempe, 1976-78, dir. psychology clinic, 1977-78; dir. childrens services Dogwood Village, Memphis, 1978; adj. prof. dept. psychology Notre Dame (Ind.) U., 1979-80; clin. psychologist dept. psychology and psychiatry The Med. Group, Michigan City, Ind., 1978—; cons. Headstart program Michigan City schs.; mem. adv. bd. Headstart, 1979—. Contbr. articles to profl. jours. Ariz. State U. faculty grantee, 1978. Mem. Am. Psychol. Assn., Assn. for Advancement Behavior Therapy, Southeastern Psychol. Assn., Sierra Club, Animal Protection Inst., Wilderness Soc., Ind. Cat Soc. Phi Kappa Phi, Phi Beta Kappa. Democrat. Office: 1225 E Coolspring Ave Michigan City IN 46360

ZEHNDER, FREDERICK JOHN, automotive executive; b. Detroit, Feb. 11, 1926; s. Frederick Ernest and Katherine Josephine (Raymann) Z.; m. Yvonne Knox, June 25, 1951 (div. Aug. 1957); 1 child, Frederick J. Jr.; m. Adele Louise Leslie, May 15, 1970; children: Leslie, John, Linda. BS, U.S. Merchant Marine Acad., 1947; MBA, U. Mich., 1951. Credit analyst Comerica Bank, Detroit, 1951-53; with Ford Dealer Ops. div. Ford Motor Co., Detroit, 1953—, budget analyst, 1953-64, with sales promotion and tng., 1964-76, used vehicle mgr. truck ops., 1976-80, ops. mgr., 1980-85; v.p. Steel City Ford, Gary, Ind., Mid-Am. Ford Truck, Tulsa, Miramar Ford Truck, San Diego, Trans West Ford, Fontana, Calif., Mid-Calif. Ford Truck, Fresno, 1985—, also bd. dirs. Served to lt. USNR, 1947-67. Mem. U. Mich. Club, Delta Sigma Pi. Republican. Lutheran. Avocations: boating, photography. Office: Ford Dealer Ops div Ford Motor Co PO Box 43308-B Detroit MI 48243

ZEHNDER, JOHN WILLIAM, restaurant executive, chef; b. Bay City, Mich., Oct. 12, 1947; s. Herman Frederick and Lenore Ruth (Eckert) Z.; m. Janet Sue Lockhart, Aug. 23, 1968; children—John Michael, Robert Matthew. B.A., Mich. State U., 1969. Food service mgr. Saga Food Service, Bloomington, Ill. and Alma, Mich., 1969-71, Catering Mgmt. Inc., Anderson, Ind. and Hiram, Ohio, 1971-73; exec. chef Zehnders of Frankenmuth, Mich., 1973—; lectr. Mich. Restaurant Assn. Mem. Round Table com., Lake Huron council Boy Scouts Am., 1980, Webelos leader, 1981-82; active Big Bros. Recipient 1st prize Pillsbury Recipe Contest, 1972, Kraft Creative Foods Contest, 1978, 1st prize Dessert of Yr. award, Nat. Frozen Food Assn., 1978, grand prize Nat. Frozen Food Assn., 1980, Procter and Gamble Cooking with Whirl, 1984, others. Mem. Saginaw Valley Restaurant Assn., Nat. Restaurant Assn., Am. Culinary Fedn., Flint-Saginaw Culinary Fedn. (trustee), Quad City Culinary Fedn., Les Amin Du Vin. Democrat. Lutheran. Avocation: Tae Kwon Do. Home: 515 Heine St Frankenmuth MI 48734 Office: Zehnder's of Frankenmuth 730 S Main St Frankenmuth MI 48734

ZEHNER, DONALD JOSEPH, JR., accountant; b. Winamac, Ind., June 26, 1958; s. Donald Joseph Sr. and Ruth Ellen (Keller) Z.; m. Pamela Sue McCune, Aug. 16, 1986; children: Benjamin Michael (dec.), Arin Shae. BS in Acctg. and Econs., St. Joseph's Coll., 1980. CPA, Ind. Staff acct. Smith, Reed and Co., Inc., Lafayette, Ind., 1980-82; sr. acct. Smith, Thompson, Wihebrink, Lafayette, 1982-84, supr., 1984-86; supr. Smith, Thompson, Wihebrink, Logansport, Ind., 1986—; instr. Ind. Vocat. Tech. Coll., Lafayette, 1983, advisor acctg. program, 1985, advisor nursing program, 1985-86; ptnr. ACME Investors, Lafayette, 1983-86. Lector., commentator St. Lawrence Ch., Lafayette, 1981-86, study group leader, 1982. Mem. Nat. Assn. Acct's. (v.p. edn. 1983-86), Am. Inst. CPA's (adv. editor jour. 1985-87, computer applications subcom. 1986-87), Ind. CPA Soc. (firm day com. 1984-85, small bus. computer com. 1986-87), Lafayette C. of C. (local gov. affairs com. 1985-86). Roman Catholic. Home: 1806 High St Logansport IN 46947 Office: Smith Thompson Wihebrink & Co Inc 300 E Broadway Suite 501 Logansport IN 46947

ZEIDLER, ROBERT BERNARD, physiological educator; b. Wheeling, W.V., Jan. 3, 1943; m. Sharon Conley, Dec. 27, 1982. B.S., West Liberty State U., 1969; Ph.D., W.V. U., 1973. Postdoctoral researcher U. Ill., Urbana, 1973-75, U. Ariz., Tucson, 1975-78; asst. prof. U. Rhodesia, Salisbury, 1978-79; research asst., prof. U. Ala., Birmingham, 1980-82, U. Mo., Columbia, 1982—. Contbr. articles to profl. jours. Grantee NIH, 1976, U. Rhodesia, 1978, Ala. Lung Assn., 1981, Nat. Lung Assn., 1984. Mem. Am. Physiol. Soc., Biophys. Soc., Red Cell Club. Home: 2809 Lynnwood Dr Columbia MO 65203 Office: U Missouri Sch Medicine Dept Anesthesiology Columbia MO 65212

ZEIMET, EDWARD JOSEPH, educator; b. Madison, Wis., Jan. 16, 1925; s. Anthony Joseph and Stella Mary (Orlowicz) Z.; B.A., U. Wis., 1948, M.S., 1950, Ph.D., 1970; m. Frances Ann Ward, May 29, 1954; children—Edward, Stephanie, Ann, Thomas, Symantha. Biology tchr. Ft. Atkinson (Wis.) High Sch., 1948-49; biologist Holtzman-Rolfsmeyer Co., Madison, 1949-52; salesman Oscar Mayer Co., Madison, 1952-54; project asst. endocrine research U. Wis. at Madison, 1954-61, zoology specialist, 1964-70; tech. rep. Spinco div. Beckman Industries, Palo Alto, Calif., 1961-64; prof. ednl. media dept. U. Wis. at LaCrosse, 1970—, dir. ednl. media program, 1975-80; chmn. Western Wis. Media Conf., 1979; community care orgn. cons. Mem. budget rev. bd. United Way, LaCrosse, 1974; campus coordinator Gene McCarthy for Pres., 1972, state alternate del., 1972; campus coordinator Alvin Baldus for U.S. Congress, 1974, 76; mem. candidate selection com. Mil. Acad.; mem. Nat. Telemedia Council; mem. adv. com. for library and info. sci. U. Wis. Extension; Served with AUS, 1943-46; PTO. Mem. Assn. Ednl. Communication Tech., Wis. Audio Visual Assn., Internat. Visual Literacy Assn., Am. Council for Better Broadcast, Wis. Acad. Sci., Arts and Letters, Phi Sigma. Democrat. Author: College Biology II, 1969; The Microslide Viewer, 1969; College Biology I, 1970; Trigger Tapes: A Tool for Teacher Education, 1975; Children's Television: Rough Stuff on Saturday; asst. editor Wis. Audiovisual Dispatch, 1975-76. Home: 445 S 19th St LaCrosse WI 54601 Office: Univ Wis-La Crosse 213 Morris Hall LaCrosse WI 54601

ZEIT, JOHN HARPER, civil engineering educator, architectural consultant; b. Cleve., Oct. 12, 1952; s. Paul Rudolph and Martha Elizabeth (Harper) Z.; m. Janet Marie Jones, May 1, 1982; 1 child, Martha Marie. BArch, Kent State U., 1978. Registered architect, Ohio. Constrn. mgr. C.M. Bldg., Inc., Akron, Ohio, 1978-81; chief designer Forest City Core Systems, Akron, 1980-81; asst. prof. civil engring. Stark Tech. Coll., Canton, Ohio, 1981—; corp. sec. Grubergrowth, Inc., Cleve., 1983—, also bd. dirs.; cons. in field. Mem. AIA, Nat. Assn. Engring. Educators. Home: 149 Spell Rd Kent OH 44240 Office: Stark Tech Coll 6200 Frank Rd NW Canton OH 44720

ZELICKSON, SUE, newspaper and cookbook editor, television reporter and host, food consultant; b. Mpls., Sept. 13, 1934; d. Harry M. and Bernice (Gross) Zipperman; m. Alvin S. Zelickson, Aug. 21, 1956; children—Barry M., Brian D. B.S. in Edn., U. Minn., 1956. Cert. elem. tchr., S.C., Minn. Tchr. various schs. Mpls., S.C., Golden Valley, Minn., 1956-79; writer, editor, columnist Mpls.-St. Paul Mag., 1980—, Buylines, Mpls., 1984—; TV-radio reporter Sta. WCCO-KSTP, Mpls, 1980—, Lifestyles with Sue Zelickson Sta. WCCO cable; restaurant developer, cons. Mpls., 1978—; v.p. Passage Tours, Mpls., 1984—. Coordinator, editor: Much Ado About Food, 1978; Minnesota Heritage Cookbook, 1979; Lee Ann Chin's Chinese Cuisine, 1981; Collins Back Room Cooking Secrets, 1981; The Governor's Table Cookbook, 1981; Chocolate Days & Chocolate Nights, 1982; Food for Show, Food on the Go, 1983; Wild Rice Star of The North, 1985; Look What's Cooking Now, 1985. Contbr. articles to Sun Newspaper, Post Publs., Mpls., Tribune. Public relations, promoter, fundraiser Mpls. Boys & Girls Club, Mpls. Inst. Arts, Hennepin County Med. Soc. Aux., Ronald McDonald House, Bonaventure Mall, Women's Assn. Minn. Symphony Orchestra, Council Jewish Women, Mt. Sinai Hosp., Brandeis U. Women, Minn. Opera Assn., Guthrie Theatre, Sholom Home, Am. Cancer Soc; bd. dirs. U. Minn. Alumni Bd., Golden Valley State Bank. Recipient Outstanding Achievement award There's Living Proof Am. Cancer Soc., Duluth, Minn., 1984; Outstanding Achievement award Boys & Girls Club Minn., 1984. Mem. Nat. Council Jewish Women, Women's Assn. Minn. Orch., numerous others. Avocations: reading, travel; writing; painting. Home and Office: 101 Ardmore Dr Minneapolis MN 55422

ZELLER, FRANCIS JOSEPH, college dean; b. Chgo., July 31, 1943; s. Charles Joseph Paul and Erma (Kile) Z.; m. Frances Joan McGrath, Aug. 3, 1968; children—Patrick, Brian. B.A. in English, Lewis U., 1967; M.A., No. Ill. U., 1970, Ed.D., 1983. Tchr., chmn. English dept. Schaumburg Dist. 54, Ill., 1967-70; asst. bus. mgr. Park Ridge Sch. Dist. 64, Ill., 1970-71; bus. mgr. Barrington Sch. Dist. 224, Ill., 1971-73; dean bus. services Ill. Valley Community Coll., Oglesby, 1973—. Exec. mem. Boy Scouts of Am., Peoria, Ill., 1983—; mem. Peoria Diocesan Pastoral Council, 1983—. Mem. Internat. Assn. Sch. Bus. Ofcls. (bd. dirs. 1985—, chmn. legal aspects com.), Ill. Assn. Sch. Bus. Ofcls., Ill. Assn. Community Coll. Bus. Adminstrs. (bd. dirs. 1984—), NEA, Delta Sigma Pi. Roman Catholic. Lodge: Rotary. Avocations: cross country skiing; tennis; hunting; distance bicycling. Office: Ill Valley Community Coll 2578 E 350th Rd Oglesby IL 61348

ZELLER, LYLE DEAN, management consultant, architect; b. Highland, Ill., Feb. 17, 1956; s. A. Gene and Mary Thelma (Willeford) Z.; m. Carla Sue Wilson, No. 6, 1976; 1 dau., Lauren Anne. A.A.S. (with honors), So. Ill. U., 1976, B.S. (with honors), 1979; M.B.A., Wash. U., St. Louis, 1983. Registered architect, Ill., Mo. Sr. archtl. technician Fischer-Stein Assocs., Carbondale, Ill., 1976-79; project architect Ralph Korte Inc., Highland, 1980-82; mgmt. cons. Peat Marwick Mitchell & Co., St. Louis, 1983-84, sr. cons., 1984-86; mgr., 1986-87, sr. mgr., 1987—. Recipient Certs. Scholastic Achievement So. Ill. U., 1976, 79. Mem. AIA (St. Louis chpt.). Office: 1010 Market St Saint Louis MO 63101

ZELLER, RICHARD ALLEN, sociology educator; b. Elgin, Ill., Oct. 5, 1944; s. Harry Knode Zeller Jr. and Juanita Ruth (Holsopple) Wagner; m. Joan Marion Brubaker; children: David Allen, Dean Leroy. BA, LaVerne Coll., 1966; MA, U. Wis., 1967, PhD, 1972. Instr. U. Minn., Morris, 1969-71; prof. sociology SUNY, Buffalo, 1971-76, Bowling Green (Ohio) State U., 1976—; sr. ptnr. Mktg. Media Research, Toledo, 1982-85; chief exec. officer Zeller Research Inc., Toledo, 1985—. Author: Statistical Analysis of Social Data, 1978, Reliability and Validity, 1979, Measurement in Social Sciences, 1980; contbr. articles to profl. jours. Mem. Am. Sociological Assn., Am. Statis. Assn. (pres. N.W. Ohio chapter 1982-83, v.p. 1981-82). Avocations: old house restoration, musical theater production. Home: 328 W Wooster Bowling Green OH 43402 Office: Bowling Green State U Sociology Dept Bowling Green OH 43402

ZELLING, DANIEL AMUNA, physician, hypnoanalyst; b. Flagy, France, Mar. 1, 1936; came to U.S., 1962, naturalized, 1968; s. Anton and Leonie Anne-Marie (Lowositz) Z.; m. Kathleen Dawn Murphy, Aug. 11, 1969; children—Martin Rudolph, Inge Sophia, Michael Patrick, Megan Anne-Marie. H.B.S.-B., Lyceum Noctua, 1956; M.D., Ryks U., Leiden, Netherlands, 1961. Intern, Ch. Homes Hosp., Balt., 1962-63; resident Barberton (Ohio) Citizens Hosp., 1963-64; gen. practice medicine, Akron, Ohio, 1964-76; exec. dir. Ohio Inst. Med. Hypnosis, Inc., Akron, 1976—; lectr. med. hypnosis Northeastern Ohio U., Rootstown, 1980—. Fellow Am. Acad. Family Physicians; mem. Soc. Med. Hypnoanalyst (pres. 1982-86), Am. Soc. Clin. Hypnosis, Internat. Soc. Hypnosis, AMA, Summit County Med. Soc., Ohio Med. Soc. Republican. Home: 255 Harmony Hills Dr Akron OH 44321 Office: 80 N Miller Rd Akron OH 44313

ZELOV, RANDOLPH D(ICKINSON), JR., architect; b. Bryn Mawr, Pa., Mar. 20, 1952; s. Randolph Dickinson and Josephine (Frank) Z.; m. Debra Rochelle Lehmkuhl, Feb. 11, 1986; children: Ryan Hopkins, Sophia Grace. B in Architecture, Cornell U., 1975; B in Theology, The Way Coll., 1979. Registered profl. architect. Coordinator design The Way Internat., New Knoxville, Ohio, 1979—. Prin. works include Performing Arts. Ctr. and Dormitory, Dayton (Masonry Inst. award of Merit 1986), Emporia (Kans.) Library Renovation (Kans. Preservation Alliance award 1986),. Mem. AIA, Am. Solar Energy Soc., Soc. Mayflower Descendents. Avocations: Bible study, philately, hunting, art, modelmaking. Home and Office: The Way Internat 19100 E Shelby Rd New Knoxville OH 45871

ZEMAITIS, BENEDICT RAMUTIS, auditor; b. Vilkaviskis, Lithuania, Mar. 13, 1933; came to U.S., 1949; s. Pius K. and Janina V. (Strimavicius) Z.; m. Vita J. Zubkus, Sept. 29, 1956. BS in Mgmt., U. Ill., 1956; MBA in Acctg., Roosevelt U., 1961. CPA, Ill.; cert. internal auditor. Internal auditor, controller, credit mgr. Aldens, Inc., Chgo., 1959-66, catalog store controller, 1968-69; sr. internal auditor Montgomery Ward Co., Chgo., 1966-67, IRS Inspection, Chgo., 1967-68; asst. chief internal auditor Ill. Dept. Revenue, Chgo., 1969-73; chief internal auditor Ill. Dept. Revenue, Springfield, 1973—. Served with U.S. Army, 1956-58. Mem. Am. Inst. CPA's, Inst. of Internal Auditors (dist. dir., chmn. membership com., chmn. internat. conf. com.). Roman Catholic. Avocations: photography, backgammon, golf, table tennis, tennis. Home: 57 Meander Pike Chatham IL 62629 Office: Ill Dept Revenue 101 W Jefferson Springfield IL 62708

ZEMBLIDGE, LAVERNE DORIS, parts manufacturing company buyer; b. Chgo., July 16, 1950; d. John Frank and Lorraine (Des Jardens) Paczesny; m. Earnest Milligan, May 20, 1969 (div. Apr., 1971); children: Lisa Marie, Tina Louise; m. Robert Lane Zemblidge, Apr. 21, 1974; 1 child, Gregg Michael. Grad. high sch., Chgo., 1968. Purchasing sec. Dee Electric Co., Chgo., 1972-74; with accounting Krano Products, Chgo., 1977-80; plant sec. Precision U-Joint, Chgo., 1980-82, purchasing sec., 1982-84; buyer Precision U-Joint, Chgo., 1984—. troop leader Girl Scouts U.S., Chgo., 1976-78; historian Mother Connelly Guild, Chgo., 1979-81. Mem. Am. Purchasing Soc. Democrat. Roman Catholic. Avocations: ceramics, interior decorating, floral arrangement, gourmet cooking. Office: Presicion Universal Joint Corp 3440 N Kedzie Chicago IL 60618

ZEMEL, DAVID MICHAEL, charitable organization administrator, human services educator; b. St. Louis, Feb. 16, 1949; s. Jack and Delores Mae (Aubuchon) Z.; m. Jane Mary Sandler, Jan. 14, 1973; 1 child, Abby Sandler. B.S. in Edn., U. Mo., 1971; M. in Social Work, Washington U., St. Louis, 1975. Tchr. Title I, St. James Schs., Mo., 1971-72; social worker II Boys Town Mo., St. James, 1972-75; program dir. St. Louis County Juvenile Court, 1975-79; dir. devel. Providence Program, Inc., St. Louis, 1979-80; devel. officer United Way Greater St. Louis, 1980-82, v.p., 1982—; assoc. prof. human services St. Louis Community Coll., 1975—; lectr. George Warren Brown Sch. Social Work, Washington U., 1987—; cons. in field. Author tng. manuals on fundraising. Mem. com. alternative edn. University City Schs., 1979—; trainer United Way Mgmt. Assistance Ctr., St. Louis, 1980—; mem. nat. profl. adv. com. Integrated Research and Devel., United Way Am., 1986—; bd. dirs. Confluence St. Louis, 1983-84, Boys Town Mo., St. Louis, 1977-79; participant Leadership St. Louis, 1987-88; mem. integrated research and devel. com. Nat. Profl. Adv. Council, United Way of Am., Alexandria, Va., 1986—. Mem. Nat. Soc. Fund Raising Execs. (chmn. legis. 1982-83), Washington U. Alumni Assn. (ann. program com.). Jewish. Home: 7015 Lindell Blvd University City MO 63130 Office: United Way Greater Saint Louis 915 Olive St Saint Louis MO 63101

ZENDER-BOYKIN, ANGELINA ELIZABETH, social services executive; b. Brighton, Mass., Apr. 19, 1933; d. Sabatino and Giovanina (Beninati) Fantasia; m. Frederick Robert Zender, Dec. 30, 1949 (div. Nov. 1982);

children: Richard, Kathryn, James, Nancy, Debra; m. Thomas Julian Boykin, Aug. 25, 1986. AS, U. Wis., Madison, 1973, BS, 1980. Waitress, 1955-66; founder Ricky Zender Meml. Home, Inc., Wausau, Wis., 1973, adminstr., daily living coordinator, 1973—; mem. Wis. State Service for Oral Exams, 1974-75; bd. dirs. Halfway House Fedn. Wis., 1980—; mem. task force Wis. Council on Devel. Disabilities, 1987—. Author: (with others) Quality of Life, 1977; mem. rev. com. Guidelines to Community Living Systems for the Developmentally Disabled. Recipient Presdl. citation for community service Apogee, 1975. Mem. Assn. Retarded Citizens (state dir.), Marathon County Assn. Retarded Citizens (treas. 1971, pres. 1973-82), Nat. Assn. Pvt. Residential Facilities for Mentally Retarded (bd. dirs. 1976-85), Nat. Soc. Autistic Children, United Comml. Travelers Aux., United Cerebral Palsy Assn., Wis. Assn. Community Human Services Programs, Am. Assn. Mental Deficiency, Wis. Assn. Residential Facilities (sec. 1982), Wis. Epilepsy Assn., Wis. Assn. Devel. Disabilities (v.p. 1981), Wausau C. of C. (mem. personnel club, chmn. interclub coordinating council), Assn. for Retarded Citizens (Hall of Honor 1980), Community Living Alliance for Mentally Retarded, Milw. Italian Community Ctr. Clubs: Toastmaster, Toastmistress (pres.). Home: 110 E Moonlite Ave Wausau WI 54401 Office: PO Box 354 Wausau WI 54401

ZENERE, RENO P., marketing executive; b. Chgo., Oct. 31, 1929; s. John and Margarita Trevisan Z.; m. Dorothy Ann Cromwell, Dec. 7, 1951; children—Mark Alan, Cheryl Ann, Marie Antoinette. Laborer, Acme Steel Corp. (formerly Interlake, Inc.), Chgo., after 1947, apprentice electrician, to 1955, project technician, 1956, engr., 1959, sales rep., 1963, mktg. specialist, 1969, product mgr., 1974, gen. mgr. mktg., 1977, v.p. mktg., 1982—. Past chmn. bd. dirs. Pullman Civic Orgn.; bd. dirs. Met. Chgo. Coalition for Aged, Pullman Found. Served to 1st lt. Ill. N.G. Democrat. Roman Catholic. Clubs: Olympia Fields Country (Olympia Fields, Ill.); KC (San Salvador).

ZENIAN, SHAHE LEVON, clinical psychologist; b. Beirut, Lebanon, Oct. 12, 1931; s. Levon Nazareth and Araxie (Bodourian) Z. Student Westminster Coll., 1949-52, Washington State Coll., 1952; B.A., U. Mich., 1958; M.A., U. Mo., 1962. Asst. clin. psychologist Student Health Service, U. Mo., Columbia, 1960-63; clin. psychologist Fulton State Hosp. (Mo.), 1963-65; supr. psychol. services Maximum Security Unit, State Hosp. No. 1, Fulton, 1965-69, chief psychologist, 1969-75; chief clin. psychologist St. Francis Community Mental Health Ctr., Cape Girardeau, Mo., 1974-76; clin. psychologist Broadlawns Med. Ctr., Des Moines, Iowa, 1976—. Served with USAF, 1952-56. Mem. Fellow Am. Orthopsychiat. Assn.; mem. Am. Psychol. Assn., Am. Assn. Counseling and Devel., Am. Assn. Correctional Psychologists, Am. Psychology-Law Soc., Law and Society Assn., Am. Correctional Assn., Iowa Corrections Assn., Nat. Jail Assn., Am. Assn. Correctional Officers. Home: PO Box 7123 Grand Station Des Moines IA 50309 Office: Broadlawns Medical Ctr 18th & Hickman Rd Des Moines IA 50314

ZENK, GEORGE EDWARD, elec. engr.; b. Erie, Pa., June 8, 1923; s. Otto John and Charlotte (Shafer) Z.; B.A., Westminster Coll., 1949; B.Sc., Carnegie Inst. Tech., 1949, M.Sc., 1950, Ph.D., 1953; m. Irma Rose Haberman, June 13, 1953. Mem. tech. staff Bell Tel. Labs., Whippany, N.J., 1953-61; sr. engr. Honeywell Aero Co., Mpls., 1962-63; cons. Control Data Corp., Mpls., 1964—. Vice pres Found. for Living, Abbott-Northwestern Hosp., Mpls., 1977-78. Served with AUS, 1943-46. NRC fellow, 1950-51; Buhl Found. fellow, 1951-52. Mem. IEEE, Sigma Xi, Tau Beta Pi, Eta Kappa Nu, Phi Kappa Phi. Patentee computer man-machine interface, spacecraft nav. system, electronic filters. Home: 6905 10th Ave S Richfield MN 55423 Office: 2300 E 88th St Bloomington MN 55420

ZENK, RONALD JAY, manufacturing executive, consultant; b. Fairmont, Minn., Sept. 17, 1958; s. Milton J. and Adeline (Czech) Z.; m. Lori Andrews, May 17, 1986. BS, St. John's U., Collegeville, Minn., 1981; MBA in Fin., U. Minn., 1982. Cons. Fox & Co., CPA's, Bloomington, Minn., 1982-83; sr. fin. mgmt. cons. Peat Marwick Main & Co. CPA's, Mpls., 1983-85; v.p. fin. Surgidyne, Inc., Eden Prairie, Minn., 1986—; fin. cons. Ordway Music Theatre, St. Paul, 1984-85, Minn. Opera, St. Paul, 1985. Home: 16469 Baywood Ln Eden Prairie MN 55344 Office: Surgidyne Inc 9600 W 76th St Eden Prairie MN 55322

ZENNER, RONALD PETER, corporate professional; b. Milw., Apr. 28, 1938; s. Peter and Irene (Schissel) Z.; m. Pamela Davidson, May 1967 (div. 1969); m. Carol B. Lundy, June 14, 1969; 1 child, Sean, Patrick. BS, Marquette U., 1961. CPA, Wis. Acct. Bucyrus Erie, Milw., 1961-63; div. controller J.I. Case, Racine, Wis., 1963-67; exec. v.p. Ozite, Libertyville, Ill., 1967-85; chief exec. officer UNR Industries, Chgo., 1985-86; v.p. Buccino & Assocs., Chgo., 1986-87; exec. v.p. Wilton Enterprises, Chgo., 1987—. Mem. Am. Inst. CPA's, Ill. Inst. CPA's. Republican. Roman Catholic. Club: University (Chgo.). Home: 932 Shoreline Rd LBS Barrington IL 60010

ZENS, JON HARDESTY, pastor; b. Barston, Calif., Apr. 25, 1945; s. Paul Henry and Goldie Pearl (Hardesty) Z.; m. Dorothea Faith Martin, June 3, 1968; children: Adam, Eve, Hannah. BA, Covenant Coll., 1969; MDiv, Westminster Theol. Sem., 1972; DMin, Calif. Grad. Sch. Theology, 1983. Pastor Nashville Reformed Bapt. Ch., Nashville, 1976-80, Malin (Oreg.) Bapt. Ch., 1981-83, Word of Life Ch., Dresser, Wis., 1983—; mem. steering com. Bapt. Council on Theology, Plano, Tex., 1980-82. Author: (book) Dipensationalism: An Inquiry Into Its Figures and Features, 1978, Studies in Theology and Ethics, 1981; editor Bapt. Reformation Rev., Nashville, 1978-81, Searching Together, St. Croix Falls, Wis., 1982—. Avocations: jogging, golf, bowling, tennis. Home: 138 Roosevelt St S Saint Croix Falls WI 54024 Office: Searching Together PO Box 548 104 Dresser St E Saint Croix Falls WI 54024

ZENSER, TERRY VERNON, biochemist; b. Port Clinton, Ohio, Aug. 1, 1945; s. Vernon S. and Hazel Z.; m. Barbara Jean Morrison, Aug. 10, 1968; children: Nathan, Jason. BS in Biol. Scis., Ohio State U., 1967; PhD in Biochemistry, U. Mo., 1971. Core coordinator VA Med. Ctr., St. Louis, 1975—; chief renal research VA Med. Ctr., Pitts., 1975-76; acting dir. Geriatric Research, Edn., and Clin. Ctr. VA Med. Ctr., St. Louis, 1979-80; biochemist U.S. Army; lectr. Hood Coll., Frederick, Md., 1974-75; adj. asst. prof. U. Pitts., 1975-76; asst., then assoc. prof. St. Louis U., 1976-85, prof. 1985—. Contbr. chpts. to books and articles to profl. jours. Served to capt. U.S. Army, 1971-75. Grantee Am. Cancer Soc., Nat. Cancer Inst., VA. Mem. Am. Fedn. for Clin. Research, Am. Soc. for Biol. Chemists, Am. Soc. for Pharmacology and Exptl. Therapeutics, Gerontol. Soc., Sigma Xi. Home: 1200 Dunloe Rd Saint Louis MO 63021 Office: VA Med Ctr 111G-JB Jefferson Barracks Div Saint Louis MO 63125

ZERBA, JANET ANN, home health care company administrator; b. Lansing, Mich., Sept. 29, 1941; d. Clare Jay and Thelma Marie (Hollenbeck) Reynolds; m. Jimmy A. Zerba, Mar. 21, 1959; divorced; remarried, Feb. 3, 1979; children: Michael, Russell, Jeffery (dec.), Melinda (dec.); m. Winton Erwin Walker, Nov. 27, 1975 (dec. Nov. 1976). LPN, Lansing Community Coll., 1970, AS in Nursing, 1976. RN, charge nurse Hayes Green Beach Hosp., Charlotte, Mich., 1976-78; RN, nursing supr. Kelly Health Care, Lansing, 1978-84; adminstr. Comprehensive Med. Home Care, Lansing, 1984-86; v.p. home care services Med. Air Equipment Supply, Lansing, 1986—; dir. clin. services Americor Home Health Services, Lansing, 1987—; profl. adv. and clin. record rev. bds., Americor Home Health Services, Lansing, 1984—; cons. Home Health Services of Mid-Mich., Midland, 1986. Mem. Assn. Career Women (bd. dirs. 1983-84), Capitol Area Discharge Planners (co-chmn. 1980-81, 84-85). Home: 4914 Hudson Dimondale MI 48821

ZERBE, KATHRYN J., psychiatrist; b. Harrisburg, Pa., Oct. 17, 1951; d. Grover Franklin and Ethel (Schreckengaust) Z. BS with BA equivalent cum laude, Duke U., 1973; MD, Temple U., 1978. Diplomate Am. Bd. Psychiatry, 1984. Resident Karl Menninger Sch. Psychiatry, Topeka, 1982; staff psychiatrist Menninger Found., Topeka, 1982—; instr. numerous sems. and courses. Author several profl. research papers; contbr. book revs. and articles to profl. jours. Probation officer Juvenile div. Dauphin County, Pa., 1973; recorder Topeka Inst. for Psychoanalysis. Seeley fellow, 1979-82; recipient ann. Laughlin Award for Merit The Nat. Psychiat. Endowment Fund, 1982, Outstanding Paper of Profl. Programs award The Menninger Found Alumni Assn., 1982, hon. mention William C. Menninger award Cen. Neuropsychiat. Assn., 1982, Writing award Topeka Inst. for Psychoanalysis, 1985. Mem. AMA, Am. Med. Women's Assn., Am. Psychiatric Assn., Assn. of Applied Psychoanalysis, Shawnee County Med. Soc., Kans. Med. Soc. Avocations: writing, reading, art history, travel. Office: The Menninger Foundation Box 829 Topeka KS 66601

ZERBI, PAUL GENOESE, thoracic and cardiovascular surgeon; b. Italy, Aug. 2, 1933; s. Domenico Genoese and Rose (Contestabile) Z.; came to U.S., 1962, naturalized, 1972; M.D., U. Modena (Italy), 1960; m. Mary Martha Berring, Jan. 11, 1964; children—Paula, Jayne, Dominic. Intern U. Hosp., U. Modena, 1960; physician with U.S. Army, Germany, 1961; resident in surgery Aultman Hosp., Canton, Ohio, 1962-63, Mercy Hosp., Canton, 1963-65, Columbus Hosp., N.Y.C., 1965-66; resident in thoracic and cardiovascular surgery Emory U. Hosps., Atlanta, 1966-68; chief surgery Central State Hosp., Milledgeville, Ga., 1968-70; practice medicine specializing in thoracic and cardiovascular surgery, Warren, Ohio, 1970—; active staff Trumbull Meml. Hosp., 1973—. Diplomate Am. Bd. Surgery, Am. Bd. Thoracic Surgery. Fellow A.C.S., Am. Coll. Chest Physicians; mem. Am., Ohio State med. assns., Trumbull County Med. Soc., Cleve. Surg. Soc., Soc. Thoracic Surgeons, Am. Heart Assn. Roman Catholic. Home: 9710 King Graves Rd Warren OH 44484 Office: 3893 E Market St Warren OH 44484

ZERKIS, STEPHEN W., corporation executive; b. N.Y.C., Aug. 28, 1939; s. Stephen and Natalie (Plescun) Z.; m. Patricia Ann Mitchell, Dec. 21, 1968; children: Gregory Francis, Christina Natalie. BS, Columbia U., 1963; MS, U. So. Calif., 1972. Cons. A.T. Kearney, Chgo., 1973-77; group mgr. Baxter Travenol Labs., Deerfield, Ill., 1977-82, Bell & Howell, Chgo., 1982-84; dir. systems Pettibone Corp., Chgo., 1982-84, corp. dir., gen. mgr., 1985—; cons. Cypress Group Inc. Served to capt. USAF, 1966-72, Korea. Roman Catholic. Avocations: sailing, golf, coaching youth sports, scouting. Home: 3154 Cherry Ln Northbrook IL 60062 Office: Pettibone Corp 5401 W Grand Ave Chicago IL 60639

ZERNER, RICHARD EGON, lawyer; b. Toledo, Aug. 27, 1947; s. Carl Egon and Erma K. (Klein) Z.; m. Nancy L. Goodman, Apr. 6, 1972; children—Loryn Brooke, Robert Egon. B.A., Hillsdale Coll., 1969; J.D., U. Toledo, 1972. Bar: Ohio 1973. Sole practice law, Toledo, 1973—; assoc. Associated Legal Group, Toledo, 1982—; bd. dirs. Westgate br. Mid-Am. Nat. Bank & Trust Co.; legal counsel Northwestern Ohio Gasoline Dealers Assn. Mem. pres.'s council Toledo Mus. Art; past trustee Maumee Valley Country Day Sch. Mem. ABA, Ohio Bar Assn., Toledo Bar Assn., Jewish Community Ctr., Maumee Valley Country Day Sch. Alumni Assn. (past pres.). Clubs: Belmont Country, Carranor Hunt & Polo, Toledo Tennis, Masons. Home: 5045 Cartagena Dr Toledo OH 43623 Office: 3223 Sylvania Ave Toledo OH 43613

ZESKIND, H. JAY, radiologist, nuclear medicine physician; b. Detroit, Jan. 6, 1948. BS, Wayne State U., Detroit, 1968, MD, 1972. Diplomate Am. Bd. Radiology, Am. Bd. Nuclear Medicine. Intern, then resident Mt. Carmel Mercy Hosp., Detroit, 1972-76, radiologist, 1976-82; radiologist Detroit Macomb Hosp., Warren, Mich., 1982—. Contbr. articles to profl. jours. Mem. AMA, Am. Coll. Radiology, Am. Coll. Nuclear Physicians, Am. Inst. Ultrasound in Medicine, Radiol. Soc. N.Am., Soc. Nuclear Medicine, Mich. State Med. Soc., Mich. Radiol. Soc., Mich. Soc. Therapeutic Radiologists, Wayne County Med. Soc., Oakland County Med. Soc., Macomb County Med. Soc. Office: Dept Radiology Macomb Hosp 11800E 12 Mile Rd Warren MI 48033

ZETTERLUND, DOREEN, film production administrator, actress; b. Madison Heights, Mich., Dec. 23, 1961; d. Walter Bernard and Josephine (Rompollo) Z. Student, Oakland U., 1980-81; BBA, Walsh Bus. Coll., 1983; MA in Mass Communication, Wayne State U., 1985. Freelance actress radio, TV, voice over comms. Detroit, 1984—; student intern Sta. WTVS-TV, Detroit, Jan. to June 1985; freelance prodn. asst. films, video Detroit, 1986—, freelance location scout, coordinator films, video, 1987—. Named Ms. Mich. Big and Beautiful, 1983. Mem. Screen Actors Guild, AFTRA, Nat. Acad. Arts and Scis., Cinema Club of Nat. Acad. Arts and Scis.

ZETTL, MANFRED PETER, executive chef, restaurant owner; b. Salzburg, Austria, Aug. 17, 1941; came to U.S., 1963; s. August and Anna (Eschbacher) Z.; m. Judith Ann Boyd, June 15, 1967; children: Peter, Victoria, Stephan, Brigitte. Grad., Hotel and Restaurant Sch., Salzburg, 1958. Exec. chef Famous-Barr Co., St. Louis, 1964-74, SS Rottedam, 1959-63; owner, pres. Slimmery Internat., St. Louis, 1974—; advisor food service Jewish Community Ctr., St. Louis, 1975—; cons. CTX div. Pet, Inc., St. Louis, 1976-79, Clipper Cruise Line, St. Louis, 1982-84, Beck Flavors, St. Louis, 1983—. Advisor Boy Scouts Am., St. Louis, 1970—. Named Chef of Yr. Les Amis De Vin, 1986, 87. Mem. Chefs de Cusine Assn. (pres. 1970-72), Am. Culinary Fedn. (Brinze medal 1985, Gold medal 1986, Silver medal 1986), Am. Sanitation Inst. (Honor award 1980), Am. Acad. Chefs, Commanderie de Bordeaux. Republican. Avocations: fishing, painting, hunting, skiing, outdoors. Office: Slimmery Internat PO Box 28742 Creve Coeur MO 63146

ZETTLE, PAULA RUTH, nurse; b. Youngstown, Ohio, Aug. 9, 1938; d. Paul Vincent and Doris Esther (Snively) Webb; R.N., St. Luke's Hosp. Sch. Nursing, 1959; postgrad. St. Joseph's Coll., 1984; m. Donald Richard Zettle; children—Peter, Lisa, Jonathan, James. Nurse, Lakewood (Ohio) Hosp., 1960-61; employee health service nurse Mt. Sinai Hosp., Hillcrest Hosp., Cleve., 1972-78; day supr., patient care coordinator Shaker Med. Center, Cleve., 1978-80; asst. dir. nursing Americana Healthcare, Mayfield Heights, Ohio, 1981; utilization rev. coordinator Kaiser Found., East Side Hosps., Cleve., 1982-84, regional utilization auditor, quality assurance coordinator, 1984—; mem. Quality Rev. Coordinators Ohio, No. Ohio Rev. Coordinators, disaster health services com. ARC, adv. bd. Upjohn Healthcare Services, also mem. clin. rev. com.; instr. CPR; cons. Leader, Girl Scouts U.S.A., 1968-73; den mother, trainer Boy Scouts Am., 1967-69. Mem. St. Luke's Hosp. and Greater Cleve. Gen. Alumni Assn., Nat. Assn. Quality Assurance Profls., Nat. Assn. Female Execs. Presbyterian. Home: 993 Professor Rd Lyndhurst OH 44124 Office: 5105 Som Ctr Rd Willoughby OH 44094

ZIARNIK, ROBERT J., municipal protective services official. Chief of police City of Milw. Office: Office of the Police Chief 749 W State St Milwaukee WI 53233 •

ZICCARELLI, MARK A., lawyer; b. Plattsburg, N.Y., July 23, 1954; s. Samuel B. and Dorcas (Winters) Z.; m. Lucinda Ann Bartholomew, Aug. 24, 1978 (div. Nov. 1979); m. Shawn Ann Haines, Nov. 9, 1985. BA, Ohio Wesleyan U., 1976; JD, Ohio State U., 1979. Sole practice Painesville, Ohio, 1979-80; ptnr. Ischie & Ziccarelli, Painesville, 1980-82; assoc. Gibson, Caito, Harkins & Brelo Co., Legal Profl. Assn., Mentor, Ohio, 1983-86, ptnr., 1986—. Vol. Legal Aid Soc., Painesville, 1985. Mem. ABA, Ohio State Bar Assn., Fla. Bar Assn., Lake County Bar Assn., Ohio Acad. Trial Lawyers, Phi Beta Kappa. Democrat. Roman Catholic. Lodge: K.C. Avocation: golf. Office: Gibson Caito Harkins & Brelo Co Local Pub Agy 8353 Mentor Ave Mentor OH 44060

ZICCARELLI, SALVATORE FRANCIS, food products executive, consultant; b. Chgo., May 1, 1936; s. Joseph and Josephine Nancy (Scibilia) Z.; m. Sheila Mae Weiss, Oct. 28, 1961; children: Mark S., Kathryn J., Matthew T., Marina M., John X. BS in Chemistry, U. Ill., Chgo., 1958; postgrad., Chgo. Tchr. Coll., 1958-59. Dir. research and devel. Newly Weds Foods Co., Chgo., 1961-68; mgr. research and devel. Beatrice Foods Co., Chgo., 1968-84; mgr. mktg. and sales Diehl Inc., Defiance, Ohio, 1984-86; div. mgr. Northland Food Co-op, Owen, Wis., 1986—. Patentee in field; contbr. articles to profl. jours. Treas. ch. sch. bd., Darien, Ill.; bd. dirs. adhoc com. sch. bd., Downers Grove. Served with USMCR. Mem. Institutional Food Tech. Assn., Am. Cereal Chemists Assn. Roman Catholic. Lodge: Cath. Order of Foresters (sec.-treas.). Office: Northland Food Co-op Spl Powders div 7550 Janes Ave Woodridge IL 60517

ZICHEK, MELVIN EDDIE, retired clergyman, educator; b. Lincoln, Nebr., May 5, 1918; s. Eddie and Agnes (Varga) Z.; A.B., Nebr. Central Coll., 1942; M.A., U. Nebr., 1953; D.Litt., McKinley-Roosevelt Ednl. Inst., 1955; m. Dorothy Virginia Patrick, May 28, 1942; 1 dau., Shannon Elaine. Ordained to ministry Christian Ch., 1942; minister Christian chs., Brock, Nebr., 1941, Ulysses, Nebr., 1942-43, Elmwood, Nebr., 1943-47, Central City, Nebr., 1947-83, ret., 1983; rural tchr., Merrick County, Nebr., 1937-40; prin. Alvo (Nebr.) Consol. High Sch., 1943-47; supt. Archer (Nebr.) Pub. Schs., 1948-57; head dept. English and speech Central City (Nebr.) High Sch., 1957-63; supt. Marquette (Nebr.) Consol. Schs., 1963-79. Served as chaplain's asst. AUS, 1942. Mem. Internat. Platform Assn., Disciples of Christ Hist. Soc., Nat. Sch. Adminstrs. Assn. Club: Buffy. Home: 2730 North Rd Grand Island NE 68803

ZICK, LEONARD O., accountant, manufacturing executive, financial consultant; b. St. Joseph, Mich., Jan. 16, 1905; s. Otto J. and Hannah (Heyn) Z.; student Western State U., Kalamazoo; m. Anna Essig, June 27, 1925 (dec. May 1976); children—Rowene (Mrs. A. C. Neidow), Arlene (Mrs. Thomas Anton), Constance Mae (Mrs. Hilary Snell), Shirley Ann (Mrs. John Vander Ley) (dec.); m. 2d, Genevieve E. Zick, Nov. 3, 1977. Sr. ptnr. firm Zick, Campbell & Rose Accts., South Bend, Ind., 1928-48; sec.-treas. C. M. Hall Lamp Co., Detroit, 1948-51, pres. 1951-54, chmn. bd., 1954-56; pres., treas., dir. Allen Electric & Equipment Co. (now Allen Group, Inc.), Kalamazoo, 1954-57, pres., treas., dir. The Lithibar Co., Holland, Mich., 1957-61; fin. v.p., treas., dir. Crampton Mfg. Co., 1961-63; mgr. corp. fin. dept. Manley, Bennett, McDonald & Co., Detroit, 1963-68; mgr. Leonard O. Zick & Assos., Holland, 1968-87; dir. Eberhard's Foods, Inc., Grand Rapids. Former mem. Mich. Republican Central Com. Mem. Nat. Assn. Accts. (past nat. v.p., dir.), Mich. Self Insurers Assn. (past pres.), Fin. Execs. Inst., Stuart Cameron McLeod Soc. (past pres.). Lutheran. Clubs: Peninsular (Grand Rapids); Holland (Mich.) Country; Union League (Chgo.); Macawtawa Yacht; East Bay Country (Largo, Fla.). Winter Home: 1609 F-225 Country Club Dr Largo FL 33541 Summer Home: 99 W 11th St Holland MI 49423

ZIEBARTH, ROBERT CHARLES, mgmt. cons.; b. Evanston, Ill., Sept. 12, 1936; s. Charles A. and Marian (Miller) Z.; m. Patience Arnold Kirkpatrick, Aug. 28, 1971; children—Dana Kirkpatrick, Scott Kirkpatrick, Christopher, Nicholas. A.B., Princeton, 1958; M.B.A., Harvard, 1964. With Bell & Howell Co., Chgo., 1964—; treas., chief fin. officer Bell & Howell Co., 1969—; mgmt. cons. Ziebarth Co., 1973—; mem. dirs. adv. bd. Arkwright Boston Ins. Co.; dir. M.B.A. Resources, Inc., Telemedia, Inc. Asso. Community Renewal Soc., Citizens council Gateway House; mem. Ill. Bd. Higher Edn., Ill. Joint Edn. Commn.; Trustee Choate Sch., Latin Sch. Chgo.; bd. dirs. Harvard Bus. Sch. Fund, U.S.O., Inc., Chgo. Maternity Center, Prentice Women's Hosp. Served to lt. USNR, 1958-62. Mem. Naval Hist. Found., Art Inst. Chgo., Chgo. Hist. Soc., Mus. Modern Art. Presbyn. Clubs: Mid-Am. (Chgo.), Racquet (Chgo.), Saddle and Cycle (Chgo.), Economic (Chgo.), Executives (Chgo.). Office: 1500 Lake Shore Dr Chicago IL 60610

ZIEGER, RICHARD DUANE, optometrist; b. Anchorage, Mar. 19, 1950; s. George Edmund and Althea Mary (Phay) Z.; m. Katherine Ann Sheppard, Aug. 25, 1973; children: Kimber Lacey, Andrew Kinan. BA, Graceland Coll., Lamoni, Iowa, 1972; postgrad., Wash. State U., Pullman, 1972-74; OD, Pacific U., Forest Grove, Oreg., 1978. Pvt. practice optometry Lamoni, 1978—, Leon, Iowa, 1984—. Mem. Am. Optometric Assn., Iowa Optometric Assn., Optometric Extension Program, Lamoni C. of C., Leon (Iowa) C. of C., RLDS Med.-Dental Assn. Reorganized Ch. of Jesus Christ of Latter-day Saints. Lodge: Lions. Avocations: fishing, handcrafts. Home: Rural Rt 2 Box 18 Lamoni IA 50140 Office: 123 N Linden St Lamoni IA 50140

ZIEGLER, CHARLES LOUIS, dentist; b. Milw., Oct. 8, 1926; s. Walter F. and Ruth Elizabeth (Bernatz) Z.; m. Ingeborg Dorothy Kummerteldt, Sept. 12, 1953; children: Ann E., Kay L., Charles L. Jr., Nancy E., James W. DDS, Marquette U., 1951. Gen. practice dentistry Milw., 1951—; assoc. prof. Marquette U. Sch. Dentistry, Milw., 1953—. V.p. Library Bd., Hales Corners, Wis., 1976-78. Served to cpl. USAF, 1944-45. Fellow Internat. Coll. Dentists (Regent 1987—); mem. ADA, Am. Acad. Restorative Dentistry, Internat. Coll. Dentists (vice regent 1983-86), Am. Acad. of Crown & Bridge Prosthodontics (pres. 1975-76), Wis. Dental Assn. (pres. 1980-81), Milw. Dental Forum (pres. 1969-70), Wis. Gnathological Soc. (pres. 1971-72), Omicron Kappa Upsilon (pres. 1967-68, Disting. Alumnus 1981). Roman Catholic. Avocations: hunting, golf, tennis. Home: 11917 Indian Trail Hales Corner WI 53130 Office: 515 Glenview Ave Wauwatosa WI 53213

ZIEGLER, DAVE ALLAN, optometrist; b. Milw., Dec. 10, 1955; s. Vernon Oscar and Dorothy Elizabeth (Ochs) Ziegler; m. Barbara Jo Tite, July 30, 1984; children: Kristen Erica Tite-Ziegler, Lauren Ashley. BS, So. Calif. Coll. Optometry, 1980, OD, 1981. Pvt. practice optometry Greenfield, Wis., 1981—; chmn. GMVSS Continuing Edn., Greenfield, 1981—; clin. investigator Allergan Pharm., Greenfield, 1985—; adj. prof. So. Coll. Optometry, Memphis, 1986—; cons. EyeCare of Wis., Milw., 1985—. Contbr. articles to profl. jours. Named Outstanding Young Man Am., 1982; Corning scholar, 1981. Fellow Am. Acad. Optometry; mem. Am. Optometric Assn., Wis. Optometric Assn., Milw. Optometric Seminar Soc. Republican. Methodist. Avocations: sports, photography. Office: 10335 W Oklahoma Ave Greenfield WI 53227

ZIEGLER, LINDA FRANCES, accountant; b. Morristown, N.J., Apr. 24, 1960; d. Charles Edwin and Barbara June (DePuy) Rogers; m. Karl Robert Ziegler, May 26, 1984; 1 child, Julie Katherine. BS in Acctg., Case Western Res. U., 1982, M Acctg., 1983. CPA, Ohio. Tax cons., auditor Touche Ross, Cleve., 1983-85; fin. tax analyst Tremco, Inc., Cleve., 1985—. Office mgr., counselor Alzheimer's Disease and Related Disorders Assn., Cleve., 1982; mem. Alzheimer's Disease Assn., Cleve., 1982—, Cleve. World Trade Assn., 1983—. Mem. Am. Inst. CPA's, Ohio Soc. CPA's, Tax Club of Cleve., Beta Alpha Psi, Sigma Psi. Club: Toastmasters (Cleve.) (v.p. 1984-85). Avocations: jazz dance, sailing, flute, piano. Home: 19533 N Sagamore Fairview Park OH 44126 Office: Tremco Inc Cleveland OH 44126

ZIEMER, JOHN ROBERT, software engineer; b. Berkley, N.J., Jan. 25, 1939; s. John Ziemer Jr. and Doris Catherine (Taylor) Rife; m. Patricia Ann Gable, June 29, 1963 (div. Nov. 1979); children: Brian A., Gary R., Wendy S; m. Sue Hayden, Dec. 29, 1979; stepchildren: Loretta Sue Boggess, Tim Kent Boggess. Student, Trenton (N.J.) State U., 1964-65, Memphis State U., 1965, U. Mo., 1971, Florissant Valley (Mo.) U., 1973-78. Enlisted USN, 1957, resigned, 1967; simulation engr. Link-Flight Simulation, Birghamton, N.Y., 1967-69, Conductron Electronics, St. Louis, 1969-72; research programmer MacDonnal Douglas Research Lab, St. Louis, 1972-81; software engr. Mastercard Internat., St. Louis, 1981—. Mem. exec. council Boy Scouts Am., St. Louis, 1976-77. Club: St. Louis Area Computer. Lodge: Mason. Avocations: camping, scuba diving, sailing, flying. Home: 1285 Swallow Ln Florissant MO 63031

ZIENTY, FERDINAND BENJAMIN, chemical company research executive, consultant; b. Chgo., Mar. 21, 1915; s. Albert Frank and Rose Cecelia (Przypyszny) Z.; B.S., U. Ill., 1935; M.S., U. Mich., 1936, Ph.D., 1938; m. Claylain Lorraine Cawiezell, Apr. 14, 1945; children—Jane Zienty Wheeler, Donald Ferd. Research chemist organic chems. div. Monsanto Co., St. Louis, 1938-40, research group leader, 1940-47, asst. dir. research, 1947-50, asso. dir. research, 1950-56, dir. research, 1956-60, dir. advanced organic chems. research, 1960-64, mgr. research and devel., 1964-79, dir. chemistry bio med program, 1979-83, dir. research Health Care div., 1983, cons., 1983—, v.p. research George Lueders & Co. subs. Monsanto Co., St. Louis, 1968-70. Recipient Hodel, Saltiel, Hodel prize for scholarship, 1935, Sesquicentennial award U. Mich., 1967; Disting. Alumnus award U. Mich. Coll. Pharmacy, 1981. Fairchild scholar, 1935, Frederick Stearns fellow, 1936-37. Fellow AAAS, N.Y. Acad. Scis.; mem. Am. Chem. Soc., Am. Inst. Chem. Engrs., Am. Pharm. Assn., Inst. Food Technologists, Mo. Acad. Sci., Soc. Chem. Industry (London). Clubs: Triple A Country, Normandie Golf. Contbr. articles to profl. jours. Patentee in field. Home and Office: 850 Rampart Dr Warson Woods MO 63122

ZIERDT, MICHAEL LEE, data processing executive; b. Humboldt, Tenn., Aug. 20, 1948; s. John Graham and Elizabeth Lee (Mathews) Z.; m. DOnna Jean Pickerill. Feb. 13, 1982. BS, Purdue U., 1971; MBA, Ind. U., 1979. Sr. programmer Inland Container Corp., Indpls., 1974-77; lead programmer Ind. U., Indpls., 1977-79, cons., 1979-80; sr. supr. MIS Allison Gas Turbine,

Indpls., 1980-84; supr. Electronic Data Systems, Indpls., 1984—. Served to 2d lt. U.S. Army, 1971. Mem. Am. Production and Inventory Control Soc., Delta Upsilon. CLub: Riveria (Indpsl.). Home: 5815 N New Jersey Indianapolis IN 46220 Office: Electronic Data Systems PO Box 420 Indianapolis IN 46206

ZIETH, RANDALL LEE, optometrist; b. Kenosha, Wis., June 16, 1952; s. Raymond and Jayne (Johansen) Z.; m. Gwyenda Teleane Vincent, June 8, 1979; one child, Caroline Reynolds Zieth. Student U. Wis.-Parkside, 1971-72; O.D., Ill. Coll. Optometry, 1972. Lic. optometrist. Resident Gesell Inst. Child Devel., New Haven, 1976-77; assoc. in pvt. practice of optometry, Watertown, Wis., Kenosha, 1978-79; gen. practice optometry, Ripon, Wis., 1979—. Chmn. United Way, Ripon, 1980. E.B. Alexander fellow Optometry Extension, Yale, U., 1977; recipient Vision Therapy Splty. award Ill. Coll. Optometry, 1976; Key Man award Ripon Jaycees, 1982. Mem. Optometric Extension Program (bd. dirs.), Wis. Optometric Assn., Am. Optometric Assn., Lake Winnebago Optometric Soc. (pres.), Coll. Optometrists for Vision Devel. (assoc.), Better Vision Inst. Lutheran. Lodges: Lions (dir. Ripon club 1983), Rotary (bd. dirs.). Avocations: karate; tennis; hunting; fishing. Home: 117 Howard St Ripon WI 54971

ZIK, JOHN JOSEPH, mechanical engineer; b. Two Rivers, Wis., Sept. 30, 1956; s. Florian Jerome and Dorothy Francis (Hunsader) Z. BS in Mech. Engring., U. Wis., 1978, MS in Mech. Engring., 1982. Licensed profl. engr., Mich. Prodn., design engr. Modine Mfg. Co., Racine, Wis., 1979-80; sr. engr. GMF Robotics Corp., Troy, Mich., 1982-86; academic staff engr. Wis. Ctr. Space Automation and Robots, Madison, 1987—. Inventor Self-Guided Welding Machine. Mem. Soc. Mfg. Engrs., Wis. Alumnus Club. Roman Catholic. Avocations: scuba diving, skiing, piano playing, reading. Office: Wis Ctr Space Automation & Robots 1357 University Ave Madison WI 53706

ZIKMUND, DOUGLAS BRUCE, pharmacist, farm owner; b. Astoria, Oreg., Apr. 10, 1945; s. Lloyd Donald and Patricia Ruth (Strong) Z.; m. Carol Joan Leininger, May 28, 1967. Student Kearney State Coll., 1964-66, U. Nebr., 1973-76, B.S. in Pharmacy, 1978. Registered pharmacist. Pharmacy intern Bradfield Drug, Lincoln, Nebr., 1974-76; pharmacist Alexander's Pharmacy, Norfolk, Nebr., 1978-79; pharmacist, owner Blevin's Drive-in Pharmacy, Columbus, Nebr., 1979—; vice chmn. Nebr. Pharmacists Polit. Action Com., Lincoln, 1981-85, chmn. 1985—. Served with USN, 1966-73, with res., 1973—. Mem. Nebr. Pharmacists Assn. (bd. dirs. 1981-85, pres. 1983-84), Nat. Assn. Retail Druggists, U. Nebr. Alumni Assn., VFW, Am. Legion. Democrat. Methodist. Lodges: Eagles, Elks. Avocations: hunting; fishing; water skiing; farming. Home: 107 S Calle Colombo Columbus NE 68601 Office: Blevins Drive-in Pharmacy 1461 28th Ave Columbus NE 68601

ZIMMER, JOHN HERMAN, lawyer; b. Sioux Falls, S.D., Dec. 30, 1922; s. John Francis and Veronica (Berke) Z.; student Augustana Coll., Sioux Falls, 1941-42, Mont. State Coll., 1943; LL.B., U. S.D., 1948; m. Deanna Langner, 1976; children by previous marriage—June, Mary Zimmer Levene, Robert Joseph, Judith Maureen Zimmer Rose. Bar: S.D. 1948. Practice law, Turner County, S.D., 1948—; ptnr. Zimmer & Duncan, Parker, S.D.; states atty. Turner County, 1955-58, 62-64; asst. prof. med. jurisprudence U. S.D.; minority counsel S.D. Senate Armed Services Com. on Strategic and Critical Materials Investigation, 1962-63; chmn. Southeastern Council Govts., 1973-75; mem. U. S.D. Law Sch. adv. council, 1973-74. Chmn. Turner County Rep. Com., 1955-56; mem. S.D. Rep. adv. com., 1959-60; alt. del. Rep. Nat. Conv., 1968; pres. S.D. Easter Seal Soc., 1986-87. Served with AUS, 1943-46; PTO. Decorated Bronze Star, Philippine Liberation ribbon. Mem. ABA, Fed., S.D. (commr. 1954-57) Bar Assns., Assn. Trial Lawyers Am., S.D. Trial Lawyers Assn. (pres. 1967-68), VFW, Am. Legion, Phi Delta Phi. Lodges: Elks, Shriners. Home: Rural Rt Parker SD 57053 Office: Zimmer & Duncan Law Bldg PO Box 547 Parker SD 57053

ZIMMER, MARY JO, pediatrician; b. Milw., Mar. 19, 1955; d. Joseph John and Alberta (Pyzyk) Z. BS, U. Wis., Milw., 1977; MD, U. Wis., Madison, 1981. Diplomate Am. Bd. Pediatrics. Intern in pediatrics Children's Hosp. Med. Ctr., Cin., 1981-82, resident in pediatrics, 1982-84, 1981-84; pediatrician Milw. Med. Clinic, 1984—. Speaker Woman to Woman Conf., Milw., 1985, vol., 1986. Fellow Am. Acad. Pediatrics; mem. Milw. Pediatric Soc., Phi Beta Kappa. Roman Catholic. Avocations: swimming, skiing, piano, cooking, traveling. Office: Milw Med Clinic 3003 W Good Hope Rd Milwaukee WI 53217

ZIMMER, RICHARD PAUL, controller; b. Detroit, July 19, 1945; s. Henry and Vera Isabel (Kouach) Z.; m. Susan Jane Scott, 1967 (div. Jan. 1978); 1 child, Wendy Sue; m. Andrea Kallman, Sept. 5, 1979. CPA, Mich. Jr. acct. Alexander Grant, CPA, Kalamazoo, 1967-69; supr. J.K. Lasser & Co, CPA's, Southfield, Mich., 1969-73; corp. controller Active Tool Mfg. Co., Roseville, Mich., 1973—. Mem. Nat. Assn. CPA's, Am. Inst. CPA's, Mich. Assn. CPA's. Republican. Club: Detroit Athletic. Avocations: golf, stained glass, woodworking. Office: Active Tool & Mfg Co 32901 Gratiot Roseville MI 48066

ZIMMERMAN, CRAIG ARTHUR, biology educator; b. Painesville, Ohio, Mar. 22, 1937; s. Ralph William and Rachel Albina (Gray) Z.; m. Jane Dean. June 17, 1962; children: Dean Arthur, Rachel Anne. BS, Baldwin-Wallace Coll., 1960; MS in Zoology, U. Mich., 1962, MS in Botany, 1964, PhD in Botany, 1969. Teaching fellow U. Mich., Ann Arbor, 1960-67; instr. biology Ctr. Coll. Ky., Danville, 1967-69, asst. prof. biology, 1969-74; researcher environ. Spindletop Research, Georgetown, Ky., 1974-75; assoc. prof. biology Aurora (Ill.) U., 1975-80, prof. biology, 1980—. Contbr. articles to profl. jours. Clk. Presbyn. Ch. Session, Georgetown, 1975, 79-81, 83-85; chmn. fellowship Community Presbyn. Ch. Session, Aurora, 1979-81, chmn. edn., 1983-85; chmn. fin. Boy Scouts Am., Aurora, 1983-85; pres. West Aurora Band Boosters, 1987—; mem. Fox Valley Symphony Orch., Aurora Summer Concert Band, 1983—. Mem. Am. Inst. Biol. Sci., Ecol. Soc. Am., Associated Colls. Chgo. Area., Sigma Xi. Home: 123 S Commonwealth Ave Aurora IL 60506 Office: Aurora U 347 S Gladstone Aurora IL 60506

ZIMMERMAN, DELANO ELMER, physician; b. Fond du Lac, Wis., Mar. 21, 1933; s. Elmer Herbert and Agatha Angeline (Freund) Z.; m. Nancy Margaret Garry, Aug. 13, 1966; children: Kate, Joseph, Nick. BS, U. Wis., 1961, MD, 1965. Intern, Hennepin County Hosp., Mpls., 1965; physician, surgeon Winnebago (Wis.) State Hosp., 1966-67; gen. practice medicine, Neenah, Wis., 1967-73; emergency room physician Community Emergency Services, Appleton, 1973-77, Meml. Med. Center, Springfield, Ill., 1977—; faculty So. Ill. U. Sch. Medicine, Springfield, 1977—. Served with USN, 1951-56. Mem. Am. Coll. Emergency Physicians, Soc. Tchrs. Emergency Medicine, Univ. Assn. for Emergency Medicine. Roman Catholic. Home: 1404 S Park Ave Springfield IL 62704 Office: Meml Med Center 800 N Rutledge Springfield IL 62781

ZIMMERMAN, DENNIS JAMES, sales professional; b. Lima, Ohio, Oct. 16, 1955; s. Clarence Andrew and Neva Joyce (Clevenger) Z. BA, Mt. Vernon Nazarene Coll., 1982. Salesman Musicland, Lima, Ohio, 1974-76, Fuller Brush, Inc., Lima, Ohio, 1976; sales rep. Cher-Beli Creations, Inc., Memphis, 1982-84; sales agt. Combined Ins. Co. Am., Chgo., 1984; sales rep. Newton Mfg. Co., Newton, Iowa, 1983—. Named one of Outstanding Young Men Am., Montgomery, 1985. Republican. Mem. United Brethren in Christ. Home: 14220 Leis Rd Spencerville OH 45887

ZIMMERMAN, FRANCES ADDIE HOWELL, government official, business and employment consultant; b. Kansas City, Mo., Oct. 10; d. Dewey J. and Louise Frances (Wydick) Howell; Asso. Degree, Park Coll., Parkville, Mo., 1944; student Rockhurst Coll., 1970, U. Mo., Kansas City, 1972, U. Mich., 1976, 77, U. Houston, 1977, U. Kans., 1979; m. Eugene R. Zimmerman, Aug. 10, 1945 (dec. Nov. 1982); children—Donald, Nancy Zimmerman Giller, Robert J., Laura. Dir. public relations program, county organizer Am. Cancer Soc., Kansas City, Mo., 1959-60; public relations Mo. Employment Service, 1962-75; instr., art dir. Regional Tng. Center, U.S. Dept. Labor, Overland Park, Kans., 1975-80, public relations and employer com. coordinator, Kansas, Mo., 1980—; instr. Mo. Div. Employment Security, 1983—, Johnson County Community coll.; cons. in field. Pres., Scarritt Sch. PTA, 1950; bd. dirs. Shawnee Mission (Kans.) High Sch., 1960; v.p. Jefferson City Women's Polit. Caucus, 1983; mem. Mo. Commn. on Status of Women, 1983. Mem. Internat. Assn. Personnel (v.p. Mo. 1975, exec. bd. internat. award of merit Mo. 1975), Am. Soc. Trainers and Developers (charter mem. orgnl. devel. media div., program com.), Nat. Assn. Female Execs., Mid-Am. Soc. Assn. Execs., Nelson Gallery Art, Kansas City C. of C., Urban League Greater Kansas City, Personal Dynamics Assn., Park Coll. Alumni Assn. Art Dirs. Club Kansas City, Nelson Gallery Art Soc. Baptist. Clubs: Kansas City Art Dirs., Overland Park Lioness. Lodge: Soroptimist. Home: 10568 Century Ln Overland Park KS 66215

ZIMMERMAN, FRANK RAYWORTH, communications executive; b. Ypsilanti, Mich., Aug. 22, 1931; s. Frank B. and Hazel (Rayworth) Z.; m. Barbara Faye Marie Kellogg, June 30, 1951; children: Deborah, Paul, Judith, John. BS, Ea. Mich. U., 1955. Mgr. traffic Mich. Bell Telephone Co., Detroit, 1955-74, gen. mgr. operator services, 1974-76, asst. v.p. revenues, 1976-78, v.p. pub. relations/revenues, 1978-83, exec. v.p., chief operating officer, 1983; sr. v.p. corp. affairs Ameritech, Chgo., 1983-87; pres., chief exec. officer, Ill. Bell Telephone Co., Chgo., 1987—, also bd. dirs.; bd. dirs. NCCJ, Dearborn Park, Ill. Prin. Chgo. United, 1987—; mem. bus. adv. council Chgo. Urban League, 1987—; bd. dirs. NCCJ, 1985—, Protestant Found. of Greater Chgo., 1987—. Recipient Bronze award Jr. Achievement, Detroit, 1982, Silver award, 1983, Disting. Alumnus award Ea. Mich. U., 1986. Republican. Methodist. Avocations: swimming, boating. Office: Ill Bell 225 W Randolph St Chicago IL 60606

ZIMMERMAN, HELENE LORETTA, business educator; b. Rochester, N.Y., Feb. 26, 1933; d. Henry Charles and Loretta Catherine (Hobert) Z. BS, SUNY, Albany, 1953, MS, 1959; PhD, U. N.D., 1969. Cert. records mgr. Bus. tchr., chmn. bus. dept. Williamson Cen. Sch., Williamson, N.Y., 1953-69; asst. prof. U. Ky., Lexington, 1969-70; prof. bus. Cen. MIch. U., Mt. Pleasant, 1970—. Author General Business, 1977; contbg. author to records mgmt. text book, 1987. Sec. Isabella County Christmas Outreach, Mt. Pleasant, 1983-87. Mem. Assn. Records Mgrs. and Adminstrn., Inst. Cert. Records Mgrs. (sec. 1985—),Internat. Soc. Bus. Edn. (internat. v.p. Eng. speaking nations 1986—), Nat. Bus. Edn. Assn., Mich. Bus. Edn. Assn. (bd. dirs. 1985—, pres. 1987—), AAUW (pres. 1984-86), Delta Kappa Gamma (state pres. 1987—). Avocations: travel, crafts. Home: 1405 Lincoln Ct Mount Pleasant MI 48858 Office: Cen Mich U Grawn 308 Mount Pleasant MI 48859

ZIMMERMAN, JO ANN, lieutenant governor, nurse; b. Van Buren Twp., Iowa, Dec. 24, 1936; d. Russell and Hazel (Ward) McIntosh; m. A. Tom Zimmerman, Aug. 26, 1956; children: Andrew, Lisa, Don and Ron (twins), Beth. Diploma in Nursing, Broadlawns Sch. of Nursing, Des Moines, 1958; BA with honors, Drake U., 1973; postgrad., Iowa State U., 1973-74. RN, Iowa. Asst. head nurse maternity dept. Broadlawns Med. Ctr., Des Moines, 1958-59, weekend supr. nursing services, 1960-61, supr. maternity dept., 1966-68; instr. maternity nursing Broadlawns Sch. Nursing, Des Moines, 1966-68; health planner, community relations assoc. Iowa Health Systems Agy., Des Moines, 1978-82; mem. Iowa Ho. Reps., 1982-86; lt. gov. State of Iowa, 1986—. Contbr. articles to profl. jours. Mem. advanced registered nurse practitioner task force on cert. nurse midwives Iowa Bd. Nursing, 1980-81, Waukee, Polk County, Iowa Health Edn. Coordinating Council, Iowa Women's Caucus, Dallas County Women's Polit. Caucus; chmn. Des Moines Area Maternity Nursing Conf. Group, 1969-70, task force on sch. health services Iowa Dept. Health, 1982, task force health edn. Iowa Dept. Pub. Instruction, 1979, adv. com. health edn. assessment tool, 1980-81, Nat. Lt. Govs. Conf. Task Force on Agrl. and Rural Devel.; co-chmn. Boone Twp. Dems., 1974-79, Dallas County Cen. Com., 1982—; bd. dirs. Iowa PTA, 1979-83, chairperson, 1980-84; bd. dirs. Waukee Community Sch. Bd., 1976-79, pres., 1978-79. Mem. Am. Nursing Assn., Iowa Nurses Assn., Iowa League for Nursing (bd. dirs. 1979-83), Family Centered Childbirth Edn. Assn. (childbirth instr., advisor), LWV, Met. Des Moines LWV (health chmn.). Mem. Christian Ch. Avocations: gardening, sewing, reading, bridge. Office: Office of Lt Gov State Capitol Bldg Des Moines IA 50319

ZIMMERMAN, JOHN MICHAEL, archivist; b. Toledo, Nov. 7, 1940; s. Ronald L. and Lillian S. (Wojiechowski) Z.; m. Dorothy Claire Uhl, Aug. 26, 1972; children: Todd Michael, Thomas Mathew, Timothy Martin. Grad. high sch., Toledo. Typesetter Owens-Ill., Toledo, 1960-68, camera operator, 1968-70, microfilm leader, 1970-78, supr. records operation, 1978-84; gen. mgr. Leonard Archives, Inc., Toledo, 1984—. Mem. Nat. Microfilm Assn. (bd. dirs. Ohio chpt. 1973, treas. 1974, sec. 1975), Am. Record Mgrs. Adminstrs. (pres. 1985-68, Mem. of Yr. Toledo chpt. 1986). Lodge: Rotary. Avocations: theatre musicals, photography. Home: 6905 S Ridgewood Dr Lambertville MI 48144 Office: Leonard Archives Inc 324 Chestnut St Toledo OH 43604

ZIMMERMAN, MARTIN JOHN, manufacturing company administrator; b. Chgo., Jan. 6, 1957; s. William Henry and Adelaide (Bolger) Z.; m. Barbara Clare Tate, Nov. 5, 1983; 1 child, John L. Gaudi III. BS, Bradley U., 1979. Design engr. Allis-Chalmers Corp., Matteson, Ill., 1979-81; field service engr. Machinery Dist., Elk Grove, Ill., 1981-84; service tng. instr. Nissan Motor Corp., Hinsdale, Ill., 1984-85; ter. sales mgr. Allen Test Products, Lombard, Ill., 1985-86; dist. service mgr. Robert Bosch Corp., Broadview, Ill., 1986—; speaker Midwest Tech. Tng. Ctr., Glen Ellyn, Ill., 1985—. Mem. Concerned Citizens for Rational Traffic Laws, Palatine, Ill., 1986. Mem. Soc. Automotive Engrs., Soc. Automotive Testers (editor The Tester 1986—), Sports Car Club Am. Roman Catholic. Avocations: race car driving, photography, reading. Home: 1044 E Fosket Palatine IL 60067 Office: Robert Bosch Corp 2800 S 25th Ave Broadview IL 60153

ZIMMERMAN, MICHAEL JAY, dentist; b. Columbus, Ohio, Jan. 22, 1943; s. Joseph Abraham and Esther Edith (Cooper) Z. m. Sydell Renee Feld, Aug. 21, 1966; 1 child, Jennifer Sue. BA, Ohio State U., 1964, DDS, 1968. Gen. practice dentistry Columbus, Ohio, 1968—. Served to lt. USN, 1968-70. Mem. ADA, Acad. Gen. Dentistry, Ohio Dental Assn., Columbus Dental Soc., Alpha Omega. Jewish. Avocations: golf, racquetball. Home: 6194 Peachtree Rd Columbus OH 43213 Office: 5320 E Main St Columbus OH 43213

ZIMMERMAN, NAOMA GIBSTINE, family therapist; b. St. Louis, Aug. 2, 1914; d. Samuel and Sadie (Cohen) Gibstine; married; children: Ann Russell, Frank. BS, U. Chgo., 1935, MSW, 1940. cert. social worker. Social worker Jewish Children's Bur., Chgo., 1937-41; family therapist Family Service South Lake County, Highland Park, Ill., 1958—; mem. summer faculty U. Chgo., 1967-71; lectr., cons. family therapy various locations, 1969—. Author: Sleepy Forest, 1943, Sleepy Village, 1943, Corky in Orbit, 1962. Mem. Nat. Assn. Social Work, Am. Orthopsychiat. Assn. Avocation: archeology. Home: 465 Drexel Glencoe IL 60022 Office: Family Service S Lake County 777 Central Ave Highland Park IL 60035

ZIMMERMAN, RAYMOND DALE, mechanical engineer, business executive; b. East Cleveland, Ohio, June 24, 1949; s. Julius Eugene and Shirley Ione (Carter) Z.; student math. Case Inst. Tech., 1966; B.S. cum laude in Mech. Engring. (scholar), U. Cin., 1972, M.S., 1978, postgrad., 1978-81. Engring. trainee Arthur G. McKee & Co., Independence, Ohio, 1968-71; project engr. Structural Dynamics Research Corp., Milford, Ohio, 1972-73, mem. tech. staff, 1973-76; research asst. U. Cin., 1976-81; exec. v.p. Quixote Measurement Dynamics, Inc., Cin., 1981-82, chmn. bd., 1981—, pres., 1982—; cons. engr., 1976—; lectr. modal analysis U. Cin., 1977—. Active Big Bros. Am., 1979-82. Structural Dynamics Research Corp. study grantee, 1976-77; Foundry Ednl. Found. grantee, 1969-71. Mem. ASME (tech. reviewer div. dynamic systems and control 1980—), Soc. Exptl. Mechanics, Sigma Xi. Contbr. articles to profl. publs. Office: PO Box 19299 Cincinnati OH 45219

ZIMMERMAN, RICHARD CARL, psychiatrist; b. Appleton, Wis., Jan. 21, 1932; s. Lawrence William and Lucille Dorothy (Risse) Z.; m. Kathleen Ancilla Dennis, Dec. 27, 1961; children: Jennifer, Beth Anne, Brian, Rebecca, Timothy, Anthony, Martha. BA cum laude, St. Felix Sem., Huntington, Ind., 1958; MD, Marquette U., 1966. Diplomate Am. Bd. Psychiatry and Neurology. Intern St. Joseph's Hosp., Milw., 1966-67; resident psychiatrist VA Hosp., Wood, Wis., 1967, Milw. Psychiat. Hosp., 1967-69; resident psychiatrist Milw. Children's Hosp., 1969-71, staff psychiatrist, 1971; practice medicine specializing in psychiatry Menomonee Falls, Wis., 1972—. Served to capt. USNR, 1977—. Fellow Am. Acad. Child and Adolescent Psychiatry; mem. Am. Psychiat. Assn., Waukesha County Med. Soc. (pres. 1983-84), Assn. Mil. Surgeons of U.S. (life), Reserve Officers Assn. (life). Republican. Roman Catholic. Office: N89 W16785 Appleton Ave Menomonee Falls WI 53051

ZIMMERMAN, ROBERT RAYMOND, management consultant; b. N.Y.C., Jan. 24, 1919; s. Isador and Nettie (Shulman) Z.; m. Helen Eugenie Sperry, Oct. 8, 1949; children—Laurence Irving, Marc Sperry. B.A. in Econs. and Indsl. Psychology, U. Minn., 1941; M.B.A. with honors in Indsl. Relations, U. Chgo., 1947. Indsl. relations mgr. Continental Can Co., Chgo., 1948-54; personnel and orgn. planning cons. to sr. assoc. Booz, Allen & Hamilton, Chgo., 1954-65; personnel v.p. Sanger Harris Dept. Store, Dallas, 1965-66; operating v.p. orgn. and key manpower planning Federated Dept. Stores, Cin., 1966-79; sr. v.p. human resources Central Bancorp., Cin., 1979-84; pres. Zimmerman Cons., Inc., also sr. v.p. Schonberg Assocs., Inc., 1984—; former lectr. mgmt. and orgn. planning Indsl. Relations Ctr. of U. Chgo.; lectr., forum leader Am. Mgmt. Assn., Conf. Bd.; mem. Orgn. Planning Council, Conf. Bd., 1975-79. Bd. dirs. South Suburban Mental Health and Family Counseling Service, Ill., 1960-65. Served to capt. Adj. Gen. Dept., U.S. Army, 1941-46. Mem. Beta Gamma Sigma. Club: Indian Hill (Ohio). Author: Auditing the Organization Structure, 1965. Office: Zimmerman Cons Inc 6340 Miami Rd Cincinnati OH 45243 Office: Schonberg Assocs Inc 1527 Madison Rd Cincinnati OH 45206

ZIMMERMAN, RUSSELL RICHARD, aerospace executive; b. Pitts., Oct. 12, 1942; s. Elwood Booth and Lois Hileman (Shultz) Z. BS, Rochester Inst. Tech., 1965. Engr. Data Corp., Dayton, 1965-67; mgr. precision lab. Data Corp., Manned Spacecraft Ctr., Tex., 1967-71; mgr. photographic engring. Mead Tech. Labs., Dayton, 1971-76, div. dir. imaging scis., 1976-78, v.p. imaging systems, 1978-81; v.p., gen. mgr. MTL Systems, Inc., Dayton, 1981—, also bd. dirs.; cons. NASA, Houston, 1967-75, USAF, Dayton, 1971—. Contbr. various tech. papers and articles to profl. jour. Mem. Soc. Photographic Scis. and Engrs., Am. Soc Photogrammetry and Remote Sensing. Methodist. Club: Engineers. Avocations: gourmet cooking, fine wines, climbing, classical music. Home: 415 N Park Pl Yellow Springs OH 45387

ZIMMERMAN, SHARON KAY, accountant; b. Peoria, Ill., Mar. 28, 1958; s. Bobby Lee Zimmerman and Beverly Darlene Lalicker. BS in Acctg., Ill. State U., 1981. CPA, Ill. Auditor State Farm Ins., Bloomington, Ill., 1981-84, acctg. and statistical analyst, 1984-87, rep. personnel employment, 1987—. Vol. re-election com. Thompson for Gov., Bloomington, 1986. Mem. Cen. Ill. CPA Soc. Republican. Presbyterian. Club: Toastmasters (Bloomington) (treas. 1987—). Avocations: tennis, golf. Home: 1008 Arlene Ct #8 Bloomington IL 61701 Office: State Farm Ins Cos 1 State Farm Plaza A-1 Bloomington IL 61701

ZIMMERMAN, SHERWOOD NELSON, state health official; b. Lynchburg, Va., Sept. 9, 1939; s. Hubert Thomas and Joyce Wentworth (Beasley) Z.; m. Patricia Ann Walker, Feb. 23, 1962; children: Sherrie Lynn, Sherwood Nelson II. BA, Lynchburg Coll., 1964. With USPHS, 1964-86; assigned to Va. State Health Dept., 1964-65, Norfolk City Health Dept., 1965-67, Ky. State Health Dept., 1967-68, Dallas City Health Dept., 1968-69, Tex. State Health Dept., 1969-71, Minn. Dept. Pub. Health, 1971-75, Ill. Dept. Pub. Health, 1975-86; with Ill. Dept. Pub. Health, Springfield, 1986—; Mem. Gov.'s Alzheimer's Disease Task force, Ill., 1986—, Ill. Diabetes Adv. Council, Springfield, 1986—, numerous other adv. bds. and coms. Trustee Village of Sherman, Ill., 1976-78, pres., 1978—, chief of police, 1978—. Served as cpl., USMC, 1957-60. Mem. Am. Pub. Health Assn., Ill. Pub. Health Assn. Baptist. Club: Nighthawks Dance (Springfield) (sec.-treas. 1986-87, pres. 1987—). Lodge: Lions (1st v.p. Frankfort, Ky., 1967). Avocations: music, boating, travel. Home: 504 Radford Dr Sherman IL 62684 Office: Ill Dept Pub Health 535 W Jefferson Springfield IL 62761

ZIMMERMAN, STEPHEN HARLEY, management consultant; b. Decatur, Ind., Oct. 17, 1941; s. Gerald Vincent and Mary Elizabeth (Pierson) Z.; m. Susan Jane Boyle, Oct. 16, 1965; children—Andrea Diane, Christopher David, Scott Nichols. Student, Purdue U., 1960-64; B.S. in Indsl. Mgmt., Ind. U., 1975. Mfg. systems staff Internat. Harvester, Fort Wayne, Ind., 1965-70; data processing mgr. Allen County, Fort Wayne, 1970-75; mgr. info. systems Zollner Corp., Fort Wayne, 1975-80, prodn. mgr., 1980-83; mgr. prodn. ops., 1983-86; pres. Stephen H. Zimmerman & Assocs., 1986— ; educator-cons. Warner Gear, Auburn, Ind., 1983. Designer plantwide mfg. systems. Mem. Fort Wayne Jaycees (bd. dirs. 1970-71, service award 1971), Common Computer Users Group (pres. 1975-77), Assn. Systems Mgmt. (pres. 1978-79, merit award 1983), Am. Prodn. and Inventory Control Soc. (pres. 1979-80), Soc. Automotive Engrs. Republican. Roman Catholic. Home and Office: 8205 Cha Ca Peta Pass Fort Wayne IN 46825 Office: Zollner Corp 2425 Coliseum Blvd S Fort Wayne IN 46803

ZIMMERMAN, TIM, manager infosystems; b. La Crosse, Kans., Jan. 14, 1953; s. Albert and Felicitas (Giebler) Z.; m. Janice Marie Mader, May 7, 1977; children: Jeffrey Galen, Kelley Dawn. BS in Bus. Data Processing, Ft. Hays U., 1976. Programmer Far Mar Co., Hutchinson, Kans., 1977-81; project leader Farmland Industries, Hutchinson, 1981-83; team leader 1st Data Resources, Omaha, 1983-84; project leader Pizza Hut, Inc., Wichita, Kans., 1984-85; mgr. pt. of sale computer systems Pizza Hut, Inc., Wichita, 1985—. Roman Catholic. Avocations: softball, basketball, music, home computers. Office: Pizza Hut Inc 9111 E Douglas Wichita KS 67207

ZIMMERMANN, GERHARDT, conductor; b. Van Wert, Ohio, June 22, 1945; s. Ervin and Ethel Jane (Allen) Z.; m. Sharon Marie Reher, Mar. 17, 1974; children—Anna Marie, Peter Karl Irum. B.Mus., Bowling Green State U.; M.F.A., U. Iowa; student, with James Dixon, Leopold Sipe, Flora Contino, Richard Lert. Tchr. in Genoa (Ohio) Pub. Schs., 1967-70; condr. orch. Augustana Coll., Rock Island, Ill., 1971-72; music dir. Clinton (Iowa) Symphony Orch., 1971-72; asst. prof. music, condr. orchs. Western Ill. U., Macomb, 1972-74; asst. condr. St. Louis Symphony Orch., 1974-78, assoc. condr., 1978-82; music dir., condr. St. Louis Youth Orch., 1975-82, Canton Symphony Orch., 1980—, N.C. Symphony Orch., Raleigh, 1982—; guest condr. Recipient (2d Prize Georg Solti Conducting Competition 1973). Mem. Am. Symphony Orch. League, Nat. Acad. Rec. Arts and Scis., Phi Mu Alpha Sinfonia. Office: NC Symphony Orch Meml Auditorium PO Box 28026 Raleigh NC 27611 Office: Canton Symphony Orch 1001 N Market Ave Canton OH 44702

ZIMMERMANN, ROBERT LAURENCE, marketing professional; b. Mpls., Jan. 1, 1932; s. Lawrence and Bertha Mabel (Foss) Z. BA, U. Minn., 1954, MA, 1965, PhD, 1970. Asst. prof. psychology U. Winnepeg, Man., Can., 1968-69; research assoc. psychiatry research unit U. Minn., Mpls., 1969-75; sr. scientist biometrics lab. George Washington U., Washington, 1975-76; pvt. cons. research design and data analysis Mpls., 1976-84; sr. research mgr. Maritz Market Research, Mpls., 1984—; clin. asst. prof. psychiatry dept. U. Minn., Mpls., 1976—; external rev. officerFDA, Washington, 1974-77. Contbr. numerous articles to profl. jours. Fellow NIMH, 1958, 61, 69-71; merit fellow State of Minn. Mem. AAAS, Am. Psychol. Assn. Democrat. Avocation: writing. Home: 1920 S First St #1104 Minneapolis MN 55454 Office: Maritz Market Research Inc 7200 France Ave S Minneapolis MN 55435

ZINCHOOK, DENNIS, advertising executive; b. Detroit, May 8, 1950; s. Walter and Helen (Scherba) Z.; m. Janice Siegel, Aug. 25, 1973. BBA, Western Mich. U., Kalamazoo, 1972. Mailroom B.B.D.O. Advt., Detroit, 1972-73; account coordinator Kenyon & Eckhardt Advt., Dearborn, Mich., 1973-77, account exec., 1973-77; account supr. Desmond & Assocs. Advt., Oak Park, Mich., 1977-81; v.p. account services Simons, Michelson & Zieve Advt., Troy, Mich., 1981—. Mem. Adcraft Club Detroit, Walnut Lake Waterski Assn. (pres. 1982—). Club: Walnut Lake Boat (commodore West Bloomfield, Mich. club 1984—). Avocations: boating, waterskiing, windsurfing, hockey, racquetball. Home: 2360 Horseshoe Dr West Bloomfield MI 48033 Office: Simons Michelson Zieve Advt 3250 W Big Beaver Rd Troy MI 48084

ZINK, DAVID CHARLES, podiatrist; b. Scranton, Pa., Sept. 14, 1955; s. Charles George Jr. and Mary Elizabeth (Bosley) Z.; m. Shauna Marie Sullivan, May 22, 1981. BS, U. Pitts., 1977; D of Podiatric Medicine, Ohio Coll. Podiatric Medicine, Cleve., 1981. Resident foot surgery St. Mary Hosp., Phila., 1981-82; pvt. practice podiatric medicine Cin., 1982—; dir. podiatric medicine Longview Hosp., Cin., 1983—, W. End Health Ctr., Cin., 1984—. Mem. Am. Podiatric Med. Assn., Ohio Podiatric Med. Assn., Southern Ohio Acad. Podiatry. Republican. Methodist. Avocations: tennis, skiing, golf. Home: 5830 Squire Hill Ct Cincinnati OH 45241 Office: 11331 Springfield Pike Cincinnati OH 45246

ZINK, ESTHER LAUREL, librarian; b. Clearwater, Fla., Jan. 18, 1941; d. Lonnie Edward and Edith Gertrude (Dukes) Owens; m. David Charles Zink, Sept. 2, 1961; children: Melodee Laurel, Dale Craig. BS, Fla. So. Coll., 1966; MLS, U. Miss., 1971; BA, Trinity Bible Coll., 1984. Cert. tchr., Fla. Head librarian Mayport (Fla.) Elem. Sch., 1967-69; head librariansch. pharmacy U. Miss., University, 1969-71; reference librarian Fla. Jr. Coll., Jacksonville, 1973-75; head librarian Trinity Bible Coll., Ellendale, N.D., 1975—; team tchr. Trinity Bible Coll., Ellendale, 1974—; presenter seminar Strawberry Lake Christian Retreat, Omega, Minn.; speaker ladies retreat Assemblies of God Chs., N.D., S.D., Minn., 1981—; team mem. library evaluation visits Am. Assn. Bible Colls., 1985-86, 86-87, presentor workshop ann. conv., 1986. Recipient Cert. of Bravery award Jacksonville Insurors Assn. and Jacksonville Fire Prevention Commn., 1967, Tchr. of Yr. award Duval County Sch. System, Mayport, 1973. Mem. ALA, Am. Theol. Library Assn., Assn. Christian Librarians (presenter ann. conf. 1987), Mountain Plains Library Assn., N.D. Library Assn. Republican. Avocations: reading, studying, cooking. Office: Trinity Bible Coll Box 420 Ellendale ND 58436

ZINSER, GEORGE L., engineering company executive; b. Schofield, Wis., Apr. 29, 1934; s. Michael and Katherine (Kmiecik) Z.; m. MaryAnn Heeren, June 18, 1960; children: Debra, Brian, Kevin, Jason. BS in Engring., Milw. Sch. Engring. Engr. Gehl Bros., West Bend, Wis., 1961-62, Tomahawk (Wis.) Boat Co., 1962-67; owner, pres. GPI Corp., Schofield, 1967—. Served with U.S. Army, 1957. Home: 2525 Weston Ave Schofield WI 54476 Office: GPI Corp PO Box 96 101 Northern Rd Schofield WI 54476

ZINSER, RICHARD WILLIAM, employee relations manager; b. Detroit, Feb. 4, 1954; s. Donald Charles and Lucille (Oswald) Z.; m. Sharon Ann Czech, Oct. 2, 1976; children: Julia, Christa, Michael. BA, Oakland U., 1976, MA, 1978; MA, Western Mich. U., 1982, postgrad. in Counseling and Personnel, 1987—. Productivity coordinator plastics div. Lear Siegler Inc, Mendon, Mich., 1982-85, tng. mgr., 1985-87; mgr. employee relations Fabri-Kal Corp., Kalamazoo, 1987—. Officer City of Portage Environ. Bd., 1980. Mem. Am. Soc. Tng. and Devel., Nat. Assn. Suggestion Systems (Performance Excellance award 1983). Avocations: stained glass, golf. Home: 1220 Woodview Portage MI 49002 Office: Fabri-Kal Corp 3303 E Cork St Kalamazoo MI 49001

ZIPSER, BURTON ALLEN, music administrator, educator; b. Cleve., Jan. 1, 1934; s. Samuel Richberger and Louise (Handelman) Z; m. Sandra Diane Cott, June 15, 1958; children: Brice, Karl, Saul, Neal. MusB, U. So. Calif., 1956; MA, Calif. State U., Los Angeles, 1965. Cert. tchr., Mich., N.Y. Tchr. Phila. Pub. Schs., 1958-59; tchr., dept. head Los Angeles County Pub. Schs., 1959-65, Oakland County Pub. Schs., 1965-73; mem. faculty Ball State U., Muncie, Ind., 1973-75; adminstr. Mich. Sinfonietta, Oak Park, 1977—; chmn. bd. S.E.M.O.R., Oak Park, 1977—. Contbr. articles to profl. jours. Pres. Soc. of Arts, Warren, Mich., 1972-73; founder Intercommunity Arts Council, West Covina, Calif., 1963. Mem. Nat. Band Assn. (state chmn. Mich. 1970-71), Nat. Assn. Jazz Educators (state chmn. Mich. 1971-72), Music Educators Nat. Conf., Am. Choral Dirs. Assn., Am. Symphony Orch. League, Conductors Guild. Jewish. Avocations: collecting stamps and coins, travel, camping, gourmet cooking, sports coaching. Home: 23451 Roanoke Oak Park MI 48237

ZIPSER, LARRY LOUIS, podiatrist; b. Columbus, Ohio, Feb. 15, 1940; s. Aladar and Bess (Gurwin) Z.; m. Jeanne Henkin, June 23, 1963; children: Marc A., Kathy Ellyn, Wendy Beth. Student, Ohio State U., 1958-59, Case Western Reserve U., Cleve., 1959; D of Podiatric Medicine, Ohio Coll. Podiatry, Cleve., 1963. Diplomate Nat. Bd. Podiatry. Intern Ohio Coll. Podiatry, Cleve., 1963-64; pvt. practice podiatry Columbus, 1964—; instr. coastal and celestial navigation The Ohio State U.,. Republican. Jewish. Clubs: U.S. Power Squadron, Bay Point Yacht. Avocations: yachting, ocean sailing. Office: 21 E State St #500 Columbus OH 43215

ZIRKEL, KIP, psychologist, consultant; b. Conn., Nov. 18, 1944; s. Clifford H. Zirkel Jr. and Sue Joe (Roberts) Northington; married. BA, U. Tex., 1967; ThM, Perkins Sch. Theology, 1970; MA, Ohio State U., 1973, PhD, 1975. Lic. psychologist, Wis. Staff psychologist Meml. U. Nfld., St. John's, Can., 1974-76; sr. staff psychologist U. Wis., La Crosse, 1976—; cons. psychologist Human Devel. Assocs., La Crosse, 1984—; psychol. cons. Luth. Social Services, La Crosse, 1980—, Family and Children's Ctr., La Crosse, 1984—. Co-author: Teaching Stress Management and Relaxation Skills: An Instructor's Manual, 1985. Bd. dirs. United Campus Ministries, La Crosse, 1976-84. Mem. Am. Psychol. Assn., Biofeedback Soc. Am. (cert.), Biofeedback Soc. Wis. Avocations: bicycling, swimming, music. Home: 1610 Madison La Crosse WI 54601 Office: U Wis La Crosse WI 54601

ZISKOVSKY, JOSEPH PAUL, automation executive; b. San Diego, Sept. 4, 1947; s. Joseph Wencelaus and Bernice (Teresa) Z.; m. Betty Ann Galaska, Dec. 23, 1969; children: Mary Beth, Joey Michael, Betsy Ann, Michael Joseph. BS, Creighton U., 1969; MBA, St. Edwards U., 1978. Mktg. mgr. automation systems Texas Instruments, Austin, 1979-82; mgr. robotics Par div. GCA Corp, St. Paul, 1982-83, dir. STD products, 1983-85; div. mgr. Productivity Inc., Mpls., 1985—; cons. in field. Author: (with others) Handbook of Industrial Robots, 1985. Mem. Robotics Internat. (sr., chmn. 1984-86), Soc. Mfg. Engrs. (Pres. award 1984-85), Boy Scouts Am. (adult, com. chmn. 1985-86). Roman Catholic. Lodge: KC (treas. Cedar Park, Tex. 1981-82). Avocations: swimming, woodworking, computers, camping. Home: 4800 Kent St Shoreview MN 55126 Office: Productivity Inc 2750 Niagara Ln N Minneapolis MN 55441

ZISOOK, EDMOND NEWTON, architect; b. Chgo., Mar. 29, 1929; s. Harry Aron and Marian (Newton) Z.; m. Lois Joan Hirsh, Dec. 22, 1956; children: Ellen Lois, Amy Joan. BArch, Ill. Inst. Tech., 1950, MArch, 1952. Archtl. designer, draftsman Skidmore Owings & Merrill, Chgo., 1954-56; pvt. practice architecture Chgo., 1956—. Prin. works include Chgo. Health Clubs, 1973—, Vertical Club of N.Y., 1980, North Shore Club, 1982. Commr. Park Dist of Highland Park, Ill., 1973-79, pres., 1975-79. Served as sgt. AUS, 1952-54. Mem. AIA. Clubs: Standard (Chgo.); Waukegan Yacht. Lodges: Masons, Shriners. Avocations: Civil War history, sailing. Home: 773 Highland Pl Highland Park IL 60035 Office: 176 W Adams St Chicago IL 60603

ZISSER, STEVEN LAWRENCE, lawyer; b. Bklyn., Mar. 12, 1953; s. Roy L. and Thelma (Nirenberg) Z.; m. Mindie Pam Stern, June 3, 1979; 1 child, Rachel Heather. BA in Polit. Sci. and Econs., U. Rochester, 1975; JD, Union U., 1978; LLM in Taxation, Georgetown U., 1982. Bar: N.Y. 1979, U.S. Tax Ct. 1980, U.S. Dist. Ct. (ea. dist.) N.Y. 1981, Ohio 1983. Assoc. Brent, Phillips, Dranoff & Davis, Nanuet, N.Y., 1978-79; atty. estate tax IRS, Washington, 1979-83; assoc. Schottenstein, Zox & Dunn, Columbus, Ohio, 1983—; lectr. Ohio Legal Ctr. Inst., Columbus, 1985—. Author: Ohio Taxation, 1985; contbr. articles to profl. jours. Mem. ABA, Ohio Bar Assn., Columbus Bar Assn., Nat. Assn. Bond Lawyers. Democrat. Jewish. Lodge: B'nai B'rith. Home: 147 N Merkle Columbus OH 43209 Office: Schottenstein Zox & Dunn 41 S High St Columbus OH 43215

ZITNIK, RALPH STERLE, cardiologist, internist; b. Chgo., June 24, 1931; s. Charles and Marjorie (Allen) Z.; B.S., Georgetown U., 1953; M.D., Loyola U., Chgo., 1957; m. Ethel Margaret Ladd, June 15, 1957; children—Ralph J., John C. (dec.), Steven J. Intern, Little Company of Mary Hosp., Evergreen Park, Ill., 1957-58, dir. dept. cardiology, 1972—, sr. attending staff, 1972—; fellow in internal medicine Mayo Grad. Sch. Medicine, Rochester, Minn., 1958-62, asst. prof. internal medicine, 1969-72, dir. heart sta. and cardiac clinics, 1969-72, chmn. cardiac and cardiovascular facilities com., 1971-72; asst. in internal medicine Peter Bent Brigham Hosp., 1962-63; research asst. Harvard Med. Sch., 1962-63; mem. attending staff VA Research Hosp., 1963-65; mem. adj. staff Passavant Meml. Hosp., 1963-65; asst. attending staff Chgo. Wesley Meml. Hosp., 1963-65, asst. dir. heart sta., 1963-65; asso. internal medicine Northwestern U., 1962-63, dir. Cardiac Clinics, 1962-63, assoc. prof. medicine, 1986—; asso. clin. prof. medicine U. Chgo., 1972-73; pres. Chgo. Med. Computers, Inc., 1972—; asso. prof. medicine Rush U., Chgo., 1974-86 ; asso. attending staff Rush-Presbyn.-St. Luke's Hosp., Chgo., 1974-86 ; mem. courtesy attending staff Hinsdale (Ill.) Sanitarium and Hosp., 1974—;attending staff Northwestern Meml. Hosp., 1986—. cons. cardiology Palos Community Hosp., Palos Heights, Ill. Bd. dirs. Chgo. Architecture Found. Aux., 1984—. Diplomate Am. Bd. Internal Medicine, also sub-bd. Cardiovascular Disease. Fellow Am. Coll. Chest Physicians, Am. Coll. Cardiology, ACP, Inst. Medicine Chgo., Am. Heart Assn. Council on Clin. Cardiology; mem. Am. Fedn. Clin. Research, Central Soc. Clin. Research, Assn. Advancement Med. Instrumentation, AAAS, Am. Inst. Ultrasound in Medicine, AMA, Ill. State Med. Soc., Chgo. Med. Soc., South Suburban Heart Assn. (dir. 1974-79, pres. 1975) Chgo. Heart Assn. (dir. 1975—, pres. 1980). Roman Catholic. Clubs: Butterfield Country, Beverly Country, Mid-America. Contbr. articles to profl. jours. Office: 2800 W 95th St Evergreen Park IL 60642

ZITSMAN, ROBERT DALE, marketing professional; b. Springfield, Ohio, July 1, 1953; s. William B. Zitsman and Corinne N. (Degan) Mansfield; m. Cheryl Ileen Blankfeld, June 19, 1977; children: Sarah, Brent. BBA, Ohio State U., 1977; MBA, Wright State U., 1984. Sales rep. Lever Bros. Co., Cin., 1977-78; application engr. Elliott Co., Dayton, Ohio, 1978-81; sales rep. Price Bros. Co., Dayton, 1981-82; mktg. analyst Grandview Hosp., Dayton, 1984-85; dir. mktg. Alton (Ill.) Meml. Hosp., 1985-86, SSM Rehab. Inst., St. Louis, 1986—. Served with USAF, 1972-73. Mem. Acad. Health Service Mktg., Soc. Hosp. Planning and Mktg. Jewish. Avocations: gourmet cooking, photography, skiing, weight-training and conditioning. Home: 5802 Dogwood Ln Godfrey IL 62035 Office: SSM Rehab Inst 8000 Bonhomme Ave Suite 310 Saint Louis MO 63105

ZITZ, JON THEODORE, food broker, retired coffee company executive; b. Hammond, Ind., Sept. 5, 1914; s. John Theodore and Veronica (Nowicki) Z.; m. Mary Virginia Kubicek, Aug. 17, 1939 (dec. 1976); children—Jay, Diane Zitz Scaletta; m. 2d, Geraldine Weber, May 17, 1978; children—Margaret Duffy, Janet Dionne, Sue Duffy. B.A. cum laude, Yankton Coll., 1937; postgrad. Northwestern U., 1938-39. Sports editor Yankton Press & Dakotan (S.D.), 1935-38; asst. sales mgr. Nat. Stamping & Electric Works, Chgo., 1939-41; with Hill Shaw Co., Chgo., 1941-84, now v.p. Mem. Nat. Coffee Assn., Nat. Assn. Food Equipment Mfrs. Republican. Roman Catholic. Club: Park Ridge Country. Contbr. articles to industry related trade papers. Home: 914 S Chester Ave Park Ridge IL 60068 Office: 914 S Chester Ave Park Ridge IL 60068

ZITZNER, JOHN STANLEY, information management consultant; b. Glen Ridge, N.J., Mar. 26, 1955; s. Arthur Stewart and Theatrice (Hazard) Z.; m. Margaret Ingersoll, June 18, 1977; children: John Bradley, Kurt Gustav. BA in Bus., Wittenberg U., 1977. Salesman Moore Corp., Cleve., 1977-78, mgr., 1978-83; pres., sr. ptnr. Bradley Co., Cleve., 1983—; pres. Mardale Corp., Cleve., 1986—; owner Accurate Word Processing, Cleve., 1983—. Contbr. articles. to profl. jours. Mem. choir Fairmount Presbyn. Ch., Cleve., 1977—, deacon, 1980-83, ruling elder, 1983—. Recipient Spl. Vol. award ARC, 1981. Mem. Bus. Forms Mgmt. Assn. Club: Indian Guides (YMCA). Lodge: Rotary. Avocations: golf, travel, handball. Home: 1084 Dorsh Rd South Euclid OH 44121 Office: Bradley Co 5241 Wilson Mills Rd #24 Cleveland OH 44143

ZIV, FEDERIC WILLIAM, telecommunications educator, writer; b. Cin., Aug. 17, 1905; s. William and Rose (Silverglade) Z. J.D., U. Mich., 1928; Litt.D., Coll. Mt. St. Joseph, 1979. D. Performing Arts (hon.), U. Cin., 1985. Founder, producer Ziv Radio and TV Co. (sold to United Artists 1961), Cin., 1930-65; programs include: Bold Venture, 1951, Favorite Story, 1947; TV shows include: Cisco Kid, 1950, Highway Patrol, 1955, Sea Hunt, 1958, Bat Masterson, 1958; chmn. bd., 1960-65; disting. prof. telecommunications U. Cin., 1967—. Author: The Valiant Muse, 1935; The Business of Writing, 1930. Home: 2330 Victory Pkwy Cincinnati OH 45206 Office: U Cin Coll Conservatory Music Clifton Ave Cincinnati OH 45221

ZIZZO, JOSEPH DANIEL, optometrist; b. Chgo., Feb. 14, 1959; s. Joseph Daniel and Peggy Doris (Guidotti) Z. Student, Loyola U., Chgo., 1977-80; BS, Ill. Coll. Optometry, 1982, OD, 1984. Pvt. practice optometry Palatine, Il., 1984—. Named one of Outstanding Young Men of Am., 1985. Mem. Am. Optometric Assn., Ill. Optometric Assn., Optometric Extension Program, Coll. Vision Devel., Palatine C. of C. Roman Catholic. Avocation: opera. Home: 1275 Baldwin #606 Palatine IL 60067 Office: 1590 N Rand Rd #N Palatine IL 60067

ZLOMEK, JOSEPH MICHAEL, newspaper publisher; b. Oneonta, N.Y., June 15, 1955; s. Frederick Mathew and Muriel Dorothy (Pyle) Z.; m. Debra Ann Chambers-Rundle, Aug. 16, 1980; 1 child, Erin Elizabeth. BJ, Utica Coll. of Syracuse U., N.Y., 1977. Reporter Manlius Pub. Co., Fayetteville, N.Y., 1977-79; reporter Oneida Pubs., Inc., Oneida, 1979-82, mng. editor, 1982-83, pub., 1983-84; gen. mgr. Northeast Pub. Co., Fall River, Mass., 1984-85; pub. Tribune-Star Pub., Terre Haute, Ind., 1985—. V.p. and bd. dirs. Vigo County chpt. Am. Cancer Soc., 1985—; bd. dirs. Hamilton Ctr., Terre Haute, 1985—, Wabash Valley Council Boy Scouts Am., 1986—, Alliance for Growth and Progress, Terre Haute, 1986-87. Recipient Internat. award Internat. Assn. Firefighters, 1981. Mem. Hoosier State Press Assn., Inland Press Assn. Roman Catholic. Lodge: Kiwanis. Avocation: book collecting. Home: 20 McKinley Blvd Terre Haute IN 47803 Office: Tribune-Star Pub Co Inc 721 Wabash Ave Terre Haute IN 47807

ZMICK, MICHELLE NAOMI, periodontist, educator; b. Chgo., July 5, 1955; d. Maurice Marc Tennant; m. Clifford Anthony Zmick, Apr. 2, 1978; children: Adam, Jordan, Tyler. BS in Biology, U. Ill., Champaign, 1975; periodontics cert., U. Ill., Chgo., 1981; DDS, Loyola U., Maywood, Ill., 1979. Lic. periodontist, Ill. Assoc. periodontist Dr. Norman Newman, Chgo., 1982-83; practice dentistry specializing in periodontics Oak Park, Ill., 1981—; assoc. prof. U. Ill., Chgo., 1981-84, adj. assoc. prof., 1984—. Mem. Chgo. Dental Soc. (west side br. correspondent dinner chmn. 1986—), Omicron Kappa Upsilon. Home: 3622 Palm Canyon Dr Northbrook IL 60062 Office: One Magnificent Smile 7020 W North Ave Chicago IL 60635

ZODROW, CHARLES F., transportation company executive; b. Milw., Oct. 4, 1922; m. Muriel Zodrow, May 5, 1945. BBA, U. Wis., 1948; JD, U. Akron, 1958. Bar: Ohio 1958. With Firestone Tire & Rubber Co., Akron, Ohio, 1949-58; mgr. fed. taxes Roadway Express, Inc., Akron, 1959-61, treas., 1962-73, v.p., treas., sec., 1974-80, exec v.p. fin. and adminstrn., 1981, chmn. bd. dirs., 1982—, also bd. dirs.; chmn. parent co. Roadway Services, Inc., Akron. Bd. dirs. Soc. Corp., Cleve., 1982—; trustee John Carroll U., Cleve., Children's Hosp. of Akron. Served with USAAF, 1943-46. Decorated D.F.C. Mem. Tax Council (bd. dirs.), Am. Trucking Assn. (v.p., bd. dirs.), Am. Inst. CPA's, ABA. Office: Roadway Services Inc 1077 Gorge Blvd Akron OH 44309 *

ZOERKLER, RAYMOND NORBERT, geologist, consultant; b. Cin., Aug. 7, 1926; s. Louis Wendell and Lisa Othelia (Weisheit) Z.; m. Phyllis Lorraine Goble, July 16, 1949; children—Cynthia Rae Zoerkler Miller, Jennifer Louise. B.S. in Geology, U. Cin., 1954. Geologist, Stanolind Oil Co., New Orleans, 1954-56, Hanley and Bird, Bradford, Pa., 1956-63, Pennzoil Co., Bradford, 1963-69; cons. petroleum cos., Marietta, Ohio, 1969—. Bd. dirs. U. Pitts., 1963—; del. Citizens Program Peoples Republic of China, 1986. Ambassador. Served with USAF, 1945-47, ETO. Mem. Am. Inst. Profl. Geologists (cert.), Am. Assn. Petroleum Geologists, Soc. Petroleum Engrs., Soc. Well Log Analysts, Delta Phi Alpha. Republican. Roman Catholic. Lodges: Rotary, Elks. Home and Office: 133 Hillcrest Dr Marietta OH 45750

ZOLL, JEFFERY MARK, lawyer; b. Evergreen Park, Ill., Sept. 25, 1954; s. Frank Earl and Earline Ruth (Abadie) Z. AB cum laude, U. Ill., 1975, JD, 1978. Bar: Ill. 1978; CPA, Ill. Tax mgr. Touche Ross and Co., Chgo., 1978-85, Arthur Andersen and Co., Chgo., 1985—. Mem. ABA, Chgo. Bar Assn., Am. Inst. CPA's, Phi Beta Kappa. Office: Arthur Andersen and Co 33 W Monroe Chicago IL 60603

ZONCA, CHARLES A., computer software engineer; b. Detroit, Oct. 19, 1943; s. Charles A. Sr. and Mary A. (Wozny) Z.; m. Barbara C. Engel, Aug. 29, 1970; children: Kimberly, Greg. BS, U. Detroit, 1965; MA, Wayne State U., 1968. Computer programmer First Fed. Savs. and Loan, Detroit, 1965-66; engring. computer applications specialist Ford Motor Co., Dearborn, Mich., 1966-83; computer specialist Gen. Motors, Warren, Mich., 1983-84; mgr. engring. Electronic Data Systems, Southfield, Mich., 1985—. Mem. IEEE, Assn. Computing Machinery, Spl. Interest Group on Graphics, Engring. Soc. Detroit. Home: 34003 Burton Ln Livonia MI 48154 Office: Electronic Data Systems 23077 Greenfield Southfield MI 48075

ZONDERVAN, PETER JOHN (PAT ZONDERVAN), publisher, religious organization executive; b. Paterson, N.J., Apr. 2, 1909; s. Louis and Nellie Petronella (Eerdmans) Z.; m. Mary Swier, May 21, 1934; children: Robert Lee, Patricia Lucille, William J., Mary Beth. Student. pub. schs., Grandville, Mich.; D.Litt. (hon.), John Brown U., 1969; Litt.D., Lee Coll., 1972; LL.D., Campbellsville Coll., Ky., 1985; L.H.D. (hon.), Taylor U, Upland, Ind., 1985. Co-founder Zondervan Pub. House, Grandville, Mich., 1931, Grand Rapids, Mich., 1932—; co-founder Zondervan Corp., Grand Rapids, 1955—; pres. Grand Rapids Camp of Gideons, 1938-41, chaplain, 1944-46, pres., 1947-48; pres. internat. trustee, 1950-52; v.p. Gideons Internat., 1952-55, pres., 1956-59, treas., 1972-75, chaplain, 1975-78; Bd. dirs. Christian Nationals Evangelism Commn., San Jose, Calif.; bd. dirs. Winona Lake Christian Assembly, Ind., 1937—, sec., 1961—; b. dir. Marantha Bible and Missionary Conf., Muskegon, Mich., 1961; organizer, 1st chmn. Christian Businessmen's Com., Grand Rapids, 1942; chmn. com. for city-wide Evangelistic meeting, 1946. Honored with declaration of P.J. Zondervan Day in Grand Rapids, Dec. 1973. Mem. Internat. Platform Assn. Clubs: Lotus (Grand Rapids) (pres. 1949, 65-67); Peninsular of Grand Rapids, Blythefield Country and Golf; Boca Golf (Boca Raton, Fla.). Office: Zondervan Corp 1415 Lake Dr SE Grand Rapids MI 49506

ZONKA, CONSTANCE ZIPPRODT, public relations executive; b Evanston, Ill., May 23, 1937; d. Herbert Edward and Agnes Irene (Turpin) Zipprodt; m. Leif B. Sorensen, June 29, 1959 (div. Mar. 1964); 1 child, Heidi Liselotte; m. Robert F. Zonka, Aug. 5, 1970 (div. June 1982) 1 son, Milo Matthew. B.A., U. Fla., 1958; student Smith Coll., 1955-56; postgrad U. Chgo., 1958-59. Dir. publicity WIND Radio, Chgo., 1962-64; Midwest asst. pub. relations dir. Time Inc., Chgo., 1964-66; account exec. D.J. Edelman, Inc., Chgo., 1966-69; pres. Connie Zonka & Assocs., Chgo., 1970—; dir. Facets Multimedia, Chgo., 1983—; coordinator Chgo. Communications, 1974—. Mem. benefit com. Midwest Women's Ctr., Chgo., 1983—. Mem. NOW, Nat. Assn. Female Execs., Nat. Assn Women Bus. Owners., Pub. Relations Soc. Am., Publicity Club Chgo. (Golden Trumpet award 1980, Merit award 1982). Democrat. Clubs: Arts, East Bank (Chgo.). Home: 1655 N Vine St Chicago IL 60614-5117 Office: Connie Zonka & Assocs 666 N Lake Shore Dr Chicago IL 60611

ZONNEVILLE, ROBERT E., trucking company executive; b. Williamson, N.Y., Jan. 23, 1925; s. Adrian J. and Matie L. Z.; student U. Buffalo, 1949-52; m. Carol A. Alliger, June 7, 1947; children—Bethann, Robin, Kim, David. Dock worker Associated Transport, Buffalo, 1952-53, terminal mgr., 1960-66; terminal mgr. Spector Redball, Cleve., 1966-68, regional mgr., Wis., Minn. and Ill., 1968-71, v.p. central area, Northfield, Ohio, 1971-82; regional mgr., Inway Nationwide, 1982-87, v.p. 1987—. Pres. local Presbyn. Ch., Home Owners Assn., Mentor Gardens Home Owners Assn., 1987—; mem. golf com. City of Euclid, Ohio, 1975, com. to elect mayor of Euclid, 1979; sec., bd. dirs. Deercreek Time Share Owners, 1986-87. Served with U.S. Army, 1943-45. Decorated Purple Heart with oak leaf cluster, Bronze Star. Recipient awards for community activities, K.C., 1979. Mem. Western Res. Traffic Club. Clubs: Elks, Masons, Scottish Rite, Shriners. Home: 7627 Buchanan Ct Mentor OH 44060 Office: 21877 Euclid Ave Room 218 Euclid OH 44117

ZOOK, LEE JAMES, social work educator; b. McVegton, Pa., Feb. 14, 1946; s. Daniel Henry and Elizabeth May Zook; m. Janice Kay Heikes, Dec. 15, 1984; 1 child, Joel Daniel. BA in Psychology, Eastern Mennonite Coll., 1968; MSW, U. Mich., 1973; PhD, Case Western Res. U., 1987. Social worker Akron Child Guidance Ctr., 1973-75; cons., counselor Ctr. Human Living, Akron, 1975-85; asst. prof. U. Akron, 1979-85, Luther Coll., Decorah, Iowa, 1985—; cons. Family Service Ctr., Alliance, Ohio, 1975-79; social worker cons. Comprecare, Decorah, 1986—. Mem. adv. bd. Akron Rape Crisis Ctr., 1983-85, Child and Adolecent Service Ctr., Canton, Ohio, 1977-78. Mem. Nat. Assn. Social Workers, Am. Assn. Marriage and Family Therapy (cert., state sec. 1977-79, state treas. 1980-82), Council Social Work Edn. Democrat. Mem. United Ch. Christ. Avocations: farming, hiking, skiing, hunting. Home: R 1 Box 113B Mabel MN 55954 Office: Luther Coll 700 Colege Dr Decorah IA 52101

ZORICK, FRANK JOHN, health sci. facility administrator; b. Cumberland, Md., Dec. 27, 1941; s. Stanley E. and Alice F. (Gogerty) Z.; m. Jean Rhian, Aug. 28, 1965 (div. July 1981); children: Ethan R., Seth R.; m. Elizabeth I. Tietz, June 17, 1984. BS, U. Md., 1963, MD, 1967. Lic. psychiatrist. Clin. dir. In Patient Services Counseling Ctr., Bangor, Maine, 1973-74, Eastern Maine Med. Ctr., Bangor, 1974-76; clin. dir. sleep disorders clinic U. Cin., 1976-78; med. dir. sleep disorder ctr. Henry Ford Hosp., Detroit, 1978—. Contbr. articles to profl. jours. Served to maj. USAF, 1971-73. Fellow Clin. Sleep Soc.; mem. AMA, AAAS, Am. Psychiat. Assn. Democrat. Home: 1300 East Lafayette Detroit MI 48207 Office: Sleep Disorders and Research Ctr Henry Ford Hosp Detroit MI 48202

ZORN, ROBERT LYNN, ednl. adminstr.; b. Youngstown, Ohio, Mar. 22, 1938; s. Robert S. and Frances L. Zorn; B.S. Ed., Kent State U., 1959; M.Ed., Westminster Coll., 1964; Ph.D., U. Pitts., 1970; m. Joan M. Wilkos, Apr. 26, 1957; children—Deborah Lynn, Patricia Lynn. Tchr., West Branch (Ohio) Schs., 1961-62; elem. prin. Poland (Ohio) Schs., 1962-67, supt. schs., 1976—; high sch. unit prin. Boardman (Ohio) Schs., 1967-70; dir. adminstrv. services Mahoning County (Ohio) Schs., 1970-73, asst. supt., 1973-76; adj. prof. edn. Youngstown State U., 1970—; chmn. Ohi Adv. Com. to State Dept. Edn.; chmn. McGuffey Hist. Soc. Nat. Educator's Hall of Fame. Chmn. Mahoning County chpt. Am. Cancer Soc.; pres. bd. trustees Poland Methodist Ch.; trustee Mahoning County chpt. Am. Heart Assn. Served to lt. USAF, 1959-61. Mem. Doctoral Assn. Educators (life), Am. Assn. Sch. Adminstrs., Ohio PTA (life; Educator of Yr. 1980-81), Phi Delta Kappa. Republican. Clubs: Fonderlac County, Rotary, Protestant Men's. Author books, the most recent being: Speed Reading, 1980; contbr. articles to profl. jours. Home: 7341 Oak Dr Poland OH 44514 Office: 53 College St Poland OH 44514

ZORNOW, WILLIAM FRANK, history educator; b. Cleve., Aug. 13, 1920; s. William Frederick Emil and Viola (Schulz) Z. A.B., Western Res. U., 1942, A.M., 1944, Ph.D., 1952. Vice pres., treas. Glenville Coal & Supply Co., Real Value Coal Corp., Zornow Coal Corp., 1941-45; dep. clk. Probate Ct., Cuyahoga County, Ohio, 1941-43; prodn. planning engr. Hickok Elec. Instrument Co., Cleve., 1943-46; teaching asst. Western Res. U., 1944-47; instr. U. Akron, 1946-47, Case Inst. Tech., 1947-50, Washburn U., 1950-51; lectr. Cleve. Coll., 1948-49; asst. prof. Kans. State U., 1951-58; asst. prof. history Kent (Ohio) State U., 1958-61, asso. prof., 1961-66, prof. history, 1966—; collection corr. Berkshire Loan and Fin. Co., Painesville (Ohio) Security Credit Acceptance Corp., Mentor, O., 1951-60; cons. Karl E. Mundt Library, Dakota State Coll., Madison, S.D. Author: Lincoln and the Party Divided, 1954, rev. edit., 1972, Kansas: A History of the Jayhawk State, 1957, America at Mid-Century, 1959; contbr.: Abraham Lincoln: A New Portrait, 1959, Kansas: The First Century, 1956; articles to encys. and profl. jours.; editor: Shawnee County (Kans.) Hist. Bull, 1950-51; abstractor: America: History and Life: Historical Abstracts, 1964—. Mem. AAUP, Am. Acad. Polit. and Social Sci., Am. Assn. State and Local History (award of merit 1958), Am. Hist. Assn., Orgn. Am. Historians, Ohio Acad. History (chmn. awards com.), Ohio Hist. Soc. (library advisory com. 1969—), Ohio Soc. N.Y., Center for Study of Presidency, Acad. Polit. Sci., Sierra Club of San Francisco, Delta Tau Delta, Pi Gamma Mu, Phi Alpha Theta, Phi Delta

Kappa. Home: 7893 Middlesex Rd Mentor OH 44060 Office: Kent State U 305 Bowman Hall Kent OH 44242

ZRULL, JOEL PETER, psychiatry educator; b. Detroit, Jan. 10, 1932; s. Arthur Benjamin and Mildred (Bazy) Z.; m. Nancy Jane Eichenlaub, June 19, 1954; children: Mark Christian, Lisa Carol. BA with honors, U. Mich., 1953, MD, 1957. Diplomate Am. Bd. Psychiatry, Am. Bd. Child Psychiatry. From instr. to assoc. prof. psychiatry U. Mich. Med. Sch., Ann Arbor, 1962-73; prof., chief child psychiatry Med. Coll. Ohio, Toledo, 1973-75, prof., chmn. dept. psychiatry, 1975—; cons. Monroe (Mich.) County Intermediate Sch. Dist., 1961—; pres. Associated Physicians MCD, Inc., Toledo, 1983-84; chief of staff Med. Coll. Hosps., Toledo, 1984-86; mem. com. on cert. in child psyhiatry ABPN, 1986—. Editor: Adult Psychiatry: New Directions in Therapy, 1983; contbr. articles to profl. jours. Grantee NIMH, 1974-76, Ohio Dept. Mental Health, 1978—. Fellow Am. Psychiat. Assn., Am. Acad. Child and Adolescent Psychiatry (chmn. com. tng. 1984—), Am. Coll. Psychiatrists, Am. Ortho-Psychiat. Assn.; mem. AMA. Republican. Roman Catholic. Avocations: tennis, bridge, golfing. Home: 6133 Wyandotte Rd W Maumee OH 43537 Office: Med Coll Ohio Caller Service 10008 Toledo OH 43699

ZSCHERNITZ, JAMES JONATHAN, aerospace communications, computer engineer; b. Marshfield, Wis., Jan. 3, 1960; s. Edmund Carl Zschernitz and Margaret Lois (Chesmore) McCormick. BS in Computer Sci., U. Wis., Madison, 1983; postgrad., U. Wis., Milw., 1985, Purdue U., 1986. Software engr. Astronautics Corp. Am., Milw., 1983-85; engr. Aerospace/Optical div. ITT Corp., Ft. Wayne, Ind., 1985—. Mem. Am. Motorcyclist Assn., Assn. Old Crows, Am. Assn. Artificial Intelligence, Mathematical Assn. of Am. Republican. Roman Catholic. Avocations: archery, bicycling, camping, computer programming, fishing. Home: 7728 Placer Run Fort Wayne IN 46815 Office: ITT Aerospace/Optical div 3700 E Pontiac St Fort Wayne IN 46801

ZUBROFF, LEONARD SAUL, surgeon; b. Minersville, Pa., Mar. 27, 1925; s. Abe and Fannie (Freedline) Z.; B.A., Wayne State U., 1945, M.D., 1949. Intern Garfield Hosp., Washington, 1949-50, resident in surgery, 1951-55, chief resident surgery, 1954-55; practice medicine specializing in surgery, 1958-76; med. dir. Chevrolet Gear and Axle Plant, Chevrolet Forge Plant, Gen. Motors Corp., Detroit, 1977-78, divisional med. dir. Detroit Diesel Allison div., 1978-87, regional med. dir. Gen. Motors Corp, 1987—; mem. staff Hutzel Hosp., Detroit Meml. Hosp. Served with USAF, 1956-58. Diplomate Am. Bd. Surgery. Fellow A.C.S.; mem. AMA, Mich. State, Wayne County med. socs., Acad. Surgery Detroit, Am. Occupational Med. Assn., Mich. Occupational Med. Assn., Detroit Occupational Physicians Assn., NAACP, Phi Lambda Kappa. Lodge: Masons (33 deg.). Home: 16233 Nine Mile Rd Apt 201 Southfield MI 48075 Office: 13400 W Outer Dr Detroit MI 48239

ZUCARO, ALDO CHARLES, insurance company executive; b. Grenoble, France, Apr. 2, 1939; s. Louis and Lucy Z.; m. Gloria J. Ward, Oct. 12, 1963; children: Lucy, Louis, Faye. B.S. in Acctg, Queens Coll., N.Y.C., 1962. C.P.A., N.Y., Ill. With Coopers & Lybrand (and predecessor), Chgo. and N.Y.C., 1962-76; exec. v.p., chief fin. officer Old Republic Internat. Corp., Chgo., 1976-81; pres., chief fin. officer, dir. Old Republic Internat. Corp., 1981—; exec. v.p., chief fin. officer, dir. Old Republic Life Ins. Co., Old Republic Life of N.Y., Old Republic Ins. Co., Internat. Bus. & Merc. Reassurance Co., Republic Mortgage Ins. Co., Title Ins. Co. Minn., Home Owners Life Ins. Co. Editor: Financial Accounting Practices of the Insurance Industry, 1975, 76. Mem. Am. Inst. C.P.A.s. Roman Catholic. Office: Old Republic Internat Corp 307 N Michigan Ave Chicago IL 60601

ZUCKER, MARK JAY, cardiologist, lawyer; b. N.Y.C., Aug. 29, 1957; s. Saul and Phyllis Z. BS, McGill U., Montreal, Que., Can., 1977; MD, Northwestern U., 1981; JD, Loyola U., Chgo., 1986. Diplomate Am. Bd. Internal Medicine, Nat. Bd. Med. Examiners; Bar: Ill., 1986. Intern Northwestern Meml. Hosp., Chgo., 1981-82, resident in internal medicine, 1982-84, fellow in cardiology, 1984-87; instr. clin. medicine Northwestern U. Med. Sch., Chgo., 1984-87; asst. prof. medicine Loyola U. Med. Sch., Maywood, Ill., 1987—. Editorial cons. Comprehensive Therapy; contbr. articles to profl. jours. Am. Soc. Anesthesiology fellow, 1978; recipient Univ. scholarship McGill U., Am. Jurisprudence award Lawyers Coop. Pub. Co., 1986. Mem. ACP, Am. Coll. Cardiology (affiliate), Am. Heart Assn. (mem. council on clin. cardiology). Avocations: skiing, carpentry, photography. Office: Loyola U Med Ctr 2160 S First St Maywood IL 60153

ZUCKER, MYRON, electrical manufacturing executive; b. N.Y.C., Jan. 28, 1905; s. William and Emily (Rose) Z.; m. Isabel Schnapper, Jan. 28, 1929; children: Ralph, Judith. BEE, Cornell U., 1925; MSEE, Union U., 1927. Registered profl. elec. engr., Mich.; cert. mfg. engr. Test engr. Gen. Electric Co., Schenectady, N.Y., 1925-30; engr. Detroit Edison Co., 1930-45; mgr. cable ops. Mackworth G. Rees Inc., Detroit, 1945-47; owner Myron Zucker Engrng. Co., Detroit, 1953—; owner, pres. Myron Zucker Inc., Detroit, 1960—. Inventor electronic controls 1935, motor speed control 1936, power cables for resistance welding 1940, power capacitor 1962, 72. Creator (with wife Isabel) City of Trees, Royal Oak, Mich. Mem. IEEE (exec. bd. 1965-67, 80—). Republican. Home and Office: 708 W Long Lake Rd Bloomfield Hills MI 48013 Office: 315 E Parent St Royal Oak MI 48067

ZUERCHER, SISTER SUZANNE, religious organization administrator; b. Evanston, Ill., July 13, 1931; d. Charles Robert and Clara (Kettenhofen) Z. AB in English, Loyola U., Chgo., 1960, MA in Clin. Psychology, 1967. Joined Benedictine Sisters, Roman Cath. Ch., 1949. Lic. psychologist, Ill. Elem. tchr. Archdiocese of Chgo., 1952-60; tchr. St. Scholastica High Sch., Chgo., 1960-64, psychologist, 1964-72; campus minister Loyola U., 1972-76, mem. staff Inst. for Spiritual Leadership, 1976-87; writing sabbatical 1987—; first councilor Benedictine Sisters, Chgo., 1969-71, formation directress, 1974-80, sec. 1986—. Mem. Ill. Psychol. Assn. Home: 7416 N Ridge Blvd Chicago IL 60645 Office: Inst for Spiritual Leadership 4906 S Greenwood Chicago IL 60645

ZUGER, WILLIAM PETER, lawyer; b. Bismarck, N.D., Sept. 16, 1946; s. John A. and Irene (Kolb) Z.; m. Mary Haunson, June 3, 1977; 2 sons, Peter William, Jack Everett. B.A., U. Minn., 1969, J.D., 1972. Bar: N.D. 1972, U.S. Dist. Ct. N.D. 1972, U.S. Ct. Appeals (8th cir.) 1972, Minn. 1985. Ptnr. Zuger & Bucklin, Bismarck, 1972-84, sr. ptnr. Zuger Kapsner & Blazer, 1984—; lectr. various med. groups, nursing schs., physician groups. Mem. ABA (nat. affiliate rep. young lawyers sect. 1975-76), N.D. Bar Assn. (chmn. law office mgmt. and procedures com. 1974-77, young lawyers sect. 1975-76, sec.-treas. 1975-76), Burleigh County Bar Assn., 4th Dist. Bar Assn. (v.p. 1976). Contbr. articles to legal jours. Home: 604 West Blvd Bismarck ND 58501 Office: 2800 N Washington St Bismarck ND 58502

ZUIDWEG, DONALD RICHARD, pharmaceutical chemical company official; b. Kalamazoo, Oct. 2, 1936; s. Adrian and Lucille Edna (Mulder) Z.; B.B.A. cum laude, Western Mich. U., 1958; M.B.A., Ind. U., 1960; m. Jean Ann Skidmore, July 21, 1956; children—Scot Richard, Alan Adrian, Lauri Marie. Various mktg., distbn. and fin. positions Upjohn Co., Kalamazoo, 1958-67, v.p. ops. lab. div., controller, 1967-73, regional distgn. mgr., 1976, corp. acctg. and fin./group mgr., 1976-79, group mgr. corp. acct'g. systems, cost acctg. and mehods and records, 1979-81, group mgr. corp. telecommunications, office automation, methods and records, 1981-83, dir. info. and telecommunication services, 1983-85, dir. mgmt. info. services, 1985—; cons. small bus. Active various sch. and ch. orgns. Served to capt. Fin. Corps, U.S. Army, 1960-66. Mem. Kalamazoo Accountants Assn. (pres. 1975), Ind. U. Sch. Bus. Alumni Assn. (life), Assn. M.B.A. Execs., Western Mich. U. Alumni Assn. (life). Office: Upjohn Pharmaceuticals 7000 Portage Rd Kalamazoo MI 49001

ZUKERMAN, PINCHAS, concert violinist; b. Tel Aviv, Israel, July 16, 1948; came to U.S., 1962, naturalized, 1976; s. Jehuda and Miriam (Lieberman) Z.; m. Eugenia Rich, May 26, 1968 (div.); 2 daus.; m. Tuesday Weld, 1985. Am.-Israel Cultural Found. scholar, Helena Rubinstein scholar, Juilliard Sch. Music, 1965-68. With impresario, Sol Hurok, 1967-76, concert and recital tours in maj. cities world-wide, 1968—, condr., soloist, English Chamber Orch., 1974, Mostly Mozart Festival, N.Y.C., 1975, guest condr., soloist, Los Angeles Philharm., Boston Symphony, Phila. Orch., N.Y. Philharm., music dir., South Bank Festival, London, 1978-80, St. Paul Chamber Orch., 1980—, tour with, Isaac Stern, mem. trio with, Daniel Barenboim and Jacqueline du Pre, recorded with, CBS, EMI, recs. Winner Internat. Levintritt Competition, 1967. Office: Care Saint Paul Chamber Orchestra 319 Landmark Center 75 West Fifth St Saint Paul MN 55102

ZUMBUSCH, PATRICK JOHN, marketing executive; b. Buffalo, June 8, 1955; s. Casper Henry and Muriel Elizabeth (Eull) Z.; m. Peggi Lou Krause, June 9, 1979; 1 child, Kara Veronica. BA in Fin. and Acctg., Augsbury Coll., 1977; M in Mgmt., U. Chgo., 1986. CPA, Minn. Acct. Ernst and Whinney, Mpls., 1977-80; internat. controller Nicolet Instrument Corp., Madison, Wis., 1980-82, corp. controller, 1982-85, mktg. mgr., 1985-86, internat. sales mgr., 1986—. Mem. Am. Inst. CPA's, Nat. Assn. Accts., Verona (Wis.) Jaycees (pres. 1985). Office: Nicolet Instrument Corp 5225 Verona Rd Madison WI 53711

ZUNG, THOMAS TSE-KWAI, architect; b. Shanghai, China, Feb. 8, 1933; s. Bate and Rose Yu-Sun (Fong) Z.; came to U.S., 1937, naturalized, 1954; student Drew U., 1950-51, (Rose scholar) Va. Poly. Inst., 1951-53, Columbia U., 1955-57; B.Arch., U. Mich., 1960; M.S. in Design Sci. (student R. Buckminster Fuller), Internat. Coll., 1982; 1 son, Thomas Ba-Tse. Project architect Edward Durell Stone, architect, N.Y.C., 1958, 60-65; architect, Cleve., 1967—; pres. Buckminster Fuller, Sadao and Zung, architects, 1979—; prin. archtl. works include City Cleve. Pub. Utilities Bldg., Cleve. State U. Sports Center Dome, Mayfran, Inc., Sawmill Creek Lodge, U. Akron Guzzetta Hall, music, speech and theater arts center, Alumni Center Bowling Green State U., U. Akron Master Plan-West, City of East Cleveland, Superior Euclid beautification plan, student recreation center at Bowling Green State U., Glenville Public Library, campus bldg. Tex. Wesleyan Coll., recreation, health and phys. edn. bdg. Wittenberg U., Medina Res. Park Office, arena, health, phys. edn. complex U. Akron, Dyke Coll., Lima State Prison, Cleve. Children's Christian Home, numerous others. Task force chmn. Greater Cleve. Growth Assn., 1970; mem. Council Human Relations, 1972, Leadership Cleve. Class '77; cubmaster local Boy Scouts Am., 1977-79; bd. dirs. Buckminster Fuller Inst., 1983—; trustee Pace Assn., 1970-73, Karamu House, 1974-80, Cleve. Inst. Music, 1979—, Ohio Arts Council, 1982-84, Chinese Cultural Assn., 1980-84. Served with Signal Corps, U.S. Army, 1953-55. Decorated 4 medals; recipient Design award Cleve. chpt. AIA, 1972, Korean Inst. Constrn. Tech., 1984; Anicka Design award U. Mich., 1959, Sr. design prize, 1960; Public Works award State of Ohio, 1971, others. Mem. AIA (dir. Cleve. chpt. 1980), Am. Soc. Planning Ofcls., English Speaking Union (trustee 1972-75), Ohio Soc. Architects, Ohio Assn. Minority Architects and Engrs. (trustee 1982—); vestryman St. Christopher-by-River, 1980-83. Clubs: Hermit, City (dir. 1972-74, v.p. 1974) (Cleve.). Lodge: Rotary. Patentee in field. Office: 1303 Prospect Ave Cleveland OH 44115

ZUNICH, MITCHELL PAUL, accountant; b. Lorain, Ohio, May 30, 1957; s. Mitchell and Violet Mae (Kobac) Z.; m. Lisa Ann Georgeff, June 2, 1984. BS in Bus. Adminstrn., Ashland Coll., 1979. Sr. auditor Coopers & Lybrand, Cleve., 1979-82; ptnr. Mitchell Zunich & Co., Elyria, Ohio, 1982—. Treas. St. George Serbian Orthodox Ch., Lorain, 1983—; dist. vice chmn. fin. Boy Scouts Am. Mem. Am. Inst. CPA's, Ohio Soc. CPA's, Lorain C. of C. Republican. Eastern Orthodox. Lodge: Rotary. Home: 766 Shadylawn Dr Amherst OH 44001 Office: Mitchell Zunich & Co 43075 N Ridge Rd Elyria OH 44035

ZÚNIGA, MARIA LUISA, nurse educator; b. Santiago, Chile, Nov. 11, 1935; d. Manuel M. and Luisa J. (Gutierrez) Arriagada; came to U.S., 1964, naturalized, 1973; m. Robert Zúniga, Mar. 20, 1965; children—Maria Luisa, Roberto Manuel. B.S. in Nursing, Catholic U. Santiago, 1957; postgrad. U. Chile Sch. Pub. Health, 1964; postgrad. (W.K. Kellogg Found. fellow), UCLA, 1964; M.A. with honors, Western Mich. U., 1977, cert. in gerontology, 1982. Nursing supr. employee's clinic Internat. Petroleum Co. Barrancabermeja, Colombia, 1958-60; instr. med.-surg. Cath. U. Santiago, 1960-64; instr. orthopedics Borgess Hosp. Sch. Nursing, Kalamazoo, 1968-69; instr. community health nursing Nazareth (Mich.) Coll., 1969-76, asst. prof. fundamentals of nursing, 1977-82, assoc. prof., 1982—; guest lectr. Borgess Med. Ctr., Nazareth Coll.; mem. adv. bd. on gerontology Western Mich. U.; apptd. mem. Kalamazoo County Commn. on Aging, mem. South Central Mich. Commn. on Aging. Named Exchange Student Am. Nurses Assn., 1960. Mem. Nat. League for Nursing, Mich. League for Nursing, Am. Pub. Health Assn., Mich. Soc. of Gerontology, Delta Kappa Gamma Soc., Alpha Iota, Alpha Psi Chpt. (Kalamazoo). Roman Catholic.

ZUPP, HOWARD LESTER, manufacturing company owner, designer; b. East Greenville, Ohio, July 14, 1919; s. Jesse Madison and Catherine Louise (Keller) Z.; m. Evelyn Mae Steiner, Jan. 21, 1942; children: Howard Bruce, Gregory Alan. Grad., Washington High Sch., Massillon, Ohio, 1937. With Republic Steel Corp. Gen. Office, Massillon, 1939-53, corp. weighing supr., 1953-56; sales engr. Revere Corp. Am., Wallingford, Conn., 1956-84; owner G.J. Routhier, Inc., Massillon, Ohio, 1984—. Served with USN, 1942-46. Mem. Internat. Soc. Weighing and Measurement (nat. pres. 1966-67, officer Lake Erie div., pub. Year Book 1961, Mark Pickell award 1971, Woody Woodland award 1979), Nat. Fedn. Ind. Bus., Nat. Rifle Assn. Republican. Lodges: Shriners, Masons. Avocations: golf, boating, fishing, collecting stamps, guns. Office: GJ Routhier Inc 604 Tremont SW Massillon OH 44646

ZURCHER, FREDERIC, manufacturing company executive; b. St. Jilien, France, Mar. 6, 1942; came to U.S., 1958; s. Jean R. and Anna C. (Steveny) Z.; m. Rayanna Weisher, June 16, 1963; children: Raymond, Sheila, Melanie. BA, Atlantic Union Coll., 1965; MA, Andrews U., 1973. Prin. Union Springs (N.Y.) Elem. Sch., 1965-69; head edn. dept. S.A.S. Coll., Madagascar, 1969-72, Collonges Coll., Collonges, France, 1973-79; v.p. prodn. Hamilton Corp., Chgo., 1979-82; pres. Geneva Creations, La Fox, Ill., 1982-86; founder several mfg. cos. in Madagascar, 1969-72, France, 1973-79. Patentee in field; contbr. articles to French mags. Mem. Soc. Glass and Ceramic Decorators. Avocations: inventions, philosophy, skiing. Home: 38W165 Joan Dr Saint Charles IL 60174 Office: Geneva Creations Inc 1N046 Linlar Dr La Fox IL 60147

ZUREK, JOHN WALTER, dentist; b. Chgo., Feb. 18, 1955; s. John Walter and Ann (Bula) Z.; m. Sandra Louise Rago, Sept. 10, 1983; 1 child, John Dominic. Student, Loyola U., Chgo., 1973-76; DDS, U. Ill., Chgo., 1980. Gen. practice dentistry Danville, Ill., 1980—. Bd. dirs. Am. Cancer Soc., Danville, 1985—. Mem. ADA, Ill. Dental Soc., Chgo. Dental Soc., Danville Dist. Dental Soc. (sec.-treas. 1983-84, v.p. 1984-85, pres. 1985-86,bd. dirs. 1986-87), Danville Jaycees. Roman Catholic. Office: 909 N Logan Danville IL 61832

ZUSKA, ALBERT JOHN, radiologist; b. San Diego, Sept. 24, 1944; s. Albert John and Appolonia (Seminara) Z.; m. Theresa Lesniak, Apr. 23, 1977; children: John Albert, Steven Frederick, Matthew Joseph. BA, Northwestern U., 1966; MD, U. Ill., 1970. Diplomate Am. Bd. Radiology, Am. Bd. Nuclear Medicine. Intern Evanston (Ill.) Hosp., 1971-72; resident U. Ill. Hosps., 1971-74; attending radiologist St. Anne's Hosp., Chgo., 1974—, co-chmn. dept. radiology, 1984—. Mem. Soc. Nuclear Medicine, Radiol. Soc. N. Am., Chgo. Med. Soc. (alternate councilor), Windham Manor Homeowners Assn. (pres. 1983-85). Republican. Congregationalist. Avocations: jogging, fishing, swimming. Office: Austin Radiology 410 Lake Oak Park IL 60302

ZUSPAN, SALLY JO, nurse; b. Cleve., Apr. 2, 1959; d. Roger Alan and Dorothy Barbara (Walker) Brown; m. Keith Alan Zuspan, Aug. 26, 1983; 1 child, Michael Alan. BS in Nursing, Armstrong State Coll., 1982. Cert. emergency nurse; cert. basic trauma life support provider, Ohio. Staff nurse St. Joseph's Hosp., Savannah, Ga., 1982-83; staff nurse Children's Hosp., Columbus, Ohio, 1983-87, trauma nurse coordinator, 1987—; instr. advanced cardiac life support Am. Heart Assn., Columbus, 1984—; lectr., Columbus, 1985—. Mem. Emergency Nurses Assn. Home: 172 E Maynard Ave Columbus OH 43202 Office: Children's Hosp 700 Children's Dr Columbus OH 43215

ZWARENSTEYN, JOHN HENDRIK, publisher; b. Zaandam, North Holland, The Netherlands, June 7, 1945; came to U.S., 1950; s. Hendrik S. and Hillegonda E. (Donker) Z.; m. Beanca J. Diana, Sept. 6, 1975. BA, Mich. State U., 1967, MBA, 1969. Advt. salesman Mich. State News, East Lansing, 1964-69; owner, pres. Zwarensteyn Enterprises, Lansing, Mich., 1968-69; v.p. Grand Rapids (Mich.) Area C. of C., 1972-79; pres. Gemini Corp., Grand Rapids, 1979-83, owner, pres., 1983—. editor, pub. Grand Rapids Mag., 1972-79. Mem. allocations bd. United Way, Grand Rapids, 1981-85; bd. dirs. Project Rehab., Grand Rapids, 1985—, strategic issues series com., 1986—, exec. com., 1987—. Mem. Pub. Relations Soc. Am. (pres. 1984-86, jud. panel 1987—, Outstanding Profl. 1980), Press Club Grand Rapids (bd. dirs. 1978-82), Assn. Area Bus. Pubs., City and Regional Mag. Assn., Grand Rapids Area C. of C., Western Mich. Soccer Assn. Unitarian. Club: Edelweiss (Grand Rapids). Avocations: photography, soccer, golf, hockey, cross-country skiing. Home: 5059 Knob Hill Grand Rapids MI 49505 Office: Gemini Corp 40 Pearl St NW #1040 Grand Rapids MI 49503

ZWART, JAY ALLEN, financial planning administrator; b. Chgo., Dec. 12, 1955. BA, Augustana Coll., Rock Island, Ill., 1977. CPA, Ill. Auditor Ernst & Whinney, Chgo., 1977-78; controller Eastern zone Am. Hosp. Supply, McGaw Park, Ill., 1978-83, nat. ops. mgr., 1984-86, dir. field ops., 1986-87; ops. mgr. Gt. Lakes area Am. Hosp. Supply, Detroit, 1983-84; dir. fin. and bus. planning Corp. Dist., Baxter-Travenol, Deerfield, Ill., 1987—. Presbyterian. Avocations: basketball, tennis, photography. Home: 1509 Oak Evanston IL 60201-4263 Office: Baxter Travenol Labs Inc 1 Baxter Pkwy Deerfield IL 60015

ZWEBEN, LARRY MICHAEL, ophthalmologist; b. Culver City, Calif., Mar. 4, 1952; s. Robert S. Zweben and Hannah (Fievisohn) Singer. ScB, Brown U., 1974; MD, U. Calif., San Diego, 1978. Intern Tucson Hosp., 1978-79; resident in ophthalmology U. Mich. Hosp., Ann Arbor, 1979-82; practice medicine specializing in ophthalmology Bellaire, Ohio, 1982-86, Sioux City, Iowa, 1986—; cons. Ohio Valley Med. Ctr., Wheeling (Ohio) Hosp., Bellaire City Hosp. E. Ohio Regional Hosp., 1982-86. Mem. Ohio State Med. Assn., Belmont County Med. Soc., Am. Acad. Ophthalmology. Democrat. Lodges: Masons, Kiwanis. Office: 401 Insurance Ctr Sioux City IA 51101

ZWIKKER, KEES, graphics company executive; b. Eindhoven, Netherlands, Apr. 29, 1927; s. Cornelius and Johanna Dorothea (Theinert) Z.; M.B.A. with honors, U. Utrecht (Netherlands), 1950; m. Marie Jean Aylward, Dec. 20, 1952 (dec.); children—Robert Kees, Jacqueline Margaret; m. Donna Jeane Kohler, June 11, 1982; stepchildren—Charles Brian, Edward Martin Testa. Advt. prodn. mgr. Lee Donneley Advt. Agy., Cleve., 1952-56; dist. sales mgr. Standard Pub. Co., Cin., 1956-62; advt. mgr. Hess & Clark div. Vick Chem. Corp., Ashland, Ohio, 1962-66; v.p. Topper Assos. Advt. Agy., Ashland, 1966-71; account exec. Cross Assos. Advt., Chagrin Falls, Ohio, 1971-72; mktg. communications mgr. Norton Co., Akron, Ohio, 1972-81; global mktg. mgr. Meistergram, Inc., Cleve., 1981-83; mktg. services specialist Gen. Electric Co., Cleve., 1984-87; mgr. mktg. services Yunker Industries, Lake Geneva, Wis., 1987—; chmn. bd. Ashland Graphic Art Co., 1963—. Mem. Aurora (Ohio) City Council, 1977-81; sec. Aurora Planning and Zoning Commn., 1974-77. Served to capt. Dutch Army, 1947-51. Mem. Nat. Advt. Assn. (cert. bus. communicator), Internat. Trade Show Exhibit Assn. (dir. 1978-83), Indsl. Marketers of Cleve., Bus. and Profl. Advt. Assn., Internat. Advt. Assn. (Cleve. chpt. v.p. 1984, pres. 1985), Internat. Mktg. Club (v.p. 1984, pres. 1985—). Republican. Roman Catholic. Club: Boating of Aurora Shores. Contbr. articles to profl. jours. Home: 3674 Nautilus Trail Aurora OH 44202 Office: Nela Park Cleveland OH 44112

ZWILLING, WILLIAM FREDERICK, orthopaedic surgeon; b. Geneva, Ill., Dec. 12, 1933; s. Daniel Frederick and Virginia Lee (Thompson) Z.; m. Martha Kreiser, Feb. 9, 1957 (div. 1968); children: Susan, Jennifer, Anthony, Pamela, Kirk; m. Diane Poppen, May 19, 1973; children: Debee, Diane, Carl, Christopher. AB, Harvard U., 1955, MD, 1959. Diplomate Am. Acad. Orthopaedic Surgeons. Practice medicine specializing in orthopaedic surgery Arlington Heights, Ill., 1969—; team physician Forest View High Sch., Arlington Heights, 1968-85, Barrington (Ill.) High Sch., 1972—, Rolling Meadows (Ill.) High Sch., 1986—. Author: Hemoglobin Toxicity Study, 1958. Served to maj. U.S. Army, 1961-68. Fellow Am. Acad. Orthopaedic Surgeons; mem. ACS, Internat. Arthroscopy Assn., Arthroscopy Assn. of N.Am., Ill. Orthopaedic Soc. Clubs: Meadow (Rolling Meadows, Ill.), Barrington Hills Country (Ill.). Home: 190 Kimberly Rd Barrington IL 60010 Office: Orthopaedic Assocs SC 1300 E Central Rd Arlington Heights IL 60005

ZYK, BERNARD ANDREW, marketing professional; b. St. Louis, Sept. 27, 1944; s. Julius Arthur and Martha (Kinzel) Z.; m. Kathleen Patricia Neary, Jan 30, 1970; children: Melissa Kathleen, Paul Bernard, Timothy Ryan. BS in Bus., U. Mo., 1967; MBA, So. Ill. U., 1974. V.p. mktg. Universal Printing Co., St. Louis, 1974—. Served with USMC, 1967-74. Mem. Assn. Young Printing Execs. Roman Catholic. Club: Craftsmen. Avocations: tennis, photography, gardening. Home: 13024 Wheatfield Farm Rd Saint Louis MO 63141 Office: Universal Printing Co 1701 Macklind Saint Louis MO 63141